W9-BNH-405
3 2109 00920 6005

WORLD TREATY INDEX

Volume 1

INTRODUCTION

MAIN ENTRY SECTION

League of Nations Treaty Series

Volume 2

MAIN ENTRY SECTION

United Nations Treaty Series: Series I, Numbers 1–6485

Volume 3

MAIN ENTRY SECTION

United Nations Treaty Series: Series I, Numbers 6486–10841; Series II, Numbers 1–657

National Treaty Collections

Volume 4

CHRONOLOGICAL SECTION

PARTY SECTION

INTERNATIONAL ORGANIZATION SECTION

UNTS SELF-INDEX SECTION

Volume 5

TOPIC SECTION

WORLD TREATY INDEX

TOPIC SECTION

VOLUME 5

PETER H. ROHN
Associate Professor of Political Science
University of Washington

Santa Barbara, California
Oxford, England

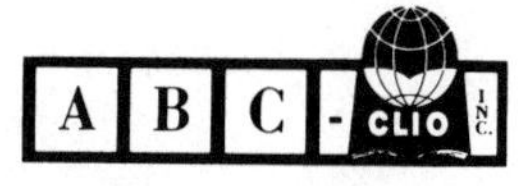

Library of Congress Catalog Card Number 73-83352
ISBN Clothbound 5-Volume Set 0-87436-125-7
ISBN Clothbound 6-Volume Set 0-87436-132-X
ISBN Clothbound Volume 5 0-87436-130-3

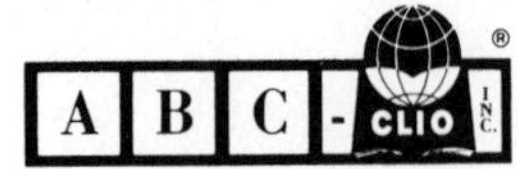

American Bibliographical Center—Clio Press, Inc.
2040 Alameda Padre Serra
Santa Barbara, California

European Bibliographical Center—Clio Press
Woodside House
Hinksey Hill
Oxford OX1 5BE, England

Designed by Barbara Monahan
Composed by Datagraphics Press
Printed and bound by Halliday Lithograph Corporation
in the United States of America

Contents

List of Abbreviations xv

TOPIC SECTION 1

User's Guide 2

League of Nations Treaty Series 3

General terms
- Change of circumstances 3
- Default remedies 3
- Treaty interpretation 3
- Treaty violation 3
- Previous treaty extension 3
- Previous treaty replacement 4
- Previous treaty renunciation 5
- Previous treaties adherence 5

General relations and amity 8
- Non-prejudice to third party 8
- Friendship and amity 8
- Non-prejudice to UN charter 9
- Peaceful relations 9
- Exchange of information and documents 10
- Frontier formalities 10
  - Visa abolition 10
  - Border traffic and migration 11
  - Passports diplomatic 12
  - Passports non-diplomatic 12
  - Denial of admission 12
  - Resident permits 12
  - Non-visa travel documents 13
  - Visas 13
  - Tourism 14
  - Frontier permits 14
  - Immigration and emigration 14
- Refugees and stateless persons 14
  - Assistance 15
  - Legal status 15
  - Refugees 15
  - Repatriation mission 15
  - Repatriation of nationals 15
  - Stateless persons 15
- Status of state 15
  - Democratic institutions 15
  - Governor-general functions 15
  - Independence maintenance 15
  - Continuity of rights and obligations 15
  - Transition period 15
  - Recognition 15
  - Re-establishment 16
  - Self-determination 16
  - Self-government 16
  - Union with other states 16

Diplomatic and consular relations 16
- Acquisition of nationality 16
- Alien registration 16
- Alien status 16
- General consular functions 17
- Diplomatic privileges 18
- Dual citizenship 18
- Consular relations establishment 18
- Diplomatic relations establishment 19
- Diplomatic relations resumption 19
- Diplomatic missions 20
- Human rights 20
- Inviolability 20
- Privileges and immunities 20
- Property 21
- Proxy diplomacy 21
- Nationality and citizenship 21
- Protection of nationals 22
- Diplomatic correspondence 23
- Non-diplomatic delegations 23
- Consular functions in shipping 23
- Consular functions in property 24
- Notarial acts and services 24

Extradition, deportation and repatriation 24
- Court procedures 25
- Extradition requests 26
- Extraditable offenses 27
- Location of crime 28
- Special factors 28
- Refusal of extradition 29
- Concurrent requests 30
- Pre-treaty crimes 30

Contents

- Limits of prosecution 30
- Provisional detainment 31
- Extradition postponement 31
- Witnesses and experts 32
- Material evidence 32

Administrative cooperation 33
- Conformity with municipal law 33
- Information centers 34
- Exchange of official publications 34
- Family law 35
- Exchange of information and documents 35
- Informational records 39
- Inspection and observation 40
- Juridical personality 40
- Expropriation 42
- Free passage and transit 42
- Legal protection and assistance 43
- Domestic legislation 45
- Operating agencies 45
- Licenses and permits 46
- Recognition and enforcement of legal decisions 47
- Incorporation of treaty provisions into national law 48
- Personnel 48
- Immovable property 48
- General property 49
- Succession 51
- Public information 51
- Jurisdiction 51
- Recognition of legal documents 51
- Private contracts 52
- Responsibility and liability 52
- Corporations 53
- Concessions 54
- Revival of treaties 54
- Prizes and arbitral awards 54
- Title and deeds 55
- Use of facilities 55
- Investigation of violations 55
- Penal sanctions 56
- Establishment of commission 56

Extraterritorial rights 58
- Abolition of treaty ports 58
- Abolition of extraterritorial rights 58

Dispute settlement 58
- Arbitration 58
- Mediation and good offices 61
- Procedure 61
- Selected disputes not subject to settlement procedures 65
- Domestic jurisdiction 65
- Existing tribunals 65
- Special tribunals 68
- Negotiation 69
- Conciliation 70
- Competence of tribunal 71

General health, education, culture, welfare and labor 73

International circulation 73

Specialists exchange 73

Sanitation 73
- Quarantine 73
- Border control 73
- Disease control 74
- Public health 74
- Insect control 74
- Narcotic drugs 74
- Nursing 74
- Pharmaceuticals 74
- Sanitation 75
- Veterinary 75
- Medical assistance and/or facilities 75

Education 75
- Recognition of degrees 75
- Exchange 75
- Commissions and foundations 75
- Teacher and student exchange 75
- Professorships 76
- Institute establishment 76
- Scholarships and grants 76
- Vocational training 76

Culture 76
- Exchange 76
- General cultural cooperation 76
- Artists 76
- Athletes 76
- Archives and objects 76

Humanitarian matters 76

ILO conventions 77
- Anti-discrimination 77
- Employment regulations 77
- Holidays and rest periods 77
- Old age and invalidity insurance 77
- Safety standards 77
- Right to organize 77
- Wages and salaries 77

Non-ILO labor relations 77
- Family allowances 78
- Administrative cooperation 78
- Old age insurance 78
- Sickness and invalidity insurance 78
- Social security 79
- Unemployment 79
- Migrant worker 79

Research and scientific projects
- Research cooperation 79
- Scientific exchange 79

General economics 79

General trade 79
- Establishment of trade relations 80
- Export quotas 82
- Import quotas 84
- Free trade 87
- Tariffs 87
- Maritime products and equipment 89
- Certificates of origin 90
- Reciprocity in trade 91
- Reexport of goods, etc. 93
- Export subsidies 94
- Trade agencies 94
- Trade procedures 94
- Embargo 95

Finances and payments 95
- Accounting procedures 95
- Attachment of funds 96
- Banking 96
- Bonds 97
- Compensation 97
- Indemnities and reimbursements 98
- Balance of payments 101

Currency 101
Monetary and gold transfers 102
Currency deposits 102
Investments 103
Exchange rates and regulations 103
Expense sharing formulae 104
Fees and exemptions 104
Financial programs 105
Funding procedures 106
Garnishment of funds 106
Inadequacy of funds 106
Internal finance 106
Interest rates 106
Payment schedules 107
Purchase authorizations 109
Non-interest rates and fees 109
Seizure funds 110
Transportation costs 110
Local currency 110
Claims, debts and assets 110
Assets 110
Claims and settlements 110
Lump sum settlements 112
Debts 112
Debt settlement 112
Assessment procedures 113
Private investment guarantee 113
Liens 113
Assets transfer 114
Commodity trade 114
Delivery guarantees 114
Delivery schedules 114
Quotas 114
Smuggling 115
Most favored nation clause 115
Taxation 118
Death duties 119
Tax credits 119
Equitable taxes 119
General 119
Taxation of immovable property 121
Taxation of professional services 121
Taxable items 121
Tax exemptions 122
Patents, copyrights and trademarks 123
Literary and artistic copyrights 123
Trademarks 123
Laws and formalities 123
Post-war adjustment 124
Recognition 124
Customs duties 124
Customs declarations 127
Customs exemptions 127
Temporary importation 129

Aid and development 129

Commodities and services
Domestic obligation 129
General technical assistance 129
Agriculture 129
Conservation
Assistance 129
Special projects 129
Specific technical assistance
General aid 129
Agricultural commodities 129
Economic assistance 129
Materials, equipment and services 129
Volunteer programs 129
Withdrawal conditions 129
Loan and credit 129
Credit provisions 129
Purchase authorization 129
Loan repayment 129
Refinance of loan
Terms of loan 130
Agricultural commodities assistance 130
Atomic energy assistance
Rights of supplier 130
Samples and testing 130
World Bank projects
Plans and standards 130
Non-bank projects
Industry 130
Irrigation 130
Natural resources 130
Hydro-electric power 130

General transportation 130

Competency certificate 131
Registration certificate 131
Passenger transport 131
Dangerous goods 132
Routes and logistics 132
Navigational conditions 132
Navigational equipment 133
Permit designation 133
Goods in transit 133
Transport of goods 133
Air transport 134
Airport facilities 135
Airport equipment 135
Airworthiness certificates 136
Conditions of airlines operating permission 136
Overflights and technical stops 137
Operating authorizations and regulations 137
Licenses and certificates of nationality 138
Water transport 139
Canal improvement 139
Innocent passage 139
Merchant vessels 139
Inland and territorial waters 140
Tonnage 141
Ports and pilotage 142
Shipwreck and salvage 144
Collision 144
Land transport 144
Commercial road vehicles 144
Driving permits 144
Railway border crossing 145
Motor vehicles and combinations 145
Railways 145
Roads and highways 146
Road rules 146
General communications 147
Amateur radio 147
Commercial and public radio 147
Bands and frequency allocation 147
Facilities and equipment 147
Communications linkage 147
Interference of broadcasts 147

Contents

Mail and money orders 147
Postal services 148
Regulations 149
Insured letters and boxes 150
Conveyance in transit 151
Money orders and postal checks 152
Parcel post 153
Rates and charges 154
Advice lists and orders 156
Telecommunications 157
Cable 157
Services 157
Telegrams 158
Radio-telephone-telegraphic communications 158
Mass media 159
Publications exchange 159
Mass media exchange 159
Information agency 159
Press and wire services 159

General military 159

Repatriation of combatants 159
Joint defense 159
Defense and security 159
Prisoners of war 159
Repatriation of civilians 159
Self-defense 160
Payment for war supplies 160
Lease of military property 160
Military assistance 160
Naval vessels 160
Return of equipment and recapture 160
Military training 160
Security of information
Surplus war property 160
Military assistance missions
Airforce-army-navy personnel ratio 160
Ranks and privileges 160
Conditions for assistance missions 160
Status of military forces
Jurisdiction 160
Procurement and logistics 160
Withdrawal of forces 160
Status of forces 161
Military installations and equipment 161
Exchange of defense information 161
Bases and facilities 161
Restrictions on transfer 161
Military service and citizenship 161
Dual nationality 161
Foreign nationals 161
Service in foreign army 162
Peace and disarmament 162
Reconversion to normalcy 162
Armistice and peace 162
Arms limitations 162
War claims and reparations 162
Loss and/or damage 162
Enemy financial interests 162
Reparations and restrictions 163
Post-war claims settlement 163
Occupation regime 163
Disarmament and demilitarization 163
Industrial controls 163
Control and occupation machinery 163
Withdrawal of occupation 163
War graves 163
Responsibility for war dead 163
Upkeep of war graves 163
Establishment of war cemeteries 163

International organizations 163

IGO constitution 163
Admission 163
Decisions 163
Subsidiary organ 163
Establishment 163
Procedure 163
Headquarters and facilities 164
Extension of functions 164
Liaison with other IGO's
Internal structure 164
IGO status
Special status 164
Status of experts 164
IGO operations
Conferences 164
IGO obligations 164
Optional clause ICJ 164
Trusteeship
Administering authority 164
Disposition of territory 164
Definition of territory 164
Respect for local customs 164
Internal travel 164

Disposition of particulars 164

Facilities and property 164
Aquisition of property 165
Boundaries of territory 165
Pasturage in frontier zones 165
Changes of territory 165
Fish, wildlife, and natural resources 165
Markers and definitions 165
Frontier peoples and personnel 166
Frontier waterways 167
Frontier crossing points 167
Continental shelf 168
Specific goods and equipment
Conservation of specific resources 168
Ocean resources 168
Wildlife
Fisheries and fishing 168
Regulation of natural resources 168
Raw materials 168

United Nations Treaty Series 169

General terms
Change of circumstances 169
Default remedies 170
Treaty interpretation 171
Annex or appendix reference 173
Treaty violation 173

Previous treaty extension 173
Previous treaty replacement 175
Previous treaty renunciation 180
Previous treaties adherence 181

General relations and amity 181

Non-prejudice to third party 181
Friendship and amity 182
Non-prejudice to UN charter 185
Peaceful relations 186
Exchange of information and documents 187
Frontier formalities 187
Visa abolition 188
Border traffic and migration 190
Passports diplomatic 192
Passports non-diplomatic 192
Denial of admission 193
Resident permits 194
Non-visa travel documents 196
Visas 197
Tourism 200
Frontier permits 200
Immigration and emigration 201
Refugees and stateless persons 201
Assistance 201
Legal status 201
Refugees 201
Repatriation mission 201
Repatriation of nationals 201
Stateless persons 202
Status of state 202
Nazi organizations 202
Democratic institutions 202
Governor-general functions 202
Independence maintenance 202
Continuity of rights and obligations 202
Transition period 202
Recognition 202
Re-establishment 203
Self-determination 203
Self-government 203
Union with other states 203
Diplomatic and consular relations 203
Acquisition of nationality 203
Alien registration 203
Alien status 203
General consular functions 204
Diplomatic privileges 205
Dual citizenship 207
Consular relations establishment 207
Diplomatic relations establishment 208
Diplomatic relations resumption 209
Diplomatic missions 209
Human rights 210
Inviolability 210
Missing persons 211
Privileges and immunities 211
Property 221
Proxy diplomacy 221
Nationality and citizenship 221
Protection of nationals 222
Diplomatic correspondence 222
Non-diplomatic delegations 223
Consular functions in shipping 223
Consular functions in property 223
Notarial acts and services 224
Extradition, deportation and repatriation 224
Court procedures 224
Extradition requests 225
Extraditable offenses 225
Location of crime 225
Special factors 226
Refusal of extradition 226
Concurrent requests 226
Pre-treaty crimes 226
Limits of prosecution 227
Provisional detainment 227
Extradition postponement 227
Witnesses and experts 227
Material evidence 228
Administrative cooperation 228
Conformity with municipal law 228
Information centers 244
Exchange of official publications 244
Family law 246
Exchange of information and documents 246
Informational records 267
Inspection and observation 272
Juridical personality 280
Expropriation 282
Free passage and transit 282
Legal protection and assistance 283
Domestic legislation 284
Operating agencies 287
Licenses and permits 290
Recognition and enforcement of legal decisions 295
Incorporation of treaty provisions into national law 296
Personnel 297
Post-colonial administration 305
Immovable property 305
General property 306
Succession 310
Public information 310
Jurisdiction 313
Waiver of immunity 313
Recognition of legal documents 313
Private contracts 316
Responsibility and liability 318
Corporations 324
Concessions 324
Revival of treaties 324
Prizes and arbitral awards 324
Technical and commercial staff 324
Title and deeds 325
Use of facilities 328
Investigation of violations 336
Penal sanctions 337
Establishment of commission 337
Extraterritorial rights 342
Abolition of treaty ports 342
Abolition of diplomatic quarters 342
Abolition of extraterritorial rights 342
Dispute settlement 342
Arbitration 343
Mediation and good offices 351
Procedure 351
Disputes disrupting normal relations 361
Domestic jurisdiction 361
Existing tribunals 361
Special tribunals 365

Contents

Negotiation 367
Conciliation 373
Advisory opinions 373
Competence of tribunal 373

General health, education, culture, welfare and labor 374
International circulation 374
Specialists exchange 375
Sanitation 376
Quarantine 377
Border control 377
Disease control 377
Public health 378
Insect control 380
Narcotic drugs 381
Nursing 381
Pharmaceuticals 381
Sanitation 381
Veterinary 382
WHO used as agency 382
Medical assistance and/or facilities 382
Education 382
Recognition of degrees 383
Exchange 384
Commissions and foundations 388
Teacher and student exchange 389
Professorships 393
Institute establishment 394
Scholarships and grants 395
Vocational training 399
Culture 403
Exchange 404
General cultural cooperation 405
Artists 408
Athletes 409
Archives and objects 411
Humanitarian matters 411
ILO conventions 411
Anti-discrimination 412
Employment regulations 412
Holidays and rest periods 413
Old age and invalidity insurance 414
Labor statistics 415
Safety standards 415
Right to organize 416
Wages and salaries 416
Non-ILO labor relations 417
Family allowances 418
Administrative cooperation 419
Old age insurance 420
Sickness and invalidity insurance 421
Social security 422
Unemployment 423
Migrant worker 424
Research and scientific projects 424
Research cooperation 426
Anthropology and archeology 427
Meteorology 428
Research results 428
Communication satellites testing 430
Nuclear research 430
Scientific exchange 430
Research and development 433

General economics 437
General trade 437
Establishment of trade relations 439
Export quotas 440
Import quotas 442
Free trade 445
Tariffs 445
Maritime products and equipment 446
Certificates of origin 446
Reciprocity in trade 447
Reexport of goods, etc. 448
Export subsidies 452
Trade agencies 452
Trade procedures 453
Embargo 455
Finances and payments 455
Accounting procedures 456
Attachment of funds 464
Banking 465
Bonds 467
Compensation 471
Indemnities and reimbursements 473
Balance of payments 480
Currency 482
Monetary and gold transfers 488
Currency deposits 490
Investments 491
Exchange rates and regulations 491
Expense sharing formulae 499
Fees and exemptions 506
Financial programs 515
Funding procedures 520
Garnishment of funds 525
Inadequacy of funds 525
Internal finance 525
Interest rates 526
Legal costs 530
Payment schedules 530
Purchase authorizations 538
Non-interest rates and fees 538
Sale of local currency 542
Seizure funds 542
Transportation costs 543
Local currency 545
Claims, debts and assets 551
Assets 551
Claims and settlements 552
Lump sum settlements 557
Debts 558
Debt settlement 559
Assessment procedures 560
Private investment guarantee 560
Liens 561
Assets transfer 561
Commodity trade 562
Delivery guarantees 564
Delivery schedules 564
Quotas 565
Smuggling 567
Most favored nation clause 567
Taxation 572
Death duties 575
Tax credits 575
Equitable taxes 576
General 577
Taxation of immovable property 579
Income taxes 579

Taxation of professional services 579
Taxable items 579
Tax exemptions 579
Patents, copyrights and trademarks 591
Compliance with domestic patent and copyright laws 591
Literary and artistic copyrights 591
Trademarks 592
Laws and formalities 592
Post-war adjustment 592
Recognition 593
Customs duties 593
Customs declarations 596
Customs exemptions 597
Customs and excise cooperation 606
Temporary importation 606

Aid and development 606

Commodities and services 607
Domestic obligation 608
General technical assistance 618
Agriculture 623
Conservation 625
Economic development 625
Assistance 625
Mutual exchange of technical knowledge 627
Special projects 627
Specific technical assistance 629
Technical cooperation 630
Technical education 630
General aid 630
Agricultural commodities 631
Economic assistance 631
Use restrictions 634
Materials, equipment and services 635
Aid missions 643
Volunteer programs 644
Surplus property 645
Relief supplies 645
Grants 646
Withdrawal conditions 646
Procurement 647
Distribution 647
Access to materials 648
Loan and credit 648
Credit provisions 650
Internal loans 652
Purchase authorization 652
Loan repayment 653
Refinance of loan 655
Terms of loan 655
Agricultural commodities assistance 660
Commodities schedule 660
Purchase authorization 662
Surplus commodities 664
Atomic energy assistance 666
Acceptance of delivery 666
General 666
Nuclear materials 667
Non-nuclear materials 668
Research facilities 669
Peaceful use 669
Rights of supplier 670
Samples and testing 670
World Bank projects 670
Loan regulations 671
Loan guarantee 675
Guarantor non-interference 679
Plans and standards 682
Non-bank projects 683
Agricultural development/credit 684
IDA development project 684
Industry 684
Irrigation 685
Natural resources 685
Hydro-electric power 685

General transportation 686

Competency certificate 687
Registration certificate 689
Passenger transport 690
Dangerous goods 691
Routes and logistics 691
Navigational conditions 696
Navigational equipment 699
Permit designation 700
Goods in transit 704
Transport of goods 704
Air transport 706
Airport facilities 710
Airport equipment 714
Airworthiness certificates 715
Conditions of airlines operating permission 718
Overflights and technical stops 722
Operating authorizations and regulations 724
Licenses and certificates of nationality 730
Water transport 732
Canal improvement 733
Innocent passage 733
Merchant vessels 733
Inland and territorial waters 735
Tonnage 736
Use of ports and territorial waters 736
Ports and pilotage 736
Shipwreck and salvage
Collision 737
Land transport 737
Agricultural vehicles and construction 738
Commercial road vehicles 738
Driving permits 738
Railway border crossing 738
Motor vehicles and combinations 739
Railways 739
Roads and highways 740
Road rules 741
General communications 741
Amateur radio 741
Commercial and public radio 742
Amateur third party message 742
Bands and frequency allocation 742
Facilities and equipment 742
Communications linkage 743
Interference of broadcasts 743
Mail and money orders 743
Postal services 744
Regulations 745
Insured letters and boxes 745
Conveyance in transit 746
Money orders and postal checks 747
Parcel post 747
Rates and charges 747
Advice lists and orders 748

Contents

Telecommunications 749
Cable 749
Satellites 749
Services 749
Telegrams 749
Radio-telephone-telegraphic communications 749
Mass media 750
Publications exchange 750
Mass media exchange 752
Information agency 753
Media guaranty 753
Press and wire services 754
Television 754

General military 754

Post-war reconstruction 755
Burial arrangements 755
Repatriation of combatants 755
Joint defense 755
Defense and security 755
Prisoners of war 758
Rearmament restrictions and controls 758
Repatriation of civilians 758
Withdrawal or relief of occupation forces 758
Military assistance 758
Atomic weapons 758
Self-defense 758
Payment for war supplies 759
Lease of military property 759
Military assistance 760
Lend lease 762
Naval vessels 762
Return of equipment and recapture 763
Military training 764
Security of information 765
Surplus war property 768
Military assistance missions 768
Airforce-army-navy personnel ratio 769
Ranks and privileges 769
Conditions for assistance missions 770
Third country military personnel 771
Status of military forces 771
Jurisdiction 772
Procurement and logistics 772
Withdrawal of forces 773
Status of forces 773
Military installations and equipment 774
Exchange of defense information 775
Testing ranges and sites 776
Bases and facilities 776
Equipment and supplies 777
Restrictions on transfer 777
Military service and citizenship 778
Dual nationality 778
Certificates of service 779
Foreign nationals 779
Service in foreign army 779
Peace and disarmament 780
Reconversion to normalcy 780
Armistice and peace 780
Arms limitations 780
War claims and reparations 780
Loss and/or damage 780
Claims arising from occupation of territories 781
Enemy financial interests 781
Reparations and restrictions 781
Post-war claims settlement 781
Occupation regime 783
Disarmament and demilitarization 783
Industrial controls 783
Control and occupation machinery 783
Withdrawal of occupation 784
War graves 784
Responsibility for war dead 784
Upkeep of war graves 784
Establishment of war cemeteries 784

International organizations 785

IGO constitution 785
Admission 785
Constitutional amendment 785
Decisions 785
Subsidiary organ 786
Establishment 787
Regional offices 787
Procedure 788
Headquarters and facilities 788
Extension of functions 789
Liaison with other IGO's 789
Internal structure 789
IGO status 790
Freedom of action 794
Freedom of meeting 794
IGO obligations 794
Security of the government 794
Special status 794
Status of experts 795
IGO operations 796
Conformity with IGO decisions 796
Assistance to United Nations 799
Conferences 799
Membership 800
UN administrative tribunal 800
Inter-agency agreements 800
Peace-keeping force 801
Recognition of specialized agency 801
Interagency requests 801
Mutual consultation 801
UN recommendations 803
IGO obligations 803
Adherence to UN Charter 804
Acceptance of UN obligations 804
Acceptance of obligations upon admittance to UN 804
Optional clause ICJ 805
Compulsory jurisdiction 805
Paragraph 2, Article 36 805
Trusteeship 806
Basic freedoms 806
Administering authority 806
Disposition of territory 806
Definition of territory 806
Socio-economic development 806
Respect for local customs 806
Internal travel 806

Disposition of particulars 807

Specific claims or waivers 807
Facilities and property 807
Aquisition of property 808

Boundaries of territory 808
- Pasturage in frontier zones 808
- Changes of territory 808
- Fish, wildlife, and natural resources 808
- Markers and definitions 808
- Frontier peoples and personnel 809
- Frontier waterways 810
- Frontier crossing points 810
- Continental shelf 810

Specific goods and equipment 810

Conservation of specific resources 811
- Ocean resources 811
- Wildlife 811
- Fisheries and fishing 811
- Regulation of natural resources 811
- Raw materials 812

Control of internal finance 812

List of Abbreviations

Accept UN Charter	Unilateral declaration accepting UN Charter obligations
Admin Cooperation	Administrative Cooperation
African Coffee Org	African Coffee Organization
African Devel Bank	African Development Bank
African Insur Org	African Insurance Organization
African Tech Org	African Technical Organization
Afromalagasy Coffee	Afro-Malagasy Coffee Organization
Afromalagasy Org	Afro-Malagasy Organization
AID (Int Devel)	Agency for International Development
Allied Milit Occup	Allied Military Occupation
Anglo-Egypt Sudan	Anglo-Egyptian Sudan
Asian Devel Bank	Asian Development Bank
Asian Productivity	Asian Productivity Organization
Bel-Lux Econ Union	Belgium-Luxembourg Economic Union
BENELUX Econ Union	Belgium-Netherlands-Luxembourg Economic Union
Bnk Int Settlement	Bank for International Settlements
British Occup Germ	British Occupied Germany
Brit Solomon Is	British Solomon Islands
Brit Virgin Is	British Virgin Islands
Central Afri Power	Central African Power Company
Central Afri Rep	Central African Republic
Central Am Bank	Central American Bank
CERN (Nuc Resrch)	European Organization for Nuclear Research
China People's Rep	People's Republic of China
Cmte Industr Devel	Committee for Industrial Development
COMECON (Econ Aid)	Council for Mutual Economic Assistance
Consul/Citizenship	Consular Matters and Citizenship
Customs Coop Coun	Customs Cooperation Council
East Afri Service	East African Common Services Organization
ECSC (Coal/Steel)	European Coal and Steel Community
EEC (Econ Commnty)	European Economic Community
EFTA (Free Trade)	European Free Trade Association
EURATOM	European Atomic Energy Commission
Eur Foot Mouth Dis	European Commission for the Control of Foot and Mouth Disease
EUROCONTROL	European Organization for the Safety of Air Navigation
Eur Plant Protect	European and Mediterranean Plant Protection Organization
Eur Space Research	European Space Research Organization
Eur Space Vehicle	European Space Vehicle Launcher Development Organization
FAO (Food Agri)	Food and Agricultural Organization of the United Nations
Fed Malay States	Federation of Malay States
Fed of Malaya	Federation of Malaya
Fed Rhod/Nyasaland	Federation of Rhodesia and Nyasaland
French Occup Germ	French Occupied Germany
Fr Equatorial Afri	French Equatorial Africa
GATT (Tariff/Trade)	General Agreement on Tariffs and Trade
Gen Communications	General Communications
General HEW	General Health, Education and Welfare

General IGO	General Intergovernmental Organizations
Hague Private IL	The Hague Conference on Private International Law
IAEA (Atom Energy)	International Atomic Energy Agency
IBRD Project	International Bank for Reconstruction and Development Project
IBRD (World Bank)	International Bank for Reconstruction and Development
ICAO (Civil Aviat)	International Civil Aviation Organization
ICJ (Int Court)	International Court of Justice
ICJ Option Clause	International Court of Justice Optional Clause Unilateral declaration accepting ICJ optional clause, or Unilateral declaration regarding UN General Assembly in connection with ICJ optional clause, or Unilateral limited declaration regarding ICJ optional clause
IDA (Devel Assoc)	International Development Association
IFC (Finance Corp)	International Finance Corporation
IGO Establishment	Intergovernmental Organization Establishment
IGO Multilat	Three or more IGO's and no State
IGO Operations	Intergovernmental Organization Operations
IGO Status/Immunit	Intergovernmental Organizational Privileges and Immunities
ILO Labor	International Labour Organization Labor Matters
ILO (Labor Org)	International Labour Organization
IMCO (Maritime Org)	Inter-Governmental Maritime Consultative Organization
IMF (Fund)	International Monetary Fund
Indo-Pac Fish Coun	Indo-Pacific Fisheries Council
Int Bureau Educ	International Bureau of Education
Int Coffee Org	International Coffee Organization
Int Coun Expl Sea	International Council for the Exploration of the Sea
Inter-Allied Com	Inter-Allied Commission
Inter-Am Devel Bnk	Inter-American Development Bank
Inter-Am Nuc Energ	Inter-American Nuclear Energy Commission
Int Exhibit Bureau	International Exhibition Bureau
Intgov Eur Migrat	Intergovernmental Committee for European Migration
Int Org Metrology	International Organization of Legal Metrology
Int Rail Transport	Central Office for International Railway Transport
Int Relief Union	International Relief Union
Int Rice Com	International Rice Commission
Int Sugar Council	International Sugar Council
Int Whaling Com	International Whaling Commission
Int Wheat Coun	International Wheat Council
Int Wine Office	International Vine and Wine Office
IRO (Refugee Org)	International Refugees Organization
It Aegean Colonies	Italian Colonies in the Aegean
ITU (Telecommun)	International Telecommunication Union
LAFTA (Free Trade)	Latin American Free Trade Association
Lat Am Nuclear Arm	Agency for the Prohibition of Nuclear Weapons in Latin America
Medit Fish Council	Mediterranean Fisheries Council
Micronesia (US)	Micronesia (US Trust Territories in the Pacific)
Milit Assistance	Military Assistance
Milit Installation	Military Installations
Milit Occupation	Military Occupation
Milit Servic/Citiz	Military Service and Citizenship
Mostfavored Nation	Most Favored Nation
NATO (North Atlan)	North Atlantic Treaty Organization
NE Atlantic Fish	Northeast Atlantic Fisheries Commission
Netherld Antilles	Netherlands Antilles
New Hebrides Is	New Hebrides Islands
Non-IBRD Project	Non-International Bank for Reconstruction and Development Project
Non-ILO Labor	Non-International Labour Organization Labor Matters
Northern Territ	Northern Territories
NW Atlantic Fish	International Commission for the Northwest Atlantic Fisheries
OAS (Am States)	Organization of American States
OAU (Afri Unity)	Organization of African Unity
OECD (Econ Coop)	Organization for Economic Co-operation and Development
Org Ctrl Am States	Organization of Central American States
Org Rail Collabor	Soviet Railroad Organization
Other HEW	Other Health, Education and Welfare
Other Party Combin	More than one State and more than one IGO, or Other combination of parties

Other Unilat Decla	Other unilateral declaration
Pan Am Health Org	Pan American Health Organization
Patents/Copyrights	Patents and Copyrights
Peace/Disarmament	Peace and Disarmament
Petrol Export Org	Organization of Petroleum Exporting Countries
Portug Colonies	Portuguese Colonies
Portug East Africa	Portuguese East Africa
Portug West Africa	Portuguese West Africa
Privil/Immunities	Privileges and Immunities
Refrigeration Inst	International Institute for Refrigeration
Rhine Navigation	Central Commission for the Navigation of the Rhine
Russ Fed Sov Rep	Russian Federation of Soviet Republics
Scientific Project	Scientific Projects
SEATO (SE Asia)	Southeast Asia Treaty Organization
Serb/Croat/Slovene	The Kingdom of the Serbs, Croats and Slovenes
South Africa	Union of South Africa
South Pacific Com	South Pacific Commission
Spanish Colonies	Spanish Colonies in Africa
Special Decla ICJ	Unilateral special declaration regarding ICJ
Specif Claim/Waive	Specific Claims and Waivers
Specif Goods/Equip	Specific Goods and Equipment
State/IGO Group	One State and mixed group of IGO-State partners, or One State and three or more IGO's, or One State and two IGO's, or Two or more States and one IGO
States Multilat	Three or more military governments and one State, or Three or more States and no IGO, or Three or more States under FAO auspices, or Three or more States under IAEA auspices, or Three or more States under ILO auspices, or Three or more States under UN auspices, or Three or more States under UNESCO auspices, or Three or more States under WHO auspices
Subsahara Tech Com	Commission for Technical Cooperation in Africa South of the Sahara
Tech Assistance	Technical Assistance
Trinidad/Tobago	Trinidad and Tobago
Turk-Caicose Is	Turk-Caicose Islands
UK Great Britain	United Kingdom of Great Britain and Northern Ireland
Ukrainian SSR	Ukrainian Soviet Socialist Republic
UN Charter	United Nations Charter
UN Emergency Fund	United Nations Emergency Fund
UNESCO (Educ/Cult)	United Nations Scientific and Cultural Organization
UN Hi Com Refugees	Office of the United Nations High Commissioner for Refugees
UNICEF (Children)	United Nations Children's Fund
UNIDO (Industrial)	United Nations Industrial Development Organization
United Arab Rep	United Arab Republic
UNKRA (Korean Rec)	United Nations Commission for the Unification and Rehabilitation of Korea
UN Mission Congo	United Nations Mission to the Congo
UN Relief Palestin	United Nations Relief and Works Agency for Palestine Refugees in the Near East
UNRRA (Relief)	United Nations Relief and Rehabilitation Association
UN Special Fund	United Nations Special Fund
UNTAB (Tech Assis)	United Nations Technical Assistance Board
UPU (Postal Union)	Universal Postal Union
US Agri Commod Aid	US Agricultural Commodity Aid
USA (United States)	United States of America
US Occup Germ	United States Occupied Germany
USSR (Soviet Union)	Union of Soviet Socialist Republics
Vatican/Holy See	The Vatican and the Holy See
WEU (West Europe)	Western European Union
WHO (World Health)	World Health Organization
WMO (Meteorology)	World Meteorological Organization
W Pacif Hi Command	West Pacific High Command

TOPIC SECTION

User's Guide

This is one of the five specialized sections of the INDEX. Each specialized section lists treaties in a different order: (1) by date of signature, (2) by party, (3) by international organizations mentioned in the treaty text, (4) by the topical categories of the UNTS Index and (5) by the topical categories of this INDEX.

Within each section there is a standard set of information per treaty: (1) parties, (2) date of signature, (3) topic, (4) citation and (5) treaty number.

In many cases a user will satisfy a query within one of the five specialized sections and will not need to go to the Main Entry Section (Volumes 1–3). It is for limited use of this kind that the present USER'S GUIDE has been designed. However, if the user is unfamiliar with the general format and search techniques of this INDEX, or if the search involves more than one specialized section, it is advisable to consult the Introduction in Volume 1.

Sample of Topic Section

PARTY ONE	PARTY TWO	DATE	CITATION	NUMBER
Change of circumstances				
Ethiopia	USA (United States)	26 Dec 57	307UNTS71	104443
Israel	Yugoslavia	11 Dec 58	386UNTS283	105548
Treaty interpretation				
Greece	ran	09 Jan 31	166UNTS323	200496
Taiwan	Dominican Republic	11 May 40	10UNTS285	200067
Ecuador	USA (United States)	02 Mar 42	105UNTS195	200332
Treaty violation				
Sweden	USA (United States)	22 Oct 63	530UNTS247	107686
Multilateral		03 Dec 63	529UNTS217	107663
Multilateral		04 Dec 65	571UNTS123	108303
Previous treaty extension				
USA (United States)	USSR (Soviet Union)	02 Aug 41	102UNTS269	200306
Colombia	USA (United States)	19 Feb 42	117UNTS185	200369
Guatemala	USA (United States)	21 Jul 42	103UNTS299	200320

Key Item. This section is ordered according to the topical categories of the INDEX. These topics are *not* in alphabetical order but are grouped together by substantive affinities, as shown in the above sample. All users, even including treaty experts, should first consult the full description of the Topic Section in the Introduction in Volume 1 for an overview of the hierarchical system and a list of topics.

Party One. In case of a bilateral treaty this column identifies one of the two parties. In case of a multilateral treaty it shows the word "Multilateral."

Party Two. In case of a bilateral treaty this column identifies the other of the two parties. In a multilateral treaty it remains blank.

Date. This column identifies the date of signature. Other dates (ratification, force, registration, accession, etc.) can be found in the Main Entry Section. Multiple dates of signature are represented only by the most recent date.

Citation. This column identifies the printed source where the full text of the treaty can be found. For details on abbreviations see Volume 1, Introduction, Thesaurus, Sources and Citations.

Treaty Number. This column identifies the serial number of each treaty under which it is listed in the Main Entry Section. See that location for all further information on any treaty.

League of Nations Treaty Series

PARTY ONE	PARTY TWO	DATE	CITATION	NUMBER
Change of circumstances				
France	UK Great Britain	09 Jul 21	6LTS341	300166
Romania	Yugoslavia	14 Dec 31	135LTS99	303106
Multilateral		23 Nov 33	192LTS389	304484
United Arab Rep	UK Great Britain	26 Aug 36	173LTS401	304031
Multilateral		23 Sep 37	190LTS299	304427
Default remedies				
Germany	Switzerland	15 Jul 31	144LTS389	303341
Belgium	France	23 Dec 31	137LTS277	303162
Treaty interpretation				
Poland	USSR (Soviet Union)	12 Oct 20	4LTS7	300101
Germany	Poland	03 Jun 22	9LTS465	300271
Czechoslovakia	Germany	02 May 23	31LTS0	300793
Germany	Lithuania	31 May 23	51LTS381	301243
Multilateral		24 Jul 23	36LTS179	300919
Turkey	USA (United States)	06 Aug 23	153LTS71	303509
Multilateral		17 Jan 25	38LTS357	300991
Czechoslovakia	Poland	23 Apr 25	48LTS383	301171
Norway	Switzerland	21 Aug 25	51LTS89	301224
Germany	USSR (Soviet Union)	12 Oct 25	53LTS7	301257
Norway	Sweden	23 Oct 25	39LTS153	301000
Norway	Sweden	25 Nov 25	60LTS295	301417
Czechoslovakia	Sweden	02 Jan 26	48LTS173	301159
Denmark	Norway	15 Jan 26	60LTS311	301418
Finland	Norway	03 Feb 26	60LTS353	301420
Romania	Switzerland	03 Feb 26	55LTS91	301306
Austria	Czechoslovakia	05 Mar 26	51LTS349	301240
Austria	Poland	16 Apr 26	62LTS329	301471
Spain	Switzerland	20 Apr 26	60LTS23	301403
Belgium	Sweden	30 Apr 26	67LTS91	301540
Italy	Spain	07 Aug 26	67LTS365	301558
Poland	Serb/Croat/Slovene	18 Sep 26	78LTS419	301800
Lithuania	USSR (Soviet Union)	28 Sep 26	60LTS145	301410
China	Finland	29 Oct 26	67LTS345	301556
Denmark	Germany	23 Feb 27	61LTS325	301444
Chile	France	24 Feb 27	69LTS277	301610
Belgium	Finland	04 Mar 27	69LTS361	301618
Belgium	Denmark	13 Mar 27	67LTS117	301542
Belgium	Portugal	09 Jul 27	74LTS39	301730
Finland	Switzerland	16 Nov 27	77LTS93	301765
Spain	Sweden	26 Apr 28	77LTS77	301764
Finland	Spain	31 May 28	82LTS229	301874

PARTY ONE	PARTY TWO	DATE	CITATION	NUMBER
Treaty interpretation (Cont.)				
Multilateral		27 Jul 29	118LTS343	302734
Canada	Germany	17 Jan 30	109LTS473	302550
Multilateral		20 Jan 30	112LTS361	302622
Greece	Spain	23 Jan 30	139LTS93	303205
Finland	France	28 Apr 30	139LTS381	303222
Belgium	Lithuania	24 Sep 30	129LTS399	302974
Greece	Turkey	30 Oct 30	125LTS9	302841
Austria	Hungary	26 Jan 31	123LTS171	302814
Netherlands	Spain	30 Mar 31	137LTS161	303153
Belgium	Bulgaria	23 Jun 31	137LTS191	303156
Afghanistan	USSR (Soviet Union)	24 Jun 31	157LTS371	303611
Bulgaria	Norway	26 Nov 31	134LTS27	303081
Greece	Poland	04 Jan 32	131LTS229	303014
Denmark	Turkey	08 Mar 32	143LTS223	303310
Netherlands	Turkey	16 Apr 32	143LTS237	303311
Norway	Turkey	16 Jan 33	161LTS173	303710
Netherlands	Yemen	12 Mar 33	146LTS359	303384
Netherlands	Norway	23 Mar 33	146LTS291	303380
Denmark	Greece	13 Apr 33	150LTS465	303478
Multilateral		11 Oct 33	150LTS431	303476
Turkey	Yugoslavia	27 Nov 33	161LTS229	303715
Multilateral		17 Mar 34	154LTS281	303554
Estonia	Latvia	14 Nov 35	166LTS83	303832
France	India	01 May 36	178LTS57	304107
France	Spain	10 Jul 39	148LTS369	303423
UK Great Britain	USA (United States)	27 Mar 41	204LTS15	304784
Treaty violation				
Bel-Lux Econ Union	Greece	22 Nov 27	69LTS341	301616
Multilateral		23 Dec 36	195LTS229	304548
Previous treaty extension				
Multilateral		12 Jan 12	4LTS281	300112
Multilateral		10 Sep 19	2LTS44	300045
Multilateral		10 Sep 19	2LTS29	300043
Muscat and Oman	UK Great Britain	11 Feb 20	5LTS59	300118
Germany	Switzerland	15 Mar 20	12LTS19	300303
Portugal	USA (United States)	14 Sep 20	7LTS253	300191
France	Netherlands	16 Sep 20	12LTS213	300312
Norway	Portugal	14 Oct 20	2LTS237	300069
Germany	UK Great Britain	31 Dec 20	8LTS241	300223
Belgium	Sweden	03 Jan 21	2LTS301	300083
Portugal	UK Great Britain	10 Jan 21	7LTS271	300194
Hungary	Switzerland	22 Mar 21	7LTS235	300189

Previous treaty extension (Cont.)

PARTY ONE	PARTY TWO	DATE	CITATION	NUMBER
Italy	Sweden	04 Jun 21	6LTS47	300148
Muscat and Oman	UK Great Britain	11 Feb 22	10LTS459	300285
Netherlands	Romania	20 Feb 22	12LTS219	300313
Iceland	UK Great Britain	01 May 22	12LTS15	300302
Denmark	UK Great Britain	01 May 22	12LTS11	300301
Norway	Spain	12 Jun 22	10LTS305	300276
Muscat and Oman	UK Great Britain	11 Feb 23	17LTS163	300433
Czechoslovakia	Romania	07 May 23	18LTS81	300455
France	USA (United States)	19 Jul 23	25LTS405	300630
Austria	USSR (Soviet Union)	08 Sep 23	20LTS153	300515
France	UK Great Britain	13 Nov 23	21LTS131	300535
Norway	USA (United States)	26 Nov 23	23LTS249	300592
Multilateral		23 Oct 24	77LTS367	301778
UK Great Britain	USA (United States)	10 Feb 25	55LTS119	301309
UK Great Britain	USA (United States)	10 Feb 25	55LTS133	301310
UK Great Britain	USA (United States)	10 Feb 25	55LTS145	301311
Muscat and Oman	UK Great Britain	11 Feb 25	35LTS233	300897
Norway	UK Great Britain	13 May 25	36LTS435	300940
Netherlands	UK Great Britain	12 Jul 25	38LTS207	300977
Great Britain	Portugal	29 Aug 25	38LTS213	300978
Czechoslovakia	Switzerland	30 Sep 25	58LTS279	301378
Norway	Sweden	23 Oct 25	39LTS153	301000
Germany	Netherlands	26 Nov 25	57LTS159	301362
Italy	UK Great Britain	20 Dec 25	50LTS281	301211
Great Britain	Iraq	13 Jan 26	47LTS419	301147
Great Britain	Muscat and Oman	11 Feb 26	57LTS13	301347
Multilateral		24 Apr 26	108LTS123	302505
Czechoslovakia	Italy	04 May 26	61LTS257	301438
Czechoslovakia	Romania	13 Jun 26	54LTS253	301288
Denmark	Switzerland	25 Aug 26	69LTS313	301613
Muscat and Oman	UK Great Britain	11 Feb 27	64LTS398	301512
Indochina	Siam	14 Jul 27	69LTS327	301614
Multilateral		18 Feb 28	132LTS275	303044
Japan	UK Great Britain	20 Aug 29	107LTS243	302481
Multilateral		17 Apr 30	126LTS201	302883
Afghanistan	UK Great Britain	06 May 30	105LTS265	302418
Portugal	UK Great Britain	14 Jun 30	107LTS275	302484
Belgium	France	23 Dec 31	137LTS277	303162
Czechoslovakia	Denmark	04 Jul 32	143LTS251	303312
Estonia	Latvia	14 Nov 32	136LTS295	303132
Austria	Hungary	21 Dec 32	169LTS161	303919
France	Hungary	03 Mar 33	140LTS177	303235
Romania	Yugoslavia	11 Mar 33	146LTS277	303378
Estonia	France	27 Apr 33	141LTS43	303260
Bel-Lux Econ Union	Poland	10 Jun 33	144LTS137	303324
Latvia	UK Great Britain	06 Jul 33	142LTS217	303294
Estonia	France	27 Jul 33	141LTS65	303261
Latvia	USSR (Soviet Union)	04 Dec 33	148LTS177	303411
Bulgaria	Turkey	21 Dec 33	148LTS9	303401
Sweden	USA (United States)	17 May 34	150LTS375	303470
Turkey	UK Great Britain	04 Jun 35	167LTS91	303860
Czechoslovakia	Germany	30 Dec 35	173LTS333	304023
Norway	Poland	14 Mar 36	171LTS371	303973
Romania	UK Great Britain	02 May 36	184LTS145	304247
Poland	Sweden	03 Jul 36	171LTS307	303968
Finland	Poland	16 Jul 36	172LTS143	303984
Brazil	Hungary	30 Jul 36	177LTS53	304079
Turkey	UK Great Britain	02 Sep 36	172LTS289	303998
Germany	Netherlands	23 Dec 36	179LTS359	304163
Multilateral		23 Dec 36	195LTS229	304548
Siam	Sweden	05 Nov 37	182LTS257	304215
Bel-Lux Econ Union	Estonia	13 Jan 38	185LTS63	304275
Italy	UK Great Britain	18 Mar 38	187LTS139	304334
Portugal	UK Great Britain	11 May 38	191LTS285	304450
Romania	UK Great Britain	11 May 39	196LTS351	304594

Previous treaty replacement

PARTY ONE	PARTY TWO	DATE	CITATION	NUMBER
Multilateral		13 Nov 08	1LTS217	300015
Germany	UK Great Britain	25 Jun 20	5LTS303	300135
Austria	UK Great Britain	22 Sep 20	5LTS309	300136
France	UK Great Britain	29 Sep 23	21LTS137	300536
Multilateral		18 Dec 23	28LTS541	300729
Japan	Mexico	08 Oct 24	36LTS259	300927
Czechoslovakia	Italy	15 Nov 24	92LTS91	302081
France	Germany	13 Apr 25	109LTS295	302546
France	Germany	14 Aug 25	75LTS103	301756
Germany	Switzerland	12 Oct 25	53LTS241	301260
Norway	Sweden	25 Nov 25	60LTS295	301417
Siam	Sweden	19 Dec 25	58LTS429	301386
Denmark	Sweden	14 Jan 26	51LTS251	301235
Denmark	Norway	15 Jan 26	60LTS311	301418
Belgium	Sweden	30 Apr 26	67LTS91	301540
Serb/Croat/Slovene	UK Great Britain	18 Jun 26	57LTS23	301349
Denmark	France	05 Jul 26	71LTS455	301684
Germany	Switzerland	14 Jul 26	59LTS87	301391
Denmark	Switzerland	25 Aug 26	69LTS313	301613
Belgium	Denmark	13 Mar 27	67LTS117	301542
France	Norway	12 Apr 27	178LTS199	304114
Belgium	Spain	19 Jul 27	80LTS17	301820
France	USA (United States)	06 Feb 28	91LTS323	302072
France	Netherlands	10 Mar 28	102LTS109	302356
Germany	Italy	23 Mar 28	93LTS165	302108
Spain	Sweden	26 Apr 28	77LTS77	301764
Belgium	Luxembourg	26 Apr 28	93LTS159	302107
Czechoslovakia	France	07 May 28	114LTS171	302663
Belgium	Luxembourg	18 May 28	89LTS207	302015
Mexico	UK Great Britain	24 Oct 28	87LTS63	301962
Norway	Spain	27 Dec 28	97LTS339	302231
Portugal	USA (United States)	01 Mar 29	99LTS375	302282
France	Germany	25 Apr 29	109LTS333	302548
UK Great Britain	USA (United States)	04 Jul 29	92LTS329	302099
Greece	Sweden	18 Oct 29	95LTS201	302174
Poland	Romania	30 Oct 29	121LTS167	302787
Austria	Germany	12 Apr 30	115LTS277	302692
Finland	Norway	14 May 30	105LTS399	302429
Denmark	Finland	14 May 30	105LTS455	302433
Finland	Sweden	14 May 30	106LTS9	302434
China	France	16 May 30	162LTS99	303738
France	Italy	03 Jun 30	153LTS135	303513
Iceland	Sweden	27 Jun 30	127LTS67	302907
Iraq	UK Great Britain	30 Jun 30	132LTS363	303048
Belgium	Romania	08 Jul 30	128LTS403	302944
Norway	Portugal	26 Jul 30	134LTS123	303087
Netherlands	UK Great Britain	01 Jan 31	115LTS509	302698
Estonia	Latvia	28 Feb 31	114LTS379	302667
Iraq	UK Great Britain	04 Mar 31	123LTS77	302807
Poland	Turkey	29 Aug 31	144LTS367	303339
UK Great Britain	Yugoslavia	23 Oct 31	126LTS209	302884
Sweden	USA (United States)	11 Jul 32	192LTS205	304473
France	Yugoslavia	29 Jul 32	144LTS313	303334
Multilateral		13 Dec 32	139LTS189	303210
Denmark	Sweden	31 Dec 32	139LTS205	303211
Multilateral		16 Feb 33	139LTS233	303213
Cuba	USA (United States)	29 May 34	150LTS95	303456
Hungary	Italy	18 Nov 34	166LTS263	303842
Belgium	France	09 May 35	162LTS437	303755
Denmark	Germany	25 May 35	159LTS389	303680
France	UK Great Britain	16 Jul 35	168LTS179	303898
Colombia	USA (United States)	13 Sep 35	170LTS293	303944
Netherlands	UK Great Britain	07 Nov 35	165LTS337	303820
Honduras	USA (United States)	18 Dec 35	167LTS313	303876

PARTY ONE	PARTY TWO	DATE	CITATION	NUMBER
Previous treaty replacement (Cont.)				
Germany	Sweden	31 Jan 36	168LTS13	303883
Germany	Sweden	31 Jan 36	168LTS19	303884
Panama	USA (United States)	02 Mar 36	200LTS17	304686
Nicaragua	USA (United States)	11 Mar 36	173LTS141	304009
Netherlands	Poland	09 Apr 36	177LTS71	304081
Guatemala	USA (United States)	24 Apr 36	170LTS345	303945
Sweden	UK Great Britain	30 Apr 36	168LTS121	303892
Brazil	Czechoslovakia	22 Jul 36	188LTS275	304363
United Arab Rep	UK Great Britain	26 Aug 36	173LTS401	304031
Australia	Bel-Lux Econ Union	03 Oct 36	177LTS271	304094
Bulgaria	Finland	27 Oct 36	179LTS309	304158
Brazil	USA (United States)	12 Nov 36	176LTS133	304057
Germany	UK Great Britain	02 Dec 36	178LTS329	304121
Estonia	Finland	18 Dec 36	178LTS41	304105
Bahamas	USA (United States)	21 Dec 36	176LTS411	304077
Chile	Netherlands	30 Dec 36	177LTS87	304082
Italy	Netherlands	01 Jan 37	178LTS415	304124
Gibralter	USA (United States)	05 Jan 37	177LTS21	304078
Multilateral		11 Feb 37	186LTS55	304303
Netherlands	Turkey	17 Feb 37	182LTS221	304213
Germany	Norway	27 Feb 37	178LTS427	304125
Brazil	Netherlands	15 Mar 37	179LTS395	304166
Finland	UK Great Britain	14 Apr 37	179LTS289	304155
Chile	Netherlands	05 May 37	182LTS385	304223
Czechoslovakia	Italy	10 May 37	190LTS397	304430
UK Great Britain		07 Jun 37	185LTS185	304282
Belgium	France	07 Jul 37	181LTS111	304182
Bel-Lux Econ Union	South Africa	13 Jul 37	182LTS247	304214
France	Luxembourg	30 Jul 37	181LTS107	304181
Netherlands	USA (United States)	20 Sep 37	184LTS319	304256
Estonia	France	16 Oct 37	183LTS41	304227
Estonia	France	16 Oct 37	183LTS37	304226
Bel-Lux Econ Union	Siam	05 Nov 37	190LTS151	304413
Siam	USA (United States)	13 Nov 37	192LTS247	304476
Norway	Siam	15 Nov 37	186LTS9	304301
Siam	UK Great Britain	23 Nov 37	188LTS333	304366
Bel-Lux Econ Union	Yugoslavia	26 Nov 37	196LTS19	304567
Italy	Siam	03 Dec 37	189LTS255	304389
France	Siam	07 Dec 37	201LTS113	304708
Italy	USA (United States)	16 Dec 37	187LTS15	304329
Bel-Lux Econ Union	Estonia	13 Jan 38	185LTS63	304275
France	Switzerland	31 Jan 38	195LTS313	304553
Chile	USA (United States)	01 Feb 38	190LTS9	304401
Netherlands	Siam	01 Feb 38	193LTS13	304485
Multilateral		10 Feb 38	192LTS59	304461
Greece	Norway	28 Feb 38	186LTS165	304309
Czechoslovakia	USA (United States)	07 Mar 38	200LTS87	304687
Italy	UK Great Britain	18 Mar 38	187LTS139	304334
Portugal	UK Great Britain	11 May 38	191LTS285	304450
Japan	USA (United States)	20 Jun 38	191LTS43	304434
France	Morocco	21 Jun 38	189LTS423	304398
Italy	Norway	21 Jun 38	190LTS193	304417
Canada	USA (United States)	28 Jul 38	192LTS125	304466
Belgium	UK Great Britain	29 Jul 38	201LTS317	304722
Ecuador	USA (United States)	06 Aug 38	193LTS85	304489
Romania	UK Great Britain	02 Sep 38	191LTS313	304453
British Guiana	USA (United States)	06 Sep 38	193LTS117	304490
Germany	UK Great Britain	10 Sep 38	194LTS313	304528
Netherlands	Romania	10 Oct 38	195LTS9	304532
Germany	Sweden	28 Oct 38	196LTS81	304570
Brazil	USA (United States)	12 Nov 38	195LTS375	304557
Greece	USA (United States)	15 Nov 38	195LTS145	304544
Canada	USA (United States)	17 Nov 38	199LTS91	304670
Iraq	USA (United States)	03 Dec 38	203LTS107	304753
Belgium	USA (United States)	15 Jan 39	199LTS321	304682

PARTY ONE	PARTY TWO	DATE	CITATION	NUMBER
Previous treaty replacement (Cont.)				
Chile	USA (United States)	24 Feb 39	197LTS217	304614
France	Norway	28 Feb 39	195LTS165	304546
Germany	USA (United States)	16 Mar 39	198LTS237	304645
Norway	Spain	26 Jul 39	198LTS87	304627
USA (United States)	Venezuela	06 Nov 39	203LTS273	304770
UK Great Britain	USSR (Soviet Union)	26 May 42	204LTS353	304813
Previous treaty renunciation				
Argentina	UK Great Britain	07 Apr 12	6LTS337	300165
Sweden	USA (United States)	29 Jun 20	2LTS153	300060
Norway	Spain	22 Nov 20	2LTS359	300089
Germany	Sweden	16 Dec 20	2LTS263	300072
Spain	Sweden	18 Dec 20	2LTS267	300073
Persia	USSR (Soviet Union)	26 Feb 21	9LTS383	300268
Multilateral		13 Mar 21	8LTS327	300232
Romania	UK Great Britain	21 Apr 21	8LTS293	300226
Brazil	UK Great Britain	16 Jul 21	10LTS407	300279
Argentina	UK Great Britain	29 Jul 21	8LTS315	300229
UK Great Britain	Uruguay	08 Aug 21	8LTS319	300230
Bolivia	UK Great Britain	11 Aug 21	8LTS323	300231
Colombia	UK Great Britain	27 Sep 21	10LTS417	300281
Portugal	UK Great Britain	04 Feb 22	9LTS187	300251
Chile	UK Great Britain	12 Apr 22	11LTS17	300287
Denmark	Germany	31 Mar 23	17LTS181	300436
Austria	Poland	13 Nov 23	34LTS399	300888
Multilateral		08 Jan 24	23LTS63	300576
China	USSR (Soviet Union)	31 May 24	37LTS175	300955
Italy	UK Great Britain	15 Jul 24	36LTS379	300936
Norway	Sweden	22 Dec 24	32LTS13	300802
Italy	Siam	09 May 26	61LTS215	301436
Bel-Lux Econ Union	Siam	13 Jul 26	62LTS287	301468
Norway	Siam	16 Jul 26	60LTS35	301404
Estonia	Latvia	05 Feb 27	62LTS319	301470
France	Norway	12 Apr 27	178LTS199	304114
Multilateral		19 May 27	68LTS407	301595
China	Denmark	12 Dec 28	91LTS207	302062
Denmark	Sweden	28 Feb 29	104LTS69	302379
Netherlands	USA (United States)	09 Jul 30	125LTS123	302851
Denmark	Estonia	16 Jan 31	112LTS215	302615
Austria	UK Great Britain	14 Jul 31	123LTS383	302824
Hungary	Italy	12 Nov 32	142LTS115	303283
France	India	28 Dec 32	140LTS36	303226
Bel-Lux Econ Union	Hungary	24 May 33	140LTS169	303234
Brazil	USA (United States)	02 Feb 35	166LTS211	303840
Germany	UK Great Britain	03 Jun 35	163LTS415	303782
France	India	04 Jan 36	170LTS97	303930
Germany	Netherlands	30 Jun 37	189LTS373	304395
France	UK Great Britain	29 Jul 37	184LTS351	304257
Bel-Lux Econ Union	Romania	24 Aug 37	193LTS189	304496
Multilateral		06 Sep 37	186LTS419	304326
France	Siam	09 Dec 37	201LTS145	304709
Germany	UK Great Britain	01 Jul 38	194LTS235	304525
Turkey	UK Great Britain	22 Nov 39	201LTS93	304705
Spain	UK Great Britain	18 Mar 40	203LTS157	304759
Romania	UK Great Britain	06 Jun 40	203LTS197	304761
Previous treaties adherence				
Czechoslovakia	France	20 Mar 20	3LTS139	300095
Netherlands	UK Great Britain	13 Apr 20	1LTS275	300021
Finland	Sweden	10 May 20	2LTS141	300058
Netherlands	Venezuela	11 May 20	7LTS85	300176
Greece	UK Great Britain	22 Sep 20	2LTS367	300090
Portugal	UK Great Britain	09 Dec 20	7LTS257	300192
Multilateral		19 Jan 21	5LTS9	300113
Czechoslovakia	Italy	23 Mar 21	32LTS183	300815
Norway	UK Great Britain	22 Apr 21	5LTS33	300114

PARTY ONE	PARTY TWO	DATE	CITATION	NUMBER
Previous treaties adherence (Cont.)				
Finland	France	13 Jul 21	29LTS445	300755
Denmark	UK Great Britain	14 Jul 21	6LTS181	300151
Austria	USA (United States)	24 Aug 21	7LTS155	300184
Germany	USA (United States)	25 Aug 21	12LTS191	300310
Italy	Switzerland	24 Sep 21	12LTS367	300330
Belgium	Netherlands	15 Oct 21	12LTS233	300315
Austria	Czechoslovakia	16 Dec 21	9LTS247	300257
Other Unilat Decla	Rhine Navigation	16 Dec 21	13LTS53	300347
Belgium	Luxembourg	27 Dec 21	12LTS253	300318
Czechoslovakia	Germany	31 Dec 21	17LTS401	300447
Estonia	France	07 Jan 22	62LTS9	301452
Multilateral		17 Mar 22	11LTS167	300296
Belgium	Switzerland	13 Jun 22	12LTS295	300321
Czechoslovakia	Serb/Croat/Slovene	31 Aug 22	13LTS231	300354
Austria	Poland	25 Sep 22	59LTS307	301400
France	UK Great Britain	26 Dec 22	16LTS213	300413
Germany	Switzerland	24 Mar 23	27LTS41	300666
Germany	Switzerland	25 Mar 23	18LTS273	300470
Persia	Russ Fed Sov Rep	25 Apr 23	110LTS323	302564
Persia	Russ Fed Sov Rep	27 Apr 23	110LTS333	302565
Multilateral		28 Apr 23	33LTS47	300832
Multilateral		03 May 23	33LTS81	300833
Austria	Denmark	30 Jun 23	18LTS189	300463
Austria	Denmark	30 Jun 23	18LTS195	300464
United Arab Rep	UK Great Britain	05 Jul 23	18LTS311	300473
Czechoslovakia	Hungary	13 Jul 23	36LTS41	300902
Czechoslovakia	Hungary	13 Jul 23	35LTS253	300899
Czechoslovakia	Hungary	13 Jul 23	36LTS13	300901
Multilateral		24 Jul 23	36LTS167	300917
Belgium	UK Great Britain	08 Aug 23	22LTS375	300566
Austria	Netherlands	05 Sep 23	20LTS147	300514
Other Unilat Decla	Greece	29 Sep 23	20LTS29	300503
Multilateral		28 Nov 23	51LTS215	301229
Multilateral		28 Nov 23	51LTS233	301232
Multilateral		28 Nov 23	51LTS221	301230
Multilateral		28 Nov 23	51LTS239	301233
Multilateral		09 Dec 23	36LTS76	300905
Multilateral		09 Dec 23	58LTS315	301380
Nepal	UK Great Britain	21 Dec 23	36LTS357	300934
Germany	UK Great Britain	05 Jan 24	36LTS365	300935
Belgium	USA (United States)	21 Jan 24	31LTS137	300791
Czechoslovakia	Italy	01 Mar 24	34LTS55	300867
Germany	Nicaragua	06 Mar 24	41LTS264	301019
Hungary	Italy	27 Mar 24	45LTS241	301102
Hungary	Italy	27 Mar 24	45LTS229	301101
Hungary	Italy	27 Mar 24	45LTS65	301099
Hungary	Romania	16 Apr 24	45LTS355	301109
Czechoslovakia	Iceland	08 May 24	46LTS419	301125
Austria	Greece	27 May 24	27LTS99	300671
Finland	Iceland	28 May 24	27LTS117	300676
China	USSR (Soviet Union)	31 May 24	37LTS193	300956
Denmark	Switzerland	06 Jun 24	34LTS175	300873
Denmark	USSR (Soviet Union)	18 Jun 24	27LTS149	300677
Hungary	Switzerland	18 Jun 24	34LTS387	300887
Spain	UK Great Britain	27 Jun 24	28LTS523	300727
Multilateral		04 Jul 24	51LTS227	301231
Austria	Germany	12 Jul 24	41LTS287	301022
Austria	Latvia	09 Aug 24	65LTS7	301516
Italy	Serb/Croat/Slovene	12 Aug 24	82LTS423	301882
Multilateral		25 Aug 24	120LTS123	302763
Austria	Switzerland	11 Oct 24	33LTS423	300862
Multilateral		12 Dec 24	37LTS113	300950
Latvia	Sweden	22 Dec 24	36LTS283	300928
Japan	USSR (Soviet Union)	20 Jan 25	34LTS31	300866
Hungary	Poland	26 Mar 25	37LTS151	300954

PARTY ONE	PARTY TWO	DATE	CITATION	NUMBER
Previous treaties adherence (Cont.)				
Czechoslovakia	Greece	08 Apr 25	38LTS291	300984
Czechoslovakia	Sweden	18 Apr 25	36LTS289	300929
Denmark	Germany	18 Apr 25	37LTS103	300949
Bulgaria	Poland	29 Apr 25	60LTS103	301408
Bulgaria	Great Britain	07 May 25	38LTS153	300973
Italy	Latvia	25 Jul 25	60LTS91	301407
Czechoslovakia	Switzerland	30 Sep 25	58LTS279	301378
Bulgaria	Czechoslovakia	16 Oct 25	56LTS265	301334
Portugal	UK Great Britain	03 Nov 25	47LTS379	301143
British Empire	Greece	26 Nov 25	63LTS167	301488
Siam	Sweden	19 Dec 25	58LTS429	301386
Bel-Lux Econ Union	Czechoslovakia	28 Dec 25	58LTS189	301372
Denmark	Siam	01 Mar 26	47LTS103	301131
Denmark	Turkey	22 Mar 26	48LTS231	301164
United Arab Rep	Greece	10 Apr 26	61LTS305	301441
Finland	Hungary	20 Apr 26	48LTS119	301154
Belgium	UK Great Britain	17 May 26	54LTS239	301287
Germany	Poland	21 Jun 26	72LTS203	301693
Finland	Germany	26 Jun 26	56LTS203	301332
Germany	Latvia	28 Jun 26	58LTS403	301385
Bel-Lux Econ Union	Siam	13 Jul 26	62LTS287	301468
Germany	Switzerland	14 Jul 26	59LTS87	301391
Austria	Netherlands	04 Aug 26	59LTS243	301394
Greece	Sweden	10 Sep 26	63LTS37	301479
Denmark	Turkey	19 Sep 26	56LTS259	301333
Bel-Lux Econ Union	Estonia	28 Sep 26	62LTS433	301475
Greece	Italy	24 Oct 26	63LTS51	301480
Germany	Netherlands	03 Nov 26	68LTS111	301575
Greece	Switzerland	29 Nov 26	63LTS27	301478
Multilateral		22 Jan 27	68LTS129	301576
Czechoslovakia	Germany	22 Jan 27	89LTS231	302019
Multilateral		22 Jan 27	68LTS149	301578
Austria	Czechoslovakia	15 Feb 27	73LTS349	301724
Czechoslovakia	Switzerland	16 Feb 27	64LTS7	301501
Multilateral		19 Feb 27	68LTS139	301577
Multilateral		24 Feb 27	68LTS159	301579
Belgium	Netherlands	28 Feb 27	68LTS169	301580
Multilateral		18 Mar 27	68LTS179	301581
Belgium	Netherlands	24 Mar 27	84LTS34	301902
Estonia	Germany	05 Apr 27	64LTS355	301508
Multilateral		02 May 27	68LTS189	301582
Greece	UK Great Britain	13 May 27	61LTS15	301425
Multilateral		10 Sep 27	75LTS7	301749
Denmark	Turkey	24 Sep 27	61LTS287	301439
Multilateral		26 Sep 27	92LTS301	302096
Persia	USSR (Soviet Union)	01 Oct 27	112LTS275	302620
Czechoslovakia	Portugal	23 Nov 27	123LTS403	302827
Siam	UK Great Britain	21 Feb 28	87LTS21	301960
Czechoslovakia	Germany	22 Mar 28	93LTS235	302113
Austria	Italy	11 May 28	100LTS375	302307
Finland	Sweden	10 Jul 28	87LTS131	301966
Germany	UK Great Britain	26 Jul 28	85LTS135	301928
Multilateral		12 Sep 28	104LTS43	302377
Multilateral		30 Nov 28	87LTS119	301965
Denmark	Sweden	13 Dec 28	104LTS55	302378
Multilateral		22 Dec 28	104LTS103	302381
Brazil	Peru	31 Dec 28	127LTS455	302931
Canada	USA (United States)	12 Jan 29	102LTS143	302359
Multilateral		14 Jan 29	87LTS169	301968
Multilateral		16 Jan 29	87LTS155	301967
Bolivia	UK Great Britain	18 Jan 29	95LTS9	302161
Multilateral		02 Feb 29	92LTS353	302100
Czechoslovakia	Germany	20 Mar 29	109LTS219	302541
Poland	Romania	30 Mar 29	123LTS147	302812
Multilateral		16 Apr 29	126LTS305	302891

PARTY ONE	PARTY TWO	DATE	CITATION	NUMBER
Previous treaties adherence (Cont.)				
Multilateral		08 May 29	91LTS337	302074
Mexico	Norway	14 Jun 29	99LTS381	302283
Multilateral		28 Jun 29	103LTS429	302374
Multilateral		28 Jun 29	103LTS377	302373
Multilateral		28 Jun 29	103LTS5	302369
Multilateral		28 Jun 29	103LTS71	302370
Multilateral		28 Jun 29	103LTS321	302372
Multilateral		28 Jun 29	103LTS249	302371
Belgium	Germany	13 Jul 29	104LTS211	302391
Persia	USSR (Soviet Union)	02 Aug 29	109LTS99	302530
Multilateral		30 Aug 29	96LTS129	302195
Multilateral		07 Sep 29	98LTS345	302255
Multilateral		25 Sep 29	98LTS361	302256
Multilateral		26 Sep 29	98LTS395	302259
Multilateral		30 Sep 29	99LTS71	302269
Multilateral		30 Sep 29	98LTS183	302246
Multilateral		01 Oct 29	98LTS197	302247
Poland	UK Great Britain	04 Oct 29	97LTS261	302227
Multilateral		08 Oct 29	98LTS409	302260
Multilateral		10 Oct 29	98LTS375	302257
Multilateral		28 Oct 29	97LTS71	302219
Multilateral		29 Oct 29	99LTS85	302270
Poland	Romania	30 Oct 29	121LTS243	302790
Multilateral		18 Nov 29	99LTS415	302287
Switzerland	UK Great Britain	10 Dec 29	99LTS53	302267
Austria	Netherlands	31 Dec 29	111LTS177	302586
UK Great Britain	USA (United States)	02 Jan 30	137LTS297	303164
Multilateral		14 Jan 30	99LTS343	302278
Multilateral		25 Feb 30	101LTS343	302335
Brazil	UK Great Britain	18 Mar 30	101LTS401	302339
France	UK Great Britain	24 Mar 30	105LTS227	302415
Romania	UK Great Britain	02 Apr 30	105LTS235	302416
Multilateral		10 Apr 30	101LTS465	302345
Multilateral		12 Apr 30	179LTS89	304137
Multilateral		12 Apr 30	179LTS115	304138
Canada	USA (United States)	09 May 30	121LTS45	302782
Poland	Romania	09 May 30	112LTS225	302617
Germany	Irish Free State	12 May 30	131LTS153	303008
Belgium	France	23 May 30	119LTS33	302738
Chile	USA (United States)	27 May 30	133LTS141	303064
Austria	Hungary	03 Jun 30	122LTS69	302799
Finland	Iceland	27 Jun 30	167LTS271	303873
France	Poland	02 Aug 30	114LTS93	302657
Poland	Portugal	27 Aug 30	115LTS127	302682
Denmark	India	16 Dec 30	114LTS73	302656
Czechoslovakia	Romania	22 Dec 30	167LTS243	303870
Norway	Turkey	16 Mar 31	138LTS41	303180
Multilateral		19 Mar 31	143LTS407	303317
Bulgaria	Poland	07 Apr 31	127LTS45	302905
Portugal	South Africa	29 Apr 31	129LTS157	302960
Multilateral		06 May 31	120LTS217	302767
Germany	Netherlands	11 Jun 31	120LTS413	302778
Bulgaria	Spain	26 Jun 31	166LTS341	303850
Italy	Netherlands	01 Jul 31	127LTS235	302923
Denmark	Iceland	11 Jul 31	141LTS323	303273
Netherlands	Yugoslavia	15 Jul 31	127LTS337	302927
Netherlands	Sweden	15 Jul 31	127LTS321	302925
Denmark	Netherlands	15 Jul 31	127LTS329	302926
Germany	Hungary	18 Jul 31	150LTS111	303458
Czechoslovakia	Netherlands	11 Aug 31	127LTS347	302928
Hungary	Romania	12 Aug 31	186LTS325	304321
Chile	USA (United States)	28 Sep 31	144LTS147	303325
Romania	Sweden	07 Oct 31	131LTS51	303003
Hungary	Poland	04 Nov 31	134LTS199	303092
Romania	Yugoslavia	14 Dec 31	135LTS99	303106

PARTY ONE	PARTY TWO	DATE	CITATION	NUMBER
Previous treaties adherence (Cont.)				
Denmark	USA (United States)	16 Jan 32	127LTS127	302913
Iceland	USA (United States)	16 Jan 32	127LTS135	302914
Brazil	Poland	03 Feb 32	147LTS113	303396
Bulgaria	Germany	24 Jun 32	147LTS211	303400
Hungary	Italy	12 Nov 32	142LTS87	303279
Hungary	Italy	12 Nov 32	142LTS115	303283
Hungary	Italy	12 Nov 32	142LTS109	303282
Panama	USA (United States)	17 Dec 32	138LTS119	303183
Romania	Yugoslavia	10 Feb 33	174LTS115	304042
Romania	Yugoslavia	10 Mar 33	146LTS245	303374
Romania	Yugoslavia	10 Mar 33	146LTS263	303376
France	Sweden	13 Mar 33	142LTS131	303285
Denmark	UK Great Britain	24 Apr 33	139LTS127	303208
Argentina	UK Great Britain	01 May 33	143LTS67	303305
Hungary	Yugoslavia	15 May 33	144LTS321	303335
Sweden	UK Great Britain	15 May 33	140LTS317	303245
Norway	UK Great Britain	15 May 33	145LTS187	303355
Iceland	UK Great Britain	19 May 33	144LTS33	303319
Multilateral		29 May 33	192LTS289	304479
Bulgaria	Czechoslovakia	29 Aug 33	148LTS15	303402
Finland	UK Great Britain	29 Sep 33	149LTS167	303438
Poland	Sweden	21 Oct 33	150LTS73	303454
Czechoslovakia	Poland	10 Feb 34	183LTS213	304238
Mexico	USA (United States)	24 Apr 34	149LTS49	303433
Spain	Turkey	19 May 34	149LTS15	303428
Bel-Lux Econ Union	Turkey	31 May 34	150LTS289	303462
Germany	Netherlands	06 Jun 34	174LTS33	304034
Czechoslovakia	Hungary	08 Jun 34	172LTS61	303979
Multilateral		09 Apr 35	163LTS177	303766
Norway	Venezuela	13 May 35	167LTS407	303882
Germany	Iraq	04 Aug 35	171LTS65	303951
Iran	USSR (Soviet Union)	27 Aug 35	176LTS299	304069
Colombia	USA (United States)	13 Sep 35	170LTS293	303944
Belgium	France	30 Dec 35	166LTS25	303826
Sweden	Turkey	27 Feb 36	167LTS75	303858
Belgium	Yugoslavia	29 Feb 36	184LTS379	304258
Iraq	Saudi Arabia	02 Apr 36	174LTS131	304044
Finland	USA (United States)	18 May 36	172LTS97	303981
Norway	Spain	13 Jun 36	170LTS199	303935
Finland	Turkey	20 Jun 36	172LTS125	303982
UK Great Britain	Yugoslavia	27 Nov 36	181LTS281	304195
Italy	Sweden	01 Dec 36	173LTS257	304017
Italy	Sweden	01 Dec 36	173LTS269	304018
Italy	Sweden	01 Dec 36	173LTS279	304019
Multilateral		23 Dec 36	188LTS75	304353
Multilateral		23 Dec 36	188LTS53	304352
Multilateral		23 Dec 36	201LTS295	304721
Italy	Netherlands	01 Jan 37	178LTS415	304124
Italy	Latvia	05 Feb 37	178LTS33	304104
France	USA (United States)	18 Feb 37	184LTS479	304269
El Salvador	USA (United States)	19 Feb 37	179LTS219	304150
Multilateral		03 Mar 37	182LTS127	304205
Italy	Norway	31 Mar 37	177LTS355	304098
Italy	Norway	31 Mar 37	177LTS349	304097
France	UK Great Britain	03 Apr 37	179LTS265	304154
Sweden	Yugoslavia	14 May 37	194LTS21	304504
Multilateral		28 May 37	180LTS5	304170
Belgium	UK Great Britain	01 Jun 37	196LTS209	304583
Estonia	Turkey	06 Jun 37	179LTS159	304143
France	Turkey	15 Jun 37	179LTS195	304147
Norway	Poland	18 Jun 37	190LTS187	304416
France	Sweden	30 Jun 37	179LTS203	304148
China	USSR (Soviet Union)	21 Aug 37	181LTS101	304180
France	Switzerland	13 Oct 37	194LTS191	304522
France	UK Great Britain	14 Oct 37	184LTS457	304266

Previous treaties adherence (Cont.)

PARTY ONE	PARTY TWO	DATE	CITATION	NUMBER
Poland	UK Great Britain	14 Oct 37	191LTS279	304449
Estonia	France	16 Oct 37	183LTS41	304227
Estonia	Germany	24 Oct 37	184LTS81	304244
Norway	Siam	15 Nov 37	186LTS9	304301
Siam	UK Great Britain	23 Nov 37	188LTS333	304366
Estonia	Greece	25 Nov 37	184LTS427	304263
Chile	UK Great Britain	26 Nov 37	186LTS285	304317
Bel-Lux Econ Union	Yugoslavia	26 Nov 37	196LTS19	304567
Sweden	Turkey	31 Dec 37	184LTS399	304260
France	Switzerland	31 Jan 38	195LTS313	304553
Greece	Sweden	01 Feb 38	185LTS217	304285
Estonia	Sweden	18 Feb 38	185LTS237	304287
Greece	Norway	28 Feb 38	186LTS165	304309
Latvia	Poland	05 Mar 38	192LTS283	304478
Cuba	USA (United States)	12 May 38	191LTS19	304432
Latvia	Poland	16 Jun 38	196LTS105	304573
Italy	Norway	21 Jun 38	190LTS193	304417
Switzerland	Yugoslavia	27 Jun 38	196LTS27	304568
Germany	UK Great Britain	01 Jul 38	194LTS235	304525
Balkan States	Bulgaria	31 Jul 38	196LTS371	304596
Estonia	Netherlands	22 Nov 38	195LTS133	304542
Iraq	USA (United States)	03 Dec 38	203LTS107	304753
Finland	Netherlands	20 Dec 38	194LTS55	304506
Chile	UK Great Britain	09 Jan 39	196LTS277	304589
Sweden	Turkey	20 Jan 39	194LTS107	304513
Sweden	Turkey	20 Jan 39	194LTS113	304514
Estonia	Sweden	30 Jan 39	194LTS131	304517
France	India	22 Mar 39	197LTS273	304619
Turkey	USA (United States)	01 Apr 39	202LTS129	304741
Latvia	Sweden	15 Apr 39	196LTS373	304597
Germany	Netherlands	17 May 39	199LTS239	304678
Hungary	Romania	19 Oct 39	201LTS415	304729
Hungary	Romania	19 Oct 39	201LTS395	304728
Romania	Switzerland	02 Nov 39	200LTS289	304699
Turkey	UK Great Britain	22 Nov 39	201LTS93	304705
Norway	UK Great Britain	02 Dec 39	201LTS97	304706
Sweden	Turkey	29 Feb 40	200LTS273	304696
Sweden	Turkey	29 Feb 40	200LTS267	304695
Spain	UK Great Britain	18 Mar 40	203LTS157	304759
United Arab Rep	UK Great Britain	17 Jul 40	202LTS97	304738
United Arab Rep	France	03 Aug 40	202LTS121	304740
Mexico	USA (United States)	28 Aug 40	203LTS357	304777

General relations and amity

PARTY ONE	PARTY TWO	DATE	CITATION	NUMBER
Muscat and Oman	UK Great Britain	11 Feb 22	10LTS459	300285
China	Denmark	12 Dec 28	91LTS207	302062
Multilateral		30 Aug 29	104LTS473	302399
Austria	Italy	06 Feb 30	105LTS97	302405
China	USSR (Soviet Union)	21 Aug 37	181LTS101	304180
Multilateral		01 Jan 42	204LTS381	304817

Non-prejudice to third party

PARTY ONE	PARTY TWO	DATE	CITATION	NUMBER
Austria-Hungary	Greece	21 Dec 04	2LTS173	300064
Germany	Hungary	01 Jun 20	7LTS207	300187
Afghanistan	Persia	22 Jun 21	33LTS285	300853
Norway	USSR (Soviet Union)	02 Sep 21	7LTS293	300196
Germany	USSR (Soviet Union)	16 Apr 22	19LTS247	300498
Austria	Germany	18 Feb 24	29LTS435	300754
China	USSR (Soviet Union)	31 May 24	37LTS175	300955
Germany	Poland	16 Dec 25	46LTS139	301117
Germany	USSR (Soviet Union)	24 Apr 26	53LTS387	301268
Multilateral		20 Feb 28	134LTS45	303082
Austria	USA (United States)	19 Jun 28	118LTS241	302728
Austria	Poland	26 Oct 32	138LTS193	303188

Non-prejudice to third party (Cont.)

PARTY ONE	PARTY TWO	DATE	CITATION	NUMBER
Denmark	Venezuela	19 Dec 33	158LTS249	303635
Belgium	Germany	10 May 35	182LTS335	304221
Norway	Venezuela	13 May 35	167LTS407	303882
Bulgaria	Denmark	07 Dec 35	182LTS183	304211
Denmark	Yugoslavia	14 Dec 35	184LTS99	304245
Panama	USA (United States)	25 Aug 39	199LTS317	304681
Multilateral		01 Jan 42	204LTS381	304817

Friendship and amity

PARTY ONE	PARTY TWO	DATE	CITATION	NUMBER
China	Persia	01 Jun 20	9LTS17	300240
Czechoslovakia	Serb/Croat/Slovene	14 Aug 20	6LTS209	300154
Japan	Paraguay	30 Nov 20	6LTS367	300169
Multilateral		19 Jan 21	5LTS9	300113
Muscat and Oman	UK Great Britain	11 Feb 21	8LTS261	300224
France	Poland	17 Feb 21	18LTS11	300449
Persia	USSR (Soviet Union)	26 Feb 21	9LTS383	300268
Poland	Romania	03 Mar 21	7LTS77	300175
UK Great Britain	USSR (Soviet Union)	16 Mar 21	4LTS127	300104
Czechoslovakia	Romania	23 Apr 21	6LTS215	300155
China	Germany	20 May 21	9LTS271	300261
Afghanistan	Persia	22 Jun 21	33LTS285	300853
Estonia	Ukrainian SSR	25 Nov 21	11LTS121	300294
Austria	Czechoslovakia	16 Dec 21	9LTS247	300257
Costa Rica	UK Great Britain	12 Jan 22	17LTS151	300432
Multilateral		17 Mar 22	11LTS167	300296
Czechoslovakia	Serb/Croat/Slovene	31 Aug 22	13LTS231	300354
Iraq	UK Great Britain	30 Apr 23	35LTS13	300890
Poland	Turkey	23 Jul 23	49LTS323	301188
Estonia	Latvia	01 Nov 23	23LTS81	300578
Hungary	Turkey	18 Dec 23	43LTS271	301062
Nepal	UK Great Britain	21 Dec 23	36LTS357	300934
Czechoslovakia	France	25 Jan 24	23LTS163	300588
Italy	Serb/Croat/Slovene	27 Jan 24	24LTS31	300596
Austria	Turkey	28 Jan 24	32LTS297	300821
Germany	Turkey	03 Mar 24	41LTS237	301017
Multilateral		14 Mar 24	25LTS423	300633
Sweden	Turkey	31 May 24	38LTS148	300972
China	USSR (Soviet Union)	31 May 24	37LTS175	300955
Czechoslovakia	Italy	05 Jul 24	26LTS21	300637
Netherlands	Turkey	16 Aug 24	39LTS148	300999
Italy	Serb/Croat/Slovene	21 Aug 24	82LTS445	301883
Spain	Turkey	27 Sep 24	43LTS307	301066
Japan	Peru	30 Sep 24	102LTS33	302351
Czechoslovakia	Turkey	11 Oct 24	38LTS317	300987
Estonia	Turkey	01 Dec 24	70LTS77	301624
Finland	Turkey	09 Dec 24	59LTS287	301398
Latvia	Turkey	03 Jan 25	59LTS81	301390
Japan	USSR (Soviet Union)	20 Jan 25	34LTS31	300866
Denmark	Turkey	26 Jan 25	36LTS317	300931
France	Siam	14 Feb 25	43LTS189	301055
Netherlands	Siam	08 Jun 25	56LTS57	301323
Siam	Spain	03 Aug 25	55LTS39	301303
Portugal	Siam	14 Aug 25	55LTS57	301304
Bulgaria	Turkey	18 Oct 25	54LTS125	301280
Turkey	USSR (Soviet Union)	17 Dec 25	157LTS353	303610
Siam	Sweden	19 Dec 25	58LTS429	301386
Chile	Turkey	30 Jan 26	59LTS249	301395
Denmark	Siam	01 Mar 26	47LTS103	301131
Afghanistan	Germany	03 Mar 26	62LTS115	301460
Germany	USSR (Soviet Union)	24 Apr 26	53LTS387	301268
Norway	Turkey	02 May 26	56LTS51	301322
Italy	Siam	09 May 26	61LTS215	301436
France	Turkey	30 May 26	54LTS195	301285
Bel-Lux Econ Union	Siam	13 Jul 26	62LTS287	301468
Norway	Siam	16 Jul 26	60LTS35	301404

PARTY ONE	PARTY TWO	DATE	CITATION	NUMBER
Friendship and amity (Cont.)				
Poland	Serb/Croat/Slovene	18 Sep 26	78LTS413	301799
China	Finland	29 Oct 26	67LTS345	301556
Hungary	Italy	05 Apr 27	67LTS399	301561
British Empire	Hedjaz	20 May 27	71LTS131	301658
Afghanistan	Poland	03 Nov 27	74LTS83	301734
Afghanistan	Latvia	16 Feb 28	78LTS99	301781
Multilateral		20 Feb 28	135LTS187	303111
Germany	Siam	07 Apr 28	85LTS337	301938
Germany	Persia	15 May 28	107LTS389	302495
Persia	Turkey	15 Jun 28	106LTS247	302449
Persia	USA (United States)	11 Jul 28	107LTS375	302494
Afghanistan	Finland	17 Jul 28	112LTS9	302601
Abyssinia	Italy	02 Aug 28	94LTS413	302158
Persia	Switzerland	28 Aug 28	107LTS397	302496
Bel-Lux Econ Union	China	22 Nov 28	87LTS287	301975
United Arab Rep	Persia	28 Nov 28	93LTS381	302127
Latvia	Persia	15 Jan 29	162LTS299	303742
Germany	Persia	17 Feb 29	111LTS19	302576
Germany	Hedjaz	26 Apr 29	115LTS265	302690
France	Persia	10 May 29	150LTS329	303465
Hedjaz	Persia	24 Aug 29	106LTS269	302450
Italy	Persia	05 Sep 29	141LTS185	303264
Lithuania	Persia	13 Jan 30	131LTS221	303013
Netherlands	Persia	12 Mar 30	111LTS387	302599
Norway	Persia	08 May 30	134LTS153	303089
Iraq	UK Great Britain	30 Jun 30	132LTS363	303048
Afghanistan	Estonia	06 Dec 30	137LTS445	303174
Afghanistan	Lithuania	09 Dec 30	138LTS29	303178
Poland	USA (United States)	15 Jun 31	139LTS395	303223
Estonia	Persia	03 Oct 31	137LTS183	303155
Turkey	USA (United States)	28 Oct 31	138LTS345	303197
Greece	Poland	04 Jan 32	131LTS229	303014
Afghanistan	Iraq	20 Dec 32	155LTS375	303588
Afghanistan	Brazil	20 Feb 33	186LTS385	304322
Netherlands	Yemen	12 Mar 33	146LTS359	303384
Italy	USSR (Soviet Union)	02 Sep 33	148LTS319	303418
Romania	Turkey	17 Oct 33	165LTS273	303814
UK Great Britain	Yemen	11 Feb 34	157LTS63	303605
Denmark	Persia	20 Feb 34	158LTS299	303640
China	Turkey	04 Apr 34	153LTS161	303515
Persia	Switzerland	25 Apr 34	159LTS235	303666
United Arab Rep	Switzerland	07 Jun 34	159LTS137	303656
Brazil	USA (United States)	02 Feb 35	166LTS211	303840
Panama	USA (United States)	02 Mar 36	200LTS17	304686
Afghanistan	USA (United States)	26 Mar 36	168LTS143	303895
Iraq	Saudi Arabia	02 Apr 36	174LTS131	304044
China	Latvia	25 Jun 36	176LTS275	304066
Finland	Mexico	02 Oct 36	179LTS303	304157
Bulgaria	Mexico	05 Nov 36	187LTS37	304331
Bulgaria	Yugoslavia	24 Jan 37	176LTS221	304063
Estonia	Mexico	28 Jan 37	185LTS39	304272
United Arab Rep	Turkey	07 Apr 37	191LTS89	304437
Iran	Iraq	18 Jul 37	190LTS259	304424
Afghanistan	Czechoslovakia	13 Oct 37	191LTS9	304431
Bel-Lux Econ Union	Siam	05 Nov 37	190LTS151	304413
Denmark	Siam	05 Nov 37	188LTS187	304358
Siam	Sweden	08 Nov 37	185LTS337	304298
Japan	Siam	08 Dec 37	188LTS375	304367
China	Estonia	21 Dec 37	194LTS123	304516
Germany	Siam	30 Dec 37	188LTS401	304368
Greece	Mexico	17 Mar 38	198LTS325	304649
Chile	USA (United States)	24 Feb 39	197LTS217	304614
Japan	Thailand	12 Jun 40	204LTS131	304791
Thailand	UK Great Britain	12 Jun 40	203LTS421	304782
UK Great Britain	USA (United States)	23 Feb 42	204LTS389	304818

PARTY ONE	PARTY TWO	DATE	CITATION	NUMBER
Friendship and amity (Cont.)				
Czechoslovakia	UK Great Britain	05 Aug 42	204LTS377	304816
China	UK Great Britain	11 Jan 43	205LTS67	304826
Non-prejudice to UN charter				
Persia	Poland	19 Mar 27	109LTS87	302529
Greece	Italy	23 Sep 28	108LTS219	302510
Greece	Serb/Croat/Slovene	27 Mar 29	108LTS201	302509
Japan	Persia	30 Mar 29	107LTS427	302499
Norway	Persia	10 May 29	107LTS403	302497
Belgium	Persia	23 May 29	110LTS369	302568
Czechoslovakia	Greece	08 Jun 29	108LTS255	302512
China	Greece	30 Sep 29	123LTS127	302811
Austria	Greece	26 Jun 30	119LTS353	302755
Lithuania	Turkey	17 Sep 30	125LTS249	302858
Czechoslovakia	Persia	29 Oct 30	121LTS53	302783
Greece	Turkey	30 Oct 30	125LTS9	302841
Afghanistan	Japan	19 Nov 30	121LTS237	302789
Austria	Hungary	26 Jan 31	123LTS171	302814
Multilateral		08 Jul 37	190LTS21	304402
Peaceful relations				
France	Switzerland	11 Jun 14	12LTS361	300329
Netherlands	Venezuela	11 May 20	7LTS85	300176
Multilateral		04 Jun 20	6LTS187	300152
France	Poland	17 Feb 21	18LTS11	300449
Persia	USSR (Soviet Union)	26 Feb 21	9LTS383	300268
UK Great Britain	USSR (Soviet Union)	16 Mar 21	4LTS127	300104
China	Germany	20 May 21	9LTS271	300261
Afghanistan	Persia	22 Jun 21	33LTS285	300853
Germany	USA (United States)	25 Aug 21	12LTS191	300310
Hungary	USA (United States)	29 Aug 21	48LTS191	301161
Afghanistan	UK Great Britain	22 Nov 21	14LTS47	300367
Estonia	Ukrainian SSR	25 Nov 21	11LTS121	300294
Austria	Czechoslovakia	16 Dec 21	9LTS247	300257
Multilateral		17 Mar 22	11LTS167	300296
Czechoslovakia	Serb/Croat/Slovene	31 Aug 22	13LTS231	300354
Iraq	UK Great Britain	30 Apr 23	35LTS13	300890
Estonia	Latvia	01 Nov 23	23LTS81	300578
Nepal	UK Great Britain	21 Dec 23	36LTS357	300934
Czechoslovakia	France	25 Jan 24	23LTS163	300588
Italy	Serb/Croat/Slovene	27 Jan 24	24LTS31	300596
Austria	Turkey	28 Jan 24	32LTS297	300821
Sweden	Turkey	31 May 24	38LTS148	300972
China	USSR (Soviet Union)	31 May 24	37LTS175	300955
Czechoslovakia	Italy	05 Jul 24	26LTS21	300637
Japan	USSR (Soviet Union)	20 Jan 25	34LTS31	300866
Denmark	Turkey	26 Jan 25	36LTS317	300931
France	Siam	14 Feb 25	43LTS189	301055
Netherlands	Siam	08 Jun 25	56LTS57	301323
Siam	Spain	03 Aug 25	55LTS39	301303
Portugal	Siam	14 Aug 25	55LTS57	301304
Switzerland	Turkey	19 Sep 25	61LTS395	301449
Multilateral		16 Oct 25	54LTS289	301292
Bulgaria	Turkey	18 Oct 25	54LTS125	301280
Turkey	USSR (Soviet Union)	17 Dec 25	157LTS353	303610
Denmark	Siam	01 Mar 26	47LTS103	301131
Poland	Romania	26 Mar 26	60LTS161	301411
France	Romania	10 Jun 26	58LTS225	301373
France	Turkey	31 Jul 26	54LTS177	301284
Italy	Yemen	02 Sep 26	67LTS383	301559
Italy	Romania	16 Sep 26	67LTS393	301560
Poland	Serb/Croat/Slovene	18 Sep 26	78LTS413	301799
Lithuania	USSR (Soviet Union)	28 Sep 26	60LTS145	301410
Albania	Italy	27 Nov 26	60LTS15	301402
Multilateral		28 Jul 27	64LTS379	301511
Afghanistan	Persia	27 Nov 27	107LTS433	302500

PARTY ONE	PARTY TWO	DATE	CITATION	NUMBER
Peaceful relations (Cont.)				
Multilateral		20 Feb 28	134LTS45	303082
Greece	Romania	21 Mar 28	108LTS187	302508
Persia	Turkey	15 Jun 28	106LTS247	302449
Italy	Persia	24 Jul 28	95LTS269	302179
United Arab Rep	Persia	28 Nov 28	93LTS381	302127
Dominican Republic	Haiti	20 Jan 29	105LTS215	302414
UK Great Britain	USSR (Soviet Union)	21 Dec 29	99LTS61	302268
Afghanistan	Lithuania	09 Dec 30	138LTS29	303178
Poland	Romania	15 Jan 31	115LTS171	302685
Greece	Poland	04 Jan 32	131LTS229	303014
Finland	USSR (Soviet Union)	21 Jan 32	157LTS393	303613
Latvia	USSR (Soviet Union)	05 Feb 32	148LTS113	303408
Estonia	USSR (Soviet Union)	04 May 32	131LTS297	303020
Poland	USSR (Soviet Union)	25 Jul 32	136LTS41	303124
France	USSR (Soviet Union)	29 Nov 32	157LTS411	303615
Afghanistan	Brazil	20 Feb 33	186LTS385	304322
Italy	USSR (Soviet Union)	02 Sep 33	148LTS319	303418
Multilateral		10 Oct 33	163LTS393	303781
Multilateral		12 Sep 34	154LTS93	303540
Czechoslovakia	USSR (Soviet Union)	16 May 35	159LTS347	303677
Panama	USA (United States)	02 Mar 36	200LTS17	304686
Afghanistan	USA (United States)	26 Mar 36	168LTS143	303895
Iraq	Saudi Arabia	02 Apr 36	174LTS131	304044
China	Latvia	25 Jun 36	176LTS275	304066
United Arab Rep	UK Great Britain	26 Aug 36	173LTS401	304031
Finland	Mexico	02 Oct 36	179LTS303	304157
Bulgaria	Mexico	05 Nov 36	187LTS37	304331
Bulgaria	Yugoslavia	24 Jan 37	176LTS221	304063
Estonia	Mexico	28 Jan 37	185LTS39	304272
Multilateral		08 Jul 37	190LTS21	304402
Iran	Iraq	18 Jul 37	190LTS259	304424
Afghanistan	Czechoslovakia	13 Oct 37	191LTS9	304431
Siam	Sweden	08 Nov 37	185LTS337	304298
Siam	USA (United States)	13 Nov 37	192LTS247	304476
Norway	Siam	15 Nov 37	186LTS9	304301
France	Siam	07 Dec 37	201LTS113	304708
China	Estonia	21 Dec 37	194LTS123	304516
Netherlands	Siam	01 Feb 38	193LTS13	304485
Multilateral		16 Apr 38	195LTS103	304538
Portugal	Siam	02 Jul 38	200LTS149	304688
Balkan States	Bulgaria	31 Jul 38	196LTS371	304596
Denmark	Germany	31 May 39	197LTS37	304603
Estonia	Germany	07 Jun 39	198LTS49	304622
Germany	Latvia	07 Jun 39	198LTS105	304629
China	UK Great Britain	11 Jan 43	205LTS67	304826
Exchange of information and documents				
Portugal	Sweden	20 Sep 21	7LTS143	300183
Frontier formalities				
Austria	Czechoslovakia	18 Jan 23	88LTS237	302000
Poland	USSR (Soviet Union)	24 Apr 24	37LTS33	300947
France	Germany	13 Apr 25	109LTS295	302546
Germany	Poland	26 Mar 27	64LTS177	301505
Czechoslovakia	Germany	27 Mar 28	90LTS151	302032
Ecuador	Germany	28 Apr 28	90LTS163	302033
Afghanistan	Persia	26 Jun 28	106LTS321	302453
Lithuania	Poland	07 Nov 28	89LTS171	302011
Norway	USA (United States)	23 Jul 29	93LTS223	302111
China	UK Great Britain	31 Oct 29	99LTS441	302289
Austria	Germany	12 Apr 30	115LTS297	302693
Hungary	Spain	19 Sep 31	124LTS353	302839
Romania	Yugoslavia	30 Jan 33	146LTS99	303362
France	Sweden	09 Jun 34	154LTS101	303541

PARTY ONE	PARTY TWO	DATE	CITATION	NUMBER
Visa abolition				
Greece	UK Great Britain	27 Jul 21	6LTS347	300167
Sweden	Switzerland	01 Jan 22	9LTS11	300239
Finland	USSR (Soviet Union)	28 Oct 22	19LTS199	300493
Finland	Norway	28 Apr 24	30LTS35	300757
Denmark	Germany	01 May 26	107LTS229	302480
Italy	Latvia	12 Jun 26	51LTS65	301222
Austria	Netherlands	01 Mar 27	68LTS75	301570
Austria	Portugal	28 Mar 27	68LTS81	301571
Finland	Germany	14 May 27	66LTS403	301533
Finland	Latvia	14 May 27	63LTS97	301482
Estonia	Finland	17 May 27	66LTS411	301534
Austria	Denmark	11 Jun 27	68LTS87	301572
Austria	Latvia	30 Jun 27	66LTS97	301526
Austria	Great Britain	18 Jul 27	68LTS97	301573
Austria	Finland	21 Jul 27	66LTS419	301535
Luxembourg	Norway	12 Sep 27	68LTS37	301566
Finland	Switzerland	14 Oct 27	71LTS205	301663
Austria	Sweden	20 Dec 27	71LTS293	301670
Germany	Norway	17 Jan 28	70LTS251	301637
Austria	Norway	08 Feb 28	71LTS211	301664
Finland	Japan	25 Feb 28	71LTS467	301685
Finland	Sweden	09 Mar 28	72LTS429	301699
Czechoslovakia	Germany	27 Mar 28	90LTS151	302032
Japan	Norway	29 Mar 28	73LTS81	301708
Austria	Czechoslovakia	30 Mar 28	73LTS87	301709
Germany	Nicaragua	30 Mar 28	93LTS123	302104
Czechoslovakia	Finland	26 Apr 28	80LTS335	301838
Ecuador	Germany	28 Apr 28	90LTS163	302033
Finland	Netherlands	07 May 28	74LTS367	301748
Czechoslovakia	Germany	11 May 28	81LTS441	301854
Finland	Italy	12 May 28	77LTS334	301775
Belgium	Finland	01 Jun 28	77LTS327	301774
Germany	Latvia	02 Jun 28	75LTS69	301752
Belgium	Czechoslovakia	26 Jun 28	80LTS9	301819
Austria	Japan	06 Jul 28	81LTS425	301851
Germany	Italy	27 Aug 28	90LTS191	302037
Germany	Uruguay	26 Oct 28	90LTS205	302039
Germany	Great Britain	15 Nov 28	90LTS213	302040
Finland	Norway	24 Nov 28	82LTS215	301872
Germany	Spain	09 Feb 29	89LTS369	302038
Germany	El Salvador	19 Feb 29	99LTS317	302274
Austria	Estonia	22 Mar 29	89LTS301	302025
Estonia	Germany	30 Apr 29	99LTS325	302275
Finland	Switzerland	22 May 29	91LTS311	302070
Finland	Switzerland	22 May 29	91LTS305	302069
Austria	Uruguay	25 May 29	93LTS229	302112
Czechoslovakia	Denmark	21 Jun 29	91LTS351	302075
Czechoslovakia	Iceland	25 Jun 29	91LTS359	302076
Germany	Siam	06 Jul 29	99LTS333	302276
Austria	Spain	23 Aug 29	97LTS353	302232
Germany	Honduras	21 Sep 29	133LTS311	303070
Czechoslovakia	Norway	11 Oct 29	96LTS211	302202
Finland	Italy	18 Oct 29	97LTS65	302218
Belgium	Ecuador	05 Dec 29	97LTS385	302237
Czechoslovakia	Latvia	24 Dec 29	99LTS9	302263
Brazil	Italy	08 Feb 30	101LTS57	302319
Austria	Panama	05 Mar 30	101LTS293	302330
Austria	Luxembourg	07 Mar 30	101LTS237	302325
Danzig	Norway	07 Apr 30	100LTS391	302308
Austria	Hungary	11 Apr 30	101LTS309	302332
Hungary	Italy	07 May 30	101LTS445	302343
Finland	Poland	15 May 30	111LTS309	302594
Austria	Italy	06 Jun 30	105LTS329	302425
Hungary	Spain	28 Aug 30	110LTS307	302562

PARTY ONE	PARTY TWO	DATE	CITATION	NUMBER
Visa abolition (Cont.)				
Albania	Austria	30 Jan 31	114LTS65	302655
Estonia	Norway	31 Jan 31	113LTS39	302633
Danzig	Finland	08 Jun 31	120LTS291	302772
Austria	Brazil	06 Jul 31	123LTS9	302801
Denmark	Poland	26 Oct 31	125LTS337	302862
Latvia	Norway	28 Jun 34	152LTS107	303488
Belgium	Norway	20 Jul 34	150LTS369	303469
Belgium	France	28 Jul 34	152LTS27	303481
Multilateral		22 Dec 34	183LTS153	304231
Multilateral		22 Dec 34	183LTS145	304230
Austria	Vatican/Holy See	23 Mar 35	167LTS385	303879
Austria	Monaco	07 Feb 36	167LTS389	303880
Finland	Hungary	03 Apr 36	172LTS167	303987
Australia	Indochina	20 May 36	170LTS221	303937
Finland	Romania	16 Nov 36	179LTS377	304164
Hungary	Norway	16 Nov 37	183LTS81	304228
Hungary	Norway	18 Feb 38	185LTS357	304299
India	Indochina	01 Mar 38	194LTS231	304524
Greece	Hungary	06 Apr 38	188LTS455	304370
Finland	Hungary	27 Mar 39	195LTS425	304563
France	UK Great Britain	08 Oct 39	201LTS59	304703
Border traffic and migration				
Multilateral		18 Mar 04	1LTS83	300011
France	Poland	03 Sep 19	1LTS337	300028
France	Italy	30 Sep 19	5LTS279	300133
Bulgaria	Greece	27 Nov 19	1LTS67	300009
Czechoslovakia	France	20 Mar 20	3LTS139	300095
Lithuania	USSR (Soviet Union)	12 Jul 20	3LTS106	300094
Austria	Germany	01 Sep 20	2LTS132	300057
Denmark	Sweden	08 Jun 21	14LTS195	300374
Denmark	Norway	21 Jul 21	13LTS357	300362
Danzig	Poland	24 Oct 21	116LTS5	302699
Finland	USSR (Soviet Union)	14 Dec 21	16LTS221	300414
Austria	Hungary	08 Feb 22	55LTS367	301320
Norway	Sweden	29 Mar 22	13LTS311	300361
Denmark	Germany	25 Apr 22	18LTS227	300466
Germany	Poland	29 Apr 22	21LTS391	300549
Germany	Poland	15 May 22	10LTS37	300273
Finland	USSR (Soviet Union)	22 Jun 22	16LTS361	300417
Belgium	Netherlands	08 Jul 22	13LTS273	300358
Austria	Poland	25 Sep 22	59LTS307	301400
Norway	UK Great Britain	22 Feb 23	15LTS159	300389
Portugal	Spain	26 Mar 23	18LTS349	300475
Liechtenstein	Switzerland	29 Mar 23	21LTS231	300545
Estonia	Germany	27 Jun 23	41LTS161	301013
Belgium	Denmark	28 Jun 23	20LTS59	300507
France	Netherlands	02 Jul 23	20LTS131	300512
Italy	Spain	15 Nov 23	39LTS49	300996
Estonia	Latvia	02 Apr 24	38LTS113	300969
Poland	Serb/Croat/Slovene	05 Apr 24	49LTS265	301185
Hungary	Romania	16 Apr 24	46LTS95	301114
Finland	Norway	28 Apr 24	30LTS35	300757
Czechoslovakia	Iceland	08 May 24	46LTS419	301125
Estonia	Netherlands	22 Jul 24	48LTS199	301162
Czechoslovakia	France	18 Aug 24	44LTS21	301080
Czechoslovakia	Netherlands	17 Oct 24	31LTS93	300786
France	Poland	09 Dec 24	44LTS127	301081
France	Saar	15 Jan 25	44LTS181	301082
Austria	Spain	03 Feb 25	43LTS313	301067
Czechoslovakia	Greece	08 Apr 25	38LTS291	300984
France	Germany	13 Apr 25	109LTS295	302546
Greece	Poland	17 Apr 25	38LTS301	300985
Bel-Lux Econ Union		07 Jul 25	54LTS267	301290
Finland	Spain	16 Jul 25	47LTS271	301135

PARTY ONE	PARTY TWO	DATE	CITATION	NUMBER
Border traffic and migration (Cont.)				
Italy	Serb/Croat/Slovene	20 Jul 25	83LTS277	301895
France	Hungary	13 Oct 25	48LTS9	301150
Germany	Italy	31 Oct 25	52LTS179	301256
Estonia	Latvia	11 Nov 25	42LTS93	301034
Norway	USSR (Soviet Union)	15 Dec 25	47LTS9	301127
Austria	Switzerland	06 Jan 26	46LTS299	301124
France	Great Britain	02 Feb 26	56LTS79	301324
Germany	Poland	27 Mar 26	64LTS249	301506
Brazil	Venezuela	13 Apr 26	80LTS283	301834
Finland	Hungary	20 Apr 26	48LTS119	301154
Germany	Spain	07 May 26	53LTS321	301264
Austria	Hungary	10 May 26	56LTS39	301321
Multilateral		21 Jun 26	78LTS229	301793
Austria	Hungary	14 Jul 26	61LTS159	301431
Austria	Hungary	14 Jul 26	61LTS123	301430
Benelux Econ Union	Germany	15 Jul 26	63LTS137	301485
Multilateral		14 Sep 26	77LTS149	301769
Hungary	Turkey	20 Dec 26	72LTS245	301696
Finland	Germany	14 May 27	66LTS403	301533
Estonia	Finland	17 May 27	66LTS411	301534
Czechoslovakia	Poland	30 May 27	98LTS233	302251
Austria	Finland	21 Jul 27	66LTS419	301535
Austria	Sweden	20 Dec 27	71LTS293	301670
Hungary	Serb/Croat/Slovene	22 Feb 28	113LTS49	302635
Finland	Japan	25 Feb 28	71LTS467	301685
Austria	Italy	11 May 28	100LTS41	302293
Estonia	Latvia	15 May 28	74LTS281	301742
Persia	USSR (Soviet Union)	31 May 28	110LTS343	302566
Germany	Latvia	02 Jun 28	75LTS69	301752
Czechoslovakia	Germany	05 Jun 28	177LTS19	302700
Lithuania	Poland	07 Nov 28	89LTS171	302011
Germany	Serb/Croat/Slovene	15 Dec 28	95LTS149	302171
Peru	UK Great Britain	31 Dec 28	100LTS431	302312
Germany	El Salvador	19 Feb 29	99LTS317	302274
Finland	USSR (Soviet Union)	13 Apr 29	96LTS93	302193
Estonia	Germany	30 Apr 29	99LTS325	302275
Finland	Switzerland	22 May 29	91LTS305	302069
Finland	Switzerland	22 May 29	91LTS311	302070
Czechoslovakia	Denmark	21 Jun 29	91LTS351	302075
Poland	Romania	30 Oct 29	121LTS243	302790
Poland	Romania	30 Oct 29	121LTS167	302787
Austria	Panama	05 Mar 30	101LTS293	302330
Austria	Luxembourg	07 Mar 30	101LTS237	302325
Austria	Hungary	11 Apr 30	101LTS309	302332
Austria	Germany	12 Apr 30	115LTS277	302692
Austria	Germany	12 Apr 30	115LTS297	302693
Denmark	Germany	03 Jul 30	105LTS427	302430
Denmark	Norway	06 Nov 30	109LTS283	302545
Czechoslovakia	Romania	22 Dec 30	168LTS209	303900
Greece	Poland	22 Apr 31	129LTS313	302966
Germany	Poland	22 Dec 31	144LTS191	303329
Finland	Hungary	07 Nov 33	142LTS179	303290
Latvia	Lithuania	01 Dec 33	148LTS87	303406
Latvia	Lithuania	01 Dec 33	148LTS97	303407
Belgium	France	30 Dec 35	166LTS25	303826
Luxembourg	Netherlands	01 Apr 36	179LTS11	304130
Austria	Germany	26 Aug 36	171LTS357	303972
Belgium	Norway	17 Dec 36	178LTS153	304110
Belgium	Netherlands	09 Jun 37	181LTS153	304186
Multilateral		08 Jul 37	190LTS21	304402
France	Switzerland	13 Oct 37	194LTS191	304522
Italy	Siam	03 Dec 37	189LTS255	304389
France	Siam	09 Dec 37	201LTS145	304709

PARTY ONE	PARTY TWO	DATE	CITATION	NUMBER
Passports diplomatic				
Cuba	Netherlands	31 Dec 13	14LTS29	300366
Norway	USSR (Soviet Union)	02 Sep 21	7LTS293	300196
Austria	Netherlands	06 Nov 22	17LTS375	300444
Denmark	USSR (Soviet Union)	23 Apr 23	18LTS15	300450
Estonia	Poland	11 Jan 24	47LTS129	301132
Finland	Netherlands	09 Mar 25	47LTS431	301148
Denmark	Germany	01 May 26	107LTS229	302480
Estonia	Poland	19 Feb 27	115LTS177	302686
Czechoslovakia	France	03 Jun 27	131LTS177	303009
Finland	Italy	12 May 28	77LTS334	301775
Germany	Honduras	21 Sep 29	133LTS311	303070
China	France	16 May 30	162LTS99	303738
France	Netherlands	25 May 36	173LTS187	304011
Finland	Romania	16 Nov 36	179LTS377	304164
Multilateral		10 Feb 37	189LTS313	304391
Estonia	Hungary	19 Jan 38	185LTS363	304300
Hungary	Norway	18 Feb 38	185LTS357	304299
Passports non-diplomatic				
Cuba	Netherlands	31 Dec 13	14LTS29	300366
Sweden	Switzerland	01 Jan 22	9LTS11	300239
Multilateral		27 Jan 22	9LTS291	300262
Denmark	Germany	25 Apr 22	18LTS227	300466
Germany	Poland	15 May 22	10LTS37	300273
Finland	USSR (Soviet Union)	28 Oct 22	19LTS153	300491
France	Netherlands	02 Jul 23	20LTS131	300512
Austria	China	19 Oct 25	55LTS9	301301
Germany	Poland	16 Jun 26	65LTS379	301522
Albania	Serb/Croat/Slovene	22 Jun 26	91LTS55	302055
Estonia	Norway	28 Jul 26	43LTS25	301045
Finland	Sweden	09 Mar 28	72LTS429	301699
Germany	Nicaragua	30 Mar 28	93LTS123	302104
Ecuador	Germany	28 Apr 28	90LTS163	302033
Finland	Italy	12 May 28	77LTS334	301775
Estonia	Latvia	15 May 28	74LTS281	301742
Germany	Italy	27 Aug 28	90LTS191	302037
Portugal	South Africa	11 Sep 28	98LTS9	302239
Germany	Uruguay	26 Oct 28	90LTS205	302039
Czechoslovakia	Serb/Croat/Slovene	07 Nov 28	98LTS297	302252
Germany	Great Britain	15 Nov 28	90LTS213	302040
Germany	El Salvador	19 Feb 29	99LTS317	302274
Estonia	Germany	30 Apr 29	99LTS325	302275
Finland	Switzerland	22 May 29	91LTS305	302069
Finland	Switzerland	22 May 29	91LTS311	302070
Austria	Uruguay	25 May 29	93LTS229	302112
Czechoslovakia	Denmark	21 Jun 29	91LTS351	302075
Germany	Siam	06 Jul 29	99LTS333	302276
Austria	Spain	23 Aug 29	97LTS353	302232
Czechoslovakia	Norway	11 Oct 29	96LTS211	302202
Finland	Italy	18 Oct 29	97LTS65	302218
Belgium	Ecuador	05 Dec 29	97LTS385	302237
Czechoslovakia	Latvia	24 Dec 29	99LTS9	302263
Austria	Panama	05 Mar 30	101LTS293	302330
Austria	Luxembourg	07 Mar 30	101LTS237	302325
Danzig	Norway	07 Apr 30	100LTS391	302308
Austria	Hungary	11 Apr 30	101LTS309	302332
Hungary	Italy	07 May 30	101LTS445	302343
Irish Free State	Italy	10 May 30	132LTS147	303034
Austria	Italy	06 Jun 30	105LTS329	302425
Hungary	Spain	28 Aug 30	110LTS307	302562
Japan	South Africa	16 Oct 30	126LTS17	302868
Albania	Austria	30 Jan 31	114LTS65	302655
Estonia	Norway	31 Jan 31	113LTS39	302633
Danzig	Finland	08 Jun 31	120LTS291	302772

PARTY ONE	PARTY TWO	DATE	CITATION	NUMBER
Passports non-diplomatic (Cont.)				
Austria	Brazil	06 Jul 31	123LTS9	302801
Hungary	Spain	19 Sep 31	124LTS353	302839
Denmark	Poland	26 Oct 31	125LTS337	302862
Poland	Romania	24 May 37	190LTS361	304428
Brazil	USA (United States)	17 Dec 37	186LTS413	304325
France	USA (United States)	14 Jan 38	191LTS213	304445
Finland	South Africa	14 Feb 38	190LTS211	304419
Lithuania	Poland	25 May 38	191LTS391	304457
Romania	USA (United States)	30 Apr 39	203LTS349	304775
Sweden	USA (United States)	05 Oct 39	203LTS353	304776
Denial of admission				
Bulgaria	Netherlands	13 Nov 20	7LTS107	300178
Finland	USSR (Soviet Union)	01 Jun 22	16LTS319	300415
Estonia	Latvia	11 Nov 25	42LTS93	301034
Denmark	Germany	01 May 26	107LTS229	302480
Germany	Sweden	14 May 26	51LTS99	301225
Italy	Latvia	12 Jun 26	51LTS65	301222
Hungary	Turkey	20 Dec 26	72LTS245	301696
Finland	Germany	14 May 27	66LTS403	301533
Finland	Latvia	14 May 27	63LTS97	301482
Estonia	Finland	17 May 27	66LTS411	301534
Austria	Denmark	11 Jun 27	68LTS87	301572
Austria	Latvia	30 Jun 27	66LTS97	301526
Austria	Great Britain	18 Jul 27	68LTS97	301573
Austria	Finland	21 Jul 27	66LTS419	301535
Austria	Sweden	20 Dec 27	71LTS293	301670
Austria	Norway	08 Feb 28	71LTS211	301664
Finland	Sweden	09 Mar 28	72LTS429	301699
Czechoslovakia	Germany	27 Mar 28	90LTS151	302032
Austria	Czechoslovakia	30 Mar 28	73LTS87	301709
Finland	Netherlands	07 May 28	74LTS367	301748
Estonia	Latvia	15 May 28	74LTS281	301742
Persia	USSR (Soviet Union)	31 May 28	110LTS343	302566
Belgium	Finland	01 Jun 28	77LTS327	301774
Germany	Latvia	02 Jun 28	75LTS69	301752
Belgium	Czechoslovakia	26 Jun 28	80LTS9	301819
Multilateral		30 Jun 28	89LTS53	302005
Belgium	France	04 Jul 28	85LTS205	301931
Germany	Persia	17 Feb 29	111LTS241	302590
Estonia	Germany	30 Apr 29	99LTS325	302275
Germany	Honduras	21 Sep 29	133LTS311	303070
Finland	Italy	18 Oct 29	97LTS65	302218
Poland	Romania	07 Dec 29	119LTS283	302752
Czechoslovakia	Latvia	24 Dec 29	99LTS9	302263
Austria	Panama	05 Mar 30	101LTS293	302330
Austria	Luxembourg	07 Mar 30	101LTS237	302325
Danzig	Norway	07 Apr 30	100LTS391	302308
Austria	Hungary	11 Apr 30	101LTS309	302332
Austria	Italy	06 Jun 30	105LTS329	302425
Czechoslovakia	Persia	29 Oct 30	121LTS59	302784
Switzerland	Turkey	13 Dec 30	129LTS331	302968
Albania	Austria	30 Jan 31	114LTS65	302655
Belgium	France	30 Mar 31	126LTS195	302882
Denmark	Poland	26 Oct 31	125LTS337	302862
Austria	Germany	07 Dec 32	137LTS69	303147
France	Sweden	09 Jun 34	154LTS101	303541
Resident permits				
Austria	Czechoslovakia	18 Jan 23	88LTS237	302000
Germany	Poland	23 Feb 24	41LTS197	301015
France	Saar	14 Dec 27	70LTS163	301631
Persia	USSR (Soviet Union)	31 May 28	110LTS343	302566
Belgium	France	04 Jul 28	85LTS205	301931
Norway	USA (United States)	25 Feb 29	134LTS81	303085
Ethiopia	Greece	23 Mar 31	153LTS127	303512

PARTY ONE	PARTY TWO	DATE	CITATION	NUMBER
Resident permits (Cont.)				
Danzig	Finland	08 Jun 31	120LTS291	302772
France	Yugoslavia	29 Jul 32	144LTS313	303334
Denmark	France	28 Jan 35	158LTS11	303619
Finland	France	26 May 37	179LTS327	304160
Belgium	Netherlands	09 Jun 37	181LTS153	304186
Lithuania	Poland	25 May 38	191LTS391	304457
Multilateral		23 May 39	202LTS159	304742
Non-visa travel documents				
France	Poland	03 Sep 19	1LTS337	300028
Czechoslovakia	France	20 Mar 20	3LTS139	300095
Germany	Poland	06 Jun 21	34LTS185	300874
Denmark	Germany	12 Jul 21	26LTS151	300645
Germany	Poland	15 May 22	10LTS37	300273
Finland	USSR (Soviet Union)	12 Aug 22	19LTS105	300489
Austria	Poland	25 Sep 22	59LTS307	301400
Finland	USSR (Soviet Union)	28 Oct 22	19LTS199	300493
Austria	Czechoslovakia	18 Jan 23	88LTS237	302000
Czechoslovakia	Hungary	08 Mar 23	48LTS257	301167
Germany	Netherlands	23 May 23	25LTS275	300617
Bulgaria	Serb/Croat/Slovene	26 Nov 23	26LTS119	300643
Estonia	Lithuania	21 May 24	62LTS55	301454
Bulgaria	Poland	29 Apr 25	60LTS103	301408
Czechoslovakia	Poland	30 May 25	50LTS243	301207
Hungary	Spain	17 Jun 25	60LTS69	301406
Denmark	Germany	20 Mar 26	53LTS377	301267
Germany	Poland	27 Mar 26	64LTS249	301506
Denmark	Germany	01 May 26	107LTS229	302480
Greece	Italy	24 Oct 26	63LTS51	301480
Germany	Turkey	12 Jan 27	73LTS133	301712
Czechoslovakia	Switzerland	16 Feb 27	64LTS7	301501
Czechoslovakia	Finland	02 Mar 27	66LTS385	301532
Denmark	Sweden	08 Mar 27	63LTS315	301498
Norway	Sweden	09 Mar 27	62LTS341	301472
Czechoslovakia	Hungary	31 May 27	65LTS61	301520
Austria	Denmark	11 Jun 27	68LTS87	301572
Czechoslovakia	Estonia	20 Jul 27	77LTS341	301776
Germany	Greece	24 Mar 28	90LTS9	302031
Czechoslovakia	Germany	27 Mar 28	90LTS151	302032
Germany	Nicaragua	30 Mar 28	93LTS123	302104
Austria	France	16 May 28	88LTS21	301986
Multilateral		30 Jun 28	89LTS53	302005
Paraguay	UK Great Britain	16 Jul 28	108LTS365	302519
Panama	UK Great Britain	25 Sep 28	90LTS311	302045
Lithuania	Poland	07 Nov 28	89LTS171	302011
Costa Rica	UK Great Britain	27 Dec 28	108LTS375	302520
Turkey	UK Great Britain	15 Jan 29	108LTS385	302521
Latvia	Poland	12 Feb 29	115LTS135	302683
Germany	El Salvador	19 Feb 29	99LTS317	302274
Estonia	Germany	30 Apr 29	99LTS325	302275
Austria	Uruguay	25 May 29	93LTS229	302112
Multilateral		14 Jun 29	94LTS275	302148
Czechoslovakia	Denmark	21 Jun 29	91LTS351	302075
Multilateral		28 Jun 29	102LTS245	302368
France	Switzerland	08 Jul 29	114LTS189	302664
China	Poland	18 Sep 29	120LTS331	302774
Czechoslovakia	Norway	11 Oct 29	96LTS211	302202
Poland	Romania	07 Dec 29	119LTS283	302752
Czechoslovakia	Latvia	24 Dec 29	99LTS9	302263
Austria	Panama	05 Mar 30	101LTS293	302330
Austria	Luxembourg	07 Mar 30	101LTS237	302325
Danzig	Norway	07 Apr 30	100LTS391	302308
Austria	Hungary	11 Apr 30	101LTS309	302332
Austria	Germany	12 Apr 30	115LTS297	302693
Austria	Italy	06 Jun 30	105LTS329	302425

PARTY ONE	PARTY TWO	DATE	CITATION	NUMBER
Non-visa travel documents (Cont.)				
Japan	South Africa	16 Oct 30	126LTS17	302868
Albania	Austria	30 Jan 31	114LTS65	302655
Multilateral		13 Apr 31	119LTS275	302751
Germany	Hungary	18 Jul 31	150LTS111	303458
Hungary	Romania	12 Aug 31	186LTS325	304321
Denmark	Poland	26 Oct 31	125LTS337	302862
Bulgaria	Germany	24 Jun 32	147LTS211	303400
Germany	Norway	03 Mar 33	138LTS179	303186
Greece	UK Great Britain	21 Apr 33	140LTS133	303230
Bulgaria	Czechoslovakia	29 Aug 33	148LTS15	303402
Brazil	Uruguay	20 Dec 33	181LTS55	304177
Czechoslovakia	Poland	10 Feb 34	183LTS213	304238
Finland	Germany	24 Mar 34	149LTS343	303442
Czechoslovakia	UK Great Britain	04 Mar 35	160LTS283	303698
Czechoslovakia	Hungary	14 Jun 35	171LTS401	303976
France	Spain	21 Dec 35	167LTS9	303856
Belgium	Italy	01 May 37	198LTS73	304624
Belgium	United Arab Rep	20 May 37	182LTS153	304207
Belgium	Sweden	15 Jun 37	198LTS77	304625
Belgium	Greece	09 Sep 37	197LTS63	304605
Belgium	Denmark	16 Sep 37	197LTS67	304606
Belgium	Czechoslovakia	16 Oct 37	184LTS73	304243
Estonia	France	16 Oct 37	183LTS41	304227
Romania	UK Great Britain	06 Dec 37	184LTS467	304267
Multilateral		10 Feb 38	192LTS59	304461
Multilateral		29 Apr 38	190LTS115	304410
Multilateral		17 May 38	192LTS319	304481
Multilateral		30 May 38	191LTS299	304451
Hungary	Norway	05 Jul 38	189LTS427	304399
Multilateral		15 Jul 38	195LTS73	304536
Multilateral		21 Aug 39	198LTS343	304652
France	UK Great Britain	08 Oct 39	201LTS59	304703
Germany	Latvia	30 Oct 39	200LTS213	304693
Multilateral		08 Jan 40	203LTS133	304756
Visas				
Denmark	Germany	12 Jul 21	26LTS151	300645
Sweden	Switzerland	01 Jan 22	9LTS11	300239
Multilateral		27 Jan 22	9LTS291	300262
Multilateral		05 Jul 22	13LTS237	300355
Denmark	Finland	12 Feb 23	18LTS71	300454
Estonia	Lithuania	21 May 24	62LTS55	301454
Czechoslovakia	Denmark	02 Jun 24	57LTS115	301357
Denmark	France	25 Feb 25	33LTS277	300852
Belgium	Germany	03 Oct 25	38LTS285	300983
Estonia	Latvia	11 Nov 25	42LTS93	301034
Austria	Denmark	19 Dec 25	57LTS121	301358
Austria	Netherlands	01 Mar 27	68LTS75	301570
Austria	Portugal	28 Mar 27	68LTS81	301571
Austria	Denmark	11 Jun 27	68LTS87	301572
Austria	Great Britain	18 Jul 27	68LTS97	301573
Luxembourg	Norway	12 Sep 27	68LTS37	301566
Denmark	Italy	26 Oct 27	68LTS229	301586
Czechoslovakia	Finland	26 Apr 28	80LTS335	301838
Finland	Italy	12 May 28	77LTS334	301775
Belgium	Finland	01 Jun 28	77LTS327	301774
Belgium	France	04 Jul 28	85LTS205	301931
Austria	Estonia	22 Mar 29	89LTS301	302025
Germany	Turkey	28 May 29	133LTS257	303069
Czechoslovakia	Denmark	21 Jun 29	91LTS351	302075
Finland	Italy	15 Aug 29	99LTS363	302280
Latvia	Norway	10 Feb 30	100LTS79	302295
Hungary	Spain	19 Sep 31	124LTS353	302839
Northern Rhodesia	South Africa	26 Sep 32	135LTS225	303113
Romania	Yugoslavia	30 Jan 33	146LTS179	303370

PARTY ONE	PARTY TWO	DATE	CITATION	NUMBER
Visas (Cont.)				
Brazil	Uruguay	20 Dec 33	181LTS55	304177
Lithuania	Spain	07 Sep 35	163LTS321	303774
Bel-Lux Econ Union	Bulgaria	01 Apr 36	169LTS23	303912
Netherlands	Romania	28 Aug 36	182LTS363	304222
Bulgaria	Sweden	07 Dec 36	173LTS393	304030
Italy	Netherlands	01 Jan 37	178LTS415	304124
South Africa	USA (United States)	24 Mar 37	189LTS113	304379
Bel-Lux Econ Union	Yugoslavia	26 Nov 37	196LTS19	304567
Bel-Lux Econ Union	Estonia	13 Jan 38	185LTS63	304275
Finland	South Africa	14 Feb 38	190LTS211	304419
Hungary	Latvia	25 Mar 38	188LTS447	304369
Multilateral		15 Apr 38	200LTS285	304698
Netherlands	Romania	10 Oct 38	195LTS9	304532
Tourism				
Japan	South Africa	16 Oct 30	126LTS17	302868
Czechoslovakia	Persia	29 Oct 30	121LTS59	302784
France	UK Great Britain	15 Dec 31	129LTS445	302976
Belgium	France	23 Dec 31	137LTS277	303162
Brazil	Uruguay	20 Dec 33	181LTS55	304177
Japan	Siam	08 Dec 37	188LTS375	304367
Germany	Siam	30 Dec 37	188LTS401	304368
Multilateral		15 Apr 38	200LTS285	304698
Multilateral		27 Jun 38	191LTS199	304443
Multilateral		06 May 39	198LTS81	304626
Frontier permits				
Austria	Czechoslovakia	10 Mar 21	9LTS333	300267
Austria	Czechoslovakia	04 May 21	15LTS13	300388
Denmark	Germany	12 Jul 21	26LTS163	300646
Denmark	Germany	12 Jul 21	26LTS151	300645
Finland	USSR (Soviet Union)	14 Dec 21	16LTS221	300414
Germany	Poland	29 Apr 22	21LTS391	300549
Germany	Poland	15 May 22	10LTS37	300273
Germany	Poland	24 Jun 22	26LTS271	300653
Italy	Serb/Croat/Slovene	23 Oct 22	18LTS413	300479
Italy	Serb/Croat/Slovene	23 Oct 22	18LTS441	300480
Multilateral		30 Dec 22	21LTS183	300542
Germany	Netherlands	23 May 23	25LTS275	300617
Estonia	Latvia	10 Jan 24	38LTS103	300968
Germany	Poland	23 Feb 24	41LTS197	301015
Estonia	Latvia	02 Apr 24	38LTS113	300969
Finland	Norway	28 Apr 24	30LTS35	300757
Latvia	Lithuania	18 Oct 24	56LTS157	301327
Germany	Poland	30 Dec 24	52LTS51	301250
Czechoslovakia	Romania	16 Apr 25	46LTS427	301126
Czechoslovakia	Poland	30 May 25	48LTS397	301172
Italy	Serb/Croat/Slovene	20 Jul 25	83LTS277	301895
Great Britain	Nejd	02 Nov 25	60LTS419	301423
Estonia	Latvia	05 Feb 26	64LTS361	301509
Denmark	Germany	01 May 26	107LTS229	302480
Multilateral		14 Sep 26	77LTS149	301769
Multilateral		13 Nov 26	77LTS249	301773
Multilateral		13 Nov 26	77LTS217	301772
Czechoslovakia	Poland	30 May 27	98LTS233	302251
Germany	Lithuania	29 Jan 28	89LTS309	302026
Sweden	Turkey	04 Feb 28	88LTS155	301994
Belgium	France	04 Jul 28	85LTS205	301931
Paraguay	UK Great Britain	16 Jul 28	108LTS365	302519
Lithuania	Poland	07 Nov 28	89LTS171	302011
Czechoslovakia	Hungary	14 Nov 28	110LTS425	302574
Austria	Czechoslovakia	12 Dec 28	108LTS9	302501
Costa Rica	UK Great Britain	27 Dec 28	108LTS375	302520
Turkey	UK Great Britain	15 Jan 29	108LTS385	302521
France	Germany	25 Apr 29	109LTS333	302548
Poland	Romania	30 Oct 29	121LTS243	302790
Frontier permits (Cont.)				
Poland	Romania	30 Oct 29	121LTS167	302787
Multilateral		09 Nov 29	125LTS205	302855
Poland	Romania	07 Dec 29	119LTS283	302752
Austria	Hungary	03 Jun 30	122LTS69	302799
Czechoslovakia	Romania	15 Jul 30	164LTS157	303793
Czechoslovakia	France	03 Oct 30	125LTS59	302846
Denmark	Norway	06 Nov 30	109LTS283	302545
Belgium	France	30 Mar 31	126LTS195	302882
Germany	Poland	22 Dec 31	144LTS191	303329
Belgium	France	23 Dec 31	137LTS277	303162
Latvia	Lithuania	01 Dec 33	148LTS87	303406
Belgium	France	09 May 35	162LTS437	303755
Belgium	Germany	10 May 35	165LTS143	303807
Bulgaria	Romania	26 Jul 35	198LTS9	304621
Belgium	France	30 Dec 35	166LTS25	303826
Austria	Germany	26 Aug 36	171LTS357	303972
Romania	Yugoslavia	13 May 37	197LTS101	304609
Belgium	Netherlands	09 Jun 37	181LTS153	304186
Bulgaria	Romania	20 Jul 37	202LTS33	304733
Norway	Sweden	20 Apr 38	189LTS153	304383
Immigration and emigration				
Danzig	Poland	09 Nov 20	6LTS189	300153
Estonia	France	07 Jan 22	62LTS9	301452
Italy	Poland	12 May 22	59LTS293	301399
Greece	Turkey	30 Jan 23	32LTS75	300807
Poland	Turkey	23 Jul 23	49LTS345	301190
Denmark	Finland	03 Aug 23	21LTS269	300547
Germany	South Africa	23 Oct 23	28LTS417	300721
Albania	Italy	29 Feb 24	44LTS343	301093
UK Great Britain	USA (United States)	03 Dec 24	43LTS41	301046
Belgium	France	24 Dec 24	78LTS367	301795
Bulgaria	Turkey	27 Dec 24	54LTS135	301281
Italy	Spain	25 Nov 25	60LTS59	301405
Multilateral		21 Jun 26	78LTS229	301793
Austria	Hungary	14 Jul 26	61LTS123	301430
Belgium	Luxembourg	20 Oct 26	78LTS375	301796
Persia	USSR (Soviet Union)	31 May 28	110LTS343	302566
Multilateral		25 Oct 28	84LTS7	301901
Germany	Uruguay	26 Oct 28	90LTS205	302039
Italy	UK Great Britain	25 Jan 29	95LTS39	302162
Germany	Persia	17 Feb 29	111LTS241	302590
Norway	USA (United States)	25 Feb 29	134LTS81	303085
Belgium	Persia	09 May 29	110LTS391	302570
Austria	Uruguay	25 May 29	93LTS229	302112
Multilateral		14 Jun 29	94LTS275	302148
Norway	USA (United States)	23 Jul 29	93LTS223	302111
Italy	Panama	16 Oct 29	138LTS355	303199
Norway	Persia	08 May 30	134LTS153	303089
Japan	South Africa	16 Oct 30	126LTS17	302868
Austria	Brazil	06 Jul 31	123LTS9	302801
Bulgaria	Germany	24 Jun 32	147LTS211	303400
Romania	Turkey	04 Sep 36	195LTS429	304564
Bel-Lux Econ Union	Uruguay	22 Feb 37	196LTS391	304600
United Arab Rep	Turkey	07 Apr 37	191LTS95	304438
Belgium	Netherlands	09 Jun 37	181LTS153	304186
France	UK Great Britain	29 Jul 37	184LTS351	304257
Estonia	France	16 Oct 37	183LTS41	304227
Latvia	Turkey	12 Jan 38	201LTS229	304716
Argentina	Netherlands	06 Sep 38	194LTS409	304531
UK Great Britain	USA (United States)	27 Mar 41	204LTS15	304784
Refugees and stateless persons				
Multilateral		12 May 26	89LTS47	302004
Multilateral		30 Jun 28	89LTS53	302005
Greece	Turkey	10 Jun 30	108LTS233	302511

PARTY ONE	PARTY TWO	DATE	CITATION	NUMBER
Assistance				
Cuba	Netherlands	31 Dec 13	14LTS29	300366
Latvia	Ukrainian SSR	03 Aug 21	17LTS295	300441
Other Unilat Decla	Greece	29 Sep 23	20LTS29	300503
Multilateral		12 May 26	89LTS47	302004
Bulgaria		09 Sep 26	58LTS245	301375
Multilateral		30 Jun 28	89LTS63	302006
Multilateral		04 Jul 36	171LTS75	303952
Multilateral		10 Feb 38	192LTS59	304461
Legal status				
Latvia	Ukrainian SSR	03 Aug 21	17LTS295	300441
Danzig	Poland	24 Oct 21	116LTS5	302699
Finland	USSR (Soviet Union)	12 Aug 22	19LTS105	300489
Other Unilat Decla	Greece	29 Sep 23	20LTS29	300503
Germany	Poland	30 Aug 24	32LTS331	300824
Multilateral		30 Jun 28	89LTS53	302005
France	Sweden	09 Jun 34	154LTS101	303541
Luxembourg	Netherlands	01 Apr 36	179LTS11	304130
Denmark	Germany	17 Jun 36	171LTS163	303958
Multilateral		04 Jul 36	171LTS75	303952
Multilateral		08 May 37	182LTS37	304202
Multilateral		10 Feb 38	192LTS59	304461
Refugees				
Latvia	USSR (Soviet Union)	11 Aug 20	2LTS195	300067
Latvia	Ukrainian SSR	03 Aug 21	17LTS317	300442
Latvia	Ukrainian SSR	03 Aug 21	17LTS295	300441
Latvia	USSR (Soviet Union)	06 Nov 21	17LTS251	300440
Multilateral		29 Sep 23	20LTS41	300504
Other Unilat Decla	Greece	29 Sep 23	20LTS29	300503
Multilateral		12 May 26	89LTS47	302004
Bulgaria		09 Sep 26	58LTS245	301375
Greece		15 Sep 27	70LTS9	301622
Multilateral		30 Jun 28	89LTS53	302005
Other Unilat Decla	Greece	14 Jan 30	108LTS349	302518
Greece	Turkey	10 Jun 30	108LTS233	302511
Multilateral		04 Jul 36	171LTS75	303952
Multilateral		10 Feb 38	192LTS59	304461
Repatriation mission				
UK Great Britain	USSR (Soviet Union)	12 Feb 20	1LTS263	300019
Multilateral		29 Sep 23	20LTS41	300504
Other Unilat Decla	Greece	29 Sep 23	20LTS29	300503
Bulgaria		09 Sep 26	58LTS245	301375
Germany	Luxembourg	28 Jun 28	90LTS183	302036
Multilateral		27 Jul 29	118LTS343	302734
Germany	Latvia	30 Oct 39	200LTS213	304693
Repatriation of nationals				
Multilateral		18 Mar 04	1LTS83	300011
France	Poland	03 Sep 19	1LTS337	300028
UK Great Britain	USSR (Soviet Union)	12 Feb 20	1LTS263	300019
Germany	Poland	12 Feb 21	9LTS149	300247
Finland	Sweden	29 Jul 21	6LTS353	300168
Czechoslovakia	Sweden	07 Sep 21	7LTS97	300177
Portugal	Sweden	20 Sep 21	7LTS143	300183
Multilateral		21 Sep 21	7LTS127	300181
France	Sweden	09 Nov 21	7LTS303	300197
Sweden	Switzerland	29 Nov 21	7LTS313	300198
Poland	Sweden	27 Dec 21	8LTS163	300220
Norway	Sweden	05 May 22	15LTS165	300390
Finland	USSR (Soviet Union)	12 Aug 22	19LTS105	300489
Austria	Sweden	04 Oct 22	9LTS317	300264
Mexico	Sweden	17 Oct 22	15LTS179	300391
Belgium	Sweden	25 Oct 22	18LTS121	300459
Greece	Turkey	30 Jan 23	32LTS75	300807

PARTY ONE	PARTY TWO	DATE	CITATION	NUMBER
Repatriation of nationals (Cont.)				
Greece	Turkey	30 Jan 23	36LTS137	300912
Hungary	Serb/Croat/Slovene	20 Mar 23	16LTS447	300422
Denmark	Sweden	13 Jul 23	18LTS143	300461
United Arab Rep	UK Great Britain	18 Jul 23	18LTS323	300474
Latvia	Lithuania	21 May 24	37LTS363	300960
Bulgaria	Czechoslovakia	06 Sep 25	50LTS253	301208
Estonia	Latvia	03 Mar 26	63LTS13	301476
France	Turkey	31 Jul 26	54LTS177	301284
Finland	Germany	18 Jun 27	71LTS361	301675
Multilateral		20 Feb 28	134LTS45	303082
Germany	Luxembourg	28 Jun 28	90LTS183	302036
Multilateral		30 Jun 28	89LTS53	302005
Multilateral		27 Jul 29	118LTS343	302734
Denmark	Finland	09 Jul 31	123LTS393	302826
France	Switzerland	09 Sep 31	142LTS205	303293
Finland	Poland	19 Dec 31	131LTS193	303010
Belgium	South Africa	04 Feb 32	127LTS121	302912
Belgium	Luxembourg	31 May 33	141LTS9	303256
Belgium	Italy	07 Feb 34	147LTS107	303395
Belgium	Netherlands	15 May 36	179LTS41	304131
Multilateral		23 Dec 36	188LTS151	304356
Multilateral		23 Dec 36	188LTS125	304355
Germany	Latvia	30 Oct 39	200LTS213	304693
Stateless persons				
Austria	Germany	11 Aug 21	29LTS429	300753
Austria	Germany	18 Feb 24	29LTS435	300754
Finland	Germany	18 Jun 27	71LTS361	301675
Multilateral		12 Apr 30	179LTS115	304138
Status of state				
France	UK Great Britain	06 Aug 14	10LTS333	300278
Other Unilat Decla	Hungary	12 Nov 21	14LTS385	300387
Multilateral		06 Apr 22	123LTS277	302818
Italy	Serb/Croat/Slovene	06 Apr 22	123LTS289	302819
Democratic institutions				
Austria-Hungary	Greece	21 Dec 04	2LTS173	300064
Governor-general functions				
France	UK Great Britain	06 Aug 14	10LTS333	300278
Independence maintenance				
Latvia	Ukrainian SSR	03 Aug 21	17LTS317	300442
Multilateral		13 Dec 21	25LTS184	300607
Multilateral		06 Feb 22	38LTS277	300982
Multilateral		04 Oct 22	12LTS385	300334
Continuity of rights and obligations				
Multilateral		19 Jan 21	5LTS9	300113
Ireland	UK Great Britain	06 Dec 21	26LTS9	300636
Denmark	Germany	10 Apr 22	10LTS73	300274
Panama	USA (United States)	02 Mar 36	200LTS17	304686
UK Great Britain	Venezuela	26 Feb 42	205LTS131	304830
Transition period				
Multilateral		10 Aug 20	28LTS225	300710
Ireland	UK Great Britain	06 Dec 21	26LTS9	300636
China	UK Great Britain	31 Oct 29	99LTS441	302289
Recognition				
Latvia	Ukrainian SSR	03 Aug 21	17LTS317	300442
Multilateral		06 Feb 22	38LTS277	300982
Multilateral		14 Mar 24	25LTS423	300633
Colombia	Nicaragua	05 May 30	105LTS337	302426
Norway	UK Great Britain	18 Nov 30	112LTS97	302609
Multilateral		10 Dec 31	129LTS177	302961
Multilateral		26 Dec 33	165LTS19	303802

PARTY ONE	PARTY TWO	DATE	CITATION	NUMBER
Re-establishment				
Multilateral		04 Oct 22	12LTS385	300334
Self-determination				
Ireland	UK Great Britain	06 Dec 21	26LTS9	300636
Multilateral		06 Feb 22	38LTS277	300982
Multilateral		14 Mar 24	25LTS423	300633
Germany	USA (United States)	21 May 25	52LTS133	301254
Self-government				
France	UK Great Britain	06 Aug 14	10LTS333	300278
Ireland	UK Great Britain	06 Dec 21	26LTS9	300636
Multilateral		06 Feb 22	38LTS277	300982
Denmark	Germany	10 Apr 22	10LTS73	300274
Union with other states				
Multilateral		19 Jan 21	5LTS9	300113
Ireland	UK Great Britain	06 Dec 21	26LTS9	300636
Diplomatic and consular relations				
Austria	Hungary	30 Sep 24	42LTS177	301040
Germany	Guatemala	04 Oct 24	52LTS19	301246
Germany	Italy	31 Oct 25	53LTS245	301261
Greece	Spain	23 Sep 26	91LTS121	302059
Austria	Persia	17 Jun 28	112LTS101	302610
Afghanistan	Finland	17 Jul 28	112LTS9	302601
Germany	Persia	17 Feb 29	111LTS19	302576
Hedjaz	Persia	24 Aug 29	106LTS269	302450
Italy	Persia	05 Sep 29	141LTS185	303264
Netherlands	Persia	12 Mar 30	111LTS387	302599
Romania	UK Great Britain	14 Jun 35	163LTS301	303772
Acquisition of nationality				
Multilateral		09 Dec 19	5LTS335	300140
Estonia	USSR (Soviet Union)	02 Feb 20	11LTS29	300289
Czechoslovakia	Germany	29 Jun 20	20LTS85	300509
Multilateral		05 Aug 20	2LTS49	300046
Multilateral		10 Aug 20	28LTS223	300711
Estonia	Latvia	19 Oct 20	17LTS189	300437
Germany	Poland	08 Dec 20	7LTS323	300199
Latvia	Lithuania	14 May 21	17LTS233	300439
Latvia	Ukrainian SSR	03 Aug 21	17LTS317	300442
Latvia	USSR (Soviet Union)	06 Nov 21	17LTS251	300440
Colombia	Peru	24 Mar 22	74LTS9	301726
Italy	Serb/Croat/Slovene	23 Oct 22	18LTS461	300481
Greece	Turkey	30 Jan 23	32LTS75	300807
Czechoslovakia	Germany	02 May 23	31LTS0	300793
France	UK Great Britain	24 Jul 23	36LTS207	300923
Multilateral		24 Jul 23	28LTS11	300701
Bulgaria	USA (United States)	23 Nov 23	25LTS238	300611
Austria	Turkey	28 Jan 24	32LTS303	300822
Bulgaria	Romania	19 Apr 24	33LTS209	300845
Multilateral		08 May 24	29LTS85	300736
Italy	UK Great Britain	15 Jul 24	36LTS379	300936
Germany	Poland	30 Aug 24	32LTS331	300824
France	Turkey	30 May 26	54LTS195	301285
Multilateral		20 Feb 28	86LTS111	301950
Czechoslovakia	USA (United States)	16 Jul 28	96LTS301	302208
United Arab Rep	Turkey	07 Apr 37	191LTS105	304439
Alien registration				
Multilateral		20 Feb 28	86LTS111	301950
Austria	Estonia	22 Mar 29	89LTS301	302025
Alien status				
Chile	Netherlands	04 Nov 13	84LTS79	301904
Germany	Poland	09 Jan 20	9LTS77	300245
Estonia	USSR (Soviet Union)	02 Feb 20	11LTS29	300289
Austria	Germany	01 Sep 20	4LTS201	300107

PARTY ONE	PARTY TWO	DATE	CITATION	NUMBER
Alien status (Cont.)				
Finland	USSR (Soviet Union)	14 Oct 20	3LTS5	300091
Poland	USSR (Soviet Union)	18 Mar 21	6LTS51	300149
Latvia	Ukrainian SSR	03 Aug 21	17LTS317	300442
Austria	Czechoslovakia	18 Feb 22	14LTS129	300371
Germany	Poland	15 Jun 22	21LTS433	300550
France	Panama	16 Aug 22	43LTS423	301075
Czechoslovakia	Serb/Croat/Slovene	17 Mar 23	30LTS185	300768
Germany	Poland	23 Jun 23	67LTS9	301537
Germany	South Africa	23 Oct 23	28LTS417	300721
Estonia	Latvia	10 Jan 24	38LTS103	300968
Iraq	UK Great Britain	25 Mar 24	35LTS131	300893
Bulgaria	Romania	19 Apr 24	33LTS221	300846
Italy	Serb/Croat/Slovene	21 Aug 24	82LTS445	301883
UK Great Britain	USA (United States)	03 Dec 24	43LTS41	301046
Belgium	France	24 Dec 24	78LTS367	301795
Bulgaria	Turkey	27 Dec 24	54LTS135	301281
UK Great Britain	USA (United States)	10 Feb 25	55LTS119	301309
UK Great Britain	USA (United States)	10 Feb 25	55LTS145	301311
UK Great Britain	USA (United States)	10 Feb 25	55LTS133	301310
France	Siam	14 Feb 25	43LTS189	301055
Germany	USSR (Soviet Union)	12 Oct 25	53LTS7	301257
Estonia	USA (United States)	23 Dec 25	50LTS13	301197
France	Poland	30 Dec 25	95LTS233	302177
Spain	Switzerland	04 Aug 26	65LTS39	301518
Hungary	USA (United States)	04 Sep 26	58LTS111	301369
China	Finland	29 Oct 26	67LTS345	301556
Bel-Lux Econ Union	Serb/Croat/Slovene	16 Dec 26	70LTS371	301647
Hungary	Turkey	20 Dec 26	72LTS245	301696
Estonia	Latvia	05 Feb 27	62LTS319	301470
Greece	Latvia	25 Feb 27	71LTS25	301652
Czechoslovakia	Germany	25 Mar 27	75LTS353	301758
Czechoslovakia	Turkey	31 May 27	75LTS79	301753
Germany	Poland	14 Jul 27	73LTS251	301718
Switzerland	Turkey	07 Aug 27	73LTS51	301706
Belgium	France	06 Oct 27	69LTS49	301599
Greece	Switzerland	01 Dec 27	84LTS271	301907
Japan	USSR (Soviet Union)	23 Jan 28	80LTS341	301839
Sweden	Turkey	04 Feb 28	88LTS155	301994
Multilateral		20 Feb 28	132LTS301	303045
Latvia	USA (United States)	20 Apr 28	80LTS35	301821
France	Persia	11 May 28	82LTS43	301858
Argentina	Sweden	14 May 28	155LTS109	303573
Italy	Persia	24 Jul 28	95LTS269	302179
Denmark	Persia	08 Sep 28	82LTS57	301859
Czechoslovakia	Serb/Croat/Slovene	19 Sep 28	87LTS309	301976
Latvia	Poland	12 Feb 29	101LTS75	302321
Germany	Persia	17 Feb 29	111LTS241	302590
Norway	USA (United States)	25 Feb 29	134LTS81	303085
Belgium	Persia	09 May 29	110LTS391	302570
Norway	Sweden	11 May 29	120LTS263	302771
France	UK Great Britain	25 May 29	95LTS55	302163
Czechoslovakia	Denmark	21 Jun 29	91LTS351	302075
Italy	Panama	16 Oct 29	138LTS355	303199
Poland	Romania	17 Dec 29	119LTS333	302754
Austria	Germany	12 Apr 30	115LTS333	302694
China	France	16 May 30	162LTS99	303738
Austria	Hungary	03 Jun 30	122LTS69	302799
Czechoslovakia	Romania	27 Jun 30	119LTS73	302742
Denmark	Finland	30 Jun 30	105LTS179	302411
El Salvador	USA (United States)	05 Sep 30	134LTS207	303093
Czechoslovakia	Persia	29 Oct 30	121LTS59	302784
Afghanistan	Japan	19 Nov 30	121LTS237	302789
Switzerland	Turkey	13 Dec 30	129LTS331	302968
Norway	Turkey	16 Mar 31	138LTS41	303180
Ethiopia	Greece	23 Mar 31	153LTS127	303512

PARTY ONE	PARTY TWO	DATE	CITATION	NUMBER
Alien status (Cont:)				
Poland	USA (United States)	15 Jun 31	139LTS395	303223
Austria	Yugoslavia	21 Jul 31	147LTS123	303397
Greece	Romania	11 Aug 31	130LTS69	302982
Poland	Turkey	29 Aug 31	144LTS367	303339
Iraq	Turkey	09 Jan 32	139LTS263	303217
France	Yugoslavia	29 Jul 32	144LTS313	303334
Argentina	Lithuania	20 Oct 32	154LTS113	303542
Romania	Yugoslavia	30 Jan 33	146LTS165	303368
Netherlands	Yemen	12 Mar 33	146LTS359	303384
Brazil	Uruguay	25 Aug 33	176LTS381	304075
Finland	USA (United States)	13 Feb 34	152LTS45	303484
Iran	USSR (Soviet Union)	27 Aug 35	176LTS299	304069
Belgium	France	30 Dec 35	166LTS25	303826
Luxembourg	Netherlands	01 Apr 36	179LTS11	304130
Finland	Switzerland	07 May 36	166LTS35	303827
United Arab Rep	UK Great Britain	09 Sep 36	182LTS317	304219
Denmark	Sweden	20 Nov 36	173LTS207	304014
Austria	Sweden	15 Jan 37	174LTS125	304043
Romania	Yugoslavia	13 May 37	197LTS145	304611
Denmark	Siam	05 Nov 37	188LTS187	304358
Belgium	Siam	05 Nov 37	190LTS163	304414
Siam	Sweden	08 Nov 37	185LTS337	304298
Siam	USA (United States)	13 Nov 37	192LTS247	304476
Siam	UK Great Britain	23 Nov 37	188LTS333	304366
France	Siam	07 Dec 37	201LTS113	304708
Japan	Siam	08 Dec 37	188LTS375	304367
Germany	Siam	30 Dec 37	188LTS401	304368
Latvia	Turkey	12 Jan 38	201LTS229	304716
Netherlands	Siam	01 Feb 38	193LTS13	304485
Romania	Switzerland	19 Jul 38	152LTS89	303486
Liberia	USA (United States)	08 Aug 38	201LTS163	304711
Sweden	USA (United States)	23 Mar 39	199LTS17	304661
Denmark	Norway	18 Jun 39	197LTS227	304615
Canada	USA (United States)	18 Jun 40	203LTS41	304748
General consular functions				
Chile	Netherlands	04 Nov 13	84LTS79	301904
Greece	Spain	06 Mar 19	3LTS81	300092
Japan	Paraguay	30 Nov 20	6LTS367	300169
Austria	Czechoslovakia	04 May 21	15LTS13	300388
China	Germany	20 May 21	9LTS271	300261
Denmark	UK Great Britain	01 Jun 21	5LTS161	300125
Estonia	Lithuania	12 Jul 21	11LTS99	300292
Latvia	Lithuania	12 Jul 21	25LTS299	300619
Estonia	Latvia	12 Jul 21	11LTS87	300291
Austria	Hungary	08 Oct 21	16LTS19	300402
Estonia	Finland	29 Oct 21	13LTS59	300348
Austria	Czechoslovakia	18 Feb 22	14LTS129	300371
Austria	Netherlands	06 Nov 22	17LTS375	300444
Denmark	USSR (Soviet Union)	23 Apr 23	18LTS15	300450
Multilateral		24 Jul 23	28LTS151	300704
Multilateral		03 Nov 23	30LTS371	300775
Germany	Hungary	06 Nov 23	45LTS253	301103
Japan	Serb/Croat/Slovene	16 Nov 23	42LTS99	301035
Hungary	Latvia	19 Nov 23	37LTS341	300959
Finland	UK Great Britain	14 Dec 23	29LTS129	300739
Multilateral		14 Dec 23	29LTS37	300732
Germany	Nicaragua	06 Mar 24	41LTS264	301019
Japan	Siam	09 Mar 24	31LTS187	300795
Denmark	Poland	22 Mar 24	31LTS13	300778
Denmark	Latvia	03 Apr 24	33LTS393	300860
Multilateral		22 May 24	35LTS175	300895
Netherlands	Poland	30 May 24	34LTS9	300865
Spain	UK Great Britain	27 Jun 24	28LTS523	300727
Latvia	Norway	14 Aug 24	36LTS211	300924

PARTY ONE	PARTY TWO	DATE	CITATION	NUMBER
General consular functions (Cont.)				
Italy	Serb/Croat/Slovene	21 Aug 24	82LTS445	301883
Hungary	Norway	16 Sep 24	33LTS103	300835
Japan	Peru	30 Sep 24	102LTS33	302351
Czechoslovakia	Netherlands	17 Oct 24	31LTS93	300786
Hungary	Netherlands	09 Dec 24	47LTS91	301130
Austria	Spain	03 Feb 25	43LTS313	301067
Albania	Italy	06 Mar 25	44LTS359	301094
Estonia	Germany	13 Mar 25	51LTS263	301236
Germany	USA (United States)	21 May 25	52LTS133	301254
Bel-Lux Econ Union		07 Jul 25	54LTS267	301290
Germany	UK Great Britain	13 Aug 25	43LTS89	301050
Germany	USSR (Soviet Union)	12 Oct 25	53LTS163	301258
Estonia	Switzerland	14 Oct 25	49LTS421	301195
Germany	Italy	31 Oct 25	52LTS179	301256
Bel-Lux Econ Union	Czechoslovakia	28 Dec 25	58LTS189	301372
France	Poland	30 Dec 25	73LTS265	301719
Estonia	UK Great Britain	18 Jan 26	48LTS209	301163
Denmark	Siam	01 Mar 26	47LTS103	301131
Netherlands	UK Great Britain	20 May 26	50LTS309	301214
Albania	Serb/Croat/Slovene	22 Jun 26	91LTS55	302055
Greece	Spain	23 Sep 26	91LTS121	302059
Austria	Estonia	15 Oct 26	93LTS137	302106
Greece	Italy	24 Oct 26	63LTS51	301480
Poland	Serb/Croat/Slovene	06 Mar 27	126LTS67	302871
Czechoslovakia	Hungary	31 May 27	65LTS61	301520
Czechoslovakia	France	03 Jun 27	131LTS177	303009
Germany	Panama	21 Nov 27	115LTS239	302689
Albania	France	15 Feb 28	107LTS307	302487
Multilateral		20 Feb 28	155LTS289	303582
Multilateral		20 Feb 28	155LTS259	303581
Germany	Siam	07 Apr 28	85LTS337	301938
Latvia	USA (United States)	20 Apr 28	80LTS35	301821
Austria	Serb/Croat/Slovene	01 May 28	96LTS373	302214
Austria	France	16 May 28	88LTS21	301986
Mexico	Panama	09 Jun 28	141LTS191	303265
Belgium	Poland	12 Jun 28	123LTS25	302803
Denmark	Greece	22 Aug 28	94LTS263	302147
Germany	South Africa	01 Sep 28	95LTS289	302181
Germany	Lithuania	30 Oct 28	90LTS255	302043
Czechoslovakia	Serb/Croat/Slovene	07 Nov 28	98LTS297	302252
Norway	USA (United States)	25 Feb 29	134LTS81	303085
Germany	Turkey	28 May 29	133LTS257	303069
Bulgaria	Germany	04 Jun 29	106LTS49	302436
Italy	Turkey	09 Sep 29	129LTS195	302962
China	Poland	18 Sep 29	120LTS331	302774
Italy	Panama	16 Oct 29	138LTS355	303199
Poland	Romania	17 Dec 29	119LTS333	302754
France	Latvia	20 Jan 30	169LTS125	303917
Estonia	USSR (Soviet Union)	20 Jan 30	102LTS225	302365
Multilateral		17 Feb 30	102LTS87	302354
Brazil	UK Great Britain	21 Feb 30	101LTS11	302315
Japan	Lithuania	02 May 30	126LTS369	302895
China	France	16 May 30	162LTS99	303738
Denmark	Turkey	31 May 30	119LTS165	302744
Sweden	UK Great Britain	28 Aug 30	114LTS9	302652
El Salvador	USA (United States)	05 Sep 30	134LTS207	303093
Finland	Sweden	16 Mar 31	118LTS71	302714
Czechoslovakia	Italy	23 May 31	126LTS185	302881
Poland	USA (United States)	15 Jun 31	139LTS395	303223
Greece	Romania	11 Aug 31	130LTS69	302982
Italy	Latvia	11 May 32	150LTS9	303450
Brazil	Uruguay	25 Aug 33	176LTS381	304075
Romania	UK Great Britain	25 Sep 33	149LTS425	303443
Brazil	Uruguay	20 Dec 33	181LTS45	304176
Finland	USA (United States)	13 Feb 34	152LTS45	303484

PARTY ONE	PARTY TWO	DATE	CITATION	NUMBER
General consular functions (Cont.)				
United Arab Rep	Switzerland	07 Jun 34	159LTS137	303656
Bulgaria	Poland	22 Dec 34	159LTS265	303671
Romania	UK Great Britain	14 Jun 35	163LTS301	303772
Iran	USSR (Soviet Union)	27 Aug 35	176LTS299	304069
Czechoslovakia	USSR (Soviet Union)	16 Nov 35	169LTS143	303918
Hungary	Poland	24 Apr 36	185LTS303	304296
France	Siam	07 Dec 37	201LTS113	304708
Liberia	USA (United States)	07 Oct 38	201LTS183	304712
UK Great Britain	USA (United States)	27 Mar 41	204LTS15	304784
Diplomatic privileges				
Chile	Netherlands	04 Nov 13	84LTS79	301904
Finland	Norway	16 Jul 21	19LTS77	300485
Afghanistan	UK Great Britain	22 Nov 21	14LTS47	300367
Peru	Venezuela	14 Mar 23	20LTS45	300505
United Arab Rep	UK Great Britain	18 Jul 23	18LTS323	300474
Latvia	Poland	03 Jan 24	42LTS451	301043
Estonia	Poland	11 Jan 24	47LTS129	301132
Poland	USSR (Soviet Union)	18 Jul 24	49LTS201	301183
Italy	Serb/Croat/Slovene	21 Aug 24	82LTS445	301883
Finland	Netherlands	09 Mar 25	47LTS431	301148
Germany	USSR (Soviet Union)	12 Oct 25	53LTS163	301258
Estonia	USA (United States)	23 Dec 25	50LTS13	301197
Cuba	USA (United States)	22 Apr 26	60LTS371	301421
Albania	Serb/Croat/Slovene	22 Jun 26	91LTS55	302055
Hungary	USA (United States)	04 Sep 26	58LTS111	301369
Austria	Estonia	15 Oct 26	93LTS137	302106
Sweden	Turkey	04 Feb 28	88LTS155	301994
Albania	France	15 Feb 28	107LTS307	302487
Latvia	USA (United States)	20 Apr 28	80LTS35	301821
Belgium	Persia	15 May 28	94LTS447	302160
Belgium	Poland	12 Jun 28	123LTS25	302803
Germany	Lithuania	30 Oct 28	90LTS255	302043
Bulgaria	Germany	04 Jun 29	106LTS49	302436
Denmark	Sweden	06 May 32	130LTS161	302989
Finland	USA (United States)	13 Feb 34	152LTS45	303484
Bulgaria	Poland	22 Dec 34	159LTS265	303671
Hungary	Poland	24 Apr 36	185LTS303	304296
Hungary	Sweden	17 Jun 36	184LTS11	304239
Dual citizenship				
Latvia	Lithuania	14 May 21	17LTS233	300439
Other Unilat Decla	Albania	02 Oct 22	9LTS173	300249
Consular relations establishment				
Chile	Netherlands	04 Nov 13	84LTS79	301904
Cuba	Netherlands	31 Dec 13	14LTS29	300366
Persia	USSR (Soviet Union)	26 Feb 21	9LTS383	300268
Czechoslovakia	Italy	23 Mar 21	32LTS183	300815
Estonia	Latvia	12 Jul 21	11LTS87	300291
Latvia	Lithuania	12 Jul 21	25LTS299	300619
Estonia	Lithuania	12 Jul 21	11LTS99	300292
Latvia	Ukrainian SSR	03 Aug 21	17LTS317	300442
Afghanistan	UK Great Britain	22 Nov 21	14LTS47	300367
Estonia	Ukrainian SSR	25 Nov 21	11LTS121	300294
Finland	Germany	21 Apr 22	19LTS87	300487
Czechoslovakia	Latvia	07 Oct 22	20LTS379	300528
Estonia	Hungary	19 Oct 22	30LTS347	300774
Austria	Netherlands	06 Nov 22	17LTS375	300444
Latvia	UK Great Britain	22 Jun 23	20LTS395	300529
Denmark	Finland	03 Aug 23	21LTS269	300547
Hungary	Latvia	19 Nov 23	37LTS341	300959
Hungary	Turkey	18 Dec 23	43LTS271	301062
Lithuania	Norway	21 Dec 23	32LTS55	300805
Latvia	Poland	03 Jan 24	42LTS451	301043
Estonia	Poland	11 Jan 24	47LTS129	301132
Czechoslovakia	Denmark	31 Jan 24	23LTS139	300585

PARTY ONE	PARTY TWO	DATE	CITATION	NUMBER
Consular relations establishment (Cont.)				
Germany	Siam	28 Feb 24	32LTS399	300828
Albania	Italy	29 Feb 24	44LTS343	301093
Czechoslovakia	Italy	01 Mar 24	34LTS55	300867
Japan	Siam	09 Mar 24	31LTS187	300795
Denmark	Latvia	03 Apr 24	33LTS393	300860
Multilateral		22 May 24	35LTS175	300895
Spain	UK Great Britain	27 Jun 24	28LTS523	300727
Poland	USSR (Soviet Union)	18 Jul 24	49LTS201	301183
Austria	Latvia	09 Aug 24	65LTS7	301516
Latvia	Norway	14 Aug 24	36LTS211	300924
Netherlands	Turkey	16 Aug 24	39LTS148	300999
Italy	Serb/Croat/Slovene	21 Aug 24	82LTS445	301883
Finland	Latvia	23 Aug 24	37LTS383	300962
Hungary	Norway	16 Sep 24	33LTS103	300835
Japan	Peru	30 Sep 24	102LTS33	302351
Czechoslovakia	Turkey	11 Oct 24	38LTS317	300987
Austria	Norway	03 Dec 24	31LTS151	300792
Latvia	Switzerland	04 Dec 24	34LTS405	300889
Japan	USSR (Soviet Union)	20 Jan 25	34LTS31	300866
France	Siam	14 Feb 25	43LTS189	301055
Finland	Netherlands	09 Mar 25	47LTS431	301148
Estonia	Germany	13 Mar 25	51LTS263	301236
Benelux Econ Union	Germany	04 Apr 25	37LTS203	300957
Germany	USA (United States)	21 May 25	52LTS133	301254
Netherlands	Siam	08 Jun 25	56LTS57	301323
Japan	Latvia	04 Jul 25	80LTS305	301836
Siam	Spain	03 Aug 25	55LTS39	301303
Germany	UK Great Britain	13 Aug 25	43LTS89	301050
Portugal	Siam	14 Aug 25	55LTS57	301304
Siam	UK Great Britain	15 Sep 25	49LTS51	301176
Germany	USSR (Soviet Union)	12 Oct 25	53LTS163	301258
Estonia	Switzerland	14 Oct 25	49LTS421	301195
Austria	China	19 Oct 25	55LTS9	301301
Norway	USSR (Soviet Union)	15 Dec 25	47LTS9	301127
Siam	Sweden	19 Dec 25	58LTS429	301386
Estonia	USA (United States)	23 Dec 25	50LTS13	301197
France	Poland	30 Dec 25	73LTS265	301719
Austria	Switzerland	06 Jan 26	46LTS299	301124
Estonia	UK Great Britain	18 Jan 26	48LTS209	301163
Chile	Turkey	30 Jan 26	59LTS249	301395
Denmark	Siam	01 Mar 26	47LTS103	301131
Finland	Hungary	20 Apr 26	48LTS119	301154
Cuba	USA (United States)	22 Apr 26	60LTS371	301421
Norway	Turkey	02 May 26	56LTS51	301322
Italy	Siam	09 May 26	61LTS215	301436
Germany	Sweden	14 May 26	51LTS99	301225
Albania	Serb/Croat/Slovene	22 Jun 26	91LTS55	302055
Bel-Lux Econ Union	Siam	13 Jul 26	62LTS287	301468
Norway	Siam	16 Jul 26	60LTS35	301404
Hungary	UK Great Britain	23 Jul 26	67LTS183	301546
Spain	Switzerland	04 Aug 26	65LTS39	301518
Hungary	USA (United States)	04 Sep 26	58LTS111	301369
Greece	Sweden	10 Sep 26	63LTS37	301479
Greece	Spain	23 Sep 26	91LTS121	302059
Austria	Estonia	15 Oct 26	93LTS137	302106
China	Finland	29 Oct 26	67LTS345	301556
Finland	Greece	18 Dec 26	70LTS89	301626
Chile	Norway	09 Feb 27	80LTS325	301837
Greece	Latvia	25 Feb 27	71LTS25	301652
Poland	Serb/Croat/Slovene	06 Mar 27	126LTS67	302871
Persia	Poland	19 Mar 27	109LTS87	302529
Serb/Croat/Slovene	UK Great Britain	12 May 27	80LTS165	301825
Greece	UK Great Britain	13 May 27	61LTS15	301425
Czechoslovakia	France	03 Jun 27	131LTS177	303009
Czechoslovakia	Estonia	20 Jul 27	77LTS341	301776

PARTY ONE	PARTY TWO	DATE	CITATION	NUMBER
Consular relations establishment (Cont.)				
Austria	Finland	08 Aug 27	70LTS349	301645
France	Germany	17 Aug 27	76LTS5	301761
Albania	France	15 Feb 28	107LTS307	302487
Multilateral		20 Feb 28	155LTS289	303582
Germany	Siam	07 Apr 28	85LTS337	301938
Latvia	USA (United States)	20 Apr 28	80LTS35	301821
Germany	Sweden	25 Apr 28	81LTS281	301844
Colombia	Vatican/Holy See	05 May 28	79LTS157	301808
Mexico	Panama	09 Jun 28	141LTS191	303265
Belgium	Poland	12 Jun 28	123LTS25	302803
Austria	USA (United States)	19 Jun 28	118LTS241	302728
Afghanistan	Finland	17 Jul 28	112LTS9	302601
Persia	Sweden	09 Aug 28	80LTS407	301841
China	Germany	17 Aug 28	91LTS93	302057
Germany	Lithuania	30 Oct 28	90LTS255	302043
Czechoslovakia	Serb/Croat/Slovene	07 Nov 28	98LTS297	302252
United Arab Rep	Persia	28 Nov 28	93LTS381	302127
Germany	Hedjaz	26 Apr 29	115LTS265	302690
Persia	Sweden	10 May 29	102LTS9	302349
France	Persia	10 May 29	150LTS329	303465
Estonia	USSR (Soviet Union)	17 May 29	94LTS323	302152
Belgium	Persia	23 May 29	110LTS369	302568
Germany	Turkey	28 May 29	133LTS257	303069
Bolivia	Netherlands	30 May 29	133LTS113	303062
Bulgaria	Germany	04 Jun 29	106LTS49	302436
Colombia	Denmark	21 Jun 29	125LTS113	302850
Serb/Croat/Slovene	Spain	27 Sep 29	98LTS319	302253
China	Greece	30 Sep 29	123LTS127	302811
Italy	Panama	16 Oct 29	138LTS355	303199
Poland	Romania	17 Dec 29	119LTS333	302754
Lithuania	Persia	13 Jan 30	131LTS221	303013
France	Latvia	20 Jan 30	169LTS125	303917
Austria	Germany	12 Apr 30	115LTS333	302694
Norway	Persia	08 May 30	134LTS153	303089
Germany	Irish Free State	12 May 30	131LTS153	303008
Romania	UK Great Britain	06 Aug 30	123LTS307	302822
El Salvador	USA (United States)	05 Sep 30	134LTS207	303093
Czechoslovakia	Persia	29 Oct 30	121LTS53	302783
Greece	Turkey	30 Oct 30	125LTS371	302866
Finland	Norway	11 Nov 30	130LTS17	302980
Afghanistan	Lithuania	09 Dec 30	138LTS29	303178
Norway	Turkey	16 Mar 31	138LTS41	303180
Siam	Switzerland	28 May 31	125LTS357	302864
Germany	Hungary	18 Jul 31	150LTS111	303458
Bolivia	Denmark	09 Nov 31	147LTS27	303387
Italy	Latvia	11 May 32	150LTS9	303450
Afghanistan	Iraq	20 Dec 32	155LTS375	303588
Latvia	USSR (Soviet Union)	04 Dec 33	148LTS145	303410
Denmark	Persia	20 Feb 34	158LTS299	303640
United Arab Rep	Switzerland	07 Jun 34	159LTS137	303656
Bulgaria	Poland	22 Dec 34	159LTS265	303671
Czechoslovakia	USSR (Soviet Union)	16 Nov 35	169LTS143	303918
Hungary	Poland	24 Apr 36	185LTS303	304296
Finland	Mexico	02 Oct 36	179LTS303	304157
Chile	Sweden	30 Oct 36	188LTS283	304364
Bulgaria	Mexico	05 Nov 36	187LTS37	304331
Estonia	Mexico	28 Jan 37	185LTS39	304272
United Arab Rep	Turkey	07 Apr 37	191LTS89	304437
Sweden	Yugoslavia	14 May 37	194LTS21	304504
France	UK Great Britain	29 Jul 37	184LTS351	304257
Denmark	Haiti	21 Oct 37	190LTS231	304422
Belgium	Siam	05 Nov 37	190LTS163	304414
Denmark	Siam	05 Nov 37	188LTS187	304358
Siam	USA (United States)	13 Nov 37	192LTS247	304476
Siam	UK Great Britain	23 Nov 37	188LTS333	304366

PARTY ONE	PARTY TWO	DATE	CITATION	NUMBER
Consular relations establishment (Cont.)				
Italy	Siam	03 Dec 37	189LTS255	304389
Greece	Latvia	15 Jan 38	195LTS19	304533
Netherlands	Siam	01 Feb 38	193LTS13	304485
Greece	Mexico	17 Mar 38	198LTS325	304649
Portugal	Siam	02 Jul 38	200LTS149	304688
Liberia	USA (United States)	07 Oct 38	201LTS183	304712
Guatemala	Norway	20 Dec 38	198LTS117	304631
Diplomatic relations establishment				
Estonia	USSR (Soviet Union)	02 Feb 20	11LTS29	300289
Germany	Latvia	15 Jul 20	2LTS91	300052
Latvia	Ukrainian SSR	03 Aug 21	17LTS317	300442
Afghanistan	UK Great Britain	22 Nov 21	14LTS47	300367
Estonia	Ukrainian SSR	25 Nov 21	11LTS121	300294
Afghanistan	France	28 Apr 22	105LTS147	302408
Latvia	Vatican/Holy See	30 May 22	17LTS365	300443
Austria	Turkey	28 Jan 24	32LTS297	300821
Germany	Turkey	03 Mar 24	41LTS237	301017
Denmark	USSR (Soviet Union)	18 Jun 24	27LTS149	300677
Netherlands	Turkey	16 Aug 24	39LTS148	300999
Czechoslovakia	Turkey	11 Oct 24	38LTS317	300987
Estonia	Turkey	01 Dec 24	70LTS77	301624
Finland	Turkey	09 Dec 24	59LTS287	301398
Latvia	Turkey	03 Jan 25	59LTS81	301390
Japan	USSR (Soviet Union)	20 Jan 25	34LTS31	300866
Switzerland	Turkey	19 Sep 25	61LTS395	301449
Chile	Turkey	30 Jan 26	59LTS249	301395
Afghanistan	Germany	03 Mar 26	62LTS115	301460
China	Finland	29 Oct 26	67LTS345	301556
Belgium	Estonia	08 Feb 27	74LTS227	301740
Afghanistan	Poland	03 Nov 27	74LTS83	301734
Afghanistan	Latvia	16 Feb 28	78LTS99	301781
Afghanistan	Switzerland	17 Feb 28	73LTS323	301722
Afghanistan	Finland	17 Jul 28	112LTS9	302601
Latvia	Persia	15 Jan 29	162LTS299	303742
Germany	Hedjaz	26 Apr 29	115LTS265	302690
Belgium	Persia	23 May 29	110LTS369	302568
China	Greece	30 Sep 29	123LTS127	302811
Lithuania	Persia	13 Jan 30	131LTS221	303013
Norway	Persia	08 May 30	134LTS153	303089
Iraq	UK Great Britain	30 Jun 30	132LTS363	303048
Lithuania	Turkey	17 Sep 30	125LTS249	302858
Czechoslovakia	Persia	29 Oct 30	121LTS53	302783
Abyssinia	Japan	15 Nov 30	133LTS135	303063
Afghanistan	Japan	19 Nov 30	121LTS237	302789
Afghanistan	Estonia	06 Dec 30	137LTS445	303174
Afghanistan	Lithuania	09 Dec 30	138LTS29	303178
Afghanistan	Iraq	20 Dec 32	155LTS375	303588
China	Turkey	04 Apr 34	153LTS161	303515
United Arab Rep	UK Great Britain	26 Aug 36	173LTS401	304031
Bulgaria	Mexico	05 Nov 36	187LTS37	304331
Estonia	Mexico	28 Jan 37	185LTS39	304272
Afghanistan	Czechoslovakia	13 Oct 37	191LTS9	304431
Diplomatic relations resumption				
Netherlands	Venezuela	11 May 20	7LTS85	300176
Lithuania	USSR (Soviet Union)	12 Jul 20	3LTS106	300094
Latvia	USSR (Soviet Union)	11 Aug 20	2LTS195	300067
China	Germany	20 May 21	9LTS271	300261
Bolivia	Germany	20 Jul 21	10LTS301	300275
Norway	USSR (Soviet Union)	02 Sep 21	7LTS293	300196
Germany	USSR (Soviet Union)	16 Apr 22	19LTS247	300498
Poland	Turkey	23 Jul 23	49LTS323	301188
Multilateral		24 Jul 23	28LTS11	300701
China	USSR (Soviet Union)	31 May 24	37LTS175	300955
Persia	Poland	19 Mar 27	109LTS87	302529

PARTY ONE	PARTY TWO	DATE	CITATION	NUMBER
Diplomatic relations resumption (Cont.)				
UK Great Britain	USSR (Soviet Union)	21 Dec 29	99LTS61	302268
Colombia	Peru	24 May 34	164LTS21	303786
Diplomatic missions				
China	Persia	01 Jun 20	9LTS17	300240
Danzig	Poland	09 Nov 20	6LTS189	300153
Germany	USSR (Soviet Union)	06 May 21	6LTS267	300159
Estonia	Latvia	12 Jul 21	11LTS87	300291
Estonia	Lithuania	12 Jul 21	11LTS99	300292
Denmark	USSR (Soviet Union)	23 Apr 23	18LTS15	300450
United Arab Rep	UK Great Britain	18 Jul 23	18LTS323	300474
Czechoslovakia	Italy	01 Mar 24	34LTS55	300867
Sweden	USSR (Soviet Union)	15 Mar 24	25LTS251	300613
Sweden	Turkey	31 May 24	38LTS148	300972
Spain	UK Great Britain	27 Jun 24	28LTS523	300727
Germany	USA (United States)	21 May 25	52LTS133	301254
Austria	Estonia	15 Oct 26	93LTS137	302106
Czechoslovakia	France	03 Jun 27	131LTS177	303009
Albania	France	15 Feb 28	107LTS307	302487
China	Germany	17 Aug 28	91LTS93	302057
Czechoslovakia	Serb/Croat/Slovene	07 Nov 28	98LTS297	302252
Bulgaria	Germany	04 Jun 29	106LTS49	302436
France	Latvia	20 Jan 30	169LTS125	303917
Czechoslovakia	USSR (Soviet Union)	16 Nov 35	169LTS143	303918
Hungary	Poland	24 Apr 36	185LTS303	304296
Multilateral		23 Dec 36	201LTS295	304721
Siam	Sweden	08 Nov 37	185LTS337	304298
Norway	Siam	15 Nov 37	186LTS9	304301
Liberia	USA (United States)	07 Oct 38	201LTS183	304712
Human rights				
France	Poland	03 Sep 19	1LTS337	300028
Bulgaria	Greece	27 Nov 19	1LTS67	300009
Multilateral		09 Dec 19	5LTS335	300140
Austria	Czechoslovakia	07 Jun 20	3LTS189	300098
Multilateral		10 Aug 20	28LTS223	300711
Danzig	Poland	09 Nov 20	6LTS189	300153
Multilateral		19 Jan 21	5LTS9	300113
Latvia	Lithuania	14 May 21	17LTS233	300439
Ireland	UK Great Britain	06 Dec 21	26LTS9	300636
Multilateral		17 Mar 22	11LTS167	300296
Other Unilat Decla	Lithuania	12 May 22	22LTS393	300569
Latvia	Vatican/Holy See	30 May 22	17LTS365	300443
Other Unilat Decla	Albania	02 Oct 22	9LTS173	300249
Greece	Turkey	30 Jan 23	32LTS75	300807
France	USA (United States)	13 Feb 23	26LTS69	300641
France	USA (United States)	13 Feb 23	26LTS53	300640
Iraq	UK Great Britain	30 Apr 23	35LTS13	300890
Multilateral		24 Jul 23	36LTS145	300913
Multilateral		24 Jul 23	28LTS215	300708
Multilateral		18 Dec 23	28LTS541	300729
Belgium	USA (United States)	21 Jan 24	31LTS137	300791
Japan	Siam	09 Mar 24	31LTS187	300795
Multilateral		08 May 24	29LTS85	300736
Poland	USSR (Soviet Union)	18 Jul 24	49LTS201	301183
Other Unilat Decla	Greece	29 Sep 24	29LTS123	300738
Other Unilat Decla	Bulgaria	29 Sep 24	29LTS117	300737
UK Great Britain	USA (United States)	03 Dec 24	43LTS41	301046
Czechoslovakia	Poland	23 Apr 25	48LTS287	301170
Netherlands	Siam	08 Jun 25	56LTS57	301323
Siam	Spain	03 Aug 25	55LTS39	301303
Portugal	Siam	14 Aug 25	55LTS57	301304
Germany	USSR (Soviet Union)	12 Oct 25	53LTS7	301257
Great Britain	Nejd	02 Nov 25	60LTS419	301423
Estonia	USA (United States)	23 Dec 25	50LTS13	301197
France	Turkey	31 Jul 26	54LTS177	301284

PARTY ONE	PARTY TWO	DATE	CITATION	NUMBER
Human rights (Cont.)				
Hungary	USA (United States)	04 Sep 26	58LTS111	301369
Multilateral		12 Jul 27	135LTS247	303115
Multilateral		28 Jul 27	64LTS379	301511
Romania	Yugoslavia	10 Mar 33	146LTS231	303373
Inviolability				
Chile	Netherlands	04 Nov 13	84LTS79	301904
Cuba	Netherlands	31 Dec 13	14LTS29	300366
Estonia	Lithuania	12 Jul 21	11LTS99	300292
Estonia	Latvia	12 Jul 21	11LTS87	300291
Latvia	Ukrainian SSR	03 Aug 21	17LTS317	300442
Mexico	UK Great Britain	17 May 22	14LTS83	300368
Austria	Netherlands	06 Nov 22	17LTS375	300444
Peru	Venezuela	14 Mar 23	20LTS45	300505
Latvia	Poland	03 Jan 24	42LTS451	301043
Estonia	Poland	11 Jan 24	47LTS129	301132
Albania	Italy	29 Feb 24	44LTS343	301093
Czechoslovakia	Italy	01 Mar 24	34LTS55	300867
Italy	Serb/Croat/Slovene	21 Aug 24	82LTS445	301883
Japan	Peru	30 Sep 24	102LTS33	302351
Germany	USSR (Soviet Union)	12 Oct 25	53LTS163	301258
France	Poland	30 Dec 25	73LTS265	301719
Albania	Serb/Croat/Slovene	22 Jun 26	91LTS55	302055
Greece	Spain	23 Sep 26	91LTS121	302059
Austria	Estonia	15 Oct 26	93LTS137	302106
Belgium	Estonia	08 Feb 27	74LTS227	301740
Poland	Serb/Croat/Slovene	06 Mar 27	126LTS67	302871
Czechoslovakia	France	03 Jun 27	131LTS177	303009
Albania	France	15 Feb 28	107LTS307	302487
Belgium	Poland	12 Jun 28	123LTS25	302803
China	Germany	17 Aug 28	91LTS93	302057
Germany	Lithuania	30 Oct 28	90LTS255	302043
Czechoslovakia	Serb/Croat/Slovene	07 Nov 28	98LTS297	302252
Norway	USA (United States)	25 Feb 29	134LTS81	303085
Bulgaria	Germany	04 Jun 29	106LTS49	302436
Poland	Romania	17 Dec 29	119LTS333	302754
France	Latvia	20 Jan 30	169LTS125	303917
Italy	Latvia	11 May 32	150LTS9	303450
Czechoslovakia	USSR (Soviet Union)	16 Nov 35	169LTS143	303918
Hungary	Poland	24 Apr 36	185LTS303	304296
Liberia	USA (United States)	07 Oct 38	201LTS183	304712
Privileges and immunities				
Chile	Netherlands	04 Nov 13	84LTS79	301904
Cuba	Netherlands	31 Dec 13	14LTS29	300366
China	Persia	01 Jun 20	9LTS17	300240
Greece	UK Great Britain	22 Sep 20	2LTS367	300090
Portugal	UK Great Britain	09 Dec 20	7LTS257	300192
Norway	UK Great Britain	22 Apr 21	5LTS33	300114
Germany	USSR (Soviet Union)	06 May 21	6LTS267	300159
China	Germany	20 May 21	9LTS271	300261
Afghanistan	Persia	22 Jun 21	33LTS285	300853
Sweden	UK Great Britain	08 Jul 21	5LTS329	300139
Estonia	Lithuania	12 Jul 21	11LTS99	300292
Latvia	Lithuania	12 Jul 21	25LTS299	300619
Estonia	Latvia	12 Jul 21	11LTS87	300291
Denmark	UK Great Britain	14 Jul 21	6LTS181	300151
Norway	USSR (Soviet Union)	02 Sep 21	7LTS293	300196
Italy	Serb/Croat/Slovene	06 Apr 22	118LTS207	302725
Latvia	Vatican/Holy See	30 May 22	17LTS365	300443
Germany	Poland	15 Jun 22	34LTS201	300875
Austria	Netherlands	06 Nov 22	17LTS375	300444
Latvia	Poland	03 Jan 24	42LTS451	301043
Estonia	Poland	11 Jan 24	47LTS129	301132
Albania	Italy	29 Feb 24	44LTS343	301093
Czechoslovakia	Italy	01 Mar 24	34LTS55	300867

PARTY ONE	PARTY TWO	DATE	CITATION	NUMBER
Privileges and immunities (Cont.)				
Poland	USSR (Soviet Union)	18 Jul 24	49LTS201	301183
Italy	Serb/Croat/Slovene	21 Aug 24	82LTS445	301883
Japan	Peru	30 Sep 24	102LTS33	302351
Finland	Netherlands	09 Mar 25	47LTS431	301148
Estonia	Germany	13 Mar 25	51LTS263	301236
France	Germany	13 Apr 25	109LTS295	302546
Czechoslovakia	Denmark	24 Jul 25	37LTS97	300948
Germany	USSR (Soviet Union)	12 Oct 25	53LTS163	301258
Estonia	USA (United States)	23 Dec 25	50LTS13	301197
France	Poland	30 Dec 25	73LTS265	301719
Afghanistan	Germany	03 Mar 26	62LTS115	301460
Cuba	USA (United States)	22 Apr 26	60LTS371	301421
Albania	Serb/Croat/Slovene	22 Jun 26	91LTS55	302055
Hungary	USA (United States)	04 Sep 26	58LTS111	301369
Greece	Spain	23 Sep 26	91LTS121	302059
Bel-Lux Econ Union	Estonia	28 Sep 26	62LTS433	301475
Austria	Estonia	15 Oct 26	93LTS137	302106
Austria	Germany	05 Feb 27	73LTS205	301714
Belgium	Estonia	08 Feb 27	74LTS227	301740
Poland	Serb/Croat/Slovene	06 Mar 27	126LTS67	302871
Persia	Poland	19 Mar 27	109LTS87	302529
Czechoslovakia	France	03 Jun 27	131LTS177	303009
Albania	France	15 Feb 28	107LTS307	302487
Multilateral		20 Feb 28	155LTS289	303582
Multilateral		20 Feb 28	155LTS259	303581
Latvia	USA (United States)	20 Apr 28	80LTS35	301821
Czechoslovakia	France	07 May 28	114LTS171	302663
France	Persia	11 May 28	82LTS43	301858
Belgium	Persia	15 May 28	94LTS447	302160
Germany	Persia	15 May 28	107LTS389	302495
Mexico	Panama	09 Jun 28	141LTS191	303265
Belgium	Poland	12 Jun 28	123LTS25	302803
Austria	Persia	17 Jun 28	112LTS101	302610
Austria	USA (United States)	19 Jun 28	118LTS241	302728
Netherlands	Persia	20 Jun 28	81LTS431	301852
Belgium	France	30 Jun 28	93LTS377	302126
Persia	USA (United States)	11 Jul 28	107LTS375	302494
Afghanistan	Finland	17 Jul 28	112LTS9	302601
Italy	Persia	24 Jul 28	95LTS269	302179
Persia	Sweden	09 Aug 28	80LTS407	301841
Persia	Switzerland	28 Aug 28	107LTS397	302496
Denmark	Persia	08 Sep 28	82LTS57	301859
Germany	Lithuania	30 Oct 28	90LTS255	302043
Czechoslovakia	Serb/Croat/Slovene	07 Nov 28	98LTS297	302252
United Arab Rep	Persia	28 Nov 28	93LTS381	302127
Italy	UK Great Britain	25 Jan 29	95LTS39	302162
Germany	Persia	17 Feb 29	111LTS19	302576
Germany	Persia	17 Feb 29	111LTS241	302590
Netherlands	Spain	27 Mar 29	101LTS479	302346
Japan	Persia	30 Mar 29	107LTS427	302499
Germany	Hedjaz	26 Apr 29	115LTS265	302690
Belgium	Persia	09 May 29	110LTS391	302570
France	Persia	10 May 29	150LTS329	303465
Norway	Persia	10 May 29	107LTS403	302497
Persia	Sweden	10 May 29	102LTS9	302349
Belgium	Persia	23 May 29	110LTS369	302568
France	UK Great Britain	25 May 29	95LTS55	302163
Persia	Sweden	27 May 29	105LTS279	302420
Germany	Turkey	28 May 29	133LTS257	303069
Bulgaria	Germany	04 Jun 29	106LTS49	302436
Italy	Turkey	09 Sep 29	129LTS195	302962
China	Greece	30 Sep 29	123LTS127	302811
Poland	Romania	17 Dec 29	119LTS333	302754
France	Latvia	20 Jan 30	169LTS125	303917
France	Luxembourg	31 Mar 30	122LTS29	302797
Privileges and immunities (Cont.)				
Czechoslovakia	Persia	29 Oct 30	121LTS53	302783
Czechoslovakia	Persia	29 Oct 30	121LTS59	302784
Afghanistan	Japan	19 Nov 30	121LTS237	302789
Poland	USA (United States)	15 Jun 31	139LTS395	303223
Multilateral		10 Nov 31	131LTS327	303023
Italy	Latvia	11 May 32	150LTS9	303450
Ethiopia	Switzerland	24 May 33	153LTS63	303508
Finland	USA (United States)	13 Feb 34	152LTS45	303484
Denmark	Persia	20 Feb 34	158LTS299	303640
Bulgaria	Poland	22 Dec 34	159LTS265	303671
Finland	Germany	25 Sep 35	172LTS359	304000
Czechoslovakia	USSR (Soviet Union)	16 Nov 35	169LTS143	303918
Afghanistan	USA (United States)	26 Mar 36	168LTS143	303895
Hungary	Poland	24 Apr 36	185LTS303	304296
Multilateral		30 Jul 36	197LTS31	304602
United Arab Rep	UK Great Britain	26 Aug 36	173LTS433	304032
United Arab Rep	UK Great Britain	26 Aug 36	173LTS401	304031
Estonia	Mexico	28 Jan 37	185LTS39	304272
Chile	Cuba	13 Mar 37	195LTS389	304558
United Arab Rep	Turkey	07 Apr 37	191LTS89	304437
Multilateral		08 May 37	182LTS37	304202
Iran	Iraq	18 Jul 37	190LTS259	304424
France	UK Great Britain	29 Jul 37	184LTS351	304257
Siam	Sweden	08 Nov 37	185LTS337	304298
Norway	Siam	15 Nov 37	186LTS9	304301
Denmark	Finland	02 Dec 37	187LTS379	304345
China	Estonia	21 Dec 37	194LTS123	304516
Greece	Latvia	15 Jan 38	195LTS19	304533
Portugal	Siam	02 Jul 38	200LTS149	304688
Liberia	USA (United States)	07 Oct 38	201LTS183	304712
El Salvador	Norway	21 Nov 38	198LTS157	304636
Multilateral		05 Feb 39	196LTS303	304592
Brazil	USA (United States)	11 Oct 40	203LTS261	304768
Property				
Estonia	Latvia	12 Jul 21	11LTS87	300291
Estonia	Lithuania	12 Jul 21	11LTS99	300292
Norway	USSR (Soviet Union)	02 Sep 21	7LTS293	300196
Czechoslovakia	Italy	01 Mar 24	34LTS55	300867
Czechoslovakia	Denmark	24 Jul 25	37LTS97	300948
Albania	Serb/Croat/Slovene	22 Jun 26	91LTS55	302055
Austria	Estonia	15 Oct 26	93LTS137	302106
Albania	France	15 Feb 28	107LTS307	302487
Belgium	Persia	15 May 28	94LTS447	302160
Germany	Lithuania	30 Oct 28	90LTS255	302043
Czechoslovakia	Serb/Croat/Slovene	07 Nov 28	98LTS297	302252
Bulgaria	Germany	04 Jun 29	106LTS49	302436
France	India	06 Jun 29	95LTS61	302164
Poland	Romania	17 Dec 29	119LTS333	302754
France	Latvia	20 Jan 30	169LTS125	303917
El Salvador	USA (United States)	05 Sep 30	134LTS207	303093
Czechoslovakia	USSR (Soviet Union)	16 Nov 35	169LTS143	303918
Hungary	Poland	24 Apr 36	185LTS303	304296
Liberia	USA (United States)	07 Oct 38	201LTS183	304712
Proxy diplomacy				
Lithuania	Poland	29 Nov 20	9LTS63	300243
Danzig	Finland	08 Jun 31	120LTS291	302772
Greece	Turkey	14 Sep 33	156LTS165	303600
Nationality and citizenship				
Greece	Spain	06 Mar 19	3LTS81	300092
Bulgaria	Greece	27 Nov 19	1LTS67	300009
Multilateral		09 Dec 19	5LTS335	300140
Estonia	USSR (Soviet Union)	02 Feb 20	11LTS29	300289
Germany	Latvia	20 Apr 20	2LTS71	300049
France	Germany	05 May 20	8LTS55	300206

PARTY ONE	PARTY TWO	DATE	CITATION	NUMBER
Nationality and citizenship (Cont.)				
Austria	Czechoslovakia	07 Jun 20	3LTS189	300098
Czechoslovakia	Germany	29 Jun 20	20LTS85	300509
Lithuania	USSR (Soviet Union)	12 Jul 20	3LTS106	300094
Multilateral		05 Aug 20	2LTS49	300046
Multilateral		10 Aug 20	28LTS223	300711
Latvia	USSR (Soviet Union)	11 Aug 20	2LTS195	300067
Poland	USSR (Soviet Union)	12 Oct 20	4LTS7	300101
Estonia	Latvia	19 Oct 20	17LTS189	300437
Germany	Poland	08 Dec 20	7LTS323	300199
Portugal	UK Great Britain	10 Jan 21	7LTS264	300193
Poland	USSR (Soviet Union)	18 Mar 21	6LTS51	300149
Norway	UK Great Britain	22 Apr 21	5LTS33	300114
Germany	USSR (Soviet Union)	06 May 21	6LTS267	300159
Latvia	Lithuania	13 May 21	17LTS211	300438
Latvia	Lithuania	14 May 21	17LTS233	300439
Denmark	UK Great Britain	14 Jul 21	6LTS181	300151
Latvia	Ukrainian SSR	03 Aug 21	17LTS317	300442
Danzig	Poland	24 Oct 21	116LTS5	302699
Latvia	USSR (Soviet Union)	06 Nov 21	17LTS251	300440
Estonia	Ukrainian SSR	25 Nov 21	11LTS143	300295
Estonia	Ukrainian SSR	25 Nov 21	11LTS121	300294
Allied Powers	Poland	01 Apr 22	9LTS325	300265
Other Unilat Decla	Lithuania	12 May 22	22LTS393	300569
Germany	Poland	15 May 22	10LTS37	300273
Austria	Germany	23 May 22	26LTS405	300660
Multilateral		05 Jul 22	13LTS237	300355
France	Saar	05 Jul 22	27LTS265	300689
Finland	USSR (Soviet Union)	12 Aug 22	19LTS105	300489
Other Unilat Decla	Albania	02 Oct 22	9LTS173	300249
Italy	Serb/Croat/Slovene	23 Oct 22	18LTS461	300481
Greece	Turkey	30 Jan 23	32LTS75	300807
Germany	Switzerland	24 Mar 23	27LTS41	300666
Czechoslovakia	Germany	02 May 23	31LTS0	300793
France	UK Great Britain	24 May 23	18LTS305	300472
Germany	Poland	23 Jun 23	67LTS9	301537
Multilateral		24 Jul 23	28LTS11	300701
France	UK Great Britain	24 Jul 23	36LTS207	300923
Bulgaria	USA (United States)	23 Nov 23	25LTS238	300611
Austria	Turkey	28 Jan 24	32LTS303	300822
Hungary	Romania	16 Apr 24	45LTS325	301106
Hungary	Romania	16 Apr 24	46LTS7	301111
Multilateral		08 May 24	29LTS85	300736
Italy	Serb/Croat/Slovene	14 Jul 24	82LTS257	301876
Italy	UK Great Britain	15 Jul 24	36LTS379	300936
Germany	Poland	30 Aug 24	32LTS331	300824
Czechoslovakia	Poland	23 Apr 25	48LTS287	301170
France	Turkey	30 May 26	54LTS195	301285
France	Switzerland	27 Aug 26	59LTS231	301392
Greece	Spain	23 Sep 26	91LTS121	302059
Albania	Greece	13 Oct 26	83LTS361	301900
Austria	Estonia	15 Oct 26	93LTS137	302106
Poland	Serb/Croat/Slovene	06 Mar 27	126LTS67	302871
Czechoslovakia	Portugal	23 Nov 27	124LTS7	302829
Multilateral		20 Feb 28	129LTS223	302963
Multilateral		20 Feb 28	86LTS111	301950
Czechoslovakia	France	07 May 28	114LTS117	302660
Belgium	Poland	12 Jun 28	123LTS25	302803
Austria	Hungary	25 Jun 28	100LTS85	302296
Belgium	France	12 Sep 28	123LTS97	302809
Belgium	France	12 Sep 28	123LTS91	302808
Germany	Lithuania	30 Oct 28	90LTS255	302043
Colombia	UK Great Britain	02 Dec 29	110LTS401	302571
Bulgaria	Turkey	23 Dec 29	122LTS17	302796
Liberia	UK Great Britain	17 Jan 30	101LTS395	302338
Estonia	Sweden	20 Jan 30	106LTS279	302451

PARTY ONE	PARTY TWO	DATE	CITATION	NUMBER
Nationality and citizenship (Cont.)				
Latvia	Sweden	30 Jan 30	110LTS139	302558
Latvia	Spain	08 Mar 30	113LTS135	302641
Austria	Sweden	24 Mar 30	105LTS313	302424
Multilateral		12 Apr 30	179LTS89	304137
Hungary	Latvia	04 May 30	101LTS449	302344
Denmark	Estonia	13 May 30	106LTS159	302443
Denmark	Poland	26 Oct 31	125LTS337	302862
Multilateral		10 Dec 31	129LTS177	302961
Albania	USA (United States)	05 Apr 32	162LTS31	303732
Austria	Germany	07 Dec 32	137LTS69	303147
Romania	Yugoslavia	30 Jan 33	146LTS173	303369
Norway	Sweden	22 Aug 33	141LTS217	303267
Denmark	Norway	11 Nov 33	143LTS25	303302
Estonia	Finland	12 Sep 36	172LTS345	303999
Hungary	UK Great Britain	22 Mar 37	190LTS59	304405
Siam	UK Great Britain	31 Mar 37	179LTS257	304153
United Arab Rep	Turkey	07 Apr 37	191LTS105	304439
Multilateral		08 May 37	182LTS37	304202
France	UK Great Britain	29 Jul 37	184LTS351	304257
Germany	Romania	03 Oct 37	190LTS369	304429
Siam	UK Great Britain	23 Nov 37	188LTS333	304366
Italy	Siam	03 Dec 37	189LTS255	304389
Estonia	Germany	23 Dec 37	189LTS333	304393
Greece	Mexico	17 Mar 38	198LTS325	304649
Belgium	Luxembourg	04 Mar 39	197LTS141	304610
Protection of nationals				
Greece	Spain	06 Mar 19	3LTS81	300092
Multilateral		09 Dec 19	5LTS335	300140
Germany	Poland	09 Jan 20	9LTS77	300245
Austria	Czechoslovakia	02 Aug 20	32LTS365	300826
Austria	Germany	01 Sep 20	4LTS201	300107
UK Great Britain	USSR (Soviet Union)	16 Mar 21	4LTS127	300104
Germany	USSR (Soviet Union)	06 May 21	6LTS267	300159
China	Germany	20 May 21	9LTS271	300261
Belgium	Luxembourg	25 Jul 21	9LTS223	300256
Austria	USA (United States)	24 Aug 21	7LTS155	300184
Estonia	France	07 Jan 22	62LTS9	301452
Czechoslovakia	Denmark	16 Jan 22	14LTS267	300378
Japan	USA (United States)	11 Feb 22	12LTS201	300311
China	Japan	28 Mar 22	13LTS213	300353
Finland	USSR (Soviet Union)	12 Aug 22	19LTS105	300489
Germany	Spain	15 Jan 23	26LTS455	300662
France	USA (United States)	13 Feb 23	26LTS69	300641
France	USA (United States)	13 Feb 23	26LTS53	300640
Iraq	UK Great Britain	30 Apr 23	35LTS13	300890
Czechoslovakia	Hungary	13 Jul 23	35LTS237	300898
Multilateral		24 Jul 23	28LTS11	300701
Multilateral		24 Jul 23	36LTS145	300913
Multilateral		24 Jul 23	36LTS167	300917
Multilateral		14 Dec 23	29LTS37	300732
Finland	UK Great Britain	14 Dec 23	23LTS125	300583
Latvia	Poland	03 Jan 24	42LTS451	301043
Estonia	Poland	11 Jan 24	47LTS129	301132
Austria	Turkey	28 Jan 24	32LTS303	300822
Iraq	UK Great Britain	25 Mar 24	35LTS131	300893
Iraq	UK Great Britain	25 Mar 24	35LTS35	300891
Hungary	Italy	27 Mar 24	45LTS65	301099
Spain	UK Great Britain	27 Jun 24	28LTS523	300727
Latvia	Norway	14 Aug 24	36LTS211	300924
Italy	Serb/Croat/Slovene	21 Aug 24	82LTS445	301883
Japan	Mexico	08 Oct 24	36LTS259	300927
UK Great Britain	USA (United States)	03 Dec 24	43LTS41	301046
Latvia	Switzerland	04 Dec 24	34LTS405	300889
Czechoslovakia	Poland	06 Mar 25	46LTS201	301120

PARTY ONE	PARTY TWO	DATE	CITATION	NUMBER
Protection of nationals (Cont.)				
Finland	Netherlands	09 Mar 25	47LTS431	301148
Denmark	UK Great Britain	04 Jun 25	36LTS131	300911
Bel-Lux Econ Union	Japan	27 Jun 25	36LTS95	300907
Germany	USSR (Soviet Union)	12 Oct 25	53LTS7	301257
Germany	USSR (Soviet Union)	12 Oct 25	53LTS163	301258
Siam	Sweden	19 Dec 25	58LTS429	301386
Estonia	USA (United States)	23 Dec 25	50LTS13	301197
France	Poland	30 Dec 25	73LTS265	301719
Italy	Siam	09 May 26	61LTS215	301436
France	Turkey	30 May 26	54LTS195	301285
Bel-Lux Econ Union	Siam	13 Jul 26	62LTS287	301468
Norway	Siam	16 Jul 26	60LTS35	301404
Spain	Switzerland	04 Aug 26	65LTS39	301518
Hungary	USA (United States)	04 Sep 26	58LTS111	301369
Austria	Estonia	15 Oct 26	93LTS137	302106
Belgium	Estonia	08 Feb 27	74LTS227	301740
Serb/Croat/Slovene	UK Great Britain	12 May 27	80LTS165	301825
Czechoslovakia	Poland	30 May 27	98LTS233	302251
Norway	Sweden	19 Nov 27	68LTS209	301584
Greece	Switzerland	01 Dec 27	84LTS271	301907
Albania	France	15 Feb 28	107LTS307	302487
Multilateral		20 Feb 28	155LTS289	303582
Latvia	USA (United States)	20 Apr 28	80LTS35	301821
Austria	Persia	17 Jun 28	112LTS101	302610
Persia	USA (United States)	11 Jul 28	107LTS375	302494
Abyssinia	Italy	02 Aug 28	94LTS413	302158
China	Germany	17 Aug 28	91LTS93	302057
Czechoslovakia	Serb/Croat/Slovene	07 Nov 28	98LTS297	302252
Bulgaria	Germany	04 Jun 29	106LTS49	302436
Poland	Romania	30 Oct 29	121LTS167	302787
Multilateral		09 Jan 30	115LTS473	302696
France	Latvia	20 Jan 30	169LTS125	303917
Multilateral		12 Apr 30	179LTS89	304137
Multilateral		12 Apr 30	179LTS115	304138
Japan	Lithuania	02 May 30	126LTS369	302895
Norway	Persia	08 May 30	134LTS153	303089
Canada	USA (United States)	09 May 30	121LTS45	302782
Irish Free State	Italy	10 May 30	132LTS147	303034
Austria	Japan	16 Aug 30	126LTS351	302894
Belgium	France	23 Aug 30	166LTS11	303825
El Salvador	USA (United States)	05 Sep 30	134LTS207	303093
Norway	Turkey	16 Mar 31	138LTS41	303180
Germany	Hungary	18 Jul 31	150LTS111	303458
Austria	Yugoslavia	21 Jul 31	147LTS123	303397
Hungary	Romania	12 Aug 31	186LTS325	304321
Bolivia	Denmark	09 Nov 31	147LTS27	303387
Bulgaria	Germany	24 Jun 32	147LTS211	303400
Romania	Yugoslavia	30 Jan 33	146LTS173	303369
Belgium	Netherlands	20 Feb 33	165LTS383	303824
Latvia	USSR (Soviet Union)	04 Dec 33	148LTS145	303410
Finland	USA (United States)	13 Feb 34	152LTS45	303484
Turkey	Yugoslavia	03 Jul 34	179LTS207	304149
Czechoslovakia	Luxembourg	01 Dec 34	168LTS287	303906
Poland	Spain	14 Dec 34	168LTS315	303908
Bulgaria	Poland	22 Dec 34	159LTS265	303671
Denmark	France	28 Jan 35	158LTS11	303619
Estonia	Italy	10 Aug 35	185LTS287	304295
Czechoslovakia	USSR (Soviet Union)	16 Nov 35	169LTS143	303918
Estonia	Lithuania	10 Dec 35	168LTS101	303889
Luxembourg	Netherlands	01 Apr 36	179LTS11	304130
China	Latvia	25 Jun 36	176LTS275	304066
United Arab Rep	UK Great Britain	26 Aug 36	173LTS401	304031
Cuba	UK Great Britain	19 Feb 37	192LTS301	304480
United Arab Rep	Turkey	07 Apr 37	191LTS95	304438
Romania	Yugoslavia	13 May 37	197LTS145	304611

PARTY ONE	PARTY TWO	DATE	CITATION	NUMBER
Protection of nationals (Cont.)				
Sweden	Yugoslavia	14 May 37	194LTS21	304504
Greece	Luxembourg	01 Sep 37	193LTS151	304491
Belgium	Siam	05 Nov 37	190LTS163	304414
Denmark	Siam	05 Nov 37	188LTS187	304358
Siam	Sweden	05 Nov 37	182LTS257	304215
Siam	Sweden	08 Nov 37	185LTS337	304298
Siam	USA (United States)	13 Nov 37	192LTS247	304476
Norway	Siam	15 Nov 37	186LTS9	304301
Italy	Siam	03 Dec 37	189LTS255	304389
France	Siam	07 Dec 37	201LTS113	304708
Japan	Siam	08 Dec 37	188LTS375	304367
Germany	Siam	30 Dec 37	188LTS401	304368
Netherlands	Siam	01 Feb 38	193LTS13	304485
Greece	Mexico	17 Mar 38	198LTS325	304649
Liberia	USA (United States)	08 Aug 38	201LTS163	304711
Latvia	Poland	29 Oct 38	195LTS169	304547
Multilateral		05 Feb 39	196LTS303	304592
Belgium	France	06 Mar 39	195LTS353	304555
Diplomatic correspondence				
Greece	Spain	06 Mar 19	3LTS81	300092
Germany	USSR (Soviet Union)	06 May 21	6LTS267	300159
Latvia	Lithuania	12 Jul 21	25LTS299	300619
Norway	USSR (Soviet Union)	02 Sep 21	7LTS293	300196
Mexico	UK Great Britain	17 May 22	14LTS83	300368
Peru	Venezuela	14 Mar 23	20LTS45	300505
Denmark	USSR (Soviet Union)	23 Apr 23	18LTS15	300450
Multilateral		03 Nov 23	30LTS371	300775
Czechoslovakia	Italy	01 Mar 24	34LTS55	300867
Multilateral		21 Jun 26	78LTS229	301793
Poland	Romania	17 Dec 29	119LTS333	302754
France	Latvia	20 Jan 30	169LTS125	303917
Brazil	Sweden	27 Jan 32	177LTS119	304086
Brazil	Poland	15 Oct 32	176LTS373	304074
Czechoslovakia	USSR (Soviet Union)	16 Nov 35	169LTS143	303918
Irish Free State	Spain	14 Jan 36	168LTS201	303899
Hungary	Poland	24 Apr 36	185LTS303	304296
Non-diplomatic delegations				
Belgium	Portugal	19 Jul 27	71LTS419	301680
Bulgaria	Germany	04 Jun 29	106LTS49	302436
Consular functions in shipping				
Chile	Netherlands	04 Nov 13	84LTS79	301904
Cuba	Netherlands	31 Dec 13	14LTS29	300366
Denmark	UK Great Britain	01 Jun 21	5LTS161	300125
Latvia	Poland	03 Jan 24	42LTS451	301043
Estonia	Poland	11 Jan 24	47LTS129	301132
Albania	Italy	29 Feb 24	44LTS343	301093
Czechoslovakia	Italy	01 Mar 24	34LTS55	300867
Poland	USSR (Soviet Union)	18 Jul 24	49LTS201	301183
Italy	Serb/Croat/Slovene	21 Aug 24	82LTS445	301883
Finland	Netherlands	09 Mar 25	47LTS431	301148
Estonia	Germany	13 Mar 25	51LTS263	301236
Germany	USA (United States)	21 May 25	52LTS133	301254
Bel-Lux Econ Union	Japan	27 Jun 25	36LTS95	300907
Bel-Lux Econ Union		07 Jul 25	54LTS267	301290
Germany	USSR (Soviet Union)	12 Oct 25	53LTS163	301258
Estonia	USA (United States)	23 Dec 25	50LTS13	301197
France	Poland	30 Dec 25	73LTS265	301719
Cuba	USA (United States)	22 Apr 26	60LTS371	301421
Albania	Serb/Croat/Slovene	22 Jun 26	91LTS55	302055
Hungary	USA (United States)	04 Sep 26	58LTS111	301369
Greece	Spain	23 Sep 26	91LTS121	302059
Austria	Estonia	15 Oct 26	93LTS137	302106
Belgium	Estonia	08 Feb 27	74LTS227	301740
Poland	Serb/Croat/Slovene	06 Mar 27	126LTS67	302871

PARTY ONE	PARTY TWO	DATE	CITATION	NUMBER
Consular functions in shipping (Cont.)				
Albania	France	15 Feb 28	107LTS307	302487
Colombia	Sweden	09 Mar 28	85LTS443	301944
Germany	Siam	07 Apr 28	85LTS337	301938
Latvia	USA (United States)	20 Apr 28	80LTS35	301821
Mexico	Panama	09 Jun 28	141LTS191	303265
Belgium	Poland	12 Jun 28	123LTS25	302803
China	Germany	17 Aug 28	91LTS93	302057
Germany	Lithuania	30 Oct 28	90LTS255	302043
Czechoslovakia	Serb/Croat/Slovene	07 Nov 28	98LTS297	302252
Norway	USA (United States)	25 Feb 29	134LTS81	303085
Estonia	USSR (Soviet Union)	17 May 29	94LTS323	302152
Germany	Turkey	28 May 29	133LTS257	303069
Italy	Turkey	09 Sep 29	129LTS195	302962
Poland	Romania	17 Dec 29	119LTS333	302754
France	Latvia	20 Jan 30	169LTS125	303917
Denmark	Lithuania	21 Jun 30	114LTS151	302662
Poland	Romania	23 Jun 30	133LTS163	303066
El Salvador	USA (United States)	05 Sep 30	134LTS207	303093
Greece	Turkey	30 Oct 30	125LTS371	302866
Estonia	Finland	11 Apr 31	124LTS217	302835
Poland	USA (United States)	15 Jun 31	139LTS395	303223
Italy	Latvia	11 May 32	150LTS9	303450
Austria	Denmark	05 Aug 32	132LTS165	303036
Finland	USA (United States)	13 Feb 34	152LTS45	303484
Bulgaria	Poland	22 Dec 34	159LTS265	303671
Czechoslovakia	USSR (Soviet Union)	16 Nov 35	169LTS143	303918
Hungary	Poland	24 Apr 36	185LTS303	304296
Liberia	USA (United States)	07 Oct 38	201LTS183	304712
Consular functions in property				
Chile	Netherlands	04 Nov 13	84LTS79	301904
Finland	UK Great Britain	14 Dec 23	23LTS125	300583
Latvia	Poland	03 Jan 24	42LTS451	301043
Estonia	Poland	11 Jan 24	47LTS129	301132
Albania	Italy	29 Feb 24	44LTS343	301093
Czechoslovakia	Italy	01 Mar 24	34LTS55	300867
Austria	Latvia	09 Aug 24	65LTS7	301516
Italy	Serb/Croat/Slovene	21 Aug 24	82LTS445	301883
France	Siam	14 Feb 25	43LTS189	301055
Estonia	Germany	13 Mar 25	51LTS263	301236
Germany	USA (United States)	21 May 25	52LTS133	301254
Netherlands	Siam	08 Jun 25	56LTS57	301323
Bel-Lux Econ Union		07 Jul 25	54LTS267	301290
Siam	Spain	03 Aug 25	55LTS39	301303
Portugal	Siam	14 Aug 25	55LTS57	301304
Austria	China	19 Oct 25	55LTS9	301301
Siam	Sweden	19 Dec 25	58LTS429	301386
Estonia	USA (United States)	23 Dec 25	50LTS13	301197
Cuba	USA (United States)	22 Apr 26	60LTS371	301421
Italy	Siam	09 May 26	61LTS215	301436
Albania	Serb/Croat/Slovene	22 Jun 26	91LTS55	302055
Bel-Lux Econ Union	Siam	13 Jul 26	62LTS287	301468
Norway	Siam	16 Jul 26	60LTS35	301404
Hungary	UK Great Britain	23 Jul 26	67LTS183	301546
Hungary	USA (United States)	04 Sep 26	58LTS111	301369
Greece	Spain	23 Sep 26	91LTS121	302059
Bel-Lux Econ Union	Estonia	28 Sep 26	62LTS433	301475
Austria	Estonia	15 Oct 26	93LTS137	302106
Austria	Germany	05 Feb 27	73LTS205	301714
Belgium	Estonia	08 Feb 27	74LTS227	301740
Greece	UK Great Britain	13 May 27	61LTS15	301425
Greece	Switzerland	01 Dec 27	84LTS271	301907
Albania	France	15 Feb 28	107LTS307	302487
Germany	Siam	07 Apr 28	85LTS337	301938
Mexico	Panama	09 Jun 28	141LTS191	303265

PARTY ONE	PARTY TWO	DATE	CITATION	NUMBER
Consular functions in property (Cont.)				
Germany	Lithuania	30 Oct 28	90LTS255	302043
Czechoslovakia	Serb/Croat/Slovene	07 Nov 28	98LTS297	302252
Norway	USA (United States)	25 Feb 29	134LTS81	303085
Germany	Turkey	28 May 29	133LTS257	303069
Bulgaria	Germany	04 Jun 29	106LTS49	302436
France	Latvia	20 Jan 30	169LTS125	303917
Latvia	UK Great Britain	24 Jul 30	107LTS301	302486
El Salvador	USA (United States)	05 Sep 30	134LTS207	303093
Poland	USA (United States)	15 Jun 31	139LTS395	303223
Bolivia	Denmark	09 Nov 31	147LTS27	303387
Finland	USA (United States)	13 Feb 34	152LTS45	303484
Denmark	Persia	20 Feb 34	158LTS299	303640
Bulgaria	Poland	22 Dec 34	159LTS265	303671
Czechoslovakia	USSR (Soviet Union)	16 Nov 35	169LTS143	303918
Hungary	Poland	24 Apr 36	185LTS303	304296
Notarial acts and services				
Estonia	Poland	11 Jan 24	47LTS129	301132
Albania	Italy	29 Feb 24	44LTS343	301093
Germany	USSR (Soviet Union)	12 Oct 25	53LTS163	301258
France	Poland	30 Dec 25	73LTS265	301719
Hungary	USA (United States)	04 Sep 26	58LTS111	301369
Belgium	Estonia	08 Feb 27	74LTS227	301740
Serb/Croat/Slovene	UK Great Britain	12 May 27	80LTS165	301825
Czechoslovakia	France	03 Jun 27	131LTS177	303009
Norway	USA (United States)	25 Feb 29	134LTS81	303085
Germany	Turkey	28 May 29	133LTS257	303069
Sweden	Turkey	24 Apr 32	129LTS325	302967
Hungary	Poland	24 Apr 36	185LTS303	304296
Extradition, deportation and repatriation				
France	UK Great Britain	06 Aug 14	10LTS333	300278
Chile	Colombia	16 Nov 14	82LTS243	301875
Portugal	UK Great Britain	10 Jan 21	7LTS264	300193
Afghanistan	Persia	22 Jun 21	33LTS285	300853
Estonia	Lithuania	12 Jul 21	43LTS179	301054
USA (United States)	Venezuela	21 Jan 22	49LTS435	301196
Finland	Germany	20 Feb 22	19LTS81	300486
Brazil	Paraguay	24 Feb 22	138LTS211	303189
Multilateral		31 Mar 22	9LTS415	300269
Czechoslovakia	Italy	06 Apr 22	55LTS171	301313
Italy	Serb/Croat/Slovene	06 Apr 22	118LTS221	302726
Poland	Serb/Croat/Slovene	04 May 23	85LTS455	301946
Multilateral		24 Jul 23	28LTS151	300704
Turkey	USA (United States)	06 Aug 23	153LTS71	303509
Estonia	USA (United States)	08 Nov 23	43LTS277	301063
Austria	Poland	19 Mar 24	56LTS95	301326
Lithuania	USA (United States)	09 Apr 24	51LTS191	301226
Hungary	Romania	16 Apr 24	42LTS145	301038
Germany	Hungary	01 May 24	41LTS282	301021
Finland	Latvia	07 Jun 24	38LTS343	300990
Italy	Serb/Croat/Slovene	21 Aug 24	82LTS445	301883
France	Latvia	29 Oct 24	93LTS265	302115
UK Great Britain	USA (United States)	03 Dec 24	43LTS41	301046
Estonia	Finland	02 Jan 25	43LTS11	301044
Estonia	Germany	09 Jan 25	42LTS13	301028
Czechoslovakia	Poland	06 Mar 25	46LTS201	301120
Czechoslovakia	Romania	07 May 25	54LTS51	301273
Czechoslovakia	USA (United States)	02 Jul 25	50LTS143	301200
Germany	Switzerland	12 Oct 25	53LTS241	301260
Finland	Norway	10 Nov 25	43LTS381	301071
Belgium	USA (United States)	18 Nov 25	50LTS225	301205
Austria	Norway	17 Dec 25	48LTS77	301152
France	Poland	30 Dec 25	95LTS217	302176
Belgium	Paraguay	20 Jan 26	97LTS197	302224
Italy	UK Great Britain	29 Jan 26	47LTS409	301145

Extradition, deportation and repatriation (Cont.)

PARTY ONE	PARTY TWO	DATE	CITATION	NUMBER
France	San Marino	30 Apr 26	89LTS9	302001
Bulgaria	Czechoslovakia	15 May 26	60LTS169	301412
Lithuania	UK Great Britain	18 May 26	61LTS401	301450
Czechoslovakia	UK Great Britain	04 Jun 26	59LTS269	301397
Albania	Serb/Croat/Slovene	22 Jun 26	91LTS81	302056
Albania	Greece	25 Jun 26	83LTS305	301898
France	Germany	28 Jun 26	53LTS435	301271
Czechoslovakia	Latvia	06 Jul 26	62LTS229	301465
Bel-Lux Econ Union	Siam	13 Jul 26	62LTS287	301468
Czechoslovakia	Estonia	17 Jul 26	63LTS255	301495
Albania	UK Great Britain	22 Jul 26	67LTS165	301545
Bel-Lux Econ Union	Estonia	28 Sep 26	62LTS433	301475
Austria	Estonia	15 Oct 26	74LTS213	301739
Liberia	Monaco	28 Oct 26	68LTS241	301588
Belgium	Estonia	11 Nov 26	65LTS405	301523
Switzerland	Uruguay	26 Nov 26	63LTS207	301491
Belgium	Latvia	11 Dec 26	63LTS299	301497
Denmark	Sweden	03 Feb 27	109LTS205	302540
Austria	Netherlands	01 Mar 27	68LTS75	301570
Austria	Portugal	28 Mar 27	68LTS81	301571
Czechoslovakia	Greece	07 Apr 27	88LTS219	301999
Greece	UK Great Britain	13 May 27	61LTS15	301425
Belgium	Lithuania	17 May 27	77LTS123	301767
Belgium	Czechoslovakia	19 Jul 27	73LTS283	301720
Latvia	Norway	12 Sep 27	71LTS303	301671
Czechoslovakia	Spain	26 Oct 27	121LTS271	302791
Poland	USA (United States)	22 Nov 27	92LTS101	302082
Czechoslovakia	Portugal	23 Nov 27	124LTS7	302829
Colombia	Panama	24 Dec 27	87LTS409	301985
Belgium	Finland	23 Jan 28	74LTS353	301747
Multilateral		20 Feb 28	86LTS111	301950
Hungary	Serb/Croat/Slovene	22 Feb 28	104LTS151	302385
Czechoslovakia	France	07 May 28	114LTS117	302660
Austria	Finland	22 Oct 28	89LTS69	302007
Multilateral		25 Oct 28	84LTS7	301901
Colombia	Nicaragua	25 Mar 29	132LTS255	303042
Multilateral		20 Apr 29	112LTS395	302624
Multilateral		20 Apr 29	112LTS371	302623
Finland	Italy	10 Jul 29	111LTS295	302593
Colombia	UK Great Britain	02 Dec 29	110LTS401	302571
Latvia	Sweden	30 Jan 30	110LTS139	302558
Latvia	Spain	08 Mar 30	113LTS135	302641
Austria	Sweden	24 Mar 30	105LTS313	302424
Poland	Romania	26 Mar 30	153LTS87	303510
Estonia	Norway	03 Apr 30	106LTS147	302442
Multilateral		17 Apr 30	126LTS201	302883
Hungary	Latvia	04 May 30	101LTS449	302344
Norway	Persia	08 May 30	134LTS153	303089
Denmark	Estonia	13 May 30	106LTS159	302443
Italy	Panama	07 Aug 30	140LTS241	303240
Czechoslovakia	Turkey	22 Aug 30	138LTS375	303196
Italy	Venezuela	23 Aug 30	128LTS377	302943
Denmark	Latvia	28 Aug 30	113LTS169	302644
Poland	Sweden	30 Aug 30	129LTS383	302973
Germany	Turkey	03 Sep 30	133LTS321	303071
Germany	Poland	21 Nov 30	139LTS351	303220
Norway	Turkey	16 Mar 31	138LTS41	303180
Czechoslovakia	Lithuania	24 Apr 31	126LTS261	302889
Greece	USA (United States)	06 May 31	138LTS293	303194
Belgium	Poland	13 May 31	131LTS109	303005
Denmark	Germany	23 Jun 31	119LTS321	302753
Hungary	Romania	12 Aug 31	186LTS325	304321
Czechoslovakia	Denmark	07 Oct 31	127LTS103	302911
Germany	Hungary	26 Oct 31	133LTS369	303074
Czechoslovakia	Sweden	17 Nov 31	134LTS135	303088
Austria	Italy	19 Nov 31	126LTS163	302879
Brazil	Italy	28 Nov 31	132LTS345	303047
Czechoslovakia	Netherlands	04 Dec 31	129LTS343	302969
UK Great Britain	USA (United States)	22 Dec 31	163LTS59	303761
Germany	Lithuania		125LTS265	302860
Austria	Latvia	05 Jan 32	133LTS59	303056
Iraq	Turkey	09 Jan 32	139LTS273	303218
Poland	UK Great Britain	11 Jan 32	148LTS221	303415
Austria	Belgium	26 Jan 32	129LTS141	302959
Iraq	UK Great Britain	02 May 32	141LTS277	303270
Brazil	Switzerland	23 Jul 32	145LTS167	303354
Austria	Germany	07 Dec 32	137LTS69	303147
Romania	Yugoslavia	30 Jan 33	146LTS113	303363
Romania	Yugoslavia	30 Jan 33	146LTS81	303361
Finland	Netherlands	21 Feb 33	139LTS365	303221
Estonia	Netherlands	08 Mar 33	146LTS319	303382
Switzerland	Turkey	01 Jun 33	159LTS329	303676
Multilateral		29 Jul 33	142LTS165	303288
Lithuania	Netherlands	01 Dec 33	150LTS337	303466
Multilateral		26 Dec 33	165LTS45	303803
Belgium	Italy	07 Feb 34	147LTS107	303395
Germany	Latvia	18 Jul 34	154LTS69	303537
Switzerland	UK Great Britain	19 Dec 34	163LTS103	303763
Denmark	Lithuania	20 Dec 34	162LTS347	303748
Multilateral		26 Jun 36	198LTS299	304648

Court procedures

PARTY ONE	PARTY TWO	DATE	CITATION	NUMBER
Czechoslovakia	Germany	29 Jun 20	20LTS85	300509
Germany	Poland	20 Sep 20	9LTS103	300246
Germany	Poland	08 Dec 20	7LTS323	300199
Estonia	Latvia	12 Jul 21	37LTS423	300964
Latvia	Lithuania	12 Jul 21	25LTS311	300620
Denmark	UK Great Britain	12 Jul 21	8LTS397	300238
Latvia	USSR (Soviet Union)	06 Nov 21	17LTS251	300440
Estonia	Ukrainian SSR	25 Nov 21	11LTS121	300294
France	UK Great Britain	02 Feb 22	10LTS448	300284
Finland	Norway	03 Mar 22	14LTS157	300372
Italy	Serb/Croat/Slovene	06 Apr 22	118LTS207	302725
Germany	Poland	12 Apr 22	21LTS327	300548
Czechoslovakia	Germany	08 May 22	23LTS171	300589
Germany	Poland	15 Jun 22	34LTS201	300875
United Arab Rep	Palestine	07 Aug 22	36LTS343	300933
Italy	Serb/Croat/Slovene	23 Oct 22	18LTS461	300481
Siam	USA (United States)	30 Dec 22	25LTS394	300629
Denmark	Finland	12 Feb 23	18LTS33	300452
Czechoslovakia	Serb/Croat/Slovene	17 Mar 23	30LTS185	300768
Poland	Serb/Croat/Slovene	04 May 23	85LTS455	301946
Turkey		24 Jul 23	36LTS161	300916
Latvia	USA (United States)	16 Oct 23	27LTS371	300698
Bulgaria	Serb/Croat/Slovene	26 Nov 23	26LTS119	300643
Finland	Sweden	29 Nov 23	23LTS41	300575
Bulgaria	USA (United States)	19 Mar 24	26LTS27	300638
Bulgaria	Romania	19 Apr 24	33LTS209	300845
Bulgaria	Romania	19 Apr 24	33LTS221	300846
Finland	UK Great Britain	30 May 24	34LTS79	300868
Denmark	Switzerland	06 Jun 24	34LTS175	300873
Norway	Sweden	27 Jun 24	28LTS309	300717
Great Britain	Latvia	16 Jul 24	37LTS369	300961
Finland	USA (United States)	01 Aug 24	34LTS103	300869
Germany	Saar	20 Sep 24	30LTS121	300765
Netherlands	USA (United States)	23 Jan 25	33LTS445	300864
Czechoslovakia	Poland	06 Mar 25	46LTS201	301120
Germany	USSR (Soviet Union)	12 Oct 25	53LTS7	301257
France	San Marino	30 Apr 26	89LTS9	302001
Austria	Germany	05 Feb 27	73LTS205	301714

PARTY ONE	PARTY TWO	DATE	CITATION	NUMBER
Court procedures (Cont.)				
Czechoslovakia	Greece	07 Apr 27	88LTS219	301999
Czechoslovakia	Spain	26 Oct 27	121LTS271	302791
Czechoslovakia	Portugal	23 Nov 27	124LTS7	302829
Colombia	Panama	24 Dec 27	87LTS409	301985
Multilateral		20 Feb 28	86LTS111	301950
Hungary	Serb/Croat/Slovene	22 Feb 28	104LTS151	302385
Czechoslovakia	France	07 May 28	114LTS171	302663
Czechoslovakia	France	07 May 28	114LTS117	302660
Mexico	Panama	23 Oct 28	194LTS137	304518
Bulgaria	Turkey	23 Dec 29	122LTS17	302796
Estonia	Sweden	20 Jan 30	106LTS279	302451
Austria	USA (United States)	30 Jan 30	106LTS379	302457
Finland	Iceland	27 Jun 30	167LTS271	303873
Germany	USA (United States)	12 Jul 30	119LTS247	302748
Sweden	UK Great Britain	28 Aug 30	114LTS9	302652
Bulgaria	Spain	26 Jun 31	166LTS341	303850
Colombia	Cuba	02 Jul 32	174LTS69	304038
Brazil	Switzerland	23 Jul 32	145LTS167	303354
Belgium	Bolivia	06 Jan 33	147LTS59	303390
Albania	USA (United States)	01 Mar 33	166LTS195	303839
Finland	USSR (Soviet Union)	04 Jul 33	149LTS83	303436
Romania	Turkey	17 Oct 33	165LTS273	303814
Czechoslovakia	Poland	10 Feb 34	178LTS159	304111
Albania	Czechoslovakia	14 Apr 34	188LTS255	304362
Belgium	UK Great Britain	02 May 34	173LTS291	304020
Iraq	USA (United States)	07 Jun 34	170LTS267	303942
Turkey	Yugoslavia	03 Jul 34	179LTS207	304149
Estonia	Hungary	08 Aug 34	167LTS153	303863
Czechoslovakia	Luxembourg	01 Dec 34	168LTS287	303906
Czechoslovakia	Monaco	22 Dec 34	171LTS27	303949
Canada	USA (United States)	15 Apr 35	162LTS73	303735
Belgium	Germany	10 May 35	182LTS335	304221
Norway	Venezuela	13 May 35	167LTS407	303882
Estonia	Italy	10 Aug 35	185LTS287	304295
Multilateral		14 Nov 35	166LTS75	303831
Bulgaria	Denmark	07 Dec 35	182LTS183	304211
Denmark	Yugoslavia	14 Dec 35	184LTS99	304245
Chile	Norway	27 Jan 36	179LTS433	304169
Greece	UK Great Britain	27 Feb 36	185LTS113	304278
Liechtenstein	USA (United States)	20 May 36	183LTS181	304235
Belgium	Liechtenstein	05 Aug 36	185LTS33	304302
Mexico	USA (United States)	06 Oct 36	180LTS33	304171
France	UK Great Britain	03 Apr 37	179LTS265	304154
Iran	Iraq	24 Jul 37	190LTS269	304425
Greece	Luxembourg	01 Sep 37	193LTS151	304491
Liberia	USA (United States)	01 Nov 37	201LTS151	304710
Poland	Switzerland	19 Nov 37	195LTS297	304552
Belgium	Turkey	09 Feb 38	198LTS181	304639
Netherlands	USA (United States)	18 Feb 38	192LTS49	304460
Greece	Switzerland	30 Mar 38	185LTS245	304288
Belgium	Mexico	22 Sep 38	198LTS399	304658
Japan	UK Great Britain	22 Mar 40	203LTS194	304760
Extradition requests				
Germany	Greece	12 Mar 07	2LTS111	300054
Chile	Colombia	16 Nov 14	82LTS243	301875
Estonia	Latvia	12 Jul 21	37LTS423	300964
Estonia	Lithuania	12 Jul 21	43LTS179	301054
Latvia	Lithuania	12 Jul 21	25LTS311	300620
Brazil	Paraguay	24 Feb 22	138LTS211	303189
Italy	Serb/Croat/Slovene	06 Apr 22	118LTS221	302726

PARTY ONE	PARTY TWO	DATE	CITATION	NUMBER
Extradition requests (Cont.)				
Czechoslovakia	Italy	06 Apr 22	55LTS171	301313
Czechoslovakia	Germany	08 May 22	23LTS171	300589
United Arab Rep	Palestine	07 Aug 22	36LTS343	300933
Siam	USA (United States)	30 Dec 22	25LTS394	300629
Denmark	Finland	12 Feb 23	18LTS33	300452
Poland	Serb/Croat/Slovene	04 May 23	85LTS455	301946
Turkey	USA (United States)	06 Aug 23	153LTS71	303509
Latvia	USA (United States)	16 Oct 23	27LTS371	300698
Bulgaria	Serb/Croat/Slovene	26 Nov 23	26LTS119	300643
Finland	Sweden	29 Nov 23	23LTS41	300575
Bulgaria	USA (United States)	19 Mar 24	26LTS27	300638
Hungary	Romania	16 Apr 24	42LTS145	301038
Bulgaria	Romania	19 Apr 24	33LTS221	300846
Finland	UK Great Britain	30 May 24	34LTS79	300868
Finland	Latvia	07 Jun 24	38LTS343	300990
Great Britain	Latvia	16 Jul 24	37LTS369	300961
Finland	USA (United States)	01 Aug 24	34LTS103	300869
France	Latvia	29 Oct 24	93LTS265	302115
Estonia	Finland	02 Jan 25	43LTS11	301044
Czechoslovakia	Poland	06 Mar 25	46LTS201	301120
Czechoslovakia	Romania	07 May 25	54LTS51	301273
Finland	Norway	10 Nov 25	43LTS381	301071
Belgium	USA (United States)	18 Nov 25	50LTS225	301205
Austria	Norway	17 Dec 25	48LTS77	301152
France	Poland	30 Dec 25	95LTS217	302176
Belgium	Paraguay	20 Jan 26	97LTS197	302224
France	San Marino	30 Apr 26	89LTS9	302001
Bulgaria	Czechoslovakia	15 May 26	60LTS169	301412
Lithuania	UK Great Britain	18 May 26	61LTS401	301450
Czechoslovakia	UK Great Britain	04 Jun 26	59LTS269	301397
Albania	Serb/Croat/Slovene	22 Jun 26	91LTS81	302056
Albania	Greece	25 Jun 26	83LTS305	301898
Czechoslovakia	Latvia	06 Jul 26	62LTS229	301465
Norway	Siam	16 Jul 26	60LTS35	301404
Czechoslovakia	Estonia	17 Jul 26	63LTS255	301495
Albania	UK Great Britain	22 Jul 26	67LTS165	301545
Austria	Estonia	15 Oct 26	74LTS213	301739
Liberia	Monaco	28 Oct 26	68LTS241	301588
Belgium	Estonia	11 Nov 26	65LTS405	301523
Switzerland	Uruguay	26 Nov 26	63LTS207	301491
Belgium	Latvia	11 Dec 26	63LTS299	301497
Czechoslovakia	Greece	07 Apr 27	88LTS219	301999
Belgium	Lithuania	17 May 27	77LTS123	301767
Belgium	Czechoslovakia	19 Jul 27	73LTS283	301720
Latvia	Norway	12 Sep 27	71LTS303	301671
Poland	USA (United States)	22 Nov 27	92LTS101	302082
Czechoslovakia	Portugal	23 Nov 27	124LTS7	302829
Colombia	Panama	24 Dec 27	87LTS409	301985
Belgium	Finland	23 Jan 28	74LTS353	301747
Hungary	Serb/Croat/Slovene	22 Feb 28	104LTS151	302385
Belgium	Portugal	28 Mar 28	92LTS185	302085
Czechoslovakia	France	07 May 28	114LTS117	302660
Austria	Finland	22 Oct 28	89LTS69	302007
Mexico	Panama	23 Oct 28	194LTS137	304518
Bulgaria	Greece	21 Feb 29	106LTS443	302461
Colombia	Nicaragua	25 Mar 29	132LTS255	303042
Finland	Italy	10 Jul 29	111LTS295	302593
Bulgaria	Turkey	23 Dec 29	122LTS17	302796
Latvia	Netherlands	27 Jan 30	117LTS343	302701
Latvia	Sweden	30 Jan 30	110LTS139	302558
Austria	USA (United States)	30 Jan 30	106LTS379	302457
Latvia	Spain	08 Mar 30	113LTS135	302641
Austria	Sweden	24 Mar 30	105LTS313	302424
Poland	Romania	26 Mar 30	153LTS87	303510
Estonia	Norway	03 Apr 30	106LTS147	302442

PARTY ONE	PARTY TWO	DATE	CITATION	NUMBER
Extradition requests (Cont.)				
Hungary	Latvia	04 May 30	101LTS449	302344
Norway	Persia	08 May 30	134LTS153	303089
Denmark	Estonia	13 May 30	106LTS159	302443
Germany	USA (United States)	12 Jul 30	119LTS247	302748
Bulgaria	Spain	17 Jul 30	114LTS41	302653
Italy	Panama	07 Aug 30	140LTS241	303240
Czechoslovakia	Turkey	22 Aug 30	138LTS375	303196
Italy	Venezuela	23 Aug 30	128LTS377	302943
Denmark	Latvia	28 Aug 30	113LTS169	302644
Poland	Sweden	30 Aug 30	129LTS383	302973
Germany	Turkey	03 Sep 30	133LTS321	303071
Germany	Poland	21 Nov 30	139LTS351	303220
Belgium	Lithuania	12 Dec 30	135LTS231	303114
Czechoslovakia	Lithuania	24 Apr 31	126LTS261	302889
Belgium	Poland	13 May 31	131LTS109	303005
Czechoslovakia	Denmark	07 Oct 31	127LTS103	302911
Czechoslovakia	Sweden	17 Nov 31	134LTS135	303088
Austria	Italy	19 Nov 31	126LTS163	302879
Brazil	Italy	28 Nov 31	132LTS345	303047
Czechoslovakia	Netherlands	04 Dec 31	129LTS343	302969
Iraq	Turkey	09 Jan 32	139LTS273	303218
Poland	UK Great Britain	11 Jan 32	148LTS221	303415
Austria	Belgium	26 Jan 32	129LTS141	302959
Iraq	UK Great Britain	02 May 32	141LTS277	303270
Colombia	Cuba	02 Jul 32	174LTS69	304038
Romania	Yugoslavia	30 Jan 33	146LTS81	303361
Finland	Netherlands	21 Feb 33	139LTS365	303221
Estonia	Netherlands	08 Mar 33	146LTS319	303382
Switzerland	Turkey	01 Jun 33	159LTS329	303676
Multilateral		26 Dec 33	165LTS45	303803
Albania	Czechoslovakia	14 Apr 34	188LTS255	304362
Estonia	Hungary	08 Aug 34	167LTS153	303863
Czechoslovakia	Luxembourg	01 Dec 34	168LTS287	303906
Denmark	Lithuania	20 Dec 34	162LTS347	303748
Czechoslovakia	Monaco	22 Dec 34	171LTS27	303949
Estonia	Italy	10 Aug 35	185LTS287	304295
Brazil	Chile	08 Nov 35	181LTS297	304197
Hungary	Poland	24 Apr 36	181LTS115	304183
Belgium	Liechtenstein	05 Aug 36	185LTS33	304302
Belgium	Siam	14 Jan 37	179LTS419	304168
Greece	Luxembourg	01 Sep 37	193LTS151	304491
Poland	Switzerland	19 Nov 37	195LTS297	304552
Belgium	Turkey	09 Feb 38	198LTS181	304639
Belgium	Mexico	22 Sep 38	198LTS399	304658
Monaco	USA (United States)	15 Feb 39	202LTS61	304735
Greece	Turkey	07 Mar 39	201LTS239	304717
Austria	Greece	28 Mar 74*	2LTS169	300063
Extraditable offenses				
Austria-Hungary	Greece	21 Dec 04	2LTS173	300064
Chile	Colombia	16 Nov 14	82LTS243	301875
Latvia	Lithuania	12 Jul 21	25LTS311	300620
USA (United States)	Venezuela	21 Jan 22	49LTS435	301196
Czechoslovakia	Italy	06 Apr 22	55LTS171	301313
Czechoslovakia	Germany	08 May 22	23LTS171	300589
UK Great Britain	USA (United States)	15 May 22	14LTS89	300369
United Arab Rep	Palestine	07 Aug 22	36LTS343	300933
Siam	USA (United States)	30 Dec 22	25LTS394	300629
Denmark	Finland	12 Feb 23	18LTS33	300452
Czechoslovakia	Serb/Croat/Slovene	17 Mar 23	30LTS185	300768
Poland	Serb/Croat/Slovene	04 May 23	85LTS455	301946

PARTY ONE	PARTY TWO	DATE	CITATION	NUMBER
Extraditable offenses (Cont.)				
Turkey	USA (United States)	06 Aug 23	153LTS71	303509
Latvia	USA (United States)	16 Oct 23	27LTS371	300698
Estonia	USA (United States)	08 Nov 23	43LTS277	301063
Bulgaria	Serb/Croat/Slovene	26 Nov 23	26LTS119	300643
Finland	Sweden	29 Nov 23	23LTS41	300575
Bulgaria	USA (United States)	19 Mar 24	26LTS27	300638
Lithuania	USA (United States)	09 Apr 24	51LTS191	301226
Hungary	Romania	16 Apr 24	42LTS145	301038
Finland	UK Great Britain	30 May 24	34LTS79	300868
Finland	Latvia	07 Jun 24	38LTS343	300990
Great Britain	Latvia	16 Jul 24	37LTS369	300961
Finland	USA (United States)	01 Aug 24	34LTS103	300869
France	Latvia	29 Oct 24	93LTS265	302115
Estonia	Finland	02 Jan 25	43LTS11	301044
Czechoslovakia	Romania	07 May 25	54LTS51	301273
Czechoslovakia	USA (United States)	02 Jul 25	50LTS143	301200
Germany	Switzerland	12 Oct 25	53LTS241	301260
Belgium	USA (United States)	18 Nov 25	50LTS225	301205
Austria	Norway	17 Dec 25	48LTS77	301152
France	Poland	30 Dec 25	95LTS217	302176
Belgium	Paraguay	20 Jan 26	97LTS197	302224
France	San Marino	30 Apr 26	89LTS9	302001
Lithuania	UK Great Britain	18 May 26	61LTS401	301450
Czechoslovakia	UK Great Britain	04 Jun 26	59LTS269	301397
Albania	Serb/Croat/Slovene	22 Jun 26	91LTS81	302056
Albania	Greece	25 Jun 26	83LTS305	301898
France	Germany	28 Jun 26	53LTS435	301271
Albania	UK Great Britain	22 Jul 26	67LTS165	301545
Austria	Estonia	15 Oct 26	74LTS213	301739
Liberia	Monaco	28 Oct 26	68LTS241	301588
Belgium	Estonia	11 Nov 26	65LTS405	301523
Switzerland	Uruguay	26 Nov 26	63LTS207	301491
Belgium	Latvia	11 Dec 26	63LTS299	301497
Czechoslovakia	Greece	07 Apr 27	88LTS219	301999
Belgium	Lithuania	17 May 27	77LTS123	301767
Belgium	Czechoslovakia	19 Jul 27	73LTS283	301720
Latvia	Norway	12 Sep 27	71LTS303	301671
Czechoslovakia	Spain	26 Oct 27	121LTS271	302791
Poland	USA (United States)	22 Nov 27	92LTS101	302082
Czechoslovakia	Portugal	23 Nov 27	124LTS7	302829
Colombia	Panama	24 Dec 27	87LTS409	301985
Belgium	Finland	23 Jan 28	74LTS353	301747
Hungary	Serb/Croat/Slovene	22 Feb 28	104LTS151	302385
Czechoslovakia	France	07 May 28	114LTS117	302660
Finland	Spain	31 May 28	82LTS229	301874
Austria	Finland	22 Oct 28	89LTS69	302007
Mexico	Panama	23 Oct 28	194LTS137	304518
Bulgaria	Greece	21 Feb 29	106LTS443	302461
Bulgaria	Turkey	23 Dec 29	122LTS17	302796
Estonia	Sweden	20 Jan 30	106LTS279	302451
Latvia	Netherlands	27 Jan 30	117LTS343	302701
Latvia	Sweden	30 Jan 30	110LTS139	302558
Austria	USA (United States)	30 Jan 30	106LTS379	302457
Latvia	Spain	08 Mar 30	113LTS135	302641
Austria	Sweden	24 Mar 30	105LTS313	302424
Hungary	Latvia	04 May 30	101LTS449	302344
Denmark	Estonia	13 May 30	106LTS159	302443
Germany	USA (United States)	12 Jul 30	119LTS247	302748
Bulgaria	Spain	17 Jul 30	114LTS41	302653
Italy	Venezuela	23 Aug 30	128LTS377	302943
Denmark	Latvia	28 Aug 30	113LTS169	302644
Germany	Turkey	03 Sep 30	133LTS321	303071
Germany	Poland	21 Nov 30	139LTS351	303220
Greece	USA (United States)	06 May 31	138LTS293	303194
Belgium	Poland	13 May 31	131LTS109	303005

PARTY ONE	PARTY TWO	DATE	CITATION	NUMBER
Extraditable offenses (Cont.)				
Czechoslovakia	Netherlands	04 Dec 31	129LTS343	302969
UK Great Britain	USA (United States)	22 Dec 31	163LTS59	303761
Poland	UK Great Britain	11 Jan 32	148LTS221	303415
Austria	Belgium	26 Jan 32	129LTS141	302959
Iraq	UK Great Britain	02 May 32	141LTS277	303270
Finland	Netherlands	21 Feb 33	139LTS365	303221
Albania	USA (United States)	01 Mar 33	166LTS195	303839
Estonia	Netherlands	08 Mar 33	146LTS319	303382
Switzerland	Turkey	01 Jun 33	159LTS329	303676
Lithuania	Netherlands	01 Dec 33	150LTS337	303466
Albania	Czechoslovakia	14 Apr 34	188LTS255	304362
Iraq	USA (United States)	07 Jun 34	170LTS267	303942
Estonia	Hungary	08 Aug 34	167LTS153	303863
Czechoslovakia	Luxembourg	01 Dec 34	168LTS287	303906
Denmark	Lithuania	20 Dec 34	162LTS347	303748
Czechoslovakia	Monaco	22 Dec 34	171LTS27	303949
Estonia	Italy	10 Aug 35	185LTS287	304295
Brazil	Chile	08 Nov 35	181LTS297	304197
Hungary	Poland	24 Apr 36	181LTS115	304183
Liechtenstein	USA (United States)	20 May 36	183LTS181	304235
Belgium	Liechtenstein	05 Aug 36	185LTS33	304302
Belgium	Siam	14 Jan 37	179LTS419	304168
Greece	Luxembourg	01 Sep 37	193LTS151	304491
Liberia	USA (United States)	01 Nov 37	201LTS151	304710
Poland	Switzerland	19 Nov 37	195LTS297	304552
Belgium	Turkey	09 Feb 38	198LTS181	304639
Belgium	Mexico	22 Sep 38	198LTS399	304658
Monaco	USA (United States)	15 Feb 39	202LTS61	304735
Greece	Turkey	07 Mar 39	201LTS239	304717
Austria	Greece	28 Mar 74*	2LTS169	300063
Location of crime				
Latvia	Lithuania	12 Jul 21	25LTS311	300620
USA (United States)	Venezuela	21 Jan 22	49LTS435	301196
Italy	Serb/Croat/Slovene	06 Apr 22	118LTS221	302726
Austria	Netherlands	06 Nov 22	17LTS375	300444
Siam	USA (United States)	30 Dec 22	25LTS394	300629
Denmark	Finland	12 Feb 23	18LTS33	300452
Finland	Sweden	29 Nov 23	23LTS41	300575
Bulgaria	USA (United States)	19 Mar 24	26LTS27	300638
Finland	UK Great Britain	30 May 24	34LTS79	300868
Belgium	USA (United States)	18 Nov 25	50LTS225	301205
Czechoslovakia	UK Great Britain	04 Jun 26	59LTS269	301397
Albania	Serb/Croat/Slovene	22 Jun 26	91LTS81	302056
Liberia	Monaco	28 Oct 26	68LTS241	301588
Switzerland	Uruguay	26 Nov 26	63LTS207	301491
Czechoslovakia	Spain	26 Oct 27	121LTS271	302791
Multilateral		20 Feb 28	86LTS111	301950
Estonia	Sweden	20 Jan 30	106LTS279	302451
Latvia	Netherlands	27 Jan 30	117LTS343	302701
Austria	USA (United States)	30 Jan 30	106LTS379	302457
Latvia	Spain	08 Mar 30	113LTS135	302641
Bulgaria	Spain	17 Jul 30	114LTS41	302653
Denmark	Latvia	28 Aug 30	113LTS169	302644
Germany	Poland	21 Nov 30	139LTS351	303220
Brazil	Italy	28 Nov 31	132LTS345	303047
Austria	Latvia	05 Jan 32	133LTS59	303056
Iraq	UK Great Britain	02 May 32	141LTS277	303270
Romania	Yugoslavia	30 Jan 33	146LTS81	303361

PARTY ONE	PARTY TWO	DATE	CITATION	NUMBER
Special factors				
Estonia	Latvia	12 Jul 21	37LTS423	300964
Latvia	Lithuania	12 Jul 21	25LTS311	300620
Italy	Serb/Croat/Slovene	06 Apr 22	118LTS221	302726
Siam	USA (United States)	30 Dec 22	25LTS394	300629
Denmark	Finland	12 Feb 23	18LTS33	300452
Poland	Serb/Croat/Slovene	04 May 23	85LTS455	301946
Turkey	USA (United States)	06 Aug 23	153LTS71	303509
Latvia	USA (United States)	16 Oct 23	27LTS371	300698
Bulgaria	Serb/Croat/Slovene	26 Nov 23	26LTS119	300643
Bulgaria	USA (United States)	19 Mar 24	26LTS27	300638
Lithuania	USA (United States)	09 Apr 24	51LTS191	301226
Bulgaria	Romania	19 Apr 24	33LTS221	300846
Finland	Latvia	07 Jun 24	38LTS343	300990
Finland	USA (United States)	01 Aug 24	34LTS103	300869
France	Latvia	29 Oct 24	93LTS265	302115
Czechoslovakia	USA (United States)	02 Jul 25	50LTS143	301200
France	Poland	30 Dec 25	95LTS217	302176
France	San Marino	30 Apr 26	89LTS9	302001
Lithuania	UK Great Britain	18 May 26	61LTS401	301450
Czechoslovakia	UK Great Britain	04 Jun 26	59LTS269	301397
Albania	Greece	25 Jun 26	83LTS305	301898
Belgium	Estonia	11 Nov 26	65LTS405	301523
Czechoslovakia	Greece	07 Apr 27	88LTS219	301999
Belgium	Lithuania	17 May 27	77LTS123	301767
Czechoslovakia	Spain	26 Oct 27	121LTS271	302791
Poland	USA (United States)	22 Nov 27	92LTS101	302082
Czechoslovakia	Portugal	23 Nov 27	124LTS7	302829
Belgium	Finland	23 Jan 28	74LTS353	301747
Hungary	Serb/Croat/Slovene	22 Feb 28	104LTS151	302385
Czechoslovakia	France	07 May 28	114LTS117	302660
Austria	Finland	22 Oct 28	89LTS69	302007
Mexico	Panama	23 Oct 28	194LTS137	304518
Finland	Italy	10 Jul 29	111LTS295	302593
Bulgaria	Turkey	23 Dec 29	122LTS17	302796
Estonia	Sweden	20 Jan 30	106LTS279	302451
Latvia	Netherlands	27 Jan 30	117LTS343	302701
Latvia	Sweden	30 Jan 30	110LTS139	302558
Austria	USA (United States)	30 Jan 30	106LTS379	302457
Latvia	Spain	08 Mar 30	113LTS135	302641
Austria	Sweden	24 Mar 30	105LTS313	302424
Estonia	Norway	03 Apr 30	106LTS147	302442
Denmark	Estonia	13 May 30	106LTS159	302443
Germany	USA (United States)	12 Jul 30	119LTS247	302748
Bulgaria	Spain	17 Jul 30	114LTS41	302653
Denmark	Latvia	28 Aug 30	113LTS169	302644
Poland	Sweden	30 Aug 30	129LTS383	302973
Germany	Turkey	03 Sep 30	133LTS321	303071
Czechoslovakia	Lithuania	24 Apr 31	126LTS261	302889
Greece	USA (United States)	06 May 31	138LTS293	303194
Belgium	Poland	13 May 31	131LTS109	303005
Czechoslovakia	Netherlands	04 Dec 31	129LTS343	302969
Poland	UK Great Britain	11 Jan 32	148LTS221	303415
Austria	Belgium	26 Jan 32	129LTS141	302959
Colombia	Cuba	02 Jul 32	174LTS69	304038
Brazil	Switzerland	23 Jul 32	145LTS167	303354
Albania	USA (United States)	01 Mar 33	166LTS195	303839
Estonia	Netherlands	08 Mar 33	146LTS319	303382
Lithuania	Netherlands	01 Dec 33	150LTS337	303466
Iraq	USA (United States)	07 Jun 34	170LTS267	303942
Denmark	Lithuania	20 Dec 34	162LTS347	303748
Liechtenstein	USA (United States)	20 May 36	183LTS181	304235
Belgium	Liechtenstein	05 Aug 36	185LTS33	304302
Belgium	Siam	14 Jan 37	179LTS419	304168

PARTY ONE	PARTY TWO	DATE	CITATION	NUMBER
Special factors (Cont.)				
Liberia	USA (United States)	01 Nov 37	201LTS151	304710
Belgium	Turkey	09 Feb 38	198LTS181	304639
Belgium	Mexico	22 Sep 38	198LTS399	304658
Monaco	USA (United States)	15 Feb 39	202LTS61	304735
Refusal of extradition				
Austria-Hungary	Greece	21 Dec 04	2LTS173	300064
Germany	Greece	12 Mar 07	2LTS111	300054
Chile	Colombia	16 Nov 14	82LTS243	301875
Estonia	Lithuania	12 Jul 21	43LTS179	301054
Estonia	Latvia	12 Jul 21	37LTS423	300964
Latvia	Lithuania	12 Jul 21	25LTS311	300620
USA (United States)	Venezuela	21 Jan 22	49LTS435	301196
Brazil	Paraguay	24 Feb 22	138LTS211	303189
Italy	Serb/Croat/Slovene	06 Apr 22	118LTS221	302726
Czechoslovakia	Italy	06 Apr 22	55LTS171	301313
Czechoslovakia	Germany	08 May 22	23LTS171	300589
United Arab Rep	Palestine	07 Aug 22	36LTS343	300933
Siam	USA (United States)	30 Dec 22	25LTS394	300629
Denmark	Finland	12 Feb 23	18LTS33	300452
Turkey	USA (United States)	06 Aug 23	153LTS71	303509
Latvia	USA (United States)	16 Oct 23	27LTS371	300698
Estonia	USA (United States)	08 Nov 23	43LTS277	301063
Bulgaria	Serb/Croat/Slovene	26 Nov 23	26LTS119	300643
Finland	Sweden	29 Nov 23	23LTS41	300575
Bulgaria	USA (United States)	19 Mar 24	26LTS27	300638
Lithuania	USA (United States)	09 Apr 24	51LTS191	301226
Hungary	Romania	16 Apr 24	42LTS145	301038
Bulgaria	Romania	19 Apr 24	33LTS221	300846
Finland	UK Great Britain	30 May 24	34LTS79	300868
Finland	Latvia	07 Jun 24	38LTS343	300990
Great Britain	Latvia	16 Jul 24	37LTS369	300961
Finland	USA (United States)	01 Aug 24	34LTS103	300869
France	Latvia	29 Oct 24	93LTS265	302115
Estonia	Finland	02 Jan 25	43LTS11	301044
Czechoslovakia	Poland	06 Mar 25	46LTS201	301120
Czechoslovakia	Romania	07 May 25	54LTS51	301273
Finland	Norway	10 Nov 25	43LTS381	301071
Belgium	USA (United States)	18 Nov 25	50LTS225	301205
Austria	Norway	17 Dec 25	48LTS77	301152
France	San Marino	30 Apr 26	89LTS9	302001
Bulgaria	Czechoslovakia	15 May 26	60LTS169	301412
Czechoslovakia	UK Great Britain	04 Jun 26	59LTS269	301397
Albania	Serb/Croat/Slovene	22 Jun 26	91LTS81	302056
Albania	Greece	25 Jun 26	83LTS305	301898
Czechoslovakia	Latvia	06 Jul 26	62LTS229	301465
Czechoslovakia	Estonia	17 Jul 26	63LTS255	301495
Albania	UK Great Britain	22 Jul 26	67LTS165	301545
Austria	Estonia	15 Oct 26	74LTS213	301739
Liberia	Monaco	28 Oct 26	68LTS241	301588
Belgium	Estonia	11 Nov 26	65LTS405	301523
Switzerland	Uruguay	26 Nov 26	63LTS207	301491
Belgium	Latvia	11 Dec 26	63LTS299	301497
Czechoslovakia	Greece	07 Apr 27	88LTS219	301999
Belgium	Lithuania	17 May 27	77LTS123	301767
Belgium	Czechoslovakia	19 Jul 27	73LTS283	301720
Latvia	Norway	12 Sep 27	71LTS303	301671
Czechoslovakia	Spain	26 Oct 27	121LTS271	302791
Poland	USA (United States)	22 Nov 27	92LTS101	302082
Czechoslovakia	Portugal	23 Nov 27	124LTS7	302829

PARTY ONE	PARTY TWO	DATE	CITATION	NUMBER
Refusal of extradition (Cont.)				
Colombia	Panama	24 Dec 27	87LTS409	301985
Belgium	Finland	23 Jan 28	74LTS353	301747
Multilateral		20 Feb 28	86LTS111	301950
Hungary	Serb/Croat/Slovene	22 Feb 28	104LTS151	302385
Czechoslovakia	France	07 May 28	114LTS117	302660
France	Spain	16 Jul 28	135LTS149	303110
Austria	Finland	22 Oct 28	89LTS69	302007
Mexico	Panama	23 Oct 28	194LTS137	304518
Bulgaria	Greece	21 Feb 29	106LTS443	302461
Colombia	Nicaragua	25 Mar 29	132LTS255	303042
Finland	Italy	10 Jul 29	111LTS295	302593
Bulgaria	Turkey	23 Dec 29	122LTS17	302796
Estonia	Sweden	20 Jan 30	106LTS279	302451
Latvia	Netherlands	27 Jan 30	117LTS343	302701
Latvia	Sweden	30 Jan 30	110LTS139	302558
Austria	USA (United States)	30 Jan 30	106LTS379	302457
Latvia	Spain	08 Mar 30	113LTS135	302641
Austria	Sweden	24 Mar 30	105LTS313	302424
Poland	Romania	26 Mar 30	153LTS87	303510
Estonia	Norway	03 Apr 30	106LTS147	302442
Hungary	Latvia	04 May 30	101LTS449	302344
Denmark	Estonia	13 May 30	106LTS159	302443
Germany	USA (United States)	12 Jul 30	119LTS247	302748
Bulgaria	Spain	17 Jul 30	114LTS41	302653
Italy	Panama	07 Aug 30	140LTS241	303240
Italy	Venezuela	23 Aug 30	128LTS377	302943
Denmark	Latvia	28 Aug 30	113LTS169	302644
Poland	Sweden	30 Aug 30	129LTS383	302973
Germany	Turkey	03 Sep 30	133LTS321	303071
Germany	Poland	21 Nov 30	139LTS351	303220
Czechoslovakia	Lithuania	24 Apr 31	126LTS261	302889
Belgium	Poland	13 May 31	131LTS109	303005
Czechoslovakia	Denmark	07 Oct 31	127LTS103	302911
Czechoslovakia	Sweden	17 Nov 31	134LTS135	303088
Brazil	Italy	28 Nov 31	132LTS345	303047
Czechoslovakia	Netherlands	04 Dec 31	129LTS343	302969
UK Great Britain	USA (United States)	22 Dec 31	163LTS59	303761
Austria	Latvia	05 Jan 32	133LTS59	303056
Iraq	Turkey	09 Jan 32	139LTS273	303218
Poland	UK Great Britain	11 Jan 32	148LTS221	303415
Austria	Belgium	26 Jan 32	129LTS141	302959
Iraq	UK Great Britain	02 May 32	141LTS277	303270
Colombia	Cuba	02 Jul 32	174LTS69	304038
Brazil	Switzerland	23 Jul 32	145LTS167	303354
Romania	Yugoslavia	30 Jan 33	146LTS81	303361
Finland	Netherlands	21 Feb 33	139LTS365	303221
Albania	USA (United States)	01 Mar 33	166LTS195	303839
Estonia	Netherlands	08 Mar 33	146LTS319	303382
Switzerland	Turkey	01 Jun 33	159LTS329	303676
Lithuania	Netherlands	01 Dec 33	150LTS337	303466
Multilateral		26 Dec 33	165LTS45	303803
Albania	Czechoslovakia	14 Apr 34	188LTS255	304362
Iraq	USA (United States)	07 Jun 34	170LTS267	303942
Germany	Latvia	18 Jul 34	154LTS69	303537
Estonia	Hungary	08 Aug 34	167LTS153	303863
Czechoslovakia	Luxembourg	01 Dec 34	168LTS287	303906
Denmark	Lithuania	20 Dec 34	162LTS347	303748
Czechoslovakia	Monaco	22 Dec 34	171LTS27	303949
Estonia	Italy	10 Aug 35	185LTS287	304295
Brazil	Chile	08 Nov 35	181LTS297	304197
Hungary	Poland	24 Apr 36	181LTS115	304183
Liechtenstein	USA (United States)	20 May 36	183LTS181	304235
Belgium	Liechtenstein	05 Aug 36	185LTS33	304302
Belgium	Siam	14 Jan 37	179LTS419	304168
Greece	Luxembourg	01 Sep 37	193LTS151	304491

PARTY ONE	PARTY TWO	DATE	CITATION	NUMBER
Refusal of extradition (Cont.)				
Poland	Switzerland	19 Nov 37	195LTS297	304552
Belgium	Turkey	09 Feb 38	198LTS181	304639
Monaco	USA (United States)	15 Feb 39	202LTS61	304735
Greece	Turkey	07 Mar 39	201LTS239	304717
Concurrent requests				
Chile	Colombia	16 Nov 14	82LTS243	301875
Estonia	Latvia	12 Jul 21	37LTS423	300964
Estonia	Lithuania	12 Jul 21	43LTS179	301054
Latvia	Lithuania	12 Jul 21	25LTS311	300620
USA (United States)	Venezuela	21 Jan 22	49LTS435	301196
Brazil	Paraguay	24 Feb 22	138LTS211	303189
Czechoslovakia	Italy	06 Apr 22	55LTS171	301313
Czechoslovakia	Germany	08 May 22	23LTS171	300589
Siam	USA (United States)	30 Dec 22	25LTS394	300629
Denmark	Finland	12 Feb 23	18LTS33	300452
Czechoslovakia	Serb/Croat/Slovene	17 Mar 23	30LTS185	300768
Poland	Serb/Croat/Slovene	04 May 23	85LTS455	301946
Latvia	USA (United States)	16 Oct 23	27LTS371	300698
Bulgaria	Serb/Croat/Slovene	26 Nov 23	26LTS119	300643
Finland	Sweden	29 Nov 23	23LTS41	300575
Bulgaria	USA (United States)	19 Mar 24	26LTS27	300638
Hungary	Romania	16 Apr 24	42LTS145	301038
Finland	UK Great Britain	30 May 24	34LTS79	300868
Great Britain	Latvia	16 Jul 24	37LTS369	300961
France	Latvia	29 Oct 24	93LTS265	302115
Czechoslovakia	Poland	06 Mar 25	46LTS201	301120
Czechoslovakia	Romania	07 May 25	54LTS51	301273
Finland	Norway	10 Nov 25	43LTS381	301071
Austria	Norway	17 Dec 25	48LTS77	301152
Belgium	Paraguay	20 Jan 26	97LTS197	302224
France	San Marino	30 Apr 26	89LTS9	302001
Bulgaria	Czechoslovakia	15 May 26	60LTS169	301412
Lithuania	UK Great Britain	18 May 26	61LTS401	301450
Czechoslovakia	UK Great Britain	04 Jun 26	59LTS269	301397
Albania	Serb/Croat/Slovene	22 Jun 26	91LTS81	302056
Albania	Greece	25 Jun 26	83LTS305	301898
Czechoslovakia	Latvia	06 Jul 26	62LTS229	301465
Czechoslovakia	Estonia	17 Jul 26	63LTS255	301495
Austria	Estonia	15 Oct 26	74LTS213	301739
Liberia	Monaco	28 Oct 26	68LTS241	301588
Belgium	Latvia	11 Dec 26	63LTS299	301497
Czechoslovakia	Greece	07 Apr 27	88LTS219	301999
Belgium	Lithuania	17 May 27	77LTS123	301767
Belgium	Czechoslovakia	19 Jul 27	73LTS283	301720
Latvia	Norway	12 Sep 27	71LTS303	301671
Czechoslovakia	Spain	26 Oct 27	121LTS271	302791
Czechoslovakia	Portugal	23 Nov 27	124LTS7	302829
Colombia	Panama	24 Dec 27	87LTS409	301985
Belgium	Finland	23 Jan 28	74LTS353	301747
Hungary	Serb/Croat/Slovene	22 Feb 28	104LTS151	302385
Austria	Finland	22 Oct 28	89LTS69	302007
Bulgaria	Greece	21 Feb 29	106LTS443	302461
Colombia	Nicaragua	25 Mar 29	132LTS255	303042
Finland	Italy	10 Jul 29	111LTS295	302593
Bulgaria	Turkey	23 Dec 29	122LTS17	302796
Estonia	Sweden	20 Jan 30	106LTS279	302451
Latvia	Netherlands	27 Jan 30	117LTS343	302701
Latvia	Sweden	30 Jan 30	110LTS139	302558
Latvia	Spain	08 Mar 30	113LTS135	302641
Austria	Sweden	24 Mar 30	105LTS313	302424
Estonia	Norway	03 Apr 30	106LTS147	302442
Hungary	Latvia	04 May 30	101LTS449	302344
Denmark	Estonia	13 May 30	106LTS159	302443
Germany	USA (United States)	12 Jul 30	119LTS247	302748

PARTY ONE	PARTY TWO	DATE	CITATION	NUMBER
Concurrent requests (Cont.)				
Bulgaria	Spain	17 Jul 30	114LTS41	302653
Czechoslovakia	Turkey	22 Aug 30	138LTS375	303196
Italy	Venezuela	23 Aug 30	128LTS377	302943
Denmark	Latvia	28 Aug 30	113LTS169	302644
Germany	Turkey	03 Sep 30	133LTS321	303071
Czechoslovakia	Lithuania	24 Apr 31	126LTS261	302889
Greece	USA (United States)	06 May 31	138LTS293	303194
Belgium	Poland	13 May 31	131LTS109	303005
Czechoslovakia	Denmark	07 Oct 31	127LTS103	302911
Czechoslovakia	Sweden	17 Nov 31	134LTS135	303088
Brazil	Italy	28 Nov 31	132LTS345	303047
Czechoslovakia	Netherlands	04 Dec 31	129LTS343	302969
Poland	UK Great Britain	11 Jan 32	148LTS221	303415
Colombia	Cuba	02 Jul 32	174LTS69	304038
Albania	USA (United States)	01 Mar 33	166LTS195	303839
Switzerland	Turkey	01 Jun 33	159LTS329	303676
Albania	Czechoslovakia	14 Apr 34	188LTS255	304362
Estonia	Hungary	08 Aug 34	167LTS153	303863
Czechoslovakia	Luxembourg	01 Dec 34	168LTS287	303906
Denmark	Lithuania	20 Dec 34	162LTS347	303748
Czechoslovakia	Monaco	22 Dec 34	171LTS27	303949
Estonia	Italy	10 Aug 35	185LTS287	304295
Hungary	Poland	24 Apr 36	181LTS115	304183
Greece	Luxembourg	01 Sep 37	193LTS151	304491
Belgium	Mexico	22 Sep 38	198LTS399	304658
Monaco	USA (United States)	15 Feb 39	202LTS61	304735
Greece	Turkey	07 Mar 39	201LTS239	304717
Pre-treaty crimes				
Poland	Serb/Croat/Slovene	04 May 23	85LTS455	301946
France	San Marino	30 Apr 26	89LTS9	302001
Albania	Serb/Croat/Slovene	22 Jun 26	91LTS81	302056
Liberia	Monaco	28 Oct 26	68LTS241	301588
Finland	Italy	10 Jul 29	111LTS295	302593
Estonia	Sweden	20 Jan 30	106LTS279	302451
Latvia	Spain	08 Mar 30	113LTS135	302641
Hungary	Latvia	04 May 30	101LTS449	302344
Bulgaria	Spain	17 Jul 30	114LTS41	302653
Italy	Panama	07 Aug 30	140LTS241	303240
Italy	Venezuela	23 Aug 30	128LTS377	302943
Poland	Sweden	30 Aug 30	129LTS383	302973
Greece	USA (United States)	06 May 31	138LTS293	303194
Brazil	Italy	28 Nov 31	132LTS345	303047
Austria	Latvia	05 Jan 32	133LTS59	303056
Brazil	Switzerland	23 Jul 32	145LTS167	303354
Estonia	Netherlands	08 Mar 33	146LTS319	303382
Germany	Latvia	18 Jul 34	154LTS69	303537
Limits of prosecution				
Czechoslovakia	Italy	06 Apr 22	55LTS171	301313
Poland	Serb/Croat/Slovene	04 May 23	85LTS455	301946
Estonia	USA (United States)	08 Nov 23	43LTS277	301063
Lithuania	USA (United States)	09 Apr 24	51LTS191	301226
Hungary	Romania	16 Apr 24	42LTS145	301038
Estonia	Finland	02 Jan 25	43LTS11	301044
Czechoslovakia	Poland	06 Mar 25	46LTS201	301120
Czechoslovakia	Romania	07 May 25	54LTS51	301273
Czechoslovakia	USA (United States)	02 Jul 25	50LTS143	301200
Austria	Norway	17 Dec 25	48LTS77	301152
Bulgaria	Czechoslovakia	15 May 26	60LTS169	301412
Lithuania	UK Great Britain	18 May 26	61LTS401	301450
Czechoslovakia	UK Great Britain	04 Jun 26	59LTS269	301397
Albania	Greece	25 Jun 26	83LTS305	301898
Czechoslovakia	Latvia	06 Jul 26	62LTS229	301465
Czechoslovakia	Estonia	17 Jul 26	63LTS255	301495
Albania	UK Great Britain	22 Jul 26	67LTS165	301545

PARTY ONE	PARTY TWO	DATE	CITATION	NUMBER
Limits of prosecution (Cont.)				
Austria	Estonia	15 Oct 26	74LTS213	301739
Belgium	Estonia	11 Nov 26	65LTS405	301523
Switzerland	Uruguay	26 Nov 26	63LTS207	301491
Austria	Finland	22 Oct 28	89LTS69	302007
Bulgaria	Greece	21 Feb 29	106LTS443	302461
Colombia	Nicaragua	25 Mar 29	132LTS255	303042
Finland	Italy	10 Jul 29	111LTS295	302593
Estonia	Sweden	20 Jan 30	106LTS279	302451
Latvia	Netherlands	27 Jan 30	117LTS343	302701
Austria	USA (United States)	30 Jan 30	106LTS379	302457
Poland	Romania	26 Mar 30	153LTS87	303510
Bulgaria	Spain	17 Jul 30	114LTS41	302653
Czechoslovakia	Turkey	22 Aug 30	138LTS375	303196
Poland	Sweden	30 Aug 30	129LTS383	302973
Czechoslovakia	Lithuania	24 Apr 31	126LTS261	302889
Czechoslovakia	Denmark	07 Oct 31	127LTS103	302911
Czechoslovakia	Netherlands	04 Dec 31	129LTS343	302969
Iraq	Turkey	09 Jan 32	139LTS273	303218
Brazil	Switzerland	23 Jul 32	145LTS167	303354
Lithuania	Netherlands	01 Dec 33	150LTS337	303466
Provisional detainment				
Chile	Colombia	16 Nov 14	82LTS243	301875
Brazil	Paraguay	24 Feb 22	138LTS211	303189
Italy	Serb/Croat/Slovene	06 Apr 22	118LTS221	302726
Czechoslovakia	Italy	06 Apr 22	55LTS171	301313
Poland	Serb/Croat/Slovene	04 May 23	85LTS455	301946
Turkey	USA (United States)	06 Aug 23	153LTS71	303509
Lithuania	USA (United States)	09 Apr 24	51LTS191	301226
Hungary	Romania	16 Apr 24	42LTS145	301038
Finland	Latvia	07 Jun 24	38LTS343	300990
France	Latvia	29 Oct 24	93LTS265	302115
Estonia	Finland	02 Jan 25	43LTS11	301044
Czechoslovakia	Poland	06 Mar 25	46LTS201	301120
Czechoslovakia	Romania	07 May 25	54LTS51	301273
Czechoslovakia	USA (United States)	02 Jul 25	50LTS143	301200
Finland	Norway	10 Nov 25	43LTS381	301071
Belgium	USA (United States)	18 Nov 25	50LTS225	301205
Austria	Norway	17 Dec 25	48LTS77	301152
Belgium	Paraguay	20 Jan 26	97LTS197	302224
Bulgaria	Czechoslovakia	15 May 26	60LTS169	301412
Czechoslovakia	UK Great Britain	04 Jun 26	59LTS269	301397
Albania	Greece	25 Jun 26	83LTS305	301898
Czechoslovakia	Latvia	06 Jul 26	62LTS229	301465
Czechoslovakia	Estonia	17 Jul 26	63LTS255	301495
Albania	UK Great Britain	22 Jul 26	67LTS165	301545
Austria	Estonia	15 Oct 26	74LTS213	301739
Liberia	Monaco	28 Oct 26	68LTS241	301588
Belgium	Lithuania	17 May 27	77LTS123	301767
Belgium	Czechoslovakia	19 Jul 27	73LTS283	301720
Latvia	Norway	12 Sep 27	71LTS303	301671
Czechoslovakia	Spain	26 Oct 27	121LTS271	302791
Czechoslovakia	Portugal	23 Nov 27	124LTS7	302829
Belgium	Finland	23 Jan 28	74LTS353	301747
Hungary	Serb/Croat/Slovene	22 Feb 28	104LTS151	302385
Czechoslovakia	France	07 May 28	114LTS117	302660
Austria	Finland	22 Oct 28	89LTS69	302007
Bulgaria	Greece	21 Feb 29	106LTS443	302461
Colombia	Nicaragua	25 Mar 29	132LTS255	303042
Finland	Italy	10 Jul 29	111LTS295	302593
Bulgaria	Turkey	23 Dec 29	122LTS17	302796
Estonia	Sweden	20 Jan 30	106LTS279	302451
Latvia	Netherlands	27 Jan 30	117LTS343	302701
Latvia	Sweden	30 Jan 30	110LTS139	302558
Austria	USA (United States)	30 Jan 30	106LTS379	302457

PARTY ONE	PARTY TWO	DATE	CITATION	NUMBER
Provisional detainment (Cont.)				
Latvia	Spain	08 Mar 30	113LTS135	302641
Austria	Sweden	24 Mar 30	105LTS313	302424
Poland	Romania	26 Mar 30	153LTS87	303510
Estonia	Norway	03 Apr 30	106LTS147	302442
Austria	Germany	12 Apr 30	115LTS297	302693
Norway	Persia	08 May 30	134LTS153	303089
Denmark	Estonia	13 May 30	106LTS159	302443
Germany	USA (United States)	12 Jul 30	119LTS247	302748
Bulgaria	Spain	17 Jul 30	114LTS41	302653
Czechoslovakia	Turkey	22 Aug 30	138LTS375	303196
Italy	Venezuela	23 Aug 30	128LTS377	302943
Denmark	Latvia	28 Aug 30	113LTS169	302644
Poland	Sweden	30 Aug 30	129LTS383	302973
Germany	Poland	21 Nov 30	139LTS351	303220
Belgium	Lithuania	12 Dec 30	135LTS231	303114
Czechoslovakia	Lithuania	24 Apr 31	126LTS261	302889
Greece	USA (United States)	06 May 31	138LTS293	303194
Czechoslovakia	Denmark	07 Oct 31	127LTS103	302911
Czechoslovakia	Sweden	17 Nov 31	134LTS135	303088
Czechoslovakia	Netherlands	04 Dec 31	129LTS343	302969
UK Great Britain	USA (United States)	22 Dec 31	163LTS59	303761
Austria	Latvia	05 Jan 32	133LTS59	303056
Iraq	Turkey	09 Jan 32	139LTS273	303218
Poland	UK Great Britain	11 Jan 32	148LTS221	303415
Austria	Belgium	26 Jan 32	129LTS141	302959
Iraq	UK Great Britain	02 May 32	141LTS277	303270
Romania	Yugoslavia	30 Jan 33	146LTS81	303361
Finland	Netherlands	21 Feb 33	139LTS365	303221
Estonia	Netherlands	08 Mar 33	146LTS319	303382
Switzerland	Turkey	01 Jun 33	159LTS329	303676
Lithuania	Netherlands	01 Dec 33	150LTS337	303466
Multilateral		26 Dec 33	165LTS45	303803
Denmark	Lithuania	20 Dec 34	162LTS347	303748
Extradition postponement				
Estonia	Lithuania	12 Jul 21	43LTS179	301054
USA (United States)	Venezuela	21 Jan 22	49LTS435	301196
Italy	Serb/Croat/Slovene	06 Apr 22	118LTS221	302726
Turkey	USA (United States)	06 Aug 23	153LTS71	303509
Estonia	USA (United States)	08 Nov 23	43LTS277	301063
Finland	Latvia	07 Jun 24	38LTS343	300990
Estonia	Finland	02 Jan 25	43LTS11	301044
Czechoslovakia	Poland	06 Mar 25	46LTS201	301120
Czechoslovakia	Romania	07 May 25	54LTS51	301273
Czechoslovakia	USA (United States)	02 Jul 25	50LTS143	301200
Finland	Norway	10 Nov 25	43LTS381	301071
Belgium	USA (United States)	18 Nov 25	50LTS225	301205
Austria	Norway	17 Dec 25	48LTS77	301152
Bulgaria	Czechoslovakia	15 May 26	60LTS169	301412
Albania	Serb/Croat/Slovene	22 Jun 26	91LTS81	302056
Czechoslovakia	Latvia	06 Jul 26	62LTS229	301465
Czechoslovakia	Estonia	17 Jul 26	63LTS255	301495
Liberia	Monaco	28 Oct 26	68LTS241	301588
Belgium	Estonia	11 Nov 26	65LTS405	301523
Switzerland	Uruguay	26 Nov 26	63LTS207	301491
Czechoslovakia	Greece	07 Apr 27	88LTS219	301999
Belgium	Lithuania	17 May 27	77LTS123	301767
Latvia	Norway	12 Sep 27	71LTS303	301671
Czechoslovakia	Spain	26 Oct 27	121LTS271	302791
Czechoslovakia	Portugal	23 Nov 27	124LTS7	302829
Hungary	Serb/Croat/Slovene	22 Feb 28	104LTS151	302385
Austria	Finland	22 Oct 28	89LTS69	302007
Bulgaria	Greece	21 Feb 29	106LTS443	302461
Finland	Italy	10 Jul 29	111LTS295	302593
Bulgaria	Turkey	23 Dec 29	122LTS17	302796

PARTY ONE	PARTY TWO	DATE	CITATION	NUMBER
Extradition postponement (Cont.)				
Latvia	Netherlands	27 Jan 30	117LTS343	302701
Austria	USA (United States)	30 Jan 30	106LTS379	302457
Latvia	Spain	08 Mar 30	113LTS135	302641
Poland	Romania	26 Mar 30	153LTS87	303510
Bulgaria	Spain	17 Jul 30	114LTS41	302653
Czechoslovakia	Turkey	22 Aug 30	138LTS375	303196
Denmark	Latvia	28 Aug 30	113LTS169	302644
Poland	Sweden	30 Aug 30	129LTS383	302973
Germany	Turkey	03 Sep 30	133LTS321	303071
Czechoslovakia	Lithuania	24 Apr 31	126LTS261	302889
Belgium	Poland	13 May 31	131LTS109	303005
Czechoslovakia	Denmark	07 Oct 31	127LTS103	302911
Czechoslovakia	Sweden	17 Nov 31	134LTS135	303088
Czechoslovakia	Netherlands	04 Dec 31	129LTS343	302969
Poland	UK Great Britain	11 Jan 32	148LTS221	303415
Romania	Yugoslavia	30 Jan 33	146LTS81	303361
Finland	Netherlands	21 Feb 33	139LTS365	303221
Switzerland	Turkey	01 Jun 33	159LTS329	303676
Witnesses and experts				
Hungary	Romania	16 Apr 24	42LTS145	301038
Estonia	Finland	02 Jan 25	43LTS11	301044
Czechoslovakia	Poland	06 Mar 25	46LTS201	301120
Czechoslovakia	Romania	07 May 25	54LTS51	301273
Finland	Norway	10 Nov 25	43LTS381	301071
Austria	Norway	17 Dec 25	48LTS77	301152
Bulgaria	Czechoslovakia	15 May 26	60LTS169	301412
Czechoslovakia	Latvia	06 Jul 26	62LTS229	301465
Czechoslovakia	Estonia	17 Jul 26	63LTS255	301495
Liberia	Monaco	28 Oct 26	68LTS241	301588
Belgium	Latvia	11 Dec 26	63LTS299	301497
Czechoslovakia	Greece	07 Apr 27	88LTS219	301999
Belgium	Lithuania	17 May 27	77LTS123	301767
Czechoslovakia	Spain	26 Oct 27	121LTS271	302791
Czechoslovakia	Portugal	23 Nov 27	124LTS7	302829
Hungary	Serb/Croat/Slovene	22 Feb 28	104LTS151	302385
Austria	Finland	22 Oct 28	89LTS69	302007
Finland	Italy	10 Jul 29	111LTS295	302593
Estonia	Sweden	20 Jan 30	106LTS279	302451
Latvia	Netherlands	27 Jan 30	117LTS343	302701
Latvia	Spain	08 Mar 30	113LTS135	302641
Estonia	Norway	03 Apr 30	106LTS147	302442
Denmark	Estonia	13 May 30	106LTS159	302443
Bulgaria	Spain	17 Jul 30	114LTS41	302653
Italy	Venezuela	23 Aug 30	128LTS377	302943
Denmark	Latvia	28 Aug 30	113LTS169	302644
Czechoslovakia	Lithuania	24 Apr 31	126LTS261	302889
Czechoslovakia	Denmark	07 Oct 31	127LTS103	302911
Czechoslovakia	Netherlands	04 Dec 31	129LTS343	302969
Austria	Belgium	26 Jan 32	129LTS141	302959
Brazil	Switzerland	23 Jul 32	145LTS167	303354
Romania	Yugoslavia	30 Jan 33	146LTS81	303361
Finland	Netherlands	21 Feb 33	139LTS365	303221
Lithuania	Netherlands	01 Dec 33	150LTS337	303466
Material evidence				
Chile	Colombia	16 Nov 14	82LTS243	301875
Estonia	Lithuania	12 Jul 21	43LTS179	301054
Italy	Serb/Croat/Slovene	06 Apr 22	118LTS221	302726
Poland	Serb/Croat/Slovene	04 May 23	85LTS455	301946
Turkey	USA (United States)	06 Aug 23	153LTS71	303509
Estonia	USA (United States)	08 Nov 23	43LTS277	301063
Lithuania	USA (United States)	09 Apr 24	51LTS191	301226
Hungary	Romania	16 Apr 24	42LTS145	301038
Finland	Latvia	07 Jun 24	38LTS343	300990
France	Latvia	29 Oct 24	93LTS265	302115

PARTY ONE	PARTY TWO	DATE	CITATION	NUMBER
Material evidence (Cont.)				
Estonia	Finland	02 Jan 25	43LTS11	301044
Czechoslovakia	Romania	07 May 25	54LTS51	301273
Czechoslovakia	USA (United States)	02 Jul 25	50LTS143	301200
Finland	Norway	10 Nov 25	43LTS381	301071
Belgium	USA (United States)	18 Nov 25	50LTS225	301205
Austria	Norway	17 Dec 25	48LTS77	301152
Bulgaria	Czechoslovakia	15 May 26	60LTS169	301412
Lithuania	UK Great Britain	18 May 26	61LTS401	301450
Czechoslovakia	UK Great Britain	04 Jun 26	59LTS269	301397
Albania	Serb/Croat/Slovene	22 Jun 26	91LTS81	302056
Albania	Greece	25 Jun 26	83LTS305	301898
Czechoslovakia	Estonia	17 Jul 26	63LTS255	301495
Albania	UK Great Britain	22 Jul 26	67LTS165	301545
Austria	Estonia	15 Oct 26	74LTS213	301739
Liberia	Monaco	28 Oct 26	68LTS241	301588
Belgium	Estonia	11 Nov 26	65LTS405	301523
Switzerland	Uruguay	26 Nov 26	63LTS207	301491
Belgium	Latvia	11 Dec 26	63LTS299	301497
Czechoslovakia	Greece	07 Apr 27	88LTS219	301999
Belgium	Lithuania	17 May 27	77LTS123	301767
Belgium	Czechoslovakia	19 Jul 27	73LTS283	301720
Latvia	Norway	12 Sep 27	71LTS303	301671
Czechoslovakia	Spain	26 Oct 27	121LTS271	302791
Czechoslovakia	Portugal	23 Nov 27	124LTS7	302829
Belgium	Finland	23 Jan 28	74LTS353	301747
Hungary	Serb/Croat/Slovene	22 Feb 28	104LTS151	302385
Czechoslovakia	France	07 May 28	114LTS117	302660
Austria	Finland	22 Oct 28	89LTS69	302007
Bulgaria	Greece	21 Feb 29	106LTS443	302461
Colombia	Nicaragua	25 Mar 29	132LTS255	303042
Finland	Italy	10 Jul 29	111LTS295	302593
Bulgaria	Turkey	23 Dec 29	122LTS17	302796
Estonia	Sweden	20 Jan 30	106LTS279	302451
Latvia	Netherlands	27 Jan 30	117LTS343	302701
Latvia	Sweden	30 Jan 30	110LTS139	302558
Austria	USA (United States)	30 Jan 30	106LTS379	302457
Latvia	Spain	08 Mar 30	113LTS135	302641
Estonia	Norway	03 Apr 30	106LTS147	302442
Hungary	Latvia	04 May 30	101LTS449	302344
Denmark	Estonia	13 May 30	106LTS159	302443
Germany	USA (United States)	12 Jul 30	119LTS247	302748
Bulgaria	Spain	17 Jul 30	114LTS41	302653
Italy	Panama	07 Aug 30	140LTS241	303240
Czechoslovakia	Turkey	22 Aug 30	138LTS375	303196
Italy	Venezuela	23 Aug 30	128LTS377	302943
Sweden	UK Great Britain	28 Aug 30	114LTS9	302652
Denmark	Latvia	28 Aug 30	113LTS169	302644
Poland	Sweden	30 Aug 30	129LTS383	302973
Germany	Turkey	03 Sep 30	133LTS321	303071
Germany	Poland	21 Nov 30	139LTS351	303220
Czechoslovakia	Lithuania	24 Apr 31	126LTS261	302889
Greece	USA (United States)	06 May 31	138LTS293	303194
Belgium	Poland	13 May 31	131LTS109	303005
Czechoslovakia	Denmark	07 Oct 31	127LTS103	302911
Czechoslovakia	Sweden	17 Nov 31	134LTS135	303088
Brazil	Italy	28 Nov 31	132LTS345	303047
Czechoslovakia	Netherlands	04 Dec 31	129LTS343	302969
UK Great Britain	USA (United States)	22 Dec 31	163LTS59	303761
Austria	Latvia	05 Jan 32	133LTS59	303056
Iraq	Turkey	09 Jan 32	139LTS273	303218
Austria	Belgium	26 Jan 32	129LTS141	302959
Iraq	UK Great Britain	02 May 32	141LTS277	303270
Brazil	Switzerland	23 Jul 32	145LTS167	303354
Denmark	UK Great Britain	29 Nov 32	139LTS9	303201
Romania	Yugoslavia	30 Jan 33	146LTS81	303361

PARTY ONE	PARTY TWO	DATE	CITATION	NUMBER
Material evidence (Cont.)				
Finland	Netherlands	21 Feb 33	139LTS365	303221
Switzerland	Turkey	01 Jun 33	159LTS329	303676
Lithuania	Netherlands	01 Dec 33	150LTS337	303466
Multilateral		26 Dec 33	165LTS45	303803
Administrative cooperation				
Austria	Germany	21 Jun 23	27LTS88	300669
France	El Salvador	25 Aug 24	93LTS365	302124
Albania	Serb/Croat/Slovene	22 Jun 26	91LTS55	302055
Czechoslovakia	Switzerland	21 Dec 26	68LTS393	301594
Czechoslovakia	Greece	07 Apr 27	88LTS187	301997
Czechoslovakia	Greece	07 Apr 27	88LTS211	301998
France	Serb/Croat/Slovene	11 Nov 27	68LTS373	301592
Germany	UK Great Britain	20 Mar 28	90LTS287	302044
Belgium	Portugal	28 Mar 28	92LTS185	302085
Austria	Hungary	25 Jun 28	100LTS85	302296
Finland	Italy	21 Aug 28	89LTS25	302002
Netherlands	Siam	27 Oct 28	93LTS131	302105
Germany	Lithuania	30 Oct 28	91LTS365	302077
Lithuania	Sweden	04 Jan 29	92LTS191	302086
Estonia	Sweden	23 Apr 29	89LTS277	302022
Brazil	Denmark	29 Apr 29	89LTS295	302024
France	UK Great Britain	25 May 29	95LTS55	302163
France	India	06 Jun 29	95LTS61	302164
Norway	Sweden	26 Jul 29	94LTS287	302149
Brazil	UK Great Britain	21 Feb 30	101LTS11	302315
Denmark	Norway	06 Nov 30	109LTS283	302545
Estonia	Latvia	17 Feb 34	150LTS103	303457
Conformity with municipal law				
Austria-Hungary	Greece	21 Dec 04	2LTS173	300064
Germany	Greece	12 Mar 07	2LTS111	300054
Multilateral		13 Nov 08	1LTS217	300015
France	Italy	30 Sep 19	5LTS279	300133
Argentina	Italy	26 Mar 20	15LTS271	300400
Belgium	Netherlands	09 Feb 21	11LTS333	300299
Latvia	Lithuania	14 May 21	17LTS233	300439
Afghanistan	Persia	22 Jun 21	33LTS285	300853
Brazil	Italy	08 Oct 21	16LTS9	300401
Afghanistan	UK Great Britain	22 Nov 21	14LTS47	300367
Belgium	France	30 Nov 21	27LTS173	300680
Czechoslovakia	Germany	12 Apr 22	22LTS329	300562
Multilateral		05 Jul 22	13LTS237	300355
United Arab Rep	Palestine	07 Aug 22	36LTS343	300933
Other Unilat Decla	Albania	02 Oct 22	9LTS173	300249
Finland	USSR (Soviet Union)	28 Oct 22	29LTS211	300743
Denmark	USSR (Soviet Union)	23 Apr 23	18LTS15	300450
Poland	Serb/Croat/Slovene	04 May 23	85LTS455	301946
Belgium	Luxembourg	17 Jul 23	27LTS235	300686
Poland	Turkey	23 Jul 23	49LTS345	301190
Multilateral		24 Jul 23	28LTS151	300704
Finland	Sweden	11 Sep 23	20LTS79	300508
Bulgaria	Serb/Croat/Slovene	26 Nov 23	26LTS141	300644
Denmark	Finland	30 Nov 23	22LTS427	300571
Multilateral		09 Dec 23	58LTS315	301380
Multilateral		09 Dec 23	36LTS76	300905
Czechoslovakia	Hungary	09 Feb 24	30LTS335	300773
Mexico	Spain	31 Mar 24	43LTS297	301065
Multilateral		31 Mar 24	27LTS211	300685
Bulgaria	Romania	19 Apr 24	33LTS209	300845
Latvia	Lithuania	21 May 24	37LTS363	300960
Multilateral		22 May 24	35LTS175	300895
Great Britain	Latvia	16 Jul 24	37LTS369	300961
Germany	Sweden	29 Aug 24	42LTS111	301036
Czechoslovakia	Netherlands	17 Oct 24	31LTS93	300786
Argentina	Belgium	20 Oct 24	137LTS381	303166
Conformity with municipal law (Cont.)				
Multilateral		23 Oct 24	77LTS367	301778
Czechoslovakia	Germany	15 Dec 24	52LTS31	301248
Czechoslovakia	Germany	15 Dec 24	52LTS41	301249
Bulgaria	Turkey	27 Dec 24	54LTS135	301281
Netherlands	Norway	09 Jan 25	48LTS247	301166
Austria	Czechoslovakia	17 Jan 25	94LTS245	302146
Finland	Netherlands	09 Mar 25	47LTS431	301148
Czechoslovakia	Romania	16 Apr 25	46LTS427	301126
Czechoslovakia	Poland	23 Apr 25	48LTS287	301170
Bel-Lux Econ Union	Japan	27 Jun 25	36LTS95	300907
Austria	China	19 Oct 25	55LTS9	301301
Estonia	Finland	10 Dec 25	50LTS335	301217
Austria	Germany	08 Jan 26	62LTS95	301459
Argentina	Austria	22 Mar 26	143LTS157	303306
Multilateral		10 Apr 26	176LTS199	304062
Cuba	USA (United States)	22 Apr 26	60LTS371	301421
Multilateral		24 Apr 26	108LTS123	302505
France	Saar	27 May 26	55LTS157	301312
Belgium	Germany	29 May 26	127LTS149	302916
Denmark	UK Great Britain	02 Jun 26	61LTS353	301445
Italy	Latvia	12 Jun 26	51LTS65	301222
Dominican Republic	USA (United States)	19 Jul 26	54LTS145	301282
Hungary	USA (United States)	04 Sep 26	58LTS111	301369
Denmark	Netherlands	23 Oct 26	72LTS13	301686
China	Finland	29 Oct 26	67LTS345	301556
Multilateral		13 Nov 26	77LTS217	301772
Hungary	Turkey	20 Dec 26	72LTS245	301696
Czechoslovakia	Switzerland	21 Dec 26	86LTS443	301956
Austria	Germany	05 Feb 27	73LTS205	301714
Czechoslovakia	Greece	07 Apr 27	88LTS211	301998
Czechoslovakia	Turkey	31 May 27	75LTS79	301753
Switzerland	Turkey	07 Aug 27	73LTS51	301706
Belgium	France	06 Oct 27	69LTS49	301599
Denmark	Iceland	13 Oct 27	67LTS411	301562
Argentina	Denmark	16 Nov 27	165LTS177	303809
Greece	Switzerland	01 Dec 27	84LTS271	301907
Australia	Norway	13 Dec 27	69LTS307	301612
France	Saar	14 Dec 27	70LTS163	301631
Germany	Switzerland	04 Feb 28	79LTS241	301814
Multilateral		20 Feb 28	132LTS301	303045
Multilateral		20 Feb 28	129LTS223	302963
Multilateral		20 Feb 28	86LTS111	301950
Belgium	Czechoslovakia	26 Jun 28	80LTS9	301819
Netherlands	Portugal	27 Jun 28	81LTS437	301853
Austria	Japan	06 Jul 28	81LTS425	301851
Abyssinia	Italy	02 Aug 28	94LTS413	302158
Czechoslovakia	Serb/Croat/Slovene	29 Sep 28	96LTS421	302215
Multilateral		25 Oct 28	84LTS7	301901
Bel-Lux Econ Union	China	22 Nov 28	87LTS287	301975
United Arab Rep	Persia	28 Nov 28	93LTS381	302127
Latvia	Persia	15 Jan 29	162LTS299	303742
Norway	Sweden	11 May 29	120LTS263	302771
Estonia	USSR (Soviet Union)	17 May 29	94LTS323	302152
Spain	UK Great Britain	27 Jun 29	101LTS375	302337
Argentina	UK Great Britain	15 Nov 29	160LTS257	303694
Germany	Italy	20 Jan 30	106LTS109	302439
Multilateral		12 Apr 30	179LTS89	304137
Irish Free State	Italy	10 May 30	132LTS147	303034
Multilateral		07 Jun 30	143LTS317	303314
Germany	USA (United States)	23 Jun 30	106LTS121	302440
Belgium	Shereefian	24 Jul 30	138LTS35	303179
Belgium	France	23 Aug 30	166LTS11	303825
El Salvador	USA (United States)	05 Sep 30	134LTS207	303093
Irish Free State	Switzerland	03 Nov 30	132LTS159	303035
Switzerland	Turkey	13 Dec 30	129LTS331	302968

PARTY ONE	PARTY TWO	DATE	CITATION	NUMBER
Conformity with municipal law (Cont.)				
Multilateral		19 Mar 31	143LTS407	303317
Czechoslovakia	Germany	21 Mar 31	143LTS177	303308
Greece	Poland	22 Apr 31	129LTS313	302966
France	Greece	05 Jun 31	31LTS201	303011
Germany	Poland	11 Jun 31	141LTS91	303263
Poland	USA (United States)	15 Jun 31	139LTS395	303223
Belgium	Germany	16 Jul 31	145LTS137	303351
Greece	Romania	11 Aug 31	130LTS69	302982
Poland	Turkey	29 Aug 31	144LTS367	303339
France	Switzerland	09 Sep 31	142LTS205	303293
Belgium	Netherlands	16 Oct 31	137LTS411	303171
Lithuania	Sweden	16 Oct 31	126LTS233	302885
Multilateral		10 Dec 31	129LTS177	302961
Finland	Poland	19 Dec 31	131LTS193	303010
Belgium	France	23 Dec 31	137LTS277	303162
Iraq	Turkey	09 Jan 32	139LTS263	303217
Germany	USA (United States)	31 May 32	133LTS409	303078
France	Yugoslavia	29 Jul 32	144LTS313	303334
Brazil	Denmark	05 Aug 32	132LTS211	303039
Austria	Czechoslovakia	18 Jan 33	142LTS41	303278
Romania	Yugoslavia	30 Jan 33	146LTS151	303367
Romania	Yugoslavia	10 Mar 33	146LTS255	303375
Netherlands	Yemen	12 Mar 33	146LTS359	303384
France	Switzerland	09 Jun 33	181LTS275	304194
Finland	UK Great Britain	11 Aug 33	149LTS131	303437
Multilateral		28 Oct 33	159LTS199	303663
Multilateral		23 Nov 33	192LTS327	304483
Multilateral		23 Nov 33	192LTS389	304484
Latvia	USSR (Soviet Union)	04 Dec 33	148LTS145	303410
Czechoslovakia	Poland	25 Jan 34	177LTS139	304088
Persia	Switzerland	25 Apr 34	160LTS173	303691
Iraq	USA (United States)	07 Jun 34	170LTS267	303942
Czechoslovakia	Luxembourg	01 Dec 34	168LTS287	303906
Latvia	Poland	20 Dec 34	162LTS361	303749
Germany	USSR (Soviet Union)	07 Mar 35	169LTS7	303911
Hungary	Netherlands	08 Jun 35	171LTS385	303975
El Salvador	Spain	15 Jun 35	165LTS321	303818
Hungary	Switzerland	18 Jun 35	174LTS7	304033
Bulgaria	USSR (Soviet Union)	10 Jul 35	168LTS275	303905
France	Hungary	23 Jul 35	173LTS243	304016
Netherlands	UK Great Britain	07 Nov 35	165LTS337	303820
Panama	USA (United States)	02 Mar 36	200LTS17	304686
France	USSR (Soviet Union)	09 Mar 36	179LTS131	304140
Luxembourg	Netherlands	01 Apr 36	179LTS11	304130
China	UK Great Britain	17 Jul 36	173LTS343	304024
Czechoslovakia	Sweden	23 Jul 36	171LTS111	303954
Sweden	Switzerland	25 Jul 36	171LTS177	303959
Estonia	Finland	12 Sep 36	172LTS345	303999
Chile	Sweden	21 Oct 36	174LTS109	304041
Germany	Greece	09 Nov 36	182LTS9	304201
Greece	USA (United States)	21 Nov 36	183LTS169	304233
France	Sweden	04 Dec 36	184LTS35	304241
Netherlands	Switzerland	27 Jan 37	186LTS433	304327
United Arab Rep	Turkey	07 Apr 37	191LTS95	304438
Multilateral		08 May 37	182LTS37	304202
Poland	Sweden	13 Sep 37	187LTS431	304348
Estonia	France	16 Oct 37	183LTS41	304227
Denmark	Siam	05 Nov 37	188LTS187	304358
Bel-Lux Econ Union	Siam	05 Nov 37	190LTS151	304413
Norway	Siam	15 Nov 37	186LTS9	304301
Japan	Siam	08 Dec 37	188LTS375	304367
Germany	Siam	30 Dec 37	188LTS401	304368
Lithuania	Poland	14 May 38	191LTS373	304456
Latvia	Poland	16 Jun 38	196LTS105	304573
Portugal	Siam	02 Jul 38	200LTS149	304688

PARTY ONE	PARTY TWO	DATE	CITATION	NUMBER
Conformity with municipal law (Cont.)				
Romania	Switzerland	19 Jul 38	152LTS89	303486
Greece	UK Great Britain	30 May 39	202LTS7	304732
France	USA (United States)	15 Jul 39	199LTS355	304683
Hungary	Romania	19 Oct 39	201LTS395	304728
Germany	Latvia	30 Oct 39	200LTS213	304693
Japan	Thailand	30 Nov 39	200LTS197	304691
Information centers				
Multilateral		18 Mar 04	1LTS83	300011
Multilateral		10 Sep 19	8LTS11	300201
Multilateral		31 Oct 20	164LTS85	303790
Multilateral		25 Jan 24	57LTS135	301360
Estonia	Finland	10 Dec 25	50LTS335	301217
Italy	Siam	09 May 26	61LTS215	301436
Germany	Turkey	03 Sep 30	133LTS321	303071
Afghanistan	USSR (Soviet Union)	06 May 35	164LTS335	303800
Albania	Italy	19 Mar 36	173LTS107	304007
Multilateral		26 Jun 36	198LTS299	304648
France	USA (United States)	12 Dec 36	176LTS403	304076
Exchange of official publications				
Paraguay	Uruguay	28 Feb 15	15LTS195	300393
Belgium	Germany	23 Apr 20	12LTS29	300305
Latvia	Lithuania	12 Jul 21	25LTS299	300619
Germany	Poland	29 Apr 22	21LTS391	300549
Belgium	UK Great Britain	21 Jun 22	24LTS91	300597
Czechoslovakia	Romania	14 Oct 22	25LTS163	300604
Belgium	Sweden	25 Oct 22	18LTS121	300459
Hungary	Sweden	26 Feb 23	17LTS35	300426
Czechoslovakia	Serb/Croat/Slovene	17 Mar 23	30LTS185	300768
Luxembourg	Sweden	11 Apr 23	16LTS453	300423
Finland	Norway	28 Apr 23	19LTS225	300496
Japan	Sweden	01 May 23	17LTS391	300446
Denmark	Sweden	13 Jul 23	18LTS143	300461
Denmark	Sweden	13 Jul 23	18LTS131	300460
Chile	Norway	27 Jul 23	33LTS249	300848
France	Norway	01 Oct 23	33LTS237	300847
Mexico	Norway	01 Oct 23	33LTS255	300849
Japan	Norway	06 Nov 23	33LTS265	300850
Bulgaria	Serb/Croat/Slovene	26 Nov 23	26LTS85	300642
Bulgaria	Serb/Croat/Slovene	26 Nov 23	26LTS119	300643
Denmark	Norway	30 Nov 23	22LTS121	300555
Hungary	Italy	27 Mar 24	45LTS65	301099
Norway	UK Great Britain	05 Jun 24	27LTS195	300683
France	El Salvador	25 Aug 24	93LTS365	302124
Estonia	Sweden	30 Aug 24	31LTS217	300797
Austria	Norway	06 Dec 24	31LTS179	300794
Norway	Sweden	22 Dec 24	32LTS13	300802
Austria	Hungary	10 May 26	56LTS39	301321
Brazil	Peru	31 Dec 28	127LTS455	302931
Finland	USSR (Soviet Union)	04 Jul 33	149LTS83	303436
Estonia	Poland	26 Sep 33	150LTS309	303464
Brazil	Uruguay	20 Dec 33	181LTS91	304179
Estonia	Latvia	17 Feb 34	150LTS391	303472
Austria	Hungary	04 Mar 35	163LTS33	303759
Germany	Hungary	28 May 36	178LTS445	304127
Peru	USA (United States)	16 Oct 36	181LTS161	304187
Multilateral		23 Dec 36	201LTS295	304721
France	Sweden	30 Jun 37	179LTS203	304148
Multilateral		14 Sep 37	181LTS137	304184
Mexico	USA (United States)	24 Sep 37	185LTS23	304270
Chile	USA (United States)	27 Oct 37	186LTS219	304314
Latvia	Poland	16 Nov 37	197LTS43	304604
Cuba	USA (United States)	12 May 38	191LTS19	304432
Mexico	USA (United States)	29 Aug 38	195LTS359	304556
Estonia	USA (United States)	06 Dec 38	198LTS361	304655

PARTY ONE	PARTY TWO	DATE	CITATION	NUMBER
Exchange of official publications (Cont.)				
Finland	USA (United States)	30 Dec 38	195LTS417	304562
Belgium	UK Great Britain	19 Jun 39	198LTS171	304637
Argentina	USA (United States)	17 Oct 39	201LTS273	304720
Nicaragua	USA (United States)	19 Feb 40	203LTS47	304749
Chile	USA (United States)	23 Apr 40	203LTS29	304747
Brazil	USA (United States)	24 Jun 40	203LTS227	304766
Honduras	USA (United States)	12 Dec 40	203LTS341	304774
Family law				
Finland	Germany	21 Apr 22	19LTS87	300487
Czechoslovakia	Serb/Croat/Slovene	17 Mar 23	30LTS185	300768
Germany	Switzerland	24 Mar 23	27LTS41	300666
Poland	Serb/Croat/Slovene	04 May 23	85LTS455	301946
Poland	Turkey	23 Jul 23	49LTS345	301190
Sweden	UK Great Britain	27 Oct 23	22LTS387	300568
Germany	Poland	05 Mar 24	49LTS251	301184
Austria	Poland	19 Mar 24	56LTS95	301326
Brazil	Switzerland	23 Jun 24	33LTS415	300861
Italy	Serb/Croat/Slovene	21 Aug 24	82LTS445	301883
Bulgaria	Turkey	27 Dec 24	54LTS135	301281
Czechoslovakia	Poland	06 Mar 25	46LTS201	301120
Czechoslovakia	Romania	07 May 25	54LTS17	301272
Albania	Serb/Croat/Slovene	22 Jun 26	91LTS81	302056
Germany	Poland	27 Oct 26	108LTS275	302513
Austria	Germany	05 Feb 27	73LTS205	301714
Austria	Germany	05 Feb 27	73LTS227	301715
Multilateral		20 Feb 28	86LTS111	301950
Hungary	Serb/Croat/Slovene	22 Feb 28	87LTS361	301982
Austria	Serb/Croat/Slovene	01 May 28	96LTS373	302214
Austria	Persia	17 Jun 28	112LTS101	302610
Multilateral		30 Jun 28	89LTS53	302005
Persia	Sweden	09 Aug 28	80LTS407	301841
Belgium	France	12 Sep 28	123LTS91	302808
Multilateral		25 Oct 28	84LTS7	301901
Luxembourg	Poland	29 Oct 28	111LTS71	302581
Estonia	Sweden	23 Apr 29	89LTS277	302022
Hungary	Yugoslavia	11 Nov 29	111LTS197	302587
Denmark	Italy	11 Dec 29	97LTS373	302235
France	Latvia	20 Jan 30	169LTS125	303917
Latvia	Sweden	30 Jan 30	110LTS139	302558
Multilateral		12 Apr 30	179LTS89	304137
Multilateral		06 Feb 31	126LTS121	302877
Multilateral		10 Feb 31	126LTS41	302870
Sweden	Turkey	24 Apr 32	129LTS325	302967
Italy	Latvia	11 May 32	150LTS9	303450
Norway	Sweden	22 Aug 33	141LTS217	303267
Bulgaria	Czechoslovakia	29 Aug 33	148LTS15	303402
Czechoslovakia	Poland	25 Jan 34	177LTS139	304088
Czechoslovakia	USSR (Soviet Union)	16 Nov 35	169LTS143	303918
Exchange of information and documents				
Austria-Hungary	Greece	21 Dec 04	2LTS173	300064
Germany	Greece	12 Mar 07	2LTS111	300054
Multilateral		12 Jan 12	4LTS281	300112
Multilateral		21 Apr 14	5LTS394	300144
Spain	USA (United States)	15 Sep 14	89LTS427	302030
Greece	Spain	06 Mar 19	3LTS81	300092
Multilateral		10 Sep 19	7LTS331	300200
France	Italy	30 Sep 19	5LTS279	300133
Multilateral		29 Feb 20	127LTS433	302930
France	Germany	01 Mar 20	1LTS367	300030
Argentina	Italy	26 Mar 20	15LTS271	300400
Belgium	Germany	23 Apr 20	12LTS29	300305
France	UK Great Britain	26 Apr 20	1LTS287	300023
France	Germany	05 May 20	8LTS55	300206
Germany	Poland	20 Sep 20	9LTS103	300246

PARTY ONE	PARTY TWO	DATE	CITATION	NUMBER
Exchange of information and documents (Cont.)				
France	UK Great Britain	20 Oct 20	2LTS323	300085
UK Great Britain	USSR (Soviet Union)	16 Mar 21	4LTS127	300104
Portugal	UK Great Britain	06 May 21	5LTS179	300128
Latvia	Lithuania	13 May 21	17LTS211	300438
Peru	USA (United States)	21 May 21	6LTS171	300150
Germany	UK Great Britain	18 Jun 21	16LTS139	300404
Norway	USA (United States)	30 Jun 21	14LTS19	300365
Latvia	Lithuania	12 Jul 21	25LTS311	300620
Denmark	UK Great Britain	12 Jul 21	8LTS397	300238
Latvia	Lithuania	12 Jul 21	25LTS299	300619
Austria	UK Great Britain	14 Jul 21	16LTS151	300405
Norway	UK Great Britain	15 Jul 21	6LTS307	300162
Belgium	Luxembourg	25 Jul 21	9LTS223	300256
Finland	Sweden	29 Jul 21	6LTS353	300168
Latvia	Ukrainian SSR	03 Aug 21	17LTS317	300442
Czechoslovakia	UK Great Britain	04 Aug 21	16LTS157	300406
Austria	Germany	17 Aug 21	19LTS237	300497
Czechoslovakia	Sweden	07 Sep 21	7LTS97	300177
Italy	Serb/Croat/Slovene	14 Sep 21	19LTS14	300482
Multilateral		21 Sep 21	7LTS127	300181
Danzig	Poland	24 Oct 21	116LTS5	302699
France	Sweden	09 Nov 21	7LTS303	300197
Greece	UK Great Britain	10 Nov 21	16LTS165	300407
Sweden	Switzerland	29 Nov 21	7LTS313	300198
Belgium	France	30 Nov 21	27LTS173	300680
Poland	Sweden	27 Dec 21	8LTS163	300220
Costa Rica	UK Great Britain	12 Jan 22	17LTS151	300432
Iraq	UK Great Britain	16 Jan 22	12LTS431	300340
Palestine	UK Great Britain	23 Jan 22	13LTS9	300342
Multilateral		06 Feb 22	38LTS277	300982
Finland	Norway	03 Mar 22	14LTS157	300372
Multilateral		17 Mar 22	11LTS167	300296
Italy	Serb/Croat/Slovene	06 Apr 22	118LTS207	302725
Germany	Poland	12 Apr 22	21LTS327	300548
Denmark	Germany	25 Apr 22	18LTS227	300466
Germany	Poland	29 Apr 22	21LTS391	300549
Norway	Sweden	05 May 22	15LTS165	300390
Czechoslovakia	Germany	08 May 22	23LTS171	300589
Germany	Poland	15 Jun 22	34LTS201	300875
Germany	Poland	18 Jun 22	34LTS235	300876
Belgium	UK Great Britain	21 Jun 22	24LTS91	300597
Germany	Poland	23 Jun 22	22LTS25	300553
Estonia	Latvia	24 Jun 22	38LTS57	300967
Latvia	USSR (Soviet Union)	24 Jun 22	38LTS9	300966
Latvia	Poland	07 Jul 22	37LTS317	300958
United Arab Rep	Palestine	07 Aug 22	36LTS343	300933
Czechoslovakia	Poland	23 Sep 22	50LTS321	301216
Austria	Sweden	04 Oct 22	9LTS317	300264
Multilateral		04 Oct 22	12LTS391	300335
Czechoslovakia	France	07 Oct 22	47LTS365	301141
Czechoslovakia	Romania	14 Oct 22	25LTS163	300604
Mexico	Sweden	17 Oct 22	15LTS179	300391
Italy	Serb/Croat/Slovene	23 Oct 22	18LTS441	300480
Belgium	Sweden	25 Oct 22	18LTS121	300459
Haiti	UK Great Britain	16 Nov 22	16LTS173	300408
Germany	Poland	18 Dec 22	34LTS301	300880
Siam	USA (United States)	30 Dec 22	25LTS394	300629
Poland	USSR (Soviet Union)	07 Feb 23	49LTS285	301186
France	USA (United States)	13 Feb 23	26LTS53	300640
France	USA (United States)	13 Feb 23	26LTS69	300641
Hungary	Sweden	26 Feb 23	17LTS35	300426
Czechoslovakia	Serb/Croat/Slovene	17 Mar 23	30LTS185	300768
Liechtenstein	Switzerland	29 Mar 23	21LTS231	300545
Luxembourg	Sweden	11 Apr 23	16LTS453	300423
Germany	Saar	21 Apr 23	27LTS295	300693

PARTY ONE	PARTY TWO	DATE	CITATION	NUMBER
Exchange of information and documents (Cont.)				
Multilateral		28 Apr 23	33LTS47	300832
Finland	Norway	28 Apr 23	19LTS225	300496
Japan	Sweden	01 May 23	17LTS391	300446
Multilateral		03 May 23	33LTS81	300833
Multilateral		03 May 23	33LTS11	300830
Poland	Serb/Croat/Slovene	04 May 23	85LTS455	301946
Germany	Poland	14 Jun 23	34LTS343	300883
Austria	Germany	21 Jun 23	27LTS88	300669
Czechoslovakia	Hungary	13 Jul 23	35LTS271	300900
Denmark	Sweden	13 Jul 23	18LTS143	300461
Denmark	Sweden	13 Jul 23	18LTS131	300460
Multilateral		24 Jul 23	28LTS11	300701
Chile	Norway	27 Jul 23	33LTS249	300848
Finland	USSR (Soviet Union)	28 Jul 23	32LTS101	300810
Czechoslovakia	Germany	15 Aug 23	27LTS94	300670
France	Norway	01 Oct 23	33LTS237	300847
Mexico	Norway	01 Oct 23	33LTS255	300849
Estonia	Latvia	01 Nov 23	23LTS81	300578
Germany	Hungary	06 Nov 23	45LTS279	301104
Japan	Norway	06 Nov 23	33LTS265	300850
Bulgaria	Serb/Croat/Slovene	26 Nov 23	26LTS85	300642
Bulgaria	Serb/Croat/Slovene	26 Nov 23	26LTS119	300643
Bulgaria	Serb/Croat/Slovene	26 Nov 23	26LTS141	300644
Finland	Sweden	29 Nov 23	23LTS41	300575
Denmark	Norway	30 Nov 23	22LTS121	300555
Nepal	UK Great Britain	21 Dec 23	36LTS357	300934
Belgium	USA (United States)	21 Jan 24	31LTS137	300791
Czechoslovakia	France	25 Jan 24	23LTS163	300588
Germany	Poland	05 Mar 24	49LTS181	301182
Bulgaria	USA (United States)	19 Mar 24	26LTS27	300638
Mexico	Spain	31 Mar 24	43LTS297	301065
Multilateral		31 Mar 24	27LTS211	300685
Hungary	Romania	16 Apr 24	45LTS341	301107
Hungary	Romania	16 Apr 24	42LTS165	301039
Hungary	Romania	16 Apr 24	45LTS325	301106
Bulgaria	Romania	19 Apr 24	33LTS209	300845
Bulgaria	Romania	19 Apr 24	33LTS221	300846
Austria	Germany	30 Apr 24	46LTS175	301119
Latvia	Lithuania	21 May 24	37LTS363	300960
Norway	UK Great Britain	05 Jun 24	27LTS195	300683
Austria	Czechoslovakia	15 Jun 24	94LTS149	302142
Austria	Serb/Croat/Slovene	18 Jun 24	115LTS25	302674
Finland	USSR (Soviet Union)	18 Jun 24	47LTS241	301134
Austria	Serb/Croat/Slovene	27 Jun 24	115LTS39	302675
Italy	Serb/Croat/Slovene	21 Aug 24	82LTS445	301883
Estonia	Sweden	30 Aug 24	31LTS217	300797
Germany	Poland	30 Aug 24	32LTS331	300824
Argentina	Norway	07 Oct 24	33LTS191	300843
Bel-Lux Econ Union	Guatemala	07 Nov 24	69LTS17	301596
Multilateral		14 Nov 24	86LTS43	301949
Multilateral		29 Nov 24	80LTS293	301835
Austria	Norway	06 Dec 24	31LTS179	300794
Hungary	Serb/Croat/Slovene	14 Dec 24	39LTS91	300997
Norway	Sweden	22 Dec 24	32LTS13	300802
Czechoslovakia	Germany	06 Feb 25	46LTS165	301118
Multilateral		11 Feb 25	51LTS337	301239
Austria	France	04 Mar 25	44LTS205	301084
Czechoslovakia	Poland	06 Mar 25	46LTS201	301120
Czechoslovakia	Poland	23 Apr 25	44LTS285	301090
Czechoslovakia	Poland	23 Apr 25	44LTS309	301091
Czechoslovakia	Poland	23 Apr 25	44LTS271	301089
Czechoslovakia	Romania	07 May 25	54LTS51	301273
Czechoslovakia	Romania	07 May 25	54LTS17	301272
Finland	Sweden	09 May 25	47LTS283	301136
Austria	Czechoslovakia	14 May 25	50LTS39	301198

PARTY ONE	PARTY TWO	DATE	CITATION	NUMBER
Exchange of information and documents (Cont.)				
France	Monaco	26 May 25	44LTS249	301086
Czechoslovakia	Poland	30 May 25	48LTS397	301172
Multilateral		09 Jun 25	49LTS9	301174
Bel-Lux Econ Union	Japan	27 Jun 25	36LTS95	300907
Italy	Serb/Croat/Slovene	20 Jul 25	83LTS241	301889
France	Spain	03 Aug 25	38LTS371	300992
France	Germany	14 Aug 25	75LTS103	301756
Czechoslovakia	Poland	05 Sep 25	58LTS143	301370
Germany	USSR (Soviet Union)	12 Oct 25	53LTS227	301259
Belgium	Hungary	05 Dec 25	43LTS173	301053
Belgium	USA (United States)	09 Dec 25	72LTS171	301690
France	Poland	30 Dec 25	48LTS139	301155
Multilateral		31 Dec 25	79LTS167	301809
Estonia	Latvia	03 Mar 26	63LTS13	301476
Cuba	USA (United States)	11 Mar 26	61LTS383	301448
Argentina	Austria	22 Mar 26	143LTS157	303306
Brazil	Venezuela	13 Apr 26	80LTS283	301834
Cuba	USA (United States)	22 Apr 26	60LTS371	301421
Multilateral		24 Apr 26	108LTS123	302505
France	San Marino	30 Apr 26	89LTS9	302001
Bulgaria	Czechoslovakia	15 May 26	60LTS203	301413
Denmark	UK Great Britain	02 Jun 26	61LTS353	301445
Czechoslovakia	UK Great Britain	11 Jun 26	48LTS425	301173
Romania	Serb/Croat/Slovene	13 Jun 26	54LTS257	301289
France	India	19 Jun 26	57LTS35	301350
Germany	Poland	21 Jun 26	72LTS203	301693
Albania	Serb/Croat/Slovene	22 Jun 26	91LTS81	302056
Czechoslovakia	Latvia	06 Jul 26	62LTS229	301465
Germany	Latvia	09 Jul 26	63LTS321	301499
Austria	Czechoslovakia	12 Jul 26	86LTS395	301952
Czechoslovakia	Estonia	17 Jul 26	63LTS255	301495
Czechoslovakia	Estonia	17 Jul 26	69LTS385	301620
France	Sweden	19 Jul 26	54LTS283	301291
Netherlands	UK Great Britain	14 Aug 26	57LTS41	301351
France	Switzerland	27 Aug 26	59LTS231	301392
Netherlands	Norway	21 Sep 26	56LTS89	301325
Austria	Estonia	15 Oct 26	74LTS213	301739
Multilateral		13 Nov 26	77LTS171	301770
Multilateral		13 Nov 26	77LTS199	301771
Czechoslovakia	Switzerland	21 Dec 26	68LTS393	301594
Czechoslovakia	Switzerland	21 Dec 26	86LTS443	301956
Germany	Poland	22 Dec 26	68LTS263	301590
Austria	Germany	05 Feb 27	73LTS205	301714
Czechoslovakia	Poland	08 Feb 27	70LTS261	301638
Czechoslovakia	Poland	08 Feb 27	70LTS299	301641
Czechoslovakia	Poland	08 Feb 27	70LTS289	301640
Czechoslovakia	Poland	08 Feb 27	70LTS275	301639
Denmark	Netherlands	19 Feb 27	60LTS271	301415
Poland	Serb/Croat/Slovene	06 Mar 27	126LTS67	302871
Belgium	Netherlands	24 Mar 27	84LTS34	301902
Czechoslovakia	Greece	07 Apr 27	88LTS211	301998
Czechoslovakia	Poland	14 Apr 27	82LTS157	301867
Belgium	UK Great Britain	03 May 27	140LTS71	303229
Belgium	UK Great Britain	06 May 27	63LTS153	301486
Czechoslovakia	Poland	30 May 27	98LTS233	302251
Czechoslovakia	Hungary	03 Jun 27	67LTS31	301538
Belgium	Germany	09 Jul 27	75LTS367	301759
Belgium	Portugal	19 Jul 27	71LTS419	301680
Belgium	Czechoslovakia	19 Jul 27	73LTS307	301721
Multilateral		28 Jul 27	64LTS379	301511
Portugal	Spain	11 Aug 27	82LTS113	301864
Italy	Spain	15 Aug 27	94LTS361	302155
Greece		15 Sep 27	70LTS9	301622
France	Germany	05 Oct 27	77LTS7	301762
Czechoslovakia	Spain	26 Oct 27	121LTS311	302793

PARTY ONE	PARTY TWO	DATE	CITATION	NUMBER
Exchange of information and documents (Cont.)				
Czechoslovakia	Spain	26 Oct 27	121LTS271	302791
Czechoslovakia	Spain	26 Oct 27	121LTS287	302792
France	Serb/Croat/Slovene	11 Nov 27	68LTS381	301593
France	Serb/Croat/Slovene	11 Nov 27	68LTS373	301592
Czechoslovakia	Portugal	23 Nov 27	124LTS7	302829
Czechoslovakia	Portugal	23 Nov 27	123LTS403	302827
Czechoslovakia	Portugal	23 Nov 27	123LTS417	302828
Germany	Poland	10 Dec 27	120LTS299	302773
Netherlands	Sweden	30 Dec 27	70LTS365	301646
Norway	USSR (Soviet Union)	16 Jan 28	70LTS239	301635
Germany	Lithuania	29 Jan 28	89LTS338	302027
Germany	USA (United States)	14 Feb 28	79LTS235	301813
Czechoslovakia	Poland	18 Feb 28	119LTS385	302758
Multilateral		20 Feb 28	129LTS223	302963
Hungary	Serb/Croat/Slovene	22 Feb 28	104LTS151	302385
Hungary	Serb/Croat/Slovene	22 Feb 28	113LTS49	302635
France	Sweden	03 Mar 28	95LTS89	302168
France	Netherlands	10 Mar 28	102LTS109	302356
Germany	UK Great Britain	20 Mar 28	90LTS287	302044
Czechoslovakia	Germany	22 Mar 28	93LTS235	302113
Belgium	Portugal	28 Mar 28	92LTS185	302085
Belgium	Luxembourg	13 Apr 28	72LTS237	301695
Belgium	Netherlands	16 Apr 28	75LTS61	301751
Chile	Germany	18 Apr 28	79LTS411	301817
Austria	Serb/Croat/Slovene	01 May 28	96LTS373	302214
Czechoslovakia	France	07 May 28	114LTS117	302660
Czechoslovakia	France	07 May 28	114LTS171	302663
Austria	Italy	11 May 28	100LTS41	302293
Belgium	Poland	12 Jun 28	123LTS25	302803
Austria	Hungary	25 Jun 28	100LTS85	302296
France	Portugal	06 Jul 28	126LTS27	302869
Czechoslovakia	USA (United States)	16 Aug 28	89LTS219	302017
Finland	Italy	21 Aug 28	84LTS265	301906
Finland	Italy	21 Aug 28	89LTS25	302002
Netherlands	Switzerland	27 Aug 28	82LTS153	301866
Portugal	South Africa	11 Sep 28	98LTS9	302239
Belgium	France	12 Sep 28	123LTS91	302808
Multilateral		26 Sep 28	93LTS343	302123
Italy	Spain	03 Oct 28	94LTS387	302156
Estonia	Latvia	19 Oct 28	97LTS359	302233
Mexico	UK Great Britain	24 Oct 28	87LTS63	301962
Multilateral		25 Oct 28	84LTS7	301901
Germany	Lithuania	30 Oct 28	91LTS365	302077
Czechoslovakia	Serb/Croat/Slovene	07 Nov 28	98LTS297	302252
Czechoslovakia	Hungary	14 Nov 28	110LTS425	302574
Poland	Romania	29 Nov 28	96LTS15	302188
Hungary	Poland	30 Nov 28	100LTS67	302294
Finland	Hungary	12 Dec 28	96LTS67	302191
Belgium	Great Britain	21 Dec 28	85LTS415	301942
Lithuania	Sweden	04 Jan 29	92LTS191	302086
United Arab Rep	Palestine	12 Jan 29	94LTS9	302132
Bulgaria	USA (United States)	21 Jan 29	93LTS331	302121
Hungary	USA (United States)	26 Jan 29	96LTS207	302201
Bulgaria	Greece	21 Feb 29	106LTS443	302461
Austria	Italy	22 Feb 29	89LTS271	302021
Bulgaria	Turkey	06 Mar 29	114LTS399	302668
Czechoslovakia	Germany	20 Mar 29	109LTS219	302541
Romania	USA (United States)	21 Mar 29	105LTS85	302403
Luxembourg	USA (United States)	06 Apr 29	106LTS469	302463
Multilateral		16 Apr 29	126LTS305	302891
Multilateral		20 Apr 29	112LTS371	302623
Estonia	Sweden	23 Apr 29	89LTS277	302022
Brazil	Denmark	29 Apr 29	89LTS295	302024
Belgium	Czechoslovakia	29 Apr 29	110LTS113	302556
Norway	Sweden	11 May 29	120LTS263	302771

PARTY ONE	PARTY TWO	DATE	CITATION	NUMBER
Exchange of information and documents (Cont.)				
Germany	Turkey	28 May 29	133LTS235	303068
Spain	UK Great Britain	27 Jun 29	101LTS375	302337
Finland	Italy	10 Jul 29	111LTS295	302593
UK Great Britain	USA (United States)	11 Jul 29	98LTS161	302245
Bulgaria	Hungary	22 Jul 29	101LTS41	302317
Estonia	USA (United States)	27 Aug 29	102LTS239	302367
Netherlands	South Africa	10 Sep 29	98LTS423	302261
Germany	Luxembourg	11 Sep 29	118LTS97	302715
Luxembourg	Netherlands	17 Sep 29	107LTS35	302466
Czechoslovakia	Switzerland	20 Sep 29	102LTS123	302357
Poland	UK Great Britain	04 Oct 29	97LTS261	302227
Germany	Switzerland	02 Nov 29	109LTS273	302544
Hungary	Yugoslavia	11 Nov 29	111LTS197	302587
France	Germany	20 Nov 29	99LTS339	302277
Estonia	Hungary	27 Nov 29	106LTS331	302454
Denmark	Italy	11 Dec 29	97LTS373	302235
Multilateral		17 Dec 29	115LTS93	302679
Poland	Romania	19 Dec 29	130LTS205	302991
Latvia	USA (United States)	14 Jan 30	105LTS307	302423
Belgium	Germany	16 Jan 30	104LTS223	302392
Austria	Belgium	18 Jan 30	104LTS231	302393
Germany	Italy	20 Jan 30	106LTS109	302439
Estonia	USSR (Soviet Union)	20 Jan 30	102LTS225	302365
Estonia	Sweden	20 Jan 30	106LTS279	302451
Latvia	Netherlands	27 Jan 30	117LTS343	302701
Austria	Luxembourg	30 Jan 30	99LTS357	302279
Austria	USA (United States)	30 Jan 30	106LTS379	302457
Brazil	UK Great Britain	21 Feb 30	101LTS11	302315
Italy	Romania	25 Feb 30	106LTS423	302459
Latvia	Spain	08 Mar 30	113LTS135	302641
Austria	Sweden	24 Mar 30	105LTS313	302424
Estonia	Norway	03 Apr 30	106LTS147	302442
Austria	Poland	10 Apr 30	108LTS289	302514
Austria	Germany	12 Apr 30	115LTS297	302693
Hungary	Latvia	04 May 30	101LTS449	302344
Denmark	Estonia	13 May 30	106LTS159	302443
Iceland	Norway	31 May 30	108LTS339	302517
United Arab Rep	France	13 Jun 30	106LTS39	302435
France	Italy	16 Jun 30	144LTS115	303323
Germany	USA (United States)	23 Jun 30	106LTS121	302440
Austria	Greece	26 Jun 30	119LTS353	302755
Belgium	Bulgaria	02 Jul 30	130LTS191	302990
Czechoslovakia	Romania	15 Jul 30	164LTS157	303793
Multilateral		01 Aug 30	128LTS9	302932
Czechoslovakia	Turkey	22 Aug 30	138LTS375	303196
Czechoslovakia	Turkey	22 Aug 30	138LTS311	303195
Sweden	UK Great Britain	28 Aug 30	114LTS9	302652
Denmark	Latvia	28 Aug 30	113LTS169	302644
Denmark	Sweden	03 Sep 30	106LTS397	302458
Germany	Turkey	03 Sep 30	133LTS321	303071
Austria	Czechoslovakia	12 Sep 30	107LTS341	302489
Austria	Belgium	01 Dec 30	112LTS37	302605
Italy	UK Great Britain	17 Dec 30	131LTS79	303004
Multilateral		22 Dec 30	126LTS341	302893
Norway	UK Great Britain	30 Jan 31	123LTS343	302823
Denmark	Italy	03 Feb 31	113LTS45	302634
Multilateral		10 Feb 31	126LTS41	302870
Czechoslovakia	Germany	21 Mar 31	143LTS177	303308
Austria	UK Great Britain	31 Mar 31	127LTS167	302918
Denmark	Spain	15 Apr 31	115LTS233	302688
Czechoslovakia	Lithuania	24 Apr 31	126LTS279	302890
France	Poland	24 Apr 31	130LTS417	303000
Czechoslovakia	Italy	23 May 31	126LTS185	302881
Belgium	Italy	11 Jul 31	136LTS9	303120
Austria	Yugoslavia	21 Jul 31	147LTS123	303397

PARTY ONE	PARTY TWO	DATE	CITATION	NUMBER
Exchange of information and documents (Cont.)				
Czechoslovakia	Germany	25 Jul 31	187LTS279	304344
Belgium	France	29 Jul 31	127LTS85	302909
Portugal	UK Great Britain	09 Aug 31	129LTS417	302975
Greece	Romania	11 Aug 31	130LTS33	302981
Hungary	Romania	12 Aug 31	186LTS325	304321
Poland	UK Great Britain	26 Aug 31	131LTS19	303002
Multilateral		24 Sep 31	155LTS349	303586
UK Great Britain	Yugoslavia	23 Oct 31	126LTS209	302884
Germany	Hungary	26 Oct 31	133LTS369	303074
Czechoslovakia	Sweden	17 Nov 31	134LTS135	303088
Germany	Lithuania	20 Nov 31	133LTS391	303077
Turkey	UK Great Britain	28 Nov 31	141LTS225	303268
Romania	Yugoslavia	14 Dec 31	135LTS31	303103
Romania	Yugoslavia	14 Dec 31	135LTS99	303106
Estonia	UK Great Britain	22 Dec 31	132LTS231	303041
Chile	Denmark	23 Dec 31	145LTS77	303346
Netherlands	Poland	24 Dec 31	131LTS269	303016
Brazil	Sweden	27 Jan 32	177LTS119	304086
Belgium	South Africa	04 Feb 32	127LTS121	302912
France	Latvia	08 Mar 32	128LTS43	302936
South Africa	Swaziland	16 Mar 32	129LTS377	302972
Multilateral		16 Mar 32	139LTS165	303209
Turkey	Yugoslavia	14 Apr 32	144LTS291	303332
Netherlands	UK Great Britain	31 May 32	140LTS287	303244
Czechoslovakia	Yugoslavia	08 Jun 32	139LTS45	303203
Brazil	Denmark	05 Aug 32	132LTS211	303039
Austria	Turkey	14 Sep 32	135LTS275	303116
Czechoslovakia	Germany	19 Sep 32	137LTS453	303175
Argentina	Lithuania	20 Oct 32	154LTS113	303542
Austria	Poland	26 Oct 32	138LTS193	303188
Denmark	UK Great Britain	29 Nov 32	139LTS9	303201
Portugal	Sweden	06 Dec 32	145LTS91	303347
Multilateral		13 Dec 32	139LTS189	303210
Romania	Yugoslavia	30 Jan 33	146LTS121	303364
Romania	Yugoslavia	30 Jan 33	146LTS99	303362
Romania	Yugoslavia	10 Feb 33	174LTS115	304042
Romania	Yugoslavia	10 Mar 33	146LTS209	303372
Netherlands	Norway	23 Mar 33	146LTS291	303380
Multilateral		12 Apr 33	161LTS65	303706
Hungary	Yugoslavia	15 May 33	144LTS321	303335
Switzerland	Turkey	01 Jun 33	159LTS329	303676
Bel-Lux Econ Union	Poland	10 Jun 33	144LTS137	303324
Finland	USSR (Soviet Union)	04 Jul 33	149LTS83	303436
Multilateral		22 Jul 33	153LTS107	303511
Austria	UK Great Britain	27 Jul 33	142LTS157	303287
Finland	UK Great Britain	11 Aug 33	149LTS131	303437
Multilateral		11 Oct 33	155LTS331	303585
Multilateral		08 Nov 33	172LTS241	303995
Multilateral		23 Nov 33	192LTS327	304483
Multilateral		20 Mar 34	175LTS5	304049
Albania	Czechoslovakia	14 Apr 34	188LTS255	304362
Mexico	USA (United States)	24 Apr 34	149LTS49	303433
France	Sweden	09 Jun 34	154LTS101	303541
Czechoslovakia	Romania	20 Jun 34	168LTS257	303903
Multilateral		25 Jul 34	177LTS59	304080
Estonia	Hungary	08 Aug 34	167LTS153	303863
Multilateral		12 Sep 34	154LTS93	303540
Belgium	Bulgaria	26 Oct 34	155LTS105	303572
Belgium	Bulgaria	26 Oct 34	155LTS99	303571
Denmark	Estonia	01 Nov 34	154LTS175	303545
Nicaragua	Spain	20 Nov 34	166LTS143	303836
Czechoslovakia	Luxembourg	01 Dec 34	168LTS287	303906
Denmark	Lithuania	20 Dec 34	155LTS237	303579
Czechoslovakia	Monaco	22 Dec 34	171LTS27	303949
Denmark	France	28 Jan 35	158LTS11	303619

PARTY ONE	PARTY TWO	DATE	CITATION	NUMBER
Exchange of information and documents (Cont.)				
Denmark	Latvia	14 Feb 35	158LTS21	303621
Multilateral		20 Feb 35	193LTS37	304486
Multilateral		20 Feb 35	186LTS173	304310
Denmark	Norway	23 Feb 35	158LTS31	303622
Denmark	Sweden	04 Mar 35	158LTS39	303623
Afghanistan	USSR (Soviet Union)	06 May 35	164LTS335	303800
Belgium	Germany	10 May 35	165LTS143	303807
Poland	Romania	17 May 35	173LTS373	304028
Belgium	Denmark	22 May 35	159LTS255	303669
Denmark	Germany	25 May 35	159LTS389	303680
Turkey	UK Great Britain	04 Jun 35	167LTS91	303860
Mexico	USA (United States)	13 Jun 35	168LTS135	303894
Hungary	Switzerland	18 Jun 35	174LTS7	304033
Bel-Lux Econ Union	Estonia	19 Jun 35	170LTS243	303940
France	Hungary	23 Jul 35	173LTS243	304016
Italy	Netherlands	29 Jul 35	165LTS329	303819
Estonia	Italy	10 Aug 35	185LTS287	304295
Denmark	France	21 Sep 35	162LTS383	303751
Bulgaria	Netherlands	23 Sep 35	166LTS51	303829
Finland	Norway	05 Nov 35	169LTS33	303913
Brazil	Chile	08 Nov 35	181LTS297	304197
Multilateral		14 Nov 35	166LTS87	303833
Finland	Romania	03 Dec 35	165LTS287	303815
Finland	Sweden	18 Dec 35	165LTS347	303821
France	Spain	30 Dec 35	172LTS217	303993
Spain	UK Great Britain	06 Jan 36	166LTS283	303844
Switzerland	USA (United States)	09 Jan 36	171LTS231	303962
China	Malaya	12 Feb 36	170LTS19	303927
Sweden	Turkey	27 Feb 36	167LTS83	303859
UK Great Britain	Yugoslavia	27 Feb 36	181LTS241	304193
Belgium	Yugoslavia	29 Feb 36	184LTS379	304258
Albania	Italy	19 Mar 36	173LTS107	304007
Multilateral		25 Mar 36	184LTS115	304246
Bel-Lux Econ Union	Bulgaria	01 Apr 36	169LTS23	303912
Hungary	Poland	24 Apr 36	181LTS115	304183
Finland	USA (United States)	18 May 36	172LTS97	303981
Finland	Turkey	20 Jun 36	172LTS135	303983
Belgium	France	16 Jul 36	171LTS287	303965
Belgium	Liechtenstein	05 Aug 36	185LTS33	304302
France	USSR (Soviet Union)	11 Aug 36	176LTS365	304073
Netherlands	Romania	28 Aug 36	182LTS363	304222
Turkey	UK Great Britain	02 Sep 36	172LTS289	303998
Romania	Turkey	04 Sep 36	195LTS429	304564
Estonia	Finland	12 Sep 36	172LTS345	303999
Multilateral		23 Sep 36	186LTS301	304319
Finland	Italy	28 Sep 36	172LTS155	303986
Canada	Germany	22 Oct 36	173LTS311	304021
Bulgaria	Finland	27 Oct 36	173LTS201	304013
Germany	Greece	09 Nov 36	182LTS9	304201
France	Sweden	04 Dec 36	184LTS35	304241
Norway	Romania	10 Dec 36	174LTS59	304037
Sweden	Turkey	14 Dec 36	174LTS51	304036
Hungary	Yugoslavia	17 Dec 36	196LTS143	304577
Multilateral		23 Dec 36	188LTS125	304355
Multilateral		23 Dec 36	188LTS99	304354
Multilateral		23 Dec 36	188LTS9	304350
Italy	Netherlands	01 Jan 37	178LTS415	304124
Greece	Turkey	15 Jan 37	202LTS107	304739
Italy	Latvia	05 Feb 37	178LTS25	304103
Netherlands	Turkey	17 Feb 37	182LTS221	304213
Brazil	Netherlands	15 Mar 37	179LTS405	304167
Hungary	UK Great Britain	22 Mar 37	190LTS59	304405
Portugal	UK Great Britain	24 Mar 37	185LTS151	304280
Italy	Norway	31 Mar 37	177LTS355	304098
United Arab Rep	Turkey	07 Apr 37	191LTS105	304439

PARTY ONE	PARTY TWO	DATE	CITATION	NUMBER
Exchange of information and documents (Cont.)				
Chile	Netherlands	05 May 37	182LTS385	304223
Finland	France	26 May 37	179LTS327	304160
Estonia	Turkey	06 Jun 37	179LTS159	304143
Multilateral		08 Jun 37	190LTS79	304406
France	Sweden	30 Jun 37	179LTS203	304148
Belgium	France	07 Jul 37	181LTS111	304182
UK Great Britain	USSR (Soviet Union)	17 Jul 37	187LTS93	304333
Germany	UK Great Britain	17 Jul 37	187LTS43	304332
Iran	Iraq	24 Jul 37	190LTS269	304425
France	Luxembourg	30 Jul 37	181LTS107	304181
Romania	USA (United States)	10 Aug 37	183LTS7	304225
Czechoslovakia	Hungary	24 Aug 37	189LTS403	304397
Bel-Lux Econ Union	Romania	24 Aug 37	193LTS189	304496
Multilateral		06 Sep 37	186LTS419	304326
Germany	Romania	03 Oct 37	190LTS369	304429
Canada	USA (United States)	09 Oct 37	185LTS33	304271
France	Greece	11 Oct 37	185LTS253	304289
Estonia	Germany	24 Oct 37	184LTS81	304244
Germany	Latvia	31 Oct 37	189LTS139	304382
Belgium	Siam	05 Nov 37	190LTS163	304414
Denmark	Siam	05 Nov 37	188LTS187	304358
Hungary	Lithuania	12 Nov 37	183LTS197	304236
Siam	USA (United States)	13 Nov 37	192LTS247	304476
Hungary	Latvia	16 Nov 37	183LTS205	304237
France	Hungary	18 Nov 37	185LTS257	304290
Chile	France	19 Nov 37	185LTS261	304291
Poland	Switzerland	19 Nov 37	195LTS297	304552
Estonia	Greece	25 Nov 37	184LTS427	304263
Estonia	Finland	01 Dec 37	187LTS413	304347
France	Switzerland	03 Dec 37	185LTS265	304292
Italy	Siam	03 Dec 37	189LTS255	304389
France	Siam	07 Dec 37	201LTS113	304708
Germany	Netherlands	18 Dec 37	190LTS29	304403
Sweden	Turkey	31 Dec 37	184LTS409	304261
Bel-Lux Econ Union	Estonia	13 Jan 38	185LTS63	304275
Netherlands	Siam	01 Feb 38	193LTS13	304485
Belgium	Netherlands	07 Feb 38	187LTS9	304328
Belgium	Turkey	09 Feb 38	198LTS181	304639
Greece	Norway	28 Feb 38	186LTS165	304309
Finland	Norway	21 Apr 38	188LTS231	304361
Poland	UK Great Britain	27 Apr 38	195LTS39	304535
Lithuania	Poland	14 May 38	191LTS373	304456
Bulgaria	Latvia	17 May 38	189LTS249	304388
Latvia	Poland	16 Jun 38	196LTS105	304573
France	Morocco	21 Jun 38	189LTS423	304398
Canada	USA (United States)	28 Jul 38	192LTS125	304466
Liberia	USA (United States)	08 Aug 38	201LTS163	304711
Romania	UK Great Britain	02 Sep 38	191LTS313	304453
Argentina	Netherlands	06 Sep 38	194LTS409	304531
Cuba	Portugal	06 Sep 38	195LTS443	304565
Germany	Switzerland	21 Sep 38	196LTS365	304595
Belgium	Mexico	22 Sep 38	198LTS399	304658
Liberia	USA (United States)	07 Oct 38	201LTS183	304712
Netherlands	Romania	10 Oct 38	195LTS9	304532
Germany	Sweden	28 Oct 38	196LTS81	304570
Aden	United Arab Rep	03 Nov 38	197LTS241	304617
Estonia	Netherlands	22 Nov 38	193LTS209	304497
Belgium	Netherlands	17 Dec 38	198LTS177	304638
Sweden	Turkey	20 Jan 39	194LTS113	304514
Burma	Siam	14 Feb 39	197LTS255	304618
Canada	USA (United States)	20 Feb 39	197LTS181	304613
France	Norway	28 Feb 39	195LTS165	304546
Belgium	Luxembourg	04 Mar 39	197LTS141	304610
Belgium	France	06 Mar 39	195LTS353	304555
Sweden	USA (United States)	23 Mar 39	199LTS17	304661
Argentina	USA (United States)	08 Apr 39	198LTS55	304623
Belgium	UK Great Britain	19 Jun 39	198LTS171	304637
France	USA (United States)	15 Jul 39	199LTS355	304683
France	USA (United States)	15 Jul 39	199LTS207	304675
Norway	Spain	26 Jul 39	198LTS87	304627
Poland	UK Great Britain	25 Aug 39	199LTS57	304665
Multilateral		19 Oct 39	200LTS167	304689
Germany	Latvia	30 Oct 39	200LTS213	304693
New Zealand	USA (United States)	28 Feb 40	203LTS11	304746
Sweden	Turkey	29 Feb 40	200LTS273	304696
Spain	UK Great Britain	18 Mar 40	203LTS157	304759
Japan	UK Great Britain	22 Mar 40	203LTS194	304760
Finland	Latvia	11 Apr 40	201LTS389	304727
Informational records				
Multilateral		29 Feb 20	127LTS433	302930
Belgium	Germany	23 Apr 20	12LTS29	300305
Allied Powers	Poland	01 Apr 22	9LTS325	300265
Italy	Serb/Croat/Slovene	06 Apr 22	118LTS207	302725
Germany	Poland	29 Apr 22	21LTS391	300549
Czechoslovakia	Germany	08 May 22	23LTS171	300589
Germany	Poland	21 Jun 22	22LTS7	300552
Czechoslovakia	France	07 Oct 22	47LTS365	301141
Latvia	UK Great Britain	17 Oct 22	16LTS397	300419
Belgium	Sweden	25 Oct 22	18LTS121	300459
Hungary	Sweden	26 Feb 23	17LTS35	300426
Czechoslovakia	Serb/Croat/Slovene	17 Mar 23	30LTS185	300768
Germany	Switzerland	25 Mar 23	18LTS273	300470
Luxembourg	Sweden	11 Apr 23	16LTS453	300423
Finland	Norway	28 Apr 23	19LTS225	300496
Japan	Sweden	01 May 23	17LTS391	300446
Poland	Serb/Croat/Slovene	04 May 23	85LTS455	301946
Germany	Poland	14 Jun 23	34LTS343	300883
Denmark	Sweden	13 Jul 23	18LTS131	300460
Denmark	Sweden	13 Jul 23	18LTS143	300461
Belgium	Luxembourg	17 Jul 23	27LTS235	300686
Bulgaria	Serb/Croat/Slovene	26 Nov 23	26LTS85	300642
Bulgaria	Serb/Croat/Slovene	26 Nov 23	26LTS119	300643
Denmark	Norway	30 Nov 23	22LTS121	300555
Multilateral		14 Dec 23	29LTS37	300732
Hungary	Italy	27 Mar 24	45LTS83	301100
Bulgaria	Romania	19 Apr 24	33LTS221	300846
Norway	UK Great Britain	05 Jun 24	27LTS195	300683
Austria	Czechoslovakia	15 Jun 24	94LTS131	302141
Finland	Sweden	27 Jun 24	29LTS19	300731
Norway	Sweden	27 Jun 24	28LTS309	300717
Poland	USSR (Soviet Union)	18 Jul 24	49LTS201	301183
Estonia	Sweden	30 Aug 24	31LTS217	300797
Other Unilat Decla	Bulgaria	29 Sep 24	29LTS117	300737
Argentina	Norway	07 Oct 24	33LTS191	300843
Multilateral		26 Nov 24	48LTS69	301151
Denmark	Germany	29 Nov 24	31LTS131	300790
Norway	Sweden	22 Dec 24	32LTS13	300802
Denmark	France	25 Feb 25	33LTS277	300852
Czechoslovakia	Poland	06 Mar 25	46LTS201	301120
Latvia	Sweden	28 Mar 25	37LTS131	300952
Germany	USA (United States)	21 May 25	52LTS133	301254
Bel-Lux Econ Union	Japan	27 Jun 25	36LTS95	300907
Germany	Poland	16 Dec 25	46LTS139	301117
Germany	Poland	27 Jan 26	64LTS113	301504
Austria	Czechoslovakia	12 Jul 26	86LTS395	301952
Germany	Poland	27 Oct 26	108LTS275	302513
Czechoslovakia	Switzerland	21 Dec 26	86LTS443	301956
Czechoslovakia	Switzerland	21 Dec 26	68LTS393	301594
Czechoslovakia	Greece	07 Apr 27	88LTS211	301998

PARTY ONE	PARTY TWO	DATE	CITATION	NUMBER
Informational records (Cont.)				
Czechoslovakia	Greece	07 Apr 27	88LTS187	301997
Belgium	Czechoslovakia	19 Jul 27	73LTS307	301721
Estonia	Latvia	22 Jul 27	73LTS333	301723
Czechoslovakia	Spain	26 Oct 27	121LTS311	302793
Czechoslovakia	Spain	26 Oct 27	121LTS287	302792
Czechoslovakia	Spain	26 Oct 27	121LTS271	302791
Multilateral		20 Feb 28	86LTS111	301950
Hungary	Serb/Croat/Slovene	22 Feb 28	104LTS151	302385
France	Netherlands	10 Mar 28	102LTS109	302356
Czechoslovakia	France	07 May 28	114LTS117	302660
Austria	Hungary	25 Jun 28	100LTS85	302296
Multilateral		30 Jun 28	89LTS53	302005
Czechoslovakia	Serb/Croat/Slovene	07 Nov 28	98LTS297	302252
Bulgaria	Turkey	06 Mar 29	114LTS399	302668
Multilateral		20 Apr 29	112LTS371	302623
United Arab Rep	UK Great Britain	07 May 29	93LTS43	302103
Spain	UK Great Britain	27 Jun 29	101LTS375	302337
Czechoslovakia	Estonia	09 Jul 29	101LTS423	302341
Finland	Italy	10 Jul 29	111LTS295	302593
Estonia	USA (United States)	27 Aug 29	102LTS239	302367
Germany	Luxembourg	11 Sep 29	118LTS97	302715
Luxembourg	Netherlands	17 Sep 29	107LTS35	302466
Czechoslovakia	Switzerland	20 Sep 29	102LTS123	302357
Bulgaria	Yugoslavia	26 Sep 29	101LTS217	302324
Hungary	Yugoslavia	11 Nov 29	111LTS197	302587
Estonia	Hungary	27 Nov 29	106LTS331	302454
Poland	Romania	19 Dec 29	130LTS205	302991
Latvia	Netherlands	27 Jan 30	117LTS343	302701
Austria	Germany	12 Apr 30	115LTS297	302693
Guatemala	Honduras	16 Jul 30	137LTS231	303159
Czechoslovakia	Turkey	22 Aug 30	138LTS311	303195
Sweden	UK Great Britain	28 Aug 30	114LTS9	302652
Norway	UK Great Britain	30 Jan 31	123LTS343	302823
Denmark	Italy	03 Feb 31	113LTS45	302634
Denmark	Spain	15 Apr 31	115LTS233	302688
Czechoslovakia	Lithuania	24 Apr 31	126LTS279	302890
Czechoslovakia	Italy	23 May 31	126LTS185	302881
Multilateral		13 Jul 31	139LTS301	303219
Multilateral		24 Sep 31	155LTS349	303586
Austria	Poland	26 Oct 32	138LTS193	303188
Finland	USSR (Soviet Union)	04 Jul 33	149LTS83	303436
Romania	Turkey	17 Oct 33	165LTS273	303814
Estonia	Latvia	17 Feb 34	150LTS391	303472
Multilateral		19 Jun 34	154LTS381	303564
Estonia	Hungary	08 Aug 34	167LTS153	303863
Finland	Sweden	18 Dec 35	165LTS347	303821
Chile	Norway	27 Jan 36	179LTS433	304169
Multilateral		23 Dec 36	188LTS53	304352
Multilateral		08 May 37	182LTS37	304202
Belgium	France	07 Jul 37	181LTS111	304182
France	Luxembourg	30 Jul 37	181LTS107	304181
Norway	Siam	15 Nov 37	186LTS9	304301
France	Hungary	18 Nov 37	185LTS257	304290
Chile	France	19 Nov 37	185LTS261	304291
France	Switzerland	03 Dec 37	185LTS265	304292
Inspection and observation				
Sweden	USA (United States)	28 May 21	6LTS41	300147
Norway	UK Great Britain	15 Jul 21	6LTS307	300162
Denmark	Germany	25 Apr 22	18LTS227	300466
Germany	Poland	15 May 22	10LTS37	300273
Germany	Poland	23 Jun 22	22LTS25	300553
Norway	Sweden	26 May 23	18LTS155	300462
France	Netherlands	02 Jul 23	20LTS131	300512
Belgium	Netherlands	14 Jul 23	20LTS119	300511

PARTY ONE	PARTY TWO	DATE	CITATION	NUMBER
Inspection and observation (Cont.)				
Multilateral		03 Nov 23	30LTS371	300775
Panama	USA (United States)	06 Jun 24	138LTS397	303200
Latvia	Switzerland	04 Dec 24	34LTS405	300889
Portugal	Spain	29 Jul 26	82LTS95	301863
Multilateral		13 Nov 26	77LTS171	301770
Multilateral		13 Nov 26	77LTS249	301773
Multilateral		13 Nov 26	77LTS199	301771
Belgium	Switzerland	05 Feb 27	68LTS45	301567
Poland	Serb/Croat/Slovene	06 Mar 27	126LTS67	302871
Germany	Lithuania	29 Jan 28	89LTS97	302009
Germany	Lithuania	29 Jan 28	89LTS338	302027
Czechoslovakia	Poland	18 Feb 28	100LTS273	302301
Multilateral		20 Feb 28	129LTS223	302963
Czechoslovakia	Germany	22 Mar 28	93LTS235	302113
Czechoslovakia	Hungary	14 Nov 28	110LTS425	302574
Austria	Czechoslovakia	12 Dec 28	108LTS9	302501
Austria	Czechoslovakia	12 Dec 28	107LTS137	302474
Italy	UK Great Britain	25 Jan 29	95LTS39	302162
Germany	Persia	17 Feb 29	111LTS241	302590
Czechoslovakia	Germany	20 Mar 29	109LTS219	302541
Multilateral		16 Apr 29	126LTS305	302891
United Arab Rep	UK Great Britain	07 May 29	93LTS43	302103
Albania	Serb/Croat/Slovene	11 Aug 29	101LTS439	302342
Italy	Serb/Croat/Slovene	16 Sep 29	101LTS127	302322
Bulgaria	Yugoslavia	26 Sep 29	101LTS217	302324
Irish Free State	Italy	10 May 30	132LTS147	303034
Chile	USA (United States)	27 May 30	133LTS141	303064
Czechoslovakia	Romania	15 Jul 30	164LTS157	303793
Czechoslovakia	Persia	29 Oct 30	121LTS59	302784
Portugal	South Africa	29 Apr 31	129LTS157	302960
Portugal	UK Great Britain	09 Aug 31	129LTS417	302975
Iraq	Turkey	09 Jan 32	139LTS273	303218
Belgium	USA (United States)	19 Apr 32	134LTS19	303080
Denmark	Sweden	31 Dec 32	139LTS205	303211
Romania	Yugoslavia	30 Jan 33	146LTS139	303366
Poland	USSR (Soviet Union)	03 Jun 33	142LTS265	303300
Finland	USSR (Soviet Union)	04 Jul 33	149LTS83	303436
Estonia	Poland	26 Sep 33	150LTS309	303464
Finland	UK Great Britain	13 Oct 33	142LTS187	303291
Finland	Hungary	07 Nov 33	142LTS179	303290
Brazil	Uruguay	20 Dec 33	181LTS69	304178
Finland	Sweden	29 Dec 33	149LTS23	303429
Finland	USSR (Soviet Union)	25 May 34	155LTS207	303578
Poland	Romania	17 May 35	173LTS373	304028
Denmark	Finland	18 Jul 35	161LTS205	303712
Multilateral		30 Oct 35	189LTS51	304375
Finland	Norway	05 Nov 35	169LTS33	303913
Bulgaria	Yugoslavia	09 Nov 35	194LTS89	304511
Canada	USA (United States)	29 Jan 37	181LTS209	304190
Multilateral		08 Jun 37	190LTS79	304406
Bulgaria	Romania	20 Jul 37	202LTS33	304733
Czechoslovakia	Hungary	24 Aug 37	189LTS403	304397
Canada	USA (United States)	07 Jan 38	184LTS305	304255
Juridical personality				
Germany	Poland	09 Jan 20	9LTS77	300245
France	Germany	05 May 20	8LTS55	300206
Czechoslovakia	Germany	29 Jun 20	17LTS69	300430
Austria	Czechoslovakia	02 Aug 20	32LTS365	300826
Multilateral		05 Aug 20	2LTS49	300046
Greece	UK Great Britain	22 Sep 20	2LTS367	300090
Czechoslovakia	Serb/Croat/Slovene	18 Oct 20	17LTS19	300424
Portugal	UK Great Britain	09 Dec 20	7LTS257	300192
Czechoslovakia	Germany	03 Feb 21	5LTS246	300132
Czechoslovakia	Italy	23 Mar 21	32LTS183	300815

PARTY ONE	PARTY TWO	DATE	CITATION	NUMBER
Juridical personality (Cont.)				
Norway	UK Great Britain	22 Apr 21	5LTS33	300114
Germany	Poland	06 Jun 21	34LTS185	300874
Multilateral		12 Jul 21	37LTS433	300965
Denmark	UK Great Britain	14 Jul 21	6LTS181	300151
Austria	USA (United States)	24 Aug 21	7LTS155	300184
Austria	Hungary	08 Oct 21	16LTS19	300402
Czechoslovakia	Germany	31 Dec 21	17LTS401	300447
France	UK Great Britain	02 Feb 22	10LTS448	300284
Germany	Poland	12 Apr 22	21LTS327	300548
Germany	Poland	26 Aug 22	26LTS365	300656
Czechoslovakia	Latvia	07 Oct 22	20LTS379	300528
Estonia	Hungary	19 Oct 22	30LTS347	300774
Japan	Poland	07 Dec 22	32LTS61	300806
Multilateral		30 Dec 22	21LTS183	300542
Germany	Poland	27 Jan 23	26LTS461	300663
Germany	Lithuania	01 Jun 23	51LTS387	301244
Austria	Germany	21 Jun 23	27LTS57	300668
Latvia	UK Great Britain	22 Jun 23	20LTS395	300529
Estonia	Germany	27 Jun 23	41LTS161	301013
Czechoslovakia	Hungary	13 Jul 23	36LTS13	300901
Czechoslovakia	UK Great Britain	14 Jul 23	29LTS377	300748
Poland	Turkey	23 Jul 23	49LTS345	301190
Turkey		24 Jul 23	36LTS161	300916
Multilateral		24 Jul 23	28LTS151	300704
Denmark	Finland	03 Aug 23	21LTS269	300547
Estonia	Latvia	01 Nov 23	25LTS354	300624
Germany	Hungary	06 Nov 23	45LTS279	301104
Finland	Poland	10 Nov 23	29LTS229	300744
Italy	Spain	15 Nov 23	39LTS49	300996
Japan	Serb/Croat/Slovene	16 Nov 23	42LTS99	301035
Hungary	Latvia	19 Nov 23	37LTS341	300959
Bulgaria	Serb/Croat/Slovene	26 Nov 23	26LTS85	300642
Multilateral		14 Dec 23	29LTS37	300732
Finland	UK Great Britain	14 Dec 23	29LTS129	300739
Latvia	Poland	03 Jan 24	42LTS451	301043
Estonia	Poland	11 Jan 24	47LTS129	301132
Germany	Siam	28 Feb 24	32LTS399	300828
Albania	Italy	29 Feb 24	44LTS343	301093
Czechoslovakia	Italy	01 Mar 24	34LTS55	300867
Japan	Siam	09 Mar 24	31LTS187	300795
Sweden	USSR (Soviet Union)	15 Mar 24	25LTS251	300613
Denmark	Poland	22 Mar 24	31LTS13	300778
Iceland	Poland	22 Mar 24	31LTS35	300779
Iraq	UK Great Britain	25 Mar 24	35LTS35	300891
Iraq	UK Great Britain	25 Mar 24	35LTS131	300893
Hungary	Italy	27 Mar 24	45LTS65	301099
Hungary	Italy	27 Mar 24	45LTS229	301101
Denmark	Latvia	03 Apr 24	33LTS393	300860
Poland	Serb/Croat/Slovene	05 Apr 24	49LTS265	301185
Bulgaria	Romania	19 Apr 24	33LTS209	300845
Multilateral		22 May 24	35LTS175	300895
Finland	Iceland	28 May 24	27LTS117	300676
Netherlands	Poland	30 May 24	34LTS9	300865
Spain	UK Great Britain	27 Jun 24	28LTS523	300727
Poland	USSR (Soviet Union)	18 Jul 24	49LTS201	301183
Latvia	Norway	14 Aug 24	36LTS211	300924
Czechoslovakia	France	18 Aug 24	44LTS21	301080
Finland	Latvia	23 Aug 24	37LTS383	300962
Czechoslovakia	Netherlands	17 Oct 24	31LTS93	300786
Finland	Italy	22 Oct 24	32LTS149	300814
Multilateral		23 Oct 24	77LTS367	301778
Austria	Hungary	08 Nov 24	44LTS407	301096
Austria	Norway	03 Dec 24	31LTS151	300792
Latvia	Switzerland	04 Dec 24	34LTS405	300889
Hungary	Netherlands	09 Dec 24	47LTS91	301130
Juridical personality (Cont.)				
France	Siam	14 Feb 25	43LTS189	301055
Benelux Econ Union	Germany	04 Apr 25	37LTS203	300957
Greece	Poland	17 Apr 25	38LTS301	300985
Czechoslovakia	Poland	23 Apr 25	44LTS285	301090
Bulgaria	Poland	29 Apr 25	60LTS103	301408
Netherlands	Siam	08 Jun 25	56LTS57	301323
Hungary	Spain	17 Jun 25	60LTS69	301406
Bel-Lux Econ Union		07 Jul 25	54LTS267	301290
Hungary	Italy	20 Jul 25	45LTS39	301098
Italy	Latvia	25 Jul 25	60LTS91	301407
Siam	Spain	03 Aug 25	55LTS39	301303
Germany	UK Great Britain	13 Aug 25	43LTS89	301050
Portugal	Siam	14 Aug 25	55LTS57	301304
Siam	UK Great Britain	15 Sep 25	49LTS51	301176
France	Hungary	13 Oct 25	48LTS9	301150
Estonia	Switzerland	14 Oct 25	49LTS421	301195
Austria	China	19 Oct 25	55LTS9	301301
Germany	Italy	31 Oct 25	52LTS179	301256
Hungary	Poland	16 Nov 25	43LTS265	301061
Norway	USSR (Soviet Union)	15 Dec 25	47LTS9	301127
Estonia	USA (United States)	23 Dec 25	50LTS13	301197
France	Poland	30 Dec 25	73LTS265	301719
Germany	Sweden	31 Dec 25	43LTS219	301056
Cuba	USA (United States)	11 Mar 26	61LTS383	301448
Finland	Hungary	20 Apr 26	48LTS119	301154
Cuba	USA (United States)	22 Apr 26	60LTS371	301421
Germany	Sweden	14 May 26	51LTS99	301225
Bel-Lux Econ Union	Siam	13 Jul 26	62LTS287	301468
Hungary	USA (United States)	04 Sep 26	58LTS111	301369
Multilateral		13 Nov 26	77LTS249	301773
Belgium	Estonia	08 Feb 27	74LTS227	301740
Multilateral		20 Feb 28	86LTS111	301950
Belgium	Persia	15 May 28	94LTS447	302160
Estonia	Sweden	11 Jun 28	81LTS277	301843
Latvia	Sweden	21 Jun 28	88LTS107	301990
Estonia	Hungary	29 Apr 29	96LTS23	302189
Belgium	Persia	09 May 29	110LTS391	302570
Persia	Sweden	10 May 29	102LTS9	302349
Multilateral		28 Jun 29	103LTS377	302373
Bulgaria	Yugoslavia	26 Sep 29	101LTS217	302324
Italy	Panama	16 Oct 29	138LTS355	303199
Denmark	Estonia	12 Dec 29	98LTS341	302254
Czechoslovakia	Germany	31 Jan 30	145LTS51	303345
Norway	Persia	08 May 30	134LTS153	303089
Germany	Irish Free State	12 May 30	131LTS153	303008
Multilateral		07 Jun 30	143LTS317	303314
Romania	Yugoslavia	19 Jun 30	140LTS229	303238
Poland	Romania	23 Jun 30	133LTS163	303066
Czechoslovakia	Romania	15 Jul 30	164LTS157	303793
France	Romania	27 Aug 30	158LTS379	303644
Norway	Turkey	16 Mar 31	138LTS41	303180
Belgium	France	16 May 31	141LTS333	303274
Germany	Switzerland	15 Jul 31	144LTS389	303341
Germany	Hungary	18 Jul 31	150LTS111	303458
Multilateral		21 Aug 31	127LTS95	302910
Romania	Sweden	07 Oct 31	131LTS51	303003
Bolivia	Denmark	09 Nov 31	147LTS27	303387
Czechoslovakia	Sweden	17 Nov 31	134LTS135	303088
Bulgaria	Germany	24 Jun 32	147LTS211	303400
Finland	UK Great Britain	13 Oct 33	142LTS187	303291
Finland	Hungary	07 Nov 33	142LTS179	303290
Latvia	Lithuania	01 Dec 33	148LTS97	303407
Latvia	USSR (Soviet Union)	04 Dec 33	148LTS145	303410
Brazil	Uruguay	20 Dec 33	181LTS69	304178
France	USSR (Soviet Union)	11 Jan 34	167LTS349	303878

PARTY ONE	PARTY TWO	DATE	CITATION	NUMBER
Juridical personality (Cont.)				
Estonia	Lithuania	13 Jan 34	148LTS337	303420
Czechoslovakia	Poland	25 Jan 34	177LTS139	304088
Czechoslovakia	Poland	10 Feb 34	178LTS159	304111
Czechoslovakia	Poland	10 Feb 34	183LTS213	304238
Denmark	Persia	20 Feb 34	158LTS299	303640
Persia	Switzerland	25 Apr 34	160LTS173	303691
Iraq	UK Great Britain	25 Jul 35	176LTS229	304064
Bulgaria	Romania	26 Jul 35	198LTS9	304621
Finland	Germany	25 Sep 35	173LTS11	304001
Czechoslovakia	Finland	21 Mar 36	179LTS295	304156
Finland	Switzerland	07 May 36	166LTS35	303827
Multilateral		04 Jul 36	171LTS75	303952
Belgium	Siam	14 Jan 37	179LTS419	304168
France	UK Great Britain	03 Apr 37	179LTS265	304154
United Arab Rep	Turkey	07 Apr 37	191LTS95	304438
Romania	Yugoslavia	13 May 37	197LTS145	304611
Bulgaria	Romania	20 Jul 37	202LTS33	304733
Greece	Luxembourg	01 Sep 37	193LTS151	304491
United Arab Rep	UK Great Britain	21 Oct 37	184LTS285	304252
Belgium	Siam	05 Nov 37	190LTS163	304414
France	Siam	07 Dec 37	201LTS113	304708
Canada	USA (United States)	07 Jan 38	184LTS305	304255
France	Switzerland	31 Jan 38	195LTS313	304553
Netherlands	Siam	01 Feb 38	193LTS13	304485
Germany	Switzerland	21 Sep 38	196LTS365	304595
Expropriation				
Poland	Turkey	23 Jul 23	49LTS345	301190
Germany	Latvia	24 Feb 24	41LTS231	301016
Bulgaria	Turkey	27 Dec 24	54LTS135	301281
Portugal	UK Great Britain	19 May 25	36LTS125	300910
Hungary	Turkey	20 Dec 26	72LTS245	301696
Greece	UK Great Britain	17 Feb 27	90LTS379	302049
Czechoslovakia	Turkey	31 May 27	75LTS79	301753
Switzerland	Turkey	07 Aug 27	73LTS51	301706
Germany	Persia	17 Feb 29	111LTS241	302590
Persia	Sweden	10 May 29	102LTS9	302349
Switzerland	Turkey	13 Dec 30	129LTS331	302968
Norway	Turkey	16 Mar 31	138LTS41	303180
Free passage and transit				
Czechoslovakia	Germany	29 Jun 20	17LTS69	300430
Germany	Switzerland	09 Jul 20	12LTS25	300304
Czechoslovakia	Serb/Croat/Slovene	18 Oct 20	17LTS19	300424
Czechoslovakia	Italy	23 Mar 21	32LTS183	300815
Czechoslovakia	Romania	23 Apr 21	15LTS235	300397
Austria	Czechoslovakia	04 May 21	15LTS13	300388
Austria	Hungary	08 Oct 21	16LTS19	300402
Estonia	Finland	29 Oct 21	13LTS59	300348
Finland	Germany	21 Apr 22	19LTS87	300487
Denmark	Germany	25 Apr 22	18LTS227	300466
Lithuania	UK Great Britain	06 May 22	13LTS25	300343
Poland	Switzerland	26 Jun 22	12LTS305	300322
Austria	Poland	25 Sep 22	59LTS307	301400
Czechoslovakia	Latvia	07 Oct 22	20LTS379	300528
Estonia	Hungary	19 Oct 22	30LTS347	300774
Denmark	Sweden	07 Nov 22	14LTS95	300370
Japan	Poland	07 Dec 22	32LTS61	300806
Canada	France	15 Dec 22	21LTS38	300532
Multilateral		30 Dec 22	21LTS183	300542
Canada	Italy	04 Jan 23	25LTS375	300626
Italy	Switzerland	27 Jan 23	25LTS21	300603
Czechoslovakia	Hungary	08 Mar 23	48LTS257	301167
Norway	Sweden	26 May 23	18LTS155	300462
Latvia	UK Great Britain	22 Jun 23	20LTS395	300529
Estonia	Germany	27 Jun 23	41LTS161	301013
Free passage and transit (Cont.)				
Belgium	Denmark	28 Jun 23	20LTS59	300507
Estonia	Sweden	07 Jul 23	20LTS189	300517
Czechoslovakia	UK Great Britain	14 Jul 23	29LTS377	300748
Denmark	Lithuania	18 Jul 23	20LTS197	300518
Poland	Turkey	23 Jul 23	49LTS329	301189
Multilateral		24 Jul 23	28LTS11	300701
Denmark	Finland	03 Aug 23	21LTS269	300547
Estonia	Iceland	07 Sep 23	23LTS131	300584
Denmark	Estonia	07 Sep 23	23LTS73	300577
Estonia	Latvia	01 Nov 23	25LTS354	300624
Finland	Poland	10 Nov 23	29LTS229	300744
Italy	Spain	15 Nov 23	39LTS49	300996
Japan	Serb/Croat/Slovene	16 Nov 23	42LTS99	301035
Hungary	Latvia	19 Nov 23	37LTS341	300959
Finland	UK Great Britain	14 Dec 23	29LTS129	300739
Multilateral		14 Dec 23	29LTS37	300732
Lithuania	Norway	21 Dec 23	32LTS55	300805
Austria	Turkey	28 Jan 24	32LTS313	300823
Czechoslovakia	Denmark	31 Jan 24	23LTS139	300585
Lithuania	Sweden	17 Feb 24	23LTS153	300587
Sweden	USSR (Soviet Union)	15 Mar 24	25LTS251	300613
Denmark	Poland	22 Mar 24	31LTS13	300778
Denmark	Latvia	03 Apr 24	33LTS393	300860
Poland	Serb/Croat/Slovene	05 Apr 24	49LTS265	301185
Hungary	Romania	16 Apr 24	46LTS95	301114
Multilateral		22 May 24	35LTS175	300895
Netherlands	Poland	30 May 24	34LTS9	300865
Finland	Japan	07 Jun 24	58LTS379	301383
Lithuania	Netherlands	10 Jun 24	34LTS373	300885
Finland	USSR (Soviet Union)	18 Jun 24	47LTS153	301133
Latvia	Netherlands	02 Jul 24	37LTS121	300951
Bel-Lux Econ Union	Canada	03 Jul 24	32LTS35	300803
Canada	Netherlands	11 Jul 24	39LTS45	300995
Italy	Serb/Croat/Slovene	14 Jul 24	82LTS257	301876
Estonia	Netherlands	22 Jul 24	48LTS199	301162
Austria	Latvia	09 Aug 24	65LTS7	301516
Czechoslovakia	France	18 Aug 24	44LTS21	301080
Netherlands	Portugal	27 Aug 24	31LTS235	300800
Multilateral		28 Aug 24	40LTS19	301002
Hungary	Norway	16 Sep 24	33LTS103	300835
Finland	Italy	22 Oct 24	32LTS149	300814
France	Latvia	30 Oct 24	37LTS399	300963
Iceland	Latvia	03 Nov 24	43LTS339	301069
Austria	Hungary	08 Nov 24	44LTS407	301096
France	Poland	09 Dec 24	44LTS127	301081
Albania	Italy	06 Mar 25	44LTS359	301094
Benelux Econ Union	Germany	04 Apr 25	37LTS203	300957
Greece	Poland	17 Apr 25	38LTS301	300985
Bulgaria	Poland	29 Apr 25	60LTS103	301408
Finland	USA (United States)	02 May 25	47LTS351	301139
Germany	USA (United States)	21 May 25	52LTS133	301254
Netherlands	Siam	08 Jun 25	56LTS57	301323
Bel-Lux Econ Union		07 Jul 25	54LTS267	301290
Hungary	Italy	20 Jul 25	45LTS39	301098
Siam	Spain	03 Aug 25	55LTS39	301303
Germany	UK Great Britain	13 Aug 25	43LTS89	301050
Portugal	Siam	14 Aug 25	55LTS57	301304
Siam	UK Great Britain	15 Sep 25	49LTS51	301176
France	Hungary	13 Oct 25	48LTS9	301150
Czechoslovakia	Japan	30 Oct 25	58LTS263	301377
Germany	Italy	31 Oct 25	52LTS179	301256
Bulgaria	UK Great Britain	12 Nov 25	43LTS165	301052
Norway	USSR (Soviet Union)	15 Dec 25	47LTS9	301127
Siam	Sweden	19 Dec 25	58LTS429	301386
Bel-Lux Econ Union	Czechoslovakia	28 Dec 25	58LTS189	301372

PARTY ONE	PARTY TWO	DATE	CITATION	NUMBER
Free passage and transit (Cont.)				
Austria	Switzerland	06 Jan 26	46LTS299	301124
Estonia	UK Great Britain	18 Jan 26	48LTS209	301163
Denmark	Siam	01 Mar 26	47LTS103	301131
Finland	Hungary	20 Apr 26	48LTS119	301154
Italy	Siam	09 May 26	61LTS215	301436
Germany	Sweden	14 May 26	51LTS99	301225
Finland	Turkey	02 Jun 26	70LTS329	301644
Finland	Germany	26 Jun 26	56LTS203	301332
Bel-Lux Econ Union	Siam	13 Jul 26	62LTS287	301468
Germany	Switzerland	14 Jul 26	59LTS87	301391
Norway	Siam	16 Jul 26	60LTS35	301404
Hungary	UK Great Britain	23 Jul 26	67LTS183	301546
Hungary	USA (United States)	04 Sep 26	58LTS111	301369
Greece	Sweden	10 Sep 26	63LTS37	301479
Albania	Greece	13 Oct 26	83LTS325	301899
Greece	Italy	24 Oct 26	63LTS51	301480
Bel-Lux Econ Union	Serb/Croat/Slovene	16 Dec 26	70LTS371	301647
Finland	Greece	18 Dec 26	70LTS89	301626
Hungary	Turkey	20 Dec 26	72LTS255	301697
Germany	Turkey	12 Jan 27	73LTS133	301712
Czechoslovakia	Switzerland	16 Feb 27	64LTS7	301501
Switzerland	Turkey	04 May 27	67LTS141	301544
Serb/Croat/Slovene	UK Great Britain	12 May 27	80LTS165	301825
Greece	UK Great Britain	13 May 27	61LTS15	301425
Czechoslovakia	Turkey	31 May 27	71LTS335	301674
Czechoslovakia	Hungary	31 May 27	65LTS61	301520
Greece	Norway	29 Jun 27	82LTS187	301869
Belgium	Portugal	21 Jul 27	71LTS439	301682
Multilateral		10 Sep 27	75LTS39	301750
Multilateral		10 Sep 27	75LTS7	301749
Italy	Lithuania	17 Sep 27	73LTS9	301701
Germany	Serb/Croat/Slovene	06 Oct 27	77LTS19	301763
Bulgaria	Turkey	12 Feb 28	81LTS383	301848
Multilateral		20 Feb 28	129LTS223	302963
Siam	UK Great Britain	21 Feb 28	87LTS21	301960
Canada	Czechoslovakia	15 Mar 28	82LTS147	301865
Belgium	Bel-Lux Econ Union	16 Aug 28	81LTS411	301849
Hungary	Serb/Croat/Slovene	19 Nov 28	97LTS101	302222
United Arab Rep	Persia	28 Nov 28	93LTS381	302127
Bolivia	UK Great Britain	18 Jan 29	95LTS9	302161
Norway	USA (United States)	25 Feb 29	134LTS81	303085
Poland	Romania	30 Mar 29	123LTS147	302812
UK Great Britain	USA (United States)	02 Apr 29	94LTS17	302133
Bolivia	Netherlands	30 May 29	133LTS113	303062
Multilateral		28 Jun 29	102LTS245	302368
UK Great Britain	USA (United States)	11 Jul 29	98LTS161	302245
Persia	USSR (Soviet Union)	02 Aug 29	109LTS99	302530
Estonia	Turkey	16 Sep 29	117LTS377	302704
Italy	Panama	16 Oct 29	138LTS355	303199
Poland	Romania	30 Oct 29	121LTS243	302790
Multilateral		09 Nov 29	125LTS205	302855
Honduras	Nicaragua	30 Jan 30	142LTS241	303297
Austria	Germany	12 Apr 30	115LTS333	302694
Hungary	Latvia	04 May 30	101LTS449	302344
Norway	Persia	08 May 30	134LTS153	303089
Germany	Irish Free State	12 May 30	131LTS153	303008
Poland	Romania	23 Jun 30	133LTS163	303066
Romania	UK Great Britain	06 Aug 30	123LTS307	302822
El Salvador	USA (United States)	05 Sep 30	134LTS207	303093
Norway	Turkey	16 Mar 31	138LTS41	303180
France	Greece	05 Jun 31	31LTS201	303011
Poland	USA (United States)	15 Jun 31	139LTS395	303223
Germany	Hungary	18 Jul 31	150LTS111	303458
Greece	Romania	11 Aug 31	130LTS33	302981
Hungary	Romania	12 Aug 31	186LTS325	304321

PARTY ONE	PARTY TWO	DATE	CITATION	NUMBER
Free passage and transit (Cont.)				
Multilateral		10 Nov 31	131LTS447	303025
Japan	USSR (Soviet Union)	23 Nov 31	132LTS133	303033
Bulgaria	Germany	24 Jun 32	147LTS211	303400
Bulgaria	Czechoslovakia	29 Aug 33	148LTS15	303402
Latvia	Lithuania	01 Dec 33	148LTS97	303407
Latvia	USSR (Soviet Union)	04 Dec 33	148LTS145	303410
Estonia	Lithuania	13 Jan 34	148LTS337	303420
Finland	USA (United States)	13 Feb 34	152LTS45	303484
Multilateral		20 Mar 34	174LTS171	304048
Finland	Germany	24 Mar 34	149LTS343	303442
Germany	USSR (Soviet Union)	07 Mar 35	169LTS7	303911
Hungary	Netherlands	08 Jun 35	171LTS385	303975
Czechoslovakia	USSR (Soviet Union)	08 Jun 35	167LTS181	303865
Hungary	Switzerland	18 Jun 35	174LTS7	304033
France	Hungary	23 Jul 35	173LTS243	304016
Germany	Iraq	04 Aug 35	171LTS65	303951
Iran	USSR (Soviet Union)	27 Aug 35	176LTS299	304069
France	USSR (Soviet Union)	09 Mar 36	179LTS131	304140
Estonia	Finland	12 Sep 36	172LTS345	303999
Germany	UK Great Britain	02 Dec 36	178LTS329	304121
Germany	Malaya	17 Dec 36	178LTS484	304129
Italy	UK Great Britain	02 Jan 37	177LTS241	304092
Hungary	UK Great Britain	22 Mar 37	190LTS59	304405
Sweden	Yugoslavia	14 May 37	194LTS21	304504
Ireland	USA (United States)	04 Nov 37	185LTS71	304276
Siam	UK Great Britain	23 Nov 37	188LTS333	304366
Multilateral		25 Oct 38	192LTS323	304482
El Salvador	Norway	21 Nov 38	198LTS157	304636
Guatemala	Norway	20 Dec 38	198LTS117	304631
Legal protection and assistance				
Multilateral		13 Nov 08	1LTS217	300015
Cuba	Netherlands	31 Dec 13	14LTS29	300366
France	Italy	30 Sep 19	5LTS279	300133
Germany	Poland	09 Jan 20	9LTS77	300245
France	Germany	05 May 20	8LTS55	300206
Czechoslovakia	Germany	29 Jun 20	20LTS85	300509
Multilateral		10 Aug 20	28LTS223	300711
Czechoslovakia	Germany	03 Feb 21	5LTS246	300132
Czechoslovakia	Italy	23 Mar 21	32LTS183	300815
China	Germany	20 May 21	9LTS271	300261
Danzig	Poland	24 Oct 21	116LTS5	302699
Czechoslovakia	Germany	20 Jan 22	26LTS201	300648
Italy	Serb/Croat/Slovene	06 Apr 22	118LTS207	302725
Czechoslovakia	Italy	06 Apr 22	55LTS189	301314
Germany	Poland	12 Apr 22	21LTS327	300548
Italy	Poland	12 May 22	59LTS293	301399
Other Unilat Decla	Lithuania	12 May 22	22LTS393	300569
Germany	Poland	15 May 22	10LTS37	300273
Finland	USSR (Soviet Union)	12 Aug 22	19LTS105	300489
Germany	Poland	26 Aug 22	26LTS365	300656
Austria	Poland	25 Sep 22	59LTS307	301400
Other Unilat Decla	Albania	02 Oct 22	9LTS173	300249
Czechoslovakia	France	07 Oct 22	47LTS365	301141
Czechoslovakia	Latvia	07 Oct 22	20LTS379	300528
Estonia	Hungary	19 Oct 22	30LTS347	300774
Germany	Poland	27 Jan 23	26LTS461	300663
Germany	Iceland	12 Feb 23	27LTS405	300700
Czechoslovakia	Serb/Croat/Slovene	17 Mar 23	30LTS185	300768
Germany	Saar	21 Apr 23	27LTS295	300693
Multilateral		28 Apr 23	33LTS47	300832
Poland	Serb/Croat/Slovene	04 May 23	85LTS455	301946
Austria	Germany	21 Jun 23	27LTS57	300668
Estonia	Germany	27 Jun 23	41LTS161	301013
Multilateral		24 Jul 23	28LTS151	300704

Legal protection and assistance (Cont.)

PARTY ONE	PARTY TWO	DATE	CITATION	NUMBER
Estonia	Latvia	01 Nov 23	25LTS354	300624
Germany	Hungary	06 Nov 23	45LTS279	301104
Japan	Serb/Croat/Slovene	16 Nov 23	42LTS99	301035
Bulgaria	Serb/Croat/Slovene	26 Nov 23	26LTS85	300642
Czechoslovakia	Italy	01 Mar 24	34LTS55	300867
Germany	Poland	05 Mar 24	49LTS181	301182
Japan	Siam	09 Mar 24	31LTS187	300795
Austria	Poland	19 Mar 24	56LTS95	301326
Mexico	Spain	31 Mar 24	43LTS297	301065
Denmark	Latvia	03 Apr 24	33LTS393	300860
Poland	Serb/Croat/Slovene	05 Apr 24	49LTS265	301185
Hungary	Romania	16 Apr 24	42LTS165	301039
Bulgaria	Romania	19 Apr 24	33LTS221	300846
Bulgaria	Romania	19 Apr 24	33LTS209	300845
Austria	Greece	27 May 24	27LTS99	300671
Netherlands	Poland	30 May 24	34LTS9	300865
Austria	Latvia	09 Aug 24	65LTS7	301516
Finland	Italy	22 Oct 24	32LTS149	300814
Latvia	Switzerland	04 Dec 24	34LTS405	300889
Hungary	Netherlands	09 Dec 24	47LTS91	301130
Czechoslovakia	Germany	15 Dec 24	52LTS41	301249
Czechoslovakia	Germany	15 Dec 24	52LTS31	301248
Bulgaria	Turkey	27 Dec 24	54LTS135	301281
France	Siam	14 Feb 25	43LTS189	301055
Austria	France	04 Mar 25	75LTS97	301755
Czechoslovakia	Poland	06 Mar 25	46LTS201	301120
Belgium	Germany	18 Apr 25	42LTS49	301031
Czechoslovakia	Poland	23 Apr 25	44LTS285	301090
Bulgaria	Poland	29 Apr 25	60LTS103	301408
Czechoslovakia	Romania	07 May 25	54LTS17	301272
Czechoslovakia	Romania	07 May 25	54LTS51	301273
Germany	USA (United States)	21 May 25	52LTS133	301254
Netherlands	Siam	08 Jun 25	56LTS57	301323
Bel-Lux Econ Union		07 Jul 25	54LTS267	301290
Italy	Latvia	25 Jul 25	60LTS91	301407
Siam	Spain	03 Aug 25	55LTS39	301303
Germany	UK Great Britain	13 Aug 25	43LTS89	301050
Portugal	Siam	14 Aug 25	55LTS57	301304
Belgium	Netherlands	28 Aug 25	93LTS431	302131
Siam	UK Great Britain	15 Sep 25	49LTS51	301176
Germany	USSR (Soviet Union)	12 Oct 25	53LTS7	301257
Germany	USSR (Soviet Union)	12 Oct 25	53LTS227	301259
Estonia	Switzerland	14 Oct 25	49LTS421	301195
Austria	China	19 Oct 25	55LTS9	301301
Czechoslovakia	Japan	30 Oct 25	58LTS263	301377
Germany	Italy	31 Oct 25	52LTS179	301256
Estonia	Germany	25 Nov 25	54LTS79	301275
Norway	USSR (Soviet Union)	15 Dec 25	47LTS9	301127
Germany	Poland	16 Dec 25	46LTS139	301117
Siam	Sweden	19 Dec 25	58LTS429	301386
Bel-Lux Econ Union	Czechoslovakia	28 Dec 25	58LTS189	301372
France	Poland	30 Dec 25	95LTS233	302177
Spain	USA (United States)	10 Feb 26	67LTS131	301543
Denmark	Siam	01 Mar 26	47LTS103	301131
Finland	Hungary	20 Apr 26	48LTS119	301154
Italy	Siam	09 May 26	61LTS215	301436
Greece	Netherlands	12 May 26	61LTS295	301440
Bulgaria	Czechoslovakia	15 May 26	60LTS169	301412
Bulgaria	Czechoslovakia	15 May 26	60LTS203	301413
Albania	Serb/Croat/Slovene	22 Jun 26	91LTS81	302056
Finland	Germany	26 Jun 26	56LTS203	301332
Germany	Latvia	28 Jun 26	58LTS403	301385
Austria	Czechoslovakia	12 Jul 26	86LTS395	301952
Bel-Lux Econ Union	Siam	13 Jul 26	62LTS287	301468
Norway	Siam	16 Jul 26	60LTS35	301404

Legal protection and assistance (Cont.)

PARTY ONE	PARTY TWO	DATE	CITATION	NUMBER
Czechoslovakia	Estonia	17 Jul 26	69LTS385	301620
Czechoslovakia	Estonia	17 Jul 26	63LTS255	301495
Hungary	UK Great Britain	23 Jul 26	67LTS183	301546
Bel-Lux Econ Union	Estonia	28 Sep 26	62LTS433	301475
Austria	Estonia	15 Oct 26	93LTS137	302106
Greece	Italy	24 Oct 26	63LTS51	301480
Germany	Turkey	12 Jan 27	73LTS187	301713
Austria	Germany	05 Feb 27	73LTS227	301715
Poland	Serb/Croat/Slovene	06 Mar 27	126LTS67	302871
Czechoslovakia	Greece	07 Apr 27	88LTS187	301997
Czechoslovakia	Greece	07 Apr 27	88LTS219	301999
Greece	UK Great Britain	13 May 27	61LTS15	301425
UK Great Britain	USA (United States)	19 May 27	64LTS101	301503
British Empire	Hedjaz	20 May 27	71LTS131	301658
Iceland	USSR (Soviet Union)	25 May 27	63LTS105	301483
Czechoslovakia	Poland	30 May 27	98LTS233	302251
Belgium	Czechoslovakia	19 Jul 27	73LTS283	301720
Switzerland	Turkey	07 Aug 27	73LTS51	301706
Belgium	France	06 Oct 27	69LTS49	301599
Germany	Saar	13 Oct 27	70LTS121	301629
Czechoslovakia	Spain	26 Oct 27	121LTS287	302792
Czechoslovakia	Spain	26 Oct 27	121LTS271	302791
Czechoslovakia	Portugal	23 Nov 27	123LTS403	302827
Czechoslovakia	Portugal	23 Nov 27	124LTS7	302829
Greece	Switzerland	01 Dec 27	84LTS271	301907
Germany	Poland	10 Dec 27	120LTS299	302773
Japan	USSR (Soviet Union)	23 Jan 28	80LTS341	301839
Multilateral		20 Feb 28	86LTS111	301950
Hungary	Serb/Croat/Slovene	22 Feb 28	104LTS151	302385
Germany	UK Great Britain	20 Mar 28	90LTS287	302044
Austria	Serb/Croat/Slovene	01 May 28	96LTS373	302214
Czechoslovakia	France	07 May 28	114LTS171	302663
Czechoslovakia	France	07 May 28	114LTS117	302660
Austria	Persia	17 Jun 28	112LTS101	302610
Austria	USA (United States)	19 Jun 28	118LTS241	302728
Austria	Hungary	25 Jun 28	100LTS85	302296
France	Spain	16 Jul 28	135LTS149	303110
Germany	Lithuania	30 Oct 28	91LTS365	302077
Czechoslovakia	Serb/Croat/Slovene	07 Nov 28	98LTS297	302252
China	Italy	27 Nov 28	93LTS173	302109
Austria	Czechoslovakia	12 Dec 28	108LTS9	302501
China	Denmark	12 Dec 28	91LTS207	302062
Germany	Persia	17 Feb 29	111LTS241	302590
Czechoslovakia	Germany	20 Mar 29	109LTS219	302541
Belgium	Persia	09 May 29	110LTS391	302570
Persia	Sweden	10 May 29	102LTS9	302349
Norway	Sweden	11 May 29	120LTS263	302771
Germany	Turkey	28 May 29	133LTS235	303068
Bolivia	Netherlands	30 May 29	133LTS113	303062
Bulgaria	Germany	04 Jun 29	106LTS49	302436
Spain	UK Great Britain	27 Jun 29	101LTS375	302337
Bulgaria	Yugoslavia	26 Sep 29	101LTS217	302324
China	Greece	30 Sep 29	123LTS127	302811
Hungary	Yugoslavia	11 Nov 29	111LTS197	302587
Poland	Romania	19 Dec 29	130LTS205	302991
Multilateral		24 Jan 30	106LTS85	302437
Multilateral		17 Feb 30	102LTS87	302354
Latvia	Spain	08 Mar 30	113LTS135	302641
Poland	Romania	26 Mar 30	153LTS87	303510
France	Luxembourg	31 Mar 30	122LTS29	302797
Austria	Germany	12 Apr 30	115LTS297	302693
Japan	Lithuania	02 May 30	126LTS369	302895
Germany	UK Great Britain	09 May 30	105LTS271	302419
Poland	Romania	23 Jun 30	133LTS163	303066
Belgium	Bulgaria	02 Jul 30	130LTS191	302990

PARTY ONE	PARTY TWO	DATE	CITATION	NUMBER
Legal protection and assistance (Cont.)				
Czechoslovakia	Romania	15 Jul 30	164LTS157	303793
Austria	Japan	16 Aug 30	126LTS351	302894
Czechoslovakia	Turkey	22 Aug 30	138LTS311	303195
Sweden	UK Great Britain	28 Aug 30	114LTS9	302652
Poland	Sweden	30 Aug 30	129LTS383	302973
Germany	Turkey	03 Sep 30	133LTS321	303071
El Salvador	USA (United States)	05 Sep 30	134LTS207	303093
Czechoslovakia	Persia	29 Oct 30	121LTS59	302784
Austria	Belgium	01 Dec 30	112LTS37	302605
Belgium	Lithuania	12 Dec 30	135LTS231	303114
Czechoslovakia	Romania	22 Dec 30	168LTS209	303900
Norway	UK Great Britain	30 Jan 31	123LTS343	302823
Multilateral		10 Feb 31	126LTS41	302870
Norway	Turkey	16 Mar 31	138LTS41	303180
Greece	Poland	22 Apr 31	129LTS313	302966
Czechoslovakia	Lithuania	24 Apr 31	126LTS261	302889
Czechoslovakia	Lithuania	24 Apr 31	126LTS279	302890
Germany	Hungary	18 Jul 31	150LTS111	303458
Greece	Romania	11 Aug 31	130LTS69	302982
Hungary	Romania	12 Aug 31	186LTS325	304321
Poland	UK Great Britain	26 Aug 31	131LTS19	303002
Czechoslovakia	Denmark	07 Oct 31	127LTS103	302911
Czechoslovakia	Netherlands	04 Dec 31	129LTS343	302969
Germany	Lithuania	05 Dec 31	125LTS265	302860
Estonia	UK Great Britain	22 Dec 31	132LTS231	303041
Austria	Belgium	26 Jan 32	129LTS141	302959
Austria	Poland	22 Apr 32	143LTS45	303304
Estonia	Spain	23 Jun 32	143LTS31	303303
Bulgaria	Germany	24 Jun 32	147LTS211	303400
Denmark	UK Great Britain	29 Nov 32	139LTS9	303201
Italy	Switzerland	03 Jan 33	142LTS17	303276
Romania	Yugoslavia	30 Jan 33	146LTS81	303361
France	Hungary	07 Apr 33	162LTS463	303756
Switzerland	Turkey	01 Jun 33	159LTS187	303662
Switzerland	Turkey	01 Jun 33	159LTS329	303676
Finland	UK Great Britain	11 Aug 33	149LTS131	303437
Bulgaria	Czechoslovakia	29 Aug 33	148LTS15	303402
Latvia	Lithuania	01 Dec 33	148LTS97	303407
Latvia	USSR (Soviet Union)	04 Dec 33	148LTS145	303410
Estonia	Lithuania	13 Jan 34	148LTS337	303420
Czechoslovakia	Poland	25 Jan 34	177LTS139	304088
Czechoslovakia	Poland	10 Feb 34	183LTS213	304238
Lithuania	UK Great Britain	24 Apr 34	169LTS373	303925
Iraq	USA (United States)	07 Jun 34	170LTS267	303942
Turkey	Yugoslavia	03 Jul 34	179LTS207	304149
Nicaragua	Spain	20 Nov 34	166LTS143	303836
Czechoslovakia	Luxembourg	01 Dec 34	168LTS287	303906
Iraq	UK Great Britain	25 Jul 35	176LTS229	304064
Bulgaria	Romania	26 Jul 35	198LTS9	304621
Iran	USSR (Soviet Union)	27 Aug 35	176LTS299	304069
Finland	Germany	25 Sep 35	173LTS11	304001
Hungary	UK Great Britain	25 Sep 35	170LTS51	303928
Brazil	Chile	08 Nov 35	181LTS297	304197
Greece	UK Great Britain	27 Feb 36	185LTS113	304278
UK Great Britain	Yugoslavia	27 Feb 36	181LTS241	304193
Belgium	Yugoslavia	29 Feb 36	184LTS379	304258
Hungary	Poland	24 Apr 36	181LTS115	304183
Multilateral		04 Jul 36	171LTS75	303952
Belgium	Liechtenstein	05 Aug 36	185LTS33	304302
Netherlands	Switzerland	27 Jan 37	186LTS433	304327
United Arab Rep	Turkey	07 Apr 37	191LTS95	304438
Sweden	Yugoslavia	14 May 37	194LTS21	304504
Bulgaria	Romania	20 Jul 37	202LTS33	304733
France	UK Great Britain	29 Jul 37	184LTS351	304257
Greece	Luxembourg	01 Sep 37	193LTS151	304491

PARTY ONE	PARTY TWO	DATE	CITATION	NUMBER
Legal protection and assistance (Cont.)				
France	Switzerland	13 Oct 37	194LTS191	304522
Estonia	France	16 Oct 37	183LTS41	304227
Liberia	USA (United States)	01 Nov 37	201LTS151	304710
Belgium	Siam	05 Nov 37	190LTS163	304414
Siam	USA (United States)	13 Nov 37	192LTS247	304476
Poland	Switzerland	19 Nov 37	195LTS297	304552
Siam	UK Great Britain	23 Nov 37	188LTS333	304366
Switzerland	UK Great Britain	03 Dec 37	194LTS223	304523
France	Siam	07 Dec 37	201LTS113	304708
Latvia	Turkey	12 Jan 38	201LTS229	304716
Greece	Switzerland	30 Mar 38	185LTS245	304288
Germany	Greece	11 May 38	197LTS75	304608
Lithuania	Poland	25 May 38	191LTS391	304457
Romania	Switzerland	19 Jul 38	152LTS89	303486
Cuba	Portugal	06 Sep 38	195LTS443	304565
Greece	UK Great Britain	30 May 39	202LTS7	304732
Norway	Spain	26 Jul 39	198LTS87	304627
Hungary	Romania	19 Oct 39	201LTS395	304728
UK Great Britain	USA (United States)	27 Mar 41	204LTS15	304784
Domestic legislation				
Austria	Czechoslovakia	07 Jun 20	3LTS189	300098
Germany	Poland	05 Mar 24	49LTS251	301184
Iraq	UK Great Britain	25 Mar 24	35LTS131	300893
Iraq	UK Great Britain	25 Mar 24	35LTS103	300892
Japan	Peru	30 Sep 24	102LTS33	302351
France	Germany	04 Jun 26	53LTS423	301270
Multilateral		20 Feb 28	155LTS259	303581
Germany	Siam	07 Apr 28	85LTS337	301938
Czechoslovakia	France	07 May 28	114LTS171	302663
Norway	Portugal	07 Feb 29	104LTS137	302383
Colombia	Nicaragua	25 Mar 29	132LTS255	303042
Belgium	Netherlands	16 Oct 31	137LTS411	303171
Belgium	France	17 Nov 31	152LTS121	303490
Romania	Yugoslavia	30 Jan 33	146LTS129	303365
Multilateral		28 Oct 33	159LTS199	303663
Sweden	UK Great Britain	30 Apr 36	168LTS121	303892
Multilateral		23 May 39	202LTS159	304742
UK Great Britain	USA (United States)	27 Mar 41	204LTS15	304784
Operating agencies				
Belgium	Luxembourg	25 Jul 21	9LTS223	300256
Italy	Serb/Croat/Slovene	14 Sep 21	19LTS14	300482
Belgium	France	30 Nov 21	27LTS173	300680
Germany	Poland	15 Jun 22	34LTS201	300875
Other Unilat Decla	Austria	04 Oct 22	12LTS405	300336
Multilateral		04 Oct 22	12LTS391	300335
Greece	Turkey	30 Jan 23	32LTS75	300807
Multilateral		29 Mar 23	23LTS256	300593
Liechtenstein	Switzerland	29 Mar 23	21LTS231	300545
Multilateral		03 May 23	33LTS25	300831
Austria	Italy	16 Jul 23	27LTS383	300699
Belgium	Luxembourg	17 Jul 23	27LTS235	300686
Estonia	Latvia	01 Nov 23	25LTS345	300623
Multilateral		18 Dec 23	28LTS541	300729
Belgium	USA (United States)	21 Jan 24	31LTS137	300791
Sweden	Switzerland	02 Jun 24	33LTS199	300844
Denmark	Switzerland	06 Jun 24	34LTS175	300873
Hungary	Switzerland	18 Jun 24	34LTS387	300887
Denmark	Finland	27 Jun 24	33LTS131	300839
Denmark	Sweden	27 Jun 24	33LTS149	300840
Finland	Sweden	27 Jun 24	29LTS19	300731
Denmark	Norway	27 Jun 24	33LTS173	300842
Other Unilat Decla	Greece	19 Sep 24	30LTS413	300776
Italy	Switzerland	20 Sep 24	33LTS91	300834
Multilateral		29 Nov 24	80LTS293	301835

PARTY ONE	PARTY TWO	DATE	CITATION	NUMBER
Operating agencies (Cont.)				
Latvia	Sweden	28 Mar 25	37LTS131	300952
Multilateral		31 Dec 25	79LTS167	301809
Dominican Republic	USA (United States)	19 Jul 26	54LTS145	301282
Austria	Germany	05 Feb 27	73LTS205	301714
Germany	Poland	11 Apr 27	69LTS419	301621
Belgium	UK Great Britain	03 May 27	140LTS71	303229
Czechoslovakia	Poland	18 Feb 28	100LTS273	302301
Bulgaria		08 Sep 28	74LTS167	301738
Austria	Czechoslovakia	12 Dec 28	107LTS137	302474
Dominican Republic	Haiti	21 Jan 29	105LTS193	302413
Brazil	Venezuela	07 Nov 29	99LTS427	302288
Brazil	UK Great Britain	18 Mar 30	101LTS401	302339
Czechoslovakia	Romania	15 Jul 30	164LTS157	303793
Czechoslovakia	Romania	22 Dec 30	167LTS243	303870
Latvia	Lithuania	25 Jan 31	118LTS175	302722
Multilateral		15 Oct 31	125LTS83	302847
Czechoslovakia	Poland	25 Jan 34	177LTS139	304088
Multilateral		09 Apr 35	163LTS177	303766
Canada	USA (United States)	29 Jan 37	181LTS209	304190
Multilateral		02 Jun 37	184LTS445	304265
Bulgaria	Romania	20 Jul 37	202LTS33	304733
Czechoslovakia	Hungary	24 Aug 37	189LTS403	304397
Canada	USA (United States)	07 Jan 38	184LTS305	304255
France	Switzerland	31 Jan 38	195LTS313	304553
Argentina	Netherlands	06 Sep 38	194LTS409	304531
Licenses and permits				
Liberia	UK Great Britain	10 Apr 13	1LTS205	300014
Multilateral		10 Sep 19	7LTS331	300200
Austria	Poland	09 Jan 20	7LTS163	300185
Germany	Hungary	01 Jun 20	7LTS207	300187
Germany	Switzerland	09 Jul 20	12LTS25	300304
Germany	Switzerland	14 Sep 20	2LTS331	300087
Czechoslovakia	Italy	23 Mar 21	32LTS183	300815
Germany	Poland	10 Apr 21	6LTS233	300158
Czechoslovakia	Romania	23 Apr 21	15LTS235	300397
Finland	UK Great Britain	10 Jun 21	16LTS133	300403
Germany	UK Great Britain	18 Jun 21	16LTS139	300404
Finland	France	13 Jul 21	29LTS445	300755
Austria	UK Great Britain	14 Jul 21	16LTS151	300405
Czechoslovakia	UK Great Britain	04 Aug 21	16LTS157	300406
Sweden	UK Great Britain	29 Aug 21	6LTS285	300160
Italy	Serb/Croat/Slovene	14 Sep 21	19LTS14	300482
Austria	Poland	23 Sep 21	7LTS181	300186
Estonia	Finland	29 Oct 21	13LTS59	300348
Greece	UK Great Britain	10 Nov 21	16LTS165	300407
Norway	UK Great Britain	16 Dec 21	16LTS187	300409
Bulgaria	UK Great Britain	05 Apr 22	16LTS191	300410
Finland	Germany	21 Apr 22	19LTS87	300487
Poland	Switzerland	26 Jun 22	12LTS305	300322
France	Panama	16 Aug 22	43LTS423	301075
Czechoslovakia	Poland	23 Sep 22	50LTS321	301216
Estonia	Hungary	19 Oct 22	30LTS347	300774
UK Great Britain	Uruguay	19 Oct 22	16LTS201	300411
Finland	USSR (Soviet Union)	21 Oct 22	29LTS197	300742
Finland	USSR (Soviet Union)	28 Oct 22	29LTS211	300743
Haiti	UK Great Britain	16 Nov 22	16LTS173	300408
Canada	France	15 Dec 22	21LTS38	300532
Belgium	Poland	30 Dec 22	21LTS201	300543
Czechoslovakia	UK Great Britain	31 Jan 23	20LTS53	300506
Colombia	UK Great Britain	08 Mar 23	17LTS167	300434
Austria	UK Great Britain	28 Mar 23	17LTS385	300445
Germany	Lithuania	01 Jun 23	51LTS387	301244
Estonia	Germany	27 Jun 23	41LTS161	301013
Belgium	Netherlands	14 Jul 23	20LTS119	300511

PARTY ONE	PARTY TWO	DATE	CITATION	NUMBER
Licenses and permits (Cont.)				
Poland	Turkey	23 Jul 23	49LTS329	301189
Multilateral		24 Jul 23	28LTS171	300705
Poland	Romania	24 Jul 23	18LTS103	300458
Multilateral		03 Nov 23	30LTS371	300775
Hungary	Latvia	19 Nov 23	37LTS341	300959
Multilateral		14 Dec 23	29LTS37	300732
Austria	Turkey	28 Jan 24	32LTS313	300823
Czechoslovakia	Denmark	31 Jan 24	23LTS139	300585
Sweden	Switzerland	20 Mar 24	25LTS243	300612
Denmark	Poland	22 Mar 24	31LTS13	300778
Denmark	Latvia	03 Apr 24	33LTS393	300860
Poland	Serb/Croat/Slovene	05 Apr 24	49LTS265	301185
France	Italy	10 Apr 24	43LTS485	301078
Netherlands	Poland	30 May 24	34LTS9	300865
Poland	USSR (Soviet Union)	18 Jul 24	49LTS201	301183
Germany	Spain	25 Jul 24	41LTS363	301023
Czechoslovakia	France	18 Aug 24	44LTS21	301080
Finland	Latvia	23 Aug 24	37LTS383	300962
Finland	Italy	22 Oct 24	32LTS149	300814
France	Latvia	30 Oct 24	37LTS399	300963
Germany	Switzerland	17 Nov 24	41LTS473	301026
Austria	Norway	03 Dec 24	31LTS151	300792
Latvia	Switzerland	04 Dec 24	34LTS405	300889
Czechoslovakia	USA (United States)	05 Dec 24	56LTS271	301335
France	Poland	09 Dec 24	44LTS127	301081
France	Saar	15 Jan 25	44LTS181	301082
Austria	Spain	03 Feb 25	43LTS313	301067
Multilateral		11 Feb 25	51LTS337	301239
Estonia	USA (United States)	02 Mar 25	43LTS289	301064
France	Portugal	04 Mar 25	44LTS197	301083
Albania	Italy	06 Mar 25	44LTS359	301094
Czechoslovakia	Greece	08 Apr 25	38LTS291	300984
Greece	Poland	17 Apr 25	38LTS301	300985
Finland	USA (United States)	02 May 25	47LTS351	301139
Spain	Sweden	04 May 25	36LTS323	300932
Germany	USA (United States)	21 May 25	52LTS133	301254
Italy	UK Great Britain	21 May 25	43LTS75	301048
Bel-Lux Econ Union		07 Jul 25	54LTS267	301290
Germany	USSR (Soviet Union)	12 Oct 25	53LTS7	301257
Germany	Italy	31 Oct 25	52LTS179	301256
Lithuania	USA (United States)	23 Dec 25	54LTS377	301300
Bel-Lux Econ Union	Czechoslovakia	28 Dec 25	58LTS189	301372
Austria	Switzerland	06 Jan 26	46LTS299	301124
Latvia	USA (United States)	01 Feb 26	55LTS33	301302
Finland	Hungary	20 Apr 26	48LTS119	301154
Germany	Sweden	14 May 26	51LTS99	301225
Hungary	USA (United States)	04 Sep 26	58LTS111	301369
Austria	Germany	05 Feb 27	73LTS205	301714
Estonia	Germany	05 Apr 27	64LTS355	301508
China	Switzerland	12 Apr 27	66LTS427	301536
France	Turkey	01 Nov 27	92LTS249	302092
Germany	Poland	10 Dec 27	120LTS299	302773
Germany	Lithuania	29 Jan 28	89LTS309	302026
Czechoslovakia	Poland	18 Feb 28	119LTS385	302758
Multilateral		20 Feb 28	129LTS223	302963
Germany	Italy	23 Mar 28	93LTS165	302108
Chile	Germany	18 Apr 28	79LTS411	301817
Czechoslovakia	Finland	26 Apr 28	80LTS335	301838
Austria	USA (United States)	19 Jun 28	118LTS241	302728
Panama	UK Great Britain	26 Sep 28	90LTS327	302046
Peru	UK Great Britain	31 Dec 28	100LTS431	302312
Ecuador	UK Great Britain	05 Jan 29	90LTS369	302048
Multilateral		16 Apr 29	126LTS305	302891
Norway	Sweden	11 May 29	120LTS263	302771
Germany	UK Great Britain	28 Dec 29	102LTS49	302352

PARTY ONE	PARTY TWO	DATE	CITATION	NUMBER
Licenses and permits (Cont.)				
Irish Free State	Italy	10 May 30	132LTS147	303034
Czechoslovakia	Romania	15 Jul 30	164LTS157	303793
Denmark	Norway	06 Nov 30	109LTS283	302545
Latvia	Lithuania	25 Jan 31	118LTS175	302722
Multilateral		30 Mar 31	138LTS149	303185
Multilateral		13 Apr 31	119LTS275	302751
Guatemala	UK Great Britain	06 Jun 31	132LTS15	303027
Multilateral		24 Sep 31	155LTS349	303586
Irish Free State	USA (United States)	18 Nov 31	131LTS279	303018
Belgium	USA (United States)	19 Apr 32	134LTS19	303080
Finland	Latvia	29 Apr 32	133LTS71	303057
Spain	UK Great Britain	26 May 32	132LTS43	303030
Sweden	USA (United States)	01 Jun 32	131LTS213	303012
Germany	Sweden	01 Jun 32	129LTS471	302979
Austria	Denmark	05 Aug 32	132LTS165	303036
Finland	USSR (Soviet Union)	25 May 34	155LTS207	303578
Czechoslovakia	Hungary	08 Jun 34	172LTS61	303979
Bel-Lux Econ Union	France	16 Jul 35	162LTS19	303731
Iran	USSR (Soviet Union)	27 Aug 35	176LTS299	304069
Romania	UK Great Britain	02 May 36	184LTS145	304247
Norway	Spain	13 Jun 36	170LTS199	303935
Germany	Greece	09 Nov 36	182LTS9	304201
UK Great Britain	Yugoslavia	27 Nov 36	181LTS281	304195
Australia	France	27 Nov 36	177LTS301	304095
Hungary	Yugoslavia	17 Dec 36	196LTS137	304576
Belgium	Norway	17 Dec 36	178LTS153	304110
Italy	Netherlands	01 Jan 37	178LTS415	304124
Brazil	Netherlands	15 Mar 37	179LTS395	304166
Hungary	UK Great Britain	22 Mar 37	190LTS59	304405
Czechoslovakia	Italy	31 Mar 37	193LTS165	304492
Italy	Norway	31 Mar 37	177LTS349	304097
Czechoslovakia	Italy	10 May 37	190LTS397	304430
Multilateral		08 Jun 37	190LTS79	304406
Bel-Lux Econ Union	Italy	30 Jun 37	197LTS23	304601
Multilateral		21 Jul 37	184LTS271	304250
Bel-Lux Econ Union	Romania	24 Aug 37	193LTS189	304496
Brazil	Lithuania	28 Sep 37	186LTS403	304324
Germany	Romania	03 Oct 37	190LTS369	304429
Canada	USA (United States)	09 Oct 37	185LTS33	304271
Bel-Lux Econ Union	Yugoslavia	26 Nov 37	196LTS19	304567
Estonia	Germany	23 Dec 37	189LTS333	304393
Belgium	Netherlands	31 Dec 37	189LTS387	304396
Canada	USA (United States)	24 Jan 38	187LTS27	304330
Estonia	Sweden	18 Feb 38	185LTS237	304287
Italy	Netherlands	26 Feb 38	194LTS75	304509
Greece	Norway	28 Feb 38	186LTS159	304308
New Zealand	Switzerland	05 May 38	189LTS167	304384
Multilateral		17 May 38	192LTS319	304481
Italy	Norway	21 Jun 38	190LTS193	304417
Switzerland	Yugoslavia	27 Jun 38	196LTS27	304568
Canada	USA (United States)	28 Jul 38	192LTS115	304465
Ecuador	USA (United States)	06 Aug 38	193LTS85	304489
Romania	UK Great Britain	02 Sep 38	191LTS313	304453
Cuba	Portugal	06 Sep 38	195LTS443	304565
Netherlands	Norway	28 Oct 38	193LTS223	304499
Estonia	Netherlands	22 Nov 38	193LTS209	304497
France	Romania	31 Mar 39	199LTS219	304677
France	USA (United States)	15 Jul 39	199LTS355	304683
Norway	Spain	26 Jul 39	198LTS87	304627
Multilateral		21 Aug 39	198LTS343	304652
Multilateral		08 Jan 40	203LTS133	304756
Recognition and enforcement of legal decisions				
France	Germany	05 May 20	8LTS55	300206
Italy	Serb/Croat/Slovene	06 Apr 22	118LTS199	302724
Recognition and enforcement of legal decisions (Cont.)				
Czechoslovakia	Italy	06 Apr 22	55LTS207	301315
Other Unilat Decla	Lithuania	12 May 22	22LTS393	300569
Latvia	Vatican/Holy See	30 May 22	17LTS365	300443
Italy	Serb/Croat/Slovene	23 Oct 22	18LTS441	300480
Poland	Serb/Croat/Slovene	04 May 23	85LTS455	301946
Germany	Hungary	06 Nov 23	45LTS279	301104
Japan	Siam	09 Mar 24	31LTS187	300795
Denmark	Latvia	03 Apr 24	33LTS393	300860
Japan	Switzerland	26 Dec 24	43LTS393	301072
Multilateral		21 Jun 26	78LTS229	301793
Albania	Serb/Croat/Slovene	22 Jun 26	91LTS9	302054
Denmark	Netherlands	23 Oct 26	72LTS13	301686
Poland	USA (United States)	14 Nov 26	58LTS97	301368
Czechoslovakia	Switzerland	21 Dec 26	86LTS443	301956
Austria	Switzerland	15 Mar 27	87LTS351	301981
Czechoslovakia	Greece	07 Apr 27	88LTS211	301998
Multilateral		26 Sep 27	92LTS301	302096
Czechoslovakia	Spain	26 Oct 27	121LTS311	302793
Czechoslovakia	Spain	26 Oct 27	121LTS287	302792
Czechoslovakia	Portugal	23 Nov 27	123LTS403	302827
Czechoslovakia	Portugal	23 Nov 27	123LTS417	302828
Hungary	Serb/Croat/Slovene	22 Feb 28	104LTS151	302385
Hungary	Serb/Croat/Slovene	22 Feb 28	87LTS361	301982
Austria	Hungary	25 Jun 28	100LTS85	302296
Finland	Italy	21 Aug 28	89LTS25	302002
Netherlands	Siam	27 Oct 28	93LTS131	302105
Hungary	Sweden	08 Nov 28	89LTS283	302023
Multilateral		30 Aug 29	104LTS473	302399
Czechoslovakia	Switzerland	20 Sep 29	102LTS123	302357
Germany	Switzerland	02 Nov 29	109LTS273	302544
Estonia	Hungary	27 Nov 29	106LTS331	302454
Greece	Hungary	05 May 30	118LTS293	302732
France	Italy	03 Jun 30	153LTS135	303513
Czechoslovakia	Romania	22 Dec 30	168LTS209	303900
Multilateral		10 Feb 31	126LTS41	302870
Czechoslovakia	Lithuania	24 Apr 31	126LTS279	302890
Multilateral		16 Mar 32	139LTS165	303209
Italy	Switzerland	03 Jan 33	142LTS17	303276
Norway	Sweden	10 Mar 33	138LTS17	303176
Japan	Netherlands	19 Apr 33	163LTS351	303778
Bel-Lux Econ Union	Hungary	24 May 33	140LTS169	303234
Multilateral		23 Nov 33	192LTS389	304484
Finland	Sweden	29 Dec 33	149LTS23	303429
France	USSR (Soviet Union)	11 Jan 34	167LTS349	303878
Czechoslovakia	Poland	10 Feb 34	178LTS159	304111
Albania	Czechoslovakia	14 Apr 34	188LTS255	304362
Lithuania	UK Great Britain	24 Apr 34	169LTS373	303925
Turkey	Yugoslavia	03 Jul 34	179LTS207	304149
Multilateral		19 Nov 34	164LTS243	303797
Canada	USA (United States)	15 Apr 35	162LTS73	303735
Iraq	UK Great Britain	25 Jul 35	176LTS229	304064
Hungary	UK Great Britain	25 Sep 35	170LTS51	303928
Finland	Germany	25 Sep 35	173LTS11	304001
Bel-Lux Econ Union	Spain	04 Apr 36	168LTS339	303909
Hungary	Poland	24 Apr 36	181LTS115	304183
Finland	Turkey	20 Jun 36	172LTS135	303983
Multilateral		26 Jun 36	198LTS299	304648
Bulgaria	France	06 Jul 36	171LTS269	303963
France	USSR (Soviet Union)	11 Aug 36	176LTS365	304073
Netherlands	Romania	28 Aug 36	182LTS363	304222
Netherlands	Turkey	17 Feb 37	182LTS221	304213
Chile	Netherlands	05 May 37	182LTS385	304223
Estonia	Turkey	06 Jun 37	179LTS159	304143
France	UK Great Britain	29 Jul 37	184LTS351	304257
Bel-Lux Econ Union	Romania	24 Aug 37	193LTS189	304496

PARTY ONE	PARTY TWO	DATE	CITATION	NUMBER
Recognition and enforcement of legal decisions (Cont.)				
Poland	Switzerland	19 Nov 37	195LTS297	304552
Estonia	Greece	25 Nov 37	184LTS427	304263
Sweden	Turkey	31 Dec 37	184LTS409	304261
Bel-Lux Econ Union	Estonia	13 Jan 38	185LTS63	304275
Belgium	Netherlands	30 Apr 38	190LTS199	304418
Germany	Greece	11 May 38	197LTS75	304608
Bulgaria	Latvia	17 May 38	189LTS249	304388
Netherlands	Romania	10 Oct 38	195LTS9	304532
Germany	Sweden	28 Oct 38	196LTS91	304571
Greece	Turkey	07 Mar 39	201LTS239	304717
Sweden	Turkey	29 Feb 40	200LTS273	304696
Incorporation of treaty provisions into national law				
Multilateral		09 Dec 19	5LTS335	300140
Greece	Turkey	30 Jan 23	32LTS75	300807
Liechtenstein	Switzerland	29 Mar 23	21LTS231	300545
Multilateral		24 Jul 23	36LTS145	300913
Multilateral		21 Jun 26	78LTS229	301793
Denmark	Sweden	03 Feb 27	109LTS205	302540
Belgium	France	21 May 27	105LTS125	302407
Iceland	Sweden	31 Oct 30	109LTS171	302535
Mexico	USA (United States)	07 Feb 36	178LTS309	304119
Multilateral		26 Jun 36	198LTS299	304648
Personnel				
Belgium	Luxembourg	25 Jul 21	9LTS223	300256
Latvia	USSR (Soviet Union)	20 Oct 21	54LTS155	301283
Germany	Saar	21 Dec 25	55LTS349	301319
Estonia	USA (United States)	23 Dec 25	50LTS13	301197
Cuba	USA (United States)	22 Apr 26	60LTS371	301421
Bulgaria		09 Sep 26	58LTS245	301375
France	Great Britain	14 Sep 27	69LTS269	301609
Bulgaria		08 Sep 28	74LTS167	301738
Multilateral		27 Jul 29	118LTS303	302733
Italy	Turkey	09 Sep 29	129LTS195	302962
Czechoslovakia	Germany	25 Jul 31	187LTS279	304344
Brazil	USA (United States)	10 May 34	150LTS445	303477
Iraq	UK Great Britain	31 Mar 36	172LTS175	303988
Brazil	USA (United States)	27 May 36	171LTS343	303971
Brazil	USA (United States)	12 Nov 36	176LTS133	304057
Lithuania	Poland	14 May 38	191LTS373	304456
Lithuania	Poland	25 May 38	191LTS391	304457
Brazil	USA (United States)	12 Nov 38	195LTS375	304557
Colombia	USA (United States)	23 Nov 38	196LTS147	304578
Colombia	USA (United States)	23 Nov 38	196LTS157	304579
Immovable property				
France	UK Great Britain	06 Aug 14	10LTS333	300278
France	UK Great Britain	26 Apr 20	1LTS287	300023
Germany	Poland	20 Sep 20	9LTS103	300246
Estonia	Latvia	19 Oct 20	17LTS189	300437
Czechoslovakia	Italy	23 Mar 21	32LTS183	300815
Latvia	Lithuania	13 May 21	17LTS211	300438
Denmark	UK Great Britain	12 Jul 21	8LTS397	300238
Finland	Norway	16 Jul 21	19LTS77	300485
Latvia	Ukrainian SSR	03 Aug 21	17LTS317	300442
Czechoslovakia	Germany	18 Mar 22	17LTS453	300448
Czechoslovakia	Italy	06 Apr 22	55LTS207	301315
Austria	Germany	28 May 22	26LTS445	300661
Latvia	Vatican/Holy See	30 May 22	17LTS365	300443
France	Saar	05 Jul 22	27LTS265	300689
Finland	USSR (Soviet Union)	12 Aug 22	19LTS105	300489
Italy	Serb/Croat/Slovene	23 Oct 22	18LTS461	300481
Greece	Turkey	30 Jan 23	32LTS75	300807
Germany	Switzerland	25 Mar 23	18LTS273	300470
Poland	Serb/Croat/Slovene	04 May 23	85LTS455	301946
Germany	Lithuania	01 Jun 23	51LTS387	301244
Immovable property (Cont.)				
Latvia	UK Great Britain	22 Jun 23	20LTS395	300529
Estonia	Germany	27 Jun 23	41LTS161	301013
Estonia	Sweden	07 Jul 23	20LTS189	300517
Poland	Turkey	23 Jul 23	49LTS345	301190
Multilateral		24 Jul 23	36LTS167	300917
Greece		24 Jul 23	36LTS153	300914
Germany	Hungary	06 Nov 23	45LTS253	301103
Germany	Hungary	26 Nov 23	45LTS309	301105
Multilateral		14 Dec 23	29LTS37	300732
Lithuania	Sweden	17 Feb 24	23LTS153	300587
Czechoslovakia	Italy	01 Mar 24	36LTS229	300925
Hungary	Italy	27 Mar 24	45LTS229	301101
Denmark	Latvia	03 Apr 24	33LTS393	300860
Poland	Serb/Croat/Slovene	05 Apr 24	49LTS265	301185
Hungary	Romania	16 Apr 24	45LTS325	301106
Hungary	Romania	16 Apr 24	46LTS27	301112
Netherlands	Poland	30 May 24	34LTS9	300865
Germany	Spain	25 Jul 24	41LTS363	301023
Czechoslovakia	France	18 Aug 24	44LTS21	301080
Germany	Poland	30 Aug 24	32LTS331	300824
Japan	Peru	30 Sep 24	102LTS33	302351
Finland	Italy	22 Oct 24	32LTS149	300814
Iceland	Latvia	03 Nov 24	43LTS339	301069
Austria	Hungary	08 Nov 24	45LTS21	301097
France	Poland	09 Dec 24	44LTS127	301081
Bulgaria	Turkey	27 Dec 24	54LTS135	301281
Austria	Spain	03 Feb 25	43LTS313	301067
Benelux Econ Union	Germany	04 Apr 25	37LTS203	300957
Czechoslovakia	Romania	16 Apr 25	46LTS427	301126
Czechoslovakia	Poland	23 Apr 25	48LTS287	301170
Czechoslovakia	Poland	23 Apr 25	44LTS271	301089
Czechoslovakia	Poland	23 Apr 25	44LTS309	301091
Spain	Sweden	04 May 25	36LTS323	300932
Czechoslovakia	Romania	07 May 25	54LTS17	301272
France	Monaco	26 May 25	44LTS249	301086
Netherlands	Siam	08 Jun 25	56LTS57	301323
Bel-Lux Econ Union		07 Jul 25	54LTS267	301290
Germany	UK Great Britain	13 Aug 25	43LTS89	301050
Siam	UK Great Britain	15 Sep 25	49LTS51	301176
Estonia	Switzerland	14 Oct 25	49LTS421	301195
Germany	Italy	31 Oct 25	52LTS179	301256
Norway	USSR (Soviet Union)	15 Dec 25	47LTS9	301127
Germany	Poland	16 Dec 25	46LTS139	301117
Estonia	USA (United States)	23 Dec 25	50LTS13	301197
France	Poland	30 Dec 25	73LTS265	301719
Estonia	UK Great Britain	18 Jan 26	48LTS209	301163
Denmark	Siam	01 Mar 26	47LTS103	301131
Germany	Portugal	20 Mar 26	53LTS361	301266
Germany	Spain	07 May 26	53LTS321	301264
Germany	Sweden	14 May 26	51LTS99	301225
Hungary	USA (United States)	04 Sep 26	58LTS111	301369
Greece	Italy	24 Oct 26	63LTS51	301480
Germany	Turkey	12 Jan 27	73LTS187	301713
UK Great Britain	USA (United States)	23 Feb 27	82LTS17	301856
Czechoslovakia	Greece	07 Apr 27	88LTS187	301997
Belgium	Germany	09 Jul 27	75LTS367	301759
Estonia	Latvia	22 Jul 27	73LTS333	301723
Belgium	France	06 Oct 27	69LTS49	301599
Greece	Switzerland	01 Dec 27	84LTS271	301907
Albania	France	15 Feb 28	107LTS307	302487
Multilateral		20 Feb 28	86LTS111	301950
Hungary	Serb/Croat/Slovene	22 Feb 28	88LTS111	301991
Germany	Siam	07 Apr 28	85LTS337	301938
Latvia	USA (United States)	20 Apr 28	80LTS35	301821
Austria	Serb/Croat/Slovene	01 May 28	96LTS373	302214

PARTY ONE	PARTY TWO	DATE	CITATION	NUMBER
Immovable property (Cont.)				
Belgium	Poland	12 Jun 28	123LTS25	302803
Austria	USA (United States)	19 Jun 28	118LTS241	302728
Lithuania	Poland	07 Nov 28	89LTS171	302011
Germany	Persia	17 Feb 29	111LTS241	302590
Belgium	Persia	09 May 29	110LTS391	302570
Persia	Sweden	10 May 29	102LTS9	302349
Hungary	Yugoslavia	11 Nov 29	111LTS197	302587
Poland	Romania	17 Dec 29	119LTS333	302754
France	Italy	03 Jun 30	153LTS135	303513
Greece	Turkey	10 Jun 30	108LTS233	302511
Hungary	Yugoslavia	27 Aug 30	113LTS163	302643
El Salvador	USA (United States)	05 Sep 30	134LTS207	303093
Czechoslovakia	Persia	29 Oct 30	121LTS59	302784
Czechoslovakia	Romania	22 Dec 30	167LTS243	303870
Latvia	Lithuania	25 Jan 31	118LTS157	302721
Poland	USA (United States)	15 Jun 31	139LTS395	303223
Romania	Yugoslavia	10 Mar 33	146LTS245	303374
Hungary	Sweden	17 Jun 36	184LTS11	304239
Hungary	Sweden	17 Jun 36	184LTS25	304240
Romania	Turkey	04 Sep 36	195LTS429	304564
Estonia	Latvia	06 Oct 36	172LTS221	303994
France	Sweden	04 Dec 36	184LTS35	304241
France	Sweden	24 Dec 36	181LTS315	304198
United Arab Rep	Turkey	07 Apr 37	191LTS95	304438
Siam	USA (United States)	13 Nov 37	192LTS247	304476
Italy	Siam	03 Dec 37	189LTS255	304389
Romania	Switzerland	19 Jul 38	152LTS89	303486
Multilateral		28 Dec 38	196LTS221	304585
UK Great Britain	USA (United States)	06 Apr 39	196LTS343	304593
Germany	Latvia	30 Oct 39	200LTS213	304693
General property				
Austria	Greece	16 Sep 04	2LTS161	300062
Germany	Greece	01 Dec 10	2LTS123	300055
Greece	Spain	06 Mar 19	3LTS81	300092
France	Italy	30 Sep 19	5LTS279	300133
Bulgaria	Greece	27 Nov 19	1LTS67	300009
Austria	Poland	09 Jan 20	7LTS163	300185
Germany	Poland	09 Jan 20	9LTS77	300245
Estonia	USSR (Soviet Union)	02 Feb 20	11LTS29	300289
France	Germany	25 Mar 20	1LTS347	300029
Lithuania	USSR (Soviet Union)	12 Jul 20	3LTS106	300094
Austria	Czechoslovakia	02 Aug 20	32LTS365	300826
Latvia	USSR (Soviet Union)	11 Aug 20	2LTS195	300067
Finland	USSR (Soviet Union)	14 Oct 20	3LTS5	300091
Estonia	Latvia	19 Oct 20	17LTS189	300437
Danzig	Poland	09 Nov 20	6LTS189	300153
Liechtenstein	Switzerland	10 Nov 20	2LTS305	300084
France	Hungary	31 Jan 21	15LTS221	300396
Germany	Poland	12 Feb 21	9LTS149	300247
UK Great Britain	USSR (Soviet Union)	16 Mar 21	4LTS127	300104
Poland	USSR (Soviet Union)	18 Mar 21	6LTS51	300149
Czechoslovakia	Italy	23 Mar 21	32LTS183	300815
Latvia	Lithuania	14 May 21	17LTS233	300439
China	Germany	20 May 21	9LTS271	300261
Germany	Saar	03 Jun 21	5LTS189	300129
Estonia	Latvia	12 Jul 21	37LTS423	300964
Latvia	Ukrainian SSR	03 Aug 21	17LTS295	300441
Latvia	Ukrainian SSR	03 Aug 21	17LTS317	300442
UK Great Britain	USA (United States)	21 Oct 21	12LTS425	300339
Danzig	Poland	24 Oct 21	116LTS5	302699
Latvia	USSR (Soviet Union)	06 Nov 21	17LTS251	300440
Estonia	Ukrainian SSR	25 Nov 21	11LTS121	300294
Hungary	UK Great Britain	20 Dec 21	10LTS437	300283
Czechoslovakia	Germany	31 Dec 21	17LTS401	300447

PARTY ONE	PARTY TWO	DATE	CITATION	NUMBER
General property (Cont.)				
France	Poland	06 Feb 22	43LTS399	301073
Multilateral		06 Feb 22	38LTS277	300982
Austria	Czechoslovakia	18 Feb 22	14LTS129	300371
Czechoslovakia	Italy	06 Apr 22	55LTS207	301315
Italy	Poland	12 May 22	59LTS293	301399
Austria	Germany	23 May 22	26LTS405	300660
Finland	USSR (Soviet Union)	07 Jul 22	19LTS99	300488
Finland	USSR (Soviet Union)	12 Aug 22	19LTS105	300489
Austria	Poland	25 Sep 22	59LTS307	301400
Austria	UK Great Britain	02 Oct 22	12LTS413	300337
Italy	Serb/Croat/Slovene	23 Oct 22	18LTS461	300481
Japan	Poland	07 Dec 22	32LTS61	300806
Belgium	Poland	30 Dec 22	21LTS201	300543
Greece	Turkey	30 Jan 23	32LTS75	300807
Denmark	Finland	12 Feb 23	18LTS33	300452
Czechoslovakia	Serb/Croat/Slovene	17 Mar 23	30LTS185	300768
Germany	Switzerland	25 Mar 23	18LTS273	300470
Belgium	UK Great Britain	28 Mar 23	16LTS439	300421
Germany	UK Great Britain	05 Apr 23	17LTS173	300435
Denmark	USSR (Soviet Union)	23 Apr 23	18LTS15	300450
Poland	Serb/Croat/Slovene	04 May 23	85LTS455	301946
Germany	Lithuania	01 Jun 23	51LTS387	301244
Latvia	UK Great Britain	22 Jun 23	20LTS395	300529
Estonia	Germany	27 Jun 23	41LTS161	301013
Estonia	Sweden	07 Jul 23	20LTS189	300517
Czechoslovakia	Hungary	13 Jul 23	36LTS41	300902
Poland	Turkey	23 Jul 23	49LTS345	301190
Multilateral		24 Jul 23	36LTS167	300917
Greece		24 Jul 23	36LTS153	300914
Multilateral		24 Jul 23	28LTS11	300701
Estonia	Iceland	07 Sep 23	23LTS131	300584
Hungary	Latvia	19 Nov 23	37LTS341	300959
Bulgaria	Serb/Croat/Slovene	26 Nov 23	26LTS119	300643
Bulgaria	Serb/Croat/Slovene	26 Nov 23	21LTS163	300540
Multilateral		14 Dec 23	29LTS37	300732
Multilateral		18 Dec 23	28LTS541	300729
Lithuania	Norway	21 Dec 23	32LTS55	300805
Czechoslovakia	Denmark	31 Jan 24	23LTS139	300585
Lithuania	Sweden	17 Feb 24	23LTS153	300587
Germany	Poland	23 Feb 24	41LTS197	301015
Hungary	Italy	27 Mar 24	45LTS241	301102
Austria	Serb/Croat/Slovene	29 Mar 24	114LTS421	302670
Mexico	Spain	31 Mar 24	43LTS297	301065
Denmark	Latvia	03 Apr 24	33LTS393	300860
Poland	Serb/Croat/Slovene	05 Apr 24	49LTS265	301185
Hungary	Romania	16 Apr 24	46LTS27	301112
Multilateral		08 May 24	29LTS85	300736
Netherlands	Poland	30 May 24	34LTS9	300865
Finland	UK Great Britain	30 May 24	34LTS79	300868
Finland	Japan	07 Jun 24	58LTS379	301383
Spain	UK Great Britain	27 Jun 24	28LTS523	300727
Germany	Spain	25 Jul 24	41LTS363	301023
Austria	Latvia	09 Aug 24	65LTS7	301516
Latvia	Norway	14 Aug 24	36LTS211	300924
Czechoslovakia	France	18 Aug 24	44LTS21	301080
Germany	Poland	30 Aug 24	32LTS331	300824
Germany	Japan	12 Sep 24	59LTS17	301387
Hungary	Norway	16 Sep 24	33LTS103	300835
Japan	Peru	30 Sep 24	102LTS33	302351
Finland	Italy	22 Oct 24	32LTS149	300814
Iceland	Latvia	03 Nov 24	43LTS339	301069
Austria	Hungary	08 Nov 24	44LTS407	301096
Austria	Hungary	08 Nov 24	45LTS21	301097
UK Great Britain	USA (United States)	03 Dec 24	43LTS41	301046
Latvia	Switzerland	04 Dec 24	34LTS405	300889

PARTY ONE	PARTY TWO	DATE	CITATION	NUMBER
General property (Cont.)				
France	Poland	09 Dec 24	44LTS127	301081
Bulgaria	Turkey	27 Dec 24	54LTS135	301281
Austria	Spain	03 Feb 25	43LTS313	301067
UK Great Britain	USA (United States)	10 Feb 25	55LTS145	301311
UK Great Britain	USA (United States)	10 Feb 25	55LTS133	301310
UK Great Britain	USA (United States)	10 Feb 25	55LTS119	301309
Benelux Econ Union	Germany	04 Apr 25	37LTS203	300957
Czechoslovakia	Poland	23 Apr 25	48LTS287	301170
Czechoslovakia	Poland	23 Apr 25	44LTS271	301089
Bulgaria	Poland	29 Apr 25	60LTS103	301408
Spain	Sweden	04 May 25	36LTS323	300932
Czechoslovakia	Romania	07 May 25	54LTS17	301272
Germany	USA (United States)	21 May 25	52LTS133	301254
France	Monaco	26 May 25	44LTS249	301086
Netherlands	Siam	08 Jun 25	56LTS57	301323
Bel-Lux Econ Union		07 Jul 25	54LTS267	301290
Hungary	Poland	22 Jul 25	48LTS167	301158
Italy	Latvia	25 Jul 25	60LTS91	301407
Germany	UK Great Britain	13 Aug 25	43LTS89	301050
Belgium	Netherlands	28 Aug 25	93LTS431	302131
Siam	UK Great Britain	15 Sep 25	49LTS51	301176
Austria	China	19 Oct 25	55LTS9	301301
Czechoslovakia	Japan	30 Oct 25	58LTS263	301377
Germany	Italy	31 Oct 25	52LTS179	301256
Germany	Italy	31 Oct 25	53LTS245	301261
Norway	USSR (Soviet Union)	15 Dec 25	47LTS9	301127
Germany	Poland	16 Dec 25	46LTS139	301117
Siam	Sweden	19 Dec 25	58LTS429	301386
Estonia	USA (United States)	23 Dec 25	50LTS13	301197
France	Poland	30 Dec 25	73LTS265	301719
Estonia	UK Great Britain	18 Jan 26	48LTS209	301163
France	Great Britain	02 Feb 26	56LTS79	301324
Denmark	Siam	01 Mar 26	47LTS103	301131
Cuba	USA (United States)	11 Mar 26	61LTS383	301448
Multilateral		10 Apr 26	120LTS187	302765
Czechoslovakia	Italy	04 May 26	61LTS257	301438
Germany	Spain	07 May 26	53LTS321	301264
Italy	Siam	09 May 26	61LTS215	301436
Germany	Sweden	14 May 26	51LTS99	301225
France	Turkey	30 May 26	54LTS195	301285
Finland	Germany	26 Jun 26	56LTS203	301332
Germany	Latvia	28 Jun 26	58LTS403	301385
Norway	Siam	16 Jul 26	60LTS35	301404
Hungary	USA (United States)	04 Sep 26	58LTS111	301369
Greece	Sweden	10 Sep 26	63LTS37	301479
Bel-Lux Econ Union	Estonia	28 Sep 26	62LTS433	301475
Austria	Estonia	15 Oct 26	93LTS137	302106
Greece	Italy	24 Oct 26	63LTS51	301480
Hungary	Turkey	20 Dec 26	72LTS245	301696
Germany	Turkey	12 Jan 27	73LTS187	301713
Greece	UK Great Britain	17 Feb 27	90LTS379	302049
UK Great Britain	USA (United States)	23 Feb 27	82LTS17	301856
Czechoslovakia	Greece	07 Apr 27	88LTS187	301997
Greece	UK Great Britain	13 May 27	61LTS15	301425
British Empire	Hedjaz	20 May 27	71LTS131	301658
Czechoslovakia	Poland	30 May 27	98LTS233	302251
Switzerland	Turkey	07 Aug 27	73LTS51	301706
France	USA (United States)	29 Aug 27	68LTS253	301589
Belgium	France	06 Oct 27	69LTS49	301599
Sweden	USSR (Soviet Union)	08 Oct 27	71LTS411	301679
Greece	Switzerland	01 Dec 27	84LTS271	301907
Multilateral		20 Feb 28	86LTS111	301950
Hungary	Serb/Croat/Slovene	22 Feb 28	88LTS111	301991
Germany	Siam	07 Apr 28	85LTS337	301938
Latvia	USA (United States)	20 Apr 28	80LTS35	301821
General property (Cont.)				
Austria	Serb/Croat/Slovene	01 May 28	96LTS373	302214
Belgium	Poland	12 Jun 28	123LTS25	302803
Austria	USA (United States)	19 Jun 28	118LTS241	302728
Abyssinia	Italy	02 Aug 28	94LTS423	302159
Czechoslovakia	Serb/Croat/Slovene	07 Nov 28	98LTS297	302252
Germany	Persia	17 Feb 29	111LTS241	302590
Norway	USA (United States)	25 Feb 29	134LTS81	303085
Netherlands	Spain	27 Mar 29	101LTS479	302346
France	Germany	25 Apr 29	109LTS333	302548
Belgium	Persia	09 May 29	110LTS391	302570
Persia	Sweden	10 May 29	102LTS9	302349
Bolivia	Netherlands	30 May 29	133LTS113	303062
Bulgaria	Germany	04 Jun 29	106LTS49	302436
Belgium	Germany	13 Jul 29	104LTS211	302391
France	UK Great Britain	02 Aug 29	100LTS459	302314
Belgium	China	31 Aug 29	123LTS105	302810
China	Greece	30 Sep 29	123LTS127	302811
Belgium	USA (United States)	04 Oct 29	105LTS189	302412
Italy	Panama	16 Oct 29	138LTS355	303199
Poland	Romania	30 Oct 29	121LTS167	302787
Hungary	Yugoslavia	11 Nov 29	111LTS197	302587
Poland	Romania	17 Dec 29	119LTS333	302754
Czechoslovakia	Poland	21 Dec 29	115LTS201	302687
Germany	UK Great Britain	28 Dec 29	102LTS49	302352
France	Germany	31 Dec 29	106LTS93	302438
Belgium	Germany	16 Jan 30	104LTS223	302392
Germany	New Zealand	17 Jan 30	109LTS485	302551
Canada	Germany	17 Jan 30	109LTS473	302550
Austria	Germany	17 Jan 30	107LTS325	302488
Austria	Belgium	18 Jan 30	104LTS231	302393
Germany	Italy	20 Jan 30	106LTS109	302439
France	Luxembourg	31 Mar 30	122LTS29	302797
China	UK Great Britain	18 Apr 30	112LTS49	302607
Hungary	Yugoslavia	27 Apr 30	113LTS153	302642
Japan	Lithuania	02 May 30	126LTS369	302895
Norway	Persia	08 May 30	134LTS153	303089
Germany	Irish Free State	12 May 30	131LTS153	303008
Netherlands	Yugoslavia	28 May 30	129LTS73	302951
Greece	Turkey	10 Jun 30	108LTS233	302511
Latvia	UK Great Britain	24 Jul 30	107LTS301	302486
Austria	Japan	16 Aug 30	126LTS351	302894
Czechoslovakia	Persia	29 Oct 30	121LTS59	302784
Multilateral		31 Oct 30	120LTS9	302760
Czechoslovakia	Romania	22 Dec 30	167LTS243	303870
Norway	Turkey	16 Mar 31	138LTS41	303180
Germany	Switzerland	15 Jul 31	144LTS389	303341
Germany	Hungary	18 Jul 31	150LTS111	303458
Greece	Romania	11 Aug 31	130LTS93	302984
Greece	Romania	11 Aug 31	130LTS69	302982
Hungary	Romania	12 Aug 31	186LTS325	304321
Romania	Sweden	07 Oct 31	131LTS51	303003
Romania	Yugoslavia	14 Dec 31	135LTS99	303106
Romania	Yugoslavia	14 Dec 31	135LTS31	303103
Bulgaria	Germany	24 Jun 32	147LTS211	303400
Germany	UK Great Britain	27 Jul 32	134LTS311	303099
Hungary	Italy	12 Nov 32	142LTS109	303282
Romania	Yugoslavia	30 Jan 33	146LTS129	303365
Albania	USA (United States)	01 Mar 33	166LTS195	303839
Romania	Yugoslavia	10 Mar 33	146LTS255	303375
Romania	Yugoslavia	11 Mar 33	146LTS277	303378
Bulgaria	Czechoslovakia	29 Aug 33	148LTS15	303402
Latvia	Lithuania	01 Dec 33	148LTS97	303407
Latvia	USSR (Soviet Union)	04 Dec 33	148LTS145	303410
Austria	Hungary	12 Jan 34	162LTS419	303754
Estonia	Lithuania	13 Jan 34	148LTS337	303420

PARTY ONE	PARTY TWO	DATE	CITATION	NUMBER
General property (Cont.)				
Albania	Czechoslovakia	14 Apr 34	188LTS255	304362
Persia	Switzerland	25 Apr 34	160LTS173	303691
Czechoslovakia	Romania	20 Jun 34	168LTS249	303902
Multilateral		19 Nov 34	164LTS243	303797
Poland	Spain	14 Dec 34	168LTS315	303908
Czechoslovakia	Monaco	22 Dec 34	171LTS27	303949
Multilateral		15 Mar 35	170LTS9	303926
France	India	31 May 35	163LTS287	303770
Estonia	Italy	10 Aug 35	185LTS287	304295
Iran	USSR (Soviet Union)	27 Aug 35	176LTS299	304069
Greece	UK Great Britain	21 Jan 36	168LTS171	303897
Czechoslovakia	Yugoslavia	24 Feb 36	187LTS185	304338
Luxembourg	Netherlands	01 Apr 36	179LTS11	304130
Hungary	Poland	24 Apr 36	181LTS115	304183
Liechtenstein	USA (United States)	20 May 36	183LTS181	304235
Hungary	Sweden	17 Jun 36	184LTS11	304239
Hungary	Sweden	17 Jun 36	184LTS25	304240
Belgium	Liechtenstein	05 Aug 36	185LTS33	304302
Romania	Turkey	04 Sep 36	195LTS429	304564
Mexico	USA (United States)	06 Oct 36	180LTS33	304171
Estonia	Latvia	06 Oct 36	172LTS221	303994
France	Sweden	24 Dec 36	181LTS315	304198
Iceland	Sweden	08 Sep 37	187LTS405	304346
France	Switzerland	13 Oct 37	194LTS191	304522
Liberia	USA (United States)	01 Nov 37	201LTS151	304710
Belgium	Siam	05 Nov 37	190LTS163	304414
Poland	Switzerland	19 Nov 37	195LTS297	304552
Siam	UK Great Britain	23 Nov 37	188LTS333	304366
Denmark	Finland	02 Dec 37	187LTS379	304345
Italy	Siam	03 Dec 37	189LTS255	304389
Latvia	Turkey	12 Jan 38	201LTS229	304716
Lithuania	Poland	25 May 38	191LTS391	304457
Romania	Switzerland	19 Jul 38	152LTS89	303486
Liberia	USA (United States)	08 Aug 38	201LTS163	304711
Multilateral		28 Dec 38	196LTS221	304585
Monaco	USA (United States)	15 Feb 39	202LTS61	304735
Greece	Turkey	07 Mar 39	201LTS239	304717
Sweden	USA (United States)	23 Mar 39	199LTS17	304661
Mexico	USA (United States)	18 Apr 39	201LTS201	304714
Germany	Latvia	30 Oct 39	200LTS213	304693
UK Great Britain	USA (United States)	27 Mar 41	204LTS15	304784
Austria	Greece	12 Jun 56*	2LTS157	300061
Succession				
Austria	Greece	16 Sep 04	2LTS161	300062
Germany	Greece	01 Dec 10	2LTS123	300055
Greece	Spain	06 Mar 19	3LTS81	300092
France	Saar	05 Jul 22	27LTS265	300689
Hungary	Romania	16 Apr 24	42LTS165	301039
Poland	USSR (Soviet Union)	18 Jul 24	49LTS201	301183
Belgium	Estonia	08 Feb 27	74LTS227	301740
Italy	Turkey	09 Sep 29	129LTS195	302962
Latvia	UK Great Britain	24 Jul 30	107LTS301	302486
Italy	Latvia	11 May 32	150LTS9	303450
France	Sweden	24 Dec 36	181LTS315	304198
Romania	UK Great Britain	02 Sep 38	191LTS313	304453
Public information				
Lithuania	USSR (Soviet Union)	12 Jul 20	3LTS106	300094
Multilateral		03 May 23	33LTS11	300830
Multilateral		30 Nov 23	102LTS153	302360
Germany	Poland	27 Oct 26	108LTS275	302513
Czechoslovakia	Greece	07 Apr 27	88LTS187	301997
Multilateral		26 Sep 28	93LTS343	302123
France	Sweden	09 Jun 34	154LTS101	303541

PARTY ONE	PARTY TWO	DATE	CITATION	NUMBER
Jurisdiction				
Belgium	Germany	23 Apr 20	12LTS29	300305
Germany	Poland	20 Sep 20	9LTS103	300246
Czechoslovakia	Germany	03 Feb 21	5LTS246	300132
Denmark	UK Great Britain	12 Jul 21	8LTS397	300238
Germany	Poland	24 Feb 22	27LTS15	300665
Germany	Poland	24 Feb 22	26LTS479	300664
Germany	Poland	12 Apr 22	21LTS327	300548
Germany	Poland	15 Jun 22	34LTS201	300875
Multilateral		15 Jun 22	21LTS463	300551
Germany	Poland	15 Jun 22	21LTS433	300550
Germany	Poland	26 Aug 22	26LTS365	300656
China	Japan	01 Dec 22	22LTS179	300559
Multilateral		18 Dec 23	28LTS541	300729
Multilateral		08 May 24	29LTS85	300736
Spain	Switzerland	04 Aug 26	65LTS39	301518
Hungary	Serb/Croat/Slovene	22 Feb 28	181LTS229	304192
Norway	Sweden	11 May 29	120LTS263	302771
Poland	Romania	30 Oct 29	121LTS167	302787
Multilateral		17 Feb 30	102LTS87	302354
Multilateral		07 Nov 33	155LTS115	303574
Multilateral		23 Nov 33	192LTS389	304484
Multilateral		26 Dec 33	165LTS19	303802
Belgium	Germany	10 May 35	182LTS323	304220
Panama	USA (United States)	02 Mar 36	200LTS17	304686
Greece	USA (United States)	21 Nov 36	183LTS169	304233
UK Great Britain	USA (United States)	27 Mar 41	204LTS15	304784
UK Great Britain	Venezuela	26 Feb 42	205LTS131	304830
Recognition of legal documents				
Greece	Spain	06 Mar 19	3LTS81	300092
Switzerland	UK Great Britain	06 Nov 19	1LTS37	300005
Multilateral		29 Feb 20	127LTS433	302930
France	Germany	05 May 20	8LTS55	300206
Denmark	UK Great Britain	23 Dec 20	2LTS249	300071
Sweden	UK Great Britain	16 Feb 21	3LTS233	300100
Multilateral		12 Jul 21	37LTS433	300965
Allied Powers	Poland	01 Apr 22	9LTS325	300265
Italy	Serb/Croat/Slovene	06 Apr 22	118LTS207	302725
Czechoslovakia	Italy	06 Apr 22	55LTS189	301314
Germany	Poland	12 Apr 22	21LTS327	300548
Belgium	UK Great Britain	21 Jun 22	24LTS91	300597
Czechoslovakia	Romania	14 Oct 22	25LTS163	300604
Italy	Serb/Croat/Slovene	23 Oct 22	18LTS441	300480
Italy	Serb/Croat/Slovene	23 Oct 22	18LTS461	300481
Czechoslovakia	Serb/Croat/Slovene	17 Mar 23	30LTS185	300768
Austria	Germany	21 Jun 23	27LTS88	300669
Austria	Germany	21 Jun 23	27LTS57	300668
United Arab Rep	UK Great Britain	05 Jul 23	18LTS311	300473
Bulgaria	Serb/Croat/Slovene	26 Nov 23	26LTS85	300642
Finland	Sweden	10 Jan 24	24LTS167	300558
Japan	UK Great Britain	21 Jan 24	25LTS11	300601
Germany	Poland	05 Mar 24	49LTS181	301182
Austria	Poland	19 Mar 24	56LTS95	301326
Hungary	Romania	16 Apr 24	42LTS165	301039
Hungary	Romania	16 Apr 24	45LTS325	301106
Bulgaria	Romania	19 Apr 24	33LTS221	300846
Belgium	Netherlands	02 May 24	27LTS113	300673
Norway	Portugal	21 Oct 24	30LTS117	300764
Denmark	UK Great Britain	18 Dec 24	32LTS287	300819
Denmark	France	25 Feb 25	33LTS277	300852
Czechoslovakia	Denmark	19 May 25	36LTS113	300908
Denmark	Hungary	04 Jun 25	36LTS119	300909
Bulgaria	Czechoslovakia	15 May 26	60LTS203	301413
Czechoslovakia	Estonia	17 Jul 26	69LTS385	301620

PARTY ONE	PARTY TWO	DATE	CITATION	NUMBER
Recognition of legal documents (Cont.)				
Multilateral		13 Nov 26	77LTS249	301773
Czechoslovakia	Greece	07 Apr 27	88LTS187	301997
Portugal	Sweden	17 May 27	64LTS373	301510
Belgium	Czechoslovakia	19 Jul 27	73LTS307	301721
Czechoslovakia	Spain	26 Oct 27	121LTS287	302792
Czechoslovakia	Portugal	23 Nov 27	123LTS403	302827
Multilateral		20 Feb 28	86LTS111	301950
Germany	UK Great Britain	20 Mar 28	90LTS287	302044
Belgium	Portugal	28 Mar 28	92LTS185	302085
Austria	Serb/Croat/Slovene	01 May 28	96LTS373	302214
Belgium	Poland	12 Jun 28	123LTS25	302803
Netherlands	Switzerland	27 Aug 28	82LTS153	301866
Germany	Lithuania	30 Oct 28	91LTS365	302077
Czechoslovakia	Serb/Croat/Slovene	07 Nov 28	98LTS297	302252
Austria	Czechoslovakia	12 Dec 28	108LTS9	302501
Spain	Sweden	02 Jan 29	94LTS353	302154
Lithuania	Sweden	04 Jan 29	92LTS191	302086
Italy	UK Great Britain	25 Jan 29	95LTS39	302162
Czechoslovakia	Germany	20 Mar 29	109LTS219	302541
Germany	Portugal	08 Apr 29	93LTS253	302114
Spain	UK Great Britain	27 Jun 29	101LTS375	302337
Greece	Sweden	18 Oct 29	95LTS201	302174
Hungary	Yugoslavia	11 Nov 29	111LTS197	302587
Poland	Romania	17 Dec 29	119LTS333	302754
Poland	Romania	19 Dec 29	130LTS205	302991
Estonia	USSR (Soviet Union)	20 Jan 30	102LTS225	302365
Multilateral		17 Feb 30	102LTS87	302354
Sweden	UK Great Britain	28 Aug 30	114LTS9	302652
Denmark	Norway	06 Nov 30	109LTS283	302545
Norway	UK Great Britain	30 Jan 31	123LTS343	302823
Poland	UK Great Britain	26 Aug 31	131LTS19	303002
Austria	Poland	26 Oct 32	138LTS193	303188
Denmark	Sweden	16 Aug 33	164LTS55	303788
Denmark	Norway	11 Nov 33	143LTS25	303302
France	UK Great Britain	18 Jan 34	171LTS183	303960
Czechoslovakia	Poland	25 Jan 34	177LTS139	304088
Czechoslovakia	Poland	10 Feb 34	178LTS159	304111
Lithuania	UK Great Britain	24 Apr 34	169LTS373	303925
Belgium	UK Great Britain	02 May 34	173LTS291	304020
Czechoslovakia	Monaco	22 Dec 34	171LTS27	303949
Iraq	UK Great Britain	25 Jul 35	176LTS229	304064
Estonia	Italy	10 Aug 35	185LTS287	304295
Hungary	UK Great Britain	25 Sep 35	170LTS51	303928
Italy	Spain	01 Oct 35	163LTS345	303777
USA (United States)	USSR (Soviet Union)	22 Nov 35	167LTS303	303875
UK Great Britain	Yugoslavia	27 Feb 36	181LTS241	304193
Greece	UK Great Britain	27 Feb 36	185LTS113	304278
Belgium	Yugoslavia	29 Feb 36	184LTS379	304258
Bolivia	Spain	13 Mar 36	170LTS179	303933
Poland	USSR (Soviet Union)	31 Mar 36	186LTS203	304312
Germany	Sweden	19 May 36	182LTS395	304224
Denmark	Germany	17 Jun 36	171LTS163	303958
Multilateral		04 Jul 36	171LTS75	303952
France	USSR (Soviet Union)	11 Aug 36	176LTS365	304073
Mexico	USA (United States)	06 Oct 36	180LTS33	304171
Germany	South Africa	16 Mar 37	189LTS107	304378
France	UK Great Britain	03 Apr 37	179LTS265	304154
Belgium	Italy	01 May 37	198LTS73	304624
Romania	Yugoslavia	13 May 37	197LTS145	304611
Belgium	Sweden	15 Jun 37	198LTS77	304625
Belgium	France	07 Jul 37	181LTS111	304182
France	Luxembourg	30 Jul 37	181LTS107	304181
Belgium	Greece	09 Sep 37	197LTS63	304605
Belgium	Denmark	16 Sep 37	197LTS67	304606
Romania	UK Great Britain	06 Dec 37	184LTS467	304267

PARTY ONE	PARTY TWO	DATE	CITATION	NUMBER
Recognition of legal documents (Cont.)				
Bulgaria	USA (United States)	05 Jan 38	191LTS207	304444
Finland	Sweden	09 Jan 38	195LTS157	304545
Belgium	Netherlands	07 Feb 38	187LTS9	304328
India	Indochina	01 Mar 38	194LTS231	304524
Greece	Switzerland	30 Mar 38	185LTS245	304288
Greece	Hungary	06 Apr 38	188LTS455	304370
Multilateral		29 Apr 38	190LTS115	304410
Germany	Greece	11 May 38	197LTS75	304608
Multilateral		17 May 38	192LTS319	304481
Multilateral		30 May 38	191LTS299	304451
Canada	USA (United States)	28 Jul 38	192LTS115	304465
Canada	USA (United States)	28 Jul 38	192LTS125	304466
Greece	Turkey	07 Mar 39	201LTS239	304717
Multilateral		21 Aug 39	198LTS343	304652
Latvia	UK Great Britain	23 Aug 39	201LTS37	304702
Canada	USA (United States)	04 Mar 40	202LTS429	304745
Germany	Greece	20 Jan 97*	2LTS107	300053
Private contracts				
Romania	UK Great Britain	22 Jan 20	1LTS257	300018
France	Germany	05 May 20	8LTS55	300206
Germany	Switzerland	06 Dec 20	2LTS343	300088
Multilateral		12 Jul 21	37LTS433	300965
France	Poland	06 Feb 22	43LTS399	301073
Germany	Poland	24 Feb 22	27LTS15	300665
Germany	Poland	24 Feb 22	26LTS479	300664
Germany	Poland	15 Jun 22	21LTS433	300550
Belgium	Poland	30 Dec 22	21LTS201	300543
Czechoslovakia	Hungary	13 Jul 23	35LTS253	300899
Italy	Turkey	24 Jul 23	36LTS195	300921
Multilateral		24 Jul 23	36LTS201	300922
Multilateral		24 Jul 23	28LTS11	300701
Sweden	UK Great Britain	27 Oct 23	22LTS387	300568
Hungary	Romania	16 Apr 24	46LTS7	301111
Multilateral		23 Oct 24	77LTS367	301778
Austria	Czechoslovakia	29 May 25	98LTS91	302242
Italy	Poland	22 Jul 25	54LTS101	301278
Multilateral		20 Feb 28	86LTS111	301950
Austria	Czechoslovakia	12 Dec 28	107LTS137	302474
Multilateral		07 Jun 30	143LTS317	303314
Multilateral		19 Mar 31	143LTS407	303317
Iran	USSR (Soviet Union)	27 Aug 35	176LTS299	304069
Multilateral		03 Mar 37	182LTS127	304205
Multilateral		09 Apr 38	191LTS119	304441
Multilateral		09 Apr 38	191LTS165	304442
Responsibility and liability				
Australia	Malay States	24 Jan 21	23LTS209	300590
Denmark	Sweden	08 Jun 21	14LTS195	300374
Denmark	Norway	21 Jul 21	13LTS357	300362
Belgium	Luxembourg	25 Jul 21	9LTS223	300256
Finland	USSR (Soviet Union)	14 Dec 21	16LTS221	300414
Czechoslovakia	Germany	31 Dec 21	17LTS401	300447
Norway	Sweden	29 Mar 22	13LTS311	300361
Italy	Serb/Croat/Slovene	06 Apr 22	118LTS207	302725
Sweden	USA (United States)	17 Apr 22	14LTS281	300380
Denmark	Germany	25 Apr 22	18LTS227	300466
Finland	Sweden	22 May 22	14LTS297	300381
Finland	Norway	23 May 22	14LTS323	300382
France	Saar	05 Jul 22	27LTS265	300689
Germany	Poland	25 Aug 22	22LTS63	300554
Finland	USSR (Soviet Union)	28 Oct 22	19LTS153	300491
Estonia	Finland	28 Nov 22	19LTS213	300494
Albania	Italy	04 Dec 22	15LTS213	300395
China	Japan	08 Dec 22	20LTS289	300522
China	Japan	08 Dec 22	20LTS233	300520

PARTY ONE	PARTY TWO	DATE	CITATION	NUMBER
Responsibility and liability (Cont.)				
China	Japan	08 Dec 22	20LTS205	300519
Netherlands	UK Great Britain	18 Jan 23	18LTS257	300469
Netherlands	UK Great Britain	23 Jan 23	16LTS425	300420
Portugal	Spain	26 Mar 23	18LTS349	300475
Multilateral		29 Mar 23	23LTS256	300593
Denmark	UK Great Britain	25 Apr 23	22LTS157	300557
Norway	Sweden	26 May 23	18LTS155	300462
Finland	USSR (Soviet Union)	05 Jun 23	18LTS203	300465
Czechoslovakia	UK Great Britain	14 Jul 23	29LTS377	300748
Multilateral		24 Jul 23	28LTS203	300707
Iceland	Norway	10 Aug 23	20LTS363	300527
France	UK Great Britain	10 Oct 23	22LTS381	300567
Multilateral		09 Dec 23	36LTS76	300905
Finland	UK Great Britain	14 Dec 23	29LTS129	300739
Japan	Siam	09 Mar 24	31LTS187	300795
Hungary	Italy	27 Mar 24	45LTS65	301099
Hungary	Romania	16 Apr 24	46LTS7	301111
Hungary	Romania	16 Apr 24	46LTS27	301112
Austria	Czechoslovakia	12 Jul 24	50LTS111	301199
Italy	Serb/Croat/Slovene	12 Aug 24	82LTS423	301882
Multilateral		25 Aug 24	120LTS123	302763
Multilateral		25 Aug 24	120LTS155	302764
Japan	Peru	30 Sep 24	102LTS33	302351
Austria	Czechoslovakia	17 Jan 25	94LTS245	302146
Canada	USA (United States)	24 Feb 25	43LTS251	301060
Austria	Czechoslovakia	14 May 25	50LTS39	301198
Paraguay	Spain	08 Jul 25	138LTS225	303190
Italy	Poland	22 Jul 25	54LTS101	301278
Siam	Spain	03 Aug 25	55LTS39	301303
Germany	UK Great Britain	13 Aug 25	43LTS89	301050
Portugal	Siam	14 Aug 25	55LTS57	301304
Siam	UK Great Britain	15 Sep 25	49LTS51	301176
Estonia	UK Great Britain	18 Jan 26	48LTS209	301163
Multilateral		10 Apr 26	176LTS199	304062
Hungary	USA (United States)	04 Sep 26	58LTS111	301369
Czechoslovakia	Hungary	30 Sep 26	57LTS87	301356
Estonia	Latvia	22 Jul 27	73LTS333	301723
Germany	Poland	07 Dec 27	92LTS203	302088
Germany	Lithuania	29 Jan 28	89LTS97	302009
Multilateral		20 Feb 28	86LTS111	301950
Multilateral		20 Feb 28	129LTS223	302963
Germany	UK Great Britain	20 Mar 28	90LTS287	302044
Germany	Siam	07 Apr 28	85LTS337	301938
Germany	Persia	17 Feb 29	111LTS241	302590
Belgium	Persia	09 May 29	110LTS391	302570
France	UK Great Britain	15 May 29	134LTS263	303097
Albania	Serb/Croat/Slovene	11 Aug 29	101LTS439	302342
France	Luxembourg	31 Mar 30	122LTS29	302797
El Salvador	USA (United States)	05 Sep 30	134LTS207	303093
Czechoslovakia	Romania	22 Dec 30	167LTS243	303870
Greece	UK Great Britain	17 Apr 31	129LTS287	302965
Mexico	Sweden	14 Sep 31	192LTS195	304472
Multilateral		10 Nov 31	131LTS447	303025
Multilateral		10 Nov 31	131LTS327	303023
France	UK Great Britain	17 Nov 31	134LTS299	303098
Japan	USSR (Soviet Union)	23 Nov 31	132LTS133	303033
France	UK Great Britain	27 Nov 31	132LTS25	303028
Multilateral		10 Dec 31	129LTS177	302961
France	UK Great Britain	28 Dec 31	133LTS79	303058
Netherlands	UK Great Britain	04 Jan 32	128LTS307	302939
Netherlands	UK Great Britain	04 Jan 32	128LTS347	302940
Hungary	UK Great Britain	10 Jun 32	132LTS53	303031
Sweden	USA (United States)	11 Jul 32	192LTS205	304473
Netherlands	UK Great Britain	13 Aug 32	134LTS317	303100
Brazil	UK Great Britain	01 Nov 32	177LTS127	304087

PARTY ONE	PARTY TWO	DATE	CITATION	NUMBER
Responsibility and liability (Cont.)				
Multilateral		23 Nov 33	192LTS327	304483
Multilateral		23 Nov 33	192LTS389	304484
Finland	Sweden	29 Dec 33	149LTS23	303429
Finland	USA (United States)	13 Feb 34	152LTS45	303484
Multilateral		20 Mar 34	175LTS5	304049
Multilateral		20 Mar 34	174LTS171	304048
Multilateral		20 Mar 34	175LTS73	304050
Multilateral		20 Mar 34	175LTS269	304051
Multilateral		20 Mar 34	175LTS363	304052
Bulgaria	Romania	26 Jul 35	198LTS9	304621
Multilateral		30 Oct 35	189LTS51	304375
Bulgaria	Yugoslavia	09 Nov 35	194LTS89	304511
Iraq	UK Great Britain	31 Mar 36	172LTS175	303988
United Arab Rep	UK Great Britain	26 Aug 36	173LTS433	304032
Germany	UK Great Britain	02 Dec 36	178LTS329	304121
Germany	Malaya	17 Dec 36	178LTS484	304129
Bahamas	USA (United States)	21 Dec 36	176LTS411	304077
Gibralter	USA (United States)	05 Jan 37	177LTS21	304078
Danzig	UK Great Britain	13 Jan 37	178LTS87	304109
El Salvador	USA (United States)	19 Feb 37	179LTS219	304150
Multilateral		03 Mar 37	182LTS127	304205
Bulgaria	Romania	20 Jul 37	202LTS33	304733
Romania	USA (United States)	10 Aug 37	183LTS7	304225
Malaya	Siam	15 Sep 37	191LTS225	304447
Netherlands	USA (United States)	20 Sep 37	184LTS319	304256
Multilateral		23 Sep 37	190LTS299	304427
Estonia	UK Great Britain	14 Dec 37	187LTS223	304343
Dominican Republic	Haiti	31 Jan 38	187LTS169	304336
Surinam	UK Great Britain	15 Mar 38	189LTS183	304385
Norway	Sweden	20 Apr 38	189LTS153	304383
Lithuania	Poland	14 May 38	191LTS373	304456
Multilateral		02 Jun 38	192LTS157	304470
USA (United States)	Yugoslavia	20 Jun 38	195LTS259	304549
Belgium	UK Great Britain	29 Jul 38	201LTS317	304722
British Guiana	USA (United States)	06 Sep 38	193LTS117	304490
Burma	United Arab Rep	30 Sep 38	203LTS373	304780
Poland	UK Great Britain	05 Oct 38	194LTS321	304529
France	UK Great Britain	26 Oct 38	194LTS371	304530
Multilateral		02 Jan 39	196LTS235	304587
Fiji Islands	USA (United States)	10 Jan 39	196LTS185	304581
Belgium	USA (United States)	15 Jan 39	199LTS321	304682
Burma	France	26 Jan 39	201LTS9	304701
Colombia	USA (United States)	07 Feb 39	196LTS53	304569
Germany	USA (United States)	16 Mar 39	198LTS237	304645
Argentina	USA (United States)	08 Apr 39	198LTS55	304623
Multilateral		23 May 39	202LTS159	304742
Barbados	USA (United States)	13 Sep 39	199LTS375	304685
Hungary	Romania	19 Oct 39	201LTS395	304728
Barbados	Martinique	21 Oct 39	201LTS65	304704
United Arab Rep	USA (United States)	13 Nov 39	198LTS419	304659
Lithuania	USA (United States)	28 Dec 39	202LTS381	304743
Corporations				
Austria	Czechoslovakia	02 Aug 20	32LTS365	300826
Finland	USSR (Soviet Union)	14 Oct 20	3LTS5	300091
Czechoslovakia	Italy	23 Mar 21	32LTS183	300815
Danzig	Poland	24 Oct 21	116LTS5	302699
Multilateral		06 Feb 22	38LTS277	300982
Italy	Poland	12 May 22	59LTS293	301399
Italy	Serb/Croat/Slovene	23 Oct 22	18LTS461	300481
Japan	Poland	07 Dec 22	32LTS61	300806
Multilateral		29 Mar 23	23LTS256	300593
Estonia	Germany	27 Jun 23	41LTS161	301013
Czechoslovakia	Hungary	13 Jul 23	36LTS13	300901
Multilateral		24 Jul 23	28LTS11	300701

PARTY ONE	PARTY TWO	DATE	CITATION	NUMBER
Corporations (Cont.)				
Italy	Spain	15 Nov 23	39LTS49	300996
Japan	Serb/Croat/Slovene	16 Nov 23	42LTS99	301035
Hungary	Italy	27 Mar 24	45LTS229	301101
Denmark	Latvia	03 Apr 24	33LTS393	300860
Poland	Serb/Croat/Slovene	05 Apr 24	49LTS265	301185
Czechoslovakia	Iceland	08 May 24	46LTS419	301125
Multilateral		22 May 24	35LTS175	300895
Netherlands	Poland	30 May 24	34LTS9	300865
Finland	Japan	07 Jun 24	58LTS379	301383
Lithuania	Netherlands	10 Jun 24	34LTS373	300885
Estonia	Netherlands	22 Jul 24	48LTS199	301162
Austria	Latvia	09 Aug 24	65LTS7	301516
Czechoslovakia	France	18 Aug 24	44LTS21	301080
Finland	Latvia	23 Aug 24	37LTS383	300962
Finland	Italy	22 Oct 24	32LTS149	300814
France	Latvia	30 Oct 24	37LTS399	300963
Iceland	Latvia	03 Nov 24	43LTS339	301069
Austria	Hungary	08 Nov 24	44LTS407	301096
Multilateral		29 Nov 24	80LTS293	301835
Latvia	Switzerland	04 Dec 24	34LTS405	300889
Hungary	Netherlands	09 Dec 24	47LTS91	301130
France	Poland	09 Dec 24	44LTS127	301081
Denmark	UK Great Britain	18 Dec 24	32LTS89	300808
Austria	Spain	03 Feb 25	43LTS313	301067
Albania	Italy	06 Mar 25	44LTS359	301094
Benelux Econ Union	Germany	04 Apr 25	37LTS203	300957
Greece	Poland	17 Apr 25	38LTS301	300985
Bulgaria	Poland	29 Apr 25	60LTS103	301408
Spain	Sweden	04 May 25	36LTS323	300932
Germany	USA (United States)	21 May 25	52LTS133	301254
Netherlands	Siam	08 Jun 25	56LTS57	301323
Bel-Lux Econ Union		07 Jul 25	54LTS267	301290
Siam	Spain	03 Aug 25	55LTS39	301303
Germany	UK Great Britain	13 Aug 25	43LTS89	301050
Portugal	Siam	14 Aug 25	55LTS57	301304
Siam	UK Great Britain	15 Sep 25	49LTS51	301176
Germany	USSR (Soviet Union)	12 Oct 25	53LTS7	301257
France	Hungary	13 Oct 25	48LTS9	301150
Austria	China	19 Oct 25	55LTS9	301301
Czechoslovakia	Japan	30 Oct 25	58LTS263	301377
Germany	Italy	31 Oct 25	52LTS179	301256
Norway	USSR (Soviet Union)	15 Dec 25	47LTS9	301127
Bel-Lux Econ Union	Czechoslovakia	28 Dec 25	58LTS189	301372
Germany	Sweden	31 Dec 25	43LTS219	301056
Austria	Switzerland	06 Jan 26	46LTS299	301124
Estonia	UK Great Britain	18 Jan 26	48LTS209	301163
Denmark	Siam	01 Mar 26	47LTS103	301131
Finland	Hungary	20 Apr 26	48LTS119	301154
Czechoslovakia	Italy	04 May 26	61LTS257	301438
Italy	Siam	09 May 26	61LTS215	301436
Greece	Netherlands	12 May 26	61LTS295	301440
Germany	Sweden	14 May 26	51LTS99	301225
Finland	Germany	26 Jun 26	56LTS203	301332
Germany	Latvia	28 Jun 26	58LTS403	301385
Bel-Lux Econ Union	Siam	13 Jul 26	62LTS287	301468
Germany	Switzerland	14 Jul 26	59LTS87	301391
Hungary	USA (United States)	04 Sep 26	58LTS111	301369
Greece	Sweden	10 Sep 26	63LTS37	301479
Bel-Lux Econ Union	Estonia	28 Sep 26	62LTS433	301475
Greece	Italy	24 Oct 26	63LTS51	301480
Hungary	Turkey	20 Dec 26	72LTS245	301696
Germany	Turkey	12 Jan 27	73LTS187	301713
Serb/Croat/Slovene	UK Great Britain	12 May 27	80LTS165	301825
Greece	UK Great Britain	13 May 27	61LTS15	301425
Czechoslovakia	Turkey	31 May 27	75LTS79	301753

PARTY ONE	PARTY TWO	DATE	CITATION	NUMBER
Corporations (Cont.)				
Czechoslovakia	Estonia	20 Jul 27	77LTS341	301776
Switzerland	Turkey	07 Aug 27	73LTS51	301706
Belgium	France	06 Oct 27	69LTS49	301599
Sweden	USSR (Soviet Union)	08 Oct 27	71LTS411	301679
Multilateral		20 Feb 28	86LTS111	301950
Norway	USSR (Soviet Union)	24 Feb 28	79LTS9	301801
Germany	Siam	07 Apr 28	85LTS337	301938
Latvia	USA (United States)	20 Apr 28	80LTS35	301821
Estonia	Sweden	11 Jun 28	81LTS277	301843
Austria	USA (United States)	19 Jun 28	118LTS241	302728
Bulgaria		08 Sep 28	74LTS167	301738
France	Germany	25 Apr 29	109LTS333	302548
Norway	Sweden	11 May 29	120LTS263	302771
France	Luxembourg	31 Mar 30	122LTS29	302797
Czechoslovakia	Persia	29 Oct 30	121LTS59	302784
Hungary	Romania	12 Aug 31	186LTS325	304321
Czechoslovakia	Poland	10 Feb 34	183LTS213	304238
Poland	Spain	14 Dec 34	168LTS315	303908
Iran	USSR (Soviet Union)	27 Aug 35	176LTS299	304069
France	Sweden	04 Dec 36	184LTS35	304241
Cuba	UK Great Britain	19 Feb 37	192LTS301	304480
United Arab Rep	Turkey	07 Apr 37	191LTS95	304438
Romania	Yugoslavia	13 May 37	197LTS145	304611
Sweden	Yugoslavia	14 May 37	194LTS21	304504
France	Switzerland	13 Oct 37	194LTS191	304522
Estonia	France	16 Oct 37	183LTS41	304227
Belgium	Siam	05 Nov 37	190LTS163	304414
Siam	USA (United States)	13 Nov 37	192LTS247	304476
Siam	UK Great Britain	23 Nov 37	188LTS333	304366
France	Siam	07 Dec 37	201LTS113	304708
Latvia	Turkey	12 Jan 38	201LTS229	304716
Sweden	USA (United States)	31 Mar 38	189LTS327	304392
Czechoslovakia	USA (United States)	18 May 38	199LTS305	304680
Liberia	USA (United States)	08 Aug 38	201LTS163	304711
El Salvador	Norway	21 Nov 38	198LTS157	304636
Guatemala	Norway	20 Dec 38	198LTS117	304631
Sweden	USA (United States)	23 Mar 39	199LTS17	304661
Denmark	Norway	18 Jun 39	197LTS227	304615
Concessions				
France	Switzerland	27 Aug 26	71LTS63	301654
France	USA (United States)	29 Aug 27	68LTS253	301589
China	UK Great Britain	18 Apr 30	112LTS49	302607
Bulgaria	Romania	22 May 37	188LTS173	304357
Portugal	South Africa	18 Jun 37	189LTS121	304380
Revival of treaties				
Multilateral		24 Jul 23	28LTS11	300701
Prizes and arbitral awards				
Argentina	Venezuela	22 Jul 11	28LTS287	300715
Norway	USA (United States)	30 Jun 21	14LTS19	300365
Multilateral		03 May 23	33LTS25	300831
Brazil	Switzerland	23 Jun 24	33LTS415	300861
Finland	Sweden	27 Jun 24	29LTS19	300731
Germany	Sweden	29 Aug 24	42LTS111	301036
Netherlands	USA (United States)	23 Jan 25	33LTS445	300864
Poland	Switzerland	07 Mar 25	50LTS261	301209
Finland	Germany	14 Mar 25	43LTS347	301070
Czechoslovakia	Poland	23 Apr 25	48LTS383	301171
Estonia	Germany	10 Aug 25	63LTS111	301484
Germany	USSR (Soviet Union)	12 Oct 25	53LTS7	301257
Poland	Sweden	03 Nov 25	62LTS263	301466
Norway	Sweden	25 Nov 25	60LTS295	301417
Denmark	Sweden	14 Jan 26	51LTS251	301235
Denmark	Norway	15 Jan 26	60LTS311	301418
Finland	Sweden	29 Jan 26	49LTS367	301192

PARTY ONE	PARTY TWO	DATE	CITATION	NUMBER
Prizes and arbitral awards (Cont.)				
Denmark	Finland	30 Jan 26	51LTS367	301242
Finland	Norway	03 Feb 26	60LTS353	301420
Cuba	USA (United States)	04 Mar 26	61LTS369	301447
Denmark	Poland	23 Apr 26	61LTS245	301437
Germany	Netherlands	20 May 26	66LTS103	301527
Poland	Serb/Croat/Slovene	18 Sep 26	78LTS419	301800
Denmark	Germany	23 Feb 27	61LTS325	301444
Chile	France	24 Feb 27	69LTS277	301610
Belgium	Finland	04 Mar 27	69LTS361	301618
Czechoslovakia	Spain	26 Oct 27	121LTS311	302793
Czechoslovakia	Portugal	23 Nov 27	123LTS417	302828
Multilateral		20 Feb 28	86LTS111	301950
Multilateral		05 Jan 29	130LTS135	302988
United Arab Rep	Palestine	12 Jan 29	94LTS9	302132
Norway	Sweden	11 May 29	120LTS263	302771
Estonia	Latvia	20 Dec 29	106LTS173	302444
France	Italy	03 Jun 30	153LTS135	303513
Finland	Iceland	27 Jun 30	167LTS271	303873
Belgium	Romania	08 Jul 30	128LTS403	302944
Belgium	Lithuania	24 Sep 30	129LTS399	302974
Netherlands	Yugoslavia	11 Mar 31	129LTS89	302952
Belgium	Bulgaria	23 Jun 31	137LTS191	303156
Bulgaria	Norway	26 Nov 31	134LTS27	303081
Portugal	Sweden	06 Dec 32	145LTS91	303347
Netherlands	Norway	23 Mar 33	146LTS291	303380
Denmark	Greece	13 Apr 33	150LTS465	303478
Romania	Turkey	17 Oct 33	165LTS273	303814
Dominican Republic	Haiti	27 Feb 35	171LTS89	303953
Canada	USA (United States)	15 Apr 35	162LTS73	303735
Belgium	Germany	10 May 35	182LTS335	304221
Norway	Venezuela	13 May 35	167LTS407	303882
Multilateral		14 Nov 35	166LTS75	303831
Bulgaria	Denmark	07 Dec 35	182LTS183	304211
Sweden	Switzerland	15 Jan 36	169LTS347	303923
Title and deeds				
Cuba	USA (United States)	02 Mar 04	127LTS143	302915
France	Germany	25 Mar 20	1LTS347	300029
France	Poland	06 Feb 22	43LTS399	301073
China	Japan	01 Dec 22	22LTS179	300559
Czechoslovakia	Serb/Croat/Slovene	17 Mar 23	30LTS185	300768
Multilateral		29 Mar 23	23LTS256	300593
Hungary	Romania	16 Apr 24	45LTS349	301108
Czechoslovakia	Romania	07 May 25	54LTS17	301272
Hungary	Poland	22 Jul 25	48LTS167	301158
Germany	Poland	16 Dec 25	46LTS139	301117
Belgium	Germany	09 Jul 27	75LTS367	301759
Hungary	Italy	10 Dec 27	78LTS403	301798
Austria	Germany	17 Jan 30	107LTS325	302488
Multilateral		10 Dec 31	129LTS177	302961
Austria	Hungary	12 Jan 34	162LTS419	303754
Multilateral		19 Nov 34	164LTS243	303797
Iraq	UK Great Britain	31 Mar 36	172LTS175	303988
Use of facilities				
Multilateral		29 Feb 20	127LTS433	302930
Denmark	Finland	27 Jul 20	19LTS71	300484
Germany	USSR (Soviet Union)	06 May 21	6LTS267	300159
Denmark	Sweden	08 Jun 21	14LTS195	300374
Denmark	Norway	21 Jul 21	13LTS357	300362
Italy	Serb/Croat/Slovene	14 Sep 21	19LTS14	300482
Norway	Sweden	29 Mar 22	13LTS311	300361
Multilateral		18 Aug 22	13LTS289	300360
Estonia	Finland	28 Nov 22	19LTS213	300494
Netherlands	UK Great Britain	23 Jan 23	16LTS425	300420
France	UK Great Britain	28 Jan 25	33LTS335	300856

PARTY ONE	PARTY TWO	DATE	CITATION	NUMBER
Use of facilities (Cont.)				
Portugal	Spain	11 Aug 27	82LTS113	301864
Germany	Poland	07 Dec 27	92LTS203	302088
Multilateral		10 Mar 28	132LTS405	303049
Multilateral		01 May 28	132LTS415	303050
Multilateral		05 Jan 29	132LTS425	303051
Multilateral		27 Jul 29	118LTS303	302733
Poland	Romania	07 Dec 29	119LTS283	302752
Czechoslovakia	Poland	21 Dec 29	115LTS201	302687
Latvia	USA (United States)	14 Jan 30	105LTS307	302423
Multilateral		26 Jun 30	133LTS9	303052
Multilateral		28 Aug 30	133LTS21	303053
China	UK Great Britain	17 Sep 30	111LTS153	302584
Germany	Poland	22 Dec 31	144LTS191	303329
Multilateral		28 Jun 32	140LTS191	303237
France	India	31 May 35	163LTS287	303770
Lithuania	Poland	25 May 38	191LTS391	304457
Investigation of violations				
Multilateral		29 Feb 20	127LTS433	302930
Belgium	Germany	23 Apr 20	12LTS29	300305
France	UK Great Britain	26 Apr 20	1LTS287	300023
France	Germany	05 May 20	8LTS55	300206
France	Germany	01 Jul 20	8LTS87	300209
Germany	Poland	20 Sep 20	9LTS103	300246
Danzig	Poland	09 Nov 20	6LTS189	300153
Germany	Switzerland	06 Dec 20	2LTS343	300088
Czechoslovakia	Germany	03 Feb 21	5LTS246	300132
Denmark	UK Great Britain	12 Jul 21	8LTS397	300238
Italy	Serb/Croat/Slovene	14 Sep 21	19LTS14	300482
Germany	Poland	12 Apr 22	21LTS327	300548
Czechoslovakia	Germany	08 May 22	23LTS171	300589
Germany	Poland	15 May 22	10LTS37	300273
Multilateral		15 Jun 22	21LTS463	300551
Germany	Poland	21 Jun 22	22LTS7	300552
Germany	Poland	26 Aug 22	26LTS365	300656
Austria	Poland	25 Sep 22	59LTS307	301400
Finland	USSR (Soviet Union)	21 Oct 22	29LTS197	300742
Italy	Serb/Croat/Slovene	23 Oct 22	18LTS441	300480
Finland	USSR (Soviet Union)	28 Oct 22	29LTS211	300743
Canada	USA (United States)	02 Mar 23	32LTS93	300809
Liechtenstein	Switzerland	29 Mar 23	21LTS231	300545
France	India	12 May 23	25LTS381	300627
Finland	USSR (Soviet Union)	28 Jul 23	32LTS101	300810
Finland	Sweden	29 Nov 23	23LTS41	300575
Bulgaria	Romania	19 Apr 24	33LTS209	300845
Sweden	USA (United States)	22 May 24	29LTS421	300752
Norway	USA (United States)	24 May 24	26LTS43	300639
Panama	USA (United States)	06 Jun 24	138LTS397	303200
Italy	Serb/Croat/Slovene	12 Aug 24	82LTS423	301882
Denmark	Germany	29 Nov 24	31LTS131	300790
France	Saar	15 Jan 25	44LTS181	301082
Finland	Sweden	09 May 25	47LTS283	301136
Bel-Lux Econ Union	Japan	27 Jun 25	36LTS95	300907
Belgium	Netherlands	28 Aug 25	93LTS431	302131
France	Hungary	13 Oct 25	48LTS9	301150
Belgium	USA (United States)	09 Dec 25	72LTS171	301690
Estonia	Latvia	02 Feb 26	64LTS413	301514
France	India	19 Jun 26	57LTS35	301350
Other Unilat Decla	Rhine Navigation	10 Sep 26	62LTS141	301462
Multilateral		13 Nov 26	77LTS249	301773
Austria	Czechoslovakia	15 Feb 27	73LTS349	301724
Austria	Switzerland	15 Mar 27	87LTS351	301981
Germany	Lithuania	29 Jan 28	89LTS309	302026
Germany	Lithuania	29 Jan 28	89LTS97	302009
Germany	Lithuania	29 Jan 28	90LTS233	302042

Investigation of violations (Cont.)

PARTY ONE	PARTY TWO	DATE	CITATION	NUMBER
Multilateral		20 Feb 28	86LTS111	301950
Austria	Serb/Croat/Slovene	01 May 28	96LTS373	302214
Austria	Italy	11 May 28	100LTS375	302307
Austria	Italy	11 May 28	100LTS41	302293
Czechoslovakia	Germany	05 Jun 28	177LTS19	302700
Austria	Czechoslovakia	12 Dec 28	108LTS9	302501
Finland	Hungary	12 Dec 28	96LTS67	302191
Germany	USSR (Soviet Union)	25 Jan 29	90LTS219	302041
Latvia	Poland	12 Feb 29	101LTS75	302321
Czechoslovakia	Germany	20 Mar 29	109LTS219	302541
Multilateral		20 Apr 29	112LTS371	302623
Bulgaria	Yugoslavia	26 Sep 29	101LTS217	302324
Poland	Romania	30 Oct 29	121LTS167	302787
Austria	Poland	10 Apr 30	108LTS289	302514
Austria	Germany	12 Apr 30	115LTS297	302693
Chile	USA (United States)	27 May 30	133LTS141	303064
Czechoslovakia	Romania	15 Jul 30	164LTS157	303793
Czechoslovakia	Romania	22 Dec 30	168LTS209	303900
Greece	UK Great Britain	17 Apr 31	129LTS287	302965
Hungary	Romania	12 Aug 31	186LTS325	304321
Multilateral		10 Dec 31	129LTS177	302961
Turkey	Yugoslavia	14 Apr 32	144LTS291	303332
France	India	28 Dec 32	140LTS36	303226
Romania	Yugoslavia	10 Feb 33	174LTS115	304042
Brazil	Portugal	26 Aug 33	179LTS63	304134
France	UK Great Britain	18 Jan 34	171LTS183	303960
Albania	Czechoslovakia	14 Apr 34	188LTS255	304362
Belgium	UK Great Britain	02 May 34	173LTS291	304020
Czechoslovakia	Romania	20 Jun 34	168LTS257	303903
Czechoslovakia	Luxembourg	01 Dec 34	168LTS287	303906
Poland	Spain	14 Dec 34	168LTS315	303908
France	South Africa	11 Feb 35	189LTS17	304372
Bulgaria	Romania	26 Jul 35	198LTS9	304621
Estonia	Italy	10 Aug 35	185LTS287	304295
Finland	Germany	25 Sep 35	173LTS11	304001
Denmark	Sweden	28 Oct 35	166LTS299	303845
Multilateral		14 Nov 35	166LTS75	303831
France	Spain	21 Dec 35	167LTS9	303856
France	India	04 Jan 36	170LTS97	303930
UK Great Britain	Yugoslavia	27 Feb 36	181LTS241	304193
Greece	UK Great Britain	27 Feb 36	185LTS113	304278
Hungary	Poland	24 Apr 36	181LTS115	304183
France	Sweden	04 Dec 36	184LTS35	304241
France	USA (United States)	12 Dec 36	176LTS403	304076
Belgium	Norway	17 Dec 36	178LTS153	304110
Greece	Turkey	15 Jan 37	202LTS107	304739
Multilateral		03 Mar 37	182LTS127	304205
Multilateral		08 Jun 37	190LTS79	304406
Canada	USA (United States)	07 Jan 38	184LTS305	304255
France	Switzerland	31 Jan 38	195LTS313	304553
Dominican Republic	Haiti	31 Jan 38	187LTS169	304336
Finland	Norway	21 Apr 38	188LTS231	304361
Finland	Norway	21 Apr 38	188LTS215	304360
Greece	Portugal	15 Aug 38	201LTS201	304707
Cuba	Portugal	06 Sep 38	195LTS443	304565
Multilateral		05 Feb 39	196LTS303	304592
Greece	Turkey	07 Mar 39	201LTS239	304717
Sweden	USA (United States)	23 Mar 39	199LTS17	304661
Multilateral		23 May 39	202LTS159	304742
Greece	UK Great Britain	30 May 39	202LTS7	304732
Latvia	UK Great Britain	23 Aug 39	201LTS37	304702
USA (United States)	Venezuela	06 Nov 39	203LTS273	304770
Japan	UK Great Britain	22 Mar 40	203LTS194	304760
Austria	Greece	28 Mar 74*	2LTS169	300063

Penal sanctions

PARTY ONE	PARTY TWO	DATE	CITATION	NUMBER
Cuba	Netherlands	31 Dec 13	14LTS29	300366
Bolivia	UK Great Britain	05 Apr 20	1LTS271	300020
Germany	USSR (Soviet Union)	19 Apr 20	2LTS63	300048
Czechoslovakia	Germany	29 Jun 20	17LTS69	300430
Germany	Poland	20 Sep 20	9LTS103	300246
Czechoslovakia	Germany	03 Feb 21	5LTS246	300132
Germany	Poland	10 Apr 21	6LTS233	300158
Denmark	UK Great Britain	12 Jul 21	8LTS397	300238
Multilateral		31 Mar 22	9LTS415	300269
Germany	Poland	12 Apr 22	21LTS327	300548
Germany	Poland	21 Jun 22	22LTS7	300552
Italy	Serb/Croat/Slovene	23 Oct 22	18LTS441	300480
Liechtenstein	Switzerland	29 Mar 23	21LTS231	300545
Austria	Germany	21 Jun 23	27LTS57	300668
Bulgaria	Serb/Croat/Slovene	26 Nov 23	26LTS119	300643
Bulgaria	Serb/Croat/Slovene	26 Nov 23	26LTS85	300642
Bulgaria	Romania	19 Apr 24	33LTS209	300845
Czechoslovakia	France	18 Aug 24	44LTS21	301080
France	Saar	15 Jan 25	44LTS181	301082
Multilateral		11 Feb 25	51LTS337	301239
Spain	USA (United States)	10 Feb 26	67LTS131	301543
United Arab Rep	Greece	10 Apr 26	61LTS305	301441
Multilateral		25 Sep 26	60LTS253	301414
Greece	UK Great Britain	13 May 27	61LTS15	301425
Multilateral		20 Feb 28	86LTS111	301950
Estonia	Latvia	15 May 28	74LTS281	301742
El Salvador	USA (United States)	05 Sep 30	134LTS207	303093
Czechoslovakia	Romania	22 Dec 30	168LTS209	303900
Hungary	Romania	12 Aug 31	186LTS325	304321
Hungary	Poland	04 Nov 31	134LTS199	303092
Spain	UK Great Britain	26 May 32	132LTS43	303030
Estonia	Spain	23 Jun 32	143LTS31	303303
Belgium	Bolivia	06 Jan 33	147LTS59	303390
Finland	UK Great Britain	13 Oct 33	142LTS187	303291
France	UK Great Britain	18 Jan 34	171LTS183	303960
Belgium	UK Great Britain	02 May 34	173LTS291	304020
Brazil	Chile	08 Nov 35	181LTS297	304197
Multilateral		14 Nov 35	166LTS75	303831
Honduras	USA (United States)	18 Dec 35	167LTS313	303876
France	Spain	21 Dec 35	167LTS9	303856
Nicaragua	USA (United States)	11 Mar 36	173LTS141	304009
Multilateral		26 Jun 36	198LTS299	304648
Greece	Portugal	15 Aug 38	201LTS201	304707
Cuba	Portugal	06 Sep 38	195LTS443	304565

Establishment of commission

PARTY ONE	PARTY TWO	DATE	CITATION	NUMBER
Argentina	Uruguay	11 Apr 18	14LTS367	300385
Brazil	UK Great Britain	04 Apr 19	5LTS45	300116
France	Italy	30 Sep 19	5LTS279	300133
Bulgaria	Greece	27 Nov 19	1LTS67	300009
France	Germany	01 Mar 20	1LTS367	300030
Estonia	Latvia	22 Mar 20	2LTS187	300066
Chile	Sweden	26 Mar 20	4LTS271	300111
France	Greece	20 Apr 20	3LTS93	300093
Austria	Czechoslovakia	07 Jun 20	3LTS189	300098
Czechoslovakia	Germany	29 Jun 20	20LTS85	300509
Lithuania	USSR (Soviet Union)	12 Jul 20	3LTS106	300094
Germany	Latvia	15 Jul 20	2LTS91	300052
Multilateral		05 Aug 20	2LTS49	300046
Multilateral		10 Aug 20	28LTS225	300710
Latvia	USSR (Soviet Union)	11 Aug 20	2LTS195	300067
Finland	USSR (Soviet Union)	14 Oct 20	3LTS5	300091
Germany	Poland	02 Nov 20	2LTS277	300081
Danzig	Poland	09 Nov 20	6LTS189	300153

Establishment of commission (Cont.)

PARTY ONE	PARTY TWO	DATE	CITATION	NUMBER
Germany	Poland	08 Dec 20	7LTS323	300199
France	UK Great Britain	23 Dec 20	22LTS353	300564
France	Hungary	31 Jan 21	15LTS221	300396
Germany	Poland	12 Feb 21	9LTS149	300247
Poland	USSR (Soviet Union)	18 Mar 21	6LTS51	300149
Latvia	Lithuania	13 May 21	17LTS211	300438
Germany	Saar	03 Jun 21	5LTS189	300129
Norway	USA (United States)	30 Jun 21	14LTS19	300365
Italy	Serb/Croat/Slovene	14 Sep 21	19LTS14	300482
Estonia	Ukrainian SSR	25 Nov 21	11LTS121	300294
France	Poland	06 Feb 22	43LTS415	301074
Colombia	Peru	24 Mar 22	74LTS9	301726
China	Japan	28 Mar 22	13LTS213	300353
Italy	UK Great Britain	11 May 22	11LTS23	300288
Finland	USSR (Soviet Union)	01 Jun 22	16LTS319	300415
Germany	Poland	15 Jun 22	34LTS201	300875
Germany	Poland	23 Jun 22	22LTS25	300553
Multilateral		04 Oct 22	12LTS391	300335
Czechoslovakia	Romania	14 Oct 22	25LTS163	300604
Italy	Serb/Croat/Slovene	23 Oct 22	18LTS461	300481
France	UK Great Britain	26 Dec 22	16LTS213	300413
Germany	Poland	27 Jan 23	26LTS461	300663
Greece	Turkey	30 Jan 23	32LTS75	300807
Greece	Turkey	30 Jan 23	36LTS137	300912
Canada	USA (United States)	02 Mar 23	32LTS93	300809
Multilateral		29 Mar 23	23LTS256	300593
Multilateral		03 May 23	33LTS25	300831
United Arab Rep	UK Great Britain	18 Jul 23	18LTS323	300474
Multilateral		24 Jul 23	28LTS11	300701
Multilateral		24 Jul 23	28LTS139	300703
Multilateral		29 Sep 23	20LTS41	300504
Other Unilat Decla	Greece	29 Sep 23	20LTS29	300503
Estonia	Latvia	01 Nov 23	25LTS354	300624
Multilateral		23 Nov 23	28LTS273	300713
Bulgaria	Serb/Croat/Slovene	26 Nov 23	26LTS85	300642
Multilateral		18 Dec 23	28LTS541	300729
Belgium	USA (United States)	21 Jan 24	31LTS137	300791
Hungary	Romania	14 Apr 24	46LTS41	301113
Hungary	Romania	16 Apr 24	46LTS27	301112
China	USSR (Soviet Union)	31 May 24	37LTS193	300956
Sweden	Switzerland	02 Jun 24	33LTS199	300844
Denmark	Switzerland	06 Jun 24	34LTS175	300873
Finland	USSR (Soviet Union)	18 Jun 24	47LTS241	301134
Hungary	Switzerland	18 Jun 24	34LTS387	300887
Denmark	Sweden	27 Jun 24	33LTS149	300840
Denmark	Finland	27 Jun 24	33LTS131	300839
Denmark	Norway	27 Jun 24	33LTS173	300842
Norway	Sweden	27 Jun 24	28LTS309	300717
Finland	Norway	27 Jun 24	29LTS403	300751
Spain	UK Great Britain	27 Jun 24	28LTS523	300727
Finland	Sweden	27 Jun 24	29LTS19	300731
Italy	UK Great Britain	15 Jul 24	36LTS379	300936
Colombia	Panama	20 Aug 24	33LTS167	300841
Other Unilat Decla	Greece	19 Sep 24	30LTS413	300776
Italy	Switzerland	20 Sep 24	33LTS91	300834
Other Unilat Decla	Bulgaria	29 Sep 24	29LTS117	300737
Other Unilat Decla	Greece	29 Sep 24	29LTS123	300738
Austria	Switzerland	11 Oct 24	33LTS423	300862
Multilateral		23 Oct 24	77LTS367	301778
Allied Powers	Germany	28 Oct 24	41LTS461	301025
Multilateral		26 Nov 24	48LTS69	301151
Multilateral		19 Feb 25	81LTS317	301845
Germany	Mexico	16 Mar 25	52LTS93	301251
Latvia	Sweden	28 Mar 25	37LTS131	300952
Multilateral		05 May 25	55LTS225	301318

Establishment of commission (Cont.)

PARTY ONE	PARTY TWO	DATE	CITATION	NUMBER
Belgium	Poland	01 Sep 25	54LTS69	301274
Estonia	Latvia	28 Oct 25	54LTS231	301286
Multilateral		31 Dec 25	79LTS167	301809
Germany	Poland	27 Jan 26	64LTS113	301504
Estonia	Latvia	05 Feb 26	64LTS361	301509
France	Turkey	30 May 26	54LTS195	301285
France	Turkey	31 Jul 26	54LTS177	301284
Denmark	Switzerland	25 Aug 26	69LTS313	301613
France	Switzerland	27 Aug 26	71LTS63	301654
Multilateral		13 Nov 26	77LTS217	301772
Other Unilat Decla	Estonia	10 Dec 26	62LTS277	301467
Estonia	Latvia	05 Feb 27	62LTS319	301470
Germany	Poland	11 Apr 27	69LTS419	301621
Brazil	UK Great Britain	22 Apr 27	92LTS311	302097
Belgium	UK Great Britain	03 May 27	140LTS71	303229
Multilateral		28 Jul 27	64LTS379	301511
Portugal	Spain	11 Aug 27	82LTS113	301864
Italy	Spain	15 Aug 27	94LTS361	302155
Germany	Lithuania	29 Jan 28	89LTS97	302009
Czechoslovakia	Poland	18 Feb 28	100LTS273	302301
Hungary	Serb/Croat/Slovene	22 Feb 28	88LTS111	301991
Hungary	Serb/Croat/Slovene	22 Feb 28	87LTS361	301982
Afghanistan	Persia	26 Jun 28	106LTS321	302453
Abyssinia	Italy	02 Aug 28	94LTS423	302159
Finland	USSR (Soviet Union)	24 Sep 28	82LTS63	301860
Multilateral		26 Sep 28	93LTS343	302123
Italy	Spain	03 Oct 28	94LTS387	302156
Brazil	Colombia	15 Nov 28	100LTS123	302299
Austria	Czechoslovakia	12 Dec 28	107LTS137	302474
Dominican Republic	Haiti	21 Jan 29	105LTS193	302413
Norway	Sweden	11 May 29	120LTS263	302771
Multilateral		30 Aug 29	104LTS473	302399
Bulgaria	Yugoslavia	26 Sep 29	101LTS217	302324
Brazil	Venezuela	07 Nov 29	99LTS427	302288
Czechoslovakia	Poland	21 Dec 29	115LTS201	302687
Multilateral		20 Jan 30	112LTS361	302622
Bulgaria	Yugoslavia	14 Feb 30	101LTS135	302323
Brazil	UK Great Britain	18 Mar 30	101LTS401	302339
Canada	USA (United States)	09 May 30	121LTS45	302782
Czechoslovakia	Romania	15 Jul 30	164LTS157	303793
China	UK Great Britain	22 Sep 30	115LTS493	302697
Czechoslovakia	Romania	22 Dec 30	167LTS243	303870
Latvia	Lithuania	25 Jan 31	118LTS175	302722
Bulgaria	Spain	26 Jun 31	166LTS341	303850
Guatemala	UK Great Britain	26 Aug 31	128LTS427	302946
Poland	Yugoslavia	02 Dec 31	139LTS119	303207
Brazil	Paraguay	09 Dec 31	136LTS427	303142
Turkey	Yugoslavia	14 Apr 32	144LTS291	303332
Panama	USA (United States)	17 Dec 32	138LTS119	303183
Romania	Yugoslavia	10 Mar 33	146LTS245	303374
Romania	Yugoslavia	11 Mar 33	146LTS277	303378
Hungary	Yugoslavia	15 May 33	144LTS321	303335
Romania	Turkey	17 Oct 33	165LTS273	303814
Multilateral		07 May 34	171LTS203	303961
Colombia	Peru	24 May 34	164LTS21	303786
Germany	Netherlands	06 Jun 34	174LTS33	304034
Hungary	Italy	18 Nov 34	166LTS263	303842
Dominican Republic	Haiti	27 Feb 35	171LTS89	303953
Multilateral		09 Apr 35	163LTS177	303766
Afghanistan	USSR (Soviet Union)	06 May 35	164LTS335	303800
Belgium	Germany	10 May 35	182LTS335	304221
Belgium	Germany	10 May 35	165LTS169	303808
Norway	Venezuela	13 May 35	167LTS407	303882
Poland	Romania	17 May 35	173LTS373	304028
Italy	Netherlands	29 Jul 35	165LTS329	303819

PARTY ONE	PARTY TWO	DATE	CITATION	NUMBER
Establishment of commission (Cont.)				
Bulgaria	Yugoslavia	09 Nov 35	194LTS89	304511
Germany	Latvia	04 Dec 35	166LTS93	303834
Bulgaria	Denmark	07 Dec 35	182LTS183	304211
Denmark	Yugoslavia	14 Dec 35	184LTS99	304245
Multilateral		20 Dec 35	167LTS141	303862
Spain	UK Great Britain	06 Jan 36	166LTS283	303844
Panama	USA (United States)	02 Mar 36	200LTS205	304692
Albania	Italy	19 Mar 36	173LTS51	304002
Iraq	UK Great Britain	31 Mar 36	172LTS175	303988
Multilateral		26 Jun 36	198LTS299	304648
Multilateral		20 Jul 36	173LTS213	304015
Romania	Turkey	04 Sep 36	195LTS429	304564
Hungary	Yugoslavia	17 Dec 36	196LTS137	304576
Multilateral		23 Dec 36	188LTS53	304352
Czechoslovakia	Italy	31 Mar 37	193LTS165	304492
Multilateral		02 Jun 37	184LTS445	304265
Bel-Lux Econ Union	Italy	30 Jun 37	197LTS23	304601
Germany	Netherlands	30 Jun 37	189LTS373	304395
Bulgaria	Romania	20 Jul 37	202LTS33	304733
Czechoslovakia	Hungary	24 Aug 37	189LTS403	304397
Bel-Lux Econ Union	Yugoslavia	26 Nov 37	196LTS19	304567
Germany	Netherlands	18 Dec 37	190LTS29	304403
Canada	USA (United States)	07 Jan 38	184LTS305	304255
France	Switzerland	31 Jan 38	195LTS313	304553
Argentina	Netherlands	06 Sep 38	194LTS409	304531
France	Romania	31 Mar 39	199LTS219	304677
Multilateral		03 Apr 39	195LTS471	304566
Romania	UK Great Britain	11 May 39	196LTS351	304594
Panama	USA (United States)	04 Jan 40	202LTS421	304744
Spain	UK Great Britain	18 Mar 40	203LTS157	304759
Canada	USA (United States)	07 Nov 40	203LTS267	304769
UK Great Britain	Venezuela	26 Feb 42	205LTS121	304829
Extraterritorial rights				
Great Britain	Japan	30 Jul 25	65LTS29	301517
Multilateral		21 Jun 26	78LTS229	301793
Netherlands	Spain	27 Mar 29	101LTS479	302346
Multilateral		17 Feb 30	102LTS87	302354
China	Norway	23 Apr 31	119LTS9	302736
Multilateral		10 Dec 31	129LTS177	302961
Multilateral		26 Jun 36	198LTS299	304648
Abolition of treaty ports				
Belgium	China	31 Aug 29	123LTS105	302810
Abolition of extraterritorial rights				
Lithuania	UK Great Britain	06 May 22	13LTS25	300343
Romania	UK Great Britain	24 May 23	18LTS301	300471
Multilateral		24 Jul 23	28LTS151	300704
Belgium	China	31 Aug 29	123LTS105	302810
Dispute settlement				
Brazil	Spain	08 Apr 09	88LTS86	301987
Spain	USA (United States)	15 Sep 14	89LTS427	302030
Multilateral		09 Dec 23	47LTS55	301129
Greece	Switzerland	21 Sep 25	87LTS187	301969
Belgium	Switzerland	05 Feb 27	68LTS45	301567
France	USA (United States)	06 Feb 28	91LTS323	302072
France	Sweden	03 Mar 28	95LTS89	302168
Italy	Turkey	30 May 28	95LTS183	302172
Denmark	USA (United States)	14 Jun 28	88LTS173	301995
Austria	USA (United States)	16 Aug 28	88LTS101	301989
Czechoslovakia	USA (United States)	16 Aug 28	89LTS219	302017
Czechoslovakia	USA (United States)	16 Aug 28	89LTS225	302018
Finland	Italy	21 Aug 28	89LTS25	302002
Multilateral		26 Sep 28	93LTS343	302123
Greece	USA (United States)	19 Jun 30	136LTS393	303137

PARTY ONE	PARTY TWO	DATE	CITATION	NUMBER
Dispute settlement (Cont.)				
Austria	Greece	26 Jun 30	119LTS353	302755
Czechoslovakia	Persia	29 Oct 30	121LTS53	302783
Hungary	Yugoslavia	30 Jan 31	120LTS105	302761
Liberia	USA (United States)	21 Aug 39	204LTS165	304795
Arbitration				
Argentina	Venezuela	22 Jul 11	28LTS287	300715
Chile	Colombia	16 Nov 14	114LTS111	302659
Peru	Uruguay	18 Jul 17	14LTS359	300384
Estonia	Latvia	22 Mar 20	2LTS187	300066
Netherlands	Venezuela	11 May 20	7LTS85	300176
Czechoslovakia	Germany	29 Jun 20	20LTS85	300509
Latvia	Lithuania	28 Sep 20	2LTS234	300068
Liechtenstein	Switzerland	10 Nov 20	2LTS305	300084
Belgium	France	14 Feb 21	12LTS245	300317
Multilateral		20 Apr 21	7LTS11	300171
Germany	Poland	21 Apr 21	12LTS61	300308
Austria	Czechoslovakia	04 May 21	15LTS13	300388
Germany	USSR (Soviet Union)	06 May 21	6LTS267	300159
Peru	USA (United States)	21 May 21	6LTS171	300150
Afghanistan	Persia	22 Jun 21	33LTS285	300853
Norway	USA (United States)	30 Jun 21	14LTS19	300365
Multilateral		12 Jul 21	11LTS111	300293
Peru	UK Great Britain	27 Aug 21	7LTS289	300195
Multilateral		15 Sep 21	30LTS141	300767
Austria	Hungary	08 Oct 21	16LTS19	300402
Estonia	Finland	29 Oct 21	13LTS59	300348
Germany	Switzerland	03 Dec 21	12LTS271	300320
Austria	Czechoslovakia	16 Dec 21	9LTS247	300257
Costa Rica	UK Great Britain	12 Jan 22	17LTS151	300432
France	Poland	06 Feb 22	43LTS399	301073
Multilateral		17 Mar 22	11LTS167	300296
Spain	Uruguay	23 Mar 22	63LTS233	301493
Colombia	Peru	24 Mar 22	74LTS9	301726
Germany	Poland	18 Jun 22	34LTS235	300876
Germany	Poland	21 Jun 22	22LTS7	300552
Germany	Poland	23 Jun 22	22LTS25	300553
Chile	Peru	20 Jul 22	21LTS141	300537
Germany	Poland	01 Aug 22	34LTS253	300877
Czechoslovakia	Latvia	07 Oct 22	20LTS379	300528
Belgium	Poland	30 Dec 22	21LTS201	300543
Uruguay	Venezuela	28 Feb 23	36LTS451	300942
Czechoslovakia	Hungary	08 Mar 23	48LTS257	301167
Germany	UK Great Britain	05 Apr 23	17LTS173	300435
Austria	Hungary	10 Apr 23	18LTS93	300457
Multilateral		03 May 23	33LTS25	300831
Multilateral		03 May 23	33LTS81	300833
Germany	Lithuania	31 May 23	51LTS381	301243
Multilateral		24 Jul 23	28LTS11	300701
Multilateral		24 Sep 23	27LTS157	300678
Austria	Poland	13 Nov 23	34LTS399	300888
Norway	USA (United States)	26 Nov 23	23LTS249	300592
Multilateral		09 Dec 23	58LTS284	301379
Czechoslovakia	France	25 Jan 24	23LTS163	300588
Iraq	UK Great Britain	25 Mar 24	35LTS35	300891
Hungary	Italy	27 Mar 24	45LTS83	301100
Hungary	Romania	28 May 24	27LTS117	300674
Hungary	Switzerland	18 Jun 24	34LTS387	300887
Sweden	USA (United States)	24 Jun 24	33LTS273	300851
France	USA (United States)	30 Jun 24	61LTS415	301451
Italy	Serb/Croat/Slovene	14 Jul 24	82LTS257	301876
Italy	Serb/Croat/Slovene	14 Jul 24	82LTS327	301877
Italy	UK Great Britain	15 Jul 24	36LTS379	300936
Austria	Romania	26 Jul 24	85LTS223	301933
Austria	Latvia	09 Aug 24	65LTS7	301516

PARTY ONE	PARTY TWO	DATE	CITATION	NUMBER
Arbitration (Cont.)				
Latvia	Norway	14 Aug 24	36LTS211	300924
Multilateral		28 Aug 24	40LTS19	301002
Germany	Sweden	29 Aug 24	42LTS111	301036
Germany	Saar	20 Sep 24	30LTS121	300765
France	Mexico	25 Sep 24	79LTS417	301818
El Salvador	Uruguay	07 Nov 24	108LTS103	302502
Multilateral		17 Jan 25	38LTS357	300991
Netherlands	USA (United States)	23 Jan 25	33LTS445	300864
Poland	Switzerland	07 Mar 25	50LTS261	301209
Finland	Germany	14 Mar 25	43LTS347	301070
Germany	Poland	14 Mar 25	95LTS239	302178
France	Switzerland	06 Apr 25	147LTS89	303393
France	Germany	13 Apr 25	109LTS295	302546
Estonia	Finland	20 Apr 25	51LTS31	301220
Czechoslovakia	Poland	23 Apr 25	48LTS383	301171
Czechoslovakia	Poland	23 Apr 25	48LTS287	301170
Multilateral		05 May 25	55LTS225	301318
Norway	UK Great Britain	13 May 25	36LTS435	300940
Great Britain	Japan	30 Jul 25	65LTS29	301517
Estonia	Germany	10 Aug 25	63LTS111	301484
Belgium	Netherlands	28 Aug 25	93LTS431	302131
Germany	USSR (Soviet Union)	12 Oct 25	53LTS7	301257
Germany	Poland	16 Oct 25	54LTS327	301295
Belgium	Germany	16 Oct 25	54LTS303	301293
France	Germany	16 Oct 25	54LTS315	301294
Czechoslovakia	Germany	16 Oct 25	54LTS341	301296
Poland	Sweden	03 Nov 25	62LTS263	301466
Norway	Sweden	25 Nov 25	60LTS295	301417
Belgium	USA (United States)	09 Dec 25	72LTS171	301690
Norway	USSR (Soviet Union)	15 Dec 25	47LTS9	301127
Czechoslovakia	Sweden	02 Jan 26	48LTS173	301159
Denmark	Sweden	14 Jan 26	51LTS251	301235
Denmark	Norway	15 Jan 26	60LTS311	301418
Finland	Sweden	29 Jan 26	49LTS367	301192
Denmark	Finland	30 Jan 26	51LTS367	301242
Finland	Norway	03 Feb 26	60LTS353	301420
Romania	Switzerland	03 Feb 26	55LTS91	301306
Austria	Czechoslovakia	05 Mar 26	51LTS349	301240
Poland	Romania	26 Mar 26	60LTS161	301411
Germany	Poland	27 Mar 26	64LTS249	301506
Austria	Poland	16 Apr 26	62LTS329	301471
Denmark	Poland	23 Apr 26	61LTS245	301437
Czechoslovakia	Italy	04 May 26	61LTS257	301438
Germany	Netherlands	20 May 26	66LTS103	301527
Belgium	Germany	29 May 26	127LTS149	302916
France	Romania	10 Jun 26	58LTS233	301374
Germany	Poland	16 Jun 26	65LTS379	301522
Portugal	South Africa	01 Jul 26	70LTS315	301643
Germany	Latvia	09 Jul 26	63LTS321	301499
Bel-Lux Econ Union	Siam	13 Jul 26	62LTS287	301468
Germany	Switzerland	14 Jul 26	59LTS87	301391
Hungary	UK Great Britain	23 Jul 26	67LTS183	301546
Italy	Spain	07 Aug 26	67LTS365	301558
France	Switzerland	27 Aug 26	71LTS63	301654
Haiti	Netherlands	07 Sep 26	71LTS219	301665
Other Unilat Decla	Rhine Navigation	10 Sep 26	62LTS141	301462
Italy	Romania	16 Sep 26	67LTS393	301560
Poland	Serb/Croat/Slovene	18 Sep 26	78LTS419	301800
Bel-Lux Econ Union	Estonia	28 Sep 26	62LTS433	301475
Albania	Greece	13 Oct 26	83LTS325	301899
Belgium	Luxembourg	20 Oct 26	78LTS375	301796
Greece	Italy	24 Oct 26	63LTS51	301480
Mexico	UK Great Britain	19 Nov 26	85LTS51	301922
Albania	Italy	27 Nov 26	60LTS15	301402
Greece	Switzerland	29 Nov 26	63LTS27	301478
Arbitration (Cont.)				
Czechoslovakia	Denmark	30 Nov 26	67LTS105	301541
Denmark	Estonia	18 Dec 26	63LTS363	301500
Germany	Italy	29 Dec 26	78LTS383	301797
Czechoslovakia	Germany	22 Jan 27	89LTS231	302019
Estonia	Latvia	05 Feb 27	62LTS319	301470
Chile	Norway	09 Feb 27	80LTS325	301837
Czechoslovakia	Switzerland	16 Feb 27	64LTS7	301501
Denmark	Germany	23 Feb 27	61LTS325	301444
Chile	France	24 Feb 27	69LTS277	301610
Belgium	Finland	04 Mar 27	69LTS361	301618
Austria	Switzerland	15 Mar 27	87LTS351	301981
Hungary	Italy	05 Apr 27	67LTS399	301561
Czechoslovakia	Greece	07 Apr 27	88LTS211	301998
Brazil	UK Great Britain	22 Apr 27	92LTS311	302097
Guatemala	Netherlands	12 May 27	85LTS323	301937
Serb/Croat/Slovene	UK Great Britain	12 May 27	80LTS165	301825
Chile	Spain	28 May 27	71LTS329	301673
Czechoslovakia	Poland	30 May 27	98LTS233	302251
Czechoslovakia	Hungary	31 May 27	65LTS61	301520
Greece	Norway	29 Jun 27	82LTS187	301869
Belgium	Portugal	09 Jul 27	74LTS39	301730
Belgium	Spain	19 Jul 27	80LTS17	301820
Czechoslovakia	Estonia	20 Jul 27	77LTS341	301776
Belgium	Portugal	20 Jul 27	71LTS431	301681
Belgium	Portugal	21 Jul 27	71LTS439	301682
France	Germany	17 Aug 27	76LTS5	301761
Colombia	Switzerland	20 Aug 27	111LTS229	302589
Italy	Lithuania	17 Sep 27	73LTS9	301701
Multilateral		26 Sep 27	92LTS301	302096
Germany	Serb/Croat/Slovene	06 Oct 27	77LTS19	301763
Latvia	USSR (Soviet Union)	10 Oct 27	84LTS47	301903
Belgium	Luxembourg	17 Oct 27	124LTS203	302834
France	Luxembourg	20 Oct 27	106LTS457	302462
Greece	Serb/Croat/Slovene	02 Nov 27	91LTS137	302060
Multilateral		08 Nov 27	97LTS391	302238
France	Serb/Croat/Slovene	11 Nov 27	68LTS381	301593
Multilateral		25 Nov 27	84LTS97	301905
Germany	Poland	07 Dec 27	92LTS203	302088
Germany	Lithuania	29 Jan 28	89LTS338	302027
Germany	Lithuania	29 Jan 28	90LTS233	302042
France	USA (United States)	06 Feb 28	91LTS323	302072
Multilateral		20 Feb 28	86LTS111	301950
Hungary	Serb/Croat/Slovene	22 Feb 28	87LTS361	301982
Hungary	Serb/Croat/Slovene	22 Feb 28	100LTS345	302306
France	Sweden	03 Mar 28	95LTS89	302168
France	Netherlands	10 Mar 28	102LTS109	302356
Denmark	Spain	14 Mar 28	74LTS93	301735
Greece	Romania	21 Mar 28	108LTS187	302508
Denmark	Haiti	05 Apr 28	99LTS19	302264
Italy	USA (United States)	19 Apr 28	113LTS183	302645
Spain	Sweden	26 Apr 28	77LTS77	301764
Germany	USA (United States)	05 May 28	90LTS177	302035
Czechoslovakia	Hungary	26 May 28	101LTS265	302328
Italy	Turkey	30 May 28	95LTS183	302172
Finland	Spain	31 May 28	82LTS229	301874
Finland	USA (United States)	07 Jun 28	87LTS9	301958
Austria	Spain	11 Jun 28	87LTS393	301984
Denmark	USA (United States)	14 Jun 28	88LTS173	301995
Luxembourg	Spain	21 Jun 28	109LTS137	302533
Hungary	Italy	04 Jul 28	92LTS117	302083
France	Portugal	06 Jul 28	126LTS27	302869
France	Spain	16 Jul 28	135LTS149	303110
Germany	UK Great Britain	26 Jul 28	85LTS135	301928
Abyssinia	Italy	02 Aug 28	94LTS413	302158
Austria	USA (United States)	16 Aug 28	88LTS95	301988

PARTY ONE	PARTY TWO	DATE	CITATION	NUMBER
Arbitration (Cont.)				
Poland	USA (United States)	16 Aug 28	99LTS409	302286
Czechoslovakia	USA (United States)	16 Aug 28	89LTS225	302018
Denmark	Greece	22 Aug 28	94LTS263	302147
Multilateral		26 Sep 28	93LTS343	302123
Portugal	Switzerland	17 Oct 28	96LTS287	302207
Albania	USA (United States)	22 Oct 28	92LTS217	302089
Sweden	USA (United States)	27 Oct 28	91LTS225	302063
Luxembourg	Poland	29 Oct 28	111LTS71	302581
Germany	Romania	10 Nov 28	91LTS101	302058
Lithuania	USA (United States)	14 Nov 28	100LTS111	302297
Czechoslovakia	Serb/Croat/Slovene	14 Nov 28	97LTS9	302216
Czechoslovakia	Hungary	14 Nov 28	110LTS425	302574
Czechoslovakia	Spain	16 Nov 28	100LTS313	302303
Hungary	Serb/Croat/Slovene	19 Nov 28	97LTS101	302222
Hungary	Poland	30 Nov 28	100LTS67	302294
Poland	Spain	03 Dec 28	101LTS501	302348
Estonia	Germany	07 Dec 28	99LTS259	302273
Switzerland	Turkey	09 Dec 28	159LTS219	303664
Austria	Estonia	11 Dec 28	92LTS229	302091
Austria	Czechoslovakia	12 Dec 28	108LTS9	302501
Finland	Hungary	12 Dec 28	96LTS67	302191
Norway	Spain	27 Dec 28	97LTS339	302231
Hungary	Turkey	05 Jan 29	100LTS137	302300
Multilateral		05 Jan 29	130LTS135	302988
Dominican Republic	Haiti	20 Jan 29	105LTS215	302414
Serb/Croat/Slovene	USA (United States)	21 Jan 29	93LTS307	302118
Bulgaria	USA (United States)	21 Jan 29	93LTS337	302122
Germany	Norway	23 Jan 29	93LTS197	302110
Hungary	USA (United States)	26 Jan 29	96LTS173	302200
Germany	Persia	17 Feb 29	111LTS19	302576
Norway	USA (United States)	20 Feb 29	91LTS413	302079
Portugal	USA (United States)	01 Mar 29	99LTS375	302282
Bulgaria	Turkey	06 Mar 29	114LTS399	302668
Czechoslovakia	Germany	20 Mar 29	109LTS219	302541
Belgium	USA (United States)	20 Mar 29	109LTS267	302543
Romania	USA (United States)	21 Mar 29	105LTS79	302402
Greece	Serb/Croat/Slovene	27 Mar 29	108LTS201	302509
Poland	Romania	30 Mar 29	123LTS147	302812
Luxembourg	USA (United States)	06 Apr 29	106LTS475	302464
Belgium	Czechoslovakia	29 Apr 29	110LTS113	302556
United Arab Rep	UK Great Britain	07 May 29	93LTS43	302103
France	Persia	10 May 29	150LTS329	303465
Hungary	Lithuania	16 May 29	96LTS333	302211
Germany	Turkey	16 May 29	109LTS451	302549
Estonia	USSR (Soviet Union)	17 May 29	94LTS323	302152
Multilateral		21 May 29	96LTS311	302210
Belgium	Persia	23 May 29	110LTS369	302568
Persia	Sweden	27 May 29	105LTS279	302420
Czechoslovakia	Greece	08 Jun 29	108LTS255	302512
Italy	Norway	10 Jun 29	105LTS161	302410
Hungary	Spain	10 Jun 29	101LTS251	302327
Multilateral		14 Jun 29	94LTS275	302148
Belgium	Greece	25 Jun 29	113LTS117	302640
Multilateral		28 Jun 29	102LTS245	302368
Czechoslovakia	Estonia	09 Jul 29	101LTS423	302341
Colombia	Spain	19 Jul 29	114LTS105	302658
Bulgaria	Hungary	22 Jul 29	101LTS41	302317
Luxembourg	Portugal	15 Aug 29	115LTS77	302678
Iceland	Spain	26 Aug 29	104LTS183	302388
Bel-Lux Econ Union	Switzerland	26 Aug 29	105LTS9	302401
Estonia	USA (United States)	27 Aug 29	102LTS233	302366
Czechoslovakia	Norway	09 Sep 29	101LTS355	302336
Germany	Luxembourg	11 Sep 29	118LTS97	302715
Czechoslovakia	Netherlands	14 Sep 29	107LTS201	302477
Luxembourg	Switzerland	16 Sep 29	107LTS23	302465

PARTY ONE	PARTY TWO	DATE	CITATION	NUMBER
Arbitration (Cont.)				
Luxembourg	Netherlands	17 Sep 29	107LTS35	302466
Czechoslovakia	Luxembourg	18 Sep 29	107LTS49	302467
Czechoslovakia	Switzerland	20 Sep 29	102LTS123	302357
Czechoslovakia	Finland	02 Oct 29	115LTS155	302684
Italy	Panama	16 Oct 29	138LTS355	303199
Poland	Romania	24 Oct 29	100LTS299	302302
Poland	Romania	30 Oct 29	121LTS243	302790
Poland	Romania	30 Oct 29	121LTS167	302787
Germany	Poland	31 Oct 29	124LTS345	302838
Germany	Switzerland	02 Nov 29	109LTS273	302544
Belgium	Germany	07 Nov 29	121LTS327	302795
Multilateral		09 Nov 29	125LTS205	302855
Estonia	Hungary	27 Nov 29	106LTS331	302454
Norway	Poland	09 Dec 29	101LTS325	302334
Estonia	Latvia	20 Dec 29	106LTS173	302444
Germany	UK Great Britain	28 Dec 29	102LTS49	302352
Bulgaria	Poland	31 Dec 29	113LTS89	302638
Netherlands	USA (United States)	13 Jan 30	107LTS69	302468
Lithuania	Persia	13 Jan 30	131LTS221	303013
Latvia	USA (United States)	14 Jan 30	105LTS301	302422
Belgium	Germany	16 Jan 30	104LTS223	302392
Canada	Germany	17 Jan 30	109LTS473	302550
Germany	New Zealand	17 Jan 30	109LTS485	302551
Austria	Belgium	18 Jan 30	104LTS231	302393
Multilateral		20 Jan 30	104LTS243	302394
Austria	Poland	20 Jan 30	133LTS223	303067
Luxembourg	Romania	22 Jan 30	110LTS151	302559
Netherlands	Romania	22 Jan 30	112LTS121	302611
Greece	Spain	23 Jan 30	139LTS93	303205
Austria	Italy	06 Feb 30	105LTS97	302405
Italy	Romania	25 Feb 30	106LTS179	302445
Denmark	Latvia	28 Feb 30	113LTS27	302632
Turkey	UK Great Britain	01 Mar 30	108LTS407	302523
Czechoslovakia	Lithuania	08 Mar 30	115LTS61	302677
Netherlands	Persia	12 Mar 30	111LTS387	302599
Brazil	UK Great Britain	18 Mar 30	101LTS401	302339
Belgium	Yugoslavia	25 Mar 30	106LTS343	302455
Austria	Poland	10 Apr 30	108LTS289	302514
Multilateral		12 Apr 30	178LTS227	304117
Multilateral		12 Apr 30	179LTS89	304137
Multilateral		12 Apr 30	179LTS115	304138
Netherlands	Poland	12 Apr 30	113LTS65	302636
Finland	France	28 Apr 30	139LTS381	303222
Greece	Hungary	05 May 30	118LTS293	302732
Norway	Persia	08 May 30	134LTS153	303089
Poland	Romania	09 May 30	112LTS225	302617
Germany	Irish Free State	12 May 30	131LTS153	303008
Iceland	USA (United States)	15 May 30	108LTS109	302503
Belgium	France	23 May 30	119LTS33	302738
Austria	Hungary	03 Jun 30	122LTS69	302799
France	Italy	03 Jun 30	153LTS135	303513
Greece	Turkey	10 Jun 30	108LTS233	302511
Poland	USA (United States)	19 Jun 30	108LTS223	302515
Poland	Romania	23 Jun 30	133LTS163	303066
Austria	Greece	26 Jun 30	119LTS353	302755
Iceland	Sweden	27 Jun 30	127LTS67	302907
Finland	Iceland	27 Jun 30	167LTS271	303873
Iceland	Norway	27 Jun 30	126LTS417	302900
Denmark	Iceland	27 Jun 30	118LTS121	302717
Belgium	Romania	08 Jul 30	128LTS403	302944
Czechoslovakia	Romania	15 Jul 30	164LTS157	303793
Guatemala	Honduras	16 Jul 30	137LTS231	303159
Norway	Portugal	26 Jul 30	134LTS123	303087
France	Poland	02 Aug 30	114LTS93	302657
Hungary	Latvia	13 Aug 30	117LTS395	302705

PARTY ONE	PARTY TWO	DATE	CITATION	NUMBER
Arbitration (Cont.)				
Italy	Venezuela	23 Aug 30	128LTS377	302943
Belgium	France	23 Aug 30	166LTS11	303825
France	Romania	27 Aug 30	158LTS379	303644
Panama	Spain	22 Sep 30	162LTS309	303743
Belgium	Lithuania	24 Sep 30	129LTS399	302974
Austria	Norway	01 Oct 30	119LTS15	302737
Greece	Turkey	30 Oct 30	125LTS9	302841
Multilateral		31 Oct 30	120LTS9	302760
Germany	Poland	21 Nov 30	139LTS351	303220
Latvia	Lithuania	24 Nov 30	112LTS405	302626
Czechoslovakia	Romania	05 Dec 30	167LTS221	303868
Czechoslovakia	Romania	05 Dec 30	167LTS205	303867
Sweden	USA (United States)	17 Dec 30	125LTS233	302856
Austria	Hungary	26 Jan 31	123LTS171	302814
Switzerland	USA (United States)	16 Feb 31	129LTS465	302978
Netherlands	Yugoslavia	11 Mar 31	129LTS89	302952
Norway	Turkey	16 Mar 31	138LTS41	303180
Czechoslovakia	Turkey	17 Mar 31	133LTS151	303065
Bulgaria	Poland	07 Apr 31	127LTS45	302905
Estonia	Finland	11 Apr 31	124LTS217	302835
Italy	Latvia	28 Apr 31	126LTS399	302898
Belgium	Bulgaria	23 Jun 31	137LTS191	303156
Czechoslovakia	Germany	25 Jul 31	187LTS279	304344
Greece	Romania	11 Aug 31	130LTS69	302982
Multilateral		21 Aug 31	127LTS95	302910
Multilateral		21 Aug 31	185LTS45	304273
Estonia	Persia	03 Oct 31	137LTS183	303155
Romania	Sweden	07 Oct 31	131LTS51	303003
Germany	Greece	10 Nov 31	133LTS385	303076
Bulgaria	Norway	26 Nov 31	134LTS27	303081
Greece	Poland	04 Jan 32	131LTS229	303014
Luxembourg	Norway	12 Feb 32	142LTS29	303277
Denmark	Turkey	08 Mar 32	143LTS223	303310
Turkey	Yugoslavia	14 Apr 32	144LTS291	303332
Italy	Luxembourg	15 Apr 32	142LTS119	303284
Bulgaria	Germany	24 Jun 32	147LTS211	303400
Greece	Spain	11 Jul 32	148LTS397	303426
Austria	UK Great Britain	16 Jul 32	144LTS9	303318
Finland	UK Great Britain	30 Sep 32	135LTS9	303101
Brazil	UK Great Britain	01 Nov 32	177LTS127	304087
Multilateral		09 Dec 32	151LTS5	303479
Norway	Turkey	16 Jan 33	161LTS173	303710
Norway	Sweden	10 Mar 33	138LTS17	303176
Netherlands	Venezuela	05 Apr 33	144LTS353	303338
Denmark	Greece	13 Apr 33	150LTS465	303478
Japan	Netherlands	19 Apr 33	163LTS351	303778
Haiti	USA (United States)	07 Aug 33	146LTS305	303381
Bulgaria	Czechoslovakia	29 Aug 33	148LTS15	303402
Finland	UK Great Britain	13 Oct 33	142LTS187	303291
Romania	Turkey	17 Oct 33	165LTS273	303814
Turkey	Yugoslavia	27 Nov 33	161LTS229	303715
Denmark	Venezuela	19 Dec 33	158LTS249	303635
Austria	Hungary	12 Jan 34	162LTS419	303754
Denmark	Persia	20 Feb 34	158LTS299	303640
Multilateral		20 Mar 34	174LTS171	304048
Persia	Switzerland	25 Apr 34	159LTS235	303666
Multilateral		12 Jun 34	155LTS367	303587
Belgium	UK Great Britain	22 Nov 34	190LTS99	304408
Poland	UK Great Britain	27 Feb 35	162LTS181	303740
Canada	USA (United States)	15 Apr 35	162LTS73	303735
Belgium	Germany	10 May 35	182LTS335	304221
Norway	Venezuela	13 May 35	167LTS407	303882
Hungary	Netherlands	08 Jun 35	171LTS385	303975
Hungary	Switzerland	18 Jun 35	174LTS7	304033
Bulgaria	Romania	26 Jul 35	198LTS9	304621

PARTY ONE	PARTY TWO	DATE	CITATION	NUMBER
Arbitration (Cont.)				
Finland	Norway	05 Nov 35	169LTS33	303913
Bulgaria	Denmark	07 Dec 35	182LTS183	304211
Denmark	Yugoslavia	14 Dec 35	184LTS99	304245
Multilateral		23 Sep 36	186LTS301	304319
Germany	Greece	09 Nov 36	182LTS9	304201
Multilateral		23 Dec 36	188LTS9	304350
Bulgaria	Romania	22 May 37	188LTS173	304357
Bulgaria	Romania	20 Jul 37	202LTS33	304733
Iran	Iraq	24 Jul 37	190LTS269	304425
Germany	Romania	03 Oct 37	190LTS369	304429
Bel-Lux Econ Union	Siam	05 Nov 37	190LTS151	304413
Italy	Siam	03 Dec 37	189LTS255	304389
Estonia	Germany	23 Dec 37	189LTS333	304393
Netherlands	USA (United States)	18 Feb 38	192LTS49	304460
Greece	Mexico	17 Mar 38	198LTS325	304649
Portugal	UK Great Britain	11 May 38	191LTS285	304450
Lithuania	Poland	25 May 38	191LTS391	304457
Guatemala	Norway	20 Dec 38	198LTS117	304631
Multilateral		23 May 39	202LTS159	304742
France	Spain	10 Jul 39	148LTS369	303423
Hungary	Romania	19 Oct 39	201LTS395	304728
United Arab Rep	UK Great Britain	17 Apr 40	201LTS253	304718
Mediation and good offices				
Poland	Romania	24 Jul 23	18LTS103	300458
Multilateral		03 Nov 23	30LTS371	300775
Norway	Sweden	27 Jun 24	28LTS309	300717
Finland	Norway	27 Jun 24	29LTS403	300751
Finland	Sweden	27 Jun 24	29LTS19	300731
Belgium	Greece	25 Jun 29	113LTS117	302640
Belgium	Lithuania	24 Sep 30	129LTS399	302974
Bulgaria	Norway	26 Nov 31	134LTS27	303081
Austria	Germany	07 Dec 32	137LTS69	303147
Norway	Venezuela	13 May 35	167LTS407	303882
Multilateral		23 Dec 36	188LTS75	304353
Procedure				
Argentina	Venezuela	22 Jul 11	28LTS287	300715
Netherlands	USA (United States)	18 Dec 13	74LTS157	301737
Colombia	USA (United States)	06 Apr 14	9LTS302	300263
Spain	USA (United States)	15 Sep 14	89LTS427	302030
Chile	Colombia	16 Nov 14	114LTS111	302659
Peru	Uruguay	18 Jul 17	14LTS359	300384
Brazil	UK Great Britain	04 Apr 19	5LTS45	300116
France	Germany	01 Mar 20	1LTS367	300030
Chile	Sweden	26 Mar 20	4LTS271	300111
Germany	Netherlands	11 May 20	3LTS153	300097
Netherlands	Venezuela	11 May 20	7LTS85	300176
Austria	Czechoslovakia	07 Jun 20	3LTS189	300098
Czechoslovakia	Germany	29 Jun 20	20LTS85	300509
France	Germany	30 Jun 20	8LTS79	300208
Multilateral		10 Aug 20	28LTS223	300711
Liechtenstein	Switzerland	10 Nov 20	2LTS305	300084
Italy	Serb/Croat/Slovene	12 Nov 20	18LTS387	300477
Bulgaria	Netherlands	13 Nov 20	7LTS107	300178
Germany	Poland	08 Dec 20	7LTS323	300199
France	UK Great Britain	23 Dec 20	22LTS353	300564
Belgium	France	14 Feb 21	12LTS245	300317
Austria	Czechoslovakia	10 Mar 21	9LTS333	300267
Czechoslovakia	Italy	23 Mar 21	32LTS183	300815
Czechoslovakia	Romania	23 Apr 21	15LTS235	300397
Peru	USA (United States)	21 May 21	6LTS171	300150
Germany	Saar	03 Jun 21	5LTS189	300129
Norway	USA (United States)	30 Jun 21	14LTS19	300365
Latvia	Ukrainian SSR	03 Aug 21	17LTS317	300442
Latvia	USSR (Soviet Union)	20 Oct 21	54LTS155	301283

PARTY ONE	PARTY TWO	DATE	CITATION	NUMBER
Procedure (Cont.)				
Estonia	Ukrainian SSR	25 Nov 21	11LTS121	300294
Belgium	France	30 Nov 21	27LTS173	300680
Germany	Switzerland	03 Dec 21	12LTS271	300320
Multilateral		13 Dec 21	25LTS184	300607
Austria	Czechoslovakia	16 Dec 21	9LTS247	300257
Costa Rica	UK Great Britain	12 Jan 22	17LTS151	300432
Multilateral		22 Feb 22	26LTS219	300649
Germany	Poland	24 Feb 22	26LTS479	300664
Germany	Poland	24 Feb 22	27LTS15	300665
Multilateral		17 Mar 22	11LTS167	300296
Colombia	Peru	24 Mar 22	74LTS9	301726
Italy	Serb/Croat/Slovene	06 Apr 22	118LTS207	302725
Other Unilat Decla	Lithuania	12 May 22	22LTS393	300569
Germany	Poland	18 Jun 22	34LTS235	300876
Belgium	UK Great Britain	21 Jun 22	24LTS91	300597
Germany	Poland	21 Jun 22	22LTS7	300552
Germany	Poland	23 Jun 22	22LTS25	300553
Latvia	Poland	07 Jul 22	37LTS317	300958
Chile	Peru	20 Jul 22	21LTS141	300537
Germany	Poland	01 Aug 22	34LTS253	300877
Other Unilat Decla	Albania	02 Oct 22	9LTS173	300249
Multilateral		04 Oct 22	12LTS391	300335
Czechoslovakia	Latvia	07 Oct 22	20LTS379	300528
Estonia	Hungary	19 Oct 22	30LTS347	300774
Germany	Poland	18 Dec 22	34LTS283	300879
France	USA (United States)	13 Feb 23	26LTS69	300641
France	USA (United States)	13 Feb 23	26LTS53	300640
France	UK Great Britain	07 Mar 23	22LTS363	300565
Germany	Switzerland	25 Mar 23	18LTS273	300470
Germany	UK Great Britain	05 Apr 23	17LTS173	300435
Austria	Hungary	10 Apr 23	18LTS93	300457
Iraq	UK Great Britain	30 Apr 23	35LTS13	300890
Multilateral		03 May 23	33LTS25	300831
Finland	USSR (Soviet Union)	05 Jun 23	18LTS203	300465
Germany	Poland	14 Jun 23	34LTS343	300883
Estonia	Germany	27 Jun 23	41LTS161	301013
Estonia	Germany	27 Jun 23	41LTS155	301012
Multilateral		24 Jul 23	28LTS139	300703
Multilateral		24 Sep 23	27LTS157	300678
Other Unilat Decla	Greece	29 Sep 23	20LTS29	300503
Estonia	Latvia	01 Nov 23	25LTS354	300624
Estonia	Latvia	01 Nov 23	23LTS81	300578
Multilateral		03 Nov 23	30LTS371	300775
Multilateral		09 Dec 23	36LTS76	300905
Multilateral		18 Dec 23	28LTS541	300729
Germany	Poland	12 Jan 24	65LTS47	301519
Belgium	USA (United States)	21 Jan 24	31LTS137	300791
UK Great Britain	USA (United States)	23 Jan 24	27LTS181	300681
Czechoslovakia	France	25 Jan 24	23LTS163	300588
Sweden	USSR (Soviet Union)	15 Mar 24	25LTS251	300613
Hungary	Italy	27 Mar 24	45LTS65	301099
Denmark	Latvia	03 Apr 24	33LTS393	300860
Hungary	Romania	14 Apr 24	46LTS41	301113
Hungary	Romania	16 Apr 24	45LTS349	301108
Hungary	Romania	16 Apr 24	46LTS7	301111
Finland	Norway	28 Apr 24	30LTS49	300758
Multilateral		08 May 24	29LTS85	300736
Norway	USA (United States)	24 May 24	26LTS43	300639
Denmark	USA (United States)	29 May 24	27LTS361	300697
Panama	USA (United States)	06 Jun 24	138LTS397	303200
Ecuador	Peru	21 Jun 24	27LTS345	300694
Sweden	USA (United States)	24 Jun 24	33LTS273	300851
Norway	Sweden	27 Jun 24	28LTS309	300717
Spain	UK Great Britain	27 Jun 24	28LTS523	300727
Finland	Sweden	27 Jun 24	29LTS19	300731

PARTY ONE	PARTY TWO	DATE	CITATION	NUMBER
Procedure (Cont.)				
Finland	Norway	27 Jun 24	29LTS403	300751
Denmark	Norway	09 Jul 24	27LTS203	300684
Austria	Czechoslovakia	12 Jul 24	50LTS111	301199
Italy	UK Great Britain	15 Jul 24	36LTS379	300936
Colombia	Panama	20 Aug 24	33LTS167	300841
Netherlands	USA (United States)	21 Aug 24	33LTS433	300863
Italy	Switzerland	20 Sep 24	33LTS91	300834
Germany	Saar	20 Sep 24	30LTS121	300765
Japan	Mexico	08 Oct 24	36LTS259	300927
Finland	Italy	22 Oct 24	32LTS149	300814
El Salvador	Uruguay	07 Nov 24	108LTS103	302502
Latvia	Switzerland	04 Dec 24	34LTS405	300889
Japan	Switzerland	26 Dec 24	43LTS393	301072
Germany	Poland	30 Dec 24	52LTS51	301250
Multilateral		17 Jan 25	38LTS357	300991
Netherlands	USA (United States)	23 Jan 25	33LTS445	300864
Finland	Norway	14 Feb 25	49LTS379	301193
Finland	Norway	14 Feb 25	49LTS391	301194
Canada	USA (United States)	24 Feb 25	43LTS251	301060
France	Germany	13 Apr 25	109LTS295	302546
Czechoslovakia	Poland	23 Apr 25	48LTS287	301170
Austria	Czechoslovakia	14 May 25	50LTS39	301198
Siam	Spain	03 Aug 25	55LTS39	301303
Germany	UK Great Britain	13 Aug 25	43LTS89	301050
France	Germany	14 Aug 25	75LTS103	301756
Portugal	Siam	14 Aug 25	55LTS57	301304
Belgium	Netherlands	28 Aug 25	93LTS431	302131
Greece	Switzerland	21 Sep 25	87LTS187	301969
Estonia	Switzerland	14 Oct 25	49LTS421	301195
Czechoslovakia	Germany	16 Oct 25	54LTS341	301296
Multilateral		16 Oct 25	54LTS289	301292
Germany	Poland	16 Oct 25	54LTS327	301295
Belgium	Germany	16 Oct 25	54LTS303	301293
France	Germany	16 Oct 25	54LTS315	301294
Germany	Italy	31 Oct 25	52LTS179	301256
France	Great Britain	02 Feb 26	56LTS79	301324
Liberia	USA (United States)	10 Feb 26	56LTS279	301336
Denmark	Siam	01 Mar 26	47LTS103	301131
France	Turkey	30 May 26	54LTS195	301285
France	Romania	10 Jun 26	58LTS225	301373
Albania	Serb/Croat/Slovene	22 Jun 26	91LTS9	302054
Germany	Latvia	28 Jun 26	58LTS403	301385
Portugal	South Africa	01 Jul 26	70LTS315	301643
Denmark	France	05 Jul 26	71LTS455	301684
Dominican Republic	USA (United States)	19 Jul 26	54LTS145	301282
Netherlands	UK Great Britain	14 Aug 26	57LTS41	301351
France	Switzerland	27 Aug 26	71LTS63	301654
Other Unilat Decla	Rhine Navigation	10 Sep 26	62LTS141	301462
Poland	Serb/Croat/Slovene	18 Sep 26	78LTS413	301799
Lithuania	USSR (Soviet Union)	28 Sep 26	60LTS145	301410
Denmark	Lithuania	11 Dec 26	67LTS333	301555
Denmark	Norway	15 Dec 26	59LTS255	301396
Belgium	Switzerland	05 Feb 27	68LTS45	301567
Czechoslovakia	Poland	08 Feb 27	70LTS275	301639
Austria	Czechoslovakia	15 Feb 27	73LTS349	301724
Germany	Poland	16 Feb 27	71LTS369	301676
Belgium	Netherlands	24 Mar 27	84LTS34	301902
Netherlands	Sweden	21 May 27	79LTS147	301807
Multilateral		12 Jul 27	135LTS247	303115
Belgium	Spain	19 Jul 27	80LTS17	301820
Estonia	USSR (Soviet Union)	08 Aug 27	70LTS401	301648
Italy	Spain	15 Aug 27	94LTS361	302155
Colombia	Switzerland	20 Aug 27	111LTS229	302589
Greece		15 Sep 27	70LTS9	301622
Persia	USSR (Soviet Union)	01 Oct 27	112LTS275	302620

PARTY ONE	PARTY TWO	DATE	CITATION	NUMBER
Procedure (Cont.)				
Sweden	USSR (Soviet Union)	08 Oct 27	71LTS411	301679
Germany	Saar	13 Oct 27	70LTS121	301629
Belgium	Luxembourg	17 Oct 27	124LTS203	302834
Finland	Switzerland	16 Nov 27	77LTS93	301765
Germany	Poland	10 Dec 27	120LTS299	302773
Hungary	Italy	10 Dec 27	78LTS403	301798
Germany	Lithuania	29 Jan 28	90LTS233	302042
France	USA (United States)	06 Feb 28	91LTS323	302072
Hungary	Serb/Croat/Slovene	22 Feb 28	87LTS361	301982
Hungary	Serb/Croat/Slovene	22 Feb 28	88LTS111	301991
France	Netherlands	10 Mar 28	102LTS109	302356
Denmark	Spain	14 Mar 28	74LTS93	301735
Germany	UK Great Britain	20 Mar 28	90LTS287	302044
Greece	Romania	21 Mar 28	108LTS187	302508
Czechoslovakia	Germany	22 Mar 28	93LTS235	302113
Spain	Sweden	26 Apr 28	77LTS77	301764
Germany	USA (United States)	05 May 28	90LTS177	302035
Germany	USA (United States)	05 May 28	90LTS171	302034
Austria	Italy	11 May 28	100LTS41	302293
Italy	Turkey	30 May 28	95LTS183	302172
Finland	USA (United States)	07 Jun 28	87LTS9	301958
Finland	USA (United States)	07 Jun 28	87LTS15	301959
Finland	Netherlands	09 Jun 28	87LTS321	301978
Austria	Spain	11 Jun 28	87LTS393	301984
Denmark	USA (United States)	14 Jun 28	88LTS173	301995
Persia	Turkey	15 Jun 28	106LTS247	302449
Luxembourg	Spain	21 Jun 28	109LTS137	302533
Afghanistan	Persia	26 Jun 28	106LTS321	302453
Germany	UK Great Britain	26 Jul 28	85LTS135	301928
Abyssinia	Italy	02 Aug 28	94LTS423	302159
Abyssinia	Italy	02 Aug 28	94LTS413	302158
Poland	USA (United States)	16 Aug 28	99LTS401	302285
Poland	USA (United States)	16 Aug 28	99LTS409	302286
Czechoslovakia	USA (United States)	16 Aug 28	89LTS225	302018
Czechoslovakia	USA (United States)	16 Aug 28	89LTS219	302017
Austria	USA (United States)	16 Aug 28	88LTS95	301988
Austria	USA (United States)	16 Aug 28	88LTS101	301989
Multilateral		27 Aug 28	94LTS57	302137
Bulgaria		08 Sep 28	74LTS167	301738
Greece	Italy	23 Sep 28	108LTS219	302510
Finland	USSR (Soviet Union)	24 Sep 28	82LTS63	301860
Multilateral		26 Sep 28	93LTS343	302123
Italy	Spain	03 Oct 28	94LTS387	302156
Portugal	Switzerland	17 Oct 28	96LTS287	302207
Albania	USA (United States)	22 Oct 28	92LTS217	302089
Sweden	USA (United States)	27 Oct 28	91LTS225	302063
Luxembourg	Poland	29 Oct 28	111LTS71	302581
Germany	Lithuania	30 Oct 28	91LTS365	302077
Multilateral		30 Oct 28	87LTS103	301963
Czechoslovakia	Serb/Croat/Slovene	07 Nov 28	95LTS101	302169
Czechoslovakia	Serb/Croat/Slovene	07 Nov 28	98LTS297	302252
Germany	Romania	10 Nov 28	91LTS101	302058
Czechoslovakia	Hungary	14 Nov 28	110LTS425	302574
Czechoslovakia	Spain	16 Nov 28	100LTS313	302303
Hungary	Poland	30 Nov 28	100LTS67	302294
Denmark	Norway	30 Nov 28	82LTS223	301873
Poland	Spain	03 Dec 28	101LTS501	302348
Switzerland	Turkey	09 Dec 28	159LTS219	303664
Finland	Hungary	12 Dec 28	96LTS67	302191
Norway	Spain	27 Dec 28	97LTS339	302231
Hungary	Turkey	05 Jan 29	100LTS137	302300
Serb/Croat/Slovene	USA (United States)	21 Jan 29	93LTS301	302117
Germany	USSR (Soviet Union)	25 Jan 29	90LTS219	302041
Bulgaria	Turkey	06 Mar 29	114LTS399	302668
Romania	USA (United States)	21 Mar 29	105LTS85	302403
Procedure (Cont.)				
Greece	Serb/Croat/Slovene	27 Mar 29	108LTS201	302509
Austria	Netherlands	28 Mar 29	109LTS39	302527
Multilateral		16 Apr 29	126LTS305	302891
Multilateral		20 Apr 29	112LTS371	302623
France	Germany	25 Apr 29	109LTS333	302548
Belgium	Czechoslovakia	29 Apr 29	110LTS113	302556
United Arab Rep	UK Great Britain	07 May 29	93LTS43	302103
Multilateral		21 May 29	96LTS311	302210
Belgium	Persia	23 May 29	110LTS369	302568
Persia	Sweden	27 May 29	105LTS279	302420
Chile	Peru	03 Jun 29	94LTS401	302157
Czechoslovakia	Greece	08 Jun 29	108LTS255	302512
Italy	Norway	10 Jun 29	105LTS161	302410
Hungary	Spain	10 Jun 29	101LTS251	302327
Multilateral		14 Jun 29	94LTS275	302148
Belgium	Greece	25 Jun 29	113LTS117	302640
Luxembourg	Portugal	15 Aug 29	115LTS77	302678
Iceland	Spain	26 Aug 29	104LTS183	302388
Multilateral		30 Aug 29	104LTS487	302400
Italy	Persia	05 Sep 29	141LTS185	303264
Czechoslovakia	Norway	09 Sep 29	101LTS355	302336
Germany	Luxembourg	11 Sep 29	118LTS97	302715
Czechoslovakia	Netherlands	14 Sep 29	107LTS201	302477
Luxembourg	Switzerland	16 Sep 29	107LTS23	302465
Luxembourg	Netherlands	17 Sep 29	107LTS35	302466
Czechoslovakia	Luxembourg	18 Sep 29	107LTS49	302467
Czechoslovakia	Switzerland	20 Sep 29	102LTS123	302357
Czechoslovakia	Finland	02 Oct 29	115LTS155	302684
Hungary	Yugoslavia	11 Nov 29	111LTS197	302587
Norway	Poland	09 Dec 29	101LTS325	302334
Czechoslovakia	Poland	21 Dec 29	115LTS201	302687
Bulgaria	Poland	31 Dec 29	113LTS89	302638
Latvia	USA (United States)	14 Jan 30	105LTS307	302423
Other Unilat Decla	Greece	14 Jan 30	108LTS349	302518
Belgium	Germany	16 Jan 30	104LTS223	302392
Austria	Belgium	18 Jan 30	104LTS231	302393
Multilateral		20 Jan 30	112LTS361	302622
Netherlands	Romania	22 Jan 30	112LTS121	302611
Luxembourg	Romania	22 Jan 30	110LTS151	302559
Greece	Spain	23 Jan 30	139LTS93	303205
Austria	Germany	05 Feb 30	119LTS201	302746
Austria	Italy	06 Feb 30	105LTS97	302405
Multilateral		17 Feb 30	102LTS87	302354
Denmark	Latvia	28 Feb 30	113LTS27	302632
Czechoslovakia	Lithuania	08 Mar 30	115LTS61	302677
Netherlands	Persia	12 Mar 30	111LTS387	302599
Brazil	UK Great Britain	18 Mar 30	101LTS401	302339
Belgium	Yugoslavia	25 Mar 30	106LTS343	302455
Multilateral		12 Apr 30	179LTS115	304138
Multilateral		12 Apr 30	179LTS89	304137
Multilateral		12 Apr 30	178LTS227	304117
Netherlands	Poland	12 Apr 30	113LTS65	302636
Finland	France	28 Apr 30	139LTS381	303222
Greece	Hungary	05 May 30	118LTS293	302732
Norway	Persia	08 May 30	134LTS153	303089
Chile	USA (United States)	27 May 30	133LTS141	303064
Greece	Turkey	10 Jun 30	108LTS233	302511
France	Italy	16 Jun 30	144LTS115	303323
Poland	Romania	23 Jun 30	133LTS163	303066
Austria	Greece	26 Jun 30	119LTS353	302755
Finland	Iceland	27 Jun 30	167LTS271	303873
China	USA (United States)	27 Jun 30	140LTS184	303236
Denmark	Iceland	27 Jun 30	118LTS121	302717
Iraq	UK Great Britain	30 Jun 30	132LTS363	303048
Italy	Poland	22 Jul 30	121LTS17	302780

PARTY ONE	PARTY TWO	DATE	CITATION	NUMBER
Procedure (Cont.)				
Hungary	Latvia	13 Aug 30	117LTS395	302705
Belgium	France	23 Aug 30	166LTS11	303825
Belgium	Lithuania	24 Sep 30	129LTS399	302974
Austria	Norway	01 Oct 30	119LTS15	302737
Multilateral		31 Oct 30	120LTS9	302760
Latvia	Lithuania	24 Nov 30	112LTS405	302626
Czechoslovakia	Romania	05 Dec 30	167LTS205	303867
Belgium	Lithuania	12 Dec 30	135LTS231	303114
Italy	UK Great Britain	17 Dec 30	131LTS79	303004
Belgium	Poland	18 Dec 30	134LTS177	303090
Latvia	Lithuania	25 Jan 31	118LTS143	302719
Austria	Hungary	26 Jan 31	123LTS171	302814
Czechoslovakia	Germany	21 Mar 31	143LTS177	303308
Netherlands	Spain	30 Mar 31	137LTS161	303153
Germany	Poland	11 Jun 31	141LTS91	303263
Belgium	Bulgaria	23 Jun 31	137LTS191	303156
Afghanistan	USSR (Soviet Union)	24 Jun 31	157LTS371	303611
Bulgaria	Spain	26 Jun 31	166LTS341	303850
Multilateral		13 Jul 31	139LTS301	303219
Germany	Switzerland	15 Jul 31	144LTS389	303341
Czechoslovakia	Germany	25 Jul 31	187LTS279	304344
Belgium	France	29 Jul 31	127LTS85	302909
France	Switzerland	09 Sep 31	142LTS205	303293
Italy	Netherlands	03 Oct 31	126LTS109	302875
Bulgaria	Norway	26 Nov 31	134LTS27	303081
Turkey	UK Great Britain	28 Nov 31	141LTS225	303268
Brazil	Paraguay	09 Dec 31	136LTS427	303142
Estonia	UK Great Britain	22 Dec 31	132LTS231	303041
Greece	Poland	04 Jan 32	131LTS229	303014
Finland	USSR (Soviet Union)	21 Jan 32	157LTS393	303613
Latvia	USSR (Soviet Union)	05 Feb 32	148LTS113	303408
Denmark	Turkey	08 Mar 32	143LTS223	303310
Poland	USSR (Soviet Union)	10 Apr 32	141LTS349	303275
Netherlands	Turkey	16 Apr 32	143LTS237	303311
Estonia	USSR (Soviet Union)	04 May 32	131LTS297	303020
Denmark	Sweden	06 May 32	130LTS161	302989
Netherlands	UK Great Britain	31 May 32	140LTS287	303244
Multilateral		28 Jun 32	140LTS191	303237
Poland	USSR (Soviet Union)	25 Jul 32	136LTS41	303124
Austria	Hungary	27 Nov 32	162LTS395	303753
France	USSR (Soviet Union)	29 Nov 32	157LTS411	303615
Portugal	Sweden	06 Dec 32	145LTS91	303347
Italy	Switzerland	03 Jan 33	142LTS17	303276
Norway	Turkey	16 Jan 33	161LTS173	303710
Austria	Czechoslovakia	18 Jan 33	142LTS41	303278
Romania	Yugoslavia	10 Mar 33	146LTS245	303374
Romania	Yugoslavia	11 Mar 33	146LTS277	303378
Netherlands	Norway	23 Mar 33	146LTS291	303380
Netherlands	Venezuela	05 Apr 33	144LTS353	303338
Denmark	Greece	13 Apr 33	150LTS465	303478
Japan	Netherlands	19 Apr 33	163LTS351	303778
Hungary	Yugoslavia	15 May 33	144LTS321	303335
Sweden	UK Great Britain	15 May 33	140LTS317	303245
Poland	USSR (Soviet Union)	03 Jun 33	142LTS265	303300
Haiti	USA (United States)	07 Aug 33	146LTS305	303381
Multilateral		10 Oct 33	163LTS393	303781
Czechoslovakia	Latvia	11 Oct 33	155LTS195	303577
Romania	Turkey	17 Oct 33	165LTS273	303814
Turkey	Yugoslavia	27 Nov 33	161LTS229	303715
Denmark	Venezuela	19 Dec 33	158LTS249	303635
Austria	Hungary	12 Jan 34	162LTS419	303754
France	UK Great Britain	18 Jan 34	171LTS183	303960
UK Great Britain	Yemen	11 Feb 34	157LTS63	303605
UK Great Britain	USSR (Soviet Union)	16 Feb 34	149LTS445	303446
Lithuania	UK Great Britain	24 Apr 34	169LTS373	303925

PARTY ONE	PARTY TWO	DATE	CITATION	NUMBER
Procedure (Cont.)				
Multilateral		26 Apr 34	164LTS63	303789
Belgium	UK Great Britain	02 May 34	173LTS291	304020
Colombia	Peru	24 May 34	164LTS21	303786
Turkey	Yugoslavia	03 Jul 34	179LTS207	304149
Multilateral		12 Sep 34	154LTS93	303540
Multilateral		20 Feb 35	193LTS59	304487
Multilateral		20 Feb 35	193LTS37	304486
Multilateral		20 Feb 35	186LTS173	304310
Belgium	Germany	10 May 35	182LTS335	304221
Belgium	Germany	10 May 35	165LTS169	303808
Hungary	Netherlands	08 Jun 35	171LTS385	303975
Hungary	Switzerland	18 Jun 35	174LTS7	304033
Bel-Lux Econ Union	Estonia	19 Jun 35	170LTS243	303940
France	Hungary	23 Jul 35	173LTS243	304016
Iraq	UK Great Britain	25 Jul 35	176LTS229	304064
Iran	USSR (Soviet Union)	27 Aug 35	176LTS299	304069
Hungary	UK Great Britain	25 Sep 35	170LTS51	303928
Finland	Germany	25 Sep 35	172LTS359	304000
Finland	Norway	05 Nov 35	169LTS33	303913
USA (United States)	USSR (Soviet Union)	22 Nov 35	167LTS303	303875
Bulgaria	Denmark	07 Dec 35	182LTS183	304211
Denmark	Yugoslavia	14 Dec 35	184LTS99	304245
Honduras	USA (United States)	18 Dec 35	167LTS313	303876
Czechoslovakia	Yugoslavia	24 Feb 36	187LTS185	304338
Greece	UK Great Britain	27 Feb 36	185LTS113	304278
UK Great Britain	Yugoslavia	27 Feb 36	181LTS241	304193
Bel-Lux Econ Union	Bulgaria	01 Apr 36	169LTS23	303912
Iraq	Saudi Arabia	02 Apr 36	174LTS131	304044
Bel-Lux Econ Union	Spain	04 Apr 36	168LTS339	303909
Hungary	Sweden	17 Jun 36	184LTS11	304239
Brazil	Denmark	30 Jul 36	194LTS81	304510
France	USSR (Soviet Union)	11 Aug 36	176LTS365	304073
United Arab Rep	UK Great Britain	26 Aug 36	173LTS401	304031
Netherlands	Romania	28 Aug 36	182LTS363	304222
Estonia	Finland	12 Sep 36	172LTS345	303999
Multilateral		23 Sep 36	186LTS301	304319
Bulgaria	Mexico	05 Nov 36	187LTS37	304331
Germany	Greece	09 Nov 36	182LTS9	304201
Australia	France	27 Nov 36	177LTS301	304095
Italy	Sweden	01 Dec 36	173LTS269	304018
Multilateral		23 Dec 36	195LTS229	304548
Multilateral		23 Dec 36	188LTS75	304353
Multilateral		23 Dec 36	188LTS9	304350
Multilateral		23 Dec 36	188LTS53	304352
Italy	Netherlands	01 Jan 37	178LTS415	304124
Estonia	Mexico	28 Jan 37	185LTS39	304272
France	USA (United States)	18 Feb 37	184LTS479	304269
Italy	Norway	31 Mar 37	177LTS355	304098
United Arab Rep	Turkey	07 Apr 37	191LTS95	304438
Multilateral		08 May 37	182LTS37	304202
Bel-Lux Econ Union	Italy	30 Jun 37	182LTS106	304203
Multilateral		08 Jul 37	190LTS21	304402
Iran	Iraq	24 Jul 37	190LTS269	304425
France	UK Great Britain	29 Jul 37	184LTS351	304257
Bel-Lux Econ Union	Romania	24 Aug 37	193LTS189	304496
Belgium	Siam	05 Nov 37	190LTS163	304414
Denmark	Siam	05 Nov 37	188LTS187	304358
Siam	Sweden	08 Nov 37	185LTS337	304298
Bel-Lux Econ Union	Yugoslavia	26 Nov 37	196LTS19	304567
Switzerland	UK Great Britain	03 Dec 37	194LTS223	304523
Italy	Siam	03 Dec 37	189LTS255	304389
France	Siam	07 Dec 37	201LTS113	304708
Estonia	Germany	23 Dec 37	189LTS333	304393
Estonia	Finland	14 Jan 38	185LTS53	304274
France	Switzerland	31 Jan 38	195LTS313	304553

PARTY ONE	PARTY TWO	DATE	CITATION	NUMBER
Procedure (Cont.)				
Netherlands	Siam	01 Feb 38	193LTS13	304485
Greece	Mexico	17 Mar 38	198LTS325	304649
Greece	Switzerland	30 Mar 38	185LTS245	304288
Germany	Greece	11 May 38	197LTS75	304608
Latvia	Poland	16 Jun 38	196LTS105	304573
Romania	Switzerland	19 Jul 38	152LTS89	303486
Canada	USA (United States)	17 Nov 38	199LTS91	304670
El Salvador	Norway	21 Nov 38	198LTS157	304636
France	Spain	10 Jul 39	148LTS369	303423
Latvia	UK Great Britain	23 Aug 39	201LTS37	304702
USA (United States)	Venezuela	06 Nov 39	203LTS273	304770
UK Great Britain	Venezuela	26 Feb 42	205LTS131	304830
UK Great Britain	Venezuela	26 Feb 42	205LTS121	304829
Selected disputes not subject to settlement procedures				
Peru	Uruguay	18 Jul 17	14LTS359	300384
Uruguay	Venezuela	28 Feb 23	36LTS451	300942
China	Germany	17 Aug 28	91LTS93	302057
Hungary	Poland	30 Nov 28	100LTS67	302294
Finland	Hungary	12 Dec 28	96LTS67	302191
Hungary	Turkey	05 Jan 29	100LTS137	302300
Multilateral		21 May 29	96LTS311	302210
Czechoslovakia	Switzerland	20 Sep 29	102LTS123	302357
Luxembourg	Romania	22 Jan 30	110LTS151	302559
France	Hungary	23 Jul 35	173LTS243	304016
Domestic jurisdiction				
Greece	Spain	06 Mar 19	3LTS81	300092
Czechoslovakia	Hungary	13 Jul 23	36LTS13	300901
Multilateral		24 Sep 23	27LTS157	300678
Estonia	Latvia	01 Nov 23	25LTS354	300624
Hungary	Latvia	19 Nov 23	37LTS341	300959
Hungary	Switzerland	18 Jun 24	34LTS387	300887
Spain	UK Great Britain	27 Jun 24	28LTS523	300727
Multilateral		17 Jan 25	38LTS357	300991
Czechoslovakia	Poland	23 Apr 25	48LTS383	301171
Estonia	Germany	10 Aug 25	63LTS111	301484
Belgium	Netherlands	28 Aug 25	93LTS431	302131
Czechoslovakia	Germany	16 Oct 25	54LTS341	301296
Germany	Poland	16 Oct 25	54LTS327	301295
France	Germany	16 Oct 25	54LTS315	301294
Belgium	Germany	16 Oct 25	54LTS303	301293
Poland	Sweden	03 Nov 25	62LTS263	301466
Romania	Switzerland	03 Feb 26	55LTS91	301306
Austria	Czechoslovakia	05 Mar 26	51LTS349	301240
Austria	Poland	16 Apr 26	62LTS329	301471
Spain	Switzerland	20 Apr 26	60LTS23	301403
Denmark	Poland	23 Apr 26	61LTS245	301437
Germany	Italy	29 Dec 26	78LTS383	301797
Chile	France	24 Feb 27	69LTS277	301610
Chile	Spain	28 May 27	71LTS329	301673
Belgium	Spain	19 Jul 27	80LTS17	301820
Italy	Lithuania	17 Sep 27	72LTS439	301700
France	Serb/Croat/Slovene	11 Nov 27	68LTS381	301593
Denmark	Haiti	05 Apr 28	99LTS19	302264
Spain	Sweden	26 Apr 28	77LTS77	301764
Germany	USA (United States)	05 May 28	90LTS177	302035
Finland	Spain	31 May 28	82LTS229	301874
Austria	Spain	11 Jun 28	87LTS393	301984
Denmark	USA (United States)	14 Jun 28	88LTS173	301995
Austria	USA (United States)	16 Aug 28	88LTS95	301988
Multilateral		26 Sep 28	93LTS343	302123
Czechoslovakia	Spain	16 Nov 28	100LTS313	302303
Poland	Spain	03 Dec 28	101LTS501	302348
Norway	Spain	27 Dec 28	97LTS339	302231
Multilateral		05 Jan 29	130LTS135	302988

PARTY ONE	PARTY TWO	DATE	CITATION	NUMBER
Domestic jurisdiction (Cont.)				
Norway	USA (United States)	20 Feb 29	91LTS413	302079
Portugal	USA (United States)	01 Mar 29	99LTS375	302282
Greece	Serb/Croat/Slovene	27 Mar 29	108LTS201	302509
Multilateral		21 May 29	96LTS311	302210
Czechoslovakia	Estonia	09 Jul 29	101LTS423	302341
Bulgaria	Hungary	22 Jul 29	101LTS41	302317
Iceland	Spain	26 Aug 29	104LTS183	302388
Czechoslovakia	Switzerland	20 Sep 29	102LTS123	302357
Poland	Romania	24 Oct 29	100LTS299	302302
Luxembourg	Romania	22 Jan 30	110LTS151	302559
Greece	Spain	23 Jan 30	139LTS93	303205
Austria	Italy	06 Feb 30	105LTS97	302405
Multilateral		17 Feb 30	102LTS87	302354
Belgium	Yugoslavia	25 Mar 30	106LTS343	302455
Finland	France	28 Apr 30	139LTS381	303222
Greece	USA (United States)	19 Jun 30	136LTS393	303137
China	USA (United States)	27 Jun 30	140LTS184	303236
Iceland	Sweden	27 Jun 30	127LTS67	302907
Iceland	Norway	27 Jun 30	126LTS417	302900
Norway	Portugal	26 Jul 30	134LTS123	303087
Panama	Spain	22 Sep 30	162LTS309	303743
Netherlands	Yugoslavia	11 Mar 31	129LTS89	302952
Italy	Latvia	28 Apr 31	126LTS399	302898
Bulgaria	Spain	26 Jun 31	166LTS341	303850
Denmark	Turkey	08 Mar 32	143LTS223	303310
Portugal	Sweden	06 Dec 32	145LTS91	303347
Brazil	Poland	27 Jan 33	142LTS255	303299
Japan	Netherlands	19 Apr 33	163LTS351	303778
Romania	Turkey	17 Oct 33	165LTS273	303814
Turkey	Yugoslavia	27 Nov 33	161LTS229	303715
Norway	Venezuela	13 May 35	167LTS407	303882
Denmark	Yugoslavia	14 Dec 35	184LTS99	304245
France	Spain	10 Jul 39	148LTS369	303423
Existing tribunals				
Netherlands	USA (United States)	18 Dec 13	74LTS157	301737
Chile	Colombia	16 Nov 14	114LTS111	302659
Danzig	Poland	09 Nov 20	6LTS189	300153
Bulgaria	Netherlands	13 Nov 20	7LTS107	300178
Czechoslovakia	Italy	23 Mar 21	32LTS261	300817
Other Unilat Decla	Lithuania	12 May 22	22LTS393	300569
Denmark	Sweden	07 Nov 22	14LTS95	300370
Belgium	Poland	30 Dec 22	21LTS201	300543
France	USA (United States)	13 Feb 23	26LTS53	300640
France	USA (United States)	13 Feb 23	26LTS69	300641
Sweden	Uruguay	24 Feb 23	63LTS239	301494
Iraq	UK Great Britain	30 Apr 23	35LTS13	300890
Norway	Sweden	26 May 23	18LTS155	300462
Multilateral		09 Dec 23	58LTS315	301380
Multilateral		18 Dec 23	28LTS541	300729
Belgium	USA (United States)	21 Jan 24	31LTS137	300791
Hungary	Italy	27 Mar 24	45LTS65	301099
Multilateral		31 Mar 24	27LTS211	300685
Denmark	Latvia	03 Apr 24	33LTS393	300860
Hungary	Romania	16 Apr 24	45LTS355	301109
Hungary	Romania	16 Apr 24	45LTS403	301110
Finland	Norway	28 Apr 24	30LTS49	300758
Sweden	USA (United States)	22 May 24	29LTS421	300752
Norway	USA (United States)	24 May 24	26LTS43	300639
Hungary	Romania	28 May 24	27LTS117	300674
Panama	USA (United States)	06 Jun 24	138LTS397	303200
Lithuania	Netherlands	10 Jun 24	34LTS373	300885
Brazil	Switzerland	23 Jun 24	33LTS415	300861
Spain	UK Great Britain	27 Jun 24	28LTS523	300727
Denmark	Norway	09 Jul 24	27LTS203	300684

PARTY ONE	PARTY TWO	DATE	CITATION	NUMBER
Existing tribunals (Cont.)				
Estonia	Netherlands	22 Jul 24	48LTS199	301162
Italy	Switzerland	20 Sep 24	33LTS91	300834
Japan	Switzerland	26 Dec 24	43LTS393	301072
Netherlands	USA (United States)	23 Jan 25	33LTS445	300864
Canada	USA (United States)	24 Feb 25	43LTS251	301060
Poland	Switzerland	07 Mar 25	50LTS261	301209
Germany	Poland	14 Mar 25	95LTS239	302178
France	Switzerland	06 Apr 25	147LTS89	303393
Czechoslovakia	Poland	23 Apr 25	48LTS383	301171
Netherlands	Siam	08 Jun 25	56LTS57	301323
Siam	Spain	03 Aug 25	55LTS39	301303
Germany	UK Great Britain	13 Aug 25	43LTS89	301050
France	Germany	14 Aug 25	75LTS103	301756
Portugal	Siam	14 Aug 25	55LTS57	301304
Norway	Switzerland	21 Aug 25	51LTS89	301224
Siam	UK Great Britain	15 Sep 25	49LTS51	301176
Germany	USSR (Soviet Union)	12 Oct 25	53LTS7	301257
Czechoslovakia	Germany	16 Oct 25	54LTS341	301296
France	Germany	16 Oct 25	54LTS315	301294
Multilateral		16 Oct 25	54LTS289	301292
Belgium	Germany	16 Oct 25	54LTS303	301293
Germany	Poland	16 Oct 25	54LTS327	301295
Great Britain	Nejd	02 Nov 25	60LTS419	301423
Poland	Sweden	03 Nov 25	62LTS263	301466
Norway	Sweden	25 Nov 25	60LTS295	301417
Siam	UK Great Britain	25 Nov 25	63LTS161	301487
Belgium	USA (United States)	09 Dec 25	72LTS171	301690
Netherlands	Switzerland	12 Dec 25	63LTS289	301496
Siam	Sweden	19 Dec 25	58LTS429	301386
Czechoslovakia	Sweden	02 Jan 26	48LTS173	301159
Austria	Switzerland	06 Jan 26	46LTS299	301124
Denmark	Sweden	14 Jan 26	51LTS251	301235
Denmark	Norway	15 Jan 26	60LTS311	301418
Finland	Sweden	29 Jan 26	49LTS367	301192
Denmark	Finland	30 Jan 26	51LTS367	301242
France	Great Britain	02 Feb 26	56LTS79	301324
Finland	Norway	03 Feb 26	60LTS353	301420
Romania	Switzerland	03 Feb 26	55LTS91	301306
Liberia	USA (United States)	10 Feb 26	56LTS279	301336
Denmark	Siam	01 Mar 26	47LTS103	301131
Cuba	USA (United States)	04 Mar 26	61LTS369	301447
Austria	Czechoslovakia	05 Mar 26	51LTS349	301240
Hungary	Italy	30 Mar 26	54LTS85	301276
Spain	Switzerland	20 Apr 26	60LTS23	301403
Belgium	Sweden	30 Apr 26	67LTS91	301540
Italy	Siam	09 May 26	61LTS215	301436
Greece	Netherlands	12 May 26	61LTS295	301440
Germany	Netherlands	20 May 26	66LTS103	301527
Austria	Sweden	28 May 26	61LTS193	301434
France	Romania	10 Jun 26	58LTS233	301374
Denmark	France	05 Jul 26	71LTS455	301684
Norway	Siam	16 Jul 26	60LTS35	301404
Italy	Spain	07 Aug 26	67LTS365	301558
Netherlands	UK Great Britain	14 Aug 26	57LTS41	301351
France	Switzerland	27 Aug 26	71LTS63	301654
Greece	Sweden	10 Sep 26	63LTS37	301479
Poland	Serb/Croat/Slovene	18 Sep 26	78LTS419	301800
Czechoslovakia	Denmark	30 Nov 26	67LTS105	301541
Other Unilat Decla	Estonia	10 Dec 26	62LTS277	301467
Denmark	Lithuania	11 Dec 26	67LTS333	301555
Denmark	Estonia	18 Dec 26	63LTS363	301500
Germany	Italy	29 Dec 26	78LTS383	301797
Belgium	Switzerland	05 Feb 27	68LTS45	301567
Denmark	Germany	23 Feb 27	61LTS325	301444
Belgium	Finland	04 Mar 27	69LTS361	301618

PARTY ONE	PARTY TWO	DATE	CITATION	NUMBER
Existing tribunals (Cont.)				
Belgium	Denmark	13 Mar 27	67LTS117	301542
Netherlands	Sweden	21 May 27	79LTS147	301807
Belgium	Portugal	09 Jul 27	74LTS39	301730
Multilateral		12 Jul 27	135LTS247	303115
Belgium	Spain	19 Jul 27	80LTS17	301820
Italy	Spain	15 Aug 27	94LTS361	302155
Colombia	Switzerland	20 Aug 27	111LTS229	302589
Brazil	France	27 Aug 27	75LTS91	301754
Italy	Lithuania	17 Sep 27	72LTS439	301700
Belgium	Luxembourg	17 Oct 27	124LTS203	302834
France	Luxembourg	20 Oct 27	106LTS457	302462
France	Serb/Croat/Slovene	11 Nov 27	68LTS381	301593
Finland	Switzerland	16 Nov 27	77LTS93	301765
Germany	Poland	10 Dec 27	120LTS299	302773
Portugal	Spain	18 Jan 28	77LTS105	301766
Germany	Lithuania	29 Jan 28	90LTS233	302042
France	Netherlands	10 Mar 28	102LTS109	302356
Denmark	Spain	14 Mar 28	74LTS93	301735
Greece	Romania	21 Mar 28	108LTS187	302508
Denmark	Haiti	05 Apr 28	99LTS19	302264
Italy	USA (United States)	19 Apr 28	113LTS183	302645
Spain	Sweden	26 Apr 28	77LTS77	301764
Italy	Turkey	30 May 28	95LTS183	302172
Finland	Spain	31 May 28	82LTS229	301874
Finland	USA (United States)	07 Jun 28	87LTS9	301958
Denmark	USA (United States)	14 Jun 28	88LTS173	301995
Luxembourg	Spain	21 Jun 28	109LTS137	302533
France	Portugal	06 Jul 28	126LTS27	302869
France	Spain	16 Jul 28	135LTS149	303110
Germany	UK Great Britain	26 Jul 28	85LTS135	301928
Poland	USA (United States)	16 Aug 28	99LTS409	302286
Poland	USA (United States)	16 Aug 28	99LTS401	302285
Austria	USA (United States)	16 Aug 28	88LTS95	301988
Czechoslovakia	USA (United States)	16 Aug 28	89LTS225	302018
Finland	Italy	21 Aug 28	89LTS25	302002
Greece	Italy	23 Sep 28	108LTS219	302510
Multilateral		26 Sep 28	93LTS343	302123
Portugal	Switzerland	17 Oct 28	96LTS287	302207
Netherlands	Siam	27 Oct 28	93LTS131	302105
Luxembourg	Poland	29 Oct 28	111LTS71	302581
Lithuania	USA (United States)	14 Nov 28	100LTS111	302297
Czechoslovakia	Spain	16 Nov 28	100LTS313	302303
Hungary	Poland	30 Nov 28	100LTS67	302294
Poland	Spain	03 Dec 28	101LTS501	302348
Switzerland	Turkey	09 Dec 28	159LTS219	303664
Norway	Spain	27 Dec 28	97LTS339	302231
Multilateral		05 Jan 29	100LTS399	302309
Serb/Croat/Slovene	USA (United States)	21 Jan 29	93LTS307	302118
Germany	Persia	17 Feb 29	111LTS19	302576
Bulgaria	Turkey	06 Mar 29	114LTS399	302668
France	Greece	11 Mar 29	95LTS401	302187
Belgium	USA (United States)	20 Mar 29	109LTS267	302543
Romania	USA (United States)	21 Mar 29	105LTS79	302402
Greece	Serb/Croat/Slovene	27 Mar 29	108LTS201	302509
Luxembourg	USA (United States)	06 Apr 29	106LTS475	302464
Multilateral		20 Apr 29	112LTS371	302623
Belgium	Czechoslovakia	29 Apr 29	110LTS113	302556
France	Persia	10 May 29	150LTS329	303465
Germany	Turkey	16 May 29	109LTS451	302549
Multilateral		21 May 29	96LTS311	302210
Belgium	Persia	23 May 29	110LTS369	302568
Persia	Sweden	27 May 29	105LTS279	302420
Bolivia	Netherlands	30 May 29	133LTS113	303062
Chile	Peru	03 Jun 29	94LTS401	302157
Czechoslovakia	Greece	08 Jun 29	108LTS255	302512

PARTY ONE	PARTY TWO	DATE	CITATION	NUMBER
Existing tribunals (Cont.)				
Hungary	Spain	10 Jun 29	101LTS251	302327
Italy	Norway	10 Jun 29	105LTS161	302410
Belgium	Greece	25 Jun 29	113LTS117	302640
Czechoslovakia	Estonia	09 Jul 29	101LTS423	302341
Bulgaria	Hungary	22 Jul 29	101LTS41	302317
Luxembourg	Portugal	15 Aug 29	115LTS77	302678
Iceland	Spain	26 Aug 29	104LTS183	302388
Estonia	USA (United States)	27 Aug 29	102LTS233	302366
Czechoslovakia	Norway	09 Sep 29	101LTS355	302336
Germany	Luxembourg	11 Sep 29	118LTS97	302715
Czechoslovakia	Netherlands	14 Sep 29	107LTS201	302477
Luxembourg	Switzerland	16 Sep 29	107LTS23	302465
Luxembourg	Netherlands	17 Sep 29	107LTS35	302466
Czechoslovakia	Luxembourg	18 Sep 29	107LTS49	302467
Czechoslovakia	Switzerland	20 Sep 29	102LTS123	302357
Czechoslovakia	Finland	02 Oct 29	115LTS155	302684
Poland	Romania	24 Oct 29	100LTS299	302302
Estonia	Hungary	27 Nov 29	106LTS331	302454
Norway	Poland	09 Dec 29	101LTS325	302334
Multilateral		18 Dec 29	104LTS27	302376
Bulgaria	Poland	31 Dec 29	113LTS89	302638
Lithuania	Persia	13 Jan 30	131LTS221	303013
Latvia	USA (United States)	14 Jan 30	105LTS301	302422
Luxembourg	Romania	22 Jan 30	110LTS151	302559
Netherlands	Romania	22 Jan 30	112LTS121	302611
Greece	Spain	23 Jan 30	139LTS93	303205
Austria	Italy	06 Feb 30	105LTS97	302405
Denmark	Latvia	28 Feb 30	113LTS27	302632
Czechoslovakia	Lithuania	08 Mar 30	115LTS61	302677
Belgium	Yugoslavia	25 Mar 30	106LTS343	302455
Multilateral		12 Apr 30	179LTS115	304138
Netherlands	Poland	12 Apr 30	113LTS65	302636
Finland	France	28 Apr 30	139LTS381	303222
Greece	Hungary	05 May 30	118LTS293	302732
Norway	Persia	08 May 30	134LTS153	303089
Belgium	France	23 May 30	119LTS33	302738
Chile	USA (United States)	27 May 30	133LTS141	303064
Netherlands	Yugoslavia	28 May 30	129LTS73	302951
Greece	Hungary	03 Jun 30	122LTS37	302798
Greece	USA (United States)	19 Jun 30	136LTS393	303137
Poland	Romania	23 Jun 30	133LTS163	303066
Austria	Greece	26 Jun 30	119LTS353	302755
Iceland	Sweden	27 Jun 30	127LTS67	302907
China	USA (United States)	27 Jun 30	140LTS184	303236
Denmark	Iceland	27 Jun 30	118LTS121	302717
Iceland	Norway	27 Jun 30	126LTS417	302900
Finland	Iceland	27 Jun 30	167LTS271	303873
Belgium	Romania	08 Jul 30	128LTS403	302944
Norway	Portugal	26 Jul 30	134LTS123	303087
Romania	UK Great Britain	06 Aug 30	123LTS307	302822
Hungary	Latvia	13 Aug 30	117LTS395	302705
Belgium	Lithuania	24 Sep 30	129LTS399	302974
Austria	Norway	01 Oct 30	119LTS15	302737
Greece	Turkey	30 Oct 30	125LTS9	302841
Latvia	Lithuania	24 Nov 30	112LTS405	302626
Iceland	USA (United States)		108LTS109	302503
Austria	Hungary	26 Jan 31	123LTS171	302814
Switzerland	USA (United States)	16 Feb 31	129LTS465	302978
Netherlands	Yugoslavia	11 Mar 31	129LTS89	302952
Czechoslovakia	Turkey	17 Mar 31	133LTS151	303065
Multilateral		30 Mar 31	138LTS149	303185
Netherlands	Spain	30 Mar 31	137LTS161	303153
Greece	UK Great Britain	17 Apr 31	129LTS287	302965
Italy	Latvia	28 Apr 31	126LTS399	302898
Belgium	Bulgaria	23 Jun 31	137LTS191	303156
Existing tribunals (Cont.)				
Bulgaria	Spain	26 Jun 31	166LTS341	303850
Multilateral		21 Aug 31	127LTS95	302910
Romania	Sweden	07 Oct 31	131LTS51	303003
Bolivia	Denmark	09 Nov 31	147LTS27	303387
Multilateral		10 Nov 31	131LTS327	303023
Bulgaria	Norway	26 Nov 31	134LTS27	303081
Romania	Yugoslavia	14 Dec 31	135LTS133	303108
Greece	Poland	04 Jan 32	131LTS229	303014
Finland	USSR (Soviet Union)	22 Jan 32	157LTS401	303614
Luxembourg	Norway	12 Feb 32	142LTS29	303277
Denmark	Turkey	08 Mar 32	143LTS223	303310
Italy	Luxembourg	15 Apr 32	142LTS119	303284
Netherlands	Turkey	16 Apr 32	143LTS237	303311
France	USSR (Soviet Union)	29 Nov 32	157LTS421	303616
Portugal	Sweden	06 Dec 32	145LTS91	303347
Panama	USA (United States)	17 Dec 32	138LTS119	303183
Norway	Turkey	16 Jan 33	161LTS173	303710
Romania	Yugoslavia	10 Mar 33	146LTS263	303376
Netherlands	Norway	23 Mar 33	146LTS291	303380
Netherlands	Venezuela	05 Apr 33	144LTS353	303338
Denmark	Greece	13 Apr 33	150LTS465	303478
Japan	Netherlands	19 Apr 33	163LTS351	303778
Argentina	UK Great Britain	01 May 33	143LTS67	303305
Norway	UK Great Britain	15 May 33	145LTS187	303355
Sweden	UK Great Britain	15 May 33	140LTS317	303245
Iceland	UK Great Britain	19 May 33	144LTS33	303319
Finland	UK Great Britain	29 Sep 33	149LTS167	303438
Multilateral		10 Oct 33	163LTS393	303781
Czechoslovakia	Latvia	11 Oct 33	155LTS195	303577
Multilateral		11 Oct 33	150LTS431	303476
Finland	UK Great Britain	13 Oct 33	142LTS187	303291
Turkey	Yugoslavia	27 Nov 33	161LTS229	303715
Denmark	Venezuela	19 Dec 33	158LTS249	303635
Denmark	Persia	20 Feb 34	158LTS299	303640
Belgium	UK Great Britain	13 Apr 34	154LTS361	303561
Multilateral		26 Apr 34	164LTS63	303789
Czechoslovakia	Romania	20 Jun 34	168LTS249	303902
Multilateral		20 Feb 35	193LTS59	304487
Multilateral		20 Feb 35	193LTS37	304486
Multilateral		20 Feb 35	186LTS173	304310
Belgium	Germany	10 May 35	182LTS335	304221
Norway	Venezuela	13 May 35	167LTS407	303882
Hungary	Switzerland	18 Jun 35	174LTS7	304033
France	Hungary	23 Jul 35	173LTS243	304016
Finland	Norway	05 Nov 35	169LTS33	303913
Bulgaria	Denmark	07 Dec 35	182LTS183	304211
Denmark	Yugoslavia	14 Dec 35	184LTS99	304245
Czechoslovakia	Finland	21 Mar 36	179LTS295	304156
Multilateral		23 Sep 36	186LTS301	304319
Hungary	UK Great Britain	22 Mar 37	190LTS59	304405
Multilateral		08 May 37	182LTS37	304202
Sweden	Yugoslavia	14 May 37	194LTS21	304504
Bulgaria	Romania	20 Jul 37	202LTS33	304733
Iran	Iraq	24 Jul 37	190LTS269	304425
Estonia	France	16 Oct 37	183LTS41	304227
Denmark	Haiti	21 Oct 37	190LTS231	304422
Denmark	Siam	05 Nov 37	188LTS187	304358
Siam	Sweden	08 Nov 37	185LTS337	304298
Norway	Siam	15 Nov 37	186LTS9	304301
Siam	UK Great Britain	23 Nov 37	188LTS333	304366
Multilateral		23 May 39	202LTS159	304742
France	Spain	10 Jul 39	148LTS369	303423
United Arab Rep	UK Great Britain	17 Jul 40	202LTS97	304738
United Arab Rep	France	03 Aug 40	202LTS121	304740

PARTY ONE	PARTY TWO	DATE	CITATION	NUMBER
Special tribunals				
Argentina	Venezuela	22 Jul 11	28LTS287	300715
Spain	USA (United States)	15 Sep 14	89LTS427	302030
Peru	Uruguay	18 Jul 17	14LTS359	300384
France	Germany	01 Mar 20	1LTS367	300030
France	Germany	25 Mar 20	1LTS347	300029
Austria	Czechoslovakia	07 Jun 20	3LTS189	300098
Czechoslovakia	Germany	29 Jun 20	20LTS85	300509
Austria	Germany	01 Sep 20	4LTS201	300107
Czechoslovakia	Italy	23 Mar 21	32LTS183	300815
Germany	Poland	21 Apr 21	12LTS61	300308
Austria	Czechoslovakia	04 May 21	15LTS13	300388
Peru	USA (United States)	21 May 21	6LTS171	300150
Belgium	Luxembourg	25 Jul 21	9LTS223	300256
Peru	UK Great Britain	27 Aug 21	7LTS289	300195
Austria	Hungary	08 Oct 21	16LTS19	300402
Estonia	Finland	29 Oct 21	13LTS167	300350
Estonia	Finland	29 Oct 21	13LTS59	300348
Belgium	France	30 Nov 21	27LTS173	300680
Germany	Switzerland	03 Dec 21	12LTS271	300320
Costa Rica	UK Great Britain	12 Jan 22	17LTS151	300432
Germany	Poland	18 Jun 22	34LTS235	300876
Germany	Poland	21 Jun 22	22LTS7	300552
Germany	Poland	23 Jun 22	22LTS25	300553
Germany	Poland	25 Aug 22	22LTS63	300554
Germany	Poland	18 Dec 22	34LTS283	300879
Sweden	Uruguay	24 Feb 23	63LTS239	301494
Uruguay	Venezuela	28 Feb 23	36LTS451	300942
Germany	Switzerland	25 Mar 23	18LTS273	300470
Multilateral		29 Mar 23	23LTS256	300593
Liechtenstein	Switzerland	29 Mar 23	21LTS231	300545
Austria	Hungary	10 Apr 23	18LTS93	300457
Multilateral		03 May 23	33LTS25	300831
Germany	Lithuania	31 May 23	51LTS381	301243
Estonia	Germany	27 Jun 23	41LTS161	301013
Czechoslovakia	Hungary	13 Jul 23	35LTS253	300899
Multilateral		24 Jul 23	28LTS11	300701
Estonia	Latvia	01 Nov 23	25LTS354	300624
Multilateral		23 Nov 23	28LTS267	300712
Multilateral		14 Dec 23	29LTS37	300732
Multilateral		18 Dec 23	28LTS541	300729
Germany	Poland	12 Jan 24	65LTS47	301519
Hungary	Italy	27 Mar 24	45LTS83	301100
Denmark	Latvia	03 Apr 24	33LTS393	300860
Hungary	Romania	16 Apr 24	46LTS7	301111
Denmark	Switzerland	06 Jun 24	34LTS175	300873
Hungary	Switzerland	18 Jun 24	34LTS387	300887
Finland	Sweden	27 Jun 24	29LTS19	300731
Norway	Sweden	27 Jun 24	28LTS309	300717
Finland	Norway	27 Jun 24	29LTS403	300751
Germany	Sweden	29 Aug 24	42LTS111	301036
Germany	Saar	20 Sep 24	30LTS121	300765
Austria	Switzerland	11 Oct 24	33LTS423	300862
Finland	Italy	22 Oct 24	32LTS149	300814
El Salvador	Uruguay	07 Nov 24	108LTS103	302502
Latvia	Switzerland	04 Dec 24	34LTS405	300889
Multilateral		17 Jan 25	38LTS357	300991
Poland	Switzerland	07 Mar 25	50LTS261	301209
Finland	Germany	14 Mar 25	43LTS347	301070
Latvia	Sweden	28 Mar 25	37LTS131	300952
France	Switzerland	06 Apr 25	147LTS89	303393
Czechoslovakia	Poland	23 Apr 25	48LTS287	301170
Czechoslovakia	Poland	23 Apr 25	48LTS383	301171
Austria	Czechoslovakia	14 May 25	50LTS39	301198
Estonia	Sweden	29 May 25	46LTS289	301123

PARTY ONE	PARTY TWO	DATE	CITATION	NUMBER
Special tribunals (Cont.)				
Lithuania	Sweden	11 Jun 25	57LTS191	301364
Bel-Lux Econ Union		07 Jul 25	54LTS267	301290
Estonia	Germany	10 Aug 25	63LTS111	301484
Norway	Switzerland	21 Aug 25	51LTS89	301224
Greece	Switzerland	21 Sep 25	87LTS187	301969
Estonia	Switzerland	14 Oct 25	49LTS421	301195
Belgium	Germany	16 Oct 25	54LTS303	301293
Czechoslovakia	Germany	16 Oct 25	54LTS341	301296
France	Germany	16 Oct 25	54LTS315	301294
Germany	Poland	16 Oct 25	54LTS327	301295
Germany	Italy	31 Oct 25	52LTS179	301256
Poland	Sweden	03 Nov 25	62LTS263	301466
Norway	Sweden	25 Nov 25	60LTS295	301417
Netherlands	Switzerland	12 Dec 25	63LTS289	301496
Czechoslovakia	Sweden	02 Jan 26	48LTS173	301159
Denmark	Norway	15 Jan 26	60LTS311	301418
Finland	Sweden	29 Jan 26	49LTS367	301192
Romania	Switzerland	03 Feb 26	55LTS91	301306
Austria	Czechoslovakia	05 Mar 26	51LTS349	301240
Austria	Poland	16 Apr 26	62LTS329	301471
Spain	Switzerland	20 Apr 26	60LTS23	301403
Denmark	Poland	23 Apr 26	61LTS245	301437
Germany	Netherlands	20 May 26	66LTS103	301527
Austria	Sweden	28 May 26	61LTS193	301434
France	Romania	10 Jun 26	58LTS233	301374
Albania	Serb/Croat/Slovene	22 Jun 26	91LTS9	302054
Denmark	France	05 Jul 26	71LTS455	301684
Italy	Spain	07 Aug 26	67LTS365	301558
Poland	Serb/Croat/Slovene	18 Sep 26	78LTS419	301800
Mexico	UK Great Britain	19 Nov 26	85LTS51	301922
Czechoslovakia	Denmark	30 Nov 26	67LTS105	301541
Denmark	Lithuania	11 Dec 26	67LTS333	301555
Denmark	Estonia	18 Dec 26	63LTS363	301500
Germany	Italy	29 Dec 26	78LTS383	301797
Belgium	Switzerland	05 Feb 27	68LTS45	301567
Chile	France	24 Feb 27	69LTS277	301610
Belgium	Finland	04 Mar 27	69LTS361	301618
Belgium	Denmark	13 Mar 27	67LTS117	301542
Netherlands	Sweden	21 May 27	79LTS147	301807
Belgium	Portugal	09 Jul 27	74LTS39	301730
Belgium	Spain	19 Jul 27	80LTS17	301820
Colombia	Switzerland	20 Aug 27	111LTS229	302589
Italy	Lithuania	17 Sep 27	72LTS439	301700
Latvia	USSR (Soviet Union)	10 Oct 27	84LTS47	301903
Belgium	Luxembourg	17 Oct 27	124LTS203	302834
France	Luxembourg	20 Oct 27	106LTS457	302462
France	Serb/Croat/Slovene	11 Nov 27	68LTS381	301593
Finland	Switzerland	16 Nov 27	77LTS93	301765
Bulgaria	Greece	09 Dec 27	87LTS199	301970
Portugal	Spain	18 Jan 28	77LTS105	301766
Germany	Lithuania	29 Jan 28	89LTS338	302027
Germany	Lithuania	29 Jan 28	90LTS233	302042
France	USA (United States)	06 Feb 28	91LTS323	302072
Multilateral		20 Feb 28	129LTS223	302963
France	Sweden	03 Mar 28	95LTS89	302168
France	Netherlands	10 Mar 28	102LTS109	302356
Denmark	Spain	14 Mar 28	74LTS93	301735
Denmark	Haiti	05 Apr 28	99LTS19	302264
Spain	Sweden	26 Apr 28	77LTS77	301764
Germany	USA (United States)	05 May 28	90LTS171	302034
Finland	Spain	31 May 28	82LTS229	301874
Finland	USA (United States)	07 Jun 28	87LTS15	301959
Finland	Netherlands	09 Jun 28	87LTS321	301978
Austria	Spain	11 Jun 28	87LTS393	301984
Luxembourg	Spain	21 Jun 28	109LTS137	302533

PARTY ONE	PARTY TWO	DATE	CITATION	NUMBER
Special tribunals (Cont.)				
France	Portugal	06 Jul 28	126LTS27	302869
Czechoslovakia	USA (United States)	16 Aug 28	89LTS219	302017
Austria	USA (United States)	16 Aug 28	88LTS101	301989
Finland	Italy	21 Aug 28	89LTS25	302002
Greece	Italy	23 Sep 28	108LTS219	302510
Multilateral		26 Sep 28	93LTS343	302123
Albania	USA (United States)	22 Oct 28	92LTS223	302090
Luxembourg	Poland	29 Oct 28	111LTS71	302581
Germany	Romania	10 Nov 28	91LTS101	302058
Lithuania	USA (United States)	14 Nov 28	100LTS117	302298
Czechoslovakia	Hungary	14 Nov 28	110LTS425	302574
Czechoslovakia	Spain	16 Nov 28	100LTS313	302303
Hungary	Poland	30 Nov 28	100LTS67	302294
Poland	Spain	03 Dec 28	101LTS501	302348
Switzerland	Turkey	09 Dec 28	159LTS219	303664
Finland	Hungary	12 Dec 28	96LTS67	302191
Austria	Czechoslovakia	12 Dec 28	108LTS9	302501
Multilateral		05 Jan 29	100LTS399	302309
Multilateral		05 Jan 29	130LTS135	302988
Serb/Croat/Slovene	USA (United States)	21 Jan 29	93LTS301	302117
Bulgaria	USA (United States)	21 Jan 29	93LTS331	302121
Germany	USSR (Soviet Union)	25 Jan 29	90LTS219	302041
Hungary	USA (United States)	26 Jan 29	96LTS207	302201
Bulgaria	Turkey	06 Mar 29	114LTS399	302668
Czechoslovakia	Germany	20 Mar 29	109LTS219	302541
Belgium	USA (United States)	20 Mar 29	109LTS261	302542
Romania	USA (United States)	21 Mar 29	105LTS85	302403
Greece	Serb/Croat/Slovene	27 Mar 29	108LTS201	302509
Luxembourg	USA (United States)	06 Apr 29	106LTS469	302463
Belgium	Czechoslovakia	29 Apr 29	110LTS113	302556
Germany	Turkey	16 May 29	109LTS451	302549
Persia	Sweden	27 May 29	105LTS279	302420
Czechoslovakia	Greece	08 Jun 29	108LTS255	302512
Hungary	Spain	10 Jun 29	101LTS251	302327
Italy	Norway	10 Jun 29	105LTS161	302410
Belgium	Greece	25 Jun 29	113LTS117	302640
Czechoslovakia	Estonia	09 Jul 29	101LTS423	302341
Bulgaria	Hungary	22 Jul 29	101LTS41	302317
Luxembourg	Portugal	15 Aug 29	115LTS77	302678
Iceland	Spain	26 Aug 29	104LTS183	302388
Estonia	USA (United States)	27 Aug 29	102LTS239	302367
Czechoslovakia	Norway	09 Sep 29	101LTS355	302336
Germany	Luxembourg	11 Sep 29	118LTS97	302715
Czechoslovakia	Netherlands	14 Sep 29	107LTS201	302477
Luxembourg	Netherlands	17 Sep 29	107LTS35	302466
Czechoslovakia	Luxembourg	18 Sep 29	107LTS49	302467
Czechoslovakia	Switzerland	20 Sep 29	102LTS123	302357
Czechoslovakia	Finland	02 Oct 29	115LTS155	302684
Chile	Poland	19 Oct 29	113LTS79	302637
Belgium	Germany	07 Nov 29	121LTS327	302795
Estonia	Hungary	27 Nov 29	106LTS331	302454
Norway	Poland	09 Dec 29	101LTS325	302334
Multilateral		18 Dec 29	104LTS27	302376
Bulgaria	Poland	31 Dec 29	113LTS89	302638
Latvia	USA (United States)	14 Jan 30	105LTS307	302423
Austria	Belgium	18 Jan 30	104LTS231	302393
Luxembourg	Romania	22 Jan 30	110LTS151	302559
Netherlands	Romania	22 Jan 30	112LTS121	302611
Greece	Spain	23 Jan 30	139LTS93	303205
Austria	Italy	06 Feb 30	105LTS97	302405
Denmark	Latvia	28 Feb 30	113LTS27	302632
Czechoslovakia	Lithuania	08 Mar 30	115LTS61	302677
Belgium	Yugoslavia	25 Mar 30	106LTS343	302455
Netherlands	Poland	12 Apr 30	113LTS65	302636
Finland	France	28 Apr 30	139LTS381	303222

PARTY ONE	PARTY TWO	DATE	CITATION	NUMBER
Special tribunals (Cont.)				
Greece	Hungary	05 May 30	118LTS293	302732
Greece	USA (United States)	19 Jun 30	136LTS399	303138
Iceland	Norway	27 Jun 30	126LTS417	302900
Finland	Iceland	27 Jun 30	167LTS271	303873
Belgium	Romania	08 Jul 30	128LTS403	302944
Guatemala	Honduras	16 Jul 30	137LTS231	303159
Norway	Portugal	26 Jul 30	134LTS123	303087
Hungary	Latvia	13 Aug 30	117LTS395	302705
Belgium	Lithuania	24 Sep 30	129LTS399	302974
Austria	Norway	01 Oct 30	119LTS15	302737
Greece	Turkey	30 Oct 30	125LTS9	302841
Latvia	Lithuania	24 Nov 30	112LTS405	302626
Austria	Hungary	26 Jan 31	123LTS171	302814
Switzerland	USA (United States)	16 Feb 31	129LTS465	302978
Netherlands	Yugoslavia	11 Mar 31	129LTS89	302952
Czechoslovakia	Turkey	17 Mar 31	133LTS151	303065
Netherlands	Spain	30 Mar 31	137LTS161	303153
Greece	Poland	22 Apr 31	129LTS313	302966
Italy	Latvia	28 Apr 31	126LTS399	302898
France	Greece	05 Jun 31	31LTS201	303011
Bulgaria	Spain	26 Jun 31	166LTS341	303850
Multilateral		13 Jul 31	139LTS301	303219
Hungary	Romania	12 Aug 31	186LTS325	304321
Bulgaria	Norway	26 Nov 31	134LTS27	303081
Chile	Denmark	23 Dec 31	145LTS77	303346
Greece	Poland	04 Jan 32	131LTS229	303014
Luxembourg	Norway	12 Feb 32	142LTS29	303277
Denmark	Turkey	08 Mar 32	143LTS223	303310
Italy	Luxembourg	15 Apr 32	142LTS119	303284
Netherlands	Turkey	16 Apr 32	143LTS237	303311
Estonia	USSR (Soviet Union)	04 May 32	131LTS297	303020
Estonia	USSR (Soviet Union)	16 Jun 32	131LTS309	303021
Latvia	USSR (Soviet Union)	18 Jun 32	148LTS129	303409
Poland	USSR (Soviet Union)	22 Nov 32	136LTS55	303125
Portugal	Sweden	06 Dec 32	145LTS91	303347
Norway	Turkey	16 Jan 33	161LTS173	303710
Brazil	Poland	27 Jan 33	142LTS255	303299
Netherlands	Norway	23 Mar 33	146LTS291	303380
Netherlands	Venezuela	05 Apr 33	144LTS353	303338
Denmark	Greece	13 Apr 33	150LTS465	303478
Czechoslovakia	Latvia	11 Oct 33	155LTS195	303577
Romania	Turkey	17 Oct 33	165LTS273	303814
Turkey	Yugoslavia	27 Nov 33	161LTS229	303715
Denmark	Venezuela	19 Dec 33	158LTS249	303635
Persia	Switzerland	25 Apr 34	159LTS235	303666
Belgium	Germany	10 May 35	182LTS335	304221
Norway	Venezuela	13 May 35	167LTS407	303882
Bulgaria	Romania	26 Jul 35	198LTS9	304621
Bulgaria	Denmark	07 Dec 35	182LTS183	304211
Denmark	Yugoslavia	14 Dec 35	184LTS99	304245
Chile	Norway	27 Jan 36	179LTS433	304169
Multilateral		23 Dec 36	188LTS53	304352
Multilateral		23 Dec 36	188LTS75	304353
Iran	Iraq	24 Jul 37	190LTS269	304425
Netherlands	USA (United States)	18 Feb 38	192LTS49	304460
Greece	Mexico	17 Mar 38	198LTS325	304649
Portugal	UK Great Britain	11 May 38	191LTS285	304450
Lithuania	Poland	25 May 38	191LTS391	304457
Greece	UK Great Britain	30 May 39	202LTS7	304732
France	Spain	10 Jul 39	148LTS369	303423
France	UK Great Britain	18 Jan 40	201LTS375	304725
Canada	USA (United States)	29 Feb 40	203LTS119	304754
Negotiation				
Germany	Switzerland	24 Mar 23	27LTS41	300666

PARTY ONE	PARTY TWO	DATE	CITATION	NUMBER
Negotiation (Cont.)				
Hungary	Romania	16 Apr 24	45LTS403	301110
Germany	Poland	30 Dec 24	52LTS51	301250
Other Unilat Decla	Rhine Navigation	10 Sep 26	62LTS141	301462
Finland	Spain	31 May 28	82LTS229	301874
Germany	Lithuania	30 Oct 28	91LTS365	302077
Spain	UK Great Britain	27 Jun 29	101LTS375	302337
Estonia	USSR (Soviet Union)	20 Jan 30	102LTS225	302365
Czechoslovakia	Persia	29 Oct 30	121LTS53	302783
Latvia	Lithuania	25 Jan 31	118LTS157	302721
France	UK Great Britain	18 Jan 34	171LTS183	303960
Belgium	UK Great Britain	02 May 34	173LTS291	304020
Iraq	UK Great Britain	25 Jul 35	176LTS229	304064
France	USSR (Soviet Union)	11 Aug 36	176LTS365	304073
Conciliation				
Netherlands	USA (United States)	18 Dec 13	74LTS157	301737
Chile	Sweden	26 Mar 20	4LTS271	300111
Germany	Switzerland	03 Dec 21	12LTS271	300320
Sweden	Switzerland	02 Jun 24	33LTS199	300844
Denmark	Switzerland	06 Jun 24	34LTS175	300873
Hungary	Switzerland	18 Jun 24	34LTS387	300887
Denmark	Sweden	27 Jun 24	33LTS149	300840
Denmark	Norway	27 Jun 24	33LTS173	300842
Denmark	Finland	27 Jun 24	33LTS131	300839
Germany	Sweden	29 Aug 24	42LTS111	301036
Italy	Switzerland	20 Sep 24	33LTS91	300834
Austria	Switzerland	11 Oct 24	33LTS423	300862
Japan	Switzerland	26 Dec 24	43LTS393	301072
Multilateral		17 Jan 25	38LTS357	300991
Poland	Switzerland	07 Mar 25	50LTS261	301209
Finland	Germany	14 Mar 25	43LTS347	301070
Latvia	Sweden	28 Mar 25	37LTS131	300952
France	Switzerland	06 Apr 25	147LTS89	303393
Czechoslovakia	Poland	23 Apr 25	48LTS383	301171
Estonia	Sweden	29 May 25	46LTS289	301123
Lithuania	Sweden	11 Jun 25	57LTS191	301364
Estonia	Germany	10 Aug 25	63LTS111	301484
Norway	Switzerland	21 Aug 25	51LTS89	301224
Greece	Switzerland	21 Sep 25	87LTS187	301969
France	Germany	16 Oct 25	54LTS315	301294
Germany	Poland	16 Oct 25	54LTS327	301295
Multilateral		16 Oct 25	54LTS289	301292
Czechoslovakia	Germany	16 Oct 25	54LTS341	301296
Belgium	Germany	16 Oct 25	54LTS303	301293
Poland	Sweden	03 Nov 25	62LTS263	301466
Netherlands	Switzerland	12 Dec 25	63LTS289	301496
Czechoslovakia	Sweden	02 Jan 26	48LTS173	301159
Romania	Switzerland	03 Feb 26	55LTS91	301306
Austria	Czechoslovakia	05 Mar 26	51LTS349	301240
Poland	Romania	26 Mar 26	60LTS161	301411
Austria	Poland	16 Apr 26	62LTS329	301471
Spain	Switzerland	20 Apr 26	60LTS23	301403
Denmark	Poland	23 Apr 26	61LTS245	301437
Belgium	Sweden	30 Apr 26	67LTS91	301540
Germany	Netherlands	20 May 26	66LTS103	301527
Austria	Sweden	28 May 26	61LTS193	301434
France	Romania	10 Jun 26	58LTS225	301373
France	Romania	10 Jun 26	58LTS233	301374
Denmark	France	05 Jul 26	71LTS455	301684
Italy	Spain	07 Aug 26	67LTS365	301558
Italy	Romania	16 Sep 26	67LTS393	301560
Poland	Serb/Croat/Slovene	18 Sep 26	78LTS419	301800
Lithuania	USSR (Soviet Union)	28 Sep 26	60LTS145	301410
Albania	Italy	27 Nov 26	60LTS15	301402
Czechoslovakia	Denmark	30 Nov 26	67LTS105	301541

PARTY ONE	PARTY TWO	DATE	CITATION	NUMBER
Conciliation (Cont.)				
Denmark	Lithuania	11 Dec 26	67LTS333	301555
Denmark	Estonia	18 Dec 26	63LTS363	301500
Germany	Italy	29 Dec 26	78LTS383	301797
Belgium	Switzerland	05 Feb 27	68LTS45	301567
Denmark	Germany	23 Feb 27	61LTS325	301444
Belgium	Denmark	13 Mar 27	67LTS117	301542
Hungary	Italy	05 Apr 27	67LTS399	301561
Netherlands	Sweden	21 May 27	79LTS147	301807
Belgium	Portugal	09 Jul 27	74LTS39	301730
Belgium	Spain	19 Jul 27	80LTS17	301820
Colombia	Switzerland	20 Aug 27	111LTS229	302589
Italy	Lithuania	17 Sep 27	72LTS439	301700
Belgium	Luxembourg	17 Oct 27	124LTS203	302834
France	Luxembourg	20 Oct 27	106LTS457	302462
Finland	Switzerland	16 Nov 27	77LTS93	301765
Portugal	Spain	18 Jan 28	77LTS105	301766
Germany	Lithuania	29 Jan 28	90LTS233	302042
France	Sweden	03 Mar 28	95LTS89	302168
France	Netherlands	10 Mar 28	102LTS109	302356
Denmark	Spain	14 Mar 28	74LTS93	301735
Greece	Romania	21 Mar 28	108LTS187	302508
Denmark	Haiti	05 Apr 28	99LTS19	302264
Spain	Sweden	26 Apr 28	77LTS77	301764
Germany	USA (United States)	05 May 28	90LTS171	302034
Italy	Turkey	30 May 28	95LTS183	302172
Finland	Spain	31 May 28	82LTS229	301874
Finland	USA (United States)	07 Jun 28	87LTS15	301959
Finland	Netherlands	09 Jun 28	87LTS321	301978
Austria	Spain	11 Jun 28	87LTS393	301984
Luxembourg	Spain	21 Jun 28	109LTS137	302533
France	Portugal	06 Jul 28	126LTS27	302869
Poland	USA (United States)	16 Aug 28	99LTS401	302285
Austria	USA (United States)	16 Aug 28	88LTS101	301989
Czechoslovakia	USA (United States)	16 Aug 28	89LTS219	302017
Finland	Italy	21 Aug 28	89LTS25	302002
Greece	Italy	23 Sep 28	108LTS219	302510
Portugal	Switzerland	17 Oct 28	96LTS287	302207
Albania	USA (United States)	22 Oct 28	92LTS223	302090
Netherlands	Siam	27 Oct 28	93LTS131	302105
Luxembourg	Poland	29 Oct 28	111LTS71	302581
Lithuania	USA (United States)	14 Nov 28	100LTS117	302298
Czechoslovakia	Spain	16 Nov 28	100LTS313	302303
Hungary	Poland	30 Nov 28	100LTS67	302294
Poland	Spain	03 Dec 28	101LTS501	302348
Switzerland	Turkey	09 Dec 28	159LTS219	303664
Finland	Hungary	12 Dec 28	96LTS67	302191
Norway	Spain	27 Dec 28	97LTS339	302231
Hungary	Turkey	05 Jan 29	100LTS137	302300
Multilateral		05 Jan 29	100LTS399	302309
Dominican Republic	Haiti	21 Jan 29	105LTS193	302413
Bulgaria	USA (United States)	21 Jan 29	93LTS331	302121
Serb/Croat/Slovene	USA (United States)	21 Jan 29	93LTS301	302117
Germany	USSR (Soviet Union)	25 Jan 29	90LTS219	302041
Hungary	USA (United States)	26 Jan 29	96LTS207	302201
Bulgaria	Turkey	06 Mar 29	114LTS399	302668
Belgium	USA (United States)	20 Mar 29	109LTS261	302542
Romania	USA (United States)	21 Mar 29	105LTS85	302403
Greece	Serb/Croat/Slovene	27 Mar 29	108LTS201	302509
Luxembourg	USA (United States)	06 Apr 29	106LTS469	302463
Belgium	Czechoslovakia	29 Apr 29	110LTS113	302556
Germany	Turkey	16 May 29	109LTS451	302549
Multilateral		21 May 29	96LTS311	302210
Czechoslovakia	Greece	08 Jun 29	108LTS255	302512
Italy	Norway	10 Jun 29	105LTS161	302410
Hungary	Spain	10 Jun 29	101LTS251	302327

PARTY ONE	PARTY TWO	DATE	CITATION	NUMBER
Conciliation (Cont.)				
Belgium	Greece	25 Jun 29	113LTS117	302640
Czechoslovakia	Estonia	09 Jul 29	101LTS423	302341
Bulgaria	Hungary	22 Jul 29	101LTS41	302317
Luxembourg	Portugal	15 Aug 29	115LTS77	302678
Iceland	Spain	26 Aug 29	104LTS183	302388
Estonia	USA (United States)	27 Aug 29	102LTS239	302367
Czechoslovakia	Norway	09 Sep 29	101LTS355	302336
Germany	Luxembourg	11 Sep 29	118LTS97	302715
Czechoslovakia	Netherlands	14 Sep 29	107LTS201	302477
Luxembourg	Switzerland	16 Sep 29	107LTS23	302465
Luxembourg	Netherlands	17 Sep 29	107LTS35	302466
Czechoslovakia	Luxembourg	18 Sep 29	107LTS49	302467
Czechoslovakia	Switzerland	20 Sep 29	102LTS123	302357
Czechoslovakia	Finland	02 Oct 29	115LTS155	302684
Chile	Poland	19 Oct 29	113LTS79	302637
Poland	Romania	24 Oct 29	100LTS299	302302
Belgium	Germany	07 Nov 29	121LTS327	302795
Estonia	Hungary	27 Nov 29	106LTS331	302454
Norway	Poland	09 Dec 29	101LTS325	302334
Multilateral		18 Dec 29	104LTS27	302376
Bulgaria	Poland	31 Dec 29	113LTS89	302638
Latvia	USA (United States)	14 Jan 30	105LTS307	302423
Netherlands	Romania	22 Jan 30	112LTS121	302611
Luxembourg	Romania	22 Jan 30	110LTS151	302559
Greece	Spain	23 Jan 30	139LTS93	303205
Austria	Italy	06 Feb 30	105LTS97	302405
Denmark	Latvia	28 Feb 30	113LTS27	302632
Czechoslovakia	Lithuania	08 Mar 30	115LTS61	302677
Belgium	Yugoslavia	25 Mar 30	106LTS343	302455
Netherlands	Poland	12 Apr 30	113LTS65	302636
Finland	France	28 Apr 30	139LTS381	303222
Greece	Hungary	05 May 30	118LTS293	302732
Greece	USA (United States)	19 Jun 30	136LTS399	303138
Austria	Greece	26 Jun 30	119LTS353	302755
Finland	Iceland	27 Jun 30	167LTS271	303873
Belgium	Romania	08 Jul 30	128LTS403	302944
Norway	Portugal	26 Jul 30	134LTS123	303087
Hungary	Latvia	13 Aug 30	117LTS395	302705
France	Romania	27 Aug 30	158LTS379	303644
Belgium	Lithuania	24 Sep 30	129LTS399	302974
Austria	Norway	01 Oct 30	119LTS15	302737
Greece	Turkey	30 Oct 30	125LTS9	302841
Latvia	Lithuania	24 Nov 30	112LTS405	302626
Austria	Hungary	26 Jan 31	123LTS171	302814
Switzerland	USA (United States)	16 Feb 31	129LTS465	302978
Netherlands	Yugoslavia	11 Mar 31	129LTS89	302952
Czechoslovakia	Turkey	17 Mar 31	133LTS151	303065
Netherlands	Spain	30 Mar 31	137LTS161	303153
Italy	Latvia	28 Apr 31	126LTS399	302898
Belgium	Bulgaria	23 Jun 31	137LTS191	303156
Bulgaria	Spain	26 Jun 31	166LTS341	303850
Bulgaria	Norway	26 Nov 31	134LTS27	303081
Multilateral		11 Dec 31	170LTS251	303941
Chile	Denmark	23 Dec 31	145LTS77	303346
Greece	Poland	04 Jan 32	131LTS229	303014
Finland	USSR (Soviet Union)	21 Jan 32	157LTS393	303613
Finland	USSR (Soviet Union)	22 Jan 32	157LTS401	303614
Latvia	USSR (Soviet Union)	05 Feb 32	148LTS113	303408
Luxembourg	Norway	12 Feb 32	142LTS29	303277
Italy	Luxembourg	15 Apr 32	142LTS119	303284
Netherlands	Turkey	16 Apr 32	143LTS237	303311
Estonia	USSR (Soviet Union)	04 May 32	131LTS297	303020
Estonia	USSR (Soviet Union)	16 Jun 32	131LTS309	303021
Latvia	USSR (Soviet Union)	18 Jun 32	148LTS129	303409
Poland	USSR (Soviet Union)	25 Jul 32	136LTS41	303124

PARTY ONE	PARTY TWO	DATE	CITATION	NUMBER
Conciliation (Cont.)				
Poland	USSR (Soviet Union)	22 Nov 32	136LTS55	303125
France	USSR (Soviet Union)	29 Nov 32	157LTS421	303616
Portugal	Sweden	06 Dec 32	145LTS91	303347
Norway	Turkey	16 Jan 33	161LTS173	303710
Brazil	Poland	27 Jan 33	142LTS255	303299
Romania	Yugoslavia	10 Mar 33	146LTS245	303374
Netherlands	Norway	23 Mar 33	146LTS291	303380
Netherlands	Venezuela	05 Apr 33	144LTS353	303338
Denmark	Greece	13 Apr 33	150LTS465	303478
Japan	Netherlands	19 Apr 33	163LTS351	303778
Italy	USSR (Soviet Union)	02 Sep 33	148LTS319	303418
Multilateral		10 Oct 33	163LTS393	303781
Czechoslovakia	Latvia	11 Oct 33	155LTS195	303577
Romania	Turkey	17 Oct 33	165LTS273	303814
Turkey	Yugoslavia	27 Nov 33	161LTS229	303715
Denmark	Venezuela	19 Dec 33	158LTS249	303635
Belgium	Germany	10 May 35	182LTS335	304221
Norway	Venezuela	13 May 35	167LTS407	303882
Bulgaria	Denmark	07 Dec 35	182LTS183	304211
Denmark	Yugoslavia	14 Dec 35	184LTS99	304245
Chile	Norway	27 Jan 36	179LTS433	304169
Estonia	Finland	12 Sep 36	172LTS345	303999
Multilateral		23 Dec 36	188LTS9	304350
Multilateral		23 Dec 36	188LTS75	304353
Iran	Iraq	24 Jul 37	190LTS269	304425
France	Spain	10 Jul 39	148LTS369	303423
Liberia	USA (United States)	21 Aug 39	204LTS165	304795
Competence of tribunal				
Argentina	Venezuela	22 Jul 11	28LTS287	300715
Netherlands	USA (United States)	18 Dec 13	74LTS157	301737
Spain	USA (United States)	15 Sep 14	89LTS427	302030
Chile	Colombia	16 Nov 14	114LTS111	302659
Peru	Uruguay	18 Jul 17	14LTS359	300384
Estonia	Latvia	22 Mar 20	2LTS187	300066
Czechoslovakia	Germany	29 Jun 20	20LTS85	300509
Latvia	Lithuania	28 Sep 20	2LTS234	300068
Germany	Switzerland	06 Dec 20	2LTS343	300088
Peru	UK Great Britain	27 Aug 21	7LTS289	300195
Germany	Switzerland	03 Dec 21	12LTS271	300320
Germany	Poland	21 Jun 22	22LTS7	300552
Uruguay	Venezuela	28 Feb 23	36LTS451	300942
Multilateral		03 May 23	33LTS25	300831
Multilateral		24 Jul 23	28LTS11	300701
Austria	Poland	13 Nov 23	34LTS399	300888
Multilateral		23 Nov 23	28LTS273	300713
Denmark	Switzerland	06 Jun 24	34LTS175	300873
Hungary	Switzerland	18 Jun 24	34LTS387	300887
Brazil	Switzerland	23 Jun 24	33LTS415	300861
Finland	Norway	27 Jun 24	29LTS403	300751
Norway	Sweden	27 Jun 24	28LTS309	300717
Finland	Sweden	27 Jun 24	29LTS19	300731
Germany	Sweden	29 Aug 24	42LTS111	301036
Italy	Switzerland	20 Sep 24	33LTS91	300834
Austria	Switzerland	11 Oct 24	33LTS423	300862
Multilateral		17 Jan 25	38LTS357	300991
Poland	Switzerland	07 Mar 25	50LTS261	301209
Finland	Germany	14 Mar 25	43LTS347	301070
Germany	Mexico	16 Mar 25	52LTS93	301251
Latvia	Sweden	28 Mar 25	37LTS131	300952
France	Switzerland	06 Apr 25	147LTS89	303393
Czechoslovakia	Poland	23 Apr 25	48LTS383	301171
Estonia	Sweden	29 May 25	46LTS289	301123
Lithuania	Sweden	11 Jun 25	57LTS191	301364
Italy	Poland	22 Jul 25	54LTS101	301278

Competence of tribunal (Cont.)

PARTY ONE	PARTY TWO	DATE	CITATION	NUMBER
Estonia	Germany	10 Aug 25	63LTS111	301484
Norway	Switzerland	21 Aug 25	51LTS89	301224
Germany	USSR (Soviet Union)	12 Oct 25	53LTS7	301257
Belgium	Germany	16 Oct 25	54LTS303	301293
Germany	Poland	16 Oct 25	54LTS327	301295
France	Germany	16 Oct 25	54LTS315	301294
Czechoslovakia	Germany	16 Oct 25	54LTS341	301296
Poland	Sweden	03 Nov 25	62LTS263	301466
Norway	Sweden	25 Nov 25	60LTS295	301417
Netherlands	Switzerland	12 Dec 25	63LTS289	301496
Czechoslovakia	Sweden	02 Jan 26	48LTS173	301159
Denmark	Norway	15 Jan 26	60LTS311	301418
Finland	Sweden	29 Jan 26	49LTS367	301192
Romania	Switzerland	03 Feb 26	55LTS91	301306
Finland	Norway	03 Feb 26	60LTS353	301420
Austria	Czechoslovakia	05 Mar 26	51LTS349	301240
Austria	Poland	16 Apr 26	62LTS329	301471
Spain	Switzerland	20 Apr 26	60LTS23	301403
Denmark	Poland	23 Apr 26	61LTS245	301437
Belgium	Sweden	30 Apr 26	67LTS91	301540
Germany	Netherlands	20 May 26	66LTS103	301527
Austria	Sweden	28 May 26	61LTS193	301434
France	Romania	10 Jun 26	58LTS233	301374
Denmark	France	05 Jul 26	71LTS455	301684
Poland	Serb/Croat/Slovene	18 Sep 26	78LTS419	301800
Czechoslovakia	Denmark	30 Nov 26	67LTS105	301541
Denmark	Lithuania	11 Dec 26	67LTS333	301555
Denmark	Estonia	18 Dec 26	63LTS363	301500
Germany	Italy	29 Dec 26	78LTS383	301797
Denmark	Germany	23 Feb 27	61LTS325	301444
Chile	France	24 Feb 27	69LTS277	301610
Belgium	Finland	04 Mar 27	69LTS361	301618
Belgium	Denmark	13 Mar 27	67LTS117	301542
Belgium	UK Great Britain	03 May 27	140LTS71	303229
Netherlands	Sweden	21 May 27	79LTS147	301807
Belgium	Portugal	09 Jul 27	74LTS39	301730
Belgium	Spain	19 Jul 27	80LTS17	301820
Colombia	Switzerland	20 Aug 27	111LTS229	302589
Italy	Lithuania	17 Sep 27	72LTS439	301700
Latvia	USSR (Soviet Union)	10 Oct 27	84LTS47	301903
Belgium	Luxembourg	17 Oct 27	124LTS203	302834
France	Luxembourg	20 Oct 27	106LTS457	302462
Finland	Switzerland	16 Nov 27	77LTS93	301765
Portugal	Spain	18 Jan 28	77LTS105	301766
France	Sweden	03 Mar 28	95LTS89	302168
France	Netherlands	10 Mar 28	102LTS109	302356
Denmark	Spain	14 Mar 28	74LTS93	301735
Greece	Romania	21 Mar 28	108LTS187	302508
Spain	Sweden	26 Apr 28	77LTS77	301764
Finland	Spain	31 May 28	82LTS229	301874
Austria	Spain	11 Jun 28	87LTS393	301984
Luxembourg	Spain	21 Jun 28	109LTS137	302533
France	Portugal	06 Jul 28	126LTS27	302869
Finland	Italy	21 Aug 28	89LTS25	302002
Greece	Italy	23 Sep 28	108LTS219	302510
Finland	USSR (Soviet Union)	24 Sep 28	82LTS63	301860
Portugal	Switzerland	17 Oct 28	96LTS287	302207
Albania	USA (United States)	22 Oct 28	92LTS217	302089
Sweden	USA (United States)	27 Oct 28	91LTS225	302063
Luxembourg	Poland	29 Oct 28	111LTS71	302581
Lithuania	USA (United States)	14 Nov 28	100LTS117	302298
Lithuania	USA (United States)	14 Nov 28	100LTS111	302297
Czechoslovakia	Spain	16 Nov 28	100LTS313	302303
Poland	Spain	03 Dec 28	101LTS501	302348
Switzerland	Turkey	09 Dec 28	159LTS219	303664

Competence of tribunal (Cont.)

PARTY ONE	PARTY TWO	DATE	CITATION	NUMBER
Finland	Hungary	12 Dec 28	96LTS67	302191
Norway	Spain	27 Dec 28	97LTS339	302231
Multilateral		05 Jan 29	130LTS135	302988
Multilateral		05 Jan 29	100LTS399	302309
Hungary	Turkey	05 Jan 29	100LTS137	302300
Dominican Republic	Haiti	20 Jan 29	105LTS215	302414
Serb/Croat/Slovene	USA (United States)	21 Jan 29	93LTS307	302118
Bulgaria	USA (United States)	21 Jan 29	93LTS337	302122
Germany	USSR (Soviet Union)	25 Jan 29	90LTS219	302041
Hungary	USA (United States)	26 Jan 29	96LTS173	302200
Portugal	USA (United States)	01 Mar 29	99LTS375	302282
Bulgaria	Turkey	06 Mar 29	114LTS399	302668
Belgium	USA (United States)	20 Mar 29	109LTS261	302542
Belgium	USA (United States)	20 Mar 29	109LTS267	302543
Romania	USA (United States)	21 Mar 29	105LTS79	302402
Greece	Serb/Croat/Slovene	27 Mar 29	108LTS201	302509
Luxembourg	USA (United States)	06 Apr 29	106LTS475	302464
Belgium	Czechoslovakia	29 Apr 29	110LTS113	302556
Germany	Turkey	16 May 29	109LTS451	302549
Czechoslovakia	Greece	08 Jun 29	108LTS255	302512
Italy	Norway	10 Jun 29	105LTS161	302410
Hungary	Spain	10 Jun 29	101LTS251	302327
Czechoslovakia	Estonia	09 Jul 29	101LTS423	302341
Colombia	Spain	19 Jul 29	114LTS105	302658
Luxembourg	Portugal	15 Aug 29	115LTS77	302678
Estonia	USA (United States)	27 Aug 29	102LTS233	302366
Czechoslovakia	Norway	09 Sep 29	101LTS355	302336
Germany	Luxembourg	11 Sep 29	118LTS97	302715
Czechoslovakia	Netherlands	14 Sep 29	107LTS201	302477
Luxembourg	Switzerland	16 Sep 29	107LTS23	302465
Luxembourg	Netherlands	17 Sep 29	107LTS35	302466
Czechoslovakia	Luxembourg	18 Sep 29	107LTS49	302467
Czechoslovakia	Switzerland	20 Sep 29	102LTS123	302357
Czechoslovakia	Finland	02 Oct 29	115LTS155	302684
Chile	Poland	19 Oct 29	113LTS79	302637
Estonia	Hungary	27 Nov 29	106LTS331	302454
Norway	Poland	09 Dec 29	101LTS325	302334
Bulgaria	Poland	31 Dec 29	113LTS89	302638
Latvia	USA (United States)	14 Jan 30	105LTS301	302422
Multilateral		20 Jan 30	104LTS243	302394
Netherlands	Romania	22 Jan 30	112LTS121	302611
Luxembourg	Romania	22 Jan 30	110LTS151	302559
Austria	Italy	06 Feb 30	105LTS97	302405
Denmark	Latvia	28 Feb 30	113LTS27	302632
Czechoslovakia	Lithuania	08 Mar 30	115LTS61	302677
Belgium	Yugoslavia	25 Mar 30	106LTS343	302455
Netherlands	Poland	12 Apr 30	113LTS65	302636
Finland	France	28 Apr 30	139LTS381	303222
Greece	Hungary	05 May 30	118LTS293	302732
France	Italy	03 Jun 30	153LTS135	303513
Greece	USA (United States)	19 Jun 30	136LTS399	303138
Austria	Greece	26 Jun 30	119LTS353	302755
Finland	Iceland	27 Jun 30	167LTS271	303873
Belgium	Romania	08 Jul 30	128LTS403	302944
Guatemala	Honduras	16 Jul 30	137LTS231	303159
Hungary	Latvia	13 Aug 30	117LTS395	302705
Austria	Norway	01 Oct 30	119LTS15	302737
Greece	Turkey	30 Oct 30	125LTS9	302841
Latvia	Lithuania	24 Nov 30	112LTS405	302626
Sweden	USA (United States)	17 Dec 30	125LTS233	302856
Austria	Hungary	26 Jan 31	123LTS171	302814
Multilateral		27 Mar 31	167LTS341	303877
Netherlands	Spain	30 Mar 31	137LTS161	303153
Italy	Latvia	28 Apr 31	126LTS399	302898
Belgium	Bulgaria	23 Jun 31	137LTS191	303156

PARTY ONE	PARTY TWO	DATE	CITATION	NUMBER
Competence of tribunal (Cont.)				
Bulgaria	Spain	26 Jun 31	166LTS341	303850
Chile	Denmark	23 Dec 31	145LTS77	303346
Finland	USSR (Soviet Union)	22 Jan 32	157LTS401	303614
Luxembourg	Norway	12 Feb 32	142LTS29	303277
Denmark	Turkey	08 Mar 32	143LTS223	303310
Italy	Luxembourg	15 Apr 32	142LTS119	303284
Netherlands	Turkey	16 Apr 32	143LTS237	303311
Latvia	USSR (Soviet Union)	18 Jun 32	148LTS129	303409
Poland	USSR (Soviet Union)	22 Nov 32	136LTS55	303125
France	USSR (Soviet Union)	29 Nov 32	157LTS421	303616
Portugal	Sweden	06 Dec 32	145LTS91	303347
Norway	Turkey	16 Jan 33	161LTS173	303710
Brazil	Poland	27 Jan 33	142LTS255	303299
Netherlands	Norway	23 Mar 33	146LTS291	303380
Netherlands	Venezuela	05 Apr 33	144LTS353	303338
Denmark	Greece	13 Apr 33	150LTS465	303478
Japan	Netherlands	19 Apr 33	163LTS351	303778
Czechoslovakia	Latvia	11 Oct 33	155LTS195	303577
Turkey	Yugoslavia	27 Nov 33	161LTS229	303715
Denmark	Venezuela	19 Dec 33	158LTS249	303635
Persia	Switzerland	25 Apr 34	159LTS235	303666
Norway	Venezuela	13 May 35	167LTS407	303882
Chile	Norway	27 Jan 36	179LTS433	304169
Multilateral		23 Dec 36	188LTS53	304352
Multilateral		08 May 37	182LTS37	304202
Iran	Iraq	24 Jul 37	190LTS269	304425
Netherlands	USA (United States)	18 Feb 38	192LTS49	304460
France	Spain	10 Jul 39	148LTS369	303423
General health, education, culture, welfare and labor				
Czechoslovakia	Poland	23 Sep 22	50LTS321	301216
Italy	UK Great Britain	21 May 25	43LTS75	301048
Paraguay	Spain	08 Jul 25	138LTS225	303190
International circulation				
Hungary	Sweden	26 Feb 23	17LTS35	300426
Luxembourg	Sweden	11 Apr 23	16LTS453	300423
Japan	Sweden	01 May 23	17LTS391	300446
Multilateral		28 Jun 29	103LTS429	302374
France	Sweden	09 Jun 34	154LTS101	303541
Bulgaria	Poland	08 Apr 35	161LTS319	303720
Specialists exchange				
Brazil	Uruguay	01 Aug 21	177LTS109	304085
Poland	Romania	24 Jul 23	18LTS103	300458
Iraq	UK Great Britain	04 Mar 31	123LTS77	302807
Denmark	France	28 Jan 35	158LTS11	303619
Finland	France	26 May 37	179LTS327	304160
Sanitation				
Finland	France	13 Jul 21	29LTS445	300755
Multilateral		03 Nov 23	30LTS371	300775
Brazil	Denmark	05 Aug 32	132LTS211	303039
Quarantine				
Multilateral		12 Jan 12	4LTS281	300112
Estonia	Latvia	24 Jun 22	38LTS57	300967
Latvia	USSR (Soviet Union)	24 Jun 22	38LTS9	300966
Latvia	Poland	07 Jul 22	37LTS317	300958
Poland	USSR (Soviet Union)	07 Feb 23	49LTS285	301186
Czechoslovakia	Poland	05 Sep 25	58LTS143	301370
Multilateral		21 Jun 26	78LTS229	301793
Germany	Latvia	09 Jul 26	63LTS321	301499
Canada	USA (United States)	23 Oct 29	96LTS167	302199
Multilateral		12 Apr 33	161LTS65	303706
Multilateral		25 Jul 34	177LTS59	304080
Iran	USSR (Soviet Union)	27 Aug 35	176LTS349	304072
Albania	Italy	19 Mar 36	173LTS107	304007

PARTY ONE	PARTY TWO	DATE	CITATION	NUMBER
Quarantine (Cont.)				
Belgium	UK Great Britain	19 Jun 39	198LTS171	304637
Border control				
Multilateral		12 Jan 12	4LTS281	300112
Multilateral		21 Apr 14	5LTS394	300144
Czechoslovakia	Italy	23 Mar 21	32LTS183	300815
Germany	Poland	10 Apr 21	6LTS233	300158
Belgium	Luxembourg	25 Jul 21	9LTS223	300256
Latvia	USSR (Soviet Union)	24 Jun 22	38LTS9	300966
Estonia	Latvia	24 Jun 22	38LTS57	300967
Latvia	Poland	07 Jul 22	37LTS317	300958
Italy	Serb/Croat/Slovene	23 Oct 22	18LTS413	300479
Canada	France	15 Dec 22	21LTS38	300532
Germany	Poland	18 Dec 22	34LTS301	300880
Poland	USSR (Soviet Union)	07 Feb 23	49LTS285	301186
Poland	Turkey	23 Jul 23	49LTS329	301189
Turkey		24 Jul 23	36LTS157	300915
Poland	Romania	24 Jul 23	18LTS103	300458
Hungary	Latvia	19 Nov 23	37LTS341	300959
Multilateral		09 Dec 23	47LTS55	301129
UK Great Britain	USA (United States)	23 Jan 24	27LTS181	300681
Czechoslovakia	Denmark	31 Jan 24	23LTS139	300585
Poland	Serb/Croat/Slovene	05 Apr 24	49LTS265	301185
Multilateral		22 May 24	35LTS175	300895
Denmark	USA (United States)	29 May 24	27LTS361	300697
Czechoslovakia	Latvia	07 Aug 24	38LTS123	300970
Italy	Serb/Croat/Slovene	12 Aug 24	83LTS19	301884
Czechoslovakia	France	18 Aug 24	44LTS21	301080
Czechoslovakia	Romania	01 Oct 24	51LTS71	301223
Multilateral		14 Nov 24	86LTS43	301949
Multilateral		01 Dec 24	78LTS351	301794
Germany	USA (United States)	21 May 25	52LTS133	301254
Multilateral		09 Jun 25	49LTS9	301174
Portugal	Siam	14 Aug 25	55LTS57	301304
Czechoslovakia	Poland	05 Sep 25	58LTS143	301370
Siam	UK Great Britain	15 Sep 25	49LTS51	301176
Germany	Italy	31 Oct 25	52LTS179	301256
Austria	Switzerland	06 Jan 26	46LTS299	301124
Latvia	USA (United States)	01 Feb 26	55LTS33	301302
Romania	USA (United States)	26 Feb 26	51LTS59	301221
Austria	Hungary	10 May 26	56LTS39	301321
Multilateral		21 Jun 26	78LTS229	301793
Germany	Latvia	09 Jul 26	63LTS321	301499
Belgium	Netherlands	24 Mar 27	84LTS34	301902
Belgium	Portugal	19 Jul 27	71LTS419	301680
Hungary	Serb/Croat/Slovene	22 Feb 28	113LTS49	302635
Persia	USSR (Soviet Union)	31 May 28	110LTS343	302566
Belgium	Netherlands	28 May 29	89LTS191	302013
Multilateral		09 Nov 29	125LTS205	302855
Italy	Romania	25 Feb 30	106LTS423	302459
Austria	Germany	12 Apr 30	115LTS277	302692
United Arab Rep	France	13 Jun 30	106LTS39	302435
Italy	Poland	22 Jul 30	121LTS17	302780
Belgium	Poland	18 Dec 30	134LTS177	303090
France	Poland	24 Apr 31	130LTS417	303000
Belgium	France	29 Jul 31	127LTS85	302909
Greece	Romania	11 Aug 31	130LTS79	302983
Germany	Lithuania	20 Nov 31	133LTS391	303077
Czechoslovakia	Germany	19 Sep 32	137LTS453	303175
Romania	Yugoslavia	10 Mar 33	146LTS209	303372
Multilateral		12 Apr 33	161LTS65	303706
Estonia	Poland	26 Sep 33	150LTS309	303464
Latvia	Lithuania	01 Dec 33	148LTS87	303406
Estonia	Latvia	17 Feb 34	150LTS391	303472
Multilateral		25 Jul 34	177LTS59	304080

PARTY ONE	PARTY TWO	DATE	CITATION	NUMBER
Border control (Cont.)				
Poland	Spain	14 Dec 34	168LTS315	303908
Multilateral		20 Feb 35	193LTS37	304486
Multilateral		20 Feb 35	193LTS59	304487
Iran	USSR (Soviet Union)	27 Aug 35	176LTS349	304072
Romania	Yugoslavia	13 May 37	197LTS161	304612
Belgium	UK Great Britain	19 Jun 39	198LTS171	304637
UK Great Britain	USA (United States)	27 Mar 41	204LTS15	304784
United Arab Rep	UK Great Britain	26 May 41	204LTS147	304793
Disease control				
Multilateral		12 Jan 12	4LTS281	300112
Multilateral		21 Apr 14	5LTS394	300144
Czechoslovakia	Italy	23 Mar 21	32LTS183	300815
Austria	Czechoslovakia	04 May 21	15LTS13	300388
Austria	Hungary	08 Oct 21	16LTS19	300402
Canada	France	15 Dec 22	21LTS38	300532
Czechoslovakia	Denmark	31 Jan 24	23LTS139	300585
Austria	Germany	30 Apr 24	46LTS175	301119
Multilateral		14 Nov 24	86LTS43	301949
Austria	Hungary	10 May 26	56LTS39	301321
Multilateral		21 Jun 26	78LTS229	301793
Germany	Latvia	09 Jul 26	63LTS321	301499
Belgium	Portugal	19 Jul 27	71LTS419	301680
Hungary	Serb/Croat/Slovene	22 Feb 28	113LTS49	302635
Belgium	Luxembourg	26 Apr 28	93LTS159	302107
Multilateral		16 Apr 29	126LTS305	302891
Belgium	Netherlands	28 May 29	89LTS191	302013
Czechoslovakia	France	03 Oct 30	125LTS59	302846
Belgium	France	29 Jul 31	127LTS85	302909
Germany	Lithuania	20 Nov 31	133LTS391	303077
Estonia	Poland	26 Sep 33	150LTS309	303464
Estonia	Latvia	17 Feb 34	150LTS391	303472
Multilateral		25 Jul 34	177LTS59	304080
Iran	USSR (Soviet Union)	27 Aug 35	176LTS344	304071
Albania	Italy	19 Mar 36	173LTS107	304007
Romania	Yugoslavia	13 May 37	197LTS161	304612
Latvia	Poland	16 Nov 37	197LTS43	304604
Denmark	Sweden	10 Jun 38	188LTS461	304371
Nigeria	Spanish Colonies	09 Dec 42	205LTS41	304825
Public health				
Multilateral		12 Jan 12	4LTS281	300112
Multilateral		21 Apr 14	5LTS394	300144
Multilateral		10 Sep 19	8LTS11	300201
Finland	Sweden	29 Jul 21	6LTS353	300168
Czechoslovakia	Sweden	07 Sep 21	7LTS97	300177
Portugal	Sweden	20 Sep 21	7LTS143	300183
Multilateral		21 Sep 21	7LTS127	300181
France	Sweden	09 Nov 21	7LTS303	300197
Sweden	Switzerland	29 Nov 21	7LTS313	300198
Other Unilat Decla	Rhine Navigation	16 Dec 21	13LTS53	300347
Poland	Sweden	27 Dec 21	8LTS163	300220
Norway	Sweden	05 May 22	15LTS165	300390
Latvia	USSR (Soviet Union)	24 Jun 22	38LTS9	300966
Estonia	Latvia	24 Jun 22	38LTS57	300967
Latvia	Poland	07 Jul 22	37LTS317	300958
Austria	Sweden	04 Oct 22	9LTS317	300264
Mexico	Sweden	17 Oct 22	15LTS179	300391
Canada	France	15 Dec 22	21LTS38	300532
Germany	Poland	18 Dec 22	34LTS301	300880
Poland	USSR (Soviet Union)	07 Feb 23	49LTS285	301186
Poland	Romania	24 Jul 23	18LTS103	300458
Chile	Norway	27 Jul 23	33LTS249	300848
Mexico	Norway	01 Oct 23	33LTS255	300849
France	Norway	01 Oct 23	33LTS237	300847
Japan	Norway	06 Nov 23	33LTS265	300850

PARTY ONE	PARTY TWO	DATE	CITATION	NUMBER
Public health (Cont.)				
Spain	UK Great Britain	27 Jun 24	28LTS523	300727
Multilateral		01 Dec 24	78LTS351	301794
Austria	Hungary	10 May 26	56LTS39	301321
Multilateral		21 Jun 26	78LTS229	301793
Belgium	Netherlands	24 Mar 27	84LTS34	301902
Belgium	Portugal	19 Jul 27	71LTS419	301680
Hungary	Serb/Croat/Slovene	22 Feb 28	110LTS411	302572
Hungary	Serb/Croat/Slovene	22 Feb 28	113LTS49	302635
Germany	Serb/Croat/Slovene	15 Dec 28	95LTS149	302171
Italy	Romania	25 Feb 30	106LTS423	302459
Irish Free State	Italy	10 May 30	132LTS147	303034
Italy	Poland	22 Jul 30	121LTS17	302780
Estonia	Latvia	17 Feb 34	150LTS391	303472
Cuba	USA (United States)	29 May 34	150LTS95	303456
Belgium	Denmark	27 Jul 34	150LTS351	303467
Belgium	Greece	01 Aug 34	153LTS273	303521
Belgium	Japan	28 Aug 34	155LTS395	303591
Belgium	Lithuania	20 Sep 34	153LTS289	303524
Belgium	Sweden	22 Sep 34	153LTS261	303519
Multilateral		22 Dec 34	183LTS145	304230
Multilateral		22 Dec 34	183LTS153	304231
Argentina	Chile	02 Jul 35	167LTS173	303864
France	Netherlands	25 May 36	173LTS187	304011
Romania	Yugoslavia	13 May 37	197LTS145	304611
Latvia	Poland	16 Nov 37	197LTS43	304604
Denmark	Sweden	10 Jun 38	188LTS461	304371
Belgium	UK Great Britain	19 Jun 39	198LTS171	304637
France	UK Great Britain	08 Oct 39	201LTS59	304703
Insect control				
Multilateral		12 Jan 12	4LTS281	300112
Multilateral		31 Oct 20	164LTS85	303790
Multilateral		20 May 26	109LTS121	302532
Afghanistan	USSR (Soviet Union)	06 May 35	164LTS335	303800
Iran	USSR (Soviet Union)	27 Aug 35	176LTS335	304070
Narcotic drugs				
Multilateral		23 Jan 12	8LTS187	300222
Finland	UK Great Britain	10 Jun 21	16LTS133	300403
Germany	UK Great Britain	18 Jun 21	16LTS139	300404
Austria	UK Great Britain	14 Jul 21	16LTS151	300405
Czechoslovakia	UK Great Britain	04 Aug 21	16LTS157	300406
Sweden	UK Great Britain	29 Aug 21	6LTS285	300160
Greece	UK Great Britain	10 Nov 21	16LTS165	300407
Norway	UK Great Britain	16 Dec 21	16LTS187	300409
Bulgaria	UK Great Britain	05 Apr 22	16LTS191	300410
UK Great Britain	Uruguay	19 Oct 22	16LTS201	300411
Haiti	UK Great Britain	16 Nov 22	16LTS173	300408
Colombia	UK Great Britain	08 Mar 23	17LTS167	300434
Netherlands	UK Great Britain	28 Sep 23	23LTS113	300581
Multilateral		11 Feb 25	51LTS337	301239
China	Switzerland	12 Apr 27	66LTS427	301536
Chile	Germany	18 Apr 28	79LTS411	301817
Multilateral		13 Jul 31	139LTS301	303219
Multilateral		27 Nov 31	177LTS373	304100
Turkey	Yugoslavia	17 Dec 34	178LTS471	304128
Argentina	Chile	02 Jul 35	167LTS173	303864
Czechoslovakia	Finland	21 Mar 36	179LTS295	304156
Multilateral		26 Jun 36	198LTS299	304648
France	India	18 Dec 36	178LTS399	304122
Nursing				
Belgium	Portugal	19 Jul 27	71LTS419	301680
Pharmaceuticals				
Czechoslovakia	Poland	23 Sep 22	50LTS321	301216
Italy	Switzerland	27 Jan 23	25LTS21	300603

PARTY ONE	PARTY TWO	DATE	CITATION	NUMBER
Pharmaceuticals (Cont.)				
Multilateral		20 Aug 29	98LTS125	302243
Multilateral		01 Aug 30	128LTS9	302932
Sanitation				
Multilateral		12 Jan 12	4LTS281	300112
Other Unilat Decla	Rhine Navigation	16 Dec 21	13LTS53	300347
Multilateral		24 Jul 23	28LTS11	300701
Italy	Serb/Croat/Slovene	14 Jul 24	82LTS257	301876
Czechoslovakia	Poland	05 Sep 25	58LTS143	301370
France	Turkey	30 May 26	54LTS195	301285
Multilateral		21 Jun 26	78LTS229	301793
Netherlands	UK Great Britain	14 Aug 26	57LTS41	301351
Bel-Lux Econ Union	Portugal	06 Jan 27	91LTS239	302065
Belgium	France	23 May 28	88LTS145	301993
Panama	UK Great Britain	25 Sep 28	90LTS311	302045
Czechoslovakia	France	03 Oct 30	125LTS59	302846
Multilateral		30 Jun 31	149LTS63	303434
Hungary	Romania	12 Aug 31	186LTS325	304321
Brazil	Uruguay	25 Aug 33	176LTS381	304075
Iran	USSR (Soviet Union)	27 Aug 35	176LTS299	304069
Colombia	USA (United States)	13 Sep 35	170LTS293	303944
Canada	USA (United States)	15 Nov 35	168LTS355	303910
Netherlands	USA (United States)	20 Dec 35	178LTS239	304118
Switzerland	USA (United States)	09 Jan 36	171LTS231	303962
France	USA (United States)	06 May 36	199LTS259	304679
Chile	Cuba	13 Mar 37	195LTS389	304558
Romania	Yugoslavia	13 May 37	197LTS161	304612
Ecuador	USA (United States)	06 Aug 38	193LTS85	304489
Veterinary				
Austria	Germany	01 Sep 20	4LTS201	300107
France	Norway	23 Apr 21	14LTS375	300386
Multilateral		25 Jan 24	57LTS135	301360
Czechoslovakia	Latvia	07 Aug 24	38LTS123	300970
Italy	Serb/Croat/Slovene	12 Aug 24	83LTS19	301884
Czechoslovakia	Romania	01 Oct 24	51LTS71	301223
Denmark	Germany	20 Mar 26	51LTS317	301237
Czechoslovakia	Poland	21 Apr 26	58LTS9	301367
Austria	Hungary	10 May 26	56LTS39	301321
Greece	USA (United States)	25 Apr 28	91LTS231	302064
Hungary	Italy	04 Jul 28	92LTS169	302084
Italy	Romania	25 Feb 30	106LTS423	302459
Poland	Romania	23 Jun 30	133LTS163	303066
Italy	Poland	22 Jul 30	121LTS17	302780
Czechoslovakia	France	03 Oct 30	125LTS59	302846
Belgium	Poland	18 Dec 30	134LTS177	303090
France	Poland	24 Apr 31	130LTS417	303000
Austria	Czechoslovakia	22 Jul 31	128LTS59	302938
Greece	Romania	11 Aug 31	130LTS79	302983
Hungary	Romania	12 Aug 31	186LTS325	304321
Romania	Yugoslavia	10 Mar 33	146LTS209	303372
Brazil	Uruguay	25 Aug 33	176LTS381	304075
Bulgaria	Czechoslovakia	29 Aug 33	148LTS15	303402
Estonia	Poland	26 Sep 33	150LTS309	303464
Multilateral		20 Feb 35	193LTS37	304486
Multilateral		20 Feb 35	193LTS59	304487
Multilateral		20 Feb 35	186LTS173	304310
Denmark	Germany	25 May 35	159LTS389	303680
Iran	USSR (Soviet Union)	27 Aug 35	176LTS349	304072
Germany	Latvia	04 Dec 35	166LTS93	303834
Albania	Italy	19 Mar 36	173LTS107	304007
Latvia	Poland	16 Nov 37	197LTS43	304604
Medical assistance and/or facilities				
France	Norway	23 Apr 21	14LTS375	300386
Austria	Germany	17 Aug 21	19LTS237	300497
Germany	Saar	13 Nov 22	27LTS273	300690

PARTY ONE	PARTY TWO	DATE	CITATION	NUMBER
Medical assistance and/or facilities (Cont.)				
Argentina	Belgium	20 Oct 24	137LTS381	303166
Multilateral		01 Dec 24	78LTS351	301794
Multilateral		27 Jul 29	118LTS303	302733
Belgium	Netherlands	15 May 36	179LTS41	304131
Education				
Multilateral		19 Jan 21	5LTS9	300113
Czechoslovakia	Hungary	13 Jul 23	35LTS237	300898
Spain	UK Great Britain	27 Jun 24	28LTS523	300727
UK Great Britain	USA (United States)	03 Dec 24	43LTS41	301046
Denmark	France	14 Jan 30	100LTS327	302304
Greece	Romania	11 Aug 31	130LTS93	302984
Romania	Yugoslavia	10 Mar 33	146LTS231	303373
Multilateral		28 Oct 33	159LTS199	303663
Brazil	Mexico	18 Dec 33	186LTS395	304323
Multilateral		02 Oct 37	182LTS263	304216
Recognition of degrees				
Colombia	Costa Rica	13 Oct 26	95LTS325	302182
Afghanistan	Belgium	16 Jun 28	97LTS97	302221
Denmark	France	14 Jan 30	100LTS327	302304
Colombia	Spain	30 Sep 35	163LTS337	303776
France	Greece	19 Dec 38	196LTS99	304572
Exchange				
Brazil	Uruguay	01 Aug 21	177LTS109	304085
Austria	Germany	17 Aug 21	19LTS237	300497
Germany	Saar	26 Aug 22	27LTS249	300688
Belgium	Poland	01 Sep 25	54LTS69	301274
Colombia	Costa Rica	13 Oct 26	95LTS325	302182
Belgium	Netherlands	26 Oct 27	89LTS37	302003
France	Norway	21 Nov 27	70LTS167	301632
France	UK Great Britain	16 May 28	80LTS257	301832
Belgium	France	30 May 28	95LTS195	302173
Denmark	France	14 Jan 30	100LTS327	302304
France	Netherlands	29 Oct 30	125LTS29	302843
Latvia	Lithuania	25 Jan 31	118LTS135	302718
Netherlands	UK Great Britain	09 Apr 31	125LTS41	302844
Poland	Yugoslavia	02 Dec 31	139LTS119	303207
Argentina	Brazil	10 Oct 33	179LTS165	304144
Argentina	Brazil	10 Oct 33	179LTS175	304145
Multilateral		11 Oct 33	155LTS331	303585
Hungary	Poland	21 Oct 34	163LTS9	303757
Austria	Hungary	04 Mar 35	163LTS33	303759
Bulgaria	Poland	08 Apr 35	161LTS319	303720
Germany	Hungary	28 May 36	178LTS445	304127
Czechoslovakia	Netherlands	25 May 37	180LTS43	304172
Estonia	Hungary	13 Oct 37	189LTS433	304400
Finland	Hungary	22 Oct 37	190LTS281	304426
Estonia	Finland	01 Dec 37	187LTS413	304347
Multilateral		10 Feb 38	192LTS59	304461
Finland	Poland	14 Feb 38	194LTS175	304520
France	Greece	19 Dec 38	196LTS99	304572
Sweden	USA (United States)	23 Mar 39	199LTS17	304661
Commissions and foundations				
Other Unilat Decla	Lithuania	12 May 22	22LTS393	300569
France	Norway	21 Nov 27	70LTS167	301632
Multilateral		03 Dec 38	200LTS249	304694
Teacher and student exchange				
China	Germany	20 May 21	9LTS271	300261
Brazil	Uruguay	01 Aug 21	177LTS109	304085
Austria	Italy	29 Mar 24	84LTS321	301911
Czechoslovakia	Denmark	02 Jun 24	57LTS115	301357
Belgium	Poland	01 Sep 25	54LTS69	301274
Austria	Denmark	19 Dec 25	57LTS121	301358
France	Norway	21 Nov 27	70LTS167	301632

PARTY ONE	PARTY TWO	DATE	CITATION	NUMBER
Teacher and student exchange (Cont.)				
Afghanistan	Belgium	16 Jun 28	97LTS97	302221
France	Yugoslavia	29 Jul 32	144LTS313	303334
Hungary	Poland	21 Oct 34	163LTS9	303757
Hungary	Italy	16 Feb 35	163LTS15	303758
Multilateral		20 Feb 35	186LTS173	304310
Austria	Hungary	04 Mar 35	163LTS33	303759
Bulgaria	Poland	08 Apr 35	161LTS319	303720
Australia	Indochina	20 May 36	170LTS221	303937
Germany	Hungary	28 May 36	178LTS445	304127
Poland	Romania	27 Nov 36	178LTS191	304113
Multilateral		23 Dec 36	188LTS125	304355
Czechoslovakia	Netherlands	25 May 37	180LTS43	304172
Belgium	Czechoslovakia	16 Oct 37	184LTS73	304243
Estonia	Finland	01 Dec 37	187LTS413	304347
Finland	Poland	14 Feb 38	194LTS175	304520
France	Greece	19 Dec 38	196LTS99	304572
France	Romania	31 Mar 39	199LTS213	304676
Professorships				
Brazil	Uruguay	01 Aug 21	177LTS109	304085
Germany	Hungary	06 Nov 23	45LTS253	301103
Austria	Hungary	08 Nov 24	44LTS407	301096
Latvia	Lithuania	25 Jan 31	118LTS135	302718
Estonia	Latvia	17 Feb 34	150LTS299	303463
Hungary	Italy	16 Feb 35	163LTS15	303758
Austria	Hungary	04 Mar 35	163LTS33	303759
Czechoslovakia	Netherlands	25 May 37	180LTS43	304172
France	Romania	31 Mar 39	199LTS213	304676
Institute establishment				
Multilateral		21 Jun 20	8LTS65	300207
Latvia	Vatican/Holy See	30 May 22	17LTS365	300443
Multilateral		24 Jul 23	36LTS179	300919
Germany	Italy	25 Feb 30	118LTS49	302713
Estonia	Latvia	17 Feb 34	150LTS299	303463
Hungary	Italy	16 Feb 35	163LTS15	303758
Multilateral		20 Feb 35	186LTS173	304310
Scholarships and grants				
Brazil	Uruguay	01 Aug 21	177LTS109	304085
Hungary	Italy	16 Feb 35	163LTS15	303758
Austria	Hungary	04 Mar 35	163LTS33	303759
Germany	Hungary	28 May 36	178LTS445	304127
Multilateral		23 Dec 36	188LTS125	304355
Multilateral		23 Dec 36	188LTS151	304356
Czechoslovakia	Netherlands	25 May 37	180LTS43	304172
Estonia	Hungary	13 Oct 37	189LTS433	304400
Finland	Hungary	22 Oct 37	190LTS281	304426
Estonia	Finland	01 Dec 37	187LTS413	304347
France	Romania	31 Mar 39	199LTS213	304676
Vocational training				
Belgium	France	30 May 28	95LTS195	302173
Multilateral		11 Oct 33	155LTS331	303585
Afghanistan	USSR (Soviet Union)	06 May 35	164LTS335	303800
Germany	Hungary	28 May 36	178LTS445	304127
France	Romania	31 Mar 39	199LTS213	304676
Culture				
Latvia	Lithuania	25 Jan 31	118LTS151	302720
Multilateral		09 Sep 86*	123LTS233	302816
Exchange				
Germany	Hungary	06 Nov 23	45LTS253	301103
France	Latvia	30 Oct 24	37LTS399	300963
Multilateral		22 Nov 28	111LTS343	302598
Poland	Yugoslavia	02 Dec 31	139LTS119	303207
Hungary	Poland	21 Oct 34	163LTS9	303757

PARTY ONE	PARTY TWO	DATE	CITATION	NUMBER
Exchange (Cont.)				
Hungary	Italy	16 Feb 35	163LTS15	303758
Austria	Hungary	04 Mar 35	163LTS33	303759
Germany	Hungary	28 May 36	178LTS445	304127
Poland	Romania	27 Nov 36	178LTS191	304113
Czechoslovakia	Netherlands	25 May 37	180LTS43	304172
Estonia	Hungary	13 Oct 37	189LTS433	304400
France	Romania	31 Mar 39	199LTS213	304676
General cultural cooperation				
France	Portugal	04 Mar 25	44LTS197	301083
Belgium	Netherlands	26 Oct 27	89LTS37	302003
Czechoslovakia	Italy	28 Mar 31	125LTS347	302863
Hungary	Italy	16 Feb 35	163LTS15	303758
Austria	Hungary	04 Mar 35	163LTS33	303759
Bulgaria	Poland	08 Apr 35	161LTS319	303720
El Salvador	Spain	15 Jun 35	165LTS321	303818
Bolivia	Spain	13 Mar 36	170LTS179	303933
Poland	Romania	27 Nov 36	178LTS191	304113
Estonia	Hungary	13 Oct 37	189LTS433	304400
Finland	Hungary	22 Oct 37	190LTS281	304426
Estonia	Finland	01 Dec 37	187LTS413	304347
Finland	Poland	14 Feb 38	194LTS175	304520
France	Greece	19 Dec 38	196LTS99	304572
Artists				
Austria	Hungary	08 Nov 24	44LTS407	301096
Brazil	Uruguay	20 Dec 33	181LTS35	304175
Austria	Hungary	04 Mar 35	163LTS33	303759
Poland	Romania	27 Nov 36	178LTS191	304113
France	Greece	19 Dec 38	196LTS99	304572
Athletes				
Multilateral		03 Feb 34	154LTS349	303560
Estonia	Hungary	13 Oct 37	189LTS433	304400
Archives and objects				
Lithuania	USSR (Soviet Union)	12 Jul 20	3LTS106	300094
Latvia	USSR (Soviet Union)	11 Aug 20	2LTS195	300067
Poland	USSR (Soviet Union)	18 Mar 21	6LTS51	300149
Bulgaria	Serb/Croat/Slovene	26 Nov 23	21LTS163	300540
Finland	USSR (Soviet Union)	18 Jun 24	47LTS241	301134
France	Portugal	04 Mar 25	44LTS197	301083
Paraguay	Spain	08 Jul 25	138LTS225	303190
Germany	Poland	16 Dec 25	46LTS139	301117
France	USA (United States)	29 Apr 26	100LTS27	302292
Germany	Poland	22 Dec 26	68LTS263	301590
Germany	Serb/Croat/Slovene	06 Oct 27	77LTS19	301763
Czechoslovakia	Italy	28 Mar 31	125LTS347	302863
Austria	Hungary	27 Nov 32	162LTS387	303752
Austria	Hungary	27 Nov 32	162LTS395	303753
Romania	Yugoslavia	30 Jan 33	146LTS183	303371
Denmark	Germany	15 Dec 33	171LTS9	303948
Multilateral		15 Apr 35	167LTS289	303874
Germany	Hungary	28 May 36	178LTS445	304127
Multilateral		09 Sep 86*	123LTS233	302816
Humanitarian matters				
Multilateral		18 Mar 04	1LTS83	300011
Belgium	France	30 Nov 21	27LTS173	300680
Multilateral		31 Mar 22	9LTS415	300269
Czechoslovakia	Germany	12 Apr 22	22LTS329	300562
Denmark	Iceland	09 Oct 22	14LTS13	300364
Czechoslovakia	Hungary	08 Mar 23	48LTS257	301167
Poland	Turkey	09 May 23	49LTS315	301187
Belgium	Luxembourg	17 Jul 23	27LTS235	300686
Bulgaria	Serb/Croat/Slovene	26 Nov 23	26LTS141	300644
Latvia	Lithuania	21 May 24	37LTS363	300960
Bulgaria	Czechoslovakia	06 Sep 25	50LTS253	301208

PARTY ONE	PARTY TWO	DATE	CITATION	NUMBER
Humanitarian matters (Cont.)				
Estonia	Latvia	03 Mar 26	63LTS13	301476
Multilateral		25 Sep 26	60LTS253	301414
Denmark	Sweden	03 Feb 27	109LTS205	302540
Austria	Germany	29 Feb 28	79LTS405	301816
Germany	Persia	17 Feb 29	111LTS19	302576
Netherlands	Yugoslavia	28 May 30	129LTS73	302951
Denmark	Finland	09 Jul 31	123LTS393	302826
France	Switzerland	09 Sep 31	142LTS205	303293
Finland	Poland	19 Dec 31	131LTS193	303010
ILO conventions				
Austria	Czechoslovakia	12 Jul 24	50LTS111	301199
Austria	Czechoslovakia	17 Jan 25	94LTS185	302145
Other Unilat Decla	USA (United States)	20 Aug 34	158LTS45	303624
United Arab Rep	ILO (Labor Org)	19 Jun 36	177LTS343	304096
Anti-discrimination				
France	Poland	03 Sep 19	1LTS337	300028
Austria	Czechoslovakia	07 Jun 20	3LTS189	300098
Multilateral		30 Jun 28	89LTS53	302005
Czechoslovakia	Serb/Croat/Slovene	19 Sep 28	87LTS309	301976
Luxembourg	Netherlands	01 Apr 36	179LTS11	304130
Employment regulations				
Czechoslovakia	France	20 Mar 20	3LTS139	300095
Multilateral		29 Mar 23	23LTS256	300593
United Arab Rep	UK Great Britain	18 Jul 23	18LTS323	300474
Finland	Poland	10 Nov 23	29LTS229	300744
Czechoslovakia	Hungary	09 Feb 24	30LTS335	300773
Iraq	UK Great Britain	25 Mar 24	35LTS35	300891
Czechoslovakia	Hungary	30 Sep 26	57LTS87	301356
Germany	Serb/Croat/Slovene	15 Dec 28	95LTS149	302171
Austria	Estonia	22 Mar 29	89LTS301	302025
Belgium	France	01 Jul 29	93LTS371	302125
Greece	UK Great Britain	17 Apr 31	129LTS287	302965
Greece	Poland	22 Apr 31	129LTS313	302966
Multilateral		10 Dec 31	129LTS177	302961
Denmark	France	28 Jan 35	158LTS11	303619
Luxembourg	Netherlands	01 Apr 36	179LTS11	304130
Multilateral		10 Feb 38	192LTS59	304461
Nigeria	Spanish Colonies	09 Dec 42	205LTS41	304825
Holidays and rest periods				
France	Poland	03 Sep 19	1LTS337	300028
Czechoslovakia	France	20 Mar 20	3LTS139	300095
Finland	UK Great Britain	14 Dec 23	23LTS125	300583
Portugal	South Africa	11 Sep 28	98LTS9	302239
Denmark	France	28 Jan 35	158LTS11	303619
Old age and invalidity insurance				
Belgium	Netherlands	09 Feb 21	11LTS333	300299
Austria	Czechoslovakia	04 May 21	15LTS13	300388
Germany	Saar	03 Jun 21	5LTS189	300129
Multilateral		29 Mar 23	23LTS256	300593
Germany	South Africa	23 Oct 23	28LTS417	300721
Multilateral		30 Nov 23	102LTS183	302361
Multilateral		30 Nov 23	102LTS153	302360
Austria	Serb/Croat/Slovene	29 Mar 24	114LTS451	302671
Austria	Czechoslovakia	29 Mar 24	94LTS75	302139
Austria	Czechoslovakia	29 Mar 24	94LTS103	302140
Austria	Czechoslovakia	15 Jun 24	94LTS131	302141
Austria	Czechoslovakia	15 Jun 24	94LTS165	302143
Austria	Serb/Croat/Slovene	18 Jun 24	114LTS481	302672
Austria	Serb/Croat/Slovene	27 Jun 24	115LTS39	302675
Austria	Italy	17 Jan 25	85LTS9	301918
Austria	Italy	17 Jan 25	85LTS19	301919
Multilateral		05 May 25	55LTS225	301318
Austria	Czechoslovakia	14 May 25	50LTS39	301198

PARTY ONE	PARTY TWO	DATE	CITATION	NUMBER
Old age and invalidity insurance (Cont.)				
Austria	Czechoslovakia	29 May 25	98LTS91	302242
Germany	USSR (Soviet Union)	12 Oct 25	53LTS7	301257
Austria	Germany	08 Jan 26	62LTS95	301459
Denmark	Netherlands	23 Oct 26	72LTS13	301686
Multilateral		24 Jan 27	70LTS453	301650
Hungary	Serb/Croat/Slovene	22 Feb 28	88LTS125	301992
Austria	Serb/Croat/Slovene	06 Jun 28	129LTS11	302950
Germany	Lithuania	30 Oct 28	89LTS127	302010
Czechoslovakia	Serb/Croat/Slovene	14 Nov 28	97LTS9	302216
Germany	Serb/Croat/Slovene	15 Dec 28	95LTS113	302170
Austria	Czechoslovakia	03 Feb 29	101LTS285	302329
Belgium	France	01 Jul 29	93LTS371	302125
Iceland	Norway	31 May 30	108LTS339	302517
Iceland	Sweden	31 Oct 30	109LTS171	302535
Romania	Yugoslavia	14 Dec 31	135LTS31	303103
Argentina	Serb/Croat/Slovene	13 Mar 35	158LTS189	303631
Safety standards				
Belgium	France	24 Dec 24	78LTS367	301795
Germany	Sweden	14 May 26	51LTS99	301225
Czechoslovakia	Serb/Croat/Slovene	19 Sep 28	87LTS309	301976
Irish Free State	Italy	10 May 30	132LTS147	303034
France	Netherlands	29 Oct 30	125LTS29	302843
Netherlands	UK Great Britain	09 Apr 31	125LTS41	302844
Irish Free State	USA (United States)	18 Nov 31	131LTS279	303018
Multilateral		10 Dec 31	129LTS177	302961
Germany	USA (United States)	16 Dec 31	129LTS129	302957
Belgium	USA (United States)	19 Apr 32	134LTS19	303080
Sweden	USA (United States)	01 Jun 32	131LTS213	303012
Multilateral		28 Oct 33	159LTS199	303663
Nigeria	Spanish Colonies	09 Dec 42	205LTS41	304825
Right to organize				
Belgium	France	24 Dec 24	78LTS367	301795
Czechoslovakia	Serb/Croat/Slovene	19 Sep 28	87LTS309	301976
Wages and salaries				
France	UK Great Britain	06 Aug 14	10LTS333	300278
France	Poland	03 Sep 19	1LTS337	300028
Czechoslovakia	France	20 Mar 20	3LTS139	300095
France	Greece	20 Apr 20	3LTS93	300093
Austria	Czechoslovakia	04 May 21	15LTS13	300388
Austria	Germany	23 May 22	26LTS405	300660
Germany	Switzerland	24 Mar 23	27LTS41	300666
Multilateral		29 Mar 23	23LTS256	300593
Germany	Hungary	06 Nov 23	45LTS253	301103
Czechoslovakia	Hungary	09 Feb 24	30LTS335	300773
Iraq	UK Great Britain	25 Mar 24	35LTS35	300891
Spain	UK Great Britain	27 Jun 24	28LTS523	300727
Austria	Hungary	08 Nov 24	44LTS407	301096
Belgium	France	24 Dec 24	78LTS367	301795
Czechoslovakia	Poland	23 Apr 25	44LTS309	301091
Germany	Saar	21 Dec 25	55LTS349	301319
Multilateral		14 Sep 26	77LTS149	301769
France	Great Britain	14 Sep 27	69LTS269	301609
Czechoslovakia	Serb/Croat/Slovene	19 Sep 28	87LTS309	301976
France	UK Great Britain	15 Dec 31	129LTS445	302976
Luxembourg	Netherlands	01 Apr 36	179LTS11	304130
Non-ILO labor relations				
France	Germany	03 Mar 20	8LTS45	300205
Austria	Italy	29 Mar 24	84LTS293	301910
Austria	Poland	29 Mar 24	130LTS251	302993
Austria	Poland	29 Mar 24	130LTS223	302992
Austria	Poland	18 Jun 24	130LTS309	302996
Austria	Italy	18 Jun 24	84LTS349	301912
Austria	Serb/Croat/Slovene	17 Jan 25	128LTS453	302949

PARTY ONE	PARTY TWO	DATE	CITATION	NUMBER
Non-ILO labor relations (Cont.)				
Austria	Poland	17 Jan 25	130LTS387	302998
Austria	Poland	17 Jan 25	130LTS327	302997
Multilateral		30 Oct 28	130LTS405	302999
Belgium	Netherlands	20 Feb 33	165LTS383	303824
Romania	Yugoslavia	10 Mar 33	146LTS255	303375
Estonia	Lithuania	13 Jan 34	148LTS337	303420
Family allowances				
Multilateral		30 Nov 23	102LTS153	302360
Austria	Hungary	30 Sep 24	42LTS177	301040
Belgium	France	24 Dec 24	78LTS367	301795
Belgium	France	21 May 27	105LTS125	302407
Administrative cooperation				
France	Italy	30 Sep 19	5LTS279	300133
Brazil	Uruguay	01 Aug 21	177LTS109	304085
Brazil	Italy	08 Oct 21	16LTS9	300401
Germany	Poland	15 May 22	10LTS37	300273
Germany	Poland	25 Aug 22	22LTS63	300554
Germany	Saar	21 Apr 23	27LTS295	300693
Austria	Italy	17 Jan 25	85LTS9	301918
Germany	Saar	13 Oct 27	70LTS121	301629
Argentina	Denmark	03 May 28	168LTS309	303907
Austria	Serb/Croat/Slovene	06 Jun 28	129LTS11	302950
Czechoslovakia	Serb/Croat/Slovene	19 Sep 28	87LTS309	301976
Austria	Germany	05 Feb 30	119LTS201	302746
France	Netherlands	29 Oct 30	125LTS29	302843
Netherlands	UK Great Britain	09 Apr 31	125LTS41	302844
Germany	Lithuania	09 Nov 31	133LTS379	303075
Argentina	Czechoslovakia	31 Mar 32	155LTS379	303589
Argentina	Lithuania	20 Oct 32	154LTS113	303542
Turkey	Yugoslavia	17 Dec 34	178LTS471	304128
Denmark	France	28 Jan 35	158LTS11	303619
Argentina	Serb/Croat/Slovene	13 Mar 35	158LTS189	303631
Argentina	Chile	02 Jul 35	167LTS173	303864
Belgium	France	06 Mar 39	195LTS353	304555
Belgium	UK Great Britain	19 Jun 39	198LTS171	304637
Old age insurance				
Belgium	France	14 Feb 21	12LTS245	300317
Germany	Poland	25 Aug 22	22LTS63	300554
Austria	Serb/Croat/Slovene	29 Mar 24	114LTS451	302671
Austria	Czechoslovakia	17 Jan 25	94LTS245	302146
Austria	Germany	08 Jan 26	62LTS95	301459
France	Saar	27 May 26	55LTS157	301312
Belgium	France	21 May 27	105LTS125	302407
Austria	Serb/Croat/Slovene	06 Jun 28	129LTS11	302950
Germany	Serb/Croat/Slovene	15 Dec 28	95LTS113	302170
Germany	Lithuania	26 Jan 29	89LTS181	302012
Czechoslovakia	Germany	21 Mar 31	143LTS177	303308
Germany	Poland	11 Jun 31	141LTS91	303263
Austria	Yugoslavia	21 Jul 31	147LTS123	303397
Belgium	Netherlands	16 Oct 31	137LTS411	303171
Austria	Czechoslovakia	18 Jan 33	142LTS41	303278
Latvia	Poland	20 Dec 34	162LTS361	303749
France	Switzerland	13 Oct 37	194LTS191	304522
Sweden	USA (United States)	23 Mar 39	199LTS17	304661
Sickness and invalidity insurance				
France	UK Great Britain	06 Aug 14	10LTS333	300278
France	Poland	03 Sep 19	1LTS337	300028
France	Italy	30 Sep 19	5LTS279	300133
Argentina	Italy	26 Mar 20	15LTS271	300400
Italy	Serb/Croat/Slovene	06 Apr 22	123LTS289	302819
Multilateral		06 Apr 22	123LTS277	302818
Germany	Poland	25 Aug 22	22LTS63	300554
Germany	Saar	21 Apr 23	27LTS295	300693

PARTY ONE	PARTY TWO	DATE	CITATION	NUMBER
Sickness and invalidity insurance (Cont.)				
Finland	Sweden	11 Sep 23	20LTS79	300508
Estonia	Latvia	01 Nov 23	25LTS354	300624
Denmark	Finland	30 Nov 23	22LTS427	300571
Iraq	UK Great Britain	25 Mar 24	35LTS35	300891
Austria	Czechoslovakia	15 Jun 24	94LTS149	302142
Austria	Serb/Croat/Slovene	18 Jun 24	115LTS25	302674
Austria	Poland	18 Jun 24	130LTS293	302995
Austria	Italy	18 Jun 24	84LTS367	301913
Austria	Poland	18 Jun 24	130LTS279	302994
Austria	Serb/Croat/Slovene	18 Jun 24	115LTS9	302673
Austria	Italy	18 Jun 24	84LTS381	301914
Austria	Serb/Croat/Slovene	27 Jun 24	115LTS49	302676
Austria	Italy	27 Sep 24	84LTS397	301915
Austria	Italy	27 Sep 24	84LTS409	301916
Austria	Hungary	30 Sep 24	42LTS177	301040
Czechoslovakia	Germany	15 Dec 24	52LTS31	301248
Czechoslovakia	Germany	15 Dec 24	52LTS41	301249
Netherlands	Norway	09 Jan 25	48LTS247	301166
Austria	Italy	17 Jan 25	84LTS419	301917
Austria	Serb/Croat/Slovene	17 Jan 25	128LTS445	302948
Austria	Italy	17 Jan 25	85LTS9	301918
Estonia	Finland	10 Dec 25	50LTS335	301217
Austria	Germany	08 Jan 26	62LTS95	301459
Argentina	Austria	22 Mar 26	143LTS157	303306
France	Saar	27 May 26	55LTS157	301312
Denmark	UK Great Britain	02 Jun 26	61LTS353	301445
Denmark	Norway	15 Dec 26	59LTS255	301396
Multilateral		24 Jan 27	70LTS453	301650
Czechoslovakia	Poland	30 May 27	98LTS233	302251
Finland	Germany	18 Jun 27	71LTS361	301675
Germany	Poland	14 Jul 27	73LTS251	301718
Germany	Saar	13 Oct 27	70LTS121	301629
Denmark	Iceland	13 Oct 27	67LTS411	301562
Argentina	Denmark	16 Nov 27	165LTS177	303809
Australia	Norway	13 Dec 27	69LTS307	301612
Argentina	Denmark	03 May 28	168LTS309	303907
Argentina	Sweden	14 May 28	155LTS109	303573
Bulgaria	Hungary	05 Jan 29	118LTS279	302730
Latvia	Poland	12 Feb 29	101LTS75	302321
Poland	Romania	30 Oct 29	121LTS167	302787
Argentina	UK Great Britain	15 Nov 29	160LTS257	303694
Austria	Germany	05 Feb 30	119LTS201	302746
Belgium	Shereefian	24 Jul 30	138LTS35	303179
Irish Free State	Switzerland	03 Nov 30	132LTS159	303035
Czechoslovakia	Germany	21 Mar 31	143LTS177	303308
Germany	Poland	11 Jun 31	141LTS91	303263
Belgium	Germany	16 Jul 31	145LTS137	303351
Austria	Yugoslavia	21 Jul 31	147LTS123	303397
Germany	Lithuania	09 Nov 31	133LTS379	303075
Multilateral		10 Dec 31	129LTS177	302961
Argentina	Czechoslovakia	31 Mar 32	155LTS379	303589
Czechoslovakia	Spain	29 Jun 32	166LTS355	303851
Argentina	Lithuania	20 Oct 32	154LTS113	303542
Austria	Czechoslovakia	18 Jan 33	142LTS41	303278
Romania	Yugoslavia	30 Jan 33	146LTS151	303367
Denmark	Germany	19 Jul 33	170LTS385	303947
Latvia	Poland	20 Dec 34	162LTS361	303749
Bulgaria	Romania	26 Jul 35	198LTS9	304621
Belgium	Netherlands	15 May 36	179LTS41	304131
Czechoslovakia	Sweden	23 Jul 36	171LTS111	303954
Sweden	Switzerland	25 Jul 36	171LTS177	303959
Netherlands	Switzerland	27 Jan 37	186LTS433	304327
Multilateral		03 Mar 37	182LTS127	304205
Multilateral		10 Feb 38	192LTS59	304461

PARTY ONE	PARTY TWO	DATE	CITATION	NUMBER
Social security				
France	Italy	30 Sep 19	5LTS279	300133
Belgium	France	14 Feb 21	12LTS245	300317
United Arab Rep	UK Great Britain	18 Jul 23	18LTS323	300474
Multilateral		24 Jul 23	28LTS11	300701
Austria	Czechoslovakia	30 Nov 23	126LTS171	302880
Austria	Serb/Croat/Slovene	29 Mar 24	114LTS421	302670
Netherlands	Poland	30 May 24	34LTS9	300865
Austria	Hungary	30 Sep 24	42LTS177	301040
Czechoslovakia	Poland	23 Apr 25	44LTS309	301091
Austria	Germany	08 Jan 26	62LTS95	301459
Germany	Poland	27 Mar 26	64LTS249	301506
Belgium	Luxembourg	20 Oct 26	78LTS375	301796
Czechoslovakia	Poland	30 May 27	98LTS233	302251
Germany	Saar	13 Oct 27	70LTS121	301629
Germany	Lithuania	29 Jan 28	89LTS83	302008
Multilateral		25 Oct 28	84LTS7	301901
Germany	Serb/Croat/Slovene	15 Dec 28	95LTS113	302170
Latvia	Poland	12 Feb 29	101LTS75	302321
Estonia	USSR (Soviet Union)	17 May 29	94LTS323	302152
Austria	Germany	05 Feb 30	119LTS201	302746
Austria	Hungary	03 Jun 30	122LTS69	302799
Multilateral		28 Oct 33	159LTS199	303663
United Arab Rep	UK Great Britain	09 Sep 36	182LTS317	304219
Unemployment				
France	UK Great Britain	06 Aug 14	10LTS333	300278
Austria	Germany	11 Aug 21	29LTS429	300753
Austria	Germany	18 Feb 24	29LTS435	300754
Germany	Poland	14 Jul 27	73LTS251	301718
Germany	Switzerland	04 Feb 28	79LTS241	301814
Austria	Germany	29 Feb 28	79LTS405	301816
Czechoslovakia	Serb/Croat/Slovene	19 Sep 28	87LTS309	301976
Switzerland	UK Great Britain	09 Nov 29	100LTS21	302291
Multilateral		10 Dec 31	129LTS177	302961
France	Switzerland	09 Jun 33	181LTS275	304194
Luxembourg	Netherlands	01 Apr 36	179LTS11	304130
Denmark	Sweden	20 Nov 36	173LTS207	304014
Austria	Sweden	15 Jan 37	174LTS125	304043
Poland	Sweden	13 Sep 37	187LTS431	304348
Migrant worker				
France	UK Great Britain	06 Aug 14	10LTS333	300278
France	Italy	30 Sep 19	5LTS279	300133
Czechoslovakia	France	20 Mar 20	3LTS139	300095
Austria	Germany	01 Sep 20	4LTS201	300107
Brazil	Italy	08 Oct 21	16LTS9	300401
Germany	Netherlands	23 May 23	25LTS275	300617
Belgium	France	24 Dec 24	78LTS367	301795
Multilateral		14 Sep 26	77LTS149	301769
Belgium	Luxembourg	20 Oct 26	78LTS375	301796
Austria	Netherlands	01 Mar 27	68LTS75	301570
Austria	Portugal	28 Mar 27	68LTS81	301571
Germany	Poland	24 Nov 27	92LTS19	302080
Czechoslovakia	Germany	27 Mar 28	90LTS151	302032
Czechoslovakia	Germany	11 May 28	81LTS441	301854
Germany	Serb/Croat/Slovene	15 Dec 28	95LTS149	302171
Germany	Serb/Croat/Slovene	15 Dec 28	95LTS113	302170
France	Luxembourg	31 Mar 30	122LTS29	302797
Danzig	Norway	07 Apr 30	100LTS391	302308
Belgium	France	23 Aug 30	166LTS11	303825
Belgium	France	30 Mar 31	126LTS195	302882
France	Sweden	09 Jun 34	154LTS101	303541
Luxembourg	Netherlands	01 Apr 36	179LTS11	304130
Finland	France	26 May 37	179LTS327	304160
Latvia	Poland	29 Oct 38	195LTS169	304547

PARTY ONE	PARTY TWO	DATE	CITATION	NUMBER
Migrant worker (Cont.)				
Nigeria	Spanish Colonies	09 Dec 42	205LTS41	304825
Research cooperation				
Afghanistan	France	09 Sep 22	105LTS153	302409
Multilateral		29 Oct 27	127LTS27	302903
Afghanistan	USSR (Soviet Union)	06 May 35	164LTS335	303800
Germany	Hungary	28 May 36	178LTS445	304127
Scientific exchange				
Poland	Yugoslavia	02 Dec 31	139LTS119	303207
Finland	Hungary	22 Oct 37	190LTS281	304426
General economics				
Germany	Hungary	01 Jun 20	7LTS207	300187
Japan	Paraguay	30 Nov 20	6LTS367	300169
Bulgaria	Germany	19 Feb 21	6LTS227	300157
Bulgaria	Sweden	14 Apr 21	5LTS240	300131
Spain	Sweden	19 Jun 21	5LTS387	300143
Bulgaria	Sweden	30 Sep 21	7LTS137	300182
Germany	Hungary	06 Nov 23	45LTS253	301103
Japan	Peru	30 Sep 24	102LTS33	302351
China	Denmark	12 Dec 28	91LTS207	302062
Belgium	Persia	23 May 29	110LTS369	302568
Sweden	UK Great Britain	28 Aug 30	114LTS9	302652
Hungary	Sweden	17 Jun 36	184LTS11	304239
General trade				
Germany	Switzerland	15 Mar 20	12LTS19	300303
Czechoslovakia	Germany	29 Jun 20	17LTS69	300430
Norway	Portugal	14 Oct 20	2LTS237	300069
Muscat and Oman	UK Great Britain	11 Feb 21	8LTS261	300224
France	Norway	23 Apr 21	14LTS375	300386
Austria	Czechoslovakia	04 May 21	15LTS13	300388
Romania	Sweden	25 Nov 21	7LTS247	300190
Netherlands	Spain	05 Jan 22	9LTS257	300259
Bulgaria	Netherlands	09 Mar 22	9LTS265	300260
Afghanistan	France	28 Apr 22	105LTS147	302408
Norway	Spain	12 Jun 22	10LTS305	300276
Poland	Switzerland	26 Jun 22	12LTS305	300322
UK Great Britain	USSR (Soviet Union)	03 Jul 22	13LTS37	300345
Bulgaria	Denmark	11 Jul 22	12LTS225	300314
Germany	Spain	15 Jan 23	26LTS455	300662
Denmark	Romania	08 May 23	17LTS31	300425
Austria	Denmark	30 Jun 23	18LTS195	300464
Austria	Denmark	30 Jun 23	18LTS189	300463
Estonia	Sweden	07 Jul 23	20LTS189	300517
Austria	Netherlands	05 Sep 23	20LTS147	300514
Estonia	Iceland	07 Sep 23	23LTS131	300584
Denmark	Estonia	07 Sep 23	23LTS73	300577
Austria	Japan	02 Oct 23	22LTS349	300563
Finland	Netherlands	01 Nov 23	23LTS33	300574
Czechoslovakia	Denmark	31 Jan 24	23LTS139	300585
Lithuania	Sweden	17 Feb 24	23LTS153	300587
Japan	Siam	09 Mar 24	31LTS187	300795
Multilateral		12 Mar 24	24LTS17	300595
Multilateral		14 Mar 24	25LTS423	300633
Denmark	USSR (Soviet Union)	18 Jun 24	27LTS149	300677
Germany	Spain	25 Jul 24	41LTS363	301023
Germany	Guatemala	04 Oct 24	52LTS19	301246
Czechoslovakia	Netherlands	17 Oct 24	31LTS93	300786
Albania	Italy	06 Mar 25	44LTS359	301094
France	Hungary	13 Oct 25	48LTS9	301150
Bulgaria	France	22 Oct 25	44LTS257	301087
Germany	Sweden	14 May 26	51LTS99	301225
Albania	Serb/Croat/Slovene	22 Jun 26	91LTS55	302055
Estonia	Norway	28 Jul 26	43LTS25	301045
Czechoslovakia	Hungary	31 May 27	65LTS61	301520

PARTY ONE	PARTY TWO	DATE	CITATION	NUMBER
General trade (Cont.)				
Denmark	Italy	26 Oct 27	68LTS229	301586
France	Turkey	01 Nov 27	92LTS249	302092
Germany	Persia	15 May 28	107LTS389	302495
Austria	USA (United States)	19 Jun 28	118LTS241	302728
Bulgaria	Latvia	22 Jun 28	97LTS379	302236
Italy	Persia	24 Jul 28	95LTS269	302179
Abyssinia	Italy	02 Aug 28	94LTS413	302158
Panama	UK Great Britain	26 Sep 28	90LTS327	302046
Bel-Lux Econ Union	China	22 Nov 28	87LTS287	301975
Multilateral		14 Dec 28	110LTS171	302560
Ecuador	UK Great Britain	05 Jan 29	90LTS369	302048
Denmark	Latvia	09 Jan 29	86LTS37	301948
Italy	UK Great Britain	25 Jan 29	95LTS39	302162
Italy	Sweden	22 Feb 29	87LTS265	301973
Japan	Persia	30 Mar 29	107LTS427	302499
Belgium	Persia	09 May 29	110LTS391	302570
Persia	Sweden	10 May 29	102LTS9	302349
Italy	Poland	22 Jul 30	121LTS17	302780
India	Turkey	03 Sep 30	109LTS25	302525
France	Greece	23 May 31	125LTS415	302867
Poland	USA (United States)	15 Jun 31	139LTS395	303223
Austria	Yugoslavia	09 Mar 32	157LTS145	303609
Germany	Spain	06 Jul 32	148LTS391	303425
New Zealand	Norway	27 Oct 33	149LTS429	303444
Bel-Lux Econ Union	New Zealand	05 Dec 33	149LTS435	303445
Netherlands	Uruguay	29 Jan 34	166LTS43	303828
UK Great Britain	USSR (Soviet Union)	16 Feb 34	149LTS445	303446
Italy	Netherlands	01 Mar 34	163LTS367	303779
Romania	Spain	21 Mar 34	159LTS171	303661
Albania	Czechoslovakia	09 Apr 34	158LTS59	303626
Multilateral		26 Apr 34	164LTS63	303789
Bulgaria	Hungary	12 Jun 34	160LTS73	303684
Netherlands	Spain	16 Jun 34	168LTS29	303885
Finland	Greece	27 Jul 34	153LTS41	303505
Netherlands	UK Great Britain	30 Jul 34	154LTS305	303557
Germany	Sweden	28 Aug 34	154LTS249	303551
Estonia	Sweden	07 Dec 34	154LTS319	303558
Spain	Uruguay	02 Jan 35	164LTS95	303791
Greece	Sweden	17 Jan 35	157LTS9	303601
Denmark	Germany	24 Jan 35	160LTS155	303689
Netherlands	South Africa	20 Feb 35	160LTS143	303688
Bel-Lux Econ Union	USA (United States)	27 Feb 35	160LTS27	303681
Poland	UK Great Britain	27 Feb 35	162LTS181	303740
Chile	Finland	01 Mar 35	159LTS113	303653
Italy	UK Great Britain	18 Mar 35	160LTS289	303699
France	Sweden	22 Mar 35	158LTS287	303639
Bulgaria	Finland	22 Mar 35	159LTS123	303654
Czechoslovakia	USSR (Soviet Union)	25 Mar 35	161LTS257	303718
Brazil	UK Great Britain	27 Mar 35	160LTS311	303700
Latvia	Lithuania	10 Apr 35	159LTS305	303674
Estonia	Spain	08 May 35	159LTS363	303678
Belgium	Luxembourg	23 May 35	161LTS335	303722
New Zealand	Sweden	24 May 35	159LTS143	303657
Sweden	USA (United States)	25 May 35	161LTS109	303707
Finland	Turkey	06 Jun 35	160LTS165	303690
Italy	Sweden	24 Jun 35	161LTS21	303702
Italy	Norway	02 Jul 35	162LTS317	303744
Italy	Norway	02 Jul 35	162LTS323	303745
Canada	Poland	03 Jul 35	172LTS69	303980
USA (United States)	USSR (Soviet Union)	15 Jul 35	162LTS91	303737
Denmark	Spain	17 Aug 35	163LTS307	303773
Spain	Sweden	23 Aug 35	162LTS331	303746
Iraq	Sweden	03 Nov 35	163LTS419	303783
Bel-Lux Econ Union	Latvia	22 Feb 36	171LTS147	303956
Japan	Siam	08 Dec 37	188LTS375	304367

PARTY ONE	PARTY TWO	DATE	CITATION	NUMBER
General trade (Cont.)				
Germany	Siam	30 Dec 37	188LTS401	304368
Turkey	UK Great Britain	03 Feb 40	203LTS399	304781
United Arab Rep	UK Great Britain	26 May 41	204LTS147	304793
Belgium	UK Great Britain	04 Jun 42	204LTS363	304814
Chile	UK Great Britain	17 Jun 42	204LTS371	304815
Establishment of trade relations				
Estonia	USSR (Soviet Union)	02 Feb 20	11LTS29	300289
UK Great Britain	USSR (Soviet Union)	16 Mar 21	4LTS127	300104
Netherlands	Spain	24 Jun 21	7LTS121	300180
Spain	UK Great Britain	31 Oct 22	28LTS339	300719
Denmark	USSR (Soviet Union)	23 Apr 23	18LTS15	300450
Germany	Portugal	28 Apr 23	32LTS385	300827
Poland	UK Great Britain	26 Nov 23	28LTS428	300722
Albania	Italy	29 Feb 24	44LTS331	301092
Other Unilat Decla	Hungary	14 Mar 24	25LTS427	300634
Italy	Serb/Croat/Slovene	14 Jul 24	82LTS257	301876
Japan	Peru	30 Sep 24	102LTS33	302351
Bel-Lux Econ Union	Guatemala	07 Nov 24	69LTS17	301596
Japan	USSR (Soviet Union)	20 Jan 25	34LTS31	300866
France	Siam	14 Feb 25	43LTS189	301055
Japan	Latvia	04 Jul 25	80LTS305	301836
Hungary	Italy	20 Jul 25	45LTS39	301098
Great Britain	Japan	30 Jul 25	65LTS29	301517
Germany	USSR (Soviet Union)	12 Oct 25	53LTS7	301257
Czechoslovakia	Poland	15 Apr 26	67LTS305	301554
Czechoslovakia	Poland	21 Apr 26	58LTS9	301367
France	Turkey	30 May 26	54LTS195	301285
Finland	Turkey	02 Jun 26	70LTS329	301644
Albania	Serb/Croat/Slovene	22 Jun 26	91LTS9	302054
Hungary	UK Great Britain	23 Jul 26	67LTS183	301546
France	Germany	05 Aug 26	73LTS105	301711
Italy	Yemen	02 Sep 26	67LTS383	301559
Hungary	USA (United States)	04 Sep 26	58LTS111	301369
Haiti	Netherlands	07 Sep 26	71LTS219	301665
Bulgaria	Hungary	10 Sep 26	69LTS333	301615
Guatemala	Italy	15 Sep 26	70LTS175	301633
Abyssinia	Netherlands	30 Sep 26	78LTS89	301780
Albania	Greece	13 Oct 26	83LTS325	301899
Greece	New Zealand	16 Nov 26	85LTS43	301921
Bel-Lux Econ Union	Serb/Croat/Slovene	16 Dec 26	70LTS371	301647
Finland	Greece	18 Dec 26	70LTS89	301626
Hungary	Turkey	20 Dec 26	72LTS255	301697
Norway	Poland	22 Dec 26	66LTS359	301530
Haiti	Italy	03 Jan 27	71LTS405	301678
Estonia	Greece	04 Jan 27	69LTS33	301598
Bel-Lux Econ Union	Portugal	06 Jan 27	91LTS239	302065
Germany	Turkey	12 Jan 27	73LTS133	301712
Chile	Norway	09 Feb 27	80LTS325	301837
United Arab Rep	Hungary	16 Feb 27	80LTS61	301822
Estonia	Poland	19 Feb 27	115LTS177	302686
Greece	Latvia	25 Feb 27	71LTS25	301652
Czechoslovakia	Finland	02 Mar 27	66LTS385	301532
Persia	Poland	19 Mar 27	109LTS53	302528
Greece	Romania	28 Mar 27	68LTS67	301569
France	Germany	31 Mar 27	66LTS7	301524
Switzerland	Turkey	04 May 27	67LTS141	301544
Guatemala	Netherlands	12 May 27	85LTS323	301937
Serb/Croat/Slovene	UK Great Britain	12 May 27	80LTS165	301825
United Arab Rep	Serb/Croat/Slovene	15 May 27	96LTS367	302213
Czechoslovakia	Turkey	31 May 27	71LTS335	301674
Latvia	USSR (Soviet Union)	02 Jun 27	68LTS321	301591
Finland	Switzerland	24 Jun 27	68LTS103	301574
Greece	Norway	29 Jun 27	82LTS187	301869
Cuba	Spain	15 Jul 27	120LTS251	302770

PARTY ONE	PARTY TWO	DATE	CITATION	NUMBER
Establishment of trade relations (Cont.)				
Belgium	Portugal	20 Jul 27	71LTS431	301681
Czechoslovakia	Estonia	20 Jul 27	77LTS341	301776
Germany	Japan	20 Jul 27	74LTS107	301736
Austria	Finland	08 Aug 27	70LTS349	301645
France	Germany	17 Aug 27	76LTS5	301761
Latvia	Poland	22 Aug 27	115LTS121	302681
Bel-Lux Econ Union	Turkey	28 Aug 27	82LTS77	301862
France	Japan	30 Aug 27	68LTS235	301587
Italy	Lithuania	17 Sep 27	73LTS9	301701
Germany	Serb/Croat/Slovene	06 Oct 27	77LTS19	301763
Greece	Serb/Croat/Slovene	02 Nov 27	91LTS137	302060
Germany	Panama	21 Nov 27	115LTS239	302689
Finland	Sweden	14 Dec 27	72LTS29	301688
Denmark	Spain	02 Jan 28	71LTS271	301668
El Salvador	UK Great Britain	07 Jan 28	80LTS231	301828
Estonia	Serb/Croat/Slovene	01 Feb 28	106LTS139	302441
Sweden	Turkey	04 Feb 28	88LTS155	301994
Bulgaria	Estonia	11 Feb 28	79LTS43	301803
Bulgaria	Turkey	12 Feb 28	81LTS383	301848
Multilateral		20 Feb 28	86LTS111	301950
Guatemala	UK Great Britain	22 Feb 28	97LTS229	302226
Haiti	UK Great Britain	25 Feb 28	85LTS91	301924
France	Italy	07 Mar 28	72LTS213	301694
Colombia	Sweden	09 Mar 28	85LTS443	301944
Estonia	Turkey	12 Mar 28	86LTS453	301957
Canada	Czechoslovakia	15 Mar 28	82LTS147	301865
Germany	Greece	24 Mar 28	90LTS9	302031
Estonia	Latvia	25 Mar 28	72LTS195	301692
Austria	Iceland	06 Apr 28	87LTS343	301980
Austria	Denmark	06 Apr 28	85LTS423	301943
Austria	France	16 May 28	88LTS21	301986
Latvia	Turkey	28 May 28	94LTS295	302150
United Arab Rep	Palestine	21 Jun 28	80LTS277	301833
Estonia	Italy	01 Jul 28	87LTS277	301974
Czechoslovakia	France	02 Jul 28	99LTS105	302272
Hungary	Italy	04 Jul 28	92LTS117	302083
Japan	New Zealand	24 Jul 28	85LTS129	301927
Netherlands	Turkey	25 Jul 28	93LTS279	302116
Belgium	Bel-Lux Econ Union	16 Aug 28	81LTS411	301849
China	Germany	17 Aug 28	91LTS93	302057
Denmark	Greece	22 Aug 28	94LTS263	302147
Germany	South Africa	01 Sep 28	95LTS289	302181
Sweden	Turkey	24 Sep 28	82LTS9	301855
Panama	UK Great Britain	25 Sep 28	90LTS311	302045
Finland	Lithuania	06 Oct 28	82LTS71	301861
Hungary	Lithuania	23 Oct 28	84LTS281	301908
Germany	Lithuania	30 Oct 28	89LTS127	302010
Hungary	Sweden	08 Nov 28	89LTS283	302023
China	Norway	12 Nov 28	87LTS381	301983
Czechoslovakia	Serb/Croat/Slovene	14 Nov 28	97LTS9	302216
Hungary	Serb/Croat/Slovene	19 Nov 28	97LTS101	302222
Estonia	Germany	07 Dec 28	99LTS259	302273
Austria	Estonia	11 Dec 28	92LTS229	302091
Bel-Lux Econ Union	Spain	15 Dec 28	84LTS287	301909
China	Portugal	19 Dec 28	107LTS93	302471
China	Sweden	20 Dec 28	107LTS81	302470
China	France	23 Dec 28	92LTS267	302095
Hungary	Japan	23 Jan 29	91LTS317	302071
Finland	Serb/Croat/Slovene	29 Jan 29	96LTS77	302192
Germany	Persia	17 Feb 29	111LTS263	302591
Belgium	Finland	19 Feb 29	111LTS31	302577
Albania	Bel-Lux Econ Union	19 Feb 29	90LTS429	302053
Persia	USSR (Soviet Union)	10 Mar 29	107LTS419	302498
France	Greece	11 Mar 29	95LTS401	302187
Estonia	France	15 Mar 29	89LTS381	302029

PARTY ONE	PARTY TWO	DATE	CITATION	NUMBER
Establishment of trade relations (Cont.)				
Austria	Netherlands	28 Mar 29	109LTS39	302527
Estonia	Hungary	29 Apr 29	96LTS23	302189
Czechoslovakia	Persia	30 Apr 29	110LTS357	302567
Bel-Lux Econ Union	Persia	09 May 29	110LTS377	302569
Hungary	Lithuania	16 May 29	96LTS333	302211
Estonia	USSR (Soviet Union)	17 May 29	94LTS323	302152
Greece	Persia	24 May 29	121LTS221	302788
Albania	Switzerland	10 Jun 29	104LTS145	302384
Romania	Turkey	11 Jun 29	112LTS139	302613
Hungary	Persia	19 Jun 29	107LTS355	302491
Colombia	Denmark	21 Jun 29	125LTS113	302850
France	Switzerland	08 Jul 29	114LTS189	302664
Japan	Turkey	31 Jul 29	111LTS289	302592
Japan	Spain	05 Aug 29	113LTS9	302629
Estonia	Portugal	22 Aug 29	98LTS225	302250
Bel-Lux Econ Union	Switzerland	26 Aug 29	105LTS9	302401
France	Turkey	29 Aug 29	123LTS193	302815
Estonia	Turkey	14 Sep 29	97LTS365	302234
Estonia	Turkey	16 Sep 29	117LTS377	302704
China	Poland	18 Sep 29	120LTS331	302774
Turkey	UK Great Britain	25 Sep 29	94LTS41	302135
Serb/Croat/Slovene	Spain	27 Sep 29	98LTS319	302253
Sweden	Turkey	29 Sep 29	119LTS53	302740
Finland	Turkey	12 Oct 29	96LTS239	302205
Latvia	Serb/Croat/Slovene	18 Oct 29	96LTS229	302204
Sweden	Turkey	19 Oct 29	96LTS221	302203
Cuba	France	06 Nov 29	114LTS345	302665
Netherlands	Turkey	21 Nov 29	99LTS397	302284
Cuba	Japan	21 Dec 29	111LTS13	302575
Poland	Portugal	28 Dec 29	117LTS363	302703
Greece	Iceland	28 Jan 30	118LTS285	302731
China	Czechoslovakia	12 Feb 30	110LTS285	302561
Portugal	UK Great Britain	18 Feb 30	108LTS393	302522
Italy	Romania	25 Feb 30	106LTS179	302445
Italy	Romania	25 Feb 30	106LTS231	302447
Denmark	France	28 Feb 30	101LTS17	302316
Turkey	UK Great Britain	01 Mar 30	108LTS407	302523
Chile	United Arab Rep	05 Mar 30	124LTS25	302830
Austria	United Arab Rep	07 Mar 30	100LTS417	302310
Finland	Portugal	08 Mar 30	105LTS441	302431
Germany	Haiti	10 Mar 30	119LTS231	302747
United Arab Rep	Yugoslavia	13 Mar 30	110LTS133	302557
Czechoslovakia	United Arab Rep	16 Mar 30	107LTS179	302475
United Arab Rep	Netherlands	17 Mar 30	105LTS91	302404
United Arab Rep	Japan	19 Mar 30	111LTS223	302588
United Arab Rep	Germany	25 Mar 30	115LTS271	302691
Greece	Poland	10 Apr 30	120LTS369	302775
Austria	Germany	12 Apr 30	115LTS333	302694
United Arab Rep	Romania	16 Apr 30	117LTS405	302706
United Arab Rep	Poland	22 Apr 30	118LTS413	302735
Denmark	United Arab Rep	07 May 30	102LTS137	302358
Irish Free State	Italy	10 May 30	132LTS147	303034
Hungary	Turkey	21 May 30	105LTS117	302406
Hungary	Turkey	21 May 30	109LTS153	302534
Germany	Turkey	27 May 30	110LTS9	302553
Belgium	Turkey	27 May 30	111LTS49	302580
United Arab Rep	Norway	27 May 30	105LTS449	302432
Denmark	Turkey	31 May 30	119LTS165	302744
Greece	Hungary	03 Jun 30	122LTS37	302798
United Arab Rep	UK Great Britain	07 Jun 30	107LTS267	302483
United Arab Rep	Sweden	07 Jun 30	102LTS207	302363
United Arab Rep	Finland	13 Jun 30	111LTS315	302595
United Arab Rep	Persia	17 Jun 30	107LTS349	302490
Germany	Romania	18 Jun 30	110LTS95	302554
Albania	Japan	20 Jun 30	123LTS295	302820

PARTY ONE	PARTY TWO	DATE	CITATION	NUMBER
Establishment of trade relations (Cont.)				
Romania	Spain	20 Jun 30	117LTS411	302707
Norway	Romania	21 Jun 30	120LTS113	302762
Denmark	Lithuania	21 Jun 30	114LTS151	302662
Iceland	Lithuania	21 Jun 30	119LTS403	302759
Czechoslovakia	Romania	27 Jun 30	119LTS73	302742
Romania	Yugoslavia	04 Aug 30	107LTS253	302482
Romania	UK Great Britain	06 Aug 30	123LTS307	302822
Hungary	Romania	10 Aug 30	107LTS185	302476
Romania	USA (United States)	20 Aug 30	115LTS115	302680
Romania	Switzerland	25 Aug 30	118LTS9	302708
Finland	Romania	28 Aug 30	118LTS193	302723
Denmark	Romania	28 Aug 30	108LTS165	302506
Bel-Lux Econ Union	Romania	28 Aug 30	107LTS221	302479
Finland	Germany	28 Aug 30	111LTS327	302597
Netherlands	Romania	29 Aug 30	108LTS177	302507
Estonia	Romania	30 Aug 30	114LTS59	302654
Austria	Romania	30 Aug 30	118LTS17	302709
El Salvador	USA (United States)	05 Sep 30	134LTS207	303093
Brazil	Netherlands	16 Sep 30	125LTS197	302854
UK Great Britain	USSR (Soviet Union)	16 Sep 30	101LTS409	302340
Bulgaria	Romania	27 Sep 30	118LTS27	302710
Japan	Romania	22 Oct 30	112LTS15	302602
Latvia	Romania	23 Oct 30	118LTS33	302711
Greece	Turkey	30 Oct 30	125LTS371	302866
Albania	Romania	03 Nov 30	118LTS39	302712
Latvia	Lithuania	24 Nov 30	112LTS417	302627
Portugal	Romania	05 Dec 30	114LTS369	302666
Estonia	Lithuania	15 Jan 31	114LTS141	302661
Romania	Sweden	21 Mar 31	106LTS237	302448
Estonia	Finland	11 Apr 31	124LTS217	302835
Chile	France	22 May 31	124LTS31	302831
Siam	Switzerland	28 May 31	125LTS357	302864
Estonia	Latvia	03 Jun 31	120LTS235	302769
Hungary	Romania	12 Aug 31	186LTS325	304321
Brazil	Sweden	16 Oct 31	125LTS51	302845
Brazil	Germany	22 Oct 31	136LTS443	303143
Brazil	Czechoslovakia	27 Nov 31	136LTS453	303144
Iraq	Turkey	10 Jan 32	152LTS17	303480
Estonia	Spain	23 Jun 32	143LTS31	303303
Czechoslovakia	Greece	30 Jul 32	156LTS159	303599
Italy	UK Great Britain	26 Nov 32	136LTS385	303136
Finland	Turkey	19 Dec 33	149LTS333	303441
France	USSR (Soviet Union)	11 Jan 34	167LTS349	303878
Finland	USA (United States)	13 Feb 34	152LTS45	303484
Finland	Germany	24 Mar 34	149LTS343	303442
Estonia	Japan	21 Jun 34	150LTS423	303475
Lithuania	UK Great Britain	06 Jul 34	155LTS9	303565
India	Japan	12 Jul 34	155LTS31	303566
Latvia	UK Great Britain	17 Jul 34	154LTS25	303536
Netherlands	UK Great Britain	30 Jul 34	154LTS305	303557
Portugal	Sweden	19 Oct 34	154LTS77	303538
Haiti	USA (United States)	28 Mar 35	161LTS157	303709
Iran	USSR (Soviet Union)	27 Aug 35	176LTS299	304069
Chile	Netherlands	05 May 37	182LTS385	304223
Bel-Lux Econ Union	Siam	05 Nov 37	190LTS151	304413
Belgium	Siam	05 Nov 37	190LTS163	304414
Siam	Sweden	08 Nov 37	185LTS337	304298
Siam	USA (United States)	13 Nov 37	192LTS247	304476
Italy	Siam	03 Dec 37	189LTS255	304389
France	Siam	07 Dec 37	201LTS113	304708
Greece	Sweden	01 Feb 38	185LTS217	304285
Portugal	Siam	02 Jul 38	200LTS149	304688
Liberia	USA (United States)	08 Aug 38	201LTS163	304711
Chile	UK Great Britain	17 Jun 42	204LTS371	304815
Chile	UK Great Britain	28 Jun 43	205LTS109	304827

PARTY ONE	PARTY TWO	DATE	CITATION	NUMBER
Export quotas				
Canada	France	19 Sep 07	1LTS95	300012
Multilateral		10 Sep 19	7LTS331	300200
Austria	Poland	09 Jan 20	7LTS163	300185
Germany	Hungary	01 Jun 20	7LTS207	300187
Czechoslovakia	Germany	29 Jun 20	17LTS69	300430
Germany	Switzerland	09 Jul 20	12LTS25	300304
Austria	Germany	01 Sep 20	4LTS201	300107
Czechoslovakia	Serb/Croat/Slovene	18 Oct 20	17LTS19	300424
Japan	Paraguay	30 Nov 20	6LTS367	300169
Persia	USSR (Soviet Union)	26 Feb 21	9LTS383	300268
Austria	Czechoslovakia	10 Mar 21	9LTS333	300267
UK Great Britain	USSR (Soviet Union)	16 Mar 21	4LTS127	300104
Czechoslovakia	Italy	23 Mar 21	32LTS183	300815
Germany	Poland	10 Apr 21	6LTS233	300158
Czechoslovakia	Romania	23 Apr 21	15LTS235	300397
Austria	Czechoslovakia	04 May 21	15LTS13	300388
Germany	USSR (Soviet Union)	06 May 21	6LTS267	300159
Finland	France	13 Jul 21	29LTS445	300755
Austria	Poland	23 Sep 21	7LTS181	300186
Austria	Hungary	08 Oct 21	16LTS19	300402
Danzig	Poland	24 Oct 21	116LTS5	302699
Estonia	Finland	29 Oct 21	13LTS59	300348
Finland	USSR (Soviet Union)	14 Dec 21	16LTS221	300414
Estonia	France	07 Jan 22	62LTS9	301452
France	Poland	06 Feb 22	43LTS415	301074
Multilateral		06 Feb 22	38LTS267	300981
France	Switzerland	20 Mar 22	12LTS377	300332
Denmark	Germany	25 Apr 22	18LTS227	300466
Italy	Poland	12 May 22	59LTS293	301399
Austria	Poland	25 Sep 22	59LTS307	301400
Czechoslovakia	Latvia	07 Oct 22	20LTS379	300528
Estonia	Hungary	19 Oct 22	30LTS347	300774
Italy	Serb/Croat/Slovene	23 Oct 22	18LTS413	300479
Italy	Serb/Croat/Slovene	23 Oct 22	18LTS441	300480
Finland	USSR (Soviet Union)	28 Oct 22	19LTS153	300491
Spain	UK Great Britain	31 Oct 22	28LTS339	300719
Japan	Poland	07 Dec 22	32LTS61	300806
Canada	France	15 Dec 22	21LTS38	300532
Czechoslovakia	Greece	10 Jan 23	21LTS217	300544
Italy	Switzerland	27 Jan 23	25LTS21	300603
Liechtenstein	Switzerland	29 Mar 23	21LTS231	300545
Norway	Portugal	11 Apr 23	16LTS379	300418
Germany	Portugal	28 Apr 23	32LTS385	300827
Germany	Lithuania	01 Jun 23	51LTS387	301244
Latvia	UK Great Britain	22 Jun 23	20LTS395	300529
Estonia	Germany	27 Jun 23	41LTS161	301013
Belgium	Denmark	28 Jun 23	20LTS59	300507
Estonia	Sweden	07 Jul 23	20LTS189	300517
Czechoslovakia	Hungary	13 Jul 23	35LTS253	300899
Czechoslovakia	UK Great Britain	14 Jul 23	29LTS377	300748
Poland	Turkey	23 Jul 23	49LTS329	301189
Multilateral		24 Jul 23	28LTS171	300705
Denmark	Finland	03 Aug 23	21LTS269	300547
Netherlands	Portugal	22 Aug 23	20LTS139	300513
Estonia	Iceland	07 Sep 23	23LTS131	300584
Multilateral		03 Nov 23	30LTS371	300775
Finland	Poland	10 Nov 23	29LTS229	300744
Italy	Spain	15 Nov 23	39LTS49	300996
Japan	Serb/Croat/Slovene	16 Nov 23	42LTS99	301035
Hungary	Latvia	19 Nov 23	37LTS341	300959
Poland	UK Great Britain	26 Nov 23	28LTS428	300722
Multilateral		14 Dec 23	29LTS37	300732
Lithuania	Norway	21 Dec 23	32LTS55	300805
Lithuania	Sweden	17 Feb 24	23LTS153	300587

PARTY ONE	PARTY TWO	DATE	CITATION	NUMBER
Export quotas (Cont.)				
Netherlands	Portugal	27 Feb 24	27LTS105	300672
Germany	Siam	28 Feb 24	32LTS399	300828
Japan	Siam	09 Mar 24	31LTS187	300795
Sweden	Switzerland	20 Mar 24	25LTS243	300612
Denmark	Poland	22 Mar 24	31LTS13	300778
Iceland	Poland	22 Mar 24	31LTS35	300779
Denmark	Latvia	03 Apr 24	33LTS393	300860
Poland	Serb/Croat/Slovene	05 Apr 24	49LTS265	301185
Hungary	Romania	16 Apr 24	46LTS7	301111
Czechoslovakia	Iceland	08 May 24	46LTS419	301125
Multilateral		22 May 24	35LTS175	300895
Finland	Iceland	28 May 24	27LTS117	300676
Netherlands	Poland	30 May 24	34LTS9	300865
Finland	Japan	07 Jun 24	58LTS379	301383
Lithuania	Netherlands	10 Jun 24	34LTS373	300885
Latvia	Netherlands	02 Jul 24	37LTS121	300951
Bel-Lux Econ Union	Canada	03 Jul 24	32LTS35	300803
Estonia	Netherlands	22 Jul 24	48LTS199	301162
Latvia	Norway	14 Aug 24	36LTS211	300924
Czechoslovakia	France	18 Aug 24	44LTS21	301080
Finland	Latvia	23 Aug 24	37LTS383	300962
Netherlands	Portugal	27 Aug 24	31LTS235	300800
Hungary	Norway	16 Sep 24	33LTS103	300835
Multilateral		30 Sep 24	30LTS135	300766
Finland	Italy	22 Oct 24	32LTS149	300814
France	Latvia	30 Oct 24	37LTS399	300963
Iceland	Latvia	03 Nov 24	43LTS339	301069
Poland	Sweden	02 Dec 24	36LTS299	300930
Latvia	Switzerland	04 Dec 24	34LTS405	300889
Czechoslovakia	USA (United States)	05 Dec 24	56LTS271	301335
Hungary	Netherlands	09 Dec 24	47LTS91	301130
France	Poland	09 Dec 24	44LTS127	301081
Austria	Spain	03 Feb 25	43LTS313	301067
Poland	USA (United States)	10 Feb 25	37LTS141	300953
Multilateral		11 Feb 25	51LTS337	301239
Estonia	USA (United States)	02 Mar 25	43LTS289	301064
France	Portugal	04 Mar 25	44LTS197	301083
Albania	Italy	06 Mar 25	44LTS359	301094
Bel-Lux Econ Union	France	04 Apr 25	44LTS213	301085
Czechoslovakia	Poland	07 Apr 25	56LTS285	301337
Czechoslovakia	Greece	08 Apr 25	38LTS291	300984
Czechoslovakia	Sweden	18 Apr 25	36LTS289	300929
Bulgaria	Poland	29 Apr 25	60LTS103	301408
Finland	USA (United States)	02 May 25	47LTS351	301139
Spain	Sweden	04 May 25	36LTS323	300932
Germany	USA (United States)	21 May 25	52LTS133	301254
Hungary	Spain	17 Jun 25	60LTS69	301406
Bel-Lux Econ Union	Japan	27 Jun 25	36LTS95	300907
Bel-Lux Econ Union		07 Jul 25	54LTS267	301290
Finland	Spain	16 Jul 25	47LTS271	301135
Czechoslovakia	Spain	19 Jul 25	60LTS329	301419
Hungary	Italy	20 Jul 25	45LTS39	301098
Italy	Latvia	25 Jul 25	60LTS91	301407
Germany	UK Great Britain	13 Aug 25	43LTS89	301050
Portugal	Siam	14 Aug 25	55LTS57	301304
Siam	UK Great Britain	15 Sep 25	49LTS51	301176
France	Hungary	13 Oct 25	48LTS9	301150
Estonia	Switzerland	14 Oct 25	49LTS421	301195
Austria	China	19 Oct 25	55LTS9	301301
Czechoslovakia	Japan	30 Oct 25	58LTS263	301377
Germany	Italy	31 Oct 25	52LTS179	301256
Bulgaria	UK Great Britain	12 Nov 25	43LTS165	301052
Germany	Netherlands	26 Nov 25	57LTS159	301362
Siam	Sweden	19 Dec 25	58LTS429	301386
Lithuania	USA (United States)	23 Dec 25	54LTS377	301300

PARTY ONE	PARTY TWO	DATE	CITATION	NUMBER
Export quotas (Cont.)				
Bel-Lux Econ Union	Czechoslovakia	28 Dec 25	58LTS189	301372
Austria	Switzerland	06 Jan 26	46LTS299	301124
Estonia	UK Great Britain	18 Jan 26	48LTS209	301163
Albania	Czechoslovakia	19 Jan 26	64LTS349	301507
Latvia	USA (United States)	01 Feb 26	55LTS33	301302
Romania	USA (United States)	26 Feb 26	51LTS59	301221
Denmark	Siam	01 Mar 26	47LTS103	301131
Denmark	Turkey	22 Mar 26	48LTS231	301164
United Arab Rep	Greece	10 Apr 26	61LTS305	301441
Finland	Hungary	20 Apr 26	48LTS119	301154
Italy	Siam	09 May 26	61LTS215	301436
Greece	Netherlands	12 May 26	61LTS295	301440
France	Italy	29 May 26	62LTS425	301474
Finland	Greece	22 Jun 26	56LTS197	301331
Finland	Germany	26 Jun 26	56LTS203	301332
Germany	Latvia	28 Jun 26	58LTS403	301385
Bel-Lux Econ Union	Siam	13 Jul 26	62LTS287	301468
Germany	Switzerland	14 Jul 26	59LTS87	301391
Norway	Siam	16 Jul 26	60LTS35	301404
Italy	Yemen	02 Sep 26	67LTS383	301559
Greece	Sweden	10 Sep 26	63LTS37	301479
Bel-Lux Econ Union	Estonia	28 Sep 26	62LTS433	301475
Greece	Italy	24 Oct 26	63LTS51	301480
Greece	Switzerland	29 Nov 26	63LTS27	301478
France	Germany	16 Feb 27	62LTS155	301463
Czechoslovakia	Switzerland	16 Feb 27	64LTS7	301501
Bulgaria	Greece	28 Feb 27	68LTS59	301568
Estonia	Germany	05 Apr 27	64LTS355	301508
Greece	UK Great Britain	13 May 27	61LTS15	301425
Hungary	Italy	25 Jul 27	74LTS53	301731
Multilateral		08 Nov 27	97LTS391	302238
Germany	Siam	07 Apr 28	85LTS337	301938
Austria	USA (United States)	19 Jun 28	118LTS241	302728
Germany	Lithuania	30 Oct 28	90LTS255	302043
China	Norway	12 Nov 28	87LTS381	301983
France	Greece	11 Mar 29	95LTS401	302187
Estonia	France	15 Mar 29	89LTS381	302029
France	Germany	25 Apr 29	109LTS333	302548
Bolivia	Netherlands	30 May 29	133LTS113	303062
Italy	Panama	16 Oct 29	138LTS355	303199
Poland	Romania	07 Dec 29	119LTS283	302752
Turkey	UK Great Britain	01 Mar 30	108LTS407	302523
Germany	Irish Free State	12 May 30	131LTS153	303008
China	France	16 May 30	162LTS99	303738
Greece	Hungary	03 Jun 30	122LTS37	302798
Czechoslovakia	Romania	27 Jun 30	119LTS73	302742
Austria	Japan	16 Aug 30	126LTS351	302894
El Salvador	USA (United States)	05 Sep 30	134LTS207	303093
Chile	Czechoslovakia	18 Sep 30	140LTS161	303233
Norway	Turkey	16 Mar 31	138LTS41	303180
Poland	USA (United States)	15 Jun 31	139LTS395	303223
Multilateral		13 Jul 31	139LTS301	303219
Germany	Hungary	18 Jul 31	150LTS111	303458
Hungary	Romania	12 Aug 31	186LTS325	304321
Romania	Sweden	07 Oct 31	131LTS51	303003
Multilateral		11 Dec 31	170LTS251	303941
Brazil	Hungary	24 Dec 31	147LTS51	303389
Brazil	Poland	03 Feb 32	147LTS113	303396
Bulgaria	Germany	24 Jun 32	147LTS211	303400
Austria	Norway	03 Sep 32	137LTS403	303170
Brazil	Uruguay	25 Aug 33	176LTS381	304075
Brazil	Portugal	26 Aug 33	179LTS63	304134
Finland	UK Great Britain	29 Sep 33	149LTS167	303438
Latvia	Lithuania	01 Dec 33	148LTS97	303407
Latvia	Lithuania	01 Dec 33	148LTS87	303406

PARTY ONE	PARTY TWO	DATE	CITATION	NUMBER
Export quotas (Cont.)				
Estonia	Lithuania	13 Jan 34	148LTS337	303420
Argentina	Bel-Lux Econ Union	16 Jan 34	147LTS79	303392
Czechoslovakia	Poland	10 Feb 34	183LTS213	304238
Germany	Netherlands	06 Jun 34	174LTS33	304034
Turkey	Yugoslavia	17 Dec 34	178LTS471	304128
France	South Africa	11 Feb 35	189LTS17	304372
Haiti	USA (United States)	28 Mar 35	161LTS157	303709
Belgium	Luxembourg	23 May 35	161LTS335	303722
Iran	USSR (Soviet Union)	27 Aug 35	176LTS299	304069
Spain	Switzerland	30 Oct 35	166LTS157	303837
Canada	USA (United States)	15 Nov 35	168LTS355	303910
Netherlands	USA (United States)	20 Dec 35	178LTS239	304118
France	Spain	21 Dec 35	167LTS9	303856
Spain	Turkey	31 Dec 35	166LTS163	303838
Sweden	Turkey	27 Feb 36	167LTS75	303858
Luxembourg	Netherlands	01 Apr 36	179LTS11	304130
Norway	Uruguay	04 Apr 36	176LTS115	304055
Romania	UK Great Britain	02 May 36	184LTS145	304247
Norway	Turkey	08 Jun 36	170LTS227	303938
Ecuador	USA (United States)	12 Jun 36	170LTS377	303946
Norway	Spain	13 Jun 36	170LTS207	303936
Finland	Turkey	20 Jun 36	172LTS125	303982
Sweden	Uruguay	13 Aug 36	183LTS161	304232
Estonia	Italy	06 Oct 36	172LTS189	303989
Bulgaria	Finland	27 Oct 36	179LTS309	304158
Chile	Sweden	30 Oct 36	188LTS283	304364
Hungary	Yugoslavia	17 Dec 36	196LTS137	304576
Bel-Lux Econ Union	Uruguay	22 Feb 37	196LTS391	304600
Chile	Cuba	13 Mar 37	195LTS389	304558
Hungary	UK Great Britain	22 Mar 37	190LTS59	304405
Chile	Netherlands	05 May 37	182LTS385	304223
Romania	Yugoslavia	13 May 37	197LTS101	304609
Sweden	Yugoslavia	14 May 37	194LTS21	304504
Ecuador	Netherlands	27 May 37	194LTS179	304521
Estonia	France	16 Oct 37	183LTS41	304227
Bel-Lux Econ Union	Siam	05 Nov 37	190LTS151	304413
Siam	Sweden	08 Nov 37	185LTS337	304298
Siam	USA (United States)	13 Nov 37	192LTS247	304476
Siam	UK Great Britain	23 Nov 37	188LTS333	304366
Sweden	Turkey	31 Dec 37	184LTS399	304260
Bel-Lux Econ Union	Estonia	13 Jan 38	185LTS63	304275
Greece	Latvia	15 Jan 38	195LTS19	304533
Greece	Sweden	01 Feb 38	185LTS217	304285
Netherlands	Siam	01 Feb 38	193LTS13	304485
Portugal	UK Great Britain	11 May 38	191LTS285	304450
Cuba	Portugal	06 Sep 38	195LTS443	304565
UK Great Britain	USA (United States)	17 Nov 38	200LTS293	304700
Iraq	USA (United States)	03 Dec 38	203LTS107	304753
Sweden	Turkey	20 Jan 39	194LTS107	304513
Turkey	USA (United States)	01 Apr 39	202LTS129	304741
Greece	Sweden	01 May 39	196LTS205	304582
UK Great Britain	USA (United States)	23 Jun 39	198LTS333	304651
Norway	Spain	26 Jul 39	198LTS87	304627
Import quotas				
Canada	France	19 Sep 07	1LTS95	300012
Multilateral		10 Sep 19	7LTS331	300200
Multilateral		10 Sep 19	8LTS11	300201
Belgium	Portugal	22 Jan 20	3LTS149	300096
France	Germany	19 May 20	1LTS383	300031
Germany	Hungary	01 Jun 20	7LTS207	300187
France	Portugal	08 Jun 20	1LTS393	300032
Czechoslovakia	Germany	29 Jun 20	17LTS69	300430
France	Italy	27 Aug 20	8LTS95	300210
Austria	Germany	01 Sep 20	4LTS201	300107

PARTY ONE	PARTY TWO	DATE	CITATION	NUMBER
Import quotas (Cont.)				
Czechoslovakia	Serb/Croat/Slovene	18 Oct 20	17LTS19	300424
Bulgaria	Netherlands	13 Nov 20	7LTS107	300178
Japan	Paraguay	30 Nov 20	6LTS367	300169
Persia	USSR (Soviet Union)	26 Feb 21	9LTS383	300268
Austria	Czechoslovakia	10 Mar 21	9LTS333	300267
UK Great Britain	USSR (Soviet Union)	16 Mar 21	4LTS127	300104
Czechoslovakia	Italy	23 Mar 21	32LTS183	300815
Germany	Poland	10 Apr 21	6LTS233	300158
Czechoslovakia	Romania	23 Apr 21	15LTS235	300397
Austria	Czechoslovakia	04 May 21	15LTS13	300388
Germany	USSR (Soviet Union)	06 May 21	6LTS267	300159
Finland	France	13 Jul 21	29LTS445	300755
Austria	Hungary	08 Oct 21	16LTS19	300402
Danzig	Poland	24 Oct 21	116LTS5	302699
Estonia	Finland	29 Oct 21	13LTS59	300348
Norway	Spain	01 Dec 21	9LTS69	300244
Finland	USSR (Soviet Union)	14 Dec 21	16LTS221	300414
Estonia	France	07 Jan 22	62LTS9	301452
France	Poland	06 Feb 22	43LTS415	301074
Multilateral		06 Feb 22	38LTS267	300981
Austria	Hungary	08 Feb 22	55LTS367	301320
France	Switzerland	20 Mar 22	12LTS377	300332
Finland	Germany	21 Apr 22	19LTS87	300487
Denmark	Germany	25 Apr 22	18LTS227	300466
Italy	Poland	12 May 22	59LTS293	301399
Austria	Poland	25 Sep 22	59LTS307	301400
Czechoslovakia	Latvia	07 Oct 22	20LTS379	300528
Estonia	Hungary	19 Oct 22	30LTS347	300774
Italy	Serb/Croat/Slovene	23 Oct 22	18LTS413	300479
Italy	Serb/Croat/Slovene	23 Oct 22	18LTS441	300480
Spain	UK Great Britain	31 Oct 22	28LTS339	300719
Japan	Poland	07 Dec 22	32LTS61	300806
Canada	France	15 Dec 22	21LTS38	300532
Czechoslovakia	Greece	10 Jan 23	21LTS217	300544
Germany	Spain	15 Jan 23	26LTS455	300662
Italy	Switzerland	27 Jan 23	25LTS21	300603
Liechtenstein	Switzerland	29 Mar 23	21LTS231	300545
Germany	Portugal	28 Apr 23	32LTS385	300827
Latvia	UK Great Britain	22 Jun 23	20LTS395	300529
Estonia	Germany	27 Jun 23	41LTS161	301013
Belgium	Denmark	28 Jun 23	20LTS59	300507
Estonia	Sweden	07 Jul 23	20LTS189	300517
Czechoslovakia	UK Great Britain	14 Jul 23	29LTS377	300748
Poland	Turkey	23 Jul 23	49LTS329	301189
Multilateral		24 Jul 23	28LTS171	300705
Denmark	Finland	03 Aug 23	21LTS269	300547
Netherlands	Portugal	22 Aug 23	20LTS139	300513
Estonia	Iceland	07 Sep 23	23LTS131	300584
Norway	Spain	07 Oct 23	59LTS47	301389
Multilateral		03 Nov 23	30LTS371	300775
Finland	Poland	10 Nov 23	29LTS229	300744
Italy	Spain	15 Nov 23	39LTS49	300996
Japan	Serb/Croat/Slovene	16 Nov 23	42LTS99	301035
Hungary	Latvia	19 Nov 23	37LTS341	300959
Poland	UK Great Britain	26 Nov 23	28LTS428	300722
Multilateral		14 Dec 23	29LTS37	300732
Lithuania	Norway	21 Dec 23	32LTS55	300805
France	Italy	10 Jan 24	43LTS431	301076
Lithuania	Sweden	17 Feb 24	23LTS153	300587
France	Greece	21 Feb 24	43LTS481	301077
Netherlands	Portugal	27 Feb 24	27LTS105	300672
Germany	Siam	28 Feb 24	32LTS399	300828
Japan	Siam	09 Mar 24	31LTS187	300795
Sweden	Switzerland	20 Mar 24	25LTS243	300612
Iceland	Poland	22 Mar 24	31LTS35	300779

PARTY ONE	PARTY TWO	DATE	CITATION	NUMBER
Import quotas (Cont.)				
Denmark	Poland	22 Mar 24	31LTS13	300778
Denmark	Latvia	03 Apr 24	33LTS393	300860
Poland	Serb/Croat/Slovene	05 Apr 24	49LTS265	301185
France	Italy	10 Apr 24	43LTS485	301078
Czechoslovakia	Iceland	08 May 24	46LTS419	301125
Multilateral		22 May 24	35LTS175	300895
Sweden	USA (United States)	22 May 24	29LTS421	300752
Norway	USA (United States)	24 May 24	26LTS43	300639
Finland	Iceland	28 May 24	27LTS117	300676
Netherlands	Poland	30 May 24	34LTS9	300865
Finland	Japan	07 Jun 24	58LTS379	301383
Lithuania	Netherlands	10 Jun 24	34LTS373	300885
Latvia	Netherlands	02 Jul 24	37LTS121	300951
Bel-Lux Econ Union	Canada	03 Jul 24	32LTS35	300803
Estonia	Netherlands	22 Jul 24	48LTS199	301162
Germany	Spain	25 Jul 24	41LTS363	301023
Latvia	Norway	14 Aug 24	36LTS211	300924
Czechoslovakia	France	18 Aug 24	44LTS21	301080
Finland	Latvia	23 Aug 24	37LTS383	300962
Netherlands	Portugal	27 Aug 24	31LTS235	300800
Hungary	Norway	16 Sep 24	33LTS103	300835
Multilateral		30 Sep 24	30LTS135	300766
Finland	Italy	22 Oct 24	32LTS149	300814
France	Latvia	30 Oct 24	37LTS399	300963
Iceland	Latvia	03 Nov 24	43LTS339	301069
Germany	Switzerland	17 Nov 24	41LTS473	301026
Poland	Sweden	02 Dec 24	36LTS299	300930
Austria	Norway	03 Dec 24	31LTS151	300792
Latvia	Switzerland	04 Dec 24	34LTS405	300889
Czechoslovakia	USA (United States)	05 Dec 24	56LTS271	301335
France	Poland	09 Dec 24	44LTS127	301081
Hungary	Netherlands	09 Dec 24	47LTS91	301130
France	Saar	15 Jan 25	44LTS181	301082
Austria	Spain	03 Feb 25	43LTS313	301067
Poland	USA (United States)	10 Feb 25	37LTS141	300953
Multilateral		11 Feb 25	51LTS337	301239
Estonia	USA (United States)	02 Mar 25	43LTS289	301064
France	Portugal	04 Mar 25	44LTS197	301083
Albania	Italy	06 Mar 25	44LTS359	301094
Bel-Lux Econ Union	France	04 Apr 25	44LTS213	301085
Czechoslovakia	Poland	07 Apr 25	56LTS285	301337
Czechoslovakia	Greece	08 Apr 25	38LTS291	300984
Czechoslovakia	Sweden	18 Apr 25	36LTS289	300929
Bulgaria	Poland	29 Apr 25	60LTS103	301408
Finland	USA (United States)	02 May 25	47LTS351	301139
Spain	Sweden	04 May 25	36LTS323	300932
Germany	Greece	15 May 25	40LTS6	301001
Germany	USA (United States)	21 May 25	52LTS133	301254
Multilateral		09 Jun 25	49LTS9	301174
Hungary	Spain	17 Jun 25	60LTS69	301406
Bel-Lux Econ Union	Japan	27 Jun 25	36LTS95	300907
Bel-Lux Econ Union		07 Jul 25	54LTS267	301290
Finland	Spain	16 Jul 25	47LTS271	301135
Czechoslovakia	Spain	19 Jul 25	60LTS329	301419
Hungary	Italy	20 Jul 25	45LTS39	301098
Italy	Latvia	25 Jul 25	60LTS91	301407
France	Spain	03 Aug 25	38LTS371	300992
Germany	UK Great Britain	13 Aug 25	43LTS89	301050
Portugal	Siam	14 Aug 25	55LTS57	301304
Siam	UK Great Britain	15 Sep 25	49LTS51	301176
Austria	Germany	03 Oct 25	52LTS171	301255
France	Hungary	13 Oct 25	48LTS9	301150
Estonia	Switzerland	14 Oct 25	49LTS421	301195
Austria	China	19 Oct 25	55LTS9	301301
Czechoslovakia	Japan	30 Oct 25	58LTS263	301377

PARTY ONE	PARTY TWO	DATE	CITATION	NUMBER
Import quotas (Cont.)				
Germany	Italy	31 Oct 25	52LTS179	301256
Germany	Switzerland	06 Nov 25	53LTS283	301262
Bulgaria	UK Great Britain	12 Nov 25	43LTS165	301052
British Empire	Greece	26 Nov 25	63LTS167	301488
Germany	Netherlands	26 Nov 25	57LTS159	301362
Norway	USSR (Soviet Union)	15 Dec 25	47LTS9	301127
Austria	Portugal	18 Dec 25	54LTS91	301277
Siam	Sweden	19 Dec 25	58LTS429	301386
Lithuania	USA (United States)	23 Dec 25	54LTS377	301300
Bel-Lux Econ Union	Czechoslovakia	28 Dec 25	58LTS189	301372
Austria	Switzerland	06 Jan 26	46LTS299	301124
Estonia	UK Great Britain	18 Jan 26	48LTS209	301163
Albania	Czechoslovakia	19 Jan 26	64LTS349	301507
Latvia	USA (United States)	01 Feb 26	55LTS33	301302
France	Germany	12 Feb 26	48LTS153	301157
Romania	USA (United States)	26 Feb 26	51LTS59	301221
Denmark	Siam	01 Mar 26	47LTS103	301131
Denmark	Germany	20 Mar 26	57LTS131	301359
Germany	Portugal	20 Mar 26	53LTS361	301266
India	Indochina	20 Mar 26	57LTS19	301348
Denmark	Turkey	22 Mar 26	48LTS231	301164
Finland	Hungary	20 Apr 26	48LTS119	301154
Italy	Siam	09 May 26	61LTS215	301436
Greece	Netherlands	12 May 26	61LTS295	301440
Austria	Germany	21 May 26	53LTS397	301269
France	Italy	29 May 26	62LTS425	301474
Finland	Greece	22 Jun 26	56LTS197	301331
Finland	Germany	26 Jun 26	56LTS203	301332
Germany	Latvia	28 Jun 26	58LTS403	301385
Bel-Lux Econ Union	Siam	13 Jul 26	62LTS287	301468
Germany	Switzerland	14 Jul 26	59LTS87	301391
Norway	Siam	16 Jul 26	60LTS35	301404
Dominican Republic	USA (United States)	19 Jul 26	54LTS145	301282
Austria	Netherlands	04 Aug 26	59LTS243	301394
Norway	Turkey	11 Aug 26	47LTS441	301149
Netherlands	Turkey	11 Aug 26	48LTS271	301168
Italy	Yemen	02 Sep 26	67LTS383	301559
Greece	Sweden	10 Sep 26	63LTS37	301479
Greece	Italy	24 Oct 26	63LTS51	301480
Greece	Switzerland	29 Nov 26	63LTS27	301478
France	Germany	16 Feb 27	62LTS155	301463
Czechoslovakia	Switzerland	16 Feb 27	64LTS7	301501
Bulgaria	Greece	28 Feb 27	68LTS59	301568
Estonia	Germany	05 Apr 27	64LTS355	301508
Hungary	Italy	25 Jul 27	74LTS53	301731
Denmark	Turkey	24 Sep 27	61LTS287	301439
Multilateral		08 Nov 27	97LTS391	302238
Germany	Siam	07 Apr 28	85LTS337	301938
Austria	USA (United States)	19 Jun 28	118LTS241	302728
Germany	Lithuania	30 Oct 28	90LTS255	302043
France	Greece	11 Mar 29	95LTS401	302187
Estonia	France	15 Mar 29	89LTS381	302029
France	Germany	25 Apr 29	109LTS333	302548
Bolivia	Netherlands	30 May 29	133LTS113	303062
Italy	Panama	16 Oct 29	138LTS355	303199
Poland	Romania	07 Dec 29	119LTS283	302752
Turkey	UK Great Britain	01 Mar 30	108LTS407	302523
Germany	Irish Free State	12 May 30	131LTS153	303008
China	France	16 May 30	162LTS99	303738
Greece	Hungary	03 Jun 30	122LTS37	302798
Poland	Romania	23 Jun 30	133LTS163	303066
Czechoslovakia	Romania	27 Jun 30	119LTS73	302742
Austria	Japan	16 Aug 30	126LTS351	302894
El Salvador	USA (United States)	05 Sep 30	134LTS207	303093
Norway	Turkey	16 Mar 31	138LTS41	303180

PARTY ONE	PARTY TWO	DATE	CITATION	NUMBER
Import quotas (Cont.)				
Czechoslovakia	Germany	20 Apr 31	141LTS307	303271
Guatemala	UK Great Britain	06 Jun 31	132LTS15	303027
Poland	USA (United States)	15 Jun 31	139LTS395	303223
Multilateral		13 Jul 31	139LTS301	303219
Germany	Hungary	18 Jul 31	150LTS111	303458
Hungary	Romania	12 Aug 31	186LTS325	304321
Romania	Sweden	07 Oct 31	131LTS51	303003
Bolivia	Denmark	09 Nov 31	147LTS27	303387
Norway	Portugal	13 Nov 31	129LTS455	302977
Brazil	Canada	04 Dec 31	139LTS241	303214
Brazil	Mexico	07 Dec 31	139LTS247	303215
Multilateral		11 Dec 31	170LTS251	303941
Bel-Lux Econ Union	Chile	14 Dec 31	126LTS247	302887
Brazil	Hungary	24 Dec 31	147LTS51	303389
Brazil	Poland	03 Feb 32	147LTS113	303396
Japan	Portugal	23 Mar 32	128LTS363	302941
Lithuania	Portugal	12 Apr 32	129LTS135	302958
Belgium	France	18 Jun 32	137LTS289	303163
Bulgaria	Germany	24 Jun 32	147LTS211	303400
Denmark	UK Great Britain	24 Apr 33	139LTS127	303208
Argentina	UK Great Britain	01 May 33	143LTS67	303305
Germany	UK Great Britain	03 May 33	140LTS139	303231
Norway	UK Great Britain	15 May 33	145LTS187	303355
Hungary	Yugoslavia	15 May 33	144LTS321	303335
Sweden	UK Great Britain	15 May 33	140LTS317	303245
Estonia	Finland	16 May 33	141LTS19	303257
Iceland	UK Great Britain	19 May 33	144LTS33	303319
Latvia	UK Great Britain	06 Jul 33	142LTS217	303294
Austria	UK Great Britain	27 Jul 33	142LTS157	303287
Brazil	Uruguay	25 Aug 33	176LTS381	304075
Brazil	Portugal	26 Aug 33	179LTS63	304134
Bulgaria	Czechoslovakia	29 Aug 33	148LTS15	303402
Estonia	Poland	26 Sep 33	150LTS309	303464
Finland	UK Great Britain	29 Sep 33	149LTS167	303438
Latvia	Lithuania	01 Dec 33	148LTS97	303407
Latvia	Lithuania	01 Dec 33	148LTS87	303406
Latvia	USSR (Soviet Union)	04 Dec 33	148LTS177	303411
France	USSR (Soviet Union)	11 Jan 34	167LTS349	303878
Estonia	Lithuania	13 Jan 34	148LTS337	303420
Argentina	Bel-Lux Econ Union	16 Jan 34	147LTS79	303392
Czechoslovakia	Poland	10 Feb 34	183LTS213	304238
Denmark	Germany	01 Mar 34	150LTS31	303451
Estonia	Germany	29 Mar 34	148LTS251	303416
Spain	Turkey	19 May 34	149LTS15	303428
Bel-Lux Econ Union	Turkey	31 May 34	150LTS289	303462
Germany	Netherlands	06 Jun 34	174LTS33	304034
Denmark	France	31 Jul 34	150LTS381	303471
Finland	Sweden	05 Sep 34	154LTS239	303550
Poland	Spain	14 Dec 34	168LTS315	303908
Brazil	USA (United States)	02 Feb 35	166LTS211	303840
France	South Africa	11 Feb 35	189LTS17	304372
Multilateral		20 Feb 35	193LTS59	304487
Haiti	USA (United States)	28 Mar 35	161LTS157	303709
Italy	South Africa	21 May 35	189LTS31	304373
Belgium	Luxembourg	23 May 35	161LTS335	303722
Turkey	UK Great Britain	04 Jun 35	167LTS91	303860
Czechoslovakia	Hungary	14 Jun 35	171LTS401	303976
UK Great Britain	Uruguay	26 Jun 35	176LTS153	304058
France	South Africa	27 Aug 35	189LTS41	304374
Iran	USSR (Soviet Union)	27 Aug 35	176LTS299	304069
Colombia	USA (United States)	13 Sep 35	170LTS293	303944
Bulgaria	Netherlands	23 Sep 35	166LTS51	303829
Canada	USA (United States)	15 Nov 35	168LTS355	303910
Germany	Latvia	04 Dec 35	166LTS93	303834
Honduras	USA (United States)	18 Dec 35	167LTS313	303876

PARTY ONE	PARTY TWO	DATE	CITATION	NUMBER
Import quotas (Cont.)				
Netherlands	USA (United States)	20 Dec 35	178LTS239	304118
France	Spain	21 Dec 35	167LTS9	303856
Czechoslovakia	Germany	30 Dec 35	173LTS333	304023
Spain	Turkey	31 Dec 35	166LTS163	303838
Switzerland	USA (United States)	09 Jan 36	171LTS231	303962
France	Sweden	18 Jan 36	167LTS197	303866
Sweden	Turkey	27 Feb 36	167LTS75	303858
Nicaragua	USA (United States)	11 Mar 36	173LTS141	304009
Albania	Italy	19 Mar 36	173LTS107	304007
Albania	Italy	19 Mar 36	173LTS131	304008
Czechoslovakia	Finland	21 Mar 36	179LTS295	304156
Finland	Latvia	28 Mar 36	171LTS155	303957
Norway	Uruguay	04 Apr 36	176LTS115	304055
Netherlands	Poland	09 Apr 36	177LTS71	304081
Guatemala	USA (United States)	24 Apr 36	170LTS345	303945
France	USA (United States)	06 May 36	199LTS259	304679
Finland	USA (United States)	18 May 36	172LTS97	303981
Norway	Turkey	08 Jun 36	170LTS227	303938
Ecuador	USA (United States)	12 Jun 36	170LTS377	303946
Norway	Spain	13 Jun 36	170LTS207	303936
Hungary	Italy	04 Jul 36	181LTS331	304199
Brazil	Norway	27 Jul 36	176LTS125	304056
Brazil	Denmark	30 Jul 36	194LTS81	304510
Brazil	Hungary	30 Jul 36	177LTS53	304079
Brazil	UK Great Britain	10 Aug 36	172LTS273	303996
Sweden	Uruguay	13 Aug 36	183LTS161	304232
Australia	Czechoslovakia	19 Aug 36	177LTS245	304093
Finland	Netherlands	25 Aug 36	172LTS151	303985
Italy	Norway	25 Aug 36	171LTS377	303974
Turkey	UK Great Britain	02 Sep 36	172LTS289	303998
Finland	Italy	28 Sep 36	172LTS155	303986
Australia	Bel-Lux Econ Union	03 Oct 36	177LTS271	304094
Estonia	Italy	06 Oct 36	172LTS189	303989
Bulgaria	Finland	27 Oct 36	179LTS309	304158
Chile	Sweden	30 Oct 36	188LTS283	304364
UK Great Britain	Yugoslavia	27 Nov 36	181LTS281	304195
Australia	France	27 Nov 36	177LTS301	304095
Costa Rica	USA (United States)	28 Nov 36	181LTS183	304189
Italy	Sweden	01 Dec 36	173LTS257	304017
Iraq	UK Great Britain	14 Dec 36	177LTS221	304091
Hungary	Yugoslavia	17 Dec 36	196LTS137	304576
Chile	Netherlands	30 Dec 36	177LTS87	304082
Czechoslovakia	South Africa	27 Jan 37	189LTS97	304377
Italy	Latvia	05 Feb 37	178LTS33	304104
Estonia	Sweden	08 Feb 37	176LTS193	304061
Netherlands	Turkey	17 Feb 37	182LTS221	304213
France	Sweden	17 Feb 37	176LTS267	304065
France	USA (United States)	18 Feb 37	184LTS479	304269
Cuba	UK Great Britain	19 Feb 37	192LTS301	304480
Bel-Lux Econ Union	Uruguay	22 Feb 37	196LTS391	304600
Brazil	Netherlands	15 Mar 37	179LTS395	304166
Hungary	UK Great Britain	22 Mar 37	190LTS59	304405
Czechoslovakia	Italy	31 Mar 37	193LTS165	304492
Italy	Norway	31 Mar 37	177LTS349	304097
Finland	UK Great Britain	14 Apr 37	179LTS289	304155
Canada	Haiti	23 Apr 37	194LTS59	304507
Chile	Netherlands	05 May 37	182LTS385	304223
Romania	Yugoslavia	13 May 37	197LTS101	304609
Sweden	Yugoslavia	14 May 37	194LTS21	304504
Sweden	Yugoslavia	14 May 37	179LTS147	304141
Ecuador	Netherlands	27 May 37	194LTS179	304521
Multilateral		28 May 37	180LTS5	304170
Estonia	Turkey	06 Jun 37	179LTS151	304142
Argentina	UK Great Britain	28 Jun 37	196LTS263	304588
Bel-Lux Econ Union	Italy	30 Jun 37	197LTS23	304601

PARTY ONE	PARTY TWO	DATE	CITATION	NUMBER
Import quotas (Cont.)				
Germany	Netherlands	30 Jun 37	189LTS373	304395
France	UK Great Britain	23 Jul 37	184LTS279	304251
Canada	Guatemala	28 Sep 37	194LTS65	304508
Estonia	France	16 Oct 37	183LTS41	304227
Germany	Latvia	31 Oct 37	189LTS139	304382
Bel-Lux Econ Union	Siam	05 Nov 37	190LTS151	304413
Siam	Sweden	08 Nov 37	185LTS337	304298
Hungary	Lithuania	12 Nov 37	183LTS197	304236
Siam	USA (United States)	13 Nov 37	192LTS247	304476
Hungary	Latvia	16 Nov 37	183LTS205	304237
Siam	UK Great Britain	23 Nov 37	188LTS333	304366
Estonia	Greece	25 Nov 37	184LTS427	304263
Bel-Lux Econ Union	Yugoslavia	26 Nov 37	196LTS19	304567
Italy	Siam	03 Dec 37	189LTS255	304389
France	Siam	09 Dec 37	201LTS145	304709
Italy	USA (United States)	16 Dec 37	187LTS15	304329
Germany	Netherlands	18 Dec 37	190LTS29	304403
Sweden	Turkey	31 Dec 37	184LTS399	304260
Latvia	Turkey	12 Jan 38	201LTS229	304716
Bel-Lux Econ Union	Estonia	13 Jan 38	185LTS63	304275
Netherlands	New Zealand	14 Jan 38	185LTS329	304297
Greece	Latvia	15 Jan 38	195LTS19	304533
France	Sweden	31 Jan 38	185LTS223	304286
Netherlands	Siam	01 Feb 38	193LTS13	304485
Chile	USA (United States)	01 Feb 38	190LTS9	304401
Greece	Sweden	01 Feb 38	185LTS217	304285
Estonia	Sweden	18 Feb 38	185LTS237	304287
Greece	Norway	28 Feb 38	186LTS159	304308
Latvia	Poland	05 Mar 38	192LTS283	304478
Czechoslovakia	USA (United States)	07 Mar 38	200LTS87	304687
Italy	UK Great Britain	18 Mar 38	187LTS139	304334
New Zealand	Switzerland	05 May 38	189LTS167	304384
Portugal	UK Great Britain	11 May 38	191LTS285	304450
Italy	Norway	21 Jun 38	190LTS193	304417
Switzerland	Yugoslavia	27 Jun 38	196LTS27	304568
Ecuador	USA (United States)	06 Aug 38	193LTS85	304489
Greece	Portugal	15 Aug 38	201LTS201	304707
Romania	UK Great Britain	02 Sep 38	191LTS313	304453
Cuba	Portugal	06 Sep 38	195LTS443	304565
Netherlands	Romania	10 Oct 38	195LTS9	304532
Greece	USA (United States)	15 Nov 38	195LTS145	304544
UK Great Britain	USA (United States)	17 Nov 38	200LTS293	304700
Canada	USA (United States)	17 Nov 38	199LTS91	304670
Estonia	Netherlands	22 Nov 38	193LTS209	304497
Australia	Switzerland	22 Nov 38	194LTS35	304505
Iraq	USA (United States)	03 Dec 38	203LTS107	304753
Guatemala	Norway	20 Dec 38	198LTS117	304631
Finland	Netherlands	20 Dec 38	194LTS55	304506
Sweden	Turkey	20 Jan 39	194LTS107	304513
Estonia	Sweden	30 Jan 39	194LTS131	304517
Multilateral		05 Feb 39	196LTS303	304592
Chile	USA (United States)	24 Feb 39	197LTS217	304614
Iceland	Norway	27 Feb 39	196LTS377	304598
Turkey	USA (United States)	01 Apr 39	202LTS129	304741
Latvia	Sweden	15 Apr 39	196LTS373	304597
Greece	Sweden	01 May 39	196LTS205	304582
Multilateral		06 May 39	198LTS81	304626
Romania	UK Great Britain	11 May 39	196LTS351	304594
Estonia	Latvia	26 May 39	198LTS99	304628
United Arab Rep	South Africa	31 May 39	198LTS295	304647
UK Great Britain	USA (United States)	23 Jun 39	198LTS333	304651
Australia	Brazil	19 Jul 39	200LTS191	304690
Norway	Spain	26 Jul 39	198LTS87	304627
USA (United States)	Venezuela	06 Nov 39	203LTS273	304770
Turkey	UK Great Britain	22 Nov 39	201LTS93	304705

PARTY ONE	PARTY TWO	DATE	CITATION	NUMBER
Import quotas (Cont.)				
Norway	UK Great Britain	02 Dec 39	201LTS97	304706
New Zealand	USA (United States)	28 Feb 40	203LTS11	304746
Sweden	Turkey	29 Feb 40	200LTS267	304695
Dominican Republic	Newfoundland	16 Mar 40	203LTS141	304757
Free trade				
France	UK Great Britain	16 Apr 02	1LTS79	300010
France	Germany	19 May 20	1LTS383	300031
Czechoslovakia	Germany	29 Jun 20	17LTS69	300430
Belgium	Luxembourg	25 Jul 21	9LTS223	300256
Italy	Spain	15 Nov 23	39LTS49	300996
Austria	Turkey	28 Jan 24	32LTS313	300823
Austria	Latvia	09 Aug 24	65LTS7	301516
Italy	Serb/Croat/Slovene	21 Aug 24	82LTS445	301883
France	Saar	15 Jan 25	44LTS181	301082
Germany	USA (United States)	21 May 25	52LTS133	301254
Bel-Lux Econ Union		07 Jul 25	54LTS267	301290
Czechoslovakia	Spain	19 Jul 25	60LTS329	301419
Hungary	Italy	20 Jul 25	45LTS39	301098
Italy	Latvia	25 Jul 25	60LTS91	301407
Estonia	USA (United States)	23 Dec 25	50LTS13	301197
Germany	Sweden	14 May 26	51LTS99	301225
Hungary	USA (United States)	04 Sep 26	58LTS111	301369
Greece	UK Great Britain	13 May 27	61LTS15	301425
Afghanistan	Switzerland	17 Feb 28	73LTS323	301722
Germany	Siam	07 Apr 28	85LTS337	301938
Latvia	USA (United States)	20 Apr 28	80LTS35	301821
Serb/Croat/Slovene	Spain	27 Sep 29	98LTS319	302253
Bel-Lux Econ Union	Turkey	31 May 34	150LTS289	303462
France	USA (United States)	18 Feb 37	184LTS479	304269
Multilateral		28 May 37	180LTS5	304170
France	UK Great Britain	23 Jul 37	184LTS279	304251
Hungary	Lithuania	12 Nov 37	183LTS197	304236
Hungary	Latvia	16 Nov 37	183LTS205	304237
Siam	UK Great Britain	23 Nov 37	188LTS333	304366
Sweden	Turkey	20 Jan 39	194LTS107	304513
Tariffs				
Canada	France	19 Sep 07	1LTS95	300012
Multilateral		10 Sep 19	8LTS11	300201
Multilateral		09 Dec 19	5LTS335	300140
Denmark	Sweden	26 Jan 20	14LTS273	300379
Belgium	Netherlands	08 Mar 20	1LTS25	300003
Austria	Germany	01 Sep 20	4LTS201	300107
Czechoslovakia	Serb/Croat/Slovene	18 Oct 20	17LTS19	300424
Australia	Malay States	24 Jan 21	23LTS209	300590
Canada	France	29 Jan 21	8LTS105	300212
Czechoslovakia	Romania	23 Apr 21	15LTS235	300397
Austria	Czechoslovakia	04 May 21	15LTS13	300388
Finland	France	13 Jul 21	29LTS445	300755
Estonia	Finland	29 Oct 21	13LTS59	300348
Finland	USSR (Soviet Union)	14 Dec 21	16LTS221	300414
Spain	Sweden	29 Dec 21	9LTS58	300242
Netherlands	Spain	05 Jan 22	9LTS257	300259
Estonia	France	07 Jan 22	62LTS9	301452
Multilateral		06 Feb 22	38LTS267	300981
Austria	Hungary	08 Feb 22	55LTS367	301320
Italy	Poland	12 May 22	59LTS293	301399
Austria	Poland	25 Sep 22	59LTS307	301400
Italy	Serb/Croat/Slovene	23 Oct 22	18LTS441	300480
Japan	Poland	07 Dec 22	32LTS61	300806
China	Japan	08 Dec 22	20LTS205	300519
Canada	France	15 Dec 22	21LTS38	300532
Czechoslovakia	Greece	10 Jan 23	21LTS217	300544
Norway	Sweden	26 May 23	18LTS155	300462
Australia	Netherlands	30 May 23	22LTS129	300556

PARTY ONE	PARTY TWO	DATE	CITATION	NUMBER
Tariffs (Cont.)				
Afghanistan	UK Great Britain	05 Jun 23	21LTS89	300533
Czechoslovakia	Hungary	13 Jul 23	35LTS253	300899
Multilateral		24 Jul 23	28LTS171	300705
Norway	Spain	07 Oct 23	59LTS47	301389
Estonia	Latvia	01 Nov 23	25LTS354	300624
Finland	Netherlands	01 Nov 23	23LTS33	300574
Multilateral		03 Nov 23	30LTS371	300775
Multilateral		09 Dec 23	47LTS55	301129
Multilateral		14 Dec 23	29LTS37	300732
France	Italy	10 Jan 24	43LTS431	301076
France	Greece	21 Feb 24	43LTS481	301077
Denmark	Latvia	03 Apr 24	33LTS393	300860
Finland	Japan	07 Jun 24	58LTS379	301383
Austria	Germany	12 Jul 24	41LTS287	301022
Austria	Latvia	09 Aug 24	65LTS7	301516
Austria	France	11 Aug 24	44LTS7	301079
Italy	Serb/Croat/Slovene	12 Aug 24	82LTS391	301880
France	Panama	15 Aug 24	93LTS425	302130
Guatemala	Nicaragua	10 Sep 24	130LTS127	302987
Multilateral		23 Oct 24	77LTS367	301778
France	Latvia	30 Oct 24	37LTS399	300963
Czechoslovakia	Italy	15 Nov 24	92LTS91	302081
Germany	Switzerland	17 Nov 24	41LTS473	301026
France	Poland	09 Dec 24	44LTS127	301081
Austria	Spain	03 Feb 25	43LTS313	301067
France	Portugal	04 Mar 25	44LTS197	301083
Bel-Lux Econ Union	France	04 Apr 25	44LTS213	301085
Czechoslovakia	Greece	08 Apr 25	38LTS291	300984
Canada	Spain	11 Apr 25	43LTS333	301068
Austria	Greece	18 Apr 25	38LTS311	300986
Greece	Hungary	04 Jun 25	39LTS139	300998
Hungary	Spain	17 Jun 25	60LTS69	301406
Czechoslovakia	Spain	19 Jul 25	60LTS329	301419
Italy	Latvia	25 Jul 25	60LTS91	301407
Siam	Spain	03 Aug 25	55LTS39	301303
Germany	UK Great Britain	13 Aug 25	43LTS89	301050
Portugal	Siam	14 Aug 25	55LTS57	301304
Germany	USSR (Soviet Union)	12 Oct 25	53LTS7	301257
France	Hungary	13 Oct 25	48LTS9	301150
Bulgaria	France	22 Oct 25	44LTS257	301087
Czechoslovakia	Japan	30 Oct 25	58LTS263	301377
Germany	Italy	31 Oct 25	52LTS179	301256
Germany	Spain	18 Nov 25	53LTS309	301263
Germany	Netherlands	26 Nov 25	57LTS159	301362
British Empire	Greece	26 Nov 25	63LTS167	301488
Siam	Sweden	19 Dec 25	58LTS429	301386
Bel-Lux Econ Union	Czechoslovakia	28 Dec 25	58LTS189	301372
Czechoslovakia	UK Great Britain	01 Feb 26	49LTS175	301181
France	Germany	12 Feb 26	48LTS153	301157
Germany	Spain	07 May 26	53LTS321	301264
Italy	Siam	09 May 26	61LTS215	301436
Greece	Netherlands	12 May 26	61LTS295	301440
France	Italy	29 May 26	62LTS425	301474
Finland	Greece	22 Jun 26	56LTS197	301331
Finland	Germany	26 Jun 26	56LTS203	301332
Bel-Lux Econ Union	Siam	13 Jul 26	62LTS287	301468
Germany	Switzerland	14 Jul 26	59LTS87	301391
Norway	Siam	16 Jul 26	60LTS35	301404
Austria	Netherlands	04 Aug 26	59LTS243	301394
Greece	Sweden	10 Sep 26	63LTS37	301479
Bel-Lux Econ Union	Estonia	28 Sep 26	62LTS433	301475
Czechoslovakia	Hungary	30 Sep 26	57LTS87	301356
Albania	Greece	13 Oct 26	83LTS325	301899
Finland	Turkey	19 Oct 26	58LTS393	301384
Greece	Italy	24 Oct 26	63LTS51	301480

PARTY ONE	PARTY TWO	DATE	CITATION	NUMBER
Tariffs (Cont.)				
Greece	New Zealand	16 Nov 26	85LTS43	301921
Greece	Switzerland	29 Nov 26	63LTS27	301478
Czechoslovakia	Switzerland	16 Feb 27	64LTS7	301501
Czechoslovakia	Germany	25 Mar 27	75LTS353	301758
France	Germany	31 Mar 27	66LTS7	301524
France	Norway	12 Apr 27	178LTS199	304114
Greece	UK Great Britain	13 May 27	61LTS15	301425
Czechoslovakia	Poland	30 May 27	98LTS233	302251
Greece	Norway	29 Jun 27	82LTS187	301869
Hungary	Italy	25 Jul 27	74LTS77	301733
Hungary	Italy	25 Jul 27	74LTS53	301731
Multilateral		08 Nov 27	97LTS391	302238
Norway	Sweden	19 Nov 27	68LTS209	301584
Multilateral		10 Mar 28	132LTS405	303049
Austria	Denmark	06 Apr 28	85LTS423	301943
Multilateral		01 May 28	132LTS415	303050
Belgium	Persia	15 May 28	94LTS447	302160
Austria	France	16 May 28	88LTS21	301986
Austria	Persia	17 Jun 28	112LTS101	302610
Netherlands	Persia	20 Jun 28	81LTS431	301852
Hungary	Italy	04 Jul 28	92LTS117	302083
China	USA (United States)	25 Jul 28	107LTS121	302472
Germany	Lithuania	30 Oct 28	89LTS127	302010
Multilateral		22 Nov 28	111LTS343	302598
China	Netherlands	19 Dec 28	111LTS161	302585
Multilateral		05 Jan 29	132LTS425	303051
Hungary	Norway	01 Feb 29	86LTS435	301955
Estonia	France	15 Mar 29	89LTS381	302029
Norway	Persia	10 May 29	107LTS403	302497
Estonia	USSR (Soviet Union)	17 May 29	94LTS323	302152
Latvia	Portugal	15 Jun 29	98LTS447	302262
Belgium	Germany	07 Nov 29	121LTS327	302795
Italy	Romania	25 Feb 30	106LTS179	302445
Estonia	Sweden	04 Apr 30	101LTS51	302318
China	Japan	06 May 30	106LTS295	302452
Germany	Irish Free State	12 May 30	131LTS153	303008
Greece	Irish Free State	15 May 30	136LTS33	303122
China	France	16 May 30	162LTS99	303738
Germany	Norway	30 May 30	107LTS129	302473
Poland	Romania	23 Jun 30	133LTS163	303066
Norway	Turkey	16 Mar 31	138LTS41	303180
Czechoslovakia	Germany	25 Jul 31	187LTS279	304344
Hungary	Romania	12 Aug 31	186LTS325	304321
Chile	USA (United States)	28 Sep 31	144LTS147	303325
France	Yugoslavia	07 Nov 31	144LTS281	303331
Bolivia	Denmark	09 Nov 31	147LTS27	303387
France	UK Great Britain	17 Nov 31	134LTS299	303098
Brazil	Czechoslovakia	27 Nov 31	136LTS453	303144
France	UK Great Britain	27 Nov 31	132LTS25	303028
Brazil	Canada	04 Dec 31	139LTS241	303214
Brazil	Romania	16 Dec 31	139LTS255	303216
Brazil	Hungary	24 Dec 31	147LTS51	303389
France	UK Great Britain	28 Dec 31	133LTS79	303058
Austria	Brazil	02 Jan 32	140LTS15	303224
Netherlands	UK Great Britain	04 Jan 32	128LTS347	302940
Brazil	Poland	03 Feb 32	147LTS113	303396
Austria	Yugoslavia	09 Mar 32	157LTS145	303609
Brazil	Yugoslavia	16 May 32	144LTS303	303333
Hungary	UK Great Britain	10 Jun 32	132LTS53	303031
Bulgaria	Germany	24 Jun 32	147LTS211	303400
Brazil	Latvia	21 Sep 32	137LTS61	303146
Brazil	Estonia	30 Sep 32	134LTS247	303095
Estonia	Latvia	14 Nov 32	136LTS295	303132
France	Hungary	03 Mar 33	140LTS177	303235
France	Sweden	13 Mar 33	142LTS131	303285

PARTY ONE	PARTY TWO	DATE	CITATION	NUMBER
Tariffs (Cont.)				
Denmark	UK Great Britain	24 Apr 33	139LTS127	303208
Estonia	France	27 Apr 33	141LTS43	303260
Germany	UK Great Britain	03 May 33	140LTS139	303231
Sweden	UK Great Britain	15 May 33	140LTS317	303245
Norway	UK Great Britain	15 May 33	145LTS187	303355
Iceland	UK Great Britain	19 May 33	144LTS33	303319
Latvia	UK Great Britain	06 Jul 33	142LTS217	303294
Brazil	Portugal	26 Aug 33	179LTS63	304134
Poland	Sweden	21 Oct 33	150LTS73	303454
Multilateral		23 Nov 33	192LTS389	304484
Latvia	Lithuania	01 Dec 33	148LTS97	303407
France	USSR (Soviet Union)	11 Jan 34	167LTS349	303878
Estonia	Lithuania	13 Jan 34	148LTS337	303420
Argentina	Bel-Lux Econ Union	16 Jan 34	147LTS79	303392
Czechoslovakia	Poland	10 Feb 34	183LTS213	304238
Denmark	Germany	01 Mar 34	150LTS31	303451
Spain	Turkey	19 May 34	149LTS15	303428
Bel-Lux Econ Union	Turkey	24 May 34	150LTS269	303460
Germany	Netherlands	06 Jun 34	174LTS33	304034
Brazil	USA (United States)	02 Feb 35	166LTS211	303840
France	South Africa	11 Feb 35	189LTS17	304372
Estonia	Poland	27 Mar 35	159LTS97	303651
Haiti	USA (United States)	28 Mar 35	161LTS157	303709
Irish Free State	Spain	04 Apr 35	166LTS391	303855
Italy	South Africa	21 May 35	189LTS31	304373
Turkey	UK Great Britain	04 Jun 35	167LTS91	303860
Czechoslovakia	Hungary	14 Jun 35	171LTS401	303976
UK Great Britain	Uruguay	26 Jun 35	176LTS153	304058
Czechoslovakia	Germany	26 Jun 35	173LTS385	304029
Bulgaria	Romania	26 Jul 35	198LTS9	304621
Germany	Iraq	04 Aug 35	171LTS65	303951
France	South Africa	27 Aug 35	189LTS41	304374
Bel-Lux Econ Union	USSR (Soviet Union)	05 Sep 35	173LTS169	304010
Colombia	USA (United States)	13 Sep 35	170LTS293	303944
Canada	USA (United States)	15 Nov 35	168LTS355	303910
Saudi Arabia	UK Great Britain	17 Nov 35	170LTS87	303929
Netherlands	USA (United States)	20 Dec 35	178LTS239	304118
France	Spain	21 Dec 35	167LTS9	303856
Czechoslovakia	Germany	30 Dec 35	173LTS333	304023
Spain	Turkey	31 Dec 35	166LTS163	303838
Switzerland	USA (United States)	09 Jan 36	171LTS231	303962
France	Sweden	18 Jan 36	167LTS197	303866
Nicaragua	USA (United States)	11 Mar 36	173LTS141	304009
Norway	Poland	14 Mar 36	171LTS371	303973
Norway	Uruguay	04 Apr 36	176LTS115	304055
Guatemala	USA (United States)	24 Apr 36	170LTS345	303945
France	USA (United States)	06 May 36	199LTS259	304679
Finland	USA (United States)	18 May 36	172LTS97	303981
Ecuador	USA (United States)	12 Jun 36	170LTS377	303946
Norway	Spain	13 Jun 36	170LTS199	303935
Finland	Turkey	20 Jun 36	172LTS125	303982
El Salvador	Sweden	23 Jun 36	171LTS291	303966
Poland	Sweden	03 Jul 36	171LTS307	303968
Hungary	Italy	04 Jul 36	181LTS331	304199
Guatemala	Sweden	11 Jul 36	171LTS299	303967
Finland	Poland	16 Jul 36	172LTS143	303984
Brazil	Czechoslovakia	22 Jul 36	188LTS275	304363
Brazil	Norway	27 Jul 36	176LTS125	304056
Brazil	Denmark	30 Jul 36	194LTS81	304510
Brazil	UK Great Britain	10 Aug 36	172LTS283	303997
Brazil	UK Great Britain	10 Aug 36	172LTS273	303996
Sweden	Uruguay	13 Aug 36	183LTS161	304232
United Arab Rep	UK Great Britain	18 Aug 36	176LTS177	304059
Australia	Czechoslovakia	19 Aug 36	177LTS245	304093
Finland	Netherlands	25 Aug 36	172LTS151	303985

PARTY ONE	PARTY TWO	DATE	CITATION	NUMBER
Tariffs (Cont.)				
Turkey	UK Great Britain	02 Sep 36	172LTS289	303998
Czechoslovakia	Guatemala	20 Sep 36	185LTS269	304293
Australia	Bel-Lux Econ Union	03 Oct 36	177LTS271	304094
Bulgaria	Finland	27 Oct 36	179LTS309	304158
Chile	Sweden	30 Oct 36	188LTS283	304364
Australia	France	27 Nov 36	177LTS301	304095
Costa Rica	USA (United States)	28 Nov 36	181LTS183	304189
Iraq	UK Great Britain	14 Dec 36	177LTS221	304091
Czechoslovakia	South Africa	27 Jan 37	189LTS97	304377
France	Sweden	17 Feb 37	176LTS267	304065
El Salvador	USA (United States)	19 Feb 37	179LTS219	304150
Cuba	UK Great Britain	19 Feb 37	192LTS301	304480
Bel-Lux Econ Union	Uruguay	22 Feb 37	196LTS391	304600
Chile	Cuba	13 Mar 37	195LTS389	304558
Brazil	Netherlands	15 Mar 37	179LTS395	304166
Finland	UK Great Britain	14 Apr 37	179LTS289	304155
Chile	Netherlands	05 May 37	182LTS385	304223
Ecuador	Netherlands	27 May 37	194LTS179	304521
Multilateral		28 May 37	180LTS5	304170
UK Great Britain		07 Jun 37	185LTS185	304282
France	Turkey	15 Jun 37	179LTS195	304147
Bel-Lux Econ Union	Italy	30 Jun 37	197LTS23	304601
Germany	Netherlands	30 Jun 37	189LTS373	304395
Denmark	Netherlands	29 Jul 37	192LTS137	304467
USA (United States)	USSR (Soviet Union)	04 Aug 37	182LTS113	304204
Poland	UK Great Britain	10 Sep 37	184LTS289	304253
Brazil	Lithuania	28 Sep 37	186LTS403	304324
Canada	Guatemala	28 Sep 37	194LTS65	304508
Poland	UK Great Britain	14 Oct 37	191LTS279	304449
Estonia	France	16 Oct 37	183LTS41	304227
Denmark	Haiti	21 Oct 37	190LTS231	304422
Italy	USA (United States)	16 Dec 37	187LTS15	304329
Greece	Latvia	15 Jan 38	195LTS19	304533
France	Sweden	31 Jan 38	185LTS223	304286
Chile	USA (United States)	01 Feb 38	190LTS9	304401
Norway	Venezuela	18 Feb 38	187LTS205	304341
Latvia	Poland	05 Mar 38	192LTS283	304478
Czechoslovakia	USA (United States)	07 Mar 38	200LTS87	304687
New Zealand	Switzerland	05 May 38	189LTS167	304384
Portugal	UK Great Britain	11 May 38	191LTS285	304450
USA (United States)	Venezuela	12 May 38	191LTS35	304433
Czechoslovakia	USA (United States)	18 May 38	199LTS305	304680
Lithuania	Poland	25 May 38	191LTS391	304457
Cuba	Portugal	06 Sep 38	195LTS443	304565
Bulgaria	Greece	16 Sep 38	195LTS27	304534
Canada	USA (United States)	17 Nov 38	199LTS91	304670
El Salvador	Norway	21 Nov 38	198LTS157	304636
Estonia	Netherlands	22 Nov 38	195LTS133	304542
Australia	Switzerland	22 Nov 38	194LTS35	304505
Iraq	USA (United States)	03 Dec 38	203LTS107	304753
Guatemala	Norway	20 Dec 38	198LTS117	304631
Chile	USA (United States)	24 Feb 39	197LTS217	304614
Turkey	USA (United States)	01 Apr 39	202LTS129	304741
Norway	Spain	26 Jul 39	198LTS87	304627
USA (United States)	Venezuela	06 Nov 39	203LTS273	304770
Dominican Republic	Newfoundland	16 Mar 40	203LTS141	304757
Maritime products and equipment				
Estonia	Hungary	19 Oct 22	30LTS347	300774
Spain	UK Great Britain	31 Oct 22	28LTS339	300719
Denmark	USA (United States)	05 Dec 22	113LTS381	302649
Poland	UK Great Britain	26 Nov 23	28LTS428	300722
Denmark	Poland	22 Mar 24	31LTS13	300778
Netherlands	Poland	30 May 24	34LTS9	300865
Guatemala	Nicaragua	10 Sep 24	130LTS127	302987

PARTY ONE	PARTY TWO	DATE	CITATION	NUMBER
Maritime products and equipment (Cont.)				
UK Great Britain	USA (United States)	16 Mar 25	113LTS105	302639
Germany	Norway	11 Apr 25	52LTS115	301252
Finland	Sweden	14 Dec 27	72LTS29	301688
Sweden	Turkey	04 Feb 28	88LTS155	301994
Austria	Iceland	06 Apr 28	87LTS343	301980
Austria	France	16 May 28	88LTS21	301986
Estonia	Italy	01 Jul 28	87LTS277	301974
France	Greece	11 Mar 29	95LTS401	302187
Czechoslovakia	Persia	30 Apr 29	110LTS357	302567
Romania	Turkey	11 Jun 29	112LTS139	302613
China	Poland	18 Sep 29	120LTS331	302774
Italy	Panama	16 Oct 29	138LTS355	303199
Norway	Sweden	18 Dec 29	98LTS389	302258
Germany	Irish Free State	12 May 30	131LTS153	303008
Hungary	Turkey	21 May 30	109LTS153	302534
Germany	Turkey	27 May 30	110LTS9	302553
Denmark	Turkey	31 May 30	119LTS165	302744
Denmark	Lithuania	21 Jun 30	114LTS151	302662
Czechoslovakia	Romania	27 Jun 30	119LTS73	302742
Irish Free State	Norway	21 Oct 30	109LTS177	302536
Latvia	Lithuania	24 Nov 30	112LTS417	302627
Brazil	Portugal	26 Aug 33	179LTS63	304134
Argentina	Netherlands	31 Jan 34	148LTS355	303421
Germany	Netherlands	18 Dec 37	190LTS29	304403
Certificates of origin				
France	UK Great Britain	16 Apr 02	1LTS79	300010
Bolivia	UK Great Britain	05 Apr 20	1LTS271	300020
France	Germany	19 May 20	1LTS383	300031
Czechoslovakia	Italy	23 Mar 21	32LTS183	300815
Germany	Poland	10 Apr 21	6LTS233	300158
France	Norway	23 Apr 21	14LTS375	300386
Austria	Czechoslovakia	04 May 21	15LTS13	300388
Finland	France	13 Jul 21	29LTS445	300755
Estonia	France	07 Jan 22	62LTS9	301452
Denmark	Germany	10 Apr 22	29LTS9	300730
Estonia	Hungary	19 Oct 22	30LTS347	300774
Canada	France	15 Dec 22	21LTS38	300532
Czechoslovakia	Greece	10 Jan 23	21LTS217	300544
Italy	Switzerland	27 Jan 23	25LTS21	300603
Poland	Turkey	23 Jul 23	49LTS329	301189
Multilateral		24 Jul 23	28LTS171	300705
Multilateral		03 Nov 23	30LTS371	300775
Italy	Spain	15 Nov 23	39LTS49	300996
France	Italy	10 Jan 24	43LTS431	301076
Austria	Turkey	28 Jan 24	32LTS313	300823
Multilateral		12 Mar 24	24LTS17	300595
Netherlands	Poland	30 May 24	34LTS9	300865
Italy	Serb/Croat/Slovene	14 Jul 24	82LTS257	301876
Czechoslovakia	France	18 Aug 24	44LTS21	301080
Finland	Latvia	23 Aug 24	37LTS383	300962
Guatemala	Nicaragua	10 Sep 24	130LTS127	302987
Finland	Italy	22 Oct 24	32LTS149	300814
France	Latvia	30 Oct 24	37LTS399	300963
Latvia	Switzerland	04 Dec 24	34LTS405	300889
France	Poland	09 Dec 24	44LTS127	301081
Austria	Spain	03 Feb 25	43LTS313	301067
Albania	Italy	06 Mar 25	44LTS359	301094
Czechoslovakia	Greece	08 Apr 25	38LTS291	300984
Austria	Greece	18 Apr 25	38LTS311	300986
Bulgaria	Poland	29 Apr 25	60LTS103	301408
Greece	Hungary	04 Jun 25	39LTS139	300998
Bel-Lux Econ Union	Japan	27 Jun 25	36LTS95	300907
Finland	Spain	16 Jul 25	47LTS271	301135
Czechoslovakia	Spain	19 Jul 25	60LTS329	301419

PARTY ONE	PARTY TWO	DATE	CITATION	NUMBER
Certificates of origin (Cont.)				
Italy	Serb/Croat/Slovene	20 Jul 25	83LTS241	301889
Hungary	Italy	20 Jul 25	45LTS39	301098
France	Hungary	13 Oct 25	48LTS9	301150
Estonia	Switzerland	14 Oct 25	49LTS421	301195
Germany	Italy	31 Oct 25	52LTS179	301256
Multilateral		06 Nov 25	74LTS319	301744
Multilateral		06 Nov 25	74LTS327	301745
Multilateral		06 Nov 25	74LTS341	301746
Austria	Portugal	18 Dec 25	54LTS91	301277
Bel-Lux Econ Union	Czechoslovakia	28 Dec 25	58LTS189	301372
Estonia	UK Great Britain	18 Jan 26	48LTS209	301163
Denmark	Siam	01 Mar 26	47LTS103	301131
Germany	Portugal	20 Mar 26	53LTS361	301266
Iceland	Poland	14 Apr 26	48LTS279	301169
Finland	Hungary	20 Apr 26	48LTS119	301154
Germany	Spain	07 May 26	53LTS321	301264
Austria	Hungary	10 May 26	56LTS39	301321
Greece	Netherlands	12 May 26	61LTS295	301440
Germany	Sweden	14 May 26	51LTS99	301225
Netherlands	UK Great Britain	20 May 26	50LTS309	301214
Finland	Turkey	02 Jun 26	70LTS329	301644
France	Norway	11 Jun 26	50LTS315	301215
Albania	Serb/Croat/Slovene	22 Jun 26	91LTS9	302054
Finland	Germany	26 Jun 26	56LTS203	301332
Germany	Switzerland	14 Jul 26	59LTS87	301391
France	Sweden	19 Jul 26	54LTS283	301291
Hungary	UK Great Britain	23 Jul 26	67LTS183	301546
Guatemala	Italy	15 Sep 26	70LTS175	301633
Albania	Greece	13 Oct 26	83LTS325	301899
Greece	Italy	24 Oct 26	63LTS51	301480
Hungary	Turkey	20 Dec 26	72LTS255	301697
Haiti	Italy	03 Jan 27	71LTS405	301678
Estonia	Greece	04 Jan 27	69LTS33	301598
Germany	Turkey	12 Jan 27	73LTS133	301712
France	Italy	26 Jan 27	79LTS49	301804
Czechoslovakia	Switzerland	16 Feb 27	64LTS7	301501
Estonia	Poland	19 Feb 27	115LTS177	302686
Greece	Latvia	25 Feb 27	71LTS25	301652
Czechoslovakia	Finland	02 Mar 27	66LTS385	301532
France	Norway	12 Apr 27	178LTS199	304114
Switzerland	Turkey	04 May 27	67LTS141	301544
Czechoslovakia	Turkey	31 May 27	71LTS335	301674
Czechoslovakia	Estonia	20 Jul 27	77LTS341	301776
France	Germany	17 Aug 27	76LTS5	301761
Latvia	Poland	22 Aug 27	115LTS121	302681
Bel-Lux Econ Union	Turkey	28 Aug 27	82LTS77	301862
Italy	Lithuania	17 Sep 27	73LTS9	301701
Germany	Serb/Croat/Slovene	06 Oct 27	77LTS19	301763
Denmark	Italy	26 Oct 27	68LTS229	301586
Germany	Panama	21 Nov 27	115LTS239	302689
Finland	Sweden	14 Dec 27	72LTS29	301688
Bulgaria	Turkey	12 Feb 28	81LTS383	301848
Bel-Lux Econ Union	France	23 Feb 28	72LTS61	301689
France	Germany	23 Feb 28	79LTS247	301815
Estonia	Latvia	25 Mar 28	72LTS195	301692
Austria	France	16 May 28	88LTS21	301986
Latvia	Turkey	28 May 28	94LTS295	302150
Hungary	Italy	04 Jul 28	92LTS117	302083
Hungary	Sweden	08 Nov 28	89LTS283	302023
Estonia	Germany	07 Dec 28	99LTS259	302273
Denmark	Latvia	09 Jan 29	86LTS37	301948
Latvia	Sweden	12 Jan 29	85LTS403	301940
Latvia	Poland	12 Feb 29	115LTS135	302683
Germany	Persia	17 Feb 29	111LTS263	302591
Italy	Sweden	22 Feb 29	87LTS265	301973

PARTY ONE	PARTY TWO	DATE	CITATION	NUMBER
Certificates of origin (Cont.)				
Estonia	France	15 Mar 29	89LTS381	302029
Austria	Netherlands	28 Mar 29	109LTS39	302527
Bel-Lux Econ Union	Persia	09 May 29	110LTS377	302569
Persia	Sweden	10 May 29	102LTS9	302349
Estonia	USSR (Soviet Union)	17 May 29	94LTS323	302152
Bolivia	Netherlands	30 May 29	133LTS113	303062
Greece	UK Great Britain	21 Jun 29	94LTS33	302134
Finland	Italy	15 Aug 29	99LTS363	302280
France	Turkey	29 Aug 29	123LTS193	302815
Estonia	Turkey	16 Sep 29	117LTS377	302704
Sweden	Turkey	29 Sep 29	119LTS53	302740
Estonia	France	07 Oct 29	104LTS193	302389
Finland	Turkey	12 Oct 29	96LTS239	302205
Italy	Panama	16 Oct 29	138LTS355	303199
Irish Free State	Portugal	29 Oct 29	131LTS145	303007
Greece	Iceland	28 Jan 30	118LTS285	302731
Honduras	Nicaragua	30 Jan 30	142LTS241	303297
Italy	Romania	25 Feb 30	106LTS179	302445
Italy	Romania	25 Feb 30	106LTS231	302447
Turkey	UK Great Britain	01 Mar 30	108LTS407	302523
Germany	Haiti	10 Mar 30	119LTS231	302747
Estonia	Sweden	04 Apr 30	101LTS51	302318
Austria	Germany	12 Apr 30	115LTS333	302694
Norway	Persia	08 May 30	134LTS153	303089
Hungary	Turkey	21 May 30	109LTS153	302534
Germany	Turkey	27 May 30	110LTS9	302553
Belgium	Turkey	27 May 30	111LTS49	302580
Denmark	Turkey	31 May 30	119LTS165	302744
Greece	Hungary	03 Jun 30	122LTS37	302798
Denmark	Lithuania	21 Jun 30	114LTS151	302662
Poland	Romania	23 Jun 30	133LTS163	303066
Czechoslovakia	Romania	27 Jun 30	119LTS73	302742
Estonia	Finland	12 Jul 30	111LTS321	302596
Italy	Norway	31 Jul 30	118LTS113	302716
Finland	Norway	11 Nov 30	130LTS17	302980
Estonia	Lithuania	15 Jan 31	114LTS141	302661
Norway	Turkey	16 Mar 31	138LTS41	303180
Poland	Sweden	16 May 31	120LTS223	302768
Bulgaria	Italy	20 May 31	129LTS361	302970
Chile	France	22 May 31	124LTS31	302831
Germany	Hungary	18 Jul 31	150LTS111	303458
Greece	Romania	11 Aug 31	130LTS33	302981
Hungary	Romania	12 Aug 31	186LTS325	304321
Romania	Sweden	07 Oct 31	131LTS51	303003
Hungary	Poland	04 Nov 31	134LTS199	303092
France	Italy	26 Dec 31	133LTS45	303055
Bulgaria	Germany	24 Jun 32	147LTS211	303400
Czechoslovakia	Denmark	04 Jul 32	143LTS251	303312
Bulgaria	Norway	05 Dec 32	136LTS281	303130
Denmark	UK Great Britain	24 Apr 33	139LTS127	303208
Brazil	Uruguay	25 Aug 33	176LTS381	304075
Brazil	Portugal	26 Aug 33	179LTS63	304134
Romania	UK Great Britain	25 Sep 33	149LTS425	303443
Estonia	Poland	26 Sep 33	150LTS309	303464
Multilateral		11 Oct 33	155LTS331	303585
Czechoslovakia	Poland	10 Feb 34	183LTS213	304238
Finland	Germany	24 Mar 34	149LTS343	303442
Bel-Lux Econ Union	Turkey	31 May 34	150LTS277	303461
France	South Africa	11 Feb 35	189LTS17	304372
Irish Free State	Spain	04 Apr 35	166LTS391	303855
Turkey	UK Great Britain	04 Jun 35	167LTS91	303860
Finland	Turkey	06 Jun 35	160LTS165	303690
Czechoslovakia	Hungary	14 Jun 35	171LTS401	303976
Romania	UK Great Britain	14 Jun 35	163LTS301	303772
Italy	Spain	01 Oct 35	163LTS345	303777

PARTY ONE	PARTY TWO	DATE	CITATION	NUMBER
Certificates of origin (Cont.)				
France	Spain	21 Dec 35	167LTS9	303856
Sweden	Turkey	27 Feb 36	167LTS75	303858
Albania	Italy	19 Mar 36	173LTS107	304007
Norway	Turkey	08 Jun 36	170LTS227	303938
Norway	Spain	13 Jun 36	170LTS199	303935
Finland	Turkey	20 Jun 36	172LTS125	303982
Turkey	UK Great Britain	02 Sep 36	172LTS289	303998
Italy	UK Great Britain	06 Nov 36	177LTS183	304090
UK Great Britain	Yugoslavia	27 Nov 36	181LTS281	304195
Australia	France	27 Nov 36	177LTS301	304095
Bulgaria	Sweden	07 Dec 36	173LTS393	304030
Estonia	Sweden	08 Feb 37	176LTS193	304061
Netherlands	Turkey	17 Feb 37	182LTS221	304213
Belgium	Norway	10 Mar 37	178LTS12	304101
Chile	Cuba	13 Mar 37	195LTS389	304558
Chile	Netherlands	05 May 37	182LTS385	304223
Romania	Yugoslavia	13 May 37	197LTS161	304612
Romania	Yugoslavia	13 May 37	197LTS145	304611
Sweden	Yugoslavia	14 May 37	194LTS21	304504
Estonia	Turkey	06 Jun 37	179LTS159	304143
Estonia	Turkey	06 Jun 37	179LTS151	304142
Lithuania	Sweden	01 Jul 37	179LTS251	304152
France	UK Great Britain	23 Jul 37	184LTS279	304251
Estonia	France	16 Oct 37	183LTS41	304227
Denmark	Haiti	21 Oct 37	190LTS231	304422
Latvia	Poland	16 Nov 37	197LTS43	304604
Estonia	Greece	25 Nov 37	184LTS427	304263
Japan	Siam	08 Dec 37	188LTS375	304367
Germany	Siam	30 Dec 37	188LTS401	304368
Sweden	Turkey	31 Dec 37	184LTS399	304260
Bulgaria	USA (United States)	05 Jan 38	191LTS207	304444
Latvia	Turkey	12 Jan 38	201LTS229	304716
Finland	Lithuania	12 Apr 38	194LTS9	304501
Bulgaria	Latvia	17 May 38	189LTS249	304388
Portugal	Siam	02 Jul 38	200LTS149	304688
Greece	Portugal	15 Aug 38	201LTS201	304707
Romania	UK Great Britain	02 Sep 38	191LTS313	304453
Cuba	Portugal	06 Sep 38	195LTS443	304565
United Arab Rep	South Africa	31 May 39	198LTS295	304647
Turkey	UK Great Britain	03 Feb 40	203LTS399	304781
Sweden	Turkey	29 Feb 40	200LTS273	304696
Sweden	Turkey	29 Feb 40	200LTS267	304695
Spain	UK Great Britain	18 Mar 40	203LTS157	304759
United Arab Rep	UK Great Britain	26 May 41	204LTS147	304793
Reciprocity in trade				
Canada	France	19 Sep 07	1LTS95	300012
Czechoslovakia	Germany	29 Jun 20	17LTS69	300430
Estonia	UK Great Britain	20 Jul 20	1LTS295	300025
Austria	Germany	01 Sep 20	4LTS201	300107
Japan	Paraguay	30 Nov 20	6LTS367	300169
Bulgaria	Germany	19 Feb 21	6LTS227	300157
Bulgaria	Hungary	03 Sep 21	7LTS229	300188
Estonia	Finland	29 Oct 21	13LTS59	300348
Ethiopia	Greece	18 Feb 22	15LTS267	300399
Lithuania	UK Great Britain	06 May 22	13LTS25	300343
Spain	UK Great Britain	31 Oct 22	28LTS339	300719
Denmark	USA (United States)	05 Dec 22	113LTS381	302649
Canada	Italy	04 Jan 23	25LTS375	300626
Estonia	Germany	27 Jun 23	41LTS161	301013
Poland	UK Great Britain	26 Nov 23	28LTS428	300722
Multilateral		09 Dec 23	58LTS284	301379
Multilateral		09 Dec 23	47LTS55	301129
Finland	UK Great Britain	14 Dec 23	29LTS129	300739
Austria	Turkey	28 Jan 24	32LTS313	300823

PARTY ONE	PARTY TWO	DATE	CITATION	NUMBER
Reciprocity in trade (Cont.)				
Japan	Siam	09 Mar 24	31LTS187	300795
Finland	Japan	07 Jun 24	58LTS379	301383
Italy	Serb/Croat/Slovene	14 Jul 24	82LTS257	301876
Italy	Serb/Croat/Slovene	12 Aug 24	82LTS391	301880
Japan	Peru	30 Sep 24	102LTS33	302351
Bel-Lux Econ Union	Guatemala	07 Nov 24	69LTS17	301596
Poland	Sweden	02 Dec 24	36LTS299	300930
Denmark	Turkey	26 Jan 25	36LTS317	300931
UK Great Britain	USA (United States)	16 Mar 25	113LTS105	302639
Latvia	USSR (Soviet Union)	19 Mar 25	38LTS141	300971
Germany	USA (United States)	20 Mar 25	119LTS185	302745
Norway	USA (United States)	24 Mar 25	67LTS417	301563
Japan	Latvia	04 Jul 25	80LTS305	301836
Hungary	Italy	20 Jul 25	45LTS39	301098
France	Spain	03 Aug 25	38LTS371	300992
Germany	UK Great Britain	13 Aug 25	43LTS89	301050
Germany	USSR (Soviet Union)	12 Oct 25	53LTS7	301257
Czechoslovakia	Japan	30 Oct 25	58LTS263	301377
Multilateral		06 Nov 25	74LTS289	301743
Hungary	Italy	25 Nov 25	74LTS251	301741
Siam	Sweden	19 Dec 25	58LTS429	301386
Norway	USSR (Soviet Union)	09 Apr 26	48LTS185	301160
Czechoslovakia	Poland	21 Apr 26	58LTS9	301367
Finland	Turkey	02 Jun 26	70LTS329	301644
Norway	Siam	16 Jul 26	60LTS35	301404
Hungary	UK Great Britain	23 Jul 26	67LTS183	301546
Hungary	USA (United States)	04 Sep 26	58LTS111	301369
Guatemala	Italy	15 Sep 26	70LTS175	301633
Abyssinia	Netherlands	30 Sep 26	78LTS89	301780
Albania	Greece	13 Oct 26	83LTS325	301899
Netherlands	USA (United States)	27 Nov 26	112LTS433	302628
Hungary	Turkey	20 Dec 26	72LTS255	301697
Norway	Poland	22 Dec 26	66LTS359	301530
Estonia	Greece	04 Jan 27	69LTS33	301598
Germany	Turkey	12 Jan 27	73LTS133	301712
Greece	Latvia	25 Feb 27	71LTS25	301652
Czechoslovakia	Finland	02 Mar 27	66LTS385	301532
Persia	Poland	19 Mar 27	109LTS53	302528
Switzerland	Turkey	04 May 27	67LTS141	301544
Guatemala	Netherlands	12 May 27	85LTS323	301937
Serb/Croat/Slovene	UK Great Britain	12 May 27	80LTS165	301825
Greece	UK Great Britain	13 May 27	61LTS15	301425
Czechoslovakia	Turkey	31 May 27	71LTS335	301674
Czechoslovakia	Hungary	31 May 27	65LTS61	301520
Greece	Norway	29 Jun 27	82LTS187	301869
Germany	Japan	20 Jul 27	74LTS107	301736
Czechoslovakia	Estonia	20 Jul 27	77LTS341	301776
Belgium	Portugal	21 Jul 27	71LTS439	301682
Austria	Finland	08 Aug 27	70LTS349	301645
France	Germany	17 Aug 27	76LTS5	301761
Latvia	Poland	22 Aug 27	115LTS121	302681
Bel-Lux Econ Union	Turkey	28 Aug 27	82LTS77	301862
Italy	Lithuania	17 Sep 27	73LTS9	301701
Denmark	Greece	29 Sep 27	62LTS219	301464
Finland	Norway	30 Sep 27	67LTS359	301557
Germany	Serb/Croat/Slovene	06 Oct 27	77LTS19	301763
Denmark	Japan	15 Oct 27	71LTS75	301655
Finland	Sweden	14 Dec 27	72LTS29	301688
Denmark	USSR (Soviet Union)	23 Dec 27	70LTS245	301636
Denmark	Spain	02 Jan 28	71LTS271	301668
Estonia	Serb/Croat/Slovene	01 Feb 28	106LTS139	302441
Bulgaria	Estonia	11 Feb 28	79LTS43	301803
Bulgaria	Turkey	12 Feb 28	81LTS383	301848
Hungary	Serb/Croat/Slovene	22 Feb 28	181LTS229	304192
Bel-Lux Econ Union	France	23 Feb 28	72LTS61	301689

PARTY ONE	PARTY TWO	DATE	CITATION	NUMBER
Reciprocity in trade (Cont.)				
Estonia	USSR (Soviet Union)	03 Mar 28	80LTS401	301840
Austria	Great Britain	13 Apr 28	80LTS247	301830
Czechoslovakia	Hungary	26 May 28	101LTS265	302328
Latvia	Turkey	28 May 28	94LTS295	302150
Bulgaria	Latvia	22 Jun 28	97LTS379	302236
Czechoslovakia	France	02 Jul 28	99LTS105	302272
Hungary	Italy	04 Jul 28	92LTS117	302083
Persia	USA (United States)	11 Jul 28	107LTS375	302494
Multilateral		15 Jul 28	79LTS133	301806
Netherlands	Turkey	25 Jul 28	93LTS279	302116
Saar	Switzerland	15 Aug 28	81LTS373	301847
Denmark	Greece	22 Aug 28	94LTS263	302147
Germany	South Africa	01 Sep 28	95LTS289	302181
Hungary	Lithuania	23 Oct 28	84LTS281	301908
Belgium	Norway	29 Oct 28	107LTS75	302469
Czechoslovakia	Serb/Croat/Slovene	14 Nov 28	97LTS9	302216
Hungary	Serb/Croat/Slovene	19 Nov 28	97LTS101	302222
Austria	Estonia	11 Dec 28	92LTS229	302091
Belgium	Denmark	12 Dec 28	107LTS363	302492
China	Portugal	19 Dec 28	107LTS93	302471
Latvia	Poland	12 Feb 29	115LTS135	302683
Germany	Persia	17 Feb 29	111LTS263	302591
Belgium	Finland	19 Feb 29	111LTS31	302577
Multilateral		20 Feb 29	124LTS357	302840
Estonia	Hungary	29 Apr 29	96LTS23	302189
Czechoslovakia	Persia	30 Apr 29	110LTS357	302567
Bel-Lux Econ Union	Persia	09 May 29	110LTS377	302569
Belgium	Sweden	13 May 29	111LTS37	302578
Estonia	USSR (Soviet Union)	17 May 29	94LTS323	302152
Bolivia	Netherlands	30 May 29	133LTS113	303062
Albania	Switzerland	10 Jun 29	104LTS145	302384
Romania	Turkey	11 Jun 29	112LTS139	302613
Canada	Denmark	18 Jun 29	95LTS81	302167
Hungary	Persia	19 Jun 29	107LTS355	302491
France	Switzerland	08 Jul 29	114LTS189	302664
Japan	Spain	05 Aug 29	113LTS9	302629
Bel-Lux Econ Union	Switzerland	26 Aug 29	105LTS9	302401
France	Turkey	29 Aug 29	123LTS193	302815
Estonia	Turkey	16 Sep 29	117LTS377	302704
Canada	Japan	21 Sep 29	96LTS143	302196
Canada	Netherlands	23 Sep 29	96LTS151	302197
Turkey	UK Great Britain	25 Sep 29	94LTS41	302135
Canada	Greece	30 Sep 29	96LTS159	302198
Belgium	France	07 Oct 29	111LTS43	302579
Finland	Turkey	12 Oct 29	96LTS239	302205
Latvia	Serb/Croat/Slovene	18 Oct 29	96LTS229	302204
Sweden	Turkey	19 Oct 29	96LTS221	302203
Cuba	France	06 Nov 29	114LTS345	302665
Norway	Sweden	18 Dec 29	98LTS389	302258
Cuba	Japan	21 Dec 29	111LTS13	302575
Portugal	UK Great Britain	18 Feb 30	108LTS393	302522
Italy	Romania	25 Feb 30	106LTS231	302447
Turkey	UK Great Britain	01 Mar 30	108LTS407	302523
Chile	United Arab Rep	05 Mar 30	124LTS25	302830
Austria	United Arab Rep	07 Mar 30	100LTS417	302310
Germany	Haiti	10 Mar 30	119LTS231	302747
United Arab Rep	Yugoslavia	13 Mar 30	110LTS133	302557
Czechoslovakia	United Arab Rep	16 Mar 30	107LTS179	302475
United Arab Rep	Japan	19 Mar 30	111LTS223	302588
Austria	Germany	12 Apr 30	115LTS333	302694
United Arab Rep	Poland	22 Apr 30	118LTS413	302735
China	Japan	06 May 30	106LTS295	302452
Denmark	United Arab Rep	07 May 30	102LTS137	302358
Germany	South Africa	12 May 30	123LTS301	302821
Germany	Irish Free State	12 May 30	131LTS153	303008

PARTY ONE	PARTY TWO	DATE	CITATION	NUMBER
Reciprocity in trade (Cont.)				
Belgium	Turkey	27 May 30	111LTS49	302580
Denmark	Turkey	31 May 30	119LTS165	302744
United Arab Rep	Hungary	12 Jun 30	106LTS437	302460
United Arab Rep	Persia	17 Jun 30	107LTS349	302490
Albania	Japan	20 Jun 30	123LTS295	302820
Iceland	Lithuania	21 Jun 30	119LTS403	302759
Denmark	Lithuania	21 Jun 30	114LTS151	302662
Poland	Romania	23 Jun 30	133LTS163	303066
Czechoslovakia	Romania	27 Jun 30	119LTS73	302742
Estonia	Finland	12 Jul 30	111LTS321	302596
Romania	Yugoslavia	04 Aug 30	107LTS253	302482
Romania	UK Great Britain	06 Aug 30	123LTS307	302822
Hungary	Romania	10 Aug 30	107LTS185	302476
Austria	Japan	16 Aug 30	126LTS351	302894
Romania	USA (United States)	20 Aug 30	115LTS115	302680
Netherlands	Romania	29 Aug 30	108LTS177	302507
Estonia	Netherlands	01 Sep 30	111LTS395	302600
India	Turkey	03 Sep 30	109LTS25	302525
UK Great Britain	USSR (Soviet Union)	16 Sep 30	101LTS409	302340
Brazil	Netherlands	16 Sep 30	125LTS197	302854
Brazil	Switzerland	29 Oct 30	140LTS265	303241
Latvia	Lithuania	24 Nov 30	112LTS417	302627
Portugal	Romania	05 Dec 30	114LTS369	302666
Estonia	Lithuania	15 Jan 31	114LTS141	302661
Norway	Turkey	16 Mar 31	138LTS41	303180
Estonia	Finland	11 Apr 31	124LTS217	302835
Belgium	Estonia	24 Apr 31	119LTS371	302756
Chile	France	22 May 31	124LTS31	302831
Greece	Norway	15 Aug 31	123LTS271	302817
Irish Free State	Sweden	08 Oct 31	125LTS23	302842
Multilateral		15 Oct 31	125LTS83	302847
Multilateral		15 Oct 31	125LTS89	302848
Brazil	Czechoslovakia	27 Nov 31	136LTS453	303144
Denmark	Finland	12 Dec 31	112LTS29	302604
Brazil	Poland	03 Feb 32	147LTS113	303396
Italy	USSR (Soviet Union)	06 May 33	158LTS51	303625
Latvia	UK Great Britain	06 Jul 33	142LTS217	303294
Germany	UK Great Britain	07 Jul 33	145LTS237	303356
Brazil	Uruguay	25 Aug 33	176LTS381	304075
Argentina	Brazil	10 Oct 33	179LTS165	304144
Latvia	USSR (Soviet Union)	04 Dec 33	148LTS145	303410
Australia	Belgium	14 Dec 33	147LTS21	303386
Finland	Turkey	19 Dec 33	149LTS333	303441
Argentina	Netherlands	31 Jan 34	148LTS355	303421
Spain	Turkey	19 May 34	149LTS15	303428
Haiti	USA (United States)	28 Mar 35	161LTS157	303709
Colombia	USA (United States)	13 Sep 35	170LTS293	303944
Denmark	Sweden	28 Oct 35	166LTS299	303845
Canada	USA (United States)	15 Nov 35	168LTS355	303910
Netherlands	USA (United States)	20 Dec 35	178LTS239	304118
Switzerland	USA (United States)	09 Jan 36	171LTS231	303962
Norway	Uruguay	04 Apr 36	176LTS115	304055
El Salvador	Sweden	23 Jun 36	171LTS291	303966
Brazil	Czechoslovakia	22 Jul 36	188LTS275	304363
Sweden	Uruguay	13 Aug 36	183LTS161	304232
Czechoslovakia	Guatemala	20 Sep 36	185LTS269	304293
Costa Rica	USA (United States)	28 Nov 36	181LTS183	304189
Bulgaria	Sweden	07 Dec 36	173LTS393	304030
El Salvador	USA (United States)	19 Feb 37	179LTS219	304150
Czechoslovakia	Italy	31 Mar 37	193LTS165	304492
Belgium	UK Great Britain	01 Jun 37	196LTS209	304583
Germany	Netherlands	30 Jun 37	189LTS373	304395
USA (United States)	USSR (Soviet Union)	04 Aug 37	182LTS113	304204
Denmark	Haiti	21 Oct 37	190LTS231	304422
Siam	Sweden	08 Nov 37	185LTS337	304298

PARTY ONE	PARTY TWO	DATE	CITATION	NUMBER
Reciprocity in trade (Cont.)				
Norway	Siam	15 Nov 37	186LTS9	304301
Bel-Lux Econ Union	Estonia	13 Jan 38	185LTS63	304275
France	Switzerland	31 Jan 38	195LTS313	304553
United Arab Rep	Iraq	16 May 38	190LTS177	304415
France	UK Great Britain	08 Nov 38	196LTS215	304584
Greece	USA (United States)	15 Nov 38	195LTS145	304544
El Salvador	Norway	21 Nov 38	198LTS157	304636
Germany	Romania	23 Mar 39	199LTS77	304668
Romania	UK Great Britain	11 May 39	196LTS351	304594
Reexport of goods, etc.				
Czechoslovakia	Serb/Croat/Slovene	18 Oct 20	17LTS19	300424
Czechoslovakia	Italy	23 Mar 21	32LTS183	300815
Czechoslovakia	Romania	23 Apr 21	15LTS235	300397
Finland	France	13 Jul 21	29LTS445	300755
Finland	Germany	21 Apr 22	19LTS87	300487
Poland	Switzerland	26 Jun 22	12LTS305	300322
Czechoslovakia	Latvia	07 Oct 22	20LTS379	300528
Estonia	Hungary	19 Oct 22	30LTS347	300774
Italy	Serb/Croat/Slovene	23 Oct 22	18LTS441	300480
Japan	Poland	07 Dec 22	32LTS61	300806
Multilateral		30 Dec 22	21LTS183	300542
Czechoslovakia	UK Great Britain	31 Jan 23	20LTS53	300506
Denmark	Finland	12 Feb 23	18LTS71	300454
Austria	UK Great Britain	28 Mar 23	17LTS385	300445
Germany	Portugal	28 Apr 23	32LTS385	300827
Latvia	UK Great Britain	22 Jun 23	20LTS395	300529
Estonia	Germany	27 Jun 23	41LTS161	301013
Poland	Turkey	23 Jul 23	49LTS329	301189
Multilateral		03 Nov 23	30LTS371	300775
Finland	Poland	10 Nov 23	29LTS229	300744
Hungary	Latvia	19 Nov 23	37LTS341	300959
Finland	UK Great Britain	14 Dec 23	29LTS129	300739
Multilateral		14 Dec 23	29LTS37	300732
Lithuania	Norway	21 Dec 23	32LTS55	300805
Austria	Turkey	28 Jan 24	32LTS313	300823
Netherlands	Portugal	27 Feb 24	27LTS105	300672
Sweden	Switzerland	20 Mar 24	25LTS243	300612
Denmark	Poland	22 Mar 24	31LTS13	300778
Denmark	Latvia	03 Apr 24	33LTS393	300860
Poland	Serb/Croat/Slovene	05 Apr 24	49LTS265	301185
Denmark	Sweden	28 Apr 24	27LTS355	300696
Multilateral		22 May 24	35LTS175	300895
Netherlands	Poland	30 May 24	34LTS9	300865
Czechoslovakia	France	18 Aug 24	44LTS21	301080
Finland	Latvia	23 Aug 24	37LTS383	300962
Netherlands	Portugal	27 Aug 24	31LTS235	300800
Hungary	Norway	16 Sep 24	33LTS103	300835
Finland	Italy	22 Oct 24	32LTS149	300814
France	Latvia	30 Oct 24	37LTS399	300963
Latvia	Switzerland	04 Dec 24	34LTS405	300889
France	Poland	09 Dec 24	44LTS127	301081
Austria	Spain	03 Feb 25	43LTS313	301067
Albania	Italy	06 Mar 25	44LTS359	301094
Bel-Lux Econ Union		07 Jul 25	54LTS267	301290
France	Hungary	13 Oct 25	48LTS9	301150
Estonia	Switzerland	14 Oct 25	49LTS421	301195
Germany	Italy	31 Oct 25	52LTS179	301256
Germany	Turkey	13 Dec 25	53LTS355	301265
Austria	Switzerland	06 Jan 26	46LTS299	301124
Estonia	UK Great Britain	18 Jan 26	48LTS209	301163
Denmark	Turkey	22 Mar 26	48LTS231	301164
Denmark	Germany	12 Apr 26	48LTS237	301165
Finland	Hungary	20 Apr 26	48LTS119	301154
Germany	Sweden	14 May 26	51LTS99	301225

PARTY ONE	PARTY TWO	DATE	CITATION	NUMBER
Reexport of goods, etc. (Cont.)				
Norway	Turkey	11 Aug 26	47LTS441	301149
Netherlands	Turkey	11 Aug 26	48LTS271	301168
Greece	Poland	22 Apr 31	129LTS313	302966
France	Greece	05 Jun 31	31LTS201	303011
Export subsidies				
France	South Africa	11 Feb 35	189LTS17	304372
Trade agencies				
Spain	UK Great Britain	31 Oct 22	28LTS339	300719
Poland	UK Great Britain	26 Nov 23	28LTS428	300722
Japan	Peru	30 Sep 24	102LTS33	302351
Austria	Serb/Croat/Slovene	06 Jun 28	129LTS11	302950
Greece	Romania	11 Aug 31	130LTS33	302981
Hungary	Romania	12 Aug 31	186LTS325	304321
Brazil	Germany	22 Oct 31	136LTS443	303143
Latvia	USSR (Soviet Union)	04 Dec 33	148LTS145	303410
Brazil	Uruguay	20 Dec 33	181LTS45	304176
France	USSR (Soviet Union)	11 Jan 34	167LTS349	303878
Turkey	Yugoslavia	17 Dec 34	178LTS471	304128
Haiti	USA (United States)	28 Mar 35	161LTS157	303709
Bel-Lux Econ Union	USSR (Soviet Union)	05 Sep 35	173LTS169	304010
United Arab Rep	UK Great Britain	18 Aug 36	176LTS177	304059
Bel-Lux Econ Union	Yugoslavia	26 Nov 37	196LTS19	304567
Trade procedures				
Bolivia	UK Great Britain	05 Apr 20	1LTS271	300020
France	Italy	27 Aug 20	8LTS95	300210
Austria	Germany	01 Sep 20	4LTS201	300107
Persia	USSR (Soviet Union)	26 Feb 21	9LTS383	300268
France	Norway	23 Apr 21	14LTS375	300386
Austria	Czechoslovakia	04 May 21	15LTS13	300388
Afghanistan	UK Great Britain	22 Nov 21	14LTS47	300367
Estonia	France	07 Jan 22	62LTS9	301452
Multilateral		06 Feb 22	38LTS277	300982
Norway	Spain	04 Apr 22	9LTS253	300258
Italy	Poland	12 May 22	59LTS293	301399
Austria	Poland	25 Sep 22	59LTS307	301400
Italy	Serb/Croat/Slovene	23 Oct 22	18LTS405	300478
Spain	UK Great Britain	31 Oct 22	28LTS339	300719
Norway	Portugal	11 Apr 23	16LTS379	300418
Germany	Portugal	28 Apr 23	32LTS385	300827
Latvia	UK Great Britain	22 Jun 23	20LTS395	300529
Netherlands	UK Great Britain	28 Sep 23	23LTS113	300581
Norway	Spain	07 Oct 23	59LTS47	301389
France	Italy	10 Apr 24	43LTS485	301078
Italy	Serb/Croat/Slovene	14 Jul 24	82LTS257	301876
Czechoslovakia	France	18 Aug 24	44LTS21	301080
Hungary	Norway	16 Sep 24	33LTS103	300835
Allied Powers	Germany	28 Oct 24	41LTS461	301025
France	Saar	15 Jan 25	44LTS181	301082
Bulgaria	Poland	29 Apr 25	60LTS103	301408
Spain	Sweden	04 May 25	36LTS323	300932
Hungary	Spain	17 Jun 25	60LTS69	301406
Czechoslovakia	Spain	19 Jul 25	60LTS329	301419
Germany	USSR (Soviet Union)	12 Oct 25	53LTS7	301257
Czechoslovakia	Japan	30 Oct 25	58LTS263	301377
Germany	Spain	18 Nov 25	53LTS309	301263
Denmark	Sweden	21 Nov 25	42LTS139	301037
Norway	USSR (Soviet Union)	15 Dec 25	47LTS9	301127
Bel-Lux Econ Union	Czechoslovakia	28 Dec 25	58LTS189	301372
Czechoslovakia	Poland	21 Apr 26	58LTS9	301367
Austria	Hungary	10 May 26	56LTS39	301321
Greece	Netherlands	12 May 26	61LTS295	301440
Austria	Czechoslovakia	12 Jul 26	86LTS383	301951
Bel-Lux Econ Union	Siam	13 Jul 26	62LTS287	301468
Germany	Switzerland	14 Jul 26	59LTS87	301391

PARTY ONE	PARTY TWO	DATE	CITATION	NUMBER
Trade procedures (Cont.)				
Bel-Lux Econ Union	Estonia	28 Sep 26	62LTS433	301475
Greece	Italy	24 Oct 26	63LTS51	301480
Greece	Switzerland	29 Nov 26	63LTS27	301478
Czechoslovakia	Switzerland	16 Feb 27	64LTS7	301501
France	Norway	12 Apr 27	178LTS199	304114
Greece	UK Great Britain	13 May 27	61LTS15	301425
Hungary	Italy	25 Jul 27	74LTS53	301731
Multilateral		08 Nov 27	97LTS391	302238
Hungary	Serb/Croat/Slovene	22 Feb 28	181LTS229	304192
France	Germany	23 Feb 28	79LTS247	301815
Bulgaria	Latvia	22 Jun 28	97LTS379	302236
Hungary	Italy	04 Jul 28	92LTS117	302083
Paraguay	UK Great Britain	16 Jul 28	108LTS365	302519
Netherlands	Turkey	25 Jul 28	93LTS279	302116
Czechoslovakia	Serb/Croat/Slovene	14 Nov 28	97LTS9	302216
Costa Rica	UK Great Britain	27 Dec 28	108LTS375	302520
Turkey	UK Great Britain	15 Jan 29	108LTS385	302521
Estonia	France	15 Mar 29	89LTS381	302029
Persia	Sweden	10 May 29	102LTS9	302349
Portugal	UK Great Britain	18 Feb 30	108LTS393	302522
Japan	Lithuania	02 May 30	126LTS369	302895
Norway	Persia	08 May 30	134LTS153	303089
China	France	16 May 30	162LTS99	303738
Switzerland	Turkey	13 Dec 30	129LTS267	302964
Iceland	Romania	08 May 31	127LTS11	302901
Germany	Hungary	18 Jul 31	150LTS111	303458
Hungary	Romania	12 Aug 31	186LTS325	304321
Brazil	Czechoslovakia	27 Nov 31	136LTS453	303144
Chile	Netherlands	17 Dec 31	127LTS79	302908
Belgium	Netherlands	29 Dec 31	127LTS163	302917
Bel-Lux Econ Union	Brazil	14 Jan 32	128LTS21	302933
Lithuania	Portugal	12 Apr 32	129LTS135	302958
Bulgaria	Germany	24 Jun 32	147LTS211	303400
Czechoslovakia	Denmark	04 Jul 32	143LTS251	303312
France	Sweden	13 Mar 33	142LTS131	303285
Germany	UK Great Britain	03 May 33	140LTS139	303231
Austria	UK Great Britain	27 Jul 33	142LTS157	303287
Brazil	Uruguay	25 Aug 33	176LTS381	304075
Brazil	Portugal	26 Aug 33	179LTS63	304134
Bulgaria	Czechoslovakia	29 Aug 33	148LTS15	303402
Estonia	Poland	26 Sep 33	150LTS309	303464
Finland	UK Great Britain	29 Sep 33	149LTS167	303438
Argentina	Brazil	10 Oct 33	179LTS165	304144
Poland	UK Great Britain	26 Oct 33	158LTS73	303628
Latvia	Lithuania	01 Dec 33	148LTS97	303407
Latvia	USSR (Soviet Union)	04 Dec 33	148LTS177	303411
Australia	Belgium	14 Dec 33	147LTS21	303386
Czechoslovakia	Poland	10 Feb 34	183LTS213	304238
Germany	Norway	06 Sep 34	161LTS187	303711
Poland	Spain	14 Dec 34	168LTS315	303908
Denmark	Germany	24 Jan 35	160LTS155	303689
Bel-Lux Econ Union	USA (United States)	27 Feb 35	160LTS27	303681
Haiti	USA (United States)	28 Mar 35	161LTS157	303709
Turkey	UK Great Britain	04 Jun 35	167LTS91	303860
Czechoslovakia	Hungary	14 Jun 35	171LTS401	303976
Iran	USSR (Soviet Union)	27 Aug 35	176LTS299	304069
Denmark	Sweden	28 Oct 35	166LTS299	303845
Honduras	USA (United States)	18 Dec 35	167LTS313	303876
France	Spain	21 Dec 35	167LTS9	303856
Nicaragua	USA (United States)	11 Mar 36	173LTS141	304009
Finland	USA (United States)	18 May 36	172LTS97	303981
Norway	Spain	13 Jun 36	170LTS199	303935
United Arab Rep	UK Great Britain	18 Aug 36	176LTS177	304059
Italy	Latvia	05 Feb 37	178LTS33	304104
Italy	Norway	31 Mar 37	177LTS349	304097

PARTY ONE	PARTY TWO	DATE	CITATION	NUMBER
Trade procedures (Cont.)				
Canada	Haiti	23 Apr 37	194LTS59	304507
Chile	Netherlands	05 May 37	182LTS385	304223
Romania	Yugoslavia	13 May 37	197LTS161	304612
Sweden	Yugoslavia	14 May 37	194LTS21	304504
Canada	Guatemala	28 Sep 37	194LTS65	304508
Brazil	Lithuania	28 Sep 37	186LTS403	304324
Estonia	France	16 Oct 37	183LTS41	304227
Latvia	Poland	16 Nov 37	197LTS43	304604
Bel-Lux Econ Union	Yugoslavia	26 Nov 37	196LTS19	304567
Germany	Netherlands	18 Dec 37	190LTS29	304403
Estonia	Sweden	18 Feb 38	185LTS237	304287
Portugal	UK Great Britain	11 May 38	191LTS285	304450
Cuba	Portugal	06 Sep 38	195LTS443	304565
Iraq	USA (United States)	03 Dec 38	203LTS107	304753
Germany	Romania	23 Mar 39	199LTS77	304668
Turkey	USA (United States)	01 Apr 39	202LTS129	304741
Romania	UK Great Britain	11 May 39	196LTS351	304594
Norway	Spain	26 Jul 39	198LTS87	304627
USA (United States)	Venezuela	06 Nov 39	203LTS273	304770
Belgium	UK Great Britain	04 Jun 42	204LTS363	304814
Chile	UK Great Britain	17 Jun 42	204LTS371	304815
Embargo				
Austria	Czechoslovakia	02 Aug 20	32LTS365	300826
France	Greece	11 Mar 29	95LTS401	302187
Finances and payments				
Danzig	Poland	24 Oct 21	116LTS5	302699
Belgium	Netherlands	28 Aug 25	93LTS431	302131
Austria	Serb/Croat/Slovene	01 May 28	96LTS373	302214
Czechoslovakia	Romania	05 Dec 30	167LTS231	303869
Multilateral		19 Mar 31	143LTS355	303316
Multilateral		19 Mar 31	143LTS407	303317
Bel-Lux Econ Union	Turkey	31 May 34	150LTS277	303461
Belgium	Netherlands	17 Dec 38	198LTS177	304638
Accounting procedures				
Denmark	Sweden	26 Jan 20	14LTS273	300379
Switzerland	UK Great Britain	28 Feb 20	6LTS9	300145
France	Germany	01 Mar 20	1LTS367	300030
China	UK Great Britain	26 Apr 20	5LTS83	300120
France	Germany	30 Jun 20	8LTS79	300208
Denmark	Germany	30 Aug 20	14LTS257	300377
Poland	USSR (Soviet Union)	12 Oct 20	4LTS7	300101
Liechtenstein	Switzerland	10 Nov 20	2LTS305	300084
Germany	Switzerland	06 Dec 20	2LTS343	300088
Australia	Malay States	24 Jan 21	23LTS209	300590
Denmark	Sweden	08 Jun 21	14LTS195	300374
Denmark	Norway	21 Jul 21	13LTS357	300362
Australia	Nauru	27 Oct 21	23LTS229	300591
Estonia	Finland	29 Oct 21	13LTS167	300350
Finland	USSR (Soviet Union)	14 Dec 21	16LTS221	300414
Iraq	UK Great Britain	16 Jan 22	12LTS431	300340
Norway	Sweden	29 Mar 22	13LTS311	300361
Sweden	USA (United States)	17 Apr 22	14LTS281	300380
Finland	Sweden	22 May 22	14LTS297	300381
Finland	Norway	23 May 22	14LTS323	300382
Finland	USSR (Soviet Union)	13 Jun 22	16LTS349	300416
Germany	Poland	15 Jun 22	34LTS201	300875
Finland	USA (United States)	21 Jul 22	13LTS243	300356
Multilateral		18 Aug 22	13LTS289	300360
Other Unilat Decla	Austria	04 Oct 22	12LTS405	300336
China	Japan	08 Dec 22	20LTS289	300522
UK Great Britain	USA (United States)	28 Dec 22	21LTS9	300531
Netherlands	UK Great Britain	18 Jan 23	18LTS257	300469
Portugal	Spain	26 Mar 23	18LTS373	300476
Multilateral		29 Mar 23	23LTS256	300593

PARTY ONE	PARTY TWO	DATE	CITATION	NUMBER
Accounting procedures (Cont.)				
Germany	UK Great Britain	05 Apr 23	17LTS173	300435
Persia	Russ Fed Sov Rep	27 Apr 23	110LTS333	302565
Australia	Netherlands	30 May 23	22LTS129	300556
Czechoslovakia	Hungary	13 Jul 23	35LTS253	300899
Czechoslovakia	Hungary	13 Jul 23	36LTS13	300901
Multilateral		24 Jul 23	28LTS203	300707
UK Great Britain	USA (United States)	08 Dec 23	23LTS93	300580
Other Unilat Decla	Hungary	14 Mar 24	25LTS427	300634
Hungary	Italy	27 Mar 24	45LTS241	301102
Austria	Czechoslovakia	12 Jul 24	50LTS111	301199
Germany	Saar	20 Sep 24	30LTS121	300765
Multilateral		23 Oct 24	77LTS367	301778
Bulgaria	Great Britain	07 May 25	38LTS153	300973
France	UK Great Britain	12 Jul 26	98LTS155	302244
Other Unilat Decla	Estonia	10 Dec 26	62LTS277	301467
Portugal	UK Great Britain	31 Dec 26	61LTS115	301429
Multilateral		10 Sep 27	75LTS39	301750
Multilateral		10 Sep 27	75LTS7	301749
Greece		15 Sep 27	70LTS9	301622
Hungary	Serb/Croat/Slovene	22 Feb 28	87LTS361	301982
Multilateral		10 Mar 28	132LTS405	303049
Multilateral		01 May 28	132LTS415	303050
Bulgaria		08 Sep 28	74LTS167	301738
Multilateral		12 Sep 28	104LTS43	302377
Multilateral		25 Oct 28	84LTS7	301901
Multilateral		27 Nov 28	92LTS321	302098
Multilateral		30 Nov 28	87LTS119	301965
Denmark	Sweden	13 Dec 28	104LTS55	302378
Multilateral		22 Dec 28	104LTS103	302381
Brazil	Peru	31 Dec 28	127LTS455	302931
Multilateral		05 Jan 29	132LTS425	303051
Multilateral		14 Jan 29	87LTS169	301968
Multilateral		16 Jan 29	87LTS155	301967
Denmark	Norway	21 Jan 29	104LTS119	302382
Multilateral		02 Feb 29	92LTS353	302100
Denmark	Sweden	28 Feb 29	104LTS69	302379
Norway	USA (United States)	30 Mar 29	91LTS383	302078
UK Great Britain	USA (United States)	02 Apr 29	94LTS17	302133
UK Great Britain	USA (United States)	06 Apr 29	99LTS27	302265
Netherlands	UK Great Britain	04 May 29	93LTS9	302101
Multilateral		08 May 29	91LTS337	302074
France	UK Great Britain	15 May 29	134LTS263	303097
Palestine	Switzerland	15 May 29	95LTS395	302186
Multilateral		28 Jun 29	103LTS429	302374
Multilateral		28 Jun 29	103LTS249	302371
Multilateral		28 Jun 29	103LTS321	302372
UK Great Britain	USA (United States)	04 Jul 29	92LTS329	302099
UK Great Britain	USA (United States)	11 Jul 29	98LTS161	302245
Persia	USSR (Soviet Union)	02 Aug 29	109LTS99	302530
Multilateral		30 Aug 29	96LTS129	302195
Multilateral		07 Sep 29	98LTS345	302255
Netherlands	South Africa	10 Sep 29	98LTS423	302261
Belgium	Irish Free State	24 Sep 29	102LTS213	302364
Multilateral		25 Sep 29	98LTS361	302256
Multilateral		26 Sep 29	98LTS395	302259
Multilateral		30 Sep 29	99LTS71	302269
Multilateral		01 Oct 29	98LTS197	302247
Poland	UK Great Britain	04 Oct 29	97LTS261	302227
Multilateral		08 Oct 29	98LTS409	302260
Multilateral		10 Oct 29	98LTS375	302257
Multilateral		28 Oct 29	97LTS71	302219
Multilateral		29 Oct 29	99LTS85	302270
Poland	Romania	30 Oct 29	121LTS167	302787
Multilateral		18 Nov 29	99LTS415	302287
Multilateral		14 Jan 30	99LTS343	302278

PARTY ONE	PARTY TWO	DATE	CITATION	NUMBER
Accounting procedures (Cont.)				
Multilateral		25 Feb 30	101LTS343	302335
Romania	UK Great Britain	02 Apr 30	105LTS235	302416
Multilateral		10 Apr 30	101LTS465	302345
UK Great Britain	USA (United States)	16 Apr 30	109LTS9	302524
Finland	Norway	14 May 30	105LTS399	302429
Denmark	Finland	14 May 30	105LTS455	302433
Latvia	UK Great Britain	24 Jul 30	107LTS301	302486
Netherlands	USA (United States)	16 Sep 30	125LTS147	302852
Denmark	India	16 Dec 30	114LTS73	302656
Mexico	Sweden	14 Sep 31	192LTS195	304472
UK Great Britain	Yugoslavia	23 Oct 31	126LTS209	302884
Multilateral		10 Nov 31	131LTS389	303024
France	UK Great Britain	17 Nov 31	134LTS299	303098
France	UK Great Britain	27 Nov 31	132LTS25	303028
Estonia	UK Great Britain	22 Dec 31	131LTS323	303022
France	UK Great Britain	28 Dec 31	133LTS79	303058
Netherlands	UK Great Britain	04 Jan 32	128LTS347	302940
Estonia	France	26 Mar 32	128LTS51	302937
Austria	Yugoslavia	20 Apr 32	132LTS217	303040
Switzerland	Yugoslavia	27 Apr 32	131LTS285	303019
Czechoslovakia	Yugoslavia	08 Jun 32	139LTS45	303203
Netherlands	South Africa	29 Jun 32	133LTS33	303054
Sweden	USA (United States)	11 Jul 32	192LTS205	304473
Bel-Lux Econ Union	Yugoslavia	07 Aug 32	139LTS223	303212
Hungary	Italy	12 Nov 32	142LTS101	303281
Chile	Sweden	08 Mar 33	142LTS147	303286
Estonia	Finland	16 May 33	141LTS19	303257
Bel-Lux Econ Union	Hungary	24 May 33	140LTS169	303234
Bel-Lux Econ Union	Bulgaria	21 Jun 33	140LTS375	303247
Multilateral		23 Nov 33	192LTS389	304484
Multilateral		23 Nov 33	192LTS327	304483
Multilateral		20 Mar 34	175LTS363	304052
Multilateral		20 Mar 34	175LTS269	304051
Multilateral		20 Mar 34	176LTS55	304054
Bulgaria	Spain	19 Nov 34	166LTS277	303843
Turkey	UK Great Britain	04 Jun 35	167LTS91	303860
Italy	Netherlands	29 Jul 35	165LTS329	303819
Bulgaria	Netherlands	23 Sep 35	166LTS51	303829
Finland	Romania	03 Dec 35	165LTS287	303815
Spain	UK Great Britain	06 Jan 36	166LTS283	303844
Greece	Sweden	11 Jan 36	165LTS299	303816
Germany	Sweden	31 Jan 36	168LTS19	303884
Sweden	Turkey	27 Feb 36	167LTS83	303859
Finland	Latvia	28 Mar 36	171LTS155	303957
Bel-Lux Econ Union	Bulgaria	01 Apr 36	169LTS23	303912
Bel-Lux Econ Union	Spain	04 Apr 36	168LTS339	303909
Romania	UK Great Britain	02 May 36	184LTS145	304247
Norway	Turkey	08 Jun 36	170LTS235	303939
Norway	Spain	13 Jun 36	170LTS207	303936
Finland	Turkey	20 Jun 36	172LTS135	303983
Italy	Norway	25 Aug 36	171LTS377	303974
Netherlands	Romania	28 Aug 36	182LTS363	304222
Turkey	UK Great Britain	02 Sep 36	172LTS289	303998
Finland	Italy	28 Sep 36	172LTS155	303986
Estonia	Italy	06 Oct 36	172LTS189	303989
Bulgaria	Finland	27 Oct 36	173LTS201	304013
Italy	UK Great Britain	06 Nov 36	177LTS183	304090
Italy	Sweden	01 Dec 36	173LTS279	304019
Italy	Sweden	01 Dec 36	173LTS269	304018
Norway	Romania	10 Dec 36	174LTS59	304037
Hungary	Yugoslavia	17 Dec 36	196LTS143	304577
Germany	Netherlands	23 Dec 36	179LTS359	304163
Greece	Sweden	31 Dec 36	174LTS87	304039
Italy	Netherlands	01 Jan 37	178LTS415	304124
Italy	Latvia	05 Feb 37	178LTS25	304103

PARTY ONE	PARTY TWO	DATE	CITATION	NUMBER
Accounting procedures (Cont.)				
Netherlands	Turkey	17 Feb 37	182LTS221	304213
Germany	Norway	27 Feb 37	178LTS427	304125
Brazil	Netherlands	15 Mar 37	179LTS405	304167
Portugal	UK Great Britain	24 Mar 37	185LTS151	304280
Italy	Norway	31 Mar 37	177LTS367	304099
Italy	Norway	31 Mar 37	177LTS355	304098
Chile	Netherlands	05 May 37	182LTS385	304223
Estonia	Turkey	06 Jun 37	179LTS159	304143
Bel-Lux Econ Union	Italy	30 Jun 37	182LTS106	304203
Bulgaria	Romania	20 Jul 37	202LTS33	304733
Bel-Lux Econ Union	Romania	24 Aug 37	193LTS189	304496
Malaya	Siam	16 Sep 37	191LTS265	304448
Multilateral		23 Sep 37	190LTS299	304427
Estonia	Germany	24 Oct 37	184LTS81	304244
Germany	Latvia	31 Oct 37	189LTS139	304382
Hungary	Lithuania	12 Nov 37	183LTS197	304236
Hungary	Latvia	16 Nov 37	183LTS205	304237
Estonia	Greece	25 Nov 37	184LTS427	304263
Germany	Netherlands	18 Dec 37	190LTS29	304403
Sweden	Turkey	31 Dec 37	184LTS409	304261
Greece	Norway	28 Feb 38	186LTS165	304309
Greece	Norway	28 Feb 38	186LTS159	304308
Finland	Lithuania	12 Apr 38	194LTS9	304501
Bulgaria	Latvia	17 May 38	189LTS249	304388
Lithuania	Poland	25 May 38	191LTS391	304457
Romania	UK Great Britain	02 Sep 38	191LTS313	304453
Netherlands	Romania	10 Oct 38	195LTS9	304532
Aden	United Arab Rep	03 Nov 38	197LTS241	304617
Colombia	USA (United States)	07 Feb 39	196LTS53	304569
Burma	Siam	14 Feb 39	197LTS255	304618
France	Romania	31 Mar 39	199LTS219	304677
Greece	Sweden	01 May 39	196LTS205	304582
Norway	Spain	26 Jul 39	198LTS87	304627
Germany	Latvia	30 Oct 39	200LTS213	304693
Sweden	Turkey	29 Feb 40	200LTS273	304696
Spain	UK Great Britain	18 Mar 40	203LTS157	304759
Finland	Latvia	11 Apr 40	201LTS389	304727
Attachment of funds				
France	Germany	30 Jun 20	8LTS79	300208
Austria	Czechoslovakia	15 Jun 24	94LTS131	302141
Austria	Serb/Croat/Slovene	18 Jun 24	114LTS481	302672
Austria	Czechoslovakia	17 Jan 25	94LTS185	302145
Netherlands	UK Great Britain	04 Jan 32	128LTS307	302939
Multilateral		29 May 33	192LTS289	304479
Banking				
China	UK Great Britain	26 Apr 20	5LTS83	300120
Austria	Czechoslovakia	02 Aug 20	32LTS365	300826
Germany	Poland	20 Sep 20	9LTS103	300246
Denmark	UK Great Britain	12 Jul 21	8LTS397	300238
Italy	Serb/Croat/Slovene	23 Oct 22	18LTS461	300481
Other Unilat Decla	Hungary	14 Mar 24	25LTS427	300634
Hungary	Italy	27 Mar 24	45LTS65	301099
Hungary	Romania	16 Apr 24	45LTS403	301110
Spain	UK Great Britain	27 Jun 24	28LTS523	300727
Other Unilat Decla	Greece	19 Sep 24	30LTS413	300776
Japan	Mexico	08 Oct 24	36LTS259	300927
Greece		15 Sep 27	70LTS9	301622
Austria	Belgium	10 Oct 27	91LTS271	302067
Italy	Spain	28 Nov 27	82LTS27	301857
Multilateral		20 Feb 28	86LTS111	301950
Bulgaria		08 Sep 28	74LTS167	301738
Germany	Romania	10 Nov 28	91LTS101	302058
Germany	Poland	14 Dec 28	113LTS311	302647
Other Unilat Decla	Greece	14 Jan 30	108LTS349	302518

PARTY ONE	PARTY TWO	DATE	CITATION	NUMBER
Banking (Cont.)				
Austria	Belgium	18 Jan 30	104LTS231	302393
Hungary	Yugoslavia	30 Jan 31	120LTS105	302761
Bel-Lux Econ Union	Hungary	26 Mar 32	136LTS405	303139
Austria	Yugoslavia	20 Apr 32	132LTS217	303040
Switzerland	Yugoslavia	27 Apr 32	131LTS285	303019
Czechoslovakia	Poland	25 Jan 34	177LTS139	304088
Multilateral		20 Mar 34	176LTS9	304053
Germany	Norway	06 Sep 34	161LTS187	303711
Finland	Germany	02 Oct 34	154LTS17	303535
Bulgaria	Spain	19 Nov 34	166LTS277	303843
Germany	Sweden	22 Dec 34	156LTS127	303596
Estonia	Spain	08 May 35	159LTS381	303679
Bel-Lux Econ Union	Estonia	19 Jun 35	170LTS243	303940
Panama	USA (United States)	02 Mar 36	200LTS17	304686
Bel-Lux Econ Union	Spain	04 Apr 36	168LTS339	303909
Norway	Turkey	08 Jun 36	170LTS227	303938
Norway	Turkey	08 Jun 36	170LTS235	303939
Finland	Turkey	20 Jun 36	172LTS135	303983
Bulgaria	France	06 Jul 36	171LTS269	303963
Brazil	Norway	27 Jul 36	176LTS125	304056
Italy	Norway	25 Aug 36	171LTS377	303974
Estonia	Italy	06 Oct 36	172LTS189	303989
Italy	UK Great Britain	06 Nov 36	177LTS183	304090
Italy	Sweden	01 Dec 36	173LTS279	304019
Norway	Romania	10 Dec 36	174LTS59	304037
Sweden	Turkey	14 Dec 36	174LTS51	304036
Hungary	Yugoslavia	17 Dec 36	196LTS143	304577
Italy	Netherlands	01 Jan 37	178LTS415	304124
Italy	Latvia	05 Feb 37	178LTS25	304103
Netherlands	Turkey	17 Feb 37	182LTS221	304213
Germany	Norway	27 Feb 37	178LTS427	304125
Brazil	Netherlands	15 Mar 37	179LTS405	304167
Italy	Norway	31 Mar 37	177LTS355	304098
Italy	Norway	31 Mar 37	177LTS367	304099
Chile	Netherlands	05 May 37	182LTS385	304223
Poland	Romania	24 May 37	190LTS361	304428
Estonia	Turkey	06 Jun 37	179LTS159	304143
Bel-Lux Econ Union	Italy	30 Jun 37	182LTS106	304203
Bel-Lux Econ Union	Romania	24 Aug 37	193LTS189	304496
Estonia	Germany	24 Oct 37	184LTS81	304244
Germany	Latvia	31 Oct 37	189LTS139	304382
Hungary	Lithuania	12 Nov 37	183LTS197	304236
Hungary	Latvia	16 Nov 37	183LTS205	304237
Germany	Netherlands	18 Dec 37	190LTS29	304403
Sweden	Turkey	31 Dec 37	184LTS409	304261
Greece	Norway	28 Feb 38	186LTS165	304309
Multilateral		09 Apr 38	191LTS119	304441
Multilateral		09 Apr 38	191LTS165	304442
Bulgaria	Latvia	17 May 38	189LTS249	304388
Switzerland	Yugoslavia	27 Jun 38	196LTS27	304568
Germany	UK Great Britain	10 Sep 38	194LTS313	304528
Netherlands	Romania	10 Oct 38	195LTS9	304532
Germany	Romania	23 Mar 39	199LTS77	304668
Norway	Spain	26 Jul 39	198LTS87	304627
Romania	Switzerland	02 Nov 39	200LTS289	304699
Bonds				
Danzig	Poland	24 Oct 21	116LTS5	302699
Austria	Czechoslovakia	17 Dec 21	22LTS401	300570
Multilateral		29 Mar 23	23LTS256	300593
Czechoslovakia	Hungary	13 Jul 23	35LTS253	300899
Czechoslovakia	Hungary	08 Mar 24	36LTS61	300904
Hungary	Italy	27 Mar 24	45LTS65	301099
Hungary	Italy	27 Mar 24	45LTS83	301100
Austria	Czechoslovakia	29 Mar 24	94LTS103	302140

PARTY ONE	PARTY TWO	DATE	CITATION	NUMBER
Bonds (Cont.)				
Hungary	Romania	16 Apr 24	46LTS7	301111
Hungary	Romania	16 Apr 24	45LTS403	301110
Austria	Czechoslovakia	15 Jun 24	94LTS149	302142
Austria	Czechoslovakia	15 Jun 24	94LTS165	302143
Austria	Romania	26 Jul 24	85LTS223	301933
Estonia	USA (United States)	28 Oct 25	62LTS63	301455
Czechoslovakia	Italy	04 May 26	61LTS257	301438
Albania	Serb/Croat/Slovene	22 Jun 26	91LTS9	302054
Dominican Republic	USA (United States)	19 Jul 26	54LTS145	301282
Poland	USA (United States)	14 Nov 26	58LTS97	301368
Bulgaria	Greece	28 Feb 27	68LTS59	301568
France	Germany	17 Aug 27	76LTS5	301761
Germany	Serb/Croat/Slovene	06 Oct 27	77LTS19	301763
Austria	Belgium	10 Oct 27	91LTS271	302067
Bulgaria	Greece	09 Dec 27	87LTS199	301970
Hungary	Serb/Croat/Slovene	22 Feb 28	87LTS361	301982
Hungary	Serb/Croat/Slovene	22 Feb 28	87LTS331	301979
Germany	Greece	24 Mar 28	90LTS9	302031
Germany	Poland	05 Jul 28	113LTS189	302646
Germany	UK Great Britain	28 Dec 29	102LTS49	302352
Other Unilat Decla	Greece	14 Jan 30	108LTS349	302518
Austria	Belgium	18 Jan 30	104LTS231	302393
Multilateral		20 Jan 30	104LTS243	302394
Germany	Haiti	10 Mar 30	119LTS231	302747
Germany	USA (United States)	23 Jun 30	106LTS121	302440
Multilateral		31 Oct 30	120LTS9	302760
Romania	Yugoslavia	14 Dec 31	135LTS89	303105
Greece	Spain	11 Jul 32	148LTS397	303426
Romania	Yugoslavia	30 Jan 33	146LTS129	303365
Argentina	UK Great Britain	01 May 33	143LTS67	303305
Austria	Hungary	12 Jan 34	162LTS419	303754
Germany	Sweden	28 Aug 34	154LTS267	303552
Germany	Sweden	22 Dec 34	156LTS145	303597
UK Great Britain	Uruguay	26 Jun 35	176LTS153	304058
Italy	Sweden	01 Dec 36	173LTS279	304019
Argentina	Netherlands	05 Feb 37	179LTS383	304165
Germany	Sweden	28 Oct 38	196LTS91	304571
Germany	Sweden	28 Oct 38	196LTS81	304570
Sweden	USA (United States)	23 Mar 39	199LTS17	304661
Canada	USA (United States)	18 Jun 40	203LTS41	304748
United Arab Rep	UK Great Britain	17 Jul 40	202LTS97	304738
United Arab Rep	France	03 Aug 40	202LTS121	304740
Compensation				
France	Germany	01 Mar 20	1LTS367	300030
France	Germany	30 Jun 20	8LTS79	300208
Germany	Latvia	15 Jul 20	2LTS91	300052
Ireland	UK Great Britain	06 Dec 21	26LTS9	300636
Finland	Norway	03 Mar 22	14LTS157	300372
Finland	USSR (Soviet Union)	28 Oct 22	19LTS153	300491
China	Japan	01 Dec 22	22LTS179	300559
Germany	Poland	27 Jan 23	26LTS461	300663
United Arab Rep	UK Great Britain	18 Jul 23	18LTS323	300474
Multilateral		30 Nov 23	102LTS183	302361
Bulgaria	USA (United States)	19 Mar 24	26LTS27	300638
Multilateral		25 Aug 24	120LTS123	302763
Germany	Saar	20 Sep 24	30LTS121	300765
Multilateral		23 Oct 24	77LTS367	301778
Finland	Germany	02 Feb 25	33LTS127	300838
Germany	Mexico	16 Mar 25	52LTS93	301251
Finland	Sweden	09 May 25	47LTS283	301136
Italy	Poland	22 Jul 25	54LTS101	301278
Spain	USA (United States)	10 Feb 26	67LTS131	301543
Multilateral		10 Apr 26	120LTS187	302765
Multilateral		24 Jan 27	70LTS453	301650

PARTY ONE	PARTY TWO	DATE	CITATION	NUMBER
Compensation (Cont.)				
Austria	Czechoslovakia	15 Feb 27	73LTS381	301725
Austria	Belgium	10 Oct 27	91LTS271	302067
Norway	Sweden	19 Nov 27	68LTS209	301584
Bulgaria	Greece	09 Dec 27	87LTS199	301970
Cuba	Germany	14 Jun 28	124LTS47	302832
Finland	Italy	21 Aug 28	89LTS25	302002
Bulgaria		08 Sep 28	74LTS167	301738
France	UK Great Britain	23 Sep 28	87LTS29	301961
Bolivia	UK Great Britain	18 Jan 29	95LTS9	302161
France	UK Great Britain	06 Mar 29	90LTS391	302050
Norway	USA (United States)	30 Mar 29	91LTS383	302078
Norway	Sweden	11 May 29	120LTS263	302771
Multilateral		28 Jun 29	103LTS5	302369
Multilateral		28 Jun 29	103LTS71	302370
Germany	UK Great Britain	17 Jul 29	100LTS439	302313
Persia	USSR (Soviet Union)	02 Aug 29	109LTS99	302530
France	UK Great Britain	02 Aug 29	100LTS459	302314
Poland	Romania	30 Oct 29	121LTS167	302787
Belgium	France	07 Nov 29	134LTS257	303096
Multilateral		09 Nov 29	125LTS205	302855
Greece	Turkey	10 Jun 30	108LTS233	302511
Italy	UK Great Britain	28 Aug 30	111LTS91	302583
Netherlands	USA (United States)	16 Sep 30	125LTS173	302853
Czechoslovakia	Romania	22 Dec 30	167LTS257	303871
France	India	28 Dec 32	140LTS36	303226
Romania	Yugoslavia	11 Mar 33	146LTS285	303379
Finland	USSR (Soviet Union)	04 Jul 33	149LTS83	303436
Finland	UK Great Britain	13 Oct 33	142LTS187	303291
Multilateral		23 Nov 33	192LTS389	304484
Multilateral		23 Nov 33	192LTS327	304483
Brazil	USA (United States)	10 May 34	150LTS445	303477
Poland	Romania	17 May 35	173LTS373	304028
Turkey	UK Great Britain	04 Jun 35	167LTS91	303860
Bulgaria	Netherlands	23 Sep 35	166LTS51	303829
Denmark	Sweden	28 Oct 35	166LTS299	303845
Estonia	Latvia	10 Dec 35	168LTS83	303888
Czechoslovakia	Finland	21 Mar 36	179LTS295	304156
Bel-Lux Econ Union	Spain	04 Apr 36	168LTS339	303909
Brazil	USA (United States)	27 May 36	171LTS343	303971
Norway	Spain	13 Jun 36	170LTS207	303936
Finland	Turkey	20 Jun 36	172LTS135	303983
Italy	Norway	25 Aug 36	171LTS377	303974
Netherlands	Romania	28 Aug 36	182LTS363	304222
Turkey	UK Great Britain	02 Sep 36	172LTS289	303998
Romania	Turkey	04 Sep 36	195LTS429	304564
Finland	Italy	28 Sep 36	172LTS155	303986
Estonia	Italy	06 Oct 36	172LTS189	303989
Estonia	Latvia	06 Oct 36	172LTS221	303994
Canada	Germany	22 Oct 36	173LTS311	304021
Bulgaria	Finland	27 Oct 36	173LTS201	304013
Brazil	USA (United States)	12 Nov 36	176LTS133	304057
Italy	Sweden	01 Dec 36	173LTS269	304018
Norway	Romania	10 Dec 36	174LTS59	304037
Sweden	Turkey	14 Dec 36	174LTS51	304036
Hungary	Yugoslavia	17 Dec 36	196LTS143	304577
Germany	Netherlands	23 Dec 36	179LTS359	304163
Italy	Netherlands	01 Jan 37	178LTS415	304124
Italy	Latvia	05 Feb 37	178LTS25	304103
Netherlands	Turkey	17 Feb 37	182LTS221	304213
Germany	Norway	27 Feb 37	178LTS427	304125
Italy	Norway	31 Mar 37	177LTS355	304098
Chile	Netherlands	05 May 37	182LTS385	304223
Estonia	Greece	25 Nov 37	184LTS427	304263
Sweden	Turkey	31 Dec 37	184LTS409	304261
Dominican Republic	Haiti	31 Jan 38	187LTS169	304336

PARTY ONE	PARTY TWO	DATE	CITATION	NUMBER
Compensation (Cont.)				
Greece	Sweden	01 Feb 38	185LTS217	304285
Netherlands	USA (United States)	18 Feb 38	192LTS49	304460
Greece	Norway	28 Feb 38	186LTS165	304309
Finland	Lithuania	12 Apr 38	194LTS9	304501
Lithuania	Poland	25 May 38	191LTS391	304457
USA (United States)	Yugoslavia	20 Jun 38	195LTS259	304549
Belgium	UK Great Britain	29 Jul 38	201LTS317	304722
Burma	United Arab Rep	30 Sep 38	203LTS373	304780
Poland	UK Great Britain	05 Oct 38	194LTS321	304529
Netherlands	Romania	10 Oct 38	195LTS9	304532
France	UK Great Britain	26 Oct 38	194LTS371	304530
Brazil	USA (United States)	12 Nov 38	195LTS375	304557
Colombia	USA (United States)	23 Nov 38	196LTS157	304579
Colombia	USA (United States)	23 Nov 38	196LTS147	304578
Multilateral		02 Jan 39	196LTS235	304587
Belgium	USA (United States)	15 Jan 39	199LTS321	304682
Sweden	Turkey	20 Jan 39	194LTS113	304514
Burma	France	26 Jan 39	201LTS9	304701
Colombia	USA (United States)	07 Feb 39	196LTS53	304569
Germany	USA (United States)	16 Mar 39	198LTS237	304645
France	India	22 Mar 39	197LTS273	304619
Guatemala	USA (United States)	28 Mar 39	199LTS181	304671
France	Romania	31 Mar 39	199LTS219	304677
Argentina	USA (United States)	08 Apr 39	198LTS55	304623
Mexico	USA (United States)	18 Apr 39	201LTS201	304714
Greece	Sweden	01 May 39	196LTS205	304582
Nicaragua	USA (United States)	22 May 39	199LTS189	304672
Multilateral		23 May 39	202LTS159	304742
Norway	Spain	26 Jul 39	198LTS87	304627
Argentina	USA (United States)	12 Sep 39	201LTS213	304715
Barbados	USA (United States)	13 Sep 39	199LTS375	304685
United Arab Rep	USA (United States)	13 Nov 39	198LTS419	304659
Turkey	UK Great Britain	22 Nov 39	201LTS93	304705
Lithuania	USA (United States)	28 Dec 39	202LTS381	304743
Sweden	Turkey	29 Feb 40	200LTS273	304696
Finland	Latvia	11 Apr 40	201LTS389	304727
Chile	USA (United States)	23 Apr 40	203LTS29	304747
Argentina	USA (United States)	29 Jun 40	203LTS57	304750
Peru	USA (United States)	31 Jul 40	203LTS91	304752
Peru	USA (United States)	31 Jul 40	203LTS75	304751
Ecuador	USA (United States)	12 Dec 40	203LTS305	304771
Ecuador	USA (United States)	12 Dec 40	203LTS327	304773
Brazil	USA (United States)	17 Jan 41	204LTS97	304788
USA (United States)	Venezuela	24 Mar 41	204LTS83	304787
Peru	USA (United States)	15 Apr 41	204LTS117	304790
Nicaragua	USA (United States)	22 May 41	204LTS283	304809
Guatemala	USA (United States)	27 May 41	204LTS185	304799
Costa Rica	USA (United States)	14 Jul 41	204LTS231	304802
Indemnities and reimbursements				
Multilateral		13 Nov 08	1LTS217	300015
Multilateral		05 Jun 12	1LTS135	300013
Chile	Colombia	16 Nov 14	82LTS243	301875
France	UK Great Britain	10 Jan 20	5LTS53	300117
Germany	USSR (Soviet Union)	19 Apr 20	2LTS63	300048
Germany	Latvia	20 Apr 20	2LTS71	300049
France	Greece	20 Apr 20	3LTS93	300093
Germany	Hungary	08 May 20	2LTS79	300050
France	Germany	01 Jul 20	8LTS87	300209
Lithuania	USSR (Soviet Union)	12 Jul 20	3LTS106	300094
Latvia	USSR (Soviet Union)	11 Aug 20	2LTS195	300067
Germany	Poland	02 Nov 20	2LTS277	300081
Danzig	Poland	09 Nov 20	6LTS189	300153
Denmark	UK Great Britain	23 Dec 20	2LTS249	300071
Czechoslovakia	Germany	03 Feb 21	5LTS246	300132

PARTY ONE	PARTY TWO	DATE	CITATION	NUMBER
Indemnities and reimbursements (Cont.)				
Latvia	USSR (Soviet Union)	20 Oct 21	54LTS155	301283
Australia	Nauru	27 Oct 21	23LTS229	300591
Germany	Switzerland	29 Oct 21	13LTS193	300351
Iraq	UK Great Britain	16 Jan 22	12LTS431	300340
Palestine	UK Great Britain	23 Jan 22	13LTS9	300342
Brazil	Paraguay	24 Feb 22	138LTS211	303189
Finland	Norway	03 Mar 22	14LTS157	300372
Colombia	Peru	24 Mar 22	74LTS9	301726
Italy	Serb/Croat/Slovene	06 Apr 22	118LTS221	302726
Italy	Serb/Croat/Slovene	06 Apr 22	118LTS207	302725
Czechoslovakia	Italy	06 Apr 22	55LTS171	301313
Germany	Poland	12 Apr 22	21LTS327	300548
Germany	Poland	18 Jun 22	34LTS235	300876
Sweden	Uruguay	24 Feb 23	63LTS239	301494
Germany	Switzerland	25 Mar 23	18LTS273	300470
Multilateral		29 Mar 23	23LTS256	300593
Germany	UK Great Britain	05 Apr 23	17LTS173	300435
Poland	Serb/Croat/Slovene	04 May 23	85LTS455	301946
Multilateral		24 Jul 23	28LTS151	300704
Multilateral		24 Jul 23	28LTS203	300707
Turkey	USA (United States)	06 Aug 23	153LTS71	303509
Iraq	UK Great Britain	25 Mar 24	35LTS145	300894
Multilateral		28 Mar 24	31LTS46	300780
Multilateral		28 Mar 24	31LTS53	300781
Austria	Czechoslovakia	29 Mar 24	94LTS103	302140
Lithuania	USA (United States)	09 Apr 24	51LTS191	301226
Hungary	Romania	16 Apr 24	42LTS145	301038
Germany	Hungary	01 May 24	41LTS282	301021
Austria	Czechoslovakia	15 Jun 24	94LTS165	302143
Finland	USSR (Soviet Union)	18 Jun 24	47LTS241	301134
Austria	Czechoslovakia	12 Jul 24	50LTS111	301199
Italy	Serb/Croat/Slovene	12 Aug 24	82LTS423	301882
Colombia	Panama	20 Aug 24	33LTS167	300841
Japan	Peru	30 Sep 24	102LTS33	302351
France	Latvia	29 Oct 24	93LTS265	302115
Hungary	Serb/Croat/Slovene	14 Dec 24	39LTS91	300997
Estonia	Finland	02 Jan 25	43LTS11	301044
Estonia	Germany	09 Jan 25	42LTS13	301028
Austria	France	04 Mar 25	44LTS205	301084
Czechoslovakia	Poland	06 Mar 25	46LTS201	301120
Germany	Poland	14 Mar 25	95LTS239	302178
Germany	Mexico	16 Mar 25	52LTS93	301251
Czechoslovakia	Romania	07 May 25	54LTS17	301272
Czechoslovakia	Romania	07 May 25	54LTS51	301273
Austria	Czechoslovakia	14 May 25	50LTS39	301198
Greece	Switzerland	21 Sep 25	87LTS187	301969
Poland	Sweden	03 Nov 25	62LTS263	301466
Finland	Norway	10 Nov 25	43LTS381	301071
Estonia	Germany	25 Nov 25	54LTS79	301275
Austria	Norway	17 Dec 25	48LTS77	301152
Austria	Denmark	19 Dec 25	57LTS121	301358
France	Poland	30 Dec 25	95LTS233	302177
France	Poland	30 Dec 25	48LTS139	301155
Multilateral		31 Dec 25	79LTS167	301809
Belgium	Paraguay	20 Jan 26	97LTS197	302224
Italy	UK Great Britain	29 Jan 26	47LTS409	301145
Brazil	Venezuela	13 Apr 26	80LTS283	301834
Bulgaria	Czechoslovakia	15 May 26	60LTS169	301412
Bulgaria	Czechoslovakia	15 May 26	60LTS203	301413
Lithuania	UK Great Britain	18 May 26	61LTS401	301450
Multilateral		20 May 26	109LTS121	302532
Czechoslovakia	UK Great Britain	04 Jun 26	59LTS269	301397
Albania	Serb/Croat/Slovene	22 Jun 26	91LTS81	302056
Albania	Greece	25 Jun 26	83LTS305	301898
Portugal	South Africa	01 Jul 26	70LTS315	301643

PARTY ONE	PARTY TWO	DATE	CITATION	NUMBER
Indemnities and reimbursements (Cont.)				
Czechoslovakia	Latvia	06 Jul 26	62LTS229	301465
Czechoslovakia	Estonia	17 Jul 26	69LTS385	301620
Czechoslovakia	Estonia	17 Jul 26	63LTS255	301495
Albania	UK Great Britain	22 Jul 26	67LTS165	301545
Lithuania	USSR (Soviet Union)	28 Sep 26	60LTS145	301410
Austria	Estonia	15 Oct 26	74LTS213	301739
Liberia	Monaco	28 Oct 26	68LTS241	301588
Multilateral		13 Nov 26	77LTS199	301771
Multilateral		13 Nov 26	77LTS171	301770
Switzerland	Uruguay	26 Nov 26	63LTS207	301491
Belgium	Latvia	11 Dec 26	63LTS299	301497
Italy	Portugal	18 Dec 26	93LTS313	302119
Germany	Turkey	12 Jan 27	73LTS187	301713
Denmark	Sweden	03 Feb 27	109LTS205	302540
France	Germany	16 Feb 27	62LTS155	301463
Finland	Latvia	14 May 27	63LTS97	301482
Belgium	Lithuania	17 May 27	77LTS123	301767
Czechoslovakia	Poland	30 May 27	98LTS233	302251
Czechoslovakia	Hungary	03 Jun 27	67LTS31	301538
Belgium	Czechoslovakia	19 Jul 27	73LTS283	301720
Belgium	Czechoslovakia	19 Jul 27	73LTS307	301721
Estonia	USSR (Soviet Union)	08 Aug 27	70LTS401	301648
France	USA (United States)	29 Aug 27	68LTS253	301589
Latvia	Norway	12 Sep 27	71LTS303	301671
Belgium	Luxembourg	17 Oct 27	124LTS203	302834
Czechoslovakia	Spain	26 Oct 27	121LTS311	302793
Czechoslovakia	Spain	26 Oct 27	121LTS271	302791
Czechoslovakia	Spain	26 Oct 27	121LTS287	302792
Poland	USA (United States)	22 Nov 27	92LTS101	302082
Czechoslovakia	Portugal	23 Nov 27	123LTS417	302828
Czechoslovakia	Portugal	23 Nov 27	124LTS7	302829
Germany	Poland	07 Dec 27	92LTS203	302088
France	Saar	14 Dec 27	70LTS155	301630
Belgium	Finland	23 Jan 28	74LTS353	301747
Germany	Lithuania	29 Jan 28	89LTS97	302009
Germany	Lithuania	29 Jan 28	90LTS233	302042
Germany	Lithuania	29 Jan 28	89LTS338	302027
Czechoslovakia	Poland	18 Feb 28	100LTS273	302301
Hungary	Serb/Croat/Slovene	22 Feb 28	104LTS151	302385
Czechoslovakia	Germany	22 Mar 28	93LTS235	302113
Austria	Serb/Croat/Slovene	01 May 28	96LTS373	302214
Czechoslovakia	France	07 May 28	114LTS171	302663
Czechoslovakia	France	07 May 28	114LTS117	302660
Finland	Netherlands	09 Jun 28	87LTS321	301978
Austria	Hungary	25 Jun 28	100LTS85	302296
Germany	Luxembourg	28 Jun 28	90LTS183	302036
Austria	Finland	22 Oct 28	89LTS69	302007
Mexico	Panama	23 Oct 28	194LTS137	304518
Multilateral		25 Oct 28	84LTS7	301901
Germany	Lithuania	30 Oct 28	91LTS365	302077
Czechoslovakia	Hungary	14 Nov 28	110LTS425	302574
Multilateral		22 Nov 28	111LTS343	302598
Bel-Lux Econ Union	China	22 Nov 28	87LTS287	301975
Hungary	Poland	30 Nov 28	100LTS67	302294
Austria	Czechoslovakia	12 Dec 28	108LTS9	302501
Austria	Czechoslovakia	12 Dec 28	107LTS137	302474
Norway	Spain	27 Dec 28	97LTS339	302231
Bulgaria	Hungary	05 Jan 29	118LTS279	302730
Dominican Republic	Haiti	21 Jan 29	105LTS193	302413
Bulgaria	Greece	21 Feb 29	106LTS443	302461
Austria	Italy	22 Feb 29	89LTS271	302021
Czechoslovakia	Germany	20 Mar 29	109LTS219	302541
Colombia	Nicaragua	25 Mar 29	132LTS255	303042
Poland	Romania	30 Mar 29	123LTS147	302812
Belgium	Czechoslovakia	29 Apr 29	110LTS113	302556

PARTY ONE	PARTY TWO	DATE	CITATION	NUMBER
Indemnities and reimbursements (Cont.)				
Norway	Sweden	11 May 29	120LTS263	302771
France	UK Great Britain	15 May 29	134LTS263	303097
Germany	Turkey	16 May 29	109LTS451	302549
Germany	Switzerland	28 May 29	104LTS19	302375
Belgium	Greece	25 Jun 29	113LTS117	302640
Multilateral		28 Jun 29	103LTS429	302374
Multilateral		28 Jun 29	103LTS321	302372
Finland	Italy	10 Jul 29	111LTS295	302593
Bulgaria	Hungary	22 Jul 29	101LTS41	302317
Norway	USA (United States)	23 Jul 29	93LTS223	302111
Luxembourg	Portugal	15 Aug 29	115LTS77	302678
Czechoslovakia	Norway	09 Sep 29	101LTS355	302336
Germany	Luxembourg	11 Sep 29	118LTS97	302715
Luxembourg	Switzerland	16 Sep 29	107LTS23	302465
Italy	Serb/Croat/Slovene	16 Sep 29	101LTS127	302322
Czechoslovakia	Luxembourg	18 Sep 29	107LTS49	302467
Czechoslovakia	Finland	02 Oct 29	115LTS155	302684
Poland	Romania	30 Oct 29	121LTS167	302787
Brazil	Venezuela	07 Nov 29	99LTS427	302288
Hungary	Yugoslavia	11 Nov 29	111LTS197	302587
Estonia	Hungary	27 Nov 29	106LTS331	302454
Poland	Romania	07 Dec 29	119LTS283	302752
Norway	Poland	09 Dec 29	101LTS325	302334
Bulgaria	Turkey	23 Dec 29	122LTS17	302796
Bulgaria	Poland	31 Dec 29	113LTS89	302638
Belgium	Germany	16 Jan 30	104LTS223	302392
Liberia	UK Great Britain	17 Jan 30	101LTS395	302338
Austria	Belgium	18 Jan 30	104LTS231	302393
Estonia	Sweden	20 Jan 30	106LTS279	302451
Latvia	Netherlands	27 Jan 30	117LTS343	302701
Austria	USA (United States)	30 Jan 30	106LTS379	302457
Austria	Germany	05 Feb 30	119LTS201	302746
Austria	Italy	06 Feb 30	105LTS97	302405
Denmark	Latvia	28 Feb 30	113LTS27	302632
Czechoslovakia	Lithuania	08 Mar 30	115LTS61	302677
Latvia	Spain	08 Mar 30	113LTS135	302641
Austria	Sweden	24 Mar 30	105LTS313	302424
Poland	Romania	26 Mar 30	153LTS87	303510
Estonia	Norway	03 Apr 30	106LTS147	302442
Netherlands	Poland	12 Apr 30	113LTS65	302636
Austria	Germany	12 Apr 30	115LTS297	302693
Hungary	Yugoslavia	27 Apr 30	113LTS153	302642
Denmark	Estonia	13 May 30	106LTS159	302443
Austria	Greece	26 Jun 30	119LTS353	302755
Belgium	Bulgaria	02 Jul 30	130LTS191	302990
Czechoslovakia	Romania	15 Jul 30	164LTS157	303793
Bulgaria	Spain	17 Jul 30	114LTS41	302653
Italy	Panama	07 Aug 30	140LTS241	303240
Czechoslovakia	Turkey	22 Aug 30	138LTS375	303196
Czechoslovakia	Turkey	22 Aug 30	138LTS311	303195
Sweden	UK Great Britain	28 Aug 30	114LTS9	302652
Denmark	Latvia	28 Aug 30	113LTS169	302644
Poland	Sweden	30 Aug 30	129LTS383	302973
Germany	Turkey	03 Sep 30	133LTS321	303071
Austria	Norway	01 Oct 30	119LTS15	302737
Greece	Turkey	30 Oct 30	125LTS9	302841
Germany	Poland	21 Nov 30	139LTS351	303220
Austria	Belgium	01 Dec 30	112LTS37	302605
Belgium	Lithuania	12 Dec 30	135LTS231	303114
Sweden	USA (United States)	17 Dec 30	125LTS233	302856
Austria	Hungary	26 Jan 31	123LTS171	302814
Norway	UK Great Britain	30 Jan 31	123LTS343	302823
France	Italy	13 Feb 31	139LTS109	303206
Czechoslovakia	Lithuania	24 Apr 31	126LTS279	302890
Czechoslovakia	Lithuania	24 Apr 31	126LTS261	302889

PARTY ONE	PARTY TWO	DATE	CITATION	NUMBER
Indemnities and reimbursements (Cont.)				
Greece	USA (United States)	06 May 31	138LTS293	303194
Belgium	Poland	13 May 31	131LTS109	303005
Denmark	Germany	23 Jun 31	119LTS321	302753
Denmark	Finland	09 Jul 31	123LTS393	302826
Czechoslovakia	Denmark	07 Oct 31	127LTS103	302911
Multilateral		10 Nov 31	131LTS389	303024
Czechoslovakia	Sweden	17 Nov 31	134LTS135	303088
Brazil	Italy	28 Nov 31	132LTS345	303047
Turkey	UK Great Britain	28 Nov 31	141LTS225	303268
Czechoslovakia	Netherlands	04 Dec 31	129LTS343	302969
Germany	Lithuania	05 Dec 31	125LTS265	302860
Austria	Latvia	05 Jan 32	133LTS59	303056
Iraq	Turkey	09 Jan 32	139LTS273	303218
Poland	UK Great Britain	11 Jan 32	148LTS221	303415
Austria	Belgium	26 Jan 32	129LTS141	302959
Iraq	UK Great Britain	02 May 32	141LTS277	303270
Latvia	USSR (Soviet Union)	18 Jun 32	148LTS129	303409
Austria	Poland	26 Oct 32	138LTS193	303188
Poland	USSR (Soviet Union)	22 Nov 32	136LTS55	303125
Italy	Switzerland	03 Jan 33	142LTS17	303276
Norway	Turkey	16 Jan 33	161LTS173	303710
Romania	Yugoslavia	30 Jan 33	146LTS113	303363
Romania	Yugoslavia	30 Jan 33	146LTS81	303361
Romania	Yugoslavia	30 Jan 33	146LTS139	303366
Romania	Yugoslavia	30 Jan 33	146LTS183	303371
Finland	Netherlands	21 Feb 33	139LTS365	303221
Estonia	Netherlands	08 Mar 33	146LTS319	303382
Romania	Yugoslavia	10 Mar 33	146LTS245	303374
Romania	Yugoslavia	11 Mar 33	146LTS277	303378
Switzerland	Turkey	01 Jun 33	159LTS187	303662
Switzerland	Turkey	01 Jun 33	159LTS329	303676
Poland	USSR (Soviet Union)	03 Jun 33	142LTS265	303300
Finland	USSR (Soviet Union)	04 Jul 33	149LTS83	303436
Finland	UK Great Britain	11 Aug 33	149LTS131	303437
Lithuania	Netherlands	01 Dec 33	150LTS337	303466
Brazil	Uruguay	20 Dec 33	181LTS35	304175
Brazil	Uruguay	20 Dec 33	181LTS69	304178
Multilateral		26 Dec 33	165LTS45	303803
Belgium	Italy	07 Feb 34	147LTS107	303395
Multilateral		20 Mar 34	175LTS5	304049
Multilateral		20 Mar 34	176LTS55	304054
Albania	Czechoslovakia	14 Apr 34	188LTS255	304362
Turkey	Yugoslavia	03 Jul 34	179LTS207	304149
Germany	Latvia	18 Jul 34	154LTS69	303537
Canada	USA (United States)	15 Apr 35	162LTS73	303735
Belgium	Germany	10 May 35	182LTS335	304221
Poland	Romania	17 May 35	173LTS373	304028
Estonia	Italy	10 Aug 35	185LTS287	304295
Multilateral		30 Oct 35	189LTS51	304375
Finland	Norway	05 Nov 35	169LTS33	303913
Brazil	Chile	08 Nov 35	181LTS297	304197
Bulgaria	Yugoslavia	09 Nov 35	194LTS89	304511
Dutch Indies	India	28 Nov 35	168LTS147	303896
Bulgaria	Denmark	07 Dec 35	182LTS183	304211
France	USA (United States)	30 Dec 35	171LTS117	303955
Chile	Norway	27 Jan 36	179LTS433	304169
Greece	UK Great Britain	27 Feb 36	185LTS113	304278
UK Great Britain	Yugoslavia	27 Feb 36	181LTS241	304193
United Arab Rep	Malaya	29 Feb 36	170LTS103	303931
Belgium	Yugoslavia	29 Feb 36	184LTS379	304258
Greece	Palestine	28 Mar 36	170LTS145	303932
Hungary	Poland	24 Apr 36	181LTS115	304183
Liechtenstein	USA (United States)	20 May 36	183LTS181	304235
France	Palestine	19 Jun 36	172LTS17	303977
Denmark	USSR (Soviet Union)	29 Jun 36	174LTS93	304040

PARTY ONE	PARTY TWO	DATE	CITATION	NUMBER
Indemnities and reimbursements (Cont.)				
Belgium	Liechtenstein	05 Aug 36	185LTS33	304302
Netherlands	Romania	28 Aug 36	182LTS363	304222
Bahamas	USA (United States)	21 Dec 36	176LTS411	304077
Multilateral		23 Dec 36	188LTS75	304353
Gibralter	USA (United States)	05 Jan 37	177LTS21	304078
Belgium	Siam	14 Jan 37	179LTS419	304168
Estonia	Sweden	16 Jan 37	178LTS49	304106
Bulgaria	Romania	20 Jul 37	202LTS33	304733
Iran	Iraq	24 Jul 37	190LTS269	304425
Czechoslovakia	Hungary	24 Aug 37	189LTS403	304397
Greece	Luxembourg	01 Sep 37	193LTS151	304491
Liberia	USA (United States)	01 Nov 37	201LTS151	304710
Poland	Switzerland	19 Nov 37	195LTS297	304552
Estonia	Finland	14 Jan 38	185LTS53	304274
Belgium	Turkey	09 Feb 38	198LTS181	304639
Netherlands	USA (United States)	18 Feb 38	192LTS49	304460
Greece	Switzerland	30 Mar 38	185LTS245	304288
Norway	Sweden	20 Apr 38	189LTS153	304383
Germany	Greece	11 May 38	197LTS75	304608
Lithuania	Poland	25 May 38	191LTS391	304457
Denmark	Sweden	10 Jun 38	188LTS461	304371
Latvia	Poland	16 Jun 38	196LTS105	304573
Germany	Switzerland	21 Sep 38	196LTS365	304595
Belgium	Mexico	22 Sep 38	198LTS399	304658
Estonia	USA (United States)	06 Dec 38	198LTS361	304655
Multilateral		28 Dec 38	196LTS221	304585
Burma	Siam	14 Feb 39	197LTS255	304618
Monaco	USA (United States)	15 Feb 39	202LTS61	304735
Greece	Turkey	07 Mar 39	201LTS239	304717
Guatemala	USA (United States)	28 Mar 39	199LTS181	304671
Nicaragua	USA (United States)	22 May 39	199LTS189	304672
Japan	UK Great Britain	22 Mar 40	203LTS194	304760
UK Great Britain	USA (United States)	02 Sep 40	203LTS201	304762
Balance of payments				
Australia	Malay States	24 Jan 21	23LTS209	300590
Netherlands	UK Great Britain	02 Jun 22	13LTS263	300357
Canada	Irish Free State	12 Oct 23	56LTS291	301338
UK Great Britain	USA (United States)	08 Dec 23	23LTS93	300580
Irish Free State	USA (United States)	31 Dec 23	56LTS303	301339
Other Unilat Decla	Hungary	14 Mar 24	25LTS427	300634
Austria	Serb/Croat/Slovene	18 Jun 24	114LTS481	302672
Germany	Irish Free State	29 Dec 24	56LTS341	301341
Estonia	Finland	20 Apr 25	51LTS31	301220
Irish Free State	New Zealand	30 Apr 25	56LTS373	301342
Irish Free State	South Africa	01 Oct 25	56LTS389	301343
Canada	Finland	18 Dec 25	47LTS319	301137
Germany	Poland	27 Mar 26	64LTS249	301506
India	Irish Free State	04 Apr 26	56LTS415	301344
Netherlands	UK Great Britain	14 Nov 27	71LTS227	301666
Finland	Turkey	19 Dec 33	149LTS333	303441
Multilateral		20 Mar 34	176LTS9	304053
Germany	UK Great Britain	01 Nov 34	163LTS79	303762
Germany	Netherlands	05 Dec 34	160LTS109	303686
Germany	Sweden	22 Dec 34	156LTS127	303596
Greece	Sweden	17 Jan 35	157LTS9	303601
Estonia	Turkey	13 Mar 35	159LTS87	303650
Italy	UK Great Britain	18 Mar 35	160LTS289	303699
Estonia	Sweden	26 Mar 35	158LTS239	303634
Latvia	Sweden	26 Mar 35	158LTS269	303637
Brazil	UK Great Britain	27 Mar 35	160LTS311	303700
Latvia	Lithuania	10 Apr 35	159LTS321	303675
Estonia	Latvia	10 Apr 35	159LTS103	303652
Estonia	Spain	08 May 35	159LTS381	303679
Finland	Turkey	06 Jun 35	160LTS165	303690

PARTY ONE	PARTY TWO	DATE	CITATION	NUMBER
Balance of payments (Cont.)				
Italy	Sweden	24 Jun 35	161LTS21	303702
Bel-Lux Econ Union	Latvia	22 Feb 36	171LTS147	303956
Currency				
China	UK Great Britain	26 Apr 20	5LTS83	300120
Austria	Czechoslovakia	02 Aug 20	32LTS365	300826
Brazil	UK Great Britain	01 Mar 21	8LTS265	300225
Czechoslovakia	Italy	23 Mar 21	32LTS261	300817
Multilateral		15 Sep 21	30LTS141	300767
UK Great Britain	USA (United States)	05 Oct 21	8LTS371	300235
Iceland	UK Great Britain	13 Oct 21	8LTS337	300234
India	Iraq	20 Oct 21	69LTS139	301601
Australia	Nauru	27 Oct 21	23LTS229	300591
Germany	Switzerland	29 Oct 21	13LTS193	300351
Palestine	UK Great Britain	23 Jan 22	13LTS9	300342
France	Switzerland	24 Jan 22	12LTS371	300331
France	Poland	06 Feb 22	43LTS415	301074
UK Great Britain	USA (United States)	22 Apr 22	20LTS415	300530
Germany	Poland	15 May 22	10LTS8	300272
Germany	Poland	18 Dec 22	34LTS283	300879
UK Great Britain	USA (United States)	28 Dec 22	21LTS9	300531
Liechtenstein	Switzerland	29 Mar 23	21LTS231	300545
Multilateral		29 Mar 23	23LTS256	300593
Netherlands	UK Great Britain	30 Apr 23	20LTS343	300525
Australia	Netherlands	30 May 23	22LTS129	300556
Germany	Lithuania	31 May 23	51LTS381	301243
Czechoslovakia	Hungary	13 Jul 23	35LTS253	300899
UK Great Britain	USA (United States)	30 Aug 23	24LTS103	300598
Netherlands	UK Great Britain	02 Oct 23	23LTS9	300573
Canada	Irish Free State	12 Oct 23	56LTS291	301338
Irish Free State	USA (United States)	31 Dec 23	56LTS303	301339
China	UK Great Britain	07 Jan 24	24LTS115	300599
Hungary	Italy	27 Mar 24	45LTS83	301100
Hungary	Italy	27 Mar 24	45LTS229	301101
Poland	Serb/Croat/Slovene	05 Apr 24	49LTS265	301185
Hungary	Romania	16 Apr 24	45LTS403	301110
Hungary	Romania	16 Apr 24	45LTS355	301109
Hungary	Romania	16 Apr 24	46LTS7	301111
Multilateral		22 May 24	35LTS175	300895
Finland	USA (United States)	26 Jun 24	30LTS9	300756
Spain	UK Great Britain	27 Jun 24	28LTS523	300727
Austria	Czechoslovakia	12 Jul 24	50LTS111	301199
Austria	Romania	26 Jul 24	85LTS223	301933
Multilateral		26 Jul 24	30LTS271	300771
Belgium	UK Great Britain	29 Jul 24	29LTS389	300749
Multilateral		25 Aug 24	120LTS123	302763
Multilateral		28 Aug 24	40LTS437	301005
Multilateral		23 Oct 24	78LTS17	301779
Austria	Czechoslovakia	27 Nov 24	42LTS201	301041
France	Poland	09 Dec 24	44LTS127	301081
Germany	Irish Free State	29 Dec 24	56LTS341	301341
Czechoslovakia	Poland	23 Apr 25	44LTS285	301090
Irish Free State	New Zealand	30 Apr 25	56LTS373	301342
Austria	Czechoslovakia	14 May 25	50LTS39	301198
Austria	Czechoslovakia	29 May 25	98LTS91	302242
Italy	Poland	22 Jul 25	54LTS101	301278
Irish Free State	South Africa	01 Oct 25	56LTS389	301343
Canada	Finland	18 Dec 25	47LTS319	301137
Hungary	UK Great Britain	28 Dec 25	49LTS125	301179
India	Irish Free State	04 Apr 26	56LTS415	301344
Czechoslovakia	Italy	04 May 26	61LTS257	301438
Australia	Germany	31 May 26	60LTS121	301409
Estonia	Great Britain	12 Oct 26	60LTS387	301422
Portugal	UK Great Britain	31 Dec 26	61LTS115	301429
Estonia	Latvia	05 Feb 27	62LTS319	301470

PARTY ONE	PARTY TWO	DATE	CITATION	NUMBER
Currency (Cont.)				
Czechoslovakia	Poland	30 May 27	98LTS233	302251
Czechoslovakia	Hungary	31 May 27	65LTS61	301520
Greece		15 Sep 27	70LTS9	301622
Austria	Belgium	10 Oct 27	91LTS271	302067
Netherlands	UK Great Britain	14 Nov 27	71LTS227	301666
Denmark	Iceland	30 Nov 27	71LTS43	301653
Netherlands	USA (United States)	30 Dec 27	72LTS179	301691
Multilateral		10 Mar 28	132LTS405	303049
Multilateral		01 May 28	132LTS415	303050
Belgium	Luxembourg	18 May 28	89LTS213	302016
Mexico	UK Great Britain	24 Oct 28	87LTS63	301962
Germany	Serb/Croat/Slovene	15 Dec 28	95LTS113	302170
Multilateral		05 Jan 29	132LTS425	303051
UK Great Britain	USA (United States)	06 Apr 29	99LTS27	302265
Multilateral		20 Apr 29	112LTS371	302623
France	UK Great Britain	15 May 29	134LTS263	303097
Netherlands	South Africa	10 Sep 29	98LTS423	302261
France	UK Great Britain	24 Mar 30	105LTS227	302415
Multilateral		14 May 30	105LTS353	302428
Finland	Norway	14 May 30	105LTS399	302429
Denmark	Finland	14 May 30	105LTS455	302433
Austria	Hungary	03 Jun 30	122LTS69	302799
Multilateral		26 Jun 30	133LTS9	303052
Portugal	UK Great Britain	27 Jun 30	107LTS281	302485
Multilateral		28 Aug 30	133LTS21	303053
France	UK Great Britain	04 Sep 30	109LTS31	302526
Netherlands	USA (United States)	16 Sep 30	125LTS173	302853
Denmark	India	16 Dec 30	114LTS73	302656
France	Italy	13 Feb 31	139LTS109	303206
Multilateral		10 Nov 31	131LTS447	303025
France	UK Great Britain	17 Nov 31	134LTS299	303098
Japan	USSR (Soviet Union)	23 Nov 31	132LTS133	303033
France	UK Great Britain	27 Nov 31	132LTS25	303028
France	UK Great Britain	28 Dec 31	133LTS79	303058
Bel-Lux Econ Union	Hungary	26 Mar 32	136LTS405	303139
Netherlands	South Africa	29 Jun 32	133LTS33	303054
France	UK Great Britain	22 Aug 32	136LTS313	303133
Austria	Norway	03 Sep 32	137LTS403	303170
Romania	Yugoslavia	30 Jan 33	146LTS129	303365
Multilateral		22 Jul 33	153LTS107	303511
Multilateral		23 Nov 33	192LTS389	304484
Finland	Turkey	19 Dec 33	149LTS333	303441
Argentina	Bel-Lux Econ Union	16 Jan 34	145LTS145	303352
Argentina	Netherlands	31 Jan 34	148LTS361	303422
Multilateral		20 Mar 34	176LTS9	304053
Irish Free State	Spain	04 Apr 35	166LTS391	303855
Bel-Lux Econ Union	Estonia	19 Jun 35	170LTS243	303940
France	UK Great Britain	16 Jul 35	168LTS179	303898
Dutch Indies	India	28 Nov 35	168LTS147	303896
Finland	Romania	03 Dec 35	165LTS287	303815
Germany	Sweden	31 Jan 36	168LTS13	303883
China	Malaya	12 Feb 36	170LTS19	303927
Bel-Lux Econ Union	Bulgaria	01 Apr 36	169LTS23	303912
Bel-Lux Econ Union	Spain	04 Apr 36	168LTS339	303909
Guatemala	USA (United States)	24 Apr 36	170LTS345	303945
Norway	Spain	13 Jun 36	170LTS207	303936
Bulgaria	France	06 Jul 36	171LTS269	303963
China	UK Great Britain	17 Jul 36	173LTS343	304024
Italy	Norway	25 Aug 36	171LTS377	303974
Turkey	UK Great Britain	02 Sep 36	172LTS289	303998
Estonia	Italy	06 Oct 36	172LTS189	303989
Norway	Romania	10 Dec 36	174LTS59	304037
Italy	Netherlands	01 Jan 37	178LTS415	304124
Germany	Norway	27 Feb 37	178LTS427	304125
Portugal	UK Great Britain	24 Mar 37	185LTS151	304280
Currency (Cont.)				
Sweden	Yugoslavia	14 May 37	179LTS147	304141
Malaya	Siam	15 Sep 37	191LTS225	304447
Multilateral		23 Sep 37	190LTS299	304427
Estonia	France	16 Oct 37	183LTS37	304226
Estonia	Greece	25 Nov 37	184LTS427	304263
Bel-Lux Econ Union	Estonia	13 Jan 38	185LTS63	304275
Bulgaria	Latvia	17 May 38	189LTS249	304388
Japan	USA (United States)	20 Jun 38	191LTS43	304434
France	Romania	31 Mar 39	199LTS219	304677
Greece	Sweden	01 May 39	196LTS205	304582
Romania	UK Great Britain	11 May 39	196LTS351	304594
Turkey	UK Great Britain	03 Feb 40	203LTS399	304781
Finland	Latvia	11 Apr 40	201LTS389	304727
Canada	USA (United States)	18 Jun 40	203LTS41	304748
United Arab Rep	UK Great Britain	17 Jul 40	202LTS97	304738
United Arab Rep	France	03 Aug 40	202LTS121	304740
Monetary and gold transfers				
China	UK Great Britain	26 Apr 20	5LTS83	300120
Peru	USA (United States)	21 May 21	6LTS171	300150
Liechtenstein	Switzerland	29 Mar 23	21LTS231	300545
Austria	Italy	16 Jul 23	27LTS383	300699
Multilateral		30 Nov 23	102LTS153	302360
Austria	Serb/Croat/Slovene	18 Jun 24	115LTS25	302674
Austria	Serb/Croat/Slovene	18 Jun 24	115LTS9	302673
Czechoslovakia	Great Britain	09 Aug 25	38LTS231	300980
Italy	UK Great Britain	20 Dec 25	49LTS79	301178
Portugal	South Africa	11 Sep 28	98LTS9	302239
Multilateral		28 Jun 29	103LTS321	302372
Bel-Lux Econ Union	Yugoslavia	07 Aug 32	139LTS223	303212
Argentina	UK Great Britain	01 May 33	143LTS67	303305
Bel-Lux Econ Union	Bulgaria	21 Jun 33	140LTS375	303247
Multilateral		22 Jul 33	153LTS107	303511
Argentina	Netherlands	31 Jan 34	148LTS361	303422
Spain	Turkey	19 May 34	149LTS15	303428
Germany	Norway	06 Sep 34	161LTS187	303711
UK Great Britain	Uruguay	26 Jun 35	176LTS153	304058
Iran	USSR (Soviet Union)	27 Aug 35	176LTS299	304069
Canada	USA (United States)	15 Nov 35	168LTS355	303910
Spain	UK Great Britain	06 Jan 36	166LTS283	303844
Greece	Sweden	11 Jan 36	165LTS299	303816
Germany	Sweden	31 Jan 36	168LTS19	303884
Bel-Lux Econ Union	Bulgaria	01 Apr 36	169LTS23	303912
Norway	Spain	13 Jun 36	170LTS207	303936
Netherlands	Romania	28 Aug 36	182LTS363	304222
Chile	Sweden	30 Oct 36	188LTS283	304364
Italy	UK Great Britain	06 Nov 36	177LTS183	304090
Italy	Sweden	01 Dec 36	173LTS269	304018
Argentina	Netherlands	05 Feb 37	179LTS383	304165
Brazil	Netherlands	15 Mar 37	179LTS395	304166
Italy	Norway	31 Mar 37	177LTS367	304099
Bel-Lux Econ Union	Yugoslavia	26 Nov 37	196LTS19	304567
Bel-Lux Econ Union	Estonia	13 Jan 38	185LTS63	304275
Greece	Sweden	01 Feb 38	185LTS217	304285
Greece	USA (United States)	15 Nov 38	195LTS145	304544
Latvia	Sweden	15 Apr 39	196LTS373	304597
Dominican Republic	Newfoundland	16 Mar 40	203LTS141	304757
Spain	UK Great Britain	18 Mar 40	203LTS157	304759
United Arab Rep	UK Great Britain	17 Jul 40	202LTS97	304738
United Arab Rep	France	03 Aug 40	202LTS121	304740
Currency deposits				
Austria	Czechoslovakia	02 Aug 20	32LTS365	300826
Germany	Switzerland	29 Oct 21	13LTS193	300351
Austria	Czechoslovakia	17 Dec 21	22LTS401	300570
Germany	Poland	24 Feb 22	26LTS479	300664

PARTY ONE	PARTY TWO	DATE	CITATION	NUMBER
Currency deposits (Cont.)				
Germany	Poland	24 Feb 22	27LTS15	300665
Finland	Germany	21 Apr 22	19LTS87	300487
Czechoslovakia	UK Great Britain	31 Jan 23	20LTS53	300506
Multilateral		28 Apr 23	33LTS47	300832
Czechoslovakia	Hungary	13 Jul 23	36LTS13	300901
Czechoslovakia	Hungary	13 Jul 23	35LTS271	300900
Czechoslovakia	Hungary	13 Jul 23	36LTS53	300903
Denmark	Estonia	27 Jul 23	19LTS253	300499
Czechoslovakia	Italy	01 Mar 24	36LTS229	300925
Czechoslovakia	Hungary	08 Mar 24	36LTS61	300904
Hungary	Italy	27 Mar 24	45LTS65	301099
Hungary	Italy	27 Mar 24	45LTS229	301101
Hungary	Romania	16 Apr 24	46LTS7	301111
Hungary	Romania	16 Apr 24	45LTS403	301110
France	Poland	09 Dec 24	44LTS127	301081
Czechoslovakia	Poland	23 Apr 25	48LTS287	301170
Germany	Italy	31 Oct 25	53LTS245	301261
Denmark	Italy	26 Oct 27	68LTS229	301586
Hungary	Serb/Croat/Slovene	22 Feb 28	87LTS331	301979
Hungary	UK Great Britain	10 Jun 32	132LTS53	303031
Romania	Yugoslavia	10 Mar 33	146LTS263	303376
Investments				
Austria	Poland	09 Jan 20	7LTS163	300185
France	UK Great Britain	24 Apr 20	1LTS281	300022
Germany	Switzerland	06 Dec 20	2LTS343	300088
Germany	Poland	10 Apr 21	6LTS233	300158
France	Poland	06 Feb 22	43LTS415	301074
France	Saar	30 Nov 22	27LTS283	300691
Belgium	Poland	30 Dec 22	21LTS201	300543
Czechoslovakia	Hungary	13 Jul 23	35LTS237	300898
Czechoslovakia	Hungary	13 Jul 23	35LTS253	300899
Czechoslovakia	Hungary	13 Jul 23	36LTS41	300902
Austria	Italy	16 Jul 23	27LTS383	300699
Hungary	Romania	16 Apr 24	45LTS403	301110
Hungary	Romania	16 Apr 24	46LTS7	301111
Italy	Serb/Croat/Slovene	14 Jul 24	82LTS257	301876
Czechoslovakia	Netherlands	17 Oct 24	31LTS93	300786
France	Poland	09 Dec 24	44LTS127	301081
Czechoslovakia	Poland	23 Apr 25	44LTS309	301091
Italy	Poland	22 Jul 25	54LTS101	301278
Germany	Italy	31 Oct 25	53LTS245	301261
Czechoslovakia	Poland	21 Apr 26	58LTS9	301367
Guatemala	Netherlands	12 May 27	85LTS323	301937
Italy	Spain	28 Nov 27	82LTS27	301857
Sweden	Turkey	29 Sep 29	119LTS53	302740
Multilateral		09 Jan 30	115LTS473	302696
Greece	Turkey	30 Oct 30	125LTS371	302866
Estonia	Finland	11 Apr 31	124LTS217	302835
Exchange rates and regulations				
China	UK Great Britain	26 Apr 20	5LTS83	300120
Germany	Switzerland	06 Dec 20	2LTS343	300088
France	Hungary	31 Jan 21	15LTS221	300396
Belgium	Netherlands	09 Feb 21	11LTS333	300299
France	Switzerland	24 Jan 22	12LTS371	300331
Czechoslovakia	Germany	12 Apr 22	22LTS329	300562
UK Great Britain	USA (United States)	22 Apr 22	20LTS415	300530
Latvia	UK Great Britain	17 Oct 22	16LTS397	300419
Germany	Saar	13 Nov 22	27LTS273	300690
China	Japan	08 Dec 22	20LTS253	300521
Germany	Switzerland	25 Mar 23	18LTS273	300470
Netherlands	UK Great Britain	30 Apr 23	20LTS343	300525
Multilateral		24 Jul 23	28LTS171	300705
Hungary	Italy	27 Mar 24	45LTS229	301101
Hungary	Italy	27 Mar 24	45LTS65	301099

PARTY ONE	PARTY TWO	DATE	CITATION	NUMBER
Exchange rates and regulations (Cont.)				
Hungary	Romania	16 Apr 24	45LTS403	301110
Multilateral		28 Aug 24	40LTS19	301002
Austria	Czechoslovakia	27 Nov 24	42LTS201	301041
Bulgaria	Great Britain	07 May 25	38LTS153	300973
Czechoslovakia	Italy	04 May 26	61LTS257	301438
Spain	UK Great Britain	19 Oct 26	61LTS79	301427
Hungary	Serb/Croat/Slovene	22 Feb 28	88LTS125	301992
Czechoslovakia	France	02 Jul 28	99LTS105	302272
Mexico	UK Great Britain	24 Oct 28	87LTS63	301962
Multilateral		28 Jun 29	103LTS321	302372
Netherlands	South Africa	10 Sep 29	98LTS423	302261
Belgium	Irish Free State	24 Sep 29	102LTS213	302364
Poland	UK Great Britain	04 Oct 29	97LTS261	302227
Austria	Poland	20 Jan 30	133LTS223	303067
Romania	UK Great Britain	02 Apr 30	105LTS235	302416
Czechoslovakia	Romania	05 Dec 30	167LTS221	303868
Austria	Czechoslovakia	22 Jul 31	128LTS59	302938
UK Great Britain	Yugoslavia	23 Oct 31	126LTS209	302884
Bel-Lux Econ Union	Hungary	26 Mar 32	136LTS405	303139
Estonia	France	26 Mar 32	128LTS51	302937
Austria	Yugoslavia	20 Apr 32	132LTS217	303040
Czechoslovakia	Yugoslavia	08 Jun 32	139LTS45	303203
Bel-Lux Econ Union	Yugoslavia	07 Aug 32	139LTS223	303212
Hungary	Italy	12 Nov 32	142LTS101	303281
Romania	Yugoslavia	30 Jan 33	146LTS129	303365
Chile	Sweden	08 Mar 33	142LTS147	303286
Estonia	Finland	16 May 33	141LTS19	303257
Bel-Lux Econ Union	Hungary	24 May 33	140LTS169	303234
Bel-Lux Econ Union	Bulgaria	21 Jun 33	140LTS375	303247
Estonia	France	27 Jul 33	141LTS65	303261
Bel-Lux Econ Union	Turkey	31 May 34	150LTS277	303461
Bulgaria	Spain	19 Nov 34	166LTS277	303843
Bel-Lux Econ Union	Estonia	19 Jun 35	170LTS243	303940
UK Great Britain	Uruguay	26 Jun 35	176LTS153	304058
Italy	Netherlands	29 Jul 35	165LTS329	303819
Spain	UK Great Britain	06 Jan 36	166LTS283	303844
Sweden	Turkey	27 Feb 36	167LTS83	303859
Nicaragua	USA (United States)	11 Mar 36	173LTS141	304009
Norway	Turkey	08 Jun 36	170LTS235	303939
Finland	Turkey	20 Jun 36	172LTS135	303983
Bulgaria	France	06 Jul 36	171LTS269	303963
Italy	Norway	25 Aug 36	171LTS377	303974
Netherlands	Romania	28 Aug 36	182LTS363	304222
Finland	Italy	28 Sep 36	172LTS155	303986
Estonia	Italy	06 Oct 36	172LTS189	303989
Canada	Germany	22 Oct 36	173LTS311	304021
Italy	UK Great Britain	06 Nov 36	177LTS183	304090
Italy	Sweden	01 Dec 36	173LTS279	304019
Norway	Romania	10 Dec 36	174LTS59	304037
Sweden	Turkey	14 Dec 36	174LTS51	304036
Hungary	Yugoslavia	17 Dec 36	196LTS143	304577
Germany	Netherlands	23 Dec 36	179LTS359	304163
Greece	Sweden	31 Dec 36	174LTS87	304039
Italy	Netherlands	01 Jan 37	178LTS415	304124
Argentina	Netherlands	05 Feb 37	179LTS383	304165
Italy	Latvia	05 Feb 37	178LTS25	304103
Netherlands	Turkey	17 Feb 37	182LTS221	304213
Brazil	Netherlands	15 Mar 37	179LTS405	304167
Italy	Norway	31 Mar 37	177LTS367	304099
Italy	Norway	31 Mar 37	177LTS355	304098
Chile	Netherlands	05 May 37	182LTS385	304223
Poland	Romania	24 May 37	190LTS361	304428
Estonia	Turkey	06 Jun 37	179LTS159	304143
UK Great Britain		07 Jun 37	185LTS185	304282
Bel-Lux Econ Union	Italy	30 Jun 37	182LTS106	304203

PARTY ONE	PARTY TWO	DATE	CITATION	NUMBER
Exchange rates and regulations (Cont.)				
Bel-Lux Econ Union	Romania	24 Aug 37	193LTS189	304496
Hungary	Lithuania	12 Nov 37	183LTS197	304236
Hungary	Latvia	16 Nov 37	183LTS205	304237
Italy	USA (United States)	16 Dec 37	187LTS15	304329
Germany	Netherlands	18 Dec 37	190LTS29	304403
Sweden	Turkey	31 Dec 37	184LTS409	304261
Greece	Sweden	01 Feb 38	185LTS217	304285
Chile	USA (United States)	01 Feb 38	190LTS9	304401
Greece	Norway	28 Feb 38	186LTS165	304309
Czechoslovakia	USA (United States)	07 Mar 38	200LTS87	304687
Finland	Lithuania	12 Apr 38	194LTS9	304501
Bulgaria	Latvia	17 May 38	189LTS249	304388
Germany	Netherlands	25 May 38	192LTS143	304468
Multilateral		27 Jun 38	191LTS199	304443
Romania	UK Great Britain	02 Sep 38	191LTS313	304453
Netherlands	Romania	10 Oct 38	195LTS9	304532
Germany	Sweden	28 Oct 38	196LTS91	304571
Sweden	Turkey	20 Jan 39	194LTS113	304514
Turkey	USA (United States)	01 Apr 39	202LTS129	304741
UK Great Britain	USA (United States)	23 Jun 39	198LTS333	304651
Norway	Spain	26 Jul 39	198LTS87	304627
USA (United States)	Venezuela	06 Nov 39	203LTS273	304770
Sweden	Turkey	29 Feb 40	200LTS273	304696
Spain	UK Great Britain	18 Mar 40	203LTS157	304759
Finland	Latvia	11 Apr 40	201LTS389	304727
Expense sharing formulae				
Austria-Hungary	Greece	21 Dec 04	2LTS173	300064
Germany	Greece	12 Mar 07	2LTS111	300054
Multilateral		10 Sep 19	2LTS35	300044
Estonia	Latvia	22 Mar 20	2LTS187	300066
Chile	Sweden	26 Mar 20	4LTS271	300111
Multilateral		21 Jun 20	8LTS65	300207
Latvia	Lithuania	28 Sep 20	2LTS234	300068
Multilateral		19 Jan 21	5LTS9	300113
France	Hungary	31 Jan 21	15LTS221	300396
Denmark	Sweden	08 Jun 21	14LTS195	300374
Estonia	Finland	29 Oct 21	13LTS167	300350
Finland	Germany	20 Feb 22	19LTS81	300486
Finland	Sweden	22 May 22	14LTS297	300381
Finland	Norway	23 May 22	14LTS323	300382
Belgium	Sweden	25 Oct 22	18LTS121	300459
Portugal	Spain	26 Mar 23	18LTS349	300475
Germany	Saar	21 Apr 23	27LTS295	300693
Panama	USA (United States)	06 Jun 24	138LTS397	303200
Finland	USA (United States)	01 Aug 24	34LTS103	300869
Belgium	Paraguay	20 Jan 26	97LTS197	302224
Czechoslovakia	Switzerland	21 Dec 26	68LTS393	301594
France	Serb/Croat/Slovene	11 Nov 27	68LTS381	301593
Norway	Sweden	19 Nov 27	68LTS209	301584
Colombia	Panama	24 Dec 27	87LTS409	301985
Hungary	Serb/Croat/Slovene	22 Feb 28	88LTS111	301991
France	Sweden	03 Mar 28	95LTS89	302168
Austria	Spain	11 Jun 28	87LTS393	301984
France	Spain	12 Jun 28	136LTS289	303131
Finland	Italy	21 Aug 28	89LTS25	302002
Multilateral		26 Sep 28	93LTS343	302123
Portugal	Switzerland	17 Oct 28	96LTS287	302207
Albania	USA (United States)	22 Oct 28	92LTS223	302090
Poland	Romania	29 Nov 28	96LTS15	302188
Finland	Hungary	12 Dec 28	96LTS67	302191
Multilateral		05 Jan 29	100LTS399	302309
Multilateral		21 May 29	96LTS311	302210
Chile	Peru	03 Jun 29	94LTS401	302157
Hungary	Latvia	04 May 30	101LTS449	302344

PARTY ONE	PARTY TWO	DATE	CITATION	NUMBER
Expense sharing formulae (Cont.)				
Poland	Romania	09 May 30	112LTS225	302617
Czechoslovakia	Romania	15 Jul 30	164LTS157	303793
Austria	Belgium	01 Dec 30	112LTS43	302606
Bulgaria	Spain	26 Jun 31	166LTS341	303850
Multilateral		11 Dec 31	170LTS251	303941
Romania	Yugoslavia	14 Dec 31	135LTS89	303105
Panama	USA (United States)	17 Dec 32	138LTS119	303183
Albania	USA (United States)	01 Mar 33	166LTS195	303839
Romania	Yugoslavia	10 Mar 33	146LTS263	303376
Multilateral		07 May 34	171LTS203	303961
Iraq	USA (United States)	07 Jun 34	170LTS267	303942
Belgium	Germany	10 May 35	182LTS323	304220
Estonia	Finland	16 Apr 36	171LTS55	303950
Bahamas	USA (United States)	21 Dec 36	176LTS411	304077
Gibralter	USA (United States)	05 Jan 37	177LTS21	304078
Norway	Sweden	20 Apr 38	189LTS153	304383
Fees and exemptions				
Liberia	UK Great Britain	10 Apr 13	1LTS205	300014
Switzerland	UK Great Britain	28 Feb 20	6LTS9	300145
Czechoslovakia	Germany	29 Jun 20	20LTS85	300509
Denmark	Finland	27 Jul 20	19LTS71	300484
France	UK Great Britain	20 Oct 20	2LTS323	300085
Liechtenstein	Switzerland	10 Nov 20	2LTS305	300084
Sweden	UK Great Britain	16 Feb 21	3LTS233	300100
Belgium	UK Great Britain	15 Mar 21	5LTS319	300138
Denmark	Germany	12 Jul 21	26LTS151	300645
Norway	UK Great Britain	15 Jul 21	6LTS307	300162
Denmark	Norway	21 Jul 21	13LTS357	300362
Multilateral		19 Sep 21	15LTS191	300392
Danzig	Poland	24 Oct 21	116LTS5	302699
Czechoslovakia	Germany	20 Jan 22	26LTS201	300648
France	UK Great Britain	02 Feb 22	10LTS448	300284
Norway	Sweden	29 Mar 22	13LTS311	300361
UK Great Britain	USA (United States)	22 Apr 22	20LTS415	300530
Belgium	UK Great Britain	21 Jun 22	24LTS91	300597
Iceland	Norway	17 Aug 22	14LTS9	300363
Czechoslovakia	France	07 Oct 22	47LTS365	301141
China	Japan	08 Dec 22	20LTS253	300521
UK Great Britain	USA (United States)	28 Dec 22	21LTS9	300531
Germany	Poland	27 Jan 23	26LTS461	300663
Multilateral		28 Apr 23	33LTS47	300832
Poland	Serb/Croat/Slovene	04 May 23	85LTS455	301946
Finland	Sweden	26 May 23	18LTS57	300453
Bulgaria	Serb/Croat/Slovene	26 Nov 23	26LTS85	300642
Latvia	Lithuania	18 Oct 24	56LTS157	301327
Germany	Poland	30 Dec 24	52LTS51	301250
Denmark	France	25 Feb 25	33LTS277	300852
Austria	France	04 Mar 25	75LTS97	301755
Czechoslovakia	Poland	23 Apr 25	44LTS285	301090
Multilateral		05 May 25	55LTS225	301318
Finland	Sweden	09 May 25	47LTS283	301136
Czechoslovakia	Poland	30 May 25	48LTS397	301172
Paraguay	Spain	08 Jul 25	138LTS225	303190
Austria	China	19 Oct 25	55LTS9	301301
Germany	Italy	31 Oct 25	53LTS245	301261
Multilateral		06 Nov 25	74LTS289	301743
Germany	Poland	16 Dec 25	46LTS139	301117
Denmark	Germany	20 Mar 26	53LTS377	301267
Multilateral		12 May 26	89LTS47	302004
Netherlands	UK Great Britain	20 May 26	50LTS309	301214
Denmark	UK Great Britain	02 Jun 26	61LTS353	301445
France	Sweden	19 Jul 26	54LTS283	301291
Finland	Switzerland	14 Oct 27	71LTS205	301663
Poland	USA (United States)	22 Nov 27	92LTS101	302082

PARTY ONE	PARTY TWO	DATE	CITATION	NUMBER
Fees and exemptions (Cont.)				
Germany	UK Great Britain	20 Mar 28	90LTS287	302044
Czechoslovakia	France	07 May 28	114LTS171	302663
Finland	Italy	12 May 28	77LTS334	301775
Belgium	Luxembourg	18 May 28	89LTS213	302016
Austria	Hungary	25 Jun 28	100LTS85	302296
Czechoslovakia	Serb/Croat/Slovene	07 Nov 28	98LTS297	302252
Brazil	Peru	31 Dec 28	127LTS455	302931
Peru	UK Great Britain	31 Dec 28	100LTS431	302312
France	UK Great Britain	06 Mar 29	90LTS391	302050
France	Germany	25 Apr 29	109LTS333	302548
Estonia	Germany	30 Apr 29	99LTS325	302275
Norway	Sweden	11 May 29	120LTS263	302771
France	UK Great Britain	15 May 29	134LTS263	303097
Spain	UK Great Britain	27 Jun 29	101LTS375	302337
UK Great Britain	USA (United States)	04 Jul 29	92LTS329	302099
Finland	Italy	15 Aug 29	99LTS363	302280
Germany	UK Great Britain	28 Dec 29	102LTS49	302352
Estonia	USSR (Soviet Union)	20 Jan 30	102LTS225	302365
Latvia	Norway	10 Feb 30	100LTS79	302295
Latvia	Spain	08 Mar 30	113LTS135	302641
Belgium	France	23 May 30	119LTS33	302738
Austria	Hungary	03 Jun 30	122LTS69	302799
Guatemala	Honduras	16 Jul 30	137LTS231	303159
France	Romania	27 Aug 30	158LTS379	303644
Netherlands	USA (United States)	16 Sep 30	125LTS147	302852
Japan	South Africa	16 Oct 30	126LTS17	302868
Multilateral		31 Oct 30	120LTS9	302760
Multilateral		10 Feb 31	126LTS41	302870
Czechoslovakia	Turkey	17 Mar 31	133LTS151	303065
Multilateral		06 May 31	120LTS217	302767
Belgium	France	16 May 31	141LTS333	303274
Guatemala	UK Great Britain	06 Jun 31	132LTS15	303027
Hungary	Spain	19 Sep 31	124LTS353	302839
France	UK Great Britain	27 Nov 31	132LTS25	303028
France	Italy	26 Dec 31	133LTS45	303055
France	UK Great Britain	28 Dec 31	133LTS79	303058
Netherlands	UK Great Britain	04 Jan 32	128LTS307	302939
Netherlands	UK Great Britain	04 Jan 32	128LTS347	302940
Hungary	UK Great Britain	10 Jun 32	132LTS53	303031
Netherlands	UK Great Britain	13 Aug 32	134LTS317	303100
Northern Rhodesia	South Africa	26 Sep 32	135LTS225	303113
Finland	UK Great Britain	30 Sep 32	135LTS9	303101
France	Hungary	07 Apr 33	162LTS463	303756
Multilateral		12 Apr 33	161LTS65	303706
Denmark	UK Great Britain	24 Apr 33	139LTS127	303208
Norway	UK Great Britain	15 May 33	145LTS187	303355
Finland	USSR (Soviet Union)	04 Jul 33	149LTS83	303436
Austria	Hungary	12 Jan 34	162LTS419	303754
Multilateral		20 Mar 34	176LTS55	304054
Multilateral		20 Mar 34	175LTS73	304050
Denmark	Germany	25 May 35	159LTS389	303680
Romania	UK Great Britain	14 Jun 35	163LTS301	303772
UK Great Britain	Uruguay	26 Jun 35	176LTS153	304058
Lithuania	Spain	07 Sep 35	163LTS321	303774
USA (United States)	USSR (Soviet Union)	22 Nov 35	167LTS303	303875
China	Malaya	12 Feb 36	170LTS19	303927
Austria	Switzerland	21 Nov 36	179LTS341	304162
Estonia	Finland	18 Dec 36	178LTS41	304105
Netherlands	Switzerland	27 Jan 37	186LTS433	304327
South Africa	USA (United States)	24 Mar 37	189LTS113	304379
Finland	Hungary	22 Oct 37	190LTS281	304426
Hungary	Lithuania	12 Nov 37	183LTS197	304236
Hungary	Norway	16 Nov 37	183LTS81	304228
Hungary	Latvia	16 Nov 37	183LTS205	304237
Brazil	USA (United States)	17 Dec 37	186LTS413	304325

PARTY ONE	PARTY TWO	DATE	CITATION	NUMBER
Fees and exemptions (Cont.)				
France	USA (United States)	14 Jan 38	191LTS213	304445
Estonia	Hungary	19 Jan 38	185LTS363	304300
Finland	South Africa	14 Feb 38	190LTS211	304419
Greece	Hungary	06 Apr 38	188LTS455	304370
Germany	Greece	11 May 38	197LTS75	304608
Lithuania	Poland	14 May 38	191LTS373	304456
France	Morocco	21 Jun 38	189LTS423	304398
Belgium	UK Great Britain	29 Jul 38	201LTS317	304722
Cuba	Portugal	06 Sep 38	195LTS443	304565
Burma	United Arab Rep	30 Sep 38	203LTS373	304780
Fiji Islands	USA (United States)	10 Jan 39	196LTS185	304581
Burma	France	26 Jan 39	201LTS9	304701
France	Norway	28 Feb 39	195LTS165	304546
Romania	USA (United States)	30 Apr 39	203LTS349	304775
Multilateral		23 May 39	202LTS159	304742
Sweden	USA (United States)	05 Oct 39	203LTS353	304776
Hungary	Romania	19 Oct 39	201LTS395	304728
Barbados	Martinique	21 Oct 39	201LTS65	304704
Lithuania	USA (United States)	28 Dec 39	202LTS381	304743
Financial programs				
France	Italy	30 Sep 19	5LTS279	300133
France	Hungary	31 Jan 21	15LTS221	300396
Germany	Saar	03 Jun 21	5LTS189	300129
Latvia	Lithuania	12 Jul 21	25LTS311	300620
Germany	Switzerland	29 Oct 21	13LTS193	300351
Czechoslovakia	Germany	08 May 22	23LTS171	300589
China	Japan	05 Dec 22	22LTS293	300560
Multilateral		29 Mar 23	23LTS256	300593
Australia	Netherlands	30 May 23	22LTS129	300556
Austria	Italy	16 Jul 23	27LTS383	300699
Bulgaria	Serb/Croat/Slovene	26 Nov 23	26LTS119	300643
Finland	Sweden	29 Nov 23	23LTS41	300575
Other Unilat Decla	Hungary	14 Mar 24	25LTS427	300634
Bulgaria	USA (United States)	19 Mar 24	26LTS27	300638
Hungary	Italy	27 Mar 24	45LTS229	301101
Austria	Serb/Croat/Slovene	29 Mar 24	114LTS451	302671
Hungary	Romania	16 Apr 24	46LTS7	301111
Hungary	Romania	16 Apr 24	45LTS403	301110
Austria	Italy	18 Jun 24	84LTS381	301914
Austria	Czechoslovakia	12 Jul 24	50LTS111	301199
Austria	Czechoslovakia	14 May 25	50LTS39	301198
Italy	Poland	22 Jul 25	54LTS101	301278
France	Saar	27 May 26	55LTS157	301312
Norway	Sweden	19 Nov 27	68LTS209	301584
Multilateral		01 May 28	132LTS415	303050
Estonia	Sweden	23 Jun 28	87LTS253	301972
Brazil	Colombia	15 Nov 28	100LTS123	302299
Brazil	Peru	31 Dec 28	127LTS455	302931
Multilateral		05 Jan 29	132LTS425	303051
Poland	Romania	30 Oct 29	121LTS167	302787
France	Yugoslavia	07 Nov 31	144LTS281	303331
Romania	Yugoslavia	14 Dec 31	135LTS31	303103
Haiti	USA (United States)	07 Aug 33	146LTS305	303381
Multilateral		28 Oct 33	159LTS199	303663
Brazil	Uruguay	20 Dec 33	181LTS45	304176
Czechoslovakia	Luxembourg	01 Dec 34	168LTS287	303906
Czechoslovakia	Monaco	22 Dec 34	171LTS27	303949
UK Great Britain	Uruguay	26 Jun 35	176LTS153	304058
Bulgaria	Netherlands	23 Sep 35	166LTS51	303829
France	India	04 Jan 36	170LTS97	303930
Albania	Italy	19 Mar 36	173LTS93	304006
Romania	UK Great Britain	02 May 36	184LTS145	304247
France	USSR (Soviet Union)	11 Aug 36	176LTS365	304073
Canada	Germany	22 Oct 36	173LTS311	304021

PARTY ONE	PARTY TWO	DATE	CITATION	NUMBER
Financial programs (Cont.)				
France	USA (United States)	12 Dec 36	176LTS403	304076
Sweden	Turkey	14 Dec 36	174LTS51	304036
Greece	Sweden	31 Dec 36	174LTS87	304039
Estonia	Sweden	08 Feb 37	176LTS193	304061
Canada	Haiti	23 Apr 37	194LTS59	304507
Multilateral		06 May 39	198LTS81	304626
Netherlands	Switzerland	01 Jul 39	198LTS195	304640
Funding procedures				
France	UK Great Britain	06 Aug 14	10LTS333	300278
Paraguay	Uruguay	28 Feb 15	15LTS195	300393
Brazil	UK Great Britain	04 Apr 19	5LTS45	300116
Norway	USA (United States)	30 Jun 21	14LTS19	300365
Latvia	Ukrainian SSR	03 Aug 21	17LTS295	300441
Germany	Poland	23 Jun 22	22LTS25	300553
United Arab Rep	Palestine	07 Aug 22	36LTS343	300933
Finland	USSR (Soviet Union)	28 Oct 22	19LTS199	300493
Germany	Saar	13 Nov 22	27LTS273	300690
Siam	USA (United States)	30 Dec 22	25LTS394	300629
Greece	Turkey	30 Jan 23	36LTS137	300912
Greece	Turkey	30 Jan 23	32LTS75	300807
Denmark	Finland	12 Feb 23	18LTS33	300452
Czechoslovakia	Serb/Croat/Slovene	17 Mar 23	30LTS185	300768
Poland	Turkey	09 May 23	49LTS315	301187
United Arab Rep	UK Great Britain	18 Jul 23	18LTS323	300474
Turkey		24 Jul 23	36LTS157	300915
Finland	USSR (Soviet Union)	28 Jul 23	32LTS101	300810
Other Unilat Decla	Greece	29 Sep 23	20LTS29	300503
Latvia	USA (United States)	16 Oct 23	27LTS371	300698
Bulgaria	Serb/Croat/Slovene	26 Nov 23	26LTS85	300642
Estonia	Latvia	10 Jan 24	38LTS103	300968
Multilateral		25 Jan 24	57LTS135	301360
Czechoslovakia	Hungary	08 Mar 24	36LTS61	300904
Austria	Italy	29 Mar 24	84LTS293	301910
Austria	Italy	29 Mar 24	84LTS321	301911
Bulgaria	Romania	19 Apr 24	33LTS221	300846
Finland	UK Great Britain	30 May 24	34LTS79	300868
Sweden	Switzerland	02 Jun 24	33LTS199	300844
Norway	UK Great Britain	05 Jun 24	27LTS195	300683
Denmark	Switzerland	06 Jun 24	34LTS175	300873
Austria	Italy	18 Jun 24	84LTS381	301914
Austria	Italy	18 Jun 24	84LTS349	301912
Hungary	Switzerland	18 Jun 24	34LTS387	300887
Austria	Italy	18 Jun 24	84LTS367	301913
Brazil	Switzerland	23 Jun 24	33LTS415	300861
Denmark	Norway	27 Jun 24	33LTS173	300842
Denmark	Sweden	27 Jun 24	33LTS149	300840
Austria	Serb/Croat/Slovene	27 Jun 24	115LTS49	302676
Finland	Sweden	27 Jun 24	29LTS19	300731
Finland	Norway	27 Jun 24	29LTS403	300751
Norway	Sweden	27 Jun 24	28LTS309	300717
Austria	Serb/Croat/Slovene	27 Jun 24	115LTS39	302675
Denmark	Finland	27 Jun 24	33LTS131	300839
Great Britain	Latvia	16 Jul 24	37LTS369	300961
Other Unilat Decla	Greece	19 Sep 24	30LTS413	300776
Italy	Switzerland	20 Sep 24	33LTS91	300834
Austria	Italy	27 Sep 24	84LTS409	301916
Austria	Italy	27 Sep 24	84LTS397	301915
Austria	Switzerland	11 Oct 24	33LTS423	300862
Czechoslovakia	Germany	15 Dec 24	52LTS41	301249
Czechoslovakia	Germany	15 Dec 24	52LTS31	301248
Norway	Sweden	22 Dec 24	32LTS13	300802
Austria	Italy	17 Jan 25	84LTS419	301917
Austria	Czechoslovakia	17 Jan 25	94LTS245	302146
Latvia	Sweden	28 Mar 25	37LTS131	300952

PARTY ONE	PARTY TWO	DATE	CITATION	NUMBER
Funding procedures (Cont.)				
Austria	Czechoslovakia	14 May 25	50LTS39	301198
Bulgaria	Czechoslovakia	06 Sep 25	50LTS253	301208
Multilateral		12 Jul 27	135LTS247	303115
Austria	Belgium	10 Oct 27	91LTS271	302067
Multilateral		29 Oct 27	127LTS27	302903
Netherlands	Sweden	24 Dec 27	71LTS391	301677
Iceland	Sweden	10 Mar 28	71LTS315	301672
Estonia	Latvia	20 Dec 29	106LTS173	302444
Latvia	Sweden	11 Jan 30	109LTS193	302539
Germany	Italy	25 Feb 30	118LTS49	302713
Latvia	Lithuania	25 Jan 31	118LTS135	302718
Multilateral		21 Aug 31	185LTS45	304273
Turkey	Yugoslavia	14 Apr 32	144LTS291	303332
Multilateral		28 Jun 32	140LTS191	303237
Colombia	Cuba	02 Jul 32	174LTS69	304038
Romania	Turkey	17 Oct 33	165LTS273	303814
Estonia	Hungary	08 Aug 34	167LTS153	303863
Norway	Venezuela	13 May 35	167LTS407	303882
Panama	USA (United States)	02 Mar 36	200LTS205	304692
Albania	Italy	19 Mar 36	173LTS51	304002
Netherlands	Romania	28 Aug 36	182LTS363	304222
UK Great Britain	Yugoslavia	27 Nov 36	181LTS281	304195
Norway	Romania	10 Dec 36	174LTS59	304037
Greece	Sweden	31 Dec 36	174LTS87	304039
Bulgaria	Latvia	17 May 38	189LTS249	304388
Romania	UK Great Britain	02 Sep 38	191LTS313	304453
Garnishment of funds				
Hungary	Latvia	25 Mar 38	188LTS447	304369
Inadequacy of funds				
Czechoslovakia	Serb/Croat/Slovene	17 Mar 23	30LTS185	300768
Bulgaria	Serb/Croat/Slovene	26 Nov 23	26LTS85	300642
Estonia	Spain	08 May 35	159LTS381	303679
Internal finance				
Hungary	Sweden	08 Nov 28	89LTS283	302023
Interest rates				
Germany	Netherlands	11 May 20	3LTS153	300097
France	Germany	30 Jun 20	8LTS79	300208
Germany	Switzerland	06 Dec 20	2LTS343	300088
France	Hungary	31 Jan 21	15LTS221	300396
France	Netherlands	16 Apr 21	11LTS341	300300
Norway	USA (United States)	30 Jun 21	14LTS19	300365
Multilateral		04 Oct 22	12LTS391	300335
Latvia	UK Great Britain	17 Oct 22	16LTS397	300419
France	Saar	30 Nov 22	27LTS283	300691
China	Japan	01 Dec 22	22LTS179	300559
China	Japan	05 Dec 22	22LTS293	300560
Germany	Switzerland	25 Mar 23	18LTS273	300470
Czechoslovakia	Hungary	13 Jul 23	35LTS253	300899
Czechoslovakia	Hungary	08 Mar 24	36LTS61	300904
Iraq	UK Great Britain	25 Mar 24	35LTS145	300894
Multilateral		28 Mar 24	31LTS46	300780
Austria	Czechoslovakia	12 Jul 24	50LTS111	301199
Multilateral		23 Oct 24	77LTS367	301778
France	Poland	09 Dec 24	44LTS127	301081
Czechoslovakia	Poland	23 Apr 25	44LTS309	301091
Estonia	USA (United States)	28 Oct 25	62LTS63	301455
Germany	Italy	31 Oct 25	53LTS245	301261
Albania	Greece	13 Oct 26	83LTS325	301899
Austria	Belgium	10 Oct 27	91LTS271	302067
Hungary	Serb/Croat/Slovene	22 Feb 28	87LTS361	301982
Germany	UK Great Britain	28 Dec 29	102LTS49	302352
Hungary	Yugoslavia	30 Jan 31	120LTS105	302761
Hungary	Italy	12 Nov 32	142LTS87	303279

PARTY ONE	PARTY TWO	DATE	CITATION	NUMBER
Interest rates (Cont.)				
Bel-Lux Econ Union	Estonia	19 Jun 35	170LTS243	303940
Albania	Italy	19 Mar 36	173LTS73	304004
Bel-Lux Econ Union	Spain	04 Apr 36	168LTS339	303909
Turkey	UK Great Britain	27 May 38	199LTS9	304660
Germany	Sweden	28 Oct 38	196LTS91	304571
Germany	Sweden	28 Oct 38	196LTS81	304570
Multilateral		27 Jan 39	196LTS287	304591
Multilateral		07 Sep 39	198LTS357	304654
Payment schedules				
Multilateral		18 Mar 04	1LTS83	300011
Multilateral		12 Jan 12	4LTS281	300112
Colombia	USA (United States)	06 Apr 14	9LTS302	300263
Paraguay	Uruguay	28 Feb 15	15LTS195	300393
Romania	UK Great Britain	22 Jan 20	1LTS257	300018
Sweden	UK Great Britain	03 Mar 20	5LTS63	300119
France	UK Great Britain	26 Apr 20	1LTS287	300023
Norway	UK Great Britain	06 Jul 20	5LTS107	300121
Belgium	France	24 Jul 20	1LTS311	300026
Austria	Czechoslovakia	02 Aug 20	32LTS365	300826
Germany	Switzerland	06 Dec 20	2LTS343	300088
Australia	Malay States	24 Jan 21	23LTS209	300590
Belgium	France	14 Feb 21	12LTS245	300317
Austria	Czechoslovakia	10 Mar 21	9LTS333	300267
Czechoslovakia	Italy	23 Mar 21	32LTS261	300817
Denmark	Sweden	08 Jun 21	14LTS195	300374
Belgium	Luxembourg	25 Jul 21	9LTS223	300256
Austria	Germany	17 Aug 21	19LTS237	300497
Danzig	Poland	24 Oct 21	116LTS5	302699
Australia	Nauru	27 Oct 21	23LTS229	300591
Germany	Switzerland	29 Oct 21	13LTS193	300351
Belgium	France	30 Nov 21	27LTS173	300680
Finland	USSR (Soviet Union)	14 Dec 21	16LTS221	300414
Hungary	UK Great Britain	20 Dec 21	10LTS437	300283
China	Japan.	04 Feb 22	10LTS309	300277
Peru	UK Great Britain	02 Mar 22	10LTS463	300286
Allied Powers	Poland	01 Apr 22	9LTS325	300265
Czechoslovakia	Germany	12 Apr 22	22LTS329	300562
Sweden	USA (United States)	17 Apr 22	14LTS281	300380
UK Great Britain	USA (United States)	22 Apr 22	20LTS415	300530
Netherlands	UK Great Britain	02 Jun 22	13LTS263	300357
Finland	USSR (Soviet Union)	13 Jun 22	16LTS349	300416
Finland	USSR (Soviet Union)	22 Jun 22	16LTS361	300417
Latvia	Poland	07 Jul 22	37LTS317	300958
Multilateral		18 Aug 22	13LTS289	300360
Germany	Poland	25 Aug 22	22LTS63	300554
Latvia	UK Great Britain	17 Oct 22	16LTS397	300419
Italy	Serb/Croat/Slovene	23 Oct 22	18LTS441	300480
Estonia	Finland	28 Nov 22	19LTS213	300494
China	Japan	01 Dec 22	22LTS179	300559
Albania	Italy	04 Dec 22	15LTS213	300395
China	Japan	05 Dec 22	22LTS293	300560
UK Great Britain	USA (United States)	28 Dec 22	21LTS9	300531
Netherlands	UK Great Britain	18 Jan 23	18LTS257	300469
Netherlands	UK Great Britain	23 Jan 23	16LTS425	300420
Poland	USSR (Soviet Union)	07 Feb 23	49LTS285	301186
Germany	Switzerland	25 Mar 23	18LTS273	300470
Portugal	Spain	26 Mar 23	18LTS349	300475
Germany	Saar	21 Apr 23	27LTS295	300693
Denmark	UK Great Britain	25 Apr 23	22LTS157	300557
Netherlands	UK Great Britain	30 Apr 23	20LTS343	300525
France	India	12 May 23	25LTS381	300627
Australia	Netherlands	30 May 23	22LTS129	300556
Belgium	Luxembourg	17 Jul 23	27LTS235	300686
Poland	Romania	24 Jul 23	18LTS103	300458

PARTY ONE	PARTY TWO	DATE	CITATION	NUMBER
Payment schedules (Cont.)				
Multilateral		23 Nov 23	28LTS267	300712
Bulgaria	Serb/Croat/Slovene	26 Nov 23	26LTS141	300644
Austria	Czechoslovakia	30 Nov 23	126LTS171	302880
UK Great Britain	USA (United States)	08 Dec 23	23LTS93	300580
Germany	Latvia	24 Feb 24	41LTS231	301016
Other Unilat Decla	Hungary	14 Mar 24	25LTS427	300634
Hungary	Italy	27 Mar 24	45LTS65	301099
Hungary	Italy	27 Mar 24	45LTS83	301100
Multilateral		28 Mar 24	31LTS53	300781
Hungary	Romania	16 Apr 24	45LTS403	301110
Hungary	Romania	16 Apr 24	45LTS355	301109
Latvia	Lithuania	21 May 24	37LTS363	300960
Denmark	USA (United States)	29 May 24	27LTS361	300697
Panama	USA (United States)	06 Jun 24	138LTS397	303200
Austria	Czechoslovakia	12 Jul 24	50LTS111	301199
Italy	UK Great Britain	15 Jul 24	36LTS379	300936
Netherlands	USA (United States)	21 Aug 24	33LTS433	300863
Canada	USA (United States)	24 Feb 25	43LTS251	301060
Multilateral		05 May 25	55LTS225	301318
Bulgaria	Great Britain	07 May 25	38LTS153	300973
Finland	Sweden	09 May 25	47LTS283	301136
Austria	Czechoslovakia	14 May 25	50LTS39	301198
Italy	Poland	22 Jul 25	54LTS101	301278
Austria	Germany	03 Oct 25	52LTS171	301255
Hungary	UK Great Britain	17 Oct 25	47LTS373	301142
Estonia	USA (United States)	28 Oct 25	62LTS63	301455
Estonia	Finland	10 Dec 25	50LTS335	301217
Estonia	Latvia	03 Mar 26	63LTS13	301476
Hungary	Italy	30 Mar 26	54LTS85	301276
Czechoslovakia	Italy	04 May 26	61LTS257	301438
France	India	19 Jun 26	57LTS35	301350
France	UK Great Britain	12 Jul 26	98LTS155	302244
Dominican Republic	USA (United States)	19 Jul 26	54LTS145	301282
Netherlands	UK Great Britain	14 Aug 26	57LTS41	301351
Poland	USA (United States)	14 Nov 26	58LTS97	301368
Germany	Saar	23 Nov 26	70LTS105	301627
Other Unilat Decla	Estonia	10 Dec 26	62LTS277	301467
Portugal	UK Great Britain	31 Dec 26	61LTS115	301429
Greece	UK Great Britain	17 Feb 27	90LTS379	302049
Finland	Sweden	10 May 27	70LTS201	301634
Hungary	Italy	21 May 27	74LTS19	301727
Czechoslovakia	Poland	30 May 27	98LTS233	302251
France	USA (United States)	29 Aug 27	68LTS253	301589
Germany	Saar	13 Oct 27	70LTS121	301629
Netherlands	USA (United States)	30 Dec 27	72LTS179	301691
Multilateral		10 Mar 28	132LTS405	303049
France	Germany	16 Mar 28	79LTS121	301805
Multilateral		01 May 28	132LTS415	303050
Czechoslovakia	Germany	11 May 28	81LTS441	301854
Cuba	Mexico	29 Jun 28	124LTS189	302833
Germany	UK Great Britain	26 Jul 28	85LTS135	301928
Mexico	UK Great Britain	24 Oct 28	87LTS63	301962
Austria	Czechoslovakia	12 Dec 28	108LTS9	302501
Multilateral		05 Jan 29	132LTS425	303051
Persia	Sweden	10 May 29	102LTS9	302349
France	UK Great Britain	15 May 29	134LTS263	303097
Multilateral		28 Jun 29	103LTS249	302371
Multilateral		28 Jun 29	102LTS245	302368
Netherlands	South Africa	10 Sep 29	98LTS423	302261
Belgium	Irish Free State	24 Sep 29	102LTS213	302364
Poland	UK Great Britain	04 Oct 29	97LTS261	302227
Belgium	Germany	07 Nov 29	121LTS327	302795
Other Unilat Decla	Greece	14 Jan 30	108LTS349	302518
Belgium	Germany	16 Jan 30	104LTS223	302392
Austria	Belgium	18 Jan 30	104LTS231	302393

PARTY ONE	PARTY TWO	DATE	CITATION	NUMBER
Payment schedules (Cont.)				
France	Poland	20 Jan 30	126LTS117	302876
Italy	Poland	20 Jan 30	127LTS41	302904
Poland	UK Great Britain	20 Jan 30	126LTS159	302878
Multilateral		20 Jan 30	113LTS389	302650
France	Yugoslavia	20 Jan 30	104LTS171	302386
Multilateral		20 Jan 30	112LTS361	302622
France	UK Great Britain	24 Mar 30	105LTS227	302415
Greece	Turkey	10 Jun 30	108LTS233	302511
Germany	USA (United States)	23 Jun 30	106LTS121	302440
Hungary	Yugoslavia	27 Aug 30	113LTS163	302643
Multilateral		28 Aug 30	133LTS21	303053
Italy	UK Great Britain	02 Sep 30	140LTS19	303225
Netherlands	USA (United States)	16 Sep 30	125LTS147	302852
China	UK Great Britain	22 Sep 30	115LTS493	302697
Czechoslovakia	Romania	05 Dec 30	167LTS205	303867
Czechoslovakia	Romania	22 Dec 30	167LTS257	303871
Hungary	Yugoslavia	30 Jan 31	120LTS105	302761
France	India	07 Mar 31	119LTS269	302750
Greece	UK Great Britain	17 Apr 31	129LTS287	302965
France	Switzerland	09 Sep 31	142LTS205	303293
Mexico	Sweden	14 Sep 31	192LTS195	304472
UK Great Britain	Yugoslavia	23 Oct 31	126LTS209	302884
Multilateral		10 Nov 31	131LTS327	303023
Multilateral		10 Nov 31	131LTS389	303024
Romania	Yugoslavia	14 Dec 31	135LTS99	303106
Romania	Yugoslavia	14 Dec 31	135LTS89	303105
Netherlands	UK Great Britain	04 Jan 32	128LTS307	302939
Netherlands	UK Great Britain	04 Jan 32	128LTS347	302940
Belgium	South Africa	04 Feb 32	127LTS121	302912
France	Latvia	08 Mar 32	128LTS43	302936
Bel-Lux Econ Union	Hungary	26 Mar 32	136LTS405	303139
Austria	Yugoslavia	20 Apr 32	132LTS217	303040
Switzerland	Yugoslavia	27 Apr 32	131LTS285	303019
Czechoslovakia	Yugoslavia	08 Jun 32	139LTS45	303203
Hungary	UK Great Britain	10 Jun 32	132LTS53	303031
Netherlands	South Africa	29 Jun 32	133LTS33	303054
Netherlands	UK Great Britain	13 Aug 32	134LTS317	303100
Hungary	Italy	12 Nov 32	142LTS101	303281
Hungary	Italy	12 Nov 32	142LTS87	303279
Panama	USA (United States)	17 Dec 32	138LTS119	303183
Austria	France	29 Dec 32	147LTS101	303394
Romania	Yugoslavia	10 Mar 33	146LTS245	303374
Estonia	Finland	16 May 33	141LTS19	303257
Bel-Lux Econ Union	Hungary	24 May 33	140LTS169	303234
Bel-Lux Econ Union	Bulgaria	21 Jun 33	140LTS375	303247
Finland	USSR (Soviet Union)	04 Jul 33	149LTS83	303436
Haiti	USA (United States)	07 Aug 33	146LTS305	303381
Argentina	Brazil	10 Oct 33	179LTS165	304144
Multilateral		23 Nov 33	192LTS389	304484
France	USSR (Soviet Union)	11 Jan 34	167LTS349	303878
Multilateral		20 Mar 34	174LTS171	304048
Multilateral		20 Mar 34	175LTS269	304051
Bel-Lux Econ Union	Turkey	24 May 34	150LTS269	303460
Bel-Lux Econ Union	Turkey	31 May 34	150LTS277	303461
Romania		21 Jun 34	168LTS265	303904
Germany	UK Great Britain	10 Aug 34	155LTS53	303568
Germany	Norway	06 Sep 34	161LTS187	303711
Finland	Germany	02 Oct 34	154LTS17	303535
Bulgaria	Spain	19 Nov 34	166LTS277	303843
Latvia	Poland	20 Dec 34	162LTS361	303749
Germany	Sweden	22 Dec 34	156LTS127	303596
France	UK Great Britain	16 Jul 35	168LTS179	303898
Italy	Netherlands	29 Jul 35	165LTS329	303819
Bulgaria	Netherlands	23 Sep 35	166LTS51	303829
Finland	Romania	03 Dec 35	165LTS287	303815

PARTY ONE	PARTY TWO	DATE	CITATION	NUMBER
Payment schedules (Cont.)				
France	USA (United States)	30 Dec 35	171LTS117	303955
Spain	Turkey	31 Dec 35	166LTS163	303838
France	India	04 Jan 36	170LTS97	303930
Spain	UK Great Britain	06 Jan 36	166LTS283	303844
Germany	Sweden	31 Jan 36	168LTS19	303884
Sweden	Turkey	27 Feb 36	167LTS83	303859
United Arab Rep	Malaya	29 Feb 36	170LTS103	303931
Albania	Italy	19 Mar 36	173LTS63	304003
Greece	Palestine	28 Mar 36	170LTS145	303932
Finland	Latvia	28 Mar 36	171LTS155	303957
Bel-Lux Econ Union	Bulgaria	01 Apr 36	169LTS23	303912
Bel-Lux Econ Union	Spain	04 Apr 36	168LTS339	303909
Romania	UK Great Britain	02 May 36	184LTS145	304247
Brazil	USA (United States)	27 May 36	171LTS343	303971
Norway	Turkey	08 Jun 36	170LTS235	303939
Norway	Spain	13 Jun 36	170LTS207	303936
France	Palestine	19 Jun 36	172LTS17	303977
Finland	Turkey	20 Jun 36	172LTS125	303982
Finland	Turkey	20 Jun 36	172LTS135	303983
Denmark	USSR (Soviet Union)	29 Jun 36	174LTS93	304040
Bulgaria	France	06 Jul 36	171LTS269	303963
Italy	Norway	25 Aug 36	171LTS377	303974
Netherlands	Romania	28 Aug 36	182LTS363	304222
Turkey	UK Great Britain	02 Sep 36	172LTS289	303998
Romania	Turkey	04 Sep 36	195LTS429	304564
Finland	Italy	28 Sep 36	172LTS155	303986
Estonia	Italy	06 Oct 36	172LTS189	303989
Bulgaria	Finland	27 Oct 36	173LTS201	304013
Italy	UK Great Britain	06 Nov 36	177LTS183	304090
Brazil	USA (United States)	12 Nov 36	176LTS133	304057
Italy	Sweden	01 Dec 36	173LTS279	304019
Italy	Sweden	01 Dec 36	173LTS269	304018
Germany	UK Great Britain	02 Dec 36	178LTS329	304121
Haiti	Jamaica	07 Dec 36	178LTS65	304108
Norway	Romania	10 Dec 36	174LTS59	304037
Sweden	Turkey	14 Dec 36	174LTS51	304036
Germany	Malaya	17 Dec 36	178LTS484	304129
Bahamas	USA (United States)	21 Dec 36	176LTS411	304077
Germany	Netherlands	23 Dec 36	179LTS359	304163
India	Nepal	23 Dec 36	178LTS405	304123
Italy	Netherlands	01 Jan 37	178LTS415	304124
Gibralter	USA (United States)	05 Jan 37	177LTS21	304078
Danzig	UK Great Britain	13 Jan 37	178LTS87	304109
Italy	Latvia	05 Feb 37	178LTS25	304103
Netherlands	Turkey	17 Feb 37	182LTS221	304213
Germany	Norway	27 Feb 37	178LTS427	304125
Malaya	Netherlands	16 Mar 37	184LTS181	304248
Italy	Norway	31 Mar 37	177LTS367	304099
Czechoslovakia	Italy	31 Mar 37	193LTS165	304492
Italy	Norway	31 Mar 37	177LTS355	304098
Chile	Netherlands	05 May 37	182LTS385	304223
Poland	Romania	24 May 37	190LTS361	304428
Estonia	Turkey	06 Jun 37	179LTS151	304142
UK Great Britain	Yugoslavia	07 Jun 37	184LTS229	304249
Bel-Lux Econ Union	Italy	30 Jun 37	182LTS106	304203
Romania	USA (United States)	10 Aug 37	183LTS7	304225
Bel-Lux Econ Union	Romania	24 Aug 37	193LTS189	304496
Malaya	Siam	15 Sep 37	191LTS225	304447
Netherlands	USA (United States)	20 Sep 37	184LTS319	304256
Estonia	France	16 Oct 37	183LTS37	304226
Estonia	Germany	24 Oct 37	184LTS81	304244
Germany	Latvia	31 Oct 37	189LTS139	304382
Hungary	Lithuania	12 Nov 37	183LTS197	304236
Hungary	Latvia	16 Nov 37	183LTS205	304237
Bel-Lux Econ Union	Yugoslavia	26 Nov 37	196LTS19	304567

PARTY ONE	PARTY TWO	DATE	CITATION	NUMBER
Payment schedules (Cont.)				
Estonia	UK Great Britain	14 Dec 37	187LTS223	304343
Germany	Netherlands	18 Dec 37	190LTS29	304403
Sweden	Turkey	31 Dec 37	184LTS409	304261
Sweden	Turkey	31 Dec 37	184LTS399	304260
Bel-Lux Econ Union	Estonia	13 Jan 38	185LTS63	304275
Dominican Republic	Haiti	31 Jan 38	187LTS169	304336
Greece	Norway	28 Feb 38	186LTS165	304309
Czechoslovakia	USA (United States)	07 Mar 38	200LTS87	304687
Surinam	UK Great Britain	15 Mar 38	189LTS183	304385
Finland	Lithuania	12 Apr 38	194LTS9	304501
Nicaragua	USA (United States)	14 Apr 38	192LTS275	304477
Norway	Sweden	20 Apr 38	189LTS153	304383
Bulgaria	Latvia	17 May 38	189LTS249	304388
Turkey	UK Great Britain	27 May 38	199LTS9	304660
Multilateral		02 Jun 38	192LTS157	304470
USA (United States)	Yugoslavia	20 Jun 38	195LTS259	304549
Switzerland	Yugoslavia	27 Jun 38	196LTS27	304568
Germany	UK Great Britain	01 Jul 38	194LTS235	304525
Romania	UK Great Britain	02 Sep 38	191LTS313	304453
British Guiana	USA (United States)	06 Sep 38	193LTS117	304490
Burma	United Arab Rep	30 Sep 38	203LTS373	304780
Poland	UK Great Britain	05 Oct 38	194LTS321	304529
Netherlands	Romania	10 Oct 38	195LTS9	304532
France	UK Great Britain	26 Oct 38	194LTS371	304530
Germany	Sweden	28 Oct 38	196LTS91	304571
Latvia	Poland	29 Oct 38	195LTS169	304547
Brazil	USA (United States)	12 Nov 38	195LTS375	304557
Greece	USA (United States)	15 Nov 38	195LTS145	304544
Colombia	USA (United States)	23 Nov 38	196LTS147	304578
Sweden	Turkey	20 Jan 39	194LTS113	304514
Burma	France	26 Jan 39	201LTS9	304701
France	India	22 Mar 39	197LTS273	304619
Germany	Romania	23 Mar 39	199LTS77	304668
France	Romania	31 Mar 39	199LTS219	304677
Turkey	USA (United States)	01 Apr 39	202LTS129	304741
Latvia	Sweden	15 Apr 39	196LTS373	304597
Multilateral		06 May 39	198LTS81	304626
Romania	UK Great Britain	11 May 39	196LTS351	304594
Multilateral		23 May 39	202LTS159	304742
Norway	Spain	26 Jul 39	198LTS87	304627
Barbados	Martinique	21 Oct 39	201LTS65	304704
Romania	Switzerland	02 Nov 39	200LTS289	304699
USA (United States)	Venezuela	06 Nov 39	203LTS273	304770
Sweden	Turkey	29 Feb 40	200LTS273	304696
Spain	UK Great Britain	18 Mar 40	203LTS157	304759
Finland	Latvia	11 Apr 40	201LTS389	304727
Romania	UK Great Britain	06 Jun 40	203LTS197	304761
United Arab Rep	UK Great Britain	17 Jul 40	202LTS97	304738
United Arab Rep	France	03 Aug 40	202LTS121	304740
Purchase authorizations				
Multilateral		21 Jun 20	8LTS65	300207
Hungary	Italy	27 Mar 24	45LTS241	301102
Greece	UK Great Britain	17 Feb 27	90LTS379	302049
Non-interest rates and fees				
Belgium	Netherlands	08 Mar 20	1LTS25	300003
Denmark	Germany	30 Aug 20	14LTS257	300377
France	Italy	12 Sep 20	1LTS397	300033
Netherlands	UK Great Britain	18 Jan 21	5LTS157	300124
Australia	Malay States	24 Jan 21	23LTS209	300590
Belgium	UK Great Britain	15 Mar 21	5LTS319	300138
Denmark	Sweden	08 Jun 21	14LTS195	300374
Denmark	Norway	21 Jul 21	13LTS357	300362
Multilateral		19 Sep 21	15LTS191	300392
Italy	Switzerland	24 Sep 21	12LTS367	300330

PARTY ONE	PARTY TWO	DATE	CITATION	NUMBER
Non-interest rates and fees (Cont.)				
Australia	Nauru	27 Oct 21	23LTS229	300591
Estonia	Finland	29 Oct 21	13LTS167	300350
Finland	USSR (Soviet Union)	14 Dec 21	16LTS221	300414
Belgium	Luxembourg	27 Dec 21	12LTS253	300318
Estonia	France	07 Jan 22	62LTS9	301452
France	Switzerland	24 Jan 22	12LTS371	300331
Multilateral		06 Feb 22	38LTS267	300981
Norway	Sweden	29 Mar 22	13LTS311	300361
India	Iraq	02 Apr 22	69LTS157	301602
Netherlands	UK Great Britain	02 Jun 22	13LTS263	300357
Finland	USSR (Soviet Union)	13 Jun 22	16LTS349	300416
Finland	USSR (Soviet Union)	22 Jun 22	16LTS361	300417
Multilateral		18 Aug 22	13LTS289	300360
Austria	Poland	25 Sep 22	59LTS307	301400
Estonia	Finland	28 Nov 22	19LTS213	300494
Albania	Italy	04 Dec 22	15LTS213	300395
UK Great Britain	USA (United States)	28 Dec 22	21LTS9	300531
Netherlands	UK Great Britain	18 Jan 23	18LTS257	300469
Netherlands	UK Great Britain	23 Jan 23	16LTS425	300420
Multilateral		29 Mar 23	23LTS256	300593
Australia	Netherlands	30 May 23	22LTS129	300556
Canada	Irish Free State	12 Oct 23	56LTS291	301338
UK Great Britain	USA (United States)	08 Dec 23	23LTS93	300580
Multilateral		09 Dec 23	58LTS284	301379
Irish Free State	USA (United States)	31 Dec 23	56LTS303	301339
Hungary	Italy	27 Mar 24	55LTS109	301308
Hungary	Italy	27 Mar 24	55LTS103	301307
Hungary	Romania	16 Apr 24	46LTS7	301111
Finland	USSR (Soviet Union)	18 Jun 24	47LTS153	301133
Italy	Serb/Croat/Slovene	12 Aug 24	82LTS423	301882
Italy	Serb/Croat/Slovene	12 Aug 24	82LTS401	301881
Multilateral		23 Oct 24	77LTS367	301778
Multilateral		12 Dec 24	37LTS113	300950
Germany	Irish Free State	29 Dec 24	56LTS341	301341
Czechoslovakia	Poland	07 Apr 25	56LTS285	301337
Irish Free State	New Zealand	30 Apr 25	56LTS373	301342
Multilateral		05 May 25	55LTS225	301318
Italy	Poland	22 Jul 25	54LTS101	301278
Irish Free State	South Africa	01 Oct 25	56LTS389	301343
Multilateral		29 Oct 25	57LTS201	301365
Germany	Netherlands	24 Mar 26	51LTS245	301234
India	Irish Free State	04 Apr 26	56LTS415	301344
Great Britain	Netherlands	27 Apr 26	50LTS295	301212
Germany	Norway	15 Jun 26	51LTS329	301238
Multilateral		01 Nov 26	78LTS109	301782
Germany	Netherlands	03 Nov 26	68LTS111	301575
Multilateral		22 Jan 27	68LTS149	301578
Multilateral		22 Jan 27	68LTS129	301576
Multilateral		19 Feb 27	68LTS139	301577
Multilateral		24 Feb 27	68LTS159	301579
Multilateral		25 Feb 27	78LTS123	301783
Belgium	Netherlands	28 Feb 27	68LTS169	301580
Multilateral		08 Mar 27	78LTS134	301784
Multilateral		18 Mar 27	68LTS179	301581
Belgium	UK Great Britain	09 Apr 27	67LTS209	301548
Multilateral		02 May 27	68LTS189	301582
France	UK Great Britain	23 May 27	67LTS227	301550
Multilateral		16 Aug 27	78LTS141	301785
Multilateral		11 Nov 27	78LTS153	301786
Multilateral		21 Nov 27	78LTS163	301787
Multilateral		07 Jan 28	78LTS187	301789
Multilateral		08 Mar 28	80LTS241	301829
Multilateral		10 Mar 28	132LTS405	303049
Multilateral		19 Mar 28	78LTS177	301788
Multilateral		23 Apr 28	78LTS197	301790

PARTY ONE	PARTY TWO	DATE	CITATION	NUMBER
Non-interest rates and fees (Cont.)				
Multilateral		25 Apr 28	78LTS207	301791
Multilateral		01 May 28	132LTS415	303050
Multilateral		09 Jun 28	78LTS219	301792
Cuba	Mexico	29 Jun 28	124LTS189	302833
Finland	Sweden	10 Jul 28	87LTS131	301966
Multilateral		12 Sep 28	104LTS43	302377
Multilateral		27 Nov 28	92LTS321	302098
Multilateral		30 Nov 28	87LTS119	301965
Denmark	Sweden	13 Dec 28	104LTS55	302378
Multilateral		22 Dec 28	104LTS103	302381
Brazil	Peru	31 Dec 28	127LTS455	302931
Multilateral		05 Jan 29	132LTS425	303051
Multilateral		14 Jan 29	87LTS169	301968
Multilateral		16 Jan 29	87LTS155	301967
Denmark	Norway	21 Jan 29	104LTS119	302382
Multilateral		02 Feb 29	92LTS353	302100
Denmark	Sweden	28 Feb 29	104LTS69	302379
Multilateral		08 May 29	91LTS337	302074
France	UK Great Britain	15 May 29	134LTS263	303097
Multilateral		30 Aug 29	96LTS129	302195
Multilateral		07 Sep 29	98LTS345	302255
Multilateral		25 Sep 29	98LTS361	302256
Multilateral		26 Sep 29	98LTS395	302259
Multilateral		30 Sep 29	99LTS71	302269
Multilateral		30 Sep 29	98LTS183	302246
Multilateral		01 Oct 29	98LTS197	302247
Multilateral		08 Oct 29	98LTS409	302260
Multilateral		10 Oct 29	98LTS375	302257
Chile	Poland	19 Oct 29	113LTS79	302637
Multilateral		28 Oct 29	97LTS71	302219
Multilateral		29 Oct 29	99LTS85	302270
Belgium	Germany	07 Nov 29	121LTS327	302795
Multilateral		18 Nov 29	99LTS415	302287
Multilateral		14 Jan 30	99LTS343	302278
Multilateral		25 Feb 30	101LTS343	302335
France	UK Great Britain	24 Mar 30	105LTS227	302415
Romania	UK Great Britain	02 Apr 30	105LTS235	302416
Multilateral		10 Apr 30	101LTS465	302345
Austria	Hungary	03 Jun 30	122LTS69	302799
Multilateral		26 Jun 30	133LTS9	303052
Estonia	Latvia	28 Feb 31	114LTS379	302667
Multilateral		10 Nov 31	131LTS389	303024
France	UK Great Britain	17 Nov 31	134LTS299	303098
Netherlands	UK Great Britain	04 Jan 32	128LTS347	302940
Netherlands	South Africa	29 Jun 32	133LTS33	303054
Netherlands	UK Great Britain	13 Aug 32	134LTS317	303100
Chile	Sweden	08 Mar 33	142LTS147	303286
Multilateral		23 Nov 33	192LTS327	304483
Greece	UK Great Britain	21 Jan 36	168LTS171	303897
Multilateral		11 Feb 37	186LTS55	304303
Bulgaria	Romania	20 Jul 37	202LTS33	304733
Multilateral		03 Dec 37	186LTS293	304318
Multilateral		23 May 39	202LTS159	304742
France	UK Great Britain	13 Sep 39	201LTS369	304724
Seizure funds				
Austria	Poland	09 Jan 20	7LTS163	300185
Hungary	Italy	27 Mar 24	45LTS241	301102
Transportation costs				
Austria	Germany	01 Sep 20	4LTS201	300107
Japan	Paraguay	30 Nov 20	6LTS367	300169
Multilateral		09 Dec 23	47LTS55	301129
Finland	USA (United States)	21 Dec 25	47LTS345	301138
Great Britain	Serb/Croat/Slovene	09 Aug 27	69LTS255	301607
Poland	Romania	29 Nov 28	96LTS15	302188

PARTY ONE	PARTY TWO	DATE	CITATION	NUMBER
Transportation costs (Cont.)				
Finland	Italy	10 Jul 29	111LTS295	302593
Bulgaria	Turkey	23 Dec 29	122LTS17	302796
Germany	USA (United States)	12 Jul 30	119LTS247	302748
Local currency				
Germany	Switzerland	06 Dec 20	2LTS343	300088
Australia	Malay States	24 Jan 21	23LTS209	300590
Australia	Netherlands	30 May 23	22LTS129	300556
Greece	Serb/Croat/Slovene	02 Nov 27	91LTS137	302060
Multilateral		10 Nov 31	131LTS389	303024
Romania	Yugoslavia	14 Dec 31	135LTS99	303106
Belgium	Netherlands	04 Aug 32	134LTS117	303086
Italy	Sweden	01 Dec 36	173LTS269	304018
Germany	UK Great Britain	01 Jul 38	194LTS235	304525
Netherlands	Romania	10 Oct 38	195LTS9	304532
Claims, debts and assets				
Multilateral		23 Oct 24	78LTS17	301779
Czechoslovakia	Serb/Croat/Slovene	07 Nov 28	95LTS101	302169
Germany	Poland	14 Dec 28	113LTS367	302648
Multilateral		01 Jul 30	121LTS153	302786
Mexico	USA (United States)	24 Apr 34	149LTS49	303433
Sweden	Turkey	19 Jun 34	150LTS413	303474
Assets				
Austria	France	03 Aug 20	5LTS355	300141
Austria	Belgium	04 Oct 20	5LTS371	300142
Other Unilat Decla	Hungary	14 Mar 24	25LTS427	300634
Germany	Greece	24 Mar 28	90LTS9	302031
Multilateral		31 Oct 30	120LTS9	302760
Czechoslovakia	Romania	22 Dec 30	167LTS243	303870
Sweden	Turkey	20 Jan 39	194LTS113	304514
Claims and settlements				
Cuba	USA (United States)	02 Mar 04	127LTS143	302915
France	Germany	25 Mar 20	1LTS347	300029
Multilateral		30 Jun 20	1LTS59	300008
Austria	Germany	01 Sep 20	2LTS132	300057
Austria	Belgium	04 Oct 20	5LTS371	300142
France	Hungary	31 Jan 21	15LTS221	300396
UK Great Britain	USSR (Soviet Union)	16 Mar 21	4LTS127	300104
UK Great Britain	Venezuela	22 Mar 21	5LTS169	300126
Czechoslovakia	Italy	23 Mar 21	32LTS261	300817
Peru	USA (United States)	21 May 21	6LTS171	300150
Multilateral		10 Jun 21	8LTS297	300227
Norway	USA (United States)	30 Jun 21	14LTS19	300365
Sweden	UK Great Britain	08 Jul 21	5LTS329	300139
Latvia	Ukrainian SSR	03 Aug 21	17LTS317	300442
Estonia	Ukrainian SSR	25 Nov 21	11LTS121	300294
Ireland	UK Great Britain	06 Dec 21	26LTS9	300636
Costa Rica	UK Great Britain	12 Jan 22	17LTS151	300432
Germany	Poland	24 Feb 22	26LTS479	300664
Germany	Poland	24 Feb 22	27LTS15	300665
Germany	Poland	15 Jun 22	21LTS433	300550
Germany	Poland	23 Jun 22	22LTS25	300553
Finland	USA (United States)	21 Jul 22	13LTS243	300356
Germany	Poland	25 Aug 22	22LTS63	300554
Finland	USSR (Soviet Union)	20 Sep 22	19LTS143	300490
Denmark	Sweden	07 Nov 22	14LTS95	300370
Germany	Poland	18 Dec 22	34LTS283	300879
Belgium	Poland	30 Dec 22	21LTS201	300543
Multilateral		29 Mar 23	23LTS256	300593
Germany	Saar	21 Apr 23	27LTS295	300693
Czechoslovakia	Hungary	13 Jul 23	36LTS13	300901
Czechoslovakia	Hungary	13 Jul 23	35LTS253	300899
Austria	Italy	16 Jul 23	27LTS383	300699
Multilateral		24 Jul 23	36LTS167	300917

PARTY ONE	PARTY TWO	DATE	CITATION	NUMBER
Claims and settlements (Cont.)				
Estonia	Latvia	01 Nov 23	25LTS341	300622
Hungary	Latvia	19 Nov 23	37LTS341	300959
Germany	UK Great Britain	05 Jan 24	36LTS365	300935
Czechoslovakia	Hungary	08 Mar 24	36LTS61	300904
Sweden	USSR (Soviet Union)	15 Mar 24	25LTS251	300613
Hungary	Italy	27 Mar 24	45LTS241	301102
Hungary	Italy	27 Mar 24	45LTS65	301099
Hungary	Italy	27 Mar 24	45LTS229	301101
Austria	Poland	29 Mar 24	130LTS251	302993
Austria	Poland	29 Mar 24	130LTS223	302992
Hungary	Romania	16 Apr 24	46LTS7	301111
Hungary	Romania	16 Apr 24	45LTS355	301109
Sweden	USA (United States)	22 May 24	29LTS421	300752
Austria	Czechoslovakia	15 Jun 24	94LTS149	302142
Austria	Poland	18 Jun 24	130LTS279	302994
Austria	Serb/Croat/Slovene	18 Jun 24	115LTS9	302673
Austria	Poland	18 Jun 24	130LTS309	302996
Austria	Poland	18 Jun 24	130LTS293	302995
Austria	Serb/Croat/Slovene	18 Jun 24	114LTS481	302672
Austria	Serb/Croat/Slovene	27 Jun 24	115LTS39	302675
Austria	Czechoslovakia	12 Jul 24	50LTS111	301199
Austria	Romania	26 Jul 24	85LTS223	301933
Austria	Romania	26 Jul 24	85LTS243	301934
Germany	Japan	12 Sep 24	59LTS17	301387
Germany	Saar	20 Sep 24	30LTS121	300765
France	Mexico	25 Sep 24	79LTS417	301818
Multilateral		23 Oct 24	77LTS367	301778
Multilateral		26 Nov 24	48LTS69	301151
Austria	Poland	17 Jan 25	130LTS387	302998
Austria	Poland	17 Jan 25	130LTS327	302997
Austria	Serb/Croat/Slovene	17 Jan 25	128LTS453	302949
Austria	Czechoslovakia	17 Jan 25	94LTS245	302146
Austria	Serb/Croat/Slovene	17 Jan 25	128LTS445	302948
Austria	Czechoslovakia	17 Jan 25	94LTS185	302145
Czechoslovakia	Poland	23 Apr 25	48LTS287	301170
Finland	Sweden	09 May 25	47LTS283	301136
Austria	Czechoslovakia	14 May 25	50LTS39	301198
Germany	Italy	31 Oct 25	53LTS245	301261
Belgium	USA (United States)	09 Dec 25	72LTS171	301690
Cuba	USA (United States)	04 Mar 26	61LTS369	301447
Hungary	Italy	30 Mar 26	54LTS85	301276
Multilateral		10 Apr 26	120LTS187	302765
Bulgaria	Czechoslovakia	15 May 26	60LTS203	301413
Dominican Republic	USA (United States)	19 Jul 26	54LTS145	301282
Belgium	Hungary	30 Sep 26	97LTS215	302225
Mexico	UK Great Britain	19 Nov 26	85LTS51	301922
Czechoslovakia	Switzerland	21 Dec 26	86LTS443	301956
Multilateral		24 Jan 27	70LTS453	301650
Austria	Switzerland	15 Mar 27	87LTS351	301981
Czechoslovakia	Greece	07 Apr 27	88LTS187	301997
UK Great Britain	USA (United States)	19 May 27	64LTS101	301503
Hungary	Italy	21 May 27	74LTS33	301729
Hungary	Italy	21 May 27	74LTS19	301727
Hungary	Italy	21 May 27	74LTS27	301728
Austria	Belgium	10 Oct 27	91LTS271	302067
Czechoslovakia	Spain	26 Oct 27	121LTS311	302793
Hungary	Italy	10 Dec 27	78LTS403	301798
Hungary	Serb/Croat/Slovene	22 Feb 28	87LTS361	301982
Hungary	Serb/Croat/Slovene	22 Feb 28	88LTS111	301991
Hungary	Serb/Croat/Slovene	22 Feb 28	110LTS411	302572
Germany	UK Great Britain	20 Mar 28	90LTS287	302044
Greece	USA (United States)	25 Apr 28	91LTS231	302064
Czechoslovakia	Hungary	26 May 28	101LTS265	302328
Austria	Hungary	25 Jun 28	100LTS85	302296
Germany	UK Great Britain	26 Jul 28	85LTS135	301928

PARTY ONE	PARTY TWO	DATE	CITATION	NUMBER
Claims and settlements (Cont.)				
France	UK Great Britain	23 Sep 28	87LTS29	301961
Czechoslovakia	Serb/Croat/Slovene	29 Sep 28	96LTS421	302215
Multilateral		30 Oct 28	130LTS405	302999
Czechoslovakia	Serb/Croat/Slovene	07 Nov 28	95LTS101	302169
Germany	Romania	10 Nov 28	91LTS101	302058
Germany	Poland	14 Dec 28	113LTS367	302648
Bulgaria	Hungary	05 Jan 29	118LTS279	302730
Austria	Czechoslovakia	03 Feb 29	101LTS285	302329
France	UK Great Britain	15 May 29	134LTS263	303097
Spain	USA (United States)	20 Jun 29	120LTS401	302776
Multilateral		28 Jun 29	103LTS249	302371
Multilateral		28 Jun 29	103LTS71	302370
Multilateral		28 Jun 29	103LTS321	302372
Belgium	Germany	13 Jul 29	104LTS201	302390
Belgium	Germany	13 Jul 29	104LTS211	302391
Germany	Poland	31 Oct 29	124LTS345	302838
Belgium	Germany	07 Nov 29	121LTS327	302795
China	UK Great Britain	09 Nov 29	99LTS453	302290
Austria	Greece	27 Dec 29	100LTS423	302311
Other Unilat Decla	Greece	14 Jan 30	108LTS349	302518
Belgium	Germany	16 Jan 30	104LTS223	302392
Austria	Belgium	18 Jan 30	104LTS231	302393
Multilateral		20 Jan 30	104LTS433	302397
Multilateral		20 Jan 30	104LTS441	302398
Multilateral		20 Jan 30	104LTS413	302395
France	Yugoslavia	20 Jan 30	104LTS177	302387
Austria	Germany	05 Feb 30	119LTS201	302746
Hungary	Yugoslavia	27 Apr 30	113LTS153	302642
Hungary	Yugoslavia	27 Aug 30	113LTS163	302643
Multilateral		31 Oct 30	120LTS9	302760
Czechoslovakia	Romania	05 Dec 30	167LTS221	303868
Sweden	USA (United States)	17 Dec 30	125LTS233	302856
Czechoslovakia	Romania	22 Dec 30	167LTS263	303872
Hungary	Yugoslavia	30 Jan 31	120LTS105	302761
Belgium	Luxembourg	09 Mar 31	137LTS267	303161
Czechoslovakia	Germany	21 Mar 31	143LTS177	303308
Belgium	France	16 May 31	141LTS333	303274
Belgium	Italy	11 Jul 31	136LTS9	303120
Romania	Yugoslavia	14 Dec 31	135LTS99	303106
Finland	Poland	19 Dec 31	131LTS193	303010
Estonia	UK Great Britain	22 Dec 31	131LTS323	303022
France	Latvia	08 Mar 32	128LTS43	302936
Austria	Yugoslavia	20 Apr 32	132LTS217	303040
Hungary	UK Great Britain	10 Jun 32	132LTS53	303031
Netherlands	UK Great Britain	13 Aug 32	134LTS317	303100
Austria	Norway	03 Sep 32	137LTS403	303170
Argentina	Lithuania	20 Oct 32	154LTS113	303542
Hungary	Italy	12 Nov 32	142LTS87	303279
Hungary	Italy	12 Nov 32	142LTS101	303281
Hungary	Italy	12 Nov 32	142LTS109	303282
Austria	Hungary	27 Nov 32	162LTS395	303753
Panama	USA (United States)	17 Dec 32	138LTS119	303183
Romania	Yugoslavia	30 Jan 33	146LTS99	303362
Chile	Sweden	08 Mar 33	142LTS147	303286
Romania	Yugoslavia	10 Mar 33	146LTS245	303374
Romania	Yugoslavia	11 Mar 33	146LTS285	303379
Romania	Yugoslavia	11 Mar 33	146LTS277	303378
Hungary	Yugoslavia	15 May 33	144LTS321	303335
Bel-Lux Econ Union	Hungary	24 May 33	140LTS169	303234
Bel-Lux Econ Union	Bulgaria	21 Jun 33	140LTS375	303247
Multilateral		23 Nov 33	192LTS389	304484
Turkey	Yugoslavia	28 Nov 33	161LTS245	303716
Austria	Hungary	12 Jan 34	162LTS419	303754
Argentina	Bel-Lux Econ Union	16 Jan 34	145LTS145	303352
Mexico	USA (United States)	24 Apr 34	156LTS81	303593

PARTY ONE	PARTY TWO	DATE	CITATION	NUMBER
Claims and settlements (Cont.)				
Sweden	Turkey	19 Jun 34	150LTS413	303474
Czechoslovakia	Romania	20 Jun 34	168LTS241	303901
Norway	UK Great Britain	05 Nov 34	154LTS231	303549
Bulgaria	Romania	26 Jul 35	198LTS9	304621
Bulgaria	Netherlands	23 Sep 35	166LTS51	303829
Finland	Romania	03 Dec 35	165LTS287	303815
Germany	Sweden	31 Jan 36	168LTS19	303884
Czechoslovakia	Yugoslavia	24 Feb 36	187LTS185	304338
Sweden	Turkey	27 Feb 36	167LTS83	303859
Albania	Italy	19 Mar 36	173LTS51	304002
Czechoslovakia	Finland	21 Mar 36	179LTS295	304156
Norway	Turkey	08 Jun 36	170LTS235	303939
Hungary	Sweden	17 Jun 36	184LTS11	304239
Italy	Norway	25 Aug 36	171LTS377	303974
Netherlands	Romania	28 Aug 36	182LTS363	304222
France	Sweden	04 Dec 36	184LTS35	304241
Norway	Romania	10 Dec 36	174LTS59	304037
Sweden	Turkey	14 Dec 36	174LTS51	304036
Hungary	Yugoslavia	17 Dec 36	196LTS137	304576
Germany	Netherlands	23 Dec 36	179LTS359	304163
Estonia	Turkey	06 Jun 37	179LTS159	304143
Bel-Lux Econ Union	Italy	30 Jun 37	197LTS23	304601
Bel-Lux Econ Union	Italy	30 Jun 37	182LTS106	304203
Bel-Lux Econ Union	Romania	24 Aug 37	193LTS189	304496
Estonia	Germany	24 Oct 37	184LTS81	304244
Germany	Latvia	31 Oct 37	189LTS139	304382
Sweden	Turkey	31 Dec 37	184LTS409	304261
Netherlands	USA (United States)	18 Feb 38	192LTS49	304460
Finland	Lithuania	12 Apr 38	194LTS9	304501
Nicaragua	USA (United States)	14 Apr 38	192LTS275	304477
Germany	Sweden	28 Oct 38	196LTS91	304571
Multilateral		02 Jan 39	196LTS235	304587
Sweden	Turkey	20 Jan 39	194LTS113	304514
Sweden	Turkey	20 Jan 39	194LTS107	304513
Burma	France	26 Jan 39	201LTS9	304701
Greece	Sweden	01 May 39	196LTS205	304582
Germany	Netherlands	17 May 39	199LTS239	304678
Barbados	USA (United States)	13 Sep 39	199LTS375	304685
Germany	Latvia	30 Oct 39	200LTS213	304693
Sweden	Turkey	29 Feb 40	200LTS273	304696
Sweden	Turkey	29 Feb 40	200LTS267	304695
United Arab Rep	UK Great Britain	17 Apr 40	201LTS253	304718
Austria	Greece	12 Jun 56*	2LTS157	300061
Lump sum settlements				
Estonia	USSR (Soviet Union)	02 Feb 20	11LTS29	300289
Poland	USSR (Soviet Union)	18 Mar 21	6LTS51	300149
UK Great Britain	Venezuela	22 Mar 21	5LTS169	300126
Multilateral		18 Dec 23	28LTS541	300729
Multilateral		28 Mar 24	31LTS46	300780
Hungary	Romania	16 Apr 24	45LTS355	301109
Austria	Czechoslovakia	15 Jun 24	94LTS131	302141
Greece	UK Great Britain	09 Apr 27	67LTS217	301549
Germany	Italy	20 Jan 30	106LTS109	302439
Bulgaria	Yugoslavia	14 Feb 30	101LTS135	302323
Czechoslovakia	Romania	22 Dec 30	167LTS263	303872
Multilateral		23 Nov 33	192LTS327	304483
UK Great Britain	Uruguay	26 Jun 35	176LTS153	304058
Albania	Italy	19 Mar 36	173LTS51	304002
Nicaragua	USA (United States)	14 Apr 38	192LTS275	304477
Sweden	Turkey	20 Jan 39	194LTS113	304514
Debts				
Austria	Poland	09 Jan 20	7LTS163	300185
Austria	France	03 Aug 20	5LTS355	300141
Austria	Germany	01 Sep 20	2LTS132	300057

PARTY ONE	PARTY TWO	DATE	CITATION	NUMBER
Debts (Cont.)				
Germany	Switzerland	06 Dec 20	2LTS343	300088
France	Hungary	31 Jan 21	15LTS221	300396
Czechoslovakia	Italy	23 Mar 21	32LTS261	300817
Germany	Switzerland	29 Oct 21	13LTS193	300351
Austria	Czechoslovakia	17 Dec 21	22LTS401	300570
Czechoslovakia	Germany	18 Mar 22	17LTS453	300448
Belgium	Poland	30 Dec 22	21LTS201	300543
Germany	Switzerland	25 Mar 23	18LTS273	300470
Czechoslovakia	Hungary	13 Jul 23	36LTS13	300901
Germany	Hungary	26 Nov 23	45LTS309	301105
Other Unilat Decla	Hungary	14 Mar 24	25LTS427	300634
Hungary	Italy	27 Mar 24	45LTS229	301101
Hungary	Italy	27 Mar 24	45LTS83	301100
Hungary	Romania	16 Apr 24	46LTS27	301112
Hungary	Romania	16 Apr 24	45LTS403	301110
Austria	Italy	18 Jun 24	84LTS381	301914
Austria	Romania	26 Jul 24	85LTS223	301933
Czechoslovakia	Poland	23 Apr 25	44LTS271	301089
Austria	Czechoslovakia	14 May 25	50LTS39	301198
Estonia	USA (United States)	28 Oct 25	62LTS63	301455
France	USA (United States)	29 Apr 26	100LTS27	302292
Poland	USA (United States)	14 Nov 26	58LTS97	301368
Greece	UK Great Britain	09 Apr 27	67LTS217	301549
Serb/Croat/Slovene		12 Aug 27	101LTS485	302347
Hungary	Serb/Croat/Slovene	22 Feb 28	88LTS111	301991
Bulgaria		08 Sep 28	74LTS167	301738
Czechoslovakia	Serb/Croat/Slovene	29 Sep 28	96LTS421	302215
Czechoslovakia	Serb/Croat/Slovene	07 Nov 28	95LTS101	302169
Germany	Poland	14 Dec 28	113LTS367	302648
Multilateral		28 Jun 29	103LTS377	302373
Germany	UK Great Britain	28 Dec 29	102LTS49	302352
France	Yugoslavia	20 Jan 30	104LTS177	302387
Hungary	Yugoslavia	27 Apr 30	113LTS153	302642
Czechoslovakia	Romania	22 Dec 30	167LTS243	303870
Hungary	Italy	12 Nov 32	142LTS109	303282
Hungary	Italy	12 Nov 32	142LTS115	303283
Romania	Yugoslavia	10 Mar 33	146LTS245	303374
Multilateral		20 Mar 34	176LTS9	304053
Chile	Netherlands	01 Jun 34	154LTS325	303559
Multilateral		19 Nov 34	164LTS243	303797
Germany	Sweden	22 Dec 34	156LTS151	303598
Estonia	Latvia	06 Oct 36	172LTS221	303994
France	Sweden	24 Dec 36	181LTS315	304198
Estonia	Germany	24 Oct 37	184LTS81	304244
Germany	Greece	11 May 38	197LTS75	304608
Debt settlement				
Greece	Spain	06 Mar 19	3LTS81	300092
France	UK Great Britain	10 Jan 20	1LTS249	300017
France	Germany	25 Mar 20	1LTS347	300029
France	Germany	30 Jun 20	8LTS79	300208
Austria	France	03 Aug 20	5LTS355	300141
Austria	Belgium	04 Oct 20	5LTS371	300142
France	Hungary	31 Jan 21	15LTS221	300396
Persia	USSR (Soviet Union)	26 Feb 21	9LTS383	300268
Poland	USSR (Soviet Union)	18 Mar 21	6LTS51	300149
Czechoslovakia	Italy	23 Mar 21	32LTS261	300817
Belgium	UK Great Britain	20 Jul 21	8LTS301	300228
Estonia	Finland	29 Oct 21	13LTS167	300350
Hungary	UK Great Britain	20 Dec 21	10LTS437	300283
Greece	UK Great Britain	03 Feb 22	9LTS191	300252
Austria	UK Great Britain	02 Oct 22	12LTS413	300337
Germany	Switzerland	25 Mar 23	18LTS273	300470
Multilateral		29 Mar 23	23LTS256	300593
Germany	UK Great Britain	05 Apr 23	17LTS173	300435

PARTY ONE	PARTY TWO	DATE	CITATION	NUMBER
Debt settlement (Cont.)				
Czechoslovakia	Hungary	13 Jul 23	35LTS271	300900
Multilateral		24 Jul 23	28LTS11	300701
Germany	Hungary	26 Nov 23	45LTS309	301105
Multilateral		30 Nov 23	102LTS153	302360
Hungary	Romania	27 Dec 23	21LTS263	300546
Germany	UK Great Britain	05 Jan 24	36LTS365	300935
Iraq	UK Great Britain	25 Mar 24	35LTS145	300894
Hungary	Italy	27 Mar 24	45LTS241	301102
Austria	Serb/Croat/Slovene	29 Mar 24	114LTS421	302670
Hungary	Romania	16 Apr 24	45LTS403	301110
Germany	Haiti	15 Oct 24	52LTS27	301247
Allied Powers	Germany	28 Oct 24	41LTS461	301025
Austria	Hungary	08 Nov 24	45LTS21	301097
Czechoslovakia	Poland	23 Apr 25	44LTS285	301090
Czechoslovakia	Poland	23 Apr 25	48LTS287	301170
Great Britain	Latvia	13 Aug 25	56LTS177	301329
Estonia	USA (United States)	28 Oct 25	62LTS63	301455
Hungary	Italy	30 Mar 26	54LTS85	301276
Poland	USA (United States)	14 Nov 26	58LTS97	301368
Czechoslovakia	Switzerland	21 Dec 26	86LTS443	301956
Portugal	UK Great Britain	31 Dec 26	61LTS115	301429
Great Britain	Serb/Croat/Slovene	09 Aug 27	69LTS255	301607
Czechoslovakia	Spain	26 Oct 27	121LTS311	302793
Hungary	Serb/Croat/Slovene	22 Feb 28	87LTS361	301982
Hungary	Serb/Croat/Slovene	22 Feb 28	100LTS345	302306
Czechoslovakia	Hungary	26 May 28	101LTS265	302328
Austria	Serb/Croat/Slovene	06 Jun 28	129LTS11	302950
Czechoslovakia	Serb/Croat/Slovene	07 Nov 28	95LTS101	302169
Bolivia	UK Great Britain	18 Jan 29	95LTS9	302161
Netherlands	UK Great Britain	22 Mar 29	90LTS421	302052
Poland	Romania	30 Oct 29	121LTS167	302787
Other Unilat Decla	Greece	14 Jan 30	108LTS349	302518
Canada	Germany	17 Jan 30	109LTS473	302550
Poland	UK Great Britain	20 Jan 30	126LTS159	302878
Austria	Poland	20 Jan 30	133LTS223	303067
Germany	Italy	20 Jan 30	106LTS109	302439
France	Poland	20 Jan 30	126LTS117	302876
France	Yugoslavia	20 Jan 30	104LTS171	302386
Italy	Poland	20 Jan 30	127LTS41	302904
Multilateral		20 Jan 30	112LTS361	302622
China	UK Great Britain	22 Sep 30	115LTS493	302697
Czechoslovakia	Romania	05 Dec 30	167LTS221	303868
Denmark	India	16 Dec 30	114LTS73	302656
Hungary	Yugoslavia	30 Jan 31	120LTS105	302761
Germany	Switzerland	15 Jul 31	144LTS389	303341
Romania	Yugoslavia	14 Dec 31	135LTS99	303106
Romania	Yugoslavia	14 Dec 31	135LTS31	303103
Romania	Yugoslavia	14 Dec 31	135LTS89	303105
Estonia	France	26 Mar 32	128LTS51	302937
Bel-Lux Econ Union	Hungary	26 Mar 32	136LTS405	303139
Austria	Yugoslavia	20 Apr 32	132LTS217	303040
South Africa	Southern Rhodesia	21 Apr 32	142LTS197	303292
Bel-Lux Econ Union	Yugoslavia	07 Aug 32	139LTS223	303212
Romania	Yugoslavia	30 Jan 33	146LTS129	303365
Estonia	Finland	16 May 33	141LTS19	303257
Bel-Lux Econ Union	Hungary	24 May 33	140LTS169	303234
Bel-Lux Econ Union	Bulgaria	21 Jun 33	140LTS375	303247
Multilateral		07 Nov 33	155LTS115	303574
Argentina	Netherlands	31 Jan 34	148LTS361	303422
Multilateral		20 Mar 34	174LTS171	304048
Bel-Lux Econ Union	Turkey	31 May 34	150LTS277	303461
Germany	USSR (Soviet Union)	07 Mar 35	169LTS7	303911
Turkey	UK Great Britain	04 Jun 35	167LTS91	303860
Bel-Lux Econ Union	Estonia	19 Jun 35	170LTS243	303940
Bulgaria	USSR (Soviet Union)	10 Jul 35	168LTS275	303905

PARTY ONE	PARTY TWO	DATE	CITATION	NUMBER
Debt settlement (Cont.)				
France	UK Great Britain	16 Jul 35	168LTS179	303898
Greece	Sweden	11 Jan 36	165LTS299	303816
China	Malaya	12 Feb 36	170LTS19	303927
Czechoslovakia	Yugoslavia	24 Feb 36	187LTS185	304338
Bel-Lux Econ Union	Spain	04 Apr 36	168LTS339	303909
Romania	UK Great Britain	02 May 36	184LTS145	304247
Norway	Turkey	08 Jun 36	170LTS227	303938
Hungary	Sweden	17 Jun 36	184LTS25	304240
Bulgaria	France	06 Jul 36	171LTS269	303963
Italy	Norway	25 Aug 36	171LTS377	303974
Finland	Italy	28 Sep 36	172LTS155	303986
Italy	UK Great Britain	06 Nov 36	177LTS183	304090
Italy	Sweden	01 Dec 36	173LTS279	304019
Italy	Sweden	01 Dec 36	173LTS269	304018
Hungary	Yugoslavia	17 Dec 36	196LTS143	304577
Greece	Sweden	31 Dec 36	174LTS87	304039
Italy	Netherlands	01 Jan 37	178LTS415	304124
Italy	Latvia	05 Feb 37	178LTS25	304103
Netherlands	Turkey	17 Feb 37	182LTS221	304213
Germany	Norway	27 Feb 37	178LTS427	304125
Brazil	Netherlands	15 Mar 37	179LTS405	304167
Italy	Norway	31 Mar 37	177LTS367	304099
Italy	Norway	31 Mar 37	177LTS355	304098
Chile	Netherlands	05 May 37	182LTS385	304223
Bel-Lux Econ Union	Italy	30 Jun 37	182LTS106	304203
Bel-Lux Econ Union	Romania	24 Aug 37	193LTS189	304496
Hungary	Lithuania	12 Nov 37	183LTS197	304236
Hungary	Latvia	16 Nov 37	183LTS205	304237
Bel-Lux Econ Union	Yugoslavia	26 Nov 37	196LTS19	304567
Germany	Netherlands	18 Dec 37	190LTS29	304403
Greece	Sweden	01 Feb 38	185LTS217	304285
Greece	Norway	28 Feb 38	186LTS165	304309
Romania	UK Great Britain	02 Sep 38	191LTS313	304453
Netherlands	Romania	10 Oct 38	195LTS9	304532
Spain	UK Great Britain	18 Mar 40	203LTS157	304759
Finland	Latvia	11 Apr 40	201LTS389	304727
Romania	UK Great Britain	06 Jun 40	203LTS197	304761
Assessment procedures				
Hungary	Sweden	08 Nov 28	89LTS283	302023
Multilateral		31 Oct 30	120LTS9	302760
Hungary	Italy	12 Nov 32	142LTS87	303279
Greece	UK Great Britain	21 Jan 36	168LTS171	303897
Estonia	Latvia	06 Oct 36	172LTS221	303994
Private investment guarantee				
Multilateral		29 Mar 23	23LTS256	300593
Bel-Lux Econ Union	Guatemala	07 Nov 24	69LTS17	301596
Finland	Turkey	02 Jun 26	70LTS329	301644
Albania	Greece	13 Oct 26	83LTS325	301899
Greece	Norway	29 Jun 27	82LTS187	301869
Italy	Lithuania	17 Sep 27	73LTS9	301701
Sweden	Turkey	04 Feb 28	88LTS155	301994
Austria	France	16 May 28	88LTS21	301986
Germany	Lithuania	30 Oct 28	89LTS127	302010
Austria	Estonia	11 Dec 28	92LTS229	302091
Greece	Hungary	03 Jun 30	122LTS37	302798
Netherlands	South Africa	29 Jun 32	133LTS33	303054
Multilateral		15 Jul 32	135LTS285	303118
Finland	Germany	24 Mar 34	149LTS343	303442
Czechoslovakia	USSR (Soviet Union)	25 Mar 35	161LTS309	303719
Liens				
France	Hungary	31 Jan 21	15LTS221	300396
Multilateral		29 Mar 23	23LTS256	300593
Other Unilat Decla	Hungary	14 Mar 24	25LTS427	300634
Multilateral		10 Apr 26	120LTS187	302765

PARTY ONE	PARTY TWO	DATE	CITATION	NUMBER
Assets transfer				
Germany	Greece	01 Dec 10	2LTS123	300055
Greece	Spain	06 Mar 19	3LTS81	300092
Romania	UK Great Britain	22 Jan 20	1LTS257	300018
France	Germany	25 Mar 20	1LTS347	300029
Austria	Czechoslovakia	02 Aug 20	32LTS365	300826
Austria	France	03 Aug 20	5LTS355	300141
Austria	Belgium	04 Oct 20	5LTS371	300142
France	Hungary	31 Jan 21	15LTS221	300396
Austria	Czechoslovakia	17 Dec 21	22LTS401	300570
Czechoslovakia	Germany	31 Dec 21	17LTS401	300447
France	Saar	05 Jul 22	27LTS265	300689
Germany	Poland	25 Aug 22	22LTS63	300554
China	Japan	05 Dec 22	22LTS293	300560
Multilateral		29 Mar 23	23LTS256	300593
France	India	12 May 23	25LTS381	300627
Czechoslovakia	Hungary	13 Jul 23	35LTS253	300899
Austria	Italy	16 Jul 23	27LTS383	300699
Multilateral		24 Jul 23	28LTS203	300707
Germany	Hungary	26 Nov 23	45LTS309	301105
Czechoslovakia	Hungary	08 Mar 24	36LTS61	300904
Hungary	Italy	27 Mar 24	45LTS241	301102
Austria	Serb/Croat/Slovene	29 Mar 24	114LTS421	302670
Hungary	Romania	16 Apr 24	46LTS27	301112
Hungary	Romania	16 Apr 24	46LTS7	301111
Hungary	Romania	16 Apr 24	45LTS403	301110
Austria	Czechoslovakia	12 Jul 24	50LTS111	301199
Austria	Romania	26 Jul 24	85LTS243	301934
Austria	Hungary	08 Nov 24	45LTS21	301097
Germany	USA (United States)	21 May 25	52LTS133	301254
Estonia	USA (United States)	28 Oct 25	62LTS63	301455
Norway	USSR (Soviet Union)	15 Dec 25	47LTS9	301127
Czechoslovakia	Italy	04 May 26	61LTS257	301438
France	India	19 Jun 26	57LTS35	301350
Denmark	Netherlands	23 Oct 26	72LTS13	301686
Multilateral		24 Jan 27	70LTS453	301650
Japan	USSR (Soviet Union)	23 Jan 28	80LTS341	301839
Multilateral		20 Feb 28	86LTS111	301950
Austria	Poland	20 Jan 30	133LTS223	303067
Multilateral		31 Oct 30	120LTS9	302760
Czechoslovakia	Romania	05 Dec 30	167LTS205	303867
Romania	Yugoslavia	14 Dec 31	135LTS99	303106
Germany	Sweden	31 Jan 36	168LTS13	303883
Commodity trade				
Costa Rica	UK Great Britain	25 Apr 23	20LTS19	300502
Germany	USA (United States)	19 May 24	41LTS271	301020
Denmark	Germany	20 Mar 26	57LTS131	301359
India	Indochina	20 Mar 26	57LTS19	301348
Italy	UK Great Britain	24 Jun 26	57LTS71	301353
France	Norway	12 Apr 27	178LTS199	304114
British Empire	Hedjaz	20 May 27	71LTS131	301658
Multilateral		11 Jul 28	95LTS373	302185
Multilateral		11 Jul 28	95LTS357	302184
Peru	UK Great Britain	31 Dec 28	100LTS431	302312
Germany	Hedjaz	26 Apr 29	115LTS265	302690
Irish Free State	Portugal	29 Oct 29	131LTS145	303007
Czechoslovakia	Germany	20 Apr 31	141LTS307	303271
Hungary	Poland	04 Nov 31	134LTS199	303092
Turkey	Yugoslavia	14 Apr 32	144LTS291	303332
Czechoslovakia	Denmark	04 Jul 32	143LTS251	303312
France	Sweden	13 Mar 33	142LTS131	303285
Multilateral		07 May 34	171LTS203	303961
Estonia	Sweden	07 Dec 34	154LTS319	303558
Poland	Spain	14 Dec 34	168LTS315	303908

PARTY ONE	PARTY TWO	DATE	CITATION	NUMBER
Commodity trade (Cont.)				
France	India	04 Jan 36	170LTS97	303930
Greece	Sweden	11 Jan 36	165LTS299	303816
Romania	Yugoslavia	13 May 37	197LTS161	304612
Norway	Poland	18 Jun 37	190LTS187	304416
Poland	UK Great Britain	10 Sep 37	184LTS289	304253
Czechoslovakia	USA (United States)	18 May 38	199LTS305	304680
France	India	22 Mar 39	197LTS273	304619
Multilateral		09 Sep 42	205LTS137	304831
Delivery guarantees				
Czechoslovakia	Germany	29 Jun 20	17LTS69	300430
Germany	Switzerland	06 Dec 20	2LTS343	300088
China	Japan	08 Dec 22	20LTS205	300519
Multilateral		11 Jul 28	95LTS373	302185
Multilateral		11 Jul 28	95LTS357	302184
Delivery schedules				
Denmark	Finland	27 Jul 20	19LTS71	300484
Germany	Switzerland	06 Dec 20	2LTS343	300088
Finland	USSR (Soviet Union)	14 Dec 21	16LTS221	300414
Quotas				
France	Greece	21 Feb 24	43LTS481	301077
Austria	France	11 Aug 24	44LTS7	301079
Czechoslovakia	France	18 Aug 24	44LTS21	301080
Finland	Italy	22 Oct 24	32LTS149	300814
France	Poland	09 Dec 24	44LTS127	301081
France	Portugal	04 Mar 25	44LTS197	301083
Czechoslovakia	Greece	08 Apr 25	38LTS291	300984
Finland	Spain	16 Jul 25	47LTS271	301135
France	Italy	29 May 26	62LTS425	301474
France	Germany	31 Mar 27	66LTS7	301524
Multilateral		26 Jun 30	133LTS9	303052
Multilateral		28 Aug 30	133LTS21	303053
Finland	Germany	28 Aug 30	111LTS327	302597
France	Greece	23 May 31	125LTS415	302867
France	Yugoslavia	07 Nov 31	144LTS281	303331
Turkey	Yugoslavia	14 Apr 32	144LTS291	303332
France	India	28 Dec 32	140LTS36	303226
Austria	France	29 Dec 32	147LTS101	303394
France	Hungary	03 Mar 33	140LTS177	303235
Denmark	UK Great Britain	24 Apr 33	139LTS127	303208
Argentina	UK Great Britain	01 May 33	143LTS67	303305
Norway	UK Great Britain	15 May 33	145LTS187	303355
Sweden	UK Great Britain	15 May 33	140LTS317	303245
Germany	UK Great Britain	07 Jul 33	145LTS237	303356
Finland	UK Great Britain	29 Sep 33	149LTS167	303438
Bulgaria	Turkey	21 Dec 33	148LTS9	303401
Multilateral		07 May 34	171LTS203	303961
France	Sweden	22 Mar 35	158LTS287	303639
Irish Free State	Spain	04 Apr 35	166LTS391	303855
Sweden	USA (United States)	25 May 35	161LTS109	303707
Czechoslovakia	Germany	26 Jun 35	173LTS385	304029
Netherlands	UK Great Britain	18 Dec 35	165LTS255	303812
France	Spain	30 Dec 35	172LTS217	303993
Norway	Spain	13 Jun 36	170LTS199	303935
El Salvador	Sweden	23 Jun 36	171LTS291	303966
Hungary	Italy	04 Jul 36	181LTS331	304199
Guatemala	Sweden	11 Jul 36	171LTS299	303967
Australia	Bel-Lux Econ Union	03 Oct 36	177LTS271	304094
Chile	Sweden	30 Oct 36	188LTS283	304364
Netherlands	New Zealand	14 Jan 38	185LTS329	304297
Estonia	Sweden	30 Jan 39	194LTS131	304517
France	India	22 Mar 39	197LTS273	304619
Multilateral		09 Sep 42	205LTS137	304831

PARTY ONE	PARTY TWO	DATE	CITATION	NUMBER
Smuggling				
Italy	Serb/Croat/Slovene	23 Oct 22	18LTS405	300478
Germany	USA (United States)	19 May 24	41LTS271	301020
Canada	USA (United States)	06 Jun 24	43LTS225	301057
France	USA (United States)	30 Jun 24	61LTS415	301451
China	Germany	31 Dec 24	42LTS7	301027
France	Saar	15 Jan 25	44LTS181	301082
Multilateral		19 Aug 25	42LTS73	301033
France	Hungary	13 Oct 25	48LTS9	301150
Belgium	USA (United States)	09 Dec 25	72LTS171	301690
Spain	USA (United States)	10 Feb 26	67LTS131	301543
Cuba	USA (United States)	04 Mar 26	61LTS369	301447
Cuba	USA (United States)	11 Mar 26	61LTS383	301448
Finland	Hungary	20 Apr 26	48LTS119	301154
Albania	Greece	13 Oct 26	83LTS325	301899
Serb/Croat/Slovene	UK Great Britain	12 May 27	80LTS165	301825
Belgium	Portugal	20 Jul 27	71LTS431	301681
Poland	USA (United States)	19 Jun 30	108LTS223	302515
Finland	Hungary	07 Nov 33	142LTS179	303290
Finland	Sweden	29 Dec 33	149LTS23	303429
Multilateral		07 May 34	171LTS203	303961
France	Spain	30 Dec 35	172LTS217	303993
Switzerland	USA (United States)	09 Jan 36	171LTS231	303962
France	USA (United States)	12 Dec 36	176LTS403	304076
Greece	Turkey	15 Jan 37	202LTS107	304739
France	Siam	09 Dec 37	201LTS145	304709
Portugal	Siam	02 Jul 38	200LTS149	304688
France	India	22 Mar 39	197LTS273	304619
Most favored nation clause				
Canada	France	19 Sep 07	1LTS95	300012
Chile	Netherlands	04 Nov 13	84LTS79	301904
Multilateral		09 Dec 19	5LTS335	300140
Germany	Hungary	01 Jun 20	7LTS207	300187
Czechoslovakia	Germany	29 Jun 20	17LTS69	300430
Estonia	UK Great Britain	20 Jul 20	1LTS295	300025
Austria	Germany	01 Sep 20	4LTS201	300107
Finland	USSR (Soviet Union)	14 Oct 20	3LTS5	300091
Czechoslovakia	Serb/Croat/Slovene	18 Oct 20	17LTS19	300424
Japan	Paraguay	30 Nov 20	6LTS367	300169
Canada	France	29 Jan 21	8LTS105	300212
Bulgaria	Germany	19 Feb 21	6LTS227	300157
Czechoslovakia	Italy	23 Mar 21	32LTS183	300815
Bulgaria	Sweden	14 Apr 21	5LTS240	300131
Czechoslovakia	Romania	23 Apr 21	15LTS235	300397
Austria	Czechoslovakia	04 May 21	15LTS13	300388
Spain	Sweden	19 Jun 21	5LTS387	300143
Bulgaria	Hungary	03 Sep 21	7LTS229	300188
Bulgaria	Sweden	30 Sep 21	7LTS137	300182
Austria	Hungary	08 Oct 21	16LTS19	300402
Estonia	Finland	29 Oct 21	13LTS59	300348
Estonia	France	07 Jan 22	62LTS9	301452
Multilateral		06 Feb 22	38LTS267	300981
Austria	Hungary	08 Feb 22	55LTS367	301320
Bulgaria	Netherlands	09 Mar 22	9LTS265	300260
Finland	Germany	21 Apr 22	19LTS87	300487
Lithuania	UK Great Britain	06 May 22	13LTS25	300343
Italy	Poland	12 May 22	59LTS293	301399
Poland	Switzerland	26 Jun 22	12LTS305	300322
Bulgaria	Denmark	11 Jul 22	12LTS225	300314
Austria	Poland	25 Sep 22	59LTS307	301400
Czechoslovakia	Latvia	07 Oct 22	20LTS379	300528
Estonia	Hungary	19 Oct 22	30LTS347	300774
Spain	UK Great Britain	31 Oct 22	28LTS339	300719
Denmark	Sweden	07 Nov 22	14LTS95	300370

PARTY ONE	PARTY TWO	DATE	CITATION	NUMBER
Most favored nation clause (Cont.)				
Canada	France	15 Dec 22	21LTS38	300532
Romania	Sweden	18 Dec 22	14LTS353	300383
Netherlands	Romania	19 Dec 22	14LTS191	300373
Multilateral		30 Dec 22	21LTS183	300542
Canada	Italy	04 Jan 23	25LTS375	300626
Italy	Switzerland	27 Jan 23	25LTS21	300603
Norway	Portugal	11 Apr 23	16LTS379	300418
Denmark	Romania	08 May 23	17LTS31	300425
Romania	UK Great Britain	24 May 23	18LTS301	300471
Norway	Sweden	26 May 23	18LTS155	300462
Finland	Sweden	26 May 23	18LTS57	300453
Germany	Lithuania	01 Jun 23	51LTS387	301244
Latvia	UK Great Britain	22 Jun 23	20LTS395	300529
Estonia	Germany	27 Jun 23	41LTS161	301013
Estonia	Sweden	07 Jul 23	20LTS189	300517
Czechoslovakia	UK Great Britain	14 Jul 23	29LTS377	300748
Iceland	Lithuania	18 Jul 23	20LTS329	300523
Denmark	Lithuania	18 Jul 23	20LTS197	300518
Poland	Turkey	23 Jul 23	49LTS329	301189
Denmark	Finland	03 Aug 23	21LTS269	300547
Netherlands	Portugal	22 Aug 23	20LTS139	300513
Estonia	Iceland	07 Sep 23	23LTS131	300584
Denmark	Estonia	07 Sep 23	23LTS73	300577
Czechoslovakia	Norway	02 Oct 23	20LTS355	300526
Austria	Japan	02 Oct 23	22LTS349	300563
Norway	Spain	07 Oct 23	59LTS47	301389
Finland	Netherlands	01 Nov 23	23LTS33	300574
Estonia	Latvia	01 Nov 23	25LTS354	300624
Finland	Poland	10 Nov 23	29LTS229	300744
Japan	Serb/Croat/Slovene	16 Nov 23	42LTS99	301035
Hungary	Latvia	19 Nov 23	37LTS341	300959
Poland	UK Great Britain	26 Nov 23	28LTS428	300722
Multilateral		14 Dec 23	29LTS37	300732
Bulgaria	Sweden	31 Dec 23	22LTS323	300561
Latvia	Poland	03 Jan 24	42LTS451	301043
Estonia	Poland	11 Jan 24	47LTS129	301132
Austria	Turkey	28 Jan 24	32LTS313	300823
Czechoslovakia	Denmark	31 Jan 24	23LTS139	300585
Lithuania	Sweden	17 Feb 24	23LTS153	300587
Netherlands	Portugal	27 Feb 24	27LTS105	300672
Germany	Siam	28 Feb 24	32LTS399	300828
Japan	Siam	09 Mar 24	31LTS187	300795
Multilateral		12 Mar 24	24LTS17	300595
Sweden	USSR (Soviet Union)	15 Mar 24	25LTS251	300613
Sweden	Switzerland	20 Mar 24	25LTS243	300612
Denmark	Poland	22 Mar 24	31LTS13	300778
Iceland	Poland	22 Mar 24	31LTS35	300779
Iraq	UK Great Britain	25 Mar 24	35LTS145	300894
Denmark	Latvia	03 Apr 24	33LTS393	300860
Poland	Serb/Croat/Slovene	05 Apr 24	49LTS265	301185
Hungary	Romania	16 Apr 24	46LTS95	301114
Czechoslovakia	Iceland	08 May 24	46LTS419	301125
Multilateral		22 May 24	35LTS175	300895
Finland	Iceland	28 May 24	27LTS117	300676
Netherlands	Poland	30 May 24	34LTS9	300865
Finland	Japan	07 Jun 24	58LTS379	301383
Lithuania	Netherlands	10 Jun 24	34LTS373	300885
Latvia	Netherlands	02 Jul 24	37LTS121	300951
Bel-Lux Econ Union	Canada	03 Jul 24	32LTS35	300803
Canada	Netherlands	11 Jul 24	39LTS45	300995
Estonia	Netherlands	22 Jul 24	48LTS199	301162
Germany	Spain	25 Jul 24	41LTS363	301023
Austria	Latvia	09 Aug 24	65LTS7	301516
Czechoslovakia	France	18 Aug 24	44LTS21	301080
Finland	Latvia	23 Aug 24	37LTS383	300962

PARTY ONE	PARTY TWO	DATE	CITATION	NUMBER
Most favored nation clause (Cont.)				
Netherlands	Portugal	27 Aug 24	31LTS235	300800
Multilateral		30 Sep 24	30LTS135	300766
Norway	Romania	01 Oct 24	29LTS397	300750
Bulgaria	Norway	02 Oct 24	30LTS103	300763
Germany	Guatemala	04 Oct 24	52LTS19	301246
Japan	Mexico	08 Oct 24	36LTS259	300927
Czechoslovakia	Netherlands	17 Oct 24	31LTS93	300786
Finland	Italy	22 Oct 24	32LTS149	300814
France	Latvia	30 Oct 24	37LTS399	300963
Iceland	Latvia	03 Nov 24	43LTS339	301069
Austria	Czechoslovakia	27 Nov 24	42LTS201	301041
Poland	Sweden	02 Dec 24	36LTS299	300930
Austria	Norway	03 Dec 24	31LTS151	300792
Czechoslovakia	USA (United States)	05 Dec 24	56LTS271	301335
Hungary	Netherlands	09 Dec 24	47LTS91	301130
France	Poland	09 Dec 24	44LTS127	301081
Latvia	Sweden	22 Dec 24	36LTS283	300928
Poland	USA (United States)	10 Feb 25	37LTS141	300953
France	Siam	14 Feb 25	43LTS189	301055
Estonia	USA (United States)	02 Mar 25	43LTS289	301064
Albania	Italy	06 Mar 25	44LTS359	301094
Hungary	Poland	26 Mar 25	37LTS151	300954
Bel-Lux Econ Union	France	04 Apr 25	44LTS213	301085
Benelux Econ Union	Germany	04 Apr 25	37LTS203	300957
Czechoslovakia	Poland	07 Apr 25	56LTS285	301337
Czechoslovakia	Greece	08 Apr 25	38LTS291	300984
Greece	Poland	17 Apr 25	38LTS301	300985
Austria	Greece	18 Apr 25	38LTS311	300986
Czechoslovakia	Sweden	18 Apr 25	36LTS289	300929
Bulgaria	Poland	29 Apr 25	60LTS103	301408
Finland	USA (United States)	02 May 25	47LTS351	301139
Spain	Sweden	04 May 25	36LTS323	300932
Germany	Greece	15 May 25	40LTS6	301001
Germany	USA (United States)	21 May 25	52LTS133	301254
Greece	Hungary	04 Jun 25	39LTS139	300998
Albania	UK Great Britain	10 Jun 25	43LTS81	301049
Hungary	Spain	17 Jun 25	60LTS69	301406
Bel-Lux Econ Union	Japan	27 Jun 25	36LTS95	300907
Bel-Lux Econ Union		07 Jul 25	54LTS267	301290
Paraguay	Spain	08 Jul 25	138LTS225	303190
Finland	Spain	16 Jul 25	47LTS271	301135
Czechoslovakia	Spain	19 Jul 25	60LTS329	301419
Hungary	Italy	20 Jul 25	45LTS39	301098
Siam	Spain	03 Aug 25	55LTS39	301303
Germany	UK Great Britain	13 Aug 25	43LTS89	301050
Siam	UK Great Britain	15 Sep 25	49LTS51	301176
Germany	USSR (Soviet Union)	12 Oct 25	53LTS7	301257
Germany	USSR (Soviet Union)	12 Oct 25	53LTS163	301258
France	Hungary	13 Oct 25	48LTS9	301150
Estonia	Switzerland	14 Oct 25	49LTS421	301195
Bulgaria	Czechoslovakia	16 Oct 25	56LTS265	301334
Denmark	France	19 Oct 25	38LTS325	300988
Czechoslovakia	Japan	30 Oct 25	58LTS263	301377
Germany	Italy	31 Oct 25	52LTS179	301256
Bulgaria	UK Great Britain	12 Nov 25	43LTS165	301052
British Empire	Greece	26 Nov 25	63LTS167	301488
Germany	Netherlands	26 Nov 25	57LTS147	301361
Germany	Turkey	13 Dec 25	53LTS355	301265
Germany	Poland	16 Dec 25	46LTS139	301117
Austria	Portugal	18 Dec 25	54LTS91	301277
Lithuania	USA (United States)	23 Dec 25	54LTS377	301300
Estonia	USA (United States)	23 Dec 25	50LTS13	301197
Austria	Switzerland	06 Jan 26	46LTS299	301124
Estonia	UK Great Britain	18 Jan 26	48LTS209	301163
Albania	Czechoslovakia	19 Jan 26	64LTS349	301507

PARTY ONE	PARTY TWO	DATE	CITATION	NUMBER
Most favored nation clause (Cont.)				
Latvia	USA (United States)	01 Feb 26	55LTS33	301302
France	Germany	12 Feb 26	48LTS153	301157
Romania	USA (United States)	26 Feb 26	51LTS59	301221
Germany	Portugal	20 Mar 26	53LTS361	301266
Denmark	Turkey	22 Mar 26	48LTS231	301164
United Arab Rep	Greece	10 Apr 26	61LTS305	301441
Finland	Hungary	20 Apr 26	48LTS119	301154
Czechoslovakia	Poland	21 Apr 26	58LTS9	301367
Czechoslovakia	Italy	04 May 26	61LTS257	301438
Germany	Spain	07 May 26	53LTS321	301264
Italy	Siam	09 May 26	61LTS215	301436
Greece	Netherlands	12 May 26	61LTS295	301440
Germany	Sweden	14 May 26	51LTS99	301225
Serb/Croat/Slovene	UK Great Britain	18 Jun 26	57LTS23	301349
Albania	Serb/Croat/Slovene	22 Jun 26	91LTS55	302055
Finland	Greece	22 Jun 26	56LTS197	301331
Finland	Germany	26 Jun 26	56LTS203	301332
Germany	Latvia	28 Jun 26	58LTS403	301385
Bel-Lux Econ Union	Siam	13 Jul 26	62LTS287	301468
Germany	Switzerland	14 Jul 26	59LTS87	301391
Norway	Siam	16 Jul 26	60LTS35	301404
Netherlands	Turkey	11 Aug 26	48LTS271	301168
Norway	Turkey	11 Aug 26	47LTS441	301149
Denmark	Turkey	19 Sep 26	56LTS259	301333
Greece	Spain	23 Sep 26	91LTS121	302059
Bel-Lux Econ Union	Estonia	28 Sep 26	62LTS433	301475
Austria	Estonia	15 Oct 26	93LTS137	302106
Finland	Turkey	19 Oct 26	58LTS393	301384
Greece	Switzerland	29 Nov 26	63LTS27	301478
Hungary	Turkey	20 Dec 26	72LTS245	301696
Belgium	Estonia	08 Feb 27	74LTS227	301740
Czechoslovakia	Switzerland	16 Feb 27	64LTS7	301501
Bulgaria	Greece	28 Feb 27	68LTS59	301568
Poland	Serb/Croat/Slovene	06 Mar 27	126LTS67	302871
Denmark	Sweden	08 Mar 27	63LTS315	301498
Norway	Sweden	09 Mar 27	62LTS341	301472
Greece	Romania	28 Mar 27	68LTS67	301569
Greece	UK Great Britain	13 May 27	61LTS15	301425
Iceland	USSR (Soviet Union)	25 May 27	63LTS105	301483
Czechoslovakia	Turkey	31 May 27	75LTS79	301753
Finland	Switzerland	24 Jun 27	68LTS103	301574
Hungary	Italy	25 Jul 27	74LTS53	301731
Switzerland	Turkey	07 Aug 27	73LTS51	301706
Italy	Spain	15 Aug 27	94LTS361	302155
Denmark	Turkey	24 Sep 27	61LTS287	301439
Denmark	Greece	29 Sep 27	62LTS219	301464
Belgium	France	06 Oct 27	69LTS49	301599
France	Turkey	01 Nov 27	92LTS249	302092
Greece	Switzerland	01 Dec 27	84LTS271	301907
Albania	France	15 Feb 28	107LTS307	302487
Siam	UK Great Britain	21 Feb 28	87LTS21	301960
France	Spain	22 Mar 28	73LTS63	301707
Germany	Siam	07 Apr 28	85LTS337	301938
Latvia	USA (United States)	20 Apr 28	80LTS35	301821
Austria	Italy	11 May 28	100LTS41	302293
Germany	Persia	15 May 28	107LTS389	302495
Belgium	Poland	12 Jun 28	123LTS25	302803
Austria	Persia	17 Jun 28	112LTS101	302610
Austria	USA (United States)	19 Jun 28	118LTS241	302728
Cuba	Mexico	29 Jun 28	124LTS189	302833
Italy	Persia	24 Jul 28	95LTS269	302179
China	USA (United States)	25 Jul 28	107LTS121	302472
Denmark	Persia	08 Sep 28	82LTS57	301859
Panama	UK Great Britain	26 Sep 28	90LTS327	302046
China	Italy	27 Nov 28	93LTS173	302109

PARTY ONE	PARTY TWO	DATE	CITATION	NUMBER
Most favored nation clause (Cont.)				
United Arab Rep	Persia	28 Nov 28	93LTS381	302127
China	Denmark	12 Dec 28	91LTS207	302062
Ecuador	UK Great Britain	05 Jan 29	90LTS369	302048
Denmark	Latvia	09 Jan 29	86LTS37	301948
Germany	Persia	17 Feb 29	111LTS19	302576
Germany	Persia	17 Feb 29	111LTS241	302590
Norway	USA (United States)	25 Feb 29	134LTS81	303085
Japan	Persia	30 Mar 29	107LTS427	302499
Germany	Hedjaz	26 Apr 29	115LTS265	302690
Norway	Persia	10 May 29	107LTS403	302497
France	Persia	10 May 29	150LTS329	303465
Persia	Sweden	10 May 29	102LTS9	302349
France	UK Great Britain	25 May 29	95LTS55	302163
Persia	Sweden	27 May 29	105LTS279	302420
Hedjaz	Persia	24 Aug 29	106LTS269	302450
Italy	Panama	16 Oct 29	138LTS355	303199
Irish Free State	Portugal	29 Oct 29	131LTS145	303007
Poland	Romania	17 Dec 29	119LTS333	302754
Lithuania	Persia	13 Jan 30	131LTS221	303013
Honduras	Nicaragua	30 Jan 30	142LTS241	303297
Netherlands	Persia	12 Mar 30	111LTS387	302599
France	Luxembourg	31 Mar 30	122LTS29	302797
Japan	Lithuania	02 May 30	126LTS369	302895
Norway	Persia	08 May 30	134LTS153	303089
Germany	Irish Free State	12 May 30	131LTS153	303008
Greece	Irish Free State	15 May 30	136LTS33	303122
Netherlands	Yugoslavia	28 May 30	129LTS73	302951
United Arab Rep	Irish Free State	28 Jul 30	137LTS421	303172
Austria	Japan	16 Aug 30	126LTS351	302894
France	Romania	27 Aug 30	158LTS379	303644
El Salvador	USA (United States)	05 Sep 30	134LTS207	303093
Chile	Czechoslovakia	18 Sep 30	140LTS161	303233
Czechoslovakia	Persia	29 Oct 30	121LTS53	302783
Brazil	Switzerland	29 Oct 30	140LTS265	303241
Czechoslovakia	Persia	29 Oct 30	121LTS59	302784
Greece	Turkey	30 Oct 30	125LTS371	302866
Finland	Norway	11 Nov 30	130LTS17	302980
Abyssinia	Japan	15 Nov 30	133LTS135	303063
Switzerland	Turkey	13 Dec 30	129LTS267	302964
Switzerland	Turkey	13 Dec 30	129LTS331	302968
China	Norway	23 Apr 31	119LTS9	302736
Finland	France	24 Apr 31	126LTS85	302872
Iceland	Romania	08 May 31	127LTS11	302901
India	Poland	18 May 31	131LTS9	303001
Bulgaria	Italy	20 May 31	129LTS371	302971
Siam	Switzerland	28 May 31	125LTS357	302864
Guatemala	UK Great Britain	06 Jun 31	132LTS15	303027
Poland	USA (United States)	15 Jun 31	139LTS395	303223
Greece	Romania	11 Aug 31	130LTS33	302981
Greece	Romania	11 Aug 31	130LTS69	302982
Hungary	Romania	12 Aug 31	186LTS325	304321
Poland	Turkey	29 Aug 31	144LTS367	303339
Brazil	UK Great Britain	11 Sep 31	130LTS103	302985
Chile	USA (United States)	28 Sep 31	144LTS147	303325
Estonia	Persia	03 Oct 31	137LTS183	303155
Romania	Sweden	07 Oct 31	131LTS51	303003
Chile	UK Great Britain	15 Oct 31	128LTS439	302947
Brazil	Irish Free State	16 Oct 31	134LTS75	303084
Turkey	USA (United States)	28 Oct 31	138LTS345	303197
Bolivia	Denmark	09 Nov 31	147LTS27	303387
Bolivia	Iceland	09 Nov 31	147LTS43	303388
Norway	Portugal	13 Nov 31	129LTS455	302977
Brazil	Finland	26 Nov 31	126LTS239	302886
Brazil	Czechoslovakia	27 Nov 31	136LTS453	303144
Brazil	Italy	28 Nov 31	131LTS273	303017

PARTY ONE	PARTY TWO	DATE	CITATION	NUMBER
Most favored nation clause (Cont.)				
Brazil	Iceland	30 Nov 31	128LTS369	302942
Brazil	Denmark	30 Nov 31	128LTS29	302934
Brazil	Canada	04 Dec 31	139LTS241	303214
Brazil	Mexico	07 Dec 31	139LTS247	303215
Brazil	Romania	16 Dec 31	139LTS255	303216
Chile	Netherlands	17 Dec 31	127LTS79	302908
Brazil	Hungary	24 Dec 31	147LTS51	303389
Brazil	Norway	31 Dec 31	126LTS385	302896
Austria	Brazil	02 Jan 32	140LTS15	303224
Iraq	Turkey	09 Jan 32	139LTS263	303217
Bel-Lux Econ Union	Brazil	14 Jan 32	128LTS21	302933
Brazil	Poland	03 Feb 32	147LTS113	303396
Japan	Portugal	23 Mar 32	128LTS363	302941
Brazil	South Africa	11 Apr 32	135LTS219	303112
Lithuania	Portugal	12 Apr 32	129LTS135	302958
Italy	Latvia	11 May 32	150LTS9	303450
Brazil	Yugoslavia	16 May 32	144LTS303	303333
Estonia	Spain	23 Jun 32	143LTS31	303303
Bulgaria	Germany	24 Jun 32	147LTS211	303400
Brazil	India	21 Jul 32	133LTS93	303059
France	Yugoslavia	29 Jul 32	144LTS313	303334
Czechoslovakia	Greece	30 Jul 32	156LTS159	303599
Bulgaria	USA (United States)	18 Aug 32	136LTS73	303126
Brazil	Latvia	21 Sep 32	137LTS61	303146
Brazil	Estonia	30 Sep 32	134LTS247	303095
Netherlands	Yemen	12 Mar 33	146LTS359	303384
Iraq	Norway	14 Mar 33	138LTS23	303177
Estonia	France	27 Apr 33	141LTS43	303260
Argentina	UK Great Britain	01 May 33	143LTS67	303305
Italy	USSR (Soviet Union)	06 May 33	158LTS51	303625
Iceland	UK Great Britain	19 May 33	144LTS33	303319
Ethiopia	Switzerland	24 May 33	153LTS63	303508
Germany	Yugoslavia	29 Jul 33	149LTS77	303435
Brazil	Uruguay	25 Aug 33	176LTS381	304075
Brazil	Portugal	26 Aug 33	179LTS63	304134
Bulgaria	Czechoslovakia	29 Aug 33	148LTS15	303402
Poland	UK Great Britain	26 Oct 33	158LTS73	303628
Latvia	USSR (Soviet Union)	04 Dec 33	148LTS145	303410
France	USSR (Soviet Union)	11 Jan 34	167LTS349	303878
Argentina	Bel-Lux Econ Union	16 Jan 34	145LTS145	303352
Argentina	Bel-Lux Econ Union	16 Jan 34	147LTS79	303392
Netherlands	Uruguay	29 Jan 34	166LTS43	303828
Argentina	Netherlands	31 Jan 34	148LTS355	303421
Argentina	Netherlands	31 Jan 34	148LTS361	303422
Czechoslovakia	Poland	10 Feb 34	183LTS213	304238
UK Great Britain	Yemen	11 Feb 34	157LTS63	303605
Finland	USA (United States)	13 Feb 34	152LTS45	303484
Denmark	Persia	20 Feb 34	158LTS299	303640
Romania	Spain	21 Mar 34	159LTS171	303661
Albania	Czechoslovakia	09 Apr 34	158LTS59	303626
Persia	Switzerland	25 Apr 34	159LTS235	303666
Persia	Switzerland	25 Apr 34	160LTS173	303691
Bel-Lux Econ Union	Turkey	24 May 34	150LTS269	303460
Netherlands	Spain	16 Jun 34	168LTS29	303885
Finland	Persia	18 Nov 34	158LTS315	303641
Bulgaria	Poland	22 Dec 34	159LTS265	303671
Spain	Uruguay	02 Jan 35	164LTS95	303791
Brazil	USA (United States)	02 Feb 35	166LTS211	303840
Netherlands	South Africa	20 Feb 35	160LTS143	303688
Poland	UK Great Britain	27 Feb 35	162LTS181	303740
Chile	Finland	01 Mar 35	159LTS113	303653
Bulgaria	Finland	22 Mar 35	159LTS123	303654
Czechoslovakia	USSR (Soviet Union)	25 Mar 35	161LTS257	303718
Latvia	Lithuania	10 Apr 35	159LTS305	303674
Estonia	Spain	08 May 35	159LTS363	303678

PARTY ONE	PARTY TWO	DATE	CITATION	NUMBER
Most favored nation clause (Cont.)				
Italy	South Africa	21 May 35	189LTS31	304373
New Zealand	Sweden	24 May 35	159LTS143	303657
Sweden	USA (United States)	25 May 35	161LTS109	303707
UK Great Britain	Uruguay	26 Jun 35	176LTS153	304058
Iran	USSR (Soviet Union)	27 Aug 35	176LTS299	304069
France	South Africa	27 Aug 35	189LTS41	304374
Bel-Lux Econ Union	USSR (Soviet Union)	05 Sep 35	173LTS169	304010
Colombia	USA (United States)	13 Sep 35	170LTS293	303944
Iraq	Sweden	03 Nov 35	163LTS419	303783
Canada	USA (United States)	15 Nov 35	168LTS355	303910
Netherlands	USA (United States)	20 Dec 35	178LTS239	304118
France	Spain	21 Dec 35	167LTS9	303856
Spain	Turkey	31 Dec 35	166LTS163	303838
Switzerland	USA (United States)	09 Jan 36	171LTS231	303962
France	Sweden	18 Jan 36	167LTS197	303866
Nicaragua	USA (United States)	11 Mar 36	173LTS141	304009
Poland	USSR (Soviet Union)	31 Mar 36	186LTS211	304313
Norway	Uruguay	04 Apr 36	176LTS115	304055
France	USA (United States)	06 May 36	199LTS259	304679
Finland	Switzerland	07 May 36	166LTS35	303827
Ecuador	USA (United States)	12 Jun 36	170LTS377	303946
El Salvador	Sweden	23 Jun 36	171LTS291	303966
Guatemala	Sweden	11 Jul 36	171LTS299	303967
Brazil	Czechoslovakia	22 Jul 36	188LTS275	304363
Brazil	Norway	27 Jul 36	176LTS125	304056
Brazil	Denmark	30 Jul 36	194LTS81	304510
Brazil	UK Great Britain	10 Aug 36	172LTS273	303996
Sweden	Uruguay	13 Aug 36	183LTS161	304232
Australia	Czechoslovakia	19 Aug 36	177LTS245	304093
Czechoslovakia	Guatemala	20 Sep 36	185LTS269	304293
Australia	Bel-Lux Econ Union	03 Oct 36	177LTS271	304094
Bulgaria	Finland	27 Oct 36	179LTS309	304158
Chile	Sweden	30 Oct 36	188LTS283	304364
Australia	France	27 Nov 36	177LTS301	304095
Norway	Romania	10 Dec 36	174LTS59	304037
Chile	Netherlands	30 Dec 36	177LTS87	304082
Czechoslovakia	South Africa	27 Jan 37	189LTS97	304377
France	Sweden	17 Feb 37	176LTS267	304065
Cuba	UK Great Britain	19 Feb 37	192LTS301	304480
Bel-Lux Econ Union	Uruguay	22 Feb 37	196LTS391	304600
Chile	Cuba	13 Mar 37	195LTS389	304558
Brazil	Netherlands	15 Mar 37	179LTS395	304166
Canada	Haiti	23 Apr 37	194LTS59	304507
Romania	Yugoslavia	13 May 37	197LTS145	304611
Sweden	Yugoslavia	14 May 37	194LTS21	304504
Ecuador	Netherlands	27 May 37	194LTS179	304521
UK Great Britain		07 Jun 37	185LTS185	304282
France	Turkey	15 Jun 37	179LTS195	304147
USA (United States)	USSR (Soviet Union)	04 Aug 37	182LTS113	304204
Brazil	Lithuania	28 Sep 37	186LTS403	304324
Canada	Guatemala	28 Sep 37	194LTS65	304508
Estonia	France	16 Oct 37	183LTS41	304227
Denmark	Haiti	21 Oct 37	190LTS231	304422
Bel-Lux Econ Union	Siam	05 Nov 37	190LTS151	304413
Siam	Sweden	08 Nov 37	185LTS337	304298
Norway	Siam	15 Nov 37	186LTS9	304301
Chile	UK Great Britain	26 Nov 37	186LTS285	304317
Greece	Lithuania	01 Dec 37	193LTS185	304495
France	Siam	07 Dec 37	201LTS113	304708
France	Siam	09 Dec 37	201LTS145	304709
Hungary	Iran	18 Dec 37	189LTS243	304387
Latvia	Turkey	12 Jan 38	201LTS229	304716
Greece	Latvia	15 Jan 38	195LTS19	304533
France	Sweden	31 Jan 38	185LTS223	304286
Chile	USA (United States)	01 Feb 38	190LTS9	304401

PARTY ONE	PARTY TWO	DATE	CITATION	NUMBER
Most favored nation clause (Cont.)				
Norway	Venezuela	18 Feb 38	187LTS205	304341
Czechoslovakia	USA (United States)	07 Mar 38	200LTS87	304687
New Zealand	Switzerland	05 May 38	189LTS167	304384
Portugal	UK Great Britain	11 May 38	191LTS285	304450
USA (United States)	Venezuela	12 May 38	191LTS35	304433
United Arab Rep	Iraq	16 May 38	190LTS177	304415
Portugal	Siam	02 Jul 38	200LTS149	304688
Romania	Switzerland	19 Jul 38	152LTS89	303486
Ecuador	USA (United States)	06 Aug 38	193LTS85	304489
Liberia	USA (United States)	08 Aug 38	201LTS163	304711
Greece	Portugal	15 Aug 38	201LTS201	304707
Cuba	Portugal	06 Sep 38	195LTS443	304565
Bulgaria	Greece	16 Sep 38	195LTS27	304534
Ecuador	Sweden	11 Nov 38	195LTS347	304554
Greece	USA (United States)	15 Nov 38	195LTS145	304544
Canada	USA (United States)	17 Nov 38	199LTS91	304670
UK Great Britain	USA (United States)	17 Nov 38	200LTS293	304700
El Salvador	Norway	21 Nov 38	198LTS157	304636
Australia	Switzerland	22 Nov 38	194LTS35	304505
Iraq	USA (United States)	03 Dec 38	203LTS107	304753
Guatemala	Norway	20 Dec 38	198LTS117	304631
Chile	UK Great Britain	09 Jan 39	196LTS277	304589
Chile	USA (United States)	24 Feb 39	197LTS217	304614
Turkey	USA (United States)	01 Apr 39	202LTS129	304741
Brazil	South Africa	18 Apr 39	198LTS289	304646
United Arab Rep	South Africa	31 May 39	198LTS295	304647
Liberia	USA (United States)	14 Jun 39	202LTS93	304737
Australia	Brazil	19 Jul 39	200LTS191	304690
Dominican Republic	Newfoundland	16 Mar 40	203LTS141	304757
Taxation				
Estonia	UK Great Britain	20 Jul 20	1LTS295	300025
Czechoslovakia	Serb/Croat/Slovene	18 Oct 20	17LTS19	300424
Czechoslovakia	Italy	23 Mar 21	32LTS261	300817
Czechoslovakia	Romania	23 Apr 21	15LTS235	300397
Austria	Hungary	08 Oct 21	16LTS19	300402
Czechoslovakia	Germany	31 Dec 21	17LTS401	300447
Austria	Czechoslovakia	11 Feb 22	152LTS175	303492
Austria	Czechoslovakia	18 Feb 22	14LTS129	300371
Austria	Germany	23 May 22	26LTS405	300660
France	Saar	05 Jul 22	27LTS265	300689
Estonia	Hungary	19 Oct 22	30LTS347	300774
Germany	Poland	21 Mar 23	34LTS315	300881
Germany	Switzerland	24 Mar 23	27LTS41	300666
Czechoslovakia	Hungary	13 Jul 23	36LTS53	300903
Czechoslovakia	UK Great Britain	14 Jul 23	29LTS377	300748
Multilateral		24 Jul 23	28LTS151	300704
Multilateral		24 Jul 23	28LTS171	300705
Estonia	Latvia	01 Nov 23	25LTS354	300624
Germany	Hungary	06 Nov 23	45LTS253	301103
Multilateral		14 Dec 23	29LTS37	300732
Austria	Turkey	28 Jan 24	32LTS313	300823
Germany	Siam	28 Feb 24	32LTS399	300828
Czechoslovakia	Italy	01 Mar 24	36LTS229	300925
Japan	Siam	09 Mar 24	31LTS187	300795
Iceland	Poland	22 Mar 24	31LTS35	300779
Denmark	Poland	22 Mar 24	31LTS13	300778
Czechoslovakia	Netherlands	17 Oct 24	31LTS93	300786
Finland	Italy	22 Oct 24	32LTS149	300814
Multilateral		23 Oct 24	78LTS17	301779
UK Great Britain	USA (United States)	16 Mar 25	113LTS105	302639
Germany	USA (United States)	20 Mar 25	119LTS185	302745
Czechoslovakia	Poland	23 Apr 25	44LTS309	301091
Germany	Italy	31 Oct 25	53LTS245	301261
Germany	Italy	31 Oct 25	52LTS179	301256

PARTY ONE	PARTY TWO	DATE	CITATION	NUMBER
Taxation (Cont.)				
Hungary	Italy	25 Nov 25	74LTS251	301741
Italy	USA (United States)	05 May 26	113LTS21	302631
Germany	Spain	07 May 26	53LTS321	301264
Irish Free State	USA (United States)	10 May 26	56LTS433	301345
Albania	Serb/Croat/Slovene	22 Jun 26	91LTS55	302055
Austria	Czechoslovakia	12 Jul 26	86LTS395	301952
Greece	Spain	23 Sep 26	91LTS121	302059
Netherlands	USA (United States)	27 Nov 26	112LTS433	302628
France	USA (United States)	08 Jul 27	114LTS413	302669
Denmark	Iceland	11 Aug 27	75LTS345	301757
Great Britain	Spain	08 Sep 27	69LTS263	301608
Austria	Switzerland	24 Oct 27	85LTS253	301935
Germany	Panama	21 Nov 27	115LTS239	302689
Denmark	Germany	14 Feb 28	71LTS285	301669
Hungary	Serb/Croat/Slovene	22 Feb 28	100LTS331	302305
Germany	Sweden	25 Apr 28	81LTS281	301844
Iceland	UK Great Britain	27 Apr 28	80LTS253	301831
Austria	Serb/Croat/Slovene	01 May 28	96LTS373	302214
Hungary	Poland	12 May 28	123LTS15	302802
Hungary	Poland	12 May 28	123LTS47	302804
Persia	Switzerland	28 Aug 28	107LTS397	302496
Canada	USA (United States)	17 Sep 28	95LTS209	302175
Belgium	Norway	29 Oct 28	107LTS75	302469
Belgium	Denmark	12 Dec 28	107LTS363	302492
Belgium	Iceland	21 Dec 28	107LTS369	302493
Belgium	Finland	19 Feb 29	111LTS31	302577
Belgium	Sweden	13 May 29	111LTS37	302578
Hungary	Lithuania	16 May 29	96LTS333	302211
Canada	Denmark	18 Jun 29	95LTS81	302167
Persia	USSR (Soviet Union)	02 Aug 29	109LTS99	302530
Belgium	France	07 Oct 29	111LTS43	302579
Multilateral		15 Mar 30	113LTS395	302651
UK Great Britain	USA (United States)	16 Apr 30	109LTS9	302524
Italy	UK Great Britain	28 Aug 30	111LTS91	302583
Greece	Netherlands	05 Dec 30	117LTS357	302702
Sweden	UK Great Britain	06 Jul 31	120LTS211	302766
Greece	Norway	15 Aug 31	123LTS271	302817
France	USA (United States)	27 Apr 32	164LTS211	303795
France	Italy	03 Oct 32	153LTS55	303507
Belgium	Netherlands	20 Feb 33	164LTS223	303796
Finland	Germany	24 Mar 34	149LTS343	303442
China	UK Great Britain	27 Oct 34	160LTS265	303695
Finland	UK Great Britain	21 Feb 35	158LTS323	303642
Netherlands	Sweden	21 Mar 35	148LTS451	303648
Germany	Sweden	14 May 35	163LTS459	303785
Death duties				
Austria	Greece	16 Sep 04	2LTS161	300062
Greece	Spain	06 Mar 19	3LTS81	300092
Latvia	Lithuania	12 Jul 21	25LTS299	300619
Austria	Czechoslovakia	18 Feb 22	14LTS129	300371
Czechoslovakia	Germany	18 Mar 22	17LTS453	300448
Austria	Germany	28 May 22	26LTS445	300661
Germany	Hungary	26 Nov 23	45LTS309	301105
Finland	UK Great Britain	14 Dec 23	23LTS125	300583
Austria	Hungary	08 Nov 24	45LTS21	301097
Czechoslovakia	Poland	23 Apr 25	44LTS271	301089
Japan	Latvia	04 Jul 25	80LTS305	301836
Austria	Poland	24 Nov 26	77LTS359	301777
Austria	Germany	05 Feb 27	73LTS205	301714
Serb/Croat/Slovene	UK Great Britain	12 May 27	80LTS165	301825
Austria	Serb/Croat/Slovene	01 May 28	96LTS373	302214
Czechoslovakia	Lithuania	24 Apr 31	126LTS279	302890
Germany	Switzerland	15 Jul 31	144LTS389	303341
South Africa	Southern Rhodesia	21 Apr 32	142LTS197	303292

PARTY ONE	PARTY TWO	DATE	CITATION	NUMBER
Death duties (Cont.)				
Czechoslovakia	Romania	20 Jun 34	168LTS249	303902
Czechoslovakia	Yugoslavia	24 Feb 36	187LTS185	304338
Hungary	Sweden	17 Jun 36	184LTS25	304240
France	Sweden	24 Dec 36	181LTS315	304198
France	Siam	07 Dec 37	201LTS113	304708
Austria	Greece	12 Jun 56*	2LTS157	300061
Tax credits				
Greece	Italy	15 Jan 32	137LTS397	303169
Spain	Sweden	23 Aug 35	162LTS331	303746
Equitable taxes				
Austria	Czechoslovakia	04 May 21	15LTS13	300388
Germany	Saar	03 Jun 21	5LTS189	300129
Austria	Hungary	08 Oct 21	16LTS19	300402
Czechoslovakia	Germany	31 Dec 21	17LTS401	300447
Austria	Germany	23 May 22	26LTS405	300660
Czechoslovakia	Hungary	13 Jul 23	35LTS237	300898
Czechoslovakia	Italy	01 Mar 24	36LTS229	300925
Poland	Sweden	02 Dec 24	36LTS299	300930
Belgium	France	24 Dec 24	78LTS367	301795
Czechoslovakia	Poland	23 Apr 25	44LTS271	301089
Germany	USSR (Soviet Union)	12 Oct 25	53LTS7	301257
France	Luxembourg	16 Jan 26	48LTS149	301156
Italy	USA (United States)	05 May 26	113LTS21	302631
Guatemala	Italy	15 Sep 26	70LTS175	301633
Finland	Greece	18 Dec 26	70LTS89	301626
Estonia	Greece	04 Jan 27	69LTS33	301598
Germany	Turkey	12 Jan 27	73LTS133	301712
Estonia	Poland	19 Feb 27	115LTS177	302686
France	USA (United States)	08 Jul 27	114LTS413	302669
Austria	Finland	08 Aug 27	70LTS349	301645
Italy	Spain	28 Nov 27	82LTS27	301857
Hungary	Serb/Croat/Slovene	22 Feb 28	100LTS331	302305
Iceland	UK Great Britain	27 Apr 28	80LTS253	301831
Hungary	Poland	12 May 28	123LTS47	302804
Austria	Hungary	25 Jun 28	100LTS85	302296
Germany	South Africa	01 Sep 28	95LTS289	302181
France	Saar	12 Nov 28	85LTS451	301945
Estonia	Germany	07 Dec 28	99LTS259	302273
Serb/Croat/Slovene	Spain	27 Sep 29	98LTS319	302253
Sweden	Turkey	29 Sep 29	119LTS53	302740
Finland	Turkey	12 Oct 29	96LTS239	302205
Czechoslovakia	Romania	27 Jun 30	119LTS73	302742
France	Italy	03 Oct 32	153LTS55	303507
Romania	Yugoslavia	10 Mar 33	146LTS263	303376
Multilateral		25 Aug 33	141LTS71	303262
Finland	UK Great Britain	21 Feb 35	158LTS323	303642
Luxembourg	Netherlands	01 Apr 36	179LTS11	304130
General				
Austria	Poland	09 Jan 20	7LTS163	300185
Austria	Czechoslovakia	02 Aug 20	32LTS365	300826
Austria	Germany	01 Sep 20	4LTS201	300107
Austria	Germany	01 Sep 20	2LTS132	300057
Estonia	Latvia	19 Oct 20	17LTS189	300437
Danzig	Poland	09 Nov 20	6LTS189	300153
Canada	France	29 Jan 21	8LTS105	300212
Poland	USSR (Soviet Union)	18 Mar 21	6LTS51	300149
Czechoslovakia	Italy	23 Mar 21	32LTS183	300815
Finland	France	13 Jul 21	29LTS445	300755
Estonia	Finland	29 Oct 21	13LTS167	300350
Multilateral		06 Feb 22	38LTS267	300981
France	Poland	06 Feb 22	43LTS415	301074
Austria	Czechoslovakia	11 Feb 22	152LTS175	303492
Austria	Czechoslovakia	18 Feb 22	14LTS129	300371
Peru	UK Great Britain	02 Mar 22	10LTS463	300286

PARTY ONE	PARTY TWO	DATE	CITATION	NUMBER
General (Cont.)				
Finland	Germany	21 Apr 22	19LTS87	300487
Italy	Poland	12 May 22	59LTS293	301399
Latvia	Vatican/Holy See	30 May 22	17LTS365	300443
Poland	Switzerland	26 Jun 22	12LTS305	300322
France	Saar	05 Jul 22	27LTS265	300689
Bulgaria	Denmark	11 Jul 22	12LTS225	300314
Germany	Poland	26 Aug 22	26LTS365	300656
Austria	Poland	25 Sep 22	59LTS307	301400
Czechoslovakia	Latvia	07 Oct 22	20LTS379	300528
Finland	USSR (Soviet Union)	21 Oct 22	29LTS197	300742
Italy	Serb/Croat/Slovene	23 Oct 22	18LTS441	300480
Italy	Serb/Croat/Slovene	23 Oct 22	18LTS413	300479
Italy	Serb/Croat/Slovene	23 Oct 22	18LTS461	300481
Denmark	Sweden	07 Nov 22	14LTS95	300370
Japan	Poland	07 Dec 22	32LTS61	300806
China	Japan	08 Dec 22	20LTS205	300519
Canada	France	15 Dec 22	21LTS38	300532
Italy	Switzerland	27 Jan 23	25LTS21	300603
Denmark	Finland	12 Feb 23	18LTS71	300454
Germany	Switzerland	25 Mar 23	18LTS273	300470
Multilateral		29 Mar 23	23LTS256	300593
France	India	12 May 23	25LTS381	300627
Finland	Sweden	26 May 23	18LTS57	300453
Germany	Lithuania	01 Jun 23	51LTS387	301244
Finland	USSR (Soviet Union)	05 Jun 23	18LTS203	300465
Latvia	UK Great Britain	22 Jun 23	20LTS395	300529
Estonia	Sweden	07 Jul 23	20LTS189	300517
Czechoslovakia	Hungary	13 Jul 23	35LTS237	300898
Poland	Turkey	23 Jul 23	49LTS329	301189
Estonia	Iceland	07 Sep 23	23LTS131	300584
Germany	Hungary	06 Nov 23	45LTS279	301104
Germany	Hungary	06 Nov 23	45LTS253	301103
Finland	Poland	10 Nov 23	29LTS229	300744
Italy	Spain	15 Nov 23	39LTS49	300996
Japan	Serb/Croat/Slovene	16 Nov 23	42LTS99	301035
Hungary	Latvia	19 Nov 23	37LTS341	300959
Finland	UK Great Britain	14 Dec 23	29LTS129	300739
Lithuania	Norway	21 Dec 23	32LTS55	300805
France	Italy	10 Jan 24	43LTS431	301076
Lithuania	Sweden	17 Feb 24	23LTS153	300587
Czechoslovakia	Italy	01 Mar 24	36LTS229	300925
Multilateral		12 Mar 24	24LTS17	300595
Other Unilat Decla	Hungary	14 Mar 24	25LTS427	300634
Hungary	Italy	27 Mar 24	45LTS65	301099
Denmark	Latvia	03 Apr 24	33LTS393	300860
Poland	Serb/Croat/Slovene	05 Apr 24	49LTS265	301185
Hungary	Romania	16 Apr 24	45LTS403	301110
Multilateral		22 May 24	35LTS175	300895
Netherlands	Poland	30 May 24	34LTS9	300865
Finland	Japan	07 Jun 24	58LTS379	301383
Lithuania	Netherlands	10 Jun 24	34LTS373	300885
Spain	UK Great Britain	27 Jun 24	28LTS523	300727
Latvia	Netherlands	02 Jul 24	37LTS121	300951
Estonia	Netherlands	22 Jul 24	48LTS199	301162
Germany	Spain	25 Jul 24	41LTS363	301023
Austria	Latvia	09 Aug 24	65LTS7	301516
Finland	Latvia	23 Aug 24	37LTS383	300962
Hungary	Norway	16 Sep 24	33LTS103	300835
Iceland	Latvia	03 Nov 24	43LTS339	301069
Austria	Hungary	08 Nov 24	44LTS407	301096
Hungary	Netherlands	09 Dec 24	47LTS91	301130
France	Poland	09 Dec 24	44LTS127	301081
Norway	UK Great Britain	18 Dec 24	32LTS9	300801
France	Saar	15 Jan 25	44LTS181	301082
Austria	Spain	03 Feb 25	43LTS313	301067

PARTY ONE	PARTY TWO	DATE	CITATION	NUMBER
General (Cont.)				
Albania	Italy	06 Mar 25	44LTS359	301094
Hungary	Poland	26 Mar 25	37LTS151	300954
Benelux Econ Union	Germany	04 Apr 25	37LTS203	300957
Czechoslovakia	Romania	16 Apr 25	46LTS427	301126
Greece	Poland	17 Apr 25	38LTS301	300985
Czechoslovakia	Poland	23 Apr 25	44LTS309	301091
Czechoslovakia	Poland	23 Apr 25	44LTS285	301090
Bulgaria	Poland	29 Apr 25	60LTS103	301408
Germany	USA (United States)	21 May 25	52LTS133	301254
Netherlands	Siam	08 Jun 25	56LTS57	301323
Hungary	Spain	17 Jun 25	60LTS69	301406
Japan	Latvia	04 Jul 25	80LTS305	301836
Bel-Lux Econ Union		07 Jul 25	54LTS267	301290
Hungary	Italy	20 Jul 25	45LTS39	301098
Italy	Latvia	25 Jul 25	60LTS91	301407
Siam	Spain	03 Aug 25	55LTS39	301303
Germany	UK Great Britain	13 Aug 25	43LTS89	301050
Portugal	Siam	14 Aug 25	55LTS57	301304
Siam	UK Great Britain	15 Sep 25	49LTS51	301176
Germany	USSR (Soviet Union)	12 Oct 25	53LTS7	301257
France	Hungary	13 Oct 25	48LTS9	301150
Austria	China	19 Oct 25	55LTS9	301301
Czechoslovakia	Japan	30 Oct 25	58LTS263	301377
Germany	Italy	31 Oct 25	53LTS245	301261
Germany	Italy	31 Oct 25	52LTS179	301256
Bulgaria	UK Great Britain	12 Nov 25	43LTS165	301052
Finland	Great Britain	18 Nov 25	42LTS445	301042
Norway	USSR (Soviet Union)	15 Dec 25	47LTS9	301127
Siam	Sweden	19 Dec 25	58LTS429	301386
Bel-Lux Econ Union	Czechoslovakia	28 Dec 25	58LTS189	301372
Austria	Switzerland	06 Jan 26	46LTS299	301124
Estonia	UK Great Britain	18 Jan 26	48LTS209	301163
France	Germany	12 Feb 26	48LTS153	301157
Denmark	Siam	01 Mar 26	47LTS103	301131
Germany	Portugal	20 Mar 26	53LTS361	301266
Germany	Poland	27 Mar 26	64LTS249	301506
Finland	Hungary	20 Apr 26	48LTS119	301154
Czechoslovakia	Poland	21 Apr 26	58LTS9	301367
Greece	Netherlands	12 May 26	61LTS295	301440
Germany	Sweden	14 May 26	51LTS99	301225
Estonia	Latvia	28 May 26	159LTS291	303672
France	India	19 Jun 26	57LTS35	301350
Finland	Germany	26 Jun 26	56LTS203	301332
Germany	Latvia	28 Jun 26	58LTS403	301385
Austria	Czechoslovakia	12 Jul 26	86LTS395	301952
Austria	Czechoslovakia	12 Jul 26	86LTS383	301951
Norway	Siam	16 Jul 26	60LTS35	301404
Greece	Sweden	10 Sep 26	63LTS37	301479
Bel-Lux Econ Union	Estonia	28 Sep 26	62LTS433	301475
Austria	Estonia	15 Oct 26	93LTS137	302106
Greece	Switzerland	29 Nov 26	63LTS27	301478
Hungary	Turkey	20 Dec 26	72LTS245	301696
Germany	Poland	22 Dec 26	68LTS263	301590
Czechoslovakia	Switzerland	16 Feb 27	64LTS7	301501
Czechoslovakia	Finland	02 Mar 27	66LTS385	301532
France	Norway	12 Apr 27	178LTS199	304114
Greece	UK Great Britain	13 May 27	61LTS15	301425
Czechoslovakia	Turkey	31 May 27	75LTS79	301753
Austria	Switzerland	24 Oct 27	85LTS253	301935
Japan	USSR (Soviet Union)	23 Jan 28	80LTS341	301839
Germany	Lithuania	29 Jan 28	89LTS338	302027
Hungary	Serb/Croat/Slovene	22 Feb 28	181LTS229	304192
Hungary	Serb/Croat/Slovene	22 Feb 28	100LTS331	302305
Bel-Lux Econ Union	France	23 Feb 28	72LTS61	301689
Germany	Greece	24 Mar 28	90LTS9	302031

PARTY ONE	PARTY TWO	DATE	CITATION	NUMBER
General (Cont.)				
Germany	Siam	07 Apr 28	85LTS337	301938
Germany	Sweden	25 Apr 28	81LTS281	301844
Hungary	Poland	12 May 28	123LTS47	302804
Latvia	Turkey	28 May 28	94LTS295	302150
Belgium	Poland	12 Jun 28	123LTS25	302803
Austria	Persia	17 Jun 28	112LTS101	302610
Austria	Hungary	25 Jun 28	100LTS85	302296
Multilateral		30 Jun 28	89LTS53	302005
Italy	Persia	24 Jul 28	95LTS269	302179
Canada	USA (United States)	17 Sep 28	95LTS209	302175
Germany	Lithuania	30 Oct 28	90LTS255	302043
Estonia	Germany	07 Dec 28	99LTS259	302273
Netherlands	Norway	11 Jan 29	85LTS409	301941
Norway	USA (United States)	25 Feb 29	134LTS81	303085
Persia	Sweden	10 May 29	102LTS9	302349
Bulgaria	Germany	04 Jun 29	106LTS49	302436
Canada	Denmark	18 Jun 29	95LTS81	302167
Italy	Panama	16 Oct 29	138LTS355	303199
Irish Free State	Portugal	29 Oct 29	131LTS145	303007
Poland	Romania	30 Oct 29	121LTS167	302787
China	UK Great Britain	31 Oct 29	99LTS441	302289
Canada	Sweden	21 Nov 29	97LTS331	302230
Honduras	Nicaragua	30 Jan 30	142LTS241	303297
Austria	Germany	12 Apr 30	115LTS297	302693
Norway	Persia	08 May 30	134LTS153	303089
Germany	Irish Free State	12 May 30	131LTS153	303008
France	Italy	16 Jun 30	144LTS115	303323
Poland	Romania	23 Jun 30	133LTS163	303066
Austria	Japan	16 Aug 30	126LTS351	302894
Finland	Norway	11 Nov 30	130LTS17	302980
Switzerland	Turkey	13 Dec 30	129LTS331	302968
Czechoslovakia	Romania	22 Dec 30	167LTS243	303870
Belgium	Luxembourg	09 Mar 31	137LTS267	303161
Finland	Sweden	16 Mar 31	118LTS71	302714
Norway	Turkey	16 Mar 31	138LTS41	303180
Multilateral		30 Mar 31	138LTS149	303185
Belgium	France	16 May 31	141LTS333	303274
Belgium	Italy	11 Jul 31	136LTS9	303120
Denmark	Iceland	11 Jul 31	141LTS323	303273
Germany	Switzerland	15 Jul 31	144LTS389	303341
Germany	Hungary	18 Jul 31	150LTS111	303458
Hungary	Romania	12 Aug 31	186LTS325	304321
Multilateral		21 Aug 31	185LTS45	304273
Bolivia	Denmark	09 Nov 31	147LTS27	303387
Belgium	France	23 Dec 31	137LTS277	303162
South Africa	Swaziland	16 Mar 32	129LTS377	302972
Austria	Poland	22 Apr 32	143LTS45	303304
France	USA (United States)	27 Apr 32	164LTS211	303795
Denmark	Sweden	06 May 32	130LTS161	302989
Belgium	France	18 Jun 32	137LTS289	303163
Bulgaria	Germany	24 Jun 32	147LTS211	303400
France	Italy	03 Oct 32	153LTS55	303507
Romania	Yugoslavia	30 Jan 33	146LTS99	303362
Belgium	Netherlands	20 Feb 33	164LTS223	303796
Norway	UK Great Britain	15 May 33	145LTS187	303355
Sweden	UK Great Britain	15 May 33	140LTS317	303245
Bulgaria	Czechoslovakia	29 Aug 33	148LTS15	303402
Finland	UK Great Britain	29 Sep 33	149LTS167	303438
Latvia	Lithuania	01 Dec 33	148LTS97	303407
Latvia	USSR (Soviet Union)	04 Dec 33	148LTS145	303410
Estonia	Lithuania	13 Jan 34	148LTS337	303420
Argentina	Bel-Lux Econ Union	16 Jan 34	147LTS79	303392
Czechoslovakia	Poland	10 Feb 34	183LTS213	304238
Finland	USA (United States)	13 Feb 34	152LTS45	303484
Finland	Germany	24 Mar 34	149LTS343	303442

PARTY ONE	PARTY TWO	DATE	CITATION	NUMBER
General (Cont.)				
Czechoslovakia	Romania	20 Jun 34	168LTS241	303901
Denmark	France	31 Jul 34	150LTS381	303471
China	UK Great Britain	27 Oct 34	160LTS265	303695
Poland	Spain	14 Dec 34	168LTS315	303908
Belgium	Germany	21 Dec 34	162LTS9	303730
Netherlands	Sweden	21 Mar 35	148LTS451	303648
Czechoslovakia	USSR (Soviet Union)	25 Mar 35	161LTS257	303718
Germany	Sweden	14 May 35	163LTS425	303784
Germany	Sweden	14 May 35	163LTS459	303785
Czechoslovakia	Hungary	14 Jun 35	171LTS401	303976
Germany	Iraq	04 Aug 35	171LTS65	303951
Belgium	Switzerland	30 Aug 35	162LTS293	303741
Finland	Germany	25 Sep 35	173LTS11	304001
Finland	Germany	25 Sep 35	172LTS359	304000
Canada	USA (United States)	15 Nov 35	168LTS355	303910
Spain	Turkey	31 Dec 35	166LTS163	303838
Switzerland	USA (United States)	09 Jan 36	171LTS231	303962
Panama	USA (United States)	02 Mar 36	200LTS17	304686
France	USA (United States)	06 May 36	199LTS259	304679
Finland	USA (United States)	18 May 36	172LTS97	303981
Hungary	Sweden	17 Jun 36	184LTS11	304239
Brazil	UK Great Britain	10 Aug 36	172LTS273	303996
Netherlands	UK Great Britain	27 Aug 36	172LTS53	303978
Romania	Turkey	04 Sep 36	195LTS429	304564
Australia	France	27 Nov 36	177LTS301	304095
Costa Rica	USA (United States)	28 Nov 36	181LTS183	304189
France	Sweden	04 Dec 36	184LTS35	304241
Canada	USA (United States)	30 Dec 36	184LTS473	304268
Czechoslovakia	South Africa	27 Jan 37	189LTS97	304377
El Salvador	USA (United States)	19 Feb 37	179LTS219	304150
United Arab Rep	Turkey	07 Apr 37	191LTS95	304438
Sweden	Yugoslavia	14 May 37	194LTS21	304504
Norway	Sweden	14 Jun 37	179LTS245	304151
Iceland	Sweden	08 Sep 37	187LTS405	304346
France	Switzerland	13 Oct 37	194LTS191	304522
Estonia	France	16 Oct 37	183LTS41	304227
Belgium	Siam	05 Nov 37	190LTS163	304414
Siam	USA (United States)	13 Nov 37	192LTS247	304476
Siam	UK Great Britain	23 Nov 37	188LTS333	304366
Denmark	Finland	02 Dec 37	187LTS379	304345
Latvia	Turkey	12 Jan 38	201LTS229	304716
Multilateral		10 Feb 38	192LTS59	304461
Lithuania	Poland	14 May 38	191LTS373	304456
Ecuador	USA (United States)	06 Aug 38	193LTS85	304489
Greece	Portugal	15 Aug 38	201LTS201	304707
Cuba	Portugal	06 Sep 38	195LTS443	304565
UK Great Britain	USA (United States)	17 Nov 38	200LTS293	304700
Canada	USA (United States)	17 Nov 38	199LTS91	304670
Guatemala	Norway	20 Dec 38	198LTS117	304631
Multilateral		05 Feb 39	196LTS303	304592
Turkey	USA (United States)	01 Apr 39	202LTS129	304741
USA (United States)	Venezuela	06 Nov 39	203LTS273	304770
United Arab Rep	UK Great Britain	17 Jul 40	202LTS97	304738
United Arab Rep	France	03 Aug 40	202LTS121	304740
Taxation of immovable property				
Czechoslovakia	Hungary	13 Jul 23	35LTS237	300898
Multilateral		30 Oct 35	189LTS51	304375
Japan	Siam	08 Dec 37	188LTS375	304367
Germany	Siam	30 Dec 37	188LTS401	304368
Taxation of professional services				
Austria	Romania	26 Jul 24	85LTS243	301934
Taxable items				
Germany	UK Great Britain	10 Nov 37	186LTS277	304316

PARTY ONE	PARTY TWO	DATE	CITATION	NUMBER
Tax exemptions				
Austria	Greece	16 Sep 04	2LTS161	300062
Cuba	Netherlands	31 Dec 13	14LTS29	300366
Greece	Spain	06 Mar 19	3LTS81	300092
Germany	Hungary	01 Jun 20	7LTS207	300187
Japan	Paraguay	30 Nov 20	6LTS367	300169
UK Great Britain	USSR (Soviet Union)	16 Mar 21	4LTS127	300104
Austria	Czechoslovakia	04 May 21	15LTS13	300388
Latvia	Lithuania	12 Jul 21	25LTS299	300619
Finland	Norway	16 Jul 21	19LTS77	300485
Austria	Germany	17 Aug 21	19LTS237	300497
Czechoslovakia	Germany	31 Dec 21	17LTS401	300447
France	Poland	06 Feb 22	43LTS415	301074
Austria	Czechoslovakia	11 Feb 22	152LTS175	303492
Austria	Czechoslovakia	18 Feb 22	14LTS129	300371
Austria	Germany	23 May 22	26LTS405	300660
Italy	Serb/Croat/Slovene	23 Oct 22	18LTS413	300479
Austria	Netherlands	06 Nov 22	17LTS375	300444
Denmark	USA (United States)	05 Dec 22	113LTS381	302649
Finland	USSR (Soviet Union)	21 Feb 23	19LTS219	300495
Germany	Poland	21 Mar 23	34LTS315	300881
Multilateral		29 Mar 23	23LTS256	300593
Germany	Netherlands	23 May 23	25LTS275	300617
Czechoslovakia	Hungary	13 Jul 23	35LTS237	300898
Austria	Italy	16 Jul 23	27LTS383	300699
Multilateral		24 Jul 23	28LTS151	300704
Multilateral		24 Jul 23	36LTS175	300918
Other Unilat Decla	Greece	29 Sep 23	20LTS29	300503
Germany	Hungary	06 Nov 23	45LTS279	301104
Finland	Poland	10 Nov 23	29LTS229	300744
Estonia	Poland	11 Jan 24	47LTS129	301132
Czechoslovakia	Italy	01 Mar 24	36LTS229	300925
Denmark	Poland	22 Mar 24	31LTS13	300778
Iraq	UK Great Britain	25 Mar 24	35LTS145	300894
Poland	USSR (Soviet Union)	18 Jul 24	49LTS201	301183
Italy	Serb/Croat/Slovene	21 Aug 24	82LTS445	301883
France	Latvia	30 Oct 24	37LTS399	300963
Austria	Hungary	08 Nov 24	44LTS407	301096
Denmark	UK Great Britain	18 Dec 24	32LTS89	300808
Norway	UK Great Britain	18 Dec 24	32LTS9	300801
Sweden	UK Great Britain	19 Dec 24	32LTS291	300820
Austria	Spain	03 Feb 25	43LTS313	301067
France	Siam	14 Feb 25	43LTS189	301055
UK Great Britain	USA (United States)	16 Mar 25	113LTS105	302639
Norway	USA (United States)	24 Mar 25	67LTS417	301563
Hungary	Poland	26 Mar 25	37LTS151	300954
Czechoslovakia	Poland	23 Apr 25	44LTS309	301091
Bel-Lux Econ Union		07 Jul 25	54LTS267	301290
Denmark	Finland	19 Oct 25	47LTS259	301140
Estonia	USA (United States)	28 Oct 25	62LTS63	301455
Germany	Italy	31 Oct 25	53LTS245	301261
Finland	Great Britain	18 Nov 25	42LTS445	301042
Hungary	Italy	25 Nov 25	74LTS251	301741
Norway	USSR (Soviet Union)	15 Dec 25	47LTS9	301127
Germany	Sweden	31 Dec 25	43LTS219	301056
Austria	Switzerland	06 Jan 26	46LTS299	301124
Germany	Poland	27 Jan 26	64LTS113	301504
Cuba	USA (United States)	22 Apr 26	60LTS371	301421
Bel-Lux Econ Union	Siam	13 Jul 26	62LTS287	301468
Benelux Econ Union	Germany	15 Jul 26	63LTS137	301485
Greece	Spain	23 Sep 26	91LTS121	302059
Poland	USA (United States)	14 Nov 26	58LTS97	301368
Bulgaria	Germany	22 Dec 26	64LTS77	301502
Portugal	UK Great Britain	31 Dec 26	61LTS115	301429
France	USA (United States)	29 Aug 27	68LTS253	301589

PARTY ONE	PARTY TWO	DATE	CITATION	NUMBER
Tax exemptions (Cont.)				
Belgium	France	06 Oct 27	69LTS49	301599
Sweden	USSR (Soviet Union)	08 Oct 27	71LTS411	301679
Denmark	Japan	15 Oct 27	71LTS75	301655
Germany	Great Britain	17 Jan 28	71LTS193	301661
Japan	USSR (Soviet Union)	23 Jan 28	80LTS341	301839
Hungary	Serb/Croat/Slovene	22 Feb 28	100LTS331	302305
Czechoslovakia	Germany	11 May 28	81LTS441	301854
Hungary	Poland	12 May 28	123LTS47	302804
Canada	USA (United States)	17 Sep 28	95LTS209	302175
Canada	Norway	02 May 29	91LTS329	302073
Estonia	USSR (Soviet Union)	17 May 29	94LTS323	302152
Bolivia	Netherlands	30 May 29	133LTS113	303062
Greece	USA (United States)	10 Jun 29	98LTS81	302241
Canada	Denmark	18 Jun 29	95LTS81	302167
Greece	UK Great Britain	31 Jul 29	95LTS67	302165
Japan	UK Great Britain	10 Aug 29	95LTS73	302166
Canada	Japan	21 Sep 29	96LTS143	302196
Canada	Netherlands	23 Sep 29	96LTS151	302197
Canada	Greece	30 Sep 29	96LTS159	302198
Italy	Panama	16 Oct 29	138LTS355	303199
Canada	Sweden	21 Nov 29	97LTS331	302230
France	Sweden	25 Jan 30	99LTS99	302271
Belgium	Spain	31 Jan 30	99LTS369	302281
France	Netherlands	28 Feb 30	101LTS303	302331
Denmark	France	28 Feb 30	101LTS17	302316
Canada	Germany	17 Apr 30	101LTS245	302326
France	Norway	02 Jun 30	102LTS27	302350
Spain	USA (United States)	10 Jun 30	120LTS407	302777
Belgium	Germany	20 Jun 30	110LTS107	302555
Germany	USA (United States)	23 Jun 30	106LTS121	302440
France	Romania	27 Aug 30	158LTS379	303644
El Salvador	USA (United States)	05 Sep 30	134LTS207	303093
Irish Free State	Norway	21 Oct 30	109LTS177	302536
Denmark	Netherlands	08 Nov 30	109LTS115	302531
Lithuania	Norway	14 Nov 30	109LTS187	302538
Czechoslovakia	Romania	05 Dec 30	167LTS205	303867
Greece	Netherlands	05 Dec 30	117LTS357	302702
Switzerland	Turkey	13 Dec 30	129LTS331	302968
Ethiopia	Greece	23 Mar 31	153LTS127	303512
Multilateral		30 Mar 31	138LTS149	303185
Estonia	Latvia	16 May 31	123LTS61	302805
Poland	USA (United States)	15 Jun 31	139LTS395	303223
Sweden	UK Great Britain	06 Jul 31	120LTS211	302766
Denmark	Norway	05 Aug 31	121LTS9	302779
Greece	Romania	11 Aug 31	130LTS69	302982
Greece	Norway	15 Aug 31	123LTS271	302817
Multilateral		21 Aug 31	127LTS95	302910
Poland	Turkey	29 Aug 31	144LTS367	303339
Irish Free State	Sweden	08 Oct 31	125LTS23	302842
Switzerland	UK Great Britain	17 Oct 31	131LTS245	303015
Greece	Sweden	19 Nov 31	126LTS411	302899
Denmark	Finland	12 Dec 31	112LTS29	302604
Romania	Yugoslavia	14 Dec 31	135LTS89	303105
Belgium	France	23 Dec 31	137LTS277	303162
Japan	Norway	23 Dec 31	127LTS21	302902
Greece	Italy	15 Jan 32	137LTS397	303169
Italy	Latvia	11 May 32	150LTS9	303450
Estonia	Spain	23 Jun 32	143LTS31	303303
France	Yugoslavia	29 Jul 32	144LTS313	303334
France	UK Great Britain	01 Oct 32	135LTS25	303102
Japan	Netherlands	26 Jan 33	138LTS185	303187
Romania	Yugoslavia	30 Jan 33	146LTS99	303362
Sweden	UK Great Britain	15 May 33	140LTS317	303245
Brazil	Uruguay	25 Aug 33	176LTS381	304075
Brazil	Uruguay	20 Dec 33	181LTS55	304177

PARTY ONE	PARTY TWO	DATE	CITATION	NUMBER
Tax exemptions (Cont.)				
Denmark	Irish Free State	25 Apr 34	149LTS31	303430
Persia	Switzerland	25 Apr 34	160LTS173	303691
Brazil	USA (United States)	02 Feb 35	166LTS211	303840
Finland	UK Great Britain	21 Feb 35	158LTS323	303642
Multilateral		15 Mar 35	170LTS9	303926
Netherlands	Sweden	21 Mar 35	148LTS451	303648
France	UK Great Britain	09 Apr 35	199LTS49	304663
Netherlands	UK Great Britain	06 Jun 35	169LTS359	303924
Colombia	USA (United States)	13 Sep 35	170LTS293	303944
Honduras	USA (United States)	18 Dec 35	167LTS313	303876
France	Spain	21 Dec 35	167LTS9	303856
Belgium	USA (United States)	28 Jan 36	166LTS333	303849
Netherlands	UK Great Britain	27 Aug 36	172LTS53	303978
United Arab Rep	UK Great Britain	09 Sep 36	182LTS317	304219
Greece	UK Great Britain	17 Sep 36	176LTS183	304060
Belgium	Norway	17 Dec 36	178LTS153	304110
Chile	Cuba	13 Mar 37	195LTS389	304558
Japan	USA (United States)	25 Mar 37	181LTS217	304191
Japan	UK Great Britain	25 Mar 37	181LTS289	304196
Canada	Haiti	23 Apr 37	194LTS59	304507
Romania	Yugoslavia	13 May 37	197LTS145	304611
Belgium	United Arab Rep	20 May 37	182LTS153	304207
Belgium	UK Great Britain	01 Jun 37	196LTS209	304583
Multilateral		02 Jun 37	184LTS445	304265
France	UK Great Britain	29 Jul 37	184LTS351	304257
Canada	Guatemala	28 Sep 37	194LTS65	304508
Denmark	Netherlands	24 Mar 38	190LTS225	304421
Sweden	USA (United States)	31 Mar 38	189LTS327	304392
Norway	Sweden	20 Apr 38	189LTS153	304383
Belgium	Netherlands	30 Apr 38	190LTS199	304418
Portugal	UK Great Britain	11 May 38	191LTS285	304450
Lithuania	Poland	14 May 38	191LTS373	304456
Belgium	Luxembourg	22 Jul 38	191LTS113	304440
Latvia	Poland	29 Oct 38	195LTS169	304547
Estonia	Lithuania	03 Dec 38	193LTS217	304498
Norway	UK Great Britain	21 Dec 38	201LTS357	304723
Estonia	Latvia	11 Jan 39	194LTS103	304512
Sweden	USA (United States)	23 Mar 39	199LTS17	304661
Dominican Republic	Newfoundland	16 Mar 40	203LTS141	304757
Patents, copyrights and trademarks				
Belgium	Lithuania	21 Jul 31	137LTS225	303158
Austria	UK Great Britain	27 Jul 33	142LTS157	303287
Poland	USA (United States)	17 Apr 34	150LTS403	303473
Bolivia	Spain	13 Mar 36	170LTS179	303933
Multilateral		09 Sep 86*	123LTS233	302816
Literary and artistic copyrights				
Italy	Sweden	24 Jun 35	161LTS27	303703
Trademarks				
Multilateral		30 Jun 20	1LTS59	300008
Austria	Czechoslovakia	04 May 21	15LTS13	300388
Finland	France	13 Jul 21	29LTS445	300755
Austria	Hungary	08 Oct 21	16LTS19	300402
Estonia	Finland	29 Oct 21	13LTS59	300348
Czechoslovakia	Latvia	07 Oct 22	20LTS379	300528
Latvia	UK Great Britain	22 Jun 23	20LTS395	300529
Estonia	Germany	27 Jun 23	41LTS161	301013
Denmark	Estonia	27 Jul 23	19LTS253	300499
Estonia	Latvia	01 Nov 23	25LTS354	300624
Germany	Siam	28 Feb 24	32LTS399	300828
Germany	Greece	21 Mar 24	30LTS257	300769
Czechoslovakia	France	18 Aug 24	44LTS21	301080
France	Latvia	30 Oct 24	37LTS399	300963
Bolivia	Germany	20 Feb 25	42LTS43	301030
Bel-Lux Econ Union		07 Jul 25	54LTS267	301290
Trademarks (Cont.)				
Portugal	Siam	14 Aug 25	55LTS57	301304
Siam	UK Great Britain	15 Sep 25	49LTS51	301176
Germany	USSR (Soviet Union)	12 Oct 25	53LTS7	301257
Austria	China	19 Oct 25	55LTS9	301301
Multilateral		06 Nov 25	74LTS341	301746
Multilateral		06 Nov 25	74LTS289	301743
Multilateral		06 Nov 25	74LTS327	301745
Norway	USSR (Soviet Union)	15 Dec 25	47LTS9	301127
Estonia	UK Great Britain	18 Jan 26	48LTS209	301163
Denmark	Siam	01 Mar 26	47LTS103	301131
Italy	UK Great Britain	24 Jun 26	57LTS71	301353
Sweden	USSR (Soviet Union)	21 Jul 26	57LTS9	301346
Chile	Norway	09 Feb 27	80LTS325	301837
Guatemala	Netherlands	12 May 27	85LTS323	301937
Serb/Croat/Slovene	UK Great Britain	12 May 27	80LTS165	301825
Italy	Lithuania	17 Sep 27	73LTS9	301701
Greece	Serb/Croat/Slovene	02 Nov 27	91LTS137	302060
Guatemala	UK Great Britain	22 Feb 28	97LTS229	302226
Austria	Great Britain	13 Apr 28	80LTS247	301830
Multilateral		15 Jul 28	79LTS133	301806
Belgium	Great Britain	21 Dec 28	85LTS415	301942
Multilateral		20 Feb 29	124LTS357	302840
Romania	Turkey	11 Jun 29	112LTS139	302613
China	Poland	18 Sep 29	120LTS331	302774
Poland	Portugal	28 Dec 29	117LTS363	302703
Germany	Persia	24 Feb 30	113LTS15	302630
Portugal	Romania	05 Dec 30	114LTS369	302666
Siam	Switzerland	28 May 31	125LTS357	302864
Italy	Netherlands	01 Jul 31	127LTS235	302923
Czechoslovakia	Netherlands	11 Aug 31	127LTS347	302928
Lithuania	Sweden	16 Oct 31	126LTS233	302885
Finland	Lithuania	19 Jun 34	153LTS49	303506
Iran	USSR (Soviet Union)	27 Aug 35	176LTS299	304069
Chile	Sweden	21 Oct 36	174LTS109	304041
Italy	UK Great Britain	06 Nov 36	177LTS169	304089
Romania	Yugoslavia	13 May 37	197LTS145	304611
France	Siam	07 Dec 37	201LTS113	304708
Denmark	Norway	18 Jun 39	197LTS227	304615
Laws and formalities				
Multilateral		13 Nov 08	1LTS217	300015
Multilateral		20 Aug 10	155LTS179	303576
Multilateral		20 Mar 14	1LTS243	300016
Sweden	USA (United States)	27 Feb 20	2LTS147	300059
Iceland	Sweden	23 Mar 21	4LTS137	300105
Brazil	Portugal	26 Sep 22	25LTS229	300610
Netherlands	USA (United States)	03 Apr 23	21LTS175	300541
Multilateral		28 Apr 23	33LTS47	300832
Hungary	Latvia	19 Nov 23	37LTS341	300959
Germany	Siam	28 Feb 24	32LTS399	300828
Multilateral		22 May 24	35LTS175	300895
Italy	Serb/Croat/Slovene	14 Jul 24	82LTS257	301876
France	Latvia	30 Oct 24	37LTS399	300963
Bolivia	Germany	20 Feb 25	42LTS43	301030
Finland	Iceland	07 Mar 25	34LTS169	300872
Japan	Latvia	04 Jul 25	80LTS305	301836
Paraguay	Spain	08 Jul 25	138LTS225	303190
Germany	UK Great Britain	13 Aug 25	43LTS89	301050
Portugal	Siam	14 Aug 25	55LTS57	301304
Hungary	UK Great Britain	23 Jul 26	67LTS183	301546
Multilateral		18 Feb 28	132LTS275	303044
Norway	USSR (Soviet Union)	24 Feb 28	79LTS9	301801
Belgium	Great Britain	21 Dec 28	85LTS415	301942
Multilateral		20 Feb 29	124LTS357	302840
France	Turkey	29 Aug 29	123LTS193	302815

PARTY ONE	PARTY TWO	DATE	CITATION	NUMBER
Laws and formalities (Cont.)				
Hungary	Yugoslavia	11 Nov 29	111LTS197	302587
Austria	Germany	15 Feb 30	109LTS501	302552
Germany	Irish Free State	12 May 30	131LTS153	303008
Argentina	USA (United States)	03 Sep 34	160LTS57	303682
Belgium	Siam	05 Nov 37	190LTS163	304414
Siam	USA (United States)	13 Nov 37	192LTS247	304476
Canada	USA (United States)	24 Jan 38	187LTS27	304330
Sweden	USA (United States)	23 Mar 39	199LTS17	304661
UK Great Britain	USA (United States)	24 Aug 42	204LTS403	304820
Post-war adjustment				
Czechoslovakia	Germany	06 Feb 25	46LTS165	301118
Recognition				
Multilateral		13 Nov 08	1LTS217	300015
Sweden	USA (United States)	27 Feb 20	2LTS147	300059
Iceland	Sweden	23 Mar 21	4LTS137	300105
France	Norway	23 Apr 21	14LTS375	300386
Finland	France	13 Jul 21	29LTS445	300755
Austria	Hungary	08 Oct 21	16LTS19	300402
Brazil	Portugal	26 Sep 22	25LTS229	300610
Czechoslovakia	Latvia	07 Oct 22	20LTS379	300528
Germany	Iceland	12 Feb 23	27LTS405	300700
Netherlands	USA (United States)	03 Apr 23	21LTS175	300541
Multilateral		28 Apr 23	33LTS47	300832
Latvia	UK Great Britain	22 Jun 23	20LTS395	300529
Denmark	Estonia	27 Jul 23	19LTS259	300500
Mexico	Spain	31 Mar 24	43LTS297	301065
Austria	Greece	27 May 24	27LTS99	300671
Austria	Latvia	09 Aug 24	65LTS7	301516
France	Portugal	04 Mar 25	44LTS197	301083
Finland	Iceland	07 Mar 25	34LTS169	300872
Czechoslovakia	Japan	30 Oct 25	58LTS263	301377
Multilateral		06 Nov 25	74LTS289	301743
Siam	Sweden	19 Dec 25	58LTS429	301386
Italy	UK Great Britain	24 Jun 26	57LTS71	301353
Germany	Latvia	28 Jun 26	58LTS403	301385
Bel-Lux Econ Union	Siam	13 Jul 26	62LTS287	301468
Greece	Spain	23 Sep 26	91LTS121	302059
Greece	Italy	24 Oct 26	63LTS51	301480
Greece	UK Great Britain	13 May 27	61LTS15	301425
Denmark	USSR (Soviet Union)	23 Dec 27	70LTS245	301636
Multilateral		18 Feb 28	132LTS275	303044
Norway	USSR (Soviet Union)	24 Feb 28	79LTS9	301801
Estonia	USSR (Soviet Union)	03 Mar 28	80LTS401	301840
Multilateral		20 Feb 29	124LTS357	302840
Persia	Sweden	10 May 29	102LTS9	302349
Germany	Persia	24 Feb 30	113LTS15	302630
Turkey	UK Great Britain	01 Mar 30	108LTS407	302523
Germany	South Africa	12 May 30	123LTS301	302821
Norway	Turkey	16 Mar 31	138LTS41	303180
Denmark	Lithuania	17 Jan 34	149LTS43	303432
Poland	USA (United States)	17 Apr 34	150LTS403	303473
Chile	Denmark	22 Aug 34	154LTS181	303546
Nicaragua	Spain	20 Nov 34	166LTS143	303836
Denmark	Norway	18 Jun 39	197LTS227	304615
UK Great Britain	USA (United States)	24 Aug 42	204LTS403	304820
Customs duties				
Liberia	UK Great Britain	10 Apr 13	1LTS205	300014
Denmark	Sweden	26 Jan 20	14LTS273	300379
France	Germany	01 Mar 20	1LTS367	300030
Germany	Switzerland	15 Mar 20	12LTS19	300303
Germany	Hungary	01 Jun 20	7LTS207	300187
France	Portugal	08 Jun 20	1LTS393	300032
Czechoslovakia	Germany	29 Jun 20	17LTS69	300430
Multilateral		10 Aug 20	28LTS225	300710

PARTY ONE	PARTY TWO	DATE	CITATION	NUMBER
Customs duties (Cont.)				
Germany	Switzerland	14 Sep 20	2LTS331	300087
Czechoslovakia	Serb/Croat/Slovene	18 Oct 20	17LTS19	300424
France	UK Great Britain	20 Oct 20	2LTS323	300085
Danzig	Poland	09 Nov 20	6LTS189	300153
Japan	Paraguay	30 Nov 20	6LTS367	300169
Denmark	UK Great Britain	23 Dec 20	2LTS249	300071
Canada	France	29 Jan 21	8LTS105	300212
Norway	USA (United States)	11 Feb 21	5LTS217	300130
Sweden	UK Great Britain	16 Feb 21	3LTS233	300100
Belgium	UK Great Britain	15 Mar 21	5LTS319	300138
Spain	Sweden	18 Mar 21	4LTS259	300109
Czechoslovakia	Italy	23 Mar 21	32LTS183	300815
Germany	Poland	10 Apr 21	6LTS233	300158
Romania	Sweden	21 Apr 21	4LTS265	300110
Czechoslovakia	Romania	23 Apr 21	15LTS235	300397
Austria	Czechoslovakia	04 May 21	15LTS13	300388
Portugal	UK Great Britain	06 May 21	5LTS179	300128
China	Germany	20 May 21	9LTS271	300261
Germany	Poland	06 Jun 21	34LTS185	300874
Finland	France	13 Jul 21	29LTS445	300755
Norway	UK Great Britain	15 Jul 21	6LTS307	300162
Belgium	Luxembourg	25 Jul 21	9LTS223	300256
Austria	Hungary	08 Oct 21	16LTS19	300402
Danzig	Poland	24 Oct 21	116LTS5	302699
Estonia	Finland	29 Oct 21	13LTS59	300348
Spain	Sweden	29 Dec 21	9LTS58	300242
Netherlands	Spain	05 Jan 22	9LTS257	300259
Multilateral		06 Feb 22	38LTS267	300981
France	Poland	06 Feb 22	43LTS415	301074
Austria	Hungary	08 Feb 22	55LTS367	301320
Austria	Czechoslovakia	18 Feb 22	14LTS129	300371
France	Switzerland	20 Mar 22	12LTS377	300332
Denmark	Germany	25 Apr 22	18LTS227	300466
Germany	Poland	29 Apr 22	21LTS391	300549
Germany	Poland	15 May 22	10LTS37	300273
Germany	Poland	15 May 22	10LTS37	300273
Poland	Switzerland	26 Jun 22	12LTS305	300322
Czechoslovakia	Latvia	07 Oct 22	20LTS379	300528
Estonia	Hungary	19 Oct 22	30LTS347	300774
Italy	Serb/Croat/Slovene	23 Oct 22	18LTS441	300480
Italy	Serb/Croat/Slovene	23 Oct 22	18LTS413	300479
Finland	USSR (Soviet Union)	28 Oct 22	19LTS153	300491
Denmark	Sweden	07 Nov 22	14LTS95	300370
France	Saar	30 Nov 22	27LTS283	300691
China	Japan	01 Dec 22	22LTS179	300559
Japan	Poland	07 Dec 22	32LTS61	300806
China	Japan	08 Dec 22	20LTS289	300522
China	Japan	08 Dec 22	20LTS233	300520
Canada	France	15 Dec 22	21LTS38	300532
Multilateral		30 Dec 22	21LTS183	300542
Germany	Spain	15 Jan 23	26LTS455	300662
Italy	Switzerland	27 Jan 23	25LTS21	300603
Norway	UK Great Britain	22 Feb 23	15LTS159	300389
Czechoslovakia	Hungary	08 Mar 23	48LTS257	301167
Multilateral		29 Mar 23	23LTS378	300594
Multilateral		29 Mar 23	23LTS256	300593
Liechtenstein	Switzerland	29 Mar 23	21LTS231	300545
Norway	Portugal	11 Apr 23	16LTS379	300418
Denmark	UK Great Britain	25 Apr 23	22LTS157	300557
Greece	Serb/Croat/Slovene	10 May 23	25LTS441	300635
Norway	Sweden	26 May 23	18LTS155	300462
Germany	Lithuania	01 Jun 23	51LTS387	301244
Finland	USSR (Soviet Union)	05 Jun 23	18LTS203	300465
Latvia	UK Great Britain	22 Jun 23	20LTS395	300529
Estonia	Germany	27 Jun 23	41LTS161	301013

PARTY ONE	PARTY TWO	DATE	CITATION	NUMBER
Customs duties (Cont.)				
Belgium	Denmark	28 Jun 23	20LTS59	300507
Estonia	Sweden	07 Jul 23	20LTS189	300517
Czechoslovakia	UK Great Britain	14 Jul 23	29LTS377	300748
Multilateral		24 Jul 23	28LTS171	300705
Netherlands	Portugal	22 Aug 23	20LTS139	300513
Estonia	Iceland	07 Sep 23	23LTS131	300584
Denmark	Estonia	07 Sep 23	23LTS73	300577
Austria	Japan	02 Oct 23	22LTS349	300563
Italy	Switzerland	22 Oct 23	65LTS301	301521
Estonia	Latvia	31 Oct 23	25LTS321	300621
Estonia	Latvia	01 Nov 23	25LTS354	300624
Multilateral		03 Nov 23	30LTS371	300775
Italy	Spain	15 Nov 23	39LTS49	300996
Japan	Serb/Croat/Slovene	16 Nov 23	42LTS99	301035
Hungary	Latvia	19 Nov 23	37LTS341	300959
Multilateral		09 Dec 23	47LTS55	301129
Finland	UK Great Britain	14 Dec 23	29LTS129	300739
Multilateral		14 Dec 23	29LTS37	300732
Multilateral		18 Dec 23	28LTS541	300729
Lithuania	Norway	21 Dec 23	32LTS55	300805
France	Italy	10 Jan 24	43LTS431	301076
Austria	Turkey	28 Jan 24	32LTS313	300823
Czechoslovakia	Denmark	31 Jan 24	23LTS139	300585
Czechoslovakia	Hungary	09 Feb 24	30LTS335	300773
Netherlands	USA (United States)	15 Feb 24	31LTS61	300783
Lithuania	Sweden	17 Feb 24	23LTS153	300587
France	Greece	21 Feb 24	43LTS481	301077
Netherlands	Portugal	27 Feb 24	27LTS105	300672
Germany	Siam	28 Feb 24	32LTS399	300828
Japan	Siam	09 Mar 24	31LTS187	300795
Multilateral		12 Mar 24	24LTS17	300595
Other Unilat Decla	Hungary	14 Mar 24	25LTS427	300634
Multilateral		14 Mar 24	25LTS423	300633
Denmark	Poland	22 Mar 24	31LTS13	300778
Iceland	Poland	22 Mar 24	31LTS35	300779
Multilateral		28 Mar 24	31LTS46	300780
Denmark	Latvia	03 Apr 24	33LTS393	300860
Poland	Serb/Croat/Slovene	05 Apr 24	49LTS265	301185
Czechoslovakia	Iceland	08 May 24	46LTS419	301125
Multilateral		22 May 24	35LTS175	300895
Finland	Iceland	28 May 24	27LTS117	300676
Lithuania	Netherlands	10 Jun 24	34LTS373	300885
Spain	UK Great Britain	27 Jun 24	28LTS523	300727
Latvia	Netherlands	02 Jul 24	37LTS121	300951
Bel-Lux Econ Union	Canada	03 Jul 24	32LTS35	300803
Italy	Serb/Croat/Slovene	14 Jul 24	82LTS257	301876
Estonia	Netherlands	22 Jul 24	48LTS199	301162
Germany	Spain	25 Jul 24	41LTS363	301023
Austria	France	11 Aug 24	44LTS7	301079
Italy	Serb/Croat/Slovene	12 Aug 24	82LTS423	301882
Czechoslovakia	France	18 Aug 24	44LTS21	301080
Netherlands	Portugal	27 Aug 24	31LTS235	300800
Multilateral		28 Aug 24	40LTS307	301004
Guatemala	Nicaragua	10 Sep 24	130LTS127	302987
Hungary	Norway	16 Sep 24	33LTS103	300835
Japan	Peru	30 Sep 24	102LTS33	302351
Japan	Mexico	08 Oct 24	36LTS259	300927
Czechoslovakia	Netherlands	17 Oct 24	31LTS93	300786
Finland	Italy	22 Oct 24	32LTS149	300814
Multilateral		23 Oct 24	77LTS367	301778
France	Latvia	30 Oct 24	37LTS399	300963
Iceland	Latvia	03 Nov 24	43LTS339	301069
Austria	Hungary	08 Nov 24	44LTS407	301096
Austria	Czechoslovakia	27 Nov 24	42LTS201	301041
Poland	Sweden	02 Dec 24	36LTS299	300930

PARTY ONE	PARTY TWO	DATE	CITATION	NUMBER
Customs duties (Cont.)				
Austria	Norway	03 Dec 24	31LTS151	300792
Latvia	Switzerland	04 Dec 24	34LTS405	300889
Hungary	Netherlands	09 Dec 24	47LTS91	301130
France	Poland	09 Dec 24	44LTS127	301081
Finland	Sweden	22 Dec 24	73LTS33	301703
Netherlands	Norway	08 Jan 25	46LTS279	301122
France	Saar	15 Jan 25	44LTS181	301082
Austria	Spain	03 Feb 25	43LTS313	301067
Poland	USA (United States)	10 Feb 25	37LTS141	300953
France	Siam	14 Feb 25	43LTS189	301055
Estonia	USA (United States)	02 Mar 25	43LTS289	301064
France	Portugal	04 Mar 25	44LTS197	301083
Albania	Italy	06 Mar 25	44LTS359	301094
Hungary	Poland	26 Mar 25	37LTS151	300954
Benelux Econ Union	Germany	04 Apr 25	37LTS203	300957
Bel-Lux Econ Union	France	04 Apr 25	44LTS213	301085
Czechoslovakia	Greece	08 Apr 25	38LTS291	300984
Germany	Norway	11 Apr 25	52LTS115	301252
France	Germany	13 Apr 25	109LTS295	302546
Greece	Poland	17 Apr 25	38LTS301	300985
Czechoslovakia	Sweden	18 Apr 25	36LTS289	300929
Austria	Greece	18 Apr 25	38LTS311	300986
Czechoslovakia	Poland	23 Apr 25	44LTS285	301090
Finland	USA (United States)	02 May 25	47LTS351	301139
Spain	Sweden	04 May 25	36LTS323	300932
Germany	Greece	15 May 25	40LTS6	301001
Germany	USA (United States)	21 May 25	52LTS133	301254
Multilateral		09 Jun 25	49LTS9	301174
Bel-Lux Econ Union	Japan	27 Jun 25	36LTS95	300907
Bel-Lux Econ Union		07 Jul 25	54LTS267	301290
Finland	Spain	16 Jul 25	47LTS271	301135
Hungary	Italy	20 Jul 25	45LTS39	301098
Germany	UK Great Britain	13 Aug 25	43LTS89	301050
Portugal	Siam	14 Aug 25	55LTS57	301304
France	Germany	14 Aug 25	75LTS103	301756
Siam	UK Great Britain	15 Sep 25	49LTS51	301176
Austria	Germany	03 Oct 25	52LTS171	301255
Germany	USSR (Soviet Union)	12 Oct 25	53LTS7	301257
France	Hungary	13 Oct 25	48LTS9	301150
Estonia	Switzerland	14 Oct 25	49LTS421	301195
Austria	China	19 Oct 25	55LTS9	301301
Germany	Italy	31 Oct 25	52LTS179	301256
Germany	Switzerland	06 Nov 25	53LTS283	301262
Bulgaria	UK Great Britain	12 Nov 25	43LTS165	301052
Germany	Spain	18 Nov 25	53LTS309	301263
Germany	Turkey	13 Dec 25	53LTS355	301265
Norway	USSR (Soviet Union)	15 Dec 25	47LTS9	301127
Austria	Portugal	18 Dec 25	54LTS91	301277
Lithuania	USA (United States)	23 Dec 25	54LTS377	301300
Austria	Switzerland	06 Jan 26	46LTS299	301124
Latvia	USA (United States)	01 Feb 26	55LTS33	301302
France	Germany	12 Feb 26	48LTS153	301157
Romania	USA (United States)	26 Feb 26	51LTS59	301221
Denmark	Siam	01 Mar 26	47LTS103	301131
Denmark	Germany	20 Mar 26	51LTS317	301237
Germany	Portugal	20 Mar 26	53LTS361	301266
Germany	Poland	27 Mar 26	64LTS249	301506
Denmark	Germany	12 Apr 26	48LTS237	301165
Czechoslovakia	Poland	15 Apr 26	67LTS305	301554
Finland	Hungary	20 Apr 26	48LTS119	301154
Germany	Spain	07 May 26	53LTS321	301264
Germany	Sweden	14 May 26	51LTS99	301225
Austria	Germany	21 May 26	53LTS397	301269
France	Turkey	30 May 26	54LTS195	301285
Germany	Poland	16 Jun 26	65LTS379	301522

PARTY ONE	PARTY TWO	DATE	CITATION	NUMBER
Customs duties (Cont.)				
Albania	Serb/Croat/Slovene	22 Jun 26	91LTS55	302055
Austria	Czechoslovakia	12 Jul 26	86LTS395	301952
Dominican Republic	USA (United States)	19 Jul 26	54LTS145	301282
Hungary	USA (United States)	04 Sep 26	58LTS111	301369
Greece	Spain	23 Sep 26	91LTS121	302059
Multilateral		13 Nov 26	77LTS249	301773
Multilateral		13 Nov 26	77LTS217	301772
France	Italy	26 Jan 27	79LTS49	301804
Germany	Poland	26 Mar 27	64LTS177	301505
Belgium	France	11 Apr 27	143LTS215	303309
Germany	Norway	27 Apr 27	69LTS57	301600
Ceylon (Sri Lanka)	Germany	02 May 27	69LTS203	301606
Latvia	USSR (Soviet Union)	02 Jun 27	68LTS321	301591
Belgium	Portugal	21 Jul 27	71LTS439	301682
Hungary	Italy	25 Jul 27	74LTS67	301732
France	Germany	17 Aug 27	76LTS5	301761
Multilateral		10 Sep 27	75LTS7	301749
Multilateral		10 Sep 27	75LTS39	301750
France	Turkey	01 Nov 27	92LTS249	302092
Denmark	Germany	08 Nov 27	70LTS83	301625
Great Britain	Latvia	16 Nov 27	71LTS185	301660
Germany	Lithuania	29 Jan 28	89LTS97	302009
Albania	France	15 Feb 28	107LTS307	302487
France	Germany	23 Feb 28	79LTS247	301815
Czechoslovakia	Germany	22 Mar 28	93LTS235	302113
Estonia	Latvia	25 Mar 28	72LTS195	301692
Latvia	Sweden	30 Mar 28	73LTS39	301704
Germany	Siam	07 Apr 28	85LTS337	301938
Germany	Netherlands	28 Apr 28	95LTS333	302183
France	Persia	11 May 28	82LTS43	301858
Germany	Persia	15 May 28	107LTS389	302495
Belgium	Persia	15 May 28	94LTS447	302160
Cuba	Germany	14 Jun 28	124LTS47	302832
Austria	Persia	17 Jun 28	112LTS101	302610
Austria	USA (United States)	19 Jun 28	118LTS241	302728
France	Spain	16 Jul 28	135LTS149	303110
Italy	Persia	24 Jul 28	95LTS269	302179
Persia	Sweden	09 Aug 28	80LTS407	301841
France	UK Great Britain	23 Sep 28	87LTS29	301961
Panama	UK Great Britain	26 Sep 28	90LTS327	302046
Czechoslovakia	Serb/Croat/Slovene	07 Nov 28	98LTS297	302252
China	Norway	12 Nov 28	87LTS381	301983
Bel-Lux Econ Union	China	22 Nov 28	87LTS287	301975
China	Italy	27 Nov 28	93LTS173	302109
China	Denmark	12 Dec 28	91LTS207	302062
Peru	UK Great Britain	31 Dec 28	100LTS431	302312
Ecuador	UK Great Britain	05 Jan 29	90LTS369	302048
Bolivia	UK Great Britain	18 Jan 29	95LTS9	302161
Germany	Persia	17 Feb 29	111LTS19	302576
France	UK Great Britain	06 Mar 29	90LTS391	302050
Persia	USSR (Soviet Union)	10 Mar 29	107LTS419	302498
Japan	Persia	30 Mar 29	107LTS427	302499
Poland	Romania	30 Mar 29	123LTS147	302812
Norway	USA (United States)	30 Mar 29	91LTS383	302078
UK Great Britain	USA (United States)	02 Apr 29	94LTS17	302133
UK Great Britain	USA (United States)	06 Apr 29	99LTS27	302265
Finland	USSR (Soviet Union)	13 Apr 29	96LTS93	302193
Persia	Sweden	10 May 29	102LTS9	302349
Belgium	Luxembourg	18 May 29	119LTS377	302757
Greece	Persia	24 May 29	121LTS221	302788
Bolivia	Netherlands	30 May 29	133LTS113	303062
Bulgaria	Germany	04 Jun 29	106LTS49	302436
Multilateral		28 Jun 29	102LTS245	302368
Multilateral		28 Jun 29	103LTS71	302370
Multilateral		28 Jun 29	103LTS5	302369

PARTY ONE	PARTY TWO	DATE	CITATION	NUMBER
Customs duties (Cont.)				
UK Great Britain	USA (United States)	04 Jul 29	92LTS329	302099
UK Great Britain	USA (United States)	11 Jul 29	98LTS161	302245
Poland	Romania	30 Oct 29	121LTS243	302790
Poland	Romania	30 Oct 29	121LTS167	302787
Belgium	Germany	07 Nov 29	121LTS327	302795
Multilateral		09 Nov 29	125LTS205	302855
Poland	Romania	07 Dec 29	119LTS283	302752
Austria	Germany	12 Apr 30	115LTS297	302693
Netherlands	Yugoslavia	28 May 30	129LTS73	302951
Multilateral		07 Jun 30	143LTS337	303315
Poland	Romania	23 Jun 30	133LTS163	303066
Czechoslovakia	Germany	27 Jun 30	112LTS169	302614
Brazil	Switzerland	29 Oct 30	140LTS265	303241
Switzerland	Turkey	13 Dec 30	129LTS267	302964
Multilateral		22 Dec 30	126LTS341	302893
Czechoslovakia	Romania	22 Dec 30	168LTS209	303900
Estonia	Finland	11 Apr 31	124LTS217	302835
Greece	Poland	22 Apr 31	129LTS313	302966
Belgium	Estonia	24 Apr 31	119LTS371	302756
Czechoslovakia	Germany	29 Apr 31	133LTS347	303072
Chile	France	22 May 31	124LTS31	302831
Estonia	Latvia	03 Jun 31	120LTS235	302769
Guatemala	UK Great Britain	06 Jun 31	132LTS15	303027
Austria	Czechoslovakia	22 Jul 31	128LTS59	302938
Mexico	Sweden	14 Sep 31	192LTS195	304472
Chile	UK Great Britain	15 Oct 31	128LTS439	302947
Multilateral		10 Nov 31	131LTS447	303025
Brazil	Iceland	30 Nov 31	128LTS369	302942
Brazil	Denmark	30 Nov 31	128LTS29	302934
Bel-Lux Econ Union	Chile	14 Dec 31	126LTS247	302887
Germany	Poland	22 Dec 31	144LTS191	303329
Netherlands	UK Great Britain	04 Jan 32	128LTS307	302939
Germany	USA (United States)	31 May 32	133LTS409	303078
Hungary	UK Great Britain	10 Jun 32	132LTS53	303031
Sweden	USA (United States)	11 Jul 32	192LTS205	304473
Netherlands	UK Great Britain	13 Aug 32	134LTS317	303100
Italy	USSR (Soviet Union)	06 May 33	158LTS51	303625
Bel-Lux Econ Union	Poland	10 Jun 33	144LTS137	303324
Estonia	France	27 Jul 33	141LTS65	303261
Netherlands	Poland	11 Dec 33	163LTS381	303780
Finland	USA (United States)	13 Feb 34	152LTS45	303484
Denmark	Persia	20 Feb 34	158LTS299	303640
Multilateral		20 Mar 34	174LTS171	304048
Denmark	Poland	01 May 34	154LTS221	303548
Finland	Poland	30 Jun 34	153LTS29	303504
Hungary	Norway	04 Jul 34	152LTS115	303489
India	Japan	12 Jul 34	155LTS31	303566
Finland	Persia	18 Nov 34	158LTS315	303641
Australia	Belgium	19 Nov 34	155LTS385	303590
Poland	Spain	14 Dec 34	168LTS315	303908
Germany	USSR (Soviet Union)	07 Mar 35	169LTS7	303911
Estonia	Poland	27 Mar 35	159LTS97	303651
Belgium	Luxembourg	23 May 35	161LTS347	303723
Sweden	USA (United States)	25 May 35	161LTS109	303707
Denmark	Germany	25 May 35	159LTS389	303680
Bulgaria	USSR (Soviet Union)	10 Jul 35	168LTS275	303905
Bulgaria	Romania	26 Jul 35	198LTS9	304621
France	Spain	21 Dec 35	167LTS9	303856
Estonia	Sweden	21 Dec 35	164LTS293	303798
France	USA (United States)	30 Dec 35	171LTS117	303955
Netherlands	UK Great Britain	30 Dec 35	165LTS263	303813
United Arab Rep	Malaya	29 Feb 36	170LTS103	303931
Albania	Italy	19 Mar 36	173LTS107	304007
Greece	Palestine	28 Mar 36	170LTS145	303932
France	India	01 May 36	178LTS57	304107

PARTY ONE	PARTY TWO	DATE	CITATION	NUMBER
Customs duties (Cont.)				
France	Palestine	19 Jun 36	172LTS17	303977
Denmark	USSR (Soviet Union)	29 Jun 36	174LTS93	304040
Germany	Greece	09 Nov 36	182LTS9	304201
Austria	Switzerland	21 Nov 36	179LTS341	304162
Germany	UK Great Britain	02 Dec 36	178LTS329	304121
Iraq	UK Great Britain	14 Dec 36	177LTS221	304091
Germany	Malaya	17 Dec 36	178LTS484	304129
Belgium	Norway	17 Dec 36	178LTS153	304110
Danzig	UK Great Britain	13 Jan 37	178LTS87	304109
Malaya	Netherlands	16 Mar 37	184LTS181	304248
Czechoslovakia	Italy	10 May 37	190LTS397	304430
Romania	Yugoslavia	13 May 37	197LTS145	304611
Denmark	Netherlands	29 Jul 37	192LTS137	304467
Romania	USA (United States)	10 Aug 37	183LTS7	304225
Netherlands	USA (United States)	20 Sep 37	184LTS319	304256
Ireland	USA (United States)	04 Nov 37	185LTS71	304276
Bel-Lux Econ Union	Siam	05 Nov 37	190LTS151	304413
Denmark	Siam	05 Nov 37	188LTS187	304358
Siam	USA (United States)	13 Nov 37	192LTS247	304476
Latvia	Poland	16 Nov 37	197LTS43	304604
Italy	Siam	03 Dec 37	189LTS255	304389
France	Siam	07 Dec 37	201LTS113	304708
France	Switzerland	31 Jan 38	195LTS313	304553
Netherlands	Siam	01 Feb 38	193LTS13	304485
Surinam	UK Great Britain	15 Mar 38	189LTS183	304385
Norway	Sweden	20 Apr 38	189LTS153	304383
Germany	Netherlands	25 May 38	192LTS143	304468
Lithuania	Poland	25 May 38	191LTS391	304457
Multilateral		02 Jun 38	192LTS157	304470
USA (United States)	Yugoslavia	20 Jun 38	195LTS259	304549
Japan	USA (United States)	20 Jun 38	191LTS43	304434
Liberia	USA (United States)	08 Aug 38	201LTS163	304711
France	UK Great Britain	26 Oct 38	194LTS371	304530
Iceland	USA (United States)	31 Oct 38	194LTS149	304519
Multilateral		05 Feb 39	196LTS303	304592
France	USA (United States)	15 Jul 39	199LTS355	304683
Hungary	Romania	19 Oct 39	201LTS395	304728
France	India	28 Jan 41	204LTS323	304811
UK Great Britain	USA (United States)	27 Mar 41	204LTS15	304784
United Arab Rep	UK Great Britain	26 May 41	204LTS147	304793
Customs declarations				
France	Germany	01 Mar 20	1LTS367	300030
Czechoslovakia	Germany	29 Jun 20	17LTS69	300430
Czechoslovakia	Serb/Croat/Slovene	18 Oct 20	17LTS19	300424
France	Norway	23 Apr 21	14LTS375	300386
Finland	USSR (Soviet Union)	14 Dec 21	16LTS221	300414
Germany	Poland	29 Apr 22	21LTS391	300549
Finland	USA (United States)	21 Jul 22	13LTS243	300356
Italy	Serb/Croat/Slovene	23 Oct 22	18LTS441	300480
Netherlands	UK Great Britain	18 Jan 23	18LTS257	300469
Czechoslovakia	UK Great Britain	31 Jan 23	20LTS53	300506
Multilateral		29 Mar 23	23LTS378	300594
Greece	Serb/Croat/Slovene	10 May 23	25LTS441	300635
Finland	USSR (Soviet Union)	05 Jun 23	18LTS203	300465
Multilateral		03 Nov 23	30LTS371	300775
Czechoslovakia	Germany	04 Mar 24	41LTS243	301018
Latvia	Norway	14 Aug 24	36LTS211	300924
Czechoslovakia	France	18 Aug 24	44LTS21	301080
Greece	Poland	17 Apr 25	38LTS301	300985
Austria	China	19 Oct 25	55LTS9	301301
Austria	Hungary	10 May 26	56LTS39	301321
Finland	Turkey	02 Jun 26	70LTS329	301644
Multilateral		14 Sep 26	77LTS149	301769
Haiti	Italy	03 Jan 27	71LTS405	301678

PARTY ONE	PARTY TWO	DATE	CITATION	NUMBER
Customs declarations (Cont.)				
France	Italy	26 Jan 27	79LTS49	301804
Switzerland	Turkey	04 May 27	67LTS141	301544
France	Germany	17 Aug 27	76LTS5	301761
Germany	Serb/Croat/Slovene	06 Oct 27	77LTS19	301763
Multilateral		20 Feb 28	129LTS223	302963
France	Italy	07 Mar 28	72LTS213	301694
France	Germany	16 Mar 28	79LTS121	301805
Germany	Netherlands	28 Apr 28	95LTS333	302183
Austria	France	16 May 28	88LTS21	301986
Japan	USA (United States)	31 May 28	101LTS63	302320
Portugal	South Africa	11 Sep 28	98LTS9	302239
China	Germany	20 Dec 28	90LTS337	302047
Switzerland	UK Great Britain	10 Dec 29	99LTS53	302267
Romania	UK Great Britain	06 Aug 30	123LTS307	302822
Multilateral		28 Mar 31	119LTS47	302739
Brazil	Germany	22 Oct 31	136LTS443	303143
Belgium	Netherlands	22 Oct 31	125LTS367	302865
Multilateral		10 Nov 31	131LTS447	303025
China	UK Great Britain	28 Apr 32	137LTS319	303165
Estonia	Spain	23 Jun 32	143LTS31	303303
Netherlands	Poland	11 Dec 33	163LTS381	303780
Denmark	Poland	01 May 34	154LTS221	303548
Hungary	Norway	04 Jul 34	152LTS115	303489
Netherlands	UK Great Britain	30 Dec 35	165LTS263	303813
Siam	Sweden	08 Nov 37	185LTS337	304298
Belgium	UK Great Britain	29 Jul 38	201LTS317	304722
Burma	United Arab Rep	30 Sep 38	203LTS373	304780
Multilateral		02 Jan 39	196LTS235	304587
Fiji Islands	USA (United States)	10 Jan 39	196LTS185	304581
Belgium	USA (United States)	15 Jan 39	199LTS321	304682
Burma	France	26 Jan 39	201LTS9	304701
Iceland	Norway	27 Feb 39	196LTS377	304598
Germany	USA (United States)	16 Mar 39	198LTS237	304645
Multilateral		23 May 39	202LTS159	304742
Barbados	USA (United States)	13 Sep 39	199LTS375	304685
United Arab Rep	USA (United States)	13 Nov 39	198LTS419	304659
Lithuania	USA (United States)	28 Dec 39	202LTS381	304743
Customs exemptions				
France	UK Great Britain	16 Apr 02	1LTS79	300010
Canada	France	19 Sep 07	1LTS95	300012
Cuba	Netherlands	31 Dec 13	14LTS29	300366
Colombia	USA (United States)	06 Apr 14	9LTS302	300263
Bulgaria	Greece	27 Nov 19	1LTS67	300009
France	Germany	01 Mar 20	1LTS367	300030
Austria	Germany	01 Sep 20	4LTS201	300107
Bulgaria	Netherlands	13 Nov 20	7LTS107	300178
Czechoslovakia	Romania	23 Apr 21	15LTS235	300397
Germany	USSR (Soviet Union)	06 May 21	6LTS267	300159
Spain	Sweden	19 Jun 21	5LTS387	300143
Norway	USSR (Soviet Union)	02 Sep 21	7LTS293	300196
Austria	Poland	23 Sep 21	7LTS181	300186
Afghanistan	UK Great Britain	22 Nov 21	14LTS47	300367
Norway	Spain	01 Dec 21	9LTS69	300244
China	Japan	04 Feb 22	10LTS309	300277
Finland	Germany	21 Apr 22	19LTS87	300487
Germany	Poland	29 Apr 22	21LTS391	300549
Italy	Poland	12 May 22	59LTS293	301399
Germany	Poland	15 May 22	10LTS37	300273
Italy	Serb/Croat/Slovene	23 Oct 22	18LTS413	300479
Finland	USSR (Soviet Union)	28 Oct 22	19LTS153	300491
Canada	France	15 Dec 22	21LTS38	300532
Multilateral		30 Dec 22	21LTS183	300542
Italy	Switzerland	27 Jan 23	25LTS21	300603
Czechoslovakia	UK Great Britain	31 Jan 23	20LTS53	300506

PARTY ONE	PARTY TWO	DATE	CITATION	NUMBER
Customs exemptions (Cont.)				
Denmark	Finland	12 Feb 23	18LTS71	300454
Austria	UK Great Britain	28 Mar 23	17LTS385	300445
Multilateral		29 Mar 23	23LTS378	300594
Multilateral		29 Mar 23	23LTS256	300593
Greece	Serb/Croat/Slovene	10 May 23	25LTS441	300635
Germany	Netherlands	23 May 23	25LTS275	300617
Germany	Lithuania	01 Jun 23	51LTS387	301244
Finland	USSR (Soviet Union)	05 Jun 23	18LTS203	300465
Poland	Turkey	23 Jul 23	49LTS329	301189
Multilateral		03 Nov 23	30LTS371	300775
Germany	Hungary	06 Nov 23	45LTS279	301104
Finland	Poland	10 Nov 23	29LTS229	300744
Italy	Spain	15 Nov 23	39LTS49	300996
Nepal	UK Great Britain	21 Dec 23	36LTS357	300934
Czechoslovakia	Germany	04 Mar 24	41LTS243	301018
Sweden	Switzerland	20 Mar 24	25LTS243	300612
Denmark	Poland	22 Mar 24	31LTS13	300778
Iraq	UK Great Britain	25 Mar 24	35LTS145	300894
Denmark	Latvia	03 Apr 24	33LTS393	300860
Denmark	Sweden	28 Apr 24	27LTS355	300696
Netherlands	Poland	30 May 24	34LTS9	300865
Spain	UK Great Britain	27 Jun 24	28LTS523	300727
Czechoslovakia	France	18 Aug 24	44LTS21	301080
Czechoslovakia	Netherlands	17 Oct 24	31LTS93	300786
Allied Powers	Germany	28 Oct 24	41LTS461	301025
Poland	Sweden	02 Dec 24	36LTS299	300930
Latvia	Switzerland	04 Dec 24	34LTS405	300889
France	Poland	09 Dec 24	44LTS127	301081
Hungary	Poland	26 Mar 25	37LTS151	300954
Czechoslovakia	Greece	08 Apr 25	38LTS291	300984
Bulgaria	Poland	29 Apr 25	60LTS103	301408
Germany	USA (United States)	21 May 25	52LTS133	301254
Bel-Lux Econ Union		07 Jul 25	54LTS267	301290
Estonia	Switzerland	14 Oct 25	49LTS421	301195
Austria	Switzerland	06 Jan 26	46LTS299	301124
Estonia	UK Great Britain	18 Jan 26	48LTS209	301163
Denmark	Germany	20 Mar 26	57LTS131	301359
Finland	Hungary	20 Apr 26	48LTS119	301154
Estonia	UK Great Britain	03 May 26	59LTS41	301388
Czechoslovakia	Italy	04 May 26	61LTS257	301438
Benelux Econ Union	Germany	15 Jul 26	63LTS137	301485
Multilateral		14 Sep 26	77LTS149	301769
Greece	Spain	23 Sep 26	91LTS121	302059
France	Germany	16 Feb 27	62LTS155	301463
Germany	Norway	27 Apr 27	69LTS57	301600
Cuba	Spain	15 Jul 27	120LTS251	302770
Hungary	Italy	25 Jul 27	74LTS67	301732
France	Germany	17 Aug 27	76LTS5	301761
Finland	Norway	30 Sep 27	67LTS359	301557
France	Turkey	01 Nov 27	92LTS249	302092
Finland	Sweden	14 Dec 27	72LTS29	301688
Haiti	UK Great Britain	13 Feb 28	85LTS63	301923
Multilateral		11 Jul 28	95LTS373	302185
Multilateral		11 Jul 28	95LTS357	302184
Turkey	UK Great Britain	15 Jan 29	108LTS385	302521
Italy	Sweden	22 Feb 29	87LTS265	301973
Norway	USA (United States)	25 Feb 29	134LTS81	303085
Persia	USSR (Soviet Union)	10 Mar 29	107LTS419	302498
Poland	Romania	30 Mar 29	123LTS147	302812
France	Germany	25 Apr 29	109LTS333	302548
Estonia	Hungary	29 Apr 29	96LTS23	302189
Estonia	USSR (Soviet Union)	17 May 29	94LTS323	302152
Belgium	Luxembourg	18 May 29	119LTS377	302757
Germany	Turkey	28 May 29	133LTS257	303069
Italy	Panama	16 Oct 29	138LTS355	303199

PARTY ONE	PARTY TWO	DATE	CITATION	NUMBER
Customs exemptions (Cont.)				
Poland	Romania	30 Oct 29	121LTS243	302790
Poland	Romania	07 Dec 29	119LTS283	302752
Czechoslovakia	Germany	22 Dec 29	110LTS417	302573
Honduras	Nicaragua	30 Jan 30	142LTS241	303297
Turkey	UK Great Britain	01 Mar 30	108LTS407	302523
Austria	Germany	12 Apr 30	115LTS277	302692
Poland	Romania	09 May 30	112LTS225	302617
Romania	UK Great Britain	06 Aug 30	123LTS307	302822
El Salvador	USA (United States)	05 Sep 30	134LTS207	303093
Bulgaria	Romania	27 Sep 30	118LTS27	302710
Bulgaria	Poland	07 Apr 31	127LTS45	302905
Greece	UK Great Britain	17 Apr 31	129LTS287	302965
Greece	Poland	22 Apr 31	129LTS313	302966
Czechoslovakia	Italy	23 May 31	126LTS185	302881
France	Greece	05 Jun 31	31LTS201	303011
Germany	Hungary	18 Jul 31	150LTS111	303458
Argentina	Finland	03 Nov 31	126LTS101	302874
Bolivia	Denmark	09 Nov 31	147LTS27	303387
Germany	Poland	22 Dec 31	144LTS191	303329
Netherlands	UK Great Britain	04 Jan 32	128LTS307	302939
Norway	USA (United States)	20 Jan 32	126LTS393	302897
Austria	Yugoslavia	09 Mar 32	157LTS145	303609
Germany	Sweden	01 Jun 32	129LTS471	302979
Hungary	UK Great Britain	10 Jun 32	132LTS53	303031
Estonia	Spain	23 Jun 32	143LTS31	303303
Bulgaria	Germany	24 Jun 32	147LTS211	303400
Multilateral		28 Jun 32	140LTS191	303237
Netherlands	UK Great Britain	13 Aug 32	134LTS317	303100
France	Hungary	03 Mar 33	140LTS177	303235
Iceland	UK Great Britain	19 May 33	144LTS33	303319
Bulgaria	Czechoslovakia	29 Aug 33	148LTS15	303402
Norway	Sweden	09 Oct 33	142LTS171	303289
Multilateral		11 Oct 33	155LTS331	303585
Poland	UK Great Britain	26 Oct 33	158LTS73	303628
Latvia	Lithuania	01 Dec 33	148LTS87	303406
Brazil	Uruguay	20 Dec 33	181LTS45	304176
Brazil	Uruguay	20 Dec 33	181LTS35	304175
Czechoslovakia	Poland	10 Feb 34	183LTS213	304238
Brazil	USA (United States)	02 Feb 35	166LTS211	303840
Czechoslovakia	USSR (Soviet Union)	25 Mar 35	161LTS257	303718
USA (United States)	USSR (Soviet Union)	15 Jul 35	162LTS91	303737
France	Netherlands	19 Oct 35	166LTS67	303830
Honduras	USA (United States)	18 Dec 35	167LTS313	303876
Estonia	Sweden	21 Dec 35	164LTS293	303798
Netherlands	UK Great Britain	30 Dec 35	165LTS263	303813
Switzerland	USA (United States)	09 Jan 36	171LTS231	303962
Guatemala	USA (United States)	24 Apr 36	170LTS345	303945
Iraq	UK Great Britain	14 Dec 36	177LTS221	304091
Chile	Cuba	13 Mar 37	195LTS389	304558
Belgium	Netherlands	26 Mar 37	179LTS52	304132
Austria	Netherlands	02 Apr 37	179LTS81	304136
Bulgaria	Romania	22 May 37	188LTS173	304357
Ecuador	Netherlands	27 May 37	194LTS179	304521
Siam	Sweden	08 Nov 37	185LTS337	304298
Switzerland	UK Great Britain	26 Jul 38	191LTS307	304452
Burma	United Arab Rep	30 Sep 38	203LTS373	304780
France	UK Great Britain	08 Nov 38	196LTS215	304584
Belgium	USA (United States)	15 Jan 39	199LTS321	304682
Multilateral		23 May 39	202LTS159	304742
Greece	UK Great Britain	30 May 39	202LTS7	304732
Netherlands	Switzerland	01 Jul 39	198LTS195	304640
Denmark	Norway	29 Aug 39	198LTS231	304644
Barbados	USA (United States)	13 Sep 39	199LTS375	304685
Hungary	Romania	19 Oct 39	201LTS395	304728
Barbados	Martinique	21 Oct 39	201LTS65	304704

PARTY ONE	PARTY TWO	DATE	CITATION	NUMBER
Customs exemptions (Cont.)				
France	India	28 Jan 41	204LTS323	304811
Denmark	USA (United States)	09 Apr 41	204LTS135	304792
Temporary importation				
Austria	Germany	01 Sep 20	4LTS201	300107
Austria	Czechoslovakia	04 May 21	15LTS13	300388
Germany	Poland	06 Jun 21	34LTS185	300874
Austria	Hungary	08 Oct 21	16LTS19	300402
Germany	Poland	15 May 22	10LTS37	300273
Multilateral		03 Nov 23	30LTS371	300775
Germany	Poland	23 Feb 24	49LTS355	301191
Germany	Poland	23 Feb 24	41LTS197	301015
Italy	Serb/Croat/Slovene	14 Jul 24	82LTS257	301876
Italy	Serb/Croat/Slovene	12 Aug 24	82LTS391	301880
Finland	Italy	22 Oct 24	32LTS149	300814
Poland	Sweden	02 Dec 24	36LTS299	300930
Hungary	Netherlands	09 Dec 24	47LTS91	301130
Germany	Poland	30 Dec 24	52LTS51	301250
Hungary	Poland	26 Mar 25	37LTS151	300954
Czechoslovakia	Poland	30 May 25	48LTS397	301172
Estonia	Latvia	05 Feb 26	64LTS361	301509
Albania	Greece	13 Oct 26	83LTS325	301899
Multilateral		13 Nov 26	77LTS249	301773
Greece	Switzerland	29 Nov 26	63LTS27	301478
Czechoslovakia	Switzerland	16 Feb 27	64LTS7	301501
Czechoslovakia	Estonia	20 Jul 27	77LTS341	301776
Germany	Poland	07 Dec 27	92LTS203	302088
Bulgaria	Turkey	12 Feb 28	81LTS383	301848
Czechoslovakia	Poland	18 Feb 28	100LTS273	302301
Panama	UK Great Britain	26 Sep 28	90LTS327	302046
Peru	UK Great Britain	31 Dec 28	100LTS431	302312
Ecuador	UK Great Britain	05 Jan 29	90LTS369	302048
Romania	UK Great Britain	06 Aug 30	123LTS307	302822
Bulgaria	Poland	07 Apr 31	127LTS45	302905
Estonia	Finland	11 Apr 31	124LTS217	302835
Austria	Yugoslavia	09 Mar 32	157LTS145	303609
Argentina	Brazil	10 Oct 33	179LTS185	304146
Denmark	Germany	13 Jan 34	144LTS379	303340
Denmark	Norway	21 Apr 34	148LTS331	303419
Finland	USSR (Soviet Union)	25 May 34	155LTS207	303578
Denmark	Germany	25 May 35	159LTS389	303680
Bel-Lux Econ Union	France	16 Jul 35	162LTS19	303731
Netherlands	UK Great Britain	30 Dec 35	165LTS263	303813
Romania	Yugoslavia	13 May 37	197LTS101	304609
France	Switzerland	31 Jan 38	195LTS313	304553
Aid and development				
UK Great Britain	USA (United States)	23 Feb 42	204LTS389	304818
Domestic obligation				
Iraq	UK Great Britain	25 Mar 24	35LTS145	300894
General technical assistance				
Multilateral		10 May 22	26LTS265	300652
Agriculture				
Multilateral		31 Oct 20	164LTS85	303790
Afghanistan	USSR (Soviet Union)	06 May 35	164LTS335	303800
Assistance				
Romania		28 Jan 33	138LTS271	303193
Special projects				
Multilateral		10 May 22	26LTS265	300652
Romania	Yugoslavia	14 Dec 31	135LTS133	303108
Albania	Italy	19 Mar 36	173LTS83	304005
General aid				
Poland	Romania	15 Jan 31	115LTS171	302685

PARTY ONE	PARTY TWO	DATE	CITATION	NUMBER
Agricultural commodities				
Romania	UK Great Britain	22 Jan 20	1LTS257	300018
Germany	Poland	10 Apr 21	6LTS233	300158
Belgium	Luxembourg	25 Jul 21	9LTS223	300256
France	Saar	15 Jan 25	44LTS181	301082
Multilateral		26 Apr 34	164LTS63	303789
Economic assistance				
Italy	Yemen	02 Sep 26	67LTS383	301559
UK Great Britain	USSR (Soviet Union)	26 May 42	204LTS353	304813
Materials, equipment and services				
Germany	Poland	23 Jun 22	22LTS25	300553
Czechoslovakia	Hungary	24 Aug 37	189LTS403	304397
France	Switzerland	31 Jan 38	195LTS313	304553
Norway	Sweden	20 Apr 38	189LTS153	304383
Latvia	Poland	16 Jun 38	196LTS105	304573
Volunteer programs				
France	Greece	20 Apr 20	3LTS93	300093
Withdrawal conditions				
Greece		15 Sep 27	70LTS9	301622
Bulgaria		08 Sep 28	74LTS167	301738
Loan and credit				
Germany	Poland	21 Mar 23	34LTS315	300881
Bulgaria		09 Sep 26	58LTS245	301375
Multilateral		07 Jun 30	143LTS257	303313
Multilateral		31 Oct 30	120LTS9	302760
Belgium	Luxembourg	23 May 35	161LTS327	303721
Albania	Italy	19 Mar 36	173LTS51	304002
Turkey	UK Great Britain	27 May 38	199LTS9	304660
Credit provisions				
Germany	Netherlands	11 May 20	3LTS153	300097
France	Netherlands	16 Apr 21	11LTS341	300300
Multilateral		04 Oct 22	12LTS391	300335
Czechoslovakia	Hungary	13 Jul 23	35LTS271	300900
Germany	UK Great Britain	05 Jan 24	36LTS365	300935
Hungary	Romania	16 Apr 24	45LTS403	301110
Austria	Czechoslovakia	14 May 25	50LTS39	301198
Other Unilat Decla	Estonia	10 Dec 26	62LTS277	301467
Greece		15 Sep 27	70LTS9	301622
Multilateral		08 Dec 27	70LTS73	301623
Multilateral		20 Feb 28	86LTS111	301950
Bulgaria		08 Sep 28	74LTS167	301738
Multilateral		07 Jun 30	143LTS337	303315
Multilateral		07 Jun 30	143LTS317	303314
Multilateral		10 Jun 30	112LTS237	302618
Netherlands	UK Great Britain	04 Jan 32	128LTS307	302939
Hungary	UK Great Britain	10 Jun 32	132LTS53	303031
Multilateral		15 Jul 32	135LTS285	303118
Netherlands	UK Great Britain	13 Aug 32	134LTS317	303100
Belgium	Luxembourg	23 May 35	161LTS327	303721
Albania	Italy	19 Mar 36	173LTS73	304004
Albania	Italy	19 Mar 36	173LTS83	304005
Belgium	Netherlands	17 Dec 38	198LTS177	304638
Multilateral		27 Jan 39	196LTS287	304591
Multilateral		07 Sep 39	198LTS357	304654
Spain	UK Great Britain	18 Mar 40	203LTS149	304758
Purchase authorization				
Other Unilat Decla	Greece	14 Jan 30	108LTS349	302518
Canada	Germany	22 Oct 36	173LTS311	304021
Loan repayment				
Germany	Netherlands	11 May 20	3LTS153	300097
France	Netherlands	16 Apr 21	11LTS341	300300
Czechoslovakia	Hungary	13 Jul 23	35LTS253	300899

PARTY ONE	PARTY TWO	DATE	CITATION	NUMBER
Loan repayment (Cont.)				
Other Unilat Decla	Hungary	14 Mar 24	25LTS427	300634
Hungary	Italy	27 Mar 24	45LTS83	301100
Hungary	Romania	16 Apr 24	45LTS403	301110
France	Poland	09 Dec 24	44LTS127	301081
Austria	Czechoslovakia	14 May 25	50LTS39	301198
China	France	23 Dec 28	92LTS267	302095
United Arab Rep	UK Great Britain	17 Mar 29	90LTS413	302051
Multilateral		10 Jun 30	112LTS237	302618
China	UK Great Britain	22 Sep 30	115LTS493	302697
Multilateral		15 Jul 32	135LTS285	303118
Romania	Yugoslavia	30 Jan 33	146LTS129	303365
Belgium	Luxembourg	23 May 35	161LTS327	303721
Albania	Italy	19 Mar 36	173LTS73	304004
Albania	Italy	19 Mar 36	173LTS83	304005
Germany	UK Great Britain	01 Jul 38	194LTS235	304525
Multilateral		07 Sep 39	198LTS357	304654
Spain	UK Great Britain	18 Mar 40	203LTS149	304758
United Arab Rep	UK Great Britain	17 Jul 40	202LTS97	304738
United Arab Rep	France	03 Aug 40	202LTS121	304740
Terms of loan				
Germany	Netherlands	11 May 20	3LTS153	300097
Italy	Poland	22 Jul 25	54LTS101	301278
Other Unilat Decla	Estonia	10 Dec 26	62LTS277	301467
Greece		15 Sep 27	70LTS9	301622
Germany	Poland	05 Jul 28	113LTS189	302646
Bulgaria		08 Sep 28	74LTS167	301738
Albania	Italy	19 Mar 36	173LTS73	304004
Netherlands	Romania	28 Aug 36	182LTS363	304222
Germany	Sweden	28 Oct 38	196LTS81	304570
United Arab Rep	UK Great Britain	17 Jul 40	202LTS97	304738
United Arab Rep	France	03 Aug 40	202LTS121	304740
Agricultural commodities assistance				
Bulgaria	France	22 Oct 25	44LTS257	301087
Rights of supplier				
France	Norway	23 Apr 21	14LTS375	300386
Albania	Italy	04 Dec 22	15LTS213	300395
Norway	Portugal	11 Apr 23	16LTS379	300418
Samples and testing				
Canada	France	15 Dec 22	21LTS38	300532
Denmark	Finland	12 Feb 23	18LTS71	300454
Germany	Lithuania	01 Jun 23	51LTS387	301244
Estonia	Germany	27 Jun 23	41LTS161	301013
Poland	Turkey	23 Jul 23	49LTS329	301189
Czechoslovakia	France	18 Aug 24	44LTS21	301080
Finland	Latvia	23 Aug 24	37LTS383	300962
France	Latvia	30 Oct 24	37LTS399	300963
France	Poland	09 Dec 24	44LTS127	301081
Austria	Spain	03 Feb 25	43LTS313	301067
Poland	USA (United States)	10 Feb 25	37LTS141	300953
Czechoslovakia	Greece	08 Apr 25	38LTS291	300984
Finland	USA (United States)	02 May 25	47LTS351	301139
Germany	USA (United States)	21 May 25	52LTS133	301254
Bel-Lux Econ Union		07 Jul 25	54LTS267	301290
Estonia	Switzerland	14 Oct 25	49LTS421	301195
Lithuania	USA (United States)	23 Dec 25	54LTS377	301300
Estonia	UK Great Britain	18 Jan 26	48LTS209	301163
Latvia	USA (United States)	01 Feb 26	55LTS33	301302
France	Germany	12 Feb 26	48LTS153	301157
Romania	USA (United States)	26 Feb 26	51LTS59	301221
Finland	Hungary	20 Apr 26	48LTS119	301154
Germany	Spain	07 May 26	53LTS321	301264
Germany	Sweden	14 May 26	51LTS99	301225
Latvia	Poland	12 Feb 29	115LTS135	302683

PARTY ONE	PARTY TWO	DATE	CITATION	NUMBER
Samples and testing (Cont.)				
Multilateral		26 Apr 34	164LTS63	303789
Plans and standards				
Portugal	Spain	11 Aug 27	82LTS113	301864
Czechoslovakia	Poland	18 Feb 28	100LTS273	302301
Czechoslovakia	Hungary	14 Nov 28	110LTS425	302574
Austria	Czechoslovakia	12 Dec 28	107LTS137	302474
Czechoslovakia	Hungary	24 Aug 37	189LTS403	304397
Norway	Sweden	20 Apr 38	189LTS153	304383
Industry				
France	Switzerland	27 Aug 26	71LTS63	301654
Irrigation				
Iraq	UK Great Britain	25 Mar 24	35LTS145	300894
Germany	Poland	14 Mar 25	95LTS239	302178
Italy	UK Great Britain	20 Dec 25	50LTS281	301211
France	Turkey	30 May 26	54LTS195	301285
United Arab Rep	UK Great Britain	07 May 29	93LTS43	302103
Romania	Yugoslavia	14 Dec 31	135LTS31	303103
Czechoslovakia	Hungary	24 Aug 37	189LTS403	304397
Natural resources				
France	UK Great Britain	24 Apr 20	1LTS281	300022
France	Poland	06 Feb 22	43LTS415	301074
Hungary	Romania	16 Apr 24	45LTS403	301110
Multilateral		05 May 25	55LTS225	301318
France	Spain	03 Aug 25	38LTS371	300992
Siam	UK Great Britain	15 Sep 25	49LTS51	301176
Romania	Yugoslavia	14 Dec 31	135LTS31	303103
Hydro-electric power				
France	UK Great Britain	23 Dec 20	22LTS353	300564
Multilateral		24 Jul 23	28LTS203	300707
Multilateral		09 Dec 23	36LTS76	300905
Multilateral		09 Dec 23	58LTS315	301380
Multilateral		05 May 25	55LTS225	301318
Italy	UK Great Britain	20 Dec 25	50LTS281	301211
Germany	Poland	27 Jan 26	64LTS113	301504
Portugal	Spain	11 Aug 27	82LTS113	301864
Austria	Czechoslovakia	12 Dec 28	108LTS9	302501
Romania	Yugoslavia	14 Dec 31	135LTS31	303103
Poland	USSR (Soviet Union)	10 Apr 32	141LTS349	303275
Canada	USA (United States)	07 Nov 40	203LTS267	304769
Canada	USA (United States)	20 May 41	204LTS199	304800
General transportation				
Germany	Hungary	01 Jun 20	7LTS207	300187
Estonia	UK Great Britain	20 Jul 20	1LTS295	300025
Bulgaria	Netherlands	13 Nov 20	7LTS107	300178
Belgium	UK Great Britain	15 Mar 21	5LTS319	300138
Multilateral		20 Apr 21	7LTS73	300174
Multilateral		20 Apr 21	7LTS11	300171
Czechoslovakia	UK Great Britain	14 Jul 23	29LTS377	300748
Finland	Poland	10 Nov 23	29LTS229	300744
Multilateral		14 Dec 23	29LTS37	300732
Sweden	Switzerland	20 Mar 24	25LTS243	300612
Denmark	Poland	22 Mar 24	31LTS13	300778
Czechoslovakia	Iceland	08 May 24	46LTS419	301125
Estonia	Lithuania	21 May 24	62LTS55	301454
China	UK Great Britain	23 May 24	28LTS481	300724
Finland	Iceland	28 May 24	27LTS117	300676
Latvia	Netherlands	02 Jul 24	37LTS121	300951
Estonia	Netherlands	22 Jul 24	48LTS199	301162
Latvia	Switzerland	04 Dec 24	34LTS405	300889
Hungary	Netherlands	09 Dec 24	47LTS91	301130
France	Saar	15 Jan 25	44LTS181	301082
Poland	USA (United States)	10 Feb 25	37LTS141	300953

PARTY ONE	PARTY TWO	DATE	CITATION	NUMBER
General transportation (Cont.)				
Estonia	USA (United States)	02 Mar 25	43LTS289	301064
Germany	Turkey	13 Dec 25	53LTS355	301265
Lithuania	USA (United States)	23 Dec 25	54LTS377	301300
Latvia	USA (United States)	01 Feb 26	55LTS33	301302
Romania	USA (United States)	26 Feb 26	51LTS59	301221
Austria	Hungary	10 May 26	56LTS39	301321
Germany	Poland	26 Mar 27	64LTS177	301505
Czechoslovakia	Hungary	31 May 27	65LTS61	301520
Austria	USA (United States)	19 Jun 28	118LTS241	302728
Bulgaria	Greece	21 Feb 29	106LTS443	302461
Persia	Sweden	10 May 29	102LTS9	302349
Estonia	Norway	03 Apr 30	106LTS147	302442
Denmark	Estonia	13 May 30	106LTS159	302443
Italy	USA (United States)	17 Aug 31	137LTS175	303154
Competency certificate				
Germany	Switzerland	14 Sep 20	2LTS331	300087
France	UK Great Britain	20 Oct 20	2LTS323	300085
Sweden	UK Great Britain	16 Feb 21	3LTS233	300100
Portugal	UK Great Britain	06 May 21	5LTS179	300128
Sweden	USA (United States)	28 May 21	6LTS41	300147
Norway	UK Great Britain	15 Jul 21	6LTS307	300162
Japan	Netherlands	12 Oct 21	12LTS239	300316
China	UK Great Britain	23 May 24	28LTS481	300724
Denmark	Iceland	30 Sep 24	32LTS355	300825
Multilateral		24 Apr 26	108LTS123	302505
Multilateral		20 Feb 28	129LTS223	302963
Portugal	Sweden	03 Jan 29	87LTS313	301977
Norway	Portugal	07 Feb 29	104LTS137	302383
Germany	Portugal	08 Apr 29	93LTS253	302114
Multilateral		31 May 29	136LTS81	303127
Denmark	Great Britain	11 Jun 29	93LTS401	302128
Denmark	Germany	14 Oct 29	98LTS211	302248
Austria	Netherlands	31 Dec 29	111LTS177	302586
Italy	USA (United States)	17 Aug 31	137LTS175	303154
Multilateral		10 Dec 31	129LTS177	302961
Germany	USA (United States)	31 May 32	133LTS409	303078
Italy	USA (United States)	01 Jun 32	140LTS273	303242
Denmark	India	08 Aug 32	140LTS369	303246
Multilateral		09 Dec 32	151LTS5	303479
Sweden	USA (United States)	09 Sep 33	144LTS183	303328
Sweden	USA (United States)	09 Sep 33	144LTS171	303327
South Africa	USA (United States)	20 Sep 33	148LTS203	303413
Norway	USA (United States)	16 Oct 33	145LTS31	303343
Denmark	USA (United States)	24 Mar 34	149LTS485	303448
Italy	UK Great Britain	17 Sep 34	155LTS85	303570
Germany	UK Great Britain	18 Sep 34	155LTS243	303580
Sweden	UK Great Britain	20 Oct 34	154LTS85	303539
UK Great Britain	USA (United States)	05 Apr 35	162LTS59	303734
Finland	UK Great Britain	03 May 35	159LTS129	303655
Germany	Norway	19 Jul 35	161LTS375	303726
Hungary	UK Great Britain	22 Mar 37	190LTS59	304405
Panama	USA (United States)	17 Aug 37	182LTS159	304208
Canada	USA (United States)	28 Jul 38	192LTS115	304465
Registration certificate				
Germany	Switzerland	14 Sep 20	2LTS331	300087
France	UK Great Britain	20 Oct 20	2LTS323	300085
Denmark	UK Great Britain	23 Dec 20	2LTS249	300071
Sweden	UK Great Britain	16 Feb 21	3LTS233	300100
Portugal	UK Great Britain	06 May 21	5LTS179	300128
Norway	UK Great Britain	15 Jul 21	6LTS307	300162
Denmark	Sweden	07 Nov 22	14LTS95	300370
British Empire	Japan	30 Nov 22	16LTS207	300412
Multilateral		29 Mar 23	23LTS256	300593
Finland	Sweden	26 May 23	18LTS57	300453

PARTY ONE	PARTY TWO	DATE	CITATION	NUMBER
Registration certificate (Cont.)				
Norway	Sweden	26 May 23	18LTS155	300462
Sweden	USSR (Soviet Union)	15 Mar 24	25LTS251	300613
Multilateral		24 Apr 26	108LTS123	302505
Multilateral		20 Feb 28	129LTS223	302963
Austria	Italy	11 May 28	100LTS41	302293
Persia	Sweden	10 May 29	102LTS9	302349
Multilateral		31 May 29	136LTS81	303127
Denmark	Great Britain	11 Jun 29	93LTS401	302128
Finland	Sweden	17 Jul 30	105LTS343	302427
Sweden	USA (United States)	29 Oct 30	109LTS181	302537
Finland	Norway	20 Nov 30	110LTS313	302563
Norway	Sweden	08 Aug 31	123LTS67	302806
Multilateral		10 Dec 31	129LTS177	302961
Denmark	India	08 Aug 32	140LTS369	303246
Denmark	Germany	09 Jan 36	166LTS135	303835
Germany	Greece	09 Nov 36	182LTS9	304201
Austria	Switzerland	21 Nov 36	179LTS341	304162
Canada	USA (United States)	28 Jul 38	192LTS94	304464
United Arab Rep	UK Great Britain	20 Feb 39	195LTS407	304560
Passenger transport				
Multilateral		20 Apr 21	7LTS11	300171
Germany	Poland	21 Apr 21	12LTS61	300308
Sweden	USA (United States)	28 May 21	6LTS41	300147
Norway	UK Great Britain	15 Jul 21	6LTS307	300162
Italy	Switzerland	24 Sep 21	12LTS367	300330
Finland	USSR (Soviet Union)	14 Dec 21	16LTS221	300414
Denmark	Germany	25 Apr 22	18LTS227	300466
Czechoslovakia	Germany	08 May 22	23LTS171	300589
Belgium	Switzerland	13 Jun 22	12LTS295	300321
Austria	Poland	25 Sep 22	59LTS307	301400
Denmark	Sweden	07 Nov 22	14LTS95	300370
Norway	Sweden	26 May 23	18LTS155	300462
Belgium	Denmark	28 Jun 23	20LTS59	300507
France	Netherlands	02 Jul 23	20LTS131	300512
China	UK Great Britain	23 May 24	28LTS481	300724
Italy	Serb/Croat/Slovene	14 Jul 24	82LTS327	301877
Czechoslovakia	Germany	25 Mar 27	75LTS353	301758
Germany	Poland	26 Mar 27	64LTS177	301505
Belgium	Portugal	21 Jul 27	71LTS439	301682
Czechoslovakia	Spain	26 Oct 27	121LTS271	302791
Czechoslovakia	Portugal	23 Nov 27	124LTS7	302829
Multilateral		20 Feb 28	129LTS223	302963
Czechoslovakia	France	07 May 28	114LTS117	302660
Italy	UK Great Britain	25 Jan 29	95LTS39	302162
Norway	Portugal	07 Feb 29	104LTS137	302383
Persia	Sweden	10 May 29	102LTS9	302349
Multilateral		31 May 29	136LTS81	303127
Canada	USA (United States)	22 Oct 29	97LTS321	302229
Poland	Romania	30 Oct 29	121LTS243	302790
Poland	Romania	30 Oct 29	121LTS167	302787
Belgium	Germany	07 Nov 29	121LTS327	302795
Multilateral		09 Nov 29	125LTS205	302855
Austria	Poland	10 Apr 30	108LTS289	302514
Irish Free State	Italy	10 May 30	132LTS147	303034
Greece	UK Great Britain	17 Apr 31	129LTS287	302965
Sweden	USA (United States)	09 Sep 33	144LTS183	303328
Latvia	USSR (Soviet Union)	04 Dec 33	148LTS145	303410
Czechoslovakia	Poland	10 Feb 34	183LTS213	304238
UK Great Britain	USA (United States)	17 Sep 34	153LTS331	303529
Czechoslovakia	Luxembourg	01 Dec 34	168LTS287	303906
Czechoslovakia	Monaco	22 Dec 34	171LTS27	303949
France	Spain	21 Dec 35	167LTS9	303856

PARTY ONE	PARTY TWO	DATE	CITATION	NUMBER
Dangerous goods				
Denmark	Sweden	07 Nov 22	14LTS95	300370
Norway	Sweden	26 May 23	18LTS155	300462
China	UK Great Britain	23 May 24	28LTS481	300724
Norway	USA (United States)	24 May 24	26LTS43	300639
Multilateral		23 Oct 24	77LTS367	301778
Siam	UK Great Britain	15 Sep 25	49LTS51	301176
Multilateral		20 Feb 28	129LTS223	302963
Multilateral		31 May 29	136LTS81	303127
Germany	Netherlands	11 Jun 31	120LTS413	302778
Austria	Netherlands	26 Jun 31	127LTS225	302922
Italy	Netherlands	01 Jul 31	127LTS235	302923
Netherlands	Sweden	15 Jul 31	127LTS321	302925
Netherlands	Yugoslavia	15 Jul 31	127LTS337	302927
Netherlands	Norway	15 Jul 31	127LTS313	302924
Denmark	Netherlands	15 Jul 31	127LTS329	302926
Netherlands	Romania	20 Jul 31	127LTS425	302929
Czechoslovakia	Netherlands	11 Aug 31	127LTS347	302928
Germany	USA (United States)	31 May 32	133LTS409	303078
Routes and logistics				
Czechoslovakia	Germany	29 Jun 20	17LTS69	300430
Bulgaria	Netherlands	13 Nov 20	7LTS107	300178
Belgium	UK Great Britain	15 Mar 21	5LTS319	300138
Portugal	UK Great Britain	06 May 21	5LTS179	300128
Norway	UK Great Britain	15 Jul 21	6LTS307	300162
Austria	Hungary	08 Oct 21	16LTS19	300402
Finland	USSR (Soviet Union)	14 Dec 21	16LTS221	300414
Germany	Poland	24 Jun 22	26LTS271	300653
Multilateral		29 Mar 23	23LTS378	300594
Afghanistan	UK Great Britain	05 Jun 23	21LTS89	300533
China	UK Great Britain	23 May 24	28LTS481	300724
Italy	Serb/Croat/Slovene	14 Jul 24	82LTS327	301877
Czechoslovakia	Poland	30 May 25	50LTS243	301207
France	Hungary	13 Oct 25	48LTS9	301150
Hungary	Romania	17 Nov 26	61LTS207	301435
Portugal	South Africa	11 Sep 28	98LTS9	302239
Belgium	Germany	07 Nov 29	121LTS327	302795
Greece	UK Great Britain	17 Apr 31	129LTS287	302965
Czechoslovakia	Germany	29 Apr 31	133LTS359	303073
Germany	Netherlands	11 Jun 31	120LTS413	302778
Italy	Netherlands	01 Jul 31	127LTS235	302923
Netherlands	Sweden	15 Jul 31	127LTS321	302925
Netherlands	Yugoslavia	15 Jul 31	127LTS337	302927
Denmark	Netherlands	15 Jul 31	127LTS329	302926
Netherlands	Norway	15 Jul 31	127LTS313	302924
Czechoslovakia	Germany	25 Jul 31	187LTS279	304344
Czechoslovakia	Netherlands	11 Aug 31	127LTS347	302928
Hungary	Netherlands	08 Jun 35	171LTS385	303975
Czechoslovakia	USSR (Soviet Union)	08 Jun 35	167LTS181	303865
Hungary	Switzerland	18 Jun 35	174LTS7	304033
Estonia	Finland	12 Sep 36	172LTS345	303999
Germany	Greece	09 Nov 36	182LTS9	304201
Austria	Switzerland	21 Nov 36	179LTS341	304162
Hungary	UK Great Britain	22 Mar 37	190LTS59	304405
Czechoslovakia	Italy	10 May 37	190LTS397	304430
Bulgaria	Romania	22 May 37	188LTS173	304357
Portugal	South Africa	18 Jun 37	189LTS121	304380
Germany	Romania	03 Oct 37	190LTS369	304429
Ireland	USA (United States)	04 Nov 37	185LTS71	304276
Multilateral		03 Dec 37	186LTS293	304318
Belgium	China	18 Dec 37	190LTS109	304409
France	Netherlands	15 Jul 38	192LTS151	304469
Lithuania	Poland	23 Jul 38	192LTS83	304462
Germany	Romania	23 Mar 39	199LTS77	304668

PARTY ONE	PARTY TWO	DATE	CITATION	NUMBER
Routes and logistics (Cont.)				
Greece	UK Great Britain	30 May 39	202LTS7	304732
Japan	Thailand	30 Nov 39	200LTS197	304691
Mexico	USA (United States)	01 Apr 41	204LTS179	304798
Navigational conditions				
Japan	UK Great Britain	12 Nov 19	6LTS333	300164
Multilateral		09 Feb 20	2LTS7	300041
Latvia	USSR (Soviet Union)	11 Aug 20	2LTS195	300067
Germany	Switzerland	14 Sep 20	2LTS331	300087
Finland	USSR (Soviet Union)	14 Oct 20	3LTS5	300091
Sweden	UK Great Britain	16 Feb 21	3LTS233	300100
Other Unilat Decla	Rhine Navigation	25 Feb 21	12LTS355	300327
Persia	USSR (Soviet Union)	26 Feb 21	9LTS383	300268
Belgium	UK Great Britain	15 Mar 21	5LTS319	300138
Germany	Poland	21 Apr 21	12LTS61	300308
Germany	USSR (Soviet Union)	06 May 21	6LTS267	300159
Portugal	UK Great Britain	06 May 21	5LTS179	300128
Serb/Croat/Slovene	UK Great Britain	29 Jul 21	10LTS411	300280
Japan	Netherlands	12 Oct 21	12LTS239	300316
Other Unilat Decla	Rhine Navigation	16 Dec 21	13LTS53	300347
Belgium	Switzerland	13 Jun 22	12LTS295	300321
Finland	USSR (Soviet Union)	28 Oct 22	19LTS153	300491
Denmark	Sweden	07 Nov 22	14LTS95	300370
Norway	Sweden	26 May 23	18LTS155	300462
Finland	USSR (Soviet Union)	05 Jun 23	18LTS203	300465
Estonia	Sweden	07 Jul 23	20LTS189	300517
Austria	Netherlands	05 Sep 23	20LTS147	300514
Denmark	Estonia	07 Sep 23	23LTS73	300577
Estonia	Iceland	07 Sep 23	23LTS131	300584
Finland	Sweden	12 Oct 23	21LTS147	300538
Italy	Spain	15 Nov 23	39LTS49	300996
Finland	UK Great Britain	14 Dec 23	29LTS129	300739
Lithuania	Norway	21 Dec 23	32LTS55	300805
Czechoslovakia	Denmark	31 Jan 24	23LTS139	300585
Lithuania	Sweden	17 Feb 24	23LTS153	300587
Germany	Siam	28 Feb 24	32LTS399	300828
Japan	Siam	09 Mar 24	31LTS187	300795
Multilateral		12 Mar 24	24LTS17	300595
Denmark	Latvia	03 Apr 24	33LTS393	300860
China	UK Great Britain	23 May 24	28LTS481	300724
Norway	USA (United States)	24 May 24	26LTS43	300639
Panama	USA (United States)	06 Jun 24	138LTS397	303200
France	USA (United States)	30 Jun 24	61LTS415	301451
Estonia	Sweden	07 Jul 24	73LTS27	301702
Czechoslovakia	France	18 Aug 24	44LTS21	301080
Japan	Peru	30 Sep 24	102LTS33	302351
Norway	Romania	01 Oct 24	29LTS397	300750
Finland	Italy	22 Oct 24	32LTS149	300814
Finland	Sweden	22 Dec 24	73LTS33	301703
France	Siam	14 Feb 25	43LTS189	301055
Albania	Italy	06 Mar 25	44LTS359	301094
Denmark	Germany	18 Apr 25	37LTS103	300949
Bulgaria	Poland	29 Apr 25	60LTS103	301408
Germany	USA (United States)	21 May 25	52LTS133	301254
Italy	Latvia	25 Jul 25	60LTS91	301407
Germany	UK Great Britain	13 Aug 25	43LTS89	301050
Estonia	USA (United States)	23 Dec 25	50LTS13	301197
Bel-Lux Econ Union	Czechoslovakia	28 Dec 25	58LTS189	301372
Cuba	USA (United States)	11 Mar 26	61LTS383	301448
Italy	Siam	09 May 26	61LTS215	301436
Greece	Netherlands	12 May 26	61LTS295	301440
Germany	Sweden	14 May 26	51LTS99	301225
Bel-Lux Econ Union	Siam	13 Jul 26	62LTS287	301468
Norway	Siam	16 Jul 26	60LTS35	301404
Estonia	Norway	28 Jul 26	43LTS25	301045

PARTY ONE	PARTY TWO	DATE	CITATION	NUMBER
Navigational conditions (Cont.)				
Denmark	Switzerland	25 Aug 26	69LTS313	301613
Greece	Sweden	10 Sep 26	63LTS37	301479
Bel-Lux Econ Union	Estonia	28 Sep 26	62LTS433	301475
Austria	Estonia	15 Oct 26	93LTS137	302106
Greece	Italy	24 Oct 26	63LTS51	301480
Greece	UK Great Britain	13 May 27	61LTS15	301425
Czechoslovakia	Poland	30 May 27	98LTS233	302251
Italy	Netherlands	28 Jun 27	68LTS203	301583
Belgium	Portugal	21 Jul 27	71LTS439	301682
Multilateral		20 Feb 28	129LTS223	302963
Siam	UK Great Britain	21 Feb 28	87LTS21	301960
Latvia	Sweden	30 Mar 28	73LTS39	301704
Germany	Siam	07 Apr 28	85LTS337	301938
Latvia	USA (United States)	20 Apr 28	80LTS35	301821
Albania	Hungary	02 Jun 28	82LTS201	301870
Greece	Hungary	28 Jun 28	82LTS209	301871
Abyssinia	Italy	02 Aug 28	94LTS423	302159
Italy	Spain	03 Oct 28	94LTS387	302156
Czechoslovakia	Serb/Croat/Slovene	07 Nov 28	98LTS297	302252
Portugal	Sweden	03 Jan 29	87LTS313	301977
Norway	Portugal	07 Feb 29	104LTS137	302383
Germany	USSR (Soviet Union)	16 Apr 29	109LTS327	302547
Germany	Hedjaz	26 Apr 29	115LTS265	302690
Persia	Sweden	10 May 29	102LTS9	302349
Multilateral		31 May 29	136LTS81	303127
Denmark	Germany	14 Oct 29	98LTS211	302248
Austria	Netherlands	31 Dec 29	111LTS177	302586
Latvia	Sweden	11 Jan 30	109LTS193	302539
UK Great Britain	USA (United States)	16 Apr 30	109LTS9	302524
Norway	Persia	08 May 30	134LTS153	303089
Germany	Irish Free State	12 May 30	131LTS153	303008
Chile	USA (United States)	27 May 30	133LTS141	303064
Poland	Romania	23 Jun 30	133LTS163	303066
Denmark	Sweden	03 Sep 30	106LTS397	302458
Chile	Czechoslovakia	18 Sep 30	140LTS161	303233
Multilateral		23 Oct 30	112LTS21	302603
Sweden	USA (United States)	29 Oct 30	109LTS181	302537
Greece	Poland	22 Apr 31	129LTS313	302966
Finland	France	24 Apr 31	126LTS85	302872
Estonia	Iceland	30 May 31	119LTS69	302741
France	Greece	05 Jun 31	31LTS201	303011
Greece	Romania	11 Aug 31	130LTS33	302981
Hungary	Romania	12 Aug 31	186LTS325	304321
Romania	Sweden	07 Oct 31	131LTS51	303003
Romania	Yugoslavia	14 Dec 31	135LTS31	303103
Germany	USA (United States)	16 Dec 31	129LTS129	302957
Germany	USA (United States)	31 May 32	133LTS409	303078
Bulgaria	Germany	24 Jun 32	147LTS211	303400
Latvia	USSR (Soviet Union)	04 Dec 33	148LTS145	303410
Estonia	Lithuania	13 Jan 34	148LTS337	303420
Czechoslovakia	Poland	10 Feb 34	183LTS213	304238
Bel-Lux Econ Union	Turkey	24 May 34	150LTS269	303460
Poland	Spain	14 Dec 34	168LTS315	303908
Hungary	Switzerland	18 Jun 35	174LTS7	304033
France	Hungary	23 Jul 35	173LTS243	304016
Iran	USSR (Soviet Union)	27 Aug 35	176LTS299	304069
France	Spain	21 Dec 35	167LTS9	303856
Sweden	Uruguay	13 Aug 36	183LTS161	304232
Estonia	Finland	12 Sep 36	172LTS345	303999
Chile	Sweden	30 Oct 36	188LTS283	304364
Germany	Greece	09 Nov 36	182LTS9	304201
Italy	UK Great Britain	02 Jan 37	177LTS241	304092
Bel-Lux Econ Union	Uruguay	22 Feb 37	196LTS391	304600
Chile	Cuba	13 Mar 37	195LTS389	304558
Sweden	Yugoslavia	14 May 37	194LTS21	304504

PARTY ONE	PARTY TWO	DATE	CITATION	NUMBER
Navigational conditions (Cont.)				
Ecuador	Netherlands	27 May 37	194LTS179	304521
Ireland	USA (United States)	04 Nov 37	185LTS71	304276
Siam	UK Great Britain	23 Nov 37	188LTS333	304366
Belgium	China	18 Dec 37	190LTS109	304409
Greece	Latvia	15 Jan 38	195LTS19	304533
Norway	Venezuela	18 Feb 38	187LTS205	304341
Sweden	USA (United States)	31 Mar 38	189LTS327	304392
Switzerland	UK Great Britain	26 Jul 38	191LTS307	304452
Greece	Portugal	15 Aug 38	201LTS201	304707
France	UK Great Britain	08 Nov 38	196LTS215	304584
Ecuador	Sweden	11 Nov 38	195LTS347	304554
El Salvador	Norway	21 Nov 38	198LTS157	304636
Iraq	USA (United States)	03 Dec 38	203LTS107	304753
Canada	USA (United States)	20 Feb 39	197LTS181	304613
France	USA (United States)	15 Jul 39	199LTS355	304683
Mexico	USA (United States)	01 Apr 41	204LTS179	304798
UK Great Britain	USA (United States)	04 Dec 42	295LTS33	304824
Navigational equipment				
Finland	Sweden	12 Oct 23	21LTS147	300538
China	UK Great Britain	23 May 24	28LTS481	300724
Multilateral		31 May 29	136LTS81	303127
Denmark	Germany	14 Oct 29	98LTS211	302248
Denmark	Sweden	03 Sep 30	106LTS397	302458
Greece	UK Great Britain	17 Apr 31	129LTS287	302965
Permit designation				
Hungary	Romania	16 Apr 24	45LTS403	301110
China	UK Great Britain	23 May 24	28LTS481	300724
Multilateral		23 Oct 24	77LTS367	301778
Italy	USA (United States)	17 Aug 31	137LTS175	303154
Italy	UK Great Britain	17 Sep 34	155LTS85	303570
Goods in transit				
Multilateral		10 Sep 19	7LTS331	300200
Italy	UK Great Britain	01 Jun 21	6LTS323	300163
Transport of goods				
Colombia	USA (United States)	06 Apr 14	9LTS302	300263
France	Germany	01 Mar 20	1LTS367	300030
Multilateral		10 Aug 20	28LTS223	300711
Belgium	Netherlands	06 Oct 20	18LTS247	300467
Italy	Netherlands	11 Oct 20	18LTS253	300468
Poland	USSR (Soviet Union)	12 Oct 20	4LTS7	300101
Finland	USSR (Soviet Union)	14 Oct 20	3LTS5	300091
Belgium	UK Great Britain	15 Mar 21	5LTS319	300138
Czechoslovakia	Italy	23 Mar 21	32LTS183	300815
Multilateral		20 Apr 21	7LTS11	300171
Germany	Poland	21 Apr 21	12LTS61	300308
Italy	Sweden	04 Jun 21	6LTS47	300148
Finland	France	13 Jul 21	29LTS445	300755
Norway	UK Great Britain	15 Jul 21	6LTS307	300162
Latvia	Ukrainian SSR	03 Aug 21	17LTS317	300442
Romania	Sweden	25 Nov 21	7LTS247	300190
Finland	USSR (Soviet Union)	14 Dec 21	16LTS221	300414
Multilateral		06 Feb 22	38LTS277	300982
Denmark	Germany	25 Apr 22	18LTS227	300466
Belgium	Switzerland	13 Jun 22	12LTS295	300321
Germany	Poland	01 Aug 22	34LTS253	300877
Austria	Poland	25 Sep 22	59LTS307	301400
Japan	Poland	07 Dec 22	32LTS61	300806
Denmark	USSR (Soviet Union)	23 Apr 23	18LTS15	300450
Greece	Serb/Croat/Slovene	10 May 23	25LTS441	300635
Multilateral		24 May 23	50LTS341	301218
Norway	Sweden	26 May 23	18LTS155	300462
Finland	USSR (Soviet Union)	05 Jun 23	18LTS203	300465
Netherlands	Serb/Croat/Slovene	15 Jun 23	20LTS337	300524

PARTY ONE	PARTY TWO	DATE	CITATION	NUMBER
Transport of goods (Cont.)				
Belgium	Denmark	28 Jun 23	20LTS59	300507
Austria	Denmark	30 Jun 23	18LTS189	300463
Austria	Denmark	30 Jun 23	18LTS195	300464
Estonia	Sweden	07 Jul 23	20LTS189	300517
Finland	Netherlands	01 Nov 23	23LTS33	300574
Italy	Spain	15 Nov 23	39LTS49	300996
UK Great Britain	USA (United States)	23 Jan 24	27LTS181	300681
Netherlands	Portugal	27 Feb 24	27LTS105	300672
Multilateral		31 Mar 24	27LTS211	300685
Norway	USA (United States)	24 May 24	26LTS43	300639
Denmark	USA (United States)	29 May 24	27LTS361	300697
Finland	USSR (Soviet Union)	18 Jun 24	47LTS153	301133
Italy	Serb/Croat/Slovene	14 Jul 24	82LTS327	301877
Latvia	Norway	14 Aug 24	36LTS211	300924
Czechoslovakia	France	18 Aug 24	44LTS21	301080
Netherlands	USA (United States)	21 Aug 24	33LTS433	300863
Finland	Latvia	23 Aug 24	37LTS383	300962
Multilateral		25 Aug 24	120LTS155	302764
Netherlands	Portugal	27 Aug 24	31LTS235	300800
Multilateral		30 Sep 24	30LTS135	300766
Japan	Peru	30 Sep 24	102LTS33	302351
Japan	Mexico	08 Oct 24	36LTS259	300927
Czechoslovakia	Netherlands	17 Oct 24	31LTS93	300786
Finland	Italy	22 Oct 24	32LTS149	300814
Multilateral		23 Oct 24	77LTS367	301778
Iceland	Latvia	03 Nov 24	43LTS339	301069
Poland	Sweden	02 Dec 24	36LTS299	300930
France	Poland	09 Dec 24	44LTS127	301081
Hungary	Netherlands	09 Dec 24	47LTS91	301130
France	Portugal	04 Mar 25	44LTS197	301083
Greece	Poland	17 Apr 25	38LTS301	300985
Czechoslovakia	Sweden	18 Apr 25	36LTS289	300929
Czechoslovakia	Poland	23 Apr 25	44LTS309	301091
Spain	Sweden	04 May 25	36LTS323	300932
Multilateral		09 Jun 25	49LTS9	301174
Germany	USSR (Soviet Union)	12 Oct 25	53LTS7	301257
France	Hungary	13 Oct 25	48LTS9	301150
Estonia	USA (United States)	23 Dec 25	50LTS13	301197
Bel-Lux Econ Union	Czechoslovakia	28 Dec 25	58LTS189	301372
Denmark	Germany	20 Mar 26	51LTS317	301237
Austria	Hungary	10 May 26	56LTS39	301321
Germany	Poland	26 Mar 27	64LTS177	301505
Belgium	Portugal	21 Jul 27	71LTS439	301682
Hungary	Italy	25 Jul 27	74LTS53	301731
Greece	Serb/Croat/Slovene	02 Nov 27	91LTS137	302060
Germany	Greece	24 Mar 28	90LTS9	302031
Austria	Denmark	06 Apr 28	85LTS423	301943
Hungary	Italy	04 Jul 28	92LTS117	302083
Germany	Lithuania	30 Oct 28	89LTS127	302010
Multilateral		22 Nov 28	111LTS343	302598
Estonia	Germany	07 Dec 28	99LTS259	302273
Austria	Estonia	11 Dec 28	92LTS229	302091
Persia	Sweden	10 May 29	102LTS9	302349
Hungary	Lithuania	16 May 29	96LTS333	302211
Estonia	USSR (Soviet Union)	17 May 29	94LTS323	302152
Denmark	Germany	14 Oct 29	98LTS211	302248
Canada	USA (United States)	22 Oct 29	97LTS321	302229
Poland	Romania	30 Oct 29	121LTS243	302790
Poland	Romania	30 Oct 29	121LTS167	302787
Belgium	Germany	07 Nov 29	121LTS327	302795
Austria	Poland	10 Apr 30	108LTS289	302514
Austria	Germany	12 Apr 30	115LTS297	302693
Japan	Lithuania	02 May 30	126LTS369	302895
Hungary	Romania	10 Aug 30	107LTS185	302476
Austria	Japan	16 Aug 30	126LTS351	302894

PARTY ONE	PARTY TWO	DATE	CITATION	NUMBER
Transport of goods (Cont.)				
Greece	UK Great Britain	17 Apr 31	129LTS287	302965
France	Greece	05 Jun 31	31LTS201	303011
Germany	Netherlands	11 Jun 31	120LTS413	302778
Hungary	Netherlands	26 Jun 31	127LTS217	302921
Austria	Netherlands	26 Jun 31	127LTS225	302922
Italy	Netherlands	01 Jul 31	127LTS235	302923
Netherlands	Norway	15 Jul 31	127LTS313	302924
Netherlands	Yugoslavia	15 Jul 31	127LTS337	302927
Denmark	Netherlands	15 Jul 31	127LTS329	302926
Netherlands	Sweden	15 Jul 31	127LTS321	302925
Netherlands	Romania	20 Jul 31	127LTS425	302929
Czechoslovakia	Netherlands	11 Aug 31	127LTS347	302928
Romania	Sweden	07 Oct 31	131LTS51	303003
Multilateral		23 Nov 33	192LTS389	304484
Czechoslovakia	Poland	10 Feb 34	183LTS213	304238
Hungary	Italy	18 Nov 34	166LTS263	303842
Bel-Lux Econ Union	France	16 Jul 35	162LTS19	303731
Colombia	USA (United States)	13 Sep 35	170LTS293	303944
Saudi Arabia	UK Great Britain	17 Nov 35	170LTS87	303929
France	Spain	30 Dec 35	172LTS217	303993
Spain	Turkey	31 Dec 35	166LTS163	303838
Norway	Uruguay	04 Apr 36	176LTS115	304055
Bulgaria	Romania	20 Jul 37	202LTS33	304733
Belgium	France	02 Oct 37	184LTS65	304242
Estonia	France	16 Oct 37	183LTS41	304227
Latvia	Poland	16 Nov 37	197LTS43	304604
Belgium	Netherlands	31 Dec 37	189LTS387	304396
Portugal	Siam	02 Jul 38	200LTS149	304688
Liberia	USA (United States)	08 Aug 38	201LTS163	304711
Multilateral		03 Apr 39	195LTS471	304566
Poland	UK Great Britain	25 Nov 39	199LTS65	304666
Air transport				
France	Switzerland	09 Dec 19	1LTS29	300004
Multilateral		01 May 20	11LTS173	300297
Belgium	UK Great Britain	05 Oct 20	5LTS147	300123
Sweden	UK Great Britain	16 Feb 21	3LTS233	300100
Norway	UK Great Britain	15 Jul 21	6LTS307	300162
Denmark	Norway	27 Jul 21	9LTS23	300241
Belgium	Netherlands	08 Jul 22	13LTS273	300358
Netherlands	UK Great Britain	11 Jul 23	33LTS111	300836
Hungary	Latvia	19 Nov 23	37LTS341	300959
Denmark	Poland	16 Dec 24	32LTS409	300829
Netherlands	Norway	08 Jan 25	46LTS279	301122
Netherlands	Switzerland	18 May 25	54LTS365	301299
Austria	Germany	19 May 25	52LTS121	301253
Netherlands	Poland	04 Sep 25	58LTS179	301371
Poland	Sweden	01 Oct 25	54LTS113	301279
Netherlands	Sweden	21 Nov 25	55LTS79	301305
Czechoslovakia	Poland	15 Apr 26	67LTS305	301554
Multilateral		22 May 26	58LTS331	301381
Denmark	Netherlands	23 Jul 26	66LTS133	301528
Multilateral		31 Mar 27	66LTS59	301525
Germany	Italy	20 May 27	79LTS179	301810
Czechoslovakia	Hungary	31 May 27	65LTS61	301520
Germany	UK Great Britain	29 Jun 27	71LTS165	301659
Germany	Spain	09 Dec 27	79LTS203	301811
Multilateral		20 Feb 28	86LTS111	301950
Saar	Switzerland	15 Aug 28	81LTS373	301847
Multilateral		12 Oct 29	137LTS11	303145
Netherlands	Spain	14 Feb 30	137LTS149	303152
Poland	Romania	02 May 31	152LTS33	303482
Italy	USA (United States)	14 Oct 31	137LTS209	303157
Belgium	Spain	27 Feb 32	137LTS129	303150
Belgium	Spain	27 Feb 32	137LTS111	303149

PARTY ONE	PARTY TWO	DATE	CITATION	NUMBER
Air transport (Cont.)				
Spain	Sweden	08 Apr 32	138LTS135	303184
Austria	UK Great Britain	16 Jul 32	144LTS9	303318
Greece	Yugoslavia	22 Jul 33	161LTS219	303714
Norway	USA (United States)	16 Oct 33	145LTS9	303342
Multilateral		07 Dec 34	158LTS91	303629
Germany	Spain	07 Jan 35	166LTS363	303852
UK Great Britain	USA (United States)	05 Apr 35	162LTS39	303733
Belgium	Italy	04 May 35	159LTS165	303660
Estonia	Sweden	20 May 35	162LTS371	303750
Hungary	Switzerland	18 Jun 35	174LTS7	304033
Portugal	UK Great Britain	24 Oct 35	167LTS133	303861
Greece	Italy	30 Jun 36	185LTS93	304277
Multilateral		20 Jul 36	173LTS213	304015
Netherlands	UK Great Britain	27 Aug 36	172LTS53	303978
Czechoslovakia	Italy	10 May 37	190LTS397	304430
Bulgaria	Romania	22 May 37	188LTS173	304357
Germany	Romania	03 Oct 37	190LTS369	304429
Multilateral		03 Dec 37	186LTS293	304318
France	Netherlands	15 Jul 38	192LTS151	304469
Canada	USA (United States)	28 Jul 38	192LTS94	304464
China	UK Great Britain	24 Jan 39	199LTS53	304664
Portugal	UK Great Britain	25 Jan 39	196LTS281	304590
Greece	UK Great Britain	30 May 39	202LTS7	304732
France	USA (United States)	15 Jul 39	199LTS207	304675
Canada	USA (United States)	18 Aug 39	199LTS367	304684
Canada	USA (United States)	02 Dec 40	203LTS219	304765
UK Great Britain	USA (United States)	27 Mar 41	204LTS15	304784
Airport facilities				
Switzerland	UK Great Britain	06 Nov 19	1LTS37	300005
France	Switzerland	09 Dec 19	1LTS29	300004
Multilateral		01 May 20	11LTS173	300297
Germany	Switzerland	14 Sep 20	2LTS331	300087
France	UK Great Britain	20 Oct 20	2LTS323	300085
Denmark	UK Great Britain	23 Dec 20	2LTS249	300071
Sweden	UK Great Britain	16 Feb 21	3LTS233	300100
Denmark	Norway	27 Jul 21	9LTS23	300241
Denmark	Germany	25 Apr 22	18LTS227	300466
Denmark	Sweden	07 Nov 22	14LTS95	300370
Multilateral		14 Dec 22	36LTS457	300943
Norway	UK Great Britain	22 Feb 23	15LTS159	300389
Belgium	Denmark	28 Jun 23	20LTS59	300507
Netherlands	UK Great Britain	11 Jul 23	33LTS111	300836
Denmark	Poland	16 Dec 24	32LTS409	300829
Netherlands	Switzerland	18 May 25	54LTS365	301299
Austria	Germany	19 May 25	52LTS121	301253
Poland	Sweden	01 Oct 25	54LTS113	301279
Netherlands	Sweden	21 Nov 25	55LTS79	301305
Belgium	Germany	29 May 26	127LTS149	302916
Denmark	Netherlands	23 Jul 26	66LTS133	301528
Czechoslovakia	Germany	22 Jan 27	89LTS231	302019
Austria	Czechoslovakia	15 Feb 27	73LTS349	301724
Germany	Italy	20 May 27	79LTS179	301810
Italy	Spain	15 Aug 27	94LTS361	302155
Multilateral		27 Oct 27	148LTS265	303417
Multilateral		20 Feb 28	129LTS223	302963
France	Spain	22 Mar 28	73LTS63	301707
Austria	Italy	11 May 28	100LTS41	302293
Germany	Netherlands	17 Aug 28	93LTS409	302129
Italy	Spain	03 Oct 28	94LTS387	302156
France	Italy	10 Mar 29	93LTS319	302120
Germany	Poland	28 Aug 29	146LTS333	303383
Austria	Netherlands	31 Dec 29	111LTS177	302586
Netherlands	Spain	14 Feb 30	137LTS149	303152
Austria	Poland	10 Apr 30	108LTS289	302514

PARTY ONE	PARTY TWO	DATE	CITATION	NUMBER
Airport facilities (Cont.)				
Czechoslovakia	Romania	20 Jun 30	150LTS63	303453
France	Poland	02 Aug 30	114LTS93	302657
Greece	UK Great Britain	17 Apr 31	129LTS287	302965
Greece	Poland	22 Apr 31	129LTS313	302966
Czechoslovakia	Germany	29 Apr 31	133LTS347	303072
Poland	Romania	02 May 31	152LTS33	303482
Multilateral		16 May 31	136LTS245	303128
France	Greece	05 Jun 31	31LTS201	303011
Italy	USA (United States)	14 Oct 31	137LTS209	303157
Belgium	Spain	27 Feb 32	137LTS111	303149
Belgium	Spain	27 Feb 32	137LTS129	303150
Spain	Sweden	08 Apr 32	138LTS135	303184
Czechoslovakia	Italy	28 Apr 32	136LTS267	303129
Germany	USA (United States)	31 May 32	133LTS409	303078
Hungary	Italy	05 Jul 32	144LTS257	303330
Austria	UK Great Britain	16 Jul 32	144LTS9	303318
Austria	Yugoslavia	14 Oct 32	147LTS173	303398
Greece	Romania	12 Jun 33	150LTS357	303468
Greece	Yugoslavia	22 Jul 33	161LTS219	303714
Sweden	USA (United States)	09 Sep 33	144LTS153	303326
South Africa	USA (United States)	20 Sep 33	148LTS189	303412
Norway	USA (United States)	16 Oct 33	145LTS9	303342
Norway	USA (United States)	16 Oct 33	145LTS43	303344
Denmark	USA (United States)	24 Mar 34	149LTS471	303447
Multilateral		07 Dec 34	158LTS91	303629
UK Great Britain	USA (United States)	05 Apr 35	162LTS39	303733
Estonia	Sweden	20 May 35	162LTS371	303750
France	Netherlands	19 Oct 35	166LTS67	303830
Portugal	UK Great Britain	24 Oct 35	167LTS133	303861
Greece	Italy	30 Jun 36	185LTS93	304277
Hungary	UK Great Britain	22 Mar 37	190LTS59	304405
Belgium	Netherlands	26 Mar 37	179LTS52	304132
Austria	Netherlands	02 Apr 37	179LTS81	304136
Portugal	South Africa	18 Jun 37	189LTS121	304380
Germany	Romania	03 Oct 37	190LTS369	304429
Estonia	Germany	23 Dec 37	189LTS333	304393
Canada	USA (United States)	28 Jul 38	192LTS94	304464
France	UK Great Britain	08 Nov 38	196LTS215	304584
Greece	UK Great Britain	30 May 39	202LTS7	304732
Airport equipment				
France	Switzerland	09 Dec 19	1LTS29	300004
Multilateral		01 May 20	11LTS173	300297
Denmark	Norway	27 Jul 21	9LTS23	300241
Netherlands	UK Great Britain	11 Jul 23	33LTS111	300836
Denmark	Poland	16 Dec 24	32LTS409	300829
Czechoslovakia	France	26 May 25	150LTS43	303452
Germany	Italy	20 May 27	79LTS179	301810
Multilateral		27 Oct 27	148LTS265	303417
Germany	Poland	28 Aug 29	146LTS333	303383
Netherlands	Spain	14 Feb 30	137LTS149	303152
Belgium	France	23 May 30	119LTS33	302738
Czechoslovakia	Romania	20 Jun 30	150LTS63	303453
Greece	UK Great Britain	17 Apr 31	129LTS287	302965
Greece	Poland	22 Apr 31	129LTS313	302966
Poland	Romania	02 May 31	152LTS33	303482
Multilateral		16 May 31	136LTS245	303128
France	Greece	05 Jun 31	31LTS201	303011
Italy	USA (United States)	14 Oct 31	137LTS209	303157
Belgium	Spain	27 Feb 32	137LTS129	303150
Belgium	Spain	27 Feb 32	137LTS111	303149
Spain	Sweden	08 Apr 32	138LTS135	303184
Czechoslovakia	Italy	28 Apr 32	136LTS267	303129
Germany	USA (United States)	31 May 32	133LTS409	303078
Hungary	Italy	05 Jul 32	144LTS257	303330

Airport equipment (Cont.)

PARTY ONE	PARTY TWO	DATE	CITATION	NUMBER
Austria	UK Great Britain	16 Jul 32	144LTS9	303318
Austria	Yugoslavia	14 Oct 32	147LTS173	303398
Multilateral		29 May 33	192LTS289	304479
Greece	Romania	12 Jun 33	150LTS357	303468
Sweden	USA (United States)	09 Sep 33	144LTS153	303326
South Africa	USA (United States)	20 Sep 33	148LTS189	303412
Norway	USA (United States)	16 Oct 33	145LTS9	303342
Denmark	USA (United States)	24 Mar 34	149LTS471	303447
Multilateral		07 Dec 34	158LTS91	303629
UK Great Britain	USA (United States)	05 Apr 35	162LTS39	303733
Estonia	Sweden	20 May 35	162LTS371	303750
Portugal	UK Great Britain	24 Oct 35	167LTS133	303861
Greece	Italy	30 Jun 36	185LTS93	304277
Canada	USA (United States)	28 Jul 38	192LTS94	304464
Greece	UK Great Britain	30 May 39	202LTS7	304732
New Zealand	USA (United States)	28 Feb 40	203LTS11	304746

Airworthiness certificates

PARTY ONE	PARTY TWO	DATE	CITATION	NUMBER
Multilateral		01 May 20	11LTS173	300297
Germany	Switzerland	14 Sep 20	2LTS331	300087
France	UK Great Britain	20 Oct 20	2LTS323	300085
Sweden	UK Great Britain	16 Feb 21	3LTS233	300100
Portugal	UK Great Britain	06 May 21	5LTS179	300128
Norway	UK Great Britain	15 Jul 21	6LTS307	300162
Denmark	Norway	27 Jul 21	9LTS23	300241
Denmark	Germany	25 Apr 22	18LTS227	300466
Belgium	Netherlands	08 Jul 22	13LTS273	300358
Denmark	Sweden	07 Nov 22	14LTS95	300370
Norway	Sweden	26 May 23	18LTS155	300462
Belgium	Denmark	28 Jun 23	20LTS59	300507
Netherlands	UK Great Britain	11 Jul 23	33LTS111	300836
Denmark	Poland	16 Dec 24	32LTS409	300829
Netherlands	Switzerland	18 May 25	54LTS365	301299
Austria	Germany	19 May 25	52LTS121	301253
Czechoslovakia	France	26 May 25	150LTS43	303452
Poland	Sweden	01 Oct 25	54LTS113	301279
Netherlands	Sweden	21 Nov 25	55LTS79	301305
Czechoslovakia	Poland	15 Apr 26	67LTS305	301554
Denmark	Netherlands	23 Jul 26	66LTS133	301528
Austria	Czechoslovakia	15 Feb 27	73LTS349	301724
Germany	Italy	20 May 27	79LTS179	301810
Germany	UK Great Britain	29 Jun 27	71LTS165	301659
Italy	Spain	15 Aug 27	94LTS361	302155
Multilateral		27 Oct 27	148LTS265	303417
Germany	Spain	09 Dec 27	79LTS203	301811
Multilateral		20 Feb 28	129LTS223	302963
France	Spain	22 Mar 28	73LTS63	301707
Austria	Italy	11 May 28	100LTS41	302293
Saar	Switzerland	15 Aug 28	81LTS373	301847
Germany	Norway	23 Jan 29	93LTS197	302110
Germany	Poland	28 Aug 29	146LTS333	303383
Multilateral		12 Oct 29	137LTS11	303145
Canada	USA (United States)	22 Oct 29	97LTS321	302229
Austria	Netherlands	31 Dec 29	111LTS177	302586
Netherlands	Spain	14 Feb 30	137LTS149	303152
Austria	Poland	10 Apr 30	108LTS289	302514
Netherlands	UK Great Britain	05 May 30	105LTS261	302417
Czechoslovakia	Romania	20 Jun 30	150LTS63	303453
Poland	Romania	02 May 31	152LTS33	303482
Multilateral		16 May 31	136LTS245	303128
Italy	Netherlands	03 Oct 31	126LTS109	302875
Italy	USA (United States)	14 Oct 31	137LTS209	303157
South Africa	USA (United States)	01 Dec 31	129LTS121	302956
Belgium	Spain	27 Feb 32	137LTS111	303149
Belgium	Spain	27 Feb 32	137LTS129	303150

Airworthiness certificates (Cont.)

PARTY ONE	PARTY TWO	DATE	CITATION	NUMBER
Germany	USA (United States)	31 May 32	133LTS427	303079
Austria	UK Great Britain	16 Jul 32	144LTS9	303318
Austria	Denmark	05 Aug 32	132LTS165	303036
Austria	Yugoslavia	14 Oct 32	147LTS173	303398
Belgium	USA (United States)	22 Oct 32	137LTS389	303167
Greece	Romania	12 Jun 33	150LTS357	303468
Greece	Yugoslavia	22 Jul 33	161LTS219	303714
Sweden	USA (United States)	09 Sep 33	144LTS183	303328
Sweden	USA (United States)	09 Sep 33	144LTS153	303326
South Africa	USA (United States)	20 Sep 33	148LTS189	303412
Norway	USA (United States)	16 Oct 33	145LTS9	303342
Norway	USA (United States)	16 Oct 33	145LTS43	303344
Denmark	USA (United States)	24 Mar 34	149LTS471	303447
Denmark	USA (United States)	24 Mar 34	149LTS493	303449
Italy	UK Great Britain	17 Sep 34	155LTS85	303570
Germany	UK Great Britain	18 Sep 34	155LTS243	303580
Multilateral		07 Dec 34	158LTS91	303629
UK Great Britain	USA (United States)	05 Apr 35	162LTS39	303733
Belgium	Italy	04 May 35	159LTS165	303660
Estonia	Sweden	20 May 35	162LTS371	303750
Hungary	Netherlands	08 Jun 35	171LTS385	303975
Hungary	Switzerland	18 Jun 35	174LTS7	304033
France	Hungary	23 Jul 35	173LTS243	304016
Portugal	UK Great Britain	24 Oct 35	167LTS133	303861
Germany	Greece	09 Nov 36	182LTS9	304201
Hungary	UK Great Britain	22 Mar 37	190LTS59	304405
Czechoslovakia	Italy	10 May 37	190LTS397	304430
Germany	Romania	03 Oct 37	190LTS369	304429
Estonia	Germany	23 Dec 37	189LTS333	304393
Lithuania	Poland	25 May 38	191LTS391	304457
Canada	USA (United States)	28 Jul 38	192LTS125	304466
Canada	USA (United States)	28 Jul 38	192LTS94	304464
Liberia	USA (United States)	14 Jun 39	202LTS93	304737
France	USA (United States)	15 Jul 39	199LTS355	304683
France	USA (United States)	15 Jul 39	199LTS207	304675
Canada	USA (United States)	18 Aug 39	199LTS367	304684
New Zealand	USA (United States)	28 Feb 40	203LTS11	304746

Conditions of airlines operating permission

PARTY ONE	PARTY TWO	DATE	CITATION	NUMBER
France	Switzerland	09 Dec 19	1LTS29	300004
Multilateral		01 May 20	11LTS173	300297
Sweden	UK Great Britain	16 Feb 21	3LTS233	300100
Austria	Czechoslovakia	04 May 21	15LTS13	300388
Denmark	Norway	27 Jul 21	9LTS23	300241
Belgium	Switzerland	13 Jun 22	12LTS295	300321
Denmark	Sweden	07 Nov 22	14LTS95	300370
Norway	Sweden	26 May 23	18LTS155	300462
France	Netherlands	02 Jul 23	20LTS131	300512
Netherlands	UK Great Britain	11 Jul 23	33LTS111	300836
Poland	UK Great Britain	13 Aug 24	31LTS213	300796
Denmark	Poland	16 Dec 24	32LTS409	300829
Austria	Poland	05 May 25	46LTS269	301121
Austria	Germany	19 May 25	52LTS121	301253
Czechoslovakia	France	26 May 25	150LTS43	303452
Netherlands	Poland	04 Sep 25	58LTS179	301371
Czechoslovakia	Poland	15 Apr 26	67LTS305	301554
Denmark	Netherlands	23 Jul 26	66LTS133	301528
Czechoslovakia	Germany	22 Jan 27	89LTS261	302020
Germany	Italy	20 May 27	79LTS179	301810
Germany	UK Great Britain	29 Jun 27	71LTS165	301659
Italy	Spain	15 Aug 27	94LTS361	302155
Germany	Spain	09 Dec 27	79LTS203	301811
France	Spain	22 Mar 28	73LTS63	301707
Saar	Switzerland	15 Aug 28	81LTS373	301847
Italy	Spain	03 Oct 28	94LTS387	302156

PARTY ONE	PARTY TWO	DATE	CITATION	NUMBER
Conditions of airlines operating permission (Cont.)				
Germany	Poland	28 Aug 29	146LTS333	303383
Multilateral		12 Oct 29	137LTS11	303145
Austria	Netherlands	31 Dec 29	111LTS177	302586
Netherlands	Spain	14 Feb 30	137LTS149	303152
Czechoslovakia	Romania	20 Jun 30	150LTS63	303453
Poland	Romania	02 May 31	152LTS33	303482
Multilateral		16 May 31	136LTS245	303128
Italy	USA (United States)	14 Oct 31	137LTS209	303157
Belgium	Spain	27 Feb 32	137LTS111	303149
Spain	Sweden	08 Apr 32	138LTS135	303184
Czechoslovakia	Italy	28 Apr 32	136LTS267	303129
Hungary	Italy	05 Jul 32	144LTS257	303330
Austria	UK Great Britain	16 Jul 32	144LTS9	303318
Austria	Yugoslavia	14 Oct 32	147LTS173	303398
Multilateral		09 Dec 32	151LTS5	303479
Greece	Romania	12 Jun 33	150LTS357	303468
Greece	Yugoslavia	22 Jul 33	161LTS219	303714
Sweden	USA (United States)	09 Sep 33	144LTS153	303326
South Africa	USA (United States)	20 Sep 33	148LTS189	303412
Norway	USA (United States)	16 Oct 33	145LTS9	303342
Denmark	USA (United States)	24 Mar 34	149LTS471	303447
Multilateral		07 Dec 34	158LTS91	303629
UK Great Britain	USA (United States)	05 Apr 35	162LTS39	303733
Estonia	Sweden	20 May 35	162LTS371	303750
Hungary	Netherlands	08 Jun 35	171LTS385	303975
Hungary	Switzerland	18 Jun 35	174LTS7	304033
France	Hungary	23 Jul 35	173LTS243	304016
Portugal	UK Great Britain	24 Oct 35	167LTS133	303861
Greece	Italy	30 Jun 36	185LTS93	304277
Estonia	Finland	12 Sep 36	172LTS345	303999
Germany	South Africa	16 Mar 37	189LTS107	304378
Hungary	UK Great Britain	22 Mar 37	190LTS59	304405
Ireland	USA (United States)	04 Nov 37	185LTS71	304276
Overflights and technical stops				
Switzerland	UK Great Britain	06 Nov 19	1LTS37	300005
France	Switzerland	09 Dec 19	1LTS29	300004
Multilateral		01 May 20	11LTS173	300297
Germany	Switzerland	14 Sep 20	2LTS331	300087
France	UK Great Britain	20 Oct 20	2LTS323	300085
Denmark	UK Great Britain	23 Dec 20	2LTS249	300071
Sweden	UK Great Britain	16 Feb 21	3LTS233	300100
Portugal	UK Great Britain	06 May 21	5LTS179	300128
Norway	UK Great Britain	15 Jul 21	6LTS307	300162
Denmark	Norway	27 Jul 21	9LTS23	300241
France	UK Great Britain	30 Jan 22	12LTS449	300341
Denmark	Germany	25 Apr 22	18LTS227	300466
Belgium	Switzerland	13 Jun 22	12LTS295	300321
Belgium	Netherlands	08 Jul 22	13LTS273	300358
Finland	USSR (Soviet Union)	28 Oct 22	19LTS199	300493
Denmark	Sweden	07 Nov 22	14LTS95	300370
Norway	Sweden	26 May 23	18LTS155	300462
Belgium	Denmark	28 Jun 23	20LTS59	300507
France	Netherlands	02 Jul 23	20LTS131	300512
Netherlands	UK Great Britain	11 Jul 23	33LTS111	300836
Denmark	Poland	16 Dec 24	32LTS409	300829
Netherlands	Norway	08 Jan 25	46LTS279	301122
Austria	Poland	05 May 25	46LTS269	301121
Netherlands	Switzerland	18 May 25	54LTS365	301299
Austria	Germany	19 May 25	52LTS121	301253
Czechoslovakia	France	26 May 25	150LTS43	303452
Netherlands	Poland	04 Sep 25	58LTS179	301371
Poland	Sweden	01 Oct 25	54LTS113	301279
Netherlands	Sweden	21 Nov 25	55LTS79	301305
Finland	Great Britain	14 Dec 25	47LTS403	301144

PARTY ONE	PARTY TWO	DATE	CITATION	NUMBER
Overflights and technical stops (Cont.)				
Czechoslovakia	Poland	15 Apr 26	67LTS305	301554
Belgium	Germany	29 May 26	127LTS149	302916
Denmark	Netherlands	23 Jul 26	66LTS133	301528
Czechoslovakia	Germany	22 Jan 27	89LTS231	302019
Austria	Czechoslovakia	15 Feb 27	73LTS349	301724
Germany	Italy	20 May 27	79LTS179	301810
Germany	UK Great Britain	29 Jun 27	71LTS165	301659
Italy	Spain	15 Aug 27	94LTS361	302155
Multilateral		27 Oct 27	148LTS265	303417
Germany	Spain	09 Dec 27	79LTS203	301811
Multilateral		20 Feb 28	129LTS223	302963
France	Spain	22 Mar 28	73LTS63	301707
Austria	Italy	11 May 28	100LTS41	302293
Saar	Switzerland	15 Aug 28	81LTS373	301847
Germany	Netherlands	17 Aug 28	93LTS409	302129
Germany	Norway	23 Jan 29	93LTS197	302110
France	Italy	10 Mar 29	93LTS319	302120
Germany	Poland	28 Aug 29	146LTS333	303383
Multilateral		12 Oct 29	137LTS11	303145
Austria	Netherlands	31 Dec 29	111LTS177	302586
Netherlands	Spain	14 Feb 30	137LTS149	303152
Austria	Poland	10 Apr 30	108LTS289	302514
Belgium	France	23 May 30	119LTS33	302738
Czechoslovakia	Romania	20 Jun 30	150LTS63	303453
France	Poland	02 Aug 30	114LTS93	302657
Bulgaria	Poland	07 Apr 31	127LTS45	302905
Greece	UK Great Britain	17 Apr 31	129LTS287	302965
Greece	Poland	22 Apr 31	129LTS313	302966
Poland	Romania	02 May 31	152LTS33	303482
Multilateral		16 May 31	136LTS245	303128
Italy	USA (United States)	14 Oct 31	137LTS209	303157
Belgium	Spain	27 Feb 32	137LTS129	303150
Belgium	Spain	27 Feb 32	137LTS111	303149
Spain	Sweden	08 Apr 32	138LTS135	303184
Czechoslovakia	Italy	28 Apr 32	136LTS267	303129
Hungary	Italy	05 Jul 32	144LTS257	303330
Austria	UK Great Britain	16 Jul 32	144LTS9	303318
Austria	Yugoslavia	14 Oct 32	147LTS173	303398
Greece	Romania	12 Jun 33	150LTS357	303468
Greece	Yugoslavia	22 Jul 33	161LTS219	303714
Sweden	USA (United States)	09 Sep 33	144LTS153	303326
South Africa	USA (United States)	20 Sep 33	148LTS189	303412
Norway	USA (United States)	16 Oct 33	145LTS9	303342
Denmark	USA (United States)	24 Mar 34	149LTS471	303447
Multilateral		07 Dec 34	158LTS91	303629
UK Great Britain	USA (United States)	05 Apr 35	162LTS39	303733
Estonia	Sweden	20 May 35	162LTS371	303750
Hungary	Netherlands	08 Jun 35	171LTS385	303975
Portugal	UK Great Britain	24 Oct 35	167LTS133	303861
Greece	Italy	30 Jun 36	185LTS93	304277
Germany	Greece	09 Nov 36	182LTS9	304201
Ireland	USA (United States)	04 Nov 37	185LTS71	304276
Estonia	Germany	23 Dec 37	189LTS333	304393
Mexico	USA (United States)	01 Apr 41	204LTS179	304798
Operating authorizations and regulations				
France	Switzerland	09 Dec 19	1LTS29	300004
Multilateral		01 May 20	11LTS173	300297
Denmark	UK Great Britain	23 Dec 20	2LTS249	300071
Sweden	UK Great Britain	16 Feb 21	3LTS233	300100
Denmark	Norway	27 Jul 21	9LTS23	300241
Greece	UK Great Britain	27 Jul 21	6LTS347	300167
Denmark	Germany	25 Apr 22	18LTS227	300466
Belgium	Switzerland	13 Jun 22	12LTS295	300321
Belgium	Netherlands	08 Jul 22	13LTS273	300358

PARTY ONE	PARTY TWO	DATE	CITATION	NUMBER
Operating authorizations and regulations (Cont.)				
Denmark	Sweden	07 Nov 22	14LTS95	300370
Norway	Sweden	26 May 23	18LTS155	300462
Belgium	Denmark	28 Jun 23	20LTS59	300507
France	Netherlands	02 Jul 23	20LTS131	300512
Netherlands	UK Great Britain	11 Jul 23	33LTS111	300836
Belgium	Netherlands	14 Jul 23	20LTS119	300511
Poland	UK Great Britain	13 Aug 24	31LTS213	300796
Denmark	Poland	16 Dec 24	32LTS409	300829
Austria	Poland	05 May 25	46LTS269	301121
Netherlands	Switzerland	18 May 25	54LTS365	301299
Austria	Germany	19 May 25	52LTS121	301253
Czechoslovakia	France	26 May 25	150LTS43	303452
Netherlands	Poland	04 Sep 25	58LTS179	301371
Netherlands	Sweden	21 Nov 25	55LTS79	301305
Czechoslovakia	Poland	15 Apr 26	67LTS305	301554
Belgium	Germany	29 May 26	127LTS149	302916
Czechoslovakia	Germany	22 Jan 27	89LTS261	302020
Czechoslovakia	Germany	22 Jan 27	89LTS231	302019
Austria	Czechoslovakia	15 Feb 27	73LTS381	301725
Multilateral		31 Mar 27	66LTS59	301525
Multilateral		19 May 27	68LTS407	301595
Germany	Italy	20 May 27	79LTS179	301810
Germany	UK Great Britain	29 Jun 27	71LTS165	301659
Italy	Spain	15 Aug 27	94LTS361	302155
Multilateral		27 Oct 27	148LTS265	303417
Germany	Spain	09 Dec 27	79LTS203	301811
Austria	Italy	11 May 28	100LTS41	302293
Austria	Italy	11 May 28	100LTS375	302307
Saar	Switzerland	15 Aug 28	81LTS373	301847
Germany	Netherlands	17 Aug 28	93LTS409	302129
Italy	Spain	03 Oct 28	94LTS387	302156
Germany	Norway	23 Jan 29	93LTS197	302110
Germany	Poland	28 Aug 29	146LTS333	303383
Multilateral		12 Oct 29	137LTS11	303145
Canada	USA (United States)	22 Oct 29	97LTS321	302229
Netherlands	Spain	14 Feb 30	137LTS149	303152
Austria	Poland	10 Apr 30	108LTS289	302514
Poland	Romania	09 May 30	112LTS225	302617
Belgium	France	23 May 30	119LTS33	302738
Netherlands	UK Great Britain	03 Jun 30	111LTS85	302582
Czechoslovakia	Romania	20 Jun 30	150LTS63	303453
France	Poland	02 Aug 30	114LTS93	302657
Bulgaria	Poland	07 Apr 31	127LTS45	302905
Greece	UK Great Britain	17 Apr 31	129LTS287	302965
Czechoslovakia	Germany	29 Apr 31	133LTS359	303073
Czechoslovakia	Germany	29 Apr 31	133LTS347	303072
Poland	Romania	02 May 31	152LTS33	303482
Multilateral		16 May 31	136LTS245	303128
Czechoslovakia	Germany	25 Jul 31	187LTS279	304344
Italy	USA (United States)	14 Oct 31	137LTS209	303157
Belgium	Spain	27 Feb 32	137LTS129	303150
Belgium	Spain	27 Feb 32	137LTS111	303149
Spain	Sweden	08 Apr 32	138LTS135	303184
Czechoslovakia	Italy	28 Apr 32	136LTS267	303129
Germany	USA (United States)	31 May 32	133LTS409	303078
Hungary	Italy	05 Jul 32	144LTS257	303330
Austria	UK Great Britain	16 Jul 32	144LTS9	303318
Austria	Yugoslavia	14 Oct 32	147LTS173	303398
Multilateral		09 Dec 32	151LTS5	303479
Multilateral		12 Apr 33	161LTS65	303706
Greece	Romania	12 Jun 33	150LTS357	303468
Greece	Yugoslavia	22 Jul 33	161LTS219	303714
Sweden	USA (United States)	09 Sep 33	144LTS153	303326
Sweden	USA (United States)	09 Sep 33	144LTS171	303327
South Africa	USA (United States)	20 Sep 33	148LTS189	303412
Operating authorizations and regulations (Cont.)				
Norway	USA (United States)	16 Oct 33	145LTS9	303342
Denmark	USA (United States)	24 Mar 34	149LTS471	303447
UK Great Britain	USA (United States)	05 Apr 35	162LTS39	303733
France	UK Great Britain	09 Apr 35	199LTS49	304663
Estonia	Sweden	20 May 35	162LTS371	303750
Hungary	Netherlands	08 Jun 35	171LTS385	303975
Hungary	Switzerland	18 Jun 35	174LTS7	304033
France	Hungary	23 Jul 35	173LTS243	304016
Portugal	UK Great Britain	24 Oct 35	167LTS133	303861
Netherlands	Poland	09 Apr 36	177LTS71	304081
Greece	Italy	30 Jun 36	185LTS93	304277
Estonia	Finland	12 Sep 36	172LTS345	303999
Netherlands	Switzerland	15 Oct 36	177LTS101	304084
Hungary	UK Great Britain	22 Mar 37	190LTS59	304405
Czechoslovakia	Italy	10 May 37	190LTS397	304430
Bulgaria	Romania	22 May 37	188LTS173	304357
Portugal	South Africa	18 Jun 37	189LTS121	304380
Germany	Romania	03 Oct 37	190LTS369	304429
Multilateral		11 Oct 37	182LTS173	304210
France	Switzerland	13 Oct 37	194LTS191	304522
Ireland	USA (United States)	04 Nov 37	185LTS71	304276
Multilateral		03 Dec 37	186LTS293	304318
Belgium	China	18 Dec 37	190LTS109	304409
Estonia	Germany	23 Dec 37	189LTS333	304393
Italy	Netherlands	26 Feb 38	194LTS75	304509
France	Netherlands	15 Jul 38	192LTS151	304469
Canada	USA (United States)	28 Jul 38	192LTS94	304464
Multilateral		25 Oct 38	192LTS323	304482
China	UK Great Britain	24 Jan 39	199LTS53	304664
Portugal	UK Great Britain	25 Jan 39	196LTS281	304590
Greece	UK Great Britain	30 May 39	202LTS7	304732
France	USA (United States)	15 Jul 39	199LTS355	304683
France	USA (United States)	15 Jul 39	199LTS207	304675
Canada	USA (United States)	18 Aug 39	199LTS367	304684
Japan	Thailand	30 Nov 39	200LTS197	304691
Licenses and certificates of nationality				
Switzerland	UK Great Britain	06 Nov 19	1LTS37	300005
France	Switzerland	09 Dec 19	1LTS29	300004
Multilateral		01 May 20	11LTS173	300297
France	UK Great Britain	20 Oct 20	2LTS323	300085
Denmark	UK Great Britain	23 Dec 20	2LTS249	300071
Sweden	UK Great Britain	16 Feb 21	3LTS233	300100
Belgium	UK Great Britain	15 Mar 21	5LTS319	300138
Portugal	UK Great Britain	06 May 21	5LTS179	300128
Norway	UK Great Britain	15 Jul 21	6LTS307	300162
Denmark	Norway	27 Jul 21	9LTS23	300241
Denmark	Germany	25 Apr 22	18LTS227	300466
Belgium	Netherlands	08 Jul 22	13LTS273	300358
Denmark	Sweden	07 Nov 22	14LTS95	300370
Belgium	Denmark	28 Jun 23	20LTS59	300507
France	Netherlands	02 Jul 23	20LTS131	300512
Netherlands	UK Great Britain	11 Jul 23	33LTS111	300836
Poland	UK Great Britain	13 Aug 24	31LTS213	300796
Denmark	Poland	16 Dec 24	32LTS409	300829
Netherlands	Norway	08 Jan 25	46LTS279	301122
Austria	Poland	05 May 25	46LTS269	301121
Netherlands	Switzerland	18 May 25	54LTS365	301299
Austria	Germany	19 May 25	52LTS121	301253
Czechoslovakia	France	26 May 25	150LTS43	303452
Netherlands	Poland	04 Sep 25	58LTS179	301371
Poland	Sweden	01 Oct 25	54LTS113	301279
Netherlands	Sweden	21 Nov 25	55LTS79	301305
Czechoslovakia	Germany	22 Jan 27	89LTS231	302019
Austria	Czechoslovakia	15 Feb 27	73LTS349	301724

PARTY ONE	PARTY TWO	DATE	CITATION	NUMBER
Licenses and certificates of nationality (Cont.)				
Multilateral		19 May 27	68LTS407	301595
Germany	UK Great Britain	29 Jun 27	71LTS165	301659
Italy	Spain	15 Aug 27	94LTS361	302155
Multilateral		27 Oct 27	148LTS265	303417
Germany	Spain	09 Dec 27	79LTS203	301811
Multilateral		20 Feb 28	129LTS223	302963
France	Spain	22 Mar 28	73LTS63	301707
Saar	Switzerland	15 Aug 28	81LTS373	301847
Germany	Netherlands	17 Aug 28	93LTS409	302129
Germany	Norway	23 Jan 29	93LTS197	302110
Germany	Poland	28 Aug 29	146LTS333	303383
Multilateral		12 Oct 29	137LTS11	303145
Canada	USA (United States)	22 Oct 29	97LTS321	302229
Austria	Netherlands	31 Dec 29	111LTS177	302586
Netherlands	Spain	14 Feb 30	137LTS149	303152
Austria	Poland	10 Apr 30	108LTS289	302514
Czechoslovakia	Romania	20 Jun 30	150LTS63	303453
Poland	Romania	02 May 31	152LTS33	303482
Multilateral		16 May 31	136LTS245	303128
Italy	USA (United States)	14 Oct 31	137LTS209	303157
Belgium	Spain	27 Feb 32	137LTS111	303149
Belgium	Spain	27 Feb 32	137LTS129	303150
Spain	Sweden	08 Apr 32	138LTS135	303184
Czechoslovakia	Italy	28 Apr 32	136LTS267	303129
Germany	USA (United States)	31 May 32	133LTS409	303078
Hungary	Italy	05 Jul 32	144LTS257	303330
Austria	UK Great Britain	16 Jul 32	144LTS9	303318
Austria	Yugoslavia	14 Oct 32	147LTS173	303398
Greece	Romania	12 Jun 33	150LTS357	303468
Greece	Yugoslavia	22 Jul 33	161LTS219	303714
Sweden	USA (United States)	09 Sep 33	144LTS153	303326
South Africa	USA (United States)	20 Sep 33	148LTS203	303413
South Africa	USA (United States)	20 Sep 33	148LTS189	303412
Norway	USA (United States)	16 Oct 33	145LTS31	303343
Denmark	USA (United States)	24 Mar 34	149LTS471	303447
Denmark	USA (United States)	24 Mar 34	149LTS485	303448
Multilateral		07 Dec 34	158LTS91	303629
UK Great Britain	USA (United States)	05 Apr 35	162LTS39	303733
Estonia	Sweden	20 May 35	162LTS371	303750
Portugal	UK Great Britain	24 Oct 35	167LTS133	303861
Greece	Italy	30 Jun 36	185LTS93	304277
Belgium	Italy	01 May 37	198LTS73	304624
Belgium	Sweden	15 Jun 37	198LTS77	304625
Multilateral		21 Jul 37	184LTS271	304250
Belgium	Denmark	16 Sep 37	197LTS67	304606
Multilateral		11 Oct 37	182LTS173	304210
Multilateral		29 Apr 38	190LTS115	304410
Multilateral		17 May 38	192LTS319	304481
Multilateral		30 May 38	191LTS299	304451
Multilateral		15 Jul 38	195LTS73	304536
Canada	USA (United States)	28 Jul 38	192LTS115	304465
Greece	UK Great Britain	30 May 39	202LTS7	304732
Liberia	USA (United States)	14 Jun 39	202LTS93	304737
France	USA (United States)	15 Jul 39	199LTS355	304683
Canada	USA (United States)	18 Aug 39	199LTS367	304684
Multilateral		21 Aug 39	198LTS343	304652
Multilateral		08 Jan 40	203LTS133	304756
Water transport				
Multilateral		10 Sep 19	7LTS331	300200
Denmark	Sweden	26 Jan 20	14LTS273	300379
Norway	Portugal	14 Oct 20	2LTS237	300069
Austria	Czechoslovakia	04 May 21	15LTS13	300388
Sweden	USA (United States)	28 May 21	6LTS41	300147
Danzig	Poland	24 Oct 21	116LTS5	302699

PARTY ONE	PARTY TWO	DATE	CITATION	NUMBER
Water transport (Cont.)				
Czechoslovakia	Hungary	13 Jul 23	35LTS237	300898
Austria	Japan	02 Oct 23	22LTS349	300563
Finland	Netherlands	01 Nov 23	23LTS33	300574
Germany	Hungary	06 Nov 23	45LTS253	301103
Finland	UK Great Britain	14 Dec 23	29LTS129	300739
Latvia	Netherlands	02 Jul 24	37LTS121	300951
Finland	Latvia	23 Aug 24	37LTS383	300962
Denmark	Iceland	30 Sep 24	32LTS355	300825
Germany	Guatemala	04 Oct 24	52LTS19	301246
Austria	Norway	03 Dec 24	31LTS151	300792
Denmark	UK Great Britain	18 Dec 24	32LTS89	300808
Sweden	UK Great Britain	19 Dec 24	32LTS291	300820
Italy	UK Great Britain	15 Jun 25	38LTS189	300976
Finland	Great Britain	18 Nov 25	42LTS445	301042
Multilateral		27 Nov 25	67LTS63	301539
Estonia	UK Great Britain	18 Jan 26	48LTS209	301163
Greece	Spain	23 Sep 26	91LTS121	302059
Germany	Persia	17 Feb 29	111LTS19	302576
Germany	Hedjaz	26 Apr 29	115LTS265	302690
Persia	Sweden	10 May 29	102LTS9	302349
Multilateral		31 May 29	136LTS81	303127
Denmark	Great Britain	11 Jun 29	93LTS401	302128
Norway	Sweden	26 Jul 29	94LTS287	302149
Greece	Sweden	18 Oct 29	95LTS201	302174
Multilateral		23 Oct 30	125LTS95	302849
Poland	USA (United States)	15 Jun 31	139LTS395	303223
Denmark	Finland	09 Jul 31	123LTS393	302826
Germany	Sweden	01 Jun 32	129LTS471	302979
UK Great Britain	USA (United States)	27 Mar 41	204LTS15	304784
Germany	Greece	20 Jan 97*	2LTS107	300053
Canal improvement				
Multilateral		23 Jul 21	26LTS173	300647
Multilateral		10 May 22	26LTS265	300652
Japan	Poland	07 Dec 22	32LTS61	300806
Finland	Italy	22 Oct 24	32LTS149	300814
Austria	Switzerland	19 Nov 24	39LTS26	300994
Romania	Yugoslavia	14 Dec 31	135LTS71	303104
Romania	Yugoslavia	14 Dec 31	135LTS133	303108
Romania	Yugoslavia	14 Dec 31	135LTS31	303103
Panama	USA (United States)	02 Mar 36	200LTS17	304686
Czechoslovakia	Hungary	24 Aug 37	189LTS403	304397
Innocent passage				
Switzerland	UK Great Britain	06 Nov 19	1LTS37	300005
Multilateral		09 Feb 20	2LTS7	300041
Germany	Switzerland	14 Sep 20	2LTS331	300087
France	UK Great Britain	20 Oct 20	2LTS323	300085
UK Great Britain	USSR (Soviet Union)	16 Mar 21	4LTS127	300104
Portugal	UK Great Britain	06 May 21	5LTS179	300128
Multilateral		24 Jul 23	28LTS115	300702
Bel-Lux Econ Union		07 Jul 25	54LTS267	301290
Netherlands	Poland	04 Sep 25	58LTS179	301371
Denmark	Netherlands	23 Jul 26	66LTS133	301528
Bel-Lux Econ Union	Estonia	28 Sep 26	62LTS433	301475
Italy	Lithuania	17 Sep 27	73LTS9	301701
Multilateral		20 Jul 36	173LTS213	304015
Italy	UK Great Britain	02 Jan 37	177LTS241	304092
Siam	USA (United States)	13 Nov 37	192LTS247	304476
Norway	Siam	15 Nov 37	186LTS9	304301
Italy	Siam	03 Dec 37	189LTS255	304389
Japan	Siam	08 Dec 37	188LTS375	304367
Germany	Siam	30 Dec 37	188LTS401	304368
Merchant vessels				
France	UK Great Britain	06 Aug 14	10LTS333	300278
Multilateral		09 Dec 19	5LTS335	300140

PARTY ONE	PARTY TWO	DATE	CITATION	NUMBER
Merchant vessels (Cont.)				
Multilateral		29 Dec 20	13LTS281	300359
Multilateral		23 Jul 21	26LTS173	300647
Norway	USSR (Soviet Union)	02 Sep 21	7LTS293	300196
Multilateral		22 Feb 22	26LTS219	300649
Finland	Germany	21 Apr 22	19LTS87	300487
Bulgaria	Denmark	11 Jul 22	12LTS225	300314
Spain	UK Great Britain	31 Oct 22	28LTS339	300719
British Empire	Japan	30 Nov 22	16LTS207	300412
Denmark	USSR (Soviet Union)	23 Apr 23	18LTS15	300450
Finland	Sweden	26 May 23	18LTS57	300453
Finland	USSR (Soviet Union)	05 Jun 23	18LTS203	300465
Estonia	Germany	27 Jun 23	41LTS161	301013
Czechoslovakia	UK Great Britain	14 Jul 23	29LTS377	300748
Belgium	Netherlands	14 Jul 23	20LTS119	300511
Multilateral		24 Jul 23	36LTS187	300920
Italy	Switzerland	22 Oct 23	65LTS301	301521
Estonia	Latvia	31 Oct 23	25LTS321	300621
Poland	UK Great Britain	26 Nov 23	28LTS428	300722
Multilateral		09 Dec 23	58LTS284	301379
Finland	UK Great Britain	14 Dec 23	29LTS129	300739
Lithuania	Norway	21 Dec 23	32LTS55	300805
Multilateral		12 Mar 24	24LTS17	300595
Sweden	USSR (Soviet Union)	15 Mar 24	25LTS251	300613
Denmark	Latvia	03 Apr 24	33LTS393	300860
Austria	Latvia	09 Aug 24	65LTS7	301516
Latvia	Norway	14 Aug 24	36LTS211	300924
Hungary	Norway	16 Sep 24	33LTS103	300835
Japan	Peru	30 Sep 24	102LTS33	302351
Finland	Italy	22 Oct 24	32LTS149	300814
Iceland	Latvia	03 Nov 24	43LTS339	301069
Bel-Lux Econ Union	Guatemala	07 Nov 24	69LTS17	301596
Poland	Sweden	02 Dec 24	36LTS299	300930
France	Poland	09 Dec 24	44LTS127	301081
Hungary	Poland	26 Mar 25	37LTS151	300954
Germany	Greece	15 May 25	40LTS6	301001
Japan	Latvia	04 Jul 25	80LTS305	301836
Germany	UK Great Britain	13 Aug 25	43LTS89	301050
Germany	USSR (Soviet Union)	12 Oct 25	53LTS7	301257
Estonia	USA (United States)	23 Dec 25	50LTS13	301197
Multilateral		28 Jan 26	51LTS9	301219
Multilateral		10 Apr 26	176LTS199	304062
Finland	Hungary	20 Apr 26	48LTS119	301154
Albania	Serb/Croat/Slovene	22 Jun 26	91LTS9	302054
Guatemala	Italy	15 Sep 26	70LTS175	301633
Albania	Greece	13 Oct 26	83LTS325	301899
Finland	Greece	18 Dec 26	70LTS89	301626
Estonia	Greece	04 Jan 27	69LTS33	301598
Czechoslovakia	Turkey	31 May 27	71LTS335	301674
Italy	Netherlands	28 Jun 27	68LTS203	301583
Greece	Norway	29 Jun 27	82LTS187	301869
France	Germany	17 Aug 27	76LTS5	301761
Bel-Lux Econ Union	Turkey	28 Aug 27	82LTS77	301862
Germany	Serb/Croat/Slovene	06 Oct 27	77LTS19	301763
Sweden	Turkey	04 Feb 28	88LTS155	301994
Bulgaria	Turkey	12 Feb 28	81LTS383	301848
Multilateral		20 Feb 28	86LTS111	301950
Germany	Greece	24 Mar 28	90LTS9	302031
Czechoslovakia	Poland	22 May 28	82LTS171	301868
Latvia	Turkey	28 May 28	94LTS295	302150
Germany	Lithuania	30 Oct 28	89LTS127	302010
Czechoslovakia	Hungary	14 Nov 28	142LTS227	303295
Norway	USA (United States)	25 Feb 29	134LTS81	303085
France	Greece	11 Mar 29	95LTS401	302187
Irish Free State	Portugal	29 Oct 29	131LTS145	303007
Irish Free State	Italy	10 May 30	132LTS147	303034

PARTY ONE	PARTY TWO	DATE	CITATION	NUMBER
Merchant vessels (Cont.)				
Denmark	Turkey	31 May 30	119LTS165	302744
El Salvador	USA (United States)	05 Sep 30	134LTS207	303093
Denmark	Norway	06 Nov 30	109LTS283	302545
Germany	Hungary	18 Jul 31	150LTS111	303458
Multilateral		24 Sep 31	155LTS349	303586
Irish Free State	USA (United States)	18 Nov 31	131LTS279	303018
Multilateral		10 Dec 31	129LTS177	302961
Latvia	Netherlands	15 Dec 31	133LTS107	303061
Germany	USA (United States)	16 Dec 31	129LTS129	302957
Iceland	USA (United States)	16 Jan 32	127LTS135	302914
Denmark	USA (United States)	16 Jan 32	127LTS127	302913
Belgium	USA (United States)	19 Apr 32	134LTS19	303080
Finland	Latvia	29 Apr 32	133LTS71	303057
Spain	UK Great Britain	26 May 32	132LTS43	303030
Sweden	USA (United States)	01 Jun 32	131LTS213	303012
Colombia	Cuba	02 Jul 32	174LTS69	304038
Denmark	Norway	08 Jul 33	140LTS149	303232
Finland	UK Great Britain	13 Oct 33	142LTS187	303291
France	USSR (Soviet Union)	11 Jan 34	167LTS349	303878
Finland	USA (United States)	13 Feb 34	152LTS45	303484
Belgium	Denmark	27 Jul 34	150LTS351	303467
Belgium	Greece	01 Aug 34	153LTS273	303521
Belgium	Lithuania	20 Sep 34	153LTS289	303524
Belgium	Sweden	22 Sep 34	153LTS261	303519
Multilateral		22 Dec 34	183LTS153	304231
Multilateral		22 Dec 34	183LTS145	304230
Denmark	Sweden	28 Oct 35	166LTS299	303845
Belgium	USA (United States)	28 Jan 36	166LTS333	303849
Poland	USSR (Soviet Union)	31 Mar 36	186LTS211	304313
Multilateral		20 Jul 36	173LTS213	304015
Brazil	Netherlands	15 Mar 37	179LTS395	304166
Romania	Yugoslavia	13 May 37	197LTS145	304611
Estonia	France	16 Oct 37	183LTS41	304227
Denmark	Siam	05 Nov 37	188LTS187	304358
Bel-Lux Econ Union	Siam	05 Nov 37	190LTS151	304413
Siam	USA (United States)	13 Nov 37	192LTS247	304476
Norway	Siam	15 Nov 37	186LTS9	304301
France	Siam	07 Dec 37	201LTS113	304708
Japan	Siam	08 Dec 37	188LTS375	304367
Germany	Siam	30 Dec 37	188LTS401	304368
Netherlands	Siam	01 Feb 38	193LTS13	304485
Liberia	USA (United States)	08 Aug 38	201LTS163	304711
Belgium	Netherlands	17 Dec 38	198LTS177	304638
France	UK Great Britain	08 Oct 39	201LTS59	304703
Poland	UK Great Britain	25 Nov 39	199LTS65	304666
Canada	USA (United States)	04 Mar 40	202LTS429	304745
UK Great Britain	USA (United States)	04 Dec 42	295LTS33	304824
Germany	Greece	20 Jan 97*	2LTS107	300053
Inland and territorial waters				
Liberia	UK Great Britain	10 Apr 13	1LTS205	300014
Germany	Hungary	01 Jun 20	7LTS207	300187
Latvia	USSR (Soviet Union)	11 Aug 20	2LTS195	300067
Muscat and Oman	UK Great Britain	11 Feb 21	8LTS261	300224
Czechoslovakia	Italy	23 Mar 21	32LTS183	300815
Germany	Poland	21 Apr 21	12LTS61	300308
Czechoslovakia	Romania	23 Apr 21	15LTS235	300397
Multilateral		23 Jul 21	26LTS173	300647
Austria	Hungary	08 Oct 21	16LTS19	300402
Danzig	Poland	24 Oct 21	116LTS5	302699
Estonia	Finland	29 Oct 21	13LTS59	300348
Multilateral		22 Feb 22	26LTS219	300649
Colombia	Peru	24 Mar 22	74LTS9	301726
Finland	Germany	21 Apr 22	19LTS87	300487
Lithuania	UK Great Britain	06 May 22	13LTS25	300343

PARTY ONE	PARTY TWO	DATE	CITATION	NUMBER
Inland and territorial waters (Cont.)				
Czechoslovakia	Latvia	07 Oct 22	20LTS379	300528
Estonia	Hungary	19 Oct 22	30LTS347	300774
Finland	USSR (Soviet Union)	21 Oct 22	29LTS197	300742
Finland	USSR (Soviet Union)	28 Oct 22	29LTS211	300743
Finland	USSR (Soviet Union)	28 Oct 22	19LTS183	300492
Japan	Poland	07 Dec 22	32LTS61	300806
Multilateral		14 Dec 22	36LTS457	300943
Multilateral		30 Dec 22	21LTS183	300542
Poland	Turkey	23 Jul 23	49LTS329	301189
Multilateral		24 Jul 23	36LTS187	300920
Multilateral		24 Jul 23	28LTS115	300702
Finland	USSR (Soviet Union)	28 Jul 23	32LTS101	300810
Denmark	Finland	03 Aug 23	21LTS269	300547
Denmark	Estonia	07 Sep 23	23LTS73	300577
Italy	Switzerland	22 Oct 23	65LTS301	301521
Estonia	Latvia	01 Nov 23	25LTS354	300624
Finland	Poland	10 Nov 23	29LTS229	300744
Italy	Spain	15 Nov 23	39LTS49	300996
Japan	Serb/Croat/Slovene	16 Nov 23	42LTS99	301035
Hungary	Latvia	19 Nov 23	37LTS341	300959
Multilateral		14 Dec 23	29LTS37	300732
UK Great Britain	USA (United States)	23 Jan 24	27LTS181	300681
Austria	Turkey	28 Jan 24	32LTS313	300823
Lithuania	Sweden	17 Feb 24	23LTS153	300587
Japan	Siam	09 Mar 24	31LTS187	300795
Denmark	Poland	22 Mar 24	31LTS13	300778
Iceland	Poland	22 Mar 24	31LTS35	300779
Denmark	Latvia	03 Apr 24	33LTS393	300860
Czechoslovakia	Iceland	08 May 24	46LTS419	301125
Finland	Iceland	28 May 24	27LTS117	300676
Denmark	USA (United States)	29 May 24	27LTS361	300697
Netherlands	Poland	30 May 24	34LTS9	300865
Finland	Japan	07 Jun 24	58LTS379	301383
Lithuania	Netherlands	10 Jun 24	34LTS373	300885
Estonia	Netherlands	22 Jul 24	48LTS199	301162
Austria	Latvia	09 Aug 24	65LTS7	301516
Netherlands	USA (United States)	21 Aug 24	33LTS433	300863
Japan	Peru	30 Sep 24	102LTS33	302351
Finland	Italy	22 Oct 24	32LTS149	300814
Austria	Switzerland	19 Nov 24	39LTS26	300994
Czechoslovakia	Germany	15 Dec 24	52LTS31	301248
Czechoslovakia	Germany	15 Dec 24	52LTS41	301249
Albania	Italy	06 Mar 25	44LTS359	301094
Germany	Poland	14 Mar 25	95LTS239	302178
Benelux Econ Union	Germany	04 Apr 25	37LTS203	300957
Netherlands	Siam	08 Jun 25	56LTS57	301323
Albania	UK Great Britain	10 Jun 25	43LTS81	301049
Bel-Lux Econ Union	Japan	27 Jun 25	36LTS95	300907
Bel-Lux Econ Union		07 Jul 25	54LTS267	301290
Siam	Spain	03 Aug 25	55LTS39	301303
Portugal	Siam	14 Aug 25	55LTS57	301304
Siam	UK Great Britain	15 Sep 25	49LTS51	301176
Germany	USSR (Soviet Union)	12 Oct 25	53LTS7	301257
France	Hungary	13 Oct 25	48LTS9	301150
Czechoslovakia	Japan	30 Oct 25	58LTS263	301377
Bulgaria	UK Great Britain	12 Nov 25	43LTS165	301052
Siam	Sweden	19 Dec 25	58LTS429	301386
Austria	Switzerland	06 Jan 26	46LTS299	301124
Estonia	UK Great Britain	18 Jan 26	48LTS209	301163
Denmark	Siam	01 Mar 26	47LTS103	301131
Multilateral		00 Apr 26	57LTS437	301366
Brazil	Venezuela	13 Apr 26	80LTS283	301834
Finland	Hungary	20 Apr 26	48LTS119	301154
Germany	Sweden	14 May 26	51LTS99	301225
Bel-Lux Econ Union	Siam	13 Jul 26	62LTS287	301468

PARTY ONE	PARTY TWO	DATE	CITATION	NUMBER
Inland and territorial waters (Cont.)				
Norway	Siam	16 Jul 26	60LTS35	301404
Greece	Spain	23 Sep 26	91LTS121	302059
Multilateral		13 Nov 26	77LTS217	301772
Germany	Poland	16 Feb 27	71LTS369	301676
Greece	UK Great Britain	13 May 27	61LTS15	301425
Greece	Serb/Croat/Slovene	02 Nov 27	91LTS137	302060
Norway	Portugal	30 Nov 27	69LTS355	301617
Siam	UK Great Britain	21 Feb 28	87LTS21	301960
Germany	Netherlands	28 Apr 28	95LTS333	302183
Czechoslovakia	Hungary	14 Nov 28	142LTS227	303295
Brazil	Colombia	15 Nov 28	100LTS123	302299
Norway	Sweden	11 May 29	120LTS263	302771
Germany	Switzerland	28 May 29	104LTS19	302375
Romania	Yugoslavia	19 Jun 30	140LTS229	303238
Estonia	Netherlands	01 Sep 30	111LTS395	302600
Multilateral		23 Oct 30	125LTS95	302849
Estonia	Latvia	28 Feb 31	114LTS379	302667
Finland	France	24 Apr 31	126LTS85	302872
Hungary	Romania	12 Aug 31	186LTS325	304321
Romania	Yugoslavia	14 Dec 31	135LTS71	303104
Multilateral		28 Jun 32	140LTS191	303237
Romania	Yugoslavia	10 Feb 33	174LTS115	304042
Finland	UK Great Britain	13 Oct 33	142LTS187	303291
Finland	Hungary	07 Nov 33	142LTS179	303290
Latvia	Lithuania	01 Dec 33	148LTS97	303407
Finland	USA (United States)	13 Feb 34	152LTS45	303484
Finland	USSR (Soviet Union)	25 May 34	155LTS207	303578
Multilateral		20 Jul 36	173LTS213	304015
Germany	Netherlands	23 Dec 36	179LTS359	304163
Czechoslovakia	Hungary	24 Aug 37	189LTS403	304397
France	Switzerland	13 Oct 37	194LTS191	304522
Siam	UK Great Britain	23 Nov 37	188LTS333	304366
Germany	Netherlands	18 Dec 37	190LTS29	304403
Lithuania	Poland	14 May 38	191LTS373	304456
Multilateral		03 Apr 39	195LTS471	304566
Tonnage				
Czechoslovakia	Italy	23 Mar 21	32LTS183	300815
Austria	Czechoslovakia	04 May 21	15LTS13	300388
Finland	USSR (Soviet Union)	14 Dec 21	16LTS221	300414
Estonia	France	07 Jan 22	62LTS9	301452
Denmark	Estonia	07 Apr 22	14LTS243	300375
Italy	Poland	12 May 22	59LTS293	301399
Denmark	Japan	22 May 22	14LTS247	300376
British Empire	Japan	30 Nov 22	16LTS207	300412
Japan	Poland	07 Dec 22	32LTS61	300806
Estonia	Germany	28 Dec 22	41LTS147	301010
Finland	Sweden	26 May 23	18LTS57	300453
Belgium	Netherlands	14 Jul 23	20LTS119	300511
Poland	Turkey	23 Jul 23	49LTS329	301189
Estonia	Latvia	01 Nov 23	25LTS354	300624
Finland	Poland	10 Nov 23	29LTS229	300744
Italy	Spain	15 Nov 23	39LTS49	300996
Japan	Serb/Croat/Slovene	16 Nov 23	42LTS99	301035
Finland	UK Great Britain	14 Dec 23	29LTS129	300739
Finland	Sweden	10 Jan 24	24LTS167	300558
Japan	UK Great Britain	21 Jan 24	25LTS11	300601
Austria	Turkey	28 Jan 24	32LTS313	300823
Denmark	Poland	22 Mar 24	31LTS13	300778
Iceland	Poland	22 Mar 24	31LTS35	300779
Denmark	Latvia	03 Apr 24	33LTS393	300860
Netherlands	Poland	30 May 24	34LTS9	300865
Finland	UK Great Britain	21 Jun 24	28LTS511	300726
Italy	Serb/Croat/Slovene	14 Jul 24	82LTS257	301876
Austria	Latvia	09 Aug 24	65LTS7	301516

PARTY ONE	PARTY TWO	DATE	CITATION	NUMBER
Tonnage (Cont.)				
Norway	Portugal	21 Oct 24	30LTS117	300764
Finland	Italy	22 Oct 24	32LTS149	300814
Poland	Sweden	02 Dec 24	36LTS299	300930
Norway	Sweden	22 Dec 24	32LTS13	300802
Belgium	Portugal	27 Feb 25	91LTS201	302061
Albania	Italy	06 Mar 25	44LTS359	301094
Latvia	USSR (Soviet Union)	19 Mar 25	38LTS141	300971
Benelux Econ Union	Germany	04 Apr 25	37LTS203	300957
Bulgaria	Poland	29 Apr 25	60LTS103	301408
Germany	USA (United States)	21 May 25	52LTS133	301254
Denmark	Finland	04 Jun 25	37LTS24	300946
Latvia	Norway	10 Jun 25	36LTS91	300906
Denmark	USSR (Soviet Union)	29 Jun 25	36LTS251	300926
Bel-Lux Econ Union		07 Jul 25	54LTS267	301290
Italy	Latvia	25 Jul 25	60LTS91	301407
Germany	UK Great Britain	13 Aug 25	43LTS89	301050
Denmark	Portugal	07 Sep 25	55LTS215	301316
Siam	UK Great Britain	15 Sep 25	49LTS51	301176
France	Hungary	13 Oct 25	48LTS9	301150
Germany	Italy	31 Oct 25	52LTS179	301256
Denmark	Sweden	21 Nov 25	42LTS139	301037
Denmark	Sweden	21 Nov 25	42LTS55	301032
Multilateral		27 Nov 25	67LTS63	301539
Norway	USSR (Soviet Union)	15 Dec 25	47LTS9	301127
Siam	Sweden	19 Dec 25	58LTS429	301386
Finland	USA (United States)	21 Dec 25	47LTS345	301138
Estonia	UK Great Britain	18 Jan 26	48LTS209	301163
Denmark	Siam	01 Mar 26	47LTS103	301131
Estonia	USSR (Soviet Union)	04 Mar 26	62LTS77	301456
Norway	USSR (Soviet Union)	09 Apr 26	48LTS185	301160
Italy	Siam	09 May 26	61LTS215	301436
Germany	Sweden	14 May 26	51LTS99	301225
Portugal	UK Great Britain	20 May 26	50LTS303	301213
Finland	Turkey	02 Jun 26	70LTS329	301644
Denmark	Japan	05 Jun 26	55LTS219	301317
Estonia	UK Great Britain	24 Jun 26	57LTS65	301352
Greece	Sweden	10 Sep 26	63LTS37	301479
Belgium	Estonia	28 Sep 26	60LTS9	301401
Bel-Lux Econ Union	Estonia	28 Sep 26	62LTS433	301475
Albania	Greece	13 Oct 26	83LTS325	301899
Greece	Italy	24 Oct 26	63LTS51	301480
Estonia	USA (United States)	30 Nov 26	62LTS313	301469
Greece	UK Great Britain	01 Dec 26	61LTS109	301428
Finland	Greece	18 Dec 26	70LTS89	301626
Norway	Poland	22 Dec 26	66LTS359	301530
Estonia	Latvia	05 Feb 27	62LTS319	301470
Estonia	Poland	19 Feb 27	115LTS177	302686
Latvia	UK Great Britain	24 Jun 27	67LTS245	301552
Greece	Norway	29 Jun 27	82LTS187	301869
Netherlands	Sweden	24 Dec 27	71LTS391	301677
Iceland	Sweden	10 Mar 28	71LTS315	301672
Germany	Latvia	13 Apr 28	73LTS46	301705
Czechoslovakia	Poland	22 May 28	82LTS171	301868
Estonia	Sweden	23 Jun 28	87LTS253	301972
Finland	Norway	23 Oct 28	85LTS211	301932
Great Britain	Portugal		71LTS199	301662
Spain	Sweden	02 Jan 29	94LTS353	302154
Norway	USA (United States)	25 Feb 29	134LTS81	303085
Germany	USSR (Soviet Union)	16 Apr 29	109LTS327	302547
Persia	Sweden	10 May 29	102LTS9	302349
Italy	Panama	16 Oct 29	138LTS355	303199
Greece	Sweden	18 Oct 29	95LTS201	302174
Latvia	Sweden	11 Jan 30	109LTS193	302539
Denmark	Turkey	31 May 30	119LTS165	302744
Poland	Portugal	27 Aug 30	115LTS127	302682

PARTY ONE	PARTY TWO	DATE	CITATION	NUMBER
Tonnage (Cont.)				
Denmark	Estonia	16 Jan 31	112LTS215	302615
Estonia	Latvia	28 Feb 31	114LTS379	302667
Norway	Turkey	16 Mar 31	138LTS41	303180
Estonia	Finland	11 Apr 31	124LTS217	302835
Estonia	Iceland	30 May 31	119LTS69	302741
Poland	USA (United States)	15 Jun 31	139LTS395	303223
Estonia	Finland	17 Jul 31	126LTS93	302873
Germany	Hungary	18 Jul 31	150LTS111	303458
Hungary	Romania	12 Aug 31	186LTS325	304321
Multilateral		15 Oct 31	125LTS83	302847
Multilateral		15 Oct 31	125LTS89	302848
Irish Free State	USA (United States)	18 Nov 31	131LTS279	303018
Multilateral		10 Dec 31	129LTS177	302961
Romania	Yugoslavia	14 Dec 31	135LTS71	303104
Latvia	Netherlands	15 Dec 31	133LTS107	303061
Germany	USA (United States)	16 Dec 31	129LTS129	302957
Denmark	USA (United States)	16 Jan 32	127LTS127	302913
Iceland	USA (United States)	16 Jan 32	127LTS135	302914
Belgium	USA (United States)	19 Apr 32	134LTS19	303080
Finland	Latvia	29 Apr 32	133LTS71	303057
Spain	UK Great Britain	26 May 32	132LTS43	303030
Italy	USA (United States)	01 Jun 32	140LTS273	303242
Sweden	USA (United States)	01 Jun 32	131LTS213	303012
Denmark	Sweden	23 Dec 32	136LTS37	303123
Norway	Sweden	10 Mar 33	138LTS17	303176
Multilateral		11 Mar 33	135LTS301	303119
Canada	USA (United States)	09 Dec 33	152LTS39	303483
Multilateral		16 Apr 34	163LTS185	303767
Poland	USA (United States)	05 Oct 34	156LTS91	303594
Poland	Spain	14 Dec 34	168LTS315	303908
Finland	UK Great Britain	03 May 35	159LTS129	303655
Germany	UK Great Britain	07 Jun 35	163LTS293	303771
Iran	USSR (Soviet Union)	27 Aug 35	176LTS299	304069
Poland	USSR (Soviet Union)	31 Mar 36	186LTS203	304312
Multilateral		20 Jul 36	173LTS213	304015
United Arab Rep	UK Great Britain	26 Aug 36	173LTS401	304031
Chile	Sweden	30 Oct 36	188LTS283	304364
Bel-Lux Econ Union	Uruguay	22 Feb 37	196LTS391	304600
Sweden	Yugoslavia	14 May 37	194LTS21	304504
Panama	USA (United States)	17 Aug 37	182LTS159	304208
Multilateral		14 Sep 37	181LTS137	304184
Estonia	France	16 Oct 37	183LTS41	304227
Finland	Sweden	09 Jan 38	195LTS157	304545
Greece	Latvia	15 Jan 38	195LTS19	304533
United Arab Rep	UK Great Britain	20 Feb 39	195LTS407	304560
Germany	Greece	20 Jan 97*	2LTS107	300053
Ports and pilotage				
Liberia	UK Great Britain	10 Apr 13	1LTS205	300014
France	Germany	01 Mar 20	1LTS367	300030
Germany	Hungary	01 Jun 20	7LTS207	300187
Austria	Germany	01 Sep 20	4LTS201	300107
Danzig	Poland	09 Nov 20	6LTS189	300153
Belgium	UK Great Britain	15 Mar 21	5LTS319	300138
Czechoslovakia	Italy	23 Mar 21	32LTS241	300816
Czechoslovakia	Italy	23 Mar 21	32LTS183	300815
Czechoslovakia	Romania	23 Apr 21	15LTS235	300397
Austria	Czechoslovakia	04 May 21	15LTS13	300388
Multilateral		23 Jul 21	26LTS173	300647
Austria	Hungary	08 Oct 21	16LTS19	300402
Estonia	Finland	29 Oct 21	13LTS59	300348
Multilateral		22 Feb 22	26LTS219	300649
Finland	Germany	21 Apr 22	19LTS87	300487
Lithuania	UK Great Britain	06 May 22	13LTS25	300343
Italy	Poland	12 May 22	59LTS293	301399

PARTY ONE	PARTY TWO	DATE	CITATION	NUMBER
Ports and pilotage (Cont.)				
Czechoslovakia	Latvia	07 Oct 22	20LTS379	300528
Estonia	Hungary	19 Oct 22	30LTS347	300774
Japan	Poland	07 Dec 22	32LTS61	300806
Multilateral		30 Dec 22	21LTS183	300542
Finland	Sweden	26 May 23	18LTS57	300453
Finland	USSR (Soviet Union)	05 Jun 23	18LTS203	300465
Latvia	UK Great Britain	22 Jun 23	20LTS395	300529
Estonia	Sweden	07 Jul 23	20LTS189	300517
Poland	Turkey	23 Jul 23	49LTS329	301189
Denmark	Finland	03 Aug 23	21LTS269	300547
Netherlands	Portugal	22 Aug 23	20LTS139	300513
Denmark	Estonia	07 Sep 23	23LTS73	300577
Estonia	Iceland	07 Sep 23	23LTS131	300584
Italy	Switzerland	22 Oct 23	65LTS301	301521
Estonia	Latvia	31 Oct 23	25LTS321	300621
Estonia	Latvia	01 Nov 23	25LTS354	300624
Finland	Poland	10 Nov 23	29LTS229	300744
Italy	Spain	15 Nov 23	39LTS49	300996
Japan	Serb/Croat/Slovene	16 Nov 23	42LTS99	301035
Hungary	Latvia	19 Nov 23	37LTS341	300959
Multilateral		09 Dec 23	58LTS284	301379
Multilateral		14 Dec 23	29LTS37	300732
Finland	UK Great Britain	14 Dec 23	29LTS129	300739
Austria	Turkey	28 Jan 24	32LTS313	300823
Lithuania	Sweden	17 Feb 24	23LTS153	300587
Czechoslovakia	Italy	01 Mar 24	34LTS55	300867
Japan	Siam	09 Mar 24	31LTS187	300795
Multilateral		12 Mar 24	24LTS17	300595
Sweden	USSR (Soviet Union)	15 Mar 24	25LTS251	300613
Denmark	Poland	22 Mar 24	31LTS13	300778
Iceland	Poland	22 Mar 24	31LTS35	300779
Denmark	Latvia	03 Apr 24	33LTS393	300860
Czechoslovakia	Iceland	08 May 24	46LTS419	301125
Sweden	USA (United States)	22 May 24	29LTS421	300752
Finland	Iceland	28 May 24	27LTS117	300676
Netherlands	Poland	30 May 24	34LTS9	300865
Finland	Japan	07 Jun 24	58LTS379	301383
Lithuania	Netherlands	10 Jun 24	34LTS373	300885
Spain	UK Great Britain	27 Jun 24	28LTS523	300727
Estonia	Sweden	07 Jul 24	73LTS27	301702
Italy	Serb/Croat/Slovene	14 Jul 24	82LTS257	301876
Estonia	Netherlands	22 Jul 24	48LTS199	301162
Latvia	Norway	14 Aug 24	36LTS211	300924
Japan	Peru	30 Sep 24	102LTS33	302351
Finland	Italy	22 Oct 24	32LTS149	300814
France	Latvia	30 Oct 24	37LTS399	300963
Iceland	Latvia	03 Nov 24	43LTS339	301069
Finland	Sweden	22 Dec 24	73LTS33	301703
Belgium	Portugal	27 Feb 25	91LTS201	302061
Albania	Italy	06 Mar 25	44LTS359	301094
Benelux Econ Union	Germany	04 Apr 25	37LTS203	300957
Greece	Poland	17 Apr 25	38LTS301	300985
Bulgaria	Poland	29 Apr 25	60LTS103	301408
Germany	USA (United States)	21 May 25	52LTS133	301254
Netherlands	Siam	08 Jun 25	56LTS57	301323
Albania	UK Great Britain	10 Jun 25	43LTS81	301049
Japan	Latvia	04 Jul 25	80LTS305	301836
Bel-Lux Econ Union		07 Jul 25	54LTS267	301290
Finland	Spain	16 Jul 25	47LTS271	301135
Italy	Latvia	25 Jul 25	60LTS91	301407
Siam	Spain	03 Aug 25	55LTS39	301303
Portugal	Siam	14 Aug 25	55LTS57	301304
Siam	UK Great Britain	15 Sep 25	49LTS51	301176
France	Hungary	13 Oct 25	48LTS9	301150
Germany	Italy	31 Oct 25	52LTS179	301256

PARTY ONE	PARTY TWO	DATE	CITATION	NUMBER
Ports and pilotage (Cont.)				
Bulgaria	UK Great Britain	12 Nov 25	43LTS165	301052
Norway	USSR (Soviet Union)	15 Dec 25	47LTS9	301127
Finland	Norway	19 Dec 25	56LTS183	301330
Siam	Sweden	19 Dec 25	58LTS429	301386
Finland	USA (United States)	21 Dec 25	47LTS345	301138
Austria	Switzerland	06 Jan 26	46LTS299	301124
Estonia	UK Great Britain	18 Jan 26	48LTS209	301163
Multilateral		28 Jan 26	51LTS9	301219
Denmark	Siam	01 Mar 26	47LTS103	301131
Finland	Hungary	20 Apr 26	48LTS119	301154
Germany	Sweden	14 May 26	51LTS99	301225
Norway	Siam	16 Jul 26	60LTS35	301404
Greece	Sweden	10 Sep 26	63LTS37	301479
Albania	Greece	13 Oct 26	83LTS325	301899
Bel-Lux Econ Union	Serb/Croat/Slovene	16 Dec 26	70LTS371	301647
Germany	Turkey	12 Jan 27	73LTS133	301712
Finland	Sweden	01 Apr 27	62LTS89	301458
Serb/Croat/Slovene	UK Great Britain	12 May 27	80LTS165	301825
Greece	UK Great Britain	13 May 27	61LTS15	301425
Czechoslovakia	Turkey	31 May 27	71LTS335	301674
Greece	Norway	29 Jun 27	82LTS187	301869
Germany	Japan	20 Jul 27	74LTS107	301736
Hungary	Italy	25 Jul 27	74LTS77	301733
Greece	Serb/Croat/Slovene	02 Nov 27	91LTS137	302060
Denmark	Spain	02 Jan 28	71LTS271	301668
Germany	Greece	24 Mar 28	90LTS9	302031
Latvia	Sweden	30 Mar 28	73LTS39	301704
Germany	Siam	07 Apr 28	85LTS337	301938
Czechoslovakia	Serb/Croat/Slovene	07 Nov 28	98LTS297	302252
Czechoslovakia	Hungary	14 Nov 28	142LTS227	303295
Finland	Serb/Croat/Slovene	29 Jan 29	96LTS77	302192
France	Greece	11 Mar 29	95LTS401	302187
Persia	Sweden	10 May 29	102LTS9	302349
Bulgaria	Germany	04 Jun 29	106LTS49	302436
Italy	Panama	16 Oct 29	138LTS355	303199
Poland	Romania	17 Dec 29	119LTS333	302754
Irish Free State	Italy	10 May 30	132LTS147	303034
Germany	Irish Free State	12 May 30	131LTS153	303008
Denmark	Estonia	16 Jan 31	112LTS215	302615
Estonia	Latvia	28 Feb 31	114LTS379	302667
Norway	Turkey	16 Mar 31	138LTS41	303180
Hungary	Romania	12 Aug 31	186LTS325	304321
Multilateral		10 Dec 31	129LTS177	302961
France	Spain	07 Mar 32	148LTS385	303424
Germany	Sweden	01 Jun 32	129LTS471	302979
Bulgaria	Germany	24 Jun 32	147LTS211	303400
Italy	Spain	30 Jul 32	149LTS9	303427
Brazil	Uruguay	25 Aug 33	176LTS381	304075
Brazil	Portugal	26 Aug 33	179LTS63	304134
Bulgaria	Czechoslovakia	29 Aug 33	148LTS15	303402
Finland	USA (United States)	13 Feb 34	152LTS45	303484
Multilateral		25 Jul 34	177LTS59	304080
Hungary	Italy	18 Nov 34	166LTS263	303842
Poland	Spain	14 Dec 34	168LTS315	303908
France	Spain	21 Dec 35	167LTS9	303856
Czechoslovakia	Finland	21 Mar 36	179LTS295	304156
Multilateral		20 Jul 36	173LTS213	304015
Sweden	Yugoslavia	14 May 37	194LTS21	304504
Siam	UK Great Britain	23 Nov 37	188LTS333	304366
France	Siam	07 Dec 37	201LTS113	304708
Japan	Siam	08 Dec 37	188LTS375	304367
Germany	Siam	30 Dec 37	188LTS401	304368
Liberia	USA (United States)	08 Aug 38	201LTS163	304711
France	India	28 Jan 41	204LTS323	304811

PARTY ONE	PARTY TWO	DATE	CITATION	NUMBER
Shipwreck and salvage				
Austria	Germany	01 Sep 20	4LTS201	300107
Czechoslovakia	Italy	23 Mar 21	32LTS183	300815
Austria	Netherlands	06 Nov 22	17LTS375	300444
Denmark	Sweden	07 Nov 22	14LTS95	300370
Finland	Sweden	26 May 23	18LTS57	300453
Norway	Sweden	26 May 23	18LTS155	300462
Finland	USSR (Soviet Union)	05 Jun 23	18LTS203	300465
Latvia	UK Great Britain	22 Jun 23	20LTS395	300529
Finland	USSR (Soviet Union)	28 Jul 23	32LTS101	300810
Denmark	Finland	03 Aug 23	21LTS269	300547
Finland	Poland	10 Nov 23	29LTS229	300744
Italy	Spain	15 Nov 23	39LTS49	300996
Finland	UK Great Britain	14 Dec 23	29LTS129	300739
Japan	Siam	09 Mar 24	31LTS187	300795
Iceland	Poland	22 Mar 24	31LTS35	300779
Denmark	Latvia	03 Apr 24	33LTS393	300860
Finland	Iceland	28 May 24	27LTS117	300676
Netherlands	Poland	30 May 24	34LTS9	300865
Italy	Serb/Croat/Slovene	14 Jul 24	82LTS257	301876
Latvia	Norway	14 Aug 24	36LTS211	300924
Finland	Latvia	23 Aug 24	37LTS383	300962
Japan	Peru	30 Sep 24	102LTS33	302351
Denmark	Sweden	28 Nov 24	32LTS41	300804
Finland	Germany	02 Feb 25	33LTS127	300838
Albania	Italy	06 Mar 25	44LTS359	301094
Bulgaria	Poland	29 Apr 25	60LTS103	301408
Germany	USA (United States)	21 May 25	52LTS133	301254
Netherlands	Siam	08 Jun 25	56LTS57	301323
Bel-Lux Econ Union	Japan	27 Jun 25	36LTS95	300907
Japan	Latvia	04 Jul 25	80LTS305	301836
Bel-Lux Econ Union		07 Jul 25	54LTS267	301290
Siam	Spain	03 Aug 25	55LTS39	301303
Germany	UK Great Britain	13 Aug 25	43LTS89	301050
Portugal	Siam	14 Aug 25	55LTS57	301304
Siam	UK Great Britain	15 Sep 25	49LTS51	301176
Germany	USSR (Soviet Union)	12 Oct 25	53LTS7	301257
Austria	China	19 Oct 25	55LTS9	301301
Germany	Italy	31 Oct 25	52LTS179	301256
Norway	USSR (Soviet Union)	15 Dec 25	47LTS9	301127
Finland	Norway	19 Dec 25	56LTS183	301330
Siam	Sweden	19 Dec 25	58LTS429	301386
Estonia	UK Great Britain	18 Jan 26	48LTS209	301163
Denmark	Siam	01 Mar 26	47LTS103	301131
Italy	Siam	09 May 26	61LTS215	301436
Germany	Sweden	14 May 26	51LTS99	301225
Finland	Turkey	02 Jun 26	70LTS329	301644
Bel-Lux Econ Union	Siam	13 Jul 26	62LTS287	301468
Norway	Siam	16 Jul 26	60LTS35	301404
Guatemala	Italy	15 Sep 26	70LTS175	301633
Bel-Lux Econ Union	Estonia	28 Sep 26	62LTS433	301475
Albania	Greece	13 Oct 26	83LTS325	301899
Greece	Italy	24 Oct 26	63LTS51	301480
Bel-Lux Econ Union	Serb/Croat/Slovene	16 Dec 26	70LTS371	301647
Finland	Greece	18 Dec 26	70LTS89	301626
Norway	Poland	22 Dec 26	66LTS359	301530
Estonia	Greece	04 Jan 27	69LTS33	301598
Germany	Turkey	12 Jan 27	73LTS133	301712
Estonia	Poland	19 Feb 27	115LTS177	302686
Greece	Latvia	25 Feb 27	71LTS25	301652
Serb/Croat/Slovene	UK Great Britain	12 May 27	80LTS165	301825
Greece	UK Great Britain	13 May 27	61LTS15	301425
Bel-Lux Econ Union	Turkey	28 Aug 27	82LTS77	301862
Germany	Serb/Croat/Slovene	06 Oct 27	77LTS19	301763
Denmark	Spain	02 Jan 28	71LTS271	301668

PARTY ONE	PARTY TWO	DATE	CITATION	NUMBER
Shipwreck and salvage (Cont.)				
Bulgaria	Turkey	12 Feb 28	81LTS383	301848
Multilateral		20 Feb 28	129LTS223	302963
Czechoslovakia	Serb/Croat/Slovene	07 Nov 28	98LTS297	302252
Estonia	Germany	07 Dec 28	99LTS259	302273
Germany	Persia	17 Feb 29	111LTS263	302591
France	Greece	11 Mar 29	95LTS401	302187
Persia	Sweden	10 May 29	102LTS9	302349
Multilateral		31 May 29	136LTS81	303127
Serb/Croat/Slovene	Spain	27 Sep 29	98LTS319	302253
Sweden	Turkey	29 Sep 29	119LTS53	302740
Finland	Turkey	12 Oct 29	96LTS239	302205
Italy	Panama	16 Oct 29	138LTS355	303199
Poland	Romania	17 Dec 29	119LTS333	302754
Austria	Germany	12 Apr 30	115LTS333	302694
Denmark	Lithuania	21 Jun 30	114LTS151	302662
Denmark	Sweden	03 Sep 30	106LTS397	302458
El Salvador	USA (United States)	05 Sep 30	134LTS207	303093
Norway	Turkey	16 Mar 31	138LTS41	303180
Hungary	Romania	12 Aug 31	186LTS325	304321
Romania	Sweden	07 Oct 31	131LTS51	303003
Multilateral		10 Dec 31	129LTS177	302961
Bulgaria	Germany	24 Jun 32	147LTS211	303400
Finland	USA (United States)	13 Feb 34	152LTS45	303484
Multilateral		12 Jun 34	155LTS367	303587
Mexico	USA (United States)	13 Jun 35	168LTS135	303894
Sweden	Yugoslavia	14 May 37	194LTS21	304504
Estonia	France	16 Oct 37	183LTS41	304227
Bel-Lux Econ Union	Siam	05 Nov 37	190LTS151	304413
Siam	USA (United States)	13 Nov 37	192LTS247	304476
Norway	Siam	15 Nov 37	186LTS9	304301
Siam	UK Great Britain	23 Nov 37	188LTS333	304366
France	Siam	07 Dec 37	201LTS113	304708
Greece	Latvia	15 Jan 38	195LTS19	304533
Collision				
Multilateral		28 Jan 26	51LTS9	301219
Multilateral		10 Apr 26	176LTS199	304062
Greece	Latvia	25 Feb 27	71LTS25	301652
Multilateral		31 May 29	136LTS81	303127
Japan	Siam	08 Dec 37	188LTS375	304367
Germany	Siam	30 Dec 37	188LTS401	304368
Multilateral		05 Feb 39	196LTS303	304592
Land transport				
Multilateral		10 Sep 19	7LTS331	300200
Finland	USSR (Soviet Union)	14 Oct 20	3LTS5	300091
Belgium	UK Great Britain	15 Mar 21	5LTS319	300138
Finland	USSR (Soviet Union)	18 Jun 24	47LTS153	301133
Finland	Sweden	28 Jun 24	28LTS327	300718
Colombia	Venezuela	20 Jul 25	39LTS15	300993
Germany	Poland	27 Mar 26	64LTS249	301506
Great Britain	Italy	10 Sep 26	57LTS77	301354
France	Saar	14 Apr 27	70LTS115	301628
Multilateral		20 Feb 28	86LTS111	301950
UK Great Britain	USA (United States)	27 Mar 41	204LTS15	304784
Commercial road vehicles				
Austria	Czechoslovakia	04 May 21	15LTS13	300388
Austria	Turkey	28 Jan 24	32LTS313	300823
Denmark	Germany	29 Nov 24	31LTS131	300790
Bel-Lux Econ Union	France	16 Jul 35	162LTS19	303731
Germany	Sweden	19 May 36	182LTS395	304224
Mexico	USA (United States)	06 Oct 36	180LTS33	304171
Driving permits				
Multilateral		24 Apr 26	108LTS123	302505
France	Saar	14 Apr 27	70LTS115	301628

PARTY ONE	PARTY TWO	DATE	CITATION	NUMBER
Driving permits (Cont.)				
Denmark	Sweden	26 Apr 30	101LTS319	302333
Denmark	Finland	30 Jun 30	105LTS179	302411
Finland	Sweden	17 Jul 30	105LTS343	302427
Denmark	Norway	06 Nov 30	109LTS283	302545
Finland	Norway	20 Nov 30	110LTS313	302563
Norway	Sweden	08 Aug 31	123LTS67	302806
Bel-Lux Econ Union	France	16 Jul 35	162LTS19	303731
Denmark	Germany	09 Jan 36	166LTS135	303835
Germany	Sweden	19 May 36	182LTS395	304224
Railway border crossing				
Italy	Switzerland	12 Nov 18	25LTS369	300625
France	Germany	01 Jul 20	8LTS87	300209
Austria	Germany	01 Sep 20	4LTS201	300107
Poland	USSR (Soviet Union)	18 Mar 21	6LTS51	300149
Germany	Poland	21 Apr 21	12LTS61	300308
Austria	Czechoslovakia	04 May 21	15LTS13	300388
Germany	Poland	06 Jun 21	34LTS185	300874
Finland	USSR (Soviet Union)	14 Dec 21	16LTS221	300414
Germany	Poland	24 Jun 22	26LTS271	300653
Germany	Saar	17 Jan 23	27LTS290	300692
Germany	Netherlands	23 May 23	25LTS275	300617
Multilateral		09 Dec 23	47LTS55	301129
Czechoslovakia	Hungary	09 Feb 24	30LTS325	300772
Czechoslovakia	Germany	04 Mar 24	41LTS243	301018
Finland	Sweden	28 Jun 24	28LTS327	300718
Italy	Serb/Croat/Slovene	14 Jul 24	82LTS327	301877
Italy	Serb/Croat/Slovene	14 Jul 24	82LTS349	301878
Italy	Serb/Croat/Slovene	12 Aug 24	82LTS423	301882
Multilateral		23 Oct 24	77LTS367	301778
Multilateral		23 Oct 24	78LTS17	301779
France	Germany	13 Apr 25	109LTS295	302546
Multilateral		05 May 25	55LTS225	301318
Belgium	Germany	01 Jul 26	62LTS127	301461
Denmark	Netherlands	23 Jul 26	66LTS133	301528
Hungary	Romania	17 Nov 26	61LTS207	301435
Germany	Poland	26 Mar 27	64LTS177	301505
Belgium	France	11 Apr 27	143LTS215	303309
Czechoslovakia	Poland	30 May 27	98LTS233	302251
Belgium	Portugal	20 Jul 27	71LTS431	301681
France	Spain	16 Jul 28	135LTS149	303110
Latvia	Poland	12 Feb 29	101LTS75	302321
Poland	Romania	30 Mar 29	123LTS147	302812
Poland	Romania	30 Oct 29	121LTS243	302790
Poland	Romania	30 Oct 29	121LTS167	302787
Multilateral		09 Nov 29	125LTS205	302855
Austria	Hungary	03 Jun 30	122LTS69	302799
France	Italy	13 Feb 31	139LTS109	303206
Netherlands	Sweden	15 Jul 31	127LTS321	302925
Netherlands	Yugoslavia	15 Jul 31	127LTS337	302927
Netherlands	Norway	15 Jul 31	127LTS313	302924
Denmark	Netherlands	15 Jul 31	127LTS329	302926
Netherlands	Romania	20 Jul 31	127LTS425	302929
Czechoslovakia	Germany	25 Jul 31	187LTS279	304344
Czechoslovakia	Poland	17 Feb 33	143LTS167	303307
Multilateral		23 Dec 36	188LTS99	304354
Bulgaria	Romania	20 Jul 37	202LTS33	304733
Lithuania	Poland	25 May 38	191LTS391	304457
Hungary	Romania	19 Oct 39	201LTS415	304729
Hungary	Romania	19 Oct 39	201LTS395	304728
Motor vehicles and combinations				
Italy	Serb/Croat/Slovene	20 Jul 25	83LTS247	301890
Multilateral		24 Apr 26	108LTS123	302505
France	Saar	14 Apr 27	70LTS115	301628
Denmark	Sweden	26 Apr 30	101LTS319	302333

PARTY ONE	PARTY TWO	DATE	CITATION	NUMBER
Motor vehicles and combinations (Cont.)				
Belgium	Germany	20 Jun 30	110LTS107	302555
Finland	Sweden	17 Jul 30	105LTS343	302427
Lithuania	Norway	14 Nov 30	109LTS187	302538
Norway	Sweden	08 Aug 31	123LTS67	302806
Finland	Netherlands	22 May 33	140LTS279	303243
Mexico	USA (United States)	06 Oct 36	180LTS33	304171
Austria	Switzerland	21 Nov 36	179LTS341	304162
Belgium	Netherlands	30 Apr 38	190LTS199	304418
Railways				
Colombia	USA (United States)	06 Apr 14	9LTS302	300263
Italy	Switzerland	12 Nov 18	25LTS369	300625
Denmark	Sweden	26 Jan 20	14LTS273	300379
Germany	Hungary	01 Jun 20	7LTS207	300187
Germany	Switzerland	09 Jul 20	12LTS25	300304
Austria	Germany	01 Sep 20	4LTS201	300107
France	Netherlands	16 Sep 20	12LTS213	300312
Belgium	Netherlands	06 Oct 20	18LTS247	300467
France	Sweden	25 Nov 20	2LTS183	300065
Belgium	Sweden	03 Jan 21	2LTS301	300083
Belgium	UK Great Britain	15 Mar 21	5LTS319	300138
Czechoslovakia	Italy	23 Mar 21	32LTS183	300815
Austria	Czechoslovakia	04 May 21	15LTS13	300388
Italy	Sweden	04 Jun 21	6LTS47	300148
Germany	Poland	06 Jun 21	34LTS185	300874
Belgium	Luxembourg	25 Jul 21	9LTS223	300256
Austria	Poland	23 Sep 21	7LTS181	300186
Italy	Switzerland	24 Sep 21	12LTS367	300330
Estonia	Finland	29 Oct 21	13LTS59	300348
Romania	Sweden	25 Nov 21	7LTS247	300190
Finland	USSR (Soviet Union)	14 Dec 21	16LTS221	300414
China	Japan	04 Feb 22	10LTS309	300277
Multilateral		06 Feb 22	38LTS277	300982
Austria	Czechoslovakia	18 Feb 22	14LTS129	300371
Netherlands	Romania	20 Feb 22	12LTS219	300313
Finland	Germany	21 Apr 22	19LTS87	300487
Italy	Poland	12 May 22	59LTS293	301399
Germany	Poland	24 Jun 22	26LTS271	300653
China	Japan	05 Dec 22	22LTS293	300560
Germany	Saar	17 Jan 23	27LTS290	300692
Czechoslovakia	Hungary	08 Mar 23	48LTS257	301167
Germany	Switzerland	24 Mar 23	27LTS41	300666
Multilateral		29 Mar 23	23LTS378	300594
Multilateral		29 Mar 23	23LTS256	300593
Netherlands	Serb/Croat/Slovene	15 Jun 23	20LTS337	300524
Estonia	Sweden	07 Jul 23	20LTS189	300517
Poland	Turkey	23 Jul 23	49LTS329	301189
Denmark	Estonia	07 Sep 23	23LTS73	300577
Estonia	Iceland	07 Sep 23	23LTS131	300584
Multilateral		03 Nov 23	30LTS371	300775
Finland	Poland	10 Nov 23	29LTS229	300744
Hungary	Latvia	19 Nov 23	37LTS341	300959
Multilateral		09 Dec 23	47LTS55	301129
Multilateral		14 Dec 23	29LTS37	300732
Finland	UK Great Britain	14 Dec 23	29LTS129	300739
Austria	Turkey	28 Jan 24	32LTS313	300823
Czechoslovakia	Denmark	31 Jan 24	23LTS139	300585
Czechoslovakia	Hungary	09 Feb 24	30LTS325	300772
Lithuania	Sweden	17 Feb 24	23LTS153	300587
Germany	Poland	23 Feb 24	49LTS355	301191
Iraq	UK Great Britain	25 Mar 24	35LTS145	300894
Austria	Serb/Croat/Slovene	29 Mar 24	114LTS421	302670
Hungary	Romania	16 Apr 24	46LTS95	301114
Czechoslovakia	Iceland	08 May 24	46LTS419	301125
China	USSR (Soviet Union)	31 May 24	37LTS193	300956

PARTY ONE	PARTY TWO	DATE	CITATION	NUMBER
Railways (Cont.)				
Finland	USSR (Soviet Union)	18 Jun 24	47LTS153	301133
Spain	UK Great Britain	27 Jun 24	28LTS523	300727
Finland	Sweden	28 Jun 24	28LTS327	300718
Italy	Serb/Croat/Slovene	14 Jul 24	82LTS327	301877
Italy	Serb/Croat/Slovene	14 Jul 24	82LTS349	301878
Austria	Latvia	09 Aug 24	65LTS7	301516
Italy	Serb/Croat/Slovene	12 Aug 24	82LTS423	301882
Finland	Latvia	23 Aug 24	37LTS383	300962
Hungary	Norway	16 Sep 24	33LTS103	300835
Multilateral		23 Oct 24	77LTS367	301778
Multilateral		23 Oct 24	78LTS17	301779
Austria	Hungary	08 Nov 24	44LTS407	301096
Czechoslovakia	Italy	15 Nov 24	92LTS91	302081
France	Poland	09 Dec 24	44LTS127	301081
Benelux Econ Union	Germany	04 Apr 25	37LTS203	300957
Multilateral		05 May 25	55LTS225	301318
Czechoslovakia	Poland	30 May 25	50LTS243	301207
Germany	USSR (Soviet Union)	12 Oct 25	53LTS7	301257
France	Hungary	13 Oct 25	48LTS9	301150
Multilateral		29 Oct 25	66LTS147	301529
Germany	Italy	31 Oct 25	52LTS179	301256
Bel-Lux Econ Union	Czechoslovakia	28 Dec 25	58LTS189	301372
Estonia	UK Great Britain	18 Jan 26	48LTS209	301163
Estonia	Latvia	02 Feb 26	64LTS413	301514
Germany	Poland	27 Mar 26	64LTS249	301506
Finland	Hungary	20 Apr 26	48LTS119	301154
Germany	Sweden	14 May 26	51LTS99	301225
Germany	Poland	16 Jun 26	65LTS379	301522
Albania	Serb/Croat/Slovene	22 Jun 26	91LTS9	302054
Germany	Latvia	28 Jun 26	58LTS403	301385
Czechoslovakia	Hungary	30 Sep 26	57LTS87	301356
Multilateral		13 Nov 26	77LTS217	301772
Hungary	Romania	17 Nov 26	61LTS207	301435
Czechoslovakia	Germany	25 Mar 27	75LTS353	301758
Germany	Poland	26 Mar 27	64LTS177	301505
Belgium	France	11 Apr 27	143LTS215	303309
Czechoslovakia	Poland	30 May 27	98LTS233	302251
Czechoslovakia	Hungary	31 May 27	65LTS61	301520
Hungary	Italy	25 Jul 27	74LTS53	301731
Sweden	Turkey	04 Feb 28	88LTS155	301994
France	Spain	16 Jul 28	135LTS149	303110
Czechoslovakia	Hungary	14 Nov 28	110LTS425	302574
Latvia	Poland	12 Feb 29	101LTS75	302321
Poland	Romania	30 Mar 29	123LTS147	302812
Poland	Romania	24 May 29	124LTS339	302837
Poland	Romania	30 Oct 29	121LTS167	302787
Poland	Romania	30 Oct 29	121LTS243	302790
Belgium	Germany	07 Nov 29	121LTS327	302795
Multilateral		09 Nov 29	125LTS205	302855
Denmark	Turkey	31 May 30	119LTS165	302744
Austria	Hungary	03 Jun 30	122LTS69	302799
Czechoslovakia	Romania	15 Jul 30	164LTS157	303793
Germany	Poland	21 Nov 30	139LTS351	303220
France	Italy	13 Feb 31	139LTS109	303206
Norway	Turkey	16 Mar 31	138LTS41	303180
Germany	Netherlands	11 Jun 31	120LTS413	302778
Austria	Netherlands	26 Jun 31	127LTS225	302922
Hungary	Netherlands	26 Jun 31	127LTS217	302921
Italy	Netherlands	01 Jul 31	127LTS235	302923
Denmark	Netherlands	15 Jul 31	127LTS329	302926
Netherlands	Sweden	15 Jul 31	127LTS321	302925
Netherlands	Norway	15 Jul 31	127LTS313	302924
Netherlands	Yugoslavia	15 Jul 31	127LTS337	302927
Germany	Hungary	18 Jul 31	150LTS111	303458
Netherlands	Romania	20 Jul 31	127LTS425	302929

PARTY ONE	PARTY TWO	DATE	CITATION	NUMBER
Railways (Cont.)				
Czechoslovakia	Germany	25 Jul 31	187LTS279	304344
Czechoslovakia	Netherlands	11 Aug 31	127LTS347	302928
Hungary	Romania	12 Aug 31	186LTS325	304321
Bulgaria	Germany	24 Jun 32	147LTS211	303400
France	Turkey	27 Oct 32	136LTS23	303121
Czechoslovakia	Poland	17 Feb 33	143LTS167	303307
Romania	Yugoslavia	10 Mar 33	146LTS271	303377
Austria	Netherlands	28 Jun 33	152LTS193	303493
Netherlands	Poland	28 Jun 33	152LTS201	303494
Germany	Netherlands	28 Jun 33	152LTS209	303495
Italy	Netherlands	06 Jul 33	152LTS247	303496
Netherlands	Norway	18 Jul 33	152LTS259	303498
Czechoslovakia	Netherlands	18 Jul 33	152LTS265	303499
Netherlands	Yugoslavia	18 Jul 33	152LTS273	303500
Denmark	Netherlands	18 Jul 33	152LTS253	303497
Brazil	Uruguay	25 Aug 33	176LTS381	304075
Multilateral		23 Nov 33	192LTS327	304483
Multilateral		23 Nov 33	192LTS389	304484
Netherlands	Sweden	29 Nov 33	153LTS11	303501
Latvia	USSR (Soviet Union)	04 Dec 33	148LTS145	303410
Czechoslovakia	Poland	10 Feb 34	183LTS213	304238
Bulgaria	Romania	26 Jul 35	198LTS9	304621
Iraq	UK Great Britain	31 Mar 36	172LTS175	303988
Cuba	UK Great Britain	19 Feb 37	192LTS301	304480
Sweden	Yugoslavia	14 May 37	194LTS21	304504
Estonia	France	16 Oct 37	183LTS41	304227
Multilateral		23 Apr 39	104LTS87	302380
Hungary	Romania	19 Oct 39	201LTS415	304729
Hungary	Romania	19 Oct 39	201LTS395	304728
Roads and highways				
Iraq	UK Great Britain	25 Mar 24	35LTS145	300894
Estonia	Latvia	02 Apr 24	38LTS113	300969
Albania	Italy	06 Mar 25	44LTS359	301094
Italy	Serb/Croat/Slovene	20 Jul 25	83LTS247	301890
Germany	Poland	02 Dec 25	70LTS427	301649
Austria	Switzerland	06 Jan 26	46LTS299	301124
Multilateral		24 Apr 26	97LTS83	302220
Greece	Italy	24 Oct 26	63LTS51	301480
Multilateral		13 Nov 26	77LTS249	301773
Multilateral		13 Nov 26	77LTS217	301772
Norway	Sweden	19 Nov 27	68LTS209	301584
Abyssinia	Italy	02 Aug 28	94LTS423	302159
Czechoslovakia	Hungary	14 Nov 28	110LTS425	302574
Austria	Czechoslovakia	12 Dec 28	108LTS9	302501
Czechoslovakia	Germany	20 Mar 29	109LTS219	302541
Honduras	Nicaragua	30 Jan 30	142LTS241	303297
Czechoslovakia	Romania	15 Jul 30	164LTS157	303793
Brazil	Uruguay	20 Dec 33	181LTS69	304178
Panama	USA (United States)	02 Mar 36	200LTS205	304692
Iraq	UK Great Britain	14 Dec 36	177LTS221	304091
Lithuania	Poland	23 Jul 38	192LTS83	304462
Panama	USA (United States)	04 Jan 40	202LTS421	304744
Road rules				
Finland	USSR (Soviet Union)	28 Oct 22	19LTS199	300493
Italy	Serb/Croat/Slovene	14 Jul 24	82LTS327	301877
Multilateral		29 Oct 25	66LTS147	301529
Multilateral		24 Apr 26	108LTS123	302505
Multilateral		24 Apr 26	97LTS83	302220
Multilateral		30 Mar 31	150LTS247	303459
Italy	Netherlands	01 Jul 31	127LTS235	302923
Czechoslovakia	Netherlands	11 Aug 31	127LTS347	302928
Czechoslovakia	Poland	17 Feb 33	143LTS167	303307
Austria	Switzerland	21 Nov 36	179LTS341	304162
Belgium	Netherlands	31 Dec 37	189LTS387	304396

PARTY ONE	PARTY TWO	DATE	CITATION	NUMBER
General communications				
Liechtenstein	Switzerland	10 Nov 20	2LTS305	300084
Poland	Serb/Croat/Slovene	04 May 23	85LTS455	301946
Multilateral		24 Jul 23	28LTS11	300701
Norway	USSR (Soviet Union)	15 Dec 25	47LTS9	301127
Germany	Poland	27 Mar 26	64LTS249	301506
Czechoslovakia	Hungary	31 May 27	65LTS61	301520
Denmark	France	01 Aug 30	108LTS115	302504
Multilateral		10 Nov 31	131LTS327	303023
Amateur radio				
Canada	USA (United States)	12 Jan 29	102LTS143	302359
Peru	USA (United States)	23 May 34	152LTS99	303487
Chile	USA (United States)	17 Aug 34	157LTS15	303602
Commercial and public radio				
Multilateral		29 Dec 20	13LTS281	300359
Denmark	Sweden	07 Nov 22	14LTS95	300370
Netherlands	Switzerland	18 May 25	54LTS365	301299
Great Britain	USA (United States)	25 Sep 25	69LTS179	301603
Poland	Sweden	01 Oct 25	54LTS113	301279
Great Britain	USA (United States)	01 Oct 25	69LTS187	301604
Netherlands	Sweden	21 Nov 25	55LTS79	301305
Multilateral		25 Nov 27	84LTS97	301905
Brazil	Peru	31 Dec 28	127LTS455	302931
Canada	USA (United States)	20 Feb 39	197LTS181	304613
Bands and frequency allocation				
Great Britain	USA (United States)	25 Sep 25	69LTS179	301603
Great Britain	USA (United States)	01 Oct 25	69LTS187	301604
Germany	UK Great Britain	19 Oct 26	67LTS203	301547
Multilateral		25 Nov 27	84LTS97	301905
Brazil	Peru	31 Dec 28	127LTS455	302931
Multilateral		28 Feb 29	97LTS301	302228
Multilateral		08 Dec 38	202LTS49	304734
Mexico	USA (United States)	28 Aug 40	203LTS357	304777
Facilities and equipment				
Multilateral		05 Jun 12	1LTS135	300013
Denmark	Sweden	08 Jun 21	14LTS195	300374
Denmark	Norway	21 Jul 21	13LTS357	300362
Estonia	Finland	29 Oct 21	13LTS167	300350
Norway	Sweden	29 Mar 22	13LTS311	300361
Denmark	Germany	25 Apr 22	18LTS227	300466
Multilateral		18 Aug 22	13LTS289	300360
Netherlands	UK Great Britain	23 Jan 23	16LTS425	300420
Norway	Sweden	26 May 23	18LTS155	300462
Belgium	Denmark	28 Jun 23	20LTS59	300507
Belgium	Netherlands	14 Jul 23	20LTS119	300511
Finland	Sweden	12 Oct 23	21LTS147	300538
Iraq	UK Great Britain	25 Mar 24	35LTS103	300892
Netherlands	Norway	08 Jan 25	46LTS279	301122
Multilateral		05 May 25	55LTS225	301318
Poland	Sweden	01 Oct 25	54LTS113	301279
Czechoslovakia	Hungary	30 Sep 26	57LTS87	301356
Spain	UK Great Britain	19 Oct 26	61LTS79	301427
Multilateral		18 Dec 26	63LTS185	301489
Multilateral		20 Feb 28	129LTS223	302963
Saar	Switzerland	15 Aug 28	81LTS373	301847
Canada	USA (United States)	12 Jan 29	102LTS143	302359
Denmark	Norway	21 Jan 29	104LTS119	302382
Multilateral		28 Feb 29	97LTS301	302228
Greece	UK Great Britain	17 Apr 31	129LTS287	302965
Romania	Yugoslavia	14 Dec 31	135LTS99	303106
Germany	USA (United States)	31 May 32	133LTS409	303078
Bulgaria	Romania	26 Jul 35	198LTS9	304621
Canada	USA (United States)	20 Feb 39	197LTS181	304613

PARTY ONE	PARTY TWO	DATE	CITATION	NUMBER
Facilities and equipment (Cont.)				
Germany	Romania	23 Mar 39	199LTS77	304668
Communications linkage				
Denmark	USSR (Soviet Union)	23 Apr 23	18LTS15	300450
Multilateral		21 Jun 26	78LTS229	301793
Interference of broadcasts				
Multilateral		29 Dec 20	13LTS281	300359
Multilateral		25 Nov 27	84LTS97	301905
Multilateral		28 Feb 29	97LTS301	302228
Multilateral		23 Sep 36	186LTS301	304319
Multilateral		08 Dec 38	202LTS49	304734
Mail and money orders				
Liechtenstein	Switzerland	10 Nov 20	2LTS305	300084
Estonia	USSR (Soviet Union)	25 Jan 21	11LTS73	300290
Brazil	UK Great Britain	01 Mar 21	8LTS265	300225
UK Great Britain	USSR (Soviet Union)	16 Mar 21	4LTS127	300104
Czechoslovakia	Romania	23 Apr 21	15LTS235	300397
Austria	Czechoslovakia	04 May 21	15LTS13	300388
Multilateral		12 Jul 21	11LTS111	300293
France	UK Great Britain	03 Sep 21	8LTS153	300218
UK Great Britain	USA (United States)	05 Oct 21	8LTS371	300235
Iceland	UK Great Britain	13 Oct 21	8LTS337	300234
Danzig	Poland	24 Oct 21	116LTS5	302699
Germany	Poland	15 May 22	10LTS8	300272
Multilateral		28 Apr 23	33LTS47	300832
UK Great Britain	USA (United States)	30 Aug 23	24LTS103	300598
Netherlands	UK Great Britain	06 Sep 23	22LTS433	300572
Luxembourg	UK Great Britain	08 Sep 23	35LTS203	300896
Netherlands	UK Great Britain	02 Oct 23	23LTS9	300573
British Empire	USA (United States)	15 Nov 23	33LTS304	300854
China	UK Great Britain	07 Jan 24	24LTS115	300599
Multilateral		26 Jul 24	30LTS271	300771
Multilateral		28 Aug 24	41LTS9	301006
Multilateral		28 Aug 24	40LTS249	301003
Great Britain	Portugal	30 Aug 24	38LTS217	300979
Finland	UK Great Britain	12 Dec 24	34LTS123	300870
China	Strait Settlements	16 Jan 25	36LTS395	300937
Finland	USSR (Soviet Union)	20 Feb 25	34LTS153	300871
United Arab Rep	Tanganyika	25 Feb 25	36LTS409	300938
France	UK Great Britain	17 Apr 25	36LTS429	300939
Great Britain	Lithuania	18 Aug 25	43LTS135	301051
Hungary	UK Great Britain	28 Dec 25	49LTS125	301179
Netherlands	UK Great Britain	30 Dec 25	61LTS9	301424
Australia	Germany	31 May 26	60LTS121	301409
Spain	UK Great Britain	19 Oct 26	61LTS79	301427
Norway	South Africa	25 Jan 27	60LTS277	301416
Netherlands	UK Great Britain	14 Nov 27	71LTS227	301666
France	UK Great Britain	12 Jun 28	85LTS109	301926
France	Spain	16 Jul 28	135LTS149	303110
India	Saudi Arabia	09 Nov 31	157LTS35	303604
Denmark	USA (United States)	28 Dec 32	140LTS453	303255
India	Iraq	13 Mar 33	140LTS43	303227
India	Iraq	31 Mar 33	140LTS63	303228
Dutch Indies	UK Great Britain	17 Jun 33	144LTS47	303320
UK Great Britain	USSR (Soviet Union)	19 Apr 34	158LTS331	303643
China	India	13 Jun 34	157LTS77	303606
Australia	Italy	22 Jun 34	165LTS107	303806
Martinique	St. Lucia	25 Aug 34	165LTS183	303810
Indochina	Malaya	07 Sep 34	155LTS73	303569
Dutch Indies	Malaya	30 Oct 34	157LTS127	303608
Multilateral		31 Dec 34	158LTS111	303630
China	Malaya	30 Mar 35	163LTS159	303765
France	Malaya	31 Aug 35	165LTS215	303811
Estonia	Finland	12 Sep 36	172LTS345	303999
Aden	United Arab Rep	25 Aug 40	204LTS297	304810

Mail and money orders (Cont.)

PARTY ONE	PARTY TWO	DATE	CITATION	NUMBER
UK Great Britain	USA (United States)	27 Mar 41	204LTS15	304784
Curacao	Trinidad/Tobago	23 Apr 42	204LTS335	304812
British Guiana	Curacao	16 Jul 42	205LTS13	304823
Postal services				
Argentina	UK Great Britain	07 Apr 12	6LTS337	300165
Denmark	Sweden	26 Jan 20	14LTS273	300379
Sweden	UK Great Britain	03 Mar 20	5LTS63	300119
Norway	UK Great Britain	06 Jul 20	5LTS107	300121
Denmark	UK Great Britain	20 Aug 20	5LTS129	300122
Belgium	UK Great Britain	05 Oct 20	5LTS147	300123
Estonia	USSR (Soviet Union)	25 Jan 21	11LTS73	300290
Norway	USA (United States)	11 Feb 21	5LTS217	300130
Persia	USSR (Soviet Union)	26 Feb 21	9LTS383	300268
Multilateral		12 Jul 21	11LTS111	300293
Multilateral		15 Sep 21	30LTS141	300767
France	UK Great Britain	10 Oct 21	9LTS181	300250
Afghanistan	UK Great Britain	22 Nov 21	14LTS47	300367
India	Iraq	02 Apr 22	69LTS157	301602
Sweden	USA (United States)	17 Apr 22	14LTS281	300380
Denmark	Germany	25 Apr 22	18LTS227	300466
Denmark	Finland	22 May 22	9LTS435	300270
Denmark	USA (United States)	08 Jun 22	11LTS311	300298
Finland	USSR (Soviet Union)	22 Jun 22	16LTS361	300417
Finland	USA (United States)	21 Jul 22	13LTS243	300356
Iceland	Norway	17 Aug 22	14LTS9	300363
Albania	Italy	05 Dec 22	15LTS203	300394
China	Japan	08 Dec 22	20LTS205	300519
China	Japan	08 Dec 22	20LTS233	300520
China	Japan	08 Dec 22	20LTS289	300522
Netherlands	UK Great Britain	18 Jan 23	18LTS257	300469
Portugal	Spain	26 Mar 23	18LTS373	300476
Portugal	Spain	26 Mar 23	18LTS349	300475
Denmark	UK Great Britain	25 Apr 23	22LTS157	300557
Persia	Russ Fed Sov Rep	25 Apr 23	110LTS323	302564
Multilateral		24 May 23	50LTS341	301218
Iceland	Norway	10 Aug 23	20LTS363	300527
Netherlands	UK Great Britain	06 Sep 23	22LTS433	300572
France	UK Great Britain	10 Oct 23	22LTS381	300567
Netherlands	USA (United States)	15 Feb 24	31LTS61	300783
Sweden	USSR (Soviet Union)	15 Mar 24	25LTS251	300613
Hungary	Italy	27 Mar 24	55LTS103	301307
Finland	USSR (Soviet Union)	18 Jun 24	29LTS313	300747
Spain	UK Great Britain	27 Jun 24	28LTS523	300727
Multilateral		26 Jul 24	30LTS271	300771
France	El Salvador	25 Aug 24	93LTS365	302124
Multilateral		28 Aug 24	40LTS249	301003
Multilateral		28 Aug 24	40LTS307	301004
Multilateral		28 Aug 24	40LTS19	301002
Sweden	USSR (Soviet Union)	12 Sep 24	31LTS75	300784
Costa Rica	UK Great Britain	29 Sep 24	31LTS121	300789
Finland	Norway	11 Oct 24	32LTS123	300812
UK Great Britain	USA (United States)	27 Oct 24	33LTS315	300855
Netherlands	Norway	08 Jan 25	46LTS279	301122
United Arab Rep	Tanganyika	25 Feb 25	36LTS409	300938
Multilateral		05 May 25	55LTS225	301318
Japan	UK Great Britain	28 Jul 25	49LTS73	301177
Siam	Strait Settlements	12 Jan 26	49LTS161	301180
Netherlands	USA (United States)	19 Jan 26	50LTS199	301202
Belgium	Netherlands	05 Mar 26	50LTS213	301203
Canada	Norway	30 Apr 26	51LTS203	301227
Norway	South Africa	25 Jan 27	60LTS277	301416
Ceylon (Sri Lanka)	Germany	02 May 27	69LTS203	301606
Iraq	Palestine	04 Aug 27	80LTS211	301826
Multilateral		10 Sep 27	75LTS7	301749

Postal services (Cont.)

PARTY ONE	PARTY TWO	DATE	CITATION	NUMBER
Multilateral		10 Sep 27	75LTS39	301750
Chile	Italy	10 Nov 27	69LTS289	301611
Haiti	UK Great Britain	13 Feb 28	85LTS63	301923
Cuba	Germany	14 Jun 28	124LTS47	302832
Estonia	Finland	20 Aug 28	85LTS195	301930
France	UK Great Britain	23 Sep 28	87LTS29	301961
Cuba	UK Great Britain	01 Dec 28	85LTS149	301929
Bolivia	UK Great Britain	18 Jan 29	95LTS9	302161
UK Great Britain	USA (United States)	06 Apr 29	99LTS27	302265
Brazil	Denmark	29 Apr 29	89LTS295	302024
Palestine	Switzerland	15 May 29	95LTS395	302186
Multilateral		28 Jun 29	102LTS245	302368
Multilateral		28 Jun 29	103LTS429	302374
Multilateral		28 Jun 29	103LTS71	302370
Multilateral		28 Jun 29	103LTS377	302373
Multilateral		28 Jun 29	103LTS5	302369
UK Great Britain	USA (United States)	11 Jul 29	98LTS161	302245
Japan	UK Great Britain	20 Aug 29	107LTS243	302481
Belgium	Germany	07 Nov 29	121LTS327	302795
Switzerland	UK Great Britain	10 Dec 29	99LTS53	302267
Netherlands	UK Great Britain	10 Feb 30	102LTS67	302353
UK Great Britain	USA (United States)	16 Apr 30	109LTS9	302524
Finland	Sweden	14 May 30	106LTS9	302434
Finland	Norway	14 May 30	105LTS399	302429
Denmark	Finland	14 May 30	105LTS455	302433
Multilateral		14 May 30	105LTS353	302428
Netherlands	UK Great Britain	03 Jun 30	111LTS85	302582
Czechoslovakia	Romania	27 Jun 30	119LTS73	302742
Netherlands	USA (United States)	09 Jul 30	125LTS123	302851
Italy	UK Great Britain	28 Aug 30	111LTS91	302583
Netherlands	USA (United States)	16 Sep 30	125LTS173	302853
Netherlands	UK Great Britain	01 Jan 31	115LTS509	302698
France	India	07 Mar 31	119LTS269	302750
Greece	UK Great Britain	17 Apr 31	129LTS287	302965
Greece	Poland	22 Apr 31	129LTS313	302966
France	Greece	05 Jun 31	31LTS201	303011
Multilateral		10 Nov 31	131LTS327	303023
France	UK Great Britain	28 Nov 31	127LTS195	302919
Netherlands	UK Great Britain	04 Jan 32	128LTS307	302939
Netherlands	UK Great Britain	04 Jan 32	128LTS347	302940
China	UK Great Britain	28 Apr 32	137LTS319	303165
Sweden	USA (United States)	11 Jul 32	192LTS205	304473
Belgium	Netherlands	04 Aug 32	134LTS117	303086
Italy	UK Great Britain	24 Aug 32	136LTS331	303134
Germany	UK Great Britain	29 Oct 32	138LTS69	303182
Italy	Palestine	06 Dec 32	139LTS59	303204
Australia	Dutch Indies	19 Sep 33	144LTS335	303337
Barbados	Curacao	10 Oct 33	145LTS245	303357
Iceland	UK Great Britain	03 Nov 33	145LTS269	303358
Finland	UK Great Britain	04 Nov 33	149LTS285	303440
Denmark	USA (United States)	11 Nov 33	145LTS113	303349
Austria	UK Great Britain	15 Dec 33	146LTS9	303360
UK Great Britain	USSR (Soviet Union)	19 Apr 34	158LTS331	303643
Australia	France	30 May 34	165LTS81	303804
Australia	United Arab Rep	08 Jun 34	165LTS95	303805
Martinique	St. Lucia	25 Aug 34	165LTS183	303810
Dutch Indies	USA (United States)	04 Oct 34	158LTS395	303646
Denmark	Malaya	23 Oct 34	155LTS141	303575
Malaya	USA (United States)	11 Dec 34	156LTS101	303595
Multilateral		31 Dec 34	158LTS111	303630
Dutch Indies	Malaya	26 Feb 35	160LTS191	303693
Italy	Malaya	09 Mar 35	163LTS113	303764
Honduras	UK Great Britain	23 Apr 35	163LTS199	303768
Switzerland	UK Great Britain	25 May 35	163LTS239	303769
USA (United States)	Windward Islands	21 Jun 35	162LTS157	303739

PARTY ONE	PARTY TWO	DATE	CITATION	NUMBER
Postal services (Cont.)				
Turkey	USA (United States)	02 Jul 35	164LTS125	303792
Bulgaria	Romania	26 Jul 35	198LTS9	304621
India	Nepal	23 Dec 36	178LTS405	304123
Portugal	UK Great Britain	24 Mar 37	185LTS175	304281
Portugal	UK Great Britain	24 Mar 37	185LTS143	304279
Czechoslovakia	Italy	10 May 37	190LTS397	304430
Portugal	South Africa	18 Jun 37	189LTS121	304380
Germany	Romania	03 Oct 37	190LTS369	304429
France	Greece	11 Oct 37	185LTS253	304289
Multilateral		03 Dec 37	186LTS293	304318
Estonia	Germany	23 Dec 37	189LTS333	304393
Lithuania	Sweden	17 May 38	192LTS237	304474
Lithuania	Poland	22 May 38	191LTS359	304455
Lithuania	Poland	25 May 38	191LTS391	304457
Belgium	UK Great Britain	29 Jul 38	201LTS317	304722
France	UK Great Britain	19 Aug 38	192LTS189	304471
Burma	United Arab Rep	30 Sep 38	203LTS373	304780
Multilateral		02 Jan 39	196LTS235	304587
Fiji Islands	USA (United States)	10 Jan 39	196LTS185	304581
Belgium	USA (United States)	15 Jan 39	199LTS321	304682
Burma	France	26 Jan 39	201LTS9	304701
Colombia	USA (United States)	07 Feb 39	196LTS53	304569
Germany	USA (United States)	16 Mar 39	198LTS237	304645
Argentina	USA (United States)	08 Apr 39	198LTS55	304623
Multilateral		23 May 39	202LTS159	304742
Greece	UK Great Britain	30 May 39	202LTS7	304732
Barbados	USA (United States)	13 Sep 39	199LTS375	304685
Hungary	Romania	19 Oct 39	201LTS395	304728
Barbados	Martinique	21 Oct 39	201LTS65	304704
United Arab Rep	USA (United States)	13 Nov 39	198LTS419	304659
Japan	Thailand	30 Nov 39	200LTS197	304691
Lithuania	USA (United States)	28 Dec 39	202LTS381	304743
Aden	United Arab Rep	25 Aug 40	204LTS297	304810
Denmark	USA (United States)	09 Apr 41	204LTS135	304792
Curacao	Trinidad/Tobago	23 Apr 42	204LTS335	304812
British Guiana	Curacao	16 Jul 42	205LTS13	304823
Regulations				
Argentina	UK Great Britain	07 Apr 12	6LTS337	300165
Switzerland	UK Great Britain	28 Feb 20	6LTS9	300145
Sweden	UK Great Britain	03 Mar 20	5LTS63	300119
Norway	UK Great Britain	06 Jul 20	5LTS107	300121
Denmark	UK Great Britain	20 Aug 20	5LTS129	300122
Liechtenstein	Switzerland	10 Nov 20	2LTS305	300084
Australia	Malay States	24 Jan 21	23LTS209	300590
Norway	USA (United States)	11 Feb 21	5LTS217	300130
Brazil	UK Great Britain	01 Mar 21	8LTS265	300225
Multilateral		12 Jul 21	11LTS111	300293
Multilateral		15 Sep 21	30LTS141	300767
UK Great Britain	USA (United States)	05 Oct 21	8LTS371	300235
France	UK Great Britain	10 Oct 21	9LTS181	300250
Iceland	UK Great Britain	13 Oct 21	8LTS337	300234
India	Iraq	20 Oct 21	69LTS139	301601
Australia	Nauru	27 Oct 21	23LTS229	300591
India	Iraq	02 Apr 22	69LTS157	301602
Sweden	USA (United States)	17 Apr 22	14LTS281	300380
UK Great Britain	USA (United States)	22 Apr 22	20LTS415	300530
Mexico	UK Great Britain	17 May 22	14LTS83	300368
Denmark	Finland	22 May 22	9LTS435	300270
Finland	Sweden	22 May 22	14LTS297	300381
Finland	Norway	23 May 22	14LTS323	300382
Netherlands	UK Great Britain	02 Jun 22	13LTS263	300357
Finland	USA (United States)	21 Jul 22	13LTS243	300356
Iceland	Norway	17 Aug 22	14LTS9	300363
Latvia	USA (United States)	14 Oct 22	38LTS331	300989

PARTY ONE	PARTY TWO	DATE	CITATION	NUMBER
Regulations (Cont.)				
Albania	Italy	05 Dec 22	15LTS203	300394
China	Japan	08 Dec 22	20LTS289	300522
China	Japan	08 Dec 22	20LTS233	300520
China	Japan	08 Dec 22	20LTS205	300519
UK Great Britain	USA (United States)	28 Dec 22	21LTS9	300531
Netherlands	UK Great Britain	18 Jan 23	18LTS257	300469
Portugal	Spain	26 Mar 23	18LTS349	300475
Portugal	Spain	26 Mar 23	18LTS373	300476
Persia	Russ Fed Sov Rep	25 Apr 23	110LTS323	302564
Multilateral		24 May 23	50LTS341	301218
Australia	Netherlands	30 May 23	22LTS129	300556
Iceland	Norway	10 Aug 23	20LTS363	300527
UK Great Britain	USA (United States)	30 Aug 23	24LTS103	300598
Netherlands	UK Great Britain	06 Sep 23	22LTS433	300572
Netherlands	UK Great Britain	02 Oct 23	23LTS9	300573
Canada	Irish Free State	12 Oct 23	56LTS291	301338
British Empire	USA (United States)	15 Nov 23	33LTS304	300854
UK Great Britain	USA (United States)	08 Dec 23	23LTS93	300580
Irish Free State	USA (United States)	31 Dec 23	56LTS303	301339
China	UK Great Britain	07 Jan 24	24LTS115	300599
Netherlands	USA (United States)	15 Feb 24	31LTS61	300783
Finland	USSR (Soviet Union)	18 Jun 24	29LTS313	300747
Multilateral		26 Jul 24	30LTS271	300771
Multilateral		28 Aug 24	40LTS19	301002
Multilateral		28 Aug 24	40LTS249	301003
Multilateral		28 Aug 24	40LTS307	301004
Great Britain	Portugal	30 Aug 24	38LTS217	300979
Sweden	USSR (Soviet Union)	12 Sep 24	31LTS75	300784
Costa Rica	UK Great Britain	29 Sep 24	31LTS121	300789
Finland	Norway	11 Oct 24	32LTS123	300812
UK Great Britain	USA (United States)	27 Oct 24	33LTS315	300855
Canada	Irish Free State	12 Nov 24	56LTS333	301340
Finland	Germany	14 Nov 24	32LTS137	300813
Germany	Irish Free State	29 Dec 24	56LTS341	301341
United Arab Rep	Tanganyika	25 Feb 25	36LTS409	300938
Irish Free State	New Zealand	30 Apr 25	56LTS373	301342
Japan	UK Great Britain	28 Jul 25	49LTS73	301177
Irish Free State	South Africa	01 Oct 25	56LTS389	301343
Siam	Strait Settlements	12 Jan 26	49LTS161	301180
India	Irish Free State	04 Apr 26	56LTS415	301344
Irish Free State	USA (United States)	10 May 26	56LTS433	301345
Australia	Germany	31 May 26	60LTS121	301409
Estonia	Great Britain	12 Oct 26	60LTS387	301422
Norway	South Africa	25 Jan 27	60LTS277	301416
Ceylon (Sri Lanka)	Germany	02 May 27	69LTS203	301606
Multilateral		10 Sep 27	75LTS39	301750
Multilateral		10 Sep 27	75LTS7	301749
Chile	Italy	10 Nov 27	69LTS289	301611
Netherlands	UK Great Britain	14 Nov 27	71LTS227	301666
Denmark	Iceland	30 Nov 27	71LTS43	301653
Haiti	UK Great Britain	13 Feb 28	85LTS63	301923
Cuba	Germany	14 Jun 28	124LTS47	302832
Estonia	Finland	20 Aug 28	85LTS195	301930
France	UK Great Britain	23 Sep 28	87LTS29	301961
Cuba	UK Great Britain	01 Dec 28	85LTS149	301929
Bolivia	UK Great Britain	18 Jan 29	95LTS9	302161
France	UK Great Britain	06 Mar 29	90LTS391	302050
Norway	USA (United States)	30 Mar 29	91LTS383	302078
UK Great Britain	USA (United States)	02 Apr 29	94LTS17	302133
UK Great Britain	USA (United States)	06 Apr 29	99LTS27	302265
Netherlands	UK Great Britain	04 May 29	93LTS9	302101
Palestine	Switzerland	15 May 29	95LTS395	302186
France	UK Great Britain	15 May 29	134LTS263	303097
Mexico	Norway	14 Jun 29	99LTS381	302283
Multilateral		28 Jun 29	103LTS377	302373

PARTY ONE	PARTY TWO	DATE	CITATION	NUMBER
Regulations (Cont.)				
Multilateral		28 Jun 29	103LTS71	302370
Multilateral		28 Jun 29	102LTS245	302368
UK Great Britain	USA (United States)	04 Jul 29	92LTS329	302099
UK Great Britain	USA (United States)	11 Jul 29	98LTS161	302245
Persia	USSR (Soviet Union)	02 Aug 29	109LTS99	302530
Japan	UK Great Britain	20 Aug 29	107LTS243	302481
Poland	Romania	30 Oct 29	121LTS243	302790
Switzerland	UK Great Britain	10 Dec 29	99LTS53	302267
UK Great Britain	USA (United States)	16 Apr 30	109LTS9	302524
Finland	Sweden	14 May 30	106LTS9	302434
Multilateral		14 May 30	105LTS353	302428
Portugal	UK Great Britain	27 Jun 30	107LTS281	302485
Netherlands	USA (United States)	09 Jul 30	125LTS123	302851
Italy	UK Great Britain	28 Aug 30	111LTS91	302583
Germany	Turkey	03 Sep 30	133LTS321	303071
Netherlands	USA (United States)	16 Sep 30	125LTS147	302852
Netherlands	USA (United States)	16 Sep 30	125LTS173	302853
Multilateral		31 Oct 30	120LTS9	302760
Netherlands	UK Great Britain	01 Jan 31	115LTS509	302698
France	India	07 Mar 31	119LTS269	302750
Mexico	Sweden	14 Sep 31	192LTS195	304472
UK Great Britain	Yugoslavia	23 Oct 31	126LTS209	302884
Multilateral		10 Nov 31	131LTS327	303023
Multilateral		10 Nov 31	131LTS389	303024
Multilateral		10 Nov 31	131LTS447	303025
Czechoslovakia	Sweden	17 Nov 31	134LTS135	303088
Japan	USSR (Soviet Union)	23 Nov 31	132LTS133	303033
Netherlands	UK Great Britain	04 Jan 32	128LTS307	302939
China	UK Great Britain	28 Apr 32	137LTS319	303165
Hungary	UK Great Britain	10 Jun 32	132LTS53	303031
Sweden	USA (United States)	11 Jul 32	192LTS205	304473
Netherlands	UK Great Britain	13 Aug 32	134LTS317	303100
France	UK Great Britain	22 Aug 32	136LTS313	303133
Italy	Palestine	06 Dec 32	139LTS59	303204
Denmark	USA (United States)	28 Dec 32	140LTS453	303255
Canada	Norway	13 Mar 33	141LTS211	303266
Finland	Netherlands	22 May 33	140LTS279	303243
Dutch Indies	UK Great Britain	17 Jun 33	144LTS47	303320
Barbados	Curacao	10 Oct 33	145LTS245	303357
Iceland	UK Great Britain	03 Nov 33	145LTS269	303358
Austria	UK Great Britain	15 Dec 33	146LTS9	303360
Multilateral		20 Mar 34	175LTS5	304049
Multilateral		20 Mar 34	175LTS73	304050
Multilateral		20 Mar 34	175LTS363	304052
UK Great Britain	USSR (Soviet Union)	19 Apr 34	158LTS331	303643
Indochina	Malaya	07 Sep 34	155LTS73	303569
Dutch Indies	USA (United States)	04 Oct 34	158LTS395	303646
Norway	USA (United States)	09 Nov 34	156LTS33	303592
Malaya	USA (United States)	11 Dec 34	156LTS101	303595
Multilateral		31 Dec 34	158LTS111	303630
Germany	USSR (Soviet Union)	07 Mar 35	169LTS7	303911
Italy	Malaya	09 Mar 35	163LTS113	303764
Honduras	UK Great Britain	23 Apr 35	163LTS199	303768
Switzerland	UK Great Britain	25 May 35	163LTS239	303769
Czechoslovakia	USSR (Soviet Union)	08 Jun 35	167LTS181	303865
USA (United States)	Windward Islands	21 Jun 35	162LTS157	303739
Multilateral		30 Oct 35	189LTS85	304376
France	USA (United States)	30 Dec 35	171LTS117	303955
China	Malaya	12 Feb 36	170LTS19	303927
United Arab Rep	Malaya	29 Feb 36	170LTS103	303931
France	USSR (Soviet Union)	09 Mar 36	179LTS131	304140
Greece	Palestine	28 Mar 36	170LTS145	303932
France	India	01 May 36	178LTS57	304107
France	Palestine	19 Jun 36	172LTS17	303977
Denmark	USSR (Soviet Union)	29 Jun 36	174LTS93	304040

PARTY ONE	PARTY TWO	DATE	CITATION	NUMBER
Regulations (Cont.)				
Germany	UK Great Britain	02 Dec 36	178LTS329	304121
Haiti	Jamaica	07 Dec 36	178LTS65	304108
Germany	Malaya	17 Dec 36	178LTS484	304129
Bahamas	USA (United States)	21 Dec 36	176LTS411	304077
India	Nepal	23 Dec 36	178LTS405	304123
Latvia	Sweden	30 Dec 36	174LTS147	304045
Gibralter	USA (United States)	05 Jan 37	177LTS21	304078
Danzig	UK Great Britain	13 Jan 37	178LTS87	304109
Malaya	Netherlands	16 Mar 37	184LTS181	304248
Portugal	UK Great Britain	24 Mar 37	185LTS151	304280
Portugal	UK Great Britain	24 Mar 37	185LTS143	304279
Portugal	UK Great Britain	24 Mar 37	185LTS175	304281
UK Great Britain	Yugoslavia	07 Jun 37	184LTS229	304249
Romania	USA (United States)	10 Aug 37	183LTS7	304225
Malaya	Siam	15 Sep 37	191LTS225	304447
Malaya	Siam	16 Sep 37	191LTS265	304448
Netherlands	USA (United States)	20 Sep 37	184LTS319	304256
France	Greece	11 Oct 37	185LTS253	304289
Estonia	UK Great Britain	14 Dec 37	187LTS223	304343
Surinam	UK Great Britain	15 Mar 38	189LTS183	304385
Norway	Sweden	20 Apr 38	189LTS153	304383
Multilateral		02 Jun 38	192LTS157	304470
USA (United States)	Yugoslavia	20 Jun 38	195LTS259	304549
Japan	USA (United States)	20 Jun 38	191LTS43	304434
Belgium	UK Great Britain	29 Jul 38	201LTS317	304722
British Guiana	USA (United States)	06 Sep 38	193LTS117	304490
Burma	United Arab Rep	30 Sep 38	203LTS373	304780
France	UK Great Britain	26 Oct 38	194LTS371	304530
Iceland	USA (United States)	31 Oct 38	194LTS149	304519
Multilateral		02 Jan 39	196LTS235	304587
Fiji Islands	USA (United States)	10 Jan 39	196LTS185	304581
Belgium	USA (United States)	15 Jan 39	199LTS321	304682
Burma	France	26 Jan 39	201LTS9	304701
Colombia	USA (United States)	07 Feb 39	196LTS53	304569
Germany	USA (United States)	16 Mar 39	198LTS237	304645
Argentina	USA (United States)	08 Apr 39	198LTS55	304623
Multilateral		23 May 39	202LTS159	304742
Barbados	USA (United States)	13 Sep 39	199LTS375	304685
Barbados	Martinique	21 Oct 39	201LTS65	304704
United Arab Rep	USA (United States)	13 Nov 39	198LTS419	304659
Lithuania	USA (United States)	28 Dec 39	202LTS381	304743
Aden	United Arab Rep	25 Aug 40	204LTS297	304810
Curacao	Trinidad/Tobago	23 Apr 42	204LTS335	304812
Insured letters and boxes				
Estonia	USSR (Soviet Union)	25 Jan 21	11LTS73	300290
Belgium	Netherlands	15 Oct 21	12LTS233	300315
Finland	Sweden	22 May 22	14LTS297	300381
Denmark	Finland	22 May 22	9LTS435	300270
Finland	Norway	23 May 22	14LTS323	300382
Netherlands	UK Great Britain	02 Jun 22	13LTS263	300357
Albania	Italy	05 Dec 22	15LTS203	300394
China	Japan	08 Dec 22	20LTS233	300520
China	Japan	08 Dec 22	20LTS289	300522
Portugal	Spain	26 Mar 23	18LTS373	300476
Multilateral		24 May 23	50LTS341	301218
Netherlands	USA (United States)	15 Feb 24	31LTS61	300783
Finland	USSR (Soviet Union)	18 Jun 24	29LTS313	300747
Multilateral		26 Jul 24	30LTS271	300771
Sweden	USSR (Soviet Union)	12 Sep 24	31LTS75	300784
Costa Rica	UK Great Britain	29 Sep 24	31LTS121	300789
Finland	Germany	14 Nov 24	32LTS137	300813
British Honduras	Mexico	25 Mar 25	43LTS61	301047
Siam	Strait Settlements	12 Jan 26	49LTS161	301180
Irish Free State	USA (United States)	10 May 26	56LTS433	301345

PARTY ONE	PARTY TWO	DATE	CITATION	NUMBER
Insured letters and boxes (Cont.)				
India	Iraq	30 Aug 26	69LTS193	301605
Norway	South Africa	25 Jan 27	60LTS277	301416
Ceylon (Sri Lanka)	Germany	02 May 27	69LTS203	301606
Multilateral		10 Sep 27	75LTS39	301750
Multilateral		10 Sep 27	75LTS7	301749
Haiti	UK Great Britain	13 Feb 28	85LTS63	301923
Cuba	Germany	14 Jun 28	124LTS47	302832
France	UK Great Britain	23 Sep 28	87LTS29	301961
Cuba	UK Great Britain	01 Dec 28	85LTS149	301929
Mexico	Norway	14 Jun 29	99LTS381	302283
Multilateral		28 Jun 29	103LTS5	302369
Multilateral		28 Jun 29	102LTS245	302368
Multilateral		28 Jun 29	103LTS71	302370
UK Great Britain	USA (United States)	11 Jul 29	98LTS161	302245
Persia	USSR (Soviet Union)	02 Aug 29	109LTS99	302530
Japan	UK Great Britain	20 Aug 29	107LTS243	302481
Switzerland	UK Great Britain	10 Dec 29	99LTS53	302267
Multilateral		14 May 30	105LTS353	302428
Finland	Sweden	14 May 30	106LTS9	302434
Finland	Norway	14 May 30	105LTS399	302429
Denmark	Finland	14 May 30	105LTS455	302433
Denmark	Turkey	31 May 30	119LTS165	302744
Portugal	UK Great Britain	14 Jun 30	107LTS275	302484
Netherlands	USA (United States)	09 Jul 30	125LTS123	302851
Italy	UK Great Britain	28 Aug 30	111LTS91	302583
Netherlands	USA (United States)	16 Sep 30	125LTS173	302853
Netherlands	UK Great Britain	01 Jan 31	115LTS509	302698
France	Greece	05 Jun 31	31LTS201	303011
France	UK Great Britain	27 Nov 31	132LTS25	303028
Netherlands	UK Great Britain	04 Jan 32	128LTS307	302939
China	UK Great Britain	28 Apr 32	137LTS319	303165
Hungary	UK Great Britain	10 Jun 32	132LTS53	303031
Netherlands	UK Great Britain	13 Aug 32	134LTS317	303100
France	UK Great Britain	22 Aug 32	136LTS313	303133
Italy	UK Great Britain	24 Aug 32	136LTS331	303134
Germany	UK Great Britain	29 Oct 32	138LTS69	303182
Canada	Norway	13 Mar 33	141LTS211	303266
Australia	Dutch Indies	19 Sep 33	144LTS335	303337
Barbados	Curacao	10 Oct 33	145LTS245	303357
Iceland	UK Great Britain	03 Nov 33	145LTS269	303358
Finland	UK Great Britain	04 Nov 33	149LTS285	303440
Austria	UK Great Britain	15 Dec 33	146LTS9	303360
UK Great Britain	USSR (Soviet Union)	19 Apr 34	158LTS331	303643
Australia	France	30 May 34	165LTS81	303804
Australia	United Arab Rep	08 Jun 34	165LTS95	303805
Martinique	St. Lucia	25 Aug 34	165LTS183	303810
Dutch Indies	USA (United States)	04 Oct 34	158LTS395	303646
Indochina	Malaya	08 Oct 34	157LTS95	303607
Norway	USA (United States)	09 Nov 34	156LTS33	303592
Dutch Indies	Malaya	26 Feb 35	160LTS191	303693
Italy	Malaya	09 Mar 35	163LTS113	303764
Honduras	UK Great Britain	23 Apr 35	163LTS199	303768
Switzerland	UK Great Britain	25 May 35	163LTS239	303769
Turkey	USA (United States)	02 Jul 35	164LTS125	303792
France	Malaya	31 Aug 35	165LTS215	303811
Belgium	UK Great Britain	29 Jul 38	201LTS317	304722
Burma	United Arab Rep	30 Sep 38	203LTS373	304780
Multilateral		02 Jan 39	196LTS235	304587
Belgium	USA (United States)	15 Jan 39	199LTS321	304682
Burma	France	26 Jan 39	201LTS9	304701
Colombia	USA (United States)	07 Feb 39	196LTS53	304569
Germany	USA (United States)	16 Mar 39	198LTS237	304645
Argentina	USA (United States)	08 Apr 39	198LTS55	304623
Barbados	USA (United States)	13 Sep 39	199LTS375	304685
Barbados	Martinique	21 Oct 39	201LTS65	304704

PARTY ONE	PARTY TWO	DATE	CITATION	NUMBER
Insured letters and boxes (Cont.)				
United Arab Rep	USA (United States)	13 Nov 39	198LTS419	304659
Lithuania	USA (United States)	28 Dec 39	202LTS381	304743
Conveyance in transit				
Chile	Colombia	16 Nov 14	82LTS243	301875
UK Great Britain	USSR (Soviet Union)	12 Feb 20	1LTS263	300019
Germany	Latvia	20 Apr 20	2LTS71	300049
China	UK Great Britain	26 Apr 20	5LTS83	300120
Germany	Hungary	08 May 20	2LTS79	300050
Estonia	Lithuania	12 Jul 21	43LTS179	301054
Multilateral		15 Sep 21	30LTS141	300767
France	UK Great Britain	10 Oct 21	9LTS181	300250
India	Iraq	02 Apr 22	69LTS157	301602
Czechoslovakia	Italy	06 Apr 22	55LTS171	301313
Finland	Sweden	22 May 22	14LTS297	300381
Finland	Norway	23 May 22	14LTS323	300382
Netherlands	UK Great Britain	02 Jun 22	13LTS263	300357
Denmark	USA (United States)	08 Jun 22	11LTS311	300298
Finland	USSR (Soviet Union)	22 Jun 22	16LTS361	300417
Albania	Italy	05 Dec 22	15LTS203	300394
China	Japan	08 Dec 22	20LTS205	300519
China	Japan	08 Dec 22	20LTS289	300522
Netherlands	UK Great Britain	18 Jan 23	18LTS257	300469
Czechoslovakia	Hungary	08 Mar 23	48LTS257	301167
Portugal	Spain	26 Mar 23	18LTS349	300475
Denmark	UK Great Britain	25 Apr 23	22LTS157	300557
Multilateral		24 May 23	50LTS341	301218
Netherlands	UK Great Britain	06 Sep 23	22LTS433	300572
France	UK Great Britain	10 Oct 23	22LTS381	300567
Netherlands	USA (United States)	15 Feb 24	31LTS61	300783
Denmark	Latvia	03 Apr 24	33LTS393	300860
Finland	Latvia	07 Jun 24	38LTS343	300990
Finland	USSR (Soviet Union)	18 Jun 24	29LTS313	300747
Finland	USSR (Soviet Union)	18 Jun 24	47LTS241	301134
Multilateral		26 Jul 24	30LTS271	300771
Multilateral		28 Aug 24	40LTS19	301002
Sweden	USSR (Soviet Union)	12 Sep 24	31LTS75	300784
Costa Rica	UK Great Britain	29 Sep 24	31LTS121	300789
Finland	Norway	11 Oct 24	32LTS123	300812
UK Great Britain	USA (United States)	27 Oct 24	33LTS315	300855
Estonia	Finland	02 Jan 25	43LTS11	301044
United Arab Rep	Tanganyika	25 Feb 25	36LTS409	300938
Czechoslovakia	Poland	06 Mar 25	46LTS201	301120
Czechoslovakia	Romania	07 May 25	54LTS51	301273
Finland	Norway	10 Nov 25	43LTS381	301071
France	Great Britain	15 Mar 26	47LTS415	301146
Canada	Norway	30 Apr 26	51LTS203	301227
Bulgaria	Czechoslovakia	15 May 26	60LTS169	301412
Albania	Greece	25 Jun 26	83LTS305	301898
Czechoslovakia	Latvia	06 Jul 26	62LTS229	301465
Czechoslovakia	Estonia	17 Jul 26	63LTS255	301495
Austria	Estonia	15 Oct 26	74LTS213	301739
Belgium	Estonia	11 Nov 26	65LTS405	301523
Switzerland	Uruguay	26 Nov 26	63LTS207	301491
Belgium	Latvia	11 Dec 26	63LTS299	301497
Czechoslovakia	Germany	22 Jan 27	89LTS261	302020
Norway	South Africa	25 Jan 27	60LTS277	301416
Austria	Czechoslovakia	15 Feb 27	73LTS349	301724
Austria	Czechoslovakia	15 Feb 27	73LTS381	301725
Belgium	Lithuania	17 May 27	77LTS123	301767
Belgium	Czechoslovakia	19 Jul 27	73LTS283	301720
Latvia	Norway	12 Sep 27	71LTS303	301671
Chile	Italy	10 Nov 27	69LTS289	301611
Belgium	Finland	23 Jan 28	74LTS353	301747
Germany	Siam	07 Apr 28	85LTS337	301938

PARTY ONE	PARTY TWO	DATE	CITATION	NUMBER
Conveyance in transit (Cont.)				
Austria	Italy	11 May 28	100LTS375	302307
Estonia	Latvia	15 May 28	74LTS281	301742
Cuba	Germany	14 Jun 28	124LTS47	302832
France	UK Great Britain	23 Sep 28	87LTS29	301961
Germany	Norway	23 Jan 29	93LTS197	302110
Poland	Romania	30 Mar 29	123LTS147	302812
Mexico	Norway	14 Jun 29	99LTS381	302283
Multilateral		28 Jun 29	102LTS245	302368
Poland	Romania	30 Oct 29	121LTS243	302790
Multilateral		09 Nov 29	125LTS205	302855
Austria	Netherlands	31 Dec 29	111LTS177	302586
Poland	Romania	26 Mar 30	153LTS87	303510
Austria	Poland	10 Apr 30	108LTS289	302514
Poland	Romania	09 May 30	112LTS225	302617
Finland	Norway	14 May 30	105LTS399	302429
Denmark	Finland	14 May 30	105LTS455	302433
Belgium	France	23 May 30	119LTS33	302738
Austria	Hungary	03 Jun 30	122LTS69	302799
Netherlands	USA (United States)	09 Jul 30	125LTS123	302851
Bulgaria	Spain	17 Jul 30	114LTS41	302653
Italy	Panama	07 Aug 30	140LTS241	303240
Czechoslovakia	Turkey	22 Aug 30	138LTS375	303196
Italy	Venezuela	23 Aug 30	128LTS377	302943
Italy	UK Great Britain	28 Aug 30	111LTS91	302583
Greece	UK Great Britain	17 Apr 31	129LTS287	302965
Czechoslovakia	Lithuania	24 Apr 31	126LTS261	302889
Czechoslovakia	Germany	29 Apr 31	133LTS347	303072
Belgium	Poland	13 May 31	131LTS109	303005
Mexico	Sweden	14 Sep 31	192LTS195	304472
Czechoslovakia	Denmark	07 Oct 31	127LTS103	302911
Multilateral		10 Nov 31	131LTS327	303023
Multilateral		10 Nov 31	131LTS447	303025
Japan	USSR (Soviet Union)	23 Nov 31	132LTS133	303033
France	UK Great Britain	28 Nov 31	127LTS195	302919
Brazil	Italy	28 Nov 31	132LTS345	303047
Czechoslovakia	Netherlands	04 Dec 31	129LTS343	302969
Netherlands	UK Great Britain	04 Jan 32	128LTS307	302939
Iraq	Turkey	09 Jan 32	139LTS273	303218
Hungary	UK Great Britain	10 Jun 32	132LTS53	303031
Netherlands	UK Great Britain	13 Aug 32	134LTS317	303100
France	UK Great Britain	22 Aug 32	136LTS313	303133
Italy	UK Great Britain	24 Aug 32	136LTS331	303134
Germany	UK Great Britain	29 Oct 32	138LTS69	303182
Italy	Palestine	06 Dec 32	139LTS59	303204
Denmark	USA (United States)	28 Dec 32	140LTS453	303255
Romania	Yugoslavia	30 Jan 33	146LTS113	303363
Finland	Netherlands	21 Feb 33	139LTS365	303221
Estonia	Netherlands	08 Mar 33	146LTS319	303382
Switzerland	Turkey	01 Jun 33	159LTS329	303676
Dutch Indies	UK Great Britain	17 Jun 33	144LTS47	303320
Australia	Dutch Indies	19 Sep 33	144LTS335	303337
Multilateral		23 Nov 33	192LTS327	304483
Lithuania	Netherlands	01 Dec 33	150LTS337	303466
Multilateral		26 Dec 33	165LTS45	303803
UK Great Britain	USSR (Soviet Union)	19 Apr 34	158LTS331	303643
Germany	Latvia	18 Jul 34	154LTS69	303537
Dutch Indies	USA (United States)	04 Oct 34	158LTS395	303646
Indochina	Malaya	08 Oct 34	157LTS95	303607
Denmark	Lithuania	20 Dec 34	162LTS347	303748
Multilateral		31 Dec 34	158LTS111	303630
Dutch Indies	Malaya	26 Feb 35	160LTS191	303693
Italy	Malaya	09 Mar 35	163LTS113	303764
Czechoslovakia	USSR (Soviet Union)	08 Jun 35	167LTS181	303865
Bulgaria	USSR (Soviet Union)	10 Jul 35	168LTS275	303905
Multilateral		30 Oct 35	189LTS85	304376

PARTY ONE	PARTY TWO	DATE	CITATION	NUMBER
Conveyance in transit (Cont.)				
France	USA (United States)	30 Dec 35	171LTS117	303955
China	Malaya	12 Feb 36	170LTS19	303927
United Arab Rep	Malaya	29 Feb 36	170LTS103	303931
France	USSR (Soviet Union)	09 Mar 36	179LTS131	304140
Greece	Palestine	28 Mar 36	170LTS145	303932
France	Palestine	19 Jun 36	172LTS17	303977
Denmark	USSR (Soviet Union)	29 Jun 36	174LTS93	304040
Haiti	Jamaica	07 Dec 36	178LTS65	304108
Estonia	Finland	18 Dec 36	178LTS41	304105
Multilateral		10 Feb 37	189LTS313	304391
Malaya	Netherlands	16 Mar 37	184LTS181	304248
UK Great Britain	Yugoslavia	07 Jun 37	184LTS229	304249
Malaya	Siam	15 Sep 37	191LTS225	304447
Netherlands	USA (United States)	20 Sep 37	184LTS319	304256
Estonia	UK Great Britain	14 Dec 37	187LTS223	304343
Surinam	UK Great Britain	15 Mar 38	189LTS183	304385
Norway	Sweden	20 Apr 38	189LTS153	304383
Lithuania	Poland	14 May 38	191LTS373	304456
Lithuania	Poland	22 May 38	191LTS359	304455
Multilateral		02 Jun 38	192LTS157	304470
USA (United States)	Yugoslavia	20 Jun 38	195LTS259	304549
Japan	USA (United States)	20 Jun 38	191LTS43	304434
France	UK Great Britain	19 Aug 38	192LTS189	304471
British Guiana	USA (United States)	06 Sep 38	193LTS117	304490
Poland	UK Great Britain	05 Oct 38	194LTS321	304529
France	UK Great Britain	26 Oct 38	194LTS371	304530
Iceland	USA (United States)	31 Oct 38	194LTS149	304519
Multilateral		02 Jan 39	196LTS235	304587
Fiji Islands	USA (United States)	10 Jan 39	196LTS185	304581
Burma	France	26 Jan 39	201LTS9	304701
Barbados	USA (United States)	13 Sep 39	199LTS375	304685
Barbados	Martinique	21 Oct 39	201LTS65	304704
Aden	United Arab Rep	25 Aug 40	204LTS297	304810
Curacao	Trinidad/Tobago	23 Apr 42	204LTS335	304812
Money orders and postal checks				
Sweden	UK Great Britain	03 Mar 20	5LTS63	300119
China	UK Great Britain	26 Apr 20	5LTS83	300120
Norway	UK Great Britain	06 Jul 20	5LTS107	300121
Denmark	UK Great Britain	20 Aug 20	5LTS129	300122
Liechtenstein	Switzerland	10 Nov 20	2LTS305	300084
Brazil	UK Great Britain	01 Mar 21	8LTS265	300225
Multilateral		12 Jul 21	11LTS111	300293
France	UK Great Britain	03 Sep 21	8LTS153	300218
UK Great Britain	USA (United States)	05 Oct 21	8LTS371	300235
Iceland	UK Great Britain	13 Oct 21	8LTS337	300234
India	Iraq	20 Oct 21	69LTS139	301601
Australia	Nauru	27 Oct 21	23LTS229	300591
Iraq	UK Great Britain	16 Jan 22	12LTS431	300340
Palestine	UK Great Britain	23 Jan 22	13LTS9	300342
UK Great Britain	USA (United States)	22 Apr 22	20LTS415	300530
Germany	Poland	15 May 22	10LTS8	300272
Latvia	USA (United States)	14 Oct 22	38LTS331	300989
Latvia	UK Great Britain	17 Oct 22	16LTS397	300419
China	Japan	08 Dec 22	20LTS253	300521
UK Great Britain	USA (United States)	28 Dec 22	21LTS9	300531
India	Iraq	08 Feb 23	85LTS37	301920
Netherlands	UK Great Britain	30 Apr 23	20LTS343	300525
Multilateral		24 May 23	50LTS341	301218
Australia	Netherlands	30 May 23	22LTS129	300556
UK Great Britain	USA (United States)	30 Aug 23	24LTS103	300598
Luxembourg	UK Great Britain	08 Sep 23	35LTS203	300896
Netherlands	UK Great Britain	02 Oct 23	23LTS9	300573
Canada	Irish Free State	12 Oct 23	56LTS291	301338
British Empire	USA (United States)	15 Nov 23	33LTS304	300854

PARTY ONE	PARTY TWO	DATE	CITATION	NUMBER
Money orders and postal checks (Cont.)				
UK Great Britain	USA (United States)	08 Dec 23	23LTS93	300580
Irish Free State	USA (United States)	31 Dec 23	56LTS303	301339
China	UK Great Britain	07 Jan 24	24LTS115	300599
Finland	USA (United States)	26 Jun 24	30LTS9	300756
Multilateral		26 Jul 24	30LTS271	300771
Multilateral		28 Aug 24	40LTS437	301005
Multilateral		28 Aug 24	40LTS19	301002
Sweden	USSR (Soviet Union)	12 Sep 24	31LTS75	300784
Finland	UK Great Britain	12 Dec 24	34LTS123	300870
Germany	Irish Free State	29 Dec 24	56LTS341	301341
China	Strait Settlements	16 Jan 25	36LTS395	300937
Finland	USSR (Soviet Union)	20 Feb 25	34LTS153	300871
France	UK Great Britain	17 Apr 25	36LTS429	300939
Irish Free State	New Zealand	30 Apr 25	56LTS373	301342
Bulgaria	Great Britain	07 May 25	38LTS153	300973
Czechoslovakia	Great Britain	09 Aug 25	38LTS231	300980
Great Britain	Lithuania	18 Aug 25	43LTS135	301051
Irish Free State	South Africa	01 Oct 25	56LTS389	301343
Canada	Finland	18 Dec 25	47LTS319	301137
Italy	UK Great Britain	20 Dec 25	49LTS79	301178
Hungary	UK Great Britain	28 Dec 25	49LTS125	301179
Netherlands	USA (United States)	19 Jan 26	50LTS199	301202
India	Irish Free State	04 Apr 26	56LTS415	301344
Australia	Germany	31 May 26	60LTS121	301409
Estonia	Great Britain	12 Oct 26	60LTS387	301422
Multilateral		30 Oct 26	61LTS65	301426
Netherlands	UK Great Britain	14 Nov 27	71LTS227	301666
Denmark	Iceland	30 Nov 27	71LTS43	301653
Netherlands	USA (United States)	30 Dec 27	72LTS179	301691
Belgium	Luxembourg	18 May 28	89LTS213	302016
France	UK Great Britain	12 Jun 28	85LTS109	301926
Cuba	Mexico	29 Jun 28	124LTS189	302833
Mexico	UK Great Britain	24 Oct 28	87LTS63	301962
Netherlands	UK Great Britain	04 May 29	93LTS9	302101
France	UK Great Britain	15 May 29	134LTS263	303097
Multilateral		28 Jun 29	103LTS377	302373
Multilateral		28 Jun 29	103LTS321	302372
Multilateral		28 Jun 29	103LTS249	302371
Germany	UK Great Britain	17 Jul 29	100LTS439	302313
Netherlands	South Africa	10 Sep 29	98LTS423	302261
Belgium	Irish Free State	24 Sep 29	102LTS213	302364
Poland	UK Great Britain	04 Oct 29	97LTS261	302227
Romania	UK Great Britain	02 Apr 30	105LTS235	302416
Multilateral		14 May 30	105LTS353	302428
Italy	UK Great Britain	28 Aug 30	111LTS91	302583
Netherlands	USA (United States)	16 Sep 30	125LTS147	302852
Denmark	India	16 Dec 30	114LTS73	302656
Netherlands	UK Great Britain	01 Jan 31	115LTS509	302698
UK Great Britain	Yugoslavia	23 Oct 31	126LTS209	302884
India	Saudi Arabia	09 Nov 31	157LTS35	303604
Multilateral		10 Nov 31	131LTS389	303024
Hungary	UK Great Britain	10 Jun 32	132LTS53	303031
Netherlands	South Africa	29 Jun 32	133LTS33	303054
Sweden	USA (United States)	11 Jul 32	192LTS205	304473
Netherlands	UK Great Britain	13 Aug 32	134LTS317	303100
India	Iraq	13 Mar 33	140LTS43	303227
Italy	South Africa	19 Jul 33	146LTS369	303385
Multilateral		20 Mar 34	175LTS269	304051
Multilateral		20 Mar 34	175LTS363	304052
Australia	Italy	22 Jun 34	165LTS107	303806
Indochina	Malaya	07 Sep 34	155LTS73	303569
Dutch Indies	Malaya	30 Oct 34	157LTS127	303608
Malaya	USA (United States)	11 Dec 34	156LTS101	303595
China	Malaya	30 Mar 35	163LTS159	303765
France	UK Great Britain	16 Jul 35	168LTS179	303898

PARTY ONE	PARTY TWO	DATE	CITATION	NUMBER
Money orders and postal checks (Cont.)				
Dutch Indies	India	28 Nov 35	168LTS147	303896
Colombia	USA (United States)	11 Jan 36	169LTS79	303914
China	UK Great Britain	17 Jul 36	173LTS343	304024
Germany	UK Great Britain	02 Dec 36	178LTS329	304121
Danzig	UK Great Britain	13 Jan 37	178LTS87	304109
Portugal	UK Great Britain	24 Mar 37	185LTS175	304281
Portugal	UK Great Britain	24 Mar 37	185LTS151	304280
Malaya	Siam	16 Sep 37	191LTS265	304448
Multilateral		23 Sep 37	190LTS299	304427
Estonia	UK Great Britain	14 Dec 37	187LTS223	304343
Aden	United Arab Rep	03 Nov 38	197LTS241	304617
Belgium	USA (United States)	15 Jan 39	199LTS321	304682
Colombia	USA (United States)	07 Feb 39	196LTS53	304569
Burma	Siam	14 Feb 39	197LTS255	304618
Lithuania	USA (United States)	28 Dec 39	202LTS381	304743
British Guiana	Curacao	16 Jul 42	205LTS13	304823
Parcel post				
Switzerland	UK Great Britain	28 Feb 20	6LTS9	300145
Sweden	UK Great Britain	03 Mar 20	5LTS63	300119
Norway	UK Great Britain	06 Jul 20	5LTS107	300121
Denmark	UK Great Britain	20 Aug 20	5LTS129	300122
Estonia	USSR (Soviet Union)	25 Jan 21	11LTS73	300290
Norway	USA (United States)	11 Feb 21	5LTS217	300130
Multilateral		12 Jul 21	11LTS111	300293
India	Iraq	02 Apr 22	69LTS157	301602
Sweden	USA (United States)	17 Apr 22	14LTS281	300380
Germany	Poland	15 May 22	10LTS37	300273
Denmark	Finland	22 May 22	9LTS435	300270
Netherlands	UK Great Britain	02 Jun 22	13LTS263	300357
Denmark	USA (United States)	08 Jun 22	11LTS311	300298
Finland	USA (United States)	21 Jul 22	13LTS243	300356
Albania	Italy	05 Dec 22	15LTS203	300394
India	Iraq	08 Feb 23	85LTS37	301920
Portugal	Spain	26 Mar 23	18LTS373	300476
Multilateral		24 May 23	50LTS341	301218
Netherlands	USA (United States)	15 Feb 24	31LTS61	300783
Finland	USSR (Soviet Union)	18 Jun 24	29LTS313	300747
Multilateral		26 Jul 24	30LTS271	300771
Austria	Latvia	09 Aug 24	65LTS7	301516
Great Britain	Portugal	30 Aug 24	38LTS217	300979
Sweden	USSR (Soviet Union)	12 Sep 24	31LTS75	300784
Costa Rica	UK Great Britain	29 Sep 24	31LTS121	300789
Finland	Norway	11 Oct 24	32LTS123	300812
UK Great Britain	USA (United States)	27 Oct 24	33LTS315	300855
Canada	Irish Free State	12 Nov 24	56LTS333	301340
Finland	Germany	14 Nov 24	32LTS137	300813
United Arab Rep	Tanganyika	25 Feb 25	36LTS409	300938
British Honduras	Mexico	25 Mar 25	43LTS61	301047
Finland	Norway	19 Dec 25	56LTS183	301330
Netherlands	UK Great Britain	30 Dec 25	61LTS9	301424
Siam	Strait Settlements	12 Jan 26	49LTS161	301180
Canada	Norway	30 Apr 26	51LTS203	301227
Irish Free State	USA (United States)	10 May 26	56LTS433	301345
Belgium	UK Great Britain	11 May 26	71LTS97	301657
India	Iraq	30 Aug 26	69LTS193	301605
Norway	South Africa	25 Jan 27	60LTS277	301416
Ceylon (Sri Lanka)	Germany	02 May 27	69LTS203	301606
Iraq	Palestine	04 Aug 27	80LTS211	301826
Multilateral		10 Sep 27	75LTS39	301750
Chile	Italy	10 Nov 27	69LTS289	301611
Denmark	Iceland	30 Nov 27	71LTS43	301653
Haiti	UK Great Britain	13 Feb 28	85LTS63	301923
Cuba	Germany	14 Jun 28	124LTS47	302832
France	Spain	16 Jul 28	135LTS149	303110

PARTY ONE	PARTY TWO	DATE	CITATION	NUMBER
Parcel post (Cont.)				
Estonia	Finland	20 Aug 28	85LTS195	301930
France	UK Great Britain	23 Sep 28	87LTS29	301961
Cuba	UK Great Britain	01 Dec 28	85LTS149	301929
Bolivia	UK Great Britain	18 Jan 29	95LTS9	302161
France	UK Great Britain	06 Mar 29	90LTS391	302050
Norway	USA (United States)	30 Mar 29	91LTS383	302078
UK Great Britain	USA (United States)	02 Apr 29	94LTS17	302133
UK Great Britain	USA (United States)	06 Apr 29	99LTS27	302265
Netherlands	UK Great Britain	04 May 29	93LTS9	302101
Palestine	Switzerland	15 May 29	95LTS395	302186
Mexico	Norway	14 Jun 29	99LTS381	302283
Multilateral		28 Jun 29	103LTS71	302370
Multilateral		28 Jun 29	102LTS245	302368
UK Great Britain	USA (United States)	04 Jul 29	92LTS329	302099
UK Great Britain	USA (United States)	11 Jul 29	98LTS161	302245
Germany	UK Great Britain	17 Jul 29	100LTS439	302313
Persia	USSR (Soviet Union)	02 Aug 29	109LTS99	302530
Japan	UK Great Britain	20 Aug 29	107LTS243	302481
Switzerland	UK Great Britain	10 Dec 29	99LTS53	302267
Netherlands	UK Great Britain	10 Feb 30	102LTS67	302353
Siam	UK Great Britain	20 Mar 30	106LTS363	302456
Multilateral		14 May 30	105LTS353	302428
Finland	Sweden	14 May 30	106LTS9	302434
Portugal	UK Great Britain	14 Jun 30	107LTS275	302484
Portugal	UK Great Britain	27 Jun 30	107LTS281	302485
Netherlands	USA (United States)	09 Jul 30	125LTS123	302851
Italy	UK Great Britain	28 Aug 30	111LTS91	302583
Netherlands	USA (United States)	16 Sep 30	125LTS173	302853
Netherlands	UK Great Britain	01 Jan 31	115LTS509	302698
Mexico	Sweden	14 Sep 31	192LTS195	304472
Multilateral		10 Nov 31	131LTS447	303025
France	UK Great Britain	17 Nov 31	134LTS299	303098
Japan	USSR (Soviet Union)	23 Nov 31	132LTS133	303033
France	UK Great Britain	27 Nov 31	132LTS25	303028
France	UK Great Britain	28 Nov 31	127LTS195	302919
Romania	Yugoslavia	14 Dec 31	135LTS31	303103
France	UK Great Britain	28 Dec 31	133LTS79	303058
Netherlands	UK Great Britain	04 Jan 32	128LTS347	302940
Netherlands	UK Great Britain	04 Jan 32	128LTS307	302939
Hungary	UK Great Britain	10 Jun 32	132LTS53	303031
Sweden	USA (United States)	11 Jul 32	192LTS205	304473
Netherlands	UK Great Britain	13 Aug 32	134LTS317	303100
France	UK Great Britain	22 Aug 32	136LTS313	303133
Italy	UK Great Britain	24 Aug 32	136LTS331	303134
Germany	UK Great Britain	29 Oct 32	138LTS69	303182
Italy	Palestine	06 Dec 32	139LTS59	303204
Denmark	USA (United States)	28 Dec 32	140LTS453	303255
Canada	Norway	13 Mar 33	141LTS211	303266
Dutch Indies	UK Great Britain	17 Jun 33	144LTS47	303320
Australia	Dutch Indies	19 Sep 33	144LTS335	303337
Barbados	Curacao	10 Oct 33	145LTS245	303357
Iceland	UK Great Britain	03 Nov 33	145LTS269	303358
Finland	UK Great Britain	04 Nov 33	149LTS285	303440
Austria	UK Great Britain	15 Dec 33	146LTS9	303360
Multilateral		20 Mar 34	175LTS73	304050
UK Great Britain	USSR (Soviet Union)	19 Apr 34	158LTS331	303643
Australia	France	30 May 34	165LTS81	303804
Australia	United Arab Rep	08 Jun 34	165LTS95	303805
China	India	13 Jun 34	157LTS77	303606
Martinique	St. Lucia	25 Aug 34	165LTS183	303810
Dutch Indies	USA (United States)	04 Oct 34	158LTS395	303646
Indochina	Malaya	08 Oct 34	157LTS95	303607
Denmark	Malaya	23 Oct 34	155LTS141	303575
Norway	USA (United States)	09 Nov 34	156LTS33	303592
Dutch Indies	Malaya	26 Feb 35	160LTS191	303693

PARTY ONE	PARTY TWO	DATE	CITATION	NUMBER
Parcel post (Cont.)				
Germany	USSR (Soviet Union)	07 Mar 35	169LTS7	303911
Italy	Malaya	09 Mar 35	163LTS113	303764
Honduras	UK Great Britain	23 Apr 35	163LTS199	303768
Switzerland	UK Great Britain	25 May 35	163LTS239	303769
Czechoslovakia	USSR (Soviet Union)	08 Jun 35	167LTS181	303865
USA (United States)	Windward Islands	21 Jun 35	162LTS157	303739
Bulgaria	USSR (Soviet Union)	10 Jul 35	168LTS275	303905
France	Malaya	31 Aug 35	165LTS215	303811
France	USSR (Soviet Union)	09 Mar 36	179LTS131	304140
Germany	UK Great Britain	02 Dec 36	178LTS329	304121
Haiti	Jamaica	07 Dec 36	178LTS65	304108
Germany	Malaya	17 Dec 36	178LTS484	304129
Bahamas	USA (United States)	21 Dec 36	176LTS411	304077
Gibralter	USA (United States)	05 Jan 37	177LTS21	304078
Danzig	UK Great Britain	13 Jan 37	178LTS87	304109
Malaya	Netherlands	16 Mar 37	184LTS181	304248
UK Great Britain	Yugoslavia	07 Jun 37	184LTS229	304249
Romania	USA (United States)	10 Aug 37	183LTS7	304225
Malaya	Siam	15 Sep 37	191LTS225	304447
Netherlands	USA (United States)	20 Sep 37	184LTS319	304256
Estonia	UK Great Britain	14 Dec 37	187LTS223	304343
Surinam	UK Great Britain	15 Mar 38	189LTS183	304385
Norway	Sweden	20 Apr 38	189LTS153	304383
Multilateral		02 Jun 38	192LTS157	304470
USA (United States)	Yugoslavia	20 Jun 38	195LTS259	304549
Japan	USA (United States)	20 Jun 38	191LTS43	304434
Belgium	UK Great Britain	29 Jul 38	201LTS317	304722
British Guiana	USA (United States)	06 Sep 38	193LTS117	304490
Burma	United Arab Rep	30 Sep 38	203LTS373	304780
Poland	UK Great Britain	05 Oct 38	194LTS321	304529
France	UK Great Britain	26 Oct 38	194LTS371	304530
Iceland	USA (United States)	31 Oct 38	194LTS149	304519
Belgium	USA (United States)	15 Jan 39	199LTS321	304682
Burma	France	26 Jan 39	201LTS9	304701
Colombia	USA (United States)	07 Feb 39	196LTS53	304569
Germany	USA (United States)	16 Mar 39	198LTS237	304645
Argentina	USA (United States)	08 Apr 39	198LTS55	304623
Barbados	USA (United States)	13 Sep 39	199LTS375	304685
Barbados	Martinique	21 Oct 39	201LTS65	304704
United Arab Rep	USA (United States)	13 Nov 39	198LTS419	304659
Lithuania	USA (United States)	28 Dec 39	202LTS381	304743
Aden	United Arab Rep	25 Aug 40	204LTS297	304810
Curacao	Trinidad/Tobago	23 Apr 42	204LTS335	304812
British Guiana	Curacao	16 Jul 42	205LTS13	304823
Rates and charges				
Switzerland	UK Great Britain	28 Feb 20	6LTS9	300145
Sweden	UK Great Britain	03 Mar 20	5LTS63	300119
Norway	UK Great Britain	06 Jul 20	5LTS107	300121
Denmark	UK Great Britain	20 Aug 20	5LTS129	300122
Belgium	UK Great Britain	05 Oct 20	5LTS147	300123
Liechtenstein	Switzerland	10 Nov 20	2LTS305	300084
Norway	USA (United States)	11 Feb 21	5LTS217	300130
Multilateral		12 Jul 21	11LTS111	300293
France	UK Great Britain	10 Oct 21	9LTS181	300250
Belgium	Netherlands	15 Oct 21	12LTS233	300315
Iraq	UK Great Britain	16 Jan 22	12LTS431	300340
Palestine	UK Great Britain	23 Jan 22	13LTS9	300342
India	Iraq	02 Apr 22	69LTS157	301602
Sweden	USA (United States)	17 Apr 22	14LTS281	300380
Finland	Sweden	22 May 22	14LTS297	300381
Finland	Norway	23 May 22	14LTS323	300382
Denmark	USA (United States)	08 Jun 22	11LTS311	300298
Finland	USA (United States)	21 Jul 22	13LTS243	300356
Iceland	Norway	17 Aug 22	14LTS9	300363

PARTY ONE	PARTY TWO	DATE	CITATION	NUMBER
Rates and charges (Cont.)				
Latvia	USA (United States)	14 Oct 22	38LTS331	300989
Latvia	UK Great Britain	17 Oct 22	16LTS397	300419
Albania	Italy	05 Dec 22	15LTS203	300394
China	Japan	08 Dec 22	20LTS233	300520
China	Japan	08 Dec 22	20LTS289	300522
China	Japan	08 Dec 22	20LTS205	300519
India	Iraq	08 Feb 23	85LTS37	301920
Portugal	Spain	26 Mar 23	18LTS373	300476
Portugal	Spain	26 Mar 23	18LTS349	300475
Persia	Russ Fed Sov Rep	25 Apr 23	110LTS323	302564
Denmark	UK Great Britain	25 Apr 23	22LTS157	300557
Persia	Russ Fed Sov Rep	27 Apr 23	110LTS333	302565
Multilateral		24 May 23	50LTS341	301218
Iceland	Norway	10 Aug 23	20LTS363	300527
Netherlands	UK Great Britain	06 Sep 23	22LTS433	300572
France	UK Great Britain	10 Oct 23	22LTS381	300567
Finland	USSR (Soviet Union)	18 Jun 24	29LTS313	300747
Multilateral		26 Jul 24	30LTS271	300771
Multilateral		28 Aug 24	41LTS9	301006
Multilateral		28 Aug 24	40LTS437	301005
Multilateral		28 Aug 24	40LTS307	301004
Multilateral		28 Aug 24	40LTS19	301002
Great Britain	Portugal	30 Aug 24	38LTS217	300979
Sweden	USSR (Soviet Union)	12 Sep 24	31LTS75	300784
Costa Rica	UK Great Britain	29 Sep 24	31LTS121	300789
Finland	Norway	11 Oct 24	32LTS123	300812
British Honduras	Mexico	25 Mar 25	43LTS61	301047
Netherlands	UK Great Britain	30 Dec 25	61LTS9	301424
Siam	Strait Settlements	12 Jan 26	49LTS161	301180
Canada	Norway	30 Apr 26	51LTS203	301227
Irish Free State	USA (United States)	10 May 26	56LTS433	301345
Belgium	UK Great Britain	11 May 26	71LTS97	301657
Multilateral		30 Oct 26	61LTS65	301426
Norway	South Africa	25 Jan 27	60LTS277	301416
Ceylon (Sri Lanka)	Germany	02 May 27	69LTS203	301606
Iraq	Palestine	04 Aug 27	80LTS211	301826
Multilateral		10 Sep 27	75LTS39	301750
Multilateral		10 Sep 27	75LTS7	301749
Chile	Italy	10 Nov 27	69LTS289	301611
Netherlands	UK Great Britain	14 Nov 27	71LTS227	301666
Denmark	Iceland	30 Nov 27	71LTS43	301653
Haiti	UK Great Britain	13 Feb 28	85LTS63	301923
Belgium	Luxembourg	18 May 28	89LTS207	302015
Cuba	Germany	14 Jun 28	124LTS47	302832
Estonia	Finland	20 Aug 28	85LTS195	301930
France	UK Great Britain	23 Sep 28	87LTS29	301961
Cuba	UK Great Britain	01 Dec 28	85LTS149	301929
Bolivia	UK Great Britain	18 Jan 29	95LTS9	302161
France	UK Great Britain	06 Mar 29	90LTS391	302050
Poland	Romania	30 Mar 29	123LTS147	302812
Norway	USA (United States)	30 Mar 29	91LTS383	302078
UK Great Britain	USA (United States)	02 Apr 29	94LTS17	302133
UK Great Britain	USA (United States)	06 Apr 29	99LTS27	302265
Netherlands	UK Great Britain	04 May 29	93LTS9	302101
Mexico	Norway	14 Jun 29	99LTS381	302283
Multilateral		28 Jun 29	103LTS429	302374
Multilateral		28 Jun 29	103LTS71	302370
Multilateral		28 Jun 29	103LTS5	302369
Multilateral		28 Jun 29	102LTS245	302368
UK Great Britain	USA (United States)	04 Jul 29	92LTS329	302099
UK Great Britain	USA (United States)	11 Jul 29	98LTS161	302245
Germany	UK Great Britain	17 Jul 29	100LTS439	302313
Persia	USSR (Soviet Union)	02 Aug 29	109LTS99	302530
Japan	UK Great Britain	20 Aug 29	107LTS243	302481
Poland	UK Great Britain	04 Oct 29	97LTS261	302227

PARTY ONE	PARTY TWO	DATE	CITATION	NUMBER
Rates and charges (Cont.)				
Poland	Romania	30 Oct 29	121LTS243	302790
Multilateral		09 Nov 29	125LTS205	302855
Switzerland	UK Great Britain	10 Dec 29	99LTS53	302267
Netherlands	UK Great Britain	10 Feb 30	102LTS67	302353
Siam	UK Great Britain	20 Mar 30	106LTS363	302456
UK Great Britain	USA (United States)	16 Apr 30	109LTS9	302524
Multilateral		14 May 30	105LTS353	302428
Finland	Sweden	14 May 30	106LTS9	302434
Denmark	Finland	14 May 30	105LTS455	302433
Finland	Norway	14 May 30	105LTS399	302429
Belgium	France	23 May 30	119LTS33	302738
Portugal	UK Great Britain	14 Jun 30	107LTS275	302484
Portugal	UK Great Britain	27 Jun 30	107LTS281	302485
Netherlands	USA (United States)	09 Jul 30	125LTS123	302851
Italy	UK Great Britain	28 Aug 30	111LTS91	302583
Netherlands	USA (United States)	16 Sep 30	125LTS173	302853
Netherlands	UK Great Britain	01 Jan 31	115LTS509	302698
Mexico	Sweden	14 Sep 31	192LTS195	304472
UK Great Britain	Yugoslavia	23 Oct 31	126LTS209	302884
Multilateral		10 Nov 31	131LTS327	303023
Multilateral		10 Nov 31	131LTS447	303025
Japan	USSR (Soviet Union)	23 Nov 31	132LTS133	303033
France	UK Great Britain	27 Nov 31	132LTS25	303028
France	UK Great Britain	28 Nov 31	127LTS195	302919
Netherlands	UK Great Britain	04 Jan 32	128LTS307	302939
China	UK Great Britain	28 Apr 32	137LTS319	303165
Hungary	UK Great Britain	10 Jun 32	132LTS53	303031
Netherlands	South Africa	29 Jun 32	133LTS33	303054
Sweden	USA (United States)	11 Jul 32	192LTS205	304473
Belgium	Netherlands	04 Aug 32	134LTS117	303086
France	UK Great Britain	22 Aug 32	136LTS313	303133
Italy	UK Great Britain	24 Aug 32	136LTS331	303134
Italy	Palestine	06 Dec 32	139LTS59	303204
Canada	Norway	13 Mar 33	141LTS211	303266
Australia	Dutch Indies	19 Sep 33	144LTS335	303337
Barbados	Curacao	10 Oct 33	145LTS245	303357
Iceland	UK Great Britain	03 Nov 33	145LTS269	303358
Finland	UK Great Britain	04 Nov 33	149LTS285	303440
Austria	UK Great Britain	15 Dec 33	146LTS9	303360
Multilateral		20 Mar 34	175LTS73	304050
Multilateral		20 Mar 34	175LTS363	304052
Multilateral		20 Mar 34	176LTS55	304054
UK Great Britain	USSR (Soviet Union)	19 Apr 34	158LTS331	303643
Australia	France	30 May 34	165LTS81	303804
Australia	United Arab Rep	08 Jun 34	165LTS95	303805
Dutch Indies	USA (United States)	04 Oct 34	158LTS395	303646
Indochina	Malaya	08 Oct 34	157LTS95	303607
Denmark	Malaya	23 Oct 34	155LTS141	303575
Multilateral		31 Dec 34	158LTS111	303630
Dutch Indies	Malaya	26 Feb 35	160LTS191	303693
Germany	USSR (Soviet Union)	07 Mar 35	169LTS7	303911
Italy	Malaya	09 Mar 35	163LTS113	303764
USA (United States)	Windward Islands	21 Jun 35	162LTS157	303739
Turkey	USA (United States)	02 Jul 35	164LTS125	303792
Bulgaria	USSR (Soviet Union)	10 Jul 35	168LTS275	303905
France	UK Great Britain	16 Jul 35	168LTS179	303898
Multilateral		30 Oct 35	189LTS85	304376
France	USA (United States)	30 Dec 35	171LTS117	303955
Colombia	USA (United States)	11 Jan 36	169LTS79	303914
China	Malaya	12 Feb 36	170LTS19	303927
United Arab Rep	Malaya	29 Feb 36	170LTS103	303931
France	USSR (Soviet Union)	09 Mar 36	179LTS131	304140
Greece	Palestine	28 Mar 36	170LTS145	303932
France	Palestine	19 Jun 36	172LTS17	303977
Denmark	USSR (Soviet Union)	29 Jun 36	174LTS93	304040

PARTY ONE	PARTY TWO	DATE	CITATION	NUMBER
Rates and charges (Cont.)				
Belgium	Netherlands	13 Jul 36	177LTS93	304083
China	UK Great Britain	17 Jul 36	173LTS343	304024
Germany	UK Great Britain	02 Dec 36	178LTS329	304121
Haiti	Jamaica	07 Dec 36	178LTS65	304108
Germany	Malaya	17 Dec 36	178LTS484	304129
Estonia	Finland	18 Dec 36	178LTS41	304105
India	Nepal	23 Dec 36	178LTS405	304123
Latvia	Sweden	30 Dec 36	174LTS147	304045
Danzig	UK Great Britain	13 Jan 37	178LTS87	304109
Estonia	Sweden	16 Jan 37	178LTS49	304106
Malaya	Netherlands	16 Mar 37	184LTS181	304248
Portugal	UK Great Britain	24 Mar 37	185LTS151	304280
Portugal	UK Great Britain	24 Mar 37	185LTS143	304279
Portugal	UK Great Britain	24 Mar 37	185LTS175	304281
Finland	Latvia	28 May 37	179LTS333	304161
UK Great Britain	Yugoslavia	07 Jun 37	184LTS229	304249
Romania	USA (United States)	10 Aug 37	183LTS7	304225
Malaya	Siam	15 Sep 37	191LTS225	304447
Malaya	Siam	16 Sep 37	191LTS265	304448
Netherlands	USA (United States)	20 Sep 37	184LTS319	304256
Multilateral		23 Sep 37	190LTS299	304427
France	Greece	11 Oct 37	185LTS253	304289
Estonia	UK Great Britain	14 Dec 37	187LTS223	304343
Surinam	UK Great Britain	15 Mar 38	189LTS183	304385
Norway	Sweden	20 Apr 38	189LTS153	304383
Lithuania	Sweden	17 May 38	192LTS237	304474
Multilateral		02 Jun 38	192LTS157	304470
Japan	USA (United States)	20 Jun 38	191LTS43	304434
USA (United States)	Yugoslavia	20 Jun 38	195LTS259	304549
Belgium	UK Great Britain	29 Jul 38	201LTS317	304722
France	UK Great Britain	19 Aug 38	192LTS189	304471
British Guiana	USA (United States)	06 Sep 38	193LTS117	304490
Burma	United Arab Rep	30 Sep 38	203LTS373	304780
Poland	UK Great Britain	05 Oct 38	194LTS321	304529
Iceland	USA (United States)	31 Oct 38	194LTS149	304519
Multilateral		02 Jan 39	196LTS235	304587
Fiji Islands	USA (United States)	10 Jan 39	196LTS185	304581
Belgium	USA (United States)	15 Jan 39	199LTS321	304682
Burma	France	26 Jan 39	201LTS9	304701
Germany	USA (United States)	16 Mar 39	198LTS237	304645
Multilateral		23 May 39	202LTS159	304742
Barbados	USA (United States)	13 Sep 39	199LTS375	304685
Barbados	Martinique	21 Oct 39	201LTS65	304704
United Arab Rep	USA (United States)	13 Nov 39	198LTS419	304659
Lithuania	USA (United States)	28 Dec 39	202LTS381	304743
Aden	United Arab Rep	25 Aug 40	204LTS297	304810
Curacao	Trinidad/Tobago	23 Apr 42	204LTS335	304812
British Guiana	Curacao	16 Jul 42	205LTS13	304823
Advice lists and orders				
Australia	Malay States	24 Jan 21	23LTS209	300590
Brazil	UK Great Britain	01 Mar 21	8LTS265	300225
UK Great Britain	USA (United States)	05 Oct 21	8LTS371	300235
Iceland	UK Great Britain	13 Oct 21	8LTS337	300234
India	Iraq	20 Oct 21	69LTS139	301601
Australia	Nauru	27 Oct 21	23LTS229	300591
India	Iraq	02 Apr 22	69LTS157	301602
UK Great Britain	USA (United States)	22 Apr 22	20LTS415	300530
Albania	Italy	05 Dec 22	15LTS203	300394
China	Japan	08 Dec 22	20LTS253	300521
UK Great Britain	USA (United States)	28 Dec 22	21LTS9	300531
Multilateral		24 May 23	50LTS341	301218
Australia	Netherlands	30 May 23	22LTS129	300556
Netherlands	UK Great Britain	02 Oct 23	23LTS9	300573
UK Great Britain	USA (United States)	08 Dec 23	23LTS93	300580

PARTY ONE	PARTY TWO	DATE	CITATION	NUMBER
Advice lists and orders (Cont.)				
Finland	USSR (Soviet Union)	18 Jun 24	29LTS313	300747
Finland	USA (United States)	26 Jun 24	30LTS9	300756
Multilateral		26 Jul 24	30LTS271	300771
United Arab Rep	Tanganyika	25 Feb 25	36LTS409	300938
Irish Free State	New Zealand	30 Apr 25	56LTS373	301342
Bulgaria	Great Britain	07 May 25	38LTS153	300973
Irish Free State	USA (United States)	10 May 26	56LTS433	301345
Australia	Germany	31 May 26	60LTS121	301409
Estonia	Great Britain	12 Oct 26	60LTS387	301422
Norway	South Africa	25 Jan 27	60LTS277	301416
Multilateral		10 Sep 27	75LTS39	301750
Chile	Italy	10 Nov 27	69LTS289	301611
Netherlands	UK Great Britain	14 Nov 27	71LTS227	301666
Denmark	Iceland	30 Nov 27	71LTS43	301653
France	UK Great Britain	15 May 29	134LTS263	303097
Multilateral		28 Jun 29	103LTS321	302372
Netherlands	South Africa	10 Sep 29	98LTS423	302261
Poland	UK Great Britain	04 Oct 29	97LTS261	302227
Romania	UK Great Britain	02 Apr 30	105LTS235	302416
Denmark	Finland	14 May 30	105LTS455	302433
Netherlands	USA (United States)	16 Sep 30	125LTS147	302852
Denmark	India	16 Dec 30	114LTS73	302656
France	India	07 Mar 31	119LTS269	302750
Mexico	Sweden	14 Sep 31	192LTS195	304472
UK Great Britain	Yugoslavia	23 Oct 31	126LTS209	302884
Multilateral		10 Nov 31	131LTS389	303024
Multilateral		10 Nov 31	131LTS327	303023
China	UK Great Britain	28 Apr 32	137LTS319	303165
Hungary	UK Great Britain	10 Jun 32	132LTS53	303031
Netherlands	South Africa	29 Jun 32	133LTS33	303054
Italy	UK Great Britain	24 Aug 32	136LTS331	303134
Germany	UK Great Britain	29 Oct 32	138LTS69	303182
Finland	UK Great Britain	04 Nov 33	149LTS285	303440
Multilateral		20 Mar 34	175LTS363	304052
UK Great Britain	USSR (Soviet Union)	19 Apr 34	158LTS331	303643
Dutch Indies	USA (United States)	04 Oct 34	158LTS395	303646
Multilateral		31 Dec 34	158LTS111	303630
Italy	Malaya	09 Mar 35	163LTS113	303764
France	UK Great Britain	16 Jul 35	168LTS179	303898
Dutch Indies	India	28 Nov 35	168LTS147	303896
France	USA (United States)	30 Dec 35	171LTS117	303955
China	Malaya	12 Feb 36	170LTS19	303927
United Arab Rep	Malaya	29 Feb 36	170LTS103	303931
Greece	Palestine	28 Mar 36	170LTS145	303932
France	Palestine	19 Jun 36	172LTS17	303977
Denmark	USSR (Soviet Union)	29 Jun 36	174LTS93	304040
China	UK Great Britain	17 Jul 36	173LTS343	304024
Germany	UK Great Britain	02 Dec 36	178LTS329	304121
Germany	Malaya	17 Dec 36	178LTS484	304129
Danzig	UK Great Britain	13 Jan 37	178LTS87	304109
Malaya	Netherlands	16 Mar 37	184LTS181	304248
Portugal	UK Great Britain	24 Mar 37	185LTS151	304280
UK Great Britain	Yugoslavia	07 Jun 37	184LTS229	304249
Romania	USA (United States)	10 Aug 37	183LTS7	304225
Malaya	Siam	15 Sep 37	191LTS225	304447
Malaya	Siam	16 Sep 37	191LTS265	304448
Estonia	UK Great Britain	14 Dec 37	187LTS223	304343
Surinam	UK Great Britain	15 Mar 38	189LTS183	304385
Norway	Sweden	20 Apr 38	189LTS153	304383
Multilateral		02 Jun 38	192LTS157	304470
Japan	USA (United States)	20 Jun 38	191LTS43	304434
British Guiana	USA (United States)	06 Sep 38	193LTS117	304490
Poland	UK Great Britain	05 Oct 38	194LTS321	304529
France	UK Great Britain	26 Oct 38	194LTS371	304530
Belgium	USA (United States)	15 Jan 39	199LTS321	304682

PARTY ONE	PARTY TWO	DATE	CITATION	NUMBER
Advice lists and orders (Cont.)				
Aden	United Arab Rep	25 Aug 40	204LTS297	304810
Curacao	Trinidad/Tobago	23 Apr 42	204LTS335	304812
Telecommunications				
Finland	USSR (Soviet Union)	14 Oct 20	3LTS5	300091
UK Great Britain	USSR (Soviet Union)	16 Mar 21	4LTS127	300104
Czechoslovakia	Romania	23 Apr 21	15LTS235	300397
Austria	Czechoslovakia	04 May 21	15LTS13	300388
Multilateral		12 Jul 21	11LTS111	300293
UK Great Britain	USSR (Soviet Union)	06 Dec 21	31LTS85	300785
Belgian Colonies	Fr Equatorial Afri	04 May 22	148LTS61	303403
Belgian Colonies	Tanganyika	10 Jul 22	148LTS71	303404
Hungary	Italy	27 Mar 24	55LTS109	301308
Finland	USSR (Soviet Union)	18 Jun 24	29LTS295	300746
Finland	USSR (Soviet Union)	18 Jun 24	29LTS265	300745
Spain	UK Great Britain	27 Jun 24	28LTS523	300727
Belgium	UK Great Britain	29 Jul 24	29LTS389	300749
Italy	Serb/Croat/Slovene	12 Aug 24	82LTS401	301881
Italy	Serb/Croat/Slovene	20 Jul 25	83LTS295	301897
Multilateral		29 Oct 25	57LTS201	301365
Czechoslovakia	Poland	21 Apr 26	58LTS9	301367
Great Britain	Netherlands	27 Apr 26	50LTS295	301212
Multilateral		01 Nov 26	78LTS109	301782
Multilateral		25 Feb 27	78LTS123	301783
Multilateral		08 Mar 27	78LTS134	301784
Netherlands	UK Great Britain	11 Mar 27	64LTS403	301513
Multilateral		15 Jun 27	69LTS375	301619
Multilateral		16 Aug 27	78LTS141	301785
Multilateral		11 Nov 27	78LTS153	301786
Multilateral		21 Nov 27	78LTS163	301787
Multilateral		25 Nov 27	84LTS97	301905
Multilateral		07 Jan 28	78LTS187	301789
Multilateral		08 Mar 28	80LTS241	301829
Multilateral		19 Mar 28	78LTS177	301788
Multilateral		23 Apr 28	78LTS197	301790
Multilateral		25 Apr 28	78LTS207	301791
Multilateral		22 May 28	85LTS99	301925
Multilateral		09 Jun 28	78LTS219	301792
Multilateral		09 Dec 32	151LTS5	303479
Gold Coast	Togo	07 Oct 33	144LTS95	303321
Belgium	Netherlands	01 Aug 34	153LTS267	303520
UK Great Britain	USA (United States)	27 Mar 41	204LTS15	304784
Cable				
Denmark	Sweden	08 Jun 21	14LTS195	300374
Denmark	Norway	21 Jul 21	13LTS357	300362
Estonia	Finland	29 Oct 21	13LTS167	300350
UK Great Britain	USSR (Soviet Union)	06 Dec 21	31LTS85	300785
China	Japan	04 Feb 22	10LTS309	300277
Norway	Sweden	29 Mar 22	13LTS311	300361
Belgian Colonies	Fr Equatorial Afri	04 May 22	148LTS61	303403
Belgian Colonies	Tanganyika	10 Jul 22	148LTS71	303404
Multilateral		18 Aug 22	13LTS289	300360
Estonia	Finland	28 Nov 22	19LTS213	300494
Albania	Italy	04 Dec 22	15LTS213	300395
Netherlands	UK Great Britain	23 Jan 23	16LTS425	300420
Italy	Serb/Croat/Slovene	12 Aug 24	82LTS401	301881
Estonia	Finland	20 Apr 25	51LTS31	301220
Multilateral		05 May 25	55LTS225	301318
Italy	Serb/Croat/Slovene	20 Jul 25	83LTS295	301897
Multilateral		30 Oct 26	61LTS65	301426
Multilateral		18 Dec 26	63LTS185	301489
Belgium	UK Great Britain	09 Apr 27	67LTS209	301548
France	UK Great Britain	23 May 27	67LTS227	301550
Multilateral		09 Dec 32	151LTS5	303479
Estonia	Finland	16 Apr 36	171LTS55	303950

PARTY ONE	PARTY TWO	DATE	CITATION	NUMBER
Services				
Multilateral		09 Feb 20	2LTS7	300041
Belgium	Netherlands	08 Mar 20	1LTS25	300003
Denmark	Sweden	08 Jun 21	14LTS195	300374
Multilateral		12 Jul 21	11LTS111	300293
Denmark	Norway	21 Jul 21	13LTS357	300362
Estonia	Finland	29 Oct 21	13LTS167	300350
UK Great Britain	USSR (Soviet Union)	06 Dec 21	31LTS85	300785
Norway	Sweden	29 Mar 22	13LTS311	300361
Belgian Colonies	Fr Equatorial Afri	04 May 22	148LTS61	303403
Belgian Colonies	Tanganyika	10 Jul 22	148LTS71	303404
Multilateral		18 Aug 22	13LTS289	300360
China	Japan	01 Dec 22	22LTS179	300559
Netherlands	UK Great Britain	23 Jan 23	16LTS425	300420
Persia	Russ Fed Sov Rep	27 Apr 23	110LTS333	302565
Finland	USSR (Soviet Union)	18 Jun 24	29LTS295	300746
Finland	USSR (Soviet Union)	18 Jun 24	29LTS265	300745
Belgium	UK Great Britain	29 Jul 24	29LTS389	300749
Italy	Serb/Croat/Slovene	12 Aug 24	82LTS401	301881
Multilateral		12 Dec 24	37LTS113	300950
Estonia	Finland	20 Apr 25	51LTS31	301220
Multilateral		05 May 25	55LTS225	301318
Multilateral		29 Oct 25	57LTS201	301365
Germany	Netherlands	24 Mar 26	51LTS245	301234
Germany	Norway	15 Jun 26	51LTS329	301238
Spain	UK Great Britain	19 Oct 26	61LTS79	301427
Multilateral		30 Oct 26	61LTS65	301426
Multilateral		01 Nov 26	78LTS109	301782
Germany	Netherlands	03 Nov 26	68LTS111	301575
Multilateral		22 Jan 27	68LTS149	301578
Multilateral		22 Jan 27	68LTS129	301576
Multilateral		19 Feb 27	68LTS139	301577
Multilateral		24 Feb 27	68LTS159	301579
Multilateral		25 Feb 27	78LTS123	301783
Belgium	Netherlands	28 Feb 27	68LTS169	301580
Multilateral		08 Mar 27	78LTS134	301784
Netherlands	UK Great Britain	11 Mar 27	64LTS403	301513
Multilateral		18 Mar 27	68LTS179	301581
Belgium	UK Great Britain	09 Apr 27	67LTS209	301548
Multilateral		02 May 27	68LTS189	301582
France	UK Great Britain	23 May 27	67LTS227	301550
Multilateral		15 Jun 27	69LTS375	301619
Multilateral		16 Aug 27	78LTS141	301785
Germany	Serb/Croat/Slovene	06 Oct 27	77LTS19	301763
Multilateral		11 Nov 27	78LTS153	301786
Multilateral		21 Nov 27	78LTS163	301787
Multilateral		07 Jan 28	78LTS187	301789
Multilateral		08 Mar 28	80LTS241	301829
Multilateral		19 Mar 28	78LTS177	301788
Multilateral		23 Apr 28	78LTS197	301790
Multilateral		25 Apr 28	78LTS207	301791
Multilateral		22 May 28	85LTS99	301925
Multilateral		09 Jun 28	78LTS219	301792
Cuba	Mexico	29 Jun 28	124LTS189	302833
Finland	Sweden	10 Jul 28	87LTS131	301966
Multilateral		12 Sep 28	104LTS43	302377
Multilateral		30 Nov 28	87LTS119	301965
Denmark	Sweden	13 Dec 28	104LTS55	302378
Multilateral		22 Dec 28	104LTS103	302381
Multilateral		14 Jan 29	87LTS169	301968
Multilateral		16 Jan 29	87LTS155	301967
Multilateral		02 Feb 29	92LTS353	302100
Poland	Romania	30 Mar 29	123LTS147	302812
Multilateral		08 May 29	91LTS337	302074
Multilateral		07 Sep 29	98LTS345	302255

PARTY ONE	PARTY TWO	DATE	CITATION	NUMBER
Services (Cont.)				
Multilateral		25 Sep 29	98LTS361	302256
Multilateral		26 Sep 29	98LTS395	302259
Multilateral		30 Sep 29	99LTS71	302269
Multilateral		30 Sep 29	98LTS183	302246
Multilateral		01 Oct 29	98LTS197	302247
Multilateral		08 Oct 29	98LTS409	302260
Multilateral		10 Oct 29	98LTS375	302257
Multilateral		29 Oct 29	99LTS85	302270
Poland	Romania	30 Oct 29	121LTS167	302787
Multilateral		18 Nov 29	99LTS415	302287
Multilateral		14 Jan 30	99LTS343	302278
Multilateral		25 Feb 30	101LTS343	302335
Multilateral		10 Apr 30	101LTS465	302345
Multilateral		09 Dec 32	151LTS5	303479
Bulgaria	Czechoslovakia	29 Aug 33	148LTS15	303402
Gold Coast	Togo	07 Oct 33	144LTS95	303321
Multilateral		30 Oct 35	189LTS51	304375
United Arab Rep	UK Great Britain	12 Aug 36	182LTS311	304218
Multilateral		11 Feb 37	186LTS55	304303
Lithuania	Poland	22 May 38	191LTS359	304455
Latvia	Poland	16 Jun 38	196LTS105	304573
Telegrams				
Belgium	Netherlands	08 Mar 20	1LTS25	300003
Denmark	Finland	27 Jul 20	19LTS71	300484
Denmark	Germany	30 Aug 20	14LTS257	300377
France	Italy	12 Sep 20	1LTS397	300033
Liechtenstein	Switzerland	10 Nov 20	2LTS305	300084
Netherlands	UK Great Britain	18 Jan 21	5LTS157	300124
Denmark	Sweden	08 Jun 21	14LTS195	300374
Multilateral		12 Jul 21	11LTS111	300293
Denmark	Norway	21 Jul 21	13LTS357	300362
Multilateral		19 Sep 21	15LTS191	300392
UK Great Britain	USSR (Soviet Union)	06 Dec 21	31LTS85	300785
Finland	USSR (Soviet Union)	14 Dec 21	16LTS221	300414
Norway	Sweden	29 Mar 22	13LTS311	300361
Belgian Colonies	Fr Equatorial Afri	04 May 22	148LTS61	303403
Finland	USSR (Soviet Union)	13 Jun 22	16LTS349	300416
Belgian Colonies	Tanganyika	10 Jul 22	148LTS71	303404
Estonia	Finland	28 Nov 22	19LTS213	300494
China	Japan	08 Dec 22	20LTS253	300521
Portugal	Spain	26 Mar 23	18LTS349	300475
Persia	Russ Fed Sov Rep	27 Apr 23	110LTS333	302565
Multilateral		24 May 23	50LTS341	301218
Sweden	USSR (Soviet Union)	15 Mar 24	25LTS251	300613
Hungary	Italy	27 Mar 24	55LTS109	301308
Finland	USSR (Soviet Union)	18 Jun 24	29LTS265	300745
Belgium	UK Great Britain	29 Jul 24	29LTS389	300749
Belgium	UK Great Britain	26 Feb 25	71LTS83	301656
Estonia	Finland	20 Apr 25	51LTS31	301220
Czechoslovakia	Poland	30 May 25	50LTS243	301207
Italy	UK Great Britain	20 Dec 25	49LTS79	301178
Hungary	UK Great Britain	28 Dec 25	49LTS125	301179
Estonia	UK Great Britain	15 Mar 26	50LTS219	301204
Germany	Netherlands	24 Mar 26	51LTS245	301234
Great Britain	Netherlands	27 Apr 26	50LTS295	301212
Estonia	Great Britain	12 Oct 26	60LTS387	301422
Spain	UK Great Britain	19 Oct 26	61LTS79	301427
Belgium	Portugal	19 Jul 27	71LTS419	301680
Brazil	Peru	31 Dec 28	127LTS455	302931
Denmark	Norway	21 Jan 29	104LTS119	302382
Denmark	Sweden	28 Feb 29	104LTS69	302379
Poland	Romania	30 Mar 29	123LTS147	302812
France	UK Great Britain	15 May 29	134LTS263	303097
Poland	Romania	30 Oct 29	121LTS167	302787

PARTY ONE	PARTY TWO	DATE	CITATION	NUMBER
Telegrams (Cont.)				
France	UK Great Britain	24 Mar 30	105LTS227	302415
Romania	UK Great Britain	02 Apr 30	105LTS235	302416
Austria	Hungary	03 Jun 30	122LTS69	302799
Multilateral		06 May 31	120LTS217	302767
Multilateral		10 Nov 31	131LTS389	303024
Germany	Lithuania	20 Nov 31	133LTS391	303077
Romania	Yugoslavia	14 Dec 31	135LTS31	303103
Multilateral		17 Feb 32	138LTS61	303181
Multilateral		09 Dec 32	151LTS5	303479
Belgium	Netherlands	01 Aug 34	153LTS267	303520
Estonia	Finland	16 Apr 36	171LTS55	303950
Multilateral		11 Feb 37	186LTS55	304303
Lithuania	Poland	25 May 38	191LTS391	304457
France	UK Great Britain	13 Sep 39	201LTS369	304724
Radio-telephone-telegraphic communications				
Multilateral		05 Jun 12	1LTS135	300013
France	UK Great Britain	10 Jan 20	5LTS53	300117
Liechtenstein	Switzerland	10 Nov 20	2LTS305	300084
Estonia	Finland	29 Oct 21	13LTS159	300349
Belgium	Luxembourg	27 Dec 21	12LTS253	300318
France	Switzerland	24 Jan 22	12LTS371	300331
Belgian Colonies	Fr Equatorial Afri	04 May 22	148LTS61	303403
Belgian Colonies	Tanganyika	10 Jul 22	148LTS71	303404
Finland	Norway	07 Sep 22	12LTS357	300328
Albania	Italy	05 Dec 22	15LTS203	300394
Finland	USSR (Soviet Union)	18 Jun 24	29LTS295	300746
Multilateral		12 Dec 24	37LTS113	300950
Multilateral		05 May 25	55LTS225	301318
Bulgaria	Great Britain	07 May 25	38LTS153	300973
Austria	Germany	19 May 25	52LTS121	301253
Multilateral		29 Oct 25	57LTS201	301365
Spain	UK Great Britain	19 Oct 26	61LTS79	301427
Multilateral		30 Oct 26	61LTS65	301426
Germany	Netherlands	03 Nov 26	68LTS111	301575
Multilateral		22 Jan 27	68LTS129	301576
Multilateral		22 Jan 27	68LTS149	301578
Multilateral		19 Feb 27	68LTS139	301577
Multilateral		24 Feb 27	68LTS159	301579
Belgium	Netherlands	28 Feb 27	68LTS169	301580
Multilateral		18 Mar 27	68LTS179	301581
Multilateral		02 May 27	68LTS189	301582
Czechoslovakia	Poland	30 May 27	98LTS233	302251
Germany	UK Great Britain	29 Jun 27	71LTS165	301659
Multilateral		25 Nov 27	84LTS97	301905
Germany	Spain	09 Dec 27	79LTS203	301811
Multilateral		10 Mar 28	132LTS405	303049
Multilateral		01 May 28	132LTS415	303050
Hungary	Italy	04 Jul 28	92LTS117	302083
Finland	Sweden	10 Jul 28	87LTS131	301966
Multilateral		12 Sep 28	104LTS43	302377
Multilateral		27 Nov 28	92LTS321	302098
Multilateral		30 Nov 28	87LTS119	301965
Denmark	Sweden	13 Dec 28	104LTS55	302378
Multilateral		22 Dec 28	104LTS103	302381
Brazil	Peru	31 Dec 28	127LTS455	302931
Multilateral		05 Jan 29	132LTS425	303051
Multilateral		14 Jan 29	87LTS169	301968
Multilateral		16 Jan 29	87LTS155	301967
Denmark	Norway	21 Jan 29	104LTS119	302382
Multilateral		02 Feb 29	92LTS353	302100
Denmark	Sweden	28 Feb 29	104LTS69	302379
Multilateral		08 May 29	91LTS337	302074
Multilateral		30 Aug 29	96LTS129	302195
Multilateral		07 Sep 29	98LTS345	302255

PARTY ONE	PARTY TWO	DATE	CITATION	NUMBER
Radio-telephone-telegraphic communications (Cont.)				
Multilateral		25 Sep 29	98LTS361	302256
Multilateral		26 Sep 29	98LTS395	302259
Multilateral		30 Sep 29	99LTS71	302269
Multilateral		30 Sep 29	98LTS183	302246
Multilateral		01 Oct 29	98LTS197	302247
Multilateral		08 Oct 29	98LTS409	302260
Multilateral		10 Oct 29	98LTS375	302257
Multilateral		28 Oct 29	97LTS71	302219
Multilateral		29 Oct 29	99LTS85	302270
Multilateral		18 Nov 29	99LTS415	302287
Estonia	Latvia	20 Dec 29	106LTS173	302444
Multilateral		14 Jan 30	99LTS343	302278
Multilateral		25 Feb 30	101LTS343	302335
France	UK Great Britain	24 Mar 30	105LTS227	302415
Multilateral		10 Apr 30	101LTS465	302345
Multilateral		26 Jun 30	133LTS9	303052
Multilateral		28 Aug 30	133LTS21	303053
Multilateral		09 Dec 32	151LTS5	303479
Gold Coast	Togo	07 Oct 33	144LTS95	303321
Chile	USA (United States)	17 Aug 34	157LTS15	303602
Multilateral		11 Feb 37	186LTS55	304303
Multilateral		08 Dec 38	202LTS49	304734
Canada	USA (United States)	20 Dec 38	196LTS171	304580
Canada	USA (United States)	20 Feb 39	197LTS181	304613
Greece	UK Great Britain	30 May 39	202LTS7	304732
Publications exchange				
Iceland	Norway	10 Aug 23	20LTS363	300527
Multilateral		11 Oct 33	155LTS331	303585
Mass media exchange				
Brazil	Peru	31 Dec 28	127LTS455	302931
Multilateral		19 Jun 33	154LTS133	303544
Multilateral		20 Mar 34	176LTS55	304054
Information agency				
Denmark	Norway	21 Jul 21	13LTS357	300362
Norway	Sweden	29 Mar 22	13LTS311	300361
Press and wire services				
Denmark	Finland	27 Jul 20	19LTS71	300484
Denmark	Germany	30 Aug 20	14LTS257	300377
Denmark	Sweden	08 Jun 21	14LTS195	300374
Denmark	Norway	21 Jul 21	13LTS357	300362
Norway	Sweden	29 Mar 22	13LTS311	300361
Brazil	Peru	31 Dec 28	127LTS455	302931
Multilateral		20 Mar 34	176LTS55	304054
General military				
Multilateral		10 Sep 19	7LTS331	300200
Multilateral		04 Jun 20	6LTS187	300152
Czechoslovakia	Italy	23 Mar 21	32LTS183	300815
Norway	Sweden	26 May 23	18LTS155	300462
Finland	USSR (Soviet Union)	05 Jun 23	18LTS203	300465
Estonia	Sweden	07 Jul 23	20LTS189	300517
Estonia	Iceland	07 Sep 23	23LTS131	300584
Italy	Spain	15 Nov 23	39LTS49	300996
Lithuania	Sweden	17 Feb 24	23LTS153	300587
Multilateral		05 May 25	55LTS225	301318
Czechoslovakia	Denmark	24 Jul 25	37LTS97	300948
Multilateral		30 Aug 29	104LTS473	302399
Greece	UK Great Britain	17 Apr 31	129LTS287	302965
Multilateral		01 Jan 42	204LTS381	304817
Repatriation of combatants				
Estonia	USSR (Soviet Union)	02 Feb 20	11LTS29	300289
UK Great Britain	USSR (Soviet Union)	12 Feb 20	1LTS263	300019
Germany	USSR (Soviet Union)	19 Apr 20	2LTS63	300048

PARTY ONE	PARTY TWO	DATE	CITATION	NUMBER
Repatriation of combatants (Cont.)				
Germany	Latvia	20 Apr 20	2LTS71	300049
Germany	USSR (Soviet Union)	07 Jul 20	2LTS85	300051
Lithuania	USSR (Soviet Union)	12 Jul 20	3LTS106	300094
Latvia	USSR (Soviet Union)	11 Aug 20	2LTS195	300067
Poland	USSR (Soviet Union)	12 Oct 20	4LTS7	300101
Germany	Poland	12 Feb 21	9LTS149	300247
Multilateral		24 Jul 23	28LTS11	300701
Multilateral		27 Jul 29	118LTS343	302734
Joint defense				
Italy	Romania	16 Sep 26	67LTS393	301560
Defense and security				
France	UK Great Britain	06 Aug 14	10LTS333	300278
Czechoslovakia	Serb/Croat/Slovene	14 Aug 20	6LTS209	300154
Multilateral		19 Jan 21	5LTS9	300113
Persia	USSR (Soviet Union)	26 Feb 21	9LTS383	300268
Poland	Romania	03 Mar 21	7LTS77	300175
Czechoslovakia	Romania	23 Apr 21	6LTS215	300155
Latvia	Ukrainian SSR	03 Aug 21	17LTS317	300442
Estonia	Ukrainian SSR	25 Nov 21	11LTS121	300294
Czechoslovakia	Serb/Croat/Slovene	31 Aug 22	13LTS231	300354
Estonia	Latvia	01 Nov 23	23LTS81	300578
Czechoslovakia	France	25 Jan 24	23LTS163	300588
Italy	Serb/Croat/Slovene	27 Jan 24	24LTS31	300596
France	Poland	16 Oct 25	54LTS353	301297
Czechoslovakia	France	16 Oct 25	54LTS359	301298
Romania	Serb/Croat/Slovene	13 Jun 26	54LTS257	301289
Albania	Italy	27 Nov 26	60LTS15	301402
Bel-Lux Econ Union	Greece	22 Nov 27	69LTS341	301616
Persia	Turkey	15 Jun 28	106LTS247	302449
Romania	Yugoslavia	27 Jun 30	107LTS215	302478
Iraq	UK Great Britain	30 Jun 30	132LTS363	303048
Multilateral		04 Jul 33	148LTS211	303414
Lithuania	USSR (Soviet Union)	05 Jul 33	148LTS79	303405
Multilateral		09 Feb 34	153LTS153	303514
France	USSR (Soviet Union)	02 May 35	167LTS395	303881
Panama	USA (United States)	02 Mar 36	200LTS17	304686
Iraq	Saudi Arabia	02 Apr 36	174LTS131	304044
United Arab Rep	UK Great Britain	26 Aug 36	173LTS401	304031
France	UK Great Britain	24 Apr 37	178LTS186	304112
China	USSR (Soviet Union)	21 Aug 37	181LTS101	304180
Multilateral		16 Apr 38	195LTS103	304538
Poland	UK Great Britain	25 Aug 39	199LTS57	304665
Multilateral		19 Oct 39	200LTS167	304689
UK Great Britain	USSR (Soviet Union)	12 Jul 41	204LTS277	304808
UK Great Britain	USA (United States)	23 Feb 42	204LTS389	304818
Prisoners of war				
Estonia	USSR (Soviet Union)	02 Feb 20	11LTS29	300289
Germany	Hungary	08 May 20	2LTS79	300050
Lithuania	Poland	29 Nov 20	9LTS63	300243
Germany	USSR (Soviet Union)	06 May 21	6LTS267	300159
Germany	Saar	13 Nov 22	27LTS273	300690
Greece	Turkey	30 Jan 23	36LTS137	300912
Multilateral		24 Jul 23	28LTS11	300701
Multilateral		24 Jul 23	36LTS145	300913
France	Turkey	31 Jul 26	54LTS177	301284
Norway	South Africa	25 Jan 27	60LTS277	301416
Multilateral		27 Jul 29	118LTS343	302734
Repatriation of civilians				
Estonia	USSR (Soviet Union)	02 Feb 20	11LTS29	300289
UK Great Britain	USSR (Soviet Union)	12 Feb 20	1LTS263	300019
Germany	USSR (Soviet Union)	19 Apr 20	2LTS63	300048
Germany	Latvia	20 Apr 20	2LTS71	300049
Germany	USSR (Soviet Union)	07 Jul 20	2LTS85	300051

PARTY ONE	PARTY TWO	DATE	CITATION	NUMBER
Repatriation of civilians (Cont.)				
Lithuania	USSR (Soviet Union)	12 Jul 20	3LTS106	300094
Latvia	USSR (Soviet Union)	11 Aug 20	2LTS195	300067
Poland	USSR (Soviet Union)	12 Oct 20	4LTS7	300101
Germany	Poland	12 Feb 21	9LTS149	300247
Multilateral		24 Jul 23	28LTS11	300701
Multilateral		27 Jul 29	118LTS343	302734
Self-defense				
Multilateral		06 Feb 22	25LTS201	300609
Poland	Turkey	23 Jul 23	49LTS329	301189
Estonia	Latvia	01 Nov 23	23LTS81	300578
Iraq	UK Great Britain	25 Mar 24	35LTS103	300892
Poland	Serb/Croat/Slovene	05 Apr 24	49LTS265	301185
Multilateral		16 Oct 25	54LTS289	301292
Poland	Romania	26 Mar 26	60LTS161	301411
Multilateral		14 Sep 37	181LTS137	304184
Denmark	USA (United States)	09 Apr 41	204LTS135	304792
Payment for war supplies				
Estonia	Latvia	01 Nov 23	25LTS341	300622
Iraq	UK Great Britain	25 Mar 24	35LTS145	300894
Multilateral		05 May 25	55LTS225	301318
Great Britain	Latvia	13 Aug 25	56LTS177	301329
Portugal	UK Great Britain	31 Dec 26	61LTS115	301429
Greece	UK Great Britain	09 Apr 27	67LTS217	301549
Lease of military property				
Iraq	UK Great Britain	25 Mar 24	35LTS103	300892
Iraq	UK Great Britain	25 Mar 24	35LTS145	300894
Japan	USA (United States)	25 Mar 37	181LTS217	304191
Japan	UK Great Britain	25 Mar 37	181LTS289	304196
Military assistance				
Poland	Romania	03 Mar 21	7LTS77	300175
Iraq	UK Great Britain	25 Mar 24	35LTS103	300892
Romania	Serb/Croat/Slovene	13 Jun 26	54LTS257	301289
Bel-Lux Econ Union	Greece	22 Nov 27	69LTS341	301616
France	USSR (Soviet Union)	02 May 35	167LTS395	303881
Germany	Romania	23 Mar 39	199LTS77	304668
Poland	UK Great Britain	25 Aug 39	199LTS57	304665
Estonia	USSR (Soviet Union)	28 Sep 39	198LTS223	304643
Latvia	USSR (Soviet Union)	05 Oct 39	198LTS381	304656
Multilateral		19 Oct 39	200LTS167	304689
UK Great Britain	USSR (Soviet Union)	26 May 42	204LTS353	304813
Norway	USA (United States)	11 Jul 42	204LTS415	304821
Naval vessels				
Multilateral		06 Feb 22	25LTS201	300609
Japan	Siam	09 Mar 24	31LTS187	300795
Brazil	Colombia	15 Nov 28	100LTS123	302299
France	Spain	07 Mar 32	148LTS385	303424
Italy	Spain	30 Jul 32	149LTS9	303427
Brazil	Germany	14 Jun 33	178LTS19	304102
Multilateral		20 Jul 36	173LTS213	304015
Multilateral		14 Sep 37	181LTS137	304184
Bel-Lux Econ Union	Siam	05 Nov 37	190LTS151	304413
Poland	UK Great Britain	25 Nov 39	199LTS65	304666
UK Great Britain	Venezuela	26 Feb 42	205LTS121	304829
Return of equipment and recapture				
Germany	USA (United States)	25 Aug 21	12LTS191	300310
Estonia	Ukrainian SSR	25 Nov 21	11LTS121	300294
Military training				
Brazil	USA (United States)	27 May 36	171LTS343	303971
Brazil	USA (United States)	12 Nov 36	176LTS133	304057
Brazil	USA (United States)	12 Nov 38	195LTS375	304557
Colombia	USA (United States)	23 Nov 38	196LTS147	304578
Colombia	USA (United States)	23 Nov 38	196LTS157	304579

PARTY ONE	PARTY TWO	DATE	CITATION	NUMBER
Military training (Cont.)				
Guatemala	USA (United States)	28 Mar 39	199LTS181	304671
Nicaragua	USA (United States)	22 May 39	199LTS189	304672
Argentina	USA (United States)	12 Sep 39	201LTS213	304715
Chile	USA (United States)	23 Apr 40	203LTS29	304747
Argentina	USA (United States)	29 Jun 40	203LTS57	304750
Peru	USA (United States)	31 Jul 40	203LTS91	304752
Peru	USA (United States)	31 Jul 40	203LTS75	304751
Ecuador	USA (United States)	12 Dec 40	203LTS327	304773
Ecuador	USA (United States)	12 Dec 40	203LTS305	304771
Brazil	USA (United States)	17 Jan 41	204LTS97	304788
USA (United States)	Venezuela	24 Mar 41	204LTS83	304787
Peru	USA (United States)	15 Apr 41	204LTS117	304790
Nicaragua	USA (United States)	22 May 41	204LTS283	304809
Guatemala	USA (United States)	27 May 41	204LTS185	304799
Costa Rica	USA (United States)	14 Jul 41	204LTS231	304802
Surplus war property				
Germany	USA (United States)	25 Aug 21	12LTS191	300310
Siam	UK Great Britain	15 Sep 25	49LTS51	301176
Norway	USA (United States)	11 Jul 42	204LTS415	304821
Airforce-army-navy personnel ratio				
Chile	USA (United States)	23 Apr 40	203LTS29	304747
Peru	USA (United States)	31 Jul 40	203LTS91	304752
Peru	USA (United States)	31 Jul 40	203LTS75	304751
Ecuador	USA (United States)	12 Dec 40	203LTS327	304773
Ecuador	USA (United States)	12 Dec 40	203LTS305	304771
Brazil	USA (United States)	17 Jan 41	204LTS97	304788
USA (United States)	Venezuela	24 Mar 41	204LTS83	304787
Costa Rica	USA (United States)	14 Jul 41	204LTS231	304802
Ranks and privileges				
Austria	Czechoslovakia	02 Aug 20	32LTS365	300826
Peru	USA (United States)	31 Jul 40	203LTS75	304751
Peru	USA (United States)	31 Jul 40	203LTS91	304752
Conditions for assistance missions				
Peru	USA (United States)	31 Jul 40	203LTS75	304751
Peru	USA (United States)	31 Jul 40	203LTS91	304752
Ecuador	USA (United States)	12 Dec 40	203LTS327	304773
Ecuador	USA (United States)	12 Dec 40	203LTS305	304771
Brazil	USA (United States)	17 Jan 41	204LTS97	304788
USA (United States)	Venezuela	24 Mar 41	204LTS83	304787
Peru	USA (United States)	15 Apr 41	204LTS117	304790
Nicaragua	USA (United States)	22 May 41	204LTS283	304809
Guatemala	USA (United States)	27 May 41	204LTS185	304799
Costa Rica	USA (United States)	14 Jul 41	204LTS231	304802
Jurisdiction				
Estonia	USSR (Soviet Union)	02 Feb 20	11LTS29	300289
United Arab Rep	UK Great Britain	21 Oct 37	184LTS285	304252
United Arab Rep	USA (United States)	02 Mar 43	204LTS425	304822
Procurement and logistics				
Spain	UK Great Britain	27 Jun 24	28LTS523	300727
Multilateral		05 May 25	55LTS225	301318
Great Britain	Italy	10 Sep 26	57LTS77	301354
Multilateral		30 Aug 29	104LTS473	302399
Withdrawal of forces				
Latvia	USSR (Soviet Union)	11 Aug 20	2LTS195	300067
China	Japan	04 Feb 22	10LTS309	300277
China	Japan	28 Mar 22	13LTS213	300353
China	Japan	01 Dec 22	22LTS179	300559
France	Turkey	31 Jul 26	54LTS177	301284
Haiti	USA (United States)	07 Aug 33	146LTS305	303381
Haiti	USA (United States)	24 Jul 34	153LTS285	303523

PARTY ONE	PARTY TWO	DATE	CITATION	NUMBER
Status of forces				
Estonia	USSR (Soviet Union)	02 Feb 20	11LTS29	300289
Brazil	USA (United States)	10 May 34	150LTS445	303477
Brazil	USA (United States)	27 May 36	171LTS343	303971
United Arab Rep	UK Great Britain	26 Aug 36	173LTS433	304032
Brazil	USA (United States)	12 Nov 36	176LTS133	304057
United Arab Rep	UK Great Britain	21 Oct 37	184LTS285	304252
UK Great Britain	USA (United States)	27 Mar 41	204LTS15	304784
United Arab Rep	USA (United States)	02 Mar 43	204LTS425	304822
Military installations and equipment				
Multilateral		06 Feb 22	25LTS201	300609
Multilateral		25 Nov 27	84LTS97	301905
Turkey	UK Great Britain	27 May 38	199LTS9	304660
Exchange of defense information				
Norway	USA (United States)	11 Jul 42	204LTS415	304821
Bases and facilities				
Multilateral		05 May 25	55LTS225	301318
Estonia	USSR (Soviet Union)	28 Sep 39	198LTS223	304643
Latvia	USSR (Soviet Union)	05 Oct 39	198LTS381	304656
UK Great Britain	USA (United States)	02 Sep 40	203LTS201	304762
UK Great Britain	USA (United States)	27 Mar 41	204LTS15	304784
Denmark	USA (United States)	09 Apr 41	204LTS135	304792
Restrictions on transfer				
Nepal	UK Great Britain	21 Dec 23	36LTS357	300934
Military service and citizenship				
Austria	Spain	03 Feb 25	43LTS313	301067
Albania	Serb/Croat/Slovene	22 Jun 26	91LTS55	302055
Greece	Spain	23 Sep 26	91LTS121	302059
Germany	Greece	24 Mar 28	90LTS9	302031
Dual nationality				
Multilateral		12 Apr 30	178LTS227	304117
Lithuania	USA (United States)	18 Oct 37	191LTS351	304454
Switzerland	USA (United States)	11 Nov 37	193LTS183	304494
Finland	USA (United States)	27 Jan 39	201LTS187	304713
Foreign nationals				
Czechoslovakia	Italy	23 Mar 21	32LTS183	300815
Austria	Czechoslovakia	04 May 21	15LTS13	300388
Italy	Poland	12 May 22	59LTS293	301399
Japan	Poland	07 Dec 22	32LTS61	300806
Denmark	Finland	21 Apr 23	17LTS57	300428
Germany	Lithuania	01 Jun 23	51LTS387	301244
Denmark	Poland	14 Jul 23	19LTS65	300483
Poland	Turkey	23 Jul 23	49LTS345	301190
Multilateral		24 Jul 23	28LTS151	300704
Germany	South Africa	23 Oct 23	28LTS417	300721
Finland	Poland	10 Nov 23	29LTS229	300744
Japan	Serb/Croat/Slovene	16 Nov 23	42LTS99	301035
Multilateral		14 Dec 23	29LTS37	300732
Finland	UK Great Britain	14 Dec 23	29LTS129	300739
Latvia	Poland	03 Jan 24	42LTS451	301043
Estonia	Poland	11 Jan 24	47LTS129	301132
Czechoslovakia	Denmark	31 Jan 24	23LTS139	300585
Albania	Italy	29 Feb 24	44LTS331	301092
Japan	Siam	09 Mar 24	31LTS187	300795
Denmark	Latvia	03 Apr 24	33LTS393	300860
Poland	Serb/Croat/Slovene	05 Apr 24	49LTS265	301185
Multilateral		08 May 24	29LTS85	300736
Multilateral		22 May 24	35LTS175	300895
Austria	Latvia	09 Aug 24	65LTS7	301516
Italy	Serb/Croat/Slovene	21 Aug 24	82LTS445	301883
Finland	Latvia	23 Aug 24	37LTS383	300962
Japan	Peru	30 Sep 24	102LTS33	302351

PARTY ONE	PARTY TWO	DATE	CITATION	NUMBER
Foreign nationals (Cont.)				
Finland	Italy	22 Oct 24	32LTS149	300814
Latvia	Switzerland	04 Dec 24	34LTS405	300889
France	Poland	09 Dec 24	44LTS127	301081
Bulgaria	Turkey	27 Dec 24	54LTS135	301281
Bulgaria	Poland	29 Apr 25	60LTS103	301408
Germany	USA (United States)	21 May 25	52LTS133	301254
Netherlands	Siam	08 Jun 25	56LTS57	301323
Japan	Latvia	04 Jul 25	80LTS305	301836
Bel-Lux Econ Union		07 Jul 25	54LTS267	301290
Siam	Spain	03 Aug 25	55LTS39	301303
Germany	UK Great Britain	13 Aug 25	43LTS89	301050
Portugal	Siam	14 Aug 25	55LTS57	301304
Siam	UK Great Britain	15 Sep 25	49LTS51	301176
Germany	USSR (Soviet Union)	12 Oct 25	53LTS7	301257
Germany	USSR (Soviet Union)	12 Oct 25	53LTS163	301258
Estonia	Switzerland	14 Oct 25	49LTS421	301195
Austria	China	19 Oct 25	55LTS9	301301
Czechoslovakia	Japan	30 Oct 25	58LTS263	301377
Germany	Italy	31 Oct 25	52LTS179	301256
Norway	USSR (Soviet Union)	15 Dec 25	47LTS9	301127
Siam	Sweden	19 Dec 25	58LTS429	301386
Estonia	USA (United States)	23 Dec 25	50LTS13	301197
Bel-Lux Econ Union	Czechoslovakia	28 Dec 25	58LTS189	301372
Estonia	UK Great Britain	18 Jan 26	48LTS209	301163
Denmark	Siam	01 Mar 26	47LTS103	301131
Finland	Hungary	20 Apr 26	48LTS119	301154
Czechoslovakia	Poland	21 Apr 26	58LTS9	301367
Italy	Siam	09 May 26	61LTS215	301436
Germany	Sweden	14 May 26	51LTS99	301225
Finland	Turkey	02 Jun 26	70LTS329	301644
Finland	Germany	26 Jun 26	56LTS203	301332
Germany	Latvia	28 Jun 26	58LTS403	301385
Bel-Lux Econ Union	Siam	13 Jul 26	62LTS287	301468
Norway	Siam	16 Jul 26	60LTS35	301404
Hungary	UK Great Britain	23 Jul 26	67LTS183	301546
Hungary	USA (United States)	04 Sep 26	58LTS111	301369
Greece	Sweden	10 Sep 26	63LTS37	301479
Guatemala	Italy	15 Sep 26	70LTS175	301633
Bel-Lux Econ Union	Estonia	28 Sep 26	62LTS433	301475
Austria	Estonia	15 Oct 26	93LTS137	302106
Greece	Italy	24 Oct 26	63LTS51	301480
Denmark	Germany	28 Oct 26	57LTS185	301363
Finland	Greece	18 Dec 26	70LTS89	301626
Hungary	Turkey	20 Dec 26	72LTS245	301696
Estonia	Latvia	05 Feb 27	62LTS319	301470
Estonia	Poland	19 Feb 27	115LTS177	302686
Greece	Latvia	25 Feb 27	71LTS25	301652
Serb/Croat/Slovene	UK Great Britain	12 May 27	80LTS165	301825
Greece	UK Great Britain	13 May 27	61LTS15	301425
Czechoslovakia	Poland	30 May 27	98LTS233	302251
Czechoslovakia	Turkey	31 May 27	75LTS79	301753
Argentina	France	26 Jun 27	62LTS85	301457
Greece	Norway	29 Jun 27	82LTS187	301869
Czechoslovakia	Estonia	20 Jul 27	77LTS341	301776
Hungary	Italy	25 Jul 27	74LTS67	301732
Switzerland	Turkey	07 Aug 27	73LTS51	301706
Germany	Serb/Croat/Slovene	06 Oct 27	77LTS19	301763
Belgium	France	06 Oct 27	69LTS49	301599
Greece	Serb/Croat/Slovene	02 Nov 27	91LTS137	302060
Germany	Panama	21 Nov 27	115LTS239	302689
Greece	Switzerland	01 Dec 27	84LTS271	301907
Sweden	Turkey	04 Feb 28	88LTS155	301994
Multilateral		20 Feb 28	132LTS301	303045
Estonia	Turkey	12 Mar 28	86LTS453	301957
Latvia	Turkey	28 May 28	94LTS295	302150

PARTY ONE	PARTY TWO	DATE	CITATION	NUMBER
Foreign nationals (Cont.)				
Austria	USA (United States)	19 Jun 28	118LTS241	302728
Italy	Persia	24 Jul 28	95LTS269	302179
Denmark	Greece	22 Aug 28	94LTS263	302147
Germany	South Africa	01 Sep 28	95LTS289	302181
Belgium	France	12 Sep 28	123LTS97	302809
Germany	Lithuania	30 Oct 28	89LTS127	302010
Czechoslovakia	Serb/Croat/Slovene	14 Nov 28	97LTS9	302216
United Arab Rep	Persia	28 Nov 28	93LTS381	302127
Estonia	Germany	07 Dec 28	99LTS259	302273
Latvia	Poland	12 Feb 29	115LTS135	302683
Germany	Persia	17 Feb 29	111LTS241	302590
Norway	USA (United States)	25 Feb 29	134LTS81	303085
Estonia	Hungary	29 Apr 29	96LTS23	302189
Persia	Sweden	10 May 29	102LTS9	302349
Hungary	Lithuania	16 May 29	96LTS333	302211
Bolivia	Netherlands	30 May 29	133LTS113	303062
Romania	Turkey	11 Jun 29	112LTS139	302613
Serb/Croat/Slovene	Spain	27 Sep 29	98LTS319	302253
Sweden	Turkey	29 Sep 29	119LTS53	302740
Finland	Turkey	12 Oct 29	96LTS239	302205
Italy	Panama	16 Oct 29	138LTS355	303199
Poland	Romania	17 Dec 29	119LTS333	302754
China	Czechoslovakia	12 Feb 30	110LTS285	302561
Italy	Romania	25 Feb 30	106LTS179	302445
Germany	Haiti	10 Mar 30	119LTS231	302747
Costa Rica	Spain	21 Mar 30	168LTS61	303886
France	Luxembourg	31 Mar 30	122LTS29	302797
Greece	Poland	10 Apr 30	120LTS369	302775
Austria	Germany	12 Apr 30	115LTS333	302694
Norway	Persia	08 May 30	134LTS153	303089
Germany	Irish Free State	12 May 30	131LTS153	303008
Greece	Hungary	03 Jun 30	122LTS37	302798
Czechoslovakia	Romania	27 Jun 30	119LTS73	302742
France	Romania	27 Aug 30	158LTS379	303644
Czechoslovakia	Persia	29 Oct 30	121LTS59	302784
Greece	Turkey	30 Oct 30	125LTS371	302866
Norway	USA (United States)	01 Nov 30	112LTS399	302625
Switzerland	Turkey	13 Dec 30	129LTS331	302968
Norway	Turkey	16 Mar 31	138LTS41	303180
Estonia	Finland	11 Apr 31	124LTS217	302835
Siam	Switzerland	28 May 31	125LTS357	302864
Germany	Hungary	18 Jul 31	150LTS111	303458
Greece	Romania	11 Aug 31	130LTS69	302982
Hungary	Romania	12 Aug 31	186LTS325	304321
Romania	Sweden	07 Oct 31	131LTS51	303003
Bolivia	Denmark	09 Nov 31	147LTS27	303387
Albania	USA (United States)	05 Apr 32	162LTS31	303732
Bulgaria	Germany	24 Jun 32	147LTS211	303400
Sweden	USA (United States)	31 Jan 33	159LTS261	303670
Bulgaria	Czechoslovakia	29 Aug 33	148LTS15	303402
Czechoslovakia	Poland	10 Feb 34	183LTS213	304238
Finland	Germany	24 Mar 34	149LTS343	303442
Persia	Switzerland	25 Apr 34	160LTS173	303691
Poland	Spain	14 Dec 34	168LTS315	303908
Iran	USSR (Soviet Union)	27 Aug 35	176LTS299	304069
United Arab Rep	Turkey	07 Apr 37	191LTS95	304438
Sweden	Yugoslavia	14 May 37	194LTS21	304504
Lithuania	USA (United States)	18 Oct 37	191LTS351	304454
Siam	USA (United States)	13 Nov 37	192LTS247	304476
Siam	UK Great Britain	23 Nov 37	188LTS333	304366
Latvia	Turkey	12 Jan 38	201LTS229	304716
Multilateral		16 Apr 38	195LTS103	304538
Mexico	UK Great Britain	18 Jul 43	205LTS115	304828
Austria	Greece	28 Mar 74*	2LTS169	300063

PARTY ONE	PARTY TWO	DATE	CITATION	NUMBER
Service in foreign army				
Czechoslovakia	Romania	23 Apr 21	15LTS235	300397
Belgium	France	04 Oct 21	8LTS157	300219
Czechoslovakia	Latvia	07 Oct 22	20LTS379	300528
Latvia	UK Great Britain	22 Jun 23	20LTS395	300529
Poland	Sweden	02 Dec 24	36LTS299	300930
Hungary	Poland	26 Mar 25	37LTS151	300954
Czechoslovakia	Sweden	18 Apr 25	36LTS289	300929
Hungary	Italy	04 Jul 28	92LTS117	302083
Germany	Lithuania	30 Oct 28	90LTS255	302043
Costa Rica	Spain	21 Mar 30	168LTS61	303886
Romania	Yugoslavia	13 May 37	197LTS145	304611
Liberia	USA (United States)	08 Aug 38	201LTS163	304711
Peace and disarmament				
Multilateral		23 Dec 36	188LTS9	304350
Reconversion to normalcy				
Allied Powers	Poland	01 Apr 22	9LTS325	300265
United Arab Rep	UK Great Britain	05 Jul 23	18LTS311	300473
Spain	UK Great Britain	27 Jun 24	28LTS523	300727
Allied Powers	Germany	28 Oct 24	41LTS461	301025
Multilateral		30 Aug 29	104LTS473	302399
Armistice and peace				
Estonia	USSR (Soviet Union)	02 Feb 20	11LTS29	300289
Lithuania	USSR (Soviet Union)	12 Jul 20	3LTS106	300094
Latvia	USSR (Soviet Union)	11 Aug 20	2LTS195	300067
Finland	USSR (Soviet Union)	14 Oct 20	3LTS5	300091
Lithuania	Poland	29 Nov 20	9LTS63	300243
Poland	USSR (Soviet Union)	18 Mar 21	6LTS51	300149
China	Germany	20 May 21	9LTS271	300261
Hungary	USA (United States)	29 Aug 21	48LTS191	301161
France	UK Great Britain	24 Jul 23	36LTS207	300923
Multilateral		24 Jul 23	28LTS11	300701
Poland	Romania	15 Jan 31	115LTS171	302685
UK Great Britain	USSR (Soviet Union)	12 Jul 41	204LTS277	304808
UK Great Britain	USSR (Soviet Union)	26 May 42	204LTS353	304813
Arms limitations				
Multilateral		06 Feb 22	25LTS201	300609
Multilateral		17 Jun 25	94LTS65	302138
Multilateral		22 May 26	58LTS331	301381
Multilateral		22 Apr 30	112LTS65	302608
Germany	UK Great Britain	18 Jun 35	161LTS9	303701
Multilateral		25 Mar 36	184LTS115	304246
UK Great Britain	USSR (Soviet Union)	17 Jul 37	187LTS93	304333
Germany	UK Great Britain	17 Jul 37	187LTS43	304332
Poland	UK Great Britain	27 Apr 38	195LTS39	304535
War claims and reparations				
Czechoslovakia	Italy	23 Mar 21	32LTS261	300817
Austria	Germany	17 Aug 21	19LTS237	300497
Germany	Romania	10 Nov 28	91LTS101	302058
Belgium	Germany	16 Jan 30	104LTS223	302392
Austria	Belgium	18 Jan 30	104LTS231	302393
China	UK Great Britain	22 Sep 30	115LTS493	302697
Loss and/or damage				
Austria	Germany	17 Aug 21	19LTS237	300497
Multilateral		06 Apr 22	20LTS11	300501
Germany	USSR (Soviet Union)	16 Apr 22	19LTS247	300498
Enemy financial interests				
Multilateral		06 Apr 22	20LTS11	300501
Belgium	Poland	30 Dec 22	21LTS201	300543
Belgium	Germany	13 Jul 29	104LTS211	302391
Germany	UK Great Britain	28 Dec 29	102LTS49	302352
Multilateral		01 Jul 30	121LTS153	302786

PARTY ONE	PARTY TWO	DATE	CITATION	NUMBER
Reparations and restrictions				
Multilateral		10 Sep 19	2LTS21	300042
France	UK Great Britain	10 Jan 20	1LTS249	300017
Austria	Germany	17 Aug 21	19LTS237	300497
Germany	Poland	01 Aug 22	34LTS253	300877
Belgium	Poland	30 Dec 22	21LTS201	300543
Multilateral		24 Jul 23	28LTS11	300701
Estonia	Latvia	01 Nov 23	25LTS341	300622
Multilateral		23 Nov 23	28LTS273	300713
Multilateral		28 Mar 24	31LTS46	300780
Germany	Romania	10 Nov 28	91LTS101	302058
Germany	UK Great Britain	28 Dec 29	102LTS49	302352
Other Unilat Decla	Greece	14 Jan 30	108LTS349	302518
Multilateral		20 Jan 30	104LTS243	302394
Multilateral		20 Jan 30	112LTS361	302622
Multilateral		01 Jul 30	121LTS153	302786
Italy	UK Great Britain	02 Sep 30	140LTS19	303225
China	UK Great Britain	22 Sep 30	115LTS493	302697
Belgium	France	17 Nov 31	152LTS121	303490
Post-war claims settlement				
France	UK Great Britain	10 Jan 20	1LTS249	300017
Estonia	USSR (Soviet Union)	02 Feb 20	11LTS29	300289
Lithuania	USSR (Soviet Union)	12 Jul 20	3LTS106	300094
Belgium	France	24 Jul 20	1LTS311	300026
Latvia	USSR (Soviet Union)	11 Aug 20	2LTS195	300067
Poland	USSR (Soviet Union)	12 Oct 20	4LTS7	300101
Poland	USSR (Soviet Union)	18 Mar 21	6LTS51	300149
Austria	Czechoslovakia	17 Dec 21	22LTS401	300570
Hungary	UK Great Britain	20 Dec 21	10LTS437	300283
Czechoslovakia	Germany	12 Apr 22	22LTS329	300562
Germany	USSR (Soviet Union)	16 Apr 22	19LTS247	300498
Belgium	Poland	30 Dec 22	21LTS201	300543
Germany	UK Great Britain	05 Apr 23	17LTS173	300435
Germany	Lithuania	31 May 23	51LTS381	301243
Multilateral		24 Jul 23	28LTS11	300701
Multilateral		23 Nov 23	28LTS267	300712
Bulgaria	Serb/Croat/Slovene	26 Nov 23	21LTS153	300539
Bulgaria	Serb/Croat/Slovene	26 Nov 23	21LTS163	300540
Hungary	Italy	27 Mar 24	45LTS65	301099
Germany	Mexico	16 Mar 25	52LTS93	301251
Greece	UK Great Britain	30 Nov 25	50LTS273	301210
France	UK Great Britain	12 Jul 26	98LTS155	302244
Great Britain	Serb/Croat/Slovene	09 Aug 27	69LTS255	301607
Netherlands	UK Great Britain	22 Mar 29	90LTS421	302052
Belgium	Germany	13 Jul 29	104LTS211	302391
Germany	UK Great Britain	28 Dec 29	102LTS49	302352
Other Unilat Decla	Greece	14 Jan 30	108LTS349	302518
Austria	Germany	17 Jan 30	107LTS325	302488
Canada	Germany	17 Jan 30	109LTS473	302550
France	Yugoslavia	20 Jan 30	104LTS171	302386
Germany	Italy	20 Jan 30	106LTS109	302439
Multilateral		20 Jan 30	113LTS389	302650
Multilateral		20 Jan 30	104LTS243	302394
Germany	USA (United States)	23 Jun 30	106LTS121	302440
Occupation regime				
Multilateral		28 Mar 24	31LTS53	300781
Multilateral		28 Mar 24	31LTS46	300780
Multilateral		30 Aug 29	104LTS487	302400
Netherlands	USA (United States)	09 Jul 30	125LTS123	302851
Netherlands	USA (United States)	16 Sep 30	125LTS173	302853
Disarmament and demilitarization				
Austria	Hungary	13 Oct 21	9LTS203	300254
Multilateral		24 Jul 23	28LTS139	300703
Multilateral		18 Dec 23	28LTS541	300729

PARTY ONE	PARTY TWO	DATE	CITATION	NUMBER
Disarmament and demilitarization (Cont.)				
Spain	UK Great Britain	27 Jun 24	28LTS523	300727
Industrial controls				
Austria	Hungary	13 Oct 21	9LTS203	300254
Multilateral		05 May 25	55LTS225	301318
Control and occupation machinery				
Multilateral		05 May 25	55LTS225	301318
Other Unilat Decla	Rhine Navigation	10 Sep 26	62LTS141	301462
Multilateral		15 Apr 35	167LTS289	303874
Withdrawal of occupation				
Multilateral		24 Jul 23	36LTS167	300917
United Arab Rep	UK Great Britain	26 Aug 36	173LTS401	304031
War graves				
Multilateral		24 Jul 23	28LTS11	300701
Multilateral		28 Dec 38	196LTS221	304585
Responsibility for war dead				
Greece	UK Great Britain	27 Aug 21	8LTS332	300233
Italy	UK Great Britain	11 May 22	11LTS23	300288
Multilateral		15 Mar 35	170LTS9	303926
Multilateral		02 Jun 37	184LTS445	304265
Upkeep of war graves				
Greece	UK Great Britain	27 Aug 21	8LTS332	300233
Italy	UK Great Britain	11 May 22	11LTS23	300288
Multilateral		15 Mar 35	170LTS9	303926
Multilateral		20 Dec 35	167LTS141	303862
Multilateral		02 Jun 37	184LTS445	304265
Establishment of war cemeteries				
Greece	UK Great Britain	27 Aug 21	8LTS332	300233
Italy	UK Great Britain	11 May 22	11LTS23	300288
France	USA (United States)	29 Aug 27	68LTS253	301589
Belgium	USA (United States)	04 Oct 29	105LTS189	302412
Multilateral		02 Jun 37	184LTS445	304265
International organizations				
Other Unilat Decla	Ethiopia	27 Sep 23	25LTS180	300606
IGO constitution				
United Arab Rep	ILO (Labor Org)	19 Jun 36	177LTS343	304096
Admission				
Multilateral		28 Jun 29	102LTS245	302368
Multilateral		23 May 39	202LTS159	304742
Decisions				
Chile	Sweden	26 Mar 20	4LTS271	300111
Multilateral		19 Jan 21	5LTS9	300113
Multilateral		23 May 39	202LTS159	304742
Subsidiary organ				
Multilateral		12 Jul 27	135LTS247	303115
Multilateral		16 Apr 29	126LTS305	302891
Multilateral		28 Jun 29	102LTS245	302368
Multilateral		16 Feb 33	139LTS233	303213
Estonia	Latvia	17 Feb 34	150LTS103	303457
Multilateral		20 Mar 34	174LTS171	304048
Multilateral		23 May 39	202LTS159	304742
Establishment				
Multilateral		28 Apr 23	33LTS47	300832
Multilateral		12 Jul 27	135LTS247	303115
Multilateral		28 Jun 29	102LTS245	302368
Multilateral		30 Oct 35	189LTS51	304375
Multilateral		23 May 39	202LTS159	304742
Procedure				
Multilateral		28 Jun 29	102LTS245	302368
Multilateral		16 Feb 33	139LTS233	303213

PARTY ONE	PARTY TWO	DATE	CITATION	NUMBER
Procedure (Cont.)				
Multilateral		25 Aug 33	141LTS71	303262
Multilateral		20 Mar 34	174LTS171	304048
Bulgaria	Poland	08 Apr 35	161LTS319	303720
Finland	Hungary	22 Oct 37	190LTS281	304426
Finland	Poland	14 Feb 38	194LTS175	304520
Belgium	France	06 Mar 39	195LTS353	304555
Headquarters and facilities				
Multilateral		19 Jan 21	5LTS9	300113
Multilateral		12 Jul 27	135LTS247	303115
Multilateral		16 Feb 33	139LTS233	303213
Extension of functions				
Multilateral		12 Jul 27	135LTS247	303115
Internal structure				
Brazil	UK Great Britain	04 Apr 19	5LTS45	300116
Chile	Sweden	26 Mar 20	4LTS271	300111
Germany	Switzerland	03 Dec 21	12LTS271	300320
Czechoslovakia	Germany	22 Feb 22	26LTS249	300650
Multilateral		28 Apr 23	33LTS47	300832
Multilateral		29 Nov 24	80LTS293	301835
Multilateral		16 Feb 33	139LTS233	303213
Romania	Turkey	17 Oct 33	165LTS273	303814
Multilateral		20 Mar 34	174LTS171	304048
Multilateral		23 May 39	202LTS159	304742
Special status				
Multilateral		12 Jul 27	135LTS247	303115
Status of experts				
Belgium	France	30 Jun 28	93LTS377	302126
Conferences				
Multilateral		19 Jan 21	5LTS9	300113
Romania	Yugoslavia	27 Jun 30	107LTS215	302478
Estonia	Latvia	17 Feb 34	150LTS103	303457
Multilateral		20 Mar 34	174LTS171	304048
Multilateral		12 Sep 34	154LTS93	303540
Multilateral		30 Oct 35	189LTS51	304375
Multilateral		30 Oct 35	189LTS85	304376
Multilateral		11 Feb 37	186LTS55	304303
IGO obligations				
Multilateral		28 Apr 23	33LTS47	300832
Optional clause ICJ				
Multilateral		27 Mar 31	167LTS341	303877
Multilateral		30 Jul 36	197LTS31	304602
Administering authority				
France	UK Great Britain	23 Dec 20	22LTS353	300564
Japan	USA (United States)	11 Feb 22	12LTS201	300311
France	USA (United States)	13 Feb 23	26LTS53	300640
France	USA (United States)	13 Feb 23	26LTS69	300641
Disposition of territory				
Cuba	USA (United States)	02 Mar 04	127LTS143	302915
France	UK Great Britain	23 Dec 20	22LTS353	300564
Belgium	USA (United States)	21 Jan 24	31LTS137	300791
Iraq	UK Great Britain	25 Mar 24	35LTS145	300894
Belgium	Portugal	22 Jul 27	71LTS449	301683
Italy	Turkey	04 Jan 32	138LTS243	303191
Definition of territory				
Multilateral		09 Feb 20	2LTS7	300041
Danzig	Poland	09 Nov 20	6LTS189	300153
France	UK Great Britain	23 Dec 20	22LTS353	300564
Japan	USA (United States)	11 Feb 22	12LTS201	300311
France	USA (United States)	13 Feb 23	26LTS69	300641
France	USA (United States)	13 Feb 23	26LTS53	300640
Iraq	UK Great Britain	25 Mar 24	35LTS145	300894

PARTY ONE	PARTY TWO	DATE	CITATION	NUMBER
Definition of territory (Cont.)				
Portugal	UK Great Britain	28 Dec 37	185LTS205	304284
UK Great Britain	USA (United States)	06 Apr 39	196LTS343	304593
Respect for local customs				
Spain	UK Great Britain	27 Jun 24	28LTS523	300727
Internal travel				
France	UK Great Britain	23 Dec 20	22LTS353	300564
Disposition of particulars				
Multilateral		09 Dec 19	5LTS335	300140
Danzig	Poland	09 Nov 20	6LTS189	300153
Germany	Poland	20 Jan 21	6LTS221	300156
Czechoslovakia	Germany	03 Feb 21	5LTS246	300132
Germany	Saar	03 Jun 21	5LTS189	300129
Multilateral		13 Dec 21	25LTS184	300607
Italy	Serb/Croat/Slovene	20 Jul 25	83LTS259	301892
Other Unilat Decla	Rhine Navigation	10 Sep 26	62LTS141	301462
Germany	Japan	20 Jul 27	74LTS107	301736
Facilities and property				
France	UK Great Britain	24 Apr 20	1LTS281	300022
France	Germany	01 Jul 20	8LTS87	300209
Multilateral		10 Aug 20	28LTS225	300710
Germany	Poland	06 Jun 21	34LTS185	300874
Germany	Poland	15 Jun 22	34LTS201	300875
Germany	Poland	01 Aug 22	34LTS253	300877
Germany	Poland	27 Jan 23	26LTS461	300663
France	India	12 May 23	25LTS381	300627
Germany	Poland	23 Jun 23	67LTS9	301537
Germany	Poland	12 Jan 24	65LTS47	301519
Czechoslovakia	Hungary	09 Feb 24	30LTS335	300773
Hungary	Romania	14 Apr 24	46LTS41	301113
Italy	Serb/Croat/Slovene	12 Aug 24	82LTS423	301882
Multilateral		29 Nov 24	80LTS293	301835
Germany	Poland	30 Dec 24	52LTS51	301250
Germany	Poland	14 Mar 25	95LTS239	302178
France	Germany	14 Aug 25	75LTS103	301756
Multilateral		31 Dec 25	79LTS167	301809
France	India	19 Jun 26	57LTS35	301350
Germany	Poland	21 Jun 26	72LTS203	301693
Portugal	South Africa	01 Jul 26	70LTS315	301643
Czechoslovakia	Hungary	30 Sep 26	57LTS87	301356
Multilateral		13 Nov 26	77LTS199	301771
Multilateral		13 Nov 26	77LTS217	301772
Multilateral		13 Nov 26	77LTS249	301773
Multilateral		13 Nov 26	77LTS171	301770
Hungary	Italy	25 Jul 27	74LTS77	301733
Germany	Lithuania	29 Jan 28	89LTS338	302027
Germany	UK Great Britain	26 Jul 28	85LTS135	301928
Czechoslovakia	Hungary	14 Nov 28	110LTS425	302574
Austria	Italy	22 Feb 29	89LTS271	302021
Czechoslovakia	Germany	20 Mar 29	109LTS219	302541
Poland	Romania	24 May 29	124LTS333	302836
Poland	Romania	24 May 29	124LTS339	302837
China	UK Great Britain	18 Apr 30	112LTS49	302607
Czechoslovakia	Romania	15 Jul 30	164LTS157	303793
Estonia	Latvia	05 Sep 30	112LTS219	302616
Latvia	Lithuania	25 Jan 31	118LTS143	302719
Denmark	Sweden	31 Dec 32	139LTS205	303211
Romania	Yugoslavia	30 Jan 33	146LTS139	303366
Finland	USSR (Soviet Union)	04 Jul 33	149LTS83	303436
Brazil	Uruguay	20 Dec 33	181LTS69	304178
Bulgaria	Romania	26 Jul 35	198LTS9	304621
Finland	Norway	05 Nov 35	169LTS33	303913
Bulgaria	Yugoslavia	09 Nov 35	194LTS89	304511
Japan	USA (United States)	25 Mar 37	181LTS217	304191

PARTY ONE	PARTY TWO	DATE	CITATION	NUMBER
Facilities and property (Cont.)				
Multilateral		02 Jun 37	184LTS445	304265
Czechoslovakia	Hungary	24 Aug 37	189LTS403	304397
Norway	Sweden	20 Apr 38	189LTS153	304383
Iceland	Norway	27 Feb 39	196LTS377	304598
Mexico	USA (United States)	18 Apr 39	201LTS201	304714
Germany	Netherlands	17 May 39	199LTS239	304678
UK Great Britain	Venezuela	26 Feb 42	205LTS131	304830
Austria	Greece	12 Jun 56*	2LTS157	300061
Aquisition of property				
Finland	USSR (Soviet Union)	15 Oct 33	149LTS243	303439
Boundaries of territory				
Cuba	USA (United States)	02 Mar 04	127LTS143	302915
Multilateral		09 Feb 20	2LTS7	300041
France	Germany	01 Mar 20	1LTS367	300030
China	Japan	04 Feb 22	10LTS309	300277
Sweden	USA (United States)	22 May 24	29LTS421	300752
Afghanistan	Persia	26 Jun 28	106LTS321	302453
Multilateral		30 Oct 28	87LTS103	301963
Chile	Peru	03 Jun 29	94LTS401	302157
Hungary	Yugoslavia	27 Apr 30	113LTS153	302642
Colombia	Nicaragua	05 May 30	105LTS337	302426
Brazil	Paraguay	09 Dec 31	136LTS427	303142
Pasturage in frontier zones				
Austria	Czechoslovakia	10 Mar 21	9LTS333	300267
Denmark	Germany	10 Apr 22	29LTS9	300730
Germany	Poland	23 Feb 24	41LTS197	301015
France	Turkey	31 Jul 26	54LTS177	301284
Multilateral		13 Nov 26	77LTS249	301773
Persia	USSR (Soviet Union)	31 May 28	110LTS343	302566
Poland	Romania	07 Dec 29	119LTS283	302752
Estonia	Latvia	05 Sep 30	112LTS219	302616
Romania	Yugoslavia	14 Dec 31	135LTS31	303103
Finland	USSR (Soviet Union)	04 Jul 33	149LTS83	303436
Finland	Norway	05 Nov 35	169LTS33	303913
Changes of territory				
Multilateral		09 Feb 20	2LTS7	300041
Multilateral		10 Aug 20	28LTS225	300710
Austria	Czechoslovakia	10 Mar 21	9LTS333	300267
Japan	USA (United States)	11 Feb 22	12LTS201	300311
Denmark	Germany	10 Apr 22	10LTS73	300274
Germany	Poland	12 Apr 22	21LTS327	300548
Germany	Poland	23 Jun 22	22LTS25	300553
Multilateral		04 Oct 22	12LTS385	300334
Multilateral		04 Oct 22	12LTS391	300335
China	Japan	01 Dec 22	22LTS179	300559
France	UK Great Britain	07 Mar 23	22LTS363	300565
Austria	Italy	16 Jul 23	27LTS383	300699
Multilateral		24 Jul 23	28LTS215	300708
Multilateral		18 Dec 23	28LTS541	300729
Hungary	Romania	16 Apr 24	46LTS27	301112
Multilateral		08 May 24	29LTS85	300736
Austria	Czechoslovakia	29 May 25	98LTS91	302242
France	Germany	14 Aug 25	75LTS103	301756
France	Great Britain	02 Feb 26	56LTS79	301324
Multilateral		13 Nov 26	77LTS249	301773
Germany	Poland	22 Dec 26	68LTS263	301590
Hungary	Serb/Croat/Slovene	22 Feb 28	88LTS111	301991
Portugal	South Africa	11 Sep 28	98LTS9	302239
Germany	Poland	14 Dec 28	113LTS311	302647
Chile	Peru	03 Jun 29	94LTS401	302157
Czechoslovakia	Germany	31 Jan 30	145LTS51	303345
Multilateral		31 Oct 30	120LTS9	302760
Czechoslovakia	Romania	22 Dec 30	167LTS243	303870

PARTY ONE	PARTY TWO	DATE	CITATION	NUMBER
Changes of territory (Cont.)				
Czechoslovakia	Romania	22 Dec 30	167LTS257	303871
Romania	Yugoslavia	14 Dec 31	135LTS89	303105
Romania	Yugoslavia	14 Dec 31	135LTS99	303106
Italy	Turkey	04 Jan 32	138LTS243	303191
Brazil	UK Great Britain	01 Nov 32	177LTS127	304087
Romania	Yugoslavia	10 Mar 33	146LTS245	303374
Belgium	Germany	10 May 35	182LTS323	304220
Czechoslovakia	Germany	27 Sep 35	182LTS267	304217
Estonia	Latvia	10 Dec 35	168LTS83	303888
Estonia	Latvia	06 Oct 36	172LTS221	303994
Portugal	UK Great Britain	28 Dec 37	185LTS205	304284
Germany	Switzerland	21 Sep 38	196LTS365	304595
UK Great Britain	USA (United States)	06 Apr 39	196LTS343	304593
Fish, wildlife, and natural resources				
Multilateral		05 Aug 20	2LTS49	300046
Afghanistan	UK Great Britain	22 Nov 21	14LTS47	300367
Germany	Poland	29 Apr 22	21LTS391	300549
Finland	USSR (Soviet Union)	28 Oct 22	19LTS153	300491
Finland	USSR (Soviet Union)	28 Oct 22	19LTS183	300492
Finland	Netherlands	01 Nov 23	23LTS33	300574
Multilateral		12 Mar 24	24LTS17	300595
Denmark	Norway	09 Jul 24	27LTS203	300684
Multilateral		05 May 25	55LTS225	301318
Finland	Sweden	09 May 25	47LTS283	301136
Estonia	Latvia	05 Feb 26	64LTS361	301509
Benelux Econ Union	Germany	15 Jul 26	63LTS137	301485
Multilateral		13 Nov 26	77LTS217	301772
Bulgaria	Germany	22 Dec 26	64LTS77	301502
Bulgaria	Turkey	12 Feb 28	81LTS383	301848
Japan	USA (United States)	31 May 28	101LTS63	302320
Czechoslovakia	Hungary	14 Nov 28	110LTS425	302574
Denmark	Sweden	09 Oct 31	126LTS255	302888
Romania	Yugoslavia	14 Dec 31	135LTS31	303103
Poland	USSR (Soviet Union)	10 Apr 32	141LTS349	303275
France	Switzerland	31 Jan 38	195LTS313	304553
Markers and definitions				
Estonia	USSR (Soviet Union)	02 Feb 20	11LTS29	300289
Estonia	Latvia	22 Mar 20	2LTS187	300066
Portugal	UK Great Britain	06 May 20	4LTS93	300103
Multilateral		05 Jul 20	2LTS241	300070
Lithuania	USSR (Soviet Union)	12 Jul 20	3LTS106	300094
Multilateral		05 Aug 20	2LTS49	300046
Latvia	USSR (Soviet Union)	11 Aug 20	2LTS195	300067
Germany	Switzerland	14 Sep 20	2LTS331	300087
Latvia	Lithuania	28 Sep 20	2LTS234	300068
Poland	USSR (Soviet Union)	12 Oct 20	4LTS7	300101
Finland	USSR (Soviet Union)	14 Oct 20	3LTS5	300091
Estonia	Latvia	19 Oct 20	17LTS189	300437
Italy	Serb/Croat/Slovene	12 Nov 20	18LTS387	300477
Allied Powers	Germany	17 Dec 20	12LTS39	300306
France	UK Great Britain	23 Dec 20	22LTS353	300564
Austria	Czechoslovakia	10 Mar 21	9LTS333	300267
Poland	USSR (Soviet Union)	18 Mar 21	6LTS51	300149
Latvia	Lithuania	13 May 21	17LTS211	300438
Multilateral		20 Oct 21	9LTS211	300255
Multilateral		09 Nov 21	12LTS381	300333
Afghanistan	UK Great Britain	22 Nov 21	14LTS47	300367
Ireland	UK Great Britain	06 Dec 21	26LTS9	300636
Colombia	Peru	24 Mar 22	74LTS9	301726
Finland	USSR (Soviet Union)	01 Jun 22	16LTS319	300415
Germany	Poland	23 Jun 22	22LTS25	300553
Denmark	Sweden	07 Nov 22	14LTS95	300370
Albania	Italy	04 Dec 22	15LTS213	300395
France	USA (United States)	13 Feb 23	26LTS53	300640

PARTY ONE	PARTY TWO	DATE	CITATION	NUMBER
Markers and definitions (Cont.)				
France	USA (United States)	13 Feb 23	26LTS69	300641
France	UK Great Britain	07 Mar 23	22LTS363	300565
Multilateral		15 Mar 23	15LTS259	300398
Germany	Switzerland	25 Mar 23	18LTS273	300470
Liechtenstein	Switzerland	29 Mar 23	21LTS231	300545
Norway	Sweden	26 May 23	18LTS155	300462
Multilateral		24 Jul 23	28LTS11	300701
Multilateral		24 Jul 23	28LTS139	300703
Estonia	Latvia	01 Nov 23	25LTS345	300623
France	UK Great Britain	21 Jan 24	28LTS461	300723
Belgium	USA (United States)	21 Jan 24	31LTS137	300791
Finland	Norway	28 Apr 24	30LTS49	300758
Italy	UK Great Britain	19 May 24	28LTS497	300725
China	USSR (Soviet Union)	31 May 24	37LTS175	300955
Ecuador	Peru	21 Jun 24	27LTS345	300694
Spain	UK Great Britain	27 Jun 24	28LTS523	300727
Italy	UK Great Britain	15 Jul 24	36LTS379	300936
Italy	Serb/Croat/Slovene	12 Aug 24	82LTS423	301882
Colombia	Panama	20 Aug 24	33LTS167	300841
Canada	USA (United States)	24 Feb 25	43LTS239	301059
Germany	Poland	14 Mar 25	95LTS239	302178
France	Germany	14 Aug 25	75LTS103	301756
Great Britain	Nejd	02 Nov 25	60LTS419	301423
Portugal	UK Great Britain	03 Nov 25	47LTS379	301143
Germany	Poland	27 Jan 26	64LTS113	301504
Belgium	UK Great Britain	17 May 26	54LTS239	301287
Germany	Poland	21 Jun 26	72LTS203	301693
Portugal	South Africa	22 Jun 26	70LTS305	301642
Belgium	Germany	01 Jul 26	62LTS127	301461
Austria	Hungary	14 Jul 26	61LTS159	301431
Austria	Hungary	14 Jul 26	61LTS123	301430
Portugal	Spain	29 Jul 26	82LTS95	301863
France	Turkey	31 Jul 26	54LTS177	301284
Germany	Poland	19 Aug 26	64LTS420	301515
Multilateral		13 Nov 26	77LTS199	301771
Multilateral		13 Nov 26	77LTS171	301770
France	Germany	22 Dec 26	77LTS141	301768
Bulgaria	Germany	22 Dec 26	64LTS77	301502
Germany	Poland	16 Feb 27	71LTS369	301676
Germany	Poland	11 Apr 27	69LTS419	301621
Brazil	UK Great Britain	22 Apr 27	92LTS311	302097
Belgium	UK Great Britain	03 May 27	140LTS71	303229
Romania	Serb/Croat/Slovene	04 Jun 27	158LTS443	303647
Belgium	Portugal	22 Jul 27	71LTS449	301683
Multilateral		28 Jul 27	64LTS379	301511
Estonia	USSR (Soviet Union)	08 Aug 27	70LTS401	301648
Portugal	South Africa	06 Oct 27	81LTS359	301846
Portugal	UK Great Britain	06 Nov 27	80LTS219	301827
Germany	Lithuania	29 Jan 28	89LTS338	302027
Germany	Lithuania	29 Jan 28	89LTS97	302009
Czechoslovakia	Poland	18 Feb 28	100LTS273	302301
Czechoslovakia	Germany	22 Mar 28	93LTS235	302113
Netherlands	UK Great Britain	26 Mar 28	108LTS331	302516
France	Spain	12 Jun 28	136LTS289	303131
Finland	USSR (Soviet Union)	24 Sep 28	82LTS63	301860
Czechoslovakia	Hungary	14 Nov 28	110LTS425	302574
Brazil	Colombia	15 Nov 28	100LTS123	302299
Austria	Czechoslovakia	12 Dec 28	107LTS137	302474
Austria	Czechoslovakia	12 Dec 28	108LTS9	302501
Multilateral		20 Dec 28	86LTS429	301954
Dominican Republic	Haiti	21 Jan 29	105LTS193	302413
Austria	Italy	22 Feb 29	89LTS271	302021
Czechoslovakia	Germany	20 Mar 29	109LTS219	302541
France	UK Great Britain	06 May 29	93LTS27	302102
Chile	Peru	03 Jun 29	94LTS401	302157

PARTY ONE	PARTY TWO	DATE	CITATION	NUMBER
Markers and definitions (Cont.)				
Albania	Serb/Croat/Slovene	11 Aug 29	101LTS439	302342
Multilateral		30 Aug 29	104LTS473	302399
Italy	Serb/Croat/Slovene	16 Sep 29	101LTS127	302322
Bulgaria	Yugoslavia	26 Sep 29	101LTS217	302324
Belgium	Germany	07 Nov 29	121LTS327	302795
Brazil	Venezuela	07 Nov 29	99LTS427	302288
Poland	Romania	07 Dec 29	119LTS283	302752
Czechoslovakia	Poland	21 Dec 29	115LTS201	302687
UK Great Britain	USA (United States)	02 Jan 30	137LTS297	303164
Liberia	UK Great Britain	17 Jan 30	101LTS395	302338
Czechoslovakia	Germany	31 Jan 30	145LTS51	303345
Brazil	UK Great Britain	18 Mar 30	101LTS401	302339
Austria	Germany	12 Apr 30	115LTS277	302692
France	Italy	08 Jul 30	137LTS93	303148
Czechoslovakia	Romania	15 Jul 30	164LTS157	303793
Denmark	Sweden	03 Sep 30	106LTS397	302458
Estonia	Latvia	05 Sep 30	112LTS219	302616
Latvia	Lithuania	25 Jan 31	118LTS143	302719
Latvia	Lithuania	25 Jan 31	118LTS157	302721
Portugal	South Africa	29 Apr 31	129LTS157	302960
Guatemala	UK Great Britain	26 Aug 31	128LTS427	302946
Brazil	Paraguay	09 Dec 31	136LTS427	303142
Romania	Yugoslavia	14 Dec 31	135LTS31	303103
Italy	Turkey	04 Jan 32	138LTS243	303191
Finland	USSR (Soviet Union)	21 Jan 32	157LTS393	303613
Denmark	Sweden	30 Jan 32	127LTS57	302906
Multilateral		14 Mar 32	131LTS135	303006
Poland	USSR (Soviet Union)	10 Apr 32	141LTS349	303275
Brazil	UK Great Britain	01 Nov 32	177LTS127	304087
Romania	Yugoslavia	30 Jan 33	146LTS139	303366
Italy	UK Great Britain	22 Nov 33	145LTS337	303359
Multilateral		01 Jun 34	154LTS373	303563
Multilateral		20 Jul 34	155LTS45	303567
Belgium	UK Great Britain	22 Nov 34	190LTS95	304407
Dominican Republic	Haiti	27 Feb 35	171LTS89	303953
Multilateral		09 Apr 35	163LTS177	303766
Belgium	Germany	10 May 35	182LTS323	304220
Belgium	Germany	10 May 35	165LTS169	303808
Belgium	Germany	10 May 35	165LTS143	303807
Poland	Romania	17 May 35	173LTS373	304028
Poland	Romania	17 May 35	173LTS363	304027
Bel-Lux Econ Union	France	16 Jul 35	162LTS19	303731
Czechoslovakia	Germany	27 Sep 35	182LTS267	304217
Finland	Norway	05 Nov 35	169LTS33	303913
Bulgaria	Yugoslavia	09 Nov 35	194LTS89	304511
China	UK Great Britain	17 Jul 36	173LTS343	304024
Australia	Netherlands	14 Sep 36	173LTS325	304022
Iran	Iraq	04 Jul 37	190LTS241	304423
Portugal	UK Great Britain	28 Dec 37	185LTS205	304284
Canada	USA (United States)	07 Jan 38	184LTS305	304255
Dominican Republic	Haiti	31 Jan 38	187LTS169	304336
El Salvador	Guatemala	09 Apr 38	189LTS275	304390
Germany	Switzerland	21 Sep 38	196LTS365	304595
Portugal	UK Great Britain	29 Oct 40	204LTS261	304807
Thailand	UK Great Britain	10 Dec 40	203LTS433	304783
Frontier peoples and personnel				
Multilateral		05 Aug 20	2LTS49	300046
Austria	Germany	01 Sep 20	4LTS201	300107
Estonia	Latvia	19 Oct 20	17LTS189	300437
Germany	Poland	29 Apr 22	21LTS391	300549
Finland	USSR (Soviet Union)	01 Jun 22	16LTS319	300415
Italy	Serb/Croat/Slovene	23 Oct 22	18LTS413	300479
Czechoslovakia	UK Great Britain	14 Jul 23	29LTS377	300748
Germany	Poland	23 Feb 24	41LTS197	301015

PARTY ONE	PARTY TWO	DATE	CITATION	NUMBER
Frontier peoples and personnel (Cont.)				
Latvia	Netherlands	02 Jul 24	37LTS121	300951
Italy	Serb/Croat/Slovene	14 Jul 24	82LTS257	301876
Latvia	Lithuania	18 Oct 24	56LTS157	301327
Germany	Poland	30 Dec 24	52LTS51	301250
Germany	Poland	14 Mar 25	95LTS239	302178
Benelux Econ Union	Germany	04 Apr 25	37LTS203	300957
Czechoslovakia	Romania	16 Apr 25	46LTS427	301126
Czechoslovakia	Poland	30 May 25	48LTS397	301172
Czechoslovakia	Poland	30 May 25	50LTS243	301207
Great Britain	Nejd	02 Nov 25	60LTS419	301423
France	Great Britain	02 Feb 26	56LTS79	301324
France	Turkey	30 May 26	54LTS195	301285
Belgium	Germany	01 Jul 26	62LTS127	301461
Germany	Switzerland	14 Jul 26	59LTS87	301391
Czechoslovakia	Hungary	30 Sep 26	57LTS87	301356
Multilateral		13 Nov 26	77LTS249	301773
Persia	USSR (Soviet Union)	31 May 28	110LTS343	302566
Afghanistan	Persia	26 Jun 28	106LTS321	302453
Bulgaria	Yugoslavia	26 Sep 29	101LTS217	302324
Czechoslovakia	Romania	15 Jul 30	164LTS157	303793
Romania	Yugoslavia	11 Mar 33	146LTS277	303378
Belgium	UK Great Britain	22 Nov 34	190LTS99	304408
Belgium	France	09 May 35	162LTS437	303755
Belgium	Germany	10 May 35	165LTS143	303807
Poland	Romania	17 May 35	173LTS373	304028
Denmark	Germany	25 May 35	159LTS389	303680
Bulgaria	Romania	26 Jul 35	198LTS9	304621
Austria	Germany	26 Aug 36	171LTS357	303972
Siam	UK Great Britain	31 Mar 37	179LTS257	304153
Romania	Yugoslavia	13 May 37	197LTS101	304609
France	Switzerland	31 Jan 38	195LTS313	304553
Belgium	Luxembourg	22 Jul 38	191LTS113	304440
Frontier waterways				
Argentina	Uruguay	11 Apr 18	14LTS367	300385
Austria	Czechoslovakia	10 Mar 21	9LTS333	300267
Germany	Netherlands	05 Jul 21	13LTS41	300346
Italy	Serb/Croat/Slovene	14 Sep 21	19LTS14	300482
Finland	USSR (Soviet Union)	28 Oct 22	19LTS183	300492
Finland	USSR (Soviet Union)	28 Jul 23	32LTS101	300810
Germany	Poland	12 Jan 24	65LTS47	301519
Hungary	Romania	14 Apr 24	46LTS41	301113
Finland	Norway	28 Apr 24	30LTS35	300757
Finland	Norway	14 Feb 25	49LTS391	301194
Finland	Norway	14 Feb 25	49LTS379	301193
Canada	USA (United States)	24 Feb 25	43LTS251	301060
Germany	Poland	14 Mar 25	95LTS239	302178
Germany	Poland	27 Jan 26	64LTS113	301504
Estonia	Latvia	05 Feb 26	64LTS361	301509
Multilateral		21 Jun 26	78LTS229	301793
Portugal	South Africa	01 Jul 26	70LTS315	301643
France	Turkey	31 Jul 26	54LTS177	301284
Germany	Poland	19 Aug 26	64LTS420	301515
Denmark	Switzerland	25 Aug 26	69LTS313	301613
Multilateral		13 Nov 26	77LTS217	301772
Multilateral		13 Nov 26	77LTS249	301773
Bulgaria	Germany	22 Dec 26	64LTS77	301502
Germany	Poland	16 Feb 27	71LTS369	301676
Germany	Poland	07 Dec 27	92LTS203	302088
Germany	Poland	10 Dec 27	120LTS299	302773
Germany	Lithuania	29 Jan 28	89LTS338	302027
Czechoslovakia	Poland	18 Feb 28	100LTS273	302301
Czechoslovakia	Poland	18 Feb 28	119LTS385	302758
Czechoslovakia	Germany	22 Mar 28	93LTS235	302113
Czechoslovakia	Hungary	14 Nov 28	110LTS425	302574

PARTY ONE	PARTY TWO	DATE	CITATION	NUMBER
Frontier waterways (Cont.)				
Austria	Czechoslovakia	12 Dec 28	108LTS9	302501
Czechoslovakia	Germany	20 Mar 29	109LTS219	302541
United Arab Rep	UK Great Britain	07 May 29	93LTS43	302103
Norway	Sweden	11 May 29	120LTS263	302771
Germany	Switzerland	28 May 29	104LTS19	302375
Czechoslovakia	Germany	31 Jan 30	145LTS51	303345
UK Great Britain	USSR (Soviet Union)	22 May 30	102LTS103	302355
Romania	Yugoslavia	19 Jun 30	140LTS229	303238
Czechoslovakia	Romania	15 Jul 30	164LTS157	303793
Latvia	Lithuania	25 Jan 31	118LTS175	302722
Italy	Turkey	04 Jan 32	138LTS243	303191
Multilateral		14 Mar 32	131LTS135	303006
Poland	USSR (Soviet Union)	10 Apr 32	141LTS349	303275
Brazil	UK Great Britain	01 Nov 32	177LTS127	304087
Denmark	Sweden	31 Dec 32	139LTS205	303211
Romania	Yugoslavia	10 Feb 33	174LTS115	304042
Multilateral		03 Feb 34	154LTS349	303560
Finland	USSR (Soviet Union)	25 May 34	155LTS207	303578
Czechoslovakia	Hungary	08 Jun 34	172LTS61	303979
Belgium	UK Great Britain	22 Nov 34	190LTS99	304408
Czechoslovakia	Germany	27 Sep 35	182LTS267	304217
Canada	USA (United States)	29 Jan 37	181LTS209	304190
Canada	USA (United States)	07 Jan 38	184LTS305	304255
Norway	Sweden	20 Apr 38	189LTS153	304383
Canada	USA (United States)	15 Sep 38	203LTS207	304763
Iceland	Norway	27 Feb 39	196LTS377	304598
Canada	USA (United States)	07 Nov 40	203LTS267	304769
Canada	USA (United States)	20 May 41	204LTS199	304800
UK Great Britain	Venezuela	26 Feb 42	205LTS121	304829
Frontier crossing points				
Estonia	Latvia	19 Oct 20	17LTS189	300437
France	UK Great Britain	20 Oct 20	2LTS323	300085
Bulgaria	Netherlands	13 Nov 20	7LTS107	300178
Denmark	UK Great Britain	23 Dec 20	2LTS249	300071
Sweden	UK Great Britain	16 Feb 21	3LTS233	300100
Austria	Czechoslovakia	10 Mar 21	9LTS333	300267
Germany	Poland	21 Apr 21	12LTS61	300308
Latvia	Lithuania	13 May 21	17LTS211	300438
Finland	France	13 Jul 21	29LTS445	300755
Belgium	Luxembourg	25 Jul 21	9LTS223	300256
Estonia	Finland	29 Oct 21	13LTS59	300348
France	UK Great Britain	30 Jan 22	12LTS449	300341
Germany	Poland	29 Apr 22	21LTS391	300549
Germany	Poland	15 May 22	10LTS37	300273
Belgium	Switzerland	13 Jun 22	12LTS295	300321
Poland	Switzerland	26 Jun 22	12LTS305	300322
Czechoslovakia	Latvia	07 Oct 22	20LTS379	300528
Italy	Serb/Croat/Slovene	23 Oct 22	18LTS441	300480
Finland	USSR (Soviet Union)	28 Oct 22	19LTS153	300491
France	Saar	30 Nov 22	27LTS283	300691
Liechtenstein	Switzerland	29 Mar 23	21LTS231	300545
Germany	Poland	23 Feb 24	41LTS197	301015
Latvia	Lithuania	18 Oct 24	56LTS157	301327
Czechoslovakia	Romania	16 Apr 25	46LTS427	301126
Finland	Sweden	09 May 25	47LTS283	301136
Czechoslovakia	Poland	30 May 25	48LTS397	301172
Germany	Poland	02 Dec 25	70LTS427	301649
Germany	Poland	27 Jan 26	64LTS113	301504
Multilateral		21 Jun 26	78LTS229	301793
Belgium	Germany	01 Jul 26	62LTS127	301461
Czechoslovakia	Hungary	30 Sep 26	57LTS87	301356
Bulgaria	Germany	22 Dec 26	64LTS77	301502
Austria	Czechoslovakia	15 Feb 27	73LTS349	301724
Belgium	Portugal	19 Jul 27	71LTS419	301680

PARTY ONE	PARTY TWO	DATE	CITATION	NUMBER
Frontier crossing points (Cont.)				
Germany	Lithuania	29 Jan 28	89LTS97	302009
France	Spain	22 Mar 28	73LTS63	301707
Austria	Czechoslovakia	12 Dec 28	108LTS9	302501
Austria	Czechoslovakia	12 Dec 28	107LTS137	302474
Poland	Romania	24 May 29	124LTS339	302837
Poland	Romania	24 May 29	124LTS333	302836
Belgium	Germany	07 Nov 29	121LTS327	302795
Poland	Romania	07 Dec 29	119LTS283	302752
Austria	Netherlands	31 Dec 29	111LTS177	302586
Poland	Romania	09 May 30	112LTS225	302617
Czechoslovakia	Romania	15 Jul 30	164LTS157	303793
Brazil	Paraguay	09 Dec 31	136LTS427	303142
Germany	Poland	22 Dec 31	144LTS191	303329
Poland	USSR (Soviet Union)	03 Jun 33	142LTS265	303300
Brazil	Uruguay	20 Dec 33	181LTS69	304178
Belgium	Germany	10 May 35	165LTS143	303807
Denmark	Germany	25 May 35	159LTS389	303680
Bel-Lux Econ Union	France	16 Jul 35	162LTS19	303731
Bulgaria	Romania	26 Jul 35	198LTS9	304621
Romania	Yugoslavia	13 May 37	197LTS101	304609
Czechoslovakia	Hungary	24 Aug 37	189LTS403	304397
Continental shelf				
Italy	Netherlands	11 Oct 20	18LTS253	300468
Conservation of specific resources				
Persia	USSR (Soviet Union)	01 Oct 27	112LTS297	302621
Ocean resources				
Multilateral		09 Feb 20	2LTS7	300041
Albania	Serb/Croat/Slovene	22 Jun 26	91LTS9	302054
Multilateral		08 Nov 33	172LTS241	303995
Multilateral		08 Jun 37	190LTS79	304406
Wildlife				
Finland	Norway	03 Mar 22	14LTS157	300372
Germany	Poland	15 Jun 22	21LTS433	300550
Finland	USSR (Soviet Union)	28 Oct 22	19LTS183	300492
Denmark	Norway	09 Jul 24	27LTS203	300684
Finland	Sweden	09 May 25	47LTS283	301136
Multilateral		13 Nov 26	77LTS249	301773
Denmark	Sweden	09 Oct 31	126LTS255	302888
Romania	Yugoslavia	14 Dec 31	135LTS31	303103
Finland	USSR (Soviet Union)	04 Jul 33	149LTS83	303436
Multilateral		08 Nov 33	172LTS241	303995
Finland	Norway	05 Nov 35	169LTS33	303913
Mexico	USA (United States)	07 Feb 36	178LTS309	304119
Fisheries and fishing				
Finland	Norway	14 Jul 20	1LTS317	300027
Persia	USSR (Soviet Union)	26 Feb 21	9LTS383	300268
Italy	Serb/Croat/Slovene	14 Sep 21	19LTS14	300482
Finland	USSR (Soviet Union)	20 Sep 22	19LTS143	300490
Finland	USSR (Soviet Union)	21 Oct 22	29LTS197	300742
Italy	Serb/Croat/Slovene	23 Oct 22	18LTS461	300481
Finland	USSR (Soviet Union)	28 Oct 22	29LTS211	300743
Canada	USA (United States)	02 Mar 23	32LTS93	300809
France	UK Great Britain	29 Sep 23	21LTS137	300536
Estonia	Latvia	28 Oct 25	54LTS231	301286
Multilateral		13 Nov 26	77LTS249	301773
Multilateral		13 Nov 26	77LTS217	301772
Greece	Italy	24 Nov 26	63LTS91	301481
Finland	Sweden	10 May 27	70LTS201	301634
Germany	Poland	10 Dec 27	120LTS299	302773
Japan	USSR (Soviet Union)	23 Jan 28	80LTS341	301839
Germany	Lithuania	29 Jan 28	89LTS309	302026
Czechoslovakia	Poland	18 Feb 28	119LTS385	302758
Czechoslovakia	Hungary	14 Nov 28	110LTS425	302574

PARTY ONE	PARTY TWO	DATE	CITATION	NUMBER
Fisheries and fishing (Cont.)				
Austria	Czechoslovakia	12 Dec 28	108LTS9	302501
Multilateral		20 Dec 28	86LTS429	301954
Multilateral		17 Dec 29	115LTS93	302679
Canada	USA (United States)	09 May 30	121LTS45	302782
UK Great Britain	USSR (Soviet Union)	22 May 30	102LTS103	302355
Czechoslovakia	Romania	15 Jul 30	164LTS157	303793
Latvia	Lithuania	25 Jan 31	118LTS175	302722
Multilateral		24 Sep 31	155LTS349	303586
Multilateral		13 Dec 32	139LTS189	303210
Denmark	Sweden	31 Dec 32	139LTS205	303211
Finland	USSR (Soviet Union)	25 May 34	155LTS207	303578
Czechoslovakia	Hungary	08 Jun 34	172LTS61	303979
Canada	USA (United States)	29 Jan 37	181LTS209	304190
Multilateral		08 Jun 37	190LTS79	304406
Multilateral		06 Sep 37	186LTS419	304326
Canada	USA (United States)	07 Jan 38	184LTS305	304255
Finland	Norway	21 Apr 38	188LTS215	304360
Finland	Norway	21 Apr 38	188LTS231	304361
Iceland	Norway	27 Feb 39	196LTS377	304598
Regulation of natural resources				
Multilateral		09 Feb 20	2LTS7	300041
Finland	Sweden	10 May 20	2LTS141	300058
Germany	Netherlands	05 Jul 21	13LTS41	300346
Peru	UK Great Britain	02 Mar 22	10LTS463	300286
Germany	Poland	15 Jun 22	21LTS433	300550
Germany	Poland	23 Jun 22	22LTS25	300553
Finland	USSR (Soviet Union)	28 Oct 22	19LTS183	300492
Finland	USSR (Soviet Union)	28 Oct 22	19LTS153	300491
France	USA (United States)	13 Feb 23	26LTS53	300640
France	USA (United States)	13 Feb 23	26LTS69	300641
Denmark	Finland	03 Aug 23	21LTS269	300547
Germany	Poland	12 Jan 24	65LTS47	301519
Belgium	USA (United States)	21 Jan 24	31LTS137	300791
Denmark	Poland	22 Mar 24	31LTS13	300778
Allied Powers	Germany	28 Oct 24	41LTS461	301025
Finland	Norway	14 Feb 25	49LTS391	301194
Finland	USA (United States)	21 Dec 25	47LTS345	301138
Belgium	Portugal	20 Jul 27	71LTS431	301681
Norway	Sweden	11 May 29	120LTS263	302771
Czechoslovakia	Romania	15 Jul 30	164LTS157	303793
Romania	Yugoslavia	14 Dec 31	135LTS31	303103
Finland	USSR (Soviet Union)	15 Oct 33	149LTS243	303439
Belgium	UK Great Britain	22 Nov 34	190LTS99	304408
Czechoslovakia	Hungary	24 Aug 37	189LTS403	304397
France	Switzerland	31 Jan 38	195LTS313	304553
Canada	USA (United States)	07 Nov 40	203LTS267	304769
Canada	USA (United States)	20 May 41	204LTS199	304800
Raw materials				
France	UK Great Britain	24 Apr 20	1LTS281	300022
Peru	UK Great Britain	27 Aug 21	7LTS289	300195
Peru	UK Great Britain	02 Mar 22	10LTS463	300286
Germany	Poland	15 Jun 22	21LTS433	300550
Germany	Poland	23 Jun 22	22LTS25	300553
Finland	USSR (Soviet Union)	28 Oct 22	19LTS153	300491
China	Japan	01 Dec 22	22LTS179	300559
Czechoslovakia	Hungary	09 Feb 24	30LTS335	300773
Finland	Norway	14 Feb 25	49LTS391	301194
Estonia	Latvia	05 Feb 26	64LTS361	301509
Germany	Poland	21 Jun 26	72LTS203	301693
Czechoslovakia	Hungary	14 Nov 28	110LTS425	302574
Romania	Yugoslavia	14 Dec 31	135LTS31	303103
Germany	Netherlands	17 May 39	199LTS239	304678

United Nations Treaty Series

PARTY ONE	PARTY TWO	DATE	CITATION	NUMBER
Change of circumstances				
Netherlands	UK Great Britain	13 Jun 39	5UNTS65	200028
Canada	USA (United States)	29 May 40	119UNTS285	200385
Canada	USA (United States)	04 Mar 43	13UNTS411	200087
Multilateral		15 Dec 44	17UNTS305	200110
Multilateral		15 Dec 44	16UNTS247	200106
Netherlands	Switzerland	24 Oct 45	3UNTS73	100025
Multilateral		31 Mar 46	17UNTS159	100274
Sweden	USA (United States)	30 Sep 46	42UNTS213	100649
Norway	USA (United States)	12 Nov 46	42UNTS227	100651
Denmark	Norway	15 Apr 47	12UNTS323	100191
Thailand	USA (United States)	08 May 47	42UNTS241	100653
Burma	Pakistan	18 Nov 47	35UNTS321	100562
Taiwan	USA (United States)	17 Mar 48	76UNTS157	100987
Italy	UK Great Britain	25 Jun 48	94UNTS239	101313
Multilateral		19 Nov 48	44UNTS277	100688
Belgium	United Arab Rep	19 Sep 49	137UNTS189	101853
Belgium	San Marino	14 Dec 49	51UNTS107	100757
Haiti	WHO (World Health)	27 Jun 50	110UNTS99	101504
WHO (World Health)	Venezuela	11 Sep 50	110UNTS237	101513
Iceland	WHO (World Health)	06 Oct 50	110UNTS127	101506
WHO (World Health)	Turkey	19 Oct 50	110UNTS215	101512
Peru	WHO (World Health)	10 Nov 50	110UNTS187	101510
Nicaragua	WHO (World Health)	10 Nov 50	110UNTS155	101508
Philippines	WHO (World Health)	28 Dec 50	110UNTS203	101511
Paraguay	WHO (World Health)	15 Feb 51	110UNTS171	101509
Multilateral		06 Mar 51	106UNTS141	101461
Indonesia	WHO (World Health)	28 Mar 51	103UNTS71	101425
Jordan	WHO (World Health)	03 Apr 51	110UNTS297	200367
Honduras	WHO (World Health)	20 Apr 51	110UNTS111	101505
Colombia	WHO (World Health)	04 May 51	110UNTS83	101503
Cambodia	WHO (World Health)	31 May 51	102UNTS279	200307
WHO (World Health)	Uruguay	11 Jun 51	128UNTS251	101724
Liberia	WHO (World Health)	11 Jun 51	103UNTS83	101426
Iraq	WHO (World Health)	01 Jul 51	110UNTS139	101507
UK Great Britain	USA (United States)	18 Jul 51	117UNTS49	101583
WHO (World Health)	Vietnam, South	21 Sep 51	107UNTS63	200352
Multilateral		20 Dec 51	163UNTS293	102151
Norway	WHO (World Health)	09 May 52	131UNTS281	101747
Germany, West	Israel	10 Sep 52	162UNTS205	102137
Belgium	New Zealand	01 Sep 53	192UNTS283	102605
Jordan	USA (United States)	21 Oct 53	222UNTS31	103020
Libya	USA (United States)	11 Jan 54	229UNTS15	103157
Norway	USA (United States)	07 May 54	231UNTS157	103215
Spain	USA (United States)	19 May 54	235UNTS87	103296
France	USA (United States)	31 May 54	236UNTS141	103321
UK Great Britain	USA (United States)	15 Jun 54	236UNTS133	103320

PARTY ONE	PARTY TWO	DATE	CITATION	NUMBER
Change of circumstances (Cont.)				
Italy	USA (United States)	24 Jun 54	235UNTS3	103290
Pakistan	USA (United States)	23 Aug 54	234UNTS243	103287
Libya	USA (United States)	03 Nov 54	238UNTS227	103366
Belgium	USA (United States)	23 Nov 54	235UNTS19	103292
Guatemala	USA (United States)	13 Dec 54	237UNTS169	103343
Turkey	USA (United States)	25 Apr 55	263UNTS299	103779
Greece	USA (United States)	27 May 55	251UNTS349	103552
USA (United States)	Yugoslavia	30 Sep 55	269UNTS89	103877
Norway	Sweden	09 Mar 56	369UNTS285	105262
Ceylon (Sri Lanka)	USA (United States)	28 Apr 56	274UNTS35	103956
Iceland	USA (United States)	06 Dec 56	265UNTS261	103818
Morocco	USA (United States)	02 Apr 57	288UNTS157	104203
Libya	USA (United States)	04 Apr 57	283UNTS181	104116
Ethiopia	USA (United States)	25 Apr 57	283UNTS205	104118
Iraq	USA (United States)	16 Jun 57	284UNTS39	104127
Germany, West	Netherlands	10 Jul 57	339UNTS97	104848
France	USA (United States)	23 Sep 57	293UNTS297	104297
Argentina	Italy	25 Nov 57	305UNTS275	104424
Ethiopia	USA (United States)	26 Dec 57	307UNTS71	104443
Israel	Yugoslavia	11 Dec 58	386UNTS283	105548
Iraq	USA (United States)	07 Jul 59	357UNTS153	105114
Norway	Sweden	28 Oct 59	427UNTS225	106157
Turkey	USA (United States)	30 Nov 59	361UNTS107	105174
Norway	USA (United States)	13 Feb 60	388UNTS255	105583
Greece	USA (United States)	15 Feb 60	377UNTS95	105397
Multilateral		26 Feb 60	418UNTS171	106022
Turkey	USA (United States)	02 Mar 60	372UNTS37	105286
Netherlands	USA (United States)	24 Mar 60	406UNTS165	105847
Denmark	USA (United States)	12 Apr 60	373UNTS9	105311
Italy	USA (United States)	07 Jul 60	380UNTS143	105455
France	USA (United States)	19 Sep 60	400UNTS21	105745
Multilateral		19 Sep 60	444UNTS259	106371
Portugal	USA (United States)	26 Sep 60	393UNTS257	105660
Togo	USA (United States)	22 Dec 60	401UNTS33	105760
Mali	USA (United States)	04 Jan 61	405UNTS165	105832
Honduras	USA (United States)	12 Apr 61	413UNTS182	105952
Sierra Leone	USA (United States)	05 May 61	409UNTS194	105885
Ivory Coast	USA (United States)	17 May 61	409UNTS241	105889
Niger	USA (United States)	26 May 61	410UNTS213	105905
Cameroon	USA (United States)	26 May 61	413UNTS195	105953
Dahomey	USA (United States)	27 May 61	445UNTS23	106373
Madagascar	USA (United States)	22 Jun 61	413UNTS219	105956
Paraguay	USA (United States)	26 Sep 61	461UNTS91	106653
El Salvador	USA (United States)	19 Dec 61	445UNTS175	106385
Costa Rica	USA (United States)	22 Dec 61	460UNTS277	106646
Dominican Republic	USA (United States)	11 Jan 62	433UNTS133	106236
Multilateral		20 Feb 62	597UNTS159	108644

PARTY ONE	PARTY TWO	DATE	CITATION	NUMBER
Change of circumstances (Cont.)				
Pakistan	USA (United States)	05 Mar 62	446UNTS57	106403
Norway	USA (United States)	05 Mar 62	446UNTS47	106402
Israel	USA (United States)	05 Mar 62	446UNTS29	106400
Peru	USA (United States)	05 Mar 62	446UNTS65	106404
Denmark	USA (United States)	05 Mar 62	446UNTS9	106398
Finland	USA (United States)	05 Mar 62	446UNTS19	106399
New Zealand	USA (United States)	05 Mar 62	446UNTS39	106401
UK Great Britain	USA (United States)	07 Mar 62	446UNTS231	106406
EEC (Econ Commnty)	USA (United States)	07 Mar 62	446UNTS81	106405
Nicaragua	USA (United States)	30 Mar 62	456UNTS241	106559
Ecuador	USA (United States)	17 Apr 62	442UNTS69	106339
Colombia	USA (United States)	23 Jul 62	458UNTS123	106595
Korea, South	IDA (Devel Assoc)	17 Aug 62	468UNTS387	200603
Central Afri Rep	USA (United States)	10 Feb 63	473UNTS83	106857
Switzerland	UK Great Britain	27 Aug 63	486UNTS183	107079
Jamaica	USA (United States)	24 Oct 63	489UNTS337	107148
Portugal	UK Great Britain	07 Apr 64	539UNTS167	107830
Malta	UK Great Britain	21 Sep 64	588UNTS55	108518
Multilateral		31 Dec 65	616UNTS317	108904
Iran	USSR (Soviet Union)	13 Jan 66	633UNTS123	109037
Israel	Kenya	25 Feb 66	582UNTS23	108455
Multilateral		05 Apr 66	640UNTS133	109159
Austria	Bulgaria	21 Apr 67	603UNTS121	108729
Ecuador	Israel	09 Aug 67	630UNTS319	108979
Bulgaria	Denmark	02 Sep 67	631UNTS71	108987
Denmark	Iran	02 Nov 67	638UNTS217	109138
Austria	Cyprus	14 Dec 67	636UNTS267	109104
Multilateral		08 Mar 68	634UNTS199	109062
Default remedies				
Multilateral		27 Dec 45	2UNTS39	100020
Multilateral		22 Jul 46	14UNTS185	100221
Multilateral		28 Aug 46	1UNTS139	200006
Taiwan	UK Great Britain	23 Jul 47	9UNTS207	100135
Netherlands	IBRD (World Bank)	07 Aug 47	152UNTS165	102015
Denmark	IBRD (World Bank)	22 Aug 47	152UNTS223	102016
Luxembourg	IBRD (World Bank)	28 Aug 47	153UNTS3	102017
Multilateral		11 Oct 47	77UNTS143	100998
Argentina	Chile	14 Dec 48	635UNTS21	109071
Brazil	IBRD (World Bank)	27 Jan 49	153UNTS264	102026
Belgium	IBRD (World Bank)	01 Mar 49	154UNTS133	102029
Multilateral		28 Apr 49	83UNTS105	101105
India	IBRD (World Bank)	18 Aug 49	154UNTS269	102031
IBRD (World Bank)	Yugoslavia	17 Sep 49	155UNTS3	102034
India	IBRD (World Bank)	29 Sep 49	154UNTS393	102033
Finland	IBRD (World Bank)	17 Oct 49	156UNTS355	200481
Iraq	IBRD (World Bank)	15 Jun 50	155UNTS267	102038
IBRD (World Bank)	Turkey	07 Jul 50	156UNTS3	102039
IBRD (World Bank)	Turkey	07 Jul 50	156UNTS75	102040
FAO (Food Agri)	United Nations	02 Aug 50	139UNTS407	200467
Ethiopia	IBRD (World Bank)	13 Sep 50	157UNTS213	102055
Ethiopia	IBRD (World Bank)	13 Sep 50	157UNTS233	102056
ILO (Labor Org)	United Nations	12 Oct 50	139UNTS395	200466
Mexico	IBRD (World Bank)	18 Oct 50	157UNTS259	102057
IBRD (World Bank)	Thailand	27 Oct 50	158UNTS25	102060
IBRD (World Bank)	Thailand	27 Oct 50	158UNTS3	102059
IBRD (World Bank)	Thailand	27 Oct 50	158UNTS43	102061
Australia	IBRD (World Bank)	14 Nov 50	156UNTS147	102041
IBRD (World Bank)	South Africa	23 Jan 51	158UNTS115	102064
Ethiopia	IBRD (World Bank)	19 Feb 51	186UNTS101	102486
ICAO (Civil Aviat)	United Nations	28 Feb 51	139UNTS429	200469
UNESCO (Educ/Cult)	United Nations	07 Mar 51	139UNTS417	200468

PARTY ONE	PARTY TWO	DATE	CITATION	NUMBER
Default remedies (Cont.)				
Colombia	IBRD (World Bank)	10 Apr 51	158UNTS155	102066
Nicaragua	IBRD (World Bank)	07 Jun 51	158UNTS277	102068
Iceland	IBRD (World Bank)	20 Jun 51	158UNTS301	102069
UK Great Britain	USA (United States)	18 Jul 51	117UNTS49	101583
Belgium	IBRD (World Bank)	13 Sep 51	158UNTS349	102071
IBRD (World Bank)	Yugoslavia	11 Oct 51	159UNTS3	102081
Nicaragua	IBRD (World Bank)	29 Oct 51	159UNTS35	102082
Iceland	IBRD (World Bank)	01 Nov 51	159UNTS55	102083
Paraguay	IBRD (World Bank)	07 Dec 51	159UNTS103	102085
Peru	IBRD (World Bank)	23 Jan 52	159UNTS163	102087
Pakistan	IBRD (World Bank)	27 Mar 52	159UNTS251	102090
Pakistan	IBRD (World Bank)	13 Jun 52	191UNTS85	102578
IBRD (World Bank)	Turkey	18 Jun 52	159UNTS269	102091
Brazil	IBRD (World Bank)	27 Jun 52	190UNTS115	102561
Australia	IBRD (World Bank)	08 Jul 52	159UNTS295	102092
Peru	IBRD (World Bank)	08 Jul 52	159UNTS321	102093
Iceland	IBRD (World Bank)	26 Aug 52	159UNTS363	102095
Colombia	IBRD (World Bank)	26 Aug 52	159UNTS339	102094
India	IBRD (World Bank)	23 Jan 53	201UNTS145	102715
IBRD (World Bank)	Yugoslavia	11 Feb 53	165UNTS231	102179
United Nations	WMO (Meteorology)	27 Mar 53	178UNTS361	200504
Brazil	IBRD (World Bank)	30 Apr 53	190UNTS133	102562
IBRD (World Bank)	South Africa	28 Aug 53	180UNTS73	102376
Nicaragua	IBRD (World Bank)	04 Sep 53	186UNTS137	102488
Nicaragua	IBRD (World Bank)	04 Sep 53	186UNTS117	102487
Colombia	IBRD (World Bank)	10 Sep 53	203UNTS3	102738
Brazil	IBRD (World Bank)	18 Dec 53	301UNTS229	104346
Australia	IBRD (World Bank)	02 Mar 54	191UNTS103	102579
Norway	IBRD (World Bank)	08 Apr 54	201UNTS131	102714
Peru	IBRD (World Bank)	12 Apr 54	190UNTS231	102567
Multilateral		12 May 54	327UNTS3	104714
Ceylon (Sri Lanka)	IBRD (World Bank)	09 Jul 54	198UNTS313	200517
El Salvador	IBRD (World Bank)	12 Oct 54	203UNTS37	102739
Multilateral		12 Mar 55	211UNTS3	102844
Australia	IBRD (World Bank)	18 Mar 55	220UNTS131	102998
Peru	IBRD (World Bank)	05 Apr 55	211UNTS115	102850
Norway	IBRD (World Bank)	19 Apr 55	211UNTS159	102852
Panama	IBRD (World Bank)	12 Jul 55	219UNTS127	102970
Guatemala	IBRD (World Bank)	29 Jul 55	229UNTS167	103165
Peru	IBRD (World Bank)	05 Aug 55	218UNTS3	102950
Lebanon	IBRD (World Bank)	25 Aug 55	230UNTS233	103188
Multilateral		12 Oct 55	560UNTS3	108165
Honduras	IBRD (World Bank)	22 Dec 55	230UNTS262	103189
Burma	IBRD (World Bank)	04 May 56	253UNTS179	103584
Haiti	IBRD (World Bank)	07 May 56	252UNTS279	103570
Chile	IBRD (World Bank)	01 Nov 56	261UNTS27	103724
Australia	IBRD (World Bank)	15 Nov 56	288UNTS117	104201
Australia	IBRD (World Bank)	03 Dec 56	288UNTS99	104200
Iran	IBRD (World Bank)	22 Jan 57	317UNTS129	104600
Ethiopia	IBRD (World Bank)	28 Jan 57	286UNTS307	104175
Multilateral		25 Mar 57	294UNTS411	104302
Multilateral		25 Mar 57	294UNTS2	104300
Lebanon	United Nations	01 May 57	266UNTS125	103827
India	IBRD (World Bank)	12 Jul 57	288UNTS135	104202
Chile	IBRD (World Bank)	24 Jul 57	282UNTS189	104099
Chile	IBRD (World Bank)	24 Jul 57	282UNTS139	104098
Belgium	IBRD (World Bank)	10 Sep 57	286UNTS291	104174
Ecuador	IBRD (World Bank)	20 Sep 57	289UNTS237	104221
IBRD (World Bank)	South Africa	01 Oct 57	280UNTS285	104065
Pakistan	IBRD (World Bank)	18 Oct 57	299UNTS303	104322
Bulgaria	Yugoslavia	21 Mar 58	386UNTS119	105541
Bulgaria	Yugoslavia	21 Mar 58	349UNTS61	105009
Belgium	Sweden	08 May 58	312UNTS145	104516
Honduras	IBRD (World Bank)	09 May 58	323UNTS4	104662
Austria	Belgium	20 Jun 58	312UNTS95	104513

PARTY ONE	PARTY TWO	DATE	CITATION	NUMBER
Default remedies (Cont.)				
IBRD (World Bank)	Sudan	21 Jul 58	323UNTS183	104669
India	IBRD (World Bank)	16 Sep 58	323UNTS235	104671
Ceylon (Sri Lanka)	IBRD (World Bank)	17 Sep 58	323UNTS51	104664
IAEA (Atom Energy)	United Nations	22 Sep 58	313UNTS323	200552
Multilateral		05 Nov 58	428UNTS73	106169
Austria	IBRD (World Bank)	02 Dec 58	340UNTS3	104856
IBRD (World Bank)	South Africa	02 Dec 58	324UNTS3	104676
El Salvador	IBRD (World Bank)	07 Jan 59	346UNTS51	104977
India	IBRD (World Bank)	08 Apr 59	348UNTS131	104998
Iran	IBRD (World Bank)	29 May 59	348UNTS103	104997
IBRD (World Bank)	South Africa	10 Jun 59	340UNTS33	104857
Greece	Yugoslavia	18 Jun 59	368UNTS27	105234
Norway	IBRD (World Bank)	08 Jul 59	344UNTS229	104952
India	IBRD (World Bank)	15 Jul 59	346UNTS33	104976
Italy	Netherlands	08 Dec 59	484UNTS309	107039
IBRD (World Bank)	Uruguay	30 Dec 59	384UNTS275	105523
ITU (Telecommun)	United Nations	14 Jan 60	348UNTS331	200566
Multilateral		26 Jan 60	439UNTS249	106333
Iran	IBRD (World Bank)	20 Feb 60	384UNTS213	105521
Costa Rica	IBRD (World Bank)	04 May 60	390UNTS201	105609
IBRD (World Bank)	Sudan	17 Jun 60	379UNTS253	105442
Panama	IBRD (World Bank)	19 Aug 60	390UNTS153	105607
Israel	IBRD (World Bank)	09 Sep 60	406UNTS3	105837
Pakistan	IBRD (World Bank)	19 Sep 60	444UNTS207	106370
Norway	IBRD (World Bank)	02 Dec 60	390UNTS131	105606
Peru	IBRD (World Bank)	19 Dec 60	417UNTS275	106010
Japan	IBRD (World Bank)	20 Dec 60	400UNTS279	105754
Ceylon (Sri Lanka)	IBRD (World Bank)	06 Jun 61	414UNTS349	105978
IBRD (World Bank)	Sudan	14 Jun 61	415UNTS26	105980
Chile	IBRD (World Bank)	28 Jun 61	426UNTS33	106129
Argentina	IBRD (World Bank)	30 Jun 61	445UNTS85	106379
Philippines	IBRD (World Bank)	26 Jul 61	414UNTS253	105976
India	IBRD (World Bank)	09 Aug 61	417UNTS297	106011
India	IBRD (World Bank)	17 Aug 61	417UNTS319	106012
Colombia	IBRD (World Bank)	28 Aug 61	416UNTS23	105993
Costa Rica	IBRD (World Bank)	13 Oct 61	430UNTS27	106202
India	IBRD (World Bank)	13 Oct 61	418UNTS3	106013
Peru	IBRD (World Bank)	03 Nov 61	430UNTS47	106203
IBRD (World Bank)	Venezuela	13 Dec 61	446UNTS371	106409
Australia	IBRD (World Bank)	23 Jan 62	430UNTS3	106201
Iceland	IBRD (World Bank)	14 Feb 62	447UNTS95	106413
Multilateral		20 Feb 62	597UNTS159	108644
Multilateral		14 Jun 62	528UNTS33	107634
Pakistan	IBRD (World Bank)	14 Sep 62	467UNTS152	106762
Israel	IBRD (World Bank)	17 Oct 62	467UNTS107	106760
IBRD (World Bank)	Uruguay	26 Oct 62	481UNTS39	106977
IBRD (World Bank)	Thailand	21 Dec 62	467UNTS63	106758
IBRD (World Bank)	Thailand	21 Dec 62	467UNTS43	106757
Nicaragua	IBRD (World Bank)	01 Mar 63	481UNTS15	106976
IBRD (World Bank)	Thailand	11 Jun 63	481UNTS227	106984
Denmark	IBRD (World Bank)	24 Jul 63	481UNTS171	106982
Taiwan	IBRD (World Bank)	27 Sep 63	483UNTS151	107012
Norway	IBRD (World Bank)	15 Oct 63	482UNTS103	106992
IBRD (World Bank)	Spain	25 Oct 63	491UNTS297	107181
New Zealand	IBRD (World Bank)	12 Nov 63	485UNTS233	107059
Niger	United Nations	20 Nov 63	536UNTS3	107793
Multilateral		30 Dec 63	568UNTS215	108270
Multilateral		30 Dec 63	568UNTS243	108272
Multilateral		30 Dec 63	568UNTS233	108271
Multilateral		30 Dec 63	551UNTS75	108035
Liberia	IBRD (World Bank)	08 Jan 64	504UNTS53	107353
New Zealand	IBRD (World Bank)	12 Mar 64	505UNTS3	107362
Peru	IBRD (World Bank)	22 Apr 64	519UNTS95	107503
Multilateral		06 May 64	514UNTS71	107442
Ecuador	IBRD (World Bank)	26 May 64	534UNTS113	107758

PARTY ONE	PARTY TWO	DATE	CITATION	NUMBER
Default remedies (Cont.)				
IBRD (World Bank)	Tunisia	05 Jun 64	539UNTS129	107827
Iran	IBRD (World Bank)	10 Jun 64	537UNTS111	107799
Gabon	IBRD (World Bank)	10 Jul 64	537UNTS63	107797
Finland	IBRD (World Bank)	10 Jul 64	516UNTS125	107474
Mexico	United Nations	17 Jul 64	533UNTS117	107738
Eur Space Research	Sweden	29 Jul 64	528UNTS81	107636
Morocco	IBRD (World Bank)	26 Aug 64	537UNTS193	107802
IBRD (World Bank)	Venezuela	28 Aug 64	520UNTS97	107512
Philippines	IBRD (World Bank)	28 Oct 64	537UNTS165	107801
IBRD (World Bank)	Thailand	25 Nov 64	537UNTS273	107805
Multilateral		02 Dec 64	572UNTS229	108317
Honduras	IBRD (World Bank)	02 Feb 65	561UNTS255	108188
Multilateral		24 Feb 65	556UNTS47	108118
IBRD (World Bank)	Uruguay	30 Mar 65	567UNTS45	108251
Iran	IBRD (World Bank)	28 Apr 65	555UNTS45	108104
Iran	IBRD (World Bank)	28 Apr 65	555UNTS21	108103
Taiwan	IBRD (World Bank)	28 Apr 65	549UNTS145	107998
India	IBRD (World Bank)	11 Jun 65	557UNTS59	108128
Peru	IBRD (World Bank)	18 Jun 65	568UNTS191	108269
Australia	Eur Space Vehicle	13 Jul 65	543UNTS183	107902
Nigeria	IBRD (World Bank)	26 Sep 65	571UNTS39	108298
Nigeria	IBRD (World Bank)	26 Sep 65	570UNTS233	108296
East Afri Service	IBRD (World Bank)	29 Sep 65	568UNTS327	200623
IBRD (World Bank)	Spain	29 Sep 65	568UNTS49	108264
Malaysia	IBRD (World Bank)	17 Nov 65	568UNTS23	108263
Multilateral		04 Dec 65	571UNTS123	108303
New Zealand	IBRD (World Bank)	17 Dec 65	567UNTS275	108260
New Zealand	IBRD (World Bank)	17 Dec 65	567UNTS255	108259
IBRD (World Bank)	Sudan	27 Dec 65	567UNTS27	108250
Belgium	Denmark	04 Feb 66	561UNTS233	108187
Guinea	IBRD (World Bank)	30 Mar 66	568UNTS3	108262
Paraguay	IBRD (World Bank)	04 Apr 66	570UNTS41	108287
Finland	IBRD (World Bank)	27 Apr 66	568UNTS107	108266
Multilateral		04 May 66	575UNTS49	108354
Peru	IBRD (World Bank)	13 May 66	570UNTS61	108288
Multilateral		20 Jun 66	572UNTS263	108318
IBRD (World Bank)	Thailand	24 Jun 66	582UNTS259	108466
Iraq	IBRD (World Bank)	22 Jul 66	584UNTS233	108480
Jamaica	IBRD (World Bank)	30 Sep 66	582UNTS179	108463
IBRD (World Bank)	Zambia	04 Oct 66	585UNTS181	108489
Greece	United Nations	14 Apr 67	595UNTS83	108613
Treaty interpretation				
Greece	Iran	09 Jan 31	166UNTS323	200496
Taiwan	Dominican Republic	11 May 40	10UNTS285	200067
Ecuador	USA (United States)	02 Mar 42	105UNTS195	200332
Taiwan	Cuba	12 Nov 42	10UNTS243	200065
Canada	USA (United States)	19 Dec 42	26UNTS363	200156
Brazil	Taiwan	20 Aug 43	14UNTS365	200094
Multilateral		15 Jan 44	161UNTS281	200489
Taiwan	Mexico	01 Aug 44	14UNTS441	200099
Multilateral		15 Dec 44	16UNTS247	200106
Multilateral		15 Dec 44	17UNTS305	200110
France	USA (United States)	28 Feb 45	76UNTS213	200247
Multilateral		07 Nov 45	2UNTS17	100018
Multilateral		16 Nov 45	4UNTS275	100052
Multilateral		27 Dec 45	2UNTS39	100020
Taiwan	Thailand	23 Jan 46	161UNTS127	102126
Canada	Netherlands	05 Feb 46	43UNTS3	100658
Greece	UK Great Britain	21 Mar 46	91UNTS149	101247

Treaty interpretation (Cont.)

PARTY ONE	PARTY TWO	DATE	CITATION	NUMBER
Multilateral		23 Apr 46	17UNTS3	100265
Multilateral		06 May 46	157UNTS85	102049
Thailand	UK Great Britain	06 May 46	99UNTS193	101380
Multilateral		22 Jul 46	14UNTS185	100221
Multilateral		30 Oct 46	27UNTS77	100401
Multilateral		07 Dec 46	157UNTS103	102050
Multilateral		11 Dec 46	12UNTS179	100186
Argentina	Taiwan	10 Feb 47	486UNTS143	107077
Multilateral		11 Oct 47	77UNTS143	100998
France	USA (United States)	30 Oct 47	125UNTS171	101676
UK Great Britain	USA (United States)	30 Oct 47	126UNTS39	101680
Netherlands	USA (United States)	30 Oct 47	76UNTS47	100978
Brazil	Netherlands	06 Nov 47	53UNTS59	100773
Brazil	Sweden	14 Nov 47	94UNTS139	101310
Brazil	Denmark	14 Nov 47	47UNTS39	100722
Brazil	Norway	14 Nov 47	44UNTS163	100684
Taiwan	Netherlands	06 Dec 47	43UNTS185	100669
Italy	USA (United States)	02 Feb 48	79UNTS171	101040
Pakistan	UK Great Britain	21 Feb 48	134UNTS128	101797
Multilateral		06 Mar 48	289UNTS3	104214
Multilateral		26 Jun 48	331UNTS217	104757
Belgium	Czechoslovakia	03 Jul 48	77UNTS137	100997
Korea, South	USA (United States)	24 Aug 48	79UNTS57	101031
Korea, South	USA (United States)	11 Sep 48	89UNTS155	101216
Multilateral		19 Nov 48	44UNTS277	100688
Multilateral		09 Dec 48	73UNTS39	100942
Greece	USA (United States)	09 Feb 49	79UNTS95	101034
Multilateral		28 Apr 49	83UNTS105	101105
Pan Am Health Org	WHO (World Health)	24 May 49	32UNTS387	200178
Multilateral		20 Jun 49	128UNTS141	101718
Multilateral		12 Aug 49	87UNTS131	101169
Iran	Netherlands	31 Oct 49	254UNTS257	103596
Afghanistan	India	04 Jan 50	81UNTS75	101064
Korea, South	USA (United States)	26 Jan 50	178UNTS97	102337
Korea, South	USA (United States)	26 Jan 50	80UNTS205	101053
Italy	Turkey	24 Mar 50	96UNTS207	101338
Iraq	Pakistan	20 Jun 50	77UNTS215	101001
Haiti	WHO (World Health)	27 Jun 50	110UNTS99	101504
Korea, South	USA (United States)	28 Jul 50	140UNTS57	101883
WHO (World Health)	Venezuela	11 Sep 50	110UNTS237	101513
Iceland	WHO (World Health)	06 Oct 50	110UNTS127	101506
Thailand	USA (United States)	17 Oct 50	79UNTS41	101030
Israel	Netherlands	23 Oct 50	189UNTS89	102543
Peru	WHO (World Health)	10 Nov 50	110UNTS187	101510
Nicaragua	WHO (World Health)	10 Nov 50	110UNTS155	101508
Multilateral		23 Dec 50	185UNTS3	102456
Philippines	WHO (World Health)	28 Dec 50	110UNTS203	101511
Paraguay	WHO (World Health)	15 Feb 51	110UNTS171	101509
Jordan	WHO (World Health)	03 Apr 51	110UNTS297	200367
Multilateral		18 Apr 51	261UNTS140	103729
Honduras	WHO (World Health)	20 Apr 51	110UNTS111	101505
Colombia	WHO (World Health)	04 May 51	110UNTS83	101503
WHO (World Health)	Uruguay	11 Jun 51	128UNTS251	101724
Iraq	WHO (World Health)	01 Jul 51	110UNTS139	101507
Burma	India	07 Jul 51	149UNTS35	101949
USA (United States)	Vietnam, South	07 Sep 51	174UNTS165	102284
Cambodia	USA (United States)	08 Sep 51	174UNTS115	102282
Laos	USA (United States)	09 Sep 51	174UNTS141	102283
India	Turkey	14 Dec 51	137UNTS15	101845
Multilateral		16 Apr 52	139UNTS35	101874
Taiwan	Japan	28 Apr 52	138UNTS3	101858
Norway	WHO (World Health)	09 May 52	131UNTS281	101747
Norway	USA (United States)	27 Jun 52	184UNTS271	102452
Multilateral		11 Jul 52	170UNTS63	102222
Multilateral		07 Nov 52	221UNTS255	103010

Treaty interpretation (Cont.)

PARTY ONE	PARTY TWO	DATE	CITATION	NUMBER
India	Iraq	10 Nov 52	172UNTS103	102242
Greece	Spain	03 Feb 53	225UNTS3	103081
Austria	Yugoslavia	19 Mar 53	467UNTS323	106768
Turkey	Yugoslavia	16 Apr 53	255UNTS99	103606
Ethiopia	USA (United States)	29 Apr 53	224UNTS121	103073
Multilateral		19 Oct 53	207UNTS189	102807
France	Greece	08 Feb 54	225UNTS121	103094
France	Greece	08 Feb 54	225UNTS107	103093
Multilateral		21 May 54	345UNTS285	104973
Saudi Arabia	UK Great Britain	30 Jul 54	201UNTS317	102722
Norway	USA (United States)	06 Aug 54	222UNTS269	103034
Multilateral		08 Sep 54	209UNTS23	102819
Germany, West	USA (United States)	29 Oct 54	273UNTS3	103943
Brazil	Italy	24 Nov 54	284UNTS325	104146
Taiwan	El Salvador	09 Dec 54	214UNTS217	102900
Iraq	Turkey	24 Feb 55	233UNTS199	103264
Multilateral		15 May 55	217UNTS223	102949
Multilateral		25 May 55	264UNTS117	103791
Multilateral		06 Jun 55	219UNTS79	102968
Belgium	Portugal	30 Jul 55	250UNTS213	103525
Multilateral		28 Sep 55	478UNTS371	106943
Liberia	USA (United States)	06 Oct 55	275UNTS87	103977
Multilateral		12 Oct 55	560UNTS3	108165
USSR (Soviet Union)	Yemen	31 Oct 55	240UNTS317	103410
Multilateral		05 Nov 55	250UNTS201	103524
Burma	China People's Rep	08 Nov 55	306UNTS11	104430
India	Japan	26 Nov 55	311UNTS243	104506
India	USA (United States)	03 Feb 56	272UNTS75	103932
Germany, West	USA (United States)	02 Mar 56	273UNTS209	103952
Germany, West	USA (United States)	07 Mar 56	271UNTS361	103926
Iran	Pakistan	09 Mar 56	449UNTS183	106460
Multilateral		13 Mar 56	427UNTS245	106158
Germany, West	Sweden	22 Mar 56	262UNTS361	103761
Korea, North	Poland	11 May 56	432UNTS161	106219
Guatemala	Honduras	22 Aug 56	263UNTS49	103767
Burma	Thailand	15 Oct 56	277UNTS87	104000
Netherlands	Switzerland	23 Oct 56	287UNTS203	104186
Japan	United Arab Rep	20 Mar 57	318UNTS345	104625
Burma	USA (United States)	21 Mar 57	300UNTS11	104327
Multilateral		29 Mar 57	283UNTS137	104113
Romania	United Arab Rep	15 Apr 57	389UNTS21	105589
Multilateral		29 Apr 57	320UNTS243	104646
Czechoslovakia	United Arab Rep	06 May 57	292UNTS317	104278
Argentina	Israel	23 May 57	280UNTS199	104059
Czechoslovakia	United Arab Rep	19 Oct 57	530UNTS181	107681
Austria	Belgium	25 Oct 57	372UNTS177	105297
Taiwan	Iran	11 Nov 57	563UNTS31	108202
Indonesia	Japan	20 Jan 58	324UNTS227	104688
Belgium	Luxembourg	28 Mar 58	303UNTS101	104372
Multilateral		10 Jun 58	454UNTS47	106539
Ethiopia	United Nations	18 Jun 58	317UNTS101	104597
Canada	USA (United States)	31 Oct 58	391UNTS219	105626
France	Israel	12 Nov 58	345UNTS79	104960
Multilateral		01 Dec 58	385UNTS137	105534
Iran	Japan	09 Dec 58	325UNTS221	104701
Korea, South	USA (United States)	18 Dec 58	325UNTS233	104702
Mongolia	Poland	23 Dec 58	432UNTS177	106220
Indonesia	Malaysia	17 Apr 59	470UNTS273	106813
Germany, West	New Zealand	20 Apr 59	402UNTS125	105782
Denmark	Sudan	11 May 59	445UNTS105	106380
Japan	Vietnam, South	13 May 59	373UNTS149	105318
Iran	Netherlands	22 May 59	474UNTS195	106882
Taiwan	Ecuador	12 Jun 59	387UNTS3	105554
Brazil	Israel	24 Jun 59	515UNTS151	107458
France	Israel	30 Jun 59	448UNTS107	106428

PARTY ONE	PARTY TWO	DATE	CITATION	NUMBER
Treaty interpretation (Cont.)				
Afghanistan	Germany, West	22 Jul 59	464UNTS177	106715
Japan	Paraguay	22 Jul 59	373UNTS85	105316
Iraq	Romania	04 Aug 59	502UNTS17	107324
Netherlands	Turkey	12 Aug 59	527UNTS181	107624
Bulgaria	Romania	21 Sep 59	387UNTS61	105558
France	USA (United States)	25 Nov 59	401UNTS75	105764
Multilateral		14 Dec 59	422UNTS57	106068
Multilateral		14 Dec 59	422UNTS33	106067
Belgium	Brazil	06 Jan 60	531UNTS149	107701
Multilateral		26 Jan 60	439UNTS249	106333
Czechoslovakia	Iraq	11 Mar 60	464UNTS267	106718
Multilateral		15 Mar 60	572UNTS133	108310
Switzerland	USA (United States)	29 Mar 60	371UNTS155	105277
Multilateral		15 Apr 60	470UNTS239	106811
Belgium	Iran	14 May 60	522UNTS249	107551
Multilateral		16 Aug 60	382UNTS8	105476
Brazil	UN Special Fund	16 Sep 60	375UNTS3	105351
Czechoslovakia	India	19 Sep 60	465UNTS67	106722
Burma	Switzerland	31 Oct 60	465UNTS97	106723
Kuwait	United Nations	31 Oct 60	391UNTS295	200581
Norway	Peru	02 Nov 60	497UNTS207	107270
Cyprus	USA (United States)	08 Dec 60	405UNTS145	105831
Netherlands	United Arab Rep	08 Dec 60	455UNTS276	106547
Multilateral		13 Dec 60	455UNTS204	106544
Multilateral		13 Dec 60	523UNTS117	107557
Japan	Pakistan	18 Dec 60	423UNTS197	106093
Ethiopia	USSR (Soviet Union)	13 Jan 61	421UNTS13	106049
Honduras	USA (United States)	18 Jan 61	402UNTS169	105785
Multilateral		18 Apr 61	500UNTS243	107312
Turkey	USSR (Soviet Union)	27 Apr 61	420UNTS307	106047
Ghana	Hungary	27 Apr 61	439UNTS17	106322
Hungary	Poland	05 Jul 61	437UNTS3	106296
Taiwan	Paraguay	18 Aug 61	438UNTS109	106314
Multilateral		18 Sep 61	500UNTS31	107305
IBRD (World Bank)	Switzerland	11 Oct 61	415UNTS396	200592
Japan	USA (United States)	16 Oct 61	433UNTS287	106250
Taiwan	El Salvador	27 Nov 61	437UNTS161	106306
Cyprus	USA (United States)	15 Jan 62	435UNTS15	106267
UNICEF (Children)	Yemen	31 Jan 62	422UNTS271	106081
Multilateral		13 Feb 62	422UNTS288	200594
Multilateral		20 Feb 62	597UNTS159	108644
Germany, West	Thailand	05 Mar 62	563UNTS165	108210
Japan	New Zealand	09 Mar 62	485UNTS351	107066
Japan	New Zealand	09 Mar 62	485UNTS339	107065
Hungary	India	30 Mar 62	519UNTS119	107504
Japan	United Arab Rep	10 May 62	498UNTS69	107278
Germany, West	Netherlands	30 Aug 62	500UNTS3	107303
Japan	Kuwait	06 Oct 62	498UNTS235	107284
Japan	UK Great Britain	14 Nov 62	478UNTS29	106934
Multilateral		10 Dec 62	521UNTS231	107525
Ghana	Mali	09 Jan 63	466UNTS165	106742
Sudan	Switzerland	18 Feb 63	563UNTS281	108215
Belgium	USA (United States)	19 Apr 63	493UNTS83	107209
Belgium	Cyprus	08 Jun 63	601UNTS311	108703
Hungary	Mongolia	10 Jul 63	519UNTS173	107508
Algeria	Tunisia	01 Sep 63	601UNTS275	108701
Niger	United Nations	20 Nov 63	536UNTS3	107793
Algeria	Czechoslovakia	09 Mar 64	601UNTS247	108700
Portugal	USA (United States)	12 Mar 64	542UNTS3	107875
USSR (Soviet Union)	Yemen	21 Mar 64	553UNTS267	108094
Germany, West	Thailand	02 Apr 64	503UNTS3	107338
Netherlands	NATO (North Atlan)	25 May 64	544UNTS237	107920
Cyprus	Hungary	02 Jun 64	602UNTS3	108704
Cyprus	Syria	22 Dec 64	602UNTS25	108705
Poland	USSR (Soviet Union)	31 Mar 65	571UNTS217	108304
Australia	France	13 Apr 65	601UNTS293	108702
Australia	Malaysia	21 Jun 65	542UNTS75	107880
Multilateral		23 Jun 65	548UNTS241	107981
Poland	USA (United States)	24 Jun 65	593UNTS147	108581
Argentina	Belgium	05 Nov 65	635UNTS229	109086
Multilateral		04 Dec 65	571UNTS123	108303
Ireland	UK Great Britain	14 Dec 65	565UNTS58	108235
Burma	Czechoslovakia	15 Dec 65	602UNTS71	108707
Multilateral		31 Dec 65	616UNTS317	108904
Argentina	Taiwan	19 Mar 66	635UNTS281	109089
Guyana	UK Great Britain	26 May 66	588UNTS143	108521
USA (United States)	Zambia	11 Aug 66	616UNTS267	108901
Multilateral		21 Jun 67	598UNTS2	108653
Treaty violation				
Multilateral		25 Jun 35	40UNTS97	100629
Multilateral		20 Jun 36	40UNTS109	100630
Multilateral		24 Jun 36	40UNTS137	100631
Multilateral		24 Oct 36	40UNTS153	100632
Multilateral		07 Nov 45	2UNTS17	100018
Multilateral		16 Nov 45	4UNTS275	100052
Multilateral		27 Dec 45	2UNTS39	100020
Multilateral		22 Jul 46	14UNTS185	100221
Multilateral		02 Sep 47	21UNTS77	100324
Multilateral		11 Oct 47	77UNTS143	100998
Netherlands	USA (United States)	29 Apr 48	32UNTS167	100498
Multilateral		28 Apr 49	83UNTS105	101105
Canada	Ecuador	10 Nov 50	231UNTS15	103199
Nicaragua	USA (United States)	31 Jan 51	160UNTS121	102105
Multilateral		18 Apr 51	261UNTS140	103729
Ceylon (Sri Lanka)	India	30 Apr 51	196UNTS199	102625
Multilateral		11 Jul 52	169UNTS3	102220
Multilateral		19 Oct 53	207UNTS189	102807
Multilateral		25 May 55	264UNTS117	103791
Multilateral		26 Oct 56	276UNTS3	103988
Multilateral		03 Oct 57	364UNTS3	105211
Multilateral		26 Jan 60	439UNTS249	106333
Multilateral		28 Jul 60	394UNTS37	105667
Ghana	Netherlands	30 Jul 60	412UNTS51	105925
Multilateral		30 Mar 61	520UNTS151	107515
Multilateral		28 Sep 62	469UNTS169	106791
Sweden	USA (United States)	22 Oct 63	530UNTS247	107686
Multilateral		03 Dec 63	529UNTS217	107663
Multilateral		04 Dec 65	571UNTS123	108303
Previous treaty extension				
Multilateral		28 Nov 19	38UNTS41	100585
Multilateral		28 Nov 19	38UNTS81	100588
Multilateral		28 Nov 19	38UNTS93	100589
Multilateral		28 Nov 19	38UNTS17	100584
Multilateral		28 Nov 19	38UNTS67	100587
Multilateral		29 Nov 19	38UNTS53	100586
Multilateral		09 Jul 20	38UNTS119	100591
Multilateral		09 Jul 20	38UNTS109	100590
Multilateral		10 Jul 20	38UNTS129	100592
Multilateral		11 Nov 21	38UNTS203	100598
Multilateral		12 Nov 21	38UNTS153	100594
Multilateral		12 Nov 21	38UNTS165	100595
Multilateral		16 Nov 21	38UNTS143	100593
Multilateral		17 Nov 21	38UNTS187	100597
Multilateral		19 Nov 21	38UNTS175	100596
Finland	USSR (Soviet Union)	28 Oct 22	67UNTS157	100874
Multilateral		05 Jun 25	38UNTS257	100602
Multilateral		08 Jun 25	38UNTS269	100603

PARTY ONE	PARTY TWO	DATE	CITATION	NUMBER
Previous treaty extension (Cont.)				
Multilateral		10 Jun 25	38UNTS229	100600
Multilateral		10 Jun 25	38UNTS243	100601
Multilateral		05 Jun 26	38UNTS281	100604
Multilateral		23 Jun 26	38UNTS315	100606
Multilateral		24 Jun 26	38UNTS295	100605
Multilateral		15 Jun 27	38UNTS343	100608
Multilateral		15 Jun 27	38UNTS327	100607
Multilateral		16 Jun 28	39UNTS3	100609
Multilateral		26 Jun 28	39UNTS15	100610
Multilateral		21 Jun 29	39UNTS27	100611
Multilateral		28 Jun 30	39UNTS55	100612
Multilateral		28 Jun 30	39UNTS85	100613
Multilateral		27 Apr 32	39UNTS103	100614
Multilateral		30 Apr 32	39UNTS133	100615
Multilateral		29 Jun 33	39UNTS211	100619
Multilateral		29 Jun 33	39UNTS235	100620
Multilateral		29 Jun 33	39UNTS259	100621
Multilateral		29 Jun 33	39UNTS189	100618
Multilateral		29 Jun 33	39UNTS285	100622
Multilateral		29 Jun 33	39UNTS151	100616
Multilateral		29 Jun 33	39UNTS165	100617
Multilateral		19 Jun 34	40UNTS3	100623
Multilateral		21 Jun 34	40UNTS19	100624
Multilateral		21 Jun 34	40UNTS33	100625
Multilateral		23 Jun 34	40UNTS45	100626
Multilateral		21 Jun 35	40UNTS63	100627
Multilateral		22 Jun 35	40UNTS73	100628
Multilateral		20 Jun 36	40UNTS109	100630
Multilateral		24 Jun 36	40UNTS137	100631
Multilateral		24 Oct 36	40UNTS205	100635
Multilateral		24 Oct 36	40UNTS153	100632
Multilateral		22 Jun 37	40UNTS217	100636
Multilateral		23 Jun 37	40UNTS233	100637
Multilateral		20 Jun 38	40UNTS255	100638
Multilateral		27 Jun 39	40UNTS311	100640
Multilateral		27 Jun 39	40UNTS281	100639
USA (United States)	USSR (Soviet Union)	02 Aug 41	102UNTS269	200306
Colombia	USA (United States)	19 Feb 42	117UNTS185	200369
Guatemala	USA (United States)	21 Jul 42	103UNTS299	200320
Colombia	USA (United States)	05 Nov 42	24UNTS227	200147
El Salvador	USA (United States)	24 Nov 42	24UNTS241	200149
Brazil	USA (United States)	10 Feb 43	102UNTS217	200304
Canada	USA (United States)	04 Mar 43	13UNTS411	200087
El Salvador	USA (United States)	25 Mar 43	13UNTS419	200088
Chile	USA (United States)	14 Apr 43	9UNTS331	200050
Argentina	USA (United States)	02 Sep 43	9UNTS363	200052
Nicaragua	USA (United States)	25 Oct 43	29UNTS383	200173
Brazil	USA (United States)	25 Nov 43	102UNTS227	200305
El Salvador	UK Great Britain	16 Dec 43	2UNTS221	200014
Peru	USA (United States)	20 Dec 43	117UNTS285	200376
Peru	USA (United States)	31 Mar 44	109UNTS165	200357
Peru	USA (United States)	02 May 44	109UNTS211	200361
Brazil	Uruguay	16 Dec 44	65UNTS305	200218
France	UK Great Britain	31 Aug 45	98UNTS249	200275
Colombia	USA (United States)	03 Dec 45	107UNTS3	101462
Brazil	Venezuela	30 Jan 46	65UNTS107	100839
Canada	Netherlands	05 Feb 46	43UNTS3	100658
Colombia	USA (United States)	19 Feb 46	166UNTS104	102187
Mexico	USA (United States)	05 Mar 46	12OUNTS3	101612
Brazil	USA (United States)	05 Apr 46	12UNTS131	100183
Italy	USA (United States)	17 Apr 46	206UNTS263	102791
USA (United States)	Uruguay	23 Apr 46	160UNTS103	102104
UK Great Britain	USA (United States)	07 May 46	6UNTS285	100082
Portugal	USA (United States)	30 May 46	174UNTS187	102285
Multilateral		27 Jun 46	164UNTS37	102157

PARTY ONE	PARTY TWO	DATE	CITATION	NUMBER
Previous treaty extension (Cont.)				
Multilateral		28 Jun 46	442UNTS235	106352
Multilateral		29 Jun 46	94UNTS11	101303
Chile	USA (United States)	30 Jul 46	7UNTS41	100090
Iran	USA (United States)	08 Aug 46	31UNTS423	100484
Peru	USA (United States)	19 Aug 46	109UNTS15	101485
Brazil	USA (United States)	17 Sep 46	7UNTS49	100091
Multilateral		09 Oct 46	38UNTS3	100583
France	USA (United States)	18 Oct 46	140UNTS23	101882
Mexico	USA (United States)	22 Oct 46	21UNTS13	100321
Peru	USA (United States)	22 Nov 46	100UNTS170	101396
Multilateral		13 Dec 46	8UNTS135	100119
El Salvador	UK Great Britain	16 Dec 46	6UNTS131	100072
Belgium	Spain	24 Jan 47	19UNTS3	100301
Paraguay	USA (United States)	03 Mar 47	135UNTS156	101819
Multilateral		03 Mar 47	11UNTS43	100148
Mexico	USA (United States)	17 Mar 47	167UNTS30	102200
Argentina	UK Great Britain	19 Mar 47	11UNTS195	100157
Mexico	USA (United States)	02 Apr 47	148UNTS104	101939
Peru	USA (United States)	19 Apr 47	136UNTS284	101840
Honduras	USA (United States)	13 May 47	166UNTS159	102189
Brazil	Ecuador	31 May 47	72UNTS25	100925
USA (United States)	Venezuela	30 Jun 47	166UNTS198	102190
Canada	Switzerland	14 Jul 47	43UNTS103	100664
Haiti	USA (United States)	27 Sep 47	136UNTS258	101839
Multilateral		12 Nov 47	53UNTS13	100770
Multilateral		12 Nov 47	46UNTS169	100709
United Arab Rep	UK Great Britain	05 Jan 48	77UNTS3	100988
Cuba	USA (United States)	27 Jan 48	67UNTS3	100862
USA (United States)	Venezuela	30 Jan 48	109UNTS25	101486
India	UK Great Britain	15 Feb 48	134UNTS70	101796
Pakistan	UK Great Britain	21 Feb 48	134UNTS128	101797
Peru	USA (United States)	02 Mar 48	109UNTS9	101484
Canada	Italy	28 Apr 48	231UNTS69	103206
Multilateral		10 Jun 48	191UNTS3	102576
Paraguay	USA (United States)	30 Jun 48	124UNTS34	101665
Multilateral		10 Jul 48	91UNTS3	101239
Bolivia	USA (United States)	14 Jul 48	136UNTS238	101838
Ireland	UK Great Britain	31 Jul 48	86UNTS37	101151
Belgium	Luxembourg	24 Aug 48	117UNTS131	101589
Netherlands	UK Great Britain	06 Sep 48	32UNTS235	100501
Ecuador	USA (United States)	21 Sep 48	80UNTS127	101048
El Salvador	USA (United States)	23 Sep 48	181UNTS101	102402
Guatemala	USA (United States)	08 Oct 48	121UNTS37	101624
Guatemala	USA (United States)	08 Oct 48	121UNTS31	101623
Multilateral		09 Dec 48	20UNTS229	100318
Brazil	USA (United States)	30 Dec 48	102UNTS3	101406
Chile	USA (United States)	21 Jan 49	160UNTS185	102107
Ecuador	USA (United States)	04 Feb 49	80UNTS137	101049
France	Norway	09 Feb 49	29UNTS13	100431
Mexico	USA (United States)	14 Feb 49	160UNTS75	102103
Multilateral		22 Feb 49	93UNTS129	101296
Multilateral		04 May 49	30UNTS23	100446
Multilateral		04 May 49	30UNTS3	100445
Ecuador	USA (United States)	17 May 49	66UNTS3	100845
Multilateral		01 Jul 49	96UNTS237	101340
El Salvador	USA (United States)	27 Jul 49	180UNTS219	102387
USA (United States)	Uruguay	27 Jul 49	151UNTS199	101995
Multilateral		12 Aug 49	75UNTS287	100973
Multilateral		12 Aug 49	75UNTS85	100971
Multilateral		12 Aug 49	75UNTS31	100970
Brazil	USA (United States)	31 Aug 49	102UNTS13	101407
Guatemala	Italy	10 Sep 49	102UNTS53	101410
Multilateral		15 Sep 49	53UNTS235	100783
Multilateral		16 Dec 49	72UNTS3	100924
Israel	UK Great Britain	10 Feb 50	86UNTS211	101161

PARTY ONE	PARTY TWO	DATE	CITATION	NUMBER
Previous treaty extension (Cont.)				
Bolivia	USA (United States)	30 Mar 50	241UNTS77	103425
Multilateral		17 Apr 50	131UNTS99	101738
ICJ Option Clause	Thailand	20 May 50	65UNTS157	100844
Peru	WHO (World Health)	26 Sep 50	104UNTS233	101444
Haiti	USA (United States)	28 Sep 50	162UNTS85	102132
Nepal	UK Great Britain	30 Oct 50	97UNTS121	101346
Colombia	USA (United States)	24 Nov 50	133UNTS49	101779
Guatemala	WHO (World Health)	28 Nov 50	103UNTS51	101423
Multilateral		29 Nov 50	88UNTS221	101194
Israel	UK Great Britain	10 Dec 50	88UNTS211	101193
El Salvador	USA (United States)	13 Dec 50	166UNTS149	102188
Brazil	USA (United States)	27 Dec 50	147UNTS33	101926
Finland	Sweden	29 Dec 50	197UNTS333	102646
Nicaragua	WHO (World Health)	02 Jan 51	103UNTS107	101428
El Salvador	WHO (World Health)	02 Jan 51	103UNTS29	101421
USA (United States)	Uruguay	07 Mar 51	165UNTS113	102173
Costa Rica	WHO (World Health)	13 Apr 51	103UNTS3	101419
Nicaragua	UK Great Britain	25 May 51	101UNTS77	101404
Austria	Sweden	29 May 51	197UNTS431	102650
Denmark	Portugal	05 Jun 51	101UNTS61	101402
Austria	UK Great Britain	28 Jun 51	117UNTS99	101586
Paraguay	USA (United States)	30 Jul 51	178UNTS163	102340
Colombia	WHO (World Health)	18 Sep 51	109UNTS45	101489
Pakistan	UK Great Britain	29 Sep 51	134UNTS183	101798
India	WHO (World Health)	23 Oct 51	109UNTS59	101491
Greece	USA (United States)	07 Jan 52	180UNTS171	102382
Austria	Canada	18 Jan 52	236UNTS245	103327
Taiwan	WHO (World Health)	07 Mar 52	128UNTS233	101723
India	WHO (World Health)	02 Apr 52	131UNTS227	101743
Czechoslovakia	Denmark	04 Apr 52	133UNTS245	101792
Multilateral		16 Apr 52	139UNTS35	101874
Mexico	WHO (World Health)	28 May 52	134UNTS319	101810
Multilateral		08 Jun 52	210UNTS317	102843
Norway	USA (United States)	27 Jun 52	184UNTS271	102452
Panama	USA (United States)	21 Jul 52	181UNTS285	102417
France	Greece	31 Jul 52	187UNTS169	102510
Denmark	Portugal	29 Aug 52	149UNTS49	101950
China People's Rep	USSR (Soviet Union)	15 Sep 52	226UNTS45	103106
Austria	Greece	20 Sep 52	187UNTS191	102512
Thailand	UK Great Britain	29 Sep 52	173UNTS31	102257
United Arab Rep	UK Great Britain	19 Oct 52	158UNTS423	102075
Multilateral		10 Nov 52	214UNTS265	102904
India	WHO (World Health)	11 Dec 52	158UNTS391	102073
Netherlands	Philippines	05 Feb 53	216UNTS99	102934
Multilateral		27 Feb 53	333UNTS3	104764
Multilateral		25 Jun 53	191UNTS143	102581
Philippines	USA (United States)	26 Jun 53	213UNTS77	102881
Canada	Germany, West	30 Oct 53	236UNTS317	103332
Multilateral		07 Dec 53	182UNTS51	102422
Multilateral		18 Feb 54	226UNTS297	103124
Ethiopia	USA (United States)	01 Jun 54	232UNTS311	103245
Italy	Yugoslavia	26 Mar 55	379UNTS3	105432
Bulgaria	Yugoslavia	17 Jun 55	375UNTS287	105370
Multilateral		22 Jun 55	249UNTS3	103498
Switzerland	USA (United States)	18 Jul 55	239UNTS311	103388
Paraguay	USA (United States)	22 Jul 55	265UNTS15	103803
Paraguay	USA (United States)	22 Jul 55	265UNTS3	103802
Bolivia	USA (United States)	09 Sep 55	256UNTS239	103633
Multilateral		29 Sep 55	222UNTS313	103037
Afghanistan	USSR (Soviet Union)	18 Dec 55	259UNTS101	103684
Italy	Switzerland	02 Feb 56	291UNTS113	104247
Nicaragua	USA (United States)	19 Mar 56	275UNTS231	103984
Austria	Yugoslavia	15 Jun 56	396UNTS117	105695
France	USA (United States)	22 Jun 56	291UNTS101	104246
Romania	Yugoslavia	04 Aug 56	395UNTS99	105682

PARTY ONE	PARTY TWO	DATE	CITATION	NUMBER
Previous treaty extension (Cont.)				
Multilateral		25 Mar 57	294UNTS2	104300
ICJ Option Clause	UK Great Britain	18 Apr 57	265UNTS221	103814
Taiwan	USA (United States)	30 Jul 57	300UNTS61	104331
New Zealand	UK Great Britain	20 Sep 57	287UNTS105	104180
Ghana	USA (United States)	12 Feb 58	442UNTS175	106348
Philippines	USA (United States)	30 Jun 58	321UNTS51	104653
France	UK Great Britain	26 Jan 59	330UNTS207	104745
Colombia	USA (United States)	08 May 59	344UNTS193	104950
Italy	USA (United States)	30 Jul 59	355UNTS393	105088
Argentina	Brazil	26 Nov 59	374UNTS31	105325
Italy	Netherlands	01 Dec 59	455UNTS241	106545
Belgium	Netherlands	20 Jan 60	373UNTS3	105310
Mexico	USA (United States)	04 Feb 60	586UNTS57	108496
United Arab Rep	USSR (Soviet Union)	27 Aug 60	399UNTS37	105733
Belgium	Netherlands	24 Feb 61	474UNTS161	106880
Congo (Brazzaville)	USA (United States)	05 Aug 61	603UNTS19	108720
Belgium	Yugoslavia	31 Oct 61	426UNTS165	106136
Mexico	USA (United States)	08 Jan 62	433UNTS163	106239
Australia	UK Great Britain	16 Aug 62	439UNTS163	106328
Trinidad/Tobago	USA (United States)	08 Oct 62	462UNTS145	106675
Dominican Republic	USA (United States)	25 Oct 62	459UNTS247	106627
Jamaica	USA (United States)	29 Nov 62	462UNTS229	106682
UN Special Fund	Uganda	19 Dec 62	449UNTS41	106451
Denmark	Germany, West	10 Jun 63	477UNTS405	106930
Multilateral		02 Sep 63	548UNTS129	107974
Czechoslovakia	USSR (Soviet Union)	27 Nov 63	496UNTS161	107250
Tanganyika	USA (United States)	09 Dec 63	526UNTS301	107612
Multilateral		08 Apr 64	501UNTS221	107320
Colombia	USA (United States)	13 May 64	530UNTS77	107673
Italy	Eur Space Research	23 May 64	528UNTS75	107635
France	Norway	16 Jul 64	510UNTS229	107417
Denmark	Tanganyika	04 Aug 64	544UNTS123	107915
Denmark	Tanganyika	04 Aug 64	544UNTS117	107914
Chile	USA (United States)	27 Oct 64	532UNTS347	107727
Multilateral		07 Nov 64	548UNTS3	107965
Austria	Hungary	11 Nov 64	576UNTS163	108368
Canada	USA (United States)	29 Jun 65	549UNTS273	108003
Multilateral		12 Nov 65	550UNTS160	108013
Chile	UNICEF (Children)	30 Nov 65	596UNTS215	108635
Tanzania	USA (United States)	06 Dec 65	592UNTS51	108568
Multilateral		22 Aug 66	571UNTS298	200624
Lesotho	United Nations	17 Nov 66	580UNTS29	108418
Multilateral		17 Nov 66	580UNTS22	108417
Multilateral		25 Jan 67	588UNTS212	108527
Previous treaty replacement				
Bolivia	Brazil	25 Feb 38	54UNTS333	200205
Brazil	France	27 Jan 40	72UNTS77	100929
Brazil	Venezuela	30 Mar 40	51UNTS291	200195
Multilateral		12 May 40	101UNTS91	101405
Canada	USA (United States)	13 Dec 40	117UNTS173	200368
Haiti	USA (United States)	13 Sep 41	103UNTS141	200311
Mexico	USA (United States)	19 Nov 41	125UNTS287	200430
Brazil	Uruguay	18 May 42	54UNTS369	200207
Netherlands	USA (United States)	08 Jul 42	103UNTS277	200318
Brazil	Paraguay	08 Oct 42	65UNTS191	200211
Taiwan	USA (United States)	11 Jan 43	10UNTS261	200066
Belgium	Taiwan	20 Oct 43	14UNTS376	200095
Brazil	Paraguay	11 Aug 44	67UNTS303	200227
Belgium	UK Great Britain	22 Aug 44	90UNTS295	200267
Multilateral		07 Dec 44	171UNTS387	200502
Canada	USA (United States)	13 Feb 45	200UNTS219	200519
Canada	USA (United States)	17 Feb 45	122UNTS261	200409
Sweden	UK Great Britain	06 Mar 45	82UNTS219	101095
France	UK Great Britain	27 Mar 45	98UNTS227	200274

PARTY ONE	PARTY TWO	DATE	CITATION	NUMBER
Previous treaty replacement (Cont.)				
Belgium	USA (United States)	19 Apr 45	139UNTS179	200455
Netherlands	USA (United States)	30 Apr 45	139UNTS319	200459
Taiwan	Netherlands	29 May 45	2UNTS307	200023
Greece	UK Great Britain	24 Jan 46	6UNTS45	100067
Canada	Netherlands	05 Feb 46	43UNTS3	100658
Taiwan	France	28 Feb 46	14UNTS113	100215
France	UK Great Britain	28 Feb 46	27UNTS173	100407
Belgium	UK Great Britain	11 Mar 46	26UNTS167	100387
Taiwan	Switzerland	13 Mar 46	14UNTS159	100218
France	USA (United States)	27 Mar 46	139UNTS114	101879
Canada	USA (United States)	30 Mar 46	7UNTS15	100089
Multilateral		05 Apr 46	231UNTS199	103221
Belgium	USA (United States)	05 Apr 46	4UNTS125	100041
Belgium	Netherlands	16 May 46	17UNTS13	100266
Canada	UK Great Britain	05 Jun 46	27UNTS207	100408
Ceylon (Sri Lanka)	India	12 Aug 46	196UNTS209	102626
Denmark	USSR (Soviet Union)	17 Aug 46	8UNTS201	100124
Brazil	USA (United States)	06 Sep 46	54UNTS197	100805
South Africa	UK Great Britain	14 Oct 46	86UNTS77	101153
Belgium	Portugal	22 Oct 46	34UNTS49	100527
Brazil	UK Great Britain	31 Oct 46	11UNTS115	100152
Canada	USA (United States)	15 Nov 46	7UNTS141	100096
Brazil	Portugal	10 Dec 46	200UNTS67	102695
Belgium	France	09 Jan 47	36UNTS145	100568
Czechoslovakia	Yugoslavia	25 Feb 47	112UNTS3	101539
Spain	UK Great Britain	28 Mar 47	66UNTS91	100849
Mexico	USA (United States)	02 Apr 47	148UNTS104	101939
France	Greece	05 May 47	76UNTS61	100980
Bulgaria	Poland	28 Jun 47	15UNTS123	100230
Romania	Yugoslavia	30 Jun 47	116UNTS57	101569
Poland	Romania	09 Aug 47	12UNTS363	100193
Hungary	Poland	28 Aug 47	15UNTS145	100231
Belgium	Netherlands	29 Aug 47	36UNTS349	100573
France	USA (United States)	01 Oct 47	148UNTS303	101940
Multilateral		02 Oct 47	193UNTS188	102616
UK Great Britain	USA (United States)	30 Oct 47	126UNTS39	101680
Belgium	USA (United States)	30 Oct 47	125UNTS103	101672
France	USA (United States)	30 Oct 47	125UNTS171	101676
Cuba	USA (United States)	30 Oct 47	119UNTS163	101611
Brazil	Netherlands	06 Nov 47	53UNTS59	100773
Brazil	Sweden	14 Nov 47	94UNTS139	101310
Ecuador	USA (United States)	14 Nov 47	149UNTS297	101959
Brazil	Norway	14 Nov 47	44UNTS163	100684
Brazil	Denmark	14 Nov 47	47UNTS39	100722
Taiwan	USA (United States)	08 Dec 47	70UNTS3	100895
Czechoslovakia	USSR (Soviet Union)	11 Dec 47	217UNTS35	102943
South Africa	USA (United States)	18 Dec 47	148UNTS85	101938
Paraguay	USA (United States)	01 Jan 48	89UNTS191	101217
France	Netherlands	02 Jan 48	70UNTS105	100899
Belgium	France	17 Jan 48	36UNTS233	100570
France	Lebanon	24 Jan 48	173UNTS99	102263
Hungary	Poland	31 Jan 48	25UNTS283	100368
Italy	USA (United States)	06 Feb 48	73UNTS113	100950
Canada	New Zealand	12 Mar 48	231UNTS219	103222
Czechoslovakia	Yugoslavia	14 Mar 48	28UNTS81	100421
Czechoslovakia	Yugoslavia	10 Apr 48	112UNTS101	101541
Multilateral		30 Apr 48	30UNTS55	100449
Ecuador	USA (United States)	14 May 48	89UNTS71	101210
Belgium	Monaco	05 Jun 48	18UNTS245	100294
France	Poland	09 Jun 48	32UNTS251	100503
Multilateral		26 Jun 48	331UNTS217	104757
Brazil	USA (United States)	30 Jun 48	125UNTS111	101673
France	Spain	23 Aug 48	28UNTS173	100425
Multilateral		17 Sep 48	97UNTS31	101345
Romania	South Africa	16 Nov 48	225UNTS71	103090

PARTY ONE	PARTY TWO	DATE	CITATION	NUMBER
Previous treaty replacement (Cont.)				
South Africa	UK Great Britain	06 Dec 48	118UNTS183	101607
Spain	UK Great Britain	15 Dec 48	87UNTS49	101165
Belgium	Sweden	21 Feb 49	95UNTS73	101317
Belgium	Luxembourg	25 Feb 49	47UNTS3	100719
Germany, West	Greece	16 Mar 49	77UNTS307	101006
Peru	USA (United States)	25 Mar 49	89UNTS15	101205
Denmark	Portugal	08 Apr 49	74UNTS209	100964
Australia	New Zealand	15 Apr 49	34UNTS225	100540
Switzerland	USA (United States)	13 May 49	51UNTS129	100761
Bulgaria	Poland	16 May 49	84UNTS313	101140
Italy	Spain	31 May 49	231UNTS251	103224
Canada	USA (United States)	04 Jun 49	122UNTS237	101649
Mexico	USA (United States)	21 Jun 49	89UNTS3	101204
France	Greece	06 Aug 49	91UNTS95	101244
Multilateral		10 Aug 49	45UNTS3	100689
Multilateral		12 Aug 49	75UNTS31	100970
Multilateral		12 Aug 49	87UNTS131	101169
Australia	Netherlands	12 Aug 49	34UNTS213	100539
Mexico	USA (United States)	15 Aug 49	66UNTS13	100846
Canada	UK Great Britain	19 Aug 49	44UNTS223	100686
Belgium	Netherlands	20 Aug 49	46UNTS133	100706
Belgium	France	29 Aug 49	93UNTS87	101293
USSR (Soviet Union)	Yugoslavia	31 Aug 49	116UNTS345	101580
Argentina	Norway	09 Sep 49	42UNTS125	100646
Multilateral		19 Sep 49	125UNTS3	101671
Colombia	USA (United States)	12 Oct 49	133UNTS15	101774
Greece	UK Great Britain	17 Oct 49	93UNTS185	101300
Multilateral		27 Oct 49	53UNTS241	100784
Italy	Norway	19 Nov 49	47UNTS75	100723
Italy	Norway	19 Nov 49	47UNTS89	100724
Norway	Portugal	28 Nov 49	47UNTS117	100726
Brazil	Spain	28 Nov 49	215UNTS303	102923
Belgium	Luxembourg	03 Dec 49	91UNTS31	101241
Denmark	Poland	07 Dec 49	81UNTS21	101059
Denmark	Germany, West	15 Dec 49	51UNTS11	100749
Czechoslovakia	Denmark	17 Dec 49	74UNTS147	100961
Czechoslovakia	Denmark	17 Dec 49	74UNTS159	100962
Guatemala	USA (United States)	20 Dec 49	70UNTS71	100897
Norway	Poland	21 Dec 49	47UNTS107	100725
Finland	Sweden	21 Dec 49	197UNTS243	102642
Haiti	USA (United States)	29 Dec 49	133UNTS21	101775
Multilateral		18 Feb 50	123UNTS45	101654
Greece	USA (United States)	20 Feb 50	196UNTS291	102630
Canada	USA (United States)	27 Feb 50	132UNTS223	101762
Honduras	USA (United States)	24 Mar 50	93UNTS11	101283
Costa Rica	USA (United States)	04 Apr 50	132UNTS177	101759
Sweden	UK Great Britain	05 Apr 50	99UNTS107	101374
Belgium	Luxembourg	06 Apr 50	65UNTS147	100843
Ireland	USA (United States)	01 May 50	222UNTS107	103026
Canada	USA (United States)	12 Jun 50	127UNTS57	101699
Spain	UK Great Britain	20 Jul 50	398UNTS101	105719
Belgium	Switzerland	28 Jul 50	71UNTS91	100911
Korea, South	USA (United States)	28 Jul 50	140UNTS57	101883
India	Nepal	31 Jul 50	104UNTS3	101430
Spain	Switzerland	03 Aug 50	254UNTS365	103600
USA (United States)	Yugoslavia	14 Aug 50	137UNTS131	101851
Czechoslovakia	USA (United States)	29 Sep 50	290UNTS3	104227
Denmark	Italy	04 Oct 50	78UNTS353	101025
Multilateral		18 Oct 50	638UNTS185	109134
Denmark	UK Great Britain	19 Oct 50	79UNTS25	101028
Taiwan	Philippines	23 Oct 50	215UNTS159	102918
Norway	UK Great Britain	06 Nov 50	88UNTS257	101197
Ceylon (Sri Lanka)	USA (United States)	07 Nov 50	92UNTS125	101265
Sweden	UK Great Britain	10 Nov 50	88UNTS265	101198
Germany, West	UK Great Britain	09 Dec 50	88UNTS247	101196

PARTY ONE	PARTY TWO	DATE	CITATION	NUMBER
Previous treaty replacement (Cont.)				
Norway	UK Great Britain	15 Dec 50	106UNTS87	101459
Brazil	USA (United States)	19 Dec 50	141UNTS3	101900
Panama	USA (United States)	20 Dec 50	92UNTS167	101269
Italy	UK Great Britain	21 Dec 50	175UNTS187	102301
Liberia	USA (United States)	22 Dec 50	92UNTS145	101267
Nicaragua	USA (United States)	23 Dec 50	92UNTS155	101268
India	USA (United States)	28 Dec 50	99UNTS39	101369
Paraguay	USA (United States)	29 Dec 50	122UNTS157	101645
Multilateral		09 Jan 51	197UNTS341	102647
Costa Rica	USA (United States)	11 Jan 51	92UNTS179	101270
Chile	USA (United States)	16 Jan 51	147UNTS11	101925
Chile	USA (United States)	16 Jan 51	151UNTS147	101990
Sweden	UK Great Britain	17 Jan 51	93UNTS225	101301
Saudi Arabia	USA (United States)	17 Jan 51	140UNTS335	101897
Denmark	Switzerland	20 Jan 51	87UNTS223	101174
Italy	Norway	22 Jan 51	88UNTS339	101202
Nepal	USA (United States)	23 Jan 51	184UNTS65	102439
Afghanistan	USA (United States)	07 Feb 51	132UNTS265	101766
Pakistan	USA (United States)	09 Feb 51	100UNTS67	101388
Denmark	Hungary	10 Feb 51	85UNTS49	101145
Dominican Republic	USA (United States)	20 Feb 51	132UNTS305	101770
Israel	USA (United States)	26 Feb 51	137UNTS57	101848
Jordan	USA (United States)	27 Feb 51	141UNTS55	101905
Colombia	USA (United States)	09 Mar 51	141UNTS15	101901
Bolivia	USA (United States)	14 Mar 51	132UNTS319	101771
Greece	Yugoslavia	15 Mar 51	187UNTS237	102516
Pakistan	UK Great Britain	02 Apr 51	168UNTS281	102219
China People's Rep	Poland	03 Apr 51	304UNTS187	104396
Haiti	USA (United States)	02 May 51	151UNTS191	101994
Ecuador	USA (United States)	03 May 51	141UNTS27	101902
United Arab Rep	USA (United States)	05 May 51	198UNTS265	102670
Iceland	USA (United States)	05 May 51	205UNTS173	102776
Belgium	UK Great Britain	08 May 51	158UNTS451	102079
India	Netherlands	24 May 51	108UNTS151	101471
Lebanon	USA (United States)	29 May 51	160UNTS49	102101
UK Great Britain	USA (United States)	03 Jun 51	137UNTS81	101850
UK Great Britain	USA (United States)	06 Jun 51	165UNTS121	102174
Ethiopia	USA (United States)	16 Jun 51	148UNTS39	101933
Cuba	USA (United States)	20 Jun 51	148UNTS3	101931
Mexico	USA (United States)	27 Jun 51	141UNTS211	101916
Greece	Netherlands	26 Jul 51	109UNTS103	101495
Multilateral		29 Jul 51	117UNTS85	101585
Greece	USA (United States)	03 Aug 51	224UNTS279	103080
France	UK Great Britain	20 Aug 51	108UNTS263	101479
Portugal	USA (United States)	06 Sep 51	237UNTS217	103348
Ethiopia	USA (United States)	07 Sep 51	206UNTS41	102785
Australia	Netherlands	25 Sep 51	128UNTS63	101713
Peru	USA (United States)	28 Sep 51	160UNTS35	102099
Pakistan	UK Great Britain	29 Sep 51	134UNTS183	101798
Denmark	USA (United States)	01 Oct 51	421UNTS105	106056
Multilateral		31 Oct 51	172UNTS193	102247
Nicaragua	USA (United States)	12 Dec 51	167UNTS151	102205
France	UK Great Britain	31 Dec 51	330UNTS145	104744
Multilateral		11 Feb 52	165UNTS77	102169
Costa Rica	USA (United States)	25 Feb 52	174UNTS233	102288
Finland	Norway	18 Mar 52	188UNTS187	102527
Sweden	Uruguay	20 Mar 52	311UNTS3	104497
Norway	Uruguay	20 Mar 52	310UNTS279	104496
Austria	Greece	22 Mar 52	187UNTS255	102517
El Salvador	USA (United States)	04 Apr 52	177UNTS219	102320
Greece	Switzerland	04 Apr 52	166UNTS271	102192
Belgium	Sweden	21 Apr 52	166UNTS9	102183
Honduras	USA (United States)	23 Apr 52	198UNTS251	102669
Belgium	Greece	24 Apr 52	166UNTS261	102191
Multilateral		10 May 52	439UNTS217	106331

PARTY ONE	PARTY TWO	DATE	CITATION	NUMBER
Previous treaty replacement (Cont.)				
Australia	USA (United States)	27 May 52	178UNTS113	102338
Ecuador	USA (United States)	29 May 52	185UNTS203	102471
Bolivia	USA (United States)	18 Jun 52	199UNTS211	102686
Iraq	UK Great Britain	10 Jul 52	151UNTS227	101998
France	Greece	23 Dec 52	187UNTS175	102511
Greece	Italy	04 Feb 53	189UNTS269	102551
Greece	Netherlands	05 Feb 53	263UNTS361	103783
Germany, West	USA (United States)	27 Feb 53	205UNTS103	102771
Canada	USA (United States)	17 Mar 53	236UNTS259	103329
Czechoslovakia	Denmark	23 Apr 53	174UNTS95	102280
Czechoslovakia	Denmark	23 Apr 53	174UNTS107	102281
Finland	Norway	20 May 53	173UNTS163	102265
El Salvador	USA (United States)	21 May 53	213UNTS15	102878
Germany, West	UK Great Britain	22 May 53	172UNTS179	102246
Japan	Thailand	19 Jun 53	174UNTS29	102276
Ethiopia	USA (United States)	25 Jun 53	212UNTS175	102869
Nicaragua	USA (United States)	30 Jun 53	215UNTS133	102917
Italy	Switzerland	02 Jul 53	257UNTS99	103653
Multilateral		20 Jul 53	227UNTS217	103140
India	UK Great Britain	20 Jul 53	196UNTS251	102628
Denmark	Uruguay	09 Sep 53	256UNTS149	103625
UNICEF (Children)	UK Great Britain	07 Oct 53	180UNTS59	102375
USA (United States)	Uruguay	30 Nov 53	229UNTS25	103158
Belgium	Lebanon	24 Dec 53	219UNTS153	102972
Netherlands	USA (United States)	22 Jan 54	190UNTS207	102565
France	Sweden	16 Feb 54	228UNTS137	103147
Multilateral		19 Feb 54	214UNTS51	102899
Multilateral		01 Mar 54	286UNTS265	104173
Bulgaria	Czechoslovakia	13 Apr 54	501UNTS3	107314
Czechoslovakia	Hungary	16 Apr 54	504UNTS231	107360
Greece	Spain	15 May 54	299UNTS261	104318
Greece	Spain	15 May 54	299UNTS277	104319
Canada	Portugal	28 May 54	391UNTS253	105631
Italy	UK Great Britain	01 Jun 54	403UNTS275	105798
Greece	Hungary	05 Jun 54	299UNTS295	104321
Belgium	Netherlands	09 Jun 54	216UNTS121	102936
Chile	UK Great Britain	31 Jul 54	618UNTS353	108934
Multilateral		19 Aug 54	201UNTS51	102710
Brazil	USA (United States)	20 Aug 54	410UNTS79	105898
El Salvador	USA (United States)	31 Aug 54	237UNTS49	103336
Guatemala	USA (United States)	01 Sep 54	199UNTS51	102677
Sweden	USSR (Soviet Union)	29 Sep 54	202UNTS259	102733
Denmark	Ireland	18 Oct 54	218UNTS295	102959
United Arab Rep	UK Great Britain	19 Oct 54	210UNTS3	102833
Netherlands	Venezuela	26 Oct 54	232UNTS103	103232
Multilateral		27 Oct 54	201UNTS95	102712
Germany, West	USA (United States)	29 Oct 54	273UNTS3	103943
Multilateral		29 Oct 54	201UNTS115	102713
Greece	Netherlands	01 Nov 54	223UNTS79	103057
Greece	Italy	10 Nov 54	227UNTS9	103128
Ethiopia	UK Great Britain	29 Nov 54	207UNTS283	102811
Denmark	USA (United States)	15 Dec 54	213UNTS273	102890
Multilateral		16 Dec 54	204UNTS323	200523
Sweden	USA (United States)	22 Dec 54	228UNTS85	103143
Italy	USA (United States)	26 Jan 55	238UNTS179	103361
South Africa	USA (United States)	22 Feb 55	247UNTS247	103473
Iraq	USA (United States)	02 Mar 55	250UNTS229	103526
France	Sweden	05 Mar 55	427UNTS133	106150
El Salvador	USA (United States)	21 Mar 55	250UNTS261	103528
Ceylon (Sri Lanka)	Germany, West	01 Apr 55	369UNTS57	105251
Taiwan	WHO (World Health)	21 Apr 55	210UNTS71	102835
Peru	USA (United States)	30 Apr 55	263UNTS309	103780
Multilateral		14 Jun 55	212UNTS263	200526
Belgium	USA (United States)	15 Jun 55	235UNTS133	103299
Multilateral		04 Jul 55	214UNTS10	102897

PARTY ONE	PARTY TWO	DATE	CITATION	NUMBER
Previous treaty replacement (Cont.)				
Libya	USA (United States)	21 Jul 55	264UNTS247	103796
Bolivia	USA (United States)	03 Aug 55	264UNTS225	103795
Iran	USA (United States)	15 Aug 55	284UNTS93	104132
Multilateral		15 Sep 55	254UNTS55	103593
Italy	Switzerland	17 Sep 55	291UNTS213	104257
Bulgaria	Yugoslavia	01 Oct 55	396UNTS223	105698
Liberia	USA (United States)	06 Oct 55	275UNTS93	103978
Guatemala	UNICEF (Children)	22 Nov 55	221UNTS305	103012
Sweden	UK Great Britain	18 Jan 56	428UNTS301	106181
Netherlands	USA (United States)	22 Jan 56	287UNTS121	104181
Austria	Italy	23 Jan 56	393UNTS97	105653
Romania	Yugoslavia	01 Feb 56	362UNTS203	105189
Multilateral		02 Feb 56	227UNTS153	103137
Hungary	Romania	03 Feb 56	362UNTS233	105190
Multilateral		10 Feb 56	228UNTS167	103150
Denmark	UK Great Britain	27 Feb 56	252UNTS83	103558
Germany, West	USA (United States)	07 Mar 56	271UNTS361	103926
Canada	Japan	20 Mar 56	517UNTS33	107482
Bulgaria	Yugoslavia	23 Mar 56	367UNTS213	105230
USA (United States)	Uruguay	23 Mar 56	376UNTS311	105386
Colombia	USA (United States)	27 Mar 56	273UNTS235	103954
Netherlands	USA (United States)	27 Mar 56	285UNTS231	104154
Sweden	USSR (Soviet Union)	31 Mar 56	259UNTS239	103691
Belgium	Germany, West	14 Apr 56	344UNTS103	104945
Indonesia	United Nations	17 Apr 56	233UNTS267	103266
Germany, West	Switzerland	02 May 56	559UNTS157	108158
Austria	Italy	07 May 56	284UNTS351	104147
Multilateral		18 May 56	339UNTS3	104844
Bulgaria	Yugoslavia	22 May 56	367UNTS119	105229
Panama	USA (United States)	25 May 56	268UNTS333	103866
Guatemala	USA (United States)	30 May 56	275UNTS271	103986
Czechoslovakia	USSR (Soviet Union)	01 Jun 56	259UNTS341	103696
Iceland	USA (United States)	04 Jun 56	275UNTS189	103982
Italy	Switzerland	04 Jun 56	378UNTS311	105429
Multilateral		07 Jun 56	381UNTS145	105470
Multilateral		08 Jun 56	247UNTS366	200541
Bulgaria	Yugoslavia	16 Jun 56	391UNTS3	105613
Multilateral		26 Jun 56	253UNTS12	103573
Multilateral		26 Jun 56	321UNTS2	104650
Argentina	UK Great Britain	30 Jun 56	269UNTS235	103884
Multilateral		02 Jul 56	248UNTS37	103484
Multilateral		02 Jul 56	540UNTS110	107846
France	UK Great Britain	10 Jul 56	326UNTS23	104708
Belgium	Germany, West	26 Jul 56	249UNTS187	103508
Austria	Sweden	14 Aug 56	262UNTS355	103760
Canada	Turkey	21 Aug 56	305UNTS89	104416
Multilateral		31 Aug 56	249UNTS158	103506
Greece	USA (United States)	07 Sep 56	278UNTS141	104030
Multilateral		11 Sep 56	266UNTS221	103832
Denmark	Finland	15 Sep 56	254UNTS3	103589
Norway	Sweden	15 Sep 56	263UNTS17	103765
Denmark	Sweden	15 Sep 56	263UNTS3	103764
Finland	Sweden	15 Sep 56	254UNTS31	103591
Finland	Norway	15 Sep 56	254UNTS17	103590
Germany, West	Netherlands	20 Sep 56	509UNTS269	107405
Canada	South Africa	28 Sep 56	299UNTS17	104304
Multilateral		05 Oct 56	251UNTS267	103545
Multilateral		05 Oct 56	251UNTS245	103544
Czechoslovakia	Hungary	13 Oct 56	300UNTS177	104337
Colombia	USA (United States)	24 Oct 56	476UNTS77	106905
Multilateral		21 Nov 56	253UNTS266	103588
Albania	Yugoslavia	23 Nov 56	386UNTS73	105539
Finland	USSR (Soviet Union)	07 Dec 56	258UNTS89	103673
Multilateral		19 Dec 56	427UNTS93	106148
France	Italy	28 Dec 56	291UNTS203	104255

PARTY ONE	PARTY TWO	DATE	CITATION	NUMBER
Previous treaty replacement (Cont.)				
Multilateral		15 Jan 57	376UNTS122	105378
Germany, West	Norway	29 Jan 57	353UNTS39	105037
Germany, West	Sweden	29 Jan 57	393UNTS113	105654
Denmark	Germany, West	29 Jan 57	302UNTS75	104354
Norway	USA (United States)	05 Feb 57	279UNTS169	104038
Australia	UK Great Britain	26 Feb 57	265UNTS197	103813
Turkey	UK Great Britain	28 Feb 57	310UNTS69	104488
Multilateral		01 Mar 57	264UNTS94	103790
Morocco	UK Great Britain	01 Mar 57	310UNTS3	104480
Belgium	Czechoslovakia	12 Mar 57	312UNTS75	104512
Netherlands	Yugoslavia	13 Mar 57	327UNTS227	104723
Liberia	USA (United States)	16 Mar 57	290UNTS59	104228
Multilateral		25 Mar 57	294UNTS411	104302
Multilateral		09 Apr 57	274UNTS172	103965
Denmark	Pakistan	10 Apr 57	302UNTS53	104353
Germany, West	Yugoslavia	10 Apr 57	463UNTS269	106708
Netherlands	Paraguay	13 Apr 57	593UNTS85	108577
Finland	USA (United States)	10 May 57	283UNTS43	104105
Iran	USSR (Soviet Union)	14 May 57	457UNTS161	106586
Denmark	Paraguay	18 May 57	286UNTS117	104163
Hungary	Netherlands	28 May 57	334UNTS291	104773
Belgium	Hungary	01 Jun 57	291UNTS17	104242
Denmark	Uruguay	04 Jun 57	286UNTS107	104162
Jordan	USA (United States)	27 Jun 57	288UNTS269	104209
Italy	USA (United States)	03 Jul 57	308UNTS195	104462
Germany, West	USA (United States)	03 Jul 57	288UNTS305	104212
Italy	United Arab Rep	06 Jul 57	302UNTS147	104357
Multilateral		09 Jul 57	274UNTS300	103972
Germany, West	Italy	12 Jul 57	291UNTS181	104252
Spain	USA (United States)	16 Aug 57	307UNTS169	104449
Italy	Switzerland	19 Sep 57	363UNTS69	105200
France	USA (United States)	23 Sep 57	293UNTS297	104297
Czechoslovakia	USSR (Soviet Union)	05 Oct 57	320UNTS129	104641
Taiwan	USA (United States)	08 Oct 57	304UNTS241	104400
Belgium	Netherlands	24 Oct 57	292UNTS199	104274
Multilateral		05 Nov 57	285UNTS301	104155
France	Italy	08 Nov 57	305UNTS393	104427
Argentina	Denmark	25 Nov 57	299UNTS83	104308
Argentina	Italy	25 Nov 57	305UNTS275	104424
Belgium	USA (United States)	03 Dec 57	303UNTS45	104370
Finland	Italy	17 Dec 57	291UNTS133	104248
Multilateral		06 Jan 58	304UNTS227	104399
Belgium	Germany, West	17 Jan 58	328UNTS173	104735
Poland	USSR (Soviet Union)	21 Jan 58	319UNTS291	104637
Czechoslovakia	Poland	31 Jan 58	431UNTS99	106214
Indonesia	WHO (World Health)	05 Feb 58	307UNTS15	104438
Bulgaria	Italy	25 Feb 58	362UNTS291	105194
Norway	Pakistan	05 Mar 58	334UNTS199	104769
Pakistan	Sweden	06 Mar 58	393UNTS181	105656
Multilateral		15 Mar 58	292UNTS273	104276
Czechoslovakia	Poland	21 Mar 58	538UNTS89	107811
Norway	South Africa	28 Mar 58	300UNTS83	104332
Denmark	South Africa	28 Mar 58	300UNTS107	104334
Netherlands	Switzerland	28 Mar 58	318UNTS175	104614
South Africa	Sweden	28 Mar 58	300UNTS95	104333
Sweden	Yugoslavia	18 Apr 58	393UNTS225	105658
Belgium	Japan	30 Apr 58	303UNTS109	104373
Albania	Italy	26 May 58	362UNTS259	105191
Austria	Netherlands	30 May 58	458UNTS147	106598
Multilateral		10 Jun 58	330UNTS3	104739
Belgium	South Africa	11 Jun 58	335UNTS63	104778
Multilateral		18 Jun 58	386UNTS355	105553
Multilateral		18 Jun 58	386UNTS345	105552
Japan	USA (United States)	19 Jun 58	325UNTS143	104699
Multilateral		19 Jun 58	306UNTS236	200550

PARTY ONE	PARTY TWO	DATE	CITATION	NUMBER
Previous treaty replacement (Cont.)				
Bulgaria	Hungary	27 Jun 58	438UNTS235	106318
Germany, West	Netherlands	30 Jun 58	315UNTS179	104568
Denmark	Sweden	21 Jul 58	320UNTS163	104642
Multilateral		25 Jul 58	352UNTS3	105035
Australia	South Africa	26 Sep 58	335UNTS121	104780
Australia	New Zealand	30 Sep 58	340UNTS61	104859
Ghana	USA (United States)	30 Sep 58	336UNTS169	104805
Hungary	Romania	07 Oct 58	416UNTS199	106004
USA (United States)	Venezuela	08 Oct 58	371UNTS69	105271
Czechoslovakia	Romania	25 Oct 58	338UNTS301	104843
Czechoslovakia	Romania	25 Oct 58	417UNTS37	106006
Multilateral		27 Oct 58	351UNTS303	105031
United Arab Rep	USA (United States)	31 Oct 58	355UNTS355	105086
Japan	USA (United States)	03 Nov 58	341UNTS83	104879
Multilateral		05 Nov 58	428UNTS73	106169
Bulgaria	Romania	03 Dec 58	417UNTS133	106007
Afghanistan	WHO (World Health)	18 Dec 58	324UNTS121	104681
Korea, South	USA (United States)	18 Dec 58	325UNTS233	104702
Muscat and Oman	USA (United States)	20 Dec 58	380UNTS181	105457
France	UK Great Britain	26 Jan 59	330UNTS213	104746
UK Great Britain	Yugoslavia	03 Feb 59	359UNTS339	105151
Czechoslovakia	United Arab Rep	07 Feb 59	372UNTS243	105301
Hungary	Poland	06 Mar 59	432UNTS3	106216
IAEA (Atom Energy)	Thailand	18 Mar 59	339UNTS307	104850
Germany, West	New Zealand	20 Apr 59	402UNTS125	105782
Multilateral		20 Apr 59	472UNTS185	106841
Multilateral		29 Apr 59	346UNTS167	104980
France	Netherlands	29 Apr 59	486UNTS379	107088
Iceland	Netherlands	30 Apr 59	487UNTS13	107091
Netherlands	Norway	30 Apr 59	487UNTS3	107090
Denmark	Netherlands	30 Apr 59	487UNTS23	107092
Hungary	Poland	20 May 59	432UNTS115	106217
South Africa	UK Great Britain	18 Jun 59	380UNTS103	105452
Czechoslovakia	Poland	04 Jul 59	363UNTS333	105210
Austria	USA (United States)	22 Jul 59	368UNTS199	105242
Netherlands	Turkey	12 Aug 59	527UNTS181	107624
New Zealand	UK Great Britain	12 Aug 59	354UNTS161	105062
Multilateral		08 Sep 59	383UNTS203	105502
South Africa	Switzerland	19 Oct 59	559UNTS257	108162
Norway	Yugoslavia	18 Nov 59	383UNTS131	105499
France	USA (United States)	25 Nov 59	401UNTS75	105764
Belgium	USA (United States)	27 Nov 59	366UNTS331	105221
Ceylon (Sri Lanka)	WHO (World Health)	21 Dec 59	349UNTS109	105011
Israel	Sweden	22 Dec 59	377UNTS277	105407
Poland	Yugoslavia	06 Feb 60	521UNTS37	107517
Australia	Canada	12 Feb 60	369UNTS89	105253
Norway	USA (United States)	13 Feb 60	388UNTS255	105583
Greece	USA (United States)	15 Feb 60	377UNTS95	105397
Turkey	USA (United States)	02 Mar 60	372UNTS37	105286
Netherlands	USA (United States)	24 Mar 60	406UNTS165	105847
Switzerland	USA (United States)	29 Mar 60	371UNTS155	105277
Ireland	UK Great Britain	29 Mar 60	371UNTS3	105267
Luxembourg	UK Great Britain	01 Apr 60	374UNTS267	105340
Netherlands	UK Great Britain	01 Apr 60	374UNTS277	105341
Belgium	UK Great Britain	01 Apr 60	361UNTS135	105177
Germany, West	Spain	28 Apr 60	465UNTS3	106720
Hungary	Yugoslavia	07 May 60	519UNTS237	107510
Cambodia	WHO (World Health)	19 May 60	372UNTS193	105298
Multilateral		04 Jun 60	360UNTS208	105159
UN Special Fund	Thailand	04 Jun 60	360UNTS97	105157
Czechoslovakia	Germany, East	16 Jun 60	415UNTS248	105988
Multilateral		17 Jun 60	536UNTS27	107794
Austria	Spain	17 Jun 60	390UNTS17	105600
Multilateral		19 Jun 60	537UNTS214	107803
Finland	USSR (Soviet Union)	23 Jun 60	379UNTS277	105443

PARTY ONE	PARTY TWO	DATE	CITATION	NUMBER
Previous treaty replacement (Cont.)				
Poland	UK Great Britain	02 Jul 60	385UNTS87	105532
Italy	USA (United States)	07 Jul 60	380UNTS143	105455
Multilateral		08 Jul 60	366UNTS310	105220
Japan	Luxembourg	21 Jul 60	384UNTS55	105510
WHO (World Health)	United Arab Rep	03 Aug 60	385UNTS3	105524
Jordan	WHO (World Health)	03 Aug 60	381UNTS133	105469
Laos	WHO (World Health)	04 Aug 60	373UNTS313	105322
WHO (World Health)	Tunisia	04 Aug 60	381UNTS335	105474
Guatemala	USA (United States)	09 Aug 60	461UNTS15	106648
France	USA (United States)	19 Sep 60	400UNTS21	105745
Hungary	UK Great Britain	25 Oct 60	419UNTS309	106034
Greece	Poland	08 Nov 60	483UNTS127	107010
Denmark	Germany, West	10 Nov 60	431UNTS21	106205
Finland	Norway	15 Nov 60	383UNTS159	105501
Canada	USA (United States)	13 Jan 61	410UNTS62	105897
Multilateral		28 Jan 61	387UNTS202	105563
Malaysia	New Zealand	03 Feb 61	447UNTS251	106418
Canada	USA (United States)	17 Feb 61	445UNTS143	106383
Belgium	USA (United States)	21 Feb 61	480UNTS149	106967
Czechoslovakia	Hungary	24 Feb 61	422UNTS15	106066
Belgium	Netherlands	24 Feb 61	474UNTS167	106881
Belgium	UK Great Britain	08 Mar 61	523UNTS17	107554
Multilateral		30 Mar 61	520UNTS151	107515
Chile	Netherlands	07 Apr 61	453UNTS239	106527
Honduras	USA (United States)	12 Apr 61	413UNTS182	105952
Turkey	USSR (Soviet Union)	27 Apr 61	420UNTS307	106047
Spain	UK Great Britain	30 May 61	562UNTS169	108198
Kuwait	UK Great Britain	19 Jun 61	399UNTS239	105743
Austria	Romania	21 Jul 61	421UNTS161	106057
Morocco	WHO (World Health)	09 Aug 61	412UNTS192	105932
Poland	UNICEF (Children)	24 Aug 61	406UNTS95	105841
Mexico	Netherlands	24 Aug 61	465UNTS291	106732
Iraq	WHO (World Health)	13 Sep 61	419UNTS69	106030
Bulgaria	Poland	19 Sep 61	483UNTS249	107018
Paraguay	USA (United States)	26 Sep 61	461UNTS91	106653
Ghana	USSR (Soviet Union)	04 Nov 61	437UNTS213	106308
Saudi Arabia	Syria	16 Nov 61	491UNTS163	107177
Cyprus	Greece	23 Nov 61	497UNTS311	107274
Finland	UK Great Britain	05 Dec 61	424UNTS217	106110
Panama	USA (United States)	11 Dec 61	445UNTS161	106384
El Salvador	USA (United States)	19 Dec 61	445UNTS175	106385
Argentina	Japan	20 Dec 61	613UNTS323	108859
Iran	USA (United States)	21 Dec 61	433UNTS269	106249
Costa Rica	USA (United States)	22 Dec 61	460UNTS277	106646
Ethiopia	WHO (World Health)	11 Jan 62	423UNTS99	106087
Poland	Romania	25 Jan 62	468UNTS3	106770
Luxembourg	USA (United States)	23 Feb 62	474UNTS3	106868
Multilateral		01 Mar 62	423UNTS122	106089
Australia	Japan	01 Mar 62	517UNTS81	107483
WHO (World Health)	Sudan	11 Mar 62	432UNTS325	106226
Multilateral		23 Mar 62	470UNTS25	106793
Nicaragua	USA (United States)	30 Mar 62	456UNTS241	106559
Mexico	USA (United States)	18 Apr 62	452UNTS3	106501
Belgium	USA (United States)	23 May 62	434UNTS133	106260
Greece	Switzerland	12 Jun 62	492UNTS47	107186
Libya	WHO (World Health)	16 Jun 62	437UNTS127	106301
Argentina	USA (United States)	22 Jun 62	458UNTS97	106594
Israel	USA (United States)	22 Jun 62	448UNTS273	106440
United Arab Rep	USSR (Soviet Union)	23 Jun 62	472UNTS43	106836
Multilateral		27 Jun 62	616UNTS79	108893
Denmark	UK Great Britain	27 Jun 62	562UNTS75	108197
Italy	USA (United States)	06 Jul 62	459UNTS123	106617
Colombia	USA (United States)	23 Jul 62	458UNTS123	106595
Indonesia	Netherlands	15 Aug 62	437UNTS273	106311
Syria	USSR (Soviet Union)	19 Aug 62	457UNTS285	106588

PARTY ONE	PARTY TWO	DATE	CITATION	NUMBER
Previous treaty replacement (Cont.)				
Austria	South Africa	31 Aug 62	443UNTS65	106359
Israel	UK Great Britain	26 Sep 62	474UNTS233	106885
Poland	Romania	05 Oct 62	521UNTS3	107516
Finland	New Zealand	12 Nov 62	485UNTS331	107064
Czechoslovakia	Poland	16 Nov 62	526UNTS3	107597
WHO (World Health)	Syria	18 Nov 62	480UNTS249	106972
Germany, West	USA (United States)	20 Nov 62	505UNTS263	107377
Australia	Fed of Malaya	26 Nov 62	453UNTS161	106523
Multilateral		12 Dec 62	457UNTS72	106578
Iceland	USA (United States)	27 Dec 62	469UNTS91	106785
India	United Nations	27 Dec 62	450UNTS3	106464
Belgium	Ecuador	10 Jan 63	457UNTS153	106585
Philippines	USA (United States)	23 Mar 63	474UNTS80	106873
Austria	Bulgaria	05 Apr 63	480UNTS3	106963
Austria	Italy	22 Apr 63	491UNTS53	107173
Philippines	USA (United States)	06 May 63	477UNTS67	106916
Portugal	South Africa	07 May 63	499UNTS49	107292
Belgium	Netherlands	13 May 63	540UNTS3	107843
Canada	Finland	05 Jun 63	472UNTS345	106846
Belgium	Cyprus	08 Jun 63	601UNTS311	108703
Korea, South	USA (United States)	18 Jun 63	487UNTS297	107112
India	USA (United States)	19 Jun 63	479UNTS175	106952
Czechoslovakia	Yugoslavia	24 Jun 63	496UNTS3	107246
Austria	USA (United States)	25 Jun 63	479UNTS223	106956
France	Israel	20 Aug 63	515UNTS173	107460
Argentina	USA (United States)	21 Aug 63	488UNTS61	107119
Switzerland	UK Great Britain	27 Aug 63	486UNTS183	107079
Multilateral		10 Sep 63	480UNTS100	106965
Denmark	Norway	12 Sep 63	613UNTS289	108857
Ecuador	USA (United States)	20 Sep 63	488UNTS147	107125
Greece	Poland	30 Sep 63	534UNTS23	107751
Czechoslovakia	Hungary	22 Oct 63	514UNTS95	107444
Multilateral		23 Oct 63	506UNTS197	107388
Iran	USA (United States)	24 Oct 63	489UNTS303	107146
Multilateral		08 Nov 63	482UNTS286	106999
Canada	USA (United States)	15 Nov 63	493UNTS67	107207
Greece	USA (United States)	13 Dec 63	494UNTS55	107226
Ceylon (Sri Lanka)	Finland	08 Jan 64	492UNTS285	107198
Czechoslovakia	Yugoslavia	20 Jan 64	538UNTS197	107816
Multilateral		28 Jan 64	502UNTS321	107336
Multilateral		10 Feb 64	496UNTS151	107249
Iceland	USA (United States)	13 Feb 64	524UNTS235	107576
Mexico	USA (United States)	14 Feb 64	524UNTS197	107574
Multilateral		20 Feb 64	491UNTS30	107172
Belgium	France	10 Mar 64	557UNTS13	108127
Spain	USA (United States)	18 Mar 64	535UNTS343	107789
Finland	USSR (Soviet Union)	24 Apr 64	537UNTS231	107804
United Arab Rep	USA (United States)	05 May 64	531UNTS229	107706
Korea, South	USA (United States)	12 May 64	529UNTS299	107667
Cyprus	Hungary	02 Jun 64	602UNTS3	108704
Finland	South Africa	12 Jun 64	505UNTS107	107367
Multilateral		20 Jun 64	539UNTS3	107819
New Zealand	USA (United States)	24 Jun 64	524UNTS101	107568
Multilateral		28 Jun 64	519UNTS14	107499
Australia	USA (United States)	28 Aug 64	510UNTS201	107415
Ceylon (Sri Lanka)	USA (United States)	29 Aug 64	531UNTS93	107695
Germany, East	Poland	06 Oct 64	552UNTS89	108051
Sweden	UK Great Britain	14 Oct 64	543UNTS135	107898
Multilateral		07 Nov 64	548UNTS3	107965
India	United Nations	25 Nov 64	519UNTS47	107501
Germany, West	UK Great Britain	26 Nov 64	603UNTS183	108734
Belgium	Germany, West	17 Dec 64	631UNTS229	108996
Cyprus	Syria	22 Dec 64	602UNTS25	108705
WHO (World Health)	Tunisia	27 Jan 65	528UNTS209	107644
Multilateral		12 Feb 65	525UNTS148	107587

PARTY ONE	PARTY TWO	DATE	CITATION	NUMBER
Previous treaty replacement (Cont.)				
Japan	UK Great Britain	22 Feb 65	560UNTS123	108171
Multilateral		23 Feb 65	527UNTS120	107622
Mexico	USA (United States)	27 Feb 65	542UNTS181	107889
UK Great Britain	Yugoslavia	01 Mar 65	548UNTS85	107972
Multilateral		05 Mar 65	527UNTS221	107627
Multilateral		08 Apr 65	533UNTS66	107733
Austria	Hungary	09 Apr 65	638UNTS53	109131
Multilateral		26 Apr 65	533UNTS50	107732
Multilateral		12 May 65	534UNTS390	107769
USA (United States)	Uruguay	17 May 65	564UNTS69	108221
Bulgaria	Czechoslovakia	22 May 65	545UNTS65	107925
Multilateral		25 May 65	535UNTS374	107791
Gambia	UNICEF (Children)	29 May 65	547UNTS29	107954
Argentina	Yugoslavia	09 Jun 65	601UNTS3	108684
Canada	USA (United States)	11 Jun 65	564UNTS83	108222
Bulgaria	Hungary	19 Aug 65	577UNTS67	108373
Multilateral		13 Sep 65	547UNTS264	107962
Multilateral		13 Sep 65	547UNTS248	107961
Czechoslovakia	USSR (Soviet Union)	17 Sep 65	549UNTS221	108001
Multilateral		21 Sep 65	547UNTS280	107963
Multilateral		21 Oct 65	547UNTS216	107959
Hungary	Yugoslavia	23 Nov 65	577UNTS89	108374
Ireland	UK Great Britain	14 Dec 65	565UNTS58	108235
Czechoslovakia	Poland	22 Jan 66	588UNTS175	108524
Brazil	UNICEF (Children)	28 Mar 66	607UNTS235	108807
Spain	USA (United States)	14 Apr 66	579UNTS173	108406
Sweden	USA (United States)	28 Jul 66	603UNTS61	108725
Bulgaria	Poland	03 Oct 66	618UNTS3	108921
Israel	Norway	02 Nov 66	630UNTS225	108972
Romania	United Arab Rep	14 Nov 66	642UNTS141	109170
Romania	United Arab Rep	14 Nov 66	642UNTS129	109169
Ghana	Romania	23 Nov 66	642UNTS63	109165
Ghana	Romania	23 Nov 66	642UNTS79	109166
UK Great Britain	USA (United States)	01 Jan 67	604UNTS3	108738
Multilateral		27 Feb 67	590UNTS156	108552
Netherlands	Romania	08 May 67	607UNTS105	108800
Multilateral		10 Jun 67	602UNTS212	108714
Multilateral		14 Jun 67	603UNTS2	108719
UK Great Britain	Yugoslavia	30 Jun 67	642UNTS325	109182
Germany, West	Romania	03 Aug 67	642UNTS47	109164
Bulgaria	Romania	22 Aug 67	631UNTS49	108986
Multilateral		12 Oct 67	607UNTS2	108792
Multilateral		12 Oct 67	607UNTS20	108793
Multilateral		14 Nov 67	614UNTS2	108860
State/IGO Group	Nigeria	20 Apr 68	636UNTS294	109106
UN Special Fund	Syria	22 Apr 68	634UNTS207	109063
State/IGO Group	Malaysia	10 May 68	636UNTS276	109105
Previous treaty renunciation				
Multilateral		20 Jan 45	140UNTS397	200471
Taiwan	France	18 Aug 45	14UNTS477	200101
Multilateral		30 Oct 46	11UNTS107	100151
Mexico	USA (United States)	15 Nov 46	105UNTS3	101450
Netherlands	USA (United States)	29 Apr 48	32UNTS167	100498
Multilateral		10 Jun 48	164UNTS113	102163
Multilateral		20 Jun 49	128UNTS141	101718
Nepal	UK Great Britain	30 Oct 50	97UNTS121	101346
Multilateral		15 Dec 50	347UNTS127	104994
Multilateral		15 Dec 50	171UNTS305	102234
Multilateral		08 Sep 51	136UNTS45	101832
Taiwan	Japan	28 Apr 52	138UNTS3	101858
Multilateral		06 Sep 52	216UNTS132	102937
Netherlands	Switzerland	03 Nov 53	293UNTS53	104285
ICJ Option Clause	Australia	06 Feb 54	186UNTS77	102484
Belgium	USA (United States)	12 Oct 54	202UNTS289	102735

PARTY ONE	PARTY TWO	DATE	CITATION	NUMBER
Previous treaty renunciation (Cont.)				
Italy	USA (United States)	30 Mar 55	257UNTS169	103654
Netherlands	USA (United States)	29 Apr 55	219UNTS105	102969
Multilateral		21 Jun 55	305UNTS265	104423
Multilateral		18 May 56	327UNTS123	104721
Multilateral		18 May 56	319UNTS21	104630
New Zealand	Switzerland	30 Dec 58	380UNTS313	105463
Sweden	UK Great Britain	28 Jul 60	404UNTS113	105808
Greece	Sweden	06 Oct 61	481UNTS137	106981
South Africa	UK Great Britain	28 May 62	443UNTS79	106361
Previous treaties adherence				
Bolivia	Brazil	25 Feb 38	51UNTS245	200192
Multilateral		12 Oct 40	161UNTS193	200485
Canada	USA (United States)	10 Nov 41	23UNTS275	200134
Panama	USA (United States)	26 May 47	138UNTS137	101866
UK Great Britain	USA (United States)	30 Sep 48	71UNTS241	100922
Multilateral		15 Dec 50	171UNTS305	102234
Czechoslovakia	Hungary	16 Apr 54	504UNTS231	107360
Multilateral		05 Oct 54	235UNTS99	103297
Austria	Yugoslavia	27 Nov 54	396UNTS75	105694
Germany, West	USA (United States)	02 Aug 55	268UNTS121	103854
Austria	USA (United States)	26 Sep 55	272UNTS31	103930
Colombia	USA (United States)	28 Nov 55	241UNTS39	103422
Czechoslovakia	Hungary	13 Oct 56	300UNTS125	104336
Multilateral		30 Sep 57	619UNTS77	108940
Germany, West	Netherlands	28 Jan 58	453UNTS183	106525
Canada	USA (United States)	07 Jan 59	391UNTS207	105624
Greece	USA (United States)	26 Apr 60	372UNTS299	105306
Belgium	USA (United States)	18 May 60	373UNTS31	105313
Canada	USA (United States)	17 Jan 61	542UNTS224	107894
Brazil	USA (United States)	13 Apr 62	445UNTS227	106391
Canada	USA (United States)	19 Apr 62	445UNTS265	106394
Australia	Fed of Malaya	26 Nov 62	453UNTS161	106523
Denmark	Netherlands	06 Jun 63	484UNTS137	107021
Multilateral		18 Jun 64	542UNTS145	107886
Poland	USSR (Soviet Union)	17 Jul 64	552UNTS175	108054
Greece	Yugoslavia	05 Nov 64	539UNTS13	107820
Germany, West	Netherlands	01 Dec 64	550UNTS123	108011
Bel-Lux Econ Union	Morocco	28 Apr 65	620UNTS171	108954
Malta	USA (United States)	15 Jan 66	579UNTS109	108402
Czechoslovakia	USSR (Soviet Union)	03 Feb 67	617UNTS267	108917
General relations and amity				
Netherlands	Yemen	12 Apr 39	79UNTS257	200249
Poland	USSR (Soviet Union)	21 Apr 45	12UNTS391	200070
Japan	Norway	28 Feb 57	280UNTS87	104054
Ceylon (Sri Lanka)	China People's Rep	19 Sep 57	337UNTS137	104821
Germany, East	USSR (Soviet Union)	27 Sep 57	292UNTS75	104268
Argentina	Denmark	25 Nov 57	299UNTS83	104308
Multilateral		16 Aug 60	382UNTS3	105475
Czechoslovakia	Poland	01 Mar 67	632UNTS255	109027
Non-prejudice to third party				
Multilateral		24 Oct 36	40UNTS187	100634
Ireland	USA (United States)	03 Feb 45	122UNTS305	200412
Taiwan	USSR (Soviet Union)	14 Aug 45	10UNTS300	200068
UK Great Britain	USA (United States)	11 Feb 46	3UNTS253	100036
France	USA (United States)	27 Mar 46	139UNTS114	101879
Belgium	Netherlands	24 May 46	31UNTS169	100477
Netherlands	Spain	13 Jul 46	4UNTS351	100055
Norway	UK Great Britain	31 Aug 46	6UNTS235	100078
Multilateral		09 Oct 46	78UNTS213	101018
Multilateral		09 Oct 46	78UNTS198	101017
Multilateral		09 Oct 46	78UNTS227	101019
USA (United States)	Uruguay	14 Dec 46	532UNTS87	107713
Taiwan	USA (United States)	20 Dec 46	22UNTS87	100332
Ecuador	USA (United States)	08 Jan 47	22UNTS119	100333

PARTY ONE	PARTY TWO	DATE	CITATION	NUMBER
Non-prejudice to third party (Cont.)				
Romania	USSR (Soviet Union)	20 Feb 47	226UNTS79	103110
Paraguay	USA (United States)	28 Feb 47	44UNTS25	100676
France	USA (United States)	04 Apr 47	24UNTS133	100353
Iraq	Jordan	14 Apr 47	23UNTS148	100345
Chile	USA (United States)	10 May 47	55UNTS21	100807
Czechoslovakia	Denmark	14 May 47	27UNTS297	100413
Czechoslovakia	Sweden	15 Oct 47	44UNTS149	100683
Austria	Netherlands	22 Jan 48	17UNTS99	100270
Multilateral		17 Mar 48	19UNTS51	100304
Argentina	Denmark	18 Mar 48	94UNTS175	101311
Pakistan	Sweden	06 May 48	36UNTS3	100564
Multilateral		26 Jun 48	331UNTS217	104757
Bulgaria	Hungary	16 Jul 48	477UNTS169	106921
France	Spain	23 Aug 48	28UNTS173	100425
Bolivia	USA (United States)	29 Sep 48	505UNTS139	107370
Netherlands	Spain	08 Oct 48	28UNTS209	100426
Mexico	Portugal	22 Oct 48	34UNTS329	100546
Argentina	Netherlands	29 Oct 48	95UNTS21	101316
Belgium	Luxembourg	14 Jan 49	36UNTS339	100572
Finland	Netherlands	25 Feb 49	53UNTS123	100777
Panama	USA (United States)	31 Mar 49	55UNTS87	100810
Multilateral		04 Apr 49	34UNTS243	100541
Canada	USA (United States)	04 Jun 49	122UNTS237	101649
Multilateral		01 Jul 49	96UNTS257	101341
Czechoslovakia	Finland	13 Jul 49	53UNTS153	100779
Dominican Republic	USA (United States)	19 Jul 49	51UNTS145	100762
Ceylon (Sri Lanka)	UK Great Britain	05 Aug 49	35UNTS137	100554
Multilateral		12 Aug 49	75UNTS31	100970
Multilateral		12 Aug 49	75UNTS85	100971
Burma	USA (United States)	28 Sep 49	55UNTS3	100806
Iran	Netherlands	31 Oct 49	254UNTS257	103596
Austria	Czechoslovakia	30 Mar 50	495UNTS85	107240
Italy	Portugal	05 Apr 50	254UNTS329	103599
Burma	Ceylon (Sri Lanka)	29 Jun 50	73UNTS3	100940
Denmark	Italy	01 Jul 50	133UNTS181	101788
Burma	Sweden	14 Sep 50	96UNTS45	101330
Luxembourg	Portugal	21 Oct 50	108UNTS67	101468
Multilateral		22 Nov 50	131UNTS25	101734
Colombia	Portugal	09 Mar 51	108UNTS87	101469
Multilateral		18 Apr 51	261UNTS140	103729
Italy	UK Great Britain	16 Jun 51	172UNTS293	102253
Cuba	Portugal	26 Jun 51	192UNTS115	102598
Burma	Denmark	30 Jul 51	108UNTS167	101472
Greece	USA (United States)	03 Aug 51	224UNTS279	103080
Burma	Netherlands	06 Sep 51	108UNTS187	101473
Ethiopia	USA (United States)	07 Sep 51	206UNTS41	102785
Italy	UK Great Britain	28 Nov 51	172UNTS27	102238
Muscat and Oman	UK Great Britain	20 Dec 51	149UNTS247	101956
Austria	UK Great Britain	12 Dec 52	172UNTS9	102237
Cuba	USA (United States)	26 May 53	224UNTS75	103070
Burma	Norway	22 Jun 53	174UNTS49	102277
Libya	UK Great Britain	29 Jul 53	186UNTS185	102491
USA (United States)	Venezuela	14 Aug 53	213UNTS99	102883
Iran	Switzerland	27 May 54	496UNTS273	107257
Iraq	Turkey	24 Feb 55	233UNTS199	103264
Brazil	Sweden	29 Apr 55	228UNTS115	103145
Syria	United Arab Rep	03 Jul 55	393UNTS67	105652
Belgium	Portugal	30 Jul 55	250UNTS213	103525
Norway	Syria	25 Feb 56	463UNTS217	106706
Ireland	USA (United States)	16 Mar 56	317UNTS195	104604
Germany, West	Sweden	22 Mar 56	262UNTS423	103763
Portugal	Venezuela	16 May 56	463UNTS239	106707
Costa Rica	USA (United States)	18 May 56	404UNTS237	105814
Cuba	USA (United States)	26 Jun 56	293UNTS257	104294
Guatemala	USA (United States)	15 Aug 56	288UNTS181	104205

PARTY ONE	PARTY TWO	DATE	CITATION	NUMBER
Non-prejudice to third party (Cont.)				
Japan	USA (United States)	23 Nov 56	324UNTS177	104685
Iran	USA (United States)	16 Jan 57	308UNTS147	104460
Iran	USA (United States)	05 Mar 57	342UNTS29	104898
Multilateral		29 Apr 57	320UNTS243	104646
Japan	USA (United States)	08 May 57	318UNTS257	104621
Ecuador	USA (United States)	31 May 57	304UNTS61	104391
Germany, West	USA (United States)	28 Jun 57	288UNTS339	104213
Czechoslovakia	United Arab Rep	30 Jun 57	411UNTS126	105917
Italy	USA (United States)	03 Jul 57	308UNTS195	104462
Germany, West	USA (United States)	03 Jul 57	288UNTS305	104212
Spain	USA (United States)	16 Aug 57	307UNTS169	104449
Italy	Switzerland	19 Sep 57	363UNTS69	105200
Sweden	UK Great Britain	20 Sep 57	310UNTS49	104486
Italy	UK Great Britain	28 Dec 57	305UNTS357	104425
Belgium	Iran	14 Apr 58	381UNTS309	105473
Germany, West	UK Great Britain	18 Apr 58	343UNTS241	104928
Multilateral		29 Apr 58	450UNTS11	106465
Japan	USA (United States)	19 Jun 58	325UNTS143	104699
Czechoslovakia	Germany, East	26 Jun 58	504UNTS221	107359
UK Great Britain	USA (United States)	03 Jul 58	326UNTS3	104707
Portugal	UK Great Britain	18 Jul 58	313UNTS109	104532
USA (United States)	Venezuela	08 Oct 58	371UNTS69	105271
Euratom	USA (United States)	08 Nov 58	338UNTS135	104835
Euratom	UK Great Britain	04 Feb 59	331UNTS125	104752
Multilateral		20 Apr 59	376UNTS85	105375
USA (United States)	Vietnam, South	22 Apr 59	347UNTS113	104993
IAEA (Atom Energy)	UK Great Britain	11 May 59	339UNTS351	104854
Germany, West	USA (United States)	01 Oct 59	358UNTS129	105130
Spain	UK Great Britain	19 Jan 60	404UNTS41	105804
Multilateral		28 Apr 60	376UNTS111	105377
Spain	UK Great Britain	13 May 60	374UNTS287	105342
Indonesia	USA (United States)	08 Jun 60	388UNTS287	105585
India	USA (United States)	13 Jun 60	377UNTS37	105394
Belgium	Burma	17 Aug 60	540UNTS185	107850
Burma	Switzerland	31 Oct 60	465UNTS97	106723
Brazil	USA (United States)	17 Mar 61	406UNTS241	105853
Poland	Syria	10 Nov 62	491UNTS228	107179
Denmark	Yugoslavia	11 Feb 64	511UNTS241	107437
Luxembourg	Netherlands	24 Mar 64	548UNTS137	107975
Switzerland	UK Great Britain	11 Aug 64	552UNTS271	108059
IAEA (Atom Energy)	Uruguay	24 Sep 65	556UNTS117	108123
IAEA (Atom Energy)	USA (United States)	26 Sep 66	589UNTS3	108532
Philippines	IAEA (Atom Energy)	28 Sep 66	589UNTS25	108533
IAEA (Atom Energy)	USA (United States)	09 Dec 66	589UNTS55	108535
UK Great Britain	USA (United States)	30 Dec 66	603UNTS273	108737
Bulgaria	Romania	15 Jun 67	634UNTS57	109051
Germany, East	Mongolia	12 Sep 68	0UNTS0	109453
Friendship and amity				
Greece	Iran	09 Jan 31	166UNTS323	200496
Netherlands	Yemen	12 Apr 39	79UNTS257	200249
Canada	USA (United States)	10 Jun 39	149UNTS332	200476
Afghanistan	Netherlands	26 Jul 39	32UNTS381	200177
Taiwan	Dominican Republic	11 May 40	10UNTS285	200067
Afghanistan	Sweden	22 Oct 40	191UNTS349	200516
Brazil	Paraguay	14 Jun 41	54UNTS249	200197
Iceland	USA (United States)	01 Jul 41	12UNTS405	200071
Brazil	Chile	18 Nov 41	67UNTS279	200225
El Salvador	USA (United States)	13 Feb 42	23UNTS293	200136
Taiwan	Iraq	16 Mar 42	14UNTS335	200091
Liberia	USA (United States)	31 Mar 42	23UNTS302	200137
Nicaragua	USA (United States)	08 Apr 42	24UNTS145	200138
Saudi Arabia	UK Great Britain	20 Apr 42	10UNTS117	200057
Brazil	Venezuela	22 Oct 42	65UNTS203	200212
Honduras	USA (United States)	26 Oct 42	24UNTS209	200145

PARTY ONE	PARTY TWO	DATE	CITATION	NUMBER
Friendship and amity (Cont.)				
Taiwan	Cuba	12 Nov 42	10UNTS243	200065
Brazil	Dominican Republic	09 Dec 42	65UNTS217	200213
Guatemala	USA (United States)	19 May 43	28UNTS377	200161
Brazil	Taiwan	20 Aug 43	14UNTS365	200094
Albania	Yugoslavia	23 Mar 44	1UNTS81	100015
Taiwan	Costa Rica	05 May 44	14UNTS427	200098
Brazil	Ecuador	24 May 44	73UNTS223	200242
Costa Rica	USA (United States)	29 May 44	124UNTS155	200417
Taiwan	Mexico	01 Aug 44	14UNTS441	200099
Bolivia	USA (United States)	07 Sep 44	162UNTS315	200494
Poland	USSR (Soviet Union)	21 Apr 45	12UNTS391	200070
Dominican Republic	USA (United States)	13 Oct 45	149UNTS361	200477
Multilateral		16 Nov 45	4UNTS275	100052
Taiwan	Ecuador	06 Jan 46	7UNTS233	100102
Taiwan	Thailand	23 Jan 46	161UNTS127	102126
Belgium	France	22 Feb 46	68UNTS157	100892
Poland	Yugoslavia	16 Mar 46	10UNTS11	100139
Jordan	UK Great Britain	22 Mar 46	6UNTS143	100074
Iraq	Turkey	29 Mar 46	37UNTS226	100580
Czechoslovakia	Yugoslavia	09 May 46	1UNTS67	100014
Belgium	Netherlands	16 May 46	17UNTS13	100266
Taiwan	USA (United States)	04 Nov 46	25UNTS69	100359
India	USA (United States)	14 Nov 46	22UNTS55	100331
Taiwan	Saudi Arabia	15 Nov 46	18UNTS197	100289
France	USA (United States)	10 Dec 46	15UNTS265	100242
Jordan	Turkey	11 Jan 47	14UNTS49	100210
Argentina	Taiwan	10 Feb 47	486UNTS143	107077
Belgium	Czechoslovakia	06 Mar 47	34UNTS77	100528
Czechoslovakia	Poland	10 Mar 47	25UNTS231	100365
Iraq	Jordan	14 Apr 47	23UNTS148	100345
Taiwan	Philippines	18 Apr 47	11UNTS361	100175
Czechoslovakia	Yugoslavia	27 Apr 47	33UNTS49	100514
France	Poland	19 May 47	12UNTS95	100181
Romania	Yugoslavia	26 Jun 47	116UNTS39	101568
Bulgaria	Poland	28 Jun 47	15UNTS123	100230
Albania	Yugoslavia	09 Jul 47	33UNTS91	100516
Italy	Philippines	09 Jul 47	44UNTS3	100674
Multilateral		02 Sep 47	21UNTS77	100324
Philippines	Spain	27 Sep 47	70UNTS133	100902
Hungary	Yugoslavia	15 Oct 47	33UNTS73	100515
Brazil	Sweden	14 Nov 47	94UNTS139	101310
Colombia	USA (United States)	22 Dec 47	51UNTS45	100751
Hungary	Romania	24 Jan 48	477UNTS155	106920
Hungary	Poland	31 Jan 48	25UNTS283	100368
Romania	USSR (Soviet Union)	04 Feb 48	48UNTS189	100745
Hungary	USSR (Soviet Union)	18 Feb 48	48UNTS163	100743
Belgium	Norway	20 Feb 48	32UNTS39	100487
Poland	Romania	27 Feb 48	46UNTS143	100707
Jordan	UK Great Britain	15 Mar 48	77UNTS77	100994
Multilateral		17 Mar 48	19UNTS51	100304
Argentina	Denmark	18 Mar 48	94UNTS175	101311
Bulgaria	USSR (Soviet Union)	18 Mar 48	48UNTS135	100741
Finland	USSR (Soviet Union)	06 Apr 48	48UNTS149	100742
Greece	USA (United States)	23 Apr 48	74UNTS107	100958
Multilateral		30 Apr 48	119UNTS3	101609
Bulgaria	Poland	29 May 48	26UNTS213	100389
Peru	USA (United States)	30 Jun 48	150UNTS45	101962
Netherlands	UK Great Britain	07 Jul 48	82UNTS259	101099
Bulgaria	Hungary	16 Jul 48	477UNTS169	106921
India	Switzerland	14 Aug 48	33UNTS3	100509
Panama	USA (United States)	24 Sep 48	150UNTS25	101961
Belgium	Italy	29 Nov 48	41UNTS3	100641
Poland	Romania	26 Jan 49	85UNTS21	101143
Panama	USA (United States)	31 Mar 49	55UNTS87	100810
Multilateral		04 Apr 49	34UNTS243	100541

PARTY ONE	PARTY TWO	DATE	CITATION	NUMBER
Friendship and amity (Cont.)				
Czechoslovakia	Hungary	16 Apr 49	477UNTS183	106922
Multilateral		05 May 49	87UNTS103	101168
Bulgaria	Poland	16 May 49	84UNTS313	101140
Norway	USA (United States)	25 May 49	32UNTS345	100507
Italy	Spain	31 May 49	231UNTS251	103224
Greece	Lebanon	10 Jun 49	178UNTS29	102334
Philippines	Thailand	14 Jun 49	81UNTS53	101062
Ecuador	Italy	24 Aug 49	72UNTS35	100926
Afghanistan	India	04 Jan 50	81UNTS75	101064
China People's Rep	USSR (Soviet Union)	14 Feb 50	226UNTS3	103103
Iran	Pakistan	18 Feb 50	161UNTS23	102119
Iraq	Pakistan	26 Feb 50	214UNTS3	102896
India	Iran	15 Mar 50	161UNTS15	102118
Italy	Turkey	24 Mar 50	96UNTS207	101338
Iraq	Pakistan	20 Jun 50	77UNTS215	101001
Luxembourg	UK Great Britain	27 Jun 50	183UNTS217	102431
India	Nepal	31 Jul 50	94UNTS3	101302
Greece	Philippines	28 Aug 50	225UNTS155	103097
Pakistan	Syria	29 Aug 50	109UNTS95	101494
Iran	Italy	24 Sep 50	281UNTS157	104077
Haiti	USA (United States)	28 Sep 50	162UNTS85	102132
Bulgaria	Romania	29 Sep 50	342UNTS141	104905
Nepal	UK Great Britain	30 Oct 50	97UNTS121	101346
Bolivia	USA (United States)	22 Nov 50	152UNTS17	102008
Albania	Poland	02 Dec 50	260UNTS131	103707
El Salvador	USA (United States)	13 Dec 50	166UNTS149	102188
Brazil	Netherlands	15 Dec 50	123UNTS101	101657
Brazil	USA (United States)	27 Dec 50	147UNTS33	101926
Albania	Poland	25 Jan 51	260UNTS217	103710
Nicaragua	USA (United States)	31 Jan 51	160UNTS121	102105
Nicaragua	USA (United States)	31 Jan 51	150UNTS3	101960
Costa Rica	USA (United States)	13 Feb 51	141UNTS169	101914
Panama	USA (United States)	26 Feb 51	160UNTS153	102106
Indonesia	Pakistan	03 Mar 51	188UNTS333	102537
India	Indonesia	03 Mar 51	167UNTS3	102197
USA (United States)	Uruguay	07 Mar 51	165UNTS113	102173
India	USA (United States)	16 Mar 51	141UNTS47	101904
Dominican Republic	USA (United States)	16 Mar 51	148UNTS15	101932
China People's Rep	Poland	03 Apr 51	304UNTS187	104396
Greece	Turkey	20 Apr 51	178UNTS17	102333
Honduras	USA (United States)	24 Apr 51	140UNTS287	101894
Netherlands	South Africa	31 May 51	188UNTS289	102533
Saudi Arabia	USA (United States)	18 Jun 51	141UNTS67	101906
India	Turkey	29 Jun 51	213UNTS183	102886
Burma	India	07 Jul 51	149UNTS35	101949
Pakistan	Turkey	26 Jul 51	188UNTS323	102536
Japan	USA (United States)	28 Aug 51	147UNTS81	101930
Pakistan	United Arab Rep	28 Aug 51	214UNTS247	102902
Ethiopia	USA (United States)	07 Sep 51	206UNTS41	102785
Greece	UK Great Britain	29 Sep 51	190UNTS260	102570
Pakistan	Saudi Arabia	25 Nov 51	177UNTS3	102304
Italy	UK Great Britain	28 Nov 51	172UNTS27	102238
India	Turkey	14 Dec 51	137UNTS15	101845
Muscat and Oman	UK Great Britain	20 Dec 51	149UNTS247	101956
France	USA (United States)	05 Jan 52	181UNTS177	102408
Iceland	USA (United States)	08 Jan 52	180UNTS183	102383
Portugal	USA (United States)	08 Jan 52	207UNTS51	102799
Germany, East	Poland	08 Jan 52	304UNTS113	104394
India	Syria	25 Feb 52	163UNTS55	102141
Italy	Jordan	24 Apr 52	281UNTS167	104078
Ethiopia	USA (United States)	15 May 52	180UNTS227	102388
New Zealand	USA (United States)	19 Jun 52	178UNTS315	102347
Burma	Pakistan	25 Jun 52	173UNTS41	102259
India	Philippines	11 Jul 52	203UNTS73	102741
Burma	Philippines	15 Aug 52	200UNTS97	102696

PARTY ONE	PARTY TWO	DATE	CITATION	NUMBER
Friendship and amity (Cont.)				
Austria	Belgium	17 Oct 52	162UNTS183	102135
Dominican Republic	Philippines	02 Nov 52	543UNTS175	107901
Chile	WHO (World Health)	04 Nov 52	150UNTS119	101966
India	Iraq	10 Nov 52	172UNTS103	102242
Ceylon (Sri Lanka)	USA (United States)	17 Nov 52	180UNTS207	102386
Ceylon (Sri Lanka)	WHO (World Health)	21 Nov 52	161UNTS315	200490
India	WHO (World Health)	11 Dec 52	158UNTS391	102073
Austria	UK Great Britain	12 Dec 52	172UNTS9	102237
Lebanon	Pakistan	16 Jan 53	284UNTS193	104137
Bolivia	Italy	31 Jan 53	281UNTS181	104079
Albania	Romania	14 Feb 53	342UNTS107	104903
Taiwan	Spain	19 Feb 53	181UNTS81	102400
Multilateral		28 Feb 53	167UNTS21	102199
Denmark	Uruguay	04 Mar 53	250UNTS51	103517
India	Muscat and Oman	15 Mar 53	190UNTS69	102559
Germany, West	USA (United States)	09 Apr 53	204UNTS79	102750
Ethiopia	USA (United States)	29 Apr 53	224UNTS121	103073
Greece	Netherlands	29 Apr 53	191UNTS235	102583
Israel	Uruguay	30 Apr 53	280UNTS269	104064
Ethiopia	USA (United States)	22 May 53	207UNTS127	102803
Germany, West	USA (United States)	02 Jun 53	231UNTS151	103214
United Arab Rep	USA (United States)	18 Jun 53	204UNTS55	102749
United Arab Rep	USA (United States)	18 Jun 53	215UNTS45	102910
Liberia	USA (United States)	23 Jun 53	213UNTS57	102880
Pakistan	Turkey	29 Jun 53	211UNTS225	102854
Pakistan	United Arab Rep	14 Nov 53	485UNTS55	107046
Finland	USSR (Soviet Union)	06 Feb 54	221UNTS143	103006
Indonesia	Thailand	03 Mar 54	213UNTS297	102893
Peru	Spain	31 Mar 54	232UNTS65	103230
Belgium	South Africa	01 Jun 54	201UNTS25	102708
Greece	Italy	11 Sep 54	284UNTS313	104145
Multilateral		02 Dec 54	226UNTS153	103112
Belgium	Greece	09 Dec 54	257UNTS243	103660
Taiwan	El Salvador	09 Dec 54	214UNTS217	102900
Multilateral		19 Dec 54	218UNTS139	102955
Peru	USA (United States)	31 Dec 54	251UNTS51	103533
Finland	USSR (Soviet Union)	24 Jan 55	240UNTS243	103406
Panama	USA (United States)	25 Jan 55	243UNTS211	103454
Iraq	Turkey	24 Feb 55	233UNTS199	103264
Multilateral		02 Mar 55	225UNTS233	103101
Chile	USA (United States)	31 Mar 55	262UNTS19	103736
Iraq	UK Great Britain	04 Apr 55	233UNTS118	103265
Japan	Thailand	06 Apr 55	230UNTS219	103187
Multilateral		06 Apr 55	261UNTS55	103725
Multilateral		14 May 55	219UNTS3	102962
Netherlands	Norway	18 May 55	252UNTS269	103569
Italy	Norway	14 Jun 55	260UNTS307	103713
Belgium	Portugal	30 Jul 55	250UNTS213	103525
Italy	Spain	11 Aug 55	267UNTS125	103839
Iran	USA (United States)	15 Aug 55	284UNTS93	104132
USA (United States)	USSR (Soviet Union)	05 Sep 55	256UNTS307	103641
Germany, East	USSR (Soviet Union)	20 Sep 55	226UNTS201	103114
Syria	United Arab Rep	20 Oct 55	247UNTS117	103461
USSR (Soviet Union)	Yemen	31 Oct 55	240UNTS317	103410
Multilateral		05 Nov 55	250UNTS201	103524
Nicaragua	USA (United States)	21 Jan 56	367UNTS3	105224
USSR (Soviet Union)	Yugoslavia	02 Feb 56	259UNTS111	103685
Iran	Pakistan	09 Mar 56	449UNTS183	106460
Turkey	UK Great Britain	12 Mar 56	313UNTS73	104530
Multilateral		13 Mar 56	427UNTS245	106158
Romania	USSR (Soviet Union)	07 Apr 56	259UNTS377	103698
Mongolia	USSR (Soviet Union)	24 Apr 56	259UNTS297	103693
Bulgaria	USSR (Soviet Union)	28 Apr 56	259UNTS363	103697
Albania	USSR (Soviet Union)	03 May 56	259UNTS391	103699
Mongolia	Romania	08 May 56	342UNTS291	104913

PARTY ONE	PARTY TWO	DATE	CITATION	NUMBER
Friendship and amity (Cont.)				
Korea, North	Poland	11 May 56	432UNTS161	106219
Korea, North	Romania	12 May 56	342UNTS189	104908
USSR (Soviet Union)	Yugoslavia	17 May 56	259UNTS145	103687
Czechoslovakia	USSR (Soviet Union)	01 Jun 56	259UNTS341	103696
Israel	USA (United States)	26 Jun 56	257UNTS55	103649
Poland	USSR (Soviet Union)	30 Jun 56	259UNTS311	103694
China People's Rep	USSR (Soviet Union)	05 Jul 56	263UNTS129	103770
Poland	Yugoslavia	06 Jul 56	281UNTS143	104076
Syria	USSR (Soviet Union)	20 Aug 56	274UNTS105	103961
Philippines	Switzerland	30 Aug 56	293UNTS43	104284
Greece	United Arab Rep	04 Sep 56	299UNTS253	104317
Korea, North	USSR (Soviet Union)	05 Sep 56	259UNTS329	103695
Belgium	Germany, West	24 Sep 56	263UNTS31	103766
Norway	USSR (Soviet Union)	12 Oct 56	308UNTS95	104457
Romania	Vietnam, North	12 Oct 56	342UNTS173	104907
Burma	Thailand	15 Oct 56	277UNTS87	104000
Romania	Yugoslavia	27 Oct 56	389UNTS55	105592
Romania	Yugoslavia	27 Oct 56	389UNTS33	105590
India	Japan	29 Oct 56	318UNTS289	104622
Ecuador	USA (United States)	31 Oct 56	283UNTS151	104114
Argentina	USA (United States)	05 Nov 56	277UNTS143	104004
Bulgaria	Yugoslavia	24 Dec 56	397UNTS3	105699
Colombia	USA (United States)	09 Jan 57	462UNTS151	106676
Czechoslovakia	Yugoslavia	29 Jan 57	300UNTS249	104339
Poland	United Arab Rep	02 Feb 57	319UNTS221	104633
Belgium	Yugoslavia	05 Feb 57	276UNTS143	103990
Taiwan	Turkey	12 Feb 57	282UNTS125	104097
USSR (Soviet Union)	Vietnam, North	15 Feb 57	274UNTS115	103962
Japan	United Arab Rep	20 Mar 57	318UNTS345	104625
India	Poland	27 Mar 57	319UNTS263	104635
Paraguay	USA (United States)	04 Apr 57	284UNTS161	104135
Poland	Vietnam, North	06 Apr 57	432UNTS255	106224
Romania	United Arab Rep	15 Apr 57	389UNTS21	105589
Iran	Japan	16 Apr 57	325UNTS113	104697
India	Romania	30 Apr 57	342UNTS251	104911
Argentina	Israel	23 May 57	280UNTS199	104059
Japan	Pakistan	27 May 57	325UNTS21	104692
Czechoslovakia	Syria	18 Jun 57	303UNTS119	104374
United Arab Rep	USSR (Soviet Union)	19 Oct 57	292UNTS151	104271
Czechoslovakia	United Arab Rep	19 Oct 57	530UNTS181	107681
Brazil	USA (United States)	05 Nov 57	303UNTS3	104368
Taiwan	Iran	11 Nov 57	563UNTS31	108202
Taiwan	Jordan	19 Nov 57	308UNTS227	104463
Israel	Norway	26 Nov 57	345UNTS99	104962
Czechoslovakia	USSR (Soviet Union)	04 Dec 57	313UNTS291	104537
Japan	USSR (Soviet Union)	06 Dec 57	325UNTS35	104694
Ethiopia	Japan	19 Dec 57	325UNTS91	104695
Belgium	Denmark	31 Dec 57	305UNTS247	104422
Multilateral		06 Jan 58	304UNTS227	104399
Japan	USA (United States)	11 Jan 58	304UNTS35	104390
Ceylon (Sri Lanka)	USSR (Soviet Union)	15 Jan 58	305UNTS235	104421
Poland	Yugoslavia	16 Jan 58	340UNTS181	104864
Israel	Philippines	26 Feb 58	507UNTS135	107398
Taiwan	Costa Rica	10 Apr 58	315UNTS165	104567
Germany, West	UK Great Britain	18 Apr 58	343UNTS241	104928
Afghanistan	USA (United States)	26 Jun 58	321UNTS67	104654
Romania	Vietnam, North	30 Jun 58	389UNTS43	105591
Muscat and Oman	UK Great Britain	25 Jul 58	312UNTS347	104524
Pakistan	Thailand	28 Aug 58	394UNTS53	105668
Czechoslovakia	Romania	25 Oct 58	338UNTS301	104843
Belgium	Spain	27 Oct 58	327UNTS107	104720
El Salvador	Israel	14 Nov 58	345UNTS67	104959
Muscat and Oman	USA (United States)	20 Dec 58	380UNTS181	105457
Mongolia	Poland	23 Dec 58	432UNTS177	106220
Belgium	Turkey	29 Dec 58	357UNTS195	105118

PARTY ONE	PARTY TWO	DATE	CITATION	NUMBER
Friendship and amity (Cont.)				
Turkey	USA (United States)	05 Mar 59	327UNTS293	104727
Israel	Liberia	09 Apr 59	448UNTS95	106427
Hungary	Iraq	11 Apr 59	439UNTS25	106323
Hungary	USSR (Soviet Union)	17 Apr 59	439UNTS41	106324
Indonesia	Malaysia	17 Apr 59	470UNTS273	106813
Iraq	USSR (Soviet Union)	05 May 59	356UNTS179	105095
Iran	UK Great Britain	06 May 59	398UNTS51	105717
Iran	Netherlands	22 May 59	474UNTS195	106882
Ethiopia	Yugoslavia	06 Jun 59	386UNTS243	105544
Finland	Hungary	10 Jun 59	439UNTS3	106321
Taiwan	Ecuador	12 Jun 59	387UNTS3	105554
Israel	Mexico	15 Jun 59	377UNTS267	105406
Greece	Yugoslavia	18 Jun 59	368UNTS137	105238
Brazil	Israel	24 Jun 59	515UNTS151	107458
Czechoslovakia	India	07 Jul 59	359UNTS259	105145
Iraq	Romania	04 Aug 59	502UNTS17	107324
Norway	Spain	19 Aug 59	376UNTS145	105379
Guinea	USA (United States)	28 Oct 59	358UNTS169	105134
Pakistan	USA (United States)	12 Nov 59	404UNTS259	105816
Czechoslovakia	Guinea	30 Nov 59	386UNTS63	105538
Czechoslovakia	USSR (Soviet Union)	02 Dec 59	374UNTS63	105330
Czechoslovakia	Ethiopia	11 Dec 59	386UNTS51	105537
Czechoslovakia	Ethiopia	11 Dec 59	399UNTS93	105736
Belgium	Brazil	06 Jan 60	531UNTS149	107701
Guinea	Hungary	12 Jan 60	519UNTS131	107505
Italy	USSR (Soviet Union)	09 Feb 60	399UNTS75	105735
Argentina	Philippines	12 Feb 60	535UNTS293	107785
Taiwan	Panama	26 Feb 60	435UNTS281	106285
Indonesia	USSR (Soviet Union)	28 Feb 60	392UNTS191	105644
Portugal	USA (United States)	19 Mar 60	371UNTS131	105275
Netherlands	Turkey	12 May 60	463UNTS207	106704
Belgium	Iran	14 May 60	522UNTS249	107551
Finland	USSR (Soviet Union)	27 May 60	379UNTS381	105444
Denmark	Poland	08 Jun 60	424UNTS37	106097
Korea, North	USSR (Soviet Union)	22 Jun 60	399UNTS3	105732
Spain	UK Great Britain	12 Jul 60	414UNTS123	105971
Japan	Pakistan	30 Jul 60	384UNTS63	105511
Mexico	USA (United States)	15 Aug 60	402UNTS177	105786
Japan	Thailand	24 Aug 60	384UNTS73	105512
Cuba	Korea, North	29 Aug 60	473UNTS117	106860
Cuba	Romania	28 Oct 60	457UNTS9	106574
Czechoslovakia	Ghana	23 Nov 60	431UNTS91	106213
Israel	Mali	24 Nov 60	413UNTS104	105945
Cambodia	Czechoslovakia	27 Nov 60	410UNTS263	105910
Cambodia	Czechoslovakia	27 Nov 60	412UNTS179	105931
Japan	UK Great Britain	03 Dec 60	414UNTS61	105966
Netherlands	United Arab Rep	08 Dec 60	455UNTS276	106547
Cuba	USSR (Soviet Union)	12 Dec 60	421UNTS3	106048
Multilateral		14 Dec 60	429UNTS93	106193
Cuba	Czechoslovakia	22 Dec 60	426UNTS145	106134
Ethiopia	USSR (Soviet Union)	13 Jan 61	421UNTS13	106049
Czechoslovakia	Hungary	24 Feb 61	422UNTS15	106066
Cuba	Poland	06 Mar 61	484UNTS123	107020
Afghanistan	Japan	15 Mar 61	450UNTS373	106480
Ceylon (Sri Lanka)	Japan	20 Mar 61	450UNTS385	106481
Cuba	Germany, East	29 Mar 61	448UNTS81	106426
India	Norway	19 Apr 61	404UNTS307	105818
Afghanistan	Czechoslovakia	23 Apr 61	437UNTS25	106297
Taiwan	Nicaragua	25 Apr 61	423UNTS139	106090
Germany, West	Netherlands	27 Apr 61	487UNTS77	107095
Ghana	Hungary	27 Apr 61	439UNTS17	106322
Taiwan	Uruguay	03 May 61	596UNTS121	108630
Czechoslovakia	Indonesia	29 May 61	479UNTS337	106962
Somalia	USSR (Soviet Union)	02 Jun 61	528UNTS147	107638
Czechoslovakia	Somalia	04 Jun 61	479UNTS291	106960

PARTY ONE	PARTY TWO	DATE	CITATION	NUMBER
Friendship and amity (Cont.)				
Nepal	USA (United States)	09 Jun 61	421UNTS223	106061
Kuwait	UK Great Britain	19 Jun 61	399UNTS239	105743
Pakistan	Philippines	15 Aug 61	522UNTS35	107534
Taiwan	Paraguay	18 Aug 61	438UNTS109	106314
Israel	Malagasy	27 Aug 61	484UNTS217	107032
Ghana	Romania	30 Sep 61	457UNTS3	106573
Taiwan	Jordan	17 Oct 61	435UNTS267	106284
Brazil	Poland	19 Oct 61	552UNTS75	108050
Switzerland	UK Great Britain	20 Oct 61	431UNTS29	106206
Guatemala	Israel	27 Nov 61	448UNTS191	106431
Taiwan	El Salvador	27 Nov 61	437UNTS161	106306
IBRD (World Bank)	South Africa	01 Dec 61	425UNTS197	106125
Ethiopia	USA (United States)	06 Dec 61	433UNTS231	106246
Argentina	Japan	20 Dec 61	613UNTS323	108859
Ghana	USA (United States)	03 Jan 62	433UNTS147	106237
Cyprus	USA (United States)	18 Jan 62	435UNTS3	106266
Ghana	USA (United States)	24 Jan 62	435UNTS23	106268
Brazil	Japan	28 Mar 62	451UNTS125	106489
Hungary	India	30 Mar 62	519UNTS119	107504
India	Japan	31 Mar 62	451UNTS143	106490
Taiwan	Malagasy	04 Apr 62	463UNTS195	106703
India	Japan	23 Apr 62	451UNTS155	106491
Gabon	Israel	15 May 62	484UNTS181	107027
United Arab Rep	USA (United States)	21 May 62	458UNTS197	106601
Denmark	USA (United States)	28 May 62	450UNTS215	106469
Senegal	USSR (Soviet Union)	14 Jun 62	437UNTS233	106309
Israel	Peru	25 Jun 62	515UNTS263	107464
Israel	Liberia	25 Jun 62	448UNTS295	106442
New Zealand	Western Samoa	01 Aug 62	453UNTS3	106515
Syria	USSR (Soviet Union)	19 Aug 62	457UNTS285	106588
Denmark	USSR (Soviet Union)	11 Sep 62	458UNTS3	106589
Cameroon	Israel	24 Oct 62	449UNTS15	106447
Germany, West	USA (United States)	20 Nov 62	505UNTS263	107377
Belgium	Tunisia	21 Dec 62	482UNTS3	106987
Iraq	USA (United States)	23 Jan 63	488UNTS163	107126
Malaysia	USA (United States)	28 Jan 63	473UNTS15	106850
Dahomey	USSR (Soviet Union)	20 Mar 63	528UNTS181	107641
Philippines	USA (United States)	23 Mar 63	474UNTS80	106873
Czechoslovakia	Tunisia	06 Apr 63	555UNTS111	108106
Belgium	Venezuela	15 May 63	470UNTS259	106812
Thailand	USA (United States)	24 May 63	477UNTS123	106918
Korea, South	USA (United States)	18 Jun 63	487UNTS297	107112
India	USA (United States)	19 Jun 63	479UNTS175	106952
Hungary	Mongolia	10 Jul 63	519UNTS173	107508
Cameroon	UK Great Britain	20 Aug 63	539UNTS233	107834
Paraguay	USA (United States)	20 Aug 63	531UNTS197	107704
Afghanistan	USA (United States)	20 Aug 63	488UNTS41	107118
Argentina	USA (United States)	21 Aug 63	488UNTS61	107119
Ecuador	USA (United States)	20 Sep 63	488UNTS147	107125
Mali	Romania	26 Sep 63	528UNTS193	107642
Iraq	Kuwait	04 Oct 63	485UNTS321	107063
Hungary	Yugoslavia	15 Oct 63	577UNTS49	108372
Iran	USA (United States)	24 Oct 63	489UNTS303	107146
Tanganyika	USSR (Soviet Union)	06 Nov 63	528UNTS157	107639
Belgium	Pakistan	14 Nov 63	535UNTS393	107792
Belgium	Poland	09 Dec 63	514UNTS195	107448
Netherlands	Tunisia	11 Feb 64	570UNTS173	108293
Iceland	USA (United States)	13 Feb 64	524UNTS235	107576
UNESCO (Educ/Cult)	Yugoslavia	27 Feb 64	489UNTS257	107143
Italy	United Nations	18 Mar 64	491UNTS21	107171
USSR (Soviet Union)	Yemen	21 Mar 64	553UNTS267	108094
Ireland	Norway	02 Apr 64	553UNTS129	108078
Mexico	Netherlands	08 Apr 64	575UNTS35	108353
Liberia	USA (United States)	08 May 64	526UNTS239	107608
Algeria	Czechoslovakia	14 May 64	538UNTS301	107817

PARTY ONE	PARTY TWO	DATE	CITATION	NUMBER
Friendship and amity (Cont.)				
Australia	USA (United States)	28 Aug 64	510UNTS201	107415
Ceylon (Sri Lanka)	USA (United States)	29 Aug 64	531UNTS93	107695
Germany, East	Poland	06 Oct 64	552UNTS89	108051
Czechoslovakia	Germany, East	06 Oct 64	545UNTS113	107927
USA (United States)	Yugoslavia	09 Nov 64	533UNTS39	107731
Belgium	Mexico	19 Nov 64	546UNTS217	107949
Taiwan	Korea, South	27 Nov 64	555UNTS3	108102
Netherlands	Nigeria	04 Dec 64	545UNTS155	107931
India	Netherlands	11 Dec 64	570UNTS165	108292
UK Great Britain	USSR (Soviet Union)	06 Jan 65	543UNTS77	107897
Peru	USA (United States)	28 Jan 65	587UNTS273	108513
Bulgaria	Czechoslovakia	22 May 65	545UNTS65	107925
Ethiopia	Hungary	25 May 65	577UNTS193	108377
China People's Rep	Romania	27 May 65	592UNTS3	108566
Uganda	USSR (Soviet Union)	24 Jul 65	596UNTS199	108633
Israel	Sierra Leone	22 Aug 65	550UNTS275	108022
Czechoslovakia	Poland	22 Jan 66	588UNTS175	108524
UK Great Britain	Yugoslavia	27 Jan 66	573UNTS243	108337
Malaysia	Philippines	07 Feb 66	608UNTS3	108809
Denmark	Iran	14 Jun 66	597UNTS283	108652
Denmark	Jordan	28 Jun 66	574UNTS3	108338
France	USSR (Soviet Union)	30 Jun 66	589UNTS99	108537
Morocco	Senegal	15 Sep 66	634UNTS105	109055
Czechoslovakia	Poland	01 Mar 67	632UNTS255	109027
Bulgaria	USSR (Soviet Union)	12 May 67	631UNTS239	108997
Bulgaria	Mongolia	21 Jul 67	610UNTS0	108839
Hungary	USSR (Soviet Union)	07 Sep 67	632UNTS89	109011
Bulgaria	Germany, East	07 Sep 67	631UNTS81	108988
Hungary	Poland	16 May 68	0UNTS0	109292
Germany, East	Mongolia	12 Sep 68	0UNTS0	109453
Non-prejudice to UN charter				
Taiwan	USSR (Soviet Union)	14 Aug 45	10UNTS300	200068
Multilateral		16 Nov 45	4UNTS275	100052
Multilateral		01 Jan 46	99UNTS131	101375
UK Great Britain	USA (United States)	27 Mar 46	4UNTS2	100039
Iraq	Turkey	29 Mar 46	37UNTS226	100580
Czechoslovakia	Yugoslavia	09 May 46	1UNTS67	100014
India	USA (United States)	16 May 46	4UNTS183	100045
France	UK Great Britain	04 Mar 47	9UNTS187	100132
Czechoslovakia	Poland	10 Mar 47	25UNTS231	100365
Philippines	USA (United States)	21 Mar 47	45UNTS47	100691
Netherlands	USA (United States)	28 May 47	17UNTS29	100267
Multilateral		02 Sep 47	21UNTS77	100324
Burma	UK Great Britain	17 Oct 47	70UNTS183	100904
Romania	Yugoslavia	19 Dec 47	116UNTS89	101571
Hungary	Romania	24 Jan 48	477UNTS155	106920
Romania	USSR (Soviet Union)	04 Feb 48	48UNTS189	100745
Hungary	USSR (Soviet Union)	18 Feb 48	48UNTS163	100743
Norway	USA (United States)	24 Feb 48	34UNTS155	100535
Multilateral		17 Mar 48	19UNTS51	100304
Bulgaria	USSR (Soviet Union)	18 Mar 48	48UNTS135	100741
Finland	USSR (Soviet Union)	06 Apr 48	48UNTS149	100742
Multilateral		30 Apr 48	119UNTS3	101609
Bulgaria	Poland	29 May 48	26UNTS213	100389
Bulgaria	Hungary	16 Jul 48	477UNTS169	106921
Czechoslovakia	USA (United States)	16 Sep 48	90UNTS35	101224
Poland	Romania	26 Jan 49	85UNTS21	101143
Israel	Lebanon	23 Mar 49	42UNTS287	100655
Israel	Jordan	03 Apr 49	42UNTS303	100656
Multilateral		04 Apr 49	34UNTS243	100541
Israel	Syria	20 Jul 49	42UNTS327	100657
Multilateral		19 Sep 49	125UNTS3	101671
Korea, South	USA (United States)	26 Jan 50	80UNTS205	101053
Italy	USA (United States)	27 Jan 50	80UNTS145	101050

PARTY ONE	PARTY TWO	DATE	CITATION	NUMBER
Non-prejudice to UN charter (Cont.)				
Netherlands	USA (United States)	27 Jan 50	80UNTS219	101054
France	USA (United States)	27 Jan 50	80UNTS171	101051
Norway	USA (United States)	27 Jan 50	80UNTS241	101055
Luxembourg	USA (United States)	27 Jan 50	80UNTS187	101052
UK Great Britain	USA (United States)	27 Jan 50	80UNTS261	101056
Belgium	USA (United States)	27 Jan 50	51UNTS213	100767
Denmark	USA (United States)	27 Jan 50	48UNTS115	100740
Iran	USA (United States)	23 May 50	81UNTS3	101057
Thailand	USA (United States)	17 Oct 50	79UNTS41	101030
Burma	USA (United States)	06 Nov 50	122UNTS81	101638
USA (United States)	Yugoslavia	21 Nov 50	93UNTS45	101286
Pakistan	USA (United States)	15 Dec 50	122UNTS89	101639
Chile	USA (United States)	04 Jan 51	165UNTS105	102172
Brazil	USA (United States)	04 Jan 51	165UNTS97	102171
Portugal	USA (United States)	05 Jan 51	133UNTS75	101782
Argentina	USA (United States)	08 Jan 51	165UNTS89	102170
Australia	USA (United States)	20 Feb 51	132UNTS297	101769
India	USA (United States)	16 Mar 51	141UNTS47	101904
USA (United States)	Yugoslavia	17 Apr 51	162UNTS173	102134
Saudi Arabia	USA (United States)	18 Jun 51	141UNTS67	101906
Philippines	USA (United States)	30 Aug 51	177UNTS133	102315
Multilateral		01 Sep 51	131UNTS83	101736
Japan	USA (United States)	08 Sep 51	136UNTS203	101834
Multilateral		08 Sep 51	136UNTS45	101832
USA (United States)	Yugoslavia	14 Nov 51	174UNTS201	102286
Portugal	USA (United States)	08 Jan 52	207UNTS51	102799
Burma	USA (United States)	09 Feb 52	179UNTS91	102357
Ecuador	USA (United States)	20 Feb 52	177UNTS43	102308
Peru	USA (United States)	22 Feb 52	165UNTS31	102166
Cuba	USA (United States)	07 Mar 52	165UNTS11	102165
Brazil	USA (United States)	15 Mar 52	199UNTS221	102687
Chile	USA (United States)	09 Apr 52	186UNTS53	102482
Colombia	USA (United States)	17 Apr 52	174UNTS215	102287
Taiwan	Japan	28 Apr 52	138UNTS3	101858
Ethiopia	USA (United States)	13 Jun 52	205UNTS17	102766
USA (United States)	Uruguay	30 Jun 52	207UNTS139	102804
Sweden	USA (United States)	01 Jul 52	187UNTS3	102497
Israel	USA (United States)	23 Jul 52	179UNTS139	102363
Dominican Republic	USA (United States)	06 Mar 53	199UNTS267	102689
Lebanon	USA (United States)	23 Mar 53	239UNTS45	103370
Philippines	USA (United States)	26 Jun 53	213UNTS77	102881
Libya	UK Great Britain	29 Jul 53	186UNTS201	102492
Spain	USA (United States)	26 Sep 53	207UNTS61	102800
Korea, South	USA (United States)	01 Oct 53	238UNTS199	103363
Japan	USA (United States)	08 Mar 54	232UNTS169	103236
Iraq	USA (United States)	21 Apr 54	222UNTS251	103032
Pakistan	USA (United States)	19 May 54	202UNTS301	102736
Honduras	USA (United States)	20 May 54	222UNTS87	103025
Guatemala	USA (United States)	30 Jul 54	234UNTS235	103286
Multilateral		09 Aug 54	211UNTS237	102855
Multilateral		08 Sep 54	209UNTS23	102819
Libya	USA (United States)	09 Sep 54	224UNTS217	103078
United Arab Rep	UK Great Britain	19 Oct 54	210UNTS3	102833
Taiwan	USA (United States)	10 Dec 54	248UNTS213	103496
Haiti	USA (United States)	28 Jan 55	270UNTS83	103894
Iraq	Turkey	24 Feb 55	233UNTS199	103264
Cambodia	USA (United States)	16 May 55	263UNTS273	103777
Guatemala	USA (United States)	18 Jun 55	262UNTS105	103740
Germany, West	USA (United States)	30 Jun 55	240UNTS47	103393
Brazil	USA (United States)	20 Sep 55	257UNTS349	103665
Syria	United Arab Rep	20 Oct 55	247UNTS117	103461
Italy	South Africa	21 May 56	255UNTS323	103616
Poland	USA (United States)	28 Jun 56	273UNTS79	103944
Ceylon (Sri Lanka)	USA (United States)	02 Nov 56	282UNTS93	104094
Saudi Arabia	USA (United States)	02 Apr 57	283UNTS97	104109

PARTY ONE	PARTY TWO	DATE	CITATION	NUMBER
Non-prejudice to UN charter (Cont.)				
Other Unilat Decla	United Arab Rep	24 Apr 57	265UNTS299	103821
Libya	USA (United States)	30 Jun 57	284UNTS177	104136
Japan	USA (United States)	14 Sep 57	293UNTS247	104293
Burma	USA (United States)	24 Jun 58	335UNTS193	104786
Indonesia	USA (United States)	13 Aug 58	335UNTS187	104785
Canada	USA (United States)	02 Sep 58	335UNTS249	104792
Iraq	USA (United States)	07 Jul 59	357UNTS153	105114
USA (United States)	Yugoslavia	25 Aug 59	357UNTS77	105106
Multilateral		14 Dec 59	368UNTS253	105245
Mali	USA (United States)	20 May 61	413UNTS205	105954
Liberia	USA (United States)	17 Jun 61	410UNTS233	105907
Dominican Republic	USA (United States)	08 Mar 62	527UNTS29	107615
El Salvador	USA (United States)	13 Apr 62	451UNTS307	106500
Bolivia	USA (United States)	26 Apr 62	461UNTS105	106654
Panama	USA (United States)	23 May 62	458UNTS225	106604
Dahomey	USA (United States)	13 Jun 62	458UNTS219	106603
Niger	USA (United States)	14 Jun 62	458UNTS233	106605
Costa Rica	USA (United States)	18 Jun 62	461UNTS155	106659
Senegal	USA (United States)	20 Jul 62	458UNTS137	106596
Jamaica	USA (United States)	06 Jun 63	477UNTS29	106913
Congo (Zaire)	USA (United States)	19 Jul 63	511UNTS47	107425
Germany, East	USSR (Soviet Union)	12 Jun 64	553UNTS249	108093
Malta	UK Great Britain	21 Sep 64	588UNTS55	108518
Bulgaria	Poland	06 Apr 67	617UNTS327	108920
Germany, East	Hungary	18 May 67	617UNTS3	108905
Hungary	USSR (Soviet Union)	07 Sep 67	632UNTS89	109011
Germany, East	Mongolia	12 Sep 68	0UNTS0	109453
Peaceful relations				
Canada	USA (United States)	10 Jun 39	149UNTS332	200476
Multilateral		29 Jan 42	93UNTS279	200271
USA (United States)	USSR (Soviet Union)	18 Apr 42	105UNTS285	200339
Belgium	USA (United States)	16 Jun 42	105UNTS159	200329
Poland	USA (United States)	01 Jul 42	103UNTS267	200317
Netherlands	USA (United States)	08 Jul 42	103UNTS277	200318
Greece	USA (United States)	10 Jul 42	103UNTS289	200319
Czechoslovakia	USA (United States)	11 Jul 42	90UNTS257	200263
Liberia	USA (United States)	08 Jun 43	117UNTS242	200373
Albania	Yugoslavia	23 Mar 44	1UNTS81	100015
Poland	USSR (Soviet Union)	21 Apr 45	12UNTS391	200070
Iraq	USA (United States)	31 Jul 45	121UNTS239	200402
Multilateral		15 Nov 45	3UNTS123	100026
Multilateral		16 Nov 45	4UNTS275	100052
Czechoslovakia	Yugoslavia	09 May 46	1UNTS67	100014
Taiwan	USA (United States)	04 Nov 46	25UNTS69	100359
Argentina	Taiwan	10 Feb 47	486UNTS143	107077
Multilateral		10 Feb 47	42UNTS3	100645
Czechoslovakia	Poland	10 Mar 47	25UNTS231	100365
Hungary	Romania	24 Jan 48	477UNTS155	106920
Romania	USSR (Soviet Union)	04 Feb 48	48UNTS189	100745
Hungary	USSR (Soviet Union)	18 Feb 48	48UNTS163	100743
Jordan	UK Great Britain	15 Mar 48	77UNTS77	100994
Bulgaria	USSR (Soviet Union)	18 Mar 48	48UNTS135	100741
Multilateral		30 Apr 48	119UNTS3	101609
Bulgaria	Poland	29 May 48	26UNTS213	100389
Bulgaria	Hungary	16 Jul 48	477UNTS169	106921
Poland	Romania	26 Jan 49	85UNTS21	101143
Israel	Lebanon	23 Mar 49	42UNTS287	100655
Israel	Jordan	03 Apr 49	42UNTS303	100656
Multilateral		04 Apr 49	34UNTS243	100541
Czechoslovakia	Hungary	16 Apr 49	477UNTS183	106922
Israel	Syria	20 Jul 49	42UNTS327	100657
China People's Rep	USSR (Soviet Union)	14 Feb 50	226UNTS3	103103
India	Pakistan	08 Apr 50	131UNTS3	101733
Czechoslovakia	Germany, East	23 Jun 50	504UNTS163	107357

PARTY ONE	PARTY TWO	DATE	CITATION	NUMBER
Peaceful relations (Cont.)				
Pakistan	USA (United States)	15 Dec 50	122UNTS89	101639
Australia	USA (United States)	20 Feb 51	132UNTS297	101769
Philippines	USA (United States)	30 Aug 51	177UNTS133	102315
Multilateral		01 Sep 51	131UNTS83	101736
Multilateral		08 Sep 51	136UNTS45	101832
Multilateral		14 Oct 51	122UNTS3	101631
Cambodia	USA (United States)	28 Dec 51	179UNTS97	102358
Thailand	USA (United States)	29 Dec 51	179UNTS113	102360
Taiwan	USA (United States)	02 Jan 52	181UNTS161	102407
France	USA (United States)	05 Jan 52	181UNTS177	102408
Austria	USA (United States)	05 Jan 52	179UNTS73	102355
Korea, South	USA (United States)	07 Jan 52	179UNTS105	102359
Italy	USA (United States)	07 Jan 52	179UNTS165	102365
Turkey	USA (United States)	07 Jan 52	179UNTS121	102361
Philippines	USA (United States)	07 Jan 52	179UNTS193	102368
Belgium	USA (United States)	07 Jan 52	179UNTS81	102356
Greece	USA (United States)	07 Jan 52	180UNTS171	102382
Portugal	USA (United States)	08 Jan 52	207UNTS51	102799
Norway	USA (United States)	08 Jan 52	179UNTS185	102367
Netherlands	USA (United States)	08 Jan 52	179UNTS175	102366
Luxembourg	USA (United States)	08 Jan 52	180UNTS191	102384
Iceland	USA (United States)	08 Jan 52	180UNTS183	102383
UK Great Britain	USA (United States)	08 Jan 52	179UNTS201	102369
Denmark	USA (United States)	08 Jan 52	179UNTS65	102354
USA (United States)	Vietnam, South	19 Jan 52	205UNTS127	102772
Burma	USA (United States)	09 Feb 52	179UNTS91	102357
Ecuador	USA (United States)	20 Feb 52	177UNTS43	102308
Peru	USA (United States)	22 Feb 52	165UNTS31	102166
Denmark	Japan	29 Feb 52	126UNTS139	101686
Cuba	USA (United States)	07 Mar 52	165UNTS11	102165
Brazil	USA (United States)	15 Mar 52	199UNTS221	102687
Colombia	USA (United States)	17 Apr 52	174UNTS215	102287
Taiwan	Japan	28 Apr 52	138UNTS3	101858
Israel	USA (United States)	23 Jul 52	179UNTS139	102363
Multilateral		28 Feb 53	167UNTS21	102199
Lebanon	USA (United States)	23 Mar 53	239UNTS45	103370
Philippines	USA (United States)	26 Jun 53	213UNTS77	102881
Spain	USA (United States)	26 Sep 53	207UNTS61	102800
Korea, South	USA (United States)	01 Oct 53	238UNTS199	103363
Pakistan	Turkey	04 Feb 54	211UNTS263	102858
Iraq	USA (United States)	21 Apr 54	222UNTS251	103032
China People's Rep	India	29 Apr 54	299UNTS57	104307
Pakistan	USA (United States)	19 May 54	202UNTS301	102736
Guatemala	USA (United States)	30 Jul 54	234UNTS235	103286
Multilateral		09 Aug 54	211UNTS237	102855
Multilateral		08 Sep 54	209UNTS23	102819
Libya	USA (United States)	09 Sep 54	224UNTS217	103078
China People's Rep	USSR (Soviet Union)	12 Oct 54	226UNTS69	103109
China People's Rep	USSR (Soviet Union)	12 Oct 54	226UNTS57	103108
Burma	Japan	05 Nov 54	251UNTS201	103542
Multilateral		02 Dec 54	226UNTS153	103112
Taiwan	El Salvador	09 Dec 54	214UNTS217	102900
Taiwan	USA (United States)	10 Dec 54	248UNTS213	103496
Iceland	USA (United States)	10 Dec 54	237UNTS191	103345
Pakistan	USA (United States)	11 Jan 55	251UNTS111	103537
Iraq	Turkey	24 Feb 55	233UNTS199	103264
Multilateral		14 May 55	219UNTS3	102962
Cambodia	USA (United States)	16 May 55	263UNTS273	103777
Guatemala	USA (United States)	18 Jun 55	262UNTS105	103740
Germany, West	USA (United States)	30 Jun 55	240UNTS47	103393
Germany, East	USSR (Soviet Union)	20 Sep 55	226UNTS201	103114
Syria	United Arab Rep	20 Oct 55	247UNTS117	103461
Japan	USSR (Soviet Union)	19 Oct 56	263UNTS99	103768
Multilateral		26 Oct 56	276UNTS3	103988
Ceylon (Sri Lanka)	USA (United States)	02 Nov 56	282UNTS93	104094

PARTY ONE	PARTY TWO	DATE	CITATION	NUMBER
Peaceful relations (Cont.)				
Japan	Poland	08 Feb 57	318UNTS251	104620
Czechoslovakia	Japan	13 Feb 57	300UNTS119	104335
Czechoslovakia	Mongolia	08 Apr 57	501UNTS171	107317
Other Unilat Decla	United Arab Rep	24 Apr 57	265UNTS299	103821
Libya	USA (United States)	30 Jun 57	284UNTS177	104136
Germany, East	Mongolia	22 Aug 57	521UNTS351	107530
Indonesia	Japan	20 Jan 58	324UNTS227	104688
Iraq	USA (United States)	07 Jul 59	357UNTS153	105114
Multilateral		16 Aug 60	397UNTS287	105712
Multilateral		16 Aug 60	382UNTS3	105475
Australia	USA (United States)	23 Aug 60	388UNTS237	105581
Czechoslovakia	Indonesia	29 May 61	479UNTS337	106962
Korea, North	USSR (Soviet Union)	06 Jul 61	420UNTS145	106045
Hungary	Indonesia	23 Aug 61	519UNTS163	107507
Dominican Republic	USA (United States)	08 Mar 62	527UNTS29	107615
Multilateral		23 Mar 62	434UNTS145	106262
Multilateral		23 Jul 62	456UNTS302	106564
New Zealand	Western Samoa	01 Aug 62	453UNTS3	106515
Belgium	Rwanda	13 Oct 62	456UNTS431	106569
Multilateral		31 Jul 63	550UNTS343	108029
Iraq	Kuwait	04 Oct 63	485UNTS321	107063
USSR (Soviet Union)	Yemen	21 Mar 64	553UNTS267	108094
Hungary	Yemen	30 May 64	577UNTS39	108371
Germany, East	USSR (Soviet Union)	12 Jun 64	553UNTS249	108093
Taiwan	Korea, South	27 Nov 64	555UNTS3	108102
Poland	USSR (Soviet Union)	08 Apr 65	540UNTS97	107845
Maldive Islands	UK Great Britain	26 Jul 65	548UNTS223	107980
Hungary	Mongolia	02 Oct 65	587UNTS35	108508
India	Pakistan	10 Jan 66	560UNTS39	108166
Mongolia	USSR (Soviet Union)	15 Jan 66	562UNTS43	108194
Iran	USSR (Soviet Union)	22 Aug 66	643UNTS203	109192
Argentina	Vatican/Holy See	10 Oct 66	601UNTS187	108696
Iran	Thailand	02 Feb 67	614UNTS251	108874
Czechoslovakia	Poland	01 Mar 67	632UNTS255	109027
Germany, East	Poland	15 Mar 67	618UNTS21	108922
Czechoslovakia	Germany, East	17 Mar 67	609UNTS187	108831
Bulgaria	Poland	06 Apr 67	617UNTS327	108920
Gambia	Senegal	19 Apr 67	640UNTS101	109156
Bulgaria	USSR (Soviet Union)	12 May 67	631UNTS239	108997
Germany, East	Hungary	18 May 67	617UNTS3	108905
Bulgaria	Mongolia	21 Jul 67	610UNTS0	108839
Bulgaria	Germany, East	07 Sep 67	631UNTS81	108988
Hungary	USSR (Soviet Union)	07 Sep 67	632UNTS89	109011
Hungary	Poland	16 May 68	0UNTS0	109292
Germany, East	Mongolia	12 Sep 68	0UNTS0	109453
Exchange of information and documents				
Germany, East	USSR (Soviet Union)	24 May 60	392UNTS205	105645
Congo (Zaire)	USA (United States)	28 Apr 64	526UNTS55	107600
Austria	Hungary	31 Oct 64	605UNTS63	108759
Frontier formalities				
Multilateral		13 Feb 46	1UNTS15	100004
Netherlands	USA (United States)	13 Mar 46	84UNTS3	101113
Czechoslovakia	Switzerland	10 Sep 47	35UNTS275	100559
France	USA (United States)	16 Sep 47	84UNTS19	101115
UK Great Britain	USA (United States)	24 Feb 48	73UNTS143	100951
Ireland	UK Great Britain	18 May 49	553UNTS209	108089
Austria	USA (United States)	12 Jul 49	84UNTS291	101138
Lebanon	Pakistan	03 Oct 50	219UNTS41	102964
Cuba	USA (United States)	17 Dec 51	152UNTS87	102012
Belgium	Germany, West	01 Apr 52	132UNTS45	101750
Australia	Germany, West	17 Dec 52	188UNTS267	102530
Belgium	France	30 Jan 53	188UNTS141	102525
France	Sweden	16 Feb 54	228UNTS137	103147
Multilateral		19 Feb 54	214UNTS51	102899

PARTY ONE	PARTY TWO	DATE	CITATION	NUMBER
Frontier formalities (Cont.)				
Austria	Romania	11 May 55	342UNTS119	104904
Czechoslovakia	Germany, East	24 Oct 55	504UNTS173	107358
Japan	Norway	28 Feb 57	280UNTS87	104054
Bulgaria	Yugoslavia	19 Apr 57	349UNTS3	105006
Austria	USSR (Soviet Union)	14 Jun 57	285UNTS169	104152
Multilateral		13 Dec 57	315UNTS139	104565
Bulgaria	Yugoslavia	04 Apr 58	367UNTS89	105228
USA (United States)	Venezuela	17 Apr 59	358UNTS83	105126
Japan	USA (United States)	19 Jan 60	373UNTS207	105321
South Africa	USA (United States)	13 Sep 60	388UNTS65	105572
Brazil	Spain	13 Oct 60	0UNTS0	109416
Argentina	Japan	20 Dec 61	451UNTS71	106485
Brazil	Colombia	02 Aug 62	0UNTS0	109422
Austria	Yugoslavia	11 Dec 62	546UNTS3	107938
Poland	USSR (Soviet Union)	22 Apr 63	493UNTS229	107217
Australia	USA (United States)	09 May 63	469UNTS55	106784
Switzerland	UK Great Britain	27 Aug 63	486UNTS183	107079
Rwanda	UN Special Fund	18 Mar 64	491UNTS3	107170
Taiwan	Philippines	25 Aug 64	511UNTS233	107436
Greece	Yugoslavia	05 Nov 64	539UNTS19	107821
Brazil	Ecuador	19 May 65	0UNTS0	109419
Denmark	Germany, West	09 Jun 65	605UNTS95	108762
Hungary	Poland	18 Jul 65	577UNTS161	108376
United Nations	Zambia	23 Oct 65	549UNTS101	107993
United Nations	United Arab Rep	26 Nov 65	551UNTS253	108046
Czechoslovakia	USSR (Soviet Union)	03 Feb 67	617UNTS267	108917
Israel	UK Great Britain	09 Feb 67	0UNTS0	109349
Benelux Econ Union	Portugal	24 May 67	601UNTS153	108693
Visa abolition				
Denmark	Norway	10 Oct 45	104UNTS335	200323
France	Netherlands	27 Mar 46	247UNTS3	103456
Monaco	Netherlands	25 Sep 46	247UNTS199	103469
France	UK Great Britain	27 Dec 46	11UNTS255	100163
Belgium	Denmark	28 Jan 47	18UNTS221	100291
Belgium	UK Great Britain	05 Feb 47	11UNTS261	100164
Luxembourg	UK Great Britain	14 Feb 47	11UNTS267	100165
Norway	UK Great Britain	26 Feb 47	11UNTS273	100166
Ireland	Sweden	19 Mar 47	553UNTS163	108083
Belgium	Sweden	20 Mar 47	34UNTS3	100522
Netherlands	Sweden	20 Mar 47	247UNTS145	103463
Denmark	UK Great Britain	20 Mar 47	11UNTS285	100168
Sweden	UK Great Britain	20 Mar 47	11UNTS291	100169
Netherlands	UK Great Britain	21 Mar 47	11UNTS297	100170
Belgium	Ireland	25 Mar 47	18UNTS227	100292
France	Ireland	22 Apr 47	553UNTS51	108068
Sweden	USA (United States)	30 Apr 47	84UNTS33	101116
Ireland	Netherlands	01 May 47	247UNTS193	103468
Denmark	Ireland	13 May 47	553UNTS37	108066
Denmark	USA (United States)	09 Jun 47	132UNTS145	101755
Ireland	Switzerland	09 Jun 47	553UNTS169	108084
Switzerland	UK Great Britain	10 Jun 47	11UNTS217	100160
Iceland	UK Great Britain	20 Jun 47	11UNTS223	100161
France	Norway	30 Jun 47	104UNTS313	101449
Belgium	Switzerland	03 Jul 47	29UNTS277	100444
Luxembourg	Norway	12 Jul 47	90UNTS59	101226
Belgium	Norway	15 Jul 47	33UNTS25	100511
Norway	USA (United States)	29 Jul 47	87UNTS343	101178
Norway	Switzerland	01 Aug 47	90UNTS65	101227
Netherlands	USA (United States)	20 Aug 47	84UNTS11	101114
Multilateral		13 Nov 47	251UNTS79	103534
France	New Zealand	22 Nov 47	15UNTS29	100228
Italy	UK Great Britain	06 Dec 47	82UNTS243	101097
Ireland	Norway	17 Dec 47	90UNTS71	101228
Belgium	Netherlands	13 Apr 48	32UNTS153	100497

PARTY ONE	PARTY TWO	DATE	CITATION	NUMBER
Visa abolition (Cont.)				
Belgium	Ireland	16 Apr 48	26UNTS159	100386
Belgium	France	23 Apr 48	19UNTS95	100307
New Zealand	Sweden	04 Jun 48	18UNTS171	100286
Monaco	Norway	16 Jul 48	90UNTS77	101229
New Zealand	Switzerland	30 Jul 48	18UNTS177	100287
Italy	USA (United States)	29 Sep 48	84UNTS43	101117
Belgium	USA (United States)	26 Oct 48	84UNTS265	101135
Monaco	UK Great Britain	10 Nov 48	81UNTS85	101065
UK Great Britain	USA (United States)	12 Nov 48	84UNTS275	101136
Ireland	Luxembourg	01 Dec 48	553UNTS111	108075
Denmark	New Zealand	13 Dec 48	92UNTS65	101261
Canada	USA (United States)	31 Jan 49	43UNTS119	100666
Netherlands	New Zealand	03 Mar 49	34UNTS207	100538
France	USA (United States)	31 Mar 49	84UNTS283	101137
Iceland	Ireland	20 May 49	553UNTS99	108073
Norway	Pakistan	08 Jun 49	90UNTS131	101231
Canada	Sweden	30 Jun 49	231UNTS37	103201
Ireland	USA (United States)	01 Aug 49	82UNTS37	101083
San Marino	UK Great Britain	12 Sep 49	87UNTS37	101164
Netherlands	Switzerland	15 Sep 49	252UNTS13	103555
USA (United States)	Uruguay	08 Nov 49	82UNTS45	101084
Belgium	Czechoslovakia	14 Nov 49	46UNTS319	100718
New Zealand	Norway	22 Nov 49	51UNTS123	100760
Canada	Luxembourg	26 Nov 49	231UNTS51	103203
Ireland	Italy	28 Nov 49	553UNTS105	108074
UK Great Britain	USA (United States)	12 Dec 49	92UNTS191	101271
Belgium	San Marino	14 Dec 49	51UNTS107	100757
Canada	Netherlands	14 Dec 49	230UNTS337	103192
Denmark	Finland	21 Dec 49	46UNTS125	100705
Finland	Norway	30 Dec 49	90UNTS175	101234
Belgium	Italy	30 Dec 49	51UNTS83	100754
Belgium	Finland	09 Feb 50	51UNTS77	100753
Portugal	USA (United States)	24 Feb 50	92UNTS219	101274
Canada	Norway	13 Mar 50	90UNTS181	101235
Belgium	Netherlands	29 Mar 50	68UNTS45	100883
Canada	France	17 Apr 50	230UNTS365	103196
UK Great Britain	USA (United States)	21 Jul 50	97UNTS193	101351
Italy	Norway	24 Jul 50	90UNTS187	101236
Belgium	Switzerland	28 Jul 50	71UNTS91	100911
UK Great Britain	USA (United States)	13 Sep 50	122UNTS51	101635
Australia	Netherlands	20 Feb 51	97UNTS283	101354
Cuba	UK Great Britain	02 Mar 51	88UNTS191	101190
Austria	Belgium	16 Mar 51	88UNTS357	101203
Israel	USA (United States)	01 Jun 51	212UNTS129	102864
Australia	Italy	19 Jun 51	184UNTS185	102447
Luxembourg	New Zealand	29 Jun 51	101UNTS71	101403
Belgium	Portugal	03 Jul 51	101UNTS17	101398
Australia	Belgium	25 Jul 51	108UNTS303	101482
Australia	Luxembourg	05 Sep 51	109UNTS31	101487
Austria	Belgium	11 Oct 51	110UNTS45	101500
Australia	Norway	19 Oct 51	128UNTS109	101716
Belgium	New Zealand	01 Nov 51	118UNTS169	101605
Belgium	Spain	04 Jan 52	121UNTS25	101622
UK Great Britain	USA (United States)	15 Jan 52	127UNTS3	101697
Spain	USA (United States)	21 Jan 52	160UNTS63	102102
Japan	USA (United States)	28 Feb 52	208UNTS255	102817
Netherlands	Portugal	14 Mar 52	309UNTS117	104470
Canada	Monaco	20 Mar 52	233UNTS123	103256
Monaco	USA (United States)	31 Mar 52	177UNTS195	102318
Monaco	New Zealand	13 Jun 52	171UNTS269	102230
Netherlands	South Africa	21 Jun 52	309UNTS123	104471
Greece	Italy	05 Jul 52	187UNTS157	102508
Multilateral		14 Jul 52	198UNTS37	102655
Greece	Turkey	05 Aug 52	187UNTS163	102509
Turkey	UK Great Britain	09 Oct 52	151UNTS233	101999

PARTY ONE	PARTY TWO	DATE	CITATION	NUMBER
Visa abolition (Cont.)				
Belgium	Turkey	16 Oct 52	149UNTS289	101958
Belgium	Germany, West	06 Dec 52	152UNTS11	102007
Australia	Germany, West	17 Dec 52	188UNTS267	102530
Germany, West	USA (United States)	09 Jan 53	212UNTS3	102859
Chile	Norway	16 Mar 53	167UNTS13	102198
Germany, West	Netherlands	17 Mar 53	293UNTS129	104290
Canada	Germany, West	15 Apr 53	236UNTS323	103333
Netherlands	Pakistan	01 May 53	293UNTS11	104281
Ethiopia	USA (United States)	22 May 53	191UNTS59	102577
Greece	UK Great Britain	01 Jun 53	172UNTS265	102250
Israel	Netherlands	16 Jun 53	220UNTS93	102993
Libya	UK Great Britain	29 Jul 53	186UNTS201	102492
Belgium	Greece	05 Aug 53	173UNTS53	102260
Greece	Netherlands	26 Sep 53	292UNTS23	104263
Germany, West	Netherlands	10 Oct 53	293UNTS115	104288
Netherlands	Turkey	04 Nov 53	293UNTS3	104280
Mexico	USA (United States)	12 Nov 53	224UNTS187	103077
Belgium	Cuba	16 Dec 53	185UNTS285	102475
Belgium	Germany, West	19 Dec 53	185UNTS277	102474
China People's Rep	India	29 Apr 54	299UNTS57	104307
Multilateral		22 May 54	199UNTS29	102675
Chile	Netherlands	18 Jun 54	292UNTS37	104265
Belgium	Israel	22 Jun 54	196UNTS245	102627
Ireland	Monaco	06 Jul 54	553UNTS117	108076
Germany, West	USA (United States)	28 Aug 54	299UNTS377	104325
Denmark	Pakistan	30 Aug 54	203UNTS59	102740
Libya	USA (United States)	09 Sep 54	224UNTS217	103078
Multilateral		23 Oct 54	332UNTS3	104760
Israel	Luxembourg	27 Oct 54	226UNTS241	103117
Finland	UK Great Britain	16 Nov 54	204UNTS177	102756
Portugal	UK Great Britain	23 Nov 54	204UNTS183	102757
Portugal	UK Great Britain	24 Nov 54	313UNTS125	104533
Netherlands	Portugal	14 Dec 54	289UNTS121	104216
Finland	Ireland	01 Feb 55	553UNTS45	108067
Belgium	Netherlands	16 Feb 55	211UNTS49	102846
Belgium	Luxembourg	04 Apr 55	211UNTS57	102847
Luxembourg	Netherlands	04 May 55	292UNTS17	104262
Germany, West	New Zealand	10 Jun 55	380UNTS307	105462
Ireland	Portugal	29 Jul 55	553UNTS135	108079
Ireland	Turkey	27 Sep 55	553UNTS193	108087
Turkey	USA (United States)	11 Oct 55	272UNTS145	103935
Greece	Netherlands	22 Nov 55	292UNTS31	104264
Austria	Italy	28 Dec 55	260UNTS345	103718
Belgium	Turkey	02 Jan 56	228UNTS203	103152
Italy	Japan	11 Jan 56	267UNTS175	103842
Australia	Turkey	10 Apr 56	247UNTS139	103462
Japan	Netherlands	16 May 56	305UNTS97	104417
Pakistan	USA (United States)	28 May 56	269UNTS15	103868
Greece	Ireland	05 Jun 56	553UNTS93	108072
UK Great Britain	USA (United States)	25 Jun 56	249UNTS59	103501
Bolivia	USA (United States)	30 Jun 56	271UNTS243	103919
Belgium	Japan	11 Jul 56	248UNTS129	103492
Belgium	Germany, West	26 Jul 56	249UNTS187	103508
Belgium	Chile	09 Oct 56	257UNTS227	103658
Belgium	Pakistan	19 Oct 56	257UNTS221	103657
Taiwan	USA (United States)	21 Nov 56	265UNTS241	103816
Japan	Luxembourg	18 Dec 56	318UNTS227	104616
Belgium	France	15 Feb 57	267UNTS3	103834
France	Netherlands	15 Feb 57	286UNTS243	104170
Belgium	Brazil	27 Feb 57	265UNTS189	103812
Dominican Republic	Japan	20 Mar 57	318UNTS245	104619
Multilateral		25 Mar 57	294UNTS2	104300
Japan	Switzerland	25 Mar 57	318UNTS239	104618
Belgium	Peru	03 May 57	274UNTS251	103970
Belgium	Colombia	24 May 57	274UNTS245	103969

PARTY ONE	PARTY TWO	DATE	CITATION	NUMBER
Visa abolition (Cont.)				
Multilateral		12 Jul 57	322UNTS245	104660
Austria	Pakistan	16 Aug 57	306UNTS3	104429
Japan	Netherlands	20 Sep 57	305UNTS105	104418
Japan	Turkey	05 Nov 57	318UNTS411	104628
Netherlands	Thailand	09 Dec 57	309UNTS291	104477
Multilateral		13 Dec 57	315UNTS139	104565
Multilateral		03 Feb 58	381UNTS165	105471
France	Israel	01 Mar 58	314UNTS87	104543
Belgium	Mexico	18 Mar 58	301UNTS291	104348
Austria	Japan	20 Mar 58	324UNTS205	104686
Belgium	Ecuador	20 Mar 58	304UNTS207	104397
Netherlands	Switzerland	29 Mar 58	330UNTS101	104741
Germany, West	Netherlands	09 Apr 58	335UNTS237	104791
Belgium	Morocco	12 Apr 58	303UNTS141	104377
Austria	New Zealand	14 May 58	317UNTS117	104598
Austria	Netherlands	30 May 58	458UNTS147	106598
New Zealand	Turkey	05 Jun 58	317UNTS123	104599
Finland	USA (United States)	15 Aug 58	314UNTS43	104540
Morocco	UK Great Britain	01 Oct 58	331UNTS119	104751
Canada	Finland	09 Dec 58	323UNTS331	104674
Finland	Japan	22 Dec 58	341UNTS41	104876
Malaysia	Netherlands	20 Jan 59	493UNTS147	107212
Greece	Pakistan	05 Mar 59	338UNTS97	104833
Ireland	Spain	17 Apr 59	553UNTS157	108082
Argentina	Belgium	09 May 59	340UNTS53	104858
Netherlands	Spain	27 May 59	458UNTS165	106599
Belgium	Spain	27 May 59	340UNTS81	104860
Australia	Monaco	07 Jul 59	354UNTS105	105057
Mexico	UK Great Britain	13 Nov 59	360UNTS3	105152
Argentina	Brazil	26 Nov 59	374UNTS51	105328
Belgium	Thailand	02 Dec 59	351UNTS89	105018
Canada	Spain	18 Dec 59	470UNTS117	106802
Turkey	UK Great Britain	01 Mar 60	374UNTS295	105343
Bolivia	UK Great Britain	18 Mar 60	374UNTS199	105335
Netherlands	UK Great Britain	01 Apr 60	374UNTS277	105341
Luxembourg	UK Great Britain	01 Apr 60	374UNTS267	105340
Belgium	UK Great Britain	01 Apr 60	361UNTS135	105177
Germany, West	Netherlands	08 Apr 60	508UNTS14	107404
Belgium	Netherlands	20 Jun 60	423UNTS19	106084
Israel	Thailand	07 Jul 60	377UNTS325	105409
Belgium	Fed of Malaya	19 Jul 60	379UNTS391	105445
Netherlands	UN Special Fund	12 Aug 60	372UNTS331	105309
Belgium	Tunisia	13 Oct 60	421UNTS71	106052
Brazil	Spain	13 Oct 60	0UNTS0	109416
Belgium	Paraguay	21 Nov 60	387UNTS237	105565
Netherlands	Paraguay	21 Nov 60	450UNTS201	106467
Japan	Pakistan	01 Dec 60	450UNTS337	106477
Israel	Philippines	14 Dec 60	449UNTS23	106448
Australia	Finland	21 Feb 61	390UNTS61	105602
Switzerland	UK Great Britain	27 Feb 61	404UNTS167	105809
Portugal	UK Great Britain	27 Feb 61	404UNTS33	105803
San Marino	UK Great Britain	08 Mar 61	414UNTS46	105964
Belgium	Chile	07 Apr 61	410UNTS255	105909
Chile	Netherlands	07 Apr 61	453UNTS239	106527
Monaco	UK Great Britain	11 Apr 61	404UNTS11	105800
Sweden	UK Great Britain	05 May 61	404UNTS105	105807
Finland	UK Great Britain	05 May 61	414UNTS101	105969
Chile	UK Great Britain	09 May 61	414UNTS37	105963
Colombia	UK Great Britain	26 May 61	414UNTS85	105967
Luxembourg	South Africa	30 May 61	412UNTS203	105933
Finland	UK Great Britain	09 Jun 61	414UNTS53	105965
Turkey	UK Great Britain	28 Jun 61	414UNTS93	105968
Israel	Liberia	03 Aug 61	484UNTS203	107030
Israel	Italy	30 Aug 61	484UNTS197	107029
Costa Rica	Israel	01 Sep 61	448UNTS247	106436

PARTY ONE	PARTY TWO	DATE	CITATION	NUMBER
Visa abolition (Cont.)				
Bolivia	Netherlands	30 Sep 61	487UNTS105	107097
Belgium	Bolivia	30 Sep 61	425UNTS53	106118
El Salvador	Israel	04 Oct 61	448UNTS253	106437
Multilateral		18 Oct 61	529UNTS89	107659
Israel	Ivory Coast	26 Oct 61	515UNTS251	107462
Iraq	Syria	03 Nov 61	489UNTS45	107134
Japan	Philippines	06 Dec 61	449UNTS29	106449
Dahomey	Israel	18 Dec 61	448UNTS259	106438
Argentina	Japan	20 Dec 61	451UNTS71	106485
Belgium	Ivory Coast	12 Feb 62	429UNTS193	106198
Ivory Coast	Netherlands	12 Feb 62	485UNTS219	107057
Central Afri Rep	Israel	14 Feb 62	484UNTS143	107022
Germany, West	Philippines	09 Mar 62	449UNTS35	106450
Netherlands	USA (United States)	24 Apr 62	436UNTS93	106289
Honduras	UK Great Britain	30 Apr 62	449UNTS159	106457
Philippines	Spain	04 Jul 62	490UNTS243	107158
Tunisia	UK Great Britain	14 Jul 62	466UNTS235	106746
Malaysia	Philippines	31 Jul 62	452UNTS223	106510
Philippines	Thailand	31 Jul 62	452UNTS235	106511
Brazil	Colombia	02 Aug 62	0UNTS0	109422
Colombia	Netherlands	03 Aug 62	485UNTS225	107058
El Salvador	UK Great Britain	20 Aug 62	453UNTS309	106532
Belgium	Colombia	27 Aug 62	449UNTS199	106461
Israel	Sierra Leone	30 Aug 62	448UNTS309	106444
Austria	South Africa	31 Aug 62	443UNTS65	106359
Multilateral		14 Sep 62	443UNTS73	106360
Honduras	Israel	10 Oct 62	484UNTS189	107028
Gabon	Israel	10 Oct 62	484UNTS175	107026
Canada	San Marino	16 Oct 62	529UNTS3	107650
Canada	Iceland	17 Oct 62	528UNTS281	107649
Japan	UK Great Britain	02 Nov 62	466UNTS277	106749
Colombia	Israel	21 Dec 62	484UNTS149	107023
Belgium	Ecuador	10 Jan 63	457UNTS153	106585
Ecuador	Netherlands	21 Jan 63	514UNTS87	107443
Bolivia	Philippines	22 Feb 63	490UNTS231	107156
France	Philippines	08 Mar 63	569UNTS77	108280
Australia	Portugal	29 Mar 63	468UNTS313	106778
Israel	Malagasy	04 May 63	484UNTS225	107033
IBRD (World Bank)	Tunisia	03 Jul 63	480UNTS209	106970
Israel	Niger	23 Jul 63	515UNTS257	107463
Ecuador	UK Great Britain	13 Sep 63	490UNTS19	107152
Israel	Tanganyika	17 Sep 63	516UNTS47	107469
Niger	United Nations	20 Nov 63	536UNTS3	107793
Multilateral		10 Feb 64	496UNTS151	107249
Congo (Zaire)	Israel	14 Apr 64	552UNTS305	108062
Multilateral		16 Apr 64	548UNTS27	107967
Multilateral		14 May 64	528UNTS13	107632
Argentina	Colombia	12 Sep 64	635UNTS149	109079
Poland	UK Great Britain	26 Sep 64	539UNTS153	107828
Norway	UK Great Britain	28 Sep 64	548UNTS63	107970
Czechoslovakia	Yugoslavia	08 Oct 64	544UNTS129	107916
Multilateral		19 Nov 64	523UNTS3	107553
Multilateral		27 Nov 64	548UNTS47	107968
Israel	Togo	09 Feb 65	550UNTS297	108024
Ivory Coast	UK Great Britain	29 Mar 65	551UNTS53	108032
Austria	Hungary	09 Apr 65	564UNTS179	108228
Brazil	Ecuador	19 May 65	0UNTS0	109419
Greece	UK Great Britain	08 Jun 65	551UNTS205	108042
Austria	Bulgaria	12 Jul 65	587UNTS45	108509
Czechoslovakia	USSR (Soviet Union)	17 Sep 65	549UNTS221	108001
Greece	Malta	01 Oct 65	550UNTS329	108027
Argentina	Spain	12 Oct 65	635UNTS221	109085
Austria	Romania	17 Nov 65	564UNTS185	108229
Israel	Paraguay	21 Nov 65	582UNTS65	108458
Hungary	Yugoslavia	23 Nov 65	577UNTS89	108374

PARTY ONE	PARTY TWO	DATE	CITATION	NUMBER
Visa abolition (Cont.)				
Finland	Malta	08 Dec 65	561UNTS205	108183
Austria	Yugoslavia	20 Dec 65	573UNTS165	108329
Malta	Sweden	29 Dec 65	561UNTS217	108185
Malta	Norway	29 Dec 65	561UNTS211	108184
Denmark	Malta	30 Dec 65	561UNTS199	108182
Panama	UK Great Britain	07 Jan 66	565UNTS25	108233
Malta	USA (United States)	15 Jan 66	579UNTS109	108402
Denmark	Israel	23 Feb 66	581UNTS187	108443
Iceland	Israel	23 Feb 66	581UNTS211	108446
Israel	Norway	23 Feb 66	581UNTS203	108445
Israel	Sweden	23 Feb 66	581UNTS195	108444
Finland	Israel	23 Feb 66	581UNTS219	108447
Romania	USSR (Soviet Union)	04 Mar 66	591UNTS327	108565
Israel	Uruguay	03 Apr 66	582UNTS73	108459
Multilateral		17 May 66	571UNTS89	108302
Guyana	UK Great Britain	26 May 66	595UNTS255	108621
Malta	Turkey	06 Jun 66	579UNTS237	108411
Ecuador	Israel	20 Jun 66	581UNTS265	108449
Gambia	Israel	11 Jul 66	582UNTS11	108453
Colombia	Israel	12 Jul 66	581UNTS181	108442
Multilateral		12 Jul 66	578UNTS23	108384
Israel	Malawi	03 Aug 66	582UNTS53	108456
Malta	Portugal	01 Sep 66	579UNTS231	108410
Ireland	Japan	01 Sep 66	608UNTS339	108822
Botswana	UK Great Britain	30 Sep 66	597UNTS211	108646
Paraguay	UK Great Britain	27 Oct 66	597UNTS229	108648
Philippines	Sweden	11 Nov 66	587UNTS3	108505
Norway	Philippines	14 Dec 66	591UNTS253	108562
Denmark	Philippines	20 Dec 66	591UNTS259	108563
Austria	Malta	21 Dec 66	595UNTS307	108625
Australia	Mexico	13 Jan 67	607UNTS77	108797
Israel	UK Great Britain	09 Feb 67	0UNTS0	109349
Argentina	UK Great Britain	17 Feb 67	617UNTS193	108913
Austria	Bulgaria	21 Apr 67	603UNTS121	108729
Israel	Switzerland	01 May 67	630UNTS313	108978
Dominican Republic	UK Great Britain	20 Jun 67	619UNTS3	108935
Ecuador	Israel	09 Aug 67	630UNTS319	108979
Bulgaria	Romania	22 Aug 67	631UNTS49	108986
Bulgaria	Denmark	02 Sep 67	631UNTS71	108987
Israel	Jamaica	05 Dec 67	632UNTS83	109010
Austria	Czechoslovakia	14 Dec 67	634UNTS51	109050
Austria	Cyprus	14 Dec 67	636UNTS267	109104
Austria	Ecuador	07 Feb 68	0UNTS0	109212
Austria	Dominican Republic	21 Feb 68	0UNTS0	109215
Multilateral		08 Mar 68	634UNTS199	109062
Jamaica	Mexico	15 Mar 68	0UNTS0	109235
Multilateral		27 Mar 68	0UNTS0	109293
Israel	Peru	01 Apr 68	0UNTS0	109354
Austria	UK Great Britain	03 Apr 68	0UNTS0	109214
Costa Rica	Israel	06 Apr 68	0UNTS0	109355
Austria	Costa Rica	30 Apr 68	0UNTS0	109324
Dominican Republic	Israel	02 May 68	0UNTS0	109357
Border traffic and migration				
Canada	USA (United States)	29 May 40	119UNTS285	200385
Brazil	Paraguay	14 Jun 41	88UNTS401	200255
Canada	USA (United States)	18 Mar 42	101UNTS205	200294
Saudi Arabia	UK Great Britain	20 Apr 42	10UNTS151	200058
Saudi Arabia	UK Great Britain	20 Apr 42	10UNTS117	200057
Australia	New Zealand	21 Jan 44	18UNTS357	200113
Belgium	France	30 Mar 45	21UNTS325	200132
Belgium	Luxembourg	28 Apr 45	41UNTS265	200181
Belgium	France	21 May 45	23UNTS215	200133
UK Great Britain	USA (United States)	10 Dec 45	3UNTS177	100030
Poland	Yugoslavia	02 Jan 46	115UNTS21	101556

PARTY ONE	PARTY TWO	DATE	CITATION	NUMBER
Border traffic and migration (Cont.)				
Taiwan	Ecuador	06 Jan 46	7UNTS233	100102
Philippines	USA (United States)	04 Jul 46	43UNTS135	100668
France	UK Great Britain	27 Dec 46	11UNTS255	100163
Belgium	USA (United States)	23 Jan 47	47UNTS23	100721
Belgium	UK Great Britain	05 Feb 47	11UNTS261	100164
Luxembourg	UK Great Britain	14 Feb 47	11UNTS267	100165
Norway	UK Great Britain	26 Feb 47	11UNTS273	100166
Sweden	UK Great Britain	20 Mar 47	11UNTS291	100169
Denmark	UK Great Britain	20 Mar 47	11UNTS285	100168
Netherlands	UK Great Britain	21 Mar 47	11UNTS297	100170
Belgium	Ireland	25 Mar 47	18UNTS227	100292
Sweden	USA (United States)	30 Apr 47	84UNTS33	101116
Iceland	UK Great Britain	20 Jun 47	11UNTS223	100161
France	Norway	30 Jun 47	104UNTS313	101449
France	New Zealand	22 Nov 47	15UNTS29	100228
Italy	UK Great Britain	06 Dec 47	82UNTS243	101097
Italy	USA (United States)	02 Feb 48	79UNTS171	101040
Belgium	France	13 Apr 48	31UNTS409	100483
Belgium	Ireland	16 Apr 48	26UNTS159	100386
France	Netherlands	02 Jun 48	204UNTS275	102762
New Zealand	Sweden	04 Jun 48	18UNTS171	100286
New Zealand	Switzerland	30 Jul 48	18UNTS177	100287
Belgium	UK Great Britain	29 Dec 48	27UNTS135	100404
Romania	Yugoslavia	31 Dec 48	116UNTS103	101572
Belgium	UK Great Britain	14 Apr 49	65UNTS117	100840
Panama	USA (United States)	14 Jun 49	89UNTS37	101207
Multilateral		01 Jul 49	120UNTS71	101616
Belgium	Luxembourg	15 Jul 49	41UNTS13	100642
Ireland	USA (United States)	01 Aug 49	82UNTS37	101083
Bulgaria	Poland	26 Sep 49	260UNTS249	103712
Bulgaria	Poland	26 Sep 49	260UNTS227	103711
Hungary	Poland	29 Oct 49	260UNTS91	103705
USA (United States)	Uruguay	08 Nov 49	82UNTS45	101084
Belgium	San Marino	14 Dec 49	51UNTS107	100757
Norway	Sweden	14 Dec 49	196UNTS19	102618
Belgium	Italy	30 Dec 49	51UNTS83	100754
Finland	Norway	30 Dec 49	90UNTS175	101234
Belgium	France	14 Mar 50	65UNTS139	100842
USA (United States)	Yugoslavia	25 Mar 50	98UNTS195	101365
India	Pakistan	08 Apr 50	131UNTS3	101733
Romania	USSR (Soviet Union)	27 May 50	221UNTS13	103000
Germany, East	Poland	23 Jun 50	304UNTS91	104393
Hungary	USSR (Soviet Union)	13 Jul 50	221UNTS35	103001
Belgium	Switzerland	28 Jul 50	71UNTS91	100911
India	Nepal	31 Jul 50	104UNTS3	101430
Luxembourg	Netherlands	25 Aug 50	81UNTS13	101058
Bulgaria	USSR (Soviet Union)	25 Aug 50	221UNTS57	103002
Belgium	France	26 Sep 50	79UNTS3	101026
Netherlands	New Zealand	16 Oct 50	83UNTS269	101111
Nepal	UK Great Britain	30 Oct 50	97UNTS121	101346
Austria	Sweden	31 Oct 50	197UNTS311	102645
Brazil	Netherlands	15 Dec 50	123UNTS101	101657
Canada	India	26 Jan 51	248UNTS89	103486
Australia	Netherlands	22 Feb 51	128UNTS115	101717
Cuba	UK Great Britain	02 Mar 51	88UNTS191	101190
Australia	Italy	29 Mar 51	131UNTS187	101741
Multilateral		18 Apr 51	261UNTS140	103729
Canada	Ceylon (Sri Lanka)	24 Apr 51	248UNTS101	103488
Multilateral		02 Jul 51	189UNTS137	102545
Greece	USA (United States)	03 Aug 51	224UNTS279	103080
Mexico	USA (United States)	11 Aug 51	162UNTS103	102133
Ethiopia	USA (United States)	07 Sep 51	206UNTS41	102785
Canada	Pakistan	23 Oct 51	248UNTS95	103487
Belgium	Spain	04 Jan 52	121UNTS25	101622
Multilateral		10 Jan 52	163UNTS3	102138

PARTY ONE	PARTY TWO	DATE	CITATION	NUMBER
Border traffic and migration (Cont.)				
Greece	Yugoslavia	02 Feb 52	188UNTS311	102535
Brazil	USA (United States)	15 Mar 52	199UNTS221	102687
United Arab Rep	USA (United States)	29 Apr 52	241UNTS3	103418
Multilateral		14 Jul 52	198UNTS47	102656
Multilateral		14 Jul 52	198UNTS37	102655
Mexico	USA (United States)	15 Jul 52	181UNTS263	102416
Australia	Germany, West	29 Aug 52	184UNTS147	102446
Austria	Yugoslavia	19 Mar 53	467UNTS323	106768
Belgium	Netherlands	26 Mar 53	165UNTS297	102180
Canada	Germany, West	15 Apr 53	236UNTS323	103333
Italy	Switzerland	02 Jul 53	257UNTS99	103653
Multilateral		19 Oct 53	207UNTS189	102807
Mexico	USA (United States)	12 Nov 53	224UNTS187	103077
Hungary	Romania	14 Dec 53	342UNTS151	104906
Belgium	UK Great Britain	04 Jan 54	247UNTS47	103459
France	Sweden	16 Feb 54	228UNTS137	103147
China People's Rep	India	29 Apr 54	299UNTS57	104307
France	Greece	13 May 54	222UNTS299	103036
Bulgaria	Romania	22 Jul 54	362UNTS101	105184
Belgium	Netherlands	13 Jan 55	210UNTS63	102834
Multilateral		19 Mar 55	228UNTS95	103144
Bulgaria	Yugoslavia	17 Jun 55	375UNTS287	105370
Germany, East	Romania	05 Aug 55	342UNTS229	104910
Philippines	UK Great Britain	29 Aug 55	221UNTS241	103009
Philippines	USA (United States)	06 Sep 55	238UNTS109	103356
Fed Rhod/Nyasaland	Netherlands	02 Nov 55	263UNTS381	103784
Belgium	Turkey	02 Jan 56	228UNTS203	103152
Czechoslovakia	Poland	13 Jan 56	265UNTS157	103811
Austria	Belgium	20 Jan 56	248UNTS3	103481
Bulgaria	Yugoslavia	22 May 56	367UNTS119	105229
Austria	Yugoslavia	15 Jun 56	396UNTS117	105695
Indonesia	Philippines	04 Jul 56	401UNTS59	105763
Australia	Netherlands	01 Aug 56	280UNTS3	104047
Romania	Yugoslavia	04 Aug 56	395UNTS99	105682
Romania	Yugoslavia	25 Sep 56	395UNTS147	105683
UK Great Britain	USA (United States)	01 Nov 56	264UNTS3	103785
UK Great Britain	USA (United States)	27 Nov 56	282UNTS43	104092
Belgium	Spain	28 Nov 56	308UNTS285	104465
Czechoslovakia	USSR (Soviet Union)	30 Nov 56	266UNTS243	103833
France	Italy	28 Dec 56	291UNTS203	104255
France	Italy	28 Feb 57	291UNTS191	104253
Multilateral		25 Mar 57	294UNTS2	104300
Australia	UK Great Britain	01 Apr 57	271UNTS235	103918
Albania	Yugoslavia	20 May 57	363UNTS99	105203
France	Netherlands	21 May 57	299UNTS43	104305
Hungary	Yugoslavia	25 May 57	477UNTS219	106924
Italy	Monaco	01 Jun 57	291UNTS197	104254
Multilateral		12 Jul 57	322UNTS245	104660
UK Great Britain	USA (United States)	01 Nov 57	299UNTS167	104312
Multilateral		13 Dec 57	315UNTS139	104565
Afghanistan	USSR (Soviet Union)	18 Jan 58	321UNTS77	104655
Multilateral		03 Feb 58	381UNTS165	105471
Germany, West	Netherlands	09 Apr 58	335UNTS237	104791
Austria	Netherlands	30 May 58	458UNTS147	106598
Germany, West	Netherlands	30 May 58	570UNTS127	108291
Australia	Germany, West	27 Aug 58	320UNTS303	104649
Germany, West	Netherlands	10 Oct 58	486UNTS345	107085
France	Italy	30 Oct 58	363UNTS3	105196
Indonesia	Malaysia	17 Apr 59	470UNTS273	106813
Multilateral		20 Apr 59	376UNTS85	105375
Czechoslovakia	Poland	04 Jul 59	363UNTS333	105210
Japan	Paraguay	22 Jul 59	373UNTS85	105316
Monaco	Netherlands	20 Oct 59	487UNTS29	107093
Guinea	UK Great Britain	22 Oct 59	351UNTS341	105033
Multilateral		14 Dec 59	422UNTS33	106067

PARTY ONE	PARTY TWO	DATE	CITATION	NUMBER
Border traffic and migration (Cont.)				
Austria	Czechoslovakia	23 Jan 60	495UNTS99	107241
Multilateral		06 Feb 60	383UNTS3	105494
Germany, West	Netherlands	08 Apr 60	508UNTS14	107404
Multilateral		11 Apr 60	374UNTS3	105323
Poland	Yugoslavia	05 May 60	423UNTS229	106095
Czechoslovakia	Poland	14 Nov 60	413UNTS4	105938
Brazil	Japan	14 Nov 60	518UNTS29	107491
Japan	UK Great Britain	03 Dec 60	414UNTS61	105966
Netherlands	Spain	08 Apr 61	482UNTS193	106996
Austria	Germany, West	19 Jul 61	414UNTS211	105974
Liberia	Switzerland	31 Aug 61	559UNTS215	108160
Belgium	Yugoslavia	31 Oct 61	426UNTS165	106136
Belgium	Luxembourg	29 Nov 61	486UNTS37	107071
Australia	UK Great Britain	28 May 62	434UNTS219	106264
Czechoslovakia	Hungary	16 Oct 62	479UNTS301	106961
Austria	France	30 Nov 62	463UNTS173	106701
Canada	USA (United States)	28 Dec 62	471UNTS13	106818
Austria	Italy	22 Apr 63	491UNTS53	107173
Multilateral		19 Jun 63	482UNTS19	106988
Multilateral		02 Sep 63	548UNTS129	107974
Tunisia	USA (United States)	18 Nov 63	494UNTS193	107233
Netherlands	Portugal	22 Nov 63	492UNTS31	107185
Greece	USA (United States)	13 Dec 63	494UNTS55	107226
Australia	Italy	31 Jan 64	488UNTS197	107129
Multilateral		10 Feb 64	496UNTS151	107249
Czechoslovakia	Yugoslavia	14 Mar 64	544UNTS147	107917
Netherlands	Turkey	19 Aug 64	521UNTS197	107523
Italy	ILO (Labor Org)	24 Oct 64	541UNTS217	107871
Austria	Hungary	09 Apr 65	638UNTS53	109131
Australia	Malta	28 Apr 65	548UNTS203	107979
Australia	Netherlands	01 Jun 65	560UNTS85	108170
Denmark	Germany, West	09 Jun 65	605UNTS95	108762
Australia	Germany, West	21 Jun 65	542UNTS53	107879
United Nations	United Arab Rep	26 Nov 65	551UNTS253	108046
Haiti	Israel	28 Mar 67	630UNTS293	108975
Austria	Bulgaria	21 Apr 67	603UNTS121	108729
Austria	Yugoslavia	26 Apr 67	603UNTS143	108731
Benelux Econ Union	Portugal	24 May 67	601UNTS153	108693
Bulgaria	Romania	15 Jun 67	634UNTS57	109051
Bulgaria	Romania	22 Aug 67	631UNTS49	108986
ILO (Labor Org)	Zambia	20 Dec 67	619UNTS293	108947
Czechoslovakia	Hungary	27 Feb 68	640UNTS49	109154
Multilateral		27 Mar 68	0UNTS0	109293
Passports diplomatic				
Lebanon	Turkey	24 Dec 46	4UNTS269	100051
Monaco	Norway	16 Jul 48	90UNTS77	101229
Greece	Lebanon	06 Oct 48	87UNTS351	101179
IRO (Refugee Org)	United Nations	07 Feb 49	26UNTS299	200153
Pakistan	Turkey	27 May 49	141UNTS325	101922
Panama	USA (United States)	14 Jun 49	89UNTS37	101207
Belgium	France	14 Mar 50	65UNTS139	100842
Pakistan	Turkey	22 Oct 51	219UNTS47	102965
Belgium	Germany, West	01 Apr 52	132UNTS45	101750
Canada	Italy	10 Oct 52	233UNTS137	103258
Belgium	Turkey	16 Oct 52	149UNTS289	101958
Netherlands	Turkey	04 Nov 53	293UNTS3	104280
China People's Rep	India	29 Apr 54	299UNTS57	104307
Belgium	Israel	22 Jun 54	196UNTS245	102627
Israel	Luxembourg	27 Oct 54	226UNTS241	103117
Austria	Italy	28 Dec 55	260UNTS345	103718
Italy	Thailand	30 Dec 55	260UNTS351	103719
Austria	Canada	19 Jun 56	305UNTS51	104412
Belgium	Brazil	27 Feb 57	265UNTS189	103812
Canada	Greece	01 Jul 57	316UNTS201	104585

PARTY ONE	PARTY TWO	DATE	CITATION	NUMBER
Passports diplomatic (Cont.)				
Multilateral		12 Jul 57	322UNTS245	104660
Austria	Israel	25 Nov 57	314UNTS81	104542
Multilateral		03 Feb 58	381UNTS165	105471
France	Israel	01 Mar 58	314UNTS87	104543
Austria	Japan	20 Mar 58	324UNTS205	104686
Multilateral		28 Jul 60	394UNTS37	105667
Brazil	Colombia	02 Aug 62	0UNTS0	109422
Austria	France	30 Nov 62	463UNTS173	106701
France	Philippines	08 Mar 63	569UNTS77	108280
Israel	Tanganyika	17 Sep 63	516UNTS47	107469
Multilateral		15 Feb 65	547UNTS3	107953
Australia	UN Special Fund	06 Feb 67	590UNTS3	108543
Algeria	ILO (Labor Org)	06 Apr 67	595UNTS99	108614
Cameroon	ILO (Labor Org)	07 May 67	596UNTS209	108634
Passports non-diplomatic				
Argentina	USA (United States)	15 Apr 41	103UNTS307	200321
Saudi Arabia	UK Great Britain	20 Apr 42	10UNTS151	200058
Belgium	Italy	23 Jun 46	19UNTS65	100305
Lebanon	Turkey	24 Dec 46	4UNTS269	100051
France	Spain	23 Aug 48	28UNTS173	100425
Belgium	USA (United States)	26 Oct 48	84UNTS265	101135
Belgium	France	28 Oct 48	25UNTS151	100360
Denmark	New Zealand	13 Dec 48	92UNTS65	101261
Italy	Yugoslavia	03 Feb 49	33UNTS105	100517
New Zealand	USA (United States)	14 Mar 49	32UNTS369	100508
Belgium	France	12 Apr 49	30UNTS45	100447
USA (United States)	Uruguay	08 Nov 49	82UNTS45	101084
Belgium	Monaco	06 Feb 50	51UNTS93	100755
Belgium	Luxembourg	06 Apr 50	65UNTS147	100843
Belgium	Switzerland	28 Jul 50	71UNTS91	100911
Japan	USA (United States)	28 Feb 52	208UNTS255	102817
Belgium	Italy	25 Jun 52	137UNTS239	101855
Turkey	UK Great Britain	09 Oct 52	151UNTS233	101999
Belgium	Turkey	16 Oct 52	149UNTS289	101958
Philippines	USA (United States)	24 Nov 52	181UNTS155	102406
Denmark	Pakistan	30 Aug 54	203UNTS59	102740
Germany, West	USA (United States)	29 Oct 54	273UNTS3	103943
Finland	UK Great Britain	16 Nov 54	204UNTS177	102756
Belgium	Israel	15 Apr 55	211UNTS43	102845
Czechoslovakia	Germany, East	24 Oct 55	504UNTS173	107358
Dominican Republic	USA (United States)	16 Dec 55	241UNTS101	103427
Austria	Italy	28 Dec 55	260UNTS345	103718
Belgium	Turkey	02 Jan 56	228UNTS203	103152
Austria	Canada	19 Jun 56	305UNTS51	104412
Denmark	Germany, West	30 Jun 56	258UNTS65	103671
Belgium	Brazil	27 Feb 57	265UNTS189	103812
France	Italy	28 Feb 57	291UNTS191	104253
Italy	Monaco	01 Jun 57	291UNTS197	104254
Austria	USSR (Soviet Union)	14 Jun 57	285UNTS169	104152
Multilateral		12 Jul 57	322UNTS245	104660
Czechoslovakia	Poland	31 Jan 58	431UNTS99	106214
Belgium	Netherlands	04 Feb 58	330UNTS83	104740
Bulgaria	Yugoslavia	21 Mar 58	386UNTS119	105541
Bulgaria	Yugoslavia	04 Apr 58	367UNTS89	105228
Austria	Netherlands	30 May 58	458UNTS147	106598
Greece	Yugoslavia	18 Jun 59	368UNTS27	105234
Bulgaria	United Arab Rep	09 Jul 59	411UNTS187	105920
Belgium	Thailand	02 Dec 59	351UNTS89	105018
France	Israel	07 Jul 60	413UNTS79	105942
Finland	Norway	15 Nov 60	383UNTS159	105501
Iceland	UK Great Britain	09 Feb 61	398UNTS259	105728
France	UK Great Britain	14 Feb 61	398UNTS267	105729
Spain	UK Great Britain	15 Feb 61	404UNTS75	105805
Germany, West	UK Great Britain	20 Feb 61	398UNTS249	105727

PARTY ONE	PARTY TWO	DATE	CITATION	NUMBER
Passports non-diplomatic (Cont.)				
Luxembourg	UK Great Britain	21 Feb 61	398UNTS243	105726
Belgium	UK Great Britain	21 Feb 61	398UNTS229	105724
Netherlands	UK Great Britain	21 Feb 61	398UNTS235	105725
Switzerland	UK Great Britain	27 Feb 61	404UNTS167	105809
Portugal	UK Great Britain	27 Feb 61	404UNTS33	105803
Italy	UK Great Britain	06 Mar 61	404UNTS3	105799
San Marino	UK Great Britain	08 Mar 61	414UNTS46	105964
Greece	UK Great Britain	06 Apr 61	403UNTS267	105797
Monaco	UK Great Britain	11 Apr 61	404UNTS11	105800
Sweden	UK Great Britain	05 May 61	404UNTS105	105807
Norway	UK Great Britain	10 May 61	414UNTS9	105960
Denmark	UK Great Britain	10 May 61	414UNTS17	105961
Finland	UK Great Britain	09 Jun 61	414UNTS53	105965
Turkey	UK Great Britain	28 Jun 61	414UNTS93	105968
Multilateral		16 Dec 61	544UNTS19	107909
Argentina	Japan	20 Dec 61	451UNTS71	106485
Hungary	Yugoslavia	09 Feb 62	577UNTS3	108370
Austria	Czechoslovakia	22 Sep 62	495UNTS157	107244
Philippines	USA (United States)	06 May 63	477UNTS67	106916
Switzerland	UK Great Britain	27 Aug 63	486UNTS183	107079
Czechoslovakia	Hungary	22 Oct 63	514UNTS95	107444
Romania	Yugoslavia	25 Dec 63	576UNTS95	108366
Israel	UK Great Britain	09 Feb 67	0UNTS0	109349
Israel	Peru	01 Apr 68	0UNTS0	109354
Costa Rica	Israel	06 Apr 68	0UNTS0	109355
Dominican Republic	Israel	02 May 68	0UNTS0	109357
Denial of admission				
Brazil	Paraguay	14 Jun 41	54UNTS303	200202
Denmark	Norway	10 Oct 45	104UNTS335	200323
Ireland	Sweden	19 Mar 47	553UNTS163	108083
Netherlands	Sweden	20 Mar 47	247UNTS145	103463
Ireland	Netherlands	01 May 47	247UNTS193	103468
Denmark	Ireland	13 May 47	553UNTS37	108066
Ireland	Switzerland	09 Jun 47	553UNTS169	108084
France	Norway	30 Jun 47	104UNTS313	101449
Ireland	Norway	17 Dec 47	90UNTS71	101228
UK Great Britain	USA (United States)	12 Nov 48	84UNTS275	101136
Ireland	Luxembourg	01 Dec 48	553UNTS111	108075
Denmark	New Zealand	13 Dec 48	92UNTS65	101261
Belgium	UK Great Britain	14 Apr 49	65UNTS117	100840
Iceland	Ireland	20 May 49	553UNTS99	108073
Canada	Sweden	30 Jun 49	231UNTS37	103201
Canada	Denmark	14 Oct 49	46UNTS97	100702
Belgium	Canada	19 Nov 49	150UNTS231	101977
Canada	Luxembourg	26 Nov 49	231UNTS51	103203
Ireland	Italy	28 Nov 49	553UNTS105	108074
Canada	Netherlands	14 Dec 49	230UNTS337	103192
Denmark	Finland	21 Dec 49	46UNTS125	100705
Finland	Norway	30 Dec 49	90UNTS175	101234
Canada	Norway	13 Mar 50	90UNTS181	101235
Belgium	Luxembourg	06 Apr 50	65UNTS147	100843
Canada	France	17 Apr 50	230UNTS365	103196
Australia	Netherlands	20 Feb 51	97UNTS283	101354
Cuba	UK Great Britain	02 Mar 51	88UNTS191	101190
Australia	Italy	19 Jun 51	184UNTS185	102447
Luxembourg	New Zealand	29 Jun 51	101UNTS71	101403
Multilateral		02 Jul 51	189UNTS137	102545
Australia	Luxembourg	05 Sep 51	109UNTS31	101487
Australia	Sweden	26 Sep 51	109UNTS39	101488
Austria	Belgium	11 Oct 51	110UNTS45	101500
Australia	Norway	19 Oct 51	128UNTS109	101716
Belgium	New Zealand	01 Nov 51	118UNTS169	101605
Spain	USA (United States)	21 Jan 52	160UNTS63	102102
Australia	Denmark	01 May 52	152UNTS3	102006

PARTY ONE	PARTY TWO	DATE	CITATION	NUMBER
Denial of admission (Cont.)				
Monaco	New Zealand	13 Jun 52	171UNTS269	102230
Netherlands	South Africa	21 Jun 52	309UNTS123	104471
Greece	Italy	05 Jul 52	187UNTS157	102508
Greece	Turkey	05 Aug 52	187UNTS163	102509
Turkey	UK Great Britain	09 Oct 52	151UNTS233	101999
Canada	Italy	10 Oct 52	233UNTS137	103258
Belgium	Turkey	16 Oct 52	149UNTS289	101958
Canada	Germany, West	15 Apr 53	236UNTS323	103333
Netherlands	Pakistan	01 May 53	293UNTS11	104281
Greece	UK Great Britain	01 Jun 53	172UNTS265	102250
Belgium	Greece	05 Aug 53	173UNTS53	102260
Greece	Netherlands	26 Sep 53	292UNTS23	104263
Germany, West	Netherlands	10 Oct 53	293UNTS115	104288
Netherlands	Turkey	04 Nov 53	293UNTS3	104280
Belgium	Cuba	16 Dec 53	185UNTS285	102475
Belgium	Germany, West	19 Dec 53	185UNTS277	102474
France	Sweden	16 Feb 54	228UNTS137	103147
Australia	Greece	24 May 54	193UNTS175	102614
Chile	Netherlands	18 Jun 54	292UNTS37	104265
Ireland	Monaco	06 Jul 54	553UNTS117	108076
Denmark	Pakistan	30 Aug 54	203UNTS59	102740
Multilateral		28 Sep 54	360UNTS117	105158
Finland	UK Great Britain	16 Nov 54	204UNTS177	102756
Portugal	UK Great Britain	23 Nov 54	204UNTS183	102757
Portugal	UK Great Britain	24 Nov 54	313UNTS125	104533
Netherlands	Portugal	14 Dec 54	289UNTS121	104216
Finland	Ireland	01 Feb 55	553UNTS45	108067
Luxembourg	Netherlands	04 May 55	292UNTS17	104262
Germany, West	New Zealand	10 Jun 55	380UNTS307	105462
Ireland	Portugal	29 Jul 55	553UNTS135	108079
Philippines	USA (United States)	06 Sep 55	238UNTS109	103356
Ireland	Turkey	27 Sep 55	553UNTS193	108087
Austria	Italy	28 Dec 55	260UNTS345	103718
Italy	Japan	11 Jan 56	267UNTS175	103842
Norway	South Africa	17 Feb 56	230UNTS213	103186
Luxembourg	Netherlands	22 Feb 56	286UNTS249	104171
Australia	Turkey	10 Apr 56	247UNTS139	103462
Japan	Netherlands	16 May 56	305UNTS97	104417
Greece	Ireland	05 Jun 56	553UNTS93	108072
Austria	Canada	19 Jun 56	305UNTS51	104412
Denmark	Germany, West	30 Jun 56	258UNTS65	103671
Belgium	Japan	11 Jul 56	248UNTS129	103492
Belgium	Germany, West	26 Jul 56	249UNTS187	103508
Canada	Turkey	21 Aug 56	305UNTS89	104416
Israel	South Africa	01 Sep 56	251UNTS161	103539
Belgium	Chile	09 Oct 56	257UNTS227	103658
Belgium	Pakistan	19 Oct 56	257UNTS221	103657
Finland	South Africa	05 Dec 56	258UNTS59	103670
Japan	Luxembourg	18 Dec 56	318UNTS227	104616
France	Netherlands	15 Feb 57	286UNTS243	104170
Belgium	Brazil	27 Feb 57	265UNTS189	103812
France	Italy	28 Feb 57	291UNTS191	104253
Dominican Republic	Japan	20 Mar 57	318UNTS245	104619
Japan	Switzerland	25 Mar 57	318UNTS239	104618
Belgium	Peru	03 May 57	274UNTS251	103970
France	Netherlands	21 May 57	299UNTS43	104305
Belgium	Colombia	24 May 57	274UNTS245	103969
Italy	Monaco	01 Jun 57	291UNTS197	104254
Austria	South Africa	11 Jun 57	272UNTS229	103941
Multilateral		12 Jul 57	322UNTS245	104660
Austria	Pakistan	16 Aug 57	306UNTS3	104429
Belgium	Netherlands	04 Feb 58	330UNTS83	104740
Belgium	Mexico	18 Mar 58	301UNTS291	104348
Austria	Japan	20 Mar 58	324UNTS205	104686
Belgium	Ecuador	20 Mar 58	304UNTS207	104397

PARTY ONE	PARTY TWO	DATE	CITATION	NUMBER
Denial of admission (Cont.)				
Netherlands	Switzerland	29 Mar 58	330UNTS101	104741
Germany, West	Netherlands	09 Apr 58	335UNTS237	104791
Belgium	Morocco	12 Apr 58	303UNTS141	104377
Israel	New Zealand	29 Apr 58	314UNTS93	104544
Austria	New Zealand	14 May 58	317UNTS117	104598
New Zealand	Turkey	05 Jun 58	317UNTS123	104599
Japan	Philippines	24 Jul 58	325UNTS103	104696
Morocco	UK Great Britain	01 Oct 58	331UNTS119	104751
Malaysia	Netherlands	20 Jan 59	493UNTS147	107212
Greece	Pakistan	05 Mar 59	338UNTS97	104833
Ireland	Spain	17 Apr 59	553UNTS157	108082
Multilateral		20 Apr 59	376UNTS85	105375
Argentina	Belgium	09 May 59	340UNTS53	104858
Netherlands	Spain	27 May 59	458UNTS165	106599
Belgium	Spain	27 May 59	340UNTS81	104860
Australia	Monaco	07 Jul 59	354UNTS105	105057
Canada	Greece	30 Sep 59	470UNTS87	106798
Mexico	UK Great Britain	13 Nov 59	360UNTS3	105152
Turkey	UK Great Britain	01 Mar 60	374UNTS295	105343
Bolivia	UK Great Britain	18 Mar 60	374UNTS199	105335
Netherlands	UK Great Britain	01 Apr 60	374UNTS277	105341
Luxembourg	UK Great Britain	01 Apr 60	374UNTS267	105340
Belgium	UK Great Britain	01 Apr 60	361UNTS135	105177
Multilateral		11 Apr 60	374UNTS3	105323
Spain	UK Great Britain	13 May 60	374UNTS287	105342
Germany, West	Netherlands	03 Jun 60	487UNTS37	107094
Belgium	Fed of Malaya	19 Jul 60	379UNTS391	105445
Japan	Luxembourg	21 Jul 60	384UNTS55	105510
Belgium	Tunisia	13 Oct 60	421UNTS71	106052
Belgium	Paraguay	21 Nov 60	387UNTS237	105565
Japan	Pakistan	01 Dec 60	450UNTS337	106477
Iceland	UK Great Britain	09 Feb 61	398UNTS259	105728
France	UK Great Britain	14 Feb 61	398UNTS267	105729
Spain	UK Great Britain	15 Feb 61	404UNTS75	105805
Germany, West	UK Great Britain	20 Feb 61	398UNTS249	105727
Netherlands	UK Great Britain	21 Feb 61	398UNTS235	105725
Belgium	UK Great Britain	21 Feb 61	398UNTS229	105724
Luxembourg	UK Great Britain	21 Feb 61	398UNTS243	105726
Australia	Finland	21 Feb 61	390UNTS61	105602
Switzerland	UK Great Britain	27 Feb 61	404UNTS167	105809
Portugal	UK Great Britain	27 Feb 61	404UNTS33	105803
Italy	UK Great Britain	06 Mar 61	404UNTS3	105799
San Marino	UK Great Britain	08 Mar 61	414UNTS46	105964
Canada	Iran	10 Mar 61	470UNTS139	106805
Greece	UK Great Britain	06 Apr 61	403UNTS267	105797
Chile	Netherlands	07 Apr 61	453UNTS239	106527
Belgium	Chile	07 Apr 61	410UNTS255	105909
Monaco	UK Great Britain	11 Apr 61	404UNTS11	105800
Multilateral		18 Apr 61	500UNTS95	107310
Finland	UK Great Britain	05 May 61	414UNTS101	105969
Sweden	UK Great Britain	05 May 61	404UNTS105	105807
Chile	UK Great Britain	09 May 61	414UNTS37	105963
Denmark	UK Great Britain	10 May 61	414UNTS17	105961
Norway	UK Great Britain	10 May 61	414UNTS9	105960
Colombia	UK Great Britain	26 May 61	414UNTS85	105967
Luxembourg	South Africa	30 May 61	412UNTS203	105933
Finland	UK Great Britain	09 Jun 61	414UNTS53	105965
Turkey	UK Great Britain	28 Jun 61	414UNTS93	105968
Australia	Spain	27 Sep 61	426UNTS159	106135
Bolivia	Netherlands	30 Sep 61	487UNTS105	107097
Belgium	Bolivia	30 Sep 61	425UNTS53	106118
New Zealand	Spain	02 Oct 61	453UNTS11	106516
Belgium	Luxembourg	29 Nov 61	486UNTS37	107071
Greece	New Zealand	06 Dec 61	486UNTS3	107067
Ivory Coast	Netherlands	12 Feb 62	485UNTS219	107057

PARTY ONE	PARTY TWO	DATE	CITATION	NUMBER
Denial of admission (Cont.)				
Belgium	Ivory Coast	12 Feb 62	429UNTS193	106198
Belgium	France	30 Mar 62	502UNTS297	107335
Honduras	UK Great Britain	30 Apr 62	449UNTS159	106457
Tunisia	UK Great Britain	14 Jul 62	466UNTS235	106746
Colombia	Netherlands	03 Aug 62	485UNTS225	107058
El Salvador	UK Great Britain	20 Aug 62	453UNTS309	106532
Austria	South Africa	31 Aug 62	443UNTS65	106359
Gabon	Israel	10 Oct 62	484UNTS175	107026
Canada	Iceland	17 Oct 62	528UNTS281	107649
Japan	UK Great Britain	02 Nov 62	466UNTS277	106749
Multilateral		29 Nov 62	457UNTS63	106577
Belgium	Ecuador	10 Jan 63	457UNTS153	106585
Ecuador	Netherlands	21 Jan 63	514UNTS87	107443
Multilateral		19 Jun 63	482UNTS19	106988
Ecuador	UK Great Britain	13 Sep 63	490UNTS19	107152
Multilateral		10 Feb 64	496UNTS151	107249
Australia	Israel	14 Apr 64	496UNTS233	107255
Multilateral		14 May 64	528UNTS3	107631
Multilateral		14 May 64	528UNTS13	107632
Czechoslovakia	Yugoslavia	08 Oct 64	544UNTS129	107916
Multilateral		19 Nov 64	523UNTS3	107553
Multilateral		27 Nov 64	548UNTS47	107968
Netherlands	Spain	10 Feb 65	545UNTS3	107922
Ivory Coast	UK Great Britain	29 Mar 65	551UNTS53	108032
Greece	UK Great Britain	08 Jun 65	551UNTS205	108042
Multilateral		08 Sep 65	578UNTS3	108382
Czechoslovakia	USSR (Soviet Union)	17 Sep 65	549UNTS221	108001
Greece	Malta	01 Oct 65	550UNTS329	108027
Argentina	Spain	12 Oct 65	635UNTS221	109085
Israel	Paraguay	21 Nov 65	582UNTS65	108458
Finland	Malta	08 Dec 65	561UNTS205	108183
Austria	Yugoslavia	20 Dec 65	573UNTS165	108329
Malta	Sweden	29 Dec 65	561UNTS217	108185
Malta	Norway	29 Dec 65	561UNTS211	108184
Denmark	Malta	30 Dec 65	561UNTS199	108182
Panama	UK Great Britain	07 Jan 66	565UNTS25	108233
Malta	Turkey	06 Jun 66	579UNTS237	108411
Multilateral		12 Jul 66	578UNTS23	108384
Malta	Portugal	01 Sep 66	579UNTS231	108410
Paraguay	UK Great Britain	27 Oct 66	597UNTS229	108648
Philippines	Sweden	11 Nov 66	587UNTS3	108505
Australia	Mexico	13 Jan 67	607UNTS77	108797
Israel	Switzerland	01 May 67	630UNTS313	108978
Dominican Republic	UK Great Britain	20 Jun 67	619UNTS3	108935
Ecuador	Israel	09 Aug 67	630UNTS319	108979
Bulgaria	Denmark	02 Sep 67	631UNTS71	108987
Austria	Cyprus	14 Dec 67	636UNTS267	109104
Resident permits				
Costa Rica	USA (United States)	29 May 44	124UNTS155	200417
Belgium	France	30 Mar 45	20UNTS297	200122
France	Netherlands	27 Mar 46	247UNTS3	103456
Philippines	USA (United States)	04 Jul 46	43UNTS135	100668
Denmark	Sweden	18 Nov 46	7UNTS251	100104
Belgium	Denmark	28 Jan 47	18UNTS221	100291
Belgium	UK Great Britain	05 Feb 47	11UNTS261	100164
Luxembourg	UK Great Britain	14 Feb 47	11UNTS267	100165
Norway	UK Great Britain	26 Feb 47	11UNTS273	100166
Sweden	UK Great Britain	20 Mar 47	11UNTS291	100169
Belgium	Sweden	20 Mar 47	34UNTS3	100522
Denmark	UK Great Britain	20 Mar 47	11UNTS285	100168
Netherlands	UK Great Britain	21 Mar 47	11UNTS297	100170
Belgium	Ireland	25 Mar 47	18UNTS227	100292
Denmark	Ireland	13 May 47	553UNTS37	108066
Belgium	Switzerland	03 Jul 47	29UNTS277	100444

PARTY ONE	PARTY TWO	DATE	CITATION	NUMBER
Resident permits (Cont.)				
Belgium	Norway	15 Jul 47	33UNTS25	100511
France	New Zealand	22 Nov 47	15UNTS29	100228
Denmark	Switzerland	21 Feb 48	14UNTS321	100224
Sweden	Switzerland	16 Mar 48	197UNTS39	102632
Belgium	Ireland	16 Apr 48	26UNTS159	100386
Philippines	Spain	20 May 48	70UNTS143	100903
New Zealand	Sweden	04 Jun 48	18UNTS171	100286
Monaco	Norway	16 Jul 48	90UNTS77	101229
New Zealand	Switzerland	30 Jul 48	18UNTS177	100287
UK Great Britain	USA (United States)	12 Nov 48	84UNTS275	101136
Denmark	New Zealand	13 Dec 48	92UNTS65	101261
Belgium	France	08 Jan 49	36UNTS151	100569
Netherlands	New Zealand	03 Mar 49	34UNTS207	100538
New Zealand	USA (United States)	14 Mar 49	32UNTS369	100508
Netherlands	Sweden	06 Jul 49	197UNTS189	102639
Netherlands	Switzerland	15 Sep 49	252UNTS13	103555
Belgium	San Marino	14 Dec 49	51UNTS107	100757
Belgium	Italy	30 Dec 49	51UNTS83	100754
Finland	Norway	30 Dec 49	90UNTS175	101234
Belgium	Monaco	06 Feb 50	51UNTS93	100755
Belgium	Finland	09 Feb 50	51UNTS77	100753
Multilateral		17 Apr 50	126UNTS285	101694
Belgium	Switzerland	28 Jul 50	71UNTS91	100911
France	Turkey	22 Dec 50	98UNTS11	101356
Canada	India	26 Jan 51	248UNTS89	103486
Cuba	UK Great Britain	02 Mar 51	88UNTS191	101190
Belgium	Finland	20 Mar 51	110UNTS27	101498
Canada	Ceylon (Sri Lanka)	24 Apr 51	248UNTS101	103488
Ethiopia	USA (United States)	02 May 51	139UNTS85	101877
Multilateral		02 Jul 51	189UNTS137	102545
Australia	Belgium	25 Jul 51	108UNTS303	101482
Belgium	Sweden	18 Sep 51	133UNTS187	101789
Austria	Belgium	11 Oct 51	110UNTS45	101500
Canada	Pakistan	23 Oct 51	248UNTS95	103487
Belgium	New Zealand	01 Nov 51	118UNTS169	101605
Belgium	Germany, West	18 Jan 52	124UNTS9	101663
Greece	Italy	05 Jul 52	187UNTS157	102508
Multilateral		14 Jul 52	198UNTS37	102655
Greece	Turkey	05 Aug 52	187UNTS163	102509
Belgium	France	29 Nov 52	160UNTS261	102110
Germany, West	USA (United States)	09 Jan 53	212UNTS3	102859
Austria	Yugoslavia	19 Mar 53	467UNTS323	106768
Germany, West	Sweden	15 May 53	227UNTS195	103139
Belgium	Greece	05 Aug 53	173UNTS53	102260
Greece	Netherlands	26 Sep 53	292UNTS23	104263
Mexico	USA (United States)	12 Nov 53	224UNTS187	103077
Multilateral		11 Dec 53	218UNTS255	102958
Belgium	Cuba	16 Dec 53	185UNTS285	102475
Belgium	Germany, West	19 Dec 53	185UNTS277	102474
Multilateral		22 May 54	199UNTS3	102674
Multilateral		22 May 54	199UNTS29	102675
Italy	Netherlands	04 Jun 54	289UNTS261	104222
France	Greece	30 Jun 54	257UNTS83	103651
Germany, West	USA (United States)	28 Aug 54	299UNTS377	104325
Denmark	Pakistan	30 Aug 54	203UNTS59	102740
Austria	Denmark	07 Sep 54	201UNTS39	102709
Multilateral		28 Sep 54	360UNTS117	105158
Austria	Netherlands	17 Nov 54	292UNTS45	104266
Portugal	UK Great Britain	23 Nov 54	204UNTS183	102757
Netherlands	Portugal	14 Dec 54	289UNTS121	104216
Germany, West	New Zealand	10 Jun 55	380UNTS307	105462
Ireland	Portugal	29 Jul 55	553UNTS135	108079
Ireland	Turkey	27 Sep 55	553UNTS193	108087
Fed Rhod/Nyasaland	Netherlands	02 Nov 55	263UNTS381	103784
Austria	Sweden	03 Nov 55	262UNTS289	103757

PARTY ONE	PARTY TWO	DATE	CITATION	NUMBER
Resident permits (Cont.)				
Austria	Italy	28 Dec 55	260UNTS345	103718
Belgium	Turkey	02 Jan 56	228UNTS203	103152
Italy	Japan	11 Jan 56	267UNTS175	103842
Multilateral		13 Mar 56	427UNTS245	106158
Multilateral		07 Jun 56	381UNTS145	105470
Denmark	Germany, West	30 Jun 56	258UNTS65	103671
Indonesia	Philippines	04 Jul 56	401UNTS59	105763
Belgium	Japan	11 Jul 56	248UNTS129	103492
Belgium	Germany, West	26 Jul 56	249UNTS187	103508
Australia	Netherlands	01 Aug 56	280UNTS3	104047
Canada	Turkey	21 Aug 56	305UNTS89	104416
Canada	France	04 Oct 56	305UNTS65	104414
Finland	South Africa	05 Dec 56	258UNTS59	103670
Japan	Luxembourg	18 Dec 56	318UNTS227	104616
Dominican Republic	Japan	20 Mar 57	318UNTS245	104619
Japan	Switzerland	25 Mar 57	318UNTS239	104618
Bulgaria	Yugoslavia	19 Apr 57	349UNTS3	105006
Belgium	Peru	03 May 57	274UNTS251	103970
Austria	South Africa	11 Jun 57	272UNTS229	103941
Multilateral		12 Jul 57	322UNTS245	104660
Hungary	USSR (Soviet Union)	24 Aug 57	318UNTS35	104608
Romania	USSR (Soviet Union)	04 Sep 57	318UNTS89	104610
Czechoslovakia	USSR (Soviet Union)	05 Oct 57	320UNTS111	104640
Japan	Turkey	05 Nov 57	318UNTS411	104628
Belgium	France	12 Nov 57	328UNTS167	104734
Multilateral		23 Nov 57	506UNTS125	107384
Italy	Spain	25 Nov 57	378UNTS289	105428
Ireland	Sweden	05 Dec 57	428UNTS221	106176
Bulgaria	USSR (Soviet Union)	12 Dec 57	302UNTS3	104351
Poland	USSR (Soviet Union)	21 Jan 58	319UNTS277	104636
Belgium	Netherlands	04 Feb 58	330UNTS83	104740
France	Israel	01 Mar 58	314UNTS87	104543
Belgium	Ecuador	20 Mar 58	304UNTS207	104397
Netherlands	Switzerland	29 Mar 58	330UNTS101	104741
Germany, West	Netherlands	09 Apr 58	335UNTS237	104791
Belgium	Morocco	12 Apr 58	303UNTS141	104377
Austria	New Zealand	14 May 58	317UNTS117	104598
Austria	Netherlands	30 May 58	458UNTS147	106598
Bulgaria	Hungary	27 Jun 58	438UNTS235	106318
Germany, West	Netherlands	30 Jun 58	315UNTS179	104568
Finland	USA (United States)	15 Aug 58	314UNTS43	104540
Mongolia	USSR (Soviet Union)	25 Aug 58	322UNTS201	104658
Canada	Finland	09 Dec 58	323UNTS331	104674
Greece	Pakistan	05 Mar 59	338UNTS97	104833
Ireland	Spain	17 Apr 59	553UNTS157	108082
Iran	UK Great Britain	06 May 59	398UNTS51	105717
Argentina	Belgium	09 May 59	340UNTS53	104858
Belgium	Spain	27 May 59	340UNTS81	104860
Netherlands	Spain	27 May 59	458UNTS165	106599
Ireland	Netherlands	28 May 59	344UNTS95	104944
Australia	Monaco	07 Jul 59	354UNTS105	105057
Monaco	Netherlands	20 Oct 59	487UNTS29	107093
Mexico	UK Great Britain	13 Nov 59	360UNTS3	105152
Canada	Spain	18 Dec 59	470UNTS117	106802
Turkey	UK Great Britain	01 Mar 60	374UNTS295	105343
Belgium	UK Great Britain	01 Apr 60	361UNTS135	105177
Multilateral		11 Apr 60	374UNTS3	105323
Israel	Thailand	07 Jul 60	377UNTS325	105409
Spain	UK Great Britain	12 Jul 60	414UNTS123	105971
Belgium	Fed of Malaya	19 Jul 60	379UNTS391	105445
Japan	Luxembourg	21 Jul 60	384UNTS55	105510
Belgium	Tunisia	13 Oct 60	421UNTS71	106052
Belgium	Paraguay	21 Nov 60	387UNTS237	105565
Italy	New Zealand	25 Jan 61	435UNTS255	106282
Iceland	UK Great Britain	09 Feb 61	398UNTS259	105728

PARTY ONE	PARTY TWO	DATE	CITATION	NUMBER
Resident permits (Cont.)				
France	UK Great Britain	14 Feb 61	398UNTS267	105729
Spain	UK Great Britain	15 Feb 61	404UNTS75	105805
Finland	Italy	18 Feb 61	434UNTS199	106263
Australia	Finland	21 Feb 61	390UNTS61	105602
Netherlands	UK Great Britain	21 Feb 61	398UNTS235	105725
Portugal	UK Great Britain	27 Feb 61	404UNTS33	105803
Switzerland	UK Great Britain	27 Feb 61	404UNTS167	105809
Italy	UK Great Britain	06 Mar 61	404UNTS3	105799
San Marino	UK Great Britain	08 Mar 61	414UNTS46	105964
Canada	Iran	10 Mar 61	470UNTS139	106805
Belgium	Chile	07 Apr 61	410UNTS255	105909
Chile	Netherlands	07 Apr 61	453UNTS239	106527
Netherlands	Spain	08 Apr 61	482UNTS193	106996
Monaco	UK Great Britain	11 Apr 61	404UNTS11	105800
Sweden	UK Great Britain	05 May 61	404UNTS105	105807
Chile	UK Great Britain	09 May 61	414UNTS37	105963
Luxembourg	South Africa	30 May 61	412UNTS203	105933
Israel	Liberia	03 Aug 61	484UNTS203	107030
Costa Rica	Israel	01 Sep 61	448UNTS247	106436
Denmark	Germany, West	12 Sep 61	516UNTS283	107478
France	USA (United States)	21 Sep 61	433UNTS243	106247
Belgium	Bolivia	30 Sep 61	425UNTS53	106118
Bolivia	Netherlands	30 Sep 61	487UNTS105	107097
New Zealand	Spain	02 Oct 61	453UNTS11	106516
El Salvador	Israel	04 Oct 61	448UNTS253	106437
Israel	Ivory Coast	26 Oct 61	515UNTS251	107462
Greece	New Zealand	06 Dec 61	486UNTS3	107067
Dahomey	Israel	18 Dec 61	448UNTS259	106438
Austria	Finland	01 Feb 62	425UNTS33	106116
Central Afri Rep	Israel	14 Feb 62	484UNTS143	107022
Germany, West	Syria	25 Jun 62	489UNTS71	107135
Colombia	Netherlands	03 Aug 62	485UNTS225	107058
Belgium	Colombia	27 Aug 62	449UNTS199	106461
Israel	Sierra Leone	30 Aug 62	448UNTS309	106444
Honduras	Israel	10 Oct 62	484UNTS189	107028
Canada	San Marino	16 Oct 62	529UNTS3	107650
Japan	UK Great Britain	02 Nov 62	466UNTS277	106749
Multilateral		29 Nov 62	457UNTS63	106577
Belgium	Ecuador	10 Jan 63	457UNTS153	106585
Ecuador	Netherlands	21 Jan 63	514UNTS87	107443
Australia	Portugal	29 Mar 63	468UNTS313	106778
Israel	Malagasy	04 May 63	484UNTS225	107033
Israel	Niger	23 Jul 63	515UNTS257	107463
Ecuador	UK Great Britain	13 Sep 63	490UNTS19	107152
Israel	Tanganyika	17 Sep 63	516UNTS47	107469
Netherlands	Portugal	22 Nov 63	492UNTS31	107185
Finland	Poland	18 Dec 63	486UNTS57	107072
Congo (Zaire)	Israel	14 Apr 64	552UNTS305	108062
Multilateral		14 May 64	528UNTS13	107632
Multilateral		14 May 64	528UNTS23	107633
Austria	Turkey	15 May 64	515UNTS109	107457
Multilateral		19 Nov 64	523UNTS3	107553
Multilateral		27 Nov 64	548UNTS47	107968
Germany, West	Jamaica	16 Dec 64	531UNTS129	107699
WMO (Meteorology)	UK Great Britain	16 Dec 64	548UNTS57	107969
Multilateral		15 Feb 65	546UNTS277	107952
Multilateral		15 Feb 65	547UNTS3	107953
Japan	Korea, South	22 Jun 65	584UNTS3	108474
Czechoslovakia	USSR (Soviet Union)	17 Sep 65	549UNTS221	108001
France	UK Great Britain	21 Sep 65	561UNTS3	108177
Austria	Yugoslavia	19 Nov 65	587UNTS239	108512
Hungary	Yugoslavia	23 Nov 65	577UNTS89	108374
Austria	Yugoslavia	20 Dec 65	573UNTS165	108329
Gambia	Israel	11 Jul 66	582UNTS11	108453
Multilateral		12 Jul 66	578UNTS23	108384

PARTY ONE	PARTY TWO	DATE	CITATION	NUMBER
Resident permits (Cont.)				
Israel	Malawi	03 Aug 66	582UNTS53	108456
Bulgaria	Romania	22 Aug 67	631UNTS49	108986
Non-visa travel documents				
Canada	USA (United States)	29 May 40	119UNTS285	200385
Belgium	France	30 Mar 45	20UNTS297	200122
Belgium	Luxembourg	28 Apr 45	41UNTS265	200181
Multilateral		13 Feb 46	1UNTS15	100004
United Nations	Switzerland	01 Jul 46	1UNTS163	200008
Multilateral		15 Oct 46	11UNTS73	100150
Multilateral		13 Dec 46	8UNTS119	100118
Multilateral		13 Dec 46	8UNTS135	100119
Multilateral		13 Dec 46	8UNTS71	100115
Greece	USA (United States)	08 Jul 47	16UNTS157	100256
Taiwan	USA (United States)	27 Oct 47	12UNTS11	100178
United Nations	WHO (World Health)	15 Nov 47	19UNTS193	200115
Multilateral		21 Nov 47	33UNTS261	100521
France	Netherlands	02 Jan 48	70UNTS105	100899
France	UNICEF (Children)	19 Feb 48	68UNTS75	100885
France	Netherlands	02 Jun 48	204UNTS275	102762
Poland	USSR (Soviet Union)	08 Jul 48	37UNTS25	100575
New Zealand	Switzerland	30 Jul 48	18UNTS177	100287
Belgium	Switzerland	01 Sep 48	23UNTS139	100344
Belgium	USA (United States)	26 Oct 48	84UNTS265	101135
Belgium	France	28 Oct 48	25UNTS151	100360
Czechoslovakia	Poland	12 Nov 48	84UNTS347	101141
WHO (World Health)	Switzerland	12 Jan 49	26UNTS331	200155
IRO (Refugee Org)	United Nations	07 Feb 49	26UNTS299	200153
New Zealand	USA (United States)	14 Mar 49	32UNTS369	100508
Belgium	France	12 Apr 49	30UNTS45	100447
ITU (Telecommun)	United Nations	26 Apr 49	30UNTS315	200175
Belgium	Denmark	31 May 49	32UNTS337	100506
Italy	Spain	31 May 49	231UNTS251	103224
Czechoslovakia	Poland	02 Jul 49	260UNTS179	103709
Belgium	Luxembourg	15 Jul 49	41UNTS13	100642
Council of Europe	France	02 Sep 49	249UNTS207	103510
Belgium	Monaco	06 Feb 50	51UNTS93	100755
Belgium	Finland	09 Feb 50	51UNTS77	100753
Spain	Sweden	18 Feb 50	166UNTS15	102184
Belgium	France	14 Mar 50	65UNTS139	100842
Belgium	Netherlands	29 Mar 50	68UNTS45	100883
Belgium	Luxembourg	06 Apr 50	65UNTS147	100843
Mexico	USA (United States)	03 May 50	98UNTS201	101366
ILO (Labor Org)	United Nations	07 Jun 50	68UNTS213	200231
Spain	UK Great Britain	20 Jul 50	398UNTS101	105719
Belgium	Switzerland	28 Jul 50	71UNTS91	100911
Spain	Switzerland	03 Aug 50	254UNTS365	103600
Belgium	France	26 Sep 50	79UNTS3	101026
Brazil	Netherlands	15 Dec 50	123UNTS101	101657
WHO (World Health)	United Arab Rep	25 Mar 51	223UNTS87	103058
Ethiopia	USA (United States)	02 May 51	139UNTS85	101877
Mexico	United Nations	20 May 51	102UNTS103	101413
Israel	USA (United States)	01 Jun 51	212UNTS129	102864
Philippines	WHO (World Health)	22 Jul 51	149UNTS197	101953
France	United Nations	17 Aug 51	122UNTS191	101647
Korea, South	United Nations	21 Sep 51	104UNTS323	200322
Philippines	Spain	06 Oct 51	215UNTS193	102920
El Salvador	USA (United States)	23 Oct 51	137UNTS43	101847
Colombia	Spain	11 Dec 51	216UNTS73	102933
Japan	USA (United States)	28 Feb 52	208UNTS255	102817
Belgium	Spain	10 Mar 52	178UNTS243	102342
Norway	Uruguay	20 Mar 52	310UNTS279	104496
Greece	Italy	05 Jul 52	187UNTS157	102508
France	WHO (World Health)	23 Jul 52	209UNTS231	102829
Japan	United Nations	25 Jul 52	135UNTS305	200443

PARTY ONE	PARTY TWO	DATE	CITATION	NUMBER
Non-visa travel documents (Cont.)				
Chile	Sweden	27 Oct 52	311UNTS63	104499
Belgium	Germany, West	14 Nov 52	160UNTS217	102108
Germany, West	USA (United States)	09 Jan 53	212UNTS3	102859
Chile	United Nations	16 Feb 53	314UNTS49	104541
Belgium	Netherlands	26 Mar 53	165UNTS297	102180
Belgium	Greece	05 Aug 53	173UNTS53	102260
ICAO (Civil Aviat)	United Arab Rep	27 Aug 53	215UNTS371	102925
Greece	Netherlands	26 Sep 53	292UNTS23	104263
Belgium	Germany, West	19 Dec 53	185UNTS277	102474
Italy	Netherlands	21 Dec 53	189UNTS25	102540
Peru	Spain	31 Mar 54	232UNTS65	103230
China People's Rep	India	29 Apr 54	299UNTS57	104307
United Nations	Thailand	26 May 54	260UNTS35	103703
Multilateral		04 Jun 54	282UNTS249	104101
France	UNESCO (Educ/Cult)	02 Jul 54	357UNTS3	105103
Belgium	UK Great Britain	05 Nov 54	209UNTS69	102822
Austria	Belgium	07 Jan 55	380UNTS219	105458
Belgium	Netherlands	13 Jan 55	210UNTS63	102834
WMO (Meteorology)	Switzerland	10 Mar 55	211UNTS277	200524
Austria	Romania	11 May 55	342UNTS119	104904
Denmark	WHO (World Health)	29 Jun 55	247UNTS168	103467
Italy	USA (United States)	30 Jun 55	258UNTS15	103667
Czechoslovakia	Germany, East	24 Oct 55	504UNTS173	107358
Austria	Israel	17 Nov 55	232UNTS153	103235
Multilateral		13 Dec 55	529UNTS141	107660
Luxembourg	Netherlands	22 Feb 56	286UNTS249	104171
Panama	USA (United States)	25 May 56	268UNTS333	103866
Belgium	Germany, West	26 Jul 56	249UNTS187	103508
United Nations	Venezuela	18 Nov 56	588UNTS243	108529
Mexico	ICAO (Civil Aviat)	20 Dec 56	497UNTS3	107259
Netherlands	Portugal	26 Mar 57	288UNTS47	104196
Bulgaria	Yugoslavia	19 Apr 57	349UNTS3	105006
Austria	USSR (Soviet Union)	14 Jun 57	285UNTS169	104152
Multilateral		12 Jul 57	322UNTS245	104660
Multilateral		23 Nov 57	506UNTS125	107384
Multilateral		13 Dec 57	315UNTS139	104565
Netherlands	Switzerland	29 Mar 58	330UNTS101	104741
Germany, West	Netherlands	09 Apr 58	335UNTS237	104791
Multilateral		13 May 58	389UNTS277	105598
Austria	Netherlands	30 May 58	458UNTS147	106598
Ethiopia	United Nations	18 Jun 58	317UNTS101	104597
Jordan	United Nations	18 Nov 58	315UNTS125	104564
Finland	USSR (Soviet Union)	21 Feb 59	338UNTS3	104830
France	Israel	19 May 59	377UNTS231	105403
Multilateral		01 Jul 59	374UNTS147	105334
Belgium	Spain	11 Sep 59	345UNTS29	104956
Monaco	Netherlands	20 Oct 59	487UNTS29	107093
Germany, West	UK Great Britain	20 Jun 60	385UNTS55	105528
Finland	Norway	15 Nov 60	383UNTS159	105501
Congo (Zaire)	United Nations	27 Nov 61	414UNTS229	105975
COMECON (Econ Aid)	USSR (Soviet Union)	07 Dec 61	506UNTS325	107392
Germany, West	United Nations	28 Jun 62	434UNTS249	200597
Austria	Czechoslovakia	22 Sep 62	495UNTS157	107244
Czechoslovakia	Poland	16 Nov 62	526UNTS3	107597
Ceylon (Sri Lanka)	ILO (Labor Org)	21 Nov 62	449UNTS263	106463
Austria	Yugoslavia	11 Dec 62	546UNTS3	107938
Poland	COMECON (Econ Aid)	22 Feb 63	506UNTS303	107391
Hungary	COMECON (Econ Aid)	28 Feb 63	506UNTS281	107390
Multilateral		19 Jun 63	482UNTS19	106988
Switzerland	UK Great Britain	27 Aug 63	486UNTS183	107079
Czechoslovakia	Hungary	22 Oct 63	514UNTS95	107444
Multilateral		10 Feb 64	496UNTS151	107249
Cyprus	United Nations	31 Mar 64	492UNTS57	107187
Multilateral		16 Apr 64	548UNTS27	107967
Multilateral		14 May 64	528UNTS13	107632

PARTY ONE	PARTY TWO	DATE	CITATION	NUMBER
Non-visa travel documents (Cont.)				
Multilateral		14 May 64	528UNTS23	107633
Multilateral		14 May 64	528UNTS3	107631
Netherlands	United Nations	27 May 64	548UNTS79	107971
Austria	United Nations	11 Jun 64	500UNTS85	107309
Iceland	UN Special Fund	10 Jul 64	502UNTS343	107337
Mexico	United Nations	17 Jul 64	533UNTS117	107738
Philippines	United Nations	15 Sep 64	510UNTS137	107410
Germany, West	Thailand	28 Oct 64	521UNTS311	107528
Germany, West	Jamaica	16 Dec 64	531UNTS129	107699
Netherlands	Spain	10 Feb 65	545UNTS3	107922
Multilateral		15 Feb 65	546UNTS277	107952
Canada	Jamaica	16 Jul 65	548UNTS265	107982
Multilateral		08 Sep 65	578UNTS3	108382
Czechoslovakia	USSR (Soviet Union)	17 Sep 65	549UNTS221	108001
Norway	Eur Space Research	21 Sep 65	579UNTS251	108413
Italy	Malta	23 Oct 65	550UNTS337	108028
Hungary	Yugoslavia	23 Nov 65	577UNTS89	108374
Austria	Yugoslavia	20 Dec 65	573UNTS165	108329
Austria	Tunisia	30 Dec 65	589UNTS119	108539
Benelux Econ Union	Portugal	24 May 67	601UNTS153	108693
Multilateral		20 Jun 67	607UNTS97	108799
Bulgaria	Romania	22 Aug 67	631UNTS49	108986
Multilateral		27 Mar 68	0UNTS0	109293
Visas				
Argentina	USA (United States)	15 Apr 41	103UNTS307	200321
Belgium	France	30 Mar 45	21UNTS325	200132
France	Netherlands	27 Mar 46	247UNTS3	103456
Belgium	Italy	23 Jun 46	19UNTS65	100305
Multilateral		15 Oct 46	11UNTS73	100150
Lebanon	Turkey	24 Dec 46	4UNTS269	100051
Belgium	USA (United States)	03 Feb 47	84UNTS255	101134
Philippines	USA (United States)	12 May 47	16UNTS123	100253
Philippines	USA (United States)	12 May 47	16UNTS137	100254
Norway	Switzerland	01 Aug 47	90UNTS65	101227
Liberia	USA (United States)	28 Oct 47	82UNTS23	101081
Multilateral		13 Nov 47	251UNTS79	103534
Iceland	USA (United States)	09 Dec 47	82UNTS31	101082
USSR (Soviet Union)	Yugoslavia	15 Dec 47	116UNTS313	101578
Belgium	Turkey	25 Feb 48	18UNTS237	100293
Poland	USSR (Soviet Union)	08 Jul 48	37UNTS107	100576
India	USA (United States)	11 Aug 48	224UNTS115	103072
France	Spain	23 Aug 48	28UNTS173	100425
Philippines	USA (United States)	27 Aug 48	44UNTS13	100675
Italy	USA (United States)	29 Sep 48	84UNTS43	101117
Argentina	Netherlands	29 Oct 48	95UNTS21	101316
Romania	Yugoslavia	31 Dec 48	116UNTS103	101572
Greece	USA (United States)	29 Jan 49	88UNTS35	101183
Canada	Turkey	28 Feb 49	231UNTS57	103204
Iraq	Pakistan	02 Mar 49	141UNTS319	101921
New Zealand	USA (United States)	14 Mar 49	32UNTS369	100508
France	USA (United States)	31 Mar 49	84UNTS283	101137
Pakistan	Turkey	27 May 49	141UNTS325	101922
Philippines	USA (United States)	07 Jun 49	45UNTS63	100692
Canada	Sweden	30 Jun 49	231UNTS37	103201
Austria	USA (United States)	12 Jul 49	84UNTS291	101138
Ireland	USA (United States)	01 Aug 49	82UNTS37	101083
Canada	Denmark	14 Oct 49	46UNTS97	100702
Belgium	Canada	19 Nov 49	150UNTS231	101977
France	Ireland	21 Nov 49	553UNTS59	108069
Canada	Luxembourg	26 Nov 49	231UNTS51	103203
Canada	Netherlands	14 Dec 49	230UNTS337	103192
Australia	USA (United States)	10 Feb 50	51UNTS167	100763
Belgium	France	14 Mar 50	65UNTS139	100842
USA (United States)	Yugoslavia	25 Mar 50	98UNTS195	101365

PARTY ONE	PARTY TWO	DATE	CITATION	NUMBER
Visas (Cont.)				
Canada	France	17 Apr 50	230UNTS365	103196
Mexico	USA (United States)	03 May 50	98UNTS201	101366
Chile	USA (United States)	29 Aug 50	122UNTS43	101634
Lebanon	Pakistan	03 Oct 50	219UNTS41	102964
Brazil	Netherlands	15 Dec 50	123UNTS101	101657
Canada	Turkey	09 Feb 51	233UNTS95	103252
Germany, West	Greece	12 Feb 51	198UNTS193	102665
Greece	Turkey	20 Apr 51	178UNTS17	102333
Ethiopia	USA (United States)	02 May 51	139UNTS85	101877
Australia	Belgium	25 Jul 51	108UNTS303	101482
Australia	Luxembourg	05 Sep 51	109UNTS31	101487
Australia	Norway	19 Oct 51	128UNTS109	101716
Pakistan	Turkey	22 Oct 51	219UNTS47	102965
Spain	USA (United States)	21 Jan 52	160UNTS63	102102
Australia	Denmark	01 May 52	152UNTS3	102006
Netherlands	South Africa	21 Jun 52	309UNTS123	104471
Belgium	Italy	25 Jun 52	137UNTS239	101855
Japan	USA (United States)	18 Sep 52	227UNTS85	103133
Canada	Italy	10 Oct 52	233UNTS137	103258
Philippines	USA (United States)	24 Nov 52	181UNTS155	102406
Belgium	France	29 Nov 52	160UNTS261	102110
Germany, West	Netherlands	13 Mar 53	293UNTS123	104289
Canada	Germany, West	15 Apr 53	236UNTS323	103333
Israel	Netherlands	18 Jun 53	220UNTS99	102994
Netherlands	Turkey	04 Nov 53	293UNTS3	104280
Mexico	USA (United States)	12 Nov 53	224UNTS187	103077
El Salvador	USA (United States)	15 Dec 53	236UNTS25	103314
UK Great Britain	USA (United States)	20 Jan 54	196UNTS95	102619
China People's Rep	India	29 Apr 54	299UNTS57	104307
Multilateral		04 Jun 54	282UNTS249	104101
Germany, West	USA (United States)	28 Aug 54	299UNTS377	104325
Guatemala	USA (United States)	01 Dec 54	237UNTS161	103342
Israel	Sweden	02 Mar 55	220UNTS105	102995
Israel	USA (United States)	02 Mar 55	220UNTS113	102996
Israel	Luxembourg	30 Mar 55	226UNTS247	103118
Belgium	Israel	15 Apr 55	211UNTS43	102845
Denmark	Israel	29 Apr 55	220UNTS87	102992
Austria	Romania	11 May 55	342UNTS119	104904
Germany, West	New Zealand	10 Jun 55	380UNTS307	105462
Canada	Japan	13 Jun 55	247UNTS151	103464
Israel	Norway	26 Jul 55	226UNTS257	103120
Canada	Israel	02 Aug 55	226UNTS265	103121
Australia	USA (United States)	20 Aug 55	268UNTS133	103855
Israel	Netherlands	21 Aug 55	299UNTS51	104306
Turkey	USA (United States)	11 Oct 55	272UNTS145	103935
Nicaragua	USA (United States)	22 Oct 55	358UNTS51	105123
Finland	Israel	16 Nov 55	257UNTS39	103647
Finland	USA (United States)	14 Dec 55	335UNTS263	104794
Dominican Republic	USA (United States)	16 Dec 55	241UNTS101	103427
Iceland	Israel	29 Dec 55	227UNTS147	103136
Italy	Thailand	30 Dec 55	260UNTS351	103719
Belgium	Turkey	02 Jan 56	228UNTS203	103152
Canada	Finland	09 Jan 56	305UNTS33	104410
Norway	South Africa	17 Feb 56	230UNTS213	103186
Australia	Austria	15 Mar 56	241UNTS331	103441
South Africa	USA (United States)	03 Apr 56	249UNTS395	103513
Australia	Turkey	10 Apr 56	247UNTS139	103462
Panama	USA (United States)	25 May 56	268UNTS333	103866
Guatemala	USA (United States)	30 May 56	275UNTS271	103986
Iceland	USA (United States)	04 Jun 56	275UNTS189	103982
Iraq	USA (United States)	06 Jun 56	275UNTS265	103985
Austria	Canada	19 Jun 56	305UNTS51	104412
Denmark	Germany, West	30 Jun 56	258UNTS65	103671
Belgium	Czechoslovakia	08 Aug 56	257UNTS215	103656
Canada	Turkey	21 Aug 56	305UNTS89	104416

PARTY ONE	PARTY TWO	DATE	CITATION	NUMBER
Visas (Cont.)				
Israel	South Africa	01 Sep 56	251UNTS161	103539
Ceylon (Sri Lanka)	USA (United States)	07 Sep 56	280UNTS35	104048
Peru	USA (United States)	09 Oct 56	288UNTS165	104204
Finland	South Africa	05 Dec 56	258UNTS59	103670
Belgium	Brazil	27 Feb 57	265UNTS189	103812
France	Italy	28 Feb 57	291UNTS191	104253
Japan	United Arab Rep	20 Mar 57	318UNTS345	104625
Japan	USA (United States)	22 Mar 57	288UNTS201	104206
Bulgaria	Yugoslavia	19 Apr 57	349UNTS3	105006
France	Netherlands	21 May 57	299UNTS43	104305
Italy	Monaco	01 Jun 57	291UNTS197	104254
Austria	South Africa	11 Jun 57	272UNTS229	103941
Canada	Greece	01 Jul 57	316UNTS201	104585
Austria	Pakistan	16 Aug 57	306UNTS3	104429
Japan	UK Great Britain	30 Aug 57	313UNTS63	104529
Austria	Israel	25 Nov 57	314UNTS81	104542
Multilateral		13 Dec 57	315UNTS139	104565
UK Great Britain	USSR (Soviet Union)	19 Dec 57	351UNTS235	105026
Canada	Portugal	24 Jan 58	392UNTS15	105634
Belgium	Ecuador	20 Mar 58	304UNTS207	104397
Bulgaria	Yugoslavia	21 Mar 58	349UNTS61	105009
Bulgaria	Yugoslavia	21 Mar 58	386UNTS119	105541
Belgium	South Africa	28 Apr 58	303UNTS131	104375
Israel	New Zealand	29 Apr 58	314UNTS93	104544
New Zealand	USA (United States)	05 May 58	317UNTS59	104594
India	USSR (Soviet Union)	02 Jun 58	393UNTS3	105650
New Zealand	Turkey	05 Jun 58	317UNTS123	104599
Philippines	USA (United States)	30 Jun 58	321UNTS51	104653
Japan	Philippines	24 Jul 58	325UNTS103	104696
Finland	USA (United States)	15 Aug 58	314UNTS43	104540
USA (United States)	USSR (Soviet Union)	20 Aug 58	336UNTS269	104809
UK Great Britain	Yugoslavia	03 Feb 59	359UNTS339	105151
Norway	Philippines	18 Feb 59	359UNTS305	105147
Morocco	UN Special Fund	04 Apr 59	354UNTS347	105069
Greece	Yugoslavia	18 Jun 59	368UNTS27	105234
Greece	Yugoslavia	18 Jun 59	388UNTS3	105570
Bulgaria	United Arab Rep	09 Jul 59	411UNTS187	105920
Italy	Philippines	14 Jul 59	490UNTS237	107157
Ghana	UN Special Fund	12 Aug 59	338UNTS203	104836
Belgium	Spain	11 Sep 59	345UNTS29	104956
Canada	Greece	30 Sep 59	470UNTS87	106798
Iran	UN Special Fund	06 Oct 59	342UNTS89	104902
Canada	Venezuela	08 Oct 59	470UNTS93	106799
Poland	UN Special Fund	15 Oct 59	344UNTS29	104941
India	UN Special Fund	20 Oct 59	344UNTS143	104946
UN Special Fund	Yugoslavia	27 Oct 59	344UNTS159	104947
Ecuador	UN Special Fund	10 Nov 59	345UNTS3	104955
Greece	UN Special Fund	13 Nov 59	345UNTS171	104966
UN Special Fund	Turkey	20 Nov 59	345UNTS105	104963
UN Special Fund	United Arab Rep	25 Nov 59	345UNTS125	104964
Israel	UN Special Fund	01 Dec 59	345UNTS197	104968
Argentina	UN Special Fund	04 Dec 59	345UNTS263	104972
Jordan	UN Special Fund	15 Dec 59	346UNTS3	104974
Canada	Spain	18 Dec 59	470UNTS117	106802
UN Special Fund	UK Great Britain	07 Jan 60	348UNTS177	105000
Peru	UN Special Fund	19 Jan 60	349UNTS83	105010
Chile	UN Special Fund	22 Jan 60	351UNTS115	105020
Colombia	UN Special Fund	04 Feb 60	355UNTS257	105080
Bolivia	UN Special Fund	09 Feb 60	351UNTS203	105024
Netherlands	Philippines	17 Feb 60	359UNTS317	105149
Luxembourg	Philippines	17 Feb 60	359UNTS311	105148
Belgium	Philippines	17 Feb 60	356UNTS303	105101
Afghanistan	UN Special Fund	21 Feb 60	351UNTS93	105019
Australia	Philippines	23 Feb 60	358UNTS139	105131
Pakistan	UN Special Fund	25 Feb 60	351UNTS141	105021

Visas (Cont.)

PARTY ONE	PARTY TWO	DATE	CITATION	NUMBER
France	UN Special Fund	17 Mar 60	354UNTS119	105059
Italy	UN Special Fund	01 Apr 60	354UNTS261	105066
Multilateral		11 Apr 60	374UNTS3	105323
UN Special Fund	Tunisia	12 Apr 60	355UNTS289	105082
Libya	UN Special Fund	19 Apr 60	356UNTS11	105090
UN Special Fund	Sudan	21 Apr 60	356UNTS213	105097
UN Special Fund	Vietnam, South	29 Apr 60	357UNTS311	200567
Laos	UN Special Fund	30 Apr 60	361UNTS171	105179
Lebanon	UN Special Fund	07 May 60	360UNTS225	105160
Iraq	UN Special Fund	19 Jun 60	376UNTS357	105389
Kuwait	UN Special Fund	29 Jun 60	369UNTS419	200575
France	Israel	07 Jul 60	413UNTS79	105942
Ethiopia	UN Special Fund	13 Jul 60	368UNTS159	105240
El Salvador	Israel	05 Sep 60	413UNTS73	105941
Brazil	UN Special Fund	16 Sep 60	375UNTS3	105351
Taiwan	UN Special Fund	20 Sep 60	375UNTS29	105352
Indonesia	UN Special Fund	07 Oct 60	378UNTS141	105424
Liberia	UN Special Fund	11 Oct 60	376UNTS341	105388
El Salvador	UN Special Fund	24 Oct 60	377UNTS171	105400
Korea, South	Philippines	11 Nov 60	490UNTS249	107159
Brazil	Japan	14 Nov 60	518UNTS29	107491
Guatemala	UN Special Fund	17 Nov 60	383UNTS67	105495
Nepal	UN Special Fund	17 Nov 60	380UNTS289	105461
Cambodia	UN Special Fund	24 Nov 60	382UNTS255	105487
Honduras	UN Special Fund	20 Dec 60	383UNTS103	105497
Kuwait	USA (United States)	27 Dec 60	401UNTS185	105771
Burma	UN Special Fund	03 Jan 61	387UNTS219	105564
Costa Rica	UN Special Fund	10 Jan 61	389UNTS253	105597
UN Special Fund	Saudi Arabia	19 Jan 61	396UNTS27	105692
Nicaragua	UN Special Fund	20 Jan 61	387UNTS15	105555
Chad	UN Special Fund	23 Jan 61	390UNTS69	105603
Italy	New Zealand	25 Jan 61	435UNTS255	106282
UN Special Fund	Somalia	28 Jan 61	388UNTS75	105573
Gabon	UN Special Fund	02 Feb 61	387UNTS289	105568
Nigeria	UN Special Fund	10 Feb 61	390UNTS85	105604
Australia	Finland	21 Feb 61	390UNTS61	105602
Mexico	UN Special Fund	23 Feb 61	388UNTS151	105576
Cyprus	UN Special Fund	24 Feb 61	389UNTS3	105588
Panama	UN Special Fund	09 Mar 61	396UNTS3	105691
Cuba	UN Special Fund	10 Mar 61	390UNTS35	105601
Canada	Iran	10 Mar 61	470UNTS139	106805
Korea, South	UN Special Fund	21 Apr 61	394UNTS231	200583
Ceylon (Sri Lanka)	UN Special Fund	03 May 61	395UNTS217	105687
Denmark	UK Great Britain	10 May 61	414UNTS17	105961
Luxembourg	South Africa	30 May 61	412UNTS203	105933
Cameroon	UN Special Fund	13 Jun 61	397UNTS297	105713
Paraguay	UN Special Fund	22 Jun 61	399UNTS117	105738
UN Special Fund	Upper Volta	26 Jun 61	400UNTS3	105744
Philippines	UN Special Fund	28 Jun 61	399UNTS141	105739
Haiti	UN Special Fund	28 Jun 61	399UNTS171	105741
Mali	UN Special Fund	21 Jul 61	401UNTS141	105768
UN Special Fund	Yemen	02 Aug 61	402UNTS43	105777
Cyprus	Israel	17 Aug 61	484UNTS169	107025
Ivory Coast	UN Special Fund	29 Aug 61	406UNTS129	105844
Liberia	Switzerland	31 Aug 61	559UNTS215	108160
France	USA (United States)	21 Sep 61	433UNTS243	106247
Australia	Spain	27 Sep 61	426UNTS159	106135
UN Special Fund	Sierra Leone	02 Oct 61	422UNTS131	106073
Mauritania	UN Special Fund	07 Nov 61	412UNTS240	105936
Congo (Brazzaville)	UN Special Fund	09 Nov 61	413UNTS58	105940
Brazil	USA (United States)	11 Nov 61	433UNTS199	106243
Greece	New Zealand	06 Dec 61	486UNTS3	107067
UN Special Fund	Venezuela	11 Dec 61	422UNTS149	106074
UN Special Fund	Senegal	16 Dec 61	425UNTS97	106121
Malagasy	UN Special Fund	05 Jan 62	419UNTS29	106028

Visas (Cont.)

PARTY ONE	PARTY TWO	DATE	CITATION	NUMBER
Hungary	Yugoslavia	09 Feb 62	577UNTS3	108370
India	United Nations	19 Feb 62	423UNTS3	106082
Niger	UN Special Fund	26 Feb 62	423UNTS83	106086
Dahomey	UN Special Fund	28 Mar 62	424UNTS55	106099
Honduras	UK Great Britain	30 Apr 62	449UNTS159	106457
UN Special Fund	Uruguay	04 May 62	429UNTS143	106196
Belgium	USA (United States)	23 May 62	434UNTS133	106260
Korea, South	USA (United States)	25 May 62	454UNTS25	106537
Romania	USA (United States)	26 May 62	456UNTS265	106561
Dominican Republic	UN Special Fund	06 Jun 62	429UNTS169	106197
Israel	Switzerland	29 Jun 62	448UNTS303	106443
Philippines	Spain	04 Jul 62	490UNTS243	107158
UN Special Fund	Syria	07 Jul 62	443UNTS3	106355
UN Special Fund	Tanganyika	17 Jul 62	435UNTS237	106281
Brazil	Colombia	02 Aug 62	0UNTS0	109422
Israel	Sierra Leone	30 Aug 62	448UNTS309	106444
Austria	Czechoslovakia	22 Sep 62	495UNTS157	107244
Canada	San Marino	16 Oct 62	529UNTS3	107650
Czechoslovakia	Yugoslavia	22 Oct 62	480UNTS267	106974
Algeria	UN Special Fund	15 Nov 62	452UNTS243	106512
Austria	Yugoslavia	11 Dec 62	546UNTS3	107938
Czechoslovakia	USA (United States)	21 Dec 62	469UNTS115	106787
Ecuador	USA (United States)	07 Jan 63	477UNTS101	106917
Poland	USA (United States)	21 Jan 63	471UNTS151	106830
United Nations	United Arab Rep	08 Feb 63	453UNTS79	106520
Bolivia	Philippines	22 Feb 63	490UNTS231	107156
UN Special Fund	Uganda	22 Mar 63	456UNTS466	106572
Australia	Portugal	29 Mar 63	468UNTS313	106778
Philippines	USA (United States)	06 May 63	477UNTS67	106916
Australia	United Nations	13 May 63	463UNTS187	106702
Jamaica	UN Special Fund	22 May 63	489UNTS191	107140
Netherlands	UN Special Fund	24 May 63	466UNTS289	106750
UN Special Fund	Western Samoa	05 Jun 63	467UNTS463	200601
Hungary	Mongolia	10 Jul 63	519UNTS173	107508
Multilateral		31 Jul 63	472UNTS220	106842
United Arab Rep	USA (United States)	01 Aug 63	488UNTS189	107128
Burundi	UN Special Fund	22 Aug 63	476UNTS49	106903
Multilateral		27 Aug 63	511UNTS210	107435
Colombia	United Nations	27 Aug 63	481UNTS3	106975
Pakistan	USSR (Soviet Union)	07 Oct 63	499UNTS161	107297
UK Great Britain	USA (United States)	11 Oct 63	483UNTS3	107005
Czechoslovakia	Hungary	22 Oct 63	514UNTS95	107444
Central Afri Rep	UN Special Fund	30 Oct 63	481UNTS247	106985
Multilateral		08 Nov 63	482UNTS286	106999
Romania	Yugoslavia	25 Dec 63	576UNTS95	108366
Multilateral		28 Jan 64	502UNTS321	107336
Italy	United Nations	18 Mar 64	491UNTS21	107171
USA (United States)	Yugoslavia	04 Apr 64	526UNTS47	107599
UK Great Britain	USSR (Soviet Union)	13 Apr 64	539UNTS197	107832
Australia	Israel	14 Apr 64	496UNTS233	107255
Afghanistan	United Nations	28 Apr 64	494UNTS77	107227
Netherlands	Yugoslavia	28 May 64	521UNTS191	107522
Ireland	UN Special Fund	03 Jun 64	496UNTS205	107253
Israel	Yugoslavia	13 Jun 64	516UNTS91	107472
United Nations	Togo	03 Jul 64	502UNTS287	107334
Dominican Republic	USA (United States)	28 Aug 64	531UNTS35	107691
UK Great Britain	Yugoslavia	20 Apr 65	551UNTS69	108034
Brazil	USA (United States)	26 May 65	549UNTS125	107995
UN Special Fund	Spain	30 Jun 65	544UNTS159	107918
United Nations	United Arab Rep	26 Nov 65	551UNTS253	108046
Austria	Yugoslavia	20 Dec 65	573UNTS165	108329
Austria	Tunisia	30 Dec 65	589UNTS119	108539
United Nations	Senegal	12 Jan 66	551UNTS147	108039
Mongolia	UN Special Fund	26 Jan 66	552UNTS201	108055
Philippines	United Nations	05 Apr 66	560UNTS191	108174

PARTY ONE	PARTY TWO	DATE	CITATION	NUMBER
Visas (Cont.)				
Japan	USA (United States)	23 Aug 66	606UNTS219	108787
Finland	United Nations	16 Jan 67	588UNTS153	108522
Romania	Sweden	01 Mar 67	642UNTS163	109172
Belgium	Hungary	20 Mar 67	601UNTS37	108686
Denmark	Tanzania	05 Apr 67	604UNTS19	108740
Romania	United Nations	08 Apr 67	594UNTS159	108602
Israel	Switzerland	01 May 67	630UNTS313	108978
Italy	USSR (Soviet Union)	16 May 67	608UNTS79	108814
Dominican Republic	UK Great Britain	20 Jun 67	619UNTS3	108935
Bulgaria	Romania	22 Aug 67	631UNTS49	108986
Belgium	Romania	22 Sep 67	637UNTS0	109109
Austria	Cyprus	14 Dec 67	636UNTS267	109104
Austria	Ecuador	07 Feb 68	0UNTS0	109212
Austria	Dominican Republic	21 Feb 68	0UNTS0	109215
Multilateral		08 Mar 68	634UNTS199	109062
Israel	Peru	01 Apr 68	0UNTS0	109354
Austria	UK Great Britain	03 Apr 68	0UNTS0	109214
Costa Rica	Israel	06 Apr 68	0UNTS0	109355
Dominican Republic	Israel	02 May 68	0UNTS0	109357
Denmark	Int Coun Expl Sea	24 Jul 68	0UNTS0	109413
Tourism				
Brazil	Paraguay	14 Jun 41	54UNTS235	200196
Austria	France	15 Mar 47	12UNTS109	100182
Czechoslovakia	Yugoslavia	27 Apr 47	33UNTS49	100514
Bulgaria	Czechoslovakia	20 Jun 47	46UNTS15	100698
Czechoslovakia	Romania	05 Sep 47	46UNTS37	100699
Liberia	USA (United States)	28 Oct 47	82UNTS23	101081
Iceland	USA (United States)	09 Dec 47	82UNTS31	101082
Belgium	Luxembourg	27 Mar 48	178UNTS265	102343
France	USA (United States)	28 Jun 48	19UNTS9	100302
Ireland	USA (United States)	28 Jun 48	24UNTS3	100349
Italy	USA (United States)	28 Jun 48	20UNTS43	100314
Denmark	USA (United States)	29 Jun 48	22UNTS217	100338
Belgium	USA (United States)	02 Jul 48	19UNTS127	100309
Greece	USA (United States)	02 Jul 48	23UNTS43	100342
Austria	USA (United States)	02 Jul 48	21UNTS29	100323
Netherlands	USA (United States)	02 Jul 48	20UNTS91	100315
Sweden	USA (United States)	03 Jul 48	23UNTS101	100343
Norway	USA (United States)	03 Jul 48	20UNTS185	100317
Luxembourg	USA (United States)	03 Jul 48	24UNTS35	100350
Iceland	USA (United States)	03 Jul 48	20UNTS141	100316
Turkey	USA (United States)	04 Jul 48	24UNTS67	100351
UK Great Britain	USA (United States)	06 Jul 48	22UNTS263	100339
France	USA (United States)	09 Jul 48	24UNTS103	100352
Multilateral		14 Jul 48	23UNTS3	100340
Portugal	USA (United States)	28 Sep 48	29UNTS213	100442
Trieste	USA (United States)	15 Oct 48	29UNTS249	100443
Luxembourg	Netherlands	26 Apr 49	182UNTS187	102425
Greece	Lebanon	10 Jun 49	178UNTS29	102334
Canada	Denmark	14 Oct 49	46UNTS97	100702
Pakistan	USA (United States)	18 Oct 49	141UNTS333	101923
Germany, West	USA (United States)	15 Dec 49	92UNTS269	101277
Denmark	Finland	21 Dec 49	46UNTS125	100705
Austria	Denmark	23 Feb 50	74UNTS269	100969
Portugal	USA (United States)	24 Feb 50	92UNTS219	101274
Mexico	USA (United States)	03 May 50	98UNTS201	101366
Luxembourg	UK Great Britain	27 Jun 50	183UNTS217	102431
Belgium	Switzerland	28 Jul 50	71UNTS91	100911
Australia	Sweden	26 Sep 51	109UNTS39	101488
Belgium	Italy	25 Jun 52	137UNTS239	101855
France	Israel	15 Sep 52	220UNTS65	102989
Belgium	Turkey	16 Oct 52	149UNTS289	101958
Austria	Belgium	17 Oct 52	162UNTS183	102135
Fed Rhod/Nyasaland	South Africa	28 Jun 53	267UNTS270	103848

PARTY ONE	PARTY TWO	DATE	CITATION	NUMBER
Tourism (Cont.)				
Mexico	USA (United States)	12 Nov 53	224UNTS187	103077
El Salvador	USA (United States)	15 Dec 53	236UNTS25	103314
Multilateral		04 Jun 54	276UNTS191	103992
Greece	Italy	11 Sep 54	284UNTS313	104145
Guatemala	USA (United States)	01 Dec 54	237UNTS161	103342
Netherlands	Norway	18 May 55	252UNTS269	103569
Italy	Lebanon	04 Nov 55	267UNTS147	103840
Netherlands	USA (United States)	27 Mar 56	285UNTS231	104154
Romania	USSR (Soviet Union)	07 Apr 56	259UNTS377	103698
Bulgaria	USSR (Soviet Union)	28 Apr 56	259UNTS363	103697
Albania	USSR (Soviet Union)	03 May 56	259UNTS391	103699
Poland	USSR (Soviet Union)	30 Jun 56	259UNTS311	103694
Greece	Yugoslavia	11 Sep 56	391UNTS117	105620
Belgium	Chile	09 Oct 56	257UNTS227	103658
Belgium	Yugoslavia	05 Feb 57	276UNTS143	103990
Taiwan	Turkey	12 Feb 57	282UNTS125	104097
Argentina	Israel	23 May 57	280UNTS199	104059
United Arab Rep	USSR (Soviet Union)	19 Oct 57	292UNTS151	104271
Belgium	Denmark	31 Dec 57	305UNTS247	104422
Canada	Portugal	24 Jan 58	392UNTS15	105634
Belgium	Spain	27 Oct 58	327UNTS107	104720
El Salvador	Israel	14 Nov 58	345UNTS67	104959
Belgium	Turkey	29 Dec 58	357UNTS195	105118
Greece	Yugoslavia	18 Jun 59	368UNTS17	105233
Brazil	Israel	24 Jun 59	515UNTS151	107458
Guinea	USA (United States)	28 Oct 59	358UNTS169	105134
USA (United States)	USSR (Soviet Union)	21 Nov 59	361UNTS35	105172
France	Israel	30 Nov 59	377UNTS237	105404
Italy	USSR (Soviet Union)	09 Feb 60	399UNTS75	105735
Finland	USSR (Soviet Union)	27 May 60	379UNTS381	105444
Spain	UK Great Britain	12 Jul 60	414UNTS123	105971
Israel	Mali	24 Nov 60	413UNTS104	105945
Romania	USA (United States)	09 Dec 60	401UNTS19	105759
Ethiopia	USSR (Soviet Union)	13 Jan 61	421UNTS13	106049
Taiwan	Jordan	17 Oct 61	435UNTS267	106284
Guatemala	Israel	27 Nov 61	448UNTS191	106431
Senegal	USSR (Soviet Union)	14 Jun 62	437UNTS233	106309
Israel	Liberia	25 Jun 62	448UNTS295	106442
Costa Rica	Israel	31 Jul 62	484UNTS155	107024
Cyprus	Greece	23 Aug 62	609UNTS15	108825
Denmark	USSR (Soviet Union)	11 Sep 62	458UNTS3	106589
Cameroon	Israel	24 Oct 62	449UNTS15	106447
Dahomey	USSR (Soviet Union)	20 Mar 63	528UNTS181	107641
Romania	USA (United States)	02 Apr 63	474UNTS95	106874
Cameroon	UK Great Britain	20 Aug 63	539UNTS233	107834
Switzerland	UK Great Britain	27 Aug 63	486UNTS183	107079
Czechoslovakia	Yugoslavia	14 Mar 64	544UNTS147	107917
Germany, East	Poland	06 Oct 64	552UNTS89	108051
Czechoslovakia	Germany, East	06 Oct 64	545UNTS113	107927
Pakistan	USSR (Soviet Union)	05 Jun 65	593UNTS115	108579
Israel	Sierra Leone	22 Aug 65	550UNTS275	108022
Argentina	Taiwan	19 Mar 66	635UNTS281	109089
Rwanda	USSR (Soviet Union)	06 May 66	633UNTS217	109039
Austria	Yugoslavia	10 Oct 66	595UNTS273	108622
UK Great Britain	USSR (Soviet Union)	24 Feb 67	606UNTS171	108785
Italy	USSR (Soviet Union)	16 May 67	608UNTS79	108814
Bulgaria	Romania	15 Jun 67	634UNTS57	109051
Italy	Romania	08 Aug 67	642UNTS191	109174
Bulgaria	Romania	22 Aug 67	631UNTS49	108986
Denmark	Romania	29 Aug 67	642UNTS357	109183
Frontier permits				
Belgium	France	21 May 45	23UNTS215	200133
Denmark	Norway	10 Oct 45	104UNTS335	200323
Multilateral		21 Nov 47	33UNTS261	100521

PARTY ONE	PARTY TWO	DATE	CITATION	NUMBER
Frontier permits (Cont.)				
Belgium	France	23 Apr 48	19UNTS95	100307
Poland	USSR (Soviet Union)	08 Jul 48	37UNTS107	100576
Belgium	UK Great Britain	29 Dec 48	27UNTS135	100404
Romania	Yugoslavia	31 Dec 48	116UNTS103	101572
Belgium	France	08 Jan 49	36UNTS151	100569
Italy	Yugoslavia	03 Feb 49	33UNTS105	100517
Belgium	UK Great Britain	14 Apr 49	65UNTS117	100840
Belgium	Luxembourg	15 Jul 49	41UNTS13	100642
San Marino	UK Great Britain	12 Sep 49	87UNTS37	101164
Norway	USSR (Soviet Union)	29 Dec 49	83UNTS291	101112
Belgium	France	14 Mar 50	65UNTS139	100842
Belgium	Netherlands	29 Mar 50	68UNTS45	100883
Belgium	Czechoslovakia	02 May 51	109UNTS3	101483
Belgium	Germany, West	18 Jan 52	243UNTS3	103443
Austria	Yugoslavia	19 Mar 53	467UNTS323	106768
Belgium	Netherlands	26 Mar 53	165UNTS297	102180
Italy	Switzerland	02 Jul 53	257UNTS99	103653
France	UK Great Britain	14 Oct 53	186UNTS151	102489
Bulgaria	Yugoslavia	20 Feb 54	397UNTS13	105700
Austria	Yugoslavia	27 Nov 54	396UNTS75	105694
Bulgaria	Yugoslavia	22 May 56	367UNTS119	105229
Bulgaria	Yugoslavia	16 Jun 56	375UNTS235	105368
Indonesia	Philippines	04 Jul 56	401UNTS59	105763
Czechoslovakia	Germany, East	06 Oct 56	501UNTS109	107315
Philippines	USA (United States)	08 Apr 57	303UNTS227	104382
Albania	Yugoslavia	29 Aug 57	391UNTS127	105621
France	Italy	27 Mar 58	305UNTS387	104426
Germany, West	Netherlands	30 May 58	570UNTS127	108291
Czechoslovakia	Poland	25 Nov 58	372UNTS205	105299
Finland	USSR (Soviet Union)	21 Feb 59	338UNTS3	104830
Greece	Yugoslavia	18 Jun 59	363UNTS133	105205
Czechoslovakia	Poland	04 Jul 59	363UNTS333	105210
Germany, West	Netherlands	03 Jun 60	487UNTS37	107094
Burma	Thailand	08 Jun 60	372UNTS321	105308
Canada	USA (United States)	17 Oct 61	426UNTS201	106138
Czechoslovakia	Hungary	16 Oct 62	479UNTS301	106961
Multilateral		16 Apr 64	548UNTS27	107967
Austria	Hungary	31 Oct 64	545UNTS241	107937
Hungary	Yugoslavia	08 Apr 65	587UNTS169	108511
Hungary	Yugoslavia	09 Aug 65	577UNTS103	108375
Italy	USSR (Soviet Union)	16 May 67	608UNTS79	108814
Immigration and emigration				
Brazil	Spain	27 Dec 60	0UNTS0	109428
Multilateral		16 Apr 64	548UNTS27	107967
Canada	Jamaica	16 Jul 65	548UNTS265	107982
Refugees and stateless persons				
UK Great Britain	USA (United States)	10 Dec 45	3UNTS177	100030
Israel	USA (United States)	07 Dec 51	157UNTS53	102046
Israel	USA (United States)	27 Feb 52	177UNTS123	102314
Austria	France	30 Nov 62	463UNTS173	106701
Cuba	USA (United States)	06 Nov 65	601UNTS81	108688
Assistance				
Multilateral		14 Jan 46	555UNTS69	108105
Multilateral		12 Aug 49	75UNTS31	100970
Netherlands	IRO (Refugee Org)	20 Jun 50	76UNTS55	100979
UN Relief Palestin	United Arab Rep	12 Sep 50	121UNTS107	101630
Brazil	Netherlands	15 Dec 50	123UNTS101	101657
Netherlands	IRO (Refugee Org)	13 Feb 51	87UNTS239	101175
Germany, West	Netherlands	29 Mar 51	149UNTS71	101952
Israel	USA (United States)	07 Dec 51	157UNTS53	102046
Israel	USA (United States)	27 Feb 52	177UNTS123	102314
Jordan	UN Relief Palestin	30 Mar 53	165UNTS317	200495
UN Relief Palestin	United Arab Rep	30 Jun 53	190UNTS3	102554
UN Relief Palestin	United Arab Rep	14 Oct 53	190UNTS13	102555

PARTY ONE	PARTY TWO	DATE	CITATION	NUMBER
Assistance (Cont.)				
Multilateral		19 Oct 53	207UNTS189	102807
Lebanon	UN Relief Palestin	26 Nov 54	202UNTS123	102728
Germany, West	Norway	18 Mar 55	209UNTS309	102832
UN Hi Com Refugees	Sweden	08 Oct 56	428UNTS307	106182
Multilateral		23 Nov 57	506UNTS125	107384
Austria	USA (United States)	03 Oct 61	426UNTS187	106137
Cuba	USA (United States)	06 Nov 65	601UNTS81	108688
Israel	UN Relief Palestin	14 Jun 67	620UNTS183	108955
Legal status				
Belgium	USA (United States)	23 Jan 47	47UNTS23	100721
Multilateral		07 Nov 49	132UNTS3	101748
Multilateral		02 Jul 51	189UNTS137	102545
Multilateral		28 Sep 54	360UNTS117	105158
Hungary	Mongolia	10 Jul 63	519UNTS173	107508
Multilateral		17 May 66	571UNTS89	108302
Refugees				
UK Great Britain	USA (United States)	10 Dec 45	3UNTS177	100030
UN Relief Palestin	United Arab Rep	12 Sep 50	121UNTS107	101630
Multilateral		02 Jul 51	189UNTS137	102545
Multilateral		23 Nov 57	506UNTS125	107384
Germany, West	Netherlands	10 Oct 58	486UNTS345	107085
Multilateral		20 Apr 59	376UNTS85	105375
Cambodia	Thailand	15 Dec 60	382UNTS315	105492
Multilateral		28 Jun 62	494UNTS271	107238
Cuba	USA (United States)	06 Nov 65	601UNTS81	108688
Multilateral		17 May 66	571UNTS89	108302
Repatriation mission				
Belgium	Netherlands	02 Jan 45	19UNTS259	200120
Belgium	Luxembourg	14 May 45	19UNTS243	200118
Belgium	Czechoslovakia	16 May 45	19UNTS251	200119
Repatriation of nationals				
Multilateral		23 Jun 26	38UNTS315	100606
Multilateral		20 Jun 36	40UNTS109	100630
Multilateral		27 Jun 39	40UNTS281	100639
Canada	USA (United States)	18 Mar 42	101UNTS205	200294
Germany, West	USA (United States)	30 Mar 42	105UNTS219	200334
Multilateral		28 Oct 44	123UNTS223	200414
Belgium	Netherlands	02 Jan 45	19UNTS259	200120
Multilateral		20 Jan 45	140UNTS397	200471
USA (United States)	USSR (Soviet Union)	11 Feb 45	68UNTS175	200229
Belgium	Luxembourg	14 May 45	19UNTS243	200118
Belgium	Czechoslovakia	16 May 45	19UNTS251	200119
Multilateral		02 Sep 45	139UNTS387	200465
Multilateral		14 Jan 46	555UNTS69	108105
Multilateral		10 Feb 47	48UNTS203	100746
Multilateral		10 Feb 47	42UNTS3	100645
Multilateral		10 Feb 47	41UNTS21	100643
Multilateral		10 Feb 47	41UNTS135	100644
France	USA (United States)	11 Mar 47	151UNTS159	101991
Italy	Netherlands	04 Dec 48	46UNTS271	100716
Israel	Lebanon	23 Mar 49	42UNTS287	100655
Israel	Jordan	03 Apr 49	42UNTS303	100656
Israel	Syria	20 Jul 49	42UNTS327	100657
Multilateral		12 Aug 49	75UNTS85	100971
Multilateral		12 Aug 49	75UNTS287	100973
Multilateral		12 Aug 49	75UNTS31	100970
Multilateral		07 Nov 49	132UNTS3	101748
Multilateral		09 Jan 51	197UNTS341	102647
Australia	Netherlands	22 Feb 51	128UNTS115	101717
Australia	Italy	29 Mar 51	131UNTS187	101741
Australia	Germany, West	29 Aug 52	184UNTS147	102446
Multilateral		11 Dec 53	218UNTS255	102958
France	Greece	13 May 54	222UNTS299	103036

PARTY ONE	PARTY TWO	DATE	CITATION	NUMBER
Repatriation of nationals (Cont.)				
Belgium	Netherlands	13 Jan 55	210UNTS63	102834
Multilateral		15 May 55	217UNTS223	102949
Fed Rhod/Nyasaland	Netherlands	02 Nov 55	263UNTS381	103784
Indonesia	Philippines	04 Jul 56	401UNTS59	105763
Australia	Netherlands	01 Aug 56	280UNTS3	104047
Belgium	Germany, West	24 Sep 56	314UNTS195	104549
Japan	USSR (Soviet Union)	19 Oct 56	263UNTS99	103768
Japan	Norway	28 Feb 57	280UNTS87	104054
Netherlands	Spain	08 Apr 61	482UNTS193	106996
Argentina	USA (United States)	16 Mar 62	454UNTS3	106535
Algeria	France	03 Jul 62	507UNTS25	107395
Netherlands	Portugal	22 Nov 63	492UNTS31	107185
Netherlands	Turkey	19 Aug 64	521UNTS197	107523
Australia	Germany, West	21 Jun 65	542UNTS53	107879
India	Pakistan	10 Jan 66	560UNTS39	108166
Stateless persons				
Multilateral		28 Sep 54	360UNTS117	105158
Multilateral		28 Jun 62	494UNTS271	107238
Status of state				
Indonesia	Netherlands	02 Nov 49	69UNTS3	100894
Fed of Malaya	UK Great Britain	08 Nov 58	327UNTS301	104728
Algeria	France	03 Jul 62	507UNTS25	107395
Malaysia	Singapore	07 Aug 65	563UNTS89	108206
Muscat and Oman	UK Great Britain	15 Nov 67	617UNTS319	108919
Nazi organizations				
Multilateral		28 Oct 44	123UNTS223	200414
Multilateral		20 Jan 45	140UNTS397	200471
Czechoslovakia	France	08 Dec 45	46UNTS77	100701
Multilateral		10 Feb 47	49UNTS3	100747
Multilateral		10 Feb 47	41UNTS21	100643
Multilateral		10 Feb 47	48UNTS203	100746
Multilateral		10 Feb 47	41UNTS135	100644
Multilateral		22 Nov 49	185UNTS307	102477
Multilateral		15 May 55	217UNTS223	102949
Democratic institutions				
Multilateral		30 Jul 40	161UNTS253	200488
France	USA (United States)	25 Aug 44	138UNTS247	200449
Multilateral		28 Jun 46	138UNTS85	101862
Multilateral		10 Feb 47	42UNTS3	100645
Multilateral		10 Feb 47	41UNTS21	100643
Multilateral		10 Feb 47	49UNTS3	100747
Multilateral		10 Feb 47	41UNTS135	100644
Multilateral		10 Feb 47	48UNTS203	100746
Multilateral		08 Apr 49	140UNTS196	101889
Multilateral		12 Aug 49	75UNTS287	100973
Indonesia	Netherlands	02 Nov 49	69UNTS3	100894
Multilateral		22 Nov 49	185UNTS307	102477
Saudi Arabia	USA (United States)	18 Jun 51	102UNTS73	101412
United Arab Rep	UK Great Britain	12 Feb 53	161UNTS157	102127
Libya	UK Great Britain	25 Mar 53	172UNTS281	102252
Multilateral		15 May 55	217UNTS223	102949
Algeria	France	03 Jul 62	507UNTS25	107395
Multilateral		26 Nov 65	598UNTS81	108655
Governor-general functions				
Italy	Norway	19 Nov 49	47UNTS89	100724
United Arab Rep	UK Great Britain	12 Feb 53	161UNTS157	102127
Czechoslovakia	UK Great Britain	15 Jan 60	374UNTS207	105336
Cyprus	UK Great Britain	16 Aug 60	382UNTS239	105485
Multilateral		26 Nov 65	598UNTS81	108655
Independence maintenance				
Bolivia	USA (United States)	10 Jun 46	13UNTS19	100197
Ethiopia	USA (United States)	04 Jul 46	13UNTS27	100198

PARTY ONE	PARTY TWO	DATE	CITATION	NUMBER
Independence maintenance (Cont.)				
Norway	USA (United States)	08 Jul 46	13UNTS35	100199
Spain	USA (United States)	11 Jul 46	13UNTS51	100201
Belgium	USA (United States)	11 Jul 46	13UNTS43	100200
United Arab Rep	USA (United States)	15 Aug 46	13UNTS59	100202
Portugal	USA (United States)	26 Aug 46	13UNTS67	100203
Denmark	USA (United States)	10 Sep 46	13UNTS75	100204
USA (United States)	Yugoslavia	03 Oct 46	13UNTS83	100205
Dominican Republic	USA (United States)	07 Oct 46	13UNTS91	100206
Libya	UK Great Britain	25 Mar 53	172UNTS281	102252
Somalia	UK Great Britain	26 Jun 60	374UNTS363	105350
Continuity of rights and obligations				
Multilateral		17 Apr 46	27UNTS103	100402
Burma	UK Great Britain	17 Oct 47	70UNTS183	100904
Germany, West	USA (United States)	15 Dec 49	92UNTS269	101277
Indonesia	USA (United States)	24 Mar 50	92UNTS387	101281
Germany, West	Netherlands	14 Dec 50	87UNTS257	101177
Libya	USA (United States)	21 Jan 52	183UNTS177	102427
Multilateral		11 Feb 52	165UNTS77	102169
India	USA (United States)	21 Oct 54	234UNTS119	103277
Fed of Malaya	UK Great Britain	12 Sep 57	279UNTS287	104046
Ghana	UK Great Britain	25 Nov 57	287UNTS233	104189
Multilateral		16 Aug 60	382UNTS8	105476
Nigeria	UK Great Britain	01 Oct 60	384UNTS207	105520
Somalia	USA (United States)	04 Feb 61	433UNTS179	106241
Sierra Leone	UK Great Britain	05 May 61	420UNTS11	106036
Multilateral		07 Aug 62	457UNTS117	106580
Multilateral		31 Aug 62	457UNTS123	106581
Trinidad/Tobago	USA (United States)	08 Oct 62	462UNTS145	106675
Jamaica	USA (United States)	29 Nov 62	462UNTS229	106682
New Zealand	Western Samoa	30 Nov 62	476UNTS3	106898
Multilateral		30 Dec 63	568UNTS243	108272
Malta	UK Great Britain	31 Dec 64	525UNTS221	107594
UN Special Fund	Singapore	31 Dec 65	552UNTS299	108061
Multilateral		31 Dec 65	552UNTS292	108060
Gambia	UK Great Britain	20 Jun 66	573UNTS203	108333
Lesotho	UN Special Fund	17 Nov 66	580UNTS17	108416
Barbados	UN Special Fund	03 Mar 67	594UNTS91	108596
Transition period				
France	USA (United States)	25 Aug 44	138UNTS247	200449
Bolivia	USA (United States)	10 Jun 46	13UNTS19	100197
Ethiopia	USA (United States)	04 Jul 46	13UNTS27	100198
Norway	USA (United States)	08 Jul 46	13UNTS35	100199
Spain	USA (United States)	11 Jul 46	13UNTS51	100201
Belgium	USA (United States)	11 Jul 46	13UNTS43	100200
United Arab Rep	USA (United States)	15 Aug 46	13UNTS59	100202
Portugal	USA (United States)	26 Aug 46	13UNTS67	100203
Denmark	USA (United States)	10 Sep 46	13UNTS75	100204
USA (United States)	Yugoslavia	03 Oct 46	13UNTS83	100205
Dominican Republic	USA (United States)	07 Oct 46	13UNTS91	100206
Indonesia	Netherlands	02 Nov 49	69UNTS3	100894
Multilateral		11 Feb 52	165UNTS77	102169
United Arab Rep	UK Great Britain	12 Feb 53	161UNTS157	102127
Somalia	UK Great Britain	26 Jun 60	374UNTS363	105350
Cyprus	UK Great Britain	16 Aug 60	382UNTS239	105485
Multilateral		19 Sep 60	419UNTS125	106032
Algeria	France	03 Jul 62	507UNTS25	107395
Recognition				
Iceland	USA (United States)	01 Jul 41	12UNTS405	200071
Lebanon	USA (United States)	08 Sep 44	124UNTS187	200419
Syria	USA (United States)	08 Sep 44	124UNTS251	200424
USA (United States)	Yemen	04 May 46	4UNTS165	100043
Philippines	USA (United States)	04 Jul 46	6UNTS335	100086
Philippines	USA (United States)	04 Jul 46	7UNTS3	100088
France	Thailand	17 Nov 46	344UNTS59	104943

PARTY ONE	PARTY TWO	DATE	CITATION	NUMBER
Recognition (Cont.)				
Burma	UK Great Britain	17 Oct 47	70UNTS183	100904
Indonesia	Netherlands	02 Nov 49	69UNTS3	100894
Multilateral		08 Sep 51	136UNTS45	101832
Multilateral		15 May 55	217UNTS223	102949
Argentina	UNICEF (Children)	19 Nov 57	300UNTS229	104338
Belgium	France	20 Sep 58	376UNTS331	105387
Pakistan	USA (United States)	11 Apr 60	372UNTS251	105302
Algeria	France	03 Jul 62	507UNTS25	107395
Multilateral		23 Jul 62	456UNTS302	106564
Malaysia	Singapore	07 Aug 65	563UNTS89	108206
Re-establishment				
France	UK Great Britain	31 Aug 45	98UNTS249	200275
Multilateral		15 May 55	217UNTS223	102949
Germany, East	USSR (Soviet Union)	12 Jun 64	553UNTS249	108093
Self-determination				
Indonesia	Netherlands	02 Nov 49	69UNTS3	100894
United Arab Rep	UK Great Britain	12 Feb 53	161UNTS157	102127
Indonesia	Netherlands	15 Aug 62	437UNTS273	106311
Multilateral		31 Jul 63	550UNTS343	108029
IBRD (World Bank)	Thailand	24 Jun 66	582UNTS259	108466
Self-government				
United Arab Rep	UK Great Britain	12 Feb 53	161UNTS157	102127
Multilateral		26 Nov 65	598UNTS81	108655
Union with other states				
Indonesia	Netherlands	02 Nov 49	69UNTS3	100894
Multilateral		15 May 55	217UNTS223	102949
Nigeria	UK Great Britain	29 May 61	478UNTS3	106931
USA (United States)	Yugoslavia	28 Nov 62	460UNTS185	106640
Diplomatic and consular relations				
Netherlands	USSR (Soviet Union)	10 Jul 42	241UNTS475	200540
Greece	USA (United States)	25 Oct 48	185UNTS103	102462
Denmark	Poland	12 May 49	87UNTS179	101172
Netherlands	UK Great Britain	30 Apr 51	91UNTS177	101250
Philippines	Vatican/Holy See	18 Jun 52	543UNTS165	107900
Bulgaria	Hungary	27 Jun 58	438UNTS235	106318
United Nations	Saudi Arabia	23 Aug 63	474UNTS155	106879
UK Great Britain	USSR (Soviet Union)	02 Dec 65	0UNTS0	109384
Sweden	USSR (Soviet Union)	30 Nov 67	0UNTS0	109385
Belgium	Israel	25 Sep 68	0UNTS0	109359
Acquisition of nationality				
Belgium	France	09 Jan 47	36UNTS145	100568
Netherlands	New Zealand	16 Oct 50	83UNTS269	101111
Multilateral		21 Dec 50	90UNTS3	101222
Multilateral		19 Oct 53	207UNTS189	102807
USSR (Soviet Union)	Yugoslavia	22 May 56	259UNTS155	103688
Poland	USSR (Soviet Union)	25 Mar 57	281UNTS121	104075
Germany, West	Netherlands	08 Apr 60	508UNTS14	107404
Multilateral		18 Apr 61	500UNTS223	107311
Hungary	USSR (Soviet Union)	21 Jan 63	577UNTS201	108378
Poland	USSR (Soviet Union)	31 Mar 65	571UNTS217	108304
Australia	Germany, West	21 Apr 65	598UNTS25	108654
Czechoslovakia	Poland	17 May 65	572UNTS181	108312
Alien registration				
Multilateral		05 Jun 26	38UNTS281	100604
Switzerland	United Arab Rep	14 Jul 60	497UNTS161	107268
Thailand	UK Great Britain	20 Nov 62	466UNTS243	106747
Alien status				
Multilateral		05 Jun 26	38UNTS281	100604
Canada	France	12 May 33	253UNTS285	200545
Taiwan	Dominican Republic	11 May 40	10UNTS285	200067
Brazil	Paraguay	14 Jun 41	54UNTS235	200196
Brazil	Venezuela	22 Oct 42	65UNTS203	200212

PARTY ONE	PARTY TWO	DATE	CITATION	NUMBER
Alien status (Cont.)				
Taiwan	Cuba	12 Nov 42	10UNTS243	200065
Brazil	Taiwan	20 Aug 43	14UNTS365	200094
Peru	USA (United States)	15 Apr 44	150UNTS317	200479
Taiwan	Costa Rica	05 May 44	14UNTS427	200098
Taiwan	Mexico	01 Aug 44	14UNTS441	200099
Syria	USA (United States)	08 Sep 44	124UNTS251	200424
Lebanon	USA (United States)	08 Sep 44	124UNTS187	200419
Dominican Republic	USA (United States)	13 Oct 45	149UNTS361	200477
Taiwan	Ecuador	06 Jan 46	7UNTS233	100102
Taiwan	Thailand	23 Jan 46	161UNTS127	102126
Taiwan	France	28 Feb 46	14UNTS137	100216
Taiwan	Switzerland	13 Mar 46	14UNTS159	100218
Argentina	Taiwan	10 Feb 47	486UNTS143	107077
Czechoslovakia	Poland	10 Mar 47	25UNTS231	100365
Austria	France	15 Mar 47	12UNTS109	100182
Taiwan	Philippines	18 Apr 47	11UNTS361	100175
Nepal	USA (United States)	25 Apr 47	16UNTS97	100251
Italy	Philippines	09 Jul 47	44UNTS3	100674
Portugal	UK Great Britain	16 Oct 47	82UNTS203	101093
Ecuador	USA (United States)	14 Nov 47	149UNTS297	101959
Italy	USA (United States)	02 Feb 48	79UNTS171	101040
Paraguay	USA (United States)	12 Mar 48	162UNTS30	102131
Philippines	Spain	20 May 48	70UNTS143	100903
India	Switzerland	14 Aug 48	33UNTS3	100509
Belgium	France	08 Jan 49	36UNTS151	100569
Philippines	Thailand	14 Jun 49	81UNTS53	101062
Multilateral		12 Aug 49	75UNTS287	100973
Ireland	USA (United States)	21 Jan 50	206UNTS269	102792
India	Nepal	31 Jul 50	94UNTS3	101302
Greece	Philippines	28 Aug 50	225UNTS155	103097
Nepal	UK Great Britain	30 Oct 50	97UNTS121	101346
Austria	Sweden	31 Oct 50	197UNTS311	102645
Nicaragua	USA (United States)	31 Jan 51	150UNTS3	101960
Norway	UK Great Britain	22 Feb 51	326UNTS209	104713
India	Indonesia	03 Mar 51	167UNTS3	102197
Honduras	USA (United States)	24 Apr 51	140UNTS287	101894
Multilateral		02 Jul 51	189UNTS137	102545
Greece	USA (United States)	03 Aug 51	224UNTS279	103080
Mexico	USA (United States)	11 Aug 51	162UNTS103	102133
Israel	USA (United States)	23 Aug 51	219UNTS237	102979
Ethiopia	USA (United States)	07 Sep 51	206UNTS41	102785
Denmark	USA (United States)	01 Oct 51	421UNTS105	106056
India	Turkey	14 Dec 51	137UNTS15	101845
Sweden	UK Great Britain	14 Mar 52	202UNTS157	102731
Italy	Jordan	24 Apr 52	281UNTS167	104078
Ethiopia	USA (United States)	15 May 52	180UNTS227	102388
India	Philippines	11 Jul 52	203UNTS73	102741
Dominican Republic	Philippines	02 Nov 52	543UNTS175	107901
India	Iraq	10 Nov 52	172UNTS103	102242
Ceylon (Sri Lanka)	USA (United States)	17 Nov 52	180UNTS207	102386
India	Muscat and Oman	15 Mar 53	190UNTS69	102559
Japan	USA (United States)	02 Apr 53	206UNTS143	102788
Greece	UK Great Britain	17 Apr 53	191UNTS151	102582
Ethiopia	USA (United States)	29 Apr 53	224UNTS121	103073
United Arab Rep	USA (United States)	18 Jun 53	204UNTS55	102749
Liberia	USA (United States)	23 Jun 53	213UNTS57	102880
Multilateral		11 Dec 53	218UNTS153	102956
Multilateral		11 Dec 53	218UNTS211	102957
Denmark	UK Great Britain	15 Dec 53	196UNTS105	102620
France	Sweden	16 Feb 54	228UNTS137	103147
Indonesia	Thailand	03 Mar 54	213UNTS297	102893
Multilateral		22 May 54	199UNTS29	102675
Germany, West	USA (United States)	29 Oct 54	273UNTS3	103943
Taiwan	El Salvador	09 Dec 54	214UNTS217	102900
Pakistan	United Arab Rep	13 Dec 54	255UNTS167	103610

PARTY ONE	PARTY TWO	DATE	CITATION	NUMBER
Alien status (Cont.)				
Multilateral		19 Dec 54	218UNTS139	102955
Peru	USA (United States)	31 Dec 54	251UNTS51	103533
Chile	USA (United States)	31 Mar 55	262UNTS19	103736
Multilateral		06 Apr 55	261UNTS55	103725
Luxembourg	Netherlands	04 May 55	292UNTS17	104262
Iran	USA (United States)	15 Aug 55	284UNTS93	104132
Multilateral		13 Dec 55	529UNTS141	107660
New Zealand	UK Great Britain	20 Dec 55	268UNTS243	103860
Austria	Belgium	20 Jan 56	248UNTS3	103481
Nicaragua	USA (United States)	21 Jan 56	367UNTS3	105224
Netherlands	USA (United States)	27 Mar 56	285UNTS231	104154
Israel	USA (United States)	26 Jun 56	257UNTS55	103649
Philippines	Switzerland	30 Aug 56	293UNTS43	104284
Burma	Thailand	15 Oct 56	277UNTS87	104000
Belgium	Spain	28 Nov 56	308UNTS285	104465
Korea, South	USA (United States)	28 Nov 56	302UNTS281	104367
France	Netherlands	15 Feb 57	286UNTS243	104170
Belgium	France	15 Feb 57	267UNTS3	103834
Multilateral		01 May 57	284UNTS201	104138
Multilateral		26 Jun 57	328UNTS247	104738
Multilateral		12 Jul 57	322UNTS245	104660
Hungary	USSR (Soviet Union)	24 Aug 57	318UNTS35	104608
Romania	USSR (Soviet Union)	04 Sep 57	318UNTS89	104610
Czechoslovakia	USSR (Soviet Union)	05 Oct 57	320UNTS111	104640
Taiwan	Jordan	19 Nov 57	308UNTS227	104463
Korea, North	USSR (Soviet Union)	16 Dec 57	292UNTS107	104269
Belgium	Denmark	31 Dec 57	305UNTS247	104422
Poland	USSR (Soviet Union)	21 Jan 58	319UNTS277	104636
Israel	Philippines	26 Feb 58	507UNTS135	107398
Mongolia	USSR (Soviet Union)	25 Aug 58	322UNTS201	104658
Pakistan	Thailand	28 Aug 58	394UNTS53	105668
Muscat and Oman	USA (United States)	20 Dec 58	380UNTS181	105457
Israel	Liberia	09 Apr 59	448UNTS95	106427
France	USA (United States)	25 Nov 59	401UNTS75	105764
Argentina	Philippines	12 Feb 60	535UNTS293	107785
Germany, West	Netherlands	08 Apr 60	508UNTS14	107404
Multilateral		11 Apr 60	374UNTS3	105323
Japan	Pakistan	30 Jul 60	384UNTS63	105511
Japan	Thailand	24 Aug 60	384UNTS73	105512
Czechoslovakia	Hungary	04 Nov 60	397UNTS227	105708
Japan	Pakistan	18 Dec 60	423UNTS197	106093
Belgium	USA (United States)	21 Feb 61	480UNTS149	106967
Afghanistan	Japan	15 Mar 61	450UNTS373	106480
Ceylon (Sri Lanka)	Japan	20 Mar 61	450UNTS385	106481
USA (United States)	Vietnam, South	03 Apr 61	424UNTS137	106106
Indonesia	Japan	01 Jul 61	517UNTS107	107484
Multilateral		26 Oct 61	496UNTS43	107247
Belgium	Italy	28 Oct 61	429UNTS199	106199
Argentina	Japan	20 Dec 61	613UNTS323	108859
Luxembourg	USA (United States)	23 Feb 62	474UNTS3	106868
Brazil	Japan	28 Mar 62	451UNTS125	106489
New Zealand	Western Samoa	01 Aug 62	453UNTS3	106515
Multilateral		29 Aug 62	443UNTS280	106366
Netherlands	Spain	17 Dec 62	499UNTS227	107301
UK Great Britain	USA (United States)	15 Jan 63	466UNTS181	106743
Australia	United Nations	13 May 63	463UNTS187	106702
Korea, South	USA (United States)	18 Jun 63	487UNTS297	107112
India	USA (United States)	19 Jun 63	479UNTS175	106952
Canada	Nigeria	03 Jul 63	529UNTS57	107656
Hungary	Mongolia	10 Jul 63	519UNTS173	107508
Afghanistan	USA (United States)	20 Aug 63	488UNTS41	107118
Colombia	United Nations	27 Aug 63	481UNTS3	106975
Malagasy	USA (United States)	07 Oct 63	494UNTS3	107221
Iran	USA (United States)	24 Oct 63	489UNTS303	107146
Tunisia	USA (United States)	18 Nov 63	494UNTS193	107233

PARTY ONE	PARTY TWO	DATE	CITATION	NUMBER
Alien status (Cont.)				
Greece	USA (United States)	13 Dec 63	494UNTS55	107226
Saudi Arabia	USA (United States)	06 Jan 64	531UNTS3	107689
Italy	United Nations	18 Mar 64	491UNTS21	107171
USSR (Soviet Union)	Yemen	21 Mar 64	553UNTS267	108094
Afghanistan	United Nations	28 Apr 64	494UNTS77	107227
Liberia	USA (United States)	08 May 64	526UNTS239	107608
United Nations	Togo	03 Jul 64	502UNTS287	107334
Belgium	Tunisia	15 Jul 64	561UNTS297	108190
Ceylon (Sri Lanka)	USA (United States)	29 Aug 64	531UNTS93	107695
Italy	ILO (Labor Org)	24 Oct 64	541UNTS217	107871
Taiwan	Korea, South	27 Nov 64	555UNTS3	108102
Netherlands	Nigeria	04 Dec 64	545UNTS155	107931
Czechoslovakia	Poland	17 May 65	572UNTS181	108312
Netherlands	Zambia	17 Dec 65	631UNTS311	109000
Finland	United Nations	16 Jan 67	588UNTS153	108522
Haiti	Israel	28 Mar 67	630UNTS293	108975
Australia	Turkey	05 Oct 67	0UNTS0	109457
General consular functions				
Greece	Iran	09 Jan 31	166UNTS331	200497
Mexico	USA (United States)	12 Aug 42	125UNTS301	200431
Taiwan	USA (United States)	11 Jan 43	10UNTS261	200066
Belgium	Taiwan	20 Oct 43	14UNTS376	200095
Canada	Taiwan	14 Apr 44	14UNTS408	200097
Taiwan	Netherlands	29 May 45	2UNTS307	200023
Taiwan	France	28 Feb 46	14UNTS113	100215
Taiwan	Denmark	20 May 46	12UNTS59	100180
Philippines	USA (United States)	14 Mar 47	45UNTS23	100690
Costa Rica	USA (United States)	12 Jan 48	70UNTS27	100896
Belgium	France	17 Jan 48	36UNTS233	100570
Philippines	Spain	20 May 48	70UNTS143	100903
Greece	Lebanon	06 Oct 48	87UNTS351	101179
Ireland	USA (United States)	01 May 50	222UNTS107	103026
Norway	UK Great Britain	22 Feb 51	326UNTS209	104713
UK Great Britain	USA (United States)	06 Jun 51	165UNTS121	102174
Panama	UNICEF (Children)	14 Jun 51	97UNTS3	101343
France	Italy	23 Aug 51	291UNTS143	104249
Australia	Netherlands	25 Sep 51	128UNTS63	101713
France	UK Great Britain	31 Dec 51	330UNTS145	104744
Sweden	UK Great Britain	14 Mar 52	202UNTS157	102731
Lebanon	Pakistan	16 Jan 53	284UNTS193	104137
Greece	UK Great Britain	17 Apr 53	191UNTS151	102582
Germany, West	USA (United States)	02 Jun 53	231UNTS151	103214
Mexico	UK Great Britain	20 Mar 54	331UNTS21	104750
Italy	UK Great Britain	01 Jun 54	403UNTS275	105798
France	Sweden	05 Mar 55	427UNTS133	106150
Germany, West	UK Great Britain	30 Jul 56	330UNTS233	104748
Germany, East	USSR (Soviet Union)	10 May 57	285UNTS135	104151
Czechoslovakia	Germany, East	24 May 57	292UNTS327	104279
Germany, East	Hungary	03 Jul 57	407UNTS186	105865
Hungary	USSR (Soviet Union)	24 Aug 57	318UNTS3	104607
Czechoslovakia	USSR (Soviet Union)	31 Aug 57	308UNTS3	104456
Romania	USSR (Soviet Union)	04 Sep 57	318UNTS55	104609
Albania	USSR (Soviet Union)	18 Sep 57	307UNTS265	104455
Czechoslovakia	USSR (Soviet Union)	05 Oct 57	320UNTS129	104641
Germany, East	Poland	25 Nov 57	340UNTS99	104862
Germany, East	USSR (Soviet Union)	28 Nov 57	305UNTS113	104419
Bulgaria	USSR (Soviet Union)	12 Dec 57	302UNTS21	104352
Korea, North	USSR (Soviet Union)	16 Dec 57	292UNTS121	104270
Poland	USSR (Soviet Union)	21 Jan 58	319UNTS291	104637
Germany, West	USSR (Soviet Union)	25 Apr 58	338UNTS49	104832
Bulgaria	Hungary	27 Jun 58	438UNTS235	106318
Germany, East	Romania	15 Jul 58	387UNTS133	105561
Mongolia	USSR (Soviet Union)	25 Aug 58	322UNTS215	104659
Poland	Yugoslavia	17 Nov 58	432UNTS267	106225

PARTY ONE	PARTY TWO	DATE	CITATION	NUMBER
General consular functions (Cont.)				
Albania	Czechoslovakia	16 Jan 59	363UNTS165	105207
Austria	USSR (Soviet Union)	28 Feb 59	356UNTS39	105091
Hungary	Romania	18 Mar 59	417UNTS3	106005
Czechoslovakia	Hungary	27 Mar 59	351UNTS57	105017
Bulgaria	Romania	23 Apr 59	387UNTS81	105559
Hungary	Poland	20 May 59	432UNTS115	106217
Bulgaria	Czechoslovakia	27 May 59	360UNTS335	105167
USSR (Soviet Union)	Vietnam, North	05 Jun 59	356UNTS111	105093
China People's Rep	USSR (Soviet Union)	23 Jun 59	356UNTS83	105092
China People's Rep	Czechoslovakia	07 May 60	402UNTS209	105787
Czechoslovakia	Poland	17 May 60	424UNTS3	106096
Czechoslovakia	Romania	21 May 60	397UNTS245	105709
Austria	UK Great Britain	24 Jun 60	502UNTS79	107327
Belgium	UK Great Britain	08 Mar 61	523UNTS17	107554
Multilateral		18 Apr 61	500UNTS95	107310
Spain	UK Great Britain	30 May 61	562UNTS169	108198
Bulgaria	Poland	19 Sep 61	483UNTS249	107018
United Nations	Saudi Arabia	16 Mar 62	456UNTS379	106566
United Nations	Tanganyika	01 Jun 62	479UNTS3	106944
Denmark	UK Great Britain	27 Jun 62	562UNTS75	108197
Poland	Romania	05 Oct 62	521UNTS3	107516
Romania	Yugoslavia	08 Nov 62	472UNTS305	106845
United Nations	Syria	17 Nov 62	456UNTS359	106565
Hungary	USSR (Soviet Union)	20 Dec 62	577UNTS245	108381
Czechoslovakia	Vietnam, North	14 Jan 63	501UNTS181	107318
Japan	USA (United States)	22 Mar 63	518UNTS179	107495
Multilateral		24 Apr 63	596UNTS261	108638
United Nations	Trinidad/Tobago	06 May 63	463UNTS109	106696
Mali	United Nations	09 May 63	463UNTS147	106699
Jamaica	United Nations	22 May 63	479UNTS19	106945
United Nations	Uganda	29 May 63	466UNTS311	106751
Czechoslovakia	Yugoslavia	24 Jun 63	496UNTS3	107246
Dominican Republic	United Nations	05 Aug 63	472UNTS353	106847
United Nations	United Arab Rep	27 Aug 63	474UNTS221	106884
Czechoslovakia	Mongolia	08 Nov 63	503UNTS125	107341
United Nations	Sierra Leone	19 Feb 64	489UNTS91	107136
United Nations	Upper Volta	26 Feb 64	489UNTS179	107139
Multilateral		03 Mar 64	516UNTS53	107470
Morocco	United Nations	03 Mar 64	490UNTS187	107154
Japan	UK Great Britain	04 May 64	561UNTS25	108179
USA (United States)	USSR (Soviet Union)	01 Jun 64	0UNTS0	109383
Mongolia	Poland	28 Oct 64	552UNTS115	108052
Greece	India	11 Feb 65	606UNTS9	108771
UK Great Britain	Yugoslavia	21 Apr 65	595UNTS189	108620
Belgium	Luxembourg	30 Sep 65	590UNTS35	108545
UK Great Britain	USSR (Soviet Union)	02 Dec 65	0UNTS0	109384
Finland	USSR (Soviet Union)	24 Jan 66	576UNTS35	108364
Japan	USSR (Soviet Union)	29 Jul 66	608UNTS93	108815
Netherlands	Norway	22 Sep 66	600UNTS227	108683
Canada	Norway	23 Nov 66	604UNTS295	108757
Singapore	UK Great Britain	01 Dec 66	605UNTS153	108763
Trinidad/Tobago	UK Great Britain	29 Dec 66	605UNTS237	108766
South Africa	Switzerland	03 Jul 67	643UNTS3	109184
Sweden	USSR (Soviet Union)	30 Nov 67	0UNTS0	109385
Belgium	Israel	25 Sep 68	0UNTS0	109359
Diplomatic privileges				
Cuba	USA (United States)	16 May 32	234UNTS283	200537
Panama	USA (United States)	31 Jan 35	234UNTS277	200536
Mexico	USA (United States)	12 Aug 42	125UNTS301	200431
Haiti	USA (United States)	24 Aug 45	139UNTS311	200458
Multilateral		13 Feb 46	1UNTS15	100004
ILO (Labor Org)	Switzerland	11 Mar 46	15UNTS377	200103
Netherlands	ICJ (Int Court)	26 Jun 46	8UNTS61	100114
United Nations	Switzerland	01 Jul 46	1UNTS163	200008

PARTY ONE	PARTY TWO	DATE	CITATION	NUMBER
Diplomatic privileges (Cont.)				
Peru	USA (United States)	27 Dec 46	152UNTS93	102013
Philippines	USA (United States)	14 Mar 47	45UNTS23	100690
Nepal	USA (United States)	25 Apr 47	16UNTS97	100251
United Nations	USA (United States)	26 Jun 47	11UNTS11	100147
Greece	USA (United States)	08 Jul 47	16UNTS157	100256
Taiwan	USA (United States)	27 Oct 47	12UNTS11	100178
Belgium	USSR (Soviet Union)	10 Nov 47	18UNTS299	100298
Multilateral		21 Nov 47	33UNTS261	100521
United Nations	USA (United States)	18 Dec 47	11UNTS347	100174
Costa Rica	USA (United States)	12 Jan 48	70UNTS27	100896
ICJ Option Clause	Honduras	02 Feb 48	15UNTS217	100236
France	UNICEF (Children)	19 Feb 48	68UNTS75	100885
Philippines	Spain	20 May 48	70UNTS143	100903
Israel	UNICEF (Children)	20 Sep 48	71UNTS17	100907
Greece	Lebanon	06 Oct 48	87UNTS351	101179
Peru	ICAO (Civil Aviat)	22 Oct 48	95UNTS3	101315
Poland	USA (United States)	30 Oct 48	15UNTS225	100238
UNICEF (Children)	Thailand	01 Dec 48	68UNTS94	100886
WHO (World Health)	Switzerland	12 Jan 49	26UNTS331	200155
Liberia	USA (United States)	22 Jul 49	232UNTS283	103242
Dominican Republic	USA (United States)	23 Jan 50	236UNTS3	103312
Burma	UNICEF (Children)	22 Apr 50	68UNTS96	100888
Ireland	USA (United States)	01 May 50	222UNTS107	103026
Chile	USA (United States)	12 May 50	177UNTS103	102312
Afghanistan	UNICEF (Children)	04 Jul 50	71UNTS3	100906
Taiwan	UNICEF (Children)	19 Jul 50	94UNTS21	101304
WHO (World Health)	United Arab Rep	25 Aug 50	92UNTS39	101259
Ceylon (Sri Lanka)	USA (United States)	07 Nov 50	92UNTS125	101265
Panama	USA (United States)	20 Dec 50	92UNTS167	101269
Liberia	USA (United States)	22 Dec 50	92UNTS145	101267
Nicaragua	USA (United States)	23 Dec 50	92UNTS155	101268
Paraguay	USA (United States)	29 Dec 50	122UNTS157	101645
Costa Rica	USA (United States)	11 Jan 51	92UNTS179	101270
Chile	USA (United States)	16 Jan 51	151UNTS147	101990
Saudi Arabia	USA (United States)	17 Jan 51	140UNTS335	101897
Paraguay	UNICEF (Children)	25 Jan 51	79UNTS9	101027
Afghanistan	USA (United States)	07 Feb 51	132UNTS265	101766
Dominican Republic	USA (United States)	20 Feb 51	132UNTS305	101770
Lebanon	USA (United States)	24 Feb 51	223UNTS121	103060
Israel	USA (United States)	26 Feb 51	137UNTS57	101848
Jordan	USA (United States)	27 Feb 51	141UNTS55	101905
Colombia	USA (United States)	09 Mar 51	141UNTS15	101901
Bolivia	USA (United States)	14 Mar 51	132UNTS319	101771
WHO (World Health)	United Arab Rep	25 Mar 51	223UNTS87	103058
Iraq	USA (United States)	10 Apr 51	151UNTS179	101993
Haiti	USA (United States)	02 May 51	151UNTS191	101994
Ecuador	USA (United States)	03 May 51	141UNTS27	101902
Belgium	Brazil	08 May 51	91UNTS75	101242
UK Great Britain	USA (United States)	06 Jun 51	165UNTS121	102174
Panama	UNICEF (Children)	14 Jun 51	97UNTS3	101343
Multilateral		15 Jun 51	148UNTS67	101936
UK Great Britain	USA (United States)	15 Jun 51	141UNTS79	101907
Ethiopia	USA (United States)	16 Jun 51	148UNTS39	101933
Burma	WHO (World Health)	09 Jul 51	104UNTS175	101439
El Salvador	USA (United States)	19 Jul 51	140UNTS259	101892
Philippines	WHO (World Health)	22 Jul 51	149UNTS197	101953
Iraq	USA (United States)	08 Aug 51	229UNTS185	103166
Belgium	Brazil	11 Aug 51	104UNTS17	101431
France	United Nations	17 Aug 51	122UNTS191	101647
Korea, South	United Nations	21 Sep 51	104UNTS323	200322
Australia	Netherlands	25 Sep 51	128UNTS63	101713
France	UK Great Britain	31 Dec 51	330UNTS145	104744
Libya	USA (United States)	21 Jan 52	183UNTS177	102427
Japan	USA (United States)	28 Feb 52	208UNTS255	102817
El Salvador	USA (United States)	04 Apr 52	177UNTS219	102320

PARTY ONE	PARTY TWO	DATE	CITATION	NUMBER
Diplomatic privileges (Cont.)				
France	WHO (World Health)	23 Jul 52	209UNTS231	102829
Belgium	Italy	22 Sep 52	157UNTS121	102051
Nicaragua	USA (United States)	09 Oct 52	184UNTS105	102442
USA (United States)	Uruguay	12 Nov 52	231UNTS145	103213
Chile	United Nations	16 Feb 53	314UNTS49	104541
ICAO (Civil Aviat)	United Arab Rep	27 Aug 53	215UNTS371	102925
Netherlands	UK Great Britain	19 Oct 53	306UNTS99	104435
Israel	USA (United States)	25 Nov 53	219UNTS205	102976
UK Great Britain	USA (United States)	20 Jan 54	196UNTS95	102619
Mexico	UK Great Britain	20 Mar 54	331UNTS21	104750
United Nations	Thailand	26 May 54	260UNTS35	103703
Italy	UK Great Britain	01 Jun 54	403UNTS275	105798
NATO (North Atlan)	USA (United States)	22 Oct 54	249UNTS175	103507
Mexico	ILO (Labor Org)	05 Jan 55	208UNTS225	102815
France	Sweden	05 Mar 55	427UNTS133	106150
WMO (Meteorology)	Switzerland	10 Mar 55	211UNTS277	200524
CERN (Nuc Resrch)	Switzerland	11 Jun 55	249UNTS405	200544
Denmark	WHO (World Health)	29 Jun 55	247UNTS168	103467
USA (United States)	Uruguay	23 Mar 56	376UNTS311	105386
Ceylon (Sri Lanka)	USA (United States)	28 Apr 56	274UNTS35	103956
Paraguay	USA (United States)	11 May 56	269UNTS33	103870
USA (United States)	Yugoslavia	21 May 56	281UNTS93	104072
Germany, West	UK Great Britain	30 Jul 56	330UNTS233	104748
United Nations	Venezuela	18 Nov 56	588UNTS243	108529
Mexico	ICAO (Civil Aviat)	20 Dec 56	497UNTS3	107259
Czechoslovakia	Germany, East	24 May 57	292UNTS327	104279
Argentina	USA (United States)	03 Jun 57	291UNTS61	104244
Ghana	USA (United States)	03 Jun 57	284UNTS63	104129
Germany, East	Hungary	03 Jul 57	407UNTS186	105865
Romania	USSR (Soviet Union)	04 Sep 57	318UNTS55	104609
Albania	USSR (Soviet Union)	18 Sep 57	307UNTS265	104455
Czechoslovakia	USSR (Soviet Union)	05 Oct 57	320UNTS129	104641
Ecuador	USA (United States)	06 Nov 57	307UNTS49	104441
Austria	IAEA (Atom Energy)	11 Dec 57	339UNTS110	104849
Bulgaria	USSR (Soviet Union)	12 Dec 57	302UNTS21	104352
Korea, North	USSR (Soviet Union)	16 Dec 57	292UNTS121	104270
Poland	USSR (Soviet Union)	21 Jan 58	319UNTS291	104637
Sudan	USA (United States)	31 Mar 58	308UNTS105	104458
Germany, West	USSR (Soviet Union)	25 Apr 58	338UNTS49	104832
El Salvador	USA (United States)	09 May 58	316UNTS29	104575
Ethiopia	United Nations	18 Jun 58	317UNTS101	104597
Mongolia	USSR (Soviet Union)	25 Aug 58	322UNTS215	104659
Iraq	USSR (Soviet Union)	11 Oct 58	328UNTS117	104731
Poland	Yugoslavia	17 Nov 58	432UNTS267	106225
Germany, West	Norway	18 Nov 58	357UNTS205	105119
Albania	Czechoslovakia	16 Jan 59	363UNTS165	105207
Austria	USSR (Soviet Union)	28 Feb 59	356UNTS39	105091
Hungary	Romania	18 Mar 59	417UNTS3	106005
Czechoslovakia	Hungary	27 Mar 59	351UNTS57	105017
Hungary	Poland	20 May 59	432UNTS115	106217
Bulgaria	Czechoslovakia	27 May 59	360UNTS335	105167
USSR (Soviet Union)	Vietnam, North	05 Jun 59	356UNTS111	105093
China People's Rep	USSR (Soviet Union)	23 Jun 59	356UNTS83	105092
Multilateral		01 Jul 59	374UNTS147	105334
Multilateral		26 Jan 60	439UNTS249	106333
Czechoslovakia	Poland	17 May 60	424UNTS3	106096
Czechoslovakia	Romania	21 May 60	397UNTS245	105709
Austria	UK Great Britain	24 Jun 60	502UNTS79	107327
Multilateral		28 Jul 60	394UNTS37	105667
Multilateral		13 Dec 60	523UNTS117	107557
Togo	USA (United States)	22 Dec 60	401UNTS33	105760
Peru	USA (United States)	13 Feb 61	406UNTS177	105848
Belgium	UK Great Britain	08 Mar 61	523UNTS17	107554
Indonesia	USA (United States)	31 Mar 61	405UNTS119	105828
Honduras	USA (United States)	12 Apr 61	413UNTS182	105952

PARTY ONE	PARTY TWO	DATE	CITATION	NUMBER
Diplomatic privileges (Cont.)				
Multilateral		18 Apr 61	500UNTS95	107310
Sierra Leone	USA (United States)	05 May 61	409UNTS194	105885
Ivory Coast	USA (United States)	17 May 61	409UNTS241	105889
Cameroon	USA (United States)	26 May 61	413UNTS195	105953
Niger	USA (United States)	26 May 61	410UNTS213	105905
Dahomey	USA (United States)	27 May 61	445UNTS23	106373
Spain	UK Great Britain	30 May 61	562UNTS169	108198
Tanganyika	USA (United States)	21 Jul 61	445UNTS33	106374
Bulgaria	Poland	19 Sep 61	483UNTS249	107018
Paraguay	USA (United States)	26 Sep 61	461UNTS91	106653
El Salvador	USA (United States)	20 Nov 61	433UNTS221	106245
Congo (Zaire)	United Nations	27 Nov 61	414UNTS229	105975
Thailand	USA (United States)	28 Nov 61	434UNTS77	106256
Panama	USA (United States)	11 Dec 61	445UNTS161	106384
El Salvador	USA (United States)	19 Dec 61	445UNTS175	106385
Iran	USA (United States)	21 Dec 61	433UNTS269	106249
Costa Rica	USA (United States)	22 Dec 61	460UNTS277	106646
Sierra Leone	USA (United States)	29 Dec 61	434UNTS43	106254
Dominican Republic	USA (United States)	11 Jan 62	433UNTS133	106236
Peru	USA (United States)	25 Jan 62	473UNTS57	106855
UK Great Britain	USA (United States)	22 Feb 62	435UNTS127	106275
Liberia	USA (United States)	08 Mar 62	445UNTS41	106375
United Nations	Saudi Arabia	16 Mar 62	456UNTS379	106566
Nicaragua	USA (United States)	30 Mar 62	456UNTS241	106559
Ecuador	USA (United States)	17 Apr 62	442UNTS69	106339
Somalia	USA (United States)	17 Apr 62	436UNTS107	106291
Ivory Coast	USA (United States)	21 Apr 62	526UNTS39	107598
Dominican Republic	USA (United States)	02 May 62	442UNTS107	106342
Ethiopia	USA (United States)	23 May 62	456UNTS293	106563
United Nations	Tanganyika	01 Jun 62	479UNTS3	106944
Bolivia	USA (United States)	19 Jun 62	458UNTS239	106606
Denmark	UK Great Britain	27 Jun 62	562UNTS75	108197
Honduras	USA (United States)	20 Jul 62	460UNTS125	106635
Niger	USA (United States)	23 Jul 62	487UNTS325	107114
Colombia	USA (United States)	23 Jul 62	458UNTS123	106595
Ecuador	USA (United States)	03 Aug 62	460UNTS133	106636
Cyprus	USA (United States)	23 Aug 62	461UNTS147	106658
Togo	USA (United States)	05 Sep 62	461UNTS47	106650
Afghanistan	USA (United States)	11 Sep 62	461UNTS169	106661
Gabon	USA (United States)	04 Oct 62	459UNTS185	106620
Poland	Romania	05 Oct 62	521UNTS3	107516
Multilateral		25 Oct 62	457UNTS129	106582
Multilateral		25 Oct 62	457UNTS137	106583
Romania	Yugoslavia	08 Nov 62	472UNTS305	106845
United Nations	Syria	17 Nov 62	456UNTS359	106565
Ceylon (Sri Lanka)	USA (United States)	21 Nov 62	462UNTS237	106683
India	USA (United States)	21 Nov 62	462UNTS255	106685
Costa Rica	USA (United States)	23 Nov 62	541UNTS67	107861
Niger	UNICEF (Children)	05 Dec 62	503UNTS195	107344
Guinea	USA (United States)	14 Dec 62	462UNTS247	106684
Guatemala	USA (United States)	29 Dec 62	474UNTS31	106869
Korea, South	USA (United States)	08 Jan 63	493UNTS105	107211
Czechoslovakia	Vietnam, North	14 Jan 63	501UNTS181	107318
Senegal	USA (United States)	17 Jan 63	493UNTS97	107210
Central Afri Rep	USA (United States)	10 Feb 63	473UNTS83	106857
Japan	USA (United States)	22 Mar 63	518UNTS179	107495
Multilateral		24 Apr 63	596UNTS261	108638
United Nations	Trinidad/Tobago	06 May 63	463UNTS109	106696
Mali	United Nations	09 May 63	463UNTS147	106699
Jamaica	United Nations	22 May 63	479UNTS19	106945
United Nations	Uganda	29 May 63	466UNTS311	106751
Czechoslovakia	Yugoslavia	24 Jun 63	496UNTS3	107246
United Nations	UK Great Britain	27 Jun 63	469UNTS145	106789
Hungary	Mongolia	10 Jul 63	519UNTS173	107508
Italy	United Nations	26 Jul 63	472UNTS173	106840

PARTY ONE	PARTY TWO	DATE	CITATION	NUMBER
Diplomatic privileges (Cont.)				
Dominican Republic	United Nations	05 Aug 63	472UNTS353	106847
United Nations	United Arab Rep	27 Aug 63	474UNTS221	106884
Jamaica	USA (United States)	24 Oct 63	489UNTS337	107148
Panama	USA (United States)	30 Oct 63	530UNTS3	107668
Czechoslovakia	Mongolia	08 Nov 63	503UNTS125	107341
United Nations	Sierra Leone	19 Feb 64	489UNTS91	107136
United Nations	Upper Volta	26 Feb 64	489UNTS179	107139
Morocco	United Nations	03 Mar 64	490UNTS187	107154
Cyprus	United Nations	31 Mar 64	492UNTS57	107187
Netherlands	United Nations	27 May 64	548UNTS79	107971
USA (United States)	USSR (Soviet Union)	01 Jun 64	0UNTS0	109383
Malaysia	UNICEF (Children)	01 Jul 64	503UNTS229	107346
Iceland	UN Special Fund	10 Jul 64	502UNTS343	107337
UN Special Fund	Zambia	15 Dec 64	522UNTS3	107532
Ethiopia	WHO (World Health)	27 Jan 65	541UNTS135	107866
WHO (World Health)	Tunisia	27 Jan 65	528UNTS209	107644
Belgium	Congo (Zaire)	06 Feb 65	540UNTS275	107853
Multilateral		23 Feb 65	527UNTS120	107622
Multilateral		05 Mar 65	527UNTS221	107627
Multilateral		08 Apr 65	533UNTS66	107733
Malawi	USA (United States)	20 Apr 65	546UNTS175	107943
UK Great Britain	Yugoslavia	21 Apr 65	595UNTS189	108620
Malta	UNICEF (Children)	22 Apr 65	533UNTS107	107737
Multilateral		26 Apr 65	533UNTS50	107732
Multilateral		12 May 65	534UNTS390	107769
Multilateral		14 May 65	550UNTS310	108026
Multilateral		25 May 65	535UNTS374	107791
Gambia	UNICEF (Children)	29 May 65	547UNTS29	107954
Austria	Petrol Export Org	24 Jun 65	589UNTS135	108540
Multilateral		20 Jul 65	541UNTS12	107857
Multilateral		13 Sep 65	547UNTS248	107961
Multilateral		21 Sep 65	547UNTS280	107963
Multilateral		12 Nov 65	550UNTS160	108013
Chile	UNICEF (Children)	30 Nov 65	596UNTS215	108635
Multilateral		04 Dec 65	571UNTS123	108303
Hungary	United Nations	04 Mar 66	559UNTS3	108151
Denmark	Italy	10 Mar 66	643UNTS349	109201
Italy	United Nations	23 May 66	565UNTS11	108231
United Nations	Tunisia	04 Aug 66	576UNTS23	108363
Multilateral		23 Sep 66	573UNTS132	108327
Israel	Norway	02 Nov 66	630UNTS225	108972
Indonesia	UNICEF (Children)	17 Nov 66	578UNTS47	108386
Greece	United Nations	14 Apr 67	595UNTS83	108613
South Africa	UK Great Britain	15 Nov 67	616UNTS277	108902
Dual citizenship				
Burma	UK Great Britain	17 Oct 47	70UNTS183	100904
Greece	Lebanon	06 Oct 48	87UNTS351	101179
USSR (Soviet Union)	Yugoslavia	22 May 56	259UNTS155	103688
Hungary	USSR (Soviet Union)	24 Aug 57	318UNTS35	104608
Romania	USSR (Soviet Union)	04 Sep 57	318UNTS89	104610
Albania	USSR (Soviet Union)	18 Sep 57	307UNTS251	104454
Czechoslovakia	USSR (Soviet Union)	05 Oct 57	320UNTS111	104640
Bulgaria	USSR (Soviet Union)	12 Dec 57	302UNTS3	104351
Korea, North	USSR (Soviet Union)	16 Dec 57	292UNTS107	104269
Poland	USSR (Soviet Union)	21 Jan 58	319UNTS277	104636
Czechoslovakia	Hungary	27 Jun 58	477UNTS321	106927
Mongolia	USSR (Soviet Union)	25 Aug 58	322UNTS201	104658
Bulgaria	Romania	21 Sep 59	387UNTS61	105558
Czechoslovakia	Hungary	04 Nov 60	397UNTS227	105708
Hungary	Poland	05 Jul 61	437UNTS3	106296
Hungary	USSR (Soviet Union)	21 Jan 63	577UNTS201	108378
Poland	USSR (Soviet Union)	31 Mar 65	571UNTS217	108304
Czechoslovakia	Poland	17 May 65	572UNTS181	108312
Bulgaria	USSR (Soviet Union)	06 Jul 66	596UNTS177	108632

PARTY ONE	PARTY TWO	DATE	CITATION	NUMBER
Consular relations establishment				
Greece	Iran	09 Jan 31	166UNTS323	200496
Canada	France	12 May 33	253UNTS285	200545
Taiwan	Dominican Republic	11 May 40	10UNTS285	200067
Finland	USSR (Soviet Union)	11 Oct 40	67UNTS139	100872
Mexico	USA (United States)	12 Aug 42	125UNTS301	200431
Taiwan	Cuba	12 Nov 42	10UNTS243	200065
Taiwan	Costa Rica	05 May 44	14UNTS427	200098
Taiwan	Mexico	01 Aug 44	14UNTS441	200099
Taiwan	Ecuador	06 Jan 46	7UNTS233	100102
Taiwan	Thailand	23 Jan 46	161UNTS127	102126
Philippines	USA (United States)	04 Jul 46	7UNTS3	100088
Taiwan	Saudi Arabia	15 Nov 46	18UNTS197	100289
Argentina	Taiwan	10 Feb 47	486UNTS143	107077
Philippines	USA (United States)	14 Mar 47	45UNTS23	100690
Taiwan	Philippines	18 Apr 47	11UNTS361	100175
Nepal	USA (United States)	25 Apr 47	16UNTS97	100251
Italy	Philippines	09 Jul 47	44UNTS3	100674
Costa Rica	USA (United States)	12 Jan 48	70UNTS27	100896
Philippines	Spain	20 May 48	70UNTS143	100903
India	Switzerland	14 Aug 48	33UNTS3	100509
Philippines	Thailand	14 Jun 49	81UNTS53	101062
Afghanistan	India	04 Jan 50	81UNTS75	101064
Iran	Pakistan	18 Feb 50	161UNTS23	102119
Iraq	Pakistan	26 Feb 50	214UNTS3	102896
India	Iran	15 Mar 50	161UNTS15	102118
Ireland	USA (United States)	01 May 50	222UNTS107	103026
India	Nepal	31 Jul 50	94UNTS3	101302
Greece	Philippines	28 Aug 50	225UNTS155	103097
Pakistan	Syria	29 Aug 50	109UNTS95	101494
Iran	Italy	24 Sep 50	281UNTS157	104077
India	Indonesia	03 Mar 51	167UNTS3	102197
UK Great Britain	USA (United States)	06 Jun 51	165UNTS121	102174
Pakistan	United Arab Rep	28 Aug 51	214UNTS247	102902
Ethiopia	USA (United States)	07 Sep 51	206UNTS41	102785
Australia	Netherlands	25 Sep 51	128UNTS63	101713
India	Turkey	14 Dec 51	137UNTS15	101845
France	UK Great Britain	31 Dec 51	330UNTS145	104744
India	Syria	25 Feb 52	163UNTS55	102141
Sweden	UK Great Britain	14 Mar 52	202UNTS157	102731
Italy	Jordan	24 Apr 52	281UNTS167	104078
Burma	Pakistan	25 Jun 52	173UNTS41	102259
India	Philippines	11 Jul 52	203UNTS73	102741
Dominican Republic	Philippines	02 Nov 52	543UNTS175	107901
India	Iraq	10 Nov 52	172UNTS103	102242
India	Muscat and Oman	15 Mar 53	190UNTS69	102559
Greece	UK Great Britain	17 Apr 53	191UNTS151	102582
Indonesia	Thailand	03 Mar 54	213UNTS297	102893
Mexico	UK Great Britain	20 Mar 54	331UNTS21	104750
Italy	UK Great Britain	01 Jun 54	403UNTS275	105798
Taiwan	El Salvador	09 Dec 54	214UNTS217	102900
France	Sweden	05 Mar 55	427UNTS133	106150
China People's Rep	Sweden	24 Jun 55	228UNTS153	103148
Iran	USA (United States)	15 Aug 55	284UNTS93	104132
Germany, West	UK Great Britain	30 Jul 56	330UNTS233	104748
Philippines	Switzerland	30 Aug 56	293UNTS43	104284
Burma	Thailand	15 Oct 56	277UNTS87	104000
Japan	USSR (Soviet Union)	19 Oct 56	263UNTS99	103768
Japan	Norway	28 Feb 57	280UNTS87	104054
Germany, East	USSR (Soviet Union)	10 May 57	285UNTS135	104151
Czechoslovakia	Germany, East	24 May 57	292UNTS327	104279
Denmark	Peru	10 Jun 57	406UNTS63	105839
Germany, East	Hungary	03 Jul 57	407UNTS186	105865
Hungary	USSR (Soviet Union)	24 Aug 57	318UNTS3	104607
Romania	USSR (Soviet Union)	04 Sep 57	318UNTS55	104609

PARTY ONE	PARTY TWO	DATE	CITATION	NUMBER
Consular relations establishment (Cont.)				
Albania	USSR (Soviet Union)	18 Sep 57	307UNTS265	104455
Czechoslovakia	USSR (Soviet Union)	05 Oct 57	320UNTS129	104641
Taiwan	Jordan	19 Nov 57	308UNTS227	104463
Germany, East	Poland	25 Nov 57	340UNTS99	104862
Bulgaria	USSR (Soviet Union)	12 Dec 57	302UNTS21	104352
Korea, North	USSR (Soviet Union)	16 Dec 57	292UNTS121	104270
Poland	USSR (Soviet Union)	21 Jan 58	319UNTS291	104637
Israel	Philippines	26 Feb 58	507UNTS135	107398
Germany, West	USSR (Soviet Union)	25 Apr 58	338UNTS49	104832
Bulgaria	Hungary	27 Jun 58	438UNTS235	106318
Mongolia	USSR (Soviet Union)	25 Aug 58	322UNTS215	104659
Pakistan	Thailand	28 Aug 58	394UNTS53	105668
Poland	Yugoslavia	17 Nov 58	432UNTS267	106225
Muscat and Oman	USA (United States)	20 Dec 58	380UNTS181	105457
Albania	Czechoslovakia	16 Jan 59	363UNTS165	105207
Austria	USSR (Soviet Union)	28 Feb 59	356UNTS39	105091
Japan	Yugoslavia	28 Feb 59	341UNTS179	104883
Hungary	Romania	18 Mar 59	417UNTS3	106005
Czechoslovakia	Hungary	27 Mar 59	351UNTS57	105017
Israel	Liberia	09 Apr 59	448UNTS95	106427
Indonesia	Malaysia	17 Apr 59	470UNTS273	106813
Bulgaria	Romania	23 Apr 59	387UNTS81	105559
Hungary	Poland	20 May 59	432UNTS115	106217
Bulgaria	Czechoslovakia	27 May 59	360UNTS335	105167
USSR (Soviet Union)	Vietnam, North	05 Jun 59	356UNTS111	105093
China People's Rep	USSR (Soviet Union)	23 Jun 59	356UNTS83	105092
Argentina	Philippines	12 Feb 60	535UNTS293	107785
China People's Rep	Czechoslovakia	07 May 60	402UNTS209	105787
Czechoslovakia	Poland	17 May 60	424UNTS3	106096
Czechoslovakia	Romania	21 May 60	397UNTS245	105709
Austria	UK Great Britain	24 Jun 60	502UNTS79	107327
Belgium	UK Great Britain	08 Mar 61	523UNTS17	107554
Multilateral		18 Apr 61	500UNTS95	107310
Spain	UK Great Britain	30 May 61	562UNTS169	108198
Israel	Malagasy	27 Aug 61	484UNTS217	107032
Bulgaria	Poland	19 Sep 61	483UNTS249	107018
Taiwan	Malagasy	04 Apr 62	463UNTS195	106703
Gabon	Israel	15 May 62	484UNTS181	107027
Denmark	UK Great Britain	27 Jun 62	562UNTS75	108197
Poland	Romania	05 Oct 62	521UNTS3	107516
Romania	Yugoslavia	08 Nov 62	472UNTS305	106845
Korea, South	USA (United States)	08 Jan 63	493UNTS105	107211
Czechoslovakia	Vietnam, North	14 Jan 63	501UNTS181	107318
Japan	USA (United States)	22 Mar 63	518UNTS179	107495
Multilateral		24 Apr 63	596UNTS261	108638
Czechoslovakia	Yugoslavia	24 Jun 63	496UNTS3	107246
Hungary	Mongolia	10 Jul 63	519UNTS173	107508
Czechoslovakia	Mongolia	08 Nov 63	503UNTS125	107341
Japan	UK Great Britain	04 May 64	561UNTS25	108179
USA (United States)	USSR (Soviet Union)	01 Jun 64	0UNTS0	109383
Mongolia	Poland	28 Oct 64	552UNTS115	108052
Taiwan	Korea, South	27 Nov 64	555UNTS3	108102
UK Great Britain	Yugoslavia	21 Apr 65	595UNTS189	108620
UK Great Britain	USSR (Soviet Union)	02 Dec 65	0UNTS0	109384
India	Pakistan	10 Jan 66	560UNTS39	108166
Finland	USSR (Soviet Union)	24 Jan 66	576UNTS35	108364
Philippines	United Nations	05 Apr 66	560UNTS191	108174
Japan	USSR (Soviet Union)	29 Jul 66	608UNTS93	108815
Romania	Spain	05 Jan 67	642UNTS103	109168
Iran	Thailand	02 Feb 67	614UNTS251	108874
Sweden	USSR (Soviet Union)	30 Nov 67	0UNTS0	109385
Diplomatic relations establishment				
Greece	Iran	09 Jan 31	166UNTS323	200496
Afghanistan	Netherlands	26 Jul 39	32UNTS381	200177

PARTY ONE	PARTY TWO	DATE	CITATION	NUMBER
Diplomatic relations establishment (Cont.)				
Taiwan	Dominican Republic	11 May 40	10UNTS285	200067
Afghanistan	Sweden	22 Oct 40	191UNTS349	200516
Taiwan	Iraq	16 Mar 42	14UNTS335	200091
Taiwan	Cuba	12 Nov 42	10UNTS243	200065
Taiwan	Mexico	01 Aug 44	14UNTS441	200099
Ethiopia	UK Great Britain	19 Dec 44	93UNTS303	200272
United Arab Rep	Yemen	27 Sep 45	9UNTS373	200053
Taiwan	Ecuador	06 Jan 46	7UNTS233	100102
Taiwan	Thailand	23 Jan 46	161UNTS127	102126
USA (United States)	Yemen	04 May 46	4UNTS165	100043
Philippines	USA (United States)	04 Jul 46	6UNTS335	100086
Philippines	USA (United States)	04 Jul 46	7UNTS3	100088
Taiwan	Saudi Arabia	15 Nov 46	18UNTS197	100289
Jordan	Turkey	11 Jan 47	14UNTS49	100210
Argentina	Taiwan	10 Feb 47	486UNTS143	107077
Taiwan	Philippines	18 Apr 47	11UNTS361	100175
Nepal	USA (United States)	25 Apr 47	16UNTS97	100251
Italy	Philippines	09 Jul 47	44UNTS3	100674
Burma	UK Great Britain	17 Oct 47	70UNTS183	100904
India	Switzerland	14 Aug 48	33UNTS3	100509
Philippines	Thailand	14 Jun 49	81UNTS53	101062
Multilateral		24 Sep 49	126UNTS237	101691
Afghanistan	India	04 Jan 50	81UNTS75	101064
Iran	Pakistan	18 Feb 50	161UNTS23	102119
Iraq	Pakistan	26 Feb 50	214UNTS3	102896
India	Iran	15 Mar 50	161UNTS15	102118
India	Nepal	31 Jul 50	94UNTS3	101302
Greece	Philippines	28 Aug 50	225UNTS155	103097
Pakistan	Syria	29 Aug 50	109UNTS95	101494
Iran	Italy	24 Sep 50	281UNTS157	104077
Nepal	UK Great Britain	30 Oct 50	97UNTS121	101346
UK Great Britain	Yemen	20 Jan 51	101UNTS39	101400
India	Indonesia	03 Mar 51	167UNTS3	102197
Pakistan	United Arab Rep	28 Aug 51	214UNTS247	102902
Ethiopia	USA (United States)	07 Sep 51	206UNTS41	102785
India	Turkey	14 Dec 51	137UNTS15	101845
India	Syria	25 Feb 52	163UNTS55	102141
Denmark	Japan	29 Feb 52	126UNTS139	101686
Italy	Jordan	24 Apr 52	281UNTS167	104078
Burma	Pakistan	25 Jun 52	173UNTS41	102259
India	Philippines	11 Jul 52	203UNTS73	102741
Dominican Republic	Philippines	02 Nov 52	543UNTS175	107901
India	Iraq	10 Nov 52	172UNTS103	102242
Indonesia	Thailand	03 Mar 54	213UNTS297	102893
Taiwan	El Salvador	09 Dec 54	214UNTS217	102900
USSR (Soviet Union)	Yemen	31 Oct 55	240UNTS317	103410
Philippines	Switzerland	30 Aug 56	293UNTS43	104284
Burma	Thailand	15 Oct 56	277UNTS87	104000
Japan	USSR (Soviet Union)	19 Oct 56	263UNTS99	103768
Japan	Poland	08 Feb 57	318UNTS251	104620
Czechoslovakia	Japan	13 Feb 57	300UNTS119	104335
Taiwan	Jordan	19 Nov 57	308UNTS227	104463
Israel	Philippines	26 Feb 58	507UNTS135	107398
Pakistan	Thailand	28 Aug 58	394UNTS53	105668
Israel	Liberia	09 Apr 59	448UNTS95	106427
Indonesia	Malaysia	17 Apr 59	470UNTS273	106813
Argentina	Philippines	12 Feb 60	535UNTS293	107785
Cuba	Korea, North	29 Aug 60	469UNTS163	106790
Multilateral		18 Apr 61	500UNTS95	107310
Israel	Malagasy	27 Aug 61	484UNTS217	107032
Gabon	Israel	15 May 62	484UNTS181	107027
Iraq	Kuwait	04 Oct 63	485UNTS321	107063
Taiwan	Korea, South	27 Nov 64	555UNTS3	108102
Gambia	UN Special Fund	09 Jun 65	538UNTS321	200612
Japan	Korea, South	22 Jun 65	583UNTS33	108471

PARTY ONE	PARTY TWO	DATE	CITATION	NUMBER
Diplomatic relations establishment (Cont.)				
India	Pakistan	10 Jan 66	560UNTS39	108166
Iran	Thailand	02 Feb 67	614UNTS251	108874
Diplomatic relations resumption				
Taiwan	Costa Rica	05 May 44	14UNTS427	200098
Chile	USA (United States)	16 Jan 51	147UNTS11	101925
Burma	India	07 Jul 51	149UNTS35	101949
Denmark	Japan	29 Feb 52	126UNTS139	101686
USSR (Soviet Union)	Vietnam, North	05 Jun 59	356UNTS111	105093
Japan	Korea, South	22 Jun 65	583UNTS33	108471
Diplomatic missions				
Multilateral		13 Feb 46	1UNTS15	100004
ILO (Labor Org)	Switzerland	11 Mar 46	15UNTS377	200103
USA (United States)	Yemen	04 May 46	4UNTS165	100043
United Nations	Switzerland	01 Jul 46	1UNTS163	200008
Multilateral		13 Dec 46	8UNTS105	100117
United Nations	USA (United States)	26 Jun 47	11UNTS11	100147
Philippines	Spain	27 Sep 47	70UNTS133	100902
Multilateral		21 Nov 47	33UNTS261	100521
United Nations	USA (United States)	18 Dec 47	11UNTS347	100174
Peru	ICAO (Civil Aviat)	22 Oct 48	95UNTS3	101315
WHO (World Health)	Switzerland	12 Jan 49	26UNTS331	200155
Multilateral		02 Sep 49	250UNTS12	103515
Council of Europe	France	02 Sep 49	249UNTS207	103510
Norway	UK Great Britain	22 Feb 51	326UNTS209	104713
Mexico	United Nations	20 May 51	102UNTS103	101413
Philippines	WHO (World Health)	22 Jul 51	149UNTS197	101953
France	United Nations	17 Aug 51	122UNTS191	101647
Multilateral		20 Sep 51	200UNTS3	102691
Sweden	UK Great Britain	14 Mar 52	202UNTS157	102731
France	WHO (World Health)	23 Jul 52	209UNTS231	102829
Greece	UK Great Britain	17 Apr 53	191UNTS151	102582
ICAO (Civil Aviat)	United Arab Rep	27 Aug 53	215UNTS371	102925
United Nations	Thailand	26 May 54	260UNTS35	103703
France	UNESCO (Educ/Cult)	02 Jul 54	357UNTS3	105103
NATO (North Atlan)	USA (United States)	22 Oct 54	249UNTS175	103507
Mexico	ILO (Labor Org)	05 Jan 55	208UNTS225	102815
WMO (Meteorology)	Switzerland	10 Mar 55	211UNTS277	200524
Turkey	USA (United States)	10 Jun 55	238UNTS149	103359
CERN (Nuc Resrch)	Switzerland	11 Jun 55	249UNTS405	200544
Canada	USA (United States)	15 Jun 55	235UNTS176	103301
Belgium	USA (United States)	15 Jun 55	235UNTS133	103299
Lebanon	USA (United States)	18 Jul 55	239UNTS247	103383
Netherlands	USA (United States)	18 Jul 55	240UNTS347	103412
Taiwan	USA (United States)	18 Jul 55	235UNTS221	103304
Colombia	USA (United States)	19 Jul 55	235UNTS233	103305
Spain	USA (United States)	19 Jul 55	239UNTS299	103387
USA (United States)	Venezuela	21 Jul 55	238UNTS121	103357
Portugal	USA (United States)	21 Jul 55	239UNTS283	103386
Denmark	USA (United States)	25 Jul 55	235UNTS245	103306
Philippines	USA (United States)	27 Jul 55	239UNTS271	103385
Italy	USA (United States)	28 Jul 55	239UNTS235	103382
Brazil	USA (United States)	03 Aug 55	235UNTS159	103300
Greece	USA (United States)	04 Aug 55	235UNTS257	103307
Chile	USA (United States)	08 Aug 55	235UNTS209	103303
Pakistan	USA (United States)	11 Aug 55	239UNTS259	103384
Japan	USA (United States)	14 Nov 55	240UNTS361	103413
USA (United States)	Uruguay	13 Jan 56	240UNTS401	103415
Sweden	USA (United States)	18 Jan 56	240UNTS413	103416
Peru	USA (United States)	25 Jan 56	240UNTS425	103417
Korea, South	USA (United States)	03 Feb 56	240UNTS129	103401
Thailand	USA (United States)	13 Mar 56	253UNTS105	103579
Austria	USA (United States)	08 Jun 56	253UNTS139	103581
New Zealand	USA (United States)	13 Jun 56	253UNTS155	103582
Dominican Republic	USA (United States)	15 Jun 56	265UNTS227	103815

PARTY ONE	PARTY TWO	DATE	CITATION	NUMBER
Diplomatic missions (Cont.)				
France	USA (United States)	19 Jun 56	281UNTS341	104087
Switzerland	USA (United States)	21 Jun 56	279UNTS41	104033
United Nations	Venezuela	18 Nov 56	588UNTS243	108529
Mexico	ICAO (Civil Aviat)	20 Dec 56	497UNTS3	107259
Lebanon	United Nations	13 Jun 58	303UNTS271	104386
Ethiopia	United Nations	18 Jun 58	317UNTS101	104597
Bulgaria	Hungary	27 Jun 58	438UNTS235	106318
Nepal	United Nations	18 Aug 58	508UNTS3	107403
Jordan	United Nations	18 Nov 58	315UNTS125	104564
Mexico	United Nations	07 Apr 59	381UNTS123	105468
United Nations	Vietnam, South	03 Jun 59	337UNTS361	200557
Panama	United Nations	24 Jun 59	507UNTS245	107402
Multilateral		01 Jul 59	374UNTS147	105334
Multilateral		18 Nov 59	390UNTS227	105610
Multilateral		14 Dec 59	368UNTS237	105244
Romania	United Nations	29 May 61	406UNTS147	105845
Congo (Zaire)	United Nations	27 Nov 61	414UNTS229	105975
United Nations	Saudi Arabia	16 Mar 62	456UNTS379	106566
United Nations	Tanganyika	01 Jun 62	479UNTS3	106944
Germany, West	United Nations	28 Jun 62	434UNTS249	200597
United Nations	Syria	17 Nov 62	456UNTS359	106565
Multilateral		24 Apr 63	596UNTS261	108638
UN Special Fund	Trinidad/Tobago	06 May 63	463UNTS93	106695
United Nations	Trinidad/Tobago	06 May 63	463UNTS109	106696
Mali	United Nations	09 May 63	463UNTS147	106699
Jamaica	United Nations	22 May 63	479UNTS19	106945
United Nations	Uganda	29 May 63	466UNTS311	106751
Hungary	Mongolia	10 Jul 63	519UNTS173	107508
Poland	United Nations	16 Jul 63	471UNTS3	106817
Italy	United Nations	26 Jul 63	472UNTS173	106840
Dominican Republic	United Nations	05 Aug 63	472UNTS353	106847
United Nations	United Arab Rep	27 Aug 63	474UNTS221	106884
WHO (World Health)	Somalia	08 Nov 63	493UNTS243	107218
WHO (World Health)	Sierra Leone	22 Nov 63	493UNTS255	107219
Brazil	Germany, West	30 Nov 63	0UNTS0	109423
Nicaragua	United Nations	03 Dec 63	482UNTS329	107002
United Nations	Sierra Leone	19 Feb 64	489UNTS91	107136
United Nations	Upper Volta	26 Feb 64	489UNTS179	107139
Morocco	United Nations	03 Mar 64	490UNTS187	107154
Cyprus	United Nations	31 Mar 64	492UNTS57	107187
Taiwan	UNICEF (Children)	08 Apr 64	500UNTS49	107306
Jamaica	UNICEF (Children)	19 May 64	500UNTS75	107308
USA (United States)	USSR (Soviet Union)	01 Jun 64	0UNTS0	109383
Austria	United Nations	11 Jun 64	500UNTS85	107309
Iceland	UN Special Fund	10 Jul 64	502UNTS343	107337
Mexico	United Nations	17 Jul 64	533UNTS117	107738
France	Eur Space Research	10 Aug 64	528UNTS135	107637
Philippines	United Nations	15 Sep 64	510UNTS137	107410
Algeria	United Nations	23 Sep 64	510UNTS217	107416
Kenya	United Nations	01 Oct 64	511UNTS199	107434
Kenya	UN Special Fund	01 Oct 64	511UNTS181	107433
Romania	UN Special Fund	24 Oct 64	519UNTS29	107500
Malawi	UN Special Fund	24 Oct 64	514UNTS235	200609
Multilateral		11 Dec 64	547UNTS297	107964
UN Special Fund	Zambia	15 Dec 64	522UNTS3	107532
WHO (World Health)	Tunisia	27 Jan 65	528UNTS209	107644
Ethiopia	WHO (World Health)	27 Jan 65	541UNTS135	107866
Multilateral		23 Feb 65	527UNTS120	107622
Multilateral		05 Mar 65	527UNTS221	107627
Multilateral		08 Apr 65	533UNTS66	107733
UK Great Britain	Yugoslavia	21 Apr 65	595UNTS189	108620
Multilateral		26 Apr 65	533UNTS50	107732
Multilateral		12 May 65	534UNTS390	107769
Multilateral		14 May 65	550UNTS310	108026
Multilateral		25 May 65	535UNTS374	107791

PARTY ONE	PARTY TWO	DATE	CITATION	NUMBER
Diplomatic missions (Cont.)				
Multilateral		20 Jul 65	541UNTS12	107857
Multilateral		13 Sep 65	547UNTS248	107961
Multilateral		21 Sep 65	547UNTS280	107963
Multilateral		12 Nov 65	550UNTS160	108013
UK Great Britain	USSR (Soviet Union)	02 Dec 65	0UNTS0	109384
Monaco	United Nations	17 Dec 65	550UNTS365	200615
Hungary	United Nations	04 Mar 66	559UNTS3	108151
Italy	United Nations	23 May 66	565UNTS11	108231
United Nations	Tunisia	04 Aug 66	576UNTS23	108363
Multilateral		23 Sep 66	573UNTS132	108327
Multilateral		25 Jan 67	588UNTS212	108527
Australia	UN Special Fund	06 Feb 67	590UNTS3	108543
Poland	United Nations	20 Feb 67	590UNTS71	108547
Algeria	ILO (Labor Org)	06 Apr 67	595UNTS99	108614
Ghana	United Nations	08 Apr 67	594UNTS149	108601
Multilateral		13 Apr 67	595UNTS60	108612
Greece	United Nations	14 Apr 67	595UNTS83	108613
Cameroon	ILO (Labor Org)	07 May 67	596UNTS209	108634
Sweden	USSR (Soviet Union)	30 Nov 67	0UNTS0	109385
Human rights				
Multilateral		30 Jul 40	161UNTS253	200488
Taiwan	Costa Rica	05 May 44	14UNTS427	200098
Multilateral		20 Jan 45	140UNTS397	200471
Multilateral		13 Dec 46	8UNTS119	100118
Multilateral		13 Dec 46	8UNTS71	100115
Multilateral		13 Dec 46	8UNTS135	100119
Multilateral		10 Feb 47	41UNTS135	100644
Multilateral		10 Feb 47	48UNTS203	100746
Multilateral		10 Feb 47	41UNTS21	100643
Multilateral		12 Aug 49	75UNTS31	100970
Multilateral		12 Aug 49	75UNTS85	100971
Indonesia	Netherlands	02 Nov 49	69UNTS3	100894
UNICEF (Children)	UK Great Britain	10 Feb 50	65UNTS86	100837
Multilateral		21 Mar 50	96UNTS271	101342
India	Pakistan	08 Apr 50	131UNTS3	101733
Multilateral		04 Nov 50	213UNTS221	102889
Multilateral		02 Jul 51	189UNTS137	102545
Israel	USA (United States)	23 Aug 51	219UNTS237	102979
Ethiopia	USA (United States)	07 Sep 51	206UNTS41	102785
Denmark	USA (United States)	01 Oct 51	421UNTS105	106056
Multilateral		31 Mar 53	193UNTS136	102613
Multilateral		28 Sep 54	360UNTS117	105158
Multilateral		15 May 55	217UNTS223	102949
Iran	USA (United States)	15 Aug 55	284UNTS93	104132
Netherlands	USA (United States)	27 Mar 56	285UNTS231	104154
Multilateral		07 Sep 56	266UNTS3	103822
Multilateral		25 Jun 57	320UNTS291	104648
Multilateral		26 Jun 57	328UNTS247	104738
Multilateral		25 Jun 58	362UNTS31	105181
Muscat and Oman	USA (United States)	20 Dec 58	380UNTS181	105457
Hungary	Poland	06 Mar 59	432UNTS3	106216
Multilateral		16 Aug 60	382UNTS8	105476
Multilateral		14 Dec 60	429UNTS93	106193
USA (United States)	Vietnam, South	03 Apr 61	424UNTS137	106106
Romania	United Nations	29 May 61	406UNTS147	105845
Mexico	United Nations	18 Aug 61	404UNTS297	105817
Luxembourg	USA (United States)	23 Feb 62	474UNTS3	106868
Multilateral		10 Dec 62	521UNTS231	107525
Colombia	United Nations	27 Aug 63	481UNTS3	106975
Italy	United Nations	18 Mar 64	491UNTS21	107171
United Nations	Togo	03 Jul 64	502UNTS287	107334
Finland	United Nations	16 Jan 67	588UNTS153	108522

PARTY ONE	PARTY TWO	DATE	CITATION	NUMBER
Inviolability				
Mexico	USA (United States)	12 Aug 42	125UNTS301	200431
Multilateral		22 Mar 45	70UNTS237	200241
Multilateral		13 Feb 46	1UNTS15	100004
ILO (Labor Org)	Switzerland	11 Mar 46	15UNTS377	200103
Netherlands	ICJ (Int Court)	26 Jun 46	8UNTS61	100114
United Nations	Switzerland	01 Jul 46	1UNTS163	200008
Mexico	UK Great Britain	27 Sep 46	91UNTS161	101248
United Nations	USA (United States)	26 Jun 47	11UNTS11	100147
Multilateral		21 Nov 47	33UNTS261	100521
United Nations	USA (United States)	18 Dec 47	11UNTS347	100174
Costa Rica	USA (United States)	12 Jan 48	70UNTS27	100896
Philippines	Spain	20 May 48	70UNTS143	100903
Multilateral		18 Aug 48	33UNTS181	100518
UNRRA (Relief)	United Nations	27 Sep 48	27UNTS349	200158
Greece	Lebanon	06 Oct 48	87UNTS351	101179
Peru	ICAO (Civil Aviat)	22 Oct 48	95UNTS3	101315
WHO (World Health)	Switzerland	12 Jan 49	26UNTS331	200155
Multilateral		02 Sep 49	250UNTS12	103515
WHO (World Health)	United Arab Rep	25 Mar 51	223UNTS87	103058
UK Great Britain	USA (United States)	06 Jun 51	165UNTS121	102174
Saudi Arabia	USA (United States)	18 Jun 51	102UNTS73	101412
Philippines	WHO (World Health)	22 Jul 51	149UNTS197	101953
Ethiopia	USA (United States)	07 Sep 51	206UNTS41	102785
Multilateral		20 Sep 51	200UNTS3	102691
Korea, South	United Nations	21 Sep 51	104UNTS323	200322
Nicaragua	USA (United States)	12 Dec 51	167UNTS151	102205
Costa Rica	USA (United States)	25 Feb 52	174UNTS233	102288
Sweden	UK Great Britain	14 Mar 52	202UNTS157	102731
France	WHO (World Health)	23 Jul 52	209UNTS231	102829
Mexico	ICAO (Civil Aviat)	28 Nov 52	164UNTS15	102156
Greece	UK Great Britain	17 Apr 53	191UNTS151	102582
ICAO (Civil Aviat)	United Arab Rep	27 Aug 53	215UNTS371	102925
United Nations	Thailand	26 May 54	260UNTS35	103703
Italy	UK Great Britain	01 Jun 54	403UNTS275	105798
France	UNESCO (Educ/Cult)	02 Jul 54	357UNTS3	105103
Multilateral		23 Oct 54	332UNTS3	104760
Mexico	ILO (Labor Org)	05 Jan 55	208UNTS225	102815
France	Sweden	05 Mar 55	427UNTS133	106150
WMO (Meteorology)	Switzerland	10 Mar 55	211UNTS277	200524
CERN (Nuc Resrch)	Switzerland	11 Jun 55	249UNTS405	200544
Denmark	WHO (World Health)	29 Jun 55	247UNTS168	103467
Iran	USA (United States)	15 Aug 55	284UNTS93	104132
Japan	Philippines	09 May 56	285UNTS3	104148
Multilateral		13 Jul 56	281UNTS3	104066
Germany, East	USSR (Soviet Union)	10 May 57	285UNTS135	104151
Czechoslovakia	Germany, East	24 May 57	292UNTS327	104279
Hungary	USSR (Soviet Union)	24 Aug 57	318UNTS3	104607
Romania	USSR (Soviet Union)	04 Sep 57	318UNTS55	104609
Albania	USSR (Soviet Union)	18 Sep 57	307UNTS265	104455
Czechoslovakia	USSR (Soviet Union)	05 Oct 57	320UNTS129	104641
Germany, East	Poland	25 Nov 57	340UNTS99	104862
Bulgaria	USSR (Soviet Union)	12 Dec 57	302UNTS21	104352
Korea, North	USSR (Soviet Union)	16 Dec 57	292UNTS121	104270
Indonesia	Japan	20 Jan 58	324UNTS247	104689
Poland	USSR (Soviet Union)	21 Jan 58	319UNTS291	104637
Germany, West	USSR (Soviet Union)	25 Apr 58	338UNTS49	104832
Bulgaria	Hungary	27 Jun 58	438UNTS235	106318
Lebanon	USA (United States)	06 Aug 58	366UNTS361	105223
Mongolia	USSR (Soviet Union)	25 Aug 58	322UNTS215	104659
Poland	Yugoslavia	17 Nov 58	432UNTS267	106225
Albania	Czechoslovakia	16 Jan 59	363UNTS165	105207
Austria	USSR (Soviet Union)	28 Feb 59	356UNTS39	105091
Hungary	Romania	18 Mar 59	417UNTS3	106005
Czechoslovakia	Hungary	27 Mar 59	351UNTS57	105017

PARTY ONE	PARTY TWO	DATE	CITATION	NUMBER
Inviolability (Cont.)				
Bulgaria	Romania	23 Apr 59	387UNTS81	105559
Hungary	Poland	20 May 59	432UNTS115	106217
Bulgaria	Czechoslovakia	27 May 59	360UNTS335	105167
USSR (Soviet Union)	Vietnam, North	05 Jun 59	356UNTS111	105093
China People's Rep	USSR (Soviet Union)	23 Jun 59	356UNTS83	105092
Multilateral		01 Jul 59	374UNTS147	105334
Multilateral		14 Dec 59	368UNTS237	105244
China People's Rep	Czechoslovakia	07 May 60	402UNTS209	105787
Czechoslovakia	Poland	17 May 60	424UNTS3	106096
Czechoslovakia	Romania	21 May 60	397UNTS245	105709
Austria	UK Great Britain	24 Jun 60	502UNTS79	107327
Multilateral		28 Jul 60	394UNTS37	105667
Multilateral		13 Dec 60	523UNTS117	107557
Multilateral		18 Apr 61	500UNTS95	107310
Bulgaria	Poland	19 Sep 61	483UNTS249	107018
Congo (Zaire)	United Nations	27 Nov 61	414UNTS229	105975
Poland	Romania	05 Oct 62	521UNTS3	107516
Romania	Yugoslavia	08 Nov 62	472UNTS305	106845
Korea, South	USA (United States)	08 Jan 63	493UNTS105	107211
Czechoslovakia	Vietnam, North	14 Jan 63	501UNTS181	107318
Japan	USA (United States)	22 Mar 63	518UNTS179	107495
Burma	Japan	29 Mar 63	518UNTS3	107490
Multilateral		24 Apr 63	596UNTS261	108638
United Nations	Trinidad/Tobago	06 May 63	463UNTS109	106696
Czechoslovakia	Yugoslavia	24 Jun 63	496UNTS3	107246
Hungary	Mongolia	10 Jul 63	519UNTS173	107508
Czechoslovakia	Mongolia	08 Nov 63	503UNTS125	107341
Niger	United Nations	20 Nov 63	536UNTS3	107793
Netherlands	NATO (North Atlan)	25 May 64	544UNTS237	107920
UK Great Britain	Yugoslavia	21 Apr 65	595UNTS189	108620
UK Great Britain	USSR (Soviet Union)	02 Dec 65	0UNTS0	109384
Guyana	UK Great Britain	26 May 66	595UNTS255	108621
Asian Devel Bank	Philippines	22 Dec 66	615UNTS375	108887
Romania	Spain	05 Jan 67	642UNTS103	109168
Sweden	USSR (Soviet Union)	30 Nov 67	0UNTS0	109385
Missing persons				
Multilateral		01 Jul 49	96UNTS257	101341
Privileges and immunities				
Multilateral		29 Jun 33	39UNTS259	100621
Multilateral		29 Jun 33	39UNTS285	100622
Taiwan	Iraq	16 Mar 42	14UNTS335	200091
Liberia	USA (United States)	31 Mar 42	23UNTS302	200137
Mexico	USA (United States)	12 Aug 42	125UNTS301	200431
Taiwan	Cuba	12 Nov 42	10UNTS243	200065
Brazil	Taiwan	20 Aug 43	14UNTS365	200094
Multilateral		15 Jan 44	161UNTS281	200489
Mexico	USA (United States)	03 Feb 44	3UNTS313	200025
Canada	Taiwan	14 Apr 44	14UNTS408	200097
Taiwan	Costa Rica	05 May 44	14UNTS427	200098
Taiwan	Mexico	01 Aug 44	14UNTS441	200099
Hungary	Yugoslavia	13 Aug 44	113UNTS233	101553
Bolivia	USA (United States)	07 Sep 44	162UNTS315	200494
Guatemala	USA (United States)	16 Sep 44	135UNTS315	200444
Taiwan	Netherlands	29 May 45	2UNTS307	200023
United Arab Rep	Yemen	27 Sep 45	9UNTS373	200053
Dominican Republic	USA (United States)	13 Oct 45	149UNTS361	200477
Multilateral		27 Dec 45	2UNTS39	100020
Taiwan	Ecuador	06 Jan 46	7UNTS233	100102
Taiwan	Thailand	23 Jan 46	161UNTS127	102126
Multilateral		13 Feb 46	1UNTS15	100004
Brazil	USA (United States)	05 Apr 46	12UNTS131	100183
USA (United States)	Yemen	04 May 46	4UNTS165	100043
Taiwan	Denmark	20 May 46	12UNTS59	100180
United Nations	Switzerland	01 Jul 46	1UNTS163	200008

PARTY ONE	PARTY TWO	DATE	CITATION	NUMBER
Privileges and immunities (Cont.)				
Philippines	USA (United States)	04 Jul 46	7UNTS3	100088
Philippines	USA (United States)	04 Jul 46	6UNTS335	100086
Multilateral		22 Jul 46	14UNTS185	100221
Denmark	USSR (Soviet Union)	17 Aug 46	8UNTS201	100124
Jordan	Turkey	11 Jan 47	14UNTS49	100210
Argentina	Taiwan	10 Feb 47	486UNTS143	107077
Burma	USA (United States)	28 Feb 47	25UNTS27	100355
Philippines	USA (United States)	14 Mar 47	45UNTS23	100690
France	ICAO (Civil Aviat)	14 Mar 47	94UNTS59	101306
Austria	France	15 Mar 47	12UNTS109	100182
Philippines	USA (United States)	21 Mar 47	45UNTS47	100691
Taiwan	Philippines	18 Apr 47	11UNTS361	100175
Nepal	USA (United States)	25 Apr 47	16UNTS97	100251
Philippines	USA (United States)	12 May 47	16UNTS137	100254
Philippines	USA (United States)	12 May 47	16UNTS109	100252
Philippines	USA (United States)	12 May 47	16UNTS123	100253
Honduras	USA (United States)	13 May 47	166UNTS159	102189
Greece	USA (United States)	20 Jun 47	7UNTS267	100105
Austria	USA (United States)	25 Jun 47	22UNTS141	100334
USA (United States)	Venezuela	30 Jun 47	166UNTS198	102190
Italy	USA (United States)	04 Jul 47	22UNTS173	100336
Greece	USA (United States)	08 Jul 47	16UNTS157	100256
Italy	Philippines	09 Jul 47	44UNTS3	100674
Hungary	USSR (Soviet Union)	15 Jul 47	216UNTS247	102940
France	UK Great Britain	13 Aug 47	91UNTS169	101249
Poland	UNICEF (Children)	23 Aug 47	65UNTS22	100815
Sweden	Yugoslavia	06 Oct 47	53UNTS107	100775
Multilateral		11 Oct 47	77UNTS143	100998
Greece	UNICEF (Children)	14 Oct 47	102UNTS39	101409
Taiwan	USA (United States)	27 Oct 47	12UNTS11	100178
Albania	UNICEF (Children)	20 Nov 47	65UNTS163	200208
UNICEF (Children)	Yugoslavia	20 Nov 47	65UNTS28	100817
Multilateral		21 Nov 47	33UNTS261	100521
Czechoslovakia	USSR (Soviet Union)	11 Dec 47	217UNTS35	102943
Guatemala	USA (United States)	05 Jan 48	135UNTS104	101817
Costa Rica	USA (United States)	12 Jan 48	70UNTS27	100896
ICJ Option Clause	Honduras	02 Feb 48	15UNTS217	100236
France	UNICEF (Children)	19 Feb 48	68UNTS75	100885
Switzerland	USSR (Soviet Union)	17 Mar 48	217UNTS87	102945
Bulgaria	USSR (Soviet Union)	01 Apr 48	217UNTS97	102946
Multilateral		30 Apr 48	119UNTS3	101609
Denmark	USA (United States)	06 May 48	26UNTS55	100377
Philippines	Spain	20 May 48	70UNTS143	100903
Taiwan	UNICEF (Children)	21 May 48	65UNTS38	100818
Multilateral		26 Jun 48	331UNTS217	104757
Ireland	USA (United States)	28 Jun 48	24UNTS3	100349
France	USA (United States)	28 Jun 48	19UNTS9	100302
Italy	USA (United States)	28 Jun 48	20UNTS43	100314
Denmark	USA (United States)	29 Jun 48	22UNTS217	100338
Greece	USA (United States)	02 Jul 48	23UNTS43	100342
Austria	USA (United States)	02 Jul 48	21UNTS29	100323
Belgium	USA (United States)	02 Jul 48	19UNTS127	100309
Netherlands	USA (United States)	02 Jul 48	20UNTS91	100315
Luxembourg	USA (United States)	03 Jul 48	24UNTS35	100350
Sweden	USA (United States)	03 Jul 48	23UNTS101	100343
Taiwan	USA (United States)	03 Jul 48	17UNTS119	100273
Iceland	USA (United States)	03 Jul 48	20UNTS141	100316
Norway	USA (United States)	03 Jul 48	20UNTS185	100317
Turkey	USA (United States)	04 Jul 48	24UNTS67	100351
UK Great Britain	USA (United States)	06 Jul 48	22UNTS263	100339
France	USA (United States)	09 Jul 48	24UNTS103	100352
Multilateral		14 Jul 48	23UNTS3	100340
Taiwan	USA (United States)	05 Aug 48	82UNTS109	101087
Multilateral		18 Aug 48	33UNTS181	100518
Philippines	USA (United States)	27 Aug 48	44UNTS13	100675

PARTY ONE	PARTY TWO	DATE	CITATION	NUMBER
Privileges and immunities (Cont.)				
Israel	UNICEF (Children)	20 Sep 48	71UNTS17	100907
UNRRA (Relief)	United Nations	27 Sep 48	27UNTS349	200158
Greece	Lebanon	06 Oct 48	87UNTS351	101179
Trieste	USA (United States)	15 Oct 48	29UNTS249	100443
Peru	ICAO (Civil Aviat)	22 Oct 48	95UNTS3	101315
UNICEF (Children)	Thailand	01 Dec 48	68UNTS94	100886
Afghanistan	UNESCO (Educ/Cult)	08 Dec 48	46UNTS3	100697
Korea, South	USA (United States)	10 Dec 48	55UNTS157	100813
Italy	USSR (Soviet Union)	11 Dec 48	217UNTS181	102948
WHO (World Health)	Switzerland	12 Jan 49	26UNTS331	200155
Chile	USA (United States)	21 Jan 49	160UNTS185	102107
Mexico	USA (United States)	14 Feb 49	160UNTS75	102103
Multilateral		28 Apr 49	83UNTS105	101105
Multilateral		05 May 49	87UNTS103	101168
Norway	USA (United States)	13 Jun 49	127UNTS163	101704
Multilateral		20 Jun 49	128UNTS141	101718
WHO (World Health)	Thailand	12 Aug 49	178UNTS347	102350
Multilateral		12 Aug 49	75UNTS287	100973
Multilateral		12 Aug 49	75UNTS85	100971
Multilateral		12 Aug 49	75UNTS31	100970
Multilateral		02 Sep 49	250UNTS12	103515
Council of Europe	France	02 Sep 49	249UNTS207	103510
Denmark	ICAO (Civil Aviat)	09 Sep 49	53UNTS341	100791
India	WHO (World Health)	09 Nov 49	67UNTS43	100865
Afghanistan	WHO (World Health)	04 Dec 49	102UNTS117	101414
Germany, West	USA (United States)	15 Dec 49	92UNTS269	101277
Norway	Sweden	17 Dec 49	197UNTS197	102640
Belgium	UK Great Britain	23 Dec 49	99UNTS61	101371
Afghanistan	India	04 Jan 50	81UNTS75	101064
Korea, South	USA (United States)	26 Jan 50	80UNTS205	101053
Norway	USA (United States)	27 Jan 50	80UNTS241	101055
Netherlands	USA (United States)	27 Jan 50	80UNTS219	101054
UK Great Britain	USA (United States)	27 Jan 50	80UNTS261	101056
France	USA (United States)	27 Jan 50	80UNTS171	101051
Italy	USA (United States)	27 Jan 50	80UNTS145	101050
Luxembourg	USA (United States)	27 Jan 50	80UNTS187	101052
Belgium	USA (United States)	27 Jan 50	51UNTS213	100767
Denmark	USA (United States)	27 Jan 50	48UNTS115	100740
United Nations	WHO (World Health)	10 Feb 50	46UNTS327	200188
UNICEF (Children)	UK Great Britain	10 Feb 50	65UNTS86	100837
Ceylon (Sri Lanka)	WHO (World Health)	17 Feb 50	102UNTS309	200309
Chile	UNICEF (Children)	03 Mar 50	126UNTS119	101685
Finland	Sweden	31 Mar 50	197UNTS285	102643
Burma	UNICEF (Children)	22 Apr 50	68UNTS96	100888
ILO (Labor Org)	United Nations	07 Jun 50	68UNTS213	200231
Brazil	UNICEF (Children)	09 Jun 50	66UNTS75	100848
Haiti	WHO (World Health)	21 Jun 50	103UNTS61	101424
Haiti	WHO (World Health)	27 Jun 50	110UNTS99	101504
Thailand	USA (United States)	01 Jul 50	81UNTS61	101063
Afghanistan	UNICEF (Children)	04 Jul 50	71UNTS3	100906
Taiwan	UNICEF (Children)	19 Jul 50	94UNTS21	101304
India	Nepal	31 Jul 50	94UNTS3	101302
Indonesia	USA (United States)	15 Aug 50	134UNTS255	101804
WHO (World Health)	United Arab Rep	25 Aug 50	92UNTS39	101259
Greece	Philippines	28 Aug 50	225UNTS155	103097
Pakistan	Syria	29 Aug 50	109UNTS95	101494
WHO (World Health)	Venezuela	11 Sep 50	110UNTS237	101513
Burma	USA (United States)	13 Sep 50	92UNTS361	101280
Thailand	USA (United States)	19 Sep 50	132UNTS199	101761
Pakistan	USA (United States)	23 Sep 50	82UNTS131	101088
Iceland	WHO (World Health)	06 Oct 50	110UNTS127	101506
Indonesia	USA (United States)	16 Oct 50	281UNTS105	104074
Thailand	USA (United States)	17 Oct 50	79UNTS41	101030
WHO (World Health)	Turkey	19 Oct 50	110UNTS215	101512
Multilateral		02 Nov 50	81UNTS160	101071

PARTY ONE	PARTY TWO	DATE	CITATION	NUMBER
Privileges and immunities (Cont.)				
Multilateral		04 Nov 50	213UNTS221	102889
Burma	USA (United States)	06 Nov 50	122UNTS81	101638
Peru	WHO (World Health)	10 Nov 50	110UNTS187	101510
Nicaragua	WHO (World Health)	10 Nov 50	110UNTS155	101508
Multilateral		24 Nov 50	81UNTS188	101072
Guatemala	WHO (World Health)	28 Nov 50	103UNTS51	101423
Multilateral		15 Dec 50	76UNTS120	100985
Philippines	WHO (World Health)	28 Dec 50	110UNTS203	101511
El Salvador	WHO (World Health)	02 Jan 51	103UNTS29	101421
Nicaragua	WHO (World Health)	02 Jan 51	103UNTS107	101428
Portugal	USA (United States)	05 Jan 51	133UNTS75	101782
United Nations	Yugoslavia	06 Jan 51	78UNTS165	101015
Multilateral		09 Jan 51	197UNTS341	102647
Chile	USA (United States)	16 Jan 51	157UNTS3	102043
Multilateral		18 Jan 51	81UNTS233	101073
Ceylon (Sri Lanka)	ILO (Labor Org)	24 Jan 51	117UNTS355	200380
Paraguay	UNICEF (Children)	25 Jan 51	79UNTS9	101027
Nicaragua	USA (United States)	31 Jan 51	160UNTS121	102105
Nicaragua	USA (United States)	31 Jan 51	150UNTS3	101960
Ethiopia	ICAO (Civil Aviat)	02 Feb 51	96UNTS123	101333
Taiwan	USA (United States)	09 Feb 51	132UNTS273	101767
Paraguay	WHO (World Health)	15 Feb 51	110UNTS171	101509
Multilateral		15 Feb 51	81UNTS245	101074
Israel	ILO (Labor Org)	19 Feb 51	100UNTS105	101391
Israel	ICAO (Civil Aviat)	19 Feb 51	96UNTS141	101334
Norway	UK Great Britain	22 Feb 51	326UNTS209	104713
Panama	USA (United States)	26 Feb 51	160UNTS153	102106
India	Indonesia	03 Mar 51	167UNTS3	102197
ILO (Labor Org)	Syria	03 Mar 51	110UNTS69	101502
Multilateral		05 Mar 51	81UNTS261	101075
Dominican Republic	USA (United States)	16 Mar 51	148UNTS15	101932
WHO (World Health)	United Arab Rep	25 Mar 51	223UNTS87	103058
Multilateral		28 Mar 51	181UNTS61	102399
Indonesia	WHO (World Health)	28 Mar 51	103UNTS71	101425
Jordan	United Nations	29 Mar 51	137UNTS267	200448
Jordan	ILO (Labor Org)	29 Mar 51	100UNTS247	200287
Liberia	ILO (Labor Org)	02 Apr 51	100UNTS117	101392
Jordan	WHO (World Health)	03 Apr 51	110UNTS297	200367
Multilateral		05 Apr 51	84UNTS299	101139
Ceylon (Sri Lanka)	ILO (Labor Org)	06 Apr 51	100UNTS235	200286
Mexico	ILO (Labor Org)	06 Apr 51	100UNTS131	101393
Guatemala	ILO (Labor Org)	13 Apr 51	126UNTS249	101692
Costa Rica	WHO (World Health)	13 Apr 51	103UNTS3	101419
Peru	ILO (Labor Org)	13 Apr 51	100UNTS31	101385
USA (United States)	Yugoslavia	17 Apr 51	162UNTS173	102134
Ecuador	ILO (Labor Org)	19 Apr 51	100UNTS77	101389
ICAO (Civil Aviat)	Thailand	19 Apr 51	96UNTS181	101336
Honduras	WHO (World Health)	20 Apr 51	110UNTS111	101505
Cuba	ILO (Labor Org)	21 Apr 51	99UNTS205	101382
Honduras	USA (United States)	24 Apr 51	140UNTS287	101894
Greece	ILO (Labor Org)	25 Apr 51	100UNTS93	101390
India	ILO (Labor Org)	26 Apr 51	100UNTS19	101384
Philippines	USA (United States)	27 Apr 51	174UNTS251	102290
Mexico	WHO (World Health)	30 Apr 51	103UNTS95	101427
WHO (World Health)	Yugoslavia	02 May 51	103UNTS117	101429
Colombia	WHO (World Health)	04 May 51	110UNTS83	101503
Pakistan	ILO (Labor Org)	16 May 51	100UNTS147	101394
Switzerland	USA (United States)	24 May 51	127UNTS227	101706
Cambodia	WHO (World Health)	31 May 51	102UNTS279	200307
Multilateral		01 Jun 51	118UNTS57	101596
UK Great Britain	USA (United States)	06 Jun 51	165UNTS121	102174
Lebanon	WHO (World Health)	07 Jun 51	126UNTS221	101690
Iceland	ICAO (Civil Aviat)	07 Jun 51	96UNTS193	101337
WHO (World Health)	Uruguay	11 Jun 51	128UNTS251	101724
Liberia	WHO (World Health)	11 Jun 51	103UNTS83	101426

Privileges and immunities (Cont.)

PARTY ONE	PARTY TWO	DATE	CITATION	NUMBER
United Nations	Thailand	11 Jun 51	90UNTS45	101225
Costa Rica	WHO (World Health)	14 Jun 51	102UNTS151	101418
Panama	UNICEF (Children)	14 Jun 51	97UNTS3	101343
Dominican Republic	ILO (Labor Org)	18 Jun 51	100UNTS3	101383
Israel	United Nations	25 Jun 51	97UNTS21	101344
Multilateral		25 Jun 51	92UNTS27	101258
ILO (Labor Org)	Vietnam, South	26 Jun 51	100UNTS223	200285
Mexico	USA (United States)	27 Jun 51	141UNTS211	101916
Multilateral		28 Jun 51	118UNTS154	101604
Iraq	WHO (World Health)	01 Jul 51	110UNTS139	101507
Ethiopia	WHO (World Health)	02 Jul 51	103UNTS39	101422
Burma	India	07 Jul 51	149UNTS35	101949
Burma	WHO (World Health)	09 Jul 51	107UNTS9	101463
Burma	WHO (World Health)	09 Jul 51	104UNTS175	101439
Burma	WHO (World Health)	09 Jul 51	104UNTS187	101440
ILO (Labor Org)	Thailand	11 Jul 51	100UNTS159	101395
Paraguay	ILO (Labor Org)	12 Jul 51	117UNTS155	101591
Philippines	WHO (World Health)	22 Jul 51	149UNTS197	101953
Multilateral		27 Jul 51	97UNTS291	200273
Iran	UNICEF (Children)	02 Aug 51	247UNTS11	103457
Multilateral		04 Aug 51	104UNTS197	101441
Israel	WHO (World Health)	07 Aug 51	104UNTS213	101442
France	United Nations	17 Aug 51	122UNTS191	101647
Japan	USA (United States)	28 Aug 51	147UNTS81	101930
France	USSR (Soviet Union)	03 Sep 51	221UNTS79	103003
UNICEF (Children)	Turkey	05 Sep 51	193UNTS55	102610
Multilateral		05 Sep 51	173UNTS15	102256
Ethiopia	USA (United States)	07 Sep 51	206UNTS41	102785
USA (United States)	Vietnam, South	07 Sep 51	174UNTS165	102284
Cambodia	USA (United States)	08 Sep 51	174UNTS115	102282
Laos	USA (United States)	09 Sep 51	174UNTS141	102283
Iraq	ICAO (Civil Aviat)	18 Sep 51	108UNTS219	101475
Korea, South	WHO (World Health)	19 Sep 51	109UNTS297	200366
Korea, South	United Nations	21 Sep 51	104UNTS323	200322
WHO (World Health)	Vietnam, South	21 Sep 51	107UNTS63	200352
Australia	Netherlands	25 Sep 51	128UNTS63	101713
Paraguay	United Nations	27 Sep 51	120UNTS105	101617
Multilateral		01 Oct 51	104UNTS249	101446
Bolivia	United Nations	01 Oct 51	104UNTS263	101447
UNICEF (Children)	UK Great Britain	02 Oct 51	104UNTS301	101448
WHO (World Health)	Thailand	04 Oct 51	109UNTS85	101493
WHO (World Health)	Thailand	04 Oct 51	109UNTS77	101492
Pakistan	WHO (World Health)	07 Oct 51	126UNTS101	101684
Ecuador	WHO (World Health)	16 Oct 51	110UNTS263	101515
India	WHO (World Health)	16 Oct 51	109UNTS49	101490
United Nations	Uruguay	17 Oct 51	122UNTS29	101633
ILO (Labor Org)	Venezuela	22 Oct 51	117UNTS139	101590
Taiwan	WHO (World Health)	25 Oct 51	126UNTS77	101683
India	WHO (World Health)	01 Nov 51	118UNTS13	101593
Panama	WHO (World Health)	09 Nov 51	118UNTS43	101595
Saudi Arabia	USA (United States)	10 Nov 51	180UNTS263	102390
Panama	ILO (Labor Org)	10 Nov 51	126UNTS269	101693
Netherlands	Switzerland	12 Nov 51	126UNTS157	101688
USA (United States)	Yugoslavia	14 Nov 51	174UNTS201	102286
Pakistan	Saudi Arabia	25 Nov 51	177UNTS3	102304
Netherlands	UK Great Britain	30 Nov 51	123UNTS177	101659
Denmark	WHO (World Health)	30 Nov 51	118UNTS3	101592
Iraq	UNICEF (Children)	10 Dec 51	126UNTS57	101682
India	Turkey	14 Dec 51	137UNTS15	101845
Mexico	WHO (World Health)	17 Dec 51	124UNTS121	101670
Guatemala	WHO (World Health)	17 Dec 51	120UNTS133	101619
India	WHO (World Health)	20 Dec 51	124UNTS109	101669
Multilateral		24 Dec 51	118UNTS290	200383
Guatemala	WHO (World Health)	29 Dec 51	124UNTS89	101668
France	UK Great Britain	31 Dec 51	330UNTS145	104744

Privileges and immunities (Cont.)

PARTY ONE	PARTY TWO	DATE	CITATION	NUMBER
India	USA (United States)	05 Jan 52	157UNTS39	102045
USA (United States)	Yugoslavia	08 Jan 52	152UNTS61	102011
Austria	WHO (World Health)	10 Jan 52	131UNTS295	200438
India	United Nations	12 Jan 52	118UNTS175	101606
Iran	USA (United States)	20 Jan 52	200UNTS191	102703
Ceylon (Sri Lanka)	United Nations	21 Jan 52	118UNTS281	200382
Costa Rica	WHO (World Health)	23 Jan 52	135UNTS265	101826
Multilateral		23 Jan 52	127UNTS269	101708
WHO (World Health)	Spain	30 Jan 52	124UNTS259	200425
UNICEF (Children)	UK Great Britain	04 Feb 52	120UNTS147	101620
ICAO (Civil Aviat)	Yugoslavia	06 Feb 52	128UNTS97	101715
Indonesia	United Nations	06 Feb 52	121UNTS3	101621
WHO (World Health)	UK Great Britain	07 Feb 52	121UNTS75	101627
Jordan	USA (United States)	12 Feb 52	168UNTS25	102211
Lebanon	ICAO (Civil Aviat)	14 Feb 52	128UNTS83	101714
Dominican Republic	WHO (World Health)	15 Feb 52	134UNTS291	101808
Dominican Republic	UNICEF (Children)	15 Feb 52	121UNTS43	101625
Multilateral		18 Feb 52	126UNTS319	200434
Burma	WHO (World Health)	18 Feb 52	127UNTS43	101698
Ecuador	USA (United States)	20 Feb 52	177UNTS43	102308
Peru	USA (United States)	22 Feb 52	165UNTS31	102166
India	Syria	25 Feb 52	163UNTS55	102141
Finland	USA (United States)	03 Mar 52	177UNTS141	102316
OAS (Am States)	USA (United States)	03 Mar 52	165UNTS67	102168
Ceylon (Sri Lanka)	WHO (World Health)	04 Mar 52	128UNTS281	200437
Greece	United Nations	05 Mar 52	123UNTS3	101650
ICAO (Civil Aviat)	United Arab Rep	06 Mar 52	151UNTS111	101986
Finland	WHO (World Health)	07 Mar 52	128UNTS269	200436
Cuba	USA (United States)	07 Mar 52	165UNTS11	102165
Sweden	UK Great Britain	14 Mar 52	202UNTS157	102731
Brazil	USA (United States)	15 Mar 52	199UNTS221	102687
Ceylon (Sri Lanka)	WHO (World Health)	26 Mar 52	134UNTS341	200442
India	United Nations	02 Apr 52	126UNTS145	101687
India	WHO (World Health)	02 Apr 52	131UNTS227	101743
Libya	UNICEF (Children)	05 Apr 52	133UNTS287	200441
Chile	USA (United States)	09 Apr 52	186UNTS53	102482
Multilateral		11 Apr 52	173UNTS2	102255
Colombia	USA (United States)	17 Apr 52	174UNTS215	102287
Liberia	UNICEF (Children)	17 Apr 52	133UNTS3	101773
India	WHO (World Health)	17 Apr 52	131UNTS241	101744
India	WHO (World Health)	19 Apr 52	131UNTS253	101745
Italy	Jordan	24 Apr 52	281UNTS167	104078
Pakistan	United Nations	28 Apr 52	128UNTS191	101720
India	ICAO (Civil Aviat)	29 Apr 52	151UNTS123	101987
Israel	USA (United States)	09 May 52	177UNTS63	102309
Norway	WHO (World Health)	09 May 52	131UNTS281	101747
Ethiopia	USA (United States)	15 May 52	180UNTS227	102388
Multilateral		22 May 52	131UNTS115	101739
Korea, South	USA (United States)	24 May 52	179UNTS23	102353
Mexico	WHO (World Health)	28 May 52	134UNTS319	101810
India	WHO (World Health)	04 Jun 52	135UNTS279	101827
Burma	WHO (World Health)	09 Jun 52	134UNTS273	101806
Brazil	WHO (World Health)	12 Jun 52	151UNTS333	102003
Belgium	UNICEF (Children)	17 Jun 52	171UNTS249	102228
Multilateral		19 Jun 52	133UNTS165	101787
India	WHO (World Health)	19 Jun 52	134UNTS307	101809
WHO (World Health)	Syria	20 Jun 52	165UNTS219	102178
OAS (Am States)	USA (United States)	22 Jun 52	181UNTS147	102405
Burma	Pakistan	25 Jun 52	173UNTS41	102259
USA (United States)	Uruguay	30 Jun 52	207UNTS139	102804
Chile	USA (United States)	30 Jun 52	199UNTS241	102688
Brazil	USA (United States)	30 Jun 52	185UNTS79	102460
Panama	USA (United States)	30 Jun 52	181UNTS121	102404
Australia	FAO (Food Agri)	07 Jul 52	184UNTS209	102449
Jordan	UNICEF (Children)	08 Jul 52	173UNTS353	200503

PARTY ONE	PARTY TWO	DATE	CITATION	NUMBER
Privileges and immunities (Cont.)				
UNICEF (Children)	Syria	10 Jul 52	136UNTS17	101830
India	Philippines	11 Jul 52	203UNTS73	102741
Chile	WHO (World Health)	11 Jul 52	137UNTS27	101846
India	WHO (World Health)	16 Jul 52	135UNTS291	101828
Colombia	United Nations	17 Jul 52	135UNTS61	101815
France	WHO (World Health)	23 Jul 52	209UNTS231	102829
UNICEF (Children)	UK Great Britain	25 Jul 52	135UNTS37	101812
Brazil	United Nations	04 Aug 52	135UNTS185	101820
Panama	USA (United States)	08 Aug 52	181UNTS257	102415
Laos	UNICEF (Children)	15 Aug 52	161UNTS323	200491
Panama	United Nations	20 Aug 52	136UNTS3	101829
Jordan	WHO (World Health)	21 Aug 52	141UNTS341	200472
Multilateral		21 Aug 52	141UNTS129	101912
UNICEF (Children)	Vietnam, South	29 Aug 52	161UNTS335	200492
Italy	ILO (Labor Org)	04 Sep 52	178UNTS371	200505
Germany, West	Israel	10 Sep 52	162UNTS205	102137
ILO (Labor Org)	Uruguay	20 Sep 52	187UNTS25	102499
United Nations	Trieste	30 Sep 52	140UNTS11	101881
Multilateral		17 Oct 52	141UNTS121	101911
Chile	WHO (World Health)	24 Oct 52	151UNTS339	102004
Dominican Republic	Philippines	02 Nov 52	543UNTS175	107901
Chile	WHO (World Health)	04 Nov 52	150UNTS119	101966
Ethiopia	USA (United States)	05 Nov 52	184UNTS139	102445
India	Iraq	10 Nov 52	172UNTS103	102242
Ceylon (Sri Lanka)	USA (United States)	17 Nov 52	180UNTS207	102386
Ceylon (Sri Lanka)	WHO (World Health)	21 Nov 52	161UNTS315	200490
Japan	WHO (World Health)	26 Nov 52	204UNTS301	200521
Mexico	ICAO (Civil Aviat)	28 Nov 52	164UNTS15	102156
India	WHO (World Health)	11 Dec 52	158UNTS391	102073
Multilateral		16 Dec 52	158UNTS407	102074
UNICEF (Children)	UK Great Britain	16 Dec 52	151UNTS359	102005
Multilateral		29 Dec 52	151UNTS317	102002
ILO (Labor Org)	UN Relief Palestin	31 Dec 52	182UNTS201	200506
Greece	USA (United States)	04 Feb 53	189UNTS3	102538
India	WHO (World Health)	11 Feb 53	163UNTS43	102140
United Nations	Sweden	11 Feb 53	160UNTS3	102096
Chile	United Nations	16 Feb 53	314UNTS49	104541
Multilateral		26 Feb 53	161UNTS31	102120
Costa Rica	United Nations	27 Feb 53	161UNTS45	102121
Nepal	United Nations	02 Mar 53	161UNTS347	200493
Denmark	Uruguay	04 Mar 53	250UNTS51	103517
Dominican Republic	USA (United States)	06 Mar 53	199UNTS267	102689
United Arab Rep	USA (United States)	12 Mar 53	204UNTS3	102747
India	Muscat and Oman	15 Mar 53	190UNTS69	102559
United Arab Rep	USA (United States)	19 Mar 53	215UNTS17	102909
France	WHO (World Health)	02 Apr 53	174UNTS83	102279
United Nations	Yemen	07 Apr 53	163UNTS73	102142
Netherlands	United Nations	09 Apr 53	163UNTS89	102143
Greece	UK Great Britain	17 Apr 53	191UNTS151	102582
Ethiopia	UNICEF (Children)	27 Apr 53	213UNTS169	102885
Ethiopia	USA (United States)	29 Apr 53	224UNTS121	103073
France	WHO (World Health)	30 Apr 53	174UNTS71	102278
El Salvador	USA (United States)	14 May 53	234UNTS71	103273
Australia	USA (United States)	14 May 53	205UNTS277	102780
United Arab Rep	USA (United States)	21 May 53	204UNTS29	102748
ICAO (Civil Aviat)	Syria	28 May 53	173UNTS199	102267
Brazil	USA (United States)	30 May 53	460UNTS89	106633
Colombia	USA (United States)	09 Jun 53	213UNTS3	102877
Ecuador	United Nations	16 Jun 53	166UNTS289	102194
United Arab Rep	USA (United States)	18 Jun 53	215UNTS45	102910
United Arab Rep	USA (United States)	18 Jun 53	204UNTS55	102749
Ethiopia	United Nations	22 Jun 53	172UNTS93	102241
Liberia	USA (United States)	23 Jun 53	213UNTS37	102879
Liberia	USA (United States)	23 Jun 53	213UNTS57	102880
Cambodia	United Nations	24 Jun 53	168UNTS309	200500

PARTY ONE	PARTY TWO	DATE	CITATION	NUMBER
Privileges and immunities (Cont.)				
Japan	United Nations	24 Jun 53	167UNTS249	200499
Pakistan	USA (United States)	25 Jun 53	205UNTS139	102773
Brazil	USA (United States)	26 Jun 53	336UNTS241	104808
Philippines	USA (United States)	26 Jun 53	213UNTS77	102881
Panama	USA (United States)	26 Jun 53	215UNTS77	102912
Chile	USA (United States)	27 Jun 53	229UNTS193	103167
Chile	USA (United States)	27 Jun 53	229UNTS53	103160
Saudi Arabia	USA (United States)	29 Jun 53	206UNTS23	102784
Afghanistan	USA (United States)	30 Jun 53	215UNTS3	102908
Nicaragua	USA (United States)	30 Jun 53	215UNTS133	102917
ICAO (Civil Aviat)	United Arab Rep	27 Aug 53	215UNTS371	102925
Belgium	USA (United States)	02 Sep 53	200UNTS127	102700
Spain	USA (United States)	26 Sep 53	207UNTS61	102800
Spain	USA (United States)	26 Sep 53	207UNTS93	102802
UNICEF (Children)	UK Great Britain	07 Oct 53	180UNTS59	102375
Multilateral		09 Oct 53	190UNTS49	102557
Multilateral		19 Oct 53	207UNTS189	102807
Jordan	USA (United States)	21 Oct 53	222UNTS31	103020
Denmark	Sweden	27 Oct 53	198UNTS111	102659
Denmark	Sweden	27 Oct 53	198UNTS71	102658
Dominican Republic	United Nations	19 Nov 53	180UNTS45	102374
Japan	UNICEF (Children)	21 Nov 53	183UNTS297	200507
Chile	USA (United States)	30 Dec 53	236UNTS41	103315
Libya	USA (United States)	11 Jan 54	229UNTS15	103157
Pakistan	United Nations	25 Jan 54	185UNTS213	102472
Brazil	WHO (World Health)	04 Feb 54	233UNTS49	103250
Multilateral		01 Mar 54	256UNTS31	103622
United Nations	Venezuela	05 Mar 54	187UNTS9	102498
Japan	USA (United States)	08 Mar 54	232UNTS169	103236
Liberia	United Nations	09 Mar 54	187UNTS61	102501
Guatemala	United Nations	10 Mar 54	191UNTS271	102587
Mexico	UK Great Britain	20 Mar 54	331UNTS21	104750
Afghanistan	USA (United States)	20 Mar 54	229UNTS7	103156
United Nations	Vietnam, South	24 Mar 54	188UNTS345	200514
Finland	Netherlands	29 Mar 54	252UNTS239	103568
Italy	USA (United States)	31 Mar 54	235UNTS293	103311
Mexico	USA (United States)	06 Apr 54	236UNTS69	103317
Japan	USA (United States)	16 Apr 54	238UNTS39	103354
Japan	USA (United States)	16 Apr 54	238UNTS3	103353
Luxembourg	USA (United States)	17 Apr 54	257UNTS255	103661
Multilateral		20 Apr 54	189UNTS11	102539
Ethiopia	USA (United States)	21 Apr 54	232UNTS299	103244
Iraq	USA (United States)	21 Apr 54	222UNTS251	103032
Bulgaria	Yugoslavia	22 Apr 54	397UNTS43	105701
China People's Rep	India	29 Apr 54	299UNTS57	104307
UNICEF (Children)	Spain	07 May 54	190UNTS357	200515
Netherlands	USA (United States)	07 May 54	213UNTS325	102895
Panama	USA (United States)	11 May 54	236UNTS107	103319
Nepal	WHO (World Health)	13 May 54	204UNTS311	200522
Pakistan	USA (United States)	19 May 54	202UNTS301	102736
Honduras	USA (United States)	20 May 54	222UNTS87	103025
Mexico	UNICEF (Children)	20 May 54	192UNTS3	102591
United Nations	Thailand	26 May 54	260UNTS35	103703
Multilateral		31 May 54	192UNTS20	102592
Multilateral		01 Jun 54	200UNTS235	200520
Italy	UK Great Britain	01 Jun 54	403UNTS275	105798
Jordan	USA (United States)	17 Jun 54	266UNTS137	103828
Italy	USA (United States)	28 Jun 54	237UNTS121	103340
Chile	USA (United States)	28 Jun 54	233UNTS3	103246
Ecuador	USA (United States)	30 Jun 54	236UNTS163	103323
Multilateral		30 Jun 54	193UNTS67	102611
France	UNESCO (Educ/Cult)	02 Jul 54	357UNTS3	105103
El Salvador	USA (United States)	16 Jul 54	237UNTS237	103350
Germany, West	USA (United States)	22 Jul 54	239UNTS3	103369
Multilateral		19 Aug 54	201UNTS51	102710

PARTY ONE	PARTY TWO	DATE	CITATION	NUMBER
Privileges and immunities (Cont.)				
Pakistan	USA (United States)	23 Aug 54	234UNTS243	103287
New Zealand	UNICEF (Children)	26 Aug 54	198UNTS173	102663
UNESCO (Educ/Cult)	UN Special Fund	29 Sep 54	363UNTS367	200572
Multilateral		06 Oct 54	201UNTS75	102711
Multilateral		23 Oct 54	332UNTS3	104760
Multilateral		27 Oct 54	201UNTS95	102712
Multilateral		29 Oct 54	201UNTS115	102713
Libya	USA (United States)	03 Nov 54	238UNTS227	103366
Lebanon	UN Relief Palestin	26 Nov 54	202UNTS123	102728
Taiwan	El Salvador	09 Dec 54	214UNTS217	102900
Guatemala	USA (United States)	13 Dec 54	237UNTS169	103343
Netherlands	USA (United States)	14 Dec 54	262UNTS35	103737
Netherlands	UNICEF (Children)	31 Dec 54	202UNTS135	102729
Mexico	ILO (Labor Org)	05 Jan 55	208UNTS225	102815
Pakistan	USA (United States)	11 Jan 55	251UNTS111	103537
Haiti	USA (United States)	28 Jan 55	270UNTS83	103894
France	Sweden	05 Mar 55	427UNTS133	106150
Mexico	USA (United States)	09 Mar 55	263UNTS247	103776
WMO (Meteorology)	Switzerland	10 Mar 55	211UNTS277	200524
El Salvador	USA (United States)	21 Mar 55	250UNTS261	103528
Italy	USA (United States)	30 Mar 55	257UNTS169	103654
Italy	USA (United States)	30 Mar 55	257UNTS199	103655
Chile	USA (United States)	31 Mar 55	262UNTS19	103736
Haiti	USA (United States)	01 Apr 55	261UNTS361	103734
Germany, West	USA (United States)	04 Apr 55	279UNTS73	104034
Multilateral		04 Apr 55	208UNTS239	102816
Taiwan	WHO (World Health)	21 Apr 55	210UNTS71	102835
Peru	USA (United States)	30 Apr 55	263UNTS309	103780
Ceylon (Sri Lanka)	Pakistan	23 May 55	286UNTS15	104159
Multilateral		25 May 55	264UNTS117	103791
CERN (Nuc Resrch)	Switzerland	11 Jun 55	249UNTS405	200544
Multilateral		14 Jun 55	212UNTS263	200526
UK Great Britain	USA (United States)	15 Jun 55	229UNTS73	103161
Guatemala	USA (United States)	18 Jun 55	262UNTS105	103740
Denmark	WHO (World Health)	29 Jun 55	247UNTS168	103467
Dominican Republic	USA (United States)	30 Jun 55	257UNTS313	103664
Germany, West	USA (United States)	30 Jun 55	240UNTS47	103393
Iran	WHO (World Health)	04 Jul 55	227UNTS65	103131
Multilateral		04 Jul 55	214UNTS10	102897
El Salvador	USA (United States)	08 Aug 55	264UNTS301	103801
Iran	USA (United States)	15 Aug 55	284UNTS93	104132
Multilateral		12 Oct 55	560UNTS3	108165
Taiwan	USA (United States)	14 Oct 55	268UNTS165	103857
Guatemala	UNICEF (Children)	22 Nov 55	221UNTS305	103012
Italy	Vatican/Holy See	16 Dec 55	260UNTS319	103715
Multilateral		02 Feb 56	227UNTS153	103137
Multilateral		10 Feb 56	228UNTS167	103150
Multilateral		10 Feb 56	228UNTS189	103151
Ethiopia	WHO (World Health)	17 Feb 56	243UNTS91	103448
Australia	Greece	15 Mar 56	241UNTS313	103438
Multilateral		30 Mar 56	604UNTS114	108748
Cambodia	UNICEF (Children)	28 Apr 56	136UNTS341	200446
Japan	Philippines	09 May 56	285UNTS3	104148
Denmark	Norway	23 May 56	271UNTS75	103910
Multilateral		31 May 56	251UNTS181	103541
Canada	Germany, West	04 Jun 56	316UNTS231	104589
Multilateral		08 Jun 56	247UNTS366	200541
Multilateral		14 Jun 56	265UNTS125	103809
Honduras	USA (United States)	25 Jun 56	279UNTS113	104036
Multilateral		26 Jun 56	321UNTS2	104650
Israel	USA (United States)	26 Jun 56	257UNTS55	103649
Multilateral		26 Jun 56	253UNTS12	103573
Multilateral		02 Jul 56	540UNTS110	107846
Multilateral		02 Jul 56	248UNTS37	103484
Lebanon	UNICEF (Children)	03 Jul 56	324UNTS145	104683

PARTY ONE	PARTY TWO	DATE	CITATION	NUMBER
Privileges and immunities (Cont.)				
Germany, West	UK Great Britain	30 Jul 56	330UNTS233	104748
UNICEF (Children)	Sudan	07 Aug 56	248UNTS307	200542
UNESCO (Educ/Cult)	UK Great Britain	09 Aug 56	256UNTS139	103624
Philippines	Switzerland	30 Aug 56	293UNTS43	104284
Multilateral		31 Aug 56	249UNTS158	103506
Denmark	WHO (World Health)	03 Sep 56	258UNTS103	103674
Multilateral		07 Sep 56	266UNTS3	103822
Multilateral		25 Sep 56	334UNTS89	104767
Multilateral		25 Sep 56	334UNTS13	104766
Norway	Sweden	27 Sep 56	261UNTS71	103726
Multilateral		05 Oct 56	251UNTS267	103545
Multilateral		05 Oct 56	251UNTS245	103544
Burma	Thailand	15 Oct 56	277UNTS87	104000
Austria	USA (United States)	25 Oct 56	299UNTS123	104310
Multilateral		26 Oct 56	276UNTS3	103988
UK Great Britain	USA (United States)	01 Nov 56	264UNTS3	103785
United Nations	Venezuela	18 Nov 56	588UNTS243	108529
Multilateral		21 Nov 56	253UNTS266	103588
UK Great Britain	USA (United States)	27 Nov 56	282UNTS43	104092
Mexico	ICAO (Civil Aviat)	20 Dec 56	497UNTS3	107259
UNESCO (Educ/Cult)	Tunisia	03 Jan 57	257UNTS21	103645
Multilateral		15 Jan 57	376UNTS122	105378
Multilateral		23 Jan 57	259UNTS426	103701
Germany, East	Poland	01 Feb 57	319UNTS115	104632
Multilateral		17 Feb 57	271UNTS2	103907
Denmark	Norway	22 Feb 57	286UNTS127	104164
Japan	Norway	28 Feb 57	280UNTS87	104054
Multilateral		01 Mar 57	264UNTS94	103790
Multilateral		25 Mar 57	294UNTS2	104300
Tunisia	USA (United States)	26 Mar 57	283UNTS117	104111
Multilateral		28 Mar 57	271UNTS30	103908
Morocco	USA (United States)	02 Apr 57	288UNTS157	104203
Multilateral		09 Apr 57	274UNTS172	103965
Lebanon	United Nations	01 May 57	266UNTS125	103827
Germany, East	USSR (Soviet Union)	10 May 57	285UNTS135	104151
Finland	USA (United States)	10 May 57	283UNTS43	104105
Czechoslovakia	Germany, East	24 May 57	292UNTS327	104279
Multilateral		24 May 57	268UNTS270	103861
Libya	USA (United States)	30 Jun 57	284UNTS177	104136
Germany, East	Hungary	03 Jul 57	407UNTS186	105865
Australia	FAO (Food Agri)	08 Jul 57	277UNTS315	104015
Multilateral		09 Jul 57	274UNTS300	103972
Denmark	United Nations	16 Jul 57	274UNTS81	103959
Canada	United Nations	29 Jul 57	274UNTS47	103957
Morocco	UNICEF (Children)	31 Jul 57	282UNTS99	104095
Brazil	United Nations	13 Aug 57	274UNTS199	103966
India	United Nations	14 Aug 57	274UNTS233	103968
Hungary	USSR (Soviet Union)	24 Aug 57	318UNTS3	104607
Czechoslovakia	USSR (Soviet Union)	31 Aug 57	308UNTS3	104456
Romania	USSR (Soviet Union)	04 Sep 57	318UNTS55	104609
Albania	USSR (Soviet Union)	18 Sep 57	307UNTS265	104455
Burma	WHO (World Health)	20 Sep 57	282UNTS113	104096
United Nations	Yugoslavia	01 Oct 57	277UNTS191	104006
Czechoslovakia	USSR (Soviet Union)	05 Oct 57	320UNTS129	104641
IAEA (Atom Energy)	United Nations	23 Oct 57	281UNTS369	200548
Germany, East	Hungary	30 Oct 57	408UNTS4	105867
UK Great Britain	USA (United States)	01 Nov 57	299UNTS167	104312
Multilateral		05 Nov 57	285UNTS301	104155
Taiwan	Jordan	19 Nov 57	308UNTS227	104463
Argentina	UNICEF (Children)	19 Nov 57	300UNTS229	104338
Germany, East	Poland	25 Nov 57	340UNTS99	104862
Germany, East	USSR (Soviet Union)	28 Nov 57	305UNTS113	104419
Bulgaria	USSR (Soviet Union)	12 Dec 57	317UNTS217	104606
Bulgaria	USSR (Soviet Union)	12 Dec 57	302UNTS21	104352
Korea, North	USSR (Soviet Union)	16 Dec 57	301UNTS301	104349

PARTY ONE	PARTY TWO	DATE	CITATION	NUMBER
Privileges and immunities (Cont.)				
Korea, North	USSR (Soviet Union)	16 Dec 57	292UNTS121	104270
Belgium	Germany, West	17 Jan 58	328UNTS173	104735
Indonesia	Japan	20 Jan 58	324UNTS247	104689
Poland	USSR (Soviet Union)	21 Jan 58	319UNTS291	104637
Ghana	WHO (World Health)	21 Jan 58	307UNTS3	104437
Multilateral		03 Feb 58	381UNTS165	105471
India	Japan	04 Feb 58	324UNTS215	104687
Indonesia	WHO (World Health)	05 Feb 58	307UNTS15	104438
Israel	Philippines	26 Feb 58	507UNTS135	107398
Multilateral		15 Mar 58	292UNTS273	104276
Sudan	USA (United States)	31 Mar 58	308UNTS105	104458
Romania	USSR (Soviet Union)	03 Apr 58	313UNTS167	104535
Israel	WHO (World Health)	11 Apr 58	307UNTS27	104439
China People's Rep	USSR (Soviet Union)	23 Apr 58	313UNTS135	104534
Germany, West	USSR (Soviet Union)	25 Apr 58	338UNTS49	104832
Lebanon	United Nations	13 Jun 58	303UNTS271	104386
Ethiopia	United Nations	18 Jun 58	317UNTS101	104597
Multilateral		19 Jun 58	306UNTS236	200550
Bulgaria	Hungary	27 Jun 58	438UNTS235	106318
Albania	USSR (Soviet Union)	30 Jun 58	328UNTS3	104729
Germany, East	Romania	15 Jul 58	395UNTS3	105681
Germany, East	Romania	15 Jul 58	387UNTS133	105561
Hungary	USSR (Soviet Union)	15 Jul 58	322UNTS3	104656
Denmark	Sweden	21 Jul 58	320UNTS163	104642
Taiwan	USA (United States)	06 Aug 58	462UNTS3	106666
Ghana	UNICEF (Children)	12 Aug 58	309UNTS103	104469
Mongolia	USSR (Soviet Union)	25 Aug 58	322UNTS105	104657
Mongolia	USSR (Soviet Union)	25 Aug 58	322UNTS215	104659
Pakistan	Thailand	28 Aug 58	394UNTS53	105668
Hungary	Romania	07 Oct 58	416UNTS199	106004
Iraq	USSR (Soviet Union)	11 Oct 58	328UNTS117	104731
Czechoslovakia	Romania	25 Oct 58	417UNTS37	106006
Poland	Yugoslavia	17 Nov 58	432UNTS267	106225
Germany, West	Norway	18 Nov 58	357UNTS205	105119
Jordan	United Nations	18 Nov 58	315UNTS125	104564
Bulgaria	Romania	03 Dec 58	417UNTS133	106007
Burma	United Nations	15 Dec 58	319UNTS3	104629
Afghanistan	WHO (World Health)	18 Dec 58	324UNTS121	104681
Muscat and Oman	USA (United States)	20 Dec 58	380UNTS181	105457
United Nations	Tunisia	23 Dec 58	321UNTS23	104651
ILO (Labor Org)	UK Great Britain	14 Jan 59	355UNTS283	105081
Albania	Czechoslovakia	16 Jan 59	363UNTS165	105207
Albania	Czechoslovakia	16 Jan 59	363UNTS195	105208
Belgium	France	20 Jan 59	361UNTS155	105178
Japan	Pakistan	17 Feb 59	341UNTS127	104880
Japan	Norway	21 Feb 59	356UNTS231	105098
Belgium	Morocco	27 Feb 59	390UNTS275	105611
Ghana	United Nations	27 Feb 59	324UNTS133	104682
Austria	USSR (Soviet Union)	28 Feb 59	356UNTS39	105091
Hungary	Poland	06 Mar 59	432UNTS3	106216
Hungary	Romania	18 Mar 59	417UNTS3	106005
IAEA (Atom Energy)	Thailand	18 Mar 59	339UNTS307	104850
Czechoslovakia	Hungary	27 Mar 59	351UNTS57	105017
Canada	Finland	28 Mar 59	355UNTS3	105072
United Nations	Sudan	28 Mar 59	327UNTS95	104719
Morocco	UN Special Fund	04 Apr 59	354UNTS347	105069
Mexico	United Nations	07 Apr 59	381UNTS123	105468
Multilateral		08 Apr 59	389UNTS69	105593
Israel	Liberia	09 Apr 59	448UNTS95	106427
Germany, West	Sweden	17 Apr 59	428UNTS155	106175
Bulgaria	Romania	23 Apr 59	387UNTS81	105559
Austria	Sweden	14 May 59	428UNTS3	106167
Hungary	Poland	20 May 59	432UNTS115	106217
Bulgaria	Czechoslovakia	27 May 59	360UNTS335	105167
United Nations	Vietnam, South	03 Jun 59	337UNTS361	200557

PARTY ONE	PARTY TWO	DATE	CITATION	NUMBER
Privileges and immunities (Cont.)				
USSR (Soviet Union)	Vietnam, North	05 Jun 59	356UNTS111	105093
Guinea	UNICEF (Children)	08 Jun 59	334UNTS277	104772
Germany, West	Netherlands	16 Jun 59	593UNTS3	108576
China People's Rep	USSR (Soviet Union)	23 Jun 59	356UNTS83	105092
Libya	United Nations	27 Jun 59	336UNTS291	104811
Multilateral		01 Jul 59	374UNTS147	105334
Laos	United Nations	06 Jul 59	337UNTS41	104814
Paraguay	United Nations	01 Aug 59	341UNTS319	104894
Ghana	UN Special Fund	12 Aug 59	338UNTS203	104836
FAO (Food Agri)	UN Special Fund	28 Sep 59	341UNTS353	200562
Iran	UN Special Fund	06 Oct 59	342UNTS89	104902
Austria	France	08 Oct 59	453UNTS95	106521
ILO (Labor Org)	UN Special Fund	12 Oct 59	343UNTS325	200563
Poland	UN Special Fund	15 Oct 59	344UNTS29	104941
Guinea	United Nations	15 Oct 59	344UNTS47	104942
India	UN Special Fund	20 Oct 59	344UNTS143	104946
UN Special Fund	Yugoslavia	27 Oct 59	344UNTS159	104947
Korea, South	United Nations	06 Nov 59	346UNTS289	200565
Ecuador	UN Special Fund	10 Nov 59	345UNTS3	104955
Greece	UN Special Fund	13 Nov 59	345UNTS171	104966
UN Special Fund	WMO (Meteorology)	17 Nov 59	345UNTS311	200564
UN Special Fund	Turkey	20 Nov 59	345UNTS105	104963
Afghanistan	United Nations	24 Nov 59	397UNTS187	105705
UN Special Fund	United Arab Rep	25 Nov 59	345UNTS125	104964
Hague Private IL	Netherlands	01 Dec 59	510UNTS191	107414
Israel	UN Special Fund	01 Dec 59	345UNTS197	104968
Guinea	UN Special Fund	02 Dec 59	345UNTS215	104969
Multilateral		03 Dec 59	348UNTS246	105003
Argentina	UN Special Fund	04 Dec 59	345UNTS263	104972
Multilateral		14 Dec 59	368UNTS237	105244
Jordan	UN Special Fund	15 Dec 59	346UNTS3	104974
Ceylon (Sri Lanka)	WHO (World Health)	21 Dec 59	349UNTS109	105011
UN Special Fund	UK Great Britain	07 Jan 60	348UNTS177	105000
Peru	UN Special Fund	19 Jan 60	349UNTS83	105010
Pakistan	WHO (World Health)	20 Jan 60	351UNTS355	105034
Chile	UN Special Fund	22 Jan 60	351UNTS115	105020
India	Japan	25 Jan 60	384UNTS31	105508
Multilateral		26 Jan 60	439UNTS249	106333
Colombia	UN Special Fund	04 Feb 60	355UNTS257	105080
Bolivia	UN Special Fund	09 Feb 60	351UNTS203	105024
Cuba	UNICEF (Children)	11 Feb 60	349UNTS277	105014
Argentina	Philippines	12 Feb 60	535UNTS293	107785
Afghanistan	UN Special Fund	21 Feb 60	351UNTS93	105019
Austria	Norway	25 Feb 60	376UNTS155	105380
Pakistan	UN Special Fund	25 Feb 60	351UNTS141	105021
France	UN Special Fund	17 Mar 60	354UNTS119	105059
Italy	UN Special Fund	01 Apr 60	354UNTS261	105066
Multilateral		12 Apr 60	359UNTS323	105150
UN Special Fund	Tunisia	12 Apr 60	355UNTS289	105082
Libya	UN Special Fund	19 Apr 60	356UNTS11	105090
ICAO (Civil Aviat)	UN Special Fund	21 Apr 60	360UNTS367	200569
UN Special Fund	Sudan	21 Apr 60	356UNTS213	105097
Cuba	Japan	22 Apr 60	442UNTS261	106354
UN Special Fund	Vietnam, South	29 Apr 60	357UNTS311	200567
Laos	UN Special Fund	30 Apr 60	361UNTS171	105179
United Nations	Togo	06 May 60	388UNTS53	105571
China People's Rep	Czechoslovakia	07 May 60	402UNTS209	105787
Lebanon	UN Special Fund	07 May 60	360UNTS225	105160
Czechoslovakia	Poland	17 May 60	424UNTS3	106096
Cambodia	WHO (World Health)	19 May 60	372UNTS193	105298
Czechoslovakia	Romania	21 May 60	397UNTS245	105709
UN Special Fund	WHO (World Health)	25 May 60	359UNTS375	200568
Multilateral		04 Jun 60	360UNTS208	105159
UN Special Fund	Togo	08 Jun 60	369UNTS401	200574
Multilateral		17 Jun 60	536UNTS27	107794

Privileges and immunities (Cont.)

PARTY ONE	PARTY TWO	DATE	CITATION	NUMBER
Multilateral		19 Jun 60	537UNTS214	107803
Iraq	UN Special Fund	19 Jun 60	376UNTS357	105389
Austria	UK Great Britain	24 Jun 60	502UNTS79	107327
Somalia	UK Great Britain	26 Jun 60	374UNTS363	105350
Kuwait	UN Special Fund	29 Jun 60	369UNTS419	200575
Multilateral		08 Jul 60	366UNTS310	105220
ITU (Telecommun)	UN Special Fund	13 Jul 60	368UNTS329	200573
Ethiopia	UN Special Fund	13 Jul 60	368UNTS159	105240
Ethiopia	United Nations	13 Jul 60	368UNTS143	105239
Multilateral		28 Jul 60	394UNTS37	105667
Jordan	WHO (World Health)	03 Aug 60	381UNTS133	105469
WHO (World Health)	United Arab Rep	03 Aug 60	385UNTS3	105524
WHO (World Health)	Tunisia	04 Aug 60	381UNTS335	105474
Laos	WHO (World Health)	04 Aug 60	373UNTS313	105322
Multilateral		01 Sep 60	403UNTS3	105792
WHO (World Health)	Saudi Arabia	06 Sep 60	395UNTS169	105684
Lebanon	WHO (World Health)	08 Sep 60	387UNTS49	105557
Iran	Japan	12 Sep 60	384UNTS43	105509
Brazil	UN Special Fund	16 Sep 60	375UNTS3	105351
Multilateral		19 Sep 60	419UNTS125	106032
Taiwan	UN Special Fund	20 Sep 60	375UNTS29	105352
Indonesia	UN Special Fund	07 Oct 60	378UNTS141	105424
Liberia	UN Special Fund	11 Oct 60	376UNTS341	105388
El Salvador	UN Special Fund	24 Oct 60	377UNTS171	105400
Kuwait	United Nations	31 Oct 60	391UNTS295	200581
UNICEF (Children)	Upper Volta	15 Nov 60	402UNTS33	105776
WHO (World Health)	Upper Volta	15 Nov 60	383UNTS91	105496
Mali	UNICEF (Children)	17 Nov 60	402UNTS23	105775
Pakistan	United Nations	17 Nov 60	380UNTS277	105460
Nepal	UN Special Fund	17 Nov 60	380UNTS289	105461
Guatemala	UN Special Fund	17 Nov 60	383UNTS67	105495
Cambodia	UN Special Fund	24 Nov 60	382UNTS255	105487
Fed of Malaya	WHO (World Health)	25 Nov 60	387UNTS37	105556
Cambodia	United Nations	30 Nov 60	383UNTS147	105500
Dahomey	WHO (World Health)	07 Dec 60	387UNTS277	105567
Congo (Brazzaville)	WHO (World Health)	12 Dec 60	399UNTS105	105737
Nepal	UNICEF (Children)	12 Dec 60	382UNTS273	105488
Multilateral		13 Dec 60	455UNTS3	106543
Multilateral		13 Dec 60	455UNTS204	106544
Bolivia	United Nations	14 Dec 60	382UNTS283	105489
Honduras	UN Special Fund	20 Dec 60	383UNTS103	105497
Burma	UN Special Fund	03 Jan 61	387UNTS219	105564
Costa Rica	UN Special Fund	10 Jan 61	389UNTS253	105597
UN Special Fund	Saudi Arabia	19 Jan 61	396UNTS27	105692
Korea, South	WHO (World Health)	20 Jan 61	406UNTS269	200589
Nicaragua	UN Special Fund	20 Jan 61	387UNTS15	105555
Chad	UN Special Fund	23 Jan 61	390UNTS69	105603
Multilateral		28 Jan 61	387UNTS202	105563
UN Special Fund	Somalia	28 Jan 61	388UNTS75	105573
Ivory Coast	WHO (World Health)	30 Jan 61	395UNTS205	105686
Gabon	UN Special Fund	02 Feb 61	387UNTS289	105568
WHO (World Health)	Togo	03 Feb 61	394UNTS207	105680
Nigeria	UN Special Fund	10 Feb 61	390UNTS85	105604
Central Afri Rep	WHO (World Health)	13 Feb 61	394UNTS149	105675
Mexico	UN Special Fund	23 Feb 61	388UNTS151	105576
Cyprus	UN Special Fund	24 Feb 61	389UNTS3	105588
Iraq	United Nations	05 Mar 61	409UNTS56	105878
Multilateral		08 Mar 61	396UNTS255	200584
Belgium	UK Great Britain	08 Mar 61	523UNTS17	107554
Panama	UN Special Fund	09 Mar 61	396UNTS3	105691
Cuba	UN Special Fund	10 Mar 61	390UNTS35	105601
Japan	United Nations	15 Mar 61	397UNTS199	105706
Kuwait	WHO (World Health)	16 Mar 61	397UNTS315	200588
Colombia	USA (United States)	04 Apr 61	405UNTS55	105822
Japan	UK Great Britain	11 Apr 61	420UNTS75	106042

Privileges and immunities (Cont.)

PARTY ONE	PARTY TWO	DATE	CITATION	NUMBER
Honduras	USA (United States)	12 Apr 61	413UNTS182	105952
Multilateral		14 Apr 61	422UNTS101	106071
Mauritania	WHO (World Health)	17 Apr 61	396UNTS301	200587
Multilateral		18 Apr 61	500UNTS95	107310
Cyprus	UNICEF (Children)	19 Apr 61	394UNTS185	105678
Korea, South	UN Special Fund	21 Apr 61	394UNTS231	200583
Mali	WHO (World Health)	27 Apr 61	407UNTS66	105860
Gabon	WHO (World Health)	27 Apr 61	397UNTS215	105707
Ceylon (Sri Lanka)	UN Special Fund	03 May 61	395UNTS217	105687
Sierra Leone	USA (United States)	05 May 61	409UNTS194	105885
Senegal	USA (United States)	13 May 61	409UNTS232	105888
Japan	Peru	15 May 61	451UNTS3	106482
Ivory Coast	USA (United States)	17 May 61	409UNTS241	105889
Niger	USA (United States)	26 May 61	410UNTS213	105905
Cameroon	USA (United States)	26 May 61	413UNTS195	105953
Dahomey	USA (United States)	27 May 61	445UNTS23	106373
South Africa	Sweden	29 May 61	442UNTS15	106335
Spain	UK Great Britain	30 May 61	562UNTS169	108198
Cameroon	UN Special Fund	13 Jun 61	397UNTS297	105713
Ethiopia	United Nations	14 Jun 61	406UNTS81	105840
Cyprus	United Nations	15 Jun 61	398UNTS39	105716
Ecuador	USA (United States)	17 Jun 61	411UNTS49	105913
Madagascar	USA (United States)	22 Jun 61	413UNTS219	105956
Paraguay	UN Special Fund	22 Jun 61	399UNTS117	105738
UN Special Fund	Upper Volta	26 Jun 61	400UNTS3	105744
Haiti	UN Special Fund	28 Jun 61	399UNTS171	105741
Haiti	United Nations	28 Jun 61	399UNTS159	105740
Philippines	UN Special Fund	28 Jun 61	399UNTS141	105739
Czechoslovakia	Poland	04 Jul 61	436UNTS189	106295
UNICEF (Children)	Saudi Arabia	04 Jul 61	413UNTS122	105947
Ghana	USA (United States)	19 Jul 61	416UNTS167	106002
Mali	UN Special Fund	21 Jul 61	401UNTS141	105768
Netherlands	Euratom	25 Jul 61	462UNTS313	106687
UN Special Fund	Yemen	02 Aug 61	402UNTS43	105777
Morocco	WHO (World Health)	09 Aug 61	412UNTS192	105932
Cameroon	UNICEF (Children)	12 Aug 61	402UNTS235	105788
Mexico	United Nations	18 Aug 61	404UNTS297	105817
Central Afri Rep	UNICEF (Children)	21 Aug 61	413UNTS48	105939
Poland	UNICEF (Children)	24 Aug 61	406UNTS95	105841
UNESCO (Educ/Cult)	Thailand	25 Aug 61	410UNTS125	105899
Chad	UNICEF (Children)	26 Aug 61	422UNTS231	106077
Lebanon	United Nations	26 Aug 61	406UNTS105	105842
Israel	Malagasy	27 Aug 61	484UNTS217	107032
Ivory Coast	UN Special Fund	29 Aug 61	406UNTS129	105844
ILO (Labor Org)	Thailand	30 Aug 61	422UNTS125	106072
Denmark	Pakistan	04 Sep 61	455UNTS305	106549
Jordan	United Nations	11 Sep 61	406UNTS255	105855
Iraq	WHO (World Health)	13 Sep 61	419UNTS69	106030
Bulgaria	Poland	19 Sep 61	483UNTS249	107018
Multilateral		20 Sep 61	407UNTS52	105859
Paraguay	USA (United States)	26 Sep 61	461UNTS91	106653
UN Special Fund	Sierra Leone	02 Oct 61	422UNTS131	106073
Greece	Sweden	06 Oct 61	481UNTS137	106981
Malagasy	WHO (World Health)	13 Oct 61	421UNTS273	106064
Multilateral		16 Oct 61	410UNTS242	105908
Austria	Denmark	23 Oct 61	425UNTS115	106122
Czechoslovakia	Hungary	02 Nov 61	438UNTS3	106313
Gabon	UNICEF (Children)	02 Nov 61	422UNTS241	106078
Multilateral		07 Nov 61	412UNTS258	105937
Mauritania	UN Special Fund	07 Nov 61	412UNTS240	105936
Congo (Brazzaville)	UN Special Fund	09 Nov 61	413UNTS58	105940
Brazil	USA (United States)	11 Nov 61	433UNTS199	106243
Malagasy	UNICEF (Children)	16 Nov 61	422UNTS251	106079
Congo (Zaire)	United Nations	27 Nov 61	414UNTS229	105975
IAEA (Atom Energy)	UN Special Fund	29 Nov 61	415UNTS408	200593

PARTY ONE	PARTY TWO	DATE	CITATION	NUMBER
Privileges and immunities (Cont.)				
Ceylon (Sri Lanka)	United Nations	04 Dec 61	415UNTS236	105987
COMECON (Econ Aid)	USSR (Soviet Union)	07 Dec 61	506UNTS325	107392
Panama	USA (United States)	11 Dec 61	445UNTS161	106384
UN Special Fund	Venezuela	11 Dec 61	422UNTS149	106074
UN Special Fund	Senegal	16 Dec 61	425UNTS97	106121
El Salvador	USA (United States)	19 Dec 61	445UNTS175	106385
Costa Rica	USA (United States)	22 Dec 61	460UNTS277	106646
Multilateral		27 Dec 61	425UNTS83	106120
Malagasy	UN Special Fund	05 Jan 62	419UNTS29	106028
Ivory Coast	UNICEF (Children)	10 Jan 62	422UNTS261	106080
Dominican Republic	USA (United States)	11 Jan 62	433UNTS133	106236
Ethiopia	WHO (World Health)	11 Jan 62	423UNTS99	106087
Multilateral		17 Jan 62	419UNTS294	106033
Multilateral		20 Jan 62	429UNTS230	200596
United Nations	Somalia	20 Jan 62	420UNTS133	106044
Poland	Romania	25 Jan 62	468UNTS3	106770
UNICEF (Children)	Yemen	31 Jan 62	422UNTS271	106081
Multilateral		13 Feb 62	422UNTS288	200594
India	United Nations	19 Feb 62	423UNTS3	106082
Multilateral		21 Feb 62	423UNTS151	106091
USSR (Soviet Union)	Yugoslavia	24 Feb 62	471UNTS195	106833
Niger	UN Special Fund	26 Feb 62	423UNTS83	106086
Multilateral		01 Mar 62	423UNTS122	106089
Dominican Republic	USA (United States)	08 Mar 62	527UNTS29	107615
WHO (World Health)	Sudan	11 Mar 62	432UNTS325	106226
United Nations	Saudi Arabia	16 Mar 62	456UNTS379	106566
Nigeria	WHO (World Health)	27 Mar 62	429UNTS123	106194
Dahomey	UN Special Fund	28 Mar 62	424UNTS55	106099
FAO (Food Agri)	USA (United States)	29 Mar 62	454UNTS13	106536
India	Japan	31 Mar 62	451UNTS143	106490
UNICEF (Children)	Somalia	01 Apr 62	431UNTS75	106211
Taiwan	Malagasy	04 Apr 62	463UNTS195	106703
Congo (Brazzaville)	UNICEF (Children)	09 Apr 62	431UNTS65	106210
Multilateral		10 Apr 62	429UNTS78	106192
UNICEF (Children)	Sierra Leone	11 Apr 62	431UNTS55	106209
Ecuador	USA (United States)	17 Apr 62	442UNTS69	106339
Multilateral		18 Apr 62	463UNTS44	106692
India	Japan	23 Apr 62	451UNTS155	106491
ILO (Labor Org)	Tanganyika	03 May 62	429UNTS73	106191
UN Special Fund	Uruguay	04 May 62	429UNTS143	106196
Israel	Sweden	15 May 62	484UNTS261	107036
Gabon	Israel	15 May 62	484UNTS181	107027
Multilateral		17 May 62	429UNTS46	106189
United Nations	Tanganyika	01 Jun 62	479UNTS3	106944
United Nations	Sweden	01 Jun 62	429UNTS135	106195
Dominican Republic	UN Special Fund	06 Jun 62	429UNTS169	106197
Multilateral		14 Jun 62	528UNTS33	107634
Libya	WHO (World Health)	16 Jun 62	437UNTS127	106301
WHO (World Health)	Sierra Leone	19 Jun 62	439UNTS151	106327
Germany, West	Syria	25 Jun 62	489UNTS71	107135
Denmark	UK Great Britain	27 Jun 62	562UNTS75	108197
Congo (Zaire)	IAEA (Atom Energy)	27 Jun 62	463UNTS31	106691
Germany, West	United Nations	28 Jun 62	434UNTS249	200597
UN Special Fund	Syria	07 Jul 62	443UNTS3	106355
UN Special Fund	Tanganyika	17 Jul 62	435UNTS237	106281
Czechoslovakia	COMECON (Econ Aid)	20 Jul 62	506UNTS345	107393
Senegal	USA (United States)	20 Jul 62	458UNTS137	106596
Colombia	USA (United States)	23 Jul 62	458UNTS123	106595
Multilateral		25 Jul 62	506UNTS177	107387
WHO (World Health)	Senegal	06 Aug 62	435UNTS179	106279
Nigeria	United Nations	07 Aug 62	435UNTS167	106278
Multilateral		12 Aug 62	443UNTS266	106365
WHO (World Health)	Western Samoa	14 Aug 62	437UNTS317	200598
Multilateral		29 Aug 62	443UNTS280	106366
Cameroon	United Nations	29 Aug 62	442UNTS3	106334

PARTY ONE	PARTY TWO	DATE	CITATION	NUMBER
Privileges and immunities (Cont.)				
Niger	United Nations	01 Oct 62	439UNTS181	106329
Chile	USA (United States)	04 Oct 62	461UNTS129	106656
Poland	Romania	05 Oct 62	521UNTS3	107516
Belgium	Rwanda	13 Oct 62	456UNTS431	106569
Austria	Luxembourg	18 Oct 62	496UNTS97	107248
Cameroon	Israel	24 Oct 62	449UNTS3	106446
Japan	UN Special Fund	31 Oct 62	444UNTS171	106368
United Nations	Western Samoa	05 Nov 62	443UNTS297	200599
Romania	Yugoslavia	08 Nov 62	472UNTS305	106845
Japan	UK Great Britain	14 Nov 62	478UNTS29	106934
Algeria	UN Special Fund	15 Nov 62	452UNTS243	106512
Multilateral		15 Nov 62	448UNTS50	106424
United Nations	Syria	17 Nov 62	456UNTS359	106565
WHO (World Health)	Syria	18 Nov 62	480UNTS249	106972
Germany, West	USA (United States)	20 Nov 62	505UNTS263	107377
Thailand	UK Great Britain	20 Nov 62	466UNTS243	106747
Algeria	UNICEF (Children)	20 Nov 62	453UNTS151	106522
Ceylon (Sri Lanka)	ILO (Labor Org)	21 Nov 62	449UNTS263	106463
Costa Rica	USA (United States)	23 Nov 62	541UNTS67	107861
Ecuador	United Nations	26 Nov 62	445UNTS3	106372
Rwanda	United Nations	28 Nov 62	450UNTS267	106473
Niger	UNICEF (Children)	05 Dec 62	503UNTS195	107344
Multilateral		06 Dec 62	450UNTS240	106471
Cameroon	WHO (World Health)	08 Dec 62	451UNTS215	106496
Ivory Coast	United Nations	10 Dec 62	451UNTS269	106498
Multilateral		12 Dec 62	457UNTS72	106578
Multilateral		17 Dec 62	486UNTS119	107076
Luxembourg	USA (United States)	18 Dec 62	532UNTS277	107723
Algeria	WHO (World Health)	20 Dec 62	463UNTS135	106698
Israel	United Nations	07 Jan 63	450UNTS229	106470
Korea, South	USA (United States)	08 Jan 63	493UNTS105	107211
Czechoslovakia	Vietnam, North	14 Jan 63	501UNTS181	107318
Mauritania	UNICEF (Children)	19 Jan 63	452UNTS271	106514
Multilateral		21 Jan 63	453UNTS20	106517
UNICEF (Children)	Tanganyika	25 Jan 63	453UNTS249	106528
Austria	United Nations	29 Jan 63	452UNTS261	106513
Japan	New Zealand	30 Jan 63	517UNTS183	107486
Multilateral		05 Feb 63	453UNTS36	106518
United Nations	United Arab Rep	08 Feb 63	453UNTS79	106520
Central Afri Rep	USA (United States)	10 Feb 63	473UNTS83	106857
Multilateral		14 Feb 63	453UNTS168	106524
Poland	COMECON (Econ Aid)	22 Feb 63	506UNTS303	107391
Hungary	COMECON (Econ Aid)	28 Feb 63	506UNTS281	107390
Japan	Thailand	01 Mar 63	475UNTS233	106895
Multilateral		06 Mar 63	455UNTS386	106552
Indonesia	USA (United States)	14 Mar 63	505UNTS79	107365
Japan	USA (United States)	22 Mar 63	518UNTS179	107495
UN Special Fund	Uganda	22 Mar 63	456UNTS466	106572
Burma	Japan	29 Mar 63	518UNTS3	107490
Ethiopia	UNICEF (Children)	01 Apr 63	457UNTS103	106579
Pakistan	United Nations	18 Apr 63	503UNTS25	107339
Multilateral		18 Apr 63	463UNTS121	106697
Multilateral		20 Apr 63	495UNTS3	107239
Multilateral		24 Apr 63	596UNTS261	108638
Norway	Spain	25 Apr 63	503UNTS41	107340
UN Special Fund	Trinidad/Tobago	06 May 63	463UNTS93	106695
United Nations	Trinidad/Tobago	06 May 63	463UNTS109	106696
Multilateral		06 May 63	463UNTS78	106694
Multilateral		09 May 63	463UNTS159	106700
Mali	United Nations	09 May 63	463UNTS147	106699
Australia	United Nations	13 May 63	463UNTS187	106702
Denmark	India	15 May 63	616UNTS23	108889
Denmark	India	15 May 63	616UNTS39	108890
Denmark	India	15 May 63	616UNTS49	108891
Jamaica	UN Special Fund	22 May 63	489UNTS191	107140

Privileges and immunities (Cont.)

PARTY ONE	PARTY TWO	DATE	CITATION	NUMBER
Multilateral		22 May 63	483UNTS72	107007
Jamaica	United Nations	22 May 63	479UNTS19	106945
Netherlands	UN Special Fund	24 May 63	466UNTS289	106750
Multilateral		24 May 63	466UNTS346	106754
United Nations	Uganda	29 May 63	466UNTS311	106751
UN Special Fund	Western Samoa	05 Jun 63	467UNTS463	200601
Jamaica	USA (United States)	06 Jun 63	477UNTS29	106913
Mongolia	WHO (World Health)	21 Jun 63	472UNTS373	106848
Czechoslovakia	Yugoslavia	24 Jun 63	496UNTS3	107246
Austria	USA (United States)	25 Jun 63	479UNTS223	106956
UNICEF (Children)	Togo	27 Jun 63	540UNTS135	107847
United Nations	UK Great Britain	27 Jun 63	469UNTS145	106789
Hungary	Mongolia	10 Jul 63	519UNTS173	107508
Poland	United Nations	16 Jul 63	471UNTS3	106817
Multilateral		23 Jul 63	471UNTS158	106831
Congo (Zaire)	UN Special Fund	26 Jul 63	474UNTS137	106878
Italy	United Nations	26 Jul 63	472UNTS173	106840
Multilateral		31 Jul 63	472UNTS220	106842
Dominican Republic	United Nations	05 Aug 63	472UNTS353	106847
UNICEF (Children)	Trinidad/Tobago	08 Aug 63	473UNTS281	106865
Burundi	WHO (World Health)	08 Aug 63	477UNTS346	106928
Cameroon	UK Great Britain	20 Aug 63	539UNTS233	107834
Burundi	UN Special Fund	22 Aug 63	476UNTS49	106903
United Nations	Saudi Arabia	23 Aug 63	474UNTS155	106879
Multilateral		27 Aug 63	511UNTS210	107435
Colombia	United Nations	27 Aug 63	481UNTS3	106975
United Nations	United Arab Rep	27 Aug 63	474UNTS221	106884
Dahomey	UNICEF (Children)	28 Aug 63	507UNTS101	107396
Multilateral		10 Sep 63	480UNTS100	106965
Multilateral		23 Sep 63	488UNTS99	107122
Jamaica	WHO (World Health)	25 Sep 63	481UNTS125	106980
Austria	Finland	08 Oct 63	490UNTS255	107160
Italy	IAEA (Atom Energy)	11 Oct 63	639UNTS25	109142
Canada	France	11 Oct 63	529UNTS71	107657
UK Great Britain	USA (United States)	11 Oct 63	483UNTS3	107005
Multilateral		23 Oct 63	506UNTS197	107388
Panama	USA (United States)	30 Oct 63	530UNTS3	107668
Central Afri Rep	UN Special Fund	30 Oct 63	481UNTS247	106985
Multilateral		30 Oct 63	480UNTS180	106968
WHO (World Health)	Tanganyika	05 Nov 63	496UNTS193	107252
Multilateral		07 Nov 63	480UNTS232	106971
Czechoslovakia	Mongolia	08 Nov 63	503UNTS125	107341
Multilateral		08 Nov 63	482UNTS286	106999
Niger	United Nations	20 Nov 63	536UNTS3	107793
Iran	UNICEF (Children)	21 Nov 63	485UNTS35	107044
Brazil	Germany, West	30 Nov 63	0UNTS0	109423
Nicaragua	United Nations	03 Dec 63	482UNTS329	107002
Iraq	UNICEF (Children)	03 Dec 63	482UNTS319	107001
Cameroon	Netherlands	18 Dec 63	521UNTS303	107527
Taiwan	USA (United States)	19 Dec 63	527UNTS69	107617
Czechoslovakia	Hungary	20 Dec 63	538UNTS127	107812
Romania	Yugoslavia	20 Dec 63	527UNTS245	107629
Burundi	UNICEF (Children)	08 Jan 64	485UNTS45	107045
Norway	Thailand	09 Jan 64	522UNTS65	107537
Czechoslovakia	Yugoslavia	20 Jan 64	538UNTS197	107816
UNICEF (Children)	Senegal	22 Jan 64	486UNTS91	107074
Multilateral		28 Jan 64	502UNTS321	107336
Iceland	USA (United States)	13 Feb 64	524UNTS235	107576
United Nations	Sierra Leone	19 Feb 64	489UNTS91	107136
Multilateral		20 Feb 64	491UNTS30	107172
United Nations	Upper Volta	26 Feb 64	489UNTS179	107139
UNESCO (Educ/Cult)	Yugoslavia	27 Feb 64	489UNTS257	107143
Morocco	United Nations	03 Mar 64	490UNTS187	107154
Italy	United Nations	18 Mar 64	491UNTS21	107171
Rwanda	UN Special Fund	18 Mar 64	491UNTS3	107170

Privileges and immunities (Cont.)

PARTY ONE	PARTY TWO	DATE	CITATION	NUMBER
Cyprus	United Nations	30 Mar 64	492UNTS261	107194
United Nations	Turkey	31 Mar 64	492UNTS273	107196
Greece	United Nations	31 Mar 64	492UNTS267	107195
Cyprus	United Nations	31 Mar 64	492UNTS57	107187
Germany, West	Thailand	02 Apr 64	503UNTS3	107338
United Nations	UK Great Britain	02 Apr 64	492UNTS279	107197
Denmark	Finland	07 Apr 64	525UNTS89	107586
Taiwan	UNICEF (Children)	08 Apr 64	500UNTS49	107306
Afghanistan	United Nations	28 Apr 64	494UNTS77	107227
Japan	UK Great Britain	04 May 64	561UNTS25	108179
Jamaica	UNICEF (Children)	19 May 64	500UNTS75	107308
Netherlands	United Nations	27 May 64	548UNTS79	107971
USA (United States)	USSR (Soviet Union)	01 Jun 64	0UNTS0	109383
Ireland	UN Special Fund	03 Jun 64	496UNTS205	107253
Ceylon (Sri Lanka)	Norway	11 Jun 64	559UNTS23	108153
Austria	United Nations	11 Jun 64	500UNTS85	107309
Rwanda	WHO (World Health)	22 Jun 64	514UNTS11	107440
Rwanda	WHO (World Health)	23 Jun 64	514UNTS157	107445
WHO (World Health)	Trinidad/Tobago	23 Jun 64	503UNTS167	107342
Multilateral		23 Jun 64	506UNTS108	107383
Multilateral		28 Jun 64	519UNTS14	107499
Malaysia	UNICEF (Children)	01 Jul 64	503UNTS229	107346
United Nations	Togo	03 Jul 64	502UNTS287	107334
Colombia	Netherlands	06 Jul 64	543UNTS289	107906
Iceland	UN Special Fund	10 Jul 64	502UNTS343	107337
Belgium	Tunisia	15 Jul 64	561UNTS297	108190
Belgium	Tunisia	15 Jul 64	560UNTS65	108169
Mexico	United Nations	17 Jul 64	533UNTS117	107738
France	Eur Space Research	10 Aug 64	528UNTS135	107637
Australia	USA (United States)	17 Aug 64	530UNTS209	107683
Taiwan	Philippines	25 Aug 64	511UNTS233	107436
Kenya	USA (United States)	26 Aug 64	531UNTS51	107692
Dominican Republic	USA (United States)	28 Aug 64	531UNTS35	107691
Canada	Japan	05 Sep 64	569UNTS99	108282
Rwanda	UNICEF (Children)	11 Sep 64	510UNTS127	107409
Philippines	United Nations	15 Sep 64	510UNTS137	107410
Norway	United Arab Rep	20 Oct 64	543UNTS3	107895
Multilateral		24 Oct 64	514UNTS220	200608
Malawi	UN Special Fund	24 Oct 64	514UNTS235	200609
Romania	UN Special Fund	24 Oct 64	519UNTS29	107500
Mongolia	Poland	28 Oct 64	552UNTS115	108052
Netherlands	Pakistan	30 Oct 64	541UNTS243	107873
Austria	Hungary	31 Oct 64	545UNTS223	107936
Multilateral		11 Nov 64	515UNTS94	107456
India	United Nations	25 Nov 64	519UNTS47	107501
France	Japan	27 Nov 64	569UNTS157	108283
Taiwan	Korea, South	27 Nov 64	555UNTS3	108102
Multilateral		01 Dec 64	550UNTS133	108012
India	Netherlands	11 Dec 64	570UNTS165	108292
Multilateral		11 Dec 64	547UNTS297	107964
Multilateral		15 Dec 64	522UNTS20	107533
UN Special Fund	Zambia	15 Dec 64	522UNTS3	107532
Germany, West	Jamaica	16 Dec 64	531UNTS129	107699
Taiwan	USA (United States)	19 Dec 64	532UNTS313	107725
Malawi	WHO (World Health)	06 Jan 65	525UNTS165	107588
Mongolia	United Nations	06 Jan 65	522UNTS45	107535
United Nations	Yugoslavia	07 Jan 65	522UNTS55	107536
Malawi	WHO (World Health)	08 Jan 65	524UNTS281	107579
Finland	Israel	21 Jan 65	581UNTS275	108450
Ethiopia	WHO (World Health)	27 Jan 65	541UNTS135	107866
WHO (World Health)	Tunisia	27 Jan 65	528UNTS209	107644
Multilateral		27 Jan 65	523UNTS102	107556
Multilateral		02 Feb 65	523UNTS256	107560
Multilateral		12 Feb 65	525UNTS148	107587
Iran	United Nations	16 Feb 65	525UNTS211	107593

Privileges and immunities (Cont.)

PARTY ONE	PARTY TWO	DATE	CITATION	NUMBER
Belgium	United Nations	20 Feb 65	535UNTS197	107780
Multilateral		23 Feb 65	527UNTS120	107622
Multilateral		05 Mar 65	527UNTS221	107627
SEATO (SE Asia)	UK Great Britain	12 Mar 65	561UNTS313	108191
Multilateral		18 Mar 65	575UNTS159	108359
Finland	United Arab Rep	01 Apr 65	562UNTS3	108193
Multilateral		08 Apr 65	533UNTS66	107733
Malawi	USA (United States)	20 Apr 65	546UNTS175	107943
UK Great Britain	Yugoslavia	21 Apr 65	595UNTS189	108620
Malta	UNICEF (Children)	22 Apr 65	533UNTS107	107737
Multilateral		26 Apr 65	533UNTS50	107732
Netherlands	Tanzania	27 Apr 65	594UNTS123	108599
Guatemala	USA (United States)	04 May 65	545UNTS163	107932
Multilateral		12 May 65	534UNTS390	107769
Multilateral		14 May 65	550UNTS310	108026
Multilateral		25 May 65	535UNTS374	107791
Gambia	UNICEF (Children)	29 May 65	547UNTS29	107954
Denmark	Thailand	01 Jun 65	551UNTS157	108040
Multilateral		02 Jun 65	537UNTS348	200611
Multilateral		02 Jun 65	551UNTS2	108030
Mongolia	UNICEF (Children)	23 Jun 65	540UNTS83	107844
Austria	Petrol Export Org	24 Jun 65	589UNTS135	108540
UN Special Fund	Spain	30 Jun 65	544UNTS159	107918
Multilateral		05 Jul 65	563UNTS104	108207
Multilateral		20 Jul 65	541UNTS12	107857
Poland	WHO (World Health)	26 Aug 65	552UNTS3	108047
Multilateral		13 Sep 65	547UNTS264	107962
Multilateral		13 Sep 65	547UNTS248	107961
France	UK Great Britain	21 Sep 65	561UNTS3	108177
Australia	Korea, South	21 Sep 65	548UNTS163	107977
Multilateral		21 Oct 65	547UNTS216	107959
United Nations	Zambia	23 Oct 65	549UNTS101	107993
Netherlands	Nigeria	28 Oct 65	578UNTS15	108383
Multilateral		12 Nov 65	550UNTS160	108013
United Nations	United Arab Rep	26 Nov 65	551UNTS253	108046
Chile	UNICEF (Children)	30 Nov 65	596UNTS215	108635
UK Great Britain	USSR (Soviet Union)	02 Dec 65	0UNTS0	109384
Multilateral		04 Dec 65	571UNTS123	108303
Monaco	United Nations	17 Dec 65	550UNTS365	200615
Multilateral		31 Dec 65	616UNTS317	108904
United Nations	Senegal	12 Jan 66	551UNTS147	108039
Multilateral		17 Jan 66	592UNTS101	108573
Finland	USSR (Soviet Union)	24 Jan 66	576UNTS35	108364
Mongolia	UN Special Fund	26 Jan 66	552UNTS201	108055
Canada	United Nations	21 Feb 66	555UNTS119	108107
Finland	United Nations	21 Feb 66	555UNTS157	108109
Denmark	United Nations	21 Feb 66	555UNTS151	108108
New Zealand	United Nations	21 Feb 66	555UNTS163	108110
United Nations	Sweden	21 Feb 66	555UNTS169	108111
Austria	United Nations	24 Feb 66	557UNTS129	108131
Israel	Kenya	25 Feb 66	582UNTS23	108455
Australia	United Nations	25 Feb 66	557UNTS85	108129
Hungary	United Nations	04 Mar 66	559UNTS3	108151
Bulgaria	UNICEF (Children)	10 Mar 66	559UNTS13	108152
Brazil	United Nations	24 Mar 66	560UNTS47	108167
Brazil	UNICEF (Children)	28 Mar 66	607UNTS235	108807
WHO (World Health)	Singapore	28 Mar 66	562UNTS59	108195
Multilateral		05 Apr 66	640UNTS133	109159
Philippines	United Nations	05 Apr 66	560UNTS191	108174
Italy	United Nations	23 May 66	565UNTS11	108231
Maldive Islands	WHO (World Health)	23 May 66	566UNTS19	108237
United Nations	Switzerland	03 Jun 66	564UNTS193	200621
Liberia	UNICEF (Children)	08 Jun 66	570UNTS31	108286
Denmark	Iran	14 Jun 66	597UNTS283	108652
Greece	United Nations	20 Jun 66	565UNTS3	108230
Denmark	Israel	27 Jun 66	581UNTS227	108448
Japan	USSR (Soviet Union)	29 Jul 66	608UNTS93	108815
United Nations	Tunisia	04 Aug 66	576UNTS23	108363
Multilateral		06 Aug 66	570UNTS178	108294
Chad	USA (United States)	31 Aug 66	606UNTS47	108773
Korea, South	USA (United States)	14 Sep 66	606UNTS55	108774
UN Special Fund	UPU (Postal Union)	21 Sep 66	573UNTS259	200626
Multilateral		23 Sep 66	573UNTS132	108327
Tunisia	USA (United States)	26 Sep 66	616UNTS259	108900
Argentina	Vatican/Holy See	10 Oct 66	601UNTS187	108696
United Nations	Sudan	08 Nov 66	576UNTS85	108365
Indonesia	UNICEF (Children)	17 Nov 66	578UNTS47	108386
Jamaica	United Nations	06 Dec 66	580UNTS211	108424
Asian Devel Bank	Philippines	22 Dec 66	615UNTS375	108887
Guinea	UNICEF (Children)	22 Dec 66	585UNTS137	108486
Romania	Spain	05 Jan 67	642UNTS103	109168
Finland	United Nations	16 Jan 67	588UNTS153	108522
Trinidad/Tobago	UK Great Britain	23 Jan 67	605UNTS277	108767
Multilateral		25 Jan 67	588UNTS212	108527
UNICEF (Children)	Zambia	02 Feb 67	589UNTS89	108536
Australia	UN Special Fund	06 Feb 67	590UNTS3	108543
Nigeria	United Nations	07 Feb 67	590UNTS25	108544
Multilateral		14 Feb 67	634UNTS281	109068
Poland	United Nations	20 Feb 67	590UNTS71	108547
Multilateral		27 Feb 67	590UNTS156	108552
Algeria	ILO (Labor Org)	06 Apr 67	595UNTS99	108614
Romania	United Nations	08 Apr 67	594UNTS159	108602
Ghana	United Nations	08 Apr 67	594UNTS149	108601
Multilateral		13 Apr 67	595UNTS60	108612
Austria	United Nations	13 Apr 67	600UNTS93	108679
Greece	United Nations	14 Apr 67	595UNTS83	108613
Multilateral		19 Apr 67	595UNTS120	108617
Hungary	UN Special Fund	28 Apr 67	595UNTS171	108619
Cameroon	ILO (Labor Org)	07 May 67	596UNTS209	108634
Malta	WHO (World Health)	10 May 67	603UNTS99	108727
Multilateral		21 Jun 67	598UNTS2	108653
Czechoslovakia	UN Special Fund	13 Jul 67	606UNTS71	108776
Barbados	WHO (World Health)	18 Jul 67	603UNTS87	108726
New Zealand	WHO (World Health)	29 Aug 67	607UNTS57	108795
Multilateral		12 Oct 67	607UNTS20	108793
Botswana	UN Special Fund	12 Oct 67	607UNTS37	108794
Denmark	Zambia	17 Oct 67	620UNTS239	108960
India	United Nations	04 Nov 67	609UNTS3	108824
Lesotho	WHO (World Health)	07 Nov 67	632UNTS143	109016
United Nations	Senegal	08 Nov 67	613UNTS255	108854
Eur Space Research	UK Great Britain	24 Nov 67	638UNTS17	109129
Sweden	USSR (Soviet Union)	30 Nov 67	0UNTS0	109385
ILO (Labor Org)	Zambia	20 Dec 67	619UNTS293	108947
Australia	UNICEF (Children)	21 Dec 67	614UNTS83	108864
Italy	United Nations	15 Jan 68	635UNTS11	109070
Iran	United Nations	15 Feb 68	631UNTS103	108990
Mauritius	UK Great Britain	12 Mar 68	0UNTS0	109269
Austria	United Nations	12 Mar 68	632UNTS131	109015
United Nations	UK Great Britain	12 Mar 68	632UNTS121	109014
Congo (Brazzaville)	United Nations	13 Mar 68	632UNTS161	109018
United Nations	Tunisia	18 Mar 68	633UNTS3	109030
State/IGO Group	Jordan	03 Apr 68	632UNTS66	109009
UN Special Fund	Syria	22 Apr 68	634UNTS207	109063
Niger	United Nations	07 May 68	639UNTS71	109145
State/IGO Group	Australia	21 May 68	636UNTS326	109108
Austria	United Nations	25 May 68	637UNTS0	109117
Botswana	UNICEF (Children)	25 Jun 68	639UNTS61	109144
Guyana	WHO (World Health)	03 Jul 68	642UNTS13	109161
India	United Nations	22 Jul 68	640UNTS121	109158
Int Wheat Coun	UK Great Britain	28 Nov 68	0UNTS0	109498

PARTY ONE	PARTY TWO	DATE	CITATION	NUMBER
Privileges and immunities (Cont.)				
Multilateral		24 Dec 68	0UNTS0	109369
ILO (Labor Org)	Trinidad/Tobago	14 Mar 69	0UNTS0	109500
UN Special Fund	Southern Yemen	04 Apr 69	0UNTS0	109456
State/IGO Group	Southern Yemen	04 Apr 69	0UNTS0	109455
Property				
Multilateral		13 Feb 46	1UNTS15	100004
ILO (Labor Org)	Switzerland	11 Mar 46	15UNTS377	200103
United Nations	Switzerland	01 Jul 46	1UNTS163	200008
United Nations	USA (United States)	26 Jun 47	11UNTS11	100147
Taiwan	Italy	30 Jul 47	12UNTS383	100195
Multilateral		21 Nov 47	33UNTS261	100521
United Nations	USA (United States)	18 Dec 47	11UNTS347	100174
Peru	ICAO (Civil Aviat)	22 Oct 48	95UNTS3	101315
WHO (World Health)	Switzerland	12 Jan 49	26UNTS331	200155
Multilateral		02 Sep 49	250UNTS12	103515
WHO (World Health)	United Arab Rep	25 Mar 51	223UNTS87	103058
Philippines	WHO (World Health)	22 Jul 51	149UNTS197	101953
Multilateral		20 Sep 51	200UNTS3	102691
Korea, South	United Nations	21 Sep 51	104UNTS323	200322
Sweden	UK Great Britain	14 Mar 52	202UNTS157	102731
France	WHO (World Health)	23 Jul 52	209UNTS231	102829
Greece	UK Great Britain	17 Apr 53	191UNTS151	102582
ICAO (Civil Aviat)	United Arab Rep	27 Aug 53	215UNTS371	102925
United Nations	Thailand	26 May 54	260UNTS35	103703
France	UNESCO (Educ/Cult)	02 Jul 54	357UNTS3	105103
Mexico	ILO (Labor Org)	05 Jan 55	208UNTS225	102815
WMO (Meteorology)	Switzerland	10 Mar 55	211UNTS277	200524
CERN (Nuc Resrch)	Switzerland	11 Jun 55	249UNTS405	200544
Denmark	WHO (World Health)	29 Jun 55	247UNTS168	103467
Bulgaria	Hungary	27 Jun 58	438UNTS235	106318
Multilateral		01 Jul 59	374UNTS147	105334
Multilateral		14 Dec 59	368UNTS237	105244
Multilateral		28 Jul 60	394UNTS37	105667
Guatemala	UN Special Fund	17 Nov 60	383UNTS67	105495
Congo (Zaire)	United Nations	27 Nov 61	414UNTS229	105975
Multilateral		24 Apr 63	596UNTS261	108638
United Nations	Trinidad/Tobago	06 May 63	463UNTS109	106696
Hungary	Mongolia	10 Jul 63	519UNTS173	107508
Kenya	United Nations	01 Oct 64	511UNTS199	107434
UK Great Britain	Yugoslavia	21 Apr 65	595UNTS189	108620
UK Great Britain	USSR (Soviet Union)	02 Dec 65	0UNTS0	109384
Sweden	USSR (Soviet Union)	30 Nov 67	0UNTS0	109385
Proxy diplomacy				
Saudi Arabia	UK Great Britain	20 Apr 42	10UNTS151	200058
Ceylon (Sri Lanka)	UK Great Britain	11 Nov 47	86UNTS25	101149
Belgium	Czechoslovakia	03 Jul 48	77UNTS137	100997
Belgium	Portugal	01 Mar 49	32UNTS49	100488
Belgium	Bolivia	26 Apr 49	34UNTS103	100530
UNICEF (Children)	UK Great Britain	17 Jun 49	65UNTS50	100820
Multilateral		16 Apr 52	139UNTS35	101874
Belgium	Greece	24 Apr 52	166UNTS261	102191
Multilateral		18 Apr 61	500UNTS95	107310
UK Great Britain	USA (United States)	26 Apr 62	445UNTS273	106395
Luxembourg	Netherlands	24 Mar 64	548UNTS137	107975
Nationality and citizenship				
Bolivia	Brazil	25 Feb 38	54UNTS333	200205
Belgium	France	30 Mar 45	20UNTS297	200122
UK Great Britain	USA (United States)	27 Mar 46	4UNTS101	100040
Albania	Yugoslavia	28 Nov 46	111UNTS143	101527
Belgium	France	09 Jan 47	36UNTS145	100568
Norway	Sweden	21 Jun 47	94UNTS107	101309
Belgium	United Arab Rep	01 Jul 47	34UNTS93	100529
Burma	UK Great Britain	17 Oct 47	70UNTS183	100904
Belgium	France	23 Apr 48	19UNTS95	100307

PARTY ONE	PARTY TWO	DATE	CITATION	NUMBER
Nationality and citizenship (Cont.)				
Philippines	Spain	20 May 48	70UNTS143	100903
Belgium	Monaco	05 Jun 48	18UNTS245	100294
Belgium	France	30 Dec 49	46UNTS111	100704
Multilateral		21 Dec 50	90UNTS3	101222
France	India	02 Feb 51	203UNTS155	102744
Belgium	USA (United States)	16 Mar 51	93UNTS109	101295
France	Sweden	16 Feb 54	228UNTS137	103147
Belgium	Netherlands	28 Jun 54	272UNTS235	103942
Multilateral		05 Oct 54	235UNTS99	103297
Sweden	Switzerland	17 Dec 54	369UNTS233	105260
Multilateral		15 Sep 55	254UNTS55	103593
Austria	USSR (Soviet Union)	17 Oct 55	240UNTS289	103409
Belgium	Sweden	18 Jan 56	293UNTS23	104283
USSR (Soviet Union)	Yugoslavia	22 May 56	259UNTS155	103688
Denmark	Norway	23 May 56	271UNTS75	103910
Switzerland	UK Great Britain	12 Jun 56	269UNTS133	103879
Belgium	Germany, West	24 Sep 56	314UNTS195	104549
Norway	Sweden	27 Sep 56	261UNTS71	103726
Italy	Sweden	20 Dec 56	369UNTS357	105265
Italy	Sweden	20 Dec 56	369UNTS305	105263
Finland	Switzerland	27 Dec 56	277UNTS7	103996
Denmark	Switzerland	14 Jan 57	286UNTS85	104161
Multilateral		20 Feb 57	309UNTS65	104468
Denmark	Netherlands	20 Feb 57	287UNTS41	104179
Denmark	Norway	22 Feb 57	286UNTS127	104164
Albania	USSR (Soviet Union)	18 Sep 57	307UNTS251	104454
Belgium	UK Great Britain	03 Oct 57	394UNTS69	105669
China People's Rep	USSR (Soviet Union)	21 Dec 57	305UNTS213	104420
Belgium	Germany, West	17 Jan 58	328UNTS173	104735
Multilateral		29 Apr 58	450UNTS11	106465
Czechoslovakia	Hungary	27 Jun 58	477UNTS321	106927
Denmark	Sweden	21 Jul 58	320UNTS163	104642
Belgium	France	20 Sep 58	376UNTS331	105387
Germany, West	Netherlands	10 Oct 58	486UNTS345	107085
Canada	USA (United States)	31 Oct 58	391UNTS219	105626
Austria	Sweden	14 May 59	428UNTS3	106167
Belgium	Spain	27 May 59	340UNTS81	104860
Germany, West	Netherlands	16 Jun 59	593UNTS3	108576
Bulgaria	Romania	21 Sep 59	387UNTS61	105558
Austria	France	08 Oct 59	453UNTS95	106521
Ethiopia	France	12 Nov 59	381UNTS3	105465
Austria	Norway	25 Feb 60	376UNTS155	105380
Romania	USA (United States)	30 Mar 60	371UNTS163	105278
Sweden	UK Great Britain	28 Jul 60	404UNTS85	105806
Multilateral		16 Aug 60	382UNTS8	105476
Sweden	Tunisia	06 Sep 60	427UNTS301	106162
Czechoslovakia	Hungary	04 Nov 60	397UNTS227	105708
Romania	UK Great Britain	10 Nov 60	385UNTS113	105533
Denmark	Germany, West	10 Nov 60	431UNTS21	106205
Iceland	UK Great Britain	09 Feb 61	398UNTS259	105728
Canada	USA (United States)	17 Feb 61	445UNTS143	106383
Germany, West	UK Great Britain	20 Feb 61	398UNTS249	105727
Belgium	UK Great Britain	21 Feb 61	398UNTS229	105724
Netherlands	UK Great Britain	21 Feb 61	398UNTS235	105725
Luxembourg	UK Great Britain	21 Feb 61	398UNTS243	105726
Switzerland	UK Great Britain	27 Feb 61	404UNTS167	105809
Morocco	Sweden	30 Mar 61	427UNTS185	106154
Belgium	Chile	07 Apr 61	410UNTS255	105909
South Africa	Sweden	29 May 61	442UNTS15	106335
Hungary	Poland	05 Jul 61	437UNTS3	106296
Austria	Germany, West	19 Jul 61	414UNTS211	105974
Italy	Norway	25 Aug 61	475UNTS269	106896
Austria	Denmark	23 Oct 61	425UNTS115	106122
Multilateral		16 Dec 61	544UNTS19	107909
Belgium	Luxembourg	30 Aug 62	485UNTS313	107062

PARTY ONE	PARTY TWO	DATE	CITATION	NUMBER
Nationality and citizenship (Cont.)				
Germany, West	Ireland	17 Oct 62	604UNTS135	108749
Austria	Luxembourg	18 Oct 62	496UNTS97	107248
Austria	France	30 Nov 62	463UNTS173	106701
Netherlands	Spain	17 Dec 62	499UNTS227	107301
Austria	Italy	22 Apr 63	491UNTS53	107173
Multilateral		24 Apr 63	596UNTS469	108639
Norway	Spain	25 Apr 63	503UNTS41	107340
Multilateral		06 May 63	634UNTS221	109065
Argentina	Belgium	11 Jun 63	635UNTS135	109077
France	UK Great Britain	21 Jun 63	540UNTS311	107855
Austria	Finland	08 Oct 63	490UNTS255	107160
Norway	Thailand	09 Jan 64	522UNTS65	107537
Norway	United Arab Rep	20 Oct 64	543UNTS3	107895
Multilateral		19 Nov 64	523UNTS3	107553
WMO (Meteorology)	UK Great Britain	16 Dec 64	548UNTS57	107969
Finland	Israel	21 Jan 65	581UNTS275	108450
Multilateral		15 Feb 65	547UNTS3	107953
Finland	United Arab Rep	01 Apr 65	562UNTS3	108193
UK Great Britain	Yugoslavia	21 Apr 65	595UNTS189	108620
Denmark	Thailand	01 Jun 65	551UNTS157	108040
Chile	UNICEF (Children)	30 Nov 65	596UNTS215	108635
UK Great Britain	USSR (Soviet Union)	02 Dec 65	0UNTS0	109384
Spain	USA (United States)	14 Apr 66	579UNTS173	108406
Multilateral		17 May 66	571UNTS89	108302
Denmark	Israel	27 Jun 66	581UNTS227	108448
Bulgaria	Italy	29 Jul 67	631UNTS33	108985
Australia	Turkey	05 Oct 67	0UNTS0	109457
Sweden	USSR (Soviet Union)	30 Nov 67	0UNTS0	109385
Protection of nationals				
Multilateral		05 Jun 26	38UNTS281	100604
Belgium	USSR (Soviet Union)	13 Mar 45	19UNTS235	200117
Taiwan	Denmark	20 May 46	12UNTS59	100180
Ireland	USA (United States)	01 May 50	222UNTS107	103026
Norway	UK Great Britain	22 Feb 51	326UNTS209	104713
UK Great Britain	USA (United States)	06 Jun 51	165UNTS121	102174
France	Italy	08 Nov 57	305UNTS393	104427
Bulgaria	Hungary	27 Jun 58	438UNTS235	106318
France	USA (United States)	25 Nov 59	401UNTS75	105764
UK Great Britain	USA (United States)	24 Jun 60	377UNTS63	105396
Spain	UK Great Britain	30 May 61	562UNTS169	108198
Austria	Czechoslovakia	10 Nov 61	455UNTS337	106550
USSR (Soviet Union)	Yugoslavia	24 Feb 62	471UNTS195	106833
Korea, South	USA (United States)	08 Jan 63	493UNTS105	107211
UK Great Britain	USSR (Soviet Union)	02 Dec 65	0UNTS0	109384
Argentina	Portugal	20 May 66	635UNTS301	109090
Sweden	USSR (Soviet Union)	30 Nov 67	0UNTS0	109385
Diplomatic correspondence				
Brazil	Uruguay	16 Dec 44	65UNTS305	200218
Brazil	Venezuela	30 Jan 46	65UNTS107	100839
Multilateral		13 Feb 46	1UNTS15	100004
ILO (Labor Org)	Switzerland	11 Mar 46	15UNTS377	200103
Norway	UK Great Britain	15 Jan 47	11UNTS187	100156
France	ICAO (Civil Aviat)	14 Mar 47	94UNTS59	101306
United Nations	USA (United States)	26 Jun 47	11UNTS11	100147
Multilateral		21 Nov 47	33UNTS261	100521
United Nations	USA (United States)	18 Dec 47	11UNTS347	100174
Costa Rica	USA (United States)	12 Jan 48	70UNTS27	100896
Peru	ICAO (Civil Aviat)	22 Oct 48	95UNTS3	101315
WHO (World Health)	Switzerland	12 Jan 49	26UNTS331	200155
ITU (Telecommun)	United Nations	26 Apr 49	30UNTS315	200175
Multilateral		02 Sep 49	250UNTS12	103515
El Salvador	WHO (World Health)	21 Apr 50	103UNTS13	101420
WHO (World Health)	United Arab Rep	25 Mar 51	223UNTS87	103058
UK Great Britain	USA (United States)	06 Jun 51	165UNTS121	102174

PARTY ONE	PARTY TWO	DATE	CITATION	NUMBER
Diplomatic correspondence (Cont.)				
Philippines	WHO (World Health)	22 Jul 51	149UNTS197	101953
France	United Nations	17 Aug 51	122UNTS191	101647
Multilateral		20 Sep 51	200UNTS3	102691
Korea, South	United Nations	21 Sep 51	104UNTS323	200322
Netherlands	UK Great Britain	30 Nov 51	123UNTS177	101659
Sweden	UK Great Britain	14 Mar 52	202UNTS157	102731
France	WHO (World Health)	23 Jul 52	209UNTS231	102829
Japan	United Nations	25 Jul 52	135UNTS305	200443
Chile	United Nations	16 Feb 53	314UNTS49	104541
Greece	UK Great Britain	17 Apr 53	191UNTS151	102582
ICAO (Civil Aviat)	United Arab Rep	27 Aug 53	215UNTS371	102925
United Nations	Thailand	26 May 54	260UNTS35	103703
Italy	UK Great Britain	01 Jun 54	403UNTS275	105798
France	UNESCO (Educ/Cult)	02 Jul 54	357UNTS3	105103
Mexico	ILO (Labor Org)	05 Jan 55	208UNTS225	102815
France	Sweden	05 Mar 55	427UNTS133	106150
WMO (Meteorology)	Switzerland	10 Mar 55	211UNTS277	200524
CERN (Nuc Resrch)	Switzerland	11 Jun 55	249UNTS405	200544
Denmark	WHO (World Health)	29 Jun 55	247UNTS168	103467
Dominican Republic	UK Great Britain	09 Aug 56	252UNTS127	103561
United Nations	Venezuela	18 Nov 56	588UNTS243	108529
Mexico	ICAO (Civil Aviat)	20 Dec 56	497UNTS3	107259
Czechoslovakia	Germany, East	24 May 57	292UNTS327	104279
Hungary	USSR (Soviet Union)	24 Aug 57	318UNTS3	104607
Romania	USSR (Soviet Union)	04 Sep 57	318UNTS55	104609
Albania	USSR (Soviet Union)	18 Sep 57	307UNTS265	104455
Czechoslovakia	USSR (Soviet Union)	05 Oct 57	320UNTS129	104641
Germany, East	Poland	25 Nov 57	340UNTS99	104862
Bulgaria	USSR (Soviet Union)	12 Dec 57	302UNTS21	104352
Korea, North	USSR (Soviet Union)	16 Dec 57	292UNTS121	104270
Poland	USSR (Soviet Union)	21 Jan 58	319UNTS291	104637
India	Japan	04 Feb 58	324UNTS215	104687
Germany, West	USSR (Soviet Union)	25 Apr 58	338UNTS49	104832
Lebanon	United Nations	13 Jun 58	303UNTS271	104386
Ethiopia	United Nations	18 Jun 58	317UNTS101	104597
Mongolia	USSR (Soviet Union)	25 Aug 58	322UNTS215	104659
Poland	Yugoslavia	17 Nov 58	432UNTS267	106225
Jordan	United Nations	18 Nov 58	315UNTS125	104564
Austria	USSR (Soviet Union)	28 Feb 59	356UNTS39	105091
Czechoslovakia	Hungary	27 Mar 59	351UNTS57	105017
Bulgaria	Romania	23 Apr 59	387UNTS81	105559
Hungary	Poland	20 May 59	432UNTS115	106217
China People's Rep	USSR (Soviet Union)	23 Jun 59	356UNTS83	105092
Multilateral		01 Jul 59	374UNTS147	105334
Multilateral		14 Dec 59	368UNTS237	105244
China People's Rep	Czechoslovakia	07 May 60	402UNTS209	105787
Czechoslovakia	Poland	17 May 60	424UNTS3	106096
Austria	UK Great Britain	24 Jun 60	502UNTS79	107327
Multilateral		28 Jul 60	394UNTS37	105667
Multilateral		18 Apr 61	500UNTS95	107310
Bulgaria	Poland	19 Sep 61	483UNTS249	107018
Romania	Yugoslavia	08 Nov 62	472UNTS305	106845
Korea, South	USA (United States)	08 Jan 63	493UNTS105	107211
Czechoslovakia	Vietnam, North	14 Jan 63	501UNTS181	107318
Japan	USA (United States)	22 Mar 63	518UNTS179	107495
Multilateral		24 Apr 63	596UNTS261	108638
Czechoslovakia	Yugoslavia	24 Jun 63	496UNTS3	107246
Hungary	Mongolia	10 Jul 63	519UNTS173	107508
Niger	United Nations	20 Nov 63	536UNTS3	107793
Nicaragua	United Nations	03 Dec 63	482UNTS329	107002
Cyprus	United Nations	31 Mar 64	492UNTS57	107187
Multilateral		11 Dec 64	547UNTS297	107964
UK Great Britain	Yugoslavia	21 Apr 65	595UNTS189	108620
Austria	Petrol Export Org	24 Jun 65	589UNTS135	108540
Multilateral		21 Sep 65	547UNTS280	107963

PARTY ONE	PARTY TWO	DATE	CITATION	NUMBER
Diplomatic correspondence (Cont.)				
Chile	UNICEF (Children)	30 Nov 65	596UNTS215	108635
Multilateral		04 Dec 65	571UNTS123	108303
Romania	Spain	05 Jan 67	642UNTS103	109168
Greece	United Nations	14 Apr 67	595UNTS83	108613
Non-diplomatic delegations				
El Salvador	USA (United States)	05 May 42	21UNTS215	200124
Hungary	USSR (Soviet Union)	15 Jul 47	216UNTS247	102940
Czechoslovakia	USSR (Soviet Union)	11 Dec 47	217UNTS35	102943
Switzerland	USSR (Soviet Union)	17 Mar 48	217UNTS87	102945
Bulgaria	USSR (Soviet Union)	01 Apr 48	217UNTS97	102946
Poland	USSR (Soviet Union)	08 Apr 48	26UNTS191	100388
Italy	USSR (Soviet Union)	11 Dec 48	217UNTS181	102948
Multilateral		12 Aug 49	75UNTS85	100971
Greece	Turkey	20 Apr 51	178UNTS17	102333
France	USSR (Soviet Union)	03 Sep 51	221UNTS79	103003
Ceylon (Sri Lanka)	WHO (World Health)	26 Mar 52	134UNTS341	200442
Germany, West	Israel	10 Sep 52	162UNTS205	102137
Liberia	USA (United States)	15 Dec 52	185UNTS45	102457
Pakistan	Turkey	29 Jun 53	211UNTS225	102854
Belgium	South Africa	01 Jun 54	201UNTS25	102708
Austria	USSR (Soviet Union)	17 Oct 55	240UNTS289	103409
Ethiopia	Italy	05 Mar 56	267UNTS189	103844
Romania	USSR (Soviet Union)	07 Apr 56	259UNTS377	103698
Mongolia	USSR (Soviet Union)	24 Apr 56	259UNTS297	103693
Bulgaria	USSR (Soviet Union)	28 Apr 56	259UNTS363	103697
Albania	USSR (Soviet Union)	03 May 56	259UNTS391	103699
Japan	Philippines	09 May 56	285UNTS3	104148
Czechoslovakia	USSR (Soviet Union)	01 Jun 56	259UNTS341	103696
Poland	USSR (Soviet Union)	30 Jun 56	259UNTS311	103694
Syria	USSR (Soviet Union)	20 Aug 56	274UNTS105	103961
Korea, North	USSR (Soviet Union)	05 Sep 56	259UNTS329	103695
USSR (Soviet Union)	Vietnam, North	15 Feb 57	274UNTS115	103962
Romania	United Arab Rep	15 Apr 57	389UNTS21	105589
Czechoslovakia	Syria	18 Jun 57	303UNTS119	104374
Germany, East	USSR (Soviet Union)	27 Sep 57	292UNTS75	104268
United Arab Rep	USSR (Soviet Union)	19 Oct 57	292UNTS151	104271
Japan	USSR (Soviet Union)	06 Dec 57	325UNTS35	104694
Ceylon (Sri Lanka)	USSR (Soviet Union)	15 Jan 58	305UNTS235	104421
Indonesia	Japan	20 Jan 58	324UNTS247	104689
Albania	USSR (Soviet Union)	15 Feb 58	313UNTS261	104536
China People's Rep	USSR (Soviet Union)	23 Apr 58	313UNTS135	104534
Germany, West	USSR (Soviet Union)	25 Apr 58	346UNTS71	104978
Romania	Vietnam, North	30 Jun 58	389UNTS43	105591
Iraq	USSR (Soviet Union)	11 Oct 58	328UNTS117	104731
Czechoslovakia	Romania	25 Oct 58	338UNTS301	104843
Hungary	Iraq	11 Apr 59	439UNTS25	106323
Iraq	USSR (Soviet Union)	05 May 59	356UNTS179	105095
Iraq	Romania	04 Aug 59	502UNTS17	107324
USA (United States)	USSR (Soviet Union)	21 Nov 59	361UNTS35	105172
Guinea	Hungary	12 Jan 60	519UNTS131	107505
Finland	USSR (Soviet Union)	27 May 60	379UNTS381	105444
Cuba	Korea, North	29 Aug 60	473UNTS117	106860
Romania	USA (United States)	09 Dec 60	401UNTS19	105759
Cuba	USSR (Soviet Union)	12 Dec 60	421UNTS3	106048
Ethiopia	USSR (Soviet Union)	13 Jan 61	421UNTS13	106049
Cuba	Germany, East	29 Mar 61	448UNTS81	106426
Cuba	Czechoslovakia	05 Apr 61	442UNTS201	106350
India	Norway	19 Apr 61	404UNTS307	105818
Czechoslovakia	Somalia	04 Jun 61	479UNTS291	106960
Denmark	USSR (Soviet Union)	11 Sep 62	458UNTS3	106589
Cameroon	Israel	24 Oct 62	449UNTS3	106446
Romania	USA (United States)	02 Apr 63	474UNTS95	106874
Hungary	Yugoslavia	15 Oct 63	577UNTS49	108372
Panama	USA (United States)	30 Oct 63	530UNTS3	107668
Non-diplomatic delegations (Cont.)				
Netherlands	Turkey	19 Aug 64	521UNTS197	107523
Czechoslovakia	United Arab Rep	26 Nov 64	545UNTS11	107923
China People's Rep	Romania	27 May 65	592UNTS3	108566
Pakistan	USSR (Soviet Union)	05 Jun 65	593UNTS115	108579
Czechoslovakia	Poland	22 Jan 66	588UNTS175	108524
Romania	Spain	05 Jan 67	642UNTS103	109168
Consular functions in shipping				
Argentina	Brazil	23 Jan 40	51UNTS281	200194
Brazil	Uruguay	08 Jan 42	54UNTS359	200206
Ireland	USA (United States)	01 May 50	222UNTS107	103026
Norway	UK Great Britain	22 Feb 51	326UNTS209	104713
Australia	Netherlands	25 Sep 51	128UNTS63	101713
France	UK Great Britain	31 Dec 51	330UNTS145	104744
Sweden	UK Great Britain	14 Mar 52	202UNTS157	102731
Greece	UK Great Britain	17 Apr 53	191UNTS151	102582
Mexico	UK Great Britain	20 Mar 54	331UNTS21	104750
Italy	UK Great Britain	01 Jun 54	403UNTS275	105798
France	Sweden	05 Mar 55	427UNTS133	106150
Germany, West	UK Great Britain	30 Jul 56	330UNTS233	104748
Bulgaria	Hungary	27 Jun 58	438UNTS235	106318
Austria	UK Great Britain	24 Jun 60	502UNTS79	107327
Belgium	UK Great Britain	08 Mar 61	523UNTS17	107554
Spain	UK Great Britain	30 May 61	562UNTS169	108198
Denmark	UK Great Britain	27 Jun 62	562UNTS75	108197
Korea, South	USA (United States)	08 Jan 63	493UNTS105	107211
Japan	USA (United States)	22 Mar 63	518UNTS179	107495
Japan	UK Great Britain	04 May 64	561UNTS25	108179
USA (United States)	USSR (Soviet Union)	01 Jun 64	0UNTS0	109383
UK Great Britain	Yugoslavia	21 Apr 65	595UNTS189	108620
UK Great Britain	USSR (Soviet Union)	02 Dec 65	0UNTS0	109384
Japan	USSR (Soviet Union)	29 Jul 66	608UNTS93	108815
Sweden	USSR (Soviet Union)	30 Nov 67	0UNTS0	109385
Consular functions in property				
Denmark	Poland	12 May 49	87UNTS179	101172
Ireland	USA (United States)	01 May 50	222UNTS107	103026
Australia	Netherlands	25 Sep 51	128UNTS63	101713
France	UK Great Britain	31 Dec 51	330UNTS145	104744
Sweden	UK Great Britain	14 Mar 52	202UNTS157	102731
Greece	UK Great Britain	17 Apr 53	191UNTS151	102582
Mexico	UK Great Britain	20 Mar 54	331UNTS21	104750
Italy	UK Great Britain	01 Jun 54	403UNTS275	105798
France	Sweden	05 Mar 55	427UNTS133	106150
Bulgaria	Yugoslavia	23 Mar 56	367UNTS213	105230
Germany, West	UK Great Britain	30 Jul 56	330UNTS233	104748
Germany, East	Poland	01 Feb 57	319UNTS115	104632
Germany, East	Hungary	30 Oct 57	408UNTS4	105867
Bulgaria	USSR (Soviet Union)	12 Dec 57	317UNTS217	104606
Bulgaria	Hungary	27 Jun 58	438UNTS235	106318
Germany, East	Romania	15 Jul 58	387UNTS133	105561
Germany, East	Romania	15 Jul 58	395UNTS3	105681
Hungary	USSR (Soviet Union)	15 Jul 58	322UNTS3	104656
Mongolia	USSR (Soviet Union)	25 Aug 58	322UNTS105	104657
Hungary	Romania	07 Oct 58	416UNTS199	106004
Czechoslovakia	Romania	25 Oct 58	417UNTS37	106006
Bulgaria	Romania	03 Dec 58	417UNTS133	106007
Albania	Czechoslovakia	16 Jan 59	363UNTS195	105208
Hungary	Poland	06 Mar 59	432UNTS3	106216
Albania	Hungary	12 Jan 60	520UNTS3	107511
Austria	UK Great Britain	24 Jun 60	502UNTS79	107327
Spain	UK Great Britain	30 May 61	562UNTS169	108198
Poland	Romania	25 Jan 62	468UNTS3	106770
USSR (Soviet Union)	Yugoslavia	24 Feb 62	471UNTS195	106833
Denmark	UK Great Britain	27 Jun 62	562UNTS75	108197
Korea, South	USA (United States)	08 Jan 63	493UNTS105	107211

PARTY ONE	PARTY TWO	DATE	CITATION	NUMBER
Consular functions in property (Cont.)				
Japan	USA (United States)	22 Mar 63	518UNTS179	107495
Czechoslovakia	Yugoslavia	20 Jan 64	538UNTS197	107816
Japan	UK Great Britain	04 May 64	561UNTS25	108179
USA (United States)	USSR (Soviet Union)	01 Jun 64	0UNTS0	109383
UK Great Britain	Yugoslavia	21 Apr 65	595UNTS189	108620
UK Great Britain	USSR (Soviet Union)	02 Dec 65	0UNTS0	109384
Panama	USA (United States)	15 Feb 66	586UNTS27	108494
Japan	USSR (Soviet Union)	29 Jul 66	608UNTS93	108815
Sweden	USSR (Soviet Union)	30 Nov 67	0UNTS0	109385
Notarial acts and services				
Greece	Lebanon	06 Oct 48	87UNTS351	101179
Ireland	USA (United States)	01 May 50	222UNTS107	103026
Luxembourg	Netherlands	08 Jul 50	135UNTS229	101824
UK Great Britain	USA (United States)	06 Jun 51	165UNTS121	102174
Sweden	UK Great Britain	14 Mar 52	202UNTS157	102731
Switzerland	UK Great Britain	16 Jan 53	196UNTS119	102621
Sweden	Switzerland	17 Dec 54	369UNTS233	105260
Multilateral		09 Jul 56	314UNTS3	104539
Germany, West	Japan	27 Jun 57	318UNTS335	104624
Italy	Monaco	06 Dec 57	363UNTS45	105198
Poland	Yugoslavia	16 Jan 58	340UNTS181	104864
Bulgaria	Hungary	27 Jun 58	438UNTS235	106318
Czechoslovakia	Poland	04 Jul 61	436UNTS189	106295
Czechoslovakia	Hungary	02 Nov 61	438UNTS3	106313
Belgium	India	16 Jul 62	453UNTS259	106529
Hungary	USSR (Soviet Union)	20 Dec 62	577UNTS245	108381
Korea, South	USA (United States)	08 Jan 63	493UNTS105	107211
Nicaragua	United Nations	03 Dec 63	482UNTS329	107002
Multilateral		03 Mar 64	516UNTS53	107470
Austria	Hungary	09 Apr 65	638UNTS135	109133
Extradition, deportation and repatriation				
Bolivia	Brazil	25 Feb 38	54UNTS333	200205
Colombia	USA (United States)	09 Sep 40	125UNTS239	200428
Belgium	Brazil	14 Jun 41	272UNTS157	103936
Jordan	UK Great Britain	19 Jul 41	9UNTS389	200055
Saudi Arabia	UK Great Britain	20 Apr 42	10UNTS99	200056
Iraq	Turkey	29 Mar 46	37UNTS369	100582
Iraq	Turkey	29 Mar 46	37UNTS333	100581
Italy	USA (United States)	17 Apr 46	206UNTS263	102791
Multilateral		12 Nov 47	53UNTS39	100771
South Africa	USA (United States)	18 Dec 47	148UNTS85	101938
Multilateral		04 May 49	92UNTS19	101257
Multilateral		21 Mar 50	96UNTS271	101342
Denmark	Hungary	10 Feb 51	85UNTS49	101145
Greece	USA (United States)	03 Aug 51	224UNTS279	103080
Jordan	Syria	23 Dec 53	204UNTS207	102759
Belgium	Lebanon	24 Dec 53	539UNTS321	107842
Belgium	Israel	08 Feb 54	188UNTS251	102528
Bulgaria	Czechoslovakia	13 Apr 54	501UNTS3	107314
Germany, West	Sweden	31 May 54	200UNTS39	102693
Denmark	Germany, West	31 May 54	200UNTS53	102694
Multilateral		23 Oct 54	332UNTS3	104760
Germany, West	Norway	18 Mar 55	209UNTS309	102832
Israel	Italy	24 Feb 56	316UNTS97	104580
Bulgaria	Yugoslavia	23 Mar 56	367UNTS213	105230
Belgium	Israel	26 Mar 56	260UNTS3	103702
Israel	Luxembourg	26 Jul 56	550UNTS239	108020
Israel	Netherlands	18 Dec 56	276UNTS153	103991
Germany, East	Poland	01 Feb 57	319UNTS115	104632
Poland	USSR (Soviet Union)	25 Mar 57	281UNTS121	104075
Czechoslovakia	USSR (Soviet Union)	31 Aug 57	308UNTS3	104456
Germany, East	Hungary	30 Oct 57	408UNTS4	105867
Germany, East	USSR (Soviet Union)	28 Nov 57	305UNTS113	104419
Bulgaria	USSR (Soviet Union)	12 Dec 57	317UNTS217	104606
Extradition, deportation and repatriation (Cont.)				
Multilateral		13 Dec 57	359UNTS273	105146
Korea, North	USSR (Soviet Union)	16 Dec 57	301UNTS301	104349
Poland	USSR (Soviet Union)	28 Dec 57	320UNTS3	104638
Belgium	Germany, West	17 Jan 58	328UNTS173	104735
Romania	USSR (Soviet Union)	03 Apr 58	313UNTS167	104535
Albania	USSR (Soviet Union)	30 Jun 58	328UNTS3	104729
Hungary	USSR (Soviet Union)	15 Jul 58	322UNTS3	104656
Germany, East	Romania	15 Jul 58	395UNTS3	105681
Mongolia	USSR (Soviet Union)	25 Aug 58	322UNTS105	104657
Hungary	Romania	07 Oct 58	416UNTS199	106004
Germany, West	Netherlands	10 Oct 58	486UNTS345	107085
Czechoslovakia	Romania	25 Oct 58	417UNTS37	106006
Bulgaria	Romania	03 Dec 58	417UNTS133	106007
Israel	Switzerland	31 Dec 58	377UNTS305	105408
Albania	Czechoslovakia	16 Jan 59	363UNTS195	105208
Belgium	Morocco	27 Feb 59	390UNTS275	105611
Greece	Yugoslavia	18 Jun 59	368UNTS81	105236
Denmark	India	16 Sep 59	405UNTS13	105820
Israel	South Africa	18 Sep 59	373UNTS47	105314
Albania	Hungary	12 Jan 60	520UNTS3	107511
Poland	Yugoslavia	06 Feb 60	521UNTS37	107517
Israel	UK Great Britain	04 Apr 60	377UNTS331	105410
Hungary	Yugoslavia	07 May 60	519UNTS237	107510
Cambodia	Thailand	15 Dec 60	382UNTS321	105493
Brazil	USA (United States)	13 Jan 61	532UNTS177	107718
Czechoslovakia	Poland	04 Jul 61	436UNTS189	106295
Austria	Germany, West	19 Jul 61	414UNTS211	105974
Austria	Israel	10 Oct 61	448UNTS161	106430
Sweden	USA (United States)	24 Oct 61	494UNTS141	107231
Czechoslovakia	Hungary	02 Nov 61	438UNTS3	106313
Argentina	Brazil	15 Nov 61	0UNTS0	109424
Bulgaria	Poland	04 Dec 61	484UNTS3	107019
Poland	Romania	25 Jan 62	468UNTS3	106770
USSR (Soviet Union)	Yugoslavia	24 Feb 62	471UNTS195	106833
Multilateral		27 Jun 62	616UNTS79	108893
Fed Rhod/Nyasaland	South Africa	19 Nov 62	458UNTS59	106592
Austria	France	30 Nov 62	463UNTS173	106701
Israel	USA (United States)	10 Dec 62	484UNTS283	107038
Sweden	UK Great Britain	26 Apr 63	590UNTS117	108551
Israel	Sweden	10 Sep 63	516UNTS3	107467
Austria	Yugoslavia	20 May 64	514UNTS3	107439
WMO (Meteorology)	UK Great Britain	16 Dec 64	548UNTS57	107969
Multilateral		15 Feb 65	547UNTS3	107953
Australia	Germany, West	21 Jun 65	542UNTS53	107879
Japan	Korea, South	22 Jun 65	584UNTS3	108474
Multilateral		03 Dec 65	572UNTS105	108309
Netherlands	Uganda	27 Jan 67	608UNTS345	108823
Multilateral		31 Jan 67	606UNTS267	108791
Kenya	Netherlands	10 Nov 67	0UNTS0	109232
Court procedures				
Multilateral		29 Jun 33	39UNTS211	100619
Multilateral		29 Jun 33	39UNTS235	100620
Multilateral		29 Jun 33	39UNTS165	100617
Multilateral		29 Jun 33	39UNTS189	100618
Colombia	USA (United States)	09 Sep 40	125UNTS239	200428
Belgium	Brazil	14 Jun 41	272UNTS157	103936
Canada	USA (United States)	09 Aug 43	29UNTS295	200168
Multilateral		27 Dec 45	2UNTS39	100020
Iraq	Turkey	29 Mar 46	37UNTS369	100582
Multilateral		12 Nov 47	46UNTS201	100710
Multilateral		09 Dec 48	78UNTS277	101021
Czechoslovakia	Poland	21 Jan 49	31UNTS205	100480
Multilateral		12 Aug 49	75UNTS287	100973
Korea, South	USA (United States)	12 Jul 50	222UNTS229	103029

PARTY ONE	PARTY TWO	DATE	CITATION	NUMBER
Court procedures (Cont.)				
UK Great Britain	USA (United States)	21 Jul 50	97UNTS193	101351
Multilateral		04 Nov 50	213UNTS221	102889
Multilateral		19 Jun 51	199UNTS67	102678
UK Great Britain	USA (United States)	15 Jan 52	127UNTS3	101697
Iraq	Switzerland	31 Mar 52	311UNTS43	104498
Ethiopia	USA (United States)	22 May 53	191UNTS59	102577
Multilateral		26 Oct 53	207UNTS237	102809
Multilateral		19 Feb 54	214UNTS51	102899
Libya	USA (United States)	09 Sep 54	224UNTS217	103078
Multilateral		23 Oct 54	332UNTS3	104760
Hungary	USSR (Soviet Union)	27 May 55	407UNTS156	105864
UK Great Britain	USA (United States)	25 Jun 56	249UNTS59	103501
Greece	USA (United States)	07 Sep 56	278UNTS141	104030
Poland	USSR (Soviet Union)	17 Dec 56	266UNTS179	103830
Germany, West	Netherlands	29 Jan 57	314UNTS173	104548
Germany, East	USSR (Soviet Union)	12 Mar 57	285UNTS105	104150
Romania	USSR (Soviet Union)	15 Apr 57	274UNTS143	103964
Multilateral		26 Jun 57	328UNTS247	104738
Poland	USSR (Soviet Union)	26 Oct 57	432UNTS221	106223
Albania	USSR (Soviet Union)	30 Jun 58	328UNTS3	104729
Japan	USA (United States)	19 Jan 60	373UNTS207	105321
Argentina	Brazil	15 Nov 61	OUNTSO	109424
Multilateral		23 Mar 62	434UNTS145	106262
Japan	UK Great Britain	14 Nov 62	478UNTS29	106934
UK Great Britain	USA (United States)	06 Apr 63	474UNTS49	106871
Australia	USA (United States)	09 May 63	469UNTS55	106784
Botswana	UK Great Britain	30 Sep 66	597UNTS211	108646
Extradition requests				
Bolivia	Brazil	25 Feb 38	54UNTS333	200205
Colombia	USA (United States)	09 Sep 40	125UNTS239	200428
Belgium	Brazil	14 Jun 41	272UNTS157	103936
Jordan	UK Great Britain	19 Jul 41	9UNTS389	200055
Jordan	Syria	23 Dec 53	204UNTS207	102759
Belgium	Lebanon	24 Dec 53	539UNTS321	107842
Bulgaria	Czechoslovakia	13 Apr 54	501UNTS3	107314
Israel	Italy	24 Feb 56	316UNTS97	104580
Bulgaria	Yugoslavia	23 Mar 56	367UNTS213	105230
Israel	Luxembourg	26 Jul 56	550UNTS239	108020
Czechoslovakia	USSR (Soviet Union)	31 Aug 57	308UNTS3	104456
Germany, East	USSR (Soviet Union)	28 Nov 57	305UNTS113	104419
Multilateral		13 Dec 57	359UNTS273	105146
Korea, North	USSR (Soviet Union)	16 Dec 57	301UNTS301	104349
Poland	USSR (Soviet Union)	28 Dec 57	320UNTS3	104638
Mongolia	USSR (Soviet Union)	25 Aug 58	322UNTS105	104657
Hungary	Romania	07 Oct 58	416UNTS199	106004
Czechoslovakia	Romania	25 Oct 58	417UNTS37	106006
Bulgaria	Romania	03 Dec 58	417UNTS133	106007
Israel	Switzerland	31 Dec 58	377UNTS305	105408
Albania	Czechoslovakia	16 Jan 59	363UNTS195	105208
Belgium	Morocco	27 Feb 59	390UNTS275	105611
Hungary	Poland	06 Mar 59	432UNTS3	106216
Greece	Yugoslavia	18 Jun 59	368UNTS81	105236
Denmark	India	16 Sep 59	405UNTS13	105820
Israel	South Africa	18 Sep 59	373UNTS47	105314
Albania	Hungary	12 Jan 60	520UNTS3	107511
Germany, West	UK Great Britain	23 Feb 60	385UNTS39	105527
Israel	UK Great Britain	04 Apr 60	377UNTS331	105410
Czechoslovakia	Poland	04 Jul 61	436UNTS189	106295
Austria	Israel	10 Oct 61	448UNTS161	106430
Sweden	USA (United States)	24 Oct 61	494UNTS141	107231
Czechoslovakia	Hungary	02 Nov 61	438UNTS3	106313
Argentina	Brazil	15 Nov 61	OUNTSO	109424
Multilateral		27 Jun 62	616UNTS79	108893
Israel	USA (United States)	10 Dec 62	484UNTS283	107038

PARTY ONE	PARTY TWO	DATE	CITATION	NUMBER
Extradition requests (Cont.)				
Sweden	UK Great Britain	26 Apr 63	590UNTS117	108551
Israel	Sweden	10 Sep 63	516UNTS3	107467
Czechoslovakia	Yugoslavia	20 Jan 64	538UNTS197	107816
Kenya	USA (United States)	19 Aug 65	574UNTS153	108348
Extraditable offenses				
Bolivia	Brazil	25 Feb 38	54UNTS333	200205
Colombia	USA (United States)	09 Sep 40	125UNTS239	200428
Belgium	Brazil	14 Jun 41	272UNTS157	103936
Jordan	UK Great Britain	19 Jul 41	9UNTS389	200055
Saudi Arabia	UK Great Britain	20 Apr 42	10UNTS99	200056
Iraq	Turkey	29 Mar 46	37UNTS369	100582
South Africa	USA (United States)	18 Dec 47	148UNTS85	101938
Multilateral		09 Dec 48	78UNTS277	101021
Sweden	USA (United States)	27 Jun 51	148UNTS77	101937
Netherlands	United Nations	09 Apr 53	163UNTS89	102143
Belgium	Lebanon	24 Dec 53	539UNTS321	107842
Bulgaria	Czechoslovakia	13 Apr 54	501UNTS3	107314
Israel	Italy	24 Feb 56	316UNTS97	104580
Bulgaria	Yugoslavia	23 Mar 56	367UNTS213	105230
Belgium	Israel	26 Mar 56	260UNTS3	103702
Israel	Luxembourg	26 Jul 56	550UNTS239	108020
Multilateral		26 Oct 56	276UNTS3	103988
Israel	Netherlands	18 Dec 56	276UNTS153	103991
Germany, East	Poland	01 Feb 57	319UNTS115	104632
Germany, East	USSR (Soviet Union)	28 Nov 57	305UNTS113	104419
Multilateral		13 Dec 57	359UNTS273	105146
Belgium	Germany, West	17 Jan 58	328UNTS173	104735
Romania	USSR (Soviet Union)	03 Apr 58	313UNTS167	104535
Hungary	USSR (Soviet Union)	15 Jul 58	322UNTS3	104656
Mongolia	USSR (Soviet Union)	25 Aug 58	322UNTS105	104657
Albania	Czechoslovakia	16 Jan 59	363UNTS195	105208
Belgium	Morocco	27 Feb 59	390UNTS275	105611
Hungary	Poland	06 Mar 59	432UNTS3	106216
Israel	South Africa	18 Sep 59	373UNTS47	105314
Israel	UK Great Britain	04 Apr 60	377UNTS331	105410
Cambodia	Thailand	15 Dec 60	382UNTS321	105493
Brazil	USA (United States)	13 Jan 61	532UNTS177	107718
Austria	Israel	10 Oct 61	448UNTS161	106430
Sweden	USA (United States)	24 Oct 61	494UNTS141	107231
Argentina	Brazil	15 Nov 61	OUNTSO	109424
Malagasy	UN Special Fund	05 Jan 62	419UNTS29	106028
USSR (Soviet Union)	Yugoslavia	24 Feb 62	471UNTS195	106833
Multilateral		27 Jun 62	616UNTS79	108893
Fed Rhod/Nyasaland	South Africa	19 Nov 62	458UNTS59	106592
Israel	USA (United States)	10 Dec 62	484UNTS283	107038
Sweden	UK Great Britain	26 Apr 63	590UNTS117	108551
Israel	Sweden	10 Sep 63	516UNTS3	107467
Ireland	UN Special Fund	03 Jun 64	496UNTS205	107253
Greece	Netherlands	13 Sep 66	596UNTS245	108637
Location of crime				
Bolivia	Brazil	25 Feb 38	54UNTS333	200205
Colombia	USA (United States)	09 Sep 40	125UNTS239	200428
Belgium	Brazil	14 Jun 41	272UNTS157	103936
Jordan	UK Great Britain	19 Jul 41	9UNTS389	200055
Multilateral		08 Aug 45	82UNTS279	200251
South Africa	USA (United States)	18 Dec 47	148UNTS85	101938
Brazil	UNICEF (Children)	09 Jun 50	66UNTS75	100848
Jordan	Syria	23 Dec 53	204UNTS207	102759
Belgium	Lebanon	24 Dec 53	539UNTS321	107842
Israel	Italy	24 Feb 56	316UNTS97	104580
Belgium	Israel	26 Mar 56	260UNTS3	103702
Israel	Luxembourg	26 Jul 56	550UNTS239	108020
Israel	Netherlands	18 Dec 56	276UNTS153	103991
Multilateral		13 Dec 57	359UNTS273	105146

PARTY ONE	PARTY TWO	DATE	CITATION	NUMBER
Location of crime (Cont.)				
Belgium	Germany, West	17 Jan 58	328UNTS173	104735
Albania	USSR (Soviet Union)	30 Jun 58	328UNTS3	104729
Israel	Switzerland	31 Dec 58	377UNTS305	105408
Belgium	Morocco	27 Feb 59	390UNTS275	105611
Greece	Yugoslavia	18 Jun 59	368UNTS81	105236
Denmark	India	16 Sep 59	405UNTS13	105820
Israel	South Africa	18 Sep 59	373UNTS47	105314
Israel	UK Great Britain	04 Apr 60	377UNTS331	105410
Brazil	USA (United States)	13 Jan 61	532UNTS177	107718
Austria	Israel	10 Oct 61	448UNTS161	106430
Sweden	USA (United States)	24 Oct 61	494UNTS141	107231
Multilateral		27 Jun 62	616UNTS79	108893
Fed Rhod/Nyasaland	South Africa	19 Nov 62	458UNTS59	106592
Israel	USA (United States)	10 Dec 62	484UNTS283	107038
Sweden	UK Great Britain	26 Apr 63	590UNTS117	108551
Israel	Sweden	10 Sep 63	516UNTS3	107467
Special factors				
Belgium	Brazil	14 Jun 41	272UNTS157	103936
Saudi Arabia	UK Great Britain	20 Apr 42	10UNTS99	200056
Iraq	Turkey	29 Mar 46	37UNTS369	100582
Multilateral		09 Dec 48	78UNTS277	101021
Jordan	Syria	23 Dec 53	204UNTS207	102759
Israel	Italy	24 Feb 56	316UNTS97	104580
Bulgaria	Yugoslavia	23 Mar 56	367UNTS213	105230
Israel	Netherlands	18 Dec 56	276UNTS153	103991
Multilateral		13 Dec 57	359UNTS273	105146
Belgium	Germany, West	17 Jan 58	328UNTS173	104735
Belgium	Morocco	27 Feb 59	390UNTS275	105611
Czechoslovakia	Poland	04 Jul 61	436UNTS189	106295
Argentina	Brazil	15 Nov 61	0UNTS0	109424
Multilateral		27 Jun 62	616UNTS79	108893
Israel	Sweden	10 Sep 63	516UNTS3	107467
Refusal of extradition				
Bolivia	Brazil	25 Feb 38	54UNTS333	200205
Colombia	USA (United States)	09 Sep 40	125UNTS239	200428
Jordan	UK Great Britain	19 Jul 41	9UNTS389	200055
Iraq	Turkey	29 Mar 46	37UNTS369	100582
South Africa	USA (United States)	18 Dec 47	148UNTS85	101938
Jordan	Syria	23 Dec 53	204UNTS207	102759
Belgium	Lebanon	24 Dec 53	539UNTS321	107842
Israel	Italy	24 Feb 56	316UNTS97	104580
Bulgaria	Yugoslavia	23 Mar 56	367UNTS213	105230
Belgium	Israel	26 Mar 56	260UNTS3	103702
Israel	Luxembourg	26 Jul 56	550UNTS239	108020
Israel	Netherlands	18 Dec 56	276UNTS153	103991
Germany, East	Poland	01 Feb 57	319UNTS115	104632
Czechoslovakia	USSR (Soviet Union)	31 Aug 57	308UNTS3	104456
Germany, East	Hungary	30 Oct 57	408UNTS4	105867
Germany, East	USSR (Soviet Union)	28 Nov 57	305UNTS113	104419
Bulgaria	USSR (Soviet Union)	12 Dec 57	317UNTS217	104606
Multilateral		13 Dec 57	359UNTS273	105146
Korea, North	USSR (Soviet Union)	16 Dec 57	301UNTS301	104349
Poland	USSR (Soviet Union)	28 Dec 57	320UNTS3	104638
Belgium	Germany, West	17 Jan 58	328UNTS173	104735
Hungary	USSR (Soviet Union)	15 Jul 58	322UNTS3	104656
Germany, East	Romania	15 Jul 58	395UNTS3	105681
Mongolia	USSR (Soviet Union)	25 Aug 58	322UNTS105	104657
Hungary	Romania	07 Oct 58	416UNTS199	106004
Czechoslovakia	Romania	25 Oct 58	417UNTS37	106006
Bulgaria	Romania	03 Dec 58	417UNTS133	106007
Israel	Switzerland	31 Dec 58	377UNTS305	105408
Belgium	Morocco	27 Feb 59	390UNTS275	105611

PARTY ONE	PARTY TWO	DATE	CITATION	NUMBER
Refusal of extradition (Cont.)				
Hungary	Poland	06 Mar 59	432UNTS3	106216
Greece	Yugoslavia	18 Jun 59	368UNTS81	105236
Denmark	India	16 Sep 59	405UNTS13	105820
Israel	South Africa	18 Sep 59	373UNTS47	105314
Albania	Hungary	12 Jan 60	520UNTS3	107511
Israel	UK Great Britain	04 Apr 60	377UNTS331	105410
Brazil	USA (United States)	13 Jan 61	532UNTS177	107718
Austria	Israel	10 Oct 61	448UNTS161	106430
Sweden	USA (United States)	24 Oct 61	494UNTS141	107231
Czechoslovakia	Hungary	02 Nov 61	438UNTS3	106313
Argentina	Brazil	15 Nov 61	0UNTS0	109424
Bulgaria	Poland	04 Dec 61	484UNTS3	107019
Poland	Romania	25 Jan 62	468UNTS3	106770
USSR (Soviet Union)	Yugoslavia	24 Feb 62	471UNTS195	106833
Fed Rhod/Nyasaland	South Africa	19 Nov 62	458UNTS59	106592
Israel	USA (United States)	10 Dec 62	484UNTS283	107038
Multilateral		10 Dec 62	521UNTS231	107525
Sweden	UK Great Britain	26 Apr 63	590UNTS117	108551
Israel	Sweden	10 Sep 63	516UNTS3	107467
Czechoslovakia	Yugoslavia	20 Jan 64	538UNTS197	107816
Multilateral		17 May 66	571UNTS89	108302
Concurrent requests				
Bolivia	Brazil	25 Feb 38	54UNTS333	200205
Colombia	USA (United States)	09 Sep 40	125UNTS239	200428
Belgium	Lebanon	24 Dec 53	539UNTS321	107842
Bulgaria	Czechoslovakia	13 Apr 54	501UNTS3	107314
Israel	Italy	24 Feb 56	316UNTS97	104580
Belgium	Israel	26 Mar 56	260UNTS3	103702
Israel	Luxembourg	26 Jul 56	550UNTS239	108020
Germany, East	Poland	01 Feb 57	319UNTS115	104632
Germany, East	Hungary	30 Oct 57	408UNTS4	105867
Germany, East	USSR (Soviet Union)	28 Nov 57	305UNTS113	104419
Multilateral		13 Dec 57	359UNTS273	105146
Korea, North	USSR (Soviet Union)	16 Dec 57	301UNTS301	104349
Poland	USSR (Soviet Union)	28 Dec 57	320UNTS3	104638
Belgium	Germany, West	17 Jan 58	328UNTS173	104735
Albania	USSR (Soviet Union)	30 Jun 58	328UNTS3	104729
Hungary	USSR (Soviet Union)	15 Jul 58	322UNTS3	104656
Germany, East	Romania	15 Jul 58	395UNTS3	105681
Mongolia	USSR (Soviet Union)	25 Aug 58	322UNTS105	104657
Hungary	Romania	07 Oct 58	416UNTS199	106004
Czechoslovakia	Romania	25 Oct 58	417UNTS37	106006
Bulgaria	Romania	03 Dec 58	417UNTS133	106007
Israel	Switzerland	31 Dec 58	377UNTS305	105408
Albania	Czechoslovakia	16 Jan 59	363UNTS195	105208
Belgium	Morocco	27 Feb 59	390UNTS275	105611
Hungary	Poland	06 Mar 59	432UNTS3	106216
Israel	South Africa	18 Sep 59	373UNTS47	105314
Albania	Hungary	12 Jan 60	520UNTS3	107511
Czechoslovakia	Poland	04 Jul 61	436UNTS189	106295
Czechoslovakia	Hungary	02 Nov 61	438UNTS3	106313
Bulgaria	Poland	04 Dec 61	484UNTS3	107019
Poland	Romania	25 Jan 62	468UNTS3	106770
USSR (Soviet Union)	Yugoslavia	24 Feb 62	471UNTS195	106833
Multilateral		27 Jun 62	616UNTS79	108893
Israel	USA (United States)	10 Dec 62	484UNTS283	107038
Israel	Sweden	10 Sep 63	516UNTS3	107467
Czechoslovakia	Yugoslavia	20 Jan 64	538UNTS197	107816
Pre-treaty crimes				
Jordan	UK Great Britain	19 Jul 41	9UNTS389	200055
South Africa	USA (United States)	18 Dec 47	148UNTS85	101938
Belgium	Lebanon	24 Dec 53	539UNTS321	107842
Ghana	USA (United States)	30 Sep 58	336UNTS169	104805
Israel	UK Great Britain	04 Apr 60	377UNTS331	105410

PARTY ONE	PARTY TWO	DATE	CITATION	NUMBER
Pre-treaty crimes (Cont.)				
Argentina	Brazil	15 Nov 61	0UNTS0	109424
Multilateral		27 Jun 62	616UNTS79	108893
Fed Rhod/Nyasaland	South Africa	19 Nov 62	458UNTS59	106592
Sweden	UK Great Britain	26 Apr 63	590UNTS117	108551
Israel	Sweden	10 Sep 63	516UNTS3	107467
Limits of prosecution				
Jordan	UK Great Britain	19 Jul 41	9UNTS389	200055
Saudi Arabia	UK Great Britain	20 Apr 42	10UNTS99	200056
Czechoslovakia	Poland	21 Jan 49	31UNTS205	100480
Belgium	Lebanon	24 Dec 53	539UNTS321	107842
Belgium	Israel	26 Mar 56	260UNTS3	103702
Israel	Luxembourg	26 Jul 56	550UNTS239	108020
Israel	Netherlands	18 Dec 56	276UNTS153	103991
Germany, East	Poland	01 Feb 57	319UNTS115	104632
Czechoslovakia	USSR (Soviet Union)	31 Aug 57	308UNTS3	104456
Germany, East	Hungary	30 Oct 57	408UNTS4	105867
Bulgaria	USSR (Soviet Union)	12 Dec 57	317UNTS217	104606
Belgium	Germany, West	17 Jan 58	328UNTS173	104735
Romania	USSR (Soviet Union)	03 Apr 58	313UNTS167	104535
Albania	USSR (Soviet Union)	30 Jun 58	328UNTS3	104729
Albania	Czechoslovakia	16 Jan 59	363UNTS195	105208
Denmark	India	16 Sep 59	405UNTS13	105820
Albania	Hungary	12 Jan 60	520UNTS3	107511
Brazil	USA (United States)	13 Jan 61	532UNTS177	107718
Czechoslovakia	Poland	04 Jul 61	436UNTS189	106295
Sweden	USA (United States)	24 Oct 61	494UNTS141	107231
Czechoslovakia	Hungary	02 Nov 61	438UNTS3	106313
Argentina	Brazil	15 Nov 61	0UNTS0	109424
Bulgaria	Poland	04 Dec 61	484UNTS3	107019
Poland	Romania	25 Jan 62	468UNTS3	106770
USSR (Soviet Union)	Yugoslavia	24 Feb 62	471UNTS195	106833
Sweden	UK Great Britain	26 Apr 63	590UNTS117	108551
Israel	Sweden	10 Sep 63	516UNTS3	107467
Czechoslovakia	Yugoslavia	20 Jan 64	538UNTS197	107816
Provisional detainment				
Bolivia	Brazil	25 Feb 38	54UNTS333	200205
Ethiopia	UK Great Britain	19 Dec 44	93UNTS303	200272
Jordan	Syria	23 Dec 53	204UNTS207	102759
Belgium	Lebanon	24 Dec 53	539UNTS321	107842
Bulgaria	Czechoslovakia	13 Apr 54	501UNTS3	107314
Israel	Italy	24 Feb 56	316UNTS97	104580
Belgium	Israel	26 Mar 56	260UNTS3	103702
Israel	Luxembourg	26 Jul 56	550UNTS239	108020
Israel	Netherlands	18 Dec 56	276UNTS153	103991
Czechoslovakia	USSR (Soviet Union)	31 Aug 57	308UNTS3	104456
Germany, East	Hungary	30 Oct 57	408UNTS4	105867
Germany, East	USSR (Soviet Union)	28 Nov 57	305UNTS113	104419
Bulgaria	USSR (Soviet Union)	12 Dec 57	317UNTS217	104606
Multilateral		13 Dec 57	359UNTS273	105146
Korea, North	USSR (Soviet Union)	16 Dec 57	301UNTS301	104349
Belgium	Germany, West	17 Jan 58	328UNTS173	104735
Romania	USSR (Soviet Union)	03 Apr 58	313UNTS167	104535
Albania	USSR (Soviet Union)	30 Jun 58	328UNTS3	104729
Germany, East	Romania	15 Jul 58	395UNTS3	105681
Hungary	USSR (Soviet Union)	15 Jul 58	322UNTS3	104656
Mongolia	USSR (Soviet Union)	25 Aug 58	322UNTS105	104657
Hungary	Romania	07 Oct 58	416UNTS199	106004
Czechoslovakia	Romania	25 Oct 58	417UNTS37	106006
Bulgaria	Romania	03 Dec 58	417UNTS133	106007
Israel	Switzerland	31 Dec 58	377UNTS305	105408
Albania	Czechoslovakia	16 Jan 59	363UNTS195	105208
Belgium	Morocco	27 Feb 59	390UNTS275	105611
Hungary	Poland	06 Mar 59	432UNTS3	106216
Denmark	India	16 Sep 59	405UNTS13	105820
Provisional detainment (Cont.)				
Norway	Sweden	28 Oct 59	427UNTS225	106157
Albania	Hungary	12 Jan 60	520UNTS3	107511
Brazil	USA (United States)	13 Jan 61	532UNTS177	107718
Czechoslovakia	Poland	04 Jul 61	436UNTS189	106295
Austria	Israel	10 Oct 61	448UNTS161	106430
Czechoslovakia	Hungary	02 Nov 61	438UNTS3	106313
Argentina	Brazil	15 Nov 61	0UNTS0	109424
Belgium	Luxembourg	29 Nov 61	486UNTS37	107071
Poland	Romania	25 Jan 62	468UNTS3	106770
USSR (Soviet Union)	Yugoslavia	24 Feb 62	471UNTS195	106833
Multilateral		27 Jun 62	616UNTS79	108893
Fed Rhod/Nyasaland	South Africa	19 Nov 62	458UNTS59	106592
Israel	USA (United States)	10 Dec 62	484UNTS283	107038
Israel	Sweden	10 Sep 63	516UNTS3	107467
Czechoslovakia	Yugoslavia	20 Jan 64	538UNTS197	107816
Extradition postponement				
Bolivia	Brazil	25 Feb 38	54UNTS333	200205
South Africa	USA (United States)	18 Dec 47	148UNTS85	101938
Belgium	Lebanon	24 Dec 53	539UNTS321	107842
Bulgaria	Czechoslovakia	13 Apr 54	501UNTS3	107314
Israel	Italy	24 Feb 56	316UNTS97	104580
Israel	Luxembourg	26 Jul 56	550UNTS239	108020
Israel	Netherlands	18 Dec 56	276UNTS153	103991
Germany, East	Poland	01 Feb 57	319UNTS115	104632
Czechoslovakia	USSR (Soviet Union)	31 Aug 57	308UNTS3	104456
Germany, East	Hungary	30 Oct 57	408UNTS4	105867
Germany, East	USSR (Soviet Union)	28 Nov 57	305UNTS113	104419
Bulgaria	USSR (Soviet Union)	12 Dec 57	317UNTS217	104606
Multilateral		13 Dec 57	359UNTS273	105146
Korea, North	USSR (Soviet Union)	16 Dec 57	301UNTS301	104349
Poland	USSR (Soviet Union)	28 Dec 57	320UNTS3	104638
Belgium	Germany, West	17 Jan 58	328UNTS173	104735
Romania	USSR (Soviet Union)	03 Apr 58	313UNTS167	104535
Albania	USSR (Soviet Union)	30 Jun 58	328UNTS3	104729
Germany, East	Romania	15 Jul 58	395UNTS3	105681
Hungary	USSR (Soviet Union)	15 Jul 58	322UNTS3	104656
Mongolia	USSR (Soviet Union)	25 Aug 58	322UNTS105	104657
Hungary	Romania	07 Oct 58	416UNTS199	106004
Czechoslovakia	Romania	25 Oct 58	417UNTS37	106006
Bulgaria	Romania	03 Dec 58	417UNTS133	106007
Israel	Switzerland	31 Dec 58	377UNTS305	105408
Albania	Czechoslovakia	16 Jan 59	363UNTS195	105208
Belgium	Morocco	27 Feb 59	390UNTS275	105611
Hungary	Poland	06 Mar 59	432UNTS3	106216
Denmark	India	16 Sep 59	405UNTS13	105820
Albania	Hungary	12 Jan 60	520UNTS3	107511
Brazil	USA (United States)	13 Jan 61	532UNTS177	107718
Czechoslovakia	Poland	04 Jul 61	436UNTS189	106295
Sweden	USA (United States)	24 Oct 61	494UNTS141	107231
Czechoslovakia	Hungary	02 Nov 61	438UNTS3	106313
Bulgaria	Poland	04 Dec 61	484UNTS3	107019
Poland	Romania	25 Jan 62	468UNTS3	106770
USSR (Soviet Union)	Yugoslavia	24 Feb 62	471UNTS195	106833
Multilateral		27 Jun 62	616UNTS79	108893
Fed Rhod/Nyasaland	South Africa	19 Nov 62	458UNTS59	106592
Israel	USA (United States)	10 Dec 62	484UNTS283	107038
Sweden	UK Great Britain	26 Apr 63	590UNTS117	108551
Czechoslovakia	Yugoslavia	20 Jan 64	538UNTS197	107816
Witnesses and experts				
Iraq	Turkey	29 Mar 46	37UNTS333	100581
Bulgaria	Czechoslovakia	13 Apr 54	501UNTS3	107314
Israel	Italy	24 Feb 56	316UNTS97	104580
France	Sweden	07 Mar 56	369UNTS155	105256
Belgium	Israel	26 Mar 56	260UNTS3	103702

PARTY ONE	PARTY TWO	DATE	CITATION	NUMBER
Witnesses and experts (Cont.)				
Israel	Luxembourg	26 Jul 56	550UNTS239	108020
Israel	Netherlands	18 Dec 56	276UNTS153	103991
Germany, East	Poland	01 Feb 57	319UNTS115	104632
Czechoslovakia	USSR (Soviet Union)	31 Aug 57	308UNTS3	104456
Germany, East	Hungary	30 Oct 57	408UNTS4	105867
Germany, East	USSR (Soviet Union)	28 Nov 57	305UNTS113	104419
Bulgaria	USSR (Soviet Union)	12 Dec 57	317UNTS217	104606
Korea, North	USSR (Soviet Union)	16 Dec 57	301UNTS301	104349
Belgium	Germany, West	17 Jan 58	328UNTS173	104735
Romania	USSR (Soviet Union)	03 Apr 58	313UNTS167	104535
Albania	USSR (Soviet Union)	30 Jun 58	328UNTS3	104729
Hungary	USSR (Soviet Union)	15 Jul 58	322UNTS3	104656
Germany, East	Romania	15 Jul 58	395UNTS3	105681
Mongolia	USSR (Soviet Union)	25 Aug 58	322UNTS105	104657
Hungary	Romania	07 Oct 58	416UNTS199	106004
Czechoslovakia	Romania	25 Oct 58	417UNTS37	106006
France	Israel	12 Nov 58	345UNTS79	104960
Bulgaria	Romania	03 Dec 58	417UNTS133	106007
Albania	Czechoslovakia	16 Jan 59	363UNTS195	105208
Belgium	Morocco	27 Feb 59	390UNTS275	105611
Czechoslovakia	Poland	04 Jul 61	436UNTS189	106295
Czechoslovakia	Hungary	02 Nov 61	438UNTS3	106313
Sweden	UK Great Britain	26 Apr 63	590UNTS117	108551
Czechoslovakia	Yugoslavia	20 Jan 64	538UNTS197	107816
Material evidence				
Czechoslovakia	Poland	21 Jan 49	31UNTS205	100480
Belgium	Israel	29 May 53	219UNTS197	102975
Belgium	Lebanon	24 Dec 53	539UNTS321	107842
Bulgaria	Czechoslovakia	13 Apr 54	501UNTS3	107314
Israel	Italy	24 Feb 56	316UNTS97	104580
Belgium	Israel	26 Mar 56	260UNTS3	103702
Israel	Luxembourg	26 Jul 56	550UNTS239	108020
Israel	Netherlands	18 Dec 56	276UNTS153	103991
Germany, East	Poland	01 Feb 57	319UNTS115	104632
Czechoslovakia	USSR (Soviet Union)	31 Aug 57	308UNTS3	104456
Germany, East	Hungary	30 Oct 57	408UNTS4	105867
Germany, East	USSR (Soviet Union)	28 Nov 57	305UNTS113	104419
Bulgaria	USSR (Soviet Union)	12 Dec 57	317UNTS217	104606
Multilateral		13 Dec 57	359UNTS273	105146
Korea, North	USSR (Soviet Union)	16 Dec 57	301UNTS301	104349
Poland	USSR (Soviet Union)	28 Dec 57	320UNTS3	104638
Belgium	Germany, West	17 Jan 58	328UNTS173	104735
Romania	USSR (Soviet Union)	03 Apr 58	313UNTS167	104535
Albania	USSR (Soviet Union)	30 Jun 58	328UNTS3	104729
Germany, East	Romania	15 Jul 58	395UNTS3	105681
Hungary	USSR (Soviet Union)	15 Jul 58	322UNTS3	104656
Mongolia	USSR (Soviet Union)	25 Aug 58	322UNTS105	104657
Hungary	Romania	07 Oct 58	416UNTS199	106004
Czechoslovakia	Romania	25 Oct 58	417UNTS37	106006
Bulgaria	Romania	03 Dec 58	417UNTS133	106007
Albania	Czechoslovakia	16 Jan 59	363UNTS195	105208
Belgium	Morocco	27 Feb 59	390UNTS275	105611
Hungary	Poland	06 Mar 59	432UNTS3	106216
Multilateral		20 Apr 59	472UNTS185	106841
Israel	South Africa	18 Sep 59	373UNTS47	105314
Albania	Hungary	12 Jan 60	520UNTS3	107511
Czechoslovakia	Poland	04 Jul 61	436UNTS189	106295
Austria	Israel	10 Oct 61	448UNTS161	106430
Czechoslovakia	Hungary	02 Nov 61	438UNTS3	106313
Argentina	Brazil	15 Nov 61	0UNTS0	109424
Bulgaria	Poland	04 Dec 61	484UNTS3	107019
Poland	Romania	25 Jan 62	468UNTS3	106770
USSR (Soviet Union)	Yugoslavia	24 Feb 62	471UNTS195	106833
Multilateral		27 Jun 62	616UNTS79	108893

PARTY ONE	PARTY TWO	DATE	CITATION	NUMBER
Material evidence (Cont.)				
Fed Rhod/Nyasaland	South Africa	19 Nov 62	458UNTS59	106592
Israel	Sweden	10 Sep 63	516UNTS3	107467
Czechoslovakia	Yugoslavia	20 Jan 64	538UNTS197	107816
Israel	UK Great Britain	05 Jul 66	630UNTS189	108971
Administrative cooperation				
Ireland	USA (United States)	21 Jan 50	206UNTS269	102792
UK Great Britain	Yemen	20 Jan 51	101UNTS39	101400
Greece	USA (United States)	03 Aug 51	224UNTS279	103080
Cuba	UK Great Britain	10 Aug 51	108UNTS243	101478
Israel	USA (United States)	23 Aug 51	219UNTS237	102979
Belgium	Netherlands	14 Nov 51	123UNTS91	101656
Japan	USA (United States)	02 Apr 53	206UNTS143	102788
Germany, West	USA (United States)	29 Oct 54	273UNTS3	103943
Netherlands	USA (United States)	27 Mar 56	285UNTS231	104154
Korea, South	USA (United States)	28 Nov 56	302UNTS281	104367
IAEA (Atom Energy)	WHO (World Health)	28 May 59	339UNTS387	200559
IAEA (Atom Energy)	OECD (Econ Coop)	24 Nov 60	396UNTS273	200585
IAEA (Atom Energy)	IMCO (Maritime Org)	13 Apr 61	425UNTS281	200595
Turkey	USSR (Soviet Union)	27 Apr 61	420UNTS307	106047
Multilateral		05 Oct 61	0UNTS0	109431
Burundi	United Nations	29 Dec 62	450UNTS279	106474
Burundi	WHO (World Health)	08 Aug 63	477UNTS346	106928
Multilateral		15 Nov 65	0UNTS0	109432
ILO (Labor Org)	OAU (Afri Unity)	25 Nov 65	550UNTS389	200617
Belgium	Israel	26 Apr 66	566UNTS187	108243
Austria	Israel	06 Jun 66	0UNTS0	109347
Austria	Israel	06 Jun 66	0UNTS0	109346
Conformity with municipal law				
Multilateral		28 Nov 19	38UNTS17	100584
Canada	France	12 May 33	253UNTS285	200545
Bolivia	Brazil	25 Feb 38	54UNTS333	200205
Brazil	France	27 Jan 40	72UNTS77	100929
Multilateral		30 Jul 40	161UNTS253	200488
Panama	USA (United States)	06 Sep 40	124UNTS209	200421
Panama	USA (United States)	28 Mar 41	103UNTS163	200312
Brazil	Paraguay	14 Jun 41	54UNTS313	200203
Brazil	Paraguay	14 Jun 41	54UNTS259	200198
Iceland	USA (United States)	21 Nov 41	124UNTS179	200418
Costa Rica	USA (United States)	16 Jan 42	23UNTS285	200135
El Salvador	USA (United States)	13 Feb 42	23UNTS293	200136
Canada	USA (United States)	04 Mar 42	124UNTS271	200426
Canada	USA (United States)	12 Mar 42	119UNTS295	200386
Nicaragua	USA (United States)	08 Apr 42	24UNTS145	200138
USA (United States)	USSR (Soviet Union)	18 Apr 42	105UNTS285	200339
Brazil	Portugal	30 Apr 42	65UNTS183	200210
Brazil	Uruguay	18 May 42	54UNTS369	200207
Belgium	USA (United States)	16 Jun 42	105UNTS159	200329
Poland	USA (United States)	01 Jul 42	103UNTS267	200317
Netherlands	USA (United States)	08 Jul 42	103UNTS277	200318
Greece	USA (United States)	10 Jul 42	103UNTS289	200319
Czechoslovakia	USA (United States)	11 Jul 42	90UNTS257	200263
Mexico	USA (United States)	04 Aug 42	148UNTS379	200475
Brazil	Paraguay	08 Oct 42	65UNTS191	200211
Honduras	USA (United States)	26 Oct 42	24UNTS209	200145
Brazil	Dominican Republic	09 Dec 42	65UNTS217	200213
Canada	USA (United States)	23 Feb 43	101UNTS243	200299
Finland	Sweden	10 Mar 43	198UNTS333	200518
UK Great Britain	USA (United States)	10 May 43	147UNTS109	200473
Guatemala	USA (United States)	19 May 43	28UNTS377	200161
Liberia	USA (United States)	08 Jun 43	117UNTS242	200373
Dominican Republic	USA (United States)	07 Jul 43	28UNTS419	200165
Brazil	Taiwan	20 Aug 43	14UNTS365	200094
France	USA (United States)	25 Sep 43	76UNTS183	200245
Iran	USA (United States)	27 Nov 43	31UNTS451	200176

Conformity with municipal law (Cont.)

PARTY ONE	PARTY TWO	DATE	CITATION	NUMBER
Multilateral		15 Jan 44	161UNTS281	200489
Canada	USA (United States)	17 Jan 44	109UNTS199	200360
Peru	USA (United States)	15 Apr 44	150UNTS317	200479
Australia	USA (United States)	10 May 44	106UNTS237	200343
Canada	USA (United States)	08 Jun 44	124UNTS297	200427
Bolivia	USA (United States)	07 Sep 44	162UNTS315	200494
Spain	USA (United States)	02 Dec 44	89UNTS345	200262
Sweden	USA (United States)	16 Dec 44	6UNTS397	200041
Denmark	USA (United States)	16 Dec 44	10UNTS213	200063
Iceland	USA (United States)	27 Jan 45	122UNTS293	200411
Ireland	USA (United States)	03 Feb 45	122UNTS305	200412
Canada	USA (United States)	13 Feb 45	200UNTS219	200519
Canada	USA (United States)	17 Feb 45	122UNTS261	200409
France	USA (United States)	20 Feb 45	76UNTS193	200246
France	USA (United States)	20 Feb 45	76UNTS223	200248
Turkey	USA (United States)	23 Feb 45	121UNTS165	200398
Sweden	UK Great Britain	06 Mar 45	82UNTS219	101095
UK Great Britain	USA (United States)	16 Apr 45	6UNTS189	100076
UK Great Britain	USA (United States)	16 Apr 45	6UNTS359	200039
Belgium	USA (United States)	17 Apr 45	139UNTS253	200454
Netherlands	USA (United States)	30 Apr 45	139UNTS341	200460
Taiwan	Netherlands	29 May 45	2UNTS307	200023
Iraq	USA (United States)	31 Jul 45	121UNTS239	200402
Switzerland	USA (United States)	03 Aug 45	51UNTS233	200191
Taiwan	France	18 Aug 45	14UNTS477	200101
France	UK Great Britain	29 Aug 45	11UNTS397	200069
Norway	USA (United States)	06 Oct 45	122UNTS319	200413
Dominican Republic	USA (United States)	13 Oct 45	149UNTS361	200477
USA (United States)	USSR (Soviet Union)	15 Oct 45	278UNTS151	200547
Guatemala	USA (United States)	25 Oct 45	139UNTS45	101875
Belgium	Canada	25 Oct 45	230UNTS127	103180
USSR (Soviet Union)	Yugoslavia	13 Nov 45	116UNTS139	101573
Greece	UK Great Britain	26 Nov 45	35UNTS161	100555
Portugal	UK Great Britain	06 Dec 45	5UNTS37	100064
Portugal	UK Great Britain	06 Dec 45	6UNTS3	100065
Portugal	USA (United States)	06 Dec 45	3UNTS139	100028
Denmark	UK Great Britain	06 Dec 45	5UNTS3	100061
Canada	UK Great Britain	21 Dec 45	27UNTS155	100405
Czechoslovakia	USA (United States)	03 Jan 46	6UNTS309	100084
United Arab Rep	USA (United States)	05 Jan 46	160UNTS27	102098
Lebanon	USA (United States)	21 Jan 46	140UNTS73	101884
Czechoslovakia	Poland	24 Jan 46	25UNTS181	100363
Canada	Mexico	08 Feb 46	230UNTS183	103183
UK Great Britain	USA (United States)	11 Feb 46	3UNTS253	100036
Netherlands	USA (United States)	11 Feb 46	3UNTS37	100023
Turkey	UK Great Britain	12 Feb 46	6UNTS79	100069
Turkey	USA (United States)	12 Feb 46	13UNTS3	100196
Belgium	France	22 Feb 46	68UNTS157	100892
France	UK Great Britain	28 Feb 46	27UNTS173	100407
Belgium	UK Great Britain	11 Mar 46	26UNTS167	100387
Poland	Yugoslavia	16 Mar 46	10UNTS11	100139
UK Great Britain	USA (United States)	27 Mar 46	4UNTS101	100040
France	USA (United States)	27 Mar 46	139UNTS114	101879
Greece	USA (United States)	27 Mar 46	15UNTS233	100239
Multilateral		31 Mar 46	17UNTS159	100274
Ireland	UK Great Britain	05 Apr 46	72UNTS57	100928
Belgium	USA (United States)	05 Apr 46	4UNTS125	100041
Netherlands	Portugal	12 Apr 46	4UNTS317	100054
Argentina	UK Great Britain	17 Apr 46	164UNTS53	102159
New Zealand	Norway	03 May 46	16UNTS211	100262
Belgium	Netherlands	16 May 46	17UNTS13	100266
France	Ireland	16 May 46	44UNTS105	100681
Belgium	Netherlands	24 May 46	31UNTS169	100477
France	USA (United States)	28 May 46	84UNTS113	101122
Ireland	Sweden	29 May 46	35UNTS231	100557

Conformity with municipal law (Cont.)

PARTY ONE	PARTY TWO	DATE	CITATION	NUMBER
Canada	UK Great Britain	05 Jun 46	27UNTS207	100408
Australia	Canada	11 Jun 46	10UNTS47	100142
United Arab Rep	USA (United States)	15 Jun 46	71UNTS157	100917
Sweden	Turkey	26 Jun 46	14UNTS21	100208
Multilateral		27 Jun 46	164UNTS37	102157
Netherlands	Spain	13 Jul 46	4UNTS351	100055
Czechoslovakia	USSR (Soviet Union)	25 Jul 46	27UNTS231	100409
France	Sweden	02 Aug 46	27UNTS251	100410
Lebanon	USA (United States)	11 Aug 46	66UNTS211	100856
Ceylon (Sri Lanka)	India	12 Aug 46	196UNTS209	102626
Netherlands	UK Great Britain	13 Aug 46	4UNTS367	100056
Taiwan	USA (United States)	30 Aug 46	12UNTS39	100179
Norway	UK Great Britain	31 Aug 46	6UNTS235	100078
Brazil	USA (United States)	06 Sep 46	54UNTS197	100805
Paraguay	USA (United States)	12 Sep 46	125UNTS179	101677
Monaco	Netherlands	25 Sep 46	247UNTS199	103469
Peru	USA (United States)	07 Oct 46	7UNTS71	100092
Greece	USA (United States)	08 Oct 46	180UNTS119	102379
France	Turkey	12 Oct 46	14UNTS33	100209
South Africa	UK Great Britain	14 Oct 46	86UNTS51	101152
South Africa	UK Great Britain	14 Oct 46	86UNTS77	101153
France	USA (United States)	18 Oct 46	140UNTS23	101882
Belgium	Portugal	22 Oct 46	34UNTS49	100527
Brazil	UK Great Britain	31 Oct 46	11UNTS115	100152
India	USA (United States)	14 Nov 46	22UNTS55	100331
Philippines	USA (United States)	16 Nov 46	7UNTS151	100097
France	Netherlands	19 Nov 46	32UNTS101	100493
Sweden	UK Great Britain	27 Nov 46	11UNTS229	100162
Albania	Yugoslavia	28 Nov 46	111UNTS163	101529
Albania	Yugoslavia	28 Nov 46	111UNTS113	101523
Albania	Yugoslavia	28 Nov 46	111UNTS93	101520
Albania	Yugoslavia	28 Nov 46	111UNTS143	101527
New Zealand	USA (United States)	03 Dec 46	7UNTS175	100099
Australia	USA (United States)	03 Dec 46	7UNTS201	100100
Portugal	Switzerland	09 Dec 46	310UNTS251	104495
Brazil	Portugal	10 Dec 46	200UNTS67	102695
South Africa	USA (United States)	13 Dec 46	167UNTS171	102207
USA (United States)	Uruguay	14 Dec 46	532UNTS87	107713
Canada	Nicaragua	19 Dec 46	236UNTS229	103326
Taiwan	USA (United States)	20 Dec 46	22UNTS87	100332
Hungary	Yugoslavia	23 Dec 46	113UNTS125	101549
Peru	USA (United States)	27 Dec 46	26UNTS227	100390
Peru	USA (United States)	27 Dec 46	152UNTS93	102013
Finland	USA (United States)	07 Jan 47	15UNTS273	100243
Ecuador	USA (United States)	08 Jan 47	22UNTS119	100333
Czechoslovakia	Ireland	29 Jan 47	27UNTS267	100411
USSR (Soviet Union)	Yugoslavia	04 Feb 47	130UNTS235	101731
Multilateral		08 Feb 47	14UNTS287	100222
France	Poland	11 Feb 47	12UNTS287	100189
Belgium	Chile	11 Feb 47	76UNTS107	100983
Thailand	USA (United States)	26 Feb 47	16UNTS17	100246
Burma	USA (United States)	28 Feb 47	25UNTS27	100355
Paraguay	USA (United States)	28 Feb 47	44UNTS25	100676
Belgium	Czechoslovakia	06 Mar 47	34UNTS77	100528
Portugal	Sweden	06 Mar 47	35UNTS243	100558
Philippines	USA (United States)	14 Mar 47	16UNTS31	100247
Austria	France	15 Mar 47	12UNTS109	100182
Netherlands	Turkey	19 Mar 47	14UNTS59	100211
Ireland	Sweden	19 Mar 47	553UNTS163	108083
Belgium	Sweden	20 Mar 47	34UNTS3	100522
Netherlands	Sweden	20 Mar 47	247UNTS145	103463
Australia	Norway	24 Mar 47	18UNTS185	100288
Belgium	Netherlands	25 Mar 47	18UNTS309	100299
France	USA (United States)	27 Mar 47	16UNTS65	100249
Taiwan	Portugal	01 Apr 47	14UNTS177	100220

Conformity with municipal law (Cont.)

PARTY ONE	PARTY TWO	DATE	CITATION	NUMBER
France	USA (United States)	04 Apr 47	24UNTS133	100353
Greece	Sweden	08 Apr 47	94UNTS73	101307
South Africa	USA (United States)	10 Apr 47	167UNTS211	102208
Greece	Netherlands	17 Apr 47	32UNTS115	100494
France	Ireland	22 Apr 47	553UNTS51	108068
New Zealand	USA (United States)	24 Apr 47	16UNTS79	100250
Canada	Portugal	25 Apr 47	94UNTS87	101308
Czechoslovakia	Yugoslavia	27 Apr 47	33UNTS49	100514
Syria	USA (United States)	28 Apr 47	262UNTS121	103741
Sweden	USA (United States)	30 Apr 47	84UNTS33	101116
Ireland	Netherlands	01 May 47	247UNTS193	103468
France	Greece	05 May 47	76UNTS61	100980
Chile	USA (United States)	10 May 47	55UNTS21	100807
Denmark	Ireland	13 May 47	553UNTS37	108066
Czechoslovakia	Denmark	14 May 47	27UNTS297	100413
ICJ Option Clause	Turkey	22 May 47	4UNTS265	100050
South Africa	USA (United States)	23 May 47	66UNTS233	100857
Poland	Yugoslavia	24 May 47	115UNTS69	101558
Panama	USA (United States)	26 May 47	138UNTS137	101866
Ireland	Switzerland	09 Jun 47	553UNTS169	108084
Greece	USA (United States)	20 Jun 47	7UNTS267	100105
Austria	USA (United States)	25 Jun 47	22UNTS141	100334
United Nations	USA (United States)	26 Jun 47	11UNTS11	100147
Canada	Sweden	27 Jun 47	27UNTS313	100414
Bulgaria	Poland	28 Jun 47	15UNTS123	100230
Iraq	Turkey	30 Jun 47	72UNTS107	100930
Romania	Yugoslavia	30 Jun 47	116UNTS57	101569
France	Norway	30 Jun 47	104UNTS313	101449
Denmark	Turkey	30 Jun 47	32UNTS301	100504
Belgium	United Arab Rep	01 Jul 47	34UNTS93	100529
Czechoslovakia	Poland	04 Jul 47	25UNTS249	100366
Italy	USA (United States)	04 Jul 47	22UNTS173	100336
Greece	USA (United States)	08 Jul 47	16UNTS157	100256
Albania	Yugoslavia	09 Jul 47	33UNTS91	100516
Turkey	USA (United States)	12 Jul 47	7UNTS299	100106
Luxembourg	Norway	12 Jul 47	90UNTS59	101226
Belgium	Norway	15 Jul 47	33UNTS25	100511
Hungary	USSR (Soviet Union)	15 Jul 47	216UNTS247	102940
France	India	16 Jul 47	27UNTS325	100415
Canada	UK Great Britain	17 Jul 47	28UNTS3	100416
Netherlands	Thailand	18 Jul 47	28UNTS27	100417
Greece	Turkey	22 Jul 47	72UNTS131	100931
Netherlands	South Africa	22 Jul 47	12UNTS257	100188
Taiwan	UK Great Britain	23 Jul 47	9UNTS207	100135
Czechoslovakia	Greece	30 Jul 47	185UNTS115	102463
Czechoslovakia	Greece	30 Jul 47	185UNTS149	102466
Norway	Switzerland	01 Aug 47	90UNTS65	101227
Netherlands	IBRD (World Bank)	07 Aug 47	152UNTS165	102015
Czechoslovakia	New Zealand	08 Aug 47	18UNTS161	100285
Canada	Ireland	08 Aug 47	28UNTS47	100419
Italy	USA (United States)	14 Aug 47	36UNTS105	100567
Denmark	IBRD (World Bank)	22 Aug 47	152UNTS223	102016
Hungary	Poland	28 Aug 47	15UNTS145	100231
Luxembourg	IBRD (World Bank)	28 Aug 47	153UNTS3	102017
Belgium	Netherlands	29 Aug 47	36UNTS349	100573
Czechoslovakia	Netherlands	01 Sep 47	32UNTS129	100495
Czechoslovakia	Switzerland	10 Sep 47	35UNTS275	100559
Greece	Lebanon	10 Sep 47	187UNTS107	102504
Lebanon	Turkey	16 Sep 47	44UNTS123	100682
Chile	UK Great Britain	16 Sep 47	133UNTS143	101786
Philippines	USA (United States)	17 Sep 47	206UNTS249	102790
Sweden	Yugoslavia	06 Oct 47	53UNTS107	100775
Hungary	Yugoslavia	15 Oct 47	33UNTS73	100515
Czechoslovakia	Sweden	15 Oct 47	44UNTS149	100683
Portugal	UK Great Britain	16 Oct 47	82UNTS203	101093

Conformity with municipal law (Cont.)

PARTY ONE	PARTY TWO	DATE	CITATION	NUMBER
Colombia	UK Great Britain	16 Oct 47	160UNTS297	102115
ICJ Option Clause	Mexico	23 Oct 47	9UNTS97	100127
Taiwan	USA (United States)	27 Oct 47	12UNTS11	100178
Brazil	Netherlands	06 Nov 47	53UNTS59	100773
Norway	Portugal	11 Nov 47	34UNTS257	100542
Brazil	Sweden	14 Nov 47	94UNTS139	101310
Ecuador	USA (United States)	14 Nov 47	149UNTS297	101959
Brazil	Norway	14 Nov 47	44UNTS163	100684
Brazil	Denmark	14 Nov 47	47UNTS39	100722
Denmark	Greece	14 Nov 47	35UNTS295	100560
Denmark	Ireland	18 Nov 47	35UNTS309	100561
Ireland	Italy	21 Nov 47	353UNTS73	105038
Italy	UK Great Britain	06 Dec 47	82UNTS243	101097
Taiwan	Netherlands	06 Dec 47	43UNTS185	100669
India	Pakistan	10 Dec 47	51UNTS173	100764
Czechoslovakia	USSR (Soviet Union)	11 Dec 47	217UNTS35	102943
USSR (Soviet Union)	Yugoslavia	15 Dec 47	116UNTS313	101578
Denmark	Portugal	15 Dec 47	35UNTS329	100563
Ireland	Norway	17 Dec 47	90UNTS71	101228
South Africa	USA (United States)	18 Dec 47	148UNTS85	101938
Peru	UK Great Britain	22 Dec 47	72UNTS143	100932
Norway	Sweden	22 Dec 47	22UNTS203	100337
Denmark	Sweden	23 Dec 47	14UNTS3	100207
UK Great Britain	USSR (Soviet Union)	27 Dec 47	82UNTS251	101098
Ethiopia	Pakistan	01 Jan 48	35UNTS3	100547
France	USA (United States)	02 Jan 48	31UNTS97	100470
Austria	USA (United States)	02 Jan 48	34UNTS141	100534
Italy	USA (United States)	03 Jan 48	31UNTS105	100471
Philippines	UK Great Britain	07 Jan 48	28UNTS63	100420
Belgium	France	17 Jan 48	36UNTS233	100570
Denmark	Norway	21 Jan 48	14UNTS307	100223
Austria	Netherlands	22 Jan 48	17UNTS99	100270
France	Lebanon	24 Jan 48	173UNTS99	102263
Hungary	Poland	31 Jan 48	25UNTS283	100368
Italy	USA (United States)	02 Feb 48	79UNTS171	101040
Italy	USA (United States)	06 Feb 48	73UNTS113	100950
Greece	United Nations	12 Feb 48	47UNTS223	100732
Poland	Romania	27 Feb 48	46UNTS143	100707
France	United Nations	10 Mar 48	47UNTS203	100731
Canada	New Zealand	12 Mar 48	231UNTS219	103222
Czechoslovakia	Yugoslavia	14 Mar 48	28UNTS81	100421
New Zealand	USA (United States)	16 Mar 48	127UNTS133	101703
Hungary	Yugoslavia	18 Mar 48	113UNTS201	101551
Argentina	Denmark	18 Mar 48	94UNTS175	101311
Cuba	UK Great Britain	19 Mar 48	175UNTS23	102294
Belgium	Luxembourg	27 Mar 48	178UNTS265	102343
Belgium	Netherlands	13 Apr 48	32UNTS153	100497
Belgium	France	13 Apr 48	31UNTS409	100483
Belgium	Ireland	16 Apr 48	26UNTS159	100386
France	UK Great Britain	19 Apr 48	83UNTS201	101109
Netherlands	USA (United States)	29 Apr 48	32UNTS167	100498
Norway	Sweden	29 Apr 48	26UNTS33	100375
Multilateral		30 Apr 48	119UNTS3	101609
Canada	France	05 May 48	231UNTS87	103209
Denmark	USA (United States)	06 May 48	26UNTS55	100377
Pakistan	Sweden	06 May 48	36UNTS3	100564
Ireland	Switzerland	06 May 48	334UNTS187	104768
Jordan	Turkey	07 May 48	32UNTS313	100505
Ireland	Netherlands	10 May 48	28UNTS121	100422
Denmark	Iceland	14 May 48	23UNTS163	100346
Guatemala	USA (United States)	18 May 48	67UNTS161	100875
Norway	Turkey	20 May 48	26UNTS137	100384
Finland	United Nations	20 May 48	47UNTS319	200189
India	Sweden	21 May 48	34UNTS285	100543
Greece	Switzerland	26 May 48	94UNTS217	101312

PARTY ONE	PARTY TWO	DATE	CITATION	NUMBER
Conformity with municipal law (Cont.)				
Luxembourg	UK Great Britain	27 May 48	53UNTS115	100776
Canada	Netherlands	02 Jun 48	32UNTS215	100499
Multilateral		19 Jun 48	310UNTS151	104492
Ireland	Norway	21 Jun 48	34UNTS317	100545
India	Pakistan	23 Jun 48	28UNTS143	100423
Italy	UK Great Britain	25 Jun 48	94UNTS239	101313
Multilateral		26 Jun 48	331UNTS217	104757
New Zealand	Pakistan	28 Jun 48	91UNTS235	101253
France	USA (United States)	28 Jun 48	19UNTS9	100302
Ireland	USA (United States)	28 Jun 48	24UNTS3	100349
Italy	USA (United States)	28 Jun 48	20UNTS43	100314
Denmark	USA (United States)	29 Jun 48	22UNTS217	100338
Peru	USA (United States)	30 Jun 48	150UNTS45	101962
Austria	USA (United States)	02 Jul 48	21UNTS29	100323
Belgium	USA (United States)	02 Jul 48	19UNTS127	100309
Greece	USA (United States)	02 Jul 48	23UNTS43	100342
Sweden	USA (United States)	03 Jul 48	23UNTS101	100343
Luxembourg	USA (United States)	03 Jul 48	24UNTS35	100350
Norway	USA (United States)	03 Jul 48	20UNTS185	100317
Taiwan	USA (United States)	03 Jul 48	17UNTS119	100273
Iceland	USA (United States)	03 Jul 48	20UNTS141	100316
Turkey	USA (United States)	04 Jul 48	24UNTS67	100351
UK Great Britain	USA (United States)	06 Jul 48	22UNTS263	100339
Netherlands	UK Great Britain	07 Jul 48	82UNTS259	101099
Multilateral		09 Jul 48	68UNTS17	100881
Multilateral		09 Jul 48	70UNTS85	100898
France	USA (United States)	09 Jul 48	24UNTS103	100352
Multilateral		14 Jul 48	23UNTS3	100340
Monaco	Norway	16 Jul 48	90UNTS77	101229
USA (United States)	Yugoslavia	19 Jul 48	89UNTS43	101208
Taiwan	USA (United States)	05 Aug 48	82UNTS109	101087
Brazil	Switzerland	10 Aug 48	94UNTS269	101314
Multilateral		18 Aug 48	33UNTS181	100518
Philippines	USA (United States)	23 Aug 48	82UNTS11	101080
France	Spain	23 Aug 48	28UNTS173	100425
Pakistan	United Nations	27 Aug 48	47UNTS269	100734
Philippines	USA (United States)	27 Aug 48	44UNTS13	100675
Greece	Lebanon	06 Sep 48	178UNTS37	102335
New Zealand	Pakistan	17 Sep 48	91UNTS275	101254
Panama	USA (United States)	24 Sep 48	150UNTS25	101961
Portugal	USA (United States)	28 Sep 48	29UNTS213	100442
Bolivia	USA (United States)	29 Sep 48	505UNTS139	107370
United Nations	Thailand	05 Oct 48	47UNTS287	100735
Czechoslovakia	United Nations	07 Oct 48	47UNTS185	100730
United Nations	San Marino	07 Oct 48	47UNTS337	200190
Netherlands	Spain	08 Oct 48	28UNTS209	100426
Australia	Denmark	08 Oct 48	22UNTS43	100330
Belgium	Luxembourg	09 Oct 48	123UNTS29	101652
Czechoslovakia	France	12 Oct 48	45UNTS81	100693
Trieste	USA (United States)	15 Oct 48	29UNTS249	100443
Sweden	Switzerland	16 Oct 48	197UNTS55	102634
France	USA (United States)	19 Oct 48	98UNTS3	101355
Philippines	USA (United States)	21 Oct 48	77UNTS197	101000
Mexico	Portugal	22 Oct 48	34UNTS329	100546
Belgium	USA (United States)	26 Oct 48	84UNTS265	101135
Belgium	USA (United States)	28 Oct 48	173UNTS67	102262
Argentina	Netherlands	29 Oct 48	95UNTS21	101316
Monaco	UK Great Britain	10 Nov 48	81UNTS85	101065
UK Great Britain	USA (United States)	12 Nov 48	84UNTS275	101136
Czechoslovakia	Poland	12 Nov 48	84UNTS347	101141
Belgium	Italy	29 Nov 48	41UNTS3	100641
Ireland	Luxembourg	01 Dec 48	553UNTS111	108075
Korea, South	USA (United States)	10 Dec 48	55UNTS157	100813
Italy	USSR (Soviet Union)	11 Dec 48	217UNTS181	102948
Denmark	New Zealand	13 Dec 48	92UNTS65	101261

PARTY ONE	PARTY TWO	DATE	CITATION	NUMBER
Conformity with municipal law (Cont.)				
Argentina	Chile	14 Dec 48	635UNTS21	109071
Argentina	Denmark	14 Dec 48	74UNTS41	100956
Argentina	Denmark	15 Dec 48	67UNTS71	100866
Denmark	Turkey	15 Dec 48	76UNTS3	100974
Ceylon (Sri Lanka)	Pakistan	15 Dec 48	91UNTS303	101255
Italy	USA (United States)	18 Dec 48	79UNTS133	101037
Ceylon (Sri Lanka)	India	21 Dec 48	28UNTS223	100427
Ceylon (Sri Lanka)	Pakistan	03 Jan 49	28UNTS247	100428
Mexico	IBRD (World Bank)	06 Jan 49	154UNTS3	102027
Mexico	IBRD (World Bank)	06 Jan 49	154UNTS81	102028
Italy	Lebanon	24 Jan 49	231UNTS241	103223
Brazil	IBRD (World Bank)	27 Jan 49	153UNTS264	102026
Switzerland	Turkey	16 Feb 49	72UNTS175	100933
Korea, South	USA (United States)	17 Feb 49	74UNTS167	100963
Finland	Netherlands	25 Feb 49	53UNTS123	100777
Belgium	IBRD (World Bank)	01 Mar 49	154UNTS133	102029
Netherlands	New Zealand	03 Mar 49	34UNTS207	100538
Netherlands	Switzerland	07 Mar 49	35UNTS69	100551
United Nations	UK Great Britain	18 Mar 49	47UNTS305	100736
Finland	USA (United States)	29 Mar 49	55UNTS59	100808
Sweden	UK Great Britain	30 Mar 49	209UNTS129	102826
Panama	USA (United States)	31 Mar 49	55UNTS87	100810
Panama	USA (United States)	31 Mar 49	55UNTS125	100811
Finland	Sweden	26 Apr 49	95UNTS83	101318
Luxembourg	Netherlands	26 Apr 49	182UNTS187	102425
Multilateral		28 Apr 49	71UNTS101	100912
Denmark	Poland	12 May 49	87UNTS179	101172
Bulgaria	Poland	16 May 49	84UNTS313	101140
Ireland	UK Great Britain	18 May 49	553UNTS209	108089
Iceland	Ireland	20 May 49	553UNTS99	108073
Italy	Spain	31 May 49	231UNTS251	103224
Australia	Pakistan	03 Jun 49	35UNTS23	100549
Canada	USA (United States)	04 Jun 49	200UNTS201	102704
Canada	USA (United States)	04 Jun 49	122UNTS237	101649
Ethiopia	India	07 Jun 49	35UNTS13	100548
Philippines	USA (United States)	07 Jun 49	45UNTS63	100692
Norway	Pakistan	08 Jun 49	90UNTS131	101231
Greece	Lebanon	10 Jun 49	178UNTS29	102334
Norway	USA (United States)	13 Jun 49	127UNTS189	101705
Lebanon	UK Great Britain	20 Jun 49	90UNTS137	101232
Belgium	Greece	21 Jun 49	137UNTS215	101854
Norway	Pakistan	23 Jun 49	35UNTS49	100550
India	Switzerland	24 Jun 49	95UNTS109	101319
Canada	Sweden	30 Jun 49	231UNTS37	103201
Multilateral		01 Jul 49	120UNTS71	101616
Czechoslovakia	Poland	02 Jul 49	260UNTS179	103709
Czechoslovakia	Poland	02 Jul 49	260UNTS149	103708
Greece	Syria	05 Jul 49	78UNTS71	101013
Australia	India	11 Jul 49	35UNTS83	100552
Iraq	Norway	12 Jul 49	53UNTS137	100778
Czechoslovakia	Finland	13 Jul 49	53UNTS153	100779
Pakistan	Philippines	16 Jul 49	35UNTS111	100553
Dominican Republic	USA (United States)	19 Jul 49	51UNTS145	100762
Netherlands	IBRD (World Bank)	26 Jul 49	154UNTS178	102030
Pakistan	UK Great Britain	27 Jul 49	44UNTS199	100685
Ireland	USA (United States)	01 Aug 49	82UNTS37	101083
Finland	IBRD (World Bank)	01 Aug 49	156UNTS289	200480
Ceylon (Sri Lanka)	UK Great Britain	05 Aug 49	35UNTS137	100554
India	IBRD (World Bank)	18 Aug 49	154UNTS269	102031
Canada	UK Great Britain	19 Aug 49	44UNTS223	100686
Colombia	IBRD (World Bank)	19 Aug 49	154UNTS329	102032
Finland	Norway	24 Aug 49	53UNTS167	100780
Denmark	Finland	26 Aug 49	53UNTS191	100781
Belgium	Canada	30 Aug 49	53UNTS221	100782
Iran	USA (United States)	01 Sep 49	79UNTS155	101039

Conformity with municipal law (Cont.)

PARTY ONE	PARTY TWO	DATE	CITATION	NUMBER
Ireland	USA (United States)	13 Sep 49	127UNTS119	101702
Ireland	USA (United States)	13 Sep 49	127UNTS89	101701
IBRD (World Bank)	Yugoslavia	17 Sep 49	155UNTS3	102034
Belgium	United Arab Rep	19 Sep 49	137UNTS189	101853
Multilateral		19 Sep 49	125UNTS3	101671
Lebanon	Netherlands	20 Sep 49	108UNTS205	101474
Burma	USA (United States)	28 Sep 49	55UNTS3	100806
India	IBRD (World Bank)	29 Sep 49	154UNTS393	102033
Greece	Philippines	08 Oct 49	187UNTS221	102515
Canada	Denmark	14 Oct 49	46UNTS97	100702
Finland	IBRD (World Bank)	17 Oct 49	156UNTS355	200481
India	Philippines	20 Oct 49	72UNTS191	100934
Iran	Netherlands	31 Oct 49	254UNTS257	103596
United Arab Rep	USA (United States)	03 Nov 49	71UNTS31	100908
Denmark	Pakistan	09 Nov 49	44UNTS255	100687
Belgium	Canada	19 Nov 49	150UNTS231	101977
New Zealand	Norway	22 Nov 49	51UNTS123	100760
Denmark	Thailand	23 Nov 49	53UNTS255	100786
Sweden	Thailand	23 Nov 49	72UNTS217	100935
Italy	Turkey	25 Nov 49	192UNTS39	102594
Norway	Thailand	26 Nov 49	53UNTS269	100787
Canada	Luxembourg	26 Nov 49	231UNTS51	103203
Australia	USA (United States)	26 Nov 49	45UNTS133	100695
Ireland	Italy	28 Nov 49	553UNTS105	108074
Brazil	Spain	28 Nov 49	215UNTS303	102923
Austria	Denmark	02 Dec 49	53UNTS281	100788
Austria	Norway	02 Dec 49	72UNTS230	100936
Austria	Sweden	02 Dec 49	108UNTS3	101465
Belgium	Luxembourg	03 Dec 49	91UNTS31	101241
Netherlands	United Arab Rep	08 Dec 49	95UNTS123	101320
Sweden	United Arab Rep	12 Dec 49	108UNTS15	101466
Colombia	UK Great Britain	13 Dec 49	88UNTS133	101189
Canada	Denmark	13 Dec 49	72UNTS247	100937
Belgium	San Marino	14 Dec 49	51UNTS107	100757
El Salvador	IBRD (World Bank)	14 Dec 49	155UNTS43	102035
Canada	Netherlands	14 Dec 49	230UNTS337	103192
Germany, West	USA (United States)	15 Dec 49	92UNTS269	101277
Norway	Sweden	17 Dec 49	197UNTS215	102641
Austria	Switzerland	19 Dec 49	254UNTS287	103597
Guatemala	USA (United States)	20 Dec 49	70UNTS71	100897
Finland	Sweden	21 Dec 49	197UNTS243	102642
USA (United States)	Yugoslavia	24 Dec 49	89UNTS209	101219
Turkey	USA (United States)	27 Dec 49	98UNTS141	101361
Australia	USA (United States)	29 Dec 49	71UNTS45	100909
France	Netherlands	30 Dec 49	203UNTS133	102743
France	Netherlands	30 Dec 49	203UNTS85	102742
Belgium	Italy	30 Dec 49	51UNTS83	100754
France	Netherlands	07 Jan 50	120UNTS25	101614
Korea, South	USA (United States)	26 Jan 50	80UNTS205	101053
Netherlands	USA (United States)	27 Jan 50	80UNTS219	101054
France	USA (United States)	27 Jan 50	80UNTS171	101051
Norway	USA (United States)	27 Jan 50	80UNTS241	101055
Italy	USA (United States)	27 Jan 50	80UNTS145	101050
Luxembourg	USA (United States)	27 Jan 50	80UNTS187	101052
Belgium	USA (United States)	27 Jan 50	51UNTS213	100767
UK Great Britain	USA (United States)	27 Jan 50	80UNTS261	101056
Denmark	USA (United States)	27 Jan 50	48UNTS115	100740
India	USA (United States)	02 Feb 50	89UNTS127	101214
UK Great Britain	Yugoslavia	09 Feb 50	88UNTS287	101200
Netherlands	Syria	13 Feb 50	108UNTS53	101467
Canada	Norway	14 Feb 50	53UNTS329	100790
Spain	Sweden	18 Feb 50	166UNTS15	102184
Greece	USA (United States)	20 Feb 50	196UNTS291	102630
Ceylon (Sri Lanka)	Thailand	24 Feb 50	72UNTS261	100938
Italy	Netherlands	04 Mar 50	254UNTS305	103598

Conformity with municipal law (Cont.)

PARTY ONE	PARTY TWO	DATE	CITATION	NUMBER
Norway	United Arab Rep	11 Mar 50	95UNTS157	101321
Canada	Norway	13 Mar 50	90UNTS181	101235
Denmark	United Arab Rep	14 Mar 50	95UNTS197	101322
Belgium	UK Great Britain	15 Mar 50	76UNTS85	100981
Multilateral		21 Mar 50	96UNTS271	101342
Denmark	Iceland	22 Mar 50	72UNTS273	100939
Iceland	Netherlands	22 Mar 50	95UNTS237	101323
Indonesia	USA (United States)	24 Mar 50	92UNTS387	101281
Denmark	UK Great Britain	27 Mar 50	68UNTS117	100891
Afghanistan	India	04 Apr 50	167UNTS105	102201
Italy	Portugal	05 Apr 50	254UNTS329	103599
Sweden	UK Great Britain	05 Apr 50	99UNTS107	101374
Turkey	United Arab Rep	12 Apr 50	128UNTS3	101711
Australia	Philippines	14 Apr 50	127UNTS281	101709
Multilateral		17 Apr 50	126UNTS285	101694
Canada	France	17 Apr 50	230UNTS365	103196
India	IBRD (World Bank)	18 Apr 50	155UNTS117	102036
Greece	United Arab Rep	24 Apr 50	163UNTS229	102149
Mexico	IBRD (World Bank)	28 Apr 50	155UNTS185	102037
Korea, South	USA (United States)	28 Apr 50	93UNTS21	101284
Israel	USA (United States)	04 May 50	132UNTS189	101760
Chile	USA (United States)	12 May 50	177UNTS103	102312
Switzerland	United Arab Rep	15 May 50	95UNTS255	101325
Brazil	IBRD (World Bank)	26 May 50	301UNTS165	104345
Austria	USA (United States)	06 Jun 50	92UNTS201	101273
Israel	USA (United States)	13 Jun 50	212UNTS93	102863
Iraq	IBRD (World Bank)	15 Jun 50	155UNTS267	102038
Iraq	Pakistan	20 Jun 50	77UNTS215	101001
Burma	Ceylon (Sri Lanka)	29 Jun 50	73UNTS3	100940
Thailand	USA (United States)	01 Jul 50	81UNTS61	101063
IBRD (World Bank)	Turkey	07 Jul 50	156UNTS3	102039
IBRD (World Bank)	Turkey	07 Jul 50	156UNTS75	102040
Spain	UK Great Britain	20 Jul 50	398UNTS101	105719
Italy	Norway	24 Jul 50	90UNTS187	101236
Ceylon (Sri Lanka)	UK Great Britain	26 Jul 50	337UNTS77	104818
Multilateral		27 Jul 50	166UNTS73	102186
France	Pakistan	31 Jul 50	96UNTS23	101329
Canada	France	01 Aug 50	73UNTS21	100941
Spain	Switzerland	03 Aug 50	254UNTS365	103600
France	United Arab Rep	08 Aug 50	127UNTS293	101710
Dominican Republic	USA (United States)	11 Aug 50	92UNTS329	101278
Indonesia	USA (United States)	15 Aug 50	134UNTS255	101804
Canada	New Zealand	16 Aug 50	77UNTS239	101002
IBRD (World Bank)	Uruguay	25 Aug 50	156UNTS203	102042
Ethiopia	IBRD (World Bank)	13 Sep 50	157UNTS233	102056
Burma	USA (United States)	13 Sep 50	92UNTS361	101280
Ethiopia	IBRD (World Bank)	13 Sep 50	157UNTS213	102055
Burma	Sweden	14 Sep 50	96UNTS45	101330
Brazil	Turkey	21 Sep 50	150UNTS299	101981
Pakistan	USA (United States)	23 Sep 50	82UNTS131	101088
Ceylon (Sri Lanka)	United Arab Rep	26 Sep 50	192UNTS53	102595
Indonesia	USA (United States)	16 Oct 50	281UNTS105	104074
Thailand	USA (United States)	17 Oct 50	79UNTS41	101030
Mexico	IBRD (World Bank)	18 Oct 50	157UNTS259	102057
Sweden	Switzerland	18 Oct 50	166UNTS49	102185
Luxembourg	Portugal	21 Oct 50	108UNTS67	101468
Belgium	Netherlands	23 Oct 50	136UNTS31	101831
Israel	Netherlands	23 Oct 50	189UNTS89	102543
Burma	USA (United States)	06 Nov 50	122UNTS81	101638
Australia	IBRD (World Bank)	14 Nov 50	156UNTS147	102041
USA (United States)	Yugoslavia	21 Nov 50	93UNTS45	101286
Multilateral		22 Nov 50	131UNTS25	101734
Bolivia	USA (United States)	22 Nov 50	152UNTS17	102008
Paraguay	USA (United States)	27 Nov 50	122UNTS147	101644
Switzerland	UK Great Britain	08 Dec 50	175UNTS55	102295

Conformity with municipal law (Cont.)

PARTY ONE	PARTY TWO	DATE	CITATION	NUMBER
Multilateral		15 Dec 50	171UNTS305	102234
Brazil	USA (United States)	19 Dec 50	140UNTS365	101899
Liberia	USA (United States)	22 Dec 50	133UNTS69	101781
France	Turkey	22 Dec 50	98UNTS11	101356
Multilateral		23 Dec 50	185UNTS3	102456
Netherlands	Norway	29 Dec 50	134UNTS19	101795
Brazil	USA (United States)	04 Jan 51	165UNTS97	102171
Chile	USA (United States)	04 Jan 51	165UNTS105	102172
Australia	Finland	04 Jan 51	80UNTS27	101042
Portugal	USA (United States)	05 Jan 51	133UNTS75	101782
USA (United States)	Yugoslavia	06 Jan 51	122UNTS137	101643
Argentina	USA (United States)	08 Jan 51	165UNTS89	102170
Chile	USA (United States)	16 Jan 51	157UNTS3	102043
Costa Rica	USA (United States)	17 Jan 51	134UNTS215	101801
Sweden	UK Great Britain	17 Jan 51	93UNTS225	101301
Panama	USA (United States)	26 Jan 51	137UNTS69	101849
Canada	India	26 Jan 51	248UNTS89	103486
Nicaragua	USA (United States)	31 Jan 51	150UNTS3	101960
Israel	Turkey	05 Feb 51	193UNTS3	102607
Canada	USA (United States)	08 Feb 51	207UNTS17	102797
Taiwan	USA (United States)	09 Feb 51	132UNTS273	101767
Australia	USA (United States)	20 Feb 51	132UNTS297	101769
Australia	Netherlands	20 Feb 51	97UNTS283	101354
Cuba	UK Great Britain	02 Mar 51	88UNTS191	101190
ILO (Labor Org)	Syria	03 Mar 51	110UNTS69	101502
Colombia	Portugal	09 Mar 51	108UNTS87	101469
Greece	Yugoslavia	15 Mar 51	187UNTS237	102516
Belgium	Netherlands	15 Mar 51	93UNTS97	101294
Dominican Republic	USA (United States)	16 Mar 51	148UNTS15	101932
India	USA (United States)	16 Mar 51	141UNTS47	101904
Canada	France	16 Mar 51	236UNTS297	103331
Canada	France	16 Mar 51	236UNTS267	103330
El Salvador	USA (United States)	19 Mar 51	134UNTS245	101803
Belgium	Finland	20 Mar 51	110UNTS27	101498
WHO (World Health)	United Arab Rep	25 Mar 51	223UNTS87	103058
United Nations	USA (United States)	28 Mar 51	108UNTS231	101476
Germany, West	Netherlands	29 Mar 51	149UNTS71	101952
Liberia	ILO (Labor Org)	02 Apr 51	100UNTS117	101392
Canada	Sweden	06 Apr 51	197UNTS393	102648
USA (United States)	Yugoslavia	17 Apr 51	162UNTS173	102134
Multilateral		18 Apr 51	261UNTS140	103729
Iraq	UK Great Britain	19 Apr 51	108UNTS121	101470
Greece	Turkey	20 Apr 51	178UNTS17	102333
Nicaragua	USA (United States)	20 Apr 51	138UNTS57	101859
Canada	Ceylon (Sri Lanka)	24 Apr 51	248UNTS101	103488
Philippines	USA (United States)	27 Apr 51	174UNTS251	102290
Norway	UK Great Britain	02 May 51	106UNTS101	101460
Ethiopia	USA (United States)	02 May 51	139UNTS85	101877
Iceland	USA (United States)	05 May 51	205UNTS173	102776
Belgium	UK Great Britain	08 May 51	158UNTS451	102079
Switzerland	USA (United States)	24 May 51	127UNTS227	101706
India	Netherlands	24 May 51	108UNTS151	101471
Greece	Norway	28 May 51	187UNTS141	102507
Netherlands	South Africa	31 May 51	188UNTS289	102533
UK Great Britain	USA (United States)	03 Jun 51	137UNTS81	101850
Italy	UK Great Britain	16 Jun 51	172UNTS293	102253
Saudi Arabia	USA (United States)	18 Jun 51	141UNTS67	101906
Multilateral		19 Jun 51	199UNTS67	102678
Australia	Italy	19 Jun 51	184UNTS185	102447
Cuba	Portugal	26 Jun 51	192UNTS115	102598
Multilateral		28 Jun 51	172UNTS159	102244
India	Turkey	29 Jun 51	213UNTS183	102886
Luxembourg	New Zealand	29 Jun 51	101UNTS71	101403
Denmark	France	30 Jun 51	151UNTS241	102000
Belgium	Portugal	03 Jul 51	101UNTS17	101398

Conformity with municipal law (Cont.)

PARTY ONE	PARTY TWO	DATE	CITATION	NUMBER
Iceland	Norway	14 Jul 51	163UNTS265	102150
Burma	Denmark	30 Jul 51	108UNTS167	101472
Canada	USA (United States)	01 Aug 51	233UNTS109	103254
Israel	Philippines	07 Aug 51	192UNTS81	102596
Lebanon	UK Great Britain	15 Aug 51	160UNTS327	102116
Iraq	USA (United States)	16 Aug 51	147UNTS65	101929
Denmark	USA (United States)	23 Aug 51	147UNTS49	101928
France	Italy	23 Aug 51	291UNTS143	104249
Japan	USA (United States)	28 Aug 51	147UNTS81	101930
Australia	Luxembourg	05 Sep 51	109UNTS31	101487
Burma	Netherlands	06 Sep 51	108UNTS187	101473
USA (United States)	Vietnam, South	07 Sep 51	174UNTS165	102284
Ethiopia	USA (United States)	07 Sep 51	206UNTS41	102785
Pakistan	United Arab Rep	08 Sep 51	133UNTS257	101793
Cambodia	USA (United States)	08 Sep 51	174UNTS115	102282
Laos	USA (United States)	09 Sep 51	174UNTS141	102283
Costa Rica	USA (United States)	11 Sep 51	234UNTS255	103288
Panama	UK Great Britain	15 Sep 51	560UNTS143	108172
Belgium	Sweden	18 Sep 51	133UNTS187	101789
Australia	Sweden	26 Sep 51	109UNTS39	101488
Pakistan	UK Great Britain	26 Sep 51	118UNTS221	101608
UK Great Britain	Yugoslavia	28 Sep 51	117UNTS107	101587
Greece	UK Great Britain	29 Sep 51	190UNTS260	102570
Philippines	Spain	06 Oct 51	215UNTS193	102920
Multilateral		09 Oct 51	220UNTS121	102997
Austria	Belgium	11 Oct 51	110UNTS45	101500
Australia	Norway	19 Oct 51	128UNTS109	101716
Greece	Luxembourg	22 Oct 51	187UNTS119	102506
Canada	Pakistan	23 Oct 51	248UNTS95	103487
El Salvador	USA (United States)	23 Oct 51	137UNTS43	101847
Belgium	New Zealand	01 Nov 51	118UNTS169	101605
USA (United States)	Yugoslavia	14 Nov 51	174UNTS201	102286
Turkey	USA (United States)	15 Nov 51	177UNTS315	102331
Finland	USA (United States)	16 Nov 51	140UNTS273	101893
Denmark	Iraq	18 Nov 51	232UNTS25	103227
Italy	UK Great Britain	28 Nov 51	172UNTS27	102238
Italy	UK Great Britain	28 Nov 51	172UNTS205	102248
India	UK Great Britain	01 Dec 51	128UNTS39	101712
Colombia	Spain	11 Dec 51	216UNTS73	102933
Finland	UK Great Britain	12 Dec 51	172UNTS45	102239
Nicaragua	USA (United States)	12 Dec 51	167UNTS151	102205
Italy	USA (United States)	12 Dec 51	137UNTS175	101852
Cambodia	USA (United States)	28 Dec 51	179UNTS97	102358
Thailand	USA (United States)	29 Dec 51	179UNTS113	102360
Laos	USA (United States)	31 Dec 51	198UNTS243	102668
Jordan	United Arab Rep	02 Jan 52	192UNTS157	102599
Taiwan	USA (United States)	02 Jan 52	181UNTS161	102407
Indonesia	USA (United States)	05 Jan 52	215UNTS121	102916
El Salvador	USA (United States)	07 Jan 52	198UNTS231	102667
Greece	USA (United States)	07 Jan 52	180UNTS171	102382
Turkey	USA (United States)	07 Jan 52	179UNTS121	102361
Korea, South	USA (United States)	07 Jan 52	179UNTS105	102359
Italy	USA (United States)	07 Jan 52	179UNTS165	102365
Belgium	USA (United States)	07 Jan 52	179UNTS81	102356
Philippines	USA (United States)	07 Jan 52	179UNTS193	102368
Greece	USA (United States)	07 Jan 52	177UNTS249	102323
Germany, East	Poland	08 Jan 52	304UNTS113	104394
UK Great Britain	USA (United States)	08 Jan 52	179UNTS201	102369
Denmark	USA (United States)	08 Jan 52	179UNTS65	102354
Norway	USA (United States)	08 Jan 52	179UNTS185	102367
Iceland	USA (United States)	08 Jan 52	180UNTS183	102383
Luxembourg	USA (United States)	08 Jan 52	180UNTS191	102384
Netherlands	USA (United States)	08 Jan 52	179UNTS175	102366
USA (United States)	Yugoslavia	08 Jan 52	152UNTS61	102011
UK Great Britain	USA (United States)	08 Jan 52	126UNTS307	101696

Conformity with municipal law (Cont.)

PARTY ONE	PARTY TWO	DATE	CITATION	NUMBER
Multilateral		10 Jan 52	163UNTS27	102139
Australia	Pakistan	16 Jan 52	151UNTS281	102001
Belgium	Germany, West	18 Jan 52	124UNTS9	101663
USA (United States)	Vietnam, South	19 Jan 52	205UNTS127	102772
Iran	USA (United States)	20 Jan 52	200UNTS191	102703
Spain	USA (United States)	21 Jan 52	160UNTS63	102102
France	USA (United States)	02 Feb 52	247UNTS223	103472
Greece	Yugoslavia	02 Feb 52	188UNTS311	102535
Austria	USA (United States)	16 Feb 52	177UNTS299	102329
Philippines	USA (United States)	19 Feb 52	177UNTS307	102330
Ecuador	USA (United States)	20 Feb 52	177UNTS43	102308
Canada	USA (United States)	21 Feb 52	205UNTS293	102781
Iraq	USA (United States)	21 Feb 52	198UNTS225	102666
Peru	USA (United States)	22 Feb 52	165UNTS31	102166
Costa Rica	USA (United States)	25 Feb 52	174UNTS233	102288
Israel	USA (United States)	27 Feb 52	177UNTS123	102314
Finland	USA (United States)	03 Mar 52	177UNTS163	102317
Cuba	USA (United States)	07 Mar 52	165UNTS11	102165
Belgium	Spain	10 Mar 52	178UNTS243	102342
Brazil	USA (United States)	15 Mar 52	199UNTS221	102687
Pakistan	Switzerland	17 Mar 52	192UNTS237	102603
Norway	Uruguay	20 Mar 52	310UNTS279	104496
Sweden	Uruguay	20 Mar 52	311UNTS3	104497
Iraq	Switzerland	31 Mar 52	311UNTS43	104498
Norway	USA (United States)	01 Apr 52	177UNTS291	102328
Chile	USA (United States)	09 Apr 52	186UNTS53	102482
Colombia	USA (United States)	17 Apr 52	174UNTS215	102287
France	Mexico	17 Apr 52	163UNTS321	102153
Honduras	USA (United States)	23 Apr 52	198UNTS251	102669
Greece	USA (United States)	23 Apr 52	177UNTS283	102327
Netherlands	Sweden	25 Apr 52	163UNTS131	102147
Denmark	Japan	28 Apr 52	166UNTS3	102182
France	Israel	29 Apr 52	189UNTS55	102542
Israel	USA (United States)	01 May 52	177UNTS89	102311
Australia	Denmark	01 May 52	152UNTS3	102006
Ethiopia	USA (United States)	15 May 52	180UNTS227	102388
Australia	USA (United States)	27 May 52	178UNTS113	102338
Ethiopia	USA (United States)	13 Jun 52	205UNTS17	102766
Monaco	New Zealand	13 Jun 52	171UNTS269	102230
Australia	United Arab Rep	14 Jun 52	173UNTS241	102269
India	United Arab Rep	14 Jun 52	173UNTS209	102268
Netherlands	South Africa	21 Jun 52	309UNTS123	104471
Denmark	UK Great Britain	23 Jun 52	151UNTS3	101982
Multilateral		26 Jun 52	196UNTS183	102624
USA (United States)	Uruguay	30 Jun 52	207UNTS139	102804
Belgium	Israel	30 Jun 52	183UNTS263	102435
Finland	USA (United States)	02 Jul 52	165UNTS203	102177
Greece	Italy	05 Jul 52	187UNTS157	102508
Australia	FAO (Food Agri)	07 Jul 52	184UNTS209	102449
Portugal	USA (United States)	09 Jul 52	180UNTS251	102389
Multilateral		11 Jul 52	170UNTS269	102223
Multilateral		11 Jul 52	170UNTS63	102222
Netherlands	Pakistan	17 Jul 52	150UNTS277	101980
Germany, West	USA (United States)	18 Jul 52	165UNTS167	102175
France	USA (United States)	22 Jul 52	181UNTS319	102420
Israel	USA (United States)	23 Jul 52	179UNTS139	102363
Greece	Turkey	05 Aug 52	187UNTS163	102509
Denmark	USA (United States)	08 Aug 52	181UNTS249	102414
Israel	USA (United States)	08 Aug 52	181UNTS37	102396
Japan	USA (United States)	11 Aug 52	212UNTS27	102862
USA (United States)	Yugoslavia	15 Aug 52	184UNTS97	102441
Multilateral		28 Aug 52	175UNTS69	102296
Ethiopia	Pakistan	29 Aug 52	150UNTS257	101979
Multilateral		05 Sep 52	247UNTS329	103479
Multilateral		06 Sep 52	216UNTS132	102937

Conformity with municipal law (Cont.)

PARTY ONE	PARTY TWO	DATE	CITATION	NUMBER
Pakistan	USA (United States)	17 Sep 52	227UNTS77	103132
Monaco	USA (United States)	24 Sep 52	186UNTS43	102481
Turkey	UK Great Britain	09 Oct 52	151UNTS233	101999
Canada	Italy	10 Oct 52	233UNTS137	103258
Austria	Luxembourg	13 Oct 52	192UNTS291	102606
Mexico	Netherlands	13 Oct 52	163UNTS341	102154
Austria	Belgium	17 Oct 52	162UNTS183	102135
Iceland	Luxembourg	23 Oct 52	193UNTS39	102609
Burma	UK Great Britain	25 Oct 52	150UNTS237	101978
Chile	Sweden	27 Oct 52	311UNTS63	104499
Chile	Denmark	27 Oct 52	271UNTS93	103911
Italy	Netherlands	28 Oct 52	289UNTS144	104218
India	Iraq	10 Nov 52	172UNTS103	102242
Denmark	Israel	14 Nov 52	160UNTS279	102113
Denmark	Israel	14 Nov 52	160UNTS289	102114
Luxembourg	Norway	17 Nov 52	311UNTS95	104500
Ceylon (Sri Lanka)	USA (United States)	17 Nov 52	180UNTS207	102386
Luxembourg	Sweden	17 Nov 52	173UNTS277	102270
Israel	Switzerland	19 Nov 52	232UNTS3	103226
Sweden	USA (United States)	20 Nov 52	177UNTS203	102319
Canada	USA (United States)	05 Dec 52	206UNTS11	102783
Belgium	Iceland	10 Dec 52	158UNTS445	102078
Austria	UK Great Britain	12 Dec 52	172UNTS9	102237
Saudi Arabia	USA (United States)	15 Dec 52	185UNTS55	102458
Saudi Arabia	USA (United States)	25 Jan 53	201UNTS3	102706
Bolivia	Italy	31 Jan 53	281UNTS181	104079
Greece	USA (United States)	04 Feb 53	189UNTS3	102538
Greece	Italy	04 Feb 53	189UNTS269	102551
Greece	Italy	04 Feb 53	189UNTS295	102552
Netherlands	Philippines	05 Feb 53	216UNTS99	102934
Japan	Netherlands	17 Feb 53	192UNTS215	102602
Japan	Sweden	20 Feb 53	173UNTS307	102272
Libya	UK Great Britain	21 Feb 53	311UNTS115	104501
Japan	Norway	23 Feb 53	192UNTS191	102601
Turkey	Yugoslavia	26 Feb 53	247UNTS54	103460
Denmark	Japan	26 Feb 53	173UNTS329	102273
Germany, West	USA (United States)	27 Feb 53	224UNTS31	103068
Germany, West	USA (United States)	27 Feb 53	223UNTS167	103065
Dominican Republic	USA (United States)	06 Mar 53	199UNTS267	102689
Belgium	France	11 Mar 53	191UNTS329	102590
France	Italy	14 Mar 53	284UNTS221	104140
Chile	Norway	16 Mar 53	167UNTS13	102198
Austria	Yugoslavia	19 Mar 53	467UNTS323	106768
Lebanon	USA (United States)	23 Mar 53	239UNTS45	103370
Belgium	Sweden	01 Apr 53	185UNTS225	102473
Germany, West	USA (United States)	09 Apr 53	204UNTS79	102750
Canada	Germany, West	15 Apr 53	236UNTS323	103333
Czechoslovakia	Denmark	23 Apr 53	174UNTS107	102281
Philippines	Thailand	27 Apr 53	174UNTS3	102274
Israel	Uruguay	30 Apr 53	280UNTS269	104064
Netherlands	Pakistan	01 May 53	293UNTS11	104281
Australia	USA (United States)	14 May 53	205UNTS237	102778
Australia	USA (United States)	14 May 53	205UNTS277	102780
Australia	USA (United States)	14 May 53	205UNTS253	102779
Germany, West	Sweden	15 May 53	227UNTS195	103139
Finland	Norway	20 May 53	173UNTS163	102265
Greece	United Arab Rep	21 May 53	256UNTS25	103621
Ethiopia	USA (United States)	22 May 53	191UNTS59	102577
Cuba	USA (United States)	26 May 53	224UNTS75	103070
Switzerland	Yugoslavia	28 May 53	232UNTS45	103228
Greece	UK Great Britain	01 Jun 53	172UNTS265	102250
Belgium	USA (United States)	18 Jun 53	222UNTS3	103019
United Arab Rep	USA (United States)	18 Jun 53	204UNTS55	102749
Japan	Thailand	19 Jun 53	174UNTS29	102276
Burma	Norway	22 Jun 53	174UNTS49	102277

Conformity with municipal law (Cont.)

PARTY ONE	PARTY TWO	DATE	CITATION	NUMBER
Liberia	USA (United States)	23 Jun 53	213UNTS57	102880
UK Great Britain	USA (United States)	24 Jun 53	224UNTS141	103074
Pakistan	USA (United States)	25 Jun 53	205UNTS139	102773
Greece	UK Great Britain	25 Jun 53	190UNTS281	102571
Philippines	USA (United States)	26 Jun 53	213UNTS77	102881
UK Great Britain	USA (United States)	26 Jun 53	183UNTS225	102432
Pakistan	Turkey	29 Jun 53	211UNTS225	102854
India	Yugoslavia	24 Jul 53	394UNTS13	105665
Canada	Mexico	27 Jul 53	192UNTS255	102604
Libya	UK Great Britain	29 Jul 53	186UNTS201	102492
Argentina	USSR (Soviet Union)	05 Aug 53	221UNTS99	103004
Belgium	Greece	05 Aug 53	173UNTS53	102260
USA (United States)	Venezuela	14 Aug 53	213UNTS99	102883
Denmark	Germany, West	14 Aug 53	202UNTS3	102725
Multilateral		27 Aug 53	213UNTS137	102884
Belgium	USA (United States)	02 Sep 53	200UNTS127	102700
Ceylon (Sri Lanka)	Netherlands	14 Sep 53	193UNTS21	102608
Greece	Netherlands	26 Sep 53	292UNTS23	104263
Spain	USA (United States)	26 Sep 53	207UNTS61	102800
Spain	USA (United States)	26 Sep 53	207UNTS93	102802
Germany, West	Netherlands	10 Oct 53	293UNTS115	104288
Denmark	USA (United States)	15 Oct 53	215UNTS111	102915
Multilateral		19 Oct 53	207UNTS189	102807
Libya	UK Great Britain	19 Oct 53	186UNTS285	102494
Jordan	USA (United States)	21 Oct 53	222UNTS31	103020
Australia	Netherlands	22 Oct 53	184UNTS193	102448
Multilateral		26 Oct 53	207UNTS237	102809
Netherlands	USA (United States)	27 Oct 53	221UNTS357	103017
Denmark	Sweden	27 Oct 53	198UNTS129	102660
Netherlands	Turkey	04 Nov 53	293UNTS3	104280
Greece	Turkey	07 Nov 53	225UNTS163	103098
Austria	Yugoslavia	11 Nov 53	363UNTS149	105206
Pakistan	United Arab Rep	14 Nov 53	485UNTS55	107046
Israel	USA (United States)	25 Nov 53	219UNTS205	102976
Cuba	USA (United States)	26 Nov 53	205UNTS213	102777
India	USSR (Soviet Union)	02 Dec 53	240UNTS143	103402
Bulgaria	Greece	05 Dec 53	225UNTS145	103096
Belgium	Cuba	16 Dec 53	185UNTS285	102475
Italy	South Africa	20 Dec 53	277UNTS293	104014
Belgium	Lebanon	24 Dec 53	219UNTS153	102972
Libya	USA (United States)	11 Jan 54	229UNTS15	103157
Bolivia	USA (United States)	15 Jan 54	229UNTS213	103168
Ethiopia	Greece	20 Jan 54	222UNTS281	103035
Japan	USA (United States)	21 Jan 54	223UNTS145	103063
Syria	UK Great Britain	30 Jan 54	449UNTS47	106452
Czechoslovakia	Greece	01 Feb 54	225UNTS95	103092
France	Greece	08 Feb 54	225UNTS107	103093
France	Greece	08 Feb 54	225UNTS121	103094
France	Sweden	16 Feb 54	228UNTS137	103147
Multilateral		19 Feb 54	214UNTS51	102899
United Arab Rep	USA (United States)	24 Feb 54	236UNTS61	103316
Japan	USA (United States)	08 Mar 54	232UNTS169	103236
Japan	USA (United States)	08 Mar 54	232UNTS227	103238
Afghanistan	USA (United States)	20 Mar 54	229UNTS7	103156
Finland	Netherlands	29 Mar 54	252UNTS185	103567
Italy	USA (United States)	31 Mar 54	235UNTS293	103311
Peru	Spain	31 Mar 54	232UNTS65	103230
Japan	USA (United States)	16 Apr 54	238UNTS39	103354
Luxembourg	USA (United States)	17 Apr 54	257UNTS255	103661
Iraq	USA (United States)	21 Apr 54	222UNTS251	103032
Italy	USA (United States)	27 Apr 54	234UNTS103	103275
Canada	USA (United States)	03 May 54	221UNTS339	103015
Netherlands	USA (United States)	07 May 54	213UNTS325	102895
Greece	Spain	15 May 54	299UNTS277	104319
Pakistan	Yugoslavia	15 May 54	286UNTS3	104158

Conformity with municipal law (Cont.)

PARTY ONE	PARTY TWO	DATE	CITATION	NUMBER
Spain	USA (United States)	19 May 54	235UNTS87	103296
Pakistan	USA (United States)	19 May 54	202UNTS301	102736
Honduras	USA (United States)	20 May 54	222UNTS87	103025
Australia	Greece	24 May 54	193UNTS175	102614
Canada	Spain	26 May 54	391UNTS273	105632
Iran	Switzerland	27 May 54	496UNTS273	107257
Canada	Portugal	28 May 54	391UNTS253	105631
Belgium	South Africa	01 Jun 54	201UNTS25	102708
Italy	Netherlands	04 Jun 54	289UNTS261	104222
Greece	Hungary	05 Jun 54	299UNTS285	104320
Greece	Hungary	05 Jun 54	299UNTS295	104321
UK Great Britain	USA (United States)	15 Jun 54	236UNTS133	103320
Lebanon	USA (United States)	18 Jun 54	233UNTS177	103262
Luxembourg	UK Great Britain	18 Jun 54	192UNTS33	102593
Italy	USA (United States)	24 Jun 54	235UNTS3	103290
Chile	USA (United States)	28 Jun 54	233UNTS3	103246
France	Greece	30 Jun 54	257UNTS83	103651
Turkey	USA (United States)	01 Jul 54	234UNTS147	103280
Ireland	Monaco	06 Jul 54	553UNTS117	108076
Germany, West	USA (United States)	22 Jul 54	239UNTS3	103369
Ireland	Luxembourg	27 Jul 54	232UNTS91	103231
Greece	USA (United States)	30 Jul 54	234UNTS43	103272
Philippines	Sweden	20 Aug 54	200UNTS121	102699
Pakistan	USA (United States)	23 Aug 54	234UNTS243	103287
Denmark	Pakistan	30 Aug 54	203UNTS59	102740
Thailand	USA (United States)	01 Sep 54	237UNTS209	103347
Austria	Denmark	07 Sep 54	201UNTS39	102709
Libya	USA (United States)	09 Sep 54	238UNTS217	103365
Greece	Italy	11 Sep 54	284UNTS313	104145
Sweden	Switzerland	25 Sep 54	262UNTS205	103746
Sweden	USSR (Soviet Union)	29 Sep 54	202UNTS259	102733
Switzerland	UK Great Britain	30 Sep 54	209UNTS197	102828
USA (United States)	Yugoslavia	18 Oct 54	273UNTS163	103951
Germany, West	UK Great Britain	18 Oct 54	218UNTS301	102960
Norway	Philippines	20 Oct 54	216UNTS11	102928
Denmark	Philippines	20 Oct 54	216UNTS3	102927
Multilateral		23 Oct 54	332UNTS3	104760
Iran	UK Great Britain	25 Oct 54	204UNTS131	102754
Netherlands	Venezuela	26 Oct 54	232UNTS103	103232
Canada	Ireland	28 Oct 54	305UNTS3	104407
Canada	Ireland	28 Oct 54	304UNTS317	104406
Greece	Netherlands	01 Nov 54	223UNTS79	103057
Libya	USA (United States)	03 Nov 54	238UNTS227	103366
Turkey	USA (United States)	15 Nov 54	238UNTS135	103358
Finland	UK Great Britain	16 Nov 54	204UNTS177	102756
Austria	Netherlands	17 Nov 54	292UNTS45	104266
Japan	USA (United States)	19 Nov 54	238UNTS207	103364
Portugal	UK Great Britain	19 Nov 54	226UNTS305	103125
USA (United States)	Vietnam, South	22 Nov 54	235UNTS11	103291
Belgium	USA (United States)	23 Nov 54	235UNTS19	103292
Portugal	UK Great Britain	23 Nov 54	204UNTS183	102757
Portugal	UK Great Britain	24 Nov 54	313UNTS125	104533
Belgium	Greece	09 Dec 54	257UNTS243	103660
Iceland	USA (United States)	10 Dec 54	237UNTS191	103345
Guatemala	USA (United States)	13 Dec 54	237UNTS169	103343
Netherlands	Portugal	14 Dec 54	289UNTS121	104216
Ecuador	Netherlands	14 Dec 54	232UNTS115	103233
India	Iran	15 Dec 54	327UNTS245	104724
Denmark	USA (United States)	15 Dec 54	213UNTS273	102890
Multilateral		19 Dec 54	218UNTS139	102955
Sweden	USA (United States)	22 Dec 54	228UNTS85	103143
Norway	Switzerland	30 Dec 54	311UNTS147	104502
Israel	South Africa	31 Dec 54	220UNTS11	102984
Austria	Belgium	07 Jan 55	380UNTS219	105458
Pakistan	USA (United States)	11 Jan 55	251UNTS111	103537

Conformity with municipal law (Cont.)

PARTY ONE	PARTY TWO	DATE	CITATION	NUMBER
Canada	Japan	12 Jan 55	311UNTS167	104503
Pakistan	USA (United States)	18 Jan 55	241UNTS53	103423
Italy	USA (United States)	26 Jan 55	238UNTS179	103361
Chile	USA (United States)	27 Jan 55	262UNTS3	103735
Haiti	USA (United States)	28 Jan 55	270UNTS83	103894
Philippines	UK Great Britain	31 Jan 55	216UNTS51	102932
Finland	Ireland	01 Feb 55	553UNTS45	108067
Italy	USA (United States)	11 Feb 55	240UNTS87	103396
Belgium	Netherlands	16 Feb 55	211UNTS49	102846
South Africa	USA (United States)	22 Feb 55	247UNTS247	103473
Costa Rica	USA (United States)	26 Feb 55	252UNTS129	103562
Greece	Japan	12 Mar 55	227UNTS33	103130
Multilateral		12 Mar 55	211UNTS3	102844
Bulgaria	Yugoslavia	16 Mar 55	397UNTS83	105702
Iraq	United Arab Rep	23 Mar 55	311UNTS199	104504
Guatemala	USA (United States)	23 Mar 55	252UNTS143	103563
Ecuador	USA (United States)	29 Mar 55	261UNTS343	103732
Italy	USA (United States)	30 Mar 55	257UNTS199	103655
Italy	USA (United States)	30 Mar 55	257UNTS169	103654
Chile	USA (United States)	31 Mar 55	262UNTS19	103736
Haiti	USA (United States)	01 Apr 55	261UNTS361	103734
Germany, West	USA (United States)	04 Apr 55	279UNTS73	104034
Multilateral		04 Apr 55	208UNTS239	102816
Belgium	Luxembourg	04 Apr 55	211UNTS57	102847
Norway	USA (United States)	06 Apr 55	269UNTS65	103874
Dominican Republic	USA (United States)	22 Apr 55	239UNTS325	103389
Argentina	USA (United States)	25 Apr 55	251UNTS283	103546
Haiti	USA (United States)	27 Apr 55	240UNTS17	103391
Israel	USA (United States)	29 Apr 55	261UNTS331	103731
Brazil	Sweden	29 Apr 55	228UNTS115	103145
Austria	Romania	11 May 55	342UNTS119	104904
USA (United States)	Yugoslavia	12 May 55	251UNTS343	103551
Austria	UK Great Britain	15 May 55	344UNTS9	104940
Cambodia	USA (United States)	16 May 55	263UNTS273	103777
Multilateral		25 May 55	264UNTS117	103791
Italy	Sweden	25 May 55	291UNTS235	104259
Pakistan	USA (United States)	26 May 55	257UNTS93	103652
Hungary	USSR (Soviet Union)	27 May 55	407UNTS156	105864
Libya	USA (United States)	30 May 55	270UNTS43	103890
Japan	USA (United States)	03 Jun 55	270UNTS51	103891
Honduras	USA (United States)	10 Jun 55	258UNTS51	103669
Germany, West	New Zealand	10 Jun 55	380UNTS307	105462
UK Great Britain	USA (United States)	15 Jun 55	214UNTS301	102905
Guatemala	USA (United States)	18 Jun 55	262UNTS105	103740
Thailand	USA (United States)	21 Jun 55	262UNTS87	103738
Turkey	USA (United States)	29 Jun 55	269UNTS97	103878
Germany, West	USA (United States)	30 Jun 55	240UNTS47	103393
France	USA (United States)	01 Jul 55	270UNTS19	103888
Germany, West	USA (United States)	07 Jul 55	275UNTS3	103973
Libya	USA (United States)	21 Jul 55	264UNTS247	103796
Germany, West	UK Great Britain	22 Jul 55	269UNTS189	103881
South Africa	Sweden	28 Jul 55	230UNTS287	103191
Australia	Taiwan	29 Jul 55	213UNTS193	102887
Philippines	UK Great Britain	29 Aug 55	221UNTS241	103009
USSR (Soviet Union)	Yugoslavia	03 Sep 55	240UNTS267	103408
Germany, East	Hungary	10 Sep 55	407UNTS132	105863
ICJ Option Clause	South Africa	12 Sep 55	216UNTS115	102935
Multilateral		21 Sep 55	269UNTS241	103885
Ireland	Turkey	27 Sep 55	553UNTS193	108087
Canada	Denmark	30 Sep 55	258UNTS115	103675
Bulgaria	Yugoslavia	01 Oct 55	396UNTS223	105698
France	Germany, West	04 Oct 55	353UNTS203	105044
India	USA (United States)	04 Oct 55	268UNTS115	103853
UK Great Britain	Vietnam, South	14 Oct 55	231UNTS193	103220
Finland	USSR (Soviet Union)	19 Oct 55	353UNTS185	105043

Conformity with municipal law (Cont.)

PARTY ONE	PARTY TWO	DATE	CITATION	NUMBER
Multilateral		20 Oct 55	378UNTS159	105425
Denmark	Syria	20 Oct 55	250UNTS61	103518
Czechoslovakia	Germany, East	24 Oct 55	504UNTS173	107358
Philippines	USA (United States)	28 Oct 55	239UNTS165	103376
Paraguay	USA (United States)	28 Oct 55	273UNTS97	103946
Pakistan	Turkey	02 Nov 55	311UNTS217	104505
Austria	Sweden	03 Nov 55	262UNTS289	103757
Netherlands	USA (United States)	04 Nov 55	269UNTS3	103867
Burma	China People's Rep	08 Nov 55	306UNTS11	104430
Israel	USA (United States)	10 Nov 55	240UNTS3	103390
Italy	Syria	10 Nov 55	267UNTS157	103841
Japan	USA (United States)	14 Nov 55	240UNTS361	103413
Bulgaria	Yugoslavia	15 Nov 55	396UNTS191	105697
UK Great Britain	USA (United States)	15 Nov 55	231UNTS185	103219
Austria	Israel	17 Nov 55	232UNTS153	103235
Colombia	USA (United States)	18 Nov 55	239UNTS173	103377
India	Japan	26 Nov 55	311UNTS243	104506
United Arab Rep	USA (United States)	14 Dec 55	240UNTS37	103392
Pakistan	Syria	18 Dec 55	320UNTS269	104647
USSR (Soviet Union)	Yugoslavia	19 Dec 55	378UNTS127	105423
Austria	Italy	28 Dec 55	260UNTS345	103718
Germany, West	USA (United States)	04 Jan 56	268UNTS143	103856
Italy	Japan	11 Jan 56	267UNTS175	103842
Czechoslovakia	Poland	13 Jan 56	265UNTS157	103811
Romania	Yugoslavia	13 Jan 56	342UNTS265	104912
USA (United States)	Yugoslavia	19 Jan 56	240UNTS121	103400
Australia	Japan	19 Jan 56	311UNTS291	104507
Austria	Italy	23 Jan 56	393UNTS97	105653
Argentina	Switzerland	25 Jan 56	559UNTS121	108157
Romania	Yugoslavia	01 Feb 56	362UNTS203	105189
India	USA (United States)	03 Feb 56	272UNTS75	103932
Hungary	Romania	03 Feb 56	362UNTS233	105190
Austria	Poland	08 Feb 56	334UNTS221	104770
Japan	USA (United States)	10 Feb 56	275UNTS105	103979
Japan	USA (United States)	10 Feb 56	275UNTS157	103980
Bulgaria	Yugoslavia	10 Feb 56	349UNTS21	105007
Netherlands	Sudan	12 Feb 56	311UNTS319	104508
Norway	South Africa	17 Feb 56	230UNTS213	103186
Norway	Syria	25 Feb 56	463UNTS217	106706
Italy	USA (United States)	27 Feb 56	291UNTS287	104260
Iran	Pakistan	09 Mar 56	449UNTS183	106460
Turkey	UK Great Britain	12 Mar 56	313UNTS73	104530
Chile	USA (United States)	13 Mar 56	275UNTS49	103975
Colombia	USA (United States)	27 Mar 56	273UNTS235	103954
Denmark	USSR (Soviet Union)	31 Mar 56	259UNTS169	103689
Norway	USSR (Soviet Union)	31 Mar 56	259UNTS205	103690
Sweden	USSR (Soviet Union)	31 Mar 56	259UNTS239	103691
Taiwan	USA (United States)	03 Apr 56	268UNTS315	103864
Australia	Turkey	10 Apr 56	247UNTS139	103462
Belgium	Germany, West	14 Apr 56	344UNTS103	104945
New Zealand	Sweden	16 Apr 56	274UNTS259	103971
Italy	USA (United States)	27 Apr 56	273UNTS149	103949
Ceylon (Sri Lanka)	USA (United States)	28 Apr 56	274UNTS35	103956
Germany, West	Switzerland	02 May 56	559UNTS157	108158
Peru	USA (United States)	03 May 56	272UNTS59	103931
Peru	USA (United States)	07 May 56	268UNTS285	103862
Portugal	Venezuela	16 May 56	463UNTS239	106707
Japan	Netherlands	16 May 56	305UNTS97	104417
Turkey	USA (United States)	18 May 56	283UNTS167	104115
Multilateral		18 May 56	339UNTS3	104844
Costa Rica	USA (United States)	18 May 56	404UNTS237	105814
Multilateral		19 May 56	399UNTS189	105742
Fed Rhod/Nyasaland	South Africa	22 May 56	254UNTS227	103595
Japan	Switzerland	24 May 56	312UNTS3	104509
Greece	Italy	26 May 56	496UNTS301	107258

Conformity with municipal law (Cont.)

PARTY ONE	PARTY TWO	DATE	CITATION	NUMBER
Netherlands	Yugoslavia	01 Jun 56	276UNTS319	103994
Canada	Germany, West	04 Jun 56	316UNTS231	104589
Italy	Switzerland	04 Jun 56	378UNTS311	105429
Greece	Ireland	05 Jun 56	553UNTS93	108072
Multilateral		07 Jun 56	381UNTS145	105470
Poland	Sweden	08 Jun 56	334UNTS257	104771
Sweden	UK Great Britain	09 Jun 56	309UNTS301	104479
India	Thailand	12 Jun 56	255UNTS341	103617
Germany, West	Ireland	12 Jun 56	353UNTS121	105040
Switzerland	UK Great Britain	12 Jun 56	269UNTS133	103879
New Zealand	USA (United States)	13 Jun 56	253UNTS155	103582
Austria	Canada	19 Jun 56	305UNTS51	104412
Canada	UK Great Britain	21 Jun 56	381UNTS111	105467
Honduras	USA (United States)	25 Jun 56	279UNTS113	104036
Indonesia	Philippines	04 Jul 56	401UNTS59	105763
Multilateral		05 Jul 56	258UNTS371	103679
Poland	Yugoslavia	06 Jul 56	281UNTS143	104076
Multilateral		09 Jul 56	314UNTS3	104539
France	UK Great Britain	10 Jul 56	326UNTS23	104708
Belgium	Japan	11 Jul 56	248UNTS129	103492
Austria	UK Great Britain	20 Jul 56	269UNTS147	103880
Belgium	Germany, West	26 Jul 56	249UNTS187	103508
Canada	Turkey	21 Aug 56	305UNTS89	104416
India	USA (United States)	29 Aug 56	278UNTS25	104019
Israel	South Africa	01 Sep 56	251UNTS161	103539
Greece	United Arab Rep	04 Sep 56	299UNTS253	104317
Italy	Spain	05 Sep 56	302UNTS195	104359
Multilateral		07 Sep 56	266UNTS3	103822
Ceylon (Sri Lanka)	India	10 Sep 56	315UNTS59	104560
Multilateral		11 Sep 56	266UNTS221	103832
Denmark	Finland	15 Sep 56	254UNTS3	103589
Denmark	Sweden	15 Sep 56	263UNTS3	103764
Belgium	Germany, West	24 Sep 56	263UNTS31	103766
Jordan	USA (United States)	24 Sep 56	278UNTS51	104020
India	USA (United States)	27 Sep 56	281UNTS289	104085
Canada	South Africa	28 Sep 56	299UNTS17	104304
Germany, West	Netherlands	28 Sep 56	327UNTS185	104722
Canada	South Africa	28 Sep 56	299UNTS3	104303
ICJ Option Clause	Israel	03 Oct 56	252UNTS301	103571
Canada	France	04 Oct 56	305UNTS65	104414
Belgium	Chile	09 Oct 56	257UNTS227	103658
Switzerland	Thailand	13 Oct 56	312UNTS43	104510
Belgium	Poland	17 Oct 56	356UNTS279	105100
Philippines	USA (United States)	18 Oct 56	280UNTS55	104050
Belgium	Pakistan	19 Oct 56	257UNTS221	103657
Norway	USSR (Soviet Union)	19 Oct 56	257UNTS3	103644
Canada	UK Great Britain	20 Oct 56	381UNTS99	105466
Colombia	USA (United States)	24 Oct 56	476UNTS77	106905
Austria	USA (United States)	25 Oct 56	299UNTS123	104310
Belgium	Turkey	25 Oct 56	380UNTS3	105447
Multilateral		26 Oct 56	276UNTS3	103988
Austria	UK Great Britain	27 Oct 56	264UNTS67	103789
Romania	Yugoslavia	27 Oct 56	389UNTS33	105590
Romania	Yugoslavia	27 Oct 56	389UNTS55	105592
India	Japan	29 Oct 56	318UNTS289	104622
Ecuador	USA (United States)	31 Oct 56	283UNTS151	104114
Argentina	USA (United States)	05 Nov 56	277UNTS143	104004
Multilateral		08 Nov 56	470UNTS171	106809
Austria	USA (United States)	21 Nov 56	290UNTS181	104237
Peru	Switzerland	23 Nov 56	411UNTS97	105916
Albania	Yugoslavia	23 Nov 56	386UNTS73	105539
Belgium	Spain	28 Nov 56	308UNTS239	104464
Belgium	Romania	04 Dec 56	317UNTS161	104602
Finland	USSR (Soviet Union)	07 Dec 56	258UNTS89	103673
Japan	Sweden	12 Dec 56	318UNTS309	104623

Conformity with municipal law (Cont.)

PARTY ONE	PARTY TWO	DATE	CITATION	NUMBER
France	USA (United States)	14 Dec 56	266UNTS117	103826
Indonesia	Yugoslavia	14 Dec 56	378UNTS117	105422
Poland	USSR (Soviet Union)	17 Dec 56	266UNTS179	103830
Japan	Luxembourg	18 Dec 56	318UNTS227	104616
Bulgaria	Yugoslavia	24 Dec 56	397UNTS3	105699
Colombia	USA (United States)	09 Jan 57	462UNTS151	106676
Denmark	Switzerland	14 Jan 57	286UNTS27	104160
Turkey	USA (United States)	15 Jan 57	280UNTS79	104053
Iran	USA (United States)	16 Jan 57	308UNTS147	104460
Iceland	Thailand	22 Jan 57	312UNTS63	104511
Italy	Netherlands	24 Jan 57	485UNTS67	107047
Germany, West	Norway	29 Jan 57	353UNTS39	105037
Italy	UK Great Britain	29 Jan 57	326UNTS119	104710
Denmark	Germany, West	29 Jan 57	302UNTS75	104354
Germany, West	Sweden	29 Jan 57	393UNTS113	105654
Korea, South	USA (United States)	30 Jan 57	278UNTS85	104024
Germany, East	Poland	01 Feb 57	319UNTS115	104632
Norway	USA (United States)	05 Feb 57	279UNTS169	104038
Belgium	Philippines	05 Feb 57	269UNTS49	103872
Taiwan	Turkey	12 Feb 57	282UNTS125	104097
France	Netherlands	15 Feb 57	286UNTS243	104170
Netherlands	USA (United States)	15 Feb 57	287UNTS239	104190
Belgium	France	15 Feb 57	267UNTS3	103834
Denmark	Norway	22 Feb 57	286UNTS127	104164
Iceland	USA (United States)	23 Feb 57	283UNTS73	104107
Canada	USA (United States)	26 Feb 57	279UNTS179	104039
Belgium	Brazil	27 Feb 57	265UNTS189	103812
France	Italy	28 Feb 57	291UNTS191	104253
Iran	USA (United States)	05 Mar 57	342UNTS29	104898
Belgium	Czechoslovakia	12 Mar 57	312UNTS75	104512
Germany, East	USSR (Soviet Union)	12 Mar 57	285UNTS105	104150
France	USA (United States)	12 Mar 57	279UNTS275	104045
Netherlands	Yugoslavia	13 Mar 57	327UNTS227	104723
Liberia	USA (United States)	16 Mar 57	290UNTS59	104228
Dominican Republic	Japan	20 Mar 57	318UNTS245	104619
Japan	Switzerland	25 Mar 57	318UNTS239	104618
Multilateral		25 Mar 57	294UNTS2	104300
Tunisia	USA (United States)	26 Mar 57	283UNTS117	104111
India	Poland	27 Mar 57	319UNTS263	104635
Morocco	USA (United States)	02 Apr 57	288UNTS157	104203
Saudi Arabia	USA (United States)	02 Apr 57	283UNTS97	104109
Netherlands	USA (United States)	03 Apr 57	410UNTS193	105904
Paraguay	USA (United States)	04 Apr 57	283UNTS193	104117
Paraguay	USA (United States)	04 Apr 57	284UNTS161	104135
Libya	USA (United States)	04 Apr 57	283UNTS181	104116
ICJ Option Clause	Sweden	06 Apr 57	264UNTS221	103794
China People's Rep	Sweden	08 Apr 57	428UNTS267	106179
Canada	USA (United States)	09 Apr 57	283UNTS217	104119
Germany, West	Yugoslavia	10 Apr 57	463UNTS269	106708
Denmark	Pakistan	10 Apr 57	302UNTS53	104353
Romania	Sweden	15 Apr 57	342UNTS325	104915
Romania	USSR (Soviet Union)	15 Apr 57	274UNTS143	103964
Bulgaria	Sweden	17 Apr 57	464UNTS3	106709
Bulgaria	Yugoslavia	19 Apr 57	349UNTS3	105006
Korea, South	USA (United States)	24 Apr 57	288UNTS219	104207
Ethiopia	USA (United States)	25 Apr 57	283UNTS205	104118
Jordan	USA (United States)	29 Apr 57	290UNTS111	104230
Israel	UK Great Britain	29 Apr 57	280UNTS227	104062
Multilateral		01 May 57	284UNTS201	104138
Belgium	Peru	03 May 57	274UNTS251	103970
Austria	USA (United States)	10 May 57	283UNTS33	104104
Belgium	Bulgaria	14 May 57	317UNTS81	104596
Ceylon (Sri Lanka)	Sweden	18 May 57	315UNTS85	104561
France	Netherlands	21 May 57	299UNTS43	104305
Czechoslovakia	Yugoslavia	22 May 57	391UNTS57	105617

PARTY ONE	PARTY TWO	DATE	CITATION	NUMBER
Conformity with municipal law (Cont.)				
Australia	Germany, West	22 May 57	357UNTS45	105105
Iraq	USA (United States)	22 May 57	284UNTS13	104125
Argentina	Israel	23 May 57	280UNTS199	104059
Belgium	Colombia	24 May 57	274UNTS245	103969
Hungary	Netherlands	28 May 57	334UNTS291	104773
Italy	Monaco	01 Jun 57	291UNTS197	104254
Belgium	Hungary	01 Jun 57	291UNTS17	104242
Austria	South Africa	11 Jun 57	272UNTS229	103941
Afghanistan	Pakistan	13 Jun 57	327UNTS51	104717
Austria	USSR (Soviet Union)	14 Jun 57	285UNTS169	104152
Iraq	USA (United States)	16 Jun 57	284UNTS39	104127
Germany, West	USA (United States)	28 Jun 57	288UNTS339	104213
Tunisia	USA (United States)	28 Jun 57	289UNTS301	104226
Jordan	USA (United States)	29 Jun 57	288UNTS263	104208
Czechoslovakia	United Arab Rep	30 Jun 57	411UNTS126	105917
Libya	USA (United States)	30 Jun 57	284UNTS177	104136
Germany, West	USA (United States)	03 Jul 57	288UNTS305	104212
Italy	United Arab Rep	06 Jul 57	302UNTS147	104357
South Africa	USA (United States)	08 Jul 57	290UNTS147	104234
Australia	FAO (Food Agri)	08 Jul 57	277UNTS315	104015
Australia	USA (United States)	12 Jul 57	290UNTS139	104233
Peru	USA (United States)	19 Jul 57	289UNTS271	104223
Norway	UK Great Britain	25 Jul 57	313UNTS3	104528
Greece	Italy	02 Aug 57	533UNTS217	107744
Hungary	Sweden	02 Aug 57	334UNTS307	104774
Austria	USA (United States)	09 Aug 57	288UNTS299	104211
Spain	USA (United States)	16 Aug 57	307UNTS169	104449
Austria	Pakistan	16 Aug 57	306UNTS3	104429
Netherlands	Romania	27 Aug 57	342UNTS309	104914
Albania	Yugoslavia	29 Aug 57	391UNTS127	105621
Czechoslovakia	USSR (Soviet Union)	31 Aug 57	308UNTS3	104456
Italy	Switzerland	19 Sep 57	363UNTS69	105200
India	USA (United States)	19 Sep 57	290UNTS175	104236
Japan	Sweden	20 Sep 57	325UNTS29	104693
Spain	USA (United States)	23 Sep 57	290UNTS261	104238
Multilateral		30 Sep 57	619UNTS77	108940
Australia	Canada	01 Oct 57	392UNTS41	105638
Italy	Pakistan	05 Oct 57	353UNTS91	105039
Taiwan	USA (United States)	08 Oct 57	304UNTS241	104400
Fed of Malaya	UK Great Britain	18 Oct 57	335UNTS3	104775
Netherlands	UK Great Britain	22 Oct 57	313UNTS309	104538
Netherlands	Sweden	23 Oct 57	306UNTS75	104433
France	Morocco	25 Oct 57	559UNTS95	108156
Poland	USSR (Soviet Union)	26 Oct 57	432UNTS221	106223
Germany, East	Hungary	30 Oct 57	408UNTS4	105867
Japan	Turkey	05 Nov 57	318UNTS411	104628
Brazil	USA (United States)	05 Nov 57	303UNTS3	104368
Belgium	France	12 Nov 57	328UNTS167	104734
Italy	Spain	25 Nov 57	378UNTS289	105428
Germany, East	USSR (Soviet Union)	28 Nov 57	305UNTS113	104419
Belgium	USA (United States)	03 Dec 57	303UNTS45	104370
Italy	Monaco	06 Dec 57	363UNTS45	105198
Italy	Yugoslavia	12 Dec 57	386UNTS293	105549
Bulgaria	USSR (Soviet Union)	12 Dec 57	317UNTS217	104606
Multilateral		13 Dec 57	359UNTS273	105146
Korea, North	USSR (Soviet Union)	16 Dec 57	301UNTS301	104349
Finland	Italy	17 Dec 57	291UNTS133	104248
UK Great Britain	USSR (Soviet Union)	19 Dec 57	351UNTS235	105026
China People's Rep	USSR (Soviet Union)	21 Dec 57	305UNTS213	104420
Poland	USSR (Soviet Union)	28 Dec 57	320UNTS3	104638
Australia	Ireland	30 Dec 57	497UNTS29	107260
Belgium	Denmark	31 Dec 57	305UNTS247	104422
Japan	USA (United States)	11 Jan 58	304UNTS35	104390
Canada	Pakistan	15 Jan 58	392UNTS35	105637
Indonesia	Japan	20 Jan 58	325UNTS13	104691

PARTY ONE	PARTY TWO	DATE	CITATION	NUMBER
Conformity with municipal law (Cont.)				
Belgium	Morocco	20 Jan 58	288UNTS3	104192
Canada	Portugal	24 Jan 58	392UNTS15	105634
Australia	USA (United States)	24 Jan 58	307UNTS105	104446
Japan	USA (United States)	25 Jan 58	304UNTS81	104392
Italy	Romania	28 Jan 58	302UNTS231	104362
Iran	Italy	29 Jan 58	302UNTS181	104358
Czechoslovakia	Poland	31 Jan 58	431UNTS99	106214
India	Japan	04 Feb 58	324UNTS215	104687
Bulgaria	Netherlands	07 Feb 58	335UNTS45	104777
Afghanistan	Turkey	08 Feb 58	464UNTS39	106711
Ceylon (Sri Lanka)	USSR (Soviet Union)	08 Feb 58	348UNTS159	104999
Albania	USSR (Soviet Union)	15 Feb 58	313UNTS261	104536
Austria	Sweden	19 Feb 58	427UNTS211	106155
UK Great Britain	USA (United States)	22 Feb 58	307UNTS207	104451
Australia	USA (United States)	25 Feb 58	317UNTS153	104601
Norway	Pakistan	05 Mar 58	334UNTS199	104769
Pakistan	Sweden	06 Mar 58	393UNTS181	105656
Belgium	Mexico	18 Mar 58	301UNTS291	104348
Austria	Japan	20 Mar 58	324UNTS205	104686
Belgium	Ecuador	20 Mar 58	304UNTS207	104397
Germany, West	Portugal	21 Mar 58	464UNTS71	106712
Bulgaria	Yugoslavia	21 Mar 58	386UNTS119	105541
Bulgaria	Yugoslavia	21 Mar 58	349UNTS61	105009
Denmark	South Africa	28 Mar 58	300UNTS107	104334
South Africa	Sweden	28 Mar 58	300UNTS95	104333
Norway	South Africa	28 Mar 58	300UNTS83	104332
Czechoslovakia	Poland	29 Mar 58	340UNTS199	104865
Sudan	USA (United States)	31 Mar 58	308UNTS105	104458
Morocco	Portugal	03 Apr 58	393UNTS203	105657
Germany, West	Netherlands	09 Apr 58	335UNTS237	104791
Belgium	Iran	14 Apr 58	381UNTS309	105473
Sweden	Yugoslavia	18 Apr 58	393UNTS225	105658
Germany, West	UK Great Britain	18 Apr 58	343UNTS241	104928
Bolivia	USA (United States)	22 Apr 58	317UNTS209	104605
Multilateral		29 Apr 58	450UNTS11	106465
Israel	New Zealand	29 Apr 58	314UNTS93	104544
Belgium	Japan	30 Apr 58	303UNTS109	104373
Saudi Arabia	USA (United States)	01 May 58	315UNTS221	104571
Austria	Netherlands	03 May 58	342UNTS3	104895
Italy	USA (United States)	08 May 58	316UNTS177	104584
Belgium	Sweden	08 May 58	312UNTS145	104516
Austria	New Zealand	14 May 58	317UNTS117	104598
Italy	Switzerland	23 May 58	363UNTS81	105201
UK Great Britain	Yugoslavia	24 May 58	326UNTS69	104709
Bulgaria	Denmark	28 May 58	312UNTS235	104521
Euratom	USA (United States)	29 May 58	335UNTS161	104783
India	USSR (Soviet Union)	02 Jun 58	393UNTS3	105650
Belgium	USSR (Soviet Union)	05 Jun 58	345UNTS145	104965
New Zealand	Turkey	05 Jun 58	317UNTS123	104599
Pakistan	Portugal	07 Jun 58	320UNTS225	104645
Denmark	Luxembourg	10 Jun 58	356UNTS193	105096
Netherlands	USSR (Soviet Union)	17 Jun 58	335UNTS77	104779
Japan	USA (United States)	19 Jun 58	325UNTS143	104699
Austria	Belgium	20 Jun 58	312UNTS95	104513
Burma	USA (United States)	24 Jun 58	335UNTS193	104786
Denmark	Romania	25 Jun 58	345UNTS231	104970
Czechoslovakia	Germany, East	26 Jun 58	504UNTS221	107359
Afghanistan	USA (United States)	26 Jun 58	321UNTS67	104654
Ecuador	USA (United States)	27 Jun 58	317UNTS51	104593
Albania	USSR (Soviet Union)	30 Jun 58	328UNTS3	104729
Philippines	USA (United States)	30 Jun 58	321UNTS51	104653
Belgium	Pakistan	04 Jul 58	387UNTS305	105569
Ethiopia	UK Great Britain	07 Jul 58	331UNTS3	104749
Fed of Malaya	USA (United States)	09 Jul 58	336UNTS79	104799
Austria	Romania	10 Jul 58	353UNTS155	105041

Conformity with municipal law (Cont.)

PARTY ONE	PARTY TWO	DATE	CITATION	NUMBER
Germany, East	Romania	15 Jul 58	395UNTS3	105681
Hungary	USSR (Soviet Union)	15 Jul 58	322UNTS3	104656
Denmark	Hungary	17 Jul 58	344UNTS281	104954
Netherlands	Yugoslavia	22 Jul 58	386UNTS263	105546
India	Sweden	30 Jul 58	369UNTS211	105259
Indonesia	USA (United States)	13 Aug 58	335UNTS187	104785
Romania	United Arab Rep	14 Aug 58	405UNTS189	105834
Finland	USA (United States)	15 Aug 58	314UNTS43	104540
Pakistan	Sweden	25 Aug 58	369UNTS183	105258
Mongolia	USSR (Soviet Union)	25 Aug 58	322UNTS105	104657
Austria	Bulgaria	12 Sep 58	353UNTS3	105036
Morocco	UK Great Britain	01 Oct 58	331UNTS119	104751
Hungary	Romania	07 Oct 58	416UNTS199	106004
USA (United States)	Venezuela	08 Oct 58	371UNTS69	105271
Iraq	USSR (Soviet Union)	11 Oct 58	328UNTS95	104730
Spain	USA (United States)	16 Oct 58	336UNTS153	104804
Czechoslovakia	Romania	25 Oct 58	417UNTS37	106006
France	Italy	30 Oct 58	363UNTS3	105196
United Arab Rep	USA (United States)	31 Oct 58	355UNTS355	105086
Multilateral		05 Nov 58	428UNTS73	106169
Euratom	USA (United States)	08 Nov 58	338UNTS135	104835
El Salvador	Israel	14 Nov 58	345UNTS67	104959
Germany, West	Norway	18 Nov 58	357UNTS205	105119
Liberia	Netherlands	28 Nov 58	393UNTS55	105651
Denmark	United Arab Rep	01 Dec 58	337UNTS69	104817
Bulgaria	Romania	03 Dec 58	417UNTS133	106007
Canada	Finland	09 Dec 58	323UNTS331	104674
Israel	Yugoslavia	11 Dec 58	386UNTS283	105548
Germany, West	USA (United States)	11 Dec 58	337UNTS31	104813
India	USA (United States)	17 Dec 58	358UNTS77	105125
Finland	Japan	22 Dec 58	341UNTS41	104876
Belgium	Turkey	29 Dec 58	357UNTS195	105118
Finland	Switzerland	07 Jan 59	353UNTS173	105042
Greece	USA (United States)	15 Jan 59	357UNTS281	105120
Albania	Czechoslovakia	16 Jan 59	363UNTS195	105208
Malaysia	Netherlands	20 Jan 59	493UNTS147	107212
Czechoslovakia	Hungary	30 Jan 59	351UNTS3	105016
UK Great Britain	Yugoslavia	03 Feb 59	359UNTS339	105151
Euratom	UK Great Britain	04 Feb 59	331UNTS125	104752
Burma	UK Great Britain	06 Feb 59	343UNTS223	104927
Japan	Pakistan	17 Feb 59	341UNTS127	104880
Japan	Norway	21 Feb 59	356UNTS231	105098
Finland	USSR (Soviet Union)	21 Feb 59	338UNTS3	104830
Canada	USA (United States)	27 Feb 59	341UNTS3	104873
Japan	Philippines	02 Mar 59	341UNTS49	104877
Greece	Pakistan	05 Mar 59	338UNTS97	104833
Hungary	Poland	06 Mar 59	432UNTS3	106216
Denmark	Japan	10 Mar 59	341UNTS55	104878
Sweden	Tunisia	19 Mar 59	497UNTS43	107261
Netherlands	Tunisia	19 Mar 59	497UNTS61	107262
Norway	Tunisia	28 Mar 59	497UNTS77	107263
Canada	Finland	28 Mar 59	355UNTS3	105072
Denmark	Tunisia	14 Apr 59	340UNTS273	104870
USA (United States)	Vietnam, South	22 Apr 59	347UNTS113	104993
Italy	United Arab Rep	29 Apr 59	363UNTS91	105202
Austria	USA (United States)	30 Apr 59	343UNTS41	104920
Ceylon (Sri Lanka)	Yugoslavia	05 May 59	391UNTS101	105618
Iraq	USSR (Soviet Union)	05 May 59	356UNTS179	105095
Austria	Netherlands	06 May 59	485UNTS153	107054
Iran	UK Great Britain	06 May 59	398UNTS51	105717
Greece	USA (United States)	06 May 59	357UNTS163	105115
France	USA (United States)	07 May 59	354UNTS83	105055
Argentina	Belgium	09 May 59	340UNTS53	104858
IAEA (Atom Energy)	USA (United States)	11 May 59	339UNTS359	104855
Japan	Vietnam, South	13 May 59	373UNTS173	105319

Conformity with municipal law (Cont.)

PARTY ONE	PARTY TWO	DATE	CITATION	NUMBER
Austria	Sweden	14 May 59	428UNTS3	106167
Panama	USA (United States)	20 May 59	346UNTS235	104983
Iran	Netherlands	22 May 59	474UNTS195	106882
Canada	USA (United States)	22 May 59	354UNTS63	105054
Fed of Malaya	USA (United States)	22 May 59	346UNTS263	104985
Netherlands	Spain	27 May 59	458UNTS165	106599
Belgium	Spain	27 May 59	340UNTS81	104860
Ireland	Netherlands	28 May 59	344UNTS95	104944
Ceylon (Sri Lanka)	Sweden	29 May 59	464UNTS109	106713
Ceylon (Sri Lanka)	Norway	29 May 59	411UNTS165	105919
Ceylon (Sri Lanka)	Denmark	29 May 59	348UNTS225	105002
Czechoslovakia	Switzerland	04 Jun 59	349UNTS121	105012
Italy	Norway	12 Jun 59	428UNTS363	106187
Israel	Mexico	15 Jun 59	377UNTS267	105406
Peru	USA (United States)	15 Jun 59	346UNTS279	104987
Germany, West	Netherlands	16 Jun 59	593UNTS3	108576
South Africa	UK Great Britain	18 Jun 59	380UNTS81	105451
South Africa	UK Great Britain	18 Jun 59	380UNTS103	105452
South Africa	UK Great Britain	18 Jun 59	380UNTS59	105450
Greece	Yugoslavia	18 Jun 59	368UNTS137	105238
Greece	Yugoslavia	18 Jun 59	368UNTS27	105234
Belgium	Japan	20 Jun 59	411UNTS3	105911
Iceland	USA (United States)	23 Jun 59	354UNTS3	105048
Brazil	Israel	24 Jun 59	515UNTS151	107458
Czechoslovakia	India	07 Jul 59	359UNTS259	105145
Australia	Monaco	07 Jul 59	354UNTS105	105057
Liberia	USA (United States)	08 Jul 59	357UNTS93	105108
Bulgaria	United Arab Rep	09 Jul 59	411UNTS187	105920
India	Italy	16 Jul 59	464UNTS129	106714
Pakistan	USA (United States)	18 Jul 59	355UNTS367	105087
India	Norway	20 Jul 59	356UNTS257	105099
Afghanistan	Germany, West	22 Jul 59	464UNTS177	106715
Austria	USA (United States)	22 Jul 59	368UNTS199	105242
Japan	Paraguay	22 Jul 59	373UNTS85	105316
Italy	USA (United States)	30 Jul 59	355UNTS393	105088
Germany, West	Iceland	12 Aug 59	411UNTS224	105921
USA (United States)	Yugoslavia	25 Aug 59	357UNTS87	105107
Canada	Germany, West	04 Sep 59	411UNTS260	105922
United Arab Rep	USA (United States)	28 Sep 59	358UNTS97	105128
Australia	Fed of Malaya	29 Sep 59	357UNTS29	105104
Austria	Netherlands	30 Sep 59	507UNTS111	107397
Canada	Greece	30 Sep 59	470UNTS87	106798
Korea, South	USA (United States)	01 Oct 59	358UNTS115	105129
Canada	Euratom	06 Oct 59	475UNTS187	106894
India	Italy	06 Oct 59	378UNTS267	105427
Canada	Venezuela	08 Oct 59	470UNTS93	106799
Austria	France	08 Oct 59	453UNTS95	106521
Nicaragua	Peru	14 Oct 59	392UNTS303	105649
South Africa	Switzerland	19 Oct 59	559UNTS257	108162
Guinea	USA (United States)	28 Oct 59	358UNTS169	105134
Mexico	UK Great Britain	13 Nov 59	360UNTS3	105152
Australia	USA (United States)	20 Nov 59	349UNTS293	105015
USA (United States)	USSR (Soviet Union)	21 Nov 59	361UNTS35	105172
France	USA (United States)	25 Nov 59	401UNTS75	105764
France	Israel	30 Nov 59	377UNTS237	105404
Italy	Netherlands	08 Dec 59	484UNTS309	107039
Liberia	Sweden	09 Dec 59	464UNTS219	106716
Czechoslovakia	Japan	15 Dec 59	383UNTS277	105505
Australia	Indonesia	17 Dec 59	354UNTS109	105058
Canada	Spain	18 Dec 59	470UNTS117	106802
Israel	Sweden	22 Dec 59	377UNTS277	105407
India	Japan	05 Jan 60	384UNTS3	105507
Guinea	Hungary	12 Jan 60	519UNTS131	107505
Czechoslovakia	UK Great Britain	15 Jan 60	374UNTS207	105336
Japan	USA (United States)	19 Jan 60	373UNTS207	105321

PARTY ONE	PARTY TWO	DATE	CITATION	NUMBER
Conformity with municipal law (Cont.)				
India	Japan	25 Jan 60	384UNTS31	105508
Multilateral		06 Feb 60	383UNTS3	105494
Italy	USSR (Soviet Union)	09 Feb 60	399UNTS75	105735
Australia	Canada	12 Feb 60	369UNTS89	105253
Germany, West	United Arab Rep	16 Feb 60	464UNTS233	106717
Denmark	USA (United States)	19 Feb 60	354UNTS151	105061
Austria	Norway	25 Feb 60	376UNTS155	105380
France	Thailand	26 Feb 60	392UNTS279	105648
Australia	Thailand	26 Feb 60	392UNTS255	105647
Indonesia	USSR (Soviet Union)	28 Feb 60	392UNTS191	105644
Turkey	UK Great Britain	01 Mar 60	374UNTS295	105343
Guinea	Netherlands	09 Mar 60	392UNTS243	105646
Finland	Iceland	10 Mar 60	497UNTS95	107264
Czechoslovakia	Iraq	11 Mar 60	464UNTS267	106718
Bulgaria	Romania	14 Mar 60	472UNTS279	106844
Austria	Guatemala	18 Mar 60	379UNTS89	105435
Bolivia	UK Great Britain	18 Mar 60	374UNTS199	105335
Portugal	USA (United States)	19 Mar 60	371UNTS131	105275
Austria	El Salvador	23 Mar 60	390UNTS3	105599
Japan	USA (United States)	23 Mar 60	372UNTS289	105305
Belgium	Switzerland	24 Mar 60	416UNTS81	105996
Luxembourg	UK Great Britain	01 Apr 60	374UNTS267	105340
Netherlands	UK Great Britain	01 Apr 60	374UNTS277	105341
Argentina	USA (United States)	01 Apr 60	371UNTS245	105281
Belgium	UK Great Britain	01 Apr 60	361UNTS135	105177
Luxembourg	Yugoslavia	09 Apr 60	464UNTS293	106719
Multilateral		11 Apr 60	374UNTS3	105323
Germany, West	UK Great Britain	20 Apr 60	449UNTS77	106453
Multilateral		22 Apr 60	418UNTS211	106023
Germany, West	Spain	28 Apr 60	465UNTS3	106720
Greece	Romania	02 May 60	485UNTS17	107043
New Zealand	Philippines	09 May 60	486UNTS65	107073
Germany, West	Ireland	11 May 60	553UNTS69	108070
Netherlands	Turkey	12 May 60	463UNTS207	106704
Australia	New Zealand	12 May 60	369UNTS119	105254
Spain	UK Great Britain	13 May 60	374UNTS287	105342
Morocco	United Arab Rep	19 May 60	563UNTS121	108208
Switzerland	Tunisia	21 May 60	497UNTS109	107265
Germany, East	USSR (Soviet Union)	24 May 60	392UNTS205	105645
Afghanistan	Czechoslovakia	28 May 60	497UNTS129	107266
UN Special Fund	Thailand	04 Jun 60	360UNTS97	105157
Cuba	Czechoslovakia	10 Jun 60	447UNTS75	106412
Luxembourg	Tunisia	13 Jun 60	497UNTS143	107267
Austria	USA (United States)	15 Jun 60	376UNTS267	105383
Iceland	Israel	15 Jun 60	377UNTS261	105405
Multilateral		22 Jun 60	546UNTS247	107951
Denmark	Peru	22 Jun 60	439UNTS113	106326
Korea, North	USSR (Soviet Union)	22 Jun 60	399UNTS3	105732
Austria	UK Great Britain	24 Jun 60	502UNTS79	107327
Poland	UK Great Britain	02 Jul 60	385UNTS87	105532
Italy	UK Great Britain	04 Jul 60	466UNTS195	106745
Spain	UK Great Britain	12 Jul 60	414UNTS123	105971
Belgium	Fed of Malaya	19 Jul 60	379UNTS391	105445
Germany, West	Pakistan	20 Jul 60	465UNTS41	106721
Spain	USA (United States)	21 Jul 60	393UNTS289	105663
Japan	Luxembourg	21 Jul 60	384UNTS55	105510
USA (United States)	Uruguay	22 Jul 60	388UNTS315	105587
Sweden	UK Great Britain	28 Jul 60	404UNTS113	105808
Sweden	UK Great Britain	28 Jul 60	404UNTS85	105806
Multilateral		28 Jul 60	394UNTS37	105667
Ghana	Netherlands	30 Jul 60	412UNTS51	105925
Japan	Pakistan	30 Jul 60	384UNTS63	105511
Ghana	USSR (Soviet Union)	04 Aug 60	421UNTS27	106050
Guatemala	USA (United States)	09 Aug 60	461UNTS15	106648
Mexico	USA (United States)	15 Aug 60	402UNTS177	105786

PARTY ONE	PARTY TWO	DATE	CITATION	NUMBER
Conformity with municipal law (Cont.)				
Germany, West	USA (United States)	16 Aug 60	418UNTS235	106024
Belgium	Burma	17 Aug 60	540UNTS185	107850
Korea, South	USA (United States)	17 Aug 60	400UNTS339	105757
Japan	Thailand	24 Aug 60	384UNTS73	105512
Ghana	United Arab Rep	29 Aug 60	412UNTS71	105926
WHO (World Health)	Saudi Arabia	06 Sep 60	395UNTS169	105684
Iran	Japan	12 Sep 60	384UNTS43	105509
Brazil	UN Special Fund	16 Sep 60	375UNTS3	105351
Czechoslovakia	India	19 Sep 60	465UNTS67	106722
Guinea	USA (United States)	30 Sep 60	394UNTS103	105671
Belgium	Tunisia	13 Oct 60	421UNTS71	106052
Belgium	Jordan	19 Oct 60	479UNTS277	106959
Hungary	UK Great Britain	25 Oct 60	419UNTS309	106034
Cuba	Romania	28 Oct 60	457UNTS9	106574
Burma	Switzerland	31 Oct 60	465UNTS97	106723
Norway	Peru	02 Nov 60	497UNTS207	107270
Australia	Italy	10 Nov 60	497UNTS247	107271
Brazil	Japan	14 Nov 60	518UNTS29	107491
Belgium	Paraguay	21 Nov 60	387UNTS237	105565
Israel	Mali	24 Nov 60	413UNTS104	105945
Japan	Pakistan	01 Dec 60	450UNTS337	106477
Japan	UK Great Britain	03 Dec 60	414UNTS61	105966
Netherlands	United Arab Rep	08 Dec 60	455UNTS276	106547
Romania	USA (United States)	09 Dec 60	401UNTS19	105759
Multilateral		13 Dec 60	523UNTS117	107557
Multilateral		14 Dec 60	429UNTS93	106193
Cambodia	Thailand	15 Dec 60	382UNTS321	105493
Canada	Pakistan	21 Dec 60	465UNTS115	106724
Togo	USA (United States)	22 Dec 60	401UNTS33	105760
Luxembourg	Thailand	29 Dec 60	465UNTS131	106725
Mali	USA (United States)	04 Jan 61	405UNTS165	105832
Jordan	Sweden	09 Jan 61	465UNTS155	106726
Brazil	USA (United States)	13 Jan 61	532UNTS177	107718
Ethiopia	USSR (Soviet Union)	13 Jan 61	421UNTS13	106049
Albania	Cuba	16 Jan 61	448UNTS67	106425
Norway	Poland	17 Jan 61	412UNTS130	105928
Germany, West	Japan	18 Jan 61	465UNTS173	106727
Australia	Japan	07 Feb 61	450UNTS343	106478
Iceland	UK Great Britain	09 Feb 61	398UNTS259	105728
France	UK Great Britain	14 Feb 61	398UNTS267	105729
Spain	UK Great Britain	15 Feb 61	404UNTS75	105805
Canada	USA (United States)	17 Feb 61	445UNTS143	106383
Finland	Italy	18 Feb 61	434UNTS199	106263
Germany, West	UK Great Britain	20 Feb 61	398UNTS249	105727
Belgium	UK Great Britain	21 Feb 61	398UNTS229	105724
Netherlands	UK Great Britain	21 Feb 61	398UNTS235	105725
Luxembourg	UK Great Britain	21 Feb 61	398UNTS243	105726
Australia	Finland	21 Feb 61	390UNTS61	105602
Belgium	Netherlands	24 Feb 61	474UNTS167	106881
Czechoslovakia	Hungary	24 Feb 61	422UNTS15	106066
Portugal	UK Great Britain	27 Feb 61	404UNTS33	105803
Switzerland	UK Great Britain	27 Feb 61	404UNTS167	105809
Cuba	Czechoslovakia	04 Mar 61	465UNTS209	106728
Cuba	Poland	06 Mar 61	484UNTS123	107020
Italy	UK Great Britain	06 Mar 61	404UNTS3	105799
Japan	Pakistan	07 Mar 61	450UNTS359	106479
San Marino	UK Great Britain	08 Mar 61	414UNTS46	105964
Canada	Iran	10 Mar 61	470UNTS139	106805
Afghanistan	Japan	15 Mar 61	450UNTS373	106480
Multilateral		16 Mar 61	638UNTS235	109139
Ceylon (Sri Lanka)	Japan	20 Mar 61	450UNTS385	106481
Cuba	Germany, East	29 Mar 61	448UNTS81	106426
Greece	UK Great Britain	06 Apr 61	403UNTS267	105797
Chile	Netherlands	07 Apr 61	453UNTS239	106527
Belgium	Chile	07 Apr 61	410UNTS255	105909

Conformity with municipal law (Cont.)

PARTY ONE	PARTY TWO	DATE	CITATION	NUMBER
Japan	UK Great Britain	11 Apr 61	420UNTS75	106042
Monaco	UK Great Britain	11 Apr 61	404UNTS11	105800
Honduras	USA (United States)	12 Apr 61	413UNTS182	105952
Multilateral		18 Apr 61	500UNTS95	107310
India	Norway	19 Apr 61	404UNTS307	105818
Germany, West	Netherlands	27 Apr 61	487UNTS77	107095
Turkey	USSR (Soviet Union)	27 Apr 61	420UNTS307	106047
Finland	UK Great Britain	05 May 61	414UNTS101	105969
Sierra Leone	USA (United States)	05 May 61	409UNTS194	105885
Sweden	UK Great Britain	05 May 61	404UNTS105	105807
Chile	UK Great Britain	09 May 61	414UNTS37	105963
Denmark	UK Great Britain	10 May 61	414UNTS17	105961
Norway	UK Great Britain	10 May 61	414UNTS9	105960
Senegal	USA (United States)	13 May 61	409UNTS232	105888
Ivory Coast	USA (United States)	17 May 61	409UNTS241	105889
Poland	Switzerland	18 May 61	559UNTS233	108161
Colombia	UK Great Britain	26 May 61	414UNTS85	105967
Niger	USA (United States)	26 May 61	410UNTS213	105905
Cameroon	USA (United States)	26 May 61	413UNTS195	105953
Dahomey	USA (United States)	27 May 61	445UNTS23	106373
Luxembourg	South Africa	30 May 61	412UNTS203	105933
Somalia	USSR (Soviet Union)	02 Jun 61	528UNTS147	107638
Czechoslovakia	Somalia	04 Jun 61	479UNTS291	106960
Czechoslovakia	Morocco	08 Jun 61	497UNTS275	107272
Finland	UK Great Britain	09 Jun 61	414UNTS53	105965
Nepal	USA (United States)	09 Jun 61	421UNTS223	106061
Cameroon	France	16 Jun 61	412UNTS148	105929
Finland	USA (United States)	16 Jun 61	413UNTS211	105955
Guinea	Sweden	17 Jun 61	465UNTS236	106729
Madagascar	USA (United States)	22 Jun 61	413UNTS219	105956
Finland	India	23 Jun 61	421UNTS49	106051
Mexico	USA (United States)	26 Jun 61	413UNTS229	105957
Turkey	UK Great Britain	28 Jun 61	414UNTS93	105968
Ghana	USA (United States)	19 Jul 61	416UNTS167	106002
Austria	Romania	21 Jul 61	421UNTS161	106057
Netherlands	Euratom	25 Jul 61	462UNTS263	106686
France	USA (United States)	27 Jul 61	433UNTS29	106229
Albania	Austria	27 Jul 61	407UNTS37	105858
Denmark	Iceland	01 Aug 61	425UNTS191	106124
Finland	Luxembourg	15 Aug 61	541UNTS45	107859
Pakistan	Philippines	15 Aug 61	522UNTS35	107534
Jordan	Norway	21 Aug 61	465UNTS275	106731
Jordan	Netherlands	24 Aug 61	466UNTS3	106733
Mexico	Netherlands	24 Aug 61	465UNTS291	106732
Italy	Norway	25 Aug 61	475UNTS269	106896
Tunisia	USSR (Soviet Union)	30 Aug 61	437UNTS243	106310
Liberia	Switzerland	31 Aug 61	559UNTS215	108160
Denmark	Pakistan	04 Sep 61	455UNTS305	106549
UK Great Britain	USA (United States)	08 Sep 61	418UNTS53	106016
Denmark	Germany, West	12 Sep 61	516UNTS283	107478
Korea, South	Thailand	15 Sep 61	413UNTS137	105948
Paraguay	USA (United States)	26 Sep 61	461UNTS91	106653
Australia	Spain	27 Sep 61	426UNTS159	106135
Pakistan	Philippines	29 Sep 61	422UNTS3	106065
Bolivia	Netherlands	30 Sep 61	487UNTS105	107097
Belgium	Bolivia	30 Sep 61	425UNTS53	106118
New Zealand	Spain	02 Oct 61	453UNTS11	106516
Multilateral		05 Oct 61	510UNTS175	107413
Greece	Sweden	06 Oct 61	481UNTS137	106981
Austria	Israel	10 Oct 61	448UNTS161	106430
Germany, West	Morocco	12 Oct 61	523UNTS289	107562
Switzerland	USA (United States)	13 Oct 61	459UNTS219	106625
Japan	Pakistan	17 Oct 61	466UNTS17	106734
Sweden	Thailand	20 Oct 61	428UNTS275	106180
Austria	Denmark	23 Oct 61	425UNTS115	106122

Conformity with municipal law (Cont.)

PARTY ONE	PARTY TWO	DATE	CITATION	NUMBER
Sweden	USA (United States)	24 Oct 61	494UNTS141	107231
Multilateral		26 Oct 61	496UNTS43	107247
Belgium	Italy	28 Oct 61	429UNTS199	106199
Ghana	USSR (Soviet Union)	04 Nov 61	437UNTS213	106308
Brazil	USA (United States)	11 Nov 61	433UNTS199	106243
Czechoslovakia	Mali	27 Nov 61	466UNTS41	106736
Guatemala	Israel	27 Nov 61	448UNTS191	106431
Congo (Zaire)	United Nations	27 Nov 61	414UNTS229	105975
Belgium	Luxembourg	29 Nov 61	486UNTS37	107071
Morocco	USA (United States)	30 Nov 61	451UNTS167	106492
Greece	New Zealand	06 Dec 61	486UNTS3	107067
Ethiopia	USA (United States)	06 Dec 61	433UNTS231	106246
Argentina	Thailand	10 Dec 61	422UNTS87	106070
Panama	USA (United States)	11 Dec 61	445UNTS161	106384
Czechoslovakia	Guinea	16 Dec 61	559UNTS49	108154
El Salvador	USA (United States)	19 Dec 61	445UNTS175	106385
Argentina	Japan	20 Dec 61	451UNTS91	106487
Austria	Japan	20 Dec 61	517UNTS155	107485
Iran	USA (United States)	21 Dec 61	433UNTS269	106249
Costa Rica	USA (United States)	22 Dec 61	460UNTS277	106646
Dominican Republic	USA (United States)	11 Jan 62	433UNTS133	106236
Thailand	USA (United States)	12 Jan 62	459UNTS95	106615
Cyprus	USA (United States)	18 Jan 62	435UNTS3	106266
Indonesia	Japan	23 Jan 62	559UNTS77	108155
Ghana	USA (United States)	24 Jan 62	435UNTS23	106268
Peru	USA (United States)	25 Jan 62	473UNTS57	106855
Luxembourg	South Africa	31 Jan 62	563UNTS153	108209
Italy	Japan	31 Jan 62	498UNTS23	107276
Austria	Finland	01 Feb 62	425UNTS33	106116
Hungary	Yugoslavia	09 Feb 62	577UNTS3	108370
Finland	Hungary	13 Feb 62	463UNTS61	106693
UK Great Britain	USA (United States)	22 Feb 62	435UNTS127	106275
Jordan	UK Great Britain	28 Feb 62	466UNTS249	106748
Germany, West	Thailand	05 Mar 62	563UNTS165	108210
Liberia	USA (United States)	08 Mar 62	445UNTS41	106375
Germany, West	Greece	08 Mar 62	533UNTS269	107747
Dominican Republic	USA (United States)	08 Mar 62	527UNTS29	107615
Australia	Germany, West	19 Mar 62	488UNTS203	107130
Brazil	Japan	28 Mar 62	451UNTS125	106489
Dahomey	UN Special Fund	28 Mar 62	424UNTS55	106099
France	Luxembourg	29 Mar 62	563UNTS227	108212
Belgium	France	30 Mar 62	502UNTS297	107335
Hungary	India	30 Mar 62	519UNTS119	107504
Nicaragua	USA (United States)	30 Mar 62	456UNTS241	106559
India	Japan	31 Mar 62	451UNTS143	106490
Ghana	USSR (Soviet Union)	06 Apr 62	498UNTS41	107277
El Salvador	USA (United States)	13 Apr 62	451UNTS307	106500
Norway	USSR (Soviet Union)	16 Apr 62	437UNTS175	106307
Ecuador	USA (United States)	17 Apr 62	442UNTS69	106339
India	Japan	23 Apr 62	451UNTS155	106491
Greece	USA (United States)	24 Apr 62	459UNTS3	106609
Bolivia	USA (United States)	26 Apr 62	461UNTS105	106654
Honduras	UK Great Britain	30 Apr 62	449UNTS159	106457
Dominican Republic	USA (United States)	02 May 62	442UNTS107	106342
Japan	United Arab Rep	10 May 62	498UNTS69	107278
Multilateral		14 May 62	544UNTS81	107911
Gabon	Israel	15 May 62	448UNTS211	106433
Belgium	USA (United States)	17 May 62	461UNTS3	106647
France	Romania	18 May 62	498UNTS115	107279
United Arab Rep	USA (United States)	21 May 62	458UNTS197	106601
Panama	USA (United States)	23 May 62	458UNTS225	106604
Ethiopia	USA (United States)	23 May 62	456UNTS293	106563
Denmark	USA (United States)	28 May 62	450UNTS215	106469
Senegal	USSR (Soviet Union)	14 Jun 62	437UNTS233	106309
France	Senegal	15 Jun 62	524UNTS3	107563

Conformity with municipal law (Cont.)

PARTY ONE	PARTY TWO	DATE	CITATION	NUMBER
Costa Rica	USA (United States)	18 Jun 62	461UNTS155	106659
Czechoslovakia	Senegal	20 Jun 62	498UNTS145	107280
Guinea	Norway	21 Jun 62	466UNTS81	106738
United Arab Rep	USSR (Soviet Union)	23 Jun 62	472UNTS19	106835
Israel	Liberia	25 Jun 62	448UNTS295	106442
Israel	Peru	25 Jun 62	515UNTS263	107464
Liberia	Norway	29 Jun 62	466UNTS95	106739
Morocco	Switzerland	05 Jul 62	498UNTS171	107281
Tunisia	UK Great Britain	14 Jul 62	466UNTS235	106746
Honduras	USA (United States)	20 Jul 62	460UNTS125	106635
Colombia	USA (United States)	23 Jul 62	458UNTS123	106595
Niger	USA (United States)	23 Jul 62	487UNTS325	107114
Ecuador	USA (United States)	03 Aug 62	460UNTS133	106636
Colombia	Netherlands	03 Aug 62	485UNTS225	107058
Syria	USSR (Soviet Union)	19 Aug 62	457UNTS285	106588
El Salvador	UK Great Britain	20 Aug 62	453UNTS309	106532
Cyprus	USA (United States)	23 Aug 62	461UNTS147	106658
Nepal	USA (United States)	24 Aug 62	460UNTS143	106637
Paraguay	USA (United States)	25 Aug 62	461UNTS207	106665
Austria	South Africa	31 Aug 62	443UNTS65	106359
Japan	UK Great Britain	04 Sep 62	475UNTS31	106888
Togo	USA (United States)	05 Sep 62	461UNTS47	106650
Multilateral		14 Sep 62	443UNTS73	106360
Ecuador	Germany, West	20 Sep 62	498UNTS199	107283
Austria	Czechoslovakia	22 Sep 62	495UNTS157	107244
Israel	UK Great Britain	26 Sep 62	474UNTS233	106885
Finland	USSR (Soviet Union)	27 Sep 62	479UNTS99	106949
Gabon	USA (United States)	04 Oct 62	459UNTS185	106620
Japan	Kuwait	06 Oct 62	498UNTS235	107284
Finland	France	12 Oct 62	498UNTS299	107285
Belgium	Rwanda	13 Oct 62	456UNTS431	106569
Czechoslovakia	Hungary	16 Oct 62	479UNTS301	106961
Austria	United Arab Rep	16 Oct 62	491UNTS63	107174
Canada	San Marino	16 Oct 62	529UNTS3	107650
Multilateral		16 Oct 62	470UNTS291	106814
Canada	Iceland	17 Oct 62	528UNTS281	107649
Hungary	Syria	18 Oct 62	491UNTS209	107178
Austria	Luxembourg	18 Oct 62	496UNTS97	107248
France	Ivory Coast	19 Oct 62	498UNTS317	107286
Czechoslovakia	Yugoslavia	22 Oct 62	480UNTS267	106974
Cameroon	Israel	24 Oct 62	449UNTS3	106446
Cameroon	Israel	24 Oct 62	449UNTS15	106447
Czechoslovakia	Norway	25 Oct 62	498UNTS335	107287
Multilateral		25 Oct 62	457UNTS137	106583
Multilateral		25 Oct 62	457UNTS129	106582
Czechoslovakia	Sweden	25 Oct 62	498UNTS343	107288
Tunisia	USA (United States)	29 Oct 62	462UNTS201	106679
Japan	UK Great Britain	02 Nov 62	466UNTS277	106749
Ethiopia	Greece	07 Nov 62	550UNTS179	108014
Poland	Syria	10 Nov 62	491UNTS228	107179
Czechoslovakia	Poland	16 Nov 62	526UNTS3	107597
Ivory Coast	Switzerland	17 Nov 62	499UNTS3	107289
Fed Rhod/Nyasaland	South Africa	19 Nov 62	458UNTS59	106592
Germany, West	USA (United States)	20 Nov 62	505UNTS263	107377
Ceylon (Sri Lanka)	USA (United States)	21 Nov 62	462UNTS237	106683
India	USA (United States)	21 Nov 62	462UNTS255	106685
Multilateral		29 Nov 62	457UNTS63	106577
Germany, West	USA (United States)	29 Nov 62	460UNTS169	106639
Multilateral		08 Dec 62	510UNTS235	107418
Austria	Yugoslavia	11 Dec 62	546UNTS3	107938
Ghana	Tunisia	11 Dec 62	563UNTS243	108213
Guinea	USA (United States)	14 Dec 62	462UNTS247	106684
Luxembourg	USA (United States)	18 Dec 62	532UNTS277	107723
Belgium	Tunisia	21 Dec 62	482UNTS3	106987
Colombia	Israel	21 Dec 62	484UNTS149	107023

Conformity with municipal law (Cont.)

PARTY ONE	PARTY TWO	DATE	CITATION	NUMBER
India	United Nations	27 Dec 62	450UNTS3	106464
Syria	United Arab Rep	27 Dec 62	491UNTS245	107180
Iceland	USA (United States)	27 Dec 62	469UNTS91	106785
Brazil	Taiwan	28 Dec 62	500UNTS61	107307
Guatemala	USA (United States)	29 Dec 62	474UNTS31	106869
Belgium	Ecuador	10 Jan 63	457UNTS153	106585
Trinidad/Tobago	USA (United States)	15 Jan 63	471UNTS141	106829
Senegal	USA (United States)	17 Jan 63	493UNTS97	107210
Japan	Philippines	19 Jan 63	517UNTS281	107489
Ecuador	Netherlands	21 Jan 63	514UNTS87	107443
Senegal	Switzerland	23 Jan 63	524UNTS23	107564
Iraq	USA (United States)	23 Jan 63	488UNTS163	107126
New Zealand	Western Samoa	24 Jan 63	499UNTS21	107290
Malaysia	USA (United States)	28 Jan 63	473UNTS15	106850
Japan	New Zealand	30 Jan 63	517UNTS183	107486
Guinea	Switzerland	01 Feb 63	499UNTS35	107291
Japan	USA (United States)	01 Feb 63	473UNTS49	106854
Mali	Senegal	07 Feb 63	524UNTS41	107565
Central Afri Rep	USA (United States)	10 Feb 63	473UNTS83	106857
Ceylon (Sri Lanka)	Denmark	16 Feb 63	486UNTS285	107083
Algeria	France	18 Feb 63	563UNTS263	108214
Japan	Thailand	01 Mar 63	475UNTS233	106895
Norway	USA (United States)	01 Mar 63	524UNTS185	107573
Austria	Czechoslovakia	08 Mar 63	495UNTS219	107245
Israel	USA (United States)	21 Mar 63	476UNTS131	106907
Philippines	USA (United States)	23 Mar 63	474UNTS80	106873
Australia	Portugal	29 Mar 63	468UNTS313	106778
Romania	USA (United States)	02 Apr 63	474UNTS95	106874
Austria	Bulgaria	05 Apr 63	480UNTS3	106963
Pakistan	United Nations	18 Apr 63	503UNTS25	107339
Belgium	USA (United States)	19 Apr 63	493UNTS83	107209
Multilateral		20 Apr 63	495UNTS3	107239
Poland	USSR (Soviet Union)	22 Apr 63	493UNTS229	107217
Japan	USA (United States)	26 Apr 63	477UNTS37	106914
Greece	Hungary	27 Apr 63	534UNTS3	107750
Algeria	Morocco	30 Apr 63	564UNTS3	108217
Philippines	USA (United States)	06 May 63	477UNTS67	106916
Portugal	South Africa	07 May 63	499UNTS49	107292
Australia	USA (United States)	09 May 63	475UNTS331	106897
New Zealand	UK Great Britain	15 May 63	486UNTS11	107068
Netherlands	Tunisia	23 May 63	523UNTS237	107558
Thailand	USA (United States)	24 May 63	477UNTS123	106918
Japan	Malaysia	04 Jun 63	517UNTS245	107488
Jamaica	USA (United States)	06 Jun 63	477UNTS29	106913
Finland	Poland	10 Jun 63	503UNTS179	107343
Korea, South	USA (United States)	18 Jun 63	487UNTS297	107112
Multilateral		19 Jun 63	482UNTS19	106988
India	USA (United States)	19 Jun 63	479UNTS175	106952
France	UK Great Britain	21 Jun 63	540UNTS311	107855
Austria	USA (United States)	25 Jun 63	479UNTS223	106956
Guinea	Ivory Coast	26 Jun 63	499UNTS71	107293
Bulgaria	USA (United States)	02 Jul 63	479UNTS245	106957
Hungary	Mongolia	10 Jul 63	519UNTS173	107508
Austria	Mongolia	15 Jul 63	496UNTS171	107251
Algeria	Mali	22 Jul 63	564UNTS29	108219
Cameroon	UK Great Britain	29 Jul 63	478UNTS148	106935
USA (United States)	Uruguay	31 Jul 63	488UNTS3	107115
Cameroon	Israel	09 Aug 63	499UNTS121	107295
Tanganyika	USSR (Soviet Union)	14 Aug 63	493UNTS195	107215
Paraguay	USA (United States)	20 Aug 63	531UNTS197	107704
Cameroon	UK Great Britain	20 Aug 63	539UNTS233	107834
Afghanistan	USA (United States)	20 Aug 63	488UNTS41	107118
France	Israel	20 Aug 63	515UNTS173	107460
Argentina	USA (United States)	21 Aug 63	488UNTS61	107119
France	Greece	21 Aug 63	533UNTS235	107746

PARTY ONE	PARTY TWO	DATE	CITATION	NUMBER
Conformity with municipal law (Cont.)				
Switzerland	UK Great Britain	27 Aug 63	486UNTS183	107079
Multilateral		02 Sep 63	548UNTS129	107974
Ecuador	USA (United States)	20 Sep 63	488UNTS147	107125
Australia	UK Great Britain	23 Sep 63	483UNTS39	107006
Austria	India	24 Sep 63	545UNTS199	107935
Pakistan	USSR (Soviet Union)	07 Oct 63	499UNTS161	107297
Malagasy	USA (United States)	07 Oct 63	494UNTS3	107221
Ivory Coast	Netherlands	09 Oct 63	499UNTS141	107296
Canada	France	11 Oct 63	529UNTS71	107657
Czechoslovakia	Hungary	22 Oct 63	514UNTS95	107444
Iran	USA (United States)	24 Oct 63	489UNTS303	107146
Jamaica	USA (United States)	24 Oct 63	489UNTS337	107148
France	UK Great Britain	05 Nov 63	539UNTS277	107838
Tanganyika	USSR (Soviet Union)	06 Nov 63	528UNTS157	107639
Belgium	Pakistan	14 Nov 63	535UNTS393	107792
Tunisia	USA (United States)	18 Nov 63	494UNTS193	107233
Netherlands	USA (United States)	26 Nov 63	388UNTS303	105586
Belgium	Poland	09 Dec 63	514UNTS195	107448
Greece	USA (United States)	13 Dec 63	494UNTS55	107226
Multilateral		14 Dec 63	507UNTS149	107399
Czechoslovakia	Romania	16 Dec 63	527UNTS285	107630
France	Israel	20 Dec 63	515UNTS165	107459
Czechoslovakia	Hungary	20 Dec 63	538UNTS127	107812
Greece	Poland	21 Dec 63	538UNTS155	107813
Romania	Yugoslavia	25 Dec 63	576UNTS95	108366
Canada	USA (United States)	27 Dec 63	494UNTS21	107223
Saudi Arabia	USA (United States)	06 Jan 64	531UNTS3	107689
Mali	Niger	15 Jan 64	499UNTS197	107299
Austria	Belgium	20 Jan 64	509UNTS275	107406
Canada	USA (United States)	22 Jan 64	530UNTS89	107674
Argentina	Paraguay	07 Feb 64	634UNTS127	109057
Paraguay	USA (United States)	10 Feb 64	511UNTS53	107426
Denmark	Yugoslavia	11 Feb 64	511UNTS241	107437
Netherlands	Tunisia	11 Feb 64	570UNTS173	108293
Iceland	USA (United States)	13 Feb 64	524UNTS235	107576
Belgium	France	10 Mar 64	557UNTS13	108127
Czechoslovakia	Yugoslavia	14 Mar 64	544UNTS147	107917
Spain	USA (United States)	18 Mar 64	535UNTS343	107789
Argentina	Yugoslavia	21 Mar 64	635UNTS153	109078
Cyprus	United Nations	31 Mar 64	492UNTS57	107187
Australia	Israel	14 Apr 64	496UNTS233	107255
United Arab Rep	USA (United States)	05 May 64	531UNTS229	107706
Liberia	USA (United States)	08 May 64	526UNTS239	107608
Austria	Turkey	15 May 64	515UNTS109	107457
Taiwan	Peru	08 Jun 64	548UNTS151	107976
Ceylon (Sri Lanka)	Norway	11 Jun 64	559UNTS23	108153
Taiwan	Ecuador	17 Jun 64	533UNTS141	107740
UK Great Britain	USA (United States)	19 Jun 64	530UNTS99	107675
New Zealand	USA (United States)	24 Jun 64	524UNTS101	107568
Denmark	USA (United States)	02 Jul 64	529UNTS277	107665
Sweden	USA (United States)	06 Jul 64	529UNTS287	107666
Ivory Coast	Mali	09 Jul 64	524UNTS121	107569
Belgium	Tunisia	15 Jul 64	560UNTS65	108169
Spain	USA (United States)	16 Jul 64	529UNTS187	107661
Mexico	USA (United States)	07 Aug 64	530UNTS123	107677
France	Eur Space Research	10 Aug 64	528UNTS135	107637
Netherlands	Turkey	19 Aug 64	521UNTS197	107523
Costa Rica	USA (United States)	24 Aug 64	531UNTS107	107696
Australia	USA (United States)	28 Aug 64	510UNTS201	107415
Ceylon (Sri Lanka)	USA (United States)	29 Aug 64	531UNTS93	107695
Argentina	Colombia	12 Sep 64	635UNTS149	109079
Multilateral		15 Sep 64	510UNTS147	107411
Taiwan	Mexico	25 Sep 64	547UNTS233	107960
Austria	Thailand	30 Sep 64	527UNTS239	107628
Czechoslovakia	Germany, East	06 Oct 64	545UNTS113	107927

PARTY ONE	PARTY TWO	DATE	CITATION	NUMBER
Conformity with municipal law (Cont.)				
Czechoslovakia	Yugoslavia	08 Oct 64	544UNTS129	107916
Sweden	UK Great Britain	14 Oct 64	543UNTS135	107898
Czechoslovakia	Hungary	17 Oct 64	545UNTS21	107924
Norway	United Arab Rep	20 Oct 64	543UNTS3	107895
Czechoslovakia	Mongolia	21 Oct 64	545UNTS91	107926
Taiwan	Ecuador	23 Oct 64	543UNTS241	107904
Germany, West	Thailand	28 Oct 64	521UNTS311	107528
Taiwan	Guatemala	08 Nov 64	543UNTS227	107903
USA (United States)	Yugoslavia	09 Nov 64	533UNTS39	107731
Austria	Hungary	11 Nov 64	576UNTS163	108368
Belgium	Mexico	19 Nov 64	546UNTS217	107949
Multilateral		19 Nov 64	523UNTS3	107553
Italy	USA (United States)	23 Nov 64	532UNTS133	107716
Germany, West	UK Great Britain	26 Nov 64	603UNTS183	108734
Multilateral		27 Nov 64	548UNTS47	107968
Japan	USA (United States)	04 Dec 64	532UNTS249	107721
Argentina	UK Great Britain	12 Jan 65	597UNTS177	108645
Finland	Israel	21 Jan 65	581UNTS275	108450
Multilateral		22 Jan 65	634UNTS239	109066
Peru	USA (United States)	28 Jan 65	587UNTS273	108513
Dominican Republic	USA (United States)	02 Feb 65	542UNTS117	107884
Belgium	Congo (Zaire)	06 Feb 65	540UNTS227	107852
Netherlands	Spain	10 Feb 65	545UNTS3	107922
Belgium	Hungary	11 Feb 65	544UNTS3	107908
Luxembourg	Portugal	12 Feb 65	571UNTS239	108305
France	UK Great Britain	25 Feb 65	543UNTS157	107899
Belgium	Luxembourg	11 Mar 65	540UNTS297	107854
Bolivia	USA (United States)	16 Mar 65	542UNTS209	107891
Denmark	Malaysia	26 Mar 65	540UNTS205	107851
Ecuador	USA (United States)	26 Mar 65	542UNTS237	107893
Finland	United Arab Rep	01 Apr 65	562UNTS3	108193
Jamaica	UK Great Britain	02 Apr 65	552UNTS219	108056
Austria	Hungary	09 Apr 65	638UNTS105	109132
Afghanistan	UK Great Britain	19 Apr 65	633UNTS45	109033
Bel-Lux Econ Union	Morocco	28 Apr 65	620UNTS171	108954
UK Great Britain	USA (United States)	10 May 65	545UNTS181	107934
Bulgaria	Czechoslovakia	22 May 65	545UNTS65	107925
Portugal	USA (United States)	26 May 65	546UNTS189	107945
China People's Rep	Romania	27 May 65	592UNTS3	108566
Denmark	Thailand	01 Jun 65	551UNTS157	108040
Australia	Netherlands	01 Jun 65	560UNTS85	108170
Saudi Arabia	USA (United States)	05 Jun 65	548UNTS285	107984
Pakistan	USSR (Soviet Union)	05 Jun 65	593UNTS115	108579
Greece	UK Great Britain	08 Jun 65	551UNTS205	108042
Canada	USA (United States)	08 Jun 65	546UNTS201	107947
Australia	Philippines	16 Jun 65	541UNTS31	107858
Belgium	USA (United States)	18 Jun 65	549UNTS95	107992
Argentina	United Arab Rep	21 Jun 65	634UNTS161	109058
Japan	Korea, South	22 Jun 65	584UNTS3	108474
Australia	USA (United States)	25 Jun 65	541UNTS155	107868
Guinea	USA (United States)	29 Jun 65	549UNTS139	107997
Malta	Yugoslavia	15 Jul 65	561UNTS223	108186
Hungary	Poland	18 Jul 65	577UNTS161	108376
Uganda	USSR (Soviet Union)	24 Jul 65	596UNTS199	108633
Luxembourg	USA (United States)	29 Jul 65	573UNTS197	108332
Peru	USA (United States)	11 Aug 65	564UNTS135	108225
Israel	Sierra Leone	22 Aug 65	550UNTS275	108022
France	UK Great Britain	21 Sep 65	561UNTS3	108177
Greece	Malta	01 Oct 65	550UNTS329	108027
Argentina	Spain	12 Oct 65	635UNTS221	109085
Philippines	USA (United States)	15 Nov 65	574UNTS205	108350
France	UK Great Britain	19 Nov 65	561UNTS19	108178
Israel	Paraguay	21 Nov 65	582UNTS65	108458
Hungary	Yugoslavia	23 Nov 65	577UNTS89	108374
Multilateral		03 Dec 65	572UNTS105	108309

PARTY ONE	PARTY TWO	DATE	CITATION	NUMBER
Conformity with municipal law (Cont.)				
Finland	Malta	08 Dec 65	561UNTS205	108183
Korea, South	Netherlands	08 Dec 65	571UNTS83	108301
Malta	Norway	29 Dec 65	561UNTS211	108184
Malta	Sweden	29 Dec 65	561UNTS217	108185
Denmark	Malta	30 Dec 65	561UNTS199	108182
Panama	UK Great Britain	07 Jan 66	565UNTS25	108233
Japan	USSR (Soviet Union)	21 Jan 66	633UNTS165	109038
Czechoslovakia	Poland	22 Jan 66	588UNTS175	108524
UK Great Britain	Yugoslavia	27 Jan 66	573UNTS243	108337
Belgium	Denmark	04 Feb 66	561UNTS233	108187
Austria	Spain	24 Mar 66	590UNTS203	108555
Paraguay	USA (United States)	11 Apr 66	578UNTS99	108389
Spain	USA (United States)	21 Apr 66	580UNTS231	108426
Multilateral		17 May 66	571UNTS89	108302
Austria	Ireland	24 May 66	636UNTS149	109102
Guyana	UK Great Britain	26 May 66	595UNTS255	108621
Malta	Turkey	06 Jun 66	579UNTS237	108411
Poland	Singapore	07 Jun 66	631UNTS189	108994
Australia	Poland	20 Jun 66	638UNTS201	109136
Denmark	Israel	27 Jun 66	581UNTS227	108448
Denmark	Jordan	28 Jun 66	574UNTS3	108338
Brazil	Denmark	08 Jul 66	581UNTS95	108435
Multilateral		12 Jul 66	578UNTS23	108384
Austria	France	15 Jul 66	604UNTS265	108755
USA (United States)	Zambia	11 Aug 66	616UNTS267	108901
Denmark	Malawi	01 Sep 66	586UNTS3	108493
Malta	Portugal	01 Sep 66	579UNTS231	108410
Netherlands	Yugoslavia	08 Sep 66	597UNTS147	108643
Paraguay	UK Great Britain	27 Oct 66	597UNTS229	108648
UK Great Britain	USA (United States)	27 Oct 66	597UNTS265	108650
Philippines	Sweden	11 Nov 66	587UNTS3	108505
Ghana	Romania	23 Nov 66	642UNTS63	109165
Kuwait	UK Great Britain	26 Nov 66	633UNTS58	109034
Guinea	Romania	01 Dec 66	642UNTS89	109167
Denmark	Singapore	20 Dec 66	593UNTS125	108580
Australia	Mexico	13 Jan 67	607UNTS77	108797
Czechoslovakia	USSR (Soviet Union)	03 Feb 67	617UNTS267	108917
Argentina	Uruguay	12 Feb 67	635UNTS125	109076
Argentina	UK Great Britain	17 Feb 67	617UNTS193	108913
Haiti	Israel	28 Mar 67	630UNTS293	108975
Austria	Bulgaria	21 Apr 67	603UNTS121	108729
Bulgaria	USSR (Soviet Union)	27 Apr 67	631UNTS3	108983
Israel	Switzerland	01 May 67	630UNTS313	108978
Liberia	IBRD (World Bank)	05 Jun 67	633UNTS13	109031
Dominican Republic	UK Great Britain	20 Jun 67	619UNTS3	108935
Denmark	Netherlands	20 Jun 67	619UNTS67	108939
UK Great Britain	Yugoslavia	30 Jun 67	642UNTS325	109182
Ecuador	Israel	09 Aug 67	630UNTS319	108979
Bulgaria	Romania	22 Aug 67	631UNTS49	108986
Bulgaria	Denmark	02 Sep 67	631UNTS71	108987
Finland	France	27 Oct 67	643UNTS75	109185
Denmark	Tanzania	01 Nov 67	619UNTS47	108938
Denmark	Iran	02 Nov 67	638UNTS217	109138
Austria	USA (United States)	21 Nov 67	634UNTS43	109049
Australia	Hungary	05 Dec 67	638UNTS209	109137
Multilateral		08 Mar 68	634UNTS199	109062
Information centers				
Multilateral		22 Jul 46	14UNTS185	100221
Multilateral		12 Aug 49	75UNTS287	100973
Multilateral		30 Jun 54	204UNTS99	102752
Bulgaria	USSR (Soviet Union)	11 Dec 59	368UNTS287	105246
Exchange of official publications				
Multilateral		27 Apr 32	39UNTS103	100614
Multilateral		20 Jun 38	40UNTS255	100638

PARTY ONE	PARTY TWO	DATE	CITATION	NUMBER
Exchange of official publications (Cont.)				
Luxembourg	UK Great Britain	29 May 39	99UNTS301	200284
Haiti	USA (United States)	05 Jun 41	101UNTS125	200289
Brazil	Paraguay	14 Jun 41	54UNTS249	200197
Mexico	USA (United States)	19 Nov 41	148UNTS367	200474
El Salvador	USA (United States)	27 Nov 41	120UNTS161	200389
Liberia	USA (United States)	15 Jan 42	117UNTS227	200372
Bolivia	USA (United States)	31 Jan 42	101UNTS137	200290
Canada	USA (United States)	04 Mar 42	124UNTS271	200426
Panama	USA (United States)	07 Mar 42	101UNTS157	200291
Iceland	USA (United States)	17 Aug 42	24UNTS163	200140
Brazil	Venezuela	22 Oct 42	65UNTS203	200212
Paraguay	USA (United States)	28 Nov 42	101UNTS173	200292
Dominican Republic	USA (United States)	10 Dec 42	24UNTS257	200151
Finland	Sweden	10 Mar 43	198UNTS333	200518
Iran	USA (United States)	21 Aug 43	101UNTS189	200293
Iraq	USA (United States)	16 Feb 44	109UNTS223	200362
Afghanistan	USA (United States)	29 Feb 44	106UNTS247	200344
Guatemala	USA (United States)	13 Apr 44	106UNTS213	200342
Canada	USA (United States)	08 Jun 44	124UNTS297	200427
Multilateral		07 Dec 44	171UNTS345	200501
Brazil	Dominican Republic	09 Apr 45	67UNTS293	200226
France	USA (United States)	14 Aug 45	73UNTS237	200243
Multilateral		27 Dec 45	2UNTS39	100020
France	Portugal	30 Apr 46	35UNTS197	100556
Canada	UK Great Britain	05 Jun 46	27UNTS207	100408
Multilateral		22 Jul 46	14UNTS185	100221
Multilateral		27 Jul 46	90UNTS229	101238
South Africa	UK Great Britain	14 Oct 46	86UNTS77	101153
South Africa	UK Great Britain	14 Oct 46	86UNTS51	101152
France	USA (United States)	18 Oct 46	140UNTS23	101882
South Africa	USA (United States)	13 Dec 46	167UNTS171	102207
Philippines	USA (United States)	14 Feb 47	16UNTS3	100245
France	ICAO (Civil Aviat)	14 Mar 47	94UNTS59	101306
South Africa	USA (United States)	10 Apr 47	167UNTS211	102208
Thailand	USA (United States)	05 Sep 47	73UNTS57	100943
Ecuador	USA (United States)	29 Oct 47	21UNTS21	100322
Sweden	USA (United States)	16 Dec 47	73UNTS65	100944
Poland	Yugoslavia	21 Jan 48	115UNTS155	101562
Canada	New Zealand	12 Mar 48	231UNTS219	103222
Norway	USA (United States)	15 Mar 48	73UNTS81	100946
New Zealand	USA (United States)	16 Mar 48	127UNTS133	101703
Burma	USA (United States)	05 Apr 48	73UNTS73	100945
Netherlands	USA (United States)	29 Apr 48	32UNTS167	100498
Denmark	USA (United States)	06 May 48	26UNTS55	100377
Philippines	USA (United States)	07 Jun 48	73UNTS89	100947
UNRRA (Relief)	United Nations	27 Sep 48	27UNTS349	200158
Netherlands	UK Great Britain	15 Oct 48	74UNTS3	100955
Belgium	USA (United States)	28 Oct 48	173UNTS67	102262
Multilateral		29 Nov 48	120UNTS13	101613
Afghanistan	UNESCO (Educ/Cult)	08 Dec 48	46UNTS3	100697
Ceylon (Sri Lanka)	USA (United States)	31 Jan 49	88UNTS21	101181
Sweden	UK Great Britain	30 Mar 49	209UNTS129	102826
Ireland	UK Great Britain	18 May 49	553UNTS209	108089
Norway	USA (United States)	13 Jun 49	127UNTS189	101705
Norway	USA (United States)	13 Jun 49	127UNTS163	101704
Colombia	USA (United States)	26 Jul 49	73UNTS106	100949
Denmark	USA (United States)	01 Aug 49	79UNTS147	101038
Multilateral		12 Aug 49	75UNTS287	100973
Ireland	USA (United States)	13 Sep 49	127UNTS89	101701
Ireland	USA (United States)	13 Sep 49	127UNTS119	101702
South Africa	USA (United States)	16 Nov 49	73UNTS97	100948
Belgium	Denmark	13 Dec 49	173UNTS193	102266
Norway	Sweden	17 Dec 49	197UNTS215	102641
France	Netherlands	30 Dec 49	203UNTS85	102742
Ireland	USA (United States)	21 Jan 50	206UNTS269	102792

PARTY ONE	PARTY TWO	DATE	CITATION	NUMBER
Exchange of official publications (Cont.)				
Israel	USA (United States)	19 Feb 50	122UNTS117	101641
Greece	USA (United States)	20 Feb 50	196UNTS291	102630
Greece	USA (United States)	20 Feb 50	196UNTS269	102629
Switzerland	USA (United States)	24 Feb 50	93UNTS3	101282
Burma	UK Great Britain	13 Mar 50	131UNTS53	101735
Honduras	USA (United States)	24 Mar 50	93UNTS11	101283
Denmark	UK Great Britain	27 Mar 50	68UNTS117	100891
Spain	USA (United States)	08 May 50	98UNTS175	101363
Indonesia	USA (United States)	07 Jun 50	98UNTS167	101362
Ceylon (Sri Lanka)	UK Great Britain	26 Jul 50	337UNTS77	104818
Greece	Philippines	28 Aug 50	225UNTS155	103097
USA (United States)	Yugoslavia	09 Oct 50	133UNTS25	101776
Greece	USA (United States)	24 Oct 50	133UNTS41	101778
Costa Rica	USA (United States)	02 Dec 50	133UNTS61	101780
Netherlands	Norway	29 Dec 50	134UNTS19	101795
India	USA (United States)	11 Jan 51	148UNTS49	101934
Canada	France	16 Mar 51	236UNTS297	103331
Canada	France	16 Mar 51	236UNTS267	103330
Canada	Sweden	06 Apr 51	197UNTS393	102648
Multilateral		18 Apr 51	261UNTS140	103729
Greece	Turkey	20 Apr 51	178UNTS17	102333
Norway	UK Great Britain	02 May 51	106UNTS101	101460
Pakistan	USA (United States)	23 May 51	134UNTS265	101805
Switzerland	USA (United States)	24 May 51	127UNTS227	101706
Switzerland	USA (United States)	09 Jul 51	165UNTS51	102167
UK Great Britain	USA (United States)	30 Jul 51	105UNTS81	101455
Multilateral		06 Dec 51	425UNTS61	106119
Finland	USA (United States)	03 Mar 52	177UNTS141	102316
Finland	USA (United States)	03 Mar 52	177UNTS163	102317
Finland	Norway	18 Mar 52	188UNTS187	102527
Netherlands	Sweden	25 Apr 52	163UNTS195	102148
Netherlands	Sweden	25 Apr 52	163UNTS131	102147
Iraq	UK Great Britain	21 Jun 52	149UNTS221	101954
Multilateral		21 Aug 52	141UNTS129	101912
Multilateral		05 Sep 52	247UNTS329	103479
Belgium	Sweden	01 Apr 53	185UNTS225	102473
Japan	USA (United States)	02 Apr 53	206UNTS143	102788
France	UK Great Britain	13 Apr 53	172UNTS173	102245
Australia	USA (United States)	14 May 53	205UNTS253	102779
Australia	USA (United States)	14 May 53	205UNTS237	102778
Australia	USA (United States)	14 May 53	205UNTS277	102780
Greece	UK Great Britain	25 Jun 53	190UNTS281	102571
Belgium	UK Great Britain	10 Sep 53	183UNTS203	102429
Denmark	Sweden	27 Oct 53	198UNTS129	102660
Denmark	Yugoslavia	27 Jan 54	193UNTS181	102615
Belgium	Finland	11 Feb 54	211UNTS63	102848
Finland	Netherlands	29 Mar 54	252UNTS239	103568
Finland	Netherlands	29 Mar 54	252UNTS185	103567
Czechoslovakia	Hungary	16 Apr 54	504UNTS231	107360
Japan	USA (United States)	16 Apr 54	238UNTS3	103353
Japan	USA (United States)	16 Apr 54	238UNTS39	103354
Multilateral		14 Jun 54	320UNTS209	104643
Germany, West	USA (United States)	22 Jul 54	239UNTS3	103369
Switzerland	UK Great Britain	30 Sep 54	209UNTS197	102828
Australia	Vietnam, South	04 Oct 54	201UNTS349	102723
Germany, West	UK Great Britain	18 Oct 54	218UNTS301	102960
Germany, West	USA (United States)	27 Oct 54	234UNTS131	103278
Canada	Ireland	28 Oct 54	304UNTS317	104406
Canada	Ireland	28 Oct 54	305UNTS3	104407
Germany, West	USA (United States)	29 Oct 54	273UNTS3	103943
Belgium	Israel	14 Dec 54	220UNTS49	102987
Italy	USA (United States)	30 Mar 55	257UNTS199	103655
Italy	USA (United States)	30 Mar 55	257UNTS169	103654
Czechoslovakia	Hungary	28 Apr 55	477UNTS197	106923
Multilateral		25 May 55	264UNTS117	103791

PARTY ONE	PARTY TWO	DATE	CITATION	NUMBER
Exchange of official publications (Cont.)				
CERN (Nuc Resrch)	Switzerland	11 Jun 55	249UNTS405	200544
Denmark	Finland	18 Jul 55	250UNTS167	103522
South Africa	Sweden	28 Jul 55	230UNTS287	103191
Canada	Denmark	30 Sep 55	258UNTS115	103675
Australia	France	27 Dec 55	241UNTS325	103440
Belgium	Sweden	18 Jan 56	293UNTS23	104283
Austria	Hungary	09 Apr 56	438UNTS123	106315
New Zealand	Sweden	16 Apr 56	274UNTS259	103971
Fed Rhod/Nyasaland	South Africa	22 May 56	254UNTS227	103595
Denmark	Norway	23 May 56	271UNTS49	103909
Canada	Germany, West	04 Jun 56	316UNTS231	104589
Honduras	USA (United States)	25 Jun 56	279UNTS113	104036
Czechoslovakia	Yugoslavia	03 Jul 56	397UNTS165	105704
Austria	UK Great Britain	20 Jul 56	269UNTS147	103880
Japan	USA (United States)	05 Sep 56	277UNTS267	104011
Ceylon (Sri Lanka)	India	10 Sep 56	315UNTS59	104560
Belgium	Germany, West	24 Sep 56	314UNTS195	104549
Canada	South Africa	28 Sep 56	299UNTS17	104304
Canada	South Africa	28 Sep 56	299UNTS3	104303
Austria	USA (United States)	25 Oct 56	299UNTS123	104310
Japan	Sweden	12 Dec 56	318UNTS309	104623
Italy	Sweden	20 Dec 56	369UNTS357	105265
Australia	Thailand	20 Dec 56	265UNTS149	103810
Denmark	Netherlands	20 Feb 57	287UNTS41	104179
Paraguay	USA (United States)	04 Apr 57	283UNTS193	104117
Germany, East	Poland	13 Jul 57	319UNTS229	104634
Australia	Canada	01 Oct 57	392UNTS41	105638
Hungary	Romania	17 Dec 57	477UNTS303	106926
Multilateral		03 Feb 58	381UNTS165	105471
Israel	Philippines	26 Feb 58	507UNTS135	107398
Belgium	Japan	18 Mar 58	303UNTS149	104378
Sweden	United Arab Rep	29 Jul 58	369UNTS323	105264
India	Sweden	30 Jul 58	369UNTS211	105259
Pakistan	Sweden	25 Aug 58	369UNTS183	105258
Germany, West	Norway	18 Nov 58	357UNTS205	105119
Czechoslovakia	Poland	25 Nov 58	372UNTS205	105299
Multilateral		03 Dec 58	416UNTS51	105995
Multilateral		03 Dec 58	398UNTS9	105715
Greece	USA (United States)	15 Jan 59	357UNTS281	105120
Belgium	France	20 Jan 59	361UNTS155	105178
Japan	Pakistan	17 Feb 59	341UNTS127	104880
Japan	Norway	21 Feb 59	356UNTS231	105098
Denmark	Japan	10 Mar 59	341UNTS55	104878
Canada	Finland	28 Mar 59	355UNTS3	105072
Bulgaria	Hungary	03 Apr 59	438UNTS269	106319
Germany, West	Sweden	17 Apr 59	428UNTS155	106175
Austria	Sweden	14 May 59	428UNTS3	106167
Germany, West	Netherlands	16 Jun 59	593UNTS3	108576
South Africa	UK Great Britain	18 Jun 59	380UNTS59	105450
South Africa	UK Great Britain	18 Jun 59	380UNTS81	105451
South Africa	UK Great Britain	18 Jun 59	380UNTS103	105452
India	Norway	20 Jul 59	356UNTS257	105099
Austria	France	08 Oct 59	453UNTS95	106521
Italy	Netherlands	01 Dec 59	455UNTS241	106545
Israel	Sweden	22 Dec 59	377UNTS277	105407
India	Japan	05 Jan 60	384UNTS3	105507
Austria	Czechoslovakia	23 Jan 60	495UNTS125	107242
Austria	Norway	25 Feb 60	376UNTS155	105380
Poland	Yugoslavia	05 May 60	423UNTS229	106095
Australia	New Zealand	12 May 60	369UNTS119	105254
Finland	USSR (Soviet Union)	23 Jun 60	379UNTS277	105443
Italy	UK Great Britain	04 Jul 60	466UNTS195	106745
Cambodia	USA (United States)	15 Jul 60	380UNTS129	105453
Sweden	UK Great Britain	28 Jul 60	404UNTS113	105808
Sweden	Tunisia	06 Sep 60	427UNTS301	106162

PARTY ONE	PARTY TWO	DATE	CITATION	NUMBER
Exchange of official publications (Cont.)				
Italy	USA (United States)	03 Dec 60	410UNTS3	105893
Canada	USA (United States)	17 Feb 61	445UNTS143	106383
Multilateral		30 Mar 61	520UNTS151	107515
Morocco	Sweden	30 Mar 61	427UNTS185	106154
USA (United States)	Vietnam, South	04 Apr 61	405UNTS77	105824
Japan	UK Great Britain	11 Apr 61	420UNTS75	106042
South Africa	Sweden	29 May 61	442UNTS15	106335
Finland	India	23 Jun 61	421UNTS49	106051
Central Afri Rep	UNICEF (Children)	21 Aug 61	413UNTS48	105939
Italy	Norway	25 Aug 61	475UNTS269	106896
Denmark	Pakistan	04 Sep 61	455UNTS305	106549
Multilateral		05 Oct 61	527UNTS181	107625
Greece	Sweden	06 Oct 61	481UNTS137	106981
Sweden	Thailand	20 Oct 61	428UNTS275	106180
Austria	Denmark	23 Oct 61	425UNTS115	106122
COMECON (Econ Aid)	USSR (Soviet Union)	07 Dec 61	506UNTS325	107392
Austria	Japan	20 Dec 61	517UNTS155	107485
Argentina	Japan	20 Dec 61	451UNTS77	106486
Austria	Czechoslovakia	13 Feb 62	455UNTS381	106551
Israel	Sweden	15 May 62	484UNTS261	107036
South Africa	UK Great Britain	28 May 62	443UNTS79	106361
Multilateral		14 Jun 62	528UNTS33	107634
Israel	Peru	25 Jun 62	515UNTS263	107464
Czechoslovakia	COMECON (Econ Aid)	20 Jul 62	506UNTS345	107393
Indonesia	Netherlands	15 Aug 62	437UNTS273	106311
Japan	UK Great Britain	04 Sep 62	475UNTS31	106888
Multilateral		11 Sep 62	455UNTS402	106553
Germany, West	UK Great Britain	20 Sep 62	453UNTS317	106533
Israel	UK Great Britain	26 Sep 62	474UNTS233	106885
Multilateral		05 Oct 62	502UNTS225	107333
Austria	United Arab Rep	16 Oct 62	491UNTS63	107174
Austria	Luxembourg	18 Oct 62	496UNTS97	107248
UK Great Britain	Vietnam, South	30 Nov 62	470UNTS51	106794
Luxembourg	USA (United States)	18 Dec 62	532UNTS277	107723
Thailand	UK Great Britain	09 Jan 63	470UNTS59	106795
Japan	New Zealand	30 Jan 63	517UNTS183	107486
Ceylon (Sri Lanka)	Denmark	16 Feb 63	486UNTS285	107083
Poland	COMECON (Econ Aid)	22 Feb 63	506UNTS303	107391
Hungary	COMECON (Econ Aid)	28 Feb 63	506UNTS281	107390
Japan	Thailand	01 Mar 63	475UNTS233	106895
Norway	Spain	25 Apr 63	503UNTS41	107340
Japan	Malaysia	04 Jun 63	517UNTS245	107488
France	UK Great Britain	21 Jun 63	540UNTS311	107855
France	Israel	20 Aug 63	515UNTS173	107460
France	Greece	21 Aug 63	533UNTS235	107746
Austria	India	24 Sep 63	545UNTS199	107935
Czechoslovakia	Yugoslavia	05 Oct 63	504UNTS151	107356
Austria	Finland	08 Oct 63	490UNTS255	107160
Norway	Thailand	09 Jan 64	522UNTS65	107537
Belgium	France	10 Mar 64	557UNTS13	108127
Cameroon	Mali	17 Mar 64	524UNTS61	107566
Denmark	Finland	07 Apr 64	525UNTS89	107586
Ceylon (Sri Lanka)	Norway	11 Jun 64	559UNTS23	108153
Sweden	UK Great Britain	14 Oct 64	543UNTS135	107898
UNESCO (Educ/Cult)	USA (United States)	16 Oct 64	550UNTS23	108006
Norway	United Arab Rep	20 Oct 64	543UNTS3	107895
Denmark	Germany, West	06 Jan 65	528UNTS201	107643
Finland	Israel	21 Jan 65	581UNTS275	108450
Benelux Econ Union	Poland	17 Feb 65	547UNTS165	107956
Finland	United Arab Rep	01 Apr 65	562UNTS3	108193
Jamaica	UK Great Britain	02 Apr 65	552UNTS219	108056
Multilateral		28 May 65	559UNTS273	108163
Denmark	Thailand	01 Jun 65	551UNTS157	108040
Gambia	UN Special Fund	09 Jun 65	538UNTS321	200612
OAU (Afri Unity)	United Nations	15 Nov 65	548UNTS315	200614

PARTY ONE	PARTY TWO	DATE	CITATION	NUMBER
Exchange of official publications (Cont.)				
Multilateral		15 Nov 65	0UNTS0	109432
Denmark	Israel	27 Jun 66	581UNTS227	108448
Germany, West	Israel	12 Sep 66	582UNTS17	108454
Korea, South	USA (United States)	24 Sep 66	607UNTS157	108803
Philippines	USA (United States)	04 Jan 67	590UNTS51	108546
Australia	UN Special Fund	06 Feb 67	590UNTS3	108543
Netherlands	Romania	20 Jul 67	633UNTS21	109032
Family law				
Multilateral		04 Nov 50	213UNTS221	102889
Multilateral		09 Jan 51	197UNTS341	102647
Bulgaria	Czechoslovakia	13 Apr 54	501UNTS3	107314
Bulgaria	Yugoslavia	23 Mar 56	367UNTS213	105230
Multilateral		26 Mar 56	259UNTS125	103686
Germany, East	Poland	01 Feb 57	319UNTS115	104632
Czechoslovakia	USSR (Soviet Union)	31 Aug 57	308UNTS3	104456
Germany, East	Hungary	30 Oct 57	408UNTS4	105867
Germany, East	USSR (Soviet Union)	28 Nov 57	305UNTS113	104419
Bulgaria	USSR (Soviet Union)	12 Dec 57	317UNTS217	104606
Korea, North	USSR (Soviet Union)	16 Dec 57	301UNTS301	104349
Poland	USSR (Soviet Union)	28 Dec 57	320UNTS3	104638
Romania	USSR (Soviet Union)	03 Apr 58	313UNTS167	104535
Pakistan	IBRD (World Bank)	23 Apr 58	323UNTS253	104672
Albania	USSR (Soviet Union)	30 Jun 58	328UNTS3	104729
Germany, East	Romania	15 Jul 58	395UNTS3	105681
Hungary	USSR (Soviet Union)	15 Jul 58	322UNTS3	104656
Mongolia	USSR (Soviet Union)	25 Aug 58	322UNTS105	104657
Hungary	Romania	07 Oct 58	416UNTS199	106004
Czechoslovakia	Romania	25 Oct 58	417UNTS37	106006
IBRD (World Bank)	South Africa	02 Dec 58	324UNTS3	104676
Bulgaria	Romania	03 Dec 58	417UNTS133	106007
Albania	Czechoslovakia	16 Jan 59	363UNTS195	105208
Hungary	Poland	06 Mar 59	432UNTS3	106216
Greece	Yugoslavia	18 Jun 59	368UNTS81	105236
Albania	Hungary	12 Jan 60	520UNTS3	107511
Poland	Yugoslavia	06 Feb 60	521UNTS37	107517
Hungary	Yugoslavia	07 May 60	519UNTS237	107510
Mexico	IBRD (World Bank)	16 Jan 61	422UNTS203	106076
Czechoslovakia	Poland	04 Jul 61	436UNTS189	106295
Multilateral		05 Oct 61	0UNTS0	109431
Czechoslovakia	Hungary	02 Nov 61	438UNTS3	106313
Bulgaria	Poland	04 Dec 61	484UNTS3	107019
Poland	Romania	25 Jan 62	468UNTS3	106770
USSR (Soviet Union)	Yugoslavia	24 Feb 62	471UNTS195	106833
Multilateral		23 Mar 62	470UNTS25	106793
Multilateral		10 Dec 62	521UNTS231	107525
Colombia	United Nations	27 Aug 63	481UNTS3	106975
Czechoslovakia	Yugoslavia	20 Jan 64	538UNTS197	107816
United Nations	Togo	03 Jul 64	502UNTS287	107334
Multilateral		24 Apr 67	634UNTS255	109067
Exchange of information and documents				
Multilateral		28 Nov 19	38UNTS17	100584
Multilateral		28 Nov 19	38UNTS41	100585
Multilateral		11 Nov 21	38UNTS203	100598
Multilateral		05 Jun 25	38UNTS257	100602
Multilateral		05 Jun 26	38UNTS281	100604
Multilateral		16 Jun 28	39UNTS3	100609
Multilateral		28 Jun 30	39UNTS55	100612
Multilateral		27 Apr 32	39UNTS103	100614
Multilateral		30 Apr 32	39UNTS133	100615
Multilateral		29 Jun 33	39UNTS151	100616
Multilateral		23 Jun 34	40UNTS45	100626
Multilateral		22 Jun 35	40UNTS73	100628
Multilateral		22 Jun 37	40UNTS217	100636
Multilateral		23 Jun 37	40UNTS233	100637

Exchange of information and documents (Cont.)

PARTY ONE	PARTY TWO	DATE	CITATION	NUMBER
Multilateral		20 Jun 38	40UNTS255	100638
Multilateral		28 Jun 39	209UNTS39	102820
Panama	USA (United States)	23 Mar 40	124UNTS195	200420
Brazil	Venezuela	30 Mar 40	51UNTS291	200195
Panama	USA (United States)	06 Sep 40	124UNTS209	200421
Multilateral		12 Oct 40	161UNTS193	200485
Multilateral		28 Nov 40	139UNTS159	200452
Brazil	Paraguay	14 Jun 41	54UNTS249	200197
Canada	USA (United States)	27 Jun 41	103UNTS205	200315
Mexico	USA (United States)	19 Nov 41	148UNTS367	200474
Canada	USA (United States)	20 Mar 42	105UNTS169	200330
Germany, West	USA (United States)	30 Mar 42	105UNTS219	200334
Canada	USA (United States)	08 Apr 42	105UNTS179	200331
Saudi Arabia	UK Great Britain	20 Apr 42	10UNTS117	200057
Peru	USA (United States)	07 May 42	103UNTS219	200316
Australia	USA (United States)	30 Sep 42	13UNTS125	200074
UK Great Britain	USA (United States)	30 Sep 42	13UNTS169	200077
New Zealand	USA (United States)	30 Sep 42	13UNTS139	200075
Netherlands	USA (United States)	30 Sep 42	13UNTS151	200076
Belgium	USA (United States)	16 Oct 42	13UNTS211	200080
South Africa	USA (United States)	31 Oct 42	105UNTS269	200338
Mexico	USA (United States)	23 Dec 42	13UNTS231	200081
Canada	USA (United States)	28 Dec 42	99UNTS241	200278
Norway	USA (United States)	16 Jan 43	13UNTS335	200082
Cuba	USA (United States)	01 Feb 43	13UNTS379	200085
Canada	USA (United States)	23 Feb 43	101UNTS243	200299
Poland	USA (United States)	25 Feb 43	13UNTS395	200086
Greece	USA (United States)	16 Mar 43	105UNTS227	200335
Multilateral		26 Mar 43	13UNTS427	200089
El Salvador	USA (United States)	31 May 43	105UNTS205	200333
UK Great Britain	USA (United States)	19 Aug 43	214UNTS341	200527
Iceland	USA (United States)	27 Sep 43	29UNTS317	200170
Czechoslovakia	USA (United States)	21 Oct 43	29UNTS369	200172
UK Great Britain	USA (United States)	01 Dec 43	3UNTS209	100033
Australia	New Zealand	21 Jan 44	18UNTS357	200113
Colombia	USA (United States)	12 Feb 44	109UNTS287	200365
Australia	USA (United States)	10 May 44	106UNTS237	200343
Brazil	Canada	24 May 44	65UNTS265	200215
Multilateral		02 Aug 44	67UNTS221	200221
Multilateral		14 Nov 44	236UNTS359	200539
Spain	USA (United States)	02 Dec 44	89UNTS345	200262
Multilateral		07 Dec 44	171UNTS345	200501
France	UK Great Britain	27 Mar 45	98UNTS227	200274
Ecuador	USA (United States)	05 Apr 45	121UNTS265	200404
UK Great Britain	USA (United States)	16 Apr 45	6UNTS189	100076
UK Great Britain	USA (United States)	16 Apr 45	6UNTS359	200039
USA (United States)	Venezuela	11 May 45	121UNTS273	200405
Chile	USA (United States)	11 Jun 45	121UNTS291	200407
Peru	USA (United States)	12 Jun 45	121UNTS283	200406
Dominican Republic	USA (United States)	13 Oct 45	149UNTS361	200477
Multilateral		07 Nov 45	2UNTS17	100018
Multilateral		16 Nov 45	4UNTS275	100052
Czechoslovakia	France	08 Dec 45	46UNTS77	100701
Canada	UK Great Britain	21 Dec 45	27UNTS155	100405
Multilateral		27 Dec 45	2UNTS39	100020
Multilateral		14 Jan 46	555UNTS69	108105
Mexico	UK Great Britain	07 Feb 46	6UNTS55	100068
France	Norway	26 Mar 46	31UNTS69	100468
France	Portugal	30 Apr 46	35UNTS197	100556
Australia	Canada	11 Jun 46	10UNTS47	100142
Netherlands	Spain	13 Jul 46	4UNTS351	100055
Multilateral		18 Jul 46	125UNTS119	101674
Multilateral		22 Jul 46	14UNTS185	100221
Hungary	USA (United States)	09 Aug 46	148UNTS313	101941
Taiwan	USA (United States)	30 Aug 46	12UNTS39	100179

Exchange of information and documents (Cont.)

PARTY ONE	PARTY TWO	DATE	CITATION	NUMBER
Albania	Yugoslavia	03 Oct 46	111UNTS87	101519
Denmark	South Africa	14 Oct 46	10UNTS29	100140
Australia	UK Great Britain	29 Oct 46	17UNTS181	100276
Multilateral		30 Oct 46	11UNTS107	100151
India	USA (United States)	14 Nov 46	22UNTS55	100331
Denmark	Sweden	18 Nov 46	7UNTS251	100104
Cuba	UK Great Britain	02 Dec 46	11UNTS161	100154
Norway	Poland	03 Dec 46	15UNTS203	100234
United Arab Rep	UK Great Britain	10 Dec 46	105UNTS15	101451
Multilateral		11 Dec 46	12UNTS179	100186
Multilateral		13 Dec 46	8UNTS71	100115
Multilateral		13 Dec 46	8UNTS135	100119
Multilateral		13 Dec 46	8UNTS165	100121
Multilateral		13 Dec 46	8UNTS91	100116
Multilateral		13 Dec 46	8UNTS119	100118
Multilateral		13 Dec 46	8UNTS151	100120
ILO (Labor Org)	United Nations	19 Dec 46	1UNTS183	200009
Australia	Netherlands	24 Jan 47	10UNTS77	100144
Hungary	Yugoslavia	25 Jan 47	130UNTS3	101726
UNESCO (Educ/Cult)	United Nations	03 Feb 47	1UNTS233	200011
Multilateral		10 Feb 47	41UNTS21	100643
Multilateral		10 Feb 47	41UNTS135	100644
Burma	USA (United States)	28 Feb 47	25UNTS27	100355
Multilateral		03 Mar 47	11UNTS43	100148
France	USA (United States)	11 Mar 47	151UNTS159	101991
Austria	France	15 Mar 47	12UNTS109	100182
Australia	Norway	24 Mar 47	18UNTS185	100288
Belgium	Netherlands	28 Apr 47	37UNTS199	100577
Philippines	USA (United States)	12 May 47	16UNTS137	100254
Philippines	USA (United States)	12 May 47	16UNTS123	100253
Philippines	USA (United States)	16 May 47	280UNTS177	104057
South Africa	USA (United States)	23 May 47	66UNTS233	100857
Czechoslovakia	UK Great Britain	16 Jun 47	46UNTS61	100700
Greece	USA (United States)	20 Jun 47	7UNTS267	100105
Bulgaria	Czechoslovakia	20 Jun 47	46UNTS15	100698
Austria	USA (United States)	21 Jun 47	67UNTS89	100868
Austria	USA (United States)	25 Jun 47	22UNTS141	100334
Belgium	United Arab Rep	01 Jul 47	34UNTS93	100529
Haiti	USA (United States)	04 Jul 47	22UNTS165	100335
Italy	USA (United States)	04 Jul 47	22UNTS173	100336
Czechoslovakia	Poland	04 Jul 47	25UNTS249	100366
Belgium	South Africa	04 Jul 47	47UNTS9	100720
Greece	USA (United States)	08 Jul 47	16UNTS157	100256
Multilateral		11 Jul 47	161UNTS113	102125
France	India	16 Jul 47	27UNTS325	100415
USSR (Soviet Union)	Yugoslavia	25 Jul 47	130UNTS315	101732
Greece	South Africa	28 Jul 47	185UNTS161	102467
Taiwan	Italy	30 Jul 47	12UNTS377	100194
Czechoslovakia	Greece	30 Jul 47	185UNTS149	102466
Iraq	UK Great Britain	13 Aug 47	9UNTS259	100136
Multilateral		14 Aug 47	138UNTS111	101863
Czechoslovakia	Romania	05 Sep 47	46UNTS37	100699
FAO (Food Agri)	ILO (Labor Org)	11 Sep 47	18UNTS335	200111
Chile	UK Great Britain	16 Sep 47	133UNTS143	101786
Multilateral		19 Sep 47	30UNTS249	100461
Sweden	Yugoslavia	06 Oct 47	53UNTS107	100775
Multilateral		11 Oct 47	77UNTS143	100998
UK Great Britain	USA (United States)	13 Oct 47	66UNTS269	100858
Chile	UK Great Britain	27 Oct 47	82UNTS209	101094
Taiwan	USA (United States)	27 Oct 47	12UNTS11	100178
Ecuador	USA (United States)	29 Oct 47	21UNTS21	100322
Multilateral		12 Nov 47	53UNTS49	100772
Finland	Norway	15 Nov 47	29UNTS179	100439
United Nations	WHO (World Health)	15 Nov 47	19UNTS193	200115
United Nations	UPU (Postal Union)	15 Nov 47	19UNTS219	200116

Exchange of information and documents (Cont.)

PARTY ONE	PARTY TWO	DATE	CITATION	NUMBER
Multilateral		18 Nov 47	17UNTS89	100269
UNICEF (Children)	Yugoslavia	20 Nov 47	65UNTS28	100817
Taiwan	USA (United States)	08 Dec 47	70UNTS3	100895
Czechoslovakia	USSR (Soviet Union)	11 Dec 47	217UNTS35	102943
Peru	UK Great Britain	22 Dec 47	72UNTS143	100932
Philippines	UK Great Britain	07 Jan 48	28UNTS63	100420
France	Lebanon	24 Jan 48	173UNTS99	102263
Cuba	USA (United States)	27 Jan 48	67UNTS3	100862
Multilateral		06 Mar 48	289UNTS3	104214
Switzerland	USSR (Soviet Union)	17 Mar 48	217UNTS87	102945
Belgium	Luxembourg	27 Mar 48	178UNTS265	102343
Bulgaria	USSR (Soviet Union)	01 Apr 48	217UNTS97	102946
Poland	USSR (Soviet Union)	08 Apr 48	26UNTS191	100388
Belgium	Italy	30 Apr 48	36UNTS305	100571
Pakistan	Sweden	06 May 48	36UNTS3	100564
Multilateral		10 May 48	140UNTS129	101887
India	Sweden	21 May 48	34UNTS285	100543
Luxembourg	UK Great Britain	27 May 48	53UNTS115	100776
France	Norway	11 Jun 48	31UNTS83	100469
Australia	Greece	16 Jun 48	18UNTS211	100290
Hungary	Poland	18 Jun 48	25UNTS319	100370
India	Pakistan	23 Jun 48	28UNTS143	100423
Italy	UK Great Britain	25 Jun 48	94UNTS239	101313
Norway	Switzerland	26 Jun 48	29UNTS193	100440
France	USA (United States)	28 Jun 48	19UNTS9	100302
Ireland	USA (United States)	28 Jun 48	24UNTS3	100349
Italy	USA (United States)	28 Jun 48	20UNTS43	100314
Denmark	USA (United States)	29 Jun 48	22UNTS217	100338
Netherlands	USA (United States)	02 Jul 48	20UNTS91	100315
Greece	USA (United States)	02 Jul 48	23UNTS43	100342
Austria	USA (United States)	02 Jul 48	21UNTS29	100323
Belgium	USA (United States)	02 Jul 48	19UNTS127	100309
Luxembourg	USA (United States)	03 Jul 48	24UNTS35	100350
Sweden	USA (United States)	03 Jul 48	23UNTS101	100343
Iceland	USA (United States)	03 Jul 48	20UNTS141	100316
Norway	USA (United States)	03 Jul 48	20UNTS185	100317
Taiwan	USA (United States)	03 Jul 48	17UNTS119	100273
Turkey	USA (United States)	04 Jul 48	24UNTS67	100351
UK Great Britain	USA (United States)	06 Jul 48	22UNTS263	100339
Poland	USSR (Soviet Union)	08 Jul 48	37UNTS25	100575
Poland	USSR (Soviet Union)	08 Jul 48	37UNTS107	100576
France	USA (United States)	09 Jul 48	24UNTS103	100352
ILO (Labor Org)	WHO (World Health)	10 Jul 48	19UNTS269	200121
Multilateral		14 Jul 48	23UNTS3	100340
UNESCO (Educ/Cult)	WHO (World Health)	15 Jul 48	44UNTS323	200184
FAO (Food Agri)	WHO (World Health)	17 Jul 48	76UNTS171	200244
USA (United States)	Yugoslavia	19 Jul 48	89UNTS43	101208
Multilateral		24 Jul 48	66UNTS25	100847
Taiwan	USA (United States)	05 Aug 48	82UNTS109	101087
FAO (Food Agri)	UNESCO (Educ/Cult)	23 Aug 48	18UNTS345	200112
France	Spain	23 Aug 48	28UNTS173	100425
Israel	UNICEF (Children)	20 Sep 48	71UNTS17	100907
Portugal	USA (United States)	28 Sep 48	29UNTS213	100442
Trieste	USA (United States)	15 Oct 48	29UNTS249	100443
France	USA (United States)	19 Oct 48	98UNTS3	101355
Czechoslovakia	Poland	12 Nov 48	84UNTS347	101141
Brazil	USA (United States)	26 Nov 48	88UNTS3	101180
Australia	Belgium	09 Dec 48	25UNTS159	100361
Finland	USSR (Soviet Union)	09 Dec 48	217UNTS135	102947
Multilateral		09 Dec 48	73UNTS39	100942
Korea, South	USA (United States)	10 Dec 48	55UNTS157	100813
Ceylon (Sri Lanka)	India	21 Dec 48	28UNTS223	100427
Ceylon (Sri Lanka)	Pakistan	03 Jan 49	28UNTS247	100428
Belgium	Luxembourg	14 Jan 49	36UNTS339	100572
Czechoslovakia	Poland	21 Jan 49	31UNTS205	100480

Exchange of information and documents (Cont.)

PARTY ONE	PARTY TWO	DATE	CITATION	NUMBER
Canada	USA (United States)	31 Jan 49	43UNTS119	100666
IRO (Refugee Org)	United Nations	07 Feb 49	26UNTS299	200153
FAO (Food Agri)	UNESCO (Educ/Cult)	09 Feb 49	43UNTS315	200182
Belgium	Luxembourg	25 Feb 49	47UNTS3	100719
Czechoslovakia	UK Great Britain	03 Mar 49	83UNTS95	101104
Belgium	Switzerland	21 Mar 49	34UNTS17	100524
Israel	Lebanon	23 Mar 49	42UNTS287	100655
Panama	USA (United States)	31 Mar 49	55UNTS87	100810
United Arab Rep	UK Great Britain	31 Mar 49	83UNTS139	101106
Israel	Jordan	03 Apr 49	42UNTS303	100656
Multilateral		08 Apr 49	140UNTS196	101889
Australia	New Zealand	15 Apr 49	34UNTS225	100540
ITU (Telecommun)	United Nations	26 Apr 49	30UNTS315	200175
Luxembourg	Netherlands	26 Apr 49	182UNTS187	102425
Multilateral		28 Apr 49	83UNTS105	101105
Multilateral		04 May 49	92UNTS19	101257
Denmark	Poland	12 May 49	87UNTS179	101172
Costa Rica	USA (United States)	31 May 49	80UNTS3	101041
Italy	Spain	31 May 49	231UNTS251	103224
Australia	Pakistan	03 Jun 49	35UNTS23	100549
Philippines	USA (United States)	07 Jun 49	45UNTS63	100692
Norway	Pakistan	23 Jun 49	35UNTS49	100550
India	Switzerland	24 Jun 49	95UNTS109	101319
Multilateral		29 Jun 49	138UNTS207	101870
Multilateral		01 Jul 49	96UNTS237	101340
Multilateral		01 Jul 49	138UNTS225	101871
Multilateral		01 Jul 49	120UNTS71	101616
Czechoslovakia	Poland	02 Jul 49	260UNTS149	103708
Czechoslovakia	Poland	02 Jul 49	260UNTS179	103709
Australia	India	11 Jul 49	35UNTS83	100552
Pakistan	Philippines	16 Jul 49	35UNTS111	100553
Israel	Syria	20 Jul 49	42UNTS327	100657
Pakistan	UK Great Britain	27 Jul 49	44UNTS199	100685
Ceylon (Sri Lanka)	UK Great Britain	05 Aug 49	35UNTS137	100554
Philippines	USA (United States)	08 Aug 49	163UNTS103	102144
Multilateral		12 Aug 49	75UNTS287	100973
Multilateral		12 Aug 49	75UNTS31	100970
Canada	UK Great Britain	19 Aug 49	44UNTS223	100686
Belgium	Netherlands	20 Aug 49	46UNTS133	100706
Greece	Italy	31 Aug 49	78UNTS89	101014
Iran	USA (United States)	01 Sep 49	79UNTS155	101039
Denmark	ICAO (Civil Aviat)	09 Sep 49	53UNTS341	100791
Multilateral		19 Sep 49	125UNTS3	101671
Belgium	United Arab Rep	19 Sep 49	137UNTS189	101853
Multilateral		24 Sep 49	126UNTS237	101691
Bulgaria	Poland	26 Sep 49	260UNTS227	103711
Bulgaria	Poland	26 Sep 49	260UNTS249	103712
Czechoslovakia	UK Great Britain	28 Sep 49	86UNTS161	101157
Finland	IBRD (World Bank)	17 Oct 49	156UNTS355	200481
India	Philippines	20 Oct 49	72UNTS191	100934
Hungary	Poland	29 Oct 49	260UNTS91	103705
Hungary	Poland	29 Oct 49	260UNTS113	103706
Iran	Netherlands	31 Oct 49	254UNTS257	103596
Denmark	Pakistan	09 Nov 49	44UNTS255	100687
France	Ireland	21 Nov 49	553UNTS59	108069
Australia	USA (United States)	26 Nov 49	45UNTS133	100695
Netherlands	United Arab Rep	08 Dec 49	95UNTS123	101320
Sweden	United Arab Rep	12 Dec 49	108UNTS15	101466
Afghanistan	India	14 Dec 49	53UNTS95	100774
Germany, West	USA (United States)	15 Dec 49	92UNTS269	101277
Turkey	USA (United States)	27 Dec 49	98UNTS141	101361
Panama	USA (United States)	26 Jan 50	132UNTS233	101763
UNICEF (Children)	UK Great Britain	10 Feb 50	65UNTS86	100837
Chile	UNICEF (Children)	03 Mar 50	126UNTS119	101685
Norway	United Arab Rep	11 Mar 50	95UNTS157	101321

PARTY ONE	PARTY TWO	DATE	CITATION	NUMBER
Exchange of information and documents (Cont.)				
Denmark	United Arab Rep	14 Mar 50	95UNTS197	101322
Indonesia	USA (United States)	24 Mar 50	92UNTS387	101281
Israel	UK Great Britain	30 Mar 50	86UNTS231	101162
Austria	Czechoslovakia	30 Mar 50	495UNTS85	107240
Sweden	UK Great Britain	05 Apr 50	99UNTS107	101374
Multilateral		06 Apr 50	119UNTS99	101610
Multilateral		08 Apr 50	66UNTS285	100860
Turkey	United Arab Rep	12 Apr 50	128UNTS3	101711
Australia	Philippines	14 Apr 50	127UNTS281	101709
Multilateral		17 Apr 50	131UNTS99	101738
Greece	United Arab Rep	24 Apr 50	163UNTS229	102149
Australia	Netherlands	26 Apr 50	54UNTS83	100796
Ireland	Spain	11 May 50	553UNTS147	108081
Switzerland	United Arab Rep	15 May 50	95UNTS255	101325
Brazil	IBRD (World Bank)	26 May 50	301UNTS165	104345
Romania	USSR (Soviet Union)	27 May 50	221UNTS13	103000
ILO (Labor Org)	OAS (Am States)	07 Jun 50	70UNTS223	200240
Iraq	Pakistan	20 Jun 50	77UNTS215	101001
Germany, East	Poland	23 Jun 50	304UNTS91	104393
Afghanistan	UNICEF (Children)	04 Jul 50	71UNTS3	100906
Hungary	USSR (Soviet Union)	13 Jul 50	221UNTS35	103001
Taiwan	UNICEF (Children)	19 Jul 50	94UNTS21	101304
Spain	UK Great Britain	20 Jul 50	398UNTS101	105719
France	Pakistan	31 Jul 50	96UNTS23	101329
India	Nepal	31 Jul 50	94UNTS3	101302
Canada	France	01 Aug 50	73UNTS21	100941
FAO (Food Agri)	United Nations	02 Aug 50	139UNTS407	200467
France	United Arab Rep	08 Aug 50	127UNTS293	101710
Canada	New Zealand	16 Aug 50	77UNTS239	101002
Brazil	USA (United States)	16 Aug 50	140UNTS223	101890
Bulgaria	USSR (Soviet Union)	25 Aug 50	221UNTS57	103002
India	Norway	29 Aug 50	73UNTS179	100952
ICJ Option Clause	Israel	04 Sep 50	108UNTS239	101477
Burma	USA (United States)	13 Sep 50	92UNTS361	101280
Ethiopia	IBRD (World Bank)	13 Sep 50	157UNTS233	102056
Ethiopia	IBRD (World Bank)	13 Sep 50	157UNTS213	102055
Thailand	USA (United States)	19 Sep 50	132UNTS199	101761
Peru	WHO (World Health)	26 Sep 50	104UNTS233	101444
Ceylon (Sri Lanka)	United Arab Rep	26 Sep 50	192UNTS53	102595
Bulgaria	Romania	29 Sep 50	342UNTS141	104905
ILO (Labor Org)	United Nations	12 Oct 50	139UNTS395	200466
Indonesia	USA (United States)	16 Oct 50	281UNTS105	104074
IBRD (World Bank)	Turkey	19 Oct 50	157UNTS333	102058
Belgium	Netherlands	23 Oct 50	136UNTS31	101831
Belgium	Italy	24 Oct 50	110UNTS39	101499
IBRD (World Bank)	Thailand	27 Oct 50	158UNTS3	102059
IBRD (World Bank)	Thailand	27 Oct 50	158UNTS25	102060
IBRD (World Bank)	Thailand	27 Oct 50	158UNTS43	102061
Multilateral		02 Nov 50	81UNTS160	101071
Ceylon (Sri Lanka)	USA (United States)	07 Nov 50	92UNTS125	101265
Australia	IBRD (World Bank)	14 Nov 50	156UNTS147	102041
Czechoslovakia	Poland	17 Nov 50	530UNTS195	107682
USA (United States)	Yugoslavia	21 Nov 50	93UNTS39	101285
Multilateral		24 Nov 50	81UNTS188	101072
Germany, West	Netherlands	14 Dec 50	87UNTS257	101177
Brazil	USA (United States)	19 Dec 50	141UNTS3	101900
Panama	USA (United States)	20 Dec 50	92UNTS167	101269
Liberia	USA (United States)	22 Dec 50	92UNTS145	101267
Nicaragua	USA (United States)	23 Dec 50	92UNTS155	101268
Italy	Yugoslavia	23 Dec 50	171UNTS291	102233
India	USA (United States)	28 Dec 50	99UNTS39	101369
Colombia	IBRD (World Bank)	28 Dec 50	158UNTS87	102063
Paraguay	USA (United States)	29 Dec 50	122UNTS157	101645
Australia	Finland	04 Jan 51	80UNTS27	101042
Multilateral		09 Jan 51	197UNTS341	102647

PARTY ONE	PARTY TWO	DATE	CITATION	NUMBER
Exchange of information and documents (Cont.)				
Costa Rica	USA (United States)	11 Jan 51	92UNTS179	101270
Chile	USA (United States)	16 Jan 51	151UNTS147	101990
Chile	USA (United States)	16 Jan 51	157UNTS3	102043
Saudi Arabia	USA (United States)	17 Jan 51	140UNTS335	101897
Netherlands	USA (United States)	19 Jan 51	141UNTS221	101917
IBRD (World Bank)	South Africa	23 Jan 51	158UNTS135	102065
Nepal	USA (United States)	23 Jan 51	184UNTS65	102439
IBRD (World Bank)	South Africa	23 Jan 51	158UNTS115	102064
Paraguay	UNICEF (Children)	25 Jan 51	79UNTS9	101027
Albania	Poland	25 Jan 51	260UNTS217	103710
Ethiopia	ICAO (Civil Aviat)	02 Feb 51	96UNTS123	101333
Afghanistan	USA (United States)	07 Feb 51	132UNTS265	101766
Pakistan	USA (United States)	09 Feb 51	100UNTS67	101388
Israel	ILO (Labor Org)	19 Feb 51	100UNTS105	101391
Ethiopia	IBRD (World Bank)	19 Feb 51	186UNTS101	102486
Dominican Republic	USA (United States)	20 Feb 51	132UNTS305	101770
Australia	Netherlands	22 Feb 51	128UNTS115	101717
Lebanon	USA (United States)	24 Feb 51	223UNTS121	103060
Israel	USA (United States)	26 Feb 51	137UNTS57	101848
Jordan	USA (United States)	27 Feb 51	141UNTS55	101905
ICAO (Civil Aviat)	United Nations	28 Feb 51	139UNTS429	200469
ILO (Labor Org)	Syria	03 Mar 51	110UNTS69	101502
UNESCO (Educ/Cult)	United Nations	07 Mar 51	139UNTS417	200468
Colombia	USA (United States)	09 Mar 51	141UNTS15	101901
Bolivia	USA (United States)	14 Mar 51	132UNTS319	101771
Greece	Yugoslavia	15 Mar 51	187UNTS237	102516
Dominican Republic	USA (United States)	16 Mar 51	148UNTS15	101932
Multilateral		28 Mar 51	181UNTS61	102399
Australia	Italy	29 Mar 51	131UNTS187	101741
Jordan	ILO (Labor Org)	29 Mar 51	100UNTS247	200287
Liberia	ILO (Labor Org)	02 Apr 51	100UNTS117	101392
Mexico	ILO (Labor Org)	06 Apr 51	100UNTS131	101393
Ceylon (Sri Lanka)	ILO (Labor Org)	06 Apr 51	100UNTS235	200286
Colombia	IBRD (World Bank)	10 Apr 51	158UNTS155	102066
United Nations	WMO (Meteorology)	10 Apr 51	103UNTS245	200415
Iraq	USA (United States)	10 Apr 51	151UNTS179	101993
Peru	ILO (Labor Org)	13 Apr 51	100UNTS31	101385
Guatemala	ILO (Labor Org)	13 Apr 51	126UNTS249	101692
Multilateral		18 Apr 51	261UNTS140	103729
Ecuador	ILO (Labor Org)	19 Apr 51	100UNTS77	101389
Iraq	UK Great Britain	19 Apr 51	108UNTS121	101470
Cuba	ILO (Labor Org)	21 Apr 51	99UNTS205	101382
Greece	ILO (Labor Org)	25 Apr 51	100UNTS93	101390
India	ILO (Labor Org)	26 Apr 51	100UNTS19	101384
Philippines	USA (United States)	27 Apr 51	174UNTS251	102290
Ceylon (Sri Lanka)	India	30 Apr 51	196UNTS199	102625
Haiti	USA (United States)	02 May 51	151UNTS191	101994
Ecuador	USA (United States)	03 May 51	141UNTS27	101902
United Arab Rep	USA (United States)	05 May 51	198UNTS265	102670
Belgium	UK Great Britain	08 May 51	158UNTS451	102079
Pakistan	ILO (Labor Org)	16 May 51	100UNTS147	101394
India	Netherlands	24 May 51	108UNTS151	101471
Multilateral		25 May 51	175UNTS215	102303
Lebanon	USA (United States)	29 May 51	160UNTS49	102101
Cambodia	WHO (World Health)	31 May 51	102UNTS279	200307
Nicaragua	IBRD (World Bank)	07 Jun 51	158UNTS215	102067
Nicaragua	IBRD (World Bank)	07 Jun 51	158UNTS277	102068
Belgium	Netherlands	14 Jun 51	101UNTS3	101397
Costa Rica	WHO (World Health)	14 Jun 51	102UNTS151	101418
Panama	UNICEF (Children)	14 Jun 51	97UNTS3	101343
UK Great Britain	USA (United States)	15 Jun 51	141UNTS79	101907
Italy	Netherlands	15 Jun 51	150UNTS103	101964
Multilateral		15 Jun 51	148UNTS67	101936
Ethiopia	USA (United States)	16 Jun 51	148UNTS39	101933
Dominican Republic	ILO (Labor Org)	18 Jun 51	100UNTS3	101383

Exchange of information and documents (Cont.)

PARTY ONE	PARTY TWO	DATE	CITATION	NUMBER
Denmark	Iran	18 Jun 51	255UNTS3	103602
Iceland	IBRD (World Bank)	20 Jun 51	158UNTS301	102069
Cuba	USA (United States)	20 Jun 51	148UNTS3	101931
ILO (Labor Org)	Vietnam, South	26 Jun 51	100UNTS223	200285
Mexico	USA (United States)	27 Jun 51	141UNTS211	101916
Multilateral		28 Jun 51	118UNTS154	101604
Multilateral		29 Jun 51	165UNTS303	102181
Ethiopia	WHO (World Health)	02 Jul 51	103UNTS39	101422
ILO (Labor Org)	Thailand	11 Jul 51	100UNTS159	101395
Paraguay	ILO (Labor Org)	12 Jul 51	117UNTS155	101591
UK Great Britain	USA (United States)	13 Jul 51	105UNTS71	101454
El Salvador	USA (United States)	19 Jul 51	140UNTS259	101892
Iran	UNICEF (Children)	02 Aug 51	247UNTS11	103457
Greece	USA (United States)	03 Aug 51	224UNTS279	103080
Israel	WHO (World Health)	07 Aug 51	104UNTS213	101442
Israel	Philippines	07 Aug 51	192UNTS81	102596
Lebanon	UK Great Britain	15 Aug 51	160UNTS327	102116
Iraq	USA (United States)	16 Aug 51	147UNTS65	101929
Denmark	USA (United States)	23 Aug 51	147UNTS49	101928
Israel	USA (United States)	23 Aug 51	219UNTS237	102979
WHO (World Health)	Saudi Arabia	29 Aug 51	110UNTS277	101516
UNICEF (Children)	Turkey	05 Sep 51	193UNTS55	102610
USA (United States)	Vietnam, South	07 Sep 51	174UNTS165	102284
Cambodia	USA (United States)	08 Sep 51	174UNTS115	102282
Laos	USA (United States)	09 Sep 51	174UNTS141	102283
Belgium	IBRD (World Bank)	13 Sep 51	158UNTS323	102070
Iraq	ICAO (Civil Aviat)	18 Sep 51	108UNTS219	101475
Belgium	Sweden	18 Sep 51	133UNTS187	101789
Denmark	USA (United States)	01 Oct 51	421UNTS105	106056
UNICEF (Children)	UK Great Britain	02 Oct 51	104UNTS301	101448
Pakistan	WHO (World Health)	07 Oct 51	126UNTS101	101684
Multilateral		09 Oct 51	220UNTS121	102997
Chile	IBRD (World Bank)	10 Oct 51	158UNTS369	102072
Italy	IBRD (World Bank)	10 Oct 51	159UNTS383	200482
IBRD (World Bank)	Yugoslavia	11 Oct 51	159UNTS3	102081
Colombia	IBRD (World Bank)	13 Oct 51	159UNTS75	102084
ILO (Labor Org)	Venezuela	22 Oct 51	117UNTS139	101590
El Salvador	USA (United States)	23 Oct 51	137UNTS43	101847
Nicaragua	IBRD (World Bank)	29 Oct 51	159UNTS35	102082
Iceland	IBRD (World Bank)	01 Nov 51	159UNTS55	102083
Panama	ILO (Labor Org)	10 Nov 51	126UNTS269	101693
Denmark	USA (United States)	16 Nov 51	180UNTS275	102391
Council of Europe	ILO (Labor Org)	23 Nov 51	126UNTS331	200435
India	UK Great Britain	01 Dec 51	128UNTS39	101712
Multilateral		06 Dec 51	425UNTS61	106119
Paraguay	IBRD (World Bank)	07 Dec 51	159UNTS103	102085
Iraq	UNICEF (Children)	10 Dec 51	126UNTS57	101682
El Salvador	Guatemala	14 Dec 51	131UNTS131	101740
Mexico	WHO (World Health)	17 Dec 51	124UNTS121	101670
Jordan	United Arab Rep	02 Jan 52	192UNTS157	102599
India	USA (United States)	05 Jan 52	157UNTS39	102045
USA (United States)	Yugoslavia	08 Jan 52	152UNTS61	102011
Mexico	IBRD (World Bank)	11 Jan 52	159UNTS129	102086
Libya	USA (United States)	21 Jan 52	183UNTS177	102427
Peru	IBRD (World Bank)	23 Jan 52	159UNTS163	102087
Greece	Yugoslavia	02 Feb 52	188UNTS311	102535
France	USA (United States)	02 Feb 52	247UNTS223	103472
Indonesia	United Nations	06 Feb 52	121UNTS3	101621
Jordan	USA (United States)	12 Feb 52	168UNTS25	102211
Dominican Republic	UNICEF (Children)	15 Feb 52	121UNTS43	101625
Canada	USA (United States)	21 Feb 52	205UNTS293	102781
IBRD (World Bank)	UK Great Britain	27 Feb 52	159UNTS181	102088
ICAO (Civil Aviat)	United Arab Rep	06 Mar 52	151UNTS111	101986
Pakistan	Switzerland	17 Mar 52	192UNTS237	102603
Netherlands	IBRD (World Bank)	20 Mar 52	159UNTS207	102089

Exchange of information and documents (Cont.)

PARTY ONE	PARTY TWO	DATE	CITATION	NUMBER
Pakistan	IBRD (World Bank)	27 Mar 52	159UNTS251	102090
Libya	UK Great Britain	31 Mar 52	151UNTS69	101984
Iraq	Switzerland	31 Mar 52	311UNTS43	104498
El Salvador	USA (United States)	04 Apr 52	177UNTS219	102320
Libya	UNICEF (Children)	05 Apr 52	133UNTS287	200441
Chile	USA (United States)	09 Apr 52	186UNTS53	102482
United Nations	Yugoslavia	10 Apr 52	141UNTS89	101908
Canada	Netherlands	10 Apr 52	233UNTS129	103257
France	Mexico	17 Apr 52	163UNTS321	102153
Liberia	UNICEF (Children)	17 Apr 52	133UNTS3	101773
India	ICAO (Civil Aviat)	29 Apr 52	151UNTS123	101987
France	Israel	29 Apr 52	189UNTS55	102542
Finland	IBRD (World Bank)	30 Apr 52	159UNTS408	200483
Israel	USA (United States)	01 May 52	177UNTS89	102311
Norway	WHO (World Health)	09 May 52	131UNTS281	101747
Israel	USA (United States)	09 May 52	177UNTS63	102309
Switzerland	UK Great Britain	13 May 52	164UNTS91	102160
Ethiopia	USA (United States)	15 May 52	180UNTS227	102388
Korea, South	USA (United States)	24 May 52	179UNTS23	102353
Pakistan	IBRD (World Bank)	13 Jun 52	191UNTS85	102578
India	United Arab Rep	14 Jun 52	173UNTS209	102268
Australia	United Arab Rep	14 Jun 52	173UNTS241	102269
Belgium	UNICEF (Children)	17 Jun 52	171UNTS249	102228
IBRD (World Bank)	Turkey	18 Jun 52	159UNTS269	102091
Multilateral		19 Jun 52	133UNTS165	101787
WHO (World Health)	Syria	20 Jun 52	165UNTS219	102178
Multilateral		26 Jun 52	196UNTS183	102624
Brazil	IBRD (World Bank)	27 Jun 52	190UNTS85	102560
Brazil	IBRD (World Bank)	27 Jun 52	190UNTS115	102561
Multilateral		28 Jun 52	210UNTS132	102838
Belgium	Israel	30 Jun 52	183UNTS263	102435
Panama	USA (United States)	30 Jun 52	181UNTS121	102404
Chile	USA (United States)	30 Jun 52	199UNTS241	102688
Australia	FAO (Food Agri)	07 Jul 52	184UNTS209	102449
Australia	IBRD (World Bank)	08 Jul 52	159UNTS295	102092
Peru	IBRD (World Bank)	08 Jul 52	159UNTS321	102093
Jordan	UNICEF (Children)	08 Jul 52	173UNTS353	200503
Portugal	USA (United States)	09 Jul 52	180UNTS251	102389
UNICEF (Children)	Syria	10 Jul 52	136UNTS17	101830
Chile	WHO (World Health)	11 Jul 52	137UNTS27	101846
Multilateral		14 Jul 52	198UNTS47	102656
India	WHO (World Health)	16 Jul 52	135UNTS291	101828
Netherlands	Pakistan	17 Jul 52	150UNTS277	101980
Chile	ILO (Labor Org)	23 Jul 52	178UNTS323	102348
UNICEF (Children)	UK Great Britain	25 Jul 52	135UNTS37	101812
Czechoslovakia	Romania	31 Jul 52	362UNTS123	105185
Laos	UNICEF (Children)	15 Aug 52	161UNTS323	200491
Panama	United Nations	20 Aug 52	136UNTS3	101829
Iceland	IBRD (World Bank)	26 Aug 52	159UNTS363	102095
Colombia	IBRD (World Bank)	26 Aug 52	159UNTS339	102094
Ethiopia	Pakistan	29 Aug 52	150UNTS257	101979
Australia	Germany, West	29 Aug 52	184UNTS147	102446
UNICEF (Children)	Vietnam, South	29 Aug 52	161UNTS335	200492
Multilateral		05 Sep 52	256UNTS3	103619
Ceylon (Sri Lanka)	Japan	06 Sep 52	314UNTS279	104552
United Nations	Trieste	30 Sep 52	140UNTS11	101881
USA (United States)	Yugoslavia	11 Oct 52	235UNTS277	103309
Multilateral		15 Oct 52	141UNTS96	101909
Iraq	USA (United States)	23 Oct 52	212UNTS201	102872
Burma	UK Great Britain	25 Oct 52	150UNTS237	101978
Ethiopia	USA (United States)	07 Nov 52	184UNTS285	102453
Saudi Arabia	USA (United States)	10 Nov 52	181UNTS307	102419
Japan	IBRD (World Bank)	12 Nov 52	354UNTS313	105068
Israel	Switzerland	19 Nov 52	232UNTS3	103226
Mexico	ICAO (Civil Aviat)	28 Nov 52	164UNTS15	102156

PARTY ONE	PARTY TWO	DATE	CITATION	NUMBER
Exchange of information and documents (Cont.)				
Saudi Arabia	USA (United States)	15 Dec 52	185UNTS67	102459
Multilateral		16 Dec 52	158UNTS407	102074
UNICEF (Children)	UK Great Britain	16 Dec 52	151UNTS359	102005
India	IBRD (World Bank)	18 Dec 52	201UNTS241	102719
Multilateral		29 Dec 52	151UNTS317	102002
ILO (Labor Org)	UN Relief Palestin	31 Dec 52	182UNTS201	200506
Switzerland	UK Great Britain	16 Jan 53	196UNTS119	102621
India	IBRD (World Bank)	23 Jan 53	201UNTS145	102715
United Nations	Sweden	11 Feb 53	160UNTS3	102096
IBRD (World Bank)	Yugoslavia	11 Feb 53	165UNTS231	102179
Taiwan	ILO (Labor Org)	13 Feb 53	178UNTS337	102349
Albania	Romania	14 Feb 53	342UNTS107	104903
Japan	Netherlands	17 Feb 53	192UNTS215	102602
Japan	Sweden	20 Feb 53	173UNTS307	102272
Libya	UK Great Britain	21 Feb 53	311UNTS115	104501
Japan	Norway	23 Feb 53	192UNTS191	102601
Multilateral		26 Feb 53	161UNTS31	102120
Denmark	Japan	26 Feb 53	173UNTS329	102273
Costa Rica	United Nations	27 Feb 53	161UNTS45	102121
Germany, West	USA (United States)	27 Feb 53	223UNTS167	103065
Nepal	United Nations	02 Mar 53	161UNTS347	200493
Denmark	Uruguay	04 Mar 53	250UNTS51	103517
IBRD (World Bank)	UK Great Britain	11 Mar 53	172UNTS115	102243
Belgium	France	11 Mar 53	191UNTS329	102590
United Arab Rep	USA (United States)	12 Mar 53	204UNTS3	102747
United Arab Rep	USA (United States)	19 Mar 53	215UNTS17	102909
France	WHO (World Health)	02 Apr 53	174UNTS83	102279
United Nations	Yemen	07 Apr 53	163UNTS73	102142
Netherlands	United Nations	09 Apr 53	163UNTS89	102143
Germany, West	USA (United States)	09 Apr 53	204UNTS79	102750
Ethiopia	UNICEF (Children)	27 Apr 53	213UNTS169	102885
Belgium	Netherlands	29 Apr 53	173UNTS61	102261
Ethiopia	USA (United States)	29 Apr 53	224UNTS121	103073
Israel	Uruguay	30 Apr 53	280UNTS269	104064
France	WHO (World Health)	30 Apr 53	174UNTS71	102278
Brazil	IBRD (World Bank)	30 Apr 53	190UNTS133	102562
Multilateral		30 Apr 53	175UNTS89	102297
Multilateral		11 May 53	456UNTS3	106555
El Salvador	USA (United States)	14 May 53	234UNTS71	103273
United Arab Rep	USA (United States)	21 May 53	204UNTS29	102748
ICAO (Civil Aviat)	Syria	28 May 53	173UNTS199	102267
Brazil	USA (United States)	30 May 53	460UNTS89	106633
Colombia	USA (United States)	09 Jun 53	213UNTS3	102877
Ecuador	United Nations	16 Jun 53	166UNTS289	102194
United Arab Rep	USA (United States)	18 Jun 53	215UNTS45	102910
France	Netherlands	20 Jun 53	187UNTS97	102503
Ethiopia	United Nations	22 Jun 53	172UNTS93	102241
Liberia	USA (United States)	23 Jun 53	213UNTS37	102879
Japan	United Nations	24 Jun 53	167UNTS249	200499
Cambodia	United Nations	24 Jun 53	168UNTS309	200500
UK Great Britain	USA (United States)	24 Jun 53	224UNTS141	103074
Pakistan	USA (United States)	25 Jun 53	205UNTS139	102773
Panama	USA (United States)	26 Jun 53	215UNTS77	102912
Brazil	USA (United States)	26 Jun 53	336UNTS241	104808
UK Great Britain	USA (United States)	26 Jun 53	183UNTS225	102432
Chile	USA (United States)	27 Jun 53	229UNTS193	103167
Chile	USA (United States)	27 Jun 53	229UNTS53	103160
Nicaragua	USA (United States)	30 Jun 53	215UNTS133	102917
UN Relief Palestin	United Arab Rep	30 Jun 53	190UNTS3	102554
Afghanistan	USA (United States)	30 Jun 53	215UNTS3	102908
ECSC (Coal/Steel)	ILO (Labor Org)	16 Jul 53	412UNTS273	200591
Brazil	IBRD (World Bank)	17 Jul 53	190UNTS149	102563
Canada	Mexico	27 Jul 53	192UNTS255	102604
Libya	UK Great Britain	29 Jul 53	186UNTS201	102492
IBRD (World Bank)	South Africa	28 Aug 53	180UNTS91	102377

PARTY ONE	PARTY TWO	DATE	CITATION	NUMBER
Exchange of information and documents (Cont.)				
IBRD (World Bank)	South Africa	28 Aug 53	180UNTS73	102376
Belgium	USA (United States)	02 Sep 53	200UNTS127	102700
Iceland	IBRD (World Bank)	04 Sep 53	188UNTS3	102519
Nicaragua	IBRD (World Bank)	04 Sep 53	186UNTS117	102487
Nicaragua	IBRD (World Bank)	04 Sep 53	186UNTS137	102488
Iceland	IBRD (World Bank)	04 Sep 53	178UNTS275	102344
IBRD (World Bank)	Turkey	10 Sep 53	187UNTS71	102502
Chile	IBRD (World Bank)	10 Sep 53	188UNTS25	102520
Colombia	IBRD (World Bank)	10 Sep 53	203UNTS3	102738
Panama	IBRD (World Bank)	25 Sep 53	188UNTS95	102522
Panama	IBRD (World Bank)	25 Sep 53	188UNTS71	102521
Spain	USA (United States)	26 Sep 53	207UNTS93	102802
Italy	IBRD (World Bank)	06 Oct 53	301UNTS135	104344
UNICEF (Children)	UK Great Britain	07 Oct 53	180UNTS59	102375
Multilateral		09 Oct 53	190UNTS49	102557
UN Relief Palestin	United Arab Rep	14 Oct 53	190UNTS13	102555
Japan	IBRD (World Bank)	15 Oct 53	187UNTS271	200511
Japan	IBRD (World Bank)	15 Oct 53	187UNTS367	200513
Japan	IBRD (World Bank)	15 Oct 53	187UNTS321	200512
Jordan	USA (United States)	21 Oct 53	222UNTS31	103020
Multilateral		26 Oct 53	207UNTS237	102809
Netherlands	USA (United States)	27 Oct 53	221UNTS357	103017
Luxembourg	Netherlands	06 Nov 53	198UNTS187	102664
Australia	Ceylon (Sri Lanka)	07 Nov 53	191UNTS249	102585
Canada	USA (United States)	12 Nov 53	223UNTS139	103062
Dominican Republic	United Nations	19 Nov 53	180UNTS45	102374
Australia	Yugoslavia	19 Nov 53	191UNTS241	102584
Japan	UNICEF (Children)	21 Nov 53	183UNTS297	200507
Israel	USA (United States)	25 Nov 53	219UNTS205	102976
Multilateral		11 Dec 53	218UNTS211	102957
Multilateral		11 Dec 53	218UNTS153	102956
Multilateral		11 Dec 53	218UNTS255	102958
Multilateral		11 Dec 53	218UNTS125	102954
Multilateral		11 Dec 53	191UNTS285	102588
Hungary	Romania	14 Dec 53	342UNTS151	104906
Brazil	IBRD (World Bank)	18 Dec 53	190UNTS179	102564
Brazil	IBRD (World Bank)	18 Dec 53	301UNTS229	104346
Jordan	Syria	23 Dec 53	204UNTS207	102759
Belgium	Lebanon	24 Dec 53	219UNTS153	102972
Chile	USA (United States)	30 Dec 53	236UNTS41	103315
USA (United States)	Yugoslavia	05 Jan 54	234UNTS267	103289
Libya	USA (United States)	11 Jan 54	229UNTS15	103157
Ethiopia	Greece	20 Jan 54	222UNTS281	103035
Japan	USA (United States)	21 Jan 54	223UNTS145	103063
Netherlands	USA (United States)	22 Jan 54	190UNTS207	102565
Syria	UK Great Britain	30 Jan 54	449UNTS47	106452
Pakistan	Turkey	04 Feb 54	211UNTS263	102858
Brazil	WHO (World Health)	04 Feb 54	233UNTS49	103250
Canada	Peru	18 Feb 54	411UNTS64	105915
Multilateral		19 Feb 54	214UNTS51	102899
Brazil	IBRD (World Bank)	24 Feb 54	301UNTS249	104347
Multilateral		25 Feb 54	215UNTS249	102922
Australia	IBRD (World Bank)	02 Mar 54	191UNTS103	102579
United Nations	Venezuela	05 Mar 54	187UNTS9	102498
Liberia	United Nations	09 Mar 54	187UNTS61	102501
Guatemala	United Nations	10 Mar 54	191UNTS271	102587
Afghanistan	USA (United States)	20 Mar 54	229UNTS7	103156
Italy	USA (United States)	31 Mar 54	235UNTS293	103311
Mexico	USA (United States)	06 Apr 54	236UNTS69	103317
Norway	IBRD (World Bank)	08 Apr 54	201UNTS131	102714
Peru	IBRD (World Bank)	12 Apr 54	190UNTS231	102567
Bulgaria	Czechoslovakia	13 Apr 54	501UNTS3	107314
USA (United States)	Yugoslavia	16 Apr 54	237UNTS77	103337
Luxembourg	USA (United States)	17 Apr 54	257UNTS255	103661
Lebanon	Yugoslavia	17 Apr 54	602UNTS199	108713

PARTY ONE	PARTY TWO	DATE	CITATION	NUMBER
Exchange of information and documents (Cont.)				
Multilateral		20 Apr 54	189UNTS11	102539
Ethiopia	USA (United States)	21 Apr 54	232UNTS299	103244
Netherlands	USA (United States)	07 May 54	213UNTS325	102895
UNICEF (Children)	Spain	07 May 54	190UNTS357	200515
Jordan	USA (United States)	13 May 54	234UNTS225	103285
Nepal	WHO (World Health)	13 May 54	204UNTS311	200522
Mexico	UNICEF (Children)	20 May 54	192UNTS3	102591
Multilateral		21 May 54	345UNTS285	104973
Multilateral		22 May 54	199UNTS3	102674
Honduras	USA (United States)	24 May 54	433UNTS155	106238
Iran	Switzerland	27 May 54	496UNTS273	107257
Multilateral		01 Jun 54	200UNTS235	200520
Pakistan	IBRD (World Bank)	02 Jun 54	324UNTS59	104678
Italy	Netherlands	04 Jun 54	289UNTS261	104222
Belgium	Netherlands	09 Jun 54	216UNTS121	102936
France	IBRD (World Bank)	10 Jun 54	210UNTS89	102836
Luxembourg	UK Great Britain	18 Jun 54	192UNTS33	102593
Lebanon	USA (United States)	18 Jun 54	233UNTS177	103262
Chile	USA (United States)	28 Jun 54	233UNTS3	103246
Italy	USA (United States)	28 Jun 54	237UNTS121	103340
Belgium	Ireland	30 Jun 54	212UNTS255	102876
Ecuador	USA (United States)	30 Jun 54	236UNTS163	103323
Multilateral		30 Jun 54	204UNTS99	102752
Ceylon (Sri Lanka)	IBRD (World Bank)	09 Jul 54	198UNTS313	200517
Bulgaria	Romania	22 Jul 54	362UNTS101	105184
Multilateral		29 Jul 54	249UNTS45	103500
Saudi Arabia	UK Great Britain	30 Jul 54	201UNTS317	102722
Chile	UK Great Britain	31 Jul 54	618UNTS353	108934
Multilateral		19 Aug 54	201UNTS51	102710
Philippines	Sweden	20 Aug 54	200UNTS121	102699
Pakistan	USA (United States)	23 Aug 54	234UNTS243	103287
New Zealand	UNICEF (Children)	26 Aug 54	198UNTS173	102663
Guatemala	USA (United States)	01 Sep 54	199UNTS51	102677
Libya	USA (United States)	09 Sep 54	224UNTS217	103078
Canada	USA (United States)	10 Sep 54	238UNTS97	103355
Greece	Italy	11 Sep 54	284UNTS313	104145
Belgium	South Africa	13 Sep 54	201UNTS15	102707
France	South Africa	17 Sep 54	216UNTS29	102930
Sweden	USSR (Soviet Union)	29 Sep 54	202UNTS259	102733
UNESCO (Educ/Cult)	UN Special Fund	29 Sep 54	363UNTS367	200572
Multilateral		06 Oct 54	201UNTS75	102711
El Salvador	IBRD (World Bank)	12 Oct 54	203UNTS37	102739
Germany, West	USA (United States)	15 Oct 54	239UNTS135	103375
USA (United States)	Yugoslavia	18 Oct 54	273UNTS163	103951
Norway	Philippines	20 Oct 54	216UNTS11	102928
Denmark	Philippines	20 Oct 54	216UNTS3	102927
Multilateral		23 Oct 54	332UNTS157	104761
Multilateral		27 Oct 54	201UNTS95	102712
Multilateral		29 Oct 54	201UNTS115	102713
Libya	USA (United States)	03 Nov 54	238UNTS227	103366
United Arab Rep	USA (United States)	06 Nov 54	237UNTS183	103344
Austria	IBRD (World Bank)	08 Nov 54	216UNTS305	200528
Poland	UK Great Britain	11 Nov 54	204UNTS137	102755
Peru	IBRD (World Bank)	12 Nov 54	209UNTS287	102831
India	IBRD (World Bank)	19 Nov 54	309UNTS159	104473
Austria	Yugoslavia	27 Nov 54	396UNTS75	105694
Guatemala	USA (United States)	13 Dec 54	237UNTS169	103343
Pakistan	United Arab Rep	13 Dec 54	255UNTS167	103610
Belgium	IBRD (World Bank)	14 Dec 54	210UNTS113	102837
Denmark	USA (United States)	15 Dec 54	213UNTS273	102890
Italy	Yugoslavia	18 Dec 54	284UNTS239	104141
Multilateral		21 Dec 54	258UNTS322	103678
Sweden	USA (United States)	22 Dec 54	228UNTS85	103143
Colombia	IBRD (World Bank)	29 Dec 54	211UNTS135	102851
Netherlands	UNICEF (Children)	31 Dec 54	202UNTS135	102729

PARTY ONE	PARTY TWO	DATE	CITATION	NUMBER
Exchange of information and documents (Cont.)				
USA (United States)	Yugoslavia	05 Jan 55	251UNTS29	103531
Pakistan	USA (United States)	11 Jan 55	251UNTS111	103537
Canada	Japan	12 Jan 55	311UNTS167	104503
Turkey	UK Great Britain	17 Jan 55	204UNTS195	102758
Pakistan	USA (United States)	18 Jan 55	241UNTS53	103423
Denmark	UK Great Britain	20 Jan 55	210UNTS303	102842
Italy	USA (United States)	26 Jan 55	238UNTS179	103361
Philippines	UK Great Britain	31 Jan 55	216UNTS51	102932
USA (United States)	Yugoslavia	09 Feb 55	241UNTS13	103419
Italy	USA (United States)	11 Feb 55	241UNTS91	103426
United Arab Rep	Yugoslavia	20 Feb 55	255UNTS199	103611
South Africa	USA (United States)	22 Feb 55	247UNTS247	103473
USA (United States)	Vietnam, South	07 Mar 55	277UNTS285	104013
Mexico	USA (United States)	09 Mar 55	263UNTS247	103776
Multilateral		12 Mar 55	211UNTS3	102844
India	IBRD (World Bank)	14 Mar 55	309UNTS129	104472
IBRD (World Bank)	UK Great Britain	15 Mar 55	265UNTS85	103808
Australia	IBRD (World Bank)	18 Mar 55	220UNTS131	102998
Multilateral		19 Mar 55	228UNTS95	103144
Iraq	United Arab Rep	23 Mar 55	311UNTS199	104504
Finland	IBRD (World Bank)	24 Mar 55	211UNTS305	200525
Colombia	IBRD (World Bank)	24 Mar 55	212UNTS217	102874
Haiti	USA (United States)	01 Apr 55	261UNTS361	103734
Germany, West	USA (United States)	04 Apr 55	279UNTS73	104034
Haiti	USA (United States)	05 Apr 55	270UNTS97	103895
Peru	IBRD (World Bank)	05 Apr 55	211UNTS115	102850
Peru	IBRD (World Bank)	19 Apr 55	221UNTS153	103007
Norway	IBRD (World Bank)	19 Apr 55	211UNTS159	102852
Taiwan	WHO (World Health)	21 Apr 55	210UNTS71	102835
Dominican Republic	USA (United States)	22 Apr 55	239UNTS325	103389
Argentina	USA (United States)	25 Apr 55	251UNTS283	103546
Philippines	USA (United States)	27 Apr 55	261UNTS351	103733
Czechoslovakia	Hungary	28 Apr 55	477UNTS197	106923
Finland	USA (United States)	06 May 55	251UNTS3	103529
USA (United States)	Vietnam, South	10 May 55	273UNTS157	103950
Netherlands	Norway	18 May 55	252UNTS269	103569
Italy	USA (United States)	23 May 55	251UNTS303	103547
Turkey	USA (United States)	26 May 55	262UNTS97	103739
Libya	USA (United States)	30 May 55	270UNTS43	103890
Korea, South	USA (United States)	31 May 55	251UNTS321	103548
Italy	IBRD (World Bank)	01 Jun 55	358UNTS203	105137
Pakistan	Sweden	04 Jun 55	228UNTS121	103146
Multilateral		06 Jun 55	219UNTS79	102968
Turkey	USA (United States)	10 Jun 55	238UNTS149	103359
Multilateral		14 Jun 55	212UNTS263	200526
Austria	USA (United States)	14 Jun 55	258UNTS37	103668
Austria	IBRD (World Bank)	14 Jun 55	221UNTS375	200531
Colombia	IBRD (World Bank)	15 Jun 55	248UNTS161	103494
Luxembourg	USA (United States)	15 Jun 55	264UNTS279	103798
Canada	USA (United States)	15 Jun 55	235UNTS201	103302
Canada	USA (United States)	15 Jun 55	235UNTS176	103301
UK Great Britain	USA (United States)	15 Jun 55	229UNTS73	103161
Belgium	USA (United States)	15 Jun 55	235UNTS133	103299
Pakistan	IBRD (World Bank)	20 Jun 55	230UNTS41	103176
Multilateral		22 Jun 55	249UNTS3	103498
Greece	USA (United States)	24 Jun 55	270UNTS361	103906
Greece	USA (United States)	24 Jun 55	270UNTS351	103905
Haiti	USA (United States)	24 Jun 55	264UNTS291	103800
Turkey	USA (United States)	29 Jun 55	269UNTS97	103878
Germany, West	USA (United States)	30 Jun 55	240UNTS47	103393
Italy	USA (United States)	30 Jun 55	258UNTS15	103667
Germany, West	USA (United States)	30 Jun 55	240UNTS69	103394
France	USA (United States)	01 Jul 55	270UNTS19	103888
Syria	United Arab Rep	03 Jul 55	393UNTS67	105652
Iran	WHO (World Health)	04 Jul 55	227UNTS65	103131

PARTY ONE	PARTY TWO	DATE	CITATION	NUMBER
Exchange of information and documents (Cont.)				
Multilateral		04 Jul 55	214UNTS10	102897
Laos	USA (United States)	08 Jul 55	278UNTS59	104021
Nicaragua	IBRD (World Bank)	08 Jul 55	229UNTS97	103162
Nicaragua	IBRD (World Bank)	08 Jul 55	229UNTS123	103163
Panama	IBRD (World Bank)	12 Jul 55	219UNTS127	102970
Israel	USA (United States)	12 Jul 55	219UNTS185	102974
Denmark	Finland	18 Jul 55	250UNTS167	103522
Netherlands	USA (United States)	18 Jul 55	240UNTS347	103412
Lebanon	USA (United States)	18 Jul 55	239UNTS247	103383
Switzerland	USA (United States)	18 Jul 55	239UNTS311	103388
Taiwan	USA (United States)	18 Jul 55	235UNTS221	103304
Colombia	USA (United States)	19 Jul 55	235UNTS233	103305
Spain	USA (United States)	19 Jul 55	239UNTS299	103387
USA (United States)	Venezuela	21 Jul 55	238UNTS121	103357
Portugal	USA (United States)	21 Jul 55	239UNTS283	103386
Libya	USA (United States)	21 Jul 55	264UNTS247	103796
Germany, West	UK Great Britain	22 Jul 55	269UNTS189	103881
Denmark	USA (United States)	25 Jul 55	235UNTS245	103306
Philippines	USA (United States)	27 Jul 55	239UNTS271	103385
Germany, East	Romania	28 Jul 55	342UNTS207	104909
Libya	USA (United States)	28 Jul 55	270UNTS269	103901
Libya	USA (United States)	28 Jul 55	270UNTS245	103900
Italy	USA (United States)	28 Jul 55	239UNTS235	103382
Libya	USA (United States)	28 Jul 55	270UNTS317	103903
Guatemala	IBRD (World Bank)	29 Jul 55	229UNTS167	103165
Argentina	USA (United States)	29 Jul 55	235UNTS121	103298
Brazil	USA (United States)	03 Aug 55	235UNTS159	103300
Greece	USA (United States)	04 Aug 55	235UNTS257	103307
Pakistan	IBRD (World Bank)	04 Aug 55	230UNTS79	103177
Peru	IBRD (World Bank)	05 Aug 55	218UNTS3	102950
Germany, East	Romania	05 Aug 55	342UNTS229	104910
Pakistan	IBRD (World Bank)	06 Aug 55	236UNTS195	103325
Chile	USA (United States)	08 Aug 55	235UNTS209	103303
IBRD (World Bank)	Thailand	09 Aug 55	221UNTS283	103011
Pakistan	USA (United States)	11 Aug 55	239UNTS259	103384
France	USA (United States)	11 Aug 55	251UNTS15	103530
Iran	USA (United States)	15 Aug 55	284UNTS93	104132
Lebanon	IBRD (World Bank)	25 Aug 55	230UNTS233	103188
Nicaragua	IBRD (World Bank)	26 Aug 55	229UNTS145	103164
France	IBRD (World Bank)	26 Aug 55	247UNTS305	103478
IBRD (World Bank)	Uruguay	29 Aug 55	243UNTS123	103450
Czechoslovakia	Germany, East	30 Aug 55	504UNTS279	107361
USSR (Soviet Union)	Yugoslavia	03 Sep 55	240UNTS267	103408
USA (United States)	USSR (Soviet Union)	05 Sep 55	256UNTS307	103641
Germany, East	Hungary	10 Sep 55	407UNTS132	105863
Bulgaria	UK Great Britain	22 Sep 55	222UNTS349	103039
France	USA (United States)	23 Sep 55	270UNTS341	103904
Bulgaria	Yugoslavia	01 Oct 55	396UNTS223	105698
France	Germany, West	04 Oct 55	353UNTS203	105044
Liberia	USA (United States)	06 Oct 55	275UNTS93	103978
Multilateral		12 Oct 55	560UNTS3	108165
Finland	USSR (Soviet Union)	19 Oct 55	353UNTS185	105043
Japan	IBRD (World Bank)	25 Oct 55	230UNTS379	200534
Fed Rhod/Nyasaland	Netherlands	02 Nov 55	263UNTS381	103784
Pakistan	Turkey	02 Nov 55	311UNTS217	104505
Netherlands	USA (United States)	04 Nov 55	269UNTS3	103867
Australia	South Africa	04 Nov 55	232UNTS143	103234
Multilateral		05 Nov 55	250UNTS201	103524
Burma	China People's Rep	08 Nov 55	306UNTS11	104430
Israel	USA (United States)	10 Nov 55	240UNTS3	103390
Japan	USA (United States)	14 Nov 55	240UNTS361	103413
Bulgaria	Yugoslavia	15 Nov 55	396UNTS191	105697
UK Great Britain	USA (United States)	15 Nov 55	231UNTS185	103219
Brazil	USA (United States)	16 Nov 55	239UNTS207	103381
Belgium	UK Great Britain	18 Nov 55	222UNTS327	103038

PARTY ONE	PARTY TWO	DATE	CITATION	NUMBER
Exchange of information and documents (Cont.)				
Guatemala	UNICEF (Children)	22 Nov 55	221UNTS305	103012
India	Japan	26 Nov 55	311UNTS243	104506
IBRD (World Bank)	South Africa	28 Nov 55	230UNTS101	103178
Bulgaria	Yugoslavia	11 Dec 55	378UNTS49	105417
United Arab Rep	USA (United States)	14 Dec 55	240UNTS37	103392
USSR (Soviet Union)	Yugoslavia	19 Dec 55	378UNTS127	105423
Costa Rica	Guatemala	20 Dec 55	280UNTS121	104056
Colombia	USA (United States)	20 Dec 55	241UNTS25	103421
Honduras	IBRD (World Bank)	22 Dec 55	230UNTS262	103189
USA (United States)	Uruguay	13 Jan 56	240UNTS401	103415
Germany, West	Sweden	17 Jan 56	262UNTS301	103758
Sweden	USA (United States)	18 Jan 56	240UNTS413	103416
Australia	Japan	19 Jan 56	311UNTS291	104507
Nicaragua	USA (United States)	21 Jan 56	367UNTS3	105224
Netherlands	USA (United States)	22 Jan 56	287UNTS121	104181
Peru	USA (United States)	25 Jan 56	240UNTS425	103417
Romania	Yugoslavia	01 Feb 56	362UNTS203	105189
Multilateral		02 Feb 56	227UNTS153	103137
Hungary	Romania	03 Feb 56	362UNTS233	105190
India	USA (United States)	03 Feb 56	272UNTS75	103932
Korea, South	USA (United States)	03 Feb 56	240UNTS129	103401
Luxembourg	Netherlands	06 Feb 56	261UNTS17	103723
Austria	USA (United States)	07 Feb 56	272UNTS117	103933
Japan	USA (United States)	10 Feb 56	275UNTS157	103980
Bulgaria	Yugoslavia	10 Feb 56	349UNTS21	105007
Multilateral		10 Feb 56	228UNTS167	103150
Multilateral		10 Feb 56	228UNTS189	103151
Czechoslovakia	Yugoslavia	11 Feb 56	397UNTS135	105703
Germany, West	USA (United States)	13 Feb 56	253UNTS119	103580
Iran	USA (United States)	20 Feb 56	272UNTS135	103934
Japan	IBRD (World Bank)	21 Feb 56	248UNTS321	200543
Indonesia	USA (United States)	02 Mar 56	271UNTS345	103925
Pakistan	USA (United States)	02 Mar 56	271UNTS371	103927
Multilateral		03 Mar 56	243UNTS169	103452
Spain	USA (United States)	05 Mar 56	271UNTS329	103924
Ethiopia	Italy	05 Mar 56	267UNTS189	103844
France	Sweden	07 Mar 56	369UNTS155	105256
Germany, West	USA (United States)	07 Mar 56	271UNTS361	103926
Turkey	USA (United States)	12 Mar 56	272UNTS21	103929
Chile	USA (United States)	13 Mar 56	275UNTS49	103975
Korea, South	USA (United States)	13 Mar 56	272UNTS3	103928
Thailand	USA (United States)	13 Mar 56	253UNTS105	103579
Colombia	USA (United States)	14 Mar 56	271UNTS303	103922
Ireland	USA (United States)	16 Mar 56	317UNTS195	104604
Germany, West	Sweden	22 Mar 56	262UNTS401	103762
Bulgaria	Yugoslavia	23 Mar 56	367UNTS213	105230
USA (United States)	Uruguay	23 Mar 56	376UNTS311	105386
France	USA (United States)	23 Mar 56	278UNTS131	104029
Ecuador	IBRD (World Bank)	26 Mar 56	292UNTS391	104277
Colombia	USA (United States)	27 Mar 56	273UNTS235	103954
Netherlands	USA (United States)	27 Mar 56	285UNTS231	104154
Sweden	USSR (Soviet Union)	31 Mar 56	259UNTS239	103691
Norway	USSR (Soviet Union)	31 Mar 56	259UNTS205	103690
Denmark	USSR (Soviet Union)	31 Mar 56	259UNTS169	103689
Taiwan	USA (United States)	03 Apr 56	268UNTS315	103864
Bulgaria	Yugoslavia	04 Apr 56	391UNTS47	105616
Belgium	Germany, West	14 Apr 56	344UNTS103	104945
Germany, West	USA (United States)	18 Apr 56	271UNTS319	103923
Bulgaria	Greece	19 Apr 56	594UNTS131	108600
Multilateral		25 Apr 56	270UNTS103	103896
Cambodia	UNICEF (Children)	28 Apr 56	136UNTS341	200446
Ceylon (Sri Lanka)	USA (United States)	28 Apr 56	274UNTS35	103956
Multilateral		30 Apr 56	310UNTS229	104494
Paraguay	USA (United States)	02 May 56	268UNTS299	103863
Germany, West	Switzerland	02 May 56	559UNTS157	108158

PARTY ONE	PARTY TWO	DATE	CITATION	NUMBER
Exchange of information and documents (Cont.)				
Norway	IBRD (World Bank)	03 May 56	243UNTS281	103455
Peru	USA (United States)	03 May 56	272UNTS59	103931
Burma	IBRD (World Bank)	04 May 56	253UNTS179	103584
Burma	IBRD (World Bank)	04 May 56	253UNTS209	103585
Haiti	IBRD (World Bank)	07 May 56	252UNTS279	103570
Peru	USA (United States)	07 May 56	268UNTS285	103862
Costa Rica	USA (United States)	18 May 56	404UNTS237	105814
Italy	South Africa	21 May 56	255UNTS323	103616
Nicaragua	IBRD (World Bank)	22 May 56	253UNTS233	103586
Bulgaria	Yugoslavia	22 May 56	367UNTS119	105229
Finland	IBRD (World Bank)	22 May 56	248UNTS57	103485
Japan	Switzerland	24 May 56	312UNTS3	104509
Portugal	USA (United States)	24 May 56	268UNTS323	103865
Greece	Italy	26 May 56	496UNTS301	107258
Fed Rhod/Nyasaland	South Africa	30 May 56	255UNTS317	103615
Multilateral		31 May 56	251UNTS181	103541
Czechoslovakia	USSR (Soviet Union)	01 Jun 56	259UNTS341	103696
Italy	Switzerland	04 Jun 56	378UNTS311	105429
Colombia	IBRD (World Bank)	06 Jun 56	248UNTS139	103493
Multilateral		07 Jun 56	381UNTS145	105470
Austria	USA (United States)	08 Jun 56	253UNTS139	103581
Multilateral		08 Jun 56	247UNTS366	200541
India	Thailand	12 Jun 56	255UNTS341	103617
Germany, West	Ireland	12 Jun 56	353UNTS121	105040
New Zealand	USA (United States)	13 Jun 56	253UNTS155	103582
Multilateral		14 Jun 56	265UNTS125	103809
Austria	Yugoslavia	15 Jun 56	396UNTS117	105695
Dominican Republic	USA (United States)	15 Jun 56	265UNTS227	103815
Czechoslovakia	Yugoslavia	16 Jun 56	552UNTS325	108064
France	USA (United States)	19 Jun 56	281UNTS341	104087
Multilateral		20 Jun 56	268UNTS3	103850
Switzerland	USA (United States)	21 Jun 56	279UNTS41	104033
IBRD (World Bank)	UK Great Britain	21 Jun 56	285UNTS355	104157
Fed Rhod/Nyasaland	IBRD (World Bank)	21 Jun 56	285UNTS317	104156
Australia	USA (United States)	22 Jun 56	283UNTS275	104123
Multilateral		26 Jun 56	321UNTS2	104650
Multilateral		26 Jun 56	253UNTS12	103573
Cuba	USA (United States)	26 Jun 56	293UNTS257	104294
India	IBRD (World Bank)	26 Jun 56	301UNTS3	104341
Israel	USA (United States)	26 Jun 56	257UNTS55	103649
Hungary	UK Great Britain	27 Jun 56	249UNTS19	103499
Italy	Switzerland	29 Jun 56	284UNTS299	104144
Poland	USSR (Soviet Union)	30 Jun 56	259UNTS311	103694
Multilateral		02 Jul 56	540UNTS110	107846
Multilateral		02 Jul 56	248UNTS37	103484
Korea, South	USA (United States)	02 Jul 56	281UNTS41	104067
Lebanon	UNICEF (Children)	03 Jul 56	324UNTS145	104683
Czechoslovakia	Yugoslavia	03 Jul 56	397UNTS165	105704
Poland	Yugoslavia	06 Jul 56	281UNTS143	104076
Multilateral		09 Jul 56	314UNTS3	104539
Ecuador	USA (United States)	19 Jul 56	372UNTS149	105295
Germany, West	UK Great Britain	31 Jul 56	252UNTS93	103559
Australia	Netherlands	01 Aug 56	280UNTS3	104047
UNICEF (Children)	Sudan	07 Aug 56	248UNTS307	200542
Pakistan	USA (United States)	07 Aug 56	281UNTS75	104071
Greece	USA (United States)	08 Aug 56	277UNTS203	104007
Taiwan	USA (United States)	14 Aug 56	281UNTS257	104083
Guatemala	USA (United States)	15 Aug 56	288UNTS181	104205
Netherlands	USA (United States)	16 Aug 56	279UNTS3	104031
Guatemala	Honduras	22 Aug 56	263UNTS49	103767
Greece	Romania	25 Aug 56	299UNTS231	104315
India	USA (United States)	29 Aug 56	278UNTS25	104019
Multilateral		31 Aug 56	249UNTS158	103506
Canada	France	04 Sep 56	305UNTS79	104415
Multilateral		07 Sep 56	266UNTS3	103822

PARTY ONE	PARTY TWO	DATE	CITATION	NUMBER
Exchange of information and documents (Cont.)				
Israel	USA (United States)	11 Sep 56	277UNTS215	104008
Greece	Yugoslavia	11 Sep 56	552UNTS311	108063
Multilateral		11 Sep 56	266UNTS221	103832
Costa Rica	IBRD (World Bank)	18 Sep 56	260UNTS369	103721
Austria	IBRD (World Bank)	21 Sep 56	259UNTS17	103681
Austria	IBRD (World Bank)	21 Sep 56	259UNTS43	103682
Belgium	Germany, West	24 Sep 56	263UNTS31	103766
Multilateral		25 Sep 56	334UNTS13	104766
Romania	Yugoslavia	25 Sep 56	395UNTS147	105683
Multilateral		25 Sep 56	334UNTS89	104767
Germany, West	Netherlands	28 Sep 56	327UNTS185	104722
Canada	France	04 Oct 56	305UNTS65	104414
Multilateral		05 Oct 56	251UNTS245	103544
Multilateral		05 Oct 56	251UNTS267	103545
Germany, West	Thailand	09 Oct 56	258UNTS143	103676
Italy	IBRD (World Bank)	11 Oct 56	359UNTS3	105138
Romania	Vietnam, North	12 Oct 56	342UNTS173	104907
IBRD (World Bank)	Thailand	12 Oct 56	261UNTS117	103728
Spain	USA (United States)	23 Oct 56	277UNTS105	104001
IBRD (World Bank)	Uruguay	25 Oct 56	265UNTS59	103807
Multilateral		26 Oct 56	276UNTS3	103988
Romania	Yugoslavia	27 Oct 56	389UNTS33	105590
Austria	UK Great Britain	27 Oct 56	264UNTS67	103789
India	Japan	29 Oct 56	318UNTS289	104622
Italy	USA (United States)	30 Oct 56	263UNTS221	103775
Chile	IBRD (World Bank)	01 Nov 56	261UNTS27	103724
USA (United States)	Yugoslavia	03 Nov 56	277UNTS119	104002
Turkey	USA (United States)	12 Nov 56	282UNTS77	104093
Australia	IBRD (World Bank)	15 Nov 56	288UNTS117	104201
Austria	USA (United States)	21 Nov 56	290UNTS181	104237
Multilateral		21 Nov 56	253UNTS266	103588
Peru	Switzerland	23 Nov 56	411UNTS97	105916
Albania	Yugoslavia	23 Nov 56	386UNTS73	105539
Korea, South	USA (United States)	28 Nov 56	302UNTS281	104367
Czechoslovakia	USSR (Soviet Union)	30 Nov 56	266UNTS243	103833
Australia	IBRD (World Bank)	03 Dec 56	288UNTS99	104200
Burma	USA (United States)	04 Dec 56	268UNTS189	103858
Finland	USSR (Soviet Union)	07 Dec 56	258UNTS89	103673
Germany, East	Romania	08 Dec 56	362UNTS189	105188
France	USA (United States)	14 Dec 56	266UNTS117	103826
Multilateral		15 Dec 56	278UNTS73	104023
India	IBRD (World Bank)	19 Dec 56	310UNTS75	104489
Japan	IBRD (World Bank)	19 Dec 56	268UNTS203	103859
Japan	IBRD (World Bank)	19 Dec 56	264UNTS179	103793
Multilateral		21 Dec 56	427UNTS81	106147
Bulgaria	Yugoslavia	24 Dec 56	397UNTS3	105699
Brazil	USA (United States)	31 Dec 56	266UNTS151	103829
UNESCO (Educ/Cult)	Tunisia	03 Jan 57	257UNTS21	103645
Colombia	USA (United States)	09 Jan 57	462UNTS151	106676
Multilateral		15 Jan 57	376UNTS122	105378
Iran	USA (United States)	16 Jan 57	308UNTS147	104460
Iran	IBRD (World Bank)	22 Jan 57	317UNTS129	104600
Iceland	Thailand	22 Jan 57	312UNTS63	104511
Multilateral		23 Jan 57	259UNTS426	103701
Ethiopia	IBRD (World Bank)	28 Jan 57	286UNTS307	104175
Denmark	Germany, West	29 Jan 57	302UNTS75	104354
Germany, West	Netherlands	29 Jan 57	314UNTS173	104548
Czechoslovakia	Yugoslavia	29 Jan 57	300UNTS249	104339
Germany, West	Sweden	29 Jan 57	393UNTS113	105654
Germany, West	Norway	29 Jan 57	353UNTS39	105037
Korea, South	USA (United States)	30 Jan 57	278UNTS85	104024
Germany, East	Poland	01 Feb 57	319UNTS115	104632
Norway	USA (United States)	05 Feb 57	279UNTS169	104038
Multilateral		09 Feb 57	314UNTS105	104546
Ecuador	USA (United States)	15 Feb 57	279UNTS155	104037

PARTY ONE	PARTY TWO	DATE	CITATION	NUMBER
Exchange of information and documents (Cont.)				
Multilateral		17 Feb 57	271UNTS2	103907
Norway	USA (United States)	25 Feb 57	284UNTS19	104126
Canada	USA (United States)	26 Feb 57	279UNTS179	104039
Chile	USA (United States)	01 Mar 57	283UNTS127	104112
Thailand	USA (United States)	04 Mar 57	279UNTS235	104043
Iran	USA (United States)	05 Mar 57	342UNTS29	104898
India	IBRD (World Bank)	05 Mar 57	272UNTS201	103939
Netherlands	Yugoslavia	13 Mar 57	327UNTS227	104723
Peru	IBRD (World Bank)	13 Mar 57	274UNTS59	103958
Burma	USA (United States)	21 Mar 57	300UNTS11	104327
Multilateral		25 Mar 57	294UNTS259	104301
Multilateral		25 Mar 57	294UNTS2	104300
Multilateral		28 Mar 57	271UNTS30	103908
Italy	UK Great Britain	29 Mar 57	310UNTS11	104481
Australia	UK Great Britain	01 Apr 57	271UNTS235	103918
Morocco	USA (United States)	02 Apr 57	288UNTS157	104203
Libya	USA (United States)	04 Apr 57	283UNTS181	104116
Poland	Vietnam, North	06 Apr 57	432UNTS255	106224
Canada	USA (United States)	09 Apr 57	283UNTS217	104119
Multilateral		09 Apr 57	274UNTS172	103965
Germany, West	Yugoslavia	10 Apr 57	463UNTS269	106708
Denmark	Pakistan	10 Apr 57	302UNTS53	104353
Iceland	USA (United States)	11 Apr 57	283UNTS107	104110
Colombia	USA (United States)	16 Apr 57	283UNTS245	104121
Peru	USA (United States)	17 Apr 57	283UNTS3	104102
Bulgaria	Yugoslavia	19 Apr 57	349UNTS3	105006
Ecuador	USA (United States)	24 Apr 57	284UNTS3	104124
Ethiopia	USA (United States)	25 Apr 57	283UNTS205	104118
Peru	USA (United States)	02 May 57	283UNTS55	104106
Austria	USA (United States)	10 May 57	283UNTS15	104103
Finland	USA (United States)	10 May 57	283UNTS43	104105
Netherlands	IBRD (World Bank)	15 May 57	274UNTS211	103967
Albania	Yugoslavia	20 May 57	363UNTS99	105203
Czechoslovakia	Yugoslavia	22 May 57	391UNTS33	105615
Australia	Germany, West	22 May 57	357UNTS45	105105
ICJ Option Clause	Pakistan	23 May 57	269UNTS77	103875
Multilateral		24 May 57	268UNTS270	103861
Hungary	Yugoslavia	25 May 57	477UNTS219	106924
India	IBRD (World Bank)	29 May 57	309UNTS201	104474
Ecuador	USA (United States)	31 May 57	304UNTS61	104391
Belgium	Hungary	01 Jun 57	291UNTS17	104242
Argentina	USA (United States)	03 Jun 57	291UNTS61	104244
Bulgaria	Czechoslovakia	03 Jun 57	292UNTS3	104261
Ghana	USA (United States)	03 Jun 57	284UNTS63	104129
Bulgaria	Yugoslavia	04 Jun 57	349UNTS35	105008
Poland	USA (United States)	07 Jun 57	291UNTS41	104243
Bolivia	USA (United States)	07 Jun 57	291UNTS77	104245
Czechoslovakia	Yugoslavia	11 Jun 57	504UNTS107	107355
Nicaragua	USA (United States)	11 Jun 57	304UNTS267	104402
Afghanistan	Pakistan	13 Jun 57	327UNTS51	104717
Italy	USA (United States)	22 Jun 57	284UNTS51	104128
Philippines	USA (United States)	25 Jun 57	289UNTS279	104224
Multilateral		26 Jun 57	325UNTS279	104704
Belgium	IBRD (World Bank)	26 Jun 57	322UNTS301	104661
Jordan	USA (United States)	27 Jun 57	288UNTS269	104209
Tunisia	USA (United States)	28 Jun 57	289UNTS301	104226
Germany, West	USA (United States)	28 Jun 57	288UNTS339	104213
Czechoslovakia	United Arab Rep	30 Jun 57	411UNTS126	105917
Pakistan	USA (United States)	01 Jul 57	344UNTS203	104951
Italy	USA (United States)	03 Jul 57	308UNTS195	104462
Germany, West	USA (United States)	03 Jul 57	288UNTS305	104212
New Zealand	UK Great Britain	04 Jul 57	402UNTS109	105780
South Africa	USA (United States)	08 Jul 57	290UNTS147	104234
Multilateral		09 Jul 57	274UNTS300	103972
Norway	UK Great Britain	12 Jul 57	310UNTS41	104485

PARTY ONE	PARTY TWO	DATE	CITATION	NUMBER
Exchange of information and documents (Cont.)				
Germany, West	Italy	12 Jul 57	291UNTS181	104252
India	IBRD (World Bank)	12 Jul 57	288UNTS135	104202
Chile	IBRD (World Bank)	24 Jul 57	282UNTS189	104099
Chile	IBRD (World Bank)	24 Jul 57	282UNTS139	104098
Morocco	UNICEF (Children)	31 Jul 57	282UNTS99	104095
Japan	IBRD (World Bank)	09 Aug 57	293UNTS59	104286
Spain	USA (United States)	16 Aug 57	307UNTS169	104449
Netherlands	Romania	27 Aug 57	342UNTS309	104914
Czechoslovakia	USSR (Soviet Union)	31 Aug 57	308UNTS3	104456
Belgium	IBRD (World Bank)	10 Sep 57	286UNTS291	104174
IBRD (World Bank)	Thailand	12 Sep 57	299UNTS349	104324
Sweden	UK Great Britain	20 Sep 57	310UNTS49	104486
Ecuador	IBRD (World Bank)	20 Sep 57	289UNTS237	104221
Burma	WHO (World Health)	20 Sep 57	282UNTS113	104096
Ecuador	IBRD (World Bank)	20 Sep 57	293UNTS135	104291
New Zealand	UK Great Britain	20 Sep 57	287UNTS105	104180
Spain	USA (United States)	23 Sep 57	290UNTS261	104238
USA (United States)	Venezuela	24 Sep 57	293UNTS307	104298
Multilateral		27 Sep 57	299UNTS211	104314
IBRD (World Bank)	South Africa	01 Oct 57	280UNTS285	104065
Belgium	UK Great Britain	03 Oct 57	394UNTS69	105669
Multilateral		03 Oct 57	366UNTS87	105216
Italy	Pakistan	05 Oct 57	353UNTS91	105039
Austria	IBRD (World Bank)	10 Oct 57	301UNTS95	104343
Cambodia	USA (United States)	17 Oct 57	299UNTS203	104313
Fed of Malaya	UK Great Britain	18 Oct 57	335UNTS3	104775
Pakistan	IBRD (World Bank)	18 Oct 57	299UNTS303	104322
Czechoslovakia	United Arab Rep	19 Oct 57	530UNTS181	107681
United Arab Rep	USSR (Soviet Union)	19 Oct 57	292UNTS151	104271
Netherlands	UK Great Britain	22 Oct 57	313UNTS309	104538
Mexico	USA (United States)	23 Oct 57	300UNTS35	104330
Germany, East	Hungary	25 Oct 57	408UNTS156	105869
Germany, East	Hungary	30 Oct 57	408UNTS4	105867
Multilateral		05 Nov 57	285UNTS301	104155
Israel	USA (United States)	07 Nov 57	302UNTS255	104365
Germany, East	Hungary	13 Nov 57	407UNTS216	105866
Pakistan	USA (United States)	15 Nov 57	303UNTS173	104380
Hungary	Yugoslavia	20 Nov 57	477UNTS267	106925
India	IBRD (World Bank)	20 Nov 57	301UNTS47	104342
Philippines	IBRD (World Bank)	22 Nov 57	293UNTS83	104287
Italy	Spain	25 Nov 57	378UNTS289	105428
Argentina	Italy	25 Nov 57	305UNTS275	104424
Argentina	Denmark	25 Nov 57	299UNTS83	104308
Belgium	IBRD (World Bank)	27 Nov 57	292UNTS175	104273
Germany, East	USSR (Soviet Union)	28 Nov 57	305UNTS113	104419
Belgium	USA (United States)	03 Dec 57	303UNTS45	104370
Czechoslovakia	USSR (Soviet Union)	04 Dec 57	313UNTS291	104537
Ireland	Sweden	05 Dec 57	428UNTS221	106176
Hungary	Yugoslavia	06 Dec 57	519UNTS215	107509
Japan	USSR (Soviet Union)	06 Dec 57	325UNTS35	104694
Italy	Monaco	06 Dec 57	363UNTS59	105199
Italy	Monaco	06 Dec 57	363UNTS45	105198
Bulgaria	USSR (Soviet Union)	12 Dec 57	317UNTS217	104606
Hungary	Romania	17 Dec 57	477UNTS303	106926
Pakistan	IBRD (World Bank)	17 Dec 57	299UNTS321	104323
Greece	USA (United States)	18 Dec 57	303UNTS159	104379
UK Great Britain	USSR (Soviet Union)	19 Dec 57	351UNTS235	105026
France	USA (United States)	27 Dec 57	307UNTS79	104444
Poland	USSR (Soviet Union)	28 Dec 57	320UNTS3	104638
Italy	UK Great Britain	28 Dec 57	305UNTS357	104425
Australia	Ireland	30 Dec 57	497UNTS29	107260
Canada	Switzerland	10 Jan 58	464UNTS21	106710
Mexico	IBRD (World Bank)	14 Jan 58	293UNTS167	104292
Poland	Yugoslavia	16 Jan 58	340UNTS181	104864
Belgium	Germany, West	17 Jan 58	328UNTS173	104735

PARTY ONE	PARTY TWO	DATE	CITATION	NUMBER
Exchange of information and documents (Cont.)				
Turkey	USA (United States)	20 Jan 58	304UNTS15	104389
Ghana	WHO (World Health)	21 Jan 58	307UNTS3	104437
Brazil	IBRD (World Bank)	22 Jan 58	323UNTS99	104666
USA (United States)	USSR (Soviet Union)	27 Jan 58	301UNTS405	104350
Spain	USA (United States)	27 Jan 58	303UNTS247	104384
Multilateral		29 Jan 58	339UNTS23	104845
Germany, West	Netherlands	30 Jan 58	315UNTS117	104563
Czechoslovakia	Poland	31 Jan 58	431UNTS99	106214
USA (United States)	Yugoslavia	03 Feb 58	304UNTS293	104404
Multilateral		03 Feb 58	381UNTS165	105471
UK Great Britain	USA (United States)	03 Feb 58	307UNTS199	104450
Indonesia	WHO (World Health)	05 Feb 58	307UNTS15	104438
Korea, South	USA (United States)	05 Feb 58	307UNTS121	104447
Bulgaria	Netherlands	07 Feb 58	335UNTS45	104777
Australia	UK Great Britain	07 Feb 58	335UNTS23	104776
Afghanistan	Turkey	08 Feb 58	464UNTS39	106711
Sudan	Sweden	17 Feb 58	393UNTS161	105655
Austria	Sweden	19 Feb 58	427UNTS211	106155
Finland	USA (United States)	21 Feb 58	304UNTS253	104401
France	USA (United States)	28 Feb 58	366UNTS343	105222
Norway	Pakistan	05 Mar 58	334UNTS199	104769
Pakistan	Sweden	06 Mar 58	393UNTS181	105656
Czechoslovakia	Hungary	12 Mar 58	408UNTS178	105870
Bulgaria	Hungary	13 Mar 58	438UNTS173	106316
Bulgaria	Hungary	13 Mar 58	438UNTS191	106317
Colombia	USA (United States)	14 Mar 58	308UNTS115	104459
Multilateral		15 Mar 58	292UNTS273	104276
Germany, West	Portugal	21 Mar 58	464UNTS71	106712
Bulgaria	Yugoslavia	21 Mar 58	386UNTS119	105541
Czechoslovakia	Romania	25 Mar 58	339UNTS77	104846
Belgium	Luxembourg	28 Mar 58	303UNTS101	104372
Czechoslovakia	Poland	29 Mar 58	340UNTS199	104865
Sudan	USA (United States)	31 Mar 58	308UNTS105	104458
Romania	USSR (Soviet Union)	03 Apr 58	313UNTS167	104535
Bulgaria	Yugoslavia	04 Apr 58	367UNTS89	105228
Peru	USA (United States)	09 Apr 58	316UNTS37	104576
Israel	WHO (World Health)	11 Apr 58	307UNTS27	104439
Belgium	Iran	14 Apr 58	381UNTS309	105473
Multilateral		15 Apr 58	539UNTS27	107822
Germany, West	Netherlands	16 Apr 58	486UNTS331	107084
Sweden	Yugoslavia	18 Apr 58	393UNTS225	105658
Taiwan	USA (United States)	18 Apr 58	308UNTS179	104461
Pakistan	IBRD (World Bank)	23 Apr 58	323UNTS253	104672
Chile	IBRD (World Bank)	28 Apr 58	359UNTS89	105140
Austria	IBRD (World Bank)	28 Apr 58	359UNTS145	105142
Saudi Arabia	USA (United States)	01 May 58	315UNTS221	104571
IBRD (World Bank)	UK Great Britain	02 May 58	324UNTS25	104677
Austria	Netherlands	03 May 58	342UNTS3	104895
Iceland	USA (United States)	03 May 58	316UNTS137	104581
Mexico	IBRD (World Bank)	05 May 58	309UNTS3	104466
Hungary	Poland	08 May 58	408UNTS212	105872
Honduras	IBRD (World Bank)	09 May 58	323UNTS4	104662
Arab League	ILO (Labor Org)	26 May 58	302UNTS343	200549
Burma	USA (United States)	27 May 58	315UNTS197	104569
India	USSR (Soviet Union)	02 Jun 58	393UNTS3	105650
Philippines	USA (United States)	03 Jun 58	316UNTS3	104573
Pakistan	Portugal	07 Jun 58	320UNTS225	104645
Belgium	South Africa	11 Jun 58	335UNTS63	104778
Japan	IBRD (World Bank)	13 Jun 58	312UNTS159	104518
Germany, East	Hungary	14 Jun 58	407UNTS78	105861
IBRD (World Bank)	UK Great Britain	16 Jun 58	309UNTS35	104467
Ceylon (Sri Lanka)	USA (United States)	18 Jun 58	316UNTS15	104574
Multilateral		19 Jun 58	306UNTS236	200550
Japan	USA (United States)	19 Jun 58	325UNTS143	104699
Austria	Belgium	20 Jun 58	312UNTS95	104513

PARTY ONE	PARTY TWO	DATE	CITATION	NUMBER
Exchange of information and documents (Cont.)				
WHO (World Health)	Sudan	21 Jun 58	307UNTS235	104453
Italy	Morocco	24 Jun 58	363UNTS23	105197
Multilateral		24 Jun 58	348UNTS275	105005
India	IBRD (World Bank)	25 Jun 58	323UNTS131	104667
Multilateral		25 Jun 58	362UNTS31	105181
India	IBRD (World Bank)	25 Jun 58	323UNTS157	104668
Multilateral		26 Jun 58	324UNTS97	104679
Albania	USSR (Soviet Union)	30 Jun 58	328UNTS3	104729
Philippines	USA (United States)	30 Jun 58	321UNTS51	104653
Netherlands	Norway	30 Jun 58	346UNTS217	104982
Ecuador	USA (United States)	30 Jun 58	336UNTS11	104796
UK Great Britain	USA (United States)	03 Jul 58	326UNTS3	104707
Belgium	Pakistan	04 Jul 58	387UNTS305	105569
EEC (Econ Commnty)	ILO (Labor Org)	07 Jul 58	312UNTS387	200551
Ethiopia	UK Great Britain	07 Jul 58	331UNTS3	104749
Hungary	USSR (Soviet Union)	15 Jul 58	322UNTS3	104656
Germany, East	Romania	15 Jul 58	395UNTS3	105681
Germany, East	Romania	15 Jul 58	387UNTS115	105560
Portugal	UK Great Britain	18 Jul 58	313UNTS109	104532
IBRD (World Bank)	Sudan	21 Jul 58	323UNTS183	104669
Netherlands	Yugoslavia	22 Jul 58	386UNTS263	105546
India	IBRD (World Bank)	23 Jul 58	317UNTS3	104590
Ghana	UNICEF (Children)	12 Aug 58	309UNTS103	104469
Romania	United Arab Rep	14 Aug 58	405UNTS189	105834
Cuba	USA (United States)	15 Aug 58	358UNTS63	105124
Japan	IBRD (World Bank)	18 Aug 58	323UNTS205	104670
Mongolia	USSR (Soviet Union)	25 Aug 58	322UNTS105	104657
Australia	Germany, West	27 Aug 58	320UNTS303	104649
Japan	IBRD (World Bank)	10 Sep 58	318UNTS133	104612
Japan	IBRD (World Bank)	10 Sep 58	323UNTS297	104673
India	IBRD (World Bank)	16 Sep 58	323UNTS235	104671
Peru	IBRD (World Bank)	17 Sep 58	323UNTS27	104663
Ceylon (Sri Lanka)	IBRD (World Bank)	17 Sep 58	323UNTS51	104664
Fed of Malaya	IBRD (World Bank)	22 Sep 58	323UNTS71	104665
Ghana	UK Great Britain	24 Sep 58	411UNTS146	105918
India	USA (United States)	26 Sep 58	336UNTS59	104798
Australia	South Africa	26 Sep 58	335UNTS121	104780
Ghana	USA (United States)	30 Sep 58	336UNTS169	104805
FAO (Food Agri)	IAEA (Atom Energy)	01 Oct 58	361UNTS211	200571
IAEA (Atom Energy)	UNESCO (Educ/Cult)	01 Oct 58	339UNTS373	200558
Brazil	IBRD (World Bank)	03 Oct 58	337UNTS177	104823
Hungary	Romania	07 Oct 58	416UNTS199	106004
USA (United States)	Venezuela	08 Oct 58	371UNTS69	105271
Ecuador	IBRD (World Bank)	09 Oct 58	337UNTS299	104827
Fed Rhod/Nyasaland	South Africa	11 Oct 58	373UNTS75	105315
Czechoslovakia	Romania	25 Oct 58	417UNTS37	106006
Czechoslovakia	Romania	25 Oct 58	338UNTS301	104843
Canada	USA (United States)	31 Oct 58	391UNTS219	105626
Multilateral		05 Nov 58	613UNTS385	200630
Multilateral		05 Nov 58	428UNTS73	106169
Israel	USA (United States)	06 Nov 58	336UNTS275	104810
Euratom	USA (United States)	08 Nov 58	338UNTS135	104835
France	Israel	12 Nov 58	345UNTS79	104960
Pakistan	USA (United States)	26 Nov 58	337UNTS3	104812
Austria	IBRD (World Bank)	02 Dec 58	340UNTS3	104856
IBRD (World Bank)	South Africa	02 Dec 58	324UNTS3	104676
Bulgaria	Romania	03 Dec 58	417UNTS133	106007
Multilateral		03 Dec 58	398UNTS9	105715
Iran	Japan	09 Dec 58	325UNTS221	104701
Germany, West	USA (United States)	11 Dec 58	337UNTS31	104813
Colombia	IBRD (World Bank)	15 Dec 58	354UNTS233	105065
Korea, South	USA (United States)	18 Dec 58	325UNTS233	104702
USA (United States)	Yugoslavia	22 Dec 58	338UNTS243	104839
United Arab Rep	USA (United States)	24 Dec 58	338UNTS221	104837
UK Great Britain	USA (United States)	30 Dec 58	338UNTS281	104841

PARTY ONE	PARTY TWO	DATE	CITATION	NUMBER
Exchange of information and documents (Cont.)				
Finland	USA (United States)	30 Dec 58	340UNTS259	104869
Finland	Switzerland	07 Jan 59	353UNTS173	105042
El Salvador	IBRD (World Bank)	07 Jan 59	346UNTS51	104977
IMCO (Maritime Org)	United Nations	13 Jan 59	324UNTS273	200553
Spain	USA (United States)	13 Jan 59	341UNTS241	104887
ILO (Labor Org)	IMCO (Maritime Org)	16 Jan 59	327UNTS309	200554
Albania	Czechoslovakia	16 Jan 59	363UNTS195	105208
Finland	Norway	21 Jan 59	325UNTS295	104705
Colombia	IBRD (World Bank)	30 Jan 59	337UNTS327	104828
UK Great Britain	Yugoslavia	03 Feb 59	359UNTS339	105151
Euratom	UK Great Britain	04 Feb 59	331UNTS125	104752
Denmark	IBRD (World Bank)	04 Feb 59	328UNTS143	104733
Costa Rica	IBRD (World Bank)	11 Feb 59	337UNTS245	104825
Turkey	USA (United States)	13 Feb 59	340UNTS235	104867
Japan	IBRD (World Bank)	17 Feb 59	337UNTS205	104824
El Salvador	IBRD (World Bank)	20 Feb 59	362UNTS75	105183
Belgium	Morocco	27 Feb 59	390UNTS275	105611
Iceland	USA (United States)	03 Mar 59	341UNTS261	104889
Hungary	Poland	06 Mar 59	432UNTS3	106216
Ceylon (Sri Lanka)	USA (United States)	13 Mar 59	342UNTS51	104900
Brazil	Netherlands	16 Mar 59	499UNTS219	107300
Iraq	USSR (Soviet Union)	16 Mar 59	346UNTS107	104979
Finland	IBRD (World Bank)	16 Mar 59	337UNTS269	104826
France	USA (United States)	21 Mar 59	342UNTS71	104901
Japan	IAEA (Atom Energy)	24 Mar 59	339UNTS327	104852
Bulgaria	Hungary	03 Apr 59	438UNTS269	106319
Morocco	UN Special Fund	04 Apr 59	354UNTS347	105069
India	IBRD (World Bank)	08 Apr 59	348UNTS131	104998
Italy	Netherlands	17 Apr 59	474UNTS207	106883
Hungary	USSR (Soviet Union)	17 Apr 59	439UNTS41	106324
Multilateral		20 Apr 59	472UNTS185	106841
Italy	IBRD (World Bank)	21 Apr 59	359UNTS191	105143
Multilateral		22 Apr 59	613UNTS391	200631
USA (United States)	Vietnam, South	22 Apr 59	347UNTS113	104993
Italy	United Arab Rep	29 Apr 59	363UNTS91	105202
Austria	USA (United States)	30 Apr 59	343UNTS41	104920
Iraq	USSR (Soviet Union)	05 May 59	356UNTS179	105095
Germany, West	USA (United States)	05 May 59	355UNTS307	105083
Austria	Netherlands	06 May 59	485UNTS153	107054
Austria	Netherlands	06 May 59	485UNTS175	107055
Netherlands	USA (United States)	06 May 59	355UNTS327	105084
IAEA (Atom Energy)	ILO (Labor Org)	08 May 59	328UNTS273	200555
Colombia	USA (United States)	08 May 59	344UNTS193	104950
Multilateral		11 May 59	527UNTS145	107623
Denmark	Sudan	11 May 59	445UNTS105	106380
Canada	Pakistan	14 May 59	426UNTS129	106133
Belgium	Sweden	18 May 59	341UNTS277	104890
Honduras	IBRD (World Bank)	20 May 59	359UNTS119	105141
Canada	USA (United States)	22 May 59	354UNTS63	105054
IAEA (Atom Energy)	WHO (World Health)	28 May 59	339UNTS387	200559
Ceylon (Sri Lanka)	Sweden	29 May 59	464UNTS109	106713
Ceylon (Sri Lanka)	Norway	29 May 59	411UNTS165	105919
Indonesia	USA (United States)	29 May 59	347UNTS85	104992
Iran	IBRD (World Bank)	29 May 59	348UNTS103	104997
Ceylon (Sri Lanka)	Denmark	29 May 59	348UNTS225	105002
Taiwan	USA (United States)	09 Jun 59	353UNTS257	105046
IBRD (World Bank)	South Africa	10 Jun 59	340UNTS33	104857
Argentina	USA (United States)	12 Jun 59	347UNTS59	104990
Brazil	IBRD (World Bank)	17 Jun 59	377UNTS111	105398
Greece	Yugoslavia	18 Jun 59	368UNTS81	105236
Greece	Yugoslavia	18 Jun 59	368UNTS3	105231
Greece	Yugoslavia	18 Jun 59	368UNTS9	105232
Greece	Yugoslavia	18 Jun 59	368UNTS27	105234
Belgium	Japan	20 Jun 59	411UNTS3	105911
IMCO (Maritime Org)	United Nations	23 Jun 59	336UNTS317	200556

PARTY ONE	PARTY TWO	DATE	CITATION	NUMBER
Exchange of information and documents (Cont.)				
Panama	USA (United States)	24 Jun 59	479UNTS145	106950
France	IBRD (World Bank)	30 Jun 59	452UNTS67	106505
Gabon	IBRD (World Bank)	30 Jun 59	452UNTS135	106507
Korea, South	USA (United States)	30 Jun 59	353UNTS297	105047
Congo (Brazzaville)	IBRD (World Bank)	30 Jun 59	452UNTS123	106506
Canada	Japan	02 Jul 59	383UNTS243	105504
Czechoslovakia	Poland	04 Jul 59	363UNTS333	105210
Multilateral		07 Jul 59	377UNTS203	105402
Norway	IBRD (World Bank)	08 Jul 59	344UNTS229	104952
Bulgaria	United Arab Rep	09 Jul 59	411UNTS187	105920
India	IBRD (World Bank)	15 Jul 59	355UNTS95	105075
India	IBRD (World Bank)	15 Jul 59	346UNTS33	104976
India	Italy	16 Jul 59	464UNTS129	106714
Austria	USA (United States)	22 Jul 59	368UNTS199	105242
Afghanistan	Germany, West	22 Jul 59	464UNTS177	106715
Subsahara Tech Com	ILO (Labor Org)	25 Jul 59	409UNTS290	200590
United Arab Rep	USA (United States)	29 Jul 59	357UNTS121	105111
Australia	Canada	04 Aug 59	391UNTS191	105623
IAEA (Atom Energy)	WMO (Meteorology)	12 Aug 59	341UNTS341	200561
Ghana	UN Special Fund	12 Aug 59	338UNTS203	104836
Germany, West	Iceland	12 Aug 59	411UNTS224	105921
Pakistan	IBRD (World Bank)	13 Aug 59	355UNTS129	105076
USA (United States)	Yugoslavia	25 Aug 59	357UNTS77	105106
Canada	Germany, West	04 Sep 59	411UNTS260	105922
Multilateral		08 Sep 59	383UNTS203	105502
Italy	IBRD (World Bank)	16 Sep 59	375UNTS159	105366
Bulgaria	Czechoslovakia	19 Sep 59	355UNTS77	105074
Pakistan	IBRD (World Bank)	25 Sep 59	355UNTS169	105077
FAO (Food Agri)	UN Special Fund	28 Sep 59	341UNTS353	200562
Australia	Fed of Malaya	29 Sep 59	357UNTS29	105104
IAEA (Atom Energy)	ICAO (Civil Aviat)	01 Oct 59	361UNTS193	200570
Colombia	USA (United States)	06 Oct 59	358UNTS145	105132
Canada	Euratom	06 Oct 59	475UNTS187	106894
Iran	UN Special Fund	06 Oct 59	342UNTS89	104902
ILO (Labor Org)	UN Special Fund	12 Oct 59	343UNTS325	200563
Poland	UN Special Fund	15 Oct 59	344UNTS29	104941
USA (United States)	Vietnam, South	16 Oct 59	360UNTS271	105163
South Africa	Switzerland	19 Oct 59	559UNTS257	108162
India	UN Special Fund	20 Oct 59	344UNTS143	104946
Guinea	UK Great Britain	22 Oct 59	351UNTS341	105033
UN Special Fund	Yugoslavia	27 Oct 59	344UNTS159	104947
Ecuador	UN Special Fund	10 Nov 59	345UNTS3	104955
Japan	IBRD (World Bank)	12 Nov 59	354UNTS279	105067
Greece	UN Special Fund	13 Nov 59	345UNTS171	104966
India	USA (United States)	13 Nov 59	360UNTS287	105164
United Arab Rep	USA (United States)	14 Nov 59	360UNTS311	105165
UN Special Fund	WMO (Meteorology)	17 Nov 59	345UNTS311	200564
UN Special Fund	Turkey	20 Nov 59	345UNTS105	104963
Australia	USA (United States)	20 Nov 59	349UNTS293	105015
Iran	IBRD (World Bank)	23 Nov 59	380UNTS245	105459
France	USA (United States)	25 Nov 59	401UNTS75	105764
UN Special Fund	United Arab Rep	25 Nov 59	345UNTS125	104964
Pakistan	IBRD (World Bank)	30 Nov 59	355UNTS203	105078
UK Great Britain	USSR (Soviet Union)	01 Dec 59	351UNTS313	105032
Israel	UN Special Fund	01 Dec 59	345UNTS197	104968
Italy	Netherlands	01 Dec 59	455UNTS241	106545
Czechoslovakia	USSR (Soviet Union)	02 Dec 59	374UNTS63	105330
Guinea	UN Special Fund	02 Dec 59	345UNTS215	104969
Multilateral		03 Dec 59	348UNTS246	105003
Argentina	UN Special Fund	04 Dec 59	345UNTS263	104972
Italy	Netherlands	08 Dec 59	484UNTS309	107039
Norway	USSR (Soviet Union)	09 Dec 59	361UNTS93	105173
France	IBRD (World Bank)	10 Dec 59	380UNTS319	105464
Czechoslovakia	Ethiopia	11 Dec 59	399UNTS93	105736
Multilateral		14 Dec 59	422UNTS33	106067

Exchange of information and documents (Cont.)

PARTY ONE	PARTY TWO	DATE	CITATION	NUMBER
Multilateral		14 Dec 59	422UNTS57	106068
Multilateral		14 Dec 59	368UNTS253	105245
Jordan	UN Special Fund	15 Dec 59	346UNTS3	104974
Germany, East	Hungary	19 Dec 59	409UNTS4	105874
Ceylon (Sri Lanka)	WHO (World Health)	21 Dec 59	349UNTS109	105011
IBRD (World Bank)	United Arab Rep	22 Dec 59	354UNTS197	105063
Turkey	USA (United States)	22 Dec 59	367UNTS57	105225
IBRD (World Bank)	Uruguay	30 Dec 59	384UNTS275	105523
Denmark	Sweden	04 Jan 60	376UNTS375	105390
Belgium	Brazil	06 Jan 60	531UNTS149	107701
UN Special Fund	UK Great Britain	07 Jan 60	348UNTS177	105000
Greece	USA (United States)	07 Jan 60	368UNTS221	105243
Guinea	Hungary	12 Jan 60	519UNTS131	107505
Albania	Hungary	12 Jan 60	520UNTS3	107511
Czechoslovakia	UK Great Britain	15 Jan 60	374UNTS207	105336
Spain	UK Great Britain	19 Jan 60	404UNTS41	105804
Peru	UN Special Fund	19 Jan 60	349UNTS83	105010
Colombia	IBRD (World Bank)	20 Jan 60	375UNTS49	105353
Chile	UN Special Fund	22 Jan 60	351UNTS115	105020
Austria	Czechoslovakia	23 Jan 60	495UNTS125	107242
Multilateral		26 Jan 60	439UNTS249	106333
El Salvador	USA (United States)	29 Jan 60	372UNTS3	105283
Germany, East	Hungary	30 Jan 60	408UNTS230	105873
Colombia	UN Special Fund	04 Feb 60	355UNTS257	105080
Poland	Yugoslavia	06 Feb 60	521UNTS37	107517
Italy	USSR (Soviet Union)	09 Feb 60	399UNTS75	105735
Bolivia	UN Special Fund	09 Feb 60	351UNTS203	105024
Cuba	UNICEF (Children)	11 Feb 60	349UNTS277	105014
Peru	USA (United States)	12 Feb 60	372UNTS83	105290
Italy	Yugoslavia	12 Feb 60	379UNTS77	105434
Germany, West	United Arab Rep	16 Feb 60	464UNTS233	106717
Iran	IBRD (World Bank)	20 Feb 60	384UNTS213	105521
Afghanistan	UN Special Fund	21 Feb 60	351UNTS93	105019
Pakistan	UN Special Fund	25 Feb 60	351UNTS141	105021
Australia	Thailand	26 Feb 60	392UNTS255	105647
Multilateral		26 Feb 60	418UNTS171	106022
Brazil	USA (United States)	27 Feb 60	384UNTS131	105515
Indonesia	USSR (Soviet Union)	28 Feb 60	392UNTS173	105643
Mauritania	IBRD (World Bank)	17 Mar 60	452UNTS211	106509
France	IBRD (World Bank)	17 Mar 60	452UNTS147	106508
Japan	IBRD (World Bank)	17 Mar 60	362UNTS43	105182
France	UN Special Fund	17 Mar 60	354UNTS119	105059
Japan	USA (United States)	23 Mar 60	372UNTS289	105305
Belgium	IBRD (World Bank)	30 Mar 60	379UNTS161	105439
Belgium	IBRD (World Bank)	30 Mar 60	379UNTS129	105438
Belgium	IBRD (World Bank)	30 Mar 60	379UNTS103	105437
Argentina	USA (United States)	01 Apr 60	371UNTS245	105281
IBRD (World Bank)	UK Great Britain	01 Apr 60	379UNTS397	105446
Italy	UN Special Fund	01 Apr 60	354UNTS261	105066
Iceland	USA (United States)	06 Apr 60	372UNTS71	105289
Germany, West	Netherlands	08 Apr 60	508UNTS14	107404
Luxembourg	Yugoslavia	09 Apr 60	464UNTS293	106719
UN Special Fund	Tunisia	12 Apr 60	355UNTS289	105082
Multilateral		12 Apr 60	359UNTS323	105150
Multilateral		15 Apr 60	470UNTS239	106811
Libya	UN Special Fund	19 Apr 60	356UNTS11	105090
Germany, West	UK Great Britain	20 Apr 60	449UNTS77	106453
UN Special Fund	Sudan	21 Apr 60	356UNTS213	105097
ICAO (Civil Aviat)	UN Special Fund	21 Apr 60	360UNTS367	200569
Multilateral		22 Apr 60	418UNTS211	106023
Germany, West	Spain	28 Apr 60	465UNTS3	106720
UN Special Fund	Vietnam, South	29 Apr 60	357UNTS311	200567
Laos	UN Special Fund	30 Apr 60	361UNTS171	105179
Greece	Romania	02 May 60	485UNTS17	107043
India	USA (United States)	04 May 60	376UNTS279	105384

Exchange of information and documents (Cont.)

PARTY ONE	PARTY TWO	DATE	CITATION	NUMBER
Costa Rica	IBRD (World Bank)	04 May 60	390UNTS201	105609
Poland	Yugoslavia	05 May 60	423UNTS229	106095
Hungary	Yugoslavia	07 May 60	519UNTS237	107510
Lebanon	UN Special Fund	07 May 60	360UNTS225	105160
Colombia	IBRD (World Bank)	10 May 60	379UNTS218	105441
Germany, West	Ireland	11 May 60	553UNTS69	108070
Morocco	United Arab Rep	19 May 60	563UNTS121	108208
Cambodia	WHO (World Health)	19 May 60	372UNTS193	105298
Denmark	UK Great Britain	20 May 60	374UNTS245	105338
Switzerland	Tunisia	21 May 60	497UNTS109	107265
Kuwait	UK Great Britain	24 May 60	412UNTS4	105923
UN Special Fund	WHO (World Health)	25 May 60	359UNTS375	200568
IBRD (World Bank)	UK Great Britain	27 May 60	375UNTS201	105367
Peru	IBRD (World Bank)	01 Jun 60	380UNTS15	105448
Multilateral		04 Jun 60	360UNTS208	105159
Indonesia	USA (United States)	08 Jun 60	388UNTS287	105585
India	USA (United States)	13 Jun 60	377UNTS37	105394
IBRD (World Bank)	Sudan	17 Jun 60	379UNTS253	105442
Multilateral		17 Jun 60	536UNTS27	107794
Iraq	UN Special Fund	19 Jun 60	376UNTS357	105389
Spain	USA (United States)	22 Jun 60	378UNTS3	105414
Nicaragua	IBRD (World Bank)	22 Jun 60	384UNTS243	105522
Somalia	UK Great Britain	26 Jun 60	374UNTS331	105346
IAEA (Atom Energy)	USA (United States)	28 Jun 60	374UNTS133	105333
Peru	IBRD (World Bank)	29 Jun 60	400UNTS99	105750
Honduras	IBRD (World Bank)	29 Jun 60	400UNTS137	105751
Denmark	USA (United States)	07 Jul 60	380UNTS39	105449
Multilateral		08 Jul 60	366UNTS310	105220
Ethiopia	UN Special Fund	13 Jul 60	368UNTS159	105240
ITU (Telecommun)	UN Special Fund	13 Jul 60	368UNTS329	200573
Switzerland	United Arab Rep	14 Jul 60	497UNTS161	107268
Germany, West	UK Great Britain	14 Jul 60	414UNTS144	105972
Poland	USA (United States)	16 Jul 60	384UNTS169	105518
Germany, West	Pakistan	20 Jul 60	465UNTS41	106721
Spain	USA (United States)	21 Jul 60	393UNTS289	105663
Poland	USA (United States)	21 Jul 60	380UNTS157	105456
France	Greece	25 Jul 60	533UNTS227	107745
Iran	USA (United States)	26 Jul 60	384UNTS141	105516
El Salvador	IBRD (World Bank)	29 Jul 60	390UNTS101	105605
India	IBRD (World Bank)	29 Jul 60	377UNTS153	105399
United Arab Rep	USA (United States)	01 Aug 60	384UNTS189	105519
WHO (World Health)	United Arab Rep	03 Aug 60	385UNTS3	105524
Jordan	WHO (World Health)	03 Aug 60	381UNTS133	105469
WHO (World Health)	Tunisia	04 Aug 60	381UNTS335	105474
Ghana	USSR (Soviet Union)	04 Aug 60	399UNTS61	105734
Laos	WHO (World Health)	04 Aug 60	373UNTS313	105322
Italy	Netherlands	06 Aug 60	455UNTS259	106546
United Arab Rep	USA (United States)	09 Aug 60	388UNTS271	105584
Guatemala	USA (United States)	09 Aug 60	461UNTS15	106648
Mexico	USA (United States)	15 Aug 60	402UNTS177	105786
Panama	IBRD (World Bank)	19 Aug 60	390UNTS153	105607
Congo (Zaire)	United Nations	23 Aug 60	373UNTS327	200576
Ghana	United Arab Rep	29 Aug 60	412UNTS71	105926
Taiwan	USA (United States)	30 Aug 60	388UNTS191	105579
Canada	USA (United States)	31 Aug 60	393UNTS247	105659
Haiti	USA (United States)	01 Sep 60	388UNTS249	105582
Lebanon	WHO (World Health)	08 Sep 60	387UNTS49	105557
Israel	IBRD (World Bank)	09 Sep 60	406UNTS3	105837
Multilateral		14 Sep 60	443UNTS247	106363
Brazil	UN Special Fund	16 Sep 60	375UNTS3	105351
Multilateral		19 Sep 60	444UNTS259	106371
Pakistan	IBRD (World Bank)	19 Sep 60	444UNTS207	106370
Multilateral		19 Sep 60	419UNTS125	106032
Czechoslovakia	India	19 Sep 60	465UNTS67	106722
Taiwan	UN Special Fund	20 Sep 60	375UNTS29	105352

PARTY ONE	PARTY TWO	DATE	CITATION	NUMBER
Exchange of information and documents (Cont.)				
Colombia	IBRD (World Bank)	20 Sep 60	390UNTS173	105608
Ecuador	USA (United States)	27 Sep 60	401UNTS115	105766
Ceylon (Sri Lanka)	USA (United States)	30 Sep 60	389UNTS221	105594
Indonesia	UN Special Fund	07 Oct 60	378UNTS141	105424
Liberia	UN Special Fund	11 Oct 60	376UNTS341	105388
Mexico	IBRD (World Bank)	18 Oct 60	422UNTS177	106075
El Salvador	UN Special Fund	24 Oct 60	377UNTS171	105400
Hungary	UK Great Britain	25 Oct 60	419UNTS309	106034
USA (United States)	Vietnam, South	28 Oct 60	401UNTS3	105758
Cuba	Romania	28 Oct 60	457UNTS9	106574
India	IBRD (World Bank)	28 Oct 60	406UNTS27	105838
Panama	USA (United States)	31 Oct 60	405UNTS63	105823
Kuwait	United Nations	31 Oct 60	391UNTS295	200581
France	USA (United States)	04 Nov 60	400UNTS323	105756
Indonesia	USA (United States)	05 Nov 60	400UNTS35	105746
Greece	USA (United States)	07 Nov 60	400UNTS57	105748
Chile	USA (United States)	08 Nov 60	405UNTS85	105825
Romania	UK Great Britain	10 Nov 60	385UNTS113	105533
Australia	Italy	10 Nov 60	497UNTS247	107271
Denmark	Germany, West	10 Nov 60	431UNTS21	106205
Czechoslovakia	Poland	14 Nov 60	413UNTS4	105938
UNICEF (Children)	Upper Volta	15 Nov 60	402UNTS33	105776
WHO (World Health)	Upper Volta	15 Nov 60	383UNTS91	105496
Nepal	UN Special Fund	17 Nov 60	380UNTS289	105461
Guatemala	UN Special Fund	17 Nov 60	383UNTS67	105495
Mali	UNICEF (Children)	17 Nov 60	402UNTS23	105775
Korea, South	USA (United States)	18 Nov 60	400UNTS49	105747
Cambodia	UN Special Fund	24 Nov 60	382UNTS255	105487
Israel	Mali	24 Nov 60	413UNTS104	105945
IAEA (Atom Energy)	OECD (Econ Coop)	24 Nov 60	396UNTS273	200585
Fed of Malaya	WHO (World Health)	25 Nov 60	387UNTS37	105556
Cambodia	Czechoslovakia	27 Nov 60	410UNTS263	105910
Norway	IBRD (World Bank)	02 Dec 60	390UNTS131	105606
Italy	USA (United States)	03 Dec 60	410UNTS3	105893
WHO (World Health)	Yemen	03 Dec 60	395UNTS187	105685
Dahomey	WHO (World Health)	07 Dec 60	387UNTS277	105567
Council of Europe	ILO (Labor Org)	08 Dec 60	389UNTS291	200579
Libya	USA (United States)	11 Dec 60	445UNTS125	106381
Congo (Brazzaville)	WHO (World Health)	12 Dec 60	399UNTS105	105737
Cuba	USSR (Soviet Union)	12 Dec 60	421UNTS3	106048
Nepal	UNICEF (Children)	12 Dec 60	382UNTS273	105488
Multilateral		13 Dec 60	523UNTS117	107557
Multilateral		14 Dec 60	429UNTS93	106193
Israel	USA (United States)	19 Dec 60	401UNTS195	105772
Peru	IBRD (World Bank)	19 Dec 60	417UNTS275	106010
Honduras	UN Special Fund	20 Dec 60	383UNTS103	105497
Japan	IBRD (World Bank)	20 Dec 60	400UNTS167	105752
Japan	IBRD (World Bank)	20 Dec 60	400UNTS279	105754
Canada	Pakistan	21 Dec 60	465UNTS115	106724
Togo	USA (United States)	22 Dec 60	401UNTS33	105760
Inter-Am Nuc Energ	IAEA (Atom Energy)	22 Dec 60	396UNTS285	200586
Cuba	Czechoslovakia	22 Dec 60	426UNTS145	106134
Niger	WHO (World Health)	28 Dec 60	394UNTS195	105679
Korea, South	USA (United States)	28 Dec 60	402UNTS3	105773
Luxembourg	Thailand	29 Dec 60	465UNTS131	106725
Finland	IAEA (Atom Energy)	30 Dec 60	395UNTS257	105690
Burma	UN Special Fund	03 Jan 61	387UNTS219	105564
Germany, West	USA (United States)	03 Jan 61	416UNTS93	105997
UK Great Britain	USSR (Soviet Union)	09 Jan 61	404UNTS175	105810
Costa Rica	UN Special Fund	10 Jan 61	389UNTS253	105597
Turkey	USA (United States)	11 Jan 61	405UNTS173	105833
Ethiopia	USSR (Soviet Union)	13 Jan 61	421UNTS13	106049
Sudan	UK Great Britain	16 Jan 61	424UNTS233	106112
Mexico	IBRD (World Bank)	16 Jan 61	422UNTS203	106076
Burma	IBRD (World Bank)	16 Jan 61	400UNTS73	105749

PARTY ONE	PARTY TWO	DATE	CITATION	NUMBER
Exchange of information and documents (Cont.)				
Germany, West	Japan	18 Jan 61	465UNTS173	106727
UN Special Fund	Saudi Arabia	19 Jan 61	396UNTS27	105692
Nicaragua	UN Special Fund	20 Jan 61	387UNTS15	105555
Korea, South	WHO (World Health)	20 Jan 61	406UNTS269	200589
Chad	UN Special Fund	23 Jan 61	390UNTS69	105603
UN Special Fund	Somalia	28 Jan 61	388UNTS75	105573
Multilateral		28 Jan 61	387UNTS202	105563
Ivory Coast	WHO (World Health)	30 Jan 61	395UNTS205	105686
Gabon	UN Special Fund	02 Feb 61	387UNTS289	105568
WHO (World Health)	Togo	03 Feb 61	394UNTS207	105680
Costa Rica	IBRD (World Bank)	03 Feb 61	414UNTS314	105977
Chad	WHO (World Health)	03 Feb 61	394UNTS161	105676
Poland	USSR (Soviet Union)	05 Feb 61	420UNTS161	106046
Nigeria	UN Special Fund	10 Feb 61	390UNTS85	105604
Central Afri Rep	WHO (World Health)	13 Feb 61	394UNTS149	105675
Finland	Italy	18 Feb 61	434UNTS199	106263
FAO (Food Agri)	UK Great Britain	20 Feb 61	642UNTS253	109178
Mexico	UN Special Fund	23 Feb 61	388UNTS151	105576
IBRD (World Bank)	Yugoslavia	23 Feb 61	415UNTS92	105982
Czechoslovakia	Hungary	24 Feb 61	422UNTS15	106066
Belgium	Netherlands	24 Feb 61	474UNTS167	106881
Cyprus	UN Special Fund	24 Feb 61	389UNTS3	105588
Panama	UN Special Fund	09 Mar 61	396UNTS3	105691
Cuba	UN Special Fund	10 Mar 61	390UNTS35	105601
Kuwait	WHO (World Health)	16 Mar 61	397UNTS315	200588
Japan	IBRD (World Bank)	16 Mar 61	400UNTS201	105753
Brazil	USA (United States)	17 Mar 61	406UNTS241	105853
USA (United States)	Vietnam, South	25 Mar 61	406UNTS187	105849
IBRD (World Bank)	UK Great Britain	29 Mar 61	415UNTS300	105990
Austria	USA (United States)	29 Mar 61	459UNTS45	106612
Cuba	Germany, East	29 Mar 61	448UNTS81	106426
Ecuador	USA (United States)	03 Apr 61	409UNTS140	105882
Cuba	Czechoslovakia	05 Apr 61	442UNTS201	106350
Iceland	USA (United States)	07 Apr 61	406UNTS203	105850
Bolivia	USA (United States)	07 Apr 61	433UNTS3	106227
Multilateral		10 Apr 61	402UNTS281	105791
Honduras	USA (United States)	12 Apr 61	413UNTS182	105952
IAEA (Atom Energy)	IMCO (Maritime Org)	13 Apr 61	425UNTS281	200595
Multilateral		14 Apr 61	422UNTS101	106071
Mauritania	WHO (World Health)	17 Apr 61	396UNTS301	200587
Cyprus	UNICEF (Children)	19 Apr 61	394UNTS185	105678
Korea, South	UN Special Fund	21 Apr 61	394UNTS231	200583
Mali	WHO (World Health)	27 Apr 61	407UNTS66	105860
Turkey	USSR (Soviet Union)	27 Apr 61	420UNTS307	106047
Gabon	WHO (World Health)	27 Apr 61	397UNTS215	105707
Ghana	Hungary	27 Apr 61	439UNTS17	106322
USA (United States)	Yugoslavia	28 Apr 61	409UNTS172	105884
IBRD (World Bank)	Thailand	28 Apr 61	415UNTS121	105983
Japan	IBRD (World Bank)	02 May 61	415UNTS144	105984
Ceylon (Sri Lanka)	UN Special Fund	03 May 61	395UNTS217	105687
Brazil	USA (United States)	04 May 61	433UNTS91	106233
Israel	USA (United States)	10 May 61	409UNTS213	105887
Honduras	IDA (Devel Assoc)	12 May 61	414UNTS180	105973
Colombia	IBRD (World Bank)	12 May 61	415UNTS172	105985
Spain	USA (United States)	22 May 61	409UNTS260	105891
Cameroon	USA (United States)	26 May 61	413UNTS195	105953
Somalia	USSR (Soviet Union)	02 Jun 61	528UNTS147	107638
Somalia	USSR (Soviet Union)	02 Jun 61	457UNTS263	106587
Czechoslovakia	Somalia	04 Jun 61	479UNTS291	106960
Ceylon (Sri Lanka)	IBRD (World Bank)	06 Jun 61	414UNTS349	105978
Nepal	USA (United States)	09 Jun 61	421UNTS223	106061
Congo (Zaire)	United Nations	12 Jun 61	494UNTS205	107234
Cameroon	UN Special Fund	13 Jun 61	397UNTS297	105713
New Zealand	UK Great Britain	13 Jun 61	497UNTS293	107273
IDA (Devel Assoc)	Sudan	14 Jun 61	415UNTS50	105981

Exchange of information and documents (Cont.)

PARTY ONE	PARTY TWO	DATE	CITATION	NUMBER
IBRD (World Bank)	Sudan	14 Jun 61	415UNTS26	105980
Multilateral		14 Jun 61	415UNTS4	105979
Ethiopia	United Nations	14 Jun 61	406UNTS81	105840
Inter-Am Devel Bnk	USA (United States)	19 Jun 61	410UNTS34	105895
India	IDA (Devel Assoc)	21 Jun 61	418UNTS61	106017
Paraguay	UN Special Fund	22 Jun 61	399UNTS117	105738
IBRD (World Bank)	UK Great Britain	23 Jun 61	415UNTS358	105991
Mexico	USA (United States)	26 Jun 61	413UNTS229	105957
UN Special Fund	Upper Volta	26 Jun 61	400UNTS3	105744
Pakistan	IBRD (World Bank)	27 Jun 61	425UNTS241	106127
Chile	IBRD (World Bank)	28 Jun 61	426UNTS33	106129
Haiti	UN Special Fund	28 Jun 61	399UNTS171	105741
Chile	IDA (Devel Assoc)	28 Jun 61	426UNTS89	106131
Philippines	UN Special Fund	28 Jun 61	399UNTS141	105739
Tunisia	USA (United States)	30 Jun 61	434UNTS85	106257
Argentina	IBRD (World Bank)	30 Jun 61	445UNTS85	106379
UNICEF (Children)	Saudi Arabia	04 Jul 61	413UNTS122	105947
Czechoslovakia	Poland	04 Jul 61	436UNTS189	106295
Argentina	Brazil	06 Jul 61	0UNTS0	109410
Bulgaria	Netherlands	07 Jul 61	489UNTS21	107133
Paraguay	USA (United States)	07 Jul 61	433UNTS53	106231
Israel	IBRD (World Bank)	11 Jul 61	429UNTS3	106188
USA (United States)	Vietnam, South	14 Jul 61	416UNTS133	105999
Germany, West	Netherlands	18 Jul 61	487UNTS95	107096
Mexico	USA (United States)	19 Jul 61	433UNTS43	106230
Mali	UN Special Fund	21 Jul 61	401UNTS141	105768
Taiwan	USA (United States)	21 Jul 61	416UNTS101	105998
Philippines	IBRD (World Bank)	26 Jul 61	414UNTS253	105976
France	USA (United States)	27 Jul 61	433UNTS29	106229
Turkey	USA (United States)	29 Jul 61	416UNTS151	106001
UN Special Fund	Yemen	02 Aug 61	402UNTS43	105777
Czechoslovakia	Ghana	02 Aug 61	465UNTS249	106730
Finland	USA (United States)	04 Aug 61	418UNTS19	106014
Morocco	WHO (World Health)	09 Aug 61	412UNTS192	105932
India	IBRD (World Bank)	09 Aug 61	417UNTS297	106011
Finland	IBRD (World Bank)	09 Aug 61	415UNTS204	105986
Cameroon	UNICEF (Children)	12 Aug 61	402UNTS235	105788
IBRD (World Bank)	UK Great Britain	16 Aug 61	426UNTS287	106143
India	IBRD (World Bank)	17 Aug 61	417UNTS319	106012
WHO (World Health)	Somalia	17 Aug 61	423UNTS111	106088
Central Afri Rep	UNICEF (Children)	21 Aug 61	413UNTS48	105939
El Salvador	USA (United States)	21 Aug 61	418UNTS35	106015
Poland	UNICEF (Children)	24 Aug 61	406UNTS95	105841
Chad	UNICEF (Children)	26 Aug 61	422UNTS231	106077
Colombia	IDA (Devel Assoc)	28 Aug 61	416UNTS3	105992
Colombia	IBRD (World Bank)	28 Aug 61	416UNTS23	105993
Ivory Coast	UN Special Fund	29 Aug 61	406UNTS129	105844
Ghana	United Nations	29 Aug 61	406UNTS117	105843
Taiwan	IDA (Devel Assoc)	30 Aug 61	416UNTS175	106003
Tunisia	USSR (Soviet Union)	30 Aug 61	437UNTS243	106310
Taiwan	IDA (Devel Assoc)	30 Aug 61	417UNTS227	106008
Liberia	Switzerland	31 Aug 61	559UNTS215	108160
Taiwan	IDA (Devel Assoc)	06 Sep 61	417UNTS253	106009
Costa Rica	IBRD (World Bank)	06 Sep 61	446UNTS345	106408
India	IDA (Devel Assoc)	06 Sep 61	418UNTS81	106018
USA (United States)	Uruguay	12 Sep 61	607UNTS175	108805
Iraq	WHO (World Health)	13 Sep 61	419UNTS69	106030
Multilateral		20 Sep 61	407UNTS52	105859
Ghana	Romania	30 Sep 61	457UNTS3	106573
Ghana	Romania	30 Sep 61	467UNTS443	106769
UN Special Fund	Sierra Leone	02 Oct 61	422UNTS131	106073
Multilateral		05 Oct 61	527UNTS181	107625
Germany, West	Morocco	12 Oct 61	523UNTS289	107562
Malagasy	WHO (World Health)	13 Oct 61	421UNTS273	106064
Switzerland	USA (United States)	13 Oct 61	459UNTS219	106625

Exchange of information and documents (Cont.)

PARTY ONE	PARTY TWO	DATE	CITATION	NUMBER
India	IBRD (World Bank)	13 Oct 61	418UNTS3	106013
Costa Rica	IBRD (World Bank)	13 Oct 61	430UNTS27	106202
Philippines	IBRD (World Bank)	13 Oct 61	415UNTS269	105989
Multilateral		16 Oct 61	410UNTS242	105908
Taiwan	Jordan	17 Oct 61	435UNTS267	106284
Japan	Pakistan	17 Oct 61	466UNTS17	106734
Multilateral		18 Oct 61	529UNTS89	107659
Pakistan	IDA (Devel Assoc)	19 Oct 61	447UNTS161	106415
Brazil	Poland	19 Oct 61	552UNTS75	108050
Indonesia	USA (United States)	26 Oct 61	433UNTS249	106248
Paraguay	IDA (Devel Assoc)	26 Oct 61	447UNTS277	106419
Belgium	Yugoslavia	31 Oct 61	426UNTS165	106136
Gabon	UNICEF (Children)	02 Nov 61	422UNTS241	106078
Czechoslovakia	Hungary	02 Nov 61	438UNTS3	106313
Peru	IBRD (World Bank)	03 Nov 61	430UNTS47	106203
Iceland	USA (United States)	06 Nov 61	426UNTS225	106140
Mauritania	UN Special Fund	07 Nov 61	412UNTS240	105936
Multilateral		07 Nov 61	412UNTS258	105937
Syria	USA (United States)	09 Nov 61	435UNTS75	106271
Congo (Brazzaville)	UN Special Fund	09 Nov 61	413UNTS58	105940
Austria	Czechoslovakia	10 Nov 61	455UNTS337	106550
Sudan	USA (United States)	14 Nov 61	434UNTS51	106255
Bolivia	USA (United States)	15 Nov 61	456UNTS192	106557
Malagasy	UNICEF (Children)	16 Nov 61	422UNTS251	106079
Congo (Zaire)	USA (United States)	18 Nov 61	433UNTS207	106244
United Nations	USA (United States)	18 Nov 61	494UNTS213	107235
India	IDA (Devel Assoc)	22 Nov 61	427UNTS3	106144
Pakistan	IDA (Devel Assoc)	22 Nov 61	447UNTS295	106420
India	IDA (Devel Assoc)	22 Nov 61	427UNTS55	106146
India	IDA (Devel Assoc)	22 Nov 61	427UNTS29	106145
Cyprus	Greece	23 Nov 61	497UNTS311	107274
Philippines	USA (United States)	24 Nov 61	433UNTS315	106251
Guatemala	Israel	27 Nov 61	448UNTS191	106431
Thailand	USA (United States)	28 Nov 61	434UNTS77	106256
Portugal	USA (United States)	28 Nov 61	434UNTS31	106253
Japan	IBRD (World Bank)	29 Nov 61	426UNTS3	106128
IBRD (World Bank)	UK Great Britain	29 Nov 61	426UNTS49	106130
IAEA (Atom Energy)	UN Special Fund	29 Nov 61	415UNTS408	200593
OAS (Am States)	USA (United States)	29 Nov 61	424UNTS119	106104
IBRD (World Bank)	South Africa	01 Dec 61	425UNTS215	106126
Taiwan	IDA (Devel Assoc)	01 Dec 61	426UNTS105	106132
Ivory Coast	USA (United States)	01 Dec 61	462UNTS221	106681
IBRD (World Bank)	South Africa	01 Dec 61	425UNTS197	106125
Bulgaria	Poland	04 Dec 61	484UNTS3	107019
Ethiopia	USA (United States)	06 Dec 61	433UNTS231	106246
COMECON (Econ Aid)	USSR (Soviet Union)	07 Dec 61	506UNTS325	107392
UN Special Fund	Venezuela	11 Dec 61	422UNTS149	106074
IBRD (World Bank)	Venezuela	13 Dec 61	446UNTS371	106409
Multilateral		15 Dec 61	424UNTS43	106098
Poland	USA (United States)	15 Dec 61	434UNTS3	106252
UN Special Fund	Senegal	16 Dec 61	425UNTS97	106121
Argentina	Japan	20 Dec 61	451UNTS77	106486
Iran	USA (United States)	21 Dec 61	433UNTS269	106249
Costa Rica	USA (United States)	22 Dec 61	460UNTS277	106646
India	IBRD (World Bank)	22 Dec 61	481UNTS85	106979
Jordan	IDA (Devel Assoc)	22 Dec 61	448UNTS21	106423
Multilateral		27 Dec 61	425UNTS83	106120
USA (United States)	Vietnam, South	27 Dec 61	433UNTS185	106242
Malagasy	UN Special Fund	05 Jan 62	419UNTS29	106028
Ivory Coast	UNICEF (Children)	10 Jan 62	422UNTS261	106080
Ethiopia	WHO (World Health)	11 Jan 62	423UNTS99	106087
Austria	Greece	15 Jan 62	498UNTS3	107275
Paraguay	USA (United States)	16 Jan 62	433UNTS169	106240
Multilateral		17 Jan 62	419UNTS294	106033
Cyprus	USA (United States)	18 Jan 62	435UNTS3	106266

PARTY ONE	PARTY TWO	DATE	CITATION	NUMBER
Exchange of information and documents (Cont.)				
United Arab Rep	USA (United States)	19 Jan 62	435UNTS107	106273
Argentina	IBRD (World Bank)	19 Jan 62	446UNTS305	106407
Multilateral		20 Jan 62	429UNTS230	200596
Australia	IBRD (World Bank)	23 Jan 62	430UNTS3	106201
Indonesia	Japan	23 Jan 62	559UNTS77	108155
Ghana	USA (United States)	24 Jan 62	435UNTS23	106268
Poland	Romania	25 Jan 62	468UNTS3	106770
Iran	USA (United States)	29 Jan 62	435UNTS53	106270
UK Great Britain	Zambia	30 Jan 62	590UNTS173	108553
UNICEF (Children)	Yemen	31 Jan 62	422UNTS271	106081
Luxembourg	South Africa	31 Jan 62	563UNTS153	108209
Italy	Japan	31 Jan 62	498UNTS23	107276
Israel	IBRD (World Bank)	01 Feb 62	435UNTS155	106277
Guinea	USA (United States)	02 Feb 62	435UNTS35	106269
Ghana	IBRD (World Bank)	08 Feb 62	449UNTS207	106462
Morocco	USA (United States)	09 Feb 62	442UNTS135	106345
Hungary	Yugoslavia	09 Feb 62	577UNTS3	108370
Bolivia	USA (United States)	12 Feb 62	451UNTS281	106499
Finland	Hungary	13 Feb 62	463UNTS61	106693
Multilateral		13 Feb 62	422UNTS288	200594
Iceland	IBRD (World Bank)	14 Feb 62	447UNTS95	106413
India	IDA (Devel Assoc)	14 Feb 62	468UNTS177	106773
Tunisia	USA (United States)	16 Feb 62	442UNTS161	106347
Indonesia	USA (United States)	19 Feb 62	435UNTS137	106276
Multilateral		20 Feb 62	597UNTS159	108644
Multilateral		21 Feb 62	423UNTS151	106091
USSR (Soviet Union)	Yugoslavia	24 Feb 62	471UNTS195	106833
Niger	UN Special Fund	26 Feb 62	423UNTS83	106086
India	IBRD (World Bank)	28 Feb 62	447UNTS3	106410
Multilateral		01 Mar 62	423UNTS122	106089
Korea, South	USA (United States)	02 Mar 62	442UNTS185	106349
Germany, West	Thailand	05 Mar 62	563UNTS165	108210
USA (United States)	USSR (Soviet Union)	08 Mar 62	460UNTS3	106630
Germany, West	Greece	08 Mar 62	533UNTS269	107747
WHO (World Health)	Sudan	11 Mar 62	432UNTS325	106226
Brazil	USA (United States)	15 Mar 62	456UNTS209	106558
Iceland	USA (United States)	16 Mar 62	445UNTS49	106376
Peru	USA (United States)	20 Mar 62	445UNTS61	106377
Nigeria	WHO (World Health)	27 Mar 62	429UNTS123	106194
Dahomey	UN Special Fund	28 Mar 62	424UNTS55	106099
Multilateral		29 Mar 62	507UNTS177	107401
UNICEF (Children)	Somalia	01 Apr 62	431UNTS75	106211
Sierra Leone	UK Great Britain	05 Apr 62	434UNTS227	106265
Belgium	Italy	06 Apr 62	490UNTS317	107161
Ghana	USSR (Soviet Union)	06 Apr 62	498UNTS41	107277
Colombia	USA (United States)	09 Apr 62	476UNTS9	106899
Congo (Brazzaville)	UNICEF (Children)	09 Apr 62	431UNTS65	106210
Multilateral		10 Apr 62	429UNTS78	106192
UNICEF (Children)	Sierra Leone	11 Apr 62	431UNTS55	106209
Liberia	USA (United States)	12 Apr 62	445UNTS213	106390
El Salvador	USA (United States)	13 Apr 62	451UNTS307	106500
Taiwan	USA (United States)	16 Apr 62	445UNTS249	106392
India	USA (United States)	16 Apr 62	445UNTS257	106393
Multilateral		18 Apr 62	463UNTS44	106692
Brazil	USA (United States)	19 Apr 62	456UNTS255	106560
UK Great Britain	USA (United States)	26 Apr 62	445UNTS273	106395
Bolivia	USA (United States)	26 Apr 62	461UNTS105	106654
USA (United States)	Uruguay	27 Apr 62	452UNTS25	106502
Taiwan	USA (United States)	27 Apr 62	436UNTS25	106287
India	USA (United States)	01 May 62	451UNTS179	106493
Israel	USA (United States)	03 May 62	442UNTS83	106340
UN Special Fund	Uruguay	04 May 62	429UNTS143	106196
Japan	United Arab Rep	10 May 62	498UNTS69	107278
Multilateral		14 May 62	544UNTS39	107910
El Salvador	USA (United States)	15 May 62	452UNTS49	106503

PARTY ONE	PARTY TWO	DATE	CITATION	NUMBER
Exchange of information and documents (Cont.)				
Multilateral		17 May 62	429UNTS46	106189
USA (United States)	Venezuela	17 May 62	456UNTS275	106562
Belgium	USA (United States)	17 May 62	461UNTS3	106647
Greece	United Nations	18 May 62	429UNTS61	106190
France	Romania	18 May 62	498UNTS115	107279
Guatemala	USA (United States)	21 May 62	451UNTS205	106495
Colombia	IBRD (World Bank)	23 May 62	447UNTS39	106411
Panama	USA (United States)	23 May 62	458UNTS225	106604
Multilateral		25 May 62	486UNTS103	107075
Greece	Tunisia	26 May 62	534UNTS163	107761
Denmark	USA (United States)	28 May 62	450UNTS215	106469
Thailand	USA (United States)	31 May 62	459UNTS135	106619
Ethiopia	IBRD (World Bank)	31 May 62	467UNTS237	106765
Dominican Republic	UN Special Fund	06 Jun 62	429UNTS169	106197
Dahomey	USA (United States)	13 Jun 62	458UNTS219	106603
Multilateral		14 Jun 62	528UNTS33	107634
France	Senegal	15 Jun 62	524UNTS3	107563
Libya	WHO (World Health)	16 Jun 62	437UNTS127	106301
Costa Rica	USA (United States)	18 Jun 62	461UNTS155	106659
WHO (World Health)	Sierra Leone	19 Jun 62	439UNTS151	106327
Mexico	IBRD (World Bank)	20 Jun 62	467UNTS205	106764
Czechoslovakia	Senegal	20 Jun 62	498UNTS145	107280
Mexico	IBRD (World Bank)	20 Jun 62	468UNTS109	106771
Argentina	USA (United States)	22 Jun 62	458UNTS97	106594
Israel	Peru	25 Jun 62	515UNTS263	107464
Germany, West	Syria	25 Jun 62	489UNTS71	107135
Congo (Zaire)	IAEA (Atom Energy)	27 Jun 62	463UNTS31	106691
India	IDA (Devel Assoc)	29 Jun 62	447UNTS221	106417
Pakistan	IDA (Devel Assoc)	29 Jun 62	447UNTS325	106421
Morocco	Switzerland	05 Jul 62	498UNTS171	107281
Morocco	Switzerland	05 Jul 62	498UNTS189	107282
UN Special Fund	Syria	07 Jul 62	443UNTS3	106355
IBRD (World Bank)	Yugoslavia	11 Jul 62	468UNTS143	106772
UN Special Fund	Tanganyika	17 Jul 62	435UNTS237	106281
India	IDA (Devel Assoc)	18 Jul 62	447UNTS191	106416
Czechoslovakia	COMECON (Econ Aid)	20 Jul 62	506UNTS345	107393
Colombia	USA (United States)	23 Jul 62	458UNTS123	106595
WHO (World Health)	Senegal	06 Aug 62	435UNTS179	106279
Multilateral		12 Aug 62	443UNTS266	106365
Ethiopia	USA (United States)	13 Aug 62	459UNTS31	106611
WHO (World Health)	Western Samoa	14 Aug 62	437UNTS317	200598
Indonesia	Netherlands	15 Aug 62	437UNTS273	106311
Finland	IBRD (World Bank)	15 Aug 62	467UNTS177	106763
Korea, South	IDA (Devel Assoc)	17 Aug 62	468UNTS387	200603
Paraguay	USA (United States)	25 Aug 62	461UNTS207	106665
Multilateral		29 Aug 62	443UNTS280	106366
Germany, West	Netherlands	30 Aug 62	500UNTS3	107303
Taiwan	USA (United States)	31 Aug 62	460UNTS247	106644
Nicaragua	IDA (Devel Assoc)	07 Sep 62	478UNTS313	106940
Morocco	USA (United States)	11 Sep 62	462UNTS207	106680
Canada	Sweden	11 Sep 62	529UNTS9	107651
Pakistan	IBRD (World Bank)	14 Sep 62	467UNTS152	106762
Pakistan	IBRD (World Bank)	14 Sep 62	467UNTS125	106761
Panama	IBRD (World Bank)	14 Sep 62	476UNTS153	106908
India	IDA (Devel Assoc)	14 Sep 62	448UNTS3	106422
India	IDA (Devel Assoc)	14 Sep 62	467UNTS265	106766
Tunisia	USA (United States)	14 Sep 62	461UNTS31	106649
IDA (Devel Assoc)	Tunisia	17 Sep 62	469UNTS33	106783
Ecuador	Germany, West	20 Sep 62	498UNTS199	107283
Multilateral		28 Sep 62	469UNTS169	106791
Sweden	USA (United States)	04 Oct 62	462UNTS31	106669
Japan	Kuwait	06 Oct 62	498UNTS235	107284
United Arab Rep	USA (United States)	08 Oct 62	462UNTS39	106670
Belgium	Romania	12 Oct 62	502UNTS31	107325
Belgium	Rwanda	13 Oct 62	456UNTS431	106569

Exchange of information and documents (Cont.)

PARTY ONE	PARTY TWO	DATE	CITATION	NUMBER
Iran	USA (United States)	15 Oct 62	473UNTS291	106866
Israel	IBRD (World Bank)	17 Oct 62	467UNTS107	106760
Hungary	Syria	18 Oct 62	491UNTS209	107178
France	Ivory Coast	19 Oct 62	498UNTS317	107286
Greece	USA (United States)	22 Oct 62	462UNTS187	106678
Czechoslovakia	Yugoslavia	22 Oct 62	480UNTS267	106974
Cameroon	Israel	24 Oct 62	449UNTS3	106446
Japan	USA (United States)	24 Oct 62	462UNTS119	106673
Dominican Republic	USA (United States)	25 Oct 62	459UNTS247	106627
IBRD (World Bank)	Uruguay	26 Oct 62	481UNTS39	106977
Japan	UN Special Fund	31 Oct 62	444UNTS171	106368
Haiti	IDA (Devel Assoc)	02 Nov 62	468UNTS205	106774
El Salvador	IDA (Devel Assoc)	02 Nov 62	468UNTS331	106780
Pakistan	IDA (Devel Assoc)	02 Nov 62	468UNTS351	106781
Korea, South	USA (United States)	07 Nov 62	462UNTS129	106674
Burma	USA (United States)	09 Nov 62	461UNTS113	106655
Poland	Syria	10 Nov 62	491UNTS228	107179
Algeria	UN Special Fund	15 Nov 62	452UNTS243	106512
Multilateral		15 Nov 62	448UNTS50	106424
Czechoslovakia	Poland	16 Nov 62	526UNTS3	107597
Ivory Coast	Switzerland	17 Nov 62	499UNTS3	107289
WHO (World Health)	Syria	18 Nov 62	480UNTS249	106972
Taiwan	USA (United States)	19 Nov 62	459UNTS263	106629
Algeria	UNICEF (Children)	20 Nov 62	453UNTS151	106522
Ceylon (Sri Lanka)	ILO (Labor Org)	21 Nov 62	449UNTS263	106463
IDA (Devel Assoc)	Turkey	23 Nov 62	469UNTS3	106782
Paraguay	USA (United States)	24 Nov 62	471UNTS49	106821
India	USA (United States)	26 Nov 62	460UNTS203	106641
India	UK Great Britain	27 Nov 62	466UNTS189	106744
USA (United States)	Yugoslavia	28 Nov 62	460UNTS185	106640
India	USA (United States)	30 Nov 62	459UNTS231	106626
Dominican Republic	USA (United States)	30 Nov 62	471UNTS25	106819
Niger	UNICEF (Children)	05 Dec 62	503UNTS195	107344
Israel	USA (United States)	06 Dec 62	460UNTS151	106638
Multilateral		06 Dec 62	450UNTS240	106471
Cameroon	WHO (World Health)	08 Dec 62	451UNTS215	106496
Multilateral		08 Dec 62	510UNTS235	107418
Nigeria	IBRD (World Bank)	10 Dec 62	468UNTS255	106776
Multilateral		12 Dec 62	552UNTS15	108048
Multilateral		12 Dec 62	457UNTS72	106578
Bolivia	USA (United States)	17 Dec 62	469UNTS121	106788
Hungary	USSR (Soviet Union)	20 Dec 62	577UNTS245	108381
Algeria	WHO (World Health)	20 Dec 62	463UNTS135	106698
Morocco	IBRD (World Bank)	21 Dec 62	478UNTS205	106937
IBRD (World Bank)	Thailand	21 Dec 62	467UNTS43	106757
IBRD (World Bank)	Thailand	21 Dec 62	467UNTS63	106758
Nigeria	USA (United States)	24 Dec 62	462UNTS180	106677
Syria	United Arab Rep	27 Dec 62	491UNTS245	107180
Thailand	UK Great Britain	09 Jan 63	470UNTS59	106795
Ghana	Mali	09 Jan 63	466UNTS165	106742
Israel	Philippines	10 Jan 63	588UNTS205	108526
Mauritania	UNICEF (Children)	19 Jan 63	452UNTS271	106514
Multilateral		21 Jan 63	453UNTS20	106517
UK Great Britain	USSR (Soviet Union)	21 Jan 63	475UNTS3	106887
Senegal	Switzerland	23 Jan 63	524UNTS23	107564
United Nations	South Pacific Com	24 Jan 63	470UNTS361	200604
UNICEF (Children)	Tanganyika	25 Jan 63	453UNTS249	106528
Malaysia	USA (United States)	28 Jan 63	473UNTS15	106850
Sudan	USA (United States)	31 Jan 63	494UNTS119	107230
Guinea	Switzerland	01 Feb 63	499UNTS35	107291
Japan	USA (United States)	01 Feb 63	473UNTS49	106854
Poland	USA (United States)	01 Feb 63	487UNTS143	107100
Bolivia	USA (United States)	04 Feb 63	473UNTS65	106856
Multilateral		05 Feb 63	453UNTS36	106518
Austria	Netherlands	06 Feb 63	570UNTS101	108290

Exchange of information and documents (Cont.)

PARTY ONE	PARTY TWO	DATE	CITATION	NUMBER
Iceland	USA (United States)	06 Feb 63	473UNTS93	106858
Mali	Senegal	07 Feb 63	524UNTS41	107565
United Nations	United Arab Rep	08 Feb 63	453UNTS79	106520
Central Afri Rep	USA (United States)	10 Feb 63	473UNTS83	106857
Pakistan	IBRD (World Bank)	13 Feb 63	467UNTS3	106756
Multilateral		14 Feb 63	453UNTS168	106524
Philippines	IBRD (World Bank)	15 Feb 63	478UNTS161	106936
UK Great Britain	Yugoslavia	16 Feb 63	507UNTS171	107400
Algeria	France	18 Feb 63	563UNTS263	108214
Sudan	Switzerland	18 Feb 63	563UNTS281	108215
United Nations	South Pacific Com	20 Feb 63	453UNTS333	200600
Turkey	USA (United States)	21 Feb 63	473UNTS311	106867
Congo (Zaire)	USA (United States)	23 Feb 63	493UNTS17	107204
Congo (Zaire)	USA (United States)	23 Feb 63	493UNTS3	107203
Ethiopia	IDA (Devel Assoc)	27 Feb 63	478UNTS289	106939
Nicaragua	IBRD (World Bank)	01 Mar 63	481UNTS15	106976
IAEA (Atom Energy)	Yugoslavia	04 Mar 63	490UNTS333	107162
Multilateral		06 Mar 63	455UNTS386	106552
IBRD (World Bank)	Thailand	07 Mar 63	467UNTS83	106759
Austria	Czechoslovakia	08 Mar 63	495UNTS219	107245
Peru	IBRD (World Bank)	13 Mar 63	478UNTS245	106938
Israel	USA (United States)	21 Mar 63	476UNTS131	106907
UN Special Fund	Uganda	22 Mar 63	456UNTS466	106572
India	IDA (Devel Assoc)	22 Mar 63	477UNTS3	106911
Colombia	USA (United States)	27 Mar 63	489UNTS289	107145
Hungary	Korea, North	29 Mar 63	577UNTS219	108379
Ethiopia	UNICEF (Children)	01 Apr 63	457UNTS103	106579
Romania	USA (United States)	02 Apr 63	474UNTS95	106874
Austria	Bulgaria	05 Apr 63	480UNTS3	106963
UK Great Britain	USA (United States)	06 Apr 63	474UNTS49	106871
Multilateral		18 Apr 63	463UNTS121	106697
Multilateral		20 Apr 63	495UNTS3	107239
Thailand	USA (United States)	25 Apr 63	476UNTS115	106906
Cyprus	Denmark	27 Apr 63	529UNTS255	107664
Greece	Hungary	27 Apr 63	550UNTS197	108016
Greece	Hungary	27 Apr 63	534UNTS3	107750
Mexico	IBRD (World Bank)	29 Apr 63	489UNTS151	107138
Algeria	Morocco	30 Apr 63	564UNTS3	108217
Austria	Bulgaria	02 May 63	535UNTS143	107778
Multilateral		06 May 63	463UNTS78	106694
El Salvador	USA (United States)	07 May 63	476UNTS35	106901
Multilateral		09 May 63	463UNTS159	106700
IBRD (World Bank)	UK Great Britain	16 May 63	477UNTS361	106929
IBRD (World Bank)	UK Great Britain	16 May 63	476UNTS211	106910
Jamaica	UN Special Fund	22 May 63	489UNTS191	107140
Guinea	USA (United States)	22 May 63	487UNTS251	107108
Multilateral		22 May 63	483UNTS72	107007
Thailand	USA (United States)	24 May 63	477UNTS123	106918
India	IDA (Devel Assoc)	24 May 63	483UNTS205	107014
Multilateral		24 May 63	466UNTS346	106754
Netherlands	UN Special Fund	24 May 63	466UNTS289	106750
Afromalagasy Org	ILO (Labor Org)	30 May 63	467UNTS482	200602
IDA (Devel Assoc)	Turkey	31 May 63	480UNTS127	106966
Colombia	IBRD (World Bank)	03 Jun 63	490UNTS199	107155
IAEA (Atom Energy)	Yugoslavia	04 Jun 63	490UNTS343	107163
India	IBRD (World Bank)	05 Jun 63	481UNTS191	106983
UN Special Fund	Western Samoa	05 Jun 63	467UNTS463	200601
Jamaica	USA (United States)	06 Jun 63	477UNTS29	106913
IBRD (World Bank)	Thailand	11 Jun 63	481UNTS227	106984
Ethiopia	USA (United States)	11 Jun 63	487UNTS269	107109
Korea, South	USA (United States)	18 Jun 63	487UNTS297	107112
Cyprus	USA (United States)	18 Jun 63	479UNTS191	106953
India	USA (United States)	19 Jun 63	479UNTS175	106952
El Salvador	IBRD (World Bank)	19 Jun 63	481UNTS59	106978
Austria	IAEA (Atom Energy)	21 Jun 63	490UNTS351	107164

Exchange of information and documents (Cont.)

PARTY ONE	PARTY TWO	DATE	CITATION	NUMBER
Mongolia	WHO (World Health)	21 Jun 63	472UNTS373	106848
IBRD (World Bank)	Yugoslavia	21 Jun 63	482UNTS43	106990
Colombia	IBRD (World Bank)	21 Jun 63	482UNTS159	106994
Guinea	Ivory Coast	26 Jun 63	499UNTS71	107293
Pakistan	IDA (Devel Assoc)	26 Jun 63	492UNTS115	107189
UNICEF (Children)	Togo	27 Jun 63	540UNTS135	107847
New Zealand	UN Special Fund	28 Jun 63	470UNTS3	106792
Colombia	IBRD (World Bank)	28 Jun 63	489UNTS113	107137
Finland	IAEA (Atom Energy)	02 Jul 63	490UNTS403	107167
Senegal	USA (United States)	03 Jul 63	527UNTS95	107620
IBRD (World Bank)	Tunisia	03 Jul 63	480UNTS209	106970
Costa Rica	IBRD (World Bank)	10 Jul 63	482UNTS69	106991
Austria	France	12 Jul 63	499UNTS91	107294
Malaysia	IBRD (World Bank)	15 Jul 63	482UNTS123	106993
Spain	USA (United States)	16 Jul 63	488UNTS77	107120
Colombia	IBRD (World Bank)	16 Jul 63	482UNTS256	106998
Austria	Denmark	17 Jul 63	479UNTS263	106958
Algeria	Mali	22 Jul 63	564UNTS29	108219
Multilateral		23 Jul 63	471UNTS158	106831
Denmark	IBRD (World Bank)	24 Jul 63	481UNTS171	106982
Pakistan	IDA (Devel Assoc)	26 Jul 63	492UNTS143	107190
Cameroon	UK Great Britain	29 Jul 63	478UNTS148	106935
Finland	IAEA (Atom Energy)	30 Jul 63	490UNTS413	107168
Multilateral		31 Jul 63	472UNTS220	106842
Malaysia	IBRD (World Bank)	07 Aug 63	485UNTS253	107060
India	USA (United States)	08 Aug 63	488UNTS21	107117
Burundi	WHO (World Health)	08 Aug 63	477UNTS346	106928
Cameroon	Israel	09 Aug 63	499UNTS121	107295
Dominican Republic	USA (United States)	13 Aug 63	492UNTS327	107202
Pakistan	IDA (Devel Assoc)	16 Aug 63	492UNTS205	107192
Pakistan	IDA (Devel Assoc)	16 Aug 63	492UNTS171	107191
Paraguay	USA (United States)	20 Aug 63	531UNTS197	107704
Afghanistan	USA (United States)	20 Aug 63	488UNTS41	107118
Argentina	USA (United States)	21 Aug 63	488UNTS61	107119
Burundi	UN Special Fund	22 Aug 63	476UNTS49	106903
Multilateral		27 Aug 63	511UNTS210	107435
Iraq	USA (United States)	27 Aug 63	489UNTS271	107144
Dahomey	UNICEF (Children)	28 Aug 63	507UNTS101	107396
IBRD (World Bank)	UK Great Britain	06 Sep 63	483UNTS173	107013
Multilateral		10 Sep 63	480UNTS100	106965
Brazil	USA (United States)	11 Sep 63	493UNTS267	107220
Finland	IBRD (World Bank)	18 Sep 63	491UNTS345	107183
IBRD (World Bank)	Venezuela	20 Sep 63	482UNTS227	106997
Mexico	IBRD (World Bank)	20 Sep 63	491UNTS317	107182
Ecuador	USA (United States)	20 Sep 63	488UNTS147	107125
IBRD (World Bank)	UK Great Britain	23 Sep 63	503UNTS247	107348
Peru	USA (United States)	23 Sep 63	488UNTS91	107121
Jamaica	WHO (World Health)	25 Sep 63	481UNTS125	106980
Germany, West	Greece	26 Sep 63	550UNTS203	108017
Mali	Romania	26 Sep 63	528UNTS193	107642
Taiwan	IBRD (World Bank)	27 Sep 63	483UNTS151	107012
Japan	IBRD (World Bank)	27 Sep 63	485UNTS283	107061
Jamaica	USA (United States)	01 Oct 63	488UNTS133	107124
El Salvador	IBRD (World Bank)	01 Oct 63	517UNTS3	107481
Czechoslovakia	Yugoslavia	05 Oct 63	504UNTS151	107356
Pakistan	USSR (Soviet Union)	07 Oct 63	499UNTS161	107297
Ivory Coast	Netherlands	09 Oct 63	499UNTS141	107296
Canada	France	11 Oct 63	529UNTS71	107657
Norway	IBRD (World Bank)	15 Oct 63	482UNTS103	106992
Hungary	Yugoslavia	15 Oct 63	577UNTS49	108372
Taiwan	USA (United States)	19 Oct 63	494UNTS27	107224
Multilateral		23 Oct 63	506UNTS197	107388
IBRD (World Bank)	Spain	25 Oct 63	491UNTS297	107181
IBRD (World Bank)	Yugoslavia	28 Oct 63	503UNTS289	107349
Multilateral		30 Oct 63	480UNTS180	106968

Exchange of information and documents (Cont.)

PARTY ONE	PARTY TWO	DATE	CITATION	NUMBER
Greece	USA (United States)	30 Oct 63	493UNTS29	107205
Central Afri Rep	UN Special Fund	30 Oct 63	481UNTS247	106985
WHO (World Health)	Tanganyika	05 Nov 63	496UNTS193	107252
Portugal	IBRD (World Bank)	06 Nov 63	492UNTS89	107188
Tanganyika	USSR (Soviet Union)	06 Nov 63	528UNTS157	107639
Portugal	IBRD (World Bank)	06 Nov 63	491UNTS137	107176
Multilateral		07 Nov 63	480UNTS232	106971
Multilateral		08 Nov 63	482UNTS286	106999
Multilateral		09 Nov 63	489UNTS209	107141
New Zealand	IBRD (World Bank)	12 Nov 63	485UNTS233	107059
Belgium	Romania	13 Nov 63	520UNTS119	107513
Paraguay	USA (United States)	14 Nov 63	505UNTS87	107366
Tunisia	USA (United States)	18 Nov 63	494UNTS193	107233
Syria	USA (United States)	18 Nov 63	494UNTS169	107232
Niger	United Nations	20 Nov 63	536UNTS3	107793
Iran	UNICEF (Children)	21 Nov 63	485UNTS35	107044
Israel	USA (United States)	22 Nov 63	494UNTS89	107228
Peru	IBRD (World Bank)	22 Nov 63	491UNTS101	107175
Netherlands	USA (United States)	26 Nov 63	388UNTS303	105586
Iraq	UNICEF (Children)	03 Dec 63	482UNTS319	107001
Multilateral		03 Dec 63	529UNTS217	107663
United Arab Rep	USA (United States)	04 Dec 63	505UNTS117	107368
Jordan	IDA (Devel Assoc)	12 Dec 63	506UNTS51	107381
Jordan	IDA (Devel Assoc)	12 Dec 63	492UNTS3	107184
Greece	USA (United States)	13 Dec 63	494UNTS55	107226
Canada	India	16 Dec 63	529UNTS45	107655
Chile	IBRD (World Bank)	18 Dec 63	504UNTS29	107352
Mexico	IAEA (Atom Energy)	18 Dec 63	490UNTS361	107165
Chile	IBRD (World Bank)	18 Dec 63	504UNTS3	107351
Netherlands	Poland	20 Dec 63	514UNTS169	107446
IDA (Devel Assoc)	Syria	24 Dec 63	534UNTS253	107764
Romania	Yugoslavia	25 Dec 63	576UNTS95	108366
Paraguay	IDA (Devel Assoc)	26 Dec 63	507UNTS3	107394
Canada	USA (United States)	27 Dec 63	494UNTS21	107223
Multilateral		30 Dec 63	568UNTS243	108272
Multilateral		30 Dec 63	568UNTS215	108270
Multilateral		30 Dec 63	568UNTS233	108271
Multilateral		30 Dec 63	551UNTS105	108036
Multilateral		30 Dec 63	551UNTS119	108037
Australia	USA (United States)	03 Jan 64	505UNTS159	107371
Burundi	UNICEF (Children)	08 Jan 64	485UNTS45	107045
Liberia	IBRD (World Bank)	08 Jan 64	504UNTS53	107353
USA (United States)	Vietnam, South	09 Jan 64	505UNTS173	107373
Mali	Niger	15 Jan 64	499UNTS197	107299
Czechoslovakia	Yugoslavia	20 Jan 64	538UNTS197	107816
Multilateral		28 Jan 64	502UNTS321	107336
Poland	USA (United States)	03 Feb 64	505UNTS245	107376
Poland	USA (United States)	03 Feb 64	505UNTS215	107375
Lebanon	Pakistan	04 Feb 64	614UNTS55	108863
IDA (Devel Assoc)	Tanganyika	05 Feb 64	506UNTS91	107382
Subsahara Tech Com	IAEA (Atom Energy)	06 Feb 64	501UNTS285	200606
Argentina	Paraguay	07 Feb 64	634UNTS127	109057
Colombia	IBRD (World Bank)	07 Feb 64	516UNTS99	107473
Paraguay	USA (United States)	10 Feb 64	511UNTS53	107426
Jordan	USA (United States)	11 Feb 64	511UNTS85	107429
Denmark	Yugoslavia	11 Feb 64	511UNTS241	107437
Iceland	USA (United States)	13 Feb 64	510UNTS295	107420
Peru	USA (United States)	13 Feb 64	511UNTS119	107431
Iceland	USA (United States)	13 Feb 64	511UNTS3	107421
Multilateral		20 Feb 64	491UNTS30	107172
USA (United States)	USSR (Soviet Union)	22 Feb 64	526UNTS131	107605
Philippines	USA (United States)	24 Feb 64	505UNTS283	107378
Denmark	USSR (Soviet Union)	27 Feb 64	509UNTS285	107407
Cyprus	USSR (Soviet Union)	29 Feb 64	602UNTS45	108706
Sudan	USA (United States)	02 Mar 64	524UNTS217	107575

PARTY ONE	PARTY TWO	DATE	CITATION	NUMBER
Exchange of information and documents (Cont.)				
Ivory Coast	USA (United States)	10 Mar 64	526UNTS285	107611
IBRD (World Bank)	Thailand	11 Mar 64	504UNTS73	107354
Nigeria	IBRD (World Bank)	12 Mar 64	516UNTS325	107480
Portugal	USA (United States)	12 Mar 64	542UNTS3	107875
New Zealand	IBRD (World Bank)	12 Mar 64	505UNTS3	107362
Czechoslovakia	Yugoslavia	14 Mar 64	544UNTS147	107917
Cameroon	Mali	17 Mar 64	524UNTS61	107566
Italy	United Nations	18 Mar 64	491UNTS21	107171
Pakistan	IDA (Devel Assoc)	25 Mar 64	534UNTS275	107765
Pakistan	IDA (Devel Assoc)	25 Mar 64	535UNTS43	107775
Bolivia	USA (United States)	25 Mar 64	532UNTS3	107710
Germany, West	Thailand	02 Apr 64	503UNTS3	107338
Malaysia	Netherlands	07 Apr 64	524UNTS81	107567
Tunisia	USA (United States)	07 Apr 64	527UNTS3	107613
Taiwan	UNICEF (Children)	08 Apr 64	500UNTS49	107306
Mexico	Netherlands	08 Apr 64	575UNTS35	108353
Norway	Yugoslavia	15 Apr 64	602UNTS177	108712
Peru	IBRD (World Bank)	22 Apr 64	519UNTS95	107503
Japan	IBRD (World Bank)	22 Apr 64	505UNTS21	107363
USA (United States)	Yugoslavia	27 Apr 64	526UNTS89	107602
USA (United States)	Yugoslavia	27 Apr 64	526UNTS73	107601
USA (United States)	Yugoslavia	28 Apr 64	526UNTS103	107603
Ethiopia	IBRD (World Bank)	08 May 64	505UNTS51	107364
Liberia	USA (United States)	08 May 64	526UNTS239	107608
Algeria	IBRD (World Bank)	14 May 64	522UNTS265	107552
Philippines	USA (United States)	14 May 64	526UNTS113	107604
Pakistan	IBRD (World Bank)	14 May 64	516UNTS145	107475
Jamaica	UNICEF (Children)	19 May 64	500UNTS75	107308
Norway	Romania	21 May 64	563UNTS45	108203
Multilateral		25 May 64	620UNTS149	108953
Ecuador	IDA (Devel Assoc)	26 May 64	534UNTS93	107757
Ecuador	IBRD (World Bank)	26 May 64	534UNTS113	107758
Multilateral		26 May 64	541UNTS271	200613
Taiwan	USA (United States)	03 Jun 64	526UNTS257	107610
Ireland	UN Special Fund	03 Jun 64	496UNTS205	107253
IBRD (World Bank)	Tunisia	05 Jun 64	539UNTS129	107827
India	IDA (Devel Assoc)	09 Jun 64	506UNTS31	107380
Iran	IBRD (World Bank)	10 Jun 64	537UNTS111	107799
Pakistan	IDA (Devel Assoc)	11 Jun 64	534UNTS309	107766
Multilateral		11 Jun 64	525UNTS61	107584
Czechoslovakia	Netherlands	11 Jun 64	556UNTS89	108120
Pakistan	IDA (Devel Assoc)	11 Jun 64	506UNTS3	107379
IAEA (Atom Energy)	USA (United States)	15 Jun 64	525UNTS3	107580
Multilateral		15 Jun 64	573UNTS85	108324
Italy	Romania	16 Jun 64	558UNTS313	108150
Multilateral		18 Jun 64	542UNTS145	107886
UK Great Britain	USA (United States)	19 Jun 64	530UNTS99	107675
Rwanda	WHO (World Health)	22 Jun 64	514UNTS11	107440
Multilateral		23 Jun 64	506UNTS108	107383
Rwanda	WHO (World Health)	23 Jun 64	514UNTS157	107445
WHO (World Health)	Trinidad/Tobago	23 Jun 64	503UNTS167	107342
Pakistan	IDA (Devel Assoc)	24 Jun 64	533UNTS191	107743
Pakistan	IDA (Devel Assoc)	24 Jun 64	533UNTS165	107742
Multilateral		28 Jun 64	519UNTS14	107499
Malaysia	UNICEF (Children)	01 Jul 64	503UNTS229	107346
India	IDA (Devel Assoc)	06 Jul 64	534UNTS49	107753
Nigeria	IBRD (World Bank)	07 Jul 64	537UNTS3	107795
Ivory Coast	Mali	09 Jul 64	524UNTS121	107569
Iceland	UN Special Fund	10 Jul 64	502UNTS343	107337
Finland	IBRD (World Bank)	10 Jul 64	516UNTS125	107474
Gabon	IBRD (World Bank)	10 Jul 64	537UNTS63	107797
IDA (Devel Assoc)	Turkey	14 Jul 64	534UNTS339	107767
Greece	USA (United States)	17 Jul 64	530UNTS13	107669
Turkey	USA (United States)	17 Jul 64	530UNTS25	107670
Poland	USSR (Soviet Union)	17 Jul 64	552UNTS175	108054
Pakistan	IDA (Devel Assoc)	21 Jul 64	534UNTS373	107768
Philippines	IBRD (World Bank)	22 Jul 64	516UNTS171	107476
Austria	Netherlands	23 Jul 64	544UNTS265	107921
Bolivia	IDA (Devel Assoc)	24 Jul 64	534UNTS171	107762
Bolivia	IDA (Devel Assoc)	24 Jul 64	534UNTS203	107763
Multilateral		28 Jul 64	555UNTS183	108113
IBRD (World Bank)	Spain	31 Jul 64	537UNTS81	107798
Switzerland	UK Great Britain	11 Aug 64	552UNTS271	108059
Kenya	IDA (Devel Assoc)	17 Aug 64	535UNTS79	107776
IBRD (World Bank)	Sierra Leone	18 Aug 64	516UNTS295	107479
Netherlands	Turkey	19 Aug 64	521UNTS197	107523
Morocco	IBRD (World Bank)	26 Aug 64	537UNTS193	107802
Pakistan	IDA (Devel Assoc)	26 Aug 64	535UNTS263	107784
IBRD (World Bank)	Venezuela	28 Aug 64	520UNTS97	107512
Australia	USA (United States)	28 Aug 64	510UNTS201	107415
IBRD (World Bank)	Venezuela	28 Aug 64	537UNTS135	107800
IDA (Devel Assoc)	Turkey	31 Aug 64	535UNTS111	107777
Paraguay	USA (United States)	05 Sep 64	530UNTS225	107685
Multilateral		18 Sep 64	555UNTS205	108114
Multilateral		18 Sep 64	556UNTS25	108117
Multilateral		21 Sep 64	555UNTS227	108115
Pakistan	IDA (Devel Assoc)	22 Sep 64	594UNTS225	108605
Iran	USA (United States)	29 Sep 64	531UNTS163	107702
USA (United States)	Vietnam, South	29 Sep 64	531UNTS183	107703
Mali	IDA (Devel Assoc)	29 Sep 64	594UNTS187	108604
Australia	UN Special Fund	30 Sep 64	510UNTS277	107419
India	USA (United States)	30 Sep 64	532UNTS321	107726
Multilateral		30 Sep 64	556UNTS3	108116
Kenya	UN Special Fund	01 Oct 64	511UNTS181	107433
USA (United States)	Yugoslavia	05 Oct 64	531UNTS63	107693
Czechoslovakia	Germany, East	06 Oct 64	545UNTS113	107927
Germany, East	Poland	06 Oct 64	552UNTS89	108051
Germany, West	Jamaica	07 Oct 64	514UNTS187	107447
Czechoslovakia	Yugoslavia	08 Oct 64	544UNTS129	107916
Colombia	USA (United States)	08 Oct 64	579UNTS3	108395
Czechoslovakia	Hungary	17 Oct 64	545UNTS21	107924
Czechoslovakia	Mongolia	21 Oct 64	545UNTS91	107926
Multilateral		24 Oct 64	514UNTS220	200608
Romania	UN Special Fund	24 Oct 64	519UNTS29	107500
Malawi	UN Special Fund	24 Oct 64	514UNTS235	200609
India	IDA (Devel Assoc)	26 Oct 64	535UNTS245	107783
Asian Productivity	ILO (Labor Org)	27 Oct 64	516UNTS367	200610
Philippines	IBRD (World Bank)	28 Oct 64	537UNTS165	107801
USA (United States)	Yugoslavia	28 Oct 64	533UNTS3	107728
USA (United States)	Yugoslavia	29 Oct 64	533UNTS17	107729
USA (United States)	Yugoslavia	05 Nov 64	550UNTS31	108007
Multilateral		07 Nov 64	548UNTS3	107965
USA (United States)	Yugoslavia	09 Nov 64	533UNTS39	107731
Austria	Hungary	11 Nov 64	576UNTS163	108368
Multilateral		11 Nov 64	515UNTS94	107456
Iran	USA (United States)	16 Nov 64	532UNTS213	107719
Greece	USA (United States)	17 Nov 64	532UNTS107	107714
USA (United States)	USSR (Soviet Union)	18 Nov 64	535UNTS307	107786
Argentina	Panama	21 Nov 64	635UNTS205	109083
Argentina	Costa Rica	23 Nov 64	635UNTS213	109084
Afghanistan	IDA (Devel Assoc)	23 Nov 64	567UNTS155	108255
Multilateral		25 Nov 64	587UNTS19	108507
IBRD (World Bank)	Thailand	25 Nov 64	537UNTS273	107805
Czechoslovakia	United Arab Rep	26 Nov 64	545UNTS11	107923
Poland	Romania	26 Nov 64	552UNTS157	108053
Argentina	IAEA (Atom Energy)	02 Dec 64	525UNTS29	107582
Multilateral		02 Dec 64	572UNTS229	108317
Kenya	USA (United States)	07 Dec 64	532UNTS263	107722
Congo (Zaire)	USA (United States)	09 Dec 64	531UNTS249	107707
India	Netherlands	11 Dec 64	570UNTS165	108292

Exchange of information and documents (Cont.)

PARTY ONE	PARTY TWO	DATE	CITATION	NUMBER
IBRD (World Bank)	Yugoslavia	11 Dec 64	537UNTS321	107807
UN Special Fund	Zambia	15 Dec 64	522UNTS3	107532
Germany, West	Jamaica	16 Dec 64	531UNTS129	107699
Paraguay	IBRD (World Bank)	16 Dec 64	549UNTS173	107999
Taiwan	IBRD (World Bank)	17 Dec 64	538UNTS3	107808
Israel	USA (United States)	22 Dec 64	532UNTS231	107720
Japan	IBRD (World Bank)	23 Dec 64	538UNTS37	107809
Mauritania	IDA (Devel Assoc)	28 Dec 64	540UNTS163	107849
Kenya	IDA (Devel Assoc)	29 Dec 64	535UNTS225	107782
Morocco	USA (United States)	29 Dec 64	593UNTS185	108584
Iceland	USA (United States)	30 Dec 64	531UNTS287	107709
Iceland	USA (United States)	30 Dec 64	542UNTS37	107878
Taiwan	USA (United States)	31 Dec 64	532UNTS59	107712
Dahomey	USA (United States)	31 Dec 64	541UNTS117	107865
Korea, South	USA (United States)	31 Dec 64	535UNTS315	107787
Taiwan	USA (United States)	31 Dec 64	532UNTS29	107711
Malawi	WHO (World Health)	06 Jan 65	525UNTS165	107588
Malawi	WHO (World Health)	08 Jan 65	524UNTS281	107579
Belgium	Sweden	11 Jan 65	533UNTS157	107741
Argentina	UK Great Britain	12 Jan 65	597UNTS177	108645
Japan	IBRD (World Bank)	13 Jan 65	537UNTS293	107806
IAEA (Atom Energy)	United Arab Rep	14 Jan 65	603UNTS45	108723
Korea, South	USA (United States)	26 Jan 65	541UNTS77	107862
Multilateral		27 Jan 65	523UNTS102	107556
Peru	USA (United States)	28 Jan 65	587UNTS273	108513
Sierra Leone	USA (United States)	29 Jan 65	542UNTS87	107882
Switzerland	USA (United States)	30 Jan 65	594UNTS55	108594
Multilateral		02 Feb 65	523UNTS256	107560
Honduras	IBRD (World Bank)	02 Feb 65	561UNTS255	108188
Mexico	IBRD (World Bank)	04 Feb 65	549UNTS189	108000
USA (United States)	USSR (Soviet Union)	05 Feb 65	541UNTS97	107863
Greece	India	11 Feb 65	606UNTS9	108771
Belgium	Hungary	11 Feb 65	544UNTS3	107908
Luxembourg	Portugal	12 Feb 65	571UNTS239	108305
Multilateral		12 Feb 65	525UNTS148	107587
Chile	IBRD (World Bank)	12 Feb 65	537UNTS35	107796
UK Great Britain	USSR (Soviet Union)	13 Feb 65	543UNTS43	107896
Tunisia	USA (United States)	17 Feb 65	542UNTS125	107885
Belgium	United Nations	20 Feb 65	535UNTS197	107780
Multilateral		24 Feb 65	556UNTS47	108118
France	UK Great Britain	25 Feb 65	543UNTS157	107899
Brazil	IBRD (World Bank)	26 Feb 65	567UNTS91	108253
Brazil	IBRD (World Bank)	26 Feb 65	553UNTS3	108065
Multilateral		26 Feb 65	556UNTS69	108119
Pakistan	USA (United States)	26 Feb 65	542UNTS103	107883
Malaysia	IBRD (World Bank)	26 Feb 65	549UNTS239	108002
Nigeria	IDA (Devel Assoc)	01 Mar 65	571UNTS3	108297
Nigeria	IDA (Devel Assoc)	01 Mar 65	563UNTS3	108201
USA (United States)	Yugoslavia	16 Mar 65	542UNTS161	107887
Dominican Republic	USA (United States)	18 Mar 65	542UNTS215	107892
IBRD (World Bank)	Thailand	22 Mar 65	538UNTS63	107810
Finland	UK Great Britain	25 Mar 65	539UNTS103	107826
Denmark	Malaysia	26 Mar 65	540UNTS205	107851
IDA (Devel Assoc)	Somalia	29 Mar 65	586UNTS101	108499
IBRD (World Bank)	Uruguay	30 Mar 65	567UNTS45	108251
Ivory Coast	USA (United States)	05 Apr 65	546UNTS143	107941
Jamaica	IBRD (World Bank)	08 Apr 65	539UNTS303	107841
Austria	Hungary	09 Apr 65	638UNTS135	109133
Afghanistan	UK Great Britain	19 Apr 65	633UNTS45	109033
Malta	UNICEF (Children)	22 Apr 65	533UNTS107	107737
Philippines	USA (United States)	23 Apr 65	546UNTS157	107942
Morocco	USA (United States)	23 Apr 65	594UNTS3	108591
Netherlands	Tanzania	27 Apr 65	594UNTS123	108599
Iran	IBRD (World Bank)	28 Apr 65	555UNTS45	108104
Taiwan	IBRD (World Bank)	28 Apr 65	549UNTS145	107998

Exchange of information and documents (Cont.)

PARTY ONE	PARTY TWO	DATE	CITATION	NUMBER
Iran	IBRD (World Bank)	28 Apr 65	555UNTS21	108103
Portugal	IBRD (World Bank)	29 Apr 65	549UNTS69	107991
Multilateral		29 Apr 65	586UNTS123	108500
Ghana	Malawi	04 May 65	541UNTS163	107869
Mauritania	Spain	11 May 65	602UNTS111	108709
Bolivia	USA (United States)	12 May 65	564UNTS143	108226
Afghanistan	USA (United States)	22 May 65	579UNTS29	108396
Bulgaria	Czechoslovakia	22 May 65	545UNTS65	107925
Ethiopia	Hungary	25 May 65	577UNTS193	108377
Japan	IBRD (World Bank)	26 May 65	550UNTS95	108010
Malaysia	Norway	26 May 65	602UNTS157	108711
USA (United States)	Vietnam, South	26 May 65	550UNTS3	108005
China People's Rep	Romania	27 May 65	592UNTS3	108566
India	IBRD (World Bank)	28 May 65	552UNTS39	108049
Gambia	UNICEF (Children)	29 May 65	547UNTS29	107954
Multilateral		02 Jun 65	537UNTS348	200611
Peru	IBRD (World Bank)	03 Jun 65	551UNTS227	108045
Finland	USSR (Soviet Union)	04 Jun 65	560UNTS169	108173
Pakistan	USSR (Soviet Union)	05 Jun 65	593UNTS115	108579
Gambia	UN Special Fund	09 Jun 65	538UNTS321	200612
India	IBRD (World Bank)	11 Jun 65	557UNTS101	108130
India	IBRD (World Bank)	11 Jun 65	557UNTS59	108128
Multilateral		18 Jun 65	573UNTS3	108320
Peru	IBRD (World Bank)	18 Jun 65	568UNTS191	108269
Multilateral		23 Jun 65	548UNTS241	107981
Mongolia	UNICEF (Children)	23 Jun 65	540UNTS83	107844
Ecuador	USA (United States)	25 Jun 65	549UNTS23	107986
Italy	IBRD (World Bank)	28 Jun 65	567UNTS127	108254
Finland	IBRD (World Bank)	30 Jun 65	550UNTS63	108009
UN Special Fund	Spain	30 Jun 65	544UNTS159	107918
ILO (Labor Org)	LAFTA (Free Trade)	02 Jul 65	563UNTS327	200619
Multilateral		02 Jul 65	592UNTS215	108575
Pakistan	IBRD (World Bank)	09 Jul 65	554UNTS39	108096
Iran	IBRD (World Bank)	12 Jul 65	554UNTS3	108095
Austria	Bulgaria	12 Jul 65	587UNTS51	108510
Mali	USA (United States)	14 Jul 65	564UNTS101	108223
USA (United States)	Yugoslavia	16 Jul 65	549UNTS111	107994
Congo (Zaire)	USA (United States)	19 Jul 65	593UNTS215	108586
Multilateral		22 Jul 65	561UNTS333	200618
ILO (Labor Org)	Org Ctrl Am States	26 Jul 65	563UNTS341	200620
Chile	USA (United States)	27 Jul 65	574UNTS83	108342
Ethiopia	USA (United States)	17 Aug 65	564UNTS119	108224
Poland	WHO (World Health)	26 Aug 65	552UNTS3	108047
Multilateral		13 Sep 65	547UNTS264	107962
Afghanistan	IAEA (Atom Energy)	24 Sep 65	556UNTS101	108121
Morocco	IAEA (Atom Energy)	24 Sep 65	556UNTS109	108122
IAEA (Atom Energy)	Uruguay	24 Sep 65	556UNTS117	108123
Multilateral		24 Sep 65	556UNTS141	108124
Nigeria	IBRD (World Bank)	26 Sep 65	571UNTS39	108298
Nigeria	IBRD (World Bank)	26 Sep 65	570UNTS233	108296
IBRD (World Bank)	Spain	29 Sep 65	568UNTS49	108264
Kenya	IBRD (World Bank)	29 Sep 65	568UNTS289	108274
IBRD (World Bank)	Uganda	29 Sep 65	568UNTS317	108276
IBRD (World Bank)	Tanzania	29 Sep 65	568UNTS309	108275
East Afri Service	IBRD (World Bank)	29 Sep 65	568UNTS327	200623
Mexico	IBRD (World Bank)	01 Oct 65	589UNTS339	108542
Chile	IBRD (World Bank)	06 Oct 65	567UNTS293	108261
Nigeria	Switzerland	11 Oct 65	602UNTS137	108710
Multilateral		21 Oct 65	547UNTS216	107959
Philippines	IBRD (World Bank)	02 Nov 65	567UNTS3	108249
Argentina	Belgium	05 Nov 65	635UNTS229	109086
OAU (Afri Unity)	United Nations	15 Nov 65	548UNTS315	200614
Multilateral		15 Nov 65	0UNTS0	109432
Malaysia	IBRD (World Bank)	17 Nov 65	568UNTS23	108263
Austria	Yugoslavia	19 Nov 65	587UNTS239	108512

Exchange of information and documents (Cont.)

PARTY ONE	PARTY TWO	DATE	CITATION	NUMBER
USA (United States)	Yugoslavia	22 Nov 65	574UNTS211	108351
ILO (Labor Org)	OAU (Afri Unity)	25 Nov 65	550UNTS389	200617
IBRD (World Bank)	Venezuela	13 Dec 65	568UNTS77	108265
Ethiopia	USA (United States)	14 Dec 65	574UNTS115	108344
Mexico	IBRD (World Bank)	15 Dec 65	568UNTS125	108267
Paraguay	IBRD (World Bank)	16 Dec 65	568UNTS165	108268
New Zealand	IBRD (World Bank)	17 Dec 65	567UNTS255	108259
New Zealand	IBRD (World Bank)	17 Dec 65	567UNTS275	108260
IBRD (World Bank)	Sudan	27 Dec 65	567UNTS27	108250
Ethiopia	IBRD (World Bank)	28 Dec 65	567UNTS229	108258
United Arab Rep	USA (United States)	03 Jan 66	579UNTS63	108399
United Arab Rep	USA (United States)	03 Jan 66	579UNTS83	108400
Liberia	USA (United States)	06 Jan 66	592UNTS101	108570
United Nations	Senegal	12 Jan 66	551UNTS147	108039
Pakistan	IDA (Devel Assoc)	13 Jan 66	567UNTS67	108252
Iran	USSR (Soviet Union)	13 Jan 66	633UNTS123	109037
IDA (Devel Assoc)	Tanzania	13 Jan 66	567UNTS177	108256
Czechoslovakia	Poland	22 Jan 66	588UNTS175	108524
Mongolia	UN Special Fund	26 Jan 66	552UNTS201	108055
UK Great Britain	Yugoslavia	27 Jan 66	573UNTS243	108337
Norway	Eur Space Research	31 Jan 66	580UNTS3	108414
Guinea	USA (United States)	04 Feb 66	579UNTS213	108409
Belgium	Denmark	04 Feb 66	561UNTS233	108187
IAEA (Atom Energy)	Turkey	08 Feb 66	573UNTS75	108323
Pakistan	IDA (Devel Assoc)	10 Feb 66	575UNTS89	108355
Multilateral		10 Feb 66	575UNTS129	108356
Austria	Finland	21 Feb 66	597UNTS273	108651
Algeria	USA (United States)	23 Feb 66	592UNTS117	108571
Brazil	Denmark	25 Feb 66	590UNTS95	108549
Multilateral		04 Mar 66	578UNTS57	108387
Korea, South	USA (United States)	07 Mar 66	579UNTS137	108404
Bulgaria	UNICEF (Children)	10 Mar 66	559UNTS13	108152
Ceylon (Sri Lanka)	USA (United States)	12 Mar 66	579UNTS117	108403
Brazil	IBRD (World Bank)	15 Mar 66	599UNTS52	108664
Argentina	Taiwan	19 Mar 66	635UNTS281	109089
Austria	Spain	24 Mar 66	590UNTS203	108555
WHO (World Health)	Singapore	28 Mar 66	562UNTS59	108195
Guinea	IBRD (World Bank)	30 Mar 66	568UNTS3	108262
Ghana	USA (United States)	01 Apr 66	579UNTS157	108405
Paraguay	IDA (Devel Assoc)	04 Apr 66	582UNTS331	108469
Paraguay	IBRD (World Bank)	04 Apr 66	570UNTS41	108287
Jordan	USA (United States)	05 Apr 66	593UNTS239	108587
Multilateral		05 Apr 66	640UNTS133	109159
Paraguay	USA (United States)	11 Apr 66	578UNTS99	108389
USA (United States)	Yugoslavia	11 Apr 66	580UNTS239	108427
Sudan	USA (United States)	13 Apr 66	586UNTS39	108495
Indonesia	USA (United States)	18 Apr 66	578UNTS106	108390
IBRD (World Bank)	Venezuela	21 Apr 66	568UNTS257	108273
Bolivia	USA (United States)	22 Apr 66	578UNTS73	108388
Romania	IAEA (Atom Energy)	22 Apr 66	603UNTS23	108721
Belgium	Israel	26 Apr 66	566UNTS187	108243
Finland	IBRD (World Bank)	27 Apr 66	568UNTS107	108266
Paraguay	USA (United States)	27 Apr 66	578UNTS121	108391
Multilateral		30 Apr 66	620UNTS191	108956
Multilateral		04 May 66	575UNTS49	108354
Rwanda	USSR (Soviet Union)	06 May 66	633UNTS217	109039
Peru	IBRD (World Bank)	13 May 66	570UNTS61	108288
IBRD (World Bank)	Tunisia	16 May 66	584UNTS155	108477
Austria	Ireland	24 May 66	636UNTS149	109102
Mexico	IBRD (World Bank)	25 May 66	596UNTS3	108627
Bulgaria	UN Special Fund	26 May 66	563UNTS71	108205
Pakistan	USA (United States)	26 May 66	594UNTS27	108592
UK Great Britain	USA (United States)	02 Jun 66	573UNTS229	108336
Austria	Israel	06 Jun 66	0UNTS0	109346
Israel	USA (United States)	06 Jun 66	593UNTS165	108583

Exchange of information and documents (Cont.)

PARTY ONE	PARTY TWO	DATE	CITATION	NUMBER
Portugal	IBRD (World Bank)	14 Jun 66	581UNTS3	108430
Portugal	IBRD (World Bank)	14 Jun 66	581UNTS29	108431
Pakistan	IDA (Devel Assoc)	17 Jun 66	582UNTS297	108468
Mexico	IAEA (Atom Energy)	20 Jun 66	573UNTS25	108321
Jamaica	IBRD (World Bank)	20 Jun 66	582UNTS145	108462
Multilateral		20 Jun 66	572UNTS263	108318
Austria	USA (United States)	23 Jun 66	601UNTS51	108687
IBRD (World Bank)	Thailand	24 Jun 66	582UNTS259	108466
Indonesia	USA (United States)	28 Jun 66	593UNTS201	108585
Denmark	Jordan	28 Jun 66	574UNTS3	108338
India	IDA (Devel Assoc)	29 Jun 66	582UNTS277	108467
India	IDA (Devel Assoc)	29 Jun 66	585UNTS101	108484
Israel	UK Great Britain	05 Jul 66	630UNTS189	108971
India	IBRD (World Bank)	07 Jul 66	595UNTS3	108610
FAO (Food Agri)	IMCO (Maritime Org)	11 Jul 66	575UNTS238	200627
Austria	France	15 Jul 66	604UNTS265	108755
Iraq	IBRD (World Bank)	22 Jul 66	584UNTS233	108480
Iran	IBRD (World Bank)	26 Jul 66	582UNTS107	108461
Malaysia	IBRD (World Bank)	26 Jul 66	586UNTS195	108504
Sweden	USA (United States)	28 Jul 66	603UNTS61	108725
IDA (Devel Assoc)	Siam	02 Aug 66	585UNTS271	108492
IDA (Devel Assoc)	Turkey	10 Aug 66	585UNTS237	108491
IBRD (World Bank)	Turkey	10 Aug 66	585UNTS199	108490
IBRD (World Bank)	Singapore	11 Aug 66	585UNTS39	108482
Kenya	IDA (Devel Assoc)	19 Aug 66	585UNTS119	108485
India	IDA (Devel Assoc)	19 Aug 66	584UNTS193	108478
Honduras	IBRD (World Bank)	25 Aug 66	582UNTS79	108460
Bulgaria	United Arab Rep	29 Aug 66	630UNTS325	108980
Romania	United Arab Rep	03 Sep 66	604UNTS73	108745
Peru	IBRD (World Bank)	07 Sep 66	585UNTS3	108481
Netherlands	Yugoslavia	08 Sep 66	597UNTS147	108643
IBRD (World Bank)	South Africa	08 Sep 66	585UNTS71	108483
UN Special Fund	UPU (Postal Union)	21 Sep 66	573UNTS259	200626
Netherlands	Norway	22 Sep 66	600UNTS227	108683
Belgium	France	23 Sep 66	588UNTS227	108528
IAEA (Atom Energy)	USA (United States)	26 Sep 66	589UNTS3	108532
Hungary	Yugoslavia	26 Sep 66	601UNTS21	108685
Philippines	IAEA (Atom Energy)	28 Sep 66	589UNTS25	108533
USSR (Soviet Union)	Yugoslavia	29 Sep 66	608UNTS219	108818
IDA (Devel Assoc)	Senegal	29 Sep 66	594UNTS277	108607
Jamaica	IBRD (World Bank)	30 Sep 66	582UNTS179	108463
Malawi	IDA (Devel Assoc)	04 Oct 66	584UNTS215	108479
IBRD (World Bank)	Zambia	04 Oct 66	585UNTS181	108489
Nicaragua	IBRD (World Bank)	05 Oct 66	582UNTS231	108465
Israel	Norway	02 Nov 66	630UNTS225	108972
IBRD (World Bank)	Singapore	04 Nov 66	585UNTS155	108488
Indonesia	UNICEF (Children)	17 Nov 66	578UNTS47	108386
Canada	Norway	23 Nov 66	604UNTS295	108757
Kuwait	UK Great Britain	26 Nov 66	633UNTS58	109034
Congo (Brazzaville)	Czechoslovakia	29 Nov 66	635UNTS3	109069
Singapore	UK Great Britain	01 Dec 66	605UNTS153	108763
India	IAEA (Atom Energy)	09 Dec 66	603UNTS35	108722
Syria	USSR (Soviet Union)	18 Dec 66	633UNTS247	109041
Brazil	IBRD (World Bank)	19 Dec 66	599UNTS177	108667
Brazil	IBRD (World Bank)	19 Dec 66	599UNTS205	108668
Brazil	IBRD (World Bank)	19 Dec 66	599UNTS107	108665
Brazil	IBRD (World Bank)	19 Dec 66	599UNTS149	108666
Denmark	Singapore	20 Dec 66	593UNTS125	108580
Philippines	USA (United States)	22 Dec 66	591UNTS219	108559
Chile	IBRD (World Bank)	23 Dec 66	595UNTS141	108618
Pakistan	IDA (Devel Assoc)	23 Dec 66	594UNTS255	108606
India	IDA (Devel Assoc)	23 Dec 66	594UNTS165	108603
Kuwait	UK Great Britain	29 Dec 66	617UNTS203	108914
Trinidad/Tobago	UK Great Britain	29 Dec 66	605UNTS237	108766
Italy	United Nations	18 Jan 67	588UNTS197	108525

PARTY ONE	PARTY TWO	DATE	CITATION	NUMBER
Exchange of information and documents (Cont.)				
Jamaica	IBRD (World Bank)	23 Jan 67	594UNTS311	108608
IBRD (World Bank)	Venezuela	26 Jan 67	596UNTS35	108628
Morocco	IBRD (World Bank)	26 Jan 67	642UNTS3	109160
UNICEF (Children)	Zambia	02 Feb 67	589UNTS89	108536
Czechoslovakia	USSR (Soviet Union)	03 Feb 67	617UNTS267	108917
Australia	UN Special Fund	06 Feb 67	590UNTS3	108543
Bulgaria	United Arab Rep	12 Feb 67	630UNTS353	108981
Bulgaria	United Arab Rep	12 Feb 67	630UNTS363	108982
Netherlands	Romania	13 Feb 67	604UNTS287	108756
Multilateral		14 Feb 67	634UNTS281	109068
Kenya	IBRD (World Bank)	17 Feb 67	599UNTS233	108669
East Afri Service	IBRD (World Bank)	17 Feb 67	599UNTS335	200629
IBRD (World Bank)	Uganda	17 Feb 67	599UNTS321	108673
IBRD (World Bank)	Tanzania	17 Feb 67	599UNTS287	108671
IBRD (World Bank)	Yugoslavia	24 Feb 67	599UNTS27	108663
Ghana	UK Great Britain	27 Feb 67	606UNTS133	108783
Trinidad/Tobago	UK Great Britain	01 Mar 67	606UNTS149	108784
Romania	Sweden	01 Mar 67	642UNTS163	109172
Romania	UK Great Britain	09 Mar 67	605UNTS195	108764
Pakistan	IBRD (World Bank)	15 Mar 67	599UNTS245	108670
Czechoslovakia	Germany, East	17 Mar 67	609UNTS187	108831
Belgium	Hungary	20 Mar 67	601UNTS37	108686
Belgium	Israel	23 Mar 67	630UNTS275	108974
IBRD (World Bank)	Thailand	24 Mar 67	599UNTS299	108672
Romania	Somalia	20 Apr 67	642UNTS155	109171
Bulgaria	USSR (Soviet Union)	27 Apr 67	631UNTS3	108983
Multilateral		04 May 67	595UNTS287	108623
Iran	IAEA (Atom Energy)	10 May 67	614UNTS93	108865
Italy	USSR (Soviet Union)	16 May 67	608UNTS79	108814
Belgium	Bulgaria	17 May 67	631UNTS215	108995
Czechoslovakia	Yugoslavia	17 May 67	617UNTS305	108918
Bulgaria	Turkey	30 May 67	631UNTS19	108984
Liberia	IBRD (World Bank)	05 Jun 67	633UNTS13	109031
Malta	USA (United States)	14 Jun 67	604UNTS231	108753
Bulgaria	Romania	15 Jun 67	634UNTS57	109051
Cameroon	UK Great Britain	16 Jun 67	618UNTS329	108933
Dominican Republic	UK Great Britain	20 Jun 67	619UNTS3	108935
IAEA (Atom Energy)	Spain	23 Jun 67	614UNTS169	108870
UK Great Britain	Yugoslavia	30 Jun 67	642UNTS325	109182
Malta	UK Great Britain	10 Jul 67	619UNTS11	108936
FAO (Food Agri)	UK Great Britain	13 Jul 67	642UNTS263	109179
Netherlands	Romania	20 Jul 67	633UNTS21	109032
Multilateral		20 Jul 67	0UNTS0	109259
Multilateral		26 Jul 67	614UNTS217	108872
Indonesia	UK Great Britain	01 Aug 67	638UNTS3	109128
Singapore	UK Great Britain	01 Aug 67	619UNTS29	108937
Mexico	IAEA (Atom Energy)	23 Aug 67	614UNTS133	108868
Belgium	Romania	22 Sep 67	637UNTS0	109109
Botswana	UN Special Fund	12 Oct 67	607UNTS37	108794
IAEA (Atom Energy)	Vietnam, South	16 Oct 67	630UNTS379	200636
Eur Space Research	UK Great Britain	24 Nov 67	638UNTS17	109129
Multilateral		08 Dec 67	620UNTS225	108959
Denmark	Malaysia	14 Dec 67	614UNTS26	108862
Iran	United Nations	15 Feb 68	631UNTS103	108990
Czechoslovakia	Hungary	27 Feb 68	640UNTS49	109154
UN Special Fund	Syria	22 Apr 68	634UNTS207	109063
Botswana	UNICEF (Children)	25 Jun 68	639UNTS61	109144
Inter-Am Devel Bnk	UN Special Fund	16 Jul 68	640UNTS305	200640
IAEA (Atom Energy)	OAU (Afri Unity)	26 Mar 69	0UNTS0	200646
Informational records				
Multilateral		12 Nov 21	38UNTS153	100594
Multilateral		30 Jul 40	161UNTS253	200488
Canada	USA (United States)	13 Dec 40	117UNTS173	200368
Germany, West	USA (United States)	30 Mar 42	105UNTS219	200334

PARTY ONE	PARTY TWO	DATE	CITATION	NUMBER
Informational records (Cont.)				
Saudi Arabia	UK Great Britain	20 Apr 42	10UNTS151	200058
USA (United States)	Uruguay	21 Jul 42	120UNTS211	200393
France	USA (United States)	25 Sep 43	76UNTS183	200245
Hungary	Yugoslavia	13 Aug 44	113UNTS233	101553
Multilateral		07 Dec 44	171UNTS345	200501
Multilateral		05 Jun 45	68UNTS189	200230
Greece	UK Great Britain	24 Jan 46	6UNTS45	100067
Mexico	UK Great Britain	07 Feb 46	6UNTS55	100068
Poland	USA (United States)	24 Apr 46	4UNTS155	100042
Hungary	USA (United States)	09 Aug 46	148UNTS313	101941
Australia	USA (United States)	03 Dec 46	7UNTS201	100100
New Zealand	USA (United States)	03 Dec 46	7UNTS175	100099
Australia	Netherlands	24 Jan 47	10UNTS77	100144
Belgium	Turkey	12 Mar 47	37UNTS215	100578
Philippines	USA (United States)	14 Mar 47	43UNTS271	100673
Australia	Norway	24 Mar 47	18UNTS185	100288
France	IBRD (World Bank)	09 May 47	152UNTS111	102014
Multilateral		19 Jun 47	171UNTS329	102235
Romania	Yugoslavia	30 Jun 47	116UNTS57	101569
Belgium	United Arab Rep	01 Jul 47	34UNTS93	100529
Belgium	South Africa	04 Jul 47	47UNTS9	100720
Greece	USA (United States)	08 Jul 47	16UNTS157	100256
Netherlands	IBRD (World Bank)	07 Aug 47	152UNTS165	102015
Iraq	UK Great Britain	13 Aug 47	9UNTS259	100136
Denmark	IBRD (World Bank)	22 Aug 47	152UNTS223	102016
Luxembourg	IBRD (World Bank)	28 Aug 47	153UNTS3	102017
Romania	Yugoslavia	30 Sep 47	116UNTS71	101570
Iran	USA (United States)	06 Oct 47	11UNTS303	100171
Greece	UNICEF (Children)	14 Oct 47	102UNTS39	101409
Taiwan	USA (United States)	27 Oct 47	12UNTS11	100178
UNICEF (Children)	Yugoslavia	20 Nov 47	65UNTS28	100817
Ethiopia	Pakistan	01 Jan 48	35UNTS3	100547
France	Lebanon	24 Jan 48	173UNTS99	102263
Multilateral		06 Mar 48	289UNTS3	104214
Czechoslovakia	Yugoslavia	14 Mar 48	28UNTS81	100421
Belgium	Monaco	05 Jun 48	18UNTS245	100294
Australia	Greece	16 Jun 48	18UNTS211	100290
Multilateral		19 Jun 48	310UNTS151	104492
Netherlands	IBRD (World Bank)	15 Jul 48	153UNTS259	102025
Netherlands	IBRD (World Bank)	15 Jul 48	153UNTS259	102022
Netherlands	IBRD (World Bank)	15 Jul 48	153UNTS259	102023
Netherlands	IBRD (World Bank)	15 Jul 48	153UNTS259	102021
Netherlands	IBRD (World Bank)	15 Jul 48	153UNTS259	102024
USA (United States)	Yugoslavia	19 Jul 48	89UNTS43	101208
Australia	Italy	02 Aug 48	28UNTS165	100424
Multilateral		18 Aug 48	33UNTS181	100518
Australia	Belgium	09 Dec 48	25UNTS159	100361
Multilateral		09 Dec 48	20UNTS229	100318
Korea, South	USA (United States)	10 Dec 48	55UNTS157	100813
Denmark	Turkey	15 Dec 48	76UNTS17	100975
Mexico	IBRD (World Bank)	06 Jan 49	154UNTS81	102028
Mexico	IBRD (World Bank)	06 Jan 49	154UNTS3	102027
Czechoslovakia	Poland	21 Jan 49	31UNTS205	100480
Norway	Turkey	24 Feb 49	29UNTS47	100433
Belgium	IBRD (World Bank)	01 Mar 49	154UNTS133	102029
Czechoslovakia	UK Great Britain	03 Mar 49	83UNTS95	101104
Chile	IBRD (World Bank)	23 Mar 49	153UNTS61	102018
Chile	IBRD (World Bank)	23 Mar 49	153UNTS141	102019
Multilateral		28 Apr 49	83UNTS105	101105
Denmark	Poland	12 May 49	87UNTS179	101172
Bulgaria	Poland	16 May 49	84UNTS313	101140
Costa Rica	USA (United States)	31 May 49	80UNTS3	101041
Ethiopia	India	07 Jun 49	35UNTS13	100548
Ireland	Sweden	25 Jun 49	558UNTS299	108148
Greece	Turkey	21 Jul 49	78UNTS55	101011

Informational records (Cont.)

PARTY ONE	PARTY TWO	DATE	CITATION	NUMBER
Netherlands	IBRD (World Bank)	26 Jul 49	154UNTS178	102030
Finland	IBRD (World Bank)	01 Aug 49	156UNTS289	200480
Multilateral		12 Aug 49	75UNTS31	100970
Multilateral		12 Aug 49	75UNTS85	100971
Multilateral		12 Aug 49	75UNTS287	100973
India	IBRD (World Bank)	18 Aug 49	154UNTS269	102031
Colombia	IBRD (World Bank)	19 Aug 49	154UNTS329	102032
IBRD (World Bank)	Yugoslavia	17 Sep 49	155UNTS3	102034
India	IBRD (World Bank)	29 Sep 49	154UNTS393	102033
Finland	IBRD (World Bank)	17 Oct 49	156UNTS355	200481
El Salvador	IBRD (World Bank)	14 Dec 49	155UNTS43	102035
UNICEF (Children)	UK Great Britain	10 Feb 50	65UNTS86	100837
Chile	UNICEF (Children)	03 Mar 50	126UNTS119	101685
Multilateral		21 Mar 50	96UNTS271	101342
Austria	Czechoslovakia	30 Mar 50	495UNTS85	107240
Israel	UK Great Britain	30 Mar 50	86UNTS231	101162
Afghanistan	India	04 Apr 50	167UNTS105	102201
India	IBRD (World Bank)	18 Apr 50	155UNTS117	102036
Australia	Netherlands	26 Apr 50	54UNTS83	100796
Mexico	IBRD (World Bank)	28 Apr 50	155UNTS185	102037
Iraq	IBRD (World Bank)	15 Jun 50	155UNTS267	102038
Germany, East	Poland	23 Jun 50	304UNTS91	104393
IBRD (World Bank)	Turkey	07 Jul 50	156UNTS75	102040
IBRD (World Bank)	Turkey	07 Jul 50	156UNTS3	102039
IBRD (World Bank)	Uruguay	25 Aug 50	156UNTS203	102042
Belgium	Japan	29 Aug 50	76UNTS113	100984
Ethiopia	IBRD (World Bank)	13 Sep 50	157UNTS213	102055
Ethiopia	IBRD (World Bank)	13 Sep 50	157UNTS233	102056
Mexico	IBRD (World Bank)	18 Oct 50	157UNTS259	102057
IBRD (World Bank)	Turkey	19 Oct 50	157UNTS333	102058
IBRD (World Bank)	Thailand	27 Oct 50	158UNTS25	102060
IBRD (World Bank)	Thailand	27 Oct 50	158UNTS43	102061
IBRD (World Bank)	Thailand	27 Oct 50	158UNTS3	102059
Australia	IBRD (World Bank)	14 Nov 50	156UNTS147	102041
Iceland	Ireland	02 Dec 50	558UNTS231	108143
Colombia	IBRD (World Bank)	28 Dec 50	158UNTS87	102063
Australia	Finland	04 Jan 51	80UNTS27	101042
Finland	Ireland	06 Jan 51	558UNTS120	108140
Chile	USA (United States)	16 Jan 51	157UNTS3	102043
IBRD (World Bank)	South Africa	23 Jan 51	158UNTS135	102065
IBRD (World Bank)	South Africa	23 Jan 51	158UNTS115	102064
Ethiopia	IBRD (World Bank)	19 Feb 51	186UNTS101	102486
Greece	Yugoslavia	15 Mar 51	187UNTS237	102516
Colombia	IBRD (World Bank)	10 Apr 51	158UNTS155	102066
Nicaragua	IBRD (World Bank)	07 Jun 51	158UNTS277	102068
Nicaragua	IBRD (World Bank)	07 Jun 51	158UNTS215	102067
Iceland	IBRD (World Bank)	20 Jun 51	158UNTS301	102069
Multilateral		18 Jul 51	102UNTS291	200308
Iran	UNICEF (Children)	02 Aug 51	247UNTS11	103457
France	USSR (Soviet Union)	03 Sep 51	221UNTS79	103003
UNICEF (Children)	Turkey	05 Sep 51	193UNTS55	102610
Belgium	IBRD (World Bank)	13 Sep 51	158UNTS323	102070
UNICEF (Children)	UK Great Britain	02 Oct 51	104UNTS301	101448
Italy	IBRD (World Bank)	10 Oct 51	159UNTS383	200482
Chile	IBRD (World Bank)	10 Oct 51	158UNTS369	102072
IBRD (World Bank)	Yugoslavia	11 Oct 51	159UNTS3	102081
Colombia	IBRD (World Bank)	13 Oct 51	159UNTS75	102084
Nicaragua	IBRD (World Bank)	29 Oct 51	159UNTS35	102082
Iceland	IBRD (World Bank)	01 Nov 51	159UNTS55	102083
Paraguay	IBRD (World Bank)	07 Dec 51	159UNTS103	102085
Iraq	UNICEF (Children)	10 Dec 51	126UNTS57	101682
Ireland	Switzerland	26 Dec 51	558UNTS305	108149
India	USA (United States)	05 Jan 52	157UNTS39	102045
Mexico	IBRD (World Bank)	11 Jan 52	159UNTS129	102086
Peru	IBRD (World Bank)	23 Jan 52	159UNTS163	102087

Informational records (Cont.)

PARTY ONE	PARTY TWO	DATE	CITATION	NUMBER
UNICEF (Children)	UK Great Britain	04 Feb 52	120UNTS147	101620
Jordan	USA (United States)	12 Feb 52	168UNTS25	102211
Dominican Republic	UNICEF (Children)	15 Feb 52	121UNTS43	101625
Canada	USA (United States)	21 Feb 52	205UNTS293	102781
IBRD (World Bank)	UK Great Britain	27 Feb 52	159UNTS181	102088
Netherlands	IBRD (World Bank)	20 Mar 52	159UNTS207	102089
Pakistan	IBRD (World Bank)	27 Mar 52	159UNTS251	102090
Libya	UNICEF (Children)	05 Apr 52	133UNTS287	200441
Canada	Netherlands	10 Apr 52	233UNTS129	103257
Liberia	UNICEF (Children)	17 Apr 52	133UNTS3	101773
Finland	IBRD (World Bank)	30 Apr 52	159UNTS408	200483
UNICEF (Children)	United Arab Rep	18 May 52	324UNTS161	104684
Korea, South	USA (United States)	24 May 52	179UNTS23	102353
Pakistan	IBRD (World Bank)	13 Jun 52	191UNTS85	102578
Belgium	UNICEF (Children)	17 Jun 52	171UNTS249	102228
IBRD (World Bank)	Turkey	18 Jun 52	159UNTS269	102091
Ethiopia	USA (United States)	24 Jun 52	181UNTS215	102411
Brazil	IBRD (World Bank)	27 Jun 52	190UNTS85	102560
Brazil	IBRD (World Bank)	27 Jun 52	190UNTS115	102561
Chile	USA (United States)	30 Jun 52	199UNTS241	102688
Panama	USA (United States)	30 Jun 52	181UNTS121	102404
Jordan	UNICEF (Children)	08 Jul 52	173UNTS353	200503
Peru	IBRD (World Bank)	08 Jul 52	159UNTS321	102093
Australia	IBRD (World Bank)	08 Jul 52	159UNTS295	102092
UNICEF (Children)	Syria	10 Jul 52	136UNTS17	101830
Chile	WHO (World Health)	11 Jul 52	137UNTS27	101846
Mexico	USA (United States)	15 Jul 52	181UNTS263	102416
UNICEF (Children)	UK Great Britain	25 Jul 52	135UNTS37	101812
Laos	UNICEF (Children)	15 Aug 52	161UNTS323	200491
Multilateral		21 Aug 52	141UNTS129	101912
Colombia	IBRD (World Bank)	26 Aug 52	159UNTS339	102094
Iceland	IBRD (World Bank)	26 Aug 52	159UNTS363	102095
UNICEF (Children)	Vietnam, South	29 Aug 52	161UNTS335	200492
Multilateral		07 Nov 52	221UNTS255	103010
UNICEF (Children)	UK Great Britain	16 Dec 52	151UNTS359	102005
India	IBRD (World Bank)	18 Dec 52	201UNTS241	102719
India	IBRD (World Bank)	23 Jan 53	201UNTS145	102715
IBRD (World Bank)	Yugoslavia	11 Feb 53	165UNTS231	102179
Turkey	Yugoslavia	26 Feb 53	247UNTS54	103460
Denmark	Uruguay	04 Mar 53	250UNTS51	103517
IBRD (World Bank)	UK Great Britain	11 Mar 53	172UNTS115	102243
United Arab Rep	USA (United States)	12 Mar 53	204UNTS3	102747
United Arab Rep	USA (United States)	19 Mar 53	215UNTS17	102909
Netherlands	United Nations	09 Apr 53	163UNTS89	102143
Ethiopia	UNICEF (Children)	27 Apr 53	213UNTS169	102885
Brazil	IBRD (World Bank)	30 Apr 53	190UNTS133	102562
United Arab Rep	USA (United States)	21 May 53	204UNTS29	102748
Switzerland	Yugoslavia	28 May 53	232UNTS45	103228
Liberia	USA (United States)	23 Jun 53	213UNTS37	102879
UK Great Britain	USA (United States)	24 Jun 53	224UNTS141	103074
Panama	USA (United States)	26 Jun 53	215UNTS77	102912
Brazil	USA (United States)	26 Jun 53	336UNTS241	104808
Chile	USA (United States)	27 Jun 53	229UNTS193	103167
Afghanistan	USA (United States)	30 Jun 53	215UNTS3	102908
Nicaragua	USA (United States)	30 Jun 53	215UNTS133	102917
Brazil	IBRD (World Bank)	17 Jul 53	190UNTS149	102563
IBRD (World Bank)	South Africa	28 Aug 53	180UNTS73	102376
IBRD (World Bank)	South Africa	28 Aug 53	180UNTS91	102377
Iceland	IBRD (World Bank)	04 Sep 53	178UNTS275	102344
Nicaragua	IBRD (World Bank)	04 Sep 53	186UNTS117	102487
Nicaragua	IBRD (World Bank)	04 Sep 53	186UNTS137	102488
IBRD (World Bank)	Turkey	10 Sep 53	187UNTS71	102502
Colombia	IBRD (World Bank)	10 Sep 53	203UNTS3	102738
UNICEF (Children)	UK Great Britain	07 Oct 53	180UNTS59	102375
Japan	IBRD (World Bank)	15 Oct 53	187UNTS367	200513

PARTY ONE	PARTY TWO	DATE	CITATION	NUMBER
Informational records (Cont.)				
Japan	IBRD (World Bank)	15 Oct 53	187UNTS321	200512
Japan	IBRD (World Bank)	15 Oct 53	187UNTS271	200511
Greece	Turkey	07 Nov 53	225UNTS163	103098
Austria	Yugoslavia	11 Nov 53	363UNTS149	105206
Japan	UNICEF (Children)	21 Nov 53	183UNTS297	200507
Brazil	IBRD (World Bank)	18 Dec 53	190UNTS179	102564
Belgium	Lebanon	24 Dec 53	539UNTS321	107842
Chile	USA (United States)	30 Dec 53	236UNTS41	103315
Multilateral		25 Feb 54	215UNTS249	102922
Australia	IBRD (World Bank)	02 Mar 54	191UNTS103	102579
Mexico	USA (United States)	06 Apr 54	236UNTS69	103317
Norway	IBRD (World Bank)	08 Apr 54	201UNTS131	102714
Peru	IBRD (World Bank)	12 Apr 54	190UNTS231	102567
Ethiopia	USA (United States)	21 Apr 54	232UNTS299	103244
UNICEF (Children)	Spain	07 May 54	190UNTS357	200515
Panama	USA (United States)	11 May 54	236UNTS107	103319
Multilateral		12 May 54	327UNTS3	104714
Mexico	UNICEF (Children)	20 May 54	192UNTS3	102591
Haiti	USA (United States)	28 May 54	233UNTS281	103267
Ethiopia	USA (United States)	01 Jun 54	232UNTS311	103245
France	IBRD (World Bank)	10 Jun 54	210UNTS89	102836
Haiti	Italy	14 Jun 54	267UNTS97	103837
Italy	USA (United States)	28 Jun 54	237UNTS121	103340
Brazil	USA (United States)	30 Jun 54	237UNTS137	103341
Ecuador	USA (United States)	30 Jun 54	236UNTS163	103323
Ceylon (Sri Lanka)	IBRD (World Bank)	09 Jul 54	198UNTS313	200517
Germany, West	Netherlands	11 Oct 54	291UNTS9	104241
El Salvador	IBRD (World Bank)	12 Oct 54	203UNTS37	102739
Belgium	France	15 Oct 54	218UNTS19	102951
Austria	IBRD (World Bank)	08 Nov 54	216UNTS305	200528
Poland	UK Great Britain	11 Nov 54	204UNTS137	102755
Peru	IBRD (World Bank)	12 Nov 54	209UNTS287	102831
India	IBRD (World Bank)	19 Nov 54	309UNTS159	104473
Belgium	IBRD (World Bank)	14 Dec 54	210UNTS113	102837
Colombia	IBRD (World Bank)	29 Dec 54	211UNTS135	102851
Netherlands	UNICEF (Children)	31 Dec 54	202UNTS135	102729
Turkey	UK Great Britain	17 Jan 55	204UNTS195	102758
Pakistan	USA (United States)	18 Jan 55	241UNTS53	103423
Italy	USA (United States)	11 Feb 55	241UNTS91	103426
Mexico	USA (United States)	09 Mar 55	263UNTS247	103776
IBRD (World Bank)	UK Great Britain	15 Mar 55	265UNTS85	103808
Australia	IBRD (World Bank)	18 Mar 55	220UNTS131	102998
Colombia	IBRD (World Bank)	24 Mar 55	212UNTS217	102874
Finland	IBRD (World Bank)	24 Mar 55	211UNTS305	200525
Peru	IBRD (World Bank)	05 Apr 55	211UNTS115	102850
Norway	IBRD (World Bank)	19 Apr 55	211UNTS159	102852
Peru	IBRD (World Bank)	19 Apr 55	221UNTS153	103007
Czechoslovakia	Hungary	28 Apr 55	477UNTS197	106923
Peru	USA (United States)	30 Apr 55	263UNTS309	103780
Austria	Romania	11 May 55	342UNTS119	104904
Multilateral		06 Jun 55	219UNTS79	102968
Austria	IBRD (World Bank)	14 Jun 55	221UNTS375	200531
Canada	USA (United States)	15 Jun 55	235UNTS201	103302
Colombia	IBRD (World Bank)	15 Jun 55	248UNTS161	103494
Pakistan	IBRD (World Bank)	20 Jun 55	230UNTS41	103176
France	USA (United States)	01 Jul 55	270UNTS19	103888
Nicaragua	IBRD (World Bank)	08 Jul 55	229UNTS123	103163
Nicaragua	IBRD (World Bank)	08 Jul 55	229UNTS97	103162
Panama	IBRD (World Bank)	12 Jul 55	219UNTS127	102970
Libya	USA (United States)	28 Jul 55	270UNTS245	103900
Libya	USA (United States)	28 Jul 55	270UNTS317	103903
Libya	USA (United States)	28 Jul 55	270UNTS269	103901
Guatemala	IBRD (World Bank)	29 Jul 55	229UNTS167	103165
Pakistan	IBRD (World Bank)	04 Aug 55	230UNTS79	103177
Peru	IBRD (World Bank)	05 Aug 55	218UNTS3	102950

PARTY ONE	PARTY TWO	DATE	CITATION	NUMBER
Informational records (Cont.)				
Pakistan	IBRD (World Bank)	06 Aug 55	236UNTS195	103325
IBRD (World Bank)	Thailand	09 Aug 55	221UNTS283	103011
Lebanon	IBRD (World Bank)	25 Aug 55	230UNTS233	103188
Nicaragua	IBRD (World Bank)	26 Aug 55	229UNTS145	103164
France	IBRD (World Bank)	26 Aug 55	247UNTS305	103478
Czechoslovakia	Germany, East	30 Aug 55	504UNTS279	107361
Bulgaria	UK Great Britain	22 Sep 55	222UNTS349	103039
Bulgaria	Yugoslavia	01 Oct 55	396UNTS223	105698
Austria	USSR (Soviet Union)	17 Oct 55	240UNTS289	103409
Japan	IBRD (World Bank)	25 Oct 55	230UNTS379	200534
Burma	China People's Rep	08 Nov 55	306UNTS11	104430
Guatemala	UNICEF (Children)	22 Nov 55	221UNTS305	103012
IBRD (World Bank)	South Africa	28 Nov 55	230UNTS101	103178
Costa Rica	Guatemala	20 Dec 55	280UNTS121	104056
Honduras	IBRD (World Bank)	22 Dec 55	230UNTS262	103189
Romania	Yugoslavia	01 Feb 56	362UNTS203	105189
Hungary	Romania	03 Feb 56	362UNTS233	105190
Austria	Poland	08 Feb 56	334UNTS221	104770
Japan	IBRD (World Bank)	21 Feb 56	248UNTS321	200543
Multilateral		03 Mar 56	243UNTS169	103452
Germany, West	USA (United States)	07 Mar 56	271UNTS361	103926
USA (United States)	Uruguay	23 Mar 56	376UNTS311	105386
Cambodia	UNICEF (Children)	28 Apr 56	136UNTS341	200446
Multilateral		30 Apr 56	310UNTS229	104494
Burma	IBRD (World Bank)	04 May 56	253UNTS179	103584
Burma	IBRD (World Bank)	04 May 56	253UNTS209	103585
Haiti	IBRD (World Bank)	07 May 56	252UNTS279	103570
Finland	IBRD (World Bank)	22 May 56	248UNTS57	103485
Nicaragua	IBRD (World Bank)	22 May 56	253UNTS233	103586
Colombia	IBRD (World Bank)	06 Jun 56	248UNTS139	103493
Poland	Sweden	08 Jun 56	334UNTS257	104771
Hungary	UK Great Britain	27 Jun 56	249UNTS19	103499
Lebanon	UNICEF (Children)	03 Jul 56	324UNTS145	104683
UNICEF (Children)	Sudan	07 Aug 56	248UNTS307	200542
Guatemala	Honduras	22 Aug 56	263UNTS49	103767
Costa Rica	IBRD (World Bank)	18 Sep 56	260UNTS369	103721
Austria	IBRD (World Bank)	21 Sep 56	259UNTS17	103681
Austria	IBRD (World Bank)	21 Sep 56	259UNTS43	103682
Costa Rica	Denmark	26 Sep 56	341UNTS305	104893
IBRD (World Bank)	Thailand	12 Oct 56	261UNTS117	103728
IBRD (World Bank)	Uruguay	25 Oct 56	265UNTS59	103807
Multilateral		26 Oct 56	276UNTS3	103988
Chile	IBRD (World Bank)	01 Nov 56	261UNTS27	103724
Australia	IBRD (World Bank)	15 Nov 56	288UNTS117	104201
Albania	Yugoslavia	23 Nov 56	386UNTS73	105539
Australia	IBRD (World Bank)	03 Dec 56	288UNTS99	104200
Japan	IBRD (World Bank)	19 Dec 56	264UNTS179	103793
India	IBRD (World Bank)	19 Dec 56	310UNTS75	104489
Japan	IBRD (World Bank)	19 Dec 56	268UNTS203	103859
UNESCO (Educ/Cult)	Tunisia	03 Jan 57	257UNTS21	103645
Iran	IBRD (World Bank)	22 Jan 57	317UNTS129	104600
Ethiopia	IBRD (World Bank)	28 Jan 57	286UNTS307	104175
India	IBRD (World Bank)	05 Mar 57	272UNTS201	103939
Peru	IBRD (World Bank)	13 Mar 57	274UNTS59	103958
Netherlands	Yugoslavia	13 Mar 57	327UNTS227	104723
Germany, West	Yugoslavia	10 Apr 57	463UNTS269	106708
Bulgaria	Sweden	17 Apr 57	464UNTS3	106709
Belgium	Bulgaria	14 May 57	317UNTS81	104596
Netherlands	IBRD (World Bank)	15 May 57	274UNTS211	103967
Hungary	Netherlands	28 May 57	334UNTS291	104773
India	IBRD (World Bank)	29 May 57	309UNTS201	104474
Belgium	Hungary	01 Jun 57	291UNTS17	104242
Argentina	USA (United States)	03 Jun 57	291UNTS61	104244
Ghana	USA (United States)	03 Jun 57	284UNTS63	104129
Denmark	Peru	10 Jun 57	406UNTS63	105839

Informational records (Cont.)

PARTY ONE	PARTY TWO	DATE	CITATION	NUMBER
Multilateral		15 Jun 57	550UNTS45	108008
Tunisia	USA (United States)	28 Jun 57	289UNTS301	104226
Chile	IBRD (World Bank)	24 Jul 57	282UNTS189	104099
Chile	IBRD (World Bank)	24 Jul 57	282UNTS139	104098
Morocco	UNICEF (Children)	31 Jul 57	282UNTS99	104095
Netherlands	Romania	27 Aug 57	342UNTS309	104914
Belgium	IBRD (World Bank)	10 Sep 57	286UNTS291	104174
Ecuador	IBRD (World Bank)	20 Sep 57	289UNTS237	104221
IBRD (World Bank)	South Africa	01 Oct 57	280UNTS285	104065
Pakistan	IBRD (World Bank)	18 Oct 57	299UNTS303	104322
Argentina	UNICEF (Children)	19 Nov 57	300UNTS229	104338
Hungary	Romania	17 Dec 57	477UNTS303	106926
Belgium	Germany, West	17 Jan 58	328UNTS173	104735
Bulgaria	Netherlands	07 Feb 58	335UNTS45	104777
Albania	USSR (Soviet Union)	15 Feb 58	313UNTS261	104536
Bulgaria	Hungary	13 Mar 58	438UNTS173	106316
Bulgaria	Yugoslavia	21 Mar 58	386UNTS119	105541
Czechoslovakia	Poland	29 Mar 58	340UNTS199	104865
Multilateral		03 Apr 58	336UNTS177	104806
Italy	Tunisia	08 Apr 58	378UNTS327	105430
Sweden	Yugoslavia	18 Apr 58	393UNTS225	105658
Germany, West	USSR (Soviet Union)	25 Apr 58	346UNTS71	104978
Japan	Poland	26 Apr 58	340UNTS221	104866
Hungary	Poland	08 May 58	408UNTS212	105872
Bulgaria	Denmark	28 May 58	312UNTS235	104521
India	USSR (Soviet Union)	02 Jun 58	393UNTS3	105650
Multilateral		10 Jun 58	454UNTS47	106539
Germany, East	Hungary	14 Jun 58	407UNTS78	105861
Denmark	El Salvador	09 Jul 58	341UNTS289	104892
Netherlands	Yugoslavia	22 Jul 58	386UNTS263	105546
Ghana	UNICEF (Children)	12 Aug 58	309UNTS103	104469
Austria	Bulgaria	12 Sep 58	353UNTS3	105036
Ceylon (Sri Lanka)	IBRD (World Bank)	17 Sep 58	323UNTS51	104664
Belgium	France	20 Sep 58	376UNTS331	105387
Canada	USA (United States)	31 Oct 58	391UNTS219	105626
IBRD (World Bank)	South Africa	02 Dec 58	324UNTS3	104676
UK Great Britain	Yugoslavia	03 Feb 59	359UNTS339	105151
Burma	UK Great Britain	06 Feb 59	343UNTS223	104927
Czechoslovakia	United Arab Rep	07 Feb 59	372UNTS243	105301
Bulgaria	Hungary	03 Apr 59	438UNTS269	106319
Morocco	UN Special Fund	04 Apr 59	354UNTS347	105069
Italy	Netherlands	17 Apr 59	474UNTS207	106883
Multilateral		20 Apr 59	472UNTS185	106841
Austria	Netherlands	06 May 59	485UNTS153	107054
Multilateral		11 May 59	527UNTS145	107623
Fed of Malaya	USA (United States)	22 May 59	346UNTS263	104985
UK Great Britain	USSR (Soviet Union)	24 May 59	374UNTS305	105344
IBRD (World Bank)	South Africa	10 Jun 59	340UNTS33	104857
Greece	Yugoslavia	18 Jun 59	368UNTS9	105232
Greece	Yugoslavia	18 Jun 59	368UNTS27	105234
Greece	Yugoslavia	18 Jun 59	368UNTS3	105231
Canada	Japan	02 Jul 59	383UNTS243	105504
Norway	IBRD (World Bank)	08 Jul 59	344UNTS229	104952
Australia	Canada	04 Aug 59	391UNTS191	105623
Ghana	UN Special Fund	12 Aug 59	338UNTS203	104836
Iran	UN Special Fund	06 Oct 59	342UNTS89	104902
Poland	UN Special Fund	15 Oct 59	344UNTS29	104941
India	UN Special Fund	20 Oct 59	344UNTS143	104946
UN Special Fund	Yugoslavia	27 Oct 59	344UNTS159	104947
Italy	Tunisia	31 Oct 59	378UNTS349	105431
Ecuador	UN Special Fund	10 Nov 59	345UNTS3	104955
Greece	UN Special Fund	13 Nov 59	345UNTS171	104966
UN Special Fund	Turkey	20 Nov 59	345UNTS105	104963
UN Special Fund	United Arab Rep	25 Nov 59	345UNTS125	104964
Czechoslovakia	Germany, East	25 Nov 59	374UNTS101	105331

Informational records (Cont.)

PARTY ONE	PARTY TWO	DATE	CITATION	NUMBER
Israel	UN Special Fund	01 Dec 59	345UNTS197	104968
Guinea	UN Special Fund	02 Dec 59	345UNTS215	104969
Argentina	UN Special Fund	04 Dec 59	345UNTS263	104972
Jordan	UN Special Fund	15 Dec 59	346UNTS3	104974
UN Special Fund	UK Great Britain	07 Jan 60	348UNTS177	105000
Peru	UN Special Fund	19 Jan 60	349UNTS83	105010
Spain	UK Great Britain	19 Jan 60	404UNTS41	105804
Chile	UN Special Fund	22 Jan 60	351UNTS115	105020
El Salvador	USA (United States)	29 Jan 60	372UNTS3	105283
Germany, East	Hungary	30 Jan 60	408UNTS230	105873
Colombia	UN Special Fund	04 Feb 60	355UNTS257	105080
Multilateral		06 Feb 60	383UNTS3	105494
Bolivia	UN Special Fund	09 Feb 60	351UNTS203	105024
Cuba	UNICEF (Children)	11 Feb 60	349UNTS277	105014
Italy	Yugoslavia	12 Feb 60	379UNTS77	105434
Iran	IBRD (World Bank)	20 Feb 60	384UNTS213	105521
Afghanistan	UN Special Fund	21 Feb 60	351UNTS93	105019
Pakistan	UN Special Fund	25 Feb 60	351UNTS141	105021
France	UN Special Fund	17 Mar 60	354UNTS119	105059
Italy	UN Special Fund	01 Apr 60	354UNTS261	105066
Germany, West	Netherlands	08 Apr 60	508UNTS14	107404
Luxembourg	Yugoslavia	09 Apr 60	464UNTS293	106719
UN Special Fund	Tunisia	12 Apr 60	355UNTS289	105082
Libya	UN Special Fund	19 Apr 60	356UNTS11	105090
UN Special Fund	Sudan	21 Apr 60	356UNTS213	105097
UN Special Fund	Vietnam, South	29 Apr 60	357UNTS311	200567
Costa Rica	IBRD (World Bank)	04 May 60	390UNTS201	105609
Denmark	UK Great Britain	20 May 60	374UNTS245	105338
Austria	Spain	17 Jun 60	390UNTS17	105600
IBRD (World Bank)	Sudan	17 Jun 60	379UNTS253	105442
Iraq	UN Special Fund	19 Jun 60	376UNTS357	105389
Korea, North	USSR (Soviet Union)	22 Jun 60	399UNTS3	105732
Panama	IBRD (World Bank)	19 Aug 60	390UNTS153	105607
Israel	IBRD (World Bank)	09 Sep 60	406UNTS3	105837
Multilateral		19 Sep 60	419UNTS125	106032
Pakistan	IBRD (World Bank)	19 Sep 60	444UNTS207	106370
Multilateral		19 Sep 60	444UNTS259	106371
Indonesia	UN Special Fund	07 Oct 60	378UNTS141	105424
Liberia	UN Special Fund	11 Oct 60	376UNTS341	105388
El Salvador	UN Special Fund	24 Oct 60	377UNTS171	105400
Hungary	UK Great Britain	25 Oct 60	419UNTS309	106034
Romania	UK Great Britain	10 Nov 60	385UNTS113	105533
UNICEF (Children)	Upper Volta	15 Nov 60	402UNTS33	105776
Guatemala	UN Special Fund	17 Nov 60	383UNTS67	105495
Mali	UNICEF (Children)	17 Nov 60	402UNTS23	105775
Cambodia	UN Special Fund	24 Nov 60	382UNTS255	105487
Norway	IBRD (World Bank)	02 Dec 60	390UNTS131	105606
Cyprus	USA (United States)	08 Dec 60	405UNTS145	105831
Nepal	UNICEF (Children)	12 Dec 60	382UNTS273	105488
Multilateral		13 Dec 60	455UNTS3	106543
Peru	IBRD (World Bank)	19 Dec 60	417UNTS275	106010
Honduras	UN Special Fund	20 Dec 60	383UNTS103	105497
Japan	IBRD (World Bank)	20 Dec 60	400UNTS279	105754
Burma	UN Special Fund	03 Jan 61	387UNTS219	105564
Costa Rica	UN Special Fund	10 Jan 61	389UNTS253	105597
UN Special Fund	Saudi Arabia	19 Jan 61	396UNTS27	105692
Nicaragua	UN Special Fund	20 Jan 61	387UNTS15	105555
Chad	UN Special Fund	23 Jan 61	390UNTS69	105603
UN Special Fund	Somalia	28 Jan 61	388UNTS75	105573
Gabon	UN Special Fund	02 Feb 61	387UNTS289	105568
Nigeria	UN Special Fund	10 Feb 61	390UNTS85	105604
Mexico	UN Special Fund	23 Feb 61	388UNTS151	105576
Cyprus	UN Special Fund	24 Feb 61	389UNTS3	105588
Panama	UN Special Fund	09 Mar 61	396UNTS3	105691
Cuba	UN Special Fund	10 Mar 61	390UNTS35	105601

PARTY ONE	PARTY TWO	DATE	CITATION	NUMBER
Informational records (Cont.)				
Multilateral		30 Mar 61	520UNTS151	107515
Cyprus	UNICEF (Children)	19 Apr 61	394UNTS185	105678
Korea, South	UN Special Fund	21 Apr 61	394UNTS231	200583
Ceylon (Sri Lanka)	UN Special Fund	03 May 61	395UNTS217	105687
Ceylon (Sri Lanka)	IBRD (World Bank)	06 Jun 61	414UNTS349	105978
Cameroon	UN Special Fund	13 Jun 61	397UNTS297	105713
IBRD (World Bank)	Sudan	14 Jun 61	415UNTS26	105980
Multilateral		14 Jun 61	415UNTS4	105979
Inter-Am Devel Bnk	USA (United States)	19 Jun 61	410UNTS34	105895
Paraguay	UN Special Fund	22 Jun 61	399UNTS117	105738
UN Special Fund	Upper Volta	26 Jun 61	400UNTS3	105744
Haiti	UN Special Fund	28 Jun 61	399UNTS171	105741
Chile	IBRD (World Bank)	28 Jun 61	426UNTS33	106129
Philippines	UN Special Fund	28 Jun 61	399UNTS141	105739
Argentina	IBRD (World Bank)	30 Jun 61	445UNTS85	106379
UNICEF (Children)	Saudi Arabia	04 Jul 61	413UNTS122	105947
Mali	UN Special Fund	21 Jul 61	401UNTS141	105768
Philippines	IBRD (World Bank)	26 Jul 61	414UNTS253	105976
UN Special Fund	Yemen	02 Aug 61	402UNTS43	105777
India	IBRD (World Bank)	09 Aug 61	417UNTS297	106011
Cameroon	UNICEF (Children)	12 Aug 61	402UNTS235	105788
India	IBRD (World Bank)	17 Aug 61	417UNTS319	106012
Central Afri Rep	UNICEF (Children)	21 Aug 61	413UNTS48	105939
Poland	UNICEF (Children)	24 Aug 61	406UNTS95	105841
Chad	UNICEF (Children)	26 Aug 61	422UNTS231	106077
Colombia	IBRD (World Bank)	28 Aug 61	416UNTS23	105993
Ivory Coast	UN Special Fund	29 Aug 61	406UNTS129	105844
UN Special Fund	Sierra Leone	02 Oct 61	422UNTS131	106073
Costa Rica	IBRD (World Bank)	13 Oct 61	430UNTS27	106202
Costa Rica	IDA (Devel Assoc)	13 Oct 61	431UNTS3	106204
India	IBRD (World Bank)	13 Oct 61	418UNTS3	106013
Pakistan	IDA (Devel Assoc)	19 Oct 61	447UNTS161	106415
Paraguay	IDA (Devel Assoc)	26 Oct 61	447UNTS277	106419
Gabon	UNICEF (Children)	02 Nov 61	422UNTS241	106078
Peru	IBRD (World Bank)	03 Nov 61	430UNTS47	106203
Mauritania	UN Special Fund	07 Nov 61	412UNTS240	105936
Congo (Brazzaville)	UN Special Fund	09 Nov 61	413UNTS58	105940
Mexico	USA (United States)	15 Nov 61	460UNTS113	106634
Malagasy	UNICEF (Children)	16 Nov 61	422UNTS251	106079
Pakistan	IDA (Devel Assoc)	22 Nov 61	447UNTS295	106420
OAS (Am States)	USA (United States)	29 Nov 61	424UNTS119	106104
UN Special Fund	Venezuela	11 Dec 61	422UNTS149	106074
IBRD (World Bank)	Venezuela	13 Dec 61	446UNTS371	106409
UN Special Fund	Senegal	16 Dec 61	425UNTS97	106121
Jordan	IDA (Devel Assoc)	22 Dec 61	448UNTS21	106423
Malagasy	UN Special Fund	05 Jan 62	419UNTS29	106028
Ivory Coast	UNICEF (Children)	10 Jan 62	422UNTS261	106080
Poland	Romania	25 Jan 62	468UNTS3	106770
UNICEF (Children)	Yemen	31 Jan 62	422UNTS271	106081
Hungary	Yugoslavia	09 Feb 62	577UNTS3	108370
Austria	Czechoslovakia	13 Feb 62	455UNTS381	106551
Finland	Hungary	13 Feb 62	463UNTS61	106693
Iceland	IBRD (World Bank)	14 Feb 62	447UNTS95	106413
India	IDA (Devel Assoc)	14 Feb 62	468UNTS177	106773
USSR (Soviet Union)	Yugoslavia	24 Feb 62	471UNTS195	106833
Niger	UN Special Fund	26 Feb 62	423UNTS83	106086
UNICEF (Children)	Somalia	01 Apr 62	431UNTS75	106211
Congo (Brazzaville)	UNICEF (Children)	09 Apr 62	431UNTS65	106210
UNICEF (Children)	Sierra Leone	11 Apr 62	431UNTS55	106209
UN Special Fund	Uruguay	04 May 62	429UNTS143	106196
Colombia	USA (United States)	15 May 62	445UNTS279	106396
Dominican Republic	UN Special Fund	06 Jun 62	429UNTS169	106197
Multilateral		14 Jun 62	528UNTS33	107634
Congo (Zaire)	IAEA (Atom Energy)	27 Jun 62	463UNTS31	106691
India	IDA (Devel Assoc)	29 Jun 62	447UNTS221	106417

PARTY ONE	PARTY TWO	DATE	CITATION	NUMBER
Informational records (Cont.)				
Pakistan	IDA (Devel Assoc)	29 Jun 62	447UNTS325	106421
UN Special Fund	Syria	07 Jul 62	443UNTS3	106355
UN Special Fund	Tanganyika	17 Jul 62	435UNTS237	106281
India	IDA (Devel Assoc)	18 Jul 62	447UNTS191	106416
Korea, South	IDA (Devel Assoc)	17 Aug 62	468UNTS387	200603
Nicaragua	IDA (Devel Assoc)	07 Sep 62	478UNTS313	106940
Pakistan	IBRD (World Bank)	14 Sep 62	467UNTS152	106762
India	IDA (Devel Assoc)	14 Sep 62	448UNTS3	106422
IDA (Devel Assoc)	Tunisia	17 Sep 62	469UNTS33	106783
Multilateral		28 Sep 62	469UNTS169	106791
Israel	IBRD (World Bank)	17 Oct 62	467UNTS107	106760
Hungary	Syria	18 Oct 62	491UNTS209	107178
IBRD (World Bank)	Uruguay	26 Oct 62	481UNTS39	106977
El Salvador	IDA (Devel Assoc)	02 Nov 62	468UNTS331	106780
Pakistan	IDA (Devel Assoc)	02 Nov 62	468UNTS351	106781
Haiti	IDA (Devel Assoc)	02 Nov 62	468UNTS205	106774
Algeria	UNICEF (Children)	20 Nov 62	453UNTS151	106522
IDA (Devel Assoc)	Turkey	23 Nov 62	469UNTS3	106782
Multilateral		08 Dec 62	510UNTS235	107418
IBRD (World Bank)	Thailand	21 Dec 62	467UNTS43	106757
IBRD (World Bank)	Thailand	21 Dec 62	467UNTS63	106758
Syria	United Arab Rep	27 Dec 62	491UNTS245	107180
Mauritania	UNICEF (Children)	19 Jan 63	452UNTS271	106514
UNICEF (Children)	Tanganyika	25 Jan 63	453UNTS249	106528
Ethiopia	IDA (Devel Assoc)	27 Feb 63	478UNTS289	106939
Nicaragua	IBRD (World Bank)	01 Mar 63	481UNTS15	106976
India	IDA (Devel Assoc)	22 Mar 63	477UNTS3	106911
UN Special Fund	Uganda	22 Mar 63	456UNTS466	106572
Hungary	Korea, North	29 Mar 63	577UNTS219	108379
Multilateral		20 Apr 63	495UNTS3	107239
Poland	USSR (Soviet Union)	22 Apr 63	493UNTS229	107217
Greece	Hungary	27 Apr 63	534UNTS3	107750
Greece	Hungary	27 Apr 63	550UNTS197	108016
Mexico	IBRD (World Bank)	29 Apr 63	489UNTS151	107138
Austria	Bulgaria	02 May 63	535UNTS143	107778
Jamaica	UN Special Fund	22 May 63	489UNTS191	107140
Netherlands	UN Special Fund	24 May 63	466UNTS289	106750
India	IDA (Devel Assoc)	24 May 63	483UNTS205	107014
IDA (Devel Assoc)	Turkey	31 May 63	480UNTS127	106966
UN Special Fund	Western Samoa	05 Jun 63	467UNTS463	200601
IBRD (World Bank)	Thailand	11 Jun 63	481UNTS227	106984
Pakistan	IDA (Devel Assoc)	26 Jun 63	492UNTS115	107189
New Zealand	UN Special Fund	28 Jun 63	470UNTS3	106792
IBRD (World Bank)	Tunisia	03 Jul 63	480UNTS209	106970
Austria	Romania	03 Jul 63	588UNTS3	108516
Hungary	Mongolia	10 Jul 63	519UNTS173	107508
Denmark	IBRD (World Bank)	24 Jul 63	481UNTS171	106982
Pakistan	IDA (Devel Assoc)	26 Jul 63	492UNTS143	107190
Pakistan	IDA (Devel Assoc)	16 Aug 63	492UNTS171	107191
Pakistan	IDA (Devel Assoc)	16 Aug 63	492UNTS205	107192
Burundi	UN Special Fund	22 Aug 63	476UNTS49	106903
Multilateral		23 Sep 63	488UNTS99	107122
Taiwan	IBRD (World Bank)	27 Sep 63	483UNTS151	107012
Czechoslovakia	Yugoslavia	05 Oct 63	504UNTS151	107356
Pakistan	USSR (Soviet Union)	07 Oct 63	499UNTS161	107297
Norway	IBRD (World Bank)	15 Oct 63	482UNTS103	106992
Multilateral		23 Oct 63	506UNTS197	107388
Central Afri Rep	UN Special Fund	30 Oct 63	481UNTS247	106985
New Zealand	IBRD (World Bank)	12 Nov 63	485UNTS233	107059
Jordan	IDA (Devel Assoc)	12 Dec 63	492UNTS3	107184
Jordan	IDA (Devel Assoc)	12 Dec 63	506UNTS51	107381
Czechoslovakia	Romania	16 Dec 63	527UNTS285	107630
IDA (Devel Assoc)	Syria	24 Dec 63	534UNTS253	107764
Paraguay	IDA (Devel Assoc)	26 Dec 63	507UNTS3	107394
Multilateral		30 Dec 63	568UNTS215	108270

PARTY ONE	PARTY TWO	DATE	CITATION	NUMBER
Informational records (Cont.)				
Multilateral		30 Dec 63	568UNTS233	108271
Multilateral		30 Dec 63	568UNTS243	108272
Liberia	IBRD (World Bank)	08 Jan 64	504UNTS53	107353
IDA (Devel Assoc)	Tanganyika	05 Feb 64	506UNTS91	107382
Denmark	Yugoslavia	11 Feb 64	511UNTS241	107437
New Zealand	IBRD (World Bank)	12 Mar 64	505UNTS3	107362
Pakistan	IDA (Devel Assoc)	25 Mar 64	535UNTS43	107775
Pakistan	IDA (Devel Assoc)	25 Mar 64	534UNTS275	107765
Peru	IBRD (World Bank)	22 Apr 64	519UNTS95	107503
Norway	Romania	21 May 64	563UNTS45	108203
Multilateral		25 May 64	620UNTS149	108953
Ecuador	IDA (Devel Assoc)	26 May 64	534UNTS93	107757
Ecuador	IBRD (World Bank)	26 May 64	534UNTS113	107758
Multilateral		26 May 64	541UNTS271	200613
Cuba	Czechoslovakia	03 Jun 64	527UNTS205	107626
France	UK Great Britain	03 Jun 64	539UNTS253	107836
Ireland	UN Special Fund	03 Jun 64	496UNTS205	107253
IBRD (World Bank)	Tunisia	05 Jun 64	539UNTS129	107827
India	IDA (Devel Assoc)	09 Jun 64	506UNTS31	107380
Iran	IBRD (World Bank)	10 Jun 64	537UNTS111	107799
Pakistan	IDA (Devel Assoc)	11 Jun 64	506UNTS3	107379
Pakistan	IDA (Devel Assoc)	11 Jun 64	534UNTS309	107766
Pakistan	IDA (Devel Assoc)	24 Jun 64	533UNTS191	107743
Niger	IDA (Devel Assoc)	24 Jun 64	554UNTS93	108098
Pakistan	IDA (Devel Assoc)	24 Jun 64	533UNTS165	107742
India	IDA (Devel Assoc)	06 Jul 64	534UNTS49	107753
Gabon	IBRD (World Bank)	10 Jul 64	537UNTS63	107797
Multilateral		10 Jul 64	613UNTS3	108851
Finland	IBRD (World Bank)	10 Jul 64	516UNTS125	107474
IDA (Devel Assoc)	Turkey	14 Jul 64	534UNTS339	107767
Pakistan	IDA (Devel Assoc)	21 Jul 64	534UNTS373	107768
Bolivia	IDA (Devel Assoc)	24 Jul 64	534UNTS203	107763
Bolivia	IDA (Devel Assoc)	24 Jul 64	534UNTS171	107762
Kenya	IDA (Devel Assoc)	17 Aug 64	535UNTS79	107776
Pakistan	IDA (Devel Assoc)	26 Aug 64	535UNTS263	107784
Morocco	IBRD (World Bank)	26 Aug 64	537UNTS193	107802
IBRD (World Bank)	Venezuela	28 Aug 64	520UNTS97	107512
IDA (Devel Assoc)	Turkey	31 Aug 64	535UNTS111	107777
Pakistan	IDA (Devel Assoc)	22 Sep 64	594UNTS225	108605
Mali	IDA (Devel Assoc)	29 Sep 64	594UNTS187	108604
Czechoslovakia	Hungary	17 Oct 64	545UNTS21	107924
India	IDA (Devel Assoc)	26 Oct 64	535UNTS245	107783
Philippines	IBRD (World Bank)	28 Oct 64	537UNTS165	107801
Afghanistan	IDA (Devel Assoc)	23 Nov 64	567UNTS155	108255
IBRD (World Bank)	Thailand	25 Nov 64	537UNTS273	107805
Mauritania	IDA (Devel Assoc)	28 Dec 64	540UNTS163	107849
Kenya	IDA (Devel Assoc)	29 Dec 64	535UNTS225	107782
Honduras	IDA (Devel Assoc)	02 Feb 65	561UNTS279	108189
Honduras	IBRD (World Bank)	02 Feb 65	561UNTS255	108188
Nigeria	IDA (Devel Assoc)	01 Mar 65	571UNTS3	108297
Nigeria	IDA (Devel Assoc)	01 Mar 65	563UNTS3	108201
Canada	USA (United States)	25 Mar 65	607UNTS141	108802
Multilateral		29 Mar 65	540UNTS145	107848
IDA (Devel Assoc)	Somalia	29 Mar 65	586UNTS101	108499
IBRD (World Bank)	Uruguay	30 Mar 65	567UNTS45	108251
IDA (Devel Assoc)	Turkey	01 Apr 65	554UNTS137	108100
Israel	UK Great Britain	15 Apr 65	551UNTS19	108031
Taiwan	IBRD (World Bank)	28 Apr 65	549UNTS145	107998
Iran	IBRD (World Bank)	28 Apr 65	555UNTS21	108103
Iran	IBRD (World Bank)	28 Apr 65	555UNTS45	108104
Multilateral		29 Apr 65	586UNTS123	108500
Malaysia	UK Great Britain	07 May 65	552UNTS259	108058
India	IBRD (World Bank)	11 Jun 65	557UNTS101	108130
India	IBRD (World Bank)	11 Jun 65	557UNTS59	108128
Peru	IBRD (World Bank)	18 Jun 65	568UNTS191	108269

PARTY ONE	PARTY TWO	DATE	CITATION	NUMBER
Informational records (Cont.)				
UN Special Fund	Spain	30 Jun 65	544UNTS159	107918
Pakistan	IDA (Devel Assoc)	30 Jun 65	554UNTS111	108099
Kenya	IDA (Devel Assoc)	30 Jun 65	554UNTS75	108097
Pakistan	IBRD (World Bank)	09 Jul 65	554UNTS39	108096
Austria	Bulgaria	12 Jul 65	587UNTS51	108510
Hungary	Poland	18 Jul 65	577UNTS161	108376
Multilateral		22 Jul 65	561UNTS333	200618
India	IDA (Devel Assoc)	11 Aug 65	562UNTS277	108199
Nigeria	IBRD (World Bank)	26 Sep 65	571UNTS39	108298
Nigeria	IBRD (World Bank)	26 Sep 65	570UNTS233	108296
IBRD (World Bank)	Spain	29 Sep 65	568UNTS49	108264
East Afri Service	IBRD (World Bank)	29 Sep 65	568UNTS327	200623
Morocco	IDA (Devel Assoc)	11 Oct 65	562UNTS299	108200
Multilateral		15 Nov 65	0UNTS0	109432
Malaysia	IBRD (World Bank)	17 Nov 65	568UNTS23	108263
New Zealand	IBRD (World Bank)	17 Dec 65	567UNTS255	108259
New Zealand	IBRD (World Bank)	17 Dec 65	567UNTS275	108260
IBRD (World Bank)	Sudan	27 Dec 65	567UNTS27	108250
Ethiopia	USA (United States)	30 Dec 65	574UNTS129	108345
IDA (Devel Assoc)	Tanzania	13 Jan 66	567UNTS177	108256
Pakistan	IDA (Devel Assoc)	13 Jan 66	567UNTS67	108252
Mongolia	UN Special Fund	26 Jan 66	552UNTS201	108055
Pakistan	IDA (Devel Assoc)	10 Feb 66	575UNTS89	108355
Austria	Finland	21 Feb 66	597UNTS273	108651
Brazil	UNICEF (Children)	28 Mar 66	607UNTS235	108807
Guinea	IBRD (World Bank)	30 Mar 66	568UNTS3	108262
Paraguay	IBRD (World Bank)	04 Apr 66	570UNTS41	108287
Paraguay	IDA (Devel Assoc)	04 Apr 66	582UNTS331	108469
Finland	IBRD (World Bank)	27 Apr 66	568UNTS107	108266
Multilateral		04 May 66	575UNTS49	108354
Peru	IBRD (World Bank)	13 May 66	570UNTS61	108288
Bulgaria	UN Special Fund	26 May 66	563UNTS71	108205
Pakistan	IDA (Devel Assoc)	17 Jun 66	582UNTS297	108468
IBRD (World Bank)	Thailand	24 Jun 66	582UNTS259	108466
India	IDA (Devel Assoc)	29 Jun 66	582UNTS277	108467
India	IDA (Devel Assoc)	29 Jun 66	585UNTS101	108484
FAO (Food Agri)	IMCO (Maritime Org)	11 Jul 66	575UNTS238	200627
Iraq	IBRD (World Bank)	22 Jul 66	584UNTS233	108480
IDA (Devel Assoc)	Siam	02 Aug 66	585UNTS271	108492
IDA (Devel Assoc)	Turkey	10 Aug 66	585UNTS237	108491
India	IDA (Devel Assoc)	19 Aug 66	584UNTS193	108478
Kenya	IDA (Devel Assoc)	19 Aug 66	585UNTS119	108485
UN Special Fund	UPU (Postal Union)	21 Sep 66	573UNTS259	200626
IDA (Devel Assoc)	Senegal	29 Sep 66	594UNTS277	108607
Jamaica	IBRD (World Bank)	30 Sep 66	582UNTS179	108463
Malawi	IDA (Devel Assoc)	04 Oct 66	584UNTS215	108479
IBRD (World Bank)	Zambia	04 Oct 66	585UNTS181	108489
India	IDA (Devel Assoc)	23 Dec 66	594UNTS165	108603
Pakistan	IDA (Devel Assoc)	23 Dec 66	594UNTS255	108606
Australia	UN Special Fund	06 Feb 67	590UNTS3	108543
East Afri Service	IBRD (World Bank)	17 Feb 67	599UNTS335	200629
United Nations	Zambia	06 Jul 67	600UNTS81	108678
Inspection and observation				
Multilateral		05 Jun 26	38UNTS281	100604
Finland	USSR (Soviet Union)	11 Oct 40	67UNTS139	100872
Honduras	USA (United States)	28 Feb 41	117UNTS205	200371
Brazil	USA (United States)	03 Sep 42	13UNTS109	200073
USA (United States)	Venezuela	14 May 43	28UNTS359	200160
Guatemala	USA (United States)	19 May 43	28UNTS377	200161
Canada	USA (United States)	03 Mar 44	109UNTS191	200359
Peru	USA (United States)	15 Apr 44	150UNTS317	200479
Dominican Republic	USA (United States)	13 Oct 45	149UNTS361	200477
USA (United States)	USSR (Soviet Union)	15 Oct 45	278UNTS151	200547
Belgium	Netherlands	24 May 46	31UNTS169	100477

Inspection and observation (Cont.)

PARTY ONE	PARTY TWO	DATE	CITATION	NUMBER
Taiwan	USA (United States)	14 Jun 46	4UNTS253	100049
Multilateral		27 Jun 46	264UNTS163	103792
Multilateral		18 Jul 46	125UNTS119	101674
Denmark	UK Great Britain	16 Aug 46	9UNTS163	100130
Philippines	USA (United States)	11 Sep 46	43UNTS231	100670
Multilateral		09 Oct 46	78UNTS227	101019
Multilateral		02 Dec 46	161UNTS72	102124
Philippines	USA (United States)	14 Feb 47	16UNTS3	100245
Philippines	USA (United States)	14 Mar 47	16UNTS31	100247
France	IBRD (World Bank)	09 May 47	152UNTS111	102014
Honduras	USA (United States)	13 May 47	166UNTS159	102189
Albania	Yugoslavia	12 Jun 47	111UNTS189	101533
Greece	USA (United States)	20 Jun 47	7UNTS267	100105
Austria	USA (United States)	21 Jun 47	67UNTS89	100868
Austria	USA (United States)	25 Jun 47	22UNTS141	100334
Italy	USA (United States)	04 Jul 47	22UNTS173	100336
Multilateral		11 Jul 47	54UNTS3	100792
Multilateral		11 Jul 47	214UNTS33	102898
Czechoslovakia	USA (United States)	25 Jul 47	90UNTS19	101223
Netherlands	IBRD (World Bank)	07 Aug 47	152UNTS165	102015
Poland	Romania	09 Aug 47	12UNTS363	100193
Denmark	IBRD (World Bank)	22 Aug 47	152UNTS223	102016
Luxembourg	IBRD (World Bank)	28 Aug 47	153UNTS3	102017
Iran	USA (United States)	06 Oct 47	11UNTS303	100171
Ecuador	USA (United States)	14 Nov 47	149UNTS297	101959
Czechoslovakia	USSR (Soviet Union)	28 Nov 47	216UNTS285	102941
Austria	USA (United States)	02 Jan 48	34UNTS141	100534
Greece	United Nations	12 Feb 48	47UNTS223	100732
UK Great Britain	USA (United States)	24 Feb 48	73UNTS143	100951
France	USA (United States)	27 Feb 48	84UNTS207	101131
Denmark	UK Great Britain	04 Mar 48	77UNTS57	100992
France	United Nations	10 Mar 48	47UNTS203	100731
Paraguay	USA (United States)	12 Mar 48	162UNTS30	102131
Belgium	France	13 Apr 48	31UNTS409	100483
IMF (Fund)	United Nations	15 Apr 48	16UNTS325	200108
Multilateral		30 Apr 48	30UNTS55	100449
Finland	United Nations	20 May 48	47UNTS319	200189
Poland	USSR (Soviet Union)	08 Jul 48	37UNTS25	100575
Poland	USSR (Soviet Union)	08 Jul 48	37UNTS107	100576
Netherlands	IBRD (World Bank)	15 Jul 48	153UNTS259	102021
Netherlands	IBRD (World Bank)	15 Jul 48	153UNTS259	102024
Netherlands	IBRD (World Bank)	15 Jul 48	153UNTS259	102022
Netherlands	IBRD (World Bank)	15 Jul 48	153UNTS259	102023
Netherlands	IBRD (World Bank)	15 Jul 48	153UNTS259	102025
Pakistan	United Nations	27 Aug 48	47UNTS269	100734
United Nations	Thailand	05 Oct 48	47UNTS287	100735
United Nations	San Marino	07 Oct 48	47UNTS337	200190
Czechoslovakia	United Nations	07 Oct 48	47UNTS185	100730
Finland	USSR (Soviet Union)	09 Dec 48	217UNTS135	102947
Korea, South	USA (United States)	10 Dec 48	55UNTS157	100813
Belgium	Denmark	30 Dec 48	25UNTS173	100362
Mexico	IBRD (World Bank)	06 Jan 49	154UNTS3	102027
Mexico	IBRD (World Bank)	06 Jan 49	154UNTS81	102028
Netherlands	USA (United States)	17 Jan 49	32UNTS241	100502
Czechoslovakia	Poland	21 Jan 49	31UNTS205	100480
Belgium	IBRD (World Bank)	01 Mar 49	154UNTS133	102029
United Nations	UK Great Britain	18 Mar 49	47UNTS305	100736
Chile	IBRD (World Bank)	23 Mar 49	153UNTS141	102019
Chile	IBRD (World Bank)	23 Mar 49	153UNTS61	102018
Israel	Lebanon	23 Mar 49	42UNTS287	100655
Israel	Jordan	03 Apr 49	42UNTS303	100656
Italy	Yugoslavia	13 Apr 49	171UNTS279	102232
Philippines	USA (United States)	07 Jun 49	45UNTS63	100692
Multilateral		20 Jun 49	128UNTS141	101718
Israel	Syria	20 Jul 49	42UNTS327	100657

Inspection and observation (Cont.)

PARTY ONE	PARTY TWO	DATE	CITATION	NUMBER
Netherlands	IBRD (World Bank)	26 Jul 49	154UNTS178	102030
Finland	IBRD (World Bank)	01 Aug 49	156UNTS289	200480
Multilateral		12 Aug 49	75UNTS85	100971
Multilateral		12 Aug 49	75UNTS287	100973
India	IBRD (World Bank)	18 Aug 49	154UNTS269	102031
Colombia	IBRD (World Bank)	19 Aug 49	154UNTS329	102032
Denmark	ICAO (Civil Aviat)	09 Sep 49	53UNTS341	100791
IBRD (World Bank)	Yugoslavia	17 Sep 49	155UNTS3	102034
Bulgaria	Poland	26 Sep 49	260UNTS249	103712
Bulgaria	Poland	26 Sep 49	260UNTS227	103711
India	IBRD (World Bank)	29 Sep 49	154UNTS393	102033
Finland	IBRD (World Bank)	17 Oct 49	156UNTS355	200481
Hungary	Poland	29 Oct 49	260UNTS91	103705
Hungary	Poland	29 Oct 49	260UNTS113	103706
United Arab Rep	USA (United States)	03 Nov 49	71UNTS31	100908
El Salvador	IBRD (World Bank)	14 Dec 49	155UNTS43	102035
Norway	USSR (Soviet Union)	29 Dec 49	83UNTS291	101112
Korea, South	USA (United States)	26 Jan 50	80UNTS205	101053
Norway	USA (United States)	27 Jan 50	80UNTS241	101055
Luxembourg	USA (United States)	27 Jan 50	80UNTS187	101052
Netherlands	USA (United States)	27 Jan 50	80UNTS219	101054
UK Great Britain	USA (United States)	27 Jan 50	80UNTS261	101056
France	USA (United States)	27 Jan 50	80UNTS171	101051
Italy	USA (United States)	27 Jan 50	80UNTS145	101050
Belgium	USA (United States)	27 Jan 50	51UNTS213	100767
Denmark	USA (United States)	27 Jan 50	48UNTS115	100740
India	USA (United States)	02 Feb 50	89UNTS127	101214
UNICEF (Children)	UK Great Britain	10 Feb 50	65UNTS86	100837
Canada	USA (United States)	27 Feb 50	132UNTS223	101762
Chile	UNICEF (Children)	03 Mar 50	126UNTS119	101685
Austria	Czechoslovakia	30 Mar 50	495UNTS85	107240
India	IBRD (World Bank)	18 Apr 50	155UNTS117	102036
Korea, South	USA (United States)	28 Apr 50	93UNTS21	101284
Mexico	IBRD (World Bank)	28 Apr 50	155UNTS185	102037
Iran	USA (United States)	23 May 50	81UNTS3	101057
Brazil	IBRD (World Bank)	26 May 50	301UNTS165	104345
Romania	USSR (Soviet Union)	27 May 50	221UNTS13	103000
Austria	USA (United States)	06 Jun 50	92UNTS201	101273
Iraq	IBRD (World Bank)	15 Jun 50	155UNTS267	102038
Germany, East	Poland	23 Jun 50	304UNTS91	104393
IBRD (World Bank)	Turkey	07 Jul 50	156UNTS75	102040
IBRD (World Bank)	Turkey	07 Jul 50	156UNTS3	102039
Hungary	USSR (Soviet Union)	13 Jul 50	221UNTS35	103001
Bulgaria	USSR (Soviet Union)	25 Aug 50	221UNTS57	103002
IBRD (World Bank)	Uruguay	25 Aug 50	156UNTS203	102042
Ethiopia	IBRD (World Bank)	13 Sep 50	157UNTS233	102056
Ethiopia	IBRD (World Bank)	13 Sep 50	157UNTS213	102055
Thailand	USA (United States)	17 Oct 50	79UNTS41	101030
Mexico	IBRD (World Bank)	18 Oct 50	157UNTS259	102057
IBRD (World Bank)	Turkey	19 Oct 50	157UNTS333	102058
IBRD (World Bank)	Thailand	27 Oct 50	158UNTS3	102059
IBRD (World Bank)	Thailand	27 Oct 50	158UNTS43	102061
IBRD (World Bank)	Thailand	27 Oct 50	158UNTS25	102060
Australia	IBRD (World Bank)	14 Nov 50	156UNTS147	102041
USA (United States)	Yugoslavia	21 Nov 50	93UNTS39	101285
Multilateral		23 Dec 50	185UNTS3	102456
Colombia	IBRD (World Bank)	28 Dec 50	158UNTS87	102063
Portugal	USA (United States)	05 Jan 51	133UNTS75	101782
USA (United States)	Yugoslavia	06 Jan 51	122UNTS137	101643
Chile	USA (United States)	16 Jan 51	157UNTS3	102043
IBRD (World Bank)	South Africa	23 Jan 51	158UNTS135	102065
IBRD (World Bank)	South Africa	23 Jan 51	158UNTS115	102064
Nicaragua	USA (United States)	31 Jan 51	150UNTS3	101960
Nicaragua	USA (United States)	31 Jan 51	160UNTS121	102105
Taiwan	USA (United States)	09 Feb 51	132UNTS273	101767

Inspection and observation (Cont.)

PARTY ONE	PARTY TWO	DATE	CITATION	NUMBER
Ethiopia	IBRD (World Bank)	19 Feb 51	186UNTS101	102486
Panama	USA (United States)	26 Feb 51	160UNTS153	102106
Dominican Republic	USA (United States)	16 Mar 51	148UNTS15	101932
Colombia	IBRD (World Bank)	10 Apr 51	158UNTS155	102066
USA (United States)	Yugoslavia	17 Apr 51	162UNTS173	102134
Honduras	USA (United States)	24 Apr 51	140UNTS287	101894
Philippines	USA (United States)	27 Apr 51	174UNTS251	102290
Multilateral		25 May 51	175UNTS215	102303
Nicaragua	IBRD (World Bank)	07 Jun 51	158UNTS215	102067
Nicaragua	IBRD (World Bank)	07 Jun 51	158UNTS277	102068
Finland	Sweden	15 Jun 51	198UNTS3	102651
Iceland	IBRD (World Bank)	20 Jun 51	158UNTS301	102069
UK Great Britain	USA (United States)	18 Jul 51	117UNTS49	101583
Iran	UNICEF (Children)	02 Aug 51	247UNTS11	103457
Mexico	USA (United States)	11 Aug 51	162UNTS103	102133
Japan	USA (United States)	28 Aug 51	147UNTS81	101930
UNICEF (Children)	Turkey	05 Sep 51	193UNTS55	102610
USA (United States)	Vietnam, South	07 Sep 51	174UNTS165	102284
Cambodia	USA (United States)	08 Sep 51	174UNTS115	102282
Laos	USA (United States)	09 Sep 51	174UNTS141	102283
Belgium	IBRD (World Bank)	13 Sep 51	158UNTS323	102070
UNICEF (Children)	UK Great Britain	02 Oct 51	104UNTS301	101448
Italy	IBRD (World Bank)	10 Oct 51	159UNTS383	200482
Chile	IBRD (World Bank)	10 Oct 51	158UNTS369	102072
IBRD (World Bank)	Yugoslavia	11 Oct 51	159UNTS3	102081
Colombia	IBRD (World Bank)	13 Oct 51	159UNTS75	102084
Nicaragua	IBRD (World Bank)	29 Oct 51	159UNTS35	102082
Iceland	IBRD (World Bank)	01 Nov 51	159UNTS55	102083
USA (United States)	Yugoslavia	14 Nov 51	174UNTS201	102286
Paraguay	IBRD (World Bank)	07 Dec 51	159UNTS103	102085
Iraq	UNICEF (Children)	10 Dec 51	126UNTS57	101682
Greece	USA (United States)	07 Jan 52	180UNTS171	102382
USA (United States)	Yugoslavia	08 Jan 52	152UNTS61	102011
Multilateral		10 Jan 52	163UNTS3	102138
Mexico	IBRD (World Bank)	11 Jan 52	159UNTS129	102086
Peru	IBRD (World Bank)	23 Jan 52	159UNTS163	102087
Canada	Spain	29 Jan 52	233UNTS117	103255
Ecuador	USA (United States)	20 Feb 52	177UNTS43	102308
Canada	USA (United States)	21 Feb 52	205UNTS293	102781
Peru	USA (United States)	22 Feb 52	165UNTS31	102166
Israel	USA (United States)	27 Feb 52	177UNTS123	102314
IBRD (World Bank)	UK Great Britain	27 Feb 52	159UNTS181	102088
Multilateral		01 Mar 52	168UNTS9	102210
Multilateral		07 Mar 52	175UNTS205	102302
Cuba	USA (United States)	07 Mar 52	165UNTS11	102165
Brazil	USA (United States)	15 Mar 52	199UNTS221	102687
Finland	Norway	18 Mar 52	188UNTS187	102527
Netherlands	IBRD (World Bank)	20 Mar 52	159UNTS207	102089
Pakistan	IBRD (World Bank)	27 Mar 52	159UNTS251	102090
Libya	UNICEF (Children)	05 Apr 52	133UNTS287	200441
United Nations	Yugoslavia	10 Apr 52	141UNTS89	101908
Colombia	USA (United States)	17 Apr 52	174UNTS215	102287
Liberia	UNICEF (Children)	17 Apr 52	133UNTS3	101773
Finland	IBRD (World Bank)	30 Apr 52	159UNTS408	200483
Multilateral		09 May 52	205UNTS65	102770
Israel	USA (United States)	09 May 52	177UNTS269	102326
Ethiopia	USA (United States)	15 May 52	180UNTS227	102388
Korea, South	USA (United States)	24 May 52	179UNTS23	102353
Pakistan	IBRD (World Bank)	13 Jun 52	191UNTS85	102578
Belgium	UNICEF (Children)	17 Jun 52	171UNTS249	102228
IBRD (World Bank)	Turkey	18 Jun 52	159UNTS269	102091
Multilateral		26 Jun 52	196UNTS183	102624
Brazil	IBRD (World Bank)	27 Jun 52	190UNTS85	102560
Brazil	IBRD (World Bank)	27 Jun 52	190UNTS115	102561
USA (United States)	Uruguay	30 Jun 52	207UNTS139	102804

Inspection and observation (Cont.)

PARTY ONE	PARTY TWO	DATE	CITATION	NUMBER
Chile	USA (United States)	30 Jun 52	199UNTS241	102688
Panama	USA (United States)	30 Jun 52	181UNTS121	102404
Finland	USA (United States)	02 Jul 52	165UNTS203	102177
Jordan	UNICEF (Children)	08 Jul 52	173UNTS353	200503
Peru	IBRD (World Bank)	08 Jul 52	159UNTS321	102093
Australia	IBRD (World Bank)	08 Jul 52	159UNTS295	102092
UNICEF (Children)	Syria	10 Jul 52	136UNTS17	101830
Germany, West	USA (United States)	18 Jul 52	165UNTS167	102175
UNICEF (Children)	UK Great Britain	25 Jul 52	135UNTS37	101812
UK Great Britain	USA (United States)	29 Jul 52	179UNTS129	102362
Laos	UNICEF (Children)	15 Aug 52	161UNTS323	200491
Colombia	IBRD (World Bank)	26 Aug 52	159UNTS339	102094
Iceland	IBRD (World Bank)	26 Aug 52	159UNTS363	102095
UNICEF (Children)	Vietnam, South	29 Aug 52	161UNTS335	200492
Ethiopia	USA (United States)	07 Nov 52	184UNTS285	102453
Japan	IBRD (World Bank)	12 Nov 52	354UNTS313	105068
Ceylon (Sri Lanka)	USA (United States)	17 Nov 52	180UNTS207	102386
Liberia	USA (United States)	15 Dec 52	185UNTS45	102457
UNICEF (Children)	UK Great Britain	16 Dec 52	151UNTS359	102005
India	IBRD (World Bank)	18 Dec 52	201UNTS241	102719
India	IBRD (World Bank)	23 Jan 53	201UNTS145	102715
Multilateral		07 Feb 53	173UNTS143	102264
IBRD (World Bank)	Yugoslavia	11 Feb 53	165UNTS231	102179
Multilateral		26 Feb 53	161UNTS31	102120
Dominican Republic	USA (United States)	06 Mar 53	199UNTS267	102689
Belgium	France	11 Mar 53	191UNTS329	102590
IBRD (World Bank)	UK Great Britain	11 Mar 53	172UNTS115	102243
United Arab Rep	USA (United States)	12 Mar 53	204UNTS3	102747
United Arab Rep	USA (United States)	19 Mar 53	215UNTS17	102909
Netherlands	United Nations	09 Apr 53	163UNTS89	102143
Ethiopia	UNICEF (Children)	27 Apr 53	213UNTS169	102885
Ethiopia	USA (United States)	29 Apr 53	224UNTS121	103073
Brazil	IBRD (World Bank)	30 Apr 53	190UNTS133	102562
El Salvador	USA (United States)	14 May 53	234UNTS71	103273
Finland	Norway	20 May 53	173UNTS163	102265
United Arab Rep	USA (United States)	21 May 53	204UNTS29	102748
Brazil	USA (United States)	30 May 53	460UNTS89	106633
Jordan	Syria	04 Jun 53	184UNTS15	102437
Canada	India	12 Jun 53	248UNTS113	103490
United Arab Rep	USA (United States)	18 Jun 53	215UNTS45	102910
United Arab Rep	USA (United States)	18 Jun 53	204UNTS55	102749
Liberia	USA (United States)	23 Jun 53	213UNTS37	102879
Liberia	USA (United States)	23 Jun 53	213UNTS57	102880
Philippines	USA (United States)	26 Jun 53	213UNTS77	102881
Panama	USA (United States)	26 Jun 53	215UNTS77	102912
Chile	USA (United States)	27 Jun 53	229UNTS193	103167
Chile	USA (United States)	27 Jun 53	229UNTS53	103160
Nicaragua	USA (United States)	30 Jun 53	215UNTS133	102917
Brazil	IBRD (World Bank)	17 Jul 53	190UNTS149	102563
IBRD (World Bank)	South Africa	28 Aug 53	180UNTS91	102377
IBRD (World Bank)	South Africa	28 Aug 53	180UNTS73	102376
Belgium	USA (United States)	02 Sep 53	200UNTS127	102700
Nicaragua	IBRD (World Bank)	04 Sep 53	186UNTS117	102487
Nicaragua	IBRD (World Bank)	04 Sep 53	186UNTS137	102488
Iceland	IBRD (World Bank)	04 Sep 53	178UNTS275	102344
Iceland	IBRD (World Bank)	04 Sep 53	188UNTS3	102519
Chile	IBRD (World Bank)	10 Sep 53	188UNTS25	102520
IBRD (World Bank)	Turkey	10 Sep 53	187UNTS71	102502
Colombia	IBRD (World Bank)	10 Sep 53	203UNTS3	102738
Panama	IBRD (World Bank)	25 Sep 53	188UNTS95	102522
Panama	IBRD (World Bank)	25 Sep 53	188UNTS71	102521
Spain	USA (United States)	26 Sep 53	207UNTS61	102800
Italy	IBRD (World Bank)	06 Oct 53	301UNTS135	104344
UNICEF (Children)	UK Great Britain	07 Oct 53	180UNTS59	102375
Japan	IBRD (World Bank)	15 Oct 53	187UNTS271	200511

Inspection and observation (Cont.)

PARTY ONE	PARTY TWO	DATE	CITATION	NUMBER
Japan	IBRD (World Bank)	15 Oct 53	187UNTS367	200513
Japan	IBRD (World Bank)	15 Oct 53	187UNTS321	200512
Jordan	USA (United States)	21 Oct 53	222UNTS31	103020
Japan	UNICEF (Children)	21 Nov 53	183UNTS297	200507
Israel	USA (United States)	25 Nov 53	219UNTS205	102976
Hungary	Romania	14 Dec 53	342UNTS151	104906
Brazil	IBRD (World Bank)	18 Dec 53	301UNTS229	104346
Brazil	IBRD (World Bank)	18 Dec 53	190UNTS179	102564
Chile	USA (United States)	30 Dec 53	236UNTS41	103315
Libya	USA (United States)	11 Jan 54	229UNTS15	103157
Pakistan	United Nations	25 Jan 54	185UNTS213	102472
Brazil	IBRD (World Bank)	24 Feb 54	301UNTS249	104347
Australia	IBRD (World Bank)	02 Mar 54	191UNTS103	102579
Japan	USA (United States)	08 Mar 54	232UNTS169	103236
Afghanistan	USA (United States)	20 Mar 54	229UNTS7	103156
Belgium	Norway	24 Mar 54	219UNTS73	102967
Italy	USA (United States)	31 Mar 54	235UNTS293	103311
Mexico	USA (United States)	06 Apr 54	233UNTS163	103261
Norway	IBRD (World Bank)	08 Apr 54	201UNTS131	102714
Peru	IBRD (World Bank)	12 Apr 54	190UNTS231	102567
Czechoslovakia	Hungary	16 Apr 54	504UNTS231	107360
Luxembourg	USA (United States)	17 Apr 54	257UNTS255	103661
Ethiopia	USA (United States)	21 Apr 54	232UNTS299	103244
Iraq	USA (United States)	21 Apr 54	222UNTS251	103032
Bulgaria	Yugoslavia	22 Apr 54	397UNTS43	105701
Canada	USA (United States)	03 May 54	221UNTS339	103015
UNICEF (Children)	Spain	07 May 54	190UNTS357	200515
Netherlands	USA (United States)	07 May 54	213UNTS325	102895
Panama	USA (United States)	11 May 54	236UNTS107	103319
Norway	Sweden	12 May 54	198UNTS157	102661
Pakistan	USA (United States)	19 May 54	202UNTS301	102736
Mexico	UNICEF (Children)	20 May 54	192UNTS3	102591
Honduras	USA (United States)	20 May 54	222UNTS87	103025
Australia	Japan	24 May 54	191UNTS125	102580
Pakistan	IBRD (World Bank)	02 Jun 54	324UNTS59	104678
France	IBRD (World Bank)	10 Jun 54	210UNTS89	102836
Chile	USA (United States)	28 Jun 54	233UNTS3	103246
Italy	USA (United States)	28 Jun 54	237UNTS121	103340
Ecuador	USA (United States)	30 Jun 54	236UNTS163	103323
Ceylon (Sri Lanka)	IBRD (World Bank)	09 Jul 54	198UNTS313	200517
UK Great Britain	USA (United States)	19 Jul 54	250UNTS193	103523
Bulgaria	Romania	22 Jul 54	362UNTS101	105184
Multilateral		29 Jul 54	249UNTS45	103500
Pakistan	USA (United States)	23 Aug 54	234UNTS243	103287
Mexico	IBRD (World Bank)	24 Aug 54	286UNTS211	104168
New Zealand	UNICEF (Children)	26 Aug 54	198UNTS173	102663
El Salvador	IBRD (World Bank)	12 Oct 54	203UNTS37	102739
USA (United States)	Yugoslavia	18 Oct 54	273UNTS163	103951
Denmark	Sweden	28 Oct 54	262UNTS211	103747
Libya	USA (United States)	03 Nov 54	238UNTS227	103366
Austria	IBRD (World Bank)	08 Nov 54	216UNTS305	200528
Peru	IBRD (World Bank)	12 Nov 54	209UNTS287	102831
India	IBRD (World Bank)	19 Nov 54	309UNTS159	104473
Belgium	IBRD (World Bank)	14 Dec 54	210UNTS113	102837
Colombia	IBRD (World Bank)	29 Dec 54	211UNTS135	102851
Netherlands	UNICEF (Children)	31 Dec 54	202UNTS135	102729
Pakistan	USA (United States)	11 Jan 55	251UNTS111	103537
Pakistan	USA (United States)	18 Jan 55	241UNTS53	103423
Haiti	USA (United States)	28 Jan 55	270UNTS83	103894
Mexico	USA (United States)	09 Mar 55	263UNTS247	103776
India	IBRD (World Bank)	14 Mar 55	309UNTS129	104472
IBRD (World Bank)	UK Great Britain	15 Mar 55	265UNTS85	103808
Australia	IBRD (World Bank)	18 Mar 55	220UNTS131	102998
Multilateral		19 Mar 55	228UNTS95	103144
Colombia	IBRD (World Bank)	24 Mar 55	212UNTS217	102874

Inspection and observation (Cont.)

PARTY ONE	PARTY TWO	DATE	CITATION	NUMBER
Finland	IBRD (World Bank)	24 Mar 55	211UNTS305	200525
Italy	Yugoslavia	26 Mar 55	379UNTS3	105432
Chile	USA (United States)	31 Mar 55	262UNTS19	103736
Haiti	USA (United States)	01 Apr 55	261UNTS361	103734
Peru	IBRD (World Bank)	05 Apr 55	211UNTS115	102850
Peru	IBRD (World Bank)	19 Apr 55	221UNTS153	103007
Norway	IBRD (World Bank)	19 Apr 55	211UNTS159	102852
Peru	USA (United States)	30 Apr 55	263UNTS309	103780
Cambodia	USA (United States)	16 May 55	263UNTS273	103777
Libya	USA (United States)	30 May 55	270UNTS43	103890
Italy	IBRD (World Bank)	01 Jun 55	358UNTS203	105137
Austria	IBRD (World Bank)	14 Jun 55	221UNTS375	200531
Canada	USA (United States)	15 Jun 55	235UNTS201	103302
Colombia	IBRD (World Bank)	15 Jun 55	248UNTS161	103494
Bulgaria	Yugoslavia	17 Jun 55	375UNTS287	105370
Guatemala	USA (United States)	18 Jun 55	262UNTS105	103740
Pakistan	IBRD (World Bank)	20 Jun 55	230UNTS41	103176
Haiti	USA (United States)	24 Jun 55	264UNTS291	103800
Turkey	USA (United States)	29 Jun 55	269UNTS97	103878
Germany, West	USA (United States)	30 Jun 55	240UNTS47	103393
Dominican Republic	USA (United States)	30 Jun 55	257UNTS313	103664
Nicaragua	IBRD (World Bank)	08 Jul 55	229UNTS123	103163
Nicaragua	IBRD (World Bank)	08 Jul 55	229UNTS97	103162
Panama	IBRD (World Bank)	12 Jul 55	219UNTS127	102970
Libya	USA (United States)	21 Jul 55	264UNTS247	103796
Guatemala	IBRD (World Bank)	29 Jul 55	229UNTS167	103165
Pakistan	IBRD (World Bank)	04 Aug 55	230UNTS79	103177
Peru	IBRD (World Bank)	05 Aug 55	218UNTS3	102950
Germany, East	Romania	05 Aug 55	342UNTS229	104910
Pakistan	IBRD (World Bank)	06 Aug 55	236UNTS195	103325
IBRD (World Bank)	Thailand	09 Aug 55	221UNTS283	103011
Lebanon	IBRD (World Bank)	25 Aug 55	230UNTS233	103188
Nicaragua	IBRD (World Bank)	26 Aug 55	229UNTS145	103164
France	IBRD (World Bank)	26 Aug 55	247UNTS305	103478
IBRD (World Bank)	Uruguay	29 Aug 55	243UNTS123	103450
Italy	Switzerland	17 Sep 55	291UNTS213	104257
Czechoslovakia	Germany, East	24 Oct 55	504UNTS173	107358
Japan	IBRD (World Bank)	25 Oct 55	230UNTS379	200534
Guatemala	UNICEF (Children)	22 Nov 55	221UNTS305	103012
IBRD (World Bank)	South Africa	28 Nov 55	230UNTS101	103178
Honduras	IBRD (World Bank)	22 Dec 55	230UNTS262	103189
Netherlands	USA (United States)	22 Jan 56	287UNTS121	104181
Italy	Switzerland	02 Feb 56	291UNTS113	104247
Japan	USA (United States)	10 Feb 56	275UNTS157	103980
Japan	IBRD (World Bank)	21 Feb 56	248UNTS321	200543
Ireland	USA (United States)	16 Mar 56	317UNTS195	104604
Ecuador	IBRD (World Bank)	26 Mar 56	292UNTS391	104277
Indonesia	United Nations	17 Apr 56	233UNTS267	103266
Bulgaria	Greece	19 Apr 56	594UNTS131	108600
Cambodia	UNICEF (Children)	28 Apr 56	136UNTS341	200446
Ceylon (Sri Lanka)	USA (United States)	28 Apr 56	274UNTS35	103956
Norway	IBRD (World Bank)	03 May 56	243UNTS281	103455
Burma	IBRD (World Bank)	04 May 56	253UNTS179	103584
Burma	IBRD (World Bank)	04 May 56	253UNTS209	103585
Haiti	IBRD (World Bank)	07 May 56	252UNTS279	103570
Costa Rica	USA (United States)	18 May 56	404UNTS237	105814
Finland	IBRD (World Bank)	22 May 56	248UNTS57	103485
Nicaragua	IBRD (World Bank)	22 May 56	253UNTS233	103586
Pakistan	USA (United States)	28 May 56	269UNTS15	103868
Germany, East	USSR (Soviet Union)	30 May 56	263UNTS143	103771
Colombia	IBRD (World Bank)	06 Jun 56	248UNTS139	103493
Austria	Yugoslavia	15 Jun 56	396UNTS117	105695
IBRD (World Bank)	UK Great Britain	21 Jun 56	285UNTS355	104157
Fed Rhod/Nyasaland	IBRD (World Bank)	21 Jun 56	285UNTS317	104156
Australia	USA (United States)	22 Jun 56	283UNTS275	104123

PARTY ONE	PARTY TWO	DATE	CITATION	NUMBER
Inspection and observation (Cont.)				
India	IBRD (World Bank)	26 Jun 56	301UNTS3	104341
Cuba	USA (United States)	26 Jun 56	293UNTS257	104294
Norway	Sweden	29 Jun 56	262UNTS335	103759
Lebanon	UNICEF (Children)	03 Jul 56	324UNTS145	104683
Romania	Yugoslavia	04 Aug 56	395UNTS99	105682
UNICEF (Children)	Sudan	07 Aug 56	248UNTS307	200542
Guatemala	USA (United States)	15 Aug 56	288UNTS181	104205
Costa Rica	IBRD (World Bank)	18 Sep 56	260UNTS369	103721
Austria	IBRD (World Bank)	21 Sep 56	259UNTS17	103681
Austria	IBRD (World Bank)	21 Sep 56	259UNTS43	103682
Romania	Yugoslavia	25 Sep 56	395UNTS147	105683
Italy	IBRD (World Bank)	11 Oct 56	359UNTS3	105138
IBRD (World Bank)	Thailand	12 Oct 56	261UNTS117	103728
Czechoslovakia	Hungary	13 Oct 56	300UNTS125	104336
Czechoslovakia	Hungary	13 Oct 56	300UNTS177	104337
IBRD (World Bank)	Uruguay	25 Oct 56	265UNTS59	103807
Ecuador	USA (United States)	31 Oct 56	283UNTS151	104114
Chile	IBRD (World Bank)	01 Nov 56	261UNTS27	103724
Argentina	USA (United States)	05 Nov 56	277UNTS143	104004
Australia	IBRD (World Bank)	15 Nov 56	288UNTS117	104201
Australia	IBRD (World Bank)	03 Dec 56	288UNTS99	104200
Japan	IBRD (World Bank)	19 Dec 56	268UNTS203	103859
India	IBRD (World Bank)	19 Dec 56	310UNTS75	104489
Japan	IBRD (World Bank)	19 Dec 56	264UNTS179	103793
Canada	USA (United States)	28 Dec 56	290UNTS103	104229
UNESCO (Educ/Cult)	Tunisia	03 Jan 57	257UNTS21	103645
Colombia	USA (United States)	09 Jan 57	462UNTS151	106676
Iceland	Thailand	22 Jan 57	312UNTS63	104511
Iran	IBRD (World Bank)	22 Jan 57	317UNTS129	104600
Ethiopia	IBRD (World Bank)	28 Jan 57	286UNTS307	104175
Germany, East	Poland	01 Feb 57	319UNTS115	104632
Multilateral		09 Feb 57	314UNTS105	104546
Iceland	USA (United States)	23 Feb 57	283UNTS73	104107
Norway	USA (United States)	25 Feb 57	284UNTS19	104126
Canada	USA (United States)	26 Feb 57	279UNTS179	104039
India	IBRD (World Bank)	05 Mar 57	272UNTS201	103939
Iran	USA (United States)	05 Mar 57	342UNTS29	104898
Dominican Republic	USA (United States)	09 Mar 57	279UNTS249	104044
Peru	IBRD (World Bank)	13 Mar 57	274UNTS59	103958
Morocco	USA (United States)	02 Apr 57	288UNTS157	104203
Libya	USA (United States)	04 Apr 57	283UNTS181	104116
Paraguay	USA (United States)	04 Apr 57	284UNTS161	104135
Multilateral		12 Apr 57	443UNTS128	106362
Ethiopia	USA (United States)	25 Apr 57	283UNTS205	104118
Austria	USA (United States)	10 May 57	283UNTS33	104104
Netherlands	IBRD (World Bank)	15 May 57	274UNTS211	103967
Albania	Yugoslavia	20 May 57	363UNTS99	105203
Hungary	Yugoslavia	25 May 57	477UNTS219	106924
India	IBRD (World Bank)	29 May 57	309UNTS201	104474
Ecuador	USA (United States)	31 May 57	304UNTS61	104391
Bulgaria	Yugoslavia	04 Jun 57	349UNTS35	105008
Nicaragua	USA (United States)	11 Jun 57	304UNTS267	104402
Belgium	IBRD (World Bank)	26 Jun 57	322UNTS301	104661
Jordan	USA (United States)	27 Jun 57	288UNTS269	104209
Finland	Norway	28 Jun 57	272UNTS191	103938
Tunisia	USA (United States)	28 Jun 57	289UNTS301	104226
Germany, West	USA (United States)	28 Jun 57	288UNTS339	104213
Libya	USA (United States)	30 Jun 57	284UNTS177	104136
Germany, West	USA (United States)	03 Jul 57	288UNTS305	104212
Italy	USA (United States)	03 Jul 57	308UNTS195	104462
South Africa	USA (United States)	08 Jul 57	290UNTS147	104234
India	IBRD (World Bank)	12 Jul 57	288UNTS135	104202
Norway	UK Great Britain	12 Jul 57	310UNTS41	104485
Chile	IBRD (World Bank)	24 Jul 57	282UNTS139	104098
Chile	IBRD (World Bank)	24 Jul 57	282UNTS189	104099

PARTY ONE	PARTY TWO	DATE	CITATION	NUMBER
Inspection and observation (Cont.)				
Morocco	UNICEF (Children)	31 Jul 57	282UNTS99	104095
Panama	USA (United States)	05 Aug 57	299UNTS113	104309
Japan	IBRD (World Bank)	09 Aug 57	293UNTS59	104286
Spain	USA (United States)	16 Aug 57	307UNTS169	104449
IBRD (World Bank)	Thailand	12 Sep 57	299UNTS349	104324
Ecuador	IBRD (World Bank)	20 Sep 57	293UNTS135	104291
Ecuador	IBRD (World Bank)	20 Sep 57	289UNTS237	104221
Sweden	UK Great Britain	20 Sep 57	310UNTS49	104486
IBRD (World Bank)	South Africa	01 Oct 57	280UNTS285	104065
Austria	IBRD (World Bank)	10 Oct 57	301UNTS95	104343
Pakistan	IBRD (World Bank)	18 Oct 57	299UNTS303	104322
Germany, East	Hungary	25 Oct 57	408UNTS156	105869
Brazil	USA (United States)	05 Nov 57	303UNTS3	104368
Argentina	UNICEF (Children)	19 Nov 57	300UNTS229	104338
India	IBRD (World Bank)	20 Nov 57	301UNTS47	104342
Philippines	IBRD (World Bank)	22 Nov 57	293UNTS83	104287
Belgium	IBRD (World Bank)	27 Nov 57	292UNTS175	104273
Pakistan	IBRD (World Bank)	17 Dec 57	299UNTS321	104323
Italy	UK Great Britain	28 Dec 57	305UNTS357	104425
Japan	USA (United States)	11 Jan 58	304UNTS35	104390
Mexico	IBRD (World Bank)	14 Jan 58	293UNTS167	104292
Brazil	IBRD (World Bank)	22 Jan 58	323UNTS99	104666
Czechoslovakia	Poland	31 Jan 58	431UNTS99	106214
Bulgaria	Hungary	13 Mar 58	438UNTS191	106317
Belgium	Luxembourg	28 Mar 58	303UNTS101	104372
Sweden	USSR (Soviet Union)	28 Mar 58	428UNTS321	106184
Austria	IBRD (World Bank)	28 Apr 58	359UNTS145	105142
Chile	IBRD (World Bank)	28 Apr 58	359UNTS89	105140
IBRD (World Bank)	UK Great Britain	02 May 58	324UNTS25	104677
Honduras	IBRD (World Bank)	09 May 58	323UNTS4	104662
Japan	IBRD (World Bank)	13 Jun 58	312UNTS159	104518
IBRD (World Bank)	UK Great Britain	16 Jun 58	309UNTS35	104467
Japan	USA (United States)	19 Jun 58	325UNTS143	104699
Multilateral		24 Jun 58	348UNTS275	105005
India	IBRD (World Bank)	25 Jun 58	323UNTS157	104668
India	IBRD (World Bank)	25 Jun 58	323UNTS131	104667
Portugal	UK Great Britain	18 Jul 58	313UNTS109	104532
IBRD (World Bank)	Sudan	21 Jul 58	323UNTS183	104669
India	IBRD (World Bank)	23 Jul 58	317UNTS3	104590
Ghana	UNICEF (Children)	12 Aug 58	309UNTS103	104469
Japan	IBRD (World Bank)	18 Aug 58	323UNTS205	104670
Japan	IBRD (World Bank)	10 Sep 58	318UNTS133	104612
Japan	IBRD (World Bank)	10 Sep 58	323UNTS297	104673
India	IBRD (World Bank)	16 Sep 58	323UNTS235	104671
Peru	IBRD (World Bank)	17 Sep 58	323UNTS27	104663
Fed of Malaya	IBRD (World Bank)	22 Sep 58	323UNTS71	104665
Brazil	IBRD (World Bank)	03 Oct 58	337UNTS177	104823
USA (United States)	Venezuela	08 Oct 58	371UNTS69	105271
Ecuador	IBRD (World Bank)	09 Oct 58	337UNTS299	104827
Spain	USA (United States)	16 Oct 58	336UNTS153	104804
France	Italy	30 Oct 58	363UNTS3	105196
Austria	IBRD (World Bank)	02 Dec 58	340UNTS3	104856
Colombia	IBRD (World Bank)	15 Dec 58	354UNTS233	105065
Korea, South	USA (United States)	18 Dec 58	325UNTS233	104702
El Salvador	IBRD (World Bank)	07 Jan 59	346UNTS51	104977
Colombia	IBRD (World Bank)	30 Jan 59	337UNTS327	104828
Costa Rica	IBRD (World Bank)	11 Feb 59	337UNTS245	104825
El Salvador	IBRD (World Bank)	20 Feb 59	362UNTS75	105183
Finland	IBRD (World Bank)	16 Mar 59	337UNTS269	104826
Morocco	UN Special Fund	04 Apr 59	354UNTS347	105069
India	IBRD (World Bank)	08 Apr 59	348UNTS131	104998
Italy	IBRD (World Bank)	21 Apr 59	359UNTS191	105143
USA (United States)	Vietnam, South	22 Apr 59	347UNTS113	104993
Canada	Pakistan	14 May 59	426UNTS129	106133
Colombia	IBRD (World Bank)	20 May 59	344UNTS251	104953

Inspection and observation (Cont.)

PARTY ONE	PARTY TWO	DATE	CITATION	NUMBER
Honduras	IBRD (World Bank)	20 May 59	359UNTS119	105141
Iran	IBRD (World Bank)	29 May 59	348UNTS103	104997
IBRD (World Bank)	South Africa	10 Jun 59	340UNTS33	104857
Brazil	IBRD (World Bank)	17 Jun 59	377UNTS111	105398
Gabon	IBRD (World Bank)	30 Jun 59	452UNTS135	106507
Congo (Brazzaville)	IBRD (World Bank)	30 Jun 59	452UNTS123	106506
France	IBRD (World Bank)	30 Jun 59	452UNTS67	106505
Canada	Japan	02 Jul 59	383UNTS243	105504
Norway	IBRD (World Bank)	08 Jul 59	344UNTS229	104952
India	IBRD (World Bank)	15 Jul 59	346UNTS33	104976
India	IBRD (World Bank)	15 Jul 59	355UNTS95	105075
Austria	USA (United States)	22 Jul 59	368UNTS199	105242
Australia	Canada	04 Aug 59	391UNTS191	105623
Mexico	USA (United States)	05 Aug 59	356UNTS3	105089
Ghana	UN Special Fund	12 Aug 59	338UNTS203	104836
Pakistan	IBRD (World Bank)	13 Aug 59	355UNTS129	105076
Italy	IBRD (World Bank)	16 Sep 59	375UNTS159	105366
Pakistan	IBRD (World Bank)	25 Sep 59	355UNTS169	105077
United Arab Rep	USA (United States)	28 Sep 59	358UNTS97	105128
Iran	UN Special Fund	06 Oct 59	342UNTS89	104902
Poland	UN Special Fund	15 Oct 59	344UNTS29	104941
India	UN Special Fund	20 Oct 59	344UNTS143	104946
UN Special Fund	Yugoslavia	27 Oct 59	344UNTS159	104947
Ecuador	UN Special Fund	10 Nov 59	345UNTS3	104955
Japan	USA (United States)	12 Nov 59	361UNTS27	105171
Greece	UN Special Fund	13 Nov 59	345UNTS171	104966
UN Special Fund	Turkey	20 Nov 59	345UNTS105	104963
Iran	IBRD (World Bank)	23 Nov 59	380UNTS245	105459
UN Special Fund	United Arab Rep	25 Nov 59	345UNTS125	104964
Pakistan	IBRD (World Bank)	30 Nov 59	355UNTS203	105078
Multilateral		01 Dec 59	402UNTS71	105778
Israel	UN Special Fund	01 Dec 59	345UNTS197	104968
Argentina	UN Special Fund	04 Dec 59	345UNTS263	104972
France	IBRD (World Bank)	10 Dec 59	380UNTS319	105464
Jordan	UN Special Fund	15 Dec 59	346UNTS3	104974
IBRD (World Bank)	United Arab Rep	22 Dec 59	354UNTS197	105063
IBRD (World Bank)	Uruguay	30 Dec 59	384UNTS275	105523
UN Special Fund	UK Great Britain	07 Jan 60	348UNTS177	105000
Spain	UK Great Britain	19 Jan 60	404UNTS41	105804
Peru	UN Special Fund	19 Jan 60	349UNTS83	105010
Colombia	IBRD (World Bank)	20 Jan 60	375UNTS49	105353
Chile	UN Special Fund	22 Jan 60	351UNTS115	105020
Colombia	UN Special Fund	04 Feb 60	355UNTS257	105080
Bolivia	UN Special Fund	09 Feb 60	351UNTS203	105024
Cuba	UNICEF (Children)	11 Feb 60	349UNTS277	105014
Iran	IBRD (World Bank)	20 Feb 60	384UNTS213	105521
Afghanistan	UN Special Fund	21 Feb 60	351UNTS93	105019
Pakistan	UN Special Fund	25 Feb 60	351UNTS141	105021
Greece	Tunisia	02 Mar 60	483UNTS89	107008
Mauritania	IBRD (World Bank)	17 Mar 60	452UNTS211	106509
France	UN Special Fund	17 Mar 60	354UNTS119	105059
France	IBRD (World Bank)	17 Mar 60	452UNTS147	106508
Japan	IBRD (World Bank)	17 Mar 60	362UNTS43	105182
Portugal	USA (United States)	19 Mar 60	371UNTS131	105275
Belgium	IBRD (World Bank)	30 Mar 60	379UNTS103	105437
Belgium	IBRD (World Bank)	30 Mar 60	379UNTS161	105439
Belgium	IBRD (World Bank)	30 Mar 60	379UNTS129	105438
Argentina	USA (United States)	01 Apr 60	371UNTS245	105281
IBRD (World Bank)	UK Great Britain	01 Apr 60	379UNTS397	105446
Italy	UN Special Fund	01 Apr 60	354UNTS261	105066
UN Special Fund	Tunisia	12 Apr 60	355UNTS289	105082
Libya	UN Special Fund	19 Apr 60	356UNTS11	105090
UN Special Fund	Sudan	21 Apr 60	356UNTS213	105097
Canada	Norway	25 Apr 60	470UNTS109	106801
UN Special Fund	Vietnam, South	29 Apr 60	357UNTS311	200567

Inspection and observation (Cont.)

PARTY ONE	PARTY TWO	DATE	CITATION	NUMBER
Laos	UN Special Fund	30 Apr 60	361UNTS171	105179
Costa Rica	IBRD (World Bank)	04 May 60	390UNTS201	105609
Poland	Yugoslavia	05 May 60	423UNTS229	106095
Lebanon	UN Special Fund	07 May 60	360UNTS225	105160
Colombia	IBRD (World Bank)	10 May 60	379UNTS218	105441
Denmark	UK Great Britain	20 May 60	374UNTS245	105338
IBRD (World Bank)	UK Great Britain	27 May 60	375UNTS201	105367
Peru	IBRD (World Bank)	01 Jun 60	380UNTS15	105448
IBRD (World Bank)	Sudan	17 Jun 60	379UNTS253	105442
Iraq	UN Special Fund	19 Jun 60	376UNTS357	105389
Belgium	Netherlands	20 Jun 60	423UNTS19	106084
Nicaragua	IBRD (World Bank)	22 Jun 60	384UNTS243	105522
Multilateral		22 Jun 60	431UNTS41	106208
Finland	USSR (Soviet Union)	23 Jun 60	379UNTS277	105443
IAEA (Atom Energy)	USA (United States)	28 Jun 60	374UNTS133	105333
Honduras	IBRD (World Bank)	29 Jun 60	400UNTS137	105751
Peru	IBRD (World Bank)	29 Jun 60	400UNTS99	105750
Ethiopia	UN Special Fund	13 Jul 60	368UNTS159	105240
USA (United States)	Uruguay	22 Jul 60	388UNTS315	105587
El Salvador	IBRD (World Bank)	29 Jul 60	390UNTS101	105605
Canada	UK Great Britain	05 Aug 60	470UNTS133	106804
Panama	IBRD (World Bank)	19 Aug 60	390UNTS153	105607
Australia	USA (United States)	23 Aug 60	388UNTS237	105581
Canada	USA (United States)	31 Aug 60	393UNTS247	105659
Haiti	USA (United States)	01 Sep 60	388UNTS249	105582
Israel	IBRD (World Bank)	09 Sep 60	406UNTS3	105837
Brazil	UN Special Fund	16 Sep 60	375UNTS3	105351
Multilateral		19 Sep 60	419UNTS125	106032
Multilateral		19 Sep 60	444UNTS259	106371
Pakistan	IBRD (World Bank)	19 Sep 60	444UNTS207	106370
Taiwan	UN Special Fund	20 Sep 60	375UNTS29	105352
Colombia	IBRD (World Bank)	20 Sep 60	390UNTS173	105608
Indonesia	UN Special Fund	07 Oct 60	378UNTS141	105424
Liberia	UN Special Fund	11 Oct 60	376UNTS341	105388
Mexico	IBRD (World Bank)	18 Oct 60	422UNTS177	106075
El Salvador	UN Special Fund	24 Oct 60	377UNTS171	105400
India	IBRD (World Bank)	28 Oct 60	406UNTS27	105838
Czechoslovakia	Poland	14 Nov 60	413UNTS4	105938
Finland	Norway	15 Nov 60	383UNTS159	105501
Nepal	UN Special Fund	17 Nov 60	380UNTS289	105461
Guatemala	UN Special Fund	17 Nov 60	383UNTS67	105495
Cambodia	UN Special Fund	24 Nov 60	382UNTS255	105487
Norway	IBRD (World Bank)	02 Dec 60	390UNTS131	105606
Cyprus	USA (United States)	08 Dec 60	405UNTS145	105831
Nepal	UNICEF (Children)	12 Dec 60	382UNTS273	105488
Peru	IBRD (World Bank)	19 Dec 60	417UNTS275	106010
Japan	IBRD (World Bank)	20 Dec 60	400UNTS167	105752
Japan	IBRD (World Bank)	20 Dec 60	400UNTS279	105754
Honduras	UN Special Fund	20 Dec 60	383UNTS103	105497
Togo	USA (United States)	22 Dec 60	401UNTS33	105760
Burma	UN Special Fund	03 Jan 61	387UNTS219	105564
Costa Rica	UN Special Fund	10 Jan 61	389UNTS253	105597
Burma	IBRD (World Bank)	16 Jan 61	400UNTS73	105749
UN Special Fund	Saudi Arabia	19 Jan 61	396UNTS27	105692
Nicaragua	UN Special Fund	20 Jan 61	387UNTS15	105555
Chad	UN Special Fund	23 Jan 61	390UNTS69	105603
UN Special Fund	Somalia	28 Jan 61	388UNTS75	105573
Gabon	UN Special Fund	02 Feb 61	387UNTS289	105568
Costa Rica	IBRD (World Bank)	03 Feb 61	414UNTS314	105977
Poland	USSR (Soviet Union)	05 Feb 61	420UNTS161	106046
Nigeria	UN Special Fund	10 Feb 61	390UNTS85	105604
IBRD (World Bank)	Yugoslavia	23 Feb 61	415UNTS92	105982
Mexico	UN Special Fund	23 Feb 61	388UNTS151	105576
Cyprus	UN Special Fund	24 Feb 61	389UNTS3	105588
Panama	UN Special Fund	09 Mar 61	396UNTS3	105691

Inspection and observation (Cont.)

PARTY ONE	PARTY TWO	DATE	CITATION	NUMBER
Cuba	UN Special Fund	10 Mar 61	390UNTS35	105601
Japan	IBRD (World Bank)	16 Mar 61	400UNTS201	105753
IBRD (World Bank)	UK Great Britain	29 Mar 61	415UNTS300	105990
Honduras	USA (United States)	12 Apr 61	413UNTS182	105952
Korea, South	UN Special Fund	21 Apr 61	394UNTS231	200583
IBRD (World Bank)	Thailand	28 Apr 61	415UNTS121	105983
Japan	IBRD (World Bank)	02 May 61	415UNTS144	105984
Ceylon (Sri Lanka)	UN Special Fund	03 May 61	395UNTS217	105687
Colombia	IBRD (World Bank)	12 May 61	415UNTS172	105985
Honduras	IDA (Devel Assoc)	12 May 61	414UNTS180	105973
Ceylon (Sri Lanka)	IBRD (World Bank)	06 Jun 61	414UNTS349	105978
Nepal	USA (United States)	09 Jun 61	421UNTS223	106061
Cameroon	UN Special Fund	13 Jun 61	397UNTS297	105713
Multilateral		14 Jun 61	415UNTS4	105979
IBRD (World Bank)	Sudan	14 Jun 61	415UNTS26	105980
IDA (Devel Assoc)	Sudan	14 Jun 61	415UNTS50	105981
Inter-Am Devel Bnk	USA (United States)	19 Jun 61	410UNTS34	105895
Paraguay	UN Special Fund	22 Jun 61	399UNTS117	105738
IBRD (World Bank)	UK Great Britain	23 Jun 61	415UNTS358	105991
UN Special Fund	Upper Volta	26 Jun 61	400UNTS3	105744
Pakistan	IBRD (World Bank)	27 Jun 61	425UNTS241	106127
Philippines	UN Special Fund	28 Jun 61	399UNTS141	105739
Chile	IBRD (World Bank)	28 Jun 61	426UNTS33	106129
Haiti	UN Special Fund	28 Jun 61	399UNTS171	105741
Argentina	IBRD (World Bank)	30 Jun 61	445UNTS85	106379
Israel	IBRD (World Bank)	11 Jul 61	429UNTS3	106188
Mali	UN Special Fund	21 Jul 61	401UNTS141	105768
Philippines	IBRD (World Bank)	26 Jul 61	414UNTS253	105976
UN Special Fund	Yemen	02 Aug 61	402UNTS43	105777
Finland	IBRD (World Bank)	09 Aug 61	415UNTS204	105986
India	IBRD (World Bank)	09 Aug 61	417UNTS297	106011
IBRD (World Bank)	UK Great Britain	16 Aug 61	426UNTS287	106143
India	IBRD (World Bank)	17 Aug 61	417UNTS319	106012
Poland	UNICEF (Children)	24 Aug 61	406UNTS95	105841
Colombia	IBRD (World Bank)	28 Aug 61	416UNTS23	105993
Ivory Coast	UN Special Fund	29 Aug 61	406UNTS129	105844
Liberia	Switzerland	31 Aug 61	559UNTS215	108160
Costa Rica	IBRD (World Bank)	06 Sep 61	446UNTS345	106408
India	IBRD (World Bank)	13 Oct 61	418UNTS3	106013
Costa Rica	IBRD (World Bank)	13 Oct 61	430UNTS27	106202
Belgium	Yugoslavia	31 Oct 61	426UNTS165	106136
Peru	IBRD (World Bank)	03 Nov 61	430UNTS47	106203
Mauritania	UN Special Fund	07 Nov 61	412UNTS240	105936
Congo (Brazzaville)	UN Special Fund	09 Nov 61	413UNTS58	105940
Denmark	UK Great Britain	15 Nov 61	420UNTS67	106041
OAS (Am States)	USA (United States)	29 Nov 61	424UNTS119	106104
IBRD (World Bank)	UK Great Britain	29 Nov 61	426UNTS49	106130
Belgium	Luxembourg	29 Nov 61	486UNTS37	107071
Japan	IBRD (World Bank)	29 Nov 61	426UNTS3	106128
IBRD (World Bank)	South Africa	01 Dec 61	425UNTS215	106126
Ethiopia	USA (United States)	06 Dec 61	433UNTS231	106246
Multilateral		06 Dec 61	473UNTS219	106864
UN Special Fund	Venezuela	11 Dec 61	422UNTS149	106074
IBRD (World Bank)	Venezuela	13 Dec 61	446UNTS371	106409
UN Special Fund	Senegal	16 Dec 61	425UNTS97	106121
Costa Rica	USA (United States)	22 Dec 61	460UNTS277	106646
Malagasy	UN Special Fund	05 Jan 62	419UNTS29	106028
Cyprus	USA (United States)	15 Jan 62	435UNTS15	106267
Cyprus	USA (United States)	18 Jan 62	435UNTS3	106266
UNESCO (Educ/Cult)	USA (United States)	19 Jan 62	435UNTS99	106272
Argentina	IBRD (World Bank)	19 Jan 62	446UNTS305	106407
Australia	IBRD (World Bank)	23 Jan 62	430UNTS3	106201
Ghana	USA (United States)	24 Jan 62	435UNTS23	106268
Ghana	IBRD (World Bank)	08 Feb 62	449UNTS207	106462
Hungary	Yugoslavia	09 Feb 62	577UNTS3	108370

Inspection and observation (Cont.)

PARTY ONE	PARTY TWO	DATE	CITATION	NUMBER
Iceland	IBRD (World Bank)	14 Feb 62	447UNTS95	106413
Niger	UN Special Fund	26 Feb 62	423UNTS83	106086
India	IBRD (World Bank)	28 Feb 62	447UNTS3	106410
Pakistan	IAEA (Atom Energy)	05 Mar 62	425UNTS17	106115
Dominican Republic	USA (United States)	08 Mar 62	527UNTS29	107615
Dahomey	UN Special Fund	28 Mar 62	424UNTS55	106099
IAEA (Atom Energy)	USA (United States)	30 Mar 62	442UNTS49	106338
Belgium	France	30 Mar 62	502UNTS297	107335
El Salvador	USA (United States)	13 Apr 62	451UNTS307	106500
Greece	USA (United States)	24 Apr 62	459UNTS3	106609
Bolivia	USA (United States)	26 Apr 62	461UNTS105	106654
UN Special Fund	Uruguay	04 May 62	429UNTS143	106196
Multilateral		15 May 62	444UNTS3	106367
Colombia	IBRD (World Bank)	23 May 62	447UNTS39	106411
Panama	USA (United States)	23 May 62	458UNTS225	106604
Denmark	USA (United States)	28 May 62	450UNTS215	106469
Ethiopia	IBRD (World Bank)	31 May 62	467UNTS237	106765
Dominican Republic	UN Special Fund	06 Jun 62	429UNTS169	106197
Niger	USA (United States)	14 Jun 62	458UNTS233	106605
Costa Rica	USA (United States)	18 Jun 62	461UNTS155	106659
Mexico	IBRD (World Bank)	20 Jun 62	467UNTS205	106764
Mexico	IBRD (World Bank)	20 Jun 62	468UNTS109	106771
Argentina	USA (United States)	22 Jun 62	458UNTS97	106594
Multilateral		27 Jun 62	463UNTS17	106690
Multilateral		27 Jun 62	463UNTS3	106688
UN Special Fund	Syria	07 Jul 62	443UNTS3	106355
IBRD (World Bank)	Yugoslavia	11 Jul 62	468UNTS143	106772
UN Special Fund	Tanganyika	17 Jul 62	435UNTS237	106281
Senegal	USA (United States)	20 Jul 62	458UNTS137	106596
Colombia	USA (United States)	23 Jul 62	458UNTS123	106595
Finland	IBRD (World Bank)	15 Aug 62	467UNTS177	106763
Philippines	USA (United States)	21 Aug 62	461UNTS163	106660
Paraguay	USA (United States)	25 Aug 62	461UNTS207	106665
Canada	Sweden	11 Sep 62	529UNTS9	107651
India	IDA (Devel Assoc)	14 Sep 62	467UNTS265	106766
Pakistan	IBRD (World Bank)	14 Sep 62	467UNTS125	106761
Panama	IBRD (World Bank)	14 Sep 62	476UNTS153	106908
Pakistan	IBRD (World Bank)	14 Sep 62	467UNTS152	106762
Finland	USSR (Soviet Union)	27 Sep 62	479UNTS99	106949
Israel	OAS (Am States)	11 Oct 62	484UNTS241	107035
Belgium	Romania	12 Oct 62	502UNTS31	107325
Israel	IBRD (World Bank)	17 Oct 62	467UNTS107	106760
Japan	USA (United States)	24 Oct 62	462UNTS119	106673
IBRD (World Bank)	Uruguay	26 Oct 62	481UNTS39	106977
Japan	UN Special Fund	31 Oct 62	444UNTS171	106368
Algeria	UN Special Fund	15 Nov 62	452UNTS243	106512
Germany, West	USA (United States)	20 Nov 62	505UNTS263	107377
India	UK Great Britain	27 Nov 62	466UNTS189	106744
Germany, West	USA (United States)	29 Nov 62	460UNTS169	106639
Nigeria	IBRD (World Bank)	10 Dec 62	468UNTS255	106776
IBRD (World Bank)	Thailand	21 Dec 62	467UNTS43	106757
Morocco	IBRD (World Bank)	21 Dec 62	478UNTS205	106937
IBRD (World Bank)	Thailand	21 Dec 62	467UNTS63	106758
Malaysia	USA (United States)	28 Jan 63	473UNTS15	106850
Central Afri Rep	USA (United States)	10 Feb 63	473UNTS83	106857
Pakistan	IBRD (World Bank)	13 Feb 63	467UNTS3	106756
Philippines	IBRD (World Bank)	15 Feb 63	478UNTS161	106936
Nicaragua	IBRD (World Bank)	01 Mar 63	481UNTS15	106976
Norway	USA (United States)	01 Mar 63	524UNTS185	107573
IAEA (Atom Energy)	Yugoslavia	04 Mar 63	490UNTS333	107162
IBRD (World Bank)	Thailand	07 Mar 63	467UNTS83	106759
Peru	IBRD (World Bank)	13 Mar 63	478UNTS245	106938
Israel	USA (United States)	21 Mar 63	476UNTS131	106907
UN Special Fund	Uganda	22 Mar 63	456UNTS466	106572
Philippines	USA (United States)	23 Mar 63	474UNTS80	106873

Inspection and observation (Cont.)

PARTY ONE	PARTY TWO	DATE	CITATION	NUMBER
UK Great Britain	USA (United States)	06 Apr 63	474UNTS49	106871
Belgium	USA (United States)	19 Apr 63	493UNTS83	107209
Thailand	USA (United States)	25 Apr 63	476UNTS115	106906
Mexico	IBRD (World Bank)	29 Apr 63	489UNTS151	107138
Australia	USA (United States)	09 May 63	475UNTS331	106897
Belgium	Netherlands	13 May 63	540UNTS3	107843
IBRD (World Bank)	UK Great Britain	16 May 63	477UNTS361	106929
IBRD (World Bank)	UK Great Britain	16 May 63	476UNTS211	106910
Netherlands	USA (United States)	20 May 63	487UNTS123	107099
Jamaica	UN Special Fund	22 May 63	489UNTS191	107140
Thailand	USA (United States)	24 May 63	477UNTS123	106918
Netherlands	UN Special Fund	24 May 63	466UNTS289	106750
Colombia	IBRD (World Bank)	03 Jun 63	490UNTS199	107155
IAEA (Atom Energy)	Yugoslavia	04 Jun 63	490UNTS343	107163
UN Special Fund	Western Samoa	05 Jun 63	467UNTS463	200601
India	IBRD (World Bank)	05 Jun 63	481UNTS191	106983
Jamaica	USA (United States)	06 Jun 63	477UNTS29	106913
Hungary	Romania	13 Jun 63	576UNTS275	108369
Korea, South	USA (United States)	18 Jun 63	487UNTS297	107112
India	USA (United States)	19 Jun 63	479UNTS175	106952
El Salvador	IBRD (World Bank)	19 Jun 63	481UNTS59	106978
IBRD (World Bank)	Yugoslavia	21 Jun 63	482UNTS43	106990
Austria	IAEA (Atom Energy)	21 Jun 63	490UNTS351	107164
Colombia	IBRD (World Bank)	21 Jun 63	482UNTS159	106994
Austria	USA (United States)	25 Jun 63	479UNTS223	106956
Colombia	IBRD (World Bank)	28 Jun 63	489UNTS113	107137
Finland	IAEA (Atom Energy)	02 Jul 63	490UNTS403	107167
Austria	Romania	03 Jul 63	588UNTS3	108516
IBRD (World Bank)	Tunisia	03 Jul 63	480UNTS209	106970
Costa Rica	IBRD (World Bank)	10 Jul 63	482UNTS69	106991
Malaysia	IBRD (World Bank)	15 Jul 63	482UNTS123	106993
Colombia	IBRD (World Bank)	16 Jul 63	482UNTS256	106998
Denmark	IBRD (World Bank)	24 Jul 63	481UNTS171	106982
Malaysia	IBRD (World Bank)	07 Aug 63	485UNTS253	107060
Paraguay	USA (United States)	20 Aug 63	531UNTS197	107704
Afghanistan	USA (United States)	20 Aug 63	488UNTS41	107118
Argentina	USA (United States)	21 Aug 63	488UNTS61	107119
Burundi	UN Special Fund	22 Aug 63	476UNTS49	106903
IBRD (World Bank)	UK Great Britain	06 Sep 63	483UNTS173	107013
Finland	IBRD (World Bank)	18 Sep 63	491UNTS345	107183
Ecuador	USA (United States)	20 Sep 63	488UNTS147	107125
IBRD (World Bank)	Venezuela	20 Sep 63	482UNTS227	106997
Mexico	IBRD (World Bank)	20 Sep 63	491UNTS317	107182
Multilateral		23 Sep 63	488UNTS99	107122
IBRD (World Bank)	UK Great Britain	23 Sep 63	503UNTS247	107348
Taiwan	IBRD (World Bank)	27 Sep 63	483UNTS151	107012
Japan	IBRD (World Bank)	27 Sep 63	485UNTS283	107061
El Salvador	IBRD (World Bank)	01 Oct 63	517UNTS3	107481
Norway	IBRD (World Bank)	15 Oct 63	482UNTS103	106992
Multilateral		17 Oct 63	525UNTS75	107585
Czechoslovakia	Hungary	22 Oct 63	514UNTS95	107444
Iran	USA (United States)	24 Oct 63	489UNTS303	107146
IBRD (World Bank)	Spain	25 Oct 63	491UNTS297	107181
IBRD (World Bank)	Yugoslavia	28 Oct 63	503UNTS289	107349
Central Afri Rep	UN Special Fund	30 Oct 63	481UNTS247	106985
Portugal	IBRD (World Bank)	06 Nov 63	492UNTS89	107188
Portugal	IBRD (World Bank)	06 Nov 63	491UNTS137	107176
New Zealand	IBRD (World Bank)	12 Nov 63	485UNTS233	107059
Tunisia	USA (United States)	18 Nov 63	494UNTS193	107233
Peru	IBRD (World Bank)	22 Nov 63	491UNTS101	107175
Romania	Yugoslavia	30 Nov 63	512UNTS2	107438
Australia	India	03 Dec 63	486UNTS279	107082
Greece	USA (United States)	13 Dec 63	494UNTS55	107226
Chile	IBRD (World Bank)	18 Dec 63	504UNTS29	107352
Mexico	IAEA (Atom Energy)	18 Dec 63	490UNTS361	107165

Inspection and observation (Cont.)

PARTY ONE	PARTY TWO	DATE	CITATION	NUMBER
Cameroon	Netherlands	18 Dec 63	521UNTS303	107527
Chile	IBRD (World Bank)	18 Dec 63	504UNTS3	107351
Multilateral		30 Dec 63	568UNTS243	108272
Multilateral		30 Dec 63	551UNTS119	108037
Multilateral		30 Dec 63	568UNTS215	108270
Multilateral		30 Dec 63	551UNTS105	108036
Liberia	IBRD (World Bank)	08 Jan 64	504UNTS53	107353
Colombia	IBRD (World Bank)	07 Feb 64	516UNTS99	107473
Paraguay	USA (United States)	10 Feb 64	511UNTS53	107426
Iceland	USA (United States)	13 Feb 64	524UNTS235	107576
IBRD (World Bank)	Thailand	11 Mar 64	504UNTS73	107354
New Zealand	IBRD (World Bank)	12 Mar 64	505UNTS3	107362
Nigeria	IBRD (World Bank)	12 Mar 64	516UNTS325	107480
Spain	USA (United States)	18 Mar 64	535UNTS343	107789
Japan	IBRD (World Bank)	22 Apr 64	505UNTS21	107363
Peru	IBRD (World Bank)	22 Apr 64	519UNTS95	107503
Finland	USSR (Soviet Union)	24 Apr 64	537UNTS231	107804
Liberia	USA (United States)	08 May 64	526UNTS239	107608
Ethiopia	IBRD (World Bank)	08 May 64	505UNTS51	107364
Pakistan	IBRD (World Bank)	14 May 64	516UNTS145	107475
Ecuador	IBRD (World Bank)	26 May 64	534UNTS113	107758
Ireland	UN Special Fund	03 Jun 64	496UNTS205	107253
IBRD (World Bank)	Tunisia	05 Jun 64	539UNTS129	107827
Iran	IBRD (World Bank)	10 Jun 64	537UNTS111	107799
IAEA (Atom Energy)	USA (United States)	15 Jun 64	525UNTS3	107580
Multilateral		15 Jun 64	573UNTS85	108324
UK Great Britain	USA (United States)	19 Jun 64	530UNTS99	107675
Denmark	USA (United States)	02 Jul 64	529UNTS277	107665
Colombia	Netherlands	06 Jul 64	543UNTS289	107906
Nigeria	IBRD (World Bank)	07 Jul 64	537UNTS3	107795
Multilateral		08 Jul 64	560UNTS201	108175
Finland	IBRD (World Bank)	10 Jul 64	516UNTS125	107474
Gabon	IBRD (World Bank)	10 Jul 64	537UNTS63	107797
Spain	USA (United States)	16 Jul 64	529UNTS187	107661
Philippines	IBRD (World Bank)	22 Jul 64	516UNTS171	107476
IBRD (World Bank)	Spain	31 Jul 64	537UNTS81	107798
Switzerland	UK Great Britain	11 Aug 64	552UNTS271	108059
IBRD (World Bank)	Sierra Leone	18 Aug 64	516UNTS295	107479
Morocco	IBRD (World Bank)	26 Aug 64	537UNTS193	107802
IBRD (World Bank)	Venezuela	28 Aug 64	520UNTS97	107512
IBRD (World Bank)	Venezuela	28 Aug 64	537UNTS135	107800
Ceylon (Sri Lanka)	USA (United States)	29 Aug 64	531UNTS93	107695
Multilateral		15 Sep 64	510UNTS147	107411
IAEA (Atom Energy)	United Arab Rep	17 Sep 64	525UNTS19	107581
Philippines	IBRD (World Bank)	28 Oct 64	537UNTS165	107801
USA (United States)	Yugoslavia	09 Nov 64	533UNTS39	107731
Austria	Hungary	11 Nov 64	576UNTS163	108368
Netherlands	Norway	17 Nov 64	579UNTS243	108412
Italy	USA (United States)	23 Nov 64	532UNTS133	107716
IBRD (World Bank)	Thailand	25 Nov 64	537UNTS273	107805
Argentina	IAEA (Atom Energy)	02 Dec 64	525UNTS29	107582
Trinidad/Tobago	USA (United States)	05 Dec 64	535UNTS331	107788
IBRD (World Bank)	Yugoslavia	11 Dec 64	537UNTS321	107807
Paraguay	IBRD (World Bank)	16 Dec 64	549UNTS173	107999
Taiwan	IBRD (World Bank)	17 Dec 64	538UNTS3	107808
Japan	IBRD (World Bank)	23 Dec 64	538UNTS37	107809
Japan	IBRD (World Bank)	13 Jan 65	537UNTS293	107806
Peru	USA (United States)	28 Jan 65	587UNTS273	108513
Honduras	IBRD (World Bank)	02 Feb 65	561UNTS255	108188
Mexico	IBRD (World Bank)	04 Feb 65	549UNTS189	108000
USA (United States)	USSR (Soviet Union)	05 Feb 65	541UNTS97	107863
Chile	IBRD (World Bank)	12 Feb 65	537UNTS35	107796
Brazil	IBRD (World Bank)	26 Feb 65	553UNTS3	108065
Brazil	IBRD (World Bank)	26 Feb 65	567UNTS91	108253
Malaysia	IBRD (World Bank)	26 Feb 65	549UNTS239	108002

PARTY ONE	PARTY TWO	DATE	CITATION	NUMBER
Inspection and observation (Cont.)				
IBRD (World Bank)	Thailand	22 Mar 65	538UNTS63	107810
IBRD (World Bank)	Uruguay	30 Mar 65	567UNTS45	108251
Hungary	Yugoslavia	08 Apr 65	587UNTS169	108511
Taiwan	USA (United States)	09 Apr 65	546UNTS81	107939
Taiwan	IBRD (World Bank)	28 Apr 65	549UNTS145	107998
Iran	IBRD (World Bank)	28 Apr 65	555UNTS45	108104
Iran	IBRD (World Bank)	28 Apr 65	555UNTS21	108103
Portugal	IBRD (World Bank)	29 Apr 65	549UNTS69	107991
UK Great Britain	USA (United States)	10 May 65	545UNTS181	107934
Japan	IBRD (World Bank)	26 May 65	550UNTS95	108010
Peru	IBRD (World Bank)	03 Jun 65	551UNTS227	108045
India	IBRD (World Bank)	11 Jun 65	557UNTS59	108128
India	IBRD (World Bank)	11 Jun 65	557UNTS101	108130
Peru	IBRD (World Bank)	18 Jun 65	568UNTS191	108269
Multilateral		18 Jun 65	573UNTS3	108320
Multilateral		23 Jun 65	548UNTS241	107981
Italy	IBRD (World Bank)	28 Jun 65	567UNTS127	108254
Guinea	USA (United States)	29 Jun 65	549UNTS139	107997
UN Special Fund	Spain	30 Jun 65	544UNTS159	107918
Finland	IBRD (World Bank)	30 Jun 65	550UNTS63	108009
Multilateral		02 Jul 65	592UNTS215	108575
Pakistan	IBRD (World Bank)	09 Jul 65	554UNTS39	108096
Iran	IBRD (World Bank)	12 Jul 65	554UNTS3	108095
Austria	Bulgaria	12 Jul 65	587UNTS51	108510
Israel	USA (United States)	20 Jul 65	549UNTS55	107989
Multilateral		22 Jul 65	561UNTS333	200618
Afghanistan	IAEA (Atom Energy)	24 Sep 65	556UNTS101	108121
Morocco	IAEA (Atom Energy)	24 Sep 65	556UNTS109	108122
IAEA (Atom Energy)	Uruguay	24 Sep 65	556UNTS117	108123
Nigeria	IBRD (World Bank)	26 Sep 65	571UNTS39	108298
Nigeria	IBRD (World Bank)	26 Sep 65	570UNTS233	108296
IBRD (World Bank)	Uganda	29 Sep 65	568UNTS317	108276
IBRD (World Bank)	Spain	29 Sep 65	568UNTS49	108264
East Afri Service	IBRD (World Bank)	29 Sep 65	568UNTS327	200623
IBRD (World Bank)	Tanzania	29 Sep 65	568UNTS309	108275
Kenya	IBRD (World Bank)	29 Sep 65	568UNTS289	108274
Mexico	IBRD (World Bank)	01 Oct 65	589UNTS339	108542
Philippines	IBRD (World Bank)	02 Nov 65	567UNTS3	108249
Multilateral		15 Nov 65	0UNTS0	109432
Malaysia	IBRD (World Bank)	17 Nov 65	568UNTS23	108263
IBRD (World Bank)	Venezuela	13 Dec 65	568UNTS77	108265
Mexico	IBRD (World Bank)	15 Dec 65	568UNTS125	108267
Paraguay	IBRD (World Bank)	16 Dec 65	568UNTS165	108268
New Zealand	IBRD (World Bank)	17 Dec 65	567UNTS255	108259
New Zealand	IBRD (World Bank)	17 Dec 65	567UNTS275	108260
IBRD (World Bank)	Sudan	27 Dec 65	567UNTS27	108250
Ethiopia	IBRD (World Bank)	28 Dec 65	567UNTS229	108258
Mongolia	UN Special Fund	26 Jan 66	552UNTS201	108055
France	Romania	14 Mar 66	604UNTS33	108741
Guinea	IBRD (World Bank)	30 Mar 66	568UNTS3	108262
Paraguay	IBRD (World Bank)	04 Apr 66	570UNTS41	108287
Paraguay	USA (United States)	11 Apr 66	578UNTS99	108389
IBRD (World Bank)	Venezuela	21 Apr 66	568UNTS257	108273
Finland	IBRD (World Bank)	27 Apr 66	568UNTS107	108266
Peru	IBRD (World Bank)	13 May 66	570UNTS61	108288
IBRD (World Bank)	Tunisia	16 May 66	584UNTS155	108477
Mexico	IBRD (World Bank)	25 May 66	596UNTS3	108627
Bulgaria	UN Special Fund	26 May 66	563UNTS71	108205
Portugal	IBRD (World Bank)	14 Jun 66	581UNTS29	108431
Portugal	IBRD (World Bank)	14 Jun 66	581UNTS3	108430
Jamaica	IBRD (World Bank)	20 Jun 66	582UNTS145	108462
India	IBRD (World Bank)	07 Jul 66	595UNTS3	108610
Iraq	IBRD (World Bank)	22 Jul 66	584UNTS233	108480
Iran	IBRD (World Bank)	26 Jul 66	582UNTS107	108461
Malaysia	IBRD (World Bank)	26 Jul 66	586UNTS195	108504

PARTY ONE	PARTY TWO	DATE	CITATION	NUMBER
Inspection and observation (Cont.)				
IBRD (World Bank)	Turkey	10 Aug 66	585UNTS199	108490
IBRD (World Bank)	Singapore	11 Aug 66	585UNTS39	108482
Honduras	IBRD (World Bank)	25 Aug 66	582UNTS79	108460
Bulgaria	United Arab Rep	29 Aug 66	630UNTS325	108980
Peru	IBRD (World Bank)	07 Sep 66	585UNTS3	108481
IBRD (World Bank)	South Africa	08 Sep 66	585UNTS71	108483
Philippines	IAEA (Atom Energy)	28 Sep 66	589UNTS25	108533
Jamaica	IBRD (World Bank)	30 Sep 66	582UNTS179	108463
IBRD (World Bank)	Zambia	04 Oct 66	585UNTS181	108489
Nicaragua	IBRD (World Bank)	05 Oct 66	582UNTS231	108465
IBRD (World Bank)	Singapore	04 Nov 66	585UNTS155	108488
IAEA (Atom Energy)	USA (United States)	09 Dec 66	589UNTS55	108535
Brazil	IBRD (World Bank)	19 Dec 66	599UNTS205	108668
Brazil	IBRD (World Bank)	19 Dec 66	599UNTS177	108667
Brazil	IBRD (World Bank)	19 Dec 66	599UNTS149	108666
Brazil	IBRD (World Bank)	19 Dec 66	599UNTS107	108665
Chile	IBRD (World Bank)	23 Dec 66	595UNTS141	108618
Jamaica	IBRD (World Bank)	23 Jan 67	594UNTS311	108608
IBRD (World Bank)	Venezuela	26 Jan 67	596UNTS35	108628
Multilateral		14 Feb 67	634UNTS281	109068
Kenya	IBRD (World Bank)	17 Feb 67	599UNTS233	108669
IBRD (World Bank)	Tanzania	17 Feb 67	599UNTS287	108671
IBRD (World Bank)	Uganda	17 Feb 67	599UNTS321	108673
Pakistan	IBRD (World Bank)	15 Mar 67	599UNTS245	108670
IBRD (World Bank)	Thailand	24 Mar 67	599UNTS299	108672
Iran	IAEA (Atom Energy)	10 May 67	614UNTS93	108865
IAEA (Atom Energy)	Spain	23 Jun 67	614UNTS169	108870
Multilateral		26 Jul 67	614UNTS217	108872
IAEA (Atom Energy)	Vietnam, South	16 Oct 67	630UNTS379	200636
Multilateral		08 Dec 67	620UNTS225	108959
Juridical personality				
Multilateral		25 Jun 36	161UNTS217	200486
Multilateral		15 Jan 44	161UNTS281	200489
Multilateral		07 Dec 44	171UNTS345	200501
Multilateral		13 Feb 46	1UNTS15	100004
ILO (Labor Org)	Switzerland	11 Mar 46	15UNTS377	200103
Belgium	Denmark	08 Apr 46	4UNTS429	100059
Denmark	Luxembourg	21 May 46	4UNTS435	100060
United Nations	Switzerland	01 Jul 46	1UNTS163	200008
Multilateral		30 Oct 46	27UNTS77	100401
Syria	UK Great Britain	02 Nov 46	11UNTS153	100153
France	ICAO (Civil Aviat)	14 Mar 47	94UNTS59	101306
Greece	Lebanon	10 Sep 47	187UNTS107	102504
Multilateral		11 Oct 47	77UNTS143	100998
Italy	USA (United States)	02 Feb 48	79UNTS171	101040
Greece	United Nations	12 Feb 48	47UNTS223	100732
France	United Nations	10 Mar 48	47UNTS203	100731
Switzerland	USSR (Soviet Union)	17 Mar 48	217UNTS73	102944
Multilateral		30 Apr 48	119UNTS3	101609
Finland	United Nations	20 May 48	47UNTS319	200189
Multilateral		09 Jul 48	68UNTS17	100881
USA (United States)	Yugoslavia	19 Jul 48	89UNTS43	101208
Pakistan	United Nations	27 Aug 48	47UNTS269	100734
United Nations	Thailand	05 Oct 48	47UNTS287	100735
Greece	Lebanon	06 Oct 48	87UNTS351	101179
Czechoslovakia	United Nations	07 Oct 48	47UNTS185	100730
United Nations	San Marino	07 Oct 48	47UNTS337	200190
Peru	ICAO (Civil Aviat)	22 Oct 48	95UNTS3	101315
WHO (World Health)	Switzerland	12 Jan 49	26UNTS331	200155
Czechoslovakia	Poland	21 Jan 49	31UNTS205	100480
United Nations	UK Great Britain	18 Mar 49	47UNTS305	100736
Multilateral		08 Apr 49	140UNTS196	101889
Denmark	Poland	12 May 49	87UNTS179	101172
Multilateral		02 Sep 49	250UNTS12	103515

PARTY ONE	PARTY TWO	DATE	CITATION	NUMBER
Juridical personality (Cont.)				
Australia	New Zealand	26 Nov 49	198UNTS161	102662
Ireland	USA (United States)	21 Jan 50	206UNTS269	102792
Afghanistan	India	04 Apr 50	167UNTS105	102201
ILO (Labor Org)	United Nations	07 Jun 50	68UNTS213	200231
Multilateral		04 Nov 50	213UNTS221	102889
WHO (World Health)	United Arab Rep	25 Mar 51	223UNTS87	103058
Multilateral		18 Apr 51	261UNTS140	103729
IBRD (World Bank)	Switzerland	29 Jun 51	216UNTS347	200529
Philippines	WHO (World Health)	22 Jul 51	149UNTS197	101953
Greece	USA (United States)	03 Aug 51	224UNTS279	103080
Israel	USA (United States)	23 Aug 51	219UNTS237	102979
France	USSR (Soviet Union)	03 Sep 51	221UNTS79	103003
Ethiopia	USA (United States)	07 Sep 51	206UNTS41	102785
Multilateral		20 Sep 51	200UNTS3	102691
Korea, South	United Nations	21 Sep 51	104UNTS323	200322
Denmark	USA (United States)	01 Oct 51	421UNTS105	106056
Multilateral		06 Dec 51	425UNTS61	106119
Germany, West	Netherlands	18 Jan 52	179UNTS147	102364
Multilateral		15 Feb 52	132UNTS51	101751
Multilateral		10 May 52	439UNTS233	106332
Chile	United Nations	16 Feb 53	314UNTS49	104541
Japan	USA (United States)	02 Apr 53	206UNTS143	102788
ICAO (Civil Aviat)	United Arab Rep	27 Aug 53	215UNTS371	102925
Multilateral		19 Oct 53	207UNTS189	102807
Czechoslovakia	Greece	01 Feb 54	225UNTS77	103091
Bulgaria	Czechoslovakia	13 Apr 54	501UNTS3	107314
France	Greece	13 May 54	222UNTS299	103036
United Nations	Thailand	26 May 54	260UNTS35	103703
Italy	UK Great Britain	01 Jun 54	312UNTS353	104525
Greece	Hungary	05 Jun 54	299UNTS285	104320
France	UNESCO (Educ/Cult)	02 Jul 54	357UNTS3	105103
Germany, West	USA (United States)	29 Oct 54	273UNTS3	103943
Mexico	ILO (Labor Org)	05 Jan 55	208UNTS225	102815
WMO (Meteorology)	Switzerland	10 Mar 55	211UNTS277	200524
Germany, West	New Zealand	30 Mar 55	271UNTS207	103916
Multilateral		25 May 55	264UNTS117	103791
CERN (Nuc Resrch)	Switzerland	11 Jun 55	249UNTS405	200544
Denmark	WHO (World Health)	29 Jun 55	247UNTS168	103467
Iran	USA (United States)	15 Aug 55	284UNTS93	104132
Austria	USSR (Soviet Union)	17 Oct 55	240UNTS289	103409
Nicaragua	USA (United States)	21 Jan 56	367UNTS3	105224
Canada	USSR (Soviet Union)	29 Feb 56	252UNTS165	103566
Bulgaria	Yugoslavia	23 Mar 56	367UNTS213	105230
Multilateral		26 Mar 56	259UNTS125	103686
Netherlands	USA (United States)	27 Mar 56	285UNTS231	104154
Multilateral		26 Oct 56	276UNTS3	103988
UK Great Britain	USA (United States)	01 Nov 56	264UNTS3	103785
UK Great Britain	USA (United States)	27 Nov 56	282UNTS43	104092
Korea, South	USA (United States)	28 Nov 56	302UNTS281	104367
Mexico	ICAO (Civil Aviat)	20 Dec 56	497UNTS3	107259
Germany, East	Poland	01 Feb 57	319UNTS115	104632
Japan	Norway	28 Feb 57	280UNTS87	104054
Multilateral		25 Mar 57	294UNTS2	104300
Czechoslovakia	USSR (Soviet Union)	31 Aug 57	308UNTS3	104456
Germany, East	USSR (Soviet Union)	27 Sep 57	292UNTS75	104268
Germany, East	Hungary	30 Oct 57	408UNTS4	105867
UK Great Britain	USA (United States)	01 Nov 57	299UNTS167	104312
Japan	USSR (Soviet Union)	06 Dec 57	325UNTS35	104694
Austria	IAEA (Atom Energy)	11 Dec 57	339UNTS110	104849
Bulgaria	USSR (Soviet Union)	12 Dec 57	317UNTS217	104606
Korea, North	USSR (Soviet Union)	16 Dec 57	301UNTS301	104349
Poland	USSR (Soviet Union)	28 Dec 57	320UNTS3	104638
Multilateral		03 Feb 58	381UNTS165	105471
Albania	USSR (Soviet Union)	15 Feb 58	313UNTS261	104536
Romania	USSR (Soviet Union)	03 Apr 58	313UNTS167	104535

PARTY ONE	PARTY TWO	DATE	CITATION	NUMBER
Juridical personality (Cont.)				
Multilateral		29 Apr 58	516UNTS205	107477
Albania	USSR (Soviet Union)	30 Jun 58	328UNTS3	104729
Germany, East	Romania	15 Jul 58	395UNTS3	105681
Hungary	USSR (Soviet Union)	15 Jul 58	322UNTS3	104656
Mongolia	USSR (Soviet Union)	25 Aug 58	322UNTS105	104657
Hungary	Romania	07 Oct 58	416UNTS199	106004
Czechoslovakia	Romania	25 Oct 58	417UNTS37	106006
Bulgaria	Romania	03 Dec 58	417UNTS133	106007
Muscat and Oman	USA (United States)	20 Dec 58	380UNTS181	105457
Albania	Czechoslovakia	16 Jan 59	363UNTS195	105208
Japan	Yugoslavia	28 Feb 59	341UNTS179	104883
Hungary	Poland	06 Mar 59	432UNTS3	106216
Greece	Yugoslavia	18 Jun 59	368UNTS81	105236
Multilateral		01 Jul 59	374UNTS147	105334
FAO (Food Agri)	UN Special Fund	28 Sep 59	341UNTS353	200562
ILO (Labor Org)	UN Special Fund	12 Oct 59	343UNTS325	200563
UN Special Fund	WMO (Meteorology)	17 Nov 59	345UNTS311	200564
Multilateral		18 Nov 59	390UNTS227	105610
Czechoslovakia	Germany, East	25 Nov 59	374UNTS101	105331
Multilateral		14 Dec 59	368UNTS253	105245
Multilateral		14 Dec 59	368UNTS237	105244
Czechoslovakia	Japan	15 Dec 59	383UNTS277	105505
Albania	Hungary	12 Jan 60	520UNTS3	107511
Multilateral		26 Jan 60	439UNTS249	106333
Poland	Yugoslavia	06 Feb 60	521UNTS37	107517
Multilateral		06 Feb 60	383UNTS3	105494
Multilateral		26 Feb 60	418UNTS171	106022
ICAO (Civil Aviat)	UN Special Fund	21 Apr 60	360UNTS367	200569
Cuba	Japan	22 Apr 60	442UNTS261	106354
Hungary	Yugoslavia	07 May 60	519UNTS237	107510
UN Special Fund	WHO (World Health)	25 May 60	359UNTS375	200568
Korea, North	USSR (Soviet Union)	22 Jun 60	399UNTS3	105732
UK Great Britain	USA (United States)	24 Jun 60	377UNTS63	105396
Multilateral		28 Jul 60	485UNTS3	107042
Multilateral		28 Jul 60	394UNTS37	105667
Multilateral		13 Dec 60	523UNTS117	107557
Multilateral		13 Dec 60	455UNTS204	106544
Japan	Pakistan	18 Dec 60	423UNTS197	106093
Belgium	USA (United States)	21 Feb 61	480UNTS149	106967
USA (United States)	Vietnam, South	03 Apr 61	424UNTS137	106106
Czechoslovakia	Poland	04 Jul 61	436UNTS189	106295
Czechoslovakia	Hungary	02 Nov 61	438UNTS3	106313
Bulgaria	Poland	04 Dec 61	484UNTS3	107019
Tanganyika	UK Great Britain	09 Dec 61	437UNTS47	106299
Paraguay	USA (United States)	16 Jan 62	433UNTS169	106240
Poland	Romania	25 Jan 62	468UNTS3	106770
Luxembourg	USA (United States)	23 Feb 62	474UNTS3	106868
USSR (Soviet Union)	Yugoslavia	24 Feb 62	471UNTS195	106833
Multilateral		26 Mar 62	539UNTS67	107825
Multilateral		29 Mar 62	507UNTS177	107401
Netherlands	USA (United States)	24 Apr 62	436UNTS93	106289
Multilateral		14 Jun 62	528UNTS33	107634
Multilateral		28 Sep 62	469UNTS169	106791
Finland	Sweden	05 Nov 62	455UNTS289	106548
Japan	UK Great Britain	14 Nov 62	478UNTS29	106934
Poland	COMECON (Econ Aid)	22 Feb 63	506UNTS303	107391
Hungary	COMECON (Econ Aid)	28 Feb 63	506UNTS281	107390
Austria	Czechoslovakia	08 Mar 63	495UNTS219	107245
Greece	Hungary	27 Apr 63	550UNTS197	108016
Austria	Bulgaria	02 May 63	535UNTS143	107778
United Nations	UK Great Britain	27 Jun 63	469UNTS145	106789
Czechoslovakia	Romania	16 Dec 63	527UNTS285	107630
Czechoslovakia	Hungary	20 Dec 63	538UNTS127	107812
Czechoslovakia	Yugoslavia	20 Jan 64	538UNTS197	107816
Canada	USA (United States)	22 Jan 64	530UNTS89	107674

PARTY ONE	PARTY TWO	DATE	CITATION	NUMBER
Juridical personality (Cont.)				
Italy	ILO (Labor Org)	24 Oct 64	541UNTS217	107871
Belgium	Congo (Zaire)	06 Feb 65	540UNTS275	107853
Austria	Petrol Export Org	24 Jun 65	589UNTS135	108540
ILO (Labor Org)	LAFTA (Free Trade)	02 Jul 65	563UNTS327	200619
Multilateral		15 Nov 65	0UNTS0	109432
Multilateral		04 Dec 65	571UNTS123	108303
Austria	United Nations	24 Feb 66	557UNTS129	108131
Australia	United Nations	25 Feb 66	557UNTS85	108129
Belgium	Israel	26 Apr 66	566UNTS187	108243
Netherlands	Tunisia	08 Jul 66	591UNTS235	108560
Colombia	Netherlands	19 Jul 66	591UNTS201	108558
Mauritania	USSR (Soviet Union)	17 Oct 66	633UNTS231	109040
Asian Devel Bank	Philippines	22 Dec 66	615UNTS375	108887
Czechoslovakia	Hungary	27 Feb 68	640UNTS49	109154
Expropriation				
Panama	USA (United States)	18 May 42	124UNTS221	200422
Mexico	USA (United States)	29 Sep 43	106UNTS265	200345
Belgium	Taiwan	20 Oct 43	14UNTS376	200095
Australia	New Zealand	21 Jan 44	18UNTS357	200113
Brazil	Paraguay	11 Aug 44	67UNTS303	200227
Mexico	UK Great Britain	07 Feb 46	6UNTS55	100068
Poland	USA (United States)	24 Apr 46	4UNTS155	100042
Taiwan	Denmark	20 May 46	12UNTS59	100180
Czechoslovakia	USA (United States)	14 Nov 46	7UNTS119	100094
Belgium	Czechoslovakia	19 Mar 47	23UNTS35	100341
Czechoslovakia	Yugoslavia	04 Sep 47	112UNTS91	101540
Poland	UK Great Britain	24 Jan 48	87UNTS3	101163
USA (United States)	Yugoslavia	19 Jul 48	89UNTS43	101208
Belgium	France	18 Feb 49	31UNTS173	100478
Denmark	Poland	12 May 49	87UNTS179	101172
Afghanistan	India	04 Apr 50	167UNTS105	102201
Germany, East	Poland	23 Jun 50	304UNTS91	104393
UK Great Britain	Yemen	20 Jan 51	101UNTS39	101400
Canada	France	26 Jan 51	233UNTS65	103251
France	UK Great Britain	11 Apr 51	106UNTS3	101456
Greece	USA (United States)	03 Aug 51	224UNTS279	103080
France	Italy	23 Aug 51	291UNTS143	104249
Israel	USA (United States)	23 Aug 51	219UNTS237	102979
Italy	USA (United States)	28 Dec 51	157UNTS63	102047
Multilateral		30 Apr 53	175UNTS89	102297
France	Sweden	16 Feb 54	228UNTS137	103147
Italy	UK Great Britain	01 Jun 54	403UNTS275	105798
Greece	Hungary	05 Jun 54	299UNTS285	104320
Hungary	UK Great Britain	19 Aug 54	199UNTS149	102681
Germany, West	USA (United States)	29 Oct 54	273UNTS3	103943
Poland	UK Great Britain	11 Nov 54	204UNTS137	102755
Iran	USA (United States)	15 Aug 55	284UNTS93	104132
Bulgaria	UK Great Britain	22 Sep 55	222UNTS349	103039
Netherlands	USA (United States)	27 Mar 56	285UNTS231	104154
Brazil	France	04 May 56	323UNTS339	104675
Netherlands	Yugoslavia	22 Jul 58	386UNTS263	105546
Greece	Yugoslavia	18 Jun 59	368UNTS3	105231
Germany, West	Pakistan	25 Nov 59	457UNTS22	106575
France	USA (United States)	25 Nov 59	401UNTS75	105764
El Salvador	USA (United States)	29 Jan 60	372UNTS3	105283
Romania	USA (United States)	30 Mar 60	371UNTS163	105278
Cuba	Japan	22 Apr 60	442UNTS261	106354
Guatemala	USA (United States)	09 Aug 60	461UNTS15	106648
Romania	UK Great Britain	10 Nov 60	385UNTS113	105533
Multilateral		13 Dec 60	523UNTS117	107557
Japan	Pakistan	18 Dec 60	423UNTS197	106093
Belgium	USA (United States)	21 Feb 61	480UNTS149	106967
Indonesia	Japan	01 Jul 61	517UNTS107	107484
Bulgaria	Netherlands	07 Jul 61	489UNTS21	107133

PARTY ONE	PARTY TWO	DATE	CITATION	NUMBER
Expropriation (Cont.)				
Japan	UK Great Britain	14 Nov 62	478UNTS29	106934
Austria	Bulgaria	02 May 63	535UNTS143	107778
Netherlands	Tunisia	23 May 63	523UNTS237	107558
Bulgaria	USA (United States)	02 Jul 63	479UNTS245	106957
Austria	Romania	03 Jul 63	588UNTS3	108516
El Salvador	Japan	19 Jul 63	518UNTS135	107494
Cameroon	UK Great Britain	29 Jul 63	478UNTS148	106935
Netherlands	Poland	20 Dec 63	514UNTS169	107446
Argentina	Yugoslavia	21 Mar 64	635UNTS153	109078
Norway	Romania	21 May 64	563UNTS45	108203
Czechoslovakia	Netherlands	11 Jun 64	556UNTS89	108120
Austria	Hungary	31 Oct 64	605UNTS3	108758
USA (United States)	Yugoslavia	05 Nov 64	550UNTS31	108007
Malta	Switzerland	20 Jan 65	548UNTS193	107978
Ivory Coast	Netherlands	26 Apr 65	634UNTS81	109053
Free passage and transit				
Ethiopia	UK Great Britain	19 Dec 44	93UNTS303	200272
Multilateral		01 Jan 46	99UNTS131	101375
Denmark	USSR (Soviet Union)	17 Aug 46	8UNTS201	100124
Multilateral		10 Feb 47	41UNTS21	100643
Multilateral		10 Feb 47	41UNTS135	100644
Multilateral		10 Feb 47	48UNTS203	100746
France	ICAO (Civil Aviat)	14 Mar 47	94UNTS59	101306
Italy	USA (United States)	02 Feb 48	79UNTS171	101040
Belgium	Switzerland	01 Sep 48	23UNTS139	100344
Belgium	France	28 Oct 48	25UNTS151	100360
Czechoslovakia	Poland	12 Nov 48	84UNTS347	101141
Italy	USSR (Soviet Union)	11 Dec 48	217UNTS181	102948
Belgium	Sweden	16 Dec 48	26UNTS3	100372
Belgium	Italy	01 Jan 49	26UNTS151	100385
Belgium	Denmark	31 May 49	32UNTS337	100506
Czechoslovakia	Poland	02 Jul 49	260UNTS179	103709
Czechoslovakia	Poland	02 Jul 49	260UNTS149	103708
Ireland	USA (United States)	21 Jan 50	206UNTS269	102792
Afghanistan	India	04 Apr 50	167UNTS105	102201
Multilateral		06 Apr 50	119UNTS99	101610
Greece	USA (United States)	03 Aug 51	224UNTS279	103080
Israel	USA (United States)	23 Aug 51	219UNTS237	102979
Denmark	USA (United States)	01 Oct 51	421UNTS105	106056
Multilateral		11 Jul 52	169UNTS3	102220
Ceylon (Sri Lanka)	WHO (World Health)	21 Nov 52	161UNTS315	200490
Japan	USA (United States)	02 Apr 53	206UNTS143	102788
Germany, West	USA (United States)	29 Oct 54	273UNTS3	103943
Multilateral		12 Mar 55	211UNTS3	102844
Costa Rica	Guatemala	20 Dec 55	280UNTS121	104056
Nicaragua	USA (United States)	21 Jan 56	367UNTS3	105224
Netherlands	USA (United States)	27 Mar 56	285UNTS231	104154
Guatemala	Honduras	22 Aug 56	263UNTS49	103767
UK Great Britain	USA (United States)	01 Nov 56	264UNTS3	103785
UK Great Britain	USA (United States)	27 Nov 56	282UNTS43	104092
Korea, South	USA (United States)	28 Nov 56	302UNTS281	104367
UK Great Britain	USA (United States)	01 Nov 57	299UNTS167	104312
Multilateral		29 Apr 58	450UNTS11	106465
Multilateral		10 Jun 58	454UNTS47	106539
Czechoslovakia	Germany, East	25 Nov 59	374UNTS101	105331
Guinea	UN Special Fund	02 Dec 59	345UNTS215	104969
Multilateral		13 Dec 60	455UNTS3	106543
Belgium	USA (United States)	21 Feb 61	480UNTS149	106967
Luxembourg	USA (United States)	23 Feb 62	474UNTS3	106868
Finland	USSR (Soviet Union)	27 Sep 62	479UNTS99	106949
Czechoslovakia	Poland	16 Nov 62	526UNTS3	107597
Czechoslovakia	Romania	16 Dec 63	527UNTS285	107630
Czechoslovakia	Hungary	20 Dec 63	538UNTS127	107812
Singapore	USSR (Soviet Union)	02 Apr 66	631UNTS125	108992

PARTY ONE	PARTY TWO	DATE	CITATION	NUMBER
Legal protection and assistance				
Canada	France	12 May 33	253UNTS285	200545
Multilateral		22 Jun 35	40UNTS73	100628
Belgium	UK Great Britain	22 Aug 44	90UNTS295	200267
Taiwan	Thailand	23 Jan 46	161UNTS127	102126
Czechoslovakia	Poland	12 Feb 46	25UNTS207	100364
Greece	UK Great Britain	21 Mar 46	91UNTS149	101247
Iraq	Turkey	29 Mar 46	37UNTS333	100581
UK Great Britain	USA (United States)	07 May 46	6UNTS285	100082
Denmark	USSR (Soviet Union)	17 Aug 46	8UNTS201	100124
Multilateral		10 Feb 47	41UNTS21	100643
Argentina	Taiwan	10 Feb 47	486UNTS143	107077
Multilateral		10 Feb 47	41UNTS135	100644
France	Poland	11 Feb 47	12UNTS287	100189
Australia	Norway	24 Mar 47	18UNTS185	100288
Hungary	USSR (Soviet Union)	15 Jul 47	216UNTS247	102940
Australia	France	28 Jul 47	97UNTS271	101353
Czechoslovakia	USSR (Soviet Union)	11 Dec 47	217UNTS35	102943
Italy	USA (United States)	02 Feb 48	79UNTS171	101040
Switzerland	USSR (Soviet Union)	17 Mar 48	217UNTS73	102944
Bulgaria	USSR (Soviet Union)	01 Apr 48	217UNTS97	102946
France	Netherlands	02 Jun 48	204UNTS275	102762
Greece	Lebanon	06 Oct 48	87UNTS351	101179
Australia	Denmark	08 Oct 48	22UNTS43	100330
Australia	Belgium	09 Dec 48	25UNTS159	100361
Italy	USSR (Soviet Union)	11 Dec 48	217UNTS181	102948
UK Great Britain	Yugoslavia	23 Dec 48	81UNTS103	101067
Belgium	France	08 Jan 49	36UNTS151	100569
Poland	UK Great Britain	14 Jan 49	83UNTS51	101101
Czechoslovakia	Poland	21 Jan 49	31UNTS205	100480
India	Pakistan	23 Apr 49	54UNTS51	100795
Multilateral		12 Aug 49	75UNTS85	100971
Multilateral		12 Aug 49	75UNTS31	100970
Ireland	USA (United States)	21 Jan 50	206UNTS269	102792
France	UK Great Britain	28 Jan 50	97UNTS155	101349
Afghanistan	India	04 Apr 50	167UNTS105	102201
India	Pakistan	08 Apr 50	131UNTS3	101733
UK Great Britain	USA (United States)	21 Jul 50	97UNTS193	101351
Multilateral		04 Nov 50	213UNTS221	102889
Multilateral		19 Jun 51	199UNTS67	102678
Multilateral		02 Jul 51	189UNTS137	102545
Greece	USA (United States)	03 Aug 51	224UNTS279	103080
Mexico	USA (United States)	11 Aug 51	162UNTS103	102133
Israel	USA (United States)	23 Aug 51	219UNTS237	102979
France	Italy	23 Aug 51	291UNTS143	104249
France	USSR (Soviet Union)	03 Sep 51	221UNTS79	103003
Ethiopia	USA (United States)	07 Sep 51	206UNTS41	102785
Multilateral		08 Sep 51	136UNTS45	101832
Denmark	USA (United States)	01 Oct 51	421UNTS105	106056
India	Turkey	14 Dec 51	137UNTS15	101845
Denmark	Norway	14 Jan 52	120UNTS119	101618
UK Great Britain	USA (United States)	15 Jan 52	127UNTS3	101697
Italy	Jordan	24 Apr 52	281UNTS167	104078
India	Muscat and Oman	15 Mar 53	190UNTS69	102559
Japan	USA (United States)	02 Apr 53	206UNTS143	102788
Libya	UK Great Britain	29 Jul 53	186UNTS201	102492
Czechoslovakia	Greece	01 Feb 54	225UNTS77	103091
France	Sweden	16 Feb 54	228UNTS137	103147
Multilateral		01 Mar 54	286UNTS265	104173
Bulgaria	Czechoslovakia	13 Apr 54	501UNTS3	107314
Greece	Hungary	05 Jun 54	299UNTS285	104320
Multilateral		28 Sep 54	360UNTS117	105158
Multilateral		23 Oct 54	332UNTS157	104761
Germany, West	USA (United States)	29 Oct 54	273UNTS3	103943
Ethiopia	UK Great Britain	29 Nov 54	207UNTS283	102811

PARTY ONE	PARTY TWO	DATE	CITATION	NUMBER
Legal protection and assistance (Cont.)				
Taiwan	El Salvador	09 Dec 54	214UNTS217	102900
Belgium	Brazil	10 Jan 55	272UNTS181	103937
Iran	USA (United States)	15 Aug 55	284UNTS93	104132
Austria	USSR (Soviet Union)	17 Oct 55	240UNTS289	103409
Burma	China People's Rep	08 Nov 55	306UNTS11	104430
Nicaragua	USA (United States)	21 Jan 56	367UNTS3	105224
Canada	USSR (Soviet Union)	29 Feb 56	252UNTS165	103566
France	Sweden	07 Mar 56	369UNTS171	105257
Bulgaria	Yugoslavia	23 Mar 56	367UNTS213	105230
Belgium	Israel	26 Mar 56	260UNTS3	103702
Netherlands	USA (United States)	27 Mar 56	285UNTS231	104154
UK Great Britain	USA (United States)	25 Jun 56	249UNTS59	103501
Israel	Luxembourg	26 Jul 56	550UNTS239	108020
Korea, South	USA (United States)	28 Nov 56	302UNTS281	104367
Bulgaria	Czechoslovakia	25 Jan 57	501UNTS149	107316
Germany, East	Poland	01 Feb 57	319UNTS115	104632
Japan	Norway	28 Feb 57	280UNTS87	104054
Dominican Republic	USA (United States)	09 Mar 57	279UNTS249	104044
Multilateral		26 Jun 57	328UNTS247	104738
Czechoslovakia	USSR (Soviet Union)	31 Aug 57	308UNTS3	104456
Germany, East	Hungary	30 Oct 57	408UNTS4	105867
Germany, East	USSR (Soviet Union)	28 Nov 57	305UNTS113	104419
Japan	USSR (Soviet Union)	06 Dec 57	325UNTS35	104694
Bulgaria	USSR (Soviet Union)	12 Dec 57	317UNTS217	104606
Korea, North	USSR (Soviet Union)	16 Dec 57	301UNTS301	104349
Poland	USSR (Soviet Union)	28 Dec 57	320UNTS3	104638
Belgium	Germany, West	17 Jan 58	328UNTS173	104735
Czechoslovakia	Poland	31 Jan 58	431UNTS99	106214
France	Italy	27 Mar 58	305UNTS409	104428
Romania	USSR (Soviet Union)	03 Apr 58	313UNTS167	104535
Hungary	USSR (Soviet Union)	24 Apr 58	408UNTS118	105868
Bulgaria	Hungary	27 Jun 58	438UNTS235	106318
Albania	USSR (Soviet Union)	30 Jun 58	328UNTS3	104729
Hungary	USSR (Soviet Union)	15 Jul 58	322UNTS3	104656
Germany, East	Romania	15 Jul 58	395UNTS3	105681
Mongolia	USSR (Soviet Union)	25 Aug 58	322UNTS105	104657
Hungary	Romania	07 Oct 58	416UNTS199	106004
Czechoslovakia	Romania	25 Oct 58	417UNTS37	106006
Bulgaria	Romania	03 Dec 58	417UNTS133	106007
Muscat and Oman	USA (United States)	20 Dec 58	380UNTS181	105457
Albania	Czechoslovakia	16 Jan 59	363UNTS195	105208
Belgium	Morocco	27 Feb 59	390UNTS275	105611
Japan	Yugoslavia	28 Feb 59	341UNTS179	104883
Hungary	Poland	06 Mar 59	432UNTS3	106216
Brazil	Netherlands	16 Mar 59	499UNTS219	107300
Greece	Yugoslavia	18 Jun 59	368UNTS81	105236
Germany, West	Pakistan	25 Nov 59	457UNTS22	106575
Czechoslovakia	Japan	15 Dec 59	383UNTS277	105505
Albania	Hungary	12 Jan 60	520UNTS3	107511
Multilateral		06 Feb 60	383UNTS3	105494
Poland	Yugoslavia	06 Feb 60	521UNTS37	107517
Argentina	Philippines	12 Feb 60	535UNTS293	107785
Cuba	Japan	22 Apr 60	442UNTS261	106354
Hungary	Yugoslavia	07 May 60	519UNTS237	107510
Germany, West	Ireland	11 May 60	553UNTS69	108070
UK Great Britain	USA (United States)	24 Jun 60	377UNTS63	105396
Multilateral		13 Dec 60	455UNTS3	106543
Japan	Pakistan	18 Dec 60	423UNTS197	106093
Germany, West	USA (United States)	03 Jan 61	416UNTS93	105997
Belgium	USA (United States)	21 Feb 61	480UNTS149	106967
Multilateral		16 Mar 61	638UNTS235	109139
USA (United States)	Vietnam, South	03 Apr 61	424UNTS137	106106
Norway	UK Great Britain	12 Jun 61	424UNTS173	106107
Indonesia	Japan	01 Jul 61	517UNTS107	107484
Czechoslovakia	Poland	04 Jul 61	436UNTS189	106295

PARTY ONE	PARTY TWO	DATE	CITATION	NUMBER
Legal protection and assistance (Cont.)				
Mexico	United Nations	18 Aug 61	404UNTS297	105817
Fed of Malaya	USA (United States)	04 Sep 61	421UNTS215	106060
Multilateral		05 Oct 61	0UNTS0	109431
Philippines	USA (United States)	31 Oct 61	424UNTS129	106105
Czechoslovakia	Hungary	02 Nov 61	438UNTS3	106313
Ghana	USSR (Soviet Union)	04 Nov 61	437UNTS213	106308
Austria	Czechoslovakia	10 Nov 61	455UNTS337	106550
Brazil	USA (United States)	11 Nov 61	433UNTS199	106243
El Salvador	USA (United States)	20 Nov 61	433UNTS221	106245
Thailand	USA (United States)	28 Nov 61	434UNTS77	106256
Bulgaria	Poland	04 Dec 61	484UNTS3	107019
Sierra Leone	USA (United States)	29 Dec 61	434UNTS43	106254
Poland	Romania	25 Jan 62	468UNTS3	106770
Luxembourg	USA (United States)	23 Feb 62	474UNTS3	106868
USSR (Soviet Union)	Yugoslavia	24 Feb 62	471UNTS195	106833
Dominican Republic	USA (United States)	02 May 62	442UNTS107	106342
Ethiopia	USA (United States)	23 May 62	456UNTS293	106563
Multilateral		27 Jun 62	616UNTS79	108893
Germany, West	Netherlands	30 Aug 62	500UNTS3	107303
Japan	UK Great Britain	14 Nov 62	478UNTS29	106934
Multilateral		08 Dec 62	510UNTS235	107418
Austria	Yugoslavia	11 Dec 62	546UNTS3	107938
Netherlands	Spain	17 Dec 62	499UNTS227	107301
Austria	Czechoslovakia	08 Mar 63	495UNTS219	107245
Netherlands	Tunisia	23 May 63	523UNTS237	107558
Hungary	Mongolia	10 Jul 63	519UNTS173	107508
El Salvador	Japan	19 Jul 63	518UNTS135	107494
Czechoslovakia	Hungary	22 Oct 63	514UNTS95	107444
Multilateral		23 Oct 63	506UNTS197	107388
Czechoslovakia	Romania	16 Dec 63	527UNTS285	107630
Czechoslovakia	Hungary	20 Dec 63	538UNTS127	107812
Czechoslovakia	Yugoslavia	20 Jan 64	538UNTS197	107816
Germany, West	Greece	16 Apr 64	609UNTS27	108826
Taiwan	USA (United States)	23 Apr 64	524UNTS141	107570
Netherlands	NATO (North Atlan)	25 May 64	544UNTS237	107920
Multilateral		25 May 64	620UNTS149	108953
Multilateral		10 Jul 64	613UNTS3	108851
Ethiopia	Netherlands	28 Oct 64	541UNTS235	107872
Multilateral		01 Dec 64	550UNTS133	108012
Austria	Hungary	09 Apr 65	638UNTS135	109133
Australia	Netherlands	01 Jun 65	560UNTS85	108170
Austria	Germany, West	17 Feb 66	614UNTS263	108875
Ireland	UK Great Britain	28 Feb 66	565UNTS33	108234
Argentina	Taiwan	19 Mar 66	635UNTS281	109089
Multilateral		17 May 66	571UNTS89	108302
Guyana	UK Great Britain	26 May 66	595UNTS255	108621
Israel	UK Great Britain	05 Jul 66	630UNTS189	108971
Botswana	UK Great Britain	30 Sep 66	597UNTS211	108646
Trinidad/Tobago	UK Great Britain	23 Jan 67	605UNTS277	108767
Haiti	Israel	28 Mar 67	630UNTS293	108975
Denmark	Tanzania	05 Apr 67	604UNTS19	108740
United Nations	Zambia	06 Jul 67	600UNTS81	108678
India	United Nations	04 Nov 67	609UNTS3	108824
United Nations	Senegal	08 Nov 67	613UNTS255	108854
Austria	Switzerland	15 Nov 67	0UNTS0	109434
Iran	United Nations	15 Feb 68	631UNTS103	108990
United Nations	Tunisia	18 Mar 68	633UNTS3	109030
Niger	United Nations	07 May 68	639UNTS71	109145
Domestic legislation				
Multilateral		28 Nov 19	38UNTS81	100588
Multilateral		28 Nov 19	38UNTS93	100589
Multilateral		28 Nov 19	38UNTS67	100587
Multilateral		10 Jul 20	38UNTS129	100592
Multilateral		11 Nov 21	38UNTS217	100599

PARTY ONE	PARTY TWO	DATE	CITATION	NUMBER
Domestic legislation (Cont.)				
Multilateral		12 Nov 21	38UNTS165	100595
Multilateral		17 Nov 21	38UNTS187	100597
Multilateral		19 Nov 21	38UNTS175	100596
Multilateral		10 Jun 25	38UNTS243	100601
Multilateral		23 Jun 26	38UNTS315	100606
Multilateral		24 Jun 26	38UNTS295	100605
Multilateral		15 Jun 27	38UNTS327	100607
Multilateral		15 Jun 27	38UNTS343	100608
Multilateral		16 Jun 28	39UNTS3	100609
Multilateral		26 Jun 28	39UNTS15	100610
Multilateral		27 Apr 32	39UNTS103	100614
Multilateral		30 Apr 32	39UNTS133	100615
Multilateral		29 Jun 33	39UNTS285	100622
Multilateral		29 Jun 33	39UNTS211	100619
Multilateral		29 Jun 33	39UNTS235	100620
Multilateral		29 Jun 33	39UNTS259	100621
Multilateral		29 Jun 33	39UNTS189	100618
Multilateral		29 Jun 33	39UNTS151	100616
Multilateral		29 Jun 33	39UNTS165	100617
Multilateral		21 Jun 34	40UNTS33	100625
Multilateral		21 Jun 34	40UNTS19	100624
Multilateral		23 Jun 34	40UNTS45	100626
Multilateral		21 Jun 35	40UNTS63	100627
Multilateral		22 Jun 35	40UNTS73	100628
Multilateral		24 Oct 36	40UNTS205	100635
Multilateral		22 Jun 37	40UNTS217	100636
Multilateral		27 Jun 39	40UNTS281	100639
Panama	USA (United States)	23 Mar 40	124UNTS195	200420
Panama	USA (United States)	06 Sep 40	124UNTS209	200421
Panama	USA (United States)	28 Mar 41	103UNTS163	200312
Canada	USA (United States)	27 Nov 41	103UNTS193	200314
Nicaragua	USA (United States)	22 May 42	105UNTS141	200328
UK Great Britain	USA (United States)	10 May 43	147UNTS109	200473
Dominican Republic	USA (United States)	19 Oct 43	21UNTS295	200130
Brazil	USA (United States)	25 Nov 43	102UNTS227	200305
UK Great Britain	USA (United States)	10 Mar 44	5UNTS205	200030
Multilateral		07 Dec 44	171UNTS345	200501
Iceland	USA (United States)	27 Jan 45	122UNTS293	200411
Ireland	USA (United States)	03 Feb 45	122UNTS305	200412
Guatemala	USA (United States)	25 Oct 45	139UNTS45	101875
Multilateral		07 Nov 45	2UNTS17	100018
Multilateral		27 Dec 45	2UNTS39	100020
UK Great Britain	USA (United States)	27 Mar 46	4UNTS101	100040
Multilateral		27 Jun 46	164UNTS37	102157
Multilateral		27 Jun 46	264UNTS163	103792
Multilateral		29 Jun 46	94UNTS11	101303
Multilateral		29 Jun 46	214UNTS233	102901
Ceylon (Sri Lanka)	India	12 Aug 46	196UNTS209	102626
India	USA (United States)	14 Nov 46	22UNTS55	100331
Denmark	Sweden	18 Nov 46	7UNTS251	100104
Philippines	USA (United States)	14 Feb 47	16UNTS3	100245
Philippines	USA (United States)	14 Mar 47	16UNTS31	100247
France	USA (United States)	27 Mar 47	16UNTS65	100249
New Zealand	USA (United States)	24 Apr 47	16UNTS79	100250
Bulgaria	Czechoslovakia	20 Jun 47	46UNTS15	100698
Multilateral		11 Jul 47	54UNTS3	100792
Multilateral		11 Jul 47	218UNTS345	102961
Canada	USA (United States)	20 Aug 47	27UNTS3	100392
Czechoslovakia	Romania	05 Sep 47	46UNTS37	100699
Multilateral		12 Nov 47	46UNTS201	100710
Multilateral		12 Nov 47	53UNTS39	100771
India	Pakistan	10 Dec 47	51UNTS173	100764
Belgium	France	17 Jan 48	36UNTS233	100570
Italy	USA (United States)	06 Feb 48	73UNTS113	100950
Paraguay	USA (United States)	12 Mar 48	162UNTS30	102131

Domestic legislation (Cont.)

PARTY ONE	PARTY TWO	DATE	CITATION	NUMBER
New Zealand	USA (United States)	16 Mar 48	127UNTS133	101703
Belgium	Luxembourg	27 Mar 48	178UNTS265	102343
Czechoslovakia	Poland	05 Apr 48	31UNTS355	100482
Poland	USSR (Soviet Union)	08 Apr 48	26UNTS191	100388
Belgium	Italy	30 Apr 48	36UNTS305	100571
France	Poland	09 Jun 48	32UNTS251	100503
France	UK Great Britain	11 Jun 48	66UNTS151	100852
Italy	UK Great Britain	25 Jun 48	94UNTS239	101313
Multilateral		26 Jun 48	331UNTS217	104757
Multilateral		09 Jul 48	81UNTS147	101070
Philippines	USA (United States)	23 Aug 48	82UNTS11	101080
Belgium	Netherlands	25 Sep 48	123UNTS81	101655
Belgium	Luxembourg	09 Oct 48	123UNTS29	101652
Czechoslovakia	France	12 Oct 48	45UNTS81	100693
Philippines	USA (United States)	21 Oct 48	77UNTS197	101000
Belgium	USA (United States)	28 Oct 48	173UNTS67	102262
Argentina	Sweden	20 Nov 48	197UNTS47	102633
Multilateral		09 Dec 48	78UNTS277	101021
Czechoslovakia	Poland	22 Jan 49	85UNTS3	101142
Italy	Lebanon	24 Jan 49	231UNTS241	103223
Mexico	USA (United States)	14 Feb 49	160UNTS75	102103
Luxembourg	Netherlands	26 Apr 49	182UNTS187	102425
Multilateral		04 May 49	98UNTS101	101358
Norway	USA (United States)	25 May 49	32UNTS345	100507
Costa Rica	USA (United States)	31 May 49	80UNTS3	101041
Norway	USA (United States)	13 Jun 49	127UNTS189	101705
Multilateral		18 Jun 49	160UNTS223	102109
Multilateral		01 Jul 49	96UNTS257	101341
Multilateral		01 Jul 49	138UNTS225	101871
Argentina	Canada	06 Aug 49	231UNTS43	103202
Multilateral		12 Aug 49	75UNTS287	100973
Ireland	USA (United States)	13 Sep 49	127UNTS89	101701
Lebanon	Netherlands	20 Sep 49	108UNTS205	101474
Bulgaria	Poland	26 Sep 49	260UNTS227	103711
Bulgaria	Poland	26 Sep 49	260UNTS249	103712
Hungary	Poland	29 Oct 49	260UNTS113	103706
Hungary	Poland	29 Oct 49	260UNTS91	103705
Belgium	Luxembourg	03 Dec 49	91UNTS31	101241
Australia	USA (United States)	29 Dec 49	71UNTS45	100909
France	Netherlands	30 Dec 49	203UNTS133	102743
France	Netherlands	07 Jan 50	120UNTS25	101614
France	UK Great Britain	28 Jan 50	97UNTS155	101349
Greece	USA (United States)	20 Feb 50	196UNTS291	102630
Multilateral		21 Mar 50	96UNTS271	101342
Argentina	Greece	21 Mar 50	187UNTS213	102514
Italy	Turkey	24 Mar 50	96UNTS207	101338
Austria	Czechoslovakia	30 Mar 50	495UNTS85	107240
Italy	Portugal	05 Apr 50	254UNTS329	103599
India	Pakistan	08 Apr 50	131UNTS3	101733
Israel	USA (United States)	04 May 50	132UNTS189	101760
Germany, East	Poland	23 Jun 50	304UNTS91	104393
Denmark	Italy	01 Jul 50	133UNTS181	101788
Argentina	USA (United States)	20 Jul 50	89UNTS63	101209
Ceylon (Sri Lanka)	UK Great Britain	26 Jul 50	337UNTS77	104818
Multilateral		27 Jul 50	166UNTS73	102186
Czechoslovakia	USA (United States)	29 Sep 50	290UNTS3	104227
France	UK Great Britain	06 Oct 50	96UNTS63	101331
Multilateral		04 Nov 50	213UNTS221	102889
Czechoslovakia	Poland	17 Nov 50	530UNTS195	107682
Multilateral		07 Dec 50	212UNTS17	102861
Multilateral		21 Dec 50	90UNTS3	101222
Liberia	USA (United States)	10 Jan 51	132UNTS255	101765
Chile	USA (United States)	16 Jan 51	157UNTS3	102043
Denmark	Norway	18 Jan 51	82UNTS153	101090
Nicaragua	USA (United States)	31 Jan 51	160UNTS121	102105

Domestic legislation (Cont.)

PARTY ONE	PARTY TWO	DATE	CITATION	NUMBER
Panama	USA (United States)	26 Feb 51	160UNTS153	102106
Germany, West	Netherlands	29 Mar 51	149UNTS71	101952
Canada	Sweden	06 Apr 51	197UNTS393	102648
Honduras	USA (United States)	24 Apr 51	140UNTS287	101894
Switzerland	USA (United States)	24 May 51	127UNTS227	101706
India	Turkey	29 Jun 51	213UNTS183	102886
Denmark	France	30 Jun 51	151UNTS241	102000
UK Great Britain	USA (United States)	18 Jul 51	117UNTS49	101583
Austria	Sweden	01 Aug 51	198UNTS13	102653
Multilateral		09 Oct 51	220UNTS121	102997
Netherlands	Switzerland	12 Nov 51	126UNTS173	101689
Finland	USA (United States)	16 Nov 51	140UNTS273	101893
Italy	UK Great Britain	28 Nov 51	172UNTS205	102248
Italy	USA (United States)	12 Dec 51	137UNTS175	101852
Jordan	USA (United States)	12 Feb 52	168UNTS25	102211
Canada	USA (United States)	21 Feb 52	205UNTS293	102781
Cuba	USA (United States)	27 Feb 52	168UNTS3	102209
Sweden	Uruguay	20 Mar 52	311UNTS3	104497
Norway	Uruguay	20 Mar 52	310UNTS279	104496
Multilateral		09 May 52	205UNTS65	102770
Israel	USA (United States)	09 May 52	177UNTS63	102309
Multilateral		20 May 52	219UNTS55	102966
Australia	USA (United States)	27 May 52	178UNTS113	102338
Belgium	Switzerland	17 Jun 52	180UNTS23	102373
Multilateral		26 Jun 52	196UNTS183	102624
Multilateral		28 Jun 52	214UNTS321	102907
Panama	USA (United States)	30 Jun 52	181UNTS121	102404
Chile	USA (United States)	30 Jun 52	199UNTS241	102688
Multilateral		11 Jul 52	170UNTS269	102223
Czechoslovakia	Romania	31 Jul 52	362UNTS123	105185
Japan	USA (United States)	11 Aug 52	212UNTS27	102862
Multilateral		06 Sep 52	216UNTS132	102937
Monaco	USA (United States)	24 Sep 52	186UNTS43	102481
Italy	Netherlands	28 Oct 52	289UNTS144	104218
Switzerland	UK Great Britain	16 Jan 53	196UNTS119	102621
United Arab Rep	USA (United States)	12 Mar 53	204UNTS3	102747
United Arab Rep	USA (United States)	19 Mar 53	215UNTS17	102909
Japan	USA (United States)	23 Mar 53	185UNTS93	102461
Jordan	UN Relief Palestin	30 Mar 53	165UNTS317	200495
Multilateral		11 May 53	456UNTS3	106555
El Salvador	USA (United States)	14 May 53	234UNTS71	103273
Australia	USA (United States)	14 May 53	205UNTS253	102779
United Arab Rep	USA (United States)	21 May 53	204UNTS29	102748
Colombia	USA (United States)	09 Jun 53	213UNTS3	102877
United Arab Rep	USA (United States)	18 Jun 53	215UNTS45	102910
Liberia	USA (United States)	23 Jun 53	213UNTS37	102879
Brazil	USA (United States)	26 Jun 53	336UNTS241	104808
Chile	USA (United States)	27 Jun 53	229UNTS193	103167
Chile	USA (United States)	27 Jun 53	229UNTS53	103160
Pakistan	Turkey	29 Jun 53	211UNTS225	102854
Afghanistan	USA (United States)	30 Jun 53	215UNTS3	102908
Nicaragua	USA (United States)	30 Jun 53	215UNTS133	102917
UN Relief Palestin	United Arab Rep	30 Jun 53	190UNTS3	102554
Multilateral		20 Jul 53	228UNTS41	103142
Luxembourg	UK Great Britain	13 Oct 53	209UNTS87	102825
Denmark	USA (United States)	15 Oct 53	215UNTS111	102915
Multilateral		17 Oct 53	184UNTS42	102438
Libya	UK Great Britain	19 Oct 53	186UNTS285	102494
Australia	Netherlands	22 Oct 53	184UNTS193	102448
Multilateral		11 Dec 53	218UNTS255	102958
Multilateral		11 Dec 53	218UNTS211	102957
Multilateral		11 Dec 53	218UNTS153	102956
Hungary	Romania	14 Dec 53	342UNTS151	104906
Chile	USA (United States)	30 Dec 53	236UNTS41	103315
Peru	Spain	31 Mar 54	232UNTS65	103230

PARTY ONE	PARTY TWO	DATE	CITATION	NUMBER
Domestic legislation (Cont.)				
Japan	USA (United States)	16 Apr 54	238UNTS39	103354
Panama	USA (United States)	11 May 54	236UNTS107	103319
Italy	UK Great Britain	01 Jun 54	312UNTS353	104525
Italy	USA (United States)	28 Jun 54	237UNTS121	103340
Chile	USA (United States)	28 Jun 54	233UNTS3	103246
Ecuador	USA (United States)	30 Jun 54	236UNTS163	103323
Bulgaria	Romania	22 Jul 54	362UNTS101	105184
Germany, West	USA (United States)	22 Jul 54	239UNTS3	103369
Multilateral		29 Jul 54	249UNTS45	103500
Netherlands	UK Great Britain	11 Aug 54	248UNTS235	103497
Multilateral		28 Sep 54	360UNTS117	105158
India	USA (United States)	21 Oct 54	234UNTS119	103277
Germany, West	Netherlands	29 Oct 54	237UNTS3	103335
Belgium	Yugoslavia	01 Nov 54	251UNTS123	103538
USA (United States)	Vietnam, South	22 Nov 54	235UNTS11	103291
India	Iran	15 Dec 54	327UNTS245	104724
Sweden	Switzerland	17 Dec 54	369UNTS233	105260
Switzerland	United Arab Rep	05 Jan 55	216UNTS41	102931
Italy	USA (United States)	30 Mar 55	257UNTS169	103654
Japan	Thailand	06 Apr 55	230UNTS219	103187
Belgium	San Marino	22 Apr 55	253UNTS41	103574
Czechoslovakia	Hungary	28 Apr 55	477UNTS197	106923
Peru	USA (United States)	30 Apr 55	263UNTS309	103780
Multilateral		15 May 55	217UNTS223	102949
Italy	Sweden	25 May 55	291UNTS235	104259
Canada	USA (United States)	08 Jun 55	247UNTS163	103466
Syria	United Arab Rep	03 Jul 55	393UNTS67	105652
Spain	USA (United States)	16 Jul 55	270UNTS211	103899
Ceylon (Sri Lanka)	USA (United States)	18 Jul 55	281UNTS295	104086
Germany, East	Romania	05 Aug 55	342UNTS229	104910
Czechoslovakia	Germany, East	30 Aug 55	504UNTS279	107361
Multilateral		15 Sep 55	254UNTS55	103593
Germany, West	Sweden	22 Mar 56	262UNTS423	103763
Bulgaria	Greece	19 Apr 56	594UNTS131	108600
Netherlands	Yugoslavia	01 Jun 56	276UNTS319	103994
Sweden	UK Great Britain	09 Jun 56	309UNTS301	104479
Honduras	USA (United States)	25 Jun 56	279UNTS113	104036
Multilateral		09 Jul 56	314UNTS3	104539
Denmark	UK Great Britain	09 Jul 56	264UNTS45	103787
France	UK Great Britain	10 Jul 56	326UNTS23	104708
Belgium	France	18 Jul 56	248UNTS121	103491
Canada	India	30 Aug 56	305UNTS59	104413
Ceylon (Sri Lanka)	India	10 Sep 56	315UNTS59	104560
Romania	Yugoslavia	25 Sep 56	395UNTS147	105683
Costa Rica	USA (United States)	19 Oct 56	278UNTS65	104022
Austria	USA (United States)	25 Oct 56	299UNTS123	104310
Belgium	United Arab Rep	31 Oct 56	257UNTS235	103659
Belgium	Spain	28 Nov 56	308UNTS239	104464
Italy	Norway	16 Dec 56	291UNTS207	104256
Multilateral		19 Dec 56	427UNTS93	106148
Italy	UK Great Britain	29 Jan 57	326UNTS119	104710
Multilateral		25 Mar 57	294UNTS2	104300
Brazil	USA (United States)	02 Apr 57	290UNTS119	104231
Paraguay	USA (United States)	04 Apr 57	283UNTS193	104117
Israel	UK Great Britain	29 Apr 57	280UNTS227	104062
Netherlands	United Arab Rep	15 May 57	288UNTS29	104194
Albania	Yugoslavia	20 May 57	363UNTS99	105203
Belgium	UK Great Britain	20 May 57	303UNTS53	104371
Czechoslovakia	Yugoslavia	22 May 57	391UNTS57	105617
Hungary	Yugoslavia	25 May 57	477UNTS219	106924
Bulgaria	Yugoslavia	04 Jun 57	349UNTS35	105008
Czechoslovakia	Yugoslavia	11 Jun 57	504UNTS107	107355
Multilateral		26 Jun 57	325UNTS279	104704
Norway	UK Great Britain	25 Jul 57	313UNTS3	104528
France	Italy	29 Jul 57	291UNTS163	104250

PARTY ONE	PARTY TWO	DATE	CITATION	NUMBER
Domestic legislation (Cont.)				
Taiwan	USA (United States)	30 Jul 57	300UNTS61	104331
Australia	Canada	01 Oct 57	392UNTS41	105638
Hungary	Yugoslavia	07 Oct 57	439UNTS61	106325
Italy	Spain	12 Oct 57	291UNTS229	104258
Germany, East	Hungary	25 Oct 57	408UNTS156	105869
France	Italy	08 Nov 57	305UNTS393	104427
Hungary	Yugoslavia	20 Nov 57	477UNTS267	106925
Hungary	Yugoslavia	06 Dec 57	519UNTS215	107509
Italy	Monaco	06 Dec 57	363UNTS45	105198
Bulgaria	Yugoslavia	18 Dec 57	376UNTS3	105372
Canada	Pakistan	15 Jan 58	392UNTS35	105637
Poland	Yugoslavia	16 Jan 58	340UNTS137	104863
Australia	UK Great Britain	29 Jan 58	292UNTS233	104275
Germany, West	Netherlands	30 Jan 58	315UNTS117	104563
Czechoslovakia	Hungary	12 Mar 58	408UNTS178	105870
Bulgaria	Hungary	13 Mar 58	438UNTS191	106317
Bulgaria	Hungary	13 Mar 58	438UNTS173	106316
Netherlands	Switzerland	28 Mar 58	318UNTS175	104614
Belgium	Greece	01 Apr 58	388UNTS93	105574
Multilateral		15 Apr 58	539UNTS27	107822
Hungary	Poland	08 May 58	408UNTS212	105872
Multilateral		13 May 58	389UNTS277	105598
UK Great Britain	Yugoslavia	24 May 58	326UNTS69	104709
Ireland	Switzerland	18 Jun 58	553UNTS183	108086
WHO (World Health)	Sudan	21 Jun 58	307UNTS235	104453
Japan	USA (United States)	03 Nov 58	341UNTS83	104879
Fed Rhod/Nyasaland	Portugal	29 Nov 58	354UNTS137	105060
Denmark	United Arab Rep	01 Dec 58	337UNTS69	104817
United Arab Rep	USA (United States)	13 Jan 59	358UNTS3	105122
Finland	Norway	21 Jan 59	325UNTS295	104705
Czechoslovakia	Hungary	30 Jan 59	351UNTS3	105016
Canada	USA (United States)	27 Feb 59	341UNTS3	104873
Bulgaria	Hungary	03 Apr 59	438UNTS269	106319
Hungary	USSR (Soviet Union)	17 Apr 59	439UNTS41	106324
Czechoslovakia	Switzerland	04 Jun 59	349UNTS121	105012
Italy	Norway	12 Jun 59	428UNTS363	106187
Multilateral		19 Jun 59	413UNTS168	105951
Bulgaria	United Arab Rep	09 Jul 59	411UNTS187	105920
Finland	UK Great Britain	28 Jul 59	355UNTS31	105073
Multilateral		08 Sep 59	383UNTS203	105502
Turkey	UK Great Britain	09 Sep 59	424UNTS267	106113
Canada	UK Great Britain	10 Dec 59	379UNTS201	105440
Multilateral		14 Dec 59	422UNTS57	106068
Multilateral		14 Dec 59	422UNTS33	106067
Germany, East	Hungary	30 Jan 60	408UNTS230	105873
Multilateral		26 Feb 60	418UNTS171	106022
Ireland	UK Great Britain	29 Mar 60	371UNTS3	105267
Germany, West	UK Great Britain	20 Apr 60	449UNTS77	106453
Germany, West	UK Great Britain	20 Apr 60	413UNTS236	105958
Poland	Yugoslavia	05 May 60	423UNTS229	106095
UN Special Fund	Thailand	04 Jun 60	360UNTS97	105157
Austria	USA (United States)	15 Jun 60	376UNTS267	105383
Multilateral		22 Jun 60	431UNTS41	106208
Korea, South	USA (United States)	17 Aug 60	400UNTS339	105757
Czechoslovakia	Poland	14 Nov 60	413UNTS4	105938
Germany, West	Netherlands	09 Mar 61	485UNTS185	107056
Multilateral		30 Mar 61	520UNTS151	107515
Bulgaria	Hungary	30 Jun 61	438UNTS287	106320
Belgium	France	07 Jul 61	406UNTS157	105846
Argentina	Japan	20 Dec 61	451UNTS91	106487
Argentina	Japan	20 Dec 61	451UNTS77	106486
Jordan	UK Great Britain	28 Feb 62	466UNTS249	106748
Multilateral		23 Mar 62	434UNTS145	106262
IAEA (Atom Energy)	USA (United States)	30 Mar 62	442UNTS49	106338
Multilateral		14 May 62	544UNTS81	107911

PARTY ONE	PARTY TWO	DATE	CITATION	NUMBER
Domestic legislation (Cont.)				
Indonesia	Netherlands	15 Aug 62	437UNTS273	106311
Italy	USA (United States)	28 Aug 62	461UNTS137	106657
Belgium	Romania	12 Oct 62	502UNTS31	107325
Austria	United Arab Rep	16 Oct 62	491UNTS63	107174
Japan	USA (United States)	24 Oct 62	462UNTS119	106673
Ethiopia	Greece	07 Nov 62	550UNTS179	108014
Ethiopia	Greece	07 Nov 62	550UNTS189	108015
Multilateral		17 Dec 62	590UNTS81	108548
Luxembourg	USA (United States)	18 Dec 62	532UNTS277	107723
Hungary	USSR (Soviet Union)	20 Dec 62	577UNTS245	108381
Iceland	USA (United States)	27 Dec 62	469UNTS91	106785
Australia	India	23 Jan 63	456UNTS185	106556
Japan	Thailand	01 Mar 63	475UNTS233	106895
Hungary	Korea, North	29 Mar 63	577UNTS219	108379
Japan	Malaysia	04 Jun 63	517UNTS245	107488
Australia	UK Great Britain	06 Jun 63	472UNTS157	106838
Multilateral		25 Jun 63	532UNTS159	107717
France	Israel	20 Aug 63	515UNTS173	107460
France	Greece	21 Aug 63	533UNTS235	107746
Czechoslovakia	Yugoslavia	05 Oct 63	504UNTS151	107356
Lebanon	UK Great Britain	24 Oct 63	535UNTS3	107772
Cuba	Czechoslovakia	03 Jun 64	527UNTS205	107626
Multilateral		08 Jul 64	560UNTS201	108175
Austria	Spain	15 Jul 64	589UNTS169	108541
France	Norway	16 Jul 64	510UNTS229	107417
Mexico	USA (United States)	07 Aug 64	530UNTS123	107677
Czechoslovakia	Mongolia	21 Oct 64	545UNTS91	107926
Austria	Hungary	11 Nov 64	576UNTS163	108368
Luxembourg	Portugal	12 Feb 65	571UNTS239	108305
Belgium	Luxembourg	11 Mar 65	540UNTS297	107854
Multilateral		18 Mar 65	575UNTS159	108359
Finland	United Arab Rep	01 Apr 65	562UNTS3	108193
Jamaica	UK Great Britain	02 Apr 65	552UNTS219	108056
Ivory Coast	Netherlands	26 Apr 65	634UNTS81	109053
Austria	Bulgaria	12 Jul 65	587UNTS51	108510
Multilateral		15 Nov 65	0UNTS0	109432
Austria	Yugoslavia	19 Nov 65	591UNTS3	108556
Austria	Brazil	21 Dec 65	595UNTS299	108624
Ireland	UK Great Britain	28 Feb 66	565UNTS33	108234
Sierra Leone	USA (United States)	06 May 66	594UNTS47	108593
Argentina	Portugal	20 May 66	635UNTS301	109090
Argentina	Bolivia	19 Dec 66	636UNTS89	109094
Romania	Sweden	01 Mar 67	642UNTS163	109172
Bulgaria	Turkey	30 May 67	631UNTS19	108984
Germany, West	Romania	03 Aug 67	642UNTS47	109164
Operating agencies				
Multilateral		10 Jul 20	38UNTS129	100592
Multilateral		10 Jun 25	38UNTS243	100601
Multilateral		29 Jun 33	39UNTS235	100620
Multilateral		29 Jun 33	39UNTS189	100618
Multilateral		29 Jun 33	39UNTS211	100619
Multilateral		29 Jun 33	39UNTS259	100621
Multilateral		29 Jun 33	39UNTS285	100622
Multilateral		29 Jun 33	39UNTS165	100617
Multilateral		24 Oct 36	40UNTS187	100634
Luxembourg	UK Great Britain	29 May 39	99UNTS301	200284
Haiti	USA (United States)	05 Jun 41	101UNTS125	200289
Haiti	USA (United States)	13 Sep 41	103UNTS141	200311
El Salvador	USA (United States)	27 Nov 41	120UNTS161	200389
Liberia	USA (United States)	15 Jan 42	117UNTS227	200372
Bolivia	USA (United States)	31 Jan 42	101UNTS137	200290
Panama	USA (United States)	07 Mar 42	101UNTS157	200291
Iceland	USA (United States)	17 Aug 42	24UNTS163	200140
Paraguay	USA (United States)	28 Nov 42	101UNTS173	200292

PARTY ONE	PARTY TWO	DATE	CITATION	NUMBER
Operating agencies (Cont.)				
Dominican Republic	USA (United States)	10 Dec 42	24UNTS257	200151
Iran	USA (United States)	21 Aug 43	101UNTS189	200293
Iraq	USA (United States)	16 Feb 44	109UNTS223	200362
Afghanistan	USA (United States)	29 Feb 44	106UNTS247	200344
Guatemala	USA (United States)	13 Apr 44	106UNTS213	200342
France	USA (United States)	14 Aug 45	73UNTS237	200243
Belgium	France	22 Feb 46	68UNTS157	100892
Poland	Yugoslavia	16 Mar 46	10UNTS11	100139
Romania	Yugoslavia	23 Dec 46	116UNTS33	101567
USSR (Soviet Union)	Yugoslavia	04 Feb 47	116UNTS171	101576
France	ICAO (Civil Aviat)	14 Mar 47	94UNTS59	101306
Philippines	USA (United States)	12 May 47	16UNTS123	100253
Philippines	USA (United States)	12 May 47	16UNTS137	100254
Philippines	USA (United States)	12 May 47	16UNTS109	100252
Romania	Yugoslavia	26 Jun 47	116UNTS39	101568
Multilateral		11 Jul 47	54UNTS3	100792
USSR (Soviet Union)	Yugoslavia	25 Jul 47	130UNTS315	101732
Thailand	USA (United States)	05 Sep 47	73UNTS57	100943
Greece	UNICEF (Children)	14 Oct 47	102UNTS39	101409
Sweden	USA (United States)	16 Dec 47	73UNTS65	100944
Poland	Romania	27 Feb 48	46UNTS143	100707
Multilateral		08 Mar 48	27UNTS117	100403
Norway	USA (United States)	15 Mar 48	73UNTS81	100946
United Nations	USA (United States)	23 Mar 48	19UNTS43	100303
Belgium	Luxembourg	27 Mar 48	178UNTS265	102343
Burma	USA (United States)	05 Apr 48	73UNTS73	100945
Greece	USA (United States)	23 Apr 48	74UNTS107	100958
Czechoslovakia	Yugoslavia	24 May 48	112UNTS215	101544
Australia	Poland	03 Jun 48	16UNTS189	100258
Philippines	USA (United States)	07 Jun 48	73UNTS89	100947
Multilateral		09 Jul 48	70UNTS85	100898
Brazil	USA (United States)	26 Nov 48	88UNTS3	101180
Finland	USSR (Soviet Union)	09 Dec 48	217UNTS135	102947
Mexico	USA (United States)	25 Jan 49	99UNTS3	101367
Ceylon (Sri Lanka)	USA (United States)	31 Jan 49	88UNTS21	101181
Multilateral		28 Feb 49	29UNTS53	100434
Luxembourg	Netherlands	26 Apr 49	182UNTS187	102425
Multilateral		04 May 49	47UNTS159	100728
Norway	USA (United States)	25 May 49	32UNTS345	100507
United Arab Rep	UK Great Britain	31 May 49	226UNTS273	103122
Lebanon	UK Great Britain	20 Jun 49	90UNTS137	101232
Colombia	USA (United States)	26 Jul 49	73UNTS106	100949
Denmark	USA (United States)	01 Aug 49	79UNTS147	101038
Mexico	USA (United States)	15 Aug 49	66UNTS13	100846
USSR (Soviet Union)	Yugoslavia	31 Aug 49	116UNTS345	101580
Belgium	Netherlands	07 Sep 49	117UNTS3	101581
Belgium	France	07 Sep 49	123UNTS13	101651
South Africa	USA (United States)	16 Nov 49	73UNTS97	100948
Belgium	Denmark	13 Dec 49	173UNTS193	102266
Israel	USA (United States)	19 Feb 50	122UNTS117	101641
Switzerland	USA (United States)	24 Feb 50	93UNTS3	101282
Honduras	USA (United States)	24 Mar 50	93UNTS11	101283
Spain	USA (United States)	08 May 50	98UNTS175	101363
Indonesia	USA (United States)	07 Jun 50	98UNTS167	101362
Luxembourg	UK Great Britain	27 Jun 50	183UNTS217	102431
Luxembourg	Netherlands	08 Jul 50	135UNTS229	101824
Multilateral		27 Jul 50	166UNTS73	102186
USA (United States)	Yugoslavia	09 Oct 50	133UNTS25	101776
Greece	USA (United States)	24 Oct 50	133UNTS41	101778
Multilateral		04 Nov 50	213UNTS221	102889
Colombia	USA (United States)	24 Nov 50	133UNTS49	101779
Costa Rica	USA (United States)	02 Dec 50	133UNTS61	101780
Albania	Poland	02 Dec 50	260UNTS131	103707
Chile	USA (United States)	16 Jan 51	157UNTS3	102043
China People's Rep	Poland	03 Apr 51	304UNTS187	104396

PARTY ONE	PARTY TWO	DATE	CITATION	NUMBER
Operating agencies (Cont.)				
Pakistan	USA (United States)	23 May 51	134UNTS265	101805
India	Turkey	29 Jun 51	213UNTS183	102886
UK Great Britain	USA (United States)	30 Jul 51	105UNTS81	101455
Panama	USA (United States)	30 Jul 51	140UNTS321	101896
Greece	UK Great Britain	29 Sep 51	190UNTS260	102570
India	WHO (World Health)	01 Nov 51	118UNTS13	101593
Saudi Arabia	USA (United States)	10 Nov 51	180UNTS263	102390
Italy	UK Great Britain	28 Nov 51	172UNTS27	102238
Denmark	WHO (World Health)	30 Nov 51	118UNTS3	101592
India	USA (United States)	05 Jan 52	157UNTS39	102045
Germany, East	Poland	08 Jan 52	304UNTS113	104394
Greece	Yugoslavia	02 Feb 52	188UNTS311	102535
UNICEF (Children)	UK Great Britain	04 Feb 52	120UNTS147	101620
Dominican Republic	UNICEF (Children)	15 Feb 52	121UNTS43	101625
Multilateral		15 Feb 52	132UNTS51	101751
OAS (Am States)	USA (United States)	03 Mar 52	165UNTS67	102168
Israel	USA (United States)	09 May 52	177UNTS63	102309
Australia	Greece	23 May 52	223UNTS17	103042
Korea, South	USA (United States)	24 May 52	179UNTS23	102353
Chile	WHO (World Health)	31 May 52	136UNTS323	101841
Brazil	USA (United States)	02 Jun 52	181UNTS109	102403
Belgium	Switzerland	17 Jun 52	180UNTS23	102373
WHO (World Health)	Syria	20 Jun 52	165UNTS219	102178
Iraq	UK Great Britain	21 Jun 52	149UNTS221	101954
Austria	UK Great Britain	30 Jun 52	138UNTS153	101867
Chile	USA (United States)	30 Jun 52	199UNTS241	102688
Panama	USA (United States)	30 Jun 52	181UNTS121	102404
Multilateral		14 Jul 52	198UNTS47	102656
Multilateral		21 Aug 52	141UNTS129	101912
Australia	Germany, West	29 Aug 52	184UNTS147	102446
Austria	Belgium	17 Oct 52	162UNTS183	102135
Iraq	USA (United States)	23 Oct 52	212UNTS201	102872
Saudi Arabia	USA (United States)	10 Nov 52	181UNTS307	102419
Netherlands	Switzerland	20 Nov 52	163UNTS121	102146
Sweden	USA (United States)	20 Nov 52	177UNTS203	102319
Austria	UK Great Britain	12 Dec 52	172UNTS9	102237
Saudi Arabia	USA (United States)	15 Dec 52	185UNTS67	102459
Bolivia	Italy	31 Jan 53	281UNTS181	104079
United Nations	Sweden	11 Feb 53	160UNTS3	102096
Albania	Romania	14 Feb 53	342UNTS107	104903
United Arab Rep	USA (United States)	12 Mar 53	204UNTS3	102747
United Arab Rep	USA (United States)	19 Mar 53	215UNTS17	102909
France	UK Great Britain	13 Apr 53	172UNTS173	102245
El Salvador	USA (United States)	14 May 53	234UNTS71	103273
Germany, West	Sweden	15 May 53	227UNTS195	103139
United Arab Rep	USA (United States)	21 May 53	204UNTS29	102748
Brazil	USA (United States)	30 May 53	460UNTS89	106633
Australia	UK Great Britain	08 Jun 53	201UNTS187	102718
Colombia	USA (United States)	09 Jun 53	213UNTS3	102877
Liberia	USA (United States)	23 Jun 53	213UNTS37	102879
UK Great Britain	USA (United States)	26 Jun 53	183UNTS225	102432
Panama	USA (United States)	26 Jun 53	215UNTS77	102912
Brazil	USA (United States)	26 Jun 53	336UNTS241	104808
Chile	USA (United States)	27 Jun 53	229UNTS53	103160
Chile	USA (United States)	27 Jun 53	229UNTS193	103167
Pakistan	Turkey	29 Jun 53	211UNTS225	102854
Ethiopia	USA (United States)	30 Jun 53	212UNTS135	102865
Afghanistan	USA (United States)	30 Jun 53	215UNTS3	102908
Nicaragua	USA (United States)	30 Jun 53	215UNTS133	102917
Multilateral		20 Jul 53	227UNTS217	103140
Denmark	Germany, West	14 Aug 53	202UNTS3	102725
Belgium	UK Great Britain	10 Sep 53	183UNTS203	102429
UN Relief Palestin	United Arab Rep	14 Oct 53	190UNTS13	102555
Chile	USA (United States)	30 Dec 53	236UNTS41	103315
Denmark	Yugoslavia	27 Jan 54	193UNTS181	102615

PARTY ONE	PARTY TWO	DATE	CITATION	NUMBER
Operating agencies (Cont.)				
Finland	USSR (Soviet Union)	06 Feb 54	221UNTS143	103006
United Arab Rep	USA (United States)	24 Feb 54	236UNTS61	103316
Mexico	USA (United States)	06 Apr 54	236UNTS69	103317
Ethiopia	USA (United States)	21 Apr 54	232UNTS299	103244
Panama	USA (United States)	11 May 54	236UNTS107	103319
Multilateral		22 May 54	199UNTS3	102674
Haiti	USA (United States)	28 May 54	233UNTS281	103267
Ethiopia	USA (United States)	01 Jun 54	232UNTS311	103245
Italy	USA (United States)	16 Jun 54	236UNTS149	103322
Jordan	USA (United States)	17 Jun 54	266UNTS137	103828
Chile	USA (United States)	28 Jun 54	233UNTS3	103246
Italy	USA (United States)	28 Jun 54	237UNTS121	103340
Ecuador	USA (United States)	30 Jun 54	236UNTS163	103323
El Salvador	USA (United States)	16 Jul 54	237UNTS237	103350
El Salvador	USA (United States)	31 Aug 54	237UNTS49	103336
Greece	Italy	11 Sep 54	284UNTS313	104145
Sweden	USSR (Soviet Union)	29 Sep 54	202UNTS259	102733
Australia	Vietnam, South	04 Oct 54	201UNTS349	102723
Germany, West	USA (United States)	27 Oct 54	234UNTS131	103278
Belgium	Greece	09 Dec 54	257UNTS243	103660
Peru	USA (United States)	31 Dec 54	251UNTS51	103533
Belgium	Brazil	10 Jan 55	272UNTS181	103937
Finland	USSR (Soviet Union)	24 Jan 55	240UNTS243	103406
Iraq	USA (United States)	02 Mar 55	250UNTS229	103526
Mexico	USA (United States)	09 Mar 55	263UNTS247	103776
El Salvador	USA (United States)	21 Mar 55	250UNTS261	103528
Japan	USA (United States)	07 Apr 55	263UNTS285	103778
Netherlands	Norway	18 May 55	252UNTS269	103569
Colombia	USA (United States)	14 Jun 55	256UNTS211	103630
Canada	USA (United States)	15 Jun 55	235UNTS201	103302
Haiti	USA (United States)	24 Jun 55	264UNTS291	103800
Dominican Republic	USA (United States)	30 Jun 55	257UNTS313	103664
Libya	USA (United States)	28 Jul 55	270UNTS269	103901
Libya	USA (United States)	28 Jul 55	270UNTS245	103900
Libya	USA (United States)	28 Jul 55	270UNTS317	103903
Brazil	USA (United States)	03 Aug 55	270UNTS71	103893
Bolivia	USA (United States)	03 Aug 55	264UNTS225	103795
El Salvador	USA (United States)	08 Aug 55	264UNTS301	103801
Colombia	USA (United States)	28 Nov 55	241UNTS39	103422
Austria	Belgium	20 Jan 56	248UNTS3	103481
USSR (Soviet Union)	Yugoslavia	02 Feb 56	259UNTS111	103685
Bulgaria	Yugoslavia	10 Feb 56	349UNTS21	105007
Turkey	UK Great Britain	12 Mar 56	313UNTS73	104530
Colombia	USA (United States)	14 Mar 56	271UNTS303	103922
France	USA (United States)	23 Mar 56	278UNTS131	104029
Albania	USSR (Soviet Union)	03 May 56	259UNTS391	103699
Mongolia	Romania	08 May 56	342UNTS291	104913
Czechoslovakia	USSR (Soviet Union)	01 Jun 56	259UNTS341	103696
Multilateral		20 Jun 56	268UNTS3	103850
Poland	USSR (Soviet Union)	30 Jun 56	259UNTS311	103694
Dominican Republic	USA (United States)	11 Aug 56	263UNTS181	103773
Netherlands	USA (United States)	16 Aug 56	279UNTS3	104031
Japan	USA (United States)	05 Sep 56	277UNTS267	104011
Czechoslovakia	Hungary	13 Oct 56	300UNTS177	104337
Denmark	Italy	26 Oct 56	267UNTS261	103847
Romania	Yugoslavia	27 Oct 56	389UNTS55	105592
India	Japan	29 Oct 56	318UNTS289	104622
UK Great Britain	USA (United States)	27 Nov 56	282UNTS43	104092
Czechoslovakia	USSR (Soviet Union)	30 Nov 56	266UNTS243	103833
Australia	Thailand	20 Dec 56	265UNTS149	103810
Multilateral		21 Dec 56	427UNTS81	106147
Belgium	Yugoslavia	05 Feb 57	276UNTS143	103990
Chile	USA (United States)	01 Mar 57	283UNTS127	104112
India	Poland	27 Mar 57	319UNTS263	104635
Ecuador	USA (United States)	24 Apr 57	284UNTS3	104124

PARTY ONE	PARTY TWO	DATE	CITATION	NUMBER
Operating agencies (Cont.)				
Ceylon (Sri Lanka)	China People's Rep	19 Sep 57	337UNTS169	104822
Poland	Yugoslavia	16 Jan 58	340UNTS181	104864
Poland	USSR (Soviet Union)	18 Mar 58	340UNTS89	104861
Belgium	Japan	18 Mar 58	303UNTS149	104378
Czechoslovakia	Poland	21 Mar 58	538UNTS89	107811
Germany, West	UK Great Britain	18 Apr 58	343UNTS241	104928
UK Great Britain	USA (United States)	30 Dec 58	338UNTS281	104841
Morocco	UN Special Fund	04 Apr 59	354UNTS347	105069
Iran	UK Great Britain	06 May 59	398UNTS51	105717
Colombia	USA (United States)	08 May 59	344UNTS193	104950
Ireland	Netherlands	28 May 59	344UNTS95	104944
Ethiopia	Yugoslavia	06 Jun 59	386UNTS243	105544
Ghana	UN Special Fund	12 Aug 59	338UNTS203	104836
Iran	UN Special Fund	06 Oct 59	342UNTS89	104902
Poland	UN Special Fund	15 Oct 59	344UNTS29	104941
India	UN Special Fund	20 Oct 59	344UNTS143	104946
UN Special Fund	Yugoslavia	27 Oct 59	344UNTS159	104947
Ecuador	UN Special Fund	10 Nov 59	345UNTS3	104955
Greece	UN Special Fund	13 Nov 59	345UNTS171	104966
UN Special Fund	Turkey	20 Nov 59	345UNTS105	104963
USA (United States)	USSR (Soviet Union)	21 Nov 59	361UNTS35	105172
UN Special Fund	United Arab Rep	25 Nov 59	345UNTS125	104964
France	Israel	30 Nov 59	377UNTS237	105404
Israel	UN Special Fund	01 Dec 59	345UNTS197	104968
Argentina	UN Special Fund	04 Dec 59	345UNTS263	104972
Jordan	UN Special Fund	15 Dec 59	346UNTS3	104974
UN Special Fund	UK Great Britain	07 Jan 60	348UNTS177	105000
Peru	UN Special Fund	19 Jan 60	349UNTS83	105010
Chile	UN Special Fund	22 Jan 60	351UNTS115	105020
Austria	Czechoslovakia	23 Jan 60	495UNTS99	107241
Colombia	UN Special Fund	04 Feb 60	355UNTS257	105080
Bolivia	UN Special Fund	09 Feb 60	351UNTS203	105024
Italy	USSR (Soviet Union)	09 Feb 60	399UNTS75	105735
Afghanistan	UN Special Fund	21 Feb 60	351UNTS93	105019
Ecuador	USA (United States)	24 Feb 60	371UNTS55	105270
Pakistan	UN Special Fund	25 Feb 60	351UNTS141	105021
France	UN Special Fund	17 Mar 60	354UNTS119	105059
Italy	UN Special Fund	01 Apr 60	354UNTS261	105066
UN Special Fund	Tunisia	12 Apr 60	355UNTS289	105082
Libya	UN Special Fund	19 Apr 60	356UNTS11	105090
UN Special Fund	Sudan	21 Apr 60	356UNTS213	105097
UN Special Fund	Vietnam, South	29 Apr 60	357UNTS311	200567
Laos	UN Special Fund	30 Apr 60	361UNTS171	105179
Lebanon	UN Special Fund	07 May 60	360UNTS225	105160
Iraq	UN Special Fund	19 Jun 60	376UNTS357	105389
Finland	USSR (Soviet Union)	23 Jun 60	379UNTS277	105443
Spain	UK Great Britain	12 Jul 60	414UNTS123	105971
Ethiopia	UN Special Fund	13 Jul 60	368UNTS159	105240
Cambodia	USA (United States)	15 Jul 60	380UNTS129	105453
South Africa	USA (United States)	13 Sep 60	388UNTS65	105572
Brazil	UN Special Fund	16 Sep 60	375UNTS3	105351
Taiwan	UN Special Fund	20 Sep 60	375UNTS29	105352
Indonesia	UN Special Fund	07 Oct 60	378UNTS141	105424
Liberia	UN Special Fund	11 Oct 60	376UNTS341	105388
El Salvador	UN Special Fund	24 Oct 60	377UNTS171	105400
Czechoslovakia	Germany, East	08 Nov 60	424UNTS71	106100
Finland	Norway	15 Nov 60	383UNTS159	105501
Guatemala	UN Special Fund	17 Nov 60	383UNTS67	105495
Nepal	UN Special Fund	17 Nov 60	380UNTS289	105461
Cambodia	UN Special Fund	24 Nov 60	382UNTS255	105487
Multilateral		01 Dec 60	414UNTS110	105970
Japan	UK Great Britain	03 Dec 60	414UNTS61	105966
Cyprus	USA (United States)	08 Dec 60	405UNTS145	105831
Honduras	UN Special Fund	20 Dec 60	383UNTS103	105497
Burma	UN Special Fund	03 Jan 61	387UNTS219	105564

PARTY ONE	PARTY TWO	DATE	CITATION	NUMBER
Operating agencies (Cont.)				
Germany, West	USA (United States)	03 Jan 61	416UNTS93	105997
Costa Rica	UN Special Fund	10 Jan 61	389UNTS253	105597
Canada	USA (United States)	17 Jan 61	542UNTS224	107894
UN Special Fund	Saudi Arabia	19 Jan 61	396UNTS27	105692
Nicaragua	UN Special Fund	20 Jan 61	387UNTS15	105555
UK Great Britain	USA (United States)	20 Jan 61	402UNTS153	105783
Chad	UN Special Fund	23 Jan 61	390UNTS69	105603
UN Special Fund	Somalia	28 Jan 61	388UNTS75	105573
Gabon	UN Special Fund	02 Feb 61	387UNTS289	105568
India	USA (United States)	07 Feb 61	462UNTS57	106671
Nigeria	UN Special Fund	10 Feb 61	390UNTS85	105604
Mexico	UN Special Fund	23 Feb 61	388UNTS151	105576
Cyprus	UN Special Fund	24 Feb 61	389UNTS3	105588
Panama	UN Special Fund	09 Mar 61	396UNTS3	105691
Cuba	UN Special Fund	10 Mar 61	390UNTS35	105601
USA (United States)	Vietnam, South	04 Apr 61	405UNTS77	105824
Korea, South	UN Special Fund	21 Apr 61	394UNTS231	200583
Ceylon (Sri Lanka)	UN Special Fund	03 May 61	395UNTS217	105687
Australia	USA (United States)	09 May 61	409UNTS203	105886
Australia	USA (United States)	22 May 61	419UNTS3	106026
Congo (Zaire)	United Nations	12 Jun 61	494UNTS205	107234
Cameroon	UN Special Fund	13 Jun 61	397UNTS297	105713
Inter-Am Devel Bnk	USA (United States)	19 Jun 61	410UNTS34	105895
Paraguay	UN Special Fund	22 Jun 61	399UNTS117	105738
UN Special Fund	Upper Volta	26 Jun 61	400UNTS3	105744
Philippines	UN Special Fund	28 Jun 61	399UNTS141	105739
Haiti	UN Special Fund	28 Jun 61	399UNTS171	105741
Mali	UN Special Fund	21 Jul 61	401UNTS141	105768
UN Special Fund	Yemen	02 Aug 61	402UNTS43	105777
Ivory Coast	UN Special Fund	29 Aug 61	406UNTS129	105844
UK Great Britain	USA (United States)	08 Sep 61	418UNTS53	106016
Germany, West	USA (United States)	29 Sep 61	424UNTS113	106103
UN Special Fund	Sierra Leone	02 Oct 61	422UNTS131	106073
Mauritania	UN Special Fund	07 Nov 61	412UNTS240	105936
Congo (Brazzaville)	UN Special Fund	09 Nov 61	413UNTS58	105940
Mexico	USA (United States)	15 Nov 61	460UNTS113	106634
UN Special Fund	Venezuela	11 Dec 61	422UNTS149	106074
UN Special Fund	Senegal	16 Dec 61	425UNTS97	106121
Ghana	USA (United States)	03 Jan 62	433UNTS147	106237
Malagasy	UN Special Fund	05 Jan 62	419UNTS29	106028
Paraguay	USA (United States)	16 Jan 62	433UNTS169	106240
Niger	UN Special Fund	26 Feb 62	423UNTS83	106086
Multilateral		05 Mar 62	425UNTS3	106114
Argentina	USA (United States)	16 Mar 62	454UNTS3	106535
Multilateral		23 Mar 62	470UNTS25	106793
Dahomey	UN Special Fund	28 Mar 62	424UNTS55	106099
Brazil	USA (United States)	13 Apr 62	445UNTS227	106391
India	Japan	23 Apr 62	451UNTS155	106491
UN Special Fund	Uruguay	04 May 62	429UNTS143	106196
Dominican Republic	UN Special Fund	06 Jun 62	429UNTS169	106197
Israel	USA (United States)	22 Jun 62	448UNTS273	106440
UN Special Fund	Syria	07 Jul 62	443UNTS3	106355
UN Special Fund	Tanganyika	17 Jul 62	435UNTS237	106281
Multilateral		25 Jul 62	506UNTS177	107387
Italy	USA (United States)	05 Sep 62	461UNTS185	106663
Multilateral		11 Sep 62	455UNTS402	106553
India	USA (United States)	09 Oct 62	471UNTS39	106820
Dominican Republic	USA (United States)	25 Oct 62	459UNTS247	106627
Japan	UN Special Fund	31 Oct 62	444UNTS171	106368
Algeria	UN Special Fund	15 Nov 62	452UNTS243	106512
UK Great Britain	Vietnam, South	30 Nov 62	470UNTS51	106794
Hungary	USSR (Soviet Union)	20 Dec 62	577UNTS245	108381
Canada	USA (United States)	28 Dec 62	471UNTS13	106818
Ethiopia	USA (United States)	25 Jan 63	473UNTS27	106851
Central Afri Rep	USA (United States)	10 Feb 63	473UNTS83	106857

PARTY ONE	PARTY TWO	DATE	CITATION	NUMBER
Operating agencies (Cont.)				
UN Special Fund	Uganda	22 Mar 63	456UNTS466	106572
Belgium	Netherlands	13 May 63	540UNTS3	107843
Jamaica	UN Special Fund	22 May 63	489UNTS191	107140
Netherlands	UN Special Fund	24 May 63	466UNTS289	106750
UN Special Fund	Western Samoa	05 Jun 63	467UNTS463	200601
Hungary	Romania	13 Jun 63	576UNTS275	108369
New Zealand	UN Special Fund	28 Jun 63	470UNTS3	106792
Burundi	UN Special Fund	22 Aug 63	476UNTS49	106903
Multilateral		17 Oct 63	525UNTS75	107585
Central Afri Rep	UN Special Fund	30 Oct 63	481UNTS247	106985
Romania	Yugoslavia	30 Nov 63	512UNTS2	107438
Finland	Poland	18 Dec 63	486UNTS57	107072
Mexico	USA (United States)	14 Feb 64	524UNTS197	107574
Multilateral		28 Feb 64	501UNTS245	107321
Spain	USA (United States)	18 Mar 64	535UNTS343	107789
Canada	USA (United States)	06 May 64	524UNTS173	107572
Austria	Turkey	15 May 64	515UNTS109	107457
Multilateral		25 May 64	620UNTS149	108953
Ireland	UN Special Fund	03 Jun 64	496UNTS205	107253
France	UK Great Britain	03 Jun 64	539UNTS253	107836
Italy	Romania	16 Jun 64	558UNTS313	108150
Multilateral		08 Jul 64	560UNTS201	108175
Poland	USSR (Soviet Union)	17 Jul 64	552UNTS175	108054
Ghana	Israel	30 Nov 64	550UNTS231	108019
Belgium	Congo (Zaire)	06 Feb 65	540UNTS275	107853
Canada	USA (United States)	25 Mar 65	607UNTS141	108802
Hungary	Yugoslavia	08 Apr 65	587UNTS169	108511
USA (United States)	Uruguay	17 May 65	564UNTS69	108221
Finland	USSR (Soviet Union)	04 Jun 65	560UNTS169	108173
UN Special Fund	Spain	30 Jun 65	544UNTS159	107918
Austria	Yugoslavia	19 Nov 65	587UNTS239	108512
Mongolia	UN Special Fund	26 Jan 66	552UNTS201	108055
Spain	USA (United States)	14 Apr 66	579UNTS173	108406
Lebanon	ILO (Labor Org)	14 May 66	600UNTS69	108676
Bulgaria	UN Special Fund	26 May 66	563UNTS71	108205
UN Special Fund	UPU (Postal Union)	21 Sep 66	573UNTS259	200626
Korea, South	USA (United States)	24 Sep 66	607UNTS157	108803
Chile	UK Great Britain	07 Oct 66	603UNTS167	108733
Australia	USA (United States)	09 Dec 66	607UNTS83	108798
ILO (Labor Org)	Senegal	09 Feb 67	600UNTS75	108677
Multilateral		17 Mar 67	594UNTS105	108598
Algeria	France	26 Dec 67	0UNTS0	109509
Licenses and permits				
Brazil	France	27 Jan 40	72UNTS77	100929
USA (United States)	Uruguay	21 Jul 42	120UNTS211	200393
Canada	USA (United States)	19 Dec 42	26UNTS363	200156
Iran	USA (United States)	08 Apr 43	106UNTS155	200340
Iceland	USA (United States)	27 Sep 43	29UNTS317	200170
UK Great Britain	USA (United States)	01 Dec 43	3UNTS209	100033
Spain	USA (United States)	02 Dec 44	89UNTS345	200262
Multilateral		07 Dec 44	171UNTS345	200501
Denmark	USA (United States)	16 Dec 44	10UNTS213	200063
Sweden	USA (United States)	16 Dec 44	6UNTS397	200041
Iceland	USA (United States)	27 Jan 45	122UNTS293	200411
Ireland	USA (United States)	03 Feb 45	122UNTS305	200412
Belgium	France	30 Mar 45	20UNTS297	200122
Switzerland	USA (United States)	03 Aug 45	51UNTS233	200191
France	UK Great Britain	29 Aug 45	11UNTS397	200069
Norway	USA (United States)	06 Oct 45	122UNTS319	200413
South Africa	UK Great Britain	26 Oct 45	72UNTS41	100927
Greece	UK Great Britain	26 Nov 45	35UNTS161	100555
Portugal	UK Great Britain	06 Dec 45	6UNTS3	100065
Portugal	UK Great Britain	06 Dec 45	5UNTS37	100064
Portugal	USA (United States)	06 Dec 45	3UNTS139	100028

PARTY ONE	PARTY TWO	DATE	CITATION	NUMBER
Licenses and permits (Cont.)				
Canada	UK Great Britain	21 Dec 45	27UNTS155	100405
Czechoslovakia	USA (United States)	03 Jan 46	6UNTS309	100084
Czechoslovakia	Poland	24 Jan 46	25UNTS181	100363
Netherlands	USA (United States)	11 Feb 46	3UNTS37	100023
UK Great Britain	USA (United States)	11 Feb 46	3UNTS253	100036
Turkey	UK Great Britain	12 Feb 46	6UNTS79	100069
Turkey	USA (United States)	12 Feb 46	13UNTS3	100196
Belgium	Norway	21 Feb 46	31UNTS435	100485
France	UK Great Britain	28 Feb 46	27UNTS173	100407
Greece	USA (United States)	27 Mar 46	15UNTS233	100239
France	USA (United States)	27 Mar 46	139UNTS114	101879
Denmark	Norway	30 Mar 46	29UNTS163	100438
Ireland	UK Great Britain	05 Apr 46	72UNTS57	100928
Belgium	USA (United States)	05 Apr 46	4UNTS125	100041
Netherlands	Portugal	12 Apr 46	4UNTS317	100054
Argentina	UK Great Britain	17 Apr 46	164UNTS53	102159
France	Ireland	16 May 46	44UNTS105	100681
France	USA (United States)	28 May 46	84UNTS151	101125
Ireland	Sweden	29 May 46	35UNTS231	100557
Australia	Canada	11 Jun 46	10UNTS47	100142
United Arab Rep	USA (United States)	15 Jun 46	71UNTS157	100917
Sweden	Turkey	26 Jun 46	14UNTS21	100208
Romania	Yugoslavia	26 Jun 46	116UNTS21	101566
Netherlands	Spain	13 Jul 46	4UNTS351	100055
Italy	Norway	20 Jul 46	30UNTS177	100456
Italy	Norway	20 Jul 46	17UNTS273	100281
Czechoslovakia	USSR (Soviet Union)	25 Jul 46	27UNTS231	100409
Multilateral		27 Jul 46	90UNTS229	101238
France	Sweden	02 Aug 46	27UNTS251	100410
Lebanon	USA (United States)	11 Aug 46	66UNTS211	100856
Netherlands	UK Great Britain	13 Aug 46	4UNTS367	100056
Hungary	Norway	27 Aug 46	31UNTS3	100465
Norway	Yugoslavia	30 Aug 46	30UNTS187	100457
Norway	UK Great Britain	31 Aug 46	6UNTS235	100078
Brazil	USA (United States)	06 Sep 46	54UNTS197	100805
Australia	Sweden	16 Sep 46	10UNTS63	100143
Canada	USA (United States)	27 Sep 46	21UNTS3	100320
France	Turkey	12 Oct 46	14UNTS33	100209
Belgium	Portugal	22 Oct 46	34UNTS49	100527
Brazil	UK Great Britain	31 Oct 46	11UNTS115	100152
Czechoslovakia	USA (United States)	14 Nov 46	7UNTS119	100094
Philippines	USA (United States)	16 Nov 46	7UNTS151	100097
Sweden	UK Great Britain	27 Nov 46	11UNTS229	100162
New Zealand	USA (United States)	03 Dec 46	7UNTS175	100099
Australia	USA (United States)	03 Dec 46	7UNTS201	100100
Norway	Poland	03 Dec 46	15UNTS203	100234
Portugal	Switzerland	09 Dec 46	310UNTS251	104495
Brazil	Portugal	10 Dec 46	200UNTS67	102695
USA (United States)	Uruguay	14 Dec 46	532UNTS87	107713
Taiwan	USA (United States)	20 Dec 46	22UNTS87	100332
Peru	USA (United States)	27 Dec 46	26UNTS227	100390
Ecuador	USA (United States)	08 Jan 47	22UNTS119	100333
Czechoslovakia	Ireland	29 Jan 47	27UNTS267	100411
USSR (Soviet Union)	Yugoslavia	04 Feb 47	130UNTS235	101731
Thailand	USA (United States)	26 Feb 47	16UNTS17	100246
Paraguay	USA (United States)	28 Feb 47	44UNTS25	100676
Portugal	Sweden	06 Mar 47	35UNTS243	100558
Netherlands	Turkey	19 Mar 47	14UNTS59	100211
Greece	Sweden	08 Apr 47	94UNTS73	101307
Austria	Norway	14 Apr 47	31UNTS21	100466
Greece	Netherlands	17 Apr 47	32UNTS115	100494
Canada	Portugal	25 Apr 47	94UNTS87	101308
Syria	USA (United States)	28 Apr 47	262UNTS121	103741
France	Greece	05 May 47	76UNTS61	100980
Bulgaria	Denmark	09 May 47	74UNTS131	100959

PARTY ONE	PARTY TWO	DATE	CITATION	NUMBER
Licenses and permits (Cont.)				
Chile	USA (United States)	10 May 47	55UNTS21	100807
Czechoslovakia	Denmark	14 May 47	27UNTS297	100413
South Africa	USA (United States)	23 May 47	66UNTS233	100857
Poland	Yugoslavia	24 May 47	115UNTS37	101557
Sweden	USA (United States)	24 Jun 47	36UNTS25	100565
Canada	Sweden	27 Jun 47	27UNTS313	100414
Denmark	Yugoslavia	28 Jun 47	78UNTS242	101020
Romania	Yugoslavia	30 Jun 47	116UNTS57	101569
Iraq	Turkey	30 Jun 47	72UNTS107	100930
Denmark	Turkey	30 Jun 47	32UNTS301	100504
Denmark	France	16 Jul 47	12UNTS3	100177
Canada	UK Great Britain	17 Jul 47	28UNTS3	100416
Netherlands	Thailand	18 Jul 47	28UNTS27	100417
Greece	Turkey	22 Jul 47	72UNTS131	100931
Netherlands	South Africa	22 Jul 47	12UNTS257	100188
Taiwan	UK Great Britain	23 Jul 47	9UNTS207	100135
Czechoslovakia	Greece	30 Jul 47	185UNTS115	102463
Poland	Romania	09 Aug 47	12UNTS363	100193
Canada	USA (United States)	20 Aug 47	27UNTS3	100392
Hungary	Poland	28 Aug 47	15UNTS145	100231
Czechoslovakia	Netherlands	01 Sep 47	32UNTS129	100495
Czechoslovakia	Switzerland	10 Sep 47	35UNTS275	100559
Lebanon	Turkey	16 Sep 47	44UNTS123	100682
Iran	USA (United States)	06 Oct 47	11UNTS303	100171
Czechoslovakia	Sweden	15 Oct 47	44UNTS149	100683
Colombia	UK Great Britain	16 Oct 47	160UNTS297	102115
Poland	Yugoslavia	07 Nov 47	115UNTS137	101561
Norway	Portugal	11 Nov 47	34UNTS257	100542
Denmark	Greece	14 Nov 47	35UNTS295	100560
Finland	Norway	15 Nov 47	29UNTS179	100439
Denmark	Ireland	18 Nov 47	35UNTS309	100561
Ireland	Italy	21 Nov 47	353UNTS73	105038
Taiwan	Netherlands	06 Dec 47	43UNTS185	100669
Denmark	Portugal	15 Dec 47	35UNTS329	100563
Austria	Netherlands	22 Jan 48	17UNTS99	100270
France	Lebanon	24 Jan 48	173UNTS99	102263
Norway	Poland	04 Feb 48	30UNTS205	100458
Italy	USA (United States)	06 Feb 48	73UNTS113	100950
Czechoslovakia	Yugoslavia	14 Mar 48	28UNTS81	100421
Hungary	Yugoslavia	18 Mar 48	113UNTS201	101551
Argentina	Denmark	18 Mar 48	94UNTS175	101311
Cuba	UK Great Britain	19 Mar 48	175UNTS23	102294
Poland	Yugoslavia	12 Apr 48	115UNTS167	101563
Norway	Sweden	29 Apr 48	26UNTS41	100376
Norway	Sweden	29 Apr 48	26UNTS33	100375
Ireland	Switzerland	06 May 48	334UNTS187	104768
Jordan	Turkey	07 May 48	32UNTS313	100505
Ireland	Netherlands	10 May 48	28UNTS121	100422
Norway	Turkey	20 May 48	26UNTS137	100384
Brazil	UK Great Britain	21 May 48	66UNTS121	100851
Czechoslovakia	Yugoslavia	24 May 48	112UNTS215	101544
Czechoslovakia	Yugoslavia	24 May 48	112UNTS111	101542
Greece	Switzerland	26 May 48	94UNTS217	101312
France	Norway	11 Jun 48	31UNTS83	100469
Ireland	Norway	21 Jun 48	34UNTS317	100545
Greece	Sweden	25 Jun 48	267UNTS337	103849
Norway	Switzerland	26 Jun 48	29UNTS193	100440
France	Norway	05 Jul 48	30UNTS281	100463
Brazil	Switzerland	10 Aug 48	94UNTS269	101314
France	Spain	23 Aug 48	28UNTS173	100425
Ireland	Netherlands	02 Sep 48	558UNTS249	108145
Greece	Lebanon	06 Sep 48	178UNTS37	102335
Bolivia	USA (United States)	29 Sep 48	505UNTS139	107370
Netherlands	Spain	08 Oct 48	28UNTS209	100426
Mexico	Portugal	22 Oct 48	34UNTS329	100546

PARTY ONE	PARTY TWO	DATE	CITATION	NUMBER
Licenses and permits (Cont.)				
Belgium	France	28 Oct 48	25UNTS151	100360
Argentina	Netherlands	29 Oct 48	95UNTS21	101316
Canada	USA (United States)	23 Nov 48	81UNTS295	101078
Austria	Denmark	29 Nov 48	74UNTS243	100967
Australia	Belgium	09 Dec 48	25UNTS159	100361
Argentina	Chile	14 Dec 48	635UNTS21	109071
Denmark	Poland	14 Dec 48	81UNTS33	101060
Denmark	Turkey	15 Dec 48	76UNTS17	100975
Belgium	Sweden	16 Dec 48	26UNTS3	100372
UK Great Britain	Yugoslavia	23 Dec 48	81UNTS133	101069
Belgium	Greece	27 Dec 48	77UNTS265	101004
Norway	Poland	31 Dec 48	29UNTS3	100430
Belgium	Italy	01 Jan 49	26UNTS151	100385
Poland	UK Great Britain	14 Jan 49	83UNTS3	101100
Poland	Yugoslavia	16 Jan 49	115UNTS241	101564
Italy	Lebanon	24 Jan 49	231UNTS241	103223
France	Norway	09 Feb 49	29UNTS13	100431
Switzerland	Turkey	16 Feb 49	72UNTS175	100933
Denmark	Greece	25 Feb 49	78UNTS325	101022
Finland	Netherlands	25 Feb 49	53UNTS123	100777
Czechoslovakia	Yugoslavia	01 Mar 49	113UNTS3	101547
Netherlands	Switzerland	07 Mar 49	35UNTS69	100551
Belgium	Norway	08 Mar 49	29UNTS83	100435
Greece	Norway	12 Mar 49	30UNTS161	100454
Germany, West	Greece	16 Mar 49	77UNTS307	101006
Finland	Greece	24 Mar 49	78UNTS13	101009
Finland	Greece	24 Mar 49	78UNTS3	101008
Finland	USA (United States)	29 Mar 49	55UNTS59	100808
Panama	USA (United States)	31 Mar 49	55UNTS87	100810
Denmark	Portugal	08 Apr 49	74UNTS209	100964
Italy	Yugoslavia	13 Apr 49	171UNTS279	102232
Finland	Sweden	26 Apr 49	95UNTS83	101318
Bulgaria	Poland	16 May 49	84UNTS313	101140
Italy	Spain	31 May 49	231UNTS251	103224
Belgium	Denmark	31 May 49	32UNTS337	100506
Canada	USA (United States)	04 Jun 49	122UNTS237	101649
Finland	Norway	13 Jun 49	34UNTS9	100523
Peru	USA (United States)	20 Jun 49	92UNTS249	101276
Belgium	Greece	21 Jun 49	137UNTS215	101854
India	Switzerland	24 Jun 49	95UNTS109	101319
Ireland	Sweden	25 Jun 49	558UNTS299	108148
Argentina	UK Great Britain	27 Jun 49	83UNTS217	101110
Korea, South	USA (United States)	29 Jun 49	55UNTS79	100809
Greece	Syria	05 Jul 49	78UNTS71	101013
Iraq	Norway	12 Jul 49	53UNTS137	100778
Czechoslovakia	Finland	13 Jul 49	53UNTS153	100779
Dominican Republic	USA (United States)	19 Jul 49	51UNTS145	100762
Multilateral		22 Jul 49	557UNTS211	108135
Brazil	UK Great Britain	03 Aug 49	86UNTS113	101154
France	Greece	06 Aug 49	91UNTS95	101244
Finland	Norway	24 Aug 49	53UNTS167	100780
Denmark	Finland	26 Aug 49	53UNTS191	100781
Belgium	Canada	30 Aug 49	53UNTS221	100782
Argentina	Norway	09 Sep 49	42UNTS125	100646
Allied Milit Occup	Norway	16 Sep 49	53UNTS3	100769
Lebanon	Netherlands	20 Sep 49	108UNTS205	101474
Czechoslovakia	UK Great Britain	28 Sep 49	86UNTS141	101156
Burma	USA (United States)	28 Sep 49	55UNTS3	100806
Greece	Philippines	08 Oct 49	187UNTS221	102515
Sweden	Thailand	23 Nov 49	72UNTS217	100935
Denmark	Thailand	23 Nov 49	53UNTS255	100786
Ireland	Netherlands	25 Nov 49	558UNTS256	108146
Italy	Turkey	25 Nov 49	192UNTS39	102594
Norway	Thailand	26 Nov 49	53UNTS269	100787
Brazil	Spain	28 Nov 49	215UNTS303	102923

PARTY ONE	PARTY TWO	DATE	CITATION	NUMBER
Licenses and permits (Cont.)				
Austria	Sweden	02 Dec 49	108UNTS3	101465
Austria	Norway	02 Dec 49	72UNTS230	100936
Austria	Denmark	02 Dec 49	53UNTS281	100788
Denmark	Poland	07 Dec 49	81UNTS21	101059
Denmark	Germany, West	15 Dec 49	51UNTS11	100749
Czechoslovakia	Denmark	17 Dec 49	74UNTS147	100961
Austria	Switzerland	19 Dec 49	254UNTS287	103597
Norway	Poland	21 Dec 49	47UNTS107	100725
USA (United States)	Yugoslavia	24 Dec 49	89UNTS209	101219
UK Great Britain	Yugoslavia	26 Dec 49	87UNTS71	101167
Greece	Portugal	31 Dec 49	92UNTS71	101262
Netherlands	Syria	13 Feb 50	108UNTS53	101467
Canada	Norway	14 Feb 50	53UNTS329	100790
Spain	Sweden	18 Feb 50	166UNTS15	102184
Austria	Denmark	23 Feb 50	74UNTS269	100969
Ceylon (Sri Lanka)	Thailand	24 Feb 50	72UNTS261	100938
Italy	Netherlands	04 Mar 50	254UNTS305	103598
Iceland	Netherlands	22 Mar 50	95UNTS237	101323
Denmark	Iceland	22 Mar 50	72UNTS273	100939
Paraguay	UK Great Britain	03 Apr 50	99UNTS81	101372
Italy	Portugal	05 Apr 50	254UNTS329	103599
Austria	Greece	11 May 50	184UNTS217	102450
Denmark	Portugal	02 Jun 50	74UNTS229	100966
Israel	USA (United States)	13 Jun 50	212UNTS93	102863
Netherlands	Spain	20 Jun 50	95UNTS303	101327
Burma	Ceylon (Sri Lanka)	29 Jun 50	73UNTS3	100940
Germany, West	Ireland	12 Jul 50	557UNTS221	108136
Spain	UK Great Britain	20 Jul 50	398UNTS101	105719
Spain	Switzerland	03 Aug 50	254UNTS365	103600
Canada	New Zealand	16 Aug 50	77UNTS239	101002
India	Norway	29 Aug 50	73UNTS179	100952
Burma	Sweden	14 Sep 50	96UNTS45	101330
Brazil	Turkey	21 Sep 50	150UNTS299	101981
Denmark	Poland	01 Oct 50	81UNTS43	101061
Sweden	Switzerland	18 Oct 50	166UNTS49	102185
Luxembourg	Portugal	21 Oct 50	108UNTS67	101468
Israel	Netherlands	23 Oct 50	189UNTS89	102543
Multilateral		22 Nov 50	131UNTS25	101734
Iceland	Ireland	02 Dec 50	558UNTS231	108143
Norway	UK Great Britain	15 Dec 50	106UNTS87	101459
Panama	USA (United States)	20 Dec 50	92UNTS167	101269
Italy	Yugoslavia	23 Dec 50	150UNTS199	101974
Finland	Ireland	06 Jan 51	558UNTS120	108140
Costa Rica	USA (United States)	17 Jan 51	134UNTS215	101801
Panama	USA (United States)	26 Jan 51	137UNTS69	101849
Colombia	Denmark	26 Jan 51	87UNTS161	101171
Israel	Turkey	05 Feb 51	193UNTS3	102607
Denmark	Hungary	10 Feb 51	85UNTS49	101145
Colombia	Portugal	09 Mar 51	108UNTS87	101469
Greece	Yugoslavia	15 Mar 51	187UNTS237	102516
El Salvador	USA (United States)	19 Mar 51	134UNTS245	101803
Nicaragua	USA (United States)	20 Apr 51	138UNTS57	101859
Greece	Norway	28 May 51	187UNTS141	102507
Cuba	Portugal	26 Jun 51	192UNTS115	102598
Ireland	Norway	02 Jul 51	100UNTS53	101387
Iceland	Norway	14 Jul 51	163UNTS265	102150
Germany, West	Ireland	23 Jul 51	558UNTS3	108137
Burma	Denmark	30 Jul 51	108UNTS167	101472
Burma	Netherlands	06 Sep 51	108UNTS187	101473
Panama	UK Great Britain	15 Sep 51	560UNTS143	108172
Denmark	Switzerland	15 Sep 51	110UNTS55	101501
Germany, West	USA (United States)	19 Sep 51	180UNTS161	102381
Burma	India	29 Sep 51	132UNTS71	101752
Philippines	Spain	06 Oct 51	215UNTS193	102920
Greece	Luxembourg	22 Oct 51	187UNTS119	102506

PARTY ONE	PARTY TWO	DATE	CITATION	NUMBER
Licenses and permits (Cont.)				
Denmark	Iraq	18 Nov 51	232UNTS25	103227
Colombia	Spain	11 Dec 51	216UNTS73	102933
Ireland	Switzerland	26 Dec 51	558UNTS305	108149
Ireland	Portugal	06 Feb 52	558UNTS289	108147
Belgium	Spain	10 Mar 52	178UNTS243	102342
Norway	Uruguay	20 Mar 52	310UNTS279	104496
Sweden	Uruguay	20 Mar 52	311UNTS3	104497
Belgium	France	21 Mar 52	137UNTS249	101856
Austria	Greece	22 Mar 52	187UNTS255	102517
Iraq	Switzerland	31 Mar 52	311UNTS43	104498
Czechoslovakia	Denmark	04 Apr 52	133UNTS245	101792
France	Mexico	17 Apr 52	163UNTS321	102153
Denmark	Japan	28 Apr 52	166UNTS3	102182
France	Israel	29 Apr 52	189UNTS55	102542
Greece	Syria	02 Jun 52	183UNTS251	102434
Denmark	Poland	09 Jun 52	135UNTS209	101822
Denmark	UK Great Britain	23 Jun 52	151UNTS3	101982
Germany, West	Greece	28 Jul 52	182UNTS85	102424
Denmark	Spain	28 Jul 52	135UNTS255	101825
France	Greece	31 Jul 52	187UNTS169	102510
Japan	USA (United States)	11 Aug 52	212UNTS27	102862
Greece	Sweden	19 Aug 52	189UNTS117	102544
Ceylon (Sri Lanka)	Japan	06 Sep 52	314UNTS279	104552
Austria	Greece	20 Sep 52	187UNTS191	102512
Austria	Luxembourg	13 Oct 52	192UNTS291	102606
Mexico	Netherlands	13 Oct 52	163UNTS341	102154
Iceland	Luxembourg	23 Oct 52	193UNTS39	102609
Chile	Sweden	27 Oct 52	311UNTS63	104499
Chile	Denmark	27 Oct 52	271UNTS93	103911
Denmark	Italy	28 Oct 52	167UNTS125	102202
United Arab Rep	UK Great Britain	30 Oct 52	172UNTS3	102236
Denmark	Israel	14 Nov 52	160UNTS279	102113
Luxembourg	Norway	17 Nov 52	311UNTS95	104500
Luxembourg	Sweden	17 Nov 52	173UNTS277	102270
Israel	Switzerland	19 Nov 52	232UNTS3	103226
France	Greece	23 Dec 52	187UNTS175	102511
UK Great Britain	USA (United States)	19 Jan 53	161UNTS3	102117
Greece	Italy	04 Feb 53	189UNTS269	102551
Greece	Italy	04 Feb 53	189UNTS295	102552
Greece	Netherlands	05 Feb 53	263UNTS361	103783
Turkey	Yugoslavia	26 Feb 53	247UNTS54	103460
Greece	Yugoslavia	28 Feb 53	252UNTS27	103557
Canada	USA (United States)	17 Mar 53	236UNTS259	103329
Czechoslovakia	Denmark	23 Apr 53	174UNTS95	102280
Greece	United Arab Rep	21 May 53	256UNTS17	103620
Cuba	USA (United States)	26 May 53	224UNTS75	103070
Switzerland	Yugoslavia	28 May 53	232UNTS45	103228
Burma	Norway	22 Jun 53	174UNTS49	102277
Burma	Yugoslavia	29 Jun 53	378UNTS83	105418
India	Yugoslavia	24 Jul 53	394UNTS13	105665
Ireland	Italy	27 Jul 53	558UNTS237	108144
Ceylon (Sri Lanka)	Yugoslavia	30 Jul 53	337UNTS103	104819
Argentina	USSR (Soviet Union)	05 Aug 53	221UNTS99	103004
USA (United States)	Venezuela	14 Aug 53	213UNTS99	102883
Ethiopia	Yugoslavia	21 Aug 53	378UNTS105	105421
Nicaragua	USA (United States)	02 Sep 53	215UNTS69	102911
Belgium	USA (United States)	02 Sep 53	200UNTS127	102700
Korea, South	Netherlands	26 Oct 53	200UNTS103	102697
Greece	Turkey	07 Nov 53	225UNTS163	103098
Austria	Yugoslavia	11 Nov 53	363UNTS149	105206
Bulgaria	Greece	05 Dec 53	225UNTS145	103096
Italy	Netherlands	21 Dec 53	189UNTS25	102540
Syria	UK Great Britain	30 Jan 54	449UNTS47	106452
Czechoslovakia	Greece	01 Feb 54	225UNTS77	103091
Italy	USA (United States)	31 Mar 54	235UNTS293	103311

PARTY ONE	PARTY TWO	DATE	CITATION	NUMBER
Licenses and permits (Cont.)				
Peru	Spain	31 Mar 54	232UNTS65	103230
Luxembourg	USA (United States)	17 Apr 54	257UNTS255	103661
Lebanon	USSR (Soviet Union)	30 Apr 54	226UNTS109	103111
Netherlands	USA (United States)	07 May 54	213UNTS325	102895
Greece	Spain	15 May 54	299UNTS261	104318
Pakistan	Yugoslavia	15 May 54	286UNTS3	104158
Greece	Hungary	05 Jun 54	299UNTS285	104320
Ireland	Luxembourg	27 Jul 54	232UNTS91	103231
USA (United States)	Yugoslavia	18 Oct 54	273UNTS163	103951
Greece	Netherlands	01 Nov 54	223UNTS79	103057
Belgium	UK Great Britain	05 Nov 54	209UNTS69	102822
Greece	Italy	10 Nov 54	227UNTS9	103128
Ceylon (Sri Lanka)	United Arab Rep	17 Nov 54	315UNTS3	104554
Netherlands	USA (United States)	14 Dec 54	262UNTS35	103737
Ecuador	Netherlands	14 Dec 54	232UNTS115	103233
Norway	Switzerland	30 Dec 54	311UNTS147	104502
Austria	Belgium	07 Jan 55	380UNTS219	105458
Turkey	UK Great Britain	17 Jan 55	204UNTS195	102758
Bulgaria	Yugoslavia	16 Mar 55	397UNTS83	105702
Italy	Yugoslavia	26 Mar 55	379UNTS3	105432
Italy	Yugoslavia	31 Mar 55	386UNTS307	105550
Ceylon (Sri Lanka)	Germany, West	01 Apr 55	369UNTS57	105251
Germany, West	USA (United States)	04 Apr 55	279UNTS73	104034
Norway	USA (United States)	06 Apr 55	269UNTS65	103874
Austria	Romania	11 May 55	342UNTS119	104904
Ceylon (Sri Lanka)	Pakistan	23 May 55	286UNTS15	104159
France	Ireland	07 Jun 55	558UNTS217	108142
Turkey	USA (United States)	29 Jun 55	269UNTS97	103878
Germany, West	USA (United States)	07 Jul 55	275UNTS3	103973
Greece	Netherlands	14 Jul 55	227UNTS27	103129
Denmark	Greece	29 Aug 55	230UNTS25	103174
Germany, East	Hungary	10 Sep 55	407UNTS132	105863
Bulgaria	Yugoslavia	01 Oct 55	396UNTS223	105698
France	Germany, West	04 Oct 55	353UNTS203	105044
Finland	USSR (Soviet Union)	19 Oct 55	353UNTS185	105043
Denmark	Syria	20 Oct 55	250UNTS61	103518
Burma	China People's Rep	08 Nov 55	306UNTS11	104430
Italy	Syria	10 Nov 55	267UNTS157	103841
Syria	USSR (Soviet Union)	16 Nov 55	259UNTS71	103683
Austria	Israel	17 Nov 55	232UNTS153	103235
Paraguay	UK Great Britain	21 Nov 55	252UNTS107	103560
Pakistan	Syria	18 Dec 55	320UNTS269	104647
Germany, West	USA (United States)	04 Jan 56	268UNTS143	103856
Austria	Italy	23 Jan 56	393UNTS97	105653
Argentina	Switzerland	25 Jan 56	559UNTS121	108157
Romania	Yugoslavia	01 Feb 56	362UNTS203	105189
Hungary	Romania	03 Feb 56	362UNTS233	105190
Austria	Poland	08 Feb 56	334UNTS221	104770
Norway	Syria	25 Feb 56	463UNTS217	106706
Burma	Sweden	06 Mar 56	369UNTS275	105261
Ceylon (Sri Lanka)	Romania	16 Mar 56	315UNTS41	104558
Denmark	USSR (Soviet Union)	31 Mar 56	259UNTS169	103689
Sweden	USSR (Soviet Union)	31 Mar 56	259UNTS239	103691
Norway	USSR (Soviet Union)	31 Mar 56	259UNTS205	103690
Belgium	Germany, West	14 Apr 56	344UNTS103	104945
Germany, West	Switzerland	02 May 56	559UNTS157	108158
Denmark	USSR (Soviet Union)	14 May 56	271UNTS125	103912
Portugal	Venezuela	16 May 56	463UNTS239	106707
Greece	Italy	26 May 56	496UNTS301	107258
Pakistan	USA (United States)	28 May 56	269UNTS15	103868
Italy	Switzerland	04 Jun 56	378UNTS311	105429
Ceylon (Sri Lanka)	Hungary	04 Jun 56	315UNTS13	104555
Poland	Sweden	08 Jun 56	334UNTS257	104771
Germany, West	Ireland	12 Jun 56	353UNTS121	105040
Bulgaria	Ceylon (Sri Lanka)	19 Jun 56	315UNTS23	104556
Czechoslovakia	Yugoslavia	03 Jul 56	397UNTS165	105704
Romania	Yugoslavia	04 Aug 56	395UNTS99	105682
Denmark	Norway	15 Sep 56	259UNTS3	103680
Multilateral		24 Sep 56	253UNTS171	103583
Romania	Yugoslavia	25 Sep 56	395UNTS147	105683
Germany, West	Netherlands	28 Sep 56	327UNTS185	104722
Switzerland	Thailand	13 Oct 56	312UNTS43	104510
Belgium	Poland	17 Oct 56	356UNTS279	105100
Colombia	USA (United States)	24 Oct 56	476UNTS77	106905
Belgium	Turkey	25 Oct 56	380UNTS3	105447
Multilateral		08 Nov 56	470UNTS171	106809
Peru	Switzerland	23 Nov 56	411UNTS97	105916
Albania	Yugoslavia	23 Nov 56	386UNTS73	105539
Belgium	Romania	04 Dec 56	317UNTS161	104602
Austria	Pakistan	24 Dec 56	316UNTS83	104579
Iran	USA (United States)	16 Jan 57	308UNTS147	104460
Iceland	Thailand	22 Jan 57	312UNTS63	104511
Germany, West	Sweden	29 Jan 57	393UNTS113	105654
Germany, West	Norway	29 Jan 57	353UNTS39	105037
Denmark	Germany, West	29 Jan 57	302UNTS75	104354
Germany, West	Sweden	13 Feb 57	428UNTS149	106174
Belgium	Czechoslovakia	12 Mar 57	312UNTS75	104512
Netherlands	Yugoslavia	13 Mar 57	327UNTS227	104723
Netherlands	Portugal	26 Mar 57	288UNTS47	104196
Netherlands	USA (United States)	03 Apr 57	410UNTS193	105904
Luxembourg	Sweden	06 Apr 57	427UNTS173	106152
Germany, West	Yugoslavia	10 Apr 57	463UNTS269	106708
Austria	Sweden	10 Apr 57	427UNTS343	106165
Romania	Sweden	15 Apr 57	342UNTS325	104915
Bulgaria	Sweden	17 Apr 57	464UNTS3	106709
Ceylon (Sri Lanka)	Italy	23 Apr 57	337UNTS115	104820
Korea, South	USA (United States)	24 Apr 57	288UNTS219	104207
France	Sweden	10 May 57	427UNTS127	106149
Belgium	Bulgaria	14 May 57	317UNTS81	104596
Hungary	Netherlands	28 May 57	334UNTS291	104773
Belgium	Hungary	01 Jun 57	291UNTS17	104242
Afghanistan	Pakistan	13 Jun 57	327UNTS51	104717
Czechoslovakia	United Arab Rep	30 Jun 57	411UNTS126	105917
Italy	United Arab Rep	06 Jul 57	302UNTS147	104357
Greece	Italy	02 Aug 57	533UNTS217	107744
Hungary	Sweden	02 Aug 57	334UNTS307	104774
Netherlands	Romania	27 Aug 57	342UNTS309	104914
Italy	Switzerland	19 Sep 57	363UNTS69	105200
Ceylon (Sri Lanka)	China People's Rep	19 Sep 57	337UNTS137	104821
Italy	Pakistan	05 Oct 57	353UNTS91	105039
France	Morocco	25 Oct 57	559UNTS95	108156
Belgium	France	12 Nov 57	328UNTS167	104734
Denmark	Netherlands	13 Nov 57	306UNTS67	104432
Norway	USSR (Soviet Union)	22 Nov 57	309UNTS269	104476
Argentina	Italy	25 Nov 57	305UNTS275	104424
China People's Rep	Denmark	01 Dec 57	309UNTS241	104475
Finland	Italy	17 Dec 57	291UNTS133	104248
UK Great Britain	USSR (Soviet Union)	19 Dec 57	351UNTS235	105026
Belgium	Morocco	20 Jan 58	288UNTS3	104192
Italy	Romania	28 Jan 58	302UNTS231	104362
Iran	Italy	29 Jan 58	302UNTS181	104358
Czechoslovakia	Poland	31 Jan 58	431UNTS99	106214
Bulgaria	Netherlands	07 Feb 58	335UNTS45	104777
Afghanistan	Turkey	08 Feb 58	464UNTS39	106711
Ceylon (Sri Lanka)	USSR (Soviet Union)	08 Feb 58	348UNTS159	104999
Austria	Sweden	19 Feb 58	427UNTS211	106155
Bulgaria	Italy	25 Feb 58	362UNTS279	105193
Luxembourg	Sweden	12 Mar 58	427UNTS179	106153
Morocco	Portugal	03 Apr 58	393UNTS203	105657
Italy	Tunisia	08 Apr 58	378UNTS327	105430

PARTY ONE	PARTY TWO	DATE	CITATION	NUMBER
Licenses and permits (Cont.)				
Italy	Sweden	14 Apr 58	427UNTS167	106151
Sweden	Yugoslavia	18 Apr 58	393UNTS225	105658
Multilateral		29 Apr 58	450UNTS11	106465
Albania	Italy	26 May 58	362UNTS259	105191
Bulgaria	Denmark	28 May 58	312UNTS235	104521
India	USSR (Soviet Union)	02 Jun 58	393UNTS3	105650
Denmark	Luxembourg	10 Jun 58	356UNTS193	105096
Netherlands	USSR (Soviet Union)	17 Jun 58	335UNTS77	104779
Multilateral		18 Jun 58	386UNTS355	105553
Austria	Belgium	20 Jun 58	312UNTS95	104513
Denmark	Romania	25 Jun 58	345UNTS231	104970
Austria	Romania	10 Jul 58	353UNTS155	105041
Denmark	Hungary	17 Jul 58	344UNTS281	104954
Romania	United Arab Rep	14 Aug 58	405UNTS189	105834
Australia	Fed of Malaya	26 Aug 58	325UNTS253	104703
Japan	New Zealand	09 Sep 58	325UNTS119	104698
Austria	Bulgaria	12 Sep 58	353UNTS3	105036
Iraq	USSR (Soviet Union)	11 Oct 58	328UNTS95	104730
Euratom	USA (United States)	08 Nov 58	338UNTS135	104835
Italy	Yugoslavia	20 Nov 58	379UNTS23	105433
Iraq	Romania	24 Dec 58	405UNTS243	105836
UK Great Britain	Yugoslavia	03 Feb 59	359UNTS339	105151
Euratom	UK Great Britain	04 Feb 59	331UNTS125	104752
Burma	UK Great Britain	06 Feb 59	343UNTS223	104927
Indonesia	USA (United States)	02 Mar 59	357UNTS145	105113
Sweden	Tunisia	19 Mar 59	497UNTS43	107261
Austria	Netherlands	19 Mar 59	485UNTS117	107048
Norway	Tunisia	28 Mar 59	497UNTS77	107263
Denmark	Tunisia	14 Apr 59	340UNTS273	104870
Germany, West	New Zealand	20 Apr 59	402UNTS125	105782
Austria	Netherlands	06 May 59	485UNTS175	107055
Austria	Netherlands	06 May 59	485UNTS153	107054
Canada	USA (United States)	22 May 59	354UNTS63	105054
UK Great Britain	USSR (Soviet Union)	24 May 59	374UNTS305	105344
Ceylon (Sri Lanka)	Sweden	29 May 59	464UNTS109	106713
Ceylon (Sri Lanka)	Norway	29 May 59	411UNTS165	105919
Ceylon (Sri Lanka)	Denmark	29 May 59	348UNTS225	105002
Ethiopia	Greece	22 Jun 59	534UNTS147	107759
Bulgaria	United Arab Rep	09 Jul 59	411UNTS187	105920
UK Great Britain	Yugoslavia	22 Jul 59	374UNTS319	105345
Canada	Euratom	06 Oct 59	475UNTS187	106894
India	Italy	06 Oct 59	378UNTS267	105427
Australia	Germany, West	14 Oct 59	345UNTS35	104957
Guinea	UK Great Britain	22 Oct 59	351UNTS341	105033
Italy	Tunisia	31 Oct 59	378UNTS349	105431
Tunisia	UK Great Britain	16 Nov 59	354UNTS367	105070
Guinea	UN Special Fund	02 Dec 59	345UNTS215	104969
Italy	Netherlands	08 Dec 59	484UNTS309	107039
Australia	Indonesia	17 Dec 59	354UNTS109	105058
Norway	USA (United States)	13 Feb 60	388UNTS255	105583
Cuba	USSR (Soviet Union)	13 Feb 60	369UNTS17	105248
France	Thailand	26 Feb 60	392UNTS279	105648
Greece	Tunisia	02 Mar 60	483UNTS89	107008
Turkey	USA (United States)	02 Mar 60	372UNTS37	105286
Finland	Iceland	10 Mar 60	497UNTS95	107264
Austria	Guatemala	18 Mar 60	379UNTS89	105435
Austria	El Salvador	23 Mar 60	390UNTS3	105599
Netherlands	USA (United States)	24 Mar 60	406UNTS165	105847
Germany, West	Netherlands	08 Apr 60	508UNTS14	107404
Luxembourg	Yugoslavia	09 Apr 60	464UNTS293	106719
Denmark	USA (United States)	12 Apr 60	373UNTS9	105311
Multilateral		28 Apr 60	376UNTS111	105377
Laos	UN Special Fund	30 Apr 60	361UNTS171	105179
Greece	Romania	02 May 60	485UNTS17	107043
Morocco	United Arab Rep	19 May 60	563UNTS121	108208

PARTY ONE	PARTY TWO	DATE	CITATION	NUMBER
Licenses and permits (Cont.)				
Switzerland	Tunisia	21 May 60	497UNTS109	107265
Afghanistan	Czechoslovakia	28 May 60	497UNTS129	107266
Cuba	Czechoslovakia	10 Jun 60	447UNTS75	106412
Luxembourg	Tunisia	13 Jun 60	497UNTS143	107267
Denmark	Peru	22 Jun 60	439UNTS113	106326
Kuwait	UN Special Fund	29 Jun 60	369UNTS419	200575
Italy	USA (United States)	07 Jul 60	380UNTS143	105455
Ethiopia	UN Special Fund	13 Jul 60	368UNTS159	105240
Ghana	USSR (Soviet Union)	04 Aug 60	421UNTS27	106050
Mexico	USA (United States)	15 Aug 60	402UNTS177	105786
Belgium	Burma	17 Aug 60	540UNTS185	107850
Austria	Czechoslovakia	14 Sep 60	495UNTS143	107243
Brazil	UN Special Fund	16 Sep 60	375UNTS3	105351
France	USA (United States)	19 Sep 60	400UNTS21	105745
Taiwan	UN Special Fund	20 Sep 60	375UNTS29	105352
Belgium	Ireland	23 Sep 60	557UNTS180	108134
Portugal	USA (United States)	26 Sep 60	393UNTS257	105660
Hungary	UK Great Britain	25 Oct 60	419UNTS309	106034
Burma	Switzerland	31 Oct 60	465UNTS97	106723
Panama	USA (United States)	31 Oct 60	405UNTS63	105823
Norway	Peru	02 Nov 60	497UNTS207	107270
Greece	Poland	08 Nov 60	483UNTS127	107010
Luxembourg	Thailand	29 Dec 60	465UNTS131	106725
Albania	Cuba	16 Jan 61	448UNTS67	106425
Norway	Poland	17 Jan 61	412UNTS130	105928
UK Great Britain	USA (United States)	20 Jan 61	402UNTS153	105783
Korea, South	Philippines	24 Feb 61	423UNTS217	106094
Multilateral		30 Mar 61	520UNTS151	107515
Somalia	USSR (Soviet Union)	02 Jun 61	493UNTS173	107214
Czechoslovakia	Morocco	08 Jun 61	497UNTS275	107272
Cameroon	France	16 Jun 61	412UNTS148	105929
Austria	Romania	21 Jul 61	421UNTS161	106057
Albania	Austria	27 Jul 61	407UNTS37	105858
Finland	Luxembourg	15 Aug 61	541UNTS45	107859
Mexico	Netherlands	24 Aug 61	465UNTS291	106732
Liberia	Switzerland	31 Aug 61	559UNTS215	108160
Ghana	Romania	30 Sep 61	467UNTS443	106769
Philippines	USA (United States)	04 Oct 61	433UNTS83	106232
Greece	Morocco	01 Nov 61	483UNTS113	107009
Iraq	Syria	03 Nov 61	489UNTS45	107134
Ghana	USSR (Soviet Union)	04 Nov 61	437UNTS213	106308
Germany, West	Thailand	13 Dec 61	541UNTS181	107870
Finland	Hungary	13 Feb 62	463UNTS61	106693
Germany, West	Greece	08 Mar 62	533UNTS269	107747
Dahomey	UN Special Fund	28 Mar 62	424UNTS55	106099
France	Romania	18 May 62	498UNTS115	107279
France	Senegal	15 Jun 62	524UNTS3	107563
United Arab Rep	USSR (Soviet Union)	23 Jun 62	472UNTS43	106836
Congo (Zaire)	IAEA (Atom Energy)	27 Jun 62	463UNTS31	106691
Morocco	Switzerland	05 Jul 62	498UNTS171	107281
Taiwan	Paraguay	11 Jul 62	458UNTS41	106591
Finland	France	12 Oct 62	498UNTS299	107285
Hungary	Syria	18 Oct 62	491UNTS209	107178
France	Ivory Coast	19 Oct 62	498UNTS317	107286
Czechoslovakia	Yugoslavia	22 Oct 62	480UNTS267	106974
Japan	UK Great Britain	14 Nov 62	478UNTS29	106934
Ivory Coast	Switzerland	17 Nov 62	499UNTS3	107289
Germany, West	USA (United States)	29 Nov 62	460UNTS169	106639
Syria	United Arab Rep	27 Dec 62	491UNTS245	107180
Brazil	Taiwan	28 Dec 62	500UNTS61	107307
Ghana	Mali	09 Jan 63	466UNTS165	106742
Greece	Pakistan	17 Jan 63	538UNTS175	107814
Senegal	Switzerland	23 Jan 63	524UNTS23	107564
Mali	Senegal	07 Feb 63	524UNTS41	107565
Algeria	France	18 Feb 63	563UNTS263	108214

PARTY ONE	PARTY TWO	DATE	CITATION	NUMBER
Licenses and permits (Cont.)				
Austria	Bulgaria	05 Apr 63	480UNTS3	106963
Greece	Hungary	27 Apr 63	534UNTS3	107750
Algeria	Morocco	30 Apr 63	564UNTS3	108217
Belgium	Cyprus	08 Jun 63	601UNTS311	108703
Guinea	Ivory Coast	26 Jun 63	499UNTS71	107293
Austria	Mongolia	15 Jul 63	496UNTS171	107251
Algeria	Mali	22 Jul 63	564UNTS29	108219
Multilateral		31 Jul 63	472UNTS220	106842
New Zealand	USSR (Soviet Union)	01 Aug 63	486UNTS27	107070
Cameroon	Israel	09 Aug 63	499UNTS121	107295
Tanganyika	USSR (Soviet Union)	14 Aug 63	493UNTS195	107215
Multilateral		27 Aug 63	511UNTS210	107435
Japan	USA (United States)	28 Aug 63	487UNTS237	107106
Algeria	Tunisia	01 Sep 63	601UNTS275	108701
Greece	Poland	30 Sep 63	534UNTS23	107751
Pakistan	USSR (Soviet Union)	07 Oct 63	499UNTS161	107297
Ivory Coast	Netherlands	09 Oct 63	499UNTS141	107296
Czechoslovakia	Hungary	22 Oct 63	514UNTS95	107444
Multilateral		08 Nov 63	482UNTS286	106999
Multilateral		18 Dec 63	490UNTS383	107166
Czechoslovakia	Hungary	20 Dec 63	538UNTS127	107812
Greece	Poland	21 Dec 63	538UNTS155	107813
Congo (Zaire)	UK Great Britain	03 Jan 64	534UNTS417	107770
Mali	Niger	15 Jan 64	499UNTS197	107299
Multilateral		28 Jan 64	502UNTS321	107336
Denmark	Yugoslavia	11 Feb 64	511UNTS241	107437
Cameroon	Mali	17 Mar 64	524UNTS61	107566
United Arab Rep	USA (United States)	05 May 64	531UNTS229	107706
Canada	USA (United States)	06 May 64	524UNTS173	107572
Austria	Romania	27 May 64	588UNTS29	108517
Cyprus	Hungary	02 Jun 64	602UNTS3	108704
Italy	Romania	16 Jun 64	558UNTS313	108150
Taiwan	Ecuador	17 Jun 64	533UNTS141	107740
New Zealand	USA (United States)	24 Jun 64	524UNTS101	107568
Sweden	USA (United States)	06 Jul 64	529UNTS287	107666
Ivory Coast	Mali	09 Jul 64	524UNTS121	107569
Costa Rica	USA (United States)	24 Aug 64	531UNTS107	107696
Austria	Thailand	30 Sep 64	527UNTS239	107628
Taiwan	Ecuador	23 Oct 64	543UNTS241	107904
Taiwan	Guatemala	08 Nov 64	543UNTS227	107903
Multilateral		02 Dec 64	525UNTS51	107583
Cyprus	Syria	22 Dec 64	602UNTS25	108705
Dominican Republic	USA (United States)	02 Feb 65	542UNTS117	107884
Bolivia	USA (United States)	16 Mar 65	542UNTS209	107891
Ecuador	USA (United States)	26 Mar 65	542UNTS237	107893
Australia	France	13 Apr 65	601UNTS293	108702
Portugal	USA (United States)	26 May 65	546UNTS189	107945
Belgium	USA (United States)	18 Jun 65	549UNTS95	107992
Australia	USA (United States)	25 Jun 65	541UNTS155	107868
Luxembourg	USA (United States)	29 Jul 65	573UNTS197	108332
Peru	USA (United States)	11 Aug 65	564UNTS135	108225
UK Great Britain	USA (United States)	26 Nov 65	561UNTS193	108181
Burma	Czechoslovakia	15 Dec 65	602UNTS71	108707
Japan	USSR (Soviet Union)	21 Jan 66	633UNTS165	109038
Belgium	Denmark	04 Feb 66	561UNTS233	108187
Austria	Germany, West	17 Feb 66	614UNTS263	108875
France	USA (United States)	05 May 66	593UNTS279	108589
Mexico	IAEA (Atom Energy)	20 Jun 66	573UNTS25	108321
Denmark	Singapore	20 Dec 66	593UNTS125	108580
UK Great Britain	USA (United States)	30 Dec 66	603UNTS245	108736
Romania	Sweden	01 Mar 67	642UNTS163	109172
Romania	UK Great Britain	09 Mar 67	605UNTS195	108764
Argentina	USA (United States)	31 Mar 67	636UNTS95	109095
Norway	USA (United States)	01 Jun 67	631UNTS119	108991
Denmark	Netherlands	20 Jun 67	619UNTS67	108939

PARTY ONE	PARTY TWO	DATE	CITATION	NUMBER
Licenses and permits (Cont.)				
Switzerland	UK Great Britain	29 Jun 67	617UNTS261	108916
Finland	Hungary	10 Nov 67	643UNTS95	109186
Austria	USA (United States)	21 Nov 67	634UNTS43	109049
France	UK Great Britain	22 Nov 67	643UNTS225	109194
Recognition and enforcement of legal decisions				
Iraq	Turkey	29 Mar 46	37UNTS333	100581
Paraguay	USA (United States)	12 Sep 46	125UNTS179	101677
Hungary	USSR (Soviet Union)	15 Jul 47	216UNTS247	102940
Czechoslovakia	USSR (Soviet Union)	11 Dec 47	217UNTS35	102943
Norway	Sweden	22 Dec 47	22UNTS203	100337
Denmark	Sweden	23 Dec 47	14UNTS3	100207
Denmark	Norway	21 Jan 48	14UNTS307	100223
Multilateral		08 Mar 48	27UNTS117	100403
Switzerland	USSR (Soviet Union)	17 Mar 48	217UNTS73	102944
Bulgaria	USSR (Soviet Union)	01 Apr 48	217UNTS97	102946
Multilateral		30 Apr 48	30UNTS55	100449
Denmark	Iceland	14 May 48	23UNTS163	100346
Poland	USSR (Soviet Union)	08 Jul 48	37UNTS107	100576
Czechoslovakia	Poland	21 Jan 49	31UNTS205	100480
Multilateral		06 Apr 50	119UNTS99	101610
Denmark	Norway	18 Jan 51	82UNTS153	101090
Multilateral		19 Jun 51	199UNTS67	102678
France	USSR (Soviet Union)	03 Sep 51	221UNTS79	103003
Japan	USA (United States)	28 Feb 52	208UNTS255	102817
Mexico	USA (United States)	26 Aug 52	264UNTS269	103797
Italy	ILO (Labor Org)	04 Sep 52	178UNTS371	200505
Multilateral		05 Sep 52	247UNTS329	103479
Jordan	Syria	23 Dec 53	204UNTS207	102759
Bulgaria	Czechoslovakia	13 Apr 54	501UNTS3	107314
Multilateral		23 Oct 54	332UNTS3	104760
Brazil	Italy	24 Nov 54	284UNTS325	104146
Haiti	USA (United States)	27 Apr 55	240UNTS17	103391
Belgium	France	01 Mar 56	337UNTS53	104815
Burma	Yugoslavia	07 Mar 56	386UNTS235	105543
Bulgaria	Yugoslavia	23 Mar 56	367UNTS213	105230
Multilateral		25 Apr 56	270UNTS103	103896
Multilateral		20 Jun 56	268UNTS3	103850
Multilateral		06 Jul 56	312UNTS109	104514
Japan	Norway	28 Feb 57	280UNTS87	104054
Czechoslovakia	USSR (Soviet Union)	31 Aug 57	308UNTS3	104456
Germany, East	USSR (Soviet Union)	27 Sep 57	292UNTS75	104268
Austria	Belgium	25 Oct 57	372UNTS177	105297
Germany, East	Hungary	30 Oct 57	408UNTS4	105867
Germany, East	USSR (Soviet Union)	28 Nov 57	305UNTS113	104419
Bulgaria	USSR (Soviet Union)	12 Dec 57	317UNTS217	104606
Korea, North	USSR (Soviet Union)	16 Dec 57	301UNTS301	104349
Poland	USSR (Soviet Union)	28 Dec 57	320UNTS3	104638
Romania	USSR (Soviet Union)	03 Apr 58	313UNTS167	104535
Multilateral		15 Apr 58	539UNTS27	107822
China People's Rep	USSR (Soviet Union)	23 Apr 58	313UNTS135	104534
Hungary	USSR (Soviet Union)	24 Apr 58	408UNTS118	105868
Germany, West	USSR (Soviet Union)	25 Apr 58	346UNTS71	104978
Japan	Poland	26 Apr 58	340UNTS221	104866
Multilateral		13 May 58	389UNTS277	105598
Multilateral		10 Jun 58	330UNTS3	104739
Belgium	Germany, West	30 Jun 58	387UNTS245	105566
Albania	USSR (Soviet Union)	30 Jun 58	328UNTS3	104729
Germany, East	Romania	15 Jul 58	395UNTS3	105681
Hungary	USSR (Soviet Union)	15 Jul 58	322UNTS3	104656
Mongolia	USSR (Soviet Union)	25 Aug 58	322UNTS105	104657
Ghana	USA (United States)	30 Sep 58	336UNTS169	104805
Hungary	Romania	07 Oct 58	416UNTS199	106004
Czechoslovakia	Romania	25 Oct 58	417UNTS37	106006
Bulgaria	Romania	03 Dec 58	417UNTS133	106007

PARTY ONE	PARTY TWO	DATE	CITATION	NUMBER
Recognition and enforcement of legal decisions (Cont.)				
Albania	Czechoslovakia	16 Jan 59	363UNTS195	105208
Italy	Netherlands	17 Apr 59	474UNTS207	106883
Belgium	Switzerland	29 Apr 59	443UNTS35	106356
Austria	Belgium	16 Jun 59	419UNTS45	106029
Greece	Yugoslavia	18 Jun 59	368UNTS69	105235
Germany, West	UK Great Britain	03 Aug 59	502UNTS197	107331
Czechoslovakia	Japan	15 Dec 59	383UNTS277	105505
Albania	Hungary	12 Jan 60	520UNTS3	107511
Poland	Yugoslavia	06 Feb 60	521UNTS37	107517
Germany, West	Netherlands	08 Apr 60	508UNTS14	107404
Hungary	Yugoslavia	07 May 60	519UNTS237	107510
Korea, North	USSR (Soviet Union)	22 Jun 60	399UNTS3	105732
Germany, West	UK Great Britain	14 Jul 60	414UNTS144	105972
Multilateral		13 Dec 60	455UNTS3	106543
Japan	Peru	15 May 61	451UNTS3	106482
Czechoslovakia	Poland	04 Jul 61	436UNTS189	106295
Austria	UK Great Britain	14 Jul 61	453UNTS267	106530
Czechoslovakia	Hungary	02 Nov 61	438UNTS3	106313
Bulgaria	Poland	04 Dec 61	484UNTS3	107019
Argentina	Japan	20 Dec 61	451UNTS77	106486
Poland	Romania	25 Jan 62	468UNTS3	106770
USSR (Soviet Union)	Yugoslavia	24 Feb 62	471UNTS195	106833
Multilateral		23 Mar 62	470UNTS25	106793
Belgium	Italy	06 Apr 62	490UNTS317	107161
Germany, West	Netherlands	30 Aug 62	547UNTS173	107957
Japan	USA (United States)	24 Oct 62	462UNTS119	106673
Multilateral		17 Dec 62	486UNTS119	107076
Austria	Netherlands	06 Feb 63	570UNTS101	108290
Austria	Czechoslovakia	08 Mar 63	495UNTS219	107245
Czechoslovakia	Yugoslavia	20 Jan 64	538UNTS197	107816
Netherlands	Norway	17 Nov 64	579UNTS243	108412
Multilateral		18 Mar 65	575UNTS159	108359
Austria	Hungary	09 Apr 65	638UNTS105	109132
Bel-Lux Econ Union	Morocco	28 Apr 65	620UNTS171	108954
Multilateral		15 Nov 65	0UNTS0	109432
France	Romania	14 Mar 66	604UNTS33	108741
Austria	Israel	06 Jun 66	0UNTS0	109347
Austria	France	15 Jul 66	604UNTS265	108755
Incorporation of treaty provisions into national law				
Multilateral		28 Nov 19	38UNTS17	100584
Multilateral		09 Jul 20	38UNTS109	100590
Multilateral		10 Jul 20	38UNTS129	100592
Multilateral		12 Nov 21	38UNTS165	100595
Multilateral		12 Nov 21	38UNTS153	100594
Multilateral		05 Jun 25	38UNTS257	100602
Multilateral		08 Jun 25	38UNTS269	100603
Multilateral		10 Jun 25	38UNTS229	100600
Multilateral		15 Jun 27	38UNTS327	100607
Multilateral		15 Jun 27	38UNTS343	100608
Multilateral		26 Jun 28	39UNTS15	100610
Multilateral		21 Jun 29	39UNTS27	100611
Multilateral		28 Jun 30	39UNTS85	100613
Multilateral		28 Jun 30	39UNTS55	100612
Multilateral		27 Apr 32	39UNTS103	100614
Multilateral		30 Apr 32	39UNTS133	100615
Multilateral		22 Jun 33	78UNTS181	101016
Multilateral		29 Jun 33	39UNTS189	100618
Multilateral		29 Jun 33	39UNTS259	100621
Multilateral		29 Jun 33	39UNTS211	100619
Multilateral		29 Jun 33	39UNTS285	100622
Multilateral		29 Jun 33	39UNTS235	100620
Multilateral		29 Jun 33	39UNTS151	100616
Multilateral		29 Jun 33	39UNTS165	100617
Multilateral		24 Oct 36	40UNTS153	100632

PARTY ONE	PARTY TWO	DATE	CITATION	NUMBER
Incorporation of treaty provisions into national law (Cont.)				
Multilateral		23 Jun 37	40UNTS233	100637
Multilateral		27 Jun 39	40UNTS281	100639
Canada	USA (United States)	19 Dec 42	26UNTS363	200156
Multilateral		27 Jun 46	264UNTS163	103792
Multilateral		09 Oct 46	78UNTS198	101017
Multilateral		09 Oct 46	78UNTS227	101019
Multilateral		09 Oct 46	78UNTS213	101018
Multilateral		11 Jul 47	54UNTS3	100792
Belgium	Netherlands	29 Aug 47	36UNTS349	100573
Canada	USA (United States)	26 Dec 47	27UNTS29	100395
India	Pakistan	31 Mar 48	54UNTS33	100793
Ceylon (Sri Lanka)	UK Great Britain	30 Apr 48	182UNTS2	102421
France	Poland	09 Jun 48	32UNTS251	100503
France	UK Great Britain	11 Jun 48	66UNTS151	100852
Multilateral		09 Jul 48	68UNTS17	100881
Multilateral		10 Jul 48	91UNTS3	101239
Czechoslovakia	France	12 Oct 48	45UNTS81	100693
Norway	Sweden	18 Dec 48	30UNTS117	100450
Multilateral		18 Jun 49	160UNTS223	102109
Multilateral		29 Jun 49	138UNTS207	101870
Multilateral		01 Jul 49	138UNTS225	101871
Multilateral		01 Jul 49	96UNTS257	101341
Multilateral		01 Jul 49	96UNTS237	101340
France	Netherlands	07 Jan 50	120UNTS25	101614
Afghanistan	UNICEF (Children)	04 Jul 50	71UNTS3	100906
Multilateral		15 Dec 50	171UNTS305	102234
Germany, West	Netherlands	29 Mar 51	149UNTS71	101952
Multilateral		28 Jun 51	172UNTS159	102244
Multilateral		29 Jun 51	165UNTS303	102181
Denmark	France	30 Jun 51	151UNTS241	102000
Italy	UK Great Britain	28 Nov 51	172UNTS205	102248
Belgium	Switzerland	17 Jun 52	180UNTS23	102373
Multilateral		28 Jun 52	210UNTS132	102838
Switzerland	UK Great Britain	16 Jan 53	196UNTS119	102621
Luxembourg	UK Great Britain	13 Oct 53	209UNTS87	102825
Greece	Romania	19 May 54	225UNTS17	103083
Italy	USA (United States)	16 Jun 54	236UNTS149	103322
Belgium	Yugoslavia	01 Nov 54	251UNTS123	103538
Peru	USA (United States)	31 Dec 54	251UNTS51	103533
Belgium	San Marino	22 Apr 55	253UNTS41	103574
UK Great Britain	USA (United States)	01 Nov 56	264UNTS3	103785
Multilateral		19 Dec 56	427UNTS93	106148
Multilateral		09 Feb 57	314UNTS105	104546
Pakistan	USA (United States)	01 Jul 57	344UNTS203	104951
Bulgaria	Yugoslavia	18 Dec 57	376UNTS3	105372
Czechoslovakia	USSR (Soviet Union)	02 Dec 59	374UNTS63	105330
Fed of Malaya	UK Great Britain	07 Jun 60	375UNTS141	105365
Somalia	UK Great Britain	26 Jun 60	374UNTS331	105346
Multilateral		23 Jan 61	530UNTS141	107679
Multilateral		22 Jun 62	494UNTS249	107237
Multilateral		28 Jun 62	494UNTS271	107238
Multilateral		23 Jul 62	456UNTS302	106564
Multilateral		25 Jun 63	532UNTS159	107717
UK Great Britain	USA (United States)	11 Oct 63	483UNTS3	107005
Multilateral		08 Jul 64	560UNTS201	108175
Austria	Spain	15 Jul 64	589UNTS169	108541
Multilateral		15 Sep 64	510UNTS147	107411
Luxembourg	Portugal	12 Feb 65	571UNTS239	108305
Personnel				
Multilateral		24 Oct 36	40UNTS187	100634
Panama	USA (United States)	23 Mar 40	124UNTS195	200420
Panama	USA (United States)	06 Sep 40	124UNTS209	200421
Brazil	USA (United States)	03 Mar 42	105UNTS99	200325
Haiti	USA (United States)	07 Apr 42	106UNTS319	200349

PARTY ONE	PARTY TWO	DATE	CITATION	NUMBER
Personnel (Cont.)				
Peru	USA (United States)	21 Apr 42	89UNTS317	200260
Honduras	USA (United States)	08 May 42	166UNTS351	200498
Peru	USA (United States)	11 May 42	136UNTS353	200447
Paraguay	USA (United States)	22 May 42	124UNTS243	200423
Bolivia	USA (United States)	16 Jul 42	13UNTS101	200072
Brazil	USA (United States)	17 Jul 42	102UNTS203	200303
Colombia	USA (United States)	23 Oct 42	105UNTS109	200326
Nicaragua	USA (United States)	27 Oct 42	99UNTS287	200283
El Salvador	USA (United States)	24 Nov 42	24UNTS241	200149
El Salvador	USA (United States)	02 Dec 42	122UNTS277	200410
Canada	USA (United States)	23 Feb 43	101UNTS243	200299
Panama	USA (United States)	02 Mar 43	107UNTS55	200351
Chile	USA (United States)	11 May 43	139UNTS295	200456
Peru	USA (United States)	20 May 43	100UNTS259	200288
Brazil	USA (United States)	25 Nov 43	102UNTS227	200305
Honduras	USA (United States)	12 Apr 44	138UNTS271	200450
Peru	USA (United States)	15 Apr 44	150UNTS317	200479
Multilateral		19 Apr 44	89UNTS279	200257
Norway	USA (United States)	16 May 44	67UNTS253	200223
Guatemala	USA (United States)	15 Jul 44	106UNTS285	200347
Multilateral		02 Aug 44	67UNTS221	200221
Spain	USA (United States)	02 Dec 44	89UNTS345	200262
Ecuador	USA (United States)	22 Jan 45	24UNTS273	200152
Dominican Republic	USA (United States)	13 Oct 45	149UNTS361	200477
USSR (Soviet Union)	Yugoslavia	13 Nov 45	116UNTS139	101573
Colombia	USA (United States)	19 Feb 46	166UNTS104	102187
France	UK Great Britain	28 Feb 46	27UNTS173	100407
Multilateral		31 Mar 46	17UNTS159	100274
Brazil	USA (United States)	05 Apr 46	12UNTS131	100183
Mexico	USA (United States)	12 Apr 46	66UNTS293	100861
USA (United States)	Uruguay	23 Apr 46	160UNTS103	102104
UK Great Britain	USA (United States)	06 May 46	99UNTS199	101381
Portugal	USA (United States)	30 May 46	174UNTS187	102285
United Arab Rep	USA (United States)	15 Jun 46	151UNTS135	101988
Czechoslovakia	USSR (Soviet Union)	25 Jul 46	27UNTS231	100409
UK Great Britain	USA (United States)	31 Jul 46	42UNTS199	100648
Mexico	UK Great Britain	27 Sep 46	91UNTS161	101248
Sweden	USA (United States)	30 Sep 46	42UNTS213	100649
Denmark	USA (United States)	01 Oct 46	42UNTS219	100650
Norway	USA (United States)	12 Nov 46	42UNTS227	100651
France	Netherlands	19 Nov 46	32UNTS101	100493
Albania	Yugoslavia	28 Nov 46	111UNTS143	101527
Albania	Yugoslavia	28 Nov 46	111UNTS127	101525
Peru	USA (United States)	27 Dec 46	152UNTS93	102013
UNESCO (Educ/Cult)	United Nations	03 Feb 47	1UNTS233	200011
FAO (Food Agri)	United Nations	03 Feb 47	1UNTS207	200010
USSR (Soviet Union)	Yugoslavia	04 Feb 47	130UNTS235	101731
Burma	USA (United States)	28 Feb 47	25UNTS27	100355
Australia	USA (United States)	10 Mar 47	10UNTS89	100145
Mexico	USA (United States)	17 Mar 47	167UNTS30	102200
Muscat and Oman	UK Great Britain	05 Apr 47	27UNTS287	100412
Czechoslovakia	Yugoslavia	27 Apr 47	33UNTS49	100514
Thailand	USA (United States)	08 May 47	42UNTS241	100653
Philippines	USA (United States)	12 May 47	16UNTS123	100253
Philippines	USA (United States)	12 May 47	16UNTS109	100252
Philippines	USA (United States)	12 May 47	16UNTS137	100254
Honduras	USA (United States)	13 May 47	166UNTS159	102189
Bolivia	USA (United States)	16 May 47	168UNTS89	102215
Brazil	Ecuador	31 May 47	72UNTS25	100925
Italy	USA (United States)	09 Jun 47	104UNTS157	101437
Greece	USA (United States)	20 Jun 47	7UNTS267	100105
Bulgaria	Poland	28 Jun 47	15UNTS123	100230
Romania	Yugoslavia	30 Jun 47	116UNTS57	101569
USA (United States)	Venezuela	30 Jun 47	166UNTS198	102190
Czechoslovakia	Poland	04 Jul 47	25UNTS249	100366

PARTY ONE	PARTY TWO	DATE	CITATION	NUMBER
Personnel (Cont.)				
Greece	USA (United States)	08 Jul 47	16UNTS157	100256
Albania	Yugoslavia	09 Jul 47	33UNTS91	100516
Turkey	USA (United States)	12 Jul 47	7UNTS299	100106
Poland	UNICEF (Children)	23 Aug 47	65UNTS22	100815
Hungary	Poland	28 Aug 47	15UNTS145	100231
FAO (Food Agri)	ILO (Labor Org)	11 Sep 47	18UNTS335	200111
Sweden	Yugoslavia	06 Oct 47	53UNTS107	100775
Greece	UNICEF (Children)	14 Oct 47	102UNTS39	101409
Hungary	Yugoslavia	15 Oct 47	33UNTS73	100515
Taiwan	USA (United States)	27 Oct 47	12UNTS11	100178
Bolivia	USA (United States)	03 Nov 47	51UNTS33	100750
Ceylon (Sri Lanka)	UK Great Britain	11 Nov 47	86UNTS31	101150
Ecuador	USA (United States)	14 Nov 47	149UNTS297	101959
United Nations	UPU (Postal Union)	15 Nov 47	19UNTS219	200116
United Nations	WHO (World Health)	15 Nov 47	19UNTS193	200115
Albania	UNICEF (Children)	20 Nov 47	65UNTS163	200208
UNICEF (Children)	Yugoslavia	20 Nov 47	65UNTS28	100817
USSR (Soviet Union)	Yugoslavia	15 Dec 47	116UNTS313	101578
Poland	Yugoslavia	21 Jan 48	115UNTS155	101562
Cuba	USA (United States)	27 Jan 48	67UNTS3	100862
Hungary	Poland	31 Jan 48	25UNTS283	100368
Norway	UK Great Britain	19 Feb 48	34UNTS33	100526
Belgium	Norway	20 Feb 48	32UNTS39	100487
Multilateral		06 Mar 48	289UNTS3	104214
Paraguay	USA (United States)	12 Mar 48	162UNTS30	102131
Czechoslovakia	Yugoslavia	14 Mar 48	28UNTS81	100421
Argentina	Denmark	18 Mar 48	94UNTS175	101311
USA (United States)	Venezuela	24 Mar 48	44UNTS57	100678
Ecuador	USA (United States)	14 May 48	89UNTS71	101210
Taiwan	UNICEF (Children)	21 May 48	65UNTS38	100818
Hungary	Poland	18 Jun 48	25UNTS319	100370
France	USA (United States)	28 Jun 48	19UNTS9	100302
Ireland	USA (United States)	28 Jun 48	24UNTS3	100349
Italy	USA (United States)	28 Jun 48	20UNTS43	100314
Denmark	USA (United States)	29 Jun 48	22UNTS217	100338
Paraguay	USA (United States)	30 Jun 48	124UNTS34	101665
Belgium	USA (United States)	02 Jul 48	19UNTS127	100309
Netherlands	USA (United States)	02 Jul 48	20UNTS91	100315
Greece	USA (United States)	02 Jul 48	23UNTS43	100342
Austria	USA (United States)	02 Jul 48	21UNTS29	100323
Sweden	USA (United States)	03 Jul 48	23UNTS101	100343
Norway	USA (United States)	03 Jul 48	20UNTS185	100317
Luxembourg	USA (United States)	03 Jul 48	24UNTS35	100350
Taiwan	USA (United States)	03 Jul 48	17UNTS119	100273
Iceland	USA (United States)	03 Jul 48	20UNTS141	100316
Turkey	USA (United States)	04 Jul 48	24UNTS67	100351
UK Great Britain	USA (United States)	06 Jul 48	22UNTS263	100339
Poland	USSR (Soviet Union)	08 Jul 48	37UNTS107	100576
France	USA (United States)	09 Jul 48	24UNTS103	100352
Multilateral		09 Jul 48	70UNTS85	100898
ILO (Labor Org)	WHO (World Health)	10 Jul 48	19UNTS269	200121
Multilateral		14 Jul 48	23UNTS3	100340
UNESCO (Educ/Cult)	WHO (World Health)	15 Jul 48	44UNTS323	200184
FAO (Food Agri)	WHO (World Health)	17 Jul 48	76UNTS171	200244
FAO (Food Agri)	UNESCO (Educ/Cult)	23 Aug 48	18UNTS345	200112
Portugal	USA (United States)	28 Sep 48	29UNTS213	100442
Trieste	USA (United States)	15 Oct 48	29UNTS249	100443
France	USA (United States)	19 Oct 48	98UNTS3	101355
Belgium	Italy	29 Nov 48	41UNTS3	100641
Afghanistan	UNESCO (Educ/Cult)	08 Dec 48	46UNTS3	100697
Korea, South	USA (United States)	10 Dec 48	55UNTS157	100813
Italy	USA (United States)	18 Dec 48	79UNTS133	101037
Brazil	USA (United States)	30 Dec 48	102UNTS3	101406
Mexico	USA (United States)	25 Jan 49	99UNTS3	101367
IRO (Refugee Org)	United Nations	07 Feb 49	26UNTS299	200153

PARTY ONE	PARTY TWO	DATE	CITATION	NUMBER
Personnel (Cont.)				
FAO (Food Agri)	UNESCO (Educ/Cult)	09 Feb 49	43UNTS315	200182
Mexico	USA (United States)	14 Feb 49	160UNTS75	102103
Multilateral		28 Feb 49	29UNTS53	100434
Austria	USA (United States)	23 Mar 49	43UNTS127	100667
Panama	USA (United States)	31 Mar 49	55UNTS141	100812
ITU (Telecommun)	United Nations	26 Apr 49	30UNTS315	200175
Bulgaria	Poland	16 May 49	84UNTS313	101140
Norway	USA (United States)	25 May 49	32UNTS345	100507
Italy	Spain	31 May 49	231UNTS251	103224
Philippines	USA (United States)	07 Jun 49	45UNTS63	100692
Korea, South	USA (United States)	29 Jun 49	55UNTS79	100809
Czechoslovakia	Poland	02 Jul 49	260UNTS179	103709
USA (United States)	Uruguay	27 Jul 49	151UNTS199	101995
Multilateral		12 Aug 49	75UNTS85	100971
WHO (World Health)	Thailand	12 Aug 49	178UNTS347	102350
Multilateral		12 Aug 49	75UNTS287	100973
Iran	USA (United States)	01 Sep 49	79UNTS155	101039
United Arab Rep	USA (United States)	03 Nov 49	71UNTS31	100908
Afghanistan	WHO (World Health)	04 Dec 49	102UNTS117	101414
Germany, West	USA (United States)	15 Dec 49	92UNTS269	101277
Turkey	USA (United States)	27 Dec 49	98UNTS141	101361
India	USA (United States)	02 Feb 50	89UNTS127	101214
UNICEF (Children)	UK Great Britain	10 Feb 50	65UNTS86	100837
Belgium	Netherlands	17 Feb 50	51UNTS101	100756
Ceylon (Sri Lanka)	WHO (World Health)	17 Feb 50	102UNTS309	200309
Multilateral		17 Apr 50	131UNTS99	101738
Korea, South	USA (United States)	28 Apr 50	93UNTS21	101284
Austria	USA (United States)	06 Jun 50	92UNTS201	101273
Haiti	WHO (World Health)	21 Jun 50	103UNTS61	101424
Haiti	WHO (World Health)	27 Jun 50	110UNTS99	101504
Thailand	USA (United States)	01 Jul 50	81UNTS61	101063
Spain	Switzerland	03 Aug 50	254UNTS365	103600
Brazil	USA (United States)	16 Aug 50	140UNTS223	101890
WHO (World Health)	Venezuela	11 Sep 50	110UNTS237	101513
Burma	USA (United States)	13 Sep 50	92UNTS361	101280
Thailand	USA (United States)	19 Sep 50	132UNTS199	101761
Pakistan	USA (United States)	23 Sep 50	82UNTS131	101088
UN Relief Palestin	WHO (World Health)	23 Sep 50	103UNTS129	200310
Peru	WHO (World Health)	26 Sep 50	104UNTS233	101444
Iceland	WHO (World Health)	06 Oct 50	110UNTS127	101506
Indonesia	USA (United States)	16 Oct 50	281UNTS105	104074
Iran	USA (United States)	19 Oct 50	92UNTS135	101266
WHO (World Health)	Turkey	19 Oct 50	110UNTS215	101512
Multilateral		02 Nov 50	81UNTS160	101071
Ceylon (Sri Lanka)	USA (United States)	07 Nov 50	92UNTS125	101265
Nicaragua	WHO (World Health)	10 Nov 50	110UNTS155	101508
Peru	WHO (World Health)	10 Nov 50	110UNTS187	101510
Multilateral		24 Nov 50	81UNTS188	101072
Germany, West	Netherlands	14 Dec 50	87UNTS257	101177
Multilateral		15 Dec 50	76UNTS120	100985
Brazil	USA (United States)	19 Dec 50	141UNTS3	101900
Panama	USA (United States)	20 Dec 50	92UNTS167	101269
Liberia	USA (United States)	22 Dec 50	92UNTS145	101267
Liberia	USA (United States)	22 Dec 50	133UNTS69	101781
Multilateral		23 Dec 50	185UNTS3	102456
Nicaragua	USA (United States)	23 Dec 50	92UNTS155	101268
Brazil	USA (United States)	27 Dec 50	147UNTS33	101926
India	USA (United States)	28 Dec 50	99UNTS39	101369
Philippines	WHO (World Health)	28 Dec 50	110UNTS203	101511
Paraguay	USA (United States)	29 Dec 50	122UNTS157	101645
United Nations	Yugoslavia	06 Jan 51	78UNTS165	101015
Costa Rica	USA (United States)	11 Jan 51	92UNTS179	101270
Chile	USA (United States)	16 Jan 51	157UNTS3	102043
Chile	USA (United States)	16 Jan 51	151UNTS147	101990
Saudi Arabia	USA (United States)	17 Jan 51	140UNTS335	101897

PARTY ONE	PARTY TWO	DATE	CITATION	NUMBER
Personnel (Cont.)				
Multilateral		18 Jan 51	81UNTS233	101073
Ceylon (Sri Lanka)	ILO (Labor Org)	24 Jan 51	117UNTS355	200380
Nicaragua	USA (United States)	31 Jan 51	150UNTS3	101960
Nicaragua	USA (United States)	31 Jan 51	160UNTS121	102105
Ethiopia	ICAO (Civil Aviat)	02 Feb 51	96UNTS123	101333
Afghanistan	USA (United States)	07 Feb 51	132UNTS265	101766
Pakistan	USA (United States)	09 Feb 51	100UNTS67	101388
Costa Rica	USA (United States)	13 Feb 51	141UNTS169	101914
Multilateral		15 Feb 51	81UNTS245	101074
Paraguay	WHO (World Health)	15 Feb 51	110UNTS171	101509
Israel	ILO (Labor Org)	19 Feb 51	100UNTS105	101391
Israel	ICAO (Civil Aviat)	19 Feb 51	96UNTS141	101334
Dominican Republic	USA (United States)	20 Feb 51	132UNTS305	101770
Lebanon	USA (United States)	24 Feb 51	223UNTS121	103060
Israel	USA (United States)	26 Feb 51	137UNTS57	101848
Panama	USA (United States)	26 Feb 51	160UNTS153	102106
ILO (Labor Org)	Syria	03 Mar 51	110UNTS69	101502
Multilateral		05 Mar 51	81UNTS261	101075
Colombia	USA (United States)	09 Mar 51	141UNTS15	101901
Bolivia	USA (United States)	14 Mar 51	132UNTS319	101771
Dominican Republic	USA (United States)	16 Mar 51	148UNTS15	101932
Multilateral		28 Mar 51	181UNTS61	102399
Indonesia	WHO (World Health)	28 Mar 51	103UNTS71	101425
Jordan	ILO (Labor Org)	29 Mar 51	100UNTS247	200287
Jordan	United Nations	29 Mar 51	137UNTS267	200448
Liberia	ILO (Labor Org)	02 Apr 51	100UNTS117	101392
Jordan	WHO (World Health)	03 Apr 51	110UNTS297	200367
Multilateral		05 Apr 51	84UNTS299	101139
Mexico	ILO (Labor Org)	06 Apr 51	100UNTS131	101393
Ceylon (Sri Lanka)	ILO (Labor Org)	06 Apr 51	100UNTS235	200286
Iraq	USA (United States)	10 Apr 51	151UNTS179	101993
United Nations	WMO (Meteorology)	10 Apr 51	103UNTS245	200415
Peru	ILO (Labor Org)	13 Apr 51	100UNTS31	101385
Guatemala	ILO (Labor Org)	13 Apr 51	126UNTS249	101692
ICAO (Civil Aviat)	Thailand	19 Apr 51	96UNTS181	101336
Ecuador	ILO (Labor Org)	19 Apr 51	100UNTS77	101389
Honduras	WHO (World Health)	20 Apr 51	110UNTS111	101505
Greece	Turkey	20 Apr 51	178UNTS17	102333
Cuba	ILO (Labor Org)	21 Apr 51	99UNTS205	101382
Honduras	USA (United States)	24 Apr 51	140UNTS287	101894
Greece	ILO (Labor Org)	25 Apr 51	100UNTS93	101390
India	ILO (Labor Org)	26 Apr 51	100UNTS19	101384
Philippines	USA (United States)	27 Apr 51	174UNTS251	102290
Mexico	WHO (World Health)	30 Apr 51	103UNTS95	101427
WHO (World Health)	Yugoslavia	02 May 51	103UNTS117	101429
Ethiopia	USA (United States)	02 May 51	139UNTS85	101877
Ecuador	USA (United States)	03 May 51	141UNTS27	101902
Colombia	WHO (World Health)	04 May 51	110UNTS83	101503
United Arab Rep	USA (United States)	05 May 51	198UNTS265	102670
Pakistan	ILO (Labor Org)	16 May 51	100UNTS147	101394
Mexico	United Nations	20 May 51	102UNTS103	101413
Nicaragua	UK Great Britain	25 May 51	101UNTS77	101404
Lebanon	USA (United States)	29 May 51	160UNTS49	102101
Cambodia	WHO (World Health)	31 May 51	102UNTS279	200307
Multilateral		01 Jun 51	118UNTS57	101596
Lebanon	WHO (World Health)	07 Jun 51	126UNTS221	101690
Liberia	WHO (World Health)	11 Jun 51	103UNTS83	101426
WHO (World Health)	Uruguay	11 Jun 51	128UNTS251	101724
United Nations	Thailand	11 Jun 51	90UNTS45	101225
Burma	WHO (World Health)	13 Jun 51	117UNTS115	101588
Costa Rica	WHO (World Health)	14 Jun 51	102UNTS151	101418
UK Great Britain	USA (United States)	15 Jun 51	141UNTS79	101907
Dominican Republic	ILO (Labor Org)	18 Jun 51	100UNTS3	101383
Cuba	USA (United States)	20 Jun 51	148UNTS3	101931
Multilateral		25 Jun 51	92UNTS27	101258

PARTY ONE	PARTY TWO	DATE	CITATION	NUMBER
Personnel (Cont.)				
Israel	United Nations	25 Jun 51	97UNTS21	101344
ILO (Labor Org)	Vietnam, South	26 Jun 51	100UNTS223	200285
Iraq	WHO (World Health)	01 Jul 51	110UNTS139	101507
Ethiopia	WHO (World Health)	02 Jul 51	103UNTS39	101422
Burma	WHO (World Health)	09 Jul 51	104UNTS187	101440
Burma	WHO (World Health)	09 Jul 51	104UNTS175	101439
ILO (Labor Org)	Thailand	11 Jul 51	100UNTS159	101395
Paraguay	ILO (Labor Org)	12 Jul 51	117UNTS155	101591
Multilateral		18 Jul 51	102UNTS291	200308
El Salvador	USA (United States)	19 Jul 51	140UNTS259	101892
El Salvador	USA (United States)	23 Jul 51	138UNTS127	101865
Panama	USA (United States)	30 Jul 51	140UNTS321	101896
Multilateral		01 Aug 51	107UNTS19	101464
Multilateral		04 Aug 51	104UNTS197	101441
Israel	WHO (World Health)	07 Aug 51	104UNTS213	101442
Iraq	USA (United States)	16 Aug 51	147UNTS65	101929
Jordan	UN Relief Palestin	20 Aug 51	120UNTS277	200394
Denmark	USA (United States)	23 Aug 51	147UNTS49	101928
Japan	USA (United States)	28 Aug 51	147UNTS81	101930
WHO (World Health)	Saudi Arabia	29 Aug 51	110UNTS277	101516
Multilateral		05 Sep 51	173UNTS15	102256
USA (United States)	Vietnam, South	07 Sep 51	174UNTS165	102284
Cambodia	USA (United States)	08 Sep 51	174UNTS115	102282
Laos	USA (United States)	09 Sep 51	174UNTS141	102283
Costa Rica	USA (United States)	11 Sep 51	234UNTS255	103288
Iraq	ICAO (Civil Aviat)	18 Sep 51	108UNTS219	101475
Korea, South	WHO (World Health)	19 Sep 51	109UNTS297	200366
WHO (World Health)	Vietnam, South	21 Sep 51	107UNTS63	200352
Paraguay	United Nations	27 Sep 51	120UNTS105	101617
Bolivia	United Nations	01 Oct 51	104UNTS263	101447
Multilateral		01 Oct 51	104UNTS249	101446
UNICEF (Children)	UK Great Britain	02 Oct 51	104UNTS301	101448
WHO (World Health)	Thailand	04 Oct 51	109UNTS85	101493
Philippines	Spain	06 Oct 51	215UNTS193	102920
Pakistan	WHO (World Health)	07 Oct 51	126UNTS101	101684
India	WHO (World Health)	11 Oct 51	118UNTS27	101594
Ecuador	WHO (World Health)	16 Oct 51	110UNTS263	101515
India	WHO (World Health)	16 Oct 51	109UNTS49	101490
United Nations	Uruguay	17 Oct 51	122UNTS29	101633
ILO (Labor Org)	Venezuela	22 Oct 51	117UNTS139	101590
El Salvador	USA (United States)	23 Oct 51	137UNTS43	101847
India	WHO (World Health)	23 Oct 51	109UNTS59	101491
Taiwan	WHO (World Health)	25 Oct 51	126UNTS77	101683
India	WHO (World Health)	01 Nov 51	118UNTS13	101593
Panama	WHO (World Health)	09 Nov 51	118UNTS43	101595
Panama	ILO (Labor Org)	10 Nov 51	126UNTS269	101693
Australia	USA (United States)	16 Nov 51	168UNTS75	102214
Denmark	WHO (World Health)	30 Nov 51	118UNTS3	101592
Colombia	Spain	11 Dec 51	216UNTS73	102933
Libya	UK Great Britain	13 Dec 51	123UNTS167	101658
Mexico	WHO (World Health)	17 Dec 51	124UNTS121	101670
India	WHO (World Health)	20 Dec 51	124UNTS109	101669
Guatemala	WHO (World Health)	29 Dec 51	124UNTS89	101668
India	USA (United States)	05 Jan 52	157UNTS39	102045
Dominican Republic	USA (United States)	07 Jan 52	174UNTS243	102289
USA (United States)	Yugoslavia	08 Jan 52	152UNTS61	102011
Austria	WHO (World Health)	10 Jan 52	131UNTS295	200438
India	United Nations	12 Jan 52	118UNTS175	101606
Costa Rica	WHO (World Health)	23 Jan 52	135UNTS265	101826
WHO (World Health)	Spain	30 Jan 52	124UNTS259	200425
Peru	USA (United States)	04 Feb 52	121UNTS255	200403
ICAO (Civil Aviat)	Yugoslavia	06 Feb 52	128UNTS97	101715
Germany, East	Poland	06 Feb 52	304UNTS131	104395
Indonesia	United Nations	06 Feb 52	121UNTS3	101621
WHO (World Health)	UK Great Britain	07 Feb 52	121UNTS75	101627

PARTY ONE	PARTY TWO	DATE	CITATION	NUMBER
Personnel (Cont.)				
Jordan	USA (United States)	12 Feb 52	168UNTS25	102211
Lebanon	ICAO (Civil Aviat)	14 Feb 52	128UNTS83	101714
Dominican Republic	WHO (World Health)	15 Feb 52	134UNTS291	101808
Burma	WHO (World Health)	18 Feb 52	127UNTS43	101698
Canada	USA (United States)	21 Feb 52	205UNTS293	102781
OAS (Am States)	USA (United States)	03 Mar 52	165UNTS67	102168
Greece	United Nations	05 Mar 52	123UNTS3	101650
ICAO (Civil Aviat)	United Arab Rep	06 Mar 52	151UNTS111	101986
Honduras	USA (United States)	07 Mar 52	233UNTS151	103260
Finland	WHO (World Health)	07 Mar 52	128UNTS269	200436
Taiwan	WHO (World Health)	07 Mar 52	128UNTS233	101723
Belgium	Spain	10 Mar 52	178UNTS243	102342
Iraq	USA (United States)	18 Mar 52	223UNTS131	103061
Ceylon (Sri Lanka)	WHO (World Health)	26 Mar 52	134UNTS341	200442
India	WHO (World Health)	02 Apr 52	131UNTS227	101743
India	United Nations	02 Apr 52	126UNTS145	101687
Peru	USA (United States)	09 Apr 52	184UNTS295	102454
Multilateral		11 Apr 52	173UNTS2	102255
India	WHO (World Health)	17 Apr 52	131UNTS241	101744
India	WHO (World Health)	19 Apr 52	131UNTS253	101745
Pakistan	United Nations	28 Apr 52	128UNTS191	101720
India	ICAO (Civil Aviat)	29 Apr 52	151UNTS123	101987
Israel	USA (United States)	01 May 52	177UNTS89	102311
Israel	USA (United States)	09 May 52	177UNTS63	102309
Norway	WHO (World Health)	09 May 52	131UNTS281	101747
Ethiopia	USA (United States)	15 May 52	180UNTS227	102388
Libya	USA (United States)	20 May 52	178UNTS155	102339
Libya	USA (United States)	20 May 52	178UNTS307	102346
Libya	USA (United States)	20 May 52	177UNTS81	102310
Iraq	USA (United States)	21 May 52	205UNTS33	102768
Iraq	USA (United States)	21 May 52	212UNTS183	102870
Multilateral		22 May 52	131UNTS115	101739
Korea, South	USA (United States)	24 May 52	179UNTS23	102353
Mexico	WHO (World Health)	28 May 52	134UNTS319	101810
Chile	WHO (World Health)	31 May 52	136UNTS323	101841
India	WHO (World Health)	04 Jun 52	135UNTS279	101827
Iraq	USA (United States)	09 Jun 52	212UNTS193	102871
Jordan	WHO (World Health)	16 Jun 52	135UNTS323	200445
Ethiopia	USA (United States)	18 Jun 52	181UNTS207	102410
India	WHO (World Health)	19 Jun 52	134UNTS307	101809
Multilateral		19 Jun 52	133UNTS165	101787
WHO (World Health)	Syria	20 Jun 52	165UNTS219	102178
Ethiopia	USA (United States)	24 Jun 52	181UNTS215	102411
Chile	USA (United States)	30 Jun 52	199UNTS241	102688
Finland	USA (United States)	02 Jul 52	165UNTS203	102177
Australia	FAO (Food Agri)	07 Jul 52	184UNTS209	102449
Chile	WHO (World Health)	11 Jul 52	137UNTS27	101846
India	WHO (World Health)	16 Jul 52	135UNTS291	101828
Colombia	United Nations	17 Jul 52	135UNTS61	101815
Germany, West	USA (United States)	18 Jul 52	165UNTS167	102175
Panama	USA (United States)	21 Jul 52	181UNTS285	102417
Chile	ILO (Labor Org)	23 Jul 52	178UNTS323	102348
Brazil	United Nations	04 Aug 52	135UNTS185	101820
Panama	USA (United States)	08 Aug 52	181UNTS257	102415
Iraq	USA (United States)	18 Aug 52	184UNTS131	102444
Panama	United Nations	20 Aug 52	136UNTS3	101829
Multilateral		21 Aug 52	141UNTS129	101912
Jordan	WHO (World Health)	21 Aug 52	141UNTS341	200472
Italy	ILO (Labor Org)	04 Sep 52	178UNTS371	200505
Pakistan	USA (United States)	17 Sep 52	227UNTS77	103132
ILO (Labor Org)	Uruguay	20 Sep 52	187UNTS25	102499
United Nations	Trieste	30 Sep 52	140UNTS11	101881
Multilateral		15 Oct 52	141UNTS96	101909
Multilateral		17 Oct 52	141UNTS121	101911
Iraq	USA (United States)	23 Oct 52	212UNTS201	102872

PARTY ONE	PARTY TWO	DATE	CITATION	NUMBER
Personnel (Cont.)				
Chile	WHO (World Health)	24 Oct 52	151UNTS339	102004
Chile	WHO (World Health)	04 Nov 52	150UNTS119	101966
Ethiopia	USA (United States)	05 Nov 52	184UNTS139	102445
Ethiopia	USA (United States)	07 Nov 52	184UNTS285	102453
Saudi Arabia	USA (United States)	10 Nov 52	181UNTS295	102418
Saudi Arabia	USA (United States)	10 Nov 52	181UNTS307	102419
Saudi Arabia	USA (United States)	10 Nov 52	181UNTS225	102412
Ceylon (Sri Lanka)	USA (United States)	17 Nov 52	180UNTS207	102386
Ceylon (Sri Lanka)	WHO (World Health)	21 Nov 52	161UNTS315	200490
Japan	WHO (World Health)	26 Nov 52	204UNTS301	200521
Mexico	ICAO (Civil Aviat)	28 Nov 52	164UNTS15	102156
India	WHO (World Health)	11 Dec 52	158UNTS391	102073
Saudi Arabia	USA (United States)	15 Dec 52	185UNTS55	102458
Liberia	USA (United States)	15 Dec 52	185UNTS45	102457
Multilateral		16 Dec 52	158UNTS407	102074
Multilateral		29 Dec 52	151UNTS317	102002
ILO (Labor Org)	UN Relief Palestin	31 Dec 52	182UNTS201	200506
Saudi Arabia	USA (United States)	25 Jan 53	201UNTS3	102706
India	WHO (World Health)	11 Feb 53	163UNTS43	102140
Taiwan	ILO (Labor Org)	13 Feb 53	178UNTS337	102349
Multilateral		26 Feb 53	161UNTS31	102120
Costa Rica	United Nations	27 Feb 53	161UNTS45	102121
Nepal	United Nations	02 Mar 53	161UNTS347	200493
France	Italy	14 Mar 53	284UNTS221	104140
United Arab Rep	USA (United States)	19 Mar 53	215UNTS17	102909
France	WHO (World Health)	02 Apr 53	174UNTS83	102279
United Nations	Yemen	07 Apr 53	163UNTS73	102142
Ethiopia	USA (United States)	29 Apr 53	224UNTS121	103073
France	WHO (World Health)	30 Apr 53	174UNTS71	102278
Multilateral		11 May 53	456UNTS3	106555
El Salvador	USA (United States)	14 May 53	234UNTS71	103273
United Arab Rep	USA (United States)	21 May 53	204UNTS29	102748
ICAO (Civil Aviat)	Syria	28 May 53	173UNTS199	102267
Brazil	USA (United States)	30 May 53	460UNTS89	106633
Ecuador	United Nations	16 Jun 53	166UNTS289	102194
United Arab Rep	USA (United States)	18 Jun 53	204UNTS55	102749
United Arab Rep	USA (United States)	18 Jun 53	215UNTS45	102910
Ethiopia	United Nations	22 Jun 53	172UNTS93	102241
Liberia	USA (United States)	23 Jun 53	213UNTS37	102879
Liberia	USA (United States)	23 Jun 53	213UNTS57	102880
Japan	United Nations	24 Jun 53	167UNTS249	200499
Cambodia	United Nations	24 Jun 53	168UNTS309	200500
Ethiopia	USA (United States)	25 Jun 53	212UNTS175	102869
Pakistan	USA (United States)	25 Jun 53	205UNTS139	102773
Brazil	USA (United States)	26 Jun 53	336UNTS241	104808
Panama	USA (United States)	26 Jun 53	215UNTS77	102912
Chile	USA (United States)	27 Jun 53	229UNTS53	103160
Chile	USA (United States)	27 Jun 53	229UNTS193	103167
Ethiopia	USA (United States)	30 Jun 53	212UNTS135	102865
Nicaragua	USA (United States)	30 Jun 53	215UNTS133	102917
Afghanistan	USA (United States)	30 Jun 53	215UNTS3	102908
UNICEF (Children)	UK Great Britain	07 Oct 53	180UNTS59	102375
Multilateral		09 Oct 53	190UNTS49	102557
Jordan	USA (United States)	21 Oct 53	222UNTS31	103020
Dominican Republic	United Nations	19 Nov 53	180UNTS45	102374
Chile	USA (United States)	30 Dec 53	236UNTS41	103315
Libya	USA (United States)	11 Jan 54	229UNTS15	103157
Bolivia	USA (United States)	15 Jan 54	229UNTS213	103168
UK Great Britain	USA (United States)	20 Jan 54	196UNTS95	102619
Pakistan	United Nations	25 Jan 54	185UNTS213	102472
Brazil	WHO (World Health)	04 Feb 54	233UNTS49	103250
United Arab Rep	USA (United States)	24 Feb 54	236UNTS61	103316
United Nations	Venezuela	05 Mar 54	187UNTS9	102498
Liberia	United Nations	09 Mar 54	187UNTS61	102501
Guatemala	United Nations	10 Mar 54	191UNTS271	102587

PARTY ONE	PARTY TWO	DATE	CITATION	NUMBER
Personnel (Cont.)				
Afghanistan	USA (United States)	20 Mar 54	229UNTS7	103156
Belgium	Norway	24 Mar 54	219UNTS73	102967
Peru	Spain	31 Mar 54	232UNTS65	103230
Mexico	USA (United States)	06 Apr 54	236UNTS69	103317
Multilateral		20 Apr 54	189UNTS11	102539
Ethiopia	USA (United States)	21 Apr 54	232UNTS299	103244
Panama	USA (United States)	11 May 54	236UNTS107	103319
Nepal	WHO (World Health)	13 May 54	204UNTS311	200522
Haiti	USA (United States)	28 May 54	233UNTS281	103267
Multilateral		31 May 54	192UNTS20	102592
Multilateral		01 Jun 54	200UNTS235	200520
Ethiopia	USA (United States)	12 Jun 54	234UNTS25	103270
Mexico	USA (United States)	17 Jun 54	237UNTS275	103352
Chile	USA (United States)	28 Jun 54	233UNTS3	103246
Italy	USA (United States)	28 Jun 54	237UNTS121	103340
Ecuador	USA (United States)	30 Jun 54	236UNTS163	103323
Brazil	USA (United States)	30 Jun 54	237UNTS137	103341
Costa Rica	USA (United States)	30 Jun 54	235UNTS35	103294
Multilateral		30 Jun 54	193UNTS67	102611
Multilateral		19 Aug 54	201UNTS51	102710
Pakistan	USA (United States)	23 Aug 54	234UNTS243	103287
El Salvador	USA (United States)	31 Aug 54	237UNTS49	103336
Guatemala	USA (United States)	01 Sep 54	199UNTS51	102677
Multilateral		06 Oct 54	201UNTS75	102711
Multilateral		27 Oct 54	201UNTS95	102712
Multilateral		29 Oct 54	201UNTS115	102713
Germany, West	USA (United States)	29 Oct 54	273UNTS3	103943
Libya	USA (United States)	03 Nov 54	238UNTS227	103366
Multilateral		01 Dec 54	210UNTS197	102839
Guatemala	USA (United States)	13 Dec 54	237UNTS169	103343
Iraq	USA (United States)	02 Mar 55	250UNTS229	103526
Mexico	USA (United States)	09 Mar 55	263UNTS247	103776
Chile	USA (United States)	31 Mar 55	262UNTS19	103736
Haiti	USA (United States)	01 Apr 55	261UNTS361	103734
Multilateral		04 Apr 55	208UNTS239	102816
Japan	USA (United States)	07 Apr 55	263UNTS285	103778
Taiwan	WHO (World Health)	21 Apr 55	210UNTS71	102835
Peru	USA (United States)	30 Apr 55	263UNTS309	103780
Austria	Romania	11 May 55	342UNTS119	104904
Pakistan	Sweden	04 Jun 55	228UNTS121	103146
Multilateral		14 Jun 55	212UNTS263	200526
Canada	USA (United States)	15 Jun 55	235UNTS201	103302
Dominican Republic	USA (United States)	30 Jun 55	257UNTS313	103664
Iran	WHO (World Health)	04 Jul 55	227UNTS65	103131
Multilateral		04 Jul 55	214UNTS10	102897
Libya	USA (United States)	21 Jul 55	264UNTS247	103796
Germany, East	Romania	28 Jul 55	342UNTS207	104909
Bolivia	USA (United States)	03 Aug 55	264UNTS225	103795
USSR (Soviet Union)	Yugoslavia	03 Sep 55	240UNTS267	103408
Italy	Switzerland	17 Sep 55	291UNTS213	104257
Liberia	USA (United States)	06 Oct 55	275UNTS93	103978
Czechoslovakia	Germany, East	24 Oct 55	504UNTS173	107358
Burma	China People's Rep	08 Nov 55	306UNTS11	104430
Multilateral		02 Feb 56	227UNTS153	103137
Austria	Poland	08 Feb 56	334UNTS221	104770
Multilateral		10 Feb 56	228UNTS167	103150
Multilateral		10 Feb 56	228UNTS189	103151
Burma	Yugoslavia	07 Mar 56	386UNTS235	105543
Multilateral		13 Mar 56	427UNTS245	106158
USA (United States)	Uruguay	23 Mar 56	376UNTS311	105386
Colombia	USA (United States)	27 Mar 56	273UNTS235	103954
Belgium	Germany, West	14 Apr 56	344UNTS103	104945
Indonesia	United Nations	17 Apr 56	233UNTS267	103266
Ceylon (Sri Lanka)	USA (United States)	28 Apr 56	274UNTS35	103956
Germany, West	Switzerland	02 May 56	559UNTS157	108158

PARTY ONE	PARTY TWO	DATE	CITATION	NUMBER
Personnel (Cont.)				
Multilateral		31 May 56	251UNTS181	103541
Poland	Sweden	08 Jun 56	334UNTS257	104771
Multilateral		08 Jun 56	247UNTS366	200541
Germany, West	Ireland	12 Jun 56	353UNTS121	105040
Multilateral		14 Jun 56	265UNTS125	103809
Israel	USA (United States)	26 Jun 56	257UNTS55	103649
Multilateral		26 Jun 56	321UNTS2	104650
Multilateral		26 Jun 56	253UNTS12	103573
Burma	USA (United States)	30 Jun 56	281UNTS65	104070
Multilateral		02 Jul 56	248UNTS37	103484
Multilateral		02 Jul 56	540UNTS110	107846
Multilateral		13 Jul 56	281UNTS3	104066
Multilateral		31 Aug 56	249UNTS158	103506
Denmark	WHO (World Health)	03 Sep 56	258UNTS103	103674
Germany, West	Netherlands	28 Sep 56	327UNTS185	104722
Multilateral		05 Oct 56	251UNTS245	103544
Multilateral		05 Oct 56	251UNTS267	103545
Belgium	Poland	17 Oct 56	356UNTS279	105100
Ecuador	USA (United States)	31 Oct 56	283UNTS151	104114
Argentina	USA (United States)	05 Nov 56	277UNTS143	104004
United Nations	Venezuela	18 Nov 56	588UNTS243	108529
Multilateral		21 Nov 56	253UNTS266	103588
Belgium	Romania	04 Dec 56	317UNTS161	104602
Multilateral		21 Dec 56	427UNTS81	106147
Colombia	USA (United States)	09 Jan 57	462UNTS151	106676
Multilateral		15 Jan 57	376UNTS122	105378
Multilateral		23 Jan 57	259UNTS426	103701
Multilateral		17 Feb 57	271UNTS2	103907
Iceland	USA (United States)	23 Feb 57	283UNTS73	104107
Canada	USA (United States)	26 Feb 57	279UNTS179	104039
Multilateral		01 Mar 57	264UNTS94	103790
Belgium	Czechoslovakia	12 Mar 57	312UNTS75	104512
Ethiopia	Sweden	16 Mar 57	304UNTS214	104398
Tunisia	USA (United States)	26 Mar 57	283UNTS117	104111
Multilateral		28 Mar 57	271UNTS30	103908
Morocco	USA (United States)	02 Apr 57	288UNTS157	104203
Libya	USA (United States)	04 Apr 57	283UNTS181	104116
Paraguay	USA (United States)	04 Apr 57	284UNTS161	104135
Canada	USA (United States)	09 Apr 57	283UNTS217	104119
Multilateral		09 Apr 57	274UNTS172	103965
Romania	Sweden	15 Apr 57	342UNTS325	104915
Bulgaria	Sweden	17 Apr 57	464UNTS3	106709
Ethiopia	USA (United States)	25 Apr 57	283UNTS205	104118
Czechoslovakia	United Arab Rep	06 May 57	292UNTS317	104278
Finland	USA (United States)	10 May 57	283UNTS43	104105
Belgium	Bulgaria	14 May 57	317UNTS81	104596
Multilateral		24 May 57	268UNTS270	103861
Hungary	Netherlands	28 May 57	334UNTS291	104773
Ghana	USA (United States)	03 Jun 57	284UNTS63	104129
Argentina	USA (United States)	03 Jun 57	291UNTS61	104244
Finland	India	14 Jun 57	277UNTS327	104016
Jordan	USA (United States)	27 Jun 57	288UNTS269	104209
Australia	FAO (Food Agri)	08 Jul 57	277UNTS315	104015
Multilateral		09 Jul 57	274UNTS300	103972
Hungary	Sweden	02 Aug 57	334UNTS307	104774
Netherlands	Romania	27 Aug 57	342UNTS309	104914
Burma	WHO (World Health)	20 Sep 57	282UNTS113	104096
New Zealand	UK Great Britain	20 Sep 57	287UNTS105	104180
USA (United States)	Venezuela	24 Sep 57	293UNTS307	104298
IAEA (Atom Energy)	United Nations	23 Oct 57	281UNTS369	200548
Multilateral		05 Nov 57	285UNTS301	104155
Brazil	USA (United States)	05 Nov 57	303UNTS3	104368
France	Italy	08 Nov 57	305UNTS393	104427
Italy	Yugoslavia	12 Dec 57	386UNTS293	105549
UK Great Britain	USSR (Soviet Union)	19 Dec 57	351UNTS235	105026

PARTY ONE	PARTY TWO	DATE	CITATION	NUMBER
Personnel (Cont.)				
Multilateral		06 Jan 58	304UNTS227	104399
Japan	USA (United States)	11 Jan 58	304UNTS35	104390
Ghana	WHO (World Health)	21 Jan 58	307UNTS3	104437
USA (United States)	USSR (Soviet Union)	27 Jan 58	301UNTS405	104350
Czechoslovakia	Poland	31 Jan 58	431UNTS99	106214
Indonesia	WHO (World Health)	05 Feb 58	307UNTS15	104438
Bulgaria	Netherlands	07 Feb 58	335UNTS45	104777
Multilateral		15 Mar 58	292UNTS273	104276
Sweden	USSR (Soviet Union)	28 Mar 58	428UNTS321	106184
Sudan	USA (United States)	31 Mar 58	308UNTS105	104458
Israel	WHO (World Health)	11 Apr 58	307UNTS27	104439
Germany, West	Netherlands	16 Apr 58	486UNTS331	107084
Saudi Arabia	USA (United States)	01 May 58	315UNTS221	104571
Ceylon (Sri Lanka)	Sweden	22 May 58	428UNTS65	106168
Bulgaria	Denmark	28 May 58	312UNTS235	104521
India	USSR (Soviet Union)	02 Jun 58	393UNTS3	105650
Netherlands	USSR (Soviet Union)	17 Jun 58	335UNTS77	104779
Multilateral		19 Jun 58	306UNTS236	200550
WHO (World Health)	Sudan	21 Jun 58	307UNTS235	104453
Denmark	Romania	25 Jun 58	345UNTS231	104970
Multilateral		25 Jun 58	362UNTS31	105181
Austria	Romania	10 Jul 58	353UNTS155	105041
Denmark	Hungary	17 Jul 58	344UNTS281	104954
Romania	United Arab Rep	14 Aug 58	405UNTS189	105834
Austria	Bulgaria	12 Sep 58	353UNTS3	105036
FAO (Food Agri)	IAEA (Atom Energy)	01 Oct 58	361UNTS211	200571
IAEA (Atom Energy)	UNESCO (Educ/Cult)	01 Oct 58	339UNTS373	200558
Spain	USA (United States)	16 Oct 58	336UNTS153	104804
Finland	Sweden	16 Oct 58	428UNTS125	106171
Burma	United Nations	15 Dec 58	319UNTS3	104629
United Nations	Tunisia	23 Dec 58	321UNTS23	104651
IMCO (Maritime Org)	United Nations	13 Jan 59	324UNTS273	200553
ILO (Labor Org)	IMCO (Maritime Org)	16 Jan 59	327UNTS309	200554
Ghana	United Nations	27 Feb 59	324UNTS133	104682
Iraq	USSR (Soviet Union)	16 Mar 59	346UNTS107	104979
IAEA (Atom Energy)	Thailand	18 Mar 59	339UNTS307	104850
United Nations	Sudan	28 Mar 59	327UNTS95	104719
Poland	UK Great Britain	03 Apr 59	351UNTS295	105030
Morocco	UN Special Fund	04 Apr 59	354UNTS347	105069
Colombia	USA (United States)	08 May 59	344UNTS193	104950
Fed of Malaya	USA (United States)	22 May 59	346UNTS263	104985
Libya	United Nations	27 Jun 59	336UNTS291	104811
Laos	United Nations	06 Jul 59	337UNTS41	104814
Bulgaria	United Arab Rep	09 Jul 59	411UNTS187	105920
Afghanistan	Germany, West	22 Jul 59	464UNTS177	106715
Paraguay	United Nations	01 Aug 59	341UNTS319	104894
Ghana	UN Special Fund	12 Aug 59	338UNTS203	104836
Germany, West	Iceland	12 Aug 59	411UNTS224	105921
Liberia	USA (United States)	13 Aug 59	357UNTS181	105116
United Arab Rep	USA (United States)	28 Sep 59	358UNTS97	105128
Germany, West	USA (United States)	01 Oct 59	358UNTS129	105130
IAEA (Atom Energy)	ICAO (Civil Aviat)	01 Oct 59	361UNTS193	200570
Iran	UN Special Fund	06 Oct 59	342UNTS89	104902
Multilateral		09 Oct 59	376UNTS382	105391
Guinea	United Nations	15 Oct 59	344UNTS47	104942
Poland	UN Special Fund	15 Oct 59	344UNTS29	104941
India	UN Special Fund	20 Oct 59	344UNTS143	104946
UN Special Fund	Yugoslavia	27 Oct 59	344UNTS159	104947
Ecuador	UN Special Fund	10 Nov 59	345UNTS3	104955
Greece	UN Special Fund	13 Nov 59	345UNTS171	104966
Multilateral		18 Nov 59	390UNTS227	105610
UN Special Fund	Turkey	20 Nov 59	345UNTS105	104963
Afghanistan	United Nations	24 Nov 59	397UNTS187	105705
UN Special Fund	United Arab Rep	25 Nov 59	345UNTS125	104964
Israel	UN Special Fund	01 Dec 59	345UNTS197	104968

PARTY ONE	PARTY TWO	DATE	CITATION	NUMBER
Personnel (Cont.)				
UK Great Britain	USSR (Soviet Union)	01 Dec 59	351UNTS313	105032
Guinea	UN Special Fund	02 Dec 59	345UNTS215	104969
Multilateral		03 Dec 59	348UNTS246	105003
Multilateral		03 Dec 59	345UNTS251	104971
Argentina	UN Special Fund	04 Dec 59	345UNTS263	104972
Jordan	UN Special Fund	15 Dec 59	346UNTS3	104974
Germany, East	Hungary	19 Dec 59	409UNTS4	105874
Ceylon (Sri Lanka)	WHO (World Health)	21 Dec 59	349UNTS109	105011
UN Special Fund	UK Great Britain	07 Jan 60	348UNTS177	105000
Czechoslovakia	UK Great Britain	15 Jan 60	374UNTS207	105336
Peru	UN Special Fund	19 Jan 60	349UNTS83	105010
Pakistan	WHO (World Health)	20 Jan 60	351UNTS355	105034
Chile	UN Special Fund	22 Jan 60	351UNTS115	105020
India	Japan	25 Jan 60	384UNTS31	105508
Germany, East	Hungary	30 Jan 60	408UNTS230	105873
Colombia	UN Special Fund	04 Feb 60	355UNTS257	105080
Bolivia	UN Special Fund	09 Feb 60	351UNTS203	105024
Afghanistan	UN Special Fund	21 Feb 60	351UNTS93	105019
Ecuador	USA (United States)	24 Feb 60	371UNTS55	105270
Pakistan	UN Special Fund	25 Feb 60	351UNTS141	105021
Multilateral		26 Feb 60	418UNTS171	106022
France	UN Special Fund	17 Mar 60	354UNTS119	105059
Portugal	USA (United States)	19 Mar 60	371UNTS131	105275
Italy	UN Special Fund	01 Apr 60	354UNTS261	105066
Multilateral		12 Apr 60	359UNTS323	105150
UN Special Fund	Tunisia	12 Apr 60	355UNTS289	105082
Libya	UN Special Fund	19 Apr 60	356UNTS11	105090
UN Special Fund	Sudan	21 Apr 60	356UNTS213	105097
Germany, West	Spain	28 Apr 60	465UNTS3	106720
UN Special Fund	Vietnam, South	29 Apr 60	357UNTS311	200567
Laos	UN Special Fund	30 Apr 60	361UNTS171	105179
United Nations	Togo	06 May 60	388UNTS53	105571
Lebanon	UN Special Fund	07 May 60	360UNTS225	105160
Cambodia	WHO (World Health)	19 May 60	372UNTS193	105298
Morocco	United Arab Rep	19 May 60	563UNTS121	108208
Afghanistan	Czechoslovakia	28 May 60	497UNTS129	107266
Multilateral		04 Jun 60	360UNTS208	105159
Iraq	UN Special Fund	19 Jun 60	376UNTS357	105389
Denmark	USA (United States)	07 Jul 60	380UNTS39	105449
Multilateral		08 Jul 60	366UNTS310	105220
Ethiopia	United Nations	13 Jul 60	368UNTS143	105239
USA (United States)	Uruguay	22 Jul 60	388UNTS315	105587
France	Greece	25 Jul 60	533UNTS227	107745
Japan	Pakistan	30 Jul 60	384UNTS63	105511
Jordan	WHO (World Health)	03 Aug 60	381UNTS133	105469
WHO (World Health)	United Arab Rep	03 Aug 60	385UNTS3	105524
Laos	WHO (World Health)	04 Aug 60	373UNTS313	105322
WHO (World Health)	Tunisia	04 Aug 60	381UNTS335	105474
Ghana	USSR (Soviet Union)	04 Aug 60	399UNTS61	105734
Japan	Thailand	24 Aug 60	384UNTS73	105512
WHO (World Health)	Saudi Arabia	06 Sep 60	395UNTS169	105684
Lebanon	WHO (World Health)	08 Sep 60	387UNTS49	105557
Iran	Japan	12 Sep 60	384UNTS43	105509
Czechoslovakia	India	19 Sep 60	465UNTS67	106722
Guinea	USA (United States)	30 Sep 60	394UNTS103	105671
Indonesia	UN Special Fund	07 Oct 60	378UNTS141	105424
Liberia	UN Special Fund	11 Oct 60	376UNTS341	105388
Nigeria	USA (United States)	19 Oct 60	394UNTS113	105672
El Salvador	UN Special Fund	24 Oct 60	377UNTS171	105400
Kuwait	United Nations	31 Oct 60	391UNTS295	200581
WHO (World Health)	Upper Volta	15 Nov 60	383UNTS91	105496
Pakistan	United Nations	17 Nov 60	380UNTS277	105460
Guatemala	UN Special Fund	17 Nov 60	383UNTS67	105495
Nepal	UN Special Fund	17 Nov 60	380UNTS289	105461
Czechoslovakia	Ghana	23 Nov 60	431UNTS85	106212

PARTY ONE	PARTY TWO	DATE	CITATION	NUMBER
Personnel (Cont.)				
Cambodia	UN Special Fund	24 Nov 60	382UNTS255	105487
Israel	Mali	24 Nov 60	413UNTS95	105944
Fed of Malaya	WHO (World Health)	25 Nov 60	387UNTS37	105556
Cambodia	United Nations	30 Nov 60	383UNTS147	105500
WHO (World Health)	Yemen	03 Dec 60	395UNTS187	105685
Dahomey	WHO (World Health)	07 Dec 60	387UNTS277	105567
Congo (Brazzaville)	WHO (World Health)	12 Dec 60	399UNTS105	105737
Multilateral		13 Dec 60	523UNTS117	107557
Bolivia	United Nations	14 Dec 60	382UNTS283	105489
Honduras	UN Special Fund	20 Dec 60	383UNTS103	105497
Togo	USA (United States)	22 Dec 60	401UNTS33	105760
Niger	WHO (World Health)	28 Dec 60	394UNTS195	105679
Burma	UN Special Fund	03 Jan 61	387UNTS219	105564
Mali	USA (United States)	04 Jan 61	405UNTS165	105832
UK Great Britain	USSR (Soviet Union)	09 Jan 61	404UNTS175	105810
Costa Rica	UN Special Fund	10 Jan 61	389UNTS253	105597
Norway	Poland	17 Jan 61	412UNTS130	105928
UN Special Fund	Saudi Arabia	19 Jan 61	396UNTS27	105692
Nicaragua	UN Special Fund	20 Jan 61	387UNTS15	105555
Korea, South	WHO (World Health)	20 Jan 61	406UNTS269	200589
Chad	UN Special Fund	23 Jan 61	390UNTS69	105603
Multilateral		28 Jan 61	387UNTS202	105563
UN Special Fund	Somalia	28 Jan 61	388UNTS75	105573
Ivory Coast	WHO (World Health)	30 Jan 61	395UNTS205	105686
Gabon	UN Special Fund	02 Feb 61	387UNTS289	105568
WHO (World Health)	Togo	03 Feb 61	394UNTS207	105680
Chad	WHO (World Health)	03 Feb 61	394UNTS161	105676
Nigeria	UN Special Fund	10 Feb 61	390UNTS85	105604
Central Afri Rep	WHO (World Health)	13 Feb 61	394UNTS149	105675
Mexico	UN Special Fund	23 Feb 61	388UNTS151	105576
Cyprus	UN Special Fund	24 Feb 61	389UNTS3	105588
Cuba	Czechoslovakia	04 Mar 61	465UNTS209	106728
Iraq	United Nations	05 Mar 61	409UNTS56	105878
Panama	UN Special Fund	09 Mar 61	396UNTS3	105691
Cuba	UN Special Fund	10 Mar 61	390UNTS35	105601
Afghanistan	Japan	15 Mar 61	450UNTS373	106480
UK Great Britain	USA (United States)	15 Mar 61	404UNTS207	105811
Kuwait	WHO (World Health)	16 Mar 61	397UNTS315	200588
Colombia	USA (United States)	04 Apr 61	405UNTS55	105822
UK Great Britain	USA (United States)	06 Apr 61	404UNTS215	105812
Honduras	USA (United States)	12 Apr 61	413UNTS182	105952
Mauritania	WHO (World Health)	17 Apr 61	396UNTS301	200587
Multilateral		18 Apr 61	500UNTS95	107310
Korea, South	UN Special Fund	21 Apr 61	394UNTS231	200583
Mali	WHO (World Health)	27 Apr 61	407UNTS66	105860
Turkey	USSR (Soviet Union)	27 Apr 61	420UNTS307	106047
Gabon	WHO (World Health)	27 Apr 61	397UNTS215	105707
Ceylon (Sri Lanka)	UN Special Fund	03 May 61	395UNTS217	105687
Sierra Leone	USA (United States)	05 May 61	409UNTS194	105885
Senegal	USA (United States)	13 May 61	409UNTS232	105888
Ivory Coast	USA (United States)	17 May 61	409UNTS241	105889
Niger	USA (United States)	26 May 61	410UNTS213	105905
Cameroon	USA (United States)	26 May 61	413UNTS195	105953
Dahomey	USA (United States)	27 May 61	445UNTS23	106373
Jamaica	UK Great Britain	01 Jun 61	478UNTS9	106932
Australia	USA (United States)	05 Jun 61	409UNTS279	105892
Czechoslovakia	Morocco	08 Jun 61	497UNTS275	107272
Nepal	USA (United States)	09 Jun 61	421UNTS223	106061
Cameroon	UN Special Fund	13 Jun 61	397UNTS297	105713
Ethiopia	United Nations	14 Jun 61	406UNTS81	105840
Cyprus	United Nations	15 Jun 61	398UNTS39	105716
Inter-Am Devel Bnk	USA (United States)	19 Jun 61	410UNTS34	105895
Paraguay	UN Special Fund	22 Jun 61	399UNTS117	105738
Madagascar	USA (United States)	22 Jun 61	413UNTS219	105956
UN Special Fund	Upper Volta	26 Jun 61	400UNTS3	105744

PARTY ONE	PARTY TWO	DATE	CITATION	NUMBER
Personnel (Cont.)				
Haiti	United Nations	28 Jun 61	399UNTS159	105740
Philippines	UN Special Fund	28 Jun 61	399UNTS141	105739
Haiti	UN Special Fund	28 Jun 61	399UNTS171	105741
Austria	Yugoslavia	30 Jun 61	443UNTS51	106358
Ghana	USA (United States)	19 Jul 61	416UNTS167	106002
Mali	UN Special Fund	21 Jul 61	401UNTS141	105768
Tanganyika	USA (United States)	21 Jul 61	445UNTS33	106374
Netherlands	Euratom	25 Jul 61	462UNTS263	106686
UN Special Fund	Yemen	02 Aug 61	402UNTS43	105777
Czechoslovakia	Ghana	02 Aug 61	465UNTS249	106730
Morocco	WHO (World Health)	09 Aug 61	412UNTS192	105932
Chile	USA (United States)	12 Aug 61	421UNTS209	106059
WHO (World Health)	Somalia	17 Aug 61	423UNTS111	106088
Mexico	United Nations	18 Aug 61	404UNTS297	105817
Lebanon	United Nations	26 Aug 61	406UNTS105	105842
Ivory Coast	UN Special Fund	29 Aug 61	406UNTS129	105844
Ghana	United Nations	29 Aug 61	406UNTS117	105843
Tunisia	USSR (Soviet Union)	30 Aug 61	437UNTS243	106310
Fed of Malaya	USA (United States)	04 Sep 61	421UNTS215	106060
Jordan	United Nations	11 Sep 61	406UNTS255	105855
Iraq	WHO (World Health)	13 Sep 61	419UNTS69	106030
Multilateral		20 Sep 61	407UNTS52	105859
Paraguay	USA (United States)	26 Sep 61	461UNTS91	106653
Dahomey	Israel	28 Sep 61	448UNTS151	106429
UN Special Fund	Sierra Leone	02 Oct 61	422UNTS131	106073
Japan	United Nations	04 Oct 61	410UNTS133	105900
Germany, West	Morocco	12 Oct 61	523UNTS289	107562
Malagasy	WHO (World Health)	13 Oct 61	421UNTS273	106064
Multilateral		16 Oct 61	410UNTS242	105908
Canada	USA (United States)	17 Oct 61	426UNTS201	106138
Belgium	Italy	28 Oct 61	429UNTS199	106199
Philippines	USA (United States)	31 Oct 61	424UNTS129	106105
Mauritania	UN Special Fund	07 Nov 61	412UNTS240	105936
Multilateral		07 Nov 61	412UNTS258	105937
Congo (Brazzaville)	UN Special Fund	09 Nov 61	413UNTS58	105940
Brazil	USA (United States)	11 Nov 61	433UNTS199	106243
United Arab Rep	UK Great Britain	14 Nov 61	449UNTS129	106455
El Salvador	USA (United States)	20 Nov 61	433UNTS221	106245
Czechoslovakia	Mali	27 Nov 61	466UNTS41	106736
Thailand	USA (United States)	28 Nov 61	434UNTS77	106256
OAS (Am States)	USA (United States)	29 Nov 61	424UNTS119	106104
Ceylon (Sri Lanka)	United Nations	04 Dec 61	415UNTS236	105987
Ethiopia	USA (United States)	06 Dec 61	433UNTS231	106246
UN Special Fund	Venezuela	11 Dec 61	422UNTS149	106074
Panama	USA (United States)	11 Dec 61	445UNTS161	106384
UN Special Fund	Senegal	16 Dec 61	425UNTS97	106121
Czechoslovakia	Guinea	16 Dec 61	559UNTS49	108154
El Salvador	USA (United States)	19 Dec 61	445UNTS175	106385
Iran	USA (United States)	21 Dec 61	433UNTS269	106249
Costa Rica	USA (United States)	22 Dec 61	460UNTS277	106646
Multilateral		27 Dec 61	425UNTS83	106120
Sierra Leone	USA (United States)	29 Dec 61	434UNTS43	106254
Ghana	USA (United States)	03 Jan 62	433UNTS147	106237
Malagasy	UN Special Fund	05 Jan 62	419UNTS29	106028
Dominican Republic	USA (United States)	11 Jan 62	433UNTS133	106236
Ethiopia	WHO (World Health)	11 Jan 62	423UNTS99	106087
Multilateral		17 Jan 62	419UNTS294	106033
Cyprus	USA (United States)	18 Jan 62	435UNTS3	106266
Multilateral		20 Jan 62	429UNTS230	200596
United Nations	Somalia	20 Jan 62	420UNTS133	106044
Ghana	USA (United States)	24 Jan 62	435UNTS23	106268
Peru	USA (United States)	25 Jan 62	473UNTS57	106855
Multilateral		13 Feb 62	422UNTS288	200594
Multilateral		21 Feb 62	423UNTS151	106091
UK Great Britain	USA (United States)	22 Feb 62	435UNTS127	106275

PARTY ONE	PARTY TWO	DATE	CITATION	NUMBER
Personnel (Cont.)				
Niger	UN Special Fund	26 Feb 62	423UNTS83	106086
Multilateral		01 Mar 62	423UNTS122	106089
Liberia	USA (United States)	08 Mar 62	445UNTS41	106375
USA (United States)	USSR (Soviet Union)	08 Mar 62	460UNTS3	106630
WHO (World Health)	Sudan	11 Mar 62	432UNTS325	106226
Nigeria	WHO (World Health)	27 Mar 62	429UNTS123	106194
Brazil	Japan	28 Mar 62	451UNTS125	106489
Nicaragua	USA (United States)	30 Mar 62	456UNTS241	106559
Belgium	France	30 Mar 62	502UNTS297	107335
India	Japan	31 Mar 62	451UNTS143	106490
Multilateral		10 Apr 62	429UNTS78	106192
Somalia	USA (United States)	17 Apr 62	436UNTS107	106291
Ecuador	USA (United States)	17 Apr 62	442UNTS69	106339
Multilateral		18 Apr 62	463UNTS44	106692
Ivory Coast	USA (United States)	21 Apr 62	526UNTS39	107598
UN Special Fund	Uruguay	04 May 62	429UNTS143	106196
Gabon	Israel	15 May 62	448UNTS211	106433
Multilateral		17 May 62	429UNTS46	106189
France	Romania	18 May 62	498UNTS115	107279
Ethiopia	USA (United States)	23 May 62	456UNTS293	106563
Ghana	Israel	25 May 62	515UNTS237	107461
Greece	Tunisia	26 May 62	534UNTS163	107761
Denmark	USA (United States)	28 May 62	450UNTS215	106469
Dominican Republic	UN Special Fund	06 Jun 62	429UNTS169	106197
Central Afri Rep	Israel	13 Jun 62	448UNTS265	106439
Libya	WHO (World Health)	16 Jun 62	437UNTS127	106301
WHO (World Health)	Sierra Leone	19 Jun 62	439UNTS151	106327
Bolivia	USA (United States)	19 Jun 62	458UNTS239	106606
Czechoslovakia	Senegal	20 Jun 62	498UNTS145	107280
Germany, West	Syria	25 Jun 62	489UNTS71	107135
Israel	Liberia	25 Jun 62	448UNTS287	106441
Congo (Zaire)	IAEA (Atom Energy)	27 Jun 62	463UNTS31	106691
Germany, West	United Nations	28 Jun 62	434UNTS249	200597
UN Special Fund	Syria	07 Jul 62	443UNTS3	106355
UN Special Fund	Tanganyika	17 Jul 62	435UNTS237	106281
Honduras	USA (United States)	20 Jul 62	460UNTS125	106635
Colombia	USA (United States)	23 Jul 62	458UNTS123	106595
Niger	USA (United States)	23 Jul 62	487UNTS325	107114
Ecuador	USA (United States)	03 Aug 62	460UNTS133	106636
WHO (World Health)	Senegal	06 Aug 62	435UNTS179	106279
Nigeria	United Nations	07 Aug 62	435UNTS167	106278
Multilateral		12 Aug 62	443UNTS266	106365
WHO (World Health)	Western Samoa	14 Aug 62	437UNTS317	200598
Nepal	USA (United States)	24 Aug 62	460UNTS143	106637
Turkey	USA (United States)	27 Aug 62	461UNTS55	106651
Cameroon	United Nations	29 Aug 62	442UNTS3	106334
Multilateral		29 Aug 62	443UNTS280	106366
Togo	USA (United States)	05 Sep 62	461UNTS47	106650
Afghanistan	USA (United States)	11 Sep 62	461UNTS169	106661
Ecuador	Germany, West	20 Sep 62	498UNTS199	107283
Austria	Czechoslovakia	22 Sep 62	495UNTS157	107244
Niger	United Nations	01 Oct 62	439UNTS181	106329
Chile	USA (United States)	04 Oct 62	461UNTS129	106656
Mali	USSR (Soviet Union)	10 Oct 62	493UNTS219	107216
Uganda	UK Great Britain	10 Oct 62	475UNTS177	106893
Belgium	Rwanda	13 Oct 62	456UNTS431	106569
Belgium	Rwanda	13 Oct 62	456UNTS425	106568
Czechoslovakia	Yugoslavia	22 Oct 62	480UNTS267	106974
Israel	Rwanda	23 Oct 62	515UNTS291	107466
Cameroon	Israel	24 Oct 62	449UNTS3	106446
Multilateral		25 Oct 62	457UNTS129	106582
Multilateral		25 Oct 62	457UNTS137	106583
United Nations	Western Samoa	05 Nov 62	443UNTS297	200599
Multilateral		15 Nov 62	448UNTS50	106424
Algeria	UN Special Fund	15 Nov 62	452UNTS243	106512

PARTY ONE	PARTY TWO	DATE	CITATION	NUMBER
Personnel (Cont.)				
WHO (World Health)	Syria	18 Nov 62	480UNTS249	106972
Germany, West	USA (United States)	20 Nov 62	505UNTS263	107377
Ceylon (Sri Lanka)	USA (United States)	21 Nov 62	462UNTS237	106683
Costa Rica	USA (United States)	23 Nov 62	541UNTS67	107861
Ecuador	United Nations	26 Nov 62	445UNTS3	106372
Rwanda	United Nations	28 Nov 62	450UNTS267	106473
Laos	USSR (Soviet Union)	01 Dec 62	472UNTS3	106834
Multilateral		06 Dec 62	450UNTS240	106471
Cameroon	WHO (World Health)	08 Dec 62	451UNTS215	106496
Ivory Coast	United Nations	10 Dec 62	451UNTS269	106498
Austria	Yugoslavia	11 Dec 62	546UNTS3	107938
Multilateral		12 Dec 62	457UNTS72	106578
Guinea	USA (United States)	14 Dec 62	462UNTS247	106684
Netherlands	Spain	17 Dec 62	499UNTS227	107301
Algeria	WHO (World Health)	20 Dec 62	463UNTS135	106698
India	United Nations	27 Dec 62	450UNTS3	106464
Guatemala	USA (United States)	29 Dec 62	474UNTS31	106869
Israel	United Nations	07 Jan 63	450UNTS229	106470
Ghana	Mali	09 Jan 63	466UNTS165	106742
Multilateral		15 Jan 63	456UNTS409	106567
UK Great Britain	USA (United States)	15 Jan 63	466UNTS181	106743
Senegal	USA (United States)	17 Jan 63	493UNTS97	107210
Multilateral		21 Jan 63	453UNTS20	106517
UK Great Britain	USSR (Soviet Union)	21 Jan 63	475UNTS3	106887
United Nations	South Pacific Com	24 Jan 63	470UNTS361	200604
New Zealand	Western Samoa	24 Jan 63	499UNTS21	107290
Malaysia	USA (United States)	28 Jan 63	473UNTS15	106850
Israel	Tanganyika	28 Jan 63	516UNTS39	107468
Austria	United Nations	29 Jan 63	452UNTS261	106513
Israel	Uganda	04 Feb 63	484UNTS273	107037
Multilateral		05 Feb 63	453UNTS36	106518
Mali	Senegal	07 Feb 63	524UNTS41	107565
United Nations	United Arab Rep	08 Feb 63	453UNTS79	106520
Central Afri Rep	USA (United States)	10 Feb 63	473UNTS83	106857
Multilateral		14 Feb 63	453UNTS168	106524
Norway	USA (United States)	01 Mar 63	524UNTS185	107573
Multilateral		06 Mar 63	455UNTS386	106552
Indonesia	USA (United States)	14 Mar 63	505UNTS79	107365
UN Special Fund	Uganda	22 Mar 63	456UNTS466	106572
Philippines	USA (United States)	23 Mar 63	474UNTS80	106873
Multilateral		18 Apr 63	463UNTS121	106697
Belgium	USA (United States)	19 Apr 63	476UNTS29	106900
Belgium	USA (United States)	19 Apr 63	493UNTS83	107209
Poland	USSR (Soviet Union)	22 Apr 63	493UNTS229	107217
Algeria	Morocco	30 Apr 63	564UNTS3	108217
Multilateral		06 May 63	463UNTS78	106694
Multilateral		09 May 63	463UNTS159	106700
Australia	United Nations	13 May 63	463UNTS187	106702
Denmark	India	15 May 63	616UNTS49	108891
Multilateral		22 May 63	483UNTS72	107007
Jamaica	UN Special Fund	22 May 63	489UNTS191	107140
Netherlands	UN Special Fund	24 May 63	466UNTS289	106750
Thailand	USA (United States)	24 May 63	477UNTS123	106918
Multilateral		24 May 63	466UNTS346	106754
UN Special Fund	Western Samoa	05 Jun 63	467UNTS463	200601
Australia	UK Great Britain	06 Jun 63	472UNTS157	106838
Korea, South	USA (United States)	18 Jun 63	487UNTS297	107112
India	USA (United States)	19 Jun 63	479UNTS175	106952
Mongolia	WHO (World Health)	21 Jun 63	472UNTS373	106848
Austria	USA (United States)	25 Jun 63	479UNTS223	106956
Algeria	Mali	22 Jul 63	564UNTS29	108219
Multilateral		23 Jul 63	471UNTS158	106831
Multilateral		31 Jul 63	472UNTS220	106842
USA (United States)	Uruguay	31 Jul 63	488UNTS3	107115
Burundi	WHO (World Health)	08 Aug 63	477UNTS346	106928

PARTY ONE	PARTY TWO	DATE	CITATION	NUMBER
Personnel (Cont.)				
Afghanistan	USA (United States)	20 Aug 63	488UNTS41	107118
Paraguay	USA (United States)	20 Aug 63	531UNTS197	107704
Argentina	USA (United States)	21 Aug 63	488UNTS61	107119
Burundi	UN Special Fund	22 Aug 63	476UNTS49	106903
Colombia	United Nations	27 Aug 63	481UNTS3	106975
Multilateral		27 Aug 63	511UNTS210	107435
Multilateral		10 Sep 63	480UNTS100	106965
Ecuador	USA (United States)	20 Sep 63	488UNTS147	107125
Jamaica	WHO (World Health)	25 Sep 63	481UNTS125	106980
Pakistan	USSR (Soviet Union)	07 Oct 63	499UNTS161	107297
UK Great Britain	USA (United States)	11 Oct 63	483UNTS3	107005
Italy	IAEA (Atom Energy)	11 Oct 63	639UNTS25	109142
Hungary	Yugoslavia	15 Oct 63	577UNTS49	108372
Multilateral		21 Oct 63	480UNTS197	106969
Czechoslovakia	Hungary	22 Oct 63	514UNTS95	107444
Iran	USA (United States)	24 Oct 63	489UNTS303	107146
Jamaica	USA (United States)	24 Oct 63	489UNTS337	107148
Multilateral		30 Oct 63	480UNTS180	106968
Central Afri Rep	UN Special Fund	30 Oct 63	481UNTS247	106985
Panama	USA (United States)	30 Oct 63	530UNTS3	107668
WHO (World Health)	Tanganyika	05 Nov 63	496UNTS193	107252
Multilateral		07 Nov 63	480UNTS232	106971
Multilateral		08 Nov 63	482UNTS286	106999
Tunisia	USA (United States)	18 Nov 63	494UNTS193	107233
Greece	USA (United States)	13 Dec 63	494UNTS55	107226
Cameroon	Netherlands	18 Dec 63	521UNTS303	107527
Laos	UK Great Britain	24 Dec 63	502UNTS189	107330
Australia	USA (United States)	03 Jan 64	505UNTS159	107371
Mali	Niger	15 Jan 64	499UNTS197	107299
Multilateral		28 Jan 64	502UNTS321	107336
Iceland	USA (United States)	13 Feb 64	524UNTS235	107576
Multilateral		20 Feb 64	491UNTS30	107172
USA (United States)	USSR (Soviet Union)	22 Feb 64	526UNTS131	107605
UNESCO (Educ/Cult)	Yugoslavia	27 Feb 64	489UNTS257	107143
Multilateral		28 Feb 64	501UNTS245	107321
Netherlands	Tunisia	03 Mar 64	533UNTS133	107739
Israel	Philippines	16 Mar 64	550UNTS269	108021
Italy	United Nations	18 Mar 64	491UNTS21	107171
Germany, West	Thailand	02 Apr 64	503UNTS3	107338
Taiwan	USA (United States)	23 Apr 64	524UNTS141	107570
Afghanistan	United Nations	28 Apr 64	494UNTS77	107227
Liberia	USA (United States)	08 May 64	526UNTS239	107608
Ireland	UN Special Fund	03 Jun 64	496UNTS205	107253
UK Great Britain	USA (United States)	19 Jun 64	530UNTS99	107675
Rwanda	WHO (World Health)	22 Jun 64	514UNTS11	107440
Rwanda	WHO (World Health)	23 Jun 64	514UNTS157	107445
Multilateral		23 Jun 64	506UNTS108	107383
WHO (World Health)	Trinidad/Tobago	23 Jun 64	503UNTS167	107342
Multilateral		28 Jun 64	519UNTS14	107499
United Nations	Togo	03 Jul 64	502UNTS287	107334
Colombia	Netherlands	06 Jul 64	543UNTS289	107906
Belgium	Tunisia	15 Jul 64	560UNTS65	108169
Belgium	Tunisia	15 Jul 64	560UNTS57	108168
Spain	USA (United States)	16 Jul 64	529UNTS187	107661
Taiwan	Philippines	25 Aug 64	511UNTS233	107436
Kenya	USA (United States)	26 Aug 64	531UNTS51	107692
Australia	USA (United States)	28 Aug 64	510UNTS201	107415
Dominican Republic	USA (United States)	28 Aug 64	531UNTS35	107691
Ceylon (Sri Lanka)	USA (United States)	29 Aug 64	531UNTS93	107695
Philippines	United Nations	15 Sep 64	510UNTS137	107410
Algeria	United Nations	23 Sep 64	510UNTS217	107416
Argentina	Paraguay	21 Oct 64	635UNTS177	109081
Multilateral		24 Oct 64	514UNTS220	200608
Ethiopia	Netherlands	28 Oct 64	541UNTS235	107872
Netherlands	Pakistan	30 Oct 64	541UNTS243	107873

PARTY ONE	PARTY TWO	DATE	CITATION	NUMBER
Personnel (Cont.)				
Multilateral		07 Nov 64	548UNTS3	107965
USA (United States)	Yugoslavia	09 Nov 64	533UNTS39	107731
Multilateral		11 Nov 64	515UNTS94	107456
Israel	Turkey	13 Nov 64	550UNTS303	108025
Netherlands	Norway	17 Nov 64	579UNTS243	108412
Multilateral		25 Nov 64	587UNTS19	108507
Ghana	Israel	30 Nov 64	550UNTS231	108019
Multilateral		11 Dec 64	547UNTS297	107964
India	Netherlands	11 Dec 64	570UNTS165	108292
Germany, West	Jamaica	16 Dec 64	531UNTS129	107699
Germany, West	Thailand	23 Dec 64	525UNTS185	107590
Malawi	WHO (World Health)	06 Jan 65	525UNTS165	107588
Malawi	WHO (World Health)	08 Jan 65	524UNTS281	107579
Ecuador	Netherlands	14 Jan 65	551UNTS129	108038
Multilateral		27 Jan 65	523UNTS102	107556
Peru	USA (United States)	28 Jan 65	587UNTS273	108513
Multilateral		02 Feb 65	523UNTS256	107560
Belgium	Congo (Zaire)	06 Feb 65	540UNTS275	107853
Multilateral		12 Feb 65	525UNTS148	107587
UK Great Britain	USSR (Soviet Union)	13 Feb 65	543UNTS43	107896
Iran	United Nations	16 Feb 65	525UNTS211	107593
Mexico	USA (United States)	27 Feb 65	542UNTS181	107889
Multilateral		18 Mar 65	575UNTS159	108359
Austria	Hungary	09 Apr 65	638UNTS53	109131
Malawi	USA (United States)	20 Apr 65	546UNTS175	107943
Netherlands	Tanzania	27 Apr 65	594UNTS123	108599
UK Great Britain	USA (United States)	10 May 65	545UNTS181	107934
Multilateral		02 Jun 65	551UNTS2	108030
Multilateral		02 Jun 65	537UNTS348	200611
Ivory Coast	Netherlands	03 Jun 65	634UNTS95	109054
UN Special Fund	Spain	30 Jun 65	544UNTS159	107918
Multilateral		05 Jul 65	563UNTS104	108207
Israel	Sierra Leone	22 Aug 65	550UNTS285	108023
Poland	WHO (World Health)	26 Aug 65	552UNTS3	108047
Multilateral		13 Sep 65	547UNTS264	107962
Multilateral		21 Oct 65	547UNTS216	107959
United Nations	United Arab Rep	26 Nov 65	551UNTS253	108046
Monaco	United Nations	17 Dec 65	550UNTS365	200615
Austria	Tunisia	30 Dec 65	589UNTS119	108539
Multilateral		31 Dec 65	552UNTS292	108060
United Nations	Senegal	12 Jan 66	551UNTS147	108039
Finland	USSR (Soviet Union)	24 Jan 66	576UNTS35	108364
Mongolia	UN Special Fund	26 Jan 66	552UNTS201	108055
Panama	USA (United States)	15 Feb 66	586UNTS27	108494
Israel	Kenya	25 Feb 66	582UNTS23	108455
Brazil	Denmark	25 Feb 66	590UNTS95	108549
WHO (World Health)	Singapore	28 Mar 66	562UNTS59	108195
Spain	USA (United States)	14 Apr 66	579UNTS173	108406
Italy	United Nations	23 May 66	565UNTS11	108231
Bulgaria	UN Special Fund	26 May 66	563UNTS71	108205
Malawi	UK Great Britain	19 Jul 66	637UNTS0	109125
United Nations	Tunisia	04 Aug 66	576UNTS23	108363
Tunisia	USA (United States)	26 Sep 66	616UNTS259	108900
Botswana	United Nations	30 Sep 66	576UNTS17	108362
Botswana	UK Great Britain	30 Sep 66	633UNTS339	109044
United Nations	Sudan	08 Nov 66	576UNTS85	108365
Malawi	UK Great Britain	21 Nov 66	637UNTS0	109126
UK Great Britain	USA (United States)	01 Jan 67	604UNTS3	108738
Finland	United Nations	16 Jan 67	588UNTS153	108522
Denmark	Tanzania	05 Apr 67	603UNTS111	108728
Denmark	Tanzania	05 Apr 67	604UNTS19	108740
Ghana	United Nations	08 Apr 67	594UNTS149	108601
Multilateral		14 Jun 67	603UNTS2	108719
Cameroon	UK Great Britain	16 Jun 67	618UNTS329	108933
Multilateral		20 Jun 67	0UNTS0	109290

PARTY ONE	PARTY TWO	DATE	CITATION	NUMBER
Personnel (Cont.)				
Multilateral		21 Jun 67	598UNTS2	108653
South Africa	Switzerland	03 Jul 67	643UNTS3	109184
Italy	Romania	08 Aug 67	642UNTS213	109175
Multilateral		12 Oct 67	607UNTS2	108792
India	United Nations	04 Nov 67	609UNTS3	108824
United Nations	Senegal	08 Nov 67	613UNTS255	108854
Multilateral		14 Nov 67	614UNTS2	108860
Chile	Denmark	15 Dec 67	643UNTS293	109199
Iran	United Nations	15 Feb 68	631UNTS103	108990
United Nations	Tunisia	18 Mar 68	633UNTS3	109030
State/IGO Group	Nigeria	20 Apr 68	636UNTS294	109106
Niger	United Nations	07 May 68	639UNTS71	109145
State/IGO Group	Malaysia	10 May 68	636UNTS276	109105
Post-colonial administration				
Multilateral		30 Jul 40	161UNTS253	200488
Ceylon (Sri Lanka)	UK Great Britain	11 Nov 47	86UNTS31	101150
Norway	IAEA (Atom Energy)	10 Apr 61	402UNTS255	105790
Tanganyika	UK Great Britain	14 Mar 62	449UNTS147	106456
Indonesia	Netherlands	15 Aug 62	437UNTS273	106311
Lesotho	UK Great Britain	17 Feb 67	632UNTS3	109004
Algeria	France	26 Dec 67	0UNTS0	109509
Immovable property				
Canada	USA (United States)	08 Jun 44	124UNTS297	200427
Denmark	UK Great Britain	06 Dec 45	5UNTS3	100061
Greece	UK Great Britain	21 Mar 46	91UNTS149	101247
Argentina	UK Great Britain	17 Sep 46	88UNTS47	101185
Taiwan	Saudi Arabia	15 Nov 46	18UNTS197	100289
Luxembourg	UK Great Britain	11 Dec 46	11UNTS167	100155
Muscat and Oman	UK Great Britain	05 Apr 47	27UNTS287	100412
Australia	Denmark	08 Oct 48	22UNTS43	100330
Italy	Yugoslavia	03 Feb 49	33UNTS105	100517
India	Pakistan	23 Apr 49	54UNTS51	100795
Denmark	Poland	12 May 49	87UNTS179	101172
Norway	USA (United States)	13 Jun 49	127UNTS189	101705
Norway	USA (United States)	13 Jun 49	127UNTS163	101704
Ireland	USA (United States)	13 Sep 49	127UNTS119	101702
Afghanistan	India	04 Apr 50	167UNTS105	102201
India	Pakistan	08 Apr 50	131UNTS3	101733
Switzerland	USA (United States)	24 May 51	127UNTS227	101706
UK Great Britain	USA (United States)	06 Jun 51	165UNTS121	102174
Multilateral		02 Jul 51	189UNTS137	102545
Denmark	USA (United States)	01 Oct 51	421UNTS105	106056
Netherlands	Switzerland	12 Nov 51	126UNTS157	101688
Netherlands	Switzerland	12 Nov 51	126UNTS173	101689
Germany, West	Netherlands	18 Jan 52	179UNTS147	102364
India	Philippines	11 Jul 52	203UNTS73	102741
India	Muscat and Oman	15 Mar 53	190UNTS69	102559
Austria	Yugoslavia	19 Mar 53	467UNTS323	106768
Austria	Yugoslavia	19 Mar 53	467UNTS293	106767
Multilateral		28 Sep 54	360UNTS117	105158
Netherlands	USA (United States)	14 Dec 54	262UNTS35	103737
Nicaragua	USA (United States)	21 Jan 56	367UNTS3	105224
Philippines	Switzerland	30 Aug 56	293UNTS43	104284
Germany, East	Poland	01 Feb 57	319UNTS115	104632
Japan	Norway	28 Feb 57	280UNTS87	104054
Czechoslovakia	USSR (Soviet Union)	31 Aug 57	308UNTS3	104456
Germany, East	USSR (Soviet Union)	28 Nov 57	305UNTS113	104419
Bulgaria	USSR (Soviet Union)	12 Dec 57	317UNTS217	104606
Korea, North	USSR (Soviet Union)	16 Dec 57	301UNTS301	104349
Poland	USSR (Soviet Union)	28 Dec 57	320UNTS3	104638
Romania	USSR (Soviet Union)	03 Apr 58	313UNTS167	104535
Hungary	USSR (Soviet Union)	15 Jul 58	322UNTS3	104656
Mongolia	USSR (Soviet Union)	25 Aug 58	322UNTS105	104657
Japan	Yugoslavia	28 Feb 59	341UNTS179	104883

PARTY ONE	PARTY TWO	DATE	CITATION	NUMBER
Immovable property (Cont.)				
Germany, West	Pakistan	25 Nov 59	457UNTS22	106575
Albania	Hungary	12 Jan 60	520UNTS3	107511
Multilateral		13 Dec 60	523UNTS117	107557
Czechoslovakia	Poland	04 Jul 61	436UNTS189	106295
Czechoslovakia	Hungary	02 Nov 61	438UNTS3	106313
Bulgaria	Poland	04 Dec 61	484UNTS3	107019
Germany, West	Israel	09 Jul 62	630UNTS87	108968
Czechoslovakia	Hungary	16 Oct 62	479UNTS301	106961
Japan	UK Great Britain	14 Nov 62	478UNTS29	106934
Multilateral		14 Nov 63	619UNTS299	108948
Taiwan	USA (United States)	23 Apr 64	524UNTS141	107570
Greece	India	11 Feb 65	606UNTS9	108771
Austria	Hungary	09 Apr 65	638UNTS105	109132
Denmark	Italy	10 Mar 66	643UNTS349	109201
Denmark	Netherlands	31 Mar 66	604UNTS209	108751
Austria	Ireland	24 May 66	636UNTS149	109102
Argentina	Germany, West	13 Jul 66	636UNTS3	109091
Netherlands	Norway	22 Sep 66	600UNTS227	108683
Singapore	UK Great Britain	01 Dec 66	605UNTS153	108763
Austria	Spain	20 Dec 66	636UNTS197	109103
Trinidad/Tobago	UK Great Britain	29 Dec 66	605UNTS237	108766
South Africa	Switzerland	03 Jul 67	643UNTS3	109184
General property				
Canada	France	12 May 33	253UNTS285	200545
Ecuador	USA (United States)	24 Feb 42	26UNTS379	200157
Brazil	USA (United States)	14 Mar 42	102UNTS195	200302
Haiti	USA (United States)	07 Apr 42	106UNTS319	200349
El Salvador	USA (United States)	05 May 42	21UNTS215	200124
Honduras	USA (United States)	08 May 42	166UNTS351	200498
Peru	USA (United States)	11 May 42	136UNTS353	200447
Nicaragua	USA (United States)	22 May 42	105UNTS141	200328
Paraguay	USA (United States)	22 May 42	124UNTS243	200423
Colombia	USA (United States)	23 Oct 42	105UNTS109	200326
Taiwan	USA (United States)	11 Jan 43	10UNTS261	200066
USA (United States)	Venezuela	18 Feb 43	21UNTS225	200125
Panama	USA (United States)	02 Mar 43	107UNTS55	200351
Chile	USA (United States)	11 May 43	139UNTS295	200456
Mexico	USA (United States)	01 Jul 43	28UNTS407	200164
Dominican Republic	USA (United States)	07 Jul 43	28UNTS419	200165
Belgium	Taiwan	20 Oct 43	14UNTS376	200095
USA (United States)	Uruguay	01 Nov 43	106UNTS311	200348
Brazil	USA (United States)	25 Nov 43	102UNTS227	200305
Liberia	USA (United States)	31 Dec 43	106UNTS199	200341
Multilateral		15 Jan 44	161UNTS281	200489
Canada	Taiwan	14 Apr 44	14UNTS408	200097
Peru	USA (United States)	15 Apr 44	150UNTS317	200479
Norway	USA (United States)	16 May 44	67UNTS253	200223
Canada	USA (United States)	07 Jun 44	99UNTS259	200280
Multilateral		02 Aug 44	67UNTS221	200221
Netherlands	UK Great Britain	02 Oct 44	231UNTS317	200535
Multilateral		28 Oct 44	123UNTS223	200414
Ecuador	USA (United States)	22 Jan 45	24UNTS273	200152
Taiwan	Netherlands	29 May 45	2UNTS307	200023
Canada	USA (United States)	06 Sep 45	99UNTS281	200282
Dominican Republic	USA (United States)	13 Oct 45	149UNTS361	200477
Denmark	UK Great Britain	06 Dec 45	5UNTS3	100061
Multilateral		27 Dec 45	2UNTS39	100020
Poland	Yugoslavia	02 Jan 46	115UNTS21	101556
Mexico	UK Great Britain	07 Feb 46	6UNTS55	100068
Netherlands	USA (United States)	11 Feb 46	3UNTS37	100023
Czechoslovakia	Poland	12 Feb 46	25UNTS207	100364
Brazil	USA (United States)	15 Feb 46	162UNTS21	102130
Taiwan	France	28 Feb 46	14UNTS113	100215
Belgium	UK Great Britain	11 Mar 46	26UNTS167	100387

PARTY ONE	PARTY TWO	DATE	CITATION	NUMBER
General property (Cont.)				
Taiwan	Switzerland	13 Mar 46	14UNTS159	100218
Greece	UK Great Britain	21 Mar 46	91UNTS149	101247
Canada	USA (United States)	30 Mar 46	7UNTS15	100089
Brazil	USA (United States)	05 Apr 46	12UNTS131	100183
Poland	USA (United States)	22 Apr 46	406UNTS215	105851
League of Nations	ILO (Labor Org)	04 May 46	19UNTS187	200114
Turkey	USA (United States)	07 May 46	6UNTS293	100083
India	USA (United States)	16 May 46	4UNTS183	100045
Greece	USA (United States)	16 May 46	184UNTS230	102451
Taiwan	Denmark	20 May 46	12UNTS59	100180
France	USA (United States)	28 May 46	84UNTS151	101125
France	USA (United States)	28 May 46	84UNTS79	101120
France	USA (United States)	28 May 46	84UNTS59	101119
Australia	USA (United States)	07 Jun 46	4UNTS237	100048
United Nations	Switzerland	01 Jul 46	1UNTS153	200007
Philippines	USA (United States)	04 Jul 46	7UNTS3	100088
New Zealand	USA (United States)	10 Jul 46	6UNTS341	100087
Multilateral		18 Jul 46	125UNTS119	101674
League of Nations	United Nations	19 Jul 46	1UNTS109	200002
Hungary	USA (United States)	09 Aug 46	148UNTS313	101941
Denmark	USSR (Soviet Union)	17 Aug 46	8UNTS201	100124
Philippines	USA (United States)	11 Sep 46	43UNTS231	100670
Greece	USA (United States)	08 Oct 46	180UNTS119	102379
Denmark	South Africa	14 Oct 46	10UNTS29	100140
Czechoslovakia	USA (United States)	14 Nov 46	7UNTS119	100094
Luxembourg	UK Great Britain	11 Dec 46	11UNTS167	100155
Denmark	India	20 Dec 46	7UNTS309	100107
Australia	Netherlands	24 Jan 47	10UNTS77	100144
Multilateral		10 Feb 47	48UNTS203	100746
Multilateral		10 Feb 47	41UNTS21	100643
Multilateral		10 Feb 47	41UNTS135	100644
Philippines	USA (United States)	14 Mar 47	43UNTS271	100673
Belgium	Czechoslovakia	19 Mar 47	23UNTS35	100341
South Africa	USA (United States)	21 Mar 47	16UNTS47	100248
Australia	Norway	24 Mar 47	18UNTS185	100288
Taiwan	Portugal	01 Apr 47	14UNTS177	100220
Taiwan	Philippines	18 Apr 47	11UNTS361	100175
Philippines	USA (United States)	12 May 47	16UNTS109	100252
Honduras	USA (United States)	13 May 47	166UNTS159	102189
Netherlands	USA (United States)	28 May 47	17UNTS29	100267
Austria	USA (United States)	21 Jun 47	67UNTS99	100869
Belgium	United Arab Rep	01 Jul 47	34UNTS93	100529
Belgium	South Africa	04 Jul 47	47UNTS9	100720
Australia	France	28 Jul 47	97UNTS271	101353
Taiwan	Italy	30 Jul 47	12UNTS383	100195
Italy	USA (United States)	14 Aug 47	36UNTS105	100567
Greece	UNICEF (Children)	14 Oct 47	102UNTS39	101409
Burma	UK Great Britain	17 Oct 47	70UNTS183	100904
Ecuador	USA (United States)	14 Nov 47	149UNTS297	101959
France	Lebanon	24 Jan 48	173UNTS99	102263
Cuba	USA (United States)	27 Jan 48	67UNTS3	100862
Italy	USA (United States)	02 Feb 48	79UNTS171	101040
Greece	United Nations	12 Feb 48	47UNTS223	100732
Denmark	Guatemala	04 Mar 48	96UNTS223	101339
France	United Nations	10 Mar 48	47UNTS203	100731
Paraguay	USA (United States)	12 Mar 48	162UNTS30	102131
Canada	France	05 May 48	231UNTS87	103209
Multilateral		10 May 48	140UNTS129	101887
Ecuador	USA (United States)	14 May 48	89UNTS71	101210
Finland	United Nations	20 May 48	47UNTS319	200189
Philippines	Spain	20 May 48	70UNTS143	100903
Multilateral		19 Jun 48	310UNTS151	104492
USA (United States)	Yugoslavia	19 Jul 48	89UNTS43	101208
USA (United States)	Yugoslavia	19 Jul 48	34UNTS195	100537
Pakistan	United Nations	27 Aug 48	47UNTS269	100734

PARTY ONE	PARTY TWO	DATE	CITATION	NUMBER
General property (Cont.)				
Korea, South	USA (United States)	11 Sep 48	89UNTS155	101216
Greece	Italy	21 Sep 48	77UNTS259	101003
United Nations	Thailand	05 Oct 48	47UNTS287	100735
Greece	Lebanon	06 Oct 48	87UNTS351	101179
United Nations	San Marino	07 Oct 48	47UNTS337	200190
Czechoslovakia	United Nations	07 Oct 48	47UNTS185	100730
Australia	Denmark	08 Oct 48	22UNTS43	100330
Australia	Belgium	09 Dec 48	25UNTS159	100361
Italy	USA (United States)	18 Dec 48	79UNTS133	101037
Poland	UK Great Britain	14 Jan 49	83UNTS51	101101
Mexico	USA (United States)	25 Jan 49	99UNTS3	101367
Italy	Yugoslavia	03 Feb 49	33UNTS105	100517
Multilateral		28 Feb 49	29UNTS53	100434
France	USA (United States)	14 Mar 49	84UNTS237	101133
United Nations	UK Great Britain	18 Mar 49	47UNTS305	100736
India	Pakistan	23 Apr 49	54UNTS51	100795
Denmark	Poland	12 May 49	87UNTS179	101172
Ethiopia	USA (United States)	20 May 49	89UNTS99	101211
Italy	Yugoslavia	23 May 49	150UNTS179	101972
Norway	USA (United States)	25 May 49	32UNTS345	100507
Philippines	Thailand	14 Jun 49	81UNTS53	101062
Multilateral		12 Aug 49	75UNTS31	100970
Multilateral		12 Aug 49	75UNTS287	100973
Mexico	USA (United States)	15 Aug 49	66UNTS13	100846
Greece	Italy	31 Aug 49	78UNTS89	101014
Czechoslovakia	UK Great Britain	28 Sep 49	86UNTS161	101157
United Arab Rep	USA (United States)	03 Nov 49	71UNTS31	100908
Ireland	USA (United States)	21 Jan 50	206UNTS269	102792
India	USA (United States)	02 Feb 50	89UNTS127	101214
Australia	Yugoslavia	22 Feb 50	51UNTS201	100766
Philippines	USA (United States)	16 Mar 50	89UNTS199	101218
Canada	Yugoslavia	29 Mar 50	230UNTS357	103195
Israel	UK Great Britain	30 Mar 50	86UNTS231	101162
Afghanistan	India	04 Apr 50	167UNTS105	102201
India	Pakistan	08 Apr 50	131UNTS3	101733
El Salvador	WHO (World Health)	21 Apr 50	103UNTS13	101420
Australia	Netherlands	26 Apr 50	54UNTS83	100796
Korea, South	USA (United States)	28 Apr 50	93UNTS21	101284
Austria	USA (United States)	06 Jun 50	92UNTS201	101273
Thailand	USA (United States)	01 Jul 50	81UNTS61	101063
Multilateral		04 Nov 50	213UNTS221	102889
Burma	USA (United States)	06 Nov 50	122UNTS81	101638
Switzerland	UK Great Britain	08 Dec 50	175UNTS55	102295
Germany, West	Netherlands	14 Dec 50	87UNTS257	101177
Brazil	Netherlands	15 Dec 50	123UNTS101	101657
Italy	Yugoslavia	23 Dec 50	150UNTS199	101974
Norway	USA (United States)	28 Dec 50	240UNTS391	103414
Chile	USA (United States)	16 Jan 51	147UNTS11	101925
Nicaragua	USA (United States)	31 Jan 51	150UNTS3	101960
New Zealand	Yugoslavia	27 Feb 51	150UNTS165	101971
Dominican Republic	USA (United States)	16 Mar 51	148UNTS15	101932
Greece	India	18 Apr 51	166UNTS305	102195
Canada	USA (United States)	18 Apr 51	134UNTS205	101800
Honduras	USA (United States)	24 Apr 51	140UNTS287	101894
Jordan	UK Great Britain	01 May 51	117UNTS19	101582
UK Great Britain	USA (United States)	06 Jun 51	165UNTS121	102174
Costa Rica	WHO (World Health)	14 Jun 51	102UNTS151	101418
Saudi Arabia	USA (United States)	18 Jun 51	102UNTS73	101412
Italy	UK Great Britain	28 Jun 51	118UNTS115	101600
Multilateral		02 Jul 51	189UNTS137	102545
Canada	France	04 Jul 51	233UNTS101	103253
Burma	WHO (World Health)	09 Jul 51	107UNTS9	101463
Multilateral		10 Jul 51	108UNTS287	101481
Multilateral		01 Aug 51	107UNTS19	101464
Multilateral		04 Aug 51	104UNTS197	101441

PARTY ONE	PARTY TWO	DATE	CITATION	NUMBER
General property (Cont.)				
Iraq	USA (United States)	16 Aug 51	147UNTS65	101929
Israel	USA (United States)	23 Aug 51	219UNTS237	102979
Denmark	USA (United States)	23 Aug 51	147UNTS49	101928
Pakistan	United Arab Rep	28 Aug 51	214UNTS247	102902
Japan	USA (United States)	28 Aug 51	147UNTS81	101930
France	USSR (Soviet Union)	03 Sep 51	221UNTS79	103003
Ethiopia	USA (United States)	07 Sep 51	206UNTS41	102785
Multilateral		08 Sep 51	136UNTS45	101832
Korea, South	WHO (World Health)	19 Sep 51	109UNTS297	200366
Australia	France	28 Sep 51	161UNTS185	102128
Denmark	USA (United States)	01 Oct 51	421UNTS105	106056
WHO (World Health)	Thailand	04 Oct 51	109UNTS77	101492
Taiwan	WHO (World Health)	25 Oct 51	126UNTS77	101683
India	WHO (World Health)	01 Nov 51	118UNTS13	101593
Italy	UK Great Britain	07 Nov 51	118UNTS133	101601
Panama	WHO (World Health)	09 Nov 51	118UNTS43	101595
Guatemala	WHO (World Health)	17 Dec 51	120UNTS133	101619
Italy	USA (United States)	28 Dec 51	157UNTS63	102047
Guatemala	WHO (World Health)	29 Dec 51	124UNTS89	101668
Indonesia	USA (United States)	05 Jan 52	215UNTS121	102916
Costa Rica	WHO (World Health)	23 Jan 52	135UNTS265	101826
UNICEF (Children)	UK Great Britain	04 Feb 52	120UNTS147	101620
Jordan	USA (United States)	12 Feb 52	168UNTS25	102211
Italy	UK Great Britain	12 Feb 52	126UNTS297	101695
Dominican Republic	WHO (World Health)	15 Feb 52	134UNTS291	101808
Dominican Republic	UNICEF (Children)	15 Feb 52	121UNTS43	101625
India	WHO (World Health)	02 Apr 52	131UNTS227	101743
Denmark	Netherlands	08 May 52	131UNTS91	101737
Israel	USA (United States)	09 May 52	177UNTS63	102309
Ethiopia	USA (United States)	15 May 52	180UNTS227	102388
Iraq	UK Great Britain	22 May 52	175UNTS97	102298
Australia	Italy	24 May 52	161UNTS65	102123
Brazil	USA (United States)	02 Jun 52	181UNTS109	102403
Burma	WHO (World Health)	09 Jun 52	134UNTS273	101806
Norway	USA (United States)	21 Jun 52	236UNTS9	103313
Chile	USA (United States)	30 Jun 52	199UNTS241	102688
Panama	USA (United States)	30 Jun 52	181UNTS121	102404
Austria	UK Great Britain	30 Jun 52	138UNTS153	101867
Finland	USA (United States)	02 Jul 52	165UNTS203	102177
India	Philippines	11 Jul 52	203UNTS73	102741
Germany, West	USA (United States)	18 Jul 52	165UNTS167	102175
Germany, West	Greece	28 Jul 52	182UNTS85	102424
Multilateral		28 Aug 52	175UNTS69	102296
Italy	Netherlands	22 Sep 52	150UNTS113	101965
Chile	WHO (World Health)	24 Oct 52	151UNTS339	102004
Chile	WHO (World Health)	04 Nov 52	150UNTS119	101966
Ceylon (Sri Lanka)	USA (United States)	17 Nov 52	180UNTS207	102386
India	WHO (World Health)	11 Dec 52	158UNTS391	102073
Saudi Arabia	USA (United States)	15 Dec 52	185UNTS67	102459
Liberia	USA (United States)	15 Dec 52	185UNTS45	102457
Greece	Spain	03 Feb 53	225UNTS3	103081
United Arab Rep	USA (United States)	12 Mar 53	204UNTS3	102747
India	Muscat and Oman	15 Mar 53	190UNTS69	102559
Austria	Yugoslavia	19 Mar 53	467UNTS323	106768
United Arab Rep	USA (United States)	19 Mar 53	215UNTS17	102909
Japan	USA (United States)	02 Apr 53	206UNTS143	102788
Ethiopia	USA (United States)	29 Apr 53	224UNTS121	103073
Multilateral		30 Apr 53	175UNTS89	102297
Germany, West	Italy	05 May 53	267UNTS9	103835
United Arab Rep	USA (United States)	21 May 53	204UNTS29	102748
Colombia	USA (United States)	09 Jun 53	213UNTS3	102877
United Arab Rep	USA (United States)	18 Jun 53	215UNTS45	102910
United Arab Rep	USA (United States)	18 Jun 53	204UNTS55	102749
Liberia	USA (United States)	23 Jun 53	213UNTS57	102880
Liberia	USA (United States)	23 Jun 53	213UNTS37	102879

PARTY ONE	PARTY TWO	DATE	CITATION	NUMBER
General property (Cont.)				
Brazil	USA (United States)	26 Jun 53	336UNTS241	104808
Panama	USA (United States)	26 Jun 53	215UNTS77	102912
Chile	USA (United States)	27 Jun 53	229UNTS53	103160
Chile	USA (United States)	27 Jun 53	229UNTS193	103167
Saudi Arabia	USA (United States)	29 Jun 53	206UNTS23	102784
Afghanistan	USA (United States)	30 Jun 53	215UNTS3	102908
India	UK Great Britain	20 Jul 53	196UNTS251	102628
Libya	UK Great Britain	29 Jul 53	186UNTS201	102492
Belgium	USA (United States)	02 Sep 53	200UNTS127	102700
Belgium	USA (United States)	17 Nov 53	251UNTS105	103536
Chile	USA (United States)	30 Dec 53	236UNTS41	103315
France	Sweden	16 Feb 54	228UNTS137	103147
Italy	USA (United States)	31 Mar 54	235UNTS293	103311
Luxembourg	USA (United States)	17 Apr 54	257UNTS255	103661
Ethiopia	USA (United States)	21 Apr 54	232UNTS299	103244
Canada	USA (United States)	03 May 54	221UNTS339	103015
Netherlands	USA (United States)	07 May 54	213UNTS325	102895
Greece	Hungary	05 Jun 54	299UNTS285	104320
Ethiopia	USA (United States)	12 Jun 54	234UNTS25	103270
Jordan	USA (United States)	17 Jun 54	266UNTS137	103828
Ecuador	USA (United States)	30 Jun 54	236UNTS163	103323
Multilateral		30 Jun 54	193UNTS67	102611
Multilateral		08 Jul 54	287UNTS27	104178
Hungary	UK Great Britain	19 Aug 54	199UNTS149	102681
Thailand	USA (United States)	01 Sep 54	237UNTS209	103347
Multilateral		28 Sep 54	360UNTS117	105158
Ethiopia	Sweden	13 Oct 54	202UNTS273	102734
Multilateral		23 Oct 54	332UNTS3	104760
Multilateral		23 Oct 54	332UNTS157	104761
Germany, West	USA (United States)	29 Oct 54	273UNTS3	103943
Poland	UK Great Britain	11 Nov 54	204UNTS137	102755
India	Iran	15 Dec 54	327UNTS245	104724
Italy	Yugoslavia	18 Dec 54	284UNTS239	104141
Peru	USA (United States)	31 Dec 54	251UNTS51	103533
Chile	USA (United States)	31 Mar 55	262UNTS19	103736
Germany, West	USA (United States)	04 Apr 55	279UNTS73	104034
Austria	UK Great Britain	15 May 55	344UNTS9	104940
Multilateral		15 May 55	217UNTS223	102949
Turkey	USA (United States)	26 May 55	262UNTS97	103739
Luxembourg	USA (United States)	15 Jun 55	264UNTS279	103798
Turkey	USA (United States)	29 Jun 55	269UNTS97	103878
Brazil	USA (United States)	03 Aug 55	270UNTS71	103893
Iran	USA (United States)	15 Aug 55	284UNTS93	104132
Finland	USSR (Soviet Union)	19 Sep 55	226UNTS187	103113
Bulgaria	UK Great Britain	22 Sep 55	222UNTS349	103039
Colombia	USA (United States)	18 Nov 55	239UNTS173	103377
Nicaragua	USA (United States)	21 Jan 56	367UNTS3	105224
Czechoslovakia	Yugoslavia	11 Feb 56	397UNTS135	105703
Canada	USSR (Soviet Union)	29 Feb 56	252UNTS165	103566
Multilateral		13 Mar 56	427UNTS245	106158
Colombia	USA (United States)	14 Mar 56	271UNTS303	103922
Germany, West	Sweden	22 Mar 56	262UNTS361	103761
Netherlands	USA (United States)	27 Mar 56	285UNTS231	104154
Argentina	Italy	23 May 56	267UNTS255	103846
Hungary	UK Great Britain	27 Jun 56	249UNTS19	103499
Poland	USA (United States)	28 Jun 56	273UNTS79	103944
Guatemala	Honduras	22 Aug 56	263UNTS49	103767
Greece	Romania	25 Aug 56	299UNTS231	104315
Philippines	Switzerland	30 Aug 56	293UNTS43	104284
Denmark	WHO (World Health)	03 Sep 56	258UNTS103	103674
Ecuador	USA (United States)	31 Oct 56	283UNTS151	104114
UK Great Britain	USA (United States)	01 Nov 56	264UNTS3	103785
Argentina	USA (United States)	05 Nov 56	277UNTS143	104004
UK Great Britain	USA (United States)	27 Nov 56	282UNTS43	104092
Korea, South	USA (United States)	28 Nov 56	302UNTS281	104367
General property (Cont.)				
Colombia	USA (United States)	09 Jan 57	462UNTS151	106676
Germany, East	Poland	01 Feb 57	319UNTS115	104632
Iceland	USA (United States)	23 Feb 57	283UNTS73	104107
Japan	Norway	28 Feb 57	280UNTS87	104054
Chile	USA (United States)	01 Mar 57	283UNTS127	104112
Ethiopia	Sweden	16 Mar 57	304UNTS214	104398
Paraguay	USA (United States)	04 Apr 57	284UNTS161	104135
Denmark	Peru	10 Jun 57	406UNTS63	105839
Multilateral		26 Jun 57	328UNTS247	104738
Czechoslovakia	USSR (Soviet Union)	31 Aug 57	308UNTS3	104456
IAEA (Atom Energy)	United Nations	23 Oct 57	281UNTS369	200548
Germany, East	Hungary	30 Oct 57	408UNTS4	105867
UK Great Britain	USA (United States)	01 Nov 57	299UNTS167	104312
Brazil	USA (United States)	05 Nov 57	303UNTS3	104368
Germany, East	USSR (Soviet Union)	28 Nov 57	305UNTS113	104419
Japan	USSR (Soviet Union)	06 Dec 57	325UNTS35	104694
Austria	IAEA (Atom Energy)	11 Dec 57	339UNTS110	104849
Bulgaria	USSR (Soviet Union)	12 Dec 57	317UNTS217	104606
Korea, North	USSR (Soviet Union)	16 Dec 57	301UNTS301	104349
Poland	USSR (Soviet Union)	28 Dec 57	320UNTS3	104638
Japan	USA (United States)	11 Jan 58	304UNTS35	104390
Czechoslovakia	Poland	29 Mar 58	340UNTS199	104865
Romania	USSR (Soviet Union)	03 Apr 58	313UNTS167	104535
Multilateral		10 Jun 58	454UNTS47	106539
Albania	USSR (Soviet Union)	30 Jun 58	328UNTS3	104729
Philippines	USA (United States)	30 Jun 58	321UNTS51	104653
Germany, East	Romania	15 Jul 58	395UNTS3	105681
Hungary	USSR (Soviet Union)	15 Jul 58	322UNTS3	104656
Taiwan	USA (United States)	06 Aug 58	462UNTS3	106666
Mongolia	USSR (Soviet Union)	25 Aug 58	322UNTS105	104657
Hungary	Romania	07 Oct 58	416UNTS199	106004
Iraq	USSR (Soviet Union)	11 Oct 58	328UNTS117	104731
Spain	USA (United States)	16 Oct 58	336UNTS153	104804
Afghanistan	WHO (World Health)	18 Dec 58	324UNTS121	104681
Austria	USA (United States)	30 Jan 59	511UNTS145	107432
Czechoslovakia	United Arab Rep	07 Feb 59	372UNTS243	105301
Japan	Yugoslavia	28 Feb 59	341UNTS179	104883
Austria	USA (United States)	22 May 59	347UNTS3	104988
Greece	Yugoslavia	18 Jun 59	368UNTS3	105231
United Arab Rep	USA (United States)	28 Sep 59	358UNTS97	105128
Austria	Netherlands	30 Sep 59	507UNTS111	107397
Germany, West	Pakistan	25 Nov 59	457UNTS22	106575
Guinea	UN Special Fund	02 Dec 59	345UNTS215	104969
Philippines	USA (United States)	07 Dec 59	359UNTS227	105144
Australia	Austria	18 Dec 59	348UNTS201	105001
Albania	Hungary	12 Jan 60	520UNTS3	107511
Poland	Yugoslavia	06 Feb 60	521UNTS37	107517
Multilateral		06 Feb 60	383UNTS3	105494
Korea, South	USA (United States)	19 Feb 60	372UNTS109	105291
Portugal	USA (United States)	19 Mar 60	371UNTS131	105275
Romania	USA (United States)	30 Mar 60	371UNTS163	105278
Cuba	Japan	22 Apr 60	442UNTS261	106354
Laos	UN Special Fund	30 Apr 60	361UNTS171	105179
Lebanon	UN Special Fund	07 May 60	360UNTS225	105160
Kuwait	UN Special Fund	29 Jun 60	369UNTS419	200575
Ethiopia	UN Special Fund	13 Jul 60	368UNTS159	105240
USA (United States)	Uruguay	22 Jul 60	388UNTS315	105587
Japan	Pakistan	30 Jul 60	384UNTS63	105511
Japan	Thailand	24 Aug 60	384UNTS73	105512
Brazil	UN Special Fund	16 Sep 60	375UNTS3	105351
Taiwan	UN Special Fund	20 Sep 60	375UNTS29	105352
UK Great Britain	USA (United States)	14 Oct 60	398UNTS165	105721
Nigeria	USA (United States)	19 Oct 60	394UNTS113	105672
Romania	UK Great Britain	10 Nov 60	385UNTS113	105533
Multilateral		13 Dec 60	523UNTS117	107557

PARTY ONE	PARTY TWO	DATE	CITATION	NUMBER
General property (Cont.)				
UK Great Britain	USA (United States)	20 Jan 61	402UNTS153	105783
Afghanistan	Japan	15 Mar 61	450UNTS373	106480
UK Great Britain	USA (United States)	15 Mar 61	404UNTS207	105811
Ceylon (Sri Lanka)	Japan	20 Mar 61	450UNTS385	106481
UK Great Britain	USA (United States)	06 Apr 61	404UNTS215	105812
Australia	USA (United States)	09 May 61	409UNTS203	105886
Japan	Peru	15 May 61	451UNTS3	106482
Cameroon	USA (United States)	26 May 61	413UNTS195	105953
Nepal	USA (United States)	09 Jun 61	421UNTS223	106061
Indonesia	UK Great Britain	29 Jun 61	443UNTS255	106364
Czechoslovakia	Poland	04 Jul 61	436UNTS189	106295
Chile	USA (United States)	12 Aug 61	421UNTS209	106059
Canada	USA (United States)	01 Sep 61	421UNTS199	106058
Czechoslovakia	Hungary	02 Nov 61	438UNTS3	106313
Iraq	Syria	03 Nov 61	489UNTS45	107134
Bulgaria	Poland	04 Dec 61	484UNTS3	107019
Ethiopia	USA (United States)	06 Dec 61	433UNTS231	106246
Costa Rica	USA (United States)	22 Dec 61	460UNTS277	106646
Paraguay	USA (United States)	16 Jan 62	433UNTS169	106240
Cyprus	USA (United States)	18 Jan 62	435UNTS3	106266
Ghana	USA (United States)	24 Jan 62	435UNTS23	106268
Luxembourg	USA (United States)	23 Feb 62	474UNTS3	106868
Argentina	USA (United States)	16 Mar 62	454UNTS3	106535
Brazil	Japan	28 Mar 62	451UNTS125	106489
Dahomey	UN Special Fund	28 Mar 62	424UNTS55	106099
India	Japan	31 Mar 62	451UNTS143	106490
India	Japan	23 Apr 62	451UNTS155	106491
Denmark	USA (United States)	28 May 62	450UNTS215	106469
Israel	USA (United States)	22 Jun 62	448UNTS273	106440
Germany, West	Israel	09 Jul 62	630UNTS87	108968
Canada	Greece	18 Jul 62	528UNTS265	107647
Colombia	USA (United States)	23 Jul 62	458UNTS123	106595
Ethiopia	USA (United States)	03 Aug 62	459UNTS79	106613
Congo (Brazzaville)	USA (United States)	01 Sep 62	459UNTS117	106616
India	USA (United States)	09 Oct 62	471UNTS39	106820
Czechoslovakia	Hungary	16 Oct 62	479UNTS301	106961
Germany, West	Ireland	17 Oct 62	604UNTS135	108749
Dominican Republic	USA (United States)	25 Oct 62	459UNTS247	106627
Saudi Arabia	USA (United States)	13 Nov 62	488UNTS175	107127
Japan	UK Great Britain	14 Nov 62	478UNTS29	106934
Canada	USA (United States)	28 Dec 62	471UNTS13	106818
UK Great Britain	USA (United States)	15 Jan 63	466UNTS181	106743
Trinidad/Tobago	USA (United States)	15 Jan 63	471UNTS141	106829
New Zealand	Western Samoa	24 Jan 63	499UNTS21	107290
Malaysia	USA (United States)	28 Jan 63	473UNTS15	106850
Philippines	USA (United States)	23 Mar 63	474UNTS80	106873
Belgium	USA (United States)	19 Apr 63	476UNTS29	106900
Greece	Hungary	27 Apr 63	550UNTS197	108016
Austria	Bulgaria	02 May 63	535UNTS143	107778
Philippines	USA (United States)	06 May 63	477UNTS67	106916
Australia	USA (United States)	09 May 63	469UNTS55	106784
Greece	UK Great Britain	09 May 63	398UNTS179	105722
Netherlands	Tunisia	23 May 63	523UNTS237	107558
Thailand	USA (United States)	24 May 63	477UNTS123	106918
Cyprus	USA (United States)	29 May 63	487UNTS283	107110
Korea, South	USA (United States)	18 Jun 63	487UNTS297	107112
India	USA (United States)	19 Jun 63	479UNTS175	106952
Austria	USA (United States)	25 Jun 63	479UNTS223	106956
Austria	Romania	03 Jul 63	588UNTS3	108516
Hungary	Mongolia	10 Jul 63	519UNTS173	107508
El Salvador	Japan	19 Jul 63	518UNTS135	107494
Malagasy	USA (United States)	26 Jul 63	487UNTS189	107104
Cameroon	UK Great Britain	29 Jul 63	478UNTS148	106935
Paraguay	USA (United States)	20 Aug 63	531UNTS197	107704
Afghanistan	USA (United States)	20 Aug 63	488UNTS41	107118

PARTY ONE	PARTY TWO	DATE	CITATION	NUMBER
General property (Cont.)				
Argentina	USA (United States)	21 Aug 63	488UNTS61	107119
Ecuador	USA (United States)	20 Sep 63	488UNTS147	107125
Malagasy	USA (United States)	07 Oct 63	494UNTS3	107221
Canada	France	11 Oct 63	529UNTS71	107657
UK Great Britain	USA (United States)	11 Oct 63	483UNTS3	107005
Iran	USA (United States)	24 Oct 63	489UNTS303	107146
Multilateral		14 Nov 63	619UNTS299	108948
Austria	Belgium	14 Nov 63	544UNTS97	107912
Tanganyika	USA (United States)	14 Nov 63	493UNTS75	107208
Tunisia	USA (United States)	18 Nov 63	494UNTS193	107233
Greece	USA (United States)	13 Dec 63	494UNTS55	107226
Chile	IBRD (World Bank)	18 Dec 63	504UNTS29	107352
New Zealand	Western Samoa	31 Dec 63	521UNTS163	107519
France	South Africa	06 Jan 64	601UNTS229	108699
Czechoslovakia	Yugoslavia	20 Jan 64	538UNTS197	107816
Canada	USA (United States)	22 Jan 64	530UNTS89	107674
Mexico	USA (United States)	14 Feb 64	524UNTS197	107574
Spain	USA (United States)	18 Mar 64	535UNTS343	107789
Kenya	USA (United States)	20 Apr 64	524UNTS165	107571
Liberia	USA (United States)	08 May 64	526UNTS239	107608
Mali	USA (United States)	09 Jun 64	530UNTS133	107678
Czechoslovakia	Netherlands	11 Jun 64	556UNTS89	108120
Belgium	Tunisia	15 Jul 64	561UNTS297	108190
Italy	USA (United States)	04 Aug 64	529UNTS205	107662
Australia	USA (United States)	28 Aug 64	510UNTS201	107415
Ceylon (Sri Lanka)	USA (United States)	29 Aug 64	531UNTS93	107695
Australia	UN Special Fund	30 Sep 64	510UNTS277	107419
Israel	USSR (Soviet Union)	07 Oct 64	516UNTS59	107471
Italy	ILO (Labor Org)	24 Oct 64	541UNTS217	107871
USA (United States)	Yugoslavia	09 Nov 64	533UNTS39	107731
Germany, West	UK Great Britain	26 Nov 64	603UNTS183	108734
Germany, West	Thailand	23 Dec 64	525UNTS201	107592
Laos	USA (United States)	29 Dec 64	542UNTS23	107876
Central Afri Rep	USA (United States)	31 Dec 64	542UNTS29	107877
Malta	Switzerland	20 Jan 65	548UNTS193	107978
Peru	USA (United States)	28 Jan 65	587UNTS273	108513
Dahomey	USA (United States)	13 Mar 65	549UNTS43	107987
Austria	Hungary	09 Apr 65	638UNTS105	109132
Australia	Germany, West	21 Apr 65	598UNTS25	108654
UK Great Britain	USA (United States)	10 May 65	545UNTS181	107934
Chad	USA (United States)	12 May 65	546UNTS183	107944
USA (United States)	Uruguay	17 May 65	564UNTS69	108221
Uganda	USA (United States)	29 May 65	546UNTS209	107948
USA (United States)	Upper Volta	18 Jun 65	549UNTS133	107996
Japan	Korea, South	22 Jun 65	584UNTS3	108474
Canada	USA (United States)	29 Jun 65	549UNTS273	108003
Multilateral		15 Nov 65	0UNTS0	109432
Panama	USA (United States)	15 Feb 66	586UNTS27	108494
Ireland	UK Great Britain	28 Feb 66	565UNTS33	108234
Netherlands	Philippines	02 Mar 66	631UNTS325	109002
Denmark	Italy	10 Mar 66	643UNTS349	109201
Austria	Ireland	24 May 66	636UNTS149	109102
Denmark	Iran	14 Jun 66	597UNTS283	108652
Argentina	Germany, West	13 Jul 66	636UNTS3	109091
Austria	France	15 Jul 66	604UNTS265	108755
Greece	UK Great Britain	12 Oct 66	578UNTS33	108385
Israel	Norway	02 Nov 66	630UNTS225	108972
Austria	Spain	20 Dec 66	636UNTS197	109103
Asian Devel Bank	Philippines	22 Dec 66	615UNTS375	108887
UK Great Britain	USA (United States)	30 Dec 66	603UNTS245	108736
UK Great Britain	USA (United States)	01 Jan 67	604UNTS3	108738
Denmark	Tanzania	05 Apr 67	604UNTS19	108740
Netherlands	Romania	08 May 67	607UNTS105	108800

PARTY ONE	PARTY TWO	DATE	CITATION	NUMBER
Succession				
Multilateral		16 Jun 28	39UNTS3	100609
Multilateral		12 Aug 49	75UNTS287	100973
Multilateral		04 Nov 50	213UNTS221	102889
Bulgaria	Czechoslovakia	13 Apr 54	501UNTS3	107314
Bulgaria	Yugoslavia	23 Mar 56	367UNTS213	105230
Germany, East	Hungary	30 Oct 57	408UNTS4	105867
Albania	USSR (Soviet Union)	30 Jun 58	328UNTS3	104729
Germany, East	Romania	15 Jul 58	395UNTS3	105681
Hungary	Romania	07 Oct 58	416UNTS199	106004
Czechoslovakia	Romania	25 Oct 58	417UNTS37	106006
Bulgaria	Romania	03 Dec 58	417UNTS133	106007
Albania	Czechoslovakia	16 Jan 59	363UNTS195	105208
Hungary	Poland	06 Mar 59	432UNTS3	106216
Albania	Hungary	12 Jan 60	520UNTS3	107511
Poland	Yugoslavia	06 Feb 60	521UNTS37	107517
Hungary	Yugoslavia	07 May 60	519UNTS237	107510
Czechoslovakia	Poland	04 Jul 61	436UNTS189	106295
Multilateral		05 Oct 61	510UNTS175	107413
Czechoslovakia	Hungary	02 Nov 61	438UNTS3	106313
Bulgaria	Poland	04 Dec 61	484UNTS3	107019
Poland	Romania	25 Jan 62	468UNTS3	106770
USSR (Soviet Union)	Yugoslavia	24 Feb 62	471UNTS195	106833
Czechoslovakia	Yugoslavia	20 Jan 64	538UNTS197	107816
Germany, West	UK Great Britain	26 Nov 64	603UNTS183	108734
Austria	Hungary	09 Apr 65	638UNTS105	109132
United Nations	Sweden	16 Jun 65	539UNTS45	107823
Public information				
Multilateral		27 Jun 39	40UNTS281	100639
Peru	USA (United States)	21 Apr 42	89UNTS317	200260
Peru	USA (United States)	07 May 42	103UNTS219	200316
USA (United States)	Uruguay	21 Jul 42	120UNTS211	200393
Ecuador	USA (United States)	29 Oct 42	89UNTS301	200259
Mexico	USA (United States)	23 Dec 42	13UNTS231	200081
Iceland	USA (United States)	27 Sep 43	29UNTS317	200170
Multilateral		16 Nov 45	4UNTS275	100052
Hungary	Norway	27 Aug 46	31UNTS3	100465
Paraguay	USA (United States)	12 Sep 46	125UNTS179	101677
Philippines	USA (United States)	21 Mar 47	45UNTS47	100691
Greece	USA (United States)	20 Jun 47	7UNTS267	100105
Austria	USA (United States)	25 Jun 47	22UNTS141	100334
Italy	USA (United States)	04 Jul 47	22UNTS173	100336
Greece	USA (United States)	08 Jul 47	16UNTS157	100256
Turkey	USA (United States)	12 Jul 47	7UNTS299	100106
Greece	UNICEF (Children)	14 Oct 47	102UNTS39	101409
Taiwan	USA (United States)	27 Oct 47	12UNTS11	100178
UNICEF (Children)	Yugoslavia	20 Nov 47	65UNTS28	100817
Italy	USA (United States)	02 Feb 48	79UNTS171	101040
Switzerland	USSR (Soviet Union)	17 Mar 48	217UNTS87	102945
France	Netherlands	02 Jun 48	204UNTS275	102762
Australia	Poland	03 Jun 48	16UNTS189	100258
Italy	USA (United States)	28 Jun 48	20UNTS43	100314
Ireland	USA (United States)	28 Jun 48	24UNTS3	100349
France	USA (United States)	28 Jun 48	19UNTS9	100302
Denmark	USA (United States)	29 Jun 48	22UNTS217	100338
Australia	Greece	01 Jul 48	22UNTS33	100329
Australia	Hungary	01 Jul 48	22UNTS3	100325
Austria	USA (United States)	02 Jul 48	21UNTS29	100323
Belgium	USA (United States)	02 Jul 48	19UNTS127	100309
Greece	USA (United States)	02 Jul 48	23UNTS43	100342
Netherlands	USA (United States)	02 Jul 48	20UNTS91	100315
Luxembourg	USA (United States)	03 Jul 48	24UNTS35	100350
Taiwan	USA (United States)	03 Jul 48	17UNTS119	100273
Sweden	USA (United States)	03 Jul 48	23UNTS101	100343

PARTY ONE	PARTY TWO	DATE	CITATION	NUMBER
Public information (Cont.)				
Iceland	USA (United States)	03 Jul 48	20UNTS141	100316
Norway	USA (United States)	03 Jul 48	20UNTS185	100317
Turkey	USA (United States)	04 Jul 48	24UNTS67	100351
UK Great Britain	USA (United States)	06 Jul 48	22UNTS263	100339
Australia	Italy	08 Jul 48	22UNTS11	100326
Australia	Yugoslavia	09 Jul 48	22UNTS17	100327
France	USA (United States)	09 Jul 48	24UNTS103	100352
Multilateral		14 Jul 48	23UNTS3	100340
Australia	Austria	19 Jul 48	22UNTS25	100328
Taiwan	USA (United States)	05 Aug 48	82UNTS109	101087
Portugal	USA (United States)	28 Sep 48	29UNTS213	100442
Trieste	USA (United States)	15 Oct 48	29UNTS249	100443
UK Great Britain	USA (United States)	01 Dec 48	81UNTS93	101066
Multilateral		09 Dec 48	73UNTS39	100942
Korea, South	USA (United States)	10 Dec 48	55UNTS157	100813
Multilateral		01 Jul 49	120UNTS71	101616
France	Greece	06 Aug 49	91UNTS95	101244
Austria	Belgium	05 Nov 49	48UNTS107	100739
Germany, West	USA (United States)	15 Dec 49	92UNTS269	101277
Korea, South	USA (United States)	26 Jan 50	80UNTS205	101053
France	USA (United States)	27 Jan 50	80UNTS171	101051
Luxembourg	USA (United States)	27 Jan 50	80UNTS187	101052
Italy	USA (United States)	27 Jan 50	80UNTS145	101050
Norway	USA (United States)	27 Jan 50	80UNTS241	101055
Belgium	USA (United States)	27 Jan 50	51UNTS213	100767
UK Great Britain	USA (United States)	27 Jan 50	80UNTS261	101056
Netherlands	USA (United States)	27 Jan 50	80UNTS219	101054
Denmark	USA (United States)	27 Jan 50	48UNTS115	100740
UNICEF (Children)	UK Great Britain	10 Feb 50	65UNTS86	100837
Chile	UNICEF (Children)	03 Mar 50	126UNTS119	101685
Multilateral		21 Mar 50	96UNTS271	101342
Multilateral		06 Apr 50	119UNTS99	101610
Iran	USA (United States)	23 May 50	81UNTS3	101057
Haiti	WHO (World Health)	27 Jun 50	110UNTS99	101504
Indonesia	USA (United States)	15 Aug 50	134UNTS255	101804
India	Norway	29 Aug 50	73UNTS179	100952
WHO (World Health)	Venezuela	11 Sep 50	110UNTS237	101513
Iceland	WHO (World Health)	06 Oct 50	110UNTS127	101506
Thailand	USA (United States)	17 Oct 50	79UNTS41	101030
Iran	USA (United States)	19 Oct 50	92UNTS135	101266
WHO (World Health)	Turkey	19 Oct 50	110UNTS215	101512
Multilateral		02 Nov 50	81UNTS160	101071
Ceylon (Sri Lanka)	USA (United States)	07 Nov 50	92UNTS125	101265
Peru	WHO (World Health)	10 Nov 50	110UNTS187	101510
Nicaragua	WHO (World Health)	10 Nov 50	110UNTS155	101508
USA (United States)	Yugoslavia	21 Nov 50	93UNTS39	101285
Multilateral		24 Nov 50	81UNTS188	101072
Brazil	USA (United States)	19 Dec 50	141UNTS3	101900
Panama	USA (United States)	20 Dec 50	92UNTS167	101269
Liberia	USA (United States)	22 Dec 50	92UNTS145	101267
Nicaragua	USA (United States)	23 Dec 50	92UNTS155	101268
India	USA (United States)	28 Dec 50	99UNTS39	101369
Philippines	WHO (World Health)	28 Dec 50	110UNTS203	101511
Paraguay	USA (United States)	29 Dec 50	122UNTS157	101645
Portugal	USA (United States)	05 Jan 51	133UNTS75	101782
USA (United States)	Yugoslavia	06 Jan 51	122UNTS137	101643
Costa Rica	USA (United States)	11 Jan 51	92UNTS179	101270
Chile	USA (United States)	16 Jan 51	147UNTS11	101925
Chile	USA (United States)	16 Jan 51	151UNTS147	101990
Saudi Arabia	USA (United States)	17 Jan 51	140UNTS335	101897
Multilateral		18 Jan 51	81UNTS233	101073
Nepal	USA (United States)	23 Jan 51	184UNTS65	102439
Ceylon (Sri Lanka)	ILO (Labor Org)	24 Jan 51	117UNTS355	200380
Ethiopia	ICAO (Civil Aviat)	02 Feb 51	96UNTS123	101333
Afghanistan	USA (United States)	07 Feb 51	132UNTS265	101766

PARTY ONE	PARTY TWO	DATE	CITATION	NUMBER
Public information (Cont.)				
Pakistan	USA (United States)	09 Feb 51	100UNTS67	101388
Paraguay	WHO (World Health)	15 Feb 51	110UNTS171	101509
Dominican Republic	USA (United States)	20 Feb 51	132UNTS305	101770
Lebanon	USA (United States)	24 Feb 51	223UNTS121	103060
Israel	USA (United States)	26 Feb 51	137UNTS57	101848
Jordan	USA (United States)	27 Feb 51	141UNTS55	101905
Colombia	USA (United States)	09 Mar 51	141UNTS15	101901
Bolivia	USA (United States)	14 Mar 51	132UNTS319	101771
Canada	USA (United States)	27 Mar 51	132UNTS333	101772
Indonesia	WHO (World Health)	28 Mar 51	103UNTS71	101425
Jordan	WHO (World Health)	03 Apr 51	110UNTS297	200367
Multilateral		05 Apr 51	84UNTS299	101139
Iraq	USA (United States)	10 Apr 51	151UNTS179	101993
USA (United States)	Yugoslavia	17 Apr 51	162UNTS173	102134
El Salvador	USA (United States)	18 Apr 51	141UNTS37	101903
Honduras	WHO (World Health)	20 Apr 51	110UNTS111	101505
Philippines	USA (United States)	27 Apr 51	174UNTS251	102290
Haiti	USA (United States)	02 May 51	151UNTS191	101994
Ecuador	USA (United States)	03 May 51	141UNTS27	101902
Colombia	WHO (World Health)	04 May 51	110UNTS83	101503
United Arab Rep	USA (United States)	05 May 51	198UNTS265	102670
Lebanon	USA (United States)	29 May 51	160UNTS49	102101
USA (United States)	Venezuela	07 Jun 51	141UNTS273	101918
Liberia	WHO (World Health)	11 Jun 51	103UNTS83	101426
WHO (World Health)	Uruguay	11 Jun 51	128UNTS251	101724
Costa Rica	WHO (World Health)	14 Jun 51	102UNTS151	101418
UK Great Britain	USA (United States)	15 Jun 51	141UNTS79	101907
Multilateral		15 Jun 51	148UNTS67	101936
Ethiopia	USA (United States)	16 Jun 51	148UNTS39	101933
Cuba	USA (United States)	20 Jun 51	148UNTS3	101931
Mexico	USA (United States)	27 Jun 51	141UNTS211	101916
Multilateral		28 Jun 51	172UNTS159	102244
Iraq	WHO (World Health)	01 Jul 51	110UNTS139	101507
UK Great Britain	USA (United States)	13 Jul 51	105UNTS71	101454
El Salvador	USA (United States)	19 Jul 51	140UNTS259	101892
Iran	UNICEF (Children)	02 Aug 51	247UNTS11	103457
France	USSR (Soviet Union)	03 Sep 51	221UNTS79	103003
UNICEF (Children)	Turkey	05 Sep 51	193UNTS55	102610
Denmark	Switzerland	15 Sep 51	110UNTS55	101501
WHO (World Health)	Vietnam, South	21 Sep 51	107UNTS63	200352
UNICEF (Children)	UK Great Britain	02 Oct 51	104UNTS301	101448
El Salvador	USA (United States)	23 Oct 51	137UNTS43	101847
USA (United States)	Yugoslavia	14 Nov 51	174UNTS201	102286
Iraq	UNICEF (Children)	10 Dec 51	126UNTS57	101682
Jordan	USA (United States)	20 Dec 51	157UNTS69	102048
USA (United States)	Yugoslavia	08 Jan 52	152UNTS61	102011
Iran	USA (United States)	20 Jan 52	200UNTS191	102703
Libya	USA (United States)	21 Jan 52	183UNTS177	102427
UNICEF (Children)	UK Great Britain	04 Feb 52	120UNTS147	101620
Dominican Republic	UNICEF (Children)	15 Feb 52	121UNTS43	101625
Ecuador	USA (United States)	20 Feb 52	177UNTS43	102308
Peru	USA (United States)	22 Feb 52	165UNTS31	102166
Cuba	USA (United States)	07 Mar 52	165UNTS11	102165
Brazil	USA (United States)	15 Mar 52	199UNTS221	102687
El Salvador	USA (United States)	04 Apr 52	177UNTS219	102320
Libya	UNICEF (Children)	05 Apr 52	133UNTS287	200441
Chile	USA (United States)	09 Apr 52	186UNTS53	102482
Colombia	USA (United States)	17 Apr 52	174UNTS215	102287
Liberia	UNICEF (Children)	17 Apr 52	133UNTS3	101773
Israel	USA (United States)	09 May 52	177UNTS269	102326
UNICEF (Children)	United Arab Rep	18 May 52	324UNTS161	104684
Korea, South	USA (United States)	24 May 52	179UNTS23	102353
Chile	WHO (World Health)	31 May 52	136UNTS323	101841
Belgium	UNICEF (Children)	17 Jun 52	171UNTS249	102228
USA (United States)	Uruguay	30 Jun 52	207UNTS139	102804

PARTY ONE	PARTY TWO	DATE	CITATION	NUMBER
Public information (Cont.)				
Jordan	UNICEF (Children)	08 Jul 52	173UNTS353	200503
UNICEF (Children)	Syria	10 Jul 52	136UNTS17	101830
UNICEF (Children)	UK Great Britain	25 Jul 52	135UNTS37	101812
Laos	UNICEF (Children)	15 Aug 52	161UNTS323	200491
UNICEF (Children)	Vietnam, South	29 Aug 52	161UNTS335	200492
Multilateral		07 Nov 52	221UNTS255	103010
UNICEF (Children)	UK Great Britain	16 Dec 52	151UNTS359	102005
UK Great Britain	USA (United States)	25 Feb 53	212UNTS157	102868
Dominican Republic	USA (United States)	06 Mar 53	199UNTS267	102689
Multilateral		31 Mar 53	435UNTS191	106280
Japan	USA (United States)	02 Apr 53	206UNTS143	102788
Ethiopia	UNICEF (Children)	27 Apr 53	213UNTS169	102885
Multilateral		30 Apr 53	175UNTS89	102297
Pakistan	USA (United States)	25 Jun 53	205UNTS139	102773
Philippines	USA (United States)	26 Jun 53	213UNTS77	102881
Spain	USA (United States)	26 Sep 53	207UNTS93	102802
Spain	USA (United States)	26 Sep 53	207UNTS61	102800
UNICEF (Children)	UK Great Britain	07 Oct 53	180UNTS59	102375
Jordan	USA (United States)	21 Oct 53	222UNTS31	103020
Netherlands	USA (United States)	27 Oct 53	221UNTS357	103017
Japan	UNICEF (Children)	21 Nov 53	183UNTS297	200507
Israel	USA (United States)	25 Nov 53	219UNTS205	102976
Belgium	Lebanon	24 Dec 53	539UNTS321	107842
Libya	USA (United States)	11 Jan 54	229UNTS15	103157
Netherlands	USA (United States)	22 Jan 54	190UNTS207	102565
Japan	USA (United States)	08 Mar 54	232UNTS169	103236
Afghanistan	USA (United States)	20 Mar 54	229UNTS7	103156
USA (United States)	Yugoslavia	16 Apr 54	237UNTS77	103337
Iraq	USA (United States)	21 Apr 54	222UNTS251	103032
UNICEF (Children)	Spain	07 May 54	190UNTS357	200515
France	Greece	13 May 54	222UNTS299	103036
Pakistan	USA (United States)	19 May 54	202UNTS301	102736
Honduras	USA (United States)	20 May 54	222UNTS87	103025
Mexico	UNICEF (Children)	20 May 54	192UNTS3	102591
Italy	USA (United States)	16 Jun 54	236UNTS149	103322
Lebanon	USA (United States)	18 Jun 54	233UNTS177	103262
Italy	USA (United States)	28 Jun 54	237UNTS121	103340
Pakistan	USA (United States)	23 Aug 54	234UNTS243	103287
New Zealand	UNICEF (Children)	26 Aug 54	198UNTS173	102663
Guatemala	USA (United States)	01 Sep 54	199UNTS51	102677
Libya	USA (United States)	03 Nov 54	238UNTS227	103366
United Arab Rep	USA (United States)	06 Nov 54	237UNTS183	103344
Guatemala	USA (United States)	13 Dec 54	237UNTS169	103343
Netherlands	UNICEF (Children)	31 Dec 54	202UNTS135	102729
Pakistan	USA (United States)	11 Jan 55	251UNTS111	103537
Haiti	USA (United States)	28 Jan 55	270UNTS83	103894
Italy	USA (United States)	11 Feb 55	240UNTS87	103396
Mexico	USA (United States)	09 Mar 55	263UNTS247	103776
Haiti	USA (United States)	01 Apr 55	261UNTS361	103734
Guatemala	USA (United States)	18 Jun 55	262UNTS105	103740
Germany, West	USA (United States)	30 Jun 55	240UNTS47	103393
Libya	USA (United States)	21 Jul 55	264UNTS247	103796
Guatemala	UNICEF (Children)	22 Nov 55	221UNTS305	103012
Japan	USA (United States)	10 Feb 56	275UNTS157	103980
USA (United States)	Uruguay	23 Mar 56	376UNTS311	105386
Italy	USA (United States)	27 Apr 56	273UNTS149	103949
Cambodia	UNICEF (Children)	28 Apr 56	136UNTS341	200446
Ceylon (Sri Lanka)	USA (United States)	28 Apr 56	274UNTS35	103956
Lebanon	UNICEF (Children)	03 Jul 56	324UNTS145	104683
UNICEF (Children)	Sudan	07 Aug 56	248UNTS307	200542
Guatemala	Honduras	22 Aug 56	263UNTS49	103767
Austria	USA (United States)	21 Nov 56	290UNTS181	104237
Belgium	Spain	28 Nov 56	308UNTS285	104465
UNESCO (Educ/Cult)	Tunisia	03 Jan 57	257UNTS21	103645
Multilateral		01 Mar 57	264UNTS94	103790

PARTY ONE	PARTY TWO	DATE	CITATION	NUMBER
Public information (Cont.)				
Burma	USA (United States)	21 Mar 57	300UNTS11	104327
Italy	UK Great Britain	29 Mar 57	310UNTS11	104481
Morocco	USA (United States)	02 Apr 57	288UNTS157	104203
Libya	USA (United States)	04 Apr 57	283UNTS181	104116
Ethiopia	USA (United States)	25 Apr 57	283UNTS205	104118
Ghana	USA (United States)	03 Jun 57	284UNTS63	104129
Argentina	USA (United States)	03 Jun 57	291UNTS61	104244
Multilateral		15 Jun 57	550UNTS45	108008
Jordan	USA (United States)	27 Jun 57	288UNTS269	104209
Tunisia	USA (United States)	28 Jun 57	289UNTS301	104226
Libya	USA (United States)	30 Jun 57	284UNTS177	104136
Peru	USA (United States)	19 Jul 57	289UNTS271	104223
Morocco	UNICEF (Children)	31 Jul 57	282UNTS99	104095
Romania	USSR (Soviet Union)	04 Sep 57	318UNTS89	104610
Czechoslovakia	USSR (Soviet Union)	05 Oct 57	320UNTS111	104640
Argentina	UNICEF (Children)	19 Nov 57	300UNTS229	104338
Multilateral		06 Jan 58	304UNTS227	104399
Poland	USSR (Soviet Union)	21 Jan 58	319UNTS277	104636
Philippines	USA (United States)	20 Feb 58	303UNTS261	104385
Sudan	USA (United States)	31 Mar 58	308UNTS105	104458
Italy	USA (United States)	08 May 58	316UNTS177	104584
Ghana	UNICEF (Children)	12 Aug 58	309UNTS103	104469
Afghanistan	WHO (World Health)	18 Dec 58	324UNTS121	104681
Morocco	UN Special Fund	04 Apr 59	354UNTS347	105069
Hungary	Iraq	11 Apr 59	439UNTS25	106323
Ghana	UN Special Fund	12 Aug 59	338UNTS203	104836
Iran	UN Special Fund	06 Oct 59	342UNTS89	104902
India	Italy	06 Oct 59	378UNTS267	105427
Poland	UN Special Fund	15 Oct 59	344UNTS29	104941
India	UN Special Fund	20 Oct 59	344UNTS143	104946
UN Special Fund	Yugoslavia	27 Oct 59	344UNTS159	104947
Ecuador	UN Special Fund	10 Nov 59	345UNTS3	104955
Japan	USA (United States)	12 Nov 59	361UNTS27	105171
Greece	UN Special Fund	13 Nov 59	345UNTS171	104966
UN Special Fund	Turkey	20 Nov 59	345UNTS105	104963
UN Special Fund	United Arab Rep	25 Nov 59	345UNTS125	104964
Israel	UN Special Fund	01 Dec 59	345UNTS197	104968
Argentina	UN Special Fund	04 Dec 59	345UNTS263	104972
Jordan	UN Special Fund	15 Dec 59	346UNTS3	104974
UN Special Fund	UK Great Britain	07 Jan 60	348UNTS177	105000
Colombia	USA (United States)	11 Jan 60	371UNTS37	105268
Guinea	Hungary	12 Jan 60	519UNTS131	107505
Peru	UN Special Fund	19 Jan 60	349UNTS83	105010
Chile	UN Special Fund	22 Jan 60	351UNTS115	105020
Colombia	UN Special Fund	04 Feb 60	355UNTS257	105080
Bolivia	UN Special Fund	09 Feb 60	351UNTS203	105024
Cuba	UNICEF (Children)	11 Feb 60	349UNTS277	105014
Afghanistan	UN Special Fund	21 Feb 60	351UNTS93	105019
Pakistan	UN Special Fund	25 Feb 60	351UNTS141	105021
Brazil	USA (United States)	27 Feb 60	384UNTS131	105515
France	UN Special Fund	17 Mar 60	354UNTS119	105059
Italy	UN Special Fund	01 Apr 60	354UNTS261	105066
UN Special Fund	Tunisia	12 Apr 60	355UNTS289	105082
Libya	UN Special Fund	19 Apr 60	356UNTS11	105090
UN Special Fund	Sudan	21 Apr 60	356UNTS213	105097
UN Special Fund	Vietnam, South	29 Apr 60	357UNTS311	200567
Laos	UN Special Fund	30 Apr 60	361UNTS171	105179
Lebanon	UN Special Fund	07 May 60	360UNTS225	105160
Iraq	UN Special Fund	19 Jun 60	376UNTS357	105389
Ethiopia	UN Special Fund	13 Jul 60	368UNTS159	105240
Brazil	UN Special Fund	16 Sep 60	375UNTS3	105351
Taiwan	UN Special Fund	20 Sep 60	375UNTS29	105352
Indonesia	UN Special Fund	07 Oct 60	378UNTS141	105424
Liberia	UN Special Fund	11 Oct 60	376UNTS341	105388
El Salvador	UN Special Fund	24 Oct 60	377UNTS171	105400

PARTY ONE	PARTY TWO	DATE	CITATION	NUMBER
Public information (Cont.)				
Cuba	Romania	28 Oct 60	457UNTS9	106574
UNICEF (Children)	Upper Volta	15 Nov 60	402UNTS33	105776
Guatemala	UN Special Fund	17 Nov 60	383UNTS67	105495
Mali	UNICEF (Children)	17 Nov 60	402UNTS23	105775
Nepal	UN Special Fund	17 Nov 60	380UNTS289	105461
Korea, South	USA (United States)	18 Nov 60	400UNTS49	105747
Cambodia	UN Special Fund	24 Nov 60	382UNTS255	105487
Nepal	UNICEF (Children)	12 Dec 60	382UNTS273	105488
Israel	USA (United States)	19 Dec 60	401UNTS195	105772
Honduras	UN Special Fund	20 Dec 60	383UNTS103	105497
Burma	UN Special Fund	03 Jan 61	387UNTS219	105564
Costa Rica	UN Special Fund	10 Jan 61	389UNTS253	105597
UN Special Fund	Saudi Arabia	19 Jan 61	396UNTS27	105692
Nicaragua	UN Special Fund	20 Jan 61	387UNTS15	105555
Chad	UN Special Fund	23 Jan 61	390UNTS69	105603
UN Special Fund	Somalia	28 Jan 61	388UNTS75	105573
Gabon	UN Special Fund	02 Feb 61	387UNTS289	105568
Nigeria	UN Special Fund	10 Feb 61	390UNTS85	105604
Mexico	UN Special Fund	23 Feb 61	388UNTS151	105576
Cyprus	UN Special Fund	24 Feb 61	389UNTS3	105588
Panama	UN Special Fund	09 Mar 61	396UNTS3	105691
Cuba	UN Special Fund	10 Mar 61	390UNTS35	105601
Honduras	USA (United States)	12 Apr 61	413UNTS182	105952
Cyprus	UNICEF (Children)	19 Apr 61	394UNTS185	105678
USA (United States)	Yugoslavia	19 Apr 61	409UNTS163	105883
Korea, South	UN Special Fund	21 Apr 61	394UNTS231	200583
Ceylon (Sri Lanka)	UN Special Fund	03 May 61	395UNTS217	105687
Cameroon	UN Special Fund	13 Jun 61	397UNTS297	105713
Paraguay	UN Special Fund	22 Jun 61	399UNTS117	105738
UN Special Fund	Upper Volta	26 Jun 61	400UNTS3	105744
Philippines	UN Special Fund	28 Jun 61	399UNTS141	105739
Haiti	UN Special Fund	28 Jun 61	399UNTS171	105741
Austria	Yugoslavia	30 Jun 61	443UNTS51	106358
UNICEF (Children)	Saudi Arabia	04 Jul 61	413UNTS122	105947
Mali	UN Special Fund	21 Jul 61	401UNTS141	105768
UN Special Fund	Yemen	02 Aug 61	402UNTS43	105777
Chile	USA (United States)	03 Aug 61	433UNTS21	106228
Cameroon	UNICEF (Children)	12 Aug 61	402UNTS235	105788
Central Afri Rep	UNICEF (Children)	21 Aug 61	413UNTS48	105939
Poland	UNICEF (Children)	24 Aug 61	406UNTS95	105841
Chad	UNICEF (Children)	26 Aug 61	422UNTS231	106077
Ivory Coast	UN Special Fund	29 Aug 61	406UNTS129	105844
UN Special Fund	Sierra Leone	02 Oct 61	422UNTS131	106073
Gabon	UNICEF (Children)	02 Nov 61	422UNTS241	106078
Czechoslovakia	Hungary	02 Nov 61	438UNTS3	106313
Mauritania	UN Special Fund	07 Nov 61	412UNTS240	105936
Congo (Brazzaville)	UN Special Fund	09 Nov 61	413UNTS58	105940
Malagasy	UNICEF (Children)	16 Nov 61	422UNTS251	106079
Guatemala	Israel	27 Nov 61	448UNTS191	106431
UN Special Fund	Venezuela	11 Dec 61	422UNTS149	106074
UN Special Fund	Senegal	16 Dec 61	425UNTS97	106121
Malagasy	UN Special Fund	05 Jan 62	419UNTS29	106028
Ivory Coast	UNICEF (Children)	10 Jan 62	422UNTS261	106080
UNICEF (Children)	Yemen	31 Jan 62	422UNTS271	106081
Niger	UN Special Fund	26 Feb 62	423UNTS83	106086
Dominican Republic	USA (United States)	08 Mar 62	527UNTS29	107615
Dahomey	UN Special Fund	28 Mar 62	424UNTS55	106099
UNICEF (Children)	Somalia	01 Apr 62	431UNTS75	106211
Congo (Brazzaville)	UNICEF (Children)	09 Apr 62	431UNTS65	106210
UNICEF (Children)	Sierra Leone	11 Apr 62	431UNTS55	106209
UN Special Fund	Uruguay	04 May 62	429UNTS143	106196
Dominican Republic	UN Special Fund	06 Jun 62	429UNTS169	106197
UN Special Fund	Syria	07 Jul 62	443UNTS3	106355
UN Special Fund	Tanganyika	17 Jul 62	435UNTS237	106281
Japan	UN Special Fund	31 Oct 62	444UNTS171	106368

PARTY ONE	PARTY TWO	DATE	CITATION	NUMBER
Public information (Cont.)				
Japan	UK Great Britain	14 Nov 62	478UNTS29	106934
Congo (Zaire)	USA (United States)	17 Nov 62	474UNTS41	106870
Algeria	UNICEF (Children)	20 Nov 62	453UNTS151	106522
Multilateral		08 Dec 62	510UNTS235	107418
Mauritania	UNICEF (Children)	19 Jan 63	452UNTS271	106514
UNICEF (Children)	Tanganyika	25 Jan 63	453UNTS249	106528
UN Special Fund	Uganda	22 Mar 63	456UNTS466	106572
Jamaica	UN Special Fund	22 May 63	489UNTS191	107140
Netherlands	UN Special Fund	24 May 63	466UNTS289	106750
UN Special Fund	Western Samoa	05 Jun 63	467UNTS463	200601
Burundi	UN Special Fund	22 Aug 63	476UNTS49	106903
Central Afri Rep	UN Special Fund	30 Oct 63	481UNTS247	106985
Somalia	USA (United States)	08 Jan 64	505UNTS165	107372
Ireland	UN Special Fund	03 Jun 64	496UNTS205	107253
Germany, East	Poland	06 Oct 64	552UNTS89	108051
Asian Productivity	ILO (Labor Org)	27 Oct 64	516UNTS367	200610
Poland	USSR (Soviet Union)	31 Mar 65	571UNTS217	108304
Afghanistan	UK Great Britain	19 Apr 65	633UNTS45	109033
Bulgaria	Czechoslovakia	22 May 65	545UNTS65	107925
China People's Rep	Romania	27 May 65	592UNTS3	108566
UN Special Fund	Spain	30 Jun 65	544UNTS159	107918
Mongolia	UN Special Fund	26 Jan 66	552UNTS201	108055
Brazil	UNICEF (Children)	28 Mar 66	607UNTS235	108807
Bulgaria	United Arab Rep	29 Aug 66	630UNTS325	108980
Kuwait	UK Great Britain	26 Nov 66	633UNTS58	109034
Australia	UNICEF (Children)	21 Dec 67	614UNTS83	108864
UN Special Fund	Syria	22 Apr 68	634UNTS207	109063
Botswana	UNICEF (Children)	25 Jun 68	639UNTS61	109144
Jurisdiction				
Multilateral		15 Jun 27	38UNTS343	100608
Multilateral		15 Jun 27	38UNTS327	100607
Poland	Yugoslavia	02 Jan 46	115UNTS21	101556
Multilateral		27 Jun 46	264UNTS163	103792
Multilateral		11 Jul 47	214UNTS33	102898
Belgium	Italy	09 Feb 48	71UNTS143	100915
Czechoslovakia	Poland	05 Apr 48	31UNTS355	100482
Italy	Netherlands	04 Dec 48	46UNTS271	100716
Czechoslovakia	Poland	21 Jan 49	31UNTS205	100480
Multilateral		01 Jul 49	96UNTS237	101340
Multilateral		12 Aug 49	75UNTS287	100973
Costa Rica	WHO (World Health)	14 Jun 51	102UNTS151	101418
Multilateral		29 Jun 51	165UNTS303	102181
IBRD (World Bank)	Switzerland	29 Jun 51	216UNTS347	200529
Tunisia	USA (United States)	28 Jun 57	289UNTS301	104226
Czechoslovakia	USSR (Soviet Union)	31 Aug 57	308UNTS3	104456
Germany, East	USSR (Soviet Union)	28 Nov 57	305UNTS113	104419
Bulgaria	USSR (Soviet Union)	12 Dec 57	317UNTS217	104606
Korea, North	USSR (Soviet Union)	16 Dec 57	301UNTS301	104349
Romania	USSR (Soviet Union)	03 Apr 58	313UNTS167	104535
Multilateral		24 Jun 58	348UNTS275	105005
Italy	USA (United States)	30 Jul 59	355UNTS393	105088
Japan	USA (United States)	12 Nov 59	361UNTS27	105171
Italy	USA (United States)	19 Jul 60	389UNTS237	105595
Cyprus	USA (United States)	08 Dec 60	405UNTS145	105831
Multilateral		18 Mar 65	575UNTS159	108359
Canada	USA (United States)	25 Mar 65	607UNTS141	108802
Austria	Hungary	09 Apr 65	638UNTS105	109132
UK Great Britain	USA (United States)	30 Dec 66	603UNTS245	108736
Czechoslovakia	Hungary	27 Feb 68	640UNTS49	109154
Waiver of immunity				
Czechoslovakia	Ireland	29 Jan 47	27UNTS267	100411
Netherlands	USA (United States)	19 Jun 53	212UNTS249	102875
Germany, West	USA (United States)	27 Jul 56	278UNTS3	104017

PARTY ONE	PARTY TWO	DATE	CITATION	NUMBER
Recognition of legal documents				
Brazil	France	27 Jan 40	72UNTS77	100929
Spain	USA (United States)	02 Dec 44	89UNTS345	200262
Denmark	USA (United States)	16 Dec 44	10UNTS213	200063
Iceland	USA (United States)	27 Jan 45	122UNTS293	200411
Ireland	USA (United States)	03 Feb 45	122UNTS305	200412
Norway	USA (United States)	06 Oct 45	122UNTS319	200413
South Africa	UK Great Britain	26 Oct 45	72UNTS41	100927
Greece	UK Great Britain	26 Nov 45	35UNTS161	100555
Portugal	UK Great Britain	06 Dec 45	6UNTS3	100065
Portugal	UK Great Britain	06 Dec 45	5UNTS37	100064
Portugal	USA (United States)	06 Dec 45	3UNTS139	100028
Canada	UK Great Britain	21 Dec 45	27UNTS155	100405
Czechoslovakia	USA (United States)	03 Jan 46	6UNTS309	100084
Czechoslovakia	Poland	24 Jan 46	25UNTS181	100363
UK Great Britain	USA (United States)	11 Feb 46	3UNTS253	100036
Turkey	UK Great Britain	12 Feb 46	6UNTS79	100069
Turkey	USA (United States)	12 Feb 46	13UNTS3	100196
France	UK Great Britain	28 Feb 46	27UNTS173	100407
France	USA (United States)	27 Mar 46	139UNTS114	101879
Greece	USA (United States)	27 Mar 46	15UNTS233	100239
Iraq	Turkey	29 Mar 46	37UNTS333	100581
Belgium	USA (United States)	05 Apr 46	4UNTS125	100041
Ireland	UK Great Britain	05 Apr 46	72UNTS57	100928
Belgium	Denmark	08 Apr 46	4UNTS429	100059
Argentina	UK Great Britain	17 Apr 46	164UNTS53	102159
France	Ireland	16 May 46	44UNTS105	100681
Denmark	Luxembourg	21 May 46	4UNTS435	100060
Ireland	Sweden	29 May 46	35UNTS231	100557
Australia	Canada	11 Jun 46	10UNTS47	100142
United Arab Rep	USA (United States)	15 Jun 46	71UNTS157	100917
Sweden	Turkey	26 Jun 46	14UNTS21	100208
Multilateral		29 Jun 46	94UNTS11	101303
Netherlands	Spain	13 Jul 46	4UNTS351	100055
Czechoslovakia	USSR (Soviet Union)	25 Jul 46	27UNTS231	100409
France	Sweden	02 Aug 46	27UNTS251	100410
Lebanon	USA (United States)	11 Aug 46	66UNTS211	100856
Norway	UK Great Britain	31 Aug 46	6UNTS235	100078
Brazil	USA (United States)	06 Sep 46	54UNTS197	100805
France	Turkey	12 Oct 46	14UNTS33	100209
Denmark	South Africa	14 Oct 46	10UNTS29	100140
Belgium	Portugal	22 Oct 46	34UNTS49	100527
Brazil	UK Great Britain	31 Oct 46	11UNTS115	100152
Philippines	USA (United States)	16 Nov 46	7UNTS151	100097
Sweden	UK Great Britain	27 Nov 46	11UNTS229	100162
New Zealand	USA (United States)	03 Dec 46	7UNTS175	100099
Australia	USA (United States)	03 Dec 46	7UNTS201	100100
Portugal	Switzerland	09 Dec 46	310UNTS251	104495
Brazil	Portugal	10 Dec 46	200UNTS67	102695
USA (United States)	Uruguay	14 Dec 46	532UNTS87	107713
Taiwan	USA (United States)	20 Dec 46	22UNTS87	100332
Ecuador	USA (United States)	08 Jan 47	22UNTS119	100333
Czechoslovakia	Ireland	29 Jan 47	27UNTS267	100411
Thailand	USA (United States)	26 Feb 47	16UNTS17	100246
Paraguay	USA (United States)	28 Feb 47	44UNTS25	100676
Portugal	Sweden	06 Mar 47	35UNTS243	100558
Netherlands	Turkey	19 Mar 47	14UNTS59	100211
Greece	Sweden	08 Apr 47	94UNTS73	101307
Greece	Netherlands	17 Apr 47	32UNTS115	100494
Canada	Portugal	25 Apr 47	94UNTS87	101308
Syria	USA (United States)	28 Apr 47	262UNTS121	103741
France	Greece	05 May 47	76UNTS61	100980
Chile	USA (United States)	10 May 47	55UNTS21	100807
Czechoslovakia	Denmark	14 May 47	27UNTS297	100413
South Africa	USA (United States)	23 May 47	66UNTS233	100857

Recognition of legal documents (Cont.)

PARTY ONE	PARTY TWO	DATE	CITATION	NUMBER
Canada	Sweden	27 Jun 47	27UNTS313	100414
Iraq	Turkey	30 Jun 47	72UNTS107	100930
Romania	Yugoslavia	30 Jun 47	116UNTS57	101569
Denmark	Turkey	30 Jun 47	32UNTS301	100504
Canada	UK Great Britain	17 Jul 47	28UNTS3	100416
Netherlands	Thailand	18 Jul 47	28UNTS27	100417
Greece	Turkey	22 Jul 47	72UNTS131	100931
Netherlands	South Africa	22 Jul 47	12UNTS257	100188
Taiwan	UK Great Britain	23 Jul 47	9UNTS207	100135
Poland	Romania	09 Aug 47	12UNTS363	100193
Hungary	Poland	28 Aug 47	15UNTS145	100231
Czechoslovakia	Netherlands	01 Sep 47	32UNTS129	100495
Czechoslovakia	Switzerland	10 Sep 47	35UNTS275	100559
Lebanon	Turkey	16 Sep 47	44UNTS123	100682
Czechoslovakia	Sweden	15 Oct 47	44UNTS149	100683
Colombia	UK Great Britain	16 Oct 47	160UNTS297	102115
Norway	Portugal	11 Nov 47	34UNTS257	100542
Denmark	Greece	14 Nov 47	35UNTS295	100560
Denmark	Ireland	18 Nov 47	35UNTS309	100561
Ireland	Italy	21 Nov 47	353UNTS73	105038
Taiwan	Netherlands	06 Dec 47	43UNTS185	100669
Denmark	Portugal	15 Dec 47	35UNTS329	100563
Austria	Netherlands	22 Jan 48	17UNTS99	100270
Italy	USA (United States)	06 Feb 48	73UNTS113	100950
Czechoslovakia	Yugoslavia	14 Mar 48	28UNTS81	100421
Argentina	Denmark	18 Mar 48	94UNTS175	101311
Cuba	UK Great Britain	19 Mar 48	175UNTS23	102294
Ireland	Switzerland	06 May 48	334UNTS187	104768
Jordan	Turkey	07 May 48	32UNTS313	100505
Ireland	Netherlands	10 May 48	28UNTS121	100422
Norway	Turkey	20 May 48	26UNTS137	100384
Greece	Switzerland	26 May 48	94UNTS217	101312
Ireland	Norway	21 Jun 48	34UNTS317	100545
France	Spain	23 Aug 48	28UNTS173	100425
Greece	Lebanon	06 Sep 48	178UNTS37	102335
Bolivia	USA (United States)	29 Sep 48	505UNTS139	107370
Netherlands	Spain	08 Oct 48	28UNTS209	100426
Mexico	Portugal	22 Oct 48	34UNTS329	100546
Argentina	Netherlands	29 Oct 48	95UNTS21	101316
Czechoslovakia	Poland	12 Nov 48	84UNTS347	101141
Italy	USSR (Soviet Union)	11 Dec 48	217UNTS181	102948
Czechoslovakia	Poland	21 Jan 49	31UNTS205	100480
Italy	Lebanon	24 Jan 49	231UNTS241	103223
Switzerland	Turkey	16 Feb 49	72UNTS175	100933
Finland	Netherlands	25 Feb 49	53UNTS123	100777
Netherlands	Switzerland	07 Mar 49	35UNTS69	100551
Finland	USA (United States)	29 Mar 49	55UNTS59	100808
Panama	USA (United States)	31 Mar 49	55UNTS87	100810
Finland	Sweden	26 Apr 49	95UNTS83	101318
Bulgaria	Poland	16 May 49	84UNTS313	101140
Italy	Spain	31 May 49	231UNTS251	103224
Canada	USA (United States)	04 Jun 49	122UNTS237	101649
Belgium	Greece	21 Jun 49	137UNTS215	101854
India	Switzerland	24 Jun 49	95UNTS109	101319
Czechoslovakia	Poland	02 Jul 49	260UNTS179	103709
Czechoslovakia	Poland	02 Jul 49	260UNTS149	103708
Greece	Syria	05 Jul 49	78UNTS71	101013
Iraq	Norway	12 Jul 49	53UNTS137	100778
Czechoslovakia	Finland	13 Jul 49	53UNTS153	100779
Dominican Republic	USA (United States)	19 Jul 49	51UNTS145	100762
Finland	Norway	24 Aug 49	53UNTS167	100780
Denmark	Finland	26 Aug 49	53UNTS191	100781
Belgium	Canada	30 Aug 49	53UNTS221	100782
Multilateral		19 Sep 49	125UNTS3	101671
Lebanon	Netherlands	20 Sep 49	108UNTS205	101474

Recognition of legal documents (Cont.)

PARTY ONE	PARTY TWO	DATE	CITATION	NUMBER
Burma	USA (United States)	28 Sep 49	55UNTS3	100806
Greece	Philippines	08 Oct 49	187UNTS221	102515
Denmark	Thailand	23 Nov 49	53UNTS255	100786
Sweden	Thailand	23 Nov 49	72UNTS217	100935
Italy	Turkey	25 Nov 49	192UNTS39	102594
Norway	Thailand	26 Nov 49	53UNTS269	100787
Austria	Norway	02 Dec 49	72UNTS230	100936
Austria	Sweden	02 Dec 49	108UNTS3	101465
Austria	Denmark	02 Dec 49	53UNTS281	100788
Austria	Switzerland	19 Dec 49	254UNTS287	103597
USA (United States)	Yugoslavia	24 Dec 49	89UNTS209	101219
Netherlands	Syria	13 Feb 50	108UNTS53	101467
Canada	Norway	14 Feb 50	53UNTS329	100790
Spain	Sweden	18 Feb 50	166UNTS15	102184
Ceylon (Sri Lanka)	Thailand	24 Feb 50	72UNTS261	100938
Italy	Netherlands	04 Mar 50	254UNTS305	103598
Denmark	Iceland	22 Mar 50	72UNTS273	100939
Iceland	Netherlands	22 Mar 50	95UNTS237	101323
Italy	Portugal	05 Apr 50	254UNTS329	103599
Israel	USA (United States)	13 Jun 50	212UNTS93	102863
Netherlands	Spain	20 Jun 50	95UNTS303	101327
Burma	Ceylon (Sri Lanka)	29 Jun 50	73UNTS3	100940
Spain	UK Great Britain	20 Jul 50	398UNTS101	105719
Spain	Switzerland	03 Aug 50	254UNTS365	103600
Canada	New Zealand	16 Aug 50	77UNTS239	101002
Burma	Sweden	14 Sep 50	96UNTS45	101330
Brazil	Turkey	21 Sep 50	150UNTS299	101981
Sweden	Switzerland	18 Oct 50	166UNTS49	102185
Luxembourg	Portugal	21 Oct 50	108UNTS67	101468
Israel	Netherlands	23 Oct 50	189UNTS89	102543
Costa Rica	USA (United States)	17 Jan 51	134UNTS215	101801
Denmark	Norway	18 Jan 51	82UNTS153	101090
Panama	USA (United States)	26 Jan 51	137UNTS69	101849
Israel	Turkey	05 Feb 51	193UNTS3	102607
Colombia	Portugal	09 Mar 51	108UNTS87	101469
Greece	Yugoslavia	15 Mar 51	187UNTS237	102516
El Salvador	USA (United States)	19 Mar 51	134UNTS245	101803
Multilateral		18 Apr 51	261UNTS140	103729
Nicaragua	USA (United States)	20 Apr 51	138UNTS57	101859
Greece	Norway	28 May 51	187UNTS141	102507
Multilateral		19 Jun 51	199UNTS67	102678
Cuba	Portugal	26 Jun 51	192UNTS115	102598
Iceland	Norway	14 Jul 51	163UNTS265	102150
Burma	Denmark	30 Jul 51	108UNTS167	101472
Burma	Netherlands	06 Sep 51	108UNTS187	101473
Panama	UK Great Britain	15 Sep 51	560UNTS143	108172
Philippines	Spain	06 Oct 51	215UNTS193	102920
Greece	Luxembourg	22 Oct 51	187UNTS119	102506
Denmark	Iraq	18 Nov 51	232UNTS25	103227
Multilateral		06 Dec 51	150UNTS67	101963
Colombia	Spain	11 Dec 51	216UNTS73	102933
France	USA (United States)	02 Feb 52	247UNTS223	103472
Belgium	Spain	10 Mar 52	178UNTS243	102342
Norway	Uruguay	20 Mar 52	310UNTS279	104496
Sweden	Uruguay	20 Mar 52	311UNTS3	104497
Belgium	France	21 Mar 52	137UNTS249	101856
Iraq	Switzerland	31 Mar 52	311UNTS43	104498
France	Mexico	17 Apr 52	163UNTS321	102153
Denmark	UK Great Britain	23 Jun 52	151UNTS3	101982
Japan	USA (United States)	11 Aug 52	212UNTS27	102862
Mexico	Netherlands	13 Oct 52	163UNTS341	102154
Austria	Luxembourg	13 Oct 52	192UNTS291	102606
Iceland	Luxembourg	23 Oct 52	193UNTS39	102609
Chile	Sweden	27 Oct 52	311UNTS63	104499
Chile	Denmark	27 Oct 52	271UNTS93	103911

PARTY ONE	PARTY TWO	DATE	CITATION	NUMBER
Recognition of legal documents (Cont.)				
Luxembourg	Sweden	17 Nov 52	173UNTS277	102270
Luxembourg	Norway	17 Nov 52	311UNTS95	104500
Israel	Switzerland	19 Nov 52	232UNTS3	103226
Ethiopia	USA (United States)	22 May 53	191UNTS59	102577
Cuba	USA (United States)	26 May 53	224UNTS75	103070
Switzerland	Yugoslavia	28 May 53	232UNTS45	103228
Burma	Norway	22 Jun 53	174UNTS49	102277
Libya	UK Great Britain	29 Jul 53	186UNTS201	102492
USA (United States)	Venezuela	14 Aug 53	213UNTS99	102883
Nicaragua	USA (United States)	02 Sep 53	215UNTS69	102911
Austria	Yugoslavia	11 Nov 53	363UNTS149	105206
Syria	UK Great Britain	30 Jan 54	449UNTS47	106452
France	Sweden	16 Feb 54	228UNTS137	103147
Peru	Spain	31 Mar 54	232UNTS65	103230
Bulgaria	Czechoslovakia	13 Apr 54	501UNTS3	107314
France	Netherlands	30 Apr 54	202UNTS115	102727
Ireland	Luxembourg	27 Jul 54	232UNTS91	103231
Saudi Arabia	UK Great Britain	30 Jul 54	201UNTS317	102722
Chile	UK Great Britain	31 Jul 54	618UNTS353	108934
Libya	USA (United States)	09 Sep 54	224UNTS217	103078
Ecuador	Netherlands	14 Dec 54	232UNTS115	103233
Denmark	USA (United States)	15 Dec 54	213UNTS273	102890
Sweden	USA (United States)	22 Dec 54	228UNTS85	103143
Norway	Switzerland	30 Dec 54	311UNTS147	104502
Austria	Belgium	07 Jan 55	380UNTS219	105458
Italy	USA (United States)	26 Jan 55	238UNTS179	103361
South Africa	USA (United States)	22 Feb 55	247UNTS247	103473
Germany, West	Norway	18 Mar 55	209UNTS309	102832
Austria	Romania	11 May 55	342UNTS119	104904
Hungary	USSR (Soviet Union)	27 May 55	407UNTS156	105864
Germany, West	USA (United States)	07 Jul 55	275UNTS3	103973
Germany, East	Romania	28 Jul 55	342UNTS207	104909
USSR (Soviet Union)	Yugoslavia	03 Sep 55	240UNTS267	103408
Germany, East	Hungary	10 Sep 55	407UNTS132	105863
Bulgaria	Yugoslavia	01 Oct 55	396UNTS223	105698
France	Germany, West	04 Oct 55	353UNTS203	105044
Finland	USSR (Soviet Union)	19 Oct 55	353UNTS185	105043
Denmark	Syria	20 Oct 55	250UNTS61	103518
Fed Rhod/Nyasaland	Netherlands	02 Nov 55	263UNTS381	103784
Netherlands	USA (United States)	04 Nov 55	269UNTS3	103867
Burma	China People's Rep	08 Nov 55	306UNTS11	104430
Austria	Israel	17 Nov 55	232UNTS153	103235
Austria	Italy	23 Jan 56	393UNTS97	105653
Argentina	Switzerland	25 Jan 56	559UNTS121	108157
Romania	Yugoslavia	01 Feb 56	362UNTS203	105189
Hungary	Romania	03 Feb 56	362UNTS233	105190
Austria	Poland	08 Feb 56	334UNTS221	104770
Norway	Syria	25 Feb 56	463UNTS217	106706
Multilateral		05 Mar 56	326UNTS181	104712
Bulgaria	Yugoslavia	23 Mar 56	367UNTS213	105230
Norway	USSR (Soviet Union)	31 Mar 56	259UNTS205	103690
Denmark	USSR (Soviet Union)	31 Mar 56	259UNTS169	103689
Sweden	USSR (Soviet Union)	31 Mar 56	259UNTS239	103691
Belgium	Germany, West	14 Apr 56	344UNTS103	104945
Germany, West	Switzerland	02 May 56	559UNTS157	108158
Portugal	Venezuela	16 May 56	463UNTS239	106707
Multilateral		19 May 56	399UNTS189	105742
Greece	Italy	26 May 56	496UNTS301	107258
Italy	Switzerland	04 Jun 56	378UNTS311	105429
Poland	Sweden	08 Jun 56	334UNTS257	104771
Germany, West	Ireland	12 Jun 56	353UNTS121	105040
Australia	Netherlands	01 Aug 56	280UNTS3	104047
Canada	France	04 Sep 56	305UNTS79	104415
Denmark	Finland	15 Sep 56	254UNTS3	103589
Denmark	Sweden	15 Sep 56	263UNTS3	103764

PARTY ONE	PARTY TWO	DATE	CITATION	NUMBER
Recognition of legal documents (Cont.)				
Switzerland	Thailand	13 Oct 56	312UNTS43	104510
Belgium	Poland	17 Oct 56	356UNTS279	105100
Colombia	USA (United States)	24 Oct 56	476UNTS77	106905
Belgium	Turkey	25 Oct 56	380UNTS3	105447
Taiwan	USA (United States)	21 Nov 56	265UNTS241	103816
Albania	Yugoslavia	23 Nov 56	386UNTS73	105539
Peru	Switzerland	23 Nov 56	411UNTS97	105916
Belgium	Romania	04 Dec 56	317UNTS161	104602
France	USA (United States)	14 Dec 56	266UNTS117	103826
Poland	USSR (Soviet Union)	17 Dec 56	266UNTS179	103830
Iran	USA (United States)	16 Jan 57	308UNTS147	104460
Iceland	Thailand	22 Jan 57	312UNTS63	104511
Denmark	Germany, West	29 Jan 57	302UNTS75	104354
Germany, West	Sweden	29 Jan 57	393UNTS113	105654
Germany, West	Norway	29 Jan 57	353UNTS39	105037
Germany, East	Poland	01 Feb 57	319UNTS115	104632
Norway	USA (United States)	05 Feb 57	279UNTS169	104038
Germany, East	USSR (Soviet Union)	12 Mar 57	285UNTS105	104150
Belgium	Czechoslovakia	12 Mar 57	312UNTS75	104512
Netherlands	Yugoslavia	13 Mar 57	327UNTS227	104723
Netherlands	USA (United States)	03 Apr 57	410UNTS193	105904
Germany, West	Yugoslavia	10 Apr 57	463UNTS269	106708
Netherlands	Venezuela	11 Apr 57	288UNTS23	104193
Romania	USSR (Soviet Union)	15 Apr 57	274UNTS143	103964
Romania	Sweden	15 Apr 57	342UNTS325	104915
Bulgaria	Sweden	17 Apr 57	464UNTS3	106709
Bulgaria	Yugoslavia	19 Apr 57	349UNTS3	105006
Belgium	Bulgaria	14 May 57	317UNTS81	104596
Czechoslovakia	Yugoslavia	22 May 57	391UNTS33	105615
Hungary	Netherlands	28 May 57	334UNTS291	104773
Belgium	Hungary	01 Jun 57	291UNTS17	104242
Italy	UK Great Britain	12 Jun 57	310UNTS35	104484
Afghanistan	Pakistan	13 Jun 57	327UNTS51	104717
Austria	USSR (Soviet Union)	14 Jun 57	285UNTS169	104152
Czechoslovakia	United Arab Rep	30 Jun 57	411UNTS126	105917
Hungary	Sweden	02 Aug 57	334UNTS307	104774
Greece	Italy	02 Aug 57	533UNTS217	107744
Netherlands	Romania	27 Aug 57	342UNTS309	104914
Czechoslovakia	USSR (Soviet Union)	31 Aug 57	308UNTS3	104456
Italy	Switzerland	19 Sep 57	363UNTS69	105200
Spain	USA (United States)	23 Sep 57	290UNTS261	104238
Italy	Pakistan	05 Oct 57	353UNTS91	105039
Netherlands	UK Great Britain	22 Oct 57	313UNTS309	104538
France	Morocco	25 Oct 57	559UNTS95	108156
Poland	USSR (Soviet Union)	26 Oct 57	432UNTS221	106223
Germany, East	Hungary	30 Oct 57	408UNTS4	105867
Germany, East	USSR (Soviet Union)	28 Nov 57	305UNTS113	104419
Belgium	USA (United States)	03 Dec 57	303UNTS45	104370
Bulgaria	USSR (Soviet Union)	12 Dec 57	317UNTS217	104606
Korea, North	USSR (Soviet Union)	16 Dec 57	301UNTS301	104349
UK Great Britain	USSR (Soviet Union)	19 Dec 57	351UNTS235	105026
Poland	Yugoslavia	16 Jan 58	340UNTS137	104863
Belgium	Morocco	20 Jan 58	288UNTS3	104192
Bulgaria	Netherlands	07 Feb 58	335UNTS45	104777
Afghanistan	Turkey	08 Feb 58	464UNTS39	106711
Bulgaria	Yugoslavia	21 Mar 58	349UNTS61	105009
Morocco	Portugal	03 Apr 58	393UNTS203	105657
Romania	USSR (Soviet Union)	03 Apr 58	313UNTS167	104535
Sweden	Yugoslavia	18 Apr 58	393UNTS225	105658
Sweden	Switzerland	30 Apr 58	427UNTS295	106161
Multilateral		13 May 58	389UNTS277	105598
Bulgaria	Denmark	28 May 58	312UNTS235	104521
India	USSR (Soviet Union)	02 Jun 58	393UNTS3	105650
Belgium	USSR (Soviet Union)	05 Jun 58	345UNTS145	104965
Denmark	Luxembourg	10 Jun 58	356UNTS193	105096

PARTY ONE	PARTY TWO	DATE	CITATION	NUMBER
Recognition of legal documents (Cont.)				
USA (United States)	Yugoslavia	16 Jun 58	317UNTS31	104591
Netherlands	USSR (Soviet Union)	17 Jun 58	335UNTS77	104779
Austria	Belgium	20 Jun 58	312UNTS95	104513
Denmark	Romania	25 Jun 58	345UNTS231	104970
Albania	USSR (Soviet Union)	30 Jun 58	328UNTS3	104729
Austria	Romania	10 Jul 58	353UNTS155	105041
Hungary	USSR (Soviet Union)	15 Jul 58	322UNTS3	104656
Germany, East	Romania	15 Jul 58	395UNTS3	105681
Denmark	Hungary	17 Jul 58	344UNTS281	104954
Romania	United Arab Rep	14 Aug 58	405UNTS189	105834
Austria	Bulgaria	12 Sep 58	353UNTS3	105036
United Arab Rep	USSR (Soviet Union)	18 Sep 58	338UNTS29	104831
Hungary	Romania	07 Oct 58	416UNTS199	106004
Czechoslovakia	Romania	25 Oct 58	417UNTS37	106006
Bulgaria	Romania	03 Dec 58	417UNTS133	106007
Germany, West	USA (United States)	11 Dec 58	337UNTS31	104813
Albania	Czechoslovakia	16 Jan 59	363UNTS195	105208
Finland	Norway	21 Jan 59	325UNTS295	104705
UK Great Britain	Yugoslavia	03 Feb 59	359UNTS339	105151
Belgium	Morocco	27 Feb 59	390UNTS275	105611
Indonesia	USA (United States)	02 Mar 59	357UNTS145	105113
Hungary	Poland	06 Mar 59	432UNTS3	106216
Sweden	Tunisia	19 Mar 59	497UNTS43	107261
Norway	Tunisia	28 Mar 59	497UNTS77	107263
Denmark	Tunisia	14 Apr 59	340UNTS273	104870
Multilateral		20 Apr 59	472UNTS185	106841
Austria	USA (United States)	30 Apr 59	343UNTS41	104920
Belgium	Sweden	18 May 59	341UNTS277	104890
Ceylon (Sri Lanka)	Denmark	29 May 59	348UNTS225	105002
Ceylon (Sri Lanka)	Sweden	29 May 59	464UNTS109	106713
Ceylon (Sri Lanka)	Norway	29 May 59	411UNTS165	105919
Greece	Yugoslavia	18 Jun 59	368UNTS81	105236
Bulgaria	United Arab Rep	09 Jul 59	411UNTS187	105920
Australia	USA (United States)	20 Nov 59	349UNTS293	105015
Albania	Hungary	12 Jan 60	520UNTS3	107511
Poland	Yugoslavia	06 Feb 60	521UNTS37	107517
France	Thailand	26 Feb 60	392UNTS279	105648
Finland	Iceland	10 Mar 60	497UNTS95	107264
Luxembourg	Yugoslavia	09 Apr 60	464UNTS293	106719
Multilateral		22 Apr 60	418UNTS211	106023
Greece	Romania	02 May 60	485UNTS17	107043
Hungary	Yugoslavia	07 May 60	519UNTS237	107510
Morocco	United Arab Rep	19 May 60	563UNTS121	108208
Switzerland	Tunisia	21 May 60	497UNTS109	107265
Afghanistan	Czechoslovakia	28 May 60	497UNTS129	107266
Luxembourg	Tunisia	13 Jun 60	497UNTS143	107267
Denmark	Peru	22 Jun 60	439UNTS113	106326
Mexico	USA (United States)	15 Aug 60	402UNTS177	105786
Belgium	Burma	17 Aug 60	540UNTS185	107850
Hungary	UK Great Britain	25 Oct 60	419UNTS309	106034
Burma	Switzerland	31 Oct 60	465UNTS97	106723
Norway	Peru	02 Nov 60	497UNTS207	107270
Luxembourg	Thailand	29 Dec 60	465UNTS131	106725
Norway	Poland	17 Jan 61	412UNTS130	105928
Czechoslovakia	Morocco	08 Jun 61	497UNTS275	107272
Cameroon	France	16 Jun 61	412UNTS148	105929
Finland	Luxembourg	15 Aug 61	541UNTS45	107859
Mexico	Netherlands	24 Aug 61	465UNTS291	106732
Liberia	Switzerland	31 Aug 61	559UNTS215	108160
Ghana	Romania	30 Sep 61	467UNTS443	106769
Switzerland	USA (United States)	13 Oct 61	459UNTS219	106625
Austria	Czechoslovakia	10 Nov 61	455UNTS337	106550
Bulgaria	Poland	04 Dec 61	484UNTS3	107019
Finland	UK Great Britain	05 Dec 61	424UNTS217	106110
Poland	Romania	25 Jan 62	468UNTS3	106770

PARTY ONE	PARTY TWO	DATE	CITATION	NUMBER
Recognition of legal documents (Cont.)				
Israel	IBRD (World Bank)	01 Feb 62	435UNTS155	106277
Hungary	Yugoslavia	09 Feb 62	577UNTS3	108370
Finland	Hungary	13 Feb 62	463UNTS61	106693
USSR (Soviet Union)	Yugoslavia	24 Feb 62	471UNTS195	106833
Ghana	USSR (Soviet Union)	06 Apr 62	498UNTS41	107277
France	Romania	18 May 62	498UNTS115	107279
France	Senegal	15 Jun 62	524UNTS3	107563
Morocco	Switzerland	05 Jul 62	498UNTS171	107281
Austria	Czechoslovakia	22 Sep 62	495UNTS157	107244
Finland	France	12 Oct 62	498UNTS299	107285
Hungary	Syria	18 Oct 62	491UNTS209	107178
France	Ivory Coast	19 Oct 62	498UNTS317	107286
Finland	New Zealand	12 Nov 62	485UNTS331	107064
Czechoslovakia	Poland	16 Nov 62	526UNTS3	107597
Ivory Coast	Switzerland	17 Nov 62	499UNTS3	107289
Ghana	Tunisia	11 Dec 62	563UNTS243	108213
Austria	Yugoslavia	11 Dec 62	546UNTS3	107938
Syria	United Arab Rep	27 Dec 62	491UNTS245	107180
Ghana	Mali	09 Jan 63	466UNTS165	106742
Senegal	Switzerland	23 Jan 63	524UNTS23	107564
Japan	USA (United States)	01 Feb 63	473UNTS49	106854
Mali	Senegal	07 Feb 63	524UNTS41	107565
Algeria	France	18 Feb 63	563UNTS263	108214
Austria	Czechoslovakia	08 Mar 63	495UNTS219	107245
Greece	Hungary	27 Apr 63	534UNTS3	107750
Algeria	Morocco	30 Apr 63	564UNTS3	108217
Australia	USA (United States)	09 May 63	469UNTS55	106784
Canada	Finland	05 Jun 63	472UNTS345	106846
Guinea	Ivory Coast	26 Jun 63	499UNTS71	107293
Algeria	Mali	22 Jul 63	564UNTS29	108219
Australia	Finland	31 Jul 63	478UNTS363	106942
Cameroon	Israel	09 Aug 63	499UNTS121	107295
Pakistan	USSR (Soviet Union)	07 Oct 63	499UNTS161	107297
Ivory Coast	Netherlands	09 Oct 63	499UNTS141	107296
Czechoslovakia	Hungary	20 Dec 63	538UNTS127	107812
Ceylon (Sri Lanka)	Finland	08 Jan 64	492UNTS285	107198
Mali	Niger	15 Jan 64	499UNTS197	107299
Czechoslovakia	Yugoslavia	20 Jan 64	538UNTS197	107816
Denmark	Yugoslavia	11 Feb 64	511UNTS241	107437
Cameroon	Mali	17 Mar 64	524UNTS61	107566
United Arab Rep	USA (United States)	05 May 64	531UNTS229	107706
Finland	South Africa	12 Jun 64	505UNTS107	107367
New Zealand	USA (United States)	24 Jun 64	524UNTS101	107568
Ivory Coast	Mali	09 Jul 64	524UNTS121	107569
Canada	Denmark	15 Oct 64	525UNTS227	107595
Denmark	India	06 Feb 65	531UNTS23	107690
Austria	Hungary	09 Apr 65	638UNTS105	109132
Austria	Hungary	09 Apr 65	638UNTS135	109133
Multilateral		15 Nov 65	0UNTS0	109432
Multilateral		05 Apr 66	640UNTS133	109159
Guyana	UK Great Britain	26 May 66	595UNTS255	108621
Austria	Israel	06 Jun 66	0UNTS0	109347
Austria	France	15 Jul 66	604UNTS265	108755
Bulgaria	United Arab Rep	29 Aug 66	630UNTS325	108980
Denmark	Singapore	20 Dec 66	593UNTS125	108580
Czechoslovakia	Yugoslavia	17 May 67	617UNTS305	108918
Private contracts				
Multilateral		24 Jun 26	38UNTS295	100605
Multilateral		27 Jun 39	40UNTS311	100640
Multilateral		27 Jun 39	40UNTS281	100639
Panama	USA (United States)	23 Mar 40	124UNTS195	200420
Canada	USA (United States)	18 Mar 42	101UNTS205	200294
Peru	USA (United States)	07 May 42	103UNTS219	200316
Canada	USA (United States)	27 Jun 42	99UNTS223	200276

PARTY ONE	PARTY TWO	DATE	CITATION	NUMBER
Private contracts (Cont.)				
USA (United States)	Uruguay	21 Jul 42	120UNTS211	200393
Canada	USA (United States)	15 Aug 42	99UNTS233	200277
Honduras	USA (United States)	26 Oct 42	24UNTS209	200145
USA (United States)	Venezuela	18 Feb 43	21UNTS225	200125
Mexico	USA (United States)	26 Apr 43	21UNTS245	200127
Liberia	USA (United States)	31 Dec 43	106UNTS199	200341
Peru	USA (United States)	15 Apr 44	150UNTS317	200479
Costa Rica	USA (United States)	29 May 44	124UNTS155	200417
Brazil	Paraguay	11 Aug 44	67UNTS303	200227
Brazil	UNRRA (Relief)	12 Oct 44	67UNTS321	200228
Dominican Republic	USA (United States)	13 Oct 45	149UNTS361	200477
Multilateral		07 Nov 45	2UNTS17	100018
Multilateral		27 Dec 45	2UNTS39	100020
Albania	Yugoslavia	01 Jul 46	111UNTS3	101517
League of Nations	United Nations	31 Jul 46	1UNTS119	200003
Multilateral		11 Jul 47	161UNTS113	102125
Multilateral		19 Sep 47	30UNTS249	100461
Burma	UK Great Britain	17 Oct 47	70UNTS183	100904
Poland	Yugoslavia	07 Nov 47	115UNTS137	101561
Ecuador	USA (United States)	14 Nov 47	149UNTS297	101959
Belgium	Italy	09 Feb 48	71UNTS143	100915
Paraguay	USA (United States)	12 Mar 48	162UNTS30	102131
France	Norway	05 Jul 48	30UNTS281	100463
Italy	Netherlands	04 Dec 48	46UNTS271	100716
Belgium	Luxembourg	14 Jan 49	36UNTS339	100572
Allied Milit Occup	Norway	17 Feb 49	30UNTS137	100451
Multilateral		29 Jun 49	138UNTS207	101870
Greece	Italy	31 Aug 49	78UNTS89	101014
Ireland	USA (United States)	21 Jan 50	206UNTS269	102792
Netherlands	New Zealand	16 Oct 50	83UNTS269	101111
Germany, West	Netherlands	14 Dec 50	87UNTS257	101177
Chile	USA (United States)	16 Jan 51	157UNTS3	102043
Costa Rica	USA (United States)	17 Jan 51	134UNTS215	101801
Panama	USA (United States)	26 Jan 51	137UNTS69	101849
Nicaragua	USA (United States)	31 Jan 51	160UNTS121	102105
Nicaragua	USA (United States)	31 Jan 51	150UNTS3	101960
Panama	USA (United States)	26 Feb 51	160UNTS153	102106
El Salvador	USA (United States)	19 Mar 51	134UNTS245	101803
Belgium	UK Great Britain	06 Apr 51	110UNTS3	101496
Multilateral		18 Apr 51	261UNTS140	103729
Nicaragua	USA (United States)	20 Apr 51	138UNTS57	101859
Honduras	USA (United States)	24 Apr 51	140UNTS287	101894
Greece	USA (United States)	03 Aug 51	224UNTS279	103080
Mexico	USA (United States)	11 Aug 51	162UNTS103	102133
Multilateral		08 Sep 51	136UNTS165	101833
Ethiopia	USA (United States)	15 May 52	180UNTS227	102388
Germany, West	Israel	10 Sep 52	162UNTS205	102137
Ceylon (Sri Lanka)	USA (United States)	17 Nov 52	180UNTS207	102386
Libya	UK Great Britain	25 Mar 53	172UNTS281	102252
Japan	USA (United States)	02 Apr 53	206UNTS143	102788
El Salvador	USA (United States)	14 May 53	234UNTS71	103273
Brazil	USA (United States)	30 May 53	460UNTS89	106633
United Arab Rep	USA (United States)	18 Jun 53	204UNTS55	102749
Liberia	USA (United States)	23 Jun 53	213UNTS57	102880
Brazil	USA (United States)	26 Jun 53	336UNTS241	104808
Chile	USA (United States)	27 Jun 53	229UNTS193	103167
Chile	USA (United States)	27 Jun 53	229UNTS53	103160
Nicaragua	USA (United States)	30 Jun 53	215UNTS133	102917
Argentina	USSR (Soviet Union)	05 Aug 53	221UNTS99	103004
Belgium	USA (United States)	02 Sep 53	200UNTS127	102700
Chile	USA (United States)	30 Dec 53	236UNTS41	103315
Bolivia	USA (United States)	15 Jan 54	229UNTS213	103168
Italy	USA (United States)	31 Mar 54	235UNTS293	103311
Luxembourg	USA (United States)	17 Apr 54	257UNTS255	103661
Ethiopia	USA (United States)	21 Apr 54	232UNTS299	103244

PARTY ONE	PARTY TWO	DATE	CITATION	NUMBER
Private contracts (Cont.)				
Netherlands	USA (United States)	07 May 54	213UNTS325	102895
Panama	USA (United States)	11 May 54	236UNTS107	103319
Italy	UK Great Britain	01 Jun 54	312UNTS353	104525
Ethiopia	USA (United States)	12 Jun 54	234UNTS25	103270
Jordan	USA (United States)	17 Jun 54	266UNTS137	103828
Chile	USA (United States)	28 Jun 54	233UNTS3	103246
Ecuador	USA (United States)	30 Jun 54	236UNTS163	103323
Costa Rica	USA (United States)	30 Jun 54	235UNTS35	103294
Greece	USA (United States)	30 Jul 54	234UNTS43	103272
USA (United States)	Yugoslavia	18 Oct 54	273UNTS163	103951
Multilateral		23 Oct 54	332UNTS3	104760
Germany, West	USA (United States)	29 Oct 54	273UNTS3	103943
Netherlands	USA (United States)	14 Dec 54	262UNTS35	103737
Mexico	USA (United States)	09 Mar 55	263UNTS247	103776
Germany, West	USA (United States)	04 Apr 55	279UNTS73	104034
Canada	USA (United States)	15 Jun 55	235UNTS201	103302
Multilateral		21 Jun 55	305UNTS265	104423
Turkey	USA (United States)	29 Jun 55	269UNTS97	103878
Greece	Netherlands	14 Jul 55	227UNTS27	103129
Nicaragua	USA (United States)	21 Jan 56	367UNTS3	105224
Ethiopia	Italy	05 Mar 56	267UNTS189	103844
Netherlands	USA (United States)	27 Mar 56	285UNTS231	104154
Canada	USA (United States)	19 Apr 56	274UNTS3	103955
Japan	Philippines	09 May 56	285UNTS3	104148
Multilateral		19 May 56	399UNTS189	105742
Pakistan	USA (United States)	28 May 56	269UNTS15	103868
Multilateral		06 Jul 56	312UNTS109	104514
Austria	UK Great Britain	09 Jul 56	310UNTS61	104487
Taiwan	USA (United States)	21 Nov 56	265UNTS241	103816
Belgium	Spain	28 Nov 56	308UNTS285	104465
Canada	USA (United States)	26 Feb 57	279UNTS179	104039
Canada	USA (United States)	09 Apr 57	283UNTS217	104119
Germany, West	USA (United States)	10 Dec 57	307UNTS59	104442
Multilateral		24 Jun 58	348UNTS275	105005
Taiwan	USA (United States)	06 Aug 58	462UNTS3	106666
Iraq	USSR (Soviet Union)	16 Mar 59	346UNTS107	104979
Multilateral		19 Jun 59	413UNTS168	105951
Japan	USA (United States)	19 Jan 60	373UNTS207	105321
Germany, West	UK Great Britain	28 Jan 60	420UNTS29	106038
Turkey	USA (United States)	02 Mar 60	372UNTS37	105286
Netherlands	USA (United States)	24 Mar 60	406UNTS165	105847
Denmark	USA (United States)	12 Apr 60	373UNTS9	105311
Norway	USA (United States)	06 Jul 60	378UNTS25	105415
Italy	USA (United States)	07 Jul 60	380UNTS143	105455
France	USA (United States)	19 Sep 60	400UNTS21	105745
Belgium	USA (United States)	21 Feb 61	480UNTS149	106967
USA (United States)	Vietnam, South	03 Apr 61	424UNTS137	106106
Netherlands	Spain	08 Apr 61	482UNTS193	106996
Argentina	Japan	20 Dec 61	613UNTS323	108859
Luxembourg	USA (United States)	23 Feb 62	474UNTS3	106868
Greece	United Nations	18 May 62	429UNTS61	106190
Belgium	Rwanda	13 Oct 62	456UNTS425	106568
Burma	Japan	29 Mar 63	518UNTS3	107490
UK Great Britain	USA (United States)	06 Apr 63	474UNTS49	106871
Netherlands	USA (United States)	20 May 63	487UNTS123	107099
El Salvador	Japan	19 Jul 63	518UNTS135	107494
UK Great Britain	USA (United States)	11 Oct 63	483UNTS3	107005
WHO (World Health)	Somalia	08 Nov 63	493UNTS243	107218
UNESCO (Educ/Cult)	United Arab Rep	09 Nov 63	489UNTS233	107142
WHO (World Health)	Sierra Leone	22 Nov 63	493UNTS255	107219
Netherlands	Portugal	22 Nov 63	492UNTS31	107185
Austria	Turkey	15 May 64	515UNTS109	107457
India	UK Great Britain	20 Nov 64	534UNTS85	107756
Italy	USA (United States)	23 Nov 64	532UNTS133	107716
Saudi Arabia	USA (United States)	05 Jun 65	548UNTS285	107984

PARTY ONE	PARTY TWO	DATE	CITATION	NUMBER
Private contracts (Cont.)				
Austria	Petrol Export Org	24 Jun 65	589UNTS135	108540
Multilateral		05 Jul 65	563UNTS104	108207
Israel	USA (United States)	20 Jul 65	549UNTS55	107989
Austria	Yugoslavia	19 Nov 65	587UNTS239	108512
IBRD (World Bank)	UK Great Britain	18 Apr 66	573UNTS209	108334
Iran	USSR (Soviet Union)	22 Aug 66	643UNTS203	109192
Romania	United Arab Rep	14 Nov 66	642UNTS141	109170
Romania	United Arab Rep	14 Nov 66	642UNTS129	109169
Ghana	Romania	23 Nov 66	642UNTS63	109165
Peru	UK Great Britain	03 Dec 66	617UNTS231	108915
Responsibility and liability				
Multilateral		27 Jun 39	40UNTS281	100639
Panama	USA (United States)	23 Mar 40	124UNTS195	200420
France	Netherlands	14 Jun 40	2UNTS263	200019
Panama	USA (United States)	06 Sep 40	124UNTS209	200421
Brazil	Paraguay	14 Jun 41	54UNTS289	200201
Canada	USA (United States)	04 Mar 42	124UNTS271	200426
Canada	USA (United States)	18 Mar 42	101UNTS205	200294
Mexico	USA (United States)	29 Apr 43	105UNTS119	200327
UK Great Britain	USA (United States)	28 Mar 44	15UNTS413	200104
UK Great Britain	USA (United States)	16 Apr 45	6UNTS189	100076
South Africa	USA (United States)	17 Apr 45	90UNTS267	200264
UK Great Britain	USA (United States)	27 Mar 46	4UNTS101	100040
UK Great Britain	USA (United States)	07 May 46	6UNTS285	100082
France	USA (United States)	28 May 46	84UNTS113	101122
Ceylon (Sri Lanka)	India	12 Aug 46	196UNTS209	102626
Denmark	UK Great Britain	16 Aug 46	9UNTS163	100130
South Africa	UK Great Britain	24 Aug 46	51UNTS187	100765
Peru	USA (United States)	07 Oct 46	7UNTS71	100092
Denmark	South Africa	14 Oct 46	10UNTS29	100140
Peru	USA (United States)	27 Dec 46	152UNTS93	102013
Australia	Netherlands	24 Jan 47	10UNTS77	100144
Netherlands	Thailand	30 Jan 47	247UNTS353	103480
Philippines	USA (United States)	14 Mar 47	45UNTS23	100690
Thailand	USA (United States)	08 May 47	42UNTS241	100653
Belgium	United Arab Rep	01 Jul 47	34UNTS93	100529
Belgium	South Africa	04 Jul 47	47UNTS9	100720
Greece	South Africa	28 Jul 47	185UNTS161	102467
Italy	USA (United States)	14 Aug 47	36UNTS53	100566
Multilateral		02 Oct 47	193UNTS188	102616
Bolivia	USA (United States)	03 Nov 47	51UNTS33	100750
Taiwan	USA (United States)	08 Dec 47	70UNTS3	100895
Costa Rica	USA (United States)	12 Jan 48	70UNTS27	100896
Italy	USA (United States)	02 Feb 48	79UNTS171	101040
India	Pakistan	31 Mar 48	54UNTS33	100793
Greece	USA (United States)	23 Apr 48	74UNTS107	100958
Netherlands	USA (United States)	29 Apr 48	32UNTS167	100498
Philippines	Spain	20 May 48	70UNTS143	100903
Australia	Greece	16 Jun 48	18UNTS211	100290
Netherlands	Spain	08 Oct 48	28UNTS209	100426
Argentina	Netherlands	29 Oct 48	95UNTS21	101316
Czechoslovakia	Poland	12 Nov 48	84UNTS347	101141
Afghanistan	UNESCO (Educ/Cult)	08 Dec 48	46UNTS3	100697
Belgium	Luxembourg	14 Jan 49	36UNTS339	100572
Austria	USA (United States)	23 Mar 49	43UNTS127	100667
Multilateral		23 Mar 49	203UNTS179	102746
Panama	USA (United States)	31 Mar 49	55UNTS141	100812
Norway	USA (United States)	25 May 49	32UNTS345	100507
Philippines	USA (United States)	07 Jun 49	45UNTS63	100692
Czechoslovakia	Poland	02 Jul 49	260UNTS149	103708
Czechoslovakia	Poland	02 Jul 49	260UNTS179	103709
Multilateral		12 Aug 49	75UNTS31	100970
Australia	Netherlands	12 Aug 49	34UNTS213	100539
WHO (World Health)	Thailand	12 Aug 49	178UNTS347	102350

PARTY ONE	PARTY TWO	DATE	CITATION	NUMBER
Responsibility and liability (Cont.)				
Multilateral		12 Aug 49	75UNTS85	100971
USSR (Soviet Union)	Yugoslavia	31 Aug 49	116UNTS345	101580
Argentina	Norway	09 Sep 49	42UNTS125	100646
Denmark	ICAO (Civil Aviat)	09 Sep 49	53UNTS341	100791
Ireland	USA (United States)	13 Sep 49	127UNTS89	101701
Multilateral		15 Sep 49	53UNTS235	100783
Multilateral		27 Oct 49	53UNTS241	100784
United Arab Rep	USA (United States)	03 Nov 49	71UNTS31	100908
Finland	UK Great Britain	28 Dec 49	86UNTS191	101159
Israel	UK Great Britain	30 Mar 50	86UNTS231	101162
El Salvador	WHO (World Health)	21 Apr 50	103UNTS13	101420
Australia	Netherlands	26 Apr 50	54UNTS83	100796
Ireland	USA (United States)	01 May 50	222UNTS107	103026
Multilateral		28 Jun 50	87UNTS153	101170
Czechoslovakia	USA (United States)	29 Sep 50	290UNTS3	104227
Ethiopia	ICAO (Civil Aviat)	02 Feb 51	96UNTS123	101333
Israel	ICAO (Civil Aviat)	19 Feb 51	96UNTS141	101334
Australia	Netherlands	22 Feb 51	128UNTS115	101717
Multilateral		06 Mar 51	106UNTS141	101461
Australia	Italy	29 Mar 51	131UNTS187	101741
ICAO (Civil Aviat)	Thailand	19 Apr 51	96UNTS181	101336
Ceylon (Sri Lanka)	India	30 Apr 51	196UNTS199	102625
Jordan	UK Great Britain	01 May 51	117UNTS19	101582
Ethiopia	USA (United States)	02 May 51	139UNTS85	101877
Lebanon	WHO (World Health)	05 Jun 51	104UNTS225	101443
UK Great Britain	USA (United States)	06 Jun 51	165UNTS121	102174
Iceland	ICAO (Civil Aviat)	07 Jun 51	96UNTS193	101337
Costa Rica	WHO (World Health)	14 Jun 51	102UNTS151	101418
Multilateral		19 Jun 51	199UNTS67	102678
Multilateral		25 Jun 51	92UNTS27	101258
Sweden	USA (United States)	27 Jun 51	148UNTS77	101937
Burma	WHO (World Health)	09 Jul 51	107UNTS9	101463
Costa Rica	USA (United States)	11 Sep 51	234UNTS255	103288
Norway	USA (United States)	17 Sep 51	140UNTS313	101895
WHO (World Health)	Vietnam, South	21 Sep 51	107UNTS63	200352
Australia	Netherlands	25 Sep 51	128UNTS63	101713
Bolivia	United Nations	01 Oct 51	104UNTS263	101447
WHO (World Health)	Thailand	04 Oct 51	109UNTS77	101492
Saudi Arabia	USA (United States)	10 Nov 51	180UNTS263	102390
France	UK Great Britain	31 Dec 51	330UNTS145	104744
Indonesia	United Nations	06 Feb 52	121UNTS3	101621
Germany, East	Poland	06 Feb 52	304UNTS131	104395
ICAO (Civil Aviat)	Yugoslavia	06 Feb 52	128UNTS97	101715
Lebanon	ICAO (Civil Aviat)	14 Feb 52	128UNTS83	101714
Ceylon (Sri Lanka)	WHO (World Health)	26 Mar 52	134UNTS341	200442
India	ICAO (Civil Aviat)	29 Apr 52	151UNTS123	101987
UNICEF (Children)	United Arab Rep	18 May 52	324UNTS161	104684
Iraq	UK Great Britain	22 May 52	175UNTS97	102298
Korea, South	USA (United States)	24 May 52	179UNTS23	102353
Australia	USA (United States)	27 May 52	178UNTS113	102338
India	WHO (World Health)	04 Jun 52	135UNTS279	101827
Burma	WHO (World Health)	09 Jun 52	134UNTS273	101806
India	WHO (World Health)	19 Jun 52	134UNTS307	101809
Finland	USA (United States)	02 Jul 52	165UNTS203	102177
Multilateral		11 Jul 52	171UNTS143	102226
Multilateral		11 Jul 52	170UNTS63	102222
Multilateral		11 Jul 52	171UNTS191	102227
Multilateral		11 Jul 52	170UNTS269	102223
Multilateral		11 Jul 52	171UNTS89	102225
Multilateral		11 Jul 52	171UNTS3	102224
Multilateral		11 Jul 52	170UNTS3	102221
Germany, West	USA (United States)	18 Jul 52	165UNTS167	102175
UK Great Britain	USA (United States)	29 Jul 52	179UNTS129	102362
Australia	Germany, West	29 Aug 52	184UNTS147	102446
Multilateral		07 Oct 52	310UNTS181	104493

Responsibility and liability (Cont.)

PARTY ONE	PARTY TWO	DATE	CITATION	NUMBER
Italy	UK Great Britain	06 Nov 52	158UNTS431	102076
Saudi Arabia	USA (United States)	10 Nov 52	181UNTS307	102419
Ceylon (Sri Lanka)	WHO (World Health)	21 Nov 52	161UNTS315	200490
South Africa	Sweden	09 Jan 53	173UNTS299	102271
Germany, West	USA (United States)	27 Feb 53	224UNTS13	103067
Germany, West	UK Great Britain	27 Feb 53	330UNTS217	104747
Germany, West	USA (United States)	27 Feb 53	205UNTS103	102771
France	Italy	14 Mar 53	284UNTS221	104140
Denmark	South Africa	30 Apr 53	174UNTS19	102275
Australia	USA (United States)	14 May 53	205UNTS237	102778
Ethiopia	USA (United States)	22 May 53	191UNTS59	102577
Israel	Switzerland	01 Jul 53	220UNTS41	102986
Germany, West	USA (United States)	20 Aug 53	224UNTS49	103069
France	USA (United States)	02 Sep 53	224UNTS153	103075
Norway	South Africa	21 Sep 53	192UNTS105	102597
Australia	Netherlands	22 Oct 53	184UNTS193	102448
Multilateral		26 Oct 53	207UNTS237	102809
Italy	South Africa	20 Dec 53	277UNTS293	104014
Belgium	Taiwan	13 Jan 54	223UNTS111	103059
France	Greece	08 Feb 54	225UNTS107	103093
France	Greece	08 Feb 54	225UNTS121	103094
Belgium	Finland	11 Feb 54	211UNTS63	102848
Germany, West	USA (United States)	12 Feb 54	223UNTS153	103064
Multilateral		19 Feb 54	214UNTS51	102899
Mexico	UK Great Britain	20 Mar 54	331UNTS21	104750
Italy	USA (United States)	31 Mar 54	235UNTS293	103311
Luxembourg	USA (United States)	17 Apr 54	257UNTS255	103661
Multilateral		20 Apr 54	189UNTS11	102539
Italy	USA (United States)	27 Apr 54	234UNTS103	103275
Netherlands	USA (United States)	07 May 54	213UNTS325	102895
Nepal	WHO (World Health)	13 May 54	204UNTS311	200522
Japan	USA (United States)	14 May 54	247UNTS273	103476
Taiwan	USA (United States)	14 May 54	231UNTS165	103216
Australia	Greece	24 May 54	191UNTS255	102586
Multilateral		31 May 54	192UNTS20	102592
Multilateral		01 Jun 54	200UNTS235	200520
Italy	UK Great Britain	01 Jun 54	403UNTS275	105798
Australia	Israel	18 Jun 54	220UNTS29	102985
Turkey	USA (United States)	01 Jul 54	234UNTS147	103280
India	USA (United States)	29 Jul 54	239UNTS69	103373
Canada	South Africa	04 Aug 54	261UNTS3	103722
Germany, West	USA (United States)	17 Aug 54	233UNTS31	103248
Multilateral		19 Aug 54	201UNTS51	102710
Libya	USA (United States)	09 Sep 54	224UNTS217	103078
Multilateral		06 Oct 54	201UNTS75	102711
Belgium	USA (United States)	12 Oct 54	202UNTS289	102735
Multilateral		23 Oct 54	332UNTS157	104761
Multilateral		27 Oct 54	201UNTS95	102712
Denmark	Sweden	28 Oct 54	262UNTS211	103747
Multilateral		29 Oct 54	201UNTS115	102713
Mexico	USA (United States)	19 Nov 54	238UNTS237	103367
Australia	Poland	25 Nov 54	521UNTS281	107526
Lebanon	UN Relief Palestin	26 Nov 54	202UNTS123	102728
Netherlands	USA (United States)	14 Dec 54	262UNTS35	103737
Australia	Austria	20 Dec 54	205UNTS157	102775
Israel	South Africa	31 Dec 54	220UNTS11	102984
Netherlands	UNICEF (Children)	31 Dec 54	202UNTS135	102729
Korea, South	USA (United States)	29 Jan 55	239UNTS53	103371
Australia	Hungary	10 Feb 55	207UNTS173	102806
France	Sweden	05 Mar 55	427UNTS133	106150
Australia	Taiwan	22 Mar 55	209UNTS3	102818
Australia	Czechoslovakia	01 Apr 55	213UNTS199	102888
Multilateral		04 Apr 55	208UNTS239	102816
Netherlands	USA (United States)	29 Apr 55	219UNTS105	102969
Iraq	UK Great Britain	30 Apr 55	226UNTS319	103126
Peru	USA (United States)	30 Apr 55	263UNTS309	103780
Hungary	USSR (Soviet Union)	27 May 55	407UNTS156	105864
Multilateral		14 Jun 55	212UNTS263	200526
Canada	USA (United States)	15 Jun 55	235UNTS176	103301
Turkey	USA (United States)	29 Jun 55	269UNTS97	103878
Multilateral		04 Jul 55	214UNTS10	102897
Iran	WHO (World Health)	04 Jul 55	227UNTS65	103131
Belgium	USA (United States)	15 Jul 55	223UNTS3	103040
Spain	USA (United States)	16 Jul 55	270UNTS211	103899
Ceylon (Sri Lanka)	USA (United States)	18 Jul 55	281UNTS295	104086
Germany, West	USA (United States)	02 Aug 55	268UNTS121	103854
Czechoslovakia	Germany, East	24 Oct 55	504UNTS173	107358
Paraguay	USA (United States)	28 Oct 55	273UNTS97	103946
Colombia	USA (United States)	18 Nov 55	239UNTS173	103377
Guatemala	UNICEF (Children)	22 Nov 55	221UNTS305	103012
Canada	Norway	20 Dec 55	305UNTS17	104408
Argentina	Switzerland	25 Jan 56	559UNTS121	108157
Multilateral		02 Feb 56	227UNTS153	103137
Multilateral		10 Feb 56	228UNTS189	103151
Multilateral		10 Feb 56	228UNTS167	103150
Germany, West	USA (United States)	13 Feb 56	253UNTS119	103580
Ireland	USA (United States)	16 Mar 56	317UNTS195	104604
Nicaragua	USA (United States)	19 Mar 56	275UNTS231	103984
Canada	Japan	20 Mar 56	517UNTS33	107482
Colombia	USA (United States)	27 Mar 56	273UNTS235	103954
Multilateral		25 Apr 56	270UNTS103	103896
Brazil	France	04 May 56	323UNTS339	104675
Multilateral		18 May 56	319UNTS21	104630
Costa Rica	USA (United States)	18 May 56	404UNTS237	105814
Multilateral		19 May 56	399UNTS189	105742
Bulgaria	Yugoslavia	22 May 56	367UNTS119	105229
Pakistan	USA (United States)	28 May 56	269UNTS15	103868
Multilateral		31 May 56	251UNTS181	103541
Austria	USA (United States)	08 Jun 56	253UNTS139	103581
Multilateral		08 Jun 56	247UNTS366	200541
New Zealand	USA (United States)	13 Jun 56	253UNTS155	103582
Multilateral		14 Jun 56	265UNTS125	103809
Dominican Republic	USA (United States)	15 Jun 56	265UNTS227	103815
France	USA (United States)	19 Jun 56	281UNTS341	104087
Cuba	USA (United States)	26 Jun 56	293UNTS257	104294
Multilateral		26 Jun 56	321UNTS2	104650
Multilateral		26 Jun 56	253UNTS12	103573
Hungary	UK Great Britain	27 Jun 56	249UNTS19	103499
Bolivia	USA (United States)	30 Jun 56	271UNTS243	103919
Multilateral		02 Jul 56	248UNTS37	103484
Multilateral		02 Jul 56	540UNTS110	107846
Lebanon	UNICEF (Children)	03 Jul 56	324UNTS145	104683
Multilateral		13 Jul 56	281UNTS3	104066
Germany, West	UK Great Britain	30 Jul 56	330UNTS233	104748
Nicaragua	USA (United States)	02 Aug 56	281UNTS99	104073
UNESCO (Educ/Cult)	UK Great Britain	09 Aug 56	256UNTS139	103624
Guatemala	USA (United States)	15 Aug 56	288UNTS181	104205
Multilateral		31 Aug 56	249UNTS158	103506
Belgium	Germany, West	24 Sep 56	314UNTS195	104549
Multilateral		25 Sep 56	334UNTS89	104767
Multilateral		25 Sep 56	334UNTS13	104766
Multilateral		05 Oct 56	251UNTS267	103545
Multilateral		05 Oct 56	251UNTS245	103544
Portugal	USA (United States)	07 Nov 56	277UNTS133	104003
Multilateral		21 Nov 56	253UNTS266	103588
Taiwan	USA (United States)	21 Nov 56	265UNTS241	103816
Japan	USA (United States)	23 Nov 56	324UNTS177	104685
Germany, West	USA (United States)	12 Dec 56	280UNTS63	104051
Germany, West	USA (United States)	12 Dec 56	280UNTS71	104052
Poland	USSR (Soviet Union)	17 Dec 56	266UNTS179	103830

PARTY ONE	PARTY TWO	DATE	CITATION	NUMBER
Responsibility and liability (Cont.)				
UNESCO (Educ/Cult)	Tunisia	03 Jan 57	257UNTS21	103645
Multilateral		15 Jan 57	376UNTS122	105378
Brazil	USA (United States)	16 Jan 57	266UNTS99	103824
Multilateral		23 Jan 57	259UNTS426	103701
Netherlands	USA (United States)	15 Feb 57	287UNTS239	104190
Multilateral		17 Feb 57	271UNTS2	103907
Canada	USA (United States)	26 Feb 57	279UNTS179	104039
Multilateral		01 Mar 57	264UNTS94	103790
Iran	USA (United States)	05 Mar 57	342UNTS29	104898
Spain	USA (United States)	09 Mar 57	283UNTS89	104108
Germany, East	USSR (Soviet Union)	12 Mar 57	285UNTS105	104150
Liberia	USA (United States)	16 Mar 57	290UNTS59	104228
Multilateral		25 Mar 57	294UNTS2	104300
India	Poland	27 Mar 57	319UNTS263	104635
Multilateral		28 Mar 57	271UNTS30	103908
Poland	Vietnam, North	06 Apr 57	432UNTS255	106224
Multilateral		09 Apr 57	274UNTS172	103965
Canada	USA (United States)	09 Apr 57	283UNTS217	104119
Romania	USSR (Soviet Union)	15 Apr 57	274UNTS143	103964
Japan	USA (United States)	08 May 57	318UNTS257	104621
Finland	USA (United States)	10 May 57	283UNTS43	104105
Germany, East	USSR (Soviet Union)	10 May 57	285UNTS135	104151
Multilateral		24 May 57	268UNTS270	103861
Ecuador	USA (United States)	31 May 57	304UNTS61	104391
Germany, West	USA (United States)	07 Jun 57	346UNTS241	104984
Finland	India	14 Jun 57	277UNTS327	104016
Germany, West	USA (United States)	28 Jun 57	288UNTS339	104213
Germany, West	USA (United States)	03 Jul 57	288UNTS305	104212
Italy	USA (United States)	03 Jul 57	308UNTS195	104462
Germany, East	Hungary	03 Jul 57	407UNTS186	105865
Australia	FAO (Food Agri)	08 Jul 57	277UNTS315	104015
South Africa	USA (United States)	08 Jul 57	290UNTS147	104234
Multilateral		09 Jul 57	274UNTS300	103972
Taiwan	USA (United States)	30 Jul 57	300UNTS61	104331
Morocco	UNICEF (Children)	31 Jul 57	282UNTS99	104095
Greece	USA (United States)	05 Aug 57	290UNTS167	104235
Spain	USA (United States)	16 Aug 57	307UNTS169	104449
Hungary	USSR (Soviet Union)	24 Aug 57	318UNTS3	104607
Italy	Switzerland	19 Sep 57	363UNTS69	105200
Burma	WHO (World Health)	20 Sep 57	282UNTS113	104096
Sweden	UK Great Britain	20 Sep 57	310UNTS49	104486
Austria	South Africa	26 Sep 57	287UNTS3	104176
Multilateral		03 Oct 57	366UNTS141	105217
Multilateral		03 Oct 57	365UNTS207	105214
Multilateral		03 Oct 57	366UNTS193	105218
Multilateral		03 Oct 57	364UNTS331	105212
Multilateral		03 Oct 57	366UNTS255	105219
Multilateral		03 Oct 57	365UNTS3	105213
Multilateral		03 Oct 57	366UNTS3	105215
Poland	USSR (Soviet Union)	26 Oct 57	432UNTS221	106223
Multilateral		05 Nov 57	285UNTS301	104155
Argentina	UNICEF (Children)	19 Nov 57	300UNTS229	104338
Germany, West	USA (United States)	10 Dec 57	307UNTS59	104442
Austria	IAEA (Atom Energy)	11 Dec 57	339UNTS110	104849
Bulgaria	USSR (Soviet Union)	12 Dec 57	302UNTS21	104352
Korea, North	USSR (Soviet Union)	16 Dec 57	292UNTS121	104270
Multilateral		06 Jan 58	304UNTS227	104399
Ghana	WHO (World Health)	21 Jan 58	307UNTS3	104437
Czechoslovakia	Poland	31 Jan 58	431UNTS99	106214
Indonesia	WHO (World Health)	05 Feb 58	307UNTS15	104438
Multilateral		15 Mar 58	292UNTS273	104276
Bulgaria	Yugoslavia	21 Mar 58	349UNTS61	105009
Israel	WHO (World Health)	11 Apr 58	307UNTS27	104439
Multilateral		15 Apr 58	539UNTS27	107822
Multilateral		29 Apr 58	450UNTS11	106465

PARTY ONE	PARTY TWO	DATE	CITATION	NUMBER
Responsibility and liability (Cont.)				
Multilateral		19 Jun 58	306UNTS236	200550
Japan	USA (United States)	19 Jun 58	325UNTS143	104699
WHO (World Health)	Sudan	21 Jun 58	307UNTS235	104453
Philippines	USA (United States)	30 Jun 58	321UNTS51	104653
UK Great Britain	USA (United States)	03 Jul 58	326UNTS3	104707
Netherlands	Yugoslavia	22 Jul 58	386UNTS263	105546
Taiwan	USA (United States)	06 Aug 58	462UNTS3	106666
Jordan	UNICEF (Children)	09 Aug 58	309UNTS297	104478
Ghana	UNICEF (Children)	12 Aug 58	309UNTS103	104469
Mongolia	USSR (Soviet Union)	25 Aug 58	322UNTS215	104659
United Arab Rep	USSR (Soviet Union)	18 Sep 58	338UNTS29	104831
USA (United States)	Venezuela	08 Oct 58	371UNTS69	105271
Iraq	USSR (Soviet Union)	11 Oct 58	328UNTS117	104731
Turkey	USA (United States)	14 Oct 58	336UNTS145	104803
Canada	USA (United States)	31 Oct 58	391UNTS219	105626
Japan	USA (United States)	03 Nov 58	341UNTS83	104879
Poland	Yugoslavia	17 Nov 58	432UNTS267	106225
France	UK Great Britain	28 Nov 58	351UNTS263	105027
Burma	United Nations	15 Dec 58	319UNTS3	104629
Afghanistan	WHO (World Health)	18 Dec 58	324UNTS121	104681
United Nations	Tunisia	23 Dec 58	321UNTS23	104651
Belgium	Turkey	29 Dec 58	357UNTS195	105118
Portugal	USA (United States)	12 Jan 59	343UNTS49	104921
United Arab Rep	USA (United States)	13 Jan 59	358UNTS3	105122
Greece	USA (United States)	15 Jan 59	357UNTS281	105120
Multilateral		15 Jan 59	348UNTS13	104996
Albania	Czechoslovakia	16 Jan 59	363UNTS165	105207
Austria	USA (United States)	30 Jan 59	511UNTS145	107432
Euratom	UK Great Britain	04 Feb 59	331UNTS125	104752
Taiwan	USA (United States)	07 Feb 59	341UNTS225	104885
Ghana	United Nations	27 Feb 59	324UNTS133	104682
Austria	USSR (Soviet Union)	28 Feb 59	356UNTS39	105091
Czechoslovakia	Hungary	27 Mar 59	351UNTS57	105017
United Nations	Sudan	28 Mar 59	327UNTS95	104719
Morocco	UN Special Fund	04 Apr 59	354UNTS347	105069
Multilateral		06 Apr 59	349UNTS167	105013
USA (United States)	Vietnam, South	22 Apr 59	347UNTS113	104993
Bulgaria	Romania	23 Apr 59	387UNTS81	105559
IAEA (Atom Energy)	UK Great Britain	11 May 59	339UNTS351	104854
IAEA (Atom Energy)	USSR (Soviet Union)	11 May 59	339UNTS341	104853
Multilateral		11 May 59	527UNTS145	107623
IAEA (Atom Energy)	USA (United States)	11 May 59	339UNTS359	104855
Thailand	USA (United States)	19 May 59	346UNTS271	104986
Hungary	Poland	20 May 59	432UNTS115	106217
Bulgaria	Czechoslovakia	27 May 59	360UNTS335	105167
USSR (Soviet Union)	Vietnam, North	05 Jun 59	356UNTS111	105093
Peru	USA (United States)	15 Jun 59	346UNTS279	104987
Greece	Yugoslavia	18 Jun 59	368UNTS9	105232
Greece	Yugoslavia	18 Jun 59	368UNTS137	105238
China People's Rep	USSR (Soviet Union)	23 Jun 59	356UNTS83	105092
Spain	USA (United States)	23 Jun 59	354UNTS11	105049
Panama	USA (United States)	24 Jun 59	479UNTS145	106950
Libya	United Nations	27 Jun 59	336UNTS291	104811
Laos	United Nations	06 Jul 59	337UNTS41	104814
Taiwan	USA (United States)	08 Jul 59	354UNTS47	105052
Paraguay	United Nations	01 Aug 59	341UNTS319	104894
Ghana	UN Special Fund	12 Aug 59	338UNTS203	104836
Italy	USA (United States)	18 Aug 59	361UNTS11	105169
Peru	USA (United States)	22 Aug 59	357UNTS99	105109
Lebanon	USA (United States)	16 Sep 59	358UNTS175	105135
Iran	UN Special Fund	06 Oct 59	342UNTS89	104902
Poland	UN Special Fund	15 Oct 59	344UNTS29	104941
Guinea	United Nations	15 Oct 59	344UNTS47	104942
Brazil	USA (United States)	19 Oct 59	372UNTS131	105293
India	UN Special Fund	20 Oct 59	344UNTS143	104946

PARTY ONE	PARTY TWO	DATE	CITATION	NUMBER
Responsibility and liability (Cont.)				
UN Special Fund	Yugoslavia	27 Oct 59	344UNTS159	104947
Norway	Sweden	28 Oct 59	427UNTS225	106157
Ecuador	UN Special Fund	10 Nov 59	345UNTS3	104955
Greece	UN Special Fund	13 Nov 59	345UNTS171	104966
UN Special Fund	Turkey	20 Nov 59	345UNTS105	104963
Afghanistan	United Nations	24 Nov 59	397UNTS187	105705
UN Special Fund	United Arab Rep	25 Nov 59	345UNTS125	104964
Belgium	USA (United States)	27 Nov 59	366UNTS331	105221
Israel	UN Special Fund	01 Dec 59	345UNTS197	104968
Taiwan	USA (United States)	02 Dec 59	361UNTS115	105175
Multilateral		03 Dec 59	348UNTS246	105003
Argentina	UN Special Fund	04 Dec 59	345UNTS263	104972
Philippines	USA (United States)	07 Dec 59	359UNTS227	105144
Multilateral		14 Dec 59	422UNTS75	106069
Ceylon (Sri Lanka)	WHO (World Health)	21 Dec 59	349UNTS109	105011
UN Special Fund	UK Great Britain	07 Jan 60	348UNTS177	105000
Colombia	USA (United States)	11 Jan 60	371UNTS37	105268
Peru	UN Special Fund	19 Jan 60	349UNTS83	105010
Pakistan	WHO (World Health)	20 Jan 60	351UNTS355	105034
Chile	UN Special Fund	22 Jan 60	351UNTS115	105020
India	Japan	25 Jan 60	384UNTS31	105508
Colombia	UN Special Fund	04 Feb 60	355UNTS257	105080
Bolivia	UN Special Fund	09 Feb 60	351UNTS203	105024
Cuba	UNICEF (Children)	11 Feb 60	349UNTS277	105014
Ecuador	USA (United States)	11 Feb 60	372UNTS141	105294
Chile	USA (United States)	19 Feb 60	371UNTS255	105282
Afghanistan	UN Special Fund	21 Feb 60	351UNTS93	105019
Pakistan	UN Special Fund	25 Feb 60	351UNTS141	105021
Peru	USA (United States)	26 Feb 60	394UNTS141	105674
Multilateral		26 Feb 60	418UNTS171	106022
Brazil	USA (United States)	27 Feb 60	384UNTS131	105515
Multilateral		15 Mar 60	572UNTS133	108310
France	UN Special Fund	17 Mar 60	354UNTS119	105059
New Zealand	USA (United States)	23 Mar 60	371UNTS147	105276
Ireland	USA (United States)	24 Mar 60	371UNTS237	105280
Italy	UN Special Fund	01 Apr 60	354UNTS261	105066
Argentina	USA (United States)	01 Apr 60	371UNTS245	105281
Colombia	USA (United States)	07 Apr 60	372UNTS27	105285
Germany, West	Netherlands	08 Apr 60	508UNTS14	107404
UN Special Fund	Tunisia	12 Apr 60	355UNTS289	105082
Multilateral		12 Apr 60	359UNTS323	105150
Ireland	South Africa	13 Apr 60	390UNTS307	105612
Multilateral		15 Apr 60	470UNTS239	106811
Libya	UN Special Fund	19 Apr 60	356UNTS11	105090
UN Special Fund	Sudan	21 Apr 60	356UNTS213	105097
Guatemala	USA (United States)	23 Apr 60	373UNTS23	105312
UN Special Fund	Vietnam, South	29 Apr 60	357UNTS311	200567
Laos	UN Special Fund	30 Apr 60	361UNTS171	105179
United Nations	Togo	06 May 60	388UNTS53	105571
Lebanon	UN Special Fund	07 May 60	360UNTS225	105160
Cambodia	WHO (World Health)	19 May 60	372UNTS193	105298
Argentina	USA (United States)	23 May 60	377UNTS3	105392
Multilateral		04 Jun 60	360UNTS208	105159
Indonesia	USA (United States)	08 Jun 60	388UNTS287	105585
India	USA (United States)	13 Jun 60	377UNTS37	105394
Iraq	UN Special Fund	19 Jun 60	376UNTS357	105389
Austria	UK Great Britain	24 Jun 60	502UNTS79	107327
IAEA (Atom Energy)	USA (United States)	28 Jun 60	374UNTS133	105333
Australia	USSR (Soviet Union)	29 Jun 60	392UNTS131	105641
Multilateral		08 Jul 60	366UNTS310	105220
Haiti	USA (United States)	08 Jul 60	380UNTS135	105454
Ethiopia	United Nations	13 Jul 60	368UNTS143	105239
Ethiopia	UN Special Fund	13 Jul 60	368UNTS159	105240
Multilateral		28 Jul 60	394UNTS37	105667
Japan	Pakistan	30 Jul 60	384UNTS63	105511

PARTY ONE	PARTY TWO	DATE	CITATION	NUMBER
Responsibility and liability (Cont.)				
Argentina	USA (United States)	02 Aug 60	384UNTS105	105514
WHO (World Health)	United Arab Rep	03 Aug 60	385UNTS3	105524
Jordan	WHO (World Health)	03 Aug 60	381UNTS133	105469
Laos	WHO (World Health)	04 Aug 60	373UNTS313	105322
WHO (World Health)	Tunisia	04 Aug 60	381UNTS335	105474
Korea, South	USA (United States)	17 Aug 60	400UNTS339	105757
Japan	Thailand	24 Aug 60	384UNTS73	105512
Canada	USA (United States)	31 Aug 60	393UNTS247	105659
WHO (World Health)	Saudi Arabia	06 Sep 60	395UNTS169	105684
Lebanon	WHO (World Health)	08 Sep 60	387UNTS49	105557
Iran	Japan	12 Sep 60	384UNTS43	105509
Taiwan	UN Special Fund	20 Sep 60	375UNTS29	105352
Indonesia	UN Special Fund	07 Oct 60	378UNTS141	105424
Liberia	UN Special Fund	11 Oct 60	376UNTS341	105388
UK Great Britain	USA (United States)	14 Oct 60	398UNTS165	105721
Nigeria	USA (United States)	19 Oct 60	394UNTS113	105672
El Salvador	UN Special Fund	24 Oct 60	377UNTS171	105400
Kuwait	United Nations	31 Oct 60	391UNTS295	200581
WHO (World Health)	Upper Volta	15 Nov 60	383UNTS91	105496
Belgium	Congo (Zaire)	15 Nov 60	394UNTS79	105670
UNICEF (Children)	Upper Volta	15 Nov 60	402UNTS33	105776
Nepal	UN Special Fund	17 Nov 60	380UNTS289	105461
Pakistan	United Nations	17 Nov 60	380UNTS277	105460
Mali	UNICEF (Children)	17 Nov 60	402UNTS23	105775
Guatemala	UN Special Fund	17 Nov 60	383UNTS67	105495
Korea, South	USA (United States)	18 Nov 60	400UNTS49	105747
Cambodia	UN Special Fund	24 Nov 60	382UNTS255	105487
Fed of Malaya	WHO (World Health)	25 Nov 60	387UNTS37	105556
Cambodia	United Nations	30 Nov 60	383UNTS147	105500
WHO (World Health)	Yemen	03 Dec 60	395UNTS187	105685
Dahomey	WHO (World Health)	07 Dec 60	387UNTS277	105567
Nepal	UNICEF (Children)	12 Dec 60	382UNTS273	105488
Congo (Brazzaville)	WHO (World Health)	12 Dec 60	399UNTS105	105737
Multilateral		13 Dec 60	523UNTS117	107557
Bolivia	United Nations	14 Dec 60	382UNTS283	105489
Israel	USA (United States)	19 Dec 60	401UNTS195	105772
Honduras	UN Special Fund	20 Dec 60	383UNTS103	105497
Niger	WHO (World Health)	28 Dec 60	394UNTS195	105679
Multilateral		30 Dec 60	395UNTS241	105689
Burma	UN Special Fund	03 Jan 61	387UNTS219	105564
Costa Rica	UN Special Fund	10 Jan 61	389UNTS253	105597
Canada	USA (United States)	17 Jan 61	542UNTS224	107894
UN Special Fund	Saudi Arabia	19 Jan 61	396UNTS27	105692
Nicaragua	UN Special Fund	20 Jan 61	387UNTS15	105555
Korea, South	WHO (World Health)	20 Jan 61	406UNTS269	200589
Chad	UN Special Fund	23 Jan 61	390UNTS69	105603
UN Special Fund	Somalia	28 Jan 61	388UNTS75	105573
Multilateral		28 Jan 61	387UNTS202	105563
Ivory Coast	WHO (World Health)	30 Jan 61	395UNTS205	105686
Gabon	UN Special Fund	02 Feb 61	387UNTS289	105568
Chad	WHO (World Health)	03 Feb 61	394UNTS161	105676
WHO (World Health)	Togo	03 Feb 61	394UNTS207	105680
Nigeria	UN Special Fund	10 Feb 61	390UNTS85	105604
Central Afri Rep	WHO (World Health)	13 Feb 61	394UNTS149	105675
Mexico	UN Special Fund	23 Feb 61	388UNTS151	105576
Cyprus	UN Special Fund	24 Feb 61	389UNTS3	105588
Iraq	United Nations	05 Mar 61	409UNTS56	105878
Panama	UN Special Fund	09 Mar 61	396UNTS3	105691
Cuba	UN Special Fund	10 Mar 61	390UNTS35	105601
Afghanistan	Japan	15 Mar 61	450UNTS373	106480
Kuwait	WHO (World Health)	16 Mar 61	397UNTS315	200588
Brazil	USA (United States)	17 Mar 61	406UNTS241	105853
Ceylon (Sri Lanka)	Japan	20 Mar 61	450UNTS385	106481
Austria	USA (United States)	29 Mar 61	459UNTS45	106612
Multilateral		10 Apr 61	402UNTS281	105791

Responsibility and liability (Cont.)

PARTY ONE	PARTY TWO	DATE	CITATION	NUMBER
Mauritania	WHO (World Health)	17 Apr 61	396UNTS301	200587
Cyprus	UNICEF (Children)	19 Apr 61	394UNTS185	105678
USA (United States)	Yugoslavia	19 Apr 61	409UNTS163	105883
Korea, South	UN Special Fund	21 Apr 61	394UNTS231	200583
Mali	WHO (World Health)	27 Apr 61	407UNTS66	105860
Turkey	USSR (Soviet Union)	27 Apr 61	420UNTS307	106047
Gabon	WHO (World Health)	27 Apr 61	397UNTS215	105707
Ceylon (Sri Lanka)	UN Special Fund	03 May 61	395UNTS217	105687
Australia	USA (United States)	09 May 61	409UNTS203	105886
Ghana	Switzerland	17 May 61	559UNTS193	108159
Multilateral		08 Jun 61	473UNTS153	106862
Cameroon	UN Special Fund	13 Jun 61	397UNTS297	105713
Ethiopia	United Nations	14 Jun 61	406UNTS81	105840
Cyprus	United Nations	15 Jun 61	398UNTS39	105716
Paraguay	UN Special Fund	22 Jun 61	399UNTS117	105738
UN Special Fund	Upper Volta	26 Jun 61	400UNTS3	105744
Haiti	UN Special Fund	28 Jun 61	399UNTS171	105741
Philippines	UN Special Fund	28 Jun 61	399UNTS141	105739
Haiti	United Nations	28 Jun 61	399UNTS159	105740
UNICEF (Children)	Saudi Arabia	04 Jul 61	413UNTS122	105947
Bulgaria	Netherlands	07 Jul 61	489UNTS21	107133
Mali	UN Special Fund	21 Jul 61	401UNTS141	105768
UN Special Fund	Yemen	02 Aug 61	402UNTS43	105777
Morocco	WHO (World Health)	09 Aug 61	412UNTS192	105932
Cameroon	UNICEF (Children)	12 Aug 61	402UNTS235	105788
Pakistan	Philippines	15 Aug 61	522UNTS35	107534
WHO (World Health)	Somalia	17 Aug 61	423UNTS111	106088
Central Afri Rep	UNICEF (Children)	21 Aug 61	413UNTS48	105939
Poland	UNICEF (Children)	24 Aug 61	406UNTS95	105841
Lebanon	United Nations	26 Aug 61	406UNTS105	105842
Chad	UNICEF (Children)	26 Aug 61	422UNTS231	106077
Ivory Coast	UN Special Fund	29 Aug 61	406UNTS129	105844
Ghana	United Nations	29 Aug 61	406UNTS117	105843
Jordan	United Nations	11 Sep 61	406UNTS255	105855
Iraq	WHO (World Health)	13 Sep 61	419UNTS69	106030
Multilateral		18 Sep 61	500UNTS31	107305
Bulgaria	Poland	19 Sep 61	483UNTS249	107018
Multilateral		20 Sep 61	407UNTS52	105859
UN Special Fund	Sierra Leone	02 Oct 61	422UNTS131	106073
IAEA (Atom Energy)	Yugoslavia	04 Oct 61	412UNTS226	105935
Multilateral		04 Oct 61	412UNTS210	105934
Malagasy	WHO (World Health)	13 Oct 61	421UNTS273	106064
Multilateral		16 Oct 61	410UNTS242	105908
Canada	USA (United States)	17 Oct 61	426UNTS201	106138
Gabon	UNICEF (Children)	02 Nov 61	422UNTS241	106078
Mauritania	UN Special Fund	07 Nov 61	412UNTS240	105936
Multilateral		07 Nov 61	412UNTS258	105937
Congo (Brazzaville)	UN Special Fund	09 Nov 61	413UNTS58	105940
Malagasy	UNICEF (Children)	16 Nov 61	422UNTS251	106079
Ceylon (Sri Lanka)	United Nations	04 Dec 61	415UNTS236	105987
Multilateral		06 Dec 61	473UNTS219	106864
UN Special Fund	Venezuela	11 Dec 61	422UNTS149	106074
UN Special Fund	Senegal	16 Dec 61	425UNTS97	106121
Multilateral		27 Dec 61	425UNTS83	106120
Malagasy	UN Special Fund	05 Jan 62	419UNTS29	106028
Ivory Coast	UNICEF (Children)	10 Jan 62	422UNTS261	106080
Ethiopia	WHO (World Health)	11 Jan 62	423UNTS99	106087
Paraguay	USA (United States)	16 Jan 62	433UNTS169	106240
Multilateral		17 Jan 62	419UNTS294	106033
Multilateral		20 Jan 62	429UNTS230	200596
United Nations	Somalia	20 Jan 62	420UNTS133	106044
UNICEF (Children)	Yemen	31 Jan 62	422UNTS271	106081
Multilateral		13 Feb 62	422UNTS288	200594
Multilateral		20 Feb 62	597UNTS159	108644
Multilateral		21 Feb 62	423UNTS151	106091

Responsibility and liability (Cont.)

PARTY ONE	PARTY TWO	DATE	CITATION	NUMBER
Niger	UN Special Fund	26 Feb 62	423UNTS83	106086
Multilateral		01 Mar 62	423UNTS122	106089
Australia	Japan	01 Mar 62	517UNTS81	107483
Multilateral		05 Mar 62	425UNTS3	106114
WHO (World Health)	Sudan	11 Mar 62	432UNTS325	106226
Australia	Germany, West	19 Mar 62	488UNTS203	107130
Nigeria	WHO (World Health)	27 Mar 62	429UNTS123	106194
Dahomey	UN Special Fund	28 Mar 62	424UNTS55	106099
Brazil	Japan	28 Mar 62	451UNTS125	106489
IAEA (Atom Energy)	USA (United States)	30 Mar 62	442UNTS49	106338
India	Japan	31 Mar 62	451UNTS143	106490
UNICEF (Children)	Somalia	01 Apr 62	431UNTS75	106211
Congo (Brazzaville)	UNICEF (Children)	09 Apr 62	431UNTS65	106210
Colombia	USA (United States)	09 Apr 62	476UNTS9	106899
Multilateral		10 Apr 62	429UNTS78	106192
UNICEF (Children)	Sierra Leone	11 Apr 62	431UNTS55	106209
Multilateral		18 Apr 62	463UNTS44	106692
India	Japan	23 Apr 62	451UNTS155	106491
Greece	USA (United States)	24 Apr 62	459UNTS3	106609
UN Special Fund	Uruguay	04 May 62	429UNTS143	106196
Multilateral		17 May 62	429UNTS46	106189
Israel	Netherlands	28 May 62	448UNTS219	106434
Thailand	USA (United States)	31 May 62	459UNTS135	106619
Dominican Republic	UN Special Fund	06 Jun 62	429UNTS169	106197
New Zealand	USA (United States)	08 Jun 62	458UNTS209	106602
Libya	WHO (World Health)	16 Jun 62	437UNTS127	106301
WHO (World Health)	Sierra Leone	19 Jun 62	439UNTS151	106327
Argentina	USA (United States)	22 Jun 62	458UNTS97	106594
Multilateral		27 Jun 62	463UNTS3	106688
Multilateral		27 Jun 62	463UNTS17	106690
UN Special Fund	Syria	07 Jul 62	443UNTS3	106355
UN Special Fund	Tanganyika	17 Jul 62	435UNTS237	106281
WHO (World Health)	Senegal	06 Aug 62	435UNTS179	106279
Nigeria	United Nations	07 Aug 62	435UNTS167	106278
Multilateral		12 Aug 62	443UNTS266	106365
WHO (World Health)	Western Samoa	14 Aug 62	437UNTS317	200598
Philippines	USA (United States)	21 Aug 62	461UNTS163	106660
Cameroon	United Nations	29 Aug 62	442UNTS3	106334
Multilateral		29 Aug 62	443UNTS280	106366
Italy	USA (United States)	05 Sep 62	461UNTS185	106663
Afghanistan	USA (United States)	11 Sep 62	461UNTS169	106661
Austria	Czechoslovakia	22 Sep 62	495UNTS157	107244
Finland	USSR (Soviet Union)	27 Sep 62	479UNTS99	106949
Niger	United Nations	01 Oct 62	439UNTS181	106329
Poland	Romania	05 Oct 62	521UNTS3	107516
Israel	OAS (Am States)	11 Oct 62	484UNTS241	107035
Multilateral		16 Oct 62	470UNTS291	106814
Dominican Republic	USA (United States)	25 Oct 62	459UNTS247	106627
Japan	UN Special Fund	31 Oct 62	444UNTS171	106368
United Nations	Western Samoa	05 Nov 62	443UNTS297	200599
Romania	Yugoslavia	08 Nov 62	472UNTS305	106845
Saudi Arabia	USA (United States)	13 Nov 62	488UNTS175	107127
Multilateral		15 Nov 62	448UNTS50	106424
Algeria	UN Special Fund	15 Nov 62	452UNTS243	106512
Czechoslovakia	Poland	16 Nov 62	526UNTS3	107597
WHO (World Health)	Syria	18 Nov 62	480UNTS249	106972
Algeria	UNICEF (Children)	20 Nov 62	453UNTS151	106522
Ecuador	United Nations	26 Nov 62	445UNTS3	106372
Rwanda	United Nations	28 Nov 62	450UNTS267	106473
Germany, West	USA (United States)	29 Nov 62	460UNTS169	106639
Multilateral		06 Dec 62	450UNTS240	106471
Cameroon	WHO (World Health)	08 Dec 62	451UNTS215	106496
Ivory Coast	United Nations	10 Dec 62	451UNTS269	106498
Austria	Yugoslavia	11 Dec 62	546UNTS3	107938
Netherlands	Spain	17 Dec 62	499UNTS227	107301

PARTY ONE	PARTY TWO	DATE	CITATION	NUMBER
Responsibility and liability (Cont.)				
Multilateral		17 Dec 62	590UNTS81	108548
Algeria	WHO (World Health)	20 Dec 62	463UNTS135	106698
India	United Nations	27 Dec 62	450UNTS3	106464
Israel	United Nations	07 Jan 63	450UNTS229	106470
Czechoslovakia	Vietnam, North	14 Jan 63	501UNTS181	107318
Pakistan	USA (United States)	16 Jan 63	471UNTS133	106828
Mauritania	UNICEF (Children)	19 Jan 63	452UNTS271	106514
Multilateral		21 Jan 63	453UNTS20	106517
United Nations	South Pacific Com	24 Jan 63	470UNTS361	200604
UNICEF (Children)	Tanganyika	25 Jan 63	453UNTS249	106528
India	USA (United States)	01 Feb 63	473UNTS37	106852
Multilateral		05 Feb 63	453UNTS36	106518
Netherlands	USA (United States)	06 Feb 63	487UNTS113	107098
United Nations	United Arab Rep	08 Feb 63	453UNTS79	106520
Multilateral		14 Feb 63	453UNTS168	106524
Norway	USA (United States)	01 Mar 63	524UNTS185	107573
Multilateral		06 Mar 63	455UNTS386	106552
Israel	USA (United States)	21 Mar 63	476UNTS131	106907
UN Special Fund	Uganda	22 Mar 63	456UNTS466	106572
Japan	USA (United States)	22 Mar 63	518UNTS179	107495
Brazil	USA (United States)	29 Mar 63	476UNTS67	106904
Hungary	Korea, North	29 Mar 63	577UNTS219	108379
UK Great Britain	USA (United States)	06 Apr 63	474UNTS49	106871
Japan	South Africa	06 Apr 63	484UNTS319	107040
Multilateral		18 Apr 63	463UNTS121	106697
Belgium	USA (United States)	19 Apr 63	493UNTS83	107209
Poland	USSR (Soviet Union)	22 Apr 63	493UNTS229	107217
Austria	Bulgaria	02 May 63	535UNTS143	107778
Multilateral		06 May 63	463UNTS78	106694
Philippines	USA (United States)	06 May 63	477UNTS67	106916
Multilateral		09 May 63	463UNTS159	106700
Multilateral		22 May 63	483UNTS72	107007
Jamaica	UN Special Fund	22 May 63	489UNTS191	107140
Multilateral		24 May 63	466UNTS346	106754
Netherlands	UN Special Fund	24 May 63	466UNTS289	106750
UN Special Fund	Western Samoa	05 Jun 63	467UNTS463	200601
Mongolia	WHO (World Health)	21 Jun 63	472UNTS373	106848
Czechoslovakia	Yugoslavia	24 Jun 63	496UNTS3	107246
Canada	Nigeria	03 Jul 63	529UNTS57	107656
Austria	Romania	03 Jul 63	588UNTS3	108516
Multilateral		23 Jul 63	471UNTS158	106831
Multilateral		31 Jul 63	472UNTS220	106842
Burundi	WHO (World Health)	08 Aug 63	477UNTS346	106928
India	USA (United States)	08 Aug 63	488UNTS21	107117
Burundi	UN Special Fund	22 Aug 63	476UNTS49	106903
Multilateral		27 Aug 63	511UNTS210	107435
Multilateral		10 Sep 63	480UNTS100	106965
Jamaica	WHO (World Health)	25 Sep 63	481UNTS125	106980
Pakistan	USSR (Soviet Union)	07 Oct 63	499UNTS161	107297
Multilateral		17 Oct 63	525UNTS75	107585
Kuwait	USA (United States)	21 Oct 63	530UNTS281	107688
Czechoslovakia	Hungary	22 Oct 63	514UNTS95	107444
Iran	USA (United States)	24 Oct 63	489UNTS303	107146
Multilateral		30 Oct 63	480UNTS180	106968
Central Afri Rep	UN Special Fund	30 Oct 63	481UNTS247	106985
WHO (World Health)	Tanganyika	05 Nov 63	496UNTS193	107252
Multilateral		07 Nov 63	480UNTS232	106971
Multilateral		08 Nov 63	482UNTS286	106999
Belgium	Romania	13 Nov 63	520UNTS119	107513
Argentina	USA (United States)	30 Nov 63	505UNTS131	107369
Romania	Yugoslavia	30 Nov 63	512UNTS2	107438
Nicaragua	United Nations	03 Dec 63	482UNTS329	107002
Multilateral		18 Dec 63	490UNTS383	107166
Taiwan	USA (United States)	19 Dec 63	527UNTS69	107617
Netherlands	Poland	20 Dec 63	514UNTS169	107446

PARTY ONE	PARTY TWO	DATE	CITATION	NUMBER
Responsibility and liability (Cont.)				
New Zealand	Western Samoa	31 Dec 63	521UNTS163	107519
Multilateral		28 Jan 64	502UNTS321	107336
Mexico	USA (United States)	14 Feb 64	524UNTS197	107574
Multilateral		20 Feb 64	491UNTS30	107172
UNESCO (Educ/Cult)	Yugoslavia	27 Feb 64	489UNTS257	107143
Multilateral		28 Feb 64	501UNTS245	107321
Netherlands	Tunisia	03 Mar 64	533UNTS133	107739
Spain	USA (United States)	18 Mar 64	535UNTS343	107789
Multilateral		08 Apr 64	501UNTS221	107320
Norway	Romania	21 May 64	563UNTS45	108203
Ireland	UN Special Fund	03 Jun 64	496UNTS205	107253
France	UK Great Britain	03 Jun 64	539UNTS253	107836
Czechoslovakia	Netherlands	11 Jun 64	556UNTS89	108120
Multilateral		11 Jun 64	525UNTS61	107584
Ireland	USA (United States)	18 Jun 64	530UNTS217	107684
UK Great Britain	USA (United States)	19 Jun 64	530UNTS99	107675
Rwanda	WHO (World Health)	22 Jun 64	514UNTS11	107440
Multilateral		23 Jun 64	506UNTS108	107383
WHO (World Health)	Trinidad/Tobago	23 Jun 64	503UNTS167	107342
Rwanda	WHO (World Health)	23 Jun 64	514UNTS157	107445
Multilateral		28 Jun 64	519UNTS14	107499
Denmark	USA (United States)	02 Jul 64	529UNTS277	107665
Sweden	USA (United States)	06 Jul 64	529UNTS287	107666
Multilateral		10 Jul 64	613UNTS3	108850
Multilateral		10 Jul 64	611UNTS387	108846
Multilateral		10 Jul 64	613UNTS193	108852
Spain	USA (United States)	16 Jul 64	529UNTS187	107661
Australia	USA (United States)	17 Aug 64	530UNTS209	107683
Multilateral		24 Oct 64	514UNTS220	200608
Ethiopia	Netherlands	28 Oct 64	541UNTS235	107872
Netherlands	Pakistan	30 Oct 64	541UNTS243	107873
Austria	Hungary	31 Oct 64	605UNTS63	108759
Multilateral		07 Nov 64	548UNTS3	107965
Multilateral		11 Nov 64	515UNTS94	107456
Italy	USA (United States)	23 Nov 64	532UNTS133	107716
Multilateral		02 Dec 64	525UNTS51	107583
Netherlands	Nigeria	04 Dec 64	545UNTS155	107931
Trinidad/Tobago	USA (United States)	05 Dec 64	535UNTS331	107788
India	Netherlands	11 Dec 64	570UNTS165	108292
Germany, West	Jamaica	16 Dec 64	531UNTS129	107699
Malawi	WHO (World Health)	06 Jan 65	525UNTS165	107588
Malawi	WHO (World Health)	08 Jan 65	524UNTS281	107579
Multilateral		27 Jan 65	523UNTS102	107556
Multilateral		02 Feb 65	523UNTS256	107560
UN Special Fund	Zambia	04 Feb 65	527UNTS115	107621
Belgium	Congo (Zaire)	06 Feb 65	540UNTS275	107853
Belgium	Congo (Zaire)	06 Feb 65	540UNTS227	107852
Multilateral		12 Feb 65	525UNTS148	107587
Multilateral		02 Jun 65	537UNTS348	200611
Multilateral		02 Jun 65	551UNTS2	108030
Saudi Arabia	USA (United States)	05 Jun 65	548UNTS285	107984
Canada	USA (United States)	11 Jun 65	564UNTS83	108222
UN Special Fund	Spain	30 Jun 65	544UNTS159	107918
Cameroon	Netherlands	06 Jul 65	571UNTS75	108300
Hungary	Poland	18 Jul 65	577UNTS161	108376
Malaysia	Singapore	07 Aug 65	563UNTS89	108206
Poland	WHO (World Health)	26 Aug 65	552UNTS3	108047
Multilateral		13 Sep 65	547UNTS264	107962
Multilateral		24 Sep 65	556UNTS141	108124
IAEA (Atom Energy)	Uruguay	24 Sep 65	556UNTS117	108123
Morocco	IAEA (Atom Energy)	24 Sep 65	556UNTS109	108122
Multilateral		21 Oct 65	547UNTS216	107959
Netherlands	Nigeria	28 Oct 65	578UNTS15	108383
Austria	Yugoslavia	19 Nov 65	591UNTS3	108556
United Nations	United Arab Rep	26 Nov 65	551UNTS253	108046

PARTY ONE	PARTY TWO	DATE	CITATION	NUMBER
Responsibility and liability (Cont.)				
Chile	UNICEF (Children)	30 Nov 65	596UNTS215	108635
Multilateral		08 Dec 65	600UNTS161	108680
UN Special Fund	Singapore	31 Dec 65	552UNTS299	108061
Mongolia	UN Special Fund	26 Jan 66	552UNTS201	108055
Austria	Finland	21 Feb 66	597UNTS273	108651
Ireland	UK Great Britain	28 Feb 66	565UNTS33	108234
WHO (World Health)	Singapore	28 Mar 66	562UNTS59	108195
Guyana	UK Great Britain	26 May 66	595UNTS255	108621
Bulgaria	UN Special Fund	26 May 66	563UNTS71	108205
United Nations	Switzerland	03 Jun 66	564UNTS193	200621
Greece	United Nations	20 Jun 66	565UNTS3	108230
Austria	France	15 Jul 66	604UNTS265	108755
Sweden	USA (United States)	28 Jul 66	603UNTS61	108725
Ivory Coast	Netherlands	01 Aug 66	591UNTS245	108561
IAEA (Atom Energy)	USA (United States)	26 Sep 66	589UNTS3	108532
Multilateral		28 Sep 66	589UNTS41	108534
Philippines	IAEA (Atom Energy)	28 Sep 66	589UNTS25	108533
UK Great Britain	USA (United States)	27 Oct 66	597UNTS265	108650
United Nations	Sudan	08 Nov 66	576UNTS85	108365
IAEA (Atom Energy)	USA (United States)	09 Dec 66	589UNTS55	108535
Syria	USSR (Soviet Union)	18 Dec 66	633UNTS247	109041
Denmark	Tanzania	05 Apr 67	604UNTS19	108740
Multilateral		13 Apr 67	595UNTS60	108612
Greece	United Nations	14 Apr 67	595UNTS83	108613
Liberia	IBRD (World Bank)	05 Jun 67	633UNTS13	109031
IAEA (Atom Energy)	USA (United States)	07 Jun 67	614UNTS109	108866
Multilateral		21 Jun 67	598UNTS2	108653
Multilateral		23 Jun 67	614UNTS185	108871
Indonesia	UK Great Britain	01 Aug 67	638UNTS3	109128
Multilateral		23 Aug 67	614UNTS145	108869
Iraq	IAEA (Atom Energy)	21 Sep 67	630UNTS41	108963
Burma	IAEA (Atom Energy)	11 Oct 67	630UNTS49	108964
IAEA (Atom Energy)	USA (United States)	16 Oct 67	630UNTS57	108965
Iran	United Nations	15 Feb 68	631UNTS103	108990
India	United Nations	22 Jul 68	640UNTS121	109158
Corporations				
Multilateral		27 Jun 39	40UNTS311	100640
Germany, West	Ireland	17 Oct 62	604UNTS135	108749
Greece	India	11 Feb 65	606UNTS9	108771
Denmark	Netherlands	31 Mar 66	604UNTS209	108751
Austria	France	15 Jul 66	604UNTS265	108755
Singapore	UK Great Britain	01 Dec 66	605UNTS153	108763
Trinidad/Tobago	UK Great Britain	29 Dec 66	605UNTS237	108766
Concessions				
Austria	Netherlands	16 Oct 59	458UNTS173	106600
Denmark	Finland	27 Mar 61	630UNTS3	108961
Japan	USA (United States)	06 Sep 66	616UNTS215	108898
Revival of treaties				
Multilateral		01 Jan 46	99UNTS131	101375
Canada	Netherlands	05 Feb 46	230UNTS199	103184
Czechoslovakia	Sweden	22 Oct 46	200UNTS31	102692
Multilateral		10 Feb 47	41UNTS21	100643
Multilateral		10 Feb 47	41UNTS135	100644
Multilateral		10 Feb 47	48UNTS203	100746
Czechoslovakia	Italy	25 Feb 48	26UNTS103	100380
Romania	USA (United States)	26 Feb 48	48UNTS9	100738
Czechoslovakia	Romania	01 Mar 48	26UNTS109	100381
Bulgaria	Czechoslovakia	05 Mar 48	26UNTS115	100382
Bulgaria	USA (United States)	08 Mar 48	29UNTS101	100437
Hungary	USA (United States)	09 Mar 48	183UNTS3	102426
Finland	UK Great Britain	12 Mar 48	104UNTS29	101433
Hungary	UK Great Britain	12 Mar 48	104UNTS35	101434
Italy	UK Great Britain	13 Mar 48	104UNTS41	101435
Romania	UK Great Britain	13 Mar 48	104UNTS117	101436

PARTY ONE	PARTY TWO	DATE	CITATION	NUMBER
Revival of treaties (Cont.)				
Italy	South Africa	01 May 48	225UNTS53	103087
Finland	South Africa	15 Nov 48	225UNTS59	103088
Hungary	South Africa	16 Nov 48	225UNTS65	103089
Australia	Italy	07 Jan 49	189UNTS239	102549
Australia	Hungary	07 Jan 49	189UNTS233	102548
Australia	Finland	07 Jan 49	189UNTS227	102547
Australia	Romania	07 Jan 49	189UNTS263	102550
Czechoslovakia	Hungary	27 Feb 49	26UNTS119	100383
Italy	Netherlands	16 Aug 49	98UNTS21	101357
Austria	Belgium	05 Nov 49	48UNTS107	100739
Austria	Belgium	22 Dec 49	46UNTS233	100712
France	Israel	03 Jun 51	219UNTS215	102977
Ireland	Norway	02 Jul 51	100UNTS53	101387
Multilateral		08 Sep 51	136UNTS45	101832
Australia	Austria	17 Nov 51	133UNTS137	101785
Germany, West	Netherlands	31 Jan 52	492UNTS295	107199
Belgium	Pakistan	20 Feb 52	133UNTS199	101790
Belgium	Germany, West	14 Aug 52	139UNTS29	101873
Japan	South Africa	27 Mar 53	173UNTS37	102258
Japan	USA (United States)	22 Apr 53	178UNTS169	102341
Japan	Pakistan	24 Apr 53	221UNTS325	103013
France	Japan	25 Apr 53	187UNTS41	102500
Australia	Japan	27 Apr 53	193UNTS78	102612
Japan	UK Great Britain	27 Apr 53	228UNTS227	103154
Belgium	Germany, West	20 May 53	180UNTS3	102370
Finland	South Africa	24 Mar 54	230UNTS121	103179
Belgium	Germany, West	30 Mar 54	190UNTS63	102558
Belgium	Germany, West	01 Apr 54	190UNTS43	102556
Belgium	Germany, West	03 Apr 54	190UNTS247	102568
Belgium	Germany, West	15 Apr 54	190UNTS253	102569
Germany, West	Netherlands	13 Aug 54	492UNTS305	107200
Belgium	Germany, West	03 Nov 54	201UNTS359	102724
Burma	Japan	05 Nov 54	251UNTS201	103542
Belgium	Germany, West	23 Nov 54	202UNTS109	102726
Burma	Japan	20 Jun 56	306UNTS61	104431
Germany, West	Netherlands	31 Oct 56	287UNTS21	104177
Germany, West	Netherlands	01 Dec 56	276UNTS127	103989
Italy	USA (United States)	03 Jul 57	308UNTS195	104462
Germany, West	UK Great Britain	23 Feb 60	385UNTS39	105527
Germany, West	Netherlands	03 Aug 61	492UNTS321	107201
Congo (Brazzaville)	USA (United States)	05 Aug 61	603UNTS19	108720
Netherlands	Norway	22 Sep 66	600UNTS227	108683
Prizes and arbitral awards				
UK Great Britain	USA (United States)	03 Nov 42	109UNTS127	200354
New Zealand	USA (United States)	28 Jan 43	121UNTS123	200395
Canada	USA (United States)	13 Aug 43	109UNTS135	200355
UK Great Britain	USA (United States)	24 Sep 43	139UNTS373	200463
Jordan	Syria	23 Dec 53	204UNTS207	102759
Germany, East	Hungary	30 Oct 57	408UNTS4	105867
Multilateral		10 Jun 58	330UNTS3	104739
Belgium	Germany, West	30 Jun 58	387UNTS245	105566
Germany, East	Romania	15 Jul 58	395UNTS3	105681
Hungary	Poland	06 Mar 59	432UNTS3	106216
Belgium	Switzerland	29 Apr 59	443UNTS35	106356
Austria	Belgium	16 Jun 59	419UNTS45	106029
Czechoslovakia	Hungary	02 Nov 61	438UNTS3	106313
Bulgaria	Poland	04 Dec 61	484UNTS3	107019
Poland	Romania	25 Jan 62	468UNTS3	106770
Multilateral		18 Mar 65	575UNTS159	108359
Canada	USA (United States)	25 Mar 65	607UNTS141	108802
Technical and commercial staff				
Peru	USA (United States)	21 Apr 42	89UNTS317	200260
Ecuador	USA (United States)	29 Oct 42	89UNTS301	200259
El Salvador	USA (United States)	02 Dec 42	122UNTS277	200410

Technical and commercial staff (Cont.)

PARTY ONE	PARTY TWO	DATE	CITATION	NUMBER
Multilateral		19 Apr 44	89UNTS279	200257
Multilateral		02 Aug 44	67UNTS221	200221
Cuba	USA (United States)	27 Jan 48	67UNTS3	100862
Peru	USA (United States)	25 Mar 49	89UNTS15	101205
Austria	Turkey	15 May 64	515UNTS109	107457
UK Great Britain	USSR (Soviet Union)	13 Feb 65	543UNTS43	107896
Denmark	Portugal	20 Feb 65	639UNTS43	109143
Austria	Yugoslavia	19 Nov 65	587UNTS239	108512

Title and deeds

PARTY ONE	PARTY TWO	DATE	CITATION	NUMBER
Canada	USA (United States)	18 Mar 42	101UNTS205	200294
Panama	USA (United States)	18 May 42	124UNTS221	200422
Taiwan	USA (United States)	02 Jun 42	14UNTS343	200092
Norway	USA (United States)	28 Aug 42	139UNTS361	200461
Taiwan	Netherlands	29 May 45	2UNTS307	200023
Taiwan	France	18 Aug 45	14UNTS477	200101
UK Great Britain	USA (United States)	27 Mar 46	4UNTS2	100039
Turkey	USA (United States)	07 May 46	6UNTS293	100083
Australia	USA (United States)	07 Jun 46	4UNTS237	100048
Brazil	USA (United States)	28 Jun 46	6UNTS327	100085
Romania	USA (United States)	28 Jun 46	148UNTS355	101944
New Zealand	USA (United States)	10 Jul 46	6UNTS341	100087
Hungary	USA (United States)	09 Aug 46	148UNTS313	101941
USSR (Soviet Union)	Yugoslavia	04 Feb 47	130UNTS235	101731
Netherlands	USA (United States)	11 Apr 47	148UNTS343	101943
Greece	USA (United States)	20 Jun 47	7UNTS267	100105
Belgium	USA (United States)	23 Jul 47	33UNTS33	100512
France	USA (United States)	01 Oct 47	148UNTS303	101940
Greece	USA (United States)	03 Dec 47	89UNTS119	101213
Austria	USA (United States)	02 Jan 48	34UNTS141	100534
Australia	Poland	03 Jun 48	16UNTS189	100258
Australia	Hungary	01 Jul 48	22UNTS3	100325
Australia	Greece	01 Jul 48	22UNTS33	100329
Australia	Italy	08 Jul 48	22UNTS11	100326
Australia	Yugoslavia	09 Jul 48	22UNTS17	100327
USA (United States)	Yugoslavia	19 Jul 48	34UNTS195	100537
Australia	Austria	19 Jul 48	22UNTS25	100328
Czechoslovakia	USA (United States)	16 Sep 48	90UNTS35	101224
Ceylon (Sri Lanka)	UK Great Britain	28 Feb 49	314UNTS269	104551
Czechoslovakia	UK Great Britain	03 Mar 49	83UNTS95	101104
Philippines	USA (United States)	16 Mar 50	89UNTS199	101218
Multilateral		02 Nov 50	81UNTS160	101071
Multilateral		24 Nov 50	81UNTS188	101072
Multilateral		15 Dec 50	76UNTS120	100985
Multilateral		23 Dec 50	185UNTS3	102456
United Nations	Yugoslavia	06 Jan 51	78UNTS165	101015
Chile	USA (United States)	16 Jan 51	157UNTS3	102043
Ethiopia	ICAO (Civil Aviat)	02 Feb 51	96UNTS123	101333
Multilateral		15 Feb 51	81UNTS245	101074
Israel	ILO (Labor Org)	19 Feb 51	100UNTS105	101391
Israel	ICAO (Civil Aviat)	19 Feb 51	96UNTS141	101334
ILO (Labor Org)	Syria	03 Mar 51	110UNTS69	101502
Multilateral		05 Mar 51	81UNTS261	101075
Luxembourg	USA (United States)	20 Mar 51	180UNTS283	102392
Multilateral		28 Mar 51	181UNTS61	102399
Jordan	United Nations	29 Mar 51	137UNTS267	200448
Jordan	ILO (Labor Org)	29 Mar 51	100UNTS247	200287
Liberia	ILO (Labor Org)	02 Apr 51	100UNTS117	101392
Multilateral		05 Apr 51	84UNTS299	101139
Ceylon (Sri Lanka)	ILO (Labor Org)	06 Apr 51	100UNTS235	200286
Mexico	ILO (Labor Org)	06 Apr 51	100UNTS131	101393
Guatemala	ILO (Labor Org)	13 Apr 51	126UNTS249	101692
Peru	ILO (Labor Org)	13 Apr 51	100UNTS31	101385
Ecuador	ILO (Labor Org)	19 Apr 51	100UNTS77	101389
ICAO (Civil Aviat)	Thailand	19 Apr 51	96UNTS181	101336

Title and deeds (Cont.)

PARTY ONE	PARTY TWO	DATE	CITATION	NUMBER
Cuba	ILO (Labor Org)	21 Apr 51	99UNTS205	101382
Greece	ILO (Labor Org)	25 Apr 51	100UNTS93	101390
India	ILO (Labor Org)	26 Apr 51	100UNTS19	101384
WHO (World Health)	Yugoslavia	02 May 51	103UNTS117	101429
Pakistan	ILO (Labor Org)	16 May 51	100UNTS147	101394
Iceland	ICAO (Civil Aviat)	07 Jun 51	96UNTS193	101337
United Nations	Thailand	11 Jun 51	90UNTS45	101225
Dominican Republic	ILO (Labor Org)	18 Jun 51	100UNTS3	101383
Israel	United Nations	25 Jun 51	97UNTS21	101344
Multilateral		25 Jun 51	92UNTS27	101258
ILO (Labor Org)	Vietnam, South	26 Jun 51	100UNTS223	200285
Multilateral		28 Jun 51	118UNTS154	101604
Ethiopia	WHO (World Health)	02 Jul 51	103UNTS39	101422
Multilateral		10 Jul 51	108UNTS287	101481
ILO (Labor Org)	Thailand	11 Jul 51	100UNTS159	101395
Paraguay	ILO (Labor Org)	12 Jul 51	117UNTS155	101591
Multilateral		27 Jul 51	97UNTS291	200273
Multilateral		29 Jul 51	117UNTS85	101585
Canada	USA (United States)	01 Aug 51	233UNTS109	103254
Multilateral		05 Sep 51	173UNTS15	102256
Japan	USA (United States)	08 Sep 51	136UNTS203	101834
Iraq	ICAO (Civil Aviat)	18 Sep 51	108UNTS219	101475
Netherlands	USA (United States)	26 Sep 51	158UNTS469	102080
Paraguay	United Nations	27 Sep 51	120UNTS105	101617
Multilateral		01 Oct 51	104UNTS249	101446
UNICEF (Children)	UK Great Britain	02 Oct 51	104UNTS301	101448
Ecuador	WHO (World Health)	16 Oct 51	110UNTS263	101515
United Nations	Uruguay	17 Oct 51	122UNTS29	101633
ILO (Labor Org)	Venezuela	22 Oct 51	117UNTS139	101590
Multilateral		31 Oct 51	172UNTS193	102247
Panama	ILO (Labor Org)	10 Nov 51	126UNTS269	101693
Denmark	USA (United States)	16 Nov 51	180UNTS275	102391
Mexico	WHO (World Health)	17 Dec 51	124UNTS121	101670
India	WHO (World Health)	20 Dec 51	124UNTS109	101669
Multilateral		24 Dec 51	118UNTS290	200383
Italy	USA (United States)	28 Dec 51	157UNTS63	102047
Greece	USA (United States)	07 Jan 52	177UNTS249	102323
Austria	WHO (World Health)	10 Jan 52	131UNTS295	200438
Ceylon (Sri Lanka)	United Nations	21 Jan 52	118UNTS281	200382
Multilateral		23 Jan 52	127UNTS269	101708
WHO (World Health)	Spain	30 Jan 52	124UNTS259	200425
ICAO (Civil Aviat)	Yugoslavia	06 Feb 52	128UNTS97	101715
WHO (World Health)	UK Great Britain	07 Feb 52	121UNTS75	101627
Lebanon	ICAO (Civil Aviat)	14 Feb 52	128UNTS83	101714
Greece	United Nations	05 Mar 52	123UNTS3	101650
ICAO (Civil Aviat)	United Arab Rep	06 Mar 52	151UNTS111	101986
Finland	WHO (World Health)	07 Mar 52	128UNTS269	200436
India	United Nations	02 Apr 52	126UNTS145	101687
United Nations	Yugoslavia	10 Apr 52	141UNTS89	101908
India	WHO (World Health)	19 Apr 52	131UNTS253	101745
Pakistan	United Nations	28 Apr 52	128UNTS191	101720
India	ICAO (Civil Aviat)	29 Apr 52	151UNTS123	101987
Iraq	USA (United States)	21 May 52	212UNTS183	102870
Multilateral		19 Jun 52	133UNTS165	101787
Panama	USA (United States)	30 Jun 52	181UNTS121	102404
Chile	USA (United States)	30 Jun 52	199UNTS241	102688
India	WHO (World Health)	16 Jul 52	135UNTS291	101828
Chile	ILO (Labor Org)	23 Jul 52	178UNTS323	102348
UNICEF (Children)	UK Great Britain	25 Jul 52	135UNTS37	101812
Panama	United Nations	20 Aug 52	136UNTS3	101829
Italy	ILO (Labor Org)	04 Sep 52	178UNTS371	200505
ILO (Labor Org)	Uruguay	20 Sep 52	187UNTS25	102499
United Nations	Trieste	30 Sep 52	140UNTS11	101881
Multilateral		15 Oct 52	141UNTS96	101909
Japan	WHO (World Health)	26 Nov 52	204UNTS301	200521

PARTY ONE	PARTY TWO	DATE	CITATION	NUMBER
Title and deeds (Cont.)				
Mexico	ICAO (Civil Aviat)	28 Nov 52	164UNTS15	102156
Multilateral		16 Dec 52	158UNTS407	102074
Multilateral		29 Dec 52	151UNTS317	102002
ILO (Labor Org)	UN Relief Palestin	31 Dec 52	182UNTS201	200506
Taiwan	ILO (Labor Org)	13 Feb 53	178UNTS337	102349
Multilateral		26 Feb 53	161UNTS31	102120
Costa Rica	United Nations	27 Feb 53	161UNTS45	102121
Nepal	United Nations	02 Mar 53	161UNTS347	200493
Austria	Yugoslavia	19 Mar 53	467UNTS293	106767
France	WHO (World Health)	02 Apr 53	174UNTS83	102279
United Nations	Yemen	07 Apr 53	163UNTS73	102142
France	WHO (World Health)	30 Apr 53	174UNTS71	102278
United Arab Rep	USA (United States)	21 May 53	204UNTS29	102748
ICAO (Civil Aviat)	Syria	28 May 53	173UNTS199	102267
Ecuador	United Nations	16 Jun 53	166UNTS289	102194
Ethiopia	United Nations	22 Jun 53	172UNTS93	102241
Liberia	USA (United States)	23 Jun 53	213UNTS37	102879
Cambodia	United Nations	24 Jun 53	168UNTS309	200500
Chile	USA (United States)	27 Jun 53	229UNTS193	103167
Chile	USA (United States)	27 Jun 53	229UNTS53	103160
Libya	UK Great Britain	29 Jul 53	186UNTS201	102492
Multilateral		27 Aug 53	213UNTS137	102884
France	USA (United States)	02 Sep 53	224UNTS153	103075
UNICEF (Children)	UK Great Britain	07 Oct 53	180UNTS59	102375
Multilateral		09 Oct 53	190UNTS49	102557
Dominican Republic	United Nations	19 Nov 53	180UNTS45	102374
Chile	USA (United States)	30 Dec 53	236UNTS41	103315
Libya	USA (United States)	11 Jan 54	229UNTS15	103157
Belgium	Taiwan	13 Jan 54	223UNTS111	103059
Pakistan	United Nations	25 Jan 54	185UNTS213	102472
Brazil	WHO (World Health)	04 Feb 54	233UNTS49	103250
United Nations	Venezuela	05 Mar 54	187UNTS9	102498
Liberia	United Nations	09 Mar 54	187UNTS61	102501
Guatemala	United Nations	10 Mar 54	191UNTS271	102587
Mexico	USA (United States)	06 Apr 54	236UNTS69	103317
Multilateral		20 Apr 54	189UNTS11	102539
Panama	USA (United States)	11 May 54	236UNTS107	103319
Nepal	WHO (World Health)	13 May 54	204UNTS311	200522
Taiwan	USA (United States)	14 May 54	231UNTS165	103216
Japan	USA (United States)	14 May 54	247UNTS273	103476
Multilateral		31 May 54	192UNTS20	102592
Ethiopia	USA (United States)	01 Jun 54	232UNTS311	103245
Multilateral		01 Jun 54	200UNTS235	200520
UK Great Britain	USA (United States)	21 Jun 54	209UNTS61	102821
Chile	USA (United States)	28 Jun 54	233UNTS3	103246
Italy	USA (United States)	28 Jun 54	237UNTS121	103340
Ecuador	USA (United States)	30 Jun 54	236UNTS163	103323
Turkey	USA (United States)	01 Jul 54	234UNTS147	103280
Netherlands	USA (United States)	13 Aug 54	251UNTS91	103535
Multilateral		19 Aug 54	201UNTS51	102710
Multilateral		06 Oct 54	201UNTS75	102711
Ethiopia	Sweden	13 Oct 54	202UNTS273	102734
Multilateral		27 Oct 54	201UNTS95	102712
Multilateral		29 Oct 54	201UNTS115	102713
Libya	USA (United States)	03 Nov 54	238UNTS227	103366
Mexico	USA (United States)	09 Mar 55	263UNTS247	103776
Multilateral		04 Apr 55	208UNTS239	102816
Taiwan	WHO (World Health)	21 Apr 55	210UNTS71	102835
Peru	USA (United States)	30 Apr 55	263UNTS309	103780
Pakistan	Sweden	04 Jun 55	228UNTS121	103146
Multilateral		14 Jun 55	212UNTS263	200526
Dominican Republic	USA (United States)	30 Jun 55	257UNTS313	103664
Multilateral		04 Jul 55	214UNTS10	102897
Iran	WHO (World Health)	04 Jul 55	227UNTS65	103131
Bolivia	USA (United States)	03 Aug 55	264UNTS225	103795

PARTY ONE	PARTY TWO	DATE	CITATION	NUMBER
Title and deeds (Cont.)				
Canada	Norway	20 Dec 55	305UNTS17	104408
Multilateral		02 Feb 56	227UNTS153	103137
Multilateral		10 Feb 56	228UNTS189	103151
Multilateral		10 Feb 56	228UNTS167	103150
France	USA (United States)	23 Mar 56	278UNTS131	104029
Multilateral		31 May 56	251UNTS181	103541
Multilateral		08 Jun 56	247UNTS366	200541
Multilateral		14 Jun 56	265UNTS125	103809
Multilateral		26 Jun 56	253UNTS12	103573
Multilateral		26 Jun 56	321UNTS2	104650
Multilateral		02 Jul 56	540UNTS110	107846
Multilateral		02 Jul 56	248UNTS37	103484
Ecuador	USA (United States)	19 Jul 56	372UNTS149	105295
UNESCO (Educ/Cult)	UK Great Britain	09 Aug 56	256UNTS139	103624
Netherlands	USA (United States)	16 Aug 56	279UNTS3	104031
Multilateral		31 Aug 56	249UNTS158	103506
Multilateral		05 Oct 56	251UNTS245	103544
Multilateral		05 Oct 56	251UNTS267	103545
Portugal	USA (United States)	07 Nov 56	277UNTS133	104003
Multilateral		21 Nov 56	253UNTS266	103588
Multilateral		15 Jan 57	376UNTS122	105378
Brazil	USA (United States)	16 Jan 57	266UNTS99	103824
Multilateral		23 Jan 57	259UNTS426	103701
Multilateral		17 Feb 57	271UNTS2	103907
Multilateral		01 Mar 57	264UNTS94	103790
Spain	USA (United States)	09 Mar 57	283UNTS89	104108
Ethiopia	Sweden	16 Mar 57	304UNTS214	104398
Multilateral		28 Mar 57	271UNTS30	103908
Multilateral		09 Apr 57	274UNTS172	103965
Peru	USA (United States)	17 Apr 57	283UNTS3	104102
Ecuador	USA (United States)	24 Apr 57	284UNTS3	104124
Germany, West	USA (United States)	01 May 57	284UNTS85	104131
Finland	USA (United States)	10 May 57	283UNTS43	104105
Multilateral		24 May 57	268UNTS270	103861
Multilateral		09 Jul 57	274UNTS300	103972
Greece	USA (United States)	05 Aug 57	290UNTS167	104235
Burma	WHO (World Health)	20 Sep 57	282UNTS113	104096
Multilateral		05 Nov 57	285UNTS301	104155
Multilateral		06 Jan 58	304UNTS227	104399
Ghana	WHO (World Health)	21 Jan 58	307UNTS3	104437
Indonesia	WHO (World Health)	05 Feb 58	307UNTS15	104438
Multilateral		15 Mar 58	292UNTS273	104276
Israel	WHO (World Health)	11 Apr 58	307UNTS27	104439
Bolivia	USA (United States)	22 Apr 58	317UNTS209	104605
Multilateral		19 Jun 58	306UNTS236	200550
WHO (World Health)	Sudan	21 Jun 58	307UNTS235	104453
Australia	New Zealand	30 Sep 58	340UNTS61	104859
Turkey	USA (United States)	14 Oct 58	336UNTS145	104803
UK Great Britain	USA (United States)	30 Dec 58	338UNTS281	104841
Taiwan	USA (United States)	07 Feb 59	341UNTS225	104885
Morocco	UN Special Fund	04 Apr 59	354UNTS347	105069
Colombia	USA (United States)	08 May 59	344UNTS193	104950
Thailand	USA (United States)	19 May 59	346UNTS271	104986
Peru	USA (United States)	15 Jun 59	346UNTS279	104987
Spain	USA (United States)	23 Jun 59	354UNTS11	105049
Taiwan	USA (United States)	08 Jul 59	354UNTS47	105052
Ghana	UN Special Fund	12 Aug 59	338UNTS203	104836
Italy	USA (United States)	18 Aug 59	361UNTS11	105169
USA (United States)	Yugoslavia	25 Aug 59	357UNTS77	105106
Iran	UN Special Fund	06 Oct 59	342UNTS89	104902
Poland	UN Special Fund	15 Oct 59	344UNTS29	104941
Brazil	USA (United States)	19 Oct 59	372UNTS131	105293
India	UN Special Fund	20 Oct 59	344UNTS143	104946
UN Special Fund	Yugoslavia	27 Oct 59	344UNTS159	104947
Korea, South	United Nations	06 Nov 59	346UNTS289	200565

Title and deeds (Cont.)

PARTY ONE	PARTY TWO	DATE	CITATION	NUMBER
Ecuador	UN Special Fund	10 Nov 59	345UNTS3	104955
Greece	UN Special Fund	13 Nov 59	345UNTS171	104966
UN Special Fund	Turkey	20 Nov 59	345UNTS105	104963
UN Special Fund	United Arab Rep	25 Nov 59	345UNTS125	104964
Israel	UN Special Fund	01 Dec 59	345UNTS197	104968
Multilateral		03 Dec 59	348UNTS246	105003
Argentina	UN Special Fund	04 Dec 59	345UNTS263	104972
Jordan	UN Special Fund	15 Dec 59	346UNTS3	104974
Ceylon (Sri Lanka)	WHO (World Health)	21 Dec 59	349UNTS109	105011
UN Special Fund	UK Great Britain	07 Jan 60	348UNTS177	105000
Peru	UN Special Fund	19 Jan 60	349UNTS83	105010
Pakistan	WHO (World Health)	20 Jan 60	351UNTS355	105034
Chile	UN Special Fund	22 Jan 60	351UNTS115	105020
Colombia	UN Special Fund	04 Feb 60	355UNTS257	105080
Bolivia	UN Special Fund	09 Feb 60	351UNTS203	105024
Ecuador	USA (United States)	11 Feb 60	372UNTS141	105294
Afghanistan	UN Special Fund	21 Feb 60	351UNTS93	105019
Ecuador	USA (United States)	24 Feb 60	371UNTS55	105270
Pakistan	UN Special Fund	25 Feb 60	351UNTS141	105021
Peru	USA (United States)	26 Feb 60	394UNTS141	105674
France	UN Special Fund	17 Mar 60	354UNTS119	105059
Argentina	USA (United States)	01 Apr 60	371UNTS245	105281
Italy	UN Special Fund	01 Apr 60	354UNTS261	105066
Colombia	USA (United States)	07 Apr 60	372UNTS27	105285
Multilateral		12 Apr 60	359UNTS323	105150
UN Special Fund	Tunisia	12 Apr 60	355UNTS289	105082
Libya	UN Special Fund	19 Apr 60	356UNTS11	105090
UN Special Fund	Sudan	21 Apr 60	356UNTS213	105097
UN Special Fund	Vietnam, South	29 Apr 60	357UNTS311	200567
Laos	UN Special Fund	30 Apr 60	361UNTS171	105179
Lebanon	UN Special Fund	07 May 60	360UNTS225	105160
Cambodia	WHO (World Health)	19 May 60	372UNTS193	105298
Multilateral		04 Jun 60	360UNTS208	105159
Iraq	UN Special Fund	19 Jun 60	376UNTS357	105389
Belgium	Netherlands	20 Jun 60	423UNTS19	106084
UK Great Britain	USA (United States)	24 Jun 60	377UNTS63	105396
Haiti	USA (United States)	08 Jul 60	380UNTS135	105454
Multilateral		08 Jul 60	366UNTS310	105220
Ethiopia	UN Special Fund	13 Jul 60	368UNTS159	105240
WHO (World Health)	United Arab Rep	03 Aug 60	385UNTS3	105524
Jordan	WHO (World Health)	03 Aug 60	381UNTS133	105469
Laos	WHO (World Health)	04 Aug 60	373UNTS313	105322
Canada	USA (United States)	31 Aug 60	393UNTS247	105659
WHO (World Health)	Saudi Arabia	06 Sep 60	395UNTS169	105684
Lebanon	WHO (World Health)	08 Sep 60	387UNTS49	105557
Iran	Japan	12 Sep 60	384UNTS43	105509
South Africa	USA (United States)	13 Sep 60	388UNTS65	105572
Brazil	UN Special Fund	16 Sep 60	375UNTS3	105351
Taiwan	UN Special Fund	20 Sep 60	375UNTS29	105352
Indonesia	UN Special Fund	07 Oct 60	378UNTS141	105424
Liberia	UN Special Fund	11 Oct 60	376UNTS341	105388
El Salvador	UN Special Fund	24 Oct 60	377UNTS171	105400
Romania	UK Great Britain	10 Nov 60	385UNTS113	105533
UNICEF (Children)	Upper Volta	15 Nov 60	402UNTS33	105776
WHO (World Health)	Upper Volta	15 Nov 60	383UNTS91	105496
Mali	UNICEF (Children)	17 Nov 60	402UNTS23	105775
Nepal	UN Special Fund	17 Nov 60	380UNTS289	105461
Guatemala	UN Special Fund	17 Nov 60	383UNTS67	105495
Cambodia	UN Special Fund	24 Nov 60	382UNTS255	105487
Fed of Malaya	WHO (World Health)	25 Nov 60	387UNTS37	105556
WHO (World Health)	Yemen	03 Dec 60	395UNTS187	105685
Dahomey	WHO (World Health)	07 Dec 60	387UNTS277	105567
Congo (Brazzaville)	WHO (World Health)	12 Dec 60	399UNTS105	105737
Honduras	UN Special Fund	20 Dec 60	383UNTS103	105497
Niger	WHO (World Health)	28 Dec 60	394UNTS195	105679

Title and deeds (Cont.)

PARTY ONE	PARTY TWO	DATE	CITATION	NUMBER
Multilateral		30 Dec 60	395UNTS241	105689
Burma	UN Special Fund	03 Jan 61	387UNTS219	105564
Costa Rica	UN Special Fund	10 Jan 61	389UNTS253	105597
UN Special Fund	Saudi Arabia	19 Jan 61	396UNTS27	105692
Korea, South	WHO (World Health)	20 Jan 61	406UNTS269	200589
Nicaragua	UN Special Fund	20 Jan 61	387UNTS15	105555
Chad	UN Special Fund	23 Jan 61	390UNTS69	105603
UN Special Fund	Somalia	28 Jan 61	388UNTS75	105573
Multilateral		28 Jan 61	387UNTS202	105563
Ivory Coast	WHO (World Health)	30 Jan 61	395UNTS205	105686
Gabon	UN Special Fund	02 Feb 61	387UNTS289	105568
Chad	WHO (World Health)	03 Feb 61	394UNTS161	105676
WHO (World Health)	Togo	03 Feb 61	394UNTS207	105680
Nigeria	UN Special Fund	10 Feb 61	390UNTS85	105604
Central Afri Rep	WHO (World Health)	13 Feb 61	394UNTS149	105675
Mexico	UN Special Fund	23 Feb 61	388UNTS151	105576
Cyprus	UN Special Fund	24 Feb 61	389UNTS3	105588
Panama	UN Special Fund	09 Mar 61	396UNTS3	105691
Cuba	UN Special Fund	10 Mar 61	390UNTS35	105601
Kuwait	WHO (World Health)	16 Mar 61	397UNTS315	200588
Multilateral		10 Apr 61	402UNTS281	105791
Mauritania	WHO (World Health)	17 Apr 61	396UNTS301	200587
Cyprus	UNICEF (Children)	19 Apr 61	394UNTS185	105678
Korea, South	UN Special Fund	21 Apr 61	394UNTS231	200583
Mali	WHO (World Health)	27 Apr 61	407UNTS66	105860
Gabon	WHO (World Health)	27 Apr 61	397UNTS215	105707
Ceylon (Sri Lanka)	UN Special Fund	03 May 61	395UNTS217	105687
Cameroon	UN Special Fund	13 Jun 61	397UNTS297	105713
Paraguay	UN Special Fund	22 Jun 61	399UNTS117	105738
Mexico	USA (United States)	26 Jun 61	413UNTS229	105957
UN Special Fund	Upper Volta	26 Jun 61	400UNTS3	105744
Philippines	UN Special Fund	28 Jun 61	399UNTS141	105739
Haiti	UN Special Fund	28 Jun 61	399UNTS171	105741
UNICEF (Children)	Saudi Arabia	04 Jul 61	413UNTS122	105947
Mali	UN Special Fund	21 Jul 61	401UNTS141	105768
UN Special Fund	Yemen	02 Aug 61	402UNTS43	105777
Morocco	WHO (World Health)	09 Aug 61	412UNTS192	105932
Cameroon	UNICEF (Children)	12 Aug 61	402UNTS235	105788
WHO (World Health)	Somalia	17 Aug 61	423UNTS111	106088
Chad	UNICEF (Children)	26 Aug 61	422UNTS231	106077
Ivory Coast	UN Special Fund	29 Aug 61	406UNTS129	105844
Iraq	WHO (World Health)	13 Sep 61	419UNTS69	106030
Multilateral		20 Sep 61	407UNTS52	105859
UN Special Fund	Sierra Leone	02 Oct 61	422UNTS131	106073
Malagasy	WHO (World Health)	13 Oct 61	421UNTS273	106064
Multilateral		16 Oct 61	410UNTS242	105908
Gabon	UNICEF (Children)	02 Nov 61	422UNTS241	106078
Mauritania	UN Special Fund	07 Nov 61	412UNTS240	105936
Multilateral		07 Nov 61	412UNTS258	105937
Congo (Brazzaville)	UN Special Fund	09 Nov 61	413UNTS58	105940
Malagasy	UNICEF (Children)	16 Nov 61	422UNTS251	106079
UN Special Fund	Venezuela	11 Dec 61	422UNTS149	106074
UN Special Fund	Senegal	16 Dec 61	425UNTS97	106121
Multilateral		27 Dec 61	425UNTS83	106120
Malagasy	UN Special Fund	05 Jan 62	419UNTS29	106028
Ivory Coast	UNICEF (Children)	10 Jan 62	422UNTS261	106080
Ethiopia	WHO (World Health)	11 Jan 62	423UNTS99	106087
Multilateral		17 Jan 62	419UNTS294	106033
Multilateral		20 Jan 62	429UNTS230	200596
UNICEF (Children)	Yemen	31 Jan 62	422UNTS271	106081
Multilateral		13 Feb 62	422UNTS288	200594
Multilateral		21 Feb 62	423UNTS151	106091
Niger	UN Special Fund	26 Feb 62	423UNTS83	106086
Multilateral		01 Mar 62	423UNTS122	106089
Cyprus	USA (United States)	02 Mar 62	445UNTS189	106386

PARTY ONE	PARTY TWO	DATE	CITATION	NUMBER
Title and deeds (Cont.)				
WHO (World Health)	Sudan	11 Mar 62	432UNTS325	106226
Nigeria	WHO (World Health)	27 Mar 62	429UNTS123	106194
Dahomey	UN Special Fund	28 Mar 62	424UNTS55	106099
UNICEF (Children)	Somalia	01 Apr 62	431UNTS75	106211
Congo (Brazzaville)	UNICEF (Children)	09 Apr 62	431UNTS65	106210
Multilateral		10 Apr 62	429UNTS78	106192
UNICEF (Children)	Sierra Leone	11 Apr 62	431UNTS55	106209
Multilateral		18 Apr 62	463UNTS44	106692
UN Special Fund	Uruguay	04 May 62	429UNTS143	106196
Multilateral		17 May 62	429UNTS46	106189
Dominican Republic	UN Special Fund	06 Jun 62	429UNTS169	106197
New Zealand	USA (United States)	08 Jun 62	458UNTS209	106602
Libya	WHO (World Health)	16 Jun 62	437UNTS127	106301
WHO (World Health)	Sierra Leone	19 Jun 62	439UNTS151	106327
Multilateral		27 Jun 62	463UNTS3	106688
Congo (Zaire)	IAEA (Atom Energy)	27 Jun 62	463UNTS31	106691
Multilateral		27 Jun 62	463UNTS17	106690
UN Special Fund	Syria	07 Jul 62	443UNTS3	106355
UN Special Fund	Tanganyika	17 Jul 62	435UNTS237	106281
WHO (World Health)	Senegal	06 Aug 62	435UNTS179	106279
Multilateral		12 Aug 62	443UNTS266	106365
WHO (World Health)	Western Samoa	14 Aug 62	437UNTS317	200598
Philippines	USA (United States)	21 Aug 62	461UNTS163	106660
Multilateral		29 Aug 62	443UNTS280	106366
Japan	UN Special Fund	31 Oct 62	444UNTS171	106368
Algeria	UN Special Fund	15 Nov 62	452UNTS243	106512
Multilateral		15 Nov 62	448UNTS50	106424
WHO (World Health)	Syria	18 Nov 62	480UNTS249	106972
Algeria	UNICEF (Children)	20 Nov 62	453UNTS151	106522
Multilateral		06 Dec 62	450UNTS240	106471
Cameroon	WHO (World Health)	08 Dec 62	451UNTS215	106496
Multilateral		12 Dec 62	457UNTS72	106578
Algeria	WHO (World Health)	20 Dec 62	463UNTS135	106698
Pakistan	USA (United States)	16 Jan 63	471UNTS133	106828
Mauritania	UNICEF (Children)	19 Jan 63	452UNTS271	106514
Multilateral		21 Jan 63	453UNTS20	106517
UNICEF (Children)	Tanganyika	25 Jan 63	453UNTS249	106528
Multilateral		05 Feb 63	453UNTS36	106518
Multilateral		14 Feb 63	453UNTS168	106524
Multilateral		06 Mar 63	455UNTS386	106552
UN Special Fund	Uganda	22 Mar 63	456UNTS466	106572
Multilateral		18 Apr 63	463UNTS121	106697
Multilateral		06 May 63	463UNTS78	106694
Australia	USA (United States)	09 May 63	475UNTS331	106897
Multilateral		09 May 63	463UNTS159	106700
Denmark	India	15 May 63	616UNTS39	108890
Denmark	India	15 May 63	616UNTS23	108889
Jamaica	UN Special Fund	22 May 63	489UNTS191	107140
Multilateral		22 May 63	483UNTS72	107007
Netherlands	UN Special Fund	24 May 63	466UNTS289	106750
Multilateral		24 May 63	466UNTS346	106754
UN Special Fund	Western Samoa	05 Jun 63	467UNTS463	200601
Mongolia	WHO (World Health)	21 Jun 63	472UNTS373	106848
Multilateral		23 Jul 63	471UNTS158	106831
Multilateral		31 Jul 63	472UNTS220	106842
Burundi	WHO (World Health)	08 Aug 63	477UNTS346	106928
Burundi	UN Special Fund	22 Aug 63	476UNTS49	106903
Multilateral		27 Aug 63	511UNTS210	107435
Mexico	USA (United States)	29 Aug 63	505UNTS185	107374
Multilateral		10 Sep 63	480UNTS100	106965
Jamaica	WHO (World Health)	25 Sep 63	481UNTS125	106980
Central Afri Rep	UN Special Fund	30 Oct 63	481UNTS247	106985
Multilateral		30 Oct 63	480UNTS180	106968
WHO (World Health)	Tanganyika	05 Nov 63	496UNTS193	107252
Multilateral		07 Nov 63	480UNTS232	106971
Title and deeds (Cont.)				
Multilateral		08 Nov 63	482UNTS286	106999
Netherlands	USA (United States)	26 Nov 63	388UNTS303	105586
Multilateral		28 Jan 64	502UNTS321	107336
Multilateral		20 Feb 64	491UNTS30	107172
Multilateral		08 Apr 64	501UNTS221	107320
Liberia	USA (United States)	14 Apr 64	526UNTS221	107606
Ireland	UN Special Fund	03 Jun 64	496UNTS205	107253
Rwanda	WHO (World Health)	22 Jun 64	514UNTS11	107440
Multilateral		23 Jun 64	506UNTS108	107383
WHO (World Health)	Trinidad/Tobago	23 Jun 64	503UNTS167	107342
Rwanda	WHO (World Health)	23 Jun 64	514UNTS157	107445
Multilateral		28 Jun 64	519UNTS14	107499
Multilateral		24 Oct 64	514UNTS220	200608
Multilateral		11 Nov 64	515UNTS94	107456
Germany, West	Thailand	23 Dec 64	525UNTS185	107590
Malawi	WHO (World Health)	06 Jan 65	525UNTS165	107588
Malawi	WHO (World Health)	08 Jan 65	524UNTS281	107579
India	USA (United States)	13 Jan 65	541UNTS107	107864
Multilateral		27 Jan 65	523UNTS102	107556
Multilateral		02 Feb 65	523UNTS256	107560
Multilateral		12 Feb 65	525UNTS148	107587
Mexico	USA (United States)	27 Feb 65	542UNTS181	107889
Multilateral		02 Jun 65	537UNTS348	200611
UN Special Fund	Spain	30 Jun 65	544UNTS159	107918
Poland	WHO (World Health)	26 Aug 65	552UNTS3	108047
Multilateral		13 Sep 65	547UNTS264	107962
Multilateral		24 Sep 65	556UNTS141	108124
Multilateral		21 Oct 65	547UNTS216	107959
Multilateral		30 Dec 65	557UNTS3	108126
Mongolia	UN Special Fund	26 Jan 66	552UNTS201	108055
IAEA (Atom Energy)	Turkey	08 Feb 66	573UNTS75	108323
WHO (World Health)	Singapore	28 Mar 66	562UNTS59	108195
Brazil	UNICEF (Children)	28 Mar 66	607UNTS235	108807
Spain	USA (United States)	14 Apr 66	579UNTS173	108406
Romania	IAEA (Atom Energy)	22 Apr 66	603UNTS23	108721
Bulgaria	UN Special Fund	26 May 66	563UNTS71	108205
Multilateral		20 Jun 66	573UNTS41	108322
India	IAEA (Atom Energy)	09 Dec 66	603UNTS35	108722
UK Great Britain	USA (United States)	30 Dec 66	603UNTS273	108737
Multilateral		23 Aug 67	614UNTS145	108869
New Zealand	WHO (World Health)	29 Aug 67	607UNTS57	108795
Iraq	IAEA (Atom Energy)	21 Sep 67	630UNTS41	108963
Burma	IAEA (Atom Energy)	11 Oct 67	630UNTS49	108964
Multilateral		12 Oct 67	607UNTS20	108793
Botswana	UN Special Fund	12 Oct 67	607UNTS37	108794
India	United Nations	04 Nov 67	609UNTS3	108824
Use of facilities				
Netherlands	USA (United States)	17 Jan 33	474UNTS119	106877
Bolivia	Brazil	25 Feb 38	88UNTS379	200254
Brazil	France	27 Jan 40	72UNTS77	100929
Panama	USA (United States)	23 Mar 40	124UNTS195	200420
Multilateral		12 May 40	101UNTS91	101405
Panama	USA (United States)	06 Sep 40	124UNTS209	200421
Multilateral		27 Mar 41	67UNTS231	200222
Haiti	USA (United States)	23 May 41	117UNTS191	200370
Brazil	Paraguay	14 Jun 41	54UNTS259	200198
Bolivia	USA (United States)	04 Sep 41	8UNTS345	200046
Multilateral		29 Jan 42	93UNTS279	200271
Peru	USA (United States)	11 Mar 42	117UNTS266	200375
Brazil	USA (United States)	07 May 42	6UNTS377	200040
Panama	USA (United States)	18 May 42	124UNTS221	200422
Colombia	USA (United States)	29 May 42	8UNTS365	200047
Canada	USA (United States)	27 Jun 42	99UNTS223	200276
Panama	USA (United States)	07 Jul 42	9UNTS289	200048

PARTY ONE	PARTY TWO	DATE	CITATION	NUMBER
Use of facilities (Cont.)				
Bolivia	USA (United States)	11 Aug 42	9UNTS309	200049
Canada	USA (United States)	15 Aug 42	99UNTS233	200277
Norway	USA (United States)	28 Aug 42	139UNTS361	200461
Nicaragua	USA (United States)	27 Oct 42	99UNTS287	200283
Dominican Republic	USA (United States)	25 Jan 43	13UNTS399	200083
Colombia	USA (United States)	29 Mar 43	124UNTS139	200416
Guatemala	USA (United States)	17 Jul 43	28UNTS431	200166
Ecuador	USA (United States)	13 Sep 43	29UNTS349	200171
Dominican Republic	USA (United States)	19 Oct 43	21UNTS295	200130
Paraguay	USA (United States)	27 Oct 43	29UNTS391	200174
Iran	USA (United States)	27 Nov 43	31UNTS451	200176
Paraguay	USA (United States)	10 Dec 43	21UNTS305	200131
USA (United States)	Venezuela	13 Jan 44	109UNTS171	200358
Canada	USA (United States)	07 Jun 44	99UNTS259	200280
Ecuador	USA (United States)	29 Jun 44	80UNTS283	200250
Peru	USA (United States)	10 Jul 44	117UNTS291	200377
Guatemala	USA (United States)	15 Jul 44	106UNTS285	200347
Brazil	USA (United States)	29 Sep 44	65UNTS271	200216
Multilateral		28 Oct 44	123UNTS223	200414
Spain	USA (United States)	02 Dec 44	89UNTS345	200262
Multilateral		07 Dec 44	84UNTS389	200252
Multilateral		07 Dec 44	171UNTS387	200502
Denmark	USA (United States)	16 Dec 44	10UNTS213	200063
Iceland	USA (United States)	27 Jan 45	122UNTS293	200411
Ireland	USA (United States)	03 Feb 45	122UNTS305	200412
Canada	USA (United States)	13 Feb 45	200UNTS219	200519
Canada	USA (United States)	17 Feb 45	122UNTS261	200409
Guatemala	USA (United States)	21 Feb 45	121UNTS133	200396
Canada	USA (United States)	26 Feb 45	99UNTS273	200281
Guatemala	USA (United States)	21 May 45	121UNTS185	200399
Chile	USA (United States)	24 May 45	121UNTS219	200401
Multilateral		05 Jun 45	68UNTS189	200230
Switzerland	USA (United States)	03 Aug 45	51UNTS233	200191
Canada	USA (United States)	06 Sep 45	99UNTS281	200282
Norway	USA (United States)	06 Oct 45	122UNTS319	200413
South Africa	UK Great Britain	26 Oct 45	72UNTS41	100927
Greece	UK Great Britain	26 Nov 45	35UNTS161	100555
Portugal	UK Great Britain	06 Dec 45	6UNTS3	100065
Portugal	USA (United States)	06 Dec 45	3UNTS139	100028
Costa Rica	USA (United States)	10 Dec 45	3UNTS157	100029
Canada	UK Great Britain	21 Dec 45	27UNTS155	100405
Honduras	USA (United States)	28 Dec 45	3UNTS185	100031
Czechoslovakia	USA (United States)	03 Jan 46	6UNTS309	100084
United Arab Rep	USA (United States)	05 Jan 46	160UNTS27	102098
Czechoslovakia	Poland	24 Jan 46	25UNTS181	100363
UK Great Britain	USA (United States)	11 Feb 46	3UNTS253	100036
Turkey	UK Great Britain	12 Feb 46	6UNTS79	100069
Turkey	USA (United States)	12 Feb 46	13UNTS3	100196
France	UK Great Britain	28 Feb 46	27UNTS173	100407
Belgium	UK Great Britain	11 Mar 46	26UNTS167	100387
Greece	USA (United States)	27 Mar 46	15UNTS233	100239
France	USA (United States)	27 Mar 46	139UNTS114	101879
Belgium	USA (United States)	05 Apr 46	4UNTS125	100041
Ireland	UK Great Britain	05 Apr 46	72UNTS57	100928
Netherlands	Portugal	12 Apr 46	4UNTS317	100054
Mexico	USA (United States)	12 Apr 46	66UNTS293	100861
Argentina	UK Great Britain	17 Apr 46	164UNTS53	102159
France	Ireland	16 May 46	44UNTS105	100681
Ireland	Sweden	29 May 46	35UNTS231	100557
Portugal	USA (United States)	30 May 46	174UNTS187	102285
USA (United States)	Venezuela	03 Jun 46	4UNTS215	100047
Australia	Canada	11 Jun 46	10UNTS47	100142
United Arab Rep	USA (United States)	15 Jun 46	71UNTS157	100917
Poland	UK Great Britain	24 Jun 46	11UNTS59	100149
Sweden	Turkey	26 Jun 46	14UNTS21	100208

PARTY ONE	PARTY TWO	DATE	CITATION	NUMBER
Use of facilities (Cont.)				
United Nations	Switzerland	01 Jul 46	1UNTS153	200007
Netherlands	Spain	13 Jul 46	4UNTS351	100055
League of Nations	United Nations	19 Jul 46	1UNTS109	200002
League of Nations	United Nations	31 Jul 46	1UNTS119	200003
France	Sweden	02 Aug 46	27UNTS251	100410
Hungary	USA (United States)	09 Aug 46	148UNTS313	101941
Lebanon	USA (United States)	11 Aug 46	66UNTS211	100856
Norway	UK Great Britain	31 Aug 46	6UNTS235	100078
Brazil	USA (United States)	06 Sep 46	54UNTS197	100805
Peru	USA (United States)	07 Oct 46	7UNTS71	100092
France	Turkey	12 Oct 46	14UNTS33	100209
Colombia	USA (United States)	14 Oct 46	7UNTS97	100093
Belgium	Portugal	22 Oct 46	34UNTS49	100527
Brazil	UK Great Britain	31 Oct 46	11UNTS115	100152
Philippines	USA (United States)	16 Nov 46	7UNTS151	100097
Sweden	UK Great Britain	27 Nov 46	11UNTS229	100162
New Zealand	USA (United States)	03 Dec 46	7UNTS175	100099
Australia	USA (United States)	03 Dec 46	7UNTS201	100100
Portugal	Switzerland	09 Dec 46	310UNTS251	104495
Brazil	Portugal	10 Dec 46	200UNTS67	102695
USA (United States)	Uruguay	14 Dec 46	532UNTS87	107713
Taiwan	USA (United States)	20 Dec 46	22UNTS87	100332
Peru	USA (United States)	27 Dec 46	152UNTS93	102013
Ecuador	USA (United States)	08 Jan 47	22UNTS119	100333
USSR (Soviet Union)	Yugoslavia	04 Feb 47	116UNTS171	101576
Multilateral		10 Feb 47	41UNTS135	100644
Multilateral		10 Feb 47	41UNTS21	100643
Thailand	USA (United States)	26 Feb 47	16UNTS17	100246
Paraguay	USA (United States)	28 Feb 47	44UNTS25	100676
Portugal	Sweden	06 Mar 47	35UNTS243	100558
Australia	USA (United States)	10 Mar 47	10UNTS89	100145
Philippines	USA (United States)	14 Mar 47	45UNTS23	100690
Philippines	USA (United States)	14 Mar 47	43UNTS271	100673
Netherlands	Turkey	19 Mar 47	14UNTS59	100211
Greece	Sweden	08 Apr 47	94UNTS73	101307
Netherlands	USA (United States)	11 Apr 47	148UNTS343	101943
Greece	Netherlands	17 Apr 47	32UNTS115	100494
Denmark	UK Great Britain	22 Apr 47	8UNTS3	100110
Canada	Portugal	25 Apr 47	94UNTS87	101308
Syria	USA (United States)	28 Apr 47	262UNTS121	103741
France	Greece	05 May 47	76UNTS61	100980
Chile	USA (United States)	10 May 47	55UNTS21	100807
Philippines	USA (United States)	12 May 47	16UNTS137	100254
Philippines	USA (United States)	12 May 47	16UNTS109	100252
Philippines	USA (United States)	12 May 47	16UNTS123	100253
Czechoslovakia	Denmark	14 May 47	27UNTS297	100413
UK Great Britain	USA (United States)	23 May 47	11UNTS211	100159
South Africa	USA (United States)	23 May 47	66UNTS233	100857
Panama	USA (United States)	26 May 47	138UNTS137	101866
Greece	UK Great Britain	05 Jun 47	9UNTS197	100133
Norway	UK Great Britain	05 Jun 47	54UNTS181	100803
Greece	USA (United States)	20 Jun 47	7UNTS267	100105
Austria	USA (United States)	21 Jun 47	67UNTS99	100869
Canada	Sweden	27 Jun 47	27UNTS313	100414
Denmark	Turkey	30 Jun 47	32UNTS301	100504
Iraq	Turkey	30 Jun 47	72UNTS107	100930
Romania	Yugoslavia	30 Jun 47	116UNTS57	101569
France	India	16 Jul 47	27UNTS325	100415
Canada	UK Great Britain	17 Jul 47	28UNTS3	100416
Netherlands	Thailand	18 Jul 47	28UNTS27	100417
Greece	Turkey	22 Jul 47	72UNTS131	100931
Netherlands	South Africa	22 Jul 47	12UNTS257	100188
Belgium	USA (United States)	23 Jul 47	33UNTS33	100512
Czechoslovakia	USA (United States)	25 Jul 47	90UNTS19	101223
Taiwan	Italy	30 Jul 47	12UNTS383	100195

PARTY ONE	PARTY TWO	DATE	CITATION	NUMBER
Use of facilities (Cont.)				
Poland	Romania	09 Aug 47	12UNTS363	100193
France	UK Great Britain	13 Aug 47	91UNTS169	101249
El Salvador	USA (United States)	19 Aug 47	51UNTS57	100752
USSR (Soviet Union)	Yugoslavia	23 Aug 47	116UNTS281	101577
Czechoslovakia	Netherlands	01 Sep 47	32UNTS129	100495
Czechoslovakia	Switzerland	10 Sep 47	35UNTS275	100559
Lebanon	Turkey	16 Sep 47	44UNTS123	100682
France	USA (United States)	01 Oct 47	148UNTS303	101940
Greece	UNICEF (Children)	14 Oct 47	102UNTS39	101409
Czechoslovakia	Sweden	15 Oct 47	44UNTS149	100683
Colombia	UK Great Britain	16 Oct 47	160UNTS297	102115
Bolivia	USA (United States)	03 Nov 47	51UNTS33	100750
Brazil	Netherlands	06 Nov 47	53UNTS59	100773
Norway	Portugal	11 Nov 47	34UNTS257	100542
Brazil	Norway	14 Nov 47	44UNTS163	100684
Denmark	Greece	14 Nov 47	35UNTS295	100560
Brazil	Sweden	14 Nov 47	94UNTS139	101310
Brazil	Denmark	14 Nov 47	47UNTS39	100722
Denmark	Ireland	18 Nov 47	35UNTS309	100561
Ireland	Italy	21 Nov 47	353UNTS73	105038
Taiwan	Netherlands	06 Dec 47	43UNTS185	100669
Denmark	Portugal	15 Dec 47	35UNTS329	100563
Costa Rica	USA (United States)	12 Jan 48	70UNTS27	100896
Austria	Netherlands	22 Jan 48	17UNTS99	100270
Italy	USA (United States)	06 Feb 48	73UNTS113	100950
UK Great Britain	USA (United States)	24 Feb 48	73UNTS143	100951
Czechoslovakia	Yugoslavia	14 Mar 48	28UNTS81	100421
Argentina	Denmark	18 Mar 48	94UNTS175	101311
Cuba	UK Great Britain	19 Mar 48	175UNTS23	102294
USA (United States)	Venezuela	24 Mar 48	44UNTS57	100678
Ireland	Switzerland	06 May 48	334UNTS187	104768
France	Ireland	06 May 48	558UNTS170	108141
Pakistan	Sweden	06 May 48	36UNTS3	100564
Jordan	Turkey	07 May 48	32UNTS313	100505
Ireland	Netherlands	10 May 48	28UNTS121	100422
Ecuador	USA (United States)	14 May 48	89UNTS71	101210
Norway	Turkey	20 May 48	26UNTS137	100384
Portugal	UK Great Britain	25 May 48	34UNTS311	100544
Greece	Switzerland	26 May 48	94UNTS217	101312
Ireland	Norway	21 Jun 48	34UNTS317	100545
India	Pakistan	23 Jun 48	28UNTS143	100423
Chile	UK Great Britain	24 Jun 48	77UNTS113	100995
Brazil	USA (United States)	29 Jul 48	80UNTS111	101047
Brazil	Switzerland	10 Aug 48	94UNTS269	101314
Multilateral		18 Aug 48	33UNTS181	100518
France	Spain	23 Aug 48	28UNTS173	100425
Philippines	USA (United States)	27 Aug 48	44UNTS13	100675
Ireland	Netherlands	02 Sep 48	558UNTS249	108145
Greece	Lebanon	06 Sep 48	178UNTS37	102335
Bolivia	USA (United States)	29 Sep 48	505UNTS139	107370
Argentina	USA (United States)	06 Oct 48	80UNTS91	101046
Netherlands	Spain	08 Oct 48	28UNTS209	100426
France	USA (United States)	19 Oct 48	98UNTS3	101355
Mexico	Portugal	22 Oct 48	34UNTS329	100546
Argentina	Netherlands	29 Oct 48	95UNTS21	101316
Brazil	USA (United States)	26 Nov 48	88UNTS3	101180
Italy	Netherlands	04 Dec 48	46UNTS271	100716
Haiti	USA (United States)	04 Jan 49	44UNTS69	100679
Italy	Lebanon	24 Jan 49	231UNTS241	103223
Switzerland	Turkey	16 Feb 49	72UNTS175	100933
Greece	USA (United States)	21 Feb 49	88UNTS29	101182
Colombia	USA (United States)	21 Feb 49	92UNTS227	101275
Colombia	USA (United States)	21 Feb 49	44UNTS83	100680
Finland	Netherlands	25 Feb 49	53UNTS123	100777
Multilateral		28 Feb 49	29UNTS53	100434

PARTY ONE	PARTY TWO	DATE	CITATION	NUMBER
Use of facilities (Cont.)				
Ceylon (Sri Lanka)	UK Great Britain	28 Feb 49	314UNTS269	104551
Netherlands	Switzerland	07 Mar 49	35UNTS69	100551
Austria	USA (United States)	23 Mar 49	43UNTS127	100667
Finland	USA (United States)	29 Mar 49	55UNTS59	100808
Panama	USA (United States)	31 Mar 49	55UNTS141	100812
Panama	USA (United States)	31 Mar 49	55UNTS87	100810
Haiti	USA (United States)	14 Apr 49	80UNTS37	101043
Finland	Sweden	26 Apr 49	95UNTS83	101318
Bulgaria	Poland	16 May 49	84UNTS313	101140
Italy	Spain	31 May 49	231UNTS251	103224
Australia	Pakistan	03 Jun 49	35UNTS23	100549
Canada	USA (United States)	04 Jun 49	122UNTS237	101649
Canada	USA (United States)	04 Jun 49	200UNTS201	102704
Belgium	Greece	21 Jun 49	137UNTS215	101854
Norway	Pakistan	23 Jun 49	35UNTS49	100550
India	Switzerland	24 Jun 49	95UNTS109	101319
Argentina	UK Great Britain	27 Jun 49	83UNTS217	101110
India	USA (United States)	04 Jul 49	200UNTS181	102702
Greece	Syria	05 Jul 49	78UNTS71	101013
Mexico	USA (United States)	05 Jul 49	68UNTS55	100884
Iraq	Norway	12 Jul 49	53UNTS137	100778
Czechoslovakia	Finland	13 Jul 49	53UNTS153	100779
Dominican Republic	USA (United States)	19 Jul 49	51UNTS145	100762
Philippines	USA (United States)	08 Aug 49	163UNTS103	102144
Finland	Norway	24 Aug 49	53UNTS167	100780
Denmark	Finland	26 Aug 49	53UNTS191	100781
Argentina	Norway	09 Sep 49	42UNTS125	100646
UK Great Britain	USA (United States)	19 Sep 49	68UNTS31	100882
Lebanon	Netherlands	20 Sep 49	108UNTS205	101474
USA (United States)	USSR (Soviet Union)	27 Sep 49	149UNTS23	101948
Burma	USA (United States)	28 Sep 49	55UNTS3	100806
Greece	Philippines	08 Oct 49	187UNTS221	102515
Denmark	Pakistan	09 Nov 49	44UNTS255	100687
Denmark	Thailand	23 Nov 49	53UNTS255	100786
Sweden	Thailand	23 Nov 49	72UNTS217	100935
Italy	Turkey	25 Nov 49	192UNTS39	102594
Norway	Thailand	26 Nov 49	53UNTS269	100787
Brazil	Spain	28 Nov 49	215UNTS303	102923
Austria	Denmark	02 Dec 49	53UNTS281	100788
Austria	Sweden	02 Dec 49	108UNTS3	101465
Austria	Norway	02 Dec 49	72UNTS230	100936
Afghanistan	WHO (World Health)	04 Dec 49	102UNTS117	101414
Canada	Denmark	13 Dec 49	72UNTS247	100937
Austria	Switzerland	19 Dec 49	254UNTS287	103597
Belgium	UK Great Britain	23 Dec 49	99UNTS61	101371
USA (United States)	Yugoslavia	24 Dec 49	89UNTS209	101219
Korea, South	USA (United States)	26 Jan 50	178UNTS97	102337
Korea, South	USA (United States)	26 Jan 50	80UNTS205	101053
France	USA (United States)	27 Jan 50	80UNTS171	101051
Norway	USA (United States)	27 Jan 50	80UNTS241	101055
Italy	USA (United States)	27 Jan 50	80UNTS145	101050
Denmark	USA (United States)	27 Jan 50	48UNTS115	100740
UK Great Britain	USA (United States)	27 Jan 50	80UNTS261	101056
Luxembourg	USA (United States)	27 Jan 50	80UNTS187	101052
Belgium	USA (United States)	27 Jan 50	51UNTS213	100767
Netherlands	USA (United States)	27 Jan 50	80UNTS219	101054
UNICEF (Children)	UK Great Britain	10 Feb 50	65UNTS86	100837
Netherlands	Syria	13 Feb 50	108UNTS53	101467
Canada	Norway	14 Feb 50	53UNTS329	100790
Ceylon (Sri Lanka)	WHO (World Health)	17 Feb 50	102UNTS309	200309
Spain	Sweden	18 Feb 50	166UNTS15	102184
Ceylon (Sri Lanka)	Thailand	24 Feb 50	72UNTS261	100938
Chile	UNICEF (Children)	03 Mar 50	126UNTS119	101685
Honduras	USA (United States)	06 Mar 50	80UNTS71	101045
Honduras	USA (United States)	06 Mar 50	80UNTS51	101044

PARTY ONE	PARTY TWO	DATE	CITATION	NUMBER
Use of facilities (Cont.)				
Philippines	USA (United States)	16 Mar 50	89UNTS199	101218
Iceland	Netherlands	22 Mar 50	95UNTS237	101323
Denmark	Iceland	22 Mar 50	72UNTS273	100939
Israel	UK Great Britain	30 Mar 50	86UNTS231	101162
Italy	Portugal	05 Apr 50	254UNTS329	103599
Iran	USA (United States)	23 May 50	81UNTS3	101057
Israel	USA (United States)	13 Jun 50	212UNTS93	102863
Iraq	Pakistan	20 Jun 50	77UNTS215	101001
Netherlands	Spain	20 Jun 50	95UNTS303	101327
Burma	Ceylon (Sri Lanka)	29 Jun 50	73UNTS3	100940
Spain	UK Great Britain	20 Jul 50	398UNTS101	105719
UK Great Britain	USA (United States)	21 Jul 50	97UNTS193	101351
Spain	Switzerland	03 Aug 50	254UNTS365	103600
Canada	New Zealand	16 Aug 50	77UNTS239	101002
USA (United States)	Venezuela	23 Aug 50	92UNTS341	101279
Burma	Sweden	14 Sep 50	96UNTS45	101330
Brazil	Turkey	21 Sep 50	150UNTS299	101981
Thailand	USA (United States)	17 Oct 50	79UNTS41	101030
Sweden	Switzerland	18 Oct 50	166UNTS49	102185
Luxembourg	Portugal	21 Oct 50	108UNTS67	101468
Israel	Netherlands	23 Oct 50	189UNTS89	102543
Multilateral		02 Nov 50	81UNTS160	101071
Multilateral		24 Nov 50	81UNTS188	101072
Colombia	USA (United States)	24 Nov 50	133UNTS49	101779
Cuba	USA (United States)	22 Dec 50	122UNTS97	101640
Liberia	USA (United States)	22 Dec 50	133UNTS69	101781
Multilateral		23 Dec 50	185UNTS3	102456
Portugal	USA (United States)	05 Jan 51	133UNTS75	101782
Liberia	USA (United States)	11 Jan 51	122UNTS125	101642
Chile	USA (United States)	16 Jan 51	157UNTS3	102043
Chile	USA (United States)	16 Jan 51	147UNTS11	101925
Multilateral		18 Jan 51	81UNTS233	101073
Ethiopia	ICAO (Civil Aviat)	02 Feb 51	96UNTS123	101333
Israel	Turkey	05 Feb 51	193UNTS3	102607
Taiwan	USA (United States)	09 Feb 51	132UNTS273	101767
Chile	USA (United States)	15 Feb 51	133UNTS95	101783
Chile	USA (United States)	15 Feb 51	133UNTS117	101784
Israel	ILO (Labor Org)	19 Feb 51	100UNTS105	101391
ILO (Labor Org)	Syria	03 Mar 51	110UNTS69	101502
Colombia	Portugal	09 Mar 51	108UNTS87	101469
Greece	Yugoslavia	15 Mar 51	187UNTS237	102516
Multilateral		28 Mar 51	181UNTS61	102399
Liberia	ILO (Labor Org)	02 Apr 51	100UNTS117	101392
Multilateral		05 Apr 51	84UNTS299	101139
USA (United States)	Yugoslavia	17 Apr 51	162UNTS173	102134
UK Great Britain	USA (United States)	25 Apr 51	99UNTS97	101373
Jordan	UK Great Britain	01 May 51	117UNTS19	101582
Iceland	USA (United States)	05 May 51	205UNTS173	102776
Multilateral		25 May 51	175UNTS215	102303
Greece	Norway	28 May 51	187UNTS141	102507
Lebanon	WHO (World Health)	07 Jun 51	126UNTS221	101690
Saudi Arabia	USA (United States)	18 Jun 51	102UNTS73	101412
Multilateral		19 Jun 51	199UNTS67	102678
Cuba	Portugal	26 Jun 51	192UNTS115	102598
Multilateral		28 Jun 51	118UNTS154	101604
Ethiopia	WHO (World Health)	02 Jul 51	103UNTS39	101422
Iceland	Norway	14 Jul 51	163UNTS265	102150
Burma	Denmark	30 Jul 51	108UNTS167	101472
Israel	WHO (World Health)	07 Aug 51	104UNTS213	101442
Israel	Philippines	07 Aug 51	192UNTS81	102596
USA (United States)	Venezuela	10 Aug 51	140UNTS345	101898
Jordan	UN Relief Palestin	20 Aug 51	120UNTS277	200394
Cuba	USA (United States)	28 Aug 51	140UNTS239	101891
Cuba	USA (United States)	28 Aug 51	134UNTS225	101802
WHO (World Health)	Saudi Arabia	29 Aug 51	110UNTS277	101516

PARTY ONE	PARTY TWO	DATE	CITATION	NUMBER
Use of facilities (Cont.)				
France	USSR (Soviet Union)	03 Sep 51	221UNTS79	103003
Burma	Netherlands	06 Sep 51	108UNTS187	101473
Portugal	USA (United States)	06 Sep 51	237UNTS217	103348
Costa Rica	USA (United States)	11 Sep 51	234UNTS255	103288
Panama	UK Great Britain	15 Sep 51	560UNTS143	108172
Iraq	ICAO (Civil Aviat)	18 Sep 51	108UNTS219	101475
WHO (World Health)	Thailand	04 Oct 51	109UNTS85	101493
Philippines	Spain	06 Oct 51	215UNTS193	102920
Pakistan	WHO (World Health)	07 Oct 51	126UNTS101	101684
Greece	Luxembourg	22 Oct 51	187UNTS119	102506
Multilateral		31 Oct 51	172UNTS193	102247
India	WHO (World Health)	01 Nov 51	118UNTS13	101593
Saudi Arabia	USA (United States)	10 Nov 51	180UNTS263	102390
USA (United States)	Yugoslavia	14 Nov 51	174UNTS201	102286
Denmark	Iraq	18 Nov 51	232UNTS25	103227
USA (United States)	Uruguay	04 Dec 51	152UNTS41	102010
Iraq	UNICEF (Children)	10 Dec 51	126UNTS57	101682
Colombia	Spain	11 Dec 51	216UNTS73	102933
India	United Nations	12 Jan 52	118UNTS175	101606
UK Great Britain	USA (United States)	15 Jan 52	127UNTS3	101697
Greece	Yugoslavia	02 Feb 52	188UNTS311	102535
UNICEF (Children)	UK Great Britain	04 Feb 52	120UNTS147	101620
Ireland	Portugal	06 Feb 52	558UNTS289	108147
Multilateral		15 Feb 52	132UNTS51	101751
Dominican Republic	UNICEF (Children)	15 Feb 52	121UNTS43	101625
Burma	WHO (World Health)	18 Feb 52	127UNTS43	101698
Ecuador	USA (United States)	20 Feb 52	177UNTS43	102308
Peru	USA (United States)	22 Feb 52	165UNTS31	102166
Japan	USA (United States)	28 Feb 52	208UNTS255	102817
ICAO (Civil Aviat)	United Arab Rep	06 Mar 52	151UNTS111	101986
Cuba	USA (United States)	07 Mar 52	165UNTS11	102165
Belgium	Spain	10 Mar 52	178UNTS243	102342
Brazil	USA (United States)	15 Mar 52	199UNTS221	102687
Pakistan	Switzerland	17 Mar 52	192UNTS237	102603
Sweden	Uruguay	20 Mar 52	311UNTS3	104497
Norway	Uruguay	20 Mar 52	310UNTS279	104496
Iraq	Switzerland	31 Mar 52	311UNTS43	104498
Libya	UNICEF (Children)	05 Apr 52	133UNTS287	200441
Chile	USA (United States)	09 Apr 52	186UNTS53	102482
France	Mexico	17 Apr 52	163UNTS321	102153
Liberia	UNICEF (Children)	17 Apr 52	133UNTS3	101773
India	ICAO (Civil Aviat)	29 Apr 52	151UNTS123	101987
Brazil	WHO (World Health)	12 Jun 52	151UNTS333	102003
WHO (World Health)	Syria	20 Jun 52	165UNTS219	102178
USA (United States)	Uruguay	30 Jun 52	207UNTS139	102804
Brazil	USA (United States)	30 Jun 52	185UNTS79	102460
Ethiopia	UK Great Britain	03 Jul 52	151UNTS207	101996
UNICEF (Children)	Syria	10 Jul 52	136UNTS17	101830
Colombia	United Nations	17 Jul 52	135UNTS61	101815
UNICEF (Children)	UK Great Britain	25 Jul 52	135UNTS37	101812
Brazil	United Nations	04 Aug 52	135UNTS185	101820
Japan	USA (United States)	11 Aug 52	212UNTS27	102862
Jordan	WHO (World Health)	21 Aug 52	141UNTS341	200472
Germany, West	Ireland	26 Sep 52	558UNTS27	108138
Austria	Luxembourg	13 Oct 52	192UNTS291	102606
Mexico	Netherlands	13 Oct 52	163UNTS341	102154
Iceland	Luxembourg	23 Oct 52	193UNTS39	102609
Chile	Sweden	27 Oct 52	311UNTS63	104499
Chile	Denmark	27 Oct 52	271UNTS93	103911
Belgium	UK Great Britain	12 Nov 52	180UNTS15	102372
Luxembourg	Norway	17 Nov 52	311UNTS95	104500
Luxembourg	Sweden	17 Nov 52	173UNTS277	102270
Israel	Switzerland	19 Nov 52	232UNTS3	103226
Nicaragua	USA (United States)	19 Nov 52	186UNTS3	102478
Portugal	UK Great Britain	21 Nov 52	404UNTS27	105802

PARTY ONE	PARTY TWO	DATE	CITATION	NUMBER
Use of facilities (Cont.)				
Canada	USA (United States)	05 Dec 52	206UNTS11	102783
USA (United States)	Venezuela	16 Jan 53	199UNTS287	102690
Japan	Netherlands	17 Feb 53	192UNTS215	102602
Japan	Sweden	20 Feb 53	173UNTS307	102272
Japan	Norway	23 Feb 53	192UNTS191	102601
Denmark	Japan	26 Feb 53	173UNTS329	102273
Germany, West	USA (United States)	27 Feb 53	223UNTS167	103065
Dominican Republic	USA (United States)	06 Mar 53	199UNTS267	102689
Belgium	Canada	30 Mar 53	181UNTS95	102401
Philippines	Thailand	27 Apr 53	174UNTS3	102274
El Salvador	USA (United States)	21 May 53	213UNTS15	102878
Ethiopia	USA (United States)	22 May 53	191UNTS59	102577
Cuba	USA (United States)	26 May 53	224UNTS75	103070
Switzerland	Yugoslavia	28 May 53	232UNTS45	103228
Japan	Thailand	19 Jun 53	174UNTS29	102276
Burma	Norway	22 Jun 53	174UNTS49	102277
Liberia	USA (United States)	23 Jun 53	213UNTS37	102879
Philippines	USA (United States)	26 Jun 53	213UNTS77	102881
India	Yugoslavia	24 Jul 53	394UNTS13	105665
Libya	UK Great Britain	29 Jul 53	186UNTS201	102492
USA (United States)	Venezuela	14 Aug 53	213UNTS99	102883
Italy	South Africa	27 Aug 53	212UNTS211	102873
Spain	USA (United States)	26 Sep 53	207UNTS61	102800
Spain	USA (United States)	26 Sep 53	207UNTS83	102801
Greece	USA (United States)	12 Oct 53	191UNTS319	102589
Multilateral		17 Oct 53	184UNTS42	102438
Austria	Yugoslavia	11 Nov 53	363UNTS149	105206
Nicaragua	USA (United States)	19 Nov 53	206UNTS117	102787
Ceylon (Sri Lanka)	Ireland	20 Nov 53	345UNTS189	104967
Pakistan	United Nations	25 Jan 54	185UNTS213	102472
Syria	UK Great Britain	30 Jan 54	449UNTS47	106452
France	Greece	08 Feb 54	225UNTS107	103093
France	Greece	08 Feb 54	225UNTS121	103094
France	Sweden	16 Feb 54	228UNTS137	103147
Multilateral		19 Feb 54	214UNTS51	102899
Japan	USA (United States)	08 Mar 54	232UNTS169	103236
Panama	USA (United States)	25 Mar 54	232UNTS289	103243
Peru	Spain	31 Mar 54	232UNTS65	103230
Iraq	USA (United States)	21 Apr 54	222UNTS251	103032
Italy	USA (United States)	27 Apr 54	234UNTS103	103275
Norway	USA (United States)	07 May 54	231UNTS157	103215
Nepal	WHO (World Health)	13 May 54	204UNTS311	200522
Spain	USA (United States)	19 May 54	235UNTS87	103296
Pakistan	USA (United States)	19 May 54	202UNTS301	102736
Honduras	USA (United States)	20 May 54	222UNTS87	103025
France	USA (United States)	31 May 54	236UNTS141	103321
Multilateral		01 Jun 54	200UNTS235	200520
UK Great Britain	USA (United States)	15 Jun 54	236UNTS133	103320
Italy	USA (United States)	24 Jun 54	235UNTS3	103290
Ireland	Luxembourg	27 Jul 54	232UNTS91	103231
Netherlands	USA (United States)	13 Aug 54	251UNTS91	103535
Libya	USA (United States)	09 Sep 54	224UNTS217	103078
El Salvador	USA (United States)	23 Sep 54	237UNTS91	103338
Sweden	USSR (Soviet Union)	29 Sep 54	202UNTS259	102733
Multilateral		06 Oct 54	201UNTS75	102711
Multilateral		23 Oct 54	332UNTS157	104761
Multilateral		23 Oct 54	332UNTS3	104760
Multilateral		27 Oct 54	201UNTS95	102712
Multilateral		29 Oct 54	201UNTS115	102713
Belgium	USA (United States)	23 Nov 54	235UNTS19	103292
Netherlands	USA (United States)	14 Dec 54	262UNTS35	103737
Ecuador	Netherlands	14 Dec 54	232UNTS115	103233
Denmark	USA (United States)	15 Dec 54	213UNTS273	102890
Multilateral		16 Dec 54	204UNTS323	200523
Sweden	USA (United States)	22 Dec 54	228UNTS85	103143

PARTY ONE	PARTY TWO	DATE	CITATION	NUMBER
Use of facilities (Cont.)				
Norway	Switzerland	30 Dec 54	311UNTS147	104502
Austria	Belgium	07 Jan 55	380UNTS219	105458
Canada	Japan	12 Jan 55	311UNTS167	104503
Italy	USA (United States)	26 Jan 55	238UNTS179	103361
Haiti	USA (United States)	28 Jan 55	270UNTS83	103894
South Africa	USA (United States)	22 Feb 55	247UNTS247	103473
Multilateral		04 Apr 55	208UNTS239	102816
Turkey	USA (United States)	25 Apr 55	263UNTS299	103779
Cambodia	USA (United States)	16 May 55	263UNTS273	103777
Hungary	USSR (Soviet Union)	27 May 55	407UNTS156	105864
Greece	USA (United States)	27 May 55	251UNTS349	103552
Multilateral		14 Jun 55	212UNTS263	200526
Belgium	USA (United States)	15 Jun 55	235UNTS133	103299
Canada	USA (United States)	15 Jun 55	235UNTS176	103301
UK Great Britain	USA (United States)	15 Jun 55	229UNTS73	103161
Guatemala	USA (United States)	18 Jun 55	262UNTS105	103740
Germany, West	USA (United States)	30 Jun 55	240UNTS47	103393
Multilateral		04 Jul 55	214UNTS10	102897
Germany, West	USA (United States)	07 Jul 55	275UNTS3	103973
Italy	USA (United States)	08 Jul 55	270UNTS29	103889
Ecuador	USA (United States)	08 Jul 55	265UNTS49	103806
Germany, West	UK Great Britain	22 Jul 55	269UNTS189	103881
Brazil	USA (United States)	03 Aug 55	270UNTS71	103893
USSR (Soviet Union)	Yugoslavia	03 Sep 55	240UNTS267	103408
USA (United States)	Yugoslavia	30 Sep 55	269UNTS89	103877
Bulgaria	Yugoslavia	01 Oct 55	396UNTS223	105698
France	Germany, West	04 Oct 55	353UNTS203	105044
Taiwan	USA (United States)	14 Oct 55	268UNTS165	103857
Finland	USSR (Soviet Union)	19 Oct 55	353UNTS185	105043
Austria	Italy	22 Oct 55	260UNTS327	103716
Czechoslovakia	Germany, East	24 Oct 55	504UNTS173	107358
Philippines	USA (United States)	28 Oct 55	239UNTS165	103376
Netherlands	USA (United States)	04 Nov 55	269UNTS3	103867
Burma	China People's Rep	08 Nov 55	306UNTS11	104430
Austria	Israel	17 Nov 55	232UNTS153	103235
India	Japan	26 Nov 55	311UNTS243	104506
Australia	Japan	19 Jan 56	311UNTS291	104507
Argentina	Switzerland	25 Jan 56	559UNTS121	108157
Romania	Yugoslavia	01 Feb 56	362UNTS203	105189
Multilateral		02 Feb 56	227UNTS153	103137
Hungary	Romania	03 Feb 56	362UNTS233	105190
India	USA (United States)	03 Feb 56	272UNTS75	103932
Austria	Poland	08 Feb 56	334UNTS221	104770
Multilateral		10 Feb 56	228UNTS167	103150
Multilateral		10 Feb 56	228UNTS189	103151
Norway	Syria	25 Feb 56	463UNTS217	106706
Multilateral		13 Mar 56	427UNTS245	106158
Colombia	USA (United States)	27 Mar 56	273UNTS235	103954
Sweden	USSR (Soviet Union)	31 Mar 56	259UNTS239	103691
Norway	USSR (Soviet Union)	31 Mar 56	259UNTS205	103690
Denmark	USSR (Soviet Union)	31 Mar 56	259UNTS169	103689
Belgium	Germany, West	14 Apr 56	344UNTS103	104945
Cambodia	UNICEF (Children)	28 Apr 56	136UNTS341	200446
Germany, West	Switzerland	02 May 56	559UNTS157	108158
Japan	Philippines	09 May 56	285UNTS3	104148
Portugal	Venezuela	16 May 56	463UNTS239	106707
Japan	Switzerland	24 May 56	312UNTS3	104509
Greece	Italy	26 May 56	496UNTS301	107258
Italy	Switzerland	04 Jun 56	378UNTS311	105429
Multilateral		08 Jun 56	247UNTS366	200541
Poland	Sweden	08 Jun 56	334UNTS257	104771
Germany, West	Ireland	12 Jun 56	353UNTS121	105040
Multilateral		14 Jun 56	265UNTS125	103809
UK Great Britain	USA (United States)	25 Jun 56	249UNTS59	103501
Multilateral		26 Jun 56	253UNTS12	103573

PARTY ONE	PARTY TWO	DATE	CITATION	NUMBER
Use of facilities (Cont.)				
Bolivia	USA (United States)	30 Jun 56	271UNTS243	103919
Multilateral		02 Jul 56	540UNTS110	107846
Multilateral		02 Jul 56	248UNTS37	103484
Multilateral		31 Aug 56	249UNTS158	103506
Multilateral		11 Sep 56	266UNTS221	103832
Argentina	USA (United States)	03 Oct 56	279UNTS13	104032
Multilateral		05 Oct 56	251UNTS267	103545
Multilateral		05 Oct 56	251UNTS245	103544
Switzerland	Thailand	13 Oct 56	312UNTS43	104510
Belgium	Poland	17 Oct 56	356UNTS279	105100
Norway	USSR (Soviet Union)	19 Oct 56	257UNTS3	103644
Colombia	USA (United States)	24 Oct 56	476UNTS77	106905
Belgium	Turkey	25 Oct 56	380UNTS3	105447
UK Great Britain	USA (United States)	01 Nov 56	264UNTS3	103785
Taiwan	USA (United States)	21 Nov 56	265UNTS241	103816
Multilateral		21 Nov 56	253UNTS266	103588
Peru	Switzerland	23 Nov 56	411UNTS97	105916
Albania	Yugoslavia	23 Nov 56	386UNTS73	105539
UK Great Britain	USA (United States)	27 Nov 56	282UNTS43	104092
Belgium	Romania	04 Dec 56	317UNTS161	104602
Dominican Republic	USA (United States)	07 Dec 56	263UNTS193	103774
Finland	USSR (Soviet Union)	07 Dec 56	258UNTS89	103673
France	USA (United States)	14 Dec 56	266UNTS117	103826
Poland	USSR (Soviet Union)	17 Dec 56	266UNTS179	103830
Australia	USA (United States)	31 Dec 56	266UNTS89	103823
Multilateral		15 Jan 57	376UNTS122	105378
Iran	USA (United States)	16 Jan 57	308UNTS147	104460
Canada	USA (United States)	17 Jan 57	266UNTS109	103825
Iceland	Thailand	22 Jan 57	312UNTS63	104511
Multilateral		23 Jan 57	259UNTS426	103701
Germany, West	Sweden	29 Jan 57	393UNTS113	105654
Germany, West	Norway	29 Jan 57	353UNTS39	105037
Denmark	Germany, West	29 Jan 57	302UNTS75	104354
Norway	USA (United States)	05 Feb 57	279UNTS169	104038
Multilateral		17 Feb 57	271UNTS2	103907
Multilateral		01 Mar 57	264UNTS94	103790
Germany, East	USSR (Soviet Union)	12 Mar 57	285UNTS105	104150
Netherlands	Yugoslavia	13 Mar 57	327UNTS227	104723
Ethiopia	Sweden	16 Mar 57	304UNTS214	104398
Multilateral		28 Mar 57	271UNTS30	103908
Saudi Arabia	USA (United States)	02 Apr 57	283UNTS97	104109
Netherlands	USA (United States)	03 Apr 57	410UNTS193	105904
Multilateral		09 Apr 57	274UNTS172	103965
Germany, West	Yugoslavia	10 Apr 57	463UNTS269	106708
Denmark	Pakistan	10 Apr 57	302UNTS53	104353
Romania	Sweden	15 Apr 57	342UNTS325	104915
Romania	USSR (Soviet Union)	15 Apr 57	274UNTS143	103964
Bulgaria	Sweden	17 Apr 57	464UNTS3	106709
Korea, South	USA (United States)	24 Apr 57	288UNTS219	104207
Czechoslovakia	United Arab Rep	06 May 57	292UNTS317	104278
Finland	USA (United States)	10 May 57	283UNTS43	104105
Australia	Germany, West	22 May 57	357UNTS45	105105
Multilateral		24 May 57	268UNTS270	103861
Hungary	Netherlands	28 May 57	334UNTS291	104773
Ghana	USA (United States)	03 Jun 57	284UNTS63	104129
Ceylon (Sri Lanka)	UK Great Britain	07 Jun 57	280UNTS107	104055
Austria	USSR (Soviet Union)	14 Jun 57	285UNTS169	104152
Finland	India	14 Jun 57	277UNTS327	104016
Iraq	USA (United States)	16 Jun 57	284UNTS39	104127
Czechoslovakia	United Arab Rep	30 Jun 57	411UNTS126	105917
Libya	USA (United States)	30 Jun 57	284UNTS177	104136
New Zealand	UK Great Britain	04 Jul 57	402UNTS109	105780
Australia	FAO (Food Agri)	08 Jul 57	277UNTS315	104015
Multilateral		09 Jul 57	274UNTS300	103972
Hungary	Sweden	02 Aug 57	334UNTS307	104774

PARTY ONE	PARTY TWO	DATE	CITATION	NUMBER
Use of facilities (Cont.)				
Netherlands	Romania	27 Aug 57	342UNTS309	104914
Burma	WHO (World Health)	20 Sep 57	282UNTS113	104096
France	USA (United States)	23 Sep 57	293UNTS297	104297
Spain	USA (United States)	23 Sep 57	290UNTS261	104238
Multilateral		03 Oct 57	366UNTS87	105216
Fed of Malaya	UK Great Britain	12 Oct 57	285UNTS59	104149
Cambodia	USA (United States)	17 Oct 57	299UNTS203	104313
Netherlands	UK Great Britain	22 Oct 57	313UNTS309	104538
Poland	USSR (Soviet Union)	26 Oct 57	432UNTS221	106223
UK Great Britain	USA (United States)	01 Nov 57	299UNTS167	104312
Multilateral		05 Nov 57	285UNTS301	104155
Taiwan	Iran	11 Nov 57	563UNTS31	108202
El Salvador	USA (United States)	21 Nov 57	303UNTS19	104369
Belgium	USA (United States)	03 Dec 57	303UNTS45	104370
Germany, West	USA (United States)	10 Dec 57	307UNTS59	104442
Ethiopia	USA (United States)	26 Dec 57	307UNTS71	104443
Canada	Switzerland	10 Jan 58	464UNTS21	106710
Indonesia	Japan	20 Jan 58	324UNTS247	104689
Belgium	Morocco	20 Jan 58	288UNTS3	104192
Czechoslovakia	Poland	31 Jan 58	431UNTS99	106214
Indonesia	WHO (World Health)	05 Feb 58	307UNTS15	104438
Bulgaria	Netherlands	07 Feb 58	335UNTS45	104777
UK Great Britain	USA (United States)	22 Feb 58	307UNTS207	104451
Norway	Pakistan	05 Mar 58	334UNTS199	104769
Pakistan	Sweden	06 Mar 58	393UNTS181	105656
Multilateral		15 Mar 58	292UNTS273	104276
Germany, West	Portugal	21 Mar 58	464UNTS71	106712
Morocco	Portugal	03 Apr 58	393UNTS203	105657
Belgium	Iran	14 Apr 58	381UNTS309	105473
Bulgaria	Denmark	28 May 58	312UNTS235	104521
India	USSR (Soviet Union)	02 Jun 58	393UNTS3	105650
Belgium	USSR (Soviet Union)	05 Jun 58	345UNTS145	104965
Denmark	Luxembourg	10 Jun 58	356UNTS193	105096
Multilateral		19 Jun 58	306UNTS236	200550
Canada	USA (United States)	20 Jun 58	317UNTS37	104592
Denmark	Romania	25 Jun 58	345UNTS231	104970
Philippines	USA (United States)	30 Jun 58	321UNTS51	104653
Austria	Romania	10 Jul 58	353UNTS155	105041
Denmark	Hungary	17 Jul 58	344UNTS281	104954
Muscat and Oman	UK Great Britain	25 Jul 58	312UNTS347	104524
Taiwan	USA (United States)	06 Aug 58	462UNTS3	106666
Romania	United Arab Rep	14 Aug 58	405UNTS189	105834
Austria	Bulgaria	12 Sep 58	353UNTS3	105036
Germany, West	USA (United States)	11 Dec 58	337UNTS31	104813
Burma	United Nations	15 Dec 58	319UNTS3	104629
Haiti	USA (United States)	24 Dec 58	338UNTS265	104840
New Zealand	USA (United States)	24 Dec 58	324UNTS111	104680
Finland	Switzerland	07 Jan 59	353UNTS173	105042
UK Great Britain	Yugoslavia	03 Feb 59	359UNTS339	105151
Indonesia	USA (United States)	02 Mar 59	357UNTS145	105113
Sweden	Tunisia	19 Mar 59	497UNTS43	107261
Netherlands	Tunisia	19 Mar 59	497UNTS61	107262
Norway	Tunisia	28 Mar 59	497UNTS77	107263
Morocco	UN Special Fund	04 Apr 59	354UNTS347	105069
Denmark	Tunisia	14 Apr 59	340UNTS273	104870
Fed of Malaya	USA (United States)	22 May 59	346UNTS263	104985
UK Great Britain	USSR (Soviet Union)	24 May 59	374UNTS305	105344
Ceylon (Sri Lanka)	Sweden	29 May 59	464UNTS109	106713
Ceylon (Sri Lanka)	Norway	29 May 59	411UNTS165	105919
Ceylon (Sri Lanka)	Denmark	29 May 59	348UNTS225	105002
Peru	USA (United States)	15 Jun 59	346UNTS279	104987
Belgium	Japan	20 Jun 59	411UNTS3	105911
Panama	USA (United States)	24 Jun 59	479UNTS145	106950
Bulgaria	United Arab Rep	09 Jul 59	411UNTS187	105920
Afghanistan	Germany, West	22 Jul 59	464UNTS177	106715

PARTY ONE	PARTY TWO	DATE	CITATION	NUMBER
Use of facilities (Cont.)				
Germany, West	Iceland	12 Aug 59	411UNTS224	105921
Ghana	UN Special Fund	12 Aug 59	338UNTS203	104836
Canada	Germany, West	04 Sep 59	411UNTS260	105922
Canada	Euratom	06 Oct 59	475UNTS187	106894
Iran	UN Special Fund	06 Oct 59	342UNTS89	104902
Multilateral		09 Oct 59	376UNTS382	105391
Nicaragua	Peru	14 Oct 59	392UNTS303	105649
Poland	UN Special Fund	15 Oct 59	344UNTS29	104941
India	UN Special Fund	20 Oct 59	344UNTS143	104946
UN Special Fund	Yugoslavia	27 Oct 59	344UNTS159	104947
Ecuador	UN Special Fund	10 Nov 59	345UNTS3	104955
Japan	USA (United States)	12 Nov 59	361UNTS27	105171
Greece	UN Special Fund	13 Nov 59	345UNTS171	104966
UN Special Fund	Turkey	20 Nov 59	345UNTS105	104963
UN Special Fund	United Arab Rep	25 Nov 59	345UNTS125	104964
Argentina	Brazil	26 Nov 59	374UNTS39	105326
Turkey	USA (United States)	30 Nov 59	361UNTS107	105174
Israel	UN Special Fund	01 Dec 59	345UNTS197	104968
Guinea	UN Special Fund	02 Dec 59	345UNTS215	104969
Argentina	UN Special Fund	04 Dec 59	345UNTS263	104972
Jordan	UN Special Fund	15 Dec 59	346UNTS3	104974
Ceylon (Sri Lanka)	WHO (World Health)	21 Dec 59	349UNTS109	105011
UN Special Fund	UK Great Britain	07 Jan 60	348UNTS177	105000
Japan	USA (United States)	19 Jan 60	373UNTS207	105321
Peru	UN Special Fund	19 Jan 60	349UNTS83	105010
Chile	UN Special Fund	22 Jan 60	351UNTS115	105020
Colombia	UN Special Fund	04 Feb 60	355UNTS257	105080
Bolivia	UN Special Fund	09 Feb 60	351UNTS203	105024
Norway	USA (United States)	13 Feb 60	388UNTS255	105583
Greece	USA (United States)	15 Feb 60	377UNTS95	105397
Afghanistan	UN Special Fund	21 Feb 60	351UNTS93	105019
Pakistan	UN Special Fund	25 Feb 60	351UNTS141	105021
Multilateral		26 Feb 60	418UNTS171	106022
France	Thailand	26 Feb 60	392UNTS279	105648
Turkey	USA (United States)	02 Mar 60	372UNTS37	105286
Finland	Iceland	10 Mar 60	497UNTS95	107264
Czechoslovakia	Iraq	11 Mar 60	464UNTS267	106718
France	UN Special Fund	17 Mar 60	354UNTS119	105059
Netherlands	USA (United States)	24 Mar 60	406UNTS165	105847
Argentina	USA (United States)	01 Apr 60	371UNTS245	105281
Italy	UN Special Fund	01 Apr 60	354UNTS261	105066
Luxembourg	Yugoslavia	09 Apr 60	464UNTS293	106719
Denmark	USA (United States)	12 Apr 60	373UNTS9	105311
Multilateral		12 Apr 60	359UNTS323	105150
UN Special Fund	Tunisia	12 Apr 60	355UNTS289	105082
Libya	UN Special Fund	19 Apr 60	356UNTS11	105090
UN Special Fund	Sudan	21 Apr 60	356UNTS213	105097
Germany, West	Spain	28 Apr 60	465UNTS3	106720
UN Special Fund	Vietnam, South	29 Apr 60	357UNTS311	200567
Laos	UN Special Fund	30 Apr 60	361UNTS171	105179
Greece	Romania	02 May 60	485UNTS17	107043
Lebanon	UN Special Fund	07 May 60	360UNTS225	105160
Morocco	United Arab Rep	19 May 60	563UNTS121	108208
Switzerland	Tunisia	21 May 60	497UNTS109	107265
Afghanistan	Czechoslovakia	28 May 60	497UNTS129	107266
Multilateral		04 Jun 60	360UNTS208	105159
Luxembourg	Tunisia	13 Jun 60	497UNTS143	107267
Canada	USA (United States)	14 Jun 60	377UNTS365	105413
Iraq	UN Special Fund	19 Jun 60	376UNTS357	105389
Denmark	Peru	22 Jun 60	439UNTS113	106326
Italy	USA (United States)	07 Jul 60	380UNTS143	105455
Multilateral		08 Jul 60	366UNTS310	105220
Ethiopia	UN Special Fund	13 Jul 60	368UNTS159	105240
Germany, West	Pakistan	20 Jul 60	465UNTS41	106721
France	Greece	25 Jul 60	533UNTS227	107745

PARTY ONE	PARTY TWO	DATE	CITATION	NUMBER
Use of facilities (Cont.)				
WHO (World Health)	Tunisia	04 Aug 60	381UNTS335	105474
Mexico	USA (United States)	15 Aug 60	402UNTS177	105786
Belgium	Burma	17 Aug 60	540UNTS185	107850
Brazil	UN Special Fund	16 Sep 60	375UNTS3	105351
Czechoslovakia	India	19 Sep 60	465UNTS67	106722
France	USA (United States)	19 Sep 60	400UNTS21	105745
Taiwan	UN Special Fund	20 Sep 60	375UNTS29	105352
Belgium	Ireland	23 Sep 60	557UNTS180	108134
Portugal	USA (United States)	26 Sep 60	393UNTS257	105660
Indonesia	UN Special Fund	07 Oct 60	378UNTS141	105424
Liberia	UN Special Fund	11 Oct 60	376UNTS341	105388
Nigeria	USA (United States)	19 Oct 60	394UNTS113	105672
El Salvador	UN Special Fund	24 Oct 60	377UNTS171	105400
Hungary	UK Great Britain	25 Oct 60	419UNTS309	106034
Burma	Switzerland	31 Oct 60	465UNTS97	106723
Norway	Peru	02 Nov 60	497UNTS207	107270
Nepal	UN Special Fund	17 Nov 60	380UNTS289	105461
Guatemala	UN Special Fund	17 Nov 60	383UNTS67	105495
Czechoslovakia	Ghana	23 Nov 60	431UNTS85	106212
Cambodia	UN Special Fund	24 Nov 60	382UNTS255	105487
Multilateral		13 Dec 60	523UNTS117	107557
Honduras	UN Special Fund	20 Dec 60	383UNTS103	105497
Luxembourg	Thailand	29 Dec 60	465UNTS131	106725
Burma	UN Special Fund	03 Jan 61	387UNTS219	105564
Costa Rica	UN Special Fund	10 Jan 61	389UNTS253	105597
Norway	Poland	17 Jan 61	412UNTS130	105928
Germany, West	Japan	18 Jan 61	465UNTS173	106727
UN Special Fund	Saudi Arabia	19 Jan 61	396UNTS27	105692
Nicaragua	UN Special Fund	20 Jan 61	387UNTS15	105555
Chad	UN Special Fund	23 Jan 61	390UNTS69	105603
UN Special Fund	Somalia	28 Jan 61	388UNTS75	105573
Gabon	UN Special Fund	02 Feb 61	387UNTS289	105568
India	USA (United States)	07 Feb 61	462UNTS57	106671
UK Great Britain	USA (United States)	10 Feb 61	409UNTS129	105880
Nigeria	UN Special Fund	10 Feb 61	390UNTS85	105604
Mexico	UN Special Fund	23 Feb 61	388UNTS151	105576
Cyprus	UN Special Fund	24 Feb 61	389UNTS3	105588
Cuba	Czechoslovakia	04 Mar 61	465UNTS209	106728
Panama	UN Special Fund	09 Mar 61	396UNTS3	105691
Cuba	UN Special Fund	10 Mar 61	390UNTS35	105601
Norway	IAEA (Atom Energy)	10 Apr 61	402UNTS255	105790
Multilateral		18 Apr 61	500UNTS95	107310
Korea, South	UN Special Fund	21 Apr 61	394UNTS231	200583
Ceylon (Sri Lanka)	UN Special Fund	03 May 61	395UNTS217	105687
Australia	USA (United States)	09 May 61	409UNTS203	105886
Australia	USA (United States)	22 May 61	419UNTS3	106026
Czechoslovakia	Somalia	04 Jun 61	480UNTS261	106973
Australia	USA (United States)	05 Jun 61	409UNTS279	105892
Czechoslovakia	Morocco	08 Jun 61	497UNTS275	107272
Cameroon	UN Special Fund	13 Jun 61	397UNTS297	105713
Paraguay	UN Special Fund	22 Jun 61	399UNTS117	105738
UN Special Fund	Upper Volta	26 Jun 61	400UNTS3	105744
Haiti	UN Special Fund	28 Jun 61	399UNTS171	105741
Philippines	UN Special Fund	28 Jun 61	399UNTS141	105739
Argentina	Brazil	06 Jul 61	0UNTS0	109410
Mali	UN Special Fund	21 Jul 61	401UNTS141	105768
Netherlands	Euratom	25 Jul 61	462UNTS263	106686
UN Special Fund	Yemen	02 Aug 61	402UNTS43	105777
Finland	Luxembourg	15 Aug 61	541UNTS45	107859
Mexico	United Nations	18 Aug 61	404UNTS297	105817
Mexico	Netherlands	24 Aug 61	465UNTS291	106732
Ivory Coast	UN Special Fund	29 Aug 61	406UNTS129	105844
UK Great Britain	USA (United States)	08 Sep 61	418UNTS53	106016
Multilateral		20 Sep 61	407UNTS52	105859
Germany, West	UK Great Britain	26 Sep 61	424UNTS201	106108

PARTY ONE	PARTY TWO	DATE	CITATION	NUMBER
Use of facilities (Cont.)				
Ghana	Romania	30 Sep 61	467UNTS443	106769
UN Special Fund	Sierra Leone	02 Oct 61	422UNTS131	106073
Germany, West	Morocco	12 Oct 61	523UNTS289	107562
Multilateral		16 Oct 61	410UNTS242	105908
Belgium	Italy	28 Oct 61	429UNTS199	106199
Iraq	Syria	03 Nov 61	489UNTS45	107134
Ghana	USSR (Soviet Union)	04 Nov 61	437UNTS213	106308
Multilateral		07 Nov 61	412UNTS258	105937
Mauritania	UN Special Fund	07 Nov 61	412UNTS240	105936
Congo (Brazzaville)	UN Special Fund	09 Nov 61	413UNTS58	105940
Malagasy	UNICEF (Children)	16 Nov 61	422UNTS251	106079
Cyprus	Greece	23 Nov 61	497UNTS311	107274
Czechoslovakia	Mali	27 Nov 61	466UNTS41	106736
Belgium	Luxembourg	29 Nov 61	486UNTS37	107071
UN Special Fund	Venezuela	11 Dec 61	422UNTS149	106074
Czechoslovakia	Guinea	16 Dec 61	559UNTS49	108154
UN Special Fund	Senegal	16 Dec 61	425UNTS97	106121
Multilateral		27 Dec 61	425UNTS83	106120
Ghana	USA (United States)	03 Jan 62	433UNTS147	106237
Malagasy	UN Special Fund	05 Jan 62	419UNTS29	106028
Austria	Greece	15 Jan 62	498UNTS3	107275
Paraguay	USA (United States)	16 Jan 62	433UNTS169	106240
Multilateral		17 Jan 62	419UNTS294	106033
Multilateral		20 Jan 62	429UNTS230	200596
Indonesia	Japan	23 Jan 62	559UNTS77	108155
Multilateral		13 Feb 62	422UNTS288	200594
Finland	Hungary	13 Feb 62	463UNTS61	106693
Multilateral		21 Feb 62	423UNTS151	106091
Niger	UN Special Fund	26 Feb 62	423UNTS83	106086
Multilateral		01 Mar 62	423UNTS122	106089
Germany, West	Thailand	05 Mar 62	563UNTS165	108210
Dominican Republic	USA (United States)	08 Mar 62	527UNTS29	107615
Argentina	USA (United States)	16 Mar 62	454UNTS3	106535
Dahomey	UN Special Fund	28 Mar 62	424UNTS55	106099
Belgium	France	30 Mar 62	502UNTS297	107335
Ghana	USSR (Soviet Union)	06 Apr 62	498UNTS41	107277
Colombia	USA (United States)	09 Apr 62	476UNTS9	106899
Multilateral		10 Apr 62	429UNTS78	106192
Multilateral		18 Apr 62	463UNTS44	106692
Netherlands	USA (United States)	24 Apr 62	436UNTS93	106289
UN Special Fund	Uruguay	04 May 62	429UNTS143	106196
Multilateral		17 May 62	429UNTS46	106189
France	Romania	18 May 62	498UNTS115	107279
Greece	United Nations	18 May 62	429UNTS61	106190
Ghana	Israel	25 May 62	515UNTS237	107461
United Nations	Sweden	01 Jun 62	429UNTS135	106195
Dominican Republic	UN Special Fund	06 Jun 62	429UNTS169	106197
United Arab Rep	USSR (Soviet Union)	23 Jun 62	472UNTS43	106836
Morocco	Switzerland	05 Jul 62	498UNTS171	107281
UN Special Fund	Syria	07 Jul 62	443UNTS3	106355
UN Special Fund	Tanganyika	17 Jul 62	435UNTS237	106281
Multilateral		12 Aug 62	443UNTS266	106365
UK Great Britain	USA (United States)	29 Aug 62	449UNTS177	106459
Italy	USA (United States)	05 Sep 62	461UNTS185	106663
Ecuador	Germany, West	20 Sep 62	498UNTS199	107283
Japan	Kuwait	06 Oct 62	498UNTS235	107284
Hungary	Syria	18 Oct 62	491UNTS209	107178
Japan	UN Special Fund	31 Oct 62	444UNTS171	106368
Poland	Syria	10 Nov 62	491UNTS228	107179
Saudi Arabia	USA (United States)	13 Nov 62	488UNTS175	107127
Algeria	UN Special Fund	15 Nov 62	452UNTS243	106512
Multilateral		15 Nov 62	448UNTS50	106424
India	UK Great Britain	27 Nov 62	466UNTS189	106744
Multilateral		06 Dec 62	450UNTS240	106471
Ghana	Tunisia	11 Dec 62	563UNTS243	108213
Use of facilities (Cont.)				
Multilateral		12 Dec 62	457UNTS72	106578
Syria	United Arab Rep	27 Dec 62	491UNTS245	107180
India	United Nations	27 Dec 62	450UNTS3	106464
Multilateral		21 Jan 63	453UNTS20	106517
United Nations	South Pacific Com	24 Jan 63	470UNTS361	200604
Ethiopia	USA (United States)	25 Jan 63	473UNTS27	106851
Austria	United Nations	29 Jan 63	452UNTS261	106513
Multilateral		05 Feb 63	453UNTS36	106518
Multilateral		14 Feb 63	453UNTS168	106524
United Nations	South Pacific Com	20 Feb 63	453UNTS333	200600
Multilateral		06 Mar 63	455UNTS386	106552
UN Special Fund	Uganda	22 Mar 63	456UNTS466	106572
Burma	Japan	29 Mar 63	518UNTS3	107490
UK Great Britain	USA (United States)	06 Apr 63	474UNTS49	106871
Multilateral		18 Apr 63	463UNTS121	106697
Multilateral		06 May 63	463UNTS78	106694
Multilateral		09 May 63	463UNTS159	106700
Jamaica	UN Special Fund	22 May 63	489UNTS191	107140
Multilateral		22 May 63	483UNTS72	107007
Multilateral		24 May 63	466UNTS346	106754
Netherlands	UN Special Fund	24 May 63	466UNTS289	106750
UN Special Fund	Western Samoa	05 Jun 63	467UNTS463	200601
Multilateral		25 Jun 63	532UNTS159	107717
IBRD (World Bank)	Tunisia	03 Jul 63	480UNTS209	106970
Multilateral		23 Jul 63	471UNTS158	106831
Multilateral		31 Jul 63	472UNTS220	106842
India	USA (United States)	08 Aug 63	488UNTS21	107117
Burundi	UN Special Fund	22 Aug 63	476UNTS49	106903
Multilateral		27 Aug 63	511UNTS210	107435
Multilateral		10 Sep 63	480UNTS100	106965
Pakistan	USSR (Soviet Union)	07 Oct 63	499UNTS161	107297
UK Great Britain	USA (United States)	11 Oct 63	483UNTS3	107005
Czechoslovakia	Hungary	22 Oct 63	514UNTS95	107444
Multilateral		30 Oct 63	480UNTS180	106968
Central Afri Rep	UN Special Fund	30 Oct 63	481UNTS247	106985
Multilateral		07 Nov 63	480UNTS232	106971
Multilateral		08 Nov 63	482UNTS286	106999
Australia	India	03 Dec 63	486UNTS279	107082
Romania	Yugoslavia	20 Dec 63	527UNTS245	107629
New Zealand	Western Samoa	31 Dec 63	521UNTS163	107519
Multilateral		28 Jan 64	502UNTS321	107336
Denmark	Yugoslavia	11 Feb 64	511UNTS241	107437
Multilateral		20 Feb 64	491UNTS30	107172
Multilateral		28 Feb 64	501UNTS245	107321
Cameroon	Mali	17 Mar 64	524UNTS61	107566
Germany, West	Thailand	02 Apr 64	503UNTS3	107338
United Arab Rep	USA (United States)	05 May 64	531UNTS229	107706
Korea, South	USA (United States)	12 May 64	529UNTS299	107667
Netherlands	NATO (North Atlan)	25 May 64	544UNTS237	107920
Ireland	UN Special Fund	03 Jun 64	496UNTS205	107253
Multilateral		23 Jun 64	506UNTS108	107383
New Zealand	USA (United States)	24 Jun 64	524UNTS101	107568
Multilateral		28 Jun 64	519UNTS14	107499
Ivory Coast	Mali	09 Jul 64	524UNTS121	107569
UK Great Britain	USA (United States)	20 Aug 64	531UNTS85	107694
Dominican Republic	USA (United States)	28 Aug 64	531UNTS35	107691
Malta	UK Great Britain	21 Sep 64	588UNTS55	108518
Australia	UN Special Fund	30 Sep 64	510UNTS277	107419
Multilateral		24 Oct 64	514UNTS220	200608
Chile	USA (United States)	27 Oct 64	532UNTS347	107727
Netherlands	Pakistan	30 Oct 64	541UNTS243	107873
Multilateral		11 Nov 64	515UNTS94	107456
India	United Nations	25 Nov 64	519UNTS47	107501
Trinidad/Tobago	USA (United States)	05 Dec 64	535UNTS331	107788
Germany, West	Jamaica	16 Dec 64	531UNTS129	107699

PARTY ONE	PARTY TWO	DATE	CITATION	NUMBER
Use of facilities (Cont.)				
Germany, West	Thailand	23 Dec 64	525UNTS177	107589
Mongolia	United Nations	06 Jan 65	522UNTS45	107535
United Nations	Yugoslavia	07 Jan 65	522UNTS55	107536
Argentina	UK Great Britain	12 Jan 65	597UNTS177	108645
India	USA (United States)	13 Jan 65	541UNTS107	107864
Denmark	Thailand	25 Jan 65	530UNTS173	107680
Multilateral		27 Jan 65	523UNTS102	107556
Multilateral		02 Feb 65	523UNTS256	107560
Multilateral		12 Feb 65	525UNTS148	107587
Iran	United Nations	16 Feb 65	525UNTS211	107593
Israel	UK Great Britain	15 Apr 65	551UNTS19	108031
Afghanistan	UK Great Britain	19 Apr 65	633UNTS45	109033
Denmark	Spain	05 May 65	543UNTS255	107905
Multilateral		02 Jun 65	537UNTS348	200611
UN Special Fund	Spain	30 Jun 65	544UNTS159	107918
Philippines	USA (United States)	12 Aug 65	579UNTS47	108397
Multilateral		13 Sep 65	547UNTS264	107962
France	UK Great Britain	21 Sep 65	561UNTS3	108177
Multilateral		21 Oct 65	547UNTS216	107959
United Nations	United Arab Rep	26 Nov 65	551UNTS253	108046
Germany, West	USA (United States)	18 Dec 65	579UNTS193	108407
Ethiopia	USA (United States)	30 Dec 65	574UNTS129	108345
Czechoslovakia	Poland	22 Jan 66	588UNTS175	108524
Mongolia	UN Special Fund	26 Jan 66	552UNTS201	108055
UK Great Britain	Yugoslavia	27 Jan 66	573UNTS243	108337
Argentina	Germany, West	01 Mar 66	635UNTS247	109087
Malta	USA (United States)	03 Aug 66	601UNTS125	108691
Tunisia	USA (United States)	26 Sep 66	616UNTS259	108900
United Nations	Sudan	08 Nov 66	576UNTS85	108365
Kuwait	UK Great Britain	26 Nov 66	633UNTS58	109034
Denmark	Singapore	20 Dec 66	593UNTS125	108580
UK Great Britain	USA (United States)	30 Dec 66	603UNTS245	108736
Romania	Spain	05 Jan 67	642UNTS103	109168
Trinidad/Tobago	UK Great Britain	23 Jan 67	605UNTS277	108767
Romania	Somalia	20 Apr 67	642UNTS155	109171
Malta	WHO (World Health)	10 May 67	603UNTS99	108727
Barbados	WHO (World Health)	18 Jul 67	603UNTS87	108726
Denmark	India	01 Sep 67	616UNTS69	108892
Italy	UK Great Britain	30 Sep 67	642UNTS271	109180
United Nations	Senegal	08 Nov 67	613UNTS255	108854
Eur Space Research	UK Great Britain	24 Nov 67	638UNTS17	109129
Iran	United Nations	15 Feb 68	631UNTS103	108990
United Nations	Tunisia	18 Mar 68	633UNTS3	109030
Niger	United Nations	07 May 68	639UNTS71	109145
State/IGO Group	Australia	21 May 68	636UNTS326	109108
Guyana	WHO (World Health)	03 Jul 68	642UNTS13	109161
India	United Nations	22 Jul 68	640UNTS121	109158
Investigation of violations				
Multilateral		10 Jul 20	38UNTS129	100592
Multilateral		24 Jun 26	38UNTS295	100605
Multilateral		16 Jun 28	39UNTS3	100609
Multilateral		21 Jun 29	39UNTS27	100611
Multilateral		28 Jun 30	39UNTS55	100612
Multilateral		28 Jun 30	39UNTS85	100613
Multilateral		27 Apr 32	39UNTS103	100614
Multilateral		30 Apr 32	39UNTS133	100615
Multilateral		29 Jun 33	39UNTS235	100620
Multilateral		29 Jun 33	39UNTS151	100616
Multilateral		29 Jun 33	39UNTS165	100617
Multilateral		29 Jun 33	39UNTS189	100618
Multilateral		29 Jun 33	39UNTS211	100619
Multilateral		24 Oct 36	40UNTS153	100632
Multilateral		28 Jun 39	209UNTS39	102820
Saudi Arabia	UK Great Britain	20 Apr 42	10UNTS151	200058

PARTY ONE	PARTY TWO	DATE	CITATION	NUMBER
Investigation of violations (Cont.)				
Mexico	USA (United States)	23 Dec 42	13UNTS231	200081
Taiwan	USA (United States)	21 May 43	14UNTS353	200093
UK Great Britain	USA (United States)	28 Mar 44	15UNTS413	200104
Multilateral		28 Oct 44	123UNTS223	200414
Spain	USA (United States)	02 Dec 44	89UNTS345	200262
Multilateral		07 Dec 44	171UNTS345	200501
Multilateral		20 Jan 45	140UNTS397	200471
Multilateral		05 Jun 45	68UNTS189	200230
Multilateral		08 Aug 45	82UNTS279	200251
United Arab Rep	USA (United States)	05 Jan 46	160UNTS27	102098
Canada	Mexico	08 Feb 46	230UNTS183	103183
UK Great Britain	USA (United States)	21 Feb 46	6UNTS137	100073
Belgium	UK Great Britain	11 Mar 46	26UNTS167	100387
France	Norway	26 Mar 46	31UNTS69	100468
Belgium	Netherlands	24 May 46	31UNTS169	100477
Belgium	Italy	23 Jun 46	19UNTS65	100305
Netherlands	Spain	13 Jul 46	4UNTS351	100055
Multilateral		09 Oct 46	78UNTS227	101019
Canada	Nicaragua	19 Dec 46	236UNTS229	103326
Multilateral		10 Feb 47	41UNTS21	100643
Multilateral		10 Feb 47	48UNTS203	100746
Multilateral		10 Feb 47	41UNTS135	100644
Philippines	USA (United States)	14 Mar 47	43UNTS271	100673
Multilateral		11 Jul 47	54UNTS3	100792
Multilateral		12 Nov 47	53UNTS49	100772
Multilateral		12 Nov 47	53UNTS39	100771
Multilateral		12 Nov 47	46UNTS201	100710
UK Great Britain	USA (United States)	24 Feb 48	73UNTS143	100951
Argentina	Denmark	18 Mar 48	94UNTS175	101311
Belgium	Netherlands	13 Apr 48	32UNTS153	100497
Multilateral		18 Aug 48	33UNTS181	100518
Philippines	USA (United States)	27 Aug 48	44UNTS13	100675
Netherlands	Spain	08 Oct 48	28UNTS209	100426
Argentina	Netherlands	29 Oct 48	95UNTS21	101316
Czechoslovakia	Poland	12 Nov 48	84UNTS347	101141
Belgium	France	08 Jan 49	36UNTS151	100569
Czechoslovakia	Poland	21 Jan 49	31UNTS205	100480
Multilateral		23 Mar 49	203UNTS179	102746
Multilateral		04 May 49	98UNTS101	101358
Multilateral		04 May 49	92UNTS19	101257
Italy	Spain	31 May 49	231UNTS251	103224
Multilateral		29 Jun 49	138UNTS207	101870
Multilateral		01 Jul 49	96UNTS237	101340
Multilateral		12 Aug 49	75UNTS85	100971
Multilateral		12 Aug 49	75UNTS287	100973
Multilateral		12 Aug 49	75UNTS31	100970
Multilateral		19 Sep 49	125UNTS3	101671
Brazil	Spain	28 Nov 49	215UNTS303	102923
Nicaragua	USA (United States)	01 Feb 50	99UNTS25	101368
Spain	Sweden	18 Feb 50	166UNTS15	102184
Multilateral		21 Mar 50	96UNTS271	101342
Netherlands	Spain	20 Jun 50	95UNTS303	101327
Korea, South	USA (United States)	12 Jul 50	222UNTS229	103029
Spain	Switzerland	03 Aug 50	254UNTS365	103600
Multilateral		04 Nov 50	213UNTS221	102889
Multilateral		19 Jun 51	199UNTS67	102678
Mexico	USA (United States)	11 Aug 51	162UNTS103	102133
Multilateral		08 Sep 51	136UNTS45	101832
Japan	USA (United States)	28 Feb 52	208UNTS255	102817
Belgium	France	21 Mar 52	137UNTS249	101856
USA (United States)	Venezuela	28 Aug 52	178UNTS51	102336
Multilateral		05 Sep 52	247UNTS329	103479
Germany, West	USA (United States)	27 Feb 53	223UNTS167	103065
Canada	USA (United States)	02 Mar 53	222UNTS77	103024
Germany, West	USA (United States)	01 Apr 53	224UNTS3	103066

PARTY ONE	PARTY TWO	DATE	CITATION	NUMBER
Investigation of violations (Cont.)				
Ethiopia	USA (United States)	22 May 53	191UNTS59	102577
Libya	UK Great Britain	29 Jul 53	186UNTS201	102492
Multilateral		19 Feb 54	214UNTS51	102899
Belgium	Germany, West	03 Mar 54	188UNTS259	102529
Multilateral		21 May 54	345UNTS285	104973
Multilateral		04 Jun 54	276UNTS191	103992
Libya	USA (United States)	09 Sep 54	224UNTS217	103078
Multilateral		23 Oct 54	332UNTS3	104760
Ethiopia	UK Great Britain	29 Nov 54	207UNTS283	102811
Hungary	USSR (Soviet Union)	27 May 55	407UNTS156	105864
France	Germany, West	04 Oct 55	353UNTS203	105044
Argentina	Switzerland	25 Jan 56	559UNTS121	108157
Multilateral		07 Jun 56	381UNTS145	105470
Australia	USA (United States)	22 Jun 56	283UNTS275	104123
Austria	USA (United States)	21 Nov 56	290UNTS181	104237
Czechoslovakia	USSR (Soviet Union)	30 Nov 56	266UNTS243	103833
Poland	USSR (Soviet Union)	17 Dec 56	266UNTS179	103830
Norway	USA (United States)	25 Feb 57	284UNTS19	104126
Germany, East	USSR (Soviet Union)	12 Mar 57	285UNTS105	104150
Romania	USSR (Soviet Union)	15 Apr 57	274UNTS143	103964
Hungary	Netherlands	28 May 57	334UNTS291	104773
Belgium	Hungary	01 Jun 57	291UNTS17	104242
Austria	USSR (Soviet Union)	14 Jun 57	285UNTS169	104152
Multilateral		26 Jun 57	325UNTS279	104704
Finland	United Nations	27 Jun 57	271UNTS135	103913
United Nations	Sweden	01 Jul 57	271UNTS187	103914
Germany, West	USA (United States)	03 Jul 57	288UNTS305	104212
Norway	United Nations	09 Jul 57	271UNTS223	103917
Spain	USA (United States)	16 Aug 57	307UNTS169	104449
Poland	USSR (Soviet Union)	26 Oct 57	432UNTS221	106223
Australia	USA (United States)	25 Feb 58	317UNTS153	104601
Belgium	Luxembourg	28 Mar 58	303UNTS101	104372
Multilateral		15 Apr 58	539UNTS27	107822
Hungary	USSR (Soviet Union)	24 Apr 58	408UNTS118	105868
Multilateral		29 Apr 58	450UNTS11	106465
Czechoslovakia	Hungary	08 May 58	407UNTS92	105862
Japan	USA (United States)	19 Jun 58	325UNTS143	104699
Hungary	USSR (Soviet Union)	21 Jul 58	408UNTS194	105871
Cuba	USA (United States)	15 Aug 58	358UNTS63	105124
USA (United States)	Venezuela	08 Oct 58	371UNTS69	105271
Multilateral		15 Jan 59	348UNTS13	104996
Austria	USA (United States)	22 Jul 59	368UNTS199	105242
Japan	USA (United States)	19 Jan 60	373UNTS207	105321
Germany, West	USA (United States)	16 Aug 60	418UNTS235	106024
Finland	Norway	15 Nov 60	383UNTS159	105501
Multilateral		13 Dec 60	523UNTS117	107557
Japan	Peru	15 May 61	451UNTS3	106482
Multilateral		08 Jun 61	473UNTS187	106863
Denmark	UK Great Britain	15 Nov 61	420UNTS67	106041
Multilateral		06 Dec 61	473UNTS219	106864
Austria	Czechoslovakia	22 Sep 62	495UNTS157	107244
Czechoslovakia	Yugoslavia	22 Oct 62	480UNTS267	106974
Japan	UK Great Britain	14 Nov 62	478UNTS29	106934
Czechoslovakia	Poland	16 Nov 62	526UNTS3	107597
Austria	Yugoslavia	11 Dec 62	546UNTS3	107938
Brazil	Taiwan	28 Dec 62	500UNTS61	107307
Poland	USSR (Soviet Union)	22 Apr 63	493UNTS229	107217
Australia	USA (United States)	09 May 63	469UNTS55	106784
Multilateral		25 Jun 63	532UNTS159	107717
Romania	Yugoslavia	25 Dec 63	576UNTS95	108366
Austria	Romania	27 May 64	588UNTS29	108517
Multilateral		15 Jun 64	573UNTS85	108324
Taiwan	Ecuador	17 Jun 64	533UNTS141	107740
Czechoslovakia	Hungary	17 Oct 64	545UNTS21	107924
Taiwan	Ecuador	23 Oct 64	543UNTS241	107904

PARTY ONE	PARTY TWO	DATE	CITATION	NUMBER
Investigation of violations (Cont.)				
Argentina	UK Great Britain	12 Jan 65	597UNTS177	108645
Multilateral		18 Jun 65	573UNTS3	108320
Hungary	Poland	18 Jul 65	577UNTS161	108376
Multilateral		15 Nov 65	0UNTS0	109432
Austria	Spain	24 Mar 66	590UNTS203	108555
Guyana	UK Great Britain	26 May 66	595UNTS255	108621
Netherlands	Yugoslavia	08 Sep 66	597UNTS147	108643
IAEA (Atom Energy)	USA (United States)	09 Dec 66	589UNTS55	108535
East Afri Service	IBRD (World Bank)	17 Feb 67	599UNTS335	200629
Penal sanctions				
Multilateral		10 Jun 25	38UNTS229	100600
Multilateral		12 Nov 47	53UNTS39	100771
Czechoslovakia	Poland	21 Jan 49	31UNTS205	100480
Denmark	France	30 Jun 51	151UNTS241	102000
Jordan	Syria	23 Dec 53	204UNTS207	102759
Multilateral		01 Mar 54	286UNTS265	104173
Multilateral		21 Jun 55	305UNTS265	104423
Multilateral		25 Jun 57	320UNTS291	104648
Multilateral		24 Jun 58	348UNTS275	105005
Belgium	Morocco	27 Feb 59	390UNTS275	105611
Cambodia	Thailand	15 Dec 60	382UNTS307	105491
Multilateral		22 Jan 65	634UNTS239	109066
Multilateral		23 Jun 67	614UNTS185	108871
Establishment of commission				
Multilateral		22 Jun 35	40UNTS73	100628
Multilateral		25 Jun 36	161UNTS217	200486
Bolivia	Brazil	25 Feb 38	51UNTS245	200192
Multilateral		17 Feb 40	161UNTS229	200487
Brazil	Venezuela	30 Mar 40	51UNTS291	200195
Brazil	Paraguay	14 Jun 41	54UNTS323	200204
Argentina	USA (United States)	14 Oct 41	119UNTS193	200384
Canada	USA (United States)	20 Mar 42	105UNTS169	200330
Brazil	USA (United States)	03 Sep 42	13UNTS109	200073
UK Great Britain	USA (United States)	03 Nov 42	109UNTS127	200354
New Zealand	USA (United States)	28 Jan 43	121UNTS123	200395
USA (United States)	Venezuela	18 Feb 43	21UNTS225	200125
Peru	USA (United States)	20 May 43	100UNTS259	200288
UK Great Britain	USA (United States)	24 Sep 43	139UNTS373	200463
Multilateral		15 Jan 44	161UNTS281	200489
Australia	New Zealand	21 Jan 44	18UNTS357	200113
Brazil	Paraguay	11 Aug 44	67UNTS303	200227
Hungary	Yugoslavia	13 Aug 44	113UNTS233	101553
Multilateral		12 Sep 44	227UNTS279	200532
Multilateral		28 Oct 44	123UNTS223	200414
Multilateral		14 Nov 44	236UNTS359	200539
Multilateral		20 Jan 45	140UNTS397	200471
Multilateral		09 Jul 45	160UNTS359	200484
Multilateral		08 Aug 45	82UNTS279	200251
UK Great Britain	USA (United States)	10 Dec 45	3UNTS177	100030
Poland	Yugoslavia	02 Jan 46	115UNTS21	101556
Multilateral		14 Jan 46	555UNTS69	108105
Czechoslovakia	Poland	12 Feb 46	25UNTS207	100364
Belgium	France	22 Feb 46	68UNTS157	100892
Belgium	UK Great Britain	11 Mar 46	26UNTS167	100387
Denmark	Norway	30 Mar 46	29UNTS163	100438
Multilateral		05 Apr 46	231UNTS199	103221
Belgium	UK Great Britain	17 Apr 46	6UNTS177	100075
Multilateral		06 May 46	99UNTS181	101379
Hungary	Yugoslavia	11 May 46	129UNTS3	101725
Afghanistan	USSR (Soviet Union)	13 Jun 46	31UNTS147	100476
Albania	Yugoslavia	01 Jul 46	111UNTS3	101517
Norway	Yugoslavia	30 Aug 46	30UNTS187	100457
Paraguay	USA (United States)	12 Sep 46	125UNTS179	101677
France	Thailand	17 Nov 46	344UNTS59	104943

PARTY ONE	PARTY TWO	DATE	CITATION	NUMBER
Establishment of commission (Cont.)				
Denmark	Sweden	18 Nov 46	7UNTS251	100104
Albania	Yugoslavia	28 Nov 46	111UNTS93	101520
Multilateral		02 Dec 46	161UNTS72	102124
UK Great Britain	USA (United States)	02 Dec 46	7UNTS163	100098
Norway	Poland	03 Dec 46	15UNTS203	100234
Netherlands	Norway	28 Jan 47	31UNTS29	100467
Finland	USSR (Soviet Union)	03 Feb 47	216UNTS231	102939
Multilateral		06 Feb 47	97UNTS227	101352
Multilateral		10 Feb 47	140UNTS111	101886
Czechoslovakia	Yugoslavia	25 Feb 47	112UNTS3	101539
Belgium	Czechoslovakia	06 Mar 47	34UNTS77	100528
Belgium	Turkey	12 Mar 47	37UNTS215	100578
Mexico	USA (United States)	17 Mar 47	167UNTS30	102200
Poland	Sweden	18 Mar 47	12UNTS295	100190
Czechoslovakia	Norway	20 Mar 47	30UNTS223	100460
Iraq	Jordan	14 Apr 47	23UNTS148	100345
Austria	Norway	14 Apr 47	31UNTS21	100466
Hungary	Yugoslavia	11 May 47	130UNTS171	101730
Bolivia	USA (United States)	16 May 47	168UNTS89	102215
France	Poland	19 May 47	12UNTS95	100181
Poland	Yugoslavia	24 May 47	115UNTS89	101560
Romania	Yugoslavia	26 Jun 47	116UNTS39	101568
Denmark	Yugoslavia	28 Jun 47	78UNTS242	101020
Norway	Switzerland	15 Jul 47	12UNTS351	100192
Hungary	Yugoslavia	24 Jul 47	114UNTS3	101554
Czechoslovakia	Greece	30 Jul 47	185UNTS115	102463
Multilateral		14 Aug 47	138UNTS111	101863
Czechoslovakia	Yugoslavia	04 Sep 47	112UNTS91	101540
Ethiopia	UK Great Britain	29 Sep 47	82UNTS191	101092
Finland	Norway	15 Nov 47	29UNTS179	100439
Multilateral		18 Nov 47	17UNTS89	100269
Norway	Poland	04 Feb 48	30UNTS205	100458
Belgium	Italy	09 Feb 48	71UNTS143	100915
Greece	United Nations	12 Feb 48	47UNTS223	100732
Poland	Romania	27 Feb 48	46UNTS143	100707
France	United Nations	10 Mar 48	47UNTS203	100731
Multilateral		17 Mar 48	19UNTS51	100304
Belgium	Luxembourg	27 Mar 48	178UNTS265	102343
Belgium	France	23 Apr 48	19UNTS95	100307
Hungary	Poland	13 May 48	25UNTS301	100369
Finland	United Nations	20 May 48	47UNTS319	200189
Czechoslovakia	Yugoslavia	24 May 48	112UNTS111	101542
Bulgaria	Poland	30 May 48	37UNTS3	100574
France	Netherlands	02 Jun 48	204UNTS275	102762
Hungary	Poland	18 Jun 48	25UNTS319	100370
Spain	UK Great Britain	23 Jun 48	66UNTS193	100854
Greece	Sweden	25 Jun 48	267UNTS337	103849
Multilateral		26 Jun 48	331UNTS217	104757
Netherlands	UK Great Britain	07 Jul 48	82UNTS259	101099
Poland	USSR (Soviet Union)	08 Jul 48	37UNTS107	100576
Multilateral		18 Aug 48	33UNTS181	100518
Pakistan	United Nations	27 Aug 48	47UNTS269	100734
Philippines	USA (United States)	27 Aug 48	44UNTS13	100675
UK Great Britain	USA (United States)	30 Sep 48	71UNTS241	100922
United Nations	Thailand	05 Oct 48	47UNTS287	100735
Czechoslovakia	United Nations	07 Oct 48	47UNTS185	100730
United Nations	San Marino	07 Oct 48	47UNTS337	200190
Austria	Denmark	29 Nov 48	74UNTS243	100967
Italy	Netherlands	04 Dec 48	46UNTS271	100716
Denmark	Poland	14 Dec 48	81UNTS33	101060
Belgium	Greece	27 Dec 48	77UNTS265	101004
Belgium	Denmark	30 Dec 48	25UNTS173	100362
Norway	Poland	31 Dec 48	29UNTS3	100430
Belgium	France	08 Jan 49	36UNTS151	100569
Mexico	USA (United States)	25 Jan 49	99UNTS3	101367

PARTY ONE	PARTY TWO	DATE	CITATION	NUMBER
Establishment of commission (Cont.)				
Multilateral		08 Feb 49	157UNTS157	102053
Denmark	Greece	25 Feb 49	78UNTS325	101022
Czechoslovakia	Yugoslavia	01 Mar 49	113UNTS3	101547
Greece	Norway	12 Mar 49	30UNTS161	100454
Germany, West	Greece	16 Mar 49	77UNTS307	101006
United Nations	UK Great Britain	18 Mar 49	47UNTS305	100736
Israel	Lebanon	23 Mar 49	42UNTS287	100655
Finland	Greece	24 Mar 49	78UNTS3	101008
Israel	Jordan	03 Apr 49	42UNTS303	100656
Multilateral		08 Apr 49	140UNTS196	101889
Canada	USA (United States)	12 Apr 49	206UNTS241	102789
India	Pakistan	23 Apr 49	54UNTS51	100795
Luxembourg	Netherlands	26 Apr 49	182UNTS187	102425
Denmark	Poland	12 May 49	87UNTS179	101172
Italy	Yugoslavia	23 May 49	150UNTS179	101972
Ireland	Sweden	25 Jun 49	558UNTS299	108148
Argentina	UK Great Britain	27 Jun 49	83UNTS217	101110
Israel	Syria	20 Jul 49	42UNTS327	100657
Greece	Turkey	21 Jul 49	78UNTS55	101011
Greece	Italy	31 Aug 49	78UNTS89	101014
Argentina	Norway	09 Sep 49	42UNTS125	100646
Bulgaria	Poland	26 Sep 49	260UNTS249	103712
Czechoslovakia	UK Great Britain	28 Sep 49	86UNTS141	101156
Italy	Norway	19 Nov 49	47UNTS75	100723
Australia	New Zealand	26 Nov 49	198UNTS161	102662
Denmark	Poland	07 Dec 49	81UNTS21	101059
Czechoslovakia	Denmark	17 Dec 49	74UNTS147	100961
Norway	Poland	21 Dec 49	47UNTS107	100725
Turkey	USA (United States)	27 Dec 49	98UNTS141	101361
Greece	Portugal	31 Dec 49	92UNTS71	101262
China People's Rep	USSR (Soviet Union)	14 Feb 50	226UNTS31	103105
Italy	Turkey	24 Mar 50	96UNTS207	101338
Multilateral		08 Apr 50	68UNTS99	100889
India	Pakistan	08 Apr 50	131UNTS3	101733
Austria	Greece	11 May 50	184UNTS217	102450
Luxembourg	UK Great Britain	27 Jun 50	183UNTS217	102431
Germany, East	Poland	06 Jul 50	319UNTS93	104631
Denmark	Spain	12 Jul 50	71UNTS135	100914
Brazil	UK Great Britain	18 Sep 50	88UNTS115	101188
Bulgaria	Romania	29 Sep 50	342UNTS141	104905
Denmark	Italy	04 Oct 50	78UNTS341	101024
Austria	Sweden	31 Oct 50	197UNTS311	102645
Multilateral		04 Nov 50	213UNTS221	102889
Czechoslovakia	Poland	17 Nov 50	530UNTS195	107682
Paraguay	USA (United States)	27 Nov 50	122UNTS147	101644
Albania	Poland	02 Dec 50	260UNTS131	103707
Germany, West	Netherlands	14 Dec 50	87UNTS257	101177
Brazil	Netherlands	15 Dec 50	123UNTS101	101657
Multilateral		15 Dec 50	157UNTS129	102052
Multilateral		15 Dec 50	171UNTS305	102234
Brazil	USA (United States)	19 Dec 50	140UNTS365	101899
Liberia	USA (United States)	22 Dec 50	133UNTS69	101781
Italy	Yugoslavia	23 Dec 50	171UNTS291	102233
UK Great Britain	Yemen	20 Jan 51	101UNTS39	101400
Albania	Poland	25 Jan 51	260UNTS217	103710
Poland	USSR (Soviet Union)	15 Feb 51	432UNTS199	106222
Canada	USA (United States)	27 Mar 51	132UNTS333	101772
China People's Rep	Poland	03 Apr 51	304UNTS187	104396
Greece	Turkey	20 Apr 51	178UNTS17	102333
Germany, West	Norway	07 May 51	92UNTS51	101260
Netherlands	South Africa	31 May 51	188UNTS289	102533
Denmark	Portugal	05 Jun 51	101UNTS61	101402
Costa Rica	WHO (World Health)	14 Jun 51	102UNTS151	101418
Multilateral		15 Jun 51	148UNTS67	101936
UK Great Britain	USA (United States)	15 Jun 51	141UNTS79	101907

Establishment of commission (Cont.)

PARTY ONE	PARTY TWO	DATE	CITATION	NUMBER
Italy	Netherlands	15 Jun 51	150UNTS103	101964
India	Turkey	29 Jun 51	213UNTS183	102886
Denmark	Spain	03 Jul 51	101UNTS51	101401
Multilateral		10 Jul 51	108UNTS287	101481
Brazil	USA (United States)	24 Jul 51	134UNTS195	101799
Multilateral		29 Jul 51	117UNTS85	101585
France	Italy	23 Aug 51	291UNTS143	104249
Greece	UK Great Britain	29 Sep 51	190UNTS260	102570
Multilateral		31 Oct 51	172UNTS193	102247
Italy	UK Great Britain	28 Nov 51	172UNTS27	102238
Denmark	WHO (World Health)	30 Nov 51	118UNTS3	101592
El Salvador	Guatemala	14 Dec 51	131UNTS131	101740
Ireland	Switzerland	26 Dec 51	558UNTS305	108149
Germany, East	Poland	08 Jan 52	304UNTS113	104394
Denmark	Norway	14 Jan 52	120UNTS119	101618
Germany, East	Poland	06 Feb 52	304UNTS131	104395
Multilateral		15 Feb 52	132UNTS51	101751
Japan	USA (United States)	28 Feb 52	208UNTS255	102817
Multilateral		07 Mar 52	175UNTS205	102302
Belgium	Pakistan	15 Mar 52	316UNTS65	104578
Finland	Norway	18 Mar 52	188UNTS187	102527
Belgium	France	21 Mar 52	137UNTS249	101856
Czechoslovakia	Denmark	04 Apr 52	133UNTS245	101792
France	Israel	29 Apr 52	189UNTS55	102542
Multilateral		09 May 52	205UNTS65	102770
Korea, South	USA (United States)	24 May 52	179UNTS23	102353
Brazil	USA (United States)	02 Jun 52	181UNTS109	102403
Greece	Syria	02 Jun 52	183UNTS251	102434
Denmark	Poland	09 Jun 52	135UNTS209	101822
Multilateral		12 Jun 52	138UNTS183	101869
Panama	USA (United States)	30 Jun 52	181UNTS121	102404
Denmark	Spain	28 Jul 52	135UNTS255	101825
USA (United States)	Venezuela	28 Aug 52	178UNTS51	102336
Denmark	Portugal	29 Aug 52	149UNTS49	101950
Germany, West	Israel	10 Sep 52	162UNTS205	102137
Austria	Belgium	17 Oct 52	162UNTS183	102135
Denmark	Italy	28 Oct 52	167UNTS125	102202
Ethiopia	USA (United States)	05 Nov 52	184UNTS139	102445
Denmark	Israel	14 Nov 52	160UNTS279	102113
Austria	UK Great Britain	12 Dec 52	172UNTS9	102237
Liberia	USA (United States)	15 Dec 52	185UNTS45	102457
France	Greece	23 Dec 52	187UNTS175	102511
UK Great Britain	USA (United States)	19 Jan 53	161UNTS3	102117
Bolivia	Italy	31 Jan 53	281UNTS181	104079
Greece	Italy	04 Feb 53	189UNTS269	102551
Greece	Netherlands	05 Feb 53	263UNTS361	103783
United Arab Rep	UK Great Britain	12 Feb 53	161UNTS157	102127
Albania	Romania	14 Feb 53	342UNTS107	104903
Turkey	Yugoslavia	26 Feb 53	247UNTS54	103460
Multilateral		26 Feb 53	161UNTS31	102120
Germany, West	USA (United States)	27 Feb 53	223UNTS167	103065
Multilateral		27 Feb 53	333UNTS3	104764
Greece	Yugoslavia	28 Feb 53	252UNTS27	103557
Canada	USA (United States)	02 Mar 53	222UNTS77	103024
Belgium	France	11 Mar 53	191UNTS329	102590
France	Italy	14 Mar 53	284UNTS221	104140
Austria	Yugoslavia	19 Mar 53	467UNTS293	106767
Germany, West	USA (United States)	09 Apr 53	204UNTS79	102750
Czechoslovakia	Denmark	23 Apr 53	174UNTS95	102280
Greece	Netherlands	29 Apr 53	191UNTS235	102583
Brazil	Ecuador	04 May 53	369UNTS37	105249
Greece	United Arab Rep	21 May 53	256UNTS17	103620
Jordan	Syria	04 Jun 53	184UNTS15	102437
United Arab Rep	USA (United States)	18 Jun 53	215UNTS45	102910
Pakistan	Turkey	29 Jun 53	211UNTS225	102854

Establishment of commission (Cont.)

PARTY ONE	PARTY TWO	DATE	CITATION	NUMBER
Multilateral		01 Jul 53	200UNTS149	102701
Italy	Switzerland	02 Jul 53	257UNTS99	103653
Argentina	USSR (Soviet Union)	05 Aug 53	221UNTS99	103004
Germany, East	USSR (Soviet Union)	22 Aug 53	221UNTS129	103005
Multilateral		27 Aug 53	213UNTS137	102884
UN Relief Palestin	United Arab Rep	14 Oct 53	190UNTS13	102555
Libya	UK Great Britain	19 Oct 53	186UNTS285	102494
Greece	Turkey	07 Nov 53	225UNTS163	103098
Canada	USA (United States)	12 Nov 53	223UNTS139	103062
Canada	USA (United States)	12 Nov 53	234UNTS97	103274
Bulgaria	Greece	05 Dec 53	225UNTS135	103095
Czechoslovakia	Greece	01 Feb 54	225UNTS77	103091
Multilateral		18 Feb 54	226UNTS297	103124
Multilateral		19 Feb 54	214UNTS51	102899
Bulgaria	Yugoslavia	20 Feb 54	397UNTS13	105700
Multilateral		22 Feb 54	188UNTS273	102531
Belgium	Norway	24 Mar 54	219UNTS73	102967
Denmark	Italy	10 Apr 54	196UNTS175	102623
Czechoslovakia	Hungary	16 Apr 54	504UNTS231	107360
Bulgaria	Yugoslavia	22 Apr 54	397UNTS43	105701
China People's Rep	India	29 Apr 54	299UNTS57	104307
India	Pakistan	08 May 54	203UNTS167	102745
France	Greece	13 May 54	222UNTS299	103036
Greece	Spain	15 May 54	299UNTS261	104318
Greece	Romania	19 May 54	225UNTS17	103083
Multilateral		21 May 54	345UNTS285	104973
Multilateral		22 May 54	199UNTS3	102674
Austria	Yugoslavia	25 May 54	227UNTS111	103135
Belgium	South Africa	01 Jun 54	201UNTS25	102708
Greece	Hungary	05 Jun 54	299UNTS285	104320
Ethiopia	USA (United States)	12 Jun 54	234UNTS25	103270
Jordan	USA (United States)	17 Jun 54	266UNTS137	103828
Italy	USA (United States)	28 Jun 54	237UNTS121	103340
France	Greece	22 Jul 54	225UNTS199	103099
Multilateral		29 Jul 54	249UNTS45	103500
Saudi Arabia	UK Great Britain	30 Jul 54	201UNTS317	102722
Multilateral		09 Aug 54	211UNTS237	102855
Multilateral		24 Aug 54	247UNTS213	103471
Multilateral		08 Sep 54	209UNTS23	102819
Canada	USA (United States)	10 Sep 54	238UNTS97	103355
Greece	Italy	11 Sep 54	284UNTS313	104145
Multilateral		23 Oct 54	332UNTS3	104760
Burma	Japan	05 Nov 54	251UNTS215	103543
Greece	Italy	10 Nov 54	227UNTS9	103128
Portugal	UK Great Britain	18 Nov 54	210UNTS265	102841
Portugal	UK Great Britain	19 Nov 54	226UNTS305	103125
Brazil	Italy	24 Nov 54	284UNTS325	104146
Austria	Yugoslavia	27 Nov 54	396UNTS75	105694
Iran	USSR (Soviet Union)	02 Dec 54	451UNTS227	106497
Belgium	Greece	09 Dec 54	257UNTS243	103660
Netherlands	USA (United States)	14 Dec 54	262UNTS35	103737
France	Netherlands	15 Dec 54	288UNTS37	104195
USSR (Soviet Union)	Yugoslavia	05 Jan 55	240UNTS207	103404
Austria	Yugoslavia	18 Jan 55	378UNTS31	105416
Iraq	Turkey	24 Feb 55	233UNTS199	103264
Greece	Japan	12 Mar 55	227UNTS33	103130
Bulgaria	Yugoslavia	16 Mar 55	397UNTS83	105702
Argentina	UK Great Britain	31 Mar 55	210UNTS223	102840
Italy	Yugoslavia	31 Mar 55	386UNTS307	105550
Italy	Yugoslavia	31 Mar 55	386UNTS317	105551
Norway	USA (United States)	06 Apr 55	269UNTS65	103874
Czechoslovakia	Hungary	28 Apr 55	477UNTS197	106923
Netherlands	USA (United States)	29 Apr 55	219UNTS105	102969
Peru	USA (United States)	30 Apr 55	263UNTS309	103780
Iraq	UK Great Britain	30 Apr 55	226UNTS319	103126

PARTY ONE	PARTY TWO	DATE	CITATION	NUMBER
Establishment of commission (Cont.)				
Korea, South	USA (United States)	02 May 55	258UNTS3	103666
Multilateral		14 May 55	219UNTS3	102962
Netherlands	Norway	18 May 55	252UNTS269	103569
Hungary	USSR (Soviet Union)	27 May 55	407UNTS156	105864
Italy	Norway	14 Jun 55	260UNTS307	103713
France	Greece	28 Jun 55	225UNTS219	103100
South Africa	UK Great Britain	30 Jun 55	248UNTS191	103495
Japan	Thailand	09 Jul 55	230UNTS13	103172
Greece	Netherlands	14 Jul 55	227UNTS27	103129
Italy	Spain	11 Aug 55	267UNTS125	103839
Multilateral		21 Sep 55	269UNTS241	103885
Syria	United Arab Rep	20 Oct 55	247UNTS117	103461
Italy	Lebanon	04 Nov 55	267UNTS147	103840
Italy	Lebanon	04 Nov 55	267UNTS113	103838
Italy	Syria	10 Nov 55	267UNTS157	103841
USSR (Soviet Union)	Yugoslavia	19 Dec 55	378UNTS127	105423
Costa Rica	Guatemala	20 Dec 55	280UNTS121	104056
Multilateral		21 Dec 55	292UNTS63	104267
Germany, West	USA (United States)	04 Jan 56	268UNTS143	103856
Bulgaria	Yugoslavia	10 Feb 56	349UNTS21	105007
Multilateral		05 Mar 56	326UNTS181	104712
Burma	Yugoslavia	07 Mar 56	386UNTS235	105543
Iran	Pakistan	09 Mar 56	449UNTS183	106460
Turkey	UK Great Britain	12 Mar 56	313UNTS73	104530
Multilateral		13 Mar 56	427UNTS245	106158
Romania	USSR (Soviet Union)	07 Apr 56	259UNTS377	103698
Austria	Hungary	09 Apr 56	438UNTS123	106315
Mongolia	USSR (Soviet Union)	24 Apr 56	259UNTS297	103693
Bulgaria	USSR (Soviet Union)	28 Apr 56	259UNTS363	103697
Albania	USSR (Soviet Union)	03 May 56	259UNTS391	103699
Peru	USA (United States)	03 May 56	272UNTS59	103931
Mongolia	Romania	08 May 56	342UNTS291	104913
Japan	Philippines	09 May 56	285UNTS3	104148
Denmark	Italy	12 May 56	260UNTS357	103720
Czechoslovakia	USSR (Soviet Union)	01 Jun 56	259UNTS341	103696
Multilateral		07 Jun 56	381UNTS145	105470
Bulgaria	Yugoslavia	16 Jun 56	375UNTS235	105368
Bulgaria	Yugoslavia	16 Jun 56	391UNTS3	105613
France	Greece	25 Jun 56	251UNTS167	103540
Poland	USSR (Soviet Union)	30 Jun 56	259UNTS311	103694
Czechoslovakia	Yugoslavia	03 Jul 56	397UNTS165	105704
China People's Rep	USSR (Soviet Union)	05 Jul 56	263UNTS129	103770
Multilateral		06 Jul 56	312UNTS109	104514
Guatemala	Honduras	22 Aug 56	263UNTS49	103767
Greece	Romania	25 Aug 56	299UNTS231	104315
Denmark	WHO (World Health)	03 Sep 56	258UNTS103	103674
Italy	Spain	05 Sep 56	302UNTS195	104359
Korea, North	USSR (Soviet Union)	05 Sep 56	259UNTS329	103695
Belgium	Germany, West	24 Sep 56	263UNTS31	103766
Romania	Yugoslavia	25 Sep 56	395UNTS147	105683
Germany, West	Thailand	09 Oct 56	258UNTS143	103676
Czechoslovakia	Hungary	13 Oct 56	300UNTS177	104337
Multilateral		26 Oct 56	276UNTS3	103988
Romania	Yugoslavia	27 Oct 56	389UNTS55	105592
India	Japan	29 Oct 56	318UNTS289	104622
Austria	USA (United States)	21 Nov 56	290UNTS181	104237
Czechoslovakia	USSR (Soviet Union)	30 Nov 56	266UNTS243	103833
Iceland	USA (United States)	06 Dec 56	265UNTS261	103818
Indonesia	Yugoslavia	14 Dec 56	378UNTS117	105422
Poland	USSR (Soviet Union)	17 Dec 56	266UNTS179	103830
Multilateral		21 Dec 56	427UNTS81	106147
Belgium	Yugoslavia	05 Feb 57	276UNTS143	103990
Multilateral		09 Feb 57	314UNTS105	104546
Norway	USSR (Soviet Union)	15 Feb 57	312UNTS289	104523
Poland	USSR (Soviet Union)	05 Mar 57	274UNTS133	103963

PARTY ONE	PARTY TWO	DATE	CITATION	NUMBER
Establishment of commission (Cont.)				
Germany, East	USSR (Soviet Union)	12 Mar 57	285UNTS105	104150
India	Poland	27 Mar 57	319UNTS263	104635
Poland	Vietnam, North	06 Apr 57	432UNTS255	106224
Romania	USSR (Soviet Union)	15 Apr 57	274UNTS143	103964
Argentina	Uruguay	27 Apr 57	635UNTS69	109072
Iran	USSR (Soviet Union)	14 May 57	457UNTS161	106586
Czechoslovakia	Yugoslavia	22 May 57	391UNTS33	105615
Hungary	Yugoslavia	25 May 57	477UNTS219	106924
Bulgaria	Yugoslavia	04 Jun 57	349UNTS35	105008
Multilateral		26 Jun 57	328UNTS247	104738
Finland	United Nations	27 Jun 57	271UNTS135	103913
Finland	Norway	28 Jun 57	272UNTS191	103938
United Nations	Sweden	01 Jul 57	271UNTS187	103914
Italy	United Arab Rep	06 Jul 57	302UNTS147	104357
Norway	United Nations	09 Jul 57	271UNTS223	103917
Denmark	Italy	12 Jul 57	291UNTS169	104251
Multilateral		12 Jul 57	322UNTS245	104660
New Zealand	UK Great Britain	20 Sep 57	287UNTS105	104180
Poland	USSR (Soviet Union)	26 Oct 57	432UNTS221	106223
France	Italy	08 Nov 57	305UNTS393	104427
Norway	USSR (Soviet Union)	22 Nov 57	309UNTS269	104476
Argentina	Italy	25 Nov 57	305UNTS275	104424
Italy	Yugoslavia	12 Dec 57	386UNTS293	105549
Hungary	Romania	17 Dec 57	477UNTS303	106926
Belgium	Denmark	31 Dec 57	305UNTS247	104422
Norway	Turkey	10 Jan 58	351UNTS229	105025
Ceylon (Sri Lanka)	USSR (Soviet Union)	15 Jan 58	305UNTS235	104421
Poland	Yugoslavia	16 Jan 58	340UNTS181	104864
Afghanistan	USSR (Soviet Union)	18 Jan 58	321UNTS77	104655
Indonesia	Japan	20 Jan 58	324UNTS247	104689
Multilateral		29 Jan 58	339UNTS23	104845
Ceylon (Sri Lanka)	USSR (Soviet Union)	08 Feb 58	348UNTS159	104999
Bulgaria	Italy	25 Feb 58	362UNTS291	105194
Brazil	Ecuador	05 Mar 58	369UNTS43	105250
Bulgaria	Yugoslavia	21 Mar 58	386UNTS119	105541
Bulgaria	Yugoslavia	04 Apr 58	367UNTS89	105228
Italy	Tunisia	08 Apr 58	378UNTS327	105430
Germany, West	UK Great Britain	18 Apr 58	343UNTS241	104928
Multilateral		29 Apr 58	559UNTS285	108164
Belgium	Sweden	08 May 58	312UNTS145	104516
Canada	USA (United States)	12 May 58	316UNTS151	104582
Philippines	USA (United States)	15 May 58	316UNTS163	104583
Lebanon	UK Great Britain	19 May 58	327UNTS43	104716
Italy	Switzerland	23 May 58	363UNTS81	105201
Brazil	Colombia	28 May 58	369UNTS141	105255
Multilateral		10 Jun 58	454UNTS47	106539
Multilateral		18 Jun 58	386UNTS345	105552
Austria	Belgium	20 Jun 58	312UNTS95	104513
Italy	Morocco	24 Jun 58	363UNTS23	105197
Multilateral		25 Jun 58	362UNTS31	105181
Afghanistan	USA (United States)	26 Jun 58	321UNTS67	104654
Romania	Vietnam, North	30 Jun 58	389UNTS43	105591
Cuba	USA (United States)	15 Aug 58	358UNTS63	105124
Canada	USA (United States)	02 Sep 58	335UNTS249	104792
Argentina	Brazil	19 Sep 58	374UNTS57	105329
Australia	New Zealand	30 Sep 58	340UNTS61	104859
Finland	Sweden	16 Oct 58	428UNTS125	106171
Belgium	Spain	27 Oct 58	327UNTS107	104720
France	Italy	30 Oct 58	363UNTS3	105196
Norway	Poland	17 Dec 58	432UNTS193	106221
Iraq	Romania	24 Dec 58	405UNTS243	105836
Belgium	Turkey	29 Dec 58	357UNTS195	105118
Cambodia	Japan	02 Mar 59	341UNTS163	104882
Hungary	Iraq	11 Apr 59	439UNTS25	106323
Multilateral		29 Apr 59	346UNTS167	104980

Establishment of commission (Cont.)

PARTY ONE	PARTY TWO	DATE	CITATION	NUMBER
Italy	United Arab Rep	29 Apr 59	363UNTS91	105202
Iran	UK Great Britain	06 May 59	398UNTS51	105717
Austria	USA (United States)	22 May 59	347UNTS3	104988
Iran	Netherlands	22 May 59	474UNTS195	106882
Ethiopia	Yugoslavia	06 Jun 59	386UNTS243	105544
Finland	Hungary	10 Jun 59	439UNTS3	106321
Greece	Yugoslavia	18 Jun 59	368UNTS137	105238
Greece	Yugoslavia	18 Jun 59	368UNTS27	105234
Greece	Yugoslavia	18 Jun 59	363UNTS133	105205
Greece	Yugoslavia	18 Jun 59	368UNTS125	105237
Panama	USA (United States)	24 Jun 59	479UNTS145	106950
Czechoslovakia	India	07 Jul 59	359UNTS259	105145
Multilateral		07 Jul 59	377UNTS203	105402
Japan	Paraguay	22 Jul 59	373UNTS85	105316
Norway	Spain	19 Aug 59	376UNTS145	105379
India	Italy	06 Oct 59	378UNTS267	105427
Guinea	UK Great Britain	22 Oct 59	351UNTS341	105033
Guinea	USA (United States)	28 Oct 59	358UNTS169	105134
Italy	Tunisia	31 Oct 59	378UNTS349	105431
Sudan	United Arab Rep	08 Nov 59	453UNTS51	106519
Austria	Denmark	14 Nov 59	630UNTS29	108962
Tunisia	UK Great Britain	16 Nov 59	354UNTS367	105070
France	Israel	30 Nov 59	377UNTS237	105404
Italy	Netherlands	01 Dec 59	455UNTS241	106545
Multilateral		14 Dec 59	422UNTS57	106068
Jordan	UN Special Fund	15 Dec 59	346UNTS3	104974
Australia	Indonesia	17 Dec 59	354UNTS109	105058
Denmark	Switzerland	21 Dec 59	633UNTS351	109045
Japan	USA (United States)	19 Jan 60	373UNTS207	105321
Austria	Czechoslovakia	23 Jan 60	495UNTS125	107242
Argentina	Mexico	26 Jan 60	635UNTS79	109073
Multilateral		06 Feb 60	383UNTS3	105494
Italy	USSR (Soviet Union)	09 Feb 60	399UNTS75	105735
India	USSR (Soviet Union)	12 Feb 60	392UNTS153	105642
Cuba	USSR (Soviet Union)	13 Feb 60	369UNTS17	105248
Greece	Tunisia	02 Mar 60	483UNTS89	107008
Austria	El Salvador	23 Mar 60	390UNTS3	105599
Germany, West	Netherlands	08 Apr 60	508UNTS14	107404
Netherlands	Turkey	12 May 60	463UNTS207	106704
Denmark	Poland	08 Jun 60	424UNTS37	106097
Cuba	Czechoslovakia	10 Jun 60	447UNTS75	106412
Czechoslovakia	Germany, East	16 Jun 60	415UNTS248	105988
Austria	Spain	17 Jun 60	390UNTS17	105600
Spain	UK Great Britain	12 Jul 60	414UNTS123	105971
Spain	USA (United States)	21 Jul 60	393UNTS289	105663
France	Greece	25 Jul 60	533UNTS227	107745
Italy	Netherlands	06 Aug 60	455UNTS259	106546
Multilateral		16 Aug 60	397UNTS287	105712
Austria	Czechoslovakia	14 Sep 60	495UNTS143	107243
Multilateral		19 Sep 60	419UNTS125	106032
Greece	Poland	08 Nov 60	483UNTS127	107010
Brazil	Japan	14 Nov 60	518UNTS29	107491
Multilateral		01 Dec 60	414UNTS110	105970
Denmark	USA (United States)	02 Dec 60	402UNTS245	105789
Japan	UK Great Britain	03 Dec 60	414UNTS61	105966
Multilateral		13 Dec 60	455UNTS3	106543
UK Great Britain	USSR (Soviet Union)	09 Jan 61	404UNTS175	105810
Canada	USA (United States)	17 Jan 61	542UNTS224	107894
Poland	USSR (Soviet Union)	05 Feb 61	420UNTS161	106046
Multilateral		30 Mar 61	520UNTS151	107515
Argentina	Uruguay	07 Apr 61	635UNTS91	109074
Netherlands	Spain	08 Apr 61	482UNTS193	106996
Norway	IAEA (Atom Energy)	10 Apr 61	402UNTS255	105790
India	Norway	19 Apr 61	404UNTS307	105818
Germany, West	Netherlands	27 Apr 61	487UNTS77	107095

Establishment of commission (Cont.)

PARTY ONE	PARTY TWO	DATE	CITATION	NUMBER
Turkey	USSR (Soviet Union)	27 Apr 61	420UNTS307	106047
Somalia	USSR (Soviet Union)	02 Jun 61	493UNTS173	107214
Ethiopia	United Nations	14 Jun 61	406UNTS81	105840
Argentina	UK Great Britain	19 Jun 61	470UNTS71	106797
Japan	USA (United States)	22 Jun 61	410UNTS53	105896
Indonesia	UK Great Britain	29 Jun 61	443UNTS255	106364
Austria	Romania	21 Jul 61	421UNTS161	106057
Netherlands	Euratom	25 Jul 61	462UNTS263	106686
Albania	Austria	27 Jul 61	407UNTS37	105858
Pakistan	Philippines	15 Aug 61	522UNTS35	107534
Belgium	Italy	28 Oct 61	429UNTS199	106199
Belgium	Yugoslavia	31 Oct 61	426UNTS165	106136
Greece	Morocco	01 Nov 61	483UNTS113	107009
Iraq	Syria	03 Nov 61	489UNTS45	107134
Denmark	UK Great Britain	15 Nov 61	420UNTS67	106041
Hungary	Yugoslavia	09 Feb 62	577UNTS3	108370
Colombia	USA (United States)	09 Apr 62	476UNTS9	106899
United Arab Rep	USSR (Soviet Union)	23 Jun 62	472UNTS43	106836
Germany, West	Syria	25 Jun 62	489UNTS71	107135
Multilateral		28 Jun 62	494UNTS271	107238
Multilateral		28 Jul 62	460UNTS219	106642
Cyprus	Greece	23 Aug 62	609UNTS15	108825
Finland	USSR (Soviet Union)	27 Sep 62	479UNTS99	106949
Sweden	USA (United States)	04 Oct 62	462UNTS31	106669
Belgium	Romania	12 Oct 62	502UNTS31	107325
Belgium	Rwanda	13 Oct 62	456UNTS431	106569
Czechoslovakia	Yugoslavia	22 Oct 62	480UNTS267	106974
France	UK Great Britain	29 Nov 62	453UNTS325	106534
Belgium	Tunisia	21 Dec 62	482UNTS3	106987
India	United Nations	27 Dec 62	450UNTS3	106464
Gabon	United Nations	11 Jan 63	450UNTS257	106472
Multilateral		15 Jan 63	456UNTS409	106567
United Nations	United Arab Rep	08 Feb 63	453UNTS79	106520
Burma	Japan	29 Mar 63	518UNTS3	107490
Austria	Bulgaria	05 Apr 63	480UNTS3	106963
UK Great Britain	USA (United States)	06 Apr 63	474UNTS49	106871
Denmark	Norway	11 May 63	613UNTS271	108856
Burma	Thailand	17 May 63	468UNTS319	106779
Multilateral		09 Jun 63	538UNTS309	107818
Austria	Mongolia	15 Jul 63	496UNTS171	107251
Cameroon	UK Great Britain	29 Jul 63	478UNTS148	106935
India	USA (United States)	08 Aug 63	488UNTS21	107117
Cameroon	UK Great Britain	20 Aug 63	539UNTS233	107834
Austria	Switzerland	02 Sep 63	548UNTS91	107973
Denmark	Norway	12 Sep 63	613UNTS289	108857
Greece	Poland	30 Sep 63	534UNTS23	107751
Czechoslovakia	Yugoslavia	05 Oct 63	504UNTS151	107356
Canada	France	11 Oct 63	529UNTS71	107657
Iran	USA (United States)	24 Oct 63	489UNTS303	107146
Belgium	Romania	13 Nov 63	520UNTS119	107513
Canada	USA (United States)	15 Nov 63	493UNTS67	107207
Romania	Yugoslavia	30 Nov 63	512UNTS2	107438
Belgium	Poland	09 Dec 63	514UNTS195	107448
Romania	Yugoslavia	20 Dec 63	527UNTS245	107629
Australia	Laos	24 Dec 63	503UNTS315	107350
Romania	Yugoslavia	25 Dec 63	576UNTS95	108366
Canada	USA (United States)	22 Jan 64	530UNTS89	107674
Multilateral		28 Feb 64	501UNTS245	107321
Spain	USA (United States)	18 Mar 64	535UNTS343	107789
Mexico	Netherlands	08 Apr 64	575UNTS35	108353
Germany, West	Greece	16 Apr 64	609UNTS27	108826
Finland	USSR (Soviet Union)	24 Apr 64	537UNTS231	107804
Japan	USA (United States)	25 Apr 64	530UNTS61	107672
Korea, South	USA (United States)	12 May 64	529UNTS299	107667
Austria	Turkey	15 May 64	515UNTS109	107457

PARTY ONE	PARTY TWO	DATE	CITATION	NUMBER
Establishment of commission (Cont.)				
Chad	France	19 May 64	0UNTSO	109440
France	UK Great Britain	03 Jun 64	539UNTS253	107836
Multilateral		11 Jun 64	525UNTS61	107584
Italy	Romania	16 Jun 64	558UNTS313	108150
Multilateral		20 Jun 64	539UNTS3	107819
Colombia	Netherlands	06 Jul 64	543UNTS289	107906
Multilateral		13 Jul 64	569UNTS65	108279
Belgium	Tunisia	15 Jul 64	560UNTS57	108168
Germany, West	UK Great Britain	27 Jul 64	539UNTS243	107835
Argentina	France	03 Oct 64	635UNTS155	109080
Argentina	Paraguay	21 Oct 64	635UNTS189	109082
Argentina	Paraguay	21 Oct 64	635UNTS177	109081
Argentina	Guatemala	30 Oct 64	601UNTS175	108695
Austria	Hungary	31 Oct 64	545UNTS223	107936
Austria	Hungary	31 Oct 64	545UNTS241	107937
Austria	Hungary	11 Nov 64	576UNTS163	108368
Argentina	Panama	21 Nov 64	635UNTS205	109083
Argentina	Costa Rica	23 Nov 64	635UNTS213	109084
India	United Nations	25 Nov 64	519UNTS47	107501
Poland	Romania	26 Nov 64	552UNTS157	108053
UK Great Britain	USSR (Soviet Union)	06 Jan 65	543UNTS77	107897
Belgium	Luxembourg	14 Jan 65	620UNTS3	108949
Denmark	Thailand	25 Jan 65	530UNTS173	107680
Belgium	Congo (Zaire)	06 Feb 65	540UNTS275	107853
Belgium	Hungary	11 Feb 65	544UNTS3	107908
Benelux Econ Union	Poland	17 Feb 65	547UNTS165	107956
Mexico	USA (United States)	27 Feb 65	542UNTS181	107889
Multilateral		18 Mar 65	575UNTS159	108359
Hungary	Yugoslavia	08 Apr 65	587UNTS169	108511
Taiwan	USA (United States)	09 Apr 65	546UNTS81	107939
Ivory Coast	Netherlands	26 Apr 65	634UNTS81	109053
USA (United States)	Uruguay	17 May 65	564UNTS69	108221
Ethiopia	Hungary	25 May 65	577UNTS193	108377
Argentina	Yugoslavia	09 Jun 65	601UNTS3	108684
Netherlands	Senegal	12 Jun 65	602UNTS231	108715
Argentina	United Arab Rep	21 Jun 65	634UNTS161	109058
Japan	Korea, South	22 Jun 65	583UNTS51	108472
Multilateral		23 Jun 65	548UNTS241	107981
Austria	Bulgaria	12 Jul 65	587UNTS51	108510
Malta	Yugoslavia	15 Jul 65	561UNTS223	108186
Multilateral		16 Jul 65	600UNTS49	108675
Hungary	Yugoslavia	09 Aug 65	577UNTS103	108375
Italy	Romania	06 Sep 65	604UNTS49	108742
France	UK Great Britain	21 Sep 65	561UNTS3	108177
Multilateral		07 Oct 65	556UNTS175	108125
Argentina	Belgium	05 Nov 65	635UNTS229	109086
Austria	Yugoslavia	19 Nov 65	587UNTS239	108512
Multilateral		30 Dec 65	557UNTS3	108126
Belgium	Denmark	04 Feb 66	561UNTS233	108187
Panama	USA (United States)	15 Feb 66	586UNTS27	108494
UK Great Britain	Venezuela	17 Feb 66	561UNTS321	108192
France	Romania	14 Mar 66	604UNTS33	108741
Argentina	Taiwan	19 Mar 66	635UNTS281	109089
Austria	Spain	24 Mar 66	590UNTS203	108555
Romania	Tunisia	21 Apr 66	604UNTS65	108744
Multilateral		30 Apr 66	620UNTS191	108956
UK Great Britain	USA (United States)	02 Jun 66	573UNTS229	108336
Bel-Lux Econ Union	Bulgaria	14 Jun 66	601UNTS167	108694
Belgium	Bulgaria	14 Jun 66	607UNTS183	108806
Multilateral		20 Jun 66	573UNTS41	108322
France	USSR (Soviet Union)	30 Jun 66	589UNTS109	108538
Belgium	Spain	19 Jul 66	575UNTS3	108352
Bulgaria	United Arab Rep	29 Aug 66	630UNTS325	108980
Netherlands	Yugoslavia	08 Sep 66	597UNTS147	108643
Morocco	Senegal	15 Sep 66	634UNTS105	109055

PARTY ONE	PARTY TWO	DATE	CITATION	NUMBER
Establishment of commission (Cont.)				
Belgium	France	23 Sep 66	588UNTS227	108528
Brazil	Netherlands	12 Oct 66	643UNTS271	109197
Romania	United Arab Rep	14 Nov 66	642UNTS129	109169
Ghana	Romania	23 Nov 66	642UNTS79	109166
Ghana	Romania	23 Nov 66	642UNTS63	109165
Argentina	Paraguay	23 Jan 67	634UNTS193	109061
Denmark	France	15 Feb 67	604UNTS247	108754
Belgium	Luxembourg	22 Feb 67	639UNTS3	109140
Belgium	Hungary	20 Mar 67	601UNTS37	108686
Belgium	Israel	23 Mar 67	630UNTS275	108974
Gambia	Senegal	19 Apr 67	640UNTS101	109156
Bulgaria	USSR (Soviet Union)	27 Apr 67	631UNTS3	108983
Czechoslovakia	Yugoslavia	17 May 67	617UNTS305	108918
Belgium	Bulgaria	17 May 67	631UNTS215	108995
Bulgaria	Turkey	30 May 67	631UNTS19	108984
Netherlands	Romania	20 Jul 67	633UNTS21	109032
Bulgaria	Italy	29 Jul 67	631UNTS33	108985
Germany, West	Romania	03 Aug 67	642UNTS47	109164
Italy	Romania	08 Aug 67	642UNTS213	109175
Italy	Romania	08 Aug 67	642UNTS191	109174
Denmark	Romania	29 Aug 67	642UNTS357	109183
Italy	UK Great Britain	30 Sep 67	642UNTS271	109180
Ecuador	Romania	10 Oct 67	642UNTS33	109163
Finland	France	27 Oct 67	643UNTS75	109185
Denmark	Poland	15 Nov 67	643UNTS383	109203
Israel	Singapore	24 Apr 68	642UNTS235	109176
Extraterritorial rights				
Greece	USA (United States)	04 Feb 53	189UNTS3	102538
Abolition of treaty ports				
Belgium	Taiwan	20 Oct 43	14UNTS376	200095
Taiwan	France	28 Feb 46	14UNTS113	100215
Taiwan	Denmark	20 May 46	12UNTS59	100180
Abolition of diplomatic quarters				
Taiwan	USA (United States)	11 Jan 43	10UNTS261	200066
Belgium	Taiwan	20 Oct 43	14UNTS376	200095
Taiwan	Netherlands	29 May 45	2UNTS307	200023
Taiwan	France	28 Feb 46	14UNTS113	100215
Taiwan	Portugal	01 Apr 47	14UNTS177	100220
Abolition of extraterritorial rights				
Taiwan	USA (United States)	11 Jan 43	10UNTS261	200066
Belgium	Taiwan	20 Oct 43	14UNTS376	200095
Canada	Taiwan	14 Apr 44	14UNTS408	200097
Taiwan	Netherlands	29 May 45	2UNTS307	200023
Taiwan	France	28 Feb 46	14UNTS113	100215
Taiwan	Denmark	20 May 46	12UNTS59	100180
Multilateral		08 Sep 51	136UNTS45	101832
Taiwan	Japan	28 Apr 52	138UNTS3	101858
Multilateral		20 Feb 62	597UNTS159	108644
Dispute settlement				
Multilateral		29 Jun 33	39UNTS211	100619
Multilateral		12 May 40	101UNTS91	101405
Brazil	Venezuela	22 Oct 42	65UNTS203	200212
Poland	Yugoslavia	02 Jan 46	115UNTS21	101556
Poland	Yugoslavia	16 Mar 46	10UNTS11	100139
France	USA (United States)	28 May 46	84UNTS161	101126
India	Netherlands	31 May 47	17UNTS65	100268
Albania	Yugoslavia	12 Jun 47	111UNTS189	101533
Multilateral		19 Jun 47	171UNTS329	102235
Bulgaria	Czechoslovakia	20 Jun 47	46UNTS15	100698
Belgium	Netherlands	29 Aug 47	36UNTS349	100573
Philippines	Spain	27 Sep 47	70UNTS133	100902
Czechoslovakia	Poland	05 Apr 48	31UNTS355	100482
France	Netherlands	02 Jun 48	204UNTS275	102762

PARTY ONE	PARTY TWO	DATE	CITATION	NUMBER
Dispute settlement (Cont.)				
France	Poland	09 Jun 48	32UNTS251	100503
Multilateral		09 Dec 48	73UNTS39	100942
Italy	USA (United States)	18 Dec 48	79UNTS133	101037
Belgium	France	08 Jan 49	36UNTS151	100569
Norway	USA (United States)	25 May 49	32UNTS345	100507
Multilateral		12 Aug 49	75UNTS85	100971
Multilateral		12 Aug 49	75UNTS287	100973
Multilateral		12 Aug 49	75UNTS31	100970
Multilateral		07 Nov 49	132UNTS31	101749
Belgium	Luxembourg	03 Dec 49	91UNTS31	101241
France	UK Great Britain	28 Jan 50	97UNTS155	101349
India	USA (United States)	02 Feb 50	89UNTS127	101214
Multilateral		17 Apr 50	126UNTS285	101694
Korea, South	USA (United States)	28 Apr 50	93UNTS21	101284
Austria	USA (United States)	06 Jun 50	92UNTS201	101273
Thailand	USA (United States)	01 Jul 50	81UNTS61	101063
Luxembourg	Netherlands	08 Jul 50	135UNTS229	101824
Multilateral		27 Jul 50	166UNTS73	102186
Pakistan	USA (United States)	23 Sep 50	82UNTS131	101088
Multilateral		22 Nov 50	131UNTS25	101734
Belgium	Finland	20 Mar 51	110UNTS27	101498
Belgium	Sweden	18 Sep 51	133UNTS187	101789
Multilateral		09 Oct 51	220UNTS121	102997
Italy	UK Great Britain	28 Nov 51	172UNTS205	102248
Belgium	Switzerland	17 Jun 52	180UNTS23	102373
Italy	Netherlands	28 Oct 52	289UNTS144	104218
Switzerland	UK Great Britain	16 Jan 53	196UNTS119	102621
Multilateral		20 Jul 53	227UNTS217	103140
Denmark	Germany, West	14 Aug 53	202UNTS3	102725
Luxembourg	UK Great Britain	13 Oct 53	209UNTS87	102825
Multilateral		11 Dec 53	218UNTS211	102957
Denmark	UK Great Britain	15 Dec 53	196UNTS105	102620
ICJ Option Clause	Finland	26 Feb 54	189UNTS223	102546
Multilateral		21 May 54	345UNTS285	104973
Italy	Netherlands	04 Jun 54	289UNTS261	104222
Netherlands	UK Great Britain	11 Aug 54	248UNTS235	103497
Austria	Denmark	07 Sep 54	201UNTS39	102709
Belgium	Yugoslavia	01 Nov 54	251UNTS123	103538
Sweden	Switzerland	17 Dec 54	369UNTS233	105260
Multilateral		19 Dec 54	218UNTS139	102955
Multilateral		14 May 55	219UNTS3	102962
Norway	Sweden	28 May 55	262UNTS151	103743
Bulgaria	Yugoslavia	17 Jun 55	375UNTS287	105370
Multilateral		12 Oct 55	560UNTS3	108165
Austria	Sweden	03 Nov 55	262UNTS289	103757
Austria	Belgium	20 Jan 56	248UNTS3	103481
Bulgaria	Greece	19 Apr 56	594UNTS131	108600
USSR (Soviet Union)	Yugoslavia	17 May 56	259UNTS145	103687
Multilateral		07 Jun 56	381UNTS145	105470
Sweden	UK Great Britain	09 Jun 56	309UNTS301	104479
Multilateral		09 Jul 56	314UNTS3	104539
Austria	Italy	12 Jul 56	378UNTS249	105426
Multilateral		07 Sep 56	266UNTS3	103822
Multilateral		11 Sep 56	266UNTS221	103832
Czechoslovakia	Hungary	13 Oct 56	300UNTS177	104337
Belgium	Spain	28 Nov 56	308UNTS239	104464
Czechoslovakia	USSR (Soviet Union)	30 Nov 56	266UNTS243	103833
Multilateral		19 Dec 56	427UNTS93	106148
Multilateral		25 Mar 57	294UNTS2	104300
Multilateral		25 Mar 57	294UNTS411	104302
Czechoslovakia	Yugoslavia	22 May 57	391UNTS57	105617
Norway	UK Great Britain	25 Jul 57	313UNTS3	104528
Multilateral		03 Oct 57	364UNTS3	105211
Hungary	Yugoslavia	07 Oct 57	439UNTS61	106325
Italy	Monaco	06 Dec 57	363UNTS45	105198

PARTY ONE	PARTY TWO	DATE	CITATION	NUMBER
Dispute settlement (Cont.)				
Hungary	Yugoslavia	06 Dec 57	519UNTS215	107509
Italy	Yugoslavia	12 Dec 57	386UNTS293	105549
Poland	Yugoslavia	16 Jan 58	340UNTS137	104863
Belgium	Greece	01 Apr 58	388UNTS93	105574
UK Great Britain	Yugoslavia	24 May 58	326UNTS69	104709
Multilateral		10 Jun 58	454UNTS47	106539
Spain	USA (United States)	16 Oct 58	336UNTS153	104804
Czechoslovakia	Hungary	30 Jan 59	351UNTS3	105016
Multilateral		29 Apr 59	346UNTS167	104980
Japan	Vietnam, South	13 May 59	373UNTS149	105318
Czechoslovakia	Switzerland	04 Jun 59	349UNTS121	105012
Finland	UK Great Britain	28 Jul 59	355UNTS31	105073
Turkey	UK Great Britain	09 Sep 59	424UNTS267	106113
Ireland	UK Great Britain	29 Mar 60	371UNTS3	105267
Germany, West	UK Great Britain	20 Apr 60	413UNTS236	105958
Germany, West	UK Great Britain	20 Apr 60	449UNTS77	106453
UN Special Fund	Thailand	04 Jun 60	360UNTS97	105157
Multilateral		14 Dec 60	429UNTS93	106193
Finland	Italy	18 Feb 61	434UNTS199	106263
Norway	IAEA (Atom Energy)	10 Apr 61	402UNTS255	105790
Honduras	IDA (Devel Assoc)	12 May 61	414UNTS180	105973
IDA (Devel Assoc)	Sudan	14 Jun 61	415UNTS50	105981
Austria	Finland	01 Feb 62	425UNTS33	106116
Pakistan	IAEA (Atom Energy)	05 Mar 62	425UNTS17	106115
Multilateral		24 Apr 63	596UNTS487	108640
Belgium	Venezuela	15 May 63	470UNTS259	106812
Niger	United Nations	20 Nov 63	536UNTS3	107793
Netherlands	Portugal	22 Nov 63	492UNTS31	107185
Multilateral		28 Feb 64	501UNTS245	107321
Multilateral		08 Apr 64	501UNTS221	107320
Algeria	Czechoslovakia	14 May 64	538UNTS301	107817
Austria	Spain	15 Jul 64	589UNTS169	108541
Netherlands	Turkey	19 Aug 64	521UNTS197	107523
Italy	ILO (Labor Org)	24 Oct 64	541UNTS217	107871
Austria	Hungary	11 Nov 64	576UNTS163	108368
Multilateral		02 Jul 65	592UNTS215	108575
Switzerland	UK Great Britain	07 Jul 65	605UNTS205	108765
Denmark	Jordan	28 Jun 66	574UNTS3	108338
Brazil	Denmark	08 Jul 66	581UNTS95	108435
Denmark	Malawi	01 Sep 66	586UNTS3	108493
Romania	United Arab Rep	03 Sep 66	604UNTS73	108745
Multilateral		02 Feb 67	606UNTS89	108777
Germany, West	Netherlands	02 Feb 67	606UNTS105	108779
Denmark	Germany, West	02 Feb 67	606UNTS97	108778
Austria	United Nations	13 Apr 67	600UNTS93	108679
Multilateral		13 Apr 67	595UNTS60	108612
Greece	United Nations	14 Apr 67	595UNTS83	108613
Arbitration				
Greece	Iran	09 Jan 31	166UNTS323	200496
Brazil	France	27 Jan 40	72UNTS77	100929
Norway	USA (United States)	28 Mar 40	88UNTS365	200253
Brazil	Venezuela	30 Mar 40	51UNTS291	200195
Haiti	USA (United States)	13 Sep 41	103UNTS141	200311
Mexico	USA (United States)	19 Nov 41	125UNTS287	200430
Taiwan	Mexico	01 Aug 44	14UNTS441	200099
Multilateral		07 Dec 44	171UNTS345	200501
Multilateral		22 Mar 45	70UNTS237	200241
South Africa	UK Great Britain	26 Oct 45	72UNTS41	100927
Portugal	UK Great Britain	06 Dec 45	6UNTS3	100065
Portugal	UK Great Britain	06 Dec 45	5UNTS37	100064
Canada	UK Great Britain	21 Dec 45	27UNTS155	100405
Multilateral		14 Jan 46	555UNTS69	108105
Czechoslovakia	Poland	24 Jan 46	25UNTS181	100363
Turkey	UK Great Britain	12 Feb 46	6UNTS79	100069

PARTY ONE	PARTY TWO	DATE	CITATION	NUMBER
Arbitration (Cont.)				
France	UK Great Britain	28 Feb 46	27UNTS173	100407
Greece	United Arab Rep	30 Mar 46	187UNTS263	102518
Ireland	UK Great Britain	05 Apr 46	72UNTS57	100928
Netherlands	Portugal	12 Apr 46	4UNTS317	100054
France	Ireland	16 May 46	44UNTS105	100681
Australia	Canada	11 Jun 46	10UNTS47	100142
Sweden	Turkey	26 Jun 46	14UNTS21	100208
United Nations	Switzerland	01 Jul 46	1UNTS153	200007
Netherlands	Spain	13 Jul 46	4UNTS351	100055
Multilateral		18 Jul 46	125UNTS119	101674
France	Sweden	02 Aug 46	27UNTS251	100410
Netherlands	UK Great Britain	13 Aug 46	4UNTS367	100056
Denmark	USSR (Soviet Union)	17 Aug 46	8UNTS201	100124
Brazil	USA (United States)	06 Sep 46	54UNTS197	100805
France	Turkey	12 Oct 46	14UNTS33	100209
Belgium	Portugal	22 Oct 46	34UNTS49	100527
Brazil	UK Great Britain	31 Oct 46	11UNTS115	100152
Portugal	Switzerland	09 Dec 46	310UNTS251	104495
Brazil	Portugal	10 Dec 46	200UNTS67	102695
USA (United States)	Uruguay	14 Dec 46	532UNTS87	107713
Czechoslovakia	Ireland	29 Jan 47	27UNTS267	100411
Multilateral		10 Feb 47	48UNTS203	100746
Romania	USSR (Soviet Union)	20 Feb 47	226UNTS79	103110
Czechoslovakia	Poland	04 Apr 47	85UNTS62	101146
Greece	Sweden	08 Apr 47	94UNTS73	101307
Greece	Netherlands	17 Apr 47	32UNTS115	100494
Canada	Portugal	25 Apr 47	94UNTS87	101308
France	Greece	05 May 47	76UNTS61	100980
Chile	USA (United States)	10 May 47	55UNTS21	100807
Hungary	Yugoslavia	11 May 47	130UNTS171	101730
Czechoslovakia	Denmark	14 May 47	27UNTS297	100413
India	Netherlands	31 May 47	17UNTS65	100268
Albania	Yugoslavia	12 Jun 47	111UNTS183	101532
Iraq	Turkey	30 Jun 47	72UNTS107	100930
Denmark	Turkey	30 Jun 47	32UNTS301	100504
Hungary	USSR (Soviet Union)	15 Jul 47	216UNTS247	102940
Canada	UK Great Britain	17 Jul 47	28UNTS3	100416
Greece	Turkey	22 Jul 47	72UNTS131	100931
Taiwan	UK Great Britain	23 Jul 47	9UNTS207	100135
Hungary	Yugoslavia	24 Jul 47	114UNTS3	101554
Netherlands	IBRD (World Bank)	07 Aug 47	152UNTS165	102015
Poland	Romania	09 Aug 47	12UNTS363	100193
Denmark	IBRD (World Bank)	22 Aug 47	152UNTS223	102016
Luxembourg	IBRD (World Bank)	28 Aug 47	153UNTS3	102017
Czechoslovakia	Switzerland	10 Sep 47	35UNTS275	100559
Chile	UK Great Britain	16 Sep 47	133UNTS143	101786
Lebanon	Turkey	16 Sep 47	44UNTS123	100682
Multilateral		02 Oct 47	193UNTS188	102616
Multilateral		11 Oct 47	77UNTS143	100998
Czechoslovakia	Sweden	15 Oct 47	44UNTS149	100683
Colombia	UK Great Britain	16 Oct 47	160UNTS297	102115
Brazil	Netherlands	06 Nov 47	53UNTS59	100773
Multilateral		12 Nov 47	53UNTS49	100772
Brazil	Sweden	14 Nov 47	94UNTS139	101310
Brazil	Denmark	14 Nov 47	47UNTS39	100722
Brazil	Norway	14 Nov 47	44UNTS163	100684
Ireland	Italy	21 Nov 47	353UNTS73	105038
Finland	USSR (Soviet Union)	01 Dec 47	217UNTS3	102942
Czechoslovakia	USSR (Soviet Union)	11 Dec 47	217UNTS35	102943
Peru	UK Great Britain	22 Dec 47	72UNTS143	100932
Philippines	UK Great Britain	07 Jan 48	28UNTS63	100420
Austria	Netherlands	22 Jan 48	17UNTS99	100270
Switzerland	USSR (Soviet Union)	17 Mar 48	217UNTS73	102944
Argentina	Denmark	18 Mar 48	94UNTS175	101311
Cuba	UK Great Britain	19 Mar 48	175UNTS23	102294

PARTY ONE	PARTY TWO	DATE	CITATION	NUMBER
Arbitration (Cont.)				
Bulgaria	USSR (Soviet Union)	01 Apr 48	217UNTS97	102946
Multilateral		30 Apr 48	30UNTS55	100449
Ireland	Switzerland	06 May 48	334UNTS187	104768
Jordan	Turkey	07 May 48	32UNTS313	100505
Multilateral		10 May 48	140UNTS129	101887
Ireland	Netherlands	10 May 48	28UNTS121	100422
Norway	Turkey	20 May 48	26UNTS137	100384
India	Sweden	21 May 48	34UNTS285	100543
Greece	Switzerland	26 May 48	94UNTS217	101312
Canada	Netherlands	02 Jun 48	32UNTS215	100499
Italy	UK Great Britain	25 Jun 48	94UNTS239	101313
Brazil	Switzerland	10 Aug 48	94UNTS269	101314
India	Switzerland	14 Aug 48	33UNTS3	100509
France	Spain	23 Aug 48	28UNTS173	100425
Greece	Lebanon	06 Sep 48	178UNTS37	102335
Iceland	ICAO (Civil Aviat)	16 Sep 48	28UNTS267	100429
Bolivia	USA (United States)	29 Sep 48	505UNTS139	107370
Greece	Lebanon	06 Oct 48	87UNTS351	101179
Netherlands	Spain	08 Oct 48	28UNTS209	100426
Mexico	Portugal	22 Oct 48	34UNTS329	100546
Argentina	Netherlands	29 Oct 48	95UNTS21	101316
Czechoslovakia	Poland	12 Nov 48	84UNTS347	101141
Italy	USSR (Soviet Union)	11 Dec 48	217UNTS181	102948
Ceylon (Sri Lanka)	India	21 Dec 48	28UNTS223	100427
Ceylon (Sri Lanka)	Pakistan	03 Jan 49	28UNTS247	100428
Mexico	IBRD (World Bank)	06 Jan 49	154UNTS81	102028
Italy	Lebanon	24 Jan 49	231UNTS241	103223
Switzerland	Turkey	16 Feb 49	72UNTS175	100933
Belgium	France	18 Feb 49	31UNTS173	100478
Belgium	IBRD (World Bank)	01 Mar 49	154UNTS133	102029
Netherlands	Switzerland	07 Mar 49	35UNTS69	100551
Panama	USA (United States)	31 Mar 49	55UNTS87	100810
Finland	Sweden	26 Apr 49	95UNTS83	101318
Multilateral		28 Apr 49	71UNTS101	100912
Denmark	Poland	12 May 49	87UNTS179	101172
United Arab Rep	UK Great Britain	31 May 49	226UNTS273	103122
Italy	Spain	31 May 49	231UNTS251	103224
Australia	Pakistan	03 Jun 49	35UNTS23	100549
Belgium	Greece	21 Jun 49	137UNTS215	101854
Norway	Pakistan	23 Jun 49	35UNTS49	100550
India	Switzerland	24 Jun 49	95UNTS109	101319
Australia	India	11 Jul 49	35UNTS83	100552
Pakistan	Philippines	16 Jul 49	35UNTS111	100553
Dominican Republic	USA (United States)	19 Jul 49	51UNTS145	100762
Netherlands	IBRD (World Bank)	26 Jul 49	154UNTS178	102030
Pakistan	UK Great Britain	27 Jul 49	44UNTS199	100685
Finland	IBRD (World Bank)	01 Aug 49	156UNTS289	200480
Ceylon (Sri Lanka)	UK Great Britain	05 Aug 49	35UNTS137	100554
WHO (World Health)	Thailand	12 Aug 49	178UNTS347	102350
India	IBRD (World Bank)	18 Aug 49	154UNTS269	102031
Colombia	IBRD (World Bank)	19 Aug 49	154UNTS329	102032
Finland	Norway	24 Aug 49	53UNTS167	100780
Denmark	Finland	26 Aug 49	53UNTS191	100781
Denmark	ICAO (Civil Aviat)	09 Sep 49	53UNTS341	100791
IBRD (World Bank)	Yugoslavia	17 Sep 49	155UNTS3	102034
Belgium	United Arab Rep	19 Sep 49	137UNTS189	101853
Lebanon	Netherlands	20 Sep 49	108UNTS205	101474
Burma	USA (United States)	28 Sep 49	55UNTS3	100806
India	IBRD (World Bank)	29 Sep 49	154UNTS393	102033
Greece	Philippines	08 Oct 49	187UNTS221	102515
India	Philippines	20 Oct 49	72UNTS191	100934
Iran	Netherlands	31 Oct 49	254UNTS257	103596
Indonesia	Netherlands	02 Nov 49	69UNTS3	100894
Multilateral		07 Nov 49	132UNTS3	101748
Sweden	Thailand	23 Nov 49	72UNTS217	100935

PARTY ONE	PARTY TWO	DATE	CITATION	NUMBER
Arbitration (Cont.)				
Denmark	Thailand	23 Nov 49	53UNTS255	100786
Italy	Turkey	25 Nov 49	192UNTS39	102594
Norway	Thailand	26 Nov 49	53UNTS269	100787
Brazil	Spain	28 Nov 49	215UNTS303	102923
Austria	Norway	02 Dec 49	72UNTS230	100936
Austria	Sweden	02 Dec 49	108UNTS3	101465
Austria	Denmark	02 Dec 49	53UNTS281	100788
Afghanistan	WHO (World Health)	04 Dec 49	102UNTS117	101414
Netherlands	United Arab Rep	08 Dec 49	95UNTS123	101320
Sweden	United Arab Rep	12 Dec 49	108UNTS15	101466
Canada	Denmark	13 Dec 49	72UNTS247	100937
El Salvador	IBRD (World Bank)	14 Dec 49	155UNTS43	102035
Austria	Switzerland	19 Dec 49	254UNTS287	103597
United Nations	WHO (World Health)	10 Feb 50	46UNTS327	200188
Ceylon (Sri Lanka)	WHO (World Health)	17 Feb 50	102UNTS309	200309
Spain	Sweden	18 Feb 50	166UNTS15	102184
Ceylon (Sri Lanka)	Thailand	24 Feb 50	72UNTS261	100938
Italy	Netherlands	04 Mar 50	254UNTS305	103598
Norway	United Arab Rep	11 Mar 50	95UNTS157	101321
Denmark	United Arab Rep	14 Mar 50	95UNTS197	101322
India	Iran	15 Mar 50	161UNTS15	102118
Denmark	Iceland	22 Mar 50	72UNTS273	100939
Iceland	Netherlands	22 Mar 50	95UNTS237	101323
Italy	Portugal	05 Apr 50	254UNTS329	103599
Sweden	UK Great Britain	05 Apr 50	99UNTS107	101374
Turkey	United Arab Rep	12 Apr 50	128UNTS3	101711
India	IBRD (World Bank)	18 Apr 50	155UNTS117	102036
Greece	United Arab Rep	24 Apr 50	163UNTS229	102149
Mexico	IBRD (World Bank)	28 Apr 50	155UNTS185	102037
Switzerland	United Arab Rep	15 May 50	95UNTS255	101325
Brazil	IBRD (World Bank)	26 May 50	301UNTS165	104345
Israel	USA (United States)	13 Jun 50	212UNTS93	102863
Iraq	IBRD (World Bank)	15 Jun 50	155UNTS267	102038
Iraq	Pakistan	20 Jun 50	77UNTS215	101001
Netherlands	Spain	20 Jun 50	95UNTS303	101327
Haiti	WHO (World Health)	27 Jun 50	110UNTS99	101504
IBRD (World Bank)	Turkey	07 Jul 50	156UNTS3	102039
IBRD (World Bank)	Turkey	07 Jul 50	156UNTS75	102040
Spain	UK Great Britain	20 Jul 50	398UNTS101	105719
France	Pakistan	31 Jul 50	96UNTS23	101329
Canada	France	01 Aug 50	73UNTS21	100941
Spain	Switzerland	03 Aug 50	254UNTS365	103600
France	United Arab Rep	08 Aug 50	127UNTS293	101710
Canada	New Zealand	16 Aug 50	77UNTS239	101002
IBRD (World Bank)	Uruguay	25 Aug 50	156UNTS203	102042
Greece	Philippines	28 Aug 50	225UNTS155	103097
WHO (World Health)	Venezuela	11 Sep 50	110UNTS237	101513
Brazil	Turkey	21 Sep 50	150UNTS299	101981
Ceylon (Sri Lanka)	United Arab Rep	26 Sep 50	192UNTS53	102595
Iceland	WHO (World Health)	06 Oct 50	110UNTS127	101506
WHO (World Health)	Turkey	19 Oct 50	110UNTS215	101512
Luxembourg	Portugal	21 Oct 50	108UNTS67	101468
Israel	Netherlands	23 Oct 50	189UNTS89	102543
Multilateral		02 Nov 50	81UNTS160	101071
Peru	WHO (World Health)	10 Nov 50	110UNTS187	101510
Nicaragua	WHO (World Health)	10 Nov 50	110UNTS155	101508
Multilateral		24 Nov 50	81UNTS188	101072
Multilateral		15 Dec 50	171UNTS305	102234
Philippines	WHO (World Health)	28 Dec 50	110UNTS203	101511
Canada	France	26 Jan 51	233UNTS65	103251
France	India	02 Feb 51	203UNTS155	102744
Israel	Turkey	05 Feb 51	193UNTS3	102607
Paraguay	WHO (World Health)	15 Feb 51	110UNTS171	101509
Israel	ILO (Labor Org)	19 Feb 51	100UNTS105	101391
ILO (Labor Org)	Syria	03 Mar 51	110UNTS69	101502

PARTY ONE	PARTY TWO	DATE	CITATION	NUMBER
Arbitration (Cont.)				
India	Indonesia	03 Mar 51	167UNTS3	102197
Colombia	Portugal	09 Mar 51	108UNTS87	101469
Greece	Yugoslavia	15 Mar 51	187UNTS237	102516
Indonesia	WHO (World Health)	28 Mar 51	103UNTS71	101425
Multilateral		28 Mar 51	181UNTS61	102399
Jordan	ILO (Labor Org)	29 Mar 51	100UNTS247	200287
Liberia	ILO (Labor Org)	02 Apr 51	100UNTS117	101392
Jordan	WHO (World Health)	03 Apr 51	110UNTS297	200367
Ceylon (Sri Lanka)	ILO (Labor Org)	06 Apr 51	100UNTS235	200286
France	UK Great Britain	11 Apr 51	106UNTS3	101456
Guatemala	ILO (Labor Org)	13 Apr 51	126UNTS249	101692
Peru	ILO (Labor Org)	13 Apr 51	100UNTS31	101385
Ecuador	ILO (Labor Org)	19 Apr 51	100UNTS77	101389
Iraq	UK Great Britain	19 Apr 51	108UNTS121	101470
Honduras	WHO (World Health)	20 Apr 51	110UNTS111	101505
Cuba	ILO (Labor Org)	21 Apr 51	99UNTS205	101382
Multilateral		25 Apr 51	91UNTS21	101240
Greece	ILO (Labor Org)	25 Apr 51	100UNTS93	101390
India	ILO (Labor Org)	26 Apr 51	100UNTS19	101384
WHO (World Health)	Yugoslavia	02 May 51	103UNTS117	101429
Colombia	WHO (World Health)	04 May 51	110UNTS83	101503
Belgium	UK Great Britain	08 May 51	158UNTS451	102079
Pakistan	ILO (Labor Org)	16 May 51	100UNTS147	101394
India	Netherlands	24 May 51	108UNTS151	101471
Greece	Norway	28 May 51	187UNTS141	102507
Cambodia	WHO (World Health)	31 May 51	102UNTS279	200307
Lebanon	WHO (World Health)	07 Jun 51	126UNTS221	101690
Liberia	WHO (World Health)	11 Jun 51	103UNTS83	101426
WHO (World Health)	Uruguay	11 Jun 51	128UNTS251	101724
Dominican Republic	ILO (Labor Org)	18 Jun 51	100UNTS3	101383
Denmark	Iran	18 Jun 51	255UNTS3	103602
Multilateral		19 Jun 51	199UNTS67	102678
Cuba	Portugal	26 Jun 51	192UNTS115	102598
ILO (Labor Org)	Vietnam, South	26 Jun 51	100UNTS223	200285
Multilateral		28 Jun 51	118UNTS154	101604
Iraq	WHO (World Health)	01 Jul 51	110UNTS139	101507
Ethiopia	WHO (World Health)	02 Jul 51	103UNTS39	101422
Burma	WHO (World Health)	09 Jul 51	104UNTS187	101440
ILO (Labor Org)	Thailand	11 Jul 51	100UNTS159	101395
Paraguay	ILO (Labor Org)	12 Jul 51	117UNTS155	101591
Iceland	Norway	14 Jul 51	163UNTS265	102150
Pakistan	Turkey	26 Jul 51	188UNTS323	102536
Burma	Denmark	30 Jul 51	108UNTS167	101472
Israel	WHO (World Health)	07 Aug 51	104UNTS213	101442
Israel	Philippines	07 Aug 51	192UNTS81	102596
Lebanon	UK Great Britain	15 Aug 51	160UNTS327	102116
WHO (World Health)	Saudi Arabia	29 Aug 51	110UNTS277	101516
Burma	Netherlands	06 Sep 51	108UNTS187	101473
Panama	UK Great Britain	15 Sep 51	560UNTS143	108172
Korea, South	WHO (World Health)	19 Sep 51	109UNTS297	200366
Canada	Italy	20 Sep 51	236UNTS251	103328
WHO (World Health)	Vietnam, South	21 Sep 51	107UNTS63	200352
Bolivia	United Nations	01 Oct 51	104UNTS263	101447
Philippines	Spain	06 Oct 51	215UNTS193	102920
Pakistan	WHO (World Health)	07 Oct 51	126UNTS101	101684
India	WHO (World Health)	11 Oct 51	118UNTS27	101594
Ecuador	WHO (World Health)	16 Oct 51	110UNTS263	101515
India	WHO (World Health)	16 Oct 51	109UNTS49	101490
Greece	Luxembourg	22 Oct 51	187UNTS119	102506
ILO (Labor Org)	Venezuela	22 Oct 51	117UNTS139	101590
Denmark	WHO (World Health)	05 Nov 51	110UNTS253	101514
Panama	WHO (World Health)	09 Nov 51	118UNTS43	101595
Panama	ILO (Labor Org)	10 Nov 51	126UNTS269	101693
Denmark	Iraq	18 Nov 51	232UNTS25	103227
India	UK Great Britain	01 Dec 51	128UNTS39	101712

PARTY ONE	PARTY TWO	DATE	CITATION	NUMBER
Arbitration (Cont.)				
Colombia	Spain	11 Dec 51	216UNTS73	102933
El Salvador	Guatemala	14 Dec 51	131UNTS131	101740
Guatemala	WHO (World Health)	17 Dec 51	120UNTS133	101619
India	WHO (World Health)	20 Dec 51	124UNTS109	101669
Multilateral		20 Dec 51	163UNTS293	102151
Italy	USA (United States)	28 Dec 51	157UNTS63	102047
Jordan	United Arab Rep	02 Jan 52	192UNTS157	102599
Austria	WHO (World Health)	10 Jan 52	131UNTS295	200438
Costa Rica	WHO (World Health)	23 Jan 52	135UNTS265	101826
Indonesia	United Nations	06 Feb 52	121UNTS3	101621
Austria	USA (United States)	16 Feb 52	177UNTS299	102329
Philippines	USA (United States)	19 Feb 52	177UNTS307	102330
India	Syria	25 Feb 52	163UNTS55	102141
Belgium	Spain	10 Mar 52	178UNTS243	102342
Pakistan	Switzerland	17 Mar 52	192UNTS237	102603
Finland	Norway	18 Mar 52	188UNTS187	102527
Sweden	Uruguay	20 Mar 52	311UNTS3	104497
Norway	Uruguay	20 Mar 52	310UNTS279	104496
Iraq	Switzerland	31 Mar 52	311UNTS43	104498
Norway	USA (United States)	01 Apr 52	177UNTS291	102328
India	WHO (World Health)	17 Apr 52	131UNTS241	101744
France	Mexico	17 Apr 52	163UNTS321	102153
India	WHO (World Health)	19 Apr 52	131UNTS253	101745
Greece	USA (United States)	23 Apr 52	177UNTS283	102327
France	Israel	29 Apr 52	189UNTS55	102542
Norway	WHO (World Health)	09 May 52	131UNTS281	101747
Multilateral		10 May 52	439UNTS233	106332
Multilateral		10 May 52	439UNTS217	106331
India	WHO (World Health)	04 Jun 52	135UNTS279	101827
Germany, West	USA (United States)	11 Jun 52	273UNTS105	103947
Australia	United Arab Rep	14 Jun 52	173UNTS241	102269
India	United Arab Rep	14 Jun 52	173UNTS209	102268
WHO (World Health)	Syria	20 Jun 52	165UNTS219	102178
Denmark	UK Great Britain	23 Jun 52	151UNTS3	101982
Taiwan	USA (United States)	25 Jun 52	136UNTS229	101837
Belgium	Israel	30 Jun 52	183UNTS263	102435
Multilateral		11 Jul 52	169UNTS3	102220
India	Philippines	11 Jul 52	203UNTS73	102741
Netherlands	Pakistan	17 Jul 52	150UNTS277	101980
Israel	USA (United States)	08 Aug 52	181UNTS37	102396
Japan	USA (United States)	11 Aug 52	212UNTS27	102862
USA (United States)	Yugoslavia	15 Aug 52	184UNTS97	102441
Ethiopia	Pakistan	29 Aug 52	150UNTS257	101979
Germany, West	Israel	10 Sep 52	162UNTS205	102137
Netherlands	Peru	22 Sep 52	255UNTS49	103604
Austria	Luxembourg	13 Oct 52	192UNTS291	102606
Mexico	Netherlands	13 Oct 52	163UNTS341	102154
Iceland	Luxembourg	23 Oct 52	193UNTS39	102609
Burma	UK Great Britain	25 Oct 52	150UNTS237	101978
Multilateral		25 Oct 52	241UNTS336	103442
Chile	Denmark	27 Oct 52	271UNTS93	103911
Chile	Sweden	27 Oct 52	311UNTS63	104499
Multilateral		07 Nov 52	221UNTS255	103010
India	Iraq	10 Nov 52	172UNTS103	102242
Belgium	UK Great Britain	12 Nov 52	180UNTS15	102372
Luxembourg	Norway	17 Nov 52	311UNTS95	104500
Luxembourg	Sweden	17 Nov 52	173UNTS277	102270
Israel	Switzerland	19 Nov 52	232UNTS3	103226
Japan	WHO (World Health)	26 Nov 52	204UNTS301	200521
ILO (Labor Org)	UN Relief Palestin	31 Dec 52	182UNTS201	200506
Japan	Netherlands	17 Feb 53	192UNTS215	102602
Japan	Sweden	20 Feb 53	173UNTS307	102272
Libya	UK Great Britain	21 Feb 53	311UNTS115	104501
Japan	Norway	23 Feb 53	192UNTS191	102601
Denmark	Japan	26 Feb 53	173UNTS329	102273

PARTY ONE	PARTY TWO	DATE	CITATION	NUMBER
Arbitration (Cont.)				
Multilateral		27 Feb 53	333UNTS3	104764
Germany, West	USA (United States)	27 Feb 53	223UNTS167	103065
Haiti	USA (United States)	13 Mar 53	212UNTS143	102866
France	Italy	14 Mar 53	284UNTS221	104140
Lebanon	Sweden	23 Mar 53	255UNTS83	103605
Philippines	Thailand	27 Apr 53	174UNTS3	102274
Cuba	USA (United States)	26 May 53	224UNTS75	103070
Switzerland	Yugoslavia	28 May 53	232UNTS45	103228
Japan	Thailand	19 Jun 53	174UNTS29	102276
Multilateral		24 Jul 53	250UNTS108	103520
Canada	Mexico	27 Jul 53	192UNTS255	102604
Libya	UK Great Britain	29 Jul 53	186UNTS201	102492
Spain	USA (United States)	26 Sep 53	207UNTS93	102802
Greece	UK Great Britain	05 Oct 53	243UNTS73	103447
Austria	Yugoslavia	11 Nov 53	363UNTS149	105206
Belgium	Lebanon	24 Dec 53	219UNTS153	102972
Ethiopia	Greece	20 Jan 54	222UNTS281	103035
Syria	UK Great Britain	30 Jan 54	449UNTS47	106452
France	Greece	08 Feb 54	225UNTS107	103093
France	Greece	08 Feb 54	225UNTS121	103094
Canada	Peru	18 Feb 54	411UNTS64	105915
Indonesia	Thailand	03 Mar 54	213UNTS297	102893
Lebanon	Switzerland	03 Mar 54	255UNTS127	103608
Japan	USA (United States)	08 Mar 54	232UNTS251	103240
Peru	Spain	31 Mar 54	232UNTS65	103230
Lebanon	Yugoslavia	17 Apr 54	602UNTS199	108713
Multilateral		12 May 54	327UNTS3	104714
Austria	Yugoslavia	25 May 54	227UNTS111	103135
Switzerland	Syria	26 May 54	255UNTS145	103609
Iran	Switzerland	27 May 54	496UNTS273	107257
Multilateral		04 Jun 54	282UNTS249	104101
Multilateral		04 Jun 54	276UNTS191	103992
Ireland	Luxembourg	27 Jul 54	232UNTS91	103231
Saudi Arabia	UK Great Britain	30 Jul 54	201UNTS317	102722
Thailand	USA (United States)	01 Sep 54	237UNTS209	103347
Libya	USA (United States)	09 Sep 54	224UNTS217	103078
Multilateral		23 Oct 54	332UNTS387	104763
Multilateral		23 Oct 54	331UNTS327	104759
Burma	Japan	05 Nov 54	251UNTS215	103543
Austria	Yugoslavia	27 Nov 54	396UNTS75	105694
Pakistan	United Arab Rep	13 Dec 54	255UNTS167	103610
Ecuador	Netherlands	14 Dec 54	232UNTS115	103233
Norway	Switzerland	30 Dec 54	311UNTS147	104502
Austria	Belgium	07 Jan 55	380UNTS219	105458
Canada	Japan	12 Jan 55	311UNTS167	104503
Philippines	UK Great Britain	31 Jan 55	216UNTS51	102932
United Arab Rep	Yugoslavia	20 Feb 55	255UNTS199	103611
Greece	UK Great Britain	24 Feb 55	209UNTS187	102827
Costa Rica	USA (United States)	26 Feb 55	252UNTS129	103562
Guatemala	USA (United States)	23 Mar 55	252UNTS143	103563
Iraq	United Arab Rep	23 Mar 55	311UNTS199	104504
Italy	Yugoslavia	26 Mar 55	379UNTS3	105432
Ecuador	USA (United States)	29 Mar 55	261UNTS343	103732
Multilateral		25 May 55	264UNTS117	103791
Pakistan	USA (United States)	26 May 55	257UNTS93	103652
Honduras	USA (United States)	10 Jun 55	258UNTS51	103669
Bulgaria	Yugoslavia	17 Jun 55	375UNTS287	105370
Syria	United Arab Rep	03 Jul 55	393UNTS67	105652
Germany, West	UK Great Britain	22 Jul 55	269UNTS189	103881
Belgium	Ireland	10 Sep 55	255UNTS235	103612
Italy	Switzerland	17 Sep 55	291UNTS213	104257
Bolivia	USA (United States)	23 Sep 55	256UNTS275	103637
France	Germany, West	04 Oct 55	353UNTS203	105044
Iceland	USA (United States)	05 Oct 55	256UNTS285	103638
Multilateral		12 Oct 55	560UNTS3	108165

PARTY ONE	PARTY TWO	DATE	CITATION	NUMBER
Arbitration (Cont.)				
Austria	USSR (Soviet Union)	17 Oct 55	240UNTS289	103409
Denmark	Syria	20 Oct 55	250UNTS61	103518
Denmark	Lebanon	21 Oct 55	248UNTS17	103482
Paraguay	USA (United States)	28 Oct 55	273UNTS97	103946
Pakistan	Turkey	02 Nov 55	311UNTS217	104505
Austria	Israel	17 Nov 55	232UNTS153	103235
India	Japan	26 Nov 55	311UNTS243	104506
Costa Rica	Guatemala	20 Dec 55	280UNTS121	104056
Austria	Italy	23 Jan 56	393UNTS97	105653
Argentina	Switzerland	25 Jan 56	559UNTS121	108157
Italy	Switzerland	02 Feb 56	291UNTS113	104247
India	USA (United States)	03 Feb 56	272UNTS75	103932
Netherlands	Sudan	12 Feb 56	311UNTS319	104508
Norway	Syria	25 Feb 56	463UNTS217	106706
Canada	USSR (Soviet Union)	29 Feb 56	252UNTS165	103566
Germany, West	Sweden	22 Mar 56	262UNTS361	103761
Belgium	Germany, West	14 Apr 56	344UNTS103	104945
Indonesia	United Nations	17 Apr 56	233UNTS267	103266
Multilateral		30 Apr 56	310UNTS229	104494
Germany, West	Switzerland	02 May 56	559UNTS157	108158
Brazil	France	04 May 56	323UNTS339	104675
Japan	Philippines	09 May 56	285UNTS3	104148
Multilateral		18 May 56	338UNTS103	104834
Multilateral		18 May 56	339UNTS3	104844
Multilateral		18 May 56	319UNTS21	104630
Multilateral		18 May 56	327UNTS123	104721
Multilateral		19 May 56	399UNTS189	105742
Japan	Switzerland	24 May 56	312UNTS3	104509
Greece	Italy	26 May 56	496UNTS301	107258
Italy	Switzerland	04 Jun 56	378UNTS311	105429
Germany, West	Ireland	12 Jun 56	353UNTS121	105040
Norway	Sweden	29 Jun 56	262UNTS335	103759
Germany, West	UK Great Britain	30 Jul 56	330UNTS233	104748
Guatemala	Honduras	22 Aug 56	263UNTS49	103767
Philippines	Switzerland	30 Aug 56	293UNTS43	104284
Jordan	USA (United States)	24 Sep 56	278UNTS51	104020
Germany, West	Netherlands	28 Sep 56	327UNTS185	104722
Switzerland	Thailand	13 Oct 56	312UNTS43	104510
Burma	Thailand	15 Oct 56	277UNTS87	104000
Colombia	USA (United States)	24 Oct 56	476UNTS77	106905
Belgium	Turkey	25 Oct 56	380UNTS3	105447
Austria	UK Great Britain	27 Oct 56	264UNTS67	103789
Peru	Switzerland	23 Nov 56	411UNTS97	105916
Luxembourg	USA (United States)	07 Dec 56	265UNTS255	103817
Multilateral		14 Dec 56	436UNTS115	106292
Multilateral		14 Dec 56	436UNTS131	106293
Mexico	ICAO (Civil Aviat)	20 Dec 56	497UNTS3	107259
Turkey	USA (United States)	15 Jan 57	280UNTS79	104053
Iceland	Thailand	22 Jan 57	312UNTS63	104511
Germany, West	Sweden	29 Jan 57	393UNTS113	105654
Denmark	Germany, West	29 Jan 57	302UNTS75	104354
Germany, West	Norway	29 Jan 57	353UNTS39	105037
Netherlands	Yugoslavia	13 Mar 57	327UNTS227	104723
Netherlands	USA (United States)	03 Apr 57	410UNTS193	105904
Denmark	Pakistan	10 Apr 57	302UNTS53	104353
Germany, West	Yugoslavia	10 Apr 57	463UNTS269	106708
Other Unilat Decla	United Arab Rep	24 Apr 57	265UNTS299	103821
Multilateral		29 Apr 57	320UNTS243	104646
Australia	Germany, West	22 May 57	357UNTS45	105105
Afghanistan	Pakistan	13 Jun 57	327UNTS51	104717
Finland	United Nations	27 Jun 57	271UNTS135	103913
Czechoslovakia	United Arab Rep	30 Jun 57	411UNTS126	105917
United Nations	Sweden	01 Jul 57	271UNTS187	103914
Norway	United Nations	09 Jul 57	271UNTS223	103917
Denmark	United Nations	16 Jul 57	274UNTS81	103959

PARTY ONE	PARTY TWO	DATE	CITATION	NUMBER
Arbitration (Cont.)				
Canada	United Nations	29 Jul 57	274UNTS47	103957
Greece	Italy	02 Aug 57	533UNTS217	107744
Brazil	United Nations	13 Aug 57	274UNTS199	103966
India	United Nations	14 Aug 57	274UNTS233	103968
Iran	USA (United States)	21 Sep 57	293UNTS287	104296
Germany, East	USSR (Soviet Union)	27 Sep 57	292UNTS75	104268
Multilateral		30 Sep 57	619UNTS77	108940
United Nations	Yugoslavia	01 Oct 57	277UNTS191	104006
Multilateral		03 Oct 57	366UNTS87	105216
Multilateral		03 Oct 57	364UNTS3	105211
Italy	Pakistan	05 Oct 57	353UNTS91	105039
Fed of Malaya	UK Great Britain	18 Oct 57	335UNTS3	104775
France	Morocco	25 Oct 57	559UNTS95	108156
USA (United States)	Vietnam, South	05 Nov 57	300UNTS23	104328
Japan	USSR (Soviet Union)	06 Dec 57	325UNTS35	104694
Italy	Yugoslavia	12 Dec 57	386UNTS293	105549
Multilateral		13 Dec 57	372UNTS159	105296
Canada	Switzerland	10 Jan 58	464UNTS21	106710
Multilateral		15 Jan 58	383UNTS229	105503
Indonesia	Japan	20 Jan 58	325UNTS13	104691
Indonesia	Japan	20 Jan 58	324UNTS247	104689
Multilateral		03 Feb 58	381UNTS165	105471
Australia	UK Great Britain	07 Feb 58	335UNTS23	104776
Afghanistan	Turkey	08 Feb 58	464UNTS39	106711
Albania	USSR (Soviet Union)	15 Feb 58	313UNTS261	104536
Sudan	Sweden	17 Feb 58	393UNTS161	105655
Norway	Pakistan	05 Mar 58	334UNTS199	104769
Pakistan	Sweden	06 Mar 58	393UNTS181	105656
Multilateral		20 Mar 58	335UNTS211	104789
Germany, West	Portugal	21 Mar 58	464UNTS71	106712
Morocco	Portugal	03 Apr 58	393UNTS203	105657
Belgium	Iran	14 Apr 58	381UNTS309	105473
Sweden	Yugoslavia	18 Apr 58	393UNTS225	105658
China People's Rep	USSR (Soviet Union)	23 Apr 58	313UNTS135	104534
Germany, West	USSR (Soviet Union)	25 Apr 58	346UNTS71	104978
Japan	Poland	26 Apr 58	340UNTS221	104866
Multilateral		10 Jun 58	454UNTS47	106539
Denmark	Luxembourg	10 Jun 58	356UNTS193	105096
Multilateral		10 Jun 58	330UNTS3	104739
Belgium	Pakistan	04 Jul 58	387UNTS305	105569
Ethiopia	UK Great Britain	07 Jul 58	331UNTS3	104749
Austria	Bulgaria	12 Sep 58	353UNTS3	105036
Ghana	UK Great Britain	24 Sep 58	411UNTS146	105918
Ghana	USA (United States)	30 Sep 58	336UNTS169	104805
Liberia	Netherlands	28 Nov 58	393UNTS55	105651
Burma	United Nations	15 Dec 58	319UNTS3	104629
United Nations	Tunisia	23 Dec 58	321UNTS23	104651
Finland	Switzerland	07 Jan 59	353UNTS173	105042
Multilateral		15 Jan 59	348UNTS13	104996
UK Great Britain	Yugoslavia	03 Feb 59	359UNTS339	105151
Ghana	United Nations	27 Feb 59	324UNTS133	104682
Sudan	USA (United States)	17 Mar 59	342UNTS13	104896
Tunisia	USA (United States)	18 Mar 59	344UNTS179	104948
IAEA (Atom Energy)	Thailand	18 Mar 59	339UNTS307	104850
Sweden	Tunisia	19 Mar 59	497UNTS43	107261
Norway	Tunisia	28 Mar 59	497UNTS77	107263
United Nations	Sudan	28 Mar 59	327UNTS95	104719
Morocco	UN Special Fund	04 Apr 59	354UNTS347	105069
Multilateral		08 Apr 59	389UNTS69	105593
Denmark	Tunisia	14 Apr 59	340UNTS273	104870
Nicaragua	USA (United States)	14 Apr 59	343UNTS119	104922
Fed of Malaya	USA (United States)	21 Apr 59	343UNTS3	104916
Denmark	Sudan	11 May 59	445UNTS105	106380
Ceylon (Sri Lanka)	Sweden	29 May 59	464UNTS109	106713
Ceylon (Sri Lanka)	Denmark	29 May 59	348UNTS225	105002

PARTY ONE	PARTY TWO	DATE	CITATION	NUMBER
Arbitration (Cont.)				
Greece	Yugoslavia	18 Jun 59	368UNTS69	105235
Greece	Yugoslavia	18 Jun 59	363UNTS133	105205
Belgium	Japan	20 Jun 59	411UNTS3	105911
Libya	United Nations	27 Jun 59	336UNTS291	104811
Laos	United Nations	06 Jul 59	337UNTS41	104814
India	Italy	16 Jul 59	464UNTS129	106714
Afghanistan	Germany, West	22 Jul 59	464UNTS177	106715
Finland	USA (United States)	22 Jul 59	354UNTS39	105051
Paraguay	United Nations	01 Aug 59	341UNTS319	104894
Germany, West	Iceland	12 Aug 59	411UNTS224	105921
Ghana	UN Special Fund	12 Aug 59	338UNTS203	104836
Canada	Germany, West	04 Sep 59	411UNTS260	105922
Australia	Fed of Malaya	29 Sep 59	357UNTS29	105104
Iran	UN Special Fund	06 Oct 59	342UNTS89	104902
Nicaragua	Peru	14 Oct 59	392UNTS303	105649
Guinea	United Nations	15 Oct 59	344UNTS47	104942
Poland	UN Special Fund	15 Oct 59	344UNTS29	104941
India	UN Special Fund	20 Oct 59	344UNTS143	104946
UN Special Fund	Yugoslavia	27 Oct 59	344UNTS159	104947
Korea, South	United Nations	06 Nov 59	346UNTS289	200565
Ecuador	UN Special Fund	10 Nov 59	345UNTS3	104955
Ethiopia	France	12 Nov 59	381UNTS3	105465
Greece	UN Special Fund	13 Nov 59	345UNTS171	104966
UN Special Fund	Turkey	20 Nov 59	345UNTS105	104963
Afghanistan	United Nations	24 Nov 59	397UNTS187	105705
Germany, West	Pakistan	25 Nov 59	457UNTS22	106575
France	USA (United States)	25 Nov 59	401UNTS75	105764
UN Special Fund	United Arab Rep	25 Nov 59	345UNTS125	104964
Israel	UN Special Fund	01 Dec 59	345UNTS197	104968
Guinea	UN Special Fund	02 Dec 59	345UNTS215	104969
Argentina	UN Special Fund	04 Dec 59	345UNTS263	104972
Liberia	Sweden	09 Dec 59	464UNTS219	106716
Norway	USSR (Soviet Union)	09 Dec 59	361UNTS93	105173
Czechoslovakia	Japan	15 Dec 59	383UNTS277	105505
Jordan	UN Special Fund	15 Dec 59	346UNTS3	104974
Argentina	USA (United States)	22 Dec 59	411UNTS42	105912
UN Special Fund	UK Great Britain	07 Jan 60	348UNTS177	105000
Czechoslovakia	UK Great Britain	15 Jan 60	374UNTS207	105336
Peru	UN Special Fund	19 Jan 60	349UNTS83	105010
Chile	UN Special Fund	22 Jan 60	351UNTS115	105020
Austria	Czechoslovakia	23 Jan 60	495UNTS125	107242
Multilateral		26 Jan 60	439UNTS249	106333
El Salvador	USA (United States)	29 Jan 60	372UNTS3	105283
Colombia	UN Special Fund	04 Feb 60	355UNTS257	105080
Bolivia	UN Special Fund	09 Feb 60	351UNTS203	105024
Germany, West	United Arab Rep	16 Feb 60	464UNTS233	106717
Korea, South	USA (United States)	19 Feb 60	372UNTS109	105291
Afghanistan	UN Special Fund	21 Feb 60	351UNTS93	105019
Pakistan	UN Special Fund	25 Feb 60	351UNTS141	105021
Multilateral		26 Feb 60	418UNTS171	106022
Australia	Thailand	26 Feb 60	392UNTS255	105647
France	Thailand	26 Feb 60	392UNTS279	105648
Guinea	Netherlands	09 Mar 60	392UNTS243	105646
Finland	Iceland	10 Mar 60	497UNTS95	107264
France	UN Special Fund	17 Mar 60	354UNTS119	105059
Belgium	Switzerland	24 Mar 60	416UNTS81	105996
Italy	UN Special Fund	01 Apr 60	354UNTS261	105066
Germany, West	Netherlands	08 Apr 60	508UNTS14	107404
Luxembourg	Yugoslavia	09 Apr 60	464UNTS293	106719
UN Special Fund	Tunisia	12 Apr 60	355UNTS289	105082
Libya	UN Special Fund	19 Apr 60	356UNTS11	105090
UN Special Fund	Sudan	21 Apr 60	356UNTS213	105097
Germany, West	Spain	28 Apr 60	465UNTS3	106720
UN Special Fund	Vietnam, South	29 Apr 60	357UNTS311	200567
Laos	UN Special Fund	30 Apr 60	361UNTS171	105179

PARTY ONE	PARTY TWO	DATE	CITATION	NUMBER
Arbitration (Cont.)				
United Nations	Togo	06 May 60	388UNTS53	105571
Lebanon	UN Special Fund	07 May 60	360UNTS225	105160
Nepal	USA (United States)	17 May 60	372UNTS313	105307
Morocco	United Arab Rep	19 May 60	563UNTS121	108208
Switzerland	Tunisia	21 May 60	497UNTS109	107265
Kuwait	UK Great Britain	24 May 60	412UNTS4	105923
Iraq	UN Special Fund	19 Jun 60	376UNTS357	105389
Korea, North	USSR (Soviet Union)	22 Jun 60	399UNTS3	105732
Denmark	Peru	22 Jun 60	439UNTS113	106326
Ireland	Portugal	24 Jun 60	412UNTS30	105924
IAEA (Atom Energy)	USA (United States)	28 Jun 60	374UNTS133	105333
Kuwait	UN Special Fund	29 Jun 60	369UNTS419	200575
Ethiopia	UN Special Fund	13 Jul 60	368UNTS159	105240
Ethiopia	United Nations	13 Jul 60	368UNTS143	105239
Switzerland	United Arab Rep	14 Jul 60	497UNTS161	107268
Germany, West	Pakistan	20 Jul 60	465UNTS41	106721
Chile	USA (United States)	29 Jul 60	405UNTS127	105829
Ghana	Netherlands	30 Jul 60	412UNTS51	105925
Guatemala	USA (United States)	09 Aug 60	461UNTS15	106648
Mexico	USA (United States)	15 Aug 60	402UNTS177	105786
Multilateral		16 Aug 60	382UNTS3	105475
Belgium	Burma	17 Aug 60	540UNTS185	107850
Ghana	United Arab Rep	29 Aug 60	412UNTS71	105926
Liberia	USA (United States)	06 Sep 60	389UNTS245	105596
Brazil	UN Special Fund	16 Sep 60	375UNTS3	105351
Pakistan	IBRD (World Bank)	19 Sep 60	444UNTS207	106370
Multilateral		19 Sep 60	444UNTS259	106371
Taiwan	UN Special Fund	20 Sep 60	375UNTS29	105352
Indonesia	UN Special Fund	07 Oct 60	378UNTS141	105424
Liberia	UN Special Fund	11 Oct 60	376UNTS341	105388
Belgium	Jordan	19 Oct 60	479UNTS277	106959
El Salvador	UN Special Fund	24 Oct 60	377UNTS171	105400
Burma	Switzerland	31 Oct 60	465UNTS97	106723
Kuwait	United Nations	31 Oct 60	391UNTS295	200581
Norway	Peru	02 Nov 60	497UNTS207	107270
Australia	Italy	10 Nov 60	497UNTS247	107271
Belgium	Congo (Zaire)	15 Nov 60	394UNTS79	105670
Nepal	UN Special Fund	17 Nov 60	380UNTS289	105461
Guatemala	UN Special Fund	17 Nov 60	383UNTS67	105495
Pakistan	United Nations	17 Nov 60	380UNTS277	105460
Indonesia	UK Great Britain	23 Nov 60	398UNTS71	105718
Cambodia	UN Special Fund	24 Nov 60	382UNTS255	105487
Cambodia	United Nations	30 Nov 60	383UNTS147	105500
Multilateral		09 Dec 60	429UNTS211	106200
Multilateral		13 Dec 60	455UNTS204	106544
Multilateral		13 Dec 60	455UNTS3	106543
Multilateral		13 Dec 60	523UNTS117	107557
Bolivia	United Nations	14 Dec 60	382UNTS283	105489
Japan	Pakistan	18 Dec 60	423UNTS197	106093
Honduras	UN Special Fund	20 Dec 60	383UNTS103	105497
Canada	Pakistan	21 Dec 60	465UNTS115	106724
Luxembourg	Thailand	29 Dec 60	465UNTS131	106725
Burma	UN Special Fund	03 Jan 61	387UNTS219	105564
Jordan	Sweden	09 Jan 61	465UNTS155	106726
Costa Rica	UN Special Fund	10 Jan 61	389UNTS253	105597
Sudan	UK Great Britain	16 Jan 61	424UNTS233	106112
Canada	USA (United States)	17 Jan 61	542UNTS224	107894
Germany, West	Japan	18 Jan 61	465UNTS173	106727
UN Special Fund	Saudi Arabia	19 Jan 61	396UNTS27	105692
Nicaragua	UN Special Fund	20 Jan 61	387UNTS15	105555
Chad	UN Special Fund	23 Jan 61	390UNTS69	105603
Panama	USA (United States)	23 Jan 61	445UNTS135	106382
Multilateral		23 Jan 61	530UNTS141	107679
UN Special Fund	Somalia	28 Jan 61	388UNTS75	105573
Gabon	UN Special Fund	02 Feb 61	387UNTS289	105568

PARTY ONE	PARTY TWO	DATE	CITATION	NUMBER
Arbitration (Cont.)				
Nigeria	UN Special Fund	10 Feb 61	390UNTS85	105604
Mexico	UN Special Fund	23 Feb 61	388UNTS151	105576
Cyprus	UN Special Fund	24 Feb 61	389UNTS3	105588
Austria	United Nations	27 Feb 61	394UNTS27	105666
Iraq	United Nations	05 Mar 61	409UNTS56	105878
Multilateral		08 Mar 61	396UNTS255	200584
Panama	UN Special Fund	09 Mar 61	396UNTS3	105691
Cuba	UN Special Fund	10 Mar 61	390UNTS35	105601
Morocco	USA (United States)	31 Mar 61	406UNTS249	105854
Multilateral		10 Apr 61	402UNTS281	105791
Multilateral		21 Apr 61	484UNTS349	107041
Korea, South	UN Special Fund	21 Apr 61	394UNTS231	200583
Ceylon (Sri Lanka)	UN Special Fund	03 May 61	395UNTS217	105687
Japan	Peru	15 May 61	451UNTS3	106482
Sierra Leone	USA (United States)	19 May 61	409UNTS251	105890
Czechoslovakia	Morocco	08 Jun 61	497UNTS275	107272
Cameroon	UN Special Fund	13 Jun 61	397UNTS297	105713
New Zealand	UK Great Britain	13 Jun 61	497UNTS293	107273
Cyprus	United Nations	15 Jun 61	398UNTS39	105716
Cameroon	France	16 Jun 61	412UNTS148	105929
Guinea	Sweden	17 Jun 61	465UNTS236	106729
Paraguay	UN Special Fund	22 Jun 61	399UNTS117	105738
UN Special Fund	Upper Volta	26 Jun 61	400UNTS3	105744
Haiti	UN Special Fund	28 Jun 61	399UNTS171	105741
Haiti	United Nations	28 Jun 61	399UNTS159	105740
Philippines	UN Special Fund	28 Jun 61	399UNTS141	105739
Mali	UN Special Fund	21 Jul 61	401UNTS141	105768
Fed of Malaya	UN Special Fund	25 Jul 61	401UNTS159	105769
Australia	New Zealand	25 Jul 61	523UNTS271	107561
Czechoslovakia	Ghana	02 Aug 61	465UNTS249	106730
UN Special Fund	Yemen	02 Aug 61	402UNTS43	105777
Finland	Luxembourg	15 Aug 61	541UNTS45	107859
Jordan	Norway	21 Aug 61	465UNTS275	106731
Jordan	Netherlands	24 Aug 61	466UNTS3	106733
Mexico	Netherlands	24 Aug 61	465UNTS291	106732
Lebanon	United Nations	26 Aug 61	406UNTS105	105842
Ivory Coast	UN Special Fund	29 Aug 61	406UNTS129	105844
Liberia	Switzerland	31 Aug 61	559UNTS215	108160
Jordan	United Nations	11 Sep 61	406UNTS255	105855
Multilateral		18 Sep 61	500UNTS31	107305
Ghana	Romania	30 Sep 61	467UNTS443	106769
UN Special Fund	Sierra Leone	02 Oct 61	422UNTS131	106073
IBRD (World Bank)	Switzerland	11 Oct 61	415UNTS396	200592
Germany, West	Morocco	12 Oct 61	523UNTS289	107562
Japan	Pakistan	17 Oct 61	466UNTS17	106734
Mauritania	UN Special Fund	07 Nov 61	412UNTS240	105936
Congo (Brazzaville)	UN Special Fund	09 Nov 61	413UNTS58	105940
Cyprus	Greece	23 Nov 61	497UNTS311	107274
Congo (Zaire)	United Nations	27 Nov 61	414UNTS229	105975
Ivory Coast	USA (United States)	01 Dec 61	462UNTS221	106681
Ceylon (Sri Lanka)	United Nations	04 Dec 61	415UNTS236	105987
Denmark	Jordan	07 Dec 61	631UNTS333	109003
UN Special Fund	Venezuela	11 Dec 61	422UNTS149	106074
Germany, West	Thailand	13 Dec 61	541UNTS181	107870
UN Special Fund	Senegal	16 Dec 61	425UNTS97	106121
Czechoslovakia	Guinea	16 Dec 61	559UNTS49	108154
Malagasy	UN Special Fund	05 Jan 62	419UNTS29	106028
Netherlands	Sweden	08 Jan 62	466UNTS65	106737
Austria	Greece	15 Jan 62	498UNTS3	107275
United Nations	Somalia	20 Jan 62	420UNTS133	106044
Indonesia	Japan	23 Jan 62	559UNTS77	108155
Italy	Japan	31 Jan 62	498UNTS23	107276
Niger	UN Special Fund	26 Feb 62	423UNTS83	106086
Germany, West	Thailand	05 Mar 62	563UNTS165	108210
United Nations	Saudi Arabia	16 Mar 62	456UNTS379	106566

PARTY ONE	PARTY TWO	DATE	CITATION	NUMBER
Arbitration (Cont.)				
Togo	USA (United States)	20 Mar 62	445UNTS79	106378
Luxembourg	Spain	26 Mar 62	563UNTS205	108211
Dahomey	UN Special Fund	28 Mar 62	424UNTS55	106099
Multilateral		29 Mar 62	507UNTS177	107401
France	Luxembourg	29 Mar 62	563UNTS227	108212
IAEA (Atom Energy)	USA (United States)	30 Mar 62	442UNTS49	106338
Sierra Leone	UK Great Britain	05 Apr 62	434UNTS227	106265
Niger	USA (United States)	26 Apr 62	459UNTS129	106618
Dominican Republic	USA (United States)	02 May 62	442UNTS99	106341
UN Special Fund	Uruguay	04 May 62	429UNTS143	106196
Japan	United Arab Rep	10 May 62	498UNTS69	107278
Greece	United Nations	18 May 62	429UNTS61	106190
United Nations	Tanganyika	01 Jun 62	479UNTS3	106944
Dominican Republic	UN Special Fund	06 Jun 62	429UNTS169	106197
France	Senegal	15 Jun 62	524UNTS3	107563
Czechoslovakia	Senegal	20 Jun 62	498UNTS145	107280
Guinea	Norway	21 Jun 62	466UNTS81	106738
Congo (Zaire)	IAEA (Atom Energy)	27 Jun 62	463UNTS31	106691
Multilateral		27 Jun 62	463UNTS17	106690
Liberia	Norway	29 Jun 62	466UNTS95	106739
Algeria	France	03 Jul 62	507UNTS25	107395
Morocco	Switzerland	05 Jul 62	498UNTS171	107281
Morocco	Switzerland	05 Jul 62	498UNTS189	107282
UN Special Fund	Syria	07 Jul 62	443UNTS3	106355
UN Special Fund	Tanganyika	17 Jul 62	435UNTS237	106281
Ethiopia	USA (United States)	03 Aug 62	459UNTS79	106613
Nigeria	United Nations	07 Aug 62	435UNTS167	106278
IAEA (Atom Energy)	USA (United States)	20 Aug 62	456UNTS447	106570
Cameroon	United Nations	29 Aug 62	442UNTS3	106334
Congo (Brazzaville)	USA (United States)	01 Sep 62	459UNTS117	106616
Multilateral		14 Sep 62	494UNTS219	107236
Ecuador	Germany, West	20 Sep 62	498UNTS199	107283
Belgium	Germany, West	21 Sep 62	502UNTS63	107326
Austria	Czechoslovakia	22 Sep 62	495UNTS157	107244
Niger	United Nations	01 Oct 62	439UNTS181	106329
Japan	Kuwait	06 Oct 62	498UNTS235	107284
Finland	France	12 Oct 62	498UNTS299	107285
Belgium	Rwanda	13 Oct 62	456UNTS425	106568
Netherlands	Norway	18 Oct 62	466UNTS145	106741
France	Ivory Coast	19 Oct 62	498UNTS317	107286
Japan	UN Special Fund	31 Oct 62	444UNTS171	106368
United Nations	Western Samoa	05 Nov 62	443UNTS297	200599
Japan	UK Great Britain	14 Nov 62	478UNTS29	106934
Algeria	UN Special Fund	15 Nov 62	452UNTS243	106512
United Nations	Syria	17 Nov 62	456UNTS359	106565
Ivory Coast	Switzerland	17 Nov 62	499UNTS3	107289
Congo (Zaire)	USA (United States)	17 Nov 62	474UNTS41	106870
Ecuador	United Nations	26 Nov 62	445UNTS3	106372
Rwanda	United Nations	28 Nov 62	450UNTS267	106473
Ivory Coast	United Nations	10 Dec 62	451UNTS269	106498
Austria	Yugoslavia	11 Dec 62	546UNTS3	107938
Nigeria	USA (United States)	24 Dec 62	462UNTS180	106677
Burundi	United Nations	29 Dec 62	450UNTS279	106474
Jamaica	USA (United States)	04 Jan 63	471UNTS119	106826
Israel	United Nations	07 Jan 63	450UNTS229	106470
Ghana	Mali	09 Jan 63	466UNTS165	106742
Trinidad/Tobago	USA (United States)	15 Jan 63	471UNTS141	106829
Senegal	Switzerland	23 Jan 63	524UNTS23	107564
Guinea	Switzerland	01 Feb 63	499UNTS35	107291
Mali	Senegal	07 Feb 63	524UNTS41	107565
Algeria	France	18 Feb 63	563UNTS263	108214
Sudan	Switzerland	18 Feb 63	563UNTS281	108215
Austria	Czechoslovakia	08 Mar 63	495UNTS219	107245
UN Special Fund	Uganda	22 Mar 63	456UNTS466	106572
Burma	Japan	29 Mar 63	518UNTS3	107490

PARTY ONE	PARTY TWO	DATE	CITATION	NUMBER
Arbitration (Cont.)				
Gabon	USA (United States)	10 Apr 63	474UNTS113	106876
Cyprus	Denmark	27 Apr 63	529UNTS255	107664
Algeria	Morocco	30 Apr 63	564UNTS3	108217
United Nations	Trinidad/Tobago	06 May 63	463UNTS109	106696
Mali	United Nations	09 May 63	463UNTS147	106699
Australia	USA (United States)	09 May 63	469UNTS55	106784
Belgium	Netherlands	13 May 63	540UNTS3	107843
Jamaica	UN Special Fund	22 May 63	489UNTS191	107140
Jamaica	United Nations	22 May 63	479UNTS19	106945
Netherlands	Tunisia	23 May 63	523UNTS237	107558
Netherlands	UN Special Fund	24 May 63	466UNTS289	106750
Multilateral		25 May 63	479UNTS39	106947
United Nations	Uganda	29 May 63	466UNTS311	106751
Cyprus	USA (United States)	29 May 63	487UNTS283	107110
UN Special Fund	Western Samoa	05 Jun 63	467UNTS463	200601
Belgium	Cyprus	08 Jun 63	601UNTS311	108703
Multilateral		09 Jun 63	538UNTS309	107818
Austria	IAEA (Atom Energy)	21 Jun 63	490UNTS351	107164
Guinea	Ivory Coast	26 Jun 63	499UNTS71	107293
United Nations	UK Great Britain	27 Jun 63	469UNTS145	106789
New Zealand	UN Special Fund	28 Jun 63	470UNTS3	106792
United Arab Rep	USA (United States)	29 Jun 63	479UNTS207	106954
Finland	IAEA (Atom Energy)	02 Jul 63	490UNTS403	107167
IBRD (World Bank)	Tunisia	03 Jul 63	480UNTS209	106970
Austria	France	12 Jul 63	499UNTS91	107294
Algeria	Mali	22 Jul 63	564UNTS29	108219
Mali	Tunisia	24 Jul 63	602UNTS91	108708
Malagasy	USA (United States)	26 Jul 63	487UNTS189	107104
Congo (Zaire)	UN Special Fund	26 Jul 63	474UNTS137	106878
Cameroon	UK Great Britain	29 Jul 63	478UNTS148	106935
Dominican Republic	United Nations	05 Aug 63	472UNTS353	106847
Cameroon	Israel	09 Aug 63	499UNTS121	107295
Burundi	UN Special Fund	22 Aug 63	476UNTS49	106903
United Nations	United Arab Rep	27 Aug 63	474UNTS221	106884
Burundi	WHO (World Health)	30 Aug 63	490UNTS423	107169
Algeria	Tunisia	01 Sep 63	601UNTS275	108701
Ivory Coast	Netherlands	09 Oct 63	499UNTS141	107296
Italy	IAEA (Atom Energy)	11 Oct 63	639UNTS25	109142
Multilateral		17 Oct 63	525UNTS75	107585
Multilateral		26 Oct 63	587UNTS9	108506
Central Afri Rep	UN Special Fund	30 Oct 63	481UNTS247	106985
Tanganyika	USA (United States)	14 Nov 63	493UNTS75	107208
Romania	Yugoslavia	30 Nov 63	512UNTS2	107438
Nicaragua	United Nations	03 Dec 63	482UNTS329	107002
Czechoslovakia	Romania	16 Dec 63	527UNTS285	107630
Multilateral		18 Dec 63	490UNTS383	107166
France	South Africa	06 Jan 64	601UNTS229	108699
Somalia	USA (United States)	08 Jan 64	505UNTS165	107372
Mali	Niger	15 Jan 64	499UNTS197	107299
Lebanon	Pakistan	04 Feb 64	614UNTS55	108863
Argentina	Paraguay	07 Feb 64	634UNTS127	109057
Denmark	Yugoslavia	11 Feb 64	511UNTS241	107437
United Nations	Sierra Leone	19 Feb 64	489UNTS91	107136
United Nations	Upper Volta	26 Feb 64	489UNTS179	107139
Morocco	United Nations	03 Mar 64	490UNTS187	107154
Multilateral		09 Mar 64	581UNTS57	108432
Cameroon	Mali	17 Mar 64	524UNTS61	107566
Malaysia	Netherlands	07 Apr 64	524UNTS81	107567
Portugal	UK Great Britain	07 Apr 64	539UNTS167	107830
Norway	Yugoslavia	15 Apr 64	602UNTS177	108712
Kenya	USA (United States)	20 Apr 64	524UNTS165	107571
United Arab Rep	USA (United States)	05 May 64	531UNTS229	107706
Multilateral		06 May 64	514UNTS71	107442
Cyprus	Hungary	02 Jun 64	602UNTS3	108704
Ireland	UN Special Fund	03 Jun 64	496UNTS205	107253

PARTY ONE	PARTY TWO	DATE	CITATION	NUMBER
Arbitration (Cont.)				
Mali	USA (United States)	09 Jun 64	530UNTS133	107678
Multilateral		11 Jun 64	525UNTS61	107584
IAEA (Atom Energy)	USA (United States)	15 Jun 64	525UNTS3	107580
Multilateral		20 Jun 64	539UNTS3	107819
New Zealand	USA (United States)	24 Jun 64	524UNTS101	107568
Mauritania	USA (United States)	03 Jul 64	532UNTS307	107724
Ivory Coast	Mali	09 Jul 64	524UNTS121	107569
Belgium	Tunisia	15 Jul 64	561UNTS297	108190
Multilateral		28 Jul 64	555UNTS183	108113
Eur Space Research	Sweden	29 Jul 64	528UNTS81	107636
France	Eur Space Research	10 Aug 64	528UNTS135	107637
IAEA (Atom Energy)	United Arab Rep	17 Sep 64	525UNTS19	107581
Multilateral		18 Sep 64	556UNTS25	108117
Multilateral		18 Sep 64	555UNTS205	108114
Multilateral		21 Sep 64	555UNTS227	108115
Algeria	United Nations	23 Sep 64	510UNTS217	107416
Multilateral		30 Sep 64	556UNTS3	108116
Kenya	United Nations	01 Oct 64	511UNTS199	107434
Malawi	UN Special Fund	24 Oct 64	514UNTS235	200609
Multilateral		01 Dec 64	550UNTS133	108012
Argentina	IAEA (Atom Energy)	02 Dec 64	525UNTS29	107582
Multilateral		02 Dec 64	572UNTS229	108317
Cyprus	Syria	22 Dec 64	602UNTS25	108705
Laos	USA (United States)	29 Dec 64	542UNTS23	107876
Central Afri Rep	USA (United States)	31 Dec 64	542UNTS29	107877
Argentina	UK Great Britain	12 Jan 65	597UNTS177	108645
IAEA (Atom Energy)	United Arab Rep	14 Jan 65	603UNTS45	108723
Malta	Switzerland	20 Jan 65	548UNTS193	107978
Ethiopia	WHO (World Health)	27 Jan 65	541UNTS135	107866
Belgium	Congo (Zaire)	06 Feb 65	540UNTS227	107852
Multilateral		23 Feb 65	527UNTS120	107622
Multilateral		24 Feb 65	556UNTS47	108118
Multilateral		26 Feb 65	556UNTS69	108119
Multilateral		05 Mar 65	527UNTS221	107627
Dahomey	USA (United States)	13 Mar 65	549UNTS43	107987
Multilateral		18 Mar 65	575UNTS159	108359
Finland	UK Great Britain	25 Mar 65	539UNTS103	107826
Denmark	Malaysia	26 Mar 65	540UNTS205	107851
Hungary	Yugoslavia	08 Apr 65	587UNTS169	108511
Multilateral		08 Apr 65	533UNTS66	107733
Australia	France	13 Apr 65	601UNTS293	108702
Ivory Coast	Netherlands	26 Apr 65	634UNTS81	109053
Multilateral		26 Apr 65	533UNTS50	107732
Bel-Lux Econ Union	Morocco	28 Apr 65	620UNTS171	108954
Ghana	Malawi	04 May 65	541UNTS163	107869
Denmark	Spain	05 May 65	543UNTS255	107905
Mauritania	Spain	11 May 65	602UNTS111	108709
Chad	USA (United States)	12 May 65	546UNTS183	107944
Multilateral		12 May 65	534UNTS390	107769
Multilateral		25 May 65	535UNTS374	107791
Malaysia	Norway	26 May 65	602UNTS157	108711
Uganda	USA (United States)	29 May 65	546UNTS209	107948
Multilateral		02 Jun 65	551UNTS2	108030
Netherlands	Senegal	12 Jun 65	602UNTS231	108715
USA (United States)	Upper Volta	18 Jun 65	549UNTS133	107996
Japan	Korea, South	22 Jun 65	583UNTS173	108473
Japan	Korea, South	22 Jun 65	583UNTS51	108472
Austria	Petrol Export Org	24 Jun 65	589UNTS135	108540
UN Special Fund	Spain	30 Jun 65	544UNTS159	107918
Multilateral		05 Jul 65	563UNTS104	108207
Switzerland	UK Great Britain	07 Jul 65	605UNTS205	108765
Australia	Eur Space Vehicle	13 Jul 65	543UNTS183	107902
Multilateral		20 Jul 65	541UNTS12	107857
France	Mauritania	22 Jul 65	0UNTS0	109329
Multilateral		13 Sep 65	547UNTS248	107961

PARTY ONE	PARTY TWO	DATE	CITATION	NUMBER
Arbitration (Cont.)				
Multilateral		21 Sep 65	547UNTS280	107963
Netherlands	UK Great Britain	06 Oct 65	595UNTS105	108615
Nigeria	Switzerland	11 Oct 65	602UNTS137	108710
Multilateral		12 Nov 65	550UNTS160	108013
Austria	Yugoslavia	19 Nov 65	591UNTS3	108556
Multilateral		04 Dec 65	571UNTS123	108303
Multilateral		08 Dec 65	600UNTS161	108680
Multilateral		16 Dec 65	570UNTS201	108295
Japan	USSR (Soviet Union)	21 Jan 66	633UNTS165	109038
Mongolia	UN Special Fund	26 Jan 66	552UNTS201	108055
Austria	Germany, West	17 Feb 66	614UNTS263	108875
Austria	Germany, West	17 Feb 66	615UNTS3	108876
Ceylon (Sri Lanka)	USA (United States)	23 Feb 66	586UNTS91	108498
Austria	United Nations	24 Feb 66	557UNTS129	108131
Australia	United Nations	25 Feb 66	557UNTS85	108129
Pakistan	IAEA (Atom Energy)	15 Mar 66	588UNTS261	108530
Singapore	USSR (Soviet Union)	02 Apr 66	631UNTS125	108992
Romania	IAEA (Atom Energy)	22 Apr 66	603UNTS23	108721
Multilateral		30 Apr 66	620UNTS191	108956
Multilateral		04 May 66	575UNTS49	108354
Multilateral		12 May 66	563UNTS54	108204
Bulgaria	UN Special Fund	26 May 66	563UNTS71	108205
IAEA (Atom Energy)	UK Great Britain	20 Jun 66	588UNTS269	108531
Multilateral		20 Jun 66	572UNTS263	108318
Euratom	UK Great Britain	11 Jul 66	639UNTS99	109147
Multilateral		28 Sep 66	589UNTS41	108534
India	IAEA (Atom Energy)	09 Dec 66	603UNTS35	108722
Denmark	Singapore	20 Dec 66	593UNTS125	108580
Asian Devel Bank	Philippines	22 Dec 66	615UNTS375	108887
Multilateral		27 Feb 67	590UNTS156	108552
Austria	Yugoslavia	08 Apr 67	0UNTS0	109216
Multilateral		13 Apr 67	595UNTS60	108612
Multilateral		19 Apr 67	595UNTS120	108617
Hungary	UN Special Fund	28 Apr 67	595UNTS171	108619
IAEA (Atom Energy)	USA (United States)	07 Jun 67	614UNTS109	108866
Multilateral		10 Jun 67	602UNTS212	108714
Denmark	Netherlands	20 Jun 67	619UNTS67	108939
Multilateral		21 Jun 67	598UNTS2	108653
Multilateral		23 Jun 67	614UNTS185	108871
Malta	UK Great Britain	10 Jul 67	619UNTS11	108936
Czechoslovakia	UN Special Fund	13 Jul 67	606UNTS71	108776
Multilateral		26 Jul 67	614UNTS217	108872
Singapore	UK Great Britain	01 Aug 67	619UNTS29	108937
Mexico	IAEA (Atom Energy)	18 Aug 67	614UNTS123	108867
Multilateral		23 Aug 67	614UNTS145	108869
Iraq	IAEA (Atom Energy)	21 Sep 67	630UNTS41	108963
Ecuador	Romania	10 Oct 67	642UNTS33	109163
Burma	IAEA (Atom Energy)	11 Oct 67	630UNTS49	108964
Botswana	UN Special Fund	12 Oct 67	607UNTS37	108794
Multilateral		12 Oct 67	607UNTS2	108792
Denmark	Iran	02 Nov 67	638UNTS217	109138
Multilateral		14 Nov 67	614UNTS2	108860
Eur Space Research	UK Great Britain	24 Nov 67	638UNTS17	109129
Denmark	Malaysia	14 Dec 67	614UNTS26	108862
Iran	United Nations	15 Feb 68	631UNTS103	108990
Denmark	Malawi	16 Dec 68	0UNTS0	109461
UN Special Fund	Southern Yemen	04 Apr 69	0UNTS0	109456
State/IGO Group	Southern Yemen	04 Apr 69	0UNTS0	109454
State/IGO Group	Southern Yemen	04 Apr 69	0UNTS0	109455
State/IGO Group	Yemen	23 Apr 69	0UNTS0	109514
Mediation and good offices				
Multilateral		22 Mar 45	70UNTS237	200241
Multilateral		13 Feb 46	1UNTS15	100004
Multilateral		30 Apr 48	30UNTS55	100449

PARTY ONE	PARTY TWO	DATE	CITATION	NUMBER
Mediation and good offices (Cont.)				
Czechoslovakia	Poland	12 Nov 48	84UNTS347	101141
WHO (World Health)	United Arab Rep	25 Aug 50	92UNTS39	101259
Greece	Philippines	28 Aug 50	225UNTS155	103097
India	Philippines	11 Jul 52	203UNTS73	102741
USA (United States)	Yugoslavia	15 Aug 52	184UNTS97	102441
Indonesia	Thailand	03 Mar 54	213UNTS297	102893
Brazil	France	04 May 56	323UNTS339	104675
Philippines	Switzerland	30 Aug 56	293UNTS43	104284
Japan	Laos	15 Oct 58	341UNTS25	104875
Germany, West	UK Great Britain	03 Aug 59	502UNTS197	107331
Argentina	Philippines	12 Feb 60	535UNTS293	107785
Multilateral		01 Dec 64	550UNTS133	108012
Japan	Korea, South	22 Jun 65	584UNTS147	108476
Procedure				
Netherlands	USA (United States)	17 Jan 33	474UNTS119	106877
Canada	France	12 May 33	253UNTS285	200545
Brazil	France	27 Jan 40	72UNTS77	100929
Norway	USA (United States)	28 Mar 40	88UNTS365	200253
Brazil	Venezuela	30 Mar 40	51UNTS291	200195
Multilateral		30 Jul 40	161UNTS253	200488
Multilateral		28 Nov 40	139UNTS159	200452
Argentina	USA (United States)	14 Oct 41	119UNTS193	200384
Brazil	Canada	17 Oct 41	67UNTS263	200224
Mexico	USA (United States)	19 Nov 41	125UNTS287	200430
Saudi Arabia	UK Great Britain	20 Apr 42	10UNTS117	200057
Peru	USA (United States)	07 May 42	103UNTS219	200316
Mexico	USA (United States)	23 Dec 42	13UNTS231	200081
Iran	USA (United States)	08 Apr 43	106UNTS155	200340
Iceland	USA (United States)	27 Sep 43	29UNTS317	200170
Mexico	USA (United States)	03 Feb 44	3UNTS313	200025
Multilateral		07 Dec 44	171UNTS345	200501
Multilateral		07 Dec 44	171UNTS387	200502
Multilateral		07 Dec 44	84UNTS389	200252
Multilateral		22 Mar 45	70UNTS237	200241
South Africa	UK Great Britain	26 Oct 45	72UNTS41	100927
Belgium	France	30 Oct 45	19UNTS87	100306
Greece	UK Great Britain	26 Nov 45	35UNTS161	100555
Portugal	UK Great Britain	06 Dec 45	6UNTS3	100065
Multilateral		27 Dec 45	2UNTS39	100020
Multilateral		14 Jan 46	555UNTS69	108105
UK Great Britain	USA (United States)	11 Feb 46	3UNTS253	100036
Turkey	UK Great Britain	12 Feb 46	6UNTS79	100069
Multilateral		13 Feb 46	1UNTS15	100004
France	UK Great Britain	28 Feb 46	27UNTS173	100407
France	Norway	26 Mar 46	31UNTS69	100468
UK Great Britain	USA (United States)	27 Mar 46	4UNTS2	100039
France	USA (United States)	27 Mar 46	139UNTS114	101879
Greece	USA (United States)	27 Mar 46	15UNTS233	100239
Iraq	Turkey	29 Mar 46	37UNTS226	100580
Greece	United Arab Rep	30 Mar 46	187UNTS263	102518
Belgium	USA (United States)	05 Apr 46	4UNTS125	100041
Ireland	UK Great Britain	05 Apr 46	72UNTS57	100928
Multilateral		17 Apr 46	27UNTS103	100402
France	Ireland	16 May 46	44UNTS105	100681
Ireland	Sweden	29 May 46	35UNTS231	100557
Australia	Canada	11 Jun 46	10UNTS47	100142
United Arab Rep	USA (United States)	15 Jun 46	71UNTS157	100917
Sweden	Turkey	26 Jun 46	14UNTS21	100208
United Nations	Switzerland	01 Jul 46	1UNTS163	200008
United Nations	Switzerland	01 Jul 46	1UNTS153	200007
Multilateral		18 Jul 46	125UNTS119	101674
France	Sweden	02 Aug 46	27UNTS251	100410
Lebanon	USA (United States)	11 Aug 46	66UNTS211	100856
Netherlands	UK Great Britain	13 Aug 46	4UNTS367	100056

PARTY ONE	PARTY TWO	DATE	CITATION	NUMBER
Procedure (Cont.)				
Denmark	USSR (Soviet Union)	17 Aug 46	8UNTS201	100124
Norway	UK Great Britain	31 Aug 46	6UNTS235	100078
Brazil	USA (United States)	06 Sep 46	54UNTS197	100805
Philippines	USA (United States)	11 Sep 46	43UNTS231	100670
Paraguay	USA (United States)	12 Sep 46	125UNTS179	101677
Belgium	USA (United States)	24 Sep 46	132UNTS80	101753
France	Turkey	12 Oct 46	14UNTS33	100209
Belgium	Portugal	22 Oct 46	34UNTS49	100527
Brazil	UK Great Britain	31 Oct 46	11UNTS115	100152
India	USA (United States)	14 Nov 46	22UNTS55	100331
Sweden	UK Great Britain	27 Nov 46	11UNTS229	100162
New Zealand	USA (United States)	03 Dec 46	7UNTS175	100099
Australia	USA (United States)	03 Dec 46	7UNTS201	100100
Portugal	Switzerland	09 Dec 46	310UNTS251	104495
Brazil	Portugal	10 Dec 46	200UNTS67	102695
Multilateral		13 Dec 46	8UNTS91	100116
USA (United States)	Uruguay	14 Dec 46	532UNTS87	107713
Taiwan	USA (United States)	20 Dec 46	22UNTS87	100332
Peru	USA (United States)	27 Dec 46	26UNTS227	100390
Thailand	UK Great Britain	06 Jan 47	99UNTS149	101376
Ecuador	USA (United States)	08 Jan 47	22UNTS119	100333
Jordan	Turkey	11 Jan 47	14UNTS49	100210
Czechoslovakia	Ireland	29 Jan 47	27UNTS267	100411
Multilateral		10 Feb 47	42UNTS3	100645
Multilateral		10 Feb 47	49UNTS3	100747
Multilateral		10 Feb 47	41UNTS135	100644
Multilateral		10 Feb 47	41UNTS21	100643
Multilateral		10 Feb 47	48UNTS203	100746
Thailand	USA (United States)	26 Feb 47	16UNTS17	100246
Paraguay	USA (United States)	28 Feb 47	44UNTS25	100676
Burma	USA (United States)	28 Feb 47	25UNTS27	100355
Portugal	Sweden	06 Mar 47	35UNTS243	100558
France	ICAO (Civil Aviat)	14 Mar 47	94UNTS59	101306
Netherlands	Turkey	19 Mar 47	14UNTS59	100211
Czechoslovakia	Poland	04 Apr 47	85UNTS62	101146
Greece	Sweden	08 Apr 47	94UNTS73	101307
Iraq	Jordan	14 Apr 47	23UNTS148	100345
Greece	Netherlands	17 Apr 47	32UNTS115	100494
Taiwan	Philippines	18 Apr 47	11UNTS361	100175
Canada	Portugal	25 Apr 47	94UNTS87	101308
Syria	USA (United States)	28 Apr 47	262UNTS121	103741
France	Greece	05 May 47	76UNTS61	100980
Chile	USA (United States)	10 May 47	55UNTS21	100807
Hungary	Yugoslavia	11 May 47	130UNTS171	101730
Czechoslovakia	Denmark	14 May 47	27UNTS297	100413
South Africa	USA (United States)	23 May 47	66UNTS233	100857
India	Netherlands	31 May 47	17UNTS65	100268
Albania	Yugoslavia	12 Jun 47	111UNTS183	101532
Canada	Sweden	27 Jun 47	27UNTS313	100414
Denmark	Turkey	30 Jun 47	32UNTS301	100504
Romania	Yugoslavia	30 Jun 47	116UNTS57	101569
Iraq	Turkey	30 Jun 47	72UNTS107	100930
Italy	Philippines	09 Jul 47	44UNTS3	100674
France	India	16 Jul 47	27UNTS325	100415
Canada	UK Great Britain	17 Jul 47	28UNTS3	100416
Greece	Turkey	22 Jul 47	72UNTS131	100931
Taiwan	UK Great Britain	23 Jul 47	9UNTS207	100135
Hungary	Yugoslavia	24 Jul 47	114UNTS3	101554
Netherlands	IBRD (World Bank)	07 Aug 47	152UNTS165	102015
Canada	Ireland	08 Aug 47	28UNTS47	100419
Poland	Romania	09 Aug 47	12UNTS363	100193
Denmark	IBRD (World Bank)	22 Aug 47	152UNTS223	102016
Hungary	Poland	28 Aug 47	15UNTS145	100231
Luxembourg	IBRD (World Bank)	28 Aug 47	153UNTS3	102017
Multilateral		02 Sep 47	21UNTS77	100324

PARTY ONE	PARTY TWO	DATE	CITATION	NUMBER
Procedure (Cont.)				
Czechoslovakia	Switzerland	10 Sep 47	35UNTS275	100559
Lebanon	Turkey	16 Sep 47	44UNTS123	100682
Chile	UK Great Britain	16 Sep 47	133UNTS143	101786
Philippines	Spain	27 Sep 47	70UNTS133	100902
Multilateral		02 Oct 47	193UNTS188	102616
Multilateral		11 Oct 47	77UNTS143	100998
Czechoslovakia	Sweden	15 Oct 47	44UNTS149	100683
Colombia	UK Great Britain	16 Oct 47	160UNTS297	102115
Burma	UK Great Britain	17 Oct 47	70UNTS183	100904
Brazil	Netherlands	06 Nov 47	53UNTS59	100773
Norway	Portugal	11 Nov 47	34UNTS257	100542
Multilateral		12 Nov 47	53UNTS49	100772
Brazil	Denmark	14 Nov 47	47UNTS39	100722
Brazil	Norway	14 Nov 47	44UNTS163	100684
Brazil	Sweden	14 Nov 47	94UNTS139	101310
Denmark	Greece	14 Nov 47	35UNTS295	100560
Denmark	Ireland	18 Nov 47	35UNTS309	100561
UNICEF (Children)	Yugoslavia	20 Nov 47	65UNTS28	100817
Ireland	Italy	21 Nov 47	353UNTS73	105038
Multilateral		21 Nov 47	33UNTS261	100521
Taiwan	Netherlands	06 Dec 47	43UNTS185	100669
Denmark	Portugal	15 Dec 47	35UNTS329	100563
Peru	UK Great Britain	22 Dec 47	72UNTS143	100932
Philippines	UK Great Britain	07 Jan 48	28UNTS63	100420
Austria	Netherlands	22 Jan 48	17UNTS99	100270
France	Lebanon	24 Jan 48	173UNTS99	102263
Italy	USA (United States)	02 Feb 48	79UNTS171	101040
Norway	Poland	04 Feb 48	30UNTS205	100458
Italy	USA (United States)	06 Feb 48	73UNTS113	100950
Multilateral		06 Mar 48	289UNTS3	104214
Czechoslovakia	Yugoslavia	14 Mar 48	28UNTS81	100421
Multilateral		17 Mar 48	19UNTS51	100304
Argentina	Denmark	18 Mar 48	94UNTS175	101311
Hungary	Yugoslavia	18 Mar 48	113UNTS141	101550
Cuba	UK Great Britain	19 Mar 48	175UNTS23	102294
Multilateral		30 Apr 48	30UNTS55	100449
Multilateral		30 Apr 48	119UNTS3	101609
India	Pakistan	04 May 48	54UNTS45	100794
Ireland	Switzerland	06 May 48	334UNTS187	104768
Pakistan	Sweden	06 May 48	36UNTS3	100564
Jordan	Turkey	07 May 48	32UNTS313	100505
Multilateral		10 May 48	140UNTS129	101887
Norway	Turkey	20 May 48	26UNTS137	100384
India	Sweden	21 May 48	34UNTS285	100543
Czechoslovakia	Yugoslavia	24 May 48	112UNTS111	101542
Greece	Switzerland	26 May 48	94UNTS217	101312
Canada	Netherlands	02 Jun 48	32UNTS215	100499
Ireland	Norway	21 Jun 48	34UNTS317	100545
India	Pakistan	23 Jun 48	28UNTS143	100423
Italy	UK Great Britain	25 Jun 48	94UNTS239	101313
Multilateral		26 Jun 48	331UNTS217	104757
Poland	USSR (Soviet Union)	08 Jul 48	37UNTS107	100576
France	UK Great Britain	15 Jul 48	71UNTS215	100920
Brazil	Switzerland	10 Aug 48	94UNTS269	101314
Multilateral		18 Aug 48	33UNTS181	100518
France	Spain	23 Aug 48	28UNTS173	100425
Greece	Lebanon	06 Sep 48	178UNTS37	102335
Bolivia	USA (United States)	29 Sep 48	505UNTS139	107370
Netherlands	Spain	08 Oct 48	28UNTS209	100426
France	USA (United States)	19 Oct 48	98UNTS3	101355
Peru	ICAO (Civil Aviat)	22 Oct 48	95UNTS3	101315
Argentina	Netherlands	29 Oct 48	95UNTS21	101316
Czechoslovakia	Poland	12 Nov 48	84UNTS347	101141
Argentina	Denmark	14 Dec 48	74UNTS41	100956
Ceylon (Sri Lanka)	India	21 Dec 48	28UNTS223	100427

PARTY ONE	PARTY TWO	DATE	CITATION	NUMBER
Procedure (Cont.)				
UK Great Britain	Yugoslavia	23 Dec 48	81UNTS133	101069
Belgium	Denmark	30 Dec 48	25UNTS173	100362
Ceylon (Sri Lanka)	Pakistan	03 Jan 49	28UNTS247	100428
Mexico	IBRD (World Bank)	06 Jan 49	154UNTS81	102028
WHO (World Health)	Switzerland	12 Jan 49	26UNTS331	200155
Italy	Lebanon	24 Jan 49	231UNTS241	103223
Italy	Yugoslavia	03 Feb 49	33UNTS105	100517
France	Norway	09 Feb 49	29UNTS13	100431
Switzerland	Turkey	16 Feb 49	72UNTS175	100933
Belgium	France	18 Feb 49	31UNTS173	100478
Finland	Netherlands	25 Feb 49	53UNTS123	100777
Czechoslovakia	Yugoslavia	01 Mar 49	113UNTS3	101547
Belgium	IBRD (World Bank)	01 Mar 49	154UNTS133	102029
Netherlands	Switzerland	07 Mar 49	35UNTS69	100551
Israel	Lebanon	23 Mar 49	42UNTS287	100655
Multilateral		23 Mar 49	203UNTS179	102746
Finland	USA (United States)	29 Mar 49	55UNTS59	100808
Panama	USA (United States)	31 Mar 49	55UNTS87	100810
Israel	Jordan	03 Apr 49	42UNTS303	100656
Italy	Yugoslavia	13 Apr 49	171UNTS279	102232
India	Pakistan	23 Apr 49	54UNTS51	100795
Finland	Sweden	26 Apr 49	95UNTS83	101318
Denmark	Poland	12 May 49	87UNTS179	101172
Switzerland	USA (United States)	13 May 49	51UNTS129	100761
Bulgaria	Poland	16 May 49	84UNTS313	101140
Netherlands	USA (United States)	17 May 49	46UNTS291	100717
Italy	Yugoslavia	23 May 49	150UNTS179	101972
Italy	Spain	31 May 49	231UNTS251	103224
Australia	Pakistan	03 Jun 49	35UNTS23	100549
Canada	USA (United States)	04 Jun 49	122UNTS237	101649
Philippines	Thailand	14 Jun 49	81UNTS53	101062
Belgium	Greece	21 Jun 49	137UNTS215	101854
Norway	Pakistan	23 Jun 49	35UNTS49	100550
India	Switzerland	24 Jun 49	95UNTS109	101319
Czechoslovakia	Poland	02 Jul 49	260UNTS179	103709
Czechoslovakia	Poland	02 Jul 49	260UNTS149	103708
Greece	Syria	05 Jul 49	78UNTS71	101013
Australia	India	11 Jul 49	35UNTS83	100552
Iraq	Norway	12 Jul 49	53UNTS137	100778
Czechoslovakia	Finland	13 Jul 49	53UNTS153	100779
Multilateral		15 Jul 49	197UNTS3	102631
Pakistan	Philippines	16 Jul 49	35UNTS111	100553
Dominican Republic	USA (United States)	19 Jul 49	51UNTS145	100762
Israel	Syria	20 Jul 49	42UNTS327	100657
Netherlands	IBRD (World Bank)	26 Jul 49	154UNTS178	102030
India	Pakistan	27 Jul 49	81UNTS273	101076
Pakistan	UK Great Britain	27 Jul 49	44UNTS199	100685
Finland	IBRD (World Bank)	01 Aug 49	156UNTS289	200480
Ceylon (Sri Lanka)	UK Great Britain	05 Aug 49	35UNTS137	100554
India	IBRD (World Bank)	18 Aug 49	154UNTS269	102031
Canada	UK Great Britain	19 Aug 49	44UNTS223	100686
Colombia	IBRD (World Bank)	19 Aug 49	154UNTS329	102032
Finland	Norway	24 Aug 49	53UNTS167	100780
Denmark	Finland	26 Aug 49	53UNTS191	100781
Belgium	Canada	30 Aug 49	53UNTS221	100782
Greece	Italy	31 Aug 49	78UNTS89	101014
Multilateral		02 Sep 49	250UNTS12	103515
Denmark	ICAO (Civil Aviat)	09 Sep 49	53UNTS341	100791
IBRD (World Bank)	Yugoslavia	17 Sep 49	155UNTS3	102034
Multilateral		19 Sep 49	125UNTS3	101671
Belgium	United Arab Rep	19 Sep 49	137UNTS189	101853
Lebanon	Netherlands	20 Sep 49	108UNTS205	101474
Burma	USA (United States)	28 Sep 49	55UNTS3	100806
India	IBRD (World Bank)	29 Sep 49	154UNTS393	102033
Greece	Philippines	08 Oct 49	187UNTS221	102515

PARTY ONE	PARTY TWO	DATE	CITATION	NUMBER
Procedure (Cont.)				
Finland	IBRD (World Bank)	17 Oct 49	156UNTS355	200481
India	Philippines	20 Oct 49	72UNTS191	100934
Iran	Netherlands	31 Oct 49	254UNTS257	103596
Indonesia	Netherlands	02 Nov 49	69UNTS3	100894
Multilateral		07 Nov 49	132UNTS3	101748
Denmark	Pakistan	09 Nov 49	44UNTS255	100687
India	WHO (World Health)	09 Nov 49	67UNTS43	100865
Denmark	Thailand	23 Nov 49	53UNTS255	100786
Sweden	Thailand	23 Nov 49	72UNTS217	100935
Italy	Turkey	25 Nov 49	192UNTS39	102594
Norway	Thailand	26 Nov 49	53UNTS269	100787
Brazil	Spain	28 Nov 49	215UNTS303	102923
Austria	Denmark	02 Dec 49	53UNTS281	100788
Austria	Sweden	02 Dec 49	108UNTS3	101465
Austria	Norway	02 Dec 49	72UNTS230	100936
Afghanistan	WHO (World Health)	04 Dec 49	102UNTS117	101414
Netherlands	United Arab Rep	08 Dec 49	95UNTS123	101320
Sweden	United Arab Rep	12 Dec 49	108UNTS15	101466
Canada	Denmark	13 Dec 49	72UNTS247	100937
El Salvador	IBRD (World Bank)	14 Dec 49	155UNTS43	102035
Austria	Switzerland	19 Dec 49	254UNTS287	103597
France	UK Great Britain	21 Dec 49	264UNTS37	103786
Ireland	USA (United States)	21 Jan 50	206UNTS269	102792
UNICEF (Children)	UK Great Britain	10 Feb 50	65UNTS86	100837
Netherlands	Syria	13 Feb 50	108UNTS53	101467
Canada	Norway	14 Feb 50	53UNTS329	100790
Ceylon (Sri Lanka)	WHO (World Health)	17 Feb 50	102UNTS309	200309
Iran	Pakistan	18 Feb 50	161UNTS23	102119
Spain	Sweden	18 Feb 50	166UNTS15	102184
Ceylon (Sri Lanka)	Thailand	24 Feb 50	72UNTS261	100938
Iraq	Pakistan	26 Feb 50	214UNTS3	102896
Chile	UNICEF (Children)	03 Mar 50	126UNTS119	101685
Italy	Netherlands	04 Mar 50	254UNTS305	103598
Norway	United Arab Rep	11 Mar 50	95UNTS157	101321
Denmark	United Arab Rep	14 Mar 50	95UNTS197	101322
India	Iran	15 Mar 50	161UNTS15	102118
Iceland	Netherlands	22 Mar 50	95UNTS237	101323
Denmark	Iceland	22 Mar 50	72UNTS273	100939
Afghanistan	India	04 Apr 50	167UNTS105	102201
Sweden	UK Great Britain	05 Apr 50	99UNTS107	101374
Italy	Portugal	05 Apr 50	254UNTS329	103599
Turkey	United Arab Rep	12 Apr 50	128UNTS3	101711
India	IBRD (World Bank)	18 Apr 50	155UNTS117	102036
Greece	United Arab Rep	24 Apr 50	163UNTS229	102149
Mexico	IBRD (World Bank)	28 Apr 50	155UNTS185	102037
Switzerland	United Arab Rep	15 May 50	95UNTS255	101325
Brazil	IBRD (World Bank)	26 May 50	301UNTS165	104345
Israel	USA (United States)	13 Jun 50	212UNTS93	102863
Iraq	IBRD (World Bank)	15 Jun 50	155UNTS267	102038
Iraq	Pakistan	20 Jun 50	77UNTS215	101001
Netherlands	Spain	20 Jun 50	95UNTS303	101327
Haiti	WHO (World Health)	27 Jun 50	110UNTS99	101504
Burma	Ceylon (Sri Lanka)	29 Jun 50	73UNTS3	100940
IBRD (World Bank)	Turkey	07 Jul 50	156UNTS3	102039
IBRD (World Bank)	Turkey	07 Jul 50	156UNTS75	102040
Spain	UK Great Britain	20 Jul 50	398UNTS101	105719
France	Pakistan	31 Jul 50	96UNTS23	101329
Canada	France	01 Aug 50	73UNTS21	100941
Spain	Switzerland	03 Aug 50	254UNTS365	103600
France	United Arab Rep	08 Aug 50	127UNTS293	101710
Canada	New Zealand	16 Aug 50	77UNTS239	101002
IBRD (World Bank)	Uruguay	25 Aug 50	156UNTS203	102042
Pakistan	Syria	29 Aug 50	109UNTS95	101494
WHO (World Health)	Venezuela	11 Sep 50	110UNTS237	101513
Burma	Sweden	14 Sep 50	96UNTS45	101330

PARTY ONE	PARTY TWO	DATE	CITATION	NUMBER
Procedure (Cont.)				
Belgium	Mexico	16 Sep 50	188UNTS119	102523
Brazil	Turkey	21 Sep 50	150UNTS299	101981
Iran	Italy	24 Sep 50	281UNTS157	104077
Ceylon (Sri Lanka)	United Arab Rep	26 Sep 50	192UNTS53	102595
Iceland	WHO (World Health)	06 Oct 50	110UNTS127	101506
Switzerland	USA (United States)	13 Oct 50	133UNTS33	101777
Sweden	Switzerland	18 Oct 50	166UNTS49	102185
WHO (World Health)	Turkey	19 Oct 50	110UNTS215	101512
Luxembourg	Portugal	21 Oct 50	108UNTS67	101468
Israel	Netherlands	23 Oct 50	189UNTS89	102543
Multilateral		02 Nov 50	81UNTS160	101071
Multilateral		04 Nov 50	213UNTS221	102889
Nicaragua	WHO (World Health)	10 Nov 50	110UNTS155	101508
Peru	WHO (World Health)	10 Nov 50	110UNTS187	101510
Multilateral		24 Nov 50	81UNTS188	101072
Multilateral		02 Dec 50	118UNTS255	200381
Germany, West	Netherlands	14 Dec 50	87UNTS257	101177
Norway	UK Great Britain	15 Dec 50	106UNTS87	101459
Multilateral		15 Dec 50	347UNTS127	104994
Philippines	WHO (World Health)	28 Dec 50	110UNTS203	101511
UK Great Britain	Yemen	20 Jan 51	101UNTS39	101400
Canada	France	26 Jan 51	233UNTS65	103251
Israel	Turkey	05 Feb 51	193UNTS3	102607
Paraguay	WHO (World Health)	15 Feb 51	110UNTS171	101509
Israel	ILO (Labor Org)	19 Feb 51	100UNTS105	101391
ILO (Labor Org)	Syria	03 Mar 51	110UNTS69	101502
Colombia	Portugal	09 Mar 51	108UNTS87	101469
Greece	Yugoslavia	15 Mar 51	187UNTS237	102516
Belgium	Netherlands	15 Mar 51	93UNTS97	101294
WHO (World Health)	United Arab Rep	25 Mar 51	223UNTS87	103058
Indonesia	WHO (World Health)	28 Mar 51	103UNTS71	101425
Multilateral		28 Mar 51	181UNTS61	102399
Jordan	ILO (Labor Org)	29 Mar 51	100UNTS247	200287
Liberia	ILO (Labor Org)	02 Apr 51	100UNTS117	101392
Jordan	WHO (World Health)	03 Apr 51	110UNTS297	200367
Ceylon (Sri Lanka)	ILO (Labor Org)	06 Apr 51	100UNTS235	200286
Mexico	ILO (Labor Org)	06 Apr 51	100UNTS131	101393
France	UK Great Britain	11 Apr 51	106UNTS3	101456
Peru	ILO (Labor Org)	13 Apr 51	100UNTS31	101385
Guatemala	ILO (Labor Org)	13 Apr 51	126UNTS249	101692
Multilateral		18 Apr 51	261UNTS140	103729
Ecuador	ILO (Labor Org)	19 Apr 51	100UNTS77	101389
Iraq	UK Great Britain	19 Apr 51	108UNTS121	101470
Honduras	WHO (World Health)	20 Apr 51	110UNTS111	101505
Cuba	ILO (Labor Org)	21 Apr 51	99UNTS205	101382
Multilateral		25 Apr 51	91UNTS21	101240
Greece	ILO (Labor Org)	25 Apr 51	100UNTS93	101390
India	ILO (Labor Org)	26 Apr 51	100UNTS19	101384
WHO (World Health)	Yugoslavia	02 May 51	103UNTS117	101429
Colombia	WHO (World Health)	04 May 51	110UNTS83	101503
Germany, West	Norway	07 May 51	92UNTS51	101260
Belgium	UK Great Britain	08 May 51	158UNTS451	102079
Pakistan	ILO (Labor Org)	16 May 51	100UNTS147	101394
India	Netherlands	24 May 51	108UNTS151	101471
Multilateral		25 May 51	175UNTS215	102303
Greece	Norway	28 May 51	187UNTS141	102507
Cambodia	WHO (World Health)	31 May 51	102UNTS279	200307
Lebanon	WHO (World Health)	07 Jun 51	126UNTS221	101690
Liberia	WHO (World Health)	11 Jun 51	103UNTS83	101426
WHO (World Health)	Uruguay	11 Jun 51	128UNTS251	101724
Italy	Netherlands	15 Jun 51	150UNTS103	101964
Dominican Republic	ILO (Labor Org)	18 Jun 51	100UNTS3	101383
Denmark	Iran	18 Jun 51	255UNTS3	103602
Multilateral		19 Jun 51	199UNTS67	102678
Cuba	Portugal	26 Jun 51	192UNTS115	102598

PARTY ONE	PARTY TWO	DATE	CITATION	NUMBER
Procedure (Cont.)				
ILO (Labor Org)	Vietnam, South	26 Jun 51	100UNTS223	200285
Multilateral		28 Jun 51	118UNTS154	101604
IBRD (World Bank)	Switzerland	29 Jun 51	216UNTS347	200529
Iraq	WHO (World Health)	01 Jul 51	110UNTS139	101507
Ethiopia	WHO (World Health)	02 Jul 51	103UNTS39	101422
Multilateral		02 Jul 51	189UNTS137	102545
Burma	India	07 Jul 51	149UNTS35	101949
ILO (Labor Org)	Thailand	11 Jul 51	100UNTS159	101395
Paraguay	ILO (Labor Org)	12 Jul 51	117UNTS155	101591
Iceland	Norway	14 Jul 51	163UNTS265	102150
Philippines	WHO (World Health)	22 Jul 51	149UNTS197	101953
Brazil	USA (United States)	24 Jul 51	134UNTS195	101799
Burma	Denmark	30 Jul 51	108UNTS167	101472
Iran	UNICEF (Children)	02 Aug 51	247UNTS11	103457
Greece	USA (United States)	03 Aug 51	224UNTS279	103080
Israel	WHO (World Health)	07 Aug 51	104UNTS213	101442
Israel	Philippines	07 Aug 51	192UNTS81	102596
Lebanon	UK Great Britain	15 Aug 51	160UNTS327	102116
France	United Nations	17 Aug 51	122UNTS191	101647
Israel	USA (United States)	23 Aug 51	219UNTS237	102979
France	Italy	23 Aug 51	291UNTS143	104249
Pakistan	United Arab Rep	28 Aug 51	214UNTS247	102902
WHO (World Health)	Saudi Arabia	29 Aug 51	110UNTS277	101516
France	USSR (Soviet Union)	03 Sep 51	221UNTS79	103003
UNICEF (Children)	Turkey	05 Sep 51	193UNTS55	102610
Burma	Netherlands	06 Sep 51	108UNTS187	101473
Ethiopia	USA (United States)	07 Sep 51	206UNTS41	102785
Multilateral		08 Sep 51	136UNTS45	101832
Panama	UK Great Britain	15 Sep 51	560UNTS143	108172
Norway	USA (United States)	17 Sep 51	140UNTS313	101895
Canada	Italy	20 Sep 51	236UNTS251	103328
Multilateral		20 Sep 51	200UNTS3	102691
Korea, South	United Nations	21 Sep 51	104UNTS323	200322
WHO (World Health)	Vietnam, South	21 Sep 51	107UNTS63	200352
Australia	Netherlands	25 Sep 51	128UNTS63	101713
Bolivia	United Nations	01 Oct 51	104UNTS263	101447
Denmark	USA (United States)	01 Oct 51	421UNTS105	106056
UNICEF (Children)	UK Great Britain	02 Oct 51	104UNTS301	101448
Philippines	Spain	06 Oct 51	215UNTS193	102920
Pakistan	WHO (World Health)	07 Oct 51	126UNTS101	101684
Ecuador	WHO (World Health)	16 Oct 51	110UNTS263	101515
India	WHO (World Health)	16 Oct 51	109UNTS49	101490
Greece	Luxembourg	22 Oct 51	187UNTS119	102506
ILO (Labor Org)	Venezuela	22 Oct 51	117UNTS139	101590
Panama	ILO (Labor Org)	10 Nov 51	126UNTS269	101693
Denmark	Iraq	18 Nov 51	232UNTS25	103227
Pakistan	Saudi Arabia	25 Nov 51	177UNTS3	102304
India	UK Great Britain	01 Dec 51	128UNTS39	101712
Multilateral		06 Dec 51	150UNTS67	101963
Iraq	UNICEF (Children)	10 Dec 51	126UNTS57	101682
Colombia	Spain	11 Dec 51	216UNTS73	102933
El Salvador	Guatemala	14 Dec 51	131UNTS131	101740
India	Turkey	14 Dec 51	137UNTS15	101845
India	WHO (World Health)	20 Dec 51	124UNTS109	101669
Multilateral		20 Dec 51	163UNTS293	102151
France	UK Great Britain	31 Dec 51	330UNTS145	104744
Jordan	United Arab Rep	02 Jan 52	192UNTS157	102599
Austria	WHO (World Health)	10 Jan 52	131UNTS295	200438
Denmark	Norway	14 Jan 52	120UNTS119	101618
Costa Rica	WHO (World Health)	23 Jan 52	135UNTS265	101826
Indonesia	United Nations	06 Feb 52	121UNTS3	101621
Japan	USA (United States)	28 Feb 52	208UNTS255	102817
Belgium	Spain	10 Mar 52	178UNTS243	102342
Sweden	UK Great Britain	14 Mar 52	202UNTS157	102731
Pakistan	Switzerland	17 Mar 52	192UNTS237	102603

PARTY ONE	PARTY TWO	DATE	CITATION	NUMBER
Procedure (Cont.)				
Sweden	Uruguay	20 Mar 52	311UNTS3	104497
Norway	Uruguay	20 Mar 52	310UNTS279	104496
Iraq	Switzerland	31 Mar 52	311UNTS43	104498
Libya	UNICEF (Children)	05 Apr 52	133UNTS287	200441
India	WHO (World Health)	17 Apr 52	131UNTS241	101744
France	Mexico	17 Apr 52	163UNTS321	102153
Liberia	UNICEF (Children)	17 Apr 52	133UNTS3	101773
India	WHO (World Health)	19 Apr 52	131UNTS253	101745
Taiwan	Japan	28 Apr 52	138UNTS3	101858
France	Israel	29 Apr 52	189UNTS55	102542
Norway	WHO (World Health)	09 May 52	131UNTS281	101747
UNICEF (Children)	United Arab Rep	18 May 52	324UNTS161	104684
Multilateral		12 Jun 52	138UNTS183	101869
Australia	United Arab Rep	14 Jun 52	173UNTS241	102269
India	United Arab Rep	14 Jun 52	173UNTS209	102268
Belgium	UNICEF (Children)	17 Jun 52	171UNTS249	102228
WHO (World Health)	Syria	20 Jun 52	165UNTS219	102178
Denmark	UK Great Britain	23 Jun 52	151UNTS3	101982
Burma	Pakistan	25 Jun 52	173UNTS41	102259
Belgium	Israel	30 Jun 52	183UNTS263	102435
Jordan	UNICEF (Children)	08 Jul 52	173UNTS353	200503
UNICEF (Children)	Syria	10 Jul 52	136UNTS17	101830
India	Philippines	11 Jul 52	203UNTS73	102741
Netherlands	Pakistan	17 Jul 52	150UNTS277	101980
France	WHO (World Health)	23 Jul 52	209UNTS231	102829
Japan	United Nations	25 Jul 52	135UNTS305	200443
UNICEF (Children)	UK Great Britain	25 Jul 52	135UNTS37	101812
Japan	USA (United States)	11 Aug 52	212UNTS27	102862
Laos	UNICEF (Children)	15 Aug 52	161UNTS323	200491
USA (United States)	Venezuela	28 Aug 52	178UNTS51	102336
Ethiopia	Pakistan	29 Aug 52	150UNTS257	101979
UNICEF (Children)	Vietnam, South	29 Aug 52	161UNTS335	200492
Multilateral		05 Sep 52	256UNTS3	103619
Germany, West	Israel	10 Sep 52	162UNTS205	102137
Netherlands	Peru	22 Sep 52	255UNTS49	103604
Austria	Luxembourg	13 Oct 52	192UNTS291	102606
Mexico	Netherlands	13 Oct 52	163UNTS341	102154
Iceland	Luxembourg	23 Oct 52	193UNTS39	102609
Burma	UK Great Britain	25 Oct 52	150UNTS237	101978
Chile	Sweden	27 Oct 52	311UNTS63	104499
Chile	Denmark	27 Oct 52	271UNTS93	103911
Multilateral		07 Nov 52	221UNTS255	103010
Belgium	UK Great Britain	12 Nov 52	180UNTS15	102372
Luxembourg	Norway	17 Nov 52	311UNTS95	104500
Luxembourg	Sweden	17 Nov 52	173UNTS277	102270
Israel	Switzerland	19 Nov 52	232UNTS3	103226
Japan	WHO (World Health)	26 Nov 52	204UNTS301	200521
UNICEF (Children)	UK Great Britain	16 Dec 52	151UNTS359	102005
ILO (Labor Org)	UN Relief Palestin	31 Dec 52	182UNTS201	200506
UK Great Britain	USA (United States)	19 Jan 53	161UNTS3	102117
Chile	United Nations	16 Feb 53	314UNTS49	104541
Japan	Netherlands	17 Feb 53	192UNTS215	102602
Japan	Sweden	20 Feb 53	173UNTS307	102272
Libya	UK Great Britain	21 Feb 53	311UNTS115	104501
Japan	Norway	23 Feb 53	192UNTS191	102601
Denmark	Japan	26 Feb 53	173UNTS329	102273
Germany, West	USA (United States)	27 Feb 53	224UNTS31	103068
Multilateral		28 Feb 53	167UNTS21	102199
France	Italy	14 Mar 53	284UNTS221	104140
Lebanon	Sweden	23 Mar 53	255UNTS83	103605
Multilateral		31 Mar 53	193UNTS136	102613
Japan	USA (United States)	02 Apr 53	206UNTS143	102788
Turkey	Yugoslavia	16 Apr 53	255UNTS99	103606
Greece	UK Great Britain	17 Apr 53	191UNTS151	102582
Philippines	Thailand	27 Apr 53	174UNTS3	102274

PARTY ONE	PARTY TWO	DATE	CITATION	NUMBER
Procedure (Cont.)				
Ethiopia	UNICEF (Children)	27 Apr 53	213UNTS169	102885
Cuba	USA (United States)	26 May 53	224UNTS75	103070
Switzerland	Yugoslavia	28 May 53	232UNTS45	103228
Japan	Thailand	19 Jun 53	174UNTS29	102276
Canada	USA (United States)	30 Jun 53	215UNTS103	102914
Multilateral		01 Jul 53	200UNTS149	102701
Canada	Mexico	27 Jul 53	192UNTS255	102604
Libya	UK Great Britain	29 Jul 53	186UNTS201	102492
USA (United States)	Venezuela	14 Aug 53	213UNTS99	102883
ICAO (Civil Aviat)	United Arab Rep	27 Aug 53	215UNTS371	102925
Multilateral		01 Oct 53	258UNTS153	103677
Greece	UK Great Britain	05 Oct 53	243UNTS73	103447
UNICEF (Children)	UK Great Britain	07 Oct 53	180UNTS59	102375
Chile	Denmark	22 Oct 53	348UNTS261	105004
Austria	Yugoslavia	11 Nov 53	363UNTS149	105206
Japan	UNICEF (Children)	21 Nov 53	183UNTS297	200507
Multilateral		11 Dec 53	191UNTS285	102588
Belgium	Lebanon	24 Dec 53	219UNTS153	102972
France	Italy	28 Dec 53	267UNTS89	103836
Ethiopia	Greece	20 Jan 54	222UNTS281	103035
Syria	UK Great Britain	30 Jan 54	449UNTS47	106452
France	Greece	08 Feb 54	225UNTS107	103093
France	Greece	08 Feb 54	225UNTS121	103094
France	Sweden	16 Feb 54	228UNTS137	103147
Canada	Peru	18 Feb 54	411UNTS64	105915
Multilateral		19 Feb 54	214UNTS51	102899
Multilateral		25 Feb 54	215UNTS249	102922
ICJ Option Clause	Finland	26 Feb 54	189UNTS223	102546
Multilateral		01 Mar 54	256UNTS31	103622
Indonesia	Thailand	03 Mar 54	213UNTS297	102893
Lebanon	Switzerland	03 Mar 54	255UNTS127	103608
Japan	USA (United States)	08 Mar 54	232UNTS251	103240
Mexico	UK Great Britain	20 Mar 54	331UNTS21	104750
Peru	Spain	31 Mar 54	232UNTS65	103230
Lebanon	Yugoslavia	17 Apr 54	602UNTS199	108713
Bulgaria	Yugoslavia	22 Apr 54	397UNTS43	105701
Canada	USA (United States)	03 May 54	221UNTS339	103015
UNICEF (Children)	Spain	07 May 54	190UNTS357	200515
Mexico	UNICEF (Children)	20 May 54	192UNTS3	102591
Switzerland	Syria	26 May 54	255UNTS145	103609
United Nations	Thailand	26 May 54	260UNTS35	103703
Iran	Switzerland	27 May 54	496UNTS273	107257
Luxembourg	UK Great Britain	18 Jun 54	192UNTS33	102593
Denmark	Italy	15 Jul 54	250UNTS43	103516
Ireland	Luxembourg	27 Jul 54	232UNTS91	103231
Chile	UK Great Britain	31 Jul 54	618UNTS353	108934
Norway	USA (United States)	06 Aug 54	222UNTS269	103034
New Zealand	UNICEF (Children)	26 Aug 54	198UNTS173	102663
Thailand	USA (United States)	01 Sep 54	237UNTS209	103347
Libya	USA (United States)	09 Sep 54	224UNTS217	103078
Multilateral		28 Sep 54	360UNTS117	105158
Ethiopia	Sweden	13 Oct 54	202UNTS273	102734
Multilateral		23 Oct 54	332UNTS387	104763
Netherlands	Venezuela	26 Oct 54	232UNTS103	103232
Burma	Japan	05 Nov 54	251UNTS201	103542
Burma	Japan	05 Nov 54	251UNTS215	103543
Brazil	Italy	24 Nov 54	284UNTS325	104146
Pakistan	United Arab Rep	13 Dec 54	255UNTS167	103610
Ecuador	Netherlands	14 Dec 54	232UNTS115	103233
India	Iran	15 Dec 54	327UNTS245	104724
Norway	Switzerland	30 Dec 54	311UNTS147	104502
Netherlands	UNICEF (Children)	31 Dec 54	202UNTS135	102729
Austria	Belgium	07 Jan 55	380UNTS219	105458
Canada	Japan	12 Jan 55	311UNTS167	104503
Denmark	UK Great Britain	20 Jan 55	210UNTS303	102842

PARTY ONE	PARTY TWO	DATE	CITATION	NUMBER
Procedure (Cont.)				
Philippines	UK Great Britain	31 Jan 55	216UNTS51	102932
United Arab Rep	Yugoslavia	20 Feb 55	255UNTS199	103611
Greece	UK Great Britain	24 Feb 55	209UNTS187	102827
Costa Rica	USA (United States)	26 Feb 55	252UNTS129	103562
France	Sweden	05 Mar 55	427UNTS133	106150
WMO (Meteorology)	Switzerland	10 Mar 55	211UNTS277	200524
Guatemala	USA (United States)	23 Mar 55	252UNTS143	103563
Iraq	United Arab Rep	23 Mar 55	311UNTS199	104504
Italy	Yugoslavia	26 Mar 55	379UNTS3	105432
Ecuador	USA (United States)	29 Mar 55	261UNTS343	103732
Brazil	UK Great Britain	05 Apr 55	403UNTS139	105793
Norway	USA (United States)	06 Apr 55	269UNTS65	103874
Multilateral		15 May 55	217UNTS223	102949
Pakistan	USA (United States)	26 May 55	257UNTS93	103652
Hungary	USSR (Soviet Union)	27 May 55	407UNTS156	105864
Honduras	USA (United States)	10 Jun 55	258UNTS51	103669
CERN (Nuc Resrch)	Switzerland	11 Jun 55	249UNTS405	200544
Denmark	WHO (World Health)	29 Jun 55	247UNTS168	103467
Syria	United Arab Rep	03 Jul 55	393UNTS67	105652
Germany, West	USA (United States)	07 Jul 55	275UNTS3	103973
Belgium	USA (United States)	15 Jul 55	223UNTS3	103040
Germany, West	UK Great Britain	22 Jul 55	269UNTS189	103881
Germany, East	Romania	28 Jul 55	342UNTS207	104909
Belgium	Ireland	10 Sep 55	255UNTS235	103612
ICJ Option Clause	South Africa	12 Sep 55	216UNTS115	102935
Italy	Switzerland	17 Sep 55	291UNTS213	104257
Bolivia	USA (United States)	23 Sep 55	256UNTS275	103637
Bulgaria	Yugoslavia	01 Oct 55	396UNTS223	105698
France	Germany, West	04 Oct 55	353UNTS203	105044
Iceland	USA (United States)	05 Oct 55	256UNTS285	103638
Denmark	Syria	20 Oct 55	250UNTS61	103518
Multilateral		20 Oct 55	378UNTS159	105425
Paraguay	USA (United States)	28 Oct 55	273UNTS97	103946
Pakistan	Turkey	02 Nov 55	311UNTS217	104505
Burma	China People's Rep	08 Nov 55	306UNTS11	104430
Austria	Israel	17 Nov 55	232UNTS153	103235
Guatemala	UNICEF (Children)	22 Nov 55	221UNTS305	103012
India	Japan	26 Nov 55	311UNTS243	104506
Multilateral		13 Dec 55	529UNTS141	107660
Costa Rica	Guatemala	20 Dec 55	280UNTS121	104056
Germany, West	USA (United States)	04 Jan 56	268UNTS143	103856
France	Japan	17 Jan 56	255UNTS275	103614
Australia	Japan	19 Jan 56	311UNTS291	104507
Austria	Italy	23 Jan 56	393UNTS97	105653
Argentina	Switzerland	25 Jan 56	559UNTS121	108157
Romania	Yugoslavia	01 Feb 56	362UNTS203	105189
India	USA (United States)	03 Feb 56	272UNTS75	103932
Hungary	Romania	03 Feb 56	362UNTS233	105190
Netherlands	Sudan	12 Feb 56	311UNTS319	104508
Norway	Syria	25 Feb 56	463UNTS217	106706
Bulgaria	Yugoslavia	23 Mar 56	367UNTS213	105230
Bulgaria	Yugoslavia	04 Apr 56	391UNTS47	105616
Belgium	Germany, West	14 Apr 56	344UNTS103	104945
Multilateral		25 Apr 56	270UNTS103	103896
Cambodia	UNICEF (Children)	28 Apr 56	136UNTS341	200446
Multilateral		30 Apr 56	310UNTS229	104494
Germany, West	Switzerland	02 May 56	559UNTS157	108158
Japan	Philippines	09 May 56	285UNTS3	104148
Portugal	Venezuela	16 May 56	463UNTS239	106707
Multilateral		18 May 56	339UNTS3	104844
Multilateral		19 May 56	399UNTS189	105742
Japan	Switzerland	24 May 56	312UNTS3	104509
Greece	Italy	26 May 56	496UNTS301	107258
Italy	Switzerland	04 Jun 56	378UNTS311	105429
Chile	Italy	04 Jun 56	362UNTS309	105195

PARTY ONE	PARTY TWO	DATE	CITATION	NUMBER
Procedure (Cont.)				
India	Thailand	12 Jun 56	255UNTS341	103617
Germany, West	Ireland	12 Jun 56	353UNTS121	105040
Multilateral		20 Jun 56	268UNTS3	103850
Lebanon	UNICEF (Children)	03 Jul 56	324UNTS145	104683
Canada	Honduras	11 Jul 56	305UNTS39	104411
Germany, West	UK Great Britain	30 Jul 56	330UNTS233	104748
Romania	Yugoslavia	04 Aug 56	395UNTS99	105682
UNICEF (Children)	Sudan	07 Aug 56	248UNTS307	200542
Jordan	USA (United States)	24 Sep 56	278UNTS51	104020
Multilateral		25 Sep 56	334UNTS13	104766
Multilateral		25 Sep 56	334UNTS89	104767
Germany, West	Netherlands	28 Sep 56	327UNTS185	104722
UN Hi Com Refugees	Sweden	08 Oct 56	428UNTS307	106182
Switzerland	Thailand	13 Oct 56	312UNTS43	104510
Burma	Thailand	15 Oct 56	277UNTS87	104000
Japan	USSR (Soviet Union)	19 Oct 56	263UNTS99	103768
Colombia	USA (United States)	24 Oct 56	476UNTS77	106905
Belgium	Turkey	25 Oct 56	380UNTS3	105447
Austria	UK Great Britain	27 Oct 56	264UNTS67	103789
Albania	Yugoslavia	23 Nov 56	386UNTS73	105539
Peru	Switzerland	23 Nov 56	411UNTS97	105916
Albania	Yugoslavia	23 Nov 56	363UNTS123	105204
Luxembourg	USA (United States)	07 Dec 56	265UNTS255	103817
Greece	Sweden	11 Dec 56	299UNTS247	104316
Poland	USSR (Soviet Union)	17 Dec 56	266UNTS179	103830
UNESCO (Educ/Cult)	Tunisia	03 Jan 57	257UNTS21	103645
Turkey	USA (United States)	15 Jan 57	280UNTS79	104053
Iran	USA (United States)	16 Jan 57	308UNTS147	104460
Iceland	Thailand	22 Jan 57	312UNTS63	104511
Germany, West	Norway	29 Jan 57	353UNTS39	105037
Germany, West	Sweden	29 Jan 57	393UNTS113	105654
Denmark	Germany, West	29 Jan 57	302UNTS75	104354
Japan	Poland	08 Feb 57	318UNTS251	104620
Czechoslovakia	Japan	13 Feb 57	300UNTS119	104335
Belgium	Czechoslovakia	12 Mar 57	312UNTS75	104512
Germany, East	USSR (Soviet Union)	12 Mar 57	285UNTS105	104150
Netherlands	Yugoslavia	13 Mar 57	327UNTS227	104723
Italy	UK Great Britain	29 Mar 57	310UNTS11	104481
Netherlands	USA (United States)	03 Apr 57	410UNTS193	105904
Denmark	Pakistan	10 Apr 57	302UNTS53	104353
Germany, West	Yugoslavia	10 Apr 57	463UNTS269	106708
Romania	USSR (Soviet Union)	15 Apr 57	274UNTS143	103964
Bulgaria	Sweden	17 Apr 57	464UNTS3	106709
Other Unilat Decla	United Arab Rep	24 Apr 57	265UNTS299	103821
Multilateral		29 Apr 57	320UNTS243	104646
Belgium	Bulgaria	14 May 57	317UNTS81	104596
Iran	USSR (Soviet Union)	14 May 57	457UNTS161	106586
Australia	Germany, West	22 May 57	357UNTS45	105105
Hungary	Yugoslavia	25 May 57	477UNTS219	106924
Hungary	Netherlands	28 May 57	334UNTS291	104773
Belgium	Hungary	01 Jun 57	291UNTS17	104242
Afghanistan	Pakistan	13 Jun 57	327UNTS51	104717
Honduras	Nicaragua	22 Jun 57	277UNTS159	104005
Finland	United Nations	27 Jun 57	271UNTS135	103913
Czechoslovakia	United Arab Rep	30 Jun 57	411UNTS126	105917
United Nations	Sweden	01 Jul 57	271UNTS187	103914
Australia	Japan	06 Jul 57	318UNTS381	104627
Norway	United Nations	09 Jul 57	271UNTS223	103917
Denmark	United Nations	16 Jul 57	274UNTS81	103959
Canada	United Nations	29 Jul 57	274UNTS47	103957
Morocco	UNICEF (Children)	31 Jul 57	282UNTS99	104095
Greece	Italy	02 Aug 57	533UNTS217	107744
Brazil	United Nations	13 Aug 57	274UNTS199	103966
India	United Nations	14 Aug 57	274UNTS233	103968
Netherlands	Romania	27 Aug 57	342UNTS309	104914

PARTY ONE	PARTY TWO	DATE	CITATION	NUMBER
Procedure (Cont.)				
Japan	USA (United States)	14 Sep 57	293UNTS247	104293
Iran	USA (United States)	21 Sep 57	293UNTS287	104296
Germany, East	USSR (Soviet Union)	27 Sep 57	292UNTS75	104268
United Nations	Yugoslavia	01 Oct 57	277UNTS191	104006
Multilateral		03 Oct 57	366UNTS87	105216
Italy	Pakistan	05 Oct 57	353UNTS91	105039
Australia	Netherlands	09 Oct 57	312UNTS225	104520
Fed of Malaya	UK Great Britain	18 Oct 57	335UNTS3	104775
France	Morocco	25 Oct 57	559UNTS95	108156
Poland	USSR (Soviet Union)	26 Oct 57	432UNTS221	106223
Philippines	USA (United States)	01 Nov 57	307UNTS39	104440
Argentina	UNICEF (Children)	19 Nov 57	300UNTS229	104338
Multilateral		23 Nov 57	506UNTS125	107384
Argentina	Italy	25 Nov 57	305UNTS275	104424
Bulgaria	USSR (Soviet Union)	12 Dec 57	302UNTS3	104351
Multilateral		13 Dec 57	372UNTS159	105296
Ethiopia	Japan	19 Dec 57	325UNTS91	104695
Australia	Ireland	30 Dec 57	497UNTS29	107260
Canada	Switzerland	10 Jan 58	464UNTS21	106710
Belgium	Germany, West	17 Jan 58	328UNTS173	104735
Indonesia	Japan	20 Jan 58	324UNTS247	104689
Indonesia	Japan	20 Jan 58	324UNTS227	104688
Belgium	Morocco	20 Jan 58	288UNTS3	104192
Multilateral		03 Feb 58	381UNTS165	105471
Australia	UK Great Britain	07 Feb 58	335UNTS23	104776
Bulgaria	Netherlands	07 Feb 58	335UNTS45	104777
Afghanistan	Turkey	08 Feb 58	464UNTS39	106711
Albania	USSR (Soviet Union)	15 Feb 58	313UNTS261	104536
Sudan	Sweden	17 Feb 58	393UNTS161	105655
Israel	Philippines	26 Feb 58	507UNTS135	107398
Norway	Pakistan	05 Mar 58	334UNTS199	104769
Pakistan	Sweden	06 Mar 58	393UNTS181	105656
Bulgaria	Hungary	13 Mar 58	438UNTS191	106317
Multilateral		20 Mar 58	335UNTS211	104789
Germany, West	Portugal	21 Mar 58	464UNTS71	106712
Belgium	Luxembourg	28 Mar 58	303UNTS101	104372
Sweden	USSR (Soviet Union)	28 Mar 58	428UNTS321	106184
Morocco	Portugal	03 Apr 58	393UNTS203	105657
Multilateral		03 Apr 58	336UNTS177	104806
Bulgaria	Yugoslavia	04 Apr 58	367UNTS89	105228
Belgium	Iran	14 Apr 58	381UNTS309	105473
Sweden	Yugoslavia	18 Apr 58	393UNTS225	105658
China People's Rep	USSR (Soviet Union)	23 Apr 58	313UNTS135	104534
Germany, West	USSR (Soviet Union)	25 Apr 58	338UNTS49	104832
Japan	Poland	26 Apr 58	340UNTS221	104866
Multilateral		29 Apr 58	559UNTS285	108164
Italy	Switzerland	23 May 58	363UNTS81	105201
Bulgaria	Denmark	28 May 58	312UNTS235	104521
India	USSR (Soviet Union)	02 Jun 58	393UNTS3	105650
Pakistan	Portugal	07 Jun 58	320UNTS225	104645
Denmark	Luxembourg	10 Jun 58	356UNTS193	105096
Multilateral		10 Jun 58	454UNTS47	106539
Ethiopia	United Nations	18 Jun 58	317UNTS101	104597
Denmark	Romania	25 Jun 58	345UNTS231	104970
Czechoslovakia	Hungary	27 Jun 58	477UNTS321	106927
Belgium	Pakistan	04 Jul 58	387UNTS305	105569
Ethiopia	UK Great Britain	07 Jul 58	331UNTS3	104749
Austria	Romania	10 Jul 58	353UNTS155	105041
Denmark	Hungary	17 Jul 58	344UNTS281	104954
Afghanistan	Austria	21 Jul 58	0UNTS0	109236
Netherlands	Yugoslavia	22 Jul 58	386UNTS263	105546
Ghana	UNICEF (Children)	12 Aug 58	309UNTS103	104469
Romania	United Arab Rep	14 Aug 58	405UNTS189	105834
Nepal	United Nations	18 Aug 58	508UNTS3	107403
Australia	Fed of Malaya	26 Aug 58	325UNTS253	104703

PARTY ONE	PARTY TWO	DATE	CITATION	NUMBER
Procedure (Cont.)				
Pakistan	Thailand	28 Aug 58	394UNTS53	105668
Japan	New Zealand	09 Sep 58	325UNTS119	104698
India	Pakistan	10 Sep 58	369UNTS81	105252
Austria	Bulgaria	12 Sep 58	353UNTS3	105036
Ghana	UK Great Britain	24 Sep 58	411UNTS146	105918
Ghana	USA (United States)	30 Sep 58	336UNTS169	104805
Belgium	Spain	27 Oct 58	327UNTS107	104720
Canada	USA (United States)	31 Oct 58	391UNTS219	105626
Liberia	Netherlands	28 Nov 58	393UNTS55	105651
Multilateral		01 Dec 58	385UNTS137	105534
Burma	United Nations	15 Dec 58	319UNTS3	104629
United Nations	Tunisia	23 Dec 58	321UNTS23	104651
Finland	Switzerland	07 Jan 59	353UNTS173	105042
UK Great Britain	Yugoslavia	03 Feb 59	359UNTS339	105151
Ghana	United Nations	27 Feb 59	324UNTS133	104682
Belgium	Morocco	27 Feb 59	390UNTS275	105611
IAEA (Atom Energy)	Thailand	18 Mar 59	339UNTS307	104850
Netherlands	Tunisia	19 Mar 59	497UNTS61	107262
Sweden	Tunisia	19 Mar 59	497UNTS43	107261
United Nations	Sudan	28 Mar 59	327UNTS95	104719
Norway	Tunisia	28 Mar 59	497UNTS77	107263
Morocco	UN Special Fund	04 Apr 59	354UNTS347	105069
Multilateral		06 Apr 59	349UNTS167	105013
Israel	Liberia	09 Apr 59	448UNTS95	106427
Denmark	Tunisia	14 Apr 59	340UNTS273	104870
Indonesia	Malaysia	17 Apr 59	470UNTS273	106813
Denmark	Sudan	11 May 59	445UNTS105	106380
Ceylon (Sri Lanka)	Norway	29 May 59	411UNTS165	105919
Ceylon (Sri Lanka)	Sweden	29 May 59	464UNTS109	106713
Ceylon (Sri Lanka)	Denmark	29 May 59	348UNTS225	105002
United Nations	Vietnam, South	03 Jun 59	337UNTS361	200557
Austria	Belgium	16 Jun 59	419UNTS45	106029
Greece	Yugoslavia	18 Jun 59	368UNTS69	105235
Greece	Yugoslavia	18 Jun 59	368UNTS81	105236
Belgium	Japan	20 Jun 59	411UNTS3	105911
Panama	United Nations	24 Jun 59	507UNTS245	107402
Libya	United Nations	27 Jun 59	336UNTS291	104811
France	Israel	30 Jun 59	448UNTS107	106428
Multilateral		01 Jul 59	374UNTS147	105334
Laos	United Nations	06 Jul 59	337UNTS41	104814
Bulgaria	United Arab Rep	09 Jul 59	411UNTS187	105920
India	Italy	16 Jul 59	464UNTS129	106714
Austria	Hungary	17 Jul 59	0UNTS0	109237
Afghanistan	Germany, West	22 Jul 59	464UNTS177	106715
Paraguay	United Nations	01 Aug 59	341UNTS319	104894
Germany, West	UK Great Britain	03 Aug 59	502UNTS197	107331
Ghana	UN Special Fund	12 Aug 59	338UNTS203	104836
Germany, West	Iceland	12 Aug 59	411UNTS224	105921
Canada	Germany, West	04 Sep 59	411UNTS260	105922
Australia	Fed of Malaya	29 Sep 59	357UNTS29	105104
Iran	UN Special Fund	06 Oct 59	342UNTS89	104902
Nicaragua	Peru	14 Oct 59	392UNTS303	105649
Poland	UN Special Fund	15 Oct 59	344UNTS29	104941
Guinea	United Nations	15 Oct 59	344UNTS47	104942
India	UN Special Fund	20 Oct 59	344UNTS143	104946
UN Special Fund	Yugoslavia	27 Oct 59	344UNTS159	104947
Korea, South	United Nations	06 Nov 59	346UNTS289	200565
Ecuador	UN Special Fund	10 Nov 59	345UNTS3	104955
Greece	UN Special Fund	13 Nov 59	345UNTS171	104966
Multilateral		18 Nov 59	390UNTS227	105610
Multilateral		19 Nov 59	410UNTS156	105902
UN Special Fund	Turkey	20 Nov 59	345UNTS105	104963
Afghanistan	United Nations	24 Nov 59	397UNTS187	105705
UN Special Fund	United Arab Rep	25 Nov 59	345UNTS125	104964
Germany, West	Pakistan	25 Nov 59	457UNTS22	106575

PARTY ONE	PARTY TWO	DATE	CITATION	NUMBER
Procedure (Cont.)				
France	USA (United States)	25 Nov 59	401UNTS75	105764
Italy	Netherlands	01 Dec 59	455UNTS241	106545
Multilateral		01 Dec 59	402UNTS71	105778
Israel	UN Special Fund	01 Dec 59	345UNTS197	104968
Guinea	UN Special Fund	02 Dec 59	345UNTS215	104969
Argentina	UN Special Fund	04 Dec 59	345UNTS263	104972
Liberia	Sweden	09 Dec 59	464UNTS219	106716
Czechoslovakia	Ethiopia	11 Dec 59	386UNTS51	105537
Czechoslovakia	Japan	15 Dec 59	383UNTS277	105505
Jordan	UN Special Fund	15 Dec 59	346UNTS3	104974
UN Special Fund	UK Great Britain	07 Jan 60	348UNTS177	105000
Czechoslovakia	UK Great Britain	15 Jan 60	374UNTS207	105336
Japan	USA (United States)	19 Jan 60	373UNTS207	105321
Peru	UN Special Fund	19 Jan 60	349UNTS83	105010
Chile	UN Special Fund	22 Jan 60	351UNTS115	105020
Colombia	UN Special Fund	04 Feb 60	355UNTS257	105080
Poland	Yugoslavia	06 Feb 60	521UNTS37	107517
Multilateral		06 Feb 60	383UNTS3	105494
Bolivia	UN Special Fund	09 Feb 60	351UNTS203	105024
Cuba	UNICEF (Children)	11 Feb 60	349UNTS277	105014
Argentina	Philippines	12 Feb 60	535UNTS293	107785
Germany, West	United Arab Rep	16 Feb 60	464UNTS233	106717
Afghanistan	UN Special Fund	21 Feb 60	351UNTS93	105019
Pakistan	UN Special Fund	25 Feb 60	351UNTS141	105021
Multilateral		26 Feb 60	418UNTS171	106022
France	Thailand	26 Feb 60	392UNTS279	105648
Australia	Thailand	26 Feb 60	392UNTS255	105647
Guinea	Netherlands	09 Mar 60	392UNTS243	105646
Finland	Iceland	10 Mar 60	497UNTS95	107264
Czechoslovakia	Iraq	11 Mar 60	464UNTS267	106718
Bulgaria	Romania	14 Mar 60	472UNTS279	106844
Multilateral		15 Mar 60	572UNTS133	108310
France	UN Special Fund	17 Mar 60	354UNTS119	105059
Belgium	Switzerland	24 Mar 60	416UNTS81	105996
Italy	UN Special Fund	01 Apr 60	354UNTS261	105066
Germany, West	Netherlands	08 Apr 60	508UNTS14	107404
Luxembourg	Yugoslavia	09 Apr 60	464UNTS293	106719
Multilateral		11 Apr 60	374UNTS3	105323
UN Special Fund	Tunisia	12 Apr 60	355UNTS289	105082
Multilateral		15 Apr 60	470UNTS239	106811
Libya	UN Special Fund	19 Apr 60	356UNTS11	105090
UN Special Fund	Sudan	21 Apr 60	356UNTS213	105097
Germany, West	Spain	28 Apr 60	465UNTS3	106720
UN Special Fund	Vietnam, South	29 Apr 60	357UNTS311	200567
Laos	UN Special Fund	30 Apr 60	361UNTS171	105179
Greece	Romania	02 May 60	485UNTS17	107043
Poland	Yugoslavia	05 May 60	423UNTS229	106095
United Nations	Togo	06 May 60	388UNTS53	105571
Hungary	Yugoslavia	07 May 60	519UNTS237	107510
Lebanon	UN Special Fund	07 May 60	360UNTS225	105160
Morocco	United Arab Rep	19 May 60	563UNTS121	108208
Switzerland	Tunisia	21 May 60	497UNTS109	107265
Kuwait	UK Great Britain	24 May 60	412UNTS4	105923
Afghanistan	Czechoslovakia	28 May 60	497UNTS129	107266
UN Special Fund	Togo	08 Jun 60	369UNTS401	200574
Luxembourg	Tunisia	13 Jun 60	497UNTS143	107267
Iraq	UN Special Fund	19 Jun 60	376UNTS357	105389
Denmark	Peru	22 Jun 60	439UNTS113	106326
Korea, North	USSR (Soviet Union)	22 Jun 60	399UNTS3	105732
Finland	USSR (Soviet Union)	23 Jun 60	379UNTS277	105443
Ireland	Portugal	24 Jun 60	412UNTS30	105924
IAEA (Atom Energy)	USA (United States)	28 Jun 60	374UNTS133	105333
Kuwait	UN Special Fund	29 Jun 60	369UNTS419	200575
Poland	UK Great Britain	02 Jul 60	385UNTS87	105532
Ethiopia	United Nations	13 Jul 60	368UNTS143	105239

PARTY ONE	PARTY TWO	DATE	CITATION	NUMBER
Procedure (Cont.)				
Ethiopia	UN Special Fund	13 Jul 60	368UNTS159	105240
Switzerland	United Arab Rep	14 Jul 60	497UNTS161	107268
Germany, West	Pakistan	20 Jul 60	465UNTS41	106721
Ghana	Netherlands	30 Jul 60	412UNTS51	105925
Guatemala	USA (United States)	09 Aug 60	461UNTS15	106648
Mexico	USA (United States)	15 Aug 60	402UNTS177	105786
Multilateral		16 Aug 60	382UNTS8	105476
Belgium	Burma	17 Aug 60	540UNTS185	107850
Ghana	United Arab Rep	29 Aug 60	412UNTS71	105926
Multilateral		01 Sep 60	403UNTS3	105792
Brazil	UN Special Fund	16 Sep 60	375UNTS3	105351
Czechoslovakia	India	19 Sep 60	465UNTS67	106722
Pakistan	IBRD (World Bank)	19 Sep 60	444UNTS207	106370
Multilateral		19 Sep 60	444UNTS259	106371
Multilateral		19 Sep 60	419UNTS125	106032
Taiwan	UN Special Fund	20 Sep 60	375UNTS29	105352
Indonesia	UN Special Fund	07 Oct 60	378UNTS141	105424
Liberia	UN Special Fund	11 Oct 60	376UNTS341	105388
Belgium	Jordan	19 Oct 60	479UNTS277	106959
El Salvador	UN Special Fund	24 Oct 60	377UNTS171	105400
Hungary	UK Great Britain	25 Oct 60	419UNTS309	106034
Kuwait	United Nations	31 Oct 60	391UNTS295	200581
Burma	Switzerland	31 Oct 60	465UNTS97	106723
Norway	Peru	02 Nov 60	497UNTS207	107270
Australia	Italy	10 Nov 60	497UNTS247	107271
Czechoslovakia	Poland	14 Nov 60	413UNTS4	105938
Guatemala	UN Special Fund	17 Nov 60	383UNTS67	105495
Pakistan	United Nations	17 Nov 60	380UNTS277	105460
Nepal	UN Special Fund	17 Nov 60	380UNTS289	105461
Indonesia	UK Great Britain	23 Nov 60	398UNTS71	105718
Cambodia	UN Special Fund	24 Nov 60	382UNTS255	105487
Cambodia	Czechoslovakia	27 Nov 60	412UNTS179	105931
Cambodia	United Nations	30 Nov 60	383UNTS147	105500
Multilateral		13 Dec 60	455UNTS204	106544
Multilateral		13 Dec 60	523UNTS117	107557
Multilateral		13 Dec 60	455UNTS3	106543
Bolivia	United Nations	14 Dec 60	382UNTS283	105489
Honduras	UN Special Fund	20 Dec 60	383UNTS103	105497
Canada	Pakistan	21 Dec 60	465UNTS115	106724
Luxembourg	Thailand	29 Dec 60	465UNTS131	106725
Multilateral		30 Dec 60	395UNTS241	105689
Finland	IAEA (Atom Energy)	30 Dec 60	395UNTS257	105690
Burma	UN Special Fund	03 Jan 61	387UNTS219	105564
Jordan	Sweden	09 Jan 61	465UNTS155	106726
Costa Rica	UN Special Fund	10 Jan 61	389UNTS253	105597
Sudan	UK Great Britain	16 Jan 61	424UNTS233	106112
Norway	Poland	17 Jan 61	412UNTS130	105928
Germany, West	Japan	18 Jan 61	465UNTS173	106727
UN Special Fund	Saudi Arabia	19 Jan 61	396UNTS27	105692
Nicaragua	UN Special Fund	20 Jan 61	387UNTS15	105555
Chad	UN Special Fund	23 Jan 61	390UNTS69	105603
UN Special Fund	Somalia	28 Jan 61	388UNTS75	105573
Gabon	UN Special Fund	02 Feb 61	387UNTS289	105568
Nigeria	UN Special Fund	10 Feb 61	390UNTS85	105604
Belgium	USA (United States)	21 Feb 61	480UNTS149	106967
Mexico	UN Special Fund	23 Feb 61	388UNTS151	105576
Cyprus	UN Special Fund	24 Feb 61	389UNTS3	105588
Cuba	Czechoslovakia	04 Mar 61	465UNTS209	106728
Iraq	United Nations	05 Mar 61	409UNTS56	105878
Multilateral		08 Mar 61	396UNTS255	200584
Belgium	UK Great Britain	08 Mar 61	523UNTS17	107554
Panama	UN Special Fund	09 Mar 61	396UNTS3	105691
Cuba	UN Special Fund	10 Mar 61	390UNTS35	105601
Iceland	UK Great Britain	11 Mar 61	397UNTS275	105710
Multilateral		14 Apr 61	422UNTS101	106071

PARTY ONE	PARTY TWO	DATE	CITATION	NUMBER
Procedure (Cont.)				
Multilateral		18 Apr 61	500UNTS243	107312
Korea, South	UN Special Fund	21 Apr 61	394UNTS231	200583
Turkey	USSR (Soviet Union)	27 Apr 61	420UNTS307	106047
Ceylon (Sri Lanka)	UN Special Fund	03 May 61	395UNTS217	105687
Japan	Peru	15 May 61	451UNTS3	106482
Poland	Switzerland	18 May 61	559UNTS233	108161
Czechoslovakia	Indonesia	29 May 61	479UNTS337	106962
Czechoslovakia	Morocco	08 Jun 61	497UNTS275	107272
Cameroon	UN Special Fund	13 Jun 61	397UNTS297	105713
New Zealand	UK Great Britain	13 Jun 61	497UNTS293	107273
Cyprus	United Nations	15 Jun 61	398UNTS39	105716
Cameroon	France	16 Jun 61	412UNTS148	105929
Guinea	Sweden	17 Jun 61	465UNTS236	106729
Paraguay	UN Special Fund	22 Jun 61	399UNTS117	105738
UN Special Fund	Upper Volta	26 Jun 61	400UNTS3	105744
Philippines	UN Special Fund	28 Jun 61	399UNTS141	105739
Haiti	United Nations	28 Jun 61	399UNTS159	105740
Haiti	UN Special Fund	28 Jun 61	399UNTS171	105741
Bulgaria	Hungary	30 Jun 61	438UNTS287	106320
Bulgaria	Poland	12 Jul 61	436UNTS147	106294
Austria	UK Great Britain	14 Jul 61	453UNTS267	106530
Mali	UN Special Fund	21 Jul 61	401UNTS141	105768
UN Special Fund	Yemen	02 Aug 61	402UNTS43	105777
Czechoslovakia	Ghana	02 Aug 61	465UNTS249	106730
Finland	Luxembourg	15 Aug 61	541UNTS45	107859
Jordan	Norway	21 Aug 61	465UNTS275	106731
Hungary	Indonesia	23 Aug 61	519UNTS163	107507
Jordan	Netherlands	24 Aug 61	466UNTS3	106733
Mexico	Netherlands	24 Aug 61	465UNTS291	106732
Lebanon	United Nations	26 Aug 61	406UNTS105	105842
Israel	Malagasy	27 Aug 61	484UNTS217	107032
Ivory Coast	UN Special Fund	29 Aug 61	406UNTS129	105844
Liberia	Switzerland	31 Aug 61	559UNTS215	108160
Jordan	United Nations	11 Sep 61	406UNTS255	105855
Bulgaria	Poland	19 Sep 61	483UNTS249	107018
Ghana	Romania	30 Sep 61	467UNTS443	106769
UN Special Fund	Sierra Leone	02 Oct 61	422UNTS131	106073
Multilateral		05 Oct 61	510UNTS175	107413
IBRD (World Bank)	Switzerland	11 Oct 61	415UNTS396	200592
Germany, West	Morocco	12 Oct 61	523UNTS289	107562
Japan	Pakistan	17 Oct 61	466UNTS17	106734
Mauritania	UN Special Fund	07 Nov 61	412UNTS240	105936
Congo (Brazzaville)	UN Special Fund	09 Nov 61	413UNTS58	105940
Argentina	Brazil	15 Nov 61	0UNTS0	109424
Cyprus	Greece	23 Nov 61	497UNTS311	107274
Czechoslovakia	Mali	27 Nov 61	466UNTS41	106736
Ivory Coast	USA (United States)	01 Dec 61	462UNTS221	106681
Ceylon (Sri Lanka)	United Nations	04 Dec 61	415UNTS236	105987
COMECON (Econ Aid)	USSR (Soviet Union)	07 Dec 61	506UNTS325	107392
UN Special Fund	Venezuela	11 Dec 61	422UNTS149	106074
Germany, West	Thailand	13 Dec 61	541UNTS181	107870
UN Special Fund	Senegal	16 Dec 61	425UNTS97	106121
Czechoslovakia	Guinea	16 Dec 61	559UNTS49	108154
Netherlands	Sweden	08 Jan 62	466UNTS65	106737
Austria	Greece	15 Jan 62	498UNTS3	107275
United Nations	Somalia	20 Jan 62	420UNTS133	106044
Indonesia	Japan	23 Jan 62	559UNTS77	108155
Italy	Japan	31 Jan 62	498UNTS23	107276
Finland	Hungary	13 Feb 62	463UNTS61	106693
Austria	Spain	19 Feb 62	0UNTS0	109238
USSR (Soviet Union)	Yugoslavia	24 Feb 62	471UNTS195	106833
Niger	UN Special Fund	26 Feb 62	423UNTS83	106086
Germany, West	Thailand	05 Mar 62	563UNTS165	108210
United Nations	Saudi Arabia	16 Mar 62	456UNTS379	106566
Luxembourg	Spain	26 Mar 62	563UNTS205	108211
Procedure (Cont.)				
Dahomey	UN Special Fund	28 Mar 62	424UNTS55	106099
Multilateral		29 Mar 62	507UNTS177	107401
France	Luxembourg	29 Mar 62	563UNTS227	108212
Taiwan	Malagasy	04 Apr 62	463UNTS195	106703
Sierra Leone	UK Great Britain	05 Apr 62	434UNTS227	106265
Ghana	USSR (Soviet Union)	06 Apr 62	498UNTS41	107277
Niger	USA (United States)	26 Apr 62	459UNTS129	106618
UN Special Fund	Uruguay	04 May 62	429UNTS143	106196
Japan	United Arab Rep	10 May 62	498UNTS69	107278
Multilateral		15 May 62	444UNTS3	106367
Gabon	Israel	15 May 62	484UNTS181	107027
Greece	United Nations	18 May 62	429UNTS61	106190
France	Romania	18 May 62	498UNTS115	107279
United Nations	Tanganyika	01 Jun 62	479UNTS3	106944
Dominican Republic	UN Special Fund	06 Jun 62	429UNTS169	106197
Multilateral		14 Jun 62	528UNTS33	107634
France	Senegal	15 Jun 62	524UNTS3	107563
Czechoslovakia	Senegal	20 Jun 62	498UNTS145	107280
Guinea	Norway	21 Jun 62	466UNTS81	106738
Multilateral		27 Jun 62	463UNTS17	106690
Congo (Zaire)	IAEA (Atom Energy)	27 Jun 62	463UNTS31	106691
Liberia	Norway	29 Jun 62	466UNTS95	106739
Morocco	Switzerland	05 Jul 62	498UNTS171	107281
Morocco	Switzerland	05 Jul 62	498UNTS189	107282
UN Special Fund	Syria	07 Jul 62	443UNTS3	106355
UN Special Fund	Tanganyika	17 Jul 62	435UNTS237	106281
Czechoslovakia	COMECON (Econ Aid)	20 Jul 62	506UNTS345	107393
Ethiopia	USA (United States)	03 Aug 62	459UNTS79	106613
Nigeria	United Nations	07 Aug 62	435UNTS167	106278
IAEA (Atom Energy)	USA (United States)	20 Aug 62	456UNTS447	106570
Cameroon	United Nations	29 Aug 62	442UNTS3	106334
Germany, West	Netherlands	30 Aug 62	500UNTS3	107303
Congo (Brazzaville)	USA (United States)	01 Sep 62	459UNTS117	106616
Multilateral		14 Sep 62	494UNTS219	107236
Ecuador	Germany, West	20 Sep 62	498UNTS199	107283
Belgium	Germany, West	21 Sep 62	502UNTS63	107326
Austria	Czechoslovakia	22 Sep 62	495UNTS157	107244
Multilateral		28 Sep 62	469UNTS169	106791
Niger	United Nations	01 Oct 62	439UNTS181	106329
Japan	Kuwait	06 Oct 62	498UNTS235	107284
Finland	France	12 Oct 62	498UNTS299	107285
Belgium	Rwanda	13 Oct 62	456UNTS425	106568
Germany, West	Ireland	17 Oct 62	604UNTS135	108749
Hungary	Syria	18 Oct 62	491UNTS209	107178
Netherlands	Norway	18 Oct 62	466UNTS145	106741
France	Ivory Coast	19 Oct 62	498UNTS317	107286
Japan	UN Special Fund	31 Oct 62	444UNTS171	106368
United Nations	Western Samoa	05 Nov 62	443UNTS297	200599
Poland	Syria	10 Nov 62	491UNTS228	107179
Algeria	UN Special Fund	15 Nov 62	452UNTS243	106512
Ivory Coast	Switzerland	17 Nov 62	499UNTS3	107289
Congo (Zaire)	USA (United States)	17 Nov 62	474UNTS41	106870
Ecuador	United Nations	26 Nov 62	445UNTS3	106372
Rwanda	United Nations	28 Nov 62	450UNTS267	106473
Ivory Coast	United Nations	10 Dec 62	451UNTS269	106498
Ghana	Tunisia	11 Dec 62	563UNTS243	108213
Austria	Yugoslavia	11 Dec 62	546UNTS3	107938
Multilateral		17 Dec 62	523UNTS93	107555
Hungary	USSR (Soviet Union)	20 Dec 62	577UNTS245	108381
Nigeria	USA (United States)	24 Dec 62	462UNTS180	106677
Syria	United Arab Rep	27 Dec 62	491UNTS245	107180
Jamaica	USA (United States)	04 Jan 63	471UNTS119	106826
Israel	United Nations	07 Jan 63	450UNTS229	106470
Korea, South	USA (United States)	08 Jan 63	493UNTS105	107211
Ghana	Mali	09 Jan 63	466UNTS165	106742

PARTY ONE	PARTY TWO	DATE	CITATION	NUMBER
Procedure (Cont.)				
Trinidad/Tobago	USA (United States)	15 Jan 63	471UNTS141	106829
Senegal	Switzerland	23 Jan 63	524UNTS23	107564
Guinea	Switzerland	01 Feb 63	499UNTS35	107291
Mali	Senegal	07 Feb 63	524UNTS41	107565
Algeria	France	18 Feb 63	563UNTS263	108214
Sudan	Switzerland	18 Feb 63	563UNTS281	108215
Poland	COMECON (Econ Aid)	22 Feb 63	506UNTS303	107391
Hungary	COMECON (Econ Aid)	28 Feb 63	506UNTS281	107390
IAEA (Atom Energy)	Yugoslavia	04 Mar 63	490UNTS333	107162
Austria	Czechoslovakia	08 Mar 63	495UNTS219	107245
UN Special Fund	Uganda	22 Mar 63	456UNTS466	106572
Burma	Japan	29 Mar 63	518UNTS3	107490
Gabon	USA (United States)	10 Apr 63	474UNTS113	106876
Brazil	USSR (Soviet Union)	20 Apr 63	0UNTS0	109257
Multilateral		20 Apr 63	495UNTS3	107239
Multilateral		24 Apr 63	596UNTS487	108640
Greece	Hungary	27 Apr 63	534UNTS3	107750
Cyprus	Denmark	27 Apr 63	529UNTS255	107664
Algeria	Morocco	30 Apr 63	564UNTS3	108217
UN Special Fund	Trinidad/Tobago	06 May 63	463UNTS93	106695
United Nations	Trinidad/Tobago	06 May 63	463UNTS109	106696
Australia	USA (United States)	09 May 63	469UNTS55	106784
Mali	United Nations	09 May 63	463UNTS147	106699
Burma	Thailand	17 May 63	468UNTS319	106779
Jamaica	UN Special Fund	22 May 63	489UNTS191	107140
Jamaica	United Nations	22 May 63	479UNTS19	106945
Netherlands	Tunisia	23 May 63	523UNTS237	107558
Netherlands	UN Special Fund	24 May 63	466UNTS289	106750
Cyprus	USA (United States)	29 May 63	487UNTS283	107110
United Nations	Uganda	29 May 63	466UNTS311	106751
IAEA (Atom Energy)	Yugoslavia	04 Jun 63	490UNTS343	107163
UN Special Fund	Western Samoa	05 Jun 63	467UNTS463	200601
Belgium	Cyprus	08 Jun 63	601UNTS311	108703
Multilateral		09 Jun 63	538UNTS309	107818
Finland	Poland	10 Jun 63	503UNTS179	107343
Guinea	Ivory Coast	26 Jun 63	499UNTS71	107293
United Nations	UK Great Britain	27 Jun 63	469UNTS145	106789
United Arab Rep	USA (United States)	29 Jun 63	479UNTS207	106954
Denmark	India	12 Jul 63	616UNTS3	108888
Austria	France	12 Jul 63	499UNTS91	107294
Algeria	Mali	22 Jul 63	564UNTS29	108219
Mali	Tunisia	24 Jul 63	602UNTS91	108708
Malagasy	USA (United States)	26 Jul 63	487UNTS189	107104
Dominican Republic	United Nations	05 Aug 63	472UNTS353	106847
Cameroon	Israel	09 Aug 63	499UNTS121	107295
Burundi	UN Special Fund	22 Aug 63	476UNTS49	106903
United Nations	United Arab Rep	27 Aug 63	474UNTS221	106884
Algeria	Tunisia	01 Sep 63	601UNTS275	108701
Multilateral		23 Sep 63	488UNTS99	107122
Pakistan	USSR (Soviet Union)	07 Oct 63	499UNTS161	107297
Ivory Coast	Netherlands	09 Oct 63	499UNTS141	107296
Multilateral		26 Oct 63	587UNTS9	108506
Central Afri Rep	UN Special Fund	30 Oct 63	481UNTS247	106985
WHO (World Health)	Somalia	08 Nov 63	493UNTS243	107218
Tanganyika	USA (United States)	14 Nov 63	493UNTS75	107208
WHO (World Health)	Sierra Leone	22 Nov 63	493UNTS255	107219
Multilateral		03 Dec 63	529UNTS217	107663
Czechoslovakia	Romania	16 Dec 63	527UNTS285	107630
Mexico	IAEA (Atom Energy)	18 Dec 63	490UNTS361	107165
France	South Africa	06 Jan 64	601UNTS229	108699
Somalia	USA (United States)	08 Jan 64	505UNTS165	107372
Mali	Niger	15 Jan 64	499UNTS197	107299
Denmark	Yugoslavia	11 Feb 64	511UNTS241	107437
United Nations	Sierra Leone	19 Feb 64	489UNTS91	107136
United Nations	Upper Volta	26 Feb 64	489UNTS179	107139

PARTY ONE	PARTY TWO	DATE	CITATION	NUMBER
Procedure (Cont.)				
Morocco	United Nations	03 Mar 64	490UNTS187	107154
Algeria	Czechoslovakia	09 Mar 64	601UNTS247	108700
Cameroon	Mali	17 Mar 64	524UNTS61	107566
USSR (Soviet Union)	Yemen	21 Mar 64	553UNTS267	108094
Cyprus	United Nations	31 Mar 64	492UNTS57	107187
Portugal	UK Great Britain	07 Apr 64	539UNTS167	107830
Malaysia	Netherlands	07 Apr 64	524UNTS81	107567
Norway	Yugoslavia	15 Apr 64	602UNTS177	108712
Kenya	USA (United States)	20 Apr 64	524UNTS165	107571
Finland	USSR (Soviet Union)	24 Apr 64	537UNTS231	107804
Japan	UK Great Britain	04 May 64	561UNTS25	108179
United Arab Rep	USA (United States)	05 May 64	531UNTS229	107706
Multilateral		06 May 64	514UNTS71	107442
Hungary	Yemen	30 May 64	577UNTS39	108371
Cyprus	Hungary	02 Jun 64	602UNTS3	108704
Mali	USA (United States)	09 Jun 64	530UNTS133	107678
Multilateral		20 Jun 64	539UNTS3	107819
New Zealand	USA (United States)	24 Jun 64	524UNTS101	107568
Ivory Coast	Mali	09 Jul 64	524UNTS121	107569
Multilateral		10 Jul 64	611UNTS7	108844
Iceland	UN Special Fund	10 Jul 64	502UNTS343	107337
Belgium	Tunisia	15 Jul 64	561UNTS297	108190
Multilateral		28 Jul 64	555UNTS183	108113
Eur Space Research	Sweden	29 Jul 64	528UNTS81	107636
France	Eur Space Research	10 Aug 64	528UNTS135	107637
Canada	Japan	05 Sep 64	569UNTS99	108282
Multilateral		18 Sep 64	555UNTS205	108114
Multilateral		21 Sep 64	555UNTS227	108115
Algeria	United Nations	23 Sep 64	510UNTS217	107416
Kenya	UN Special Fund	01 Oct 64	511UNTS181	107433
Kenya	United Nations	01 Oct 64	511UNTS199	107434
Romania	UN Special Fund	24 Oct 64	519UNTS29	107500
Malawi	UN Special Fund	24 Oct 64	514UNTS235	200609
Italy	ILO (Labor Org)	24 Oct 64	541UNTS217	107871
France	Japan	27 Nov 64	569UNTS157	108283
Multilateral		01 Dec 64	550UNTS133	108012
Multilateral		02 Dec 64	572UNTS229	108317
State/IGO Group	IAEA (Atom Energy)	04 Dec 64	637UNTS0	109111
UN Special Fund	Zambia	15 Dec 64	522UNTS3	107532
Cyprus	Syria	22 Dec 64	602UNTS25	108705
Laos	USA (United States)	29 Dec 64	542UNTS23	107876
Central Afri Rep	USA (United States)	31 Dec 64	542UNTS29	107877
Argentina	UK Great Britain	12 Jan 65	597UNTS177	108645
Malta	Switzerland	20 Jan 65	548UNTS193	107978
Ethiopia	WHO (World Health)	27 Jan 65	541UNTS135	107866
Belgium	Congo (Zaire)	06 Feb 65	540UNTS227	107852
Multilateral		23 Feb 65	527UNTS120	107622
Multilateral		24 Feb 65	556UNTS47	108118
Multilateral		26 Feb 65	556UNTS69	108119
Multilateral		05 Mar 65	527UNTS221	107627
Dahomey	USA (United States)	13 Mar 65	549UNTS43	107987
Multilateral		18 Mar 65	575UNTS159	108359
Finland	UK Great Britain	25 Mar 65	539UNTS103	107826
Denmark	Malaysia	26 Mar 65	540UNTS205	107851
Multilateral		08 Apr 65	533UNTS66	107733
Australia	France	13 Apr 65	601UNTS293	108702
Ivory Coast	Netherlands	26 Apr 65	634UNTS81	109053
Multilateral		26 Apr 65	533UNTS50	107732
Ghana	Malawi	04 May 65	541UNTS163	107869
Denmark	Spain	05 May 65	543UNTS255	107905
Mauritania	Spain	11 May 65	602UNTS111	108709
Chad	USA (United States)	12 May 65	546UNTS183	107944
Canada	USA (United States)	12 May 65	545UNTS169	107933
Multilateral		12 May 65	534UNTS390	107769
Multilateral		14 May 65	550UNTS310	108026

PARTY ONE	PARTY TWO	DATE	CITATION	NUMBER
Procedure (Cont.)				
Multilateral		25 May 65	535UNTS374	107791
Malaysia	Norway	26 May 65	602UNTS157	108711
British Guiana	USA (United States)	29 May 65	605UNTS87	108761
Uganda	USA (United States)	29 May 65	546UNTS209	107948
Multilateral		02 Jun 65	551UNTS2	108030
Saudi Arabia	USA (United States)	05 Jun 65	548UNTS285	107984
Ivory Coast	Sweden	07 Jun 65	0UNTS0	109240
Netherlands	Senegal	12 Jun 65	602UNTS231	108715
USA (United States)	Upper Volta	18 Jun 65	549UNTS133	107996
Japan	Korea, South	22 Jun 65	584UNTS147	108476
UN Special Fund	Spain	30 Jun 65	544UNTS159	107918
Multilateral		05 Jul 65	563UNTS104	108207
Switzerland	UK Great Britain	07 Jul 65	605UNTS205	108765
Cameroon	France	10 Jul 65	0UNTS0	109433
Australia	Eur Space Vehicle	13 Jul 65	543UNTS183	107902
Multilateral		20 Jul 65	541UNTS12	107857
France	Mauritania	22 Jul 65	0UNTS0	109329
Multilateral		13 Sep 65	547UNTS248	107961
Multilateral		21 Sep 65	547UNTS280	107963
IAEA (Atom Energy)	Uruguay	24 Sep 65	556UNTS117	108123
Nigeria	Switzerland	11 Oct 65	602UNTS137	108710
Cuba	USA (United States)	06 Nov 65	601UNTS81	108688
Multilateral		12 Nov 65	550UNTS160	108013
Austria	Yugoslavia	19 Nov 65	591UNTS3	108556
Multilateral		31 Dec 65	616UNTS317	108904
Iran	USSR (Soviet Union)	13 Jan 66	633UNTS123	109037
Multilateral		17 Jan 66	592UNTS101	108573
Japan	USSR (Soviet Union)	21 Jan 66	633UNTS165	109038
Mongolia	UN Special Fund	26 Jan 66	552UNTS201	108055
New Zealand	United Nations	21 Feb 66	555UNTS163	108110
Canada	United Nations	21 Feb 66	555UNTS119	108107
United Nations	UK Great Britain	21 Feb 66	555UNTS177	108112
Finland	United Nations	21 Feb 66	555UNTS157	108109
United Nations	Sweden	21 Feb 66	555UNTS169	108111
Denmark	United Nations	21 Feb 66	555UNTS151	108108
Austria	United Nations	24 Feb 66	557UNTS129	108131
Australia	United Nations	25 Feb 66	557UNTS85	108129
Pakistan	IAEA (Atom Energy)	15 Mar 66	588UNTS261	108530
Denmark	Netherlands	31 Mar 66	604UNTS209	108751
Singapore	USSR (Soviet Union)	02 Apr 66	631UNTS125	108992
Multilateral		28 Apr 66	604UNTS219	108752
Bulgaria	UN Special Fund	26 May 66	563UNTS71	108205
Ivory Coast	Norway	07 Jun 66	0UNTS0	109249
Canada	USA (United States)	15 Jun 66	594UNTS83	108595
Mexico	IAEA (Atom Energy)	20 Jun 66	573UNTS25	108321
Multilateral		20 Jun 66	572UNTS263	108318
Romania	USSR (Soviet Union)	21 Jun 66	604UNTS81	108746
Austria	USA (United States)	23 Jun 66	601UNTS51	108687
Austria	France	15 Jul 66	604UNTS265	108755
Philippines	IAEA (Atom Energy)	28 Sep 66	589UNTS25	108533
Multilateral		28 Sep 66	589UNTS41	108534
Argentina	Vatican/Holy See	10 Oct 66	601UNTS187	108696
IAEA (Atom Energy)	Turkey	08 Dec 66	608UNTS69	108813
Norway	Singapore	20 Dec 66	0UNTS0	109242
Denmark	Singapore	20 Dec 66	593UNTS125	108580
Iran	Thailand	02 Feb 67	614UNTS251	108874
Czechoslovakia	USSR (Soviet Union)	03 Feb 67	617UNTS267	108917
Australia	UN Special Fund	06 Feb 67	590UNTS3	108543
Japan	Singapore	14 Feb 67	0UNTS0	109244
Algeria	Ivory Coast	16 Feb 67	0UNTS0	109245
Multilateral		27 Feb 67	590UNTS156	108552
Trinidad/Tobago	UK Great Britain	01 Mar 67	606UNTS149	108784
Australia	Austria	22 Mar 67	0UNTS0	109246
Austria	Yugoslavia	08 Apr 67	0UNTS0	109216
Denmark	Norway	20 Apr 67	604UNTS103	108747

PARTY ONE	PARTY TWO	DATE	CITATION	NUMBER
Procedure (Cont.)				
Iran	IAEA (Atom Energy)	10 May 67	614UNTS93	108865
IAEA (Atom Energy)	USA (United States)	07 Jun 67	614UNTS109	108866
Multilateral		10 Jun 67	602UNTS212	108714
Netherlands	Sierra Leone	13 Jun 67	0UNTS0	109247
Malta	USA (United States)	14 Jun 67	604UNTS231	108753
Multilateral		14 Jun 67	603UNTS2	108719
State/IGO Group	IAEA (Atom Energy)	19 Jun 67	637UNTS0	109112
Denmark	Peru	20 Jun 67	0UNTS0	109446
Multilateral		21 Jun 67	598UNTS2	108653
IAEA (Atom Energy)	Spain	23 Jun 67	614UNTS169	108870
Multilateral		23 Jun 67	614UNTS185	108871
Multilateral		03 Jul 67	0UNTS0	109248
Czechoslovakia	UN Special Fund	13 Jul 67	606UNTS71	108776
Malaysia	UK Great Britain	01 Aug 67	633UNTS93	109036
Denmark	Ghana	09 Aug 67	610UNTS0	108842
Ceylon (Sri Lanka)	IBRD (World Bank)	24 Aug 67	632UNTS217	109025
IAEA (Atom Energy)	Vietnam, South	16 Oct 67	630UNTS379	200636
IAEA (Atom Energy)	USA (United States)	16 Oct 67	630UNTS57	108965
Denmark	Zambia	17 Oct 67	620UNTS239	108960
Multilateral		27 Oct 67	608UNTS37	108811
Multilateral		14 Nov 67	614UNTS2	108860
Austria	Switzerland	15 Nov 67	0UNTS0	109434
State/IGO Group	IAEA (Atom Energy)	05 Jan 68	637UNTS0	109114
Czechoslovakia	Hungary	27 Feb 68	640UNTS49	109154
State/IGO Group	IAEA (Atom Energy)	28 Feb 68	637UNTS0	109115
Multilateral		18 Mar 68	0UNTS0	109262
Denmark	India	25 Mar 68	0UNTS0	109229
State/IGO Group	Jordan	03 Apr 68	632UNTS66	109009
State/IGO Group	Nigeria	20 Apr 68	636UNTS294	109106
Denmark	India	29 Apr 68	0UNTS0	109230
State/IGO Group	IBRD (World Bank)	02 May 68	637UNTS0	109110
State/IGO Group	Malaysia	10 May 68	636UNTS276	109105
State/IGO Group	Sierra Leone	29 May 68	637UNTS0	109120
Denmark	Tunisia	07 Jun 68	0UNTS0	109407
Honduras	IDA (Devel Assoc)	12 Jun 68	0UNTS0	109409
Denmark	Int Coun Expl Sea	24 Jul 68	0UNTS0	109413
Denmark	Senegal	03 Aug 68	0UNTS0	109282
Multilateral		28 Sep 68	0UNTS0	109296
Denmark	Morocco	05 Nov 68	0UNTS0	109415
Denmark	Malawi	16 Dec 68	0UNTS0	109461
Multilateral		24 Dec 68	0UNTS0	109369
State/IGO Group	Southern Yemen	04 Apr 69	0UNTS0	109454
UN Special Fund	Southern Yemen	04 Apr 69	0UNTS0	109456
State/IGO Group	Southern Yemen	04 Apr 69	0UNTS0	109455
State/IGO Group	Yemen	23 Apr 69	0UNTS0	109514
Disputes disrupting normal relations				
Multilateral		26 Oct 56	276UNTS3	103988
Domestic jurisdiction				
Brazil	Venezuela	30 Mar 40	51UNTS291	200195
Multilateral		12 Nov 47	46UNTS201	100710
Philippines	Thailand	14 Jun 49	81UNTS53	101062
Canada	UK Great Britain	19 Aug 49	44UNTS223	100686
Denmark	ICAO (Civil Aviat)	09 Sep 49	53UNTS341	100791
Italy	Turkey	24 Mar 50	96UNTS207	101338
Germany, West	USA (United States)	11 Jun 52	273UNTS105	103947
India	Philippines	11 Jul 52	203UNTS73	102741
Indonesia	Thailand	03 Mar 54	213UNTS297	102893
Brazil	Italy	24 Nov 54	284UNTS325	104146
Multilateral		29 Apr 57	320UNTS243	104646
Czechoslovakia	Romania	16 Dec 63	527UNTS285	107630
Existing tribunals				
Canada	France	12 May 33	253UNTS285	200545
Brazil	France	27 Jan 40	72UNTS77	100929
Norway	USA (United States)	28 Mar 40	88UNTS365	200253

Existing tribunals (Cont.)

PARTY ONE	PARTY TWO	DATE	CITATION	NUMBER
Brazil	Venezuela	30 Mar 40	51UNTS291	200195
Greece	UK Great Britain	26 Nov 45	35UNTS161	100555
Portugal	UK Great Britain	06 Dec 45	6UNTS3	100065
Portugal	UK Great Britain	06 Dec 45	5UNTS37	100064
Canada	UK Great Britain	21 Dec 45	27UNTS155	100405
Czechoslovakia	Poland	24 Jan 46	25UNTS181	100363
UK Great Britain	USA (United States)	11 Feb 46	3UNTS253	100036
Turkey	UK Great Britain	12 Feb 46	6UNTS79	100069
France	UK Great Britain	28 Feb 46	27UNTS173	100407
France	USA (United States)	27 Mar 46	139UNTS114	101879
Greece	USA (United States)	27 Mar 46	15UNTS233	100239
Ireland	UK Great Britain	05 Apr 46	72UNTS57	100928
Belgium	USA (United States)	05 Apr 46	4UNTS125	100041
Netherlands	Portugal	12 Apr 46	4UNTS317	100054
France	Ireland	16 May 46	44UNTS105	100681
Ireland	Sweden	29 May 46	35UNTS231	100557
Australia	Canada	11 Jun 46	10UNTS47	100142
Sweden	Turkey	26 Jun 46	14UNTS21	100208
United Nations	Switzerland	01 Jul 46	1UNTS163	200008
Netherlands	Spain	13 Jul 46	4UNTS351	100055
Canada	Newfoundland	29 Jul 46	17UNTS169	100275
France	Sweden	02 Aug 46	27UNTS251	100410
Lebanon	USA (United States)	11 Aug 46	66UNTS211	100856
Netherlands	UK Great Britain	13 Aug 46	4UNTS367	100056
Norway	UK Great Britain	31 Aug 46	6UNTS235	100078
Brazil	USA (United States)	06 Sep 46	54UNTS197	100805
France	Turkey	12 Oct 46	14UNTS33	100209
Belgium	Portugal	22 Oct 46	34UNTS49	100527
Brazil	UK Great Britain	31 Oct 46	11UNTS115	100152
India	USA (United States)	14 Nov 46	22UNTS55	100331
Sweden	UK Great Britain	27 Nov 46	11UNTS229	100162
New Zealand	USA (United States)	03 Dec 46	7UNTS175	100099
Australia	USA (United States)	03 Dec 46	7UNTS201	100100
Portugal	Switzerland	09 Dec 46	310UNTS251	104495
Brazil	Portugal	10 Dec 46	200UNTS67	102695
Multilateral		13 Dec 46	8UNTS165	100121
Multilateral		13 Dec 46	8UNTS151	100120
Multilateral		13 Dec 46	8UNTS119	100118
Multilateral		13 Dec 46	8UNTS105	100117
Multilateral		13 Dec 46	8UNTS135	100119
USA (United States)	Uruguay	14 Dec 46	532UNTS87	107713
Taiwan	USA (United States)	20 Dec 46	22UNTS87	100332
Peru	USA (United States)	27 Dec 46	26UNTS227	100390
Ecuador	USA (United States)	08 Jan 47	22UNTS119	100333
Czechoslovakia	Ireland	29 Jan 47	27UNTS267	100411
UNESCO (Educ/Cult)	United Nations	03 Feb 47	1UNTS233	200011
FAO (Food Agri)	United Nations	03 Feb 47	1UNTS207	200010
Thailand	USA (United States)	26 Feb 47	16UNTS17	100246
Paraguay	USA (United States)	28 Feb 47	44UNTS25	100676
Portugal	Sweden	06 Mar 47	35UNTS243	100558
France	ICAO (Civil Aviat)	14 Mar 47	94UNTS59	101306
Netherlands	Turkey	19 Mar 47	14UNTS59	100211
Greece	Netherlands	17 Apr 47	32UNTS115	100494
Canada	Portugal	25 Apr 47	94UNTS87	101308
Syria	USA (United States)	28 Apr 47	262UNTS121	103741
France	Greece	05 May 47	76UNTS61	100980
Chile	USA (United States)	10 May 47	55UNTS21	100807
Czechoslovakia	Denmark	14 May 47	27UNTS297	100413
Canada	Sweden	27 Jun 47	27UNTS313	100414
Iraq	Turkey	30 Jun 47	72UNTS107	100930
Denmark	Turkey	30 Jun 47	32UNTS301	100504
France	India	16 Jul 47	27UNTS325	100415
Canada	UK Great Britain	17 Jul 47	28UNTS3	100416
Netherlands	Thailand	18 Jul 47	28UNTS27	100417
Greece	Turkey	22 Jul 47	72UNTS131	100931

Existing tribunals (Cont.)

PARTY ONE	PARTY TWO	DATE	CITATION	NUMBER
Taiwan	UK Great Britain	23 Jul 47	9UNTS207	100135
Canada	Ireland	08 Aug 47	28UNTS47	100419
Poland	Romania	09 Aug 47	12UNTS363	100193
Multilateral		02 Sep 47	21UNTS77	100324
Czechoslovakia	Switzerland	10 Sep 47	35UNTS275	100559
Lebanon	Turkey	16 Sep 47	44UNTS123	100682
Chile	UK Great Britain	16 Sep 47	133UNTS143	101786
Czechoslovakia	Sweden	15 Oct 47	44UNTS149	100683
Colombia	UK Great Britain	16 Oct 47	160UNTS297	102115
Burma	UK Great Britain	17 Oct 47	70UNTS183	100904
Norway	Portugal	11 Nov 47	34UNTS257	100542
Multilateral		12 Nov 47	46UNTS201	100710
Multilateral		12 Nov 47	53UNTS49	100772
Denmark	Greece	14 Nov 47	35UNTS295	100560
Denmark	Ireland	18 Nov 47	35UNTS309	100561
Albania	UNICEF (Children)	20 Nov 47	65UNTS163	200208
Multilateral		21 Nov 47	33UNTS261	100521
Denmark	Portugal	15 Dec 47	35UNTS329	100563
Peru	UK Great Britain	22 Dec 47	72UNTS143	100932
Philippines	UK Great Britain	07 Jan 48	28UNTS63	100420
France	Lebanon	24 Jan 48	173UNTS99	102263
France	UNICEF (Children)	19 Feb 48	68UNTS75	100885
Cuba	UK Great Britain	19 Mar 48	175UNTS23	102294
Pakistan	Sweden	06 May 48	36UNTS3	100564
Ireland	Switzerland	06 May 48	334UNTS187	104768
Jordan	Turkey	07 May 48	32UNTS313	100505
Ireland	Netherlands	10 May 48	28UNTS121	100422
Norway	Turkey	20 May 48	26UNTS137	100384
India	Sweden	21 May 48	34UNTS285	100543
Greece	Switzerland	26 May 48	94UNTS217	101312
Canada	Netherlands	02 Jun 48	32UNTS215	100499
Ireland	Norway	21 Jun 48	34UNTS317	100545
India	Pakistan	23 Jun 48	28UNTS143	100423
Italy	UK Great Britain	25 Jun 48	94UNTS239	101313
Ireland	USA (United States)	28 Jun 48	24UNTS3	100349
France	USA (United States)	28 Jun 48	19UNTS9	100302
Denmark	USA (United States)	29 Jun 48	22UNTS217	100338
Austria	USA (United States)	02 Jul 48	21UNTS29	100323
Belgium	USA (United States)	02 Jul 48	19UNTS127	100309
Greece	USA (United States)	02 Jul 48	23UNTS43	100342
Netherlands	USA (United States)	02 Jul 48	20UNTS91	100315
Sweden	USA (United States)	03 Jul 48	23UNTS101	100343
Taiwan	USA (United States)	03 Jul 48	17UNTS119	100273
Luxembourg	USA (United States)	03 Jul 48	24UNTS35	100350
Norway	USA (United States)	03 Jul 48	20UNTS185	100317
Iceland	USA (United States)	03 Jul 48	20UNTS141	100316
Turkey	USA (United States)	04 Jul 48	24UNTS67	100351
UK Great Britain	USA (United States)	06 Jul 48	22UNTS263	100339
France	UK Great Britain	15 Jul 48	71UNTS215	100920
Greece	Lebanon	06 Sep 48	178UNTS37	102335
Portugal	USA (United States)	28 Sep 48	29UNTS213	100442
Greece	Lebanon	06 Oct 48	87UNTS351	101179
France	USA (United States)	19 Oct 48	98UNTS3	101355
Mexico	Portugal	22 Oct 48	34UNTS329	100546
Peru	ICAO (Civil Aviat)	22 Oct 48	95UNTS3	101315
Australia	Belgium	09 Dec 48	25UNTS159	100361
Multilateral		09 Dec 48	78UNTS277	101021
Denmark	Poland	14 Dec 48	81UNTS33	101060
Argentina	Chile	14 Dec 48	635UNTS21	109071
Ceylon (Sri Lanka)	India	21 Dec 48	28UNTS223	100427
Ceylon (Sri Lanka)	Pakistan	03 Jan 49	28UNTS247	100428
IRO (Refugee Org)	United Nations	07 Feb 49	26UNTS299	200153
Switzerland	Turkey	16 Feb 49	72UNTS175	100933
Belgium	France	18 Feb 49	31UNTS173	100478
Finland	Netherlands	25 Feb 49	53UNTS123	100777

PARTY ONE	PARTY TWO	DATE	CITATION	NUMBER
Existing tribunals (Cont.)				
Netherlands	Switzerland	07 Mar 49	35UNTS69	100551
Finland	Sweden	26 Apr 49	95UNTS83	101318
ITU (Telecommun)	United Nations	26 Apr 49	30UNTS315	200175
Multilateral		28 Apr 49	71UNTS101	100912
Australia	Pakistan	03 Jun 49	35UNTS23	100549
Belgium	Greece	21 Jun 49	137UNTS215	101854
Norway	Pakistan	23 Jun 49	35UNTS49	100550
India	Switzerland	24 Jun 49	95UNTS109	101319
Greece	Syria	05 Jul 49	78UNTS71	101013
Australia	India	11 Jul 49	35UNTS83	100552
Iraq	Norway	12 Jul 49	53UNTS137	100778
Pakistan	Philippines	16 Jul 49	35UNTS111	100553
Pakistan	UK Great Britain	27 Jul 49	44UNTS199	100685
Ceylon (Sri Lanka)	UK Great Britain	05 Aug 49	35UNTS137	100554
Canada	UK Great Britain	19 Aug 49	44UNTS223	100686
Finland	Norway	24 Aug 49	53UNTS167	100780
Denmark	Finland	26 Aug 49	53UNTS191	100781
Belgium	Canada	30 Aug 49	53UNTS221	100782
Guatemala	Italy	10 Sep 49	102UNTS53	101410
Belgium	United Arab Rep	19 Sep 49	137UNTS189	101853
Lebanon	Netherlands	20 Sep 49	108UNTS205	101474
Greece	Philippines	08 Oct 49	187UNTS221	102515
India	Philippines	20 Oct 49	72UNTS191	100934
Iran	Netherlands	31 Oct 49	254UNTS257	103596
Denmark	Pakistan	09 Nov 49	44UNTS255	100687
Denmark	Thailand	23 Nov 49	53UNTS255	100786
Sweden	Thailand	23 Nov 49	72UNTS217	100935
Norway	Thailand	26 Nov 49	53UNTS269	100787
Austria	Norway	02 Dec 49	72UNTS230	100936
Austria	Sweden	02 Dec 49	108UNTS3	101465
Austria	Denmark	02 Dec 49	53UNTS281	100788
Netherlands	United Arab Rep	08 Dec 49	95UNTS123	101320
Sweden	United Arab Rep	12 Dec 49	108UNTS15	101466
Canada	Denmark	13 Dec 49	72UNTS247	100937
Denmark	Germany, West	15 Dec 49	51UNTS11	100749
Austria	Switzerland	19 Dec 49	254UNTS287	103597
Ireland	USA (United States)	21 Jan 50	206UNTS269	102792
Netherlands	Syria	13 Feb 50	108UNTS53	101467
Canada	Norway	14 Feb 50	53UNTS329	100790
Ceylon (Sri Lanka)	Thailand	24 Feb 50	72UNTS261	100938
Chile	UNICEF (Children)	03 Mar 50	126UNTS119	101685
Norway	United Arab Rep	11 Mar 50	95UNTS157	101321
Denmark	United Arab Rep	14 Mar 50	95UNTS197	101322
Multilateral		21 Mar 50	96UNTS271	101342
Denmark	Iceland	22 Mar 50	72UNTS273	100939
Iceland	Netherlands	22 Mar 50	95UNTS237	101323
Italy	Turkey	24 Mar 50	96UNTS207	101338
Italy	Portugal	05 Apr 50	254UNTS329	103599
Multilateral		06 Apr 50	119UNTS99	101610
Turkey	United Arab Rep	12 Apr 50	128UNTS3	101711
Greece	United Arab Rep	24 Apr 50	163UNTS229	102149
Switzerland	United Arab Rep	15 May 50	95UNTS255	101325
Iraq	Pakistan	20 Jun 50	77UNTS215	101001
France	Pakistan	31 Jul 50	96UNTS23	101329
France	United Arab Rep	08 Aug 50	127UNTS293	101710
Canada	New Zealand	16 Aug 50	77UNTS239	101002
Greece	Philippines	28 Aug 50	225UNTS155	103097
Ceylon (Sri Lanka)	United Arab Rep	26 Sep 50	192UNTS53	102595
Sweden	Switzerland	18 Oct 50	166UNTS49	102185
Luxembourg	Portugal	21 Oct 50	108UNTS67	101468
Multilateral		07 Dec 50	212UNTS17	102861
Norway	UK Great Britain	15 Dec 50	106UNTS87	101459
France	UK Great Britain	29 Dec 50	118UNTS149	101603
Canada	France	26 Jan 51	233UNTS65	103251
Nicaragua	USA (United States)	31 Jan 51	150UNTS3	101960
Existing tribunals (Cont.)				
Colombia	Portugal	09 Mar 51	108UNTS87	101469
France	UK Great Britain	11 Apr 51	106UNTS3	101456
Iraq	UK Great Britain	19 Apr 51	108UNTS121	101470
Belgium	UK Great Britain	08 May 51	158UNTS451	102079
India	Netherlands	24 May 51	108UNTS151	101471
Multilateral		25 May 51	175UNTS215	102303
Greece	Norway	28 May 51	187UNTS141	102507
Denmark	Iran	18 Jun 51	255UNTS3	103602
Cuba	Portugal	26 Jun 51	192UNTS115	102598
Burma	WHO (World Health)	09 Jul 51	104UNTS187	101440
Iran	UNICEF (Children)	02 Aug 51	247UNTS11	103457
Greece	USA (United States)	03 Aug 51	224UNTS279	103080
Lebanon	UK Great Britain	15 Aug 51	160UNTS327	102116
Israel	USA (United States)	23 Aug 51	219UNTS237	102979
UNICEF (Children)	Turkey	05 Sep 51	193UNTS55	102610
Multilateral		08 Sep 51	136UNTS45	101832
Korea, South	United Nations	21 Sep 51	104UNTS323	200322
Denmark	USA (United States)	01 Oct 51	421UNTS105	106056
Philippines	Spain	06 Oct 51	215UNTS193	102920
Greece	Luxembourg	22 Oct 51	187UNTS119	102506
Denmark	Iraq	18 Nov 51	232UNTS25	103227
India	UK Great Britain	01 Dec 51	128UNTS39	101712
Iraq	UNICEF (Children)	10 Dec 51	126UNTS57	101682
Colombia	Spain	11 Dec 51	216UNTS73	102933
Jordan	USA (United States)	20 Dec 51	157UNTS69	102048
Jordan	United Arab Rep	02 Jan 52	192UNTS157	102599
Multilateral		10 Jan 52	163UNTS3	102138
Multilateral		10 Jan 52	163UNTS27	102139
Belgium	Spain	10 Mar 52	178UNTS243	102342
Sweden	UK Great Britain	14 Mar 52	202UNTS157	102731
Iraq	Switzerland	31 Mar 52	311UNTS43	104498
Libya	UNICEF (Children)	05 Apr 52	133UNTS287	200441
Liberia	UNICEF (Children)	17 Apr 52	133UNTS3	101773
Israel	USA (United States)	09 May 52	177UNTS269	102326
India	WHO (World Health)	04 Jun 52	135UNTS279	101827
Australia	United Arab Rep	14 Jun 52	173UNTS241	102269
India	United Arab Rep	14 Jun 52	173UNTS209	102268
Belgium	UNICEF (Children)	17 Jun 52	171UNTS249	102228
Denmark	UK Great Britain	23 Jun 52	151UNTS3	101982
Jordan	UNICEF (Children)	08 Jul 52	173UNTS353	200503
UNICEF (Children)	Syria	10 Jul 52	136UNTS17	101830
India	Philippines	11 Jul 52	203UNTS73	102741
Netherlands	Pakistan	17 Jul 52	150UNTS277	101980
Japan	United Nations	25 Jul 52	135UNTS305	200443
Laos	UNICEF (Children)	15 Aug 52	161UNTS323	200491
Ethiopia	Pakistan	29 Aug 52	150UNTS257	101979
Iceland	Luxembourg	23 Oct 52	193UNTS39	102609
Chile	Denmark	27 Oct 52	271UNTS93	103911
Chile	Sweden	27 Oct 52	311UNTS63	104499
Multilateral		07 Nov 52	221UNTS255	103010
Luxembourg	Norway	17 Nov 52	311UNTS95	104500
Luxembourg	Sweden	17 Nov 52	173UNTS277	102270
Multilateral		31 Mar 53	193UNTS136	102613
Japan	USA (United States)	02 Apr 53	206UNTS143	102788
Netherlands	United Nations	09 Apr 53	163UNTS89	102143
Greece	UK Great Britain	17 Apr 53	191UNTS151	102582
Philippines	Thailand	27 Apr 53	174UNTS3	102274
Ethiopia	UNICEF (Children)	27 Apr 53	213UNTS169	102885
Germany, West	Italy	05 May 53	267UNTS9	103835
Japan	UNICEF (Children)	21 Nov 53	183UNTS297	200507
Multilateral		11 Dec 53	218UNTS255	102958
Multilateral		11 Dec 53	218UNTS153	102956
Multilateral		11 Dec 53	218UNTS211	102957
Belgium	Lebanon	24 Dec 53	219UNTS153	102972
Ethiopia	Greece	20 Jan 54	222UNTS281	103035

PARTY ONE	PARTY TWO	DATE	CITATION	NUMBER
Existing tribunals (Cont.)				
Syria	UK Great Britain	30 Jan 54	449UNTS47	106452
France	Sweden	16 Feb 54	228UNTS137	103147
Canada	Peru	18 Feb 54	411UNTS64	105915
ICJ Option Clause	Finland	26 Feb 54	189UNTS223	102546
Indonesia	Thailand	03 Mar 54	213UNTS297	102893
Japan	USA (United States)	08 Mar 54	232UNTS251	103240
Mexico	UK Great Britain	20 Mar 54	331UNTS21	104750
Peru	Spain	31 Mar 54	232UNTS65	103230
UNICEF (Children)	Spain	07 May 54	190UNTS357	200515
Multilateral		12 May 54	327UNTS3	104714
Mexico	UNICEF (Children)	20 May 54	192UNTS3	102591
Switzerland	Syria	26 May 54	255UNTS145	103609
Iran	Switzerland	27 May 54	496UNTS273	107257
Italy	UK Great Britain	01 Jun 54	403UNTS275	105798
Ireland	Luxembourg	27 Jul 54	232UNTS91	103231
New Zealand	UNICEF (Children)	26 Aug 54	198UNTS173	102663
Thailand	USA (United States)	01 Sep 54	237UNTS209	103347
Germany, West	USA (United States)	29 Oct 54	273UNTS3	103943
Burma	Japan	05 Nov 54	251UNTS201	103542
Brazil	Italy	24 Nov 54	284UNTS325	104146
Pakistan	United Arab Rep	13 Dec 54	255UNTS167	103610
Ecuador	Netherlands	14 Dec 54	232UNTS115	103233
Norway	Switzerland	30 Dec 54	311UNTS147	104502
Netherlands	UNICEF (Children)	31 Dec 54	202UNTS135	102729
Philippines	UK Great Britain	31 Jan 55	216UNTS51	102932
Costa Rica	USA (United States)	26 Feb 55	252UNTS129	103562
France	Sweden	05 Mar 55	427UNTS133	106150
WMO (Meteorology)	Switzerland	10 Mar 55	211UNTS277	200524
Guatemala	USA (United States)	23 Mar 55	252UNTS143	103563
Iraq	United Arab Rep	23 Mar 55	311UNTS199	104504
Ecuador	USA (United States)	29 Mar 55	261UNTS343	103732
Pakistan	USA (United States)	26 May 55	257UNTS93	103652
Norway	Sweden	28 May 55	262UNTS151	103743
Honduras	USA (United States)	10 Jun 55	258UNTS51	103669
Syria	United Arab Rep	03 Jul 55	393UNTS67	105652
Iran	USA (United States)	15 Aug 55	284UNTS93	104132
Belgium	Ireland	10 Sep 55	255UNTS235	103612
Italy	Switzerland	17 Sep 55	291UNTS213	104257
Multilateral		12 Oct 55	560UNTS3	108165
Denmark	Syria	20 Oct 55	250UNTS61	103518
Multilateral		20 Oct 55	378UNTS159	105425
Paraguay	USA (United States)	28 Oct 55	273UNTS97	103946
Pakistan	Turkey	02 Nov 55	311UNTS217	104505
Guatemala	UNICEF (Children)	22 Nov 55	221UNTS305	103012
Nicaragua	USA (United States)	21 Jan 56	367UNTS3	105224
Norway	Syria	25 Feb 56	463UNTS217	106706
Netherlands	USA (United States)	27 Mar 56	285UNTS231	104154
Cambodia	UNICEF (Children)	28 Apr 56	136UNTS341	200446
Multilateral		30 Apr 56	310UNTS229	104494
Portugal	Venezuela	16 May 56	463UNTS239	106707
Italy	Switzerland	04 Jun 56	378UNTS311	105429
Multilateral		20 Jun 56	268UNTS3	103850
Lebanon	UNICEF (Children)	03 Jul 56	324UNTS145	104683
France	UK Great Britain	10 Jul 56	326UNTS23	104708
Germany, West	UK Great Britain	30 Jul 56	330UNTS233	104748
UNICEF (Children)	Sudan	07 Aug 56	248UNTS307	200542
Philippines	Switzerland	30 Aug 56	293UNTS43	104284
Multilateral		07 Sep 56	266UNTS3	103822
Multilateral		25 Sep 56	334UNTS13	104766
Multilateral		25 Sep 56	334UNTS89	104767
Switzerland	Thailand	13 Oct 56	312UNTS43	104510
Belgium	Turkey	25 Oct 56	380UNTS3	105447
Multilateral		26 Oct 56	276UNTS3	103988
Austria	UK Great Britain	27 Oct 56	264UNTS67	103789
Peru	Switzerland	23 Nov 56	411UNTS97	105916

PARTY ONE	PARTY TWO	DATE	CITATION	NUMBER
Existing tribunals (Cont.)				
Korea, South	USA (United States)	28 Nov 56	302UNTS281	104367
Greece	Sweden	11 Dec 56	299UNTS247	104316
UNESCO (Educ/Cult)	Tunisia	03 Jan 57	257UNTS21	103645
Turkey	USA (United States)	15 Jan 57	280UNTS79	104053
Iceland	Thailand	22 Jan 57	312UNTS63	104511
Multilateral		20 Feb 57	309UNTS65	104468
Japan	Norway	28 Feb 57	280UNTS87	104054
Belgium	Netherlands	07 Mar 57	282UNTS241	104100
Dominican Republic	USA (United States)	09 Mar 57	279UNTS249	104044
Italy	UK Great Britain	29 Mar 57	310UNTS11	104481
Denmark	Pakistan	10 Apr 57	302UNTS53	104353
Other Unilat Decla	United Arab Rep	24 Apr 57	265UNTS299	103821
Multilateral		29 Apr 57	320UNTS243	104646
Afghanistan	Pakistan	13 Jun 57	327UNTS51	104717
Honduras	Nicaragua	22 Jun 57	277UNTS159	104005
Morocco	UNICEF (Children)	31 Jul 57	282UNTS99	104095
Iran	USA (United States)	21 Sep 57	293UNTS287	104296
Germany, East	USSR (Soviet Union)	27 Sep 57	292UNTS75	104268
Italy	Pakistan	05 Oct 57	353UNTS91	105039
Fed of Malaya	UK Great Britain	18 Oct 57	335UNTS3	104775
IAEA (Atom Energy)	United Nations	23 Oct 57	281UNTS369	200548
USA (United States)	Vietnam, South	05 Nov 57	300UNTS23	104328
Argentina	UNICEF (Children)	19 Nov 57	300UNTS229	104338
Multilateral		23 Nov 57	506UNTS125	107384
Canada	Switzerland	10 Jan 58	464UNTS21	106710
Indonesia	Japan	20 Jan 58	324UNTS227	104688
Norway	Pakistan	05 Mar 58	334UNTS199	104769
Pakistan	Sweden	06 Mar 58	393UNTS181	105656
Belgium	Iran	14 Apr 58	381UNTS309	105473
China People's Rep	USSR (Soviet Union)	23 Apr 58	313UNTS135	104534
Multilateral		29 Apr 58	450UNTS169	106466
Pakistan	Portugal	07 Jun 58	320UNTS225	104645
Denmark	Luxembourg	10 Jun 58	356UNTS193	105096
Belgium	Pakistan	04 Jul 58	387UNTS305	105569
Ghana	UNICEF (Children)	12 Aug 58	309UNTS103	104469
Liberia	Netherlands	28 Nov 58	393UNTS55	105651
Finland	Switzerland	07 Jan 59	353UNTS173	105042
IMCO (Maritime Org)	United Nations	13 Jan 59	324UNTS273	200553
Ceylon (Sri Lanka)	Denmark	29 May 59	348UNTS225	105002
Ceylon (Sri Lanka)	Norway	29 May 59	411UNTS165	105919
Ceylon (Sri Lanka)	Sweden	29 May 59	464UNTS109	106713
India	Italy	16 Jul 59	464UNTS129	106714
Germany, West	UK Great Britain	03 Aug 59	502UNTS197	107331
Nicaragua	Peru	14 Oct 59	392UNTS303	105649
India	Pakistan	23 Oct 59	362UNTS3	105180
Germany, West	Pakistan	25 Nov 59	457UNTS22	106575
Liberia	Sweden	09 Dec 59	464UNTS219	106716
El Salvador	USA (United States)	29 Jan 60	372UNTS3	105283
Cuba	UNICEF (Children)	11 Feb 60	349UNTS277	105014
Korea, South	USA (United States)	19 Feb 60	372UNTS109	105291
Guinea	Netherlands	09 Mar 60	392UNTS243	105646
Belgium	Switzerland	24 Mar 60	416UNTS81	105996
Nepal	USA (United States)	17 May 60	372UNTS313	105307
Kuwait	UK Great Britain	24 May 60	412UNTS4	105923
Korea, North	USSR (Soviet Union)	22 Jun 60	399UNTS3	105732
Denmark	Peru	22 Jun 60	439UNTS113	106326
Austria	UK Great Britain	24 Jun 60	502UNTS79	107327
Switzerland	United Arab Rep	14 Jul 60	497UNTS161	107268
Ghana	Netherlands	30 Jul 60	412UNTS51	105925
Guatemala	USA (United States)	09 Aug 60	461UNTS15	106648
Ghana	United Arab Rep	29 Aug 60	412UNTS71	105926
Belgium	Jordan	19 Oct 60	479UNTS277	106959
Norway	Peru	02 Nov 60	497UNTS207	107270
Japan	Pakistan	18 Dec 60	423UNTS197	106093
Canada	Pakistan	21 Dec 60	465UNTS115	106724

PARTY ONE	PARTY TWO	DATE	CITATION	NUMBER
Existing tribunals (Cont.)				
Luxembourg	Thailand	29 Dec 60	465UNTS131	106725
Canada	USA (United States)	17 Jan 61	542UNTS224	107894
Belgium	USA (United States)	21 Feb 61	480UNTS149	106967
Belgium	UK Great Britain	08 Mar 61	523UNTS17	107554
USA (United States)	Vietnam, South	03 Apr 61	424UNTS137	106106
Multilateral		18 Apr 61	500UNTS243	107312
Spain	UK Great Britain	30 May 61	562UNTS169	108198
Guinea	Sweden	17 Jun 61	465UNTS236	106729
Netherlands	Euratom	25 Jul 61	462UNTS263	106686
Finland	Luxembourg	15 Aug 61	541UNTS45	107859
Jordan	Netherlands	24 Aug 61	466UNTS3	106733
Liberia	Switzerland	31 Aug 61	559UNTS215	108160
Multilateral		04 Oct 61	412UNTS210	105934
IAEA (Atom Energy)	Yugoslavia	04 Oct 61	412UNTS226	105935
Ivory Coast	USA (United States)	01 Dec 61	462UNTS221	106681
Germany, West	Thailand	13 Dec 61	541UNTS181	107870
Luxembourg	USA (United States)	23 Feb 62	474UNTS3	106868
Multilateral		05 Mar 62	425UNTS3	106114
Taiwan	Malagasy	04 Apr 62	463UNTS195	106703
Niger	USA (United States)	26 Apr 62	459UNTS129	106618
Multilateral		14 Jun 62	528UNTS33	107634
Guinea	Norway	21 Jun 62	466UNTS81	106738
Denmark	UK Great Britain	27 Jun 62	562UNTS75	108197
Liberia	Norway	29 Jun 62	466UNTS95	106739
Ethiopia	USA (United States)	03 Aug 62	459UNTS79	106613
IAEA (Atom Energy)	USA (United States)	20 Aug 62	456UNTS447	106570
Congo (Brazzaville)	USA (United States)	01 Sep 62	459UNTS117	106616
Japan	UK Great Britain	14 Nov 62	478UNTS29	106934
Congo (Zaire)	USA (United States)	17 Nov 62	474UNTS41	106870
Ghana	Tunisia	11 Dec 62	563UNTS243	108213
Nigeria	USA (United States)	24 Dec 62	462UNTS180	106677
Jamaica	USA (United States)	04 Jan 63	471UNTS119	106826
Ghana	Mali	09 Jan 63	466UNTS165	106742
Trinidad/Tobago	USA (United States)	15 Jan 63	471UNTS141	106829
Gabon	USA (United States)	10 Apr 63	474UNTS113	106876
Multilateral		20 Apr 63	495UNTS3	107239
Netherlands	Tunisia	23 May 63	523UNTS237	107558
Cyprus	USA (United States)	29 May 63	487UNTS283	107110
United Arab Rep	USA (United States)	29 Jun 63	479UNTS207	106954
Malagasy	USA (United States)	26 Jul 63	487UNTS189	107104
Cameroon	UK Great Britain	29 Jul 63	478UNTS148	106935
Multilateral		26 Oct 63	587UNTS9	108506
Tanganyika	USA (United States)	14 Nov 63	493UNTS75	107208
Niger	United Nations	20 Nov 63	536UNTS3	107793
Multilateral		03 Dec 63	529UNTS217	107663
IAEA (Atom Energy)	Yugoslavia	07 Dec 63	501UNTS273	107322
Czechoslovakia	Romania	16 Dec 63	527UNTS285	107630
Somalia	USA (United States)	08 Jan 64	505UNTS165	107372
Multilateral		28 Feb 64	501UNTS245	107321
Malaysia	Netherlands	07 Apr 64	524UNTS81	107567
Norway	Yugoslavia	15 Apr 64	602UNTS177	108712
Kenya	USA (United States)	20 Apr 64	524UNTS165	107571
Japan	UK Great Britain	04 May 64	561UNTS25	108179
Mali	USA (United States)	09 Jun 64	530UNTS133	107678
Australia	UN Special Fund	30 Sep 64	510UNTS277	107419
Laos	USA (United States)	29 Dec 64	542UNTS23	107876
Central Afri Rep	USA (United States)	31 Dec 64	542UNTS29	107877
Multilateral		23 Feb 65	527UNTS120	107622
Multilateral		05 Mar 65	527UNTS221	107627
Dahomey	USA (United States)	13 Mar 65	549UNTS43	107987
Denmark	Malaysia	26 Mar 65	540UNTS205	107851
Multilateral		08 Apr 65	533UNTS66	107733
Ghana	Malawi	04 May 65	541UNTS163	107869
Chad	USA (United States)	12 May 65	546UNTS183	107944
Multilateral		14 May 65	550UNTS310	108026

PARTY ONE	PARTY TWO	DATE	CITATION	NUMBER
Existing tribunals (Cont.)				
Uganda	USA (United States)	29 May 65	546UNTS209	107948
Netherlands	Senegal	12 Jun 65	602UNTS231	108715
USA (United States)	Upper Volta	18 Jun 65	549UNTS133	107996
Switzerland	UK Great Britain	07 Jul 65	605UNTS205	108765
United Nations	UK Great Britain	21 Feb 66	555UNTS177	108112
Multilateral		30 Apr 66	620UNTS191	108956
Denmark	Singapore	20 Dec 66	593UNTS125	108580
Multilateral		02 Feb 67	606UNTS89	108777
Germany, West	Netherlands	02 Feb 67	606UNTS105	108779
Denmark	Germany, West	02 Feb 67	606UNTS97	108778
Multilateral		14 Feb 67	634UNTS281	109068
Greece	United Nations	14 Apr 67	595UNTS83	108613
Multilateral		10 Jun 67	602UNTS212	108714
Iraq	IAEA (Atom Energy)	21 Sep 67	630UNTS41	108963
Burma	IAEA (Atom Energy)	11 Oct 67	630UNTS49	108964
Multilateral		14 Nov 67	614UNTS2	108860
Eur Space Research	UK Great Britain	24 Nov 67	638UNTS17	109129
Special tribunals				
Greece	Iran	09 Jan 31	166UNTS323	200496
Argentina	USA (United States)	14 Oct 41	119UNTS193	200384
Multilateral		07 Dec 44	171UNTS345	200501
South Africa	UK Great Britain	26 Oct 45	72UNTS41	100927
Greece	UK Great Britain	26 Nov 45	35UNTS161	100555
Ireland	UK Great Britain	05 Apr 46	72UNTS57	100928
France	Ireland	16 May 46	44UNTS105	100681
Ireland	Sweden	29 May 46	35UNTS231	100557
United Arab Rep	USA (United States)	15 Jun 46	71UNTS157	100917
Paraguay	USA (United States)	28 Feb 47	44UNTS25	100676
Portugal	Sweden	06 Mar 47	35UNTS243	100558
Greece	Sweden	08 Apr 47	94UNTS73	101307
South Africa	USA (United States)	23 May 47	66UNTS233	100857
Albania	Yugoslavia	12 Jun 47	111UNTS201	101535
Netherlands	South Africa	22 Jul 47	12UNTS257	100188
Hungary	Yugoslavia	24 Jul 47	114UNTS3	101554
Poland	Romania	09 Aug 47	12UNTS363	100193
Czechoslovakia	Switzerland	10 Sep 47	35UNTS275	100559
Lebanon	Turkey	16 Sep 47	44UNTS123	100682
Philippines	Spain	27 Sep 47	70UNTS133	100902
Czechoslovakia	Sweden	15 Oct 47	44UNTS149	100683
Denmark	Greece	14 Nov 47	35UNTS295	100560
Denmark	Ireland	18 Nov 47	35UNTS309	100561
Ireland	Italy	21 Nov 47	353UNTS73	105038
Taiwan	Netherlands	06 Dec 47	43UNTS185	100669
Denmark	Portugal	15 Dec 47	35UNTS329	100563
Italy	USA (United States)	06 Feb 48	73UNTS113	100950
Multilateral		30 Apr 48	119UNTS3	101609
Pakistan	Sweden	06 May 48	36UNTS3	100564
Bolivia	USA (United States)	29 Sep 48	505UNTS139	107370
WHO (World Health)	Switzerland	12 Jan 49	26UNTS331	200155
Finland	Netherlands	25 Feb 49	53UNTS123	100777
Finland	USA (United States)	29 Mar 49	55UNTS59	100808
Panama	USA (United States)	31 Mar 49	55UNTS87	100810
Switzerland	USA (United States)	13 May 49	51UNTS129	100761
Canada	USA (United States)	04 Jun 49	122UNTS237	101649
Iraq	Norway	12 Jul 49	53UNTS137	100778
Czechoslovakia	Finland	13 Jul 49	53UNTS153	100779
Dominican Republic	USA (United States)	19 Jul 49	51UNTS145	100762
Pakistan	UK Great Britain	27 Jul 49	44UNTS199	100685
Ceylon (Sri Lanka)	UK Great Britain	05 Aug 49	35UNTS137	100554
Canada	UK Great Britain	19 Aug 49	44UNTS223	100686
Burma	USA (United States)	28 Sep 49	55UNTS3	100806
Denmark	Pakistan	09 Nov 49	44UNTS255	100687
Italy	Turkey	25 Nov 49	192UNTS39	102594
Italy	Netherlands	04 Mar 50	254UNTS305	103598

PARTY ONE	PARTY TWO	DATE	CITATION	NUMBER
Special tribunals (Cont.)				
Sweden	UK Great Britain	05 Apr 50	99UNTS107	101374
Multilateral		06 Apr 50	119UNTS99	101610
Israel	USA (United States)	13 Jun 50	212UNTS93	102863
Burma	Ceylon (Sri Lanka)	29 Jun 50	73UNTS3	100940
Spain	UK Great Britain	20 Jul 50	398UNTS101	105719
Spain	Switzerland	03 Aug 50	254UNTS365	103600
France	United Arab Rep	08 Aug 50	127UNTS293	101710
Burma	Sweden	14 Sep 50	96UNTS45	101330
Sweden	Switzerland	18 Oct 50	166UNTS49	102185
Israel	Netherlands	23 Oct 50	189UNTS89	102543
Israel	Turkey	05 Feb 51	193UNTS3	102607
WHO (World Health)	United Arab Rep	25 Mar 51	223UNTS87	103058
Multilateral		18 Apr 51	261UNTS140	103729
Denmark	Iran	18 Jun 51	255UNTS3	103602
Philippines	WHO (World Health)	22 Jul 51	149UNTS197	101953
Burma	Denmark	30 Jul 51	108UNTS167	101472
Israel	Philippines	07 Aug 51	192UNTS81	102596
Burma	Netherlands	06 Sep 51	108UNTS187	101473
Panama	UK Great Britain	15 Sep 51	560UNTS143	108172
Philippines	Spain	06 Oct 51	215UNTS193	102920
Colombia	Spain	11 Dec 51	216UNTS73	102933
Belgium	Spain	10 Mar 52	178UNTS243	102342
Pakistan	Switzerland	17 Mar 52	192UNTS237	102603
France	Israel	29 Apr 52	189UNTS55	102542
Germany, West	USA (United States)	11 Jun 52	273UNTS105	103947
Belgium	Israel	30 Jun 52	183UNTS263	102435
Japan	USA (United States)	11 Aug 52	212UNTS27	102862
Netherlands	Peru	22 Sep 52	255UNTS49	103604
Mexico	Netherlands	13 Oct 52	163UNTS341	102154
Burma	UK Great Britain	25 Oct 52	150UNTS237	101978
Multilateral		10 Nov 52	214UNTS265	102904
Israel	Switzerland	19 Nov 52	232UNTS3	103226
Japan	Netherlands	17 Feb 53	192UNTS215	102602
Japan	Sweden	20 Feb 53	173UNTS307	102272
Libya	UK Great Britain	21 Feb 53	311UNTS115	104501
Japan	Norway	23 Feb 53	192UNTS191	102601
France	Italy	14 Mar 53	284UNTS221	104140
Cuba	USA (United States)	26 May 53	224UNTS75	103070
Switzerland	Yugoslavia	28 May 53	232UNTS45	103228
Japan	Thailand	19 Jun 53	174UNTS29	102276
Burma	Norway	22 Jun 53	174UNTS49	102277
Canada	Mexico	27 Jul 53	192UNTS255	102604
USA (United States)	Venezuela	14 Aug 53	213UNTS99	102883
Peru	Spain	31 Mar 54	232UNTS65	103230
Austria	Yugoslavia	25 May 54	227UNTS111	103135
Saudi Arabia	UK Great Britain	30 Jul 54	201UNTS317	102722
Norway	USA (United States)	06 Aug 54	222UNTS269	103034
Multilateral		23 Oct 54	331UNTS327	104759
Multilateral		23 Oct 54	332UNTS219	104762
Austria	Yugoslavia	27 Nov 54	396UNTS75	105694
Canada	Japan	12 Jan 55	311UNTS167	104503
Austria	Yugoslavia	18 Jan 55	378UNTS31	105416
CERN (Nuc Resrch)	Switzerland	11 Jun 55	249UNTS405	200544
Denmark	WHO (World Health)	29 Jun 55	247UNTS168	103467
Germany, West	USA (United States)	07 Jul 55	275UNTS3	103973
Germany, West	UK Great Britain	22 Jul 55	269UNTS189	103881
France	Germany, West	04 Oct 55	353UNTS203	105044
Austria	USSR (Soviet Union)	17 Oct 55	240UNTS289	103409
Austria	Israel	17 Nov 55	232UNTS153	103235
India	Japan	26 Nov 55	311UNTS243	104506
Australia	Japan	19 Jan 56	311UNTS291	104507
Argentina	Switzerland	25 Jan 56	559UNTS121	108157
India	USA (United States)	03 Feb 56	272UNTS75	103932
Belgium	Germany, West	14 Apr 56	344UNTS103	104945
Germany, West	Switzerland	02 May 56	559UNTS157	108158

PARTY ONE	PARTY TWO	DATE	CITATION	NUMBER
Special tribunals (Cont.)				
Multilateral		18 May 56	339UNTS3	104844
Japan	Switzerland	24 May 56	312UNTS3	104509
Greece	Italy	26 May 56	496UNTS301	107258
Germany, West	Ireland	12 Jun 56	353UNTS121	105040
Norway	Sweden	29 Jun 56	262UNTS335	103759
Multilateral		06 Jul 56	312UNTS109	104514
Germany, West	Netherlands	28 Sep 56	327UNTS185	104722
Colombia	USA (United States)	24 Oct 56	476UNTS77	106905
Iran	USA (United States)	16 Jan 57	308UNTS147	104460
Germany, West	Sweden	29 Jan 57	393UNTS113	105654
Germany, West	Norway	29 Jan 57	353UNTS39	105037
Denmark	Germany, West	29 Jan 57	302UNTS75	104354
Netherlands	Yugoslavia	13 Mar 57	327UNTS227	104723
Multilateral		25 Mar 57	294UNTS411	104302
Netherlands	USA (United States)	03 Apr 57	410UNTS193	105904
Germany, West	Yugoslavia	10 Apr 57	463UNTS269	106708
Australia	Germany, West	22 May 57	357UNTS45	105105
Greece	Italy	02 Aug 57	533UNTS217	107744
Multilateral		03 Oct 57	366UNTS87	105216
France	Morocco	25 Oct 57	559UNTS95	108156
Austria	IAEA (Atom Energy)	11 Dec 57	339UNTS110	104849
Multilateral		13 Dec 57	372UNTS159	105296
Australia	Ireland	30 Dec 57	497UNTS29	107260
Australia	UK Great Britain	07 Feb 58	335UNTS23	104776
Afghanistan	Turkey	08 Feb 58	464UNTS39	106711
Sudan	Sweden	17 Feb 58	393UNTS161	105655
Germany, West	Portugal	21 Mar 58	464UNTS71	106712
Morocco	Portugal	03 Apr 58	393UNTS203	105657
Sweden	Yugoslavia	18 Apr 58	393UNTS225	105658
Multilateral		10 Jun 58	454UNTS47	106539
Ethiopia	United Nations	18 Jun 58	317UNTS101	104597
Ethiopia	UK Great Britain	07 Jul 58	331UNTS3	104749
Ghana	USA (United States)	30 Sep 58	336UNTS169	104805
UK Great Britain	Yugoslavia	03 Feb 59	359UNTS339	105151
Japan	IAEA (Atom Energy)	24 Mar 59	339UNTS327	104852
Canada	IAEA (Atom Energy)	24 Mar 59	339UNTS315	104851
Denmark	Sudan	11 May 59	445UNTS105	106380
Greece	Yugoslavia	18 Jun 59	368UNTS69	105235
Greece	Yugoslavia	18 Jun 59	363UNTS133	105205
Belgium	Japan	20 Jun 59	411UNTS3	105911
Afghanistan	Germany, West	22 Jul 59	464UNTS177	106715
Germany, West	Iceland	12 Aug 59	411UNTS224	105921
Canada	Germany, West	04 Sep 59	411UNTS260	105922
Australia	Fed of Malaya	29 Sep 59	357UNTS29	105104
Germany, West	Pakistan	25 Nov 59	457UNTS22	106575
Norway	USSR (Soviet Union)	09 Dec 59	361UNTS93	105173
Czechoslovakia	UK Great Britain	15 Jan 60	374UNTS207	105336
El Salvador	USA (United States)	29 Jan 60	372UNTS3	105283
Multilateral		06 Feb 60	383UNTS3	105494
Germany, West	United Arab Rep	16 Feb 60	464UNTS233	106717
Korea, South	USA (United States)	19 Feb 60	372UNTS109	105291
Multilateral		26 Feb 60	418UNTS171	106022
Australia	Thailand	26 Feb 60	392UNTS255	105647
Finland	Iceland	10 Mar 60	497UNTS95	107264
Germany, West	Netherlands	08 Apr 60	508UNTS14	107404
Luxembourg	Yugoslavia	09 Apr 60	464UNTS293	106719
Germany, West	Spain	28 Apr 60	465UNTS3	106720
Nepal	USA (United States)	17 May 60	372UNTS313	105307
Morocco	United Arab Rep	19 May 60	563UNTS121	108208
Ireland	Portugal	24 Jun 60	412UNTS30	105924
Germany, West	Pakistan	20 Jul 60	465UNTS41	106721
Mexico	USA (United States)	15 Aug 60	402UNTS177	105786
Multilateral		16 Aug 60	382UNTS8	105476
Belgium	Burma	17 Aug 60	540UNTS185	107850
Burma	Switzerland	31 Oct 60	465UNTS97	106723

PARTY ONE	PARTY TWO	DATE	CITATION	NUMBER
Special tribunals (Cont.)				
Australia	Italy	10 Nov 60	497UNTS247	107271
Indonesia	UK Great Britain	23 Nov 60	398UNTS71	105718
Multilateral		13 Dec 60	523UNTS117	107557
Multilateral		13 Dec 60	455UNTS3	106543
Multilateral		30 Dec 60	395UNTS241	105689
Jordan	Sweden	09 Jan 61	465UNTS155	106726
Germany, West	Japan	18 Jan 61	465UNTS173	106727
Multilateral		10 Apr 61	402UNTS281	105791
Czechoslovakia	Morocco	08 Jun 61	497UNTS275	107272
New Zealand	UK Great Britain	13 Jun 61	497UNTS293	107273
Cameroon	France	16 Jun 61	412UNTS148	105929
Czechoslovakia	Ghana	02 Aug 61	465UNTS249	106730
Jordan	Norway	21 Aug 61	465UNTS275	106731
Mexico	Netherlands	24 Aug 61	465UNTS291	106732
Ghana	Romania	30 Sep 61	467UNTS443	106769
Germany, West	Morocco	12 Oct 61	523UNTS289	107562
Japan	Pakistan	17 Oct 61	466UNTS17	106734
Cyprus	Greece	23 Nov 61	497UNTS311	107274
Congo (Zaire)	United Nations	27 Nov 61	414UNTS229	105975
Czechoslovakia	Guinea	16 Dec 61	559UNTS49	108154
Netherlands	Sweden	08 Jan 62	466UNTS65	106737
Austria	Greece	15 Jan 62	498UNTS3	107275
Indonesia	Japan	23 Jan 62	559UNTS77	108155
Italy	Japan	31 Jan 62	498UNTS23	107276
Germany, West	Thailand	05 Mar 62	563UNTS165	108210
Luxembourg	Spain	26 Mar 62	563UNTS205	108211
France	Luxembourg	29 Mar 62	563UNTS227	108212
IAEA (Atom Energy)	USA (United States)	30 Mar 62	442UNTS49	106338
Sierra Leone	UK Great Britain	05 Apr 62	434UNTS227	106265
Dominican Republic	USA (United States)	02 May 62	442UNTS99	106341
Japan	United Arab Rep	10 May 62	498UNTS69	107278
France	Senegal	15 Jun 62	524UNTS3	107563
Czechoslovakia	Senegal	20 Jun 62	498UNTS145	107280
Morocco	Switzerland	05 Jul 62	498UNTS171	107281
Morocco	Switzerland	05 Jul 62	498UNTS189	107282
Ecuador	Germany, West	20 Sep 62	498UNTS199	107283
Austria	Czechoslovakia	22 Sep 62	495UNTS157	107244
Multilateral		28 Sep 62	469UNTS169	106791
Japan	Kuwait	06 Oct 62	498UNTS235	107284
Finland	France	12 Oct 62	498UNTS299	107285
Netherlands	Norway	18 Oct 62	466UNTS145	106741
France	Ivory Coast	19 Oct 62	498UNTS317	107286
Ivory Coast	Switzerland	17 Nov 62	499UNTS3	107289
Austria	Yugoslavia	11 Dec 62	546UNTS3	107938
Multilateral		12 Dec 62	552UNTS15	108048
Ghana	Mali	09 Jan 63	466UNTS165	106742
Senegal	Switzerland	23 Jan 63	524UNTS23	107564
Guinea	Switzerland	01 Feb 63	499UNTS35	107291
Mali	Senegal	07 Feb 63	524UNTS41	107565
Sudan	Switzerland	18 Feb 63	563UNTS281	108215
Algeria	France	18 Feb 63	563UNTS263	108214
Cyprus	Denmark	27 Apr 63	529UNTS255	107664
Algeria	Morocco	30 Apr 63	564UNTS3	108217
Belgium	Cyprus	08 Jun 63	601UNTS311	108703
Austria	IAEA (Atom Energy)	21 Jun 63	490UNTS351	107164
Guinea	Ivory Coast	26 Jun 63	499UNTS71	107293
Finland	IAEA (Atom Energy)	02 Jul 63	490UNTS403	107167
Austria	France	12 Jul 63	499UNTS91	107294
Algeria	Mali	22 Jul 63	564UNTS29	108219
Mali	Tunisia	24 Jul 63	602UNTS91	108708
Cameroon	UK Great Britain	29 Jul 63	478UNTS148	106935
Cameroon	Israel	09 Aug 63	499UNTS121	107295
Algeria	Tunisia	01 Sep 63	601UNTS275	108701
Ivory Coast	Netherlands	09 Oct 63	499UNTS141	107296
Multilateral		17 Oct 63	525UNTS75	107585

PARTY ONE	PARTY TWO	DATE	CITATION	NUMBER
Special tribunals (Cont.)				
Nicaragua	United Nations	03 Dec 63	482UNTS329	107002
Multilateral		18 Dec 63	490UNTS383	107166
Mali	Niger	15 Jan 64	499UNTS197	107299
Denmark	Yugoslavia	11 Feb 64	511UNTS241	107437
Cameroon	Mali	17 Mar 64	524UNTS61	107566
Cyprus	United Nations	31 Mar 64	492UNTS57	107187
Norway	Yugoslavia	15 Apr 64	602UNTS177	108712
United Arab Rep	USA (United States)	05 May 64	531UNTS229	107706
Cyprus	Hungary	02 Jun 64	602UNTS3	108704
Multilateral		11 Jun 64	525UNTS61	107584
Multilateral		15 Jun 64	573UNTS85	108324
IAEA (Atom Energy)	USA (United States)	15 Jun 64	525UNTS3	107580
New Zealand	USA (United States)	24 Jun 64	524UNTS101	107568
Ivory Coast	Mali	09 Jul 64	524UNTS121	107569
Belgium	Tunisia	15 Jul 64	561UNTS297	108190
Eur Space Research	Sweden	29 Jul 64	528UNTS81	107636
IAEA (Atom Energy)	United Arab Rep	17 Sep 64	525UNTS19	107581
Argentina	IAEA (Atom Energy)	02 Dec 64	525UNTS29	107582
Cyprus	Syria	22 Dec 64	602UNTS25	108705
Argentina	UK Great Britain	12 Jan 65	597UNTS177	108645
Malta	Switzerland	20 Jan 65	548UNTS193	107978
Belgium	Congo (Zaire)	06 Feb 65	540UNTS227	107852
Multilateral		18 Mar 65	575UNTS159	108359
Canada	USA (United States)	25 Mar 65	607UNTS141	108802
Finland	UK Great Britain	25 Mar 65	539UNTS103	107826
Australia	France	13 Apr 65	601UNTS293	108702
Multilateral		26 Apr 65	533UNTS50	107732
Bel-Lux Econ Union	Morocco	28 Apr 65	620UNTS171	108954
Ghana	Malawi	04 May 65	541UNTS163	107869
Denmark	Spain	05 May 65	543UNTS255	107905
Mauritania	Spain	11 May 65	602UNTS111	108709
Malaysia	Norway	26 May 65	602UNTS157	108711
British Guiana	USA (United States)	29 May 65	605UNTS87	108761
Netherlands	Senegal	12 Jun 65	602UNTS231	108715
Multilateral		18 Jun 65	573UNTS3	108320
Multilateral		23 Jun 65	548UNTS241	107981
India	Pakistan	30 Jun 65	548UNTS277	107983
Switzerland	UK Great Britain	07 Jul 65	605UNTS205	108765
Afghanistan	IAEA (Atom Energy)	24 Sep 65	556UNTS101	108121
Multilateral		24 Sep 65	556UNTS141	108124
Morocco	IAEA (Atom Energy)	24 Sep 65	556UNTS109	108122
Nigeria	Switzerland	11 Oct 65	602UNTS137	108710
IAEA (Atom Energy)	Turkey	08 Feb 66	573UNTS75	108323
United Nations	UK Great Britain	21 Feb 66	555UNTS177	108112
Multilateral		20 Jun 66	573UNTS41	108322
Austria	USA (United States)	23 Jun 66	601UNTS51	108687
IAEA (Atom Energy)	USA (United States)	26 Sep 66	589UNTS3	108532
Multilateral		28 Sep 66	589UNTS41	108534
Congo (Brazzaville)	Denmark	27 Feb 67	600UNTS189	108681
Trinidad/Tobago	UK Great Britain	01 Mar 67	606UNTS149	108784
Negotiation				
Brazil	France	27 Jan 40	72UNTS77	100929
Haiti	USA (United States)	13 Sep 41	103UNTS141	200311
Mexico	USA (United States)	19 Nov 41	148UNTS367	200474
Multilateral		22 Apr 42	8UNTS237	200044
Multilateral		26 Mar 43	13UNTS427	200089
Guatemala	USA (United States)	19 May 43	28UNTS377	200161
Canada	USA (United States)	08 Jun 44	124UNTS297	200427
Multilateral		07 Dec 44	84UNTS389	200252
Multilateral		07 Dec 44	171UNTS387	200502
South Africa	UK Great Britain	26 Oct 45	72UNTS41	100927
Poland	Yugoslavia	23 Nov 45	115UNTS3	101555
Mexico	UK Great Britain	07 Feb 46	6UNTS55	100068
France	Ireland	16 May 46	44UNTS105	100681

PARTY ONE	PARTY TWO	DATE	CITATION	NUMBER
Negotiation (Cont.)				
Sweden	Turkey	26 Jun 46	14UNTS21	100208
Czechoslovakia	USSR (Soviet Union)	25 Jul 46	27UNTS231	100409
Denmark	USSR (Soviet Union)	17 Aug 46	8UNTS201	100124
Argentina	UK Great Britain	17 Sep 46	88UNTS47	101185
France	Turkey	12 Oct 46	14UNTS33	100209
France	USA (United States)	18 Oct 46	140UNTS23	101882
Belgium	Portugal	22 Oct 46	34UNTS49	100527
Multilateral		07 Dec 46	157UNTS103	102050
Portugal	Switzerland	09 Dec 46	310UNTS251	104495
Denmark	Norway	30 Dec 46	8UNTS21	100111
Czechoslovakia	Yugoslavia	25 Feb 47	112UNTS3	101539
Burma	USA (United States)	28 Feb 47	25UNTS27	100355
Canada	USA (United States)	18 Mar 47	117UNTS79	101584
Netherlands	Turkey	19 Mar 47	14UNTS59	100211
France	Greece	05 May 47	76UNTS61	100980
Romania	Yugoslavia	30 Jun 47	116UNTS57	101569
Iraq	Turkey	30 Jun 47	72UNTS107	100930
Denmark	Turkey	30 Jun 47	32UNTS301	100504
Italy	Philippines	09 Jul 47	44UNTS3	100674
Canada	UK Great Britain	17 Jul 47	28UNTS3	100416
Hungary	Yugoslavia	24 Jul 47	114UNTS3	101554
Canada	Ireland	08 Aug 47	28UNTS47	100419
Hungary	Poland	28 Aug 47	15UNTS145	100231
Czechoslovakia	Switzerland	10 Sep 47	35UNTS275	100559
Chile	UK Great Britain	16 Sep 47	133UNTS143	101786
Lebanon	Turkey	16 Sep 47	44UNTS123	100682
Czechoslovakia	Sweden	15 Oct 47	44UNTS149	100683
Colombia	UK Great Britain	16 Oct 47	160UNTS297	102115
Peru	UK Great Britain	22 Dec 47	72UNTS143	100932
Philippines	UK Great Britain	07 Jan 48	28UNTS63	100420
Multilateral		06 Mar 48	289UNTS3	104214
Bulgaria	USSR (Soviet Union)	01 Apr 48	217UNTS97	102946
Netherlands	USA (United States)	29 Apr 48	32UNTS167	100498
Pakistan	Sweden	06 May 48	36UNTS3	100564
Ireland	Switzerland	06 May 48	334UNTS187	104768
Denmark	USA (United States)	06 May 48	26UNTS55	100377
Jordan	Turkey	07 May 48	32UNTS313	100505
India	Sweden	21 May 48	34UNTS285	100543
Greece	Switzerland	26 May 48	94UNTS217	101312
Canada	Netherlands	02 Jun 48	32UNTS215	100499
India	Pakistan	23 Jun 48	28UNTS143	100423
Italy	UK Great Britain	25 Jun 48	94UNTS239	101313
Belgium	Czechoslovakia	03 Jul 48	77UNTS137	100997
India	Switzerland	14 Aug 48	33UNTS3	100509
Multilateral		18 Aug 48	33UNTS181	100518
Greece	Lebanon	06 Sep 48	178UNTS37	102335
Belgium	Netherlands	25 Sep 48	123UNTS81	101655
Belgium	Luxembourg	09 Oct 48	123UNTS29	101652
France	USA (United States)	19 Oct 48	98UNTS3	101355
Argentina	Denmark	14 Dec 48	74UNTS41	100956
UK Great Britain	Yugoslavia	23 Dec 48	81UNTS133	101069
Ceylon (Sri Lanka)	Pakistan	03 Jan 49	28UNTS247	100428
Poland	UK Great Britain	14 Jan 49	83UNTS3	101100
Italy	Lebanon	24 Jan 49	231UNTS241	103223
Switzerland	Turkey	16 Feb 49	72UNTS175	100933
Czechoslovakia	Yugoslavia	01 Mar 49	113UNTS3	101547
Netherlands	Switzerland	07 Mar 49	35UNTS69	100551
Finland	Sweden	26 Apr 49	95UNTS83	101318
Denmark	Poland	12 May 49	87UNTS179	101172
Bulgaria	Poland	16 May 49	84UNTS313	101140
United Arab Rep	UK Great Britain	31 May 49	226UNTS273	103122
Australia	Pakistan	03 Jun 49	35UNTS23	100549
Norway	USA (United States)	13 Jun 49	127UNTS163	101704
Norway	USA (United States)	13 Jun 49	127UNTS189	101705
Belgium	Greece	21 Jun 49	137UNTS215	101854

PARTY ONE	PARTY TWO	DATE	CITATION	NUMBER
Negotiation (Cont.)				
Norway	Pakistan	23 Jun 49	35UNTS49	100550
India	Switzerland	24 Jun 49	95UNTS109	101319
Greece	Syria	05 Jul 49	78UNTS71	101013
Australia	India	11 Jul 49	35UNTS83	100552
Pakistan	Philippines	16 Jul 49	35UNTS111	100553
Pakistan	UK Great Britain	27 Jul 49	44UNTS199	100685
Multilateral		05 Aug 49	88UNTS229	101195
Ceylon (Sri Lanka)	UK Great Britain	05 Aug 49	35UNTS137	100554
Multilateral		10 Aug 49	45UNTS3	100689
Finland	Norway	24 Aug 49	53UNTS167	100780
Denmark	Finland	26 Aug 49	53UNTS191	100781
Belgium	Canada	30 Aug 49	53UNTS221	100782
Belgium	United Arab Rep	19 Sep 49	137UNTS189	101853
Multilateral		19 Sep 49	125UNTS3	101671
Lebanon	Netherlands	20 Sep 49	108UNTS205	101474
Greece	Philippines	08 Oct 49	187UNTS221	102515
India	Philippines	20 Oct 49	72UNTS191	100934
Iran	Netherlands	31 Oct 49	254UNTS257	103596
Multilateral		07 Nov 49	132UNTS3	101748
Denmark	Pakistan	09 Nov 49	44UNTS255	100687
Italy	Turkey	25 Nov 49	192UNTS39	102594
Afghanistan	WHO (World Health)	04 Dec 49	102UNTS117	101414
Netherlands	United Arab Rep	08 Dec 49	95UNTS123	101320
Sweden	United Arab Rep	12 Dec 49	108UNTS15	101466
Canada	Denmark	13 Dec 49	72UNTS247	100937
Austria	Switzerland	19 Dec 49	254UNTS287	103597
Norway	Poland	21 Dec 49	47UNTS107	100725
Norway	USSR (Soviet Union)	29 Dec 49	83UNTS291	101112
Belgium	France	30 Dec 49	46UNTS111	100704
Afghanistan	India	04 Jan 50	81UNTS75	101064
Netherlands	Syria	13 Feb 50	108UNTS53	101467
Ceylon (Sri Lanka)	WHO (World Health)	17 Feb 50	102UNTS309	200309
Italy	Netherlands	04 Mar 50	254UNTS305	103598
Norway	United Arab Rep	11 Mar 50	95UNTS157	101321
Denmark	United Arab Rep	14 Mar 50	95UNTS197	101322
Iceland	Netherlands	22 Mar 50	95UNTS237	101323
Afghanistan	India	04 Apr 50	167UNTS105	102201
Sweden	UK Great Britain	05 Apr 50	99UNTS107	101374
Multilateral		08 Apr 50	68UNTS99	100889
Turkey	United Arab Rep	12 Apr 50	128UNTS3	101711
Greece	United Arab Rep	24 Apr 50	163UNTS229	102149
Switzerland	United Arab Rep	15 May 50	95UNTS255	101325
Haiti	WHO (World Health)	27 Jun 50	110UNTS99	101504
Spain	UK Great Britain	20 Jul 50	398UNTS101	105719
Spain	Switzerland	03 Aug 50	254UNTS365	103600
Canada	New Zealand	16 Aug 50	77UNTS239	101002
WHO (World Health)	Venezuela	11 Sep 50	110UNTS237	101513
Ceylon (Sri Lanka)	United Arab Rep	26 Sep 50	192UNTS53	102595
Iceland	WHO (World Health)	06 Oct 50	110UNTS127	101506
Switzerland	USA (United States)	13 Oct 50	133UNTS33	101777
Sweden	Switzerland	18 Oct 50	166UNTS49	102185
WHO (World Health)	Turkey	19 Oct 50	110UNTS215	101512
Luxembourg	Portugal	21 Oct 50	108UNTS67	101468
Israel	Netherlands	23 Oct 50	189UNTS89	102543
Philippines	USA (United States)	06 Nov 50	122UNTS63	101637
Nicaragua	WHO (World Health)	10 Nov 50	110UNTS155	101508
Peru	WHO (World Health)	10 Nov 50	110UNTS187	101510
Multilateral		15 Dec 50	347UNTS127	104994
Multilateral		15 Dec 50	171UNTS305	102234
Philippines	WHO (World Health)	28 Dec 50	110UNTS203	101511
Canada	France	26 Jan 51	233UNTS65	103251
France	India	02 Feb 51	203UNTS155	102744
Israel	Turkey	05 Feb 51	193UNTS3	102607
Denmark	Hungary	10 Feb 51	85UNTS49	101145
Paraguay	WHO (World Health)	15 Feb 51	110UNTS171	101509

PARTY ONE	PARTY TWO	DATE	CITATION	NUMBER
Negotiation (Cont.)				
India	Indonesia	03 Mar 51	167UNTS3	102197
Canada	France	16 Mar 51	236UNTS267	103330
Indonesia	WHO (World Health)	28 Mar 51	103UNTS71	101425
Jordan	WHO (World Health)	03 Apr 51	110UNTS297	200367
France	UK Great Britain	11 Apr 51	106UNTS3	101456
Iraq	UK Great Britain	19 Apr 51	108UNTS121	101470
Honduras	WHO (World Health)	20 Apr 51	110UNTS111	101505
Colombia	WHO (World Health)	04 May 51	110UNTS83	101503
Belgium	UK Great Britain	08 May 51	158UNTS451	102079
Switzerland	USA (United States)	24 May 51	127UNTS227	101706
India	Netherlands	24 May 51	108UNTS151	101471
Cambodia	WHO (World Health)	31 May 51	102UNTS279	200307
WHO (World Health)	Uruguay	11 Jun 51	128UNTS251	101724
Liberia	WHO (World Health)	11 Jun 51	103UNTS83	101426
Denmark	Iran	18 Jun 51	255UNTS3	103602
Iraq	WHO (World Health)	01 Jul 51	110UNTS139	101507
Switzerland	USA (United States)	09 Jul 51	165UNTS51	102167
Iceland	Norway	14 Jul 51	163UNTS265	102150
Israel	Philippines	07 Aug 51	192UNTS81	102596
Mexico	USA (United States)	11 Aug 51	162UNTS103	102133
Lebanon	UK Great Britain	15 Aug 51	160UNTS327	102116
Panama	UK Great Britain	15 Sep 51	560UNTS143	108172
WHO (World Health)	Vietnam, South	21 Sep 51	107UNTS63	200352
Bolivia	United Nations	01 Oct 51	104UNTS263	101447
UNICEF (Children)	UK Great Britain	02 Oct 51	104UNTS301	101448
India	WHO (World Health)	11 Oct 51	118UNTS27	101594
India	WHO (World Health)	16 Oct 51	109UNTS49	101490
Greece	Luxembourg	22 Oct 51	187UNTS119	102506
India	UK Great Britain	01 Dec 51	128UNTS39	101712
Colombia	Spain	11 Dec 51	216UNTS73	102933
Multilateral		20 Dec 51	163UNTS293	102151
India	WHO (World Health)	20 Dec 51	124UNTS109	101669
Italy	USA (United States)	28 Dec 51	157UNTS63	102047
Jordan	United Arab Rep	02 Jan 52	192UNTS157	102599
USA (United States)	Yugoslavia	08 Jan 52	152UNTS61	102011
Multilateral		10 Jan 52	163UNTS27	102139
Multilateral		10 Jan 52	163UNTS3	102138
Belgium	Germany, West	18 Jan 52	124UNTS9	101663
Indonesia	United Nations	06 Feb 52	121UNTS3	101621
India	Syria	25 Feb 52	163UNTS55	102141
Belgium	Spain	10 Mar 52	178UNTS243	102342
Belgium	Pakistan	15 Mar 52	316UNTS65	104578
Pakistan	Switzerland	17 Mar 52	192UNTS237	102603
Iraq	Switzerland	31 Mar 52	311UNTS43	104498
France	Mexico	17 Apr 52	163UNTS321	102153
India	WHO (World Health)	17 Apr 52	131UNTS241	101744
India	WHO (World Health)	19 Apr 52	131UNTS253	101745
Greece	USA (United States)	23 Apr 52	177UNTS283	102327
Netherlands	Sweden	25 Apr 52	163UNTS131	102147
Taiwan	Japan	28 Apr 52	138UNTS3	101858
France	Israel	29 Apr 52	189UNTS55	102542
Norway	WHO (World Health)	09 May 52	131UNTS281	101747
Multilateral		22 May 52	131UNTS115	101739
Germany, West	USA (United States)	11 Jun 52	273UNTS105	103947
Australia	United Arab Rep	14 Jun 52	173UNTS241	102269
India	United Arab Rep	14 Jun 52	173UNTS209	102268
Denmark	UK Great Britain	23 Jun 52	151UNTS3	101982
Norway	USA (United States)	27 Jun 52	184UNTS271	102452
Belgium	Israel	30 Jun 52	183UNTS263	102435
Netherlands	Pakistan	17 Jul 52	150UNTS277	101980
UNICEF (Children)	UK Great Britain	25 Jul 52	135UNTS37	101812
Israel	USA (United States)	08 Aug 52	181UNTS37	102396
USA (United States)	Yugoslavia	15 Aug 52	184UNTS97	102441
UNICEF (Children)	Vietnam, South	29 Aug 52	161UNTS335	200492
Ethiopia	Pakistan	29 Aug 52	150UNTS257	101979

PARTY ONE	PARTY TWO	DATE	CITATION	NUMBER
Negotiation (Cont.)				
Multilateral		06 Sep 52	216UNTS132	102937
Netherlands	Peru	22 Sep 52	255UNTS49	103604
Iceland	Luxembourg	23 Oct 52	193UNTS39	102609
Burma	UK Great Britain	25 Oct 52	150UNTS237	101978
Multilateral		07 Nov 52	221UNTS255	103010
India	Iraq	10 Nov 52	172UNTS103	102242
Luxembourg	Norway	17 Nov 52	311UNTS95	104500
Luxembourg	Sweden	17 Nov 52	173UNTS277	102270
Israel	Switzerland	19 Nov 52	232UNTS3	103226
UNICEF (Children)	UK Great Britain	16 Dec 52	151UNTS359	102005
Japan	Netherlands	17 Feb 53	192UNTS215	102602
Japan	Sweden	20 Feb 53	173UNTS307	102272
Libya	UK Great Britain	21 Feb 53	311UNTS115	104501
Japan	Norway	23 Feb 53	192UNTS191	102601
Germany, West	USA (United States)	27 Feb 53	224UNTS31	103068
Lebanon	Sweden	23 Mar 53	255UNTS83	103605
Multilateral		31 Mar 53	193UNTS136	102613
Philippines	Thailand	27 Apr 53	174UNTS3	102274
Australia	USA (United States)	14 May 53	205UNTS277	102780
Japan	Thailand	19 Jun 53	174UNTS29	102276
Canada	Mexico	27 Jul 53	192UNTS255	102604
Spain	USA (United States)	26 Sep 53	207UNTS93	102802
UNICEF (Children)	UK Great Britain	07 Oct 53	180UNTS59	102375
Denmark	Sweden	27 Oct 53	198UNTS71	102658
Denmark	Sweden	27 Oct 53	198UNTS111	102659
Belgium	Lebanon	24 Dec 53	219UNTS153	102972
Ethiopia	Greece	20 Jan 54	222UNTS281	103035
Syria	UK Great Britain	30 Jan 54	449UNTS47	106452
Belgium	Finland	11 Feb 54	211UNTS63	102848
Canada	Peru	18 Feb 54	411UNTS64	105915
Multilateral		19 Feb 54	214UNTS51	102899
Bulgaria	Yugoslavia	20 Feb 54	397UNTS13	105700
Multilateral		25 Feb 54	215UNTS249	102922
Lebanon	Switzerland	03 Mar 54	255UNTS127	103608
Japan	USA (United States)	08 Mar 54	232UNTS251	103240
Finland	Netherlands	29 Mar 54	252UNTS239	103568
Peru	Spain	31 Mar 54	232UNTS65	103230
Japan	USA (United States)	16 Apr 54	238UNTS39	103354
Japan	USA (United States)	16 Apr 54	238UNTS3	103353
Lebanon	Yugoslavia	17 Apr 54	602UNTS199	108713
Switzerland	Syria	26 May 54	255UNTS145	103609
Multilateral		04 Jun 54	282UNTS249	104101
Multilateral		04 Jun 54	276UNTS191	103992
Multilateral		30 Jun 54	193UNTS67	102611
Germany, West	USA (United States)	22 Jul 54	239UNTS3	103369
Ireland	Luxembourg	27 Jul 54	232UNTS91	103231
Brazil	USA (United States)	20 Aug 54	410UNTS79	105898
Thailand	USA (United States)	01 Sep 54	237UNTS209	103347
Austria	UK Great Britain	14 Oct 54	204UNTS87	102751
Multilateral		23 Oct 54	332UNTS387	104763
Burma	Japan	05 Nov 54	251UNTS201	103542
Pakistan	United Arab Rep	13 Dec 54	255UNTS167	103610
India	Iran	15 Dec 54	327UNTS245	104724
Norway	Switzerland	30 Dec 54	311UNTS147	104502
Austria	Belgium	07 Jan 55	380UNTS219	105458
Canada	Japan	12 Jan 55	311UNTS167	104503
Philippines	UK Great Britain	31 Jan 55	216UNTS51	102932
United Arab Rep	Yugoslavia	20 Feb 55	255UNTS199	103611
Costa Rica	USA (United States)	26 Feb 55	252UNTS129	103562
Iraq	United Arab Rep	23 Mar 55	311UNTS199	104504
Guatemala	USA (United States)	23 Mar 55	252UNTS143	103563
Ecuador	USA (United States)	29 Mar 55	261UNTS343	103732
Italy	USA (United States)	30 Mar 55	257UNTS169	103654
Italy	USA (United States)	30 Mar 55	257UNTS199	103655
Pakistan	USA (United States)	26 May 55	257UNTS93	103652

PARTY ONE	PARTY TWO	DATE	CITATION	NUMBER
Negotiation (Cont.)				
Honduras	USA (United States)	10 Jun 55	258UNTS51	103669
Syria	United Arab Rep	03 Jul 55	393UNTS67	105652
Germany, West	UK Great Britain	22 Jul 55	269UNTS189	103881
Germany, East	Romania	28 Jul 55	342UNTS207	104909
Belgium	Ireland	10 Sep 55	255UNTS235	103612
Bolivia	USA (United States)	23 Sep 55	256UNTS275	103637
Bulgaria	Yugoslavia	01 Oct 55	396UNTS223	105698
Iceland	USA (United States)	05 Oct 55	256UNTS285	103638
Denmark	Syria	20 Oct 55	250UNTS61	103518
Paraguay	USA (United States)	28 Oct 55	273UNTS97	103946
Pakistan	Turkey	02 Nov 55	311UNTS217	104505
Burma	China People's Rep	08 Nov 55	306UNTS11	104430
Austria	Israel	17 Nov 55	232UNTS153	103235
India	Japan	26 Nov 55	311UNTS243	104506
Bulgaria	Yugoslavia	11 Dec 55	378UNTS49	105417
Czechoslovakia	Poland	13 Jan 56	265UNTS157	103811
France	Japan	17 Jan 56	255UNTS275	103614
Belgium	Sweden	18 Jan 56	293UNTS23	104283
Australia	Japan	19 Jan 56	311UNTS291	104507
Austria	Italy	23 Jan 56	393UNTS97	105653
Romania	Yugoslavia	01 Feb 56	362UNTS203	105189
Netherlands	Sudan	12 Feb 56	311UNTS319	104508
Norway	Syria	25 Feb 56	463UNTS217	106706
Multilateral		01 Mar 56	343UNTS129	104923
Germany, West	USA (United States)	02 Mar 56	273UNTS209	103952
Norway	Sweden	09 Mar 56	369UNTS285	105262
Ceylon (Sri Lanka)	Romania	16 Mar 56	315UNTS51	104559
Indonesia	United Nations	17 Apr 56	233UNTS267	103266
Multilateral		30 Apr 56	310UNTS229	104494
Multilateral		18 May 56	338UNTS103	104834
Multilateral		18 May 56	339UNTS3	104844
Multilateral		18 May 56	327UNTS123	104721
Multilateral		18 May 56	319UNTS21	104630
Multilateral		19 May 56	399UNTS189	105742
Japan	Switzerland	24 May 56	312UNTS3	104509
Italy	Switzerland	04 Jun 56	378UNTS311	105429
Canada	Germany, West	04 Jun 56	316UNTS231	104589
Austria	Yugoslavia	15 Jun 56	396UNTS117	105695
Honduras	USA (United States)	25 Jun 56	279UNTS113	104036
Multilateral		16 Aug 56	287UNTS223	104188
IBRD (World Bank)	Switzerland	17 Sep 56	340UNTS311	200560
Multilateral		25 Sep 56	334UNTS89	104767
Multilateral		25 Sep 56	334UNTS13	104766
Norway	Sweden	27 Sep 56	261UNTS71	103726
Switzerland	Thailand	13 Oct 56	312UNTS43	104510
Czechoslovakia	Hungary	13 Oct 56	300UNTS177	104337
Belgium	Turkey	25 Oct 56	380UNTS3	105447
Austria	USA (United States)	25 Oct 56	299UNTS123	104310
Austria	UK Great Britain	27 Oct 56	264UNTS67	103789
Peru	Switzerland	23 Nov 56	411UNTS97	105916
Albania	Yugoslavia	23 Nov 56	386UNTS73	105539
Luxembourg	USA (United States)	07 Dec 56	265UNTS255	103817
Japan	Sweden	12 Dec 56	318UNTS309	104623
Multilateral		14 Dec 56	436UNTS115	106292
Multilateral		14 Dec 56	436UNTS131	106293
Italy	Sweden	20 Dec 56	369UNTS357	105265
Turkey	USA (United States)	15 Jan 57	280UNTS79	104053
Iran	USA (United States)	16 Jan 57	308UNTS147	104460
Italy	Netherlands	24 Jan 57	485UNTS67	107047
Denmark	Norway	22 Feb 57	286UNTS127	104164
Australia	UK Great Britain	26 Feb 57	265UNTS197	103813
Belgium	Czechoslovakia	12 Mar 57	312UNTS75	104512
Netherlands	Yugoslavia	13 Mar 57	327UNTS227	104723
Paraguay	USA (United States)	04 Apr 57	283UNTS193	104117
Denmark	Pakistan	10 Apr 57	302UNTS53	104353

PARTY ONE	PARTY TWO	DATE	CITATION	NUMBER
Negotiation (Cont.)				
Belgium	Bulgaria	14 May 57	317UNTS81	104596
Hungary	Yugoslavia	25 May 57	477UNTS219	106924
Hungary	Netherlands	28 May 57	334UNTS291	104773
Belgium	Hungary	01 Jun 57	291UNTS17	104242
Czechoslovakia	Yugoslavia	11 Jun 57	504UNTS107	107355
Afghanistan	Pakistan	13 Jun 57	327UNTS51	104717
Austria	USSR (Soviet Union)	14 Jun 57	285UNTS169	104152
Czechoslovakia	United Arab Rep	30 Jun 57	411UNTS126	105917
Australia	Japan	06 Jul 57	318UNTS381	104627
Netherlands	Romania	27 Aug 57	342UNTS309	104914
Iran	USA (United States)	21 Sep 57	293UNTS287	104296
Multilateral		30 Sep 57	619UNTS77	108940
Multilateral		03 Oct 57	366UNTS87	105216
Italy	Pakistan	05 Oct 57	353UNTS91	105039
Fed of Malaya	UK Great Britain	18 Oct 57	335UNTS3	104775
USA (United States)	Vietnam, South	05 Nov 57	300UNTS23	104328
Germany, East	Hungary	13 Nov 57	407UNTS216	105866
Argentina	Italy	25 Nov 57	305UNTS275	104424
Argentina	Denmark	25 Nov 57	299UNTS83	104308
Multilateral		13 Dec 57	372UNTS159	105296
Australia	Ireland	30 Dec 57	497UNTS29	107260
Canada	Switzerland	10 Jan 58	464UNTS21	106710
Multilateral		15 Jan 58	383UNTS229	105503
Indonesia	Japan	20 Jan 58	324UNTS227	104688
Belgium	Morocco	20 Jan 58	288UNTS3	104192
Australia	UK Great Britain	07 Feb 58	335UNTS23	104776
Bulgaria	Netherlands	07 Feb 58	335UNTS45	104777
Afghanistan	Turkey	08 Feb 58	464UNTS39	106711
Sudan	Sweden	17 Feb 58	393UNTS161	105655
Austria	Sweden	18 Feb 58	427UNTS349	106166
Norway	Pakistan	05 Mar 58	334UNTS199	104769
Pakistan	Sweden	06 Mar 58	393UNTS181	105656
Czechoslovakia	Hungary	12 Mar 58	408UNTS178	105870
Multilateral		20 Mar 58	335UNTS211	104789
Belgium	Iran	14 Apr 58	381UNTS309	105473
Sweden	Yugoslavia	18 Apr 58	393UNTS225	105658
Bulgaria	Denmark	28 May 58	312UNTS235	104521
India	USSR (Soviet Union)	02 Jun 58	393UNTS3	105650
Pakistan	Portugal	07 Jun 58	320UNTS225	104645
Denmark	Luxembourg	10 Jun 58	356UNTS193	105096
Denmark	Romania	25 Jun 58	345UNTS231	104970
Belgium	Pakistan	04 Jul 58	387UNTS305	105569
Ethiopia	UK Great Britain	07 Jul 58	331UNTS3	104749
Austria	Romania	10 Jul 58	353UNTS155	105041
Denmark	Hungary	17 Jul 58	344UNTS281	104954
Romania	United Arab Rep	14 Aug 58	405UNTS189	105834
Australia	Fed of Malaya	26 Aug 58	325UNTS253	104703
Japan	New Zealand	09 Sep 58	325UNTS119	104698
Ghana	UK Great Britain	24 Sep 58	411UNTS146	105918
Germany, West	Norway	18 Nov 58	357UNTS205	105119
Liberia	Netherlands	28 Nov 58	393UNTS55	105651
United Nations	Tunisia	23 Dec 58	321UNTS23	104651
Finland	Switzerland	07 Jan 59	353UNTS173	105042
Multilateral		15 Jan 59	348UNTS13	104996
UK Great Britain	Yugoslavia	03 Feb 59	359UNTS339	105151
Burma	UK Great Britain	06 Feb 59	343UNTS223	104927
Japan	Pakistan	17 Feb 59	341UNTS127	104880
Japan	Norway	21 Feb 59	356UNTS231	105098
Ghana	United Nations	27 Feb 59	324UNTS133	104682
Denmark	Japan	10 Mar 59	341UNTS55	104878
Netherlands	Tunisia	19 Mar 59	497UNTS61	107262
Sweden	Tunisia	19 Mar 59	497UNTS43	107261
Canada	IAEA (Atom Energy)	24 Mar 59	339UNTS315	104851
Japan	IAEA (Atom Energy)	24 Mar 59	339UNTS327	104852
Norway	Tunisia	28 Mar 59	497UNTS77	107263

PARTY ONE	PARTY TWO	DATE	CITATION	NUMBER
Negotiation (Cont.)				
Canada	Finland	28 Mar 59	355UNTS3	105072
United Nations	Sudan	28 Mar 59	327UNTS95	104719
Morocco	UN Special Fund	04 Apr 59	354UNTS347	105069
Denmark	Tunisia	14 Apr 59	340UNTS273	104870
Germany, West	Sweden	17 Apr 59	428UNTS155	106175
Denmark	Sudan	11 May 59	445UNTS105	106380
Austria	Sweden	14 May 59	428UNTS3	106167
Belgium	Japan	20 Jun 59	411UNTS3	105911
Libya	United Nations	27 Jun 59	336UNTS291	104811
Laos	United Nations	06 Jul 59	337UNTS41	104814
Bulgaria	United Arab Rep	09 Jul 59	411UNTS187	105920
Paraguay	United Nations	01 Aug 59	341UNTS319	104894
Ghana	UN Special Fund	12 Aug 59	338UNTS203	104836
Australia	Fed of Malaya	29 Sep 59	357UNTS29	105104
Iran	UN Special Fund	06 Oct 59	342UNTS89	104902
Austria	France	08 Oct 59	453UNTS95	106521
Multilateral		09 Oct 59	376UNTS382	105391
Nicaragua	Peru	14 Oct 59	392UNTS303	105649
Guinea	United Nations	15 Oct 59	344UNTS47	104942
Poland	UN Special Fund	15 Oct 59	344UNTS29	104941
India	UN Special Fund	20 Oct 59	344UNTS143	104946
UN Special Fund	Yugoslavia	27 Oct 59	344UNTS159	104947
Ecuador	UN Special Fund	10 Nov 59	345UNTS3	104955
Greece	UN Special Fund	13 Nov 59	345UNTS171	104966
UN Special Fund	Turkey	20 Nov 59	345UNTS105	104963
Afghanistan	United Nations	24 Nov 59	397UNTS187	105705
UN Special Fund	United Arab Rep	25 Nov 59	345UNTS125	104964
Israel	UN Special Fund	01 Dec 59	345UNTS197	104968
Guinea	UN Special Fund	02 Dec 59	345UNTS215	104969
Argentina	UN Special Fund	04 Dec 59	345UNTS263	104972
Liberia	Sweden	09 Dec 59	464UNTS219	106716
Jordan	UN Special Fund	15 Dec 59	346UNTS3	104974
India	Japan	05 Jan 60	384UNTS3	105507
UN Special Fund	UK Great Britain	07 Jan 60	348UNTS177	105000
Czechoslovakia	UK Great Britain	15 Jan 60	374UNTS207	105336
Japan	USA (United States)	19 Jan 60	373UNTS207	105321
Peru	UN Special Fund	19 Jan 60	349UNTS83	105010
Chile	UN Special Fund	22 Jan 60	351UNTS115	105020
Austria	Czechoslovakia	23 Jan 60	495UNTS125	107242
El Salvador	USA (United States)	29 Jan 60	372UNTS3	105283
Colombia	UN Special Fund	04 Feb 60	355UNTS257	105080
Multilateral		06 Feb 60	383UNTS3	105494
Bolivia	UN Special Fund	09 Feb 60	351UNTS203	105024
Argentina	Philippines	12 Feb 60	535UNTS293	107785
Korea, South	USA (United States)	19 Feb 60	372UNTS109	105291
Afghanistan	UN Special Fund	21 Feb 60	351UNTS93	105019
Austria	Norway	25 Feb 60	376UNTS155	105380
Pakistan	UN Special Fund	25 Feb 60	351UNTS141	105021
Multilateral		26 Feb 60	418UNTS171	106022
Australia	Thailand	26 Feb 60	392UNTS255	105647
France	Thailand	26 Feb 60	392UNTS279	105648
Guinea	Netherlands	09 Mar 60	392UNTS243	105646
Finland	Iceland	10 Mar 60	497UNTS95	107264
Czechoslovakia	Iraq	11 Mar 60	464UNTS267	106718
Multilateral		15 Mar 60	572UNTS133	108310
France	UN Special Fund	17 Mar 60	354UNTS119	105059
Belgium	Switzerland	24 Mar 60	416UNTS81	105996
Italy	UN Special Fund	01 Apr 60	354UNTS261	105066
Luxembourg	Yugoslavia	09 Apr 60	464UNTS293	106719
UN Special Fund	Tunisia	12 Apr 60	355UNTS289	105082
Libya	UN Special Fund	19 Apr 60	356UNTS11	105090
UN Special Fund	Sudan	21 Apr 60	356UNTS213	105097
UN Special Fund	Vietnam, South	29 Apr 60	357UNTS311	200567
Laos	UN Special Fund	30 Apr 60	361UNTS171	105179
Greece	Romania	02 May 60	485UNTS17	107043

PARTY ONE	PARTY TWO	DATE	CITATION	NUMBER
Negotiation (Cont.)				
Poland	Yugoslavia	05 May 60	423UNTS229	106095
United Nations	Togo	06 May 60	388UNTS53	105571
Lebanon	UN Special Fund	07 May 60	360UNTS225	105160
Nepal	USA (United States)	17 May 60	372UNTS313	105307
Switzerland	Tunisia	21 May 60	497UNTS109	107265
Kuwait	UK Great Britain	24 May 60	412UNTS4	105923
Afghanistan	Czechoslovakia	28 May 60	497UNTS129	107266
Luxembourg	Tunisia	13 Jun 60	497UNTS143	107267
Iraq	UN Special Fund	19 Jun 60	376UNTS357	105389
Denmark	Peru	22 Jun 60	439UNTS113	106326
Finland	USSR (Soviet Union)	23 Jun 60	379UNTS277	105443
Ireland	Portugal	24 Jun 60	412UNTS30	105924
Kuwait	UN Special Fund	29 Jun 60	369UNTS419	200575
Poland	UK Great Britain	02 Jul 60	385UNTS87	105532
Ethiopia	UN Special Fund	13 Jul 60	368UNTS159	105240
Ethiopia	United Nations	13 Jul 60	368UNTS143	105239
Switzerland	United Arab Rep	14 Jul 60	497UNTS161	107268
Ghana	Netherlands	30 Jul 60	412UNTS51	105925
Guatemala	USA (United States)	09 Aug 60	461UNTS15	106648
Multilateral		16 Aug 60	382UNTS8	105476
Ghana	United Arab Rep	29 Aug 60	412UNTS71	105926
Sweden	Tunisia	06 Sep 60	427UNTS301	106162
Brazil	UN Special Fund	16 Sep 60	375UNTS3	105351
Czechoslovakia	India	19 Sep 60	465UNTS67	106722
Multilateral		19 Sep 60	444UNTS259	106371
Taiwan	UN Special Fund	20 Sep 60	375UNTS29	105352
Multilateral		06 Oct 60	473UNTS131	106861
Indonesia	UN Special Fund	07 Oct 60	378UNTS141	105424
Liberia	UN Special Fund	11 Oct 60	376UNTS341	105388
Belgium	Jordan	19 Oct 60	479UNTS277	106959
El Salvador	UN Special Fund	24 Oct 60	377UNTS171	105400
Hungary	UK Great Britain	25 Oct 60	419UNTS309	106034
Norway	Peru	02 Nov 60	497UNTS207	107270
Australia	Italy	10 Nov 60	497UNTS247	107271
Romania	UK Great Britain	10 Nov 60	385UNTS113	105533
Czechoslovakia	Poland	14 Nov 60	413UNTS4	105938
Guatemala	UN Special Fund	17 Nov 60	383UNTS67	105495
Nepal	UN Special Fund	17 Nov 60	380UNTS289	105461
Pakistan	United Nations	17 Nov 60	380UNTS277	105460
Indonesia	UK Great Britain	23 Nov 60	398UNTS71	105718
Cambodia	UN Special Fund	24 Nov 60	382UNTS255	105487
Cambodia	United Nations	30 Nov 60	383UNTS147	105500
Multilateral		09 Dec 60	429UNTS211	106200
Multilateral		13 Dec 60	523UNTS117	107557
Bolivia	United Nations	14 Dec 60	382UNTS283	105489
Honduras	UN Special Fund	20 Dec 60	383UNTS103	105497
Canada	Pakistan	21 Dec 60	465UNTS115	106724
Luxembourg	Thailand	29 Dec 60	465UNTS131	106725
Burma	UN Special Fund	03 Jan 61	387UNTS219	105564
Jordan	Sweden	09 Jan 61	465UNTS155	106726
Costa Rica	UN Special Fund	10 Jan 61	389UNTS253	105597
Sudan	UK Great Britain	16 Jan 61	424UNTS233	106112
Norway	Poland	17 Jan 61	412UNTS130	105928
UN Special Fund	Saudi Arabia	19 Jan 61	396UNTS27	105692
Nicaragua	UN Special Fund	20 Jan 61	387UNTS15	105555
Chad	UN Special Fund	23 Jan 61	390UNTS69	105603
UN Special Fund	Somalia	28 Jan 61	388UNTS75	105573
Gabon	UN Special Fund	02 Feb 61	387UNTS289	105568
Nigeria	UN Special Fund	10 Feb 61	390UNTS85	105604
Canada	USA (United States)	17 Feb 61	445UNTS143	106383
Mexico	UN Special Fund	23 Feb 61	388UNTS151	105576
Cyprus	UN Special Fund	24 Feb 61	389UNTS3	105588
Cuba	Czechoslovakia	04 Mar 61	465UNTS209	106728
Iraq	United Nations	05 Mar 61	409UNTS56	105878
Panama	UN Special Fund	09 Mar 61	396UNTS3	105691

PARTY ONE	PARTY TWO	DATE	CITATION	NUMBER
Negotiation (Cont.)				
Cuba	UN Special Fund	10 Mar 61	390UNTS35	105601
Japan	UK Great Britain	11 Apr 61	420UNTS75	106042
Korea, South	UN Special Fund	21 Apr 61	394UNTS231	200583
Ceylon (Sri Lanka)	UN Special Fund	03 May 61	395UNTS217	105687
Poland	Switzerland	18 May 61	559UNTS233	108161
Multilateral		08 Jun 61	473UNTS153	106862
Multilateral		08 Jun 61	473UNTS187	106863
New Zealand	UK Great Britain	13 Jun 61	497UNTS293	107273
Cameroon	UN Special Fund	13 Jun 61	397UNTS297	105713
Cyprus	United Nations	15 Jun 61	398UNTS39	105716
Cameroon	France	16 Jun 61	412UNTS148	105929
Guinea	Sweden	17 Jun 61	465UNTS236	106729
Paraguay	UN Special Fund	22 Jun 61	399UNTS117	105738
UN Special Fund	Upper Volta	26 Jun 61	400UNTS3	105744
Haiti	United Nations	28 Jun 61	399UNTS159	105740
Philippines	UN Special Fund	28 Jun 61	399UNTS141	105739
Haiti	UN Special Fund	28 Jun 61	399UNTS171	105741
Mali	UN Special Fund	21 Jul 61	401UNTS141	105768
Czechoslovakia	Ghana	02 Aug 61	465UNTS249	106730
UN Special Fund	Yemen	02 Aug 61	402UNTS43	105777
Finland	Luxembourg	15 Aug 61	541UNTS45	107859
Jordan	Norway	21 Aug 61	465UNTS275	106731
Jordan	Netherlands	24 Aug 61	466UNTS3	106733
Italy	Norway	25 Aug 61	475UNTS269	106896
Lebanon	United Nations	26 Aug 61	406UNTS105	105842
Ivory Coast	UN Special Fund	29 Aug 61	406UNTS129	105844
Liberia	Switzerland	31 Aug 61	559UNTS215	108160
Jordan	United Nations	11 Sep 61	406UNTS255	105855
Ghana	Romania	30 Sep 61	467UNTS443	106769
UN Special Fund	Sierra Leone	02 Oct 61	422UNTS131	106073
Greece	Sweden	06 Oct 61	481UNTS137	106981
Japan	Pakistan	17 Oct 61	466UNTS17	106734
Mauritania	UN Special Fund	07 Nov 61	412UNTS240	105936
Congo (Brazzaville)	UN Special Fund	09 Nov 61	413UNTS58	105940
Cyprus	Greece	23 Nov 61	497UNTS311	107274
Czechoslovakia	Mali	27 Nov 61	466UNTS41	106736
Ivory Coast	USA (United States)	01 Dec 61	462UNTS221	106681
Ceylon (Sri Lanka)	United Nations	04 Dec 61	415UNTS236	105987
Denmark	Jordan	07 Dec 61	631UNTS333	109003
UN Special Fund	Venezuela	11 Dec 61	422UNTS149	106074
Czechoslovakia	Guinea	16 Dec 61	559UNTS49	108154
UN Special Fund	Senegal	16 Dec 61	425UNTS97	106121
Austria	Japan	20 Dec 61	517UNTS155	107485
Malagasy	UN Special Fund	05 Jan 62	419UNTS29	106028
Netherlands	Sweden	08 Jan 62	466UNTS65	106737
Austria	Greece	15 Jan 62	498UNTS3	107275
United Nations	Somalia	20 Jan 62	420UNTS133	106044
Indonesia	Japan	23 Jan 62	559UNTS77	108155
Italy	Japan	31 Jan 62	498UNTS23	107276
Finland	Hungary	13 Feb 62	463UNTS61	106693
Niger	UN Special Fund	26 Feb 62	423UNTS83	106086
Multilateral		07 Mar 62	445UNTS205	106389
Luxembourg	Spain	26 Mar 62	563UNTS205	108211
Dahomey	UN Special Fund	28 Mar 62	424UNTS55	106099
France	Luxembourg	29 Mar 62	563UNTS227	108212
IAEA (Atom Energy)	USA (United States)	30 Mar 62	442UNTS49	106338
Sierra Leone	UK Great Britain	05 Apr 62	434UNTS227	106265
Ghana	USSR (Soviet Union)	06 Apr 62	498UNTS41	107277
Netherlands	USA (United States)	24 Apr 62	436UNTS93	106289
Niger	USA (United States)	26 Apr 62	459UNTS129	106618
Dominican Republic	USA (United States)	02 May 62	442UNTS99	106341
UN Special Fund	Uruguay	04 May 62	429UNTS143	106196
Japan	United Arab Rep	10 May 62	498UNTS69	107278
Greece	United Nations	18 May 62	429UNTS61	106190
Dominican Republic	UN Special Fund	06 Jun 62	429UNTS169	106197

PARTY ONE	PARTY TWO	DATE	CITATION	NUMBER
Negotiation (Cont.)				
Czechoslovakia	Senegal	20 Jun 62	498UNTS145	107280
Guinea	Norway	21 Jun 62	466UNTS81	106738
Congo (Zaire)	IAEA (Atom Energy)	27 Jun 62	463UNTS31	106691
Multilateral		27 Jun 62	463UNTS17	106690
Liberia	Norway	29 Jun 62	466UNTS95	106739
UN Special Fund	Syria	07 Jul 62	443UNTS3	106355
UN Special Fund	Tanganyika	17 Jul 62	435UNTS237	106281
Ethiopia	USA (United States)	03 Aug 62	459UNTS79	106613
Nigeria	United Nations	07 Aug 62	435UNTS167	106278
Cameroon	United Nations	29 Aug 62	442UNTS3	106334
Congo (Brazzaville)	USA (United States)	01 Sep 62	459UNTS117	106616
Niger	United Nations	01 Oct 62	439UNTS181	106329
Japan	Kuwait	06 Oct 62	498UNTS235	107284
Austria	United Arab Rep	16 Oct 62	491UNTS63	107174
Austria	Luxembourg	18 Oct 62	496UNTS97	107248
Hungary	Syria	18 Oct 62	491UNTS209	107178
Netherlands	Norway	18 Oct 62	466UNTS145	106741
Japan	UN Special Fund	31 Oct 62	444UNTS171	106368
United Nations	Western Samoa	05 Nov 62	443UNTS297	200599
Poland	Syria	10 Nov 62	491UNTS228	107179
Algeria	UN Special Fund	15 Nov 62	452UNTS243	106512
Congo (Zaire)	USA (United States)	17 Nov 62	474UNTS41	106870
Ecuador	United Nations	26 Nov 62	445UNTS3	106372
Rwanda	United Nations	28 Nov 62	450UNTS267	106473
Multilateral		08 Dec 62	510UNTS235	107418
Multilateral		10 Dec 62	521UNTS231	107525
Ivory Coast	United Nations	10 Dec 62	451UNTS269	106498
Nigeria	USA (United States)	24 Dec 62	462UNTS180	106677
Syria	United Arab Rep	27 Dec 62	491UNTS245	107180
Jamaica	USA (United States)	04 Jan 63	471UNTS119	106826
Israel	United Nations	07 Jan 63	450UNTS229	106470
Trinidad/Tobago	USA (United States)	15 Jan 63	471UNTS141	106829
Japan	New Zealand	30 Jan 63	517UNTS183	107486
Sudan	Switzerland	18 Feb 63	563UNTS281	108215
Algeria	France	18 Feb 63	563UNTS263	108214
Japan	Thailand	01 Mar 63	475UNTS233	106895
IAEA (Atom Energy)	Yugoslavia	04 Mar 63	490UNTS333	107162
UN Special Fund	Uganda	22 Mar 63	456UNTS466	106572
Gabon	USA (United States)	10 Apr 63	474UNTS113	106876
Norway	Spain	25 Apr 63	503UNTS41	107340
Greece	Hungary	27 Apr 63	534UNTS3	107750
Cyprus	Denmark	27 Apr 63	529UNTS255	107664
Jamaica	UN Special Fund	22 May 63	489UNTS191	107140
Netherlands	UN Special Fund	24 May 63	466UNTS289	106750
Cyprus	USA (United States)	29 May 63	487UNTS283	107110
Japan	Malaysia	04 Jun 63	517UNTS245	107488
IAEA (Atom Energy)	Yugoslavia	04 Jun 63	490UNTS343	107163
UN Special Fund	Western Samoa	05 Jun 63	467UNTS463	200601
Belgium	Cyprus	08 Jun 63	601UNTS311	108703
Finland	Poland	10 Jun 63	503UNTS179	107343
Austria	IAEA (Atom Energy)	21 Jun 63	490UNTS351	107164
New Zealand	UN Special Fund	28 Jun 63	470UNTS3	106792
United Arab Rep	USA (United States)	29 Jun 63	479UNTS207	106954
Mali	Tunisia	24 Jul 63	602UNTS91	108708
Argentina	USA (United States)	24 Jul 63	487UNTS183	107103
Malagasy	USA (United States)	26 Jul 63	487UNTS189	107104
Finland	IAEA (Atom Energy)	30 Jul 63	490UNTS413	107168
Cameroon	Israel	09 Aug 63	499UNTS121	107295
France	Israel	20 Aug 63	515UNTS173	107460
Burundi	UN Special Fund	22 Aug 63	476UNTS49	106903
Algeria	Tunisia	01 Sep 63	601UNTS275	108701
Pakistan	USSR (Soviet Union)	07 Oct 63	499UNTS161	107297
Austria	Finland	08 Oct 63	490UNTS255	107160
Central Afri Rep	UN Special Fund	30 Oct 63	481UNTS247	106985
Tanganyika	USA (United States)	14 Nov 63	493UNTS75	107208

PARTY ONE	PARTY TWO	DATE	CITATION	NUMBER
Negotiation (Cont.)				
Romania	Yugoslavia	30 Nov 63	512UNTS2	107438
Multilateral		18 Dec 63	490UNTS383	107166
Somalia	USA (United States)	08 Jan 64	505UNTS165	107372
Norway	Thailand	09 Jan 64	522UNTS65	107537
Denmark	Yugoslavia	11 Feb 64	511UNTS241	107437
Belgium	France	10 Mar 64	557UNTS13	108127
Denmark	Finland	07 Apr 64	525UNTS89	107586
Malaysia	Netherlands	07 Apr 64	524UNTS81	107567
Norway	Yugoslavia	15 Apr 64	602UNTS177	108712
Kenya	USA (United States)	20 Apr 64	524UNTS165	107571
Netherlands	NATO (North Atlan)	25 May 64	544UNTS237	107920
Cyprus	Hungary	02 Jun 64	602UNTS3	108704
Ireland	UN Special Fund	03 Jun 64	496UNTS205	107253
Mali	USA (United States)	09 Jun 64	530UNTS133	107678
Ceylon (Sri Lanka)	Norway	11 Jun 64	559UNTS23	108153
Multilateral		15 Jun 64	573UNTS85	108324
Spain	USA (United States)	16 Jul 64	529UNTS187	107661
IAEA (Atom Energy)	United Arab Rep	17 Sep 64	525UNTS19	107581
Norway	United Arab Rep	20 Oct 64	543UNTS3	107895
Cyprus	Syria	22 Dec 64	602UNTS25	108705
Laos	USA (United States)	29 Dec 64	542UNTS23	107876
Central Afri Rep	USA (United States)	31 Dec 64	542UNTS29	107877
Malta	Switzerland	20 Jan 65	548UNTS193	107978
Finland	Israel	21 Jan 65	581UNTS275	108450
Dahomey	USA (United States)	13 Mar 65	549UNTS43	107987
Finland	UK Great Britain	25 Mar 65	539UNTS103	107826
Denmark	Malaysia	26 Mar 65	540UNTS205	107851
Finland	United Arab Rep	01 Apr 65	562UNTS3	108193
Australia	France	13 Apr 65	601UNTS293	108702
Bel-Lux Econ Union	Morocco	28 Apr 65	620UNTS171	108954
Denmark	Spain	05 May 65	543UNTS255	107905
Chad	USA (United States)	12 May 65	546UNTS183	107944
British Guiana	USA (United States)	29 May 65	605UNTS87	108761
Uganda	USA (United States)	29 May 65	546UNTS209	107948
Denmark	Thailand	01 Jun 65	551UNTS157	108040
Multilateral		02 Jun 65	551UNTS2	108030
USA (United States)	Upper Volta	18 Jun 65	549UNTS133	107996
UN Special Fund	Spain	30 Jun 65	544UNTS159	107918
Multilateral		05 Jul 65	563UNTS104	108207
Multilateral		24 Sep 65	556UNTS141	108124
Netherlands	UK Great Britain	06 Oct 65	595UNTS113	108616
Mongolia	UN Special Fund	26 Jan 66	552UNTS201	108055
Norway	Eur Space Research	31 Jan 66	580UNTS3	108414
IAEA (Atom Energy)	Turkey	08 Feb 66	573UNTS75	108323
UK Great Britain	USA (United States)	05 Apr 66	592UNTS61	108569
Bulgaria	Turkey	18 Apr 66	631UNTS263	108999
Multilateral		30 Apr 66	620UNTS191	108956
Multilateral		04 May 66	575UNTS49	108354
Multilateral		20 Jun 66	573UNTS41	108322
Mexico	IAEA (Atom Energy)	20 Jun 66	573UNTS25	108321
Austria	USA (United States)	23 Jun 66	601UNTS51	108687
Denmark	Israel	27 Jun 66	581UNTS227	108448
Israel	UK Great Britain	05 Jul 66	630UNTS189	108971
IAEA (Atom Energy)	USA (United States)	26 Sep 66	589UNTS3	108532
IAEA (Atom Energy)	USA (United States)	09 Dec 66	589UNTS55	108535
Denmark	Singapore	20 Dec 66	593UNTS125	108580
Argentina	Paraguay	23 Jan 67	634UNTS181	109060
Korea, South	New Zealand	31 Jan 67	598UNTS91	108656
Trinidad/Tobago	UK Great Britain	01 Mar 67	606UNTS149	108784
Bulgaria	Turkey	30 May 67	631UNTS19	108984
Denmark	Netherlands	20 Jun 67	619UNTS67	108939
Multilateral		21 Jun 67	598UNTS2	108653
Malta	UK Great Britain	10 Jul 67	619UNTS11	108936
Singapore	UK Great Britain	01 Aug 67	619UNTS29	108937
Malaysia	UK Great Britain	01 Aug 67	633UNTS93	109036

PARTY ONE	PARTY TWO	DATE	CITATION	NUMBER
Negotiation (Cont.)				
Iraq	IAEA (Atom Energy)	21 Sep 67	630UNTS41	108963
Burma	IAEA (Atom Energy)	11 Oct 67	630UNTS49	108964
IAEA (Atom Energy)	Vietnam, South	16 Oct 67	630UNTS379	200636
Iran	United Nations	15 Feb 68	631UNTS103	108990
Conciliation				
Brazil	Venezuela	30 Mar 40	51UNTS291	200195
France	Thailand	17 Nov 46	344UNTS59	104943
Multilateral		10 Feb 47	48UNTS203	100746
Multilateral		10 Feb 47	41UNTS21	100643
Multilateral		17 Mar 48	19UNTS51	100304
Multilateral		30 Apr 48	30UNTS55	100449
Multilateral		18 Aug 48	33UNTS181	100518
Finland	Sweden	17 Feb 49	197UNTS123	102636
Multilateral		28 Apr 49	71UNTS101	100912
Greece	Italy	31 Aug 49	78UNTS89	101014
Italy	Turkey	24 Mar 50	96UNTS207	101338
Spain	Switzerland	03 Aug 50	254UNTS365	103600
Multilateral		15 Dec 50	347UNTS127	104994
Italy	USA (United States)	13 Feb 51	148UNTS57	101935
Italy	Netherlands	15 Jun 51	150UNTS103	101964
Multilateral		19 Feb 54	214UNTS51	102899
Brazil	Italy	24 Nov 54	284UNTS325	104146
Costa Rica	Guatemala	20 Dec 55	280UNTS121	104056
Multilateral		01 Mar 56	343UNTS129	104923
Philippines	Switzerland	30 Aug 56	293UNTS43	104284
Multilateral		29 Apr 57	320UNTS243	104646
Multilateral		29 Apr 58	450UNTS169	106466
Ethiopia	France	12 Nov 59	381UNTS3	105465
Argentina	Philippines	12 Feb 60	535UNTS293	107785
Multilateral		18 Apr 61	500UNTS243	107312
Algeria	France	03 Jul 62	507UNTS25	107395
Italy	IAEA (Atom Energy)	11 Oct 63	639UNTS25	109142
Lebanon	Pakistan	04 Feb 64	614UNTS55	108863
IAEA (Atom Energy)	United Arab Rep	14 Jan 65	603UNTS45	108723
Multilateral		18 Mar 65	575UNTS159	108359
Austria	Hungary	09 Apr 65	638UNTS53	109131
Japan	Korea, South	22 Jun 65	584UNTS147	108476
Switzerland	UK Great Britain	07 Jul 65	605UNTS205	108765
Austria	Germany, West	17 Feb 66	614UNTS263	108875
Austria	Germany, West	17 Feb 66	615UNTS3	108876
Romania	IAEA (Atom Energy)	22 Apr 66	603UNTS23	108721
India	IAEA (Atom Energy)	09 Dec 66	603UNTS35	108722
Asian Devel Bank	Philippines	22 Dec 66	615UNTS375	108887
Romania	Sweden	01 Mar 67	642UNTS163	109172
Iran	IAEA (Atom Energy)	10 May 67	614UNTS93	108865
IAEA (Atom Energy)	USA (United States)	07 Jun 67	614UNTS109	108866
Multilateral		23 Jun 67	614UNTS185	108871
Multilateral		26 Jul 67	614UNTS217	108872
Mexico	IAEA (Atom Energy)	18 Aug 67	614UNTS123	108867
Mexico	IAEA (Atom Energy)	23 Aug 67	614UNTS133	108868
Multilateral		23 Aug 67	614UNTS145	108869
Multilateral		12 Oct 67	607UNTS2	108792
Botswana	UN Special Fund	12 Oct 67	607UNTS37	108794
Denmark	Iran	02 Nov 67	638UNTS217	109138
Multilateral		14 Nov 67	614UNTS2	108860
Denmark	Malaysia	14 Dec 67	614UNTS26	108862
Advisory opinions				
Brazil	Venezuela	30 Mar 40	51UNTS291	200195
Competence of tribunal				
Brazil	France	27 Jan 40	72UNTS77	100929
Norway	USA (United States)	28 Mar 40	88UNTS365	200253
Multilateral		07 Dec 44	171UNTS345	200501
Ethiopia	UK Great Britain	19 Dec 44	93UNTS303	200272
Portugal	UK Great Britain	06 Dec 45	5UNTS37	100064

PARTY ONE	PARTY TWO	DATE	CITATION	NUMBER
Competence of tribunal (Cont.)				
Portugal	UK Great Britain	06 Dec 45	6UNTS3	100065
UK Great Britain	USA (United States)	11 Feb 46	3UNTS253	100036
Belgium	USA (United States)	05 Apr 46	4UNTS125	100041
United Arab Rep	USA (United States)	15 Jun 46	71UNTS157	100917
Lebanon	USA (United States)	11 Aug 46	66UNTS211	100856
Norway	UK Great Britain	31 Aug 46	6UNTS235	100078
Brazil	USA (United States)	06 Sep 46	54UNTS197	100805
Syria	UK Great Britain	02 Nov 46	11UNTS153	100153
Australia	USA (United States)	03 Dec 46	7UNTS201	100100
Brazil	Portugal	10 Dec 46	200UNTS67	102695
USA (United States)	Uruguay	14 Dec 46	532UNTS87	107713
Peru	USA (United States)	27 Dec 46	26UNTS227	100390
Ecuador	USA (United States)	08 Jan 47	22UNTS119	100333
Multilateral		10 Feb 47	48UNTS203	100746
Multilateral		10 Feb 47	41UNTS21	100643
Multilateral		10 Feb 47	41UNTS135	100644
Thailand	USA (United States)	26 Feb 47	16UNTS17	100246
Paraguay	USA (United States)	28 Feb 47	44UNTS25	100676
Syria	USA (United States)	28 Apr 47	262UNTS121	103741
Chile	USA (United States)	10 May 47	55UNTS21	100807
South Africa	USA (United States)	23 May 47	66UNTS233	100857
Canada	Sweden	27 Jun 47	27UNTS313	100414
Taiwan	Netherlands	06 Dec 47	43UNTS185	100669
Italy	USA (United States)	06 Feb 48	73UNTS113	100950
Cuba	UK Great Britain	19 Mar 48	175UNTS23	102294
Multilateral		18 Aug 48	33UNTS181	100518
Bolivia	USA (United States)	29 Sep 48	505UNTS139	107370
Netherlands	Spain	08 Oct 48	28UNTS209	100426
Argentina	Netherlands	29 Oct 48	95UNTS21	101316
Finland	USA (United States)	29 Mar 49	55UNTS59	100808
Panama	USA (United States)	31 Mar 49	55UNTS87	100810
Multilateral		28 Apr 49	71UNTS101	100912
Switzerland	USA (United States)	13 May 49	51UNTS129	100761
Canada	USA (United States)	04 Jun 49	122UNTS237	101649
Czechoslovakia	Finland	13 Jul 49	53UNTS153	100779
Dominican Republic	USA (United States)	19 Jul 49	51UNTS145	100762
Burma	USA (United States)	28 Sep 49	55UNTS3	100806
Canada	Norway	14 Feb 50	53UNTS329	100790
Iceland	Netherlands	22 Mar 50	95UNTS237	101323
Israel	USA (United States)	13 Jun 50	212UNTS93	102863
Netherlands	Spain	20 Jun 50	95UNTS303	101327
Haiti	WHO (World Health)	27 Jun 50	110UNTS99	101504
Burma	Ceylon (Sri Lanka)	29 Jun 50	73UNTS3	100940
WHO (World Health)	Venezuela	11 Sep 50	110UNTS237	101513
Burma	Sweden	14 Sep 50	96UNTS45	101330
Iceland	WHO (World Health)	06 Oct 50	110UNTS127	101506
WHO (World Health)	Turkey	19 Oct 50	110UNTS215	101512
Nicaragua	WHO (World Health)	10 Nov 50	110UNTS155	101508
Peru	WHO (World Health)	10 Nov 50	110UNTS187	101510
Philippines	WHO (World Health)	28 Dec 50	110UNTS203	101511
Paraguay	WHO (World Health)	15 Feb 51	110UNTS171	101509
Indonesia	WHO (World Health)	28 Mar 51	103UNTS71	101425
Jordan	WHO (World Health)	03 Apr 51	110UNTS297	200367
Honduras	WHO (World Health)	20 Apr 51	110UNTS111	101505
Multilateral		25 Apr 51	91UNTS21	101240
Colombia	WHO (World Health)	04 May 51	110UNTS83	101503
Cambodia	WHO (World Health)	31 May 51	102UNTS279	200307
WHO (World Health)	Uruguay	11 Jun 51	128UNTS251	101724
Liberia	WHO (World Health)	11 Jun 51	103UNTS83	101426
Iraq	WHO (World Health)	01 Jul 51	110UNTS139	101507
Burma	Denmark	30 Jul 51	108UNTS167	101472
Multilateral		08 Sep 51	136UNTS45	101832
Panama	UK Great Britain	15 Sep 51	560UNTS143	108172
WHO (World Health)	Vietnam, South	21 Sep 51	107UNTS63	200352
Philippines	Spain	06 Oct 51	215UNTS193	102920

PARTY ONE	PARTY TWO	DATE	CITATION	NUMBER
Competence of tribunal (Cont.)				
France	Mexico	17 Apr 52	163UNTS321	102153
Norway	WHO (World Health)	09 May 52	131UNTS281	101747
Germany, West	USA (United States)	11 Jun 52	273UNTS105	103947
Cuba	USA (United States)	26 May 53	224UNTS75	103070
Switzerland	Yugoslavia	28 May 53	232UNTS45	103228
Burma	Norway	22 Jun 53	174UNTS49	102277
USA (United States)	Venezuela	14 Aug 53	213UNTS99	102883
Saudi Arabia	UK Great Britain	30 Jul 54	201UNTS317	102722
Norway	USA (United States)	06 Aug 54	222UNTS269	103034
Germany, West	USA (United States)	07 Jul 55	275UNTS3	103973
India	USA (United States)	03 Feb 56	272UNTS75	103932
Multilateral		18 May 56	339UNTS3	104844
Germany, West	Ireland	12 Jun 56	353UNTS121	105040
Iran	USA (United States)	16 Jan 57	308UNTS147	104460
Germany, West	Norway	29 Jan 57	353UNTS39	105037
Netherlands	Yugoslavia	13 Mar 57	327UNTS227	104723
Netherlands	USA (United States)	03 Apr 57	410UNTS193	105904
Fed of Malaya	UK Great Britain	04 Mar 58	314UNTS253	104550
Multilateral		10 Jun 58	330UNTS3	104739
Italy	Netherlands	17 Apr 59	474UNTS207	106883
Germany, West	Netherlands	08 Apr 60	508UNTS14	107404
Ghana	UK Great Britain	05 Jul 60	402UNTS17	105774
Germany, West	UK Great Britain	14 Jul 60	414UNTS144	105972
Mexico	USA (United States)	15 Aug 60	402UNTS177	105786
Belgium	Burma	17 Aug 60	540UNTS185	107850
Burma	Switzerland	31 Oct 60	465UNTS97	106723
Czechoslovakia	Poland	04 Jul 61	436UNTS189	106295
Germany, West	Netherlands	30 Aug 62	547UNTS173	107957
Austria	Czechoslovakia	22 Sep 62	495UNTS157	107244
Austria	Yugoslavia	11 Dec 62	546UNTS3	107938
Austria	Netherlands	06 Feb 63	570UNTS101	108290
Tanganyika	UK Great Britain	03 Apr 63	478UNTS23	106933
Algeria	Morocco	30 Apr 63	564UNTS3	108217
Algeria	Mali	22 Jul 63	564UNTS29	108219
Portugal	UK Great Britain	07 Apr 64	539UNTS167	107830
United Arab Rep	USA (United States)	05 May 64	531UNTS229	107706
New Zealand	USA (United States)	24 Jun 64	524UNTS101	107568
Multilateral		18 Mar 65	575UNTS159	108359
British Guiana	USA (United States)	29 May 65	605UNTS87	108761
Switzerland	UK Great Britain	07 Jul 65	605UNTS205	108765
Sierra Leone	USA (United States)	06 May 66	594UNTS47	108593
Trinidad/Tobago	UK Great Britain	01 Mar 67	606UNTS149	108784
General health, education, culture, welfare and labor				
Multilateral		22 Mar 45	70UNTS237	200241
Multilateral		22 Jul 46	9UNTS3	100125
Multilateral		14 May 54	249UNTS215	103511
Multilateral		08 Sep 54	209UNTS23	102819
Iraq	USA (United States)	02 Mar 55	250UNTS229	103526
Haiti	USA (United States)	27 Apr 55	240UNTS17	103391
Libya	USA (United States)	28 Jul 55	270UNTS269	103901
Czechoslovakia	Yugoslavia	22 May 57	391UNTS33	105615
UK Great Britain	USA (United States)	24 Jun 60	377UNTS63	105396
Multilateral		05 Oct 61	0UNTS0	109431
UK Great Britain	USSR (Soviet Union)	24 Feb 67	606UNTS171	108785
Austria	Switzerland	15 Nov 67	0UNTS0	109434
International circulation				
Taiwan	USA (United States)	05 Aug 48	82UNTS109	101087
South Africa	USA (United States)	26 Mar 52	165UNTS187	102176
Denmark	Sweden	28 Oct 54	262UNTS211	103747
Czechoslovakia	United Arab Rep	19 Oct 57	530UNTS181	107681
Multilateral		28 Apr 60	376UNTS111	105377
Multilateral		05 Oct 61	0UNTS0	109431
Multilateral		14 May 62	544UNTS39	107910
Multilateral		14 Sep 62	494UNTS219	107236

PARTY ONE	PARTY TWO	DATE	CITATION	NUMBER
International circulation (Cont.)				
Pakistan	USSR (Soviet Union)	07 Oct 63	499UNTS161	107297
Romania	USA (United States)	23 Dec 64	535UNTS359	107790
Hungary	Yugoslavia	26 Sep 66	601UNTS21	108685
Specialists exchange				
Mexico	USA (United States)	19 Nov 41	148UNTS367	200474
Ecuador	USA (United States)	24 Feb 42	26UNTS379	200157
Brazil	USA (United States)	14 Mar 42	102UNTS195	200302
Haiti	USA (United States)	07 Apr 42	106UNTS319	200349
El Salvador	USA (United States)	05 May 42	21UNTS215	200124
Honduras	USA (United States)	08 May 42	166UNTS351	200498
Peru	USA (United States)	11 May 42	136UNTS353	200447
Paraguay	USA (United States)	22 May 42	124UNTS243	200423
Nicaragua	USA (United States)	22 May 42	105UNTS141	200328
Bolivia	USA (United States)	16 Jul 42	13UNTS101	200072
Colombia	USA (United States)	23 Oct 42	105UNTS109	200326
Mexico	USA (United States)	18 Nov 42	120UNTS183	200392
Brazil	Dominican Republic	09 Dec 42	65UNTS217	200213
Panama	USA (United States)	02 Mar 43	107UNTS55	200351
Chile	USA (United States)	11 May 43	139UNTS295	200456
Mexico	USA (United States)	01 Jul 43	28UNTS407	200164
Dominican Republic	USA (United States)	07 Jul 43	28UNTS419	200165
USA (United States)	Uruguay	01 Nov 43	106UNTS311	200348
Honduras	USA (United States)	12 Apr 44	138UNTS271	200450
Peru	USA (United States)	15 Apr 44	150UNTS317	200479
Multilateral		02 Aug 44	67UNTS221	200221
Ecuador	USA (United States)	22 Jan 45	24UNTS273	200152
Dominican Republic	USA (United States)	13 Oct 45	149UNTS361	200477
Greece	UK Great Britain	24 Jan 46	6UNTS45	100067
Brazil	USA (United States)	15 Feb 46	162UNTS21	102130
Colombia	USA (United States)	19 Feb 46	166UNTS104	102187
USA (United States)	Uruguay	23 Apr 46	160UNTS103	102104
Bulgaria	Czechoslovakia	20 Jun 47	46UNTS15	100698
Czechoslovakia	Romania	05 Sep 47	46UNTS37	100699
Ecuador	USA (United States)	14 Nov 47	149UNTS297	101959
Czechoslovakia	USSR (Soviet Union)	28 Nov 47	216UNTS285	102941
Colombia	USA (United States)	22 Dec 47	51UNTS45	100751
Paraguay	USA (United States)	12 Mar 48	162UNTS30	102131
Belgium	Luxembourg	27 Mar 48	178UNTS265	102343
Poland	USSR (Soviet Union)	08 Apr 48	26UNTS191	100388
Hungary	Poland	18 Jun 48	25UNTS319	100370
Brazil	USA (United States)	26 Nov 48	88UNTS3	101180
Czechoslovakia	Poland	22 Jan 49	85UNTS3	101142
Luxembourg	Netherlands	26 Apr 49	182UNTS187	102425
Bulgaria	Poland	26 Sep 49	260UNTS227	103711
Hungary	Poland	29 Oct 49	260UNTS91	103705
Czechoslovakia	Poland	17 Nov 50	530UNTS195	107682
Colombia	WHO (World Health)	05 Jan 51	102UNTS139	101417
Nicaragua	USA (United States)	31 Jan 51	150UNTS3	101960
Costa Rica	USA (United States)	13 Feb 51	141UNTS169	101914
Dominican Republic	USA (United States)	16 Mar 51	148UNTS15	101932
Greece	Turkey	20 Apr 51	178UNTS17	102333
Honduras	USA (United States)	24 Apr 51	140UNTS287	101894
Nicaragua	UK Great Britain	25 May 51	101UNTS77	101404
Brazil	USA (United States)	29 Jun 51	184UNTS303	102455
Burma	WHO (World Health)	09 Jul 51	107UNTS9	101463
Japan	USA (United States)	28 Aug 51	147UNTS81	101930
Korea, South	WHO (World Health)	19 Sep 51	109UNTS297	200366
Greece	UK Great Britain	29 Sep 51	190UNTS260	102570
WHO (World Health)	Thailand	04 Oct 51	109UNTS77	101492
India	WHO (World Health)	23 Oct 51	109UNTS59	101491
Taiwan	WHO (World Health)	25 Oct 51	126UNTS77	101683
Panama	WHO (World Health)	09 Nov 51	118UNTS43	101595
El Salvador	USA (United States)	12 Dec 51	132UNTS287	101768
Guatemala	WHO (World Health)	17 Dec 51	120UNTS133	101619
Specialists exchange (Cont.)				
Guatemala	WHO (World Health)	29 Dec 51	124UNTS89	101668
Germany, East	Poland	08 Jan 52	304UNTS113	104394
Colombia	USA (United States)	12 Jan 52	168UNTS109	102216
Costa Rica	WHO (World Health)	23 Jan 52	135UNTS265	101826
Dominican Republic	WHO (World Health)	15 Feb 52	134UNTS291	101808
Burma	WHO (World Health)	18 Feb 52	127UNTS43	101698
Taiwan	WHO (World Health)	07 Mar 52	128UNTS233	101723
Mexico	WHO (World Health)	28 May 52	134UNTS319	101810
Burma	WHO (World Health)	09 Jun 52	134UNTS273	101806
Brazil	WHO (World Health)	12 Jun 52	151UNTS333	102003
Finland	USA (United States)	02 Jul 52	165UNTS203	102177
Germany, West	USA (United States)	18 Jul 52	165UNTS167	102175
Chile	WHO (World Health)	04 Nov 52	150UNTS119	101966
Ethiopia	USA (United States)	05 Nov 52	184UNTS139	102445
India	WHO (World Health)	11 Dec 52	158UNTS391	102073
Saudi Arabia	USA (United States)	25 Jan 53	201UNTS3	102706
Bolivia	Italy	31 Jan 53	281UNTS181	104079
Albania	Romania	14 Feb 53	342UNTS107	104903
Israel	Uruguay	30 Apr 53	280UNTS269	104064
Saudi Arabia	USA (United States)	29 Jun 53	206UNTS23	102784
Hungary	Romania	14 Dec 53	342UNTS151	104906
Bulgaria	Romania	22 Jul 54	362UNTS101	105184
Greece	Italy	11 Sep 54	284UNTS313	104145
Peru	USA (United States)	31 Dec 54	251UNTS51	103533
Czechoslovakia	Hungary	28 Apr 55	477UNTS197	106923
Netherlands	Norway	18 May 55	252UNTS269	103569
Italy	Norway	14 Jun 55	260UNTS307	103713
UK Great Britain	USA (United States)	15 Jun 55	229UNTS73	103161
Belgium	Portugal	30 Jul 55	250UNTS213	103525
Brazil	USA (United States)	03 Aug 55	270UNTS71	103893
Germany, East	Romania	05 Aug 55	342UNTS229	104910
Italy	Lebanon	04 Nov 55	267UNTS147	103840
Bulgaria	Yugoslavia	11 Dec 55	378UNTS49	105417
Bulgaria	Yugoslavia	10 Feb 56	349UNTS21	105007
Burma	Yugoslavia	07 Mar 56	386UNTS235	105543
Bulgaria	Greece	19 Apr 56	594UNTS131	108600
Bulgaria	USSR (Soviet Union)	28 Apr 56	259UNTS363	103697
Korea, North	Romania	12 May 56	342UNTS189	104908
USSR (Soviet Union)	Yugoslavia	17 May 56	259UNTS145	103687
Germany, East	USSR (Soviet Union)	30 May 56	263UNTS143	103771
Czechoslovakia	USSR (Soviet Union)	01 Jun 56	259UNTS341	103696
Austria	Yugoslavia	15 Jun 56	396UNTS117	105695
Czechoslovakia	Yugoslavia	16 Jun 56	552UNTS325	108064
Czechoslovakia	Yugoslavia	03 Jul 56	397UNTS165	105704
Poland	Yugoslavia	06 Jul 56	281UNTS143	104076
Korea, North	USSR (Soviet Union)	05 Sep 56	259UNTS329	103695
Greece	Yugoslavia	11 Sep 56	552UNTS311	108063
Belgium	Germany, West	24 Sep 56	263UNTS31	103766
Romania	Yugoslavia	25 Sep 56	395UNTS147	105683
Romania	Vietnam, North	12 Oct 56	342UNTS173	104907
Norway	USSR (Soviet Union)	12 Oct 56	308UNTS95	104457
Multilateral		26 Oct 56	276UNTS3	103988
Poland	United Arab Rep	02 Feb 57	319UNTS221	104633
Belgium	Yugoslavia	05 Feb 57	276UNTS143	103990
USSR (Soviet Union)	Vietnam, North	15 Feb 57	274UNTS115	103962
Poland	Vietnam, North	06 Apr 57	432UNTS255	106224
Czechoslovakia	Yugoslavia	22 May 57	391UNTS33	105615
Argentina	Israel	23 May 57	280UNTS199	104059
Hungary	Yugoslavia	25 May 57	477UNTS219	106924
Bulgaria	Czechoslovakia	03 Jun 57	292UNTS3	104261
Bulgaria	Yugoslavia	04 Jun 57	349UNTS35	105008
Czechoslovakia	Yugoslavia	11 Jun 57	504UNTS107	107355
Germany, East	Hungary	13 Nov 57	407UNTS216	105866
Hungary	Yugoslavia	20 Nov 57	477UNTS267	106925
Czechoslovakia	USSR (Soviet Union)	04 Dec 57	313UNTS291	104537

PARTY ONE	PARTY TWO	DATE	CITATION	NUMBER
Specialists exchange (Cont.)				
Hungary	Yugoslavia	06 Dec 57	519UNTS215	107509
Hungary	Romania	17 Dec 57	477UNTS303	106926
Norway	Turkey	10 Jan 58	351UNTS229	105025
USA (United States)	USSR (Soviet Union)	27 Jan 58	301UNTS405	104350
Czechoslovakia	Hungary	12 Mar 58	408UNTS178	105870
Czechoslovakia	Romania	25 Mar 58	339UNTS77	104846
Taiwan	Costa Rica	10 Apr 58	315UNTS165	104567
Germany, West	UK Great Britain	18 Apr 58	343UNTS241	104928
Afghanistan	USA (United States)	26 Jun 58	321UNTS67	104654
Czechoslovakia	Romania	25 Oct 58	338UNTS301	104843
Norway	Poland	17 Dec 58	432UNTS193	106221
Afghanistan	WHO (World Health)	18 Dec 58	324UNTS121	104681
Mongolia	Poland	23 Dec 58	432UNTS177	106220
Belgium	Turkey	29 Dec 58	357UNTS195	105118
Hungary	Poland	14 Feb 59	431UNTS157	106215
Bulgaria	Hungary	03 Apr 59	438UNTS269	106319
Hungary	USSR (Soviet Union)	17 Apr 59	439UNTS41	106324
Ceylon (Sri Lanka)	Yugoslavia	05 May 59	391UNTS101	105618
Iraq	USSR (Soviet Union)	05 May 59	356UNTS179	105095
Iran	UK Great Britain	06 May 59	398UNTS51	105717
Fed of Malaya	USA (United States)	22 May 59	346UNTS263	104985
Taiwan	Ecuador	12 Jun 59	387UNTS3	105554
Brazil	Israel	24 Jun 59	515UNTS151	107458
Iraq	Romania	04 Aug 59	502UNTS17	107324
Guinea	USA (United States)	28 Oct 59	358UNTS169	105134
USA (United States)	USSR (Soviet Union)	21 Nov 59	361UNTS35	105172
UK Great Britain	USSR (Soviet Union)	01 Dec 59	351UNTS313	105032
Czechoslovakia	Ethiopia	11 Dec 59	399UNTS93	105736
Czechoslovakia	Ethiopia	11 Dec 59	386UNTS45	105536
Multilateral		14 Dec 59	422UNTS33	106067
Multilateral		14 Dec 59	422UNTS57	106068
Germany, East	Hungary	19 Dec 59	409UNTS4	105874
Belgium	Brazil	06 Jan 60	531UNTS149	107701
Italy	USSR (Soviet Union)	09 Feb 60	399UNTS75	105735
Taiwan	Panama	26 Feb 60	435UNTS281	106285
Spain	USA (United States)	18 Mar 60	372UNTS13	105284
Mexico	USA (United States)	12 Apr 60	372UNTS47	105287
Poland	Yugoslavia	05 May 60	423UNTS229	106095
Netherlands	Turkey	12 May 60	463UNTS207	106704
Multilateral		19 Jun 60	537UNTS214	107803
Czechoslovakia	Poland	14 Nov 60	413UNTS4	105938
Czechoslovakia	Ghana	23 Nov 60	431UNTS91	106213
Cambodia	Czechoslovakia	27 Nov 60	410UNTS263	105910
Japan	UK Great Britain	03 Dec 60	414UNTS61	105966
Cuba	USSR (Soviet Union)	12 Dec 60	421UNTS3	106048
Cuba	Czechoslovakia	22 Dec 60	426UNTS145	106134
Thailand	USA (United States)	23 Dec 60	405UNTS135	105830
UK Great Britain	USSR (Soviet Union)	09 Jan 61	404UNTS175	105810
Ethiopia	USSR (Soviet Union)	13 Jan 61	421UNTS13	106049
Czechoslovakia	Hungary	24 Feb 61	422UNTS15	106066
Cuba	Poland	06 Mar 61	484UNTS123	107020
Cuba	Germany, East	29 Mar 61	448UNTS81	106426
India	Norway	19 Apr 61	404UNTS307	105818
Afghanistan	Czechoslovakia	23 Apr 61	437UNTS25	106297
Germany, West	Netherlands	27 Apr 61	487UNTS77	107095
Ghana	Hungary	27 Apr 61	439UNTS17	106322
Czechoslovakia	Somalia	04 Jun 61	479UNTS291	106960
Taiwan	Paraguay	18 Aug 61	438UNTS109	106314
Multilateral		18 Oct 61	529UNTS89	107659
United Arab Rep	UK Great Britain	14 Nov 61	449UNTS129	106455
Argentina	Japan	20 Dec 61	451UNTS77	106486
Ghana	USA (United States)	03 Jan 62	433UNTS147	106237
USA (United States)	USSR (Soviet Union)	08 Mar 62	460UNTS3	106630
Hungary	India	30 Mar 62	519UNTS119	107504
United Arab Rep	USA (United States)	21 May 62	458UNTS197	106601

PARTY ONE	PARTY TWO	DATE	CITATION	NUMBER
Specialists exchange (Cont.)				
Multilateral		14 Jun 62	528UNTS33	107634
Senegal	USSR (Soviet Union)	14 Jun 62	437UNTS233	106309
Israel	Liberia	25 Jun 62	448UNTS295	106442
Syria	USSR (Soviet Union)	19 Aug 62	457UNTS285	106588
Denmark	USSR (Soviet Union)	11 Sep 62	458UNTS3	106589
Multilateral		14 Sep 62	494UNTS219	107236
Multilateral		28 Sep 62	469UNTS169	106791
Cameroon	Israel	24 Oct 62	449UNTS15	106447
Ceylon (Sri Lanka)	USA (United States)	21 Nov 62	462UNTS237	106683
Belgium	Tunisia	21 Dec 62	482UNTS3	106987
UK Great Britain	USSR (Soviet Union)	21 Jan 63	475UNTS3	106887
Iraq	USA (United States)	23 Jan 63	488UNTS163	107126
Hungary	Korea, North	29 Mar 63	577UNTS219	108379
Czechoslovakia	Tunisia	06 Apr 63	555UNTS111	108106
Belgium	Venezuela	15 May 63	470UNTS259	106812
Paraguay	USA (United States)	20 Aug 63	531UNTS197	107704
Czechoslovakia	Yugoslavia	05 Oct 63	504UNTS151	107356
Hungary	Yugoslavia	15 Oct 63	577UNTS49	108372
Belgium	Romania	13 Nov 63	520UNTS119	107513
Belgium	Pakistan	14 Nov 63	535UNTS393	107792
Belgium	Poland	09 Dec 63	514UNTS195	107448
USA (United States)	USSR (Soviet Union)	22 Feb 64	526UNTS131	107605
Multilateral		28 Feb 64	501UNTS245	107321
Czechoslovakia	Yugoslavia	14 Mar 64	544UNTS147	107917
Taiwan	USA (United States)	23 Apr 64	524UNTS141	107570
Algeria	Czechoslovakia	14 May 64	538UNTS301	107817
Cuba	Czechoslovakia	03 Jun 64	527UNTS205	107626
Italy	Romania	16 Jun 64	558UNTS313	108150
Australia	USA (United States)	17 Aug 64	530UNTS209	107683
Germany, East	Poland	06 Oct 64	552UNTS89	108051
Czechoslovakia	Germany, East	06 Oct 64	545UNTS113	107927
Czechoslovakia	Mongolia	21 Oct 64	545UNTS91	107926
Austria	Hungary	11 Nov 64	576UNTS163	108368
Belgium	Mexico	19 Nov 64	546UNTS217	107949
India	United Nations	25 Nov 64	519UNTS47	107501
Poland	Romania	26 Nov 64	552UNTS157	108053
Czechoslovakia	United Arab Rep	26 Nov 64	545UNTS11	107923
Romania	USA (United States)	23 Dec 64	535UNTS359	107790
Germany, West	Thailand	23 Dec 64	525UNTS177	107589
UK Great Britain	USSR (Soviet Union)	06 Jan 65	543UNTS77	107897
Ecuador	Netherlands	14 Jan 65	551UNTS129	108038
Peru	USA (United States)	28 Jan 65	587UNTS273	108513
Germany, West	Jamaica	03 Feb 65	531UNTS143	107700
UK Great Britain	USSR (Soviet Union)	13 Feb 65	543UNTS43	107896
Bulgaria	Czechoslovakia	22 May 65	545UNTS65	107925
Ethiopia	Hungary	25 May 65	577UNTS193	108377
Pakistan	USSR (Soviet Union)	05 Jun 65	593UNTS115	108579
Multilateral		02 Jul 65	592UNTS215	108575
Austria	Bulgaria	12 Jul 65	587UNTS51	108510
Czechoslovakia	Poland	22 Jan 66	588UNTS175	108524
UK Great Britain	Yugoslavia	27 Jan 66	573UNTS243	108337
FAO (Food Agri)	IMCO (Maritime Org)	11 Jul 66	575UNTS238	200627
Multilateral		02 Aug 66	582UNTS59	108457
Multilateral		23 Sep 66	573UNTS132	108327
Hungary	Yugoslavia	26 Sep 66	601UNTS21	108685
United Nations	Sudan	08 Nov 66	576UNTS85	108365
Romania	UK Great Britain	09 Mar 67	605UNTS195	108764
Greece	United Nations	14 Apr 67	595UNTS83	108613
Czechoslovakia	Mongolia	31 Mar 68	0UNTS0	109279
Sanitation				
Belgium	UK Great Britain	05 Oct 44	5UNTS227	200031
Multilateral		30 Oct 46	27UNTS77	100401
Panama	USA (United States)	31 Mar 49	55UNTS87	100810
Greece	Yugoslavia	02 Feb 52	188UNTS311	102535

PARTY ONE	PARTY TWO	DATE	CITATION	NUMBER
Sanitation (Cont.)				
Jordan	USA (United States)	12 Feb 52	168UNTS25	102211
Mexico	USA (United States)	26 Aug 52	264UNTS269	103797
Saudi Arabia	USA (United States)	15 Dec 52	185UNTS55	102458
Mexico	USA (United States)	30 Jul 54	269UNTS39	103871
Libya	USA (United States)	11 Dec 60	445UNTS125	106381
Thailand	USA (United States)	23 Dec 60	405UNTS135	105830
Multilateral		18 Oct 61	529UNTS89	107659
Hungary	Yugoslavia	26 Sep 66	601UNTS21	108685
Bulgaria	Poland	06 Apr 67	617UNTS327	108920
Quarantine				
Multilateral		07 Dec 44	171UNTS345	200501
Canada	USA (United States)	17 Feb 45	122UNTS261	200409
Multilateral		22 Jul 46	14UNTS185	100221
Mexico	USA (United States)	17 Mar 47	167UNTS30	102200
Czechoslovakia	USSR (Soviet Union)	28 Nov 47	216UNTS285	102941
Poland	USSR (Soviet Union)	08 Apr 48	26UNTS191	100388
Czechoslovakia	Poland	22 Jan 49	85UNTS3	101142
Canada	USA (United States)	04 Jun 49	122UNTS237	101649
Belgium	Canada	30 Aug 49	53UNTS221	100782
Bulgaria	Poland	26 Sep 49	260UNTS227	103711
Hungary	Poland	29 Oct 49	260UNTS91	103705
Canada	Denmark	13 Dec 49	72UNTS247	100937
Canada	Norway	14 Feb 50	53UNTS329	100790
Romania	USSR (Soviet Union)	27 May 50	221UNTS13	103000
Germany, East	Poland	23 Jun 50	304UNTS91	104393
Hungary	USSR (Soviet Union)	13 Jul 50	221UNTS35	103001
Canada	New Zealand	16 Aug 50	77UNTS239	101002
Bulgaria	USSR (Soviet Union)	25 Aug 50	221UNTS57	103002
Multilateral		25 May 51	175UNTS215	102303
Czechoslovakia	Romania	31 Jul 52	362UNTS123	105185
Mexico	USA (United States)	26 Aug 52	264UNTS269	103797
Saudi Arabia	USA (United States)	29 Jun 53	206UNTS23	102784
Multilateral		11 Dec 53	191UNTS285	102588
Hungary	Romania	14 Dec 53	342UNTS151	104906
Bulgaria	Romania	22 Jul 54	362UNTS101	105184
Multilateral		29 Jul 54	249UNTS45	103500
Multilateral		19 Mar 55	228UNTS95	103144
Germany, East	Romania	05 Aug 55	342UNTS229	104910
Bulgaria	Greece	19 Apr 56	594UNTS131	108600
Germany, East	USSR (Soviet Union)	30 May 56	263UNTS143	103771
Greece	Yugoslavia	11 Sep 56	552UNTS311	108063
Albania	Yugoslavia	20 May 57	363UNTS99	105203
Bulgaria	Yugoslavia	04 Jun 57	349UNTS35	105008
New Zealand	UK Great Britain	20 Sep 57	287UNTS105	104180
Germany, East	Hungary	25 Oct 57	408UNTS156	105869
Hungary	Yugoslavia	20 Nov 57	477UNTS267	106925
Czechoslovakia	USSR (Soviet Union)	04 Dec 57	313UNTS291	104537
Hungary	Yugoslavia	06 Dec 57	519UNTS215	107509
Hungary	USSR (Soviet Union)	17 Apr 59	439UNTS41	106324
Multilateral		14 Dec 59	422UNTS33	106067
Australia	Fed of Malaya	26 Nov 62	453UNTS161	106523
Cuba	Czechoslovakia	03 Jun 64	527UNTS205	107626
Multilateral		07 Nov 64	548UNTS3	107965
Austria	Hungary	11 Nov 64	576UNTS163	108368
Austria	Bulgaria	12 Jul 65	587UNTS51	108510
Czechoslovakia	Mongolia	09 Dec 66	637UNTS0	109124
Border control				
Multilateral		15 Dec 44	16UNTS247	200106
Multilateral		15 Dec 44	17UNTS305	200110
United Arab Rep	USA (United States)	05 Jan 46	160UNTS27	102098
Albania	Yugoslavia	11 Jul 46	4UNTS407	100058
Multilateral		22 Jul 46	14UNTS185	100221
Czechoslovakia	USSR (Soviet Union)	28 Nov 47	216UNTS285	102941
Poland	USSR (Soviet Union)	08 Apr 48	26UNTS191	100388

PARTY ONE	PARTY TWO	DATE	CITATION	NUMBER
Border control (Cont.)				
Canada	USA (United States)	30 Apr 48	77UNTS191	100999
Czechoslovakia	Poland	22 Jan 49	85UNTS3	101142
Austria	Czechoslovakia	30 Mar 50	495UNTS85	107240
Romania	USSR (Soviet Union)	27 May 50	221UNTS13	103000
Multilateral		25 May 51	175UNTS215	102303
Ethiopia	USA (United States)	07 Sep 51	206UNTS41	102785
India	WHO (World Health)	14 Apr 52	131UNTS265	101746
Austria	Yugoslavia	19 Mar 53	467UNTS323	106768
Japan	USA (United States)	02 Apr 53	206UNTS143	102788
Mexico	USA (United States)	30 Jul 54	269UNTS39	103871
Italy	Yugoslavia	26 Mar 55	379UNTS3	105432
Czechoslovakia	Germany, East	30 Aug 55	504UNTS279	107361
Bulgaria	Yugoslavia	11 Dec 55	378UNTS49	105417
Italy	Switzerland	02 Feb 56	291UNTS113	104247
Hungary	Romania	03 Feb 56	362UNTS233	105190
Bulgaria	Greece	19 Apr 56	594UNTS131	108600
Bulgaria	Yugoslavia	22 May 56	367UNTS119	105229
Germany, East	USSR (Soviet Union)	30 May 56	263UNTS143	103771
Austria	Yugoslavia	15 Jun 56	396UNTS117	105695
Czechoslovakia	Yugoslavia	16 Jun 56	552UNTS325	108064
Greece	Yugoslavia	11 Sep 56	552UNTS311	108063
Hungary	Yugoslavia	25 May 57	477UNTS219	106924
Czechoslovakia	Yugoslavia	11 Jun 57	504UNTS107	107355
Germany, East	Hungary	25 Oct 57	408UNTS156	105869
Hungary	Yugoslavia	20 Nov 57	477UNTS267	106925
Hungary	Yugoslavia	06 Dec 57	519UNTS215	107509
Bulgaria	Hungary	13 Mar 58	438UNTS191	106317
Germany, West	Netherlands	16 Apr 58	486UNTS331	107084
Italy	Netherlands	01 Dec 59	455UNTS241	106545
Multilateral		14 Dec 59	422UNTS57	106068
Poland	Yugoslavia	05 May 60	423UNTS229	106095
Czechoslovakia	Poland	14 Nov 60	413UNTS4	105938
Belgium	Yugoslavia	31 Oct 61	426UNTS165	106136
Belgium	Romania	12 Oct 62	502UNTS31	107325
Austria	Hungary	11 Nov 64	576UNTS163	108368
Austria	Bulgaria	12 Jul 65	587UNTS51	108510
Czechoslovakia	Mongolia	09 Dec 66	637UNTS0	109124
UK Great Britain	USA (United States)	30 Dec 66	603UNTS245	108736
Bulgaria	Turkey	30 May 67	631UNTS19	108984
Netherlands	Romania	20 Jul 67	633UNTS21	109032
Czechoslovakia	Romania	17 Nov 67	0UNTS0	109280
Disease control				
Brazil	USA (United States)	14 Mar 42	102UNTS195	200302
El Salvador	USA (United States)	05 May 42	21UNTS215	200124
Honduras	USA (United States)	08 May 42	166UNTS351	200498
Bolivia	USA (United States)	16 Jul 42	13UNTS101	200072
Brazil	USA (United States)	17 Jul 42	102UNTS203	200303
Colombia	USA (United States)	23 Oct 42	105UNTS109	200326
Brazil	USA (United States)	10 Feb 43	102UNTS217	200304
Panama	USA (United States)	02 Mar 43	107UNTS55	200351
Multilateral		07 Dec 44	171UNTS345	200501
Multilateral		15 Dec 44	17UNTS305	200110
Multilateral		15 Dec 44	16UNTS247	200106
Multilateral		22 Jul 46	14UNTS185	100221
Mexico	USA (United States)	17 Mar 47	167UNTS30	102200
Czechoslovakia	USSR (Soviet Union)	28 Nov 47	216UNTS285	102941
Poland	USSR (Soviet Union)	08 Apr 48	26UNTS191	100388
Multilateral		24 Jul 48	66UNTS25	100847
Czechoslovakia	Poland	22 Jan 49	85UNTS3	101142
Multilateral		12 Aug 49	75UNTS31	100970
Bulgaria	Poland	26 Sep 49	260UNTS249	103712
Bulgaria	Poland	26 Sep 49	260UNTS227	103711
Hungary	Poland	29 Oct 49	260UNTS113	103706
Hungary	Poland	29 Oct 49	260UNTS91	103705

PARTY ONE	PARTY TWO	DATE	CITATION	NUMBER
Disease control (Cont.)				
Austria	Czechoslovakia	30 Mar 50	495UNTS85	107240
Multilateral		17 Apr 50	131UNTS99	101738
El Salvador	WHO (World Health)	21 Apr 50	103UNTS13	101420
Romania	USSR (Soviet Union)	27 May 50	221UNTS13	103000
Haiti	WHO (World Health)	21 Jun 50	103UNTS61	101424
Germany, East	Poland	23 Jun 50	304UNTS91	104393
Hungary	USSR (Soviet Union)	13 Jul 50	221UNTS35	103001
Bulgaria	USSR (Soviet Union)	25 Aug 50	221UNTS57	103002
Peru	WHO (World Health)	26 Sep 50	104UNTS233	101444
Haiti	USA (United States)	28 Sep 50	162UNTS85	102132
Guatemala	WHO (World Health)	28 Nov 50	103UNTS51	101423
El Salvador	USA (United States)	13 Dec 50	166UNTS149	102188
Brazil	USA (United States)	27 Dec 50	147UNTS33	101926
Nicaragua	WHO (World Health)	02 Jan 51	103UNTS107	101428
El Salvador	WHO (World Health)	02 Jan 51	103UNTS29	101421
Colombia	WHO (World Health)	05 Jan 51	102UNTS139	101417
Bolivia	WHO (World Health)	07 Feb 51	104UNTS167	101438
Costa Rica	USA (United States)	13 Feb 51	141UNTS169	101914
Denmark	WHO (World Health)	14 Feb 51	104UNTS243	101445
USA (United States)	Uruguay	07 Mar 51	165UNTS113	102173
Costa Rica	WHO (World Health)	13 Apr 51	103UNTS3	101419
Multilateral		25 May 51	175UNTS215	102303
Nicaragua	UK Great Britain	25 May 51	101UNTS77	101404
Burma	WHO (World Health)	13 Jun 51	117UNTS115	101588
Taiwan	WHO (World Health)	25 Oct 51	126UNTS77	101683
Multilateral		06 Dec 51	150UNTS67	101963
Guatemala	WHO (World Health)	29 Dec 51	124UNTS89	101668
Greece	Yugoslavia	02 Feb 52	188UNTS311	102535
Dominican Republic	WHO (World Health)	15 Feb 52	134UNTS291	101808
India	WHO (World Health)	02 Apr 52	131UNTS227	101743
Mexico	WHO (World Health)	28 May 52	134UNTS319	101810
Czechoslovakia	Romania	31 Jul 52	362UNTS123	105185
Mexico	USA (United States)	26 Aug 52	264UNTS269	103797
Dominican Republic	WHO (World Health)	10 Oct 52	150UNTS133	101967
India	WHO (World Health)	11 Dec 52	158UNTS391	102073
Ethiopia	USA (United States)	29 Apr 53	224UNTS121	103073
Ethiopia	USA (United States)	22 May 53	191UNTS59	102577
United Arab Rep	USA (United States)	18 Jun 53	215UNTS45	102910
Ethiopia	USA (United States)	30 Jun 53	212UNTS135	102865
Multilateral		11 Dec 53	191UNTS285	102588
Hungary	Romania	14 Dec 53	342UNTS151	104906
Belgium	UK Great Britain	04 Jan 54	247UNTS47	103459
Bulgaria	Romania	22 Jul 54	362UNTS101	105184
Multilateral		29 Jul 54	249UNTS45	103500
Multilateral		23 Oct 54	332UNTS3	104760
Denmark	Sweden	28 Oct 54	262UNTS211	103747
Italy	Yugoslavia	26 Mar 55	379UNTS3	105432
Germany, East	Romania	05 Aug 55	342UNTS229	104910
Czechoslovakia	Germany, East	30 Aug 55	504UNTS279	107361
Taiwan	USA (United States)	14 Oct 55	268UNTS165	103857
Bulgaria	Yugoslavia	11 Dec 55	378UNTS49	105417
Italy	Switzerland	02 Feb 56	291UNTS113	104247
Bulgaria	Greece	19 Apr 56	594UNTS131	108600
Germany, East	USSR (Soviet Union)	30 May 56	263UNTS143	103771
Czechoslovakia	Yugoslavia	16 Jun 56	552UNTS325	108064
Romania	Yugoslavia	04 Aug 56	395UNTS99	105682
Denmark	WHO (World Health)	03 Sep 56	258UNTS103	103674
Greece	Yugoslavia	11 Sep 56	552UNTS311	108063
Romania	Yugoslavia	25 Sep 56	395UNTS147	105683
Albania	Yugoslavia	20 May 57	363UNTS99	105203
Hungary	Yugoslavia	25 May 57	477UNTS219	106924
Bulgaria	Czechoslovakia	03 Jun 57	292UNTS3	104261
Bulgaria	Yugoslavia	04 Jun 57	349UNTS35	105008
Czechoslovakia	Yugoslavia	11 Jun 57	504UNTS107	107355
New Zealand	UK Great Britain	20 Sep 57	287UNTS105	104180

PARTY ONE	PARTY TWO	DATE	CITATION	NUMBER
Disease control (Cont.)				
Germany, East	Hungary	25 Oct 57	408UNTS156	105869
Hungary	Yugoslavia	20 Nov 57	477UNTS267	106925
Hungary	Yugoslavia	06 Dec 57	519UNTS215	107509
Hungary	Romania	17 Dec 57	477UNTS303	106926
Czechoslovakia	Hungary	12 Mar 58	408UNTS178	105870
Bulgaria	Hungary	13 Mar 58	438UNTS191	106317
Bulgaria	Hungary	13 Mar 58	438UNTS173	106316
Germany, West	Netherlands	16 Apr 58	486UNTS331	107084
SEATO (SE Asia)	USA (United States)	29 May 59	347UNTS77	104991
Italy	Netherlands	01 Dec 59	455UNTS241	106545
Multilateral		14 Dec 59	422UNTS57	106068
Multilateral		14 Dec 59	422UNTS33	106067
Poland	Yugoslavia	05 May 60	423UNTS229	106095
Czechoslovakia	Poland	14 Nov 60	413UNTS4	105938
Cuba	Czechoslovakia	05 Apr 61	442UNTS201	106350
Belgium	Yugoslavia	31 Oct 61	426UNTS165	106136
Argentina	Japan	20 Dec 61	451UNTS77	106486
Finland	Hungary	13 Feb 62	463UNTS61	106693
USA (United States)	USSR (Soviet Union)	08 Mar 62	460UNTS3	106630
Japan	USA (United States)	24 Oct 62	462UNTS119	106673
Australia	Fed of Malaya	26 Nov 62	453UNTS161	106523
Hungary	Korea, North	29 Mar 63	577UNTS219	108379
Denmark	India	15 May 63	616UNTS49	108891
Austria	Hungary	09 Jul 63	482UNTS29	106989
USA (United States)	USSR (Soviet Union)	22 Feb 64	526UNTS131	107605
Cuba	Czechoslovakia	03 Jun 64	527UNTS205	107626
Czechoslovakia	Mongolia	21 Oct 64	545UNTS91	107926
Multilateral		07 Nov 64	548UNTS3	107965
Austria	Hungary	11 Nov 64	576UNTS163	108368
Austria	Bulgaria	12 Jul 65	587UNTS51	108510
Romania	United Arab Rep	03 Sep 66	604UNTS73	108745
Turkey	USSR (Soviet Union)	24 Feb 67	643UNTS153	109190
Netherlands	Vietnam, South	24 Mar 67	610UNTS0	108834
Bulgaria	Turkey	30 May 67	631UNTS19	108984
Netherlands	Romania	20 Jul 67	633UNTS21	109032
Denmark	India	10 Jun 68	0UNTS0	109219
Public health				
Multilateral		11 Nov 21	38UNTS217	100599
Multilateral		10 Jun 25	38UNTS229	100600
Multilateral		15 Jun 27	38UNTS327	100607
Multilateral		15 Jun 27	38UNTS343	100608
Multilateral		27 Apr 32	39UNTS103	100614
Multilateral		20 Jun 36	40UNTS109	100630
Multilateral		24 Oct 36	40UNTS187	100634
Multilateral		23 Jun 37	40UNTS233	100637
Multilateral		27 Jun 39	40UNTS281	100639
Ecuador	USA (United States)	24 Feb 42	26UNTS379	200157
Brazil	USA (United States)	14 Mar 42	102UNTS195	200302
Germany, West	USA (United States)	30 Mar 42	105UNTS219	200334
Haiti	USA (United States)	07 Apr 42	106UNTS319	200349
El Salvador	USA (United States)	05 May 42	21UNTS215	200124
Honduras	USA (United States)	08 May 42	166UNTS351	200498
Peru	USA (United States)	11 May 42	136UNTS353	200447
Nicaragua	USA (United States)	22 May 42	105UNTS141	200328
Paraguay	USA (United States)	22 May 42	124UNTS243	200423
Bolivia	USA (United States)	16 Jul 42	13UNTS101	200072
Brazil	USA (United States)	17 Jul 42	102UNTS203	200303
Colombia	USA (United States)	23 Oct 42	105UNTS109	200326
Brazil	USA (United States)	10 Feb 43	102UNTS217	200304
USA (United States)	Venezuela	18 Feb 43	21UNTS225	200125
Panama	USA (United States)	02 Mar 43	107UNTS55	200351
Mexico	USA (United States)	26 Apr 43	21UNTS245	200127
Chile	USA (United States)	11 May 43	139UNTS295	200456
Mexico	USA (United States)	01 Jul 43	28UNTS407	200164

PARTY ONE	PARTY TWO	DATE	CITATION	NUMBER
Public health (Cont.)				
Dominican Republic	USA (United States)	07 Jul 43	28UNTS419	200165
USA (United States)	Uruguay	01 Nov 43	106UNTS311	200348
Brazil	USA (United States)	25 Nov 43	102UNTS227	200305
Costa Rica	USA (United States)	29 May 44	124UNTS155	200417
Multilateral		15 Dec 44	17UNTS305	200110
Multilateral		15 Dec 44	16UNTS247	200106
Colombia	USA (United States)	19 Feb 46	166UNTS104	102187
USA (United States)	Uruguay	23 Apr 46	160UNTS103	102104
Belgium	Italy	23 Jun 46	19UNTS65	100305
Multilateral		27 Jun 46	264UNTS163	103792
Multilateral		29 Jun 46	214UNTS233	102901
Multilateral		22 Jul 46	14UNTS185	100221
Multilateral		09 Oct 46	78UNTS213	101018
Multilateral		09 Oct 46	78UNTS198	101017
Philippines	USA (United States)	14 Mar 47	43UNTS271	100673
Belgium	Poland	24 Mar 47	18UNTS279	100297
Peru	USA (United States)	19 Apr 47	136UNTS284	101840
Honduras	USA (United States)	13 May 47	166UNTS159	102189
Ecuador	USA (United States)	21 Jun 47	26UNTS275	100391
USA (United States)	Venezuela	30 Jun 47	166UNTS198	102190
Belgium	Netherlands	29 Aug 47	36UNTS349	100573
Haiti	USA (United States)	27 Sep 47	136UNTS258	101839
Austria	USA (United States)	08 Oct 47	25UNTS3	100354
Portugal	UK Great Britain	16 Oct 47	82UNTS203	101093
Czechoslovakia	Poland	05 Apr 48	31UNTS355	100482
Paraguay	USA (United States)	30 Jun 48	124UNTS34	101665
Bolivia	USA (United States)	14 Jul 48	136UNTS238	101838
Taiwan	USA (United States)	05 Aug 48	82UNTS109	101087
El Salvador	USA (United States)	23 Sep 48	181UNTS101	102402
Brazil	USA (United States)	30 Dec 48	102UNTS3	101406
Chile	USA (United States)	21 Jan 49	160UNTS185	102107
Mexico	USA (United States)	14 Feb 49	160UNTS75	102103
Philippines	USA (United States)	07 Jun 49	45UNTS63	100692
Multilateral		01 Jul 49	120UNTS71	101616
USA (United States)	Uruguay	27 Jul 49	151UNTS199	101995
El Salvador	USA (United States)	27 Jul 49	180UNTS219	102387
Multilateral		12 Aug 49	75UNTS85	100971
Multilateral		12 Aug 49	75UNTS287	100973
WHO (World Health)	Thailand	12 Aug 49	178UNTS347	102350
Multilateral		12 Aug 49	75UNTS31	100970
Brazil	USA (United States)	31 Aug 49	102UNTS13	101407
Multilateral		07 Nov 49	132UNTS3	101748
UNICEF (Children)	UK Great Britain	10 Feb 50	65UNTS86	100837
Haiti	WHO (World Health)	21 Jun 50	103UNTS61	101424
Multilateral		27 Jul 50	166UNTS73	102186
UN Relief Palestin	WHO (World Health)	23 Sep 50	103UNTS129	200310
Haiti	USA (United States)	28 Sep 50	162UNTS85	102132
Austria	Sweden	31 Oct 50	197UNTS311	102645
El Salvador	USA (United States)	13 Dec 50	166UNTS149	102188
Brazil	USA (United States)	27 Dec 50	147UNTS33	101926
Nicaragua	USA (United States)	31 Jan 51	160UNTS121	102105
Bolivia	WHO (World Health)	07 Feb 51	104UNTS167	101438
Costa Rica	USA (United States)	13 Feb 51	141UNTS169	101914
Panama	USA (United States)	26 Feb 51	160UNTS153	102106
USA (United States)	Uruguay	07 Mar 51	165UNTS113	102173
Costa Rica	WHO (World Health)	13 Apr 51	103UNTS3	101419
Nicaragua	UK Great Britain	25 May 51	101UNTS77	101404
Multilateral		25 May 51	175UNTS215	102303
Burma	WHO (World Health)	13 Jun 51	117UNTS115	101588
Saudi Arabia	USA (United States)	18 Jun 51	102UNTS73	101412
Brazil	USA (United States)	29 Jun 51	184UNTS303	102455
Ethiopia	WHO (World Health)	02 Jul 51	103UNTS39	101422
Burma	WHO (World Health)	09 Jul 51	107UNTS9	101463
Burma	WHO (World Health)	09 Jul 51	104UNTS187	101440
Multilateral		01 Aug 51	107UNTS19	101464

PARTY ONE	PARTY TWO	DATE	CITATION	NUMBER
Public health (Cont.)				
Multilateral		04 Aug 51	104UNTS197	101441
Israel	WHO (World Health)	07 Aug 51	104UNTS213	101442
Korea, South	WHO (World Health)	19 Sep 51	109UNTS297	200366
WHO (World Health)	Thailand	04 Oct 51	109UNTS77	101492
WHO (World Health)	Thailand	04 Oct 51	109UNTS85	101493
India	WHO (World Health)	11 Oct 51	118UNTS27	101594
India	WHO (World Health)	01 Nov 51	118UNTS13	101593
Denmark	WHO (World Health)	05 Nov 51	110UNTS253	101514
Panama	WHO (World Health)	09 Nov 51	118UNTS43	101595
Denmark	WHO (World Health)	30 Nov 51	118UNTS3	101592
Guatemala	WHO (World Health)	17 Dec 51	120UNTS133	101619
Costa Rica	WHO (World Health)	23 Jan 52	135UNTS265	101826
UNICEF (Children)	UK Great Britain	04 Feb 52	120UNTS147	101620
Burma	WHO (World Health)	18 Feb 52	127UNTS43	101698
Ceylon (Sri Lanka)	WHO (World Health)	26 Mar 52	134UNTS341	200442
Denmark	WHO (World Health)	26 Mar 52	134UNTS285	101807
India	WHO (World Health)	14 Apr 52	131UNTS265	101746
Chile	WHO (World Health)	31 May 52	136UNTS323	101841
India	WHO (World Health)	04 Jun 52	135UNTS279	101827
Burma	WHO (World Health)	09 Jun 52	134UNTS273	101806
Iraq	USA (United States)	09 Jun 52	212UNTS193	102871
Jordan	WHO (World Health)	16 Jun 52	135UNTS323	200445
India	WHO (World Health)	19 Jun 52	134UNTS307	101809
Multilateral		28 Jun 52	210UNTS132	102838
Jordan	WHO (World Health)	21 Aug 52	141UNTS341	200472
Dominican Republic	WHO (World Health)	10 Oct 52	150UNTS133	101967
Chile	WHO (World Health)	04 Nov 52	150UNTS119	101966
Japan	WHO (World Health)	26 Nov 52	204UNTS301	200521
India	WHO (World Health)	11 Dec 52	158UNTS391	102073
Saudi Arabia	USA (United States)	15 Dec 52	185UNTS67	102459
Austria	Yugoslavia	19 Mar 53	467UNTS323	106768
United Arab Rep	USA (United States)	19 Mar 53	215UNTS17	102909
Ethiopia	USA (United States)	29 Apr 53	224UNTS121	103073
United Arab Rep	USA (United States)	18 Jun 53	215UNTS45	102910
Saudi Arabia	USA (United States)	29 Jun 53	206UNTS23	102784
Afghanistan	USA (United States)	30 Jun 53	215UNTS3	102908
Multilateral		20 Jul 53	227UNTS217	103140
Multilateral		20 Jul 53	228UNTS41	103142
Multilateral		11 Dec 53	218UNTS255	102958
Belgium	Norway	24 Mar 54	219UNTS73	102967
France	Greece	13 May 54	222UNTS299	103036
Italy	USA (United States)	28 Jun 54	237UNTS121	103340
Mexico	USA (United States)	30 Jul 54	269UNTS39	103871
Libya	USA (United States)	09 Sep 54	224UNTS217	103078
Mexico	USA (United States)	19 Nov 54	238UNTS237	103367
Czechoslovakia	Hungary	28 Apr 55	477UNTS197	106923
Canada	USA (United States)	15 Jun 55	235UNTS176	103301
Canada	USA (United States)	15 Jun 55	235UNTS201	103302
Philippines	UK Great Britain	29 Aug 55	221UNTS241	103009
USA (United States)	USSR (Soviet Union)	05 Sep 55	256UNTS307	103641
Bulgaria	Yugoslavia	15 Nov 55	396UNTS179	105696
Multilateral		13 Mar 56	427UNTS245	106158
Multilateral		09 Jul 56	314UNTS3	104539
Denmark	WHO (World Health)	03 Sep 56	258UNTS103	103674
UN Hi Com Refugees	Sweden	08 Oct 56	428UNTS307	106182
UK Great Britain	USA (United States)	01 Nov 56	264UNTS3	103785
UK Great Britain	USA (United States)	27 Nov 56	282UNTS43	104092
Multilateral		19 Dec 56	427UNTS93	106148
Multilateral		21 Dec 56	427UNTS81	106147
Ethiopia	Sweden	16 Mar 57	304UNTS214	104398
Australia	UK Great Britain	01 Apr 57	271UNTS235	103918
Czechoslovakia	Yugoslavia	22 May 57	391UNTS33	105615
Belgium	Colombia	24 May 57	274UNTS245	103969
Italy	UK Great Britain	12 Jun 57	310UNTS35	104484
New Zealand	UK Great Britain	20 Sep 57	287UNTS105	104180

PARTY ONE	PARTY TWO	DATE	CITATION	NUMBER
Public health (Cont.)				
IAEA (Atom Energy)	United Nations	23 Oct 57	281UNTS369	200548
UK Great Britain	USA (United States)	01 Nov 57	299UNTS167	104312
Hungary	Yugoslavia	20 Nov 57	477UNTS267	106925
Czechoslovakia	USSR (Soviet Union)	04 Dec 57	313UNTS291	104537
Hungary	Romania	17 Dec 57	477UNTS303	106926
Canada	Switzerland	10 Jan 58	464UNTS21	106710
Poland	Yugoslavia	16 Jan 58	340UNTS181	104864
Bulgaria	Hungary	13 Mar 58	438UNTS173	106316
Czechoslovakia	Romania	25 Mar 58	339UNTS77	104846
Albania	Yugoslavia	28 Apr 58	386UNTS103	105540
Hungary	Poland	08 May 58	408UNTS212	105872
UK Great Britain	Yugoslavia	24 May 58	326UNTS69	104709
Germany, East	Hungary	14 Jun 58	407UNTS78	105861
Multilateral		24 Jun 58	348UNTS275	105005
Philippines	USA (United States)	30 Jun 58	321UNTS51	104653
Australia	Germany, West	27 Aug 58	320UNTS303	104649
Multilateral		15 Dec 58	351UNTS159	105022
Mongolia	Poland	23 Dec 58	432UNTS177	106220
IAEA (Atom Energy)	Thailand	18 Mar 59	339UNTS307	104850
Bulgaria	Hungary	03 Apr 59	438UNTS269	106319
Hungary	USSR (Soviet Union)	17 Apr 59	439UNTS41	106324
SEATO (SE Asia)	USA (United States)	29 May 59	347UNTS77	104991
Czechoslovakia	Korea, North	04 Jun 59	338UNTS291	104842
Multilateral		19 Jun 59	413UNTS158	105950
Panama	USA (United States)	24 Jun 59	479UNTS145	106950
Bulgaria	Czechoslovakia	19 Sep 59	355UNTS77	105074
USA (United States)	USSR (Soviet Union)	21 Nov 59	361UNTS35	105172
Czechoslovakia	USSR (Soviet Union)	02 Dec 59	374UNTS63	105330
Canada	UK Great Britain	10 Dec 59	379UNTS201	105440
Germany, East	USSR (Soviet Union)	24 May 60	392UNTS205	105645
Multilateral		22 Jun 60	431UNTS41	106208
Somalia	UK Great Britain	26 Jun 60	374UNTS331	105346
Italy	Netherlands	06 Aug 60	455UNTS259	106546
Finland	IAEA (Atom Energy)	30 Dec 60	395UNTS257	105690
Cuba	Czechoslovakia	05 Apr 61	442UNTS201	106350
Norway	IAEA (Atom Energy)	10 Apr 61	402UNTS255	105790
Ghana	Hungary	27 Apr 61	439UNTS17	106322
Somalia	USSR (Soviet Union)	02 Jun 61	528UNTS147	107638
Czechoslovakia	Somalia	04 Jun 61	479UNTS291	106960
Germany, West	Netherlands	18 Jul 61	487UNTS95	107096
IAEA (Atom Energy)	Yugoslavia	04 Oct 61	412UNTS226	105935
Multilateral		18 Oct 61	529UNTS89	107659
Ghana	USA (United States)	03 Jan 62	433UNTS147	106237
Colombia	USA (United States)	09 Apr 62	476UNTS9	106899
Multilateral		14 May 62	544UNTS39	107910
Senegal	USSR (Soviet Union)	14 Jun 62	437UNTS233	106309
Syria	USSR (Soviet Union)	19 Aug 62	457UNTS285	106588
Israel	Rwanda	23 Oct 62	515UNTS291	107466
Cameroon	Israel	24 Oct 62	449UNTS3	106446
Japan	USA (United States)	24 Oct 62	462UNTS119	106673
Multilateral		17 Dec 62	486UNTS119	107076
Israel	Tanganyika	28 Jan 63	516UNTS39	107468
India	USA (United States)	01 Feb 63	473UNTS37	106852
Israel	Uganda	04 Feb 63	484UNTS273	107037
Dahomey	USSR (Soviet Union)	20 Mar 63	528UNTS181	107641
Hungary	Korea, North	29 Mar 63	577UNTS219	108379
Australia	UK Great Britain	06 Jun 63	472UNTS157	106838
Finland	IAEA (Atom Energy)	02 Jul 63	490UNTS403	107167
Finland	IAEA (Atom Energy)	30 Jul 63	490UNTS413	107168
India	USA (United States)	08 Aug 63	488UNTS21	107117
Czechoslovakia	Yugoslavia	05 Oct 63	504UNTS151	107356
UK Great Britain	USA (United States)	11 Oct 63	483UNTS3	107005
Multilateral		17 Oct 63	525UNTS75	107585
Tanganyika	USSR (Soviet Union)	06 Nov 63	528UNTS157	107639
IAEA (Atom Energy)	Yugoslavia	07 Dec 63	501UNTS273	107322

PARTY ONE	PARTY TWO	DATE	CITATION	NUMBER
Public health (Cont.)				
Chile	IBRD (World Bank)	18 Dec 63	504UNTS29	107352
Multilateral		28 Feb 64	501UNTS245	107321
Multilateral		11 Jun 64	525UNTS61	107584
Multilateral		08 Jul 64	560UNTS201	108175
Multilateral		08 Jul 64	602UNTS259	108718
Netherlands	Turkey	19 Aug 64	521UNTS197	107523
IAEA (Atom Energy)	United Arab Rep	17 Sep 64	525UNTS19	107581
Ethiopia	Netherlands	28 Oct 64	541UNTS235	107872
Multilateral		07 Nov 64	548UNTS3	107965
Netherlands	Norway	17 Nov 64	579UNTS243	108412
IAEA (Atom Energy)	United Arab Rep	14 Jan 65	603UNTS45	108723
China People's Rep	Romania	27 May 65	592UNTS3	108566
Pakistan	USSR (Soviet Union)	05 Jun 65	593UNTS115	108579
Australia	Malaysia	21 Jun 65	542UNTS75	107880
Multilateral		23 Jun 65	614UNTS239	108873
Uganda	USSR (Soviet Union)	24 Jul 65	596UNTS199	108633
Israel	Sierra Leone	22 Aug 65	550UNTS285	108023
IAEA (Atom Energy)	Uruguay	24 Sep 65	556UNTS117	108123
Afghanistan	IAEA (Atom Energy)	24 Sep 65	556UNTS101	108121
Morocco	IAEA (Atom Energy)	24 Sep 65	556UNTS109	108122
Ethiopia	USA (United States)	30 Dec 65	574UNTS129	108345
IAEA (Atom Energy)	Turkey	08 Feb 66	573UNTS75	108323
Belgium	Bulgaria	14 Jun 66	607UNTS183	108806
Mexico	IAEA (Atom Energy)	20 Jun 66	573UNTS25	108321
Belgium	France	23 Sep 66	588UNTS227	108528
Hungary	Yugoslavia	26 Sep 66	601UNTS21	108685
Philippines	IAEA (Atom Energy)	28 Sep 66	589UNTS25	108533
UK Great Britain	USSR (Soviet Union)	24 Feb 67	606UNTS171	108785
Netherlands	Vietnam, South	24 Mar 67	610UNTS0	108834
Czechoslovakia	Romania	17 Nov 67	0UNTS0	109280
Congo (Zaire)	Denmark	25 May 68	0UNTS0	109289
Insect control				
Multilateral		15 Dec 44	16UNTS247	200106
Czechoslovakia	USSR (Soviet Union)	28 Nov 47	216UNTS285	102941
Poland	USSR (Soviet Union)	08 Apr 48	26UNTS191	100388
Czechoslovakia	Poland	22 Jan 49	85UNTS3	101142
Multilateral		22 Feb 49	93UNTS129	101296
Bulgaria	Poland	26 Sep 49	260UNTS227	103711
Hungary	Poland	29 Oct 49	260UNTS91	103705
Austria	Czechoslovakia	30 Mar 50	495UNTS85	107240
Multilateral		17 Apr 50	131UNTS99	101738
Romania	USSR (Soviet Union)	27 May 50	221UNTS13	103000
Germany, East	Poland	23 Jun 50	304UNTS91	104393
Hungary	USSR (Soviet Union)	13 Jul 50	221UNTS35	103001
Bulgaria	USSR (Soviet Union)	25 Aug 50	221UNTS57	103002
Peru	WHO (World Health)	26 Sep 50	104UNTS233	101444
Czechoslovakia	Poland	17 Nov 50	530UNTS195	107682
Guatemala	WHO (World Health)	28 Nov 50	103UNTS51	101423
Nicaragua	WHO (World Health)	02 Jan 51	103UNTS107	101428
El Salvador	WHO (World Health)	02 Jan 51	103UNTS29	101421
Costa Rica	USA (United States)	13 Feb 51	141UNTS169	101914
Costa Rica	WHO (World Health)	13 Apr 51	103UNTS3	101419
Multilateral		25 May 51	175UNTS215	102303
Burma	WHO (World Health)	13 Jun 51	117UNTS115	101588
Taiwan	WHO (World Health)	25 Oct 51	126UNTS77	101683
Dominican Republic	WHO (World Health)	15 Feb 52	134UNTS291	101808
Czechoslovakia	Romania	31 Jul 52	362UNTS123	105185
Ethiopia	USA (United States)	05 Nov 52	184UNTS139	102445
Ethiopia	USA (United States)	29 Apr 53	224UNTS121	103073
United Arab Rep	USA (United States)	18 Jun 53	215UNTS45	102910
Hungary	Romania	14 Dec 53	342UNTS151	104906
Bulgaria	Romania	22 Jul 54	362UNTS101	105184
Multilateral		29 Jul 54	249UNTS45	103500
Germany, East	Romania	05 Aug 55	342UNTS229	104910

PARTY ONE	PARTY TWO	DATE	CITATION	NUMBER
Insect control (Cont.)				
Italy	Switzerland	02 Feb 56	291UNTS113	104247
Bulgaria	Greece	19 Apr 56	594UNTS131	108600
Germany, East	USSR (Soviet Union)	30 May 56	263UNTS143	103771
Czechoslovakia	Yugoslavia	16 Jun 56	552UNTS325	108064
Greece	Yugoslavia	11 Sep 56	552UNTS311	108063
Romania	Yugoslavia	25 Sep 56	395UNTS147	105683
Albania	Yugoslavia	20 May 57	363UNTS99	105203
Bulgaria	Yugoslavia	04 Jun 57	349UNTS35	105008
Czechoslovakia	Yugoslavia	11 Jun 57	504UNTS107	107355
Germany, East	Hungary	25 Oct 57	408UNTS156	105869
Hungary	Yugoslavia	06 Dec 57	519UNTS215	107509
Multilateral		14 Dec 59	422UNTS33	106067
Multilateral		14 May 62	544UNTS81	107911
USA (United States)	USSR (Soviet Union)	22 Feb 64	526UNTS131	107605
Cuba	Czechoslovakia	03 Jun 64	527UNTS205	107626
Australia	UN Special Fund	30 Sep 64	510UNTS277	107419
Czechoslovakia	United Arab Rep	26 Nov 64	545UNTS11	107923
Multilateral		02 Jul 65	592UNTS215	108575
Czechoslovakia	Mongolia	09 Dec 66	637UNTS0	109124
Narcotic drugs				
Haiti	USA (United States)	07 Apr 42	106UNTS319	200349
Multilateral		11 Dec 46	12UNTS179	100186
Lebanon	Turkey	16 Sep 47	44UNTS123	100682
Multilateral		19 Nov 48	44UNTS277	100688
Nicaragua	USA (United States)	28 Feb 50	132UNTS169	101758
USA (United States)	Uruguay	07 Mar 51	165UNTS113	102173
Multilateral		11 May 53	456UNTS3	106555
Germany, West	USA (United States)	07 Mar 56	271UNTS361	103926
Multilateral		30 Mar 61	520UNTS151	107515
Nursing				
Nicaragua	USA (United States)	31 Jan 51	160UNTS121	102105
Costa Rica	USA (United States)	13 Feb 51	141UNTS169	101914
Panama	USA (United States)	26 Feb 51	160UNTS153	102106
Nicaragua	UK Great Britain	25 May 51	101UNTS77	101404
Costa Rica	WHO (World Health)	14 Jun 51	102UNTS151	101418
Burma	WHO (World Health)	09 Jul 51	102UNTS131	101416
Burma	WHO (World Health)	09 Jul 51	104UNTS175	101439
India	WHO (World Health)	23 Oct 51	109UNTS59	101491
Taiwan	WHO (World Health)	07 Mar 52	128UNTS233	101723
India	WHO (World Health)	04 Jun 52	135UNTS279	101827
India	WHO (World Health)	19 Jun 52	134UNTS307	101809
India	WHO (World Health)	11 Feb 53	163UNTS43	102140
Ethiopia	USA (United States)	29 Apr 53	224UNTS121	103073
United Arab Rep	USA (United States)	18 Jun 53	215UNTS45	102910
Multilateral		13 Mar 56	427UNTS245	106158
Multilateral		07 Nov 64	548UNTS3	107965
Pharmaceuticals				
Multilateral		20 May 52	219UNTS55	102966
Czechoslovakia	Hungary	28 Apr 55	477UNTS197	106923
Austria	Italy	19 Nov 56	284UNTS293	104143
Hungary	Romania	17 Dec 57	477UNTS303	106926
Hungary	Poland	08 May 58	408UNTS212	105872
Bulgaria	Hungary	03 Apr 59	438UNTS269	106319
Cuba	Czechoslovakia	03 Jun 64	527UNTS205	107626
Hungary	Yugoslavia	26 Sep 66	601UNTS21	108685
Congo (Zaire)	Denmark	25 May 68	0UNTS0	109289
Sanitation				
Netherlands	UK Great Britain	13 Jun 39	5UNTS65	200028
Ecuador	USA (United States)	24 Feb 42	26UNTS379	200157
Brazil	USA (United States)	03 Mar 42	105UNTS91	200324
Brazil	USA (United States)	14 Mar 42	102UNTS195	200302
El Salvador	USA (United States)	05 May 42	21UNTS215	200124
Honduras	USA (United States)	08 May 42	166UNTS351	200498

PARTY ONE	PARTY TWO	DATE	CITATION	NUMBER
Sanitation (Cont.)				
Nicaragua	USA (United States)	22 May 42	105UNTS141	200328
Paraguay	USA (United States)	22 May 42	124UNTS243	200423
Bolivia	USA (United States)	16 Jul 42	13UNTS101	200072
Brazil	USA (United States)	17 Jul 42	102UNTS203	200303
Colombia	USA (United States)	23 Oct 42	105UNTS109	200326
Brazil	USA (United States)	10 Feb 43	102UNTS217	200304
USA (United States)	Venezuela	18 Feb 43	21UNTS225	200125
Panama	USA (United States)	02 Mar 43	107UNTS55	200351
Chile	USA (United States)	11 May 43	139UNTS295	200456
Mexico	USA (United States)	01 Jul 43	28UNTS407	200164
Dominican Republic	USA (United States)	07 Jul 43	28UNTS419	200165
USA (United States)	Uruguay	01 Nov 43	106UNTS311	200348
Brazil	USA (United States)	25 Nov 43	102UNTS227	200305
Multilateral		15 Dec 44	17UNTS305	200110
Multilateral		15 Dec 44	16UNTS247	200106
Colombia	USA (United States)	19 Feb 46	166UNTS104	102187
USA (United States)	Uruguay	23 Apr 46	160UNTS103	102104
Hungary	USA (United States)	09 Aug 46	148UNTS313	101941
Netherlands	USA (United States)	11 Apr 47	148UNTS343	101943
Honduras	USA (United States)	13 May 47	166UNTS159	102189
Ecuador	USA (United States)	21 Jun 47	26UNTS275	100391
USA (United States)	Venezuela	30 Jun 47	166UNTS198	102190
Belgium	USA (United States)	23 Jul 47	33UNTS33	100512
France	USA (United States)	01 Oct 47	148UNTS303	101940
Canada	USA (United States)	30 Apr 48	77UNTS191	100999
Paraguay	USA (United States)	30 Jun 48	124UNTS34	101665
Taiwan	USA (United States)	05 Aug 48	82UNTS109	101087
El Salvador	USA (United States)	23 Sep 48	181UNTS101	102402
Brazil	USA (United States)	30 Dec 48	102UNTS3	101406
Chile	USA (United States)	21 Jan 49	160UNTS185	102107
Mexico	USA (United States)	14 Feb 49	160UNTS75	102103
Panama	USA (United States)	31 Mar 49	55UNTS87	100810
Multilateral		18 Jun 49	160UNTS223	102109
USA (United States)	Uruguay	27 Jul 49	151UNTS199	101995
El Salvador	USA (United States)	27 Jul 49	180UNTS219	102387
Multilateral		12 Aug 49	75UNTS287	100973
Brazil	USA (United States)	31 Aug 49	102UNTS13	101407
Haiti	USA (United States)	28 Sep 50	162UNTS85	102132
Iran	USA (United States)	19 Oct 50	92UNTS135	101266
El Salvador	USA (United States)	13 Dec 50	166UNTS149	102188
Brazil	USA (United States)	27 Dec 50	147UNTS33	101926
Nicaragua	USA (United States)	31 Jan 51	160UNTS121	102105
Costa Rica	USA (United States)	13 Feb 51	141UNTS169	101914
Panama	USA (United States)	26 Feb 51	160UNTS153	102106
Multilateral		25 May 51	175UNTS215	102303
Multilateral		31 Oct 51	172UNTS193	102247
Jordan	USA (United States)	12 Feb 52	168UNTS25	102211
Iraq	USA (United States)	09 Jun 52	212UNTS193	102871
Chile	WHO (World Health)	24 Oct 52	151UNTS339	102004
Ceylon (Sri Lanka)	WHO (World Health)	21 Nov 52	161UNTS315	200490
United Arab Rep	USA (United States)	19 Mar 53	215UNTS17	102909
Ethiopia	USA (United States)	29 Apr 53	224UNTS121	103073
Afghanistan	USA (United States)	30 Jun 53	215UNTS3	102908
Libya	UK Great Britain	29 Jul 53	186UNTS201	102492
Multilateral		11 Dec 53	191UNTS285	102588
Belgium	UK Great Britain	04 Jan 54	247UNTS47	103459
Multilateral		29 Jul 54	249UNTS45	103500
Multilateral		19 Mar 55	228UNTS95	103144
Canada	USA (United States)	15 Jun 55	235UNTS201	103302
France	USA (United States)	01 Jul 55	270UNTS19	103888
Korea, South	United Nations	06 Nov 59	346UNTS289	200565
USA (United States)	USSR (Soviet Union)	08 Mar 62	460UNTS3	106630
Japan	USA (United States)	24 Oct 62	462UNTS119	106673
USA (United States)	USSR (Soviet Union)	22 Feb 64	526UNTS131	107605
Philippines	IBRD (World Bank)	22 Jul 64	516UNTS171	107476

PARTY ONE	PARTY TWO	DATE	CITATION	NUMBER
Sanitation (Cont.)				
Multilateral		07 Nov 64	548UNTS3	107965
IBRD (World Bank)	Venezuela	21 Apr 66	568UNTS257	108273
Belgium	Bulgaria	14 Jun 66	607UNTS183	108806
Veterinary				
Mexico	USA (United States)	17 Mar 47	167UNTS30	102200
Italy	Yugoslavia	03 Feb 49	33UNTS105	100517
Bulgaria	Poland	26 Sep 49	260UNTS249	103712
Hungary	Poland	29 Oct 49	260UNTS113	103706
Multilateral		25 May 51	175UNTS215	102303
Greece	Yugoslavia	02 Feb 52	188UNTS311	102535
Panama	USA (United States)	21 Jul 52	181UNTS285	102417
Austria	Yugoslavia	19 Mar 53	467UNTS323	106768
Multilateral		11 Dec 53	191UNTS285	102588
Italy	Yugoslavia	26 Mar 55	379UNTS3	105432
Bulgaria	Yugoslavia	17 Jun 55	375UNTS287	105370
Czechoslovakia	Germany, East	30 Aug 55	504UNTS279	107361
Italy	Switzerland	02 Feb 56	291UNTS113	104247
Bulgaria	Yugoslavia	22 May 56	367UNTS119	105229
Austria	Yugoslavia	15 Jun 56	396UNTS117	105695
Romania	Yugoslavia	04 Aug 56	395UNTS99	105682
Germany, East	Romania	08 Dec 56	362UNTS189	105188
Hungary	Yugoslavia	25 May 57	477UNTS219	106924
Bulgaria	Czechoslovakia	03 Jun 57	292UNTS3	104261
Czechoslovakia	Yugoslavia	11 Jun 57	504UNTS107	107355
Germany, East	Hungary	13 Nov 57	407UNTS216	105866
Czechoslovakia	Hungary	12 Mar 58	408UNTS178	105870
Bulgaria	Hungary	13 Mar 58	438UNTS173	106316
Bulgaria	Hungary	13 Mar 58	438UNTS191	106317
Germany, West	Netherlands	16 Apr 58	486UNTS331	107084
Italy	Netherlands	01 Dec 59	455UNTS241	106545
Multilateral		14 Dec 59	422UNTS57	106068
Germany, West	Netherlands	08 Apr 60	508UNTS14	107404
Poland	Yugoslavia	05 May 60	423UNTS229	106095
Czechoslovakia	Poland	14 Nov 60	413UNTS4	105938
Belgium	Yugoslavia	31 Oct 61	426UNTS165	106136
Argentina	Japan	20 Dec 61	451UNTS77	106486
Belgium	Romania	12 Oct 62	502UNTS31	107325
Cuba	Czechoslovakia	03 Jun 64	527UNTS205	107626
Jordan	UK Great Britain	31 Aug 64	541UNTS3	107856
Czechoslovakia	Mongolia	21 Oct 64	545UNTS91	107926
Austria	Hungary	11 Nov 64	576UNTS163	108368
Germany, West	Thailand	23 Dec 64	525UNTS201	107592
Ecuador	Netherlands	14 Jan 65	551UNTS129	108038
Austria	Bulgaria	12 Jul 65	587UNTS51	108510
Netherlands	Nigeria	28 Oct 65	578UNTS15	108383
Belgium	Bulgaria	14 Jun 66	607UNTS183	108806
Bulgaria	United Arab Rep	29 Aug 66	630UNTS325	108980
Argentina	Bolivia	19 Dec 66	636UNTS75	109092
Netherlands	Romania	20 Jul 67	633UNTS21	109032
WHO used as agency				
Multilateral		23 Apr 46	16UNTS179	100257
Multilateral		23 Apr 46	17UNTS3	100265
Multilateral		11 Dec 46	12UNTS179	100186
Multilateral		19 Nov 48	44UNTS277	100688
WHO (World Health)	Thailand	12 Aug 49	178UNTS347	102350
Multilateral		17 Apr 50	131UNTS99	101738
El Salvador	WHO (World Health)	21 Apr 50	103UNTS13	101420
Haiti	WHO (World Health)	21 Jun 50	103UNTS61	101424
UN Relief Palestin	WHO (World Health)	23 Sep 50	103UNTS129	200310
Peru	WHO (World Health)	26 Sep 50	104UNTS233	101444
Guatemala	WHO (World Health)	28 Nov 50	103UNTS51	101423
Nicaragua	WHO (World Health)	02 Jan 51	103UNTS107	101428
El Salvador	WHO (World Health)	02 Jan 51	103UNTS29	101421
Colombia	WHO (World Health)	05 Jan 51	102UNTS139	101417

PARTY ONE	PARTY TWO	DATE	CITATION	NUMBER
WHO used as agency (Cont.)				
Bolivia	WHO (World Health)	07 Feb 51	104UNTS167	101438
Denmark	WHO (World Health)	14 Feb 51	104UNTS243	101445
Costa Rica	WHO (World Health)	13 Apr 51	103UNTS3	101419
Multilateral		25 May 51	175UNTS215	102303
Lebanon	WHO (World Health)	05 Jun 51	104UNTS225	101443
Burma	WHO (World Health)	13 Jun 51	117UNTS115	101588
Costa Rica	WHO (World Health)	14 Jun 51	102UNTS151	101418
Burma	WHO (World Health)	09 Jul 51	104UNTS175	101439
Burma	WHO (World Health)	09 Jul 51	107UNTS9	101463
Burma	WHO (World Health)	09 Jul 51	104UNTS187	101440
Multilateral		01 Aug 51	107UNTS19	101464
Multilateral		04 Aug 51	104UNTS197	101441
Korea, South	WHO (World Health)	19 Sep 51	109UNTS297	200366
WHO (World Health)	Thailand	04 Oct 51	109UNTS77	101492
India	WHO (World Health)	11 Oct 51	118UNTS27	101594
India	WHO (World Health)	23 Oct 51	109UNTS59	101491
Taiwan	WHO (World Health)	25 Oct 51	126UNTS77	101683
Denmark	WHO (World Health)	05 Nov 51	110UNTS253	101514
Panama	WHO (World Health)	09 Nov 51	118UNTS43	101595
Denmark	WHO (World Health)	30 Nov 51	118UNTS3	101592
Guatemala	WHO (World Health)	17 Dec 51	120UNTS133	101619
Guatemala	WHO (World Health)	29 Dec 51	124UNTS89	101668
Costa Rica	WHO (World Health)	23 Jan 52	135UNTS265	101826
Dominican Republic	WHO (World Health)	15 Feb 52	134UNTS291	101808
Burma	WHO (World Health)	18 Feb 52	127UNTS43	101698
Taiwan	WHO (World Health)	07 Mar 52	128UNTS233	101723
Ceylon (Sri Lanka)	WHO (World Health)	26 Mar 52	134UNTS341	200442
Denmark	WHO (World Health)	26 Mar 52	134UNTS285	101807
India	WHO (World Health)	02 Apr 52	131UNTS227	101743
India	WHO (World Health)	14 Apr 52	131UNTS265	101746
Multilateral		20 May 52	219UNTS55	102966
Mexico	WHO (World Health)	28 May 52	134UNTS319	101810
Chile	WHO (World Health)	31 May 52	136UNTS323	101841
Burma	WHO (World Health)	09 Jun 52	134UNTS273	101806
Brazil	WHO (World Health)	12 Jun 52	151UNTS333	102003
India	WHO (World Health)	19 Jun 52	134UNTS307	101809
Dominican Republic	WHO (World Health)	10 Oct 52	150UNTS133	101967
Chile	WHO (World Health)	24 Oct 52	151UNTS339	102004
Chile	WHO (World Health)	04 Nov 52	150UNTS119	101966
Ceylon (Sri Lanka)	WHO (World Health)	21 Nov 52	161UNTS315	200490
India	WHO (World Health)	11 Dec 52	158UNTS391	102073
Saudi Arabia	USA (United States)	29 Jun 53	206UNTS23	102784
Denmark	WHO (World Health)	03 Sep 56	258UNTS103	103674
USA (United States)	USSR (Soviet Union)	21 Nov 59	361UNTS35	105172
Multilateral		30 Mar 61	520UNTS151	107515
Multilateral		07 Nov 64	548UNTS3	107965
Netherlands	Norway	17 Nov 64	579UNTS243	108412
Medical assistance and/or facilities				
India	WHO (World Health)	09 Nov 49	67UNTS43	100865
Dominican Republic	WHO (World Health)	10 Oct 52	150UNTS133	101967
Multilateral		14 Sep 62	494UNTS219	107236
Multilateral		23 Jun 65	614UNTS239	108873
Hungary	Yugoslavia	26 Sep 66	601UNTS21	108685
Czechoslovakia	Mongolia	31 Mar 68	0UNTS0	109279
Denmark	India	10 Jun 68	0UNTS0	109219
Education				
Multilateral		30 Jul 40	161UNTS253	200488
Multilateral		16 Nov 45	4UNTS275	100052
Multilateral		30 Oct 46	27UNTS77	100401
Multilateral		30 Apr 48	119UNTS3	101609
Greece	Lebanon	06 Oct 48	87UNTS351	101179
Italy	USA (United States)	18 Dec 48	79UNTS133	101037
Multilateral		21 Mar 50	96UNTS271	101342
Austria	Czechoslovakia	30 Mar 50	495UNTS85	107240

PARTY ONE	PARTY TWO	DATE	CITATION	NUMBER
Education (Cont.)				
Iran	USA (United States)	19 Oct 50	92UNTS135	101266
Liberia	ILO (Labor Org)	02 Apr 51	100UNTS117	101392
Honduras	USA (United States)	24 Apr 51	140UNTS287	101894
Mexico	WHO (World Health)	30 Apr 51	103UNTS95	101427
Multilateral		02 Jul 51	189UNTS137	102545
Multilateral		06 Dec 51	425UNTS61	106119
Jordan	USA (United States)	12 Feb 52	168UNTS25	102211
India	United Nations	02 Apr 52	126UNTS145	101687
WHO (World Health)	Syria	20 Jun 52	165UNTS219	102178
Sweden	USA (United States)	20 Nov 52	177UNTS203	102319
France	WHO (World Health)	02 Apr 53	174UNTS83	102279
Haiti	USA (United States)	28 May 54	233UNTS281	103267
Italy	USA (United States)	28 Jun 54	237UNTS121	103340
Austria	Denmark	07 Sep 54	201UNTS39	102709
Peru	USA (United States)	31 Dec 54	251UNTS51	103533
Haiti	USA (United States)	27 Apr 55	240UNTS17	103391
Libya	USA (United States)	28 Jul 55	270UNTS245	103900
Philippines	USA (United States)	28 Oct 55	239UNTS165	103376
Multilateral		15 Dec 56	278UNTS73	104023
Czechoslovakia	USSR (Soviet Union)	04 Dec 57	313UNTS291	104537
Germany, West	Netherlands	30 Jun 58	315UNTS179	104568
UK Great Britain	Yugoslavia	12 Apr 60	360UNTS79	105155
Costa Rica	IBRD (World Bank)	04 May 60	390UNTS201	105609
Libya	USA (United States)	11 Dec 60	445UNTS125	106381
Multilateral		14 Dec 60	429UNTS93	106193
Multilateral		23 Mar 62	434UNTS145	106262
Israel	USA (United States)	22 Jun 62	448UNTS273	106440
Italy	USA (United States)	28 Aug 62	461UNTS137	106657
IDA (Devel Assoc)	Tunisia	17 Sep 62	469UNTS33	106783
India	USA (United States)	09 Oct 62	471UNTS39	106820
Israel	Rwanda	23 Oct 62	515UNTS291	107466
UK Great Britain	USSR (Soviet Union)	21 Jan 63	475UNTS3	106887
Israel	Tanganyika	28 Jan 63	516UNTS39	107468
Israel	Uganda	04 Feb 63	484UNTS273	107037
Pakistan	IDA (Devel Assoc)	25 Mar 64	534UNTS275	107765
Pakistan	IDA (Devel Assoc)	25 Mar 64	535UNTS43	107775
Denmark	Kenya	26 Jun 64	573UNTS107	108325
Afghanistan	IDA (Devel Assoc)	23 Nov 64	567UNTS155	108255
UK Great Britain	USSR (Soviet Union)	13 Feb 65	543UNTS43	107896
Nigeria	IDA (Devel Assoc)	01 Mar 65	571UNTS3	108297
France	USA (United States)	07 May 65	573UNTS183	108331
USA (United States)	Uruguay	17 May 65	564UNTS69	108221
Israel	Sierra Leone	22 Aug 65	550UNTS285	108023
Morocco	IDA (Devel Assoc)	11 Oct 65	562UNTS299	108200
Netherlands	Nigeria	28 Oct 65	578UNTS15	108383
Burma	USA (United States)	01 Jun 66	580UNTS253	108428
Ivory Coast	Netherlands	01 Aug 66	591UNTS245	108561
Netherlands	Yugoslavia	11 Aug 66	602UNTS243	108716
Kenya	IDA (Devel Assoc)	19 Aug 66	585UNTS119	108485
Romania	United Arab Rep	03 Sep 66	604UNTS73	108745
UK Great Britain	USSR (Soviet Union)	24 Feb 67	606UNTS171	108785
Germany, East	Poland	15 Mar 67	618UNTS21	108922
Bulgaria	Poland	06 Apr 67	617UNTS327	108920
Recognition of degrees				
Brazil	Paraguay	14 Jun 41	54UNTS235	200196
Brazil	Venezuela	22 Oct 42	65UNTS203	200212
Brazil	Dominican Republic	09 Dec 42	65UNTS217	200213
Brazil	Ecuador	24 May 44	73UNTS223	200242
Poland	Yugoslavia	16 Mar 46	10UNTS11	100139
Belgium	UK Great Britain	17 Apr 46	6UNTS177	100075
Belgium	Netherlands	16 May 46	17UNTS13	100266
France	USA (United States)	10 Dec 46	15UNTS265	100242
Belgium	Czechoslovakia	06 Mar 47	34UNTS77	100528
Austria	France	15 Mar 47	12UNTS109	100182
Recognition of degrees (Cont.)				
Czechoslovakia	Yugoslavia	27 Apr 47	33UNTS49	100514
France	Poland	19 May 47	12UNTS95	100181
Czechoslovakia	UK Great Britain	16 Jun 47	46UNTS61	100700
Bulgaria	Czechoslovakia	20 Jun 47	46UNTS15	100698
Romania	Yugoslavia	26 Jun 47	116UNTS39	101568
Bulgaria	Poland	28 Jun 47	15UNTS123	100230
Czechoslovakia	Poland	04 Jul 47	25UNTS249	100366
Albania	Yugoslavia	09 Jul 47	33UNTS91	100516
Czechoslovakia	Romania	05 Sep 47	46UNTS37	100699
Hungary	Yugoslavia	15 Oct 47	33UNTS73	100515
USSR (Soviet Union)	Yugoslavia	15 Dec 47	116UNTS313	101578
Norway	UK Great Britain	19 Feb 48	34UNTS33	100526
Belgium	Norway	20 Feb 48	32UNTS39	100487
Poland	Romania	27 Feb 48	46UNTS143	100707
Belgium	Luxembourg	27 Mar 48	178UNTS265	102343
Netherlands	UK Great Britain	07 Jul 48	82UNTS259	101099
Luxembourg	Netherlands	26 Apr 49	182UNTS187	102425
Greece	Lebanon	10 Jun 49	178UNTS29	102334
Luxembourg	UK Great Britain	27 Jun 50	183UNTS217	102431
Greece	Turkey	20 Apr 51	178UNTS17	102333
India	Turkey	29 Jun 51	213UNTS183	102886
Greece	UK Great Britain	29 Sep 51	190UNTS260	102570
Italy	UK Great Britain	28 Nov 51	172UNTS27	102238
Austria	Belgium	17 Oct 52	162UNTS183	102135
Austria	UK Great Britain	12 Dec 52	172UNTS9	102237
Bolivia	Italy	31 Jan 53	281UNTS181	104079
Pakistan	Turkey	29 Jun 53	211UNTS225	102854
Pakistan	United Arab Rep	14 Nov 53	485UNTS55	107046
Multilateral		11 Dec 53	218UNTS125	102954
Ireland	UK Great Britain	06 Apr 54	553UNTS197	108088
Greece	Italy	11 Sep 54	284UNTS313	104145
Belgium	France	15 Oct 54	218UNTS19	102951
Belgium	Greece	09 Dec 54	257UNTS243	103660
Japan	Thailand	06 Apr 55	230UNTS219	103187
Netherlands	Norway	18 May 55	252UNTS269	103569
Italy	Spain	11 Aug 55	267UNTS125	103839
Iran	Pakistan	09 Mar 56	449UNTS183	106460
Turkey	UK Great Britain	12 Mar 56	313UNTS73	104530
Romania	USSR (Soviet Union)	07 Apr 56	259UNTS377	103698
Austria	Italy	09 May 56	267UNTS227	103845
Czechoslovakia	USSR (Soviet Union)	01 Jun 56	259UNTS341	103696
Greece	United Arab Rep	04 Sep 56	299UNTS253	104317
Belgium	Germany, West	24 Sep 56	263UNTS31	103766
Multilateral		15 Dec 56	278UNTS73	104023
Poland	United Arab Rep	02 Feb 57	319UNTS221	104633
Japan	United Arab Rep	20 Mar 57	318UNTS345	104625
India	Poland	27 Mar 57	319UNTS263	104635
Multilateral		12 Apr 57	443UNTS128	106362
Romania	United Arab Rep	15 Apr 57	389UNTS21	105589
Japan	Pakistan	27 May 57	325UNTS21	104692
Czechoslovakia	United Arab Rep	19 Oct 57	530UNTS181	107681
United Arab Rep	USSR (Soviet Union)	19 Oct 57	292UNTS151	104271
Czechoslovakia	USSR (Soviet Union)	04 Dec 57	313UNTS291	104537
Belgium	Denmark	31 Dec 57	305UNTS247	104422
Germany, West	UK Great Britain	18 Apr 58	343UNTS241	104928
Belgium	Spain	27 Oct 58	327UNTS107	104720
Belgium	Turkey	29 Dec 58	357UNTS195	105118
Hungary	Iraq	11 Apr 59	439UNTS25	106323
Iran	UK Great Britain	06 May 59	398UNTS51	105717
Czechoslovakia	India	07 Jul 59	359UNTS259	105145
Iraq	Romania	04 Aug 59	502UNTS17	107324
Czechoslovakia	Guinea	30 Nov 59	386UNTS63	105538
France	Israel	30 Nov 59	377UNTS237	105404
Czechoslovakia	Ethiopia	11 Dec 59	399UNTS93	105736
Multilateral		14 Dec 59	444UNTS193	106369

PARTY ONE	PARTY TWO	DATE	CITATION	NUMBER
Recognition of degrees (Cont.)				
Germany, East	Hungary	19 Dec 59	409UNTS4	105874
Guinea	Hungary	12 Jan 60	519UNTS131	107505
Italy	USSR (Soviet Union)	09 Feb 60	399UNTS75	105735
Indonesia	USSR (Soviet Union)	28 Feb 60	392UNTS191	105644
Spain	UK Great Britain	12 Jul 60	414UNTS123	105971
Czechoslovakia	Ghana	23 Nov 60	431UNTS91	106213
Japan	UK Great Britain	03 Dec 60	414UNTS61	105966
Netherlands	United Arab Rep	08 Dec 60	455UNTS276	106547
Cuba	Czechoslovakia	22 Dec 60	426UNTS145	106134
Czechoslovakia	Hungary	24 Feb 61	422UNTS15	106066
India	Norway	19 Apr 61	404UNTS307	105818
Afghanistan	Czechoslovakia	23 Apr 61	437UNTS25	106297
Germany, West	Netherlands	27 Apr 61	487UNTS77	107095
Ghana	Hungary	27 Apr 61	439UNTS17	106322
Pakistan	Philippines	15 Aug 61	522UNTS35	107534
Ghana	United Nations	29 Aug 61	406UNTS117	105843
Argentina	Japan	20 Dec 61	451UNTS77	106486
Austria	Czechoslovakia	13 Feb 62	455UNTS381	106551
USA (United States)	USSR (Soviet Union)	08 Mar 62	460UNTS3	106630
Hungary	India	30 Mar 62	519UNTS119	107504
Senegal	USSR (Soviet Union)	14 Jun 62	437UNTS233	106309
Syria	USSR (Soviet Union)	19 Aug 62	457UNTS285	106588
Belgium	Tunisia	21 Dec 62	482UNTS3	106987
Dahomey	USSR (Soviet Union)	20 Mar 63	528UNTS181	107641
Cameroon	UK Great Britain	20 Aug 63	539UNTS233	107834
Belgium	Romania	13 Nov 63	520UNTS119	107513
Belgium	Pakistan	14 Nov 63	535UNTS393	107792
Belgium	Poland	09 Dec 63	514UNTS195	107448
Netherlands	Tunisia	11 Feb 64	570UNTS173	108293
USA (United States)	USSR (Soviet Union)	22 Feb 64	526UNTS131	107605
Spain	USA (United States)	18 Mar 64	535UNTS343	107789
Algeria	Czechoslovakia	14 May 64	538UNTS301	107817
Czechoslovakia	Germany, East	06 Oct 64	545UNTS113	107927
Belgium	Mexico	19 Nov 64	546UNTS217	107949
Argentina	Panama	21 Nov 64	635UNTS205	109083
Argentina	Costa Rica	23 Nov 64	635UNTS213	109084
Belgium	Hungary	11 Feb 65	544UNTS3	107908
Bulgaria	Czechoslovakia	22 May 65	545UNTS65	107925
China People's Rep	Romania	27 May 65	592UNTS3	108566
Pakistan	USSR (Soviet Union)	05 Jun 65	593UNTS115	108579
Uganda	USSR (Soviet Union)	24 Jul 65	596UNTS199	108633
Argentina	Belgium	05 Nov 65	635UNTS229	109086
Austria	Finland	09 Dec 65	0UNTS0	109462
Argentina	Taiwan	19 Mar 66	635UNTS281	109089
Tunisia	USA (United States)	26 Sep 66	616UNTS259	108900
Bulgaria	Poland	03 Oct 66	618UNTS3	108921
Netherlands	Romania	13 Feb 67	604UNTS287	108756
Belgium	Israel	23 Mar 67	630UNTS275	108974
Eur Space Research	UK Great Britain	24 Nov 67	638UNTS17	109129
Exchange				
Brazil	Paraguay	14 Jun 41	54UNTS235	200196
Brazil	Chile	18 Nov 41	67UNTS279	200225
Peru	USA (United States)	24 Aug 42	24UNTS153	200139
Honduras	USA (United States)	12 Apr 44	138UNTS271	200450
Peru	USA (United States)	15 Apr 44	150UNTS317	200479
Brazil	Ecuador	24 May 44	73UNTS223	200242
Bolivia	USA (United States)	07 Sep 44	162UNTS315	200494
Guatemala	USA (United States)	16 Sep 44	135UNTS315	200444
Panama	USA (United States)	14 Nov 44	139UNTS367	200462
Ecuador	USA (United States)	22 Jan 45	24UNTS273	200152
El Salvador	USA (United States)	09 Jun 45	149UNTS379	200478
Dominican Republic	USA (United States)	13 Oct 45	149UNTS361	200477
Czechoslovakia	France	08 Dec 45	46UNTS77	100701
Brazil	USA (United States)	15 Feb 46	162UNTS21	102130

PARTY ONE	PARTY TWO	DATE	CITATION	NUMBER
Exchange (Cont.)				
Belgium	France	22 Feb 46	68UNTS157	100892
Brazil	USA (United States)	05 Apr 46	12UNTS131	100183
Belgium	Netherlands	16 May 46	17UNTS13	100266
India	USA (United States)	16 May 46	4UNTS183	100045
France	USA (United States)	28 May 46	84UNTS59	101119
Australia	USA (United States)	07 Jun 46	4UNTS237	100048
New Zealand	USA (United States)	10 Jul 46	6UNTS341	100087
Taiwan	USA (United States)	30 Aug 46	12UNTS39	100179
Philippines	USA (United States)	11 Sep 46	43UNTS231	100670
France	Netherlands	19 Nov 46	32UNTS101	100493
France	USA (United States)	10 Dec 46	15UNTS265	100242
Multilateral		13 Dec 46	8UNTS105	100117
Multilateral		13 Dec 46	8UNTS151	100120
Multilateral		13 Dec 46	8UNTS91	100116
Belgium	Czechoslovakia	06 Mar 47	34UNTS77	100528
Czechoslovakia	Yugoslavia	27 Apr 47	33UNTS49	100514
France	Poland	19 May 47	12UNTS95	100181
Czechoslovakia	UK Great Britain	16 Jun 47	46UNTS61	100700
Bulgaria	Czechoslovakia	20 Jun 47	46UNTS15	100698
Bulgaria	Poland	28 Jun 47	15UNTS123	100230
Czechoslovakia	Poland	04 Jul 47	25UNTS249	100366
Albania	Yugoslavia	09 Jul 47	33UNTS91	100516
Czechoslovakia	Romania	05 Sep 47	46UNTS37	100699
Hungary	Yugoslavia	15 Oct 47	33UNTS73	100515
Ecuador	USA (United States)	14 Nov 47	149UNTS297	101959
USSR (Soviet Union)	Yugoslavia	15 Dec 47	116UNTS313	101578
Guatemala	USA (United States)	05 Jan 48	135UNTS104	101817
Hungary	Poland	31 Jan 48	25UNTS283	100368
Belgium	Norway	20 Feb 48	32UNTS39	100487
Poland	Romania	27 Feb 48	46UNTS143	100707
France	UK Great Britain	02 Mar 48	77UNTS33	100990
Paraguay	USA (United States)	12 Mar 48	162UNTS30	102131
Philippines	USA (United States)	23 Mar 48	43UNTS247	100671
Belgium	Luxembourg	27 Mar 48	178UNTS265	102343
Greece	USA (United States)	23 Apr 48	74UNTS107	100958
Hungary	Poland	18 Jun 48	25UNTS319	100370
Peru	USA (United States)	30 Jun 48	150UNTS45	101962
Taiwan	USA (United States)	05 Aug 48	82UNTS109	101087
New Zealand	USA (United States)	14 Sep 48	18UNTS251	100295
UK Great Britain	USA (United States)	22 Sep 48	71UNTS64	100910
Panama	USA (United States)	24 Sep 48	150UNTS25	101961
Multilateral		08 Oct 48	19UNTS113	100308
Belgium	Italy	29 Nov 48	41UNTS3	100641
Afghanistan	UNESCO (Educ/Cult)	08 Dec 48	46UNTS3	100697
Italy	USA (United States)	18 Dec 48	79UNTS133	101037
Luxembourg	Netherlands	26 Apr 49	182UNTS187	102425
Bolivia	USA (United States)	16 May 49	162UNTS3	102129
Netherlands	USA (United States)	17 May 49	46UNTS291	100717
Ethiopia	USA (United States)	20 May 49	89UNTS99	101211
Norway	USA (United States)	25 May 49	32UNTS345	100507
Multilateral		15 Jul 49	197UNTS3	102631
United Arab Rep	USA (United States)	03 Nov 49	71UNTS31	100908
Australia	USA (United States)	26 Nov 49	45UNTS133	100695
Turkey	USA (United States)	27 Dec 49	98UNTS141	101361
India	USA (United States)	02 Feb 50	89UNTS127	101214
Korea, South	USA (United States)	28 Apr 50	93UNTS21	101284
Austria	USA (United States)	06 Jun 50	92UNTS201	101273
Luxembourg	UK Great Britain	27 Jun 50	183UNTS217	102431
Thailand	USA (United States)	01 Jul 50	81UNTS61	101063
Pakistan	USA (United States)	23 Sep 50	82UNTS131	101088
Haiti	USA (United States)	28 Sep 50	162UNTS85	102132
Czechoslovakia	Poland	17 Nov 50	530UNTS195	107682
Bolivia	USA (United States)	22 Nov 50	152UNTS17	102008
Albania	Poland	02 Dec 50	260UNTS131	103707
El Salvador	USA (United States)	13 Dec 50	166UNTS149	102188

PARTY ONE	PARTY TWO	DATE	CITATION	NUMBER
Exchange (Cont.)				
Colombia	WHO (World Health)	05 Jan 51	102UNTS139	101417
Nicaragua	USA (United States)	31 Jan 51	150UNTS3	101960
Costa Rica	USA (United States)	13 Feb 51	141UNTS169	101914
USA (United States)	Uruguay	07 Mar 51	165UNTS113	102173
Dominican Republic	USA (United States)	16 Mar 51	148UNTS15	101932
China People's Rep	Poland	03 Apr 51	304UNTS187	104396
Honduras	USA (United States)	24 Apr 51	140UNTS287	101894
Netherlands	South Africa	31 May 51	188UNTS289	102533
Costa Rica	WHO (World Health)	14 Jun 51	102UNTS151	101418
India	Turkey	29 Jun 51	213UNTS183	102886
Burma	WHO (World Health)	09 Jul 51	104UNTS187	101440
Burma	WHO (World Health)	09 Jul 51	102UNTS131	101416
Multilateral		18 Jul 51	102UNTS291	200308
Panama	USA (United States)	30 Jul 51	140UNTS321	101896
Multilateral		04 Aug 51	104UNTS197	101441
Denmark	USA (United States)	23 Aug 51	147UNTS49	101928
Japan	USA (United States)	28 Aug 51	147UNTS81	101930
Panama	USA (United States)	23 Oct 51	140UNTS3	101880
India	WHO (World Health)	23 Oct 51	109UNTS59	101491
El Salvador	USA (United States)	12 Dec 51	132UNTS287	101768
Mexico	WHO (World Health)	17 Dec 51	124UNTS121	101670
Germany, East	Poland	08 Jan 52	304UNTS113	104394
Colombia	USA (United States)	12 Jan 52	168UNTS109	102216
WHO (World Health)	Spain	30 Jan 52	124UNTS259	200425
Peru	USA (United States)	04 Feb 52	121UNTS255	200403
Finland	WHO (World Health)	07 Mar 52	128UNTS269	200436
Ceylon (Sri Lanka)	WHO (World Health)	26 Mar 52	134UNTS341	200442
South Africa	USA (United States)	26 Mar 52	165UNTS187	102176
India	WHO (World Health)	17 Apr 52	131UNTS241	101744
India	WHO (World Health)	19 Apr 52	131UNTS253	101745
Pakistan	United Nations	28 Apr 52	128UNTS191	101720
Ethiopia	USA (United States)	15 May 52	180UNTS227	102388
Libya	USA (United States)	20 May 52	177UNTS81	102310
Iraq	USA (United States)	21 May 52	205UNTS25	102767
Ethiopia	USA (United States)	18 Jun 52	181UNTS207	102410
India	WHO (World Health)	19 Jun 52	134UNTS307	101809
Multilateral		19 Jun 52	133UNTS165	101787
Finland	USA (United States)	02 Jul 52	165UNTS203	102177
Australia	FAO (Food Agri)	07 Jul 52	184UNTS209	102449
India	WHO (World Health)	16 Jul 52	135UNTS291	101828
Germany, West	USA (United States)	18 Jul 52	165UNTS167	102175
Chile	ILO (Labor Org)	23 Jul 52	178UNTS323	102348
Panama	United Nations	20 Aug 52	136UNTS3	101829
Italy	ILO (Labor Org)	04 Sep 52	178UNTS371	200505
Multilateral		15 Oct 52	141UNTS96	101909
Austria	Belgium	17 Oct 52	162UNTS183	102135
Ceylon (Sri Lanka)	USA (United States)	17 Nov 52	180UNTS207	102386
Sweden	USA (United States)	20 Nov 52	177UNTS203	102319
Ceylon (Sri Lanka)	WHO (World Health)	21 Nov 52	161UNTS315	200490
Mexico	ICAO (Civil Aviat)	28 Nov 52	164UNTS15	102156
Multilateral		16 Dec 52	158UNTS407	102074
Multilateral		29 Dec 52	151UNTS317	102002
Saudi Arabia	USA (United States)	25 Jan 53	201UNTS3	102706
Bolivia	Italy	31 Jan 53	281UNTS181	104079
United Nations	Sweden	11 Feb 53	160UNTS3	102096
India	WHO (World Health)	11 Feb 53	163UNTS43	102140
Taiwan	ILO (Labor Org)	13 Feb 53	178UNTS337	102349
UK Great Britain	USA (United States)	25 Feb 53	212UNTS157	102868
Multilateral		26 Feb 53	161UNTS31	102120
Germany, West	USA (United States)	27 Feb 53	205UNTS103	102771
Costa Rica	United Nations	27 Feb 53	161UNTS45	102121
Nepal	United Nations	02 Mar 53	161UNTS347	200493
United Arab Rep	USA (United States)	19 Mar 53	215UNTS17	102909
France	WHO (World Health)	02 Apr 53	174UNTS83	102279
United Nations	Yemen	07 Apr 53	163UNTS73	102142

PARTY ONE	PARTY TWO	DATE	CITATION	NUMBER
Exchange (Cont.)				
Ethiopia	USA (United States)	29 Apr 53	224UNTS121	103073
Greece	Netherlands	29 Apr 53	191UNTS235	102583
France	WHO (World Health)	30 Apr 53	174UNTS71	102278
ICAO (Civil Aviat)	Syria	28 May 53	173UNTS199	102267
Ecuador	United Nations	16 Jun 53	166UNTS289	102194
United Arab Rep	USA (United States)	18 Jun 53	204UNTS55	102749
Ethiopia	United Nations	22 Jun 53	172UNTS93	102241
Liberia	USA (United States)	23 Jun 53	213UNTS57	102880
Cambodia	United Nations	24 Jun 53	168UNTS309	200500
Ethiopia	USA (United States)	25 Jun 53	212UNTS175	102869
UK Great Britain	USA (United States)	26 Jun 53	183UNTS225	102432
Saudi Arabia	USA (United States)	29 Jun 53	206UNTS23	102784
Pakistan	Turkey	29 Jun 53	211UNTS225	102854
Multilateral		09 Oct 53	190UNTS49	102557
Dominican Republic	United Nations	19 Nov 53	180UNTS45	102374
Brazil	WHO (World Health)	04 Feb 54	233UNTS49	103250
United Nations	Venezuela	05 Mar 54	187UNTS9	102498
Liberia	United Nations	09 Mar 54	187UNTS61	102501
Guatemala	United Nations	10 Mar 54	191UNTS271	102587
Ireland	UK Great Britain	06 Apr 54	553UNTS197	108088
Multilateral		20 Apr 54	189UNTS11	102539
Nepal	WHO (World Health)	13 May 54	204UNTS311	200522
Multilateral		01 Jun 54	200UNTS235	200520
Belgium	South Africa	01 Jun 54	201UNTS25	102708
Brazil	USA (United States)	30 Jun 54	237UNTS137	103341
Multilateral		19 Aug 54	201UNTS51	102710
Austria	Denmark	07 Sep 54	201UNTS39	102709
Multilateral		06 Oct 54	201UNTS75	102711
Ethiopia	Sweden	13 Oct 54	202UNTS273	102734
Multilateral		27 Oct 54	201UNTS95	102712
Multilateral		29 Oct 54	201UNTS115	102713
Portugal	UK Great Britain	19 Nov 54	226UNTS305	103125
Belgium	Greece	09 Dec 54	257UNTS243	103660
Multilateral		19 Dec 54	218UNTS139	102955
Chile	USA (United States)	31 Mar 55	262UNTS19	103736
Multilateral		04 Apr 55	208UNTS239	102816
Taiwan	WHO (World Health)	21 Apr 55	210UNTS71	102835
Netherlands	Norway	18 May 55	252UNTS269	103569
Multilateral		14 Jun 55	212UNTS263	200526
Italy	Norway	14 Jun 55	260UNTS307	103713
Colombia	USA (United States)	14 Jun 55	256UNTS211	103630
Iran	WHO (World Health)	04 Jul 55	227UNTS65	103131
Multilateral		04 Jul 55	214UNTS10	102897
Belgium	Portugal	30 Jul 55	250UNTS213	103525
Czechoslovakia	Germany, East	30 Aug 55	504UNTS279	107361
Bulgaria	Yugoslavia	11 Dec 55	378UNTS49	105417
Multilateral		02 Feb 56	227UNTS153	103137
Multilateral		10 Feb 56	228UNTS167	103150
Multilateral		10 Feb 56	228UNTS189	103151
Iran	Pakistan	09 Mar 56	449UNTS183	106460
Turkey	UK Great Britain	12 Mar 56	313UNTS73	104530
Romania	USSR (Soviet Union)	07 Apr 56	259UNTS377	103698
Mongolia	USSR (Soviet Union)	24 Apr 56	259UNTS297	103693
Germany, East	USSR (Soviet Union)	26 Apr 56	259UNTS279	103692
Bulgaria	USSR (Soviet Union)	28 Apr 56	259UNTS363	103697
Peru	USA (United States)	03 May 56	272UNTS59	103931
Albania	USSR (Soviet Union)	03 May 56	259UNTS391	103699
Mongolia	Romania	08 May 56	342UNTS291	104913
Korea, North	Poland	11 May 56	432UNTS161	106219
Korea, North	Romania	12 May 56	342UNTS189	104908
USSR (Soviet Union)	Yugoslavia	17 May 56	259UNTS145	103687
Multilateral		31 May 56	251UNTS181	103541
Czechoslovakia	USSR (Soviet Union)	01 Jun 56	259UNTS341	103696
Multilateral		08 Jun 56	247UNTS366	200541
Multilateral		14 Jun 56	265UNTS125	103809

PARTY ONE	PARTY TWO	DATE	CITATION	NUMBER
Exchange (Cont.)				
Multilateral		26 Jun 56	321UNTS2	104650
Israel	USA (United States)	26 Jun 56	257UNTS55	103649
Multilateral		26 Jun 56	253UNTS12	103573
Poland	USSR (Soviet Union)	30 Jun 56	259UNTS311	103694
Multilateral		02 Jul 56	540UNTS110	107846
Multilateral		02 Jul 56	248UNTS37	103484
China People's Rep	USSR (Soviet Union)	05 Jul 56	263UNTS129	103770
Poland	Yugoslavia	06 Jul 56	281UNTS143	104076
Syria	USSR (Soviet Union)	20 Aug 56	274UNTS105	103961
Multilateral		31 Aug 56	249UNTS158	103506
Korea, North	USSR (Soviet Union)	05 Sep 56	259UNTS329	103695
Multilateral		05 Oct 56	251UNTS245	103544
Multilateral		05 Oct 56	251UNTS267	103545
Germany, West	Thailand	09 Oct 56	258UNTS143	103676
Romania	Vietnam, North	12 Oct 56	342UNTS173	104907
Norway	USSR (Soviet Union)	12 Oct 56	308UNTS95	104457
Denmark	Italy	26 Oct 56	267UNTS261	103847
Romania	Yugoslavia	27 Oct 56	389UNTS33	105590
India	Japan	29 Oct 56	318UNTS289	104622
Ecuador	USA (United States)	31 Oct 56	283UNTS151	104114
Argentina	USA (United States)	05 Nov 56	277UNTS143	104004
Multilateral		21 Nov 56	253UNTS266	103588
Bulgaria	Yugoslavia	24 Dec 56	397UNTS3	105699
Colombia	USA (United States)	09 Jan 57	462UNTS151	106676
Multilateral		15 Jan 57	376UNTS122	105378
Multilateral		23 Jan 57	259UNTS426	103701
Czechoslovakia	Yugoslavia	29 Jan 57	300UNTS249	104339
Poland	United Arab Rep	02 Feb 57	319UNTS221	104633
Belgium	Yugoslavia	05 Feb 57	276UNTS143	103990
USSR (Soviet Union)	Vietnam, North	15 Feb 57	274UNTS115	103962
Multilateral		17 Feb 57	271UNTS2	103907
Iceland	USA (United States)	23 Feb 57	283UNTS73	104107
Multilateral		01 Mar 57	264UNTS94	103790
Japan	United Arab Rep	20 Mar 57	318UNTS345	104625
India	Poland	27 Mar 57	319UNTS263	104635
Multilateral		28 Mar 57	271UNTS30	103908
Paraguay	USA (United States)	04 Apr 57	284UNTS161	104135
Poland	Vietnam, North	06 Apr 57	432UNTS255	106224
Multilateral		09 Apr 57	274UNTS172	103965
Multilateral		12 Apr 57	443UNTS128	106362
Iran	Japan	16 Apr 57	325UNTS113	104697
India	Romania	30 Apr 57	342UNTS251	104911
Finland	USA (United States)	10 May 57	283UNTS43	104105
Multilateral		24 May 57	268UNTS270	103861
Czechoslovakia	Syria	18 Jun 57	303UNTS119	104374
Multilateral		09 Jul 57	274UNTS300	103972
Burma	WHO (World Health)	20 Sep 57	282UNTS113	104096
Czechoslovakia	United Arab Rep	19 Oct 57	530UNTS181	107681
United Arab Rep	USSR (Soviet Union)	19 Oct 57	292UNTS151	104271
Brazil	USA (United States)	05 Nov 57	303UNTS3	104368
Multilateral		05 Nov 57	285UNTS301	104155
Taiwan	Iran	11 Nov 57	563UNTS31	108202
Israel	Norway	26 Nov 57	345UNTS99	104962
Czechoslovakia	USSR (Soviet Union)	04 Dec 57	313UNTS291	104537
Belgium	Denmark	31 Dec 57	305UNTS247	104422
Norway	Turkey	10 Jan 58	351UNTS229	105025
Japan	USA (United States)	11 Jan 58	304UNTS35	104390
Ceylon (Sri Lanka)	USSR (Soviet Union)	15 Jan 58	305UNTS235	104421
Poland	Yugoslavia	16 Jan 58	340UNTS181	104864
Ghana	WHO (World Health)	21 Jan 58	307UNTS3	104437
USA (United States)	USSR (Soviet Union)	27 Jan 58	301UNTS405	104350
Indonesia	WHO (World Health)	05 Feb 58	307UNTS15	104438
Czechoslovakia	Hungary	12 Mar 58	408UNTS178	105870
Bulgaria	Hungary	13 Mar 58	438UNTS173	106316
Multilateral		15 Mar 58	292UNTS273	104276

PARTY ONE	PARTY TWO	DATE	CITATION	NUMBER
Exchange (Cont.)				
Czechoslovakia	Romania	25 Mar 58	339UNTS77	104846
Taiwan	Costa Rica	10 Apr 58	315UNTS165	104567
Israel	WHO (World Health)	11 Apr 58	307UNTS27	104439
Hungary	Poland	08 May 58	408UNTS212	105872
Germany, East	Hungary	14 Jun 58	407UNTS78	105861
Multilateral		19 Jun 58	306UNTS236	200550
WHO (World Health)	Sudan	21 Jun 58	307UNTS235	104453
Germany, West	Netherlands	30 Jun 58	315UNTS179	104568
Germany, East	Romania	15 Jul 58	387UNTS115	105560
Muscat and Oman	UK Great Britain	25 Jul 58	312UNTS347	104524
Spain	USA (United States)	16 Oct 58	336UNTS153	104804
Czechoslovakia	Romania	25 Oct 58	338UNTS301	104843
Belgium	Spain	27 Oct 58	327UNTS107	104720
Iran	Japan	09 Dec 58	325UNTS221	104701
Norway	Poland	17 Dec 58	432UNTS193	106221
Mongolia	Poland	23 Dec 58	432UNTS177	106220
Hungary	Iraq	11 Apr 59	439UNTS25	106323
Iran	Netherlands	22 May 59	474UNTS195	106882
Finland	Hungary	10 Jun 59	439UNTS3	106321
Taiwan	Ecuador	12 Jun 59	387UNTS3	105554
Czechoslovakia	India	07 Jul 59	359UNTS259	105145
Norway	Spain	19 Aug 59	376UNTS145	105379
Bulgaria	Czechoslovakia	19 Sep 59	355UNTS77	105074
United Arab Rep	USA (United States)	28 Sep 59	358UNTS97	105128
USA (United States)	USSR (Soviet Union)	21 Nov 59	361UNTS35	105172
Czechoslovakia	Guinea	30 Nov 59	386UNTS63	105538
France	Israel	30 Nov 59	377UNTS237	105404
UK Great Britain	USSR (Soviet Union)	01 Dec 59	351UNTS313	105032
Multilateral		03 Dec 59	348UNTS246	105003
Czechoslovakia	Ethiopia	11 Dec 59	399UNTS93	105736
Germany, East	Hungary	19 Dec 59	409UNTS4	105874
Ceylon (Sri Lanka)	WHO (World Health)	21 Dec 59	349UNTS109	105011
Belgium	Brazil	06 Jan 60	531UNTS149	107701
Pakistan	WHO (World Health)	20 Jan 60	351UNTS355	105034
India	USSR (Soviet Union)	12 Feb 60	392UNTS153	105642
Japan	USA (United States)	18 Feb 60	372UNTS117	105292
Indonesia	USSR (Soviet Union)	28 Feb 60	392UNTS191	105644
Portugal	USA (United States)	19 Mar 60	371UNTS131	105275
Japan	USA (United States)	23 Mar 60	372UNTS289	105305
Multilateral		12 Apr 60	359UNTS323	105150
Netherlands	Turkey	12 May 60	463UNTS207	106704
Belgium	Iran	14 May 60	522UNTS249	107551
Cambodia	WHO (World Health)	19 May 60	372UNTS193	105298
Finland	USSR (Soviet Union)	27 May 60	379UNTS381	105444
Multilateral		04 Jun 60	360UNTS208	105159
Denmark	Poland	08 Jun 60	424UNTS37	106097
Multilateral		08 Jul 60	366UNTS310	105220
USA (United States)	Uruguay	22 Jul 60	388UNTS315	105587
France	Greece	25 Jul 60	533UNTS227	107745
Jordan	WHO (World Health)	03 Aug 60	381UNTS133	105469
WHO (World Health)	United Arab Rep	03 Aug 60	385UNTS3	105524
WHO (World Health)	Tunisia	04 Aug 60	381UNTS335	105474
Laos	WHO (World Health)	04 Aug 60	373UNTS313	105322
Cuba	Korea, North	29 Aug 60	473UNTS117	106860
Israel	UK Great Britain	31 Aug 60	385UNTS71	105530
WHO (World Health)	Saudi Arabia	06 Sep 60	395UNTS169	105684
Lebanon	WHO (World Health)	08 Sep 60	387UNTS49	105557
Cuba	Romania	28 Oct 60	457UNTS9	106574
Czechoslovakia	Germany, East	08 Nov 60	424UNTS71	106100
WHO (World Health)	Upper Volta	15 Nov 60	383UNTS91	105496
Czechoslovakia	Ghana	23 Nov 60	431UNTS91	106213
Fed of Malaya	WHO (World Health)	25 Nov 60	387UNTS37	105556
Cambodia	Czechoslovakia	27 Nov 60	410UNTS263	105910
WHO (World Health)	Yemen	03 Dec 60	395UNTS187	105685
Dahomey	WHO (World Health)	07 Dec 60	387UNTS277	105567

PARTY ONE	PARTY TWO	DATE	CITATION	NUMBER
Exchange (Cont.)				
Netherlands	United Arab Rep	08 Dec 60	455UNTS276	106547
Romania	USA (United States)	09 Dec 60	401UNTS19	105759
Cuba	USSR (Soviet Union)	12 Dec 60	421UNTS3	106048
Congo (Brazzaville)	WHO (World Health)	12 Dec 60	399UNTS105	105737
Cuba	Czechoslovakia	22 Dec 60	426UNTS145	106134
Niger	WHO (World Health)	28 Dec 60	394UNTS195	105679
UK Great Britain	USSR (Soviet Union)	09 Jan 61	404UNTS175	105810
Ethiopia	USSR (Soviet Union)	13 Jan 61	421UNTS13	106049
Korea, South	WHO (World Health)	20 Jan 61	406UNTS269	200589
Multilateral		28 Jan 61	387UNTS202	105563
Ivory Coast	WHO (World Health)	30 Jan 61	395UNTS205	105686
Chad	WHO (World Health)	03 Feb 61	394UNTS161	105676
WHO (World Health)	Togo	03 Feb 61	394UNTS207	105680
Central Afri Rep	WHO (World Health)	13 Feb 61	394UNTS149	105675
Czechoslovakia	Hungary	24 Feb 61	422UNTS15	106066
Cuba	Poland	06 Mar 61	484UNTS123	107020
Kuwait	WHO (World Health)	16 Mar 61	397UNTS315	200588
Cuba	Germany, East	29 Mar 61	448UNTS81	106426
Mauritania	WHO (World Health)	17 Apr 61	396UNTS301	200587
India	Norway	19 Apr 61	404UNTS307	105818
Afghanistan	Czechoslovakia	23 Apr 61	437UNTS25	106297
Taiwan	Nicaragua	25 Apr 61	423UNTS139	106090
Ghana	Hungary	27 Apr 61	439UNTS17	106322
Mali	WHO (World Health)	27 Apr 61	407UNTS66	105860
Gabon	WHO (World Health)	27 Apr 61	397UNTS215	105707
Taiwan	Uruguay	03 May 61	596UNTS121	108630
Somalia	USSR (Soviet Union)	02 Jun 61	528UNTS147	107638
Czechoslovakia	Somalia	04 Jun 61	479UNTS291	106960
Nepal	USA (United States)	09 Jun 61	421UNTS223	106061
Ethiopia	United Nations	14 Jun 61	406UNTS81	105840
Morocco	WHO (World Health)	09 Aug 61	412UNTS192	105932
Pakistan	Philippines	15 Aug 61	522UNTS35	107534
WHO (World Health)	Somalia	17 Aug 61	423UNTS111	106088
Taiwan	Paraguay	18 Aug 61	438UNTS109	106314
Mexico	United Nations	18 Aug 61	404UNTS297	105817
Iraq	WHO (World Health)	13 Sep 61	419UNTS69	106030
Multilateral		20 Sep 61	407UNTS52	105859
Ghana	Romania	30 Sep 61	457UNTS3	106573
Japan	United Nations	04 Oct 61	410UNTS133	105900
Malagasy	WHO (World Health)	13 Oct 61	421UNTS273	106064
Multilateral		16 Oct 61	410UNTS242	105908
Taiwan	Jordan	17 Oct 61	435UNTS267	106284
Brazil	Poland	19 Oct 61	552UNTS75	108050
Multilateral		07 Nov 61	412UNTS258	105937
United Arab Rep	UK Great Britain	14 Nov 61	449UNTS129	106455
Taiwan	El Salvador	27 Nov 61	437UNTS161	106306
Ethiopia	USA (United States)	06 Dec 61	433UNTS231	106246
Multilateral		27 Dec 61	425UNTS83	106120
Ethiopia	WHO (World Health)	11 Jan 62	423UNTS99	106087
Multilateral		17 Jan 62	419UNTS294	106033
Cyprus	USA (United States)	18 Jan 62	435UNTS3	106266
Multilateral		20 Jan 62	429UNTS230	200596
Ghana	USA (United States)	24 Jan 62	435UNTS23	106268
Multilateral		13 Feb 62	422UNTS288	200594
Multilateral		21 Feb 62	423UNTS151	106091
Multilateral		01 Mar 62	423UNTS122	106089
USA (United States)	USSR (Soviet Union)	08 Mar 62	460UNTS3	106630
WHO (World Health)	Sudan	11 Mar 62	432UNTS325	106226
Nigeria	WHO (World Health)	27 Mar 62	429UNTS123	106194
Hungary	India	30 Mar 62	519UNTS119	107504
Multilateral		10 Apr 62	429UNTS78	106192
Multilateral		18 Apr 62	463UNTS44	106692
Multilateral		17 May 62	429UNTS46	106189
Denmark	USA (United States)	28 May 62	450UNTS215	106469
Senegal	USSR (Soviet Union)	14 Jun 62	437UNTS233	106309

PARTY ONE	PARTY TWO	DATE	CITATION	NUMBER
Exchange (Cont.)				
Libya	WHO (World Health)	16 Jun 62	437UNTS127	106301
WHO (World Health)	Sierra Leone	19 Jun 62	439UNTS151	106327
Israel	USA (United States)	22 Jun 62	448UNTS273	106440
WHO (World Health)	Senegal	06 Aug 62	435UNTS179	106279
Multilateral		12 Aug 62	443UNTS266	106365
WHO (World Health)	Western Samoa	14 Aug 62	437UNTS317	200598
Syria	USSR (Soviet Union)	19 Aug 62	457UNTS285	106588
Multilateral		29 Aug 62	443UNTS280	106366
Denmark	USSR (Soviet Union)	11 Sep 62	458UNTS3	106589
Cameroon	Israel	24 Oct 62	449UNTS3	106446
Multilateral		15 Nov 62	448UNTS50	106424
WHO (World Health)	Syria	18 Nov 62	480UNTS249	106972
Germany, West	USA (United States)	20 Nov 62	505UNTS263	107377
Multilateral		06 Dec 62	450UNTS240	106471
Cameroon	WHO (World Health)	08 Dec 62	451UNTS215	106496
Multilateral		12 Dec 62	457UNTS72	106578
Algeria	WHO (World Health)	20 Dec 62	463UNTS135	106698
Belgium	Tunisia	21 Dec 62	482UNTS3	106987
Multilateral		21 Jan 63	453UNTS20	106517
Iraq	USA (United States)	23 Jan 63	488UNTS163	107126
Malaysia	USA (United States)	28 Jan 63	473UNTS15	106850
Multilateral		05 Feb 63	453UNTS36	106518
Multilateral		14 Feb 63	453UNTS168	106524
Multilateral		06 Mar 63	455UNTS386	106552
Dahomey	USSR (Soviet Union)	20 Mar 63	528UNTS181	107641
Philippines	USA (United States)	23 Mar 63	474UNTS80	106873
Hungary	Korea, North	29 Mar 63	577UNTS219	108379
Romania	USA (United States)	02 Apr 63	474UNTS95	106874
Czechoslovakia	Tunisia	06 Apr 63	555UNTS111	108106
Multilateral		18 Apr 63	463UNTS121	106697
Multilateral		06 May 63	463UNTS78	106694
Multilateral		09 May 63	463UNTS159	106700
Australia	United Nations	13 May 63	463UNTS187	106702
Belgium	Venezuela	15 May 63	470UNTS259	106812
Multilateral		22 May 63	483UNTS72	107007
Thailand	USA (United States)	24 May 63	477UNTS123	106918
Multilateral		24 May 63	466UNTS346	106754
Korea, South	USA (United States)	18 Jun 63	487UNTS297	107112
India	USA (United States)	19 Jun 63	479UNTS175	106952
Mongolia	WHO (World Health)	21 Jun 63	472UNTS373	106848
Austria	USA (United States)	25 Jun 63	479UNTS223	106956
IBRD (World Bank)	Tunisia	03 Jul 63	480UNTS209	106970
Multilateral		23 Jul 63	471UNTS158	106831
Multilateral		31 Jul 63	472UNTS220	106842
Burundi	WHO (World Health)	08 Aug 63	477UNTS346	106928
Cameroon	UK Great Britain	20 Aug 63	539UNTS233	107834
Paraguay	USA (United States)	20 Aug 63	531UNTS197	107704
Afghanistan	USA (United States)	20 Aug 63	488UNTS41	107118
Argentina	USA (United States)	21 Aug 63	488UNTS61	107119
Multilateral		27 Aug 63	511UNTS210	107435
Colombia	United Nations	27 Aug 63	481UNTS3	106975
Multilateral		10 Sep 63	480UNTS100	106965
Ecuador	USA (United States)	20 Sep 63	488UNTS147	107125
Mali	Romania	26 Sep 63	528UNTS193	107642
Czechoslovakia	Yugoslavia	05 Oct 63	504UNTS151	107356
Hungary	Yugoslavia	15 Oct 63	577UNTS49	108372
Iran	USA (United States)	24 Oct 63	489UNTS303	107146
Multilateral		30 Oct 63	480UNTS180	106968
WHO (World Health)	Tanganyika	05 Nov 63	496UNTS193	107252
Tanganyika	USSR (Soviet Union)	06 Nov 63	528UNTS157	107639
Multilateral		07 Nov 63	480UNTS232	106971
Multilateral		08 Nov 63	482UNTS286	106999
Belgium	Romania	13 Nov 63	520UNTS119	107513
Belgium	Pakistan	14 Nov 63	535UNTS393	107792
Tunisia	USA (United States)	18 Nov 63	494UNTS193	107233

PARTY ONE	PARTY TWO	DATE	CITATION	NUMBER
Exchange (Cont.)				
Greece	USA (United States)	13 Dec 63	494UNTS55	107226
Multilateral		28 Jan 64	502UNTS321	107336
Netherlands	Tunisia	11 Feb 64	570UNTS173	108293
Iceland	USA (United States)	13 Feb 64	524UNTS235	107576
Multilateral		20 Feb 64	491UNTS30	107172
USA (United States)	USSR (Soviet Union)	22 Feb 64	526UNTS131	107605
UNESCO (Educ/Cult)	Yugoslavia	27 Feb 64	489UNTS257	107143
Spain	USA (United States)	18 Mar 64	535UNTS343	107789
Ireland	Norway	02 Apr 64	553UNTS129	108078
Mexico	Netherlands	08 Apr 64	575UNTS35	108353
Taiwan	USA (United States)	23 Apr 64	524UNTS141	107570
Afghanistan	United Nations	28 Apr 64	494UNTS77	107227
Liberia	USA (United States)	08 May 64	526UNTS239	107608
Algeria	Czechoslovakia	14 May 64	538UNTS301	107817
Cuba	Czechoslovakia	03 Jun 64	527UNTS205	107626
Rwanda	WHO (World Health)	22 Jun 64	514UNTS11	107440
Multilateral		23 Jun 64	506UNTS108	107383
Rwanda	WHO (World Health)	23 Jun 64	514UNTS157	107445
WHO (World Health)	Trinidad/Tobago	23 Jun 64	503UNTS167	107342
Denmark	Kenya	26 Jun 64	573UNTS107	108325
Multilateral		28 Jun 64	519UNTS14	107499
United Nations	Togo	03 Jul 64	502UNTS287	107334
Australia	USA (United States)	28 Aug 64	510UNTS201	107415
Ceylon (Sri Lanka)	USA (United States)	29 Aug 64	531UNTS93	107695
Argentina	France	03 Oct 64	635UNTS155	109080
Germany, East	Poland	06 Oct 64	552UNTS89	108051
Czechoslovakia	Germany, East	06 Oct 64	545UNTS113	107927
Czechoslovakia	Mongolia	21 Oct 64	545UNTS91	107926
Multilateral		24 Oct 64	514UNTS220	200608
Philippines	IBRD (World Bank)	28 Oct 64	537UNTS165	107801
USA (United States)	Yugoslavia	09 Nov 64	533UNTS39	107731
Multilateral		11 Nov 64	515UNTS94	107456
Belgium	Mexico	19 Nov 64	546UNTS217	107949
Argentina	Panama	21 Nov 64	635UNTS205	109083
Argentina	Costa Rica	23 Nov 64	635UNTS213	109084
Czechoslovakia	United Arab Rep	26 Nov 64	545UNTS11	107923
Netherlands	Nigeria	04 Dec 64	545UNTS155	107931
Malawi	WHO (World Health)	06 Jan 65	525UNTS165	107588
Malawi	WHO (World Health)	08 Jan 65	524UNTS281	107579
Belgium	Sweden	11 Jan 65	533UNTS157	107741
Multilateral		27 Jan 65	523UNTS102	107556
Peru	USA (United States)	28 Jan 65	587UNTS273	108513
Multilateral		02 Feb 65	523UNTS256	107560
Belgium	Hungary	11 Feb 65	544UNTS3	107908
Multilateral		12 Feb 65	525UNTS148	107587
UK Great Britain	USSR (Soviet Union)	13 Feb 65	543UNTS43	107896
Benelux Econ Union	Poland	17 Feb 65	547UNTS165	107956
France	USA (United States)	07 May 65	573UNTS183	108331
UK Great Britain	USA (United States)	10 May 65	545UNTS181	107934
USA (United States)	Uruguay	17 May 65	564UNTS69	108221
Bulgaria	Czechoslovakia	22 May 65	545UNTS65	107925
Ethiopia	Hungary	25 May 65	577UNTS193	108377
China People's Rep	Romania	27 May 65	592UNTS3	108566
Multilateral		02 Jun 65	537UNTS348	200611
Pakistan	USSR (Soviet Union)	05 Jun 65	593UNTS115	108579
Uganda	USSR (Soviet Union)	24 Jul 65	596UNTS199	108633
Poland	WHO (World Health)	26 Aug 65	552UNTS3	108047
Multilateral		13 Sep 65	547UNTS264	107962
Multilateral		21 Oct 65	547UNTS216	107959
Argentina	Belgium	05 Nov 65	635UNTS229	109086
Brazil	El Salvador	30 Nov 65	0UNTS0	109430
Italy	USA (United States)	12 Jan 66	587UNTS309	108515
United Nations	Senegal	12 Jan 66	551UNTS147	108039
Czechoslovakia	Poland	22 Jan 66	588UNTS175	108524
Brazil	Denmark	25 Feb 66	590UNTS95	108549

PARTY ONE	PARTY TWO	DATE	CITATION	NUMBER
Exchange (Cont.)				
Argentina	Germany, West	01 Mar 66	635UNTS247	109087
WHO (World Health)	Singapore	28 Mar 66	562UNTS59	108195
Romania	Tunisia	21 Apr 66	604UNTS65	108744
Romania	Tunisia	21 Apr 66	604UNTS57	108743
Rwanda	USSR (Soviet Union)	06 May 66	633UNTS217	109039
Denmark	Iran	14 Jun 66	597UNTS283	108652
Ivory Coast	Netherlands	01 Aug 66	591UNTS245	108561
Iran	USSR (Soviet Union)	22 Aug 66	643UNTS203	109192
Romania	United Arab Rep	03 Sep 66	604UNTS73	108745
Jamaica	IBRD (World Bank)	30 Sep 66	582UNTS179	108463
Bulgaria	Poland	03 Oct 66	618UNTS3	108921
Brazil	Netherlands	12 Oct 66	643UNTS271	109197
IAEA (Atom Energy)	Turkey	08 Dec 66	608UNTS69	108813
Argentina	Bolivia	19 Dec 66	636UNTS83	109093
Finland	United Nations	16 Jan 67	588UNTS153	108522
Israel	Philippines	20 Feb 67	597UNTS139	108642
Belgium	Luxembourg	22 Feb 67	639UNTS3	109140
Romania	UK Great Britain	09 Mar 67	605UNTS195	108764
Belgium	Israel	23 Mar 67	630UNTS275	108974
Kuwait	USSR (Soviet Union)	27 Mar 67	643UNTS135	109189
Czechoslovakia	Poland	26 Apr 67	610UNTS0	108832
Belgium	Bulgaria	17 May 67	631UNTS215	108995
Italy	Romania	08 Aug 67	642UNTS191	109174
Denmark	Romania	29 Aug 67	642UNTS357	109183
Denmark	Thailand	16 Oct 68	0UNTS0	109463
IAEA (Atom Energy)	OAU (Afri Unity)	26 Mar 69	0UNTS0	200646
Commissions and foundations				
Paraguay	USA (United States)	22 May 42	124UNTS243	200423
Peru	USA (United States)	15 Apr 44	150UNTS317	200479
Dominican Republic	USA (United States)	13 Oct 45	149UNTS361	200477
Multilateral		16 Nov 45	4UNTS275	100052
Czechoslovakia	France	08 Dec 45	46UNTS77	100701
Poland	Yugoslavia	16 Mar 46	10UNTS11	100139
Belgium	UK Great Britain	17 Apr 46	6UNTS177	100075
Belgium	Netherlands	16 May 46	17UNTS13	100266
Taiwan	USA (United States)	30 Aug 46	12UNTS39	100179
France	Netherlands	19 Nov 46	32UNTS101	100493
Burma	USA (United States)	28 Feb 47	25UNTS27	100355
Austria	France	15 Mar 47	12UNTS109	100182
Czechoslovakia	Yugoslavia	27 Apr 47	33UNTS49	100514
France	Poland	19 May 47	12UNTS95	100181
Czechoslovakia	UK Great Britain	16 Jun 47	46UNTS61	100700
Bulgaria	Poland	28 Jun 47	15UNTS123	100230
Albania	Yugoslavia	09 Jul 47	33UNTS91	100516
Czechoslovakia	Romania	05 Sep 47	46UNTS37	100699
Hungary	Yugoslavia	15 Oct 47	33UNTS73	100515
Ecuador	USA (United States)	14 Nov 47	149UNTS297	101959
Guatemala	USA (United States)	05 Jan 48	135UNTS104	101817
Hungary	Poland	31 Jan 48	25UNTS283	100368
Norway	UK Great Britain	19 Feb 48	34UNTS33	100526
Belgium	Norway	20 Feb 48	32UNTS39	100487
Paraguay	USA (United States)	12 Mar 48	162UNTS30	102131
Philippines	USA (United States)	23 Mar 48	43UNTS247	100671
Greece	USA (United States)	23 Apr 48	74UNTS107	100958
New Zealand	USA (United States)	14 Sep 48	18UNTS251	100295
UK Great Britain	USA (United States)	22 Sep 48	71UNTS64	100910
Multilateral		08 Oct 48	19UNTS113	100308
Belgium	Italy	29 Nov 48	41UNTS3	100641
Italy	USA (United States)	18 Dec 48	79UNTS133	101037
Netherlands	USA (United States)	17 May 49	46UNTS291	100717
Norway	USA (United States)	25 May 49	32UNTS345	100507
Iran	USA (United States)	01 Sep 49	79UNTS155	101039
United Arab Rep	USA (United States)	03 Nov 49	71UNTS31	100908
Australia	USA (United States)	26 Nov 49	45UNTS133	100695

PARTY ONE	PARTY TWO	DATE	CITATION	NUMBER
Commissions and foundations (Cont.)				
India	USA (United States)	02 Feb 50	89UNTS127	101214
Korea, South	USA (United States)	28 Apr 50	93UNTS21	101284
Austria	USA (United States)	06 Jun 50	92UNTS201	101273
Thailand	USA (United States)	01 Jul 50	81UNTS61	101063
Pakistan	USA (United States)	23 Sep 50	82UNTS131	101088
Nicaragua	USA (United States)	31 Jan 51	150UNTS3	101960
Dominican Republic	USA (United States)	16 Mar 51	148UNTS15	101932
Honduras	USA (United States)	24 Apr 51	140UNTS287	101894
Nicaragua	UK Great Britain	25 May 51	101UNTS77	101404
Iraq	USA (United States)	16 Aug 51	147UNTS65	101929
Denmark	USA (United States)	23 Aug 51	147UNTS49	101928
Japan	USA (United States)	28 Aug 51	147UNTS81	101930
South Africa	USA (United States)	26 Mar 52	165UNTS187	102176
Ethiopia	USA (United States)	15 May 52	180UNTS227	102388
Finland	USA (United States)	02 Jul 52	165UNTS203	102177
Germany, West	USA (United States)	18 Jul 52	165UNTS167	102175
Chile	WHO (World Health)	24 Oct 52	151UNTS339	102004
Ceylon (Sri Lanka)	USA (United States)	17 Nov 52	180UNTS207	102386
Sweden	USA (United States)	20 Nov 52	177UNTS203	102319
United Arab Rep	USA (United States)	18 Jun 53	204UNTS55	102749
Liberia	USA (United States)	23 Jun 53	213UNTS57	102880
Pakistan	United Arab Rep	14 Nov 53	485UNTS55	107046
Chile	USA (United States)	31 Mar 55	262UNTS19	103736
Israel	USA (United States)	26 Jun 56	257UNTS55	103649
Denmark	Italy	26 Oct 56	267UNTS261	103847
Ecuador	USA (United States)	31 Oct 56	283UNTS151	104114
Argentina	USA (United States)	05 Nov 56	277UNTS143	104004
Colombia	USA (United States)	09 Jan 57	462UNTS151	106676
Iceland	USA (United States)	23 Feb 57	283UNTS73	104107
Paraguay	USA (United States)	04 Apr 57	284UNTS161	104135
Brazil	USA (United States)	05 Nov 57	303UNTS3	104368
Japan	USA (United States)	11 Jan 58	304UNTS35	104390
Spain	USA (United States)	16 Oct 58	336UNTS153	104804
Bulgaria	Czechoslovakia	19 Sep 59	355UNTS77	105074
United Arab Rep	USA (United States)	28 Sep 59	358UNTS97	105128
Portugal	USA (United States)	19 Mar 60	371UNTS131	105275
USA (United States)	Uruguay	22 Jul 60	388UNTS315	105587
Multilateral		28 Jul 60	485UNTS3	107042
Nepal	USA (United States)	09 Jun 61	421UNTS223	106061
Ethiopia	USA (United States)	06 Dec 61	433UNTS231	106246
Cyprus	USA (United States)	18 Jan 62	435UNTS3	106266
Ghana	USA (United States)	24 Jan 62	435UNTS23	106268
USA (United States)	USSR (Soviet Union)	08 Mar 62	460UNTS3	106630
Multilateral		26 Mar 62	539UNTS67	107825
Denmark	USA (United States)	28 May 62	450UNTS215	106469
Israel	USA (United States)	22 Jun 62	448UNTS273	106440
Multilateral		22 Jun 62	494UNTS249	107237
Dominican Republic	USA (United States)	25 Oct 62	459UNTS247	106627
Germany, West	USA (United States)	20 Nov 62	505UNTS263	107377
Malaysia	USA (United States)	28 Jan 63	473UNTS15	106850
Philippines	USA (United States)	23 Mar 63	474UNTS80	106873
Thailand	USA (United States)	24 May 63	477UNTS123	106918
Korea, South	USA (United States)	18 Jun 63	487UNTS297	107112
India	USA (United States)	19 Jun 63	479UNTS175	106952
Austria	USA (United States)	25 Jun 63	479UNTS223	106956
Afghanistan	USA (United States)	20 Aug 63	488UNTS41	107118
Paraguay	USA (United States)	20 Aug 63	531UNTS197	107704
Argentina	USA (United States)	21 Aug 63	488UNTS61	107119
Ecuador	USA (United States)	20 Sep 63	488UNTS147	107125
Hungary	Yugoslavia	15 Oct 63	577UNTS49	108372
Greece	USA (United States)	13 Dec 63	494UNTS55	107226
Iceland	USA (United States)	13 Feb 64	524UNTS235	107576
USA (United States)	USSR (Soviet Union)	22 Feb 64	526UNTS131	107605
Taiwan	USA (United States)	23 Apr 64	524UNTS141	107570
Liberia	USA (United States)	08 May 64	526UNTS239	107608

PARTY ONE	PARTY TWO	DATE	CITATION	NUMBER
Commissions and foundations (Cont.)				
Australia	USA (United States)	28 Aug 64	510UNTS201	107415
Ceylon (Sri Lanka)	USA (United States)	29 Aug 64	531UNTS93	107695
USA (United States)	Yugoslavia	09 Nov 64	533UNTS39	107731
Peru	USA (United States)	28 Jan 65	587UNTS273	108513
UK Great Britain	USA (United States)	10 May 65	545UNTS181	107934
USA (United States)	Uruguay	17 May 65	564UNTS69	108221
East Afri Service	United Nations	27 Nov 65	550UNTS375	200616
Denmark	Iran	14 Jun 66	597UNTS283	108652
Multilateral		23 Sep 66	573UNTS132	108327
Netherlands	Romania	13 Feb 67	604UNTS287	108756
Poland	United Nations	20 Feb 67	590UNTS71	108547
Multilateral		07 Feb 68	0UNTS0	109513
Teacher and student exchange				
Brazil	Paraguay	14 Jun 41	54UNTS235	200196
Brazil	Chile	18 Nov 41	67UNTS279	200225
Canada	USA (United States)	04 Mar 42	124UNTS271	200426
Brazil	Venezuela	22 Oct 42	65UNTS203	200212
Brazil	Dominican Republic	09 Dec 42	65UNTS217	200213
Brazil	Ecuador	24 May 44	73UNTS223	200242
UK Great Britain	USA (United States)	16 Apr 45	6UNTS189	100076
Dominican Republic	USA (United States)	13 Oct 45	149UNTS361	200477
Multilateral		16 Nov 45	4UNTS275	100052
Czechoslovakia	France	08 Dec 45	46UNTS77	100701
Belgium	France	22 Feb 46	68UNTS157	100892
Poland	Yugoslavia	16 Mar 46	10UNTS11	100139
Brazil	USA (United States)	05 Apr 46	12UNTS131	100183
Belgium	UK Great Britain	17 Apr 46	6UNTS177	100075
Belgium	Netherlands	16 May 46	17UNTS13	100266
Canada	UK Great Britain	05 Jun 46	27UNTS207	100408
Australia	UK Great Britain	29 Oct 46	17UNTS181	100276
France	Netherlands	19 Nov 46	32UNTS101	100493
France	USA (United States)	10 Dec 46	15UNTS265	100242
South Africa	USA (United States)	13 Dec 46	167UNTS171	102207
Belgium	Czechoslovakia	06 Mar 47	34UNTS77	100528
Austria	France	15 Mar 47	12UNTS109	100182
Czechoslovakia	Yugoslavia	27 Apr 47	33UNTS49	100514
France	Poland	19 May 47	12UNTS95	100181
Czechoslovakia	UK Great Britain	16 Jun 47	46UNTS61	100700
Bulgaria	Czechoslovakia	20 Jun 47	46UNTS15	100698
Romania	Yugoslavia	26 Jun 47	116UNTS39	101568
Bulgaria	Poland	28 Jun 47	15UNTS123	100230
Czechoslovakia	Poland	04 Jul 47	25UNTS249	100366
Albania	Yugoslavia	09 Jul 47	33UNTS91	100516
Czechoslovakia	Romania	05 Sep 47	46UNTS37	100699
Hungary	Yugoslavia	15 Oct 47	33UNTS73	100515
Ecuador	USA (United States)	14 Nov 47	149UNTS297	101959
USSR (Soviet Union)	Yugoslavia	15 Dec 47	116UNTS313	101578
Colombia	USA (United States)	22 Dec 47	51UNTS45	100751
France	Netherlands	02 Jan 48	70UNTS105	100899
Hungary	Poland	31 Jan 48	25UNTS283	100368
Norway	UK Great Britain	19 Feb 48	34UNTS33	100526
Belgium	Norway	20 Feb 48	32UNTS39	100487
Poland	Romania	27 Feb 48	46UNTS143	100707
France	UK Great Britain	02 Mar 48	77UNTS33	100990
Canada	New Zealand	12 Mar 48	231UNTS219	103222
Paraguay	USA (United States)	12 Mar 48	162UNTS30	102131
New Zealand	USA (United States)	16 Mar 48	127UNTS133	101703
Philippines	USA (United States)	23 Mar 48	43UNTS247	100671
Belgium	Luxembourg	27 Mar 48	178UNTS265	102343
Netherlands	USA (United States)	29 Apr 48	32UNTS167	100498
Denmark	USA (United States)	06 May 48	26UNTS55	100377
Hungary	Poland	18 Jun 48	25UNTS319	100370
Netherlands	UK Great Britain	07 Jul 48	82UNTS259	101099
New Zealand	USA (United States)	14 Sep 48	18UNTS251	100295

PARTY ONE	PARTY TWO	DATE	CITATION	NUMBER
Teacher and student exchange (Cont.)				
UK Great Britain	USA (United States)	22 Sep 48	71UNTS64	100910
Multilateral		08 Oct 48	19UNTS113	100308
Belgium	USA (United States)	28 Oct 48	173UNTS67	102262
Belgium	Italy	29 Nov 48	41UNTS3	100641
Italy	USA (United States)	18 Dec 48	79UNTS133	101037
Sweden	UK Great Britain	30 Mar 49	209UNTS129	102826
Luxembourg	Netherlands	26 Apr 49	182UNTS187	102425
Netherlands	USA (United States)	17 May 49	46UNTS291	100717
Greece	Lebanon	10 Jun 49	178UNTS29	102334
Norway	USA (United States)	13 Jun 49	127UNTS189	101705
Ireland	USA (United States)	13 Sep 49	127UNTS89	101701
United Arab Rep	USA (United States)	03 Nov 49	71UNTS31	100908
France	Netherlands	30 Dec 49	203UNTS85	102742
India	USA (United States)	02 Feb 50	89UNTS127	101214
Greece	USA (United States)	20 Feb 50	196UNTS291	102630
Burma	UK Great Britain	13 Mar 50	131UNTS53	101735
Denmark	UK Great Britain	27 Mar 50	68UNTS117	100891
Korea, South	USA (United States)	28 Apr 50	93UNTS21	101284
Austria	USA (United States)	06 Jun 50	92UNTS201	101273
Canada	USA (United States)	12 Jun 50	127UNTS67	101700
Luxembourg	UK Great Britain	27 Jun 50	183UNTS217	102431
Thailand	USA (United States)	01 Jul 50	81UNTS61	101063
Ceylon (Sri Lanka)	UK Great Britain	26 Jul 50	337UNTS77	104818
Pakistan	USA (United States)	23 Sep 50	82UNTS131	101088
Czechoslovakia	Poland	17 Nov 50	530UNTS195	107682
Albania	Poland	02 Dec 50	260UNTS131	103707
Netherlands	Norway	29 Dec 50	134UNTS19	101795
Nicaragua	USA (United States)	31 Jan 51	150UNTS3	101960
Canada	France	16 Mar 51	236UNTS267	103330
Canada	Sweden	06 Apr 51	197UNTS393	102648
Greece	Turkey	20 Apr 51	178UNTS17	102333
Honduras	USA (United States)	24 Apr 51	140UNTS287	101894
Norway	UK Great Britain	02 May 51	106UNTS101	101460
Switzerland	USA (United States)	24 May 51	127UNTS227	101706
Netherlands	South Africa	31 May 51	188UNTS289	102533
India	Turkey	29 Jun 51	213UNTS183	102886
Burma	WHO (World Health)	09 Jul 51	104UNTS187	101440
Iraq	USA (United States)	16 Aug 51	147UNTS65	101929
Denmark	USA (United States)	23 Aug 51	147UNTS49	101928
Japan	USA (United States)	28 Aug 51	147UNTS81	101930
Greece	UK Great Britain	29 Sep 51	190UNTS260	102570
Italy	UK Great Britain	28 Nov 51	172UNTS27	102238
Italy	Netherlands	05 Dec 51	0UNTS0	109323
Finland	UK Great Britain	12 Dec 51	172UNTS45	102239
Colombia	USA (United States)	12 Jan 52	168UNTS109	102216
Belgium	Germany, West	18 Jan 52	124UNTS9	101663
Peru	USA (United States)	04 Feb 52	121UNTS255	200403
Finland	USA (United States)	03 Mar 52	177UNTS163	102317
South Africa	USA (United States)	26 Mar 52	165UNTS187	102176
Netherlands	Sweden	25 Apr 52	163UNTS131	102147
Germany, West	USA (United States)	18 Jul 52	165UNTS167	102175
Austria	Belgium	17 Oct 52	162UNTS183	102135
Chile	WHO (World Health)	24 Oct 52	151UNTS339	102004
Chile	WHO (World Health)	04 Nov 52	150UNTS119	101966
Ceylon (Sri Lanka)	USA (United States)	17 Nov 52	180UNTS207	102386
Austria	UK Great Britain	12 Dec 52	172UNTS9	102237
Saudi Arabia	USA (United States)	25 Jan 53	201UNTS3	102706
Bolivia	Italy	31 Jan 53	281UNTS181	104079
Germany, West	USA (United States)	09 Apr 53	204UNTS79	102750
Greece	Netherlands	29 Apr 53	191UNTS235	102583
Ethiopia	USA (United States)	29 Apr 53	224UNTS121	103073
Israel	Uruguay	30 Apr 53	280UNTS269	104064
Australia	USA (United States)	14 May 53	205UNTS253	102779
United Arab Rep	USA (United States)	18 Jun 53	204UNTS55	102749
Liberia	USA (United States)	23 Jun 53	213UNTS57	102880

PARTY ONE	PARTY TWO	DATE	CITATION	NUMBER
Teacher and student exchange (Cont.)				
Greece	UK Great Britain	25 Jun 53	190UNTS281	102571
Pakistan	Turkey	29 Jun 53	211UNTS225	102854
Denmark	Sweden	27 Oct 53	198UNTS71	102658
Pakistan	United Arab Rep	14 Nov 53	485UNTS55	107046
Belgium	Finland	11 Feb 54	211UNTS63	102848
Finland	Netherlands	29 Mar 54	252UNTS185	103567
Japan	USA (United States)	16 Apr 54	238UNTS39	103354
Belgium	South Africa	01 Jun 54	201UNTS25	102708
Germany, West	USA (United States)	22 Jul 54	239UNTS3	103369
Austria	Denmark	07 Sep 54	201UNTS39	102709
Greece	Italy	11 Sep 54	284UNTS313	104145
Switzerland	UK Great Britain	30 Sep 54	209UNTS197	102828
Ethiopia	Sweden	13 Oct 54	202UNTS273	102734
Germany, West	UK Great Britain	18 Oct 54	218UNTS301	102960
Canada	Ireland	28 Oct 54	304UNTS317	104406
France	Sweden	05 Nov 54	262UNTS229	103748
Portugal	UK Great Britain	19 Nov 54	226UNTS305	103125
Belgium	Greece	09 Dec 54	257UNTS243	103660
Italy	USA (United States)	30 Mar 55	257UNTS169	103654
Chile	USA (United States)	31 Mar 55	262UNTS19	103736
Ceylon (Sri Lanka)	Germany, West	01 Apr 55	369UNTS57	105251
Japan	Thailand	06 Apr 55	230UNTS219	103187
Czechoslovakia	Hungary	28 Apr 55	477UNTS197	106923
Netherlands	Norway	18 May 55	252UNTS269	103569
Pakistan	Sweden	04 Jun 55	228UNTS121	103146
South Africa	Sweden	28 Jul 55	230UNTS287	103191
Belgium	Portugal	30 Jul 55	250UNTS213	103525
Italy	Spain	11 Aug 55	267UNTS125	103839
Czechoslovakia	Germany, East	30 Aug 55	504UNTS279	107361
Canada	Denmark	30 Sep 55	258UNTS115	103675
Burma	Yugoslavia	07 Mar 56	386UNTS235	105543
Iran	Pakistan	09 Mar 56	449UNTS183	106460
Turkey	UK Great Britain	12 Mar 56	313UNTS73	104530
Romania	USSR (Soviet Union)	07 Apr 56	259UNTS377	103698
New Zealand	Sweden	16 Apr 56	274UNTS259	103971
Mongolia	USSR (Soviet Union)	24 Apr 56	259UNTS297	103693
Germany, East	USSR (Soviet Union)	26 Apr 56	259UNTS279	103692
Bulgaria	USSR (Soviet Union)	28 Apr 56	259UNTS363	103697
Albania	USSR (Soviet Union)	03 May 56	259UNTS391	103699
Peru	USA (United States)	03 May 56	272UNTS59	103931
Mongolia	Romania	08 May 56	342UNTS291	104913
Korea, North	Poland	11 May 56	432UNTS161	106219
Korea, North	Romania	12 May 56	342UNTS189	104908
USSR (Soviet Union)	Yugoslavia	17 May 56	259UNTS145	103687
Fed Rhod/Nyasaland	South Africa	22 May 56	254UNTS227	103595
Czechoslovakia	USSR (Soviet Union)	01 Jun 56	259UNTS341	103696
Canada	Germany, West	04 Jun 56	316UNTS231	104589
Honduras	USA (United States)	25 Jun 56	279UNTS113	104036
Israel	USA (United States)	26 Jun 56	257UNTS55	103649
Poland	USSR (Soviet Union)	30 Jun 56	259UNTS311	103694
Burma	USA (United States)	30 Jun 56	281UNTS65	104070
China People's Rep	USSR (Soviet Union)	05 Jul 56	263UNTS129	103770
Poland	Yugoslavia	06 Jul 56	281UNTS143	104076
Austria	UK Great Britain	20 Jul 56	269UNTS147	103880
Austria	Sweden	14 Aug 56	262UNTS355	103760
Greece	United Arab Rep	04 Sep 56	299UNTS253	104317
Korea, North	USSR (Soviet Union)	05 Sep 56	259UNTS329	103695
Belgium	Germany, West	24 Sep 56	263UNTS31	103766
Canada	South Africa	28 Sep 56	299UNTS17	104304
Austria	USA (United States)	25 Oct 56	299UNTS123	104310
Denmark	Italy	26 Oct 56	267UNTS261	103847
India	Japan	29 Oct 56	318UNTS289	104622
Ecuador	USA (United States)	31 Oct 56	283UNTS151	104114
Argentina	USA (United States)	05 Nov 56	277UNTS143	104004
Germany, East	Romania	08 Dec 56	362UNTS189	105188

Teacher and student exchange (Cont.)

PARTY ONE	PARTY TWO	DATE	CITATION	NUMBER
Japan	Sweden	12 Dec 56	318UNTS309	104623
Multilateral		15 Dec 56	278UNTS73	104023
Italy	Sweden	20 Dec 56	369UNTS357	105265
Italy	Netherlands	24 Jan 57	485UNTS67	107047
Czechoslovakia	Yugoslavia	29 Jan 57	300UNTS249	104339
Poland	United Arab Rep	02 Feb 57	319UNTS221	104633
Belgium	Yugoslavia	05 Feb 57	276UNTS143	103990
Taiwan	Turkey	12 Feb 57	282UNTS125	104097
USSR (Soviet Union)	Vietnam, North	15 Feb 57	274UNTS115	103962
Denmark	Netherlands	20 Feb 57	287UNTS41	104179
Denmark	Norway	22 Feb 57	286UNTS127	104164
Multilateral		22 Feb 57	274UNTS93	103960
Iceland	USA (United States)	23 Feb 57	283UNTS73	104107
Japan	United Arab Rep	20 Mar 57	318UNTS345	104625
Paraguay	USA (United States)	04 Apr 57	283UNTS193	104117
Paraguay	USA (United States)	04 Apr 57	284UNTS161	104135
Poland	Vietnam, North	06 Apr 57	432UNTS255	106224
Romania	United Arab Rep	15 Apr 57	389UNTS21	105589
Iran	Japan	16 Apr 57	325UNTS113	104697
India	Romania	30 Apr 57	342UNTS251	104911
Ceylon (Sri Lanka)	Sweden	18 May 57	315UNTS85	104561
Argentina	Israel	23 May 57	280UNTS199	104059
Japan	Pakistan	27 May 57	325UNTS21	104692
Bulgaria	Czechoslovakia	03 Jun 57	292UNTS3	104261
Czechoslovakia	Yugoslavia	11 Jun 57	504UNTS107	107355
Czechoslovakia	Syria	18 Jun 57	303UNTS119	104374
Australia	FAO (Food Agri)	08 Jul 57	277UNTS315	104015
Australia	Canada	01 Oct 57	392UNTS41	105638
United Arab Rep	USSR (Soviet Union)	19 Oct 57	292UNTS151	104271
Czechoslovakia	United Arab Rep	19 Oct 57	530UNTS181	107681
Brazil	USA (United States)	05 Nov 57	303UNTS3	104368
Taiwan	Iran	11 Nov 57	563UNTS31	108202
Germany, East	Hungary	13 Nov 57	407UNTS216	105866
Hungary	Romania	17 Dec 57	477UNTS303	106926
Belgium	Denmark	31 Dec 57	305UNTS247	104422
Norway	Turkey	10 Jan 58	351UNTS229	105025
Japan	USA (United States)	11 Jan 58	304UNTS35	104390
USA (United States)	USSR (Soviet Union)	27 Jan 58	301UNTS405	104350
Czechoslovakia	Romania	25 Mar 58	339UNTS77	104846
Taiwan	Costa Rica	10 Apr 58	315UNTS165	104567
Germany, West	UK Great Britain	18 Apr 58	343UNTS241	104928
Hungary	Poland	08 May 58	408UNTS212	105872
Afghanistan	USA (United States)	26 Jun 58	321UNTS67	104654
Germany, East	Romania	15 Jul 58	387UNTS115	105560
Denmark	Sweden	21 Jul 58	320UNTS163	104642
Sweden	United Arab Rep	29 Jul 58	369UNTS323	105264
India	Sweden	30 Jul 58	369UNTS211	105259
Pakistan	Sweden	25 Aug 58	369UNTS183	105258
Czechoslovakia	Romania	25 Oct 58	338UNTS301	104843
El Salvador	Israel	14 Nov 58	345UNTS67	104959
Germany, West	Norway	18 Nov 58	357UNTS205	105119
Iran	Japan	09 Dec 58	325UNTS221	104701
Mongolia	Poland	23 Dec 58	432UNTS177	106220
Belgium	Turkey	29 Dec 58	357UNTS195	105118
Japan	Pakistan	17 Feb 59	341UNTS127	104880
Japan	Norway	21 Feb 59	356UNTS231	105098
Denmark	Japan	10 Mar 59	341UNTS55	104878
Canada	Finland	28 Mar 59	355UNTS3	105072
Bulgaria	Hungary	03 Apr 59	438UNTS269	106319
Hungary	Iraq	11 Apr 59	439UNTS25	106323
Germany, West	Sweden	17 Apr 59	428UNTS155	106175
Hungary	USSR (Soviet Union)	17 Apr 59	439UNTS41	106324
Iraq	USSR (Soviet Union)	05 May 59	356UNTS179	105095
Iran	UK Great Britain	06 May 59	398UNTS51	105717
Austria	Sweden	14 May 59	428UNTS3	106167

Teacher and student exchange (Cont.)

PARTY ONE	PARTY TWO	DATE	CITATION	NUMBER
Iran	Netherlands	22 May 59	474UNTS195	106882
Finland	Hungary	10 Jun 59	439UNTS3	106321
Taiwan	Ecuador	12 Jun 59	387UNTS3	105554
Israel	Mexico	15 Jun 59	377UNTS267	105406
Germany, West	Netherlands	16 Jun 59	593UNTS3	108576
South Africa	UK Great Britain	18 Jun 59	380UNTS103	105452
South Africa	UK Great Britain	18 Jun 59	380UNTS59	105450
South Africa	UK Great Britain	18 Jun 59	380UNTS81	105451
Brazil	Israel	24 Jun 59	515UNTS151	107458
Czechoslovakia	India	07 Jul 59	359UNTS259	105145
India	Norway	20 Jul 59	356UNTS257	105099
Iraq	Romania	04 Aug 59	502UNTS17	107324
Bulgaria	Czechoslovakia	19 Sep 59	355UNTS77	105074
United Arab Rep	USA (United States)	28 Sep 59	358UNTS97	105128
Austria	France	08 Oct 59	453UNTS95	106521
Guinea	USA (United States)	28 Oct 59	358UNTS169	105134
USA (United States)	USSR (Soviet Union)	21 Nov 59	361UNTS35	105172
Czechoslovakia	Guinea	30 Nov 59	386UNTS63	105538
France	Israel	30 Nov 59	377UNTS237	105404
UK Great Britain	USSR (Soviet Union)	01 Dec 59	351UNTS313	105032
Multilateral		03 Dec 59	345UNTS251	104971
Czechoslovakia	Ethiopia	11 Dec 59	399UNTS93	105736
Multilateral		14 Dec 59	422UNTS57	106068
Multilateral		14 Dec 59	422UNTS33	106067
Germany, East	Hungary	19 Dec 59	409UNTS4	105874
Israel	Sweden	22 Dec 59	377UNTS277	105407
India	Japan	05 Jan 60	384UNTS3	105507
Belgium	Brazil	06 Jan 60	531UNTS149	107701
Italy	USSR (Soviet Union)	09 Feb 60	399UNTS75	105735
India	USSR (Soviet Union)	12 Feb 60	392UNTS153	105642
Austria	Norway	25 Feb 60	376UNTS155	105380
Taiwan	Panama	26 Feb 60	435UNTS281	106285
Indonesia	USSR (Soviet Union)	28 Feb 60	392UNTS191	105644
Portugal	USA (United States)	19 Mar 60	371UNTS131	105275
Australia	New Zealand	12 May 60	369UNTS119	105254
Netherlands	Turkey	12 May 60	463UNTS207	106704
Finland	USSR (Soviet Union)	27 May 60	379UNTS381	105444
Italy	UK Great Britain	04 Jul 60	466UNTS195	106745
Spain	UK Great Britain	12 Jul 60	414UNTS123	105971
USA (United States)	Uruguay	22 Jul 60	388UNTS315	105587
Sweden	UK Great Britain	28 Jul 60	404UNTS113	105808
Cuba	Korea, North	29 Aug 60	473UNTS117	106860
Czechoslovakia	Ghana	23 Nov 60	431UNTS91	106213
Israel	Mali	24 Nov 60	413UNTS104	105945
Cambodia	Czechoslovakia	27 Nov 60	410UNTS263	105910
Japan	UK Great Britain	03 Dec 60	414UNTS61	105966
Netherlands	United Arab Rep	08 Dec 60	455UNTS276	106547
Romania	USA (United States)	09 Dec 60	401UNTS19	105759
Cuba	Czechoslovakia	22 Dec 60	426UNTS145	106134
UK Great Britain	USSR (Soviet Union)	09 Jan 61	404UNTS175	105810
Ethiopia	USSR (Soviet Union)	13 Jan 61	421UNTS13	106049
Czechoslovakia	Hungary	24 Feb 61	422UNTS15	106066
Cuba	Poland	06 Mar 61	484UNTS123	107020
Cuba	Germany, East	29 Mar 61	448UNTS81	106426
Cuba	Czechoslovakia	05 Apr 61	442UNTS201	106350
Japan	UK Great Britain	11 Apr 61	420UNTS75	106042
India	Norway	19 Apr 61	404UNTS307	105818
Afghanistan	Czechoslovakia	23 Apr 61	437UNTS25	106297
Taiwan	Nicaragua	25 Apr 61	423UNTS139	106090
Ghana	Hungary	27 Apr 61	439UNTS17	106322
Germany, West	Netherlands	27 Apr 61	487UNTS77	107095
Taiwan	Uruguay	03 May 61	596UNTS121	108630
Somalia	USSR (Soviet Union)	02 Jun 61	528UNTS147	107638
Finland	India	23 Jun 61	421UNTS49	106051
Netherlands	Euratom	25 Jul 61	462UNTS263	106686

Teacher and student exchange (Cont.)

PARTY ONE	PARTY TWO	DATE	CITATION	NUMBER
Pakistan	Philippines	15 Aug 61	522UNTS35	107534
Taiwan	Paraguay	18 Aug 61	438UNTS109	106314
Italy	Norway	25 Aug 61	475UNTS269	106896
Tunisia	USSR (Soviet Union)	30 Aug 61	437UNTS243	106310
Denmark	Pakistan	04 Sep 61	455UNTS305	106549
China People's Rep	Denmark	23 Sep 61	446UNTS3	106397
Ghana	Romania	30 Sep 61	457UNTS3	106573
Japan	United Nations	04 Oct 61	410UNTS133	105900
Greece	Sweden	06 Oct 61	481UNTS137	106981
Brazil	Poland	19 Oct 61	552UNTS75	108050
Sweden	Thailand	20 Oct 61	428UNTS275	106180
Austria	Denmark	23 Oct 61	425UNTS115	106122
United Arab Rep	UK Great Britain	14 Nov 61	449UNTS129	106455
Austria	Japan	20 Dec 61	517UNTS155	107485
Argentina	Japan	20 Dec 61	451UNTS77	106486
USA (United States)	USSR (Soviet Union)	08 Mar 62	460UNTS3	106630
Multilateral		26 Mar 62	539UNTS67	107825
Hungary	India	30 Mar 62	519UNTS119	107504
United Arab Rep	USA (United States)	21 May 62	458UNTS197	106601
South Africa	UK Great Britain	28 May 62	443UNTS79	106361
Senegal	USSR (Soviet Union)	14 Jun 62	437UNTS233	106309
Israel	USA (United States)	22 Jun 62	448UNTS273	106440
Israel	Liberia	25 Jun 62	448UNTS295	106442
Israel	Peru	25 Jun 62	515UNTS263	107464
Costa Rica	Israel	31 Jul 62	484UNTS155	107024
Syria	USSR (Soviet Union)	19 Aug 62	457UNTS285	106588
Japan	UK Great Britain	04 Sep 62	475UNTS31	106888
Denmark	USSR (Soviet Union)	11 Sep 62	458UNTS3	106589
Israel	UK Great Britain	26 Sep 62	474UNTS233	106885
India	USA (United States)	09 Oct 62	471UNTS39	106820
Austria	United Arab Rep	16 Oct 62	491UNTS63	107174
Austria	Luxembourg	18 Oct 62	496UNTS97	107248
Cameroon	Israel	24 Oct 62	449UNTS15	106447
Germany, West	USA (United States)	20 Nov 62	505UNTS263	107377
Luxembourg	USA (United States)	18 Dec 62	532UNTS277	107723
Belgium	Tunisia	21 Dec 62	482UNTS3	106987
UK Great Britain	USSR (Soviet Union)	21 Jan 63	475UNTS3	106887
Iraq	USA (United States)	23 Jan 63	488UNTS163	107126
Japan	New Zealand	30 Jan 63	517UNTS183	107486
Ceylon (Sri Lanka)	Denmark	16 Feb 63	486UNTS285	107083
Japan	Thailand	01 Mar 63	475UNTS233	106895
Dahomey	USSR (Soviet Union)	20 Mar 63	528UNTS181	107641
Philippines	USA (United States)	23 Mar 63	474UNTS80	106873
Romania	USA (United States)	02 Apr 63	474UNTS95	106874
Czechoslovakia	Tunisia	06 Apr 63	555UNTS111	108106
Norway	Spain	25 Apr 63	503UNTS41	107340
Philippines	USA (United States)	06 May 63	477UNTS67	106916
Belgium	Venezuela	15 May 63	470UNTS259	106812
Japan	Malaysia	04 Jun 63	517UNTS245	107488
Austria	USA (United States)	25 Jun 63	479UNTS223	106956
Paraguay	USA (United States)	20 Aug 63	531UNTS197	107704
Afghanistan	USA (United States)	20 Aug 63	488UNTS41	107118
Cameroon	UK Great Britain	20 Aug 63	539UNTS233	107834
France	Israel	20 Aug 63	515UNTS173	107460
Argentina	USA (United States)	21 Aug 63	488UNTS61	107119
France	Greece	21 Aug 63	533UNTS235	107746
Ecuador	USA (United States)	20 Sep 63	488UNTS147	107125
Austria	India	24 Sep 63	545UNTS199	107935
Czechoslovakia	Yugoslavia	05 Oct 63	504UNTS151	107356
Austria	Finland	08 Oct 63	490UNTS255	107160
Hungary	Yugoslavia	15 Oct 63	577UNTS49	108372
Multilateral		21 Oct 63	480UNTS197	106969
Iran	USA (United States)	24 Oct 63	489UNTS303	107146
Tanganyika	USSR (Soviet Union)	06 Nov 63	528UNTS157	107639
Belgium	Romania	13 Nov 63	520UNTS119	107513

Teacher and student exchange (Cont.)

PARTY ONE	PARTY TWO	DATE	CITATION	NUMBER
Belgium	Pakistan	14 Nov 63	535UNTS393	107792
Tunisia	USA (United States)	18 Nov 63	494UNTS193	107233
Belgium	Poland	09 Dec 63	514UNTS195	107448
Greece	USA (United States)	13 Dec 63	494UNTS55	107226
Norway	Thailand	09 Jan 64	522UNTS65	107537
Netherlands	Tunisia	11 Feb 64	570UNTS173	108293
Iceland	USA (United States)	13 Feb 64	524UNTS235	107576
USA (United States)	USSR (Soviet Union)	22 Feb 64	526UNTS131	107605
Multilateral		28 Feb 64	501UNTS245	107321
Belgium	France	10 Mar 64	557UNTS13	108127
Spain	USA (United States)	18 Mar 64	535UNTS343	107789
Germany, West	Thailand	02 Apr 64	503UNTS3	107338
Denmark	Finland	07 Apr 64	525UNTS89	107586
Mexico	Netherlands	08 Apr 64	575UNTS35	108353
Taiwan	USA (United States)	23 Apr 64	524UNTS141	107570
Liberia	USA (United States)	08 May 64	526UNTS239	107608
Algeria	Czechoslovakia	14 May 64	538UNTS301	107817
Australia	USA (United States)	28 Aug 64	510UNTS201	107415
Ceylon (Sri Lanka)	USA (United States)	29 Aug 64	531UNTS93	107695
Canada	Japan	05 Sep 64	569UNTS99	108282
Germany, East	Poland	06 Oct 64	552UNTS89	108051
Czechoslovakia	Germany, East	06 Oct 64	545UNTS113	107927
Norway	United Arab Rep	20 Oct 64	543UNTS3	107895
USA (United States)	Yugoslavia	09 Nov 64	533UNTS39	107731
Belgium	Mexico	19 Nov 64	546UNTS217	107949
Czechoslovakia	United Arab Rep	26 Nov 64	545UNTS11	107923
Poland	Romania	26 Nov 64	552UNTS157	108053
France	Japan	27 Nov 64	569UNTS157	108283
Netherlands	Nigeria	04 Dec 64	545UNTS155	107931
Belgium	Sweden	11 Jan 65	533UNTS157	107741
Finland	Israel	21 Jan 65	581UNTS275	108450
Peru	USA (United States)	28 Jan 65	587UNTS273	108513
Belgium	Hungary	11 Feb 65	544UNTS3	107908
UK Great Britain	USSR (Soviet Union)	13 Feb 65	543UNTS43	107896
Finland	United Arab Rep	01 Apr 65	562UNTS3	108193
Jamaica	UK Great Britain	02 Apr 65	552UNTS219	108056
France	USA (United States)	07 May 65	573UNTS183	108331
UK Great Britain	USA (United States)	10 May 65	545UNTS181	107934
USA (United States)	Uruguay	17 May 65	564UNTS69	108221
Bulgaria	Czechoslovakia	22 May 65	545UNTS65	107925
China People's Rep	Romania	27 May 65	592UNTS3	108566
Denmark	Thailand	01 Jun 65	551UNTS157	108040
Pakistan	USSR (Soviet Union)	05 Jun 65	593UNTS115	108579
Uganda	USSR (Soviet Union)	24 Jul 65	596UNTS199	108633
Israel	Sierra Leone	22 Aug 65	550UNTS275	108022
United Arab Rep	UK Great Britain	29 Sep 65	0UNTS0	109444
East Afri Service	United Nations	27 Nov 65	550UNTS375	200616
Brazil	El Salvador	30 Nov 65	0UNTS0	109430
Austria	Finland	09 Dec 65	0UNTS0	109462
UK Great Britain	Yugoslavia	27 Jan 66	573UNTS243	108337
France	Yugoslavia	08 Feb 66	0UNTS0	109503
Romania	Tunisia	21 Apr 66	604UNTS57	108743
Romania	Tunisia	21 Apr 66	604UNTS65	108744
Rwanda	USSR (Soviet Union)	06 May 66	633UNTS217	109039
Denmark	Israel	27 Jun 66	581UNTS227	108448
Netherlands	Yugoslavia	11 Aug 66	602UNTS243	108716
Hungary	Yugoslavia	26 Sep 66	601UNTS21	108685
Bulgaria	Poland	03 Oct 66	618UNTS3	108921
United Nations	Sudan	08 Nov 66	576UNTS85	108365
Kuwait	UK Great Britain	26 Nov 66	633UNTS58	109034
IAEA (Atom Energy)	Turkey	08 Dec 66	608UNTS69	108813
Denmark	France	15 Feb 67	604UNTS247	108754
UK Great Britain	USSR (Soviet Union)	24 Feb 67	606UNTS171	108785
Belgium	Israel	23 Mar 67	630UNTS275	108974
Czechoslovakia	Poland	26 Apr 67	610UNTS0	108832

PARTY ONE	PARTY TWO	DATE	CITATION	NUMBER
Teacher and student exchange (Cont.)				
Belgium	Canada	08 May 67	637UNTSO	109119
Czechoslovakia	Mongolia	31 Mar 68	OUNTSO	109279
Professorships				
Multilateral		22 Jun 33	78UNTS181	101016
Brazil	Paraguay	14 Jun 41	54UNTS235	200196
Brazil	Chile	18 Nov 41	67UNTS279	200225
Peru	USA (United States)	24 Aug 42	24UNTS153	200139
Peru	USA (United States)	15 Apr 44	150UNTS317	200479
Brazil	Ecuador	24 May 44	73UNTS223	200242
Czechoslovakia	France	08 Dec 45	46UNTS77	100701
Belgium	France	22 Feb 46	68UNTS157	100892
Poland	Yugoslavia	16 Mar 46	10UNTS11	100139
Belgium	Netherlands	16 May 46	17UNTS13	100266
France	Netherlands	19 Nov 46	32UNTS101	100493
France	USA (United States)	10 Dec 46	15UNTS265	100242
Austria	France	15 Mar 47	12UNTS109	100182
Czechoslovakia	Yugoslavia	27 Apr 47	33UNTS49	100514
France	Poland	19 May 47	12UNTS95	100181
Czechoslovakia	UK Great Britain	16 Jun 47	46UNTS61	100700
Bulgaria	Czechoslovakia	20 Jun 47	46UNTS15	100698
Romania	Yugoslavia	26 Jun 47	116UNTS39	101568
Bulgaria	Poland	28 Jun 47	15UNTS123	100230
Czechoslovakia	Poland	04 Jul 47	25UNTS249	100366
Albania	Yugoslavia	09 Jul 47	33UNTS91	100516
Czechoslovakia	Romania	05 Sep 47	46UNTS37	100699
Hungary	Yugoslavia	15 Oct 47	33UNTS73	100515
Ecuador	USA (United States)	14 Nov 47	149UNTS297	101959
Hungary	Poland	31 Jan 48	25UNTS283	100368
Norway	UK Great Britain	19 Feb 48	34UNTS33	100526
Belgium	Norway	20 Feb 48	32UNTS39	100487
Poland	Romania	27 Feb 48	46UNTS143	100707
Greece	USA (United States)	23 Apr 48	74UNTS107	100958
Netherlands	UK Great Britain	07 Jul 48	82UNTS259	101099
Belgium	Italy	29 Nov 48	41UNTS3	100641
Italy	USA (United States)	18 Dec 48	79UNTS133	101037
Greece	Lebanon	10 Jun 49	178UNTS29	102334
Bulgaria	Poland	26 Sep 49	260UNTS249	103712
Hungary	Poland	29 Oct 49	260UNTS113	103706
India	USA (United States)	02 Feb 50	89UNTS127	101214
Korea, South	USA (United States)	28 Apr 50	93UNTS21	101284
Austria	USA (United States)	06 Jun 50	92UNTS201	101273
Haiti	WHO (World Health)	21 Jun 50	103UNTS61	101424
Thailand	USA (United States)	01 Jul 50	81UNTS61	101063
Pakistan	USA (United States)	23 Sep 50	82UNTS131	101088
Multilateral		02 Nov 50	81UNTS160	101071
Multilateral		24 Nov 50	81UNTS188	101072
Albania	Poland	02 Dec 50	260UNTS131	103707
Multilateral		18 Jan 51	81UNTS233	101073
Ethiopia	ICAO (Civil Aviat)	02 Feb 51	96UNTS123	101333
Multilateral		15 Feb 51	81UNTS245	101074
Multilateral		05 Mar 51	81UNTS261	101075
China People's Rep	Poland	03 Apr 51	304UNTS187	104396
Multilateral		05 Apr 51	84UNTS299	101139
ICAO (Civil Aviat)	Thailand	19 Apr 51	96UNTS181	101336
Greece	Turkey	20 Apr 51	178UNTS17	102333
Cuba	ILO (Labor Org)	21 Apr 51	99UNTS205	101382
Iceland	ICAO (Civil Aviat)	07 Jun 51	96UNTS193	101337
United Nations	Thailand	11 Jun 51	90UNTS45	101225
Israel	United Nations	25 Jun 51	97UNTS21	101344
Multilateral		25 Jun 51	92UNTS27	101258
India	Turkey	29 Jun 51	213UNTS183	102886
Burma	WHO (World Health)	09 Jul 51	104UNTS187	101440
Multilateral		27 Jul 51	97UNTS291	200273
Iraq	USA (United States)	16 Aug 51	147UNTS65	101929

PARTY ONE	PARTY TWO	DATE	CITATION	NUMBER
Professorships (Cont.)				
Denmark	USA (United States)	23 Aug 51	147UNTS49	101928
Greece	UK Great Britain	29 Sep 51	190UNTS260	102570
Italy	UK Great Britain	28 Nov 51	172UNTS27	102238
India	WHO (World Health)	20 Dec 51	124UNTS109	101669
Germany, East	Poland	08 Jan 52	304UNTS113	104394
Peru	USA (United States)	04 Feb 52	121UNTS255	200403
India	WHO (World Health)	17 Apr 52	131UNTS241	101744
Finland	USA (United States)	02 Jul 52	165UNTS203	102177
Germany, West	USA (United States)	18 Jul 52	165UNTS167	102175
Chile	WHO (World Health)	24 Oct 52	151UNTS339	102004
Austria	UK Great Britain	12 Dec 52	172UNTS9	102237
Bolivia	Italy	31 Jan 53	281UNTS181	104079
Israel	Uruguay	30 Apr 53	280UNTS269	104064
Pakistan	Turkey	29 Jun 53	211UNTS225	102854
Pakistan	United Arab Rep	14 Nov 53	485UNTS55	107046
Greece	Italy	11 Sep 54	284UNTS313	104145
Japan	Thailand	06 Apr 55	230UNTS219	103187
Netherlands	Norway	18 May 55	252UNTS269	103569
Belgium	Portugal	30 Jul 55	250UNTS213	103525
Italy	Spain	11 Aug 55	267UNTS125	103839
Iran	Pakistan	09 Mar 56	449UNTS183	106460
Turkey	UK Great Britain	12 Mar 56	313UNTS73	104530
Germany, East	USSR (Soviet Union)	26 Apr 56	259UNTS279	103692
Czechoslovakia	USSR (Soviet Union)	01 Jun 56	259UNTS341	103696
Greece	United Arab Rep	04 Sep 56	299UNTS253	104317
Denmark	Italy	26 Oct 56	267UNTS261	103847
Taiwan	Turkey	12 Feb 57	282UNTS125	104097
Japan	United Arab Rep	20 Mar 57	318UNTS345	104625
Iran	Japan	16 Apr 57	325UNTS113	104697
Japan	Pakistan	27 May 57	325UNTS21	104692
Finland	India	14 Jun 57	277UNTS327	104016
Germany, West	UK Great Britain	18 Apr 58	343UNTS241	104928
Germany, East	Romania	15 Jul 58	387UNTS115	105560
Belgium	Spain	27 Oct 58	327UNTS107	104720
Afghanistan	WHO (World Health)	18 Dec 58	324UNTS121	104681
Belgium	Turkey	29 Dec 58	357UNTS195	105118
Iraq	USSR (Soviet Union)	05 May 59	356UNTS179	105095
Iran	UK Great Britain	06 May 59	398UNTS51	105717
Finland	Hungary	10 Jun 59	439UNTS3	106321
Brazil	Israel	24 Jun 59	515UNTS151	107458
Iraq	Romania	04 Aug 59	502UNTS17	107324
France	Israel	30 Nov 59	377UNTS237	105404
Germany, East	Hungary	19 Dec 59	409UNTS4	105874
Guinea	Hungary	12 Jan 60	519UNTS131	107505
Argentina	Mexico	26 Jan 60	635UNTS79	109073
Italy	USSR (Soviet Union)	09 Feb 60	399UNTS75	105735
Spain	UK Great Britain	12 Jul 60	414UNTS123	105971
Cuba	Romania	28 Oct 60	457UNTS9	106574
Israel	Mali	24 Nov 60	413UNTS95	105944
Japan	UK Great Britain	03 Dec 60	414UNTS61	105966
Czechoslovakia	Hungary	24 Feb 61	422UNTS15	106066
Denmark	Germany, West	12 Sep 61	516UNTS283	107478
Taiwan	Jordan	17 Oct 61	435UNTS267	106284
United Arab Rep	UK Great Britain	14 Nov 61	449UNTS129	106455
India	United Nations	19 Feb 62	423UNTS3	106082
USA (United States)	USSR (Soviet Union)	08 Mar 62	460UNTS3	106630
United Arab Rep	USA (United States)	21 May 62	458UNTS197	106601
Israel	Peru	25 Jun 62	515UNTS263	107464
Syria	USSR (Soviet Union)	19 Aug 62	457UNTS285	106588
Germany, West	USA (United States)	20 Nov 62	505UNTS263	107377
Iraq	USA (United States)	23 Jan 63	488UNTS163	107126
Paraguay	USA (United States)	20 Aug 63	531UNTS197	107704
Argentina	USA (United States)	21 Aug 63	488UNTS61	107119
Ecuador	USA (United States)	20 Sep 63	488UNTS147	107125
Hungary	Yugoslavia	15 Oct 63	577UNTS49	108372

PARTY ONE	PARTY TWO	DATE	CITATION	NUMBER
Professorships (Cont.)				
Tunisia	USA (United States)	18 Nov 63	494UNTS193	107233
Greece	USA (United States)	13 Dec 63	494UNTS55	107226
Finland	Poland	18 Dec 63	486UNTS57	107072
Iceland	USA (United States)	13 Feb 64	524UNTS235	107576
USA (United States)	USSR (Soviet Union)	22 Feb 64	526UNTS131	107605
Mexico	Netherlands	08 Apr 64	575UNTS35	108353
Australia	USA (United States)	28 Aug 64	510UNTS201	107415
Ceylon (Sri Lanka)	USA (United States)	29 Aug 64	531UNTS93	107695
Argentina	France	03 Oct 64	635UNTS155	109080
Czechoslovakia	Germany, East	06 Oct 64	545UNTS113	107927
USA (United States)	Yugoslavia	09 Nov 64	533UNTS39	107731
Poland	Romania	26 Nov 64	552UNTS157	108053
Netherlands	Nigeria	04 Dec 64	545UNTS155	107931
Belgium	Sweden	11 Jan 65	533UNTS157	107741
Peru	USA (United States)	28 Jan 65	587UNTS273	108513
France	USA (United States)	07 May 65	573UNTS183	108331
UK Great Britain	USA (United States)	10 May 65	545UNTS181	107934
Bulgaria	Czechoslovakia	22 May 65	545UNTS65	107925
Multilateral		21 Oct 65	547UNTS216	107959
East Afri Service	United Nations	27 Nov 65	550UNTS375	200616
Czechoslovakia	Poland	22 Jan 66	588UNTS175	108524
UK Great Britain	Yugoslavia	27 Jan 66	573UNTS243	108337
Argentina	Taiwan	19 Mar 66	635UNTS281	109089
Ivory Coast	Netherlands	01 Aug 66	591UNTS245	108561
Netherlands	Yugoslavia	11 Aug 66	602UNTS243	108716
Hungary	Yugoslavia	26 Sep 66	601UNTS21	108685
Brazil	Netherlands	12 Oct 66	643UNTS271	109197
United Nations	Sudan	08 Nov 66	576UNTS85	108365
Netherlands	Poland	22 Aug 67	0UNTS0	109275
Institute establishment				
Brazil	Dominican Republic	09 Apr 45	67UNTS293	200226
Poland	Yugoslavia	16 Mar 46	10UNTS11	100139
Multilateral		22 Jul 46	14UNTS185	100221
Austria	France	15 Mar 47	12UNTS109	100182
Czechoslovakia	Yugoslavia	27 Apr 47	33UNTS49	100514
Czechoslovakia	UK Great Britain	16 Jun 47	46UNTS61	100700
Bulgaria	Czechoslovakia	20 Jun 47	46UNTS15	100698
Romania	Yugoslavia	26 Jun 47	116UNTS39	101568
Bulgaria	Poland	28 Jun 47	15UNTS123	100230
Czechoslovakia	Poland	04 Jul 47	25UNTS249	100366
Albania	Yugoslavia	09 Jul 47	33UNTS91	100516
Czechoslovakia	Romania	05 Sep 47	46UNTS37	100699
Hungary	Yugoslavia	15 Oct 47	33UNTS73	100515
Hungary	Poland	31 Jan 48	25UNTS283	100368
Norway	UK Great Britain	19 Feb 48	34UNTS33	100526
Poland	Romania	27 Feb 48	46UNTS143	100707
Netherlands	UK Great Britain	07 Jul 48	82UNTS259	101099
Greece	Italy	21 Sep 48	77UNTS259	101003
Belgium	Italy	29 Nov 48	41UNTS3	100641
Norway	USA (United States)	25 May 49	32UNTS345	100507
Bulgaria	Poland	26 Sep 49	260UNTS249	103712
Hungary	Poland	29 Oct 49	260UNTS113	103706
Denmark	WHO (World Health)	14 Feb 51	104UNTS243	101445
Greece	Turkey	20 Apr 51	178UNTS17	102333
Nicaragua	UK Great Britain	25 May 51	101UNTS77	101404
Multilateral		01 Jun 51	118UNTS57	101596
Burma	WHO (World Health)	13 Jun 51	117UNTS115	101588
India	Turkey	29 Jun 51	213UNTS183	102886
Burma	WHO (World Health)	09 Jul 51	107UNTS9	101463
Multilateral		18 Jul 51	102UNTS291	200308
Greece	UK Great Britain	29 Sep 51	190UNTS260	102570
Italy	UK Great Britain	28 Nov 51	172UNTS27	102238
Multilateral		06 Dec 51	425UNTS61	106119
India	WHO (World Health)	20 Dec 51	124UNTS109	101669

PARTY ONE	PARTY TWO	DATE	CITATION	NUMBER
Institute establishment (Cont.)				
Guatemala	WHO (World Health)	29 Dec 51	124UNTS89	101668
OAS (Am States)	USA (United States)	03 Mar 52	165UNTS67	102168
Taiwan	WHO (World Health)	07 Mar 52	128UNTS233	101723
Ethiopia	USA (United States)	15 May 52	180UNTS227	102388
Burma	WHO (World Health)	09 Jun 52	134UNTS273	101806
Multilateral		21 Aug 52	141UNTS129	101912
Austria	Belgium	17 Oct 52	162UNTS183	102135
Chile	WHO (World Health)	24 Oct 52	151UNTS339	102004
Ethiopia	USA (United States)	07 Nov 52	184UNTS285	102453
Ceylon (Sri Lanka)	USA (United States)	17 Nov 52	180UNTS207	102386
India	WHO (World Health)	11 Dec 52	158UNTS391	102073
Austria	UK Great Britain	12 Dec 52	172UNTS9	102237
Bolivia	Italy	31 Jan 53	281UNTS181	104079
United Arab Rep	USA (United States)	19 Mar 53	215UNTS17	102909
Israel	Uruguay	30 Apr 53	280UNTS269	104064
United Arab Rep	USA (United States)	18 Jun 53	204UNTS55	102749
Liberia	USA (United States)	23 Jun 53	213UNTS57	102880
Pakistan	Turkey	29 Jun 53	211UNTS225	102854
Saudi Arabia	USA (United States)	29 Jun 53	206UNTS23	102784
Pakistan	United Nations	25 Jan 54	185UNTS213	102472
Mexico	USA (United States)	06 Apr 54	236UNTS69	103317
Greece	Italy	11 Sep 54	284UNTS313	104145
Ethiopia	Sweden	13 Oct 54	202UNTS273	102734
Portugal	UK Great Britain	19 Nov 54	226UNTS305	103125
Belgium	Greece	09 Dec 54	257UNTS243	103660
Pakistan	Sweden	04 Jun 55	228UNTS121	103146
Italy	Spain	11 Aug 55	267UNTS125	103839
Burma	Yugoslavia	07 Mar 56	386UNTS235	105543
Iran	Pakistan	09 Mar 56	449UNTS183	106460
Turkey	UK Great Britain	12 Mar 56	313UNTS73	104530
Israel	USA (United States)	26 Jun 56	257UNTS55	103649
Greece	United Arab Rep	04 Sep 56	299UNTS253	104317
Belgium	Germany, West	24 Sep 56	263UNTS31	103766
Czechoslovakia	Yugoslavia	29 Jan 57	300UNTS249	104339
Multilateral		22 Feb 57	274UNTS93	103960
Ethiopia	Sweden	16 Mar 57	304UNTS214	104398
Japan	United Arab Rep	20 Mar 57	318UNTS345	104625
India	Poland	27 Mar 57	319UNTS263	104635
Australia	FAO (Food Agri)	08 Jul 57	277UNTS315	104015
Belgium	Denmark	31 Dec 57	305UNTS247	104422
Germany, West	UK Great Britain	18 Apr 58	343UNTS241	104928
FAO (Food Agri)	UK Great Britain	24 Apr 58	642UNTS245	109177
Afghanistan	USA (United States)	26 Jun 58	321UNTS67	104654
Belgium	Spain	27 Oct 58	327UNTS107	104720
Afghanistan	WHO (World Health)	18 Dec 58	324UNTS121	104681
Belgium	Turkey	29 Dec 58	357UNTS195	105118
India	Netherlands	16 Jan 59	506UNTS153	107386
Iran	UK Great Britain	06 May 59	398UNTS51	105717
Iran	Netherlands	22 May 59	474UNTS195	106882
Brazil	Israel	24 Jun 59	515UNTS151	107458
Czechoslovakia	India	07 Jul 59	359UNTS259	105145
Lebanon	USA (United States)	16 Sep 59	358UNTS175	105135
France	Israel	30 Nov 59	377UNTS237	105404
India	Japan	25 Jan 60	384UNTS31	105508
Netherlands	Turkey	12 May 60	463UNTS207	106704
Japan	Pakistan	30 Jul 60	384UNTS63	105511
Japan	Thailand	24 Aug 60	384UNTS73	105512
Iran	Japan	12 Sep 60	384UNTS43	105509
Japan	UK Great Britain	03 Dec 60	414UNTS61	105966
Afghanistan	Japan	15 Mar 61	450UNTS373	106480
Ceylon (Sri Lanka)	Japan	20 Mar 61	450UNTS385	106481
Cuba	Germany, East	29 Mar 61	448UNTS81	106426
Germany, West	Netherlands	27 Apr 61	487UNTS77	107095
Ethiopia	United Nations	14 Jun 61	406UNTS81	105840
Pakistan	Philippines	15 Aug 61	522UNTS35	107534

PARTY ONE	PARTY TWO	DATE	CITATION	NUMBER
Institute establishment (Cont.)				
Ghana	United Nations	29 Aug 61	406UNTS117	105843
Tunisia	USSR (Soviet Union)	30 Aug 61	437UNTS243	106310
Brazil	Japan	28 Mar 62	451UNTS125	106489
Hungary	India	30 Mar 62	519UNTS119	107504
India	Japan	31 Mar 62	451UNTS143	106490
India	Japan	23 Apr 62	451UNTS155	106491
United Arab Rep	USA (United States)	21 May 62	458UNTS197	106601
Israel	Peru	25 Jun 62	515UNTS263	107464
Multilateral		28 Sep 62	469UNTS169	106791
United Nations	South Pacific Com	24 Jan 63	470UNTS361	200604
United Nations	United Arab Rep	08 Feb 63	453UNTS79	106520
Cameroon	UK Great Britain	20 Aug 63	539UNTS233	107834
Italy	IAEA (Atom Energy)	11 Oct 63	639UNTS25	109142
Belgium	Pakistan	14 Nov 63	535UNTS393	107792
Netherlands	Tunisia	03 Mar 64	533UNTS133	107739
Germany, West	Thailand	02 Apr 64	503UNTS3	107338
Taiwan	Philippines	25 Aug 64	511UNTS233	107436
Germany, East	Poland	06 Oct 64	552UNTS89	108051
Italy	ILO (Labor Org)	24 Oct 64	541UNTS217	107871
Argentina	Guatemala	30 Oct 64	601UNTS175	108695
Netherlands	Pakistan	30 Oct 64	541UNTS243	107873
Belgium	Mexico	19 Nov 64	546UNTS217	107949
India	Netherlands	11 Dec 64	570UNTS165	108292
Germany, West	Jamaica	16 Dec 64	531UNTS129	107699
Cameroon	Netherlands	06 Jul 65	571UNTS75	108300
Bulgaria	Hungary	19 Aug 65	577UNTS67	108373
East Afri Service	United Nations	27 Nov 65	550UNTS375	200616
UK Great Britain	Yugoslavia	27 Jan 66	573UNTS243	108337
Netherlands	Philippines	02 Mar 66	631UNTS325	109002
Argentina	Taiwan	19 Mar 66	635UNTS281	109089
Multilateral		23 Sep 66	573UNTS132	108327
Denmark	Uganda	03 Jul 68	0UNTS0	109467
Denmark	Malawi	03 Sep 68	0UNTS0	109414
Int Wheat Coun	UK Great Britain	28 Nov 68	0UNTS0	109498
ILO (Labor Org)	Trinidad/Tobago	14 Mar 69	0UNTS0	109500
Scholarships and grants				
Brazil	Paraguay	14 Jun 41	54UNTS235	200196
Brazil	Chile	18 Nov 41	67UNTS279	200225
Peru	USA (United States)	24 Aug 42	24UNTS153	200139
Brazil	Dominican Republic	09 Dec 42	65UNTS217	200213
Peru	USA (United States)	15 Apr 44	150UNTS317	200479
Brazil	Ecuador	24 May 44	73UNTS223	200242
Dominican Republic	USA (United States)	13 Oct 45	149UNTS361	200477
Czechoslovakia	France	08 Dec 45	46UNTS77	100701
Belgium	France	22 Feb 46	68UNTS157	100892
Poland	Yugoslavia	16 Mar 46	10UNTS11	100139
Brazil	USA (United States)	05 Apr 46	12UNTS131	100183
Belgium	UK Great Britain	17 Apr 46	6UNTS177	100075
France	USA (United States)	10 Dec 46	15UNTS265	100242
Belgium	Czechoslovakia	06 Mar 47	34UNTS77	100528
Austria	France	15 Mar 47	12UNTS109	100182
Czechoslovakia	Yugoslavia	27 Apr 47	33UNTS49	100514
France	Poland	19 May 47	12UNTS95	100181
Czechoslovakia	UK Great Britain	16 Jun 47	46UNTS61	100700
Bulgaria	Czechoslovakia	20 Jun 47	46UNTS15	100698
Romania	Yugoslavia	26 Jun 47	116UNTS39	101568
Bulgaria	Poland	28 Jun 47	15UNTS123	100230
Albania	Yugoslavia	09 Jul 47	33UNTS91	100516
Czechoslovakia	Romania	05 Sep 47	46UNTS37	100699
Hungary	Yugoslavia	15 Oct 47	33UNTS73	100515
Ecuador	USA (United States)	14 Nov 47	149UNTS297	101959
USSR (Soviet Union)	Yugoslavia	15 Dec 47	116UNTS313	101578
Hungary	Poland	31 Jan 48	25UNTS283	100368
Norway	UK Great Britain	19 Feb 48	34UNTS33	100526

PARTY ONE	PARTY TWO	DATE	CITATION	NUMBER
Scholarships and grants (Cont.)				
Belgium	Norway	20 Feb 48	32UNTS39	100487
Poland	Romania	27 Feb 48	46UNTS143	100707
Philippines	USA (United States)	23 Mar 48	43UNTS247	100671
Belgium	Luxembourg	27 Mar 48	178UNTS265	102343
Greece	USA (United States)	23 Apr 48	74UNTS107	100958
Netherlands	UK Great Britain	07 Jul 48	82UNTS259	101099
UK Great Britain	USA (United States)	22 Sep 48	71UNTS64	100910
Belgium	Italy	29 Nov 48	41UNTS3	100641
Italy	USA (United States)	18 Dec 48	79UNTS133	101037
Luxembourg	Netherlands	26 Apr 49	182UNTS187	102425
Netherlands	USA (United States)	17 May 49	46UNTS291	100717
Norway	USA (United States)	25 May 49	32UNTS345	100507
Greece	Lebanon	10 Jun 49	178UNTS29	102334
Bulgaria	Poland	26 Sep 49	260UNTS249	103712
Hungary	Poland	29 Oct 49	260UNTS113	103706
United Arab Rep	USA (United States)	03 Nov 49	71UNTS31	100908
India	USA (United States)	02 Feb 50	89UNTS127	101214
Korea, South	USA (United States)	28 Apr 50	93UNTS21	101284
Austria	USA (United States)	06 Jun 50	92UNTS201	101273
Luxembourg	UK Great Britain	27 Jun 50	183UNTS217	102431
Thailand	USA (United States)	01 Jul 50	81UNTS61	101063
Pakistan	USA (United States)	23 Sep 50	82UNTS131	101088
Austria	Sweden	31 Oct 50	197UNTS311	102645
Multilateral		02 Nov 50	81UNTS160	101071
Multilateral		24 Nov 50	81UNTS188	101072
Albania	Poland	02 Dec 50	260UNTS131	103707
Multilateral		15 Dec 50	76UNTS120	100985
United Nations	Yugoslavia	06 Jan 51	78UNTS165	101015
Multilateral		18 Jan 51	81UNTS233	101073
Nicaragua	USA (United States)	31 Jan 51	150UNTS3	101960
Nicaragua	USA (United States)	31 Jan 51	160UNTS121	102105
Ethiopia	ICAO (Civil Aviat)	02 Feb 51	96UNTS123	101333
Israel	ILO (Labor Org)	19 Feb 51	100UNTS105	101391
Israel	ICAO (Civil Aviat)	19 Feb 51	96UNTS141	101334
ILO (Labor Org)	Syria	03 Mar 51	110UNTS69	101502
Multilateral		28 Mar 51	181UNTS61	102399
Jordan	United Nations	29 Mar 51	137UNTS267	200448
Jordan	ILO (Labor Org)	29 Mar 51	100UNTS247	200287
Liberia	ILO (Labor Org)	02 Apr 51	100UNTS117	101392
China People's Rep	Poland	03 Apr 51	304UNTS187	104396
Multilateral		05 Apr 51	84UNTS299	101139
Mexico	ILO (Labor Org)	06 Apr 51	100UNTS131	101393
Ceylon (Sri Lanka)	ILO (Labor Org)	06 Apr 51	100UNTS235	200286
Peru	ILO (Labor Org)	13 Apr 51	100UNTS31	101385
Guatemala	ILO (Labor Org)	13 Apr 51	126UNTS249	101692
ICAO (Civil Aviat)	Thailand	19 Apr 51	96UNTS181	101336
Ecuador	ILO (Labor Org)	19 Apr 51	100UNTS77	101389
Greece	Turkey	20 Apr 51	178UNTS17	102333
Greece	ILO (Labor Org)	25 Apr 51	100UNTS93	101390
India	ILO (Labor Org)	26 Apr 51	100UNTS19	101384
Mexico	WHO (World Health)	30 Apr 51	103UNTS95	101427
WHO (World Health)	Yugoslavia	02 May 51	103UNTS117	101429
Pakistan	ILO (Labor Org)	16 May 51	100UNTS147	101394
Multilateral		01 Jun 51	118UNTS57	101596
Lebanon	WHO (World Health)	07 Jun 51	126UNTS221	101690
Costa Rica	WHO (World Health)	14 Jun 51	102UNTS151	101418
Dominican Republic	ILO (Labor Org)	18 Jun 51	100UNTS3	101383
ILO (Labor Org)	Vietnam, South	26 Jun 51	100UNTS223	200285
Multilateral		28 Jun 51	118UNTS154	101604
India	Turkey	29 Jun 51	213UNTS183	102886
Ethiopia	WHO (World Health)	02 Jul 51	103UNTS39	101422
ILO (Labor Org)	Thailand	11 Jul 51	100UNTS159	101395
Paraguay	ILO (Labor Org)	12 Jul 51	117UNTS155	101591
Multilateral		04 Aug 51	104UNTS197	101441
Israel	WHO (World Health)	07 Aug 51	104UNTS213	101442

Scholarships and grants (Cont.)

PARTY ONE	PARTY TWO	DATE	CITATION	NUMBER
Iraq	USA (United States)	16 Aug 51	147UNTS65	101929
Denmark	USA (United States)	23 Aug 51	147UNTS49	101928
WHO (World Health)	Saudi Arabia	29 Aug 51	110UNTS277	101516
Multilateral		05 Sep 51	173UNTS15	102256
Iraq	ICAO (Civil Aviat)	18 Sep 51	108UNTS219	101475
Korea, South	WHO (World Health)	19 Sep 51	109UNTS297	200366
Paraguay	United Nations	27 Sep 51	120UNTS105	101617
Greece	UK Great Britain	29 Sep 51	190UNTS260	102570
Bolivia	United Nations	01 Oct 51	104UNTS263	101447
Multilateral		01 Oct 51	104UNTS249	101446
Pakistan	WHO (World Health)	07 Oct 51	126UNTS101	101684
Ecuador	WHO (World Health)	16 Oct 51	110UNTS263	101515
United Nations	Uruguay	17 Oct 51	122UNTS29	101633
ILO (Labor Org)	Venezuela	22 Oct 51	117UNTS139	101590
Panama	WHO (World Health)	09 Nov 51	118UNTS43	101595
Panama	ILO (Labor Org)	10 Nov 51	126UNTS269	101693
Italy	UK Great Britain	28 Nov 51	172UNTS27	102238
Mexico	WHO (World Health)	17 Dec 51	124UNTS121	101670
Guatemala	WHO (World Health)	17 Dec 51	120UNTS133	101619
Multilateral		24 Dec 51	118UNTS290	200383
Guatemala	WHO (World Health)	29 Dec 51	124UNTS89	101668
Germany, East	Poland	08 Jan 52	304UNTS113	104394
Austria	WHO (World Health)	10 Jan 52	131UNTS295	200438
Ceylon (Sri Lanka)	United Nations	21 Jan 52	118UNTS281	200382
Multilateral		23 Jan 52	127UNTS269	101708
Costa Rica	WHO (World Health)	23 Jan 52	135UNTS265	101826
WHO (World Health)	Spain	30 Jan 52	124UNTS259	200425
Peru	USA (United States)	04 Feb 52	121UNTS255	200403
ICAO (Civil Aviat)	Yugoslavia	06 Feb 52	128UNTS97	101715
WHO (World Health)	UK Great Britain	07 Feb 52	121UNTS75	101627
Lebanon	ICAO (Civil Aviat)	14 Feb 52	128UNTS83	101714
Multilateral		18 Feb 52	126UNTS319	200434
Greece	United Nations	05 Mar 52	123UNTS3	101650
ICAO (Civil Aviat)	United Arab Rep	06 Mar 52	151UNTS111	101986
Taiwan	WHO (World Health)	07 Mar 52	128UNTS233	101723
South Africa	USA (United States)	26 Mar 52	165UNTS187	102176
Denmark	WHO (World Health)	26 Mar 52	134UNTS285	101807
India	United Nations	02 Apr 52	126UNTS145	101687
Peru	USA (United States)	09 Apr 52	184UNTS295	102454
Multilateral		11 Apr 52	173UNTS2	102255
India	ICAO (Civil Aviat)	29 Apr 52	151UNTS123	101987
Multilateral		22 May 52	131UNTS115	101739
India	WHO (World Health)	04 Jun 52	135UNTS279	101827
Burma	WHO (World Health)	09 Jun 52	134UNTS273	101806
India	WHO (World Health)	19 Jun 52	134UNTS307	101809
Multilateral		19 Jun 52	133UNTS165	101787
WHO (World Health)	Syria	20 Jun 52	165UNTS219	102178
Brazil	USA (United States)	30 Jun 52	185UNTS79	102460
Finland	USA (United States)	02 Jul 52	165UNTS203	102177
Chile	WHO (World Health)	11 Jul 52	137UNTS27	101846
India	WHO (World Health)	16 Jul 52	135UNTS291	101828
Germany, West	USA (United States)	18 Jul 52	165UNTS167	102175
Chile	ILO (Labor Org)	23 Jul 52	178UNTS323	102348
Panama	United Nations	20 Aug 52	136UNTS3	101829
Jordan	WHO (World Health)	21 Aug 52	141UNTS341	200472
Italy	ILO (Labor Org)	04 Sep 52	178UNTS371	200505
ILO (Labor Org)	Uruguay	20 Sep 52	187UNTS25	102499
Multilateral		15 Oct 52	141UNTS96	101909
Austria	Belgium	17 Oct 52	162UNTS183	102135
Chile	WHO (World Health)	24 Oct 52	151UNTS339	102004
Chile	WHO (World Health)	04 Nov 52	150UNTS119	101966
Sweden	USA (United States)	20 Nov 52	177UNTS203	102319
Japan	WHO (World Health)	26 Nov 52	204UNTS301	200521
Mexico	ICAO (Civil Aviat)	28 Nov 52	164UNTS15	102156
Austria	UK Great Britain	12 Dec 52	172UNTS9	102237

Scholarships and grants (Cont.)

PARTY ONE	PARTY TWO	DATE	CITATION	NUMBER
Multilateral		16 Dec 52	158UNTS407	102074
Multilateral		29 Dec 52	151UNTS317	102002
ILO (Labor Org)	UN Relief Palestin	31 Dec 52	182UNTS201	200506
Saudi Arabia	USA (United States)	25 Jan 53	201UNTS3	102706
Bolivia	Italy	31 Jan 53	281UNTS181	104079
India	WHO (World Health)	11 Feb 53	163UNTS43	102140
Taiwan	ILO (Labor Org)	13 Feb 53	178UNTS337	102349
Albania	Romania	14 Feb 53	342UNTS107	104903
Multilateral		26 Feb 53	161UNTS31	102120
Costa Rica	United Nations	27 Feb 53	161UNTS45	102121
Nepal	United Nations	02 Mar 53	161UNTS347	200493
France	WHO (World Health)	02 Apr 53	174UNTS83	102279
United Nations	Yemen	07 Apr 53	163UNTS73	102142
Germany, West	USA (United States)	09 Apr 53	204UNTS79	102750
Ethiopia	USA (United States)	29 Apr 53	224UNTS121	103073
Greece	Netherlands	29 Apr 53	191UNTS235	102583
France	WHO (World Health)	30 Apr 53	174UNTS71	102278
ICAO (Civil Aviat)	Syria	28 May 53	173UNTS199	102267
Ecuador	United Nations	16 Jun 53	166UNTS289	102194
United Arab Rep	USA (United States)	18 Jun 53	215UNTS45	102910
Ethiopia	United Nations	22 Jun 53	172UNTS93	102241
Liberia	USA (United States)	23 Jun 53	213UNTS37	102879
Cambodia	United Nations	24 Jun 53	168UNTS309	200500
Pakistan	Turkey	29 Jun 53	211UNTS225	102854
Saudi Arabia	USA (United States)	29 Jun 53	206UNTS23	102784
Afghanistan	USA (United States)	30 Jun 53	215UNTS3	102908
Multilateral		09 Oct 53	190UNTS49	102557
Netherlands	USA (United States)	27 Oct 53	221UNTS357	103017
Dominican Republic	United Nations	19 Nov 53	180UNTS45	102374
Brazil	WHO (World Health)	04 Feb 54	233UNTS49	103250
United Nations	Venezuela	05 Mar 54	187UNTS9	102498
Liberia	United Nations	09 Mar 54	187UNTS61	102501
Guatemala	United Nations	10 Mar 54	191UNTS271	102587
Multilateral		20 Apr 54	189UNTS11	102539
Nepal	WHO (World Health)	13 May 54	204UNTS311	200522
Multilateral		31 May 54	192UNTS20	102592
Belgium	South Africa	01 Jun 54	201UNTS25	102708
Multilateral		01 Jun 54	200UNTS235	200520
Multilateral		19 Aug 54	201UNTS51	102710
Greece	Italy	11 Sep 54	284UNTS313	104145
Multilateral		06 Oct 54	201UNTS75	102711
Ethiopia	Sweden	13 Oct 54	202UNTS273	102734
Multilateral		27 Oct 54	201UNTS95	102712
Multilateral		29 Oct 54	201UNTS115	102713
Portugal	UK Great Britain	19 Nov 54	226UNTS305	103125
Belgium	Greece	09 Dec 54	257UNTS243	103660
Chile	USA (United States)	31 Mar 55	262UNTS19	103736
Multilateral		04 Apr 55	208UNTS239	102816
Japan	Thailand	06 Apr 55	230UNTS219	103187
Taiwan	WHO (World Health)	21 Apr 55	210UNTS71	102835
Netherlands	Norway	18 May 55	252UNTS269	103569
Pakistan	Sweden	04 Jun 55	228UNTS121	103146
Italy	Norway	14 Jun 55	260UNTS307	103713
Multilateral		14 Jun 55	212UNTS263	200526
Iran	WHO (World Health)	04 Jul 55	227UNTS65	103131
Multilateral		04 Jul 55	214UNTS10	102897
Belgium	Portugal	30 Jul 55	250UNTS213	103525
Italy	Spain	11 Aug 55	267UNTS125	103839
USSR (Soviet Union)	Yugoslavia	19 Dec 55	378UNTS127	105423
Multilateral		02 Feb 56	227UNTS153	103137
Multilateral		10 Feb 56	228UNTS189	103151
Multilateral		10 Feb 56	228UNTS167	103150
Iran	Pakistan	09 Mar 56	449UNTS183	106460
Turkey	UK Great Britain	12 Mar 56	313UNTS73	104530
Korea, North	Poland	11 May 56	432UNTS161	106219

PARTY ONE	PARTY TWO	DATE	CITATION	NUMBER
Scholarships and grants (Cont.)				
USSR (Soviet Union)	Yugoslavia	17 May 56	259UNTS145	103687
Multilateral		31 May 56	251UNTS181	103541
Multilateral		08 Jun 56	247UNTS366	200541
Multilateral		14 Jun 56	265UNTS125	103809
Multilateral		26 Jun 56	253UNTS12	103573
Multilateral		26 Jun 56	321UNTS2	104650
Multilateral		02 Jul 56	248UNTS37	103484
Multilateral		02 Jul 56	540UNTS110	107846
Poland	Yugoslavia	06 Jul 56	281UNTS143	104076
Syria	USSR (Soviet Union)	20 Aug 56	274UNTS105	103961
Multilateral		31 Aug 56	249UNTS158	103506
Greece	United Arab Rep	04 Sep 56	299UNTS253	104317
Belgium	Germany, West	24 Sep 56	263UNTS31	103766
Multilateral		05 Oct 56	251UNTS245	103544
Multilateral		05 Oct 56	251UNTS267	103545
Germany, West	Thailand	09 Oct 56	258UNTS143	103676
Romania	Vietnam, North	12 Oct 56	342UNTS173	104907
Romania	Yugoslavia	27 Oct 56	389UNTS33	105590
India	Japan	29 Oct 56	318UNTS289	104622
Ecuador	USA (United States)	31 Oct 56	283UNTS151	104114
Argentina	USA (United States)	05 Nov 56	277UNTS143	104004
Multilateral		21 Nov 56	253UNTS266	103588
Bulgaria	Yugoslavia	24 Dec 56	397UNTS3	105699
Colombia	USA (United States)	09 Jan 57	462UNTS151	106676
Multilateral		23 Jan 57	259UNTS426	103701
Czechoslovakia	Yugoslavia	29 Jan 57	300UNTS249	104339
Poland	United Arab Rep	02 Feb 57	319UNTS221	104633
Belgium	Yugoslavia	05 Feb 57	276UNTS143	103990
Taiwan	Turkey	12 Feb 57	282UNTS125	104097
USSR (Soviet Union)	Vietnam, North	15 Feb 57	274UNTS115	103962
Multilateral		17 Feb 57	271UNTS2	103907
Multilateral		22 Feb 57	274UNTS93	103960
Iceland	USA (United States)	23 Feb 57	283UNTS73	104107
Multilateral		01 Mar 57	264UNTS94	103790
Japan	United Arab Rep	20 Mar 57	318UNTS345	104625
India	Poland	27 Mar 57	319UNTS263	104635
Multilateral		28 Mar 57	271UNTS30	103908
Paraguay	USA (United States)	04 Apr 57	284UNTS161	104135
Multilateral		09 Apr 57	274UNTS172	103965
Romania	United Arab Rep	15 Apr 57	389UNTS21	105589
Iran	Japan	16 Apr 57	325UNTS113	104697
Czechoslovakia	United Arab Rep	06 May 57	292UNTS317	104278
Finland	USA (United States)	10 May 57	283UNTS43	104105
Multilateral		24 May 57	268UNTS270	103861
Japan	Pakistan	27 May 57	325UNTS21	104692
Multilateral		09 Jul 57	274UNTS300	103972
Burma	WHO (World Health)	20 Sep 57	282UNTS113	104096
United Arab Rep	USSR (Soviet Union)	19 Oct 57	292UNTS151	104271
Czechoslovakia	United Arab Rep	19 Oct 57	530UNTS181	107681
IAEA (Atom Energy)	United Nations	23 Oct 57	281UNTS369	200548
Multilateral		05 Nov 57	285UNTS301	104155
Brazil	USA (United States)	05 Nov 57	303UNTS3	104368
Taiwan	Iran	11 Nov 57	563UNTS31	108202
Israel	Norway	26 Nov 57	345UNTS99	104962
Belgium	Denmark	31 Dec 57	305UNTS247	104422
Norway	Turkey	10 Jan 58	351UNTS229	105025
Japan	USA (United States)	11 Jan 58	304UNTS35	104390
Poland	Yugoslavia	16 Jan 58	340UNTS181	104864
Ghana	WHO (World Health)	21 Jan 58	307UNTS3	104437
Indonesia	WHO (World Health)	05 Feb 58	307UNTS15	104438
Multilateral		15 Mar 58	292UNTS273	104276
Israel	WHO (World Health)	11 Apr 58	307UNTS27	104439
Germany, West	UK Great Britain	18 Apr 58	343UNTS241	104928
Germany, East	Hungary	14 Jun 58	407UNTS78	105861
Multilateral		19 Jun 58	306UNTS236	200550

PARTY ONE	PARTY TWO	DATE	CITATION	NUMBER
Scholarships and grants (Cont.)				
WHO (World Health)	Sudan	21 Jun 58	307UNTS235	104453
Afghanistan	USA (United States)	26 Jun 58	321UNTS67	104654
Spain	USA (United States)	16 Oct 58	336UNTS153	104804
Belgium	Spain	27 Oct 58	327UNTS107	104720
Norway	Poland	17 Dec 58	432UNTS193	106221
Afghanistan	WHO (World Health)	18 Dec 58	324UNTS121	104681
Belgium	Turkey	29 Dec 58	357UNTS195	105118
Hungary	Iraq	11 Apr 59	439UNTS25	106323
Iraq	USSR (Soviet Union)	05 May 59	356UNTS179	105095
Iran	UK Great Britain	06 May 59	398UNTS51	105717
Iran	Netherlands	22 May 59	474UNTS195	106882
Finland	Hungary	10 Jun 59	439UNTS3	106321
Greece	Yugoslavia	18 Jun 59	368UNTS137	105238
Brazil	Israel	24 Jun 59	515UNTS151	107458
Czechoslovakia	India	07 Jul 59	359UNTS259	105145
Iraq	Romania	04 Aug 59	502UNTS17	107324
Norway	Spain	19 Aug 59	376UNTS145	105379
United Arab Rep	USA (United States)	28 Sep 59	358UNTS97	105128
Multilateral		09 Oct 59	376UNTS382	105391
Guinea	USA (United States)	28 Oct 59	358UNTS169	105134
Czechoslovakia	Guinea	30 Nov 59	386UNTS63	105538
France	Israel	30 Nov 59	377UNTS237	105404
Multilateral		03 Dec 59	345UNTS251	104971
Multilateral		03 Dec 59	348UNTS246	105003
Czechoslovakia	Ethiopia	11 Dec 59	399UNTS93	105736
Czechoslovakia	Ethiopia	11 Dec 59	386UNTS45	105536
Ceylon (Sri Lanka)	WHO (World Health)	21 Dec 59	349UNTS109	105011
Belgium	Brazil	06 Jan 60	531UNTS149	107701
Guinea	Hungary	12 Jan 60	519UNTS131	107505
Pakistan	WHO (World Health)	20 Jan 60	351UNTS355	105034
Portugal	USA (United States)	19 Mar 60	371UNTS131	105275
Multilateral		12 Apr 60	359UNTS323	105150
Netherlands	Turkey	12 May 60	463UNTS207	106704
Belgium	Iran	14 May 60	522UNTS249	107551
Cambodia	WHO (World Health)	19 May 60	372UNTS193	105298
Multilateral		04 Jun 60	360UNTS208	105159
Denmark	Poland	08 Jun 60	424UNTS37	106097
Multilateral		19 Jun 60	537UNTS214	107803
Multilateral		08 Jul 60	366UNTS310	105220
Spain	UK Great Britain	12 Jul 60	414UNTS123	105971
USA (United States)	Uruguay	22 Jul 60	388UNTS315	105587
France	Greece	25 Jul 60	533UNTS227	107745
Jordan	WHO (World Health)	03 Aug 60	381UNTS133	105469
WHO (World Health)	United Arab Rep	03 Aug 60	385UNTS3	105524
WHO (World Health)	Tunisia	04 Aug 60	381UNTS335	105474
Laos	WHO (World Health)	04 Aug 60	373UNTS313	105322
Japan	Thailand	24 Aug 60	384UNTS73	105512
United Arab Rep	USSR (Soviet Union)	27 Aug 60	399UNTS37	105733
WHO (World Health)	Saudi Arabia	06 Sep 60	395UNTS169	105684
Lebanon	WHO (World Health)	08 Sep 60	387UNTS49	105557
Cuba	Romania	28 Oct 60	457UNTS9	106574
WHO (World Health)	Upper Volta	15 Nov 60	383UNTS91	105496
Czechoslovakia	Ghana	23 Nov 60	431UNTS91	106213
Fed of Malaya	WHO (World Health)	25 Nov 60	387UNTS37	105556
WHO (World Health)	Yemen	03 Dec 60	395UNTS187	105685
Japan	UK Great Britain	03 Dec 60	414UNTS61	105966
Dahomey	WHO (World Health)	07 Dec 60	387UNTS277	105567
Netherlands	United Arab Rep	08 Dec 60	455UNTS276	106547
Congo (Brazzaville)	WHO (World Health)	12 Dec 60	399UNTS105	105737
Cuba	USSR (Soviet Union)	12 Dec 60	421UNTS3	106048
Cuba	Czechoslovakia	22 Dec 60	426UNTS145	106134
Niger	WHO (World Health)	28 Dec 60	394UNTS195	105679
Ethiopia	USSR (Soviet Union)	13 Jan 61	421UNTS13	106049
Korea, South	WHO (World Health)	20 Jan 61	406UNTS269	200589
Multilateral		28 Jan 61	387UNTS202	105563

Scholarships and grants (Cont.)

PARTY ONE	PARTY TWO	DATE	CITATION	NUMBER
Ivory Coast	WHO (World Health)	30 Jan 61	395UNTS205	105686
WHO (World Health)	Togo	03 Feb 61	394UNTS207	105680
Chad	WHO (World Health)	03 Feb 61	394UNTS161	105676
Central Afri Rep	WHO (World Health)	13 Feb 61	394UNTS149	105675
Cuba	Poland	06 Mar 61	484UNTS123	107020
Kuwait	WHO (World Health)	16 Mar 61	397UNTS315	200588
Mauritania	WHO (World Health)	17 Apr 61	396UNTS301	200587
Afghanistan	Czechoslovakia	23 Apr 61	437UNTS25	106297
Ghana	Hungary	27 Apr 61	439UNTS17	106322
Gabon	WHO (World Health)	27 Apr 61	397UNTS215	105707
Germany, West	Netherlands	27 Apr 61	487UNTS77	107095
Mali	WHO (World Health)	27 Apr 61	407UNTS66	105860
Somalia	USSR (Soviet Union)	02 Jun 61	528UNTS147	107638
Czechoslovakia	Somalia	04 Jun 61	479UNTS291	106960
Nepal	USA (United States)	09 Jun 61	421UNTS223	106061
Israel	Upper Volta	11 Jun 61	413UNTS113	105946
Ethiopia	United Nations	14 Jun 61	406UNTS81	105840
Morocco	WHO (World Health)	09 Aug 61	412UNTS192	105932
Pakistan	Philippines	15 Aug 61	522UNTS35	107534
WHO (World Health)	Somalia	17 Aug 61	423UNTS111	106088
Israel	Malagasy	27 Aug 61	413UNTS86	105943
Ghana	United Nations	29 Aug 61	406UNTS117	105843
Iraq	WHO (World Health)	13 Sep 61	419UNTS69	106030
Multilateral		20 Sep 61	407UNTS52	105859
Dahomey	Israel	28 Sep 61	448UNTS151	106429
Ghana	Romania	30 Sep 61	457UNTS3	106573
Japan	United Nations	04 Oct 61	410UNTS133	105900
Malagasy	WHO (World Health)	13 Oct 61	421UNTS273	106064
Multilateral		16 Oct 61	410UNTS242	105908
Taiwan	Jordan	17 Oct 61	435UNTS267	106284
Brazil	Poland	19 Oct 61	552UNTS75	108050
Belgium	Italy	28 Oct 61	429UNTS199	106199
Multilateral		07 Nov 61	412UNTS258	105937
United Arab Rep	UK Great Britain	14 Nov 61	449UNTS129	106455
Ethiopia	USA (United States)	06 Dec 61	433UNTS231	106246
Multilateral		27 Dec 61	425UNTS83	106120
Ethiopia	WHO (World Health)	11 Jan 62	423UNTS99	106087
Multilateral		17 Jan 62	419UNTS294	106033
Cyprus	USA (United States)	18 Jan 62	435UNTS3	106266
Multilateral		20 Jan 62	429UNTS230	200596
Ghana	USA (United States)	24 Jan 62	435UNTS23	106268
Multilateral		13 Feb 62	422UNTS288	200594
Multilateral		21 Feb 62	423UNTS151	106091
Multilateral		01 Mar 62	423UNTS122	106089
USA (United States)	USSR (Soviet Union)	08 Mar 62	460UNTS3	106630
WHO (World Health)	Sudan	11 Mar 62	432UNTS325	106226
Nigeria	WHO (World Health)	27 Mar 62	429UNTS123	106194
Multilateral		10 Apr 62	429UNTS78	106192
Multilateral		18 Apr 62	463UNTS44	106692
Gabon	Israel	15 May 62	448UNTS211	106433
Multilateral		17 May 62	429UNTS46	106189
United Arab Rep	USA (United States)	21 May 62	458UNTS197	106601
Ghana	Israel	25 May 62	515UNTS237	107461
Greece	Tunisia	26 May 62	534UNTS163	107761
Denmark	USA (United States)	28 May 62	450UNTS215	106469
Central Afri Rep	Israel	13 Jun 62	448UNTS265	106439
Senegal	USSR (Soviet Union)	14 Jun 62	437UNTS233	106309
Libya	WHO (World Health)	16 Jun 62	437UNTS127	106301
WHO (World Health)	Sierra Leone	19 Jun 62	439UNTS151	106327
Israel	USA (United States)	22 Jun 62	448UNTS273	106440
Israel	Liberia	25 Jun 62	448UNTS287	106441
WHO (World Health)	Senegal	06 Aug 62	435UNTS179	106279
Multilateral		12 Aug 62	443UNTS266	106365
WHO (World Health)	Western Samoa	14 Aug 62	437UNTS317	200598
Syria	USSR (Soviet Union)	19 Aug 62	457UNTS285	106588

Scholarships and grants (Cont.)

PARTY ONE	PARTY TWO	DATE	CITATION	NUMBER
Multilateral		29 Aug 62	443UNTS280	106366
Israel	OAS (Am States)	11 Oct 62	484UNTS241	107035
Belgium	Rwanda	13 Oct 62	456UNTS431	106569
Belgium	Rwanda	13 Oct 62	456UNTS425	106568
Israel	Rwanda	23 Oct 62	515UNTS291	107466
Cameroon	Israel	24 Oct 62	449UNTS15	106447
Cameroon	Israel	24 Oct 62	449UNTS3	106446
Multilateral		15 Nov 62	448UNTS50	106424
WHO (World Health)	Syria	18 Nov 62	480UNTS249	106972
Multilateral		06 Dec 62	450UNTS240	106471
Cameroon	WHO (World Health)	08 Dec 62	451UNTS215	106496
Multilateral		12 Dec 62	457UNTS72	106578
Algeria	WHO (World Health)	20 Dec 62	463UNTS135	106698
Belgium	Tunisia	21 Dec 62	482UNTS3	106987
India	United Nations	27 Dec 62	450UNTS3	106464
Multilateral		21 Jan 63	453UNTS20	106517
UK Great Britain	USSR (Soviet Union)	21 Jan 63	475UNTS3	106887
Iraq	USA (United States)	23 Jan 63	488UNTS163	107126
Malaysia	USA (United States)	28 Jan 63	473UNTS15	106850
Israel	Tanganyika	28 Jan 63	516UNTS39	107468
Israel	Uganda	04 Feb 63	484UNTS273	107037
Multilateral		05 Feb 63	453UNTS36	106518
United Nations	United Arab Rep	08 Feb 63	453UNTS79	106520
Multilateral		14 Feb 63	453UNTS168	106524
Multilateral		06 Mar 63	455UNTS386	106552
Dahomey	USSR (Soviet Union)	20 Mar 63	528UNTS181	107641
Philippines	USA (United States)	23 Mar 63	474UNTS80	106873
Brazil	USA (United States)	29 Mar 63	476UNTS67	106904
Czechoslovakia	Tunisia	06 Apr 63	555UNTS111	108106
Multilateral		18 Apr 63	463UNTS121	106697
Multilateral		06 May 63	463UNTS78	106694
Multilateral		09 May 63	463UNTS159	106700
Belgium	Venezuela	15 May 63	470UNTS259	106812
Multilateral		22 May 63	483UNTS72	107007
Multilateral		24 May 63	466UNTS346	106754
Thailand	USA (United States)	24 May 63	477UNTS123	106918
Korea, South	USA (United States)	18 Jun 63	487UNTS297	107112
India	USA (United States)	19 Jun 63	479UNTS175	106952
Mongolia	WHO (World Health)	21 Jun 63	472UNTS373	106848
Austria	USA (United States)	25 Jun 63	479UNTS223	106956
Multilateral		23 Jul 63	471UNTS158	106831
Multilateral		31 Jul 63	472UNTS220	106842
Burundi	WHO (World Health)	08 Aug 63	477UNTS346	106928
Afghanistan	USA (United States)	20 Aug 63	488UNTS41	107118
Cameroon	UK Great Britain	20 Aug 63	539UNTS233	107834
Multilateral		27 Aug 63	511UNTS210	107435
Multilateral		10 Sep 63	480UNTS100	106965
Jamaica	WHO (World Health)	25 Sep 63	481UNTS125	106980
Mali	Romania	26 Sep 63	528UNTS193	107642
Hungary	Yugoslavia	15 Oct 63	577UNTS49	108372
Multilateral		21 Oct 63	480UNTS197	106969
Iran	USA (United States)	24 Oct 63	489UNTS303	107146
Multilateral		30 Oct 63	480UNTS180	106968
WHO (World Health)	Tanganyika	05 Nov 63	496UNTS193	107252
Tanganyika	USSR (Soviet Union)	06 Nov 63	528UNTS157	107639
Multilateral		07 Nov 63	480UNTS232	106971
Multilateral		08 Nov 63	482UNTS286	106999
Belgium	Romania	13 Nov 63	520UNTS119	107513
Belgium	Pakistan	14 Nov 63	535UNTS393	107792
Belgium	Poland	09 Dec 63	514UNTS195	107448
Multilateral		28 Jan 64	502UNTS321	107336
Netherlands	Tunisia	11 Feb 64	570UNTS173	108293
Multilateral		20 Feb 64	491UNTS30	107172
USA (United States)	USSR (Soviet Union)	22 Feb 64	526UNTS131	107605
Multilateral		28 Feb 64	501UNTS245	107321

PARTY ONE	PARTY TWO	DATE	CITATION	NUMBER
Scholarships and grants (Cont.)				
Mexico	Netherlands	08 Apr 64	575UNTS35	108353
Taiwan	USA (United States)	23 Apr 64	524UNTS141	107570
Liberia	USA (United States)	08 May 64	526UNTS239	107608
Algeria	Czechoslovakia	14 May 64	538UNTS301	107817
Multilateral		11 Jun 64	525UNTS61	107584
Italy	Romania	16 Jun 64	558UNTS313	108150
Rwanda	WHO (World Health)	22 Jun 64	514UNTS11	107440
WHO (World Health)	Trinidad/Tobago	23 Jun 64	503UNTS167	107342
Rwanda	WHO (World Health)	23 Jun 64	514UNTS157	107445
Multilateral		23 Jun 64	506UNTS108	107383
Multilateral		28 Jun 64	519UNTS14	107499
Belgium	Tunisia	15 Jul 64	560UNTS57	108168
Argentina	France	03 Oct 64	635UNTS155	109080
Chad	Israel	07 Oct 64	630UNTS175	108969
Italy	ILO (Labor Org)	24 Oct 64	541UNTS217	107871
Multilateral		24 Oct 64	514UNTS220	200608
Netherlands	Pakistan	30 Oct 64	541UNTS243	107873
Argentina	Guatemala	30 Oct 64	601UNTS175	108695
Multilateral		11 Nov 64	515UNTS94	107456
Belgium	Mexico	19 Nov 64	546UNTS217	107949
Argentina	Panama	21 Nov 64	635UNTS205	109083
Argentina	Costa Rica	23 Nov 64	635UNTS213	109084
India	United Nations	25 Nov 64	519UNTS47	107501
India	Netherlands	11 Dec 64	570UNTS165	108292
Germany, West	Thailand	23 Dec 64	525UNTS201	107592
Germany, West	Thailand	23 Dec 64	525UNTS177	107589
Malawi	WHO (World Health)	06 Jan 65	525UNTS165	107588
Malawi	WHO (World Health)	08 Jan 65	524UNTS281	107579
Denmark	Thailand	25 Jan 65	530UNTS173	107680
Multilateral		27 Jan 65	523UNTS102	107556
Multilateral		02 Feb 65	523UNTS256	107560
Belgium	Hungary	11 Feb 65	544UNTS3	107908
Multilateral		12 Feb 65	525UNTS148	107587
USA (United States)	Uruguay	17 May 65	564UNTS69	108221
Ethiopia	Hungary	25 May 65	577UNTS193	108377
China People's Rep	Romania	27 May 65	592UNTS3	108566
Multilateral		02 Jun 65	537UNTS348	200611
Uganda	USSR (Soviet Union)	24 Jul 65	596UNTS199	108633
Israel	Sierra Leone	22 Aug 65	550UNTS285	108023
Poland	WHO (World Health)	26 Aug 65	552UNTS3	108047
Multilateral		13 Sep 65	547UNTS264	107962
Multilateral		21 Oct 65	547UNTS216	107959
Netherlands	Nigeria	28 Oct 65	578UNTS15	108383
Argentina	Belgium	05 Nov 65	635UNTS229	109086
East Afri Service	United Nations	27 Nov 65	550UNTS375	200616
UK Great Britain	Yugoslavia	27 Jan 66	573UNTS243	108337
Brazil	Denmark	25 Feb 66	590UNTS95	108549
WHO (World Health)	Singapore	28 Mar 66	562UNTS59	108195
Romania	Tunisia	21 Apr 66	604UNTS57	108743
Romania	Tunisia	21 Apr 66	604UNTS65	108744
Rwanda	USSR (Soviet Union)	06 May 66	633UNTS217	109039
Denmark	Iran	14 Jun 66	597UNTS283	108652
Romania	United Arab Rep	03 Sep 66	604UNTS73	108745
Multilateral		23 Sep 66	573UNTS132	108327
United Nations	Sudan	08 Nov 66	576UNTS85	108365
Congo (Brazzaville)	Czechoslovakia	29 Nov 66	635UNTS3	109069
Netherlands	Romania	13 Feb 67	604UNTS287	108756
Denmark	France	15 Feb 67	604UNTS247	108754
Belgium	Israel	23 Mar 67	630UNTS275	108974
Multilateral		20 Jun 67	0UNTS0	109290
Italy	Romania	08 Aug 67	642UNTS191	109174
Denmark	Romania	29 Aug 67	642UNTS357	109183
Vocational training				
Brazil	Paraguay	14 Jun 41	54UNTS235	200196

PARTY ONE	PARTY TWO	DATE	CITATION	NUMBER
Vocational training (Cont.)				
Brazil	Chile	18 Nov 41	67UNTS279	200225
El Salvador	USA (United States)	05 May 42	21UNTS215	200124
Paraguay	USA (United States)	22 May 42	124UNTS243	200423
Nicaragua	USA (United States)	22 May 42	105UNTS141	200328
Bolivia	USA (United States)	16 Jul 42	13UNTS101	200072
Peru	USA (United States)	24 Aug 42	24UNTS153	200139
Colombia	USA (United States)	23 Oct 42	105UNTS109	200326
El Salvador	USA (United States)	02 Dec 42	122UNTS277	200410
Mexico	USA (United States)	14 Jun 43	66UNTS331	200220
USA (United States)	Uruguay	01 Nov 43	106UNTS311	200348
Peru	USA (United States)	04 Apr 44	89UNTS291	200258
Multilateral		19 Apr 44	89UNTS279	200257
Brazil	Ecuador	24 May 44	73UNTS223	200242
Bolivia	USA (United States)	07 Sep 44	162UNTS315	200494
Brazil	Dominican Republic	09 Apr 45	67UNTS293	200226
Dominican Republic	USA (United States)	13 Oct 45	149UNTS361	200477
Czechoslovakia	France	08 Dec 45	46UNTS77	100701
Colombia	USA (United States)	19 Feb 46	166UNTS104	102187
Brazil	USA (United States)	05 Apr 46	12UNTS131	100183
Belgium	Netherlands	16 May 46	17UNTS13	100266
Multilateral		27 Jun 46	164UNTS37	102157
France	USA (United States)	10 Dec 46	15UNTS265	100242
Austria	France	15 Mar 47	12UNTS109	100182
Philippines	USA (United States)	12 May 47	16UNTS123	100253
Philippines	USA (United States)	12 May 47	16UNTS137	100254
Philippines	USA (United States)	12 May 47	16UNTS109	100252
Czechoslovakia	UK Great Britain	16 Jun 47	46UNTS61	100700
Bulgaria	Czechoslovakia	20 Jun 47	46UNTS15	100698
Romania	Yugoslavia	26 Jun 47	116UNTS39	101568
Bulgaria	Poland	28 Jun 47	15UNTS123	100230
USA (United States)	Venezuela	30 Jun 47	166UNTS198	102190
Multilateral		11 Jul 47	218UNTS345	102961
USSR (Soviet Union)	Yugoslavia	25 Jul 47	130UNTS315	101732
Czechoslovakia	Romania	05 Sep 47	46UNTS37	100699
Austria	USA (United States)	08 Oct 47	25UNTS3	100354
Ecuador	USA (United States)	14 Nov 47	149UNTS297	101959
Norway	UK Great Britain	19 Feb 48	34UNTS33	100526
Belgium	Norway	20 Feb 48	32UNTS39	100487
Paraguay	USA (United States)	12 Mar 48	162UNTS30	102131
Peru	USA (United States)	30 Jun 48	150UNTS45	101962
Panama	USA (United States)	24 Sep 48	150UNTS25	101961
Belgium	Italy	29 Nov 48	41UNTS3	100641
Afghanistan	UNESCO (Educ/Cult)	08 Dec 48	46UNTS3	100697
Belgium	France	08 Jan 49	36UNTS151	100569
Korea, North	USSR (Soviet Union)	17 Mar 49	221UNTS3	102999
Peru	USA (United States)	25 Mar 49	89UNTS15	101205
Mexico	USA (United States)	21 Jun 49	89UNTS3	101204
WHO (World Health)	Thailand	12 Aug 49	178UNTS347	102350
Bulgaria	Poland	26 Sep 49	260UNTS249	103712
Hungary	Poland	29 Oct 49	260UNTS113	103706
France	Ireland	21 Nov 49	553UNTS59	108069
UNICEF (Children)	UK Great Britain	10 Feb 50	65UNTS86	100837
Multilateral		17 Apr 50	131UNTS99	101738
Luxembourg	UK Great Britain	27 Jun 50	183UNTS217	102431
Pakistan	USA (United States)	23 Sep 50	82UNTS131	101088
Peru	WHO (World Health)	26 Sep 50	104UNTS233	101444
Iran	USA (United States)	19 Oct 50	92UNTS135	101266
Multilateral		02 Nov 50	81UNTS160	101071
Czechoslovakia	Poland	17 Nov 50	530UNTS195	107682
Bolivia	USA (United States)	22 Nov 50	152UNTS17	102008
Multilateral		24 Nov 50	81UNTS188	101072
Colombia	USA (United States)	24 Nov 50	133UNTS49	101779
Guatemala	WHO (World Health)	28 Nov 50	103UNTS51	101423
France	Turkey	22 Dec 50	98UNTS11	101356
El Salvador	WHO (World Health)	02 Jan 51	103UNTS29	101421

PARTY ONE	PARTY TWO	DATE	CITATION	NUMBER
Vocational training (Cont.)				
Nicaragua	WHO (World Health)	02 Jan 51	103UNTS107	101428
Colombia	WHO (World Health)	05 Jan 51	102UNTS139	101417
United Nations	Yugoslavia	06 Jan 51	78UNTS165	101015
Chile	USA (United States)	16 Jan 51	157UNTS3	102043
Multilateral		18 Jan 51	81UNTS233	101073
Albania	Poland	25 Jan 51	260UNTS217	103710
Nicaragua	USA (United States)	31 Jan 51	160UNTS121	102105
Ethiopia	ICAO (Civil Aviat)	02 Feb 51	96UNTS123	101333
Multilateral		15 Feb 51	81UNTS245	101074
Israel	ILO (Labor Org)	19 Feb 51	100UNTS105	101391
Israel	ICAO (Civil Aviat)	19 Feb 51	96UNTS141	101334
ILO (Labor Org)	Syria	03 Mar 51	110UNTS69	101502
Multilateral		05 Mar 51	81UNTS261	101075
Dominican Republic	USA (United States)	16 Mar 51	148UNTS15	101932
Multilateral		28 Mar 51	181UNTS61	102399
Jordan	ILO (Labor Org)	29 Mar 51	100UNTS247	200287
Jordan	United Nations	29 Mar 51	137UNTS267	200448
Multilateral		05 Apr 51	84UNTS299	101139
Mexico	ILO (Labor Org)	06 Apr 51	100UNTS131	101393
Ceylon (Sri Lanka)	ILO (Labor Org)	06 Apr 51	100UNTS235	200286
Peru	ILO (Labor Org)	13 Apr 51	100UNTS31	101385
Guatemala	ILO (Labor Org)	13 Apr 51	126UNTS249	101692
Costa Rica	WHO (World Health)	13 Apr 51	103UNTS3	101419
El Salvador	USA (United States)	18 Apr 51	141UNTS37	101903
Multilateral		18 Apr 51	261UNTS140	103729
Ecuador	ILO (Labor Org)	19 Apr 51	100UNTS77	101389
ICAO (Civil Aviat)	Thailand	19 Apr 51	96UNTS181	101336
Greece	Turkey	20 Apr 51	178UNTS17	102333
Cuba	ILO (Labor Org)	21 Apr 51	99UNTS205	101382
Honduras	USA (United States)	24 Apr 51	140UNTS287	101894
Greece	ILO (Labor Org)	25 Apr 51	100UNTS93	101390
India	ILO (Labor Org)	26 Apr 51	100UNTS19	101384
WHO (World Health)	Yugoslavia	02 May 51	103UNTS117	101429
United Arab Rep	USA (United States)	05 May 51	198UNTS265	102670
Pakistan	ILO (Labor Org)	16 May 51	100UNTS147	101394
Nicaragua	UK Great Britain	25 May 51	101UNTS77	101404
Lebanon	USA (United States)	29 May 51	160UNTS49	102101
USA (United States)	Venezuela	07 Jun 51	141UNTS273	101918
Iceland	ICAO (Civil Aviat)	07 Jun 51	96UNTS193	101337
United Nations	Thailand	11 Jun 51	90UNTS45	101225
Burma	WHO (World Health)	13 Jun 51	117UNTS115	101588
Costa Rica	WHO (World Health)	14 Jun 51	102UNTS151	101418
Dominican Republic	ILO (Labor Org)	18 Jun 51	100UNTS3	101383
Multilateral		25 Jun 51	92UNTS27	101258
Israel	United Nations	25 Jun 51	97UNTS21	101344
ILO (Labor Org)	Vietnam, South	26 Jun 51	100UNTS223	200285
Multilateral		28 Jun 51	118UNTS154	101604
Brazil	USA (United States)	29 Jun 51	184UNTS303	102455
India	Turkey	29 Jun 51	213UNTS183	102886
Ethiopia	WHO (World Health)	02 Jul 51	103UNTS39	101422
Burma	WHO (World Health)	09 Jul 51	104UNTS187	101440
ILO (Labor Org)	Thailand	11 Jul 51	100UNTS159	101395
Paraguay	ILO (Labor Org)	12 Jul 51	117UNTS155	101591
Multilateral		27 Jul 51	97UNTS291	200273
Panama	USA (United States)	30 Jul 51	140UNTS321	101896
Multilateral		01 Aug 51	107UNTS19	101464
Multilateral		04 Aug 51	104UNTS197	101441
Israel	WHO (World Health)	07 Aug 51	104UNTS213	101442
Japan	USA (United States)	28 Aug 51	147UNTS81	101930
WHO (World Health)	Saudi Arabia	29 Aug 51	110UNTS277	101516
Multilateral		05 Sep 51	173UNTS15	102256
Portugal	USA (United States)	06 Sep 51	237UNTS217	103348
Iraq	ICAO (Civil Aviat)	18 Sep 51	108UNTS219	101475
Korea, South	WHO (World Health)	19 Sep 51	109UNTS297	200366
Paraguay	United Nations	27 Sep 51	120UNTS105	101617

PARTY ONE	PARTY TWO	DATE	CITATION	NUMBER
Vocational training (Cont.)				
Multilateral		01 Oct 51	104UNTS249	101446
WHO (World Health)	Thailand	04 Oct 51	109UNTS77	101492
WHO (World Health)	Thailand	04 Oct 51	109UNTS85	101493
Pakistan	WHO (World Health)	07 Oct 51	126UNTS101	101684
Ecuador	WHO (World Health)	16 Oct 51	110UNTS263	101515
United Nations	Uruguay	17 Oct 51	122UNTS29	101633
ILO (Labor Org)	Venezuela	22 Oct 51	117UNTS139	101590
India	WHO (World Health)	23 Oct 51	109UNTS59	101491
Taiwan	WHO (World Health)	25 Oct 51	126UNTS77	101683
Panama	WHO (World Health)	09 Nov 51	118UNTS43	101595
Panama	ILO (Labor Org)	10 Nov 51	126UNTS269	101693
Australia	USA (United States)	16 Nov 51	168UNTS75	102214
Italy	UK Great Britain	28 Nov 51	172UNTS27	102238
El Salvador	USA (United States)	12 Dec 51	132UNTS287	101768
Mexico	WHO (World Health)	17 Dec 51	124UNTS121	101670
Guatemala	WHO (World Health)	17 Dec 51	120UNTS133	101619
India	WHO (World Health)	20 Dec 51	124UNTS109	101669
Multilateral		24 Dec 51	118UNTS290	200383
Guatemala	WHO (World Health)	29 Dec 51	124UNTS89	101668
Austria	WHO (World Health)	10 Jan 52	131UNTS295	200438
Colombia	USA (United States)	12 Jan 52	168UNTS109	102216
Ceylon (Sri Lanka)	United Nations	21 Jan 52	118UNTS281	200382
Multilateral		23 Jan 52	127UNTS269	101708
Costa Rica	WHO (World Health)	23 Jan 52	135UNTS265	101826
WHO (World Health)	Spain	30 Jan 52	124UNTS259	200425
Peru	USA (United States)	04 Feb 52	121UNTS255	200403
ICAO (Civil Aviat)	Yugoslavia	06 Feb 52	128UNTS97	101715
WHO (World Health)	UK Great Britain	07 Feb 52	121UNTS75	101627
Jordan	USA (United States)	12 Feb 52	168UNTS25	102211
Lebanon	ICAO (Civil Aviat)	14 Feb 52	128UNTS83	101714
Dominican Republic	WHO (World Health)	15 Feb 52	134UNTS291	101808
Burma	WHO (World Health)	18 Feb 52	127UNTS43	101698
Greece	United Nations	05 Mar 52	123UNTS3	101650
ICAO (Civil Aviat)	United Arab Rep	06 Mar 52	151UNTS111	101986
Taiwan	WHO (World Health)	07 Mar 52	128UNTS233	101723
Finland	WHO (World Health)	07 Mar 52	128UNTS269	200436
India	United Nations	02 Apr 52	126UNTS145	101687
United Nations	Yugoslavia	10 Apr 52	141UNTS89	101908
India	WHO (World Health)	17 Apr 52	131UNTS241	101744
India	WHO (World Health)	19 Apr 52	131UNTS253	101745
Pakistan	United Nations	28 Apr 52	128UNTS191	101720
India	ICAO (Civil Aviat)	29 Apr 52	151UNTS123	101987
Israel	USA (United States)	09 May 52	177UNTS63	102309
Ethiopia	USA (United States)	15 May 52	180UNTS227	102388
Libya	USA (United States)	20 May 52	178UNTS155	102339
Libya	USA (United States)	20 May 52	177UNTS81	102310
Iraq	USA (United States)	21 May 52	205UNTS25	102767
Iraq	USA (United States)	21 May 52	205UNTS33	102768
Chile	WHO (World Health)	31 May 52	136UNTS323	101841
India	WHO (World Health)	04 Jun 52	135UNTS279	101827
Iraq	USA (United States)	09 Jun 52	212UNTS193	102871
Brazil	WHO (World Health)	12 Jun 52	151UNTS333	102003
Ethiopia	USA (United States)	18 Jun 52	181UNTS207	102410
India	WHO (World Health)	19 Jun 52	134UNTS307	101809
Multilateral		19 Jun 52	133UNTS165	101787
WHO (World Health)	Syria	20 Jun 52	165UNTS219	102178
Ethiopia	USA (United States)	24 Jun 52	181UNTS215	102411
Panama	USA (United States)	30 Jun 52	181UNTS121	102404
Chile	USA (United States)	30 Jun 52	199UNTS241	102688
Brazil	USA (United States)	30 Jun 52	185UNTS79	102460
Australia	FAO (Food Agri)	07 Jul 52	184UNTS209	102449
Chile	WHO (World Health)	11 Jul 52	137UNTS27	101846
India	WHO (World Health)	16 Jul 52	135UNTS291	101828
Chile	ILO (Labor Org)	23 Jul 52	178UNTS323	102348
Iraq	USA (United States)	18 Aug 52	184UNTS131	102444

PARTY ONE	PARTY TWO	DATE	CITATION	NUMBER
Vocational training (Cont.)				
Panama	United Nations	20 Aug 52	136UNTS3	101829
Multilateral		21 Aug 52	141UNTS129	101912
Italy	ILO (Labor Org)	04 Sep 52	178UNTS371	200505
ILO (Labor Org)	Uruguay	20 Sep 52	187UNTS25	102499
United Nations	Trieste	30 Sep 52	140UNTS11	101881
Multilateral		15 Oct 52	141UNTS96	101909
Iraq	USA (United States)	23 Oct 52	212UNTS201	102872
Chile	WHO (World Health)	24 Oct 52	151UNTS339	102004
Chile	WHO (World Health)	04 Nov 52	150UNTS119	101966
Ethiopia	USA (United States)	05 Nov 52	184UNTS139	102445
Ethiopia	USA (United States)	07 Nov 52	184UNTS285	102453
Saudi Arabia	USA (United States)	10 Nov 52	181UNTS295	102418
Saudi Arabia	USA (United States)	10 Nov 52	181UNTS225	102412
Ceylon (Sri Lanka)	USA (United States)	17 Nov 52	180UNTS207	102386
Japan	WHO (World Health)	26 Nov 52	204UNTS301	200521
Mexico	ICAO (Civil Aviat)	28 Nov 52	164UNTS15	102156
India	WHO (World Health)	11 Dec 52	158UNTS391	102073
Austria	UK Great Britain	12 Dec 52	172UNTS9	102237
Saudi Arabia	USA (United States)	15 Dec 52	185UNTS55	102458
Saudi Arabia	USA (United States)	15 Dec 52	185UNTS67	102459
Multilateral		16 Dec 52	158UNTS407	102074
Multilateral		29 Dec 52	151UNTS317	102002
ILO (Labor Org)	UN Relief Palestin	31 Dec 52	182UNTS201	200506
Saudi Arabia	USA (United States)	25 Jan 53	201UNTS3	102706
India	WHO (World Health)	11 Feb 53	163UNTS43	102140
Taiwan	ILO (Labor Org)	13 Feb 53	178UNTS337	102349
Multilateral		26 Feb 53	161UNTS31	102120
Costa Rica	United Nations	27 Feb 53	161UNTS45	102121
Nepal	United Nations	02 Mar 53	161UNTS347	200493
United Arab Rep	USA (United States)	12 Mar 53	204UNTS3	102747
Japan	USA (United States)	18 Mar 53	212UNTS149	102867
France	WHO (World Health)	02 Apr 53	174UNTS83	102279
United Nations	Yemen	07 Apr 53	163UNTS73	102142
Ethiopia	USA (United States)	29 Apr 53	224UNTS121	103073
France	WHO (World Health)	30 Apr 53	174UNTS71	102278
United Arab Rep	USA (United States)	21 May 53	204UNTS29	102748
ICAO (Civil Aviat)	Syria	28 May 53	173UNTS199	102267
Brazil	USA (United States)	30 May 53	460UNTS89	106633
Ecuador	United Nations	16 Jun 53	166UNTS289	102194
United Arab Rep	USA (United States)	18 Jun 53	215UNTS45	102910
United Arab Rep	USA (United States)	18 Jun 53	204UNTS55	102749
Ethiopia	United Nations	22 Jun 53	172UNTS93	102241
Liberia	USA (United States)	23 Jun 53	213UNTS57	102880
Cambodia	United Nations	24 Jun 53	168UNTS309	200500
Ethiopia	USA (United States)	25 Jun 53	212UNTS175	102869
Panama	USA (United States)	26 Jun 53	215UNTS77	102912
Chile	USA (United States)	27 Jun 53	229UNTS53	103160
Chile	USA (United States)	27 Jun 53	229UNTS193	103167
Saudi Arabia	USA (United States)	29 Jun 53	206UNTS23	102784
Ethiopia	USA (United States)	30 Jun 53	212UNTS135	102865
Afghanistan	USA (United States)	30 Jun 53	215UNTS3	102908
Nicaragua	USA (United States)	30 Jun 53	215UNTS133	102917
Multilateral		09 Oct 53	190UNTS49	102557
Dominican Republic	United Nations	19 Nov 53	180UNTS45	102374
Brazil	WHO (World Health)	04 Feb 54	233UNTS49	103250
United Nations	Venezuela	05 Mar 54	187UNTS9	102498
Liberia	United Nations	09 Mar 54	187UNTS61	102501
Guatemala	United Nations	10 Mar 54	191UNTS271	102587
Mexico	USA (United States)	06 Apr 54	236UNTS69	103317
Ireland	UK Great Britain	06 Apr 54	553UNTS197	108088
Multilateral		20 Apr 54	189UNTS11	102539
Nepal	WHO (World Health)	13 May 54	204UNTS311	200522
Multilateral		31 May 54	192UNTS20	102592
Multilateral		01 Jun 54	200UNTS235	200520
Italy	Netherlands	04 Jun 54	289UNTS261	104222

PARTY ONE	PARTY TWO	DATE	CITATION	NUMBER
Vocational training (Cont.)				
Ethiopia	USA (United States)	12 Jun 54	234UNTS25	103270
Costa Rica	USA (United States)	30 Jun 54	235UNTS35	103294
Ecuador	USA (United States)	30 Jun 54	236UNTS163	103323
Multilateral		19 Aug 54	201UNTS51	102710
Greece	Italy	11 Sep 54	284UNTS313	104145
Multilateral		06 Oct 54	201UNTS75	102711
Ethiopia	Sweden	13 Oct 54	202UNTS273	102734
Multilateral		27 Oct 54	201UNTS95	102712
Multilateral		29 Oct 54	201UNTS115	102713
Austria	Netherlands	17 Nov 54	292UNTS45	104266
Belgium	Greece	09 Dec 54	257UNTS243	103660
Mexico	USA (United States)	09 Mar 55	263UNTS247	103776
Ceylon (Sri Lanka)	Germany, West	01 Apr 55	369UNTS57	105251
Multilateral		04 Apr 55	208UNTS239	102816
Japan	USA (United States)	07 Apr 55	263UNTS285	103778
Taiwan	WHO (World Health)	21 Apr 55	210UNTS71	102835
Czechoslovakia	Hungary	28 Apr 55	477UNTS197	106923
Pakistan	Sweden	04 Jun 55	228UNTS121	103146
Multilateral		14 Jun 55	212UNTS263	200526
Bulgaria	Yugoslavia	17 Jun 55	375UNTS287	105370
Multilateral		04 Jul 55	214UNTS10	102897
Iran	WHO (World Health)	04 Jul 55	227UNTS65	103131
Czechoslovakia	Germany, East	30 Aug 55	504UNTS279	107361
Austria	Sweden	03 Nov 55	262UNTS289	103757
Italy	Lebanon	04 Nov 55	267UNTS147	103840
Multilateral		02 Feb 56	227UNTS153	103137
Multilateral		10 Feb 56	228UNTS167	103150
Multilateral		10 Feb 56	228UNTS189	103151
Iran	Pakistan	09 Mar 56	449UNTS183	106460
Multilateral		13 Mar 56	427UNTS245	106158
Mongolia	USSR (Soviet Union)	24 Apr 56	259UNTS297	103693
Germany, East	USSR (Soviet Union)	26 Apr 56	259UNTS279	103692
Korea, North	Romania	12 May 56	342UNTS189	104908
Multilateral		31 May 56	251UNTS181	103541
Czechoslovakia	USSR (Soviet Union)	01 Jun 56	259UNTS341	103696
Multilateral		08 Jun 56	247UNTS366	200541
Multilateral		14 Jun 56	265UNTS125	103809
Israel	USA (United States)	26 Jun 56	257UNTS55	103649
Multilateral		26 Jun 56	321UNTS2	104650
Multilateral		26 Jun 56	253UNTS12	103573
Multilateral		02 Jul 56	248UNTS37	103484
Multilateral		02 Jul 56	540UNTS110	107846
Multilateral		31 Aug 56	249UNTS158	103506
Belgium	Germany, West	24 Sep 56	263UNTS31	103766
Canada	France	04 Oct 56	305UNTS65	104414
Multilateral		05 Oct 56	251UNTS267	103545
Multilateral		05 Oct 56	251UNTS245	103544
UN Hi Com Refugees	Sweden	08 Oct 56	428UNTS307	106182
Germany, West	Thailand	09 Oct 56	258UNTS143	103676
Romania	Yugoslavia	27 Oct 56	389UNTS55	105592
Multilateral		21 Nov 56	253UNTS266	103588
UK Great Britain	USA (United States)	27 Nov 56	282UNTS43	104092
Germany, East	Romania	08 Dec 56	362UNTS189	105188
Multilateral		15 Jan 57	376UNTS122	105378
Multilateral		23 Jan 57	259UNTS426	103701
Multilateral		17 Feb 57	271UNTS2	103907
Multilateral		01 Mar 57	264UNTS94	103790
India	Poland	27 Mar 57	319UNTS263	104635
Multilateral		28 Mar 57	271UNTS30	103908
Multilateral		09 Apr 57	274UNTS172	103965
India	Romania	30 Apr 57	342UNTS251	104911
Czechoslovakia	United Arab Rep	06 May 57	292UNTS317	104278
Finland	USA (United States)	10 May 57	283UNTS43	104105
Multilateral		24 May 57	268UNTS270	103861
Bulgaria	Czechoslovakia	03 Jun 57	292UNTS3	104261

Vocational training (Cont.)

PARTY ONE	PARTY TWO	DATE	CITATION	NUMBER
Czechoslovakia	Yugoslavia	11 Jun 57	504UNTS107	107355
Multilateral		26 Jun 57	328UNTS247	104738
Multilateral		09 Jul 57	274UNTS300	103972
Greece	Italy	02 Aug 57	533UNTS217	107744
Burma	WHO (World Health)	20 Sep 57	282UNTS113	104096
New Zealand	UK Great Britain	20 Sep 57	287UNTS105	104180
UK Great Britain	USA (United States)	01 Nov 57	299UNTS167	104312
Multilateral		05 Nov 57	285UNTS301	104155
Germany, East	Hungary	13 Nov 57	407UNTS216	105866
Italy	Spain	25 Nov 57	378UNTS289	105428
Ireland	Sweden	05 Dec 57	428UNTS221	106176
Ceylon (Sri Lanka)	USSR (Soviet Union)	15 Jan 58	305UNTS235	104421
Poland	Yugoslavia	16 Jan 58	340UNTS181	104864
Ghana	WHO (World Health)	21 Jan 58	307UNTS3	104437
Indonesia	WHO (World Health)	05 Feb 58	307UNTS15	104438
Czechoslovakia	Hungary	12 Mar 58	408UNTS178	105870
Multilateral		15 Mar 58	292UNTS273	104276
Czechoslovakia	Romania	25 Mar 58	339UNTS77	104846
Israel	WHO (World Health)	11 Apr 58	307UNTS27	104439
Hungary	Poland	08 May 58	408UNTS212	105872
Germany, East	Hungary	14 Jun 58	407UNTS78	105861
Multilateral		19 Jun 58	306UNTS236	200550
WHO (World Health)	Sudan	21 Jun 58	307UNTS235	104453
Multilateral		25 Jun 58	362UNTS31	105181
Germany, East	Romania	15 Jul 58	387UNTS115	105560
Iran	Japan	09 Dec 58	325UNTS221	104701
Burma	United Nations	15 Dec 58	319UNTS3	104629
Afghanistan	WHO (World Health)	18 Dec 58	324UNTS121	104681
United Nations	Tunisia	23 Dec 58	321UNTS23	104651
Mongolia	Poland	23 Dec 58	432UNTS177	106220
Ghana	United Nations	27 Feb 59	324UNTS133	104682
United Nations	Sudan	28 Mar 59	327UNTS95	104719
Bulgaria	Hungary	03 Apr 59	438UNTS269	106319
Hungary	USSR (Soviet Union)	17 Apr 59	439UNTS41	106324
Brazil	Israel	24 Jun 59	515UNTS151	107458
Libya	United Nations	27 Jun 59	336UNTS291	104811
Laos	United Nations	06 Jul 59	337UNTS41	104814
Paraguay	United Nations	01 Aug 59	341UNTS319	104894
Bulgaria	Czechoslovakia	19 Sep 59	355UNTS77	105074
Canada	Euratom	06 Oct 59	475UNTS187	106894
Guinea	United Nations	15 Oct 59	344UNTS47	104942
USA (United States)	USSR (Soviet Union)	21 Nov 59	361UNTS35	105172
Multilateral		03 Dec 59	348UNTS246	105003
Czechoslovakia	Ethiopia	11 Dec 59	386UNTS45	105536
Germany, East	Hungary	19 Dec 59	409UNTS4	105874
Ceylon (Sri Lanka)	WHO (World Health)	21 Dec 59	349UNTS109	105011
Pakistan	WHO (World Health)	20 Jan 60	351UNTS355	105034
India	Japan	25 Jan 60	384UNTS31	105508
Ecuador	USA (United States)	24 Feb 60	371UNTS55	105270
Indonesia	USSR (Soviet Union)	28 Feb 60	392UNTS173	105643
Japan	USA (United States)	23 Mar 60	372UNTS289	105305
Multilateral		12 Apr 60	359UNTS323	105150
United Nations	Togo	06 May 60	388UNTS53	105571
Cambodia	WHO (World Health)	19 May 60	372UNTS193	105298
Multilateral		04 Jun 60	360UNTS208	105159
Multilateral		19 Jun 60	537UNTS214	107803
Multilateral		08 Jul 60	366UNTS310	105220
Ethiopia	United Nations	13 Jul 60	368UNTS143	105239
France	Greece	25 Jul 60	533UNTS227	107745
Japan	Pakistan	30 Jul 60	384UNTS63	105511
WHO (World Health)	United Arab Rep	03 Aug 60	385UNTS3	105524
Jordan	WHO (World Health)	03 Aug 60	381UNTS133	105469
Laos	WHO (World Health)	04 Aug 60	373UNTS313	105322
Ghana	USSR (Soviet Union)	04 Aug 60	399UNTS61	105734
WHO (World Health)	Tunisia	04 Aug 60	381UNTS335	105474

Vocational training (Cont.)

PARTY ONE	PARTY TWO	DATE	CITATION	NUMBER
Japan	Thailand	24 Aug 60	384UNTS73	105512
WHO (World Health)	Saudi Arabia	06 Sep 60	395UNTS169	105684
Lebanon	WHO (World Health)	08 Sep 60	387UNTS49	105557
Iran	Japan	12 Sep 60	384UNTS43	105509
WHO (World Health)	Upper Volta	15 Nov 60	383UNTS91	105496
Pakistan	United Nations	17 Nov 60	380UNTS277	105460
Fed of Malaya	WHO (World Health)	25 Nov 60	387UNTS37	105556
Cambodia	United Nations	30 Nov 60	383UNTS147	105500
WHO (World Health)	Yemen	03 Dec 60	395UNTS187	105685
Dahomey	WHO (World Health)	07 Dec 60	387UNTS277	105567
Congo (Brazzaville)	WHO (World Health)	12 Dec 60	399UNTS105	105737
Multilateral		13 Dec 60	523UNTS117	107557
Bolivia	United Nations	14 Dec 60	382UNTS283	105489
Niger	WHO (World Health)	28 Dec 60	394UNTS195	105679
Ethiopia	USSR (Soviet Union)	13 Jan 61	421UNTS13	106049
Korea, South	WHO (World Health)	20 Jan 61	406UNTS269	200589
Multilateral		28 Jan 61	387UNTS202	105563
Ivory Coast	WHO (World Health)	30 Jan 61	395UNTS205	105686
Chad	WHO (World Health)	03 Feb 61	394UNTS161	105676
WHO (World Health)	Togo	03 Feb 61	394UNTS207	105680
Central Afri Rep	WHO (World Health)	13 Feb 61	394UNTS149	105675
Finland	Italy	18 Feb 61	434UNTS199	106263
Iraq	United Nations	05 Mar 61	409UNTS56	105878
Cuba	Poland	06 Mar 61	484UNTS123	107020
Afghanistan	Japan	15 Mar 61	450UNTS373	106480
Kuwait	WHO (World Health)	16 Mar 61	397UNTS315	200588
Ceylon (Sri Lanka)	Japan	20 Mar 61	450UNTS385	106481
Cuba	Germany, East	29 Mar 61	448UNTS81	106426
Cuba	Czechoslovakia	05 Apr 61	442UNTS201	106350
Mauritania	WHO (World Health)	17 Apr 61	396UNTS301	200587
Gabon	WHO (World Health)	27 Apr 61	397UNTS215	105707
Mali	WHO (World Health)	27 Apr 61	407UNTS66	105860
Somalia	USSR (Soviet Union)	02 Jun 61	457UNTS263	106587
Czechoslovakia	Somalia	04 Jun 61	479UNTS291	106960
Cyprus	United Nations	15 Jun 61	398UNTS39	105716
Haiti	United Nations	28 Jun 61	399UNTS159	105740
Morocco	WHO (World Health)	09 Aug 61	412UNTS192	105932
Pakistan	Philippines	15 Aug 61	522UNTS35	107534
WHO (World Health)	Somalia	17 Aug 61	423UNTS111	106088
Lebanon	United Nations	26 Aug 61	406UNTS105	105842
Ghana	United Nations	29 Aug 61	406UNTS117	105843
Tunisia	USSR (Soviet Union)	30 Aug 61	437UNTS243	106310
Jordan	United Nations	11 Sep 61	406UNTS255	105855
Iraq	WHO (World Health)	13 Sep 61	419UNTS69	106030
Multilateral		20 Sep 61	407UNTS52	105859
Japan	United Nations	04 Oct 61	410UNTS133	105900
Malagasy	WHO (World Health)	13 Oct 61	421UNTS273	106064
Multilateral		16 Oct 61	410UNTS242	105908
Multilateral		18 Oct 61	529UNTS89	107659
Multilateral		07 Nov 61	412UNTS258	105937
Ceylon (Sri Lanka)	United Nations	04 Dec 61	415UNTS236	105987
Argentina	Japan	20 Dec 61	451UNTS77	106486
Multilateral		27 Dec 61	425UNTS83	106120
Ghana	USA (United States)	03 Jan 62	433UNTS147	106237
Ethiopia	WHO (World Health)	11 Jan 62	423UNTS99	106087
Multilateral		17 Jan 62	419UNTS294	106033
United Nations	Somalia	20 Jan 62	420UNTS133	106044
Multilateral		20 Jan 62	429UNTS230	200596
Multilateral		13 Feb 62	422UNTS288	200594
Multilateral		21 Feb 62	423UNTS151	106091
Multilateral		01 Mar 62	423UNTS122	106089
USA (United States)	USSR (Soviet Union)	08 Mar 62	460UNTS3	106630
WHO (World Health)	Sudan	11 Mar 62	432UNTS325	106226
Nigeria	WHO (World Health)	27 Mar 62	429UNTS123	106194
Brazil	Japan	28 Mar 62	451UNTS125	106489

PARTY ONE	PARTY TWO	DATE	CITATION	NUMBER
Vocational training (Cont.)				
India	Japan	31 Mar 62	451UNTS143	106490
Multilateral		10 Apr 62	429UNTS78	106192
Multilateral		18 Apr 62	463UNTS44	106692
India	Japan	23 Apr 62	451UNTS155	106491
Multilateral		17 May 62	429UNTS46	106189
Greece	Tunisia	26 May 62	534UNTS163	107761
Senegal	USSR (Soviet Union)	14 Jun 62	437UNTS233	106309
Libya	WHO (World Health)	16 Jun 62	437UNTS127	106301
WHO (World Health)	Sierra Leone	19 Jun 62	439UNTS151	106327
Multilateral		22 Jun 62	494UNTS249	107237
WHO (World Health)	Senegal	06 Aug 62	435UNTS179	106279
Nigeria	United Nations	07 Aug 62	435UNTS167	106278
Multilateral		12 Aug 62	443UNTS266	106365
WHO (World Health)	Western Samoa	14 Aug 62	437UNTS317	200598
Italy	USA (United States)	28 Aug 62	461UNTS137	106657
Cameroon	United Nations	29 Aug 62	442UNTS3	106334
Multilateral		29 Aug 62	443UNTS280	106366
Italy	USA (United States)	05 Sep 62	461UNTS185	106663
Niger	United Nations	01 Oct 62	439UNTS181	106329
Belgium	Rwanda	13 Oct 62	456UNTS431	106569
Belgium	Rwanda	13 Oct 62	456UNTS425	106568
Israel	Rwanda	23 Oct 62	515UNTS291	107466
Cameroon	Israel	24 Oct 62	449UNTS3	106446
United Nations	Western Samoa	05 Nov 62	443UNTS297	200599
Multilateral		15 Nov 62	448UNTS50	106424
WHO (World Health)	Syria	18 Nov 62	480UNTS249	106972
Ecuador	United Nations	26 Nov 62	445UNTS3	106372
Rwanda	United Nations	28 Nov 62	450UNTS267	106473
Laos	USSR (Soviet Union)	01 Dec 62	472UNTS3	106834
Multilateral		06 Dec 62	450UNTS240	106471
Cameroon	WHO (World Health)	08 Dec 62	451UNTS215	106496
Ivory Coast	United Nations	10 Dec 62	451UNTS269	106498
Multilateral		12 Dec 62	457UNTS72	106578
Algeria	WHO (World Health)	20 Dec 62	463UNTS135	106698
Belgium	Tunisia	21 Dec 62	482UNTS3	106987
India	United Nations	27 Dec 62	450UNTS3	106464
Israel	United Nations	07 Jan 63	450UNTS229	106470
UK Great Britain	USA (United States)	15 Jan 63	466UNTS181	106743
Multilateral		21 Jan 63	453UNTS20	106517
UK Great Britain	USSR (Soviet Union)	21 Jan 63	475UNTS3	106887
United Nations	South Pacific Com	24 Jan 63	470UNTS361	200604
New Zealand	Western Samoa	24 Jan 63	499UNTS21	107290
Ethiopia	USA (United States)	25 Jan 63	473UNTS27	106851
Israel	Tanganyika	28 Jan 63	516UNTS39	107468
Israel	Uganda	04 Feb 63	484UNTS273	107037
Multilateral		05 Feb 63	453UNTS36	106518
Multilateral		14 Feb 63	453UNTS168	106524
Multilateral		06 Mar 63	455UNTS386	106552
Dahomey	USSR (Soviet Union)	20 Mar 63	528UNTS181	107641
Hungary	Korea, North	29 Mar 63	577UNTS219	108379
Romania	USA (United States)	02 Apr 63	474UNTS95	106874
Multilateral		18 Apr 63	463UNTS121	106697
Multilateral		06 May 63	463UNTS78	106694
Multilateral		09 May 63	463UNTS159	106700
Denmark	India	15 May 63	616UNTS23	108889
Multilateral		22 May 63	483UNTS72	107007
Multilateral		24 May 63	466UNTS346	106754
Mongolia	WHO (World Health)	21 Jun 63	472UNTS373	106848
Multilateral		23 Jul 63	471UNTS158	106831
Multilateral		31 Jul 63	472UNTS220	106842
Burundi	WHO (World Health)	08 Aug 63	477UNTS346	106928
Multilateral		27 Aug 63	511UNTS210	107435
Multilateral		10 Sep 63	480UNTS100	106965
Jamaica	WHO (World Health)	25 Sep 63	481UNTS125	106980
Hungary	Yugoslavia	15 Oct 63	577UNTS49	108372

PARTY ONE	PARTY TWO	DATE	CITATION	NUMBER
Vocational training (Cont.)				
Multilateral		30 Oct 63	480UNTS180	106968
WHO (World Health)	Tanganyika	05 Nov 63	496UNTS193	107252
Multilateral		07 Nov 63	480UNTS232	106971
Multilateral		08 Nov 63	482UNTS286	106999
Belgium	Pakistan	14 Nov 63	535UNTS393	107792
Cameroon	Netherlands	18 Dec 63	521UNTS303	107527
Multilateral		28 Jan 64	502UNTS321	107336
Iceland	USA (United States)	13 Feb 64	524UNTS235	107576
Multilateral		20 Feb 64	491UNTS30	107172
USA (United States)	USSR (Soviet Union)	22 Feb 64	526UNTS131	107605
Germany, West	Thailand	02 Apr 64	503UNTS3	107338
Cuba	Czechoslovakia	03 Jun 64	527UNTS205	107626
Rwanda	WHO (World Health)	22 Jun 64	514UNTS11	107440
WHO (World Health)	Trinidad/Tobago	23 Jun 64	503UNTS167	107342
Rwanda	WHO (World Health)	23 Jun 64	514UNTS157	107445
Multilateral		23 Jun 64	506UNTS108	107383
Multilateral		28 Jun 64	519UNTS14	107499
Taiwan	Philippines	25 Aug 64	511UNTS233	107436
Czechoslovakia	Mongolia	21 Oct 64	545UNTS91	107926
Italy	ILO (Labor Org)	24 Oct 64	541UNTS217	107871
Multilateral		24 Oct 64	514UNTS220	200608
Asian Productivity	ILO (Labor Org)	27 Oct 64	516UNTS367	200610
Multilateral		07 Nov 64	548UNTS3	107965
Multilateral		11 Nov 64	515UNTS94	107456
Israel	Turkey	13 Nov 64	550UNTS303	108025
India	United Nations	25 Nov 64	519UNTS47	107501
Czechoslovakia	United Arab Rep	26 Nov 64	545UNTS11	107923
Poland	Romania	26 Nov 64	552UNTS157	108053
Ghana	Israel	30 Nov 64	550UNTS231	108019
Germany, West	Jamaica	16 Dec 64	531UNTS129	107699
Germany, West	Thailand	23 Dec 64	525UNTS177	107589
Malawi	WHO (World Health)	06 Jan 65	525UNTS165	107588
Malawi	WHO (World Health)	08 Jan 65	524UNTS281	107579
Ecuador	Netherlands	14 Jan 65	551UNTS129	108038
Multilateral		27 Jan 65	523UNTS102	107556
Multilateral		02 Feb 65	523UNTS256	107560
Germany, West	Jamaica	03 Feb 65	531UNTS143	107700
Multilateral		12 Feb 65	525UNTS148	107587
Benelux Econ Union	Poland	17 Feb 65	547UNTS165	107956
Mexico	USA (United States)	27 Feb 65	546UNTS135	107940
Multilateral		02 Jun 65	537UNTS348	200611
Multilateral		02 Jun 65	551UNTS2	108030
Pakistan	USSR (Soviet Union)	05 Jun 65	593UNTS115	108579
Multilateral		02 Jul 65	592UNTS215	108575
Uganda	USSR (Soviet Union)	24 Jul 65	596UNTS199	108633
Israel	Sierra Leone	22 Aug 65	550UNTS285	108023
Poland	WHO (World Health)	26 Aug 65	552UNTS3	108047
Multilateral		13 Sep 65	547UNTS264	107962
Chile	IBRD (World Bank)	06 Oct 65	567UNTS293	108261
East Afri Service	United Nations	27 Nov 65	550UNTS375	200616
Israel	Kenya	25 Feb 66	582UNTS23	108455
WHO (World Health)	Singapore	28 Mar 66	562UNTS59	108195
Denmark	Iran	14 Jun 66	597UNTS283	108652
Multilateral		23 Sep 66	573UNTS132	108327
Argentina	Bolivia	19 Dec 66	636UNTS75	109092
Multilateral		21 Jun 67	598UNTS2	108653
Denmark	Zambia	17 Oct 67	620UNTS239	108960
Culture				
Multilateral		30 Apr 48	119UNTS3	101609
Australia	Denmark	08 Oct 48	22UNTS43	100330
Netherlands	South Africa	31 May 51	188UNTS289	102533
Pakistan	United Arab Rep	14 Nov 53	485UNTS55	107046
Hungary	USSR (Soviet Union)	28 Jun 56	259UNTS405	103700
Germany, West	Japan	14 Feb 57	318UNTS361	104626

PARTY ONE	PARTY TWO	DATE	CITATION	NUMBER
Culture (Cont.)				
Iraq	Poland	02 Apr 59	432UNTS147	106218
UK Great Britain	Yugoslavia	12 Apr 60	360UNTS79	105155
Brazil	Spain	25 Jun 60	0UNTS0	109427
Ghana	Poland	17 Jan 61	572UNTS209	108314
Brazil	Japan	23 Jan 61	569UNTS81	108281
Argentina	UK Great Britain	19 Jun 61	470UNTS71	106797
Algeria	France	03 Jul 62	507UNTS25	107395
Mali	Poland	02 Nov 62	572UNTS219	108315
Chad	France	19 May 64	0UNTS0	109442
Argentina	Guatemala	30 Oct 64	601UNTS175	108695
Brazil	Costa Rica	19 Nov 64	0UNTS0	109429
United Arab Rep	UK Great Britain	29 Sep 65	0UNTS0	109444
Brazil	El Salvador	30 Nov 65	0UNTS0	109430
Brazil	Chile	18 Mar 66	0UNTS0	109418
Algeria	France	08 Apr 66	0UNTS0	109508
Czechoslovakia	USSR (Soviet Union)	23 Apr 66	566UNTS159	108242
Netherlands	Yugoslavia	11 Aug 66	602UNTS243	108716
Netherlands	Romania	13 Feb 67	604UNTS287	108756
Denmark	France	15 Feb 67	604UNTS247	108754
UK Great Britain	USSR (Soviet Union)	24 Feb 67	606UNTS171	108785
Bulgaria	Poland	06 Apr 67	617UNTS327	108920
Belgium	Canada	08 May 67	637UNTS0	109119
Belgium	United Arab Rep	17 May 67	0UNTS0	109501
Germany, East	Hungary	18 May 67	617UNTS3	108905
France	USSR (Soviet Union)	08 Jul 67	0UNTS0	109378
France	Ireland	04 Nov 67	0UNTS0	109291
Czechoslovakia	France	06 Mar 68	0UNTS0	109379
Hungary	Poland	16 May 68	0UNTS0	109292
Multilateral		01 Aug 68	0UNTS0	109368
Exchange				
Brazil	Paraguay	14 Jun 41	54UNTS235	200196
Brazil	Chile	18 Nov 41	67UNTS279	200225
Brazil	Venezuela	22 Oct 42	65UNTS203	200212
Brazil	Dominican Republic	09 Dec 42	65UNTS217	200213
Brazil	Ecuador	24 May 44	73UNTS223	200242
Brazil	Canada	24 May 44	65UNTS265	200215
Multilateral		22 Mar 45	70UNTS237	200241
Brazil	Dominican Republic	09 Apr 45	67UNTS293	200226
Multilateral		16 Nov 45	4UNTS275	100052
Czechoslovakia	France	08 Dec 45	46UNTS77	100701
Belgium	France	22 Feb 46	68UNTS157	100892
Belgium	UK Great Britain	17 Apr 46	6UNTS177	100075
France	USA (United States)	10 Dec 46	15UNTS265	100242
Belgium	Czechoslovakia	06 Mar 47	34UNTS77	100528
France	Poland	19 May 47	12UNTS95	100181
Bulgaria	Czechoslovakia	20 Jun 47	46UNTS15	100698
Romania	Yugoslavia	26 Jun 47	116UNTS39	101568
Czechoslovakia	Romania	05 Sep 47	46UNTS37	100699
Colombia	USA (United States)	22 Dec 47	51UNTS45	100751
Norway	UK Great Britain	19 Feb 48	34UNTS33	100526
France	UK Great Britain	02 Mar 48	77UNTS33	100990
Belgium	Luxembourg	27 Mar 48	178UNTS265	102343
Hungary	Poland	18 Jun 48	25UNTS319	100370
Belgium	Italy	29 Nov 48	41UNTS3	100641
Luxembourg	Netherlands	26 Apr 49	182UNTS187	102425
Greece	Lebanon	10 Jun 49	178UNTS29	102334
Multilateral		15 Jul 49	197UNTS3	102631
Mexico	USA (United States)	30 Aug 49	98UNTS183	101364
Indonesia	Netherlands	02 Nov 49	69UNTS3	100894
Belgium	United Arab Rep	28 Nov 49	76UNTS91	100982
Luxembourg	UK Great Britain	27 Jun 50	183UNTS217	102431
Multilateral		18 Jan 51	81UNTS233	101073
China People's Rep	Poland	03 Apr 51	304UNTS187	104396
Greece	Turkey	20 Apr 51	178UNTS17	102333

PARTY ONE	PARTY TWO	DATE	CITATION	NUMBER
Exchange (Cont.)				
India	Turkey	29 Jun 51	213UNTS183	102886
Greece	UK Great Britain	29 Sep 51	190UNTS260	102570
Italy	Netherlands	05 Dec 51	0UNTS0	109323
Germany, East	Poland	08 Jan 52	304UNTS113	104394
Austria	Belgium	17 Oct 52	162UNTS183	102135
Bolivia	Italy	31 Jan 53	281UNTS181	104079
Germany, West	USA (United States)	09 Apr 53	204UNTS79	102750
Greece	Netherlands	29 Apr 53	191UNTS235	102583
Israel	Uruguay	30 Apr 53	280UNTS269	104064
Pakistan	United Arab Rep	14 Nov 53	485UNTS55	107046
Belgium	South Africa	01 Jun 54	201UNTS25	102708
Ethiopia	Greece	31 Jul 54	241UNTS319	103439
Greece	Italy	11 Sep 54	284UNTS313	104145
Portugal	UK Great Britain	19 Nov 54	226UNTS305	103125
Belgium	Greece	09 Dec 54	257UNTS243	103660
Multilateral		19 Dec 54	218UNTS139	102955
Netherlands	Norway	18 May 55	252UNTS269	103569
Italy	Norway	14 Jun 55	260UNTS307	103713
Belgium	Portugal	30 Jul 55	250UNTS213	103525
Italy	Spain	11 Aug 55	267UNTS125	103839
Romania	USSR (Soviet Union)	07 Apr 56	259UNTS377	103698
Mongolia	USSR (Soviet Union)	24 Apr 56	259UNTS297	103693
Germany, East	USSR (Soviet Union)	26 Apr 56	259UNTS279	103692
Bulgaria	USSR (Soviet Union)	28 Apr 56	259UNTS363	103697
Albania	USSR (Soviet Union)	03 May 56	259UNTS391	103699
Mongolia	Romania	08 May 56	342UNTS291	104913
Korea, North	Poland	11 May 56	432UNTS161	106219
Korea, North	Romania	12 May 56	342UNTS189	104908
Czechoslovakia	USSR (Soviet Union)	01 Jun 56	259UNTS341	103696
Poland	USSR (Soviet Union)	30 Jun 56	259UNTS311	103694
China People's Rep	USSR (Soviet Union)	05 Jul 56	263UNTS129	103770
Poland	Yugoslavia	06 Jul 56	281UNTS143	104076
Syria	USSR (Soviet Union)	20 Aug 56	274UNTS105	103961
Greece	United Arab Rep	04 Sep 56	299UNTS253	104317
Korea, North	USSR (Soviet Union)	05 Sep 56	259UNTS329	103695
Belgium	Germany, West	24 Sep 56	263UNTS31	103766
Romania	Vietnam, North	12 Oct 56	342UNTS173	104907
Norway	USSR (Soviet Union)	12 Oct 56	308UNTS95	104457
Denmark	Italy	26 Oct 56	267UNTS261	103847
Romania	Yugoslavia	27 Oct 56	389UNTS33	105590
India	Japan	29 Oct 56	318UNTS289	104622
Bulgaria	Yugoslavia	24 Dec 56	397UNTS3	105699
Belgium	Yugoslavia	05 Feb 57	276UNTS143	103990
Taiwan	Spain	07 Feb 57	314UNTS161	104547
Taiwan	Turkey	12 Feb 57	282UNTS125	104097
USSR (Soviet Union)	Vietnam, North	15 Feb 57	274UNTS115	103962
Japan	United Arab Rep	20 Mar 57	318UNTS345	104625
India	Poland	27 Mar 57	319UNTS263	104635
Poland	Vietnam, North	06 Apr 57	432UNTS255	106224
Iran	Japan	16 Apr 57	325UNTS113	104697
India	Romania	30 Apr 57	342UNTS251	104911
Czechoslovakia	Yugoslavia	22 May 57	391UNTS33	105615
Argentina	Israel	23 May 57	280UNTS199	104059
Japan	Pakistan	27 May 57	325UNTS21	104692
Czechoslovakia	Syria	18 Jun 57	303UNTS119	104374
United Arab Rep	USSR (Soviet Union)	19 Oct 57	292UNTS151	104271
Israel	Norway	26 Nov 57	345UNTS99	104962
Belgium	Denmark	31 Dec 57	305UNTS247	104422
Norway	Turkey	10 Jan 58	351UNTS229	105025
Ceylon (Sri Lanka)	USSR (Soviet Union)	15 Jan 58	305UNTS235	104421
USA (United States)	USSR (Soviet Union)	27 Jan 58	301UNTS405	104350
Taiwan	Costa Rica	10 Apr 58	315UNTS165	104567
Afghanistan	USA (United States)	26 Jun 58	321UNTS67	104654
Germany, East	Romania	15 Jul 58	387UNTS115	105560
Czechoslovakia	Romania	25 Oct 58	338UNTS301	104843

PARTY ONE	PARTY TWO	DATE	CITATION	NUMBER
Exchange (Cont.)				
El Salvador	Israel	14 Nov 58	345UNTS67	104959
Norway	Poland	17 Dec 58	432UNTS193	106221
Mongolia	Poland	23 Dec 58	432UNTS177	106220
Belgium	Turkey	29 Dec 58	357UNTS195	105118
Hungary	Iraq	11 Apr 59	439UNTS25	106323
Iraq	USSR (Soviet Union)	05 May 59	356UNTS179	105095
Taiwan	Ecuador	12 Jun 59	387UNTS3	105554
Israel	Mexico	15 Jun 59	377UNTS267	105406
Greece	Yugoslavia	18 Jun 59	368UNTS137	105238
Brazil	Israel	24 Jun 59	515UNTS151	107458
Czechoslovakia	India	07 Jul 59	359UNTS259	105145
Norway	Spain	19 Aug 59	376UNTS145	105379
Guinea	USA (United States)	28 Oct 59	358UNTS169	105134
Czechoslovakia	Guinea	30 Nov 59	386UNTS63	105538
France	Israel	30 Nov 59	377UNTS237	105404
Czechoslovakia	Ethiopia	11 Dec 59	399UNTS93	105736
Iraq	UK Great Britain	14 Dec 59	374UNTS253	105339
Germany, East	Hungary	19 Dec 59	409UNTS4	105874
Belgium	Brazil	06 Jan 60	531UNTS149	107701
Argentina	Mexico	26 Jan 60	635UNTS79	109073
Italy	USSR (Soviet Union)	09 Feb 60	399UNTS75	105735
India	USSR (Soviet Union)	12 Feb 60	392UNTS153	105642
Taiwan	Panama	26 Feb 60	435UNTS281	106285
Netherlands	Turkey	12 May 60	463UNTS207	106704
Belgium	Iran	14 May 60	522UNTS249	107551
Finland	USSR (Soviet Union)	27 May 60	379UNTS381	105444
Denmark	Poland	08 Jun 60	424UNTS37	106097
Brazil	Spain	25 Jun 60	0UNTS0	109427
Cuba	Korea, North	29 Aug 60	473UNTS117	106860
Cuba	Romania	28 Oct 60	457UNTS9	106574
Czechoslovakia	Ghana	23 Nov 60	431UNTS91	106213
Israel	Mali	24 Nov 60	413UNTS104	105945
Cambodia	Czechoslovakia	27 Nov 60	410UNTS263	105910
Netherlands	United Arab Rep	08 Dec 60	455UNTS276	106547
Romania	USA (United States)	09 Dec 60	401UNTS19	105759
Cuba	USSR (Soviet Union)	12 Dec 60	421UNTS3	106048
Cuba	Czechoslovakia	22 Dec 60	426UNTS145	106134
Ethiopia	USSR (Soviet Union)	13 Jan 61	421UNTS13	106049
Ghana	Poland	17 Jan 61	572UNTS209	108314
Brazil	Japan	23 Jan 61	569UNTS81	108281
New Zealand	United Nations	02 Feb 61	391UNTS23	105614
Cuba	Poland	06 Mar 61	484UNTS123	107020
India	Norway	19 Apr 61	404UNTS307	105818
Afghanistan	Czechoslovakia	23 Apr 61	437UNTS25	106297
Taiwan	Nicaragua	25 Apr 61	423UNTS139	106090
Somalia	USSR (Soviet Union)	02 Jun 61	528UNTS147	107638
Czechoslovakia	Somalia	04 Jun 61	479UNTS291	106960
Argentina	UK Great Britain	19 Jun 61	470UNTS71	106797
Pakistan	Philippines	15 Aug 61	522UNTS35	107534
Taiwan	Paraguay	18 Aug 61	438UNTS109	106314
Ghana	Romania	30 Sep 61	457UNTS3	106573
Taiwan	Jordan	17 Oct 61	435UNTS267	106284
Brazil	Poland	19 Oct 61	552UNTS75	108050
Multilateral		26 Oct 61	496UNTS43	107247
Guatemala	Israel	27 Nov 61	448UNTS191	106431
Taiwan	El Salvador	27 Nov 61	437UNTS161	106306
USA (United States)	USSR (Soviet Union)	08 Mar 62	460UNTS3	106630
Hungary	India	30 Mar 62	519UNTS119	107504
Israel	Peru	25 Jun 62	515UNTS263	107464
Israel	Liberia	25 Jun 62	448UNTS295	106442
Costa Rica	Israel	31 Jul 62	484UNTS155	107024
Syria	USSR (Soviet Union)	19 Aug 62	457UNTS285	106588
Denmark	USSR (Soviet Union)	11 Sep 62	458UNTS3	106589
Cameroon	Israel	24 Oct 62	449UNTS15	106447
Mali	Poland	02 Nov 62	572UNTS219	108315

PARTY ONE	PARTY TWO	DATE	CITATION	NUMBER
Exchange (Cont.)				
Multilateral		12 Dec 62	552UNTS15	108048
Belgium	Tunisia	21 Dec 62	482UNTS3	106987
UK Great Britain	USSR (Soviet Union)	21 Jan 63	475UNTS3	106887
Iraq	USA (United States)	23 Jan 63	488UNTS163	107126
Dahomey	USSR (Soviet Union)	20 Mar 63	528UNTS181	107641
Romania	USA (United States)	02 Apr 63	474UNTS95	106874
Belgium	Venezuela	15 May 63	470UNTS259	106812
Taiwan	Liberia	15 Jun 63	521UNTS361	107531
Austria	USA (United States)	25 Jun 63	479UNTS223	106956
Cameroon	UK Great Britain	20 Aug 63	539UNTS233	107834
Hungary	Yugoslavia	15 Oct 63	577UNTS49	108372
Tanganyika	USSR (Soviet Union)	06 Nov 63	528UNTS157	107639
Belgium	Romania	13 Nov 63	520UNTS119	107513
Belgium	Pakistan	14 Nov 63	535UNTS393	107792
Belgium	Poland	09 Dec 63	514UNTS195	107448
USA (United States)	USSR (Soviet Union)	22 Feb 64	526UNTS131	107605
Ireland	Norway	02 Apr 64	553UNTS129	108078
Taiwan	USA (United States)	23 Apr 64	524UNTS141	107570
Algeria	Czechoslovakia	14 May 64	538UNTS301	107817
Chad	France	19 May 64	0UNTS0	109442
Czechoslovakia	Germany, East	06 Oct 64	545UNTS113	107927
Argentina	Guatemala	30 Oct 64	601UNTS175	108695
Brazil	Costa Rica	19 Nov 64	0UNTS0	109429
Argentina	Panama	21 Nov 64	635UNTS205	109083
Argentina	Costa Rica	23 Nov 64	635UNTS213	109084
Poland	Romania	26 Nov 64	552UNTS157	108053
Romania	USA (United States)	23 Dec 64	535UNTS359	107790
Belgium	Hungary	11 Feb 65	544UNTS3	107908
UK Great Britain	USSR (Soviet Union)	13 Feb 65	543UNTS43	107896
UK Great Britain	USA (United States)	10 May 65	545UNTS181	107934
Bulgaria	Czechoslovakia	22 May 65	545UNTS65	107925
Ethiopia	Hungary	25 May 65	577UNTS193	108377
Israel	Sierra Leone	22 Aug 65	550UNTS275	108022
Brazil	El Salvador	30 Nov 65	0UNTS0	109430
Argentina	Taiwan	19 Mar 66	635UNTS281	109089
Algeria	France	08 Apr 66	0UNTS0	109508
Romania	Tunisia	21 Apr 66	604UNTS57	108743
Czechoslovakia	USSR (Soviet Union)	23 Apr 66	566UNTS159	108242
Netherlands	Yugoslavia	11 Aug 66	602UNTS243	108716
Multilateral		03 Oct 66	610UNTS169	108841
Kuwait	UK Great Britain	26 Nov 66	633UNTS58	109034
Congo (Brazzaville)	Czechoslovakia	29 Nov 66	635UNTS3	109069
Bulgaria	United Arab Rep	12 Feb 67	630UNTS353	108981
Kuwait	USSR (Soviet Union)	27 Mar 67	643UNTS135	109189
Belgium	Canada	08 May 67	637UNTS0	109119
Belgium	United Arab Rep	17 May 67	0UNTS0	109501
France	USSR (Soviet Union)	08 Jul 67	0UNTS0	109378
Italy	Romania	08 Aug 67	642UNTS191	109174
Netherlands	Poland	22 Aug 67	0UNTS0	109275
Czechoslovakia	France	06 Mar 68	0UNTS0	109379
General cultural cooperation				
Brazil	Dominican Republic	09 Dec 42	65UNTS217	200213
Brazil	Canada	24 May 44	65UNTS265	200215
Brazil	Dominican Republic	09 Apr 45	67UNTS293	200226
Poland	Yugoslavia	16 Mar 46	10UNTS11	100139
Belgium	UK Great Britain	17 Apr 46	6UNTS177	100075
India	USA (United States)	16 May 46	4UNTS183	100045
Belgium	Netherlands	16 May 46	17UNTS13	100266
Australia	USA (United States)	07 Jun 46	4UNTS237	100048
New Zealand	USA (United States)	10 Jul 46	6UNTS341	100087
Philippines	USA (United States)	11 Sep 46	43UNTS231	100670
France	Netherlands	19 Nov 46	32UNTS101	100493
Belgium	Czechoslovakia	06 Mar 47	34UNTS77	100528
Czechoslovakia	Poland	10 Mar 47	25UNTS231	100365

PARTY ONE	PARTY TWO	DATE	CITATION	NUMBER
General cultural cooperation (Cont.)				
Austria	France	15 Mar 47	12UNTS109	100182
Czechoslovakia	Yugoslavia	27 Apr 47	33UNTS49	100514
France	Poland	19 May 47	12UNTS95	100181
Romania	Yugoslavia	26 Jun 47	116UNTS39	101568
Bulgaria	Poland	28 Jun 47	15UNTS123	100230
Czechoslovakia	Poland	04 Jul 47	25UNTS249	100366
Albania	Yugoslavia	09 Jul 47	33UNTS91	100516
Hungary	Yugoslavia	15 Oct 47	33UNTS73	100515
Colombia	USA (United States)	22 Dec 47	51UNTS45	100751
Hungary	Poland	31 Jan 48	25UNTS283	100368
Hungary	USSR (Soviet Union)	18 Feb 48	48UNTS163	100743
Norway	UK Great Britain	19 Feb 48	34UNTS33	100526
Belgium	Norway	20 Feb 48	32UNTS39	100487
Poland	Romania	27 Feb 48	46UNTS143	100707
France	UK Great Britain	02 Mar 48	77UNTS33	100990
Multilateral		17 Mar 48	19UNTS51	100304
Bulgaria	USSR (Soviet Union)	18 Mar 48	48UNTS135	100741
Belgium	Luxembourg	27 Mar 48	178UNTS265	102343
Finland	USSR (Soviet Union)	06 Apr 48	48UNTS149	100742
Bulgaria	Poland	29 May 48	26UNTS213	100389
Hungary	Poland	18 Jun 48	25UNTS319	100370
Netherlands	UK Great Britain	07 Jul 48	82UNTS259	101099
Greece	Italy	21 Sep 48	77UNTS259	101003
Belgium	Italy	29 Nov 48	41UNTS3	100641
Poland	Romania	26 Jan 49	85UNTS21	101143
Korea, North	USSR (Soviet Union)	17 Mar 49	221UNTS3	102999
Multilateral		04 Apr 49	34UNTS243	100541
Greece	Lebanon	10 Jun 49	178UNTS29	102334
Mexico	USA (United States)	30 Aug 49	98UNTS183	101364
Belgium	United Arab Rep	28 Nov 49	76UNTS91	100982
Afghanistan	India	04 Jan 50	81UNTS75	101064
Luxembourg	UK Great Britain	27 Jun 50	183UNTS217	102431
Multilateral		22 Nov 50	131UNTS25	101734
Albania	Poland	02 Dec 50	260UNTS131	103707
China People's Rep	Poland	03 Apr 51	304UNTS187	104396
Greece	Turkey	20 Apr 51	178UNTS17	102333
India	Turkey	29 Jun 51	213UNTS183	102886
Greece	UK Great Britain	29 Sep 51	190UNTS260	102570
Italy	UK Great Britain	28 Nov 51	172UNTS27	102238
Italy	Netherlands	05 Dec 51	0UNTS0	109323
Germany, East	Poland	08 Jan 52	304UNTS113	104394
India	Syria	25 Feb 52	163UNTS55	102141
Austria	Belgium	17 Oct 52	162UNTS183	102135
Austria	UK Great Britain	12 Dec 52	172UNTS9	102237
Bolivia	Italy	31 Jan 53	281UNTS181	104079
Albania	Romania	14 Feb 53	342UNTS107	104903
Germany, West	USA (United States)	09 Apr 53	204UNTS79	102750
Greece	Netherlands	29 Apr 53	191UNTS235	102583
Israel	Uruguay	30 Apr 53	280UNTS269	104064
Pakistan	Turkey	29 Jun 53	211UNTS225	102854
Belgium	South Africa	01 Jun 54	201UNTS25	102708
Greece	Italy	11 Sep 54	284UNTS313	104145
Portugal	UK Great Britain	19 Nov 54	226UNTS305	103125
Guatemala	USA (United States)	01 Dec 54	237UNTS161	103342
Belgium	Greece	09 Dec 54	257UNTS243	103660
Multilateral		19 Dec 54	218UNTS139	102955
Japan	Thailand	06 Apr 55	230UNTS219	103187
Netherlands	Norway	18 May 55	252UNTS269	103569
Italy	Norway	14 Jun 55	260UNTS307	103713
Belgium	Portugal	30 Jul 55	250UNTS213	103525
Italy	Spain	11 Aug 55	267UNTS125	103839
Iran	Pakistan	09 Mar 56	449UNTS183	106460
Turkey	UK Great Britain	12 Mar 56	313UNTS73	104530
Romania	USSR (Soviet Union)	07 Apr 56	259UNTS377	103698
Mongolia	USSR (Soviet Union)	24 Apr 56	259UNTS297	103693

PARTY ONE	PARTY TWO	DATE	CITATION	NUMBER
General cultural cooperation (Cont.)				
Germany, East	USSR (Soviet Union)	26 Apr 56	259UNTS279	103692
Bulgaria	USSR (Soviet Union)	28 Apr 56	259UNTS363	103697
Albania	USSR (Soviet Union)	03 May 56	259UNTS391	103699
Mongolia	Romania	08 May 56	342UNTS291	104913
Korea, North	Poland	11 May 56	432UNTS161	106219
Korea, North	Romania	12 May 56	342UNTS189	104908
USSR (Soviet Union)	Yugoslavia	17 May 56	259UNTS145	103687
Czechoslovakia	USSR (Soviet Union)	01 Jun 56	259UNTS341	103696
Hungary	USSR (Soviet Union)	28 Jun 56	259UNTS405	103700
Poland	USSR (Soviet Union)	30 Jun 56	259UNTS311	103694
China People's Rep	USSR (Soviet Union)	05 Jul 56	263UNTS129	103770
Poland	Yugoslavia	06 Jul 56	281UNTS143	104076
Syria	USSR (Soviet Union)	20 Aug 56	274UNTS105	103961
Greece	United Arab Rep	04 Sep 56	299UNTS253	104317
Korea, North	USSR (Soviet Union)	05 Sep 56	259UNTS329	103695
Italy	Spain	05 Sep 56	302UNTS195	104359
Belgium	Germany, West	24 Sep 56	263UNTS31	103766
Norway	USSR (Soviet Union)	12 Oct 56	308UNTS95	104457
Romania	Vietnam, North	12 Oct 56	342UNTS173	104907
Denmark	Italy	26 Oct 56	267UNTS261	103847
Romania	Yugoslavia	27 Oct 56	389UNTS33	105590
India	Japan	29 Oct 56	318UNTS289	104622
Bulgaria	Yugoslavia	24 Dec 56	397UNTS3	105699
Czechoslovakia	Yugoslavia	29 Jan 57	300UNTS249	104339
Poland	United Arab Rep	02 Feb 57	319UNTS221	104633
Belgium	Yugoslavia	05 Feb 57	276UNTS143	103990
Taiwan	Turkey	12 Feb 57	282UNTS125	104097
USSR (Soviet Union)	Vietnam, North	15 Feb 57	274UNTS115	103962
Japan	United Arab Rep	20 Mar 57	318UNTS345	104625
India	Poland	27 Mar 57	319UNTS263	104635
Poland	Vietnam, North	06 Apr 57	432UNTS255	106224
Czechoslovakia	Mongolia	08 Apr 57	501UNTS171	107317
Romania	United Arab Rep	15 Apr 57	389UNTS21	105589
Iran	Japan	16 Apr 57	325UNTS113	104697
India	Romania	30 Apr 57	342UNTS251	104911
Argentina	Israel	23 May 57	280UNTS199	104059
Japan	Pakistan	27 May 57	325UNTS21	104692
Czechoslovakia	Syria	18 Jun 57	303UNTS119	104374
Germany, East	Poland	13 Jul 57	319UNTS229	104634
Czechoslovakia	United Arab Rep	19 Oct 57	530UNTS181	107681
United Arab Rep	USSR (Soviet Union)	19 Oct 57	292UNTS151	104271
Taiwan	Iran	11 Nov 57	563UNTS31	108202
Israel	Norway	26 Nov 57	345UNTS99	104962
Belgium	Denmark	31 Dec 57	305UNTS247	104422
Norway	Turkey	10 Jan 58	351UNTS229	105025
Ceylon (Sri Lanka)	USSR (Soviet Union)	15 Jan 58	305UNTS235	104421
Taiwan	Costa Rica	10 Apr 58	315UNTS165	104567
Germany, West	UK Great Britain	18 Apr 58	343UNTS241	104928
Afghanistan	USA (United States)	26 Jun 58	321UNTS67	104654
Finland	Sweden	16 Oct 58	428UNTS125	106171
Belgium	Spain	27 Oct 58	327UNTS107	104720
Norway	Poland	17 Dec 58	432UNTS193	106221
Mongolia	Poland	23 Dec 58	432UNTS177	106220
Belgium	Turkey	29 Dec 58	357UNTS195	105118
Hungary	Poland	14 Feb 59	431UNTS157	106215
Hungary	Iraq	11 Apr 59	439UNTS25	106323
Indonesia	Malaysia	17 Apr 59	470UNTS273	106813
Iraq	USSR (Soviet Union)	05 May 59	356UNTS179	105095
Iran	UK Great Britain	06 May 59	398UNTS51	105717
Iran	Netherlands	22 May 59	474UNTS195	106882
Finland	Hungary	10 Jun 59	439UNTS3	106321
Taiwan	Ecuador	12 Jun 59	387UNTS3	105554
Israel	Mexico	15 Jun 59	377UNTS267	105406
Greece	Yugoslavia	18 Jun 59	368UNTS137	105238
Brazil	Israel	24 Jun 59	515UNTS151	107458

PARTY ONE	PARTY TWO	DATE	CITATION	NUMBER
General cultural cooperation (Cont.)				
Czechoslovakia	India	07 Jul 59	359UNTS259	105145
Iraq	Romania	04 Aug 59	502UNTS17	107324
Norway	Spain	19 Aug 59	376UNTS145	105379
Guinea	USA (United States)	28 Oct 59	358UNTS169	105134
USA (United States)	USSR (Soviet Union)	21 Nov 59	361UNTS35	105172
Czechoslovakia	Guinea	30 Nov 59	386UNTS63	105538
France	Israel	30 Nov 59	377UNTS237	105404
UK Great Britain	USSR (Soviet Union)	01 Dec 59	351UNTS313	105032
Czechoslovakia	Ethiopia	11 Dec 59	399UNTS93	105736
Iraq	UK Great Britain	14 Dec 59	374UNTS253	105339
Belgium	Brazil	06 Jan 60	531UNTS149	107701
Guinea	Hungary	12 Jan 60	519UNTS131	107505
Argentina	Mexico	26 Jan 60	635UNTS79	109073
Italy	USSR (Soviet Union)	09 Feb 60	399UNTS75	105735
Argentina	Philippines	12 Feb 60	535UNTS293	107785
India	USSR (Soviet Union)	12 Feb 60	392UNTS153	105642
Taiwan	Panama	26 Feb 60	435UNTS281	106285
Indonesia	USSR (Soviet Union)	28 Feb 60	392UNTS191	105644
Finland	Sweden	13 Apr 60	428UNTS131	106172
Netherlands	Turkey	12 May 60	463UNTS207	106704
Belgium	Iran	14 May 60	522UNTS249	107551
Finland	USSR (Soviet Union)	27 May 60	379UNTS381	105444
Denmark	Poland	08 Jun 60	424UNTS37	106097
Brazil	Spain	25 Jun 60	0UNTS0	109427
Spain	UK Great Britain	12 Jul 60	414UNTS123	105971
Multilateral		28 Jul 60	485UNTS3	107042
Cuba	Korea, North	29 Aug 60	473UNTS117	106860
Cuba	Romania	28 Oct 60	457UNTS9	106574
Czechoslovakia	Ghana	23 Nov 60	431UNTS91	106213
Israel	Mali	24 Nov 60	413UNTS104	105945
Cambodia	Czechoslovakia	27 Nov 60	410UNTS263	105910
Japan	UK Great Britain	03 Dec 60	414UNTS61	105966
Netherlands	United Arab Rep	08 Dec 60	455UNTS276	106547
Romania	USA (United States)	09 Dec 60	401UNTS19	105759
Cuba	USSR (Soviet Union)	12 Dec 60	421UNTS3	106048
Cuba	Czechoslovakia	22 Dec 60	426UNTS145	106134
UK Great Britain	USSR (Soviet Union)	09 Jan 61	404UNTS175	105810
Ethiopia	USSR (Soviet Union)	13 Jan 61	421UNTS13	106049
Ghana	Poland	17 Jan 61	572UNTS209	108314
Brazil	Japan	23 Jan 61	569UNTS81	108281
Czechoslovakia	Hungary	24 Feb 61	422UNTS15	106066
Cuba	Poland	06 Mar 61	484UNTS123	107020
Cuba	Germany, East	29 Mar 61	448UNTS81	106426
India	Norway	19 Apr 61	404UNTS307	105818
Afghanistan	Czechoslovakia	23 Apr 61	437UNTS25	106297
Taiwan	Nicaragua	25 Apr 61	423UNTS139	106090
Germany, West	Netherlands	27 Apr 61	487UNTS77	107095
Ghana	Hungary	27 Apr 61	439UNTS17	106322
Taiwan	Uruguay	03 May 61	596UNTS121	108630
Somalia	USSR (Soviet Union)	02 Jun 61	528UNTS147	107638
Czechoslovakia	Somalia	04 Jun 61	479UNTS291	106960
UK Great Britain	Yugoslavia	08 Jun 61	437UNTS111	106300
Argentina	UK Great Britain	19 Jun 61	470UNTS71	106797
Pakistan	Philippines	15 Aug 61	522UNTS35	107534
Taiwan	Paraguay	18 Aug 61	438UNTS109	106314
Ghana	Romania	30 Sep 61	457UNTS3	106573
Taiwan	Jordan	17 Oct 61	435UNTS267	106284
Brazil	Poland	19 Oct 61	552UNTS75	108050
Guatemala	Israel	27 Nov 61	448UNTS191	106431
Taiwan	El Salvador	27 Nov 61	437UNTS161	106306
Multilateral		23 Mar 62	434UNTS145	106262
Hungary	India	30 Mar 62	519UNTS119	107504
United Arab Rep	USA (United States)	21 May 62	458UNTS197	106601
Senegal	USSR (Soviet Union)	14 Jun 62	437UNTS233	106309
Israel	Peru	25 Jun 62	515UNTS263	107464

PARTY ONE	PARTY TWO	DATE	CITATION	NUMBER
General cultural cooperation (Cont.)				
Israel	Liberia	25 Jun 62	448UNTS295	106442
Syria	USSR (Soviet Union)	19 Aug 62	457UNTS285	106588
Denmark	USSR (Soviet Union)	11 Sep 62	458UNTS3	106589
Cameroon	Israel	24 Oct 62	449UNTS15	106447
Mali	Poland	02 Nov 62	572UNTS219	108315
Belgium	Tunisia	21 Dec 62	482UNTS3	106987
Iraq	USA (United States)	23 Jan 63	488UNTS163	107126
Indonesia	USA (United States)	14 Mar 63	505UNTS79	107365
Dahomey	USSR (Soviet Union)	20 Mar 63	528UNTS181	107641
Romania	USA (United States)	02 Apr 63	474UNTS95	106874
Czechoslovakia	Tunisia	06 Apr 63	555UNTS111	108106
Belgium	Venezuela	15 May 63	470UNTS259	106812
Taiwan	Liberia	15 Jun 63	521UNTS361	107531
Cameroon	UK Great Britain	20 Aug 63	539UNTS233	107834
Mali	Romania	26 Sep 63	528UNTS193	107642
Tanganyika	USSR (Soviet Union)	06 Nov 63	528UNTS157	107639
Belgium	Romania	13 Nov 63	520UNTS119	107513
Belgium	Pakistan	14 Nov 63	535UNTS393	107792
Belgium	Poland	09 Dec 63	514UNTS195	107448
Netherlands	Tunisia	11 Feb 64	570UNTS173	108293
Spain	USA (United States)	18 Mar 64	535UNTS343	107789
Ireland	Norway	02 Apr 64	553UNTS129	108078
Mexico	Netherlands	08 Apr 64	575UNTS35	108353
Algeria	Czechoslovakia	14 May 64	538UNTS301	107817
Chad	France	19 May 64	0UNTS0	109442
Argentina	France	03 Oct 64	635UNTS155	109080
Germany, East	Poland	06 Oct 64	552UNTS89	108051
Czechoslovakia	Germany, East	06 Oct 64	545UNTS113	107927
Brazil	Costa Rica	19 Nov 64	0UNTS0	109429
Belgium	Mexico	19 Nov 64	546UNTS217	107949
Argentina	Panama	21 Nov 64	635UNTS205	109083
Argentina	Costa Rica	23 Nov 64	635UNTS213	109084
Romania	USA (United States)	23 Dec 64	535UNTS359	107790
Belgium	Sweden	11 Jan 65	533UNTS157	107741
Belgium	Hungary	11 Feb 65	544UNTS3	107908
UK Great Britain	USSR (Soviet Union)	13 Feb 65	543UNTS43	107896
Poland	USSR (Soviet Union)	08 Apr 65	540UNTS97	107845
Afghanistan	UK Great Britain	19 Apr 65	633UNTS45	109033
Bulgaria	Czechoslovakia	22 May 65	545UNTS65	107925
China People's Rep	Romania	27 May 65	592UNTS3	108566
Pakistan	USSR (Soviet Union)	05 Jun 65	593UNTS115	108579
Japan	Korea, South	22 Jun 65	584UNTS49	108475
Uganda	USSR (Soviet Union)	24 Jul 65	596UNTS199	108633
Israel	Sierra Leone	22 Aug 65	550UNTS275	108022
United Arab Rep	UK Great Britain	29 Sep 65	0UNTS0	109444
Argentina	Belgium	05 Nov 65	635UNTS229	109086
Brazil	El Salvador	30 Nov 65	0UNTS0	109430
Austria	Brazil	21 Dec 65	595UNTS299	108624
Czechoslovakia	Poland	22 Jan 66	588UNTS175	108524
UK Great Britain	Yugoslavia	27 Jan 66	573UNTS243	108337
Brazil	Chile	18 Mar 66	0UNTS0	109418
Argentina	Taiwan	19 Mar 66	635UNTS281	109089
Algeria	France	08 Apr 66	0UNTS0	109508
Romania	Tunisia	21 Apr 66	604UNTS57	108743
Czechoslovakia	USSR (Soviet Union)	23 Apr 66	566UNTS159	108242
Rwanda	USSR (Soviet Union)	06 May 66	633UNTS217	109039
Netherlands	Yugoslavia	11 Aug 66	602UNTS243	108716
Iran	USSR (Soviet Union)	22 Aug 66	643UNTS203	109192
Multilateral		03 Oct 66	610UNTS169	108841
Bulgaria	Poland	03 Oct 66	618UNTS3	108921
Brazil	Netherlands	12 Oct 66	643UNTS271	109197
Kuwait	UK Great Britain	26 Nov 66	633UNTS58	109034
Congo (Brazzaville)	Czechoslovakia	29 Nov 66	635UNTS3	109069
Netherlands	Romania	13 Feb 67	604UNTS287	108756
Denmark	France	15 Feb 67	604UNTS247	108754

PARTY ONE	PARTY TWO	DATE	CITATION	NUMBER
General cultural cooperation (Cont.)				
Belgium	Luxembourg	22 Feb 67	639UNTS3	109140
Germany, East	Poland	15 Mar 67	618UNTS21	108922
Kuwait	USSR (Soviet Union)	27 Mar 67	643UNTS135	109189
Belgium	Canada	08 May 67	637UNTS0	109119
Belgium	United Arab Rep	17 May 67	0UNTS0	109501
Belgium	Bulgaria	17 May 67	631UNTS215	108995
France	USSR (Soviet Union)	08 Jul 67	0UNTS0	109378
Bulgaria	Mongolia	21 Jul 67	610UNTS0	108839
Italy	Romania	08 Aug 67	642UNTS191	109174
Netherlands	Poland	22 Aug 67	0UNTS0	109275
Denmark	Romania	29 Aug 67	642UNTS357	109183
Bulgaria	Germany, East	07 Sep 67	631UNTS81	108988
France	Ireland	04 Nov 67	0UNTS0	109291
Czechoslovakia	France	06 Mar 68	0UNTS0	109379
Multilateral		01 Aug 68	0UNTS0	109368
Artists				
Brazil	Chile	18 Nov 41	67UNTS279	200225
Brazil	Venezuela	22 Oct 42	65UNTS203	200212
Brazil	Ecuador	24 May 44	73UNTS223	200242
Brazil	Dominican Republic	09 Apr 45	67UNTS293	200226
Belgium	France	22 Feb 46	68UNTS157	100892
Poland	Yugoslavia	16 Mar 46	10UNTS11	100139
Belgium	UK Great Britain	17 Apr 46	6UNTS177	100075
Belgium	Netherlands	16 May 46	17UNTS13	100266
France	Netherlands	19 Nov 46	32UNTS101	100493
France	USA (United States)	10 Dec 46	15UNTS265	100242
Belgium	Czechoslovakia	06 Mar 47	34UNTS77	100528
Austria	France	15 Mar 47	12UNTS109	100182
Czechoslovakia	Yugoslavia	27 Apr 47	33UNTS49	100514
France	Poland	19 May 47	12UNTS95	100181
Czechoslovakia	UK Great Britain	16 Jun 47	46UNTS61	100700
Bulgaria	Czechoslovakia	20 Jun 47	46UNTS15	100698
Romania	Yugoslavia	26 Jun 47	116UNTS39	101568
Czechoslovakia	Poland	04 Jul 47	25UNTS249	100366
Albania	Yugoslavia	09 Jul 47	33UNTS91	100516
Czechoslovakia	Romania	05 Sep 47	46UNTS37	100699
Hungary	Yugoslavia	15 Oct 47	33UNTS73	100515
Colombia	USA (United States)	22 Dec 47	51UNTS45	100751
Norway	UK Great Britain	19 Feb 48	34UNTS33	100526
Belgium	Norway	20 Feb 48	32UNTS39	100487
Poland	Romania	27 Feb 48	46UNTS143	100707
France	UK Great Britain	02 Mar 48	77UNTS33	100990
Belgium	Luxembourg	27 Mar 48	178UNTS265	102343
Hungary	Poland	18 Jun 48	25UNTS319	100370
Belgium	Italy	29 Nov 48	41UNTS3	100641
Luxembourg	Netherlands	26 Apr 49	182UNTS187	102425
Greece	Lebanon	10 Jun 49	178UNTS29	102334
Belgium	United Arab Rep	28 Nov 49	76UNTS91	100982
Luxembourg	UK Great Britain	27 Jun 50	183UNTS217	102431
Albania	Poland	02 Dec 50	260UNTS131	103707
India	Turkey	29 Jun 51	213UNTS183	102886
Greece	UK Great Britain	29 Sep 51	190UNTS260	102570
Italy	UK Great Britain	28 Nov 51	172UNTS27	102238
Italy	Netherlands	05 Dec 51	0UNTS0	109323
Germany, East	Poland	08 Jan 52	304UNTS113	104394
Austria	Belgium	17 Oct 52	162UNTS183	102135
Austria	UK Great Britain	12 Dec 52	172UNTS9	102237
Albania	Romania	14 Feb 53	342UNTS107	104903
Germany, West	USA (United States)	09 Apr 53	204UNTS79	102750
Greece	Netherlands	29 Apr 53	191UNTS235	102583
Israel	Uruguay	30 Apr 53	280UNTS269	104064
Pakistan	United Arab Rep	14 Nov 53	485UNTS55	107046
Belgium	South Africa	01 Jun 54	201UNTS25	102708
Greece	Italy	11 Sep 54	284UNTS313	104145

PARTY ONE	PARTY TWO	DATE	CITATION	NUMBER
Artists (Cont.)				
Portugal	UK Great Britain	19 Nov 54	226UNTS305	103125
Belgium	Greece	09 Dec 54	257UNTS243	103660
Netherlands	Norway	18 May 55	252UNTS269	103569
Italy	Norway	14 Jun 55	260UNTS307	103713
Belgium	Portugal	30 Jul 55	250UNTS213	103525
Italy	Spain	11 Aug 55	267UNTS125	103839
Iran	Pakistan	09 Mar 56	449UNTS183	106460
Romania	USSR (Soviet Union)	07 Apr 56	259UNTS377	103698
Mongolia	USSR (Soviet Union)	24 Apr 56	259UNTS297	103693
Germany, East	USSR (Soviet Union)	26 Apr 56	259UNTS279	103692
Bulgaria	USSR (Soviet Union)	28 Apr 56	259UNTS363	103697
Albania	USSR (Soviet Union)	03 May 56	259UNTS391	103699
Mongolia	Romania	08 May 56	342UNTS291	104913
Korea, North	Romania	12 May 56	342UNTS189	104908
USSR (Soviet Union)	Yugoslavia	17 May 56	259UNTS145	103687
Czechoslovakia	USSR (Soviet Union)	01 Jun 56	259UNTS341	103696
Poland	USSR (Soviet Union)	30 Jun 56	259UNTS311	103694
China People's Rep	USSR (Soviet Union)	05 Jul 56	263UNTS129	103770
Poland	Yugoslavia	06 Jul 56	281UNTS143	104076
Syria	USSR (Soviet Union)	20 Aug 56	274UNTS105	103961
Greece	United Arab Rep	04 Sep 56	299UNTS253	104317
Korea, North	USSR (Soviet Union)	05 Sep 56	259UNTS329	103695
Belgium	Germany, West	24 Sep 56	263UNTS31	103766
Norway	USSR (Soviet Union)	12 Oct 56	308UNTS95	104457
Romania	Vietnam, North	12 Oct 56	342UNTS173	104907
Denmark	Italy	26 Oct 56	267UNTS261	103847
Romania	Yugoslavia	27 Oct 56	389UNTS33	105590
India	Japan	29 Oct 56	318UNTS289	104622
Czechoslovakia	Yugoslavia	29 Jan 57	300UNTS249	104339
Poland	United Arab Rep	02 Feb 57	319UNTS221	104633
Belgium	Yugoslavia	05 Feb 57	276UNTS143	103990
Taiwan	Turkey	12 Feb 57	282UNTS125	104097
USSR (Soviet Union)	Vietnam, North	15 Feb 57	274UNTS115	103962
Japan	United Arab Rep	20 Mar 57	318UNTS345	104625
India	Poland	27 Mar 57	319UNTS263	104635
Poland	Vietnam, North	06 Apr 57	432UNTS255	106224
Romania	United Arab Rep	15 Apr 57	389UNTS21	105589
Iran	Japan	16 Apr 57	325UNTS113	104697
India	Romania	30 Apr 57	342UNTS251	104911
Argentina	Israel	23 May 57	280UNTS199	104059
Japan	Pakistan	27 May 57	325UNTS21	104692
Czechoslovakia	Syria	18 Jun 57	303UNTS119	104374
United Arab Rep	USSR (Soviet Union)	19 Oct 57	292UNTS151	104271
Taiwan	Iran	11 Nov 57	563UNTS31	108202
Belgium	Denmark	31 Dec 57	305UNTS247	104422
Norway	Turkey	10 Jan 58	351UNTS229	105025
Ceylon (Sri Lanka)	USSR (Soviet Union)	15 Jan 58	305UNTS235	104421
Germany, West	UK Great Britain	18 Apr 58	343UNTS241	104928
Afghanistan	USA (United States)	26 Jun 58	321UNTS67	104654
Germany, East	Romania	15 Jul 58	387UNTS115	105560
Czechoslovakia	Romania	25 Oct 58	338UNTS301	104843
El Salvador	Israel	14 Nov 58	345UNTS67	104959
Norway	Poland	17 Dec 58	432UNTS193	106221
Mongolia	Poland	23 Dec 58	432UNTS177	106220
Belgium	Turkey	29 Dec 58	357UNTS195	105118
Hungary	Iraq	11 Apr 59	439UNTS25	106323
Iraq	USSR (Soviet Union)	05 May 59	356UNTS179	105095
Iran	Netherlands	22 May 59	474UNTS195	106882
Finland	Hungary	10 Jun 59	439UNTS3	106321
Taiwan	Ecuador	12 Jun 59	387UNTS3	105554
Israel	Mexico	15 Jun 59	377UNTS267	105406
Greece	Yugoslavia	18 Jun 59	368UNTS137	105238
Brazil	Israel	24 Jun 59	515UNTS151	107458
Czechoslovakia	India	07 Jul 59	359UNTS259	105145
Iraq	Romania	04 Aug 59	502UNTS17	107324

PARTY ONE	PARTY TWO	DATE	CITATION	NUMBER
Artists (Cont.)				
Norway	Spain	19 Aug 59	376UNTS145	105379
Guinea	USA (United States)	28 Oct 59	358UNTS169	105134
USA (United States)	USSR (Soviet Union)	21 Nov 59	361UNTS35	105172
Czechoslovakia	Guinea	30 Nov 59	386UNTS63	105538
France	Israel	30 Nov 59	377UNTS237	105404
UK Great Britain	USSR (Soviet Union)	01 Dec 59	351UNTS313	105032
Czechoslovakia	Ethiopia	11 Dec 59	399UNTS93	105736
Germany, East	Hungary	19 Dec 59	409UNTS4	105874
Belgium	Brazil	06 Jan 60	531UNTS149	107701
Guinea	Hungary	12 Jan 60	519UNTS131	107505
Italy	USSR (Soviet Union)	09 Feb 60	399UNTS75	105735
India	USSR (Soviet Union)	12 Feb 60	392UNTS153	105642
Taiwan	Panama	26 Feb 60	435UNTS281	106285
Indonesia	USSR (Soviet Union)	28 Feb 60	392UNTS191	105644
Netherlands	Turkey	12 May 60	463UNTS207	106704
Belgium	Iran	14 May 60	522UNTS249	107551
Finland	USSR (Soviet Union)	27 May 60	379UNTS381	105444
Denmark	Poland	08 Jun 60	424UNTS37	106097
Cuba	Korea, North	29 Aug 60	473UNTS117	106860
Cuba	Romania	28 Oct 60	457UNTS9	106574
Czechoslovakia	Ghana	23 Nov 60	431UNTS91	106213
Israel	Mali	24 Nov 60	413UNTS104	105945
Cambodia	Czechoslovakia	27 Nov 60	410UNTS263	105910
Netherlands	United Arab Rep	08 Dec 60	455UNTS276	106547
Romania	USA (United States)	09 Dec 60	401UNTS19	105759
Cuba	Czechoslovakia	22 Dec 60	426UNTS145	106134
UK Great Britain	USSR (Soviet Union)	09 Jan 61	404UNTS175	105810
Ethiopia	USSR (Soviet Union)	13 Jan 61	421UNTS13	106049
Ghana	Poland	17 Jan 61	572UNTS209	108314
Brazil	Japan	23 Jan 61	569UNTS81	108281
Czechoslovakia	Hungary	24 Feb 61	422UNTS15	106066
Cuba	Poland	06 Mar 61	484UNTS123	107020
Cuba	Germany, East	29 Mar 61	448UNTS81	106426
India	Norway	19 Apr 61	404UNTS307	105818
Afghanistan	Czechoslovakia	23 Apr 61	437UNTS25	106297
Germany, West	Netherlands	27 Apr 61	487UNTS77	107095
Ghana	Hungary	27 Apr 61	439UNTS17	106322
Taiwan	Uruguay	03 May 61	596UNTS121	108630
Somalia	USSR (Soviet Union)	02 Jun 61	528UNTS147	107638
Czechoslovakia	Somalia	04 Jun 61	479UNTS291	106960
Pakistan	Philippines	15 Aug 61	522UNTS35	107534
Taiwan	Paraguay	18 Aug 61	438UNTS109	106314
Ghana	Romania	30 Sep 61	457UNTS3	106573
Taiwan	Jordan	17 Oct 61	435UNTS267	106284
Brazil	Poland	19 Oct 61	552UNTS75	108050
Taiwan	El Salvador	27 Nov 61	437UNTS161	106306
Guatemala	Israel	27 Nov 61	448UNTS191	106431
USA (United States)	USSR (Soviet Union)	08 Mar 62	460UNTS3	106630
Hungary	India	30 Mar 62	519UNTS119	107504
United Arab Rep	USA (United States)	21 May 62	458UNTS197	106601
Senegal	USSR (Soviet Union)	14 Jun 62	437UNTS233	106309
Israel	Peru	25 Jun 62	515UNTS263	107464
Costa Rica	Israel	31 Jul 62	484UNTS155	107024
Syria	USSR (Soviet Union)	19 Aug 62	457UNTS285	106588
Denmark	USSR (Soviet Union)	11 Sep 62	458UNTS3	106589
Cameroon	Israel	24 Oct 62	449UNTS15	106447
Mali	Poland	02 Nov 62	572UNTS219	108315
Belgium	Tunisia	21 Dec 62	482UNTS3	106987
UK Great Britain	USSR (Soviet Union)	21 Jan 63	475UNTS3	106887
Iraq	USA (United States)	23 Jan 63	488UNTS163	107126
Dahomey	USSR (Soviet Union)	20 Mar 63	528UNTS181	107641
Romania	USA (United States)	02 Apr 63	474UNTS95	106874
Czechoslovakia	Tunisia	06 Apr 63	555UNTS111	108106
Belgium	Venezuela	15 May 63	470UNTS259	106812
Taiwan	Liberia	15 Jun 63	521UNTS361	107531

PARTY ONE	PARTY TWO	DATE	CITATION	NUMBER
Artists (Cont.)				
Cameroon	UK Great Britain	20 Aug 63	539UNTS233	107834
Mali	Romania	26 Sep 63	528UNTS193	107642
Hungary	Yugoslavia	15 Oct 63	577UNTS49	108372
Tanganyika	USSR (Soviet Union)	06 Nov 63	528UNTS157	107639
Belgium	Romania	13 Nov 63	520UNTS119	107513
Belgium	Pakistan	14 Nov 63	535UNTS393	107792
Belgium	Poland	09 Dec 63	514UNTS195	107448
USA (United States)	USSR (Soviet Union)	22 Feb 64	526UNTS131	107605
Ireland	Norway	02 Apr 64	553UNTS129	108078
Mexico	Netherlands	08 Apr 64	575UNTS35	108353
Algeria	Czechoslovakia	14 May 64	538UNTS301	107817
Argentina	France	03 Oct 64	635UNTS155	109080
Czechoslovakia	Germany, East	06 Oct 64	545UNTS113	107927
Germany, East	Poland	06 Oct 64	552UNTS89	108051
Belgium	Mexico	19 Nov 64	546UNTS217	107949
Poland	Romania	26 Nov 64	552UNTS157	108053
Romania	USA (United States)	23 Dec 64	535UNTS359	107790
Belgium	Sweden	11 Jan 65	533UNTS157	107741
Belgium	Hungary	11 Feb 65	544UNTS3	107908
UK Great Britain	USSR (Soviet Union)	13 Feb 65	543UNTS43	107896
Bulgaria	Czechoslovakia	22 May 65	545UNTS65	107925
Ethiopia	Hungary	25 May 65	577UNTS193	108377
China People's Rep	Romania	27 May 65	592UNTS3	108566
Pakistan	USSR (Soviet Union)	05 Jun 65	593UNTS115	108579
Japan	Korea, South	22 Jun 65	584UNTS49	108475
Uganda	USSR (Soviet Union)	24 Jul 65	596UNTS199	108633
Israel	Sierra Leone	22 Aug 65	550UNTS275	108022
Argentina	Belgium	05 Nov 65	635UNTS229	109086
Czechoslovakia	Poland	22 Jan 66	588UNTS175	108524
UK Great Britain	Yugoslavia	27 Jan 66	573UNTS243	108337
Brazil	Chile	18 Mar 66	0UNTS0	109418
Romania	Tunisia	21 Apr 66	604UNTS57	108743
Czechoslovakia	USSR (Soviet Union)	23 Apr 66	566UNTS159	108242
Netherlands	Yugoslavia	11 Aug 66	602UNTS243	108716
Netherlands	Romania	13 Feb 67	604UNTS287	108756
Denmark	France	15 Feb 67	604UNTS247	108754
UK Great Britain	USSR (Soviet Union)	24 Feb 67	606UNTS171	108785
Belgium	Bulgaria	17 May 67	631UNTS215	108995
Indonesia	UK Great Britain	01 Aug 67	638UNTS3	109128
Denmark	Romania	29 Aug 67	642UNTS357	109183
France	Ireland	04 Nov 67	0UNTS0	109291
Athletes				
Poland	Yugoslavia	16 Mar 46	10UNTS11	100139
Austria	France	15 Mar 47	12UNTS109	100182
Czechoslovakia	Yugoslavia	27 Apr 47	33UNTS49	100514
France	Poland	19 May 47	12UNTS95	100181
Bulgaria	Czechoslovakia	20 Jun 47	46UNTS15	100698
Romania	Yugoslavia	26 Jun 47	116UNTS39	101568
Bulgaria	Poland	28 Jun 47	15UNTS123	100230
Czechoslovakia	Poland	04 Jul 47	25UNTS249	100366
Albania	Yugoslavia	09 Jul 47	33UNTS91	100516
Hungary	Yugoslavia	15 Oct 47	33UNTS73	100515
Colombia	USA (United States)	22 Dec 47	51UNTS45	100751
Poland	Romania	27 Feb 48	46UNTS143	100707
France	UK Great Britain	02 Mar 48	77UNTS33	100990
Hungary	Poland	18 Jun 48	25UNTS319	100370
Greece	Lebanon	10 Jun 49	178UNTS29	102334
Belgium	United Arab Rep	28 Nov 49	76UNTS91	100982
India	Turkey	29 Jun 51	213UNTS183	102886
Italy	Netherlands	05 Dec 51	0UNTS0	109323
Albania	Romania	14 Feb 53	342UNTS107	104903
Greece	Netherlands	29 Apr 53	191UNTS235	102583
Israel	Uruguay	30 Apr 53	280UNTS269	104064
Pakistan	Turkey	29 Jun 53	211UNTS225	102854

PARTY ONE	PARTY TWO	DATE	CITATION	NUMBER
Athletes (Cont.)				
Pakistan	United Arab Rep	14 Nov 53	485UNTS55	107046
Greece	Italy	11 Sep 54	284UNTS313	104145
Turkey	UK Great Britain	12 Mar 56	313UNTS73	104530
Romania	USSR (Soviet Union)	07 Apr 56	259UNTS377	103698
Mongolia	USSR (Soviet Union)	24 Apr 56	259UNTS297	103693
Germany, East	USSR (Soviet Union)	26 Apr 56	259UNTS279	103692
Bulgaria	USSR (Soviet Union)	28 Apr 56	259UNTS363	103697
Albania	USSR (Soviet Union)	03 May 56	259UNTS391	103699
USSR (Soviet Union)	Yugoslavia	17 May 56	259UNTS145	103687
Czechoslovakia	USSR (Soviet Union)	01 Jun 56	259UNTS341	103696
Poland	USSR (Soviet Union)	30 Jun 56	259UNTS311	103694
China People's Rep	USSR (Soviet Union)	05 Jul 56	263UNTS129	103770
Poland	Yugoslavia	06 Jul 56	281UNTS143	104076
Belgium	Czechoslovakia	08 Aug 56	257UNTS215	103656
Syria	USSR (Soviet Union)	20 Aug 56	274UNTS105	103961
Greece	United Arab Rep	04 Sep 56	299UNTS253	104317
Korea, North	USSR (Soviet Union)	05 Sep 56	259UNTS329	103695
India	Japan	29 Oct 56	318UNTS289	104622
Poland	United Arab Rep	02 Feb 57	319UNTS221	104633
Taiwan	Turkey	12 Feb 57	282UNTS125	104097
USSR (Soviet Union)	Vietnam, North	15 Feb 57	274UNTS115	103962
Japan	United Arab Rep	20 Mar 57	318UNTS345	104625
India	Poland	27 Mar 57	319UNTS263	104635
Poland	Vietnam, North	06 Apr 57	432UNTS255	106224
Romania	United Arab Rep	15 Apr 57	389UNTS21	105589
Iran	Japan	16 Apr 57	325UNTS113	104697
India	Romania	30 Apr 57	342UNTS251	104911
Czechoslovakia	Syria	18 Jun 57	303UNTS119	104374
Czechoslovakia	United Arab Rep	19 Oct 57	530UNTS181	107681
United Arab Rep	USSR (Soviet Union)	19 Oct 57	292UNTS151	104271
Taiwan	Iran	11 Nov 57	563UNTS31	108202
Ceylon (Sri Lanka)	USSR (Soviet Union)	15 Jan 58	305UNTS235	104421
USA (United States)	USSR (Soviet Union)	27 Jan 58	301UNTS405	104350
Taiwan	Costa Rica	10 Apr 58	315UNTS165	104567
Germany, East	Romania	15 Jul 58	387UNTS115	105560
Spain	USA (United States)	16 Oct 58	336UNTS153	104804
Czechoslovakia	Romania	25 Oct 58	338UNTS301	104843
El Salvador	Israel	14 Nov 58	345UNTS67	104959
Mongolia	Poland	23 Dec 58	432UNTS177	106220
Hungary	Iraq	11 Apr 59	439UNTS25	106323
Iraq	USSR (Soviet Union)	05 May 59	356UNTS179	105095
Iran	UK Great Britain	06 May 59	398UNTS51	105717
Iran	Netherlands	22 May 59	474UNTS195	106882
Taiwan	Ecuador	12 Jun 59	387UNTS3	105554
Brazil	Israel	24 Jun 59	515UNTS151	107458
Czechoslovakia	India	07 Jul 59	359UNTS259	105145
Iraq	Romania	04 Aug 59	502UNTS17	107324
USA (United States)	USSR (Soviet Union)	21 Nov 59	361UNTS35	105172
Czechoslovakia	Guinea	30 Nov 59	386UNTS63	105538
UK Great Britain	USSR (Soviet Union)	01 Dec 59	351UNTS313	105032
Czechoslovakia	Ethiopia	11 Dec 59	399UNTS93	105736
Germany, East	Hungary	19 Dec 59	409UNTS4	105874
Guinea	Hungary	12 Jan 60	519UNTS131	107505
Italy	USSR (Soviet Union)	09 Feb 60	399UNTS75	105735
India	USSR (Soviet Union)	12 Feb 60	392UNTS153	105642
Taiwan	Panama	26 Feb 60	435UNTS281	106285
Indonesia	USSR (Soviet Union)	28 Feb 60	392UNTS191	105644
Netherlands	Turkey	12 May 60	463UNTS207	106704
Finland	USSR (Soviet Union)	27 May 60	379UNTS381	105444
Cuba	Korea, North	29 Aug 60	473UNTS117	106860
Cuba	Romania	28 Oct 60	457UNTS9	106574
Czechoslovakia	Ghana	23 Nov 60	431UNTS91	106213
Cambodia	Czechoslovakia	27 Nov 60	410UNTS263	105910
Romania	USA (United States)	09 Dec 60	401UNTS19	105759
Cuba	USSR (Soviet Union)	12 Dec 60	421UNTS3	106048

PARTY ONE	PARTY TWO	DATE	CITATION	NUMBER
Athletes (Cont.)				
Cuba	Czechoslovakia	22 Dec 60	426UNTS145	106134
UK Great Britain	USSR (Soviet Union)	09 Jan 61	404UNTS175	105810
Ethiopia	USSR (Soviet Union)	13 Jan 61	421UNTS13	106049
Ghana	Poland	17 Jan 61	572UNTS209	108314
Brazil	Japan	23 Jan 61	569UNTS81	108281
Czechoslovakia	Hungary	24 Feb 61	422UNTS15	106066
Cuba	Poland	06 Mar 61	484UNTS123	107020
Cuba	Germany, East	29 Mar 61	448UNTS81	106426
Afghanistan	Czechoslovakia	23 Apr 61	437UNTS25	106297
Taiwan	Nicaragua	25 Apr 61	423UNTS139	106090
Ghana	Hungary	27 Apr 61	439UNTS17	106322
Taiwan	Uruguay	03 May 61	596UNTS121	108630
Somalia	USSR (Soviet Union)	02 Jun 61	528UNTS147	107638
Czechoslovakia	Somalia	04 Jun 61	479UNTS291	106960
Pakistan	Philippines	15 Aug 61	522UNTS35	107534
Taiwan	Paraguay	18 Aug 61	438UNTS109	106314
Taiwan	Jordan	17 Oct 61	435UNTS267	106284
Brazil	Poland	19 Oct 61	552UNTS75	108050
Taiwan	El Salvador	27 Nov 61	437UNTS161	106306
USA (United States)	USSR (Soviet Union)	08 Mar 62	460UNTS3	106630
Hungary	India	30 Mar 62	519UNTS119	107504
Senegal	USSR (Soviet Union)	14 Jun 62	437UNTS233	106309
Israel	Peru	25 Jun 62	515UNTS263	107464
Israel	Liberia	25 Jun 62	448UNTS295	106442
Syria	USSR (Soviet Union)	19 Aug 62	457UNTS285	106588
Denmark	USSR (Soviet Union)	11 Sep 62	458UNTS3	106589
Mali	Poland	02 Nov 62	572UNTS219	108315
Belgium	Tunisia	21 Dec 62	482UNTS3	106987
UK Great Britain	USSR (Soviet Union)	21 Jan 63	475UNTS3	106887
Dahomey	USSR (Soviet Union)	20 Mar 63	528UNTS181	107641
Romania	USA (United States)	02 Apr 63	474UNTS95	106874
Cameroon	UK Great Britain	20 Aug 63	539UNTS233	107834
Mali	Romania	26 Sep 63	528UNTS193	107642
Hungary	Yugoslavia	15 Oct 63	577UNTS49	108372
Tanganyika	USSR (Soviet Union)	06 Nov 63	528UNTS157	107639
Belgium	Romania	13 Nov 63	520UNTS119	107513
Belgium	Pakistan	14 Nov 63	535UNTS393	107792
Netherlands	Tunisia	11 Feb 64	570UNTS173	108293
USA (United States)	USSR (Soviet Union)	22 Feb 64	526UNTS131	107605
Algeria	Czechoslovakia	14 May 64	538UNTS301	107817
Germany, East	Poland	06 Oct 64	552UNTS89	108051
Czechoslovakia	Germany, East	06 Oct 64	545UNTS113	107927
Poland	Romania	26 Nov 64	552UNTS157	108053
Romania	USA (United States)	23 Dec 64	535UNTS359	107790
Belgium	Hungary	11 Feb 65	544UNTS3	107908
UK Great Britain	USSR (Soviet Union)	13 Feb 65	543UNTS43	107896
Afghanistan	UK Great Britain	19 Apr 65	633UNTS45	109033
Bulgaria	Czechoslovakia	22 May 65	545UNTS65	107925
Ethiopia	Hungary	25 May 65	577UNTS193	108377
China People's Rep	Romania	27 May 65	592UNTS3	108566
Pakistan	USSR (Soviet Union)	05 Jun 65	593UNTS115	108579
Pakistan	IDA (Devel Assoc)	30 Jun 65	554UNTS111	108099
Uganda	USSR (Soviet Union)	24 Jul 65	596UNTS199	108633
Bulgaria	Hungary	19 Aug 65	577UNTS67	108373
Czechoslovakia	Poland	22 Jan 66	588UNTS175	108524
Argentina	Taiwan	19 Mar 66	635UNTS281	109089
Romania	Tunisia	21 Apr 66	604UNTS57	108743
Czechoslovakia	USSR (Soviet Union)	23 Apr 66	566UNTS159	108242
Rwanda	USSR (Soviet Union)	06 May 66	633UNTS217	109039
Iran	USSR (Soviet Union)	22 Aug 66	643UNTS203	109192
Congo (Brazzaville)	Czechoslovakia	29 Nov 66	635UNTS3	109069
Netherlands	Romania	13 Feb 67	604UNTS287	108756
UK Great Britain	USSR (Soviet Union)	24 Feb 67	606UNTS171	108785
Belgium	Bulgaria	17 May 67	631UNTS215	108995
France	Romania	26 Jun 67	642UNTS181	109173

PARTY ONE	PARTY TWO	DATE	CITATION	NUMBER
Athletes (Cont.)				
Italy	Romania	08 Aug 67	642UNTS191	109174
Denmark	Romania	29 Aug 67	642UNTS357	109183
France	Ireland	04 Nov 67	0UNTS0	109291
Archives and objects				
Multilateral		28 Oct 44	123UNTS223	200414
Multilateral		20 Jan 45	140UNTS397	200471
Multilateral		10 Feb 47	48UNTS203	100746
Multilateral		10 Feb 47	41UNTS135	100644
Multilateral		10 Feb 47	41UNTS21	100643
Pakistan	Switzerland	17 Mar 52	192UNTS237	102603
Italy	Yugoslavia	18 Dec 54	284UNTS239	104141
France	Ireland	04 Nov 67	0UNTS0	109291
Humanitarian matters				
Multilateral		21 Jun 29	39UNTS27	100611
Germany, West	USA (United States)	30 Mar 42	105UNTS219	200334
Belgium	USSR (Soviet Union)	13 Mar 45	19UNTS235	200117
Czechoslovakia	USSR (Soviet Union)	25 Jul 46	27UNTS231	100409
France	USA (United States)	11 Mar 47	151UNTS159	101991
Romania	Yugoslavia	30 Jun 47	116UNTS57	101569
Hungary	Poland	28 Aug 47	15UNTS145	100231
Austria	USA (United States)	08 Oct 47	25UNTS3	100354
Greece	UNICEF (Children)	14 Oct 47	102UNTS39	101409
Greece	United Nations	12 Feb 48	47UNTS223	100732
France	United Nations	10 Mar 48	47UNTS203	100731
France	UK Great Britain	19 Apr 48	83UNTS201	101109
Iceland	United Nations	19 Apr 48	47UNTS251	100733
Finland	United Nations	20 May 48	47UNTS319	200189
Multilateral		10 Jun 48	191UNTS3	102576
Multilateral		10 Jun 48	164UNTS113	102163
Pakistan	United Nations	27 Aug 48	47UNTS269	100734
Canada	United Nations	27 Aug 48	47UNTS167	100729
United Nations	Thailand	05 Oct 48	47UNTS287	100735
United Nations	San Marino	07 Oct 48	47UNTS337	200190
Czechoslovakia	United Nations	07 Oct 48	47UNTS185	100730
Czechoslovakia	Poland	12 Nov 48	84UNTS347	101141
Multilateral		09 Dec 48	78UNTS277	101021
Canada	USA (United States)	31 Jan 49	43UNTS119	100666
United Nations	UK Great Britain	18 Mar 49	47UNTS305	100736
Bulgaria	Poland	16 May 49	84UNTS313	101140
Multilateral		12 Aug 49	75UNTS31	100970
Multilateral		12 Aug 49	75UNTS287	100973
Multilateral		12 Aug 49	75UNTS85	100971
Multilateral		04 Nov 50	213UNTS221	102889
Multilateral		09 Jan 51	197UNTS341	102647
Saudi Arabia	USA (United States)	18 Jun 51	102UNTS73	101412
Sweden	USA (United States)	27 Jun 51	148UNTS77	101937
Norway	USA (United States)	17 Sep 51	140UNTS313	101895
UNICEF (Children)	UK Great Britain	04 Feb 52	120UNTS147	101620
Dominican Republic	UNICEF (Children)	15 Feb 52	121UNTS43	101625
Canada	USA (United States)	21 Feb 52	205UNTS293	102781
Switzerland	Yugoslavia	28 May 53	232UNTS45	103228
Germany, West	USA (United States)	12 Feb 54	223UNTS153	103064
Greece	Romania	19 May 54	225UNTS27	103084
Sweden	USSR (Soviet Union)	29 Sep 54	202UNTS259	102733
Germany, West	USA (United States)	06 Jun 55	315UNTS155	104566
Germany, East	Hungary	10 Sep 55	407UNTS132	105863
Finland	USSR (Soviet Union)	19 Oct 55	353UNTS185	105043
Czechoslovakia	Germany, East	24 Oct 55	504UNTS173	107358
Multilateral		13 Dec 55	250UNTS3	103514
Multilateral		04 Jan 56	256UNTS171	103627
Romania	Yugoslavia	01 Feb 56	362UNTS203	105189
Hungary	Romania	03 Feb 56	362UNTS233	105190
Norway	USSR (Soviet Union)	31 Mar 56	259UNTS205	103690
Denmark	USSR (Soviet Union)	31 Mar 56	259UNTS169	103689

PARTY ONE	PARTY TWO	DATE	CITATION	NUMBER
Humanitarian matters (Cont.)				
Sweden	USSR (Soviet Union)	31 Mar 56	259UNTS239	103691
Multilateral		07 Sep 56	266UNTS3	103822
Multilateral		11 Sep 56	266UNTS221	103832
Czechoslovakia	Germany, East	06 Oct 56	501UNTS109	107315
Norway	USSR (Soviet Union)	19 Oct 56	257UNTS3	103644
Israel	UN Relief Palestin	09 Nov 56	280UNTS261	104063
Finland	USSR (Soviet Union)	07 Dec 56	258UNTS89	103673
Multilateral		21 Dec 56	427UNTS81	106147
Belgium	Czechoslovakia	12 Mar 57	312UNTS75	104512
Germany, West	Yugoslavia	10 Apr 57	463UNTS269	106708
Bulgaria	Sweden	17 Apr 57	464UNTS3	106709
Hungary	Netherlands	28 May 57	334UNTS291	104773
Hungary	Sweden	02 Aug 57	334UNTS307	104774
Netherlands	Romania	27 Aug 57	342UNTS309	104914
UK Great Britain	USSR (Soviet Union)	19 Dec 57	351UNTS235	105026
Germany, West	Netherlands	30 Jan 58	315UNTS117	104563
Bulgaria	Netherlands	07 Feb 58	335UNTS45	104777
Multilateral		29 Apr 58	450UNTS11	106465
Bulgaria	Denmark	28 May 58	312UNTS235	104521
India	USSR (Soviet Union)	02 Jun 58	393UNTS3	105650
Belgium	USSR (Soviet Union)	05 Jun 58	345UNTS145	104965
Netherlands	USSR (Soviet Union)	17 Jun 58	335UNTS77	104779
Austria	Romania	10 Jul 58	353UNTS155	105041
Denmark	Hungary	17 Jul 58	344UNTS281	104954
Romania	United Arab Rep	14 Aug 58	405UNTS189	105834
Austria	Bulgaria	12 Sep 58	353UNTS3	105036
UK Great Britain	Yugoslavia	03 Feb 59	359UNTS339	105151
Bulgaria	United Arab Rep	09 Jul 59	411UNTS187	105920
Greece	Romania	02 May 60	485UNTS17	107043
Multilateral		17 Jun 60	536UNTS27	107794
Hungary	UK Great Britain	25 Oct 60	419UNTS309	106034
Multilateral		13 Dec 60	523UNTS117	107557
Norway	Poland	17 Jan 61	412UNTS130	105928
Liberia	Switzerland	31 Aug 61	559UNTS215	108160
Ghana	Romania	30 Sep 61	467UNTS443	106769
Mexico	USA (United States)	08 Jan 62	433UNTS163	106239
Finland	Hungary	13 Feb 62	463UNTS61	106693
Ghana	USSR (Soviet Union)	06 Apr 62	498UNTS41	107277
France	Romania	18 May 62	498UNTS115	107279
Morocco	Switzerland	05 Jul 62	498UNTS189	107282
Austria	Czechoslovakia	22 Sep 62	495UNTS157	107244
Hungary	Syria	18 Oct 62	491UNTS209	107178
Czechoslovakia	Poland	16 Nov 62	526UNTS3	107597
Austria	Yugoslavia	11 Dec 62	546UNTS3	107938
Syria	United Arab Rep	27 Dec 62	491UNTS245	107180
Greece	Hungary	27 Apr 63	534UNTS3	107750
Pakistan	USSR (Soviet Union)	07 Oct 63	499UNTS161	107297
Denmark	Yugoslavia	11 Feb 64	511UNTS241	107437
Multilateral		27 Jan 67	610UNTS205	108843
ILO conventions				
Multilateral		28 Nov 19	38UNTS17	100584
Multilateral		28 Nov 19	38UNTS93	100589
Multilateral		28 Nov 19	38UNTS81	100588
Multilateral		28 Nov 19	38UNTS67	100587
Multilateral		28 Nov 19	38UNTS41	100585
Multilateral		29 Nov 19	38UNTS53	100586
Multilateral		09 Jul 20	38UNTS119	100591
Multilateral		09 Jul 20	38UNTS109	100590
Multilateral		10 Jul 20	38UNTS129	100592
Multilateral		11 Nov 21	38UNTS203	100598
Multilateral		11 Nov 21	38UNTS217	100599
Multilateral		12 Nov 21	38UNTS165	100595
Multilateral		12 Nov 21	38UNTS153	100594
Multilateral		16 Nov 21	38UNTS143	100593

PARTY ONE	PARTY TWO	DATE	CITATION	NUMBER
ILO conventions (Cont.)				
Multilateral		17 Nov 21	38UNTS187	100597
Multilateral		19 Nov 21	38UNTS175	100596
Multilateral		05 Jun 25	38UNTS257	100602
Multilateral		08 Jun 25	38UNTS269	100603
Multilateral		10 Jun 25	38UNTS229	100600
Multilateral		10 Jun 25	38UNTS243	100601
Multilateral		05 Jun 26	38UNTS281	100604
Multilateral		23 Jun 26	38UNTS315	100606
Multilateral		24 Jun 26	38UNTS295	100605
Multilateral		15 Jun 27	38UNTS327	100607
Multilateral		15 Jun 27	38UNTS343	100608
Multilateral		16 Jun 28	39UNTS3	100609
Multilateral		26 Jun 28	39UNTS15	100610
Multilateral		28 Jun 30	39UNTS85	100613
Multilateral		28 Jun 30	39UNTS55	100612
Multilateral		27 Apr 32	39UNTS103	100614
Multilateral		30 Apr 32	39UNTS133	100615
Multilateral		22 Jun 33	78UNTS181	101016
Multilateral		29 Jun 33	39UNTS211	100619
Multilateral		29 Jun 33	39UNTS285	100622
Multilateral		29 Jun 33	39UNTS235	100620
Multilateral		29 Jun 33	39UNTS151	100616
Multilateral		29 Jun 33	39UNTS259	100621
Multilateral		29 Jun 33	39UNTS189	100618
Multilateral		29 Jun 33	39UNTS165	100617
Multilateral		19 Jun 34	40UNTS3	100623
Multilateral		21 Jun 34	40UNTS33	100625
Multilateral		21 Jun 34	40UNTS19	100624
Multilateral		23 Jun 34	40UNTS45	100626
Multilateral		21 Jun 35	40UNTS63	100627
Multilateral		22 Jun 35	40UNTS73	100628
Multilateral		22 Jun 35	271UNTS199	103915
Multilateral		25 Jun 35	40UNTS97	100629
Multilateral		20 Jun 36	40UNTS109	100630
Multilateral		24 Jun 36	40UNTS137	100631
Multilateral		24 Oct 36	40UNTS187	100634
Multilateral		24 Oct 36	40UNTS153	100632
Multilateral		24 Oct 36	40UNTS205	100635
Multilateral		24 Oct 36	40UNTS169	100633
Multilateral		22 Jun 37	40UNTS217	100636
Multilateral		23 Jun 37	40UNTS233	100637
Multilateral		20 Jun 38	40UNTS255	100638
Multilateral		27 Jun 39	40UNTS281	100639
Multilateral		27 Jun 39	40UNTS311	100640
Multilateral		28 Jun 39	209UNTS39	102820
Multilateral		27 Jun 46	264UNTS163	103792
Multilateral		27 Jun 46	164UNTS37	102157
Multilateral		28 Jun 46	442UNTS235	106352
Multilateral		29 Jun 46	94UNTS11	101303
Multilateral		29 Jun 46	214UNTS233	102901
Multilateral		09 Oct 46	78UNTS227	101019
Multilateral		09 Oct 46	38UNTS3	100583
Multilateral		09 Oct 46	78UNTS198	101017
Multilateral		09 Oct 46	78UNTS213	101018
Multilateral		19 Jun 47	171UNTS329	102235
Multilateral		11 Jul 47	161UNTS113	102125
Multilateral		11 Jul 47	214UNTS33	102898
Multilateral		11 Jul 47	218UNTS345	102961
Multilateral		11 Jul 47	54UNTS3	100792
Multilateral		09 Jul 48	70UNTS85	100898
Multilateral		09 Jul 48	68UNTS17	100881
Multilateral		09 Jul 48	81UNTS147	101070
Multilateral		10 Jul 48	91UNTS3	101239
Multilateral		18 Jun 49	160UNTS223	102109
Multilateral		18 Jun 49	605UNTS295	108768

PARTY ONE	PARTY TWO	DATE	CITATION	NUMBER
ILO conventions (Cont.)				
Multilateral		29 Jun 49	138UNTS207	101870
Multilateral		01 Jul 49	120UNTS71	101616
Multilateral		01 Jul 49	96UNTS237	101340
Multilateral		01 Jul 49	138UNTS225	101871
Multilateral		01 Jul 49	96UNTS257	101341
Multilateral		28 Jun 51	172UNTS159	102244
Multilateral		29 Jun 51	165UNTS303	102181
Denmark	France	30 Jun 51	151UNTS241	102000
Multilateral		26 Jun 52	196UNTS183	102624
Multilateral		28 Jun 52	210UNTS132	102838
Multilateral		28 Jun 52	214UNTS321	102907
Multilateral		21 Jun 55	305UNTS265	104423
Multilateral		19 Dec 56	427UNTS93	106148
Multilateral		25 Jun 57	320UNTS291	104648
Multilateral		26 Jun 57	325UNTS279	104704
Multilateral		26 Jun 57	328UNTS247	104738
Multilateral		13 May 58	389UNTS277	105598
Arab League	ILO (Labor Org)	26 May 58	302UNTS343	200549
Multilateral		24 Jun 58	348UNTS275	105005
Multilateral		25 Jun 58	362UNTS31	105181
Multilateral		19 Jun 59	413UNTS148	105949
Multilateral		19 Jun 59	413UNTS168	105951
Multilateral		19 Jun 59	413UNTS158	105950
Multilateral		22 Jun 60	431UNTS41	106208
Austria	Finland	01 Feb 62	425UNTS33	106116
Multilateral		22 Jun 62	494UNTS249	107237
Multilateral		28 Jun 62	494UNTS271	107238
Multilateral		25 Jun 63	532UNTS159	107717
Multilateral		08 Jul 64	560UNTS201	108175
Multilateral		08 Jul 64	602UNTS259	108718
Multilateral		13 Jul 64	569UNTS65	108279
Multilateral		21 Jun 66	0UNTS0	109298
Anti-discrimination				
Multilateral		05 Jun 25	38UNTS257	100602
Mexico	USA (United States)	29 Apr 43	105UNTS119	200327
Multilateral		11 Jul 47	218UNTS345	102961
Multilateral		30 Apr 48	119UNTS3	101609
Multilateral		01 Jul 49	96UNTS257	101341
Multilateral		29 Jun 51	165UNTS303	102181
Multilateral		02 Jul 51	189UNTS137	102545
ICJ Option Clause	Laos	24 Oct 52	149UNTS285	101957
ICJ Option Clause	Finland	26 Feb 54	189UNTS223	102546
Multilateral		28 Sep 54	360UNTS117	105158
Multilateral		21 Jun 55	305UNTS265	104423
Norway	USSR (Soviet Union)	19 Oct 56	257UNTS3	103644
Multilateral		25 Mar 57	294UNTS2	104300
Czechoslovakia	Yugoslavia	22 May 57	391UNTS33	105615
Multilateral		25 Jun 57	320UNTS291	104648
Multilateral		26 Jun 57	328UNTS247	104738
Multilateral		24 Jun 58	348UNTS275	105005
Multilateral		25 Jun 58	362UNTS31	105181
Czechoslovakia	USSR (Soviet Union)	02 Dec 59	374UNTS63	105330
Bulgaria	Poland	12 Jul 61	436UNTS147	106294
Multilateral		18 Oct 61	529UNTS89	107659
Multilateral		22 Jun 62	494UNTS249	107237
Multilateral		28 Jun 62	494UNTS271	107238
Multilateral		08 Jul 64	602UNTS259	108718
Multilateral		13 Jul 64	569UNTS65	108279
Multilateral		07 Mar 66	0UNTS0	109464
Employment regulations				
Multilateral		28 Nov 19	38UNTS93	100589
Multilateral		28 Nov 19	38UNTS67	100587
Multilateral		28 Nov 19	38UNTS81	100588
Multilateral		29 Nov 19	38UNTS53	100586

PARTY ONE	PARTY TWO	DATE	CITATION	NUMBER
Employment regulations (Cont.)				
Multilateral		09 Jul 20	38UNTS109	100590
Multilateral		10 Jul 20	38UNTS129	100592
Multilateral		11 Nov 21	38UNTS203	100598
Multilateral		11 Nov 21	38UNTS217	100599
Multilateral		16 Nov 21	38UNTS143	100593
Multilateral		19 Nov 21	38UNTS175	100596
Multilateral		24 Jun 26	38UNTS295	100605
Multilateral		28 Jun 30	39UNTS55	100612
Multilateral		28 Jun 30	39UNTS85	100613
Multilateral		30 Apr 32	39UNTS133	100615
Multilateral		22 Jun 33	78UNTS181	101016
Multilateral		29 Jun 33	39UNTS151	100616
Multilateral		19 Jun 34	40UNTS3	100623
Multilateral		21 Jun 35	40UNTS63	100627
Multilateral		20 Jun 36	40UNTS109	100630
Multilateral		24 Jun 36	40UNTS137	100631
Multilateral		24 Oct 36	40UNTS205	100635
Multilateral		22 Jun 37	40UNTS217	100636
Multilateral		27 Jun 39	40UNTS281	100639
Mexico	USA (United States)	29 Apr 43	105UNTS119	200327
Costa Rica	USA (United States)	29 May 44	124UNTS155	200417
Multilateral		27 Jun 46	164UNTS37	102157
Multilateral		29 Jun 46	214UNTS233	102901
Multilateral		09 Oct 46	78UNTS227	101019
Multilateral		09 Oct 46	78UNTS198	101017
Multilateral		09 Oct 46	78UNTS213	101018
Denmark	UK Great Britain	20 Jan 47	118UNTS73	101597
Philippines	USA (United States)	16 May 47	280UNTS177	104057
Switzerland	UK Great Britain	10 Jun 47	11UNTS217	100160
Multilateral		11 Jul 47	54UNTS3	100792
Belgium	Italy	09 Feb 48	71UNTS143	100915
Denmark	Switzerland	21 Feb 48	14UNTS321	100224
France	Netherlands	02 Jun 48	204UNTS275	102762
Multilateral		09 Jul 48	81UNTS147	101070
Multilateral		09 Jul 48	70UNTS85	100898
Multilateral		10 Jul 48	91UNTS3	101239
New Zealand	Switzerland	30 Jul 48	18UNTS177	100287
Italy	Netherlands	04 Dec 48	46UNTS271	100716
Multilateral		18 Jun 49	605UNTS295	108768
Multilateral		29 Jun 49	138UNTS207	101870
Multilateral		01 Jul 49	96UNTS237	101340
Multilateral		01 Jul 49	96UNTS257	101341
France	Netherlands	20 Jul 49	204UNTS287	102763
France	Ireland	21 Nov 49	553UNTS59	108069
Multilateral		17 Apr 50	126UNTS285	101694
Italy	UK Great Britain	28 Jul 50	101UNTS25	101399
Luxembourg	Netherlands	25 Aug 50	81UNTS13	101058
Netherlands	New Zealand	16 Oct 50	83UNTS269	101111
Austria	Sweden	31 Oct 50	197UNTS311	102645
France	Turkey	22 Dec 50	98UNTS11	101356
Belgium	Finland	20 Mar 51	110UNTS27	101498
Multilateral		18 Apr 51	261UNTS140	103729
Multilateral		02 Jul 51	189UNTS137	102545
Mexico	USA (United States)	11 Aug 51	162UNTS103	102133
Belgium	Sweden	18 Sep 51	133UNTS187	101789
Belgium	Germany, West	18 Jan 52	124UNTS9	101663
Netherlands	Switzerland	20 Nov 52	163UNTS121	102146
Germany, West	Sweden	15 May 53	227UNTS195	103139
Belgium	Germany, West	28 May 54	249UNTS387	103512
Italy	Netherlands	04 Jun 54	289UNTS261	104222
France	Greece	30 Jun 54	257UNTS83	103651
Austria	Denmark	07 Sep 54	201UNTS39	102709
Multilateral		28 Sep 54	360UNTS117	105158
Austria	Netherlands	17 Nov 54	292UNTS45	104266
Philippines	UK Great Britain	29 Aug 55	221UNTS241	103009

PARTY ONE	PARTY TWO	DATE	CITATION	NUMBER
Employment regulations (Cont.)				
Austria	Sweden	03 Nov 55	262UNTS289	103757
Austria	Belgium	20 Jan 56	248UNTS3	103481
Multilateral		07 Jun 56	381UNTS145	105470
Austria	Italy	12 Jul 56	378UNTS249	105426
Multilateral		07 Sep 56	266UNTS3	103822
Canada	France	04 Oct 56	305UNTS65	104414
Italy	UK Great Britain	12 Jun 57	310UNTS35	104484
Multilateral		25 Jun 57	320UNTS291	104648
Multilateral		26 Jun 57	328UNTS247	104738
Italy	Spain	25 Nov 57	378UNTS289	105428
Ireland	Sweden	05 Dec 57	428UNTS221	106176
Multilateral		03 Apr 58	336UNTS177	104806
Multilateral		24 Jun 58	348UNTS275	105005
Multilateral		01 Dec 58	385UNTS137	105534
Multilateral		19 Jun 59	413UNTS148	105949
Multilateral		19 Jun 59	413UNTS168	105951
Fed of Malaya	UK Great Britain	27 Jul 59	374UNTS21	105324
Germany, West	Ireland	11 May 60	553UNTS69	108070
Multilateral		22 Jun 60	431UNTS41	106208
Somalia	UK Great Britain	26 Jun 60	374UNTS339	105347
Somalia	UK Great Britain	26 Jun 60	374UNTS347	105348
Italy	Netherlands	06 Aug 60	455UNTS259	106546
Multilateral		01 Sep 60	403UNTS3	105792
Finland	Italy	18 Feb 61	434UNTS199	106263
Denmark	Germany, West	12 Sep 61	516UNTS283	107478
Multilateral		18 Oct 61	529UNTS89	107659
Belgium	Italy	28 Oct 61	429UNTS199	106199
UK Great Britain	Zambia	30 Jan 62	590UNTS173	108553
Austria	Finland	01 Feb 62	425UNTS33	106116
Multilateral		20 Apr 63	495UNTS3	107239
UK Great Britain	USA (United States)	11 Oct 63	483UNTS3	107005
Finland	Poland	18 Dec 63	486UNTS57	107072
Austria	Turkey	15 May 64	515UNTS109	107457
Multilateral		08 Jul 64	602UNTS259	108718
Multilateral		10 Jul 64	613UNTS127	108853
Multilateral		13 Jul 64	569UNTS65	108279
Netherlands	Turkey	19 Aug 64	521UNTS197	107523
Australia	Germany, West	21 Jun 65	542UNTS53	107879
Multilateral		22 Jun 65	610UNTS0	108836
Austria	Yugoslavia	19 Nov 65	587UNTS239	108512
Denmark	Netherlands	20 Jun 67	619UNTS67	108939
Philippines	USA (United States)	27 May 68	0UNTS0	109435
Holidays and rest periods				
Multilateral		28 Nov 19	38UNTS17	100584
Multilateral		28 Nov 19	38UNTS93	100589
Multilateral		28 Nov 19	38UNTS67	100587
Multilateral		29 Nov 19	38UNTS53	100586
Multilateral		09 Jul 20	38UNTS109	100590
Multilateral		16 Nov 21	38UNTS143	100593
Multilateral		17 Nov 21	38UNTS187	100597
Multilateral		08 Jun 25	38UNTS269	100603
Multilateral		16 Jun 28	39UNTS3	100609
Multilateral		28 Jun 30	39UNTS55	100612
Multilateral		28 Jun 30	39UNTS85	100613
Multilateral		30 Apr 32	39UNTS133	100615
Multilateral		19 Jun 34	40UNTS3	100623
Multilateral		21 Jun 34	40UNTS33	100625
Multilateral		22 Jun 35	271UNTS199	103915
Multilateral		25 Jun 35	40UNTS97	100629
Multilateral		24 Oct 36	40UNTS169	100633
Multilateral		28 Jun 39	209UNTS39	102820
Canada	USA (United States)	04 Nov 42	24UNTS217	200146
Multilateral		09 Oct 46	78UNTS227	101019
Philippines	USA (United States)	16 May 47	280UNTS177	104057

Holidays and rest periods (Cont.)

PARTY ONE	PARTY TWO	DATE	CITATION	NUMBER
Multilateral		09 Jul 48	81UNTS147	101070
Multilateral		10 Jul 48	91UNTS3	101239
Multilateral		18 Jun 49	605UNTS295	108768
Multilateral		29 Jun 49	138UNTS207	101870
FAO (Food Agri)	United Nations	02 Aug 50	139UNTS407	200467
ILO (Labor Org)	United Nations	12 Oct 50	139UNTS395	200466
ICAO (Civil Aviat)	United Nations	28 Feb 51	139UNTS429	200469
UNESCO (Educ/Cult)	United Nations	07 Mar 51	139UNTS417	200468
Multilateral		26 Jun 52	196UNTS183	102624
Multilateral		28 Jun 52	210UNTS132	102838
Multilateral		28 Jun 52	214UNTS321	102907
United Nations	WMO (Meteorology)	27 Mar 53	178UNTS361	200504
Multilateral		21 May 54	345UNTS285	104973
Multilateral		26 Jun 57	325UNTS279	104704
France	Italy	01 Aug 57	302UNTS221	104360
Poland	Yugoslavia	16 Jan 58	340UNTS181	104864
France	Italy	27 Mar 58	305UNTS387	104426
Multilateral		24 Jun 58	348UNTS275	105005
IAEA (Atom Energy)	United Nations	22 Sep 58	313UNTS323	200552
ITU (Telecommun)	United Nations	14 Jan 60	348UNTS331	200566
IMF (Fund)	United Nations	22 Dec 60	384UNTS315	200578
IBRD (World Bank)	United Nations	05 Jan 61	384UNTS303	200577
Sierra Leone	UK Great Britain	05 May 61	420UNTS17	106037
Jamaica	UK Great Britain	01 Jun 61	478UNTS9	106932
Netherlands	Spain	17 Dec 62	499UNTS227	107301
Netherlands	Portugal	22 Nov 63	492UNTS31	107185
Philippines	USA (United States)	27 May 68	0UNTS0	109435
Philippines	USA (United States)	28 Dec 68	0UNTS0	109436

Old age and invalidity insurance

PARTY ONE	PARTY TWO	DATE	CITATION	NUMBER
Multilateral		28 Nov 19	38UNTS41	100585
Multilateral		12 Nov 21	38UNTS165	100595
Multilateral		05 Jun 25	38UNTS257	100602
Multilateral		10 Jun 25	38UNTS229	100600
Multilateral		21 Jun 29	39UNTS27	100611
Multilateral		29 Jun 33	39UNTS211	100619
Multilateral		29 Jun 33	39UNTS189	100618
Multilateral		29 Jun 33	39UNTS235	100620
Multilateral		29 Jun 33	39UNTS259	100621
Multilateral		29 Jun 33	39UNTS165	100617
Multilateral		29 Jun 33	39UNTS285	100622
Multilateral		21 Jun 34	40UNTS19	100624
Multilateral		22 Jun 35	40UNTS73	100628
Multilateral		24 Oct 36	40UNTS187	100634
Canada	USA (United States)	04 Nov 42	24UNTS217	200146
Dominican Republic	USA (United States)	19 Oct 43	21UNTS295	200130
Multilateral		28 Jun 46	442UNTS235	106352
Multilateral		30 Oct 46	27UNTS77	100401
Belgium	Poland	24 Mar 47	18UNTS279	100297
Belgium	Netherlands	29 Aug 47	36UNTS349	100573
Belgium	France	17 Jan 48	36UNTS233	100570
Czechoslovakia	Poland	05 Apr 48	31UNTS355	100482
Belgium	Italy	30 Apr 48	36UNTS305	100571
France	Poland	09 Jun 48	32UNTS251	100503
France	UK Great Britain	11 Jun 48	66UNTS151	100852
Czechoslovakia	France	12 Oct 48	45UNTS81	100693
Australia	New Zealand	15 Apr 49	34UNTS225	100540
WHO (World Health)	Thailand	12 Aug 49	178UNTS347	102350
Belgium	Luxembourg	03 Dec 49	91UNTS31	101241
France	Netherlands	07 Jan 50	120UNTS25	101614
France	UK Great Britain	28 Jan 50	97UNTS155	101349
Israel	UK Great Britain	30 Mar 50	86UNTS231	101162
Luxembourg	Netherlands	08 Jul 50	135UNTS229	101824
Multilateral		27 Jul 50	166UNTS73	102186
Germany, West	Netherlands	29 Mar 51	149UNTS71	101952

Old age and invalidity insurance (Cont.)

PARTY ONE	PARTY TWO	DATE	CITATION	NUMBER
Multilateral		18 Apr 51	261UNTS140	103729
Denmark	France	30 Jun 51	151UNTS241	102000
Mexico	USA (United States)	11 Aug 51	162UNTS103	102133
Italy	UK Great Britain	28 Nov 51	172UNTS205	102248
Belgium	Switzerland	17 Jun 52	180UNTS23	102373
Multilateral		28 Jun 52	210UNTS132	102838
Italy	Netherlands	28 Oct 52	289UNTS144	104218
Switzerland	UK Great Britain	16 Jan 53	196UNTS119	102621
Germany, West	Italy	05 May 53	267UNTS9	103835
Australia	UK Great Britain	08 Jun 53	201UNTS187	102718
Multilateral		20 Jul 53	228UNTS41	103142
Denmark	Germany, West	14 Aug 53	202UNTS3	102725
Luxembourg	UK Great Britain	13 Oct 53	209UNTS87	102825
Multilateral		11 Dec 53	218UNTS211	102957
Multilateral		11 Dec 53	218UNTS153	102956
Denmark	UK Great Britain	15 Dec 53	196UNTS105	102620
Netherlands	UK Great Britain	11 Aug 54	248UNTS235	103497
Belgium	Yugoslavia	01 Nov 54	251UNTS123	103538
Sweden	Switzerland	17 Dec 54	369UNTS233	105260
Belgium	San Marino	22 Apr 55	253UNTS41	103574
Italy	Sweden	25 May 55	291UNTS235	104259
Multilateral		15 Sep 55	254UNTS55	103593
New Zealand	UK Great Britain	20 Dec 55	268UNTS243	103860
Netherlands	Yugoslavia	01 Jun 56	276UNTS319	103994
Sweden	UK Great Britain	09 Jun 56	309UNTS301	104479
Netherlands	UK Great Britain	12 Jun 56	250UNTS81	103519
Multilateral		09 Jul 56	314UNTS3	104539
Denmark	UK Great Britain	09 Jul 56	264UNTS45	103787
France	UK Great Britain	10 Jul 56	326UNTS23	104708
Belgium	Spain	28 Nov 56	308UNTS239	104464
Italy	UK Great Britain	29 Jan 57	326UNTS119	104710
Israel	UK Great Britain	29 Apr 57	280UNTS227	104062
Czechoslovakia	Romania	02 May 57	387UNTS167	105562
Belgium	UK Great Britain	20 May 57	303UNTS53	104371
Czechoslovakia	Yugoslavia	22 May 57	391UNTS57	105617
Norway	UK Great Britain	25 Jul 57	313UNTS3	104528
Hungary	Yugoslavia	07 Oct 57	439UNTS61	106325
Italy	Monaco	06 Dec 57	363UNTS59	105199
Italy	Monaco	06 Dec 57	363UNTS45	105198
Bulgaria	Yugoslavia	18 Dec 57	376UNTS3	105372
Poland	Yugoslavia	16 Jan 58	340UNTS137	104863
Australia	UK Great Britain	29 Jan 58	292UNTS233	104275
France	Italy	27 Mar 58	305UNTS387	104426
Netherlands	Switzerland	28 Mar 58	318UNTS175	104614
Belgium	Greece	01 Apr 58	388UNTS93	105574
UK Great Britain	Yugoslavia	24 May 58	326UNTS69	104709
Multilateral		24 Jun 58	348UNTS275	105005
Fed Rhod/Nyasaland	South Africa	11 Oct 58	373UNTS75	105315
Czechoslovakia	Hungary	30 Jan 59	351UNTS3	105016
Czechoslovakia	Switzerland	04 Jun 59	349UNTS121	105012
Finland	UK Great Britain	28 Jul 59	355UNTS31	105073
Denmark	UK Great Britain	27 Aug 59	360UNTS11	105153
Turkey	UK Great Britain	09 Sep 59	424UNTS267	106113
Czechoslovakia	USSR (Soviet Union)	02 Dec 59	374UNTS63	105330
Ireland	UK Great Britain	29 Mar 60	371UNTS3	105267
Germany, West	UK Great Britain	20 Apr 60	413UNTS236	105958
UN Special Fund	Thailand	04 Jun 60	360UNTS97	105157
Somalia	UK Great Britain	26 Jun 60	374UNTS331	105346
Bulgaria	Hungary	30 Jun 61	438UNTS287	106320
Bulgaria	Poland	12 Jul 61	436UNTS147	106294
Hungary	Romania	07 Sep 61	519UNTS141	107506
Multilateral		18 Oct 61	529UNTS89	107659
IBRD (World Bank)	South Africa	01 Dec 61	425UNTS197	106125
Multilateral		28 Jun 62	494UNTS271	107238
Multilateral		08 Jul 64	602UNTS259	108718

PARTY ONE	PARTY TWO	DATE	CITATION	NUMBER
Old age and invalidity insurance (Cont.)				
Austria	Spain	15 Jul 64	589UNTS169	108541
Luxembourg	Portugal	12 Feb 65	571UNTS239	108305
Belgium	Poland	26 Nov 65	620UNTS13	108950
Argentina	Portugal	20 May 66	635UNTS301	109090
Multilateral		24 Feb 67	596UNTS133	108631
Labor statistics				
Multilateral		28 Nov 19	38UNTS81	100588
Multilateral		28 Nov 19	38UNTS17	100584
Multilateral		28 Nov 19	38UNTS67	100587
Multilateral		28 Nov 19	38UNTS41	100585
Multilateral		10 Jul 20	38UNTS129	100592
Multilateral		11 Nov 21	38UNTS203	100598
Multilateral		17 Nov 21	38UNTS187	100597
Multilateral		19 Nov 21	38UNTS175	100596
Multilateral		24 Jun 26	38UNTS295	100605
Multilateral		16 Jun 28	39UNTS3	100609
Multilateral		28 Jun 30	39UNTS55	100612
Multilateral		28 Jun 30	39UNTS85	100613
Multilateral		22 Jun 35	40UNTS73	100628
Multilateral		25 Jun 35	40UNTS97	100629
Multilateral		24 Jun 36	40UNTS137	100631
Multilateral		24 Oct 36	40UNTS153	100632
Multilateral		24 Oct 36	40UNTS205	100635
Multilateral		22 Jun 37	40UNTS217	100636
Multilateral		20 Jun 38	40UNTS255	100638
Multilateral		27 Jun 39	40UNTS281	100639
Multilateral		28 Jun 39	209UNTS39	102820
Belgium	Italy	23 Jun 46	19UNTS65	100305
Multilateral		27 Jun 46	264UNTS163	103792
Multilateral		09 Oct 46	78UNTS213	101018
Multilateral		09 Oct 46	78UNTS198	101017
Multilateral		09 Oct 46	78UNTS227	101019
ILO (Labor Org)	United Nations	19 Dec 46	1UNTS183	200009
UNESCO (Educ/Cult)	United Nations	03 Feb 47	1UNTS233	200011
FAO (Food Agri)	United Nations	03 Feb 47	1UNTS207	200010
Multilateral		11 Jul 47	54UNTS3	100792
FAO (Food Agri)	ILO (Labor Org)	11 Sep 47	18UNTS335	200111
United Nations	WHO (World Health)	15 Nov 47	19UNTS193	200115
United Nations	UPU (Postal Union)	15 Nov 47	19UNTS219	200116
Albania	UNICEF (Children)	20 Nov 47	65UNTS163	200208
Multilateral		09 Jul 48	70UNTS85	100898
ILO (Labor Org)	WHO (World Health)	10 Jul 48	19UNTS269	200121
Multilateral		10 Jul 48	91UNTS3	101239
UNESCO (Educ/Cult)	WHO (World Health)	15 Jul 48	44UNTS323	200184
FAO (Food Agri)	WHO (World Health)	17 Jul 48	76UNTS171	200244
FAO (Food Agri)	UNESCO (Educ/Cult)	23 Aug 48	18UNTS345	200112
UNRRA (Relief)	United Nations	27 Sep 48	27UNTS349	200158
IRO (Refugee Org)	United Nations	07 Feb 49	26UNTS299	200153
FAO (Food Agri)	UNESCO (Educ/Cult)	09 Feb 49	43UNTS315	200182
ITU (Telecommun)	United Nations	26 Apr 49	30UNTS315	200175
Multilateral		29 Jun 49	138UNTS207	101870
Multilateral		01 Jul 49	96UNTS237	101340
ILO (Labor Org)	OAS (Am States)	07 Jun 50	70UNTS223	200240
United Nations	WMO (Meteorology)	10 Apr 51	103UNTS245	200415
Mexico	USA (United States)	11 Aug 51	162UNTS103	102133
Council of Europe	ILO (Labor Org)	23 Nov 51	126UNTS331	200435
Multilateral		26 Jun 52	196UNTS183	102624
ECSC (Coal/Steel)	ILO (Labor Org)	16 Jul 53	412UNTS273	200591
Multilateral		22 May 54	199UNTS3	102674
Belgium	Germany, West	28 May 54	249UNTS387	103512
France	Greece	30 Jun 54	257UNTS83	103651
Belgium	San Marino	22 Apr 55	253UNTS41	103574
Argentina	USA (United States)	29 Jul 55	235UNTS121	103298
Multilateral		04 Jan 56	256UNTS171	103627

PARTY ONE	PARTY TWO	DATE	CITATION	NUMBER
Labor statistics (Cont.)				
Sweden	USA (United States)	18 Jan 56	240UNTS413	103416
Germany, West	UK Great Britain	31 Jul 56	252UNTS93	103559
Multilateral		25 Mar 57	294UNTS2	104300
Multilateral		25 Mar 57	294UNTS259	104301
Multilateral		13 May 58	389UNTS277	105598
IAEA (Atom Energy)	UNESCO (Educ/Cult)	01 Oct 58	339UNTS373	200558
FAO (Food Agri)	IAEA (Atom Energy)	01 Oct 58	361UNTS211	200571
IMCO (Maritime Org)	United Nations	13 Jan 59	324UNTS273	200553
ILO (Labor Org)	IMCO (Maritime Org)	16 Jan 59	327UNTS309	200554
IAEA (Atom Energy)	ILO (Labor Org)	08 May 59	328UNTS273	200555
Multilateral		19 Jun 59	413UNTS168	105951
Subsahara Tech Com	ILO (Labor Org)	25 Jul 59	409UNTS290	200590
IAEA (Atom Energy)	WMO (Meteorology)	12 Aug 59	341UNTS341	200561
IAEA (Atom Energy)	ICAO (Civil Aviat)	01 Oct 59	361UNTS193	200570
ITU (Telecommun)	United Nations	14 Jan 60	348UNTS331	200566
IMF (Fund)	United Nations	22 Dec 60	384UNTS315	200578
IBRD (World Bank)	United Nations	05 Jan 61	384UNTS303	200577
Euratom	ILO (Labor Org)	26 Jan 61	390UNTS323	200580
Taiwan	UNICEF (Children)	08 Apr 64	500UNTS49	107306
France	Eur Space Research	10 Aug 64	528UNTS135	107637
FAO (Food Agri)	IMCO (Maritime Org)	11 Jul 66	575UNTS238	200627
Multilateral		13 Apr 67	595UNTS60	108612
Safety standards				
Multilateral		28 Nov 19	38UNTS17	100584
Multilateral		29 Nov 19	38UNTS53	100586
Multilateral		11 Nov 21	38UNTS217	100599
Multilateral		19 Nov 21	38UNTS175	100596
Multilateral		08 Jun 25	38UNTS269	100603
Multilateral		21 Jun 29	39UNTS27	100611
Multilateral		28 Jun 30	39UNTS55	100612
Multilateral		27 Apr 32	39UNTS103	100614
Multilateral		23 Jun 37	40UNTS233	100637
Multilateral		28 Jun 39	209UNTS39	102820
Canada	USA (United States)	04 Nov 42	24UNTS217	200146
Mexico	USA (United States)	29 Apr 43	105UNTS119	200327
Costa Rica	USA (United States)	29 May 44	124UNTS155	200417
USSR (Soviet Union)	Yugoslavia	13 Nov 45	116UNTS139	101573
Multilateral		09 Oct 46	78UNTS198	101017
Multilateral		09 Oct 46	78UNTS213	101018
Albania	Yugoslavia	28 Nov 46	111UNTS163	101529
Philippines	USA (United States)	16 May 47	280UNTS177	104057
Multilateral		11 Jul 47	218UNTS345	102961
Multilateral		11 Jul 47	54UNTS3	100792
Italy	Netherlands	04 Dec 48	46UNTS271	100716
Belgium	France	08 Jan 49	36UNTS151	100569
Multilateral		18 Jun 49	160UNTS223	102109
Multilateral		29 Jun 49	138UNTS207	101870
Multilateral		01 Jul 49	120UNTS71	101616
Netherlands	New Zealand	16 Oct 50	83UNTS269	101111
Belgium	Finland	20 Mar 51	110UNTS27	101498
Mexico	USA (United States)	11 Aug 51	162UNTS103	102133
France	Greece	13 May 54	222UNTS299	103036
Multilateral		21 May 54	345UNTS285	104973
Philippines	UK Great Britain	29 Aug 55	221UNTS241	103009
Austria	Belgium	20 Jan 56	248UNTS3	103481
Multilateral		07 Jun 56	381UNTS145	105470
Multilateral		26 Jun 57	325UNTS279	104704
Multilateral		24 Jun 58	348UNTS275	105005
Multilateral		19 Jun 59	413UNTS148	105949
Multilateral		19 Jun 59	413UNTS158	105950
Italy	Netherlands	06 Aug 60	455UNTS259	106546
Finland	Italy	18 Feb 61	434UNTS199	106263
Netherlands	Spain	08 Apr 61	482UNTS193	106996
Multilateral		25 Jun 63	532UNTS159	107717

PARTY ONE	PARTY TWO	DATE	CITATION	NUMBER
Safety standards (Cont.)				
Netherlands	Portugal	22 Nov 63	492UNTS31	107185
Multilateral		08 Jul 64	560UNTS201	108175
Multilateral		22 Jun 65	610UNTS0	108836
Austria	Yugoslavia	19 Nov 65	587UNTS239	108512
Multilateral		21 Jun 66	0UNTS0	109298
Philippines	USA (United States)	27 May 68	0UNTS0	109435
Multilateral		24 Dec 68	0UNTS0	109369
Philippines	USA (United States)	28 Dec 68	0UNTS0	109436
Right to organize				
Multilateral		12 Nov 21	38UNTS153	100594
Multilateral		19 Jun 47	171UNTS329	102235
Multilateral		09 Jul 48	68UNTS17	100881
Belgium	France	08 Jan 49	36UNTS151	100569
Multilateral		01 Jul 49	96UNTS257	101341
Multilateral		01 Jul 49	120UNTS71	101616
Mexico	USA (United States)	11 Aug 51	162UNTS103	102133
Multilateral		25 Mar 57	294UNTS2	104300
Multilateral		24 Jun 58	348UNTS275	105005
Multilateral		25 Jun 58	362UNTS31	105181
Multilateral		18 Oct 61	529UNTS89	107659
IMCO (Maritime Org)	United Nations	11 Feb 64	489UNTS357	200605
Philippines	USA (United States)	27 May 68	0UNTS0	109435
Wages and salaries				
Peru	USA (United States)	21 Apr 42	89UNTS317	200260
Mexico	USA (United States)	24 Oct 42	21UNTS189	200123
Nicaragua	USA (United States)	27 Oct 42	99UNTS287	200283
Canada	USA (United States)	04 Nov 42	24UNTS217	200146
Mexico	USA (United States)	26 Apr 43	21UNTS245	200127
Mexico	USA (United States)	29 Apr 43	105UNTS119	200327
USA (United States)	Venezuela	14 May 43	28UNTS359	200160
Peru	USA (United States)	20 May 43	100UNTS259	200288
Costa Rica	USA (United States)	29 May 44	124UNTS155	200417
UK Great Britain	USA (United States)	16 Apr 45	6UNTS189	100076
Denmark	UK Great Britain	24 Oct 45	93UNTS143	101297
USSR (Soviet Union)	Yugoslavia	13 Nov 45	116UNTS139	101573
Belgium	Italy	23 Jun 46	19UNTS65	100305
Multilateral		28 Jun 46	442UNTS235	106352
South Africa	UK Great Britain	14 Oct 46	86UNTS77	101153
Albania	Yugoslavia	28 Nov 46	111UNTS163	101529
Philippines	USA (United States)	16 May 47	280UNTS177	104057
Multilateral		11 Jul 47	218UNTS345	102961
Denmark	Switzerland	21 Feb 48	14UNTS321	100224
Costa Rica	USA (United States)	27 Feb 48	135UNTS74	101816
Sweden	Switzerland	16 Mar 48	197UNTS39	102632
New Zealand	USA (United States)	16 Mar 48	127UNTS133	101703
Belgium	Luxembourg	25 Mar 48	18UNTS323	100300
Netherlands	USA (United States)	29 Apr 48	32UNTS167	100498
Denmark	USA (United States)	06 May 48	26UNTS55	100377
France	Netherlands	02 Jun 48	204UNTS275	102762
Netherlands	UK Great Britain	15 Oct 48	74UNTS3	100955
Italy	Netherlands	04 Dec 48	46UNTS271	100716
Belgium	France	08 Jan 49	36UNTS151	100569
Norway	USA (United States)	13 Jun 49	127UNTS189	101705
Multilateral		18 Jun 49	605UNTS295	108768
Multilateral		01 Jul 49	138UNTS225	101871
Multilateral		01 Jul 49	120UNTS71	101616
Netherlands	Sweden	06 Jul 49	197UNTS189	102639
Ireland	USA (United States)	13 Sep 49	127UNTS89	101701
Multilateral		07 Nov 49	132UNTS31	101749
France	Ireland	21 Nov 49	553UNTS59	108069
Denmark	UK Great Britain	27 Mar 50	68UNTS117	100891
Canada	USA (United States)	12 Jun 50	127UNTS67	101700
Luxembourg	Netherlands	25 Aug 50	81UNTS13	101058
Colombia	USA (United States)	24 Nov 50	133UNTS49	101779

PARTY ONE	PARTY TWO	DATE	CITATION	NUMBER
Wages and salaries (Cont.)				
France	Turkey	22 Dec 50	98UNTS11	101356
Switzerland	USA (United States)	24 May 51	127UNTS227	101706
Multilateral		28 Jun 51	172UNTS159	102244
Multilateral		29 Jun 51	165UNTS303	102181
Mexico	USA (United States)	11 Aug 51	162UNTS103	102133
WHO (World Health)	Thailand	04 Oct 51	109UNTS85	101493
India	WHO (World Health)	01 Nov 51	118UNTS13	101593
Netherlands	Switzerland	12 Nov 51	126UNTS173	101689
Dominican Republic	USA (United States)	07 Jan 52	174UNTS243	102289
Multilateral		26 Jun 52	196UNTS183	102624
Multilateral		28 Jun 52	210UNTS132	102838
Italy	Netherlands	28 Oct 52	289UNTS144	104218
Netherlands	Switzerland	20 Nov 52	163UNTS121	102146
Germany, West	Italy	05 May 53	267UNTS9	103835
Germany, West	Sweden	15 May 53	227UNTS195	103139
Australia	UK Great Britain	08 Jun 53	201UNTS187	102718
Multilateral		21 May 54	345UNTS285	104973
Italy	Netherlands	04 Jun 54	289UNTS261	104222
Saudi Arabia	UK Great Britain	30 Jul 54	201UNTS317	102722
Netherlands	UK Great Britain	11 Aug 54	248UNTS235	103497
Austria	Denmark	07 Sep 54	201UNTS39	102709
Germany, West	Netherlands	29 Oct 54	237UNTS3	103335
Belgium	Yugoslavia	01 Nov 54	251UNTS123	103538
Austria	Netherlands	17 Nov 54	292UNTS45	104266
Mexico	USA (United States)	19 Nov 54	238UNTS237	103367
Brazil	Italy	24 Nov 54	284UNTS325	104146
Multilateral		01 Dec 54	210UNTS197	102839
Sweden	Switzerland	17 Dec 54	369UNTS233	105260
Belgium	San Marino	22 Apr 55	253UNTS41	103574
Italy	Sweden	25 May 55	291UNTS235	104259
Norway	Sweden	28 May 55	262UNTS151	103743
Multilateral		15 Sep 55	254UNTS55	103593
Austria	Sweden	03 Nov 55	262UNTS289	103757
New Zealand	UK Great Britain	20 Dec 55	268UNTS243	103860
Austria	Belgium	20 Jan 56	248UNTS3	103481
France	Italy	03 Mar 56	267UNTS181	103843
Indonesia	United Nations	17 Apr 56	233UNTS267	103266
Netherlands	Yugoslavia	01 Jun 56	276UNTS319	103994
Multilateral		07 Jun 56	381UNTS145	105470
Sweden	UK Great Britain	09 Jun 56	309UNTS301	104479
Netherlands	UK Great Britain	12 Jun 56	250UNTS81	103519
Multilateral		09 Jul 56	314UNTS3	104539
Denmark	UK Great Britain	09 Jul 56	264UNTS45	103787
France	UK Great Britain	10 Jul 56	326UNTS23	104708
Austria	Italy	12 Jul 56	378UNTS249	105426
Multilateral		13 Jul 56	281UNTS3	104066
Australia	Netherlands	01 Aug 56	280UNTS3	104047
Canada	France	04 Oct 56	305UNTS65	104414
Belgium	Spain	28 Nov 56	308UNTS239	104464
Israel	UK Great Britain	29 Apr 57	280UNTS227	104062
Belgium	UK Great Britain	20 May 57	303UNTS53	104371
Czechoslovakia	Yugoslavia	22 May 57	391UNTS57	105617
Multilateral		25 Jun 57	320UNTS291	104648
Multilateral		26 Jun 57	325UNTS279	104704
Norway	UK Great Britain	25 Jul 57	313UNTS3	104528
France	Italy	01 Aug 57	302UNTS221	104360
Hungary	Yugoslavia	07 Oct 57	439UNTS61	106325
Italy	Spain	25 Nov 57	378UNTS289	105428
Ireland	Sweden	05 Dec 57	428UNTS221	106176
Italy	Monaco	06 Dec 57	363UNTS59	105199
Italy	Monaco	06 Dec 57	363UNTS45	105198
Bulgaria	Yugoslavia	18 Dec 57	376UNTS3	105372
Poland	Yugoslavia	16 Jan 58	340UNTS137	104863
Australia	UK Great Britain	29 Jan 58	292UNTS233	104275
Netherlands	Switzerland	28 Mar 58	318UNTS175	104614

PARTY ONE	PARTY TWO	DATE	CITATION	NUMBER
Wages and salaries (Cont.)				
Belgium	Greece	01 Apr 58	388UNTS93	105574
UK Great Britain	Yugoslavia	24 May 58	326UNTS69	104709
Multilateral		24 Jun 58	348UNTS275	105005
Fed Rhod/Nyasaland	South Africa	11 Oct 58	373UNTS75	105315
Finland	Norway	21 Jan 59	325UNTS295	104705
Czechoslovakia	Hungary	30 Jan 59	351UNTS3	105016
Ireland	Netherlands	28 May 59	344UNTS95	104944
Czechoslovakia	Switzerland	04 Jun 59	349UNTS121	105012
Italy	Norway	12 Jun 59	428UNTS363	106187
Fed of Malaya	UK Great Britain	27 Jul 59	374UNTS21	105324
Finland	UK Great Britain	28 Jul 59	355UNTS31	105073
Multilateral		08 Sep 59	383UNTS203	105502
Turkey	UK Great Britain	09 Sep 59	424UNTS267	106113
Czechoslovakia	USSR (Soviet Union)	02 Dec 59	374UNTS63	105330
Canada	UK Great Britain	10 Dec 59	379UNTS201	105440
Ireland	UK Great Britain	29 Mar 60	371UNTS3	105267
Germany, West	UK Great Britain	20 Apr 60	449UNTS77	106453
Germany, West	UK Great Britain	20 Apr 60	413UNTS236	105958
Germany, West	Ireland	11 May 60	553UNTS69	108070
Germany, East	USSR (Soviet Union)	24 May 60	392UNTS205	105645
UN Special Fund	Thailand	04 Jun 60	360UNTS97	105157
Somalia	UK Great Britain	26 Jun 60	374UNTS331	105346
Somalia	UK Great Britain	26 Jun 60	374UNTS339	105347
Somalia	UK Great Britain	26 Jun 60	374UNTS347	105348
Italy	Netherlands	06 Aug 60	455UNTS259	106546
Finland	Italy	18 Feb 61	434UNTS199	106263
Netherlands	Spain	08 Apr 61	482UNTS193	106996
Denmark	Germany, West	12 Sep 61	516UNTS283	107478
IBRD (World Bank)	South Africa	01 Dec 61	425UNTS197	106125
UK Great Britain	Zambia	30 Jan 62	590UNTS173	108553
Multilateral		22 Jun 62	494UNTS249	107237
Germany, West	Israel	09 Jul 62	630UNTS87	108968
Denmark	India	15 May 63	616UNTS39	108890
Netherlands	Portugal	22 Nov 63	492UNTS31	107185
Austria	Spain	15 Jul 64	589UNTS169	108541
Australia	USA (United States)	17 Aug 64	530UNTS209	107683
Chad	Israel	07 Oct 64	630UNTS175	108969
Luxembourg	Portugal	12 Feb 65	571UNTS239	108305
France	UK Great Britain	25 Feb 65	543UNTS157	107899
Bel-Lux Econ Union	Morocco	28 Apr 65	620UNTS171	108954
France	UK Great Britain	19 Nov 65	561UNTS19	108178
Austria	Ireland	24 May 66	636UNTS149	109102
Argentina	Germany, West	13 Jul 66	636UNTS3	109091
Botswana	UK Great Britain	30 Sep 66	633UNTS339	109044
Austria	Spain	20 Dec 66	636UNTS197	109103
Denmark	Netherlands	20 Jun 67	619UNTS67	108939
Denmark	Zambia	17 Oct 67	620UNTS239	108960
Philippines	USA (United States)	27 May 68	0UNTS0	109435
Philippines	USA (United States)	28 Dec 68	0UNTS0	109436
Non-ILO labor relations				
Canada	USA (United States)	12 Mar 42	119UNTS295	200386
Mexico	USA (United States)	04 Aug 42	148UNTS379	200475
Canada	USA (United States)	04 Nov 42	24UNTS217	200146
Mexico	USA (United States)	26 Apr 43	21UNTS245	200127
Mexico	USA (United States)	29 Apr 43	105UNTS119	200327
Dominican Republic	USA (United States)	19 Oct 43	21UNTS295	200130
Costa Rica	USA (United States)	29 May 44	124UNTS155	200417
Belgium	Italy	23 Jun 46	19UNTS65	100305
Canada	Newfoundland	29 Jul 46	17UNTS169	100275
Mexico	USA (United States)	15 Nov 46	105UNTS3	101450
Denmark	Sweden	18 Nov 46	7UNTS251	100104
Albania	Yugoslavia	28 Nov 46	111UNTS163	101529
Belgium	Poland	24 Mar 47	18UNTS279	100297
Philippines	USA (United States)	16 May 47	280UNTS177	104057

PARTY ONE	PARTY TWO	DATE	CITATION	NUMBER
Non-ILO labor relations (Cont.)				
Canada	USA (United States)	19 May 47	43UNTS97	100663
Italy	UK Great Britain	30 May 47	54UNTS131	100800
France	UK Great Britain	13 Aug 47	91UNTS169	101249
Belgium	Netherlands	29 Aug 47	36UNTS349	100573
France	USA (United States)	25 Oct 47	89UNTS111	101212
Norway	Sweden	22 Dec 47	22UNTS203	100337
Denmark	Sweden	23 Dec 47	14UNTS3	100207
Belgium	France	17 Jan 48	36UNTS233	100570
Denmark	Norway	21 Jan 48	14UNTS307	100223
Belgium	Italy	09 Feb 48	71UNTS143	100915
Denmark	Switzerland	21 Feb 48	14UNTS321	100224
Sweden	Switzerland	16 Mar 48	197UNTS39	102632
Czechoslovakia	Poland	05 Apr 48	31UNTS355	100482
Belgium	Italy	30 Apr 48	36UNTS305	100571
Denmark	Iceland	14 May 48	23UNTS163	100346
France	Netherlands	02 Jun 48	204UNTS275	102762
France	Poland	09 Jun 48	32UNTS251	100503
France	UK Great Britain	11 Jun 48	66UNTS151	100852
Czechoslovakia	France	12 Oct 48	45UNTS81	100693
Italy	Netherlands	04 Dec 48	46UNTS271	100716
Norway	Sweden	18 Dec 48	30UNTS117	100450
Belgium	France	08 Jan 49	36UNTS151	100569
Australia	New Zealand	15 Apr 49	34UNTS225	100540
Netherlands	Sweden	06 Jul 49	197UNTS189	102639
Multilateral		27 Aug 49	47UNTS127	100727
Multilateral		07 Nov 49	132UNTS31	101749
France	Ireland	21 Nov 49	553UNTS59	108069
Belgium	Luxembourg	03 Dec 49	91UNTS31	101241
France	Netherlands	07 Jan 50	120UNTS25	101614
France	UK Great Britain	28 Jan 50	97UNTS155	101349
Multilateral		17 Apr 50	126UNTS285	101694
Luxembourg	Netherlands	08 Jul 50	135UNTS229	101824
Multilateral		27 Jul 50	166UNTS73	102186
Italy	UK Great Britain	28 Jul 50	101UNTS25	101399
Luxembourg	Netherlands	25 Aug 50	81UNTS13	101058
Austria	Sweden	31 Oct 50	197UNTS311	102645
France	Turkey	22 Dec 50	98UNTS11	101356
Denmark	Norway	18 Jan 51	82UNTS153	101090
Belgium	Finland	20 Mar 51	110UNTS27	101498
Germany, West	Netherlands	29 Mar 51	149UNTS71	101952
Denmark	France	30 Jun 51	151UNTS241	102000
Mexico	USA (United States)	11 Aug 51	162UNTS103	102133
Multilateral		28 Aug 51	198UNTS17	102654
Canada	USA (United States)	11 Sep 51	206UNTS311	102793
Belgium	Sweden	18 Sep 51	133UNTS187	101789
Italy	UK Great Britain	28 Nov 51	172UNTS205	102248
Belgium	Switzerland	17 Jun 52	180UNTS23	102373
Italy	Netherlands	28 Oct 52	289UNTS144	104218
Netherlands	Switzerland	20 Nov 52	163UNTS121	102146
Switzerland	UK Great Britain	16 Jan 53	196UNTS119	102621
Belgium	France	27 Feb 53	164UNTS49	102158
Germany, West	Italy	05 May 53	267UNTS9	103835
Germany, West	Sweden	15 May 53	227UNTS195	103139
Australia	UK Great Britain	08 Jun 53	201UNTS187	102718
Multilateral		20 Jul 53	228UNTS3	103141
Multilateral		20 Jul 53	228UNTS41	103142
Multilateral		20 Jul 53	227UNTS217	103140
Denmark	Germany, West	14 Aug 53	202UNTS3	102725
Luxembourg	UK Great Britain	13 Oct 53	209UNTS87	102825
Multilateral		11 Dec 53	218UNTS211	102957
Multilateral		11 Dec 53	218UNTS153	102956
Multilateral		11 Dec 53	218UNTS255	102958
Denmark	UK Great Britain	15 Dec 53	196UNTS105	102620
Multilateral		01 Mar 54	256UNTS31	103622
France	Greece	13 May 54	222UNTS299	103036

PARTY ONE	PARTY TWO	DATE	CITATION	NUMBER
Non-ILO labor relations (Cont.)				
Multilateral		21 May 54	345UNTS285	104973
Multilateral		22 May 54	199UNTS3	102674
Belgium	Germany, West	28 May 54	249UNTS387	103512
Italy	Netherlands	04 Jun 54	289UNTS261	104222
France	Greece	30 Jun 54	257UNTS83	103651
Netherlands	UK Great Britain	11 Aug 54	248UNTS235	103497
Austria	Denmark	07 Sep 54	201UNTS39	102709
Multilateral		23 Oct 54	332UNTS3	104760
Germany, West	Netherlands	29 Oct 54	237UNTS3	103335
Belgium	Yugoslavia	01 Nov 54	251UNTS123	103538
Austria	Netherlands	17 Nov 54	292UNTS45	104266
Mexico	USA (United States)	19 Nov 54	238UNTS237	103367
Sweden	Switzerland	17 Dec 54	369UNTS233	105260
Peru	USA (United States)	31 Dec 54	251UNTS51	103533
Italy	USA (United States)	11 Feb 55	240UNTS87	103396
Belgium	San Marino	22 Apr 55	253UNTS41	103574
Italy	Sweden	25 May 55	291UNTS235	104259
El Salvador	USA (United States)	08 Aug 55	264UNTS301	103801
Philippines	UK Great Britain	29 Aug 55	221UNTS241	103009
Multilateral		15 Sep 55	254UNTS55	103593
Fed Rhod/Nyasaland	Netherlands	02 Nov 55	263UNTS381	103784
Austria	Sweden	03 Nov 55	262UNTS289	103757
New Zealand	UK Great Britain	20 Dec 55	268UNTS243	103860
Austria	Belgium	20 Jan 56	248UNTS3	103481
France	Italy	03 Mar 56	267UNTS181	103843
Canada	USA (United States)	23 Apr 56	300UNTS29	104329
Netherlands	Yugoslavia	01 Jun 56	276UNTS319	103994
Multilateral		07 Jun 56	381UNTS145	105470
Sweden	UK Great Britain	09 Jun 56	309UNTS301	104479
Netherlands	UK Great Britain	12 Jun 56	250UNTS81	103519
Denmark	UK Great Britain	09 Jul 56	264UNTS45	103787
Austria	UK Great Britain	09 Jul 56	310UNTS61	104487
Multilateral		09 Jul 56	314UNTS3	104539
France	UK Great Britain	10 Jul 56	326UNTS23	104708
Austria	Italy	12 Jul 56	378UNTS249	105426
Belgium	France	18 Jul 56	248UNTS121	103491
Australia	Netherlands	01 Aug 56	280UNTS3	104047
Canada	France	04 Oct 56	305UNTS65	104414
Belgium	Spain	28 Nov 56	308UNTS285	104465
Belgium	Spain	28 Nov 56	308UNTS239	104464
Multilateral		19 Dec 56	427UNTS93	106148
France	Italy	28 Dec 56	291UNTS203	104255
Australia	UK Great Britain	01 Apr 57	271UNTS235	103918
Germany, West	UK Great Britain	11 Apr 57	331UNTS173	104753
Israel	UK Great Britain	29 Apr 57	280UNTS227	104062
Belgium	UK Great Britain	20 May 57	303UNTS53	104371
Czechoslovakia	Yugoslavia	22 May 57	391UNTS57	105617
Italy	UK Great Britain	12 Jun 57	310UNTS35	104484
Norway	UK Great Britain	25 Jul 57	313UNTS3	104528
France	Italy	01 Aug 57	302UNTS221	104360
France	Italy	19 Sep 57	302UNTS225	104361
Hungary	Yugoslavia	07 Oct 57	439UNTS61	106325
Belgium	France	12 Nov 57	328UNTS167	104734
Italy	Spain	25 Nov 57	378UNTS289	105428
Ireland	Sweden	05 Dec 57	428UNTS221	106176
Italy	Monaco	06 Dec 57	363UNTS45	105198
Italy	Monaco	06 Dec 57	363UNTS59	105199
Bulgaria	Yugoslavia	18 Dec 57	376UNTS3	105372
Poland	Yugoslavia	16 Jan 58	340UNTS137	104863
Poland	Yugoslavia	16 Jan 58	340UNTS181	104864
Australia	UK Great Britain	29 Jan 58	292UNTS233	104275
France	Italy	27 Mar 58	305UNTS409	104428
Netherlands	Switzerland	28 Mar 58	318UNTS175	104614
Belgium	Greece	01 Apr 58	388UNTS93	105574
UK Great Britain	Yugoslavia	24 May 58	326UNTS69	104709

PARTY ONE	PARTY TWO	DATE	CITATION	NUMBER
Non-ILO labor relations (Cont.)				
Germany, West	Netherlands	30 Jun 58	315UNTS179	104568
Australia	Germany, West	27 Aug 58	320UNTS303	104649
Fed Rhod/Nyasaland	South Africa	11 Oct 58	373UNTS75	105315
Finland	Norway	21 Jan 59	325UNTS295	104705
Czechoslovakia	Hungary	30 Jan 59	351UNTS3	105016
Ireland	Netherlands	28 May 59	344UNTS95	104944
Czechoslovakia	Switzerland	04 Jun 59	349UNTS121	105012
Italy	Norway	12 Jun 59	428UNTS363	106187
Fed of Malaya	UK Great Britain	27 Jul 59	374UNTS21	105324
Finland	UK Great Britain	28 Jul 59	355UNTS31	105073
Multilateral		08 Sep 59	383UNTS203	105502
Turkey	UK Great Britain	09 Sep 59	424UNTS267	106113
Czechoslovakia	USSR (Soviet Union)	02 Dec 59	374UNTS63	105330
Canada	UK Great Britain	10 Dec 59	379UNTS201	105440
Japan	USA (United States)	19 Jan 60	373UNTS207	105321
Ireland	UK Great Britain	29 Mar 60	371UNTS3	105267
Germany, West	UK Great Britain	20 Apr 60	413UNTS236	105958
Germany, West	UK Great Britain	20 Apr 60	449UNTS77	106453
Germany, West	Ireland	11 May 60	553UNTS69	108070
Germany, East	USSR (Soviet Union)	24 May 60	392UNTS205	105645
UN Special Fund	Thailand	04 Jun 60	360UNTS97	105157
Somalia	UK Great Britain	26 Jun 60	374UNTS347	105348
Somalia	UK Great Britain	26 Jun 60	374UNTS339	105347
Somalia	UK Great Britain	26 Jun 60	374UNTS331	105346
Italy	Netherlands	06 Aug 60	455UNTS259	106546
Finland	Italy	18 Feb 61	434UNTS199	106263
Netherlands	Spain	08 Apr 61	482UNTS193	106996
Denmark	Germany, West	12 Sep 61	516UNTS283	107478
IBRD (World Bank)	South Africa	01 Dec 61	425UNTS197	106125
UK Great Britain	Zambia	30 Jan 62	590UNTS173	108553
Austria	Finland	01 Feb 62	425UNTS33	106116
Multilateral		23 Mar 62	434UNTS145	106262
Australia	UK Great Britain	16 Aug 62	439UNTS163	106328
Netherlands	Portugal	22 Nov 63	492UNTS31	107185
Finland	Poland	18 Dec 63	486UNTS57	107072
Australia	Italy	31 Jan 64	488UNTS197	107129
Austria	Turkey	15 May 64	515UNTS109	107457
Austria	Spain	15 Jul 64	589UNTS169	108541
Brazil	Spain	11 Aug 64	0UNTS0	109417
Netherlands	Turkey	19 Aug 64	521UNTS197	107523
France	UK Great Britain	25 Feb 65	543UNTS157	107899
France	UK Great Britain	19 Nov 65	561UNTS19	108178
Austria	Yugoslavia	19 Nov 65	587UNTS239	108512
Korea, South	USA (United States)	09 Feb 67	0UNTS0	109605
Family allowances				
Mexico	USA (United States)	26 Apr 43	21UNTS245	200127
Mexico	USA (United States)	29 Apr 43	105UNTS119	200327
Belgium	Italy	23 Jun 46	19UNTS65	100305
Belgium	Netherlands	29 Aug 47	36UNTS349	100573
Greece	UNICEF (Children)	14 Oct 47	102UNTS39	101409
Czechoslovakia	Poland	05 Apr 48	31UNTS355	100482
Belgium	Italy	30 Apr 48	36UNTS305	100571
France	UK Great Britain	11 Jun 48	66UNTS151	100852
Czechoslovakia	France	12 Oct 48	45UNTS81	100693
Multilateral		01 Jul 49	120UNTS71	101616
Belgium	Luxembourg	03 Dec 49	91UNTS31	101241
France	Yugoslavia	05 Jan 50	0UNTS0	109502
France	Netherlands	07 Jan 50	120UNTS25	101614
Luxembourg	Netherlands	08 Jul 50	135UNTS229	101824
Multilateral		27 Jul 50	166UNTS73	102186
Netherlands	New Zealand	16 Oct 50	83UNTS269	101111
Belgium	Finland	20 Mar 51	110UNTS27	101498
Mexico	USA (United States)	11 Aug 51	162UNTS103	102133
Multilateral		28 Aug 51	198UNTS17	102654

PARTY ONE	PARTY TWO	DATE	CITATION	NUMBER
Family allowances (Cont.)				
Italy	UK Great Britain	28 Nov 51	172UNTS205	102248
Italy	Netherlands	28 Oct 52	289UNTS144	104218
Australia	UK Great Britain	08 Jun 53	201UNTS187	102718
Denmark	Germany, West	14 Aug 53	202UNTS3	102725
Luxembourg	UK Great Britain	13 Oct 53	209UNTS87	102825
Netherlands	UK Great Britain	11 Aug 54	248UNTS235	103497
Belgium	Yugoslavia	01 Nov 54	251UNTS123	103538
Belgium	San Marino	22 Apr 55	253UNTS41	103574
Czechoslovakia	Hungary	28 Apr 55	477UNTS197	106923
Italy	Sweden	25 May 55	291UNTS235	104259
Multilateral		15 Sep 55	254UNTS55	103593
New Zealand	UK Great Britain	20 Dec 55	268UNTS243	103860
Netherlands	Yugoslavia	01 Jun 56	276UNTS319	103994
Sweden	UK Great Britain	09 Jun 56	309UNTS301	104479
Netherlands	UK Great Britain	12 Jun 56	250UNTS81	103519
France	UK Great Britain	10 Jul 56	326UNTS23	104708
Belgium	Spain	28 Nov 56	308UNTS239	104464
Israel	UK Great Britain	29 Apr 57	280UNTS227	104062
Belgium	UK Great Britain	20 May 57	303UNTS53	104371
Czechoslovakia	Yugoslavia	22 May 57	391UNTS57	105617
Norway	UK Great Britain	25 Jul 57	313UNTS3	104528
Hungary	Yugoslavia	07 Oct 57	439UNTS61	106325
Italy	Monaco	06 Dec 57	363UNTS59	105199
Bulgaria	Yugoslavia	18 Dec 57	376UNTS3	105372
Poland	Yugoslavia	16 Jan 58	340UNTS137	104863
Australia	UK Great Britain	29 Jan 58	292UNTS233	104275
France	Italy	27 Mar 58	305UNTS409	104428
UK Great Britain	Yugoslavia	24 May 58	326UNTS69	104709
Czechoslovakia	Hungary	30 Jan 59	351UNTS3	105016
Hungary	Poland	14 Feb 59	431UNTS157	106215
Italy	Norway	12 Jun 59	428UNTS363	106187
Fed of Malaya	UK Great Britain	27 Jul 59	374UNTS21	105324
Finland	UK Great Britain	28 Jul 59	355UNTS31	105073
Turkey	UK Great Britain	09 Sep 59	424UNTS267	106113
Canada	UK Great Britain	10 Dec 59	379UNTS201	105440
Germany, East	Hungary	30 Jan 60	408UNTS230	105873
Ireland	UK Great Britain	29 Mar 60	371UNTS3	105267
Germany, West	UK Great Britain	20 Apr 60	413UNTS236	105958
Germany, East	USSR (Soviet Union)	24 May 60	392UNTS205	105645
UN Special Fund	Thailand	04 Jun 60	360UNTS97	105157
Somalia	UK Great Britain	26 Jun 60	374UNTS339	105347
Argentina	Italy	12 Apr 61	0UNTS0	109522
IBRD (World Bank)	South Africa	01 Dec 61	425UNTS197	106125
Italy	USA (United States)	28 Aug 62	461UNTS137	106657
Netherlands	Spain	17 Dec 62	499UNTS227	107301
Israel	USA (United States)	21 Mar 63	476UNTS131	106907
Austria	Spain	15 Jul 64	589UNTS169	108541
Luxembourg	Portugal	12 Feb 65	571UNTS239	108305
France	UK Great Britain	25 Feb 65	543UNTS157	107899
France	Mauritania	22 Jul 65	0UNTS0	109329
France	UK Great Britain	19 Nov 65	561UNTS19	108178
Belgium	Poland	26 Nov 65	620UNTS13	108950
Ireland	UK Great Britain	28 Feb 66	565UNTS33	108234
Denmark	Jordan	28 Jun 66	574UNTS3	108338
Netherlands	Portugal	12 Oct 66	0UNTS0	109273
Austria	Switzerland	15 Nov 67	0UNTS0	109434
Administrative cooperation				
Multilateral		28 Nov 19	38UNTS41	100585
Multilateral		09 Jul 20	38UNTS109	100590
Multilateral		09 Jul 20	38UNTS119	100591
Multilateral		10 Jul 20	38UNTS129	100592
Multilateral		17 Nov 21	38UNTS187	100597
Multilateral		19 Nov 21	38UNTS175	100596
Multilateral		05 Jun 25	38UNTS257	100602

PARTY ONE	PARTY TWO	DATE	CITATION	NUMBER
Administrative cooperation (Cont.)				
Multilateral		08 Jun 25	38UNTS269	100603
Multilateral		24 Jun 26	38UNTS295	100605
Multilateral		15 Jun 27	38UNTS327	100607
Multilateral		15 Jun 27	38UNTS343	100608
Multilateral		28 Jun 39	209UNTS39	102820
Albania	Yugoslavia	28 Nov 46	111UNTS163	101529
Multilateral		11 Jul 47	214UNTS33	102898
France	UK Great Britain	13 Aug 47	91UNTS169	101249
Belgium	Netherlands	29 Aug 47	36UNTS349	100573
France	USA (United States)	25 Oct 47	89UNTS111	101212
Sweden	Switzerland	16 Mar 48	197UNTS39	102632
France	Netherlands	02 Jun 48	204UNTS275	102762
France	UK Great Britain	11 Jun 48	66UNTS151	100852
Czechoslovakia	France	12 Oct 48	45UNTS81	100693
Ireland	Switzerland	14 Mar 49	553UNTS175	108085
Multilateral		01 Jul 49	120UNTS71	101616
Multilateral		01 Jul 49	138UNTS225	101871
Netherlands	Sweden	06 Jul 49	197UNTS189	102639
France	Ireland	21 Nov 49	553UNTS59	108069
Belgium	Luxembourg	03 Dec 49	91UNTS31	101241
France	Yugoslavia	05 Jan 50	0UNTS0	109502
France	Netherlands	07 Jan 50	120UNTS25	101614
France	UK Great Britain	28 Jan 50	97UNTS155	101349
Multilateral		17 Apr 50	126UNTS285	101694
Luxembourg	Netherlands	08 Jul 50	135UNTS229	101824
Multilateral		27 Jul 50	166UNTS73	102186
Luxembourg	Netherlands	25 Aug 50	81UNTS13	101058
France	Turkey	22 Dec 50	98UNTS11	101356
Australia	Netherlands	22 Feb 51	128UNTS115	101717
Germany, West	Netherlands	29 Mar 51	149UNTS71	101952
Australia	Italy	29 Mar 51	131UNTS187	101741
Denmark	France	30 Jun 51	151UNTS241	102000
Mexico	USA (United States)	11 Aug 51	162UNTS103	102133
Multilateral		28 Aug 51	198UNTS17	102654
Belgium	Sweden	18 Sep 51	133UNTS187	101789
Italy	UK Great Britain	28 Nov 51	172UNTS205	102248
Belgium	Switzerland	17 Jun 52	180UNTS23	102373
Multilateral		28 Jun 52	214UNTS321	102907
Multilateral		28 Jun 52	210UNTS132	102838
Australia	Germany, West	29 Aug 52	184UNTS147	102446
Netherlands	Switzerland	20 Nov 52	163UNTS121	102146
Germany, West	Italy	05 May 53	267UNTS9	103835
Germany, West	Sweden	15 May 53	227UNTS195	103139
Australia	UK Great Britain	08 Jun 53	201UNTS187	102718
Denmark	Germany, West	14 Aug 53	202UNTS3	102725
Luxembourg	UK Great Britain	13 Oct 53	209UNTS87	102825
Multilateral		22 May 54	199UNTS3	102674
Belgium	Germany, West	28 May 54	249UNTS387	103512
Italy	Netherlands	04 Jun 54	289UNTS261	104222
France	Greece	30 Jun 54	257UNTS83	103651
Netherlands	UK Great Britain	11 Aug 54	248UNTS235	103497
Belgium	Yugoslavia	01 Nov 54	251UNTS123	103538
Sweden	Switzerland	17 Dec 54	369UNTS233	105260
Peru	USA (United States)	31 Dec 54	251UNTS51	103533
Belgium	San Marino	22 Apr 55	253UNTS41	103574
Italy	Sweden	25 May 55	291UNTS235	104259
El Salvador	USA (United States)	08 Aug 55	264UNTS301	103801
Multilateral		15 Sep 55	254UNTS55	103593
Fed Rhod/Nyasaland	Netherlands	02 Nov 55	263UNTS381	103784
Austria	Sweden	03 Nov 55	262UNTS289	103757
Italy	Lebanon	04 Nov 55	267UNTS147	103840
New Zealand	UK Great Britain	20 Dec 55	268UNTS243	103860
Austria	Belgium	20 Jan 56	248UNTS3	103481
Multilateral		07 Jun 56	381UNTS145	105470
Sweden	UK Great Britain	09 Jun 56	309UNTS301	104479

PARTY ONE	PARTY TWO	DATE	CITATION	NUMBER
Administrative cooperation (Cont.)				
Multilateral		09 Jul 56	314UNTS3	104539
France	UK Great Britain	10 Jul 56	326UNTS23	104708
Austria	Italy	12 Jul 56	378UNTS249	105426
Australia	Netherlands	01 Aug 56	280UNTS3	104047
Canada	France	04 Oct 56	305UNTS65	104414
Belgium	Spain	28 Nov 56	308UNTS239	104464
Australia	UK Great Britain	01 Apr 57	271UNTS235	103918
Czechoslovakia	Romania	02 May 57	387UNTS167	105562
Belgium	UK Great Britain	20 May 57	303UNTS53	104371
Czechoslovakia	Yugoslavia	22 May 57	391UNTS57	105617
Norway	UK Great Britain	25 Jul 57	313UNTS3	104528
Albania	Yugoslavia	29 Aug 57	391UNTS127	105621
Hungary	Yugoslavia	07 Oct 57	439UNTS61	106325
Italy	Spain	25 Nov 57	378UNTS289	105428
Ireland	Sweden	05 Dec 57	428UNTS221	106176
Bulgaria	Yugoslavia	18 Dec 57	376UNTS3	105372
Poland	Yugoslavia	16 Jan 58	340UNTS137	104863
Australia	UK Great Britain	29 Jan 58	292UNTS233	104275
France	Italy	27 Mar 58	305UNTS409	104428
Netherlands	Switzerland	28 Mar 58	318UNTS175	104614
Belgium	Greece	01 Apr 58	388UNTS93	105574
Arab League	ILO (Labor Org)	26 May 58	302UNTS343	200549
Germany, West	Netherlands	30 Jun 58	315UNTS179	104568
Australia	Germany, West	27 Aug 58	320UNTS303	104649
Fed Rhod/Nyasaland	South Africa	11 Oct 58	373UNTS75	105315
Hungary	Poland	14 Feb 59	431UNTS157	106215
Ireland	Netherlands	28 May 59	344UNTS95	104944
Italy	Norway	12 Jun 59	428UNTS363	106187
Finland	UK Great Britain	28 Jul 59	355UNTS31	105073
Turkey	UK Great Britain	09 Sep 59	424UNTS267	106113
Czechoslovakia	USSR (Soviet Union)	02 Dec 59	374UNTS63	105330
Ireland	UK Great Britain	29 Mar 60	371UNTS3	105267
Germany, West	UK Great Britain	20 Apr 60	449UNTS77	106453
Germany, West	UK Great Britain	20 Apr 60	413UNTS236	105958
Germany, West	Ireland	11 May 60	553UNTS69	108070
Germany, East	USSR (Soviet Union)	24 May 60	392UNTS205	105645
UN Special Fund	Thailand	04 Jun 60	360UNTS97	105157
Somalia	UK Great Britain	26 Jun 60	374UNTS331	105346
Italy	Netherlands	06 Aug 60	455UNTS259	106546
Finland	Italy	18 Feb 61	434UNTS199	106263
Netherlands	Spain	08 Apr 61	482UNTS193	106996
Argentina	Italy	12 Apr 61	0UNTS0	109522
Denmark	Germany, West	12 Sep 61	516UNTS283	107478
Austria	Finland	01 Feb 62	425UNTS33	106116
Netherlands	Spain	17 Dec 62	499UNTS227	107301
Netherlands	Portugal	22 Nov 63	492UNTS31	107185
Finland	Poland	18 Dec 63	486UNTS57	107072
Austria	Turkey	15 May 64	515UNTS109	107457
Brazil	Spain	11 Aug 64	0UNTS0	109417
Netherlands	Turkey	19 Aug 64	521UNTS197	107523
Benelux Econ Union	Poland	17 Feb 65	547UNTS165	107956
France	UK Great Britain	25 Feb 65	543UNTS157	107899
Australia	Netherlands	01 Jun 65	560UNTS85	108170
France	Mauritania	22 Jul 65	0UNTS0	109329
Ireland	UK Great Britain	28 Feb 66	565UNTS33	108234
Netherlands	Portugal	12 Oct 66	0UNTS0	109273
Austria	Switzerland	15 Nov 67	0UNTS0	109434
Old age insurance				
France	Portugal	30 Apr 46	35UNTS197	100556
Belgium	Netherlands	29 Aug 47	36UNTS349	100573
Belgium	France	17 Jan 48	36UNTS233	100570
Belgium	Italy	30 Apr 48	36UNTS305	100571
France	Poland	09 Jun 48	32UNTS251	100503
France	UK Great Britain	11 Jun 48	66UNTS151	100852
Old age insurance (Cont.)				
Czechoslovakia	France	12 Oct 48	45UNTS81	100693
Australia	New Zealand	15 Apr 49	34UNTS225	100540
Multilateral		27 Aug 49	47UNTS127	100727
Belgium	Luxembourg	03 Dec 49	91UNTS31	101241
France	Yugoslavia	05 Jan 50	0UNTS0	109502
France	Netherlands	07 Jan 50	120UNTS25	101614
France	UK Great Britain	28 Jan 50	97UNTS155	101349
United Nations	WHO (World Health)	20 Apr 50	139UNTS445	200470
Luxembourg	Netherlands	08 Jul 50	135UNTS229	101824
Multilateral		27 Jul 50	166UNTS73	102186
Germany, West	Netherlands	29 Mar 51	149UNTS71	101952
Denmark	France	30 Jun 51	151UNTS241	102000
Italy	UK Great Britain	28 Nov 51	172UNTS205	102248
Belgium	Switzerland	17 Jun 52	180UNTS23	102373
Italy	Netherlands	28 Oct 52	289UNTS144	104218
Switzerland	UK Great Britain	16 Jan 53	196UNTS119	102621
Belgium	France	27 Feb 53	164UNTS49	102158
Germany, West	Italy	05 May 53	267UNTS9	103835
Australia	UK Great Britain	08 Jun 53	201UNTS187	102718
Multilateral		20 Jul 53	228UNTS41	103142
Denmark	Germany, West	14 Aug 53	202UNTS3	102725
Luxembourg	UK Great Britain	13 Oct 53	209UNTS87	102825
Multilateral		11 Dec 53	218UNTS211	102957
Multilateral		11 Dec 53	218UNTS153	102956
Netherlands	UK Great Britain	11 Aug 54	248UNTS235	103497
Belgium	Yugoslavia	01 Nov 54	251UNTS123	103538
Belgium	San Marino	22 Apr 55	253UNTS41	103574
Italy	Sweden	25 May 55	291UNTS235	104259
Multilateral		15 Sep 55	254UNTS55	103593
New Zealand	UK Great Britain	20 Dec 55	268UNTS243	103860
Netherlands	Yugoslavia	01 Jun 56	276UNTS319	103994
Sweden	UK Great Britain	09 Jun 56	309UNTS301	104479
France	UK Great Britain	10 Jul 56	326UNTS23	104708
Belgium	France	18 Jul 56	248UNTS121	103491
Belgium	Spain	28 Nov 56	308UNTS239	104464
Israel	UK Great Britain	29 Apr 57	280UNTS227	104062
Belgium	UK Great Britain	20 May 57	303UNTS53	104371
Czechoslovakia	Yugoslavia	22 May 57	391UNTS57	105617
Germany, East	Poland	13 Jul 57	319UNTS229	104634
Norway	UK Great Britain	25 Jul 57	313UNTS3	104528
Hungary	Yugoslavia	07 Oct 57	439UNTS61	106325
Bulgaria	Yugoslavia	18 Dec 57	376UNTS3	105372
Poland	Yugoslavia	16 Jan 58	340UNTS137	104863
Australia	UK Great Britain	29 Jan 58	292UNTS233	104275
France	Italy	27 Mar 58	305UNTS409	104428
Netherlands	Switzerland	28 Mar 58	318UNTS175	104614
Belgium	Greece	01 Apr 58	388UNTS93	105574
UK Great Britain	Yugoslavia	24 May 58	326UNTS69	104709
Czechoslovakia	Hungary	30 Jan 59	351UNTS3	105016
Hungary	Poland	14 Feb 59	431UNTS157	106215
Czechoslovakia	Switzerland	04 Jun 59	349UNTS121	105012
Italy	Norway	12 Jun 59	428UNTS363	106187
Fed of Malaya	UK Great Britain	27 Jul 59	374UNTS21	105324
Finland	UK Great Britain	28 Jul 59	355UNTS31	105073
Turkey	UK Great Britain	09 Sep 59	424UNTS267	106113
Czechoslovakia	USSR (Soviet Union)	02 Dec 59	374UNTS63	105330
Germany, East	Hungary	30 Jan 60	408UNTS230	105873
Ireland	UK Great Britain	29 Mar 60	371UNTS3	105267
Germany, West	UK Great Britain	20 Apr 60	413UNTS236	105958
UN Special Fund	Thailand	04 Jun 60	360UNTS97	105157
Somalia	UK Great Britain	26 Jun 60	374UNTS331	105346
Somalia	UK Great Britain	26 Jun 60	374UNTS339	105347
IMF (Fund)	United Nations	22 Dec 60	384UNTS315	200578
IBRD (World Bank)	United Nations	05 Jan 61	384UNTS303	200577
Germany, West	Netherlands	09 Mar 61	485UNTS185	107056

PARTY ONE	PARTY TWO	DATE	CITATION	NUMBER
Old age insurance (Cont.)				
Argentina	Italy	12 Apr 61	0UNTS0	109522
Multilateral		18 Oct 61	529UNTS89	107659
IBRD (World Bank)	South Africa	01 Dec 61	425UNTS197	106125
Netherlands	Spain	17 Dec 62	499UNTS227	107301
Israel	Netherlands	25 Apr 63	484UNTS231	107034
Austria	Spain	15 Jul 64	589UNTS169	108541
Luxembourg	Portugal	12 Feb 65	571UNTS239	108305
France	Mauritania	22 Jul 65	0UNTS0	109329
Belgium	Poland	26 Nov 65	620UNTS13	108950
France	Israel	17 Dec 65	581UNTS311	108451
Ireland	UK Great Britain	28 Feb 66	565UNTS33	108234
Netherlands	Turkey	05 Apr 66	0UNTS0	109204
Argentina	Portugal	20 May 66	635UNTS301	109090
Botswana	UK Great Britain	30 Sep 66	633UNTS339	109044
Netherlands	Portugal	12 Oct 66	0UNTS0	109273
Canada	UK Great Britain	13 Dec 66	0UNTS0	109274
Austria	Switzerland	15 Nov 67	0UNTS0	109434
Sickness and invalidity insurance				
Multilateral		29 Nov 19	38UNTS53	100586
Multilateral		10 Jun 25	38UNTS243	100601
Multilateral		15 Jun 27	38UNTS343	100608
Multilateral		15 Jun 27	38UNTS327	100607
Multilateral		29 Jun 33	39UNTS211	100619
Multilateral		29 Jun 33	39UNTS165	100617
Multilateral		29 Jun 33	39UNTS189	100618
Multilateral		29 Jun 33	39UNTS259	100621
Multilateral		29 Jun 33	39UNTS285	100622
Multilateral		29 Jun 33	39UNTS235	100620
Multilateral		22 Jun 35	40UNTS73	100628
Canada	USA (United States)	04 Nov 42	24UNTS217	200146
Dominican Republic	USA (United States)	19 Oct 43	21UNTS295	200130
Costa Rica	USA (United States)	29 May 44	124UNTS155	200417
Poland	Yugoslavia	02 Jan 46	115UNTS21	101556
France	Portugal	30 Apr 46	35UNTS197	100556
Albania	Yugoslavia	28 Nov 46	111UNTS163	101529
Belgium	Poland	24 Mar 47	18UNTS279	100297
Philippines	USA (United States)	16 May 47	280UNTS177	104057
Italy	UK Great Britain	30 May 47	54UNTS131	100800
Belgium	Netherlands	29 Aug 47	36UNTS349	100573
Norway	Sweden	22 Dec 47	22UNTS203	100337
Denmark	Sweden	23 Dec 47	14UNTS3	100207
Belgium	France	17 Jan 48	36UNTS233	100570
Denmark	Norway	21 Jan 48	14UNTS307	100223
Czechoslovakia	Poland	05 Apr 48	31UNTS355	100482
Belgium	Italy	30 Apr 48	36UNTS305	100571
Denmark	Iceland	14 May 48	23UNTS163	100346
France	Poland	09 Jun 48	32UNTS251	100503
France	UK Great Britain	11 Jun 48	66UNTS151	100852
Czechoslovakia	France	12 Oct 48	45UNTS81	100693
Netherlands	UK Great Britain	15 Oct 48	74UNTS3	100955
Australia	New Zealand	15 Apr 49	34UNTS225	100540
Multilateral		01 Jul 49	120UNTS71	101616
Multilateral		07 Nov 49	132UNTS3	101748
Multilateral		07 Nov 49	132UNTS31	101749
Belgium	Luxembourg	03 Dec 49	91UNTS31	101241
France	Yugoslavia	05 Jan 50	0UNTS0	109502
France	Netherlands	07 Jan 50	120UNTS25	101614
Ireland	USA (United States)	21 Jan 50	206UNTS269	102792
France	UK Great Britain	28 Jan 50	97UNTS155	101349
Netherlands	IRO (Refugee Org)	20 Jun 50	76UNTS55	100979
Luxembourg	Netherlands	08 Jul 50	135UNTS229	101824
Multilateral		27 Jul 50	166UNTS73	102186
Italy	UK Great Britain	28 Jul 50	101UNTS25	101399
Germany, West	Netherlands	29 Mar 51	149UNTS71	101952

PARTY ONE	PARTY TWO	DATE	CITATION	NUMBER
Sickness and invalidity insurance (Cont.)				
Denmark	France	30 Jun 51	151UNTS241	102000
Mexico	USA (United States)	11 Aug 51	162UNTS103	102133
Italy	UK Great Britain	28 Nov 51	172UNTS205	102248
Belgium	Switzerland	17 Jun 52	180UNTS23	102373
Multilateral		28 Jun 52	214UNTS321	102907
Multilateral		28 Jun 52	210UNTS132	102838
Italy	Netherlands	28 Oct 52	289UNTS144	104218
Switzerland	UK Great Britain	16 Jan 53	196UNTS119	102621
Germany, West	Italy	05 May 53	267UNTS9	103835
Australia	UK Great Britain	08 Jun 53	201UNTS187	102718
Multilateral		20 Jul 53	228UNTS3	103141
Multilateral		20 Jul 53	227UNTS217	103140
Multilateral		20 Jul 53	228UNTS41	103142
Denmark	Germany, West	14 Aug 53	202UNTS3	102725
Luxembourg	UK Great Britain	13 Oct 53	209UNTS87	102825
Multilateral		11 Dec 53	218UNTS211	102957
Multilateral		11 Dec 53	218UNTS153	102956
Denmark	UK Great Britain	15 Dec 53	196UNTS105	102620
Netherlands	UK Great Britain	11 Aug 54	248UNTS235	103497
Belgium	Yugoslavia	01 Nov 54	251UNTS123	103538
Mexico	USA (United States)	19 Nov 54	238UNTS237	103367
Sweden	Switzerland	17 Dec 54	369UNTS233	105260
Belgium	San Marino	22 Apr 55	253UNTS41	103574
Italy	Sweden	25 May 55	291UNTS235	104259
Multilateral		15 Sep 55	254UNTS55	103593
New Zealand	UK Great Britain	20 Dec 55	268UNTS243	103860
France	Italy	03 Mar 56	267UNTS181	103843
Netherlands	Yugoslavia	01 Jun 56	276UNTS319	103994
Sweden	UK Great Britain	09 Jun 56	309UNTS301	104479
Netherlands	UK Great Britain	12 Jun 56	250UNTS81	103519
Denmark	UK Great Britain	09 Jul 56	264UNTS45	103787
Multilateral		09 Jul 56	314UNTS3	104539
France	UK Great Britain	10 Jul 56	326UNTS23	104708
Belgium	Spain	28 Nov 56	308UNTS239	104464
Multilateral		19 Dec 56	427UNTS93	106148
Italy	UK Great Britain	29 Jan 57	326UNTS119	104710
Australia	UK Great Britain	01 Apr 57	271UNTS235	103918
Israel	UK Great Britain	29 Apr 57	280UNTS227	104062
Czechoslovakia	Romania	02 May 57	387UNTS167	105562
Belgium	UK Great Britain	20 May 57	303UNTS53	104371
Czechoslovakia	Yugoslavia	22 May 57	391UNTS57	105617
Germany, East	Poland	13 Jul 57	319UNTS229	104634
Norway	UK Great Britain	25 Jul 57	313UNTS3	104528
Hungary	Yugoslavia	07 Oct 57	439UNTS61	106325
Czechoslovakia	USSR (Soviet Union)	04 Dec 57	313UNTS291	104537
Italy	Monaco	06 Dec 57	363UNTS45	105198
Italy	Monaco	06 Dec 57	363UNTS59	105199
Bulgaria	Yugoslavia	18 Dec 57	376UNTS3	105372
Poland	Yugoslavia	16 Jan 58	340UNTS137	104863
Australia	UK Great Britain	29 Jan 58	292UNTS233	104275
Netherlands	Switzerland	28 Mar 58	318UNTS175	104614
Belgium	Greece	01 Apr 58	388UNTS93	105574
UK Great Britain	Yugoslavia	24 May 58	326UNTS69	104709
Multilateral		24 Jun 58	348UNTS275	105005
Australia	Germany, West	27 Aug 58	320UNTS303	104649
Fed Rhod/Nyasaland	South Africa	11 Oct 58	373UNTS75	105315
Czechoslovakia	Hungary	30 Jan 59	351UNTS3	105016
Hungary	Poland	14 Feb 59	431UNTS157	106215
Hungary	USSR (Soviet Union)	17 Apr 59	439UNTS41	106324
Czechoslovakia	Switzerland	04 Jun 59	349UNTS121	105012
Italy	Norway	12 Jun 59	428UNTS363	106187
Fed of Malaya	UK Great Britain	27 Jul 59	374UNTS21	105324
Finland	UK Great Britain	28 Jul 59	355UNTS31	105073
Turkey	UK Great Britain	09 Sep 59	424UNTS267	106113
Czechoslovakia	USSR (Soviet Union)	02 Dec 59	374UNTS63	105330

PARTY ONE	PARTY TWO	DATE	CITATION	NUMBER
Sickness and invalidity insurance (Cont.)				
Germany, East	Hungary	30 Jan 60	408UNTS230	105873
Bulgaria	Romania	14 Mar 60	472UNTS279	106844
Ireland	UK Great Britain	29 Mar 60	371UNTS3	105267
Germany, West	UK Great Britain	20 Apr 60	413UNTS236	105958
Germany, East	USSR (Soviet Union)	24 May 60	392UNTS205	105645
UN Special Fund	Thailand	04 Jun 60	360UNTS97	105157
Somalia	UK Great Britain	26 Jun 60	374UNTS331	105346
Somalia	UK Great Britain	26 Jun 60	374UNTS339	105347
Korea, South	USA (United States)	17 Aug 60	400UNTS339	105757
Brazil	Japan	14 Nov 60	518UNTS29	107491
IMF (Fund)	United Nations	22 Dec 60	384UNTS315	200578
IBRD (World Bank)	United Nations	05 Jan 61	384UNTS303	200577
Argentina	Italy	12 Apr 61	0UNTS0	109522
Bulgaria	Hungary	30 Jun 61	438UNTS287	106320
Bulgaria	Poland	12 Jul 61	436UNTS147	106294
Multilateral		18 Oct 61	529UNTS89	107659
IBRD (World Bank)	South Africa	01 Dec 61	425UNTS197	106125
Multilateral		14 May 62	544UNTS81	107911
Multilateral		28 Jun 62	494UNTS271	107238
Multilateral		17 Dec 62	486UNTS119	107076
Netherlands	Spain	17 Dec 62	499UNTS227	107301
Hungary	USSR (Soviet Union)	20 Dec 62	577UNTS245	108381
Multilateral		08 Jul 64	602UNTS259	108718
Austria	Spain	15 Jul 64	589UNTS169	108541
Luxembourg	Portugal	12 Feb 65	571UNTS239	108305
Australia	Germany, West	21 Jun 65	542UNTS53	107879
France	Mauritania	22 Jul 65	0UNTS0	109329
Austria	Yugoslavia	19 Nov 65	591UNTS3	108556
France	Israel	17 Dec 65	581UNTS311	108451
France	Yugoslavia	08 Feb 66	0UNTS0	109503
Ireland	UK Great Britain	28 Feb 66	565UNTS33	108234
Netherlands	Turkey	05 Apr 66	0UNTS0	109204
Multilateral		28 Apr 66	604UNTS219	108752
Argentina	Portugal	20 May 66	635UNTS301	109090
Greece	Netherlands	13 Sep 66	596UNTS245	108637
Netherlands	Portugal	12 Oct 66	0UNTS0	109273
Austria	Switzerland	15 Nov 67	0UNTS0	109434
Social security				
Multilateral		09 Jul 20	38UNTS119	100591
France	Portugal	30 Apr 46	35UNTS197	100556
Denmark	Sweden	18 Nov 46	7UNTS251	100104
Belgium	Poland	24 Mar 47	18UNTS279	100297
Multilateral		11 Jul 47	218UNTS345	102961
France	UK Great Britain	13 Aug 47	91UNTS169	101249
Belgium	Netherlands	29 Aug 47	36UNTS349	100573
Ceylon (Sri Lanka)	UK Great Britain	11 Nov 47	86UNTS31	101150
Belgium	France	17 Jan 48	36UNTS233	100570
Czechoslovakia	Poland	05 Apr 48	31UNTS355	100482
Belgium	Italy	30 Apr 48	36UNTS305	100571
France	Netherlands	02 Jun 48	204UNTS275	102762
France	Poland	09 Jun 48	32UNTS251	100503
France	UK Great Britain	11 Jun 48	66UNTS151	100852
Czechoslovakia	France	12 Oct 48	45UNTS81	100693
Australia	New Zealand	15 Apr 49	34UNTS225	100540
Multilateral		01 Jul 49	120UNTS71	101616
Multilateral		07 Nov 49	132UNTS3	101748
Multilateral		07 Nov 49	132UNTS31	101749
Belgium	Luxembourg	03 Dec 49	91UNTS31	101241
France	Yugoslavia	05 Jan 50	0UNTS0	109502
France	Netherlands	07 Jan 50	120UNTS25	101614
France	UK Great Britain	28 Jan 50	97UNTS155	101349
Luxembourg	Netherlands	08 Jul 50	135UNTS229	101824
Multilateral		27 Jul 50	166UNTS73	102186
Luxembourg	Netherlands	25 Aug 50	81UNTS13	101058

PARTY ONE	PARTY TWO	DATE	CITATION	NUMBER
Social security (Cont.)				
Netherlands	New Zealand	16 Oct 50	83UNTS269	101111
Germany, West	Netherlands	29 Mar 51	149UNTS71	101952
Denmark	France	30 Jun 51	151UNTS241	102000
Multilateral		02 Jul 51	189UNTS137	102545
Greece	USA (United States)	03 Aug 51	224UNTS279	103080
Israel	USA (United States)	23 Aug 51	219UNTS237	102979
Denmark	USA (United States)	01 Oct 51	421UNTS105	106056
Italy	UK Great Britain	28 Nov 51	172UNTS205	102248
Belgium	Switzerland	17 Jun 52	180UNTS23	102373
Multilateral		28 Jun 52	210UNTS132	102838
Italy	Netherlands	28 Oct 52	289UNTS144	104218
Netherlands	Switzerland	20 Nov 52	163UNTS121	102146
Switzerland	UK Great Britain	16 Jan 53	196UNTS119	102621
Japan	USA (United States)	02 Apr 53	206UNTS143	102788
Germany, West	Italy	05 May 53	267UNTS9	103835
Australia	UK Great Britain	08 Jun 53	201UNTS187	102718
Multilateral		20 Jul 53	227UNTS217	103140
Denmark	Germany, West	14 Aug 53	202UNTS3	102725
Luxembourg	UK Great Britain	13 Oct 53	209UNTS87	102825
Multilateral		11 Dec 53	218UNTS255	102958
Multilateral		11 Dec 53	218UNTS153	102956
Multilateral		11 Dec 53	218UNTS211	102957
France	Greece	30 Jun 54	257UNTS83	103651
Netherlands	UK Great Britain	11 Aug 54	248UNTS235	103497
Austria	Denmark	07 Sep 54	201UNTS39	102709
Multilateral		28 Sep 54	360UNTS117	105158
Belgium	Yugoslavia	01 Nov 54	251UNTS123	103538
Sweden	Switzerland	17 Dec 54	369UNTS233	105260
Italy	Sweden	25 May 55	291UNTS235	104259
Multilateral		15 Sep 55	254UNTS55	103593
New Zealand	UK Great Britain	20 Dec 55	268UNTS243	103860
Austria	Belgium	20 Jan 56	248UNTS3	103481
Netherlands	Yugoslavia	01 Jun 56	276UNTS319	103994
Sweden	UK Great Britain	09 Jun 56	309UNTS301	104479
Netherlands	UK Great Britain	12 Jun 56	250UNTS81	103519
Multilateral		09 Jul 56	314UNTS3	104539
France	UK Great Britain	10 Jul 56	326UNTS23	104708
Australia	Netherlands	01 Aug 56	280UNTS3	104047
Belgium	Spain	28 Nov 56	308UNTS285	104465
Belgium	Spain	28 Nov 56	308UNTS239	104464
Korea, South	USA (United States)	28 Nov 56	302UNTS281	104367
Bulgaria	Czechoslovakia	25 Jan 57	501UNTS149	107316
Argentina	Uruguay	27 Apr 57	635UNTS69	109072
Israel	UK Great Britain	29 Apr 57	280UNTS227	104062
Czechoslovakia	Romania	02 May 57	387UNTS167	105562
Belgium	UK Great Britain	20 May 57	303UNTS53	104371
Czechoslovakia	Yugoslavia	22 May 57	391UNTS57	105617
Czechoslovakia	Yugoslavia	22 May 57	391UNTS33	105615
Multilateral		26 Jun 57	328UNTS247	104738
Norway	UK Great Britain	25 Jul 57	313UNTS3	104528
Hungary	Yugoslavia	07 Oct 57	439UNTS61	106325
Italy	Monaco	06 Dec 57	363UNTS59	105199
Austria	IAEA (Atom Energy)	11 Dec 57	339UNTS110	104849
Bulgaria	Yugoslavia	18 Dec 57	376UNTS3	105372
Poland	Yugoslavia	16 Jan 58	340UNTS181	104864
Poland	Yugoslavia	16 Jan 58	340UNTS137	104863
Germany, West	Netherlands	28 Jan 58	453UNTS183	106525
Australia	UK Great Britain	29 Jan 58	292UNTS233	104275
Netherlands	Switzerland	28 Mar 58	318UNTS175	104614
Belgium	Greece	01 Apr 58	388UNTS93	105574
UK Great Britain	Yugoslavia	24 May 58	326UNTS69	104709
Czechoslovakia	Hungary	30 Jan 59	351UNTS3	105016
Hungary	Poland	14 Feb 59	431UNTS157	106215
Czechoslovakia	Switzerland	04 Jun 59	349UNTS121	105012
Italy	Norway	12 Jun 59	428UNTS363	106187

PARTY ONE	PARTY TWO	DATE	CITATION	NUMBER
Social security (Cont.)				
Finland	UK Great Britain	28 Jul 59	355UNTS31	105073
Turkey	UK Great Britain	09 Sep 59	424UNTS267	106113
Czechoslovakia	USSR (Soviet Union)	02 Dec 59	374UNTS63	105330
Canada	UK Great Britain	10 Dec 59	379UNTS201	105440
Bulgaria	USSR (Soviet Union)	11 Dec 59	368UNTS287	105246
ITU (Telecommun)	United Nations	14 Jan 60	348UNTS331	200566
Germany, East	Hungary	30 Jan 60	408UNTS230	105873
Bulgaria	Romania	14 Mar 60	472UNTS279	106844
Ireland	UK Great Britain	29 Mar 60	371UNTS3	105267
Germany, West	UK Great Britain	20 Apr 60	413UNTS236	105958
Germany, East	USSR (Soviet Union)	24 May 60	392UNTS205	105645
UN Special Fund	Thailand	04 Jun 60	360UNTS97	105157
Somalia	UK Great Britain	26 Jun 60	374UNTS331	105346
Italy	Netherlands	06 Aug 60	455UNTS259	106546
Romania	USSR (Soviet Union)	24 Dec 60	472UNTS245	106843
Argentina	Italy	12 Apr 61	0UNTS0	109522
Multilateral		18 Apr 61	500UNTS95	107310
Albania	Romania	03 May 61	592UNTS21	108567
Bulgaria	Hungary	30 Jun 61	438UNTS287	106320
Bulgaria	Poland	12 Jul 61	436UNTS147	106294
Hungary	Romania	07 Sep 61	519UNTS141	107506
Multilateral		05 Oct 61	0UNTS0	109431
Multilateral		18 Oct 61	529UNTS89	107659
Multilateral		14 May 62	544UNTS81	107911
Multilateral		22 Jun 62	494UNTS249	107237
Multilateral		28 Jun 62	494UNTS271	107238
Australia	UK Great Britain	16 Aug 62	439UNTS163	106328
Uganda	UK Great Britain	10 Oct 62	475UNTS177	106893
Netherlands	Spain	17 Dec 62	499UNTS227	107301
Hungary	USSR (Soviet Union)	20 Dec 62	577UNTS245	108381
Korea, South	USA (United States)	08 Jan 63	493UNTS105	107211
Israel	Netherlands	25 Apr 63	484UNTS231	107034
Philippines	USA (United States)	30 Aug 63	489UNTS323	107147
Kenya	UK Great Britain	16 Jan 64	502UNTS213	107332
Malaysia	UK Great Britain	09 Jul 64	522UNTS213	107547
Malaysia	UK Great Britain	09 Jul 64	522UNTS189	107545
Malaysia	UK Great Britain	09 Jul 64	522UNTS201	107546
Austria	Spain	15 Jul 64	589UNTS169	108541
Brazil	Spain	11 Aug 64	0UNTS0	109417
Dominican Republic	USA (United States)	28 Aug 64	531UNTS35	107691
Luxembourg	Portugal	12 Feb 65	571UNTS239	108305
Gambia	UK Great Britain	05 Jun 65	551UNTS193	108041
Austria	Petrol Export Org	24 Jun 65	589UNTS135	108540
France	Mauritania	22 Jul 65	0UNTS0	109329
Austria	Yugoslavia	19 Nov 65	587UNTS239	108512
Austria	Yugoslavia	19 Nov 65	591UNTS3	108556
Belgium	Poland	26 Nov 65	620UNTS13	108950
France	Israel	17 Dec 65	581UNTS311	108451
France	Israel	17 Dec 65	582UNTS3	108452
Ireland	UK Great Britain	28 Feb 66	565UNTS33	108234
Netherlands	Turkey	05 Apr 66	0UNTS0	109204
Argentina	Portugal	20 May 66	635UNTS301	109090
Guyana	UK Great Britain	26 May 66	588UNTS143	108521
UK Great Britain	Zambia	28 Jul 66	590UNTS191	108554
Netherlands	Norway	22 Sep 66	600UNTS227	108683
Botswana	UK Great Britain	30 Sep 66	633UNTS339	109044
Netherlands	Portugal	12 Oct 66	0UNTS0	109273
Austria	United Nations	13 Apr 67	600UNTS93	108679
Australia	Turkey	05 Oct 67	0UNTS0	109457
Austria	Switzerland	15 Nov 67	0UNTS0	109434
Belgium	Netherlands	21 Mar 68	0UNTS0	109363
Unemployment				
Multilateral		28 Nov 19	38UNTS41	100585
Multilateral		10 Jul 20	38UNTS129	100592

PARTY ONE	PARTY TWO	DATE	CITATION	NUMBER
Unemployment (Cont.)				
Multilateral		12 Nov 21	38UNTS165	100595
Multilateral		23 Jun 34	40UNTS45	100626
Canada	USA (United States)	12 Mar 42	119UNTS295	200386
Canada	USA (United States)	04 Nov 42	24UNTS217	200146
France	Portugal	30 Apr 46	35UNTS197	100556
Belgium	Netherlands	29 Aug 47	36UNTS349	100573
Belgium	Italy	09 Feb 48	71UNTS143	100915
Czechoslovakia	Poland	05 Apr 48	31UNTS355	100482
Belgium	Italy	30 Apr 48	36UNTS305	100571
France	Netherlands	02 Jun 48	204UNTS275	102762
Norway	Sweden	18 Dec 48	30UNTS117	100450
Australia	New Zealand	15 Apr 49	34UNTS225	100540
France	Yugoslavia	05 Jan 50	0UNTS0	109502
Denmark	Norway	18 Jan 51	82UNTS153	101090
Canada	USA (United States)	11 Sep 51	206UNTS311	102793
Multilateral		28 Jun 52	210UNTS132	102838
Italy	Netherlands	28 Oct 52	289UNTS144	104218
Australia	UK Great Britain	08 Jun 53	201UNTS187	102718
Germany, West	Netherlands	29 Oct 54	237UNTS3	103335
Belgium	Yugoslavia	01 Nov 54	251UNTS123	103538
Belgium	San Marino	22 Apr 55	253UNTS41	103574
Italy	Sweden	25 May 55	291UNTS235	104259
Multilateral		15 Sep 55	254UNTS55	103593
New Zealand	UK Great Britain	20 Dec 55	268UNTS243	103860
Canada	USA (United States)	23 Apr 56	300UNTS29	104329
Netherlands	Yugoslavia	01 Jun 56	276UNTS319	103994
Multilateral		07 Jun 56	381UNTS145	105470
Sweden	UK Great Britain	09 Jun 56	309UNTS301	104479
Netherlands	UK Great Britain	12 Jun 56	250UNTS81	103519
Belgium	Spain	28 Nov 56	308UNTS239	104464
Bulgaria	Czechoslovakia	25 Jan 57	501UNTS149	107316
Italy	UK Great Britain	29 Jan 57	326UNTS119	104710
Australia	UK Great Britain	01 Apr 57	271UNTS235	103918
Belgium	UK Great Britain	20 May 57	303UNTS53	104371
Germany, East	Poland	13 Jul 57	319UNTS229	104634
Norway	UK Great Britain	25 Jul 57	313UNTS3	104528
Hungary	Yugoslavia	07 Oct 57	439UNTS61	106325
Italy	Spain	25 Nov 57	378UNTS289	105428
Bulgaria	Yugoslavia	18 Dec 57	376UNTS3	105372
Australia	UK Great Britain	29 Jan 58	292UNTS233	104275
Belgium	Greece	01 Apr 58	388UNTS93	105574
UK Great Britain	Yugoslavia	24 May 58	326UNTS69	104709
Australia	Germany, West	27 Aug 58	320UNTS303	104649
Finland	Norway	21 Jan 59	325UNTS295	104705
Hungary	Poland	14 Feb 59	431UNTS157	106215
Italy	Norway	12 Jun 59	428UNTS363	106187
Finland	UK Great Britain	28 Jul 59	355UNTS31	105073
Multilateral		08 Sep 59	383UNTS203	105502
Turkey	UK Great Britain	09 Sep 59	424UNTS267	106113
Canada	UK Great Britain	10 Dec 59	379UNTS201	105440
Germany, East	Hungary	30 Jan 60	408UNTS230	105873
Ireland	UK Great Britain	29 Mar 60	371UNTS3	105267
Germany, West	UK Great Britain	20 Apr 60	413UNTS236	105958
Germany, West	UK Great Britain	20 Apr 60	449UNTS77	106453
UN Special Fund	Thailand	04 Jun 60	360UNTS97	105157
Finland	Italy	18 Feb 61	434UNTS199	106263
Argentina	Italy	12 Apr 61	0UNTS0	109522
Multilateral		18 Oct 61	529UNTS89	107659
Multilateral		28 Jun 62	494UNTS271	107238
Netherlands	Spain	17 Dec 62	499UNTS227	107301
Finland	Poland	18 Dec 63	486UNTS57	107072
Austria	Spain	15 Jul 64	589UNTS169	108541
Brazil	Spain	11 Aug 64	0UNTS0	109417
Luxembourg	Portugal	12 Feb 65	571UNTS239	108305
France	Mauritania	22 Jul 65	0UNTS0	109329

PARTY ONE	PARTY TWO	DATE	CITATION	NUMBER
Unemployment (Cont.)				
Austria	Yugoslavia	19 Nov 65	587UNTS239	108512
Austria	Yugoslavia	19 Nov 65	591UNTS3	108556
Ireland	UK Great Britain	14 Dec 65	565UNTS58	108235
Ireland	UK Great Britain	28 Feb 66	565UNTS33	108234
Netherlands	Turkey	05 Apr 66	0UNTS0	109204
Greece	Netherlands	13 Sep 66	596UNTS245	108637
Netherlands	Portugal	12 Oct 66	0UNTS0	109273
Austria	Switzerland	15 Nov 67	0UNTS0	109434
Belgium	Netherlands	21 Mar 68	0UNTS0	109363
Migrant worker				
Multilateral		29 Jun 33	39UNTS285	100622
Multilateral		29 Jun 33	39UNTS235	100620
Multilateral		29 Jun 33	39UNTS259	100621
Multilateral		29 Jun 33	39UNTS189	100618
Multilateral		20 Jun 36	40UNTS109	100630
Panama	USA (United States)	18 May 42	124UNTS221	200422
Mexico	USA (United States)	04 Aug 42	148UNTS379	200475
Mexico	USA (United States)	26 Apr 43	21UNTS245	200127
Mexico	USA (United States)	29 Apr 43	105UNTS119	200327
Mexico	USA (United States)	01 Jul 43	28UNTS407	200164
Costa Rica	USA (United States)	29 May 44	124UNTS155	200417
France	Portugal	30 Apr 46	35UNTS197	100556
Belgium	Italy	23 Jun 46	19UNTS65	100305
Denmark	Sweden	18 Nov 46	7UNTS251	100104
Multilateral		11 Jul 47	218UNTS345	102961
France	UK Great Britain	13 Aug 47	91UNTS169	101249
France	USA (United States)	25 Oct 47	89UNTS111	101212
Belgium	Italy	09 Feb 48	71UNTS143	100915
Sweden	Switzerland	16 Mar 48	197UNTS39	102632
Italy	Netherlands	04 Dec 48	46UNTS271	100716
Ireland	Switzerland	14 Mar 49	553UNTS175	108085
Multilateral		01 Jul 49	120UNTS71	101616
Netherlands	Sweden	06 Jul 49	197UNTS189	102639
France	Ireland	21 Nov 49	553UNTS59	108069
Luxembourg	Netherlands	25 Aug 50	81UNTS13	101058
Austria	Sweden	31 Oct 50	197UNTS311	102645
France	Turkey	22 Dec 50	98UNTS11	101356
Multilateral		18 Apr 51	261UNTS140	103729
Mexico	USA (United States)	11 Aug 51	162UNTS103	102133
Germany, West	USA (United States)	28 Dec 51	181UNTS45	102397
Austria	USA (United States)	05 Jan 52	179UNTS73	102355
Belgium	USA (United States)	07 Jan 52	179UNTS81	102356
Italy	USA (United States)	07 Jan 52	179UNTS165	102365
Greece	USA (United States)	07 Jan 52	180UNTS171	102382
Denmark	USA (United States)	08 Jan 52	179UNTS65	102354
Netherlands	USA (United States)	08 Jan 52	179UNTS175	102366
Iceland	USA (United States)	08 Jan 52	180UNTS183	102383
Norway	USA (United States)	08 Jan 52	179UNTS185	102367
Luxembourg	USA (United States)	08 Jan 52	180UNTS191	102384
Belgium	Germany, West	18 Jan 52	243UNTS3	103443
Germany, West	Sweden	15 May 53	227UNTS195	103139
Italy	Netherlands	04 Jun 54	289UNTS261	104222
France	Greece	30 Jun 54	257UNTS83	103651
Austria	Netherlands	17 Nov 54	292UNTS45	104266
Philippines	UK Great Britain	29 Aug 55	221UNTS241	103009
Austria	Sweden	03 Nov 55	262UNTS289	103757
Czechoslovakia	Poland	13 Jan 56	265UNTS157	103811
Austria	Belgium	20 Jan 56	248UNTS3	103481
France	Italy	03 Mar 56	267UNTS181	103843
Austria	Italy	12 Jul 56	378UNTS249	105426
Canada	France	04 Oct 56	305UNTS65	104414
Multilateral		25 Mar 57	294UNTS2	104300
Germany, East	Poland	13 Jul 57	319UNTS229	104634
France	Italy	01 Aug 57	302UNTS221	104360
Migrant worker (Cont.)				
France	Italy	19 Sep 57	302UNTS225	104361
Belgium	France	12 Nov 57	328UNTS167	104734
Italy	Spain	25 Nov 57	378UNTS289	105428
Ireland	Sweden	05 Dec 57	428UNTS221	106176
France	Italy	27 Mar 58	305UNTS409	104428
Multilateral		24 Jun 58	348UNTS275	105005
Germany, West	Netherlands	30 Jun 58	315UNTS179	104568
Ireland	Netherlands	28 May 59	344UNTS95	104944
India	Italy	06 Oct 59	378UNTS267	105427
Germany, West	Ireland	11 May 60	553UNTS69	108070
Italy	Netherlands	06 Aug 60	455UNTS259	106546
Finland	Italy	18 Feb 61	434UNTS199	106263
Netherlands	Spain	08 Apr 61	482UNTS193	106996
Denmark	Germany, West	12 Sep 61	516UNTS283	107478
Multilateral		18 Oct 61	529UNTS89	107659
Austria	Finland	01 Feb 62	425UNTS33	106116
Multilateral		22 Jun 62	494UNTS249	107237
Netherlands	Portugal	22 Nov 63	492UNTS31	107185
Finland	Poland	18 Dec 63	486UNTS57	107072
Austria	Turkey	15 May 64	515UNTS109	107457
Brazil	Spain	11 Aug 64	0UNTS0	109417
Netherlands	Turkey	19 Aug 64	521UNTS197	107523
France	UK Great Britain	25 Feb 65	543UNTS157	107899
Ivory Coast	Netherlands	03 Jun 65	634UNTS95	109054
Australia	Germany, West	21 Jun 65	542UNTS53	107879
Austria	Yugoslavia	19 Nov 65	587UNTS239	108512
France	UK Great Britain	19 Nov 65	561UNTS19	108178
Netherlands	Zambia	17 Dec 65	631UNTS311	109000
Ireland	UK Great Britain	28 Feb 66	565UNTS33	108234
Multilateral		28 Apr 66	604UNTS219	108752
Kenya	Netherlands	09 Feb 67	610UNTS0	108833
Australia	Turkey	05 Oct 67	0UNTS0	109457
Research and scientific projects				
Multilateral		12 May 40	101UNTS91	101405
Peru	USA (United States)	21 Apr 42	89UNTS317	200260
Nicaragua	USA (United States)	27 Oct 42	99UNTS287	200283
Ecuador	USA (United States)	29 Oct 42	89UNTS301	200259
El Salvador	USA (United States)	02 Dec 42	122UNTS277	200410
Mexico	USA (United States)	14 Jun 43	66UNTS331	200220
UK Great Britain	USA (United States)	01 Dec 43	3UNTS209	100033
Peru	USA (United States)	04 Apr 44	89UNTS291	200258
Multilateral		19 Apr 44	89UNTS279	200257
Guatemala	USA (United States)	15 Jul 44	106UNTS285	200347
Multilateral		02 Aug 44	67UNTS221	200221
USSR (Soviet Union)	Yugoslavia	13 Nov 45	116UNTS139	101573
Multilateral		31 Mar 46	17UNTS159	100274
Mexico	USA (United States)	12 Apr 46	66UNTS293	100861
Philippines	USA (United States)	12 May 47	16UNTS137	100254
Philippines	USA (United States)	12 May 47	16UNTS109	100252
USSR (Soviet Union)	Yugoslavia	25 Jul 47	130UNTS315	101732
Paraguay	USA (United States)	01 Jan 48	89UNTS191	101217
Ecuador	USA (United States)	14 May 48	89UNTS71	101210
Multilateral		18 Aug 48	33UNTS181	100518
Brazil	USA (United States)	26 Nov 48	88UNTS3	101180
Multilateral		09 Dec 48	20UNTS229	100318
Multilateral		09 Dec 48	73UNTS39	100942
Mexico	USA (United States)	25 Jan 49	99UNTS3	101367
Multilateral		28 Feb 49	29UNTS53	100434
Peru	USA (United States)	25 Mar 49	89UNTS15	101205
Mexico	USA (United States)	15 Aug 49	66UNTS13	100846
Canada	USA (United States)	22 Jun 50	70UNTS115	100900
Spain	Sweden	12 Oct 50	197UNTS305	102644
Multilateral		02 Nov 50	81UNTS160	101071
Multilateral		24 Nov 50	81UNTS188	101072

PARTY ONE	PARTY TWO	DATE	CITATION	NUMBER
Research and scientific projects (Cont.)				
Colombia	USA (United States)	24 Nov 50	133UNTS49	101779
Multilateral		15 Dec 50	76UNTS120	100985
Multilateral		18 Jan 51	81UNTS233	101073
Ethiopia	ICAO (Civil Aviat)	02 Feb 51	96UNTS123	101333
Multilateral		15 Feb 51	81UNTS245	101074
Israel	ICAO (Civil Aviat)	19 Feb 51	96UNTS141	101334
Multilateral		05 Mar 51	81UNTS261	101075
Multilateral		28 Mar 51	181UNTS61	102399
Jordan	United Nations	29 Mar 51	137UNTS267	200448
Multilateral		05 Apr 51	84UNTS299	101139
ICAO (Civil Aviat)	Thailand	19 Apr 51	96UNTS181	101336
Mexico	WHO (World Health)	30 Apr 51	103UNTS95	101427
WHO (World Health)	Yugoslavia	02 May 51	103UNTS117	101429
Lebanon	WHO (World Health)	05 Jun 51	104UNTS225	101443
Iceland	ICAO (Civil Aviat)	07 Jun 51	96UNTS193	101337
Lebanon	WHO (World Health)	07 Jun 51	126UNTS221	101690
Israel	United Nations	25 Jun 51	97UNTS21	101344
Multilateral		25 Jun 51	92UNTS27	101258
Multilateral		28 Jun 51	118UNTS154	101604
Ethiopia	WHO (World Health)	02 Jul 51	103UNTS39	101422
Israel	WHO (World Health)	07 Aug 51	104UNTS213	101442
WHO (World Health)	Saudi Arabia	29 Aug 51	110UNTS277	101516
Iraq	ICAO (Civil Aviat)	18 Sep 51	108UNTS219	101475
Paraguay	United Nations	27 Sep 51	120UNTS105	101617
Multilateral		01 Oct 51	104UNTS249	101446
WHO (World Health)	Thailand	04 Oct 51	109UNTS85	101493
Pakistan	WHO (World Health)	07 Oct 51	126UNTS101	101684
Ecuador	WHO (World Health)	16 Oct 51	110UNTS263	101515
India	WHO (World Health)	01 Nov 51	118UNTS13	101593
Saudi Arabia	USA (United States)	10 Nov 51	180UNTS263	102390
Denmark	WHO (World Health)	30 Nov 51	118UNTS3	101592
Multilateral		06 Dec 51	425UNTS61	106119
Multilateral		24 Dec 51	118UNTS290	200383
Ceylon (Sri Lanka)	United Nations	21 Jan 52	118UNTS281	200382
Multilateral		23 Jan 52	127UNTS269	101708
ICAO (Civil Aviat)	Yugoslavia	06 Feb 52	128UNTS97	101715
WHO (World Health)	UK Great Britain	07 Feb 52	121UNTS75	101627
Lebanon	ICAO (Civil Aviat)	14 Feb 52	128UNTS83	101714
Multilateral		15 Feb 52	132UNTS51	101751
Burma	WHO (World Health)	18 Feb 52	127UNTS43	101698
ICAO (Civil Aviat)	United Arab Rep	06 Mar 52	151UNTS111	101986
Denmark	WHO (World Health)	26 Mar 52	134UNTS285	101807
India	WHO (World Health)	17 Apr 52	131UNTS241	101744
India	ICAO (Civil Aviat)	29 Apr 52	151UNTS123	101987
Brazil	USA (United States)	02 Jun 52	181UNTS109	102403
Brazil	WHO (World Health)	12 Jun 52	151UNTS333	102003
Japan	WHO (World Health)	26 Nov 52	204UNTS301	200521
Multilateral		31 May 54	192UNTS20	102592
Norway	Sweden	28 May 55	262UNTS151	103743
Brazil	USA (United States)	03 Aug 55	270UNTS71	103893
UK Great Britain	USA (United States)	15 Nov 55	231UNTS185	103219
Colombia	USA (United States)	14 Mar 56	271UNTS303	103922
Romania	Yugoslavia	27 Oct 56	389UNTS55	105592
UK Great Britain	USA (United States)	01 Nov 56	264UNTS3	103785
UK Great Britain	USA (United States)	27 Nov 56	282UNTS43	104092
Chile	USA (United States)	01 Mar 57	283UNTS127	104112
UK Great Britain	USA (United States)	01 Nov 57	299UNTS167	104312
Argentina	Paraguay	23 Jan 58	0UNTS0	109294
Lebanon	USA (United States)	16 Sep 59	358UNTS175	105135
Taiwan	USA (United States)	02 Dec 59	361UNTS115	105175
Austria	Czechoslovakia	23 Jan 60	495UNTS99	107241
Mexico	USA (United States)	04 Feb 60	586UNTS57	108496
Chile	USA (United States)	19 Feb 60	371UNTS255	105282
New Zealand	USA (United States)	23 Mar 60	371UNTS147	105276
Ireland	USA (United States)	24 Mar 60	371UNTS237	105280

PARTY ONE	PARTY TWO	DATE	CITATION	NUMBER
Research and scientific projects (Cont.)				
Chile	USA (United States)	28 Mar 60	401UNTS105	105765
Guatemala	USA (United States)	23 Apr 60	373UNTS23	105312
Argentina	USA (United States)	23 May 60	377UNTS3	105392
Canada	USA (United States)	14 Jun 60	377UNTS365	105413
France	Greece	25 Jul 60	533UNTS227	107745
Canada	USA (United States)	24 Aug 60	388UNTS225	105580
Nigeria	USA (United States)	19 Oct 60	394UNTS113	105672
Czechoslovakia	Ghana	23 Nov 60	431UNTS85	106212
Multilateral		01 Dec 60	414UNTS110	105970
UK Great Britain	USA (United States)	20 Jan 61	402UNTS153	105783
India	USA (United States)	07 Feb 61	462UNTS57	106671
Multilateral		08 Mar 61	396UNTS255	200584
UK Great Britain	USA (United States)	15 Mar 61	404UNTS207	105811
Multilateral		30 Mar 61	520UNTS151	107515
UK Great Britain	USA (United States)	06 Apr 61	404UNTS215	105812
Norway	IAEA (Atom Energy)	10 Apr 61	402UNTS255	105790
Australia	USA (United States)	22 May 61	419UNTS3	106026
Czechoslovakia	Somalia	04 Jun 61	480UNTS261	106973
Netherlands	Euratom	25 Jul 61	462UNTS263	106686
Chile	USA (United States)	12 Aug 61	421UNTS209	106059
UK Great Britain	USA (United States)	08 Sep 61	418UNTS53	106016
UK Great Britain	USA (United States)	26 Sep 61	421UNTS99	106055
Germany, West	USA (United States)	29 Sep 61	424UNTS113	106103
Ghana	USA (United States)	03 Jan 62	433UNTS147	106237
Paraguay	USA (United States)	16 Jan 62	433UNTS169	106240
Multilateral		26 Mar 62	539UNTS67	107825
Multilateral		14 May 62	544UNTS39	107910
Multilateral		25 May 62	486UNTS103	107075
Greece	Tunisia	26 May 62	534UNTS163	107761
Italy	USA (United States)	05 Sep 62	461UNTS185	106663
India	USA (United States)	09 Oct 62	471UNTS39	106820
Dominican Republic	USA (United States)	25 Oct 62	459UNTS247	106627
France	UK Great Britain	29 Nov 62	453UNTS325	106534
India	United Nations	27 Dec 62	450UNTS3	106464
Canada	USA (United States)	28 Dec 62	471UNTS13	106818
UK Great Britain	USA (United States)	15 Jan 63	466UNTS181	106743
Ethiopia	USA (United States)	25 Jan 63	473UNTS27	106851
India	USA (United States)	01 Feb 63	473UNTS37	106852
Brazil	USA (United States)	29 Mar 63	476UNTS67	106904
UK Great Britain	USA (United States)	11 Oct 63	483UNTS3	107005
Argentina	USA (United States)	30 Nov 63	505UNTS131	107369
New Zealand	Western Samoa	31 Dec 63	521UNTS163	107519
France	South Africa	06 Jan 64	601UNTS229	108699
Mexico	USA (United States)	14 Feb 64	524UNTS197	107574
Canada	USA (United States)	06 May 64	524UNTS173	107572
France	UK Great Britain	03 Jun 64	539UNTS253	107836
Peru	USA (United States)	07 Jul 64	530UNTS113	107676
Multilateral		15 Jul 64	610UNTS143	108840
Australia	USA (United States)	17 Aug 64	530UNTS209	107683
Dominican Republic	USA (United States)	28 Aug 64	531UNTS35	107691
Australia	UN Special Fund	30 Sep 64	510UNTS277	107419
USA (United States)	Western Samoa	03 Nov 64	521UNTS181	107521
India	United Nations	25 Nov 64	519UNTS47	107501
India	Netherlands	11 Dec 64	570UNTS165	108292
Germany, West	Thailand	23 Dec 64	525UNTS177	107589
UK Great Britain	USSR (Soviet Union)	06 Jan 65	543UNTS77	107897
Germany, West	Jamaica	03 Feb 65	531UNTS143	107700
Mexico	USA (United States)	27 Feb 65	546UNTS135	107940
Canada	USA (United States)	11 Jun 65	564UNTS83	108222
Canada	USA (United States)	29 Jun 65	549UNTS273	108003
Panama	USA (United States)	15 Feb 66	586UNTS27	108494
Israel	Kenya	25 Feb 66	582UNTS23	108455
Spain	USA (United States)	14 Apr 66	586UNTS79	108497
Bel-Lux Econ Union	Bulgaria	14 Jun 66	601UNTS167	108694
France	USA (United States)	17 Jun 66	601UNTS113	108690

PARTY ONE	PARTY TWO	DATE	CITATION	NUMBER
Research and scientific projects (Cont.)				
France	USSR (Soviet Union)	30 Jun 66	589UNTS99	108537
Hungary	Yugoslavia	26 Sep 66	601UNTS21	108685
United Nations	Sudan	08 Nov 66	576UNTS85	108365
Trinidad/Tobago	UK Great Britain	23 Jan 67	605UNTS277	108767
Multilateral		27 Jan 67	610UNTS205	108843
UK Great Britain	USSR (Soviet Union)	24 Feb 67	606UNTS171	108785
Multilateral		20 Jul 67	0UNTS0	109259
Multilateral		28 Dec 67	0UNTS0	109322
Israel	USA (United States)	22 May 68	0UNTS0	109356
New Zealand	USA (United States)	09 Jul 68	0UNTS0	109208
United Nations	United Arab Rep	14 Nov 68	0UNTS0	109371
Australia	USA (United States)	13 Jan 69	0UNTS0	109460
Research cooperation				
Multilateral		12 May 40	101UNTS91	101405
Nicaragua	USA (United States)	11 Jan 41	117UNTS253	200374
Costa Rica	USA (United States)	18 Jun 41	103UNTS173	200313
Peru	USA (United States)	21 Apr 42	89UNTS317	200260
Mexico	USA (United States)	24 Oct 42	21UNTS189	200123
Ecuador	USA (United States)	29 Oct 42	89UNTS301	200259
Mexico	USA (United States)	10 Nov 42	66UNTS307	200219
El Salvador	USA (United States)	02 Dec 42	122UNTS277	200410
Costa Rica	USA (United States)	03 Apr 43	13UNTS463	200090
Mexico	USA (United States)	14 Jun 43	66UNTS331	200220
Multilateral		15 Jan 44	161UNTS281	200489
Guatemala	USA (United States)	15 Jul 44	106UNTS285	200347
Multilateral		02 Aug 44	67UNTS221	200221
Haiti	USA (United States)	08 Jan 45	121UNTS153	200397
Czechoslovakia	France	08 Dec 45	46UNTS77	100701
Mexico	USA (United States)	12 Apr 46	66UNTS293	100861
Belgium	Netherlands	24 May 46	31UNTS169	100477
Multilateral		02 Dec 46	161UNTS72	102124
Austria	France	15 Mar 47	12UNTS109	100182
Philippines	USA (United States)	12 May 47	16UNTS123	100253
Czechoslovakia	UK Great Britain	16 Jun 47	46UNTS61	100700
Bulgaria	Czechoslovakia	20 Jun 47	46UNTS15	100698
Romania	Yugoslavia	26 Jun 47	116UNTS39	101568
Bulgaria	Poland	28 Jun 47	15UNTS123	100230
Czechoslovakia	Romania	05 Sep 47	46UNTS37	100699
Paraguay	USA (United States)	01 Jan 48	89UNTS191	101217
Cuba	USA (United States)	27 Jan 48	67UNTS3	100862
Hungary	Poland	31 Jan 48	25UNTS283	100368
Norway	UK Great Britain	19 Feb 48	34UNTS33	100526
Belgium	Norway	20 Feb 48	32UNTS39	100487
Poland	Romania	27 Feb 48	46UNTS143	100707
Multilateral		29 Nov 48	120UNTS13	101613
Multilateral		08 Feb 49	157UNTS157	102053
Multilateral		28 Feb 49	29UNTS53	100434
Mexico	USA (United States)	15 Aug 49	66UNTS13	100846
United Arab Rep	UK Great Britain	20 Mar 50	226UNTS287	103123
Canada	USA (United States)	22 Jun 50	70UNTS115	100900
Albania	Poland	02 Dec 50	260UNTS131	103707
Lebanon	WHO (World Health)	05 Jun 51	104UNTS225	101443
Denmark	WHO (World Health)	30 Nov 51	118UNTS3	101592
Multilateral		06 Dec 51	425UNTS61	106119
Germany, East	Poland	08 Jan 52	304UNTS113	104394
Multilateral		01 Mar 52	168UNTS9	102210
Denmark	WHO (World Health)	26 Mar 52	134UNTS285	101807
Mexico	USA (United States)	26 Aug 52	264UNTS269	103797
Ceylon (Sri Lanka)	USA (United States)	17 Nov 52	180UNTS207	102386
Bolivia	Italy	31 Jan 53	281UNTS181	104079
Israel	Uruguay	30 Apr 53	280UNTS269	104064
United Arab Rep	USA (United States)	18 Jun 53	204UNTS55	102749
Liberia	USA (United States)	23 Jun 53	213UNTS57	102880
Pakistan	Turkey	29 Jun 53	211UNTS225	102854

PARTY ONE	PARTY TWO	DATE	CITATION	NUMBER
Research cooperation (Cont.)				
Greece	Italy	11 Sep 54	284UNTS313	104145
Belgium	Greece	09 Dec 54	257UNTS243	103660
Netherlands	Norway	18 May 55	252UNTS269	103569
Norway	Sweden	28 May 55	262UNTS151	103743
Canada	USA (United States)	15 Jun 55	235UNTS176	103301
Multilateral		12 Oct 55	560UNTS3	108165
Netherlands	USA (United States)	22 Jan 56	287UNTS121	104181
Turkey	UK Great Britain	12 Mar 56	313UNTS73	104530
Colombia	USA (United States)	14 Mar 56	271UNTS303	103922
Ireland	USA (United States)	16 Mar 56	317UNTS195	104604
France	USA (United States)	23 Mar 56	278UNTS131	104029
Multilateral		26 Mar 56	259UNTS125	103686
Chile	USA (United States)	20 Apr 56	293UNTS277	104295
Switzerland	USA (United States)	21 Jun 56	279UNTS41	104033
Australia	USA (United States)	22 Jun 56	283UNTS275	104123
Cuba	USA (United States)	26 Jun 56	293UNTS257	104294
Poland	USSR (Soviet Union)	30 Jun 56	259UNTS311	103694
Poland	Yugoslavia	06 Jul 56	281UNTS143	104076
Dominican Republic	USA (United States)	11 Aug 56	263UNTS181	103773
Guatemala	USA (United States)	15 Aug 56	288UNTS181	104205
Netherlands	USA (United States)	16 Aug 56	279UNTS3	104031
Greece	United Arab Rep	04 Sep 56	299UNTS253	104317
Multilateral		26 Oct 56	276UNTS3	103988
Bulgaria	Yugoslavia	24 Dec 56	397UNTS3	105699
Czechoslovakia	Yugoslavia	29 Jan 57	300UNTS249	104339
Poland	United Arab Rep	02 Feb 57	319UNTS221	104633
Belgium	Yugoslavia	05 Feb 57	276UNTS143	103990
Multilateral		09 Feb 57	314UNTS105	104546
Taiwan	Turkey	12 Feb 57	282UNTS125	104097
Norway	USA (United States)	25 Feb 57	284UNTS19	104126
Multilateral		25 Mar 57	294UNTS259	104301
Iran	Japan	16 Apr 57	325UNTS113	104697
Peru	USA (United States)	17 Apr 57	283UNTS3	104102
Ecuador	USA (United States)	24 Apr 57	284UNTS3	104124
Argentina	Israel	23 May 57	280UNTS199	104059
Japan	Pakistan	27 May 57	325UNTS21	104692
Ecuador	USA (United States)	31 May 57	304UNTS61	104391
Czechoslovakia	Syria	18 Jun 57	303UNTS119	104374
Germany, West	USA (United States)	28 Jun 57	288UNTS339	104213
Italy	USA (United States)	03 Jul 57	308UNTS195	104462
Germany, West	USA (United States)	03 Jul 57	288UNTS305	104212
South Africa	USA (United States)	08 Jul 57	290UNTS147	104234
Norway	UK Great Britain	12 Jul 57	310UNTS41	104485
Spain	USA (United States)	16 Aug 57	307UNTS169	104449
Sweden	UK Great Britain	20 Sep 57	310UNTS49	104486
Hungary	Yugoslavia	20 Nov 57	477UNTS267	106925
Norway	USSR (Soviet Union)	22 Nov 57	309UNTS269	104476
Austria	IAEA (Atom Energy)	11 Dec 57	339UNTS110	104849
Italy	UK Great Britain	28 Dec 57	305UNTS357	104425
UK Great Britain	USA (United States)	20 Jan 58	304UNTS3	104387
Argentina	Paraguay	23 Jan 58	0UNTS0	109294
Australia	USA (United States)	25 Feb 58	317UNTS153	104601
FAO (Food Agri)	UK Great Britain	24 Apr 58	642UNTS245	109177
Japan	USA (United States)	19 Jun 58	325UNTS143	104699
UK Great Britain	USA (United States)	03 Jul 58	326UNTS3	104707
Portugal	UK Great Britain	18 Jul 58	313UNTS109	104532
USA (United States)	Venezuela	08 Oct 58	371UNTS69	105271
Euratom	USA (United States)	08 Nov 58	338UNTS135	104835
El Salvador	Israel	14 Nov 58	345UNTS67	104959
Belgium	Turkey	29 Dec 58	357UNTS195	105118
UK Great Britain	USA (United States)	30 Dec 58	338UNTS281	104841
Euratom	UK Great Britain	04 Feb 59	331UNTS125	104752
Iran	UK Great Britain	06 May 59	398UNTS51	105717
Canada	USA (United States)	22 May 59	354UNTS63	105054
SEATO (SE Asia)	USA (United States)	29 May 59	347UNTS77	104991

PARTY ONE	PARTY TWO	DATE	CITATION	NUMBER
Research cooperation (Cont.)				
Canada	Japan	02 Jul 59	383UNTS243	105504
USA (United States)	USSR (Soviet Union)	21 Nov 59	361UNTS35	105172
Germany, West	Pakistan	25 Nov 59	457UNTS22	106575
France	Israel	30 Nov 59	377UNTS237	105404
Multilateral		01 Dec 59	402UNTS71	105778
Multilateral		14 Dec 59	368UNTS253	105245
Ecuador	USA (United States)	24 Feb 60	371UNTS55	105270
Spain	USA (United States)	18 Mar 60	372UNTS13	105284
Chile	USA (United States)	28 Mar 60	401UNTS105	105765
Mexico	USA (United States)	12 Apr 60	372UNTS47	105287
Fed of Malaya	UK Great Britain	07 Jun 60	375UNTS141	105365
India	USA (United States)	13 Jun 60	377UNTS37	105394
Nigeria	USA (United States)	19 Oct 60	394UNTS113	105672
Romania	USA (United States)	09 Dec 60	401UNTS19	105759
Thailand	USA (United States)	23 Dec 60	405UNTS135	105830
Finland	IAEA (Atom Energy)	30 Dec 60	395UNTS257	105690
Multilateral		30 Dec 60	395UNTS241	105689
USA (United States)	Yugoslavia	19 Jan 61	402UNTS163	105784
Czechoslovakia	Hungary	24 Feb 61	422UNTS15	106066
Multilateral		08 Mar 61	396UNTS255	200584
UK Great Britain	USA (United States)	15 Mar 61	404UNTS207	105811
Brazil	USA (United States)	17 Mar 61	406UNTS241	105853
UK Great Britain	USA (United States)	06 Apr 61	404UNTS215	105812
Multilateral		10 Apr 61	402UNTS281	105791
Netherlands	Euratom	25 Jul 61	462UNTS263	106686
Italy	United Nations	23 Aug 61	405UNTS3	105819
UK Great Britain	USA (United States)	26 Sep 61	421UNTS99	106055
IAEA (Atom Energy)	Yugoslavia	04 Oct 61	412UNTS226	105935
Japan	United Nations	04 Oct 61	410UNTS133	105900
Japan	Thailand	25 Nov 61	451UNTS55	106484
Argentina	USA (United States)	16 Mar 62	454UNTS3	106535
Multilateral		26 Mar 62	539UNTS67	107825
Multilateral		14 May 62	544UNTS81	107911
Multilateral		14 Jun 62	528UNTS33	107634
Argentina	USA (United States)	22 Jun 62	458UNTS97	106594
Multilateral		17 Dec 62	486UNTS119	107076
India	United Nations	27 Dec 62	450UNTS3	106464
Israel	Philippines	10 Jan 63	588UNTS205	108526
IAEA (Atom Energy)	Yugoslavia	04 Mar 63	490UNTS333	107162
IAEA (Atom Energy)	Yugoslavia	04 Jun 63	490UNTS343	107163
Austria	IAEA (Atom Energy)	21 Jun 63	490UNTS351	107164
Finland	IAEA (Atom Energy)	02 Jul 63	490UNTS403	107167
Finland	IAEA (Atom Energy)	30 Jul 63	490UNTS413	107168
Malagasy	USA (United States)	07 Oct 63	494UNTS3	107221
Multilateral		17 Oct 63	525UNTS75	107585
Multilateral		03 Dec 63	529UNTS217	107663
Mexico	IAEA (Atom Energy)	18 Dec 63	490UNTS361	107165
France	South Africa	06 Jan 64	601UNTS229	108699
Netherlands	Tunisia	11 Feb 64	570UNTS173	108293
Mexico	Netherlands	08 Apr 64	575UNTS35	108353
Multilateral		11 Jun 64	525UNTS61	107584
Switzerland	UK Great Britain	11 Aug 64	552UNTS271	108059
IAEA (Atom Energy)	United Arab Rep	17 Sep 64	525UNTS19	107581
USA (United States)	USSR (Soviet Union)	18 Nov 64	535UNTS307	107786
Japan	USA (United States)	25 Nov 64	533UNTS31	107730
India	United Nations	25 Nov 64	519UNTS47	107501
Czechoslovakia	United Arab Rep	26 Nov 64	545UNTS11	107923
Argentina	IAEA (Atom Energy)	02 Dec 64	525UNTS29	107582
Germany, West	Thailand	23 Dec 64	525UNTS201	107592
Ecuador	Netherlands	14 Jan 65	551UNTS129	108038
Switzerland	USA (United States)	30 Jan 65	594UNTS55	108594
Mexico	USA (United States)	27 Feb 65	542UNTS181	107889
Mexico	USA (United States)	27 Feb 65	546UNTS135	107940
Canada	USA (United States)	11 Jun 65	564UNTS83	108222
Multilateral		02 Jul 65	592UNTS215	108575

PARTY ONE	PARTY TWO	DATE	CITATION	NUMBER
Research cooperation (Cont.)				
IAEA (Atom Energy)	Uruguay	24 Sep 65	556UNTS117	108123
Multilateral		07 Oct 65	556UNTS175	108125
Ethiopia	USA (United States)	30 Dec 65	574UNTS129	108345
UK Great Britain	Yugoslavia	27 Jan 66	573UNTS243	108337
Norway	Eur Space Research	31 Jan 66	580UNTS3	108414
Multilateral		30 Mar 66	593UNTS261	108588
Spain	USA (United States)	14 Apr 66	579UNTS173	108406
Czechoslovakia	USSR (Soviet Union)	23 Apr 66	566UNTS159	108242
Denmark	Iran	14 Jun 66	597UNTS283	108652
France	USA (United States)	17 Jun 66	601UNTS113	108690
Mexico	IAEA (Atom Energy)	20 Jun 66	573UNTS25	108321
Multilateral		20 Jun 66	573UNTS41	108322
France	USSR (Soviet Union)	30 Jun 66	589UNTS109	108538
Tunisia	USA (United States)	26 Sep 66	616UNTS259	108900
Philippines	IAEA (Atom Energy)	28 Sep 66	589UNTS25	108533
Brazil	Netherlands	12 Oct 66	643UNTS271	109197
IAEA (Atom Energy)	Turkey	08 Dec 66	608UNTS69	108813
Australia	USA (United States)	09 Dec 66	607UNTS83	108798
Australia	USA (United States)	09 Dec 66	607UNTS83	108798
UK Great Britain	USA (United States)	30 Dec 66	603UNTS245	108736
UK Great Britain	USA (United States)	01 Jan 67	604UNTS3	108738
Trinidad/Tobago	UK Great Britain	23 Jan 67	605UNTS277	108767
Israel	Philippines	20 Feb 67	597UNTS139	108642
Belgium	Luxembourg	22 Feb 67	639UNTS3	109140
Kuwait	USSR (Soviet Union)	27 Mar 67	643UNTS135	109189
Romania	Somalia	20 Apr 67	642UNTS155	109171
Bulgaria	USSR (Soviet Union)	27 Apr 67	631UNTS3	108983
Multilateral		20 Jul 67	0UNTS0	109259
Netherlands	Romania	20 Jul 67	633UNTS21	109032
Italy	Romania	08 Aug 67	642UNTS191	109174
Hungary	UK Great Britain	09 Aug 67	632UNTS39	109006
Denmark	Romania	29 Aug 67	642UNTS357	109183
Multilateral		22 Sep 67	0UNTS0	109258
Chile	Denmark	15 Dec 67	643UNTS293	109199
Multilateral		28 Dec 67	0UNTS0	109322
UK Great Britain	USSR (Soviet Union)	19 Jan 68	0UNTS0	109277
Mauritius	UK Great Britain	12 Mar 68	0UNTS0	109270
Netherlands	Yugoslavia	13 Mar 68	0UNTS0	109297
France	South Africa	27 Mar 68	643UNTS343	109200
Israel	USA (United States)	22 May 68	0UNTS0	109356
New Zealand	USA (United States)	09 Jul 68	0UNTS0	109208
Denmark	Thailand	16 Oct 68	0UNTS0	109463
Australia	UK Great Britain	16 Oct 68	0UNTS0	109459
United Nations	United Arab Rep	14 Nov 68	0UNTS0	109371
Australia	USA (United States)	13 Jan 69	0UNTS0	109460
Anthropology and archeology				
Peru	USA (United States)	04 Apr 44	89UNTS291	200258
Multilateral		19 Apr 44	89UNTS279	200257
Peru	USA (United States)	25 Mar 49	89UNTS15	101205
Mexico	USA (United States)	21 Jun 49	89UNTS3	101204
Colombia	USA (United States)	24 Nov 50	133UNTS49	101779
Greece	Turkey	20 Apr 51	178UNTS17	102333
Pakistan	Turkey	29 Jun 53	211UNTS225	102854
Greece	Italy	11 Sep 54	284UNTS313	104145
Iran	Pakistan	09 Mar 56	449UNTS183	106460
Greece	United Arab Rep	04 Sep 56	299UNTS253	104317
Poland	Vietnam, North	06 Apr 57	432UNTS255	106224
India	Romania	30 Apr 57	342UNTS251	104911
Hungary	Iraq	11 Apr 59	439UNTS25	106323
Iraq	USSR (Soviet Union)	05 May 59	356UNTS179	105095
Iran	UK Great Britain	06 May 59	398UNTS51	105717
Finland	Hungary	10 Jun 59	439UNTS3	106321
France	Israel	30 Nov 59	377UNTS237	105404
Netherlands	United Arab Rep	08 Dec 60	455UNTS276	106547

Anthropology and archeology (Cont.)

PARTY ONE	PARTY TWO	DATE	CITATION	NUMBER
India	Norway	19 Apr 61	404UNTS307	105818
Pakistan	Philippines	15 Aug 61	522UNTS35	107534
United Arab Rep	USA (United States)	21 May 62	458UNTS197	106601
Israel	Peru	25 Jun 62	515UNTS263	107464
Iraq	USA (United States)	23 Jan 63	488UNTS163	107126
UNESCO (Educ/Cult)	United Arab Rep	09 Nov 63	489UNTS233	107142
Netherlands	Tunisia	11 Feb 64	570UNTS173	108293
Japan	Korea, South	22 Jun 65	584UNTS49	108475

Meteorology

PARTY ONE	PARTY TWO	DATE	CITATION	NUMBER
Multilateral		12 May 40	101UNTS91	101405
Mexico	USA (United States)	10 Nov 42	66UNTS307	200219
Mexico	USA (United States)	14 Jun 43	66UNTS331	200220
Multilateral		02 Aug 44	67UNTS221	200221
Multilateral		07 Dec 44	171UNTS345	200501
Poland	Yugoslavia	16 Mar 46	10UNTS11	100139
Mexico	USA (United States)	12 Apr 46	66UNTS293	100861
Sweden	USA (United States)	30 Sep 46	42UNTS213	100649
Denmark	USA (United States)	01 Oct 46	42UNTS219	100650
USSR (Soviet Union)	Yugoslavia	04 Feb 47	130UNTS235	101731
Australia	USA (United States)	10 Mar 47	10UNTS89	100145
Thailand	USA (United States)	08 May 47	42UNTS241	100653
Philippines	USA (United States)	12 May 47	16UNTS123	100253
Italy	USA (United States)	09 Jun 47	104UNTS157	101437
Multilateral		11 Oct 47	77UNTS143	100998
France	Lebanon	24 Jan 48	173UNTS99	102263
Cuba	USA (United States)	27 Jan 48	67UNTS3	100862
Multilateral		10 Jun 48	164UNTS113	102163
France	USA (United States)	19 Oct 48	98UNTS3	101355
Multilateral		28 Feb 49	29UNTS53	100434
Mexico	USA (United States)	15 Aug 49	66UNTS13	100846
Denmark	ICAO (Civil Aviat)	09 Sep 49	53UNTS341	100791
Philippines	USA (United States)	16 Mar 50	89UNTS199	101218
United Arab Rep	UK Great Britain	20 Mar 50	226UNTS287	103123
Ireland	Spain	11 May 50	553UNTS147	108081
Canada	USA (United States)	22 Jun 50	70UNTS115	100900
Spain	Sweden	12 Oct 50	197UNTS305	102644
Greece	USA (United States)	25 Jun 52	181UNTS53	102398
Multilateral		25 Feb 54	215UNTS249	102922
Belgium	Ireland	30 Jun 54	212UNTS255	102876
Multilateral		23 Oct 54	332UNTS3	104760
Norway	Sweden	28 May 55	262UNTS151	103743
USSR (Soviet Union)	Yugoslavia	03 Sep 55	240UNTS267	103408
UK Great Britain	USA (United States)	15 Nov 55	231UNTS185	103219
Colombia	USA (United States)	14 Mar 56	271UNTS303	103922
France	USA (United States)	23 Mar 56	278UNTS131	104029
Denmark	USSR (Soviet Union)	31 Mar 56	259UNTS169	103689
Norway	USSR (Soviet Union)	31 Mar 56	259UNTS205	103690
Sweden	USSR (Soviet Union)	31 Mar 56	259UNTS239	103691
Dominican Republic	USA (United States)	11 Aug 56	263UNTS181	103773
Netherlands	USA (United States)	16 Aug 56	279UNTS3	104031
Multilateral		25 Sep 56	334UNTS13	104766
Multilateral		25 Sep 56	334UNTS89	104767
USSR (Soviet Union)	Vietnam, North	15 Feb 57	274UNTS115	103962
Chile	USA (United States)	01 Mar 57	283UNTS127	104112
Peru	USA (United States)	17 Apr 57	283UNTS3	104102
Ecuador	USA (United States)	24 Apr 57	284UNTS3	104124
UK Great Britain	USA (United States)	20 Jan 58	304UNTS3	104387
Australia	USA (United States)	25 Feb 58	317UNTS153	104601
Argentina	USA (United States)	28 Apr 58	315UNTS211	104570
UK Great Britain	USA (United States)	30 Dec 58	338UNTS281	104841
Colombia	USA (United States)	08 May 59	344UNTS193	104950
Japan	USA (United States)	19 Jan 60	373UNTS207	105321
Mexico	USA (United States)	04 Feb 60	586UNTS57	108496
Canada	USA (United States)	14 Jun 60	377UNTS365	105413

Meteorology (Cont.)

PARTY ONE	PARTY TWO	DATE	CITATION	NUMBER
India	USA (United States)	07 Feb 61	462UNTS57	106671
Australia	USA (United States)	09 May 61	409UNTS203	105886
Chile	USA (United States)	12 Aug 61	421UNTS209	106059
UK Great Britain	USA (United States)	26 Sep 61	421UNTS99	106055
Multilateral		05 Mar 62	425UNTS3	106114
USA (United States)	USSR (Soviet Union)	08 Mar 62	460UNTS3	106630
India	USA (United States)	09 Oct 62	471UNTS39	106820
Canada	USA (United States)	28 Dec 62	471UNTS13	106818
UK Great Britain	USA (United States)	15 Jan 63	466UNTS181	106743
New Zealand	USA (United States)	15 May 63	477UNTS55	106915
New Zealand	Western Samoa	31 Dec 63	521UNTS163	107519
Mexico	USA (United States)	14 Feb 64	524UNTS197	107574
USA (United States)	USSR (Soviet Union)	22 Feb 64	526UNTS131	107605
Peru	USA (United States)	07 Jul 64	530UNTS113	107676
France	Norway	16 Jul 64	510UNTS229	107417
USA (United States)	Western Samoa	03 Nov 64	521UNTS181	107521
India	Netherlands	11 Dec 64	570UNTS165	108292
Mexico	USA (United States)	27 Feb 65	546UNTS135	107940
Canada	USA (United States)	11 Jun 65	564UNTS83	108222
Multilateral		08 Dec 65	600UNTS161	108680
Spain	USA (United States)	14 Apr 66	586UNTS79	108497
France	USA (United States)	17 Jun 66	601UNTS113	108690
France	USSR (Soviet Union)	30 Jun 66	589UNTS99	108537
Israel	USA (United States)	22 May 68	0UNTS0	109356
Australia	USA (United States)	13 Jan 69	0UNTS0	109460

Research results

PARTY ONE	PARTY TWO	DATE	CITATION	NUMBER
Peru	USA (United States)	21 Apr 42	89UNTS317	200260
Nicaragua	USA (United States)	27 Oct 42	99UNTS287	200283
Ecuador	USA (United States)	29 Oct 42	89UNTS301	200259
El Salvador	USA (United States)	02 Dec 42	122UNTS277	200410
UK Great Britain	USA (United States)	19 Aug 43	214UNTS341	200527
UK Great Britain	USA (United States)	01 Dec 43	3UNTS209	100033
Peru	USA (United States)	04 Apr 44	89UNTS291	200258
Multilateral		19 Apr 44	89UNTS279	200257
Guatemala	USA (United States)	15 Jul 44	106UNTS285	200347
Multilateral		15 Dec 44	16UNTS247	200106
Multilateral		15 Dec 44	17UNTS305	200110
Multilateral		15 Nov 45	3UNTS123	100026
Czechoslovakia	France	08 Dec 45	46UNTS77	100701
Multilateral		31 Mar 46	17UNTS159	100274
Mexico	USA (United States)	12 Apr 46	66UNTS293	100861
Multilateral		02 Dec 46	161UNTS72	102124
Austria	France	15 Mar 47	12UNTS109	100182
Philippines	USA (United States)	12 May 47	16UNTS123	100253
Philippines	USA (United States)	12 May 47	16UNTS109	100252
Philippines	USA (United States)	12 May 47	16UNTS137	100254
Poland	Yugoslavia	24 May 47	115UNTS89	101560
Hungary	Poland	31 Jan 48	25UNTS283	100368
Poland	USSR (Soviet Union)	08 Apr 48	26UNTS191	100388
Ecuador	USA (United States)	14 May 48	89UNTS71	101210
Hungary	Poland	18 Jun 48	25UNTS319	100370
Multilateral		24 Jul 48	66UNTS25	100847
Multilateral		18 Aug 48	33UNTS181	100518
Multilateral		19 Nov 48	44UNTS277	100688
Brazil	USA (United States)	26 Nov 48	88UNTS3	101180
Multilateral		09 Dec 48	73UNTS39	100942
Czechoslovakia	Poland	22 Jan 49	85UNTS3	101142
Mexico	USA (United States)	25 Jan 49	99UNTS3	101367
Multilateral		08 Feb 49	157UNTS157	102053
Multilateral		22 Feb 49	93UNTS129	101296
Peru	USA (United States)	25 Mar 49	89UNTS15	101205
Costa Rica	USA (United States)	31 May 49	80UNTS3	101041
Mexico	USA (United States)	21 Jun 49	89UNTS3	101204
Multilateral		24 Sep 49	126UNTS237	101691

PARTY ONE	PARTY TWO	DATE	CITATION	NUMBER
Research results (Cont.)				
Bulgaria	Poland	26 Sep 49	260UNTS249	103712
Bulgaria	Poland	26 Sep 49	260UNTS227	103711
Hungary	Poland	29 Oct 49	260UNTS91	103705
Hungary	Poland	29 Oct 49	260UNTS113	103706
United Arab Rep	UK Great Britain	20 Mar 50	226UNTS287	103123
Multilateral		17 Apr 50	131UNTS99	101738
El Salvador	WHO (World Health)	21 Apr 50	103UNTS13	101420
Romania	USSR (Soviet Union)	27 May 50	221UNTS13	103000
Haiti	WHO (World Health)	21 Jun 50	103UNTS61	101424
Hungary	USSR (Soviet Union)	13 Jul 50	221UNTS35	103001
Bulgaria	USSR (Soviet Union)	25 Aug 50	221UNTS57	103002
Peru	WHO (World Health)	26 Sep 50	104UNTS233	101444
Colombia	USA (United States)	24 Nov 50	133UNTS49	101779
Guatemala	WHO (World Health)	28 Nov 50	103UNTS51	101423
El Salvador	WHO (World Health)	02 Jan 51	103UNTS29	101421
Nicaragua	WHO (World Health)	02 Jan 51	103UNTS107	101428
Colombia	WHO (World Health)	05 Jan 51	102UNTS139	101417
Lebanon	USA (United States)	24 Feb 51	223UNTS121	103060
China People's Rep	Poland	03 Apr 51	304UNTS187	104396
Greece	Turkey	20 Apr 51	178UNTS17	102333
Multilateral		01 Aug 51	107UNTS19	101464
Guatemala	WHO (World Health)	29 Dec 51	124UNTS89	101668
Dominican Republic	WHO (World Health)	15 Feb 52	134UNTS291	101808
Multilateral		01 Mar 52	168UNTS9	102210
Taiwan	WHO (World Health)	07 Mar 52	128UNTS233	101723
India	WHO (World Health)	02 Apr 52	131UNTS227	101743
Mexico	WHO (World Health)	28 May 52	134UNTS319	101810
Chile	WHO (World Health)	31 May 52	136UNTS323	101841
Brazil	USA (United States)	02 Jun 52	181UNTS109	102403
Chile	WHO (World Health)	24 Oct 52	151UNTS339	102004
India	WHO (World Health)	11 Dec 52	158UNTS391	102073
Czechoslovakia	Hungary	28 Apr 55	477UNTS197	106923
Turkey	USA (United States)	10 Jun 55	238UNTS149	103359
Canada	USA (United States)	15 Jun 55	235UNTS176	103301
UK Great Britain	USA (United States)	15 Jun 55	214UNTS301	102905
Israel	USA (United States)	12 Jul 55	219UNTS185	102974
Taiwan	USA (United States)	18 Jul 55	235UNTS221	103304
Switzerland	USA (United States)	18 Jul 55	239UNTS311	103388
Lebanon	USA (United States)	18 Jul 55	239UNTS247	103383
Colombia	USA (United States)	19 Jul 55	235UNTS233	103305
Spain	USA (United States)	19 Jul 55	239UNTS299	103387
Portugal	USA (United States)	21 Jul 55	239UNTS283	103386
USA (United States)	Venezuela	21 Jul 55	238UNTS121	103357
Denmark	USA (United States)	25 Jul 55	235UNTS245	103306
Philippines	USA (United States)	27 Jul 55	239UNTS271	103385
Italy	USA (United States)	28 Jul 55	239UNTS235	103382
Argentina	USA (United States)	29 Jul 55	235UNTS121	103298
Brazil	USA (United States)	03 Aug 55	235UNTS159	103300
Greece	USA (United States)	04 Aug 55	235UNTS257	103307
Chile	USA (United States)	08 Aug 55	235UNTS209	103303
Pakistan	USA (United States)	11 Aug 55	239UNTS259	103384
UK Great Britain	USA (United States)	15 Nov 55	231UNTS185	103219
USSR (Soviet Union)	Yugoslavia	19 Dec 55	378UNTS127	105423
USA (United States)	Uruguay	13 Jan 56	240UNTS401	103415
Sweden	USA (United States)	18 Jan 56	240UNTS413	103416
Netherlands	USA (United States)	22 Jan 56	287UNTS121	104181
Peru	USA (United States)	25 Jan 56	240UNTS425	103417
Korea, South	USA (United States)	03 Feb 56	240UNTS129	103401
Germany, West	USA (United States)	13 Feb 56	253UNTS119	103580
Thailand	USA (United States)	13 Mar 56	253UNTS105	103579
Multilateral		26 Mar 56	259UNTS125	103686
Germany, East	USSR (Soviet Union)	26 Apr 56	259UNTS279	103692
Albania	USSR (Soviet Union)	03 May 56	259UNTS391	103699
Korea, North	Poland	11 May 56	432UNTS161	106219
Korea, North	Romania	12 May 56	342UNTS189	104908

PARTY ONE	PARTY TWO	DATE	CITATION	NUMBER
Research results (Cont.)				
Costa Rica	USA (United States)	18 May 56	404UNTS237	105814
Austria	USA (United States)	08 Jun 56	253UNTS139	103581
New Zealand	USA (United States)	13 Jun 56	253UNTS155	103582
Dominican Republic	USA (United States)	15 Jun 56	265UNTS227	103815
Czechoslovakia	Yugoslavia	16 Jun 56	552UNTS325	108064
France	USA (United States)	19 Jun 56	281UNTS341	104087
Australia	USA (United States)	22 Jun 56	283UNTS275	104123
China People's Rep	USSR (Soviet Union)	05 Jul 56	263UNTS129	103770
Guatemala	USA (United States)	15 Aug 56	288UNTS181	104205
Greece	Yugoslavia	11 Sep 56	552UNTS311	108063
Romania	Vietnam, North	12 Oct 56	342UNTS173	104907
Multilateral		26 Oct 56	276UNTS3	103988
Romania	Yugoslavia	27 Oct 56	389UNTS55	105592
Bulgaria	Yugoslavia	24 Dec 56	397UNTS3	105699
USSR (Soviet Union)	Vietnam, North	15 Feb 57	274UNTS115	103962
Norway	USA (United States)	25 Feb 57	284UNTS19	104126
Multilateral		25 Mar 57	294UNTS259	104301
India	Romania	30 Apr 57	342UNTS251	104911
Albania	Yugoslavia	20 May 57	363UNTS99	105203
Bulgaria	Czechoslovakia	03 Jun 57	292UNTS3	104261
Czechoslovakia	Yugoslavia	11 Jun 57	504UNTS107	107355
South Africa	USA (United States)	08 Jul 57	290UNTS147	104234
United Arab Rep	USSR (Soviet Union)	19 Oct 57	292UNTS151	104271
IAEA (Atom Energy)	United Nations	23 Oct 57	281UNTS369	200548
Germany, East	Hungary	25 Oct 57	408UNTS156	105869
Germany, East	Hungary	13 Nov 57	407UNTS216	105866
Hungary	Yugoslavia	20 Nov 57	477UNTS267	106925
Czechoslovakia	USSR (Soviet Union)	04 Dec 57	313UNTS291	104537
Hungary	Romania	17 Dec 57	477UNTS303	106926
Czechoslovakia	Hungary	12 Mar 58	408UNTS178	105870
Czechoslovakia	Romania	25 Mar 58	339UNTS77	104846
Hungary	Poland	08 May 58	408UNTS212	105872
UK Great Britain	USA (United States)	03 Jul 58	326UNTS3	104707
Germany, East	Romania	15 Jul 58	387UNTS115	105560
Bulgaria	Hungary	03 Apr 59	438UNTS269	106319
Hungary	USSR (Soviet Union)	17 Apr 59	439UNTS41	106324
Ceylon (Sri Lanka)	Yugoslavia	05 May 59	391UNTS101	105618
Greece	Yugoslavia	18 Jun 59	368UNTS137	105238
Multilateral		07 Jul 59	377UNTS203	105402
Lebanon	USA (United States)	16 Sep 59	358UNTS175	105135
Bulgaria	Czechoslovakia	19 Sep 59	355UNTS77	105074
New Zealand	USA (United States)	30 Oct 59	361UNTS21	105170
Czechoslovakia	Guinea	30 Nov 59	386UNTS63	105538
Taiwan	USA (United States)	02 Dec 59	361UNTS115	105175
Multilateral		14 Dec 59	422UNTS33	106067
Multilateral		14 Dec 59	422UNTS57	106068
Spain	UK Great Britain	19 Jan 60	404UNTS41	105804
Chile	USA (United States)	19 Feb 60	371UNTS255	105282
Australia	USA (United States)	26 Feb 60	354UNTS95	105056
New Zealand	USA (United States)	23 Mar 60	371UNTS147	105276
Ireland	USA (United States)	24 Mar 60	371UNTS237	105280
Guatemala	USA (United States)	23 Apr 60	373UNTS23	105312
Argentina	USA (United States)	23 May 60	377UNTS3	105392
France	Greece	25 Jul 60	533UNTS227	107745
UK Great Britain	USA (United States)	14 Oct 60	398UNTS165	105721
Nigeria	USA (United States)	19 Oct 60	394UNTS113	105672
Italy	USA (United States)	03 Dec 60	410UNTS3	105893
Netherlands	United Arab Rep	08 Dec 60	455UNTS276	106547
Thailand	USA (United States)	23 Dec 60	405UNTS135	105830
UK Great Britain	USSR (Soviet Union)	09 Jan 61	404UNTS175	105810
Multilateral		08 Mar 61	396UNTS255	200584
UK Great Britain	USA (United States)	15 Mar 61	404UNTS207	105811
Cuba	Czechoslovakia	05 Apr 61	442UNTS201	106350
Australia	USA (United States)	05 Jun 61	409UNTS279	105892
UK Great Britain	USA (United States)	08 Sep 61	418UNTS53	106016

PARTY ONE	PARTY TWO	DATE	CITATION	NUMBER
Research results (Cont.)				
IAEA (Atom Energy)	Yugoslavia	04 Oct 61	412UNTS226	105935
Japan	Thailand	25 Nov 61	451UNTS55	106484
Pakistan	IAEA (Atom Energy)	05 Mar 62	425UNTS17	106115
Argentina	USA (United States)	16 Mar 62	454UNTS3	106535
Argentina	USA (United States)	22 Jun 62	458UNTS97	106594
Costa Rica	Israel	31 Jul 62	484UNTS155	107024
Multilateral		28 Sep 62	469UNTS169	106791
Dominican Republic	USA (United States)	25 Oct 62	459UNTS247	106627
UK Great Britain	USSR (Soviet Union)	21 Jan 63	475UNTS3	106887
India	USA (United States)	01 Feb 63	473UNTS37	106852
IAEA (Atom Energy)	Yugoslavia	04 Mar 63	490UNTS333	107162
Brazil	USA (United States)	29 Mar 63	476UNTS67	106904
IAEA (Atom Energy)	Yugoslavia	04 Jun 63	490UNTS343	107163
Austria	IAEA (Atom Energy)	21 Jun 63	490UNTS351	107164
Finland	IAEA (Atom Energy)	02 Jul 63	490UNTS403	107167
IBRD (World Bank)	Tunisia	03 Jul 63	480UNTS209	106970
Finland	IAEA (Atom Energy)	30 Jul 63	490UNTS413	107168
Hungary	Yugoslavia	15 Oct 63	577UNTS49	108372
Belgium	Romania	13 Nov 63	520UNTS119	107513
Argentina	USA (United States)	30 Nov 63	505UNTS131	107369
Multilateral		03 Dec 63	529UNTS217	107663
Mexico	IAEA (Atom Energy)	18 Dec 63	490UNTS361	107165
Multilateral		08 Apr 64	501UNTS221	107320
Canada	USA (United States)	06 May 64	524UNTS173	107572
Multilateral		11 Jun 64	525UNTS61	107584
Multilateral		15 Jun 64	573UNTS85	108324
Italy	Romania	16 Jun 64	558UNTS313	108150
Multilateral		18 Jun 64	542UNTS145	107886
Switzerland	UK Great Britain	11 Aug 64	552UNTS271	108059
Australia	USA (United States)	17 Aug 64	530UNTS209	107683
IAEA (Atom Energy)	United Arab Rep	17 Sep 64	525UNTS19	107581
Australia	UN Special Fund	30 Sep 64	510UNTS277	107419
USA (United States)	USSR (Soviet Union)	18 Nov 64	535UNTS307	107786
India	United Nations	25 Nov 64	519UNTS47	107501
Japan	USA (United States)	25 Nov 64	533UNTS31	107730
Poland	Romania	26 Nov 64	552UNTS157	108053
Argentina	IAEA (Atom Energy)	02 Dec 64	525UNTS29	107582
UK Great Britain	USSR (Soviet Union)	06 Jan 65	543UNTS77	107897
Switzerland	USA (United States)	30 Jan 65	594UNTS55	108594
Mexico	USA (United States)	27 Feb 65	542UNTS181	107889
Ethiopia	Hungary	25 May 65	577UNTS193	108377
Multilateral		18 Jun 65	573UNTS3	108320
Canada	USA (United States)	29 Jun 65	549UNTS273	108003
Multilateral		02 Jul 65	592UNTS215	108575
Afghanistan	IAEA (Atom Energy)	24 Sep 65	556UNTS101	108121
IAEA (Atom Energy)	Uruguay	24 Sep 65	556UNTS117	108123
Morocco	IAEA (Atom Energy)	24 Sep 65	556UNTS109	108122
Ethiopia	USA (United States)	30 Dec 65	574UNTS129	108345
IAEA (Atom Energy)	Turkey	08 Feb 66	573UNTS75	108323
Philippines	United Nations	05 Apr 66	560UNTS191	108174
Bulgaria	UN Special Fund	26 May 66	563UNTS71	108205
Mexico	IAEA (Atom Energy)	20 Jun 66	573UNTS25	108321
France	USSR (Soviet Union)	30 Jun 66	589UNTS99	108537
Philippines	IAEA (Atom Energy)	28 Sep 66	589UNTS25	108533
Israel	Philippines	20 Feb 67	597UNTS139	108642
Australia	UK Great Britain	16 Oct 68	0UNTS0	109459
Australia	USA (United States)	13 Jan 69	0UNTS0	109460
Communication satellites testing				
Mexico	USA (United States)	12 Apr 46	66UNTS293	100861
Mexico	USA (United States)	25 Jan 49	99UNTS3	101367
Panama	USA (United States)	30 Jun 52	181UNTS121	102404
UN Relief Palestin	United Arab Rep	14 Oct 53	190UNTS13	102555
UK Great Britain	USA (United States)	01 Nov 56	264UNTS3	103785
Spain	USA (United States)	18 Mar 60	372UNTS13	105284

PARTY ONE	PARTY TWO	DATE	CITATION	NUMBER
Communication satellites testing (Cont.)				
Mexico	USA (United States)	12 Apr 60	372UNTS47	105287
Canada	USA (United States)	24 Aug 60	388UNTS225	105580
UK Great Britain	USA (United States)	14 Oct 60	398UNTS165	105721
Nigeria	USA (United States)	19 Oct 60	394UNTS113	105672
Multilateral		01 Dec 60	414UNTS110	105970
UK Great Britain	USA (United States)	20 Jan 61	402UNTS153	105783
UK Great Britain	USA (United States)	29 Mar 61	405UNTS107	105826
France	USA (United States)	31 Mar 61	409UNTS136	105881
Australia	USA (United States)	05 Jun 61	409UNTS279	105892
Germany, West	USA (United States)	29 Sep 61	424UNTS113	106103
Brazil	USA (United States)	27 Oct 61	433UNTS113	106234
Argentina	USA (United States)	16 Mar 62	454UNTS3	106535
India	USA (United States)	09 Oct 62	471UNTS39	106820
Canada	USA (United States)	28 Dec 62	471UNTS13	106818
Malagasy	USA (United States)	07 Oct 63	494UNTS3	107221
Multilateral		17 Oct 63	525UNTS75	107585
Canada	USA (United States)	06 May 64	524UNTS173	107572
Spain	USA (United States)	26 Jan 65	542UNTS81	107881
France	USSR (Soviet Union)	30 Jun 66	589UNTS99	108537
Nuclear research				
Multilateral		15 Feb 52	132UNTS51	101751
Brazil	USA (United States)	03 Aug 55	270UNTS71	103893
Multilateral		26 Mar 56	259UNTS125	103686
Multilateral		26 Oct 56	276UNTS3	103988
Multilateral		25 Mar 57	294UNTS259	104301
IAEA (Atom Energy)	United Nations	23 Oct 57	281UNTS369	200548
Italy	UK Great Britain	28 Dec 57	305UNTS357	104425
New Zealand	USA (United States)	24 Dec 58	324UNTS111	104680
Euratom	UK Great Britain	04 Feb 59	331UNTS125	104752
Canada	USA (United States)	22 May 59	354UNTS63	105054
Panama	USA (United States)	24 Jun 59	479UNTS145	106950
Canada	Euratom	06 Oct 59	475UNTS187	106894
Brazil	USA (United States)	17 Mar 61	406UNTS241	105853
Norway	IAEA (Atom Energy)	10 Apr 61	402UNTS255	105790
Australia	USA (United States)	09 May 61	409UNTS203	105886
Netherlands	Euratom	25 Jul 61	462UNTS263	106686
IAEA (Atom Energy)	Yugoslavia	04 Oct 61	412UNTS226	105935
Multilateral		05 Mar 62	425UNTS3	106114
Pakistan	IAEA (Atom Energy)	05 Mar 62	425UNTS17	106115
USA (United States)	USSR (Soviet Union)	08 Mar 62	460UNTS3	106630
Colombia	USA (United States)	09 Apr 62	476UNTS9	106899
India	USA (United States)	01 Feb 63	473UNTS37	106852
Brazil	USA (United States)	29 Mar 63	476UNTS67	106904
India	USA (United States)	08 Aug 63	488UNTS21	107117
Argentina	USA (United States)	30 Nov 63	505UNTS131	107369
IAEA (Atom Energy)	Yugoslavia	07 Dec 63	501UNTS273	107322
Mexico	IAEA (Atom Energy)	18 Dec 63	490UNTS361	107165
USA (United States)	USSR (Soviet Union)	22 Feb 64	526UNTS131	107605
Multilateral		08 Apr 64	501UNTS221	107320
USA (United States)	USSR (Soviet Union)	18 Nov 64	535UNTS307	107786
Canada	USA (United States)	29 Jun 65	549UNTS273	108003
IAEA (Atom Energy)	Uruguay	24 Sep 65	556UNTS117	108123
Multilateral		30 Mar 66	593UNTS261	108588
IAEA (Atom Energy)	UK Great Britain	20 Jun 66	588UNTS269	108531
Multilateral		20 Jun 66	573UNTS41	108322
Israel	Philippines	20 Feb 67	597UNTS139	108642
Scientific exchange				
Multilateral		12 May 40	101UNTS91	101405
Brazil	Paraguay	14 Jun 41	54UNTS235	200196
Brazil	Paraguay	14 Jun 41	54UNTS249	200197
Brazil	Chile	18 Nov 41	67UNTS279	200225
Brazil	Venezuela	22 Oct 42	65UNTS203	200212
Brazil	Dominican Republic	09 Dec 42	65UNTS217	200213
UK Great Britain	USA (United States)	19 Aug 43	214UNTS341	200527

PARTY ONE	PARTY TWO	DATE	CITATION	NUMBER
Scientific exchange (Cont.)				
Brazil	Canada	24 May 44	65UNTS265	200215
Brazil	Ecuador	24 May 44	73UNTS223	200242
Brazil	Dominican Republic	09 Apr 45	67UNTS293	200226
Multilateral		15 Nov 45	3UNTS123	100026
Czechoslovakia	France	08 Dec 45	46UNTS77	100701
Belgium	France	22 Feb 46	68UNTS157	100892
Poland	Yugoslavia	16 Mar 46	10UNTS11	100139
Belgium	Netherlands	16 May 46	17UNTS13	100266
France	Netherlands	19 Nov 46	32UNTS101	100493
France	USA (United States)	10 Dec 46	15UNTS265	100242
Belgium	Czechoslovakia	06 Mar 47	34UNTS77	100528
Czechoslovakia	Yugoslavia	27 Apr 47	33UNTS49	100514
France	Poland	19 May 47	12UNTS95	100181
Poland	Yugoslavia	24 May 47	115UNTS89	101560
Czechoslovakia	UK Great Britain	16 Jun 47	46UNTS61	100700
Bulgaria	Czechoslovakia	20 Jun 47	46UNTS15	100698
Romania	Yugoslavia	26 Jun 47	116UNTS39	101568
Bulgaria	Poland	28 Jun 47	15UNTS123	100230
Czechoslovakia	Poland	04 Jul 47	25UNTS249	100366
Albania	Yugoslavia	09 Jul 47	33UNTS91	100516
Czechoslovakia	Romania	05 Sep 47	46UNTS37	100699
Multilateral		11 Oct 47	77UNTS143	100998
Hungary	Yugoslavia	15 Oct 47	33UNTS73	100515
Colombia	USA (United States)	22 Dec 47	51UNTS45	100751
Hungary	Poland	31 Jan 48	25UNTS283	100368
Norway	UK Great Britain	19 Feb 48	34UNTS33	100526
Belgium	Norway	20 Feb 48	32UNTS39	100487
Poland	Romania	27 Feb 48	46UNTS143	100707
Belgium	Luxembourg	27 Mar 48	178UNTS265	102343
Hungary	Poland	18 Jun 48	25UNTS319	100370
Netherlands	UK Great Britain	07 Jul 48	82UNTS259	101099
Belgium	Italy	29 Nov 48	41UNTS3	100641
Multilateral		29 Nov 48	120UNTS13	101613
Luxembourg	Netherlands	26 Apr 49	182UNTS187	102425
Costa Rica	USA (United States)	31 May 49	80UNTS3	101041
Greece	Lebanon	10 Jun 49	178UNTS29	102334
Multilateral		15 Jul 49	197UNTS3	102631
Multilateral		24 Sep 49	126UNTS237	101691
Austria	Czechoslovakia	30 Mar 50	495UNTS85	107240
Luxembourg	UK Great Britain	27 Jun 50	183UNTS217	102431
Bulgaria	Romania	29 Sep 50	342UNTS141	104905
Spain	Sweden	12 Oct 50	197UNTS305	102644
Czechoslovakia	Poland	17 Nov 50	530UNTS195	107682
Albania	Poland	02 Dec 50	260UNTS131	103707
Albania	Poland	25 Jan 51	260UNTS217	103710
China People's Rep	Poland	03 Apr 51	304UNTS187	104396
Greece	Turkey	20 Apr 51	178UNTS17	102333
Netherlands	South Africa	31 May 51	188UNTS289	102533
India	Turkey	29 Jun 51	213UNTS183	102886
Greece	UK Great Britain	29 Sep 51	190UNTS260	102570
Saudi Arabia	USA (United States)	10 Nov 51	180UNTS263	102390
Multilateral		06 Dec 51	425UNTS61	106119
El Salvador	USA (United States)	12 Dec 51	132UNTS287	101768
Germany, East	Poland	08 Jan 52	304UNTS113	104394
Burma	WHO (World Health)	18 Feb 52	127UNTS43	101698
Israel	USA (United States)	09 May 52	177UNTS63	102309
Brazil	USA (United States)	02 Jun 52	181UNTS109	102403
Germany, West	USA (United States)	18 Jul 52	165UNTS167	102175
Czechoslovakia	Romania	31 Jul 52	362UNTS123	105185
Albania	Romania	14 Feb 53	342UNTS107	104903
Germany, West	USA (United States)	09 Apr 53	204UNTS79	102750
Israel	Uruguay	30 Apr 53	280UNTS269	104064
Pakistan	United Arab Rep	14 Nov 53	485UNTS55	107046
Hungary	Romania	14 Dec 53	342UNTS151	104906
UK Great Britain	Yugoslavia	31 Dec 53	190UNTS335	102574

PARTY ONE	PARTY TWO	DATE	CITATION	NUMBER
Scientific exchange (Cont.)				
Canada	USA (United States)	03 May 54	221UNTS339	103015
Belgium	South Africa	01 Jun 54	201UNTS25	102708
Bulgaria	Romania	22 Jul 54	362UNTS101	105184
Greece	Italy	11 Sep 54	284UNTS313	104145
Belgium	Greece	09 Dec 54	257UNTS243	103660
UK Great Britain	Yugoslavia	31 Dec 54	209UNTS81	102824
Japan	Thailand	06 Apr 55	230UNTS219	103187
Czechoslovakia	Hungary	28 Apr 55	477UNTS197	106923
Netherlands	Norway	18 May 55	252UNTS269	103569
Turkey	USA (United States)	10 Jun 55	238UNTS149	103359
Italy	Norway	14 Jun 55	260UNTS307	103713
UK Great Britain	USA (United States)	15 Jun 55	229UNTS73	103161
Canada	USA (United States)	15 Jun 55	235UNTS176	103301
Belgium	USA (United States)	15 Jun 55	235UNTS133	103299
UK Great Britain	USA (United States)	15 Jun 55	214UNTS301	102905
Bulgaria	Yugoslavia	17 Jun 55	375UNTS287	105370
Multilateral		22 Jun 55	249UNTS3	103498
Israel	USA (United States)	12 Jul 55	219UNTS185	102974
Netherlands	USA (United States)	18 Jul 55	240UNTS347	103412
Taiwan	USA (United States)	18 Jul 55	235UNTS221	103304
Lebanon	USA (United States)	18 Jul 55	239UNTS247	103383
Switzerland	USA (United States)	18 Jul 55	239UNTS311	103388
Colombia	USA (United States)	19 Jul 55	235UNTS233	103305
Spain	USA (United States)	19 Jul 55	239UNTS299	103387
USA (United States)	Venezuela	21 Jul 55	238UNTS121	103357
Portugal	USA (United States)	21 Jul 55	239UNTS283	103386
Denmark	USA (United States)	25 Jul 55	235UNTS245	103306
Philippines	USA (United States)	27 Jul 55	239UNTS271	103385
Italy	USA (United States)	28 Jul 55	239UNTS235	103382
Argentina	USA (United States)	29 Jul 55	235UNTS121	103298
Belgium	Portugal	30 Jul 55	250UNTS213	103525
Brazil	USA (United States)	03 Aug 55	235UNTS159	103300
Greece	USA (United States)	04 Aug 55	235UNTS257	103307
Chile	USA (United States)	08 Aug 55	235UNTS209	103303
Italy	Spain	11 Aug 55	267UNTS125	103839
Pakistan	USA (United States)	11 Aug 55	239UNTS259	103384
Czechoslovakia	Germany, East	30 Aug 55	504UNTS279	107361
Japan	USA (United States)	14 Nov 55	240UNTS361	103413
Belgium	UK Great Britain	18 Nov 55	222UNTS327	103038
USSR (Soviet Union)	Yugoslavia	19 Dec 55	378UNTS127	105423
USA (United States)	Uruguay	13 Jan 56	240UNTS401	103415
Sweden	USA (United States)	18 Jan 56	240UNTS413	103416
Peru	USA (United States)	25 Jan 56	240UNTS425	103417
Korea, South	USA (United States)	03 Feb 56	240UNTS129	103401
Bulgaria	Yugoslavia	10 Feb 56	349UNTS21	105007
Germany, West	USA (United States)	13 Feb 56	253UNTS119	103580
Thailand	USA (United States)	13 Mar 56	253UNTS105	103579
Multilateral		26 Mar 56	259UNTS125	103686
Romania	USSR (Soviet Union)	07 Apr 56	259UNTS377	103698
Bulgaria	Greece	19 Apr 56	594UNTS131	108600
Chile	USA (United States)	20 Apr 56	293UNTS277	104295
Mongolia	USSR (Soviet Union)	24 Apr 56	259UNTS297	103693
Germany, East	USSR (Soviet Union)	26 Apr 56	259UNTS279	103692
Bulgaria	USSR (Soviet Union)	28 Apr 56	259UNTS363	103697
Albania	USSR (Soviet Union)	03 May 56	259UNTS391	103699
Mongolia	Romania	08 May 56	342UNTS291	104913
Korea, North	Poland	11 May 56	432UNTS161	106219
Korea, North	Romania	12 May 56	342UNTS189	104908
Czechoslovakia	USSR (Soviet Union)	01 Jun 56	259UNTS341	103696
Austria	USA (United States)	08 Jun 56	253UNTS139	103581
New Zealand	USA (United States)	13 Jun 56	253UNTS155	103582
Austria	Yugoslavia	15 Jun 56	396UNTS117	105695
Dominican Republic	USA (United States)	15 Jun 56	265UNTS227	103815
Czechoslovakia	Yugoslavia	16 Jun 56	552UNTS325	108064
France	USA (United States)	19 Jun 56	281UNTS341	104087

PARTY ONE	PARTY TWO	DATE	CITATION	NUMBER
Scientific exchange (Cont.)				
Switzerland	USA (United States)	21 Jun 56	279UNTS41	104033
Hungary	USSR (Soviet Union)	28 Jun 56	259UNTS405	103700
Poland	USSR (Soviet Union)	30 Jun 56	259UNTS311	103694
Czechoslovakia	Yugoslavia	03 Jul 56	397UNTS165	105704
China People's Rep	USSR (Soviet Union)	05 Jul 56	263UNTS129	103770
Poland	Yugoslavia	06 Jul 56	281UNTS143	104076
Germany, West	UK Great Britain	31 Jul 56	252UNTS93	103559
Syria	USSR (Soviet Union)	20 Aug 56	274UNTS105	103961
Greece	United Arab Rep	04 Sep 56	299UNTS253	104317
Korea, North	USSR (Soviet Union)	05 Sep 56	259UNTS329	103695
Romania	Yugoslavia	25 Sep 56	395UNTS147	105683
Romania	Vietnam, North	12 Oct 56	342UNTS173	104907
Norway	USSR (Soviet Union)	12 Oct 56	308UNTS95	104457
Multilateral		26 Oct 56	276UNTS3	103988
Denmark	Italy	26 Oct 56	267UNTS261	103847
Romania	Yugoslavia	27 Oct 56	389UNTS55	105592
Romania	Yugoslavia	27 Oct 56	389UNTS33	105590
Germany, East	Romania	08 Dec 56	362UNTS189	105188
Bulgaria	Yugoslavia	24 Dec 56	397UNTS3	105699
Czechoslovakia	Yugoslavia	29 Jan 57	300UNTS249	104339
Poland	United Arab Rep	02 Feb 57	319UNTS221	104633
Belgium	Yugoslavia	05 Feb 57	276UNTS143	103990
Taiwan	Turkey	12 Feb 57	282UNTS125	104097
Japan	United Arab Rep	20 Mar 57	318UNTS345	104625
Multilateral		25 Mar 57	294UNTS259	104301
India	Poland	27 Mar 57	319UNTS263	104635
Romania	United Arab Rep	15 Apr 57	389UNTS21	105589
Iran	Japan	16 Apr 57	325UNTS113	104697
India	Romania	30 Apr 57	342UNTS251	104911
Albania	Yugoslavia	20 May 57	363UNTS99	105203
Czechoslovakia	Yugoslavia	22 May 57	391UNTS33	105615
Argentina	Israel	23 May 57	280UNTS199	104059
Hungary	Yugoslavia	25 May 57	477UNTS219	106924
Japan	Pakistan	27 May 57	325UNTS21	104692
Czechoslovakia	Yugoslavia	11 Jun 57	504UNTS107	107355
Czechoslovakia	Syria	18 Jun 57	303UNTS119	104374
United Arab Rep	USSR (Soviet Union)	19 Oct 57	292UNTS151	104271
Czechoslovakia	United Arab Rep	19 Oct 57	530UNTS181	107681
Germany, East	Hungary	25 Oct 57	408UNTS156	105869
Taiwan	Iran	11 Nov 57	563UNTS31	108202
Germany, East	Hungary	13 Nov 57	407UNTS216	105866
Hungary	Yugoslavia	20 Nov 57	477UNTS267	106925
Israel	Norway	26 Nov 57	345UNTS99	104962
Czechoslovakia	USSR (Soviet Union)	04 Dec 57	313UNTS291	104537
Hungary	Yugoslavia	06 Dec 57	519UNTS215	107509
Hungary	Romania	17 Dec 57	477UNTS303	106926
Belgium	Denmark	31 Dec 57	305UNTS247	104422
Norway	Turkey	10 Jan 58	351UNTS229	105025
Ceylon (Sri Lanka)	USSR (Soviet Union)	15 Jan 58	305UNTS235	104421
Argentina	Paraguay	23 Jan 58	0UNTS0	109294
USA (United States)	USSR (Soviet Union)	27 Jan 58	301UNTS405	104350
India	Japan	04 Feb 58	324UNTS215	104687
Czechoslovakia	Hungary	12 Mar 58	408UNTS178	105870
Czechoslovakia	Romania	25 Mar 58	339UNTS77	104846
Taiwan	Costa Rica	10 Apr 58	315UNTS165	104567
Hungary	Poland	08 May 58	408UNTS212	105872
Germany, East	Hungary	14 Jun 58	407UNTS78	105861
Afghanistan	USA (United States)	26 Jun 58	321UNTS67	104654
Romania	Vietnam, North	30 Jun 58	389UNTS43	105591
Germany, East	Romania	15 Jul 58	387UNTS115	105560
Czechoslovakia	Romania	25 Oct 58	338UNTS301	104843
El Salvador	Israel	14 Nov 58	345UNTS67	104959
Iran	Japan	09 Dec 58	325UNTS221	104701
Haiti	Japan	17 Dec 58	518UNTS91	107492
Norway	Poland	17 Dec 58	432UNTS193	106221

PARTY ONE	PARTY TWO	DATE	CITATION	NUMBER
Scientific exchange (Cont.)				
Mongolia	Poland	23 Dec 58	432UNTS177	106220
Belgium	Turkey	29 Dec 58	357UNTS195	105118
Bulgaria	Hungary	03 Apr 59	438UNTS269	106319
Hungary	Iraq	11 Apr 59	439UNTS25	106323
Ceylon (Sri Lanka)	Yugoslavia	05 May 59	391UNTS101	105618
Iraq	USSR (Soviet Union)	05 May 59	356UNTS179	105095
Iran	Netherlands	22 May 59	474UNTS195	106882
SEATO (SE Asia)	USA (United States)	29 May 59	347UNTS77	104991
Finland	Hungary	10 Jun 59	439UNTS3	106321
Taiwan	Ecuador	12 Jun 59	387UNTS3	105554
Israel	Mexico	15 Jun 59	377UNTS267	105406
Greece	Yugoslavia	18 Jun 59	368UNTS137	105238
Brazil	Israel	24 Jun 59	515UNTS151	107458
Panama	USA (United States)	24 Jun 59	479UNTS145	106950
Czechoslovakia	India	07 Jul 59	359UNTS259	105145
Iraq	Romania	04 Aug 59	502UNTS17	107324
Norway	Spain	19 Aug 59	376UNTS145	105379
Bulgaria	Czechoslovakia	19 Sep 59	355UNTS77	105074
Canada	Euratom	06 Oct 59	475UNTS187	106894
Guinea	USA (United States)	28 Oct 59	358UNTS169	105134
Pakistan	USA (United States)	12 Nov 59	404UNTS259	105816
USA (United States)	USSR (Soviet Union)	21 Nov 59	361UNTS35	105172
Germany, West	Pakistan	25 Nov 59	457UNTS22	106575
Czechoslovakia	Guinea	30 Nov 59	386UNTS63	105538
France	Israel	30 Nov 59	377UNTS237	105404
Multilateral		01 Dec 59	402UNTS71	105778
UK Great Britain	USSR (Soviet Union)	01 Dec 59	351UNTS313	105032
Czechoslovakia	Ethiopia	11 Dec 59	399UNTS93	105736
Czechoslovakia	Ethiopia	11 Dec 59	386UNTS45	105536
Multilateral		14 Dec 59	422UNTS33	106067
Multilateral		14 Dec 59	422UNTS57	106068
Germany, East	Hungary	19 Dec 59	409UNTS4	105874
Belgium	Brazil	06 Jan 60	531UNTS149	107701
Colombia	USA (United States)	11 Jan 60	371UNTS37	105268
Guinea	Hungary	12 Jan 60	519UNTS131	107505
Austria	Czechoslovakia	23 Jan 60	495UNTS99	107241
Italy	USSR (Soviet Union)	09 Feb 60	399UNTS75	105735
India	USSR (Soviet Union)	12 Feb 60	392UNTS153	105642
Ecuador	USA (United States)	24 Feb 60	371UNTS55	105270
Taiwan	Panama	26 Feb 60	435UNTS281	106285
Indonesia	USSR (Soviet Union)	28 Feb 60	392UNTS191	105644
Poland	Yugoslavia	05 May 60	423UNTS229	106095
Netherlands	Turkey	12 May 60	463UNTS207	106704
Denmark	Poland	08 Jun 60	424UNTS37	106097
Cuba	Korea, North	29 Aug 60	473UNTS117	106860
Multilateral		19 Sep 60	419UNTS125	106032
Cuba	Romania	28 Oct 60	457UNTS9	106574
Czechoslovakia	Poland	14 Nov 60	413UNTS4	105938
Czechoslovakia	Ghana	23 Nov 60	431UNTS91	106213
Czechoslovakia	Ghana	23 Nov 60	431UNTS85	106212
Israel	Mali	24 Nov 60	413UNTS104	105945
Cambodia	Czechoslovakia	27 Nov 60	410UNTS263	105910
Multilateral		01 Dec 60	414UNTS110	105970
Netherlands	United Arab Rep	08 Dec 60	455UNTS276	106547
Romania	USA (United States)	09 Dec 60	401UNTS19	105759
Cuba	USSR (Soviet Union)	12 Dec 60	421UNTS3	106048
Cuba	Czechoslovakia	22 Dec 60	426UNTS145	106134
Thailand	USA (United States)	23 Dec 60	405UNTS135	105830
UK Great Britain	USSR (Soviet Union)	09 Jan 61	404UNTS175	105810
Ethiopia	USSR (Soviet Union)	13 Jan 61	421UNTS13	106049
India	USA (United States)	07 Feb 61	462UNTS57	106671
Czechoslovakia	Hungary	24 Feb 61	422UNTS15	106066
Cuba	Poland	06 Mar 61	484UNTS123	107020
Multilateral		08 Mar 61	396UNTS255	200584
Cuba	Germany, East	29 Mar 61	448UNTS81	106426

PARTY ONE	PARTY TWO	DATE	CITATION	NUMBER
Scientific exchange (Cont.)				
Cuba	Czechoslovakia	05 Apr 61	442UNTS201	106350
India	Norway	19 Apr 61	404UNTS307	105818
Afghanistan	Czechoslovakia	23 Apr 61	437UNTS25	106297
Ghana	Hungary	27 Apr 61	439UNTS17	106322
Australia	USA (United States)	22 May 61	419UNTS3	106026
Somalia	USSR (Soviet Union)	02 Jun 61	528UNTS147	107638
Czechoslovakia	Somalia	04 Jun 61	479UNTS291	106960
Czechoslovakia	Somalia	04 Jun 61	480UNTS261	106973
Taiwan	Paraguay	18 Aug 61	438UNTS109	106314
Italy	United Nations	23 Aug 61	405UNTS3	105819
UK Great Britain	USA (United States)	08 Sep 61	418UNTS53	106016
Ghana	Romania	30 Sep 61	457UNTS3	106573
Taiwan	Jordan	17 Oct 61	435UNTS267	106284
Brazil	Poland	19 Oct 61	552UNTS75	108050
Guatemala	Israel	27 Nov 61	448UNTS191	106431
Taiwan	El Salvador	27 Nov 61	437UNTS161	106306
Argentina	Japan	20 Dec 61	451UNTS77	106486
Ghana	USA (United States)	03 Jan 62	433UNTS147	106237
USA (United States)	USSR (Soviet Union)	08 Mar 62	460UNTS3	106630
Argentina	USA (United States)	16 Mar 62	454UNTS3	106535
Multilateral		26 Mar 62	539UNTS67	107825
Multilateral		29 Mar 62	507UNTS177	107401
Hungary	India	30 Mar 62	519UNTS119	107504
Colombia	USA (United States)	09 Apr 62	476UNTS9	106899
United Arab Rep	USA (United States)	21 May 62	458UNTS197	106601
Senegal	USSR (Soviet Union)	14 Jun 62	437UNTS233	106309
Israel	Peru	25 Jun 62	515UNTS263	107464
Israel	Liberia	25 Jun 62	448UNTS295	106442
Costa Rica	Israel	31 Jul 62	484UNTS155	107024
Syria	USSR (Soviet Union)	19 Aug 62	457UNTS285	106588
Italy	USA (United States)	05 Sep 62	461UNTS185	106663
Denmark	USSR (Soviet Union)	11 Sep 62	458UNTS3	106589
Cameroon	Israel	24 Oct 62	449UNTS15	106447
Multilateral		12 Dec 62	552UNTS15	108048
Belgium	Tunisia	21 Dec 62	482UNTS3	106987
Israel	Philippines	10 Jan 63	588UNTS205	108526
UK Great Britain	USSR (Soviet Union)	21 Jan 63	475UNTS3	106887
Ethiopia	USA (United States)	25 Jan 63	473UNTS27	106851
Dahomey	USSR (Soviet Union)	20 Mar 63	528UNTS181	107641
Hungary	Korea, North	29 Mar 63	577UNTS219	108379
Romania	USA (United States)	02 Apr 63	474UNTS95	106874
Czechoslovakia	Tunisia	06 Apr 63	555UNTS111	108106
Belgium	Venezuela	15 May 63	470UNTS259	106812
India	USA (United States)	08 Aug 63	488UNTS21	107117
Mali	Romania	26 Sep 63	528UNTS193	107642
Czechoslovakia	Yugoslavia	05 Oct 63	504UNTS151	107356
Hungary	Yugoslavia	15 Oct 63	577UNTS49	108372
Tanganyika	USSR (Soviet Union)	06 Nov 63	528UNTS157	107639
Belgium	Romania	13 Nov 63	520UNTS119	107513
Belgium	Pakistan	14 Nov 63	535UNTS393	107792
Multilateral		03 Dec 63	529UNTS217	107663
Belgium	Poland	09 Dec 63	514UNTS195	107448
Greece	USA (United States)	13 Dec 63	494UNTS55	107226
Netherlands	Tunisia	11 Feb 64	570UNTS173	108293
USA (United States)	USSR (Soviet Union)	22 Feb 64	526UNTS131	107605
UNESCO (Educ/Cult)	Yugoslavia	27 Feb 64	489UNTS257	107143
Ireland	Norway	02 Apr 64	553UNTS129	108078
Mexico	Netherlands	08 Apr 64	575UNTS35	108353
Canada	USA (United States)	06 May 64	524UNTS173	107572
Algeria	Czechoslovakia	14 May 64	538UNTS301	107817
Cuba	Czechoslovakia	03 Jun 64	527UNTS205	107626
Multilateral		11 Jun 64	525UNTS61	107584
Italy	Romania	16 Jun 64	558UNTS313	108150
Multilateral		18 Jun 64	542UNTS145	107886
Multilateral		15 Jul 64	610UNTS143	108840

PARTY ONE	PARTY TWO	DATE	CITATION	NUMBER
Scientific exchange (Cont.)				
Switzerland	UK Great Britain	11 Aug 64	552UNTS271	108059
Australia	USA (United States)	17 Aug 64	530UNTS209	107683
Dominican Republic	USA (United States)	28 Aug 64	531UNTS35	107691
Germany, East	Poland	06 Oct 64	552UNTS89	108051
Czechoslovakia	Germany, East	06 Oct 64	545UNTS113	107927
Chad	Israel	07 Oct 64	630UNTS175	108969
Czechoslovakia	Mongolia	21 Oct 64	545UNTS91	107926
USA (United States)	USSR (Soviet Union)	18 Nov 64	535UNTS307	107786
Poland	Romania	26 Nov 64	552UNTS157	108053
Czechoslovakia	United Arab Rep	26 Nov 64	545UNTS11	107923
UK Great Britain	USSR (Soviet Union)	06 Jan 65	543UNTS77	107897
Belgium	Sweden	11 Jan 65	533UNTS157	107741
USA (United States)	USSR (Soviet Union)	05 Feb 65	541UNTS97	107863
Belgium	Hungary	11 Feb 65	544UNTS3	107908
UK Great Britain	USSR (Soviet Union)	13 Feb 65	543UNTS43	107896
Ethiopia	Hungary	25 May 65	577UNTS193	108377
China People's Rep	Romania	27 May 65	592UNTS3	108566
Pakistan	USSR (Soviet Union)	05 Jun 65	593UNTS115	108579
Uganda	USSR (Soviet Union)	24 Jul 65	596UNTS199	108633
Israel	Sierra Leone	22 Aug 65	550UNTS275	108022
Argentina	Belgium	05 Nov 65	635UNTS229	109086
Czechoslovakia	Poland	22 Jan 66	588UNTS175	108524
UK Great Britain	Yugoslavia	27 Jan 66	573UNTS243	108337
Netherlands	Philippines	02 Mar 66	631UNTS325	109002
Romania	Tunisia	21 Apr 66	604UNTS65	108744
Czechoslovakia	USSR (Soviet Union)	23 Apr 66	566UNTS159	108242
Rwanda	USSR (Soviet Union)	06 May 66	633UNTS217	109039
France	USSR (Soviet Union)	30 Jun 66	589UNTS99	108537
Hungary	Yugoslavia	26 Sep 66	601UNTS21	108685
Bulgaria	Poland	03 Oct 66	618UNTS3	108921
Netherlands	Nigeria	18 Oct 66	603UNTS53	108724
Morocco	USSR (Soviet Union)	27 Oct 66	608UNTS197	108816
IAEA (Atom Energy)	Turkey	08 Dec 66	608UNTS69	108813
Syria	USSR (Soviet Union)	18 Dec 66	633UNTS247	109041
Israel	Philippines	20 Feb 67	597UNTS139	108642
UK Great Britain	USSR (Soviet Union)	24 Feb 67	606UNTS171	108785
Romania	Somalia	20 Apr 67	642UNTS155	109171
Bulgaria	USSR (Soviet Union)	27 Apr 67	631UNTS3	108983
Belgium	Bulgaria	17 May 67	631UNTS215	108995
Bulgaria	Turkey	30 May 67	631UNTS19	108984
Hungary	UK Great Britain	09 Aug 67	632UNTS39	109006
Czechoslovakia	UK Great Britain	26 Mar 68	0UNTS0	109278
United Nations	United Arab Rep	14 Nov 68	0UNTS0	109371
IAEA (Atom Energy)	OAU (Afri Unity)	26 Mar 69	0UNTS0	200646
Research and development				
Honduras	USA (United States)	28 Feb 41	117UNTS205	200371
Ecuador	USA (United States)	24 Feb 42	26UNTS379	200157
Brazil	USA (United States)	14 Mar 42	102UNTS195	200302
Haiti	USA (United States)	07 Apr 42	106UNTS319	200349
Peru	USA (United States)	21 Apr 42	89UNTS317	200260
El Salvador	USA (United States)	05 May 42	21UNTS215	200124
Honduras	USA (United States)	08 May 42	166UNTS351	200498
Paraguay	USA (United States)	22 May 42	124UNTS243	200423
Nicaragua	USA (United States)	22 May 42	105UNTS141	200328
Bolivia	USA (United States)	16 Jul 42	13UNTS101	200072
Brazil	USA (United States)	17 Jul 42	102UNTS203	200303
Colombia	USA (United States)	23 Oct 42	105UNTS109	200326
Nicaragua	USA (United States)	27 Oct 42	99UNTS287	200283
Ecuador	USA (United States)	29 Oct 42	89UNTS301	200259
El Salvador	USA (United States)	02 Dec 42	122UNTS277	200410
USA (United States)	Venezuela	18 Feb 43	21UNTS225	200125
Panama	USA (United States)	02 Mar 43	107UNTS55	200351
Mexico	USA (United States)	14 Jun 43	66UNTS331	200220
Mexico	USA (United States)	01 Jul 43	28UNTS407	200164

Research and development (Cont.)

PARTY ONE	PARTY TWO	DATE	CITATION	NUMBER
Dominican Republic	USA (United States)	07 Jul 43	28UNTS419	200165
USA (United States)	Uruguay	01 Nov 43	106UNTS311	200348
Brazil	USA (United States)	25 Nov 43	102UNTS227	200305
Peru	USA (United States)	15 Apr 44	150UNTS317	200479
Guatemala	USA (United States)	15 Jul 44	106UNTS285	200347
Multilateral		02 Aug 44	67UNTS221	200221
El Salvador	USA (United States)	09 Jun 45	149UNTS379	200478
Dominican Republic	USA (United States)	13 Oct 45	149UNTS361	200477
Albania	Yugoslavia	28 Nov 46	111UNTS93	101520
Mexico	USA (United States)	17 Mar 47	167UNTS30	102200
Philippines	USA (United States)	12 May 47	16UNTS109	100252
Honduras	USA (United States)	13 May 47	166UNTS159	102189
Bolivia	USA (United States)	16 May 47	168UNTS89	102215
Multilateral		11 Oct 47	77UNTS143	100998
Ecuador	USA (United States)	14 Nov 47	149UNTS297	101959
Czechoslovakia	USSR (Soviet Union)	28 Nov 47	216UNTS285	102941
Paraguay	USA (United States)	01 Jan 48	89UNTS191	101217
Cuba	USA (United States)	27 Jan 48	67UNTS3	100862
Paraguay	USA (United States)	12 Mar 48	162UNTS30	102131
Ecuador	USA (United States)	14 May 48	89UNTS71	101210
Brazil	USA (United States)	26 Nov 48	88UNTS3	101180
France	USA (United States)	27 Nov 48	168UNTS119	102217
Multilateral		09 Dec 48	20UNTS229	100318
Italy	USA (United States)	18 Dec 48	79UNTS133	101037
Multilateral		08 Feb 49	157UNTS157	102053
Multilateral		22 Feb 49	93UNTS129	101296
Costa Rica	USA (United States)	31 May 49	80UNTS3	101041
Mexico	USA (United States)	21 Jun 49	89UNTS3	101204
Mexico	USA (United States)	15 Aug 49	66UNTS13	100846
United Arab Rep	USA (United States)	03 Nov 49	71UNTS31	100908
Canada	USA (United States)	22 Jun 50	70UNTS115	100900
Thailand	USA (United States)	01 Jul 50	81UNTS61	101063
Brazil	USA (United States)	16 Aug 50	140UNTS223	101890
Czechoslovakia	Poland	17 Nov 50	530UNTS195	107682
Guatemala	WHO (World Health)	28 Nov 50	103UNTS51	101423
El Salvador	WHO (World Health)	02 Jan 51	103UNTS29	101421
Nicaragua	WHO (World Health)	02 Jan 51	103UNTS107	101428
Colombia	WHO (World Health)	05 Jan 51	102UNTS139	101417
United Nations	Yugoslavia	06 Jan 51	78UNTS165	101015
Chile	USA (United States)	16 Jan 51	157UNTS3	102043
Albania	Poland	25 Jan 51	260UNTS217	103710
Nicaragua	USA (United States)	31 Jan 51	160UNTS121	102105
Nicaragua	USA (United States)	31 Jan 51	150UNTS3	101960
Costa Rica	USA (United States)	13 Feb 51	141UNTS169	101914
Denmark	WHO (World Health)	14 Feb 51	104UNTS243	101445
Lebanon	USA (United States)	24 Feb 51	223UNTS121	103060
Dominican Republic	USA (United States)	16 Mar 51	148UNTS15	101932
Honduras	USA (United States)	24 Apr 51	140UNTS287	101894
Nicaragua	UK Great Britain	25 May 51	101UNTS77	101404
Netherlands	South Africa	31 May 51	188UNTS289	102533
Lebanon	WHO (World Health)	05 Jun 51	104UNTS225	101443
Burma	WHO (World Health)	13 Jun 51	117UNTS115	101588
El Salvador	USA (United States)	19 Jul 51	140UNTS259	101892
Multilateral		01 Aug 51	107UNTS19	101464
Iraq	USA (United States)	16 Aug 51	147UNTS65	101929
Denmark	USA (United States)	23 Aug 51	147UNTS49	101928
Japan	USA (United States)	28 Aug 51	147UNTS81	101930
Korea, South	WHO (World Health)	19 Sep 51	109UNTS297	200366
WHO (World Health)	Thailand	04 Oct 51	109UNTS85	101493
WHO (World Health)	Thailand	04 Oct 51	109UNTS77	101492
Taiwan	WHO (World Health)	25 Oct 51	126UNTS77	101683
India	WHO (World Health)	01 Nov 51	118UNTS13	101593
Panama	WHO (World Health)	09 Nov 51	118UNTS43	101595
Saudi Arabia	USA (United States)	10 Nov 51	180UNTS263	102390
Italy	UK Great Britain	28 Nov 51	172UNTS27	102238

Research and development (Cont.)

PARTY ONE	PARTY TWO	DATE	CITATION	NUMBER
Denmark	WHO (World Health)	30 Nov 51	118UNTS3	101592
Guatemala	WHO (World Health)	17 Dec 51	120UNTS133	101619
Guatemala	WHO (World Health)	29 Dec 51	124UNTS89	101668
Costa Rica	WHO (World Health)	23 Jan 52	135UNTS265	101826
WHO (World Health)	Spain	30 Jan 52	124UNTS259	200425
Jordan	USA (United States)	12 Feb 52	168UNTS25	102211
Multilateral		15 Feb 52	132UNTS51	101751
Dominican Republic	WHO (World Health)	15 Feb 52	134UNTS291	101808
Burma	WHO (World Health)	18 Feb 52	127UNTS43	101698
Greece	United Nations	05 Mar 52	123UNTS3	101650
Finland	WHO (World Health)	07 Mar 52	128UNTS269	200436
Taiwan	WHO (World Health)	07 Mar 52	128UNTS233	101723
Iraq	USA (United States)	18 Mar 52	223UNTS131	103061
Denmark	WHO (World Health)	26 Mar 52	134UNTS285	101807
India	WHO (World Health)	02 Apr 52	131UNTS227	101743
India	United Nations	02 Apr 52	126UNTS145	101687
Peru	USA (United States)	09 Apr 52	184UNTS295	102454
Pakistan	United Nations	28 Apr 52	128UNTS191	101720
Iraq	USA (United States)	21 May 52	212UNTS183	102870
Mexico	WHO (World Health)	28 May 52	134UNTS319	101810
Chile	WHO (World Health)	31 May 52	136UNTS323	101841
Brazil	USA (United States)	02 Jun 52	181UNTS109	102403
Brazil	WHO (World Health)	12 Jun 52	151UNTS333	102003
Multilateral		19 Jun 52	133UNTS165	101787
Ethiopia	USA (United States)	24 Jun 52	181UNTS215	102411
Finland	USA (United States)	02 Jul 52	165UNTS203	102177
India	WHO (World Health)	16 Jul 52	135UNTS291	101828
Germany, West	USA (United States)	18 Jul 52	165UNTS167	102175
Chile	ILO (Labor Org)	23 Jul 52	178UNTS323	102348
Panama	United Nations	20 Aug 52	136UNTS3	101829
Mexico	USA (United States)	26 Aug 52	264UNTS269	103797
Italy	ILO (Labor Org)	04 Sep 52	178UNTS371	200505
Multilateral		15 Oct 52	141UNTS96	101909
Austria	Belgium	17 Oct 52	162UNTS183	102135
Saudi Arabia	USA (United States)	10 Nov 52	181UNTS307	102419
Saudi Arabia	USA (United States)	10 Nov 52	181UNTS225	102412
Ceylon (Sri Lanka)	USA (United States)	17 Nov 52	180UNTS207	102386
Sweden	USA (United States)	20 Nov 52	177UNTS203	102319
Mexico	ICAO (Civil Aviat)	28 Nov 52	164UNTS15	102156
Austria	UK Great Britain	12 Dec 52	172UNTS9	102237
Multilateral		16 Dec 52	158UNTS407	102074
Multilateral		29 Dec 52	151UNTS317	102002
Saudi Arabia	USA (United States)	25 Jan 53	201UNTS3	102706
Taiwan	ILO (Labor Org)	13 Feb 53	178UNTS337	102349
UK Great Britain	USA (United States)	25 Feb 53	212UNTS157	102868
Costa Rica	United Nations	27 Feb 53	161UNTS45	102121
Nepal	United Nations	02 Mar 53	161UNTS347	200493
United Arab Rep	USA (United States)	12 Mar 53	204UNTS3	102747
United Arab Rep	USA (United States)	19 Mar 53	215UNTS17	102909
France	WHO (World Health)	02 Apr 53	174UNTS83	102279
United Nations	Yemen	07 Apr 53	163UNTS73	102142
France	WHO (World Health)	30 Apr 53	174UNTS71	102278
United Arab Rep	USA (United States)	21 May 53	204UNTS29	102748
Ecuador	United Nations	16 Jun 53	166UNTS289	102194
United Arab Rep	USA (United States)	18 Jun 53	204UNTS55	102749
Ethiopia	United Nations	22 Jun 53	172UNTS93	102241
Liberia	USA (United States)	23 Jun 53	213UNTS57	102880
Liberia	USA (United States)	23 Jun 53	213UNTS37	102879
Cambodia	United Nations	24 Jun 53	168UNTS309	200500
Afghanistan	USA (United States)	30 Jun 53	215UNTS3	102908
UN Relief Palestin	United Arab Rep	30 Jun 53	190UNTS3	102554
Multilateral		09 Oct 53	190UNTS49	102557
Dominican Republic	United Nations	19 Nov 53	180UNTS45	102374
Multilateral		11 Dec 53	191UNTS285	102588
UK Great Britain	USA (United States)	20 Jan 54	196UNTS95	102619

PARTY ONE	PARTY TWO	DATE	CITATION	NUMBER
Research and development (Cont.)				
Brazil	WHO (World Health)	04 Feb 54	233UNTS49	103250
United Nations	Venezuela	05 Mar 54	187UNTS9	102498
Liberia	United Nations	09 Mar 54	187UNTS61	102501
Guatemala	United Nations	10 Mar 54	191UNTS271	102587
Multilateral		20 Apr 54	189UNTS11	102539
Nepal	WHO (World Health)	13 May 54	204UNTS311	200522
Multilateral		01 Jun 54	200UNTS235	200520
Italy	USA (United States)	28 Jun 54	237UNTS121	103340
Costa Rica	USA (United States)	30 Jun 54	235UNTS35	103294
Multilateral		29 Jul 54	249UNTS45	103500
Multilateral		19 Aug 54	201UNTS51	102710
Multilateral		06 Oct 54	201UNTS75	102711
Multilateral		27 Oct 54	201UNTS95	102712
Multilateral		29 Oct 54	201UNTS115	102713
Chile	USA (United States)	31 Mar 55	262UNTS19	103736
Multilateral		04 Apr 55	208UNTS239	102816
Taiwan	WHO (World Health)	21 Apr 55	210UNTS71	102835
Czechoslovakia	Hungary	28 Apr 55	477UNTS197	106923
Multilateral		14 Jun 55	212UNTS263	200526
Iran	WHO (World Health)	04 Jul 55	227UNTS65	103131
Multilateral		04 Jul 55	214UNTS10	102897
Brazil	USA (United States)	03 Aug 55	270UNTS71	103893
Multilateral		12 Oct 55	560UNTS3	108165
Italy	Lebanon	04 Nov 55	267UNTS147	103840
Bulgaria	Yugoslavia	11 Dec 55	378UNTS49	105417
Multilateral		02 Feb 56	227UNTS153	103137
Multilateral		10 Feb 56	228UNTS167	103150
Multilateral		10 Feb 56	228UNTS189	103151
Burma	Yugoslavia	07 Mar 56	386UNTS235	105543
Colombia	USA (United States)	14 Mar 56	271UNTS303	103922
Romania	USSR (Soviet Union)	07 Apr 56	259UNTS377	103698
Germany, East	USSR (Soviet Union)	30 May 56	263UNTS143	103771
Multilateral		31 May 56	251UNTS181	103541
Multilateral		08 Jun 56	247UNTS366	200541
Multilateral		14 Jun 56	265UNTS125	103809
Czechoslovakia	Yugoslavia	16 Jun 56	552UNTS325	108064
Multilateral		26 Jun 56	321UNTS2	104650
Israel	USA (United States)	26 Jun 56	257UNTS55	103649
Multilateral		26 Jun 56	253UNTS12	103573
Multilateral		02 Jul 56	540UNTS110	107846
Multilateral		02 Jul 56	248UNTS37	103484
China People's Rep	USSR (Soviet Union)	05 Jul 56	263UNTS129	103770
Multilateral		31 Aug 56	249UNTS158	103506
Denmark	WHO (World Health)	03 Sep 56	258UNTS103	103674
Multilateral		05 Oct 56	251UNTS245	103544
Multilateral		05 Oct 56	251UNTS267	103545
Romania	Vietnam, North	12 Oct 56	342UNTS173	104907
Multilateral		26 Oct 56	276UNTS3	103988
Romania	Yugoslavia	27 Oct 56	389UNTS55	105592
Romania	Yugoslavia	27 Oct 56	389UNTS33	105590
Ecuador	USA (United States)	31 Oct 56	283UNTS151	104114
Argentina	USA (United States)	05 Nov 56	277UNTS143	104004
Multilateral		21 Nov 56	253UNTS266	103588
UK Great Britain	USA (United States)	27 Nov 56	282UNTS43	104092
Multilateral		15 Jan 57	376UNTS122	105378
Multilateral		23 Jan 57	259UNTS426	103701
Multilateral		17 Feb 57	271UNTS2	103907
Iceland	USA (United States)	23 Feb 57	283UNTS73	104107
Chile	USA (United States)	01 Mar 57	283UNTS127	104112
Multilateral		01 Mar 57	264UNTS94	103790
Multilateral		28 Mar 57	271UNTS30	103908
Paraguay	USA (United States)	04 Apr 57	284UNTS161	104135
Multilateral		09 Apr 57	274UNTS172	103965
Romania	United Arab Rep	15 Apr 57	389UNTS21	105589
Czechoslovakia	United Arab Rep	06 May 57	292UNTS317	104278

PARTY ONE	PARTY TWO	DATE	CITATION	NUMBER
Research and development (Cont.)				
Finland	USA (United States)	10 May 57	283UNTS43	104105
Multilateral		24 May 57	268UNTS270	103861
Czechoslovakia	Yugoslavia	11 Jun 57	504UNTS107	107355
Multilateral		09 Jul 57	274UNTS300	103972
Burma	WHO (World Health)	20 Sep 57	282UNTS113	104096
New Zealand	UK Great Britain	20 Sep 57	287UNTS105	104180
USA (United States)	Venezuela	24 Sep 57	293UNTS307	104298
Cambodia	USA (United States)	17 Oct 57	299UNTS203	104313
IAEA (Atom Energy)	United Nations	23 Oct 57	281UNTS369	200548
UK Great Britain	USA (United States)	01 Nov 57	299UNTS167	104312
Brazil	USA (United States)	05 Nov 57	303UNTS3	104368
Multilateral		05 Nov 57	285UNTS301	104155
Hungary	Yugoslavia	20 Nov 57	477UNTS267	106925
Czechoslovakia	USSR (Soviet Union)	04 Dec 57	313UNTS291	104537
Hungary	Romania	17 Dec 57	477UNTS303	106926
Japan	USA (United States)	11 Jan 58	304UNTS35	104390
Ghana	WHO (World Health)	21 Jan 58	307UNTS3	104437
Argentina	Paraguay	23 Jan 58	0UNTS0	109294
Indonesia	WHO (World Health)	05 Feb 58	307UNTS15	104438
Multilateral		15 Mar 58	292UNTS273	104276
Czechoslovakia	Romania	25 Mar 58	339UNTS77	104846
Israel	WHO (World Health)	11 Apr 58	307UNTS27	104439
Germany, West	UK Great Britain	18 Apr 58	343UNTS241	104928
Hungary	Poland	08 May 58	408UNTS212	105872
Germany, East	Hungary	14 Jun 58	407UNTS78	105861
Multilateral		19 Jun 58	306UNTS236	200550
WHO (World Health)	Sudan	21 Jun 58	307UNTS235	104453
Spain	USA (United States)	16 Oct 58	336UNTS153	104804
New Zealand	USA (United States)	24 Dec 58	324UNTS111	104680
Iraq	USSR (Soviet Union)	16 Mar 59	346UNTS107	104979
Bulgaria	Hungary	03 Apr 59	438UNTS269	106319
Hungary	USSR (Soviet Union)	17 Apr 59	439UNTS41	106324
Israel	Mexico	15 Jun 59	377UNTS267	105406
Greece	Yugoslavia	18 Jun 59	368UNTS137	105238
Lebanon	USA (United States)	16 Sep 59	358UNTS175	105135
Bulgaria	Czechoslovakia	19 Sep 59	355UNTS77	105074
United Arab Rep	USA (United States)	28 Sep 59	358UNTS97	105128
New Zealand	USA (United States)	30 Oct 59	361UNTS21	105170
Afghanistan	United Nations	24 Nov 59	397UNTS187	105705
Multilateral		01 Dec 59	402UNTS71	105778
Taiwan	USA (United States)	02 Dec 59	361UNTS115	105175
Multilateral		03 Dec 59	348UNTS246	105003
Multilateral		14 Dec 59	422UNTS33	106067
Multilateral		14 Dec 59	422UNTS57	106068
Ceylon (Sri Lanka)	WHO (World Health)	21 Dec 59	349UNTS109	105011
Belgium	Brazil	06 Jan 60	531UNTS149	107701
Pakistan	WHO (World Health)	20 Jan 60	351UNTS355	105034
Chile	USA (United States)	19 Feb 60	371UNTS255	105282
Indonesia	USSR (Soviet Union)	28 Feb 60	392UNTS173	105643
Indonesia	USSR (Soviet Union)	28 Feb 60	392UNTS191	105644
Portugal	USA (United States)	19 Mar 60	371UNTS131	105275
New Zealand	USA (United States)	23 Mar 60	371UNTS147	105276
Ireland	USA (United States)	24 Mar 60	371UNTS237	105280
Chile	USA (United States)	28 Mar 60	401UNTS105	105765
Multilateral		12 Apr 60	359UNTS323	105150
Guatemala	USA (United States)	23 Apr 60	373UNTS23	105312
Poland	Yugoslavia	05 May 60	423UNTS229	106095
Cambodia	WHO (World Health)	19 May 60	372UNTS193	105298
Argentina	USA (United States)	23 May 60	377UNTS3	105392
Multilateral		04 Jun 60	360UNTS208	105159
IAEA (Atom Energy)	USA (United States)	28 Jun 60	374UNTS133	105333
Multilateral		08 Jul 60	366UNTS310	105220
USA (United States)	Uruguay	22 Jul 60	388UNTS315	105587
Japan	Pakistan	30 Jul 60	384UNTS63	105511
WHO (World Health)	United Arab Rep	03 Aug 60	385UNTS3	105524

PARTY ONE	PARTY TWO	DATE	CITATION	NUMBER
Research and development (Cont.)				
Jordan	WHO (World Health)	03 Aug 60	381UNTS133	105469
Ghana	USSR (Soviet Union)	04 Aug 60	399UNTS61	105734
WHO (World Health)	Tunisia	04 Aug 60	381UNTS335	105474
Laos	WHO (World Health)	04 Aug 60	373UNTS313	105322
Canada	USA (United States)	24 Aug 60	388UNTS225	105580
United Arab Rep	USSR (Soviet Union)	27 Aug 60	399UNTS37	105733
WHO (World Health)	Saudi Arabia	06 Sep 60	395UNTS169	105684
Lebanon	WHO (World Health)	08 Sep 60	387UNTS49	105557
UK Great Britain	USA (United States)	14 Oct 60	398UNTS165	105721
Nigeria	USA (United States)	19 Oct 60	394UNTS113	105672
Cuba	Romania	28 Oct 60	457UNTS9	106574
WHO (World Health)	Upper Volta	15 Nov 60	383UNTS91	105496
Fed of Malaya	WHO (World Health)	25 Nov 60	387UNTS37	105556
WHO (World Health)	Yemen	03 Dec 60	395UNTS187	105685
Dahomey	WHO (World Health)	07 Dec 60	387UNTS277	105567
Netherlands	United Arab Rep	08 Dec 60	455UNTS276	106547
Congo (Brazzaville)	WHO (World Health)	12 Dec 60	399UNTS105	105737
Thailand	USA (United States)	23 Dec 60	405UNTS135	105830
Niger	WHO (World Health)	28 Dec 60	394UNTS195	105679
UK Great Britain	USSR (Soviet Union)	09 Jan 61	404UNTS175	105810
Korea, South	WHO (World Health)	20 Jan 61	406UNTS269	200589
UK Great Britain	USA (United States)	20 Jan 61	402UNTS153	105783
Multilateral		28 Jan 61	387UNTS202	105563
Ivory Coast	WHO (World Health)	30 Jan 61	395UNTS205	105686
WHO (World Health)	Togo	03 Feb 61	394UNTS207	105680
Chad	WHO (World Health)	03 Feb 61	394UNTS161	105676
India	USA (United States)	07 Feb 61	462UNTS57	106671
Central Afri Rep	WHO (World Health)	13 Feb 61	394UNTS149	105675
Cuba	Poland	06 Mar 61	484UNTS123	107020
Multilateral		08 Mar 61	396UNTS255	200584
Afghanistan	Japan	15 Mar 61	450UNTS373	106480
UK Great Britain	USA (United States)	15 Mar 61	404UNTS207	105811
Kuwait	WHO (World Health)	16 Mar 61	397UNTS315	200588
Ceylon (Sri Lanka)	Japan	20 Mar 61	450UNTS385	106481
UK Great Britain	USA (United States)	29 Mar 61	405UNTS107	105826
France	USA (United States)	31 Mar 61	409UNTS136	105881
UK Great Britain	USA (United States)	06 Apr 61	404UNTS215	105812
Mauritania	WHO (World Health)	17 Apr 61	396UNTS301	200587
Mali	WHO (World Health)	27 Apr 61	407UNTS66	105860
Gabon	WHO (World Health)	27 Apr 61	397UNTS215	105707
Australia	USA (United States)	09 May 61	409UNTS203	105886
Australia	USA (United States)	22 May 61	419UNTS3	106026
Somalia	USSR (Soviet Union)	02 Jun 61	457UNTS263	106587
Australia	USA (United States)	05 Jun 61	409UNTS279	105892
Netherlands	Euratom	25 Jul 61	462UNTS263	106686
Morocco	WHO (World Health)	09 Aug 61	412UNTS192	105932
WHO (World Health)	Somalia	17 Aug 61	423UNTS111	106088
Tunisia	USSR (Soviet Union)	30 Aug 61	437UNTS243	106310
UK Great Britain	USA (United States)	08 Sep 61	418UNTS53	106016
Iraq	WHO (World Health)	13 Sep 61	419UNTS69	106030
Multilateral		20 Sep 61	407UNTS52	105859
Dahomey	Israel	28 Sep 61	448UNTS151	106429
Germany, West	USA (United States)	29 Sep 61	424UNTS113	106103
IAEA (Atom Energy)	Yugoslavia	04 Oct 61	412UNTS226	105935
Multilateral		04 Oct 61	412UNTS210	105934
Malagasy	WHO (World Health)	13 Oct 61	421UNTS273	106064
Multilateral		16 Oct 61	410UNTS242	105908
Brazil	Poland	19 Oct 61	552UNTS75	108050
Multilateral		07 Nov 61	412UNTS258	105937
United Arab Rep	UK Great Britain	14 Nov 61	449UNTS129	106455
Guatemala	Israel	27 Nov 61	448UNTS191	106431
Multilateral		27 Dec 61	425UNTS83	106120
Ghana	USA (United States)	03 Jan 62	433UNTS147	106237
Ethiopia	WHO (World Health)	11 Jan 62	423UNTS99	106087
Paraguay	USA (United States)	16 Jan 62	433UNTS169	106240

PARTY ONE	PARTY TWO	DATE	CITATION	NUMBER
Research and development (Cont.)				
Multilateral		17 Jan 62	419UNTS294	106033
Multilateral		20 Jan 62	429UNTS230	200596
Multilateral		13 Feb 62	422UNTS288	200594
Multilateral		21 Feb 62	423UNTS151	106091
Multilateral		01 Mar 62	423UNTS122	106089
Pakistan	IAEA (Atom Energy)	05 Mar 62	425UNTS17	106115
USA (United States)	USSR (Soviet Union)	08 Mar 62	460UNTS3	106630
WHO (World Health)	Sudan	11 Mar 62	432UNTS325	106226
Argentina	USA (United States)	16 Mar 62	454UNTS3	106535
Nigeria	WHO (World Health)	27 Mar 62	429UNTS123	106194
Brazil	Japan	28 Mar 62	451UNTS125	106489
Multilateral		10 Apr 62	429UNTS78	106192
Multilateral		18 Apr 62	463UNTS44	106692
Multilateral		14 May 62	544UNTS39	107910
Gabon	Israel	15 May 62	448UNTS211	106433
Multilateral		17 May 62	429UNTS46	106189
United Arab Rep	USA (United States)	21 May 62	458UNTS197	106601
Central Afri Rep	Israel	13 Jun 62	448UNTS265	106439
Libya	WHO (World Health)	16 Jun 62	437UNTS127	106301
WHO (World Health)	Sierra Leone	19 Jun 62	439UNTS151	106327
Israel	USA (United States)	22 Jun 62	448UNTS273	106440
Israel	Peru	25 Jun 62	515UNTS263	107464
Germany, West	Syria	25 Jun 62	489UNTS71	107135
Israel	Liberia	25 Jun 62	448UNTS295	106442
Israel	Liberia	25 Jun 62	448UNTS287	106441
WHO (World Health)	Senegal	06 Aug 62	435UNTS179	106279
Multilateral		12 Aug 62	443UNTS266	106365
WHO (World Health)	Western Samoa	14 Aug 62	437UNTS317	200598
Multilateral		29 Aug 62	443UNTS280	106366
Italy	USA (United States)	05 Sep 62	461UNTS185	106663
Iran	United Nations	05 Sep 62	442UNTS249	106353
Israel	Rwanda	23 Oct 62	515UNTS291	107466
Cameroon	Israel	24 Oct 62	449UNTS15	106447
Multilateral		15 Nov 62	448UNTS50	106424
WHO (World Health)	Syria	18 Nov 62	480UNTS249	106972
Germany, West	USA (United States)	20 Nov 62	505UNTS263	107377
France	UK Great Britain	29 Nov 62	453UNTS325	106534
Multilateral		06 Dec 62	450UNTS240	106471
Cameroon	WHO (World Health)	08 Dec 62	451UNTS215	106496
Multilateral		12 Dec 62	457UNTS72	106578
Algeria	WHO (World Health)	20 Dec 62	463UNTS135	106698
Belgium	Tunisia	21 Dec 62	482UNTS3	106987
India	United Nations	27 Dec 62	450UNTS3	106464
Canada	USA (United States)	28 Dec 62	471UNTS13	106818
UK Great Britain	USSR (Soviet Union)	21 Jan 63	475UNTS3	106887
Multilateral		21 Jan 63	453UNTS20	106517
Iraq	USA (United States)	23 Jan 63	488UNTS163	107126
Ethiopia	USA (United States)	25 Jan 63	473UNTS27	106851
Israel	Tanganyika	28 Jan 63	516UNTS39	107468
India	USA (United States)	01 Feb 63	473UNTS37	106852
Multilateral		05 Feb 63	453UNTS36	106518
United Nations	United Arab Rep	08 Feb 63	453UNTS79	106520
Multilateral		14 Feb 63	453UNTS168	106524
Multilateral		06 Mar 63	455UNTS386	106552
Multilateral		18 Apr 63	463UNTS121	106697
Multilateral		06 May 63	463UNTS78	106694
Multilateral		09 May 63	463UNTS159	106700
Belgium	Venezuela	15 May 63	470UNTS259	106812
Multilateral		22 May 63	483UNTS72	107007
Multilateral		24 May 63	466UNTS346	106754
Mongolia	WHO (World Health)	21 Jun 63	472UNTS373	106848
Austria	USA (United States)	25 Jun 63	479UNTS223	106956
Multilateral		23 Jul 63	471UNTS158	106831
Multilateral		31 Jul 63	472UNTS220	106842
Burundi	WHO (World Health)	08 Aug 63	477UNTS346	106928

PARTY ONE	PARTY TWO	DATE	CITATION	NUMBER
Research and development (Cont.)				
Cameroon	UK Great Britain	20 Aug 63	539UNTS233	107834
Afghanistan	USA (United States)	20 Aug 63	488UNTS41	107118
Argentina	USA (United States)	21 Aug 63	488UNTS61	107119
Multilateral		27 Aug 63	511UNTS210	107435
Multilateral		10 Sep 63	480UNTS100	106965
Ecuador	USA (United States)	20 Sep 63	488UNTS147	107125
Jamaica	WHO (World Health)	25 Sep 63	481UNTS125	106980
Czechoslovakia	Yugoslavia	05 Oct 63	504UNTS151	107356
UK Great Britain	USA (United States)	11 Oct 63	483UNTS3	107005
Hungary	Yugoslavia	15 Oct 63	577UNTS49	108372
Multilateral		30 Oct 63	480UNTS180	106968
WHO (World Health)	Tanganyika	05 Nov 63	496UNTS193	107252
Multilateral		07 Nov 63	480UNTS232	106971
Multilateral		08 Nov 63	482UNTS286	106999
UNESCO (Educ/Cult)	United Arab Rep	09 Nov 63	489UNTS233	107142
Belgium	Romania	13 Nov 63	520UNTS119	107513
Argentina	USA (United States)	30 Nov 63	505UNTS131	107369
Multilateral		03 Dec 63	529UNTS217	107663
IAEA (Atom Energy)	Yugoslavia	07 Dec 63	501UNTS273	107322
Belgium	Poland	09 Dec 63	514UNTS195	107448
New Zealand	Western Samoa	31 Dec 63	521UNTS163	107519
Finland	IAEA (Atom Energy)	27 Jan 64	501UNTS213	107319
Multilateral		28 Jan 64	502UNTS321	107336
Multilateral		20 Feb 64	491UNTS30	107172
USA (United States)	USSR (Soviet Union)	22 Feb 64	526UNTS131	107605
Multilateral		28 Feb 64	501UNTS245	107321
Spain	USA (United States)	18 Mar 64	535UNTS343	107789
Canada	USA (United States)	06 May 64	524UNTS173	107572
France	UK Great Britain	03 Jun 64	539UNTS253	107836
Cuba	Czechoslovakia	03 Jun 64	527UNTS205	107626
Rwanda	WHO (World Health)	22 Jun 64	514UNTS11	107440
Multilateral		23 Jun 64	506UNTS108	107383
Rwanda	WHO (World Health)	23 Jun 64	514UNTS157	107445
WHO (World Health)	Trinidad/Tobago	23 Jun 64	503UNTS167	107342
Multilateral		28 Jun 64	519UNTS14	107499
Australia	USA (United States)	17 Aug 64	530UNTS209	107683
Dominican Republic	USA (United States)	28 Aug 64	531UNTS35	107691
Australia	USA (United States)	28 Aug 64	510UNTS201	107415
Australia	UN Special Fund	30 Sep 64	510UNTS277	107419
Czechoslovakia	Mongolia	21 Oct 64	545UNTS91	107926
Multilateral		24 Oct 64	514UNTS220	200608
Asian Productivity	ILO (Labor Org)	27 Oct 64	516UNTS367	200610
Multilateral		07 Nov 64	548UNTS3	107965
Multilateral		11 Nov 64	515UNTS94	107456
Belgium	Mexico	19 Nov 64	546UNTS217	107949
India	United Nations	25 Nov 64	519UNTS47	107501
Germany, West	Thailand	23 Dec 64	525UNTS177	107589
Germany, West	Thailand	23 Dec 64	525UNTS201	107592
UK Great Britain	USSR (Soviet Union)	06 Jan 65	543UNTS77	107897
Malawi	WHO (World Health)	06 Jan 65	525UNTS165	107588
Malawi	WHO (World Health)	08 Jan 65	524UNTS281	107579
Ecuador	Netherlands	14 Jan 65	551UNTS129	108038
Denmark	Thailand	25 Jan 65	530UNTS173	107680
Spain	USA (United States)	26 Jan 65	542UNTS81	107881
Multilateral		27 Jan 65	523UNTS102	107556
Multilateral		02 Feb 65	523UNTS256	107560
Germany, West	Jamaica	03 Feb 65	531UNTS143	107700
Multilateral		12 Feb 65	525UNTS148	107587
UK Great Britain	USSR (Soviet Union)	13 Feb 65	543UNTS43	107896
Mexico	USA (United States)	27 Feb 65	546UNTS135	107940
UK Great Britain	USA (United States)	10 May 65	545UNTS181	107934
USA (United States)	Uruguay	17 May 65	564UNTS69	108221
Bulgaria	Czechoslovakia	22 May 65	545UNTS65	107925
Multilateral		02 Jun 65	537UNTS348	200611
Canada	USA (United States)	29 Jun 65	549UNTS273	108003

PARTY ONE	PARTY TWO	DATE	CITATION	NUMBER
Research and development (Cont.)				
Multilateral		02 Jul 65	592UNTS215	108575
Israel	Sierra Leone	22 Aug 65	550UNTS285	108023
Poland	WHO (World Health)	26 Aug 65	552UNTS3	108047
Multilateral		13 Sep 65	547UNTS264	107962
Multilateral		21 Oct 65	547UNTS216	107959
East Afri Service	United Nations	27 Nov 65	550UNTS375	200616
Panama	USA (United States)	15 Feb 66	586UNTS27	108494
Brazil	Denmark	25 Feb 66	590UNTS95	108549
Israel	Kenya	25 Feb 66	582UNTS23	108455
WHO (World Health)	Singapore	28 Mar 66	562UNTS59	108195
Spain	USA (United States)	14 Apr 66	586UNTS79	108497
Denmark	Iran	14 Jun 66	597UNTS283	108652
France	USSR (Soviet Union)	30 Jun 66	589UNTS99	108537
Morocco	USSR (Soviet Union)	27 Oct 66	608UNTS197	108816
United Nations	Sudan	08 Nov 66	576UNTS85	108365
Multilateral		28 Dec 67	0UNTS0	109322
New Zealand	USA (United States)	09 Jul 68	0UNTS0	109208
Australia	USA (United States)	13 Jan 69	0UNTS0	109460
General economics				
Taiwan	USA (United States)	02 Jun 42	14UNTS343	200092
USA (United States)	Yugoslavia	24 Jul 42	34UNTS361	200179
Multilateral		22 Mar 45	70UNTS237	200241
France	USA (United States)	28 May 46	84UNTS167	101127
Denmark	USSR (Soviet Union)	17 Aug 46	8UNTS201	100124
Czechoslovakia	Poland	04 Apr 47	85UNTS62	101146
Multilateral		17 Mar 48	19UNTS51	100304
Multilateral		18 Apr 51	261UNTS140	103729
Ethiopia	Yugoslavia	21 Aug 53	378UNTS105	105421
Guatemala	Honduras	22 Aug 56	263UNTS49	103767
Indonesia	UK Great Britain	29 Jun 61	443UNTS255	106364
Ivory Coast	Netherlands	26 Apr 65	634UNTS81	109053
Italy	Romania	06 Sep 65	604UNTS49	108742
Argentina	Germany, West	01 Mar 66	635UNTS247	109087
Bel-Lux Econ Union	Bulgaria	14 Jun 66	601UNTS167	108694
USSR (Soviet Union)	Zambia	26 May 67	643UNTS179	109191
Multilateral		20 Jul 67	0UNTS0	109259
Germany, West	Romania	03 Aug 67	642UNTS47	109164
Netherlands	Poland	22 Aug 67	0UNTS0	109276
Denmark	Poland	15 Nov 67	643UNTS383	109203
Austria	Canada	28 Feb 68	636UNTS141	109101
Netherlands	Yugoslavia	13 Mar 68	0UNTS0	109297
General trade				
Canada	USA (United States)	13 Dec 40	117UNTS173	200368
UK Great Britain	USSR (Soviet Union)	16 Aug 41	91UNTS341	200269
Panama	USA (United States)	18 May 42	124UNTS221	200422
Taiwan	USA (United States)	02 Jun 42	14UNTS343	200092
USA (United States)	Venezuela	13 Oct 42	138UNTS282	200451
Mexico	USA (United States)	18 Nov 42	120UNTS183	200392
Canada	Taiwan	22 Mar 44	14UNTS397	200096
Canada	Czechoslovakia	01 Mar 45	45UNTS283	200185
Multilateral		20 Mar 45	2UNTS299	200022
Canada	Norway	25 Jun 45	45UNTS297	200186
Belgium	Canada	25 Oct 45	230UNTS127	103180
UK Great Britain	USA (United States)	06 Dec 45	126UNTS13	101679
Canada	Netherlands	05 Feb 46	43UNTS3	100658
Canada	Taiwan	07 Feb 46	43UNTS23	100659
Canada	UK Great Britain	06 Mar 46	20UNTS13	100312
Denmark	Norway	30 Mar 46	29UNTS163	100438
Canada	France	09 Apr 46	43UNTS43	100660
Bolivia	USA (United States)	10 Jun 46	13UNTS19	100197
Romania	Yugoslavia	26 Jun 46	116UNTS21	101566
Luxembourg	USA (United States)	03 Jul 46	32UNTS85	100491
Ethiopia	USA (United States)	04 Jul 46	13UNTS27	100198
Norway	USA (United States)	08 Jul 46	13UNTS35	100199

PARTY ONE	PARTY TWO	DATE	CITATION	NUMBER
General trade (Cont.)				
Belgium	USA (United States)	11 Jul 46	13UNTS43	100200
Spain	USA (United States)	11 Jul 46	13UNTS51	100201
United Arab Rep	USA (United States)	15 Aug 46	13UNTS59	100202
Portugal	USA (United States)	26 Aug 46	13UNTS67	100203
Denmark	USA (United States)	10 Sep 46	13UNTS75	100204
USA (United States)	Yugoslavia	03 Oct 46	13UNTS83	100205
Dominican Republic	USA (United States)	07 Oct 46	13UNTS91	100206
Multilateral		30 Oct 46	27UNTS77	100401
Czechoslovakia	Poland	10 Mar 47	25UNTS231	100365
Poland	Sweden	18 Mar 47	12UNTS295	100190
Sweden	USA (United States)	24 Jun 47	36UNTS25	100565
Haiti	USA (United States)	04 Jul 47	22UNTS165	100335
Hungary	Yugoslavia	24 Jul 47	114UNTS3	101554
Czechoslovakia	Greece	30 Jul 47	185UNTS115	102463
Multilateral		19 Sep 47	30UNTS269	100462
South Africa	UK Great Britain	09 Oct 47	17UNTS239	100278
Finland	Norway	15 Nov 47	29UNTS179	100439
Hungary	USSR (Soviet Union)	18 Feb 48	48UNTS163	100743
Bulgaria	USSR (Soviet Union)	18 Mar 48	48UNTS135	100741
Hungary	Yugoslavia	18 Mar 48	113UNTS219	101552
Czechoslovakia	Poland	05 Apr 48	31UNTS325	100481
Finland	USSR (Soviet Union)	06 Apr 48	48UNTS149	100742
Norway	Sweden	29 Apr 48	26UNTS33	100375
Norway	Sweden	29 Apr 48	26UNTS41	100376
Bulgaria	Poland	29 May 48	26UNTS213	100389
Netherlands	UK Great Britain	11 Jun 48	66UNTS183	100853
Spain	UK Great Britain	23 Jun 48	66UNTS193	100854
France	USA (United States)	28 Jun 48	31UNTS115	100472
Greece	USA (United States)	02 Jul 48	31UNTS131	100474
Netherlands	USA (United States)	02 Jul 48	32UNTS77	100490
Turkey	USA (United States)	04 Jul 48	34UNTS185	100536
France	USA (United States)	09 Jul 48	32UNTS93	100492
Multilateral		14 Jul 48	31UNTS123	100473
USA (United States)	Yugoslavia	19 Jul 48	89UNTS43	101208
Portugal	USA (United States)	28 Sep 48	31UNTS139	100475
Denmark	Poland	14 Dec 48	81UNTS33	101060
Argentina	Denmark	14 Dec 48	74UNTS41	100956
Norway	Poland	31 Dec 48	29UNTS3	100430
Poland	Romania	26 Jan 49	85UNTS21	101143
Allied Milit Occup	Norway	17 Feb 49	30UNTS137	100451
Denmark	Greece	25 Feb 49	78UNTS335	101023
Multilateral		16 Mar 49	29UNTS95	100436
Multilateral		23 Mar 49	203UNTS179	102746
Multilateral		04 Apr 49	34UNTS243	100541
Multilateral		20 Jun 49	128UNTS141	101718
Argentina	UK Great Britain	27 Jun 49	83UNTS217	101110
Belgium	Chile	23 Aug 49	46UNTS163	100708
Argentina	Norway	09 Sep 49	42UNTS125	100646
Denmark	Poland	07 Dec 49	81UNTS21	101059
Paraguay	UK Great Britain	03 Apr 50	99UNTS81	101372
Denmark	Finland	08 Jul 50	73UNTS191	100953
Denmark	Spain	12 Jul 50	71UNTS135	100914
Denmark	Italy	04 Oct 50	78UNTS341	101024
Colombia	Denmark	26 Jan 51	87UNTS161	101171
Canada	Spain	29 Jan 52	233UNTS117	103255
Denmark	Spain	28 Jul 52	135UNTS255	101825
USA (United States)	Venezuela	28 Aug 52	178UNTS51	102336
Canada	United Arab Rep	03 Dec 52	233UNTS145	103259
Germany, West	USA (United States)	27 Feb 53	224UNTS13	103067
Brazil	Ecuador	04 May 53	369UNTS37	105249
Germany, West	USA (United States)	02 Jun 53	231UNTS151	103214
Argentina	USSR (Soviet Union)	05 Aug 53	221UNTS99	103004
Ethiopia	Yugoslavia	21 Aug 53	378UNTS105	105421
Denmark	Uruguay	09 Sep 53	256UNTS149	103625
Brazil	UK Great Britain	01 Oct 53	183UNTS207	102430

PARTY ONE	PARTY TWO	DATE	CITATION	NUMBER
General trade (Cont.)				
Canada	USA (United States)	12 Nov 53	223UNTS139	103062
Bulgaria	Greece	05 Dec 53	225UNTS145	103096
Czechoslovakia	Greece	01 Feb 54	225UNTS95	103092
Multilateral		01 Mar 54	256UNTS31	103622
Greece	Romania	19 May 54	225UNTS27	103084
Greece	Hungary	05 Jun 54	299UNTS295	104321
Hungary	UK Great Britain	19 Aug 54	199UNTS149	102681
USSR (Soviet Union)	Yugoslavia	05 Jan 55	240UNTS225	103405
Turkey	UK Great Britain	17 Jan 55	204UNTS195	102758
Argentina	UK Great Britain	31 Mar 55	210UNTS223	102840
Bulgaria	UK Great Britain	22 Sep 55	222UNTS349	103039
Austria	USSR (Soviet Union)	17 Oct 55	240UNTS289	103409
Syria	USSR (Soviet Union)	16 Nov 55	259UNTS71	103683
Denmark	UK Great Britain	27 Feb 56	252UNTS83	103558
Burma	Israel	05 Mar 56	280UNTS209	104060
Burma	Yugoslavia	07 Mar 56	386UNTS207	105542
Argentina	UK Great Britain	30 Jun 56	269UNTS235	103884
Canada	Honduras	11 Jul 56	305UNTS39	104411
Costa Rica	Denmark	26 Sep 56	341UNTS305	104893
Poland	United Arab Rep	02 Feb 57	319UNTS221	104633
Turkey	UK Great Britain	28 Feb 57	310UNTS69	104488
Denmark	Paraguay	18 May 57	286UNTS117	104163
Denmark	Uruguay	04 Jun 57	286UNTS107	104162
Argentina	Italy	25 Nov 57	305UNTS275	104424
Brazil	Ecuador	05 Mar 58	369UNTS43	105250
USSR (Soviet Union)	Vietnam, North	12 Mar 58	356UNTS149	105094
Multilateral		03 Apr 58	336UNTS177	104806
China People's Rep	USSR (Soviet Union)	23 Apr 58	313UNTS135	104534
Multilateral		18 Jun 58	386UNTS355	105553
Multilateral		01 Dec 58	385UNTS137	105534
Czechoslovakia	Japan	15 Dec 59	383UNTS277	105505
Multilateral		16 Aug 60	382UNTS8	105476
Greece	Poland	08 Nov 60	483UNTS141	107011
USA (United States)	Upper Volta	01 Jun 61	410UNTS223	105906
Japan	USA (United States)	22 Jun 61	410UNTS53	105896
Indonesia	UK Great Britain	29 Jun 61	443UNTS255	106364
Sweden	USA (United States)	05 Mar 62	459UNTS17	106610
EEC (Econ Commnty)	USA (United States)	07 Mar 62	445UNTS195	106387
Netherlands	USA (United States)	24 Apr 62	436UNTS93	106289
Multilateral		15 May 62	444UNTS3	106367
UK Great Britain	USA (United States)	10 Dec 62	471UNTS91	106824
Spain	USA (United States)	31 Dec 62	471UNTS99	106825
South Africa	Spain	08 Feb 63	458UNTS79	106593
Austria	Bulgaria	02 May 63	535UNTS143	107778
Austria	Mongolia	15 Jul 63	496UNTS171	107251
Korea, South	USA (United States)	18 Mar 64	524UNTS263	107578
Morocco	USA (United States)	29 Dec 64	593UNTS185	108584
Greece	Japan	09 Apr 65	632UNTS61	109008
Argentina	Brazil	23 Apr 65	0UNTS0	109411
Multilateral		28 May 65	559UNTS273	108163
Argentina	Yugoslavia	09 Jun 65	601UNTS3	108684
Multilateral		08 Jul 65	597UNTS3	108641
Italy	Romania	06 Sep 65	604UNTS49	108742
Argentina	India	26 Mar 66	601UNTS201	108697
Bulgaria	Singapore	05 May 66	631UNTS165	108993
Australia	Poland	20 Jun 66	638UNTS201	109136
Argentina	USA (United States)	08 Aug 66	606UNTS209	108786
Japan	USA (United States)	06 Sep 66	616UNTS215	108898
Romania	United Arab Rep	14 Nov 66	642UNTS129	109169
Ghana	Romania	23 Nov 66	642UNTS63	109165
Guinea	Romania	01 Dec 66	642UNTS89	109167
Czechoslovakia	Germany, East	17 Mar 67	609UNTS187	108831
Denmark	Paraguay	03 May 67	608UNTS55	108812
Australia	Romania	18 May 67	642UNTS25	109162
Germany, East	Hungary	18 May 67	617UNTS3	108905

PARTY ONE	PARTY TWO	DATE	CITATION	NUMBER
General trade (Cont.)				
Ecuador	Romania	10 Oct 67	642UNTS33	109163
Australia	Hungary	05 Dec 67	638UNTS209	109137
Hungary	Poland	16 May 68	0UNTS0	109292
Establishment of trade relations				
Brazil	Paraguay	14 Jun 41	88UNTS401	200255
USA (United States)	Uruguay	21 Jul 42	120UNTS211	200393
Brazil	UNRRA (Relief)	12 Oct 44	67UNTS321	200228
Poland	Yugoslavia	23 Nov 45	115UNTS3	101555
Italy	USA (United States)	06 Dec 45	3UNTS131	100027
Belgium	Norway	21 Feb 46	31UNTS435	100485
USA (United States)	Yemen	04 May 46	4UNTS165	100043
Italy	Norway	20 Jul 46	30UNTS177	100456
Hungary	Norway	27 Aug 46	31UNTS3	100465
Norway	Yugoslavia	30 Aug 46	30UNTS187	100457
Australia	Sweden	16 Sep 46	10UNTS63	100143
Taiwan	USA (United States)	04 Nov 46	25UNTS69	100359
Hungary	Yugoslavia	01 Jan 47	113UNTS63	101548
Norway	USSR (Soviet Union)	19 Feb 47	30UNTS293	100464
Belgium	Turkey	12 Mar 47	37UNTS215	100578
Austria	Norway	14 Apr 47	31UNTS21	100466
Denmark	Yugoslavia	28 Jun 47	78UNTS242	101020
Multilateral		30 Oct 47	55UNTS188	100814
Finland	USSR (Soviet Union)	01 Dec 47	217UNTS3	102942
UK Great Britain	USSR (Soviet Union)	27 Dec 47	91UNTS113	101245
Norway	Poland	04 Feb 48	30UNTS205	100458
Denmark	Guatemala	04 Mar 48	96UNTS223	101339
Hungary	Poland	13 May 48	25UNTS301	100369
Greece	Lebanon	06 Oct 48	87UNTS351	101179
Multilateral		22 Jul 49	557UNTS211	108135
Mexico	Netherlands	27 Jan 50	123UNTS197	101661
Belgium	Mexico	16 Sep 50	188UNTS119	102523
Multilateral		18 Apr 51	261UNTS140	103729
Norway	Pakistan	21 May 51	318UNTS163	104613
France	USSR (Soviet Union)	03 Sep 51	221UNTS79	103003
Ireland	Spain	19 Dec 51	0UNTS0	109228
Czechoslovakia	Romania	31 Jul 52	362UNTS123	105185
Denmark	Israel	14 Nov 52	160UNTS279	102113
Denmark	Uruguay	04 Mar 53	250UNTS51	103517
Multilateral		24 Jul 53	250UNTS108	103520
Ceylon (Sri Lanka)	Yugoslavia	30 Jul 53	337UNTS103	104819
Argentina	USSR (Soviet Union)	05 Aug 53	221UNTS99	103004
Ethiopia	Yugoslavia	21 Aug 53	378UNTS105	105421
Ceylon (Sri Lanka)	Ireland	20 Nov 53	345UNTS189	104967
Germany, West	Ireland	02 Dec 53	558UNTS38	108139
Cuba	UK Great Britain	18 Dec 53	186UNTS157	102490
Lebanon	USSR (Soviet Union)	30 Apr 54	226UNTS109	103111
Greece	Hungary	05 Jun 54	299UNTS285	104320
Germany, West	USA (United States)	29 Oct 54	273UNTS3	103943
Ceylon (Sri Lanka)	United Arab Rep	17 Nov 54	315UNTS3	104554
Multilateral		21 Dec 54	258UNTS322	103678
USSR (Soviet Union)	Yugoslavia	05 Jan 55	240UNTS207	103404
Bulgaria	Yugoslavia	16 Mar 55	397UNTS83	105702
Turkey	USA (United States)	10 Jun 55	238UNTS149	103359
Belgium	USA (United States)	15 Jun 55	235UNTS133	103299
Canada	USA (United States)	15 Jun 55	235UNTS176	103301
Israel	USA (United States)	12 Jul 55	219UNTS185	102974
Switzerland	USA (United States)	18 Jul 55	239UNTS311	103388
Taiwan	USA (United States)	18 Jul 55	235UNTS221	103304
Netherlands	USA (United States)	18 Jul 55	240UNTS347	103412
Lebanon	USA (United States)	18 Jul 55	239UNTS247	103383
Colombia	USA (United States)	19 Jul 55	235UNTS233	103305
Spain	USA (United States)	19 Jul 55	239UNTS299	103387
USA (United States)	Venezuela	21 Jul 55	238UNTS121	103357
Portugal	USA (United States)	21 Jul 55	239UNTS283	103386

PARTY ONE	PARTY TWO	DATE	CITATION	NUMBER
Establishment of trade relations (Cont.)				
Denmark	USA (United States)	25 Jul 55	235UNTS245	103306
Philippines	USA (United States)	27 Jul 55	239UNTS271	103385
Italy	USA (United States)	28 Jul 55	239UNTS235	103382
Argentina	USA (United States)	29 Jul 55	235UNTS121	103298
Brazil	USA (United States)	03 Aug 55	235UNTS159	103300
Greece	USA (United States)	04 Aug 55	235UNTS257	103307
Chile	USA (United States)	08 Aug 55	235UNTS209	103303
Pakistan	USA (United States)	11 Aug 55	239UNTS259	103384
Iran	USA (United States)	15 Aug 55	284UNTS93	104132
USSR (Soviet Union)	Yemen	31 Oct 55	240UNTS317	103410
Italy	Lebanon	04 Nov 55	267UNTS113	103838
Italy	Syria	10 Nov 55	267UNTS157	103841
Japan	USA (United States)	14 Nov 55	240UNTS361	103413
Syria	USSR (Soviet Union)	16 Nov 55	259UNTS71	103683
USA (United States)	Uruguay	13 Jan 56	240UNTS401	103415
Sweden	USA (United States)	18 Jan 56	240UNTS413	103416
Peru	USA (United States)	25 Jan 56	240UNTS425	103417
Korea, South	USA (United States)	03 Feb 56	240UNTS129	103401
Germany, West	USA (United States)	13 Feb 56	253UNTS119	103580
Canada	USSR (Soviet Union)	29 Feb 56	252UNTS165	103566
Thailand	USA (United States)	13 Mar 56	253UNTS105	103579
Ceylon (Sri Lanka)	Romania	16 Mar 56	315UNTS41	104558
Ceylon (Sri Lanka)	Hungary	04 Jun 56	315UNTS13	104555
Austria	USA (United States)	08 Jun 56	253UNTS139	103581
New Zealand	USA (United States)	13 Jun 56	253UNTS155	103582
Bulgaria	Ceylon (Sri Lanka)	19 Jun 56	315UNTS23	104556
France	USA (United States)	19 Jun 56	281UNTS341	104087
Switzerland	USA (United States)	21 Jun 56	279UNTS41	104033
Multilateral		07 Sep 56	266UNTS3	103822
Multilateral		25 Mar 57	294UNTS2	104300
Ceylon (Sri Lanka)	Italy	23 Apr 57	337UNTS115	104820
Denmark	Peru	10 Jun 57	406UNTS63	105839
Ceylon (Sri Lanka)	China People's Rep	19 Sep 57	337UNTS137	104821
China People's Rep	Denmark	01 Dec 57	309UNTS241	104475
Japan	USSR (Soviet Union)	06 Dec 57	325UNTS35	104694
Canada	Fed Rhod/Nyasaland	06 Feb 58	392UNTS27	105636
Ceylon (Sri Lanka)	USSR (Soviet Union)	08 Feb 58	348UNTS159	104999
USSR (Soviet Union)	Vietnam, North	12 Mar 58	356UNTS149	105094
Germany, West	UK Great Britain	18 Apr 58	343UNTS241	104928
Germany, West	USSR (Soviet Union)	25 Apr 58	346UNTS71	104978
Japan	Poland	26 Apr 58	340UNTS221	104866
Iraq	USSR (Soviet Union)	11 Oct 58	328UNTS95	104730
Israel	Yugoslavia	11 Dec 58	386UNTS271	105547
Haiti	Japan	17 Dec 58	518UNTS91	107492
Iraq	Romania	24 Dec 58	405UNTS243	105836
Multilateral		30 Jan 59	0UNTS0	109234
Japan	Yugoslavia	28 Feb 59	341UNTS179	104883
United Arab Rep	UK Great Britain	28 Feb 59	343UNTS159	104925
Poland	USA (United States)	10 Jun 59	347UNTS41	104989
Guinea	UK Great Britain	22 Oct 59	351UNTS341	105033
Czechoslovakia	Japan	15 Dec 59	383UNTS277	105505
Multilateral		04 Jan 60	370UNTS3	105266
Cuba	USSR (Soviet Union)	13 Feb 60	369UNTS17	105248
Fed of Malaya	Japan	10 May 60	383UNTS293	105506
Fed Rhod/Nyasaland	South Africa	16 May 60	376UNTS217	105381
Brazil	Greece	30 Jul 60	607UNTS245	108808
New Zealand	Yugoslavia	09 Sep 60	402UNTS119	105781
Tunisia	UK Great Britain	17 Jan 61	566UNTS2	108236
Honduras	USA (United States)	18 Jan 61	402UNTS169	105785
USA (United States)	Yugoslavia	19 Jan 61	402UNTS163	105784
Korea, South	Philippines	24 Feb 61	423UNTS217	106094
Austria	USA (United States)	29 Mar 61	459UNTS45	106612
Ghana	USSR (Soviet Union)	02 Jul 61	0UNTS0	109380
Argentina	Japan	20 Dec 61	613UNTS323	108859
Argentina	USA (United States)	22 Jun 62	458UNTS97	106594

PARTY ONE	PARTY TWO	DATE	CITATION	NUMBER
Establishment of trade relations (Cont.)				
Algeria	France	03 Jul 62	507UNTS25	107395
Chile	Netherlands	13 Jul 62	466UNTS109	106740
Cameroon	Greece	29 Oct 62	538UNTS185	107815
Brazil	USSR (Soviet Union)	20 Apr 63	0UNTS0	109256
Brazil	USSR (Soviet Union)	20 Apr 63	0UNTS0	109257
Multilateral		30 Apr 63	570UNTS23	108285
India	USSR (Soviet Union)	10 Jun 63	0UNTS0	109382
Dahomey	USSR (Soviet Union)	10 Jul 63	528UNTS167	107640
Cameroon	UK Great Britain	29 Jul 63	478UNTS148	106935
Multilateral		13 Aug 63	592UNTS139	108572
Tanganyika	USSR (Soviet Union)	14 Aug 63	493UNTS195	107215
Multilateral		23 Oct 63	506UNTS197	107388
USSR (Soviet Union)	Yemen	21 Mar 64	553UNTS267	108094
Taiwan	Peru	08 Jun 64	548UNTS151	107976
Taiwan	Ecuador	17 Jun 64	533UNTS141	107740
Japan	Korea, South	22 Jun 65	583UNTS33	108471
Singapore	USSR (Soviet Union)	02 Apr 66	631UNTS125	108992
Poland	Singapore	07 Jun 66	631UNTS189	108994
Belgium	Bulgaria	14 Jun 66	607UNTS183	108806
Australia	Bulgaria	22 Jun 66	607UNTS69	108796
Taiwan	Thailand	23 Nov 66	581UNTS125	108436
Bulgaria	USSR (Soviet Union)	27 Apr 67	631UNTS3	108983
Chad	USSR (Soviet Union)	22 Jun 67	643UNTS121	109188
Bulgaria	New Zealand	03 Nov 67	0UNTS0	109207
Israel	Singapore	24 Apr 68	642UNTS235	109176
Multilateral		24 Dec 68	0UNTS0	109369
Export quotas				
Bolivia	Brazil	25 Feb 38	51UNTS245	200192
Netherlands	UK Great Britain	14 Jun 40	2UNTS251	200018
Multilateral		12 Oct 40	161UNTS193	200485
Argentina	USA (United States)	14 Oct 41	119UNTS193	200384
Brazil	USA (United States)	03 Mar 42	105UNTS91	200324
Peru	USA (United States)	07 May 42	103UNTS219	200316
USA (United States)	Uruguay	21 Jul 42	120UNTS211	200393
Canada	USA (United States)	09 Nov 42	101UNTS233	200298
Mexico	USA (United States)	18 Nov 42	120UNTS183	200392
Mexico	USA (United States)	23 Dec 42	13UNTS231	200081
Multilateral		21 Dec 43	65UNTS231	200214
Dominican Republic	USA (United States)	11 Feb 44	109UNTS251	200363
Argentina	USA (United States)	09 May 45	139UNTS227	200453
Canada	Mexico	08 Feb 46	230UNTS183	103183
Belgium	Norway	21 Feb 46	31UNTS435	100485
Denmark	Norway	30 Mar 46	29UNTS163	100438
Multilateral		06 May 46	99UNTS181	101379
Romania	Yugoslavia	26 Jun 46	116UNTS21	101566
Albania	Yugoslavia	01 Jul 46	111UNTS3	101517
Italy	Norway	20 Jul 46	30UNTS177	100456
Norway	Yugoslavia	30 Aug 46	30UNTS187	100457
Paraguay	USA (United States)	12 Sep 46	125UNTS179	101677
Taiwan	USA (United States)	04 Nov 46	25UNTS69	100359
Czechoslovakia	USA (United States)	14 Nov 46	7UNTS119	100094
Norway	USSR (Soviet Union)	27 Dec 46	17UNTS283	100282
Netherlands	Norway	28 Jan 47	31UNTS29	100467
Romania	USSR (Soviet Union)	20 Feb 47	226UNTS79	103110
Poland	Sweden	18 Mar 47	12UNTS295	100190
Czechoslovakia	Norway	20 Mar 47	30UNTS223	100460
Belgium	Netherlands	28 Apr 47	37UNTS199	100577
Denmark	Yugoslavia	28 Jun 47	78UNTS242	101020
Czechoslovakia	Greece	30 Jul 47	185UNTS149	102466
Czechoslovakia	Greece	30 Jul 47	185UNTS143	102465
Multilateral		05 Oct 47	34UNTS23	100525
Greece	UNICEF (Children)	14 Oct 47	102UNTS39	101409
Multilateral		30 Oct 47	55UNTS188	100814
Finland	Norway	15 Nov 47	29UNTS179	100439

PARTY ONE	PARTY TWO	DATE	CITATION	NUMBER
Export quotas (Cont.)				
France	Lebanon	24 Jan 48	173UNTS99	102263
Italy	USA (United States)	02 Feb 48	79UNTS171	101040
Norway	Poland	04 Feb 48	30UNTS205	100458
Hungary	Yugoslavia	18 Mar 48	113UNTS201	101551
Norway	Sweden	29 Apr 48	26UNTS33	100375
Hungary	Poland	13 May 48	25UNTS301	100369
Norway	Switzerland	26 Jun 48	29UNTS193	100440
Ireland	UK Great Britain	31 Jul 48	86UNTS37	101151
UK Great Britain	USA (United States)	30 Sep 48	71UNTS241	100922
South Africa	UK Great Britain	06 Dec 48	118UNTS183	101607
Denmark	Turkey	15 Dec 48	76UNTS17	100975
Norway	Poland	31 Dec 48	29UNTS3	100430
Poland	UK Great Britain	14 Jan 49	83UNTS3	101100
Italy	Yugoslavia	03 Feb 49	33UNTS105	100517
France	Norway	09 Feb 49	29UNTS13	100431
Netherlands	Norway	26 Feb 49	29UNTS33	100432
Greece	Norway	12 Mar 49	30UNTS161	100454
Ireland	Sweden	25 Jun 49	558UNTS299	108148
Belgium	Netherlands	20 Aug 49	46UNTS133	100706
Czechoslovakia	UK Great Britain	28 Sep 49	86UNTS141	101156
Ireland	Netherlands	25 Nov 49	558UNTS256	108146
Ireland	USA (United States)	21 Jan 50	206UNTS269	102792
Chile	UNICEF (Children)	03 Mar 50	126UNTS119	101685
Afghanistan	India	04 Apr 50	167UNTS105	102201
Multilateral		31 May 50	74UNTS95	100957
Denmark	Finland	08 Jul 50	73UNTS191	100953
Denmark	Spain	12 Jul 50	71UNTS135	100914
India	Nepal	31 Jul 50	104UNTS3	101430
Brazil	UK Great Britain	18 Sep 50	88UNTS115	101188
Denmark	Poland	01 Oct 50	81UNTS43	101061
Multilateral		23 Dec 50	185UNTS3	102456
Finland	Ireland	06 Jan 51	558UNTS120	108140
Iran	UNICEF (Children)	02 Aug 51	247UNTS11	103457
Greece	USA (United States)	03 Aug 51	224UNTS279	103080
UNICEF (Children)	Turkey	05 Sep 51	193UNTS55	102610
Ethiopia	USA (United States)	07 Sep 51	206UNTS41	102785
Denmark	USA (United States)	01 Oct 51	421UNTS105	106056
Iraq	UNICEF (Children)	10 Dec 51	126UNTS57	101682
El Salvador	Guatemala	14 Dec 51	131UNTS131	101740
Jordan	USA (United States)	20 Dec 51	157UNTS69	102048
Ireland	Switzerland	26 Dec 51	558UNTS305	108149
UK Great Britain	USA (United States)	18 Jan 52	184UNTS79	102440
UNICEF (Children)	UK Great Britain	04 Feb 52	120UNTS147	101620
India	Syria	25 Feb 52	163UNTS55	102141
Austria	Greece	22 Mar 52	187UNTS255	102517
Libya	UNICEF (Children)	05 Apr 52	133UNTS287	200441
Liberia	UNICEF (Children)	17 Apr 52	133UNTS3	101773
UNICEF (Children)	United Arab Rep	18 May 52	324UNTS161	104684
Korea, South	USA (United States)	24 May 52	179UNTS23	102353
Greece	Syria	02 Jun 52	183UNTS251	102434
Belgium	UNICEF (Children)	17 Jun 52	171UNTS249	102228
Norway	USA (United States)	27 Jun 52	184UNTS271	102452
Jordan	UNICEF (Children)	08 Jul 52	173UNTS353	200503
UNICEF (Children)	Syria	10 Jul 52	136UNTS17	101830
Greece	Israel	22 Jul 52	219UNTS231	102978
UNICEF (Children)	UK Great Britain	25 Jul 52	135UNTS37	101812
Denmark	Spain	28 Jul 52	135UNTS255	101825
Laos	UNICEF (Children)	15 Aug 52	161UNTS323	200491
UNICEF (Children)	Vietnam, South	29 Aug 52	161UNTS335	200492
Ceylon (Sri Lanka)	Japan	06 Sep 52	314UNTS279	104552
Denmark	Israel	14 Nov 52	160UNTS275	102112
UNICEF (Children)	UK Great Britain	16 Dec 52	151UNTS359	102005
India	Pakistan	20 Feb 53	164UNTS3	102155
Turkey	Yugoslavia	26 Feb 53	247UNTS54	103460
Germany, West	UK Great Britain	27 Feb 53	330UNTS217	104747

PARTY ONE	PARTY TWO	DATE	CITATION	NUMBER
Export quotas (Cont.)				
Greece	Yugoslavia	28 Feb 53	252UNTS27	103557
Japan	USA (United States)	02 Apr 53	206UNTS143	102788
Netherlands	United Nations	09 Apr 53	163UNTS89	102143
Czechoslovakia	Denmark	23 Apr 53	174UNTS95	102280
Ethiopia	UNICEF (Children)	27 Apr 53	213UNTS169	102885
Belgium	USA (United States)	18 Jun 53	222UNTS3	103019
Fed Rhod/Nyasaland	South Africa	28 Jun 53	267UNTS270	103848
Burma	Yugoslavia	29 Jun 53	378UNTS83	105418
Italy	Switzerland	02 Jul 53	257UNTS99	103653
Multilateral		24 Jul 53	250UNTS108	103520
Argentina	USSR (Soviet Union)	05 Aug 53	221UNTS99	103004
UNICEF (Children)	UK Great Britain	07 Oct 53	180UNTS59	102375
Greece	Turkey	07 Nov 53	225UNTS163	103098
Ceylon (Sri Lanka)	Ireland	20 Nov 53	345UNTS189	104967
Japan	UNICEF (Children)	21 Nov 53	183UNTS297	200507
India	USSR (Soviet Union)	02 Dec 53	240UNTS143	103402
Bulgaria	Greece	05 Dec 53	225UNTS135	103095
Cuba	UK Great Britain	18 Dec 53	186UNTS157	102490
Czechoslovakia	Greece	01 Feb 54	225UNTS77	103091
Multilateral		01 Mar 54	256UNTS31	103622
Japan	USA (United States)	08 Mar 54	232UNTS169	103236
Afghanistan	USA (United States)	20 Mar 54	229UNTS7	103156
Lebanon	USSR (Soviet Union)	30 Apr 54	226UNTS109	103111
UNICEF (Children)	Spain	07 May 54	190UNTS357	200515
Greece	Spain	15 May 54	299UNTS261	104318
Greece	Romania	19 May 54	225UNTS17	103083
Mexico	UNICEF (Children)	20 May 54	192UNTS3	102591
Afghanistan	USA (United States)	29 May 54	234UNTS3	103268
Haiti	Italy	14 Jun 54	267UNTS97	103837
France	Greece	22 Jul 54	225UNTS199	103099
Thailand	USA (United States)	11 Aug 54	234UNTS155	103281
New Zealand	UNICEF (Children)	26 Aug 54	198UNTS173	102663
Denmark	Sweden	28 Oct 54	262UNTS211	103747
Germany, West	USA (United States)	29 Oct 54	273UNTS3	103943
Netherlands	UNICEF (Children)	31 Dec 54	202UNTS135	102729
USSR (Soviet Union)	Yugoslavia	05 Jan 55	240UNTS225	103405
Turkey	UK Great Britain	17 Jan 55	204UNTS195	102758
Greece	Japan	12 Mar 55	227UNTS33	103130
Italy	Yugoslavia	31 Mar 55	386UNTS317	105551
France	Greece	28 Jun 55	225UNTS219	103100
Greece	Netherlands	14 Jul 55	227UNTS27	103129
Iran	USA (United States)	15 Aug 55	284UNTS93	104132
Denmark	Greece	29 Aug 55	230UNTS25	103174
Italy	Lebanon	04 Nov 55	267UNTS113	103838
Guatemala	UNICEF (Children)	22 Nov 55	221UNTS305	103012
Pakistan	Syria	18 Dec 55	320UNTS269	104647
Nicaragua	USA (United States)	21 Jan 56	367UNTS3	105224
Italy	Switzerland	02 Feb 56	291UNTS113	104247
Italy	USA (United States)	27 Feb 56	291UNTS287	104260
Canada	USSR (Soviet Union)	29 Feb 56	252UNTS165	103566
Ethiopia	Italy	05 Mar 56	267UNTS189	103844
Turkey	UK Great Britain	12 Mar 56	313UNTS73	104530
USA (United States)	Uruguay	23 Mar 56	376UNTS311	105386
Netherlands	USA (United States)	27 Mar 56	285UNTS231	104154
Cambodia	UNICEF (Children)	28 Apr 56	136UNTS341	200446
Denmark	Italy	12 May 56	260UNTS357	103720
France	Greece	25 Jun 56	251UNTS167	103540
Indonesia	UK Great Britain	02 Jul 56	265UNTS285	103820
Indonesia	UK Great Britain	02 Jul 56	265UNTS271	103819
UNICEF (Children)	Sudan	07 Aug 56	248UNTS307	200542
Guatemala	Honduras	22 Aug 56	263UNTS49	103767
Denmark	Greece	04 Sep 56	256UNTS319	103643
Korea, South	USA (United States)	28 Nov 56	302UNTS281	104367
Indonesia	Yugoslavia	14 Dec 56	378UNTS117	105422
UNESCO (Educ/Cult)	Tunisia	03 Jan 57	257UNTS21	103645

PARTY ONE	PARTY TWO	DATE	CITATION	NUMBER
Export quotas (Cont.)				
Multilateral		25 Mar 57	294UNTS2	104300
Ghana	USA (United States)	03 Jun 57	284UNTS63	104129
Denmark	Uruguay	04 Jun 57	286UNTS107	104162
Iraq	USA (United States)	16 Jun 57	284UNTS39	104127
Italy	USA (United States)	22 Jun 57	284UNTS51	104128
Australia	Japan	06 Jul 57	318UNTS381	104627
Morocco	UNICEF (Children)	31 Jul 57	282UNTS99	104095
Ceylon (Sri Lanka)	China People's Rep	19 Sep 57	337UNTS137	104821
France	USA (United States)	23 Sep 57	293UNTS297	104297
Japan	USSR (Soviet Union)	06 Dec 57	325UNTS35	104694
Belgium	Denmark	31 Dec 57	305UNTS247	104422
Multilateral		03 Feb 58	381UNTS165	105471
India	Japan	04 Feb 58	324UNTS215	104687
Ceylon (Sri Lanka)	USSR (Soviet Union)	08 Feb 58	348UNTS159	104999
Greece	India	14 Feb 58	609UNTS94	108827
Italy	Tunisia	08 Apr 58	378UNTS327	105430
Germany, West	USSR (Soviet Union)	25 Apr 58	346UNTS71	104978
Multilateral		10 Jun 58	454UNTS47	106539
Ghana	UNICEF (Children)	12 Aug 58	309UNTS103	104469
Australia	Fed of Malaya	26 Aug 58	325UNTS253	104703
Japan	New Zealand	09 Sep 58	325UNTS119	104698
Multilateral		01 Dec 58	385UNTS137	105534
Burma	UK Great Britain	06 Feb 59	343UNTS223	104927
Argentina	Sweden	12 Jun 59	427UNTS337	106164
Korea, South	USA (United States)	25 Sep 59	358UNTS163	105133
India	Italy	06 Oct 59	378UNTS267	105427
Norway	Sweden	28 Oct 59	427UNTS225	106157
Italy	Tunisia	31 Oct 59	378UNTS349	105431
Tunisia	UK Great Britain	16 Nov 59	354UNTS367	105070
Czechoslovakia	Japan	15 Dec 59	383UNTS277	105505
Denmark	Switzerland	21 Dec 59	633UNTS351	109045
Multilateral		04 Jan 60	370UNTS3	105266
Cuba	UNICEF (Children)	11 Feb 60	349UNTS277	105014
Ecuador	USA (United States)	24 Feb 60	371UNTS55	105270
Greece	Tunisia	02 Mar 60	483UNTS89	107008
Austria	Guatemala	18 Mar 60	379UNTS89	105435
Cuba	Japan	22 Apr 60	442UNTS261	106354
Lebanon	UN Special Fund	07 May 60	360UNTS225	105160
Korea, North	USSR (Soviet Union)	22 Jun 60	399UNTS3	105732
Ghana	USSR (Soviet Union)	04 Aug 60	421UNTS27	106050
Multilateral		01 Sep 60	403UNTS3	105792
Greece	Poland	08 Nov 60	483UNTS127	107010
Multilateral		13 Dec 60	455UNTS3	106543
Japan	Pakistan	18 Dec 60	423UNTS197	106093
Tunisia	UK Great Britain	17 Jan 61	566UNTS2	108236
Korea, South	Philippines	24 Feb 61	423UNTS217	106094
Multilateral		16 Mar 61	638UNTS235	109139
USA (United States)	Vietnam, South	03 Apr 61	424UNTS137	106106
Japan	Peru	15 May 61	451UNTS3	106482
Somalia	USSR (Soviet Union)	02 Jun 61	493UNTS173	107214
Indonesia	Japan	01 Jul 61	517UNTS107	107484
Austria	Romania	21 Jul 61	421UNTS161	106057
Central Afri Rep	UNICEF (Children)	21 Aug 61	413UNTS48	105939
Poland	UNICEF (Children)	24 Aug 61	406UNTS95	105841
Korea, South	Thailand	15 Sep 61	413UNTS137	105948
Pakistan	Philippines	29 Sep 61	422UNTS3	106065
Iraq	Syria	03 Nov 61	489UNTS45	107134
Ghana	USSR (Soviet Union)	04 Nov 61	437UNTS213	106308
Canada	Italy	18 Dec 61	470UNTS153	106807
India	USA (United States)	16 Apr 62	445UNTS257	106393
Brazil	USA (United States)	19 Apr 62	456UNTS255	106560
Multilateral		15 May 62	444UNTS3	106367
United Arab Rep	USSR (Soviet Union)	23 Jun 62	472UNTS43	106836
Italy	USA (United States)	06 Jul 62	459UNTS123	106617
Cyprus	Greece	23 Aug 62	609UNTS15	108825

PARTY ONE	PARTY TWO	DATE	CITATION	NUMBER
Export quotas (Cont.)				
Multilateral		28 Sep 62	469UNTS169	106791
Cameroon	Greece	29 Oct 62	538UNTS185	107815
Japan	UK Great Britain	14 Nov 62	478UNTS29	106934
Australia	Fed of Malaya	26 Nov 62	453UNTS161	106523
Laos	USSR (Soviet Union)	01 Dec 62	458UNTS21	106590
Brazil	Taiwan	28 Dec 62	500UNTS61	107307
Greece	Pakistan	17 Jan 63	538UNTS175	107814
Japan	USA (United States)	01 Feb 63	473UNTS49	106854
Austria	Czechoslovakia	08 Mar 63	495UNTS219	107245
Multilateral		02 Apr 63	475UNTS121	106889
Burma	UK Great Britain	02 Apr 63	475UNTS139	106890
Brazil	USSR (Soviet Union)	20 Apr 63	0UNTS0	109257
Multilateral		30 Apr 63	570UNTS23	108285
Denmark	Norway	11 May 63	613UNTS271	108856
India	USSR (Soviet Union)	10 Jun 63	0UNTS0	109382
Spain	USA (United States)	16 Jul 63	488UNTS77	107120
El Salvador	Japan	19 Jul 63	518UNTS135	107494
Multilateral		13 Aug 63	592UNTS139	108572
Tanganyika	USSR (Soviet Union)	14 Aug 63	493UNTS195	107215
Greece	Poland	30 Sep 63	534UNTS23	107751
Jamaica	USA (United States)	01 Oct 63	488UNTS133	107124
Canada	France	11 Oct 63	529UNTS71	107657
Taiwan	USA (United States)	19 Oct 63	494UNTS27	107224
Israel	USA (United States)	22 Nov 63	494UNTS89	107228
Czechoslovakia	Romania	16 Dec 63	527UNTS285	107630
Cameroon	Netherlands	18 Dec 63	521UNTS303	107527
Greece	Poland	21 Dec 63	538UNTS155	107813
Taiwan	Ecuador	17 Jun 64	533UNTS141	107740
Turkey	USA (United States)	17 Jul 64	530UNTS25	107670
Greece	USA (United States)	17 Jul 64	530UNTS13	107669
Syria	UK Great Britain	31 Aug 64	539UNTS259	107837
Finland	UK Great Britain	12 Sep 64	535UNTS13	107773
Denmark	UK Great Britain	16 Sep 64	534UNTS427	107771
Taiwan	Mexico	25 Sep 64	547UNTS233	107960
Greece	Norway	25 Sep 64	610UNTS0	108835
Austria	Thailand	30 Sep 64	527UNTS239	107628
USA (United States)	Yugoslavia	05 Oct 64	531UNTS63	107693
Czechoslovakia	Germany, East	06 Oct 64	545UNTS113	107927
Canada	USA (United States)	16 Jan 65	606UNTS31	108772
Malta	Switzerland	20 Jan 65	548UNTS193	107978
Korea, South	USA (United States)	26 Jan 65	541UNTS77	107862
Pakistan	USA (United States)	26 Feb 65	542UNTS103	107883
Bulgaria	Czechoslovakia	22 May 65	545UNTS65	107925
Argentina	Yugoslavia	09 Jun 65	601UNTS3	108684
Argentina	United Arab Rep	21 Jun 65	634UNTS161	109058
Multilateral		16 Jul 65	600UNTS49	108675
Israel	USA (United States)	20 Jul 65	549UNTS55	107989
Australia	New Zealand	31 Aug 65	554UNTS169	108101
Australia	Korea, South	21 Sep 65	548UNTS163	107977
Poland	USA (United States)	27 Sep 65	564UNTS169	108227
Australia	USSR (Soviet Union)	15 Oct 65	553UNTS239	108092
Finland	USA (United States)	03 Nov 65	573UNTS175	108330
Ireland	UK Great Britain	14 Dec 65	565UNTS58	108235
Multilateral		31 Dec 65	616UNTS317	108904
Japan	USSR (Soviet Union)	21 Jan 66	633UNTS165	109038
Austria	Germany, West	17 Feb 66	614UNTS263	108875
Romania	UK Great Britain	22 Mar 66	571UNTS281	108307
Argentina	India	26 Mar 66	601UNTS201	108697
Singapore	USSR (Soviet Union)	02 Apr 66	631UNTS125	108992
Poland	Singapore	07 Jun 66	631UNTS189	108994
Belgium	Bulgaria	14 Jun 66	607UNTS183	108806
Australia	Poland	20 Jun 66	638UNTS201	109136
Ivory Coast	Netherlands	01 Aug 66	591UNTS245	108561
Bulgaria	United Arab Rep	29 Aug 66	630UNTS325	108980
Mauritania	USSR (Soviet Union)	17 Oct 66	633UNTS231	109040

PARTY ONE	PARTY TWO	DATE	CITATION	NUMBER
Export quotas (Cont.)				
Romania	United Arab Rep	14 Nov 66	642UNTS129	109169
Guinea	Romania	01 Dec 66	642UNTS89	109167
Korea, South	New Zealand	31 Jan 67	598UNTS91	108656
Bulgaria	USSR (Soviet Union)	27 Apr 67	631UNTS3	108983
Malta	USA (United States)	14 Jun 67	604UNTS231	108753
Chad	USSR (Soviet Union)	22 Jun 67	643UNTS121	109188
Netherlands	Romania	20 Jul 67	633UNTS21	109032
Israel	USA (United States)	04 Aug 67	0UNTS0	109351
Ecuador	Romania	10 Oct 67	642UNTS33	109163
Bulgaria	New Zealand	03 Nov 67	0UNTS0	109207
Australia	Hungary	05 Dec 67	638UNTS209	109137
Israel	Singapore	24 Apr 68	642UNTS235	109176
Import quotas				
Netherlands	UK Great Britain	14 Jun 40	2UNTS251	200018
Multilateral		12 Oct 40	161UNTS193	200485
Argentina	USA (United States)	14 Oct 41	119UNTS193	200384
Brazil	Canada	17 Oct 41	67UNTS263	200224
Peru	USA (United States)	07 May 42	103UNTS219	200316
USA (United States)	Uruguay	21 Jul 42	120UNTS211	200393
Mexico	USA (United States)	23 Dec 42	13UNTS231	200081
UK Great Britain	USA (United States)	30 Apr 43	28UNTS341	200159
Argentina	USA (United States)	09 May 45	139UNTS227	200453
Belgium	Canada	25 Oct 45	230UNTS127	103180
Finland	Norway	27 Nov 45	17UNTS247	100279
UK Great Britain	USA (United States)	06 Dec 45	126UNTS13	101679
Greece	UK Great Britain	24 Jan 46	6UNTS45	100067
Canada	Mexico	08 Feb 46	230UNTS183	103183
Belgium	Norway	21 Feb 46	31UNTS435	100485
Canada	UK Great Britain	06 Mar 46	20UNTS13	100312
Denmark	Norway	30 Mar 46	29UNTS163	100438
Poland	USA (United States)	24 Apr 46	4UNTS155	100042
Thailand	UK Great Britain	01 May 46	99UNTS169	101377
Multilateral		06 May 46	99UNTS181	101379
France	USA (United States)	28 May 46	84UNTS161	101126
Albania	Yugoslavia	01 Jul 46	111UNTS3	101517
Italy	Norway	20 Jul 46	17UNTS273	100281
Italy	Norway	20 Jul 46	30UNTS177	100456
Denmark	USSR (Soviet Union)	17 Aug 46	8UNTS201	100124
Norway	Yugoslavia	30 Aug 46	30UNTS187	100457
Paraguay	USA (United States)	12 Sep 46	125UNTS179	101677
Taiwan	USA (United States)	04 Nov 46	25UNTS69	100359
Czechoslovakia	USA (United States)	14 Nov 46	7UNTS119	100094
UK Great Britain	USA (United States)	02 Dec 46	7UNTS163	100098
Hungary	Yugoslavia	23 Dec 46	113UNTS125	101549
Austria	UK Great Britain	23 Dec 46	88UNTS93	101186
Norway	USSR (Soviet Union)	27 Dec 46	17UNTS283	100282
Netherlands	Norway	28 Jan 47	31UNTS29	100467
Romania	USSR (Soviet Union)	20 Feb 47	226UNTS79	103110
Poland	Sweden	18 Mar 47	12UNTS295	100190
Czechoslovakia	Norway	20 Mar 47	30UNTS223	100460
Denmark	Yugoslavia	28 Jun 47	78UNTS242	101020
Multilateral		05 Oct 47	34UNTS23	100525
Multilateral		30 Oct 47	55UNTS188	100814
Belgium	USSR (Soviet Union)	10 Nov 47	18UNTS299	100298
Finland	Norway	15 Nov 47	29UNTS179	100439
France	Lebanon	24 Jan 48	173UNTS99	102263
Italy	USA (United States)	02 Feb 48	79UNTS171	101040
Norway	Poland	04 Feb 48	30UNTS205	100458
Denmark	Hungary	28 Feb 48	85UNTS35	101144
Norway	Sweden	29 Apr 48	26UNTS33	100375
France	Ireland	06 May 48	558UNTS170	108141
Hungary	Poland	13 May 48	25UNTS301	100369
Brazil	UK Great Britain	21 May 48	66UNTS121	100851
Norway	Switzerland	26 Jun 48	29UNTS193	100440

PARTY ONE	PARTY TWO	DATE	CITATION	NUMBER
Import quotas (Cont.)				
Ireland	UK Great Britain	31 Jul 48	86UNTS37	101151
France	USA (United States)	16 Sep 48	84UNTS185	101129
Canada	USA (United States)	23 Nov 48	81UNTS295	101078
South Africa	UK Great Britain	06 Dec 48	118UNTS183	101607
Denmark	Turkey	15 Dec 48	76UNTS17	100975
Norway	Poland	31 Dec 48	29UNTS3	100430
Poland	UK Great Britain	14 Jan 49	83UNTS3	101100
Italy	Yugoslavia	03 Feb 49	33UNTS105	100517
France	Norway	09 Feb 49	29UNTS13	100431
Netherlands	Norway	26 Feb 49	29UNTS33	100432
Greece	Norway	12 Mar 49	30UNTS161	100454
Finland	Greece	24 Mar 49	78UNTS13	101009
Greece	Turkey	02 Apr 49	78UNTS23	101010
Greece	Turkey	21 Jul 49	78UNTS65	101012
Multilateral		10 Aug 49	45UNTS3	100689
Denmark	UK Great Britain	13 Aug 49	68UNTS105	100890
Czechoslovakia	UK Great Britain	28 Sep 49	86UNTS141	101156
Ireland	Netherlands	25 Nov 49	558UNTS256	108146
Denmark	Germany, West	15 Dec 49	51UNTS11	100749
Czechoslovakia	Denmark	17 Dec 49	74UNTS147	100961
Ireland	USA (United States)	21 Jan 50	206UNTS269	102792
Afghanistan	India	04 Apr 50	167UNTS105	102201
Multilateral		31 May 50	74UNTS95	100957
Denmark	Finland	08 Jul 50	73UNTS191	100953
Denmark	Spain	12 Jul 50	71UNTS135	100914
India	Nepal	31 Jul 50	104UNTS3	101430
Brazil	UK Great Britain	18 Sep 50	88UNTS115	101188
Denmark	Poland	01 Oct 50	81UNTS43	101061
Austria	Ireland	06 Oct 50	557UNTS173	108133
Multilateral		22 Nov 50	131UNTS25	101734
Iceland	Ireland	02 Dec 50	558UNTS231	108143
Multilateral		23 Dec 50	185UNTS3	102456
Finland	Ireland	06 Jan 51	558UNTS120	108140
Germany, West	Ireland	23 Jul 51	558UNTS3	108137
Greece	USA (United States)	03 Aug 51	224UNTS279	103080
Ethiopia	USA (United States)	07 Sep 51	206UNTS41	102785
Greece	UK Great Britain	29 Sep 51	190UNTS260	102570
Denmark	USA (United States)	01 Oct 51	421UNTS105	106056
Multilateral		06 Dec 51	150UNTS67	101963
El Salvador	Guatemala	14 Dec 51	131UNTS131	101740
UK Great Britain	USA (United States)	18 Jan 52	184UNTS79	102440
Iran	USA (United States)	20 Jan 52	200UNTS191	102703
Ireland	Portugal	06 Feb 52	558UNTS289	108147
India	Syria	25 Feb 52	163UNTS55	102141
Austria	Greece	22 Mar 52	187UNTS255	102517
Greece	Syria	02 Jun 52	183UNTS251	102434
Greece	Israel	22 Jul 52	219UNTS231	102978
Denmark	Spain	28 Jul 52	135UNTS255	101825
Ceylon (Sri Lanka)	Japan	06 Sep 52	314UNTS279	104552
Germany, West	Ireland	26 Sep 52	558UNTS27	108138
Multilateral		07 Nov 52	221UNTS255	103010
Denmark	Israel	14 Nov 52	160UNTS275	102112
Turkey	Yugoslavia	26 Feb 53	247UNTS54	103460
Germany, West	UK Great Britain	27 Feb 53	330UNTS217	104747
Germany, West	USA (United States)	27 Feb 53	224UNTS13	103067
Greece	Yugoslavia	28 Feb 53	252UNTS27	103557
Japan	USA (United States)	02 Apr 53	206UNTS143	102788
Fed Rhod/Nyasaland	South Africa	28 Jun 53	267UNTS270	103848
Burma	Yugoslavia	29 Jun 53	378UNTS83	105418
Italy	Switzerland	02 Jul 53	257UNTS99	103653
Multilateral		24 Jul 53	250UNTS108	103520
Ireland	Italy	27 Jul 53	558UNTS237	108144
Argentina	USSR (Soviet Union)	05 Aug 53	221UNTS99	103004
Multilateral		01 Oct 53	258UNTS153	103677
UNICEF (Children)	UK Great Britain	07 Oct 53	180UNTS59	102375

PARTY ONE	PARTY TWO	DATE	CITATION	NUMBER
Import quotas (Cont.)				
UN Relief Palestin	United Arab Rep	14 Oct 53	190UNTS13	102555
Denmark	Greece	19 Oct 53	225UNTS9	103082
Greece	Turkey	07 Nov 53	225UNTS163	103098
India	USSR (Soviet Union)	02 Dec 53	240UNTS143	103402
Bulgaria	Greece	05 Dec 53	225UNTS135	103095
Cuba	UK Great Britain	18 Dec 53	186UNTS157	102490
UK Great Britain	Yugoslavia	31 Dec 53	190UNTS335	102574
Czechoslovakia	Greece	01 Feb 54	225UNTS77	103091
Canada	Japan	31 Mar 54	236UNTS329	103334
Lebanon	USSR (Soviet Union)	30 Apr 54	226UNTS109	103111
Greece	Spain	15 May 54	299UNTS261	104318
Greece	Spain	15 May 54	299UNTS277	104319
Greece	Romania	19 May 54	225UNTS17	103083
France	Greece	22 Jul 54	225UNTS199	103099
Denmark	Sweden	28 Oct 54	262UNTS211	103747
Germany, West	USA (United States)	29 Oct 54	273UNTS3	103943
Greece	Netherlands	01 Nov 54	223UNTS79	103057
UK Great Britain	Yugoslavia	31 Dec 54	209UNTS81	102824
Turkey	UK Great Britain	17 Jan 55	204UNTS195	102758
Greece	Japan	12 Mar 55	227UNTS33	103130
Italy	Yugoslavia	31 Mar 55	386UNTS317	105551
Ceylon (Sri Lanka)	Germany, West	01 Apr 55	369UNTS57	105251
Philippines	USA (United States)	27 Apr 55	261UNTS351	103733
Canada	Ethiopia	03 Jun 55	247UNTS157	103465
France	Ireland	07 Jun 55	558UNTS217	108142
France	Greece	28 Jun 55	225UNTS219	103100
Greece	Netherlands	14 Jul 55	227UNTS27	103129
Germany, East	Romania	28 Jul 55	342UNTS207	104909
Iran	USA (United States)	15 Aug 55	284UNTS93	104132
Denmark	Greece	29 Aug 55	230UNTS25	103174
Italy	Lebanon	04 Nov 55	267UNTS113	103838
Italy	Syria	10 Nov 55	267UNTS157	103841
Pakistan	Syria	18 Dec 55	320UNTS269	104647
Nicaragua	USA (United States)	21 Jan 56	367UNTS3	105224
Canada	USSR (Soviet Union)	29 Feb 56	252UNTS165	103566
Ethiopia	Italy	05 Mar 56	267UNTS189	103844
USA (United States)	Uruguay	23 Mar 56	376UNTS311	105386
Netherlands	USA (United States)	27 Mar 56	285UNTS231	104154
Germany, West	USA (United States)	26 Apr 56	283UNTS267	104122
Denmark	Italy	12 May 56	260UNTS357	103720
France	Greece	25 Jun 56	251UNTS167	103540
Hungary	UK Great Britain	27 Jun 56	249UNTS19	103499
Indonesia	UK Great Britain	02 Jul 56	265UNTS271	103819
Indonesia	UK Great Britain	02 Jul 56	265UNTS285	103820
Guatemala	Honduras	22 Aug 56	263UNTS49	103767
Denmark	Greece	04 Sep 56	256UNTS319	103643
Denmark	Italy	26 Oct 56	267UNTS261	103847
Korea, South	USA (United States)	28 Nov 56	302UNTS281	104367
Indonesia	Yugoslavia	14 Dec 56	378UNTS117	105422
Multilateral		15 Jan 57	376UNTS122	105378
Multilateral		25 Mar 57	294UNTS2	104300
Ghana	USA (United States)	03 Jun 57	284UNTS63	104129
Iraq	USA (United States)	16 Jun 57	284UNTS39	104127
Italy	USA (United States)	22 Jun 57	284UNTS51	104128
Australia	Japan	06 Jul 57	318UNTS381	104627
Ceylon (Sri Lanka)	China People's Rep	19 Sep 57	337UNTS137	104821
Japan	USSR (Soviet Union)	06 Dec 57	325UNTS35	104694
Multilateral		03 Feb 58	381UNTS165	105471
India	Japan	04 Feb 58	324UNTS215	104687
Ceylon (Sri Lanka)	USSR (Soviet Union)	08 Feb 58	348UNTS159	104999
Greece	India	14 Feb 58	609UNTS94	108827
Sweden	USSR (Soviet Union)	28 Mar 58	428UNTS321	106184
USA (United States)	Yugoslavia	05 Apr 58	338UNTS233	104838
Italy	Tunisia	08 Apr 58	378UNTS327	105430
Germany, West	USSR (Soviet Union)	25 Apr 58	346UNTS71	104978

PARTY ONE	PARTY TWO	DATE	CITATION	NUMBER
Import quotas (Cont.)				
Multilateral		10 Jun 58	454UNTS47	106539
Multilateral		25 Jul 58	352UNTS3	105035
Australia	Fed of Malaya	26 Aug 58	325UNTS253	104703
Japan	New Zealand	09 Sep 58	325UNTS119	104698
Iraq	USSR (Soviet Union)	11 Oct 58	328UNTS95	104730
Burma	UK Great Britain	06 Feb 59	343UNTS223	104927
Australia	Italy	12 Feb 59	328UNTS133	104732
Morocco	UN Special Fund	04 Apr 59	354UNTS347	105069
Germany, West	New Zealand	20 Apr 59	402UNTS125	105782
Iran	UK Great Britain	06 May 59	398UNTS51	105717
Iceland	USA (United States)	23 Jun 59	354UNTS3	105048
Ghana	UN Special Fund	12 Aug 59	338UNTS203	104836
Korea, South	USA (United States)	01 Oct 59	358UNTS115	105129
India	Italy	06 Oct 59	378UNTS267	105427
Iran	UN Special Fund	06 Oct 59	342UNTS89	104902
Poland	UN Special Fund	15 Oct 59	344UNTS29	104941
India	UN Special Fund	20 Oct 59	344UNTS143	104946
USA (United States)	Yugoslavia	22 Oct 59	360UNTS259	105161
Guinea	UK Great Britain	22 Oct 59	351UNTS341	105033
UN Special Fund	Yugoslavia	27 Oct 59	344UNTS159	104947
Norway	Sweden	28 Oct 59	427UNTS225	106157
Italy	Tunisia	31 Oct 59	378UNTS349	105431
Ecuador	UN Special Fund	10 Nov 59	345UNTS3	104955
Greece	UN Special Fund	13 Nov 59	345UNTS171	104966
Tunisia	UK Great Britain	16 Nov 59	354UNTS367	105070
UN Special Fund	Turkey	20 Nov 59	345UNTS105	104963
UN Special Fund	United Arab Rep	25 Nov 59	345UNTS125	104964
Israel	UN Special Fund	01 Dec 59	345UNTS197	104968
Guinea	UN Special Fund	02 Dec 59	345UNTS215	104969
Argentina	UN Special Fund	04 Dec 59	345UNTS263	104972
Czechoslovakia	Japan	15 Dec 59	383UNTS277	105505
Jordan	UN Special Fund	15 Dec 59	346UNTS3	104974
Denmark	Switzerland	21 Dec 59	633UNTS351	109045
Multilateral		04 Jan 60	370UNTS3	105266
UN Special Fund	UK Great Britain	07 Jan 60	348UNTS177	105000
Peru	UN Special Fund	19 Jan 60	349UNTS83	105010
Chile	UN Special Fund	22 Jan 60	351UNTS115	105020
Colombia	UN Special Fund	04 Feb 60	355UNTS257	105080
Bolivia	UN Special Fund	09 Feb 60	351UNTS203	105024
Afghanistan	UN Special Fund	21 Feb 60	351UNTS93	105019
Ecuador	USA (United States)	24 Feb 60	371UNTS55	105270
Pakistan	UN Special Fund	25 Feb 60	351UNTS141	105021
Greece	Tunisia	02 Mar 60	483UNTS89	107008
France	UN Special Fund	17 Mar 60	354UNTS119	105059
Austria	Guatemala	18 Mar 60	379UNTS89	105435
Italy	UN Special Fund	01 Apr 60	354UNTS261	105066
UK Great Britain	Yugoslavia	12 Apr 60	360UNTS79	105155
UN Special Fund	Tunisia	12 Apr 60	355UNTS289	105082
Libya	UN Special Fund	19 Apr 60	356UNTS11	105090
UN Special Fund	Sudan	21 Apr 60	356UNTS213	105097
Cuba	Japan	22 Apr 60	442UNTS261	106354
Multilateral		22 Apr 60	418UNTS211	106023
UN Special Fund	Vietnam, South	29 Apr 60	357UNTS311	200567
Laos	UN Special Fund	30 Apr 60	361UNTS171	105179
Cuba	Czechoslovakia	10 Jun 60	447UNTS75	106412
Iraq	UN Special Fund	19 Jun 60	376UNTS357	105389
Korea, North	USSR (Soviet Union)	22 Jun 60	399UNTS3	105732
Kuwait	UN Special Fund	29 Jun 60	369UNTS419	200575
Spain	UK Great Britain	12 Jul 60	414UNTS123	105971
Ethiopia	UN Special Fund	13 Jul 60	368UNTS159	105240
Ghana	USSR (Soviet Union)	04 Aug 60	421UNTS27	106050
Congo (Zaire)	United Nations	23 Aug 60	373UNTS327	200576
Israel	UK Great Britain	31 Aug 60	385UNTS71	105530
Brazil	UN Special Fund	16 Sep 60	375UNTS3	105351
Taiwan	UN Special Fund	20 Sep 60	375UNTS29	105352

PARTY ONE	PARTY TWO	DATE	CITATION	NUMBER
Import quotas (Cont.)				
Indonesia	UN Special Fund	07 Oct 60	378UNTS141	105424
Liberia	UN Special Fund	11 Oct 60	376UNTS341	105388
El Salvador	UN Special Fund	24 Oct 60	377UNTS171	105400
Greece	Poland	08 Nov 60	483UNTS127	107010
Guatemala	UN Special Fund	17 Nov 60	383UNTS67	105495
Nepal	UN Special Fund	17 Nov 60	380UNTS289	105461
Cambodia	UN Special Fund	24 Nov 60	382UNTS255	105487
Multilateral		13 Dec 60	455UNTS3	106543
Japan	Pakistan	18 Dec 60	423UNTS197	106093
Honduras	UN Special Fund	20 Dec 60	383UNTS103	105497
Iceland	USA (United States)	30 Dec 60	401UNTS43	105761
Burma	UN Special Fund	03 Jan 61	387UNTS219	105564
Costa Rica	UN Special Fund	10 Jan 61	389UNTS253	105597
UK Great Britain	USSR (Soviet Union)	12 Jan 61	398UNTS157	105720
Tunisia	UK Great Britain	17 Jan 61	566UNTS2	108236
UN Special Fund	Saudi Arabia	19 Jan 61	396UNTS27	105692
Nicaragua	UN Special Fund	20 Jan 61	387UNTS15	105555
Chad	UN Special Fund	23 Jan 61	390UNTS69	105603
UN Special Fund	Somalia	28 Jan 61	388UNTS75	105573
Gabon	UN Special Fund	02 Feb 61	387UNTS289	105568
Nigeria	UN Special Fund	10 Feb 61	390UNTS85	105604
Mexico	UN Special Fund	23 Feb 61	388UNTS151	105576
Korea, South	Philippines	24 Feb 61	423UNTS217	106094
Cyprus	UN Special Fund	24 Feb 61	389UNTS3	105588
Panama	UN Special Fund	09 Mar 61	396UNTS3	105691
Cuba	UN Special Fund	10 Mar 61	390UNTS35	105601
Multilateral		16 Mar 61	638UNTS235	109139
USA (United States)	Vietnam, South	03 Apr 61	424UNTS137	106106
Korea, South	UN Special Fund	21 Apr 61	394UNTS231	200583
Ceylon (Sri Lanka)	UN Special Fund	03 May 61	395UNTS217	105687
Japan	Peru	15 May 61	451UNTS3	106482
Ghana	Switzerland	17 May 61	559UNTS193	108159
Somalia	USSR (Soviet Union)	02 Jun 61	493UNTS173	107214
Multilateral		08 Jun 61	473UNTS187	106863
Cameroon	UN Special Fund	13 Jun 61	397UNTS297	105713
Paraguay	UN Special Fund	22 Jun 61	399UNTS117	105738
UN Special Fund	Upper Volta	26 Jun 61	400UNTS3	105744
Philippines	UN Special Fund	28 Jun 61	399UNTS141	105739
Haiti	UN Special Fund	28 Jun 61	399UNTS171	105741
Indonesia	Japan	01 Jul 61	517UNTS107	107484
Austria	Romania	21 Jul 61	421UNTS161	106057
Mali	UN Special Fund	21 Jul 61	401UNTS141	105768
UN Special Fund	Yemen	02 Aug 61	402UNTS43	105777
Ivory Coast	UN Special Fund	29 Aug 61	406UNTS129	105844
Korea, South	Thailand	15 Sep 61	413UNTS137	105948
Pakistan	Philippines	29 Sep 61	422UNTS3	106065
UN Special Fund	Sierra Leone	02 Oct 61	422UNTS131	106073
Iraq	Syria	03 Nov 61	489UNTS45	107134
Ghana	USSR (Soviet Union)	04 Nov 61	437UNTS213	106308
Mauritania	UN Special Fund	07 Nov 61	412UNTS240	105936
Congo (Brazzaville)	UN Special Fund	09 Nov 61	413UNTS58	105940
UN Special Fund	Venezuela	11 Dec 61	422UNTS149	106074
UN Special Fund	Senegal	16 Dec 61	425UNTS97	106121
Malagasy	UN Special Fund	05 Jan 62	419UNTS29	106028
UK Great Britain	Yugoslavia	13 Feb 62	431UNTS35	106207
Niger	UN Special Fund	26 Feb 62	423UNTS83	106086
Dahomey	UN Special Fund	28 Mar 62	424UNTS55	106099
India	USA (United States)	16 Apr 62	445UNTS257	106393
Brazil	USA (United States)	19 Apr 62	456UNTS255	106560
Ireland	USA (United States)	03 May 62	442UNTS117	106343
UN Special Fund	Uruguay	04 May 62	429UNTS143	106196
Multilateral		15 May 62	444UNTS3	106367
Guatemala	USA (United States)	21 May 62	451UNTS205	106495
Dominican Republic	UN Special Fund	06 Jun 62	429UNTS169	106197
UN Special Fund	Syria	07 Jul 62	443UNTS3	106355

PARTY ONE	PARTY TWO	DATE	CITATION	NUMBER
Import quotas (Cont.)				
UN Special Fund	Tanganyika	17 Jul 62	435UNTS237	106281
Cyprus	Greece	23 Aug 62	609UNTS15	108825
Multilateral		28 Sep 62	469UNTS169	106791
Cameroon	Greece	29 Oct 62	538UNTS185	107815
Japan	UN Special Fund	31 Oct 62	444UNTS171	106368
Japan	UK Great Britain	14 Nov 62	478UNTS29	106934
Australia	Fed of Malaya	26 Nov 62	453UNTS161	106523
Laos	USSR (Soviet Union)	01 Dec 62	458UNTS21	106590
Brazil	Taiwan	28 Dec 62	500UNTS61	107307
Greece	Pakistan	17 Jan 63	538UNTS175	107814
Austria	Czechoslovakia	08 Mar 63	495UNTS219	107245
Indonesia	USA (United States)	14 Mar 63	505UNTS79	107365
UN Special Fund	Uganda	22 Mar 63	456UNTS466	106572
Burma	UK Great Britain	02 Apr 63	475UNTS139	106890
Multilateral		02 Apr 63	475UNTS121	106889
Brazil	USSR (Soviet Union)	20 Apr 63	0UNTS0	109257
Australia	New Zealand	29 Apr 63	483UNTS241	107017
Multilateral		30 Apr 63	570UNTS23	108285
Denmark	Norway	11 May 63	613UNTS271	108856
Laos	UK Great Britain	17 May 63	475UNTS155	106891
Jamaica	UN Special Fund	22 May 63	489UNTS191	107140
Netherlands	UN Special Fund	24 May 63	466UNTS289	106750
UN Special Fund	Western Samoa	05 Jun 63	467UNTS463	200601
India	USSR (Soviet Union)	10 Jun 63	0UNTS0	109382
El Salvador	Japan	19 Jul 63	518UNTS135	107494
Multilateral		31 Jul 63	472UNTS220	106842
Multilateral		13 Aug 63	592UNTS139	108572
Tanganyika	USSR (Soviet Union)	14 Aug 63	493UNTS195	107215
Burundi	UN Special Fund	22 Aug 63	476UNTS49	106903
Multilateral		27 Aug 63	511UNTS210	107435
Greece	Poland	30 Sep 63	534UNTS23	107751
Multilateral		23 Oct 63	506UNTS197	107388
Jamaica	USA (United States)	24 Oct 63	489UNTS337	107148
Central Afri Rep	UN Special Fund	30 Oct 63	481UNTS247	106985
Multilateral		08 Nov 63	482UNTS286	106999
Czechoslovakia	Romania	16 Dec 63	527UNTS285	107630
Cameroon	Netherlands	18 Dec 63	521UNTS303	107527
Greece	Poland	21 Dec 63	538UNTS155	107813
Multilateral		28 Jan 64	502UNTS321	107336
Ireland	UN Special Fund	03 Jun 64	496UNTS205	107253
Taiwan	Ecuador	17 Jun 64	533UNTS141	107740
Colombia	Netherlands	06 Jul 64	543UNTS289	107906
Greece	Norway	25 Sep 64	610UNTS0	108835
Taiwan	Mexico	25 Sep 64	547UNTS233	107960
Austria	Thailand	30 Sep 64	527UNTS239	107628
Canada	USA (United States)	16 Jan 65	606UNTS31	108772
Netherlands	Tanzania	27 Apr 65	594UNTS123	108599
Argentina	Yugoslavia	09 Jun 65	601UNTS3	108684
UN Special Fund	Spain	30 Jun 65	544UNTS159	107918
Multilateral		16 Jul 65	600UNTS49	108675
Australia	New Zealand	31 Aug 65	554UNTS169	108101
Australia	Korea, South	21 Sep 65	548UNTS163	107977
Poland	USA (United States)	27 Sep 65	564UNTS169	108227
Australia	USSR (Soviet Union)	15 Oct 65	553UNTS239	108092
Finland	USA (United States)	03 Nov 65	573UNTS175	108330
Ireland	UK Great Britain	14 Dec 65	565UNTS58	108235
Japan	USSR (Soviet Union)	21 Jan 66	633UNTS165	109038
Mongolia	UN Special Fund	26 Jan 66	552UNTS201	108055
Austria	Germany, West	17 Feb 66	614UNTS263	108875
Argentina	India	26 Mar 66	601UNTS201	108697
Singapore	USSR (Soviet Union)	02 Apr 66	631UNTS125	108992
Poland	Singapore	07 Jun 66	631UNTS189	108994
Australia	Poland	20 Jun 66	638UNTS201	109136
Ivory Coast	Netherlands	01 Aug 66	591UNTS245	108561
Bulgaria	United Arab Rep	29 Aug 66	630UNTS325	108980

PARTY ONE	PARTY TWO	DATE	CITATION	NUMBER
Import quotas (Cont.)				
Mauritania	USSR (Soviet Union)	17 Oct 66	633UNTS231	109040
Romania	United Arab Rep	14 Nov 66	642UNTS129	109169
Guinea	Romania	01 Dec 66	642UNTS89	109167
Korea, South	New Zealand	31 Jan 67	598UNTS91	108656
Bulgaria	USSR (Soviet Union)	27 Apr 67	631UNTS3	108983
Malta	USA (United States)	14 Jun 67	604UNTS231	108753
Chad	USSR (Soviet Union)	22 Jun 67	643UNTS121	109188
Netherlands	Romania	20 Jul 67	633UNTS21	109032
Israel	USA (United States)	04 Aug 67	0UNTS0	109351
Ecuador	Romania	10 Oct 67	642UNTS33	109163
Bulgaria	New Zealand	03 Nov 67	0UNTS0	109207
Australia	Hungary	05 Dec 67	638UNTS209	109137
Israel	Singapore	24 Apr 68	642UNTS235	109176
Free trade				
USA (United States)	Uruguay	21 Jul 42	120UNTS211	200393
UK Great Britain	USA (United States)	21 Feb 46	6UNTS137	100073
Poland	Yugoslavia	12 Apr 48	115UNTS167	101563
Ireland	USA (United States)	21 Jan 50	206UNTS269	102792
Austria	Denmark	23 Feb 50	74UNTS269	100969
Multilateral		18 Apr 51	261UNTS140	103729
Greece	USA (United States)	03 Aug 51	224UNTS279	103080
Israel	USA (United States)	23 Aug 51	219UNTS237	102979
Ethiopia	USA (United States)	07 Sep 51	206UNTS41	102785
Denmark	USA (United States)	01 Oct 51	421UNTS105	106056
El Salvador	Guatemala	14 Dec 51	131UNTS131	101740
Denmark	Israel	14 Nov 52	160UNTS279	102113
Japan	USA (United States)	02 Apr 53	206UNTS143	102788
Multilateral		09 Dec 53	249UNTS197	103509
Switzerland	Syria	26 May 54	255UNTS145	103609
Iran	USA (United States)	15 Aug 55	284UNTS93	104132
Costa Rica	Guatemala	20 Dec 55	280UNTS121	104056
Multilateral		21 Dec 55	292UNTS63	104267
Nicaragua	USA (United States)	21 Jan 56	367UNTS3	105224
Netherlands	USA (United States)	27 Mar 56	285UNTS231	104154
Portugal	USA (United States)	24 May 56	268UNTS323	103865
Multilateral		16 Aug 56	287UNTS223	104188
Guatemala	Honduras	22 Aug 56	263UNTS49	103767
Korea, South	USA (United States)	28 Nov 56	302UNTS281	104367
Multilateral		25 Mar 57	294UNTS2	104300
Multilateral		03 Feb 58	381UNTS165	105471
Albania	USSR (Soviet Union)	15 Feb 58	313UNTS261	104536
Multilateral		10 Jun 58	454UNTS47	106539
Muscat and Oman	USA (United States)	20 Dec 58	380UNTS181	105457
Italy	Tunisia	31 Oct 59	378UNTS349	105431
Multilateral		04 Jan 60	370UNTS3	105266
Multilateral		06 Feb 60	383UNTS3	105494
Multilateral		13 Dec 60	455UNTS3	106543
USA (United States)	Vietnam, South	03 Apr 61	424UNTS137	106106
Belgium	Italy	28 Oct 61	429UNTS199	106199
Multilateral		23 Mar 62	434UNTS145	106262
Iceland	USA (United States)	06 Feb 63	473UNTS93	106858
Ethiopia	USA (United States)	11 Jun 63	487UNTS269	107109
Canada	France	11 Oct 63	529UNTS71	107657
Iceland	USA (United States)	13 Feb 64	511UNTS3	107421
Taiwan	USA (United States)	03 Jun 64	526UNTS257	107610
Dahomey	USA (United States)	31 Dec 64	541UNTS117	107865
Ireland	UK Great Britain	14 Dec 65	565UNTS58	108235
Tariffs				
Canada	France	12 May 33	253UNTS285	200545
Argentina	Brazil	23 Jan 40	51UNTS281	200194
Brazil	Uruguay	08 Jan 42	54UNTS359	200206
Haiti	USA (United States)	19 Feb 42	105UNTS238	200336
Dominican Republic	USA (United States)	14 Nov 42	24UNTS233	200148
Turkey	USA (United States)	22 Apr 44	109UNTS279	200364

PARTY ONE	PARTY TWO	DATE	CITATION	NUMBER
Tariffs (Cont.)				
Colombia	USA (United States)	17 Apr 45	139UNTS303	200457
Multilateral		04 Dec 45	9UNTS101	100128
USA (United States)	USSR (Soviet Union)	24 May 46	4UNTS201	100046
Bolivia	USA (United States)	10 Jun 46	13UNTS19	100197
Luxembourg	USA (United States)	03 Jul 46	32UNTS85	100491
Ethiopia	USA (United States)	04 Jul 46	13UNTS27	100198
Norway	USA (United States)	08 Jul 46	13UNTS35	100199
Spain	USA (United States)	11 Jul 46	13UNTS51	100201
Belgium	USA (United States)	11 Jul 46	13UNTS43	100200
United Arab Rep	USA (United States)	15 Aug 46	13UNTS59	100202
Portugal	USA (United States)	26 Aug 46	13UNTS67	100203
Denmark	USA (United States)	10 Sep 46	13UNTS75	100204
USA (United States)	Yugoslavia	03 Oct 46	13UNTS83	100205
Dominican Republic	USA (United States)	07 Oct 46	13UNTS91	100206
Multilateral		30 Oct 47	55UNTS188	100814
Multilateral		22 Dec 47	32UNTS143	100496
Czechoslovakia	Poland	05 Apr 48	31UNTS325	100481
France	USA (United States)	28 Jun 48	31UNTS115	100472
Italy	USA (United States)	28 Jun 48	25UNTS45	100356
Denmark	USA (United States)	29 Jun 48	27UNTS35	100396
Belgium	USA (United States)	02 Jul 48	27UNTS43	100397
Greece	USA (United States)	02 Jul 48	31UNTS131	100474
Netherlands	USA (United States)	02 Jul 48	32UNTS77	100490
Austria	USA (United States)	02 Jul 48	25UNTS53	100357
Sweden	USA (United States)	03 Jul 48	27UNTS69	100400
Iceland	USA (United States)	03 Jul 48	27UNTS49	100398
Norway	USA (United States)	03 Jul 48	27UNTS59	100399
Turkey	USA (United States)	04 Jul 48	34UNTS185	100536
UK Great Britain	USA (United States)	06 Jul 48	25UNTS61	100358
Multilateral		14 Sep 48	18UNTS267	100296
Portugal	USA (United States)	28 Sep 48	31UNTS139	100475
South Africa	UK Great Britain	06 Dec 48	118UNTS183	101607
Multilateral		12 Feb 49	189UNTS33	102541
Belgium	Chile	23 Aug 49	46UNTS163	100708
Finland	USA (United States)	18 Jan 50	92UNTS197	101272
Multilateral		15 Dec 50	347UNTS127	104994
Denmark	Iran	18 Jun 51	255UNTS3	103602
Denmark	Italy	24 Oct 51	118UNTS91	101598
Mexico	UK Great Britain	12 Jun 52	196UNTS149	102622
Lebanon	Yugoslavia	17 Apr 54	602UNTS199	108713
Lebanon	USSR (Soviet Union)	30 Apr 54	226UNTS109	103111
Austria	USSR (Soviet Union)	09 Nov 55	255UNTS247	103613
Denmark	UK Great Britain	27 Feb 56	252UNTS83	103558
Bulgaria	Yugoslavia	22 May 56	367UNTS119	105229
India	Thailand	12 Jun 56	255UNTS341	103617
Finland	USSR (Soviet Union)	14 Sep 56	255UNTS365	103618
Turkey	UK Great Britain	28 Feb 57	310UNTS29	104483
Multilateral		25 Mar 57	294UNTS2	104300
Albania	Yugoslavia	29 Aug 57	391UNTS167	105622
Multilateral		25 Nov 57	403UNTS169	105795
Ceylon (Sri Lanka)	India	13 Jan 58	315UNTS107	104562
Canada	USA (United States)	09 Mar 59	340UNTS295	104872
New Zealand	UK Great Britain	12 Aug 59	354UNTS161	105062
Multilateral		01 Sep 59	454UNTS289	106542
Argentina	Brazil	26 Nov 59	374UNTS45	105327
Australia	Canada	12 Feb 60	369UNTS89	105253
Belgium	Netherlands	20 Jun 60	423UNTS19	106084
Multilateral		08 Oct 60	450UNTS309	106476
Malaysia	New Zealand	03 Feb 61	447UNTS251	106418
Denmark	Jordan	07 Dec 61	631UNTS333	109003
Portugal	USA (United States)	05 Mar 62	436UNTS101	106290
EEC (Econ Commnty)	USA (United States)	07 Mar 62	436UNTS49	106288
Canada	USA (United States)	07 Mar 62	436UNTS3	106286
Multilateral		07 Mar 62	445UNTS205	106389
Japan	New Zealand	09 Mar 62	485UNTS351	107066

PARTY ONE	PARTY TWO	DATE	CITATION	NUMBER
Tariffs (Cont.)				
Haiti	USA (United States)	06 Jun 62	452UNTS59	106504
Spain	USA (United States)	31 Dec 62	471UNTS99	106825
New Zealand	UK Great Britain	15 May 63	486UNTS11	107068
Belgium	Cyprus	08 Jun 63	601UNTS311	108703
Switzerland	USA (United States)	11 Jul 63	487UNTS177	107102
Iceland	USA (United States)	15 Jul 63	527UNTS45	107616
Argentina	USA (United States)	24 Jul 63	487UNTS183	107103
Lebanon	Pakistan	04 Feb 64	614UNTS55	108863
Argentina	Paraguay	07 Feb 64	634UNTS127	109057
Norway	Yugoslavia	15 Apr 64	602UNTS177	108712
Cyprus	Hungary	02 Jun 64	602UNTS3	108704
Ireland	Vietnam, South	01 Dec 64	553UNTS233	108091
Canada	USA (United States)	16 Jan 65	606UNTS31	108772
Mauritania	Spain	11 May 65	602UNTS111	108709
Malaysia	Norway	26 May 65	602UNTS157	108711
Australia	Philippines	16 Jun 65	541UNTS31	107858
Australia	New Zealand	31 Aug 65	554UNTS169	108101
Nigeria	Switzerland	11 Oct 65	602UNTS137	108710
Ireland	UK Great Britain	14 Dec 65	565UNTS58	108235
Burma	Czechoslovakia	15 Dec 65	602UNTS71	108707
Canada	USA (United States)	17 Dec 65	574UNTS49	108341
UK Great Britain	USA (United States)	05 Apr 66	592UNTS61	108569
Bulgaria	Turkey	18 Apr 66	631UNTS263	108999
Austria	USA (United States)	23 Jun 66	601UNTS51	108687
Argentina	USA (United States)	08 Aug 66	606UNTS209	108786
Denmark	Norway	23 Dec 66	613UNTS265	108855
Congo (Brazzaville)	Denmark	27 Feb 67	600UNTS189	108681
Trinidad/Tobago	UK Great Britain	01 Mar 67	606UNTS149	108784
Malta	USA (United States)	14 Jun 67	604UNTS231	108753
Malta	UK Great Britain	10 Jul 67	619UNTS11	108936
Singapore	UK Great Britain	01 Aug 67	619UNTS29	108937
Malaysia	UK Great Britain	01 Aug 67	633UNTS93	109036
Denmark	Malaysia	14 Dec 67	614UNTS26	108862
Austria	Romania	28 Apr 68	0UNTS0	109377
Multilateral		24 Dec 68	0UNTS0	109369
Maritime products and equipment				
Multilateral		30 Oct 46	11UNTS107	100151
Canada	USA (United States)	30 Apr 48	77UNTS191	100999
Ethiopia	USA (United States)	07 Sep 51	206UNTS41	102785
Denmark	Israel	14 Nov 52	160UNTS279	102113
Multilateral		29 Nov 54	287UNTS209	104187
Multilateral		16 Aug 56	287UNTS223	104188
Japan	Norway	28 Feb 57	280UNTS87	104054
USSR (Soviet Union)	Vietnam, North	12 Mar 58	356UNTS149	105094
Multilateral		04 Jan 60	370UNTS3	105266
Fed of Malaya	Japan	10 May 60	383UNTS293	105506
Brazil	USSR (Soviet Union)	20 Apr 63	0UNTS0	109256
Iran	USA (United States)	29 Sep 64	531UNTS163	107702
Certificates of origin				
Belgium	Denmark	08 Apr 46	4UNTS429	100059
Denmark	Luxembourg	21 May 46	4UNTS435	100060
Multilateral		30 Oct 47	55UNTS188	100814
Argentina	Norway	09 Sep 49	42UNTS125	100646
Indonesia	USA (United States)	02 Mar 56	271UNTS345	103925
Austria	Czechoslovakia	14 Sep 60	495UNTS143	107243
Iraq	Syria	03 Nov 61	489UNTS45	107134
Multilateral		28 Sep 62	469UNTS169	106791
Brazil	Taiwan	28 Dec 62	500UNTS61	107307
Multilateral		13 Aug 63	592UNTS139	108572
Tanganyika	USSR (Soviet Union)	14 Aug 63	493UNTS195	107215
Czechoslovakia	Romania	16 Dec 63	527UNTS285	107630
Czechoslovakia	Hungary	20 Dec 63	538UNTS127	107812
Taiwan	Peru	08 Jun 64	548UNTS151	107976
Taiwan	Ecuador	17 Jun 64	533UNTS141	107740

PARTY ONE	PARTY TWO	DATE	CITATION	NUMBER
Certificates of origin (Cont.)				
Taiwan	Ecuador	23 Oct 64	543UNTS241	107904
Taiwan	Guatemala	08 Nov 64	543UNTS227	107903
Haiti	Israel	28 Mar 67	630UNTS293	108975
Netherlands	Romania	20 Jul 67	633UNTS21	109032
Reciprocity in trade				
Brazil	Canada	17 Oct 41	67UNTS263	200224
Peru	USA (United States)	07 May 42	103UNTS219	200316
USA (United States)	Uruguay	21 Jul 42	120UNTS211	200393
Iran	USA (United States)	08 Apr 43	106UNTS155	200340
Chile	USA (United States)	30 Jul 45	6UNTS409	200042
France	USA (United States)	08 Nov 45	76UNTS151	100986
Poland	Yugoslavia	23 Nov 45	115UNTS3	101555
Canada	Mexico	08 Feb 46	230UNTS183	103183
Poland	USA (United States)	24 Apr 46	4UNTS155	100042
Paraguay	USA (United States)	12 Sep 46	125UNTS179	101677
Canada	Taiwan	26 Sep 46	14UNTS167	100219
Taiwan	USA (United States)	04 Nov 46	25UNTS69	100359
Canada	Nicaragua	19 Dec 46	236UNTS229	103326
Belgium	Turkey	12 Mar 47	37UNTS221	100579
Hungary	USSR (Soviet Union)	15 Jul 47	216UNTS247	102940
Multilateral		30 Oct 47	55UNTS188	100814
Czechoslovakia	USSR (Soviet Union)	11 Dec 47	217UNTS35	102943
Norway	Poland	04 Feb 48	30UNTS205	100458
Canada	Turkey	15 Mar 48	231UNTS63	103205
Bulgaria	USSR (Soviet Union)	01 Apr 48	217UNTS97	102946
Canada	Italy	28 Apr 48	231UNTS69	103206
Norway	Switzerland	26 Jun 48	29UNTS193	100440
Ireland	USA (United States)	28 Jun 48	32UNTS69	100489
Italy	USSR (Soviet Union)	11 Dec 48	217UNTS181	102948
Argentina	Denmark	14 Dec 48	74UNTS41	100956
Norway	Poland	31 Dec 48	29UNTS3	100430
Argentina	Norway	09 Sep 49	42UNTS125	100646
Italy	Norway	19 Nov 49	47UNTS75	100723
Denmark	Poland	07 Dec 49	81UNTS21	101059
Ireland	USA (United States)	21 Jan 50	206UNTS269	102792
Denmark	Spain	12 Jul 50	71UNTS135	100914
Canada	Venezuela	11 Oct 50	231UNTS3	103198
Canada	Ecuador	10 Nov 50	231UNTS15	103199
Canada	Costa Rica	18 Nov 50	231UNTS25	103200
Norway	Pakistan	21 May 51	318UNTS163	104613
Greece	USA (United States)	03 Aug 51	224UNTS279	103080
Israel	USA (United States)	23 Aug 51	219UNTS237	102979
Denmark	USA (United States)	01 Oct 51	421UNTS105	106056
Denmark	Italy	24 Oct 51	118UNTS91	101598
El Salvador	Guatemala	14 Dec 51	131UNTS131	101740
Ireland	Spain	19 Dec 51	0UNTS0	109228
Denmark	Poland	09 Jun 52	135UNTS209	101822
Greece	Israel	22 Jul 52	219UNTS231	102978
Japan	USA (United States)	02 Apr 53	206UNTS143	102788
Multilateral		24 Jul 53	250UNTS108	103520
Ceylon (Sri Lanka)	Yugoslavia	30 Jul 53	337UNTS103	104819
Argentina	USSR (Soviet Union)	05 Aug 53	221UNTS99	103004
Canada	Japan	31 Mar 54	236UNTS329	103334
Denmark	USA (United States)	15 Dec 54	213UNTS273	102890
India	Iran	15 Dec 54	327UNTS245	104724
USSR (Soviet Union)	Yugoslavia	05 Jan 55	240UNTS207	103404
Canada	Ethiopia	03 Jun 55	247UNTS157	103465
Austria	USSR (Soviet Union)	17 Oct 55	240UNTS289	103409
USSR (Soviet Union)	Yemen	31 Oct 55	240UNTS317	103410
Italy	Lebanon	04 Nov 55	267UNTS113	103838
Italy	Syria	10 Nov 55	267UNTS157	103841
Syria	USSR (Soviet Union)	16 Nov 55	259UNTS71	103683
Paraguay	UK Great Britain	21 Nov 55	252UNTS107	103560
Costa Rica	Guatemala	20 Dec 55	280UNTS121	104056

PARTY ONE	PARTY TWO	DATE	CITATION	NUMBER
Reciprocity in trade (Cont.)				
Nicaragua	USA (United States)	21 Jan 56	367UNTS3	105224
Canada	USSR (Soviet Union)	29 Feb 56	252UNTS165	103566
Canada	Honduras	11 Jul 56	305UNTS39	104411
Multilateral		16 Aug 56	287UNTS223	104188
Costa Rica	Denmark	26 Sep 56	341UNTS305	104893
Taiwan	Philippines	18 Oct 56	541UNTS57	107860
Japan	Norway	28 Feb 57	280UNTS87	104054
Multilateral		25 Mar 57	294UNTS2	104300
Ceylon (Sri Lanka)	Italy	23 Apr 57	337UNTS115	104820
Multilateral		27 Jun 57	284UNTS139	104133
UK Great Britain	USA (United States)	27 Jun 57	284UNTS75	104130
Australia	Japan	06 Jul 57	318UNTS381	104627
Germany, East	USSR (Soviet Union)	27 Sep 57	292UNTS75	104268
Argentina	Denmark	25 Nov 57	299UNTS83	104308
Argentina	Italy	25 Nov 57	305UNTS275	104424
Japan	USSR (Soviet Union)	06 Dec 57	325UNTS35	104694
China People's Rep	USSR (Soviet Union)	21 Dec 57	305UNTS213	104420
India	Japan	04 Feb 58	324UNTS215	104687
Albania	USSR (Soviet Union)	15 Feb 58	313UNTS261	104536
Denmark	El Salvador	09 Jul 58	341UNTS289	104892
Japan	New Zealand	09 Sep 58	325UNTS119	104698
Fed Rhod/Nyasaland	Portugal	29 Nov 58	354UNTS137	105060
Haiti	Japan	17 Dec 58	518UNTS91	107492
Multilateral		15 Jan 59	348UNTS13	104996
Japan	Yugoslavia	28 Feb 59	341UNTS179	104883
UK Great Britain	USSR (Soviet Union)	24 May 59	374UNTS305	105344
New Zealand	UK Great Britain	12 Aug 59	354UNTS161	105062
Czechoslovakia	Germany, East	25 Nov 59	374UNTS101	105331
Czechoslovakia	Japan	15 Dec 59	383UNTS277	105505
Multilateral		06 Feb 60	383UNTS3	105494
Australia	Canada	12 Feb 60	369UNTS89	105253
Greece	Tunisia	02 Mar 60	483UNTS89	107008
Multilateral		13 Dec 60	455UNTS3	106543
Tunisia	UK Great Britain	17 Jan 61	566UNTS2	108236
USA (United States)	Vietnam, South	03 Apr 61	424UNTS137	106106
Japan	Peru	15 May 61	451UNTS3	106482
Korea, South	Thailand	15 Sep 61	413UNTS137	105948
Argentina	Thailand	10 Dec 61	422UNTS87	106070
Argentina	Japan	20 Dec 61	613UNTS323	108859
Israel	Vietnam, South	11 Apr 62	448UNTS205	106432
Brazil	USA (United States)	19 Apr 62	456UNTS255	106560
Taiwan	Paraguay	11 Jul 62	458UNTS41	106591
Cyprus	Greece	23 Aug 62	609UNTS15	108825
Laos	USSR (Soviet Union)	01 Dec 62	458UNTS21	106590
Austria	Czechoslovakia	08 Mar 63	495UNTS219	107245
Brazil	USSR (Soviet Union)	20 Apr 63	0UNTS0	109257
Brazil	USSR (Soviet Union)	20 Apr 63	0UNTS0	109256
El Salvador	USA (United States)	07 May 63	476UNTS35	106901
India	USA (United States)	09 May 63	476UNTS43	106902
France	Japan	14 May 63	518UNTS111	107493
India	USSR (Soviet Union)	10 Jun 63	0UNTS0	109382
India	USA (United States)	27 Jun 63	479UNTS215	106955
El Salvador	Japan	19 Jul 63	518UNTS135	107494
New Zealand	USSR (Soviet Union)	01 Aug 63	486UNTS27	107070
Dominican Republic	USA (United States)	13 Aug 63	492UNTS327	107202
Multilateral		13 Aug 63	592UNTS139	108572
Tanganyika	USSR (Soviet Union)	14 Aug 63	493UNTS195	107215
Iraq	USA (United States)	27 Aug 63	489UNTS271	107144
Paraguay	USA (United States)	16 Sep 63	494UNTS101	107229
Peru	USA (United States)	23 Sep 63	488UNTS91	107121
Czechoslovakia	Romania	16 Dec 63	527UNTS285	107630
Taiwan	Ecuador	17 Jun 64	533UNTS141	107740
Greece	Norway	25 Sep 64	610UNTS0	108835
Argentina	Yugoslavia	09 Jun 65	601UNTS3	108684
Australia	Philippines	16 Jun 65	541UNTS31	107858

PARTY ONE	PARTY TWO	DATE	CITATION	NUMBER
Reciprocity in trade (Cont.)				
Argentina	United Arab Rep	21 Jun 65	634UNTS161	109058
Australia	USSR (Soviet Union)	15 Oct 65	553UNTS239	108092
Ireland	UK Great Britain	14 Dec 65	565UNTS58	108235
Singapore	USA (United States)	30 Aug 66	616UNTS242	108899
Ghana	Romania	23 Nov 66	642UNTS63	109165
Korea, South	New Zealand	31 Jan 67	598UNTS91	108656
Bulgaria	USSR (Soviet Union)	12 May 67	631UNTS239	108997
Australia	Romania	18 May 67	642UNTS25	109162
Bulgaria	New Zealand	03 Nov 67	0UNTS0	109207
Reexport of goods, etc.				
USA (United States)	Yugoslavia	24 Jul 42	34UNTS361	200179
Iran	USA (United States)	08 Apr 43	106UNTS155	200340
USA (United States)	USSR (Soviet Union)	15 Oct 45	278UNTS151	200547
Netherlands	Portugal	12 Apr 46	4UNTS317	100054
Netherlands	Spain	13 Jul 46	4UNTS351	100055
Czechoslovakia	USSR (Soviet Union)	25 Jul 46	27UNTS231	100409
Netherlands	UK Great Britain	13 Aug 46	4UNTS367	100056
Netherlands	Turkey	19 Mar 47	14UNTS59	100211
Greece	Netherlands	17 Apr 47	32UNTS115	100494
France	Greece	05 May 47	76UNTS61	100980
Albania	Yugoslavia	22 Jun 47	111UNTS207	101536
Hungary	USSR (Soviet Union)	15 Jul 47	216UNTS247	102940
France	India	16 Jul 47	27UNTS325	100415
Netherlands	Thailand	18 Jul 47	28UNTS27	100417
Netherlands	South Africa	22 Jul 47	12UNTS257	100188
Netherlands	IBRD (World Bank)	07 Aug 47	152UNTS165	102015
Denmark	IBRD (World Bank)	22 Aug 47	152UNTS223	102016
Luxembourg	IBRD (World Bank)	28 Aug 47	153UNTS3	102017
Czechoslovakia	Netherlands	01 Sep 47	32UNTS129	100495
Taiwan	Netherlands	06 Dec 47	43UNTS185	100669
Czechoslovakia	USSR (Soviet Union)	11 Dec 47	217UNTS35	102943
Austria	Netherlands	22 Jan 48	17UNTS99	100270
Italy	USA (United States)	02 Feb 48	79UNTS171	101040
Argentina	Denmark	18 Mar 48	94UNTS175	101311
Bulgaria	USSR (Soviet Union)	01 Apr 48	217UNTS97	102946
Pakistan	Sweden	06 May 48	36UNTS3	100564
Ireland	Netherlands	10 May 48	28UNTS121	100422
India	Sweden	21 May 48	34UNTS285	100543
Greece	Switzerland	26 May 48	94UNTS217	101312
India	Pakistan	23 Jun 48	28UNTS143	100423
France	Spain	23 Aug 48	28UNTS173	100425
Greece	Lebanon	06 Sep 48	178UNTS37	102335
Netherlands	Spain	08 Oct 48	28UNTS209	100426
Mexico	Portugal	22 Oct 48	34UNTS329	100546
Argentina	Netherlands	29 Oct 48	95UNTS21	101316
Korea, South	USA (United States)	10 Dec 48	55UNTS157	100813
Italy	USSR (Soviet Union)	11 Dec 48	217UNTS181	102948
Ceylon (Sri Lanka)	Pakistan	03 Jan 49	28UNTS247	100428
Italy	Lebanon	24 Jan 49	231UNTS241	103223
France	Norway	09 Feb 49	29UNTS13	100431
Finland	Netherlands	25 Feb 49	53UNTS123	100777
Belgium	IBRD (World Bank)	01 Mar 49	154UNTS133	102029
Netherlands	Switzerland	07 Mar 49	35UNTS69	100551
Italy	Spain	31 May 49	231UNTS251	103224
Australia	Pakistan	03 Jun 49	35UNTS23	100549
Belgium	Greece	21 Jun 49	137UNTS215	101854
Norway	Pakistan	23 Jun 49	35UNTS49	100550
Pakistan	Philippines	16 Jul 49	35UNTS111	100553
Greece	Turkey	21 Jul 49	78UNTS55	101011
Pakistan	UK Great Britain	27 Jul 49	44UNTS199	100685
Brazil	UK Great Britain	03 Aug 49	86UNTS113	101154
Argentina	Norway	09 Sep 49	42UNTS125	100646
Lebanon	Netherlands	20 Sep 49	108UNTS205	101474
Finland	IBRD (World Bank)	17 Oct 49	156UNTS355	200481

PARTY ONE	PARTY TWO	DATE	CITATION	NUMBER
Reexport of goods, etc. (Cont.)				
Denmark	Pakistan	09 Nov 49	44UNTS255	100687
Sweden	Thailand	23 Nov 49	72UNTS217	100935
Denmark	Thailand	23 Nov 49	53UNTS255	100786
Norway	Thailand	26 Nov 49	53UNTS269	100787
Brazil	Spain	28 Nov 49	215UNTS303	102923
Austria	Sweden	02 Dec 49	108UNTS3	101465
Austria	Norway	02 Dec 49	72UNTS230	100936
Spain	Sweden	18 Feb 50	166UNTS15	102184
Ceylon (Sri Lanka)	Thailand	24 Feb 50	72UNTS261	100938
Italy	Netherlands	04 Mar 50	254UNTS305	103598
Iceland	Netherlands	22 Mar 50	95UNTS237	101323
Austria	Czechoslovakia	30 Mar 50	495UNTS85	107240
Italy	Portugal	05 Apr 50	254UNTS329	103599
Netherlands	Spain	20 Jun 50	95UNTS303	101327
Iraq	Pakistan	20 Jun 50	77UNTS215	101001
France	Pakistan	31 Jul 50	96UNTS23	101329
India	Nepal	31 Jul 50	104UNTS3	101430
Brazil	UK Great Britain	18 Sep 50	88UNTS115	101188
Israel	Netherlands	23 Oct 50	189UNTS89	102543
Multilateral		22 Nov 50	131UNTS25	101734
Cuba	USA (United States)	22 Dec 50	122UNTS97	101640
Norway	USA (United States)	28 Dec 50	240UNTS391	103414
India	USA (United States)	28 Dec 50	99UNTS39	101369
Nepal	USA (United States)	23 Jan 51	184UNTS65	102439
Colombia	Portugal	09 Mar 51	108UNTS87	101469
United Arab Rep	USA (United States)	05 May 51	198UNTS265	102670
Cuba	Portugal	26 Jun 51	192UNTS115	102598
Burma	Netherlands	06 Sep 51	108UNTS187	101473
Greece	Luxembourg	22 Oct 51	187UNTS119	102506
Denmark	USA (United States)	16 Nov 51	180UNTS275	102391
Greece	USA (United States)	07 Jan 52	177UNTS249	102323
Pakistan	Switzerland	17 Mar 52	192UNTS237	102603
France	Mexico	17 Apr 52	163UNTS321	102153
France	Israel	29 Apr 52	189UNTS55	102542
Belgium	Italy	25 Jun 52	137UNTS239	101855
Portugal	USA (United States)	09 Jul 52	180UNTS251	102389
Czechoslovakia	Romania	31 Jul 52	362UNTS123	105185
Ethiopia	Pakistan	29 Aug 52	150UNTS257	101979
Denmark	Portugal	29 Aug 52	149UNTS49	101950
Germany, West	Israel	10 Sep 52	162UNTS205	102137
Austria	Luxembourg	13 Oct 52	192UNTS291	102606
Burma	UK Great Britain	25 Oct 52	150UNTS237	101978
Multilateral		07 Nov 52	221UNTS255	103010
Philippines	Thailand	27 Apr 53	174UNTS3	102274
Greece	United Arab Rep	21 May 53	256UNTS17	103620
UN Relief Palestin	United Arab Rep	14 Oct 53	190UNTS13	102555
Greece	Turkey	07 Nov 53	225UNTS163	103098
Belgium	USA (United States)	17 Nov 53	251UNTS105	103536
Hungary	Romania	14 Dec 53	342UNTS151	104906
France	Sweden	16 Feb 54	228UNTS137	103147
Multilateral		19 Feb 54	214UNTS51	102899
United Arab Rep	USA (United States)	24 Feb 54	236UNTS61	103316
Japan	USA (United States)	08 Mar 54	232UNTS215	103237
Honduras	USA (United States)	24 May 54	433UNTS155	106238
Luxembourg	USA (United States)	07 Jul 54	233UNTS23	103247
Bulgaria	Romania	22 Jul 54	362UNTS101	105184
Denmark	Sweden	28 Oct 54	262UNTS211	103747
Burma	Japan	05 Nov 54	251UNTS215	103543
Turkey	USA (United States)	15 Nov 54	238UNTS135	103358
Ecuador	Netherlands	14 Dec 54	232UNTS115	103233
USA (United States)	Yugoslavia	05 Jan 55	251UNTS29	103531
Austria	Belgium	07 Jan 55	380UNTS219	105458
Haiti	USA (United States)	05 Apr 55	270UNTS97	103895
Dominican Republic	USA (United States)	22 Apr 55	239UNTS325	103389
Finland	USA (United States)	06 May 55	251UNTS3	103529

Reexport of goods, etc. (Cont.)

PARTY ONE	PARTY TWO	DATE	CITATION	NUMBER
USA (United States)	Vietnam, South	10 May 55	273UNTS157	103950
Italy	USA (United States)	23 May 55	251UNTS303	103547
Turkey	USA (United States)	26 May 55	262UNTS97	103739
Korea, South	USA (United States)	31 May 55	251UNTS321	103548
Austria	USA (United States)	14 Jun 55	258UNTS37	103668
UK Great Britain	USA (United States)	15 Jun 55	229UNTS73	103161
Canada	USA (United States)	15 Jun 55	235UNTS176	103301
Bulgaria	Yugoslavia	17 Jun 55	375UNTS287	105370
Greece	USA (United States)	24 Jun 55	270UNTS351	103905
Greece	USA (United States)	24 Jun 55	270UNTS361	103906
Germany, West	USA (United States)	30 Jun 55	240UNTS69	103394
Germany, East	Romania	05 Aug 55	342UNTS229	104910
France	USA (United States)	11 Aug 55	251UNTS15	103530
France	USA (United States)	23 Sep 55	270UNTS341	103904
France	Germany, West	04 Oct 55	353UNTS203	105044
Brazil	USA (United States)	16 Nov 55	239UNTS207	103381
Austria	Israel	17 Nov 55	232UNTS153	103235
Belgium	UK Great Britain	18 Nov 55	222UNTS327	103038
Argentina	USA (United States)	21 Dec 55	240UNTS329	103411
Austria	Italy	23 Jan 56	393UNTS97	105653
Argentina	Switzerland	25 Jan 56	559UNTS121	108157
Italy	Switzerland	02 Feb 56	291UNTS113	104247
Austria	USA (United States)	07 Feb 56	272UNTS117	103933
Netherlands	Sudan	12 Feb 56	311UNTS319	104508
Iran	USA (United States)	20 Feb 56	272UNTS135	103934
Pakistan	USA (United States)	02 Mar 56	271UNTS371	103927
Spain	USA (United States)	05 Mar 56	271UNTS329	103924
Ethiopia	Italy	05 Mar 56	267UNTS189	103844
Turkey	USA (United States)	12 Mar 56	272UNTS21	103929
Korea, South	USA (United States)	13 Mar 56	272UNTS3	103928
Taiwan	USA (United States)	03 Apr 56	268UNTS315	103864
Paraguay	USA (United States)	02 May 56	268UNTS299	103863
Japan	Philippines	09 May 56	285UNTS3	104148
Greece	Italy	26 May 56	496UNTS301	107258
Italy	Switzerland	04 Jun 56	378UNTS311	105429
Korea, South	USA (United States)	02 Jul 56	281UNTS41	104067
Lebanon	UNICEF (Children)	03 Jul 56	324UNTS145	104683
Pakistan	USA (United States)	07 Aug 56	281UNTS75	104071
Greece	USA (United States)	08 Aug 56	277UNTS203	104007
Taiwan	USA (United States)	14 Aug 56	281UNTS257	104083
India	USA (United States)	29 Aug 56	278UNTS25	104019
Israel	USA (United States)	11 Sep 56	277UNTS215	104008
Romania	Yugoslavia	25 Sep 56	395UNTS147	105683
Germany, West	Netherlands	28 Sep 56	327UNTS185	104722
Italy	USA (United States)	30 Oct 56	263UNTS221	103775
Ceylon (Sri Lanka)	USA (United States)	02 Nov 56	282UNTS93	104094
USA (United States)	Yugoslavia	03 Nov 56	277UNTS119	104002
Multilateral		08 Nov 56	470UNTS171	106809
Burma	USA (United States)	04 Dec 56	268UNTS189	103858
Brazil	USA (United States)	31 Dec 56	266UNTS151	103829
Iceland	Thailand	22 Jan 57	312UNTS63	104511
Denmark	Germany, West	29 Jan 57	302UNTS75	104354
Korea, South	USA (United States)	30 Jan 57	278UNTS85	104024
Ecuador	USA (United States)	15 Feb 57	279UNTS155	104037
Thailand	USA (United States)	04 Mar 57	279UNTS235	104043
Belgium	Czechoslovakia	12 Mar 57	312UNTS75	104512
Netherlands	USA (United States)	03 Apr 57	410UNTS193	105904
Iceland	USA (United States)	11 Apr 57	283UNTS107	104110
Colombia	USA (United States)	16 Apr 57	283UNTS245	104121
Peru	USA (United States)	02 May 57	283UNTS55	104106
Austria	USA (United States)	10 May 57	283UNTS15	104103
Belgium	Bulgaria	14 May 57	317UNTS81	104596
Albania	Yugoslavia	20 May 57	363UNTS99	105203
Belgium	Hungary	01 Jun 57	291UNTS17	104242
Bulgaria	Yugoslavia	04 Jun 57	349UNTS35	105008

Reexport of goods, etc. (Cont.)

PARTY ONE	PARTY TWO	DATE	CITATION	NUMBER
Poland	USA (United States)	07 Jun 57	291UNTS41	104243
Bolivia	USA (United States)	07 Jun 57	291UNTS77	104245
Philippines	USA (United States)	25 Jun 57	289UNTS279	104224
Greece	Italy	02 Aug 57	533UNTS217	107744
Netherlands	Romania	27 Aug 57	342UNTS309	104914
Multilateral		03 Oct 57	366UNTS87	105216
Italy	Pakistan	05 Oct 57	353UNTS91	105039
Mexico	USA (United States)	23 Oct 57	300UNTS35	104330
Germany, East	Hungary	25 Oct 57	408UNTS156	105869
Israel	USA (United States)	07 Nov 57	302UNTS255	104365
Pakistan	USA (United States)	15 Nov 57	303UNTS173	104380
Argentina	UNICEF (Children)	19 Nov 57	300UNTS229	104338
Greece	USA (United States)	18 Dec 57	303UNTS159	104379
France	USA (United States)	27 Dec 57	307UNTS79	104444
Turkey	USA (United States)	20 Jan 58	304UNTS15	104389
Indonesia	Japan	20 Jan 58	324UNTS247	104689
Spain	USA (United States)	27 Jan 58	303UNTS247	104384
UK Great Britain	USA (United States)	03 Feb 58	307UNTS199	104450
USA (United States)	Yugoslavia	03 Feb 58	304UNTS293	104404
India	Japan	04 Feb 58	324UNTS215	104687
Korea, South	USA (United States)	05 Feb 58	307UNTS121	104447
Bulgaria	Netherlands	07 Feb 58	335UNTS45	104777
Poland	USA (United States)	15 Feb 58	307UNTS217	104452
Finland	USA (United States)	21 Feb 58	304UNTS253	104401
France	USA (United States)	28 Feb 58	366UNTS343	105222
Norway	Pakistan	05 Mar 58	334UNTS199	104769
Pakistan	Sweden	06 Mar 58	393UNTS181	105656
Colombia	USA (United States)	14 Mar 58	308UNTS115	104459
Germany, West	Portugal	21 Mar 58	464UNTS71	106712
Belgium	Luxembourg	28 Mar 58	303UNTS101	104372
Morocco	Portugal	03 Apr 58	393UNTS203	105657
Peru	USA (United States)	09 Apr 58	316UNTS37	104576
Taiwan	USA (United States)	18 Apr 58	308UNTS179	104461
China People's Rep	USSR (Soviet Union)	23 Apr 58	313UNTS135	104534
Iceland	USA (United States)	03 May 58	316UNTS137	104581
Burma	USA (United States)	27 May 58	315UNTS197	104569
India	USSR (Soviet Union)	02 Jun 58	393UNTS3	105650
Philippines	USA (United States)	03 Jun 58	316UNTS3	104573
Netherlands	USSR (Soviet Union)	17 Jun 58	335UNTS77	104779
Ceylon (Sri Lanka)	USA (United States)	18 Jun 58	316UNTS15	104574
Ecuador	USA (United States)	30 Jun 58	336UNTS11	104796
India	USA (United States)	26 Sep 58	336UNTS59	104798
Israel	USA (United States)	06 Nov 58	336UNTS275	104810
Pakistan	USA (United States)	26 Nov 58	337UNTS3	104812
Liberia	Netherlands	28 Nov 58	393UNTS55	105651
USA (United States)	Yugoslavia	22 Dec 58	338UNTS243	104839
Iraq	Romania	24 Dec 58	405UNTS243	105836
United Arab Rep	USA (United States)	24 Dec 58	338UNTS221	104837
Finland	USA (United States)	30 Dec 58	340UNTS259	104869
Spain	USA (United States)	13 Jan 59	341UNTS241	104887
Turkey	USA (United States)	13 Feb 59	340UNTS235	104867
Iceland	USA (United States)	03 Mar 59	341UNTS261	104889
Ceylon (Sri Lanka)	USA (United States)	13 Mar 59	342UNTS51	104900
Netherlands	Tunisia	19 Mar 59	497UNTS61	107262
Sweden	Tunisia	19 Mar 59	497UNTS43	107261
France	USA (United States)	21 Mar 59	342UNTS71	104901
Norway	Tunisia	28 Mar 59	497UNTS77	107263
Denmark	Tunisia	14 Apr 59	340UNTS273	104870
Ceylon (Sri Lanka)	Denmark	29 May 59	348UNTS225	105002
Ceylon (Sri Lanka)	Norway	29 May 59	411UNTS165	105919
Ceylon (Sri Lanka)	Sweden	29 May 59	464UNTS109	106713
Indonesia	USA (United States)	29 May 59	347UNTS85	104992
Taiwan	USA (United States)	09 Jun 59	353UNTS257	105046
Argentina	USA (United States)	12 Jun 59	347UNTS59	104990
Korea, South	USA (United States)	30 Jun 59	353UNTS297	105047

Reexport of goods, etc. (Cont.)

PARTY ONE	PARTY TWO	DATE	CITATION	NUMBER
India	Italy	16 Jul 59	464UNTS129	106714
United Arab Rep	USA (United States)	29 Jul 59	357UNTS121	105111
Colombia	USA (United States)	06 Oct 59	358UNTS145	105132
USA (United States)	Vietnam, South	16 Oct 59	360UNTS271	105163
Turkey	USA (United States)	13 Nov 59	361UNTS3	105168
India	USA (United States)	13 Nov 59	360UNTS287	105164
United Arab Rep	USA (United States)	14 Nov 59	360UNTS311	105165
Czechoslovakia	Germany, East	25 Nov 59	374UNTS101	105331
Belgium	USA (United States)	27 Nov 59	366UNTS331	105221
Liberia	Sweden	09 Dec 59	464UNTS219	106716
Turkey	USA (United States)	22 Dec 59	367UNTS57	105225
Denmark	Sweden	04 Jan 60	376UNTS375	105390
Greece	USA (United States)	07 Jan 60	368UNTS221	105243
Czechoslovakia	UK Great Britain	15 Jan 60	374UNTS207	105336
Peru	USA (United States)	12 Feb 60	372UNTS83	105290
Cuba	USSR (Soviet Union)	13 Feb 60	369UNTS17	105248
Greece	USA (United States)	15 Feb 60	377UNTS95	105397
France	Thailand	26 Feb 60	392UNTS279	105648
Guinea	Netherlands	09 Mar 60	392UNTS243	105646
Iceland	USA (United States)	06 Apr 60	372UNTS71	105289
Pakistan	USA (United States)	11 Apr 60	372UNTS251	105302
Laos	UN Special Fund	30 Apr 60	361UNTS171	105179
India	USA (United States)	04 May 60	376UNTS279	105384
Lebanon	UN Special Fund	07 May 60	360UNTS225	105160
Morocco	United Arab Rep	19 May 60	563UNTS121	108208
Afghanistan	Czechoslovakia	28 May 60	497UNTS129	107266
Cuba	Czechoslovakia	10 Jun 60	447UNTS75	106412
Spain	USA (United States)	22 Jun 60	378UNTS3	105414
Denmark	Peru	22 Jun 60	439UNTS113	106326
Korea, North	USSR (Soviet Union)	22 Jun 60	399UNTS3	105732
Ireland	Portugal	24 Jun 60	412UNTS30	105924
Kuwait	UN Special Fund	29 Jun 60	369UNTS419	200575
Ethiopia	UN Special Fund	13 Jul 60	368UNTS159	105240
Poland	USA (United States)	21 Jul 60	380UNTS157	105456
Iran	USA (United States)	26 Jul 60	384UNTS141	105516
United Arab Rep	USA (United States)	01 Aug 60	384UNTS189	105519
United Arab Rep	USA (United States)	09 Aug 60	388UNTS271	105584
Taiwan	USA (United States)	30 Aug 60	388UNTS191	105579
Brazil	UN Special Fund	16 Sep 60	375UNTS3	105351
Taiwan	UN Special Fund	20 Sep 60	375UNTS29	105352
Ecuador	USA (United States)	27 Sep 60	401UNTS115	105766
Ceylon (Sri Lanka)	USA (United States)	30 Sep 60	389UNTS221	105594
Belgium	Jordan	19 Oct 60	479UNTS277	106959
Hungary	UK Great Britain	25 Oct 60	419UNTS309	106034
USA (United States)	Vietnam, South	28 Oct 60	401UNTS3	105758
Norway	Peru	02 Nov 60	497UNTS207	107270
France	USA (United States)	04 Nov 60	400UNTS323	105756
Indonesia	USA (United States)	05 Nov 60	400UNTS35	105746
Greece	USA (United States)	07 Nov 60	400UNTS57	105748
Chile	USA (United States)	08 Nov 60	405UNTS85	105825
Canada	Pakistan	21 Dec 60	465UNTS115	106724
Korea, South	USA (United States)	28 Dec 60	402UNTS3	105773
Jordan	Sweden	09 Jan 61	465UNTS155	106726
Turkey	USA (United States)	11 Jan 61	405UNTS173	105833
Albania	Cuba	16 Jan 61	448UNTS67	106425
Cuba	Czechoslovakia	04 Mar 61	465UNTS209	106728
USA (United States)	Vietnam, South	25 Mar 61	406UNTS187	105849
Multilateral		30 Mar 61	520UNTS151	107515
Ecuador	USA (United States)	03 Apr 61	409UNTS140	105882
Bolivia	USA (United States)	07 Apr 61	433UNTS3	106227
Iceland	USA (United States)	07 Apr 61	406UNTS203	105850
USA (United States)	Yugoslavia	28 Apr 61	409UNTS172	105884
Brazil	USA (United States)	04 May 61	433UNTS91	106233
Israel	USA (United States)	10 May 61	409UNTS213	105887
Poland	Switzerland	18 May 61	559UNTS233	108161

Reexport of goods, etc. (Cont.)

PARTY ONE	PARTY TWO	DATE	CITATION	NUMBER
Spain	USA (United States)	22 May 61	409UNTS260	105891
Czechoslovakia	Morocco	08 Jun 61	497UNTS275	107272
New Zealand	UK Great Britain	13 Jun 61	497UNTS293	107273
Cameroon	France	16 Jun 61	412UNTS148	105929
Guinea	Sweden	17 Jun 61	465UNTS236	106729
Tunisia	USA (United States)	30 Jun 61	434UNTS85	106257
Paraguay	USA (United States)	07 Jul 61	433UNTS53	106231
USA (United States)	Vietnam, South	14 Jul 61	416UNTS133	105999
Taiwan	USA (United States)	21 Jul 61	416UNTS101	105998
Turkey	USA (United States)	29 Jul 61	416UNTS151	106001
Finland	USA (United States)	04 Aug 61	418UNTS19	106014
El Salvador	USA (United States)	21 Aug 61	418UNTS35	106015
Jordan	Norway	21 Aug 61	465UNTS275	106731
Japan	Pakistan	17 Oct 61	466UNTS17	106734
Indonesia	USA (United States)	26 Oct 61	433UNTS249	106248
Iraq	Syria	03 Nov 61	489UNTS45	107134
Iceland	USA (United States)	06 Nov 61	426UNTS225	106140
Syria	USA (United States)	09 Nov 61	435UNTS75	106271
Sudan	USA (United States)	14 Nov 61	434UNTS51	106255
Bolivia	USA (United States)	15 Nov 61	456UNTS192	106557
Congo (Zaire)	USA (United States)	18 Nov 61	433UNTS207	106244
Cyprus	Greece	23 Nov 61	497UNTS311	107274
Philippines	USA (United States)	24 Nov 61	433UNTS315	106251
Czechoslovakia	Mali	27 Nov 61	466UNTS41	106736
Portugal	USA (United States)	28 Nov 61	434UNTS31	106253
Poland	USA (United States)	15 Dec 61	434UNTS3	106252
Czechoslovakia	Guinea	16 Dec 61	559UNTS49	108154
USA (United States)	Vietnam, South	27 Dec 61	433UNTS185	106242
Netherlands	Sweden	08 Jan 62	466UNTS65	106737
Austria	Greece	15 Jan 62	498UNTS3	107275
United Arab Rep	USA (United States)	19 Jan 62	435UNTS107	106273
Iran	USA (United States)	29 Jan 62	435UNTS53	106270
Italy	Japan	31 Jan 62	498UNTS23	107276
Guinea	USA (United States)	02 Feb 62	435UNTS35	106269
Morocco	USA (United States)	09 Feb 62	442UNTS135	106345
Bolivia	USA (United States)	12 Feb 62	451UNTS281	106499
Tunisia	USA (United States)	16 Feb 62	442UNTS161	106347
Indonesia	USA (United States)	19 Feb 62	435UNTS137	106276
Korea, South	USA (United States)	02 Mar 62	442UNTS185	106349
Germany, West	Greece	08 Mar 62	533UNTS269	107747
Brazil	USA (United States)	15 Mar 62	456UNTS209	106558
Iceland	USA (United States)	16 Mar 62	445UNTS49	106376
Peru	USA (United States)	20 Mar 62	445UNTS61	106377
Luxembourg	Spain	26 Mar 62	563UNTS205	108211
Dahomey	UN Special Fund	28 Mar 62	424UNTS55	106099
France	Luxembourg	29 Mar 62	563UNTS227	108212
Sierra Leone	UK Great Britain	05 Apr 62	434UNTS227	106265
Liberia	USA (United States)	12 Apr 62	445UNTS213	106390
Taiwan	USA (United States)	16 Apr 62	445UNTS249	106392
UK Great Britain	USA (United States)	26 Apr 62	445UNTS273	106395
Taiwan	USA (United States)	27 Apr 62	436UNTS25	106287
USA (United States)	Uruguay	27 Apr 62	452UNTS25	106502
India	USA (United States)	01 May 62	451UNTS179	106493
Israel	USA (United States)	03 May 62	442UNTS83	106340
Colombia	USA (United States)	15 May 62	445UNTS279	106396
El Salvador	USA (United States)	15 May 62	452UNTS49	106503
France	Romania	18 May 62	498UNTS115	107279
Guatemala	USA (United States)	21 May 62	451UNTS205	106495
Germany, West	USA (United States)	25 May 62	458UNTS259	106608
France	Senegal	15 Jun 62	524UNTS3	107563
Czechoslovakia	Senegal	20 Jun 62	498UNTS145	107280
Guinea	Norway	21 Jun 62	466UNTS81	106738
United Arab Rep	USSR (Soviet Union)	23 Jun 62	472UNTS43	106836
Liberia	Norway	29 Jun 62	466UNTS95	106739
Morocco	Switzerland	05 Jul 62	498UNTS171	107281

Reexport of goods, etc. (Cont.)

PARTY ONE	PARTY TWO	DATE	CITATION	NUMBER
Chile	USA (United States)	07 Aug 62	461UNTS61	106652
Ethiopia	USA (United States)	13 Aug 62	459UNTS31	106611
IAEA (Atom Energy)	USA (United States)	20 Aug 62	456UNTS447	106570
Taiwan	USA (United States)	31 Aug 62	460UNTS247	106644
Afghanistan	USA (United States)	11 Sep 62	461UNTS169	106661
Tunisia	USA (United States)	14 Sep 62	461UNTS31	106649
Ecuador	Germany, West	20 Sep 62	498UNTS199	107283
Multilateral		28 Sep 62	469UNTS169	106791
United Arab Rep	USA (United States)	08 Oct 62	462UNTS39	106670
Belgium	Romania	12 Oct 62	502UNTS31	107325
Finland	France	12 Oct 62	498UNTS299	107285
Iran	USA (United States)	15 Oct 62	473UNTS291	106866
Netherlands	Norway	18 Oct 62	466UNTS145	106741
France	Ivory Coast	19 Oct 62	498UNTS317	107286
Greece	USA (United States)	22 Oct 62	462UNTS187	106678
Czechoslovakia	Yugoslavia	22 Oct 62	480UNTS267	106974
Japan	UN Special Fund	31 Oct 62	444UNTS171	106368
Korea, South	USA (United States)	07 Nov 62	462UNTS129	106674
Burma	USA (United States)	09 Nov 62	461UNTS113	106655
Poland	Syria	10 Nov 62	491UNTS228	107179
Algeria	UN Special Fund	15 Nov 62	452UNTS243	106512
Ivory Coast	Switzerland	17 Nov 62	499UNTS3	107289
Taiwan	USA (United States)	19 Nov 62	459UNTS263	106629
Ceylon (Sri Lanka)	USA (United States)	21 Nov 62	462UNTS237	106683
Paraguay	USA (United States)	24 Nov 62	471UNTS49	106821
India	USA (United States)	26 Nov 62	460UNTS203	106641
USA (United States)	Yugoslavia	28 Nov 62	460UNTS185	106640
Dominican Republic	USA (United States)	30 Nov 62	471UNTS25	106819
India	USA (United States)	30 Nov 62	459UNTS231	106626
Israel	USA (United States)	06 Dec 62	460UNTS151	106638
Austria	Yugoslavia	11 Dec 62	546UNTS3	107938
Ghana	Tunisia	11 Dec 62	563UNTS243	108213
Bolivia	USA (United States)	17 Dec 62	469UNTS121	106788
Syria	United Arab Rep	27 Dec 62	491UNTS245	107180
Senegal	Switzerland	23 Jan 63	524UNTS23	107564
Sudan	USA (United States)	31 Jan 63	494UNTS119	107230
Poland	USA (United States)	01 Feb 63	487UNTS143	107100
Mali	Senegal	07 Feb 63	524UNTS41	107565
Algeria	France	18 Feb 63	563UNTS263	108214
Turkey	USA (United States)	21 Feb 63	473UNTS311	106867
Congo (Zaire)	USA (United States)	23 Feb 63	493UNTS3	107203
Congo (Zaire)	USA (United States)	23 Feb 63	493UNTS17	107204
Austria	Czechoslovakia	08 Mar 63	495UNTS219	107245
Colombia	USA (United States)	27 Mar 63	489UNTS289	107145
Burma	Japan	29 Mar 63	518UNTS3	107490
Ecuador	USA (United States)	05 Apr 63	477UNTS135	106919
Cyprus	Denmark	27 Apr 63	529UNTS255	107664
Algeria	Morocco	30 Apr 63	564UNTS3	108217
El Salvador	USA (United States)	07 May 63	476UNTS35	106901
India	USA (United States)	09 May 63	476UNTS43	106902
Guinea	USA (United States)	22 May 63	487UNTS251	107108
Finland	Poland	10 Jun 63	503UNTS179	107343
Cyprus	USA (United States)	18 Jun 63	479UNTS191	106953
Guinea	Ivory Coast	26 Jun 63	499UNTS71	107293
Senegal	USA (United States)	03 Jul 63	527UNTS95	107620
Austria	France	12 Jul 63	499UNTS91	107294
Algeria	Mali	22 Jul 63	564UNTS29	108219
Cameroon	Israel	09 Aug 63	499UNTS121	107295
Dominican Republic	USA (United States)	13 Aug 63	492UNTS327	107202
Tanganyika	USSR (Soviet Union)	14 Aug 63	493UNTS195	107215
Iraq	USA (United States)	27 Aug 63	489UNTS271	107144
Brazil	USA (United States)	11 Sep 63	493UNTS267	107220
Paraguay	USA (United States)	16 Sep 63	494UNTS101	107229
Peru	USA (United States)	23 Sep 63	488UNTS91	107121
Greece	Poland	30 Sep 63	534UNTS23	107751

Reexport of goods, etc. (Cont.)

PARTY ONE	PARTY TWO	DATE	CITATION	NUMBER
Pakistan	USSR (Soviet Union)	07 Oct 63	499UNTS161	107297
Ivory Coast	Netherlands	09 Oct 63	499UNTS141	107296
Greece	USA (United States)	30 Oct 63	493UNTS29	107205
Paraguay	USA (United States)	14 Nov 63	505UNTS87	107366
Syria	USA (United States)	18 Nov 63	494UNTS169	107232
Netherlands	USA (United States)	26 Nov 63	388UNTS303	105586
USA (United States)	Vietnam, South	09 Jan 64	505UNTS173	107373
Mali	Niger	15 Jan 64	499UNTS197	107299
Poland	USA (United States)	03 Feb 64	505UNTS215	107375
Poland	USA (United States)	03 Feb 64	505UNTS245	107376
Jordan	USA (United States)	11 Feb 64	511UNTS85	107429
Peru	USA (United States)	13 Feb 64	511UNTS119	107431
Iceland	USA (United States)	13 Feb 64	510UNTS295	107420
Sudan	USA (United States)	02 Mar 64	524UNTS217	107575
Netherlands	Tunisia	03 Mar 64	533UNTS133	107739
Ivory Coast	USA (United States)	10 Mar 64	526UNTS285	107611
Cameroon	Mali	17 Mar 64	524UNTS61	107566
Bolivia	USA (United States)	25 Mar 64	532UNTS3	107710
Malaysia	Netherlands	07 Apr 64	524UNTS81	107567
Portugal	UK Great Britain	07 Apr 64	539UNTS167	107830
Tunisia	USA (United States)	07 Apr 64	527UNTS3	107613
USA (United States)	Yugoslavia	27 Apr 64	526UNTS73	107601
USA (United States)	Yugoslavia	27 Apr 64	526UNTS89	107602
USA (United States)	Yugoslavia	28 Apr 64	526UNTS103	107603
Congo (Zaire)	USA (United States)	28 Apr 64	526UNTS55	107600
Philippines	USA (United States)	14 May 64	526UNTS113	107604
Multilateral		20 Jun 64	539UNTS3	107819
Colombia	Netherlands	06 Jul 64	543UNTS289	107906
Ivory Coast	Mali	09 Jul 64	524UNTS121	107569
Paraguay	USA (United States)	05 Sep 64	530UNTS225	107685
USA (United States)	Vietnam, South	29 Sep 64	531UNTS183	107703
India	USA (United States)	30 Sep 64	532UNTS321	107726
Colombia	USA (United States)	08 Oct 64	579UNTS3	108395
Czechoslovakia	Hungary	17 Oct 64	545UNTS21	107924
USA (United States)	Yugoslavia	28 Oct 64	533UNTS3	107728
USA (United States)	Yugoslavia	29 Oct 64	533UNTS17	107729
Iran	USA (United States)	16 Nov 64	532UNTS213	107719
Greece	USA (United States)	17 Nov 64	532UNTS107	107714
Kenya	USA (United States)	07 Dec 64	532UNTS263	107722
Congo (Zaire)	USA (United States)	09 Dec 64	531UNTS249	107707
Israel	USA (United States)	22 Dec 64	532UNTS231	107720
Iceland	USA (United States)	30 Dec 64	531UNTS287	107709
Iceland	USA (United States)	30 Dec 64	542UNTS37	107878
Taiwan	USA (United States)	31 Dec 64	532UNTS59	107712
Korea, South	USA (United States)	31 Dec 64	535UNTS315	107787
Taiwan	USA (United States)	31 Dec 64	532UNTS29	107711
Argentina	UK Great Britain	12 Jan 65	597UNTS177	108645
Sierra Leone	USA (United States)	29 Jan 65	542UNTS87	107882
Tunisia	USA (United States)	17 Feb 65	542UNTS125	107885
USA (United States)	Yugoslavia	16 Mar 65	542UNTS161	107887
Dominican Republic	USA (United States)	18 Mar 65	542UNTS215	107892
Finland	UK Great Britain	25 Mar 65	539UNTS103	107826
Ivory Coast	USA (United States)	05 Apr 65	546UNTS143	107941
Philippines	USA (United States)	23 Apr 65	546UNTS157	107942
Morocco	USA (United States)	23 Apr 65	594UNTS3	108591
Netherlands	Tanzania	27 Apr 65	594UNTS123	108599
Ghana	Malawi	04 May 65	541UNTS163	107869
Denmark	Spain	05 May 65	543UNTS255	107905
Bolivia	USA (United States)	12 May 65	564UNTS143	108226
Afghanistan	USA (United States)	22 May 65	579UNTS29	108396
USA (United States)	Vietnam, South	26 May 65	550UNTS3	108005
Ecuador	USA (United States)	25 Jun 65	549UNTS23	107986
Mali	USA (United States)	14 Jul 65	564UNTS101	108223
USA (United States)	Yugoslavia	16 Jul 65	549UNTS111	107994
Congo (Zaire)	USA (United States)	19 Jul 65	593UNTS215	108586

PARTY ONE	PARTY TWO	DATE	CITATION	NUMBER
Reexport of goods, etc. (Cont.)				
Chile	USA (United States)	27 Jul 65	574UNTS83	108342
Bolivia	USA (United States)	17 Aug 65	587UNTS289	108514
Ethiopia	USA (United States)	17 Aug 65	564UNTS119	108224
Australia	New Zealand	31 Aug 65	554UNTS169	108101
USA (United States)	Yugoslavia	22 Nov 65	574UNTS211	108351
Ethiopia	USA (United States)	14 Dec 65	574UNTS115	108344
Ireland	UK Great Britain	14 Dec 65	565UNTS58	108235
United Arab Rep	USA (United States)	03 Jan 66	579UNTS63	108399
Liberia	USA (United States)	06 Jan 66	592UNTS101	108570
Guinea	USA (United States)	04 Feb 66	579UNTS213	108409
Algeria	USA (United States)	23 Feb 66	592UNTS117	108571
Brazil	Denmark	25 Feb 66	590UNTS95	108549
Multilateral		04 Mar 66	578UNTS57	108387
Korea, South	USA (United States)	07 Mar 66	579UNTS137	108404
Ceylon (Sri Lanka)	USA (United States)	12 Mar 66	579UNTS117	108403
Ghana	USA (United States)	01 Apr 66	579UNTS157	108405
Jordan	USA (United States)	05 Apr 66	593UNTS239	108587
USA (United States)	Yugoslavia	11 Apr 66	580UNTS239	108427
Sudan	USA (United States)	13 Apr 66	586UNTS39	108495
Indonesia	USA (United States)	18 Apr 66	578UNTS106	108390
Bolivia	USA (United States)	22 Apr 66	578UNTS73	108388
Paraguay	USA (United States)	27 Apr 66	578UNTS121	108391
Pakistan	USA (United States)	26 May 66	594UNTS27	108592
Indonesia	USA (United States)	28 Jun 66	593UNTS201	108585
Mauritania	USSR (Soviet Union)	17 Oct 66	633UNTS231	109040
Denmark	Singapore	20 Dec 66	593UNTS125	108580
Philippines	USA (United States)	22 Dec 66	591UNTS219	108559
Israel	USA (United States)	29 Mar 68	0UNTS0	109352
Multilateral		24 Dec 68	0UNTS0	109369
Export subsidies				
Multilateral		27 Dec 45	2UNTS39	100020
USA (United States)	Venezuela	29 Mar 46	124UNTS57	101666
Multilateral		30 Oct 47	55UNTS188	100814
El Salvador	Guatemala	14 Dec 51	131UNTS131	101740
Multilateral		01 Oct 53	258UNTS153	103677
Paraguay	UK Great Britain	21 Nov 55	252UNTS107	103560
Costa Rica	Guatemala	20 Dec 55	280UNTS121	104056
Philippines	USA (United States)	18 Oct 56	280UNTS55	104050
Multilateral		25 Mar 57	294UNTS2	104300
Austria	Denmark	14 Nov 59	630UNTS29	108962
Multilateral		04 Jan 60	370UNTS3	105266
Multilateral		13 Dec 60	455UNTS3	106543
Australia	New Zealand	29 Apr 63	483UNTS241	107017
Denmark	Norway	11 May 63	613UNTS271	108856
Ireland	UK Great Britain	30 Jun 64	522UNTS141	107541
Australia	New Zealand	31 Aug 65	554UNTS169	108101
Multilateral		31 Dec 65	616UNTS317	108904
Belgium	Bulgaria	14 Jun 66	607UNTS183	108806
Israel	USA (United States)	29 Mar 68	0UNTS0	109352
Multilateral		24 Dec 68	0UNTS0	109369
Trade agencies				
Multilateral		28 Nov 40	139UNTS159	200452
Brazil	Paraguay	14 Jun 41	54UNTS259	200198
Peru	USA (United States)	07 May 42	103UNTS219	200316
USA (United States)	Venezuela	13 Oct 42	138UNTS282	200451
Argentina	USA (United States)	09 May 45	139UNTS227	200453
Multilateral		06 May 46	99UNTS181	101379
France	USA (United States)	28 May 46	84UNTS151	101125
Italy	Norway	20 Jul 46	30UNTS177	100456
Denmark	USSR (Soviet Union)	17 Aug 46	8UNTS201	100124
Paraguay	USA (United States)	12 Sep 46	125UNTS179	101677
Albania	Yugoslavia	03 Oct 46	111UNTS227	101537
Taiwan	USA (United States)	04 Nov 46	25UNTS69	100359
Canada	Nicaragua	19 Dec 46	236UNTS229	103326
Trade agencies (Cont.)				
Hungary	Yugoslavia	01 Jan 47	113UNTS63	101548
Czechoslovakia	Yugoslavia	25 Feb 47	112UNTS3	101539
Albania	Yugoslavia	22 Jun 47	111UNTS207	101536
Hungary	Yugoslavia	24 Jul 47	114UNTS3	101554
Multilateral		30 Oct 47	55UNTS188	100814
Poland	Yugoslavia	07 Nov 47	115UNTS137	101561
Finland	USSR (Soviet Union)	01 Dec 47	217UNTS3	102942
Hungary	Yugoslavia	18 Mar 48	113UNTS141	101550
Poland	Yugoslavia	12 Apr 48	115UNTS167	101563
France	Norway	11 Jun 48	31UNTS83	100469
France	Norway	05 Jul 48	30UNTS281	100463
Argentina	Denmark	14 Dec 48	74UNTS41	100956
Norway	Poland	31 Dec 48	29UNTS3	100430
Poland	Yugoslavia	16 Jan 49	115UNTS241	101564
Multilateral		23 Mar 49	203UNTS179	102746
Argentina	Norway	09 Sep 49	42UNTS125	100646
Afghanistan	India	04 Jan 50	81UNTS75	101064
Mexico	Netherlands	27 Jan 50	123UNTS197	101661
Brazil	UK Great Britain	18 Sep 50	88UNTS115	101188
Finland	Ireland	06 Jan 51	558UNTS120	108140
Colombia	Denmark	26 Jan 51	87UNTS161	101171
Ceylon (Sri Lanka)	India	30 Apr 51	196UNTS199	102625
Ireland	Norway	02 Jul 51	100UNTS53	101387
El Salvador	Guatemala	14 Dec 51	131UNTS131	101740
Ireland	Switzerland	26 Dec 51	558UNTS305	108149
Ireland	Portugal	06 Feb 52	558UNTS289	108147
Germany, West	Ireland	26 Sep 52	558UNTS27	108138
Fed Rhod/Nyasaland	South Africa	28 Jun 53	267UNTS270	103848
India	Yugoslavia	24 Jul 53	394UNTS13	105665
Ireland	Italy	27 Jul 53	558UNTS237	108144
Spain	USA (United States)	30 Jul 54	235UNTS45	103295
Brazil	USA (United States)	20 Aug 54	410UNTS79	105898
Multilateral		29 Nov 54	287UNTS209	104187
Thailand	USA (United States)	14 Nov 55	239UNTS201	103380
Multilateral		21 Dec 55	292UNTS63	104267
Argentina	USA (United States)	21 Dec 55	240UNTS329	103411
Burma	Yugoslavia	07 Mar 56	386UNTS207	105542
Canada	Hungary	08 Mar 56	305UNTS27	104409
Ceylon (Sri Lanka)	Romania	16 Mar 56	315UNTS41	104558
Germany, West	Italy	19 Apr 56	281UNTS195	104080
Guatemala	Honduras	22 Aug 56	263UNTS49	103767
Australia	Japan	06 Jul 57	318UNTS381	104627
Belgium	Luxembourg	28 Mar 58	303UNTS101	104372
Burma	UK Great Britain	06 Feb 59	343UNTS223	104927
Czechoslovakia	Germany, East	25 Nov 59	374UNTS101	105331
Czechoslovakia	Japan	15 Dec 59	383UNTS277	105505
Denmark	Sweden	04 Jan 60	376UNTS375	105390
Cuba	Czechoslovakia	10 Jun 60	447UNTS75	106412
Korea, North	USSR (Soviet Union)	22 Jun 60	399UNTS3	105732
Ghana	USSR (Soviet Union)	04 Aug 60	421UNTS27	106050
Belgium	Ireland	23 Sep 60	557UNTS180	108134
Albania	Cuba	16 Jan 61	448UNTS67	106425
Ghana	USSR (Soviet Union)	02 Jul 61	0UNTS0	109380
Ghana	USSR (Soviet Union)	04 Nov 61	437UNTS213	106308
United Arab Rep	USSR (Soviet Union)	23 Jun 62	472UNTS43	106836
South Africa	Spain	08 Feb 63	458UNTS79	106593
Burma	UK Great Britain	02 Apr 63	475UNTS139	106890
Multilateral		02 Apr 63	475UNTS121	106889
Brazil	USSR (Soviet Union)	20 Apr 63	0UNTS0	109256
Brazil	USSR (Soviet Union)	20 Apr 63	0UNTS0	109257
India	USSR (Soviet Union)	10 Jun 63	0UNTS0	109382
Canada	Poland	05 Nov 63	529UNTS81	107658
United Arab Rep	USA (United States)	04 Dec 63	505UNTS117	107368
Greece	Poland	21 Dec 63	538UNTS155	107813
Australia	USA (United States)	17 Feb 64	511UNTS17	107422

PARTY ONE	PARTY TWO	DATE	CITATION	NUMBER
Trade agencies (Cont.)				
Philippines	USA (United States)	24 Feb 64	505UNTS283	107378
Portugal	USA (United States)	12 Mar 64	542UNTS3	107875
Mexico	USA (United States)	14 May 64	526UNTS228	107607
Ireland	UK Great Britain	25 Jun 64	553UNTS221	108090
Turkey	USA (United States)	17 Jul 64	530UNTS25	107670
Greece	USA (United States)	17 Jul 64	530UNTS13	107669
Austria	Thailand	30 Sep 64	527UNTS239	107628
USA (United States)	Yugoslavia	05 Oct 64	531UNTS63	107693
Morocco	USA (United States)	29 Dec 64	593UNTS185	108584
Korea, South	USA (United States)	26 Jan 65	541UNTS77	107862
Taiwan	USA (United States)	09 Apr 65	546UNTS81	107939
Argentina	Yugoslavia	09 Jun 65	601UNTS3	108684
Australia	Korea, South	21 Sep 65	548UNTS163	107977
Japan	USSR (Soviet Union)	21 Jan 66	633UNTS165	109038
Singapore	USSR (Soviet Union)	02 Apr 66	631UNTS125	108992
Poland	Singapore	07 Jun 66	631UNTS189	108994
Mauritania	USSR (Soviet Union)	17 Oct 66	633UNTS231	109040
Ghana	Romania	23 Nov 66	642UNTS63	109165
Romania	Spain	05 Jan 67	642UNTS103	109168
Bulgaria	USSR (Soviet Union)	27 Apr 67	631UNTS3	108983
Israel	Singapore	24 Apr 68	642UNTS235	109176
Multilateral		24 Dec 68	0UNTS0	109369
Trade procedures				
Brazil	Canada	17 Oct 41	67UNTS263	200224
Peru	USA (United States)	07 May 42	103UNTS219	200316
Mexico	USA (United States)	23 Dec 42	13UNTS231	200081
Iran	USA (United States)	08 Apr 43	106UNTS155	200340
Iceland	USA (United States)	27 Sep 43	29UNTS317	200170
Multilateral		21 Dec 43	65UNTS231	200214
Netherlands	Switzerland	24 Oct 45	3UNTS73	100025
Canada	Mexico	08 Feb 46	230UNTS183	103183
Poland	USA (United States)	24 Apr 46	4UNTS155	100042
France	USA (United States)	28 May 46	84UNTS151	101125
Romania	Yugoslavia	26 Jun 46	116UNTS21	101566
Albania	Yugoslavia	01 Jul 46	111UNTS3	101517
Philippines	USA (United States)	04 Jul 46	43UNTS135	100668
Norway	Portugal	16 Aug 46	30UNTS215	100459
Hungary	Norway	27 Aug 46	31UNTS3	100465
Paraguay	USA (United States)	12 Sep 46	125UNTS179	101677
Australia	Sweden	16 Sep 46	10UNTS63	100143
Argentina	USA (United States)	19 Sep 46	7UNTS131	100095
Taiwan	USA (United States)	04 Nov 46	25UNTS69	100359
Czechoslovakia	USA (United States)	14 Nov 46	7UNTS119	100094
Canada	Nicaragua	19 Dec 46	236UNTS229	103326
Norway	USSR (Soviet Union)	27 Dec 46	17UNTS283	100282
Hungary	Yugoslavia	01 Jan 47	113UNTS63	101548
Norway	USSR (Soviet Union)	19 Feb 47	30UNTS293	100464
Belgium	Turkey	12 Mar 47	37UNTS215	100578
Albania	Yugoslavia	22 Jun 47	111UNTS207	101536
Sweden	USA (United States)	24 Jun 47	36UNTS25	100565
Denmark	Yugoslavia	28 Jun 47	78UNTS242	101020
Hungary	USSR (Soviet Union)	15 Jul 47	216UNTS247	102940
Norway	Switzerland	15 Jul 47	12UNTS351	100192
Czechoslovakia	Greece	30 Jul 47	185UNTS115	102463
Multilateral		30 Oct 47	55UNTS188	100814
Poland	Yugoslavia	07 Nov 47	115UNTS137	101561
Finland	USSR (Soviet Union)	01 Dec 47	217UNTS3	102942
Czechoslovakia	USSR (Soviet Union)	11 Dec 47	217UNTS35	102943
Switzerland	USSR (Soviet Union)	17 Mar 48	217UNTS87	102945
Hungary	Yugoslavia	18 Mar 48	113UNTS201	101551
Hungary	Yugoslavia	18 Mar 48	113UNTS141	101550
Bulgaria	USSR (Soviet Union)	01 Apr 48	217UNTS97	102946
Czechoslovakia	Yugoslavia	10 Apr 48	112UNTS101	101541
Poland	Yugoslavia	12 Apr 48	115UNTS167	101563

PARTY ONE	PARTY TWO	DATE	CITATION	NUMBER
Trade procedures (Cont.)				
Norway	Sweden	29 Apr 48	26UNTS41	100376
Canada	USA (United States)	30 Apr 48	77UNTS191	100999
Czechoslovakia	Yugoslavia	24 May 48	112UNTS111	101542
Greece	Sweden	25 Jun 48	267UNTS337	103849
Ireland	UK Great Britain	31 Jul 48	86UNTS37	101151
Ireland	Netherlands	02 Sep 48	558UNTS249	108145
Austria	Denmark	29 Nov 48	74UNTS243	100967
Italy	USSR (Soviet Union)	11 Dec 48	217UNTS181	102948
Argentina	Denmark	14 Dec 48	74UNTS41	100956
UK Great Britain	Yugoslavia	23 Dec 48	81UNTS133	101069
Belgium	Greece	27 Dec 48	77UNTS265	101004
Poland	UK Great Britain	14 Jan 49	83UNTS3	101100
Denmark	Greece	25 Feb 49	78UNTS325	101022
Finland	Greece	24 Mar 49	78UNTS3	101008
Ireland	Sweden	25 Jun 49	558UNTS299	108148
Greece	Turkey	21 Jul 49	78UNTS55	101011
Argentina	Norway	09 Sep 49	42UNTS125	100646
Allied Milit Occup	Norway	16 Sep 49	53UNTS3	100769
Bulgaria	Poland	26 Sep 49	260UNTS249	103712
Bulgaria	Poland	26 Sep 49	260UNTS227	103711
Czechoslovakia	UK Great Britain	28 Sep 49	86UNTS141	101156
Hungary	Poland	29 Oct 49	260UNTS113	103706
Hungary	Poland	29 Oct 49	260UNTS91	103705
Greece	Portugal	31 Dec 49	92UNTS71	101262
Mexico	Netherlands	27 Jan 50	123UNTS197	101661
Austria	Denmark	23 Feb 50	74UNTS269	100969
Austria	Czechoslovakia	30 Mar 50	495UNTS85	107240
Germany, East	Poland	23 Jun 50	304UNTS91	104393
Belgium	Japan	29 Aug 50	82UNTS147	101089
Austria	Ireland	06 Oct 50	557UNTS173	108133
Switzerland	USA (United States)	13 Oct 50	133UNTS33	101777
Canada	Ecuador	10 Nov 50	231UNTS15	103199
Iceland	Ireland	02 Dec 50	558UNTS231	108143
Finland	Ireland	06 Jan 51	558UNTS120	108140
Colombia	Denmark	26 Jan 51	87UNTS161	101171
Germany, West	Greece	12 Feb 51	198UNTS193	102665
Multilateral		18 Apr 51	261UNTS140	103729
Ceylon (Sri Lanka)	India	30 Apr 51	196UNTS199	102625
Germany, West	Ireland	23 Jul 51	558UNTS3	108137
Ethiopia	USA (United States)	07 Sep 51	206UNTS41	102785
Denmark	Italy	24 Oct 51	118UNTS91	101598
El Salvador	Guatemala	14 Dec 51	131UNTS131	101740
Ireland	Spain	19 Dec 51	0UNTS0	109228
Ireland	Switzerland	26 Dec 51	558UNTS305	108149
Ireland	Portugal	06 Feb 52	558UNTS289	108147
Czechoslovakia	Romania	31 Jul 52	362UNTS123	105185
Greece	Sweden	19 Aug 52	189UNTS117	102544
USA (United States)	Venezuela	28 Aug 52	178UNTS51	102336
Denmark	Portugal	29 Aug 52	149UNTS49	101950
Denmark	Greece	15 Sep 52	187UNTS207	102513
Austria	Greece	20 Sep 52	187UNTS191	102512
Germany, West	Ireland	26 Sep 52	558UNTS27	108138
Multilateral		07 Nov 52	221UNTS255	103010
Denmark	Israel	14 Nov 52	160UNTS279	102113
Denmark	Israel	14 Nov 52	160UNTS275	102112
Greece	Italy	04 Feb 53	189UNTS269	102551
Greece	Netherlands	05 Feb 53	263UNTS361	103783
Turkey	Yugoslavia	26 Feb 53	247UNTS54	103460
Multilateral		11 May 53	456UNTS3	106555
Greece	United Arab Rep	21 May 53	256UNTS17	103620
Fed Rhod/Nyasaland	South Africa	28 Jun 53	267UNTS270	103848
Burma	Yugoslavia	29 Jun 53	378UNTS83	105418
Greece	Sweden	24 Jul 53	189UNTS309	102553
Ireland	Italy	27 Jul 53	558UNTS237	108144
Ceylon (Sri Lanka)	Yugoslavia	30 Jul 53	337UNTS103	104819

PARTY ONE	PARTY TWO	DATE	CITATION	NUMBER
Trade procedures (Cont.)				
Argentina	USSR (Soviet Union)	05 Aug 53	221UNTS99	103004
Denmark	Greece	19 Oct 53	225UNTS9	103082
Greece	Turkey	07 Nov 53	225UNTS163	103098
Canada	USA (United States)	12 Nov 53	223UNTS139	103062
Multilateral		09 Dec 53	249UNTS197	103509
Hungary	Romania	14 Dec 53	342UNTS151	104906
UK Great Britain	Yugoslavia	31 Dec 53	190UNTS335	102574
Canada	Japan	31 Mar 54	236UNTS329	103334
Denmark	Italy	10 Apr 54	196UNTS175	102623
China People's Rep	India	29 Apr 54	299UNTS57	104307
Pakistan	Yugoslavia	15 May 54	286UNTS3	104158
Canada	Spain	26 May 54	391UNTS273	105632
Bulgaria	Romania	22 Jul 54	362UNTS101	105184
France	Greece	22 Jul 54	225UNTS199	103099
Spain	USA (United States)	30 Jul 54	235UNTS45	103295
Hungary	UK Great Britain	19 Aug 54	199UNTS149	102681
Greece	Netherlands	01 Nov 54	223UNTS79	103057
Greece	Italy	10 Nov 54	227UNTS9	103128
Turkey	USA (United States)	15 Nov 54	238UNTS135	103358
Multilateral		29 Nov 54	287UNTS209	104187
UK Great Britain	Yugoslavia	31 Dec 54	209UNTS81	102824
Greece	Japan	12 Mar 55	227UNTS33	103130
Italy	Yugoslavia	26 Mar 55	379UNTS3	105432
Italy	Yugoslavia	31 Mar 55	386UNTS317	105551
Argentina	UK Great Britain	31 Mar 55	210UNTS223	102840
Ceylon (Sri Lanka)	Germany, West	01 Apr 55	369UNTS57	105251
Ceylon (Sri Lanka)	Pakistan	23 May 55	286UNTS15	104159
Canada	Ethiopia	03 Jun 55	247UNTS157	103465
France	Ireland	07 Jun 55	558UNTS217	108142
Bulgaria	Yugoslavia	17 Jun 55	375UNTS287	105370
France	Greece	28 Jun 55	225UNTS219	103100
Greece	Netherlands	14 Jul 55	227UNTS27	103129
Switzerland	USA (United States)	18 Jul 55	239UNTS311	103388
Germany, East	Romania	05 Aug 55	342UNTS229	104910
Denmark	Greece	29 Aug 55	230UNTS25	103174
Austria	USSR (Soviet Union)	17 Oct 55	240UNTS289	103409
Italy	Lebanon	04 Nov 55	267UNTS113	103838
Italy	Syria	10 Nov 55	267UNTS157	103841
Multilateral		21 Dec 55	292UNTS63	104267
Ceylon (Sri Lanka)	Romania	16 Mar 56	315UNTS41	104558
Netherlands	USA (United States)	27 Mar 56	285UNTS231	104154
Bulgaria	Greece	19 Apr 56	594UNTS131	108600
Germany, West	Italy	19 Apr 56	281UNTS195	104080
Denmark	Italy	12 May 56	260UNTS357	103720
Germany, East	USSR (Soviet Union)	30 May 56	263UNTS143	103771
Ceylon (Sri Lanka)	Hungary	04 Jun 56	315UNTS13	104555
Austria	Yugoslavia	15 Jun 56	396UNTS117	105695
Bulgaria	Ceylon (Sri Lanka)	19 Jun 56	315UNTS23	104556
France	Greece	25 Jun 56	251UNTS167	103540
Romania	Yugoslavia	04 Aug 56	395UNTS99	105682
Guatemala	Honduras	22 Aug 56	263UNTS49	103767
Denmark	Greece	04 Sep 56	256UNTS319	103643
Romania	Yugoslavia	25 Sep 56	395UNTS147	105683
Germany, East	Romania	08 Dec 56	362UNTS189	105188
Indonesia	Yugoslavia	14 Dec 56	378UNTS117	105422
Austria	Pakistan	24 Dec 56	316UNTS83	104579
Australia	UK Great Britain	26 Feb 57	265UNTS197	103813
Multilateral		25 Mar 57	294UNTS2	104300
Ceylon (Sri Lanka)	Italy	23 Apr 57	337UNTS115	104820
Albania	Yugoslavia	20 May 57	363UNTS99	105203
Hungary	Yugoslavia	25 May 57	477UNTS219	106924
Bulgaria	Yugoslavia	04 Jun 57	349UNTS35	105008
Czechoslovakia	Yugoslavia	11 Jun 57	504UNTS107	107355
Australia	Japan	06 Jul 57	318UNTS381	104627
Denmark	Italy	12 Jul 57	291UNTS169	104251

PARTY ONE	PARTY TWO	DATE	CITATION	NUMBER
Trade procedures (Cont.)				
Germany, East	Hungary	25 Oct 57	408UNTS156	105869
Germany, East	Hungary	13 Nov 57	407UNTS216	105866
Denmark	UK Great Britain	18 Nov 57	403UNTS153	105794
Hungary	Yugoslavia	06 Dec 57	519UNTS215	107509
China People's Rep	USSR (Soviet Union)	21 Dec 57	305UNTS213	104420
India	Japan	04 Feb 58	324UNTS215	104687
Ceylon (Sri Lanka)	USSR (Soviet Union)	08 Feb 58	348UNTS159	104999
Czechoslovakia	Hungary	12 Mar 58	408UNTS178	105870
Bulgaria	Hungary	13 Mar 58	438UNTS191	106317
Bulgaria	Hungary	13 Mar 58	438UNTS173	106316
Belgium	Luxembourg	28 Mar 58	303UNTS101	104372
Italy	Tunisia	08 Apr 58	378UNTS327	105430
Japan	Poland	26 Apr 58	340UNTS221	104866
Multilateral		10 Jun 58	454UNTS47	106539
Multilateral		18 Jun 58	386UNTS345	105552
Italy	Morocco	24 Jun 58	363UNTS23	105197
Australia	Fed of Malaya	26 Aug 58	325UNTS253	104703
Japan	New Zealand	09 Sep 58	325UNTS119	104698
Iraq	USSR (Soviet Union)	11 Oct 58	328UNTS117	104731
Iraq	USSR (Soviet Union)	11 Oct 58	328UNTS95	104730
Fed Rhod/Nyasaland	Portugal	29 Nov 58	354UNTS137	105060
Multilateral		15 Dec 58	351UNTS159	105022
Iraq	Romania	24 Dec 58	405UNTS243	105836
Burma	UK Great Britain	06 Feb 59	343UNTS223	104927
Germany, West	New Zealand	20 Apr 59	402UNTS125	105782
UK Great Britain	USSR (Soviet Union)	24 May 59	374UNTS305	105344
Argentina	Sweden	12 Jun 59	427UNTS337	106164
New Zealand	UK Great Britain	12 Aug 59	354UNTS161	105062
Korea, South	USA (United States)	25 Sep 59	358UNTS163	105133
India	Italy	06 Oct 59	378UNTS267	105427
Australia	Germany, West	14 Oct 59	345UNTS35	104957
Guinea	UK Great Britain	22 Oct 59	351UNTS341	105033
Italy	Tunisia	31 Oct 59	378UNTS349	105431
Tunisia	UK Great Britain	16 Nov 59	354UNTS367	105070
Argentina	Brazil	26 Nov 59	374UNTS31	105325
Italy	Netherlands	01 Dec 59	455UNTS241	106545
Multilateral		14 Dec 59	422UNTS57	106068
Czechoslovakia	Japan	15 Dec 59	383UNTS277	105505
Australia	Indonesia	17 Dec 59	354UNTS109	105058
Denmark	Sweden	04 Jan 60	376UNTS375	105390
Multilateral		06 Feb 60	383UNTS3	105494
Australia	Canada	12 Feb 60	369UNTS89	105253
Greece	Tunisia	02 Mar 60	483UNTS89	107008
Austria	Guatemala	18 Mar 60	379UNTS89	105435
Finland	USA (United States)	23 Mar 60	371UNTS117	105274
Switzerland	USA (United States)	29 Mar 60	371UNTS155	105277
UK Great Britain	Yugoslavia	12 Apr 60	360UNTS79	105155
Cuba	Japan	22 Apr 60	442UNTS261	106354
Multilateral		28 Apr 60	376UNTS111	105377
Poland	Yugoslavia	05 May 60	423UNTS229	106095
Austria	Spain	17 Jun 60	390UNTS17	105600
Ghana	USSR (Soviet Union)	04 Aug 60	421UNTS27	106050
Israel	UK Great Britain	31 Aug 60	385UNTS71	105530
Multilateral		08 Oct 60	450UNTS309	106476
Czechoslovakia	Poland	14 Nov 60	413UNTS4	105938
Multilateral		13 Dec 60	455UNTS3	106543
Malaysia	New Zealand	03 Feb 61	447UNTS251	106418
Multilateral		16 Mar 61	638UNTS235	109139
Multilateral		30 Mar 61	520UNTS151	107515
USA (United States)	Vietnam, South	03 Apr 61	424UNTS137	106106
Japan	Peru	15 May 61	451UNTS3	106482
Ghana	USSR (Soviet Union)	02 Jul 61	0UNTS0	109380
Austria	Romania	21 Jul 61	421UNTS161	106057
Korea, South	Thailand	15 Sep 61	413UNTS137	105948
Pakistan	Philippines	29 Sep 61	422UNTS3	106065

PARTY ONE	PARTY TWO	DATE	CITATION	NUMBER
Trade procedures (Cont.)				
Belgium	Yugoslavia	31 Oct 61	426UNTS165	106136
Greece	Morocco	01 Nov 61	483UNTS113	107009
Ghana	USSR (Soviet Union)	04 Nov 61	437UNTS213	106308
Argentina	Thailand	10 Dec 61	422UNTS87	106070
Argentina	Japan	20 Dec 61	451UNTS77	106486
Portugal	USA (United States)	05 Mar 62	436UNTS101	106290
Multilateral		07 Mar 62	445UNTS199	106388
Multilateral		07 Mar 62	445UNTS205	106389
EEC (Econ Commnty)	USA (United States)	07 Mar 62	436UNTS49	106288
Canada	USA (United States)	07 Mar 62	436UNTS3	106286
USA (United States)	USSR (Soviet Union)	08 Mar 62	460UNTS3	106630
Japan	New Zealand	09 Mar 62	485UNTS339	107065
Japan	New Zealand	09 Mar 62	485UNTS351	107066
Taiwan	USA (United States)	16 Apr 62	445UNTS249	106392
UK Great Britain	USA (United States)	26 Apr 62	445UNTS273	106395
El Salvador	USA (United States)	15 May 62	452UNTS49	106503
Colombia	USA (United States)	15 May 62	445UNTS279	106396
Haiti	USA (United States)	06 Jun 62	452UNTS59	106504
United Arab Rep	USSR (Soviet Union)	23 Jun 62	472UNTS43	106836
IAEA (Atom Energy)	USA (United States)	20 Aug 62	456UNTS447	106570
Multilateral		28 Sep 62	469UNTS169	106791
Belgium	Romania	12 Oct 62	502UNTS31	107325
Japan	USA (United States)	24 Oct 62	462UNTS119	106673
Brazil	Taiwan	28 Dec 62	500UNTS61	107307
Greece	Pakistan	17 Jan 63	538UNTS175	107814
South Africa	Spain	08 Feb 63	458UNTS79	106593
Burma	UK Great Britain	02 Apr 63	475UNTS139	106890
Multilateral		02 Apr 63	475UNTS121	106889
Brazil	USSR (Soviet Union)	20 Apr 63	0UNTS0	109257
Brazil	USSR (Soviet Union)	20 Apr 63	0UNTS0	109256
Multilateral		09 Jun 63	538UNTS309	107818
India	USSR (Soviet Union)	10 Jun 63	0UNTS0	109382
Multilateral		13 Aug 63	592UNTS139	108572
Denmark	Greece	26 Sep 63	534UNTS43	107752
Greece	Poland	30 Sep 63	534UNTS23	107751
USA (United States)	USSR (Soviet Union)	22 Feb 64	526UNTS131	107605
Cuba	Czechoslovakia	03 Jun 64	527UNTS205	107626
Multilateral		20 Jun 64	539UNTS3	107819
Ireland	UK Great Britain	30 Jun 64	522UNTS141	107541
Greece	Norway	25 Sep 64	610UNTS0	108835
Czechoslovakia	Mongolia	21 Oct 64	545UNTS91	107926
Austria	Hungary	11 Nov 64	576UNTS163	108368
Greece	Japan	09 Apr 65	632UNTS61	109008
Argentina	Brazil	23 Apr 65	0UNTS0	109411
Argentina	Yugoslavia	09 Jun 65	601UNTS3	108684
Austria	Bulgaria	12 Jul 65	587UNTS51	108510
Australia	New Zealand	31 Aug 65	554UNTS169	108101
Australia	Korea, South	21 Sep 65	548UNTS163	107977
Ireland	UK Great Britain	14 Dec 65	565UNTS58	108235
Canada	USA (United States)	17 Dec 65	574UNTS49	108341
Multilateral		31 Dec 65	616UNTS317	108904
Czechoslovakia	Poland	22 Jan 66	588UNTS175	108524
UK Great Britain	USA (United States)	05 Apr 66	592UNTS61	108569
Australia	Bulgaria	22 Jun 66	607UNTS69	108796
Mauritania	USSR (Soviet Union)	17 Oct 66	633UNTS231	109040
Romania	United Arab Rep	14 Nov 66	642UNTS129	109169
Guinea	Romania	01 Dec 66	642UNTS89	109167
Korea, South	New Zealand	31 Jan 67	598UNTS91	108656
Romania	Sweden	01 Mar 67	642UNTS163	109172
Denmark	Paraguay	03 May 67	608UNTS55	108812
Australia	Romania	18 May 67	642UNTS25	109162
Bulgaria	Turkey	30 May 67	631UNTS19	108984
Israel	USA (United States)	04 Aug 67	0UNTS0	109351
Malaysia	Philippines	01 Sep 67	608UNTS13	108810
Ecuador	Romania	10 Oct 67	642UNTS33	109163

PARTY ONE	PARTY TWO	DATE	CITATION	NUMBER
Trade procedures (Cont.)				
Israel	USA (United States)	29 Mar 68	0UNTS0	109352
Israel	Singapore	24 Apr 68	642UNTS235	109176
Austria	Romania	28 Apr 68	0UNTS0	109377
Multilateral		24 Dec 68	0UNTS0	109369
Embargo				
Germany, West	USA (United States)	18 Feb 55	247UNTS257	103474
USA (United States)	Vietnam, South	14 Jul 61	416UNTS133	105999
Finances and payments				
France	Netherlands	09 Apr 46	3UNTS57	100024
Multilateral		19 Jul 46	1UNTS97	200001
Spain	USA (United States)	03 May 48	132UNTS155	101756
Turkey	UK Great Britain	16 Oct 48	83UNTS85	101103
Argentina	Denmark	14 Dec 48	74UNTS41	100956
Czechoslovakia	UK Great Britain	28 Sep 49	86UNTS141	101156
Indonesia	Netherlands	02 Nov 49	69UNTS3	100894
Chile	USA (United States)	16 Jan 51	147UNTS11	101925
France	United Nations	17 Aug 51	122UNTS191	101647
Iraq	UK Great Britain	10 Jul 52	151UNTS227	101998
Ethiopia	UK Great Britain	06 Sep 52	149UNTS57	101951
Libya	UK Great Britain	29 Jul 53	186UNTS277	102493
Multilateral		01 Oct 53	258UNTS153	103677
Jordan	Syria	23 Dec 53	204UNTS207	102759
Multilateral		01 Mar 54	256UNTS31	103622
Hungary	UK Great Britain	19 Aug 54	199UNTS149	102681
Argentina	UK Great Britain	31 Mar 55	210UNTS223	102840
Multilateral		25 May 55	264UNTS117	103791
Multilateral		29 Sep 55	222UNTS313	103037
Austria	USSR (Soviet Union)	09 Nov 55	255UNTS247	103613
Multilateral		30 Mar 56	604UNTS114	108748
Multilateral		25 Apr 56	270UNTS103	103896
Italy	Switzerland	29 Jun 56	284UNTS299	104144
Austria	IAEA (Atom Energy)	11 Dec 57	339UNTS110	104849
Multilateral		01 Dec 58	385UNTS137	105534
Mongolia	Poland	23 Dec 58	432UNTS177	106220
Multilateral		01 Sep 60	403UNTS3	105792
Ethiopia	USSR (Soviet Union)	13 Jan 61	421UNTS13	106049
Cuba	Germany, East	29 Mar 61	448UNTS81	106426
Brazil	Poland	19 Oct 61	552UNTS75	108050
Belgium	Cyprus	08 Jun 63	601UNTS311	108703
Algeria	Tunisia	01 Sep 63	601UNTS275	108701
Belgium	Romania	13 Nov 63	520UNTS119	107513
Cyprus	Hungary	02 Jun 64	602UNTS3	108704
Germany, East	Poland	06 Oct 64	552UNTS89	108051
Czechoslovakia	Germany, East	06 Oct 64	545UNTS113	107927
Austria	Hungary	31 Oct 64	605UNTS3	108758
Cyprus	Syria	22 Dec 64	602UNTS25	108705
Morocco	USA (United States)	29 Dec 64	593UNTS185	108584
Greece	India	11 Feb 65	606UNTS9	108771
Australia	France	13 Apr 65	601UNTS293	108702
Bulgaria	Czechoslovakia	22 May 65	545UNTS65	107925
British Guiana	USA (United States)	29 May 65	605UNTS87	108761
Argentina	Yugoslavia	09 Jun 65	601UNTS3	108684
Multilateral		08 Dec 65	600UNTS161	108680
Multilateral		17 Jan 66	592UNTS101	108573
Denmark	Netherlands	31 Mar 66	604UNTS209	108751
Romania	USSR (Soviet Union)	21 Jun 66	604UNTS81	108746
Singapore	UK Great Britain	01 Dec 66	605UNTS153	108763
Trinidad/Tobago	UK Great Britain	29 Dec 66	605UNTS237	108766
Trinidad/Tobago	UK Great Britain	23 Jan 67	605UNTS277	108767
Austria	United Nations	13 Apr 67	600UNTS93	108679
Jordan	UK Great Britain	02 May 67	610UNTS0	108837
Germany, West	UK Great Britain	05 May 67	613UNTS313	108858

PARTY ONE	PARTY TWO	DATE	CITATION	NUMBER
Accounting procedures				
Netherlands	UK Great Britain	13 Jun 39	5UNTS65	200028
Anglo-Egypt Sudan	Fr Equatorial Afri	02 Nov 39	2UNTS209	200012
France	Netherlands	14 Jun 40	2UNTS263	200019
Brazil	Paraguay	14 Jun 41	54UNTS235	200196
UK Great Britain	USSR (Soviet Union)	16 Aug 41	91UNTS341	200269
Haiti	USA (United States)	13 Sep 41	103UNTS141	200311
Brazil	Chile	18 Nov 41	67UNTS279	200225
Mexico	USA (United States)	19 Nov 41	148UNTS367	200474
Iceland	USA (United States)	21 Nov 41	124UNTS179	200418
Brazil	USA (United States)	17 Jul 42	102UNTS203	200303
Australia	USA (United States)	03 Sep 42	24UNTS195	200143
New Zealand	USA (United States)	03 Sep 42	24UNTS185	200142
France	USA (United States)	03 Sep 42	24UNTS177	200141
USA (United States)	Venezuela	18 Feb 43	21UNTS225	200125
Canada	USA (United States)	23 Feb 43	101UNTS243	200299
Mexico	USA (United States)	26 Apr 43	21UNTS245	200127
Mexico	USA (United States)	29 Apr 43	105UNTS119	200327
France	USA (United States)	25 Sep 43	76UNTS183	200245
Multilateral		21 Oct 43	2UNTS281	200021
Brazil	USA (United States)	25 Nov 43	102UNTS227	200305
Multilateral		15 Jan 44	161UNTS281	200489
Canada	Taiwan	22 Mar 44	14UNTS397	200096
Peru	USA (United States)	15 Apr 44	150UNTS317	200479
Brazil	Ecuador	24 May 44	73UNTS223	200242
Bolivia	USA (United States)	07 Sep 44	162UNTS315	200494
UK Great Britain	USSR (Soviet Union)	23 Sep 44	10UNTS171	200060
Belgium	UK Great Britain	05 Oct 44	5UNTS227	200031
Brazil	UNRRA (Relief)	12 Oct 44	67UNTS321	200228
Multilateral		07 Dec 44	171UNTS345	200501
Ecuador	USA (United States)	22 Jan 45	24UNTS273	200152
France	USA (United States)	28 Feb 45	76UNTS213	200247
Canada	Czechoslovakia	01 Mar 45	45UNTS283	200185
Sweden	UK Great Britain	06 Mar 45	5UNTS241	200032
Sweden	UK Great Britain	06 Mar 45	82UNTS219	101095
France	UK Great Britain	27 Mar 45	98UNTS227	200274
Belgium	USA (United States)	19 Apr 45	139UNTS179	200455
Canada	Norway	25 Jun 45	45UNTS297	200186
Denmark	UK Great Britain	16 Aug 45	5UNTS251	200033
Netherlands	UK Great Britain	07 Sep 45	2UNTS325	200024
Dominican Republic	USA (United States)	13 Oct 45	149UNTS361	200477
Belgium	Norway	23 Oct 45	16UNTS311	200107
Netherlands	Switzerland	24 Oct 45	3UNTS73	100025
Belgium	Canada	25 Oct 45	230UNTS127	103180
Czechoslovakia	UK Great Britain	01 Nov 45	5UNTS15	100062
Netherlands	Norway	06 Nov 45	2UNTS5	100017
Multilateral		07 Nov 45	2UNTS17	100018
Norway	UK Great Britain	08 Nov 45	5UNTS27	100063
Finland	Norway	27 Nov 45	17UNTS247	100279
Netherlands	Sweden	30 Nov 45	2UNTS27	100019
Denmark	UK Great Britain	06 Dec 45	5UNTS3	100061
UK Great Britain	USA (United States)	06 Dec 45	126UNTS13	101679
Czechoslovakia	Norway	13 Dec 45	17UNTS261	100280
Multilateral		27 Dec 45	2UNTS39	100020
Multilateral		14 Jan 46	555UNTS69	108105
Poland	Yugoslavia	18 Jan 46	115UNTS83	101559
Lebanon	USA (United States)	21 Jan 46	140UNTS73	101884
Greece	UK Great Britain	24 Jan 46	6UNTS45	100067
Denmark	Netherlands	31 Jan 46	3UNTS3	100021
Canada	Netherlands	05 Feb 46	43UNTS3	100658
Canada	Taiwan	07 Feb 46	43UNTS23	100659
Netherlands	USA (United States)	11 Feb 46	3UNTS37	100023
Colombia	USA (United States)	19 Feb 46	166UNTS104	102187
Switzerland	UK Great Britain	12 Mar 46	6UNTS107	100070
Brazil	USA (United States)	05 Apr 46	12UNTS131	100183

PARTY ONE	PARTY TWO	DATE	CITATION	NUMBER
Accounting procedures (Cont.)				
Belgium	Denmark	08 Apr 46	4UNTS429	100059
Canada	France	09 Apr 46	43UNTS43	100660
Portugal	UK Great Britain	16 Apr 46	6UNTS119	100071
France	Greece	24 Apr 46	91UNTS83	101243
France	UK Great Britain	29 Apr 46	98UNTS123	101360
Denmark	Luxembourg	21 May 46	4UNTS435	100060
France	USA (United States)	28 May 46	84UNTS141	101124
France	USA (United States)	28 May 46	84UNTS121	101123
Belgium	Italy	23 Jun 46	19UNTS65	100305
Poland	UK Great Britain	24 Jun 46	11UNTS59	100149
Romania	Yugoslavia	26 Jun 46	116UNTS21	101566
Belgium	Canada	13 Jul 46	230UNTS159	103181
Italy	Norway	20 Jul 46	17UNTS273	100281
Multilateral		22 Jul 46	14UNTS185	100221
Norway	Yugoslavia	30 Aug 46	15UNTS163	100232
Philippines	USA (United States)	17 Sep 46	15UNTS249	100240
Albania	Yugoslavia	03 Oct 46	111UNTS87	101519
Greece	USA (United States)	08 Oct 46	180UNTS119	102379
Denmark	South Africa	14 Oct 46	10UNTS29	100140
Multilateral		30 Oct 46	27UNTS77	100401
Peru	USA (United States)	22 Nov 46	100UNTS170	101396
Norway	Sweden	22 Nov 46	15UNTS171	100233
Norway	Poland	03 Dec 46	15UNTS203	100234
France	USA (United States)	10 Dec 46	15UNTS265	100242
United Arab Rep	UK Great Britain	10 Dec 46	105UNTS15	101451
ILO (Labor Org)	United Nations	19 Dec 46	1UNTS183	200009
Denmark	India	20 Dec 46	7UNTS309	100107
Hungary	Yugoslavia	23 Dec 46	113UNTS125	101549
Norway	USSR (Soviet Union)	27 Dec 46	17UNTS283	100282
Australia	Netherlands	24 Jan 47	10UNTS77	100144
UNESCO (Educ/Cult)	United Nations	03 Feb 47	1UNTS233	200011
FAO (Food Agri)	United Nations	03 Feb 47	1UNTS207	200010
Norway	USSR (Soviet Union)	19 Feb 47	30UNTS293	100464
Mexico	USA (United States)	17 Mar 47	167UNTS30	102200
Spain	UK Great Britain	28 Mar 47	66UNTS91	100849
Bulgaria	Denmark	09 May 47	74UNTS139	100960
Honduras	USA (United States)	13 May 47	166UNTS159	102189
Poland	Yugoslavia	24 May 47	115UNTS69	101558
New Zealand	UK Great Britain	27 May 47	17UNTS211	100277
Albania	Yugoslavia	12 Jun 47	111UNTS195	101534
Austria	USA (United States)	21 Jun 47	67UNTS89	100868
Ecuador	USA (United States)	21 Jun 47	26UNTS275	100391
Albania	Yugoslavia	22 Jun 47	111UNTS207	101536
Austria	USA (United States)	25 Jun 47	22UNTS141	100334
Romania	Yugoslavia	26 Jun 47	116UNTS39	101568
United Arab Rep	UK Great Britain	30 Jun 47	93UNTS165	101299
USA (United States)	Venezuela	30 Jun 47	166UNTS198	102190
Belgium	United Arab Rep	01 Jul 47	34UNTS93	100529
France	New Zealand	02 Jul 47	16UNTS219	100263
Italy	USA (United States)	04 Jul 47	22UNTS173	100336
Czechoslovakia	Poland	04 Jul 47	25UNTS249	100366
Haiti	USA (United States)	04 Jul 47	22UNTS165	100335
Greece	USA (United States)	08 Jul 47	16UNTS157	100256
Norway	Switzerland	15 Jul 47	12UNTS351	100192
UK Great Britain	Uruguay	15 Jul 47	71UNTS179	100918
Czechoslovakia	USA (United States)	25 Jul 47	90UNTS19	101223
USSR (Soviet Union)	Yugoslavia	25 Jul 47	130UNTS315	101732
Taiwan	Italy	30 Jul 47	12UNTS377	100194
Czechoslovakia	Greece	30 Jul 47	185UNTS149	102466
Netherlands	IBRD (World Bank)	07 Aug 47	152UNTS165	102015
Multilateral		14 Aug 47	138UNTS111	101863
India	UK Great Britain	14 Aug 47	11UNTS371	100176
Denmark	IBRD (World Bank)	22 Aug 47	152UNTS223	102016
Luxembourg	IBRD (World Bank)	28 Aug 47	153UNTS3	102017
Multilateral		19 Sep 47	30UNTS269	100462

Accounting procedures (Cont.)

PARTY ONE	PARTY TWO	DATE	CITATION	NUMBER
Romania	Yugoslavia	30 Sep 47	116UNTS71	101570
Multilateral		02 Oct 47	193UNTS188	102616
Multilateral		05 Oct 47	34UNTS23	100525
UK Great Britain	USA (United States)	09 Oct 47	34UNTS129	100533
South Africa	UK Great Britain	09 Oct 47	17UNTS239	100278
Multilateral		11 Oct 47	77UNTS143	100998
Taiwan	USA (United States)	27 Oct 47	12UNTS11	100178
Bolivia	USA (United States)	03 Nov 47	51UNTS33	100750
Ecuador	USA (United States)	14 Nov 47	149UNTS297	101959
United Nations	WHO (World Health)	15 Nov 47	19UNTS193	200115
United Nations	UPU (Postal Union)	15 Nov 47	19UNTS219	200116
Multilateral		18 Nov 47	17UNTS89	100269
USSR (Soviet Union)	Yugoslavia	15 Dec 47	116UNTS313	101578
UK Great Britain	USSR (Soviet Union)	27 Dec 47	82UNTS251	101098
United Arab Rep	UK Great Britain	05 Jan 48	77UNTS3	100988
Guatemala	USA (United States)	05 Jan 48	135UNTS104	101817
Czechoslovakia	New Zealand	22 Jan 48	16UNTS229	100264
France	Lebanon	24 Jan 48	173UNTS99	102263
Hungary	Poland	31 Jan 48	25UNTS283	100368
Greece	United Nations	12 Feb 48	47UNTS223	100732
India	UK Great Britain	15 Feb 48	134UNTS70	101796
Pakistan	UK Great Britain	21 Feb 48	134UNTS128	101797
Denmark	Hungary	28 Feb 48	85UNTS35	101144
Poland	UK Great Britain	02 Mar 48	77UNTS47	100991
France	United Nations	10 Mar 48	47UNTS203	100731
Paraguay	USA (United States)	12 Mar 48	162UNTS30	102131
Hungary	Yugoslavia	18 Mar 48	113UNTS219	101552
Hungary	Yugoslavia	18 Mar 48	113UNTS201	101551
USA (United States)	Venezuela	24 Mar 48	44UNTS57	100678
India	Pakistan	31 Mar 48	54UNTS33	100793
Poland	Yugoslavia	12 Apr 48	115UNTS167	101563
Hungary	Yugoslavia	17 Apr 48	130UNTS101	101727
Denmark	Norway	21 Apr 48	18UNTS139	100284
Greece	USA (United States)	23 Apr 48	74UNTS107	100958
Norway	Sweden	29 Apr 48	26UNTS11	100374
Multilateral		30 Apr 48	119UNTS3	101609
Multilateral		10 May 48	140UNTS129	101887
Multilateral		11 May 48	500UNTS267	107313
Finland	United Nations	20 May 48	47UNTS319	200189
Brazil	UK Great Britain	21 May 48	66UNTS121	100851
Czechoslovakia	Yugoslavia	24 May 48	112UNTS183	101543
Czechoslovakia	Yugoslavia	24 May 48	112UNTS225	101545
Chile	UK Great Britain	24 Jun 48	77UNTS113	100995
Multilateral		26 Jun 48	331UNTS217	104757
France	USA (United States)	28 Jun 48	19UNTS9	100302
Italy	USA (United States)	28 Jun 48	20UNTS43	100314
Ireland	USA (United States)	28 Jun 48	24UNTS3	100349
Denmark	USA (United States)	29 Jun 48	22UNTS217	100338
India	Pakistan	30 Jun 48	29UNTS199	100441
Peru	USA (United States)	30 Jun 48	150UNTS45	101962
Greece	USA (United States)	02 Jul 48	23UNTS43	100342
Austria	USA (United States)	02 Jul 48	21UNTS29	100323
Netherlands	USA (United States)	02 Jul 48	20UNTS91	100315
Belgium	USA (United States)	02 Jul 48	19UNTS127	100309
Norway	USA (United States)	03 Jul 48	20UNTS185	100317
Iceland	USA (United States)	03 Jul 48	20UNTS141	100316
Luxembourg	USA (United States)	03 Jul 48	24UNTS35	100350
Taiwan	USA (United States)	03 Jul 48	17UNTS119	100273
UK Great Britain	USA (United States)	06 Jul 48	22UNTS263	100339
France	USA (United States)	09 Jul 48	24UNTS103	100352
France	UK Great Britain	12 Jul 48	90UNTS83	101230
Multilateral		14 Jul 48	23UNTS3	100340
Peru	UK Great Britain	20 Jul 48	66UNTS197	100855
Taiwan	USA (United States)	05 Aug 48	82UNTS109	101087
Pakistan	United Nations	27 Aug 48	47UNTS269	100734

Accounting procedures (Cont.)

PARTY ONE	PARTY TWO	DATE	CITATION	NUMBER
Korea, South	USA (United States)	11 Sep 48	89UNTS155	101216
New Zealand	Pakistan	17 Sep 48	91UNTS275	101254
Israel	UNICEF (Children)	20 Sep 48	71UNTS17	100907
Panama	USA (United States)	24 Sep 48	150UNTS25	101961
UNRRA (Relief)	United Nations	27 Sep 48	27UNTS349	200158
United Nations	Thailand	05 Oct 48	47UNTS287	100735
Czechoslovakia	United Nations	07 Oct 48	47UNTS185	100730
United Nations	San Marino	07 Oct 48	47UNTS337	200190
Belgium	Netherlands	11 Oct 48	26UNTS95	100379
Trieste	USA (United States)	15 Oct 48	29UNTS249	100443
Italy	USA (United States)	26 Nov 48	79UNTS71	101032
Austria	Denmark	29 Nov 48	74UNTS257	100968
UK Great Britain	USA (United States)	01 Dec 48	81UNTS93	101066
UNICEF (Children)	Thailand	01 Dec 48	68UNTS94	100886
Korea, South	USA (United States)	10 Dec 48	55UNTS157	100813
Argentina	Denmark	14 Dec 48	74UNTS41	100956
Denmark	Poland	14 Dec 48	81UNTS33	101060
Denmark	Turkey	15 Dec 48	76UNTS3	100974
Spain	UK Great Britain	15 Dec 48	87UNTS49	101165
Multilateral		16 Dec 48	79UNTS85	101033
Italy	USA (United States)	18 Dec 48	79UNTS133	101037
France	USA (United States)	23 Dec 48	67UNTS171	100876
Belgium	Greece	27 Dec 48	77UNTS293	101005
USSR (Soviet Union)	Yugoslavia	27 Dec 48	116UNTS327	101579
Poland	UK Great Britain	14 Jan 49	83UNTS3	101100
Belgium	Luxembourg	14 Jan 49	36UNTS339	100572
Netherlands	USA (United States)	17 Jan 49	32UNTS241	100502
Chile	USA (United States)	21 Jan 49	160UNTS185	102107
Austria	Norway	28 Jan 49	30UNTS145	100452
France	USA (United States)	07 Feb 49	67UNTS189	100877
IRO (Refugee Org)	United Nations	07 Feb 49	26UNTS299	200153
Denmark	Sweden	08 Feb 49	33UNTS227	100519
Multilateral		08 Feb 49	157UNTS157	102053
Greece	USA (United States)	09 Feb 49	79UNTS95	101034
Austria	USA (United States)	11 Feb 49	79UNTS113	101035
Trieste	USA (United States)	11 Feb 49	79UNTS123	101036
Mexico	USA (United States)	14 Feb 49	160UNTS75	102103
Multilateral		22 Feb 49	93UNTS129	101296
Norway	Turkey	24 Feb 49	30UNTS151	100453
Denmark	Greece	25 Feb 49	78UNTS335	101023
Multilateral		28 Feb 49	29UNTS53	100434
Czechoslovakia	Yugoslavia	01 Mar 49	112UNTS241	101546
Belgium	IBRD (World Bank)	01 Mar 49	154UNTS133	102029
Belgium	Portugal	01 Mar 49	32UNTS49	100488
Greece	Norway	12 Mar 49	33UNTS13	100510
Canada	USA (United States)	14 Mar 49	82UNTS3	101079
Multilateral		16 Mar 49	29UNTS95	100436
Germany, West	Greece	16 Mar 49	77UNTS327	101007
United Nations	UK Great Britain	18 Mar 49	47UNTS305	100736
Denmark	Finland	22 Mar 49	33UNTS247	100520
Austria	USA (United States)	23 Mar 49	43UNTS127	100667
Finland	Greece	24 Mar 49	78UNTS13	101009
United Arab Rep	UK Great Britain	31 Mar 49	83UNTS139	101106
Panama	USA (United States)	31 Mar 49	55UNTS141	100812
Greece	Turkey	02 Apr 49	78UNTS23	101010
Denmark	Portugal	08 Apr 49	74UNTS221	100965
India	Pakistan	23 Apr 49	54UNTS51	100795
Netherlands	USA (United States)	26 Apr 49	70UNTS123	100901
ITU (Telecommun)	United Nations	26 Apr 49	30UNTS315	200175
Belgium	Bolivia	26 Apr 49	34UNTS103	100530
Multilateral		28 Apr 49	83UNTS105	101105
Pan Am Health Org	WHO (World Health)	24 May 49	32UNTS387	200178
Norway	USA (United States)	25 May 49	32UNTS345	100507
Multilateral		20 Jun 49	128UNTS141	101718
Argentina	UK Great Britain	27 Jun 49	83UNTS217	101110

Accounting procedures (Cont.)

PARTY ONE	PARTY TWO	DATE	CITATION	NUMBER
Greece	UK Great Britain	29 Jun 49	86UNTS203	101160
Greece	Turkey	21 Jul 49	78UNTS65	101012
Multilateral		05 Aug 49	88UNTS229	101195
Multilateral		10 Aug 49	45UNTS3	100689
WHO (World Health)	Thailand	12 Aug 49	178UNTS347	102350
Czechoslovakia	UK Great Britain	18 Aug 49	86UNTS129	101155
India	IBRD (World Bank)	18 Aug 49	154UNTS269	102031
Brazil	USA (United States)	31 Aug 49	102UNTS13	101407
Greece	Italy	31 Aug 49	78UNTS89	101014
Iran	USA (United States)	01 Sep 49	79UNTS155	101039
Argentina	Norway	09 Sep 49	42UNTS125	100646
Denmark	ICAO (Civil Aviat)	09 Sep 49	53UNTS341	100791
IBRD (World Bank)	Yugoslavia	17 Sep 49	155UNTS3	102034
India	IBRD (World Bank)	29 Sep 49	154UNTS393	102033
Greece	UK Great Britain	17 Oct 49	93UNTS185	101300
Finland	IBRD (World Bank)	17 Oct 49	156UNTS355	200481
Norway	USA (United States)	31 Oct 49	68UNTS3	100879
United Arab Rep	USA (United States)	03 Nov 49	71UNTS31	100908
Italy	Norway	19 Nov 49	47UNTS89	100724
Norway	Portugal	28 Nov 49	47UNTS117	100726
Colombia	UK Great Britain	13 Dec 49	88UNTS133	101189
Afghanistan	India	14 Dec 49	53UNTS95	100774
Denmark	Germany, West	15 Dec 49	51UNTS11	100749
Germany, West	USA (United States)	15 Dec 49	92UNTS269	101277
Norway	Poland	21 Dec 49	47UNTS107	100725
Sweden	UK Great Britain	30 Dec 49	87UNTS59	101166
Greece	Portugal	31 Dec 49	92UNTS83	101263
Canada	USA (United States)	24 Jan 50	151UNTS171	101992
Austria	UK Great Britain	26 Jan 50	97UNTS183	101350
India	USA (United States)	02 Feb 50	89UNTS127	101214
UK Great Britain	Yugoslavia	09 Feb 50	88UNTS287	101200
China People's Rep	USSR (Soviet Union)	14 Feb 50	226UNTS21	103104
Canada	Norway	18 Mar 50	230UNTS349	103194
Canada	Denmark	25 Mar 50	230UNTS343	103193
Canada	Yugoslavia	29 Mar 50	230UNTS357	103195
Paraguay	UK Great Britain	03 Apr 50	99UNTS81	101372
India	IBRD (World Bank)	18 Apr 50	155UNTS117	102036
El Salvador	WHO (World Health)	21 Apr 50	103UNTS13	101420
Burma	UNICEF (Children)	22 Apr 50	68UNTS96	100888
Australia	Netherlands	26 Apr 50	54UNTS83	100796
Korea, South	USA (United States)	28 Apr 50	93UNTS21	101284
Austria	USA (United States)	06 Jun 50	92UNTS201	101273
Iraq	IBRD (World Bank)	15 Jun 50	155UNTS267	102038
Thailand	USA (United States)	01 Jul 50	81UNTS61	101063
Afghanistan	UNICEF (Children)	04 Jul 50	71UNTS3	100906
IBRD (World Bank)	Turkey	07 Jul 50	156UNTS75	102040
IBRD (World Bank)	Turkey	07 Jul 50	156UNTS3	102039
Denmark	Spain	12 Jul 50	71UNTS129	100913
Korea, South	USA (United States)	28 Jul 50	140UNTS57	101883
FAO (Food Agri)	United Nations	02 Aug 50	139UNTS407	200467
Belgium	Japan	29 Aug 50	76UNTS113	100984
Ethiopia	IBRD (World Bank)	13 Sep 50	157UNTS213	102055
Ethiopia	IBRD (World Bank)	13 Sep 50	157UNTS233	102056
Pakistan	USA (United States)	23 Sep 50	82UNTS131	101088
Canada	USSR (Soviet Union)	29 Sep 50	230UNTS371	103197
Denmark	Italy	04 Oct 50	78UNTS353	101025
Netherlands	USA (United States)	07 Oct 50	79UNTS33	101029
ILO (Labor Org)	United Nations	12 Oct 50	139UNTS395	200466
IBRD (World Bank)	Turkey	19 Oct 50	157UNTS333	102058
IBRD (World Bank)	Thailand	27 Oct 50	158UNTS25	102060
IBRD (World Bank)	Thailand	27 Oct 50	158UNTS43	102061
IBRD (World Bank)	Thailand	27 Oct 50	158UNTS3	102059
Australia	IBRD (World Bank)	14 Nov 50	156UNTS147	102041
Switzerland	UK Great Britain	08 Dec 50	175UNTS55	102295
Multilateral		15 Dec 50	76UNTS120	100985

Accounting procedures (Cont.)

PARTY ONE	PARTY TWO	DATE	CITATION	NUMBER
Multilateral		15 Dec 50	160UNTS267	102111
Italy	UK Great Britain	21 Dec 50	175UNTS187	102301
Italy	Yugoslavia	23 Dec 50	150UNTS191	101973
Sweden	UK Great Britain	17 Jan 51	93UNTS225	101301
Netherlands	USA (United States)	19 Jan 51	141UNTS221	101917
Denmark	Switzerland	20 Jan 51	87UNTS223	101174
Italy	Norway	22 Jan 51	88UNTS339	101202
IBRD (World Bank)	South Africa	23 Jan 51	158UNTS115	102064
Colombia	Denmark	26 Jan 51	87UNTS161	101171
Nicaragua	USA (United States)	31 Jan 51	150UNTS3	101960
Nicaragua	USA (United States)	31 Jan 51	160UNTS121	102105
Ethiopia	ICAO (Civil Aviat)	02 Feb 51	96UNTS123	101333
France	UK Great Britain	17 Feb 51	88UNTS199	101191
Ethiopia	IBRD (World Bank)	19 Feb 51	186UNTS101	102486
Australia	Netherlands	22 Feb 51	128UNTS115	101717
Panama	USA (United States)	26 Feb 51	160UNTS153	102106
ICAO (Civil Aviat)	United Nations	28 Feb 51	139UNTS429	200469
UNESCO (Educ/Cult)	United Nations	07 Mar 51	139UNTS417	200468
Australia	Italy	29 Mar 51	131UNTS187	101741
China People's Rep	Poland	03 Apr 51	304UNTS187	104396
United Nations	WMO (Meteorology)	10 Apr 51	103UNTS245	200415
Colombia	IBRD (World Bank)	10 Apr 51	158UNTS155	102066
Canada	USA (United States)	18 Apr 51	134UNTS205	101800
Honduras	USA (United States)	24 Apr 51	140UNTS287	101894
UK Great Britain	Yugoslavia	10 May 51	102UNTS29	101408
Italy	USA (United States)	16 May 51	206UNTS325	102795
Mexico	United Nations	20 May 51	102UNTS103	101413
India	UK Great Britain	05 Jun 51	135UNTS3	101811
Nicaragua	IBRD (World Bank)	07 Jun 51	158UNTS277	102068
Saudi Arabia	USA (United States)	18 Jun 51	141UNTS67	101906
Iceland	IBRD (World Bank)	20 Jun 51	158UNTS301	102069
Sweden	USA (United States)	27 Jun 51	148UNTS77	101937
United Arab Rep	UK Great Britain	01 Jul 51	249UNTS125	103503
Canada	France	04 Jul 51	233UNTS101	103253
UK Great Britain	USA (United States)	18 Jul 51	117UNTS49	101583
Multilateral		01 Aug 51	107UNTS19	101464
Iraq	USA (United States)	16 Aug 51	147UNTS65	101929
Denmark	USA (United States)	23 Aug 51	147UNTS49	101928
Japan	USA (United States)	28 Aug 51	147UNTS81	101930
Japan	UK Great Britain	31 Aug 51	108UNTS273	101480
Costa Rica	USA (United States)	11 Sep 51	234UNTS255	103288
Belgium	IBRD (World Bank)	13 Sep 51	158UNTS349	102071
Norway	USA (United States)	17 Sep 51	140UNTS313	101895
Pakistan	UK Great Britain	26 Sep 51	118UNTS221	101608
UK Great Britain	Yugoslavia	28 Sep 51	117UNTS107	101587
Pakistan	UK Great Britain	29 Sep 51	134UNTS183	101798
IBRD (World Bank)	Yugoslavia	11 Oct 51	159UNTS3	102081
Iceland	IBRD (World Bank)	01 Nov 51	159UNTS55	102083
South Africa	USA (United States)	09 Nov 51	160UNTS41	102100
Turkey	USA (United States)	15 Nov 51	177UNTS315	102331
Israel	USA (United States)	07 Dec 51	157UNTS53	102046
Paraguay	IBRD (World Bank)	07 Dec 51	159UNTS103	102085
Jordan	USA (United States)	20 Dec 51	157UNTS69	102048
Spain	UK Great Britain	20 Dec 51	123UNTS187	101660
Taiwan	USA (United States)	02 Jan 52	181UNTS161	102407
Austria	USA (United States)	05 Jan 52	179UNTS73	102355
Belgium	USA (United States)	07 Jan 52	179UNTS81	102356
Italy	USA (United States)	07 Jan 52	179UNTS165	102365
Greece	USA (United States)	07 Jan 52	180UNTS171	102382
Greece	USA (United States)	07 Jan 52	177UNTS249	102323
Turkey	USA (United States)	07 Jan 52	179UNTS121	102361
Iceland	USA (United States)	08 Jan 52	180UNTS183	102383
Luxembourg	USA (United States)	08 Jan 52	180UNTS191	102384
Germany, East	Poland	08 Jan 52	304UNTS113	104394
Norway	USA (United States)	08 Jan 52	179UNTS185	102367

Accounting procedures (Cont.)

PARTY ONE	PARTY TWO	DATE	CITATION	NUMBER
Netherlands	USA (United States)	08 Jan 52	179UNTS175	102366
USA (United States)	Yugoslavia	08 Jan 52	152UNTS61	102011
UK Great Britain	USA (United States)	08 Jan 52	179UNTS201	102369
Denmark	USA (United States)	08 Jan 52	179UNTS65	102354
Peru	IBRD (World Bank)	23 Jan 52	159UNTS163	102087
Jordan	USA (United States)	12 Feb 52	168UNTS25	102211
Dominican Republic	WHO (World Health)	15 Feb 52	134UNTS291	101808
Austria	USA (United States)	16 Feb 52	177UNTS299	102329
Philippines	USA (United States)	19 Feb 52	177UNTS307	102330
Israel	USA (United States)	27 Feb 52	177UNTS123	102314
Japan	USA (United States)	28 Feb 52	208UNTS255	102817
Pakistan	IBRD (World Bank)	27 Mar 52	159UNTS251	102090
Norway	USA (United States)	01 Apr 52	177UNTS291	102328
Greece	Switzerland	04 Apr 52	166UNTS271	102192
Peru	USA (United States)	09 Apr 52	184UNTS295	102454
Canada	Netherlands	10 Apr 52	233UNTS129	103257
Greece	USA (United States)	23 Apr 52	177UNTS283	102327
Belgium	Greece	24 Apr 52	166UNTS261	102191
Israel	USA (United States)	09 May 52	177UNTS269	102326
Israel	USA (United States)	09 May 52	177UNTS63	102309
Ethiopia	USA (United States)	15 May 52	180UNTS227	102388
Netherlands	USA (United States)	15 May 52	177UNTS233	102321
Germany, West	Netherlands	19 May 52	134UNTS3	101794
Korea, South	USA (United States)	24 May 52	179UNTS23	102353
Pakistan	IBRD (World Bank)	13 Jun 52	191UNTS85	102578
IBRD (World Bank)	Turkey	18 Jun 52	159UNTS269	102091
Germany, West	Netherlands	20 Jun 52	136UNTS221	101836
South Africa	USA (United States)	24 Jun 52	177UNTS241	102322
Brazil	IBRD (World Bank)	27 Jun 52	190UNTS85	102560
Finland	USA (United States)	02 Jul 52	165UNTS203	102177
Australia	IBRD (World Bank)	08 Jul 52	159UNTS295	102092
Peru	IBRD (World Bank)	08 Jul 52	159UNTS321	102093
Iraq	UK Great Britain	10 Jul 52	151UNTS227	101998
Multilateral		11 Jul 52	170UNTS269	102223
Multilateral		11 Jul 52	171UNTS143	102226
Multilateral		11 Jul 52	171UNTS3	102224
Germany, West	USA (United States)	18 Jul 52	165UNTS167	102175
Pakistan	UK Great Britain	22 Jul 52	157UNTS185	102054
Israel	USA (United States)	23 Jul 52	179UNTS139	102363
Germany, West	Greece	28 Jul 52	182UNTS85	102424
Colombia	IBRD (World Bank)	26 Aug 52	159UNTS339	102094
Mexico	USA (United States)	26 Aug 52	264UNTS269	103797
Iceland	IBRD (World Bank)	26 Aug 52	159UNTS363	102095
Multilateral		28 Aug 52	175UNTS69	102296
Australia	Germany, West	29 Aug 52	184UNTS147	102446
Germany, West	Israel	10 Sep 52	162UNTS205	102137
Pakistan	USA (United States)	17 Sep 52	227UNTS77	103132
United Arab Rep	UK Great Britain	30 Oct 52	172UNTS3	102236
Denmark	Israel	14 Nov 52	160UNTS289	102114
Ceylon (Sri Lanka)	USA (United States)	17 Nov 52	180UNTS207	102386
Mexico	ICAO (Civil Aviat)	28 Nov 52	164UNTS15	102156
Liberia	USA (United States)	15 Dec 52	185UNTS45	102457
India	IBRD (World Bank)	23 Jan 53	201UNTS145	102715
Greece	Italy	04 Feb 53	189UNTS295	102552
IBRD (World Bank)	Yugoslavia	11 Feb 53	165UNTS231	102179
United Nations	WMO (Meteorology)	27 Mar 53	178UNTS361	200504
Czechoslovakia	Denmark	23 Apr 53	174UNTS107	102281
Syria	Turkey	28 Apr 53	204UNTS255	102760
Ethiopia	USA (United States)	29 Apr 53	224UNTS121	103073
Brazil	IBRD (World Bank)	30 Apr 53	190UNTS133	102562
Greece	United Arab Rep	21 May 53	256UNTS25	103621
United Arab Rep	USA (United States)	18 Jun 53	204UNTS55	102749
United Arab Rep	USA (United States)	18 Jun 53	215UNTS45	102910
Liberia	USA (United States)	23 Jun 53	213UNTS57	102880
UK Great Britain	USA (United States)	24 Jun 53	224UNTS141	103074

Accounting procedures (Cont.)

PARTY ONE	PARTY TWO	DATE	CITATION	NUMBER
Pakistan	USA (United States)	25 Jun 53	205UNTS139	102773
Israel	Switzerland	01 Jul 53	220UNTS41	102986
Brazil	IBRD (World Bank)	17 Jul 53	190UNTS149	102563
India	UK Great Britain	20 Jul 53	196UNTS251	102628
Multilateral		30 Jul 53	215UNTS97	102913
Ceylon (Sri Lanka)	Yugoslavia	30 Jul 53	337UNTS103	104819
Argentina	USSR (Soviet Union)	05 Aug 53	221UNTS99	103004
IBRD (World Bank)	South Africa	28 Aug 53	180UNTS73	102376
Nicaragua	IBRD (World Bank)	04 Sep 53	186UNTS137	102488
Nicaragua	IBRD (World Bank)	04 Sep 53	186UNTS117	102487
Denmark	Uruguay	09 Sep 53	256UNTS149	103625
IBRD (World Bank)	Turkey	10 Sep 53	187UNTS71	102502
Colombia	IBRD (World Bank)	10 Sep 53	203UNTS3	102738
Spain	USA (United States)	26 Sep 53	207UNTS93	102802
UN Relief Palestin	United Arab Rep	14 Oct 53	190UNTS13	102555
Jordan	USA (United States)	21 Oct 53	222UNTS31	103020
Australia	Netherlands	22 Oct 53	184UNTS193	102448
Israel	USA (United States)	25 Nov 53	219UNTS205	102976
France	Netherlands	27 Nov 53	302UNTS245	104363
India	USSR (Soviet Union)	02 Dec 53	240UNTS143	103402
Bulgaria	Greece	05 Dec 53	225UNTS145	103096
Multilateral		11 Dec 53	191UNTS285	102588
Brazil	IBRD (World Bank)	18 Dec 53	301UNTS229	104346
Italy	South Africa	20 Dec 53	277UNTS293	104014
Japan	UK Great Britain	29 Jan 54	190UNTS319	102572
Czechoslovakia	Greece	01 Feb 54	225UNTS95	103092
Czechoslovakia	Greece	01 Feb 54	225UNTS77	103091
Germany, West	USA (United States)	12 Feb 54	223UNTS153	103064
Australia	IBRD (World Bank)	02 Mar 54	191UNTS103	102579
Japan	USA (United States)	08 Mar 54	232UNTS267	103241
Mexico	USA (United States)	06 Apr 54	233UNTS163	103261
Norway	IBRD (World Bank)	08 Apr 54	201UNTS131	102714
Peru	IBRD (World Bank)	12 Apr 54	190UNTS231	102567
USA (United States)	Yugoslavia	16 Apr 54	237UNTS77	103337
Lebanon	USSR (Soviet Union)	30 Apr 54	226UNTS109	103111
France	Netherlands	30 Apr 54	202UNTS115	102727
Greece	Spain	15 May 54	299UNTS277	104319
Greece	Romania	19 May 54	225UNTS27	103084
Australia	Greece	24 May 54	191UNTS255	102586
Greece	Hungary	05 Jun 54	299UNTS285	104320
Greece	Hungary	05 Jun 54	299UNTS295	104321
Netherlands	Norway	09 Jun 54	287UNTS179	104184
Australia	Israel	18 Jun 54	220UNTS29	102985
France	Netherlands	09 Jul 54	287UNTS169	104183
Ceylon (Sri Lanka)	IBRD (World Bank)	09 Jul 54	198UNTS313	200517
Multilateral		29 Jul 54	249UNTS45	103500
Canada	South Africa	04 Aug 54	261UNTS3	103722
Brazil	USA (United States)	20 Aug 54	410UNTS79	105898
Pakistan	USA (United States)	23 Aug 54	234UNTS243	103287
New Zealand	UNICEF (Children)	26 Aug 54	198UNTS173	102663
El Salvador	USA (United States)	31 Aug 54	237UNTS49	103336
UNESCO (Educ/Cult)	UN Special Fund	29 Sep 54	363UNTS367	200572
El Salvador	IBRD (World Bank)	12 Oct 54	203UNTS37	102739
Multilateral		23 Oct 54	332UNTS157	104761
Iran	UK Great Britain	25 Oct 54	204UNTS131	102754
Poland	UK Great Britain	11 Nov 54	204UNTS137	102755
Turkey	USA (United States)	15 Nov 54	238UNTS135	103358
Portugal	UK Great Britain	18 Nov 54	210UNTS265	102841
Australia	Poland	25 Nov 54	521UNTS281	107526
Guatemala	USA (United States)	13 Dec 54	237UNTS169	103343
Belgium	IBRD (World Bank)	14 Dec 54	210UNTS113	102837
Netherlands	USA (United States)	14 Dec 54	262UNTS35	103737
Australia	Austria	20 Dec 54	205UNTS157	102775
Iceland	Netherlands	28 Dec 54	287UNTS159	104182
Israel	South Africa	31 Dec 54	220UNTS11	102984

Accounting procedures (Cont.)

PARTY ONE	PARTY TWO	DATE	CITATION	NUMBER
Peru	USA (United States)	31 Dec 54	251UNTS51	103533
USSR (Soviet Union)	Yugoslavia	05 Jan 55	240UNTS225	103405
Pakistan	USA (United States)	11 Jan 55	251UNTS111	103537
Turkey	UK Great Britain	17 Jan 55	204UNTS195	102758
Pakistan	USA (United States)	18 Jan 55	241UNTS53	103423
Chile	USA (United States)	27 Jan 55	262UNTS3	103735
Australia	Hungary	10 Feb 55	207UNTS173	102806
Italy	USA (United States)	11 Feb 55	240UNTS87	103396
USA (United States)	Vietnam, South	07 Mar 55	277UNTS285	104013
Mexico	USA (United States)	09 Mar 55	263UNTS247	103776
Australia	IBRD (World Bank)	18 Mar 55	220UNTS131	102998
Australia	Taiwan	22 Mar 55	209UNTS3	102818
Argentina	UK Great Britain	31 Mar 55	210UNTS223	102840
Chile	USA (United States)	31 Mar 55	262UNTS19	103736
Haiti	USA (United States)	01 Apr 55	261UNTS361	103734
Ceylon (Sri Lanka)	Germany, West	01 Apr 55	369UNTS57	105251
Australia	Czechoslovakia	01 Apr 55	213UNTS199	102888
Peru	IBRD (World Bank)	05 Apr 55	211UNTS115	102850
Norway	IBRD (World Bank)	19 Apr 55	211UNTS159	102852
Philippines	USA (United States)	27 Apr 55	261UNTS351	103733
Israel	USA (United States)	29 Apr 55	261UNTS331	103731
Multilateral		25 May 55	264UNTS117	103791
Norway	Sweden	28 May 55	262UNTS151	103743
Pakistan	Sweden	04 Jun 55	228UNTS121	103146
Austria	IBRD (World Bank)	14 Jun 55	221UNTS375	200531
Colombia	IBRD (World Bank)	15 Jun 55	248UNTS161	103494
Colombia	USA (United States)	23 Jun 55	263UNTS337	103781
Haiti	USA (United States)	24 Jun 55	264UNTS291	103800
Italy	USA (United States)	30 Jun 55	258UNTS15	103667
Multilateral		04 Jul 55	214UNTS10	102897
Panama	IBRD (World Bank)	12 Jul 55	219UNTS127	102970
Belgium	USA (United States)	15 Jul 55	223UNTS3	103040
Guatemala	IBRD (World Bank)	29 Jul 55	229UNTS167	103165
Peru	IBRD (World Bank)	05 Aug 55	218UNTS3	102950
Greece	USSR (Soviet Union)	23 Aug 55	233UNTS39	103249
Lebanon	IBRD (World Bank)	25 Aug 55	230UNTS233	103188
Austria	USSR (Soviet Union)	17 Oct 55	0UNTS0	109255
Austria	USSR (Soviet Union)	09 Nov 55	255UNTS247	103613
Bulgaria	Yugoslavia	15 Nov 55	396UNTS191	105697
Syria	USSR (Soviet Union)	16 Nov 55	259UNTS71	103683
IBRD (World Bank)	South Africa	28 Nov 55	230UNTS101	103178
Korea, North	Romania	05 Dec 55	362UNTS141	105186
Argentina	USA (United States)	21 Dec 55	240UNTS329	103411
Honduras	IBRD (World Bank)	22 Dec 55	230UNTS262	103189
Romania	Yugoslavia	13 Jan 56	342UNTS265	104912
Germany, West	Sweden	17 Jan 56	262UNTS301	103758
Denmark	Netherlands	31 Jan 56	286UNTS255	104172
Multilateral		02 Feb 56	227UNTS153	103137
Multilateral		10 Feb 56	228UNTS189	103151
Japan	USA (United States)	10 Feb 56	275UNTS105	103979
Multilateral		10 Feb 56	228UNTS167	103150
Italy	USA (United States)	27 Feb 56	291UNTS287	104260
Ethiopia	Italy	05 Mar 56	267UNTS189	103844
Burma	Yugoslavia	07 Mar 56	386UNTS207	105542
Ceylon (Sri Lanka)	Romania	16 Mar 56	315UNTS51	104559
Canada	Japan	20 Mar 56	517UNTS33	107482
Romania	USSR (Soviet Union)	07 Apr 56	259UNTS377	103698
Austria	Hungary	09 Apr 56	438UNTS123	106315
Mongolia	USSR (Soviet Union)	24 Apr 56	259UNTS297	103693
Bulgaria	USSR (Soviet Union)	28 Apr 56	259UNTS363	103697
Ceylon (Sri Lanka)	USA (United States)	28 Apr 56	274UNTS35	103956
Albania	USSR (Soviet Union)	03 May 56	259UNTS391	103699
Brazil	France	04 May 56	323UNTS339	104675
Haiti	IBRD (World Bank)	07 May 56	252UNTS279	103570
Austria	Italy	07 May 56	284UNTS351	104147

Accounting procedures (Cont.)

PARTY ONE	PARTY TWO	DATE	CITATION	NUMBER
Germany, East	USSR (Soviet Union)	30 May 56	263UNTS143	103771
Czechoslovakia	USSR (Soviet Union)	01 Jun 56	259UNTS341	103696
Colombia	IBRD (World Bank)	06 Jun 56	248UNTS139	103493
Bulgaria	Ceylon (Sri Lanka)	19 Jun 56	315UNTS33	104557
Canada	UK Great Britain	21 Jun 56	381UNTS111	105467
Israel	USA (United States)	26 Jun 56	257UNTS55	103649
Italy	Netherlands	29 Jun 56	287UNTS193	104185
Italy	Switzerland	29 Jun 56	284UNTS299	104144
Poland	USSR (Soviet Union)	30 Jun 56	259UNTS311	103694
China People's Rep	USSR (Soviet Union)	05 Jul 56	263UNTS129	103770
Poland	Yugoslavia	06 Jul 56	281UNTS143	104076
Greece	Romania	25 Aug 56	299UNTS231	104315
Korea, North	USSR (Soviet Union)	05 Sep 56	259UNTS329	103695
Multilateral		11 Sep 56	266UNTS221	103832
Belgium	Germany, West	24 Sep 56	263UNTS31	103766
Multilateral		25 Sep 56	334UNTS89	104767
Multilateral		25 Sep 56	334UNTS13	104766
India	Poland	29 Sep 56	276UNTS305	103993
Canada	UK Great Britain	20 Oct 56	381UNTS99	105466
Multilateral		26 Oct 56	276UNTS3	103988
Ecuador	USA (United States)	31 Oct 56	283UNTS151	104114
Argentina	USA (United States)	05 Nov 56	277UNTS143	104004
Australia	IBRD (World Bank)	15 Nov 56	288UNTS117	104201
Canada	UK Great Britain	16 Nov 56	412UNTS166	105930
Australia	IBRD (World Bank)	03 Dec 56	288UNTS99	104200
Multilateral		21 Dec 56	427UNTS81	106147
France	Italy	28 Dec 56	291UNTS203	104255
Colombia	USA (United States)	09 Jan 57	462UNTS151	106676
Iran	IBRD (World Bank)	22 Jan 57	317UNTS129	104600
Ethiopia	IBRD (World Bank)	28 Jan 57	286UNTS307	104175
Sweden	USSR (Soviet Union)	28 Jan 57	428UNTS315	106183
Iceland	USA (United States)	23 Feb 57	283UNTS73	104107
Multilateral		01 Mar 57	264UNTS94	103790
Burma	India	12 Mar 57	312UNTS131	104515
Tunisia	USA (United States)	26 Mar 57	283UNTS117	104111
France	Japan	27 Mar 57	318UNTS233	104617
Australia	UK Great Britain	01 Apr 57	271UNTS235	103918
Morocco	USA (United States)	02 Apr 57	288UNTS157	104203
Paraguay	USA (United States)	04 Apr 57	284UNTS161	104135
Libya	USA (United States)	04 Apr 57	283UNTS181	104116
Netherlands	Paraguay	13 Apr 57	593UNTS85	108577
Ethiopia	USA (United States)	25 Apr 57	283UNTS205	104118
Austria	USA (United States)	10 May 57	283UNTS33	104104
Denmark	Paraguay	18 May 57	286UNTS117	104163
Jordan	USA (United States)	27 Jun 57	288UNTS269	104209
India	IBRD (World Bank)	12 Jul 57	288UNTS135	104202
Germany, West	Italy	12 Jul 57	291UNTS181	104252
Albania	Yugoslavia	29 Aug 57	391UNTS167	105622
Ceylon (Sri Lanka)	China People's Rep	19 Sep 57	337UNTS137	104821
Ceylon (Sri Lanka)	China People's Rep	19 Sep 57	337UNTS169	104822
Ecuador	IBRD (World Bank)	20 Sep 57	289UNTS237	104221
Austria	South Africa	26 Sep 57	287UNTS3	104176
Multilateral		03 Oct 57	366UNTS3	105215
Multilateral		03 Oct 57	366UNTS193	105218
Multilateral		03 Oct 57	364UNTS3	105211
Taiwan	USA (United States)	08 Oct 57	304UNTS241	104400
Pakistan	IBRD (World Bank)	18 Oct 57	299UNTS303	104322
United Arab Rep	USSR (Soviet Union)	19 Oct 57	292UNTS151	104271
Brazil	USA (United States)	05 Nov 57	303UNTS3	104368
Argentina	Denmark	25 Nov 57	299UNTS83	104308
Argentina	Italy	25 Nov 57	305UNTS275	104424
UK Great Britain	USSR (Soviet Union)	19 Dec 57	351UNTS235	105026
Brazil	Italy	08 Jan 58	362UNTS273	105192
Japan	USA (United States)	11 Jan 58	304UNTS35	104390
Poland	Yugoslavia	16 Jan 58	340UNTS181	104864

Accounting procedures (Cont.)

PARTY ONE	PARTY TWO	DATE	CITATION	NUMBER
Indonesia	Japan	20 Jan 58	325UNTS3	104690
Bulgaria	Italy	25 Feb 58	362UNTS279	105193
Sweden	USSR (Soviet Union)	28 Mar 58	428UNTS321	106184
USA (United States)	Yugoslavia	05 Apr 58	338UNTS233	104838
Honduras	IBRD (World Bank)	09 May 58	323UNTS4	104662
Bulgaria	Denmark	28 May 58	312UNTS235	104521
Multilateral		18 Jun 58	386UNTS355	105553
IBRD (World Bank)	Sudan	21 Jul 58	323UNTS183	104669
Netherlands	Yugoslavia	22 Jul 58	386UNTS263	105546
Australia	Netherlands	23 Jul 58	328UNTS227	104736
Burma	USA (United States)	25 Aug 58	336UNTS3	104795
Australia	Germany, West	27 Aug 58	320UNTS303	104649
India	IBRD (World Bank)	16 Sep 58	323UNTS235	104671
Ceylon (Sri Lanka)	IBRD (World Bank)	17 Sep 58	323UNTS51	104664
Iraq	USSR (Soviet Union)	11 Oct 58	328UNTS95	104730
Finland	Sweden	16 Oct 58	428UNTS125	106171
Spain	USA (United States)	16 Oct 58	336UNTS153	104804
Multilateral		27 Oct 58	351UNTS303	105031
United Arab Rep	USA (United States)	31 Oct 58	355UNTS355	105086
Turkey	UK Great Britain	25 Nov 58	327UNTS35	104715
IBRD (World Bank)	South Africa	02 Dec 58	324UNTS3	104676
Israel	Yugoslavia	11 Dec 58	386UNTS283	105548
El Salvador	IBRD (World Bank)	07 Jan 59	346UNTS51	104977
IMCO (Maritime Org)	United Nations	13 Jan 59	324UNTS273	200553
Burma	UK Great Britain	06 Feb 59	343UNTS223	104927
Iraq	USSR (Soviet Union)	16 Mar 59	346UNTS107	104979
India	IBRD (World Bank)	08 Apr 59	348UNTS131	104998
Italy	United Arab Rep	29 Apr 59	363UNTS91	105202
Austria	USA (United States)	22 May 59	347UNTS3	104988
Iran	IBRD (World Bank)	29 May 59	348UNTS103	104997
IBRD (World Bank)	South Africa	10 Jun 59	340UNTS33	104857
IMCO (Maritime Org)	United Nations	23 Jun 59	336UNTS317	200556
Norway	IBRD (World Bank)	08 Jul 59	344UNTS229	104952
India	IBRD (World Bank)	15 Jul 59	346UNTS33	104976
New Zealand	UK Great Britain	21 Sep 59	401UNTS51	105762
FAO (Food Agri)	UN Special Fund	28 Sep 59	341UNTS353	200562
United Arab Rep	USA (United States)	28 Sep 59	358UNTS97	105128
Multilateral		09 Oct 59	376UNTS382	105391
ILO (Labor Org)	UN Special Fund	12 Oct 59	343UNTS325	200563
Guinea	UK Great Britain	22 Oct 59	351UNTS341	105033
UN Special Fund	WMO (Meteorology)	17 Nov 59	345UNTS311	200564
Norway	Yugoslavia	18 Nov 59	383UNTS131	105499
Multilateral		18 Nov 59	390UNTS227	105610
USA (United States)	USSR (Soviet Union)	21 Nov 59	361UNTS35	105172
Pakistan	IBRD (World Bank)	30 Nov 59	355UNTS203	105078
Multilateral		14 Dec 59	368UNTS253	105245
Multilateral		14 Dec 59	422UNTS75	106069
Australia	Austria	18 Dec 59	348UNTS201	105001
IBRD (World Bank)	Uruguay	30 Dec 59	384UNTS275	105523
Denmark	Sweden	04 Jan 60	376UNTS375	105390
Cuba	USSR (Soviet Union)	13 Feb 60	369UNTS17	105248
Cuba	USSR (Soviet Union)	13 Feb 60	369UNTS3	105247
Iran	IBRD (World Bank)	20 Feb 60	384UNTS213	105521
Indonesia	USSR (Soviet Union)	28 Feb 60	392UNTS173	105643
Portugal	USA (United States)	19 Mar 60	371UNTS131	105275
Ireland	South Africa	13 Apr 60	390UNTS307	105612
ICAO (Civil Aviat)	UN Special Fund	21 Apr 60	360UNTS367	200569
Laos	UN Special Fund	30 Apr 60	361UNTS171	105179
Costa Rica	IBRD (World Bank)	04 May 60	390UNTS201	105609
UN Special Fund	WHO (World Health)	25 May 60	359UNTS375	200568
USA (United States)	Yugoslavia	03 Jun 60	376UNTS243	105382
IBRD (World Bank)	Sudan	17 Jun 60	379UNTS253	105442
Australia	USSR (Soviet Union)	29 Jun 60	392UNTS131	105641
ITU (Telecommun)	UN Special Fund	13 Jul 60	368UNTS329	200573
Ethiopia	UN Special Fund	13 Jul 60	368UNTS159	105240

Accounting procedures (Cont.)

PARTY ONE	PARTY TWO	DATE	CITATION	NUMBER
USA (United States)	Uruguay	22 Jul 60	388UNTS315	105587
Multilateral		28 Jul 60	485UNTS3	107042
India	IBRD (World Bank)	29 Jul 60	377UNTS153	105399
Ghana	USSR (Soviet Union)	04 Aug 60	399UNTS61	105734
Ghana	USSR (Soviet Union)	04 Aug 60	421UNTS27	106050
Panama	IBRD (World Bank)	19 Aug 60	390UNTS153	105607
Congo (Zaire)	United Nations	23 Aug 60	373UNTS327	200576
Israel	UK Great Britain	31 Aug 60	385UNTS71	105530
Israel	IBRD (World Bank)	09 Sep 60	406UNTS3	105837
Brazil	UN Special Fund	16 Sep 60	375UNTS3	105351
Pakistan	IBRD (World Bank)	19 Sep 60	444UNTS207	106370
Multilateral		19 Sep 60	444UNTS259	106371
Taiwan	UN Special Fund	20 Sep 60	375UNTS29	105352
Guinea	USA (United States)	30 Sep 60	394UNTS103	105671
Netherlands	Romania	30 Sep 60	479UNTS91	106948
Chile	USA (United States)	28 Oct 60	401UNTS177	105770
Greece	Poland	08 Nov 60	483UNTS141	107011
Norway	IBRD (World Bank)	02 Dec 60	390UNTS131	105606
Multilateral		13 Dec 60	455UNTS204	106544
Peru	IBRD (World Bank)	19 Dec 60	417UNTS275	106010
Japan	IBRD (World Bank)	20 Dec 60	400UNTS279	105754
Togo	USA (United States)	22 Dec 60	401UNTS33	105760
Mali	USA (United States)	04 Jan 61	405UNTS165	105832
Australia	Japan	07 Feb 61	450UNTS343	106478
Philippines	USA (United States)	12 Mar 61	288UNTS285	104210
Cuba	Czechoslovakia	05 Apr 61	442UNTS201	106350
Honduras	USA (United States)	12 Apr 61	413UNTS182	105952
Turkey	USSR (Soviet Union)	27 Apr 61	420UNTS307	106047
Sierra Leone	USA (United States)	05 May 61	409UNTS194	105885
Senegal	USA (United States)	13 May 61	409UNTS232	105888
Ivory Coast	USA (United States)	17 May 61	409UNTS241	105889
Niger	USA (United States)	26 May 61	410UNTS213	105905
Cameroon	USA (United States)	26 May 61	413UNTS195	105953
Dahomey	USA (United States)	27 May 61	445UNTS23	106373
Somalia	USSR (Soviet Union)	02 Jun 61	493UNTS173	107214
Somalia	USSR (Soviet Union)	02 Jun 61	457UNTS263	106587
Ceylon (Sri Lanka)	IBRD (World Bank)	06 Jun 61	414UNTS349	105978
Nepal	USA (United States)	09 Jun 61	421UNTS223	106061
Congo (Zaire)	United Nations	12 Jun 61	494UNTS205	107234
Ethiopia	United Nations	14 Jun 61	406UNTS81	105840
IBRD (World Bank)	Sudan	14 Jun 61	415UNTS26	105980
Finland	USA (United States)	16 Jun 61	413UNTS211	105955
Inter-Am Devel Bnk	USA (United States)	19 Jun 61	410UNTS34	105895
Madagascar	USA (United States)	22 Jun 61	413UNTS219	105956
Chile	IBRD (World Bank)	28 Jun 61	426UNTS33	106129
Argentina	IBRD (World Bank)	30 Jun 61	445UNTS85	106379
Philippines	IBRD (World Bank)	26 Jul 61	414UNTS253	105976
India	IBRD (World Bank)	09 Aug 61	417UNTS297	106011
India	IBRD (World Bank)	17 Aug 61	417UNTS319	106012
Colombia	IBRD (World Bank)	28 Aug 61	416UNTS23	105993
Tunisia	USSR (Soviet Union)	30 Aug 61	437UNTS243	106310
Austria	USA (United States)	03 Oct 61	426UNTS187	106137
IBRD (World Bank)	Switzerland	11 Oct 61	415UNTS396	200592
Costa Rica	IBRD (World Bank)	13 Oct 61	430UNTS27	106202
Costa Rica	IDA (Devel Assoc)	13 Oct 61	431UNTS3	106204
India	IBRD (World Bank)	13 Oct 61	418UNTS3	106013
Pakistan	IDA (Devel Assoc)	19 Oct 61	447UNTS161	106415
Paraguay	IDA (Devel Assoc)	26 Oct 61	447UNTS277	106419
Iraq	Syria	03 Nov 61	489UNTS45	107134
Peru	IBRD (World Bank)	03 Nov 61	430UNTS47	106203
United Nations	USA (United States)	18 Nov 61	494UNTS213	107235
Pakistan	IDA (Devel Assoc)	22 Nov 61	447UNTS295	106420
IAEA (Atom Energy)	UN Special Fund	29 Nov 61	415UNTS408	200593
OAS (Am States)	USA (United States)	29 Nov 61	424UNTS119	106104
Morocco	USA (United States)	30 Nov 61	451UNTS167	106492

PARTY ONE	PARTY TWO	DATE	CITATION	NUMBER
Accounting procedures (Cont.)				
Ethiopia	USA (United States)	06 Dec 61	433UNTS231	106246
Panama	USA (United States)	11 Dec 61	445UNTS161	106384
IBRD (World Bank)	Venezuela	13 Dec 61	446UNTS371	106409
Iran	USA (United States)	21 Dec 61	433UNTS269	106249
Jordan	IDA (Devel Assoc)	22 Dec 61	448UNTS21	106423
Dominican Republic	USA (United States)	11 Jan 62	433UNTS133	106236
Thailand	USA (United States)	12 Jan 62	459UNTS95	106615
Cyprus	USA (United States)	15 Jan 62	435UNTS15	106267
Cyprus	USA (United States)	18 Jan 62	435UNTS3	106266
UNESCO (Educ/Cult)	USA (United States)	19 Jan 62	435UNTS99	106272
Australia	IBRD (World Bank)	23 Jan 62	430UNTS3	106201
Ghana	USA (United States)	24 Jan 62	435UNTS23	106268
Iceland	IBRD (World Bank)	14 Feb 62	447UNTS95	106413
India	IDA (Devel Assoc)	14 Feb 62	468UNTS177	106773
Jordan	UK Great Britain	28 Feb 62	466UNTS249	106748
Australia	Japan	01 Mar 62	517UNTS81	107483
Australia	Germany, West	19 Mar 62	488UNTS203	107130
Dahomey	UN Special Fund	28 Mar 62	424UNTS55	106099
Multilateral		29 Mar 62	507UNTS177	107401
Ghana	USSR (Soviet Union)	06 Apr 62	498UNTS41	107277
Israel	Netherlands	28 May 62	448UNTS219	106434
Denmark	USA (United States)	28 May 62	450UNTS215	106469
Multilateral		14 Jun 62	528UNTS33	107634
Israel	USA (United States)	22 Jun 62	448UNTS273	106440
United Arab Rep	USSR (Soviet Union)	23 Jun 62	472UNTS19	106835
Pakistan	IDA (Devel Assoc)	29 Jun 62	447UNTS325	106421
India	IDA (Devel Assoc)	29 Jun 62	447UNTS221	106417
Israel	Switzerland	29 Jun 62	448UNTS303	106443
India	IDA (Devel Assoc)	18 Jul 62	447UNTS191	106416
Multilateral		25 Jul 62	506UNTS177	107387
Indonesia	Netherlands	15 Aug 62	437UNTS273	106311
Korea, South	IDA (Devel Assoc)	17 Aug 62	468UNTS387	200603
Nicaragua	IDA (Devel Assoc)	07 Sep 62	478UNTS313	106940
Pakistan	IBRD (World Bank)	14 Sep 62	467UNTS152	106762
India	IDA (Devel Assoc)	14 Sep 62	448UNTS3	106422
IDA (Devel Assoc)	Tunisia	17 Sep 62	469UNTS33	106783
Multilateral		28 Sep 62	469UNTS169	106791
Multilateral		16 Oct 62	470UNTS321	106815
Multilateral		16 Oct 62	470UNTS291	106814
Israel	IBRD (World Bank)	17 Oct 62	467UNTS107	106760
IBRD (World Bank)	Uruguay	26 Oct 62	481UNTS39	106977
El Salvador	IDA (Devel Assoc)	02 Nov 62	468UNTS331	106780
Haiti	IDA (Devel Assoc)	02 Nov 62	468UNTS205	106774
Pakistan	IDA (Devel Assoc)	02 Nov 62	468UNTS351	106781
Algeria	UN Special Fund	15 Nov 62	452UNTS243	106512
IDA (Devel Assoc)	Turkey	23 Nov 62	469UNTS3	106782
Laos	USSR (Soviet Union)	01 Dec 62	472UNTS3	106834
Laos	USSR (Soviet Union)	01 Dec 62	471UNTS181	106832
Niger	UNICEF (Children)	05 Dec 62	503UNTS195	107344
Australia	UK Great Britain	06 Dec 62	457UNTS145	106584
Multilateral		08 Dec 62	510UNTS235	107418
IBRD (World Bank)	Thailand	21 Dec 62	467UNTS43	106757
IBRD (World Bank)	Thailand	21 Dec 62	467UNTS63	106758
Malaysia	USA (United States)	28 Jan 63	473UNTS15	106850
Central Afri Rep	USA (United States)	10 Feb 63	473UNTS83	106857
India	New Zealand	22 Feb 63	486UNTS19	107069
Ethiopia	IDA (Devel Assoc)	27 Feb 63	478UNTS289	106939
Nicaragua	IBRD (World Bank)	01 Mar 63	481UNTS15	106976
India	IDA (Devel Assoc)	22 Mar 63	477UNTS3	106911
Philippines	USA (United States)	23 Mar 63	474UNTS80	106873
Ethiopia	UNICEF (Children)	01 Apr 63	457UNTS103	106579
UK Great Britain	USA (United States)	06 Apr 63	474UNTS49	106871
Multilateral		20 Apr 63	495UNTS3	107239
Brazil	USSR (Soviet Union)	20 Apr 63	0UNTS0	109256
Greece	Hungary	27 Apr 63	550UNTS197	108016

PARTY ONE	PARTY TWO	DATE	CITATION	NUMBER
Accounting procedures (Cont.)				
Austria	Bulgaria	02 May 63	535UNTS143	107778
Laos	UK Great Britain	17 May 63	475UNTS155	106891
Thailand	USA (United States)	24 May 63	477UNTS123	106918
India	IDA (Devel Assoc)	24 May 63	483UNTS205	107014
IDA (Devel Assoc)	Turkey	31 May 63	480UNTS127	106966
Australia	UK Great Britain	06 Jun 63	472UNTS157	106838
Finland	Poland	10 Jun 63	503UNTS179	107343
IBRD (World Bank)	Thailand	11 Jun 63	481UNTS227	106984
Korea, South	USA (United States)	18 Jun 63	487UNTS297	107112
India	USA (United States)	19 Jun 63	479UNTS175	106952
Austria	USA (United States)	25 Jun 63	479UNTS223	106956
Pakistan	IDA (Devel Assoc)	26 Jun 63	492UNTS115	107189
UNICEF (Children)	Togo	27 Jun 63	540UNTS135	107847
IBRD (World Bank)	Tunisia	03 Jul 63	480UNTS209	106970
Austria	Romania	03 Jul 63	588UNTS3	108516
Denmark	IBRD (World Bank)	24 Jul 63	481UNTS171	106982
Pakistan	IDA (Devel Assoc)	26 Jul 63	492UNTS143	107190
Pakistan	IDA (Devel Assoc)	16 Aug 63	492UNTS171	107191
Pakistan	IDA (Devel Assoc)	16 Aug 63	492UNTS205	107192
Afghanistan	USA (United States)	20 Aug 63	488UNTS41	107118
Paraguay	USA (United States)	20 Aug 63	531UNTS197	107704
Argentina	USA (United States)	21 Aug 63	488UNTS61	107119
Dahomey	UNICEF (Children)	28 Aug 63	507UNTS101	107396
Denmark	Norway	12 Sep 63	613UNTS289	108857
Ecuador	USA (United States)	20 Sep 63	488UNTS147	107125
Australia	UK Great Britain	23 Sep 63	483UNTS39	107006
Taiwan	IBRD (World Bank)	27 Sep 63	483UNTS151	107012
Pakistan	USSR (Soviet Union)	07 Oct 63	499UNTS161	107297
Canada	France	11 Oct 63	529UNTS71	107657
Norway	IBRD (World Bank)	15 Oct 63	482UNTS103	106992
Multilateral		23 Oct 63	506UNTS197	107388
Iran	USA (United States)	24 Oct 63	489UNTS303	107146
IBRD (World Bank)	Spain	25 Oct 63	491UNTS297	107181
New Zealand	IBRD (World Bank)	12 Nov 63	485UNTS233	107059
Tunisia	USA (United States)	18 Nov 63	494UNTS193	107233
Iran	UNICEF (Children)	21 Nov 63	485UNTS35	107044
Romania	Yugoslavia	30 Nov 63	512UNTS2	107438
Iraq	UNICEF (Children)	03 Dec 63	482UNTS319	107001
Jordan	IDA (Devel Assoc)	12 Dec 63	506UNTS51	107381
Jordan	IDA (Devel Assoc)	12 Dec 63	492UNTS3	107184
Greece	USA (United States)	13 Dec 63	494UNTS55	107226
Netherlands	Poland	20 Dec 63	514UNTS169	107446
IDA (Devel Assoc)	Syria	24 Dec 63	534UNTS253	107764
Paraguay	IDA (Devel Assoc)	26 Dec 63	507UNTS3	107394
Multilateral		30 Dec 63	568UNTS215	108270
Multilateral		30 Dec 63	568UNTS243	108272
Multilateral		30 Dec 63	568UNTS233	108271
Congo (Zaire)	UK Great Britain	03 Jan 64	534UNTS417	107770
Liberia	IBRD (World Bank)	08 Jan 64	504UNTS53	107353
Burundi	UNICEF (Children)	08 Jan 64	485UNTS45	107045
IDA (Devel Assoc)	Tanganyika	05 Feb 64	506UNTS91	107382
Cyprus	USSR (Soviet Union)	29 Feb 64	602UNTS45	108706
New Zealand	IBRD (World Bank)	12 Mar 64	505UNTS3	107362
Spain	USA (United States)	18 Mar 64	535UNTS343	107789
Pakistan	IDA (Devel Assoc)	25 Mar 64	535UNTS43	107775
Pakistan	IDA (Devel Assoc)	25 Mar 64	534UNTS275	107765
Taiwan	UNICEF (Children)	08 Apr 64	500UNTS49	107306
Peru	IBRD (World Bank)	22 Apr 64	519UNTS95	107503
Liberia	USA (United States)	08 May 64	526UNTS239	107608
Jamaica	UNICEF (Children)	19 May 64	500UNTS75	107308
Multilateral		26 May 64	541UNTS271	200613
Ecuador	IBRD (World Bank)	26 May 64	534UNTS113	107758
Ecuador	IDA (Devel Assoc)	26 May 64	534UNTS93	107757
India	IDA (Devel Assoc)	09 Jun 64	506UNTS31	107380
Iran	IBRD (World Bank)	10 Jun 64	537UNTS111	107799

PARTY ONE	PARTY TWO	DATE	CITATION	NUMBER
Accounting procedures (Cont.)				
Pakistan	IDA (Devel Assoc)	11 Jun 64	534UNTS309	107766
Czechoslovakia	Netherlands	11 Jun 64	556UNTS89	108120
Pakistan	IDA (Devel Assoc)	11 Jun 64	506UNTS3	107379
Niger	IDA (Devel Assoc)	24 Jun 64	554UNTS93	108098
Pakistan	IDA (Devel Assoc)	24 Jun 64	533UNTS191	107743
Pakistan	IDA (Devel Assoc)	24 Jun 64	533UNTS165	107742
Malaysia	UNICEF (Children)	01 Jul 64	503UNTS229	107346
India	IDA (Devel Assoc)	06 Jul 64	534UNTS49	107753
Finland	IBRD (World Bank)	10 Jul 64	516UNTS125	107474
Gabon	IBRD (World Bank)	10 Jul 64	537UNTS63	107797
Iceland	UN Special Fund	10 Jul 64	502UNTS343	107337
IDA (Devel Assoc)	Turkey	14 Jul 64	534UNTS339	107767
Pakistan	IDA (Devel Assoc)	21 Jul 64	534UNTS373	107768
Bolivia	IDA (Devel Assoc)	24 Jul 64	534UNTS171	107762
Bolivia	IDA (Devel Assoc)	24 Jul 64	534UNTS203	107763
Multilateral		28 Jul 64	555UNTS183	108113
Kenya	IDA (Devel Assoc)	17 Aug 64	535UNTS79	107776
Pakistan	IDA (Devel Assoc)	26 Aug 64	535UNTS263	107784
Morocco	IBRD (World Bank)	26 Aug 64	537UNTS193	107802
IBRD (World Bank)	Venezuela	28 Aug 64	520UNTS97	107512
Australia	USA (United States)	28 Aug 64	510UNTS201	107415
IDA (Devel Assoc)	Turkey	31 Aug 64	535UNTS111	107777
Rwanda	UNICEF (Children)	11 Sep 64	510UNTS127	107409
Multilateral		18 Sep 64	556UNTS25	108117
Multilateral		18 Sep 64	555UNTS205	108114
Pakistan	IDA (Devel Assoc)	22 Sep 64	594UNTS225	108605
Mali	IDA (Devel Assoc)	29 Sep 64	594UNTS187	108604
Multilateral		30 Sep 64	556UNTS3	108116
India	IDA (Devel Assoc)	26 Oct 64	535UNTS245	107783
Philippines	IBRD (World Bank)	28 Oct 64	537UNTS165	107801
Multilateral		07 Nov 64	548UNTS3	107965
USA (United States)	Yugoslavia	09 Nov 64	533UNTS39	107731
Afghanistan	IDA (Devel Assoc)	23 Nov 64	567UNTS155	108255
IBRD (World Bank)	Thailand	25 Nov 64	537UNTS273	107805
Czechoslovakia	United Arab Rep	26 Nov 64	545UNTS11	107923
Ghana	Israel	30 Nov 64	550UNTS231	108019
Multilateral		02 Dec 64	572UNTS229	108317
Mauritania	IDA (Devel Assoc)	28 Dec 64	540UNTS163	107849
Kenya	IDA (Devel Assoc)	29 Dec 64	535UNTS225	107782
Peru	USA (United States)	28 Jan 65	587UNTS273	108513
Honduras	IBRD (World Bank)	02 Feb 65	561UNTS255	108188
Honduras	IDA (Devel Assoc)	02 Feb 65	561UNTS279	108189
Belgium	Congo (Zaire)	06 Feb 65	540UNTS275	107853
Belgium	Congo (Zaire)	06 Feb 65	540UNTS227	107852
Belgium	United Nations	20 Feb 65	535UNTS191	107779
Japan	UK Great Britain	22 Feb 65	560UNTS123	108171
Multilateral		24 Feb 65	556UNTS47	108118
Multilateral		26 Feb 65	556UNTS69	108119
Nigeria	IDA (Devel Assoc)	01 Mar 65	571UNTS3	108297
Nigeria	IDA (Devel Assoc)	01 Mar 65	563UNTS3	108201
IDA (Devel Assoc)	Somalia	29 Mar 65	586UNTS101	108499
IDA (Devel Assoc)	Turkey	01 Apr 65	554UNTS137	108100
Jamaica	IBRD (World Bank)	08 Apr 65	539UNTS303	107841
Taiwan	USA (United States)	09 Apr 65	546UNTS81	107939
Malta	UNICEF (Children)	22 Apr 65	533UNTS107	107737
Taiwan	IBRD (World Bank)	28 Apr 65	549UNTS145	107998
Iran	IBRD (World Bank)	28 Apr 65	555UNTS21	108103
Iran	IBRD (World Bank)	28 Apr 65	555UNTS45	108104
UK Great Britain	USA (United States)	10 May 65	545UNTS181	107934
Multilateral		28 May 65	559UNTS273	108163
Gambia	UNICEF (Children)	29 May 65	547UNTS29	107954
Saudi Arabia	USA (United States)	05 Jun 65	548UNTS285	107984
India	IBRD (World Bank)	11 Jun 65	557UNTS101	108130
India	IBRD (World Bank)	11 Jun 65	557UNTS59	108128
Peru	IBRD (World Bank)	18 Jun 65	568UNTS191	108269

PARTY ONE	PARTY TWO	DATE	CITATION	NUMBER
Accounting procedures (Cont.)				
Mongolia	UNICEF (Children)	23 Jun 65	540UNTS83	107844
Multilateral		23 Jun 65	548UNTS241	107981
Pakistan	IDA (Devel Assoc)	30 Jun 65	554UNTS111	108099
Kenya	IDA (Devel Assoc)	30 Jun 65	554UNTS75	108097
Multilateral		02 Jul 65	592UNTS215	108575
Australia	Germany, West	08 Jul 65	543UNTS305	107907
Israel	USA (United States)	20 Jul 65	549UNTS55	107989
India	IDA (Devel Assoc)	11 Aug 65	562UNTS277	108199
Nigeria	IBRD (World Bank)	26 Sep 65	570UNTS233	108296
Nigeria	IBRD (World Bank)	26 Sep 65	571UNTS39	108298
IBRD (World Bank)	Spain	29 Sep 65	568UNTS49	108264
East Afri Service	IBRD (World Bank)	29 Sep 65	568UNTS327	200623
Morocco	IDA (Devel Assoc)	11 Oct 65	562UNTS299	108200
Malaysia	IBRD (World Bank)	17 Nov 65	568UNTS23	108263
Saudi Arabia	USA (United States)	19 Nov 65	580UNTS35	108419
Multilateral		04 Dec 65	571UNTS123	108303
New Zealand	IBRD (World Bank)	17 Dec 65	567UNTS255	108259
New Zealand	IBRD (World Bank)	17 Dec 65	567UNTS275	108260
IBRD (World Bank)	Sudan	27 Dec 65	567UNTS27	108250
Italy	USA (United States)	12 Jan 66	587UNTS309	108515
Pakistan	IDA (Devel Assoc)	13 Jan 66	567UNTS67	108252
IDA (Devel Assoc)	Tanzania	13 Jan 66	567UNTS177	108256
Argentina	Uruguay	07 Mar 66	635UNTS275	109088
Bulgaria	UNICEF (Children)	10 Mar 66	559UNTS13	108152
Guinea	IBRD (World Bank)	30 Mar 66	568UNTS3	108262
Paraguay	IDA (Devel Assoc)	04 Apr 66	582UNTS331	108469
Paraguay	IBRD (World Bank)	04 Apr 66	570UNTS41	108287
IBRD (World Bank)	UK Great Britain	18 Apr 66	573UNTS209	108334
Finland	IBRD (World Bank)	27 Apr 66	568UNTS107	108266
Multilateral		04 May 66	575UNTS49	108354
Peru	IBRD (World Bank)	13 May 66	570UNTS61	108288
Bulgaria	UN Special Fund	26 May 66	563UNTS71	108205
Pakistan	IDA (Devel Assoc)	17 Jun 66	582UNTS297	108468
Multilateral		20 Jun 66	572UNTS263	108318
IBRD (World Bank)	Thailand	24 Jun 66	582UNTS259	108466
Denmark	Jordan	28 Jun 66	574UNTS3	108338
India	IDA (Devel Assoc)	29 Jun 66	582UNTS277	108467
India	IDA (Devel Assoc)	29 Jun 66	585UNTS101	108484
Brazil	Denmark	08 Jul 66	581UNTS95	108435
Iraq	IBRD (World Bank)	22 Jul 66	584UNTS233	108480
Turkey	UK Great Britain	29 Jul 66	597UNTS241	108649
IDA (Devel Assoc)	Siam	02 Aug 66	585UNTS271	108492
IDA (Devel Assoc)	Turkey	10 Aug 66	585UNTS237	108491
Kenya	IDA (Devel Assoc)	19 Aug 66	585UNTS119	108485
Denmark	Malawi	01 Sep 66	586UNTS3	108493
Germany, West	Israel	12 Sep 66	582UNTS17	108454
UN Special Fund	UPU (Postal Union)	21 Sep 66	573UNTS259	200626
IDA (Devel Assoc)	Senegal	29 Sep 66	594UNTS277	108607
USSR (Soviet Union)	Yugoslavia	29 Sep 66	608UNTS219	108818
Jamaica	IBRD (World Bank)	30 Sep 66	582UNTS179	108463
Malawi	IDA (Devel Assoc)	04 Oct 66	584UNTS215	108479
IBRD (World Bank)	Zambia	04 Oct 66	585UNTS181	108489
IBRD (World Bank)	IFC (Finance Corp)	28 Oct 66	586UNTS225	200628
Romania	United Arab Rep	14 Nov 66	642UNTS141	109170
Indonesia	UNICEF (Children)	17 Nov 66	578UNTS47	108386
Ghana	Romania	23 Nov 66	642UNTS79	109166
Guinea	Romania	01 Dec 66	642UNTS89	109167
Peru	UK Great Britain	03 Dec 66	617UNTS231	108915
Syria	USSR (Soviet Union)	18 Dec 66	633UNTS247	109041
India	IDA (Devel Assoc)	23 Dec 66	594UNTS165	108603
Pakistan	IDA (Devel Assoc)	23 Dec 66	594UNTS255	108606
UNICEF (Children)	Zambia	02 Feb 67	589UNTS89	108536
Australia	UN Special Fund	06 Feb 67	590UNTS3	108543
East Afri Service	IBRD (World Bank)	17 Feb 67	599UNTS335	200629
Cameroon	UK Great Britain	16 Jun 67	618UNTS329	108933

PARTY ONE	PARTY TWO	DATE	CITATION	NUMBER
Accounting procedures (Cont.)				
Multilateral		23 Jun 67	614UNTS185	108871
UK Great Britain	Yugoslavia	30 Jun 67	642UNTS325	109182
Denmark	Tanzania	01 Nov 67	619UNTS47	108938
Denmark	Iran	02 Nov 67	638UNTS217	109138
Australia	UNICEF (Children)	21 Dec 67	614UNTS83	108864
UK Great Britain	USSR (Soviet Union)	05 Jan 68	638UNTS41	109130
Denmark	Malaysia	29 Feb 68	640UNTS29	109153
Inter-Am Devel Bnk	UN Special Fund	16 Jul 68	640UNTS305	200640
Attachment of funds				
Multilateral		29 Jun 33	39UNTS285	100622
Denmark	UK Great Britain	06 Dec 45	5UNTS3	100061
Multilateral		14 Jan 46	555UNTS69	108105
Mexico	UK Great Britain	07 Feb 46	6UNTS55	100068
Hungary	Yugoslavia	18 Mar 48	113UNTS141	101550
Multilateral		19 Jun 48	310UNTS151	104492
Italy	New Zealand	19 Apr 50	67UNTS81	100867
Israel	USA (United States)	07 Dec 51	157UNTS53	102046
Jordan	USA (United States)	20 Dec 51	157UNTS69	102048
Laos	USA (United States)	31 Dec 51	198UNTS243	102668
Indonesia	USA (United States)	05 Jan 52	215UNTS121	102916
India	USA (United States)	05 Jan 52	157UNTS39	102045
El Salvador	USA (United States)	07 Jan 52	198UNTS231	102667
Dominican Republic	USA (United States)	07 Jan 52	174UNTS243	102289
Guatemala	USA (United States)	08 Jan 52	181UNTS31	102395
UK Great Britain	USA (United States)	08 Jan 52	126UNTS307	101696
Iran	USA (United States)	20 Jan 52	200UNTS191	102703
Jordan	USA (United States)	12 Feb 52	168UNTS25	102211
Israel	USA (United States)	27 Feb 52	177UNTS123	102314
Honduras	USA (United States)	07 Mar 52	233UNTS151	103260
Israel	USA (United States)	09 May 52	177UNTS63	102309
Israel	USA (United States)	09 May 52	177UNTS269	102326
Korea, South	USA (United States)	24 May 52	179UNTS23	102353
Chile	USA (United States)	30 Jun 52	199UNTS241	102688
Panama	USA (United States)	30 Jun 52	181UNTS121	102404
Multilateral		11 Jul 52	169UNTS3	102220
Denmark	Germany, West	26 Feb 53	178UNTS3	102332
United Arab Rep	USA (United States)	12 Mar 53	204UNTS3	102747
United Arab Rep	USA (United States)	19 Mar 53	215UNTS17	102909
El Salvador	USA (United States)	14 May 53	234UNTS71	103273
United Arab Rep	USA (United States)	21 May 53	204UNTS29	102748
Colombia	USA (United States)	09 Jun 53	213UNTS3	102877
Liberia	USA (United States)	23 Jun 53	213UNTS37	102879
Spain	USA (United States)	26 Sep 53	207UNTS93	102802
Israel	USA (United States)	25 Nov 53	219UNTS205	102976
Bolivia	USA (United States)	15 Jan 54	229UNTS213	103168
United Arab Rep	USA (United States)	24 Feb 54	236UNTS61	103316
Ethiopia	USA (United States)	01 Jun 54	232UNTS311	103245
Ethiopia	USA (United States)	12 Jun 54	234UNTS25	103270
Italy	USA (United States)	28 Jun 54	237UNTS121	103340
Guatemala	USA (United States)	01 Sep 54	199UNTS51	102677
Peru	USA (United States)	30 Apr 55	263UNTS309	103780
Libya	USA (United States)	21 Jul 55	264UNTS247	103796
Thailand	USA (United States)	14 Nov 55	239UNTS201	103380
USA (United States)	Uruguay	23 Mar 56	376UNTS311	105386
Ceylon (Sri Lanka)	USA (United States)	28 Apr 56	274UNTS35	103956
Libya	USA (United States)	04 Apr 57	283UNTS181	104116
Ethiopia	USA (United States)	25 Apr 57	283UNTS205	104118
Argentina	USA (United States)	03 Jun 57	291UNTS61	104244
Ghana	USA (United States)	03 Jun 57	284UNTS63	104129
Finland	Sweden	16 Oct 58	428UNTS125	106171
Czechoslovakia	Romania	25 Oct 58	338UNTS301	104843
Peru	UN Special Fund	19 Jan 60	349UNTS83	105010
Iraq	UN Special Fund	19 Jun 60	376UNTS357	105389
Indonesia	UN Special Fund	07 Oct 60	378UNTS141	105424

PARTY ONE	PARTY TWO	DATE	CITATION	NUMBER
Attachment of funds (Cont.)				
Liberia	UN Special Fund	11 Oct 60	376UNTS341	105388
El Salvador	UN Special Fund	24 Oct 60	377UNTS171	105400
Greece	Poland	08 Nov 60	483UNTS141	107011
Guatemala	UN Special Fund	17 Nov 60	383UNTS67	105495
Nepal	UN Special Fund	17 Nov 60	380UNTS289	105461
Cambodia	UN Special Fund	24 Nov 60	382UNTS255	105487
Honduras	UN Special Fund	20 Dec 60	383UNTS103	105497
Togo	USA (United States)	22 Dec 60	401UNTS33	105760
Burma	UN Special Fund	03 Jan 61	387UNTS219	105564
Costa Rica	UN Special Fund	10 Jan 61	389UNTS253	105597
UN Special Fund	Saudi Arabia	19 Jan 61	396UNTS27	105692
Nicaragua	UN Special Fund	20 Jan 61	387UNTS15	105555
Chad	UN Special Fund	23 Jan 61	390UNTS69	105603
UN Special Fund	Somalia	28 Jan 61	388UNTS75	105573
Gabon	UN Special Fund	02 Feb 61	387UNTS289	105568
Nigeria	UN Special Fund	10 Feb 61	390UNTS85	105604
Mexico	UN Special Fund	23 Feb 61	388UNTS151	105576
Panama	UN Special Fund	09 Mar 61	396UNTS3	105691
Cuba	UN Special Fund	10 Mar 61	390UNTS35	105601
Cyprus	UNICEF (Children)	19 Apr 61	394UNTS185	105678
Korea, South	UN Special Fund	21 Apr 61	394UNTS231	200583
Ceylon (Sri Lanka)	UN Special Fund	03 May 61	395UNTS217	105687
Sierra Leone	USA (United States)	05 May 61	409UNTS194	105885
Senegal	USA (United States)	13 May 61	409UNTS232	105888
Ivory Coast	USA (United States)	17 May 61	409UNTS241	105889
Niger	USA (United States)	26 May 61	410UNTS213	105905
Cameroon	USA (United States)	26 May 61	413UNTS195	105953
Dahomey	USA (United States)	27 May 61	445UNTS23	106373
Cameroon	UN Special Fund	13 Jun 61	397UNTS297	105713
Madagascar	USA (United States)	22 Jun 61	413UNTS219	105956
Paraguay	UN Special Fund	22 Jun 61	399UNTS117	105738
UN Special Fund	Upper Volta	26 Jun 61	400UNTS3	105744
Philippines	UN Special Fund	28 Jun 61	399UNTS141	105739
Haiti	UN Special Fund	28 Jun 61	399UNTS171	105741
Mali	UN Special Fund	21 Jul 61	401UNTS141	105768
UN Special Fund	Yemen	02 Aug 61	402UNTS43	105777
Chad	UNICEF (Children)	26 Aug 61	422UNTS231	106077
Ivory Coast	UN Special Fund	29 Aug 61	406UNTS129	105844
UN Special Fund	Sierra Leone	02 Oct 61	422UNTS131	106073
Gabon	UNICEF (Children)	02 Nov 61	422UNTS241	106078
Mauritania	UN Special Fund	07 Nov 61	412UNTS240	105936
Congo (Brazzaville)	UN Special Fund	09 Nov 61	413UNTS58	105940
Malagasy	UNICEF (Children)	16 Nov 61	422UNTS251	106079
UN Special Fund	Venezuela	11 Dec 61	422UNTS149	106074
UN Special Fund	Senegal	16 Dec 61	425UNTS97	106121
Iran	USA (United States)	21 Dec 61	433UNTS269	106249
Malagasy	UN Special Fund	05 Jan 62	419UNTS29	106028
Ivory Coast	UNICEF (Children)	10 Jan 62	422UNTS261	106080
UNICEF (Children)	Yemen	31 Jan 62	422UNTS271	106081
Niger	UN Special Fund	26 Feb 62	423UNTS83	106086
UNICEF (Children)	Somalia	01 Apr 62	431UNTS75	106211
Congo (Brazzaville)	UNICEF (Children)	09 Apr 62	431UNTS65	106210
UNICEF (Children)	Sierra Leone	11 Apr 62	431UNTS55	106209
UN Special Fund	Uruguay	04 May 62	429UNTS143	106196
Dominican Republic	UN Special Fund	06 Jun 62	429UNTS169	106197
UN Special Fund	Syria	07 Jul 62	443UNTS3	106355
UN Special Fund	Tanganyika	17 Jul 62	435UNTS237	106281
Algeria	UNICEF (Children)	20 Nov 62	453UNTS151	106522
Multilateral		12 Dec 62	552UNTS15	108048
Mauritania	UNICEF (Children)	19 Jan 63	452UNTS271	106514
UNICEF (Children)	Tanganyika	25 Jan 63	453UNTS249	106528
Central Afri Rep	USA (United States)	10 Feb 63	473UNTS83	106857
UN Special Fund	Uganda	22 Mar 63	456UNTS466	106572
Jamaica	UN Special Fund	22 May 63	489UNTS191	107140
Netherlands	UN Special Fund	24 May 63	466UNTS289	106750

PARTY ONE	PARTY TWO	DATE	CITATION	NUMBER
Attachment of funds (Cont.)				
UN Special Fund	Western Samoa	05 Jun 63	467UNTS463	200601
Burundi	UN Special Fund	22 Aug 63	476UNTS49	106903
Central Afri Rep	UN Special Fund	30 Oct 63	481UNTS247	106985
Ireland	UN Special Fund	03 Jun 64	496UNTS205	107253
Argentina	Guatemala	30 Oct 64	601UNTS175	108695
UN Special Fund	Spain	30 Jun 65	544UNTS159	107918
Mongolia	UN Special Fund	26 Jan 66	552UNTS201	108055
Czechoslovakia	Germany, East	17 Mar 67	609UNTS187	108831
Banking				
France	Netherlands	14 Jun 40	2UNTS263	200019
Netherlands	UK Great Britain	25 Jul 40	2UNTS275	200020
Brazil	Paraguay	14 Apr 41	54UNTS269	200199
Brazil	Paraguay	14 Jun 41	54UNTS313	200203
UK Great Britain	USSR (Soviet Union)	16 Aug 41	91UNTS341	200269
Haiti	USA (United States)	13 Sep 41	103UNTS141	200311
Belgium	UK Great Britain	05 Oct 44	5UNTS227	200031
Canada	Czechoslovakia	01 Mar 45	45UNTS283	200185
Sweden	UK Great Britain	06 Mar 45	5UNTS241	200032
Sweden	UK Great Britain	06 Mar 45	82UNTS219	101095
France	UK Great Britain	27 Mar 45	98UNTS227	200274
Canada	Norway	25 Jun 45	45UNTS297	200186
Denmark	UK Great Britain	16 Aug 45	5UNTS251	200033
Netherlands	UK Great Britain	07 Sep 45	2UNTS325	200024
Belgium	Norway	23 Oct 45	183UNTS337	200510
Belgium	Norway	23 Oct 45	16UNTS311	200107
Netherlands	Switzerland	24 Oct 45	3UNTS73	100025
Belgium	Canada	25 Oct 45	230UNTS127	103180
Czechoslovakia	UK Great Britain	01 Nov 45	5UNTS15	100062
Netherlands	Norway	06 Nov 45	2UNTS5	100017
Norway	UK Great Britain	08 Nov 45	5UNTS27	100063
Poland	Yugoslavia	23 Nov 45	115UNTS3	101555
Finland	Norway	27 Nov 45	17UNTS247	100279
Netherlands	Sweden	30 Nov 45	2UNTS27	100019
Denmark	UK Great Britain	06 Dec 45	5UNTS3	100061
Czechoslovakia	Norway	13 Dec 45	17UNTS261	100280
Belgium	Portugal	07 Jan 46	19UNTS159	100310
Poland	Yugoslavia	18 Jan 46	115UNTS83	101559
Greece	UK Great Britain	24 Jan 46	6UNTS45	100067
Denmark	Netherlands	31 Jan 46	3UNTS3	100021
Canada	Netherlands	05 Feb 46	43UNTS3	100658
Canada	Taiwan	07 Feb 46	43UNTS23	100659
Belgium	Norway	21 Feb 46	31UNTS199	100479
Switzerland	UK Great Britain	12 Mar 46	6UNTS107	100070
Belgium	Denmark	08 Apr 46	4UNTS429	100059
Canada	France	09 Apr 46	43UNTS43	100660
Portugal	UK Great Britain	16 Apr 46	6UNTS119	100071
France	Greece	24 Apr 46	91UNTS83	101243
France	UK Great Britain	29 Apr 46	98UNTS123	101360
Denmark	Luxembourg	21 May 46	4UNTS435	100060
Poland	UK Great Britain	24 Jun 46	11UNTS59	100149
Romania	Yugoslavia	26 Jun 46	116UNTS21	101566
Albania	Yugoslavia	01 Jul 46	111UNTS3	101517
Italy	Norway	20 Jul 46	17UNTS273	100281
Norway	Yugoslavia	30 Aug 46	15UNTS163	100232
Argentina	UK Great Britain	17 Sep 46	88UNTS47	101185
Philippines	USA (United States)	17 Sep 46	15UNTS249	100240
Albania	Yugoslavia	03 Oct 46	111UNTS227	101537
Greece	USA (United States)	08 Oct 46	180UNTS119	102379
Denmark	South Africa	14 Oct 46	10UNTS29	100140
Norway	Sweden	22 Nov 46	15UNTS171	100233
Albania	Yugoslavia	28 Nov 46	111UNTS143	101527
Norway	Poland	03 Dec 46	15UNTS203	100234
Hungary	Yugoslavia	23 Dec 46	113UNTS125	101549
Norway	USSR (Soviet Union)	27 Dec 46	17UNTS283	100282

PARTY ONE	PARTY TWO	DATE	CITATION	NUMBER
Banking (Cont.)				
Australia	Netherlands	24 Jan 47	10UNTS77	100144
Norway	USSR (Soviet Union)	19 Feb 47	30UNTS293	100464
Czechoslovakia	Yugoslavia	25 Feb 47	112UNTS3	101539
Netherlands	UK Great Britain	26 Feb 47	11UNTS279	100167
Belgium	Turkey	12 Mar 47	33UNTS43	100513
Mexico	USA (United States)	17 Mar 47	167UNTS30	102200
Spain	UK Great Britain	28 Mar 47	66UNTS91	100849
Bulgaria	Denmark	09 May 47	74UNTS139	100960
Poland	Yugoslavia	24 May 47	115UNTS69	101558
New Zealand	UK Great Britain	27 May 47	17UNTS211	100277
Albania	Yugoslavia	12 Jun 47	111UNTS195	101534
Albania	Yugoslavia	22 Jun 47	111UNTS207	101536
United Arab Rep	UK Great Britain	30 Jun 47	93UNTS165	101299
Belgium	United Arab Rep	01 Jul 47	34UNTS93	100529
France	New Zealand	02 Jul 47	16UNTS219	100263
Haiti	USA (United States)	04 Jul 47	22UNTS165	100335
UK Great Britain	Uruguay	15 Jul 47	71UNTS179	100918
Norway	Switzerland	15 Jul 47	12UNTS351	100192
Taiwan	Italy	30 Jul 47	12UNTS377	100194
India	UK Great Britain	14 Aug 47	11UNTS371	100176
Bulgaria	Yugoslavia	22 Aug 47	111UNTS241	101538
Multilateral		19 Sep 47	30UNTS269	100462
Romania	Yugoslavia	30 Sep 47	116UNTS71	101570
Multilateral		05 Oct 47	34UNTS23	100525
South Africa	UK Great Britain	09 Oct 47	17UNTS239	100278
Multilateral		30 Oct 47	55UNTS188	100814
Poland	Yugoslavia	07 Nov 47	115UNTS137	101561
UK Great Britain	USSR (Soviet Union)	27 Dec 47	82UNTS251	101098
Czechoslovakia	New Zealand	22 Jan 48	16UNTS229	100264
France	Lebanon	24 Jan 48	173UNTS99	102263
India	UK Great Britain	15 Feb 48	134UNTS70	101796
Denmark	Hungary	28 Feb 48	85UNTS35	101144
Poland	UK Great Britain	02 Mar 48	77UNTS47	100991
Hungary	Yugoslavia	18 Mar 48	113UNTS201	101551
Hungary	Yugoslavia	18 Mar 48	113UNTS141	101550
India	Pakistan	31 Mar 48	54UNTS33	100793
Denmark	Norway	21 Apr 48	18UNTS139	100284
Norway	Sweden	29 Apr 48	26UNTS11	100374
Brazil	UK Great Britain	21 May 48	66UNTS121	100851
Czechoslovakia	Yugoslavia	24 May 48	112UNTS225	101545
Czechoslovakia	Yugoslavia	24 May 48	112UNTS183	101543
Chile	UK Great Britain	24 Jun 48	77UNTS113	100995
India	Pakistan	30 Jun 48	29UNTS199	100441
Netherlands	IBRD (World Bank)	15 Jul 48	153UNTS211	102020
Peru	UK Great Britain	20 Jul 48	66UNTS197	100855
Australia	Denmark	08 Oct 48	22UNTS43	100330
Argentina	Denmark	14 Dec 48	74UNTS41	100956
Denmark	Poland	14 Dec 48	81UNTS33	101060
Denmark	Turkey	15 Dec 48	76UNTS3	100974
Spain	UK Great Britain	15 Dec 48	87UNTS49	101165
Belgium	Greece	27 Dec 48	77UNTS293	101005
USSR (Soviet Union)	Yugoslavia	27 Dec 48	116UNTS327	101579
Poland	UK Great Britain	14 Jan 49	83UNTS3	101100
Austria	Norway	28 Jan 49	30UNTS145	100452
Denmark	Sweden	08 Feb 49	33UNTS227	100519
Norway	Turkey	24 Feb 49	30UNTS151	100453
Denmark	Greece	25 Feb 49	78UNTS335	101023
Netherlands	Norway	26 Feb 49	29UNTS33	100432
Belgium	Portugal	01 Mar 49	32UNTS49	100488
Czechoslovakia	Yugoslavia	01 Mar 49	112UNTS241	101546
Greece	Norway	12 Mar 49	33UNTS13	100510
Germany, West	Greece	16 Mar 49	77UNTS327	101007
Denmark	Finland	22 Mar 49	33UNTS247	100520
Finland	Greece	24 Mar 49	78UNTS13	101009
United Arab Rep	UK Great Britain	31 Mar 49	83UNTS139	101106

Banking (Cont.)

PARTY ONE	PARTY TWO	DATE	CITATION	NUMBER
Greece	Turkey	02 Apr 49	78UNTS23	101010
Denmark	Portugal	08 Apr 49	74UNTS221	100965
India	Pakistan	23 Apr 49	54UNTS51	100795
Belgium	Bolivia	26 Apr 49	34UNTS103	100530
Argentina	UK Great Britain	27 Jun 49	83UNTS217	101110
Greece	Turkey	21 Jul 49	78UNTS65	101012
Multilateral		05 Aug 49	88UNTS229	101195
Multilateral		10 Aug 49	45UNTS3	100689
Czechoslovakia	UK Great Britain	18 Aug 49	86UNTS129	101155
Argentina	Norway	09 Sep 49	42UNTS125	100646
Italy	Norway	19 Nov 49	47UNTS89	100724
Norway	Portugal	28 Nov 49	47UNTS117	100726
Denmark	Germany, West	15 Dec 49	51UNTS11	100749
Norway	Poland	21 Dec 49	47UNTS107	100725
Sweden	UK Great Britain	30 Dec 49	87UNTS59	101166
Greece	Portugal	31 Dec 49	92UNTS83	101263
Austria	UK Great Britain	26 Jan 50	97UNTS183	101350
Nicaragua	USA (United States)	01 Feb 50	99UNTS25	101368
Paraguay	UK Great Britain	03 Apr 50	99UNTS81	101372
Australia	Netherlands	26 Apr 50	54UNTS83	100796
Denmark	Spain	12 Jul 50	71UNTS129	100913
Brazil	UK Great Britain	18 Sep 50	88UNTS115	101188
Denmark	Italy	04 Oct 50	78UNTS353	101025
Denmark	UK Great Britain	19 Oct 50	79UNTS25	101028
Norway	UK Great Britain	06 Nov 50	88UNTS257	101197
Sweden	UK Great Britain	10 Nov 50	88UNTS265	101198
Germany, West	UK Great Britain	09 Dec 50	88UNTS247	101196
Italy	UK Great Britain	21 Dec 50	175UNTS187	102301
Italy	Yugoslavia	23 Dec 50	150UNTS191	101973
Chile	USA (United States)	16 Jan 51	147UNTS11	101925
Denmark	Switzerland	20 Jan 51	87UNTS223	101174
Italy	Norway	22 Jan 51	88UNTS339	101202
Colombia	Denmark	26 Jan 51	87UNTS161	101171
Austria	UK Great Britain	31 Jan 51	88UNTS107	101187
United Arab Rep	UK Great Britain	01 Jul 51	249UNTS143	103504
United Arab Rep	UK Great Britain	01 Jul 51	249UNTS125	103503
Portugal	UK Great Britain	20 Jul 51	105UNTS61	101453
Japan	UK Great Britain	31 Aug 51	108UNTS273	101480
UK Great Britain	Yugoslavia	28 Sep 51	117UNTS107	101587
Pakistan	UK Great Britain	29 Sep 51	134UNTS183	101798
Denmark	Italy	24 Oct 51	118UNTS91	101598
El Salvador	Guatemala	14 Dec 51	131UNTS131	101740
Belgium	Norway	21 Jan 52	123UNTS39	101653
Canada	Spain	29 Jan 52	233UNTS117	103255
Austria	Greece	22 Mar 52	187UNTS255	102517
Greece	Switzerland	04 Apr 52	166UNTS271	102192
Canada	Netherlands	10 Apr 52	233UNTS129	103257
Belgium	Greece	24 Apr 52	166UNTS261	102191
Germany, West	Greece	28 Jul 52	182UNTS85	102424
UK Great Britain	Yugoslavia	20 Aug 52	158UNTS439	102077
Multilateral		28 Aug 52	175UNTS69	102296
Greece	Italy	04 Feb 53	189UNTS295	102552
Denmark	Germany, West	26 Feb 53	178UNTS3	102332
Germany, West	USA (United States)	27 Feb 53	224UNTS13	103067
Germany, West	USA (United States)	27 Feb 53	223UNTS167	103065
Czechoslovakia	Denmark	23 Apr 53	174UNTS107	102281
Greece	United Arab Rep	21 May 53	256UNTS25	103621
Germany, West	UK Great Britain	22 May 53	172UNTS179	102246
India	UK Great Britain	20 Jul 53	196UNTS251	102628
Argentina	USSR (Soviet Union)	05 Aug 53	221UNTS99	103004
Denmark	Uruguay	09 Sep 53	256UNTS149	103625
Brazil	UK Great Britain	01 Oct 53	183UNTS207	102430
India	USSR (Soviet Union)	02 Dec 53	240UNTS143	103402
Bulgaria	Greece	05 Dec 53	225UNTS145	103096
Japan	UK Great Britain	29 Jan 54	190UNTS319	102572

Banking (Cont.)

PARTY ONE	PARTY TWO	DATE	CITATION	NUMBER
Czechoslovakia	Greece	01 Feb 54	225UNTS95	103092
Greece	Spain	15 May 54	299UNTS277	104319
Greece	Romania	19 May 54	225UNTS27	103084
Greece	Hungary	05 Jun 54	299UNTS295	104321
Netherlands	Norway	09 Jun 54	287UNTS179	104184
Haiti	Italy	14 Jun 54	267UNTS97	103837
Multilateral		08 Jul 54	287UNTS27	104178
France	Netherlands	09 Jul 54	287UNTS169	104183
Belgium	Italy	12 Jul 54	288UNTS59	104198
Brazil	USA (United States)	20 Aug 54	410UNTS79	105898
Iceland	Netherlands	28 Dec 54	287UNTS159	104182
USSR (Soviet Union)	Yugoslavia	05 Jan 55	240UNTS225	103405
Turkey	UK Great Britain	17 Jan 55	204UNTS195	102758
Argentina	UK Great Britain	31 Mar 55	210UNTS223	102840
Multilateral		25 May 55	264UNTS117	103791
Syria	USSR (Soviet Union)	16 Nov 55	259UNTS71	103683
Argentina	USA (United States)	21 Dec 55	240UNTS329	103411
Denmark	Netherlands	31 Jan 56	286UNTS255	104172
Burma	Yugoslavia	07 Mar 56	386UNTS207	105542
Canada	Hungary	08 Mar 56	305UNTS27	104409
Ceylon (Sri Lanka)	Romania	16 Mar 56	315UNTS51	104559
Austria	Italy	07 May 56	284UNTS351	104147
Bulgaria	Ceylon (Sri Lanka)	19 Jun 56	315UNTS33	104557
Hungary	UK Great Britain	27 Jun 56	249UNTS19	103499
Italy	Netherlands	29 Jun 56	287UNTS193	104185
Guatemala	Honduras	22 Aug 56	263UNTS49	103767
Argentina	UK Great Britain	31 Oct 56	269UNTS229	103883
Sweden	USSR (Soviet Union)	28 Jan 57	428UNTS315	106183
Burma	India	12 Mar 57	312UNTS131	104515
Tunisia	USA (United States)	26 Mar 57	283UNTS117	104111
Netherlands	Paraguay	13 Apr 57	593UNTS85	108577
Denmark	Paraguay	18 May 57	286UNTS117	104163
Denmark	Uruguay	04 Jun 57	286UNTS107	104162
Italy	United Arab Rep	06 Jul 57	302UNTS147	104357
Germany, West	Italy	12 Jul 57	291UNTS181	104252
Ceylon (Sri Lanka)	China People's Rep	19 Sep 57	337UNTS137	104821
Multilateral		03 Oct 57	366UNTS193	105218
Argentina	Italy	25 Nov 57	305UNTS275	104424
Argentina	Denmark	25 Nov 57	299UNTS83	104308
China People's Rep	Denmark	01 Dec 57	309UNTS241	104475
Finland	Italy	17 Dec 57	291UNTS133	104248
Italy	Romania	28 Jan 58	302UNTS231	104362
Multilateral		18 Jun 58	386UNTS355	105553
Netherlands	Yugoslavia	22 Jul 58	386UNTS263	105546
Burma	USA (United States)	25 Aug 58	336UNTS3	104795
Canada	USA (United States)	31 Oct 58	391UNTS219	105626
Israel	Yugoslavia	11 Dec 58	386UNTS283	105548
Iraq	Romania	24 Dec 58	405UNTS243	105836
Austria	UK Great Britain	14 Mar 59	343UNTS263	104930
Netherlands	Switzerland	14 Apr 59	486UNTS367	107086
Italy	UK Great Britain	14 Apr 59	343UNTS289	104934
Sweden	UK Great Britain	18 Apr 59	360UNTS89	105156
Belgium	Netherlands	28 Apr 59	485UNTS123	107049
France	Netherlands	29 Apr 59	486UNTS379	107088
Netherlands	Sweden	30 Apr 59	485UNTS147	107053
Netherlands	Norway	30 Apr 59	487UNTS3	107090
Netherlands	Portugal	30 Apr 59	485UNTS129	107050
Germany, West	Netherlands	30 Apr 59	485UNTS141	107052
Iceland	Netherlands	30 Apr 59	487UNTS13	107091
Multilateral		11 May 59	527UNTS145	107623
Turkey	UK Great Britain	13 Jun 59	551UNTS59	108033
Netherlands	Turkey	12 Aug 59	527UNTS181	107624
Norway	Yugoslavia	18 Nov 59	383UNTS131	105499
Denmark	Sweden	04 Jan 60	376UNTS375	105390
Cuba	USSR (Soviet Union)	13 Feb 60	369UNTS17	105248

PARTY ONE	PARTY TWO	DATE	CITATION	NUMBER
Banking (Cont.)				
Cuba	USSR (Soviet Union)	13 Feb 60	369UNTS3	105247
Indonesia	USSR (Soviet Union)	28 Feb 60	392UNTS173	105643
Ghana	USSR (Soviet Union)	04 Aug 60	399UNTS61	105734
Ghana	USSR (Soviet Union)	04 Aug 60	421UNTS27	106050
Netherlands	Romania	30 Sep 60	479UNTS91	106948
Guinea	USA (United States)	30 Sep 60	394UNTS103	105671
Greece	Poland	08 Nov 60	483UNTS141	107011
Belgium	Congo (Zaire)	15 Nov 60	394UNTS79	105670
Multilateral		13 Dec 60	455UNTS204	106544
Multilateral		13 Dec 60	455UNTS3	106543
USA (United States)	Yugoslavia	19 Jan 61	402UNTS163	105784
Sierra Leone	USA (United States)	05 May 61	409UNTS194	105885
Senegal	USA (United States)	13 May 61	409UNTS232	105888
Ivory Coast	USA (United States)	17 May 61	409UNTS241	105889
Niger	USA (United States)	26 May 61	410UNTS213	105905
Cameroon	USA (United States)	26 May 61	413UNTS195	105953
Dahomey	USA (United States)	27 May 61	445UNTS23	106373
Somalia	USSR (Soviet Union)	02 Jun 61	493UNTS173	107214
Madagascar	USA (United States)	22 Jun 61	413UNTS219	105956
Tunisia	USSR (Soviet Union)	30 Aug 61	437UNTS243	106310
Iraq	Syria	03 Nov 61	489UNTS45	107134
Panama	USA (United States)	11 Dec 61	445UNTS161	106384
United Arab Rep	USSR (Soviet Union)	23 Jun 62	472UNTS43	106836
United Arab Rep	USSR (Soviet Union)	23 Jun 62	472UNTS19	106835
Laos	USSR (Soviet Union)	01 Dec 62	471UNTS181	106832
Multilateral		08 Dec 62	510UNTS235	107418
Indonesia	USA (United States)	14 Mar 63	505UNTS79	107365
Burma	UK Great Britain	02 Apr 63	475UNTS139	106890
Multilateral		02 Apr 63	475UNTS121	106889
Brazil	USSR (Soviet Union)	20 Apr 63	0UNTS0	109256
Austria	Bulgaria	02 May 63	535UNTS143	107778
Austria	Romania	03 Jul 63	588UNTS3	108516
Multilateral		13 Aug 63	592UNTS139	108572
Multilateral		23 Oct 63	506UNTS197	107388
Netherlands	Poland	20 Dec 63	514UNTS169	107446
Multilateral		10 Jul 64	613UNTS193	108852
IDA (Devel Assoc)	Turkey	31 Aug 64	535UNTS111	107777
Austria	Hungary	31 Oct 64	605UNTS63	108759
Belgium	Congo (Zaire)	06 Feb 65	540UNTS275	107853
Belgium	Congo (Zaire)	06 Feb 65	540UNTS227	107852
IDA (Devel Assoc)	Turkey	01 Apr 65	554UNTS137	108100
Taiwan	USA (United States)	09 Apr 65	546UNTS81	107939
Pakistan	IDA (Devel Assoc)	30 Jun 65	554UNTS111	108099
Philippines	USA (United States)	15 Nov 65	574UNTS205	108350
Austria	Finland	21 Feb 66	597UNTS273	108651
Denmark	Netherlands	31 Mar 66	604UNTS209	108751
USSR (Soviet Union)	Yugoslavia	29 Sep 66	608UNTS219	108818
Ghana	UK Great Britain	27 Feb 67	606UNTS133	108783
Israel	USA (United States)	04 Aug 67	0UNTS0	109351
Bulgaria	New Zealand	03 Nov 67	0UNTS0	109207
Bonds				
Multilateral		15 Jun 27	38UNTS327	100607
Multilateral		15 Jun 27	38UNTS343	100608
France	Netherlands	14 Jun 40	2UNTS263	200019
Netherlands	UK Great Britain	14 Jun 40	2UNTS251	200018
Mexico	USA (United States)	19 Nov 41	125UNTS287	200430
Mexico	USA (United States)	26 Apr 43	21UNTS245	200127
Mexico	USA (United States)	29 Apr 43	105UNTS119	200327
Canada	Czechoslovakia	01 Mar 45	45UNTS283	200185
Canada	Norway	25 Jun 45	45UNTS297	200186
Belgium	Canada	25 Oct 45	230UNTS127	103180
Denmark	UK Great Britain	06 Dec 45	5UNTS3	100061
Canada	Netherlands	05 Feb 46	43UNTS3	100658
Canada	Taiwan	07 Feb 46	43UNTS23	100659

PARTY ONE	PARTY TWO	DATE	CITATION	NUMBER
Bonds (Cont.)				
Greece	UK Great Britain	21 Mar 46	91UNTS149	101247
Belgium	Denmark	08 Apr 46	4UNTS429	100059
Canada	France	09 Apr 46	43UNTS43	100660
Denmark	Luxembourg	21 May 46	4UNTS435	100060
Denmark	New Zealand	18 Sep 46	10UNTS39	100141
Denmark	South Africa	14 Oct 46	10UNTS29	100140
Luxembourg	UK Great Britain	11 Dec 46	11UNTS167	100155
Australia	Netherlands	24 Jan 47	10UNTS77	100144
Muscat and Oman	UK Great Britain	05 Apr 47	27UNTS287	100412
Philippines	USA (United States)	16 May 47	280UNTS177	104057
New Zealand	UK Great Britain	27 May 47	17UNTS211	100277
USSR (Soviet Union)	Yugoslavia	25 Jul 47	130UNTS315	101732
Netherlands	IBRD (World Bank)	07 Aug 47	152UNTS165	102015
Denmark	IBRD (World Bank)	22 Aug 47	152UNTS223	102016
Luxembourg	IBRD (World Bank)	28 Aug 47	153UNTS3	102017
Hungary	Poland	28 Aug 47	15UNTS145	100231
South Africa	UK Great Britain	09 Oct 47	17UNTS239	100278
France	Lebanon	24 Jan 48	173UNTS99	102263
Denmark	Hungary	28 Feb 48	85UNTS35	101144
Czechoslovakia	Yugoslavia	14 Mar 48	28UNTS81	100421
India	Pakistan	30 Jun 48	29UNTS199	100441
Australia	Denmark	08 Oct 48	22UNTS43	100330
Australia	Belgium	09 Dec 48	25UNTS159	100361
Belgium	France	18 Feb 49	31UNTS173	100478
Netherlands	Norway	26 Feb 49	29UNTS33	100432
Belgium	IBRD (World Bank)	01 Mar 49	154UNTS133	102029
India	Pakistan	23 Apr 49	54UNTS51	100795
Italy	Yugoslavia	23 May 49	150UNTS179	101972
Netherlands	IBRD (World Bank)	26 Jul 49	154UNTS178	102030
Finland	IBRD (World Bank)	01 Aug 49	156UNTS289	200480
India	IBRD (World Bank)	18 Aug 49	154UNTS269	102031
Colombia	IBRD (World Bank)	19 Aug 49	154UNTS329	102032
IBRD (World Bank)	Yugoslavia	17 Sep 49	155UNTS3	102034
India	IBRD (World Bank)	29 Sep 49	154UNTS393	102033
Finland	IBRD (World Bank)	17 Oct 49	156UNTS355	200481
El Salvador	IBRD (World Bank)	14 Dec 49	155UNTS43	102035
Czechoslovakia	Denmark	17 Dec 49	74UNTS159	100962
Australia	Ceylon (Sri Lanka)	12 Jan 50	53UNTS295	100789
Israel	UK Great Britain	30 Mar 50	86UNTS231	101162
India	IBRD (World Bank)	18 Apr 50	155UNTS117	102036
Mexico	IBRD (World Bank)	28 Apr 50	155UNTS185	102037
Brazil	IBRD (World Bank)	26 May 50	301UNTS165	104345
Iraq	IBRD (World Bank)	15 Jun 50	155UNTS267	102038
IBRD (World Bank)	Turkey	07 Jul 50	156UNTS75	102040
IBRD (World Bank)	Turkey	07 Jul 50	156UNTS3	102039
IBRD (World Bank)	Uruguay	25 Aug 50	156UNTS203	102042
Belgium	Japan	29 Aug 50	76UNTS113	100984
Ethiopia	IBRD (World Bank)	13 Sep 50	157UNTS213	102055
Ethiopia	IBRD (World Bank)	13 Sep 50	157UNTS233	102056
Mexico	IBRD (World Bank)	18 Oct 50	157UNTS259	102057
IBRD (World Bank)	Thailand	27 Oct 50	158UNTS3	102059
IBRD (World Bank)	Thailand	27 Oct 50	158UNTS25	102060
IBRD (World Bank)	Thailand	27 Oct 50	158UNTS43	102061
Colombia	IBRD (World Bank)	02 Nov 50	158UNTS59	102062
Australia	IBRD (World Bank)	14 Nov 50	156UNTS147	102041
Colombia	IBRD (World Bank)	28 Dec 50	158UNTS87	102063
Chile	USA (United States)	16 Jan 51	147UNTS11	101925
IBRD (World Bank)	South Africa	23 Jan 51	158UNTS115	102064
Ethiopia	IBRD (World Bank)	19 Feb 51	186UNTS101	102486
Multilateral		06 Mar 51	106UNTS141	101461
Colombia	IBRD (World Bank)	10 Apr 51	158UNTS155	102066
Nicaragua	IBRD (World Bank)	07 Jun 51	158UNTS215	102067
Nicaragua	IBRD (World Bank)	07 Jun 51	158UNTS277	102068
Iceland	IBRD (World Bank)	20 Jun 51	158UNTS301	102069
Belgium	IBRD (World Bank)	13 Sep 51	158UNTS323	102070

PARTY ONE	PARTY TWO	DATE	CITATION	NUMBER
Bonds (Cont.)				
Belgium	IBRD (World Bank)	13 Sep 51	158UNTS349	102071
IBRD (World Bank)	Yugoslavia	11 Oct 51	159UNTS3	102081
Colombia	IBRD (World Bank)	13 Oct 51	159UNTS75	102084
Nicaragua	IBRD (World Bank)	29 Oct 51	159UNTS35	102082
Iceland	IBRD (World Bank)	01 Nov 51	159UNTS55	102083
Paraguay	IBRD (World Bank)	07 Dec 51	159UNTS103	102085
Mexico	IBRD (World Bank)	11 Jan 52	159UNTS129	102086
Peru	IBRD (World Bank)	23 Jan 52	159UNTS163	102087
IBRD (World Bank)	UK Great Britain	27 Feb 52	159UNTS181	102088
Canada	Netherlands	10 Apr 52	233UNTS129	103257
Pakistan	IBRD (World Bank)	13 Jun 52	191UNTS85	102578
IBRD (World Bank)	Turkey	18 Jun 52	159UNTS269	102091
Brazil	IBRD (World Bank)	27 Jun 52	190UNTS85	102560
Brazil	IBRD (World Bank)	27 Jun 52	190UNTS115	102561
Australia	IBRD (World Bank)	08 Jul 52	159UNTS295	102092
Peru	IBRD (World Bank)	08 Jul 52	159UNTS321	102093
Iceland	IBRD (World Bank)	26 Aug 52	159UNTS363	102095
Colombia	IBRD (World Bank)	26 Aug 52	159UNTS339	102094
Japan	IBRD (World Bank)	12 Nov 52	354UNTS313	105068
India	IBRD (World Bank)	18 Dec 52	201UNTS241	102719
India	IBRD (World Bank)	23 Jan 53	201UNTS145	102715
IBRD (World Bank)	Yugoslavia	11 Feb 53	165UNTS231	102179
Germany, West	USA (United States)	27 Feb 53	224UNTS31	103068
Germany, West	USA (United States)	27 Feb 53	224UNTS13	103067
IBRD (World Bank)	UK Great Britain	11 Mar 53	172UNTS115	102243
Germany, West	USA (United States)	01 Apr 53	224UNTS3	103066
Brazil	IBRD (World Bank)	30 Apr 53	190UNTS133	102562
Brazil	IBRD (World Bank)	17 Jul 53	190UNTS149	102563
IBRD (World Bank)	South Africa	28 Aug 53	180UNTS73	102376
IBRD (World Bank)	South Africa	28 Aug 53	180UNTS91	102377
Nicaragua	IBRD (World Bank)	04 Sep 53	186UNTS137	102488
Iceland	IBRD (World Bank)	04 Sep 53	188UNTS3	102519
Nicaragua	IBRD (World Bank)	04 Sep 53	186UNTS117	102487
Iceland	IBRD (World Bank)	04 Sep 53	178UNTS275	102344
IBRD (World Bank)	Turkey	10 Sep 53	187UNTS71	102502
Colombia	IBRD (World Bank)	10 Sep 53	203UNTS3	102738
Chile	IBRD (World Bank)	10 Sep 53	188UNTS25	102520
Panama	IBRD (World Bank)	25 Sep 53	188UNTS95	102522
Panama	IBRD (World Bank)	25 Sep 53	188UNTS71	102521
Italy	IBRD (World Bank)	06 Oct 53	301UNTS135	104344
Japan	IBRD (World Bank)	15 Oct 53	187UNTS367	200513
Brazil	IBRD (World Bank)	18 Dec 53	190UNTS179	102564
Brazil	IBRD (World Bank)	18 Dec 53	301UNTS229	104346
Brazil	IBRD (World Bank)	24 Feb 54	301UNTS249	104347
Australia	IBRD (World Bank)	02 Mar 54	191UNTS103	102579
Norway	IBRD (World Bank)	08 Apr 54	201UNTS131	102714
Peru	IBRD (World Bank)	12 Apr 54	190UNTS231	102567
Pakistan	IBRD (World Bank)	02 Jun 54	324UNTS59	104678
Italy	Netherlands	04 Jun 54	289UNTS261	104222
France	IBRD (World Bank)	10 Jun 54	210UNTS89	102836
Multilateral		08 Jul 54	287UNTS27	104178
Ceylon (Sri Lanka)	IBRD (World Bank)	09 Jul 54	198UNTS313	200517
Mexico	IBRD (World Bank)	24 Aug 54	286UNTS211	104168
El Salvador	IBRD (World Bank)	12 Oct 54	203UNTS37	102739
Austria	IBRD (World Bank)	08 Nov 54	216UNTS305	200528
Peru	IBRD (World Bank)	12 Nov 54	209UNTS287	102831
India	IBRD (World Bank)	19 Nov 54	309UNTS159	104473
Belgium	IBRD (World Bank)	14 Dec 54	210UNTS113	102837
Iceland	Netherlands	28 Dec 54	287UNTS159	104182
Colombia	IBRD (World Bank)	29 Dec 54	211UNTS135	102851
Mexico	USA (United States)	09 Mar 55	263UNTS247	103776
India	IBRD (World Bank)	14 Mar 55	309UNTS129	104472
IBRD (World Bank)	UK Great Britain	15 Mar 55	265UNTS85	103808
Australia	IBRD (World Bank)	18 Mar 55	220UNTS131	102998
Colombia	IBRD (World Bank)	24 Mar 55	212UNTS217	102874

PARTY ONE	PARTY TWO	DATE	CITATION	NUMBER
Bonds (Cont.)				
Finland	IBRD (World Bank)	24 Mar 55	211UNTS305	200525
Peru	IBRD (World Bank)	05 Apr 55	211UNTS115	102850
Norway	IBRD (World Bank)	19 Apr 55	211UNTS159	102852
Peru	IBRD (World Bank)	19 Apr 55	221UNTS153	103007
Italy	IBRD (World Bank)	01 Jun 55	358UNTS203	105137
Nicaragua	IBRD (World Bank)	08 Jul 55	229UNTS97	103162
Nicaragua	IBRD (World Bank)	08 Jul 55	229UNTS123	103163
Panama	IBRD (World Bank)	12 Jul 55	219UNTS127	102970
Guatemala	IBRD (World Bank)	29 Jul 55	229UNTS167	103165
Pakistan	IBRD (World Bank)	04 Aug 55	230UNTS79	103177
Peru	IBRD (World Bank)	05 Aug 55	218UNTS3	102950
Pakistan	IBRD (World Bank)	06 Aug 55	236UNTS195	103325
IBRD (World Bank)	Thailand	09 Aug 55	221UNTS283	103011
France	IBRD (World Bank)	26 Aug 55	247UNTS305	103478
Nicaragua	IBRD (World Bank)	26 Aug 55	229UNTS145	103164
IBRD (World Bank)	Uruguay	29 Aug 55	243UNTS123	103450
Japan	IBRD (World Bank)	25 Oct 55	230UNTS379	200534
IBRD (World Bank)	South Africa	28 Nov 55	230UNTS101	103178
Honduras	IBRD (World Bank)	22 Dec 55	230UNTS262	103189
Denmark	Netherlands	31 Jan 56	286UNTS255	104172
Japan	IBRD (World Bank)	21 Feb 56	248UNTS321	200543
Germany, West	USA (United States)	02 Mar 56	273UNTS209	103952
Ecuador	IBRD (World Bank)	26 Mar 56	292UNTS391	104277
Norway	IBRD (World Bank)	03 May 56	243UNTS281	103455
Burma	IBRD (World Bank)	04 May 56	253UNTS179	103584
Brazil	France	04 May 56	323UNTS339	104675
Burma	IBRD (World Bank)	04 May 56	253UNTS209	103585
Haiti	IBRD (World Bank)	07 May 56	252UNTS279	103570
Nicaragua	IBRD (World Bank)	22 May 56	253UNTS233	103586
Finland	IBRD (World Bank)	22 May 56	248UNTS57	103485
Colombia	IBRD (World Bank)	06 Jun 56	248UNTS139	103493
IBRD (World Bank)	UK Great Britain	21 Jun 56	285UNTS355	104157
Fed Rhod/Nyasaland	IBRD (World Bank)	21 Jun 56	285UNTS317	104156
India	IBRD (World Bank)	26 Jun 56	301UNTS3	104341
Italy	Netherlands	29 Jun 56	287UNTS193	104185
Italy	Switzerland	29 Jun 56	284UNTS299	104144
Costa Rica	IBRD (World Bank)	18 Sep 56	260UNTS369	103721
Austria	IBRD (World Bank)	21 Sep 56	259UNTS17	103681
Austria	IBRD (World Bank)	21 Sep 56	259UNTS43	103682
Italy	IBRD (World Bank)	11 Oct 56	359UNTS3	105138
IBRD (World Bank)	Thailand	12 Oct 56	261UNTS117	103728
IBRD (World Bank)	Uruguay	25 Oct 56	265UNTS59	103807
Chile	IBRD (World Bank)	01 Nov 56	261UNTS27	103724
Australia	IBRD (World Bank)	15 Nov 56	288UNTS117	104201
Austria	USA (United States)	21 Nov 56	290UNTS181	104237
Australia	IBRD (World Bank)	03 Dec 56	288UNTS99	104200
Japan	IBRD (World Bank)	19 Dec 56	268UNTS203	103859
India	IBRD (World Bank)	19 Dec 56	310UNTS75	104489
Iran	IBRD (World Bank)	22 Jan 57	317UNTS129	104600
Ethiopia	IBRD (World Bank)	28 Jan 57	286UNTS307	104175
India	IBRD (World Bank)	05 Mar 57	272UNTS201	103939
Peru	IBRD (World Bank)	13 Mar 57	274UNTS59	103958
Ethiopia	Sweden	16 Mar 57	304UNTS214	104398
Netherlands	IBRD (World Bank)	15 May 57	274UNTS211	103967
India	IBRD (World Bank)	29 May 57	309UNTS201	104474
Belgium	IBRD (World Bank)	26 Jun 57	322UNTS301	104661
India	IBRD (World Bank)	12 Jul 57	288UNTS135	104202
Chile	IBRD (World Bank)	24 Jul 57	282UNTS189	104099
Chile	IBRD (World Bank)	24 Jul 57	282UNTS139	104098
Japan	IBRD (World Bank)	09 Aug 57	293UNTS59	104286
Belgium	IBRD (World Bank)	10 Sep 57	286UNTS291	104174
IBRD (World Bank)	Thailand	12 Sep 57	299UNTS349	104324
Ecuador	IBRD (World Bank)	20 Sep 57	293UNTS135	104291
Ecuador	IBRD (World Bank)	20 Sep 57	289UNTS237	104221
IBRD (World Bank)	South Africa	01 Oct 57	280UNTS285	104065

PARTY ONE	PARTY TWO	DATE	CITATION	NUMBER
Bonds (Cont.)				
Multilateral		03 Oct 57	365UNTS207	105214
Austria	IBRD (World Bank)	10 Oct 57	301UNTS95	104343
Pakistan	IBRD (World Bank)	18 Oct 57	299UNTS303	104322
India	IBRD (World Bank)	20 Nov 57	301UNTS47	104342
Philippines	IBRD (World Bank)	22 Nov 57	293UNTS83	104287
Belgium	IBRD (World Bank)	27 Nov 57	292UNTS175	104273
Pakistan	IBRD (World Bank)	17 Dec 57	299UNTS321	104323
Mexico	IBRD (World Bank)	14 Jan 58	293UNTS167	104292
Brazil	IBRD (World Bank)	22 Jan 58	323UNTS99	104666
Bulgaria	Hungary	13 Mar 58	438UNTS173	106316
Pakistan	IBRD (World Bank)	23 Apr 58	323UNTS253	104672
Austria	IBRD (World Bank)	28 Apr 58	359UNTS145	105142
Chile	IBRD (World Bank)	28 Apr 58	359UNTS89	105140
IBRD (World Bank)	UK Great Britain	02 May 58	324UNTS25	104677
Mexico	IBRD (World Bank)	05 May 58	309UNTS3	104466
Honduras	IBRD (World Bank)	09 May 58	323UNTS4	104662
Japan	IBRD (World Bank)	13 Jun 58	312UNTS159	104518
IBRD (World Bank)	UK Great Britain	16 Jun 58	309UNTS35	104467
India	IBRD (World Bank)	25 Jun 58	323UNTS157	104668
India	IBRD (World Bank)	25 Jun 58	323UNTS131	104667
IBRD (World Bank)	Sudan	21 Jul 58	323UNTS183	104669
India	IBRD (World Bank)	23 Jul 58	317UNTS3	104590
Japan	IBRD (World Bank)	18 Aug 58	323UNTS205	104670
Japan	IBRD (World Bank)	10 Sep 58	318UNTS133	104612
Japan	IBRD (World Bank)	10 Sep 58	323UNTS297	104673
India	IBRD (World Bank)	16 Sep 58	323UNTS235	104671
Ceylon (Sri Lanka)	IBRD (World Bank)	17 Sep 58	323UNTS51	104664
Peru	IBRD (World Bank)	17 Sep 58	323UNTS27	104663
Fed of Malaya	IBRD (World Bank)	22 Sep 58	323UNTS71	104665
Brazil	IBRD (World Bank)	03 Oct 58	337UNTS177	104823
Ecuador	IBRD (World Bank)	09 Oct 58	337UNTS299	104827
Canada	USA (United States)	31 Oct 58	391UNTS219	105626
Austria	IBRD (World Bank)	02 Dec 58	340UNTS3	104856
IBRD (World Bank)	South Africa	02 Dec 58	324UNTS3	104676
Colombia	IBRD (World Bank)	15 Dec 58	354UNTS233	105065
El Salvador	IBRD (World Bank)	07 Jan 59	346UNTS51	104977
Colombia	IBRD (World Bank)	30 Jan 59	337UNTS327	104828
Denmark	IBRD (World Bank)	04 Feb 59	328UNTS143	104733
Costa Rica	IBRD (World Bank)	11 Feb 59	337UNTS245	104825
El Salvador	IBRD (World Bank)	20 Feb 59	362UNTS75	105183
Finland	IBRD (World Bank)	16 Mar 59	337UNTS269	104826
India	IBRD (World Bank)	08 Apr 59	348UNTS131	104998
Italy	IBRD (World Bank)	21 Apr 59	359UNTS191	105143
Iceland	Netherlands	30 Apr 59	487UNTS13	107091
Netherlands	Norway	30 Apr 59	487UNTS3	107090
Colombia	IBRD (World Bank)	20 May 59	344UNTS251	104953
Honduras	IBRD (World Bank)	20 May 59	359UNTS119	105141
Iran	IBRD (World Bank)	29 May 59	348UNTS103	104997
IBRD (World Bank)	South Africa	10 Jun 59	340UNTS33	104857
Brazil	IBRD (World Bank)	17 Jun 59	377UNTS111	105398
France	IBRD (World Bank)	30 Jun 59	452UNTS67	106505
Congo (Brazzaville)	IBRD (World Bank)	30 Jun 59	452UNTS123	106506
Gabon	IBRD (World Bank)	30 Jun 59	452UNTS135	106507
Norway	IBRD (World Bank)	08 Jul 59	344UNTS229	104952
India	IBRD (World Bank)	15 Jul 59	346UNTS33	104976
India	IBRD (World Bank)	15 Jul 59	355UNTS95	105075
Pakistan	IBRD (World Bank)	13 Aug 59	355UNTS129	105076
Italy	IBRD (World Bank)	16 Sep 59	375UNTS159	105366
Pakistan	IBRD (World Bank)	25 Sep 59	355UNTS169	105077
Japan	IBRD (World Bank)	12 Nov 59	354UNTS279	105067
Ethiopia	France	12 Nov 59	381UNTS3	105465
Iran	IBRD (World Bank)	23 Nov 59	380UNTS245	105459
Pakistan	IBRD (World Bank)	30 Nov 59	355UNTS203	105078
France	IBRD (World Bank)	10 Dec 59	380UNTS319	105464
IBRD (World Bank)	United Arab Rep	22 Dec 59	354UNTS197	105063

PARTY ONE	PARTY TWO	DATE	CITATION	NUMBER
Bonds (Cont.)				
IBRD (World Bank)	Uruguay	30 Dec 59	384UNTS275	105523
Colombia	IBRD (World Bank)	20 Jan 60	375UNTS49	105353
Iran	IBRD (World Bank)	20 Feb 60	384UNTS213	105521
Japan	IBRD (World Bank)	17 Mar 60	362UNTS43	105182
Mauritania	IBRD (World Bank)	17 Mar 60	452UNTS211	106509
France	IBRD (World Bank)	17 Mar 60	452UNTS147	106508
Belgium	IBRD (World Bank)	30 Mar 60	379UNTS161	105439
Belgium	IBRD (World Bank)	30 Mar 60	379UNTS129	105438
Belgium	IBRD (World Bank)	30 Mar 60	379UNTS103	105437
IBRD (World Bank)	UK Great Britain	01 Apr 60	379UNTS397	105446
Multilateral		15 Apr 60	470UNTS239	106811
Costa Rica	IBRD (World Bank)	04 May 60	390UNTS201	105609
Colombia	IBRD (World Bank)	10 May 60	379UNTS218	105441
IBRD (World Bank)	UK Great Britain	27 May 60	375UNTS201	105367
Peru	IBRD (World Bank)	01 Jun 60	380UNTS15	105448
IBRD (World Bank)	Sudan	17 Jun 60	379UNTS253	105442
Nicaragua	IBRD (World Bank)	22 Jun 60	384UNTS243	105522
Honduras	IBRD (World Bank)	29 Jun 60	400UNTS137	105751
Peru	IBRD (World Bank)	29 Jun 60	400UNTS99	105750
El Salvador	IBRD (World Bank)	29 Jul 60	390UNTS101	105605
India	IBRD (World Bank)	29 Jul 60	377UNTS153	105399
Germany, West	USA (United States)	16 Aug 60	418UNTS235	106024
Panama	IBRD (World Bank)	19 Aug 60	390UNTS153	105607
Israel	IBRD (World Bank)	09 Sep 60	406UNTS3	105837
Pakistan	IBRD (World Bank)	19 Sep 60	444UNTS207	106370
Colombia	IBRD (World Bank)	20 Sep 60	390UNTS173	105608
Mexico	IBRD (World Bank)	18 Oct 60	422UNTS177	106075
India	IBRD (World Bank)	28 Oct 60	406UNTS27	105838
Belgium	Congo (Zaire)	15 Nov 60	394UNTS79	105670
Norway	IBRD (World Bank)	02 Dec 60	390UNTS131	105606
Multilateral		13 Dec 60	455UNTS204	106544
Peru	IBRD (World Bank)	19 Dec 60	417UNTS275	106010
Japan	IBRD (World Bank)	20 Dec 60	400UNTS279	105754
Japan	IBRD (World Bank)	20 Dec 60	400UNTS167	105752
Burma	IBRD (World Bank)	16 Jan 61	400UNTS73	105749
Mexico	IBRD (World Bank)	16 Jan 61	422UNTS203	106076
Costa Rica	IBRD (World Bank)	03 Feb 61	414UNTS314	105977
IBRD (World Bank)	Yugoslavia	23 Feb 61	415UNTS92	105982
Japan	IBRD (World Bank)	16 Mar 61	400UNTS201	105753
IBRD (World Bank)	UK Great Britain	29 Mar 61	415UNTS300	105990
IBRD (World Bank)	Thailand	28 Apr 61	415UNTS121	105983
Japan	IBRD (World Bank)	02 May 61	415UNTS144	105984
Colombia	IBRD (World Bank)	12 May 61	415UNTS172	105985
Ceylon (Sri Lanka)	IBRD (World Bank)	06 Jun 61	414UNTS349	105978
IBRD (World Bank)	Sudan	14 Jun 61	415UNTS26	105980
IBRD (World Bank)	UK Great Britain	23 Jun 61	415UNTS358	105991
Pakistan	IBRD (World Bank)	27 Jun 61	425UNTS241	106127
Chile	IBRD (World Bank)	28 Jun 61	426UNTS33	106129
Argentina	IBRD (World Bank)	30 Jun 61	445UNTS85	106379
Israel	IBRD (World Bank)	11 Jul 61	429UNTS3	106188
Philippines	IBRD (World Bank)	26 Jul 61	414UNTS253	105976
India	IBRD (World Bank)	09 Aug 61	417UNTS297	106011
Finland	IBRD (World Bank)	09 Aug 61	415UNTS204	105986
IBRD (World Bank)	UK Great Britain	16 Aug 61	426UNTS287	106143
India	IBRD (World Bank)	17 Aug 61	417UNTS319	106012
UK Great Britain	USA (United States)	28 Aug 61	434UNTS103	106258
Colombia	IBRD (World Bank)	28 Aug 61	416UNTS23	105993
Costa Rica	IBRD (World Bank)	06 Sep 61	446UNTS345	106408
India	IBRD (World Bank)	13 Oct 61	418UNTS3	106013
Costa Rica	IBRD (World Bank)	13 Oct 61	430UNTS27	106202
Philippines	IBRD (World Bank)	13 Oct 61	415UNTS269	105989
Peru	IBRD (World Bank)	03 Nov 61	430UNTS47	106203
IBRD (World Bank)	UK Great Britain	29 Nov 61	426UNTS49	106130
IBRD (World Bank)	South Africa	01 Dec 61	425UNTS215	106126
IBRD (World Bank)	Venezuela	13 Dec 61	446UNTS371	106409

Bonds (Cont.)

PARTY ONE	PARTY TWO	DATE	CITATION	NUMBER
India	IBRD (World Bank)	22 Dec 61	481UNTS85	106979
Argentina	IBRD (World Bank)	19 Jan 62	446UNTS305	106407
Australia	IBRD (World Bank)	23 Jan 62	430UNTS3	106201
Israel	IBRD (World Bank)	01 Feb 62	435UNTS155	106277
Ghana	IBRD (World Bank)	08 Feb 62	449UNTS207	106462
Iceland	IBRD (World Bank)	14 Feb 62	447UNTS95	106413
India	IBRD (World Bank)	28 Feb 62	447UNTS3	106410
Colombia	IBRD (World Bank)	23 May 62	447UNTS39	106411
Ethiopia	IBRD (World Bank)	31 May 62	467UNTS237	106765
Mexico	IBRD (World Bank)	20 Jun 62	467UNTS205	106764
Mexico	IBRD (World Bank)	20 Jun 62	468UNTS109	106771
Italy	USA (United States)	06 Jul 62	459UNTS123	106617
IBRD (World Bank)	Yugoslavia	11 Jul 62	468UNTS143	106772
Finland	IBRD (World Bank)	15 Aug 62	467UNTS177	106763
Pakistan	IBRD (World Bank)	14 Sep 62	467UNTS152	106762
Panama	IBRD (World Bank)	14 Sep 62	476UNTS153	106908
India	IDA (Devel Assoc)	14 Sep 62	467UNTS265	106766
Pakistan	IBRD (World Bank)	14 Sep 62	467UNTS125	106761
IBRD (World Bank)	Uruguay	26 Oct 62	481UNTS39	106977
Multilateral		08 Dec 62	510UNTS235	107418
Nigeria	IBRD (World Bank)	10 Dec 62	468UNTS255	106776
IBRD (World Bank)	Thailand	21 Dec 62	467UNTS43	106757
Morocco	IBRD (World Bank)	21 Dec 62	478UNTS205	106937
IBRD (World Bank)	Thailand	21 Dec 62	467UNTS63	106758
Pakistan	IBRD (World Bank)	13 Feb 63	467UNTS3	106756
Philippines	IBRD (World Bank)	15 Feb 63	478UNTS161	106936
Nicaragua	IBRD (World Bank)	01 Mar 63	481UNTS15	106976
IBRD (World Bank)	Thailand	07 Mar 63	467UNTS83	106759
Peru	IBRD (World Bank)	13 Mar 63	478UNTS245	106938
Thailand	USA (United States)	25 Apr 63	476UNTS115	106906
Greece	Hungary	27 Apr 63	550UNTS197	108016
Mexico	IBRD (World Bank)	29 Apr 63	489UNTS151	107138
Austria	Bulgaria	02 May 63	535UNTS143	107778
IBRD (World Bank)	UK Great Britain	16 May 63	476UNTS211	106910
IBRD (World Bank)	UK Great Britain	16 May 63	477UNTS361	106929
Colombia	IBRD (World Bank)	03 Jun 63	490UNTS199	107155
India	IBRD (World Bank)	05 Jun 63	481UNTS191	106983
IBRD (World Bank)	Thailand	11 Jun 63	481UNTS227	106984
El Salvador	IBRD (World Bank)	19 Jun 63	481UNTS59	106978
IBRD (World Bank)	Yugoslavia	21 Jun 63	482UNTS43	106990
Colombia	IBRD (World Bank)	21 Jun 63	482UNTS159	106994
Colombia	IBRD (World Bank)	28 Jun 63	489UNTS113	107137
Costa Rica	IBRD (World Bank)	10 Jul 63	482UNTS69	106991
Malaysia	IBRD (World Bank)	15 Jul 63	482UNTS123	106993
Colombia	IBRD (World Bank)	16 Jul 63	482UNTS256	106998
Denmark	IBRD (World Bank)	24 Jul 63	481UNTS171	106982
Malaysia	IBRD (World Bank)	07 Aug 63	485UNTS253	107060
IBRD (World Bank)	UK Great Britain	06 Sep 63	483UNTS173	107013
Finland	IBRD (World Bank)	18 Sep 63	491UNTS345	107183
IBRD (World Bank)	Venezuela	20 Sep 63	482UNTS227	106997
Mexico	IBRD (World Bank)	20 Sep 63	491UNTS317	107182
IBRD (World Bank)	UK Great Britain	23 Sep 63	503UNTS247	107348
Taiwan	IBRD (World Bank)	27 Sep 63	483UNTS151	107012
Japan	IBRD (World Bank)	27 Sep 63	485UNTS283	107061
El Salvador	IBRD (World Bank)	01 Oct 63	517UNTS3	107481
Norway	IBRD (World Bank)	15 Oct 63	482UNTS103	106992
IBRD (World Bank)	Spain	25 Oct 63	491UNTS297	107181
IBRD (World Bank)	Yugoslavia	28 Oct 63	503UNTS289	107349
Portugal	IBRD (World Bank)	06 Nov 63	491UNTS137	107176
Portugal	IBRD (World Bank)	06 Nov 63	492UNTS89	107188
New Zealand	IBRD (World Bank)	12 Nov 63	485UNTS233	107059
Peru	IBRD (World Bank)	22 Nov 63	491UNTS101	107175
Chile	IBRD (World Bank)	18 Dec 63	504UNTS3	107351
Netherlands	Poland	20 Dec 63	514UNTS169	107446
Multilateral		30 Dec 63	568UNTS243	108272

Bonds (Cont.)

PARTY ONE	PARTY TWO	DATE	CITATION	NUMBER
Multilateral		30 Dec 63	551UNTS119	108037
Multilateral		30 Dec 63	568UNTS233	108271
Multilateral		30 Dec 63	568UNTS215	108270
Multilateral		30 Dec 63	551UNTS105	108036
Multilateral		30 Dec 63	551UNTS75	108035
Liberia	IBRD (World Bank)	08 Jan 64	504UNTS53	107353
Colombia	IBRD (World Bank)	07 Feb 64	516UNTS99	107473
IBRD (World Bank)	Thailand	11 Mar 64	504UNTS73	107354
Nigeria	IBRD (World Bank)	12 Mar 64	516UNTS325	107480
New Zealand	IBRD (World Bank)	12 Mar 64	505UNTS3	107362
Japan	IBRD (World Bank)	22 Apr 64	505UNTS21	107363
Peru	IBRD (World Bank)	22 Apr 64	519UNTS95	107503
Ethiopia	IBRD (World Bank)	08 May 64	505UNTS51	107364
Algeria	IBRD (World Bank)	14 May 64	522UNTS265	107552
Pakistan	IBRD (World Bank)	14 May 64	516UNTS145	107475
Ecuador	IBRD (World Bank)	26 May 64	534UNTS113	107758
France	Italy	02 Jun 64	634UNTS117	109056
IBRD (World Bank)	Tunisia	05 Jun 64	539UNTS129	107827
Iran	IBRD (World Bank)	10 Jun 64	537UNTS111	107799
Nigeria	IBRD (World Bank)	07 Jul 64	537UNTS3	107795
Finland	IBRD (World Bank)	10 Jul 64	516UNTS125	107474
Gabon	IBRD (World Bank)	10 Jul 64	537UNTS63	107797
Philippines	IBRD (World Bank)	22 Jul 64	516UNTS171	107476
IBRD (World Bank)	Spain	31 Jul 64	537UNTS81	107798
IBRD (World Bank)	Sierra Leone	18 Aug 64	516UNTS295	107479
Morocco	IBRD (World Bank)	26 Aug 64	537UNTS193	107802
IBRD (World Bank)	Venezuela	28 Aug 64	520UNTS97	107512
IBRD (World Bank)	Venezuela	28 Aug 64	537UNTS135	107800
Philippines	IBRD (World Bank)	28 Oct 64	537UNTS165	107801
Austria	Hungary	31 Oct 64	605UNTS3	108758
IBRD (World Bank)	Thailand	25 Nov 64	537UNTS273	107805
IBRD (World Bank)	Yugoslavia	11 Dec 64	537UNTS321	107807
Paraguay	IBRD (World Bank)	16 Dec 64	549UNTS173	107999
Taiwan	IBRD (World Bank)	17 Dec 64	538UNTS3	107808
Japan	IBRD (World Bank)	23 Dec 64	538UNTS37	107809
Japan	IBRD (World Bank)	13 Jan 65	537UNTS293	107806
Mexico	IBRD (World Bank)	04 Feb 65	549UNTS189	108000
Belgium	Congo (Zaire)	06 Feb 65	540UNTS275	107853
Belgium	Congo (Zaire)	06 Feb 65	540UNTS227	107852
Chile	IBRD (World Bank)	12 Feb 65	537UNTS35	107796
Malaysia	IBRD (World Bank)	26 Feb 65	549UNTS239	108002
Brazil	IBRD (World Bank)	26 Feb 65	553UNTS3	108065
IBRD (World Bank)	Thailand	22 Mar 65	538UNTS63	107810
IBRD (World Bank)	Uruguay	30 Mar 65	567UNTS45	108251
Jamaica	IBRD (World Bank)	08 Apr 65	539UNTS303	107841
Taiwan	IBRD (World Bank)	28 Apr 65	549UNTS145	107998
Iran	IBRD (World Bank)	28 Apr 65	555UNTS21	108103
Iran	IBRD (World Bank)	28 Apr 65	555UNTS45	108104
Portugal	IBRD (World Bank)	29 Apr 65	549UNTS69	107991
Malaysia	UK Great Britain	07 May 65	552UNTS259	108058
Japan	IBRD (World Bank)	26 May 65	550UNTS95	108010
Peru	IBRD (World Bank)	03 Jun 65	551UNTS227	108045
India	IBRD (World Bank)	11 Jun 65	557UNTS59	108128
India	IBRD (World Bank)	11 Jun 65	557UNTS101	108130
Peru	IBRD (World Bank)	18 Jun 65	568UNTS191	108269
Italy	IBRD (World Bank)	28 Jun 65	567UNTS127	108254
Finland	IBRD (World Bank)	30 Jun 65	550UNTS63	108009
Pakistan	IBRD (World Bank)	09 Jul 65	554UNTS39	108096
Iran	IBRD (World Bank)	12 Jul 65	554UNTS3	108095
Nigeria	IBRD (World Bank)	26 Sep 65	570UNTS233	108296
Nigeria	IBRD (World Bank)	26 Sep 65	571UNTS39	108298
IBRD (World Bank)	Tanzania	29 Sep 65	568UNTS309	108275
East Afri Service	IBRD (World Bank)	29 Sep 65	568UNTS327	200623
Kenya	IBRD (World Bank)	29 Sep 65	568UNTS289	108274
IBRD (World Bank)	Spain	29 Sep 65	568UNTS49	108264

PARTY ONE	PARTY TWO	DATE	CITATION	NUMBER
Bonds (Cont.)				
IBRD (World Bank)	Uganda	29 Sep 65	568UNTS317	108276
Mexico	IBRD (World Bank)	01 Oct 65	589UNTS339	108542
Chile	IBRD (World Bank)	06 Oct 65	567UNTS293	108261
Philippines	IBRD (World Bank)	02 Nov 65	567UNTS3	108249
Malaysia	IBRD (World Bank)	17 Nov 65	568UNTS23	108263
IBRD (World Bank)	Venezuela	13 Dec 65	568UNTS77	108265
Mexico	IBRD (World Bank)	15 Dec 65	568UNTS125	108267
Paraguay	IBRD (World Bank)	16 Dec 65	568UNTS165	108268
New Zealand	IBRD (World Bank)	17 Dec 65	567UNTS255	108259
New Zealand	IBRD (World Bank)	17 Dec 65	567UNTS275	108260
IBRD (World Bank)	Sudan	27 Dec 65	567UNTS27	108250
Ethiopia	IBRD (World Bank)	28 Dec 65	567UNTS229	108258
Pakistan	IDA (Devel Assoc)	10 Feb 66	575UNTS89	108355
Brazil	IBRD (World Bank)	15 Mar 66	599UNTS52	108664
Guinea	IBRD (World Bank)	30 Mar 66	568UNTS3	108262
Paraguay	IBRD (World Bank)	04 Apr 66	570UNTS41	108287
IBRD (World Bank)	Venezuela	21 Apr 66	568UNTS257	108273
Finland	IBRD (World Bank)	27 Apr 66	568UNTS107	108266
Peru	IBRD (World Bank)	13 May 66	570UNTS61	108288
IBRD (World Bank)	Tunisia	16 May 66	584UNTS155	108477
Colombia	IBRD (World Bank)	16 May 66	608UNTS249	108819
Mexico	IBRD (World Bank)	25 May 66	596UNTS3	108627
Morocco	IBRD (World Bank)	13 Jun 66	615UNTS205	108881
Portugal	IBRD (World Bank)	14 Jun 66	581UNTS29	108431
Portugal	IBRD (World Bank)	14 Jun 66	581UNTS3	108430
Jamaica	IBRD (World Bank)	20 Jun 66	582UNTS145	108462
IBRD (World Bank)	Thailand	24 Jun 66	582UNTS259	108466
India	IBRD (World Bank)	07 Jul 66	595UNTS3	108610
Iraq	IBRD (World Bank)	22 Jul 66	584UNTS233	108480
Iran	IBRD (World Bank)	26 Jul 66	582UNTS107	108461
Malaysia	IBRD (World Bank)	26 Jul 66	586UNTS195	108504
IBRD (World Bank)	Turkey	10 Aug 66	585UNTS199	108490
IBRD (World Bank)	Singapore	11 Aug 66	585UNTS39	108482
India	IDA (Devel Assoc)	19 Aug 66	584UNTS193	108478
Honduras	IBRD (World Bank)	25 Aug 66	582UNTS79	108460
Peru	IBRD (World Bank)	07 Sep 66	585UNTS3	108481
IBRD (World Bank)	South Africa	08 Sep 66	585UNTS71	108483
Jamaica	IBRD (World Bank)	30 Sep 66	582UNTS179	108463
IBRD (World Bank)	Zambia	04 Oct 66	585UNTS181	108489
Nicaragua	IBRD (World Bank)	05 Oct 66	582UNTS231	108465
IBRD (World Bank)	Singapore	04 Nov 66	585UNTS155	108488
Brazil	IBRD (World Bank)	19 Dec 66	599UNTS107	108665
Brazil	IBRD (World Bank)	19 Dec 66	599UNTS205	108668
Brazil	IBRD (World Bank)	19 Dec 66	599UNTS177	108667
Brazil	IBRD (World Bank)	19 Dec 66	599UNTS149	108666
Chile	IBRD (World Bank)	23 Dec 66	595UNTS141	108618
Jamaica	IBRD (World Bank)	23 Jan 67	594UNTS311	108608
IBRD (World Bank)	Venezuela	26 Jan 67	596UNTS35	108628
East Afri Service	IBRD (World Bank)	17 Feb 67	599UNTS335	200629
IBRD (World Bank)	Tanzania	17 Feb 67	599UNTS287	108671
IBRD (World Bank)	Tunisia	21 Feb 67	618UNTS39	108923
IBRD (World Bank)	Yugoslavia	24 Feb 67	599UNTS27	108663
Guatemala	IBRD (World Bank)	10 Mar 67	616UNTS139	108894
IBRD (World Bank)	Trinidad/Tobago	10 Mar 67	599UNTS3	108662
Cameroon	IBRD (World Bank)	28 Mar 67	618UNTS89	108925
IBRD (World Bank)	UK Great Britain	24 Apr 67	600UNTS3	108674
IBRD (World Bank)	Senegal	01 May 67	615UNTS267	108883
Cyprus	IBRD (World Bank)	16 May 67	617UNTS21	108906
Honduras	IBRD (World Bank)	26 May 67	615UNTS145	108879
Pakistan	IBRD (World Bank)	26 May 67	616UNTS167	108895
Multilateral		12 Jun 67	615UNTS321	108885
China	IBRD (World Bank)	14 Jun 67	615UNTS243	108882
Colombia	IBRD (World Bank)	15 Jun 67	615UNTS47	108877
Malaysia	IBRD (World Bank)	15 Jun 67	618UNTS235	108930
Other Party Combin	Ecuador	19 Jun 67	615UNTS75	108878

PARTY ONE	PARTY TWO	DATE	CITATION	NUMBER
Bonds (Cont.)				
Colombia	IBRD (World Bank)	29 Jun 67	619UNTS99	108941
IBRD (World Bank)	Singapore	05 Jul 67	618UNTS189	108928
IBRD (World Bank)	Yugoslavia	18 Jul 67	615UNTS343	108886
Argentina	IBRD (World Bank)	31 Jul 67	633UNTS289	109042
Taiwan	IBRD (World Bank)	02 Aug 67	618UNTS301	108932
IBRD (World Bank)	Spain	04 Aug 67	619UNTS209	108944
Taiwan	IBRD (World Bank)	07 Aug 67	620UNTS113	108952
Pakistan	IBRD (World Bank)	10 Aug 67	618UNTS261	108931
Madagascar	IBRD (World Bank)	23 Aug 67	618UNTS215	108929
Peru	IBRD (World Bank)	11 Sep 67	619UNTS171	108943
IBRD (World Bank)	Tunisia	14 Sep 67	639UNTS147	109149
IBRD (World Bank)	Singapore	15 Sep 67	615UNTS295	108884
India	IBRD (World Bank)	19 Sep 67	615UNTS165	108880
IBRD (World Bank)	Thailand	19 Sep 67	619UNTS275	108946
Brazil	IBRD (World Bank)	23 Sep 67	620UNTS77	108951
Israel	IBRD (World Bank)	15 Nov 67	619UNTS129	108942
Ceylon (Sri Lanka)	IBRD (World Bank)	22 Nov 67	639UNTS221	109151
IBRD (World Bank)	Tanzania	13 Dec 67	619UNTS239	108945
Argentina	IBRD (World Bank)	25 Jan 68	639UNTS187	109150
Mexico	IBRD (World Bank)	26 Jan 68	640UNTS3	109152
Korea, South	IBRD (World Bank)	31 Jan 68	639UNTS263	200638
Compensation				
Multilateral		27 Mar 41	67UNTS231	200222
Haiti	USA (United States)	23 May 41	117UNTS191	200370
Brazil	Paraguay	14 Jun 41	54UNTS289	200201
Bolivia	USA (United States)	04 Sep 41	8UNTS345	200046
Peru	USA (United States)	11 Mar 42	117UNTS266	200375
Brazil	USA (United States)	07 May 42	6UNTS377	200040
Colombia	USA (United States)	29 May 42	8UNTS365	200047
Panama	USA (United States)	07 Jul 42	9UNTS289	200048
Bolivia	USA (United States)	11 Aug 42	9UNTS309	200049
Dominican Republic	USA (United States)	25 Jan 43	13UNTS399	200083
Guatemala	USA (United States)	17 Jul 43	28UNTS431	200166
Ecuador	USA (United States)	13 Sep 43	29UNTS349	200171
Paraguay	USA (United States)	27 Oct 43	29UNTS391	200174
Iran	USA (United States)	27 Nov 43	31UNTS451	200176
Paraguay	USA (United States)	10 Dec 43	21UNTS305	200131
USA (United States)	Venezuela	13 Jan 44	109UNTS171	200358
Ecuador	USA (United States)	29 Jun 44	80UNTS283	200250
Peru	USA (United States)	10 Jul 44	117UNTS291	200377
Brazil	Paraguay	11 Aug 44	67UNTS303	200227
Brazil	USA (United States)	29 Sep 44	65UNTS271	200216
Multilateral		08 Oct 44	45UNTS311	200187
Multilateral		20 Jan 45	140UNTS397	200471
USA (United States)	USSR (Soviet Union)	11 Feb 45	68UNTS175	200229
Guatemala	USA (United States)	21 Feb 45	121UNTS133	200396
Guatemala	USA (United States)	21 May 45	121UNTS185	200399
Chile	USA (United States)	24 May 45	121UNTS219	200401
Portugal	UK Great Britain	01 Jul 45	5UNTS263	200034
Denmark	UK Great Britain	06 Dec 45	5UNTS3	100061
Costa Rica	USA (United States)	10 Dec 45	3UNTS157	100029
Honduras	USA (United States)	28 Dec 45	3UNTS185	100031
Multilateral		01 Jan 46	99UNTS131	101375
Greece	UK Great Britain	24 Jan 46	6UNTS45	100067
Mexico	UK Great Britain	07 Feb 46	6UNTS55	100068
France	Norway	26 Mar 46	31UNTS69	100468
UK Great Britain	USA (United States)	27 Mar 46	4UNTS2	100039
Poland	USA (United States)	24 Apr 46	4UNTS155	100042
USA (United States)	Venezuela	03 Jun 46	4UNTS215	100047
Multilateral		18 Jul 46	125UNTS119	101674
Ceylon (Sri Lanka)	India	12 Aug 46	196UNTS209	102626
Argentina	UK Great Britain	17 Sep 46	88UNTS47	101185
Peru	USA (United States)	07 Oct 46	7UNTS71	100092
Colombia	USA (United States)	14 Oct 46	7UNTS97	100093

Compensation (Cont.)

PARTY ONE	PARTY TWO	DATE	CITATION	NUMBER
Canada	Netherlands	30 Dec 46	230UNTS205	103185
Multilateral		10 Feb 47	49UNTS3	100747
Belgium	Czechoslovakia	19 Mar 47	23UNTS35	100341
Belgium	South Africa	04 Jul 47	47UNTS9	100720
Belgium	USA (United States)	23 Jul 47	33UNTS33	100512
Greece	South Africa	28 Jul 47	185UNTS161	102467
Italy	USA (United States)	14 Aug 47	36UNTS53	100566
El Salvador	USA (United States)	19 Aug 47	51UNTS57	100752
Iran	USA (United States)	06 Oct 47	11UNTS303	100171
Bolivia	USA (United States)	03 Nov 47	51UNTS33	100750
Poland	UK Great Britain	24 Jan 48	87UNTS3	101163
Italy	USA (United States)	02 Feb 48	79UNTS171	101040
Belgium	UK Great Britain	07 Jun 48	20UNTS33	100313
Australia	Greece	16 Jun 48	18UNTS211	100290
Brazil	USA (United States)	29 Jul 48	80UNTS111	101047
Argentina	USA (United States)	06 Oct 48	80UNTS91	101046
Czechoslovakia	Poland	12 Nov 48	84UNTS347	101141
Ceylon (Sri Lanka)	Pakistan	15 Dec 48	91UNTS303	101255
Haiti	USA (United States)	04 Jan 49	44UNTS69	100679
Belgium	France	18 Feb 49	31UNTS173	100478
Colombia	USA (United States)	21 Feb 49	92UNTS227	101275
Colombia	USA (United States)	21 Feb 49	44UNTS83	100680
Haiti	USA (United States)	14 Apr 49	80UNTS37	101043
Denmark	Poland	12 May 49	87UNTS179	101172
Italy	Spain	31 May 49	231UNTS251	103224
Peru	USA (United States)	20 Jun 49	92UNTS249	101276
Czechoslovakia	Poland	02 Jul 49	260UNTS149	103708
Czechoslovakia	Poland	02 Jul 49	260UNTS179	103709
Mexico	USA (United States)	05 Jul 49	68UNTS55	100884
Greece	Turkey	21 Jul 49	78UNTS65	101012
Denmark	ICAO (Civil Aviat)	09 Sep 49	53UNTS341	100791
Czechoslovakia	UK Great Britain	28 Sep 49	86UNTS161	101157
Finland	USA (United States)	01 Nov 49	68UNTS11	100880
Belgium	Canada	16 Nov 49	51UNTS3	100748
France	UK Great Britain	23 Jan 50	97UNTS149	101348
Korea, South	USA (United States)	26 Jan 50	178UNTS97	102337
Belgium	Netherlands	17 Feb 50	51UNTS101	100756
Spain	Sweden	18 Feb 50	166UNTS15	102184
Honduras	USA (United States)	06 Mar 50	80UNTS51	101044
Honduras	USA (United States)	06 Mar 50	80UNTS71	101045
Italy	New Zealand	19 Apr 50	67UNTS81	100867
Australia	Netherlands	26 Apr 50	54UNTS83	100796
Netherlands	Spain	20 Jun 50	95UNTS303	101327
UK Great Britain	USA (United States)	21 Jul 50	97UNTS193	101351
Spain	Switzerland	03 Aug 50	254UNTS365	103600
USA (United States)	Venezuela	23 Aug 50	92UNTS341	101279
Czechoslovakia	USA (United States)	29 Sep 50	290UNTS3	104227
Cuba	USA (United States)	22 Dec 50	122UNTS97	101640
Australia	Finland	04 Jan 51	80UNTS27	101042
Liberia	USA (United States)	11 Jan 51	122UNTS125	101642
Canada	France	26 Jan 51	233UNTS65	103251
Chile	USA (United States)	15 Feb 51	133UNTS117	101784
Chile	USA (United States)	15 Feb 51	133UNTS95	101783
Belgium	Netherlands	15 Mar 51	93UNTS97	101294
Belgium	USA (United States)	16 Mar 51	93UNTS109	101295
France	UK Great Britain	11 Apr 51	106UNTS3	101456
Germany, West	Norway	07 May 51	92UNTS51	101260
Italy	Netherlands	15 Jun 51	150UNTS103	101964
Saudi Arabia	USA (United States)	18 Jun 51	102UNTS73	101412
Multilateral		19 Jun 51	199UNTS67	102678
Denmark	France	30 Jun 51	151UNTS241	102000
USA (United States)	Venezuela	10 Aug 51	140UNTS345	101898
Israel	USA (United States)	23 Aug 51	219UNTS237	102979
Cuba	USA (United States)	28 Aug 51	134UNTS225	101802
Cuba	USA (United States)	28 Aug 51	140UNTS239	101891

Compensation (Cont.)

PARTY ONE	PARTY TWO	DATE	CITATION	NUMBER
Multilateral		08 Sep 51	136UNTS45	101832
USA (United States)	Uruguay	04 Dec 51	152UNTS41	102010
Italy	USA (United States)	28 Dec 51	157UNTS63	102047
UK Great Britain	USA (United States)	15 Jan 52	127UNTS3	101697
Canada	Netherlands	10 Apr 52	233UNTS129	103257
Israel	USA (United States)	09 May 52	177UNTS269	102326
Australia	USA (United States)	27 May 52	178UNTS113	102338
Multilateral		11 Jul 52	170UNTS63	102222
Japan	USA (United States)	12 Nov 52	184UNTS111	102443
Nicaragua	USA (United States)	19 Nov 52	186UNTS3	102478
Canada	USA (United States)	05 Dec 52	206UNTS11	102783
United Arab Rep	UK Great Britain	05 Jan 53	207UNTS277	102810
USA (United States)	Venezuela	16 Jan 53	199UNTS287	102690
El Salvador	USA (United States)	21 May 53	213UNTS15	102878
Ethiopia	USA (United States)	22 May 53	191UNTS59	102577
Libya	UK Great Britain	29 Jul 53	186UNTS201	102492
Greece	USA (United States)	12 Oct 53	191UNTS319	102589
Australia	Netherlands	22 Oct 53	184UNTS193	102448
Nicaragua	USA (United States)	19 Nov 53	206UNTS117	102787
Belgium	Taiwan	13 Jan 54	223UNTS111	103059
Italy	USA (United States)	27 Apr 54	234UNTS103	103275
Japan	USA (United States)	14 May 54	247UNTS273	103476
Taiwan	USA (United States)	14 May 54	231UNTS165	103216
Australia	Greece	24 May 54	191UNTS255	102586
Italy	UK Great Britain	01 Jun 54	403UNTS275	105798
Turkey	USA (United States)	01 Jul 54	234UNTS147	103280
UK Great Britain	USA (United States)	21 Jul 54	222UNTS243	103031
India	USA (United States)	29 Jul 54	239UNTS69	103373
Libya	USA (United States)	09 Sep 54	224UNTS217	103078
El Salvador	USA (United States)	23 Sep 54	237UNTS91	103338
Belgium	USA (United States)	12 Oct 54	202UNTS289	102735
France	Netherlands	15 Dec 54	288UNTS37	104195
Australia	Austria	20 Dec 54	205UNTS157	102775
Korea, South	USA (United States)	29 Jan 55	239UNTS53	103371
Australia	Hungary	10 Feb 55	207UNTS173	102806
Australia	Taiwan	22 Mar 55	209UNTS3	102818
Australia	Czechoslovakia	01 Apr 55	213UNTS199	102888
Netherlands	USA (United States)	29 Apr 55	219UNTS105	102969
Hungary	USSR (Soviet Union)	27 May 55	407UNTS156	105864
Japan	Thailand	09 Jul 55	230UNTS13	103172
Spain	USA (United States)	16 Jul 55	270UNTS211	103899
Ceylon (Sri Lanka)	USA (United States)	18 Jul 55	281UNTS295	104086
Czechoslovakia	Germany, East	24 Oct 55	504UNTS173	107358
Canada	Norway	20 Dec 55	305UNTS17	104408
Belgium	Switzerland	05 Jan 56	228UNTS159	103149
Luxembourg	Netherlands	06 Feb 56	261UNTS17	103723
Multilateral		19 May 56	399UNTS189	105742
UK Great Britain	USA (United States)	25 Jun 56	249UNTS59	103501
Bolivia	USA (United States)	30 Jun 56	271UNTS243	103919
Greece	Romania	25 Aug 56	299UNTS231	104315
Multilateral		25 Sep 56	334UNTS13	104766
Argentina	USA (United States)	03 Oct 56	279UNTS13	104032
Portugal	USA (United States)	07 Nov 56	277UNTS133	104003
Austria	USA (United States)	21 Nov 56	290UNTS181	104237
Dominican Republic	USA (United States)	07 Dec 56	263UNTS193	103774
Sweden	UK Great Britain	08 Dec 56	264UNTS61	103788
Poland	USSR (Soviet Union)	17 Dec 56	266UNTS179	103830
Brazil	USA (United States)	16 Jan 57	266UNTS99	103824
Germany, West	Netherlands	29 Jan 57	314UNTS173	104548
Spain	USA (United States)	09 Mar 57	283UNTS89	104108
Germany, East	USSR (Soviet Union)	12 Mar 57	285UNTS105	104150
Liberia	USA (United States)	16 Mar 57	290UNTS59	104228
Italy	UK Great Britain	29 Mar 57	310UNTS11	104481
Romania	USSR (Soviet Union)	15 Apr 57	274UNTS143	103964
Other Unilat Decla	United Arab Rep	24 Apr 57	265UNTS299	103821

PARTY ONE	PARTY TWO	DATE	CITATION	NUMBER
Compensation (Cont.)				
Germany, West	USA (United States)	01 May 57	284UNTS85	104131
Finland	USA (United States)	10 May 57	283UNTS43	104105
Taiwan	USA (United States)	30 Jul 57	300UNTS61	104331
Greece	USA (United States)	05 Aug 57	290UNTS167	104235
Japan	Sweden	20 Sep 57	325UNTS29	104693
Multilateral		03 Oct 57	365UNTS3	105213
Poland	USSR (Soviet Union)	26 Oct 57	432UNTS221	106223
Philippines	USA (United States)	01 Nov 57	307UNTS39	104440
El Salvador	USA (United States)	21 Nov 57	303UNTS19	104369
Philippines	USA (United States)	20 Feb 58	303UNTS261	104385
Australia	USA (United States)	25 Feb 58	317UNTS153	104601
Bulgaria	Yugoslavia	21 Mar 58	386UNTS119	105541
Multilateral		29 Apr 58	450UNTS11	106465
Lebanon	UK Great Britain	19 May 58	327UNTS43	104716
Netherlands	Norway	30 Jun 58	346UNTS217	104982
Netherlands	Yugoslavia	22 Jul 58	386UNTS263	105546
Australia	Netherlands	23 Jul 58	328UNTS227	104736
Denmark	USA (United States)	28 Aug 58	335UNTS133	104781
Turkey	USA (United States)	14 Oct 58	336UNTS145	104803
Japan	USA (United States)	03 Nov 58	341UNTS83	104879
Burma	United Nations	15 Dec 58	319UNTS3	104629
United Nations	Tunisia	23 Dec 58	321UNTS23	104651
Portugal	USA (United States)	12 Jan 59	343UNTS49	104921
United Arab Rep	USA (United States)	13 Jan 59	358UNTS3	105122
Greece	USA (United States)	15 Jan 59	357UNTS281	105120
Taiwan	USA (United States)	07 Feb 59	341UNTS225	104885
Ghana	United Nations	27 Feb 59	324UNTS133	104682
United Nations	Sudan	28 Mar 59	327UNTS95	104719
France	USA (United States)	07 May 59	354UNTS83	105055
Thailand	USA (United States)	19 May 59	346UNTS271	104986
Peru	USA (United States)	15 Jun 59	346UNTS279	104987
Greece	Yugoslavia	18 Jun 59	368UNTS27	105234
Spain	USA (United States)	23 Jun 59	354UNTS11	105049
Libya	United Nations	27 Jun 59	336UNTS291	104811
Laos	United Nations	06 Jul 59	337UNTS41	104814
Taiwan	USA (United States)	08 Jul 59	354UNTS47	105052
Denmark	Yugoslavia	13 Jul 59	386UNTS251	105545
Paraguay	United Nations	01 Aug 59	341UNTS319	104894
Italy	USA (United States)	18 Aug 59	361UNTS11	105169
Guinea	United Nations	15 Oct 59	344UNTS47	104942
Brazil	USA (United States)	19 Oct 59	372UNTS131	105293
Norway	Sweden	28 Oct 59	427UNTS225	106157
Korea, South	United Nations	06 Nov 59	346UNTS289	200565
Afghanistan	United Nations	24 Nov 59	397UNTS187	105705
France	USA (United States)	25 Nov 59	401UNTS75	105764
Germany, West	Pakistan	25 Nov 59	457UNTS22	106575
Ecuador	USA (United States)	11 Feb 60	372UNTS141	105294
Peru	USA (United States)	26 Feb 60	394UNTS141	105674
Multilateral		15 Mar 60	572UNTS133	108310
Argentina	USA (United States)	01 Apr 60	371UNTS245	105281
Colombia	USA (United States)	07 Apr 60	372UNTS27	105285
United Nations	Togo	06 May 60	388UNTS53	105571
Haiti	USA (United States)	08 Jul 60	380UNTS135	105454
Ethiopia	United Nations	13 Jul 60	368UNTS143	105239
Peru	USA (United States)	15 Jul 60	384UNTS159	105517
Spain	USA (United States)	21 Jul 60	393UNTS289	105663
Argentina	USA (United States)	02 Aug 60	384UNTS105	105514
Korea, South	USA (United States)	17 Aug 60	400UNTS339	105757
Australia	USA (United States)	23 Aug 60	388UNTS237	105581
Canada	USA (United States)	31 Aug 60	393UNTS247	105659
Kuwait	United Nations	31 Oct 60	391UNTS295	200581
Pakistan	United Nations	17 Nov 60	380UNTS277	105460
Cambodia	United Nations	30 Nov 60	383UNTS147	105500
Bolivia	United Nations	14 Dec 60	382UNTS283	105489
Iraq	United Nations	05 Mar 61	409UNTS56	105878

PARTY ONE	PARTY TWO	DATE	CITATION	NUMBER
Compensation (Cont.)				
Somalia	USSR (Soviet Union)	02 Jun 61	457UNTS263	106587
Cyprus	United Nations	15 Jun 61	398UNTS39	105716
Haiti	United Nations	28 Jun 61	399UNTS159	105740
Lebanon	United Nations	26 Aug 61	406UNTS105	105842
Jordan	United Nations	11 Sep 61	406UNTS255	105855
Japan	IBRD (World Bank)	29 Nov 61	426UNTS3	106128
Ceylon (Sri Lanka)	United Nations	04 Dec 61	415UNTS236	105987
United Nations	Somalia	20 Jan 62	420UNTS133	106044
Thailand	USA (United States)	31 May 62	459UNTS135	106619
Nigeria	United Nations	07 Aug 62	435UNTS167	106278
Cameroon	United Nations	29 Aug 62	442UNTS3	106334
Belgium	Germany, West	21 Sep 62	502UNTS63	107326
Austria	Czechoslovakia	22 Sep 62	495UNTS157	107244
Niger	United Nations	01 Oct 62	439UNTS181	106329
Sweden	USA (United States)	04 Oct 62	462UNTS31	106669
Mali	USSR (Soviet Union)	10 Oct 62	493UNTS219	107216
Israel	OAS (Am States)	11 Oct 62	484UNTS241	107035
Belgium	Rwanda	13 Oct 62	456UNTS431	106569
United Nations	Western Samoa	05 Nov 62	443UNTS297	200599
Czechoslovakia	Poland	16 Nov 62	526UNTS3	107597
Ecuador	United Nations	26 Nov 62	445UNTS3	106372
Ivory Coast	United Nations	10 Dec 62	451UNTS269	106498
Austria	Yugoslavia	11 Dec 62	546UNTS3	107938
Israel	United Nations	07 Jan 63	450UNTS229	106470
Pakistan	USA (United States)	16 Jan 63	471UNTS133	106828
Norway	USA (United States)	01 Mar 63	524UNTS185	107573
Germany, West	USA (United States)	14 Mar 63	474UNTS71	106872
Multilateral		02 Apr 63	475UNTS121	106889
Burma	UK Great Britain	02 Apr 63	475UNTS139	106890
Belgium	USA (United States)	19 Apr 63	493UNTS83	107209
Japan	USA (United States)	26 Apr 63	477UNTS37	106914
Australia	USA (United States)	09 May 63	475UNTS331	106897
Netherlands	Tunisia	23 May 63	523UNTS237	107558
El Salvador	IBRD (World Bank)	19 Jun 63	481UNTS59	106978
Bulgaria	USA (United States)	02 Jul 63	479UNTS245	106957
Multilateral		17 Oct 63	525UNTS75	107585
Multilateral		21 Oct 63	480UNTS197	106969
Czechoslovakia	Hungary	22 Oct 63	514UNTS95	107444
Multilateral		14 Nov 63	619UNTS299	108948
Netherlands	Poland	20 Dec 63	514UNTS169	107446
Belgium	Netherlands	06 Jan 64	531UNTS119	107698
Argentina	Yugoslavia	21 Mar 64	635UNTS153	109078
Germany, West	Thailand	02 Apr 64	503UNTS3	107338
Ireland	USA (United States)	18 Jun 64	530UNTS217	107684
UK Great Britain	USA (United States)	19 Jun 64	530UNTS99	107675
Sweden	USA (United States)	06 Jul 64	529UNTS287	107666
Spain	USA (United States)	16 Jul 64	529UNTS187	107661
Eur Space Research	Sweden	29 Jul 64	528UNTS81	107636
France	Eur Space Research	10 Aug 64	528UNTS135	107637
Chile	USA (United States)	27 Oct 64	532UNTS347	107727
Ethiopia	Netherlands	28 Oct 64	541UNTS235	107872
Netherlands	Pakistan	30 Oct 64	541UNTS243	107873
Italy	USA (United States)	23 Nov 64	532UNTS133	107716
Trinidad/Tobago	USA (United States)	05 Dec 64	535UNTS331	107788
Belgium	Luxembourg	14 Jan 65	620UNTS3	108949
Australia	Germany, West	21 Apr 65	598UNTS25	108654
Ivory Coast	Netherlands	26 Apr 65	634UNTS81	109053
Multilateral		02 Jun 65	551UNTS2	108030
Multilateral		05 Jul 65	563UNTS104	108207
Australia	Germany, West	08 Jul 65	543UNTS305	107907
Botswana	UK Great Britain	30 Sep 66	597UNTS211	108646
Multilateral		21 Jun 67	598UNTS2	108653
Indemnities and reimbursements				
Multilateral		23 Jun 26	38UNTS315	100606

PARTY ONE	PARTY TWO	DATE	CITATION	NUMBER
Indemnities and reimbursements (Cont.)				
Multilateral		22 Jun 35	40UNTS73	100628
Multilateral		20 Jun 36	40UNTS109	100630
Bolivia	Brazil	25 Feb 38	88UNTS379	200254
Bolivia	Brazil	25 Feb 38	54UNTS333	200205
Luxembourg	UK Great Britain	29 May 39	99UNTS301	200284
Panama	USA (United States)	23 Mar 40	124UNTS195	200420
Norway	USA (United States)	28 Mar 40	88UNTS365	200253
Multilateral		30 Jul 40	161UNTS253	200488
Multilateral		27 Mar 41	67UNTS231	200222
Haiti	USA (United States)	23 May 41	117UNTS191	200370
Haiti	USA (United States)	05 Jun 41	101UNTS125	200289
Jordan	UK Great Britain	19 Jul 41	9UNTS381	200054
Bolivia	USA (United States)	04 Sep 41	8UNTS345	200046
El Salvador	USA (United States)	27 Nov 41	120UNTS161	200389
Liberia	USA (United States)	15 Jan 42	117UNTS227	200372
Bolivia	USA (United States)	31 Jan 42	101UNTS137	200290
Panama	USA (United States)	07 Mar 42	101UNTS157	200291
Peru	USA (United States)	11 Mar 42	117UNTS266	200375
Peru	USA (United States)	21 Apr 42	89UNTS317	200260
Brazil	USA (United States)	07 May 42	6UNTS377	200040
Honduras	USA (United States)	08 May 42	166UNTS351	200498
Colombia	USA (United States)	29 May 42	8UNTS365	200047
Panama	USA (United States)	07 Jul 42	9UNTS289	200048
Bolivia	USA (United States)	11 Aug 42	9UNTS309	200049
Iceland	USA (United States)	17 Aug 42	24UNTS163	200140
Ecuador	USA (United States)	29 Oct 42	89UNTS301	200259
Paraguay	USA (United States)	28 Nov 42	101UNTS173	200292
Dominican Republic	USA (United States)	10 Dec 42	24UNTS257	200151
Dominican Republic	USA (United States)	25 Jan 43	13UNTS399	200083
Finland	Sweden	10 Mar 43	198UNTS333	200518
Multilateral		26 Mar 43	13UNTS427	200089
Colombia	USA (United States)	29 Mar 43	124UNTS139	200416
Canada	USA (United States)	26 May 43	7UNTS345	200043
Guatemala	USA (United States)	17 Jul 43	28UNTS431	200166
Canada	USA (United States)	09 Aug 43	29UNTS295	200168
Iran	USA (United States)	21 Aug 43	101UNTS189	200293
Ecuador	USA (United States)	13 Sep 43	29UNTS349	200171
France	USA (United States)	25 Sep 43	76UNTS183	200245
Paraguay	USA (United States)	27 Oct 43	29UNTS391	200174
Iran	USA (United States)	27 Nov 43	31UNTS451	200176
Paraguay	USA (United States)	10 Dec 43	21UNTS305	200131
USA (United States)	Venezuela	13 Jan 44	109UNTS171	200358
Mexico	USA (United States)	03 Feb 44	3UNTS313	200025
Iraq	USA (United States)	16 Feb 44	109UNTS223	200362
Afghanistan	USA (United States)	29 Feb 44	106UNTS247	200344
UK Great Britain	USA (United States)	28 Mar 44	15UNTS413	200104
Guatemala	USA (United States)	13 Apr 44	106UNTS213	200342
Multilateral		19 Apr 44	89UNTS279	200257
Ecuador	USA (United States)	29 Jun 44	80UNTS283	200250
Peru	USA (United States)	10 Jul 44	117UNTS291	200377
Belgium	UK Great Britain	22 Aug 44	90UNTS295	200267
Brazil	USA (United States)	29 Sep 44	65UNTS271	200216
Guatemala	USA (United States)	21 Feb 45	121UNTS133	200396
Belgium	USA (United States)	17 Apr 45	139UNTS253	200454
Netherlands	USA (United States)	30 Apr 45	139UNTS341	200460
Guatemala	USA (United States)	21 May 45	121UNTS185	200399
Chile	USA (United States)	24 May 45	121UNTS219	200401
Denmark	UK Great Britain	24 Oct 45	93UNTS143	101297
Poland	Yugoslavia	23 Nov 45	115UNTS3	101555
Czechoslovakia	France	08 Dec 45	46UNTS77	100701
Costa Rica	USA (United States)	10 Dec 45	3UNTS157	100029
Netherlands	UK Great Britain	20 Dec 45	4UNTS303	100053
Honduras	USA (United States)	28 Dec 45	3UNTS185	100031
Multilateral		14 Jan 46	555UNTS69	108105
Netherlands	USA (United States)	11 Feb 46	3UNTS37	100023

PARTY ONE	PARTY TWO	DATE	CITATION	NUMBER
Indemnities and reimbursements (Cont.)				
Czechoslovakia	Poland	12 Feb 46	25UNTS207	100364
Brazil	USA (United States)	15 Feb 46	162UNTS21	102130
Colombia	USA (United States)	19 Feb 46	166UNTS104	102187
Belgium	UK Great Britain	11 Mar 46	26UNTS167	100387
Poland	Yugoslavia	16 Mar 46	10UNTS11	100139
UK Great Britain	USA (United States)	27 Mar 46	4UNTS101	100040
Iraq	Turkey	29 Mar 46	37UNTS333	100581
Brazil	USA (United States)	05 Apr 46	12UNTS131	100183
Multilateral		17 Apr 46	27UNTS103	100402
Hungary	Yugoslavia	11 May 46	129UNTS3	101725
France	USA (United States)	28 May 46	84UNTS121	101123
France	USA (United States)	28 May 46	84UNTS93	101121
France	USA (United States)	28 May 46	84UNTS113	101122
USA (United States)	Venezuela	03 Jun 46	4UNTS215	100047
United Nations	Switzerland	01 Jul 46	1UNTS153	200007
Albania	Yugoslavia	01 Jul 46	111UNTS81	101518
Multilateral		18 Jul 46	125UNTS119	101674
Czechoslovakia	USSR (Soviet Union)	25 Jul 46	27UNTS231	100409
League of Nations	United Nations	31 Jul 46	1UNTS119	200003
Hungary	USA (United States)	09 Aug 46	148UNTS313	101941
Ceylon (Sri Lanka)	India	12 Aug 46	196UNTS209	102626
Denmark	UK Great Britain	16 Aug 46	9UNTS163	100130
Poland	USA (United States)	29 Aug 46	160UNTS11	102097
Norway	UK Great Britain	27 Sep 46	6UNTS259	100079
Peru	USA (United States)	07 Oct 46	7UNTS71	100092
Philippines	USA (United States)	19 Oct 46	43UNTS263	100672
France	Netherlands	19 Nov 46	32UNTS101	100493
Albania	Yugoslavia	28 Nov 46	111UNTS109	101522
Albania	Yugoslavia	28 Nov 46	111UNTS163	101529
UK Great Britain	USA (United States)	02 Dec 46	7UNTS163	100098
Netherlands	UK Great Britain	04 Dec 46	12UNTS241	100187
Romania	Yugoslavia	23 Dec 46	116UNTS33	101567
Peru	USA (United States)	27 Dec 46	152UNTS93	102013
Belgium	UK Great Britain	16 Jan 47	54UNTS97	100797
Australia	Netherlands	24 Jan 47	10UNTS77	100144
Philippines	USA (United States)	14 Mar 47	43UNTS271	100673
Greece	UK Great Britain	07 Apr 47	11UNTS201	100158
France	South Africa	18 Apr 47	225UNTS35	103085
Denmark	UK Great Britain	22 Apr 47	8UNTS3	100110
Philippines	USA (United States)	12 May 47	16UNTS109	100252
France	Poland	19 May 47	12UNTS95	100181
South Africa	USA (United States)	23 May 47	66UNTS233	100857
Austria	USA (United States)	21 Jun 47	67UNTS99	100869
Bulgaria	Poland	28 Jun 47	15UNTS123	100230
USSR (Soviet Union)	Yugoslavia	25 Jul 47	130UNTS315	101732
Greece	South Africa	28 Jul 47	185UNTS161	102467
Australia	France	28 Jul 47	97UNTS271	101353
Poland	Romania	09 Aug 47	12UNTS363	100193
France	UK Great Britain	13 Aug 47	91UNTS169	101249
Multilateral		14 Aug 47	138UNTS111	101863
El Salvador	USA (United States)	19 Aug 47	51UNTS57	100752
France	USA (United States)	01 Oct 47	148UNTS303	101940
Iran	USA (United States)	06 Oct 47	11UNTS303	100171
Greece	UNICEF (Children)	14 Oct 47	102UNTS39	101409
France	USA (United States)	25 Oct 47	89UNTS111	101212
Bolivia	USA (United States)	03 Nov 47	51UNTS33	100750
Taiwan	USA (United States)	08 Dec 47	70UNTS3	100895
USSR (Soviet Union)	Yugoslavia	15 Dec 47	116UNTS313	101578
Sweden	USA (United States)	16 Dec 47	73UNTS65	100944
South Africa	USA (United States)	18 Dec 47	148UNTS85	101938
Guatemala	USA (United States)	05 Jan 48	135UNTS104	101817
UK Great Britain	USA (United States)	24 Feb 48	73UNTS143	100951
France	USA (United States)	27 Feb 48	84UNTS207	101131
Paraguay	USA (United States)	12 Mar 48	162UNTS30	102131
Norway	USA (United States)	15 Mar 48	73UNTS81	100946

Indemnities and reimbursements (Cont.)

PARTY ONE	PARTY TWO	DATE	CITATION	NUMBER
USA (United States)	Venezuela	24 Mar 48	44UNTS57	100678
Burma	USA (United States)	05 Apr 48	73UNTS73	100945
Belgium	Netherlands	13 Apr 48	32UNTS153	100497
Philippines	USA (United States)	07 Jun 48	73UNTS89	100947
Multilateral		19 Jun 48	310UNTS151	104492
Australia	Hungary	01 Jul 48	22UNTS3	100325
Australia	Greece	01 Jul 48	22UNTS33	100329
Australia	Italy	08 Jul 48	22UNTS11	100326
Australia	Yugoslavia	09 Jul 48	22UNTS17	100327
Austria	Austria	19 Jul 48	22UNTS25	100328
Brazil	USA (United States)	29 Jul 48	80UNTS111	101047
Greece	UK Great Britain	07 Sep 48	180UNTS144	102380
Argentina	USA (United States)	06 Oct 48	80UNTS91	101046
New Zealand	UK Great Britain	12 Nov 48	162UNTS197	102136
Czechoslovakia	Poland	12 Nov 48	84UNTS347	101141
Taiwan	USA (United States)	18 Nov 48	198UNTS287	102672
Italy	USA (United States)	26 Nov 48	79UNTS71	101032
UK Great Britain	USA (United States)	01 Dec 48	81UNTS93	101066
Afghanistan	UNESCO (Educ/Cult)	08 Dec 48	46UNTS3	100697
Multilateral		16 Dec 48	79UNTS85	101033
Italy	USA (United States)	18 Dec 48	79UNTS133	101037
France	USA (United States)	23 Dec 48	67UNTS171	100876
Haiti	USA (United States)	04 Jan 49	44UNTS69	100679
Netherlands	USA (United States)	17 Jan 49	32UNTS241	100502
Chile	USA (United States)	21 Jan 49	160UNTS185	102107
Mexico	USA (United States)	25 Jan 49	99UNTS3	101367
France	USA (United States)	07 Feb 49	67UNTS189	100877
Austria	USA (United States)	11 Feb 49	79UNTS113	101035
Trieste	USA (United States)	11 Feb 49	79UNTS123	101036
Mexico	USA (United States)	14 Feb 49	160UNTS75	102103
Colombia	USA (United States)	21 Feb 49	92UNTS227	101275
Colombia	USA (United States)	21 Feb 49	44UNTS83	100680
Ceylon (Sri Lanka)	UK Great Britain	28 Feb 49	314UNTS269	104551
Czechoslovakia	UK Great Britain	03 Mar 49	83UNTS95	101104
United Nations	UK Great Britain	18 Mar 49	47UNTS305	100736
Israel	Lebanon	23 Mar 49	42UNTS287	100655
Austria	USA (United States)	23 Mar 49	43UNTS127	100667
Finland	USA (United States)	29 Mar 49	55UNTS59	100808
Panama	USA (United States)	31 Mar 49	55UNTS87	100810
Panama	USA (United States)	31 Mar 49	55UNTS141	100812
Israel	Jordan	03 Apr 49	42UNTS303	100656
Haiti	USA (United States)	14 Apr 49	80UNTS37	101043
Multilateral		04 May 49	92UNTS19	101257
Canada	Netherlands	09 May 49	46UNTS263	100715
Switzerland	USA (United States)	13 May 49	51UNTS129	100761
Canada	USA (United States)	04 Jun 49	122UNTS237	101649
Philippines	USA (United States)	07 Jun 49	45UNTS63	100692
Italy	UK Great Britain	14 Jun 49	135UNTS49	101813
Peru	USA (United States)	20 Jun 49	92UNTS249	101276
Mexico	USA (United States)	21 Jun 49	89UNTS3	101204
Czechoslovakia	Poland	02 Jul 49	260UNTS179	103709
Czechoslovakia	Poland	02 Jul 49	260UNTS149	103708
India	USA (United States)	04 Jul 49	200UNTS181	102702
Mexico	USA (United States)	05 Jul 49	68UNTS55	100884
Dominican Republic	USA (United States)	19 Jul 49	51UNTS145	100762
Israel	Syria	20 Jul 49	42UNTS327	100657
Colombia	USA (United States)	26 Jul 49	73UNTS106	100949
USA (United States)	Uruguay	27 Jul 49	151UNTS199	101995
Philippines	USA (United States)	08 Aug 49	163UNTS103	102144
WHO (World Health)	Thailand	12 Aug 49	178UNTS347	102350
Multilateral		12 Aug 49	87UNTS131	101169
Mexico	USA (United States)	15 Aug 49	66UNTS13	100846
Greece	Italy	31 Aug 49	78UNTS89	101014
Denmark	ICAO (Civil Aviat)	09 Sep 49	53UNTS341	100791
Norway	USA (United States)	31 Oct 49	68UNTS3	100879

Indemnities and reimbursements (Cont.)

PARTY ONE	PARTY TWO	DATE	CITATION	NUMBER
United Arab Rep	USA (United States)	03 Nov 49	71UNTS31	100908
Multilateral		07 Nov 49	132UNTS3	101748
South Africa	USA (United States)	16 Nov 49	73UNTS97	100948
Australia	New Zealand	26 Nov 49	198UNTS161	102662
Australia	USA (United States)	26 Nov 49	45UNTS133	100695
Korea, South	USA (United States)	26 Jan 50	178UNTS97	102337
France	USA (United States)	27 Jan 50	80UNTS171	101051
UK Great Britain	USA (United States)	27 Jan 50	80UNTS261	101056
Luxembourg	USA (United States)	27 Jan 50	80UNTS187	101052
Norway	USA (United States)	27 Jan 50	80UNTS241	101055
Netherlands	USA (United States)	27 Jan 50	80UNTS219	101054
Italy	USA (United States)	27 Jan 50	80UNTS145	101050
Denmark	USA (United States)	27 Jan 50	48UNTS115	100740
India	USA (United States)	02 Feb 50	89UNTS127	101214
Ceylon (Sri Lanka)	WHO (World Health)	17 Feb 50	102UNTS309	200309
Israel	USA (United States)	19 Feb 50	122UNTS117	101641
Honduras	USA (United States)	06 Mar 50	80UNTS71	101045
Honduras	USA (United States)	06 Mar 50	80UNTS51	101044
Honduras	USA (United States)	24 Mar 50	93UNTS11	101283
Italy	New Zealand	19 Apr 50	67UNTS81	100867
Korea, South	USA (United States)	28 Apr 50	93UNTS21	101284
Spain	USA (United States)	08 May 50	98UNTS175	101363
Austria	USA (United States)	06 Jun 50	92UNTS201	101273
Indonesia	USA (United States)	07 Jun 50	98UNTS167	101362
Burma	Ceylon (Sri Lanka)	29 Jun 50	73UNTS3	100940
Korea, South	USA (United States)	28 Jul 50	140UNTS57	101883
USA (United States)	Venezuela	23 Aug 50	92UNTS341	101279
Burma	Sweden	14 Sep 50	96UNTS45	101330
Pakistan	USA (United States)	23 Sep 50	82UNTS131	101088
Czechoslovakia	USA (United States)	29 Sep 50	290UNTS3	104227
USA (United States)	Yugoslavia	09 Oct 50	133UNTS25	101776
Netherlands	New Zealand	16 Oct 50	83UNTS269	101111
Thailand	USA (United States)	17 Oct 50	79UNTS41	101030
Greece	USA (United States)	24 Oct 50	133UNTS41	101778
Costa Rica	USA (United States)	02 Dec 50	133UNTS61	101780
Germany, West	Netherlands	14 Dec 50	87UNTS257	101177
Cuba	USA (United States)	22 Dec 50	122UNTS97	101640
Brazil	USA (United States)	27 Dec 50	147UNTS33	101926
Portugal	USA (United States)	05 Jan 51	133UNTS75	101782
Multilateral		09 Jan 51	197UNTS341	102647
Liberia	USA (United States)	11 Jan 51	122UNTS125	101642
Netherlands	USA (United States)	19 Jan 51	141UNTS221	101917
Nicaragua	USA (United States)	31 Jan 51	160UNTS121	102105
Nicaragua	USA (United States)	31 Jan 51	150UNTS3	101960
Israel	Turkey	05 Feb 51	193UNTS3	102607
Poland	USSR (Soviet Union)	15 Feb 51	432UNTS199	106222
Chile	USA (United States)	15 Feb 51	133UNTS95	101783
Chile	USA (United States)	15 Feb 51	133UNTS117	101784
Panama	USA (United States)	26 Feb 51	160UNTS153	102106
Greece	Yugoslavia	15 Mar 51	187UNTS237	102516
Dominican Republic	USA (United States)	16 Mar 51	148UNTS15	101932
Belgium	UK Great Britain	06 Apr 51	110UNTS3	101496
USA (United States)	Yugoslavia	17 Apr 51	162UNTS173	102134
Honduras	USA (United States)	24 Apr 51	140UNTS287	101894
Ethiopia	USA (United States)	02 May 51	139UNTS85	101877
Ceylon (Sri Lanka)	USA (United States)	14 May 51	141UNTS159	101913
Pakistan	USA (United States)	23 May 51	134UNTS265	101805
Burma	WHO (World Health)	13 Jun 51	117UNTS115	101588
Saudi Arabia	USA (United States)	18 Jun 51	141UNTS67	101906
Multilateral		19 Jun 51	199UNTS67	102678
Sweden	USA (United States)	27 Jun 51	148UNTS77	101937
Burma	WHO (World Health)	09 Jul 51	107UNTS9	101463
Panama	USA (United States)	30 Jul 51	140UNTS321	101896
UK Great Britain	USA (United States)	30 Jul 51	105UNTS81	101455
Burma	Denmark	30 Jul 51	108UNTS167	101472

Indemnities and reimbursements (Cont.)

PARTY ONE	PARTY TWO	DATE	CITATION	NUMBER
Canada	USA (United States)	01 Aug 51	233UNTS109	103254
Multilateral		01 Aug 51	107UNTS19	101464
Multilateral		04 Aug 51	104UNTS197	101441
USA (United States)	Venezuela	10 Aug 51	140UNTS345	101898
Iraq	USA (United States)	16 Aug 51	147UNTS65	101929
Jordan	UN Relief Palestin	20 Aug 51	120UNTS277	200394
Denmark	USA (United States)	23 Aug 51	147UNTS49	101928
Multilateral		28 Aug 51	198UNTS17	102654
Japan	USA (United States)	28 Aug 51	147UNTS81	101930
Cuba	USA (United States)	28 Aug 51	140UNTS239	101891
Cuba	USA (United States)	28 Aug 51	134UNTS225	101802
UNICEF (Children)	Turkey	05 Sep 51	193UNTS55	102610
Burma	Netherlands	06 Sep 51	108UNTS187	101473
Japan	USA (United States)	08 Sep 51	136UNTS203	101834
Costa Rica	USA (United States)	11 Sep 51	234UNTS255	103288
Norway	USA (United States)	17 Sep 51	140UNTS313	101895
Korea, South	WHO (World Health)	19 Sep 51	109UNTS297	200366
UNICEF (Children)	UK Great Britain	02 Oct 51	104UNTS301	101448
WHO (World Health)	Thailand	04 Oct 51	109UNTS77	101492
El Salvador	USA (United States)	23 Oct 51	137UNTS43	101847
India	WHO (World Health)	23 Oct 51	109UNTS59	101491
Panama	WHO (World Health)	09 Nov 51	118UNTS43	101595
Italy	UK Great Britain	12 Nov 51	135UNTS55	101814
USA (United States)	Yugoslavia	14 Nov 51	174UNTS201	102286
USA (United States)	Uruguay	04 Dec 51	152UNTS41	102010
Guatemala	WHO (World Health)	17 Dec 51	120UNTS133	101619
Multilateral		20 Dec 51	163UNTS309	102152
Germany, West	USA (United States)	28 Dec 51	181UNTS45	102397
Guatemala	WHO (World Health)	29 Dec 51	124UNTS89	101668
Mexico	IBRD (World Bank)	11 Jan 52	159UNTS129	102086
Colombia	USA (United States)	12 Jan 52	168UNTS109	102216
Iran	USA (United States)	20 Jan 52	200UNTS191	102703
Costa Rica	WHO (World Health)	23 Jan 52	135UNTS265	101826
Greece	Yugoslavia	02 Feb 52	188UNTS311	102535
Peru	USA (United States)	04 Feb 52	121UNTS255	200403
UNICEF (Children)	UK Great Britain	04 Feb 52	120UNTS147	101620
Dominican Republic	WHO (World Health)	15 Feb 52	134UNTS291	101808
Dominican Republic	UNICEF (Children)	15 Feb 52	121UNTS43	101625
Ecuador	USA (United States)	20 Feb 52	177UNTS43	102308
Peru	USA (United States)	22 Feb 52	165UNTS31	102166
Honduras	USA (United States)	07 Mar 52	233UNTS151	103260
Cuba	USA (United States)	07 Mar 52	165UNTS11	102165
Taiwan	WHO (World Health)	07 Mar 52	128UNTS233	101723
France	USA (United States)	13 Mar 52	177UNTS21	102306
Brazil	USA (United States)	15 Mar 52	199UNTS221	102687
Iraq	USA (United States)	18 Mar 52	223UNTS131	103061
Ceylon (Sri Lanka)	WHO (World Health)	26 Mar 52	134UNTS341	200442
Denmark	WHO (World Health)	26 Mar 52	134UNTS285	101807
India	WHO (World Health)	02 Apr 52	131UNTS227	101743
Colombia	USA (United States)	17 Apr 52	174UNTS215	102287
Israel	USA (United States)	01 May 52	177UNTS89	102311
Israel	USA (United States)	09 May 52	177UNTS269	102326
Netherlands	USA (United States)	15 May 52	177UNTS233	102321
Korea, South	USA (United States)	24 May 52	179UNTS23	102353
Australia	Italy	24 May 52	161UNTS65	102123
Australia	USA (United States)	27 May 52	178UNTS113	102338
Mexico	WHO (World Health)	28 May 52	134UNTS319	101810
India	WHO (World Health)	04 Jun 52	135UNTS279	101827
Burma	WHO (World Health)	09 Jun 52	134UNTS273	101806
Belgium	UNICEF (Children)	17 Jun 52	171UNTS249	102228
India	WHO (World Health)	19 Jun 52	134UNTS307	101809
Norway	USA (United States)	21 Jun 52	236UNTS9	103313
Iraq	UK Great Britain	21 Jun 52	149UNTS221	101954
South Africa	USA (United States)	24 Jun 52	177UNTS241	102322
Norway	USA (United States)	27 Jun 52	184UNTS271	102452

Indemnities and reimbursements (Cont.)

PARTY ONE	PARTY TWO	DATE	CITATION	NUMBER
USA (United States)	Uruguay	30 Jun 52	207UNTS139	102804
Brazil	USA (United States)	30 Jun 52	185UNTS79	102460
Ethiopia	UK Great Britain	03 Jul 52	151UNTS207	101996
Jordan	UNICEF (Children)	08 Jul 52	173UNTS353	200503
Multilateral		11 Jul 52	170UNTS63	102222
Multilateral		11 Jul 52	171UNTS89	102225
UK Great Britain	USA (United States)	29 Jul 52	179UNTS129	102362
Japan	USA (United States)	11 Aug 52	212UNTS27	102862
Laos	UNICEF (Children)	15 Aug 52	161UNTS323	200491
UNICEF (Children)	Vietnam, South	29 Aug 52	161UNTS335	200492
Australia	Germany, West	29 Aug 52	184UNTS147	102446
Multilateral		05 Sep 52	247UNTS329	103479
Pakistan	USA (United States)	17 Sep 52	227UNTS77	103132
Mexico	Netherlands	13 Oct 52	163UNTS341	102154
Iraq	USA (United States)	23 Oct 52	212UNTS201	102872
Chile	WHO (World Health)	24 Oct 52	151UNTS339	102004
Burma	UK Great Britain	25 Oct 52	150UNTS237	101978
Chile	WHO (World Health)	04 Nov 52	150UNTS119	101966
Ethiopia	USA (United States)	05 Nov 52	184UNTS139	102445
Ceylon (Sri Lanka)	USA (United States)	17 Nov 52	180UNTS207	102386
Israel	Switzerland	19 Nov 52	232UNTS3	103226
Nicaragua	USA (United States)	19 Nov 52	186UNTS3	102478
Ceylon (Sri Lanka)	WHO (World Health)	21 Nov 52	161UNTS315	200490
USA (United States)	Yugoslavia	03 Dec 52	185UNTS183	102469
India	WHO (World Health)	11 Dec 52	158UNTS391	102073
United Arab Rep	UK Great Britain	05 Jan 53	207UNTS277	102810
USA (United States)	Venezuela	16 Jan 53	199UNTS287	102690
Saudi Arabia	USA (United States)	25 Jan 53	201UNTS3	102706
Dominican Republic	USA (United States)	06 Mar 53	199UNTS267	102689
France	Italy	14 Mar 53	284UNTS221	104140
Lebanon	USA (United States)	23 Mar 53	239UNTS45	103370
Japan	USA (United States)	23 Mar 53	185UNTS93	102461
Netherlands	United Nations	09 Apr 53	163UNTS89	102143
Ethiopia	UNICEF (Children)	27 Apr 53	213UNTS169	102885
Ethiopia	USA (United States)	29 Apr 53	224UNTS121	103073
El Salvador	USA (United States)	21 May 53	213UNTS15	102878
Ethiopia	USA (United States)	22 May 53	191UNTS59	102577
Cuba	USA (United States)	26 May 53	224UNTS75	103070
Switzerland	Yugoslavia	28 May 53	232UNTS45	103228
United Arab Rep	USA (United States)	18 Jun 53	204UNTS55	102749
Burma	Norway	22 Jun 53	174UNTS49	102277
Liberia	USA (United States)	23 Jun 53	213UNTS57	102880
Philippines	USA (United States)	26 Jun 53	213UNTS77	102881
Saudi Arabia	USA (United States)	29 Jun 53	206UNTS23	102784
Canada	USA (United States)	30 Jun 53	215UNTS103	102914
Multilateral		20 Jul 53	228UNTS41	103142
Multilateral		20 Jul 53	228UNTS3	103141
Canada	Mexico	27 Jul 53	192UNTS255	102604
USA (United States)	Venezuela	14 Aug 53	213UNTS99	102883
Germany, West	USA (United States)	20 Aug 53	224UNTS49	103069
Germany, East	USSR (Soviet Union)	22 Aug 53	221UNTS129	103005
Spain	USA (United States)	26 Sep 53	207UNTS61	102800
UNICEF (Children)	UK Great Britain	07 Oct 53	180UNTS59	102375
Greece	USA (United States)	12 Oct 53	191UNTS319	102589
Multilateral		17 Oct 53	184UNTS42	102438
Nicaragua	USA (United States)	19 Nov 53	206UNTS117	102787
Germany, West	USA (United States)	23 Nov 53	224UNTS107	103071
Multilateral		11 Dec 53	218UNTS255	102958
Belgium	Lebanon	24 Dec 53	539UNTS321	107842
Chile	USA (United States)	30 Dec 53	236UNTS41	103315
Belgium	Taiwan	13 Jan 54	223UNTS111	103059
UK Great Britain	USA (United States)	20 Jan 54	196UNTS95	102619
Japan	USA (United States)	21 Jan 54	223UNTS145	103063
Pakistan	United Nations	25 Jan 54	185UNTS213	102472
Denmark	Yugoslavia	27 Jan 54	193UNTS181	102615

PARTY ONE	PARTY TWO	DATE	CITATION	NUMBER
Indemnities and reimbursements (Cont.)				
France	Greece	08 Feb 54	225UNTS121	103094
France	Greece	08 Feb 54	225UNTS107	103093
Germany, West	USA (United States)	12 Feb 54	223UNTS153	103064
Multilateral		19 Feb 54	214UNTS51	102899
Multilateral		25 Feb 54	215UNTS249	102922
Multilateral		01 Mar 54	286UNTS265	104173
Japan	USA (United States)	08 Mar 54	232UNTS169	103236
Panama	USA (United States)	25 Mar 54	232UNTS289	103243
Italy	USA (United States)	31 Mar 54	235UNTS293	103311
Bulgaria	Czechoslovakia	13 Apr 54	501UNTS3	107314
Czechoslovakia	Hungary	16 Apr 54	504UNTS231	107360
Lebanon	Yugoslavia	17 Apr 54	602UNTS199	108713
Ethiopia	USA (United States)	21 Apr 54	232UNTS299	103244
Iraq	USA (United States)	21 Apr 54	222UNTS251	103032
Italy	USA (United States)	27 Apr 54	234UNTS103	103275
France	Netherlands	30 Apr 54	202UNTS115	102727
UNICEF (Children)	Spain	07 May 54	190UNTS357	200515
Netherlands	USA (United States)	07 May 54	213UNTS325	102895
Japan	USA (United States)	14 May 54	247UNTS273	103476
Pakistan	USA (United States)	19 May 54	202UNTS301	102736
Honduras	USA (United States)	20 May 54	222UNTS87	103025
Mexico	UNICEF (Children)	20 May 54	192UNTS3	102591
Multilateral		14 Jun 54	320UNTS209	104643
Jordan	USA (United States)	17 Jun 54	266UNTS137	103828
Turkey	USA (United States)	23 Jun 54	233UNTS189	103263
Chile	USA (United States)	28 Jun 54	233UNTS3	103246
Turkey	USA (United States)	01 Jul 54	234UNTS147	103280
Bulgaria	Romania	22 Jul 54	362UNTS101	105184
Multilateral		29 Jul 54	249UNTS45	103500
Greece	USA (United States)	30 Jul 54	234UNTS43	103272
Saudi Arabia	UK Great Britain	30 Jul 54	201UNTS317	102722
Norway	USA (United States)	06 Aug 54	222UNTS269	103034
Netherlands	USA (United States)	13 Aug 54	251UNTS91	103535
Ceylon (Sri Lanka)	USA (United States)	23 Aug 54	314UNTS297	104553
New Zealand	UNICEF (Children)	26 Aug 54	198UNTS173	102663
Libya	USA (United States)	09 Sep 54	224UNTS217	103078
El Salvador	USA (United States)	23 Sep 54	237UNTS91	103338
Multilateral		28 Sep 54	360UNTS117	105158
Australia	Vietnam, South	04 Oct 54	201UNTS349	102723
Germany, West	Netherlands	11 Oct 54	291UNTS9	104241
Germany, West	USA (United States)	15 Oct 54	239UNTS135	103375
USA (United States)	Yugoslavia	18 Oct 54	273UNTS163	103951
Canada	UK Great Britain	19 Oct 54	214UNTS309	102906
Multilateral		23 Oct 54	332UNTS157	104761
Germany, West	USA (United States)	27 Oct 54	234UNTS131	103278
Lebanon	UN Relief Palestin	26 Nov 54	202UNTS123	102728
Belgium	Israel	14 Dec 54	220UNTS49	102987
Netherlands	UNICEF (Children)	31 Dec 54	202UNTS135	102729
USSR (Soviet Union)	Yugoslavia	05 Jan 55	240UNTS225	103405
Peru	USA (United States)	07 Jan 55	261UNTS321	103730
Pakistan	USA (United States)	11 Jan 55	251UNTS111	103537
Austria	Yugoslavia	18 Jan 55	378UNTS31	105416
Korea, South	USA (United States)	29 Jan 55	239UNTS53	103371
Italy	USA (United States)	11 Feb 55	240UNTS87	103396
Germany, West	USA (United States)	18 Feb 55	247UNTS257	103474
Greece	UK Great Britain	24 Feb 55	209UNTS187	102827
Germany, West	Norway	18 Mar 55	209UNTS309	102832
Germany, West	USA (United States)	04 Apr 55	279UNTS73	104034
Germany, West	USA (United States)	14 Apr 55	263UNTS351	103782
USA (United States)	Vietnam, South	23 Apr 55	277UNTS279	104012
Czechoslovakia	Hungary	28 Apr 55	477UNTS197	106923
Cambodia	USA (United States)	16 May 55	263UNTS273	103777
Korea, South	USA (United States)	29 May 55	256UNTS263	103636
Japan	USA (United States)	03 Jun 55	270UNTS51	103891
Germany, West	USA (United States)	06 Jun 55	315UNTS155	104566

PARTY ONE	PARTY TWO	DATE	CITATION	NUMBER
Indemnities and reimbursements (Cont.)				
Guatemala	USA (United States)	18 Jun 55	262UNTS105	103740
Turkey	USA (United States)	29 Jun 55	269UNTS97	103878
Italy	USA (United States)	08 Jul 55	270UNTS29	103889
Ecuador	USA (United States)	08 Jul 55	265UNTS49	103806
Belgium	USA (United States)	15 Jul 55	223UNTS3	103040
Spain	USA (United States)	16 Jul 55	270UNTS211	103899
Germany, East	Romania	05 Aug 55	342UNTS229	104910
Czechoslovakia	Germany, East	30 Aug 55	504UNTS279	107361
Belgium	USA (United States)	31 Aug 55	223UNTS111	103041
Multilateral		15 Sep 55	254UNTS55	103593
Multilateral		29 Sep 55	222UNTS313	103037
Czechoslovakia	Germany, East	24 Oct 55	504UNTS173	107358
Philippines	USA (United States)	28 Oct 55	239UNTS165	103376
Austria	Israel	17 Nov 55	232UNTS153	103235
Guatemala	UNICEF (Children)	22 Nov 55	221UNTS305	103012
Bulgaria	Yugoslavia	11 Dec 55	378UNTS49	105417
Canada	Norway	20 Dec 55	305UNTS17	104408
Multilateral		04 Jan 56	256UNTS171	103627
Cuba	USA (United States)	10 Jan 56	240UNTS101	103398
Austria	Italy	23 Jan 56	393UNTS97	105653
Hungary	Romania	03 Feb 56	362UNTS233	105190
India	USA (United States)	03 Feb 56	272UNTS75	103932
Israel	Italy	24 Feb 56	316UNTS97	104580
Italy	USA (United States)	27 Feb 56	291UNTS287	104260
Nicaragua	USA (United States)	19 Mar 56	275UNTS231	103984
Bulgaria	Yugoslavia	23 Mar 56	367UNTS213	105230
France	USA (United States)	23 Mar 56	278UNTS131	104029
Belgium	Israel	26 Mar 56	260UNTS3	103702
Japan	USA (United States)	13 Apr 56	273UNTS223	103953
Belgium	Germany, West	14 Apr 56	344UNTS103	104945
Bulgaria	Greece	19 Apr 56	594UNTS131	108600
Japan	Philippines	09 May 56	285UNTS3	104148
Multilateral		19 May 56	399UNTS189	105742
Pakistan	USA (United States)	28 May 56	269UNTS15	103868
Bulgaria	Yugoslavia	16 Jun 56	391UNTS3	105613
Norway	Sweden	29 Jun 56	262UNTS335	103759
Burma	USA (United States)	30 Jun 56	281UNTS65	104070
Bolivia	USA (United States)	30 Jun 56	271UNTS243	103919
Israel	Luxembourg	26 Jul 56	550UNTS239	108020
Netherlands	USA (United States)	16 Aug 56	279UNTS3	104031
Guatemala	Honduras	22 Aug 56	263UNTS49	103767
Denmark	WHO (World Health)	03 Sep 56	258UNTS103	103674
Italy	Spain	05 Sep 56	302UNTS195	104359
Japan	USA (United States)	05 Sep 56	277UNTS267	104011
Pakistan	USA (United States)	10 Sep 56	277UNTS259	104010
Multilateral		11 Sep 56	266UNTS221	103832
Multilateral		25 Sep 56	334UNTS13	104766
Multilateral		25 Sep 56	334UNTS89	104767
Germany, West	Netherlands	28 Sep 56	327UNTS185	104722
Argentina	USA (United States)	03 Oct 56	279UNTS13	104032
Czechoslovakia	Germany, East	06 Oct 56	501UNTS109	107315
Czechoslovakia	Hungary	13 Oct 56	300UNTS177	104337
Portugal	USA (United States)	07 Nov 56	277UNTS133	104003
Austria	USA (United States)	21 Nov 56	290UNTS181	104237
Japan	USA (United States)	23 Nov 56	324UNTS177	104685
Dominican Republic	USA (United States)	07 Dec 56	263UNTS193	103774
Germany, East	Romania	08 Dec 56	362UNTS189	105188
Canada	Germany, West	10 Dec 56	392UNTS3	105633
Germany, West	USA (United States)	12 Dec 56	280UNTS63	104051
Germany, West	USA (United States)	12 Dec 56	280UNTS71	104052
Israel	Netherlands	18 Dec 56	276UNTS153	103991
Australia	Thailand	20 Dec 56	265UNTS149	103810
Multilateral		21 Dec 56	427UNTS81	106147
Australia	USA (United States)	31 Dec 56	266UNTS89	103823
Iran	USA (United States)	16 Jan 57	308UNTS147	104460

Indemnities and reimbursements (Cont.)

PARTY ONE	PARTY TWO	DATE	CITATION	NUMBER
Germany, West	Norway	29 Jan 57	353UNTS39	105037
Germany, West	Netherlands	29 Jan 57	314UNTS173	104548
Germany, East	Poland	01 Feb 57	319UNTS115	104632
Multilateral		09 Feb 57	314UNTS105	104546
Netherlands	USA (United States)	15 Feb 57	287UNTS239	104190
Poland	USSR (Soviet Union)	05 Mar 57	274UNTS133	103963
Spain	USA (United States)	09 Mar 57	283UNTS89	104108
Dominican Republic	USA (United States)	09 Mar 57	279UNTS249	104044
Netherlands	Yugoslavia	13 Mar 57	327UNTS227	104723
Netherlands	USA (United States)	03 Apr 57	410UNTS193	105904
Canada	Netherlands	13 Apr 57	316UNTS223	104588
Canada	Denmark	17 Apr 57	316UNTS207	104586
Canada	Norway	17 Apr 57	316UNTS215	104587
Peru	USA (United States)	17 Apr 57	283UNTS3	104102
Ecuador	USA (United States)	24 Apr 57	284UNTS3	104124
Germany, West	USA (United States)	01 May 57	284UNTS85	104131
Japan	USA (United States)	08 May 57	318UNTS257	104621
Austria	USA (United States)	10 May 57	283UNTS33	104104
Hungary	Netherlands	28 May 57	334UNTS291	104773
Belgium	Hungary	01 Jun 57	291UNTS17	104242
Bulgaria	Czechoslovakia	03 Jun 57	292UNTS3	104261
Bulgaria	Yugoslavia	04 Jun 57	349UNTS35	105008
Germany, West	USA (United States)	07 Jun 57	346UNTS241	104984
Finland	India	14 Jun 57	277UNTS327	104016
Multilateral		15 Jun 57	550UNTS45	108008
Iraq	USA (United States)	16 Jun 57	284UNTS39	104127
Jordan	USA (United States)	27 Jun 57	288UNTS269	104209
Finland	United Nations	27 Jun 57	271UNTS135	103913
United Nations	Sweden	01 Jul 57	271UNTS187	103914
New Zealand	UK Great Britain	04 Jul 57	402UNTS109	105780
Norway	United Nations	09 Jul 57	271UNTS223	103917
Germany, West	Netherlands	10 Jul 57	339UNTS97	104848
Denmark	United Nations	16 Jul 57	274UNTS81	103959
Canada	United Nations	29 Jul 57	274UNTS47	103957
Taiwan	USA (United States)	30 Jul 57	300UNTS61	104331
Morocco	UNICEF (Children)	31 Jul 57	282UNTS99	104095
Greece	USA (United States)	05 Aug 57	290UNTS167	104235
Brazil	United Nations	13 Aug 57	274UNTS199	103966
India	United Nations	14 Aug 57	274UNTS233	103968
Turkey	UK Great Britain	16 Aug 57	310UNTS21	104482
Czechoslovakia	USSR (Soviet Union)	31 Aug 57	308UNTS3	104456
Ceylon (Sri Lanka)	China People's Rep	19 Sep 57	337UNTS169	104822
New Zealand	UK Great Britain	20 Sep 57	287UNTS105	104180
France	USA (United States)	23 Sep 57	293UNTS297	104297
United Nations	Yugoslavia	01 Oct 57	277UNTS191	104006
Germany, East	Hungary	25 Oct 57	408UNTS156	105869
Germany, East	Hungary	30 Oct 57	408UNTS4	105867
Germany, East	Hungary	13 Nov 57	407UNTS216	105866
Hungary	Yugoslavia	20 Nov 57	477UNTS267	106925
El Salvador	USA (United States)	21 Nov 57	303UNTS19	104369
Norway	USSR (Soviet Union)	22 Nov 57	309UNTS269	104476
Germany, East	USSR (Soviet Union)	28 Nov 57	305UNTS113	104419
Czechoslovakia	USSR (Soviet Union)	04 Dec 57	313UNTS291	104537
Hungary	Yugoslavia	06 Dec 57	519UNTS215	107509
Germany, West	USA (United States)	10 Dec 57	307UNTS59	104442
Italy	Yugoslavia	12 Dec 57	386UNTS293	105549
Bulgaria	USSR (Soviet Union)	12 Dec 57	317UNTS217	104606
Multilateral		13 Dec 57	359UNTS273	105146
Korea, North	USSR (Soviet Union)	16 Dec 57	301UNTS301	104349
Hungary	Romania	17 Dec 57	477UNTS303	106926
Ethiopia	USA (United States)	26 Dec 57	307UNTS71	104443
Poland	USSR (Soviet Union)	28 Dec 57	320UNTS3	104638
Belgium	Germany, West	17 Jan 58	328UNTS173	104735
Czechoslovakia	Poland	31 Jan 58	431UNTS99	106214
Belgium	Netherlands	04 Feb 58	330UNTS83	104740

Indemnities and reimbursements (Cont.)

PARTY ONE	PARTY TWO	DATE	CITATION	NUMBER
Bulgaria	Netherlands	07 Feb 58	335UNTS45	104777
Czechoslovakia	Hungary	12 Mar 58	408UNTS178	105870
Bulgaria	Hungary	13 Mar 58	438UNTS173	106316
Poland	USSR (Soviet Union)	18 Mar 58	340UNTS89	104861
Belgium	Japan	18 Mar 58	303UNTS149	104378
Czechoslovakia	Romania	25 Mar 58	339UNTS77	104846
Sweden	USSR (Soviet Union)	28 Mar 58	428UNTS321	106184
Romania	USSR (Soviet Union)	03 Apr 58	313UNTS167	104535
Hungary	USSR (Soviet Union)	24 Apr 58	408UNTS118	105868
Hungary	Poland	08 May 58	408UNTS212	105872
Italy	USA (United States)	08 May 58	316UNTS177	104584
Canada	USA (United States)	12 May 58	316UNTS151	104582
Lebanon	UK Great Britain	19 May 58	327UNTS43	104716
Germany, East	Hungary	14 Jun 58	407UNTS78	105861
Multilateral		26 Jun 58	324UNTS97	104679
Ecuador	USA (United States)	27 Jun 58	317UNTS51	104593
Albania	USSR (Soviet Union)	30 Jun 58	328UNTS3	104729
Philippines	USA (United States)	30 Jun 58	321UNTS51	104653
Germany, East	Romania	15 Jul 58	395UNTS3	105681
Hungary	USSR (Soviet Union)	15 Jul 58	322UNTS3	104656
Mongolia	USSR (Soviet Union)	25 Aug 58	322UNTS105	104657
Austria	Bulgaria	12 Sep 58	353UNTS3	105036
United Arab Rep	USSR (Soviet Union)	18 Sep 58	338UNTS29	104831
Hungary	Romania	07 Oct 58	416UNTS199	106004
Turkey	USA (United States)	14 Oct 58	336UNTS145	104803
Czechoslovakia	Romania	25 Oct 58	417UNTS37	106006
Japan	USA (United States)	03 Nov 58	341UNTS83	104879
France	Israel	12 Nov 58	345UNTS79	104960
Bulgaria	Romania	03 Dec 58	417UNTS133	106007
Multilateral		03 Dec 58	416UNTS51	105995
Multilateral		15 Dec 58	351UNTS159	105022
Korea, South	USA (United States)	18 Dec 58	325UNTS233	104702
Haiti	USA (United States)	24 Dec 58	338UNTS265	104840
UK Great Britain	USA (United States)	30 Dec 58	338UNTS281	104841
Israel	Switzerland	31 Dec 58	377UNTS305	105408
Portugal	USA (United States)	12 Jan 59	343UNTS49	104921
United Arab Rep	USA (United States)	13 Jan 59	358UNTS3	105122
Albania	Czechoslovakia	16 Jan 59	363UNTS195	105208
Hungary	Poland	06 Mar 59	432UNTS3	106216
Iraq	USSR (Soviet Union)	16 Mar 59	346UNTS107	104979
Bulgaria	Hungary	03 Apr 59	438UNTS269	106319
Ghana	USA (United States)	09 Apr 59	342UNTS21	104897
Italy	Netherlands	17 Apr 59	474UNTS207	106883
Hungary	USSR (Soviet Union)	17 Apr 59	439UNTS41	106324
IAEA (Atom Energy)	USSR (Soviet Union)	11 May 59	339UNTS341	104853
IAEA (Atom Energy)	USA (United States)	11 May 59	339UNTS359	104855
IAEA (Atom Energy)	UK Great Britain	11 May 59	339UNTS351	104854
Japan	Vietnam, South	13 May 59	373UNTS149	105318
Ethiopia	Yugoslavia	06 Jun 59	386UNTS243	105544
Peru	USA (United States)	15 Jun 59	346UNTS279	104987
Greece	Yugoslavia	18 Jun 59	368UNTS81	105236
Iceland	USA (United States)	23 Jun 59	354UNTS3	105048
Germany, West	UK Great Britain	03 Aug 59	502UNTS197	107331
Italy	USA (United States)	18 Aug 59	361UNTS11	105169
Denmark	India	16 Sep 59	405UNTS13	105820
Israel	South Africa	18 Sep 59	373UNTS47	105314
Bulgaria	Czechoslovakia	19 Sep 59	355UNTS77	105074
New Zealand	UK Great Britain	21 Sep 59	401UNTS51	105762
Korea, South	USA (United States)	01 Oct 59	358UNTS115	105129
Multilateral		09 Oct 59	376UNTS382	105391
Belgium	USA (United States)	27 Nov 59	366UNTS331	105221
Turkey	USA (United States)	30 Nov 59	361UNTS107	105174
Taiwan	USA (United States)	02 Dec 59	361UNTS115	105175
Multilateral		14 Dec 59	422UNTS33	106067
Multilateral		14 Dec 59	422UNTS57	106068

PARTY ONE	PARTY TWO	DATE	CITATION	NUMBER
Indemnities and reimbursements (Cont.)				
Colombia	USA (United States)	11 Jan 60	371UNTS37	105268
Albania	Hungary	12 Jan 60	520UNTS3	107511
Japan	USA (United States)	19 Jan 60	373UNTS207	105321
Austria	Czechoslovakia	23 Jan 60	495UNTS99	107241
Poland	Yugoslavia	06 Feb 60	521UNTS37	107517
Italy	Yugoslavia	12 Feb 60	379UNTS77	105434
Spain	USA (United States)	13 Feb 60	371UNTS185	105279
Greece	USA (United States)	15 Feb 60	377UNTS95	105397
Chile	USA (United States)	19 Feb 60	371UNTS255	105282
Brazil	USA (United States)	27 Feb 60	384UNTS131	105515
Indonesia	USSR (Soviet Union)	28 Feb 60	392UNTS173	105643
Turkey	USA (United States)	02 Mar 60	372UNTS37	105286
Germany, West	USA (United States)	16 Mar 60	371UNTS101	105272
New Zealand	USA (United States)	23 Mar 60	371UNTS147	105276
Belgium	Switzerland	24 Mar 60	416UNTS81	105996
Ireland	USA (United States)	24 Mar 60	371UNTS237	105280
Argentina	USA (United States)	01 Apr 60	371UNTS245	105281
Denmark	USA (United States)	12 Apr 60	373UNTS9	105311
Japan	USA (United States)	15 Apr 60	372UNTS267	105303
Guatemala	USA (United States)	23 Apr 60	373UNTS23	105312
Canada	Norway	25 Apr 60	470UNTS109	106801
Poland	Yugoslavia	05 May 60	423UNTS229	106095
Lebanon	UN Special Fund	07 May 60	360UNTS225	105160
Argentina	USA (United States)	23 May 60	377UNTS3	105392
Germany, East	USSR (Soviet Union)	24 May 60	392UNTS205	105645
Belgium	Netherlands	20 Jun 60	423UNTS19	106084
Somalia	UK Great Britain	26 Jun 60	374UNTS347	105348
IAEA (Atom Energy)	USA (United States)	28 Jun 60	374UNTS133	105333
Norway	USA (United States)	06 Jul 60	378UNTS25	105415
Italy	USA (United States)	07 Jul 60	380UNTS143	105455
Switzerland	United Arab Rep	14 Jul 60	497UNTS161	107268
Cambodia	USA (United States)	15 Jul 60	380UNTS129	105453
Spain	USA (United States)	21 Jul 60	393UNTS289	105663
Japan	Pakistan	30 Jul 60	384UNTS63	105511
Argentina	USA (United States)	02 Aug 60	384UNTS105	105514
Ghana	USSR (Soviet Union)	04 Aug 60	399UNTS61	105734
Canada	UK Great Britain	05 Aug 60	470UNTS133	106804
Mexico	USA (United States)	15 Aug 60	402UNTS177	105786
Cyprus	UK Great Britain	16 Aug 60	382UNTS207	105481
Japan	Thailand	24 Aug 60	384UNTS73	105512
Canada	USA (United States)	31 Aug 60	393UNTS247	105659
Multilateral		19 Sep 60	444UNTS259	106371
Multilateral		19 Sep 60	419UNTS125	106032
France	USA (United States)	19 Sep 60	400UNTS21	105745
Portugal	USA (United States)	26 Sep 60	393UNTS257	105660
UK Great Britain	USA (United States)	14 Oct 60	398UNTS165	105721
Nigeria	USA (United States)	19 Oct 60	394UNTS113	105672
Cuba	Romania	28 Oct 60	457UNTS9	106574
Kuwait	United Nations	31 Oct 60	391UNTS295	200581
Czechoslovakia	Germany, East	08 Nov 60	424UNTS71	106100
Korea, South	USA (United States)	18 Nov 60	400UNTS49	105747
Finland	Sweden	21 Nov 60	383UNTS125	105498
Argentina	Uruguay	23 Nov 60	0UNTS0	109519
Norway	USA (United States)	29 Nov 60	404UNTS251	105815
Nepal	UNICEF (Children)	12 Dec 60	382UNTS273	105488
Multilateral		13 Dec 60	523UNTS117	107557
Israel	USA (United States)	19 Dec 60	401UNTS195	105772
UK Great Britain	USA (United States)	20 Jan 61	402UNTS153	105783
Brazil	USA (United States)	17 Mar 61	406UNTS241	105853
Multilateral		30 Mar 61	520UNTS151	107515
USA (United States)	Vietnam, South	04 Apr 61	405UNTS77	105824
Cuba	Czechoslovakia	05 Apr 61	442UNTS201	106350
UK Great Britain	USA (United States)	06 Apr 61	404UNTS215	105812
Netherlands	Spain	08 Apr 61	482UNTS193	106996
USA (United States)	Yugoslavia	19 Apr 61	409UNTS163	105883

PARTY ONE	PARTY TWO	DATE	CITATION	NUMBER
Indemnities and reimbursements (Cont.)				
Australia	USA (United States)	05 Jun 61	409UNTS279	105892
Multilateral		14 Jun 61	415UNTS4	105979
Czechoslovakia	Poland	04 Jul 61	436UNTS189	106295
Austria	Germany, West	19 Jul 61	414UNTS211	105974
Mexico	United Nations	18 Aug 61	404UNTS297	105817
Ghana	United Nations	29 Aug 61	406UNTS117	105843
Tunisia	USSR (Soviet Union)	30 Aug 61	437UNTS243	106310
Liberia	Switzerland	31 Aug 61	559UNTS215	108160
Hungary	Romania	07 Sep 61	519UNTS141	107506
Canada	USA (United States)	23 Sep 61	421UNTS79	106053
Germany, West	UK Great Britain	26 Sep 61	424UNTS201	106108
Japan	United Nations	04 Oct 61	410UNTS133	105900
Austria	Israel	10 Oct 61	448UNTS161	106430
Canada	USA (United States)	17 Oct 61	426UNTS201	106138
Sweden	USA (United States)	24 Oct 61	494UNTS141	107231
Czechoslovakia	Hungary	02 Nov 61	438UNTS3	106313
Austria	Czechoslovakia	10 Nov 61	455UNTS337	106550
United Arab Rep	UK Great Britain	14 Nov 61	449UNTS129	106455
Bulgaria	Poland	04 Dec 61	484UNTS3	107019
Poland	Romania	25 Jan 62	468UNTS3	106770
UK Great Britain	Zambia	30 Jan 62	590UNTS173	108553
Multilateral		20 Feb 62	597UNTS159	108644
USSR (Soviet Union)	Yugoslavia	24 Feb 62	471UNTS195	106833
Cyprus	USA (United States)	02 Mar 62	445UNTS189	106386
Multilateral		23 Mar 62	470UNTS25	106793
IAEA (Atom Energy)	USA (United States)	30 Mar 62	442UNTS49	106338
Netherlands	USA (United States)	24 Apr 62	436UNTS93	106289
Multilateral		14 May 62	544UNTS81	107911
Multilateral		14 May 62	544UNTS39	107910
Greece	United Nations	18 May 62	429UNTS61	106190
New Zealand	USA (United States)	08 Jun 62	458UNTS209	106602
Multilateral		27 Jun 62	463UNTS3	106688
Multilateral		27 Jun 62	463UNTS17	106690
Multilateral		25 Jul 62	506UNTS177	107387
Costa Rica	Israel	31 Jul 62	484UNTS155	107024
Indonesia	Netherlands	15 Aug 62	437UNTS273	106311
UK Great Britain	USA (United States)	29 Aug 62	449UNTS177	106459
Germany, West	Netherlands	30 Aug 62	500UNTS3	107303
Austria	Czechoslovakia	22 Sep 62	495UNTS157	107244
Denmark	Germany, West	03 Oct 62	450UNTS291	106475
Dominican Republic	USA (United States)	25 Oct 62	459UNTS247	106627
Saudi Arabia	USA (United States)	13 Nov 62	488UNTS175	107127
Japan	UK Great Britain	14 Nov 62	478UNTS29	106934
Czechoslovakia	Poland	16 Nov 62	526UNTS3	107597
France	UK Great Britain	29 Nov 62	453UNTS325	106534
UK Great Britain	Vietnam, South	30 Nov 62	470UNTS51	106794
Austria	France	30 Nov 62	463UNTS173	106701
Laos	USSR (Soviet Union)	01 Dec 62	472UNTS3	106834
Israel	USA (United States)	10 Dec 62	484UNTS283	107038
Austria	Yugoslavia	11 Dec 62	546UNTS3	107938
Multilateral		17 Dec 62	486UNTS119	107076
New Zealand	Western Samoa	24 Jan 63	499UNTS21	107290
Ethiopia	USA (United States)	25 Jan 63	473UNTS27	106851
Hungary	Korea, North	29 Mar 63	577UNTS219	108379
Romania	USA (United States)	02 Apr 63	474UNTS95	106874
UK Great Britain	USA (United States)	06 Apr 63	474UNTS49	106871
Sweden	UK Great Britain	26 Apr 63	590UNTS117	108551
Australia	USA (United States)	09 May 63	475UNTS331	106897
Australia	USA (United States)	09 May 63	469UNTS55	106784
Greece	UK Great Britain	09 May 63	398UNTS179	105722
Belgium	Netherlands	13 May 63	540UNTS3	107843
Australia	United Nations	13 May 63	463UNTS187	106702
Denmark	India	15 May 63	616UNTS23	108889
Denmark	India	15 May 63	616UNTS49	108891
Denmark	India	15 May 63	616UNTS39	108890

PARTY ONE	PARTY TWO	DATE	CITATION	NUMBER
Indemnities and reimbursements (Cont.)				
Laos	UK Great Britain	17 May 63	475UNTS155	106891
Australia	UK Great Britain	06 Jun 63	472UNTS157	106838
Multilateral		19 Jun 63	482UNTS19	106988
Canada	Nigeria	03 Jul 63	529UNTS57	107656
IBRD (World Bank)	Tunisia	03 Jul 63	480UNTS209	106970
Mexico	USA (United States)	29 Aug 63	505UNTS185	107374
Multilateral		23 Sep 63	488UNTS99	107122
Germany, West	Greece	26 Sep 63	550UNTS203	108017
Czechoslovakia	Yugoslavia	05 Oct 63	504UNTS151	107356
Multilateral		17 Oct 63	525UNTS75	107585
Czechoslovakia	Hungary	22 Oct 63	514UNTS95	107444
Netherlands	Portugal	22 Nov 63	492UNTS31	107185
Romania	Yugoslavia	30 Nov 63	512UNTS2	107438
Australia	India	03 Dec 63	486UNTS279	107082
IAEA (Atom Energy)	Yugoslavia	07 Dec 63	501UNTS273	107322
Chile	IBRD (World Bank)	18 Dec 63	504UNTS29	107352
New Zealand	Western Samoa	31 Dec 63	521UNTS163	107519
Czechoslovakia	Yugoslavia	20 Jan 64	538UNTS197	107816
Canada	USA (United States)	22 Jan 64	530UNTS89	107674
Finland	IAEA (Atom Energy)	27 Jan 64	501UNTS213	107319
Mexico	USA (United States)	14 Feb 64	524UNTS197	107574
UNESCO (Educ/Cult)	Yugoslavia	27 Feb 64	489UNTS257	107143
Multilateral		28 Feb 64	501UNTS245	107321
Canada	USA (United States)	06 Mar 64	524UNTS255	107577
Italy	United Nations	18 Mar 64	491UNTS21	107171
Multilateral		08 Apr 64	501UNTS221	107320
Norway	Yugoslavia	15 Apr 64	602UNTS177	108712
Afghanistan	United Nations	28 Apr 64	494UNTS77	107227
Germany, West	Ireland	13 May 64	553UNTS87	108071
Multilateral		25 May 64	620UNTS149	108953
Netherlands	NATO (North Atlan)	25 May 64	544UNTS237	107920
Multilateral		26 May 64	541UNTS271	200613
Cuba	Czechoslovakia	03 Jun 64	527UNTS205	107626
Multilateral		15 Jun 64	573UNTS85	108324
IAEA (Atom Energy)	USA (United States)	15 Jun 64	525UNTS3	107580
United Nations	Togo	03 Jul 64	502UNTS287	107334
Multilateral		10 Jul 64	613UNTS127	108853
Austria	Netherlands	23 Jul 64	544UNTS265	107921
Netherlands	Turkey	19 Aug 64	521UNTS197	107523
Chad	Israel	07 Oct 64	630UNTS175	108969
Israel	USSR (Soviet Union)	07 Oct 64	516UNTS59	107471
UNESCO (Educ/Cult)	USA (United States)	16 Oct 64	550UNTS23	108006
Argentina	Paraguay	21 Oct 64	635UNTS177	109081
Czechoslovakia	Mongolia	21 Oct 64	545UNTS91	107926
Chile	USA (United States)	27 Oct 64	532UNTS347	107727
Multilateral		07 Nov 64	548UNTS3	107965
Ethiopia	USA (United States)	25 Nov 64	532UNTS125	107715
Czechoslovakia	United Arab Rep	26 Nov 64	545UNTS11	107923
Netherlands	Nigeria	04 Dec 64	545UNTS155	107931
Trinidad/Tobago	USA (United States)	05 Dec 64	535UNTS331	107788
Denmark	Pakistan	12 Dec 64	636UNTS313	109107
Germany, West	Thailand	23 Dec 64	525UNTS177	107589
Germany, West	Thailand	23 Dec 64	525UNTS201	107592
UK Great Britain	USSR (Soviet Union)	06 Jan 65	543UNTS77	107897
Belgium	Sweden	11 Jan 65	533UNTS157	107741
Belgium	Luxembourg	14 Jan 65	620UNTS3	108949
Germany, West	Jamaica	03 Feb 65	531UNTS143	107700
Mexico	USA (United States)	27 Feb 65	542UNTS181	107889
Mexico	USA (United States)	27 Feb 65	546UNTS135	107940
Multilateral		18 Mar 65	575UNTS159	108359
Canada	USA (United States)	25 Mar 65	607UNTS141	108802
Austria	Hungary	09 Apr 65	638UNTS135	109133
Australia	Germany, West	21 Apr 65	598UNTS25	108654
Multilateral		02 Jun 65	551UNTS2	108030
Finland	USSR (Soviet Union)	04 Jun 65	560UNTS169	108173

PARTY ONE	PARTY TWO	DATE	CITATION	NUMBER
Indemnities and reimbursements (Cont.)				
Saudi Arabia	USA (United States)	05 Jun 65	548UNTS285	107984
Multilateral		18 Jun 65	573UNTS3	108320
Multilateral		23 Jun 65	548UNTS241	107981
Multilateral		02 Jul 65	592UNTS215	108575
Multilateral		24 Sep 65	556UNTS141	108124
Austria	Yugoslavia	19 Nov 65	591UNTS3	108556
France	UK Great Britain	19 Nov 65	561UNTS19	108178
Netherlands	Zambia	17 Dec 65	631UNTS311	109000
Germany, West	USA (United States)	18 Dec 65	579UNTS193	108407
Italy	USA (United States)	27 Dec 65	574UNTS145	108347
Panama	USA (United States)	15 Feb 66	586UNTS27	108494
Spain	USA (United States)	14 Apr 66	579UNTS173	108406
Romania	Tunisia	21 Apr 66	604UNTS65	108744
Spain	USA (United States)	21 Apr 66	580UNTS231	108426
Multilateral		04 May 66	575UNTS49	108354
Multilateral		17 May 66	571UNTS89	108302
Denmark	Iran	14 Jun 66	597UNTS283	108652
Argentina	Bolivia	15 Jun 66	0UNTS0	109518
Multilateral		20 Jun 66	573UNTS41	108322
Israel	UK Great Britain	05 Jul 66	630UNTS189	108971
Korea, South	USA (United States)	24 Sep 66	607UNTS157	108803
Tunisia	USA (United States)	26 Sep 66	616UNTS259	108900
IAEA (Atom Energy)	USA (United States)	26 Sep 66	589UNTS3	108532
Greece	UK Great Britain	12 Oct 66	578UNTS33	108385
IAEA (Atom Energy)	USA (United States)	09 Dec 66	589UNTS55	108535
UK Great Britain	USA (United States)	30 Dec 66	603UNTS273	108737
UK Great Britain	USA (United States)	30 Dec 66	603UNTS245	108736
UK Great Britain	USA (United States)	01 Jan 67	604UNTS3	108738
Finland	United Nations	16 Jan 67	588UNTS153	108522
Trinidad/Tobago	UK Great Britain	23 Jan 67	605UNTS277	108767
Denmark	France	15 Feb 67	604UNTS247	108754
Denmark	Tanzania	05 Apr 67	604UNTS19	108740
Argentina	Uruguay	30 May 67	0UNTS0	109521
Multilateral		21 Jun 67	598UNTS2	108653
Netherlands	Romania	20 Jul 67	633UNTS21	109032
Italy	Romania	08 Aug 67	642UNTS213	109175
Denmark	Zambia	17 Oct 67	620UNTS239	108960
Iran	United Nations	15 Feb 68	631UNTS103	108990
Czechoslovakia	Hungary	27 Feb 68	640UNTS49	109154
Inter-Am Devel Bnk	UN Special Fund	16 Jul 68	640UNTS305	200640
Balance of payments				
Netherlands	UK Great Britain	14 Jun 40	2UNTS251	200018
France	Netherlands	14 Jun 40	2UNTS263	200019
Netherlands	UK Great Britain	25 Jul 40	2UNTS275	200020
UK Great Britain	USSR (Soviet Union)	16 Aug 41	91UNTS341	200269
Multilateral		21 Oct 43	2UNTS281	200021
Brazil	USA (United States)	25 Nov 43	102UNTS227	200305
Belgium	UK Great Britain	05 Oct 44	5UNTS227	200031
Sweden	UK Great Britain	06 Mar 45	5UNTS241	200032
Sweden	UK Great Britain	06 Mar 45	82UNTS219	101095
France	UK Great Britain	27 Mar 45	98UNTS227	200274
Denmark	UK Great Britain	16 Aug 45	5UNTS251	200033
Netherlands	UK Great Britain	07 Sep 45	2UNTS325	200024
Belgium	Norway	23 Oct 45	16UNTS311	200107
Netherlands	Switzerland	24 Oct 45	3UNTS73	100025
Czechoslovakia	UK Great Britain	01 Nov 45	5UNTS15	100062
Norway	UK Great Britain	08 Nov 45	5UNTS27	100063
Finland	Norway	27 Nov 45	17UNTS247	100279
Netherlands	Sweden	30 Nov 45	2UNTS27	100019
UK Great Britain	USA (United States)	06 Dec 45	126UNTS13	101679
Czechoslovakia	Norway	13 Dec 45	17UNTS261	100280
Multilateral		27 Dec 45	2UNTS39	100020
Denmark	Netherlands	31 Jan 46	3UNTS3	100021
Canada	UK Great Britain	06 Mar 46	20UNTS13	100312

PARTY ONE	PARTY TWO	DATE	CITATION	NUMBER
Balance of payments (Cont.)				
France	Norway	06 Mar 46	15UNTS13	100227
Switzerland	UK Great Britain	12 Mar 46	6UNTS107	100070
Portugal	UK Great Britain	16 Apr 46	6UNTS119	100071
France	Greece	24 Apr 46	91UNTS83	101243
France	USA (United States)	28 May 46	84UNTS151	101125
Norway	Yugoslavia	30 Aug 46	15UNTS163	100232
Czechoslovakia	USA (United States)	14 Nov 46	7UNTS119	100094
Norway	Sweden	22 Nov 46	15UNTS171	100233
Norway	Poland	03 Dec 46	15UNTS203	100234
Hungary	Yugoslavia	23 Dec 46	113UNTS125	101549
Norway	USSR (Soviet Union)	27 Dec 46	17UNTS283	100282
Spain	UK Great Britain	28 Mar 47	66UNTS91	100849
Denmark	Norway	15 Apr 47	12UNTS323	100191
Bulgaria	Denmark	09 May 47	74UNTS139	100960
Poland	Yugoslavia	24 May 47	115UNTS37	101557
Poland	Yugoslavia	24 May 47	115UNTS69	101558
New Zealand	UK Great Britain	27 May 47	17UNTS211	100277
Sweden	USA (United States)	24 Jun 47	36UNTS25	100565
United Arab Rep	UK Great Britain	30 Jun 47	93UNTS165	101299
UK Great Britain	Uruguay	15 Jul 47	71UNTS179	100918
Norway	Switzerland	15 Jul 47	12UNTS351	100192
Hungary	Yugoslavia	24 Jul 47	114UNTS3	101554
Czechoslovakia	Greece	30 Jul 47	185UNTS115	102463
Taiwan	Italy	30 Jul 47	12UNTS377	100194
Bulgaria	Yugoslavia	22 Aug 47	111UNTS241	101538
Multilateral		19 Sep 47	30UNTS269	100462
Romania	Yugoslavia	30 Sep 47	116UNTS71	101570
Multilateral		05 Oct 47	34UNTS23	100525
Multilateral		30 Oct 47	55UNTS188	100814
Belgium	UK Great Britain	14 Nov 47	25UNTS269	100367
Multilateral		18 Nov 47	17UNTS89	100269
United Arab Rep	UK Great Britain	05 Jan 48	77UNTS3	100988
Pakistan	UK Great Britain	21 Feb 48	134UNTS128	101797
Denmark	Hungary	28 Feb 48	85UNTS35	101144
Hungary	Yugoslavia	18 Mar 48	113UNTS219	101552
Hungary	Yugoslavia	18 Mar 48	113UNTS201	101551
India	Pakistan	31 Mar 48	54UNTS33	100793
Poland	Yugoslavia	12 Apr 48	115UNTS167	101563
Denmark	Norway	21 Apr 48	18UNTS139	100284
Ceylon (Sri Lanka)	UK Great Britain	30 Apr 48	182UNTS2	102421
France	Ireland	06 May 48	558UNTS170	108141
Brazil	UK Great Britain	21 May 48	66UNTS121	100851
Czechoslovakia	Yugoslavia	24 May 48	112UNTS183	101543
Peru	UK Great Britain	20 Jul 48	66UNTS197	100855
Ireland	UK Great Britain	31 Jul 48	86UNTS37	101151
Ireland	Netherlands	02 Sep 48	558UNTS249	108145
France	USA (United States)	16 Sep 48	84UNTS185	101129
Burma	UK Great Britain	12 Oct 48	71UNTS255	100923
Austria	Denmark	29 Nov 48	74UNTS257	100968
Argentina	Denmark	14 Dec 48	74UNTS41	100956
Denmark	Turkey	15 Dec 48	76UNTS3	100974
UK Great Britain	Yugoslavia	23 Dec 48	81UNTS133	101069
Belgium	Greece	27 Dec 48	77UNTS293	101005
Poland	Yugoslavia	16 Jan 49	115UNTS241	101564
Denmark	Sweden	08 Feb 49	33UNTS227	100519
France	Norway	09 Feb 49	29UNTS13	100431
Norway	Turkey	24 Feb 49	30UNTS151	100453
Denmark	Greece	25 Feb 49	78UNTS335	101023
Czechoslovakia	Yugoslavia	01 Mar 49	112UNTS241	101546
Belgium	Portugal	01 Mar 49	32UNTS49	100488
Greece	Norway	12 Mar 49	33UNTS13	100510
Denmark	Finland	22 Mar 49	33UNTS247	100520
Multilateral		23 Mar 49	203UNTS179	102746
Finland	Greece	24 Mar 49	78UNTS13	101009
Greece	Turkey	02 Apr 49	78UNTS23	101010

PARTY ONE	PARTY TWO	DATE	CITATION	NUMBER
Balance of payments (Cont.)				
Denmark	Portugal	08 Apr 49	74UNTS221	100965
Belgium	Bolivia	26 Apr 49	34UNTS103	100530
Argentina	UK Great Britain	27 Jun 49	83UNTS217	101110
Greece	Turkey	21 Jul 49	78UNTS65	101012
Brazil	UK Great Britain	03 Aug 49	86UNTS113	101154
Multilateral		05 Aug 49	88UNTS229	101195
Multilateral		10 Aug 49	45UNTS3	100689
Argentina	Norway	09 Sep 49	42UNTS125	100646
Italy	Norway	19 Nov 49	47UNTS89	100724
Norway	Portugal	28 Nov 49	47UNTS117	100726
Denmark	Germany, West	15 Dec 49	51UNTS11	100749
Czechoslovakia	Denmark	17 Dec 49	74UNTS159	100962
Sweden	UK Great Britain	30 Dec 49	87UNTS59	101166
Greece	Portugal	31 Dec 49	92UNTS83	101263
Austria	Denmark	23 Feb 50	74UNTS269	100969
Israel	UK Great Britain	30 Mar 50	86UNTS231	101162
Paraguay	UK Great Britain	03 Apr 50	99UNTS81	101372
Costa Rica	USA (United States)	04 Apr 50	132UNTS177	101759
Austria	Greece	11 May 50	184UNTS217	102450
Multilateral		31 May 50	74UNTS95	100957
Denmark	Spain	12 Jul 50	71UNTS129	100913
Belgium	Japan	29 Aug 50	76UNTS113	100984
Brazil	UK Great Britain	18 Sep 50	88UNTS115	101188
Denmark	Italy	04 Oct 50	78UNTS353	101025
Colombia	Denmark	26 Jan 51	87UNTS161	101171
Ceylon (Sri Lanka)	India	30 Apr 51	196UNTS199	102625
Pakistan	UK Great Britain	29 Sep 51	134UNTS183	101798
Germany, West	Greece	28 Jul 52	182UNTS85	102424
Austria	Greece	20 Sep 52	187UNTS191	102512
USA (United States)	Yugoslavia	11 Oct 52	235UNTS277	103309
United Arab Rep	UK Great Britain	30 Oct 52	172UNTS3	102236
Denmark	Israel	14 Nov 52	160UNTS289	102114
Czechoslovakia	Denmark	23 Apr 53	174UNTS107	102281
Israel	UK Great Britain	13 May 53	175UNTS179	102300
Argentina	USSR (Soviet Union)	05 Aug 53	221UNTS99	103004
Denmark	Uruguay	09 Sep 53	256UNTS149	103625
USA (United States)	Yugoslavia	05 Jan 54	234UNTS267	103289
Czechoslovakia	Greece	01 Feb 54	225UNTS95	103092
Canada	Japan	31 Mar 54	236UNTS329	103334
Greece	Spain	15 May 54	299UNTS277	104319
Greece	Romania	19 May 54	225UNTS27	103084
Canada	Spain	26 May 54	391UNTS273	105632
Canada	Portugal	28 May 54	391UNTS253	105631
Greece	Hungary	05 Jun 54	299UNTS295	104321
USSR (Soviet Union)	Yugoslavia	05 Jan 55	240UNTS225	103405
Turkey	UK Great Britain	17 Jan 55	204UNTS195	102758
Argentina	UK Great Britain	31 Mar 55	210UNTS223	102840
Canada	Ethiopia	03 Jun 55	247UNTS157	103465
Argentina	USA (United States)	21 Dec 55	240UNTS329	103411
Denmark	Netherlands	31 Jan 56	286UNTS255	104172
Canada	USSR (Soviet Union)	29 Feb 56	252UNTS165	103566
Ceylon (Sri Lanka)	Romania	16 Mar 56	315UNTS51	104559
Multilateral		25 Apr 56	270UNTS103	103896
UNESCO (Educ/Cult)	UK Great Britain	09 Aug 56	256UNTS139	103624
Multilateral		25 Mar 57	294UNTS2	104300
Australia	Japan	06 Jul 57	318UNTS381	104627
Ceylon (Sri Lanka)	China People's Rep	19 Sep 57	337UNTS137	104821
Japan	USSR (Soviet Union)	06 Dec 57	325UNTS35	104694
Indonesia	Japan	20 Jan 58	325UNTS3	104690
Multilateral		03 Apr 58	336UNTS177	104806
Japan	Poland	26 Apr 58	340UNTS221	104866
Multilateral		18 Jun 58	386UNTS355	105553
Australia	Fed of Malaya	26 Aug 58	325UNTS253	104703
Multilateral		01 Dec 58	385UNTS137	105534
Israel	Yugoslavia	11 Dec 58	386UNTS283	105548

PARTY ONE	PARTY TWO	DATE	CITATION	NUMBER
Balance of payments (Cont.)				
Haiti	Japan	17 Dec 58	518UNTS91	107492
Multilateral		06 Apr 59	349UNTS167	105013
Turkey	UK Great Britain	13 Jun 59	551UNTS59	108033
Greece	Yugoslavia	18 Jun 59	368UNTS3	105231
Australia	Germany, West	14 Oct 59	345UNTS35	104957
Norway	Yugoslavia	18 Nov 59	383UNTS131	105499
Argentina	Brazil	26 Nov 59	374UNTS39	105326
Czechoslovakia	Japan	15 Dec 59	383UNTS277	105505
Cuba	USSR (Soviet Union)	13 Feb 60	369UNTS17	105248
Iran	USA (United States)	12 Apr 60	372UNTS63	105288
Multilateral		01 Sep 60	403UNTS3	105792
Greece	Poland	08 Nov 60	483UNTS141	107011
Multilateral		13 Dec 60	455UNTS3	106543
Malaysia	New Zealand	03 Feb 61	447UNTS251	106418
Indonesia	Japan	01 Jul 61	517UNTS107	107484
Switzerland	UK Great Britain	20 Oct 61	431UNTS29	106206
Luxembourg	USA (United States)	23 Feb 62	474UNTS3	106868
Multilateral		15 May 62	444UNTS3	106367
Algeria	France	03 Jul 62	507UNTS25	107395
Burma	UK Great Britain	02 Apr 63	475UNTS139	106890
Multilateral		02 Apr 63	475UNTS121	106889
Brazil	USSR (Soviet Union)	20 Apr 63	0UNTS0	109256
Austria	Romania	03 Jul 63	588UNTS3	108516
Tanganyika	USSR (Soviet Union)	14 Aug 63	493UNTS195	107215
Denmark	Norway	12 Sep 63	613UNTS289	108857
Multilateral		23 Oct 63	506UNTS197	107388
Canada	UK Great Britain	15 Apr 64	515UNTS39	107452
UK Great Britain	USA (United States)	15 Apr 64	515UNTS55	107453
Australia	UK Great Britain	15 Apr 64	515UNTS23	107451
Argentina	UK Great Britain	15 Apr 64	515UNTS3	107450
South Africa	UK Great Britain	22 Jun 64	515UNTS71	107454
Sweden	UK Great Britain	30 Jun 64	515UNTS83	107455
Cyprus	UK Great Britain	02 Jul 64	522UNTS129	107540
Germany, West	UK Great Britain	27 Jul 64	539UNTS243	107835
India	UK Great Britain	31 Jul 64	522UNTS153	107542
Multilateral		20 Aug 64	514UNTS25	107441
Kenya	UK Great Britain	25 Aug 64	522UNTS165	107543
Malawi	UK Great Britain	01 Sep 64	522UNTS117	107539
Tanganyika	UK Great Britain	02 Sep 64	522UNTS177	107544
Malta	Switzerland	20 Jan 65	548UNTS193	107978
New Zealand	Poland	07 Jul 65	548UNTS19	107966
Multilateral		16 Jul 65	600UNTS49	108675
Australia	New Zealand	31 Aug 65	554UNTS169	108101
Australia	USSR (Soviet Union)	15 Oct 65	553UNTS239	108092
Ireland	UK Great Britain	14 Dec 65	565UNTS58	108235
Multilateral		28 Apr 66	604UNTS219	108752
Korea, South	New Zealand	31 Jan 67	598UNTS91	108656
Germany, West	UK Great Britain	05 May 67	613UNTS313	108858
Israel	USA (United States)	04 Aug 67	0UNTS0	109351
Bulgaria	New Zealand	03 Nov 67	0UNTS0	109207
Germany, West	UK Great Britain	11 Apr 68	0UNTS0	109288
Ireland	UK Great Britain	23 Sep 68	0UNTS0	109374
Currency				
Netherlands	UK Great Britain	13 Jun 39	5UNTS65	200028
Netherlands	UK Great Britain	14 Jun 40	2UNTS251	200018
UK Great Britain	USSR (Soviet Union)	16 Aug 41	91UNTS341	200269
Mexico	USA (United States)	19 Nov 41	148UNTS367	200474
Mexico	USA (United States)	23 Dec 42	13UNTS231	200081
Mexico	USA (United States)	29 Sep 43	106UNTS265	200345
Multilateral		21 Oct 43	2UNTS281	200021
Honduras	USA (United States)	12 Apr 44	138UNTS271	200450
Peru	USA (United States)	15 Apr 44	150UNTS317	200479
Guatemala	USA (United States)	16 Sep 44	135UNTS315	200444
Multilateral		20 Jan 45	140UNTS397	200471

PARTY ONE	PARTY TWO	DATE	CITATION	NUMBER
Currency (Cont.)				
Ecuador	USA (United States)	22 Jan 45	24UNTS273	200152
France	USA (United States)	28 Feb 45	76UNTS213	200247
Canada	Czechoslovakia	01 Mar 45	45UNTS283	200185
Sweden	UK Great Britain	06 Mar 45	5UNTS241	200032
Sweden	UK Great Britain	06 Mar 45	82UNTS219	101095
France	UK Great Britain	27 Mar 45	98UNTS227	200274
Argentina	USA (United States)	09 May 45	139UNTS227	200453
Canada	Norway	25 Jun 45	45UNTS297	200186
USA (United States)	USSR (Soviet Union)	15 Oct 45	278UNTS151	200547
Belgium	Norway	23 Oct 45	16UNTS311	200107
Netherlands	Switzerland	24 Oct 45	3UNTS73	100025
Czechoslovakia	UK Great Britain	01 Nov 45	5UNTS15	100062
Netherlands	Norway	06 Nov 45	2UNTS5	100017
Norway	UK Great Britain	08 Nov 45	5UNTS27	100063
Poland	Yugoslavia	23 Nov 45	115UNTS3	101555
Finland	Norway	27 Nov 45	17UNTS247	100279
Multilateral		04 Dec 45	9UNTS101	100128
Czechoslovakia	Norway	13 Dec 45	17UNTS261	100280
Romania	Yugoslavia	15 Dec 45	116UNTS3	101565
Netherlands	UK Great Britain	20 Dec 45	4UNTS303	100053
Multilateral		27 Dec 45	2UNTS39	100020
Greece	UK Great Britain	24 Jan 46	6UNTS45	100067
Denmark	Netherlands	31 Jan 46	3UNTS3	100021
Canada	Netherlands	05 Feb 46	43UNTS3	100658
Mexico	UK Great Britain	07 Feb 46	6UNTS55	100068
Canada	Taiwan	07 Feb 46	43UNTS23	100659
Colombia	USA (United States)	19 Feb 46	166UNTS104	102187
Belgium	Norway	21 Feb 46	31UNTS199	100479
France	Norway	06 Mar 46	15UNTS13	100227
Switzerland	UK Great Britain	12 Mar 46	6UNTS107	100070
Canada	France	09 Apr 46	43UNTS43	100660
Portugal	UK Great Britain	16 Apr 46	6UNTS119	100071
France	Greece	24 Apr 46	91UNTS83	101243
France	USA (United States)	28 May 46	84UNTS121	101123
Albania	Yugoslavia	01 Jul 46	111UNTS81	101518
Albania	Yugoslavia	01 Jul 46	111UNTS3	101517
Philippines	USA (United States)	04 Jul 46	43UNTS135	100668
Italy	Norway	20 Jul 46	17UNTS273	100281
Norway	Yugoslavia	30 Aug 46	15UNTS163	100232
Australia	Sweden	16 Sep 46	10UNTS63	100143
Argentina	USA (United States)	19 Sep 46	7UNTS131	100095
Albania	Yugoslavia	03 Oct 46	111UNTS227	101537
Norway	Sweden	22 Nov 46	15UNTS171	100233
France	UK Great Britain	03 Dec 46	54UNTS117	100798
Denmark	India	20 Dec 46	7UNTS309	100107
Hungary	Yugoslavia	23 Dec 46	113UNTS125	101549
Norway	USSR (Soviet Union)	27 Dec 46	17UNTS283	100282
Australia	Netherlands	24 Jan 47	10UNTS77	100144
USSR (Soviet Union)	Yugoslavia	04 Feb 47	130UNTS235	101731
Multilateral		10 Feb 47	49UNTS3	100747
Belgium	Turkey	12 Mar 47	33UNTS43	100513
Spain	UK Great Britain	28 Mar 47	66UNTS91	100849
Greece	UK Great Britain	07 Apr 47	11UNTS201	100158
Denmark	Norway	15 Apr 47	12UNTS323	100191
Bulgaria	Denmark	09 May 47	74UNTS139	100960
Bulgaria	Denmark	09 May 47	74UNTS131	100959
Honduras	USA (United States)	13 May 47	166UNTS159	102189
New Zealand	UK Great Britain	27 May 47	17UNTS211	100277
Albania	Yugoslavia	12 Jun 47	111UNTS189	101533
Austria	USA (United States)	21 Jun 47	67UNTS89	100868
Albania	Yugoslavia	22 Jun 47	111UNTS207	101536
USA (United States)	Venezuela	30 Jun 47	166UNTS198	102190
Belgium	United Arab Rep	01 Jul 47	34UNTS93	100529
France	New Zealand	02 Jul 47	16UNTS219	100263
Norway	Switzerland	15 Jul 47	12UNTS351	100192

PARTY ONE	PARTY TWO	DATE	CITATION	NUMBER
Currency (Cont.)				
UK Great Britain	Uruguay	15 Jul 47	71UNTS179	100918
Hungary	Yugoslavia	24 Jul 47	114UNTS3	101554
Czechoslovakia	USA (United States)	25 Jul 47	90UNTS19	101223
Australia	France	28 Jul 47	97UNTS271	101353
Czechoslovakia	Greece	30 Jul 47	185UNTS149	102466
Multilateral		04 Aug 47	28UNTS41	100418
Belgium	India	04 Aug 47	76UNTS23	100976
Netherlands	IBRD (World Bank)	07 Aug 47	152UNTS165	102015
Italy	USA (United States)	14 Aug 47	36UNTS105	100567
Denmark	IBRD (World Bank)	22 Aug 47	152UNTS223	102016
Luxembourg	IBRD (World Bank)	28 Aug 47	153UNTS3	102017
Romania	Yugoslavia	30 Sep 47	116UNTS71	101570
Multilateral		05 Oct 47	34UNTS23	100525
South Africa	UK Great Britain	09 Oct 47	17UNTS239	100278
Multilateral		30 Oct 47	55UNTS188	100814
Belgium	UK Great Britain	14 Nov 47	25UNTS269	100367
Ecuador	USA (United States)	14 Nov 47	149UNTS297	101959
Guatemala	USA (United States)	05 Jan 48	135UNTS104	101817
Czechoslovakia	New Zealand	22 Jan 48	16UNTS229	100264
France	Lebanon	24 Jan 48	173UNTS99	102263
Italy	USA (United States)	06 Feb 48	73UNTS113	100950
Denmark	Hungary	28 Feb 48	85UNTS35	101144
Poland	UK Great Britain	02 Mar 48	77UNTS47	100991
Paraguay	USA (United States)	12 Mar 48	162UNTS30	102131
Hungary	Yugoslavia	18 Mar 48	113UNTS201	101551
Hungary	Yugoslavia	18 Mar 48	113UNTS219	101552
Denmark	Norway	21 Apr 48	18UNTS139	100284
Greece	USA (United States)	23 Apr 48	74UNTS107	100958
Norway	Sweden	29 Apr 48	26UNTS11	100374
Brazil	UK Great Britain	21 May 48	66UNTS121	100851
Czechoslovakia	Yugoslavia	24 May 48	112UNTS183	101543
Chile	UK Great Britain	24 Jun 48	77UNTS113	100995
India	Pakistan	30 Jun 48	29UNTS199	100441
Peru	USA (United States)	30 Jun 48	150UNTS45	101962
UK Great Britain	Uruguay	12 Jul 48	71UNTS199	100919
USA (United States)	Yugoslavia	19 Jul 48	34UNTS195	100537
USA (United States)	Yugoslavia	19 Jul 48	89UNTS43	101208
Peru	UK Great Britain	20 Jul 48	66UNTS197	100855
New Zealand	Pakistan	17 Sep 48	91UNTS275	101254
El Salvador	USA (United States)	23 Sep 48	181UNTS101	102402
Panama	USA (United States)	24 Sep 48	150UNTS25	101961
Australia	Denmark	08 Oct 48	22UNTS43	100330
France	USA (United States)	22 Oct 48	84UNTS173	101128
Austria	Denmark	29 Nov 48	74UNTS257	100968
Argentina	Denmark	14 Dec 48	74UNTS41	100956
Spain	UK Great Britain	15 Dec 48	87UNTS49	101165
Denmark	Turkey	15 Dec 48	76UNTS3	100974
Italy	USA (United States)	18 Dec 48	79UNTS133	101037
Belgium	Greece	27 Dec 48	77UNTS293	101005
Poland	UK Great Britain	14 Jan 49	83UNTS51	101101
Poland	UK Great Britain	14 Jan 49	83UNTS3	101100
Chile	USA (United States)	21 Jan 49	160UNTS185	102107
Denmark	Sweden	08 Feb 49	33UNTS227	100519
Norway	Turkey	24 Feb 49	30UNTS151	100453
Denmark	Greece	25 Feb 49	78UNTS325	101022
Denmark	Greece	25 Feb 49	78UNTS335	101023
Netherlands	Norway	26 Feb 49	29UNTS33	100432
Belgium	IBRD (World Bank)	01 Mar 49	154UNTS133	102029
Czechoslovakia	Yugoslavia	01 Mar 49	112UNTS241	101546
Belgium	Portugal	01 Mar 49	32UNTS49	100488
Greece	Norway	12 Mar 49	33UNTS13	100510
Germany, West	Greece	16 Mar 49	77UNTS327	101007
Denmark	Finland	22 Mar 49	33UNTS247	100520
Finland	Greece	24 Mar 49	78UNTS3	101008
United Arab Rep	UK Great Britain	31 Mar 49	83UNTS139	101106

PARTY ONE	PARTY TWO	DATE	CITATION	NUMBER
Currency (Cont.)				
Greece	Turkey	02 Apr 49	78UNTS23	101010
Denmark	Portugal	08 Apr 49	74UNTS221	100965
Belgium	Bolivia	26 Apr 49	34UNTS103	100530
Canada	Netherlands	09 May 49	46UNTS263	100715
Norway	USA (United States)	25 May 49	32UNTS345	100507
Finland	Norway	13 Jun 49	34UNTS9	100523
Argentina	UK Great Britain	27 Jun 49	83UNTS217	101110
Austria	USA (United States)	12 Jul 49	84UNTS291	101138
Greece	Turkey	21 Jul 49	78UNTS65	101012
El Salvador	USA (United States)	27 Jul 49	180UNTS219	102387
USA (United States)	Uruguay	27 Jul 49	151UNTS199	101995
Finland	IBRD (World Bank)	01 Aug 49	156UNTS289	200480
Multilateral		05 Aug 49	88UNTS229	101195
Multilateral		10 Aug 49	45UNTS3	100689
Multilateral		12 Aug 49	87UNTS131	101169
WHO (World Health)	Thailand	12 Aug 49	178UNTS347	102350
Czechoslovakia	UK Great Britain	18 Aug 49	86UNTS129	101155
India	IBRD (World Bank)	18 Aug 49	154UNTS269	102031
Denmark	ICAO (Civil Aviat)	09 Sep 49	53UNTS341	100791
IBRD (World Bank)	Yugoslavia	17 Sep 49	155UNTS3	102034
India	IBRD (World Bank)	29 Sep 49	154UNTS393	102033
Finland	IBRD (World Bank)	17 Oct 49	156UNTS355	200481
Multilateral		27 Oct 49	53UNTS241	100784
United Arab Rep	USA (United States)	03 Nov 49	71UNTS31	100908
Norway	Portugal	28 Nov 49	47UNTS117	100726
Denmark	Germany, West	15 Dec 49	51UNTS11	100749
Norway	USSR (Soviet Union)	29 Dec 49	83UNTS291	101112
Sweden	UK Great Britain	30 Dec 49	87UNTS59	101166
Greece	Portugal	31 Dec 49	92UNTS83	101263
Austria	UK Great Britain	26 Jan 50	97UNTS183	101350
India	USA (United States)	02 Feb 50	89UNTS127	101214
China People's Rep	USSR (Soviet Union)	14 Feb 50	226UNTS31	103105
Paraguay	UK Great Britain	03 Apr 50	99UNTS81	101372
India	IBRD (World Bank)	18 Apr 50	155UNTS117	102036
Korea, South	USA (United States)	28 Apr 50	93UNTS21	101284
Austria	Greece	11 May 50	184UNTS217	102450
Austria	USA (United States)	06 Jun 50	92UNTS201	101273
Iraq	IBRD (World Bank)	15 Jun 50	155UNTS267	102038
Thailand	USA (United States)	01 Jul 50	81UNTS61	101063
IBRD (World Bank)	Turkey	07 Jul 50	156UNTS3	102039
IBRD (World Bank)	Turkey	07 Jul 50	156UNTS75	102040
Korea, South	USA (United States)	28 Jul 50	140UNTS57	101883
Belgium	Japan	29 Aug 50	76UNTS113	100984
Belgium	Japan	29 Aug 50	82UNTS147	101089
Netherlands	USA (United States)	07 Oct 50	79UNTS33	101029
IBRD (World Bank)	Turkey	19 Oct 50	157UNTS333	102058
Colombia	IBRD (World Bank)	02 Nov 50	158UNTS59	102062
Norway	UK Great Britain	06 Nov 50	88UNTS257	101197
Philippines	USA (United States)	06 Nov 50	122UNTS63	101637
Sweden	UK Great Britain	10 Nov 50	88UNTS265	101198
Bolivia	USA (United States)	22 Nov 50	152UNTS17	102008
Germany, West	UK Great Britain	09 Dec 50	88UNTS247	101196
El Salvador	USA (United States)	13 Dec 50	166UNTS149	102188
Italy	UK Great Britain	21 Dec 50	175UNTS187	102301
Brazil	USA (United States)	27 Dec 50	147UNTS33	101926
Colombia	IBRD (World Bank)	28 Dec 50	158UNTS87	102063
Colombia	WHO (World Health)	05 Jan 51	102UNTS139	101417
Finland	Ireland	06 Jan 51	558UNTS120	108140
Sweden	UK Great Britain	17 Jan 51	93UNTS225	101301
Italy	Norway	22 Jan 51	88UNTS339	101202
Nicaragua	USA (United States)	31 Jan 51	150UNTS3	101960
Nicaragua	USA (United States)	31 Jan 51	160UNTS121	102105
Austria	UK Great Britain	31 Jan 51	88UNTS107	101187
Panama	USA (United States)	26 Feb 51	160UNTS153	102106
France	UK Great Britain	11 Apr 51	106UNTS3	101456

PARTY ONE	PARTY TWO	DATE	CITATION	NUMBER
Currency (Cont.)				
Honduras	USA (United States)	24 Apr 51	140UNTS287	101894
Nicaragua	IBRD (World Bank)	07 Jun 51	158UNTS277	102068
Sweden	USA (United States)	27 Jun 51	148UNTS77	101937
United Arab Rep	UK Great Britain	01 Jul 51	249UNTS143	103504
Portugal	UK Great Britain	20 Jul 51	105UNTS61	101453
Multilateral		04 Aug 51	104UNTS197	101441
India	United Nations	14 Aug 51	98UNTS115	101359
Iraq	USA (United States)	16 Aug 51	147UNTS65	101929
Denmark	USA (United States)	23 Aug 51	147UNTS49	101928
Japan	USA (United States)	28 Aug 51	147UNTS81	101930
Japan	UK Great Britain	31 Aug 51	108UNTS273	101480
Pakistan	United Arab Rep	08 Sep 51	133UNTS257	101793
Norway	USA (United States)	17 Sep 51	140UNTS313	101895
Panama	WHO (World Health)	09 Nov 51	118UNTS43	101595
El Salvador	Guatemala	14 Dec 51	131UNTS131	101740
Spain	UK Great Britain	20 Dec 51	123UNTS187	101660
Portugal	USA (United States)	08 Jan 52	207UNTS51	102799
UK Great Britain	USA (United States)	18 Jan 52	184UNTS79	102440
Japan	USA (United States)	28 Feb 52	208UNTS255	102817
Finland	Norway	18 Mar 52	188UNTS187	102527
Austria	Greece	22 Mar 52	187UNTS255	102517
Belgium	USA (United States)	07 Apr 52	205UNTS3	102765
Ethiopia	USA (United States)	15 May 52	180UNTS227	102388
Denmark	Poland	09 Jun 52	135UNTS221	101823
Taiwan	USA (United States)	25 Jun 52	136UNTS229	101837
Belgium	Italy	25 Jun 52	137UNTS239	101855
Austria	UK Great Britain	30 Jun 52	138UNTS153	101867
Finland	USA (United States)	02 Jul 52	165UNTS203	102177
Multilateral		11 Jul 52	171UNTS143	102226
Multilateral		11 Jul 52	171UNTS3	102224
Germany, West	USA (United States)	18 Jul 52	165UNTS167	102175
UK Great Britain	Yugoslavia	20 Aug 52	158UNTS439	102077
Multilateral		28 Aug 52	175UNTS69	102296
Chile	WHO (World Health)	04 Nov 52	150UNTS119	101966
Denmark	Israel	14 Nov 52	160UNTS289	102114
Ceylon (Sri Lanka)	USA (United States)	17 Nov 52	180UNTS207	102386
Sweden	USA (United States)	20 Nov 52	177UNTS203	102319
Japan	UK Great Britain	21 Nov 52	172UNTS303	102254
Liberia	USA (United States)	15 Dec 52	185UNTS45	102457
Belgium	Germany, West	23 Dec 52	186UNTS69	102483
Greece	Italy	04 Feb 53	189UNTS269	102551
Denmark	Germany, West	26 Feb 53	178UNTS3	102332
Germany, West	USA (United States)	27 Feb 53	205UNTS103	102771
Multilateral		27 Feb 53	333UNTS3	104764
Germany, West	USA (United States)	27 Feb 53	224UNTS13	103067
Portugal	USA (United States)	01 Apr 53	205UNTS41	102769
Czechoslovakia	Denmark	23 Apr 53	174UNTS107	102281
Ethiopia	USA (United States)	29 Apr 53	224UNTS121	103073
Israel	UK Great Britain	13 May 53	175UNTS179	102300
Greece	United Arab Rep	21 May 53	256UNTS25	103621
Ethiopia	USA (United States)	22 May 53	191UNTS59	102577
Germany, West	UK Great Britain	22 May 53	172UNTS179	102246
Japan	Syria	08 Jun 53	184UNTS3	102436
United Arab Rep	USA (United States)	18 Jun 53	204UNTS55	102749
United Arab Rep	USA (United States)	18 Jun 53	215UNTS45	102910
Liberia	USA (United States)	23 Jun 53	213UNTS57	102880
India	Yugoslavia	24 Jul 53	394UNTS13	105665
Ceylon (Sri Lanka)	Yugoslavia	30 Jul 53	337UNTS103	104819
Argentina	USSR (Soviet Union)	05 Aug 53	221UNTS99	103004
Denmark	Uruguay	09 Sep 53	256UNTS149	103625
IBRD (World Bank)	Turkey	10 Sep 53	187UNTS71	102502
Brazil	UK Great Britain	01 Oct 53	183UNTS207	102430
Multilateral		01 Oct 53	258UNTS153	103677
Nicaragua	USA (United States)	19 Nov 53	206UNTS117	102787
India	USSR (Soviet Union)	02 Dec 53	240UNTS143	103402

PARTY ONE	PARTY TWO	DATE	CITATION	NUMBER
Currency (Cont.)				
Germany, West	Ireland	02 Dec 53	558UNTS38	108139
Japan	USA (United States)	24 Dec 53	222UNTS193	103028
Japan	UK Great Britain	29 Jan 54	190UNTS319	102572
Czechoslovakia	Greece	01 Feb 54	225UNTS95	103092
Germany, West	USA (United States)	12 Feb 54	223UNTS153	103064
Multilateral		19 Feb 54	214UNTS51	102899
Multilateral		01 Mar 54	256UNTS31	103622
Belgium	Germany, West	03 Mar 54	188UNTS259	102529
Japan	USA (United States)	08 Mar 54	232UNTS267	103241
Japan	USA (United States)	08 Mar 54	232UNTS251	103240
Greece	Spain	15 May 54	299UNTS277	104319
Greece	Romania	19 May 54	225UNTS27	103084
Canada	Portugal	28 May 54	391UNTS253	105631
Greece	Hungary	05 Jun 54	299UNTS295	104321
Netherlands	Norway	09 Jun 54	287UNTS179	104184
Haiti	Italy	14 Jun 54	267UNTS97	103837
Belgium	Ireland	30 Jun 54	212UNTS255	102876
France	Netherlands	09 Jul 54	287UNTS169	104183
Belgium	Italy	12 Jul 54	288UNTS59	104198
Switzerland	UK Great Britain	16 Jul 54	199UNTS197	102685
Thailand	USA (United States)	11 Aug 54	234UNTS155	103281
Thailand	USA (United States)	01 Sep 54	237UNTS209	103347
Libya	USA (United States)	09 Sep 54	224UNTS217	103078
Multilateral		28 Sep 54	207UNTS293	102812
UNESCO (Educ/Cult)	UN Special Fund	29 Sep 54	363UNTS367	200572
Multilateral		23 Oct 54	332UNTS3	104760
Iran	UK Great Britain	25 Oct 54	204UNTS131	102754
Denmark	Sweden	28 Oct 54	262UNTS211	103747
Netherlands	USA (United States)	14 Dec 54	262UNTS35	103737
USA (United States)	Yugoslavia	05 Jan 55	251UNTS29	103531
USSR (Soviet Union)	Yugoslavia	05 Jan 55	240UNTS225	103405
Peru	USA (United States)	07 Jan 55	261UNTS321	103730
Costa Rica	USA (United States)	26 Feb 55	252UNTS129	103562
Peru	USA (United States)	16 Mar 55	252UNTS151	103564
Guatemala	USA (United States)	23 Mar 55	252UNTS143	103563
Ecuador	USA (United States)	29 Mar 55	261UNTS343	103732
Argentina	UK Great Britain	31 Mar 55	210UNTS223	102840
Chile	USA (United States)	31 Mar 55	262UNTS19	103736
Pakistan	USA (United States)	26 May 55	257UNTS93	103652
Honduras	USA (United States)	10 Jun 55	258UNTS51	103669
Austria	USA (United States)	14 Jun 55	258UNTS37	103668
Ecuador	USA (United States)	08 Jul 55	265UNTS49	103806
Belgium	USA (United States)	15 Jul 55	223UNTS3	103040
Switzerland	USA (United States)	18 Jul 55	239UNTS311	103388
Germany, West	UK Great Britain	22 Jul 55	269UNTS189	103881
Italy	Switzerland	23 Jul 55	284UNTS279	104142
Thailand	USA (United States)	09 Sep 55	264UNTS285	103799
Multilateral		12 Oct 55	560UNTS3	108165
Austria	USSR (Soviet Union)	17 Oct 55	0UNTS0	109255
Czechoslovakia	Germany, East	24 Oct 55	504UNTS173	107358
Paraguay	USA (United States)	28 Oct 55	273UNTS97	103946
Italy	Lebanon	04 Nov 55	267UNTS113	103838
Italy	Syria	10 Nov 55	267UNTS157	103841
Thailand	USA (United States)	14 Nov 55	239UNTS201	103380
Syria	USSR (Soviet Union)	16 Nov 55	259UNTS71	103683
Korea, North	Romania	05 Dec 55	362UNTS141	105186
Argentina	USA (United States)	21 Dec 55	240UNTS329	103411
Cuba	USA (United States)	10 Jan 56	240UNTS101	103398
Denmark	Netherlands	31 Jan 56	286UNTS255	104172
Norway	Syria	25 Feb 56	463UNTS217	106706
Burma	Yugoslavia	07 Mar 56	386UNTS235	105543
Burma	Yugoslavia	07 Mar 56	386UNTS207	105542
Korea, South	USA (United States)	13 Mar 56	272UNTS3	103928
Ceylon (Sri Lanka)	Romania	16 Mar 56	315UNTS51	104559
Brazil	France	04 May 56	323UNTS339	104675

PARTY ONE	PARTY TWO	DATE	CITATION	NUMBER
Currency (Cont.)				
Austria	Italy	07 May 56	284UNTS351	104147
Turkey	USA (United States)	18 May 56	283UNTS167	104115
Multilateral		19 May 56	399UNTS189	105742
Bulgaria	Ceylon (Sri Lanka)	19 Jun 56	315UNTS33	104557
Canada	UK Great Britain	21 Jun 56	381UNTS111	105467
Israel	USA (United States)	26 Jun 56	257UNTS55	103649
Italy	Switzerland	29 Jun 56	284UNTS299	104144
Bolivia	USA (United States)	30 Jun 56	271UNTS243	103919
Denmark	WHO (World Health)	03 Sep 56	258UNTS103	103674
Pakistan	USA (United States)	10 Sep 56	277UNTS259	104010
Belgium	Germany, West	24 Sep 56	314UNTS195	104549
Multilateral		25 Sep 56	334UNTS89	104767
Multilateral		25 Sep 56	334UNTS13	104766
Czechoslovakia	Hungary	13 Oct 56	300UNTS177	104337
Canada	UK Great Britain	20 Oct 56	381UNTS99	105466
Ecuador	USA (United States)	31 Oct 56	283UNTS151	104114
Argentina	USA (United States)	05 Nov 56	277UNTS143	104004
France	USA (United States)	08 Nov 56	280UNTS189	104058
Japan	USA (United States)	23 Nov 56	324UNTS177	104685
Dominican Republic	USA (United States)	07 Dec 56	263UNTS193	103774
Austria	Pakistan	24 Dec 56	316UNTS83	104579
Australia	USA (United States)	31 Dec 56	266UNTS89	103823
Colombia	USA (United States)	09 Jan 57	462UNTS151	106676
Denmark	Germany, West	29 Jan 57	302UNTS75	104354
Germany, West	Sweden	29 Jan 57	393UNTS113	105654
Iceland	USA (United States)	23 Feb 57	283UNTS73	104107
France	USA (United States)	12 Mar 57	279UNTS275	104045
Multilateral		29 Mar 57	283UNTS137	104113
Paraguay	USA (United States)	04 Apr 57	284UNTS161	104135
Netherlands	Paraguay	13 Apr 57	593UNTS85	108577
Ceylon (Sri Lanka)	Italy	23 Apr 57	337UNTS115	104820
Denmark	Uruguay	04 Jun 57	286UNTS107	104162
Czechoslovakia	Yugoslavia	11 Jun 57	504UNTS107	107355
Italy	United Arab Rep	06 Jul 57	302UNTS147	104357
Germany, West	Italy	12 Jul 57	291UNTS181	104252
India	USA (United States)	19 Sep 57	290UNTS175	104236
Ceylon (Sri Lanka)	China People's Rep	19 Sep 57	337UNTS137	104821
Multilateral		03 Oct 57	366UNTS3	105215
Multilateral		03 Oct 57	366UNTS141	105217
Multilateral		03 Oct 57	365UNTS207	105214
Taiwan	USA (United States)	08 Oct 57	304UNTS241	104400
USA (United States)	Vietnam, South	05 Nov 57	300UNTS23	104328
Brazil	USA (United States)	05 Nov 57	303UNTS3	104368
Argentina	Denmark	25 Nov 57	299UNTS83	104308
Argentina	Italy	25 Nov 57	305UNTS275	104424
Norway	USSR (Soviet Union)	18 Dec 57	312UNTS257	104522
Japan	USA (United States)	11 Jan 58	304UNTS35	104390
Australia	USA (United States)	24 Jan 58	307UNTS105	104446
Italy	Romania	28 Jan 58	302UNTS231	104362
Iran	Italy	29 Jan 58	302UNTS181	104358
Czechoslovakia	Poland	31 Jan 58	431UNTS99	106214
Poland	USA (United States)	15 Feb 58	307UNTS217	104452
Canada	India	20 Feb 58	391UNTS231	105628
Bulgaria	Italy	25 Feb 58	362UNTS279	105193
Colombia	USA (United States)	14 Mar 58	308UNTS115	104459
Bulgaria	Yugoslavia	21 Mar 58	386UNTS119	105541
Peru	USA (United States)	09 Apr 58	316UNTS37	104576
Belgium	Japan	30 Apr 58	303UNTS109	104373
Iceland	USA (United States)	03 May 58	316UNTS137	104581
Albania	Italy	26 May 58	362UNTS259	105191
Burma	USA (United States)	27 May 58	315UNTS197	104569
USA (United States)	Vietnam, South	17 Jun 58	321UNTS35	104652
Multilateral		18 Jun 58	386UNTS355	105553
Burma	USA (United States)	25 Aug 58	336UNTS3	104795
Iraq	USSR (Soviet Union)	11 Oct 58	328UNTS95	104730
Spain	USA (United States)	16 Oct 58	336UNTS153	104804
Canada	India	22 Oct 58	392UNTS21	105635
United Arab Rep	USA (United States)	31 Oct 58	355UNTS355	105086
Canada	USA (United States)	31 Oct 58	391UNTS219	105626
Canada	Ceylon (Sri Lanka)	05 Nov 58	391UNTS225	105627
Turkey	UK Great Britain	25 Nov 58	327UNTS35	104715
Netherlands	Turkey	29 Nov 58	335UNTS229	104790
Multilateral		01 Dec 58	385UNTS137	105534
Israel	Yugoslavia	11 Dec 58	386UNTS283	105548
Korea, South	USA (United States)	18 Dec 58	325UNTS233	104702
Afghanistan	WHO (World Health)	18 Dec 58	324UNTS121	104681
Iraq	Romania	24 Dec 58	405UNTS243	105836
Haiti	USA (United States)	24 Dec 58	338UNTS265	104840
Burma	UK Great Britain	06 Feb 59	343UNTS223	104927
Cambodia	Japan	02 Mar 59	341UNTS163	104882
Iraq	USSR (Soviet Union)	16 Mar 59	346UNTS107	104979
Sudan	USA (United States)	17 Mar 59	342UNTS13	104896
Tunisia	USA (United States)	18 Mar 59	344UNTS179	104948
Germany, West	UK Great Britain	10 Apr 59	343UNTS295	104935
Nicaragua	USA (United States)	14 Apr 59	343UNTS119	104922
Sweden	UK Great Britain	18 Apr 59	360UNTS89	105156
Fed of Malaya	USA (United States)	21 Apr 59	343UNTS3	104916
Germany, West	Netherlands	30 Apr 59	485UNTS141	107052
Netherlands	Sweden	30 Apr 59	485UNTS147	107053
Netherlands	UK Great Britain	30 Apr 59	343UNTS307	104937
Fed of Malaya	UK Great Britain	01 May 59	345UNTS57	104958
Switzerland	UK Great Britain	06 May 59	343UNTS315	104938
Multilateral		11 May 59	527UNTS145	107623
Japan	Vietnam, South	13 May 59	373UNTS173	105319
Greece	UK Great Britain	21 May 59	344UNTS3	104939
Ceylon (Sri Lanka)	Norway	29 May 59	411UNTS165	105919
Ceylon (Sri Lanka)	Sweden	29 May 59	464UNTS109	106713
Ethiopia	Yugoslavia	06 Jun 59	386UNTS243	105544
Greece	Yugoslavia	18 Jun 59	368UNTS27	105234
Greece	Yugoslavia	18 Jun 59	368UNTS3	105231
Finland	USA (United States)	22 Jul 59	354UNTS39	105051
Taiwan	USA (United States)	22 Jul 59	357UNTS293	105121
Netherlands	Turkey	12 Aug 59	527UNTS181	107624
United Arab Rep	USA (United States)	28 Sep 59	358UNTS97	105128
FAO (Food Agri)	UN Special Fund	28 Sep 59	341UNTS353	200562
Austria	Netherlands	30 Sep 59	507UNTS111	107397
ILO (Labor Org)	UN Special Fund	12 Oct 59	343UNTS325	200563
Sudan	United Arab Rep	08 Nov 59	453UNTS51	106519
Ethiopia	France	12 Nov 59	381UNTS3	105465
Turkey	USA (United States)	13 Nov 59	361UNTS3	105168
UN Special Fund	WMO (Meteorology)	17 Nov 59	345UNTS311	200564
Norway	Yugoslavia	18 Nov 59	383UNTS131	105499
Argentina	USA (United States)	22 Dec 59	411UNTS42	105912
Denmark	Sweden	04 Jan 60	376UNTS375	105390
Israel	USA (United States)	07 Jan 60	368UNTS181	105241
Japan	USA (United States)	19 Jan 60	373UNTS207	105321
Multilateral		26 Jan 60	439UNTS249	106333
Multilateral		06 Feb 60	383UNTS3	105494
Cuba	USSR (Soviet Union)	13 Feb 60	369UNTS17	105248
Cuba	USSR (Soviet Union)	13 Feb 60	369UNTS3	105247
Korea, South	USA (United States)	19 Feb 60	372UNTS109	105291
Denmark	USA (United States)	19 Feb 60	354UNTS151	105061
Multilateral		26 Feb 60	418UNTS171	106022
Austria	Guatemala	18 Mar 60	379UNTS89	105435
Portugal	USA (United States)	19 Mar 60	371UNTS131	105275
Finland	USA (United States)	23 Mar 60	371UNTS117	105274
Austria	El Salvador	23 Mar 60	390UNTS3	105599
ICAO (Civil Aviat)	UN Special Fund	21 Apr 60	360UNTS367	200569
Nepal	USA (United States)	17 May 60	372UNTS313	105307
Kuwait	UK Great Britain	24 May 60	412UNTS4	105923

PARTY ONE	PARTY TWO	DATE	CITATION	NUMBER
Currency (Cont.)				
UN Special Fund	WHO (World Health)	25 May 60	359UNTS375	200568
Chile	USA (United States)	02 Jun 60	377UNTS11	105393
Belgium	Netherlands	20 Jun 60	423UNTS19	106084
Somalia	UK Great Britain	26 Jun 60	374UNTS363	105350
ITU (Telecommun)	UN Special Fund	13 Jul 60	368UNTS329	200573
Chile	USA (United States)	29 Jul 60	405UNTS127	105829
Ghana	Netherlands	30 Jul 60	412UNTS51	105925
Ghana	USSR (Soviet Union)	04 Aug 60	421UNTS27	106050
Guatemala	USA (United States)	09 Aug 60	461UNTS15	106648
Congo (Zaire)	United Nations	23 Aug 60	373UNTS327	200576
Israel	UK Great Britain	31 Aug 60	385UNTS71	105530
Multilateral		01 Sep 60	403UNTS3	105792
Liberia	USA (United States)	06 Sep 60	389UNTS245	105596
Multilateral		19 Sep 60	444UNTS259	106371
Multilateral		21 Sep 60	394UNTS3	105664
Netherlands	Romania	30 Sep 60	479UNTS91	106948
Portugal	USA (United States)	31 Oct 60	394UNTS127	105673
Greece	Poland	08 Nov 60	483UNTS127	107010
Belgium	Congo (Zaire)	15 Nov 60	394UNTS79	105670
Multilateral		13 Dec 60	455UNTS3	106543
Multilateral		13 Dec 60	523UNTS117	107557
Multilateral		13 Dec 60	455UNTS204	106544
Panama	USA (United States)	23 Jan 61	445UNTS135	106382
Australia	Japan	07 Feb 61	450UNTS343	106478
Korea, South	USA (United States)	08 Feb 61	405UNTS37	105821
UK Great Britain	USA (United States)	10 Feb 61	409UNTS68	105879
Japan	Pakistan	07 Mar 61	450UNTS359	106479
Philippines	USA (United States)	12 Mar 61	288UNTS285	104210
Morocco	USA (United States)	31 Mar 61	406UNTS249	105854
Turkey	USSR (Soviet Union)	27 Apr 61	420UNTS307	106047
Honduras	IDA (Devel Assoc)	12 May 61	414UNTS180	105973
Sierra Leone	USA (United States)	19 May 61	409UNTS251	105890
USA (United States)	Upper Volta	01 Jun 61	410UNTS223	105906
Somalia	USSR (Soviet Union)	02 Jun 61	493UNTS173	107214
Nepal	USA (United States)	09 Jun 61	421UNTS223	106061
IDA (Devel Assoc)	Sudan	14 Jun 61	415UNTS50	105981
Finland	USA (United States)	16 Jun 61	413UNTS211	105955
Inter-Am Devel Bnk	USA (United States)	19 Jun 61	410UNTS34	105895
India	IDA (Devel Assoc)	21 Jun 61	418UNTS61	106017
Indonesia	UK Great Britain	29 Jun 61	443UNTS255	106364
Bulgaria	Netherlands	07 Jul 61	489UNTS21	107133
Albania	Austria	27 Jul 61	407UNTS37	105858
Colombia	IDA (Devel Assoc)	28 Aug 61	416UNTS3	105992
Taiwan	IDA (Devel Assoc)	30 Aug 61	416UNTS175	106003
Taiwan	IDA (Devel Assoc)	30 Aug 61	417UNTS227	106008
United Arab Rep	USA (United States)	02 Sep 61	421UNTS251	106063
India	IDA (Devel Assoc)	06 Sep 61	418UNTS81	106018
Taiwan	IDA (Devel Assoc)	06 Sep 61	417UNTS253	106009
Paraguay	USA (United States)	26 Sep 61	461UNTS91	106653
Pakistan	Philippines	29 Sep 61	422UNTS3	106065
IBRD (World Bank)	Switzerland	11 Oct 61	415UNTS396	200592
Pakistan	USA (United States)	14 Oct 61	426UNTS237	106141
Greece	USA (United States)	18 Oct 61	426UNTS209	106139
Switzerland	UK Great Britain	20 Oct 61	431UNTS29	106206
Greece	Morocco	01 Nov 61	483UNTS113	107009
Iraq	Syria	03 Nov 61	489UNTS45	107134
India	IDA (Devel Assoc)	22 Nov 61	427UNTS29	106145
India	IDA (Devel Assoc)	22 Nov 61	427UNTS55	106146
India	IDA (Devel Assoc)	22 Nov 61	427UNTS3	106144
IAEA (Atom Energy)	UN Special Fund	29 Nov 61	415UNTS408	200593
Morocco	USA (United States)	30 Nov 61	451UNTS167	106492
Taiwan	IDA (Devel Assoc)	01 Dec 61	426UNTS105	106132
Ivory Coast	USA (United States)	01 Dec 61	462UNTS221	106681
Ethiopia	USA (United States)	06 Dec 61	433UNTS231	106246
Denmark	Jordan	07 Dec 61	631UNTS333	109003

PARTY ONE	PARTY TWO	DATE	CITATION	NUMBER
Currency (Cont.)				
USA (United States)	Yugoslavia	28 Dec 61	434UNTS111	106259
Thailand	USA (United States)	12 Jan 62	459UNTS95	106615
Cyprus	USA (United States)	18 Jan 62	435UNTS3	106266
UNESCO (Educ/Cult)	USA (United States)	19 Jan 62	435UNTS99	106272
Ghana	USA (United States)	24 Jan 62	435UNTS23	106268
Hungary	Yugoslavia	09 Feb 62	577UNTS3	108370
IDA (Devel Assoc)	UK Great Britain	13 Mar 62	466UNTS331	106753
Togo	USA (United States)	20 Mar 62	445UNTS79	106378
Niger	USA (United States)	26 Apr 62	459UNTS129	106618
Dominican Republic	USA (United States)	02 May 62	442UNTS99	106341
Denmark	USA (United States)	28 May 62	450UNTS215	106469
Germany, West	Israel	01 Jun 62	448UNTS227	106435
United Arab Rep	USSR (Soviet Union)	23 Jun 62	472UNTS19	106835
Algeria	France	03 Jul 62	507UNTS25	107395
Ceylon (Sri Lanka)	USA (United States)	19 Jul 62	454UNTS31	106538
Ethiopia	USA (United States)	03 Aug 62	459UNTS79	106613
Chile	USA (United States)	07 Aug 62	461UNTS61	106652
Ethiopia	USA (United States)	13 Aug 62	459UNTS31	106611
IAEA (Atom Energy)	USA (United States)	20 Aug 62	456UNTS447	106570
Congo (Brazzaville)	USA (United States)	01 Sep 62	459UNTS117	106616
Morocco	USA (United States)	11 Sep 62	462UNTS207	106680
Multilateral		28 Sep 62	469UNTS169	106791
Multilateral		16 Oct 62	470UNTS321	106815
Cameroon	Greece	29 Oct 62	538UNTS185	107815
Congo (Zaire)	USA (United States)	17 Nov 62	474UNTS41	106870
Germany, West	USA (United States)	20 Nov 62	505UNTS263	107377
USA (United States)	Vietnam, South	21 Nov 62	469UNTS101	106786
Dominican Republic	USA (United States)	30 Nov 62	471UNTS25	106819
Laos	USSR (Soviet Union)	01 Dec 62	472UNTS3	106834
Laos	USSR (Soviet Union)	01 Dec 62	471UNTS181	106832
Australia	UK Great Britain	06 Dec 62	457UNTS145	106584
Multilateral		08 Dec 62	510UNTS235	107418
Nigeria	USA (United States)	24 Dec 62	462UNTS180	106677
Brazil	Taiwan	28 Dec 62	500UNTS61	107307
Trinidad/Tobago	USA (United States)	15 Jan 63	471UNTS141	106829
Greece	Pakistan	17 Jan 63	538UNTS175	107814
Malaysia	USA (United States)	28 Jan 63	473UNTS15	106850
Bolivia	USA (United States)	04 Feb 63	473UNTS65	106856
South Africa	Spain	08 Feb 63	458UNTS79	106593
India	New Zealand	22 Feb 63	486UNTS19	107069
Congo (Zaire)	USA (United States)	23 Feb 63	493UNTS3	107203
Israel	USA (United States)	21 Mar 63	476UNTS131	106907
Philippines	USA (United States)	23 Mar 63	474UNTS80	106873
Colombia	USA (United States)	27 Mar 63	489UNTS289	107145
Burma	UK Great Britain	02 Apr 63	475UNTS139	106890
Multilateral		02 Apr 63	475UNTS121	106889
Gabon	USA (United States)	10 Apr 63	474UNTS113	106876
Brazil	USSR (Soviet Union)	20 Apr 63	0UNTS0	109257
Brazil	USSR (Soviet Union)	20 Apr 63	0UNTS0	109256
Belgium	Netherlands	13 May 63	540UNTS3	107843
Canada	India	14 May 63	529UNTS31	107653
Thailand	USA (United States)	24 May 63	477UNTS123	106918
India	IDA (Devel Assoc)	24 May 63	483UNTS205	107014
Cyprus	USA (United States)	29 May 63	487UNTS283	107110
IDA (Devel Assoc)	Turkey	31 May 63	480UNTS127	106966
Argentina	UK Great Britain	05 Jun 63	482UNTS353	107004
Australia	UK Great Britain	06 Jun 63	472UNTS157	106838
Korea, South	USA (United States)	18 Jun 63	487UNTS297	107112
India	USA (United States)	19 Jun 63	479UNTS175	106952
Pakistan	IDA (Devel Assoc)	26 Jun 63	492UNTS115	107189
India	USA (United States)	27 Jun 63	479UNTS215	106955
United Arab Rep	USA (United States)	29 Jun 63	479UNTS207	106954
Finland	IAEA (Atom Energy)	02 Jul 63	490UNTS403	107167
Senegal	USA (United States)	03 Jul 63	527UNTS95	107620
Austria	Mongolia	15 Jul 63	496UNTS171	107251

PARTY ONE	PARTY TWO	DATE	CITATION	NUMBER
Currency (Cont.)				
Mali	Tunisia	24 Jul 63	602UNTS91	108708
Malagasy	USA (United States)	26 Jul 63	487UNTS189	107104
Pakistan	IDA (Devel Assoc)	26 Jul 63	492UNTS143	107190
New Zealand	USSR (Soviet Union)	01 Aug 63	486UNTS27	107070
Tanganyika	USSR (Soviet Union)	14 Aug 63	493UNTS195	107215
Pakistan	IDA (Devel Assoc)	16 Aug 63	492UNTS171	107191
Pakistan	IDA (Devel Assoc)	16 Aug 63	492UNTS205	107192
Afghanistan	USA (United States)	20 Aug 63	488UNTS41	107118
Australia	UK Great Britain	23 Sep 63	483UNTS39	107006
Greece	Poland	30 Sep 63	534UNTS23	107751
UK Great Britain	USA (United States)	11 Oct 63	483UNTS3	107005
Kuwait	USA (United States)	21 Oct 63	530UNTS281	107688
Multilateral		23 Oct 63	506UNTS197	107388
Iran	USA (United States)	24 Oct 63	489UNTS303	107146
UNESCO (Educ/Cult)	United Arab Rep	09 Nov 63	489UNTS233	107142
Tanganyika	USA (United States)	14 Nov 63	493UNTS75	107208
Iran	USA (United States)	17 Nov 63	530UNTS41	107671
Syria	USA (United States)	18 Nov 63	494UNTS169	107232
Tunisia	USA (United States)	18 Nov 63	494UNTS193	107233
Jordan	IDA (Devel Assoc)	12 Dec 63	492UNTS3	107184
Greece	USA (United States)	13 Dec 63	494UNTS55	107226
Multilateral		18 Dec 63	490UNTS383	107166
Netherlands	Poland	20 Dec 63	514UNTS169	107446
Greece	Poland	21 Dec 63	538UNTS155	107813
IDA (Devel Assoc)	Syria	24 Dec 63	534UNTS253	107764
Paraguay	IDA (Devel Assoc)	26 Dec 63	507UNTS3	107394
Congo (Zaire)	UK Great Britain	03 Jan 64	534UNTS417	107770
Somalia	USA (United States)	08 Jan 64	505UNTS165	107372
IDA (Devel Assoc)	Tanganyika	05 Feb 64	506UNTS91	107382
Iceland	USA (United States)	13 Feb 64	511UNTS3	107421
Iceland	USA (United States)	13 Feb 64	524UNTS235	107576
Korea, South	USA (United States)	18 Mar 64	524UNTS263	107578
Pakistan	IDA (Devel Assoc)	25 Mar 64	535UNTS43	107775
Pakistan	IDA (Devel Assoc)	25 Mar 64	534UNTS275	107765
Malaysia	Netherlands	07 Apr 64	524UNTS81	107567
Liberia	USA (United States)	14 Apr 64	526UNTS221	107606
Kenya	USA (United States)	20 Apr 64	524UNTS165	107571
Taiwan	USA (United States)	23 Apr 64	524UNTS141	107570
USA (United States)	Yugoslavia	27 Apr 64	526UNTS73	107601
Liberia	USA (United States)	08 May 64	526UNTS239	107608
Taiwan	Peru	08 Jun 64	548UNTS151	107976
India	IDA (Devel Assoc)	09 Jun 64	506UNTS31	107380
Mali	USA (United States)	09 Jun 64	530UNTS133	107678
Pakistan	IDA (Devel Assoc)	11 Jun 64	506UNTS3	107379
Pakistan	IDA (Devel Assoc)	11 Jun 64	534UNTS309	107766
Guinea	USA (United States)	13 Jun 64	531UNTS263	107708
Taiwan	Ecuador	17 Jun 64	533UNTS141	107740
Pakistan	IDA (Devel Assoc)	24 Jun 64	533UNTS191	107743
Niger	IDA (Devel Assoc)	24 Jun 64	554UNTS93	108098
Pakistan	IDA (Devel Assoc)	24 Jun 64	533UNTS165	107742
Mauritania	USA (United States)	03 Jul 64	532UNTS307	107724
Sweden	USA (United States)	06 Jul 64	529UNTS287	107666
India	IDA (Devel Assoc)	06 Jul 64	534UNTS49	107753
Multilateral		10 Jul 64	613UNTS3	108851
IDA (Devel Assoc)	Turkey	14 Jul 64	534UNTS339	107767
Pakistan	IDA (Devel Assoc)	21 Jul 64	534UNTS373	107768
Bolivia	IDA (Devel Assoc)	24 Jul 64	534UNTS203	107763
Bolivia	IDA (Devel Assoc)	24 Jul 64	534UNTS171	107762
Kenya	IDA (Devel Assoc)	17 Aug 64	535UNTS79	107776
Pakistan	IDA (Devel Assoc)	26 Aug 64	535UNTS263	107784
Ceylon (Sri Lanka)	USA (United States)	29 Aug 64	531UNTS93	107695
IDA (Devel Assoc)	Turkey	31 Aug 64	535UNTS111	107777
Pakistan	IDA (Devel Assoc)	22 Sep 64	594UNTS225	108605
Taiwan	Mexico	25 Sep 64	547UNTS233	107960
Mali	IDA (Devel Assoc)	29 Sep 64	594UNTS187	108604

PARTY ONE	PARTY TWO	DATE	CITATION	NUMBER
Currency (Cont.)				
Brazil	UK Great Britain	14 Oct 64	539UNTS289	107840
Taiwan	Ecuador	23 Oct 64	543UNTS241	107904
India	IDA (Devel Assoc)	26 Oct 64	535UNTS245	107783
USA (United States)	Yugoslavia	05 Nov 64	550UNTS31	108007
Greece	Yugoslavia	05 Nov 64	539UNTS13	107820
Taiwan	Guatemala	08 Nov 64	543UNTS227	107903
USA (United States)	Yugoslavia	09 Nov 64	533UNTS39	107731
Afghanistan	IDA (Devel Assoc)	23 Nov 64	567UNTS155	108255
Mauritania	IDA (Devel Assoc)	28 Dec 64	540UNTS163	107849
Kenya	IDA (Devel Assoc)	29 Dec 64	535UNTS225	107782
Laos	USA (United States)	29 Dec 64	542UNTS23	107876
Morocco	USA (United States)	29 Dec 64	593UNTS185	108584
Central Afri Rep	USA (United States)	31 Dec 64	542UNTS29	107877
Honduras	IDA (Devel Assoc)	02 Feb 65	561UNTS279	108189
Belgium	Congo (Zaire)	06 Feb 65	540UNTS227	107852
Japan	UK Great Britain	22 Feb 65	560UNTS123	108171
Nigeria	IDA (Devel Assoc)	01 Mar 65	563UNTS3	108201
Nigeria	IDA (Devel Assoc)	01 Mar 65	571UNTS3	108297
Dahomey	USA (United States)	13 Mar 65	549UNTS43	107987
Denmark	Malaysia	26 Mar 65	540UNTS205	107851
Multilateral		29 Mar 65	540UNTS145	107848
IDA (Devel Assoc)	Somalia	29 Mar 65	586UNTS101	108499
IDA (Devel Assoc)	Turkey	01 Apr 65	554UNTS137	108100
Jamaica	IBRD (World Bank)	08 Apr 65	539UNTS303	107841
Philippines	USA (United States)	23 Apr 65	546UNTS157	107942
UK Great Britain	USA (United States)	10 May 65	545UNTS181	107934
Chad	USA (United States)	12 May 65	546UNTS183	107944
Bolivia	USA (United States)	12 May 65	564UNTS143	108226
India	IBRD (World Bank)	28 May 65	552UNTS39	108049
Uganda	USA (United States)	29 May 65	546UNTS209	107948
USA (United States)	Upper Volta	18 Jun 65	549UNTS133	107996
Austria	Petrol Export Org	24 Jun 65	589UNTS135	108540
Pakistan	IDA (Devel Assoc)	30 Jun 65	554UNTS111	108099
Kenya	IDA (Devel Assoc)	30 Jun 65	554UNTS75	108097
New Zealand	Poland	07 Jul 65	548UNTS19	107966
Mali	USA (United States)	14 Jul 65	564UNTS101	108223
Malta	Yugoslavia	15 Jul 65	561UNTS223	108186
Multilateral		22 Jul 65	561UNTS333	200618
Israel	USA (United States)	26 Jul 65	549UNTS49	107988
India	IDA (Devel Assoc)	11 Aug 65	562UNTS277	108199
Morocco	IDA (Devel Assoc)	11 Oct 65	562UNTS299	108200
Australia	USSR (Soviet Union)	15 Oct 65	553UNTS239	108092
Turkey	UK Great Britain	21 Oct 65	561UNTS185	108180
Chile	UK Great Britain	23 Nov 65	560UNTS215	108176
Multilateral		04 Dec 65	571UNTS123	108303
Italy	USA (United States)	27 Dec 65	574UNTS145	108347
Multilateral		31 Dec 65	616UNTS317	108904
IDA (Devel Assoc)	Tanzania	13 Jan 66	567UNTS177	108256
Pakistan	IDA (Devel Assoc)	13 Jan 66	567UNTS67	108252
Multilateral		17 Jan 66	592UNTS101	108573
Japan	USSR (Soviet Union)	21 Jan 66	633UNTS165	109038
IDA (Devel Assoc)	UK Great Britain	08 Feb 66	567UNTS207	108257
Multilateral		10 Feb 66	575UNTS129	108356
Pakistan	IDA (Devel Assoc)	10 Feb 66	575UNTS89	108355
Colombia	USA (United States)	10 Mar 66	0UNTS0	109604
USA (United States)	Vietnam, South	21 Mar 66	578UNTS165	108394
Singapore	USA (United States)	25 Mar 66	580UNTS221	108425
Paraguay	IDA (Devel Assoc)	04 Apr 66	582UNTS331	108469
Israel	USA (United States)	06 Jun 66	578UNTS143	108392
Pakistan	IDA (Devel Assoc)	17 Jun 66	582UNTS297	108468
Multilateral		20 Jun 66	573UNTS41	108322
India	IDA (Devel Assoc)	29 Jun 66	585UNTS101	108484
India	IDA (Devel Assoc)	29 Jun 66	582UNTS277	108467
Brazil	Denmark	08 Jul 66	581UNTS95	108435
Turkey	UK Great Britain	29 Jul 66	597UNTS241	108649

PARTY ONE	PARTY TWO	DATE	CITATION	NUMBER
Currency (Cont.)				
Tunisia	USA (United States)	30 Jul 66	601UNTS133	108692
IDA (Devel Assoc)	Siam	02 Aug 66	585UNTS271	108492
IDA (Devel Assoc)	Turkey	10 Aug 66	585UNTS237	108491
USA (United States)	Zambia	11 Aug 66	616UNTS267	108901
India	IDA (Devel Assoc)	19 Aug 66	584UNTS193	108478
Kenya	IDA (Devel Assoc)	19 Aug 66	585UNTS119	108485
Denmark	Malawi	01 Sep 66	586UNTS3	108493
UN Special Fund	UPU (Postal Union)	21 Sep 66	573UNTS259	200626
IDA (Devel Assoc)	Senegal	29 Sep 66	594UNTS277	108607
Malawi	IDA (Devel Assoc)	04 Oct 66	584UNTS215	108479
IBRD (World Bank)	IFC (Finance Corp)	28 Oct 66	586UNTS225	200628
Romania	United Arab Rep	14 Nov 66	642UNTS141	109170
Guinea	Romania	01 Dec 66	642UNTS89	109167
Pakistan	IDA (Devel Assoc)	23 Dec 66	594UNTS255	108606
India	IDA (Devel Assoc)	23 Dec 66	594UNTS165	108603
Trinidad/Tobago	UK Great Britain	23 Jan 67	605UNTS277	108767
Korea, South	New Zealand	31 Jan 67	598UNTS91	108656
Germany, West	UK Great Britain	05 May 67	613UNTS313	108858
Ecuador	Romania	10 Oct 67	642UNTS33	109163
Denmark	India	25 Mar 68	0UNTS0	109229
Germany, West	UK Great Britain	11 Apr 68	0UNTS0	109288
Denmark	India	29 Apr 68	0UNTS0	109230
Inter-Am Devel Bnk	UN Special Fund	16 Jul 68	640UNTS305	200640
Ireland	UK Great Britain	23 Sep 68	0UNTS0	109374
Monetary and gold transfers				
Netherlands	UK Great Britain	14 Jun 40	2UNTS251	200018
UK Great Britain	USSR (Soviet Union)	16 Aug 41	91UNTS341	200269
Multilateral		26 Mar 43	13UNTS427	200089
Multilateral		21 Oct 43	2UNTS281	200021
Belgium	UK Great Britain	05 Oct 44	5UNTS227	200031
Canada	Czechoslovakia	01 Mar 45	45UNTS283	200185
Sweden	UK Great Britain	06 Mar 45	5UNTS241	200032
Sweden	UK Great Britain	06 Mar 45	82UNTS219	101095
France	UK Great Britain	27 Mar 45	98UNTS227	200274
Canada	Norway	25 Jun 45	45UNTS297	200186
Denmark	UK Great Britain	16 Aug 45	5UNTS251	200033
Netherlands	UK Great Britain	07 Sep 45	2UNTS325	200024
Belgium	Norway	23 Oct 45	16UNTS311	200107
Netherlands	Switzerland	24 Oct 45	3UNTS73	100025
Belgium	Canada	25 Oct 45	230UNTS127	103180
Czechoslovakia	UK Great Britain	01 Nov 45	5UNTS15	100062
Netherlands	Norway	06 Nov 45	2UNTS5	100017
Norway	UK Great Britain	08 Nov 45	5UNTS27	100063
Netherlands	Sweden	30 Nov 45	2UNTS27	100019
UK Great Britain	USA (United States)	06 Dec 45	126UNTS13	101679
Denmark	UK Great Britain	06 Dec 45	5UNTS3	100061
Czechoslovakia	Norway	13 Dec 45	17UNTS261	100280
Multilateral		27 Dec 45	2UNTS39	100020
Denmark	Netherlands	31 Jan 46	3UNTS3	100021
Canada	Netherlands	05 Feb 46	43UNTS3	100658
Canada	Mexico	08 Feb 46	230UNTS183	103183
France	Norway	06 Mar 46	15UNTS13	100227
Switzerland	UK Great Britain	12 Mar 46	6UNTS107	100070
Portugal	UK Great Britain	16 Apr 46	6UNTS119	100071
France	Greece	24 Apr 46	91UNTS83	101243
France	UK Great Britain	29 Apr 46	98UNTS123	101360
France	USA (United States)	28 May 46	84UNTS59	101119
Poland	UK Great Britain	24 Jun 46	11UNTS59	100149
Philippines	USA (United States)	04 Jul 46	43UNTS135	100668
Norway	Sweden	22 Nov 46	15UNTS171	100233
France	UK Great Britain	03 Dec 46	54UNTS117	100798
Norway	Poland	03 Dec 46	15UNTS203	100234
Canada	Nicaragua	19 Dec 46	236UNTS229	103326
Norway	USSR (Soviet Union)	27 Dec 46	17UNTS283	100282

PARTY ONE	PARTY TWO	DATE	CITATION	NUMBER
Monetary and gold transfers (Cont.)				
Multilateral		10 Feb 47	42UNTS3	100645
Netherlands	UK Great Britain	26 Feb 47	11UNTS279	100167
Belgium	Turkey	12 Mar 47	33UNTS43	100513
Spain	UK Great Britain	28 Mar 47	66UNTS91	100849
Denmark	Norway	15 Apr 47	12UNTS323	100191
New Zealand	UK Great Britain	27 May 47	17UNTS211	100277
Austria	USA (United States)	21 Jun 47	67UNTS99	100869
Sweden	USA (United States)	24 Jun 47	36UNTS25	100565
United Arab Rep	UK Great Britain	30 Jun 47	93UNTS165	101299
Belgium	South Africa	04 Jul 47	47UNTS9	100720
UK Great Britain	Uruguay	15 Jul 47	71UNTS179	100918
Norway	Switzerland	15 Jul 47	12UNTS351	100192
Taiwan	Italy	30 Jul 47	12UNTS377	100194
India	UK Great Britain	14 Aug 47	11UNTS371	100176
Bulgaria	Yugoslavia	22 Aug 47	111UNTS241	101538
South Africa	UK Great Britain	09 Oct 47	17UNTS239	100278
Multilateral		30 Oct 47	55UNTS188	100814
Multilateral		04 Nov 47	93UNTS61	101288
Multilateral		16 Dec 47	82UNTS237	101096
UK Great Britain	USSR (Soviet Union)	27 Dec 47	82UNTS251	101098
United Arab Rep	UK Great Britain	05 Jan 48	77UNTS3	100988
Denmark	Hungary	28 Feb 48	85UNTS35	101144
India	Pakistan	31 Mar 48	54UNTS33	100793
Denmark	Norway	21 Apr 48	18UNTS139	100284
Norway	Sweden	29 Apr 48	26UNTS11	100374
Multilateral		13 May 48	140UNTS187	101888
Czechoslovakia	Yugoslavia	24 May 48	112UNTS225	101545
India	Pakistan	30 Jun 48	29UNTS199	100441
Peru	UK Great Britain	20 Jul 48	66UNTS197	100855
Korea, South	USA (United States)	11 Sep 48	89UNTS155	101216
UK Great Britain	USA (United States)	22 Sep 48	71UNTS64	100910
Argentina	Denmark	14 Dec 48	74UNTS41	100956
Spain	UK Great Britain	15 Dec 48	87UNTS49	101165
Denmark	Turkey	15 Dec 48	76UNTS3	100974
Belgium	Greece	27 Dec 48	77UNTS293	101005
Denmark	Sweden	08 Feb 49	33UNTS227	100519
Netherlands	Norway	26 Feb 49	29UNTS33	100432
Belgium	Portugal	01 Mar 49	32UNTS49	100488
Finland	Greece	24 Mar 49	78UNTS13	101009
United Arab Rep	UK Great Britain	31 Mar 49	83UNTS139	101106
India	Pakistan	23 Apr 49	54UNTS51	100795
Belgium	Bolivia	26 Apr 49	34UNTS103	100530
Netherlands	USA (United States)	17 May 49	46UNTS291	100717
UNICEF (Children)	UK Great Britain	17 Jun 49	65UNTS50	100820
Multilateral		05 Aug 49	88UNTS229	101195
Czechoslovakia	UK Great Britain	18 Aug 49	86UNTS129	101155
Argentina	Norway	09 Sep 49	42UNTS125	100646
Czechoslovakia	Denmark	17 Dec 49	74UNTS159	100962
Sweden	UK Great Britain	30 Dec 49	87UNTS59	101166
Austria	UK Great Britain	26 Jan 50	97UNTS183	101350
Israel	UK Great Britain	30 Mar 50	86UNTS231	101162
Paraguay	UK Great Britain	03 Apr 50	99UNTS81	101372
Italy	New Zealand	19 Apr 50	67UNTS81	100867
Denmark	Spain	12 Jul 50	71UNTS129	100913
Denmark	UK Great Britain	19 Oct 50	79UNTS25	101028
Norway	UK Great Britain	06 Nov 50	88UNTS257	101197
Germany, West	UK Great Britain	09 Dec 50	88UNTS247	101196
Italy	UK Great Britain	21 Dec 50	175UNTS187	102301
Austria	UK Great Britain	31 Jan 51	88UNTS107	101187
New Zealand	Yugoslavia	27 Feb 51	150UNTS165	101971
Multilateral		18 Apr 51	261UNTS140	103729
Ceylon (Sri Lanka)	India	30 Apr 51	196UNTS199	102625
Austria	USA (United States)	15 May 51	139UNTS79	101876
United Arab Rep	UK Great Britain	01 Jul 51	249UNTS143	103504
Portugal	UK Great Britain	20 Jul 51	105UNTS61	101453

Monetary and gold transfers (Cont.)

PARTY ONE	PARTY TWO	DATE	CITATION	NUMBER
France	UK Great Britain	20 Aug 51	108UNTS263	101479
Japan	UK Great Britain	31 Aug 51	108UNTS273	101480
Ethiopia	USA (United States)	07 Sep 51	206UNTS41	102785
Pakistan	UK Great Britain	29 Sep 51	134UNTS183	101798
Denmark	Italy	24 Oct 51	118UNTS91	101598
Spain	UK Great Britain	20 Dec 51	123UNTS187	101660
UK Great Britain	USA (United States)	08 Jan 52	179UNTS201	102369
UK Great Britain	USA (United States)	08 Jan 52	126UNTS307	101696
Netherlands	USA (United States)	15 May 52	177UNTS233	102321
South Africa	USA (United States)	24 Jun 52	177UNTS241	102322
Taiwan	USA (United States)	25 Jun 52	136UNTS229	101837
Iraq	UK Great Britain	10 Jul 52	151UNTS227	101998
Multilateral		11 Jul 52	169UNTS3	102220
UK Great Britain	Yugoslavia	20 Aug 52	158UNTS439	102077
Australia	Germany, West	29 Aug 52	184UNTS147	102446
Ceylon (Sri Lanka)	Japan	06 Sep 52	314UNTS279	104552
United Arab Rep	UK Great Britain	30 Oct 52	172UNTS3	102236
Libya	UK Great Britain	21 Feb 53	311UNTS115	104501
Turkey	Yugoslavia	26 Feb 53	247UNTS54	103460
Multilateral		27 Feb 53	333UNTS3	104764
Israel	UK Great Britain	13 May 53	175UNTS179	102300
Germany, West	UK Great Britain	22 May 53	172UNTS179	102246
Japan	Syria	08 Jun 53	184UNTS3	102436
UK Great Britain	USA (United States)	24 Jun 53	224UNTS141	103074
Ethiopia	USA (United States)	25 Jun 53	212UNTS175	102869
Multilateral		20 Jul 53	227UNTS217	103140
India	UK Great Britain	20 Jul 53	196UNTS251	102628
Ceylon (Sri Lanka)	Yugoslavia	30 Jul 53	337UNTS103	104819
Argentina	USSR (Soviet Union)	05 Aug 53	221UNTS99	103004
Denmark	Germany, West	14 Aug 53	202UNTS3	102725
Japan	UK Great Britain	29 Jan 54	190UNTS319	102572
France	Greece	13 May 54	222UNTS299	103036
Pakistan	Yugoslavia	15 May 54	286UNTS3	104158
Multilateral		08 Jul 54	287UNTS27	104178
Switzerland	UK Great Britain	16 Jul 54	199UNTS197	102685
Multilateral		28 Sep 54	207UNTS293	102812
Greece	Netherlands	01 Nov 54	223UNTS79	103057
Mexico	USA (United States)	19 Nov 54	238UNTS237	103367
Netherlands	USA (United States)	25 May 55	289UNTS227	104220
Libya	USA (United States)	30 May 55	270UNTS43	103890
Germany, West	UK Great Britain	22 Jul 55	269UNTS189	103881
Philippines	UK Great Britain	29 Aug 55	221UNTS241	103009
Austria	USSR (Soviet Union)	17 Oct 55	0UNTS0	109255
Denmark	Syria	20 Oct 55	250UNTS61	103518
Italy	Syria	10 Nov 55	267UNTS157	103841
Bulgaria	Yugoslavia	15 Nov 55	396UNTS191	105697
Syria	USSR (Soviet Union)	16 Nov 55	259UNTS71	103683
Paraguay	UK Great Britain	21 Nov 55	252UNTS107	103560
Costa Rica	Guatemala	20 Dec 55	280UNTS121	104056
Norway	Syria	25 Feb 56	463UNTS217	106706
Guatemala	Honduras	22 Aug 56	263UNTS49	103767
Austria	UK Great Britain	27 Oct 56	264UNTS67	103789
Belgium	Spain	28 Nov 56	308UNTS285	104465
Indonesia	Yugoslavia	14 Dec 56	378UNTS117	105422
Multilateral		19 Dec 56	427UNTS93	106148
Austria	Pakistan	24 Dec 56	316UNTS83	104579
Germany, West	Sweden	29 Jan 57	393UNTS113	105654
Germany, West	Norway	29 Jan 57	353UNTS39	105037
Denmark	Germany, West	29 Jan 57	302UNTS75	104354
Ceylon (Sri Lanka)	Italy	23 Apr 57	337UNTS115	104820
Belgium	Hungary	01 Jun 57	291UNTS17	104242
Czechoslovakia	United Arab Rep	30 Jun 57	411UNTS126	105917
France	Italy	01 Aug 57	302UNTS221	104360
Ceylon (Sri Lanka)	China People's Rep	19 Sep 57	337UNTS137	104821
France	Italy	19 Sep 57	302UNTS225	104361

Monetary and gold transfers (Cont.)

PARTY ONE	PARTY TWO	DATE	CITATION	NUMBER
Multilateral		03 Oct 57	366UNTS87	105216
Multilateral		03 Oct 57	366UNTS193	105218
Fed of Malaya	UK Great Britain	18 Oct 57	335UNTS3	104775
Argentina	Italy	25 Nov 57	305UNTS275	104424
Italy	Monaco	06 Dec 57	363UNTS45	105198
Poland	Yugoslavia	16 Jan 58	340UNTS137	104863
Netherlands	Switzerland	28 Mar 58	318UNTS175	104614
Czechoslovakia	Poland	29 Mar 58	340UNTS199	104865
Bulgaria	Denmark	28 May 58	312UNTS235	104521
India	USSR (Soviet Union)	02 Jun 58	393UNTS3	105650
Multilateral		10 Jun 58	454UNTS47	106539
Denmark	Romania	25 Jun 58	345UNTS231	104970
Ethiopia	UK Great Britain	07 Jul 58	331UNTS3	104749
Denmark	Hungary	17 Jul 58	344UNTS281	104954
Lebanon	USA (United States)	03 Sep 58	336UNTS91	104801
Ghana	UK Great Britain	24 Sep 58	411UNTS146	105918
Iraq	USSR (Soviet Union)	11 Oct 58	328UNTS95	104730
Multilateral		27 Oct 58	351UNTS303	105031
Netherlands	Turkey	29 Nov 58	335UNTS229	104790
Czechoslovakia	Hungary	30 Jan 59	351UNTS3	105016
Poland	UK Great Britain	03 Apr 59	351UNTS295	105030
Austria	USA (United States)	22 May 59	347UNTS3	104988
Ceylon (Sri Lanka)	Norway	29 May 59	411UNTS165	105919
Ceylon (Sri Lanka)	Denmark	29 May 59	348UNTS225	105002
Czechoslovakia	Switzerland	04 Jun 59	349UNTS121	105012
Multilateral		04 Jan 60	370UNTS3	105266
Czechoslovakia	UK Great Britain	15 Jan 60	374UNTS207	105336
Multilateral		26 Jan 60	439UNTS249	106333
Belgium	Switzerland	24 Mar 60	416UNTS81	105996
Switzerland	Tunisia	21 May 60	497UNTS109	107265
Kuwait	UK Great Britain	24 May 60	412UNTS4	105923
Austria	Spain	17 Jun 60	390UNTS17	105600
Ireland	Portugal	24 Jun 60	412UNTS30	105924
Poland	UK Great Britain	02 Jul 60	385UNTS87	105532
Ghana	Netherlands	30 Jul 60	412UNTS51	105925
Belgium	Burma	17 Aug 60	540UNTS185	107850
Ghana	United Arab Rep	29 Aug 60	412UNTS71	105926
Argentina	Bolivia	07 Sep 60	0UNTS0	109516
Hungary	UK Great Britain	25 Oct 60	419UNTS309	106034
Burma	Switzerland	31 Oct 60	465UNTS97	106723
Indonesia	UK Great Britain	23 Nov 60	398UNTS71	105718
Multilateral		13 Dec 60	523UNTS117	107557
Jordan	Sweden	09 Jan 61	465UNTS155	106726
Netherlands	Spain	08 Apr 61	482UNTS193	106996
Somalia	USSR (Soviet Union)	02 Jun 61	493UNTS173	107214
New Zealand	UK Great Britain	13 Jun 61	497UNTS293	107273
Inter-Am Devel Bnk	USA (United States)	19 Jun 61	410UNTS34	105895
Indonesia	Japan	01 Jul 61	517UNTS107	107484
Albania	Austria	27 Jul 61	407UNTS37	105858
Czechoslovakia	Ghana	02 Aug 61	465UNTS249	106730
Jordan	Norway	21 Aug 61	465UNTS275	106731
Liberia	Switzerland	31 Aug 61	559UNTS215	108160
Ghana	Romania	30 Sep 61	467UNTS443	106769
Belgium	Italy	28 Oct 61	429UNTS199	106199
Iraq	Syria	03 Nov 61	489UNTS45	107134
Czechoslovakia	Guinea	16 Dec 61	559UNTS49	108154
Netherlands	Sweden	08 Jan 62	466UNTS65	106737
Multilateral		23 Mar 62	434UNTS145	106262
Luxembourg	Spain	26 Mar 62	563UNTS205	108211
France	Luxembourg	29 Mar 62	563UNTS227	108212
Sierra Leone	UK Great Britain	05 Apr 62	434UNTS227	106265
Multilateral		25 May 62	486UNTS103	107075
Czechoslovakia	Senegal	20 Jun 62	498UNTS145	107280
United Arab Rep	USSR (Soviet Union)	23 Jun 62	472UNTS19	106835
Netherlands	Norway	18 Oct 62	466UNTS145	106741

PARTY ONE	PARTY TWO	DATE	CITATION	NUMBER
Monetary and gold transfers (Cont.)				
Ghana	Tunisia	11 Dec 62	563UNTS243	108213
Syria	United Arab Rep	27 Dec 62	491UNTS245	107180
Senegal	Switzerland	23 Jan 63	524UNTS23	107564
Cyprus	Denmark	27 Apr 63	529UNTS255	107664
Multilateral		23 Oct 63	506UNTS197	107388
Multilateral		09 Nov 63	489UNTS209	107141
Netherlands	Portugal	22 Nov 63	492UNTS31	107185
Malaysia	Netherlands	07 Apr 64	524UNTS81	107567
Austria	Turkey	15 May 64	515UNTS109	107457
Finland	UK Great Britain	25 Mar 65	539UNTS103	107826
Denmark	Malaysia	26 Mar 65	540UNTS205	107851
Ghana	Malawi	04 May 65	541UNTS163	107869
Denmark	Spain	05 May 65	543UNTS255	107905
Multilateral		04 Dec 65	571UNTS123	108303
Denmark	Singapore	20 Dec 66	593UNTS125	108580
Israel	USA (United States)	04 Aug 67	0UNTS0	109351
Denmark	Malaysia	14 Dec 67	614UNTS26	108862
Currency deposits				
Netherlands	UK Great Britain	14 Jun 40	2UNTS251	200018
France	Netherlands	14 Jun 40	2UNTS263	200019
Haiti	USA (United States)	13 Sep 41	103UNTS141	200311
Netherlands	Sweden	30 Nov 45	2UNTS27	100019
Czechoslovakia	Norway	13 Dec 45	17UNTS261	100280
Greece	UK Great Britain	24 Jan 46	6UNTS45	100067
Taiwan	USA (United States)	30 Aug 46	12UNTS39	100179
Denmark	New Zealand	18 Sep 46	10UNTS39	100141
Albania	Yugoslavia	03 Oct 46	111UNTS87	101519
Burma	USA (United States)	28 Feb 47	25UNTS27	100355
Spain	UK Great Britain	28 Mar 47	66UNTS91	100849
Bulgaria	Denmark	09 May 47	74UNTS139	100960
Poland	UK Great Britain	02 Mar 48	77UNTS47	100991
India	Pakistan	31 Mar 48	54UNTS33	100793
Denmark	Norway	21 Apr 48	18UNTS139	100284
Norway	Sweden	29 Apr 48	26UNTS11	100374
India	Pakistan	30 Jun 48	29UNTS199	100441
Taiwan	USA (United States)	03 Jul 48	17UNTS119	100273
Korea, South	USA (United States)	10 Dec 48	55UNTS157	100813
Spain	UK Great Britain	15 Dec 48	87UNTS49	101165
Denmark	Turkey	15 Dec 48	76UNTS3	100974
Belgium	Luxembourg	14 Jan 49	36UNTS339	100572
Belgium	Portugal	01 Mar 49	32UNTS49	100488
Denmark	Finland	22 Mar 49	33UNTS247	100520
United Arab Rep	UK Great Britain	31 Mar 49	83UNTS139	101106
Greece	Turkey	21 Jul 49	78UNTS65	101012
Multilateral		05 Aug 49	88UNTS229	101195
Czechoslovakia	UK Great Britain	18 Aug 49	86UNTS129	101155
Norway	Portugal	28 Nov 49	47UNTS117	100726
Turkey	USA (United States)	27 Dec 49	98UNTS141	101361
Sweden	UK Great Britain	30 Dec 49	87UNTS59	101166
Austria	UK Great Britain	26 Jan 50	97UNTS183	101350
Ceylon (Sri Lanka)	WHO (World Health)	17 Feb 50	102UNTS309	200309
Israel	UK Great Britain	30 Mar 50	86UNTS231	101162
Brazil	USA (United States)	16 Aug 50	140UNTS223	101890
Denmark	Italy	04 Oct 50	78UNTS353	101025
Colombia	Denmark	26 Jan 51	87UNTS161	101171
Austria	USA (United States)	15 May 51	139UNTS79	101876
UK Great Britain	USA (United States)	18 Jul 51	117UNTS49	101583
Jordan	USA (United States)	20 Dec 51	157UNTS69	102048
India	USA (United States)	05 Jan 52	157UNTS39	102045
UK Great Britain	USA (United States)	08 Jan 52	126UNTS307	101696
Iran	USA (United States)	20 Jan 52	200UNTS191	102703
Libya	USA (United States)	21 Jan 52	183UNTS177	102427
Jordan	USA (United States)	12 Feb 52	168UNTS25	102211
Peru	USA (United States)	09 Apr 52	184UNTS295	102454

PARTY ONE	PARTY TWO	DATE	CITATION	NUMBER
Currency deposits (Cont.)				
Israel	USA (United States)	09 May 52	177UNTS269	102326
Israel	USA (United States)	09 May 52	177UNTS63	102309
Bolivia	USA (United States)	18 Jun 52	199UNTS211	102686
Ethiopia	USA (United States)	18 Jun 52	181UNTS207	102410
Ethiopia	USA (United States)	24 Jun 52	181UNTS215	102411
Chile	USA (United States)	30 Jun 52	199UNTS241	102688
Panama	USA (United States)	30 Jun 52	181UNTS121	102404
Ethiopia	USA (United States)	07 Nov 52	184UNTS285	102453
United Arab Rep	USA (United States)	12 Mar 53	204UNTS3	102747
United Arab Rep	USA (United States)	19 Mar 53	215UNTS17	102909
El Salvador	USA (United States)	14 May 53	234UNTS71	103273
United Arab Rep	USA (United States)	21 May 53	204UNTS29	102748
United Arab Rep	USA (United States)	18 Jun 53	215UNTS45	102910
Liberia	USA (United States)	23 Jun 53	213UNTS37	102879
Ethiopia	USA (United States)	25 Jun 53	212UNTS175	102869
Brazil	USA (United States)	26 Jun 53	336UNTS241	104808
Chile	USA (United States)	27 Jun 53	229UNTS193	103167
Chile	USA (United States)	27 Jun 53	229UNTS53	103160
Nicaragua	USA (United States)	30 Jun 53	215UNTS133	102917
Ethiopia	USA (United States)	30 Jun 53	212UNTS135	102865
Chile	USA (United States)	30 Dec 53	236UNTS41	103315
Japan	USA (United States)	08 Mar 54	232UNTS227	103238
Afghanistan	USA (United States)	20 Mar 54	229UNTS7	103156
Panama	USA (United States)	11 May 54	236UNTS107	103319
Ethiopia	USA (United States)	12 Jun 54	234UNTS25	103270
Jordan	USA (United States)	17 Jun 54	266UNTS137	103828
Italy	USA (United States)	28 Jun 54	237UNTS121	103340
Chile	USA (United States)	28 Jun 54	233UNTS3	103246
Ecuador	USA (United States)	30 Jun 54	236UNTS163	103323
Germany, West	UK Great Britain	10 Jul 54	199UNTS135	102680
Germany, West	USA (United States)	29 Oct 54	273UNTS3	103943
Pakistan	USA (United States)	18 Jan 55	241UNTS53	103423
Chile	USA (United States)	27 Jan 55	262UNTS3	103735
Peru	USA (United States)	07 Feb 55	241UNTS63	103424
USA (United States)	Vietnam, South	07 Mar 55	277UNTS285	104013
Mexico	USA (United States)	09 Mar 55	263UNTS247	103776
Israel	USA (United States)	29 Apr 55	261UNTS331	103731
Peru	USA (United States)	30 Apr 55	263UNTS309	103780
Italy	USA (United States)	19 May 55	269UNTS83	103876
Multilateral		25 May 55	264UNTS117	103791
Thailand	USA (United States)	21 Jun 55	262UNTS87	103738
Colombia	USA (United States)	23 Jun 55	263UNTS337	103781
Laos	USA (United States)	08 Jul 55	278UNTS59	104021
Israel	USA (United States)	10 Nov 55	240UNTS3	103390
United Arab Rep	USA (United States)	14 Dec 55	240UNTS37	103392
Colombia	USA (United States)	20 Dec 55	241UNTS25	103421
Germany, West	USA (United States)	23 Dec 55	240UNTS79	103395
Italy	USA (United States)	27 Feb 56	291UNTS287	104260
Chile	USA (United States)	13 Mar 56	275UNTS49	103975
Peru	USA (United States)	07 May 56	268UNTS285	103862
Burma	USA (United States)	30 Jun 56	281UNTS65	104070
Netherlands	USA (United States)	07 Aug 56	281UNTS57	104069
Pakistan	USA (United States)	07 Aug 56	281UNTS75	104071
Greece	USA (United States)	08 Aug 56	277UNTS203	104007
Taiwan	USA (United States)	14 Aug 56	281UNTS257	104083
India	USA (United States)	29 Aug 56	278UNTS25	104019
Israel	USA (United States)	11 Sep 56	277UNTS215	104008
Spain	USA (United States)	23 Oct 56	277UNTS105	104001
USA (United States)	Yugoslavia	03 Nov 56	277UNTS119	104002
Turkey	USA (United States)	12 Nov 56	282UNTS77	104093
Turkey	USA (United States)	23 Nov 56	290UNTS273	104239
Korea, South	USA (United States)	30 Jan 57	278UNTS85	104024
Ecuador	USA (United States)	15 Feb 57	279UNTS155	104037
Thailand	USA (United States)	04 Mar 57	279UNTS235	104043
Tunisia	USA (United States)	26 Mar 57	283UNTS117	104111

PARTY ONE	PARTY TWO	DATE	CITATION	NUMBER
Currency deposits (Cont.)				
Libya	USA (United States)	04 Apr 57	283UNTS181	104116
Iceland	USA (United States)	11 Apr 57	283UNTS107	104110
Colombia	USA (United States)	16 Apr 57	283UNTS245	104121
Other Unilat Decla	United Arab Rep	24 Apr 57	265UNTS299	103821
Ethiopia	USA (United States)	25 Apr 57	283UNTS205	104118
Peru	USA (United States)	02 May 57	283UNTS55	104106
Austria	USA (United States)	10 May 57	283UNTS33	104104
Austria	USA (United States)	10 May 57	283UNTS15	104103
Bolivia	USA (United States)	07 Jun 57	291UNTS77	104245
Philippines	USA (United States)	25 Jun 57	289UNTS279	104224
Jordan	USA (United States)	27 Jun 57	288UNTS269	104209
Multilateral		03 Oct 57	366UNTS193	105218
Mexico	USA (United States)	23 Oct 57	300UNTS35	104330
Bulgaria	Yugoslavia	04 Apr 58	367UNTS89	105228
USA (United States)	Vietnam, South	17 Jun 58	321UNTS35	104652
Burma	USA (United States)	25 Aug 58	336UNTS3	104795
Australia	New Zealand	30 Sep 58	340UNTS61	104859
Japan	Laos	15 Oct 58	341UNTS25	104875
Iraq	USSR (Soviet Union)	16 Mar 59	346UNTS107	104979
Turkey	USA (United States)	26 May 59	354UNTS57	105053
Germany, West	UK Great Britain	03 Aug 59	502UNTS197	107331
Colombia	USA (United States)	06 Oct 59	358UNTS145	105132
Multilateral		09 Oct 59	376UNTS382	105391
USA (United States)	Yugoslavia	22 Oct 59	360UNTS259	105161
Israel	UK Great Britain	31 Aug 60	385UNTS71	105530
Belgium	Congo (Zaire)	15 Nov 60	394UNTS79	105670
Togo	USA (United States)	22 Dec 60	401UNTS33	105760
Iceland	USA (United States)	30 Dec 60	401UNTS43	105761
Mali	USA (United States)	04 Jan 61	405UNTS165	105832
Somalia	USSR (Soviet Union)	02 Jun 61	457UNTS263	106587
Congo (Zaire)	United Nations	12 Jun 61	494UNTS205	107234
Austria	USA (United States)	03 Oct 61	426UNTS187	106137
United Nations	USA (United States)	18 Nov 61	494UNTS213	107235
Morocco	USA (United States)	09 Feb 62	442UNTS135	106345
Dominican Republic	USA (United States)	02 May 62	442UNTS99	106341
Senegal	Switzerland	23 Jan 63	524UNTS23	107564
Central Afri Rep	USA (United States)	10 Feb 63	473UNTS83	106857
Multilateral		23 Oct 63	506UNTS197	107388
IBRD (World Bank)	Tunisia	05 Jun 64	539UNTS129	107827
IBRD (World Bank)	Venezuela	28 Aug 64	520UNTS97	107512
Morocco	USA (United States)	23 Apr 65	594UNTS3	108591
Philippines	USA (United States)	23 Apr 65	546UNTS157	107942
Iran	IBRD (World Bank)	28 Apr 65	555UNTS45	108104
Congo (Zaire)	USA (United States)	19 Jul 65	593UNTS215	108586
Multilateral		04 Dec 65	571UNTS123	108303
Jordan	USA (United States)	05 Apr 66	593UNTS239	108587
Pakistan	USA (United States)	26 May 66	594UNTS27	108592
Israel	USA (United States)	06 Jun 66	593UNTS165	108583
Ireland	UK Great Britain	23 Sep 68	0UNTS0	109374
Investments				
Netherlands	UK Great Britain	14 Jun 40	2UNTS251	200018
Denmark	UK Great Britain	16 Aug 45	5UNTS251	200033
Netherlands	UK Great Britain	07 Sep 45	2UNTS325	200024
Czechoslovakia	UK Great Britain	01 Nov 45	5UNTS15	100062
Netherlands	Norway	06 Nov 45	2UNTS5	100017
France	USA (United States)	08 Nov 45	76UNTS151	100986
Costa Rica	USA (United States)	10 Dec 45	3UNTS157	100029
Denmark	New Zealand	18 Sep 46	10UNTS39	100141
Taiwan	USA (United States)	04 Nov 46	25UNTS69	100359
USSR (Soviet Union)	Yugoslavia	04 Feb 47	130UNTS235	101731
Spain	UK Great Britain	28 Mar 47	66UNTS91	100849
Poland	UK Great Britain	02 Mar 48	77UNTS47	100991
India	Pakistan	30 Jun 48	29UNTS199	100441
ILO (Labor Org)	WHO (World Health)	10 Jul 48	19UNTS269	200121

PARTY ONE	PARTY TWO	DATE	CITATION	NUMBER
Investments (Cont.)				
Israel	UNICEF (Children)	20 Sep 48	71UNTS17	100907
Spain	UK Great Britain	15 Dec 48	87UNTS49	101165
Belgium	Portugal	01 Mar 49	32UNTS49	100488
Multilateral		23 Mar 49	203UNTS179	102746
Multilateral		05 Aug 49	88UNTS229	101195
Czechoslovakia	UK Great Britain	18 Aug 49	86UNTS129	101155
Sweden	UK Great Britain	30 Dec 49	87UNTS59	101166
Austria	UK Great Britain	26 Jan 50	97UNTS183	101350
Multilateral		18 Apr 51	261UNTS140	103729
El Salvador	Guatemala	14 Dec 51	131UNTS131	101740
Italy	USA (United States)	28 Dec 51	157UNTS63	102047
India	UK Great Britain	20 Jul 53	196UNTS251	102628
Multilateral		08 Jul 54	287UNTS27	104178
Germany, West	USA (United States)	29 Oct 54	273UNTS3	103943
Iraq	UK Great Britain	30 Apr 55	226UNTS319	103126
Multilateral		25 May 55	264UNTS117	103791
Iran	USA (United States)	15 Aug 55	284UNTS93	104132
Multilateral		12 Oct 55	560UNTS3	108165
Guatemala	Honduras	22 Aug 56	263UNTS49	103767
Cuba	USA (United States)	04 Feb 57	302UNTS273	104366
Afghanistan	USA (United States)	09 Jun 57	307UNTS97	104445
France	Italy	08 Nov 57	305UNTS393	104427
China People's Rep	USSR (Soviet Union)	23 Apr 58	313UNTS135	104534
Ghana	USA (United States)	30 Sep 58	336UNTS169	104805
ILO (Labor Org)	IMCO (Maritime Org)	16 Jan 59	327UNTS309	200554
Sudan	USA (United States)	17 Mar 59	342UNTS13	104896
Tunisia	USA (United States)	18 Mar 59	344UNTS179	104948
Nicaragua	USA (United States)	14 Apr 59	343UNTS119	104922
Fed of Malaya	USA (United States)	21 Apr 59	343UNTS3	104916
Finland	USA (United States)	22 Jul 59	354UNTS39	105051
Argentina	USA (United States)	22 Dec 59	411UNTS42	105912
Chile	USA (United States)	29 Jul 60	405UNTS127	105829
Multilateral		19 Sep 60	444UNTS259	106371
Multilateral		13 Dec 60	455UNTS204	106544
Panama	USA (United States)	23 Jan 61	445UNTS135	106382
Morocco	USA (United States)	31 Mar 61	406UNTS249	105854
Sierra Leone	USA (United States)	19 May 61	409UNTS251	105890
Togo	USA (United States)	20 Mar 62	445UNTS79	106378
Greece	Tunisia	26 May 62	534UNTS163	107761
Netherlands	Tunisia	23 May 63	523UNTS237	107558
Brazil	Germany, West	30 Nov 63	0UNTS0	109425
Romania	Yugoslavia	30 Nov 63	512UNTS2	107438
Belgium	Tunisia	15 Jul 64	560UNTS57	108168
Belgium	Tunisia	15 Jul 64	561UNTS297	108190
Ivory Coast	Netherlands	26 Apr 65	634UNTS81	109053
Bel-Lux Econ Union	Morocco	28 Apr 65	620UNTS171	108954
British Guiana	USA (United States)	29 May 65	605UNTS87	108761
USA (United States)	Zambia	11 Aug 66	616UNTS267	108901
Exchange rates and regulations				
Netherlands	UK Great Britain	14 Jun 40	2UNTS251	200018
France	Netherlands	14 Jun 40	2UNTS263	200019
Netherlands	UK Great Britain	25 Jul 40	2UNTS275	200020
Multilateral		27 Mar 41	67UNTS231	200222
Haiti	USA (United States)	23 May 41	117UNTS191	200370
UK Great Britain	USSR (Soviet Union)	16 Aug 41	91UNTS341	200269
Bolivia	USA (United States)	04 Sep 41	8UNTS345	200046
Ecuador	USA (United States)	02 Mar 42	105UNTS195	200332
Peru	USA (United States)	11 Mar 42	117UNTS266	200375
Brazil	USA (United States)	07 May 42	6UNTS377	200040
Colombia	USA (United States)	29 May 42	8UNTS365	200047
Panama	USA (United States)	07 Jul 42	9UNTS289	200048
Bolivia	USA (United States)	11 Aug 42	9UNTS309	200049
Dominican Republic	USA (United States)	25 Jan 43	13UNTS399	200083
Guatemala	USA (United States)	17 Jul 43	28UNTS431	200166

PARTY ONE	PARTY TWO	DATE	CITATION	NUMBER
Exchange rates and regulations (Cont.)				
Ecuador	USA (United States)	13 Sep 43	29UNTS349	200171
Multilateral		21 Oct 43	2UNTS281	200021
Paraguay	USA (United States)	27 Oct 43	29UNTS391	200174
Iran	USA (United States)	27 Nov 43	31UNTS451	200176
USA (United States)	Venezuela	13 Jan 44	109UNTS171	200358
Ecuador	USA (United States)	29 Jun 44	80UNTS283	200250
Peru	USA (United States)	10 Jul 44	117UNTS291	200377
Belgium	UK Great Britain	22 Aug 44	90UNTS295	200267
Brazil	USA (United States)	29 Sep 44	65UNTS271	200216
Belgium	UK Great Britain	05 Oct 44	5UNTS227	200031
Guatemala	USA (United States)	21 Feb 45	121UNTS133	200396
Canada	Czechoslovakia	01 Mar 45	45UNTS283	200185
Sweden	UK Great Britain	06 Mar 45	82UNTS219	101095
France	UK Great Britain	27 Mar 45	98UNTS227	200274
Guatemala	USA (United States)	21 May 45	121UNTS185	200399
Chile	USA (United States)	24 May 45	121UNTS219	200401
Canada	Norway	25 Jun 45	45UNTS297	200186
Denmark	UK Great Britain	16 Aug 45	5UNTS251	200033
Netherlands	UK Great Britain	07 Sep 45	2UNTS325	200024
Dominican Republic	USA (United States)	13 Oct 45	149UNTS361	200477
Belgium	Norway	23 Oct 45	16UNTS311	200107
Netherlands	Switzerland	24 Oct 45	3UNTS73	100025
Belgium	Canada	25 Oct 45	230UNTS127	103180
Czechoslovakia	UK Great Britain	01 Nov 45	5UNTS15	100062
Netherlands	Norway	06 Nov 45	2UNTS5	100017
Norway	UK Great Britain	08 Nov 45	5UNTS27	100063
Finland	Norway	27 Nov 45	17UNTS247	100279
Netherlands	Sweden	30 Nov 45	2UNTS27	100019
Denmark	UK Great Britain	06 Dec 45	5UNTS3	100061
UK Great Britain	USA (United States)	06 Dec 45	126UNTS13	101679
Czechoslovakia	Norway	13 Dec 45	17UNTS261	100280
Netherlands	UK Great Britain	20 Dec 45	4UNTS303	100053
Multilateral		27 Dec 45	2UNTS39	100020
Honduras	USA (United States)	28 Dec 45	3UNTS185	100031
Lebanon	USA (United States)	21 Jan 46	140UNTS73	101884
Greece	UK Great Britain	24 Jan 46	6UNTS45	100067
Denmark	Netherlands	31 Jan 46	3UNTS3	100021
Canada	Netherlands	05 Feb 46	43UNTS3	100658
Canada	UK Great Britain	06 Mar 46	20UNTS13	100312
Switzerland	UK Great Britain	12 Mar 46	6UNTS107	100070
Belgium	Denmark	08 Apr 46	4UNTS429	100059
Portugal	UK Great Britain	16 Apr 46	6UNTS119	100071
Poland	USA (United States)	22 Apr 46	406UNTS215	105851
France	Greece	24 Apr 46	91UNTS83	101243
France	UK Great Britain	29 Apr 46	98UNTS123	101360
New Zealand	Norway	03 May 46	16UNTS211	100262
Greece	USA (United States)	16 May 46	184UNTS230	102451
India	USA (United States)	16 May 46	4UNTS183	100045
Denmark	Luxembourg	21 May 46	4UNTS435	100060
France	USA (United States)	28 May 46	84UNTS141	101124
USA (United States)	Venezuela	03 Jun 46	4UNTS215	100047
Australia	USA (United States)	07 Jun 46	4UNTS237	100048
Romania	Yugoslavia	26 Jun 46	116UNTS21	101566
Albania	Yugoslavia	01 Jul 46	111UNTS3	101517
Luxembourg	USA (United States)	03 Jul 46	32UNTS85	100491
New Zealand	USA (United States)	10 Jul 46	6UNTS341	100087
Italy	Norway	20 Jul 46	17UNTS273	100281
Taiwan	USA (United States)	30 Aug 46	12UNTS39	100179
Argentina	USA (United States)	19 Sep 46	7UNTS131	100095
Albania	Yugoslavia	03 Oct 46	111UNTS227	101537
Peru	USA (United States)	07 Oct 46	7UNTS71	100092
Colombia	USA (United States)	14 Oct 46	7UNTS97	100093
Norway	Sweden	22 Nov 46	15UNTS171	100233
UK Great Britain	USA (United States)	02 Dec 46	7UNTS163	100098
Hungary	Yugoslavia	23 Dec 46	113UNTS125	101549

PARTY ONE	PARTY TWO	DATE	CITATION	NUMBER
Exchange rates and regulations (Cont.)				
Norway	USSR (Soviet Union)	27 Dec 46	17UNTS283	100282
Australia	Netherlands	24 Jan 47	10UNTS77	100144
Multilateral		10 Feb 47	41UNTS135	100644
Multilateral		10 Feb 47	41UNTS21	100643
Czechoslovakia	Yugoslavia	25 Feb 47	112UNTS3	101539
Burma	USA (United States)	28 Feb 47	25UNTS27	100355
Australia	Norway	24 Mar 47	18UNTS185	100288
Spain	UK Great Britain	28 Mar 47	66UNTS91	100849
Denmark	Norway	15 Apr 47	12UNTS323	100191
France	South Africa	18 Apr 47	225UNTS35	103085
Bulgaria	Denmark	09 May 47	74UNTS139	100960
Hungary	Yugoslavia	11 May 47	130UNTS171	101730
New Zealand	UK Great Britain	27 May 47	17UNTS211	100277
Netherlands	USA (United States)	28 May 47	17UNTS29	100267
Albania	Yugoslavia	12 Jun 47	111UNTS195	101534
Belgium	United Arab Rep	01 Jul 47	34UNTS93	100529
Norway	Switzerland	15 Jul 47	12UNTS351	100192
UK Great Britain	Uruguay	15 Jul 47	71UNTS179	100918
Czechoslovakia	USA (United States)	25 Jul 47	90UNTS19	101223
Greece	South Africa	28 Jul 47	185UNTS161	102467
Taiwan	Italy	30 Jul 47	12UNTS377	100194
Czechoslovakia	Greece	30 Jul 47	185UNTS149	102466
Czechoslovakia	New Zealand	08 Aug 47	18UNTS161	100285
El Salvador	USA (United States)	19 Aug 47	51UNTS57	100752
Multilateral		29 Sep 47	45UNTS125	100694
Multilateral		05 Oct 47	34UNTS23	100525
Iran	USA (United States)	06 Oct 47	11UNTS303	100171
South Africa	UK Great Britain	09 Oct 47	17UNTS239	100278
Greece	UNICEF (Children)	14 Oct 47	102UNTS39	101409
Multilateral		30 Oct 47	55UNTS188	100814
Poland	Yugoslavia	07 Nov 47	115UNTS137	101561
Ecuador	USA (United States)	14 Nov 47	149UNTS297	101959
Belgium	UK Great Britain	14 Nov 47	25UNTS269	100367
France	Lebanon	24 Jan 48	173UNTS99	102263
Norway	USA (United States)	24 Feb 48	34UNTS155	100535
Denmark	Hungary	28 Feb 48	85UNTS35	101144
Poland	UK Great Britain	02 Mar 48	77UNTS47	100991
Paraguay	USA (United States)	12 Mar 48	162UNTS30	102131
Philippines	USA (United States)	23 Mar 48	43UNTS247	100671
India	Pakistan	31 Mar 48	54UNTS33	100793
Czechoslovakia	Poland	05 Apr 48	31UNTS325	100481
Hungary	Yugoslavia	17 Apr 48	130UNTS101	101727
Denmark	Norway	21 Apr 48	18UNTS139	100284
Norway	Sweden	29 Apr 48	26UNTS11	100374
Brazil	UK Great Britain	21 May 48	66UNTS121	100851
France	Poland	09 Jun 48	32UNTS251	100503
France	USA (United States)	28 Jun 48	19UNTS9	100302
France	USA (United States)	28 Jun 48	31UNTS115	100472
Denmark	USA (United States)	29 Jun 48	27UNTS35	100396
India	Pakistan	30 Jun 48	29UNTS199	100441
Greece	USA (United States)	02 Jul 48	31UNTS131	100474
Netherlands	USA (United States)	02 Jul 48	32UNTS77	100490
Greece	USA (United States)	02 Jul 48	23UNTS43	100342
Turkey	USA (United States)	04 Jul 48	34UNTS185	100536
France	UK Great Britain	12 Jul 48	90UNTS83	101230
Peru	UK Great Britain	20 Jul 48	66UNTS197	100855
Brazil	USA (United States)	29 Jul 48	80UNTS111	101047
Korea, South	USA (United States)	11 Sep 48	89UNTS155	101216
New Zealand	USA (United States)	14 Sep 48	18UNTS251	100295
Czechoslovakia	USA (United States)	16 Sep 48	90UNTS35	101224
Portugal	USA (United States)	28 Sep 48	31UNTS139	100475
Argentina	USA (United States)	06 Oct 48	80UNTS91	101046
Multilateral		08 Oct 48	19UNTS113	100308
Australia	Belgium	09 Dec 48	25UNTS159	100361
Argentina	Denmark	14 Dec 48	74UNTS41	100956

PARTY ONE	PARTY TWO	DATE	CITATION	NUMBER
Exchange rates and regulations (Cont.)				
Denmark	Poland	14 Dec 48	81UNTS33	101060
Denmark	Turkey	15 Dec 48	76UNTS3	100974
Spain	UK Great Britain	15 Dec 48	87UNTS49	101165
Italy	USA (United States)	18 Dec 48	79UNTS133	101037
Belgium	Greece	27 Dec 48	77UNTS293	101005
Haiti	USA (United States)	04 Jan 49	44UNTS69	100679
Belgium	France	08 Jan 49	36UNTS151	100569
Denmark	Sweden	08 Feb 49	33UNTS227	100519
Colombia	USA (United States)	21 Feb 49	44UNTS83	100680
Colombia	USA (United States)	21 Feb 49	92UNTS227	101275
Norway	Turkey	24 Feb 49	30UNTS151	100453
Denmark	Greece	25 Feb 49	78UNTS335	101023
Belgium	Portugal	01 Mar 49	32UNTS49	100488
Czechoslovakia	Yugoslavia	01 Mar 49	112UNTS241	101546
Greece	Norway	12 Mar 49	33UNTS13	100510
Denmark	Finland	22 Mar 49	33UNTS247	100520
Finland	Greece	24 Mar 49	78UNTS13	101009
United Arab Rep	UK Great Britain	31 Mar 49	83UNTS139	101106
Greece	Turkey	02 Apr 49	78UNTS23	101010
Denmark	Portugal	08 Apr 49	74UNTS221	100965
Haiti	USA (United States)	14 Apr 49	80UNTS37	101043
Belgium	Bolivia	26 Apr 49	34UNTS103	100530
Netherlands	USA (United States)	26 Apr 49	70UNTS123	100901
Netherlands	USA (United States)	17 May 49	46UNTS291	100717
Ethiopia	USA (United States)	20 May 49	89UNTS99	101211
Finland	Norway	13 Jun 49	34UNTS9	100523
Peru	USA (United States)	20 Jun 49	92UNTS249	101276
Lebanon	UK Great Britain	20 Jun 49	90UNTS137	101232
Argentina	UK Great Britain	27 Jun 49	83UNTS217	101110
Mexico	USA (United States)	05 Jul 49	68UNTS55	100884
Greece	Turkey	21 Jul 49	78UNTS65	101012
Multilateral		05 Aug 49	88UNTS229	101195
Multilateral		10 Aug 49	45UNTS3	100689
Multilateral		12 Aug 49	87UNTS131	101169
WHO (World Health)	Thailand	12 Aug 49	178UNTS347	102350
Czechoslovakia	UK Great Britain	18 Aug 49	86UNTS129	101155
Greece	Italy	31 Aug 49	78UNTS89	101014
Belgium	UK Great Britain	07 Sep 49	106UNTS61	101457
Denmark	ICAO (Civil Aviat)	09 Sep 49	53UNTS341	100791
Argentina	Norway	09 Sep 49	42UNTS125	100646
Italy	Norway	19 Nov 49	47UNTS89	100724
Norway	Portugal	28 Nov 49	47UNTS117	100726
Afghanistan	WHO (World Health)	04 Dec 49	102UNTS117	101414
Colombia	UK Great Britain	13 Dec 49	88UNTS133	101189
Denmark	Germany, West	15 Dec 49	51UNTS11	100749
Czechoslovakia	Denmark	17 Dec 49	74UNTS159	100962
Norway	Poland	21 Dec 49	47UNTS107	100725
Turkey	USA (United States)	27 Dec 49	98UNTS141	101361
Sweden	UK Great Britain	30 Dec 49	87UNTS59	101166
Greece	Portugal	31 Dec 49	92UNTS83	101263
Ireland	USA (United States)	21 Jan 50	206UNTS269	102792
Austria	UK Great Britain	26 Jan 50	97UNTS183	101350
Korea, South	USA (United States)	26 Jan 50	178UNTS97	102337
India	USA (United States)	02 Feb 50	89UNTS127	101214
UK Great Britain	Yugoslavia	09 Feb 50	88UNTS287	101200
Honduras	USA (United States)	06 Mar 50	80UNTS71	101045
Honduras	USA (United States)	06 Mar 50	80UNTS51	101044
Canada	Norway	18 Mar 50	230UNTS349	103194
Canada	Denmark	25 Mar 50	230UNTS343	103193
Canada	Yugoslavia	29 Mar 50	230UNTS357	103195
Israel	UK Great Britain	30 Mar 50	86UNTS231	101162
Paraguay	UK Great Britain	03 Apr 50	99UNTS81	101372
Korea, South	USA (United States)	28 Apr 50	93UNTS21	101284
Austria	USA (United States)	06 Jun 50	92UNTS201	101273
Thailand	USA (United States)	01 Jul 50	81UNTS61	101063

PARTY ONE	PARTY TWO	DATE	CITATION	NUMBER
Exchange rates and regulations (Cont.)				
Denmark	Spain	12 Jul 50	71UNTS129	100913
USA (United States)	Venezuela	23 Aug 50	92UNTS341	101279
WHO (World Health)	United Arab Rep	25 Aug 50	92UNTS39	101259
Pakistan	USA (United States)	23 Sep 50	82UNTS131	101088
Denmark	Italy	04 Oct 50	78UNTS353	101025
Canada	Venezuela	11 Oct 50	231UNTS3	103198
Denmark	UK Great Britain	19 Oct 50	79UNTS25	101028
IBRD (World Bank)	Turkey	19 Oct 50	157UNTS333	102058
Norway	UK Great Britain	06 Nov 50	88UNTS257	101197
Philippines	USA (United States)	06 Nov 50	122UNTS63	101637
Sweden	UK Great Britain	10 Nov 50	88UNTS265	101198
Multilateral		24 Nov 50	81UNTS188	101072
Germany, West	UK Great Britain	09 Dec 50	88UNTS247	101196
Cuba	USA (United States)	22 Dec 50	122UNTS97	101640
Italy	Yugoslavia	23 Dec 50	150UNTS191	101973
Australia	Finland	04 Jan 51	80UNTS27	101042
Liberia	USA (United States)	11 Jan 51	122UNTS125	101642
Chile	USA (United States)	16 Jan 51	157UNTS3	102043
Multilateral		18 Jan 51	81UNTS233	101073
Denmark	Switzerland	20 Jan 51	87UNTS223	101174
Italy	Norway	22 Jan 51	88UNTS339	101202
Nicaragua	USA (United States)	31 Jan 51	160UNTS121	102105
Nicaragua	USA (United States)	31 Jan 51	150UNTS3	101960
Ethiopia	ICAO (Civil Aviat)	02 Feb 51	96UNTS123	101333
Chile	USA (United States)	15 Feb 51	133UNTS117	101784
Chile	USA (United States)	15 Feb 51	133UNTS95	101783
Israel	ILO (Labor Org)	19 Feb 51	100UNTS105	101391
Israel	ICAO (Civil Aviat)	19 Feb 51	96UNTS141	101334
Panama	USA (United States)	26 Feb 51	160UNTS153	102106
ILO (Labor Org)	Syria	03 Mar 51	110UNTS69	101502
Multilateral		06 Mar 51	106UNTS141	101461
Colombia	USA (United States)	09 Mar 51	141UNTS15	101901
Multilateral		28 Mar 51	181UNTS61	102399
Jordan	ILO (Labor Org)	29 Mar 51	100UNTS247	200287
Liberia	ILO (Labor Org)	02 Apr 51	100UNTS117	101392
Multilateral		05 Apr 51	84UNTS299	101139
Ceylon (Sri Lanka)	ILO (Labor Org)	06 Apr 51	100UNTS235	200286
Guatemala	ILO (Labor Org)	13 Apr 51	126UNTS249	101692
Peru	ILO (Labor Org)	13 Apr 51	100UNTS31	101385
USA (United States)	Yugoslavia	17 Apr 51	162UNTS173	102134
Ecuador	ILO (Labor Org)	19 Apr 51	100UNTS77	101389
Cuba	ILO (Labor Org)	21 Apr 51	99UNTS205	101382
Honduras	USA (United States)	24 Apr 51	140UNTS287	101894
Greece	ILO (Labor Org)	25 Apr 51	100UNTS93	101390
India	ILO (Labor Org)	26 Apr 51	100UNTS19	101384
Ethiopia	USA (United States)	02 May 51	139UNTS85	101877
Pakistan	ILO (Labor Org)	16 May 51	100UNTS147	101394
Iceland	ICAO (Civil Aviat)	07 Jun 51	96UNTS193	101337
Dominican Republic	ILO (Labor Org)	18 Jun 51	100UNTS3	101383
ILO (Labor Org)	Vietnam, South	26 Jun 51	100UNTS223	200285
Multilateral		28 Jun 51	118UNTS154	101604
United Arab Rep	UK Great Britain	01 Jul 51	249UNTS143	103504
Ethiopia	WHO (World Health)	02 Jul 51	103UNTS39	101422
Canada	France	04 Jul 51	233UNTS101	103253
ILO (Labor Org)	Thailand	11 Jul 51	100UNTS159	101395
Paraguay	ILO (Labor Org)	12 Jul 51	117UNTS155	101591
Portugal	UK Great Britain	20 Jul 51	105UNTS61	101453
Greece	USA (United States)	03 Aug 51	224UNTS279	103080
Israel	WHO (World Health)	07 Aug 51	104UNTS213	101442
USA (United States)	Venezuela	10 Aug 51	140UNTS345	101898
Iraq	USA (United States)	16 Aug 51	147UNTS65	101929
Jordan	UN Relief Palestin	20 Aug 51	120UNTS277	200394
France	UK Great Britain	20 Aug 51	108UNTS263	101479
Denmark	USA (United States)	23 Aug 51	147UNTS49	101928
Israel	USA (United States)	23 Aug 51	219UNTS237	102979

Exchange rates and regulations (Cont.)

PARTY ONE	PARTY TWO	DATE	CITATION	NUMBER
Cuba	USA (United States)	28 Aug 51	140UNTS239	101891
Cuba	USA (United States)	28 Aug 51	134UNTS225	101802
WHO (World Health)	Saudi Arabia	29 Aug 51	110UNTS277	101516
Japan	UK Great Britain	31 Aug 51	108UNTS273	101480
Ethiopia	USA (United States)	07 Sep 51	206UNTS41	102785
Iraq	ICAO (Civil Aviat)	18 Sep 51	108UNTS219	101475
Denmark	USA (United States)	01 Oct 51	421UNTS105	106056
ILO (Labor Org)	Venezuela	22 Oct 51	117UNTS139	101590
Panama	ILO (Labor Org)	10 Nov 51	126UNTS269	101693
USA (United States)	Uruguay	04 Dec 51	152UNTS41	102010
El Salvador	Guatemala	14 Dec 51	131UNTS131	101740
Spain	UK Great Britain	20 Dec 51	123UNTS187	101660
Jordan	USA (United States)	20 Dec 51	157UNTS69	102048
USA (United States)	Yugoslavia	08 Jan 52	152UNTS61	102011
Iran	USA (United States)	20 Jan 52	200UNTS191	102703
UNICEF (Children)	UK Great Britain	04 Feb 52	120UNTS147	101620
ICAO (Civil Aviat)	Yugoslavia	06 Feb 52	128UNTS97	101715
Jordan	USA (United States)	12 Feb 52	168UNTS25	102211
Lebanon	ICAO (Civil Aviat)	14 Feb 52	128UNTS83	101714
Dominican Republic	UNICEF (Children)	15 Feb 52	121UNTS43	101625
Israel	USA (United States)	27 Feb 52	177UNTS123	102314
Japan	USA (United States)	28 Feb 52	208UNTS255	102817
ICAO (Civil Aviat)	United Arab Rep	06 Mar 52	151UNTS111	101986
Honduras	USA (United States)	07 Mar 52	233UNTS151	103260
Greece	Switzerland	04 Apr 52	166UNTS271	102192
India	ICAO (Civil Aviat)	29 Apr 52	151UNTS123	101987
Israel	USA (United States)	09 May 52	177UNTS63	102309
Israel	USA (United States)	09 May 52	177UNTS269	102326
Ethiopia	USA (United States)	15 May 52	180UNTS227	102388
Korea, South	USA (United States)	24 May 52	179UNTS23	102353
Panama	USA (United States)	30 Jun 52	181UNTS121	102404
Chile	USA (United States)	30 Jun 52	199UNTS241	102688
Finland	USA (United States)	02 Jul 52	165UNTS203	102177
Multilateral		11 Jul 52	170UNTS269	102223
Multilateral		11 Jul 52	169UNTS3	102220
Germany, West	USA (United States)	18 Jul 52	165UNTS167	102175
Pakistan	UK Great Britain	22 Jul 52	157UNTS185	102054
Iraq	USA (United States)	23 Oct 52	212UNTS201	102872
Denmark	Israel	14 Nov 52	160UNTS289	102114
Ceylon (Sri Lanka)	USA (United States)	17 Nov 52	180UNTS207	102386
Mexico	ICAO (Civil Aviat)	28 Nov 52	164UNTS15	102156
ILO (Labor Org)	UN Relief Palestin	31 Dec 52	182UNTS201	200506
USA (United States)	Venezuela	16 Jan 53	199UNTS287	102690
Chile	United Nations	16 Feb 53	314UNTS49	104541
Multilateral		27 Feb 53	333UNTS3	104764
Germany, West	USA (United States)	27 Feb 53	205UNTS103	102771
United Arab Rep	USA (United States)	12 Mar 53	204UNTS3	102747
United Arab Rep	USA (United States)	19 Mar 53	215UNTS17	102909
Lebanon	Sweden	23 Mar 53	255UNTS83	103605
Japan	USA (United States)	02 Apr 53	206UNTS143	102788
Czechoslovakia	Denmark	23 Apr 53	174UNTS107	102281
Ethiopia	USA (United States)	29 Apr 53	224UNTS121	103073
Germany, West	Italy	05 May 53	267UNTS9	103835
Israel	UK Great Britain	13 May 53	175UNTS179	102300
United Arab Rep	USA (United States)	21 May 53	204UNTS29	102748
El Salvador	USA (United States)	21 May 53	213UNTS15	102878
Greece	United Arab Rep	21 May 53	256UNTS25	103621
United Arab Rep	USA (United States)	18 Jun 53	204UNTS55	102749
United Arab Rep	USA (United States)	18 Jun 53	215UNTS45	102910
Liberia	USA (United States)	23 Jun 53	213UNTS57	102880
Chile	USA (United States)	27 Jun 53	229UNTS193	103167
Nicaragua	USA (United States)	30 Jun 53	215UNTS133	102917
Argentina	USSR (Soviet Union)	05 Aug 53	221UNTS99	103004
Denmark	Germany, West	14 Aug 53	202UNTS3	102725
Brazil	UK Great Britain	01 Oct 53	183UNTS207	102430

Exchange rates and regulations (Cont.)

PARTY ONE	PARTY TWO	DATE	CITATION	NUMBER
Greece	UK Great Britain	05 Oct 53	243UNTS73	103447
Nicaragua	USA (United States)	19 Nov 53	206UNTS117	102787
Israel	USA (United States)	25 Nov 53	219UNTS205	102976
France	Netherlands	27 Nov 53	302UNTS245	104363
India	USSR (Soviet Union)	02 Dec 53	240UNTS143	103402
Bulgaria	Greece	05 Dec 53	225UNTS145	103096
Chile	USA (United States)	30 Dec 53	236UNTS41	103315
Bolivia	USA (United States)	15 Jan 54	229UNTS213	103168
Japan	UK Great Britain	29 Jan 54	190UNTS319	102572
Czechoslovakia	Greece	01 Feb 54	225UNTS95	103092
Finland	USSR (Soviet Union)	06 Feb 54	221UNTS143	103006
Turkey	UK Great Britain	11 Feb 54	190UNTS343	102575
Multilateral		19 Feb 54	214UNTS51	102899
United Arab Rep	USA (United States)	24 Feb 54	236UNTS61	103316
Multilateral		01 Mar 54	256UNTS31	103622
United Nations	Venezuela	05 Mar 54	187UNTS9	102498
Japan	USA (United States)	08 Mar 54	232UNTS227	103238
Canada	Japan	31 Mar 54	236UNTS329	103334
ECSC (Coal/Steel)	USA (United States)	23 Apr 54	229UNTS229	103170
Lebanon	USSR (Soviet Union)	30 Apr 54	226UNTS109	103111
Panama	USA (United States)	11 May 54	236UNTS107	103319
Nepal	WHO (World Health)	13 May 54	204UNTS311	200522
Greece	Spain	15 May 54	299UNTS277	104319
Greece	Romania	19 May 54	225UNTS27	103084
Canada	Portugal	28 May 54	391UNTS253	105631
Ethiopia	USA (United States)	01 Jun 54	232UNTS311	103245
Multilateral		01 Jun 54	200UNTS235	200520
Greece	Hungary	05 Jun 54	299UNTS295	104321
Ethiopia	USA (United States)	12 Jun 54	234UNTS25	103270
Jordan	USA (United States)	17 Jun 54	266UNTS137	103828
Italy	USA (United States)	28 Jun 54	237UNTS121	103340
Chile	USA (United States)	28 Jun 54	233UNTS3	103246
Ecuador	USA (United States)	30 Jun 54	236UNTS163	103323
Netherlands	UK Great Britain	09 Jul 54	199UNTS157	102682
Austria	UK Great Britain	09 Jul 54	201UNTS277	102720
Belgium	UK Great Britain	09 Jul 54	201UNTS299	102721
Germany, West	UK Great Britain	10 Jul 54	199UNTS135	102680
Portugal	UK Great Britain	10 Jul 54	199UNTS169	102683
Belgium	Italy	12 Jul 54	288UNTS59	104198
Switzerland	UK Great Britain	16 Jul 54	199UNTS197	102685
Sweden	UK Great Britain	28 Jul 54	199UNTS181	102684
Guatemala	USA (United States)	01 Sep 54	199UNTS51	102677
El Salvador	USA (United States)	23 Sep 54	237UNTS91	103338
UNESCO (Educ/Cult)	UN Special Fund	29 Sep 54	363UNTS367	200572
Multilateral		27 Oct 54	201UNTS95	102712
Turkey	USA (United States)	15 Nov 54	238UNTS135	103358
Korea, South	USA (United States)	17 Nov 54	256UNTS251	103635
Guatemala	USA (United States)	13 Dec 54	237UNTS169	103343
Netherlands	USA (United States)	14 Dec 54	262UNTS35	103737
Multilateral		16 Dec 54	204UNTS323	200523
Belgium	Greece	16 Dec 54	223UNTS73	103056
Italy	Yugoslavia	18 Dec 54	284UNTS239	104141
USA (United States)	Yugoslavia	05 Jan 55	251UNTS29	103531
Pakistan	USA (United States)	11 Jan 55	251UNTS111	103537
Finland	USSR (Soviet Union)	24 Jan 55	240UNTS243	103406
Chile	USA (United States)	27 Jan 55	262UNTS3	103735
Peru	USA (United States)	07 Feb 55	241UNTS63	103424
USA (United States)	Vietnam, South	07 Mar 55	277UNTS285	104013
Mexico	USA (United States)	09 Mar 55	263UNTS247	103776
Multilateral		04 Apr 55	208UNTS239	102816
Israel	USA (United States)	29 Apr 55	261UNTS331	103731
Peru	USA (United States)	30 Apr 55	263UNTS309	103780
Finland	USA (United States)	06 May 55	251UNTS3	103529
Italy	USA (United States)	19 May 55	269UNTS83	103876
Italy	USA (United States)	23 May 55	251UNTS303	103547

PARTY ONE	PARTY TWO	DATE	CITATION	NUMBER
Exchange rates and regulations (Cont.)				
Multilateral		25 May 55	264UNTS117	103791
Korea, South	USA (United States)	31 May 55	251UNTS321	103548
UK Great Britain	USA (United States)	07 Jun 55	265UNTS27	103804
Multilateral		14 Jun 55	212UNTS263	200526
Austria	USA (United States)	14 Jun 55	258UNTS37	103668
Canada	USA (United States)	15 Jun 55	235UNTS201	103302
Thailand	USA (United States)	21 Jun 55	262UNTS87	103738
Colombia	USA (United States)	23 Jun 55	263UNTS337	103781
Greece	USA (United States)	24 Jun 55	270UNTS361	103906
Greece	USA (United States)	24 Jun 55	270UNTS351	103905
Multilateral		04 Jul 55	214UNTS10	102897
Laos	USA (United States)	08 Jul 55	278UNTS59	104021
Japan	Thailand	09 Jul 55	230UNTS13	103172
Libya	USA (United States)	21 Jul 55	264UNTS247	103796
France	USA (United States)	11 Aug 55	251UNTS15	103530
Thailand	USA (United States)	09 Sep 55	264UNTS285	103799
Multilateral		29 Sep 55	222UNTS313	103037
Italy	Syria	10 Nov 55	267UNTS157	103841
Israel	USA (United States)	10 Nov 55	240UNTS3	103390
Thailand	USA (United States)	14 Nov 55	239UNTS201	103380
Syria	USSR (Soviet Union)	16 Nov 55	259UNTS71	103683
Pakistan	Syria	18 Dec 55	320UNTS269	104647
Costa Rica	Guatemala	20 Dec 55	280UNTS121	104056
Germany, West	USA (United States)	23 Dec 55	240UNTS79	103395
Nicaragua	USA (United States)	21 Jan 56	367UNTS3	105224
Denmark	Netherlands	31 Jan 56	286UNTS255	104172
USSR (Soviet Union)	Yugoslavia	02 Feb 56	259UNTS111	103685
Multilateral		02 Feb 56	227UNTS153	103137
Austria	USA (United States)	07 Feb 56	272UNTS117	103933
Multilateral		10 Feb 56	228UNTS167	103150
Multilateral		10 Feb 56	228UNTS189	103151
Iran	USA (United States)	20 Feb 56	272UNTS135	103934
Italy	USA (United States)	27 Feb 56	291UNTS287	104260
Pakistan	USA (United States)	02 Mar 56	271UNTS371	103927
Indonesia	USA (United States)	02 Mar 56	271UNTS345	103925
Spain	USA (United States)	05 Mar 56	271UNTS329	103924
Turkey	USA (United States)	12 Mar 56	272UNTS21	103929
Korea, South	USA (United States)	13 Mar 56	272UNTS3	103928
Japan	Netherlands	13 Mar 56	252UNTS3	103554
USA (United States)	Uruguay	23 Mar 56	376UNTS311	105386
Netherlands	USA (United States)	27 Mar 56	285UNTS231	104154
Ceylon (Sri Lanka)	USA (United States)	28 Apr 56	274UNTS35	103956
Paraguay	USA (United States)	02 May 56	268UNTS299	103863
Brazil	France	04 May 56	323UNTS339	104675
Austria	Italy	07 May 56	284UNTS351	104147
Peru	USA (United States)	07 May 56	268UNTS285	103862
Multilateral		19 May 56	399UNTS189	105742
Portugal	USA (United States)	24 May 56	268UNTS323	103865
Multilateral		31 May 56	251UNTS181	103541
UK Great Britain	USA (United States)	05 Jun 56	247UNTS205	103470
Multilateral		08 Jun 56	247UNTS366	200541
Canada	UK Great Britain	21 Jun 56	381UNTS111	105467
Multilateral		26 Jun 56	321UNTS2	104650
Multilateral		26 Jun 56	253UNTS12	103573
Burma	USA (United States)	30 Jun 56	281UNTS65	104070
Bolivia	USA (United States)	30 Jun 56	271UNTS243	103919
Multilateral		02 Jul 56	540UNTS110	107846
Multilateral		02 Jul 56	248UNTS37	103484
Netherlands	USA (United States)	07 Aug 56	281UNTS57	104069
Greece	USA (United States)	08 Aug 56	277UNTS203	104007
Taiwan	USA (United States)	14 Aug 56	281UNTS257	104083
India	USA (United States)	29 Aug 56	278UNTS25	104019
Israel	USA (United States)	11 Sep 56	277UNTS215	104008
Multilateral		25 Sep 56	334UNTS13	104766
Multilateral		25 Sep 56	334UNTS89	104767

PARTY ONE	PARTY TWO	DATE	CITATION	NUMBER
Exchange rates and regulations (Cont.)				
Argentina	USA (United States)	03 Oct 56	279UNTS13	104032
Multilateral		05 Oct 56	251UNTS245	103544
Multilateral		05 Oct 56	251UNTS267	103545
Canada	UK Great Britain	20 Oct 56	381UNTS99	105466
Spain	USA (United States)	23 Oct 56	277UNTS105	104001
Italy	USA (United States)	30 Oct 56	263UNTS221	103775
Ecuador	USA (United States)	31 Oct 56	283UNTS151	104114
Argentina	UK Great Britain	31 Oct 56	269UNTS229	103883
USA (United States)	Yugoslavia	03 Nov 56	277UNTS119	104002
Argentina	USA (United States)	05 Nov 56	277UNTS143	104004
Turkey	USA (United States)	12 Nov 56	282UNTS77	104093
Multilateral		21 Nov 56	253UNTS266	103588
Korea, South	USA (United States)	28 Nov 56	302UNTS281	104367
Burma	USA (United States)	04 Dec 56	268UNTS189	103858
Dominican Republic	USA (United States)	07 Dec 56	263UNTS193	103774
Brazil	USA (United States)	31 Dec 56	266UNTS151	103829
Colombia	USA (United States)	09 Jan 57	462UNTS151	106676
Multilateral		23 Jan 57	259UNTS426	103701
Germany, West	Norway	29 Jan 57	353UNTS39	105037
Denmark	Germany, West	29 Jan 57	302UNTS75	104354
Korea, South	USA (United States)	30 Jan 57	278UNTS85	104024
Ecuador	USA (United States)	15 Feb 57	279UNTS155	104037
Multilateral		17 Feb 57	271UNTS2	103907
Iceland	USA (United States)	23 Feb 57	283UNTS73	104107
Multilateral		01 Mar 57	264UNTS94	103790
Thailand	USA (United States)	04 Mar 57	279UNTS235	104043
Multilateral		25 Mar 57	294UNTS2	104300
Tunisia	USA (United States)	26 Mar 57	283UNTS117	104111
Multilateral		28 Mar 57	271UNTS30	103908
Paraguay	USA (United States)	04 Apr 57	284UNTS161	104135
Libya	USA (United States)	04 Apr 57	283UNTS181	104116
Multilateral		09 Apr 57	274UNTS172	103965
Iceland	USA (United States)	11 Apr 57	283UNTS107	104110
Netherlands	Paraguay	13 Apr 57	593UNTS85	108577
Colombia	USA (United States)	16 Apr 57	283UNTS245	104121
Ethiopia	USA (United States)	25 Apr 57	283UNTS205	104118
Peru	USA (United States)	02 May 57	283UNTS55	104106
Finland	USA (United States)	10 May 57	283UNTS43	104105
Austria	USA (United States)	10 May 57	283UNTS15	104103
Denmark	Paraguay	18 May 57	286UNTS117	104163
Multilateral		24 May 57	268UNTS270	103861
Argentina	USA (United States)	03 Jun 57	291UNTS61	104244
Ghana	USA (United States)	03 Jun 57	284UNTS63	104129
Poland	USA (United States)	07 Jun 57	291UNTS41	104243
Bolivia	USA (United States)	07 Jun 57	291UNTS77	104245
Philippines	USA (United States)	25 Jun 57	289UNTS279	104224
Jordan	USA (United States)	27 Jun 57	288UNTS269	104209
Australia	Japan	06 Jul 57	318UNTS381	104627
Multilateral		09 Jul 57	274UNTS300	103972
Germany, West	Italy	12 Jul 57	291UNTS181	104252
Ceylon (Sri Lanka)	China People's Rep	19 Sep 57	337UNTS137	104821
Burma	WHO (World Health)	20 Sep 57	282UNTS113	104096
Multilateral		03 Oct 57	366UNTS3	105215
Taiwan	USA (United States)	08 Oct 57	304UNTS241	104400
Mexico	USA (United States)	23 Oct 57	300UNTS35	104330
Brazil	USA (United States)	05 Nov 57	303UNTS3	104368
Multilateral		05 Nov 57	285UNTS301	104155
Israel	USA (United States)	07 Nov 57	302UNTS255	104365
Pakistan	USA (United States)	15 Nov 57	303UNTS173	104380
El Salvador	USA (United States)	21 Nov 57	303UNTS19	104369
Argentina	Denmark	25 Nov 57	299UNTS83	104308
China People's Rep	Denmark	01 Dec 57	309UNTS241	104475
Greece	USA (United States)	18 Dec 57	303UNTS159	104379
France	USA (United States)	27 Dec 57	307UNTS79	104444
Multilateral		06 Jan 58	304UNTS227	104399

Exchange rates and regulations (Cont.)

PARTY ONE	PARTY TWO	DATE	CITATION	NUMBER
Japan	USA (United States)	11 Jan 58	304UNTS35	104390
Turkey	USA (United States)	20 Jan 58	304UNTS15	104389
Spain	USA (United States)	27 Jan 58	303UNTS247	104384
USA (United States)	Yugoslavia	03 Feb 58	304UNTS293	104404
UK Great Britain	USA (United States)	03 Feb 58	307UNTS199	104450
Indonesia	WHO (World Health)	05 Feb 58	307UNTS15	104438
Korea, South	USA (United States)	05 Feb 58	307UNTS121	104447
Greece	India	14 Feb 58	609UNTS94	108827
Finland	USA (United States)	21 Feb 58	304UNTS253	104401
France	USA (United States)	28 Feb 58	366UNTS343	105222
Colombia	USA (United States)	14 Mar 58	308UNTS115	104459
Multilateral		15 Mar 58	292UNTS273	104276
Sudan	USA (United States)	31 Mar 58	308UNTS105	104458
Peru	USA (United States)	09 Apr 58	316UNTS37	104576
Taiwan	USA (United States)	18 Apr 58	308UNTS179	104461
Belgium	Japan	30 Apr 58	303UNTS109	104373
Saudi Arabia	USA (United States)	01 May 58	315UNTS221	104571
Iceland	USA (United States)	03 May 58	316UNTS137	104581
Burma	USA (United States)	27 May 58	315UNTS197	104569
Philippines	USA (United States)	03 Jun 58	316UNTS3	104573
Multilateral		18 Jun 58	386UNTS355	105553
Ceylon (Sri Lanka)	USA (United States)	18 Jun 58	316UNTS15	104574
Multilateral		19 Jun 58	306UNTS236	200550
Denmark	Romania	25 Jun 58	345UNTS231	104970
Ecuador	USA (United States)	30 Jun 58	336UNTS11	104796
Burma	USA (United States)	25 Aug 58	336UNTS3	104795
Australia	Fed of Malaya	26 Aug 58	325UNTS253	104703
Ghana	UK Great Britain	24 Sep 58	411UNTS146	105918
India	USA (United States)	26 Sep 58	336UNTS59	104798
Spain	USA (United States)	16 Oct 58	336UNTS153	104804
Multilateral		27 Oct 58	351UNTS303	105031
United Arab Rep	USA (United States)	31 Oct 58	355UNTS355	105086
Israel	USA (United States)	06 Nov 58	336UNTS275	104810
Pakistan	USA (United States)	26 Nov 58	337UNTS3	104812
Afghanistan	WHO (World Health)	18 Dec 58	324UNTS121	104681
Muscat and Oman	USA (United States)	20 Dec 58	380UNTS181	105457
USA (United States)	Yugoslavia	22 Dec 58	338UNTS243	104839
United Arab Rep	USA (United States)	24 Dec 58	338UNTS221	104837
Finland	USA (United States)	30 Dec 58	340UNTS259	104869
Spain	USA (United States)	13 Jan 59	341UNTS241	104887
Turkey	USA (United States)	13 Feb 59	340UNTS235	104867
Iceland	USA (United States)	03 Mar 59	341UNTS261	104889
India	USA (United States)	03 Mar 59	341UNTS235	104886
France	UK Great Britain	05 Mar 59	343UNTS277	104932
Ceylon (Sri Lanka)	USA (United States)	13 Mar 59	342UNTS51	104900
Iraq	USSR (Soviet Union)	16 Mar 59	346UNTS107	104979
France	USA (United States)	21 Mar 59	342UNTS71	104901
Morocco	UN Special Fund	04 Apr 59	354UNTS347	105069
Germany, West	UK Great Britain	10 Apr 59	343UNTS295	104935
Italy	UK Great Britain	14 Apr 59	343UNTS289	104934
Sweden	UK Great Britain	18 Apr 59	360UNTS89	105156
Belgium	UK Great Britain	23 Apr 59	343UNTS271	104931
Norway	UK Great Britain	23 Apr 59	343UNTS283	104933
France	Netherlands	29 Apr 59	486UNTS379	107088
Netherlands	UK Great Britain	30 Apr 59	343UNTS307	104937
Switzerland	UK Great Britain	06 May 59	343UNTS315	104938
Iceland	UK Great Britain	14 May 59	343UNTS301	104936
Greece	UK Great Britain	21 May 59	344UNTS3	104939
Austria	USA (United States)	22 May 59	347UNTS3	104988
Ceylon (Sri Lanka)	Denmark	29 May 59	348UNTS225	105002
Indonesia	USA (United States)	29 May 59	347UNTS85	104992
Taiwan	USA (United States)	09 Jun 59	353UNTS257	105046
Poland	USA (United States)	10 Jun 59	347UNTS41	104989
Argentina	USA (United States)	12 Jun 59	347UNTS59	104990
Korea, South	USA (United States)	30 Jun 59	353UNTS297	105047

Exchange rates and regulations (Cont.)

PARTY ONE	PARTY TWO	DATE	CITATION	NUMBER
United Arab Rep	USA (United States)	29 Jul 59	357UNTS121	105111
Ghana	UN Special Fund	12 Aug 59	338UNTS203	104836
FAO (Food Agri)	UN Special Fund	28 Sep 59	341UNTS353	200562
United Arab Rep	USA (United States)	28 Sep 59	358UNTS97	105128
Colombia	USA (United States)	06 Oct 59	358UNTS145	105132
Iran	UN Special Fund	06 Oct 59	342UNTS89	104902
ILO (Labor Org)	UN Special Fund	12 Oct 59	343UNTS325	200563
Poland	UN Special Fund	15 Oct 59	344UNTS29	104941
USA (United States)	Vietnam, South	16 Oct 59	360UNTS271	105163
India	UN Special Fund	20 Oct 59	344UNTS143	104946
UN Special Fund	Yugoslavia	27 Oct 59	344UNTS159	104947
Ecuador	UN Special Fund	10 Nov 59	345UNTS3	104955
Ethiopia	France	12 Nov 59	381UNTS3	105465
India	USA (United States)	13 Nov 59	360UNTS287	105164
Greece	UN Special Fund	13 Nov 59	345UNTS171	104966
United Arab Rep	USA (United States)	14 Nov 59	360UNTS311	105165
UN Special Fund	WMO (Meteorology)	17 Nov 59	345UNTS311	200564
Norway	Yugoslavia	18 Nov 59	383UNTS131	105499
UN Special Fund	Turkey	20 Nov 59	345UNTS105	104963
France	USA (United States)	25 Nov 59	401UNTS75	105764
UN Special Fund	United Arab Rep	25 Nov 59	345UNTS125	104964
Israel	UN Special Fund	01 Dec 59	345UNTS197	104968
Guinea	UN Special Fund	02 Dec 59	345UNTS215	104969
Multilateral		03 Dec 59	348UNTS246	105003
Argentina	UN Special Fund	04 Dec 59	345UNTS263	104972
Jordan	UN Special Fund	15 Dec 59	346UNTS3	104974
Ceylon (Sri Lanka)	WHO (World Health)	21 Dec 59	349UNTS109	105011
Turkey	USA (United States)	22 Dec 59	367UNTS57	105225
Greece	USA (United States)	07 Jan 60	368UNTS221	105243
UN Special Fund	UK Great Britain	07 Jan 60	348UNTS177	105000
Peru	UN Special Fund	19 Jan 60	349UNTS83	105010
Chile	UN Special Fund	22 Jan 60	351UNTS115	105020
Multilateral		26 Jan 60	439UNTS249	106333
Colombia	UN Special Fund	04 Feb 60	355UNTS257	105080
Bolivia	UN Special Fund	09 Feb 60	351UNTS203	105024
Peru	USA (United States)	12 Feb 60	372UNTS83	105290
Cuba	USSR (Soviet Union)	13 Feb 60	369UNTS3	105247
Afghanistan	UN Special Fund	21 Feb 60	351UNTS93	105019
Pakistan	UN Special Fund	25 Feb 60	351UNTS141	105021
Multilateral		26 Feb 60	418UNTS171	106022
Indonesia	USSR (Soviet Union)	28 Feb 60	392UNTS173	105643
France	UN Special Fund	17 Mar 60	354UNTS119	105059
Portugal	USA (United States)	19 Mar 60	371UNTS131	105275
Austria	El Salvador	23 Mar 60	390UNTS3	105599
Italy	UN Special Fund	01 Apr 60	354UNTS261	105066
Iceland	USA (United States)	06 Apr 60	372UNTS71	105289
Pakistan	USA (United States)	11 Apr 60	372UNTS251	105302
UK Great Britain	Yugoslavia	12 Apr 60	360UNTS79	105155
Multilateral		12 Apr 60	359UNTS323	105150
UN Special Fund	Tunisia	12 Apr 60	355UNTS289	105082
Libya	UN Special Fund	19 Apr 60	356UNTS11	105090
ICAO (Civil Aviat)	UN Special Fund	21 Apr 60	360UNTS367	200569
UN Special Fund	Sudan	21 Apr 60	356UNTS213	105097
UN Special Fund	Vietnam, South	29 Apr 60	357UNTS311	200567
Laos	UN Special Fund	30 Apr 60	361UNTS171	105179
India	USA (United States)	04 May 60	376UNTS279	105384
Lebanon	UN Special Fund	07 May 60	360UNTS225	105160
UN Special Fund	WHO (World Health)	25 May 60	359UNTS375	200568
Multilateral		04 Jun 60	360UNTS208	105159
Iraq	UN Special Fund	19 Jun 60	376UNTS357	105389
Spain	USA (United States)	22 Jun 60	378UNTS3	105414
Ireland	Portugal	24 Jun 60	412UNTS30	105924
Somalia	UK Great Britain	26 Jun 60	374UNTS339	105347
Kuwait	UN Special Fund	29 Jun 60	369UNTS419	200575
Multilateral		08 Jul 60	366UNTS310	105220

Exchange rates and regulations (Cont.)

PARTY ONE	PARTY TWO	DATE	CITATION	NUMBER
ITU (Telecommun)	UN Special Fund	13 Jul 60	368UNTS329	200573
Ethiopia	UN Special Fund	13 Jul 60	368UNTS159	105240
Poland	USA (United States)	21 Jul 60	380UNTS157	105456
USA (United States)	Uruguay	22 Jul 60	388UNTS315	105587
Iran	USA (United States)	26 Jul 60	384UNTS141	105516
Ghana	Netherlands	30 Jul 60	412UNTS51	105925
United Arab Rep	USA (United States)	01 Aug 60	384UNTS189	105519
Argentina	USA (United States)	02 Aug 60	384UNTS105	105514
Ghana	USSR (Soviet Union)	04 Aug 60	421UNTS27	106050
Ghana	USSR (Soviet Union)	04 Aug 60	399UNTS61	105734
United Arab Rep	USA (United States)	09 Aug 60	388UNTS271	105584
Belgium	Burma	17 Aug 60	540UNTS185	107850
Congo (Zaire)	United Nations	23 Aug 60	373UNTS327	200576
Taiwan	USA (United States)	30 Aug 60	388UNTS191	105579
Multilateral		01 Sep 60	403UNTS3	105792
Brazil	UN Special Fund	16 Sep 60	375UNTS3	105351
Multilateral		19 Sep 60	444UNTS259	106371
Taiwan	UN Special Fund	20 Sep 60	375UNTS29	105352
Ecuador	USA (United States)	27 Sep 60	401UNTS115	105766
Ceylon (Sri Lanka)	USA (United States)	30 Sep 60	389UNTS221	105594
Guinea	USA (United States)	30 Sep 60	394UNTS103	105671
Indonesia	UN Special Fund	07 Oct 60	378UNTS141	105424
Liberia	UN Special Fund	11 Oct 60	376UNTS341	105388
El Salvador	UN Special Fund	24 Oct 60	377UNTS171	105400
Hungary	UK Great Britain	25 Oct 60	419UNTS309	106034
Chile	USA (United States)	28 Oct 60	401UNTS177	105770
USA (United States)	Vietnam, South	28 Oct 60	401UNTS3	105758
Burma	Switzerland	31 Oct 60	465UNTS97	106723
France	USA (United States)	04 Nov 60	400UNTS323	105756
Indonesia	USA (United States)	05 Nov 60	400UNTS35	105746
Greece	USA (United States)	07 Nov 60	400UNTS57	105748
Greece	Poland	08 Nov 60	483UNTS141	107011
Chile	USA (United States)	08 Nov 60	405UNTS85	105825
Guatemala	UN Special Fund	17 Nov 60	383UNTS67	105495
Nepal	UN Special Fund	17 Nov 60	380UNTS289	105461
Indonesia	UK Great Britain	23 Nov 60	398UNTS71	105718
Cambodia	UN Special Fund	24 Nov 60	382UNTS255	105487
Multilateral		13 Dec 60	455UNTS3	106543
Multilateral		13 Dec 60	455UNTS204	106544
Honduras	UN Special Fund	20 Dec 60	383UNTS103	105497
Togo	USA (United States)	22 Dec 60	401UNTS33	105760
Korea, South	USA (United States)	28 Dec 60	402UNTS3	105773
Burma	UN Special Fund	03 Jan 61	387UNTS219	105564
Mali	USA (United States)	04 Jan 61	405UNTS165	105832
Jordan	Sweden	09 Jan 61	465UNTS155	106726
Costa Rica	UN Special Fund	10 Jan 61	389UNTS253	105597
Turkey	USA (United States)	11 Jan 61	405UNTS173	105833
UN Special Fund	Saudi Arabia	19 Jan 61	396UNTS27	105692
Nicaragua	UN Special Fund	20 Jan 61	387UNTS15	105555
Chad	UN Special Fund	23 Jan 61	390UNTS69	105603
UN Special Fund	Somalia	28 Jan 61	388UNTS75	105573
Gabon	UN Special Fund	02 Feb 61	387UNTS289	105568
Australia	Japan	07 Feb 61	450UNTS343	106478
Nigeria	UN Special Fund	10 Feb 61	390UNTS85	105604
Belgium	USA (United States)	21 Feb 61	480UNTS149	106967
Mexico	UN Special Fund	23 Feb 61	388UNTS151	105576
Cyprus	UN Special Fund	24 Feb 61	389UNTS3	105588
Japan	Pakistan	07 Mar 61	450UNTS359	106479
Panama	UN Special Fund	09 Mar 61	396UNTS3	105691
Cuba	UN Special Fund	10 Mar 61	390UNTS35	105601
Philippines	USA (United States)	12 Mar 61	288UNTS285	104210
USA (United States)	Vietnam, South	25 Mar 61	406UNTS187	105849
USA (United States)	Vietnam, South	03 Apr 61	424UNTS137	106106
Ecuador	USA (United States)	03 Apr 61	409UNTS140	105882
Bolivia	USA (United States)	07 Apr 61	433UNTS3	106227

Exchange rates and regulations (Cont.)

PARTY ONE	PARTY TWO	DATE	CITATION	NUMBER
Iceland	USA (United States)	07 Apr 61	406UNTS203	105850
Honduras	USA (United States)	12 Apr 61	413UNTS182	105952
Korea, South	UN Special Fund	21 Apr 61	394UNTS231	200583
USA (United States)	Yugoslavia	28 Apr 61	409UNTS172	105884
Ceylon (Sri Lanka)	UN Special Fund	03 May 61	395UNTS217	105687
Brazil	USA (United States)	04 May 61	433UNTS91	106233
Sierra Leone	USA (United States)	05 May 61	409UNTS194	105885
Israel	USA (United States)	10 May 61	409UNTS213	105887
Senegal	USA (United States)	13 May 61	409UNTS232	105888
Ivory Coast	USA (United States)	17 May 61	409UNTS241	105889
Spain	USA (United States)	22 May 61	409UNTS260	105891
Niger	USA (United States)	26 May 61	410UNTS213	105905
Cameroon	USA (United States)	26 May 61	413UNTS195	105953
Dahomey	USA (United States)	27 May 61	445UNTS23	106373
Somalia	USSR (Soviet Union)	02 Jun 61	457UNTS263	106587
Cameroon	UN Special Fund	13 Jun 61	397UNTS297	105713
Madagascar	USA (United States)	22 Jun 61	413UNTS219	105956
Paraguay	UN Special Fund	22 Jun 61	399UNTS117	105738
UN Special Fund	Upper Volta	26 Jun 61	400UNTS3	105744
Haiti	UN Special Fund	28 Jun 61	399UNTS171	105741
Philippines	UN Special Fund	28 Jun 61	399UNTS141	105739
Tunisia	USA (United States)	30 Jun 61	434UNTS85	106257
Bulgaria	Netherlands	07 Jul 61	489UNTS21	107133
Paraguay	USA (United States)	07 Jul 61	433UNTS53	106231
UK Great Britain	Yugoslavia	21 Jul 61	420UNTS61	106040
Taiwan	USA (United States)	21 Jul 61	416UNTS101	105998
Mali	UN Special Fund	21 Jul 61	401UNTS141	105768
Turkey	USA (United States)	29 Jul 61	416UNTS151	106001
UN Special Fund	Yemen	02 Aug 61	402UNTS43	105777
Finland	USA (United States)	04 Aug 61	418UNTS19	106014
El Salvador	USA (United States)	21 Aug 61	418UNTS35	106015
Ivory Coast	UN Special Fund	29 Aug 61	406UNTS129	105844
Tunisia	USSR (Soviet Union)	30 Aug 61	437UNTS243	106310
Multilateral		20 Sep 61	407UNTS52	105859
Paraguay	USA (United States)	26 Sep 61	461UNTS91	106653
UN Special Fund	Sierra Leone	02 Oct 61	422UNTS131	106073
Multilateral		16 Oct 61	410UNTS242	105908
Indonesia	USA (United States)	26 Oct 61	433UNTS249	106248
Iceland	USA (United States)	06 Nov 61	426UNTS225	106140
Multilateral		07 Nov 61	412UNTS258	105937
Mauritania	UN Special Fund	07 Nov 61	412UNTS240	105936
Syria	USA (United States)	09 Nov 61	435UNTS75	106271
Congo (Brazzaville)	UN Special Fund	09 Nov 61	413UNTS58	105940
Brazil	USA (United States)	11 Nov 61	433UNTS199	106243
Sudan	USA (United States)	14 Nov 61	434UNTS51	106255
Bolivia	USA (United States)	15 Nov 61	456UNTS192	106557
Congo (Zaire)	USA (United States)	18 Nov 61	433UNTS207	106244
El Salvador	USA (United States)	20 Nov 61	433UNTS221	106245
Philippines	USA (United States)	24 Nov 61	433UNTS315	106251
Portugal	USA (United States)	28 Nov 61	434UNTS31	106253
IAEA (Atom Energy)	UN Special Fund	29 Nov 61	415UNTS408	200593
Morocco	USA (United States)	30 Nov 61	451UNTS167	106492
UN Special Fund	Venezuela	11 Dec 61	422UNTS149	106074
Germany, West	Thailand	13 Dec 61	541UNTS181	107870
Poland	USA (United States)	15 Dec 61	434UNTS3	106252
UN Special Fund	Senegal	16 Dec 61	425UNTS97	106121
El Salvador	USA (United States)	19 Dec 61	445UNTS175	106385
Iran	USA (United States)	21 Dec 61	433UNTS269	106249
Costa Rica	USA (United States)	22 Dec 61	460UNTS277	106646
USA (United States)	Vietnam, South	27 Dec 61	433UNTS185	106242
Multilateral		27 Dec 61	425UNTS83	106120
Sierra Leone	USA (United States)	29 Dec 61	434UNTS43	106254
Malagasy	UN Special Fund	05 Jan 62	419UNTS29	106028
Netherlands	Sweden	08 Jan 62	466UNTS65	106737
Japan	USA (United States)	09 Jan 62	451UNTS97	106488

PARTY ONE	PARTY TWO	DATE	CITATION	NUMBER
Exchange rates and regulations (Cont.)				
Dominican Republic	USA (United States)	11 Jan 62	433UNTS133	106236
Thailand	USA (United States)	12 Jan 62	459UNTS95	106615
Multilateral		17 Jan 62	419UNTS294	106033
Cyprus	USA (United States)	18 Jan 62	435UNTS3	106266
United Arab Rep	USA (United States)	19 Jan 62	435UNTS107	106273
Multilateral		20 Jan 62	429UNTS230	200596
Iran	USA (United States)	29 Jan 62	435UNTS53	106270
Guinea	USA (United States)	02 Feb 62	435UNTS35	106269
Morocco	USA (United States)	09 Feb 62	442UNTS135	106345
Bolivia	USA (United States)	12 Feb 62	451UNTS281	106499
Multilateral		13 Feb 62	422UNTS288	200594
Tunisia	USA (United States)	16 Feb 62	442UNTS161	106347
Indonesia	USA (United States)	19 Feb 62	435UNTS137	106276
Multilateral		21 Feb 62	423UNTS151	106091
Luxembourg	USA (United States)	23 Feb 62	474UNTS3	106868
Niger	UN Special Fund	26 Feb 62	423UNTS83	106086
Jordan	UK Great Britain	28 Feb 62	466UNTS249	106748
Multilateral		01 Mar 62	423UNTS122	106089
Korea, South	USA (United States)	02 Mar 62	442UNTS185	106349
IDA (Devel Assoc)	UK Great Britain	13 Mar 62	466UNTS331	106753
Brazil	USA (United States)	15 Mar 62	456UNTS209	106558
Iceland	USA (United States)	16 Mar 62	445UNTS49	106376
Peru	USA (United States)	20 Mar 62	445UNTS61	106377
Dahomey	UN Special Fund	28 Mar 62	424UNTS55	106099
Nicaragua	USA (United States)	30 Mar 62	456UNTS241	106559
Sierra Leone	UK Great Britain	05 Apr 62	434UNTS227	106265
Multilateral		10 Apr 62	429UNTS78	106192
Somalia	USA (United States)	17 Apr 62	436UNTS107	106291
Multilateral		18 Apr 62	463UNTS44	106692
Ivory Coast	USA (United States)	21 Apr 62	526UNTS39	107598
Taiwan	USA (United States)	27 Apr 62	436UNTS25	106287
USA (United States)	Uruguay	27 Apr 62	452UNTS25	106502
India	USA (United States)	01 May 62	451UNTS179	106493
Dominican Republic	USA (United States)	02 May 62	442UNTS107	106342
Israel	USA (United States)	03 May 62	442UNTS83	106340
UN Special Fund	Uruguay	04 May 62	429UNTS143	106196
USA (United States)	Venezuela	17 May 62	456UNTS275	106562
Multilateral		17 May 62	429UNTS46	106189
Ethiopia	USA (United States)	23 May 62	456UNTS293	106563
Pakistan	USA (United States)	31 May 62	460UNTS75	106631
Dominican Republic	UN Special Fund	06 Jun 62	429UNTS169	106197
Bolivia	USA (United States)	19 Jun 62	458UNTS239	106606
United Arab Rep	USSR (Soviet Union)	23 Jun 62	472UNTS19	106835
UN Special Fund	Syria	07 Jul 62	443UNTS3	106355
UN Special Fund	Tanganyika	17 Jul 62	435UNTS237	106281
Honduras	USA (United States)	20 Jul 62	460UNTS125	106635
Colombia	USA (United States)	23 Jul 62	458UNTS123	106595
Niger	USA (United States)	23 Jul 62	487UNTS325	107114
Multilateral		12 Aug 62	443UNTS266	106365
Cyprus	USA (United States)	23 Aug 62	461UNTS147	106658
Nepal	USA (United States)	24 Aug 62	460UNTS143	106637
Multilateral		29 Aug 62	443UNTS280	106366
Togo	USA (United States)	05 Sep 62	461UNTS47	106650
Morocco	USA (United States)	11 Sep 62	462UNTS207	106680
Tunisia	USA (United States)	14 Sep 62	461UNTS31	106649
Gabon	USA (United States)	04 Oct 62	459UNTS185	106620
United Arab Rep	USA (United States)	08 Oct 62	462UNTS39	106670
Iran	USA (United States)	15 Oct 62	473UNTS291	106866
Netherlands	Norway	18 Oct 62	466UNTS145	106741
Greece	USA (United States)	22 Oct 62	462UNTS187	106678
Japan	UN Special Fund	31 Oct 62	444UNTS171	106368
Korea, South	USA (United States)	07 Nov 62	462UNTS129	106674
Burma	USA (United States)	09 Nov 62	461UNTS113	106655
Algeria	UN Special Fund	15 Nov 62	452UNTS243	106512
Multilateral		15 Nov 62	448UNTS50	106424

PARTY ONE	PARTY TWO	DATE	CITATION	NUMBER
Exchange rates and regulations (Cont.)				
Taiwan	USA (United States)	19 Nov 62	459UNTS263	106629
Germany, West	USA (United States)	20 Nov 62	505UNTS263	107377
Ceylon (Sri Lanka)	USA (United States)	21 Nov 62	462UNTS237	106683
Costa Rica	USA (United States)	23 Nov 62	541UNTS67	107861
Paraguay	USA (United States)	24 Nov 62	471UNTS49	106821
India	USA (United States)	26 Nov 62	460UNTS203	106641
UK Great Britain	Yugoslavia	28 Nov 62	470UNTS65	106796
USA (United States)	Yugoslavia	28 Nov 62	460UNTS185	106640
India	USA (United States)	30 Nov 62	459UNTS231	106626
Laos	USSR (Soviet Union)	01 Dec 62	471UNTS181	106832
Israel	USA (United States)	06 Dec 62	460UNTS151	106638
Multilateral		06 Dec 62	450UNTS240	106471
Ghana	Tunisia	11 Dec 62	563UNTS243	108213
Multilateral		12 Dec 62	457UNTS72	106578
Guinea	USA (United States)	14 Dec 62	462UNTS247	106684
Bolivia	USA (United States)	17 Dec 62	469UNTS121	106788
Multilateral		21 Jan 63	453UNTS20	106517
Sudan	USA (United States)	31 Jan 63	494UNTS119	107230
Poland	USA (United States)	01 Feb 63	487UNTS143	107100
Guinea	Switzerland	01 Feb 63	499UNTS35	107291
Multilateral		05 Feb 63	453UNTS36	106518
Iceland	USA (United States)	06 Feb 63	473UNTS93	106858
Central Afri Rep	USA (United States)	10 Feb 63	473UNTS83	106857
Multilateral		14 Feb 63	453UNTS168	106524
Turkey	USA (United States)	21 Feb 63	473UNTS311	106867
Congo (Zaire)	USA (United States)	23 Feb 63	493UNTS17	107204
Congo (Zaire)	USA (United States)	23 Feb 63	493UNTS3	107203
Multilateral		06 Mar 63	455UNTS386	106552
UN Special Fund	Uganda	22 Mar 63	456UNTS466	106572
Multilateral		18 Apr 63	463UNTS121	106697
Cyprus	Denmark	27 Apr 63	529UNTS255	107664
Multilateral		06 May 63	463UNTS78	106694
Multilateral		09 May 63	463UNTS159	106700
Guinea	USA (United States)	22 May 63	487UNTS251	107108
Jamaica	UN Special Fund	22 May 63	489UNTS191	107140
Multilateral		22 May 63	483UNTS72	107007
Netherlands	UN Special Fund	24 May 63	466UNTS289	106750
Multilateral		24 May 63	466UNTS346	106754
UN Special Fund	Western Samoa	05 Jun 63	467UNTS463	200601
Ethiopia	USA (United States)	11 Jun 63	487UNTS269	107109
Cyprus	USA (United States)	18 Jun 63	479UNTS191	106953
Senegal	USA (United States)	03 Jul 63	527UNTS95	107620
Multilateral		23 Jul 63	471UNTS158	106831
Multilateral		31 Jul 63	472UNTS220	106842
Burundi	UN Special Fund	22 Aug 63	476UNTS49	106903
Multilateral		27 Aug 63	511UNTS210	107435
Multilateral		10 Sep 63	480UNTS100	106965
Brazil	USA (United States)	11 Sep 63	493UNTS267	107220
Denmark	Norway	12 Sep 63	613UNTS289	108857
Jamaica	USA (United States)	24 Oct 63	489UNTS337	107148
Central Afri Rep	UN Special Fund	30 Oct 63	481UNTS247	106985
Greece	USA (United States)	30 Oct 63	493UNTS29	107205
Multilateral		30 Oct 63	480UNTS180	106968
Multilateral		07 Nov 63	480UNTS232	106971
Multilateral		08 Nov 63	482UNTS286	106999
Paraguay	USA (United States)	14 Nov 63	505UNTS87	107366
Tunisia	USA (United States)	18 Nov 63	494UNTS193	107233
Greece	USA (United States)	13 Dec 63	494UNTS55	107226
Cameroon	Netherlands	18 Dec 63	521UNTS303	107527
Australia	Laos	24 Dec 63	503UNTS315	107350
USA (United States)	Vietnam, South	09 Jan 64	505UNTS173	107373
Multilateral		28 Jan 64	502UNTS321	107336
Poland	USA (United States)	03 Feb 64	505UNTS215	107375
Poland	USA (United States)	03 Feb 64	505UNTS245	107376
Jordan	USA (United States)	11 Feb 64	511UNTS85	107429

Exchange rates and regulations (Cont.)

PARTY ONE	PARTY TWO	DATE	CITATION	NUMBER
Iceland	USA (United States)	13 Feb 64	510UNTS295	107420
Peru	USA (United States)	13 Feb 64	511UNTS119	107431
Iceland	USA (United States)	13 Feb 64	524UNTS235	107576
Multilateral		20 Feb 64	491UNTS30	107172
Sudan	USA (United States)	02 Mar 64	524UNTS217	107575
Ivory Coast	USA (United States)	10 Mar 64	526UNTS285	107611
Bolivia	USA (United States)	25 Mar 64	532UNTS3	107710
Malaysia	Netherlands	07 Apr 64	524UNTS81	107567
Tunisia	USA (United States)	07 Apr 64	527UNTS3	107613
USA (United States)	Yugoslavia	27 Apr 64	526UNTS73	107601
Congo (Zaire)	USA (United States)	28 Apr 64	526UNTS55	107600
Philippines	USA (United States)	14 May 64	526UNTS113	107604
Ireland	UN Special Fund	03 Jun 64	496UNTS205	107253
Taiwan	USA (United States)	03 Jun 64	526UNTS257	107610
Multilateral		23 Jun 64	506UNTS108	107383
Multilateral		28 Jun 64	519UNTS14	107499
Colombia	Netherlands	06 Jul 64	543UNTS289	107906
Paraguay	USA (United States)	05 Sep 64	530UNTS225	107685
USA (United States)	Vietnam, South	29 Sep 64	531UNTS183	107703
Iran	USA (United States)	29 Sep 64	531UNTS163	107702
India	USA (United States)	30 Sep 64	532UNTS321	107726
Colombia	USA (United States)	08 Oct 64	579UNTS3	108395
Multilateral		24 Oct 64	514UNTS220	200608
Chile	USA (United States)	27 Oct 64	532UNTS347	107727
Multilateral		11 Nov 64	515UNTS94	107456
Kenya	USA (United States)	07 Dec 64	532UNTS263	107722
Congo (Zaire)	USA (United States)	09 Dec 64	531UNTS249	107707
Israel	USA (United States)	22 Dec 64	532UNTS231	107720
Iceland	USA (United States)	30 Dec 64	542UNTS37	107878
Korea, South	USA (United States)	31 Dec 64	535UNTS315	107787
Dahomey	USA (United States)	31 Dec 64	541UNTS117	107865
Taiwan	USA (United States)	31 Dec 64	532UNTS29	107711
Multilateral		27 Jan 65	523UNTS102	107556
Multilateral		02 Feb 65	523UNTS256	107560
Multilateral		12 Feb 65	525UNTS148	107587
Tunisia	USA (United States)	17 Feb 65	542UNTS125	107885
Japan	UK Great Britain	22 Feb 65	560UNTS123	108171
Finland	UK Great Britain	25 Mar 65	539UNTS103	107826
Denmark	Malaysia	26 Mar 65	540UNTS205	107851
Malawi	USA (United States)	20 Apr 65	546UNTS175	107943
Morocco	USA (United States)	23 Apr 65	594UNTS3	108591
Ghana	Malawi	04 May 65	541UNTS163	107869
Denmark	Spain	05 May 65	543UNTS255	107905
UK Great Britain	USA (United States)	10 May 65	545UNTS181	107934
Bolivia	USA (United States)	12 May 65	564UNTS143	108226
USA (United States)	Uruguay	17 May 65	564UNTS69	108221
Afghanistan	USA (United States)	22 May 65	579UNTS29	108396
USA (United States)	Vietnam, South	26 May 65	550UNTS3	108005
Multilateral		02 Jun 65	551UNTS2	108030
Multilateral		02 Jun 65	537UNTS348	200611
UN Special Fund	Spain	30 Jun 65	544UNTS159	107918
Mali	USA (United States)	14 Jul 65	564UNTS101	108223
Congo (Zaire)	USA (United States)	19 Jul 65	593UNTS215	108586
Chile	USA (United States)	27 Jul 65	574UNTS83	108342
Multilateral		13 Sep 65	547UNTS264	107962
Multilateral		21 Oct 65	547UNTS216	107959
United Arab Rep	USA (United States)	03 Jan 66	579UNTS63	108399
Mongolia	UN Special Fund	26 Jan 66	552UNTS201	108055
Guinea	USA (United States)	04 Feb 66	579UNTS213	108409
Multilateral		04 Mar 66	578UNTS57	108387
Korea, South	USA (United States)	07 Mar 66	579UNTS137	108404
Ceylon (Sri Lanka)	USA (United States)	12 Mar 66	579UNTS117	108403
Ghana	USA (United States)	01 Apr 66	579UNTS157	108405
Jordan	USA (United States)	05 Apr 66	593UNTS239	108587
USA (United States)	Yugoslavia	11 Apr 66	580UNTS239	108427

Exchange rates and regulations (Cont.)

PARTY ONE	PARTY TWO	DATE	CITATION	NUMBER
Sudan	USA (United States)	13 Apr 66	586UNTS39	108495
Bolivia	USA (United States)	22 Apr 66	578UNTS73	108388
Pakistan	USA (United States)	26 May 66	594UNTS27	108592
Israel	USA (United States)	06 Jun 66	593UNTS165	108583
IBRD (World Bank)	IFC (Finance Corp)	28 Oct 66	586UNTS225	200628
Denmark	Singapore	20 Dec 66	593UNTS125	108580
Korea, South	USA (United States)	09 Feb 67	0UNTS0	109605
Multilateral		21 Jun 67	598UNTS2	108653
UK Great Britain	Yugoslavia	30 Jun 67	642UNTS325	109182
Malta	UK Great Britain	10 Jul 67	619UNTS11	108936
Singapore	UK Great Britain	01 Aug 67	619UNTS29	108937
Bel-Lux Econ Union	Czechoslovakia	10 Oct 67	0UNTS0	109362
Inter-Am Devel Bnk	UN Special Fund	16 Jul 68	640UNTS305	200640

Expense sharing formulae

PARTY ONE	PARTY TWO	DATE	CITATION	NUMBER
Norway	USA (United States)	28 Mar 40	88UNTS365	200253
Multilateral		12 May 40	101UNTS91	101405
Multilateral		27 Mar 41	67UNTS231	200222
Haiti	USA (United States)	23 May 41	117UNTS191	200370
Bolivia	USA (United States)	04 Sep 41	8UNTS345	200046
Costa Rica	USA (United States)	16 Jan 42	23UNTS285	200135
El Salvador	USA (United States)	13 Feb 42	23UNTS293	200136
Ecuador	USA (United States)	24 Feb 42	26UNTS379	200157
Peru	USA (United States)	11 Mar 42	117UNTS266	200375
Brazil	USA (United States)	14 Mar 42	102UNTS195	200302
Nicaragua	USA (United States)	08 Apr 42	24UNTS145	200138
El Salvador	USA (United States)	05 May 42	21UNTS215	200124
Honduras	USA (United States)	08 May 42	166UNTS351	200498
Nicaragua	USA (United States)	22 May 42	105UNTS141	200328
Paraguay	USA (United States)	22 May 42	124UNTS243	200423
Colombia	USA (United States)	29 May 42	8UNTS365	200047
Panama	USA (United States)	07 Jul 42	9UNTS289	200048
Bolivia	USA (United States)	16 Jul 42	13UNTS101	200072
Bolivia	USA (United States)	11 Aug 42	9UNTS309	200049
Honduras	USA (United States)	26 Oct 42	24UNTS209	200145
Nicaragua	USA (United States)	27 Oct 42	99UNTS287	200283
El Salvador	USA (United States)	02 Dec 42	122UNTS277	200410
Dominican Republic	USA (United States)	25 Jan 43	13UNTS399	200083
Brazil	USA (United States)	10 Feb 43	102UNTS217	200304
USA (United States)	Venezuela	18 Feb 43	21UNTS225	200125
Panama	USA (United States)	02 Mar 43	107UNTS55	200351
Chile	USA (United States)	11 May 43	139UNTS295	200456
Guatemala	USA (United States)	19 May 43	28UNTS377	200161
Panama	USA (United States)	07 Jun 43	21UNTS269	200128
Mexico	USA (United States)	14 Jun 43	66UNTS331	200220
Mexico	USA (United States)	01 Jul 43	28UNTS407	200164
Dominican Republic	USA (United States)	07 Jul 43	28UNTS419	200165
Guatemala	USA (United States)	17 Jul 43	28UNTS431	200166
Ecuador	USA (United States)	13 Sep 43	29UNTS349	200171
Paraguay	USA (United States)	27 Oct 43	29UNTS391	200174
USA (United States)	Uruguay	01 Nov 43	106UNTS311	200348
Brazil	USA (United States)	25 Nov 43	102UNTS227	200305
Iran	USA (United States)	27 Nov 43	31UNTS451	200176
Paraguay	USA (United States)	10 Dec 43	21UNTS305	200131
USA (United States)	Venezuela	13 Jan 44	109UNTS171	200358
Multilateral		15 Jan 44	161UNTS281	200489
Honduras	USA (United States)	12 Apr 44	138UNTS271	200450
Peru	USA (United States)	15 Apr 44	150UNTS317	200479
Ecuador	USA (United States)	29 Jun 44	80UNTS283	200250
Peru	USA (United States)	10 Jul 44	117UNTS291	200377
Guatemala	USA (United States)	15 Jul 44	106UNTS285	200347
Multilateral		02 Aug 44	67UNTS221	200221
Bolivia	USA (United States)	07 Sep 44	162UNTS315	200494
Brazil	USA (United States)	29 Sep 44	65UNTS271	200216
Ecuador	USA (United States)	22 Jan 45	24UNTS273	200152

PARTY ONE	PARTY TWO	DATE	CITATION	NUMBER
Expense sharing formulae (Cont.)				
Guatemala	USA (United States)	21 Feb 45	121UNTS133	200396
Guatemala	USA (United States)	21 May 45	121UNTS185	200399
Chile	USA (United States)	24 May 45	121UNTS219	200401
El Salvador	USA (United States)	09 Jun 45	149UNTS379	200478
Dominican Republic	USA (United States)	13 Oct 45	149UNTS361	200477
Netherlands	Switzerland	24 Oct 45	3UNTS73	100025
Multilateral		04 Dec 45	9UNTS101	100128
Costa Rica	USA (United States)	10 Dec 45	3UNTS157	100029
Honduras	USA (United States)	28 Dec 45	3UNTS185	100031
Brazil	USA (United States)	15 Feb 46	162UNTS21	102130
Colombia	USA (United States)	19 Feb 46	166UNTS104	102187
Poland	Yugoslavia	16 Mar 46	10UNTS11	100139
France	Norway	26 Mar 46	31UNTS69	100468
UK Great Britain	USA (United States)	27 Mar 46	4UNTS2	100039
Brazil	USA (United States)	05 Apr 46	12UNTS131	100183
Mexico	USA (United States)	12 Apr 46	66UNTS293	100861
Multilateral		17 Apr 46	27UNTS103	100402
UK Great Britain	USA (United States)	06 May 46	99UNTS199	101381
France	USA (United States)	28 May 46	84UNTS79	101120
USA (United States)	Venezuela	03 Jun 46	4UNTS215	100047
Taiwan	USA (United States)	14 Jun 46	4UNTS253	100049
Albania	Yugoslavia	03 Oct 46	111UNTS227	101537
Peru	USA (United States)	07 Oct 46	7UNTS71	100092
Colombia	USA (United States)	14 Oct 46	7UNTS97	100093
Albania	Yugoslavia	28 Nov 46	111UNTS93	101520
USSR (Soviet Union)	Yugoslavia	04 Feb 47	116UNTS171	101576
Mexico	USA (United States)	17 Mar 47	167UNTS30	102200
Philippines	USA (United States)	21 Mar 47	45UNTS47	100691
Australia	Norway	24 Mar 47	18UNTS185	100288
Honduras	USA (United States)	13 May 47	166UNTS159	102189
Netherlands	USA (United States)	28 May 47	17UNTS29	100267
Ecuador	USA (United States)	21 Jun 47	26UNTS275	100391
USA (United States)	Venezuela	30 Jun 47	166UNTS198	102190
Poland	Romania	09 Aug 47	12UNTS363	100193
El Salvador	USA (United States)	19 Aug 47	51UNTS57	100752
Iran	USA (United States)	06 Oct 47	11UNTS303	100171
Greece	UNICEF (Children)	14 Oct 47	102UNTS39	101409
Ecuador	USA (United States)	14 Nov 47	149UNTS297	101959
Guatemala	USA (United States)	05 Jan 48	135UNTS104	101817
Cuba	USA (United States)	27 Jan 48	67UNTS3	100862
Greece	United Nations	12 Feb 48	47UNTS223	100732
France	United Nations	10 Mar 48	47UNTS203	100731
Paraguay	USA (United States)	12 Mar 48	162UNTS30	102131
Philippines	USA (United States)	23 Mar 48	43UNTS247	100671
France	UK Great Britain	19 Apr 48	83UNTS201	101109
Ecuador	USA (United States)	14 May 48	89UNTS71	101210
Finland	United Nations	20 May 48	47UNTS319	200189
Multilateral		26 Jun 48	331UNTS217	104757
Peru	USA (United States)	30 Jun 48	150UNTS45	101962
Brazil	USA (United States)	29 Jul 48	80UNTS111	101047
Pakistan	United Nations	27 Aug 48	47UNTS269	100734
El Salvador	USA (United States)	23 Sep 48	181UNTS101	102402
Panama	USA (United States)	24 Sep 48	150UNTS25	101961
Bolivia	USA (United States)	29 Sep 48	505UNTS139	107370
United Nations	Thailand	05 Oct 48	47UNTS287	100735
Argentina	USA (United States)	06 Oct 48	80UNTS91	101046
United Nations	San Marino	07 Oct 48	47UNTS337	200190
Czechoslovakia	United Nations	07 Oct 48	47UNTS185	100730
Afghanistan	UNESCO (Educ/Cult)	08 Dec 48	46UNTS3	100697
Brazil	USA (United States)	30 Dec 48	102UNTS3	101406
Haiti	USA (United States)	04 Jan 49	44UNTS69	100679
Chile	USA (United States)	21 Jan 49	160UNTS185	102107
Multilateral		08 Feb 49	157UNTS157	102053
Colombia	USA (United States)	21 Feb 49	44UNTS83	100680
Colombia	USA (United States)	21 Feb 49	92UNTS227	101275

PARTY ONE	PARTY TWO	DATE	CITATION	NUMBER
Expense sharing formulae (Cont.)				
Multilateral		22 Feb 49	93UNTS129	101296
Multilateral		28 Feb 49	29UNTS53	100434
United Nations	UK Great Britain	18 Mar 49	47UNTS305	100736
Peru	USA (United States)	25 Mar 49	89UNTS15	101205
Haiti	USA (United States)	14 Apr 49	80UNTS37	101043
Multilateral		28 Apr 49	83UNTS105	101105
Multilateral		05 May 49	87UNTS103	101168
Netherlands	USA (United States)	17 May 49	46UNTS291	100717
UNICEF (Children)	UK Great Britain	17 Jun 49	65UNTS50	100820
Peru	USA (United States)	20 Jun 49	92UNTS249	101276
Mexico	USA (United States)	05 Jul 49	68UNTS55	100884
Greece	Turkey	21 Jul 49	78UNTS55	101011
El Salvador	USA (United States)	27 Jul 49	180UNTS219	102387
USA (United States)	Uruguay	27 Jul 49	151UNTS199	101995
WHO (World Health)	Thailand	12 Aug 49	178UNTS347	102350
Brazil	USA (United States)	31 Aug 49	102UNTS13	101407
Belgium	France	07 Sep 49	123UNTS13	101651
Belgium	Netherlands	07 Sep 49	117UNTS3	101581
Denmark	ICAO (Civil Aviat)	09 Sep 49	53UNTS341	100791
Afghanistan	WHO (World Health)	04 Dec 49	102UNTS117	101414
Korea, South	USA (United States)	26 Jan 50	178UNTS97	102337
Ceylon (Sri Lanka)	WHO (World Health)	17 Feb 50	102UNTS309	200309
Honduras	USA (United States)	06 Mar 50	80UNTS71	101045
Honduras	USA (United States)	06 Mar 50	80UNTS51	101044
Multilateral		17 Apr 50	131UNTS99	101738
El Salvador	WHO (World Health)	21 Apr 50	103UNTS13	101420
Haiti	WHO (World Health)	21 Jun 50	103UNTS61	101424
USA (United States)	Venezuela	23 Aug 50	92UNTS341	101279
UN Relief Palestin	WHO (World Health)	23 Sep 50	103UNTS129	200310
Peru	WHO (World Health)	26 Sep 50	104UNTS233	101444
Haiti	USA (United States)	28 Sep 50	162UNTS85	102132
Netherlands	New Zealand	16 Oct 50	83UNTS269	101111
Iran	USA (United States)	19 Oct 50	92UNTS135	101266
Multilateral		02 Nov 50	81UNTS160	101071
Bolivia	USA (United States)	22 Nov 50	152UNTS17	102008
Colombia	USA (United States)	24 Nov 50	133UNTS49	101779
Multilateral		24 Nov 50	81UNTS188	101072
Guatemala	WHO (World Health)	28 Nov 50	103UNTS51	101423
El Salvador	USA (United States)	13 Dec 50	166UNTS149	102188
Brazil	USA (United States)	19 Dec 50	140UNTS365	101899
Cuba	USA (United States)	22 Dec 50	122UNTS97	101640
Brazil	USA (United States)	27 Dec 50	147UNTS33	101926
Nicaragua	WHO (World Health)	02 Jan 51	103UNTS107	101428
El Salvador	WHO (World Health)	02 Jan 51	103UNTS29	101421
Colombia	WHO (World Health)	05 Jan 51	102UNTS139	101417
United Nations	Yugoslavia	06 Jan 51	78UNTS165	101015
Liberia	USA (United States)	11 Jan 51	122UNTS125	101642
Chile	USA (United States)	16 Jan 51	157UNTS3	102043
Costa Rica	USA (United States)	17 Jan 51	134UNTS215	101801
Multilateral		18 Jan 51	81UNTS233	101073
Ceylon (Sri Lanka)	ILO (Labor Org)	24 Jan 51	117UNTS355	200380
Panama	USA (United States)	26 Jan 51	137UNTS69	101849
Nicaragua	USA (United States)	31 Jan 51	160UNTS121	102105
Nicaragua	USA (United States)	31 Jan 51	150UNTS3	101960
Ethiopia	ICAO (Civil Aviat)	02 Feb 51	96UNTS123	101333
Chile	USA (United States)	15 Feb 51	133UNTS117	101784
Chile	USA (United States)	15 Feb 51	133UNTS95	101783
Multilateral		15 Feb 51	81UNTS245	101074
Israel	ICAO (Civil Aviat)	19 Feb 51	96UNTS141	101334
Israel	ILO (Labor Org)	19 Feb 51	100UNTS105	101391
Panama	USA (United States)	26 Feb 51	160UNTS153	102106
ILO (Labor Org)	Syria	03 Mar 51	110UNTS69	101502
Multilateral		05 Mar 51	81UNTS261	101075
Dominican Republic	USA (United States)	16 Mar 51	148UNTS15	101932
El Salvador	USA (United States)	19 Mar 51	134UNTS245	101803

PARTY ONE	PARTY TWO	DATE	CITATION	NUMBER
Expense sharing formulae (Cont.)				
Canada	USA (United States)	27 Mar 51	132UNTS333	101772
Multilateral		28 Mar 51	181UNTS61	102399
Jordan	United Nations	29 Mar 51	137UNTS267	200448
Jordan	ILO (Labor Org)	29 Mar 51	100UNTS247	200287
Liberia	ILO (Labor Org)	02 Apr 51	100UNTS117	101392
Multilateral		05 Apr 51	84UNTS299	101139
Ceylon (Sri Lanka)	ILO (Labor Org)	06 Apr 51	100UNTS235	200286
Mexico	ILO (Labor Org)	06 Apr 51	100UNTS131	101393
Guatemala	ILO (Labor Org)	13 Apr 51	126UNTS249	101692
Costa Rica	WHO (World Health)	13 Apr 51	103UNTS3	101419
Peru	ILO (Labor Org)	13 Apr 51	100UNTS31	101385
ICAO (Civil Aviat)	Thailand	19 Apr 51	96UNTS181	101336
Ecuador	ILO (Labor Org)	19 Apr 51	100UNTS77	101389
Nicaragua	USA (United States)	20 Apr 51	138UNTS57	101859
Cuba	ILO (Labor Org)	21 Apr 51	99UNTS205	101382
Honduras	USA (United States)	24 Apr 51	140UNTS287	101894
Greece	ILO (Labor Org)	25 Apr 51	100UNTS93	101390
India	ILO (Labor Org)	26 Apr 51	100UNTS19	101384
Mexico	WHO (World Health)	30 Apr 51	103UNTS95	101427
Ethiopia	USA (United States)	02 May 51	139UNTS85	101877
WHO (World Health)	Yugoslavia	02 May 51	103UNTS117	101429
United Arab Rep	USA (United States)	05 May 51	198UNTS265	102670
Pakistan	ILO (Labor Org)	16 May 51	100UNTS147	101394
Lebanon	USA (United States)	29 May 51	160UNTS49	102101
Lebanon	WHO (World Health)	07 Jun 51	126UNTS221	101690
Iceland	ICAO (Civil Aviat)	07 Jun 51	96UNTS193	101337
United Nations	Thailand	11 Jun 51	90UNTS45	101225
Burma	WHO (World Health)	13 Jun 51	117UNTS115	101588
Dominican Republic	ILO (Labor Org)	18 Jun 51	100UNTS3	101383
Israel	United Nations	25 Jun 51	97UNTS21	101344
Multilateral		25 Jun 51	92UNTS27	101258
ILO (Labor Org)	Vietnam, South	26 Jun 51	100UNTS223	200285
Multilateral		28 Jun 51	118UNTS154	101604
Brazil	USA (United States)	29 Jun 51	184UNTS303	102455
Burma	WHO (World Health)	09 Jul 51	107UNTS9	101463
Burma	WHO (World Health)	09 Jul 51	104UNTS175	101439
Burma	WHO (World Health)	09 Jul 51	104UNTS187	101440
ILO (Labor Org)	Thailand	11 Jul 51	100UNTS159	101395
Paraguay	ILO (Labor Org)	12 Jul 51	117UNTS155	101591
UK Great Britain	USA (United States)	13 Jul 51	105UNTS71	101454
El Salvador	USA (United States)	19 Jul 51	140UNTS259	101892
El Salvador	USA (United States)	23 Jul 51	138UNTS127	101865
Multilateral		27 Jul 51	97UNTS291	200273
Panama	USA (United States)	30 Jul 51	140UNTS321	101896
Canada	USA (United States)	01 Aug 51	233UNTS109	103254
Multilateral		01 Aug 51	107UNTS19	101464
Multilateral		04 Aug 51	104UNTS197	101441
Israel	WHO (World Health)	07 Aug 51	104UNTS213	101442
USA (United States)	Venezuela	10 Aug 51	140UNTS345	101898
Cuba	USA (United States)	28 Aug 51	140UNTS239	101891
Cuba	USA (United States)	28 Aug 51	134UNTS225	101802
WHO (World Health)	Saudi Arabia	29 Aug 51	110UNTS277	101516
Multilateral		05 Sep 51	173UNTS15	102256
Japan	USA (United States)	08 Sep 51	136UNTS203	101834
Panama	UK Great Britain	15 Sep 51	560UNTS143	108172
Iraq	ICAO (Civil Aviat)	18 Sep 51	108UNTS219	101475
Korea, South	WHO (World Health)	19 Sep 51	109UNTS297	200366
Canada	Italy	20 Sep 51	236UNTS251	103328
Paraguay	United Nations	27 Sep 51	120UNTS105	101617
Multilateral		01 Oct 51	104UNTS249	101446
Bolivia	United Nations	01 Oct 51	104UNTS263	101447
WHO (World Health)	Thailand	04 Oct 51	109UNTS77	101492
Pakistan	WHO (World Health)	07 Oct 51	126UNTS101	101684
Ecuador	WHO (World Health)	16 Oct 51	110UNTS263	101515
India	WHO (World Health)	16 Oct 51	109UNTS49	101490

PARTY ONE	PARTY TWO	DATE	CITATION	NUMBER
Expense sharing formulae (Cont.)				
United Nations	Uruguay	17 Oct 51	122UNTS29	101633
ILO (Labor Org)	Venezuela	22 Oct 51	117UNTS139	101590
India	WHO (World Health)	23 Oct 51	109UNTS59	101491
Taiwan	WHO (World Health)	25 Oct 51	126UNTS77	101683
India	WHO (World Health)	01 Nov 51	118UNTS13	101593
Saudi Arabia	USA (United States)	10 Nov 51	180UNTS263	102390
Panama	ILO (Labor Org)	10 Nov 51	126UNTS269	101693
USA (United States)	Uruguay	04 Dec 51	152UNTS41	102010
El Salvador	USA (United States)	12 Dec 51	132UNTS287	101768
Mexico	WHO (World Health)	17 Dec 51	124UNTS121	101670
Multilateral		24 Dec 51	118UNTS290	200383
Guatemala	WHO (World Health)	29 Dec 51	124UNTS89	101668
Austria	WHO (World Health)	10 Jan 52	131UNTS295	200438
India	United Nations	12 Jan 52	118UNTS175	101606
Ceylon (Sri Lanka)	United Nations	21 Jan 52	118UNTS281	200382
Costa Rica	WHO (World Health)	23 Jan 52	135UNTS265	101826
Multilateral		23 Jan 52	127UNTS269	101708
WHO (World Health)	Spain	30 Jan 52	124UNTS259	200425
UNICEF (Children)	UK Great Britain	04 Feb 52	120UNTS147	101620
ICAO (Civil Aviat)	Yugoslavia	06 Feb 52	128UNTS97	101715
WHO (World Health)	UK Great Britain	07 Feb 52	121UNTS75	101627
Lebanon	ICAO (Civil Aviat)	14 Feb 52	128UNTS83	101714
Dominican Republic	WHO (World Health)	15 Feb 52	134UNTS291	101808
Multilateral		18 Feb 52	126UNTS319	200434
Greece	United Nations	05 Mar 52	123UNTS3	101650
ICAO (Civil Aviat)	United Arab Rep	06 Mar 52	151UNTS111	101986
Taiwan	WHO (World Health)	07 Mar 52	128UNTS233	101723
Finland	WHO (World Health)	07 Mar 52	128UNTS269	200436
Ceylon (Sri Lanka)	WHO (World Health)	26 Mar 52	134UNTS341	200442
Libya	UK Great Britain	31 Mar 52	151UNTS69	101984
India	United Nations	02 Apr 52	126UNTS145	101687
India	WHO (World Health)	02 Apr 52	131UNTS227	101743
Peru	USA (United States)	09 Apr 52	184UNTS295	102454
Multilateral		11 Apr 52	173UNTS2	102255
India	WHO (World Health)	17 Apr 52	131UNTS241	101744
Pakistan	United Nations	28 Apr 52	128UNTS191	101720
India	ICAO (Civil Aviat)	29 Apr 52	151UNTS123	101987
Ethiopia	USA (United States)	15 May 52	180UNTS227	102388
Multilateral		22 May 52	131UNTS115	101739
Mexico	WHO (World Health)	28 May 52	134UNTS319	101810
Ecuador	USA (United States)	29 May 52	185UNTS203	102471
India	WHO (World Health)	04 Jun 52	135UNTS279	101827
Burma	WHO (World Health)	09 Jun 52	134UNTS273	101806
Bolivia	USA (United States)	18 Jun 52	199UNTS211	102686
Ethiopia	USA (United States)	18 Jun 52	181UNTS207	102410
Multilateral		19 Jun 52	133UNTS165	101787
WHO (World Health)	Syria	20 Jun 52	165UNTS219	102178
Ethiopia	USA (United States)	24 Jun 52	181UNTS215	102411
Finland	USA (United States)	02 Jul 52	165UNTS203	102177
Australia	FAO (Food Agri)	07 Jul 52	184UNTS209	102449
India	WHO (World Health)	16 Jul 52	135UNTS291	101828
Colombia	United Nations	17 Jul 52	135UNTS61	101815
Germany, West	USA (United States)	18 Jul 52	165UNTS167	102175
Chile	ILO (Labor Org)	23 Jul 52	178UNTS323	102348
Brazil	United Nations	04 Aug 52	135UNTS185	101820
Iraq	USA (United States)	18 Aug 52	184UNTS131	102444
Panama	United Nations	20 Aug 52	136UNTS3	101829
Multilateral		21 Aug 52	141UNTS129	101912
Jordan	WHO (World Health)	21 Aug 52	141UNTS341	200472
Italy	ILO (Labor Org)	04 Sep 52	178UNTS371	200505
ILO (Labor Org)	Uruguay	20 Sep 52	187UNTS25	102499
United Nations	Trieste	30 Sep 52	140UNTS11	101881
Multilateral		15 Oct 52	141UNTS96	101909
Chile	WHO (World Health)	24 Oct 52	151UNTS339	102004
Chile	WHO (World Health)	04 Nov 52	150UNTS119	101966

PARTY ONE	PARTY TWO	DATE	CITATION	NUMBER
Expense sharing formulae (Cont.)				
Ethiopia	USA (United States)	05 Nov 52	184UNTS139	102445
Saudi Arabia	USA (United States)	10 Nov 52	181UNTS307	102419
Saudi Arabia	USA (United States)	10 Nov 52	181UNTS295	102418
Belgium	UK Great Britain	12 Nov 52	180UNTS15	102372
Ceylon (Sri Lanka)	WHO (World Health)	21 Nov 52	161UNTS315	200490
Japan	WHO (World Health)	26 Nov 52	204UNTS301	200521
Mexico	ICAO (Civil Aviat)	28 Nov 52	164UNTS15	102156
India	WHO (World Health)	11 Dec 52	158UNTS391	102073
Saudi Arabia	USA (United States)	15 Dec 52	185UNTS67	102459
Saudi Arabia	USA (United States)	15 Dec 52	185UNTS55	102458
Multilateral		16 Dec 52	158UNTS407	102074
Multilateral		29 Dec 52	151UNTS317	102002
ILO (Labor Org)	UN Relief Palestin	31 Dec 52	182UNTS201	200506
USA (United States)	Venezuela	16 Jan 53	199UNTS287	102690
Saudi Arabia	USA (United States)	25 Jan 53	201UNTS3	102706
India	WHO (World Health)	11 Feb 53	163UNTS43	102140
Taiwan	ILO (Labor Org)	13 Feb 53	178UNTS337	102349
Costa Rica	United Nations	27 Feb 53	161UNTS45	102121
Germany, West	USA (United States)	27 Feb 53	223UNTS167	103065
Nepal	United Nations	02 Mar 53	161UNTS347	200493
United Arab Rep	USA (United States)	12 Mar 53	204UNTS3	102747
France	Italy	14 Mar 53	284UNTS221	104140
United Arab Rep	USA (United States)	19 Mar 53	215UNTS17	102909
Japan	USA (United States)	23 Mar 53	185UNTS93	102461
France	WHO (World Health)	02 Apr 53	174UNTS83	102279
United Nations	Yemen	07 Apr 53	163UNTS73	102142
Ethiopia	USA (United States)	29 Apr 53	224UNTS121	103073
France	WHO (World Health)	30 Apr 53	174UNTS71	102278
United Arab Rep	USA (United States)	21 May 53	204UNTS29	102748
El Salvador	USA (United States)	21 May 53	213UNTS15	102878
ICAO (Civil Aviat)	Syria	28 May 53	173UNTS199	102267
Brazil	USA (United States)	30 May 53	460UNTS89	106633
Ecuador	United Nations	16 Jun 53	166UNTS289	102194
United Arab Rep	USA (United States)	18 Jun 53	215UNTS45	102910
Ethiopia	United Nations	22 Jun 53	172UNTS93	102241
Cambodia	United Nations	24 Jun 53	168UNTS309	200500
Japan	United Nations	24 Jun 53	167UNTS249	200499
Pakistan	USA (United States)	25 Jun 53	205UNTS139	102773
Brazil	USA (United States)	26 Jun 53	336UNTS241	104808
Panama	USA (United States)	26 Jun 53	215UNTS77	102912
Saudi Arabia	USA (United States)	29 Jun 53	206UNTS23	102784
Nicaragua	USA (United States)	30 Jun 53	215UNTS133	102917
Afghanistan	USA (United States)	30 Jun 53	215UNTS3	102908
Ethiopia	USA (United States)	30 Jun 53	212UNTS135	102865
Multilateral		09 Oct 53	190UNTS49	102557
Austria	Yugoslavia	11 Nov 53	363UNTS149	105206
Nicaragua	USA (United States)	19 Nov 53	206UNTS117	102787
Dominican Republic	United Nations	19 Nov 53	180UNTS45	102374
Libya	USA (United States)	11 Jan 54	229UNTS15	103157
Pakistan	United Nations	25 Jan 54	185UNTS213	102472
Brazil	WHO (World Health)	04 Feb 54	233UNTS49	103250
United Nations	Venezuela	05 Mar 54	187UNTS9	102498
Liberia	United Nations	09 Mar 54	187UNTS61	102501
Guatemala	United Nations	10 Mar 54	191UNTS271	102587
USA (United States)	USSR (Soviet Union)	26 Mar 54	247UNTS263	103475
Mexico	USA (United States)	06 Apr 54	236UNTS69	103317
Multilateral		20 Apr 54	189UNTS11	102539
Ethiopia	USA (United States)	21 Apr 54	232UNTS299	103244
Canada	USA (United States)	03 May 54	221UNTS339	103015
Norway	USA (United States)	07 May 54	231UNTS157	103215
Nepal	WHO (World Health)	13 May 54	204UNTS311	200522
Multilateral		31 May 54	192UNTS20	102592
Multilateral		01 Jun 54	200UNTS235	200520
Multilateral		30 Jun 54	193UNTS67	102611
Multilateral		29 Jul 54	249UNTS45	103500

PARTY ONE	PARTY TWO	DATE	CITATION	NUMBER
Expense sharing formulae (Cont.)				
Netherlands	USA (United States)	13 Aug 54	251UNTS91	103535
Multilateral		19 Aug 54	201UNTS51	102710
El Salvador	USA (United States)	23 Sep 54	237UNTS91	103338
Multilateral		06 Oct 54	201UNTS75	102711
Ethiopia	Sweden	13 Oct 54	202UNTS273	102734
Multilateral		23 Oct 54	332UNTS157	104761
Multilateral		27 Oct 54	201UNTS95	102712
Multilateral		29 Oct 54	201UNTS115	102713
Libya	USA (United States)	03 Nov 54	238UNTS227	103366
United Arab Rep	USA (United States)	06 Nov 54	237UNTS183	103344
Multilateral		01 Dec 54	210UNTS197	102839
Guatemala	USA (United States)	13 Dec 54	237UNTS169	103343
USA (United States)	USSR (Soviet Union)	22 Dec 54	251UNTS41	103532
Peru	USA (United States)	31 Dec 54	251UNTS51	103533
Austria	Belgium	07 Jan 55	380UNTS219	105458
Greece	UK Great Britain	24 Feb 55	209UNTS187	102827
Mexico	USA (United States)	09 Mar 55	263UNTS247	103776
Haiti	USA (United States)	01 Apr 55	261UNTS361	103734
Multilateral		04 Apr 55	208UNTS239	102816
Japan	USA (United States)	07 Apr 55	263UNTS285	103778
Taiwan	WHO (World Health)	21 Apr 55	210UNTS71	102835
Peru	USA (United States)	30 Apr 55	263UNTS309	103780
Multilateral		25 May 55	264UNTS117	103791
USA (United States)	USSR (Soviet Union)	26 May 55	270UNTS61	103892
Norway	Sweden	28 May 55	262UNTS151	103743
Multilateral		14 Jun 55	212UNTS263	200526
Canada	USA (United States)	15 Jun 55	235UNTS201	103302
Iran	WHO (World Health)	04 Jul 55	227UNTS65	103131
Multilateral		04 Jul 55	214UNTS10	102897
Belgium	USA (United States)	31 Aug 55	223UNTS111	103041
France	Germany, West	04 Oct 55	353UNTS203	105044
Canada	Norway	20 Dec 55	305UNTS17	104408
Multilateral		04 Jan 56	256UNTS171	103627
Multilateral		02 Feb 56	227UNTS153	103137
Multilateral		10 Feb 56	228UNTS167	103150
Multilateral		10 Feb 56	228UNTS189	103151
Norway	Sweden	09 Mar 56	369UNTS285	105262
Multilateral		13 Mar 56	427UNTS245	106158
Colombia	USA (United States)	14 Mar 56	271UNTS303	103922
Canada	USA (United States)	23 Apr 56	300UNTS29	104329
Germany, West	Switzerland	02 May 56	559UNTS157	108158
Multilateral		31 May 56	251UNTS181	103541
Multilateral		08 Jun 56	247UNTS366	200541
Germany, West	Ireland	12 Jun 56	353UNTS121	105040
Multilateral		14 Jun 56	265UNTS125	103809
Multilateral		26 Jun 56	321UNTS2	104650
Israel	USA (United States)	26 Jun 56	257UNTS55	103649
Multilateral		26 Jun 56	253UNTS12	103573
Bolivia	USA (United States)	30 Jun 56	271UNTS243	103919
Multilateral		02 Jul 56	540UNTS110	107846
Multilateral		02 Jul 56	248UNTS37	103484
UNESCO (Educ/Cult)	UK Great Britain	09 Aug 56	256UNTS139	103624
Multilateral		31 Aug 56	249UNTS158	103506
Denmark	WHO (World Health)	03 Sep 56	258UNTS103	103674
Italy	Spain	05 Sep 56	302UNTS195	104359
Multilateral		25 Sep 56	334UNTS89	104767
Multilateral		25 Sep 56	334UNTS13	104766
Argentina	USA (United States)	03 Oct 56	279UNTS13	104032
Multilateral		05 Oct 56	251UNTS267	103545
Multilateral		05 Oct 56	251UNTS245	103544
Colombia	USA (United States)	24 Oct 56	476UNTS77	106905
Multilateral		26 Oct 56	276UNTS3	103988
Ecuador	USA (United States)	31 Oct 56	283UNTS151	104114
Argentina	USA (United States)	05 Nov 56	277UNTS143	104004
Multilateral		21 Nov 56	253UNTS266	103588

PARTY ONE	PARTY TWO	DATE	CITATION	NUMBER
Expense sharing formulae (Cont.)				
Dominican Republic	USA (United States)	07 Dec 56	263UNTS193	103774
Colombia	USA (United States)	09 Jan 57	462UNTS151	106676
Multilateral		15 Jan 57	376UNTS122	105378
Multilateral		23 Jan 57	259UNTS426	103701
Germany, West	Norway	29 Jan 57	353UNTS39	105037
Denmark	Germany, West	29 Jan 57	302UNTS75	104354
Multilateral		17 Feb 57	271UNTS2	103907
Multilateral		22 Feb 57	274UNTS93	103960
Iceland	USA (United States)	23 Feb 57	283UNTS73	104107
Chile	USA (United States)	01 Mar 57	283UNTS127	104112
Multilateral		01 Mar 57	264UNTS94	103790
Ethiopia	Sweden	16 Mar 57	304UNTS214	104398
Multilateral		28 Mar 57	271UNTS30	103908
Australia	UK Great Britain	01 Apr 57	271UNTS235	103918
Paraguay	USA (United States)	04 Apr 57	284UNTS161	104135
Libya	USA (United States)	04 Apr 57	283UNTS181	104116
Multilateral		09 Apr 57	274UNTS172	103965
Finland	USA (United States)	10 May 57	283UNTS43	104105
Australia	Germany, West	22 May 57	357UNTS45	105105
Multilateral		24 May 57	268UNTS270	103861
Bulgaria	Czechoslovakia	03 Jun 57	292UNTS3	104261
Germany, West	USA (United States)	07 Jun 57	346UNTS241	104984
Tunisia	USA (United States)	28 Jun 57	289UNTS301	104226
Australia	FAO (Food Agri)	08 Jul 57	277UNTS315	104015
Multilateral		09 Jul 57	274UNTS300	103972
Germany, West	Netherlands	10 Jul 57	339UNTS97	104848
Greece	Italy	02 Aug 57	533UNTS217	107744
New Zealand	UK Great Britain	20 Sep 57	287UNTS105	104180
Burma	WHO (World Health)	20 Sep 57	282UNTS113	104096
Multilateral		03 Oct 57	366UNTS87	105216
IAEA (Atom Energy)	United Nations	23 Oct 57	281UNTS369	200548
France	Morocco	25 Oct 57	559UNTS95	108156
Brazil	USA (United States)	05 Nov 57	303UNTS3	104368
Multilateral		05 Nov 57	285UNTS301	104155
France	Italy	08 Nov 57	305UNTS393	104427
El Salvador	USA (United States)	21 Nov 57	303UNTS19	104369
Czechoslovakia	USSR (Soviet Union)	04 Dec 57	313UNTS291	104537
Italy	Yugoslavia	12 Dec 57	386UNTS293	105549
Finland	Italy	17 Dec 57	291UNTS133	104248
Japan	USA (United States)	11 Jan 58	304UNTS35	104390
Ghana	WHO (World Health)	21 Jan 58	307UNTS3	104437
Japan	USA (United States)	25 Jan 58	304UNTS81	104392
Indonesia	WHO (World Health)	05 Feb 58	307UNTS15	104438
Afghanistan	Turkey	08 Feb 58	464UNTS39	106711
Multilateral		15 Mar 58	292UNTS273	104276
Germany, West	Portugal	21 Mar 58	464UNTS71	106712
Morocco	Portugal	03 Apr 58	393UNTS203	105657
Israel	WHO (World Health)	11 Apr 58	307UNTS27	104439
Sweden	Yugoslavia	18 Apr 58	393UNTS225	105658
Multilateral		19 Jun 58	306UNTS236	200550
WHO (World Health)	Sudan	21 Jun 58	307UNTS235	104453
Australia	Germany, West	27 Aug 58	320UNTS303	104649
Austria	Bulgaria	12 Sep 58	353UNTS3	105036
Finland	Sweden	22 Sep 58	428UNTS119	106170
Finland	Sweden	16 Oct 58	428UNTS125	106171
Spain	USA (United States)	16 Oct 58	336UNTS153	104804
Burma	United Nations	15 Dec 58	319UNTS3	104629
Afghanistan	WHO (World Health)	18 Dec 58	324UNTS121	104681
United Nations	Tunisia	23 Dec 58	321UNTS23	104651
Haiti	USA (United States)	24 Dec 58	338UNTS265	104840
Finland	Switzerland	07 Jan 59	353UNTS173	105042
UK Great Britain	Yugoslavia	03 Feb 59	359UNTS339	105151
Ghana	United Nations	27 Feb 59	324UNTS133	104682
United Nations	Sudan	28 Mar 59	327UNTS95	104719
Morocco	UN Special Fund	04 Apr 59	354UNTS347	105069

PARTY ONE	PARTY TWO	DATE	CITATION	NUMBER
Expense sharing formulae (Cont.)				
Colombia	USA (United States)	08 May 59	344UNTS193	104950
Denmark	USA (United States)	08 May 59	344UNTS185	104949
Fed of Malaya	USA (United States)	22 May 59	346UNTS263	104985
Libya	United Nations	27 Jun 59	336UNTS291	104811
Laos	United Nations	06 Jul 59	337UNTS41	104814
Afghanistan	Germany, West	22 Jul 59	464UNTS177	106715
Paraguay	United Nations	01 Aug 59	341UNTS319	104894
Germany, West	Iceland	12 Aug 59	411UNTS224	105921
Ghana	UN Special Fund	12 Aug 59	338UNTS203	104836
Canada	Germany, West	04 Sep 59	411UNTS260	105922
Bulgaria	Czechoslovakia	19 Sep 59	355UNTS77	105074
United Arab Rep	USA (United States)	28 Sep 59	358UNTS97	105128
Iran	UN Special Fund	06 Oct 59	342UNTS89	104902
Multilateral		09 Oct 59	376UNTS382	105391
Poland	UN Special Fund	15 Oct 59	344UNTS29	104941
Guinea	United Nations	15 Oct 59	344UNTS47	104942
India	UN Special Fund	20 Oct 59	344UNTS143	104946
UN Special Fund	Yugoslavia	27 Oct 59	344UNTS159	104947
Ecuador	UN Special Fund	10 Nov 59	345UNTS3	104955
Japan	USA (United States)	12 Nov 59	361UNTS27	105171
Greece	UN Special Fund	13 Nov 59	345UNTS171	104966
UN Special Fund	Turkey	20 Nov 59	345UNTS105	104963
Afghanistan	United Nations	24 Nov 59	397UNTS187	105705
UN Special Fund	United Arab Rep	25 Nov 59	345UNTS125	104964
Israel	UN Special Fund	01 Dec 59	345UNTS197	104968
Guinea	UN Special Fund	02 Dec 59	345UNTS215	104969
Multilateral		03 Dec 59	348UNTS246	105003
Multilateral		03 Dec 59	345UNTS251	104971
Argentina	UN Special Fund	04 Dec 59	345UNTS263	104972
Jordan	UN Special Fund	15 Dec 59	346UNTS3	104974
Ceylon (Sri Lanka)	WHO (World Health)	21 Dec 59	349UNTS109	105011
UN Special Fund	UK Great Britain	07 Jan 60	348UNTS177	105000
Peru	UN Special Fund	19 Jan 60	349UNTS83	105010
Pakistan	WHO (World Health)	20 Jan 60	351UNTS355	105034
Chile	UN Special Fund	22 Jan 60	351UNTS115	105020
India	Japan	25 Jan 60	384UNTS31	105508
Colombia	UN Special Fund	04 Feb 60	355UNTS257	105080
Bolivia	UN Special Fund	09 Feb 60	351UNTS203	105024
Germany, West	United Arab Rep	16 Feb 60	464UNTS233	106717
Afghanistan	UN Special Fund	21 Feb 60	351UNTS93	105019
Pakistan	UN Special Fund	25 Feb 60	351UNTS141	105021
Finland	Iceland	10 Mar 60	497UNTS95	107264
France	UN Special Fund	17 Mar 60	354UNTS119	105059
Portugal	USA (United States)	19 Mar 60	371UNTS131	105275
Japan	USA (United States)	23 Mar 60	372UNTS289	105305
Italy	UN Special Fund	01 Apr 60	354UNTS261	105066
Germany, West	Netherlands	08 Apr 60	508UNTS14	107404
Luxembourg	Yugoslavia	09 Apr 60	464UNTS293	106719
Multilateral		12 Apr 60	359UNTS323	105150
UN Special Fund	Tunisia	12 Apr 60	355UNTS289	105082
Multilateral		15 Apr 60	470UNTS239	106811
Libya	UN Special Fund	19 Apr 60	356UNTS11	105090
UN Special Fund	Sudan	21 Apr 60	356UNTS213	105097
Germany, West	Spain	28 Apr 60	465UNTS3	106720
UN Special Fund	Vietnam, South	29 Apr 60	357UNTS311	200567
United Nations	Togo	06 May 60	388UNTS53	105571
Lebanon	UN Special Fund	07 May 60	360UNTS225	105160
Morocco	United Arab Rep	19 May 60	563UNTS121	108208
Cambodia	WHO (World Health)	19 May 60	372UNTS193	105298
Multilateral		04 Jun 60	360UNTS208	105159
Iraq	UN Special Fund	19 Jun 60	376UNTS357	105389
Multilateral		08 Jul 60	366UNTS310	105220
Ethiopia	United Nations	13 Jul 60	368UNTS143	105239
Germany, West	Pakistan	20 Jul 60	465UNTS41	106721
Argentina	USA (United States)	02 Aug 60	384UNTS105	105514

PARTY ONE	PARTY TWO	DATE	CITATION	NUMBER
Expense sharing formulae (Cont.)				
WHO (World Health)	United Arab Rep	03 Aug 60	385UNTS3	105524
Jordan	WHO (World Health)	03 Aug 60	381UNTS133	105469
WHO (World Health)	Tunisia	04 Aug 60	381UNTS335	105474
Laos	WHO (World Health)	04 Aug 60	373UNTS313	105322
Italy	Netherlands	06 Aug 60	455UNTS259	106546
Belgium	Burma	17 Aug 60	540UNTS185	107850
Australia	USA (United States)	23 Aug 60	388UNTS237	105581
WHO (World Health)	Saudi Arabia	06 Sep 60	395UNTS169	105684
Lebanon	WHO (World Health)	08 Sep 60	387UNTS49	105557
Iran	Japan	12 Sep 60	384UNTS43	105509
Brazil	UN Special Fund	16 Sep 60	375UNTS3	105351
Taiwan	UN Special Fund	20 Sep 60	375UNTS29	105352
Guinea	USA (United States)	30 Sep 60	394UNTS103	105671
Indonesia	UN Special Fund	07 Oct 60	378UNTS141	105424
Liberia	UN Special Fund	11 Oct 60	376UNTS341	105388
El Salvador	UN Special Fund	24 Oct 60	377UNTS171	105400
Kuwait	United Nations	31 Oct 60	391UNTS295	200581
Burma	Switzerland	31 Oct 60	465UNTS97	106723
WHO (World Health)	Upper Volta	15 Nov 60	383UNTS91	105496
Guatemala	UN Special Fund	17 Nov 60	383UNTS67	105495
Pakistan	United Nations	17 Nov 60	380UNTS277	105460
Nepal	UN Special Fund	17 Nov 60	380UNTS289	105461
Israel	Mali	24 Nov 60	413UNTS95	105944
Cambodia	UN Special Fund	24 Nov 60	382UNTS255	105487
Fed of Malaya	WHO (World Health)	25 Nov 60	387UNTS37	105556
Cambodia	United Nations	30 Nov 60	383UNTS147	105500
Multilateral		01 Dec 60	414UNTS110	105970
WHO (World Health)	Yemen	03 Dec 60	395UNTS187	105685
Dahomey	WHO (World Health)	07 Dec 60	387UNTS277	105567
Cyprus	USA (United States)	08 Dec 60	405UNTS145	105831
Congo (Brazzaville)	WHO (World Health)	12 Dec 60	399UNTS105	105737
Bolivia	United Nations	14 Dec 60	382UNTS283	105489
Honduras	UN Special Fund	20 Dec 60	383UNTS103	105497
Niger	WHO (World Health)	28 Dec 60	394UNTS195	105679
Burma	UN Special Fund	03 Jan 61	387UNTS219	105564
Costa Rica	UN Special Fund	10 Jan 61	389UNTS253	105597
Germany, West	Japan	18 Jan 61	465UNTS173	106727
UN Special Fund	Saudi Arabia	19 Jan 61	396UNTS27	105692
Korea, South	WHO (World Health)	20 Jan 61	406UNTS269	200589
Nicaragua	UN Special Fund	20 Jan 61	387UNTS15	105555
Chad	UN Special Fund	23 Jan 61	390UNTS69	105603
Multilateral		28 Jan 61	387UNTS202	105563
UN Special Fund	Somalia	28 Jan 61	388UNTS75	105573
Ivory Coast	WHO (World Health)	30 Jan 61	395UNTS205	105686
Gabon	UN Special Fund	02 Feb 61	387UNTS289	105568
Chad	WHO (World Health)	03 Feb 61	394UNTS161	105676
WHO (World Health)	Togo	03 Feb 61	394UNTS207	105680
Nigeria	UN Special Fund	10 Feb 61	390UNTS85	105604
Central Afri Rep	WHO (World Health)	13 Feb 61	394UNTS149	105675
Mexico	UN Special Fund	23 Feb 61	388UNTS151	105576
Belgium	Netherlands	24 Feb 61	474UNTS167	106881
Cyprus	UN Special Fund	24 Feb 61	389UNTS3	105588
Iraq	United Nations	05 Mar 61	409UNTS56	105878
Panama	UN Special Fund	09 Mar 61	396UNTS3	105691
Cuba	UN Special Fund	10 Mar 61	390UNTS35	105601
Afghanistan	Japan	15 Mar 61	450UNTS373	106480
Kuwait	WHO (World Health)	16 Mar 61	397UNTS315	200588
Ceylon (Sri Lanka)	Japan	20 Mar 61	450UNTS385	106481
Mauritania	WHO (World Health)	17 Apr 61	396UNTS301	200587
Korea, South	UN Special Fund	21 Apr 61	394UNTS231	200583
Mali	WHO (World Health)	27 Apr 61	407UNTS66	105860
Gabon	WHO (World Health)	27 Apr 61	397UNTS215	105707
Ceylon (Sri Lanka)	UN Special Fund	03 May 61	395UNTS217	105687
Czechoslovakia	Morocco	08 Jun 61	497UNTS275	107272
Nepal	USA (United States)	09 Jun 61	421UNTS223	106061

PARTY ONE	PARTY TWO	DATE	CITATION	NUMBER
Expense sharing formulae (Cont.)				
Israel	Upper Volta	11 Jun 61	413UNTS113	105946
Cameroon	UN Special Fund	13 Jun 61	397UNTS297	105713
Ethiopia	United Nations	14 Jun 61	406UNTS81	105840
Cyprus	United Nations	15 Jun 61	398UNTS39	105716
Cameroon	France	16 Jun 61	412UNTS148	105929
Paraguay	UN Special Fund	22 Jun 61	399UNTS117	105738
UN Special Fund	Upper Volta	26 Jun 61	400UNTS3	105744
Haiti	United Nations	28 Jun 61	399UNTS159	105740
Haiti	UN Special Fund	28 Jun 61	399UNTS171	105741
Philippines	UN Special Fund	28 Jun 61	399UNTS141	105739
Mali	UN Special Fund	21 Jul 61	401UNTS141	105768
UN Special Fund	Yemen	02 Aug 61	402UNTS43	105777
Morocco	WHO (World Health)	09 Aug 61	412UNTS192	105932
WHO (World Health)	Somalia	17 Aug 61	423UNTS111	106088
Mexico	United Nations	18 Aug 61	404UNTS297	105817
Mexico	Netherlands	24 Aug 61	465UNTS291	106732
Lebanon	United Nations	26 Aug 61	406UNTS105	105842
Ivory Coast	UN Special Fund	29 Aug 61	406UNTS129	105844
Jordan	United Nations	11 Sep 61	406UNTS255	105855
Iraq	WHO (World Health)	13 Sep 61	419UNTS69	106030
Multilateral		20 Sep 61	407UNTS52	105859
Canada	USA (United States)	27 Sep 61	421UNTS85	106054
Dahomey	Israel	28 Sep 61	448UNTS151	106429
UN Special Fund	Sierra Leone	02 Oct 61	422UNTS131	106073
Austria	USA (United States)	03 Oct 61	426UNTS187	106137
Germany, West	Morocco	12 Oct 61	523UNTS289	107562
Malagasy	WHO (World Health)	13 Oct 61	421UNTS273	106064
Multilateral		16 Oct 61	410UNTS242	105908
Belgium	Italy	28 Oct 61	429UNTS199	106199
Mauritania	UN Special Fund	07 Nov 61	412UNTS240	105936
Multilateral		07 Nov 61	412UNTS258	105937
Congo (Brazzaville)	UN Special Fund	09 Nov 61	413UNTS58	105940
Cyprus	Greece	23 Nov 61	497UNTS311	107274
Ceylon (Sri Lanka)	United Nations	04 Dec 61	415UNTS236	105987
Ethiopia	USA (United States)	06 Dec 61	433UNTS231	106246
UN Special Fund	Venezuela	11 Dec 61	422UNTS149	106074
UN Special Fund	Senegal	16 Dec 61	425UNTS97	106121
Multilateral		27 Dec 61	425UNTS83	106120
Malagasy	UN Special Fund	05 Jan 62	419UNTS29	106028
Ethiopia	WHO (World Health)	11 Jan 62	423UNTS99	106087
Austria	Greece	15 Jan 62	498UNTS3	107275
Multilateral		17 Jan 62	419UNTS294	106033
Cyprus	USA (United States)	18 Jan 62	435UNTS3	106266
Multilateral		20 Jan 62	429UNTS230	200596
United Nations	Somalia	20 Jan 62	420UNTS133	106044
Ghana	USA (United States)	24 Jan 62	435UNTS23	106268
Multilateral		13 Feb 62	422UNTS288	200594
Multilateral		21 Feb 62	423UNTS151	106091
Niger	UN Special Fund	26 Feb 62	423UNTS83	106086
Multilateral		01 Mar 62	423UNTS122	106089
Germany, West	Thailand	05 Mar 62	563UNTS165	108210
WHO (World Health)	Sudan	11 Mar 62	432UNTS325	106226
Nigeria	WHO (World Health)	27 Mar 62	429UNTS123	106194
Brazil	Japan	28 Mar 62	451UNTS125	106489
Dahomey	UN Special Fund	28 Mar 62	424UNTS55	106099
India	Japan	31 Mar 62	451UNTS143	106490
Multilateral		10 Apr 62	429UNTS78	106192
Multilateral		18 Apr 62	463UNTS44	106692
India	Japan	23 Apr 62	451UNTS155	106491
UN Special Fund	Uruguay	04 May 62	429UNTS143	106196
Multilateral		09 May 62	453UNTS299	106531
Multilateral		14 May 62	544UNTS81	107911
Multilateral		17 May 62	429UNTS46	106189
Ghana	Israel	25 May 62	515UNTS237	107461
Denmark	USA (United States)	28 May 62	450UNTS215	106469

Expense sharing formulae (Cont.)

PARTY ONE	PARTY TWO	DATE	CITATION	NUMBER
Australia	UK Great Britain	28 May 62	434UNTS219	106264
Dominican Republic	UN Special Fund	06 Jun 62	429UNTS169	106197
France	Senegal	15 Jun 62	524UNTS3	107563
Libya	WHO (World Health)	16 Jun 62	437UNTS127	106301
WHO (World Health)	Sierra Leone	19 Jun 62	439UNTS151	106327
Germany, West	Syria	25 Jun 62	489UNTS71	107135
Morocco	Switzerland	05 Jul 62	498UNTS171	107281
Morocco	Switzerland	05 Jul 62	498UNTS189	107282
UN Special Fund	Syria	07 Jul 62	443UNTS3	106355
UN Special Fund	Tanganyika	17 Jul 62	435UNTS237	106281
WHO (World Health)	Senegal	06 Aug 62	435UNTS179	106279
Nigeria	United Nations	07 Aug 62	435UNTS167	106278
Multilateral		12 Aug 62	443UNTS266	106365
WHO (World Health)	Western Samoa	14 Aug 62	437UNTS317	200598
Multilateral		29 Aug 62	443UNTS280	106366
Cameroon	United Nations	29 Aug 62	442UNTS3	106334
Ecuador	Germany, West	20 Sep 62	498UNTS199	107283
Niger	United Nations	01 Oct 62	439UNTS181	106329
India	USA (United States)	09 Oct 62	471UNTS39	106820
Finland	France	12 Oct 62	498UNTS299	107285
Belgium	Rwanda	13 Oct 62	456UNTS431	106569
France	Ivory Coast	19 Oct 62	498UNTS317	107286
Israel	Rwanda	23 Oct 62	515UNTS291	107466
Cameroon	Israel	24 Oct 62	449UNTS3	106446
Japan	UN Special Fund	31 Oct 62	444UNTS171	106368
United Nations	Western Samoa	05 Nov 62	443UNTS297	200599
Algeria	UN Special Fund	15 Nov 62	452UNTS243	106512
Multilateral		15 Nov 62	448UNTS50	106424
Ivory Coast	Switzerland	17 Nov 62	499UNTS3	107289
WHO (World Health)	Syria	18 Nov 62	480UNTS249	106972
Germany, West	USA (United States)	20 Nov 62	505UNTS263	107377
Ecuador	United Nations	26 Nov 62	445UNTS3	106372
Rwanda	United Nations	28 Nov 62	450UNTS267	106473
Multilateral		06 Dec 62	450UNTS240	106471
Cameroon	WHO (World Health)	08 Dec 62	451UNTS215	106496
Ivory Coast	United Nations	10 Dec 62	451UNTS269	106498
Austria	Yugoslavia	11 Dec 62	546UNTS3	107938
Ghana	Tunisia	11 Dec 62	563UNTS243	108213
Multilateral		12 Dec 62	457UNTS72	106578
Algeria	WHO (World Health)	20 Dec 62	463UNTS135	106698
Israel	United Nations	07 Jan 63	450UNTS229	106470
Ghana	Mali	09 Jan 63	466UNTS165	106742
Multilateral		15 Jan 63	456UNTS409	106567
Multilateral		21 Jan 63	453UNTS20	106517
Senegal	Switzerland	23 Jan 63	524UNTS23	107564
United Nations	South Pacific Com	24 Jan 63	470UNTS361	200604
Malaysia	USA (United States)	28 Jan 63	473UNTS15	106850
Guinea	Switzerland	01 Feb 63	499UNTS35	107291
Multilateral		05 Feb 63	453UNTS36	106518
Mali	Senegal	07 Feb 63	524UNTS41	107565
Multilateral		14 Feb 63	453UNTS168	106524
Algeria	France	18 Feb 63	563UNTS263	108214
United Nations	South Pacific Com	20 Feb 63	453UNTS333	200600
Multilateral		06 Mar 63	455UNTS386	106552
Israel	USA (United States)	21 Mar 63	476UNTS131	106907
UN Special Fund	Uganda	22 Mar 63	456UNTS466	106572
Philippines	USA (United States)	23 Mar 63	474UNTS80	106873
Hungary	Korea, North	29 Mar 63	577UNTS219	108379
UK Great Britain	USA (United States)	06 Apr 63	474UNTS49	106871
Multilateral		18 Apr 63	463UNTS121	106697
Cyprus	Denmark	27 Apr 63	529UNTS255	107664
Multilateral		06 May 63	463UNTS78	106694
Australia	USA (United States)	09 May 63	469UNTS55	106784
Multilateral		09 May 63	463UNTS159	106700
Australia	United Nations	13 May 63	463UNTS187	106702

Expense sharing formulae (Cont.)

PARTY ONE	PARTY TWO	DATE	CITATION	NUMBER
Multilateral		22 May 63	483UNTS72	107007
Jamaica	UN Special Fund	22 May 63	489UNTS191	107140
Multilateral		24 May 63	466UNTS346	106754
Netherlands	UN Special Fund	24 May 63	466UNTS289	106750
Thailand	USA (United States)	24 May 63	477UNTS123	106918
UN Special Fund	Western Samoa	05 Jun 63	467UNTS463	200601
Korea, South	USA (United States)	18 Jun 63	487UNTS297	107112
India	USA (United States)	19 Jun 63	479UNTS175	106952
Mongolia	WHO (World Health)	21 Jun 63	472UNTS373	106848
Guinea	Ivory Coast	26 Jun 63	499UNTS71	107293
Canada	Nigeria	03 Jul 63	529UNTS57	107656
Austria	France	12 Jul 63	499UNTS91	107294
Multilateral		23 Jul 63	471UNTS158	106831
Multilateral		31 Jul 63	472UNTS220	106842
Burundi	WHO (World Health)	08 Aug 63	477UNTS346	106928
Cameroon	Israel	09 Aug 63	499UNTS121	107295
Burundi	UN Special Fund	22 Aug 63	476UNTS49	106903
Multilateral		27 Aug 63	511UNTS210	107435
Multilateral		10 Sep 63	480UNTS100	106965
Jamaica	WHO (World Health)	25 Sep 63	481UNTS125	106980
Ivory Coast	Netherlands	09 Oct 63	499UNTS141	107296
Canada	France	11 Oct 63	529UNTS71	107657
Multilateral		21 Oct 63	480UNTS197	106969
Central Afri Rep	UN Special Fund	30 Oct 63	481UNTS247	106985
Multilateral		30 Oct 63	480UNTS180	106968
WHO (World Health)	Tanganyika	05 Nov 63	496UNTS193	107252
Multilateral		07 Nov 63	480UNTS232	106971
Multilateral		08 Nov 63	482UNTS286	106999
New Zealand	Western Samoa	31 Dec 63	521UNTS163	107519
Mali	Niger	15 Jan 64	499UNTS197	107299
Multilateral		28 Jan 64	502UNTS321	107336
Denmark	Yugoslavia	11 Feb 64	511UNTS241	107437
Iceland	USA (United States)	13 Feb 64	524UNTS235	107576
Multilateral		20 Feb 64	491UNTS30	107172
UNESCO (Educ/Cult)	Yugoslavia	27 Feb 64	489UNTS257	107143
Multilateral		28 Feb 64	501UNTS245	107321
Israel	Philippines	16 Mar 64	550UNTS269	108021
Cameroon	Mali	17 Mar 64	524UNTS61	107566
Italy	United Nations	18 Mar 64	491UNTS21	107171
Afghanistan	United Nations	28 Apr 64	494UNTS77	107227
United Arab Rep	USA (United States)	05 May 64	531UNTS229	107706
Liberia	USA (United States)	08 May 64	526UNTS239	107608
Austria	Yugoslavia	20 May 64	514UNTS3	107439
Multilateral		26 May 64	541UNTS271	200613
Ireland	UN Special Fund	03 Jun 64	496UNTS205	107253
Rwanda	WHO (World Health)	22 Jun 64	514UNTS11	107440
Rwanda	WHO (World Health)	23 Jun 64	514UNTS157	107445
WHO (World Health)	Trinidad/Tobago	23 Jun 64	503UNTS167	107342
Multilateral		23 Jun 64	506UNTS108	107383
New Zealand	USA (United States)	24 Jun 64	524UNTS101	107568
Multilateral		28 Jun 64	519UNTS14	107499
United Nations	Togo	03 Jul 64	502UNTS287	107334
Ivory Coast	Mali	09 Jul 64	524UNTS121	107569
Belgium	Tunisia	15 Jul 64	560UNTS57	108168
Taiwan	Philippines	25 Aug 64	511UNTS233	107436
Australia	USA (United States)	28 Aug 64	510UNTS201	107415
Multilateral		24 Oct 64	514UNTS220	200608
Chile	USA (United States)	27 Oct 64	532UNTS347	107727
Multilateral		07 Nov 64	548UNTS3	107965
Multilateral		11 Nov 64	515UNTS94	107456
Israel	Turkey	13 Nov 64	550UNTS303	108025
Japan	USA (United States)	04 Dec 64	532UNTS249	107721
Germany, West	Jamaica	16 Dec 64	531UNTS129	107699
Germany, West	Thailand	23 Dec 64	525UNTS201	107592
Malawi	WHO (World Health)	06 Jan 65	525UNTS165	107588

PARTY ONE	PARTY TWO	DATE	CITATION	NUMBER
Expense sharing formulae (Cont.)				
Malawi	WHO (World Health)	08 Jan 65	524UNTS281	107579
Argentina	UK Great Britain	12 Jan 65	597UNTS177	108645
India	USA (United States)	13 Jan 65	541UNTS107	107864
Denmark	Thailand	25 Jan 65	530UNTS173	107680
Multilateral		27 Jan 65	523UNTS102	107556
Multilateral		02 Feb 65	523UNTS256	107560
Multilateral		12 Feb 65	525UNTS148	107587
Belgium	United Nations	20 Feb 65	535UNTS191	107779
Ghana	Malawi	04 May 65	541UNTS163	107869
UK Great Britain	USA (United States)	10 May 65	545UNTS181	107934
British Guiana	USA (United States)	29 May 65	605UNTS87	108761
Multilateral		02 Jun 65	551UNTS2	108030
Multilateral		02 Jun 65	537UNTS348	200611
UN Special Fund	Spain	30 Jun 65	544UNTS159	107918
Multilateral		02 Jul 65	592UNTS215	108575
Multilateral		05 Jul 65	563UNTS104	108207
Poland	WHO (World Health)	26 Aug 65	552UNTS3	108047
Multilateral		13 Sep 65	547UNTS264	107962
Multilateral		21 Oct 65	547UNTS216	107959
Multilateral		04 Dec 65	571UNTS123	108303
Austria	Tunisia	30 Dec 65	589UNTS119	108539
Mongolia	UN Special Fund	26 Jan 66	552UNTS201	108055
Israel	Kenya	25 Feb 66	582UNTS23	108455
Brazil	Denmark	25 Feb 66	590UNTS95	108549
WHO (World Health)	Singapore	28 Mar 66	562UNTS59	108195
Denmark	Iran	14 Jun 66	597UNTS283	108652
Finland	United Nations	16 Jan 67	588UNTS153	108522
Multilateral		21 Jun 67	598UNTS2	108653
Israel	USA (United States)	04 Aug 67	0UNTS0	109351
Fees and exemptions				
Canada	France	12 May 33	253UNTS285	200545
Argentina	Brazil	23 Jan 40	51UNTS281	200194
Brazil	France	27 Jan 40	72UNTS77	100929
Panama	USA (United States)	23 Mar 40	124UNTS195	200420
Panama	USA (United States)	06 Sep 40	124UNTS209	200421
Brazil	Paraguay	14 Jun 41	54UNTS289	200201
Brazil	Uruguay	08 Jan 42	54UNTS359	200206
Canada	USA (United States)	18 Mar 42	101UNTS205	200294
Brazil	USA (United States)	17 Jul 42	102UNTS203	200303
Brazil	Venezuela	22 Oct 42	65UNTS203	200212
Brazil	Dominican Republic	09 Dec 42	65UNTS217	200213
Brazil	USA (United States)	25 Nov 43	102UNTS227	200305
Multilateral		15 Jan 44	161UNTS281	200489
Canada	Taiwan	14 Apr 44	14UNTS408	200097
Brazil	Ecuador	24 May 44	73UNTS223	200242
Multilateral		07 Dec 44	171UNTS387	200502
Multilateral		07 Dec 44	171UNTS345	200501
Multilateral		07 Dec 44	84UNTS389	200252
Sweden	USA (United States)	16 Dec 44	6UNTS397	200041
Denmark	USA (United States)	16 Dec 44	10UNTS213	200063
Ecuador	USA (United States)	22 Jan 45	24UNTS273	200152
Iceland	USA (United States)	27 Jan 45	122UNTS293	200411
Ireland	USA (United States)	03 Feb 45	122UNTS305	200412
Canada	USA (United States)	17 Feb 45	122UNTS261	200409
Belgium	France	30 Mar 45	20UNTS297	200122
Iceland	USA (United States)	11 Apr 45	16UNTS241	200105
Panama	USA (United States)	13 May 45	89UNTS273	200256
Taiwan	Netherlands	29 May 45	2UNTS307	200023
Portugal	UK Great Britain	01 Jul 45	5UNTS263	200034
Switzerland	USA (United States)	03 Aug 45	51UNTS233	200191
Norway	USA (United States)	06 Oct 45	122UNTS319	200413
Dominican Republic	USA (United States)	13 Oct 45	149UNTS361	200477
South Africa	UK Great Britain	26 Oct 45	72UNTS41	100927
Greece	UK Great Britain	26 Nov 45	35UNTS161	100555

PARTY ONE	PARTY TWO	DATE	CITATION	NUMBER
Fees and exemptions (Cont.)				
Denmark	UK Great Britain	06 Dec 45	5UNTS3	100061
Portugal	USA (United States)	06 Dec 45	3UNTS139	100028
Portugal	UK Great Britain	06 Dec 45	5UNTS37	100064
Portugal	UK Great Britain	06 Dec 45	6UNTS3	100065
Canada	UK Great Britain	21 Dec 45	27UNTS155	100405
Czechoslovakia	USA (United States)	03 Jan 46	6UNTS309	100084
Czechoslovakia	Poland	24 Jan 46	25UNTS181	100363
UK Great Britain	USA (United States)	11 Feb 46	3UNTS253	100036
Turkey	USA (United States)	12 Feb 46	13UNTS3	100196
Turkey	UK Great Britain	12 Feb 46	6UNTS79	100069
France	UK Great Britain	28 Feb 46	27UNTS173	100407
Taiwan	France	28 Feb 46	14UNTS113	100215
Canada	UK Great Britain	06 Mar 46	20UNTS13	100312
Netherlands	USA (United States)	13 Mar 46	84UNTS3	101113
Greece	UK Great Britain	21 Mar 46	91UNTS149	101247
Greece	USA (United States)	27 Mar 46	15UNTS233	100239
France	USA (United States)	27 Mar 46	139UNTS114	101879
Multilateral		31 Mar 46	17UNTS159	100274
Ireland	UK Great Britain	05 Apr 46	72UNTS57	100928
Belgium	USA (United States)	05 Apr 46	4UNTS125	100041
Netherlands	Portugal	12 Apr 46	4UNTS317	100054
Argentina	UK Great Britain	17 Apr 46	164UNTS53	102159
France	Ireland	16 May 46	44UNTS105	100681
Taiwan	Denmark	20 May 46	12UNTS59	100180
Ireland	Sweden	29 May 46	35UNTS231	100557
Australia	Canada	11 Jun 46	10UNTS47	100142
United Arab Rep	USA (United States)	15 Jun 46	71UNTS157	100917
Sweden	Turkey	26 Jun 46	14UNTS21	100208
Netherlands	Spain	13 Jul 46	4UNTS351	100055
Canada	Newfoundland	29 Jul 46	17UNTS169	100275
France	Sweden	02 Aug 46	27UNTS251	100410
Lebanon	USA (United States)	11 Aug 46	66UNTS211	100856
Netherlands	UK Great Britain	13 Aug 46	4UNTS367	100056
Norway	UK Great Britain	31 Aug 46	6UNTS235	100078
Brazil	USA (United States)	06 Sep 46	54UNTS197	100805
Philippines	USA (United States)	11 Sep 46	43UNTS231	100670
Mexico	UK Great Britain	27 Sep 46	91UNTS161	101248
Sweden	USA (United States)	30 Sep 46	42UNTS213	100649
France	Turkey	12 Oct 46	14UNTS33	100209
Multilateral		15 Oct 46	11UNTS73	100150
Belgium	Portugal	22 Oct 46	34UNTS49	100527
Brazil	UK Great Britain	31 Oct 46	11UNTS115	100152
Norway	USA (United States)	12 Nov 46	42UNTS227	100651
India	USA (United States)	14 Nov 46	22UNTS55	100331
Philippines	USA (United States)	16 Nov 46	7UNTS151	100097
Sweden	UK Great Britain	27 Nov 46	11UNTS229	100162
New Zealand	USA (United States)	03 Dec 46	7UNTS175	100099
Australia	USA (United States)	03 Dec 46	7UNTS201	100100
Portugal	Switzerland	09 Dec 46	310UNTS251	104495
France	USA (United States)	10 Dec 46	15UNTS265	100242
Brazil	Portugal	10 Dec 46	200UNTS67	102695
Luxembourg	UK Great Britain	11 Dec 46	11UNTS167	100155
USA (United States)	Uruguay	14 Dec 46	532UNTS87	107713
Taiwan	USA (United States)	20 Dec 46	22UNTS87	100332
Peru	USA (United States)	27 Dec 46	26UNTS227	100390
Ecuador	USA (United States)	08 Jan 47	22UNTS119	100333
Czechoslovakia	Ireland	29 Jan 47	27UNTS267	100411
Thailand	USA (United States)	26 Feb 47	16UNTS17	100246
Paraguay	USA (United States)	28 Feb 47	44UNTS25	100676
Portugal	Sweden	06 Mar 47	35UNTS243	100558
Australia	USA (United States)	10 Mar 47	10UNTS89	100145
Netherlands	Turkey	19 Mar 47	14UNTS59	100211
Muscat and Oman	UK Great Britain	05 Apr 47	27UNTS287	100412
Greece	Sweden	08 Apr 47	94UNTS73	101307
Greece	Netherlands	17 Apr 47	32UNTS115	100494

PARTY ONE	PARTY TWO	DATE	CITATION	NUMBER
Fees and exemptions (Cont.)				
Canada	Portugal	25 Apr 47	94UNTS87	101308
Syria	USA (United States)	28 Apr 47	262UNTS121	103741
Sweden	USA (United States)	30 Apr 47	84UNTS33	101116
France	Greece	05 May 47	76UNTS61	100980
Thailand	USA (United States)	08 May 47	42UNTS241	100653
France	IBRD (World Bank)	09 May 47	152UNTS111	102014
Chile	USA (United States)	10 May 47	55UNTS21	100807
Honduras	USA (United States)	13 May 47	166UNTS159	102189
Czechoslovakia	Denmark	14 May 47	27UNTS297	100413
South Africa	USA (United States)	23 May 47	66UNTS233	100857
Italy	USA (United States)	09 Jun 47	104UNTS157	101437
Denmark	USA (United States)	09 Jun 47	132UNTS145	101755
Canada	Sweden	27 Jun 47	27UNTS313	100414
USA (United States)	Venezuela	30 Jun 47	166UNTS198	102190
Iraq	Turkey	30 Jun 47	72UNTS107	100930
Romania	Yugoslavia	30 Jun 47	116UNTS57	101569
Denmark	Turkey	30 Jun 47	32UNTS301	100504
Belgium	South Africa	04 Jul 47	47UNTS9	100720
Canada	UK Great Britain	17 Jul 47	28UNTS3	100416
Netherlands	Thailand	18 Jul 47	28UNTS27	100417
Greece	Turkey	22 Jul 47	72UNTS131	100931
Netherlands	South Africa	22 Jul 47	12UNTS257	100188
Taiwan	UK Great Britain	23 Jul 47	9UNTS207	100135
Norway	USA (United States)	29 Jul 47	87UNTS343	101178
Netherlands	IBRD (World Bank)	07 Aug 47	152UNTS165	102015
Poland	Romania	09 Aug 47	12UNTS363	100193
Denmark	IBRD (World Bank)	22 Aug 47	152UNTS223	102016
Luxembourg	IBRD (World Bank)	28 Aug 47	153UNTS3	102017
Hungary	Poland	28 Aug 47	15UNTS145	100231
Czechoslovakia	Netherlands	01 Sep 47	32UNTS129	100495
Czechoslovakia	Switzerland	10 Sep 47	35UNTS275	100559
FAO (Food Agri)	ILO (Labor Org)	11 Sep 47	18UNTS335	200111
France	USA (United States)	16 Sep 47	84UNTS19	101115
Lebanon	Turkey	16 Sep 47	44UNTS123	100682
Czechoslovakia	Sweden	15 Oct 47	44UNTS149	100683
Colombia	UK Great Britain	16 Oct 47	160UNTS297	102115
Liberia	USA (United States)	28 Oct 47	82UNTS23	101081
Norway	Portugal	11 Nov 47	34UNTS257	100542
Multilateral		13 Nov 47	251UNTS79	103534
Ecuador	USA (United States)	14 Nov 47	149UNTS297	101959
Brazil	Sweden	14 Nov 47	94UNTS139	101310
Brazil	Denmark	14 Nov 47	47UNTS39	100722
Brazil	Norway	14 Nov 47	44UNTS163	100684
Denmark	Greece	14 Nov 47	35UNTS295	100560
Denmark	Ireland	18 Nov 47	35UNTS309	100561
Ireland	Italy	21 Nov 47	353UNTS73	105038
Taiwan	Netherlands	06 Dec 47	43UNTS185	100669
Iceland	USA (United States)	09 Dec 47	82UNTS31	101082
Denmark	Portugal	15 Dec 47	35UNTS329	100563
Costa Rica	USA (United States)	12 Jan 48	70UNTS27	100896
Belgium	France	17 Jan 48	36UNTS233	100570
Austria	Netherlands	22 Jan 48	17UNTS99	100270
Italy	USA (United States)	02 Feb 48	79UNTS171	101040
Italy	USA (United States)	06 Feb 48	73UNTS113	100950
UK Great Britain	USA (United States)	24 Feb 48	73UNTS143	100951
Czechoslovakia	Yugoslavia	14 Mar 48	28UNTS81	100421
Argentina	Denmark	18 Mar 48	94UNTS175	101311
Cuba	UK Great Britain	19 Mar 48	175UNTS23	102294
Belgium	Italy	30 Apr 48	36UNTS305	100571
Canada	France	05 May 48	231UNTS87	103209
Ireland	Switzerland	06 May 48	334UNTS187	104768
Jordan	Turkey	07 May 48	32UNTS313	100505
Ireland	Netherlands	10 May 48	28UNTS121	100422
Guatemala	USA (United States)	18 May 48	67UNTS161	100875
Norway	Turkey	20 May 48	26UNTS137	100384

PARTY ONE	PARTY TWO	DATE	CITATION	NUMBER
Fees and exemptions (Cont.)				
Greece	Switzerland	26 May 48	94UNTS217	101312
Belgium	Monaco	05 Jun 48	18UNTS245	100294
France	Poland	09 Jun 48	32UNTS251	100503
France	UK Great Britain	11 Jun 48	66UNTS151	100852
Multilateral		19 Jun 48	310UNTS151	104492
Ireland	Norway	21 Jun 48	34UNTS317	100545
Belgium	USA (United States)	02 Jul 48	27UNTS43	100397
Poland	USSR (Soviet Union)	08 Jul 48	37UNTS107	100576
Netherlands	IBRD (World Bank)	15 Jul 48	153UNTS259	102022
Netherlands	IBRD (World Bank)	15 Jul 48	153UNTS259	102023
Netherlands	IBRD (World Bank)	15 Jul 48	153UNTS259	102024
Netherlands	IBRD (World Bank)	15 Jul 48	153UNTS259	102025
Netherlands	IBRD (World Bank)	15 Jul 48	153UNTS259	102021
Brazil	Switzerland	10 Aug 48	94UNTS269	101314
India	USA (United States)	11 Aug 48	224UNTS115	103072
Multilateral		18 Aug 48	33UNTS181	100518
France	Spain	23 Aug 48	28UNTS173	100425
Philippines	USA (United States)	27 Aug 48	44UNTS13	100675
Greece	Lebanon	06 Sep 48	178UNTS37	102335
Bolivia	USA (United States)	29 Sep 48	505UNTS139	107370
Greece	Lebanon	06 Oct 48	87UNTS351	101179
Netherlands	Spain	08 Oct 48	28UNTS209	100426
Australia	Denmark	08 Oct 48	22UNTS43	100330
France	USA (United States)	19 Oct 48	98UNTS3	101355
Mexico	Portugal	22 Oct 48	34UNTS329	100546
Belgium	USA (United States)	26 Oct 48	84UNTS265	101135
Argentina	Netherlands	29 Oct 48	95UNTS21	101316
Panama	USA (United States)	05 Nov 48	89UNTS27	101206
Czechoslovakia	Poland	12 Nov 48	84UNTS347	101141
Brazil	USA (United States)	26 Nov 48	88UNTS3	101180
Belgium	UK Great Britain	29 Dec 48	27UNTS135	100404
Romania	Yugoslavia	31 Dec 48	116UNTS103	101572
Mexico	IBRD (World Bank)	06 Jan 49	154UNTS81	102028
Mexico	IBRD (World Bank)	06 Jan 49	154UNTS3	102027
Belgium	France	08 Jan 49	36UNTS151	100569
Italy	Lebanon	24 Jan 49	231UNTS241	103223
Brazil	IBRD (World Bank)	27 Jan 49	153UNTS264	102026
Greece	USA (United States)	29 Jan 49	88UNTS35	101183
Switzerland	Turkey	16 Feb 49	72UNTS175	100933
Belgium	Luxembourg	25 Feb 49	47UNTS3	100719
Finland	Netherlands	25 Feb 49	53UNTS123	100777
Belgium	IBRD (World Bank)	01 Mar 49	154UNTS133	102029
Netherlands	Switzerland	07 Mar 49	35UNTS69	100551
Belgium	Switzerland	21 Mar 49	34UNTS17	100524
Chile	IBRD (World Bank)	23 Mar 49	153UNTS141	102019
Chile	IBRD (World Bank)	23 Mar 49	153UNTS61	102018
Finland	USA (United States)	29 Mar 49	55UNTS59	100808
Panama	USA (United States)	31 Mar 49	55UNTS87	100810
Belgium	UK Great Britain	14 Apr 49	65UNTS117	100840
Finland	Sweden	26 Apr 49	95UNTS83	101318
Bulgaria	Poland	16 May 49	84UNTS313	101140
Norway	USA (United States)	25 May 49	32UNTS345	100507
Canada	USA (United States)	04 Jun 49	122UNTS237	101649
Finland	Norway	13 Jun 49	34UNTS9	100523
Belgium	Greece	21 Jun 49	137UNTS215	101854
India	Switzerland	24 Jun 49	95UNTS109	101319
Korea, South	USA (United States)	29 Jun 49	55UNTS79	100809
Canada	Sweden	30 Jun 49	231UNTS37	103201
Czechoslovakia	Poland	02 Jul 49	260UNTS149	103708
Czechoslovakia	Poland	02 Jul 49	260UNTS179	103709
Greece	Syria	05 Jul 49	78UNTS71	101013
Australia	India	11 Jul 49	35UNTS83	100552
Iraq	Norway	12 Jul 49	53UNTS137	100778
Czechoslovakia	Finland	13 Jul 49	53UNTS153	100779
Dominican Republic	USA (United States)	19 Jul 49	51UNTS145	100762

PARTY ONE	PARTY TWO	DATE	CITATION	NUMBER
Fees and exemptions (Cont.)				
Netherlands	IBRD (World Bank)	26 Jul 49	154UNTS178	102030
Finland	IBRD (World Bank)	01 Aug 49	156UNTS289	200480
Ireland	USA (United States)	01 Aug 49	82UNTS37	101083
India	IBRD (World Bank)	18 Aug 49	154UNTS269	102031
Colombia	IBRD (World Bank)	19 Aug 49	154UNTS329	102032
Finland	Norway	24 Aug 49	53UNTS167	100780
Denmark	Finland	26 Aug 49	53UNTS191	100781
Denmark	ICAO (Civil Aviat)	09 Sep 49	53UNTS341	100791
IBRD (World Bank)	Yugoslavia	17 Sep 49	155UNTS3	102034
Lebanon	Netherlands	20 Sep 49	108UNTS205	101474
Burma	USA (United States)	28 Sep 49	55UNTS3	100806
India	IBRD (World Bank)	29 Sep 49	154UNTS393	102033
Greece	Philippines	08 Oct 49	187UNTS221	102515
Finland	IBRD (World Bank)	17 Oct 49	156UNTS355	200481
Pakistan	USA (United States)	18 Oct 49	141UNTS333	101923
USA (United States)	Uruguay	08 Nov 49	82UNTS45	101084
Belgium	Canada	19 Nov 49	150UNTS231	101977
Sweden	Thailand	23 Nov 49	72UNTS217	100935
Denmark	Thailand	23 Nov 49	53UNTS255	100786
Italy	Turkey	25 Nov 49	192UNTS39	102594
Canada	Luxembourg	26 Nov 49	231UNTS51	103203
Norway	Thailand	26 Nov 49	53UNTS269	100787
Brazil	Spain	28 Nov 49	215UNTS303	102923
Austria	Sweden	02 Dec 49	108UNTS3	101465
Austria	Norway	02 Dec 49	72UNTS230	100936
Austria	Denmark	02 Dec 49	53UNTS281	100788
Canada	Denmark	13 Dec 49	72UNTS247	100937
Canada	Netherlands	14 Dec 49	230UNTS337	103192
El Salvador	IBRD (World Bank)	14 Dec 49	155UNTS43	102035
Austria	Switzerland	19 Dec 49	254UNTS287	103597
Guatemala	USA (United States)	20 Dec 49	70UNTS71	100897
USA (United States)	Yugoslavia	24 Dec 49	89UNTS209	101219
Australia	USA (United States)	10 Feb 50	51UNTS167	100763
Netherlands	Syria	13 Feb 50	108UNTS53	101467
Canada	Norway	14 Feb 50	53UNTS329	100790
Spain	Sweden	18 Feb 50	166UNTS15	102184
Australia	Yugoslavia	22 Feb 50	51UNTS201	100766
Portugal	USA (United States)	24 Feb 50	92UNTS219	101274
Ceylon (Sri Lanka)	Thailand	24 Feb 50	72UNTS261	100938
Canada	Norway	13 Mar 50	90UNTS181	101235
Philippines	USA (United States)	16 Mar 50	89UNTS199	101218
Iceland	Netherlands	22 Mar 50	95UNTS237	101323
Italy	Portugal	05 Apr 50	254UNTS329	103599
Multilateral		06 Apr 50	119UNTS99	101610
Canada	France	17 Apr 50	230UNTS365	103196
India	IBRD (World Bank)	18 Apr 50	155UNTS117	102036
Mexico	IBRD (World Bank)	28 Apr 50	155UNTS185	102037
Mexico	USA (United States)	03 May 50	98UNTS201	101366
Brazil	IBRD (World Bank)	26 May 50	301UNTS165	104345
Israel	USA (United States)	13 Jun 50	212UNTS93	102863
Iraq	IBRD (World Bank)	15 Jun 50	155UNTS267	102038
Netherlands	Spain	20 Jun 50	95UNTS303	101327
Burma	Ceylon (Sri Lanka)	29 Jun 50	73UNTS3	100940
IBRD (World Bank)	Turkey	07 Jul 50	156UNTS3	102039
IBRD (World Bank)	Turkey	07 Jul 50	156UNTS75	102040
Luxembourg	Netherlands	08 Jul 50	135UNTS229	101824
Spain	UK Great Britain	20 Jul 50	398UNTS101	105719
Multilateral		27 Jul 50	166UNTS73	102186
Spain	Switzerland	03 Aug 50	254UNTS365	103600
Dominican Republic	USA (United States)	11 Aug 50	92UNTS329	101278
Canada	New Zealand	16 Aug 50	77UNTS239	101002
IBRD (World Bank)	Uruguay	25 Aug 50	156UNTS203	102042
Chile	USA (United States)	29 Aug 50	122UNTS43	101634
Ethiopia	IBRD (World Bank)	13 Sep 50	157UNTS213	102055
Ethiopia	IBRD (World Bank)	13 Sep 50	157UNTS233	102056

PARTY ONE	PARTY TWO	DATE	CITATION	NUMBER
Fees and exemptions (Cont.)				
Burma	Sweden	14 Sep 50	96UNTS45	101330
Brazil	Turkey	21 Sep 50	150UNTS299	101981
Lebanon	Pakistan	03 Oct 50	219UNTS41	102964
Sweden	Switzerland	18 Oct 50	166UNTS49	102185
Mexico	IBRD (World Bank)	18 Oct 50	157UNTS259	102057
IBRD (World Bank)	Turkey	19 Oct 50	157UNTS333	102058
Luxembourg	Portugal	21 Oct 50	108UNTS67	101468
Israel	Netherlands	23 Oct 50	189UNTS89	102543
IBRD (World Bank)	Thailand	27 Oct 50	158UNTS25	102060
IBRD (World Bank)	Thailand	27 Oct 50	158UNTS43	102061
IBRD (World Bank)	Thailand	27 Oct 50	158UNTS3	102059
Australia	IBRD (World Bank)	14 Nov 50	156UNTS147	102041
Norway	UK Great Britain	15 Dec 50	106UNTS87	101459
Colombia	IBRD (World Bank)	28 Dec 50	158UNTS87	102063
Costa Rica	USA (United States)	17 Jan 51	134UNTS215	101801
IBRD (World Bank)	South Africa	23 Jan 51	158UNTS115	102064
IBRD (World Bank)	South Africa	23 Jan 51	158UNTS135	102065
Panama	USA (United States)	26 Jan 51	137UNTS69	101849
Nicaragua	USA (United States)	31 Jan 51	150UNTS3	101960
Israel	Turkey	05 Feb 51	193UNTS3	102607
Ethiopia	IBRD (World Bank)	19 Feb 51	186UNTS101	102486
Australia	Netherlands	20 Feb 51	97UNTS283	101354
Colombia	Portugal	09 Mar 51	108UNTS87	101469
Greece	Yugoslavia	15 Mar 51	187UNTS237	102516
El Salvador	USA (United States)	19 Mar 51	134UNTS245	101803
Colombia	IBRD (World Bank)	10 Apr 51	158UNTS155	102066
Greece	Turkey	20 Apr 51	178UNTS17	102333
Nicaragua	USA (United States)	20 Apr 51	138UNTS57	101859
Netherlands	UK Great Britain	30 Apr 51	91UNTS177	101250
Greece	Norway	28 May 51	187UNTS141	102507
Israel	USA (United States)	01 Jun 51	212UNTS129	102864
UK Great Britain	USA (United States)	06 Jun 51	165UNTS121	102174
Nicaragua	IBRD (World Bank)	07 Jun 51	158UNTS215	102067
Nicaragua	IBRD (World Bank)	07 Jun 51	158UNTS277	102068
Australia	Italy	19 Jun 51	184UNTS185	102447
Iceland	IBRD (World Bank)	20 Jun 51	158UNTS301	102069
Cuba	Portugal	26 Jun 51	192UNTS115	102598
Ireland	Norway	02 Jul 51	100UNTS53	101387
Multilateral		02 Jul 51	189UNTS137	102545
Iceland	Norway	14 Jul 51	163UNTS265	102150
Australia	Belgium	25 Jul 51	108UNTS303	101482
Burma	Denmark	30 Jul 51	108UNTS167	101472
Greece	USA (United States)	03 Aug 51	224UNTS279	103080
Israel	Philippines	07 Aug 51	192UNTS81	102596
Israel	USA (United States)	23 Aug 51	219UNTS237	102979
Australia	Luxembourg	05 Sep 51	109UNTS31	101487
Burma	Netherlands	06 Sep 51	108UNTS187	101473
Belgium	IBRD (World Bank)	13 Sep 51	158UNTS349	102071
Belgium	IBRD (World Bank)	13 Sep 51	158UNTS323	102070
Panama	UK Great Britain	15 Sep 51	560UNTS143	108172
Australia	Sweden	26 Sep 51	109UNTS39	101488
UNICEF (Children)	UK Great Britain	02 Oct 51	104UNTS301	101448
Philippines	Spain	06 Oct 51	215UNTS193	102920
Chile	IBRD (World Bank)	10 Oct 51	158UNTS369	102072
Italy	IBRD (World Bank)	10 Oct 51	159UNTS383	200482
Austria	Belgium	11 Oct 51	110UNTS45	101500
IBRD (World Bank)	Yugoslavia	11 Oct 51	159UNTS3	102081
Colombia	IBRD (World Bank)	13 Oct 51	159UNTS75	102084
Australia	Norway	19 Oct 51	128UNTS109	101716
Greece	Luxembourg	22 Oct 51	187UNTS119	102506
Nicaragua	IBRD (World Bank)	29 Oct 51	159UNTS35	102082
Iceland	IBRD (World Bank)	01 Nov 51	159UNTS55	102083
Belgium	Netherlands	14 Nov 51	123UNTS91	101656
Denmark	Iraq	18 Nov 51	232UNTS25	103227
Italy	UK Great Britain	28 Nov 51	172UNTS205	102248

PARTY ONE	PARTY TWO	DATE	CITATION	NUMBER
Fees and exemptions (Cont.)				
Paraguay	IBRD (World Bank)	07 Dec 51	159UNTS103	102085
Colombia	Spain	11 Dec 51	216UNTS73	102933
Cuba	USA (United States)	17 Dec 51	152UNTS87	102012
Mexico	IBRD (World Bank)	11 Jan 52	159UNTS129	102086
Spain	USA (United States)	21 Jan 52	160UNTS63	102102
Peru	IBRD (World Bank)	23 Jan 52	159UNTS163	102087
Germany, East	Poland	06 Feb 52	304UNTS131	104395
IBRD (World Bank)	UK Great Britain	27 Feb 52	159UNTS181	102088
Belgium	Spain	10 Mar 52	178UNTS243	102342
France	USA (United States)	13 Mar 52	177UNTS21	102306
Pakistan	Switzerland	17 Mar 52	192UNTS237	102603
Norway	Uruguay	20 Mar 52	310UNTS279	104496
Canada	Monaco	20 Mar 52	233UNTS123	103256
Sweden	Uruguay	20 Mar 52	311UNTS3	104497
Netherlands	IBRD (World Bank)	20 Mar 52	159UNTS207	102089
Belgium	France	21 Mar 52	137UNTS249	101856
Pakistan	IBRD (World Bank)	27 Mar 52	159UNTS251	102090
Iraq	Switzerland	31 Mar 52	311UNTS43	104498
Monaco	USA (United States)	31 Mar 52	177UNTS195	102318
Belgium	Germany, West	01 Apr 52	132UNTS45	101750
France	Mexico	17 Apr 52	163UNTS321	102153
Finland	IBRD (World Bank)	30 Apr 52	159UNTS408	200483
Australia	Denmark	01 May 52	152UNTS3	102006
Pakistan	IBRD (World Bank)	13 Jun 52	191UNTS85	102578
Belgium	Switzerland	17 Jun 52	180UNTS23	102373
IBRD (World Bank)	Turkey	18 Jun 52	159UNTS269	102091
Netherlands	South Africa	21 Jun 52	309UNTS123	104471
Belgium	Italy	25 Jun 52	137UNTS239	101855
Brazil	IBRD (World Bank)	27 Jun 52	190UNTS115	102561
Brazil	IBRD (World Bank)	27 Jun 52	190UNTS85	102560
Greece	Italy	05 Jul 52	187UNTS157	102508
Australia	IBRD (World Bank)	08 Jul 52	159UNTS295	102092
Peru	IBRD (World Bank)	08 Jul 52	159UNTS321	102093
Mexico	USA (United States)	15 Jul 52	181UNTS263	102416
Japan	USA (United States)	11 Aug 52	212UNTS27	102862
Iceland	IBRD (World Bank)	26 Aug 52	159UNTS363	102095
Colombia	IBRD (World Bank)	26 Aug 52	159UNTS339	102094
Japan	USA (United States)	18 Sep 52	227UNTS85	103133
Canada	Italy	10 Oct 52	233UNTS137	103258
Austria	Luxembourg	13 Oct 52	192UNTS291	102606
Mexico	Netherlands	13 Oct 52	163UNTS341	102154
Iceland	Luxembourg	23 Oct 52	193UNTS39	102609
Chile	Sweden	27 Oct 52	311UNTS63	104499
Chile	Denmark	27 Oct 52	271UNTS93	103911
Japan	IBRD (World Bank)	12 Nov 52	354UNTS313	105068
Luxembourg	Norway	17 Nov 52	311UNTS95	104500
Luxembourg	Sweden	17 Nov 52	173UNTS277	102270
Israel	Switzerland	19 Nov 52	232UNTS3	103226
Philippines	USA (United States)	24 Nov 52	181UNTS155	102406
Belgium	France	29 Nov 52	160UNTS261	102110
India	WHO (World Health)	11 Dec 52	158UNTS391	102073
India	IBRD (World Bank)	18 Dec 52	201UNTS241	102719
Germany, West	USA (United States)	09 Jan 53	212UNTS3	102859
Switzerland	UK Great Britain	16 Jan 53	196UNTS119	102621
India	IBRD (World Bank)	23 Jan 53	201UNTS145	102715
IBRD (World Bank)	Yugoslavia	11 Feb 53	165UNTS231	102179
Japan	Netherlands	17 Feb 53	192UNTS215	102602
Japan	Sweden	20 Feb 53	173UNTS307	102272
Japan	Norway	23 Feb 53	192UNTS191	102601
Denmark	Japan	26 Feb 53	173UNTS329	102273
Germany, West	Netherlands	13 Mar 53	293UNTS123	104289
Chile	Norway	16 Mar 53	167UNTS13	102198
Lebanon	Sweden	23 Mar 53	255UNTS83	103605
Canada	Germany, West	15 Apr 53	236UNTS323	103333
Turkey	Yugoslavia	16 Apr 53	255UNTS99	103606

PARTY ONE	PARTY TWO	DATE	CITATION	NUMBER
Fees and exemptions (Cont.)				
Philippines	Thailand	27 Apr 53	174UNTS3	102274
Belgium	Netherlands	29 Apr 53	173UNTS61	102261
Brazil	IBRD (World Bank)	30 Apr 53	190UNTS133	102562
Finland	Norway	20 May 53	173UNTS163	102265
Cuba	USA (United States)	26 May 53	224UNTS75	103070
Switzerland	Yugoslavia	28 May 53	232UNTS45	103228
Japan	Thailand	19 Jun 53	174UNTS29	102276
Burma	Norway	22 Jun 53	174UNTS49	102277
Pakistan	Turkey	29 Jun 53	211UNTS225	102854
Brazil	IBRD (World Bank)	17 Jul 53	190UNTS149	102563
Belgium	Greece	05 Aug 53	173UNTS53	102260
USA (United States)	Venezuela	14 Aug 53	213UNTS99	102883
IBRD (World Bank)	South Africa	28 Aug 53	180UNTS73	102376
IBRD (World Bank)	South Africa	28 Aug 53	180UNTS91	102377
Nicaragua	USA (United States)	02 Sep 53	215UNTS69	102911
Iceland	IBRD (World Bank)	04 Sep 53	188UNTS3	102519
Nicaragua	IBRD (World Bank)	04 Sep 53	186UNTS117	102487
Nicaragua	IBRD (World Bank)	04 Sep 53	186UNTS137	102488
Iceland	IBRD (World Bank)	04 Sep 53	178UNTS275	102344
Colombia	IBRD (World Bank)	10 Sep 53	203UNTS3	102738
IBRD (World Bank)	Turkey	10 Sep 53	187UNTS71	102502
Chile	IBRD (World Bank)	10 Sep 53	188UNTS25	102520
Panama	IBRD (World Bank)	25 Sep 53	188UNTS71	102521
Panama	IBRD (World Bank)	25 Sep 53	188UNTS95	102522
Italy	IBRD (World Bank)	06 Oct 53	301UNTS135	104344
UNICEF (Children)	UK Great Britain	07 Oct 53	180UNTS59	102375
Luxembourg	UK Great Britain	13 Oct 53	209UNTS87	102825
Japan	IBRD (World Bank)	15 Oct 53	187UNTS321	200512
Japan	IBRD (World Bank)	15 Oct 53	187UNTS271	200511
Japan	IBRD (World Bank)	15 Oct 53	187UNTS367	200513
Austria	Yugoslavia	11 Nov 53	363UNTS149	105206
Cuba	USA (United States)	26 Nov 53	205UNTS213	102777
El Salvador	USA (United States)	15 Dec 53	236UNTS25	103314
Brazil	IBRD (World Bank)	18 Dec 53	301UNTS229	104346
Brazil	IBRD (World Bank)	18 Dec 53	190UNTS179	102564
Jordan	Syria	23 Dec 53	204UNTS207	102759
Syria	UK Great Britain	30 Jan 54	449UNTS47	106452
Brazil	IBRD (World Bank)	24 Feb 54	301UNTS249	104347
Multilateral		25 Feb 54	215UNTS249	102922
Australia	IBRD (World Bank)	02 Mar 54	191UNTS103	102579
Lebanon	Switzerland	03 Mar 54	255UNTS127	103608
Peru	Spain	31 Mar 54	232UNTS65	103230
Ireland	UK Great Britain	06 Apr 54	553UNTS197	108088
Norway	IBRD (World Bank)	08 Apr 54	201UNTS131	102714
Peru	IBRD (World Bank)	12 Apr 54	190UNTS231	102567
Bulgaria	Czechoslovakia	13 Apr 54	501UNTS3	107314
Australia	Greece	24 May 54	193UNTS175	102614
Belgium	Germany, West	28 May 54	249UNTS387	103512
Pakistan	IBRD (World Bank)	02 Jun 54	324UNTS59	104678
Greece	Hungary	05 Jun 54	299UNTS295	104321
France	IBRD (World Bank)	10 Jun 54	210UNTS89	102836
Chile	Netherlands	18 Jun 54	292UNTS37	104265
Ceylon (Sri Lanka)	IBRD (World Bank)	09 Jul 54	198UNTS313	200517
Belgium	Italy	12 Jul 54	288UNTS59	104198
Ireland	Luxembourg	27 Jul 54	232UNTS91	103231
Brazil	USA (United States)	20 Aug 54	410UNTS79	105898
Mexico	IBRD (World Bank)	24 Aug 54	286UNTS211	104168
Germany, West	USA (United States)	28 Aug 54	299UNTS377	104325
Denmark	Pakistan	30 Aug 54	203UNTS59	102740
Greece	Italy	11 Sep 54	284UNTS313	104145
El Salvador	IBRD (World Bank)	12 Oct 54	203UNTS37	102739
Multilateral		23 Oct 54	332UNTS157	104761
Austria	IBRD (World Bank)	08 Nov 54	216UNTS305	200528
Poland	UK Great Britain	11 Nov 54	204UNTS137	102755
Peru	IBRD (World Bank)	12 Nov 54	209UNTS287	102831

PARTY ONE	PARTY TWO	DATE	CITATION	NUMBER
Fees and exemptions (Cont.)				
India	IBRD (World Bank)	19 Nov 54	309UNTS159	104473
Guatemala	USA (United States)	01 Dec 54	237UNTS161	103342
Multilateral		01 Dec 54	210UNTS197	102839
Ecuador	Netherlands	14 Dec 54	232UNTS115	103233
Belgium	IBRD (World Bank)	14 Dec 54	210UNTS113	102837
Colombia	IBRD (World Bank)	29 Dec 54	211UNTS135	102851
Norway	Switzerland	30 Dec 54	311UNTS147	104502
Peru	USA (United States)	31 Dec 54	251UNTS51	103533
Austria	Belgium	07 Jan 55	380UNTS219	105458
Belgium	Brazil	10 Jan 55	272UNTS181	103937
Canada	Japan	12 Jan 55	311UNTS167	104503
Israel	USA (United States)	02 Mar 55	220UNTS113	102996
Israel	Sweden	02 Mar 55	220UNTS105	102995
India	IBRD (World Bank)	14 Mar 55	309UNTS129	104472
IBRD (World Bank)	UK Great Britain	15 Mar 55	265UNTS85	103808
Australia	IBRD (World Bank)	18 Mar 55	220UNTS131	102998
Finland	IBRD (World Bank)	24 Mar 55	211UNTS305	200525
Colombia	IBRD (World Bank)	24 Mar 55	212UNTS217	102874
Israel	Luxembourg	30 Mar 55	226UNTS247	103118
Peru	IBRD (World Bank)	05 Apr 55	211UNTS115	102850
Peru	IBRD (World Bank)	19 Apr 55	221UNTS153	103007
Norway	IBRD (World Bank)	19 Apr 55	211UNTS159	102852
Belgium	San Marino	22 Apr 55	253UNTS41	103574
Denmark	Israel	29 Apr 55	220UNTS87	102992
Austria	Romania	11 May 55	342UNTS119	104904
Netherlands	USA (United States)	25 May 55	289UNTS227	104220
Italy	IBRD (World Bank)	01 Jun 55	358UNTS203	105137
Germany, West	New Zealand	10 Jun 55	380UNTS307	105462
Canada	Japan	13 Jun 55	247UNTS151	103464
Austria	IBRD (World Bank)	14 Jun 55	221UNTS375	200531
Colombia	IBRD (World Bank)	15 Jun 55	248UNTS161	103494
Pakistan	IBRD (World Bank)	20 Jun 55	230UNTS41	103176
Germany, West	USA (United States)	07 Jul 55	275UNTS3	103973
Nicaragua	IBRD (World Bank)	08 Jul 55	229UNTS97	103162
Nicaragua	IBRD (World Bank)	08 Jul 55	229UNTS123	103163
Panama	IBRD (World Bank)	12 Jul 55	219UNTS127	102970
Germany, West	UK Great Britain	22 Jul 55	269UNTS189	103881
Israel	Norway	26 Jul 55	226UNTS257	103120
Guatemala	IBRD (World Bank)	29 Jul 55	229UNTS167	103165
Canada	Israel	02 Aug 55	226UNTS265	103121
Pakistan	IBRD (World Bank)	04 Aug 55	230UNTS79	103177
Peru	IBRD (World Bank)	05 Aug 55	218UNTS3	102950
Pakistan	IBRD (World Bank)	06 Aug 55	236UNTS195	103325
IBRD (World Bank)	Thailand	09 Aug 55	221UNTS283	103011
Italy	Spain	11 Aug 55	267UNTS125	103839
Australia	USA (United States)	20 Aug 55	268UNTS133	103855
Israel	Netherlands	21 Aug 55	299UNTS51	104306
Lebanon	IBRD (World Bank)	25 Aug 55	230UNTS233	103188
France	IBRD (World Bank)	26 Aug 55	247UNTS305	103478
Nicaragua	IBRD (World Bank)	26 Aug 55	229UNTS145	103164
IBRD (World Bank)	Uruguay	29 Aug 55	243UNTS123	103450
USSR (Soviet Union)	Yugoslavia	03 Sep 55	240UNTS267	103408
Bulgaria	Yugoslavia	01 Oct 55	396UNTS223	105698
France	Germany, West	04 Oct 55	353UNTS203	105044
Turkey	USA (United States)	11 Oct 55	272UNTS145	103935
Denmark	Syria	20 Oct 55	250UNTS61	103518
Nicaragua	USA (United States)	22 Oct 55	358UNTS51	105123
Czechoslovakia	Germany, East	24 Oct 55	504UNTS173	107358
Japan	IBRD (World Bank)	25 Oct 55	230UNTS379	200534
Burma	China People's Rep	08 Nov 55	306UNTS11	104430
Austria	USSR (Soviet Union)	09 Nov 55	255UNTS247	103613
Thailand	USA (United States)	14 Nov 55	239UNTS201	103380
Bulgaria	Yugoslavia	15 Nov 55	396UNTS191	105697
Finland	Israel	16 Nov 55	257UNTS39	103647
Austria	Israel	17 Nov 55	232UNTS153	103235

PARTY ONE	PARTY TWO	DATE	CITATION	NUMBER
Fees and exemptions (Cont.)				
IBRD (World Bank)	South Africa	28 Nov 55	230UNTS101	103178
Finland	USA (United States)	14 Dec 55	335UNTS263	104794
Honduras	IBRD (World Bank)	22 Dec 55	230UNTS262	103189
Austria	Italy	28 Dec 55	260UNTS345	103718
Iceland	Israel	29 Dec 55	227UNTS147	103136
Italy	Thailand	30 Dec 55	260UNTS351	103719
Canada	Finland	09 Jan 56	305UNTS33	104410
Italy	Japan	11 Jan 56	267UNTS175	103842
France	Japan	17 Jan 56	255UNTS275	103614
Australia	Japan	19 Jan 56	311UNTS291	104507
Nicaragua	USA (United States)	21 Jan 56	367UNTS3	105224
Austria	Italy	23 Jan 56	393UNTS97	105653
Argentina	Switzerland	25 Jan 56	559UNTS121	108157
Romania	Yugoslavia	01 Feb 56	362UNTS203	105189
India	USA (United States)	03 Feb 56	272UNTS75	103932
Austria	Poland	08 Feb 56	334UNTS221	104770
Norway	South Africa	17 Feb 56	230UNTS213	103186
Taiwan	USA (United States)	20 Feb 56	275UNTS73	103976
Japan	IBRD (World Bank)	21 Feb 56	248UNTS321	200543
Norway	Syria	25 Feb 56	463UNTS217	106706
Norway	Sweden	09 Mar 56	369UNTS285	105262
Germany, West	Sweden	22 Mar 56	262UNTS423	103763
USA (United States)	Uruguay	23 Mar 56	376UNTS311	105386
Bulgaria	Yugoslavia	23 Mar 56	367UNTS213	105230
Ecuador	IBRD (World Bank)	26 Mar 56	292UNTS391	104277
South Africa	USA (United States)	03 Apr 56	249UNTS395	103513
Australia	Turkey	10 Apr 56	247UNTS139	103462
Belgium	Germany, West	14 Apr 56	344UNTS103	104945
Germany, West	Switzerland	02 May 56	559UNTS157	108158
Norway	IBRD (World Bank)	03 May 56	243UNTS281	103455
Burma	IBRD (World Bank)	04 May 56	253UNTS209	103585
Burma	IBRD (World Bank)	04 May 56	253UNTS179	103584
Haiti	IBRD (World Bank)	07 May 56	252UNTS279	103570
Portugal	Venezuela	16 May 56	463UNTS239	106707
Multilateral		18 May 56	339UNTS3	104844
Multilateral		19 May 56	399UNTS189	105742
Nicaragua	IBRD (World Bank)	22 May 56	253UNTS233	103586
Finland	IBRD (World Bank)	22 May 56	248UNTS57	103485
Japan	Switzerland	24 May 56	312UNTS3	104509
Panama	USA (United States)	25 May 56	268UNTS333	103866
Greece	Italy	26 May 56	496UNTS301	107258
Guatemala	USA (United States)	30 May 56	275UNTS271	103986
Italy	Switzerland	04 Jun 56	378UNTS311	105429
Colombia	IBRD (World Bank)	06 Jun 56	248UNTS139	103493
Poland	Sweden	08 Jun 56	334UNTS257	104771
Germany, West	Ireland	12 Jun 56	353UNTS121	105040
India	Thailand	12 Jun 56	255UNTS341	103617
Austria	Canada	19 Jun 56	305UNTS51	104412
Fed Rhod/Nyasaland	IBRD (World Bank)	21 Jun 56	285UNTS317	104156
IBRD (World Bank)	UK Great Britain	21 Jun 56	285UNTS355	104157
India	IBRD (World Bank)	26 Jun 56	301UNTS3	104341
Belgium	Czechoslovakia	08 Aug 56	257UNTS215	103656
Canada	Turkey	21 Aug 56	305UNTS89	104416
Israel	South Africa	01 Sep 56	251UNTS161	103539
Ceylon (Sri Lanka)	USA (United States)	07 Sep 56	280UNTS35	104048
Finland	USSR (Soviet Union)	14 Sep 56	255UNTS365	103618
Denmark	Sweden	15 Sep 56	263UNTS3	103764
Norway	Sweden	15 Sep 56	263UNTS17	103765
Denmark	Finland	15 Sep 56	254UNTS3	103589
Finland	Norway	15 Sep 56	254UNTS17	103590
Finland	Sweden	15 Sep 56	254UNTS31	103591
Costa Rica	IBRD (World Bank)	18 Sep 56	260UNTS369	103721
Austria	IBRD (World Bank)	21 Sep 56	259UNTS17	103681
Austria	IBRD (World Bank)	21 Sep 56	259UNTS43	103682
Multilateral		25 Sep 56	334UNTS13	104766

PARTY ONE	PARTY TWO	DATE	CITATION	NUMBER
Fees and exemptions (Cont.)				
Multilateral		25 Sep 56	334UNTS89	104767
Germany, West	Netherlands	28 Sep 56	327UNTS185	104722
Italy	IBRD (World Bank)	11 Oct 56	359UNTS3	105138
IBRD (World Bank)	Thailand	12 Oct 56	261UNTS117	103728
Switzerland	Thailand	13 Oct 56	312UNTS43	104510
Belgium	Poland	17 Oct 56	356UNTS279	105100
Colombia	USA (United States)	24 Oct 56	476UNTS77	106905
Belgium	Turkey	25 Oct 56	380UNTS3	105447
Chile	IBRD (World Bank)	01 Nov 56	261UNTS27	103724
Australia	IBRD (World Bank)	15 Nov 56	288UNTS117	104201
Peru	Switzerland	23 Nov 56	411UNTS97	105916
Albania	Yugoslavia	23 Nov 56	386UNTS73	105539
Australia	Netherlands	29 Nov 56	302UNTS141	104356
Australia	IBRD (World Bank)	03 Dec 56	288UNTS99	104200
Belgium	Romania	04 Dec 56	317UNTS161	104602
Finland	South Africa	05 Dec 56	258UNTS59	103670
Japan	IBRD (World Bank)	19 Dec 56	268UNTS203	103859
Japan	IBRD (World Bank)	19 Dec 56	264UNTS179	103793
Iran	USA (United States)	16 Jan 57	308UNTS147	104460
Iceland	Thailand	22 Jan 57	312UNTS63	104511
Iran	IBRD (World Bank)	22 Jan 57	317UNTS129	104600
Ethiopia	IBRD (World Bank)	28 Jan 57	286UNTS307	104175
Germany, West	Sweden	29 Jan 57	393UNTS113	105654
Germany, West	Norway	29 Jan 57	353UNTS39	105037
Denmark	Germany, West	29 Jan 57	302UNTS75	104354
Belgium	Brazil	27 Feb 57	265UNTS189	103812
India	IBRD (World Bank)	05 Mar 57	272UNTS201	103939
Belgium	Czechoslovakia	12 Mar 57	312UNTS75	104512
Peru	IBRD (World Bank)	13 Mar 57	274UNTS59	103958
Japan	USA (United States)	22 Mar 57	288UNTS201	104206
Multilateral		25 Mar 57	294UNTS2	104300
Poland	USSR (Soviet Union)	25 Mar 57	281UNTS121	104075
Germany, West	Yugoslavia	10 Apr 57	463UNTS269	106708
Denmark	Pakistan	10 Apr 57	302UNTS53	104353
Romania	Sweden	15 Apr 57	342UNTS325	104915
Bulgaria	Sweden	17 Apr 57	464UNTS3	106709
Korea, South	USA (United States)	24 Apr 57	288UNTS219	104207
Netherlands	IBRD (World Bank)	15 May 57	274UNTS211	103967
Australia	Germany, West	22 May 57	357UNTS45	105105
Hungary	Netherlands	28 May 57	334UNTS291	104773
India	IBRD (World Bank)	29 May 57	309UNTS201	104474
Austria	South Africa	11 Jun 57	272UNTS229	103941
Austria	USSR (Soviet Union)	14 Jun 57	285UNTS169	104152
Multilateral		15 Jun 57	583UNTS3	108470
Belgium	IBRD (World Bank)	26 Jun 57	322UNTS301	104661
Czechoslovakia	United Arab Rep	30 Jun 57	411UNTS126	105917
India	IBRD (World Bank)	12 Jul 57	288UNTS135	104202
Chile	IBRD (World Bank)	24 Jul 57	282UNTS189	104099
Chile	IBRD (World Bank)	24 Jul 57	282UNTS139	104098
Greece	Italy	02 Aug 57	533UNTS217	107744
Hungary	Sweden	02 Aug 57	334UNTS307	104774
Japan	IBRD (World Bank)	09 Aug 57	293UNTS59	104286
Austria	Pakistan	16 Aug 57	306UNTS3	104429
Netherlands	Romania	27 Aug 57	342UNTS309	104914
Japan	UK Great Britain	30 Aug 57	313UNTS63	104529
Belgium	IBRD (World Bank)	10 Sep 57	286UNTS291	104174
IBRD (World Bank)	Thailand	12 Sep 57	299UNTS349	104324
Italy	Switzerland	19 Sep 57	363UNTS69	105200
Ecuador	IBRD (World Bank)	20 Sep 57	289UNTS237	104221
Ecuador	IBRD (World Bank)	20 Sep 57	293UNTS135	104291
Multilateral		27 Sep 57	299UNTS211	104314
IBRD (World Bank)	South Africa	01 Oct 57	280UNTS285	104065
Multilateral		03 Oct 57	366UNTS87	105216
Austria	IBRD (World Bank)	10 Oct 57	301UNTS95	104343
Pakistan	IBRD (World Bank)	18 Oct 57	299UNTS303	104322

PARTY ONE	PARTY TWO	DATE	CITATION	NUMBER
Fees and exemptions (Cont.)				
Belgium	Netherlands	24 Oct 57	489UNTS11	107132
Belgium	Netherlands	24 Oct 57	489UNTS3	107131
France	Morocco	25 Oct 57	559UNTS95	108156
India	IBRD (World Bank)	20 Nov 57	301UNTS47	104342
Philippines	IBRD (World Bank)	22 Nov 57	293UNTS83	104287
Belgium	IBRD (World Bank)	27 Nov 57	292UNTS175	104273
Korea, North	USSR (Soviet Union)	16 Dec 57	301UNTS301	104349
Pakistan	IBRD (World Bank)	17 Dec 57	299UNTS321	104323
China People's Rep	USSR (Soviet Union)	21 Dec 57	305UNTS213	104420
Australia	Ireland	30 Dec 57	497UNTS29	107260
Canada	Switzerland	10 Jan 58	464UNTS21	106710
Mexico	IBRD (World Bank)	14 Jan 58	293UNTS167	104292
Belgium	Morocco	20 Jan 58	288UNTS3	104192
Brazil	IBRD (World Bank)	22 Jan 58	323UNTS99	104666
Canada	Portugal	24 Jan 58	392UNTS15	105634
Czechoslovakia	Poland	31 Jan 58	431UNTS99	106214
Bulgaria	Netherlands	07 Feb 58	335UNTS45	104777
Belgium	Mexico	18 Mar 58	301UNTS291	104348
Austria	Japan	20 Mar 58	324UNTS205	104686
Belgium	Ecuador	20 Mar 58	304UNTS207	104397
Germany, West	Portugal	21 Mar 58	464UNTS71	106712
Morocco	Portugal	03 Apr 58	393UNTS203	105657
Bulgaria	Yugoslavia	04 Apr 58	367UNTS89	105228
Belgium	Iran	14 Apr 58	381UNTS309	105473
Sweden	Yugoslavia	18 Apr 58	393UNTS225	105658
Pakistan	IBRD (World Bank)	23 Apr 58	323UNTS253	104672
Austria	IBRD (World Bank)	28 Apr 58	359UNTS145	105142
Chile	IBRD (World Bank)	28 Apr 58	359UNTS89	105140
Israel	New Zealand	29 Apr 58	314UNTS93	104544
IBRD (World Bank)	UK Great Britain	02 May 58	324UNTS25	104677
New Zealand	USA (United States)	05 May 58	317UNTS59	104594
Mexico	IBRD (World Bank)	05 May 58	309UNTS3	104466
Belgium	Sweden	08 May 58	312UNTS145	104516
Honduras	IBRD (World Bank)	09 May 58	323UNTS4	104662
Italy	Switzerland	23 May 58	363UNTS81	105201
Bulgaria	Denmark	28 May 58	312UNTS235	104521
Austria	Netherlands	30 May 58	458UNTS147	106598
India	USSR (Soviet Union)	02 Jun 58	393UNTS3	105650
New Zealand	Turkey	05 Jun 58	317UNTS123	104599
Denmark	Luxembourg	10 Jun 58	356UNTS193	105096
Japan	IBRD (World Bank)	13 Jun 58	312UNTS159	104518
IBRD (World Bank)	UK Great Britain	16 Jun 58	309UNTS35	104467
Denmark	Romania	25 Jun 58	345UNTS231	104970
India	IBRD (World Bank)	25 Jun 58	323UNTS131	104667
India	IBRD (World Bank)	25 Jun 58	323UNTS157	104668
Czechoslovakia	Hungary	27 Jun 58	477UNTS321	106927
Austria	Romania	10 Jul 58	353UNTS155	105041
Denmark	Hungary	17 Jul 58	344UNTS281	104954
IBRD (World Bank)	Sudan	21 Jul 58	323UNTS183	104669
India	IBRD (World Bank)	23 Jul 58	317UNTS3	104590
Romania	United Arab Rep	14 Aug 58	405UNTS189	105834
Japan	IBRD (World Bank)	18 Aug 58	323UNTS205	104670
USA (United States)	USSR (Soviet Union)	20 Aug 58	336UNTS269	104809
Japan	IBRD (World Bank)	10 Sep 58	318UNTS133	104612
Japan	IBRD (World Bank)	10 Sep 58	323UNTS297	104673
Austria	Bulgaria	12 Sep 58	353UNTS3	105036
India	IBRD (World Bank)	16 Sep 58	323UNTS235	104671
Peru	IBRD (World Bank)	17 Sep 58	323UNTS27	104663
Ceylon (Sri Lanka)	IBRD (World Bank)	17 Sep 58	323UNTS51	104664
Fed of Malaya	IBRD (World Bank)	22 Sep 58	323UNTS71	104665
Brazil	IBRD (World Bank)	03 Oct 58	337UNTS177	104823
Ecuador	IBRD (World Bank)	09 Oct 58	337UNTS299	104827
Canada	USA (United States)	31 Oct 58	391UNTS219	105626
France	Israel	12 Nov 58	345UNTS79	104960
Austria	IBRD (World Bank)	02 Dec 58	340UNTS3	104856

PARTY ONE	PARTY TWO	DATE	CITATION	NUMBER
Fees and exemptions (Cont.)				
Colombia	IBRD (World Bank)	15 Dec 58	354UNTS233	105065
El Salvador	IBRD (World Bank)	07 Jan 59	346UNTS51	104977
Belgium	France	20 Jan 59	361UNTS155	105178
Colombia	IBRD (World Bank)	30 Jan 59	337UNTS327	104828
UK Great Britain	Yugoslavia	03 Feb 59	359UNTS339	105151
Costa Rica	IBRD (World Bank)	11 Feb 59	337UNTS245	104825
Japan	IBRD (World Bank)	17 Feb 59	337UNTS205	104824
Norway	Philippines	18 Feb 59	359UNTS305	105147
El Salvador	IBRD (World Bank)	20 Feb 59	362UNTS75	105183
Indonesia	USA (United States)	02 Mar 59	357UNTS145	105113
Brazil	Netherlands	16 Mar 59	499UNTS219	107300
Finland	IBRD (World Bank)	16 Mar 59	337UNTS269	104826
Sweden	Tunisia	19 Mar 59	497UNTS43	107261
Netherlands	Tunisia	19 Mar 59	497UNTS61	107262
Norway	Tunisia	28 Mar 59	497UNTS77	107263
India	IBRD (World Bank)	08 Apr 59	348UNTS131	104998
Netherlands	Switzerland	14 Apr 59	486UNTS367	107086
Denmark	Tunisia	14 Apr 59	340UNTS273	104870
Italy	IBRD (World Bank)	21 Apr 59	359UNTS191	105143
France	Netherlands	29 Apr 59	486UNTS379	107088
Netherlands	Norway	30 Apr 59	487UNTS3	107090
Netherlands	Portugal	30 Apr 59	485UNTS129	107050
Iceland	Netherlands	30 Apr 59	487UNTS13	107091
Netherlands	Sweden	30 Apr 59	485UNTS147	107053
Greece	Netherlands	30 Apr 59	485UNTS135	107051
Belgium	Sweden	18 May 59	341UNTS277	104890
Honduras	IBRD (World Bank)	20 May 59	359UNTS119	105141
Colombia	IBRD (World Bank)	20 May 59	344UNTS251	104953
Fed of Malaya	USA (United States)	22 May 59	346UNTS263	104985
Netherlands	Spain	27 May 59	458UNTS165	106599
Ceylon (Sri Lanka)	Sweden	29 May 59	464UNTS109	106713
Ceylon (Sri Lanka)	Norway	29 May 59	411UNTS165	105919
Ceylon (Sri Lanka)	Denmark	29 May 59	348UNTS225	105002
Iran	IBRD (World Bank)	29 May 59	348UNTS103	104997
IBRD (World Bank)	South Africa	10 Jun 59	340UNTS33	104857
Brazil	IBRD (World Bank)	17 Jun 59	377UNTS111	105398
Greece	Yugoslavia	18 Jun 59	368UNTS81	105236
Belgium	Japan	20 Jun 59	411UNTS3	105911
Congo (Brazzaville)	IBRD (World Bank)	30 Jun 59	452UNTS123	106506
France	IBRD (World Bank)	30 Jun 59	452UNTS67	106505
Gabon	IBRD (World Bank)	30 Jun 59	452UNTS135	106507
Norway	IBRD (World Bank)	08 Jul 59	344UNTS229	104952
Bulgaria	United Arab Rep	09 Jul 59	411UNTS187	105920
Italy	Philippines	14 Jul 59	490UNTS237	107157
India	IBRD (World Bank)	15 Jul 59	355UNTS95	105075
India	IBRD (World Bank)	15 Jul 59	346UNTS33	104976
Afghanistan	Germany, West	22 Jul 59	464UNTS177	106715
Germany, West	Iceland	12 Aug 59	411UNTS224	105921
Pakistan	IBRD (World Bank)	13 Aug 59	355UNTS129	105076
Canada	Germany, West	04 Sep 59	411UNTS260	105922
Belgium	Spain	11 Sep 59	345UNTS29	104956
Italy	IBRD (World Bank)	16 Sep 59	375UNTS159	105366
Pakistan	IBRD (World Bank)	25 Sep 59	355UNTS169	105077
Canada	Greece	30 Sep 59	470UNTS87	106798
Canada	Venezuela	08 Oct 59	470UNTS93	106799
Multilateral		09 Oct 59	376UNTS382	105391
Nicaragua	Peru	14 Oct 59	392UNTS303	105649
Japan	IBRD (World Bank)	12 Nov 59	354UNTS279	105067
Iran	IBRD (World Bank)	23 Nov 59	380UNTS245	105459
Guinea	UN Special Fund	02 Dec 59	345UNTS215	104969
France	IBRD (World Bank)	10 Dec 59	380UNTS319	105464
Multilateral		14 Dec 59	422UNTS75	106069
Canada	Spain	18 Dec 59	470UNTS117	106802
IBRD (World Bank)	United Arab Rep	22 Dec 59	354UNTS197	105063
IBRD (World Bank)	Uruguay	30 Dec 59	384UNTS275	105523

PARTY ONE	PARTY TWO	DATE	CITATION	NUMBER
Fees and exemptions (Cont.)				
Albania	Hungary	12 Jan 60	520UNTS3	107511
Colombia	IBRD (World Bank)	20 Jan 60	375UNTS49	105353
Multilateral		26 Jan 60	439UNTS249	106333
Luxembourg	Philippines	17 Feb 60	359UNTS311	105148
Netherlands	Philippines	17 Feb 60	359UNTS317	105149
Belgium	Philippines	17 Feb 60	356UNTS303	105101
Iran	IBRD (World Bank)	20 Feb 60	384UNTS213	105521
Australia	Philippines	23 Feb 60	358UNTS139	105131
Ecuador	USA (United States)	24 Feb 60	371UNTS55	105270
Finland	Iceland	10 Mar 60	497UNTS95	107264
Czechoslovakia	Iraq	11 Mar 60	464UNTS267	106718
France	IBRD (World Bank)	17 Mar 60	452UNTS147	106508
Mauritania	IBRD (World Bank)	17 Mar 60	452UNTS211	106509
Japan	IBRD (World Bank)	17 Mar 60	362UNTS43	105182
Belgium	IBRD (World Bank)	30 Mar 60	379UNTS103	105437
Belgium	IBRD (World Bank)	30 Mar 60	379UNTS129	105438
Belgium	IBRD (World Bank)	30 Mar 60	379UNTS161	105439
IBRD (World Bank)	UK Great Britain	01 Apr 60	379UNTS397	105446
Luxembourg	Yugoslavia	09 Apr 60	464UNTS293	106719
Germany, West	Spain	28 Apr 60	465UNTS3	106720
Laos	UN Special Fund	30 Apr 60	361UNTS171	105179
Greece	Romania	02 May 60	485UNTS17	107043
Costa Rica	IBRD (World Bank)	04 May 60	390UNTS201	105609
Hungary	Yugoslavia	07 May 60	519UNTS237	107510
Colombia	IBRD (World Bank)	10 May 60	379UNTS218	105441
Germany, West	Ireland	11 May 60	553UNTS69	108070
Morocco	United Arab Rep	19 May 60	563UNTS121	108208
Switzerland	Tunisia	21 May 60	497UNTS109	107265
IBRD (World Bank)	UK Great Britain	27 May 60	375UNTS201	105367
Afghanistan	Czechoslovakia	28 May 60	497UNTS129	107266
Peru	IBRD (World Bank)	01 Jun 60	380UNTS15	105448
Luxembourg	Tunisia	13 Jun 60	497UNTS143	107267
IBRD (World Bank)	Sudan	17 Jun 60	379UNTS253	105442
Denmark	Peru	22 Jun 60	439UNTS113	106326
Nicaragua	IBRD (World Bank)	22 Jun 60	384UNTS243	105522
Kuwait	UN Special Fund	29 Jun 60	369UNTS419	200575
Honduras	IBRD (World Bank)	29 Jun 60	400UNTS137	105751
Peru	IBRD (World Bank)	29 Jun 60	400UNTS99	105750
Ethiopia	UN Special Fund	13 Jul 60	368UNTS159	105240
Germany, West	Pakistan	20 Jul 60	465UNTS41	106721
Japan	Luxembourg	21 Jul 60	384UNTS55	105510
El Salvador	IBRD (World Bank)	29 Jul 60	390UNTS101	105605
Mexico	USA (United States)	15 Aug 60	402UNTS177	105786
Belgium	Burma	17 Aug 60	540UNTS185	107850
Panama	IBRD (World Bank)	19 Aug 60	390UNTS153	105607
El Salvador	Israel	05 Sep 60	413UNTS73	105941
Israel	IBRD (World Bank)	09 Sep 60	406UNTS3	105837
Brazil	UN Special Fund	16 Sep 60	375UNTS3	105351
Pakistan	IBRD (World Bank)	19 Sep 60	444UNTS207	106370
Colombia	IBRD (World Bank)	20 Sep 60	390UNTS173	105608
Taiwan	UN Special Fund	20 Sep 60	375UNTS29	105352
Mexico	IBRD (World Bank)	18 Oct 60	422UNTS177	106075
Belgium	Jordan	19 Oct 60	479UNTS277	106959
Hungary	UK Great Britain	25 Oct 60	419UNTS309	106034
India	IBRD (World Bank)	28 Oct 60	406UNTS27	105838
Burma	Switzerland	31 Oct 60	465UNTS97	106723
Norway	Peru	02 Nov 60	497UNTS207	107270
Greece	Poland	08 Nov 60	483UNTS141	107011
Australia	Italy	10 Nov 60	497UNTS247	107271
Korea, South	Philippines	11 Nov 60	490UNTS249	107159
Finland	Norway	15 Nov 60	383UNTS159	105501
Norway	IBRD (World Bank)	02 Dec 60	390UNTS131	105606
Multilateral		13 Dec 60	523UNTS117	107557
Peru	IBRD (World Bank)	19 Dec 60	417UNTS275	106010
Japan	IBRD (World Bank)	20 Dec 60	400UNTS279	105754

PARTY ONE	PARTY TWO	DATE	CITATION	NUMBER
Fees and exemptions (Cont.)				
Japan	IBRD (World Bank)	20 Dec 60	400UNTS167	105752
Kuwait	USA (United States)	27 Dec 60	401UNTS185	105771
Luxembourg	Thailand	29 Dec 60	465UNTS131	106725
Mexico	IBRD (World Bank)	16 Jan 61	422UNTS203	106076
Burma	IBRD (World Bank)	16 Jan 61	400UNTS73	105749
Norway	Poland	17 Jan 61	412UNTS130	105928
Germany, West	Japan	18 Jan 61	465UNTS173	106727
UK Great Britain	USA (United States)	20 Jan 61	402UNTS153	105783
Costa Rica	IBRD (World Bank)	03 Feb 61	414UNTS314	105977
Belgium	USA (United States)	21 Feb 61	480UNTS149	106967
Australia	Finland	21 Feb 61	390UNTS61	105602
IBRD (World Bank)	Yugoslavia	23 Feb 61	415UNTS92	105982
Belgium	Netherlands	24 Feb 61	474UNTS167	106881
Cuba	Czechoslovakia	04 Mar 61	465UNTS209	106728
Canada	Iran	10 Mar 61	470UNTS139	106805
Japan	IBRD (World Bank)	16 Mar 61	400UNTS201	105753
IBRD (World Bank)	UK Great Britain	29 Mar 61	415UNTS300	105990
IBRD (World Bank)	Thailand	28 Apr 61	415UNTS121	105983
Japan	IBRD (World Bank)	02 May 61	415UNTS144	105984
Colombia	IBRD (World Bank)	12 May 61	415UNTS172	105985
Poland	Switzerland	18 May 61	559UNTS233	108161
Luxembourg	South Africa	30 May 61	412UNTS203	105933
Ceylon (Sri Lanka)	IBRD (World Bank)	06 Jun 61	414UNTS349	105978
Czechoslovakia	Morocco	08 Jun 61	497UNTS275	107272
New Zealand	UK Great Britain	13 Jun 61	497UNTS293	107273
IBRD (World Bank)	Sudan	14 Jun 61	415UNTS26	105980
Cameroon	France	16 Jun 61	412UNTS148	105929
IBRD (World Bank)	UK Great Britain	23 Jun 61	415UNTS358	105991
Pakistan	IBRD (World Bank)	27 Jun 61	425UNTS241	106127
Chile	IBRD (World Bank)	28 Jun 61	426UNTS33	106129
Argentina	IBRD (World Bank)	30 Jun 61	445UNTS85	106379
Hungary	Poland	05 Jul 61	437UNTS3	106296
Israel	IBRD (World Bank)	11 Jul 61	429UNTS3	106188
Philippines	IBRD (World Bank)	26 Jul 61	414UNTS253	105976
India	IBRD (World Bank)	09 Aug 61	417UNTS297	106011
Finland	IBRD (World Bank)	09 Aug 61	415UNTS204	105986
Finland	Luxembourg	15 Aug 61	541UNTS45	107859
IBRD (World Bank)	UK Great Britain	16 Aug 61	426UNTS287	106143
Cyprus	Israel	17 Aug 61	484UNTS169	107025
India	IBRD (World Bank)	17 Aug 61	417UNTS319	106012
Jordan	Netherlands	24 Aug 61	466UNTS3	106733
Mexico	Netherlands	24 Aug 61	465UNTS291	106732
Colombia	IBRD (World Bank)	28 Aug 61	416UNTS23	105993
Costa Rica	IBRD (World Bank)	06 Sep 61	446UNTS345	106408
Denmark	Germany, West	12 Sep 61	516UNTS283	107478
France	USA (United States)	21 Sep 61	433UNTS243	106247
Australia	Spain	27 Sep 61	426UNTS159	106135
Ghana	Romania	30 Sep 61	467UNTS443	106769
New Zealand	Spain	02 Oct 61	453UNTS11	106516
Germany, West	Morocco	12 Oct 61	523UNTS289	107562
Costa Rica	IBRD (World Bank)	13 Oct 61	430UNTS27	106202
India	IBRD (World Bank)	13 Oct 61	418UNTS3	106013
Philippines	IBRD (World Bank)	13 Oct 61	415UNTS269	105989
Philippines	USA (United States)	31 Oct 61	424UNTS129	106105
Peru	IBRD (World Bank)	03 Nov 61	430UNTS47	106203
Brazil	USA (United States)	11 Nov 61	433UNTS199	106243
El Salvador	USA (United States)	20 Nov 61	433UNTS221	106245
Cyprus	Greece	23 Nov 61	497UNTS311	107274
Czechoslovakia	Mali	27 Nov 61	466UNTS41	106736
Japan	IBRD (World Bank)	29 Nov 61	426UNTS3	106128
IBRD (World Bank)	UK Great Britain	29 Nov 61	426UNTS49	106130
IBRD (World Bank)	South Africa	01 Dec 61	425UNTS215	106126
Greece	New Zealand	06 Dec 61	486UNTS3	107067
IBRD (World Bank)	Venezuela	13 Dec 61	446UNTS371	106409
Czechoslovakia	Guinea	16 Dec 61	559UNTS49	108154

PARTY ONE	PARTY TWO	DATE	CITATION	NUMBER
Fees and exemptions (Cont.)				
India	IBRD (World Bank)	22 Dec 61	481UNTS85	106979
Sierra Leone	USA (United States)	29 Dec 61	434UNTS43	106254
Austria	Greece	15 Jan 62	498UNTS3	107275
Argentina	IBRD (World Bank)	19 Jan 62	446UNTS305	106407
Indonesia	Japan	23 Jan 62	559UNTS77	108155
Australia	IBRD (World Bank)	23 Jan 62	430UNTS3	106201
Peru	USA (United States)	25 Jan 62	473UNTS57	106855
Poland	Romania	25 Jan 62	468UNTS3	106770
Luxembourg	South Africa	31 Jan 62	563UNTS153	108209
Italy	Japan	31 Jan 62	498UNTS23	107276
Ghana	IBRD (World Bank)	08 Feb 62	449UNTS207	106462
Iceland	IBRD (World Bank)	14 Feb 62	447UNTS95	106413
Multilateral		20 Feb 62	597UNTS159	108644
India	IBRD (World Bank)	28 Feb 62	447UNTS3	106410
Germany, West	Thailand	05 Mar 62	563UNTS165	108210
Luxembourg	Spain	26 Mar 62	563UNTS205	108211
Dahomey	UN Special Fund	28 Mar 62	424UNTS55	106099
France	Luxembourg	29 Mar 62	563UNTS227	108212
Sierra Leone	UK Great Britain	05 Apr 62	434UNTS227	106265
Ghana	USSR (Soviet Union)	06 Apr 62	498UNTS41	107277
Japan	United Arab Rep	10 May 62	498UNTS69	107278
Multilateral		14 May 62	544UNTS39	107910
France	Romania	18 May 62	498UNTS115	107279
Ethiopia	USA (United States)	23 May 62	456UNTS293	106563
Colombia	IBRD (World Bank)	23 May 62	447UNTS39	106411
Belgium	USA (United States)	23 May 62	434UNTS133	106260
Korea, South	USA (United States)	25 May 62	454UNTS25	106537
Ethiopia	IBRD (World Bank)	31 May 62	467UNTS237	106765
Pakistan	USA (United States)	31 May 62	460UNTS75	106631
France	Senegal	15 Jun 62	524UNTS3	107563
Bolivia	USA (United States)	19 Jun 62	458UNTS239	106606
Czechoslovakia	Senegal	20 Jun 62	498UNTS145	107280
Mexico	IBRD (World Bank)	20 Jun 62	468UNTS109	106771
Mexico	IBRD (World Bank)	20 Jun 62	467UNTS205	106764
Guinea	Norway	21 Jun 62	466UNTS81	106738
United Arab Rep	USSR (Soviet Union)	23 Jun 62	472UNTS19	106835
Liberia	Norway	29 Jun 62	466UNTS95	106739
Philippines	Spain	04 Jul 62	490UNTS243	107158
Morocco	Switzerland	05 Jul 62	498UNTS171	107281
IBRD (World Bank)	Yugoslavia	11 Jul 62	468UNTS143	106772
Canada	USA (United States)	13 Jul 62	460UNTS83	106632
Niger	USA (United States)	23 Jul 62	487UNTS325	107114
Malaysia	Philippines	31 Jul 62	452UNTS223	106510
Philippines	Thailand	31 Jul 62	452UNTS235	106511
Ecuador	USA (United States)	03 Aug 62	460UNTS133	106636
Finland	IBRD (World Bank)	15 Aug 62	467UNTS177	106763
Cyprus	USA (United States)	23 Aug 62	461UNTS147	106658
Nepal	USA (United States)	24 Aug 62	460UNTS143	106637
Turkey	USA (United States)	27 Aug 62	461UNTS55	106651
Germany, West	Netherlands	30 Aug 62	500UNTS3	107303
Israel	Sierra Leone	30 Aug 62	448UNTS309	106444
Togo	USA (United States)	05 Sep 62	461UNTS47	106650
Panama	IBRD (World Bank)	14 Sep 62	476UNTS153	106908
Pakistan	IBRD (World Bank)	14 Sep 62	467UNTS125	106761
India	IDA (Devel Assoc)	14 Sep 62	467UNTS265	106766
Pakistan	IBRD (World Bank)	14 Sep 62	467UNTS152	106762
Multilateral		14 Sep 62	443UNTS73	106360
Ecuador	Germany, West	20 Sep 62	498UNTS199	107283
Austria	Czechoslovakia	22 Sep 62	495UNTS157	107244
Gabon	USA (United States)	04 Oct 62	459UNTS185	106620
Japan	Kuwait	06 Oct 62	498UNTS235	107284
Finland	France	12 Oct 62	498UNTS299	107285
Canada	San Marino	16 Oct 62	529UNTS3	107650
Israel	IBRD (World Bank)	17 Oct 62	467UNTS107	106760
Hungary	Syria	18 Oct 62	491UNTS209	107178

PARTY ONE	PARTY TWO	DATE	CITATION	NUMBER
Fees and exemptions (Cont.)				
Netherlands	Norway	18 Oct 62	466UNTS145	106741
France	Ivory Coast	19 Oct 62	498UNTS317	107286
Multilateral		25 Oct 62	457UNTS137	106583
Dominican Republic	USA (United States)	25 Oct 62	459UNTS247	106627
Multilateral		25 Oct 62	457UNTS129	106582
IBRD (World Bank)	Uruguay	26 Oct 62	481UNTS39	106977
Japan	UN Special Fund	31 Oct 62	444UNTS171	106368
Poland	Syria	10 Nov 62	491UNTS228	107179
Algeria	UN Special Fund	15 Nov 62	452UNTS243	106512
Czechoslovakia	Poland	16 Nov 62	526UNTS3	107597
Ivory Coast	Switzerland	17 Nov 62	499UNTS3	107289
Ceylon (Sri Lanka)	USA (United States)	21 Nov 62	462UNTS237	106683
Rwanda	United Nations	28 Nov 62	450UNTS267	106473
Laos	USSR (Soviet Union)	01 Dec 62	471UNTS181	106832
Nigeria	IBRD (World Bank)	10 Dec 62	468UNTS255	106776
Austria	Yugoslavia	11 Dec 62	546UNTS3	107938
Guinea	USA (United States)	14 Dec 62	462UNTS247	106684
Morocco	IBRD (World Bank)	21 Dec 62	478UNTS205	106937
IBRD (World Bank)	Thailand	21 Dec 62	467UNTS43	106757
IBRD (World Bank)	Thailand	21 Dec 62	467UNTS63	106758
Syria	United Arab Rep	27 Dec 62	491UNTS245	107180
Ecuador	USA (United States)	07 Jan 63	477UNTS101	106917
Ghana	Mali	09 Jan 63	466UNTS165	106742
Poland	USA (United States)	21 Jan 63	471UNTS151	106830
Mali	Senegal	07 Feb 63	524UNTS41	107565
Pakistan	IBRD (World Bank)	13 Feb 63	467UNTS3	106756
Philippines	IBRD (World Bank)	15 Feb 63	478UNTS161	106936
Algeria	France	18 Feb 63	563UNTS263	108214
Sudan	Switzerland	18 Feb 63	563UNTS281	108215
Bolivia	Philippines	22 Feb 63	490UNTS231	107156
Nicaragua	IBRD (World Bank)	01 Mar 63	481UNTS15	106976
IBRD (World Bank)	Thailand	07 Mar 63	467UNTS83	106759
Peru	IBRD (World Bank)	13 Mar 63	478UNTS245	106938
Australia	Portugal	29 Mar 63	468UNTS313	106778
Thailand	USA (United States)	25 Apr 63	476UNTS115	106906
Cyprus	Denmark	27 Apr 63	529UNTS255	107664
Mexico	IBRD (World Bank)	29 Apr 63	489UNTS151	107138
Algeria	Morocco	30 Apr 63	564UNTS3	108217
IBRD (World Bank)	UK Great Britain	16 May 63	477UNTS361	106929
IBRD (World Bank)	UK Great Britain	16 May 63	476UNTS211	106910
Colombia	IBRD (World Bank)	03 Jun 63	490UNTS199	107155
India	IBRD (World Bank)	05 Jun 63	481UNTS191	106983
Finland	Poland	10 Jun 63	503UNTS179	107343
IBRD (World Bank)	Thailand	11 Jun 63	481UNTS227	106984
Colombia	IBRD (World Bank)	21 Jun 63	482UNTS159	106994
IBRD (World Bank)	Yugoslavia	21 Jun 63	482UNTS43	106990
Guinea	Ivory Coast	26 Jun 63	499UNTS71	107293
Colombia	IBRD (World Bank)	28 Jun 63	489UNTS113	107137
Costa Rica	IBRD (World Bank)	10 Jul 63	482UNTS69	106991
Austria	France	12 Jul 63	499UNTS91	107294
Malaysia	IBRD (World Bank)	15 Jul 63	482UNTS123	106993
Colombia	IBRD (World Bank)	16 Jul 63	482UNTS256	106998
Algeria	Mali	22 Jul 63	564UNTS29	108219
Denmark	IBRD (World Bank)	24 Jul 63	481UNTS171	106982
USA (United States)	Uruguay	31 Jul 63	488UNTS3	107115
United Arab Rep	USA (United States)	01 Aug 63	488UNTS189	107128
Malaysia	IBRD (World Bank)	07 Aug 63	485UNTS253	107060
Cameroon	Israel	09 Aug 63	499UNTS121	107295
IBRD (World Bank)	UK Great Britain	06 Sep 63	483UNTS173	107013
Finland	IBRD (World Bank)	18 Sep 63	491UNTS345	107183
Mexico	IBRD (World Bank)	20 Sep 63	491UNTS317	107182
IBRD (World Bank)	Venezuela	20 Sep 63	482UNTS227	106997
IBRD (World Bank)	UK Great Britain	23 Sep 63	503UNTS247	107348
Japan	IBRD (World Bank)	27 Sep 63	485UNTS283	107061
Taiwan	IBRD (World Bank)	27 Sep 63	483UNTS151	107012

PARTY ONE	PARTY TWO	DATE	CITATION	NUMBER
Fees and exemptions (Cont.)				
El Salvador	IBRD (World Bank)	01 Oct 63	517UNTS3	107481
Pakistan	USSR (Soviet Union)	07 Oct 63	499UNTS161	107297
Ivory Coast	Netherlands	09 Oct 63	499UNTS141	107296
Norway	IBRD (World Bank)	15 Oct 63	482UNTS103	106992
Czechoslovakia	Hungary	22 Oct 63	514UNTS95	107444
IBRD (World Bank)	Spain	25 Oct 63	491UNTS297	107181
IBRD (World Bank)	Yugoslavia	28 Oct 63	503UNTS289	107349
Portugal	IBRD (World Bank)	06 Nov 63	492UNTS89	107188
Portugal	IBRD (World Bank)	06 Nov 63	491UNTS137	107176
New Zealand	IBRD (World Bank)	12 Nov 63	485UNTS233	107059
Peru	IBRD (World Bank)	22 Nov 63	491UNTS101	107175
Canada	Denmark	28 Nov 63	496UNTS223	107254
Chile	IBRD (World Bank)	18 Dec 63	504UNTS3	107351
Multilateral		30 Dec 63	568UNTS215	108270
Multilateral		30 Dec 63	568UNTS243	108272
Multilateral		30 Dec 63	568UNTS233	108271
Multilateral		30 Dec 63	551UNTS105	108036
Multilateral		30 Dec 63	551UNTS119	108037
Liberia	IBRD (World Bank)	08 Jan 64	504UNTS53	107353
Mali	Niger	15 Jan 64	499UNTS197	107299
Czechoslovakia	Yugoslavia	20 Jan 64	538UNTS197	107816
Colombia	IBRD (World Bank)	07 Feb 64	516UNTS99	107473
Denmark	Yugoslavia	11 Feb 64	511UNTS241	107437
Mexico	USA (United States)	14 Feb 64	524UNTS197	107574
Cyprus	USSR (Soviet Union)	29 Feb 64	602UNTS45	108706
Multilateral		03 Mar 64	516UNTS53	107470
IBRD (World Bank)	Thailand	11 Mar 64	504UNTS73	107354
New Zealand	IBRD (World Bank)	12 Mar 64	505UNTS3	107362
Nigeria	IBRD (World Bank)	12 Mar 64	516UNTS325	107480
Cameroon	Mali	17 Mar 64	524UNTS61	107566
USA (United States)	Yugoslavia	04 Apr 64	526UNTS47	107599
Malaysia	Netherlands	07 Apr 64	524UNTS81	107567
Portugal	UK Great Britain	07 Apr 64	539UNTS167	107830
UK Great Britain	USSR (Soviet Union)	13 Apr 64	539UNTS197	107832
Australia	Israel	14 Apr 64	496UNTS233	107255
UK Great Britain	USA (United States)	15 Apr 64	515UNTS55	107453
Argentina	UK Great Britain	15 Apr 64	515UNTS3	107450
Australia	UK Great Britain	15 Apr 64	515UNTS23	107451
Canada	UK Great Britain	15 Apr 64	515UNTS39	107452
Japan	IBRD (World Bank)	22 Apr 64	505UNTS21	107363
Peru	IBRD (World Bank)	22 Apr 64	519UNTS95	107503
United Arab Rep	USA (United States)	05 May 64	531UNTS229	107706
Canada	USA (United States)	06 May 64	524UNTS173	107572
Ethiopia	IBRD (World Bank)	08 May 64	505UNTS51	107364
Algeria	IBRD (World Bank)	14 May 64	522UNTS265	107552
Pakistan	IBRD (World Bank)	14 May 64	516UNTS145	107475
Ecuador	IBRD (World Bank)	26 May 64	534UNTS113	107758
Netherlands	Yugoslavia	28 May 64	521UNTS191	107522
IBRD (World Bank)	Tunisia	05 Jun 64	539UNTS129	107827
Iran	IBRD (World Bank)	10 Jun 64	537UNTS111	107799
Israel	Yugoslavia	13 Jun 64	516UNTS91	107472
South Africa	UK Great Britain	22 Jun 64	515UNTS71	107454
New Zealand	USA (United States)	24 Jun 64	524UNTS101	107568
Sweden	UK Great Britain	30 Jun 64	515UNTS83	107455
Cyprus	UK Great Britain	02 Jul 64	522UNTS129	107540
Nigeria	IBRD (World Bank)	07 Jul 64	537UNTS3	107795
Ivory Coast	Mali	09 Jul 64	524UNTS121	107569
Finland	IBRD (World Bank)	10 Jul 64	516UNTS125	107474
Gabon	IBRD (World Bank)	10 Jul 64	537UNTS63	107797
Philippines	IBRD (World Bank)	22 Jul 64	516UNTS171	107476
IBRD (World Bank)	Spain	31 Jul 64	537UNTS81	107798
India	UK Great Britain	31 Jul 64	522UNTS153	107542
IBRD (World Bank)	Sierra Leone	18 Aug 64	516UNTS295	107479
Multilateral		20 Aug 64	514UNTS25	107441
Kenya	UK Great Britain	25 Aug 64	522UNTS165	107543

PARTY ONE	PARTY TWO	DATE	CITATION	NUMBER
Fees and exemptions (Cont.)				
Morocco	IBRD (World Bank)	26 Aug 64	537UNTS193	107802
IBRD (World Bank)	Venezuela	28 Aug 64	520UNTS97	107512
Dominican Republic	USA (United States)	28 Aug 64	531UNTS35	107691
IBRD (World Bank)	Venezuela	28 Aug 64	537UNTS135	107800
Syria	UK Great Britain	31 Aug 64	539UNTS259	107837
Malawi	UK Great Britain	01 Sep 64	522UNTS117	107539
Tanganyika	UK Great Britain	02 Sep 64	522UNTS177	107544
Finland	UK Great Britain	12 Sep 64	535UNTS13	107773
Denmark	UK Great Britain	16 Sep 64	534UNTS427	107771
Philippines	IBRD (World Bank)	28 Oct 64	537UNTS165	107801
IBRD (World Bank)	Thailand	25 Nov 64	537UNTS273	107805
Multilateral		25 Nov 64	587UNTS19	108507
IBRD (World Bank)	Yugoslavia	11 Dec 64	537UNTS321	107807
India	Netherlands	11 Dec 64	570UNTS165	108292
Paraguay	IBRD (World Bank)	16 Dec 64	549UNTS173	107999
Taiwan	IBRD (World Bank)	17 Dec 64	538UNTS3	107808
Japan	IBRD (World Bank)	23 Dec 64	538UNTS37	107809
Argentina	UK Great Britain	12 Jan 65	597UNTS177	108645
Japan	IBRD (World Bank)	13 Jan 65	537UNTS293	107806
Honduras	IBRD (World Bank)	02 Feb 65	561UNTS255	108188
Mexico	IBRD (World Bank)	04 Feb 65	549UNTS189	108000
Chile	IBRD (World Bank)	12 Feb 65	537UNTS35	107796
Brazil	IBRD (World Bank)	26 Feb 65	553UNTS3	108065
Brazil	IBRD (World Bank)	26 Feb 65	567UNTS91	108253
Malaysia	IBRD (World Bank)	26 Feb 65	549UNTS239	108002
IBRD (World Bank)	Thailand	22 Mar 65	538UNTS63	107810
Finland	UK Great Britain	25 Mar 65	539UNTS103	107826
Denmark	Malaysia	26 Mar 65	540UNTS205	107851
IBRD (World Bank)	Uruguay	30 Mar 65	567UNTS45	108251
UK Great Britain	Yugoslavia	20 Apr 65	551UNTS69	108034
Iran	IBRD (World Bank)	28 Apr 65	555UNTS21	108103
Taiwan	IBRD (World Bank)	28 Apr 65	549UNTS145	107998
Iran	IBRD (World Bank)	28 Apr 65	555UNTS45	108104
Portugal	IBRD (World Bank)	29 Apr 65	549UNTS69	107991
Ghana	Malawi	04 May 65	541UNTS163	107869
Denmark	Spain	05 May 65	543UNTS255	107905
Japan	IBRD (World Bank)	26 May 65	550UNTS95	108010
Brazil	USA (United States)	26 May 65	549UNTS125	107995
Peru	IBRD (World Bank)	03 Jun 65	551UNTS227	108045
India	IBRD (World Bank)	11 Jun 65	557UNTS59	108128
India	IBRD (World Bank)	11 Jun 65	557UNTS101	108130
Peru	IBRD (World Bank)	18 Jun 65	568UNTS191	108269
Australia	Germany, West	21 Jun 65	542UNTS53	107879
Italy	IBRD (World Bank)	28 Jun 65	567UNTS127	108254
Finland	IBRD (World Bank)	30 Jun 65	550UNTS63	108009
Pakistan	IBRD (World Bank)	09 Jul 65	554UNTS39	108096
Iran	IBRD (World Bank)	12 Jul 65	554UNTS3	108095
Nigeria	IBRD (World Bank)	26 Sep 65	570UNTS233	108296
Nigeria	IBRD (World Bank)	26 Sep 65	571UNTS39	108298
IBRD (World Bank)	Uganda	29 Sep 65	568UNTS317	108276
Kenya	IBRD (World Bank)	29 Sep 65	568UNTS289	108274
IBRD (World Bank)	Tanzania	29 Sep 65	568UNTS309	108275
IBRD (World Bank)	Spain	29 Sep 65	568UNTS49	108264
East Afri Service	IBRD (World Bank)	29 Sep 65	568UNTS327	200623
Mexico	IBRD (World Bank)	01 Oct 65	589UNTS339	108542
Chile	IBRD (World Bank)	06 Oct 65	567UNTS293	108261
Netherlands	Nigeria	28 Oct 65	578UNTS15	108383
Philippines	IBRD (World Bank)	02 Nov 65	567UNTS3	108249
Malaysia	IBRD (World Bank)	17 Nov 65	568UNTS23	108263
Austria	Yugoslavia	19 Nov 65	591UNTS3	108556
Hungary	Yugoslavia	23 Nov 65	577UNTS89	108374
IBRD (World Bank)	Venezuela	13 Dec 65	568UNTS77	108265
Mexico	IBRD (World Bank)	15 Dec 65	568UNTS125	108267
Paraguay	IBRD (World Bank)	16 Dec 65	568UNTS165	108268
New Zealand	IBRD (World Bank)	17 Dec 65	567UNTS255	108259

PARTY ONE	PARTY TWO	DATE	CITATION	NUMBER
Fees and exemptions (Cont.)				
New Zealand	IBRD (World Bank)	17 Dec 65	567UNTS275	108260
France	Israel	17 Dec 65	581UNTS311	108451
Austria	Yugoslavia	20 Dec 65	573UNTS165	108329
IBRD (World Bank)	Sudan	27 Dec 65	567UNTS27	108250
Ethiopia	IBRD (World Bank)	28 Dec 65	567UNTS229	108258
Belgium	Denmark	04 Feb 66	561UNTS233	108187
Austria	Germany, West	17 Feb 66	614UNTS263	108875
Guinea	IBRD (World Bank)	30 Mar 66	568UNTS3	108262
Paraguay	IBRD (World Bank)	04 Apr 66	570UNTS41	108287
IBRD (World Bank)	Venezuela	21 Apr 66	568UNTS257	108273
Finland	IBRD (World Bank)	27 Apr 66	568UNTS107	108266
Peru	IBRD (World Bank)	13 May 66	570UNTS61	108288
IBRD (World Bank)	Tunisia	16 May 66	584UNTS155	108477
Mexico	IBRD (World Bank)	25 May 66	596UNTS3	108627
Portugal	IBRD (World Bank)	14 Jun 66	581UNTS3	108430
Portugal	IBRD (World Bank)	14 Jun 66	581UNTS29	108431
Jamaica	IBRD (World Bank)	20 Jun 66	582UNTS145	108462
IBRD (World Bank)	Thailand	24 Jun 66	582UNTS259	108466
India	IBRD (World Bank)	07 Jul 66	595UNTS3	108610
Iraq	IBRD (World Bank)	22 Jul 66	584UNTS233	108480
Malaysia	IBRD (World Bank)	26 Jul 66	586UNTS195	108504
Iran	IBRD (World Bank)	26 Jul 66	582UNTS107	108461
IBRD (World Bank)	Turkey	10 Aug 66	585UNTS199	108490
IBRD (World Bank)	Singapore	11 Aug 66	585UNTS39	108482
Japan	USA (United States)	23 Aug 66	606UNTS219	108787
Honduras	IBRD (World Bank)	25 Aug 66	582UNTS79	108460
Peru	IBRD (World Bank)	07 Sep 66	585UNTS3	108481
IBRD (World Bank)	South Africa	08 Sep 66	585UNTS71	108483
Greece	Netherlands	13 Sep 66	596UNTS245	108637
Jamaica	IBRD (World Bank)	30 Sep 66	582UNTS179	108463
IBRD (World Bank)	Zambia	04 Oct 66	585UNTS181	108489
Nicaragua	IBRD (World Bank)	05 Oct 66	582UNTS231	108465
IBRD (World Bank)	Singapore	04 Nov 66	585UNTS155	108488
Denmark	Singapore	20 Dec 66	593UNTS125	108580
Chile	IBRD (World Bank)	23 Dec 66	595UNTS141	108618
Australia	Mexico	13 Jan 67	607UNTS77	108797
Jamaica	IBRD (World Bank)	23 Jan 67	594UNTS311	108608
IBRD (World Bank)	Venezuela	26 Jan 67	596UNTS35	108628
Romania	United Nations	08 Apr 67	594UNTS159	108602
Austria	Bulgaria	21 Apr 67	603UNTS121	108729
Financial programs				
Bolivia	Brazil	25 Feb 38	51UNTS245	200192
Panama	USA (United States)	23 Mar 40	124UNTS195	200420
France	Netherlands	14 Jun 40	2UNTS263	200019
Panama	USA (United States)	06 Sep 40	124UNTS209	200421
Ecuador	USA (United States)	24 Feb 42	26UNTS379	200157
Brazil	USA (United States)	03 Mar 42	105UNTS99	200325
Brazil	USA (United States)	14 Mar 42	102UNTS195	200302
Honduras	USA (United States)	08 May 42	166UNTS351	200498
Paraguay	USA (United States)	22 May 42	124UNTS243	200423
Nicaragua	USA (United States)	22 May 42	105UNTS141	200328
Peru	USA (United States)	24 Aug 42	24UNTS153	200139
Brazil	USA (United States)	03 Sep 42	13UNTS109	200073
Brazil	USA (United States)	10 Feb 43	102UNTS217	200304
USA (United States)	Venezuela	18 Feb 43	21UNTS225	200125
Chile	USA (United States)	11 May 43	139UNTS295	200456
USA (United States)	Venezuela	14 May 43	28UNTS359	200160
Peru	USA (United States)	20 May 43	100UNTS259	200288
Liberia	USA (United States)	31 Dec 43	106UNTS199	200341
Honduras	USA (United States)	12 Apr 44	138UNTS271	200450
Peru	USA (United States)	15 Apr 44	150UNTS317	200479
Bolivia	USA (United States)	07 Sep 44	162UNTS315	200494
Dominican Republic	USA (United States)	13 Oct 45	149UNTS361	200477
Belgium	Norway	23 Oct 45	16UNTS311	200107

PARTY ONE	PARTY TWO	DATE	CITATION	NUMBER
Financial programs (Cont.)				
Netherlands	Switzerland	24 Oct 45	3UNTS73	100025
Multilateral		07 Nov 45	2UNTS17	100018
Multilateral		16 Nov 45	4UNTS275	100052
UK Great Britain	USA (United States)	06 Dec 45	126UNTS13	101679
Multilateral		27 Dec 45	2UNTS39	100020
Greece	UK Great Britain	24 Jan 46	6UNTS45	100067
Mexico	UK Great Britain	07 Feb 46	6UNTS55	100068
Brazil	USA (United States)	15 Feb 46	162UNTS21	102130
Colombia	USA (United States)	19 Feb 46	166UNTS104	102187
France	UK Great Britain	29 Apr 46	98UNTS123	101360
UK Great Britain	USA (United States)	07 May 46	6UNTS285	100082
India	USA (United States)	16 May 46	4UNTS183	100045
France	USA (United States)	28 May 46	84UNTS141	101124
France	USA (United States)	28 May 46	84UNTS121	101123
Portugal	USA (United States)	30 May 46	174UNTS187	102285
Australia	USA (United States)	07 Jun 46	4UNTS237	100048
Albania	Yugoslavia	01 Jul 46	111UNTS81	101518
Albania	Yugoslavia	01 Jul 46	111UNTS3	101517
Australia	Sweden	16 Sep 46	10UNTS63	100143
Philippines	USA (United States)	17 Sep 46	15UNTS249	100240
Greece	USA (United States)	08 Oct 46	180UNTS119	102379
Colombia	USA (United States)	14 Oct 46	7UNTS97	100093
Multilateral		30 Oct 46	27UNTS77	100401
Peru	USA (United States)	22 Nov 46	100UNTS170	101396
Albania	Yugoslavia	28 Nov 46	111UNTS143	101527
Austria	UK Great Britain	23 Dec 46	88UNTS93	101186
Peru	USA (United States)	27 Dec 46	152UNTS93	102013
Hungary	Yugoslavia	01 Jan 47	113UNTS63	101548
USSR (Soviet Union)	Yugoslavia	04 Feb 47	116UNTS171	101576
Paraguay	USA (United States)	03 Mar 47	135UNTS156	101819
Philippines	USA (United States)	14 Mar 47	16UNTS31	100247
Hungary	Yugoslavia	11 May 47	130UNTS171	101730
Honduras	USA (United States)	13 May 47	166UNTS159	102189
New Zealand	UK Great Britain	27 May 47	17UNTS211	100277
Ecuador	USA (United States)	21 Jun 47	26UNTS275	100391
Albania	Yugoslavia	22 Jun 47	111UNTS207	101536
Sweden	USA (United States)	24 Jun 47	36UNTS25	100565
USA (United States)	Venezuela	30 Jun 47	166UNTS198	102190
United Arab Rep	UK Great Britain	30 Jun 47	93UNTS165	101299
Hungary	Yugoslavia	24 Jul 47	114UNTS3	101554
Multilateral		04 Aug 47	28UNTS41	100418
Czechoslovakia	Yugoslavia	04 Sep 47	112UNTS91	101540
Sweden	Yugoslavia	06 Oct 47	53UNTS107	100775
UK Great Britain	USA (United States)	09 Oct 47	34UNTS129	100533
Greece	UNICEF (Children)	14 Oct 47	102UNTS39	101409
Bolivia	USA (United States)	03 Nov 47	51UNTS33	100750
Ecuador	USA (United States)	14 Nov 47	149UNTS297	101959
Haiti	USA (United States)	19 Dec 47	135UNTS130	101818
Guatemala	USA (United States)	05 Jan 48	135UNTS104	101817
France	Lebanon	24 Jan 48	173UNTS99	102263
Italy	USA (United States)	02 Feb 48	79UNTS171	101040
Paraguay	USA (United States)	12 Mar 48	162UNTS30	102131
United Nations	USA (United States)	23 Mar 48	19UNTS43	100303
USA (United States)	Venezuela	24 Mar 48	44UNTS57	100678
IMF (Fund)	United Nations	15 Apr 48	16UNTS325	200108
Greece	USA (United States)	23 Apr 48	74UNTS107	100958
Ceylon (Sri Lanka)	UK Great Britain	30 Apr 48	182UNTS2	102421
Guatemala	USA (United States)	18 May 48	67UNTS161	100875
Czechoslovakia	Yugoslavia	24 May 48	112UNTS183	101543
Peru	USA (United States)	30 Jun 48	150UNTS45	101962
Australia	Hungary	01 Jul 48	22UNTS3	100325
Australia	Greece	01 Jul 48	22UNTS33	100329
Australia	Italy	08 Jul 48	22UNTS11	100326
Australia	Yugoslavia	09 Jul 48	22UNTS17	100327
Australia	Austria	19 Jul 48	22UNTS25	100328

PARTY ONE	PARTY TWO	DATE	CITATION	NUMBER
Financial programs (Cont.)				
Philippines	USA (United States)	27 Aug 48	44UNTS13	100675
El Salvador	USA (United States)	23 Sep 48	181UNTS101	102402
Panama	USA (United States)	24 Sep 48	150UNTS25	101961
Brazil	USA (United States)	26 Nov 48	88UNTS3	101180
Denmark	Poland	14 Dec 48	81UNTS33	101060
Argentina	Denmark	14 Dec 48	74UNTS41	100956
Italy	USA (United States)	18 Dec 48	79UNTS133	101037
Brazil	USA (United States)	30 Dec 48	102UNTS3	101406
Poland	UK Great Britain	14 Jan 49	83UNTS3	101100
Multilateral		08 Feb 49	157UNTS157	102053
France	Norway	09 Feb 49	29UNTS13	100431
Mexico	USA (United States)	14 Feb 49	160UNTS75	102103
Netherlands	Norway	26 Feb 49	29UNTS33	100432
Austria	USA (United States)	23 Mar 49	43UNTS127	100667
Pan Am Health Org	WHO (World Health)	24 May 49	32UNTS387	200178
Norway	USA (United States)	25 May 49	32UNTS345	100507
Multilateral		05 Aug 49	88UNTS229	101195
Brazil	USA (United States)	31 Aug 49	102UNTS13	101407
Belgium	Netherlands	07 Sep 49	117UNTS3	101581
Belgium	UK Great Britain	07 Sep 49	106UNTS61	101457
Belgium	France	07 Sep 49	123UNTS13	101651
United Arab Rep	USA (United States)	03 Nov 49	71UNTS31	100908
Australia	New Zealand	26 Nov 49	198UNTS161	102662
UNICEF (Children)	UK Great Britain	19 Dec 49	65UNTS64	100828
UK Great Britain	Yugoslavia	26 Dec 49	87UNTS71	101167
Costa Rica	UNICEF (Children)	14 Jan 50	65UNTS70	100830
India	USA (United States)	02 Feb 50	89UNTS127	101214
UNICEF (Children)	UK Great Britain	10 Feb 50	65UNTS86	100837
Austria	Denmark	23 Feb 50	74UNTS269	100969
Chile	UNICEF (Children)	03 Mar 50	126UNTS119	101685
Israel	UK Great Britain	30 Mar 50	86UNTS231	101162
Multilateral		17 Apr 50	131UNTS99	101738
El Salvador	WHO (World Health)	21 Apr 50	103UNTS13	101420
Korea, South	USA (United States)	28 Apr 50	93UNTS21	101284
Austria	USA (United States)	06 Jun 50	92UNTS201	101273
Haiti	WHO (World Health)	21 Jun 50	103UNTS61	101424
Haiti	WHO (World Health)	27 Jun 50	110UNTS99	101504
Multilateral		28 Jun 50	87UNTS153	101170
Thailand	USA (United States)	01 Jul 50	81UNTS61	101063
Brazil	USA (United States)	16 Aug 50	140UNTS223	101890
WHO (World Health)	Venezuela	11 Sep 50	110UNTS237	101513
Pakistan	USA (United States)	23 Sep 50	82UNTS131	101088
UN Relief Palestin	WHO (World Health)	23 Sep 50	103UNTS129	200310
Peru	WHO (World Health)	26 Sep 50	104UNTS233	101444
Haiti	USA (United States)	28 Sep 50	162UNTS85	102132
Denmark	Poland	01 Oct 50	81UNTS43	101061
Iceland	WHO (World Health)	06 Oct 50	110UNTS127	101506
WHO (World Health)	Turkey	19 Oct 50	110UNTS215	101512
Norway	UK Great Britain	06 Nov 50	88UNTS257	101197
Nicaragua	WHO (World Health)	10 Nov 50	110UNTS155	101508
Peru	WHO (World Health)	10 Nov 50	110UNTS187	101510
Bolivia	USA (United States)	22 Nov 50	152UNTS17	102008
Guatemala	WHO (World Health)	28 Nov 50	103UNTS51	101423
Germany, West	UK Great Britain	09 Dec 50	88UNTS247	101196
El Salvador	USA (United States)	13 Dec 50	166UNTS149	102188
Brazil	Netherlands	15 Dec 50	123UNTS101	101657
Multilateral		15 Dec 50	157UNTS129	102052
Multilateral		15 Dec 50	76UNTS120	100985
Brazil	USA (United States)	19 Dec 50	141UNTS3	101900
Italy	UK Great Britain	21 Dec 50	175UNTS187	102301
Liberia	USA (United States)	22 Dec 50	133UNTS69	101781
Liberia	USA (United States)	22 Dec 50	92UNTS145	101267
Nicaragua	USA (United States)	23 Dec 50	92UNTS155	101268
India	USA (United States)	28 Dec 50	99UNTS39	101369
Philippines	WHO (World Health)	28 Dec 50	110UNTS203	101511

PARTY ONE	PARTY TWO	DATE	CITATION	NUMBER
Financial programs (Cont.)				
UK Great Britain	Yugoslavia	28 Dec 50	88UNTS329	101201
Paraguay	USA (United States)	29 Dec 50	122UNTS157	101645
El Salvador	WHO (World Health)	02 Jan 51	103UNTS29	101421
Nicaragua	WHO (World Health)	02 Jan 51	103UNTS107	101428
Colombia	WHO (World Health)	05 Jan 51	102UNTS139	101417
Costa Rica	USA (United States)	11 Jan 51	92UNTS179	101270
Costa Rica	USA (United States)	17 Jan 51	134UNTS215	101801
Saudi Arabia	USA (United States)	17 Jan 51	140UNTS335	101897
Panama	USA (United States)	26 Jan 51	137UNTS69	101849
Nicaragua	USA (United States)	31 Jan 51	150UNTS3	101960
Nicaragua	USA (United States)	31 Jan 51	160UNTS121	102105
Afghanistan	USA (United States)	07 Feb 51	132UNTS265	101766
Pakistan	USA (United States)	09 Feb 51	100UNTS67	101388
Paraguay	WHO (World Health)	15 Feb 51	110UNTS171	101509
Poland	USSR (Soviet Union)	15 Feb 51	432UNTS199	106222
Dominican Republic	USA (United States)	20 Feb 51	132UNTS305	101770
Lebanon	USA (United States)	24 Feb 51	223UNTS121	103060
Israel	USA (United States)	26 Feb 51	137UNTS57	101848
Panama	USA (United States)	26 Feb 51	160UNTS153	102106
Multilateral		06 Mar 51	106UNTS141	101461
USA (United States)	Uruguay	07 Mar 51	165UNTS113	102173
Bolivia	USA (United States)	14 Mar 51	132UNTS319	101771
Dominican Republic	USA (United States)	16 Mar 51	148UNTS15	101932
El Salvador	USA (United States)	19 Mar 51	134UNTS245	101803
Indonesia	WHO (World Health)	28 Mar 51	103UNTS71	101425
Australia	Italy	29 Mar 51	131UNTS187	101741
Jordan	WHO (World Health)	03 Apr 51	110UNTS297	200367
Costa Rica	WHO (World Health)	13 Apr 51	103UNTS3	101419
Multilateral		18 Apr 51	261UNTS140	103729
Honduras	WHO (World Health)	20 Apr 51	110UNTS111	101505
Nicaragua	USA (United States)	20 Apr 51	138UNTS57	101859
Honduras	USA (United States)	24 Apr 51	140UNTS287	101894
Mexico	WHO (World Health)	30 Apr 51	103UNTS95	101427
Ethiopia	USA (United States)	02 May 51	139UNTS85	101877
Colombia	WHO (World Health)	04 May 51	110UNTS83	101503
Austria	USA (United States)	15 May 51	139UNTS79	101876
Cambodia	WHO (World Health)	31 May 51	102UNTS279	200307
Multilateral		01 Jun 51	118UNTS57	101596
Liberia	WHO (World Health)	11 Jun 51	103UNTS83	101426
WHO (World Health)	Uruguay	11 Jun 51	128UNTS251	101724
UK Great Britain	USA (United States)	15 Jun 51	141UNTS79	101907
Multilateral		15 Jun 51	148UNTS67	101936
Iraq	WHO (World Health)	01 Jul 51	110UNTS139	101507
Ethiopia	WHO (World Health)	02 Jul 51	103UNTS39	101422
Burma	WHO (World Health)	09 Jul 51	102UNTS131	101416
Burma	WHO (World Health)	09 Jul 51	104UNTS175	101439
Burma	WHO (World Health)	17 Jul 51	102UNTS127	101415
Multilateral		04 Aug 51	104UNTS197	101441
Japan	USA (United States)	28 Aug 51	147UNTS81	101930
Japan	UK Great Britain	31 Aug 51	149UNTS227	101955
UNICEF (Children)	Turkey	05 Sep 51	193UNTS55	102610
Canada	India	10 Sep 51	391UNTS237	105629
Costa Rica	USA (United States)	11 Sep 51	234UNTS255	103288
WHO (World Health)	Vietnam, South	21 Sep 51	107UNTS63	200352
El Salvador	USA (United States)	23 Oct 51	137UNTS43	101847
Panama	USA (United States)	23 Oct 51	140UNTS3	101880
India	WHO (World Health)	23 Oct 51	109UNTS59	101491
Taiwan	WHO (World Health)	25 Oct 51	126UNTS77	101683
Panama	WHO (World Health)	09 Nov 51	118UNTS43	101595
Israel	USA (United States)	07 Dec 51	157UNTS53	102046
Iraq	UNICEF (Children)	10 Dec 51	126UNTS57	101682
Libya	UK Great Britain	13 Dec 51	123UNTS167	101658
Guatemala	WHO (World Health)	17 Dec 51	120UNTS133	101619
Jordan	USA (United States)	20 Dec 51	157UNTS69	102048
UK Great Britain	USA (United States)	08 Jan 52	126UNTS307	101696

PARTY ONE	PARTY TWO	DATE	CITATION	NUMBER
Financial programs (Cont.)				
Portugal	USA (United States)	08 Jan 52	207UNTS51	102799
Iran	USA (United States)	20 Jan 52	200UNTS191	102703
Libya	USA (United States)	21 Jan 52	183UNTS177	102427
UNICEF (Children)	UK Great Britain	04 Feb 52	120UNTS147	101620
Indonesia	United Nations	06 Feb 52	121UNTS3	101621
Dominican Republic	UNICEF (Children)	15 Feb 52	121UNTS43	101625
Israel	USA (United States)	27 Feb 52	177UNTS123	102314
Iraq	USA (United States)	18 Mar 52	223UNTS131	103061
Finland	Norway	18 Mar 52	188UNTS187	102527
Greece	Switzerland	04 Apr 52	166UNTS271	102192
Libya	UNICEF (Children)	05 Apr 52	133UNTS287	200441
Canada	Netherlands	10 Apr 52	233UNTS129	103257
Liberia	UNICEF (Children)	17 Apr 52	133UNTS3	101773
India	WHO (World Health)	19 Apr 52	131UNTS253	101745
Belgium	Greece	24 Apr 52	166UNTS261	102191
Israel	USA (United States)	01 May 52	177UNTS89	102311
Norway	WHO (World Health)	09 May 52	131UNTS281	101747
Belgium	USA (United States)	12 May 52	179UNTS15	102352
Ethiopia	USA (United States)	15 May 52	180UNTS227	102388
UNICEF (Children)	United Arab Rep	18 May 52	324UNTS161	104684
Libya	USA (United States)	20 May 52	177UNTS81	102310
Libya	USA (United States)	20 May 52	178UNTS307	102346
Libya	USA (United States)	20 May 52	178UNTS155	102339
Iraq	USA (United States)	21 May 52	205UNTS33	102768
Iraq	USA (United States)	21 May 52	212UNTS183	102870
Iraq	USA (United States)	21 May 52	205UNTS25	102767
Mexico	WHO (World Health)	28 May 52	134UNTS319	101810
Iraq	USA (United States)	09 Jun 52	212UNTS193	102871
Finland	USA (United States)	02 Jul 52	165UNTS203	102177
UNICEF (Children)	Syria	10 Jul 52	136UNTS17	101830
Chile	WHO (World Health)	11 Jul 52	137UNTS27	101846
Canada	Ceylon (Sri Lanka)	11 Jul 52	391UNTS245	105630
Germany, West	USA (United States)	18 Jul 52	165UNTS167	102175
UNICEF (Children)	UK Great Britain	25 Jul 52	135UNTS37	101812
Panama	USA (United States)	08 Aug 52	181UNTS257	102415
UNICEF (Children)	Vietnam, South	29 Aug 52	161UNTS335	200492
Multilateral		17 Oct 52	141UNTS121	101911
Iraq	USA (United States)	23 Oct 52	212UNTS201	102872
Chile	WHO (World Health)	24 Oct 52	151UNTS339	102004
United Arab Rep	UK Great Britain	30 Oct 52	172UNTS3	102236
Ethiopia	USA (United States)	07 Nov 52	184UNTS285	102453
Saudi Arabia	USA (United States)	10 Nov 52	181UNTS225	102412
Ceylon (Sri Lanka)	USA (United States)	17 Nov 52	180UNTS207	102386
Liberia	USA (United States)	15 Dec 52	185UNTS45	102457
Greece	Italy	04 Feb 53	189UNTS295	102552
United Nations	Sweden	11 Feb 53	160UNTS3	102096
Multilateral		26 Feb 53	161UNTS31	102120
Germany, West	USA (United States)	27 Feb 53	224UNTS13	103067
Germany, West	UK Great Britain	27 Feb 53	330UNTS217	104747
Germany, West	USA (United States)	27 Feb 53	205UNTS103	102771
Multilateral		27 Feb 53	333UNTS3	104764
Germany, West	USA (United States)	27 Feb 53	224UNTS31	103068
Jordan	UN Relief Palestin	30 Mar 53	165UNTS317	200495
Netherlands	United Nations	09 Apr 53	163UNTS89	102143
Czechoslovakia	Denmark	23 Apr 53	174UNTS107	102281
Ethiopia	UNICEF (Children)	27 Apr 53	213UNTS169	102885
Ethiopia	USA (United States)	29 Apr 53	224UNTS121	103073
Germany, West	UK Great Britain	22 May 53	172UNTS179	102246
Jordan	Syria	04 Jun 53	184UNTS15	102437
Colombia	USA (United States)	09 Jun 53	213UNTS3	102877
United Arab Rep	USA (United States)	18 Jun 53	204UNTS55	102749
United Arab Rep	USA (United States)	18 Jun 53	215UNTS45	102910
Liberia	USA (United States)	23 Jun 53	213UNTS57	102880
Ethiopia	USA (United States)	25 Jun 53	212UNTS175	102869
UK Great Britain	USA (United States)	26 Jun 53	183UNTS225	102432

PARTY ONE	PARTY TWO	DATE	CITATION	NUMBER
Financial programs (Cont.)				
Chile	USA (United States)	27 Jun 53	229UNTS53	103160
Chile	USA (United States)	27 Jun 53	229UNTS193	103167
UN Relief Palestin	United Arab Rep	30 Jun 53	190UNTS3	102554
India	UK Great Britain	20 Jul 53	196UNTS251	102628
Nicaragua	USA (United States)	02 Sep 53	215UNTS69	102911
Multilateral		01 Oct 53	258UNTS153	103677
Libya	UK Great Britain	19 Oct 53	186UNTS285	102494
India	USSR (Soviet Union)	02 Dec 53	240UNTS143	103402
Bulgaria	Greece	05 Dec 53	225UNTS145	103096
Multilateral		11 Dec 53	191UNTS285	102588
Bolivia	USA (United States)	15 Jan 54	229UNTS213	103168
UK Great Britain	USA (United States)	20 Jan 54	196UNTS95	102619
Japan	UK Great Britain	29 Jan 54	190UNTS319	102572
Czechoslovakia	Greece	01 Feb 54	225UNTS95	103092
Germany, West	USA (United States)	12 Feb 54	223UNTS153	103064
Multilateral		01 Mar 54	256UNTS31	103622
Japan	USA (United States)	08 Mar 54	232UNTS227	103238
UNICEF (Children)	Spain	07 May 54	190UNTS357	200515
Greece	Spain	15 May 54	299UNTS277	104319
Mexico	UNICEF (Children)	20 May 54	192UNTS3	102591
Netherlands	Norway	09 Jun 54	287UNTS179	104184
Italy	USA (United States)	16 Jun 54	236UNTS149	103322
Jordan	USA (United States)	17 Jun 54	266UNTS137	103828
Italy	USA (United States)	28 Jun 54	237UNTS121	103340
Costa Rica	USA (United States)	30 Jun 54	235UNTS35	103294
Brazil	USA (United States)	30 Jun 54	237UNTS137	103341
France	Netherlands	09 Jul 54	287UNTS169	104183
Belgium	Italy	12 Jul 54	288UNTS59	104198
Switzerland	UK Great Britain	16 Jul 54	199UNTS197	102685
El Salvador	USA (United States)	16 Jul 54	237UNTS237	103350
New Zealand	UNICEF (Children)	26 Aug 54	198UNTS173	102663
El Salvador	USA (United States)	31 Aug 54	237UNTS49	103336
Libya	USA (United States)	09 Sep 54	238UNTS217	103365
Poland	UK Great Britain	11 Nov 54	204UNTS137	102755
Turkey	USA (United States)	15 Nov 54	238UNTS135	103358
Portugal	UK Great Britain	18 Nov 54	210UNTS265	102841
Lebanon	UN Relief Palestin	26 Nov 54	202UNTS123	102728
Austria	Yugoslavia	27 Nov 54	396UNTS75	105694
Iceland	Netherlands	28 Dec 54	287UNTS159	104182
Netherlands	UNICEF (Children)	31 Dec 54	202UNTS135	102729
Peru	USA (United States)	31 Dec 54	251UNTS51	103533
USSR (Soviet Union)	Yugoslavia	05 Jan 55	240UNTS225	103405
Pakistan	USA (United States)	11 Jan 55	251UNTS111	103537
Turkey	UK Great Britain	17 Jan 55	204UNTS195	102758
Peru	USA (United States)	07 Feb 55	241UNTS63	103424
Iraq	USA (United States)	02 Mar 55	250UNTS229	103526
USA (United States)	Vietnam, South	07 Mar 55	277UNTS285	104013
El Salvador	USA (United States)	21 Mar 55	250UNTS261	103528
Argentina	UK Great Britain	31 Mar 55	210UNTS223	102840
Chile	USA (United States)	31 Mar 55	262UNTS19	103736
USA (United States)	Vietnam, South	23 Apr 55	277UNTS279	104012
Finland	USA (United States)	06 May 55	251UNTS3	103529
USA (United States)	Yugoslavia	12 May 55	251UNTS337	103550
USA (United States)	Yugoslavia	12 May 55	251UNTS343	103551
Multilateral		25 May 55	264UNTS117	103791
Libya	USA (United States)	30 May 55	270UNTS43	103890
Pakistan	Sweden	04 Jun 55	228UNTS121	103146
UK Great Britain	USA (United States)	07 Jun 55	265UNTS27	103804
Thailand	USA (United States)	21 Jun 55	262UNTS87	103738
Haiti	USA (United States)	24 Jun 55	264UNTS291	103800
Dominican Republic	USA (United States)	30 Jun 55	257UNTS313	103664
Germany, West	USA (United States)	07 Jul 55	275UNTS3	103973
Belgium	USA (United States)	15 Jul 55	223UNTS3	103040
Libya	USA (United States)	28 Jul 55	270UNTS245	103900
Libya	USA (United States)	28 Jul 55	270UNTS269	103901

PARTY ONE	PARTY TWO	DATE	CITATION	NUMBER
Financial programs (Cont.)				
Libya	USA (United States)	28 Jul 55	270UNTS317	103903
Bolivia	USA (United States)	03 Aug 55	264UNTS225	103795
El Salvador	USA (United States)	08 Aug 55	264UNTS301	103801
Italy	Switzerland	17 Sep 55	291UNTS213	104257
Austria	USA (United States)	26 Sep 55	272UNTS31	103930
Multilateral		29 Sep 55	222UNTS313	103037
Liberia	USA (United States)	06 Oct 55	275UNTS93	103978
Syria	USSR (Soviet Union)	16 Nov 55	259UNTS71	103683
Guatemala	UNICEF (Children)	22 Nov 55	221UNTS305	103012
Argentina	USA (United States)	21 Dec 55	240UNTS329	103411
Italy	Switzerland	22 Dec 55	260UNTS339	103717
USA (United States)	Yugoslavia	19 Jan 56	240UNTS121	103400
Japan	USA (United States)	10 Feb 56	275UNTS105	103979
Ceylon (Sri Lanka)	Romania	16 Mar 56	315UNTS51	104559
Colombia	USA (United States)	27 Mar 56	273UNTS235	103954
Austria	Hungary	09 Apr 56	438UNTS123	106315
Cambodia	UNICEF (Children)	28 Apr 56	136UNTS341	200446
Peru	USA (United States)	03 May 56	272UNTS59	103931
Austria	Italy	07 May 56	284UNTS351	104147
UK Great Britain	USA (United States)	05 Jun 56	247UNTS205	103470
Bulgaria	Ceylon (Sri Lanka)	19 Jun 56	315UNTS33	104557
Israel	USA (United States)	26 Jun 56	257UNTS55	103649
Libya	USA (United States)	27 Jun 56	273UNTS89	103945
Norway	Sweden	29 Jun 56	262UNTS335	103759
Italy	Switzerland	29 Jun 56	284UNTS299	104144
Italy	Netherlands	29 Jun 56	287UNTS193	104185
Multilateral		13 Jul 56	281UNTS3	104066
Australia	Netherlands	01 Aug 56	280UNTS3	104047
Multilateral		26 Oct 56	276UNTS3	103988
Ecuador	USA (United States)	31 Oct 56	283UNTS151	104114
Argentina	USA (United States)	05 Nov 56	277UNTS143	104004
Colombia	USA (United States)	09 Jan 57	462UNTS151	106676
Sweden	USSR (Soviet Union)	28 Jan 57	428UNTS315	106183
Iceland	USA (United States)	23 Feb 57	283UNTS73	104107
Poland	USSR (Soviet Union)	05 Mar 57	274UNTS133	103963
Multilateral		25 Mar 57	294UNTS259	104301
Multilateral		25 Mar 57	294UNTS411	104302
Paraguay	USA (United States)	04 Apr 57	284UNTS161	104135
Jordan	USA (United States)	29 Apr 57	290UNTS111	104230
Japan	USA (United States)	08 May 57	318UNTS257	104621
Denmark	Uruguay	04 Jun 57	286UNTS107	104162
Finland	India	14 Jun 57	277UNTS327	104016
UK Great Britain	USA (United States)	27 Jun 57	290UNTS133	104232
Finland	Norway	28 Jun 57	272UNTS191	103938
Jordan	USA (United States)	29 Jun 57	288UNTS263	104208
Germany, West	Italy	12 Jul 57	291UNTS181	104252
Morocco	UNICEF (Children)	31 Jul 57	282UNTS99	104095
Brazil	USA (United States)	05 Nov 57	303UNTS3	104368
Argentina	Italy	25 Nov 57	305UNTS275	104424
Argentina	UK Great Britain	25 Nov 57	313UNTS95	104531
Argentina	Denmark	25 Nov 57	299UNTS83	104308
China People's Rep	Denmark	01 Dec 57	309UNTS241	104475
Multilateral		06 Jan 58	304UNTS227	104399
Japan	USA (United States)	11 Jan 58	304UNTS35	104390
Iran	Italy	29 Jan 58	302UNTS181	104358
Canada	India	20 Feb 58	391UNTS231	105628
Poland	USSR (Soviet Union)	18 Mar 58	340UNTS89	104861
Jordan	UK Great Britain	26 Mar 58	312UNTS373	104526
Bolivia	USA (United States)	22 Apr 58	317UNTS209	104605
Belgium	Japan	30 Apr 58	303UNTS109	104373
Jordan	UK Great Britain	07 May 58	312UNTS379	104527
Multilateral		18 Jun 58	386UNTS355	105553
Ecuador	USA (United States)	27 Jun 58	317UNTS51	104593
Philippines	USA (United States)	30 Jun 58	321UNTS51	104653
Lebanon	USA (United States)	03 Sep 58	336UNTS91	104801

PARTY ONE	PARTY TWO	DATE	CITATION	NUMBER
Financial programs (Cont.)				
Germany, West	UK Great Britain	03 Oct 58	398UNTS293	105731
Spain	USA (United States)	16 Oct 58	336UNTS153	104804
Finland	Sweden	16 Oct 58	428UNTS125	106171
Canada	UK Great Britain	18 Oct 58	392UNTS61	105639
Canada	India	22 Oct 58	392UNTS21	105635
Canada	Ceylon (Sri Lanka)	05 Nov 58	391UNTS225	105627
Euratom	USA (United States)	08 Nov 58	338UNTS135	104835
Netherlands	Turkey	29 Nov 58	335UNTS229	104790
Afghanistan	WHO (World Health)	18 Dec 58	324UNTS121	104681
India	USA (United States)	03 Mar 59	341UNTS235	104886
France	UK Great Britain	05 Mar 59	343UNTS277	104932
Austria	UK Great Britain	14 Mar 59	343UNTS263	104930
Morocco	UN Special Fund	04 Apr 59	354UNTS347	105069
Germany, West	UK Great Britain	10 Apr 59	343UNTS295	104935
Italy	UK Great Britain	14 Apr 59	343UNTS289	104934
Netherlands	Switzerland	14 Apr 59	486UNTS367	107086
Sweden	UK Great Britain	18 Apr 59	360UNTS89	105156
Norway	UK Great Britain	23 Apr 59	343UNTS283	104933
Belgium	UK Great Britain	23 Apr 59	343UNTS271	104931
India	Netherlands	27 Apr 59	506UNTS141	107385
Belgium	Netherlands	28 Apr 59	485UNTS123	107049
Austria	Netherlands	29 Apr 59	486UNTS373	107087
Italy	United Arab Rep	29 Apr 59	363UNTS91	105202
Italy	Netherlands	29 Apr 59	486UNTS387	107089
France	Netherlands	29 Apr 59	486UNTS379	107088
Netherlands	Portugal	30 Apr 59	485UNTS129	107050
Germany, West	Netherlands	30 Apr 59	485UNTS141	107052
Netherlands	Norway	30 Apr 59	487UNTS3	107090
Netherlands	UK Great Britain	30 Apr 59	343UNTS307	104937
Iceland	Netherlands	30 Apr 59	487UNTS13	107091
Denmark	Netherlands	30 Apr 59	487UNTS23	107092
Switzerland	UK Great Britain	06 May 59	343UNTS315	104938
Multilateral		11 May 59	527UNTS145	107623
Japan	Vietnam, South	13 May 59	373UNTS173	105319
Japan	Vietnam, South	13 May 59	373UNTS149	105318
Iceland	UK Great Britain	14 May 59	343UNTS301	104936
Libya	USA (United States)	21 May 59	361UNTS123	105176
Greece	UK Great Britain	21 May 59	344UNTS3	104939
Fed of Malaya	USA (United States)	22 May 59	346UNTS263	104985
Turkey	USA (United States)	26 May 59	354UNTS57	105053
Jordan	UK Great Britain	11 Jun 59	351UNTS283	105028
Turkey	UK Great Britain	13 Jun 59	551UNTS59	108033
Iceland	USA (United States)	23 Jun 59	354UNTS3	105048
Burma	USA (United States)	24 Jun 59	358UNTS91	105127
USA (United States)	Yemen	30 Jun 59	357UNTS137	105112
Ghana	UN Special Fund	12 Aug 59	338UNTS203	104836
United Arab Rep	USA (United States)	28 Sep 59	358UNTS97	105128
Iran	UN Special Fund	06 Oct 59	342UNTS89	104902
Poland	UN Special Fund	15 Oct 59	344UNTS29	104941
India	UN Special Fund	20 Oct 59	344UNTS143	104946
UN Special Fund	Yugoslavia	27 Oct 59	344UNTS159	104947
Ecuador	UN Special Fund	10 Nov 59	345UNTS3	104955
Greece	UN Special Fund	13 Nov 59	345UNTS171	104966
UN Special Fund	Turkey	20 Nov 59	345UNTS105	104963
UN Special Fund	United Arab Rep	25 Nov 59	345UNTS125	104964
Israel	UN Special Fund	01 Dec 59	345UNTS197	104968
Argentina	UN Special Fund	04 Dec 59	345UNTS263	104972
Jordan	UN Special Fund	15 Dec 59	346UNTS3	104974
Denmark	Sweden	04 Jan 60	376UNTS375	105390
UN Special Fund	UK Great Britain	07 Jan 60	348UNTS177	105000
Peru	UN Special Fund	19 Jan 60	349UNTS83	105010
Chile	UN Special Fund	22 Jan 60	351UNTS115	105020
Colombia	UN Special Fund	04 Feb 60	355UNTS257	105080
Bolivia	UN Special Fund	09 Feb 60	351UNTS203	105024
Cuba	USSR (Soviet Union)	13 Feb 60	369UNTS17	105248

PARTY ONE	PARTY TWO	DATE	CITATION	NUMBER
Financial programs (Cont.)				
Afghanistan	UN Special Fund	21 Feb 60	351UNTS93	105019
Ecuador	USA (United States)	24 Feb 60	371UNTS55	105270
Pakistan	UN Special Fund	25 Feb 60	351UNTS141	105021
Brazil	USA (United States)	27 Feb 60	384UNTS131	105515
France	UN Special Fund	17 Mar 60	354UNTS119	105059
Portugal	USA (United States)	19 Mar 60	371UNTS131	105275
Italy	UN Special Fund	01 Apr 60	354UNTS261	105066
UN Special Fund	Tunisia	12 Apr 60	355UNTS289	105082
Libya	UN Special Fund	19 Apr 60	356UNTS11	105090
UN Special Fund	Sudan	21 Apr 60	356UNTS213	105097
UN Special Fund	Vietnam, South	29 Apr 60	357UNTS311	200567
Laos	UN Special Fund	30 Apr 60	361UNTS171	105179
Jordan	UK Great Britain	04 May 60	385UNTS81	105531
Lebanon	UN Special Fund	07 May 60	360UNTS225	105160
Japan	USA (United States)	31 May 60	376UNTS301	105385
Cuba	Czechoslovakia	10 Jun 60	447UNTS75	106412
Iraq	UN Special Fund	19 Jun 60	376UNTS357	105389
IAEA (Atom Energy)	USA (United States)	28 Jun 60	374UNTS133	105333
Ethiopia	UN Special Fund	13 Jul 60	368UNTS159	105240
Italy	USA (United States)	19 Jul 60	389UNTS237	105595
USA (United States)	Uruguay	22 Jul 60	388UNTS315	105587
India	IBRD (World Bank)	29 Jul 60	377UNTS153	105399
Cyprus	UK Great Britain	16 Aug 60	382UNTS231	105484
Congo (Zaire)	United Nations	23 Aug 60	373UNTS327	200576
Guinea	USA (United States)	30 Sep 60	394UNTS103	105671
Indonesia	UN Special Fund	07 Oct 60	378UNTS141	105424
Liberia	UN Special Fund	11 Oct 60	376UNTS341	105388
El Salvador	UN Special Fund	24 Oct 60	377UNTS171	105400
Chile	USA (United States)	28 Oct 60	401UNTS177	105770
Greece	Poland	08 Nov 60	483UNTS141	107011
Brazil	Japan	14 Nov 60	518UNTS29	107491
Guatemala	UN Special Fund	17 Nov 60	383UNTS67	105495
Nepal	UN Special Fund	17 Nov 60	380UNTS289	105461
Finland	Sweden	21 Nov 60	383UNTS125	105498
Cambodia	UN Special Fund	24 Nov 60	382UNTS255	105487
Multilateral		13 Dec 60	523UNTS117	107557
Honduras	UN Special Fund	20 Dec 60	383UNTS103	105497
Iceland	USA (United States)	30 Dec 60	401UNTS43	105761
Burma	UN Special Fund	03 Jan 61	387UNTS219	105564
Costa Rica	UN Special Fund	10 Jan 61	389UNTS253	105597
USA (United States)	Yugoslavia	19 Jan 61	402UNTS163	105784
UN Special Fund	Saudi Arabia	19 Jan 61	396UNTS27	105692
Nicaragua	UN Special Fund	20 Jan 61	387UNTS15	105555
Chad	UN Special Fund	23 Jan 61	390UNTS69	105603
UN Special Fund	Somalia	28 Jan 61	388UNTS75	105573
Gabon	UN Special Fund	02 Feb 61	387UNTS289	105568
Nigeria	UN Special Fund	10 Feb 61	390UNTS85	105604
Mexico	UN Special Fund	23 Feb 61	388UNTS151	105576
Cyprus	UN Special Fund	24 Feb 61	389UNTS3	105588
Panama	UN Special Fund	09 Mar 61	396UNTS3	105691
Cuba	UN Special Fund	10 Mar 61	390UNTS35	105601
Austria	USA (United States)	29 Mar 61	459UNTS45	106612
USA (United States)	Yugoslavia	19 Apr 61	409UNTS163	105883
Korea, South	UN Special Fund	21 Apr 61	394UNTS231	200583
Ceylon (Sri Lanka)	UN Special Fund	03 May 61	395UNTS217	105687
Honduras	IDA (Devel Assoc)	12 May 61	414UNTS180	105973
Senegal	USA (United States)	13 May 61	409UNTS232	105888
Ghana	Switzerland	17 May 61	559UNTS193	108159
Nepal	USA (United States)	09 Jun 61	421UNTS223	106061
Congo (Zaire)	United Nations	12 Jun 61	494UNTS205	107234
Cameroon	UN Special Fund	13 Jun 61	397UNTS297	105713
IDA (Devel Assoc)	Sudan	14 Jun 61	415UNTS50	105981
Finland	USA (United States)	16 Jun 61	413UNTS211	105955
Paraguay	UN Special Fund	22 Jun 61	399UNTS117	105738
UN Special Fund	Upper Volta	26 Jun 61	400UNTS3	105744

PARTY ONE	PARTY TWO	DATE	CITATION	NUMBER
Financial programs (Cont.)				
Haiti	UN Special Fund	28 Jun 61	399UNTS171	105741
Philippines	UN Special Fund	28 Jun 61	399UNTS141	105739
Mali	UN Special Fund	21 Jul 61	401UNTS141	105768
UN Special Fund	Yemen	02 Aug 61	402UNTS43	105777
Chile	USA (United States)	03 Aug 61	433UNTS21	106228
Colombia	IDA (Devel Assoc)	28 Aug 61	416UNTS3	105992
Ivory Coast	UN Special Fund	29 Aug 61	406UNTS129	105844
Taiwan	IDA (Devel Assoc)	30 Aug 61	416UNTS175	106003
UN Special Fund	Sierra Leone	02 Oct 61	422UNTS131	106073
Iraq	Syria	03 Nov 61	489UNTS45	107134
Mauritania	UN Special Fund	07 Nov 61	412UNTS240	105936
Congo (Brazzaville)	UN Special Fund	09 Nov 61	413UNTS58	105940
Ivory Coast	USA (United States)	01 Dec 61	462UNTS221	106681
Ethiopia	USA (United States)	06 Dec 61	433UNTS231	106246
UN Special Fund	Venezuela	11 Dec 61	422UNTS149	106074
Germany, West	Thailand	13 Dec 61	541UNTS181	107870
UN Special Fund	Senegal	16 Dec 61	425UNTS97	106121
Malagasy	UN Special Fund	05 Jan 62	419UNTS29	106028
Cyprus	USA (United States)	15 Jan 62	435UNTS15	106267
Cyprus	USA (United States)	18 Jan 62	435UNTS3	106266
Ghana	USA (United States)	24 Jan 62	435UNTS23	106268
Niger	UN Special Fund	26 Feb 62	423UNTS83	106086
IDA (Devel Assoc)	UK Great Britain	13 Mar 62	466UNTS331	106753
Brazil	USA (United States)	13 Apr 62	445UNTS227	106391
UN Special Fund	Uruguay	04 May 62	429UNTS143	106196
El Salvador	USA (United States)	15 May 62	452UNTS49	106503
Greece	United Nations	18 May 62	429UNTS61	106190
Denmark	USA (United States)	28 May 62	450UNTS215	106469
Germany, West	UK Great Britain	06 Jun 62	437UNTS39	106298
Dominican Republic	UN Special Fund	06 Jun 62	429UNTS169	106197
UN Special Fund	Syria	07 Jul 62	443UNTS3	106355
UN Special Fund	Tanganyika	17 Jul 62	435UNTS237	106281
Italy	USA (United States)	28 Aug 62	461UNTS137	106657
Israel	OAS (Am States)	11 Oct 62	484UNTS241	107035
Belgium	Rwanda	13 Oct 62	456UNTS425	106568
Tunisia	USA (United States)	29 Oct 62	462UNTS201	106679
Germany, West	USA (United States)	20 Nov 62	505UNTS263	107377
Nigeria	USA (United States)	24 Dec 62	462UNTS180	106677
New Zealand	Western Samoa	24 Jan 63	499UNTS21	107290
Malaysia	USA (United States)	28 Jan 63	473UNTS15	106850
Austria	United Nations	29 Jan 63	452UNTS261	106513
Indonesia	USA (United States)	14 Mar 63	505UNTS79	107365
UN Special Fund	Uganda	22 Mar 63	456UNTS466	106572
Philippines	USA (United States)	23 Mar 63	474UNTS80	106873
Brazil	USA (United States)	29 Mar 63	476UNTS67	106904
Belgium	Netherlands	13 May 63	540UNTS3	107843
Canada	India	14 May 63	529UNTS31	107653
Denmark	India	15 May 63	616UNTS23	108889
Laos	UK Great Britain	17 May 63	475UNTS155	106891
Jamaica	UN Special Fund	22 May 63	489UNTS191	107140
Thailand	USA (United States)	24 May 63	477UNTS123	106918
Netherlands	UN Special Fund	24 May 63	466UNTS289	106750
UN Special Fund	Western Samoa	05 Jun 63	467UNTS463	200601
Australia	UK Great Britain	06 Jun 63	472UNTS157	106838
Korea, South	USA (United States)	18 Jun 63	487UNTS297	107112
India	USA (United States)	19 Jun 63	479UNTS175	106952
Austria	USA (United States)	25 Jun 63	479UNTS223	106956
New Zealand	UN Special Fund	28 Jun 63	470UNTS3	106792
Bulgaria	USA (United States)	02 Jul 63	479UNTS245	106957
IBRD (World Bank)	Tunisia	03 Jul 63	480UNTS209	106970
Paraguay	USA (United States)	20 Aug 63	531UNTS197	107704
Afghanistan	USA (United States)	20 Aug 63	488UNTS41	107118
Argentina	USA (United States)	21 Aug 63	488UNTS61	107119
Burundi	UN Special Fund	22 Aug 63	476UNTS49	106903
Mexico	USA (United States)	29 Aug 63	505UNTS185	107374

PARTY ONE	PARTY TWO	DATE	CITATION	NUMBER
Financial programs (Cont.)				
Finland	IBRD (World Bank)	18 Sep 63	491UNTS345	107183
Ecuador	USA (United States)	20 Sep 63	488UNTS147	107125
Canada	France	11 Oct 63	529UNTS71	107657
Iran	USA (United States)	24 Oct 63	489UNTS303	107146
Central Afri Rep	UN Special Fund	30 Oct 63	481UNTS247	106985
Multilateral		09 Nov 63	489UNTS209	107141
UNESCO (Educ/Cult)	United Arab Rep	09 Nov 63	489UNTS233	107142
Tunisia	USA (United States)	18 Nov 63	494UNTS193	107233
Greece	USA (United States)	13 Dec 63	494UNTS55	107226
Cameroon	Netherlands	18 Dec 63	521UNTS303	107527
Chile	IBRD (World Bank)	18 Dec 63	504UNTS29	107352
Netherlands	Poland	20 Dec 63	514UNTS169	107446
Laos	UK Great Britain	24 Dec 63	502UNTS189	107330
Iceland	USA (United States)	13 Feb 64	524UNTS235	107576
Spain	USA (United States)	18 Mar 64	535UNTS343	107789
Liberia	USA (United States)	08 May 64	526UNTS239	107608
Multilateral		26 May 64	541UNTS271	200613
Ireland	UN Special Fund	03 Jun 64	496UNTS205	107253
Colombia	Netherlands	06 Jul 64	543UNTS289	107906
Multilateral		10 Jul 64	611UNTS7	108844
Belgium	Tunisia	15 Jul 64	560UNTS65	108169
IDA (Devel Assoc)	UK Great Britain	31 Jul 64	535UNTS205	107781
Ceylon (Sri Lanka)	USA (United States)	29 Aug 64	531UNTS93	107695
Australia	UN Special Fund	30 Sep 64	510UNTS277	107419
Italy	ILO (Labor Org)	24 Oct 64	541UNTS217	107871
USA (United States)	Yugoslavia	09 Nov 64	533UNTS39	107731
Peru	USA (United States)	28 Jan 65	587UNTS273	108513
Iran	United Nations	16 Feb 65	525UNTS211	107593
Belgium	United Nations	20 Feb 65	535UNTS197	107780
Mexico	USA (United States)	27 Feb 65	542UNTS181	107889
Multilateral		18 Mar 65	575UNTS159	108359
Australia	Malta	28 Apr 65	548UNTS203	107979
Multilateral		29 Apr 65	586UNTS123	108500
Finland	IBRD (World Bank)	30 Jun 65	550UNTS63	108009
UN Special Fund	Spain	30 Jun 65	544UNTS159	107918
Multilateral		05 Jul 65	563UNTS104	108207
Multilateral		22 Jul 65	561UNTS333	200618
Saudi Arabia	USA (United States)	19 Nov 65	580UNTS35	108419
Mongolia	UN Special Fund	26 Jan 66	552UNTS201	108055
IDA (Devel Assoc)	UK Great Britain	08 Feb 66	567UNTS207	108257
Philippines	United Nations	05 Apr 66	560UNTS191	108174
Multilateral		04 May 66	575UNTS49	108354
Rwanda	USSR (Soviet Union)	06 May 66	633UNTS217	109039
Bulgaria	UN Special Fund	26 May 66	563UNTS71	108205
Canada	USA (United States)	09 Jun 66	580UNTS263	108429
FAO (Food Agri)	IMCO (Maritime Org)	11 Jul 66	575UNTS238	200627
Netherlands	Norway	22 Sep 66	600UNTS227	108683
Asian Devel Bank	Philippines	22 Dec 66	615UNTS375	108887
IBRD (World Bank)	Trinidad/Tobago	10 Mar 67	599UNTS3	108662
Multilateral		17 Mar 67	594UNTS105	108598
Greece	United Nations	14 Apr 67	595UNTS83	108613
Multilateral		26 Jul 67	614UNTS217	108872
Bulgaria	Italy	29 Jul 67	631UNTS33	108985
New Zealand	WHO (World Health)	29 Aug 67	607UNTS57	108795
Multilateral		12 Oct 67	607UNTS20	108793
India	United Nations	04 Nov 67	609UNTS3	108824
United Nations	Senegal	08 Nov 67	613UNTS255	108854
Eur Space Research	UK Great Britain	24 Nov 67	638UNTS17	109129
Chile	Denmark	15 Dec 67	643UNTS293	109199
Iran	United Nations	15 Feb 68	631UNTS103	108990
United Nations	Tunisia	18 Mar 68	633UNTS3	109030
State/IGO Group	Australia	21 May 68	636UNTS326	109108
Funding procedures				
Bolivia	Brazil	25 Feb 38	88UNTS379	200254

Funding procedures (Cont.)

PARTY ONE	PARTY TWO	DATE	CITATION	NUMBER
Honduras	USA (United States)	28 Feb 41	117UNTS205	200371
Brazil	Paraguay	14 Jun 41	54UNTS289	200201
Costa Rica	USA (United States)	18 Jun 41	103UNTS173	200313
Brazil	USA (United States)	03 Mar 42	105UNTS91	200324
El Salvador	USA (United States)	05 May 42	21UNTS215	200124
Honduras	USA (United States)	08 May 42	166UNTS351	200498
Peru	USA (United States)	11 May 42	136UNTS353	200447
Bolivia	USA (United States)	16 Jul 42	13UNTS101	200072
Peru	USA (United States)	24 Aug 42	24UNTS153	200139
Brazil	USA (United States)	10 Feb 43	102UNTS217	200304
USA (United States)	Venezuela	18 Feb 43	21UNTS225	200125
USA (United States)	Venezuela	14 May 43	28UNTS359	200160
Mexico	USA (United States)	01 Jul 43	28UNTS407	200164
Dominican Republic	USA (United States)	07 Jul 43	28UNTS419	200165
France	USA (United States)	25 Sep 43	76UNTS183	200245
Multilateral		15 Jan 44	161UNTS281	200489
Mexico	USA (United States)	27 Jan 44	106UNTS275	200346
Honduras	USA (United States)	12 Apr 44	138UNTS271	200450
Peru	USA (United States)	15 Apr 44	150UNTS317	200479
Belgium	UK Great Britain	22 Aug 44	90UNTS295	200267
Bolivia	USA (United States)	07 Sep 44	162UNTS315	200494
Guatemala	USA (United States)	16 Sep 44	135UNTS315	200444
Brazil	UNRRA (Relief)	12 Oct 44	67UNTS321	200228
Multilateral		07 Dec 44	171UNTS345	200501
Haiti	USA (United States)	08 Jan 45	121UNTS153	200397
Ecuador	USA (United States)	22 Jan 45	24UNTS273	200152
El Salvador	USA (United States)	09 Jun 45	149UNTS379	200478
France	UK Great Britain	31 Aug 45	98UNTS249	200275
Dominican Republic	USA (United States)	13 Oct 45	149UNTS361	200477
Denmark	UK Great Britain	24 Oct 45	93UNTS143	101297
UK Great Britain	USA (United States)	05 Nov 45	138UNTS75	101861
Multilateral		07 Nov 45	2UNTS17	100018
Multilateral		16 Nov 45	4UNTS275	100052
Netherlands	UK Great Britain	20 Dec 45	4UNTS303	100053
Multilateral		27 Dec 45	2UNTS39	100020
Brazil	USA (United States)	15 Feb 46	162UNTS21	102130
Colombia	USA (United States)	19 Feb 46	166UNTS104	102187
Canada	UK Great Britain	06 Mar 46	20UNTS13	100312
Brazil	USA (United States)	05 Apr 46	12UNTS131	100183
Multilateral		23 Apr 46	16UNTS179	100257
USA (United States)	Uruguay	23 Apr 46	160UNTS103	102104
France	UK Great Britain	29 Apr 46	98UNTS123	101360
Multilateral		19 Jul 46	1UNTS97	200001
Multilateral		22 Jul 46	14UNTS185	100221
Taiwan	USA (United States)	30 Aug 46	12UNTS39	100179
Argentina	UK Great Britain	17 Sep 46	88UNTS47	101185
Multilateral		30 Oct 46	27UNTS77	100401
Albania	Yugoslavia	28 Nov 46	111UNTS151	101528
Albania	Yugoslavia	28 Nov 46	111UNTS143	101527
Albania	Yugoslavia	28 Nov 46	111UNTS171	101530
UK Great Britain	USA (United States)	02 Dec 46	7UNTS163	100098
ILO (Labor Org)	United Nations	19 Dec 46	1UNTS183	200009
Australia	Netherlands	24 Jan 47	10UNTS77	100144
FAO (Food Agri)	United Nations	03 Feb 47	1UNTS207	200010
UNESCO (Educ/Cult)	United Nations	03 Feb 47	1UNTS233	200011
USSR (Soviet Union)	Yugoslavia	04 Feb 47	130UNTS235	101731
Multilateral		06 Feb 47	97UNTS227	101352
Burma	USA (United States)	28 Feb 47	25UNTS27	100355
Mexico	USA (United States)	17 Mar 47	167UNTS30	102200
Honduras	USA (United States)	13 May 47	166UNTS159	102189
Albania	Yugoslavia	12 Jun 47	111UNTS195	101534
Ecuador	USA (United States)	21 Jun 47	26UNTS275	100391
Austria	USA (United States)	25 Jun 47	22UNTS141	100334
USA (United States)	Venezuela	30 Jun 47	166UNTS198	102190
Italy	USA (United States)	04 Jul 47	22UNTS173	100336

Funding procedures (Cont.)

PARTY ONE	PARTY TWO	DATE	CITATION	NUMBER
India	UK Great Britain	14 Aug 47	11UNTS371	100176
Multilateral		11 Oct 47	77UNTS143	100998
Greece	UNICEF (Children)	14 Oct 47	102UNTS39	101409
Ecuador	USA (United States)	14 Nov 47	149UNTS297	101959
United Nations	WHO (World Health)	15 Nov 47	19UNTS193	200115
United Nations	UPU (Postal Union)	15 Nov 47	19UNTS219	200116
Albania	UNICEF (Children)	20 Nov 47	65UNTS163	200208
Guatemala	USA (United States)	05 Jan 48	135UNTS104	101817
France	UNICEF (Children)	19 Feb 48	68UNTS75	100885
Costa Rica	USA (United States)	27 Feb 48	135UNTS74	101816
Denmark	Hungary	28 Feb 48	85UNTS35	101144
Multilateral		06 Mar 48	289UNTS3	104214
Paraguay	USA (United States)	12 Mar 48	162UNTS30	102131
Greece	USA (United States)	23 Apr 48	74UNTS107	100958
Multilateral		30 Apr 48	119UNTS3	101609
France	USA (United States)	28 Jun 48	19UNTS9	100302
Ireland	USA (United States)	28 Jun 48	24UNTS3	100349
Italy	USA (United States)	28 Jun 48	20UNTS43	100314
Denmark	USA (United States)	29 Jun 48	22UNTS217	100338
Peru	USA (United States)	30 Jun 48	150UNTS45	101962
Belgium	USA (United States)	02 Jul 48	19UNTS127	100309
Netherlands	USA (United States)	02 Jul 48	20UNTS91	100315
Greece	USA (United States)	02 Jul 48	23UNTS43	100342
Austria	USA (United States)	02 Jul 48	21UNTS29	100323
Iceland	USA (United States)	03 Jul 48	20UNTS141	100316
Norway	USA (United States)	03 Jul 48	20UNTS185	100317
Luxembourg	USA (United States)	03 Jul 48	24UNTS35	100350
UK Great Britain	USA (United States)	06 Jul 48	22UNTS263	100339
ICJ Option Clause	Switzerland	06 Jul 48	17UNTS111	100271
France	USA (United States)	09 Jul 48	24UNTS103	100352
Multilateral		14 Jul 48	23UNTS3	100340
UNESCO (Educ/Cult)	WHO (World Health)	15 Jul 48	44UNTS323	200184
FAO (Food Agri)	WHO (World Health)	17 Jul 48	76UNTS171	200244
Taiwan	USA (United States)	05 Aug 48	82UNTS109	101087
Multilateral		18 Aug 48	33UNTS181	100518
FAO (Food Agri)	UNESCO (Educ/Cult)	23 Aug 48	18UNTS345	200112
Philippines	USA (United States)	27 Aug 48	44UNTS13	100675
El Salvador	USA (United States)	23 Sep 48	181UNTS101	102402
Panama	USA (United States)	24 Sep 48	150UNTS25	101961
UNRRA (Relief)	United Nations	27 Sep 48	27UNTS349	200158
Trieste	USA (United States)	15 Oct 48	29UNTS249	100443
Brazil	USA (United States)	26 Nov 48	88UNTS3	101180
Multilateral		29 Nov 48	120UNTS13	101613
Afghanistan	UNESCO (Educ/Cult)	08 Dec 48	46UNTS3	100697
Italy	USA (United States)	18 Dec 48	79UNTS133	101037
Brazil	USA (United States)	30 Dec 48	102UNTS3	101406
Belgium	Luxembourg	14 Jan 49	36UNTS339	100572
Chile	USA (United States)	21 Jan 49	160UNTS185	102107
IRO (Refugee Org)	United Nations	07 Feb 49	26UNTS299	200153
Multilateral		08 Feb 49	157UNTS157	102053
FAO (Food Agri)	UNESCO (Educ/Cult)	09 Feb 49	43UNTS315	200182
Mexico	USA (United States)	14 Feb 49	160UNTS75	102103
United Arab Rep	UK Great Britain	31 Mar 49	83UNTS139	101106
Belgium	Bolivia	26 Apr 49	34UNTS103	100530
ITU (Telecommun)	United Nations	26 Apr 49	30UNTS315	200175
Multilateral		28 Apr 49	83UNTS105	101105
Multilateral		05 May 49	87UNTS103	101168
Pan Am Health Org	WHO (World Health)	24 May 49	32UNTS387	200178
Norway	USA (United States)	25 May 49	32UNTS345	100507
Costa Rica	USA (United States)	31 May 49	80UNTS3	101041
Multilateral		20 Jun 49	128UNTS141	101718
El Salvador	USA (United States)	27 Jul 49	180UNTS219	102387
Iran	USA (United States)	01 Sep 49	79UNTS155	101039
Belgium	Netherlands	07 Sep 49	117UNTS3	101581
Belgium	France	07 Sep 49	123UNTS13	101651

Funding procedures (Cont.)

PARTY ONE	PARTY TWO	DATE	CITATION	NUMBER
Belgium	UK Great Britain	07 Sep 49	106UNTS61	101457
Denmark	ICAO (Civil Aviat)	09 Sep 49	53UNTS341	100791
Multilateral		15 Sep 49	53UNTS235	100783
Multilateral		24 Sep 49	126UNTS237	101691
Czechoslovakia	UK Great Britain	28 Sep 49	86UNTS141	101156
Multilateral		27 Oct 49	53UNTS241	100784
United Arab Rep	USA (United States)	03 Nov 49	71UNTS31	100908
Australia	USA (United States)	26 Nov 49	45UNTS133	100695
Germany, West	USA (United States)	15 Dec 49	92UNTS269	101277
UK Great Britain	Yugoslavia	26 Dec 49	87UNTS71	101167
Turkey	USA (United States)	27 Dec 49	98UNTS141	101361
Norway	Sweden	28 Jan 50	202UNTS151	102730
India	USA (United States)	02 Feb 50	89UNTS127	101214
UNICEF (Children)	UK Great Britain	10 Feb 50	65UNTS86	100837
United Nations	WHO (World Health)	10 Feb 50	46UNTS327	200188
ICJ Option Clause	Liechtenstein	10 Mar 50	51UNTS115	100758
Indonesia	USA (United States)	24 Mar 50	92UNTS387	101281
Korea, South	USA (United States)	28 Apr 50	93UNTS21	101284
Austria	USA (United States)	06 Jun 50	92UNTS201	101273
Brazil	UNICEF (Children)	09 Jun 50	66UNTS75	100848
Netherlands	IRO (Refugee Org)	20 Jun 50	76UNTS55	100979
Multilateral		28 Jun 50	87UNTS153	101170
Thailand	USA (United States)	01 Jul 50	81UNTS61	101063
Taiwan	UNICEF (Children)	19 Jul 50	94UNTS21	101304
Brazil	USA (United States)	16 Aug 50	140UNTS223	101890
WHO (World Health)	United Arab Rep	25 Aug 50	92UNTS39	101259
Pakistan	USA (United States)	23 Sep 50	82UNTS131	101088
UN Relief Palestin	WHO (World Health)	23 Sep 50	103UNTS129	200310
Haiti	USA (United States)	28 Sep 50	162UNTS85	102132
Sweden	UK Great Britain	10 Nov 50	88UNTS265	101198
Bolivia	USA (United States)	22 Nov 50	152UNTS17	102008
Paraguay	USA (United States)	27 Nov 50	122UNTS147	101644
El Salvador	USA (United States)	13 Dec 50	166UNTS149	102188
Multilateral		15 Dec 50	76UNTS120	100985
Italy	Yugoslavia	23 Dec 50	150UNTS199	101974
Italy	Yugoslavia	23 Dec 50	150UNTS191	101973
Brazil	USA (United States)	27 Dec 50	147UNTS33	101926
Colombia	WHO (World Health)	05 Jan 51	102UNTS139	101417
USA (United States)	Yugoslavia	06 Jan 51	122UNTS137	101643
Chile	USA (United States)	16 Jan 51	151UNTS147	101990
Nicaragua	USA (United States)	31 Jan 51	150UNTS3	101960
Nicaragua	USA (United States)	31 Jan 51	160UNTS121	102105
Italy	USA (United States)	13 Feb 51	148UNTS57	101935
Panama	USA (United States)	26 Feb 51	160UNTS153	102106
Jordan	USA (United States)	27 Feb 51	141UNTS55	101905
USA (United States)	Uruguay	07 Mar 51	165UNTS113	102173
Dominican Republic	USA (United States)	16 Mar 51	148UNTS15	101932
Belgium	UK Great Britain	06 Apr 51	110UNTS3	101496
Iraq	USA (United States)	10 Apr 51	151UNTS179	101993
United Nations	WMO (Meteorology)	10 Apr 51	103UNTS245	200415
Multilateral		18 Apr 51	261UNTS140	103729
Honduras	USA (United States)	24 Apr 51	140UNTS287	101894
Haiti	USA (United States)	02 May 51	151UNTS191	101994
Ecuador	USA (United States)	03 May 51	141UNTS27	101902
UK Great Britain	Yugoslavia	10 May 51	102UNTS29	101408
UK Great Britain	USA (United States)	15 Jun 51	141UNTS79	101907
Ethiopia	USA (United States)	16 Jun 51	148UNTS39	101933
Cuba	USA (United States)	20 Jun 51	148UNTS3	101931
Mexico	USA (United States)	27 Jun 51	141UNTS211	101916
Burma	WHO (World Health)	09 Jul 51	104UNTS187	101440
Iraq	USA (United States)	16 Aug 51	147UNTS65	101929
Jordan	UN Relief Palestin	20 Aug 51	120UNTS277	200394
Denmark	USA (United States)	23 Aug 51	147UNTS49	101928
Japan	USA (United States)	28 Aug 51	147UNTS81	101930
Bolivia	United Nations	01 Oct 51	104UNTS263	101447

Funding procedures (Cont.)

PARTY ONE	PARTY TWO	DATE	CITATION	NUMBER
Multilateral		09 Oct 51	220UNTS121	102997
Council of Europe	ILO (Labor Org)	23 Nov 51	126UNTS331	200435
Multilateral		06 Dec 51	425UNTS61	106119
Multilateral		20 Dec 51	163UNTS309	102152
India	USA (United States)	05 Jan 52	157UNTS39	102045
Dominican Republic	USA (United States)	07 Jan 52	174UNTS243	102289
USA (United States)	Yugoslavia	08 Jan 52	152UNTS61	102011
Colombia	USA (United States)	12 Jan 52	168UNTS109	102216
Iran	USA (United States)	20 Jan 52	200UNTS191	102703
Indonesia	United Nations	06 Feb 52	121UNTS3	101621
Jordan	USA (United States)	12 Feb 52	168UNTS25	102211
Multilateral		15 Feb 52	132UNTS51	101751
Multilateral		01 Mar 52	168UNTS9	102210
OAS (Am States)	USA (United States)	03 Mar 52	165UNTS67	102168
El Salvador	USA (United States)	04 Apr 52	177UNTS219	102320
Peru	USA (United States)	09 Apr 52	184UNTS295	102454
Belgium	Greece	24 Apr 52	166UNTS261	102191
Israel	USA (United States)	09 May 52	177UNTS63	102309
Multilateral		09 May 52	205UNTS65	102770
Ethiopia	USA (United States)	15 May 52	180UNTS227	102388
Netherlands	USA (United States)	15 May 52	177UNTS233	102321
Ecuador	USA (United States)	29 May 52	185UNTS203	102471
Chile	WHO (World Health)	31 May 52	136UNTS323	101841
Bolivia	USA (United States)	18 Jun 52	199UNTS211	102686
South Africa	USA (United States)	24 Jun 52	177UNTS241	102322
Panama	USA (United States)	30 Jun 52	181UNTS121	102404
Chile	USA (United States)	30 Jun 52	199UNTS241	102688
Finland	USA (United States)	02 Jul 52	165UNTS203	102177
Multilateral		11 Jul 52	169UNTS3	102220
Mexico	USA (United States)	15 Jul 52	181UNTS263	102416
Germany, West	USA (United States)	18 Jul 52	165UNTS167	102175
Ceylon (Sri Lanka)	USA (United States)	17 Nov 52	180UNTS207	102386
Sweden	USA (United States)	20 Nov 52	177UNTS203	102319
Liberia	USA (United States)	15 Dec 52	185UNTS45	102457
Saudi Arabia	USA (United States)	15 Dec 52	185UNTS67	102459
UK Great Britain	USA (United States)	25 Feb 53	212UNTS157	102868
Germany, West	USA (United States)	27 Feb 53	205UNTS103	102771
United Arab Rep	USA (United States)	12 Mar 53	204UNTS3	102747
United Arab Rep	USA (United States)	19 Mar 53	215UNTS17	102909
Ethiopia	USA (United States)	29 Apr 53	224UNTS121	103073
El Salvador	USA (United States)	14 May 53	234UNTS71	103273
United Arab Rep	USA (United States)	21 May 53	204UNTS29	102748
Jordan	Syria	04 Jun 53	184UNTS15	102437
United Arab Rep	USA (United States)	18 Jun 53	204UNTS55	102749
United Arab Rep	USA (United States)	18 Jun 53	215UNTS45	102910
Liberia	USA (United States)	23 Jun 53	213UNTS37	102879
Liberia	USA (United States)	23 Jun 53	213UNTS57	102880
UK Great Britain	USA (United States)	24 Jun 53	224UNTS141	103074
Ethiopia	USA (United States)	25 Jun 53	212UNTS175	102869
UK Great Britain	USA (United States)	26 Jun 53	183UNTS225	102432
Brazil	USA (United States)	26 Jun 53	336UNTS241	104808
Chile	USA (United States)	27 Jun 53	229UNTS193	103167
Chile	USA (United States)	27 Jun 53	229UNTS53	103160
Saudi Arabia	USA (United States)	29 Jun 53	206UNTS23	102784
Nicaragua	USA (United States)	30 Jun 53	215UNTS133	102917
Afghanistan	USA (United States)	30 Jun 53	215UNTS3	102908
ECSC (Coal/Steel)	ILO (Labor Org)	16 Jul 53	412UNTS273	200591
Spain	USA (United States)	26 Sep 53	207UNTS93	102802
UN Relief Palestin	United Arab Rep	14 Oct 53	190UNTS13	102555
Libya	UK Great Britain	19 Oct 53	186UNTS285	102494
Multilateral		19 Oct 53	207UNTS189	102807
Bulgaria	Greece	05 Dec 53	225UNTS145	103096
Multilateral		11 Dec 53	191UNTS285	102588
Chile	USA (United States)	30 Dec 53	236UNTS41	103315
Bolivia	USA (United States)	15 Jan 54	229UNTS213	103168

PARTY ONE	PARTY TWO	DATE	CITATION	NUMBER
Funding procedures (Cont.)				
Netherlands	USA (United States)	22 Jan 54	190UNTS207	102565
United Arab Rep	USA (United States)	24 Feb 54	236UNTS61	103316
USA (United States)	Yugoslavia	16 Apr 54	237UNTS77	103337
ECSC (Coal/Steel)	USA (United States)	23 Apr 54	229UNTS229	103170
Panama	USA (United States)	11 May 54	236UNTS107	103319
Haiti	USA (United States)	28 May 54	233UNTS281	103267
Ethiopia	USA (United States)	01 Jun 54	232UNTS311	103245
Italy	USA (United States)	16 Jun 54	236UNTS149	103322
Mexico	USA (United States)	17 Jun 54	237UNTS275	103352
Chile	USA (United States)	28 Jun 54	233UNTS3	103246
Ecuador	USA (United States)	30 Jun 54	236UNTS163	103323
Brazil	USA (United States)	30 Jun 54	237UNTS137	103341
Multilateral		30 Jun 54	193UNTS67	102611
El Salvador	USA (United States)	16 Jul 54	237UNTS237	103350
Multilateral		29 Jul 54	249UNTS45	103500
Pakistan	USA (United States)	23 Aug 54	234UNTS243	103287
El Salvador	USA (United States)	31 Aug 54	237UNTS49	103336
Guatemala	USA (United States)	01 Sep 54	199UNTS51	102677
Canada	USA (United States)	10 Sep 54	238UNTS97	103355
UNESCO (Educ/Cult)	UN Special Fund	29 Sep 54	363UNTS367	200572
Pakistan	USA (United States)	11 Jan 55	251UNTS111	103537
Italy	USA (United States)	11 Feb 55	241UNTS91	103426
Iraq	USA (United States)	02 Mar 55	250UNTS229	103526
Mexico	USA (United States)	09 Mar 55	263UNTS247	103776
El Salvador	USA (United States)	21 Mar 55	250UNTS261	103528
Chile	USA (United States)	31 Mar 55	262UNTS19	103736
Philippines	USA (United States)	27 Apr 55	261UNTS351	103733
Peru	USA (United States)	30 Apr 55	263UNTS309	103780
Multilateral		25 May 55	264UNTS117	103791
Canada	USA (United States)	15 Jun 55	235UNTS201	103302
Haiti	USA (United States)	24 Jun 55	264UNTS291	103800
Italy	USA (United States)	30 Jun 55	258UNTS15	103667
Dominican Republic	USA (United States)	30 Jun 55	257UNTS313	103664
Libya	USA (United States)	21 Jul 55	264UNTS247	103796
Libya	USA (United States)	28 Jul 55	270UNTS245	103900
Libya	USA (United States)	28 Jul 55	270UNTS317	103903
Libya	USA (United States)	28 Jul 55	270UNTS269	103901
Brazil	USA (United States)	03 Aug 55	270UNTS71	103893
Bolivia	USA (United States)	03 Aug 55	264UNTS225	103795
El Salvador	USA (United States)	08 Aug 55	264UNTS301	103801
Multilateral		12 Oct 55	560UNTS3	108165
Multilateral		20 Oct 55	378UNTS159	105425
USSR (Soviet Union)	Yugoslavia	19 Dec 55	378UNTS127	105423
Haiti	USA (United States)	28 Dec 55	240UNTS95	103397
USA (United States)	Uruguay	23 Mar 56	376UNTS311	105386
Multilateral		26 Mar 56	259UNTS125	103686
Austria	Hungary	09 Apr 56	438UNTS123	106315
Ceylon (Sri Lanka)	USA (United States)	28 Apr 56	274UNTS35	103956
Peru	USA (United States)	03 May 56	272UNTS59	103931
Multilateral		20 Jun 56	268UNTS3	103850
Israel	USA (United States)	26 Jun 56	257UNTS55	103649
Burma	USA (United States)	30 Jun 56	281UNTS65	104070
Belgium	Germany, West	24 Sep 56	314UNTS195	104549
UN Hi Com Refugees	Sweden	08 Oct 56	428UNTS307	106182
Multilateral		26 Oct 56	276UNTS3	103988
Ecuador	USA (United States)	31 Oct 56	283UNTS151	104114
Argentina	USA (United States)	05 Nov 56	277UNTS143	104004
United Nations	Venezuela	18 Nov 56	588UNTS243	108529
Colombia	USA (United States)	09 Jan 57	462UNTS151	106676
Norway	USSR (Soviet Union)	15 Feb 57	312UNTS289	104523
Iceland	USA (United States)	23 Feb 57	283UNTS73	104107
Canada	USA (United States)	26 Feb 57	279UNTS179	104039
Multilateral		25 Mar 57	294UNTS2	104300
Morocco	USA (United States)	02 Apr 57	288UNTS157	104203
Paraguay	USA (United States)	04 Apr 57	284UNTS161	104135

PARTY ONE	PARTY TWO	DATE	CITATION	NUMBER
Funding procedures (Cont.)				
Canada	USA (United States)	09 Apr 57	283UNTS217	104119
Multilateral		12 Apr 57	443UNTS128	106362
Ethiopia	USA (United States)	25 Apr 57	283UNTS205	104118
Ghana	USA (United States)	03 Jun 57	284UNTS63	104129
Argentina	USA (United States)	03 Jun 57	291UNTS61	104244
Jordan	USA (United States)	27 Jun 57	288UNTS269	104209
France	USA (United States)	23 Sep 57	293UNTS297	104297
USA (United States)	Venezuela	24 Sep 57	293UNTS307	104298
Brazil	USA (United States)	05 Nov 57	303UNTS3	104368
Argentina	Denmark	25 Nov 57	299UNTS83	104308
Japan	USA (United States)	11 Jan 58	304UNTS35	104390
Bulgaria	Yugoslavia	04 Apr 58	367UNTS89	105228
Saudi Arabia	USA (United States)	01 May 58	315UNTS221	104571
Philippines	USA (United States)	30 Jun 58	321UNTS51	104653
Australia	New Zealand	30 Sep 58	340UNTS61	104859
FAO (Food Agri)	IAEA (Atom Energy)	01 Oct 58	361UNTS211	200571
IAEA (Atom Energy)	UNESCO (Educ/Cult)	01 Oct 58	339UNTS373	200558
Spain	USA (United States)	16 Oct 58	336UNTS153	104804
Finland	Sweden	16 Oct 58	428UNTS125	106171
IMCO (Maritime Org)	United Nations	13 Jan 59	324UNTS273	200553
Mexico	United Nations	07 Apr 59	381UNTS123	105468
Hungary	USSR (Soviet Union)	17 Apr 59	439UNTS41	106324
IAEA (Atom Energy)	ILO (Labor Org)	08 May 59	328UNTS273	200555
IMCO (Maritime Org)	United Nations	23 Jun 59	336UNTS317	200556
IAEA (Atom Energy)	WMO (Meteorology)	12 Aug 59	341UNTS341	200561
Peru	USA (United States)	22 Aug 59	357UNTS99	105109
FAO (Food Agri)	UN Special Fund	28 Sep 59	341UNTS353	200562
United Arab Rep	USA (United States)	28 Sep 59	358UNTS97	105128
IAEA (Atom Energy)	ICAO (Civil Aviat)	01 Oct 59	361UNTS193	200570
Multilateral		09 Oct 59	376UNTS382	105391
ILO (Labor Org)	UN Special Fund	12 Oct 59	343UNTS325	200563
Sudan	United Arab Rep	08 Nov 59	453UNTS51	106519
UN Special Fund	WMO (Meteorology)	17 Nov 59	345UNTS311	200564
Multilateral		18 Nov 59	390UNTS227	105610
Multilateral		19 Nov 59	410UNTS156	105902
Guinea	UN Special Fund	02 Dec 59	345UNTS215	104969
Multilateral		14 Dec 59	368UNTS253	105245
Colombia	USA (United States)	11 Jan 60	371UNTS37	105268
ITU (Telecommun)	United Nations	14 Jan 60	348UNTS331	200566
Multilateral		26 Jan 60	439UNTS249	106333
Multilateral		06 Feb 60	383UNTS3	105494
Multilateral		26 Feb 60	418UNTS171	106022
Portugal	USA (United States)	19 Mar 60	371UNTS131	105275
ICAO (Civil Aviat)	UN Special Fund	21 Apr 60	360UNTS367	200569
UN Special Fund	WHO (World Health)	25 May 60	359UNTS375	200568
Multilateral		19 Jun 60	537UNTS214	107803
Belgium	Netherlands	20 Jun 60	423UNTS19	106084
ITU (Telecommun)	UN Special Fund	13 Jul 60	368UNTS329	200573
USA (United States)	Uruguay	22 Jul 60	388UNTS315	105587
Congo (Zaire)	United Nations	23 Aug 60	373UNTS327	200576
Korea, South	USA (United States)	18 Nov 60	400UNTS49	105747
Multilateral		13 Dec 60	455UNTS204	106544
Israel	USA (United States)	19 Dec 60	401UNTS195	105772
Togo	USA (United States)	22 Dec 60	401UNTS33	105760
Inter-Am Nuc Energ	IAEA (Atom Energy)	22 Dec 60	396UNTS285	200586
Thailand	USA (United States)	23 Dec 60	405UNTS135	105830
Belgium	Netherlands	24 Feb 61	474UNTS167	106881
Multilateral		27 Mar 61	420UNTS109	106043
Norway	IAEA (Atom Energy)	10 Apr 61	402UNTS255	105790
Multilateral		14 Apr 61	422UNTS101	106071
Ivory Coast	USA (United States)	17 May 61	409UNTS241	105889
Australia	USA (United States)	22 May 61	419UNTS3	106026
Cameroon	USA (United States)	26 May 61	413UNTS195	105953
Niger	USA (United States)	26 May 61	410UNTS213	105905
Dahomey	USA (United States)	27 May 61	445UNTS23	106373

Funding procedures (Cont.)

PARTY ONE	PARTY TWO	DATE	CITATION	NUMBER
Nepal	USA (United States)	09 Jun 61	421UNTS223	106061
Congo (Zaire)	United Nations	12 Jun 61	494UNTS205	107234
Inter-Am Devel Bnk	USA (United States)	19 Jun 61	410UNTS34	105895
Madagascar	USA (United States)	22 Jun 61	413UNTS219	105956
Netherlands	Euratom	25 Jul 61	462UNTS263	106686
Ghana	United Nations	29 Aug 61	406UNTS117	105843
Fed of Malaya	USA (United States)	04 Sep 61	421UNTS215	106060
Paraguay	USA (United States)	26 Sep 61	461UNTS91	106653
Austria	USA (United States)	03 Oct 61	426UNTS187	106137
Brazil	USA (United States)	11 Nov 61	433UNTS199	106243
United Arab Rep	UK Great Britain	14 Nov 61	449UNTS129	106455
El Salvador	USA (United States)	20 Nov 61	433UNTS221	106245
OAS (Am States)	USA (United States)	29 Nov 61	424UNTS119	106104
IAEA (Atom Energy)	UN Special Fund	29 Nov 61	415UNTS408	200593
Ethiopia	USA (United States)	06 Dec 61	433UNTS231	106246
COMECON (Econ Aid)	USSR (Soviet Union)	07 Dec 61	506UNTS325	107392
Tanganyika	UK Great Britain	09 Dec 61	437UNTS47	106299
Panama	USA (United States)	11 Dec 61	445UNTS161	106384
El Salvador	USA (United States)	19 Dec 61	445UNTS175	106385
Costa Rica	USA (United States)	22 Dec 61	460UNTS277	106646
Sierra Leone	USA (United States)	29 Dec 61	434UNTS43	106254
Ghana	USA (United States)	03 Jan 62	433UNTS147	106237
Dominican Republic	USA (United States)	11 Jan 62	433UNTS133	106236
Cyprus	USA (United States)	18 Jan 62	435UNTS3	106266
UNESCO (Educ/Cult)	USA (United States)	19 Jan 62	435UNTS99	106272
Ghana	USA (United States)	24 Jan 62	435UNTS23	106268
Multilateral		20 Feb 62	597UNTS159	108644
IDA (Devel Assoc)	UK Great Britain	13 Mar 62	466UNTS331	106753
Multilateral		29 Mar 62	507UNTS177	107401
Brazil	USA (United States)	13 Apr 62	445UNTS227	106391
Ecuador	USA (United States)	17 Apr 62	442UNTS69	106339
Ivory Coast	USA (United States)	21 Apr 62	526UNTS39	107598
Dominican Republic	USA (United States)	02 May 62	442UNTS107	106342
Ethiopia	USA (United States)	23 May 62	456UNTS293	106563
Multilateral		25 May 62	486UNTS103	107075
Australia	UK Great Britain	28 May 62	434UNTS219	106264
Denmark	USA (United States)	28 May 62	450UNTS215	106469
Pakistan	USA (United States)	31 May 62	460UNTS75	106631
Multilateral		14 Jun 62	528UNTS33	107634
Bolivia	USA (United States)	19 Jun 62	458UNTS239	106606
Israel	USA (United States)	22 Jun 62	448UNTS273	106440
Germany, West	United Nations	28 Jun 62	434UNTS249	200597
Honduras	USA (United States)	20 Jul 62	460UNTS125	106635
Czechoslovakia	COMECON (Econ Aid)	20 Jul 62	506UNTS345	107393
Colombia	USA (United States)	23 Jul 62	458UNTS123	106595
Niger	USA (United States)	23 Jul 62	487UNTS325	107114
Cyprus	USA (United States)	23 Aug 62	461UNTS147	106658
Nepal	USA (United States)	24 Aug 62	460UNTS143	106637
Italy	USA (United States)	28 Aug 62	461UNTS137	106657
Togo	USA (United States)	05 Sep 62	461UNTS47	106650
Iran	United Nations	05 Sep 62	442UNTS249	106353
Afghanistan	USA (United States)	11 Sep 62	461UNTS169	106661
Austria	Czechoslovakia	22 Sep 62	495UNTS157	107244
Multilateral		28 Sep 62	469UNTS169	106791
Gabon	USA (United States)	04 Oct 62	459UNTS185	106620
Multilateral		05 Oct 62	502UNTS225	107333
Tunisia	USA (United States)	29 Oct 62	462UNTS201	106679
Czechoslovakia	Poland	16 Nov 62	526UNTS3	107597
Germany, West	USA (United States)	20 Nov 62	505UNTS263	107377
Ceylon (Sri Lanka)	USA (United States)	21 Nov 62	462UNTS237	106683
India	USA (United States)	21 Nov 62	462UNTS255	106685
Costa Rica	USA (United States)	23 Nov 62	541UNTS67	107861
Multilateral		12 Dec 62	552UNTS15	108048
Guinea	USA (United States)	14 Dec 62	462UNTS247	106684
Canada	USA (United States)	28 Dec 62	471UNTS13	106818

Funding procedures (Cont.)

PARTY ONE	PARTY TWO	DATE	CITATION	NUMBER
Malaysia	USA (United States)	28 Jan 63	473UNTS15	106850
India	USA (United States)	01 Feb 63	473UNTS37	106852
Central Afri Rep	USA (United States)	10 Feb 63	473UNTS83	106857
Poland	COMECON (Econ Aid)	22 Feb 63	506UNTS303	107391
Hungary	COMECON (Econ Aid)	28 Feb 63	506UNTS281	107390
Israel	USA (United States)	21 Mar 63	476UNTS131	106907
Philippines	USA (United States)	23 Mar 63	474UNTS80	106873
Brazil	USA (United States)	29 Mar 63	476UNTS67	106904
Multilateral		20 Apr 63	495UNTS3	107239
Jordan	UK Great Britain	27 Apr 63	475UNTS169	106892
Algeria	Morocco	30 Apr 63	564UNTS3	108217
El Salvador	USA (United States)	07 May 63	476UNTS35	106901
Thailand	USA (United States)	24 May 63	477UNTS123	106918
Australia	UK Great Britain	06 Jun 63	472UNTS157	106838
Korea, South	USA (United States)	18 Jun 63	487UNTS297	107112
India	USA (United States)	19 Jun 63	479UNTS175	106952
Austria	USA (United States)	25 Jun 63	479UNTS223	106956
Poland	United Nations	16 Jul 63	471UNTS3	106817
Algeria	Mali	22 Jul 63	564UNTS29	108219
Italy	United Nations	26 Jul 63	472UNTS173	106840
USA (United States)	Uruguay	31 Jul 63	488UNTS3	107115
Afghanistan	USA (United States)	20 Aug 63	488UNTS41	107118
Paraguay	USA (United States)	20 Aug 63	531UNTS197	107704
Argentina	USA (United States)	21 Aug 63	488UNTS61	107119
Ecuador	USA (United States)	20 Sep 63	488UNTS147	107125
Hungary	Yugoslavia	15 Oct 63	577UNTS49	108372
Czechoslovakia	Hungary	22 Oct 63	514UNTS95	107444
Multilateral		23 Oct 63	506UNTS197	107388
Jamaica	USA (United States)	24 Oct 63	489UNTS337	107148
Iran	USA (United States)	24 Oct 63	489UNTS303	107146
Panama	USA (United States)	30 Oct 63	530UNTS3	107668
UNESCO (Educ/Cult)	United Arab Rep	09 Nov 63	489UNTS233	107142
Tunisia	USA (United States)	18 Nov 63	494UNTS193	107233
Romania	Yugoslavia	30 Nov 63	512UNTS2	107438
Multilateral		03 Dec 63	529UNTS217	107663
Greece	USA (United States)	13 Dec 63	494UNTS55	107226
Cameroon	Netherlands	18 Dec 63	521UNTS303	107527
Chile	IBRD (World Bank)	18 Dec 63	504UNTS29	107352
Subsahara Tech Com	IAEA (Atom Energy)	06 Feb 64	501UNTS285	200606
IMCO (Maritime Org)	United Nations	11 Feb 64	489UNTS357	200605
Iceland	USA (United States)	13 Feb 64	524UNTS235	107576
Italy	United Nations	18 Mar 64	491UNTS21	107171
Spain	USA (United States)	18 Mar 64	535UNTS343	107789
Liberia	USA (United States)	08 May 64	526UNTS239	107608
Austria	United Nations	11 Jun 64	500UNTS85	107309
Colombia	Netherlands	06 Jul 64	543UNTS289	107906
Mexico	United Nations	17 Jul 64	533UNTS117	107738
Multilateral		28 Jul 64	555UNTS183	108113
Australia	USA (United States)	28 Aug 64	510UNTS201	107415
Ceylon (Sri Lanka)	USA (United States)	29 Aug 64	531UNTS93	107695
Multilateral		18 Sep 64	556UNTS25	108117
Multilateral		18 Sep 64	555UNTS205	108114
Multilateral		21 Sep 64	555UNTS227	108115
Australia	UN Special Fund	30 Sep 64	510UNTS277	107419
Multilateral		30 Sep 64	556UNTS3	108116
Czechoslovakia	Mongolia	21 Oct 64	545UNTS91	107926
USA (United States)	Yugoslavia	09 Nov 64	533UNTS39	107731
Multilateral		25 Nov 64	587UNTS19	108507
Multilateral		02 Dec 64	572UNTS229	108317
WHO (World Health)	Tunisia	27 Jan 65	528UNTS209	107644
Peru	USA (United States)	28 Jan 65	587UNTS273	108513
Belgium	Congo (Zaire)	06 Feb 65	540UNTS275	107853
Multilateral		24 Feb 65	556UNTS47	108118
Multilateral		26 Feb 65	556UNTS69	108119
Malawi	USA (United States)	20 Apr 65	546UNTS175	107943

PARTY ONE	PARTY TWO	DATE	CITATION	NUMBER
Funding procedures (Cont.)				
UK Great Britain	USA (United States)	10 May 65	545UNTS181	107934
Multilateral		04 Dec 65	571UNTS123	108303
Monaco	United Nations	17 Dec 65	550UNTS365	200615
IDA (Devel Assoc)	UK Great Britain	08 Feb 66	567UNTS207	108257
Italy	United Nations	23 May 66	565UNTS11	108231
Multilateral		20 Jun 66	572UNTS263	108318
United Nations	Tunisia	04 Aug 66	576UNTS23	108363
Multilateral		23 Sep 66	573UNTS132	108327
Indonesia	USA (United States)	30 Sep 66	616UNTS199	108897
Multilateral		25 Jan 67	588UNTS212	108527
Multilateral		17 Mar 67	594UNTS105	108598
Ghana	United Nations	08 Apr 67	594UNTS149	108601
Garnishment of funds				
Nepal	USA (United States)	23 Jan 51	184UNTS65	102439
Israel	USA (United States)	07 Dec 51	157UNTS53	102046
Jordan	USA (United States)	20 Dec 51	157UNTS69	102048
Germany, West	USA (United States)	28 Dec 51	181UNTS45	102397
Cambodia	USA (United States)	28 Dec 51	179UNTS97	102358
Thailand	USA (United States)	29 Dec 51	179UNTS113	102360
Laos	USA (United States)	31 Dec 51	198UNTS243	102668
Taiwan	USA (United States)	02 Jan 52	181UNTS161	102407
Austria	USA (United States)	05 Jan 52	179UNTS73	102355
Indonesia	USA (United States)	05 Jan 52	215UNTS121	102916
India	USA (United States)	05 Jan 52	157UNTS39	102045
Korea, South	USA (United States)	07 Jan 52	179UNTS105	102359
Italy	USA (United States)	07 Jan 52	179UNTS165	102365
Greece	USA (United States)	07 Jan 52	180UNTS171	102382
El Salvador	USA (United States)	07 Jan 52	198UNTS231	102667
Philippines	USA (United States)	07 Jan 52	179UNTS193	102368
Belgium	USA (United States)	07 Jan 52	179UNTS81	102356
Turkey	USA (United States)	07 Jan 52	179UNTS121	102361
Dominican Republic	USA (United States)	07 Jan 52	174UNTS243	102289
UK Great Britain	USA (United States)	08 Jan 52	179UNTS201	102369
Netherlands	USA (United States)	08 Jan 52	179UNTS175	102366
UK Great Britain	USA (United States)	08 Jan 52	126UNTS307	101696
Guatemala	USA (United States)	08 Jan 52	181UNTS31	102395
Denmark	USA (United States)	08 Jan 52	179UNTS65	102354
Luxembourg	USA (United States)	08 Jan 52	180UNTS191	102384
Iceland	USA (United States)	08 Jan 52	180UNTS183	102383
Norway	USA (United States)	08 Jan 52	179UNTS185	102367
USA (United States)	Vietnam, South	19 Jan 52	205UNTS127	102772
Ecuador	USA (United States)	20 Feb 52	177UNTS43	102308
Peru	USA (United States)	22 Feb 52	165UNTS31	102166
Israel	USA (United States)	27 Feb 52	177UNTS123	102314
Honduras	USA (United States)	07 Mar 52	233UNTS151	103260
Cuba	USA (United States)	07 Mar 52	165UNTS11	102165
Chile	USA (United States)	09 Apr 52	186UNTS53	102482
Colombia	USA (United States)	17 Apr 52	174UNTS215	102287
Israel	USA (United States)	09 May 52	177UNTS269	102326
Israel	USA (United States)	09 May 52	177UNTS63	102309
Ethiopia	USA (United States)	15 May 52	180UNTS227	102388
Korea, South	USA (United States)	24 May 52	179UNTS23	102353
Brazil	USA (United States)	30 Jun 52	185UNTS79	102460
Chile	USA (United States)	30 Jun 52	199UNTS241	102688
Panama	USA (United States)	30 Jun 52	181UNTS121	102404
USA (United States)	Uruguay	30 Jun 52	207UNTS139	102804
Ethiopia	USA (United States)	07 Nov 52	184UNTS285	102453
Dominican Republic	USA (United States)	06 Mar 53	199UNTS267	102689
United Arab Rep	USA (United States)	12 Mar 53	204UNTS3	102747
United Arab Rep	USA (United States)	19 Mar 53	215UNTS17	102909
El Salvador	USA (United States)	14 May 53	234UNTS71	103273
United Arab Rep	USA (United States)	21 May 53	204UNTS29	102748
Colombia	USA (United States)	09 Jun 53	213UNTS3	102877
Liberia	USA (United States)	23 Jun 53	213UNTS37	102879

PARTY ONE	PARTY TWO	DATE	CITATION	NUMBER
Garnishment of funds (Cont.)				
Philippines	USA (United States)	26 Jun 53	213UNTS77	102881
Spain	USA (United States)	26 Sep 53	207UNTS61	102800
Spain	USA (United States)	26 Sep 53	207UNTS93	102802
Israel	USA (United States)	25 Nov 53	219UNTS205	102976
Bolivia	USA (United States)	15 Jan 54	229UNTS213	103168
United Arab Rep	USA (United States)	24 Feb 54	236UNTS61	103316
Japan	USA (United States)	08 Mar 54	232UNTS169	103236
Iraq	USA (United States)	21 Apr 54	222UNTS251	103032
Pakistan	USA (United States)	19 May 54	202UNTS301	102736
Honduras	USA (United States)	20 May 54	222UNTS87	103025
Ethiopia	USA (United States)	01 Jun 54	232UNTS311	103245
Ethiopia	USA (United States)	12 Jun 54	234UNTS25	103270
Italy	USA (United States)	28 Jun 54	237UNTS121	103340
Guatemala	USA (United States)	01 Sep 54	199UNTS51	102677
Pakistan	USA (United States)	11 Jan 55	251UNTS111	103537
Haiti	USA (United States)	28 Jan 55	270UNTS83	103894
Peru	USA (United States)	30 Apr 55	263UNTS309	103780
Multilateral		25 May 55	264UNTS117	103791
Guatemala	USA (United States)	18 Jun 55	262UNTS105	103740
Germany, West	USA (United States)	30 Jun 55	240UNTS47	103393
Libya	USA (United States)	21 Jul 55	264UNTS247	103796
Ethiopia	Italy	05 Mar 56	267UNTS189	103844
USA (United States)	Uruguay	23 Mar 56	376UNTS311	105386
Ceylon (Sri Lanka)	USA (United States)	28 Apr 56	274UNTS35	103956
Libya	USA (United States)	04 Apr 57	283UNTS181	104116
Ethiopia	USA (United States)	25 Apr 57	283UNTS205	104118
Argentina	USA (United States)	03 Jun 57	291UNTS61	104244
Ghana	USA (United States)	03 Jun 57	284UNTS63	104129
Libya	USA (United States)	30 Jun 57	284UNTS177	104136
Multilateral		26 Jan 60	439UNTS249	106333
Togo	USA (United States)	22 Dec 60	401UNTS33	105760
Italy	New Zealand	25 Jan 61	435UNTS255	106282
Sierra Leone	USA (United States)	05 May 61	409UNTS194	105885
Senegal	USA (United States)	13 May 61	409UNTS232	105888
Ivory Coast	USA (United States)	17 May 61	409UNTS241	105889
Cameroon	USA (United States)	26 May 61	413UNTS195	105953
Niger	USA (United States)	26 May 61	410UNTS213	105905
Dahomey	USA (United States)	27 May 61	445UNTS23	106373
Madagascar	USA (United States)	22 Jun 61	413UNTS219	105956
Iran	USA (United States)	21 Dec 61	433UNTS269	106249
Dominican Republic	USA (United States)	08 Mar 62	527UNTS29	107615
Central Afri Rep	USA (United States)	10 Feb 63	473UNTS83	106857
Inadequacy of funds				
Multilateral		27 Dec 45	2UNTS39	100020
Albania	Yugoslavia	03 Oct 46	111UNTS227	101537
Colombia	IBRD (World Bank)	02 Nov 50	158UNTS59	102062
Colombia	USA (United States)	09 Mar 51	141UNTS15	101901
Greece	Italy	04 Feb 53	189UNTS295	102552
Czechoslovakia	Denmark	23 Apr 53	174UNTS107	102281
Czechoslovakia	Greece	01 Feb 54	225UNTS95	103092
Multilateral		25 Feb 54	215UNTS249	102922
Greece	Spain	15 May 54	299UNTS277	104319
Greece	Romania	19 May 54	225UNTS27	103084
Greece	Hungary	05 Jun 54	299UNTS295	104321
USSR (Soviet Union)	Yugoslavia	05 Jan 55	240UNTS225	103405
Argentina	UK Great Britain	31 Mar 55	210UNTS223	102840
Israel	Yugoslavia	11 Dec 58	386UNTS283	105548
Nicaragua	USA (United States)	30 Mar 62	456UNTS241	106559
United Arab Rep	USSR (Soviet Union)	23 Jun 62	472UNTS19	106835
Multilateral		08 Dec 62	510UNTS235	107418
Internal finance				
Guatemala	USA (United States)	19 May 43	28UNTS377	200161
Belgium	UK Great Britain	05 Oct 44	5UNTS227	200031
Sweden	UK Great Britain	06 Mar 45	82UNTS219	101095

PARTY ONE	PARTY TWO	DATE	CITATION	NUMBER
Internal finance (Cont.)				
Belgium	Norway	23 Oct 45	16UNTS311	200107
Norway	UK Great Britain	08 Nov 45	5UNTS27	100063
Multilateral		27 Dec 45	2UNTS39	100020
Greece	UK Great Britain	24 Jan 46	6UNTS45	100067
Switzerland	UK Great Britain	12 Mar 46	6UNTS107	100070
Portugal	UK Great Britain	16 Apr 46	6UNTS119	100071
Argentina	UK Great Britain	17 Sep 46	88UNTS47	101185
Spain	UK Great Britain	28 Mar 47	66UNTS91	100849
Austria	USA (United States)	23 Mar 49	43UNTS127	100667
Panama	USA (United States)	31 Mar 49	55UNTS141	100812
Norway	Portugal	28 Nov 49	47UNTS117	100726
Sweden	UK Great Britain	30 Dec 49	87UNTS59	101166
Costa Rica	USA (United States)	04 Apr 50	132UNTS177	101759
Denmark	UK Great Britain	19 Oct 50	79UNTS25	101028
Multilateral		06 Mar 51	106UNTS141	101461
Portugal	UK Great Britain	20 Jul 51	105UNTS61	101453
Multilateral		20 Dec 51	163UNTS309	102152
Germany, West	USA (United States)	27 Feb 53	224UNTS13	103067
Germany, West	USA (United States)	27 Feb 53	223UNTS167	103065
Germany, West	UK Great Britain	22 May 53	172UNTS179	102246
Bulgaria	Yugoslavia	15 Nov 55	396UNTS191	105697
Spain	USA (United States)	27 Jan 58	303UNTS247	104384
Congo (Zaire)	United Nations	12 Jun 61	494UNTS205	107234
Laos	UK Great Britain	24 Dec 63	502UNTS189	107330
Multilateral		31 Dec 65	616UNTS317	108904
Pakistan	IDA (Devel Assoc)	17 Jun 66	582UNTS297	108468
Interest rates				
Bolivia	Brazil	25 Feb 38	88UNTS379	200254
Bolivia	Brazil	25 Feb 38	51UNTS245	200192
Netherlands	UK Great Britain	13 Jun 39	5UNTS65	200028
Netherlands	UK Great Britain	14 Jun 40	2UNTS251	200018
France	Netherlands	14 Jun 40	2UNTS263	200019
Brazil	Paraguay	14 Apr 41	54UNTS269	200199
UK Great Britain	USSR (Soviet Union)	16 Aug 41	91UNTS341	200269
Mexico	USA (United States)	19 Nov 41	148UNTS367	200474
Mexico	USA (United States)	19 Nov 41	125UNTS287	200430
Mexico	USA (United States)	29 Sep 43	106UNTS265	200345
Multilateral		21 Oct 43	2UNTS281	200021
UK Great Britain	USSR (Soviet Union)	23 Sep 44	10UNTS171	200060
Canada	Czechoslovakia	01 Mar 45	45UNTS283	200185
France	UK Great Britain	27 Mar 45	98UNTS227	200274
Canada	Norway	25 Jun 45	45UNTS297	200186
Netherlands	Switzerland	24 Oct 45	3UNTS73	100025
Belgium	Canada	25 Oct 45	230UNTS127	103180
Netherlands	Norway	06 Nov 45	2UNTS5	100017
Finland	Norway	27 Nov 45	17UNTS247	100279
Netherlands	Sweden	30 Nov 45	2UNTS27	100019
UK Great Britain	USA (United States)	06 Dec 45	126UNTS13	101679
Multilateral		27 Dec 45	2UNTS39	100020
Greece	UK Great Britain	24 Jan 46	6UNTS45	100067
Denmark	Netherlands	31 Jan 46	3UNTS3	100021
Canada	Netherlands	05 Feb 46	43UNTS3	100658
Mexico	UK Great Britain	07 Feb 46	6UNTS55	100068
Canada	Taiwan	07 Feb 46	43UNTS23	100659
Canada	UK Great Britain	06 Mar 46	20UNTS13	100312
Canada	France	09 Apr 46	43UNTS43	100660
Poland	USA (United States)	22 Apr 46	406UNTS215	105851
France	UK Great Britain	29 Apr 46	98UNTS123	101360
Greece	USA (United States)	16 May 46	184UNTS230	102451
France	USA (United States)	28 May 46	84UNTS59	101119
Taiwan	USA (United States)	14 Jun 46	4UNTS253	100049
Romania	Yugoslavia	26 Jun 46	116UNTS21	101566
Albania	Yugoslavia	01 Jul 46	111UNTS81	101518
Italy	Norway	20 Jul 46	17UNTS273	100281

PARTY ONE	PARTY TWO	DATE	CITATION	NUMBER
Interest rates (Cont.)				
Denmark	New Zealand	18 Sep 46	10UNTS39	100141
Norway	Sweden	22 Nov 46	15UNTS171	100233
Norway	Poland	03 Dec 46	15UNTS203	100234
Hungary	Yugoslavia	23 Dec 46	113UNTS125	101549
Australia	Netherlands	24 Jan 47	10UNTS77	100144
Belgium	Czechoslovakia	19 Mar 47	23UNTS35	100341
Bulgaria	Denmark	09 May 47	74UNTS139	100960
Poland	Yugoslavia	24 May 47	115UNTS69	101558
New Zealand	UK Great Britain	27 May 47	17UNTS211	100277
Netherlands	USA (United States)	28 May 47	17UNTS29	100267
Albania	Yugoslavia	12 Jun 47	111UNTS195	101534
Albania	Yugoslavia	22 Jun 47	111UNTS207	101536
France	New Zealand	02 Jul 47	16UNTS219	100263
Haiti	USA (United States)	04 Jul 47	22UNTS165	100335
UK Great Britain	Uruguay	15 Jul 47	71UNTS179	100918
Norway	Switzerland	15 Jul 47	12UNTS351	100192
USSR (Soviet Union)	Yugoslavia	25 Jul 47	130UNTS315	101732
Netherlands	IBRD (World Bank)	07 Aug 47	152UNTS165	102015
Denmark	IBRD (World Bank)	22 Aug 47	152UNTS223	102016
USSR (Soviet Union)	Yugoslavia	23 Aug 47	116UNTS281	101577
Luxembourg	IBRD (World Bank)	28 Aug 47	153UNTS3	102017
Multilateral		19 Sep 47	30UNTS269	100462
Multilateral		19 Sep 47	30UNTS249	100461
Romania	Yugoslavia	30 Sep 47	116UNTS71	101570
Multilateral		05 Oct 47	34UNTS23	100525
South Africa	UK Great Britain	09 Oct 47	17UNTS239	100278
Brazil	Netherlands	06 Nov 47	53UNTS59	100773
Greece	Norway	08 Dec 47	30UNTS171	100455
Czechoslovakia	New Zealand	22 Jan 48	16UNTS229	100264
France	Lebanon	24 Jan 48	173UNTS99	102263
Denmark	Hungary	28 Feb 48	85UNTS35	101144
Netherlands	UK Great Britain	11 Mar 48	77UNTS69	100993
Hungary	Yugoslavia	18 Mar 48	113UNTS201	101551
Denmark	Norway	21 Apr 48	18UNTS139	100284
Norway	Sweden	29 Apr 48	26UNTS11	100374
Czechoslovakia	Yugoslavia	24 May 48	112UNTS225	101545
Czechoslovakia	Yugoslavia	24 May 48	112UNTS183	101543
Chile	UK Great Britain	24 Jun 48	77UNTS113	100995
France	UK Great Britain	12 Jul 48	90UNTS83	101230
Korea, South	USA (United States)	11 Sep 48	89UNTS155	101216
France	USA (United States)	22 Oct 48	84UNTS173	101128
Austria	Denmark	29 Nov 48	74UNTS257	100968
Argentina	Denmark	14 Dec 48	74UNTS41	100956
Denmark	Poland	14 Dec 48	81UNTS33	101060
Belgium	Greece	27 Dec 48	77UNTS293	101005
Denmark	Greece	25 Feb 49	78UNTS335	101023
Belgium	Portugal	01 Mar 49	32UNTS49	100488
Belgium	IBRD (World Bank)	01 Mar 49	154UNTS133	102029
Germany, West	Greece	16 Mar 49	77UNTS327	101007
Denmark	Finland	22 Mar 49	33UNTS247	100520
Finland	Greece	24 Mar 49	78UNTS13	101009
Denmark	Portugal	08 Apr 49	74UNTS221	100965
Belgium	Bolivia	26 Apr 49	34UNTS103	100530
Denmark	Poland	12 May 49	87UNTS179	101172
Greece	Turkey	21 Jul 49	78UNTS65	101012
Multilateral		10 Aug 49	45UNTS3	100689
India	IBRD (World Bank)	18 Aug 49	154UNTS269	102031
Belgium	Netherlands	07 Sep 49	117UNTS3	101581
Belgium	France	07 Sep 49	123UNTS13	101651
Belgium	UK Great Britain	07 Sep 49	106UNTS61	101457
Argentina	Norway	09 Sep 49	42UNTS125	100646
IBRD (World Bank)	Yugoslavia	17 Sep 49	155UNTS3	102034
India	IBRD (World Bank)	29 Sep 49	154UNTS393	102033
Finland	IBRD (World Bank)	17 Oct 49	156UNTS355	200481
Italy	Norway	19 Nov 49	47UNTS89	100724

PARTY ONE	PARTY TWO	DATE	CITATION	NUMBER
Interest rates (Cont.)				
Denmark	Germany, West	15 Dec 49	51UNTS11	100749
Czechoslovakia	Denmark	17 Dec 49	74UNTS159	100962
Norway	Poland	21 Dec 49	47UNTS107	100725
Greece	Portugal	31 Dec 49	92UNTS83	101263
Australia	Ceylon (Sri Lanka)	12 Jan 50	53UNTS295	100789
China People's Rep	USSR (Soviet Union)	14 Feb 50	226UNTS21	103104
Israel	UK Great Britain	30 Mar 50	86UNTS231	101162
India	IBRD (World Bank)	18 Apr 50	155UNTS117	102036
Iraq	IBRD (World Bank)	15 Jun 50	155UNTS267	102038
Multilateral		28 Jun 50	87UNTS153	101170
IBRD (World Bank)	Turkey	07 Jul 50	156UNTS75	102040
IBRD (World Bank)	Turkey	07 Jul 50	156UNTS3	102039
Ethiopia	IBRD (World Bank)	13 Sep 50	157UNTS233	102056
Ethiopia	IBRD (World Bank)	13 Sep 50	157UNTS213	102055
Canada	USSR (Soviet Union)	29 Sep 50	230UNTS371	103197
Denmark	Italy	04 Oct 50	78UNTS353	101025
IBRD (World Bank)	Thailand	27 Oct 50	158UNTS25	102060
IBRD (World Bank)	Thailand	27 Oct 50	158UNTS3	102059
IBRD (World Bank)	Thailand	27 Oct 50	158UNTS43	102061
Philippines	USA (United States)	06 Nov 50	122UNTS63	101637
Australia	IBRD (World Bank)	14 Nov 50	156UNTS147	102041
Italy	Yugoslavia	23 Dec 50	150UNTS191	101973
UK Great Britain	Yugoslavia	28 Dec 50	88UNTS329	101201
Ethiopia	IBRD (World Bank)	19 Feb 51	186UNTS101	102486
Colombia	IBRD (World Bank)	10 Apr 51	158UNTS155	102066
France	UK Great Britain	11 Apr 51	106UNTS3	101456
UK Great Britain	Yugoslavia	10 May 51	102UNTS29	101408
Nicaragua	IBRD (World Bank)	07 Jun 51	158UNTS277	102068
Iceland	IBRD (World Bank)	20 Jun 51	158UNTS301	102069
UK Great Britain	USA (United States)	18 Jul 51	117UNTS49	101583
Belgium	IBRD (World Bank)	13 Sep 51	158UNTS349	102071
Chile	IBRD (World Bank)	10 Oct 51	158UNTS369	102072
Nicaragua	IBRD (World Bank)	29 Oct 51	159UNTS35	102082
Iceland	IBRD (World Bank)	01 Nov 51	159UNTS55	102083
Paraguay	IBRD (World Bank)	07 Dec 51	159UNTS103	102085
Multilateral		20 Dec 51	163UNTS309	102152
Peru	IBRD (World Bank)	23 Jan 52	159UNTS163	102087
Pakistan	IBRD (World Bank)	27 Mar 52	159UNTS251	102090
Greece	Switzerland	04 Apr 52	166UNTS271	102192
Canada	Netherlands	10 Apr 52	233UNTS129	103257
Germany, West	Netherlands	19 May 52	134UNTS3	101794
Pakistan	IBRD (World Bank)	13 Jun 52	191UNTS85	102578
IBRD (World Bank)	Turkey	18 Jun 52	159UNTS269	102091
Brazil	IBRD (World Bank)	27 Jun 52	190UNTS115	102561
Australia	IBRD (World Bank)	08 Jul 52	159UNTS295	102092
Peru	IBRD (World Bank)	08 Jul 52	159UNTS321	102093
Multilateral		11 Jul 52	170UNTS269	102223
Colombia	IBRD (World Bank)	26 Aug 52	159UNTS339	102094
Iceland	IBRD (World Bank)	26 Aug 52	159UNTS363	102095
Denmark	Israel	14 Nov 52	160UNTS289	102114
India	IBRD (World Bank)	23 Jan 53	201UNTS145	102715
Greece	Italy	04 Feb 53	189UNTS295	102552
IBRD (World Bank)	Yugoslavia	11 Feb 53	165UNTS231	102179
Denmark	Germany, West	26 Feb 53	178UNTS3	102332
Germany, West	USA (United States)	27 Feb 53	205UNTS103	102771
Germany, West	USA (United States)	27 Feb 53	224UNTS13	103067
Libya	UK Great Britain	25 Mar 53	172UNTS281	102252
Czechoslovakia	Denmark	23 Apr 53	174UNTS107	102281
Brazil	IBRD (World Bank)	30 Apr 53	190UNTS133	102562
El Salvador	USA (United States)	14 May 53	234UNTS71	103273
Greece	United Arab Rep	21 May 53	256UNTS25	103621
UK Great Britain	USA (United States)	26 Jun 53	183UNTS225	102432
Brazil	USA (United States)	26 Jun 53	336UNTS241	104808
IBRD (World Bank)	South Africa	28 Aug 53	180UNTS73	102376
Nicaragua	IBRD (World Bank)	04 Sep 53	186UNTS117	102487

PARTY ONE	PARTY TWO	DATE	CITATION	NUMBER
Interest rates (Cont.)				
Nicaragua	IBRD (World Bank)	04 Sep 53	186UNTS137	102488
Colombia	IBRD (World Bank)	10 Sep 53	203UNTS3	102738
Bulgaria	Greece	05 Dec 53	225UNTS145	103096
Brazil	IBRD (World Bank)	18 Dec 53	190UNTS179	102564
Brazil	IBRD (World Bank)	18 Dec 53	301UNTS229	104346
Czechoslovakia	Greece	01 Feb 54	225UNTS95	103092
Finland	USSR (Soviet Union)	06 Feb 54	221UNTS143	103006
Australia	IBRD (World Bank)	02 Mar 54	191UNTS103	102579
Norway	IBRD (World Bank)	08 Apr 54	201UNTS131	102714
Peru	IBRD (World Bank)	12 Apr 54	190UNTS231	102567
ECSC (Coal/Steel)	USA (United States)	23 Apr 54	229UNTS229	103170
Greece	Romania	19 May 54	225UNTS27	103084
Greece	Hungary	05 Jun 54	299UNTS295	104321
Netherlands	Norway	09 Jun 54	287UNTS179	104184
Italy	USA (United States)	16 Jun 54	236UNTS149	103322
Chile	USA (United States)	28 Jun 54	233UNTS3	103246
Austria	UK Great Britain	09 Jul 54	201UNTS277	102720
Netherlands	UK Great Britain	09 Jul 54	199UNTS157	102682
France	Netherlands	09 Jul 54	287UNTS169	104183
Ceylon (Sri Lanka)	IBRD (World Bank)	09 Jul 54	198UNTS313	200517
Belgium	UK Great Britain	09 Jul 54	201UNTS299	102721
Portugal	UK Great Britain	10 Jul 54	199UNTS169	102683
Belgium	Italy	12 Jul 54	288UNTS59	104198
Switzerland	UK Great Britain	16 Jul 54	199UNTS197	102685
Sweden	UK Great Britain	28 Jul 54	199UNTS181	102684
Brazil	USA (United States)	20 Aug 54	410UNTS79	105898
El Salvador	IBRD (World Bank)	12 Oct 54	203UNTS37	102739
Belgium	IBRD (World Bank)	14 Dec 54	210UNTS113	102837
UK Great Britain	Yugoslavia	22 Dec 54	207UNTS227	102808
Iceland	Netherlands	28 Dec 54	287UNTS159	104182
USSR (Soviet Union)	Yugoslavia	05 Jan 55	240UNTS225	103405
Finland	USSR (Soviet Union)	24 Jan 55	240UNTS243	103406
Australia	IBRD (World Bank)	18 Mar 55	220UNTS131	102998
Peru	IBRD (World Bank)	05 Apr 55	211UNTS115	102850
Germany, West	USA (United States)	14 Apr 55	263UNTS351	103782
Norway	IBRD (World Bank)	19 Apr 55	211UNTS159	102852
Panama	IBRD (World Bank)	12 Jul 55	219UNTS127	102970
Guatemala	IBRD (World Bank)	29 Jul 55	229UNTS167	103165
Peru	IBRD (World Bank)	05 Aug 55	218UNTS3	102950
Multilateral		29 Sep 55	222UNTS313	103037
Brazil	USA (United States)	16 Nov 55	239UNTS207	103381
IBRD (World Bank)	South Africa	28 Nov 55	230UNTS101	103178
Honduras	IBRD (World Bank)	22 Dec 55	230UNTS262	103189
USA (United States)	Yugoslavia	19 Jan 56	240UNTS121	103400
Denmark	Netherlands	31 Jan 56	286UNTS255	104172
USSR (Soviet Union)	Yugoslavia	02 Feb 56	259UNTS111	103685
Japan	USA (United States)	10 Feb 56	275UNTS105	103979
Chile	USA (United States)	13 Mar 56	275UNTS49	103975
Ceylon (Sri Lanka)	Romania	16 Mar 56	315UNTS51	104559
Burma	IBRD (World Bank)	04 May 56	253UNTS179	103584
Haiti	IBRD (World Bank)	07 May 56	252UNTS279	103570
Multilateral		19 May 56	399UNTS189	105742
Colombia	IBRD (World Bank)	06 Jun 56	248UNTS139	103493
Bulgaria	Ceylon (Sri Lanka)	19 Jun 56	315UNTS33	104557
Italy	Switzerland	29 Jun 56	284UNTS299	104144
Italy	Netherlands	29 Jun 56	287UNTS193	104185
Multilateral		31 Aug 56	249UNTS158	103506
IBRD (World Bank)	Switzerland	17 Sep 56	340UNTS311	200560
Australia	IBRD (World Bank)	15 Nov 56	288UNTS117	104201
Australia	IBRD (World Bank)	03 Dec 56	288UNTS99	104200
India	IBRD (World Bank)	19 Dec 56	310UNTS75	104489
Iran	IBRD (World Bank)	22 Jan 57	317UNTS129	104600
Ethiopia	IBRD (World Bank)	28 Jan 57	286UNTS307	104175
Burma	India	12 Mar 57	312UNTS131	104515
Netherlands	Paraguay	13 Apr 57	593UNTS85	108577

PARTY ONE	PARTY TWO	DATE	CITATION	NUMBER
Interest rates (Cont.)				
Denmark	Uruguay	04 Jun 57	286UNTS107	104162
Poland	USA (United States)	07 Jun 57	291UNTS41	104243
Jordan	USA (United States)	27 Jun 57	288UNTS269	104209
India	IBRD (World Bank)	12 Jul 57	288UNTS135	104202
Turkey	UK Great Britain	16 Aug 57	310UNTS21	104482
Belgium	IBRD (World Bank)	10 Sep 57	286UNTS291	104174
Ecuador	IBRD (World Bank)	20 Sep 57	289UNTS237	104221
IBRD (World Bank)	South Africa	01 Oct 57	280UNTS285	104065
Multilateral		03 Oct 57	366UNTS193	105218
Pakistan	IBRD (World Bank)	18 Oct 57	299UNTS303	104322
Argentina	UK Great Britain	25 Nov 57	313UNTS95	104531
France	USA (United States)	30 Jan 58	304UNTS9	104388
Canada	India	20 Feb 58	391UNTS231	105628
Multilateral		18 Jun 58	386UNTS355	105553
Ecuador	USA (United States)	27 Jun 58	317UNTS51	104593
Netherlands	Norway	30 Jun 58	346UNTS217	104982
IBRD (World Bank)	Sudan	21 Jul 58	323UNTS183	104669
India	IBRD (World Bank)	16 Sep 58	323UNTS235	104671
Ceylon (Sri Lanka)	IBRD (World Bank)	17 Sep 58	323UNTS51	104664
Germany, West	UK Great Britain	03 Oct 58	398UNTS293	105731
Canada	India	22 Oct 58	392UNTS21	105635
Canada	Ceylon (Sri Lanka)	05 Nov 58	391UNTS225	105627
Turkey	UK Great Britain	25 Nov 58	327UNTS35	104715
Netherlands	Turkey	29 Nov 58	335UNTS229	104790
IBRD (World Bank)	South Africa	02 Dec 58	324UNTS3	104676
Israel	Yugoslavia	11 Dec 58	386UNTS283	105548
El Salvador	IBRD (World Bank)	07 Jan 59	346UNTS51	104977
UK Great Britain	Yugoslavia	03 Feb 59	343UNTS153	104924
Denmark	IBRD (World Bank)	04 Feb 59	328UNTS143	104733
France	UK Great Britain	05 Mar 59	343UNTS277	104932
Austria	UK Great Britain	14 Mar 59	343UNTS263	104930
India	IBRD (World Bank)	08 Apr 59	348UNTS131	104998
Italy	UK Great Britain	14 Apr 59	343UNTS289	104934
Netherlands	Switzerland	14 Apr 59	486UNTS367	107086
Sweden	UK Great Britain	18 Apr 59	360UNTS89	105156
Belgium	UK Great Britain	23 Apr 59	343UNTS271	104931
Norway	UK Great Britain	23 Apr 59	343UNTS283	104933
Belgium	Netherlands	28 Apr 59	485UNTS123	107049
Austria	Netherlands	29 Apr 59	486UNTS373	107087
Italy	Netherlands	29 Apr 59	486UNTS387	107089
Netherlands	Portugal	30 Apr 59	485UNTS129	107050
Iceland	Netherlands	30 Apr 59	487UNTS13	107091
Netherlands	Norway	30 Apr 59	487UNTS3	107090
Netherlands	Sweden	30 Apr 59	485UNTS147	107053
Netherlands	UK Great Britain	30 Apr 59	343UNTS307	104937
Germany, West	Netherlands	30 Apr 59	485UNTS141	107052
Greece	Netherlands	30 Apr 59	485UNTS135	107051
Denmark	Netherlands	30 Apr 59	487UNTS23	107092
Fed of Malaya	UK Great Britain	01 May 59	345UNTS57	104958
Switzerland	UK Great Britain	06 May 59	343UNTS315	104938
Multilateral		11 May 59	527UNTS145	107623
Japan	Vietnam, South	13 May 59	373UNTS149	105318
Iceland	UK Great Britain	14 May 59	343UNTS301	104936
Greece	UK Great Britain	21 May 59	344UNTS3	104939
Iran	IBRD (World Bank)	29 May 59	348UNTS103	104997
Ethiopia	Yugoslavia	06 Jun 59	386UNTS243	105544
IBRD (World Bank)	South Africa	10 Jun 59	340UNTS33	104857
Jordan	UK Great Britain	11 Jun 59	351UNTS283	105028
Turkey	UK Great Britain	13 Jun 59	551UNTS59	108033
Iceland	USA (United States)	23 Jun 59	354UNTS3	105048
Norway	IBRD (World Bank)	08 Jul 59	344UNTS229	104952
India	IBRD (World Bank)	15 Jul 59	346UNTS33	104976
Netherlands	Turkey	12 Aug 59	527UNTS181	107624
Ethiopia	France	12 Nov 59	381UNTS3	105465
Norway	Yugoslavia	18 Nov 59	383UNTS131	105499

PARTY ONE	PARTY TWO	DATE	CITATION	NUMBER
Interest rates (Cont.)				
IBRD (World Bank)	Uruguay	30 Dec 59	384UNTS275	105523
Denmark	Sweden	04 Jan 60	376UNTS375	105390
Cuba	USSR (Soviet Union)	13 Feb 60	369UNTS3	105247
Cuba	USSR (Soviet Union)	13 Feb 60	369UNTS17	105248
Iran	IBRD (World Bank)	20 Feb 60	384UNTS213	105521
Indonesia	USSR (Soviet Union)	28 Feb 60	392UNTS173	105643
Costa Rica	IBRD (World Bank)	04 May 60	390UNTS201	105609
Jordan	UK Great Britain	04 May 60	385UNTS81	105531
IBRD (World Bank)	Sudan	17 Jun 60	379UNTS253	105442
Belgium	Netherlands	20 Jun 60	423UNTS19	106084
India	IBRD (World Bank)	29 Jul 60	377UNTS153	105399
Ghana	USSR (Soviet Union)	04 Aug 60	399UNTS61	105734
Panama	IBRD (World Bank)	19 Aug 60	390UNTS153	105607
United Arab Rep	USSR (Soviet Union)	27 Aug 60	399UNTS37	105733
Israel	IBRD (World Bank)	09 Sep 60	406UNTS3	105837
Pakistan	IBRD (World Bank)	19 Sep 60	444UNTS207	106370
Norway	IBRD (World Bank)	02 Dec 60	390UNTS131	105606
Peru	IBRD (World Bank)	19 Dec 60	417UNTS275	106010
Japan	IBRD (World Bank)	20 Dec 60	400UNTS279	105754
Honduras	IDA (Devel Assoc)	12 May 61	414UNTS180	105973
Ceylon (Sri Lanka)	IBRD (World Bank)	06 Jun 61	414UNTS349	105978
IBRD (World Bank)	Sudan	14 Jun 61	415UNTS26	105980
IDA (Devel Assoc)	Sudan	14 Jun 61	415UNTS50	105981
Inter-Am Devel Bnk	USA (United States)	19 Jun 61	410UNTS34	105895
India	IDA (Devel Assoc)	21 Jun 61	418UNTS61	106017
Chile	IDA (Devel Assoc)	28 Jun 61	426UNTS89	106131
Chile	IBRD (World Bank)	28 Jun 61	426UNTS33	106129
Argentina	IBRD (World Bank)	30 Jun 61	445UNTS85	106379
Jordan	UK Great Britain	17 Jul 61	420UNTS53	106039
Brazil	UK Great Britain	21 Jul 61	414UNTS26	105962
UK Great Britain	Yugoslavia	21 Jul 61	420UNTS61	106040
Philippines	IBRD (World Bank)	26 Jul 61	414UNTS253	105976
India	IBRD (World Bank)	09 Aug 61	417UNTS297	106011
India	IBRD (World Bank)	17 Aug 61	417UNTS319	106012
Colombia	IBRD (World Bank)	28 Aug 61	416UNTS23	105993
Colombia	IDA (Devel Assoc)	28 Aug 61	416UNTS3	105992
Taiwan	IDA (Devel Assoc)	30 Aug 61	416UNTS175	106003
Taiwan	IDA (Devel Assoc)	30 Aug 61	417UNTS227	106008
Tunisia	USSR (Soviet Union)	30 Aug 61	437UNTS243	106310
India	IDA (Devel Assoc)	06 Sep 61	418UNTS81	106018
Taiwan	IDA (Devel Assoc)	06 Sep 61	417UNTS253	106009
IBRD (World Bank)	Switzerland	11 Oct 61	415UNTS396	200592
India	IBRD (World Bank)	13 Oct 61	418UNTS3	106013
Costa Rica	IDA (Devel Assoc)	13 Oct 61	431UNTS3	106204
Costa Rica	IBRD (World Bank)	13 Oct 61	430UNTS27	106202
Pakistan	IDA (Devel Assoc)	19 Oct 61	447UNTS161	106415
Switzerland	UK Great Britain	20 Oct 61	431UNTS29	106206
Paraguay	IDA (Devel Assoc)	26 Oct 61	447UNTS277	106419
Peru	IBRD (World Bank)	03 Nov 61	430UNTS47	106203
India	IDA (Devel Assoc)	22 Nov 61	427UNTS29	106145
India	IDA (Devel Assoc)	22 Nov 61	427UNTS55	106146
Pakistan	IDA (Devel Assoc)	22 Nov 61	447UNTS295	106420
India	IDA (Devel Assoc)	22 Nov 61	427UNTS3	106144
Taiwan	IDA (Devel Assoc)	01 Dec 61	426UNTS105	106132
IBRD (World Bank)	Venezuela	13 Dec 61	446UNTS371	106409
Jordan	IDA (Devel Assoc)	22 Dec 61	448UNTS21	106423
Japan	USA (United States)	09 Jan 62	451UNTS97	106488
Australia	IBRD (World Bank)	23 Jan 62	430UNTS3	106201
India	IDA (Devel Assoc)	14 Feb 62	468UNTS177	106773
Iceland	IBRD (World Bank)	14 Feb 62	447UNTS95	106413
Jordan	UK Great Britain	30 May 62	449UNTS167	106458
United Arab Rep	USSR (Soviet Union)	23 Jun 62	472UNTS19	106835
Pakistan	IDA (Devel Assoc)	29 Jun 62	447UNTS325	106421
India	IDA (Devel Assoc)	29 Jun 62	447UNTS221	106417
India	IDA (Devel Assoc)	18 Jul 62	447UNTS191	106416

PARTY ONE	PARTY TWO	DATE	CITATION	NUMBER
Interest rates (Cont.)				
Korea, South	IDA (Devel Assoc)	17 Aug 62	468UNTS387	200603
IAEA (Atom Energy)	USA (United States)	20 Aug 62	456UNTS447	106570
Nicaragua	IDA (Devel Assoc)	07 Sep 62	478UNTS313	106940
India	IDA (Devel Assoc)	14 Sep 62	448UNTS3	106422
Pakistan	IBRD (World Bank)	14 Sep 62	467UNTS152	106762
IDA (Devel Assoc)	Tunisia	17 Sep 62	469UNTS33	106783
Germany, West	Ireland	17 Oct 62	604UNTS135	108749
Israel	IBRD (World Bank)	17 Oct 62	467UNTS107	106760
IBRD (World Bank)	Uruguay	26 Oct 62	481UNTS39	106977
El Salvador	IDA (Devel Assoc)	02 Nov 62	468UNTS331	106780
Haiti	IDA (Devel Assoc)	02 Nov 62	468UNTS205	106774
Pakistan	IDA (Devel Assoc)	02 Nov 62	468UNTS351	106781
IDA (Devel Assoc)	Turkey	23 Nov 62	469UNTS3	106782
Laos	USSR (Soviet Union)	01 Dec 62	472UNTS3	106834
Laos	USSR (Soviet Union)	01 Dec 62	471UNTS181	106832
IBRD (World Bank)	Thailand	21 Dec 62	467UNTS43	106757
IBRD (World Bank)	Thailand	21 Dec 62	467UNTS63	106758
India	New Zealand	22 Feb 63	486UNTS19	107069
Ethiopia	IDA (Devel Assoc)	27 Feb 63	478UNTS289	106939
Nicaragua	IBRD (World Bank)	01 Mar 63	481UNTS15	106976
India	IDA (Devel Assoc)	22 Mar 63	477UNTS3	106911
Jordan	UK Great Britain	27 Apr 63	475UNTS169	106892
Austria	Bulgaria	02 May 63	535UNTS143	107778
Canada	India	14 May 63	529UNTS31	107653
India	IDA (Devel Assoc)	24 May 63	483UNTS205	107014
IDA (Devel Assoc)	Turkey	31 May 63	480UNTS127	106966
Argentina	UK Great Britain	05 Jun 63	482UNTS353	107004
Pakistan	IDA (Devel Assoc)	26 Jun 63	492UNTS115	107189
Austria	Romania	03 Jul 63	588UNTS3	108516
Denmark	India	12 Jul 63	616UNTS3	108888
Denmark	IBRD (World Bank)	24 Jul 63	481UNTS171	106982
Pakistan	IDA (Devel Assoc)	26 Jul 63	492UNTS143	107190
Pakistan	IDA (Devel Assoc)	16 Aug 63	492UNTS171	107191
Pakistan	IDA (Devel Assoc)	16 Aug 63	492UNTS205	107192
Taiwan	IBRD (World Bank)	27 Sep 63	483UNTS151	107012
Norway	IBRD (World Bank)	15 Oct 63	482UNTS103	106992
Multilateral		23 Oct 63	506UNTS197	107388
IBRD (World Bank)	Spain	25 Oct 63	491UNTS297	107181
New Zealand	IBRD (World Bank)	12 Nov 63	485UNTS233	107059
Romania	Yugoslavia	30 Nov 63	512UNTS2	107438
Jordan	IDA (Devel Assoc)	12 Dec 63	492UNTS3	107184
Jordan	IDA (Devel Assoc)	12 Dec 63	506UNTS51	107381
Chile	IBRD (World Bank)	18 Dec 63	504UNTS29	107352
IDA (Devel Assoc)	Syria	24 Dec 63	534UNTS253	107764
Paraguay	IDA (Devel Assoc)	26 Dec 63	507UNTS3	107394
Multilateral		30 Dec 63	568UNTS233	108271
Multilateral		30 Dec 63	568UNTS215	108270
Multilateral		30 Dec 63	568UNTS243	108272
Liberia	IBRD (World Bank)	08 Jan 64	504UNTS53	107353
IDA (Devel Assoc)	Tanganyika	05 Feb 64	506UNTS91	107382
Australia	USA (United States)	05 Feb 64	511UNTS103	107430
New Zealand	IBRD (World Bank)	12 Mar 64	505UNTS3	107362
Pakistan	IDA (Devel Assoc)	25 Mar 64	535UNTS43	107775
Pakistan	IDA (Devel Assoc)	25 Mar 64	534UNTS275	107765
Peru	IBRD (World Bank)	22 Apr 64	519UNTS95	107503
Ecuador	IDA (Devel Assoc)	26 May 64	534UNTS93	107757
India	IDA (Devel Assoc)	09 Jun 64	506UNTS31	107380
Pakistan	IDA (Devel Assoc)	11 Jun 64	506UNTS3	107379
Pakistan	IDA (Devel Assoc)	11 Jun 64	534UNTS309	107766
Pakistan	IDA (Devel Assoc)	24 Jun 64	533UNTS165	107742
Niger	IDA (Devel Assoc)	24 Jun 64	554UNTS93	108098
Pakistan	IDA (Devel Assoc)	24 Jun 64	533UNTS191	107743
India	IDA (Devel Assoc)	06 Jul 64	534UNTS49	107753
Finland	IBRD (World Bank)	10 Jul 64	516UNTS125	107474
Gabon	IBRD (World Bank)	10 Jul 64	537UNTS63	107797

PARTY ONE	PARTY TWO	DATE	CITATION	NUMBER
Interest rates (Cont.)				
IDA (Devel Assoc)	Turkey	14 Jul 64	534UNTS339	107767
Pakistan	IDA (Devel Assoc)	21 Jul 64	534UNTS373	107768
New Zealand	Western Samoa	23 Jul 64	521UNTS173	107520
Bolivia	IDA (Devel Assoc)	24 Jul 64	534UNTS203	107763
Bolivia	IDA (Devel Assoc)	24 Jul 64	534UNTS171	107762
Kenya	IDA (Devel Assoc)	17 Aug 64	535UNTS79	107776
Morocco	IBRD (World Bank)	26 Aug 64	537UNTS193	107802
Pakistan	IDA (Devel Assoc)	26 Aug 64	535UNTS263	107784
IDA (Devel Assoc)	Turkey	31 Aug 64	535UNTS111	107777
Jordan	UK Great Britain	31 Aug 64	541UNTS3	107856
Pakistan	IDA (Devel Assoc)	22 Sep 64	594UNTS225	108605
Mali	IDA (Devel Assoc)	29 Sep 64	594UNTS187	108604
Israel	USSR (Soviet Union)	07 Oct 64	516UNTS59	107471
Brazil	UK Great Britain	14 Oct 64	539UNTS289	107840
India	IDA (Devel Assoc)	26 Oct 64	535UNTS245	107783
Philippines	IBRD (World Bank)	28 Oct 64	537UNTS165	107801
India	UK Great Britain	20 Nov 64	534UNTS85	107756
Afghanistan	IDA (Devel Assoc)	23 Nov 64	567UNTS155	108255
IBRD (World Bank)	Thailand	25 Nov 64	537UNTS273	107805
Mauritania	IDA (Devel Assoc)	28 Dec 64	540UNTS163	107849
Kenya	IDA (Devel Assoc)	29 Dec 64	535UNTS225	107782
Honduras	IDA (Devel Assoc)	02 Feb 65	561UNTS279	108189
Honduras	IBRD (World Bank)	02 Feb 65	561UNTS255	108188
Greece	India	11 Feb 65	606UNTS9	108771
Nigeria	IDA (Devel Assoc)	01 Mar 65	563UNTS3	108201
Nigeria	IDA (Devel Assoc)	01 Mar 65	571UNTS3	108297
IDA (Devel Assoc)	Somalia	29 Mar 65	586UNTS101	108499
IBRD (World Bank)	Uruguay	30 Mar 65	567UNTS45	108251
IDA (Devel Assoc)	Turkey	01 Apr 65	554UNTS137	108100
Jamaica	IBRD (World Bank)	08 Apr 65	539UNTS303	107841
Iran	IBRD (World Bank)	28 Apr 65	555UNTS21	108103
Taiwan	IBRD (World Bank)	28 Apr 65	549UNTS145	107998
India	IBRD (World Bank)	28 May 65	552UNTS39	108049
India	IBRD (World Bank)	11 Jun 65	557UNTS101	108130
India	IBRD (World Bank)	11 Jun 65	557UNTS59	108128
Peru	IBRD (World Bank)	18 Jun 65	568UNTS191	108269
Kenya	IDA (Devel Assoc)	30 Jun 65	554UNTS75	108097
Pakistan	IDA (Devel Assoc)	30 Jun 65	554UNTS111	108099
India	IDA (Devel Assoc)	11 Aug 65	562UNTS277	108199
Multilateral		24 Sep 65	556UNTS141	108124
Nigeria	IBRD (World Bank)	26 Sep 65	570UNTS233	108296
Nigeria	IBRD (World Bank)	26 Sep 65	571UNTS39	108298
IBRD (World Bank)	Spain	29 Sep 65	568UNTS49	108264
East Afri Service	IBRD (World Bank)	29 Sep 65	568UNTS327	200623
Morocco	IDA (Devel Assoc)	11 Oct 65	562UNTS299	108200
Turkey	UK Great Britain	21 Oct 65	561UNTS185	108180
Chile	UK Great Britain	23 Nov 65	560UNTS215	108176
New Zealand	IBRD (World Bank)	17 Dec 65	567UNTS255	108259
New Zealand	IBRD (World Bank)	17 Dec 65	567UNTS275	108260
IBRD (World Bank)	Sudan	27 Dec 65	567UNTS27	108250
Liberia	USA (United States)	06 Jan 66	592UNTS101	108570
Pakistan	IDA (Devel Assoc)	13 Jan 66	567UNTS67	108252
IDA (Devel Assoc)	Tanzania	13 Jan 66	567UNTS177	108256
Multilateral		10 Feb 66	575UNTS129	108356
Pakistan	IDA (Devel Assoc)	10 Feb 66	575UNTS89	108355
Algeria	USA (United States)	23 Feb 66	592UNTS117	108571
Brazil	IBRD (World Bank)	15 Mar 66	599UNTS52	108664
Guinea	IBRD (World Bank)	30 Mar 66	568UNTS3	108262
Denmark	Netherlands	31 Mar 66	604UNTS209	108751
Paraguay	IBRD (World Bank)	04 Apr 66	570UNTS41	108287
Paraguay	IDA (Devel Assoc)	04 Apr 66	582UNTS331	108469
Finland	IBRD (World Bank)	27 Apr 66	568UNTS107	108266
Peru	IBRD (World Bank)	13 May 66	570UNTS61	108288
Burma	USA (United States)	01 Jun 66	580UNTS253	108428
Pakistan	IDA (Devel Assoc)	17 Jun 66	582UNTS297	108468

PARTY ONE	PARTY TWO	DATE	CITATION	NUMBER
Interest rates (Cont.)				
Multilateral		20 Jun 66	573UNTS41	108322
IBRD (World Bank)	Thailand	24 Jun 66	582UNTS259	108466
Denmark	Jordan	28 Jun 66	574UNTS3	108338
Indonesia	USA (United States)	28 Jun 66	593UNTS201	108585
India	IDA (Devel Assoc)	29 Jun 66	585UNTS101	108484
India	IDA (Devel Assoc)	29 Jun 66	582UNTS277	108467
Brazil	Denmark	08 Jul 66	581UNTS95	108435
Argentina	Germany, West	13 Jul 66	636UNTS3	109091
Iraq	IBRD (World Bank)	22 Jul 66	584UNTS233	108480
Jordan	UK Great Britain	26 Jul 66	597UNTS219	108647
IDA (Devel Assoc)	Siam	02 Aug 66	585UNTS271	108492
IDA (Devel Assoc)	Turkey	10 Aug 66	585UNTS237	108491
India	IDA (Devel Assoc)	19 Aug 66	584UNTS193	108478
Kenya	IDA (Devel Assoc)	19 Aug 66	585UNTS119	108485
Denmark	Malawi	01 Sep 66	586UNTS3	108493
Argentina	UK Great Britain	15 Sep 66	603UNTS151	108732
Netherlands	Norway	22 Sep 66	600UNTS227	108683
Philippines	IBRD (World Bank)	23 Sep 66	596UNTS71	108629
USSR (Soviet Union)	Yugoslavia	29 Sep 66	608UNTS219	108818
IDA (Devel Assoc)	Senegal	29 Sep 66	594UNTS277	108607
Jamaica	IBRD (World Bank)	30 Sep 66	582UNTS179	108463
IBRD (World Bank)	Zambia	04 Oct 66	585UNTS181	108489
Malawi	IDA (Devel Assoc)	04 Oct 66	584UNTS215	108479
IBRD (World Bank)	IFC (Finance Corp)	28 Oct 66	586UNTS225	200628
Singapore	UK Great Britain	01 Dec 66	605UNTS153	108763
Syria	USSR (Soviet Union)	18 Dec 66	633UNTS247	109041
Brazil	IBRD (World Bank)	19 Dec 66	599UNTS107	108665
Brazil	IBRD (World Bank)	19 Dec 66	599UNTS149	108666
Brazil	IBRD (World Bank)	19 Dec 66	599UNTS177	108667
Brazil	IBRD (World Bank)	19 Dec 66	599UNTS205	108668
Philippines	USA (United States)	22 Dec 66	591UNTS219	108559
India	IDA (Devel Assoc)	23 Dec 66	594UNTS165	108603
Pakistan	IDA (Devel Assoc)	23 Dec 66	594UNTS255	108606
Trinidad/Tobago	UK Great Britain	29 Dec 66	605UNTS237	108766
East Afri Service	IBRD (World Bank)	17 Feb 67	599UNTS335	200629
IBRD (World Bank)	Tanzania	17 Feb 67	599UNTS287	108671
IBRD (World Bank)	Uganda	17 Feb 67	599UNTS321	108673
IBRD (World Bank)	Yugoslavia	24 Feb 67	599UNTS27	108663
Ghana	UK Great Britain	27 Feb 67	606UNTS133	108783
IBRD (World Bank)	Trinidad/Tobago	10 Mar 67	599UNTS3	108662
IBRD (World Bank)	Thailand	24 Mar 67	599UNTS299	108672
IBRD (World Bank)	UK Great Britain	24 Apr 67	600UNTS3	108674
USSR (Soviet Union)	Zambia	26 May 67	643UNTS179	109191
Indonesia	UK Great Britain	01 Aug 67	638UNTS3	109128
Denmark	Tanzania	01 Nov 67	619UNTS47	108938
Denmark	Iran	02 Nov 67	638UNTS217	109138
Austria	Canada	28 Feb 68	636UNTS141	109101
Denmark	Malaysia	29 Feb 68	640UNTS29	109153
Legal costs				
Multilateral		25 May 55	264UNTS117	103791
Payment schedules				
Bolivia	Brazil	25 Feb 38	51UNTS245	200192
Bolivia	Brazil	25 Feb 38	88UNTS379	200254
France	Netherlands	14 Jun 40	2UNTS263	200019
Netherlands	UK Great Britain	14 Jun 40	2UNTS251	200018
Brazil	Paraguay	14 Apr 41	54UNTS269	200199
Brazil	Paraguay	14 Jun 41	54UNTS289	200201
UK Great Britain	USSR (Soviet Union)	16 Aug 41	91UNTS341	200269
Peru	USA (United States)	07 May 42	103UNTS219	200316
USA (United States)	Uruguay	21 Jul 42	120UNTS211	200393
Haiti	USA (United States)	30 Sep 42	24UNTS205	200144
Mexico	USA (United States)	23 Dec 42	13UNTS231	200081
Iran	USA (United States)	08 Apr 43	106UNTS155	200340
UK Great Britain	USA (United States)	10 May 43	147UNTS109	200473

PARTY ONE	PARTY TWO	DATE	CITATION	NUMBER
Payment schedules (Cont.)				
France	USA (United States)	25 Sep 43	76UNTS183	200245
Iceland	USA (United States)	27 Sep 43	29UNTS317	200170
Mexico	USA (United States)	29 Sep 43	106UNTS265	200345
Multilateral		21 Oct 43	2UNTS281	200021
Liberia	USA (United States)	31 Dec 43	106UNTS199	200341
Turkey	UK Great Britain	23 Mar 44	2UNTS227	200015
Brazil	Paraguay	11 Aug 44	67UNTS303	200227
UK Great Britain	USSR (Soviet Union)	23 Sep 44	10UNTS171	200060
Belgium	UK Great Britain	05 Oct 44	5UNTS227	200031
Multilateral		08 Oct 44	45UNTS311	200187
France	USA (United States)	20 Feb 45	76UNTS193	200246
Canada	Czechoslovakia	01 Mar 45	45UNTS283	200185
Sweden	UK Great Britain	06 Mar 45	5UNTS241	200032
Sweden	UK Great Britain	06 Mar 45	82UNTS219	101095
France	UK Great Britain	27 Mar 45	98UNTS227	200274
South Africa	USA (United States)	17 Apr 45	90UNTS267	200264
Argentina	USA (United States)	09 May 45	139UNTS227	200453
Canada	Norway	25 Jun 45	45UNTS297	200186
Denmark	UK Great Britain	16 Aug 45	5UNTS251	200033
Netherlands	UK Great Britain	07 Sep 45	2UNTS325	200024
USA (United States)	USSR (Soviet Union)	15 Oct 45	278UNTS151	200547
Belgium	Norway	23 Oct 45	16UNTS311	200107
Netherlands	Switzerland	24 Oct 45	3UNTS73	100025
Guatemala	USA (United States)	25 Oct 45	139UNTS45	101875
Czechoslovakia	UK Great Britain	01 Nov 45	5UNTS15	100062
Netherlands	Norway	06 Nov 45	2UNTS5	100017
France	USA (United States)	08 Nov 45	76UNTS151	100986
Norway	UK Great Britain	08 Nov 45	5UNTS27	100063
Finland	Norway	27 Nov 45	17UNTS247	100279
Netherlands	Sweden	30 Nov 45	2UNTS27	100019
UK Great Britain	USA (United States)	06 Dec 45	126UNTS13	101679
Denmark	UK Great Britain	06 Dec 45	5UNTS3	100061
Czechoslovakia	Norway	13 Dec 45	17UNTS261	100280
Romania	Yugoslavia	15 Dec 45	116UNTS3	101565
Multilateral		27 Dec 45	2UNTS39	100020
Belgium	Portugal	07 Jan 46	19UNTS159	100310
Poland	Yugoslavia	18 Jan 46	115UNTS83	101559
Lebanon	USA (United States)	21 Jan 46	140UNTS73	101884
Denmark	Netherlands	31 Jan 46	3UNTS3	100021
Canada	Netherlands	05 Feb 46	43UNTS3	100658
Canada	Taiwan	07 Feb 46	43UNTS23	100659
France	USA (United States)	07 Feb 46	3UNTS239	100034
Mexico	UK Great Britain	07 Feb 46	6UNTS55	100068
Netherlands	USA (United States)	09 Feb 46	3UNTS247	100035
Netherlands	USA (United States)	11 Feb 46	3UNTS37	100023
Belgium	Norway	21 Feb 46	31UNTS199	100479
Canada	UK Great Britain	06 Mar 46	20UNTS13	100312
France	Norway	06 Mar 46	15UNTS13	100227
Switzerland	UK Great Britain	12 Mar 46	6UNTS107	100070
Greece	UK Great Britain	21 Mar 46	91UNTS149	101247
France	Norway	26 Mar 46	31UNTS69	100468
UK Great Britain	USA (United States)	27 Mar 46	4UNTS101	100040
Multilateral		31 Mar 46	17UNTS159	100274
Belgium	Denmark	08 Apr 46	4UNTS429	100059
Canada	France	09 Apr 46	43UNTS43	100660
Portugal	UK Great Britain	16 Apr 46	6UNTS119	100071
France	Greece	24 Apr 46	91UNTS83	101243
USSR (Soviet Union)	Yugoslavia	26 Apr 46	116UNTS163	101575
France	UK Great Britain	29 Apr 46	98UNTS123	101360
UK Great Britain	USA (United States)	07 May 46	6UNTS285	100082
Turkey	USA (United States)	07 May 46	6UNTS293	100083
Haiti	USA (United States)	14 May 46	4UNTS179	100044
Greece	USA (United States)	16 May 46	184UNTS230	102451
France	USA (United States)	28 May 46	84UNTS59	101119
Taiwan	USA (United States)	14 Jun 46	4UNTS253	100049

PARTY ONE	PARTY TWO	DATE	CITATION	NUMBER
Payment schedules (Cont.)				
Poland	UK Great Britain	24 Jun 46	11UNTS59	100149
Romania	Yugoslavia	26 Jun 46	116UNTS21	101566
Albania	Yugoslavia	01 Jul 46	111UNTS3	101517
Albania	Yugoslavia	01 Jul 46	111UNTS81	101518
Italy	Norway	20 Jul 46	17UNTS273	100281
Ceylon (Sri Lanka)	India	12 Aug 46	196UNTS209	102626
Hungary	UK Great Britain	12 Aug 46	89UNTS219	101220
South Africa	UK Great Britain	24 Aug 46	51UNTS187	100765
Norway	Yugoslavia	30 Aug 46	15UNTS163	100232
Norway	Yugoslavia	30 Aug 46	30UNTS187	100457
Paraguay	USA (United States)	12 Sep 46	125UNTS179	101677
Netherlands	UK Great Britain	16 Sep 46	4UNTS401	100057
Argentina	UK Great Britain	17 Sep 46	88UNTS47	101185
Taiwan	USA (United States)	04 Nov 46	25UNTS69	100359
Norway	Sweden	22 Nov 46	15UNTS171	100233
Norway	Poland	03 Dec 46	15UNTS203	100234
United Arab Rep	UK Great Britain	10 Dec 46	105UNTS15	101451
Hungary	Yugoslavia	23 Dec 46	113UNTS125	101549
Norway	USSR (Soviet Union)	27 Dec 46	17UNTS283	100282
Australia	Netherlands	24 Jan 47	10UNTS77	100144
Finland	USSR (Soviet Union)	03 Feb 47	216UNTS231	102939
Norway	USSR (Soviet Union)	19 Feb 47	30UNTS293	100464
Czechoslovakia	Yugoslavia	25 Feb 47	112UNTS3	101539
Netherlands	UK Great Britain	26 Feb 47	11UNTS279	100167
Paraguay	USA (United States)	03 Mar 47	135UNTS156	101819
Belgium	Turkey	12 Mar 47	37UNTS215	100578
Belgium	Turkey	12 Mar 47	33UNTS43	100513
Austria	France	15 Mar 47	12UNTS109	100182
Poland	Sweden	18 Mar 47	12UNTS295	100190
Belgium	Czechoslovakia	19 Mar 47	23UNTS35	100341
Czechoslovakia	Norway	20 Mar 47	30UNTS223	100460
South Africa	USA (United States)	21 Mar 47	16UNTS47	100248
Australia	Norway	24 Mar 47	18UNTS185	100288
Belgium	Poland	24 Mar 47	18UNTS279	100297
Spain	UK Great Britain	28 Mar 47	66UNTS91	100849
Austria	Norway	14 Apr 47	31UNTS21	100466
Austria	Norway	14 Apr 47	15UNTS211	100235
Denmark	Norway	15 Apr 47	12UNTS323	100191
Italy	UK Great Britain	17 Apr 47	54UNTS149	100801
Austria	UK Great Britain	28 Apr 47	93UNTS53	101287
Bulgaria	Denmark	09 May 47	74UNTS139	100960
Bulgaria	Denmark	09 May 47	74UNTS131	100959
Poland	Yugoslavia	24 May 47	115UNTS69	101558
Poland	Yugoslavia	24 May 47	115UNTS37	101557
New Zealand	UK Great Britain	27 May 47	17UNTS211	100277
Netherlands	USA (United States)	28 May 47	17UNTS29	100267
Albania	Yugoslavia	12 Jun 47	111UNTS195	101534
Austria	USA (United States)	21 Jun 47	67UNTS99	100869
Albania	Yugoslavia	22 Jun 47	111UNTS207	101536
Denmark	Yugoslavia	28 Jun 47	78UNTS242	101020
Belgium	United Arab Rep	01 Jul 47	34UNTS93	100529
France	New Zealand	02 Jul 47	16UNTS219	100263
Haiti	USA (United States)	04 Jul 47	22UNTS165	100335
Greece	USA (United States)	08 Jul 47	16UNTS157	100256
Norway	Switzerland	15 Jul 47	12UNTS351	100192
UK Great Britain	Uruguay	15 Jul 47	71UNTS179	100918
Hungary	Yugoslavia	24 Jul 47	114UNTS3	101554
USSR (Soviet Union)	Yugoslavia	25 Jul 47	130UNTS315	101732
Australia	France	28 Jul 47	97UNTS271	101353
Czechoslovakia	Greece	30 Jul 47	185UNTS133	102464
Taiwan	Italy	30 Jul 47	12UNTS377	100194
Czechoslovakia	Greece	30 Jul 47	185UNTS115	102463
India	UK Great Britain	14 Aug 47	11UNTS371	100176
Italy	USA (United States)	14 Aug 47	36UNTS105	100567
Poland	UNICEF (Children)	23 Aug 47	65UNTS22	100815

PARTY ONE	PARTY TWO	DATE	CITATION	NUMBER
Payment schedules (Cont.)				
Belgium	Netherlands	29 Aug 47	36UNTS349	100573
Multilateral		19 Sep 47	30UNTS269	100462
Multilateral		29 Sep 47	45UNTS125	100694
Romania	Yugoslavia	30 Sep 47	116UNTS71	101570
Multilateral		05 Oct 47	34UNTS23	100525
Burma	UK Great Britain	17 Oct 47	70UNTS183	100904
Taiwan	USA (United States)	27 Oct 47	12UNTS11	100178
Multilateral		30 Oct 47	55UNTS188	100814
Poland	Yugoslavia	07 Nov 47	115UNTS137	101561
Multilateral		18 Nov 47	17UNTS89	100269
Norway	Sweden	22 Dec 47	22UNTS203	100337
Denmark	Sweden	23 Dec 47	14UNTS3	100207
UK Great Britain	USSR (Soviet Union)	27 Dec 47	82UNTS251	101098
United Arab Rep	UK Great Britain	05 Jan 48	77UNTS3	100988
Denmark	Norway	21 Jan 48	14UNTS307	100223
Czechoslovakia	New Zealand	22 Jan 48	16UNTS229	100264
France	Lebanon	24 Jan 48	173UNTS99	102263
Poland	UK Great Britain	02 Mar 48	77UNTS47	100991
Netherlands	UK Great Britain	11 Mar 48	77UNTS69	100993
Hungary	Yugoslavia	18 Mar 48	113UNTS219	101552
Hungary	Yugoslavia	18 Mar 48	113UNTS201	101551
Hungary	Yugoslavia	18 Mar 48	113UNTS141	101550
USA (United States)	Venezuela	24 Mar 48	44UNTS57	100678
Czechoslovakia	Poland	05 Apr 48	31UNTS355	100482
Poland	Yugoslavia	12 Apr 48	115UNTS167	101563
IMF (Fund)	United Nations	15 Apr 48	16UNTS325	200108
Hungary	Yugoslavia	17 Apr 48	130UNTS101	101727
Denmark	Norway	21 Apr 48	18UNTS139	100284
Norway	Sweden	29 Apr 48	26UNTS11	100374
Belgium	Italy	30 Apr 48	36UNTS305	100571
Ceylon (Sri Lanka)	UK Great Britain	30 Apr 48	182UNTS2	102421
Denmark	Iceland	14 May 48	23UNTS163	100346
Brazil	UK Great Britain	21 May 48	66UNTS121	100851
Czechoslovakia	Yugoslavia	24 May 48	112UNTS183	101543
Czechoslovakia	Yugoslavia	24 May 48	112UNTS111	101542
Czechoslovakia	Yugoslavia	24 May 48	112UNTS225	101545
France	Poland	09 Jun 48	32UNTS251	100503
Netherlands	UK Great Britain	11 Jun 48	66UNTS183	100853
France	UK Great Britain	11 Jun 48	66UNTS151	100852
Burma	Pakistan	22 Jun 48	91UNTS197	101252
Spain	UK Great Britain	23 Jun 48	66UNTS193	100854
Greece	Sweden	25 Jun 48	267UNTS337	103849
Norway	Switzerland	26 Jun 48	29UNTS193	100440
New Zealand	Pakistan	28 Jun 48	91UNTS235	101253
France	UK Great Britain	12 Jul 48	90UNTS83	101230
UK Great Britain	Uruguay	12 Jul 48	71UNTS199	100919
Peru	UK Great Britain	20 Jul 48	66UNTS197	100855
Ireland	Netherlands	02 Sep 48	558UNTS249	108145
Greece	UK Great Britain	07 Sep 48	180UNTS144	102380
Korea, South	USA (United States)	11 Sep 48	89UNTS155	101216
Iceland	ICAO (Civil Aviat)	16 Sep 48	28UNTS267	100429
New Zealand	Pakistan	17 Sep 48	91UNTS275	101254
Australia	Denmark	08 Oct 48	22UNTS43	100330
Czechoslovakia	France	12 Oct 48	45UNTS81	100693
Taiwan	USA (United States)	18 Nov 48	198UNTS287	102672
Italy	USA (United States)	26 Nov 48	79UNTS71	101032
Austria	Denmark	29 Nov 48	74UNTS257	100968
Austria	Denmark	29 Nov 48	74UNTS243	100967
Italy	Netherlands	04 Dec 48	46UNTS271	100716
Australia	Belgium	09 Dec 48	25UNTS159	100361
Denmark	Poland	14 Dec 48	81UNTS33	101060
Argentina	Denmark	14 Dec 48	74UNTS41	100956
Spain	UK Great Britain	15 Dec 48	87UNTS49	101165
Denmark	Turkey	15 Dec 48	76UNTS17	100975
Denmark	Turkey	15 Dec 48	76UNTS3	100974

PARTY ONE	PARTY TWO	DATE	CITATION	NUMBER
Payment schedules (Cont.)				
Multilateral		16 Dec 48	79UNTS85	101033
UK Great Britain	Yugoslavia	23 Dec 48	81UNTS121	101068
Belgium	Greece	27 Dec 48	77UNTS265	101004
USSR (Soviet Union)	Yugoslavia	27 Dec 48	116UNTS327	101579
Belgium	Luxembourg	14 Jan 49	36UNTS339	100572
Poland	UK Great Britain	14 Jan 49	83UNTS3	101100
Poland	Yugoslavia	16 Jan 49	115UNTS241	101564
Netherlands	USA (United States)	17 Jan 49	32UNTS241	100502
Denmark	Sweden	08 Feb 49	33UNTS227	100519
Greece	USA (United States)	09 Feb 49	79UNTS95	101034
France	Norway	09 Feb 49	29UNTS13	100431
Trieste	USA (United States)	11 Feb 49	79UNTS123	101036
Austria	USA (United States)	11 Feb 49	79UNTS113	101035
Norway	Turkey	24 Feb 49	30UNTS151	100453
Norway	Turkey	24 Feb 49	29UNTS47	100433
Denmark	Greece	25 Feb 49	78UNTS325	101022
Denmark	Greece	25 Feb 49	78UNTS335	101023
Multilateral		28 Feb 49	29UNTS53	100434
Czechoslovakia	Yugoslavia	01 Mar 49	112UNTS241	101546
Czechoslovakia	Yugoslavia	01 Mar 49	113UNTS3	101547
Belgium	Portugal	01 Mar 49	32UNTS49	100488
Greece	Norway	12 Mar 49	33UNTS13	100510
Greece	Norway	12 Mar 49	30UNTS161	100454
France	USA (United States)	14 Mar 49	84UNTS237	101133
Germany, West	Greece	16 Mar 49	77UNTS327	101007
Germany, West	Greece	16 Mar 49	77UNTS307	101006
Multilateral		16 Mar 49	29UNTS95	100436
Denmark	Finland	22 Mar 49	33UNTS247	100520
Austria	USA (United States)	23 Mar 49	43UNTS127	100667
Finland	Greece	24 Mar 49	78UNTS13	101009
Finland	Greece	24 Mar 49	78UNTS3	101008
Panama	USA (United States)	31 Mar 49	55UNTS141	100812
United Arab Rep	UK Great Britain	31 Mar 49	83UNTS139	101106
Greece	Turkey	02 Apr 49	78UNTS23	101010
Denmark	Portugal	08 Apr 49	74UNTS221	100965
Denmark	Portugal	08 Apr 49	74UNTS209	100964
Italy	Yugoslavia	13 Apr 49	171UNTS279	102232
Australia	New Zealand	15 Apr 49	34UNTS225	100540
Canada	Netherlands	09 May 49	46UNTS263	100715
Ethiopia	USA (United States)	20 May 49	89UNTS99	101211
UNICEF (Children)	UK Great Britain	17 Jun 49	65UNTS50	100820
Argentina	UK Great Britain	27 Jun 49	83UNTS217	101110
Greece	Turkey	21 Jul 49	78UNTS55	101011
Greece	Turkey	21 Jul 49	78UNTS65	101012
Multilateral		22 Jul 49	557UNTS211	108135
Brazil	UK Great Britain	03 Aug 49	86UNTS113	101154
Multilateral		05 Aug 49	88UNTS229	101195
Multilateral		10 Aug 49	45UNTS3	100689
Australia	Netherlands	12 Aug 49	34UNTS213	100539
Czechoslovakia	UK Great Britain	18 Aug 49	86UNTS129	101155
Multilateral		27 Aug 49	47UNTS127	100727
Greece	Italy	31 Aug 49	78UNTS89	101014
Belgium	Netherlands	07 Sep 49	117UNTS3	101581
Belgium	France	07 Sep 49	123UNTS13	101651
Belgium	UK Great Britain	07 Sep 49	106UNTS61	101457
Argentina	Norway	09 Sep 49	42UNTS125	100646
Denmark	ICAO (Civil Aviat)	09 Sep 49	53UNTS341	100791
Czechoslovakia	UK Great Britain	28 Sep 49	86UNTS141	101156
Czechoslovakia	UK Great Britain	28 Sep 49	86UNTS161	101157
Greece	UK Great Britain	17 Oct 49	93UNTS185	101300
Multilateral		07 Nov 49	132UNTS31	101749
Italy	Norway	19 Nov 49	47UNTS75	100723
Italy	Norway	19 Nov 49	47UNTS89	100724
Norway	Portugal	28 Nov 49	47UNTS117	100726
Belgium	Luxembourg	03 Dec 49	91UNTS31	101241

PARTY ONE	PARTY TWO	DATE	CITATION	NUMBER
Payment schedules (Cont.)				
Denmark	Poland	07 Dec 49	81UNTS21	101059
Colombia	UK Great Britain	13 Dec 49	88UNTS133	101189
Denmark	Germany, West	15 Dec 49	51UNTS11	100749
Czechoslovakia	Denmark	17 Dec 49	74UNTS147	100961
Czechoslovakia	Denmark	17 Dec 49	74UNTS159	100962
Norway	Poland	21 Dec 49	47UNTS107	100725
UK Great Britain	Yugoslavia	26 Dec 49	87UNTS71	101167
Greece	Portugal	31 Dec 49	92UNTS83	101263
Greece	Portugal	31 Dec 49	92UNTS71	101262
France	Netherlands	07 Jan 50	120UNTS25	101614
Australia	Ceylon (Sri Lanka)	12 Jan 50	53UNTS295	100789
Austria	UK Great Britain	26 Jan 50	97UNTS183	101350
France	UK Great Britain	28 Jan 50	97UNTS155	101349
UK Great Britain	Yugoslavia	09 Feb 50	88UNTS287	101200
China People's Rep	USSR (Soviet Union)	14 Feb 50	226UNTS21	103104
Canada	Yugoslavia	29 Mar 50	230UNTS357	103195
Israel	UK Great Britain	30 Mar 50	86UNTS231	101162
Paraguay	UK Great Britain	03 Apr 50	99UNTS81	101372
Austria	Greece	11 May 50	184UNTS217	102450
Denmark	Portugal	02 Jun 50	74UNTS229	100966
Multilateral		28 Jun 50	87UNTS153	101170
Finland	UK Great Britain	07 Jul 50	138UNTS171	101868
Luxembourg	Netherlands	08 Jul 50	135UNTS229	101824
Denmark	Spain	12 Jul 50	71UNTS129	100913
Germany, West	Ireland	12 Jul 50	557UNTS221	108136
Multilateral		27 Jul 50	166UNTS73	102186
USA (United States)	Yugoslavia	14 Aug 50	137UNTS131	101851
Belgium	Japan	29 Aug 50	76UNTS113	100984
Brazil	UK Great Britain	18 Sep 50	88UNTS115	101188
Czechoslovakia	USA (United States)	29 Sep 50	290UNTS3	104227
Canada	USSR (Soviet Union)	29 Sep 50	230UNTS371	103197
Denmark	Poland	01 Oct 50	81UNTS43	101061
Denmark	Italy	04 Oct 50	78UNTS353	101025
Denmark	Italy	04 Oct 50	78UNTS341	101024
Austria	Ireland	06 Oct 50	557UNTS173	108133
Netherlands	USA (United States)	07 Oct 50	79UNTS33	101029
Denmark	UK Great Britain	19 Oct 50	79UNTS25	101028
Philippines	USA (United States)	06 Nov 50	122UNTS63	101637
Norway	UK Great Britain	06 Nov 50	88UNTS257	101197
Canada	Ecuador	10 Nov 50	231UNTS15	103199
Italy	UK Great Britain	21 Dec 50	175UNTS187	102301
Italy	Yugoslavia	23 Dec 50	150UNTS191	101973
UK Great Britain	Yugoslavia	28 Dec 50	88UNTS329	101201
Finland	Ireland	06 Jan 51	558UNTS120	108140
Sweden	UK Great Britain	17 Jan 51	93UNTS225	101301
Denmark	Norway	18 Jan 51	82UNTS153	101090
Denmark	Switzerland	20 Jan 51	87UNTS223	101174
Italy	Norway	22 Jan 51	88UNTS339	101202
Austria	UK Great Britain	31 Jan 51	88UNTS107	101187
Denmark	Hungary	10 Feb 51	85UNTS49	101145
India	USA (United States)	16 Mar 51	141UNTS47	101904
Germany, West	Netherlands	29 Mar 51	149UNTS71	101952
Belgium	UK Great Britain	06 Apr 51	110UNTS3	101496
Jordan	UK Great Britain	01 May 51	117UNTS19	101582
United Arab Rep	USA (United States)	05 May 51	198UNTS265	102670
UK Great Britain	Yugoslavia	10 May 51	102UNTS29	101408
UK Great Britain	USA (United States)	03 Jun 51	137UNTS81	101850
India	UK Great Britain	05 Jun 51	135UNTS3	101811
Saudi Arabia	USA (United States)	18 Jun 51	141UNTS67	101906
Denmark	France	30 Jun 51	151UNTS241	102000
United Arab Rep	UK Great Britain	01 Jul 51	249UNTS143	103504
Ireland	Norway	02 Jul 51	100UNTS53	101387
UK Great Britain	USA (United States)	18 Jul 51	117UNTS49	101583
Portugal	UK Great Britain	20 Jul 51	105UNTS61	101453
France	UK Great Britain	20 Aug 51	108UNTS263	101479

PARTY ONE	PARTY TWO	DATE	CITATION	NUMBER
Payment schedules (Cont.)				
Multilateral		28 Aug 51	198UNTS17	102654
Japan	UK Great Britain	31 Aug 51	108UNTS273	101480
Japan	UK Great Britain	31 Aug 51	149UNTS227	101955
Pakistan	United Arab Rep	08 Sep 51	133UNTS257	101793
Denmark	Switzerland	15 Sep 51	110UNTS55	101501
UK Great Britain	Yugoslavia	28 Sep 51	117UNTS107	101587
Pakistan	UK Great Britain	29 Sep 51	134UNTS183	101798
South Africa	USA (United States)	09 Nov 51	160UNTS41	102100
Italy	UK Great Britain	28 Nov 51	172UNTS205	102248
Spain	UK Great Britain	20 Dec 51	123UNTS187	101660
Ireland	Switzerland	26 Dec 51	558UNTS305	108149
Australia	Pakistan	16 Jan 52	151UNTS281	102001
UK Great Britain	USA (United States)	18 Jan 52	184UNTS79	102440
Belgium	Norway	21 Jan 52	123UNTS39	101653
Ireland	Portugal	06 Feb 52	558UNTS289	108147
Israel	USA (United States)	27 Feb 52	177UNTS123	102314
Belgium	Pakistan	15 Mar 52	316UNTS65	104578
Czechoslovakia	Denmark	04 Apr 52	133UNTS245	101792
Greece	Switzerland	04 Apr 52	166UNTS271	102192
Belgium	Greece	24 Apr 52	166UNTS261	102191
Italy	Jordan	24 Apr 52	281UNTS167	104078
United Arab Rep	USA (United States)	29 Apr 52	241UNTS3	103418
Germany, West	Netherlands	19 May 52	134UNTS3	101794
Greece	Syria	02 Jun 52	183UNTS251	102434
Denmark	Poland	09 Jun 52	135UNTS221	101823
Denmark	Poland	09 Jun 52	135UNTS209	101822
Belgium	Switzerland	17 Jun 52	180UNTS23	102373
Multilateral		11 Jul 52	171UNTS143	102226
Multilateral		11 Jul 52	170UNTS63	102222
Multilateral		11 Jul 52	171UNTS89	102225
Multilateral		11 Jul 52	171UNTS3	102224
Multilateral		11 Jul 52	170UNTS269	102223
Israel	USA (United States)	23 Jul 52	179UNTS139	102363
Germany, West	Greece	28 Jul 52	182UNTS85	102424
USA (United States)	Venezuela	28 Aug 52	178UNTS51	102336
Ceylon (Sri Lanka)	Japan	06 Sep 52	314UNTS279	104552
Germany, West	Israel	10 Sep 52	162UNTS205	102137
Austria	Greece	20 Sep 52	187UNTS191	102512
Germany, West	Ireland	26 Sep 52	558UNTS27	108138
Italy	Netherlands	28 Oct 52	289UNTS144	104218
Denmark	Italy	28 Oct 52	167UNTS125	102202
Denmark	Israel	14 Nov 52	160UNTS279	102113
Denmark	Israel	14 Nov 52	160UNTS289	102114
Nicaragua	USA (United States)	19 Nov 52	186UNTS3	102478
Sweden	USA (United States)	20 Nov 52	177UNTS203	102319
France	Greece	23 Dec 52	187UNTS175	102511
Switzerland	UK Great Britain	16 Jan 53	196UNTS119	102621
Greece	Italy	04 Feb 53	189UNTS295	102552
Greece	Italy	04 Feb 53	189UNTS269	102551
Greece	Netherlands	05 Feb 53	263UNTS361	103783
Denmark	Germany, West	26 Feb 53	178UNTS3	102332
Turkey	Yugoslavia	26 Feb 53	247UNTS54	103460
Multilateral		27 Feb 53	333UNTS3	104764
Germany, West	UK Great Britain	27 Feb 53	330UNTS217	104747
Germany, West	USA (United States)	27 Feb 53	205UNTS103	102771
Germany, West	USA (United States)	27 Feb 53	224UNTS13	103067
Belgium	France	27 Feb 53	164UNTS49	102158
Greece	Yugoslavia	28 Feb 53	252UNTS27	103557
Haiti	USA (United States)	13 Mar 53	212UNTS143	102866
Libya	UK Great Britain	25 Mar 53	172UNTS281	102252
Italy	UK Great Britain	13 Apr 53	172UNTS271	102251
Czechoslovakia	Denmark	23 Apr 53	174UNTS107	102281
Czechoslovakia	Denmark	23 Apr 53	174UNTS95	102280
Germany, West	Italy	05 May 53	267UNTS9	103835
Greece	United Arab Rep	21 May 53	256UNTS25	103621

PARTY ONE	PARTY TWO	DATE	CITATION	NUMBER
Payment schedules (Cont.)				
Greece	United Arab Rep	21 May 53	256UNTS17	103620
Germany, West	UK Great Britain	22 May 53	172UNTS179	102246
Australia	UK Great Britain	08 Jun 53	201UNTS187	102718
Japan	Syria	08 Jun 53	184UNTS3	102436
UK Great Britain	USA (United States)	26 Jun 53	183UNTS225	102432
Fed Rhod/Nyasaland	South Africa	28 Jun 53	267UNTS270	103848
Multilateral		20 Jul 53	227UNTS217	103140
Multilateral		20 Jul 53	228UNTS41	103142
India	Yugoslavia	24 Jul 53	394UNTS13	105665
Ireland	Italy	27 Jul 53	558UNTS237	108144
Libya	UK Great Britain	29 Jul 53	186UNTS277	102493
Ceylon (Sri Lanka)	Yugoslavia	30 Jul 53	337UNTS103	104819
Argentina	USSR (Soviet Union)	05 Aug 53	221UNTS99	103004
Denmark	Germany, West	14 Aug 53	202UNTS3	102725
Denmark	Uruguay	09 Sep 53	256UNTS149	103625
Luxembourg	UK Great Britain	13 Oct 53	209UNTS87	102825
Australia	Netherlands	22 Oct 53	184UNTS193	102448
Greece	Turkey	07 Nov 53	225UNTS163	103098
Germany, West	USA (United States)	23 Nov 53	224UNTS107	103071
India	USSR (Soviet Union)	02 Dec 53	240UNTS143	103402
Bulgaria	Greece	05 Dec 53	225UNTS145	103096
Bulgaria	Greece	05 Dec 53	225UNTS135	103095
Multilateral		09 Dec 53	249UNTS197	103509
Multilateral		11 Dec 53	218UNTS153	102956
Multilateral		11 Dec 53	218UNTS211	102957
Denmark	UK Great Britain	15 Dec 53	196UNTS105	102620
Japan	UK Great Britain	29 Jan 54	190UNTS319	102572
Czechoslovakia	Greece	01 Feb 54	225UNTS95	103092
Czechoslovakia	Greece	01 Feb 54	225UNTS77	103091
Finland	USSR (Soviet Union)	06 Feb 54	221UNTS143	103006
France	Greece	08 Feb 54	225UNTS107	103093
France	Greece	08 Feb 54	225UNTS121	103094
Turkey	UK Great Britain	11 Feb 54	190UNTS343	102575
Multilateral		25 Feb 54	215UNTS249	102922
Denmark	Italy	10 Apr 54	196UNTS175	102623
Czechoslovakia	Hungary	16 Apr 54	504UNTS231	107360
ECSC (Coal/Steel)	USA (United States)	23 Apr 54	229UNTS229	103170
Lebanon	USSR (Soviet Union)	30 Apr 54	226UNTS109	103111
Greece	Spain	15 May 54	299UNTS261	104318
Pakistan	Yugoslavia	15 May 54	286UNTS3	104158
Greece	Spain	15 May 54	299UNTS277	104319
Greece	Romania	19 May 54	225UNTS17	103083
Greece	Hungary	05 Jun 54	299UNTS285	104320
Greece	Hungary	05 Jun 54	299UNTS295	104321
Netherlands	Norway	09 Jun 54	287UNTS179	104184
Haiti	Italy	14 Jun 54	267UNTS97	103837
Belgium	Ireland	30 Jun 54	212UNTS255	102876
Multilateral		08 Jul 54	287UNTS27	104178
France	Netherlands	09 Jul 54	287UNTS169	104183
Belgium	UK Great Britain	09 Jul 54	201UNTS299	102721
Austria	UK Great Britain	09 Jul 54	201UNTS277	102720
Netherlands	UK Great Britain	09 Jul 54	199UNTS157	102682
Germany, West	UK Great Britain	10 Jul 54	199UNTS135	102680
Portugal	UK Great Britain	10 Jul 54	199UNTS169	102683
Belgium	Italy	12 Jul 54	288UNTS59	104198
Switzerland	UK Great Britain	16 Jul 54	199UNTS197	102685
Finland	USSR (Soviet Union)	17 Jul 54	240UNTS173	103403
France	Greece	22 Jul 54	225UNTS199	103099
Sweden	UK Great Britain	28 Jul 54	199UNTS181	102684
India	USA (United States)	29 Jul 54	239UNTS69	103373
Guatemala	USA (United States)	30 Jul 54	234UNTS235	103286
Thailand	USA (United States)	11 Aug 54	234UNTS155	103281
Netherlands	UK Great Britain	11 Aug 54	248UNTS235	103497
Hungary	UK Great Britain	19 Aug 54	199UNTS149	102681
Greece	USSR (Soviet Union)	02 Sep 54	230UNTS33	103175

PARTY ONE	PARTY TWO	DATE	CITATION	NUMBER
Payment schedules (Cont.)				
Multilateral		28 Sep 54	207UNTS293	102812
Germany, West	USA (United States)	15 Oct 54	239UNTS135	103375
Iran	UK Great Britain	25 Oct 54	204UNTS131	102754
Germany, West	Netherlands	29 Oct 54	237UNTS3	103335
Greece	Netherlands	01 Nov 54	223UNTS79	103057
Belgium	Yugoslavia	01 Nov 54	251UNTS123	103538
Burma	Japan	05 Nov 54	251UNTS215	103543
Greece	Italy	10 Nov 54	227UNTS9	103128
Poland	UK Great Britain	11 Nov 54	204UNTS137	102755
Turkey	USA (United States)	15 Nov 54	238UNTS135	103358
Belgium	Greece	16 Dec 54	223UNTS73	103056
Sweden	Switzerland	17 Dec 54	369UNTS233	105260
Italy	Yugoslavia	18 Dec 54	284UNTS239	104141
Iceland	Netherlands	28 Dec 54	287UNTS159	104182
USSR (Soviet Union)	Yugoslavia	05 Jan 55	240UNTS225	103405
USA (United States)	Yugoslavia	05 Jan 55	251UNTS29	103531
Turkey	UK Great Britain	17 Jan 55	204UNTS195	102758
Finland	USSR (Soviet Union)	24 Jan 55	240UNTS243	103406
Australia	Hungary	10 Feb 55	207UNTS173	102806
Greece	Japan	12 Mar 55	227UNTS33	103130
Bulgaria	Yugoslavia	16 Mar 55	397UNTS83	105702
Italy	Yugoslavia	31 Mar 55	386UNTS317	105551
Argentina	UK Great Britain	31 Mar 55	210UNTS223	102840
Ceylon (Sri Lanka)	Germany, West	01 Apr 55	369UNTS57	105251
Germany, West	USA (United States)	14 Apr 55	263UNTS351	103782
India	Pakistan	15 Apr 55	247UNTS25	103458
Belgium	San Marino	22 Apr 55	253UNTS41	103574
Finland	USA (United States)	06 May 55	251UNTS3	103529
USA (United States)	Yugoslavia	12 May 55	251UNTS337	103550
Italy	USA (United States)	19 May 55	269UNTS83	103876
Italy	Sweden	25 May 55	291UNTS235	104259
Korea, South	USA (United States)	31 May 55	251UNTS321	103548
France	Ireland	07 Jun 55	558UNTS217	108142
India	Pakistan	12 Jun 55	228UNTS211	103153
Austria	USA (United States)	14 Jun 55	258UNTS37	103668
France	Greece	28 Jun 55	225UNTS219	103100
Italy	USA (United States)	30 Jun 55	258UNTS15	103667
Spain	USA (United States)	16 Jul 55	270UNTS211	103899
Switzerland	USA (United States)	18 Jul 55	239UNTS311	103388
Ceylon (Sri Lanka)	USA (United States)	18 Jul 55	281UNTS295	104086
Italy	Switzerland	23 Jul 55	284UNTS279	104142
Greece	USSR (Soviet Union)	23 Aug 55	233UNTS39	103249
Belgium	USA (United States)	31 Aug 55	223UNTS111	103041
Thailand	USA (United States)	09 Sep 55	264UNTS285	103799
Bulgaria	UK Great Britain	22 Sep 55	222UNTS349	103039
Italy	Lebanon	04 Nov 55	267UNTS113	103838
Austria	USSR (Soviet Union)	09 Nov 55	255UNTS247	103613
Italy	Syria	10 Nov 55	267UNTS157	103841
Thailand	USA (United States)	14 Nov 55	239UNTS201	103380
Syria	USSR (Soviet Union)	16 Nov 55	259UNTS71	103683
Pakistan	Syria	18 Dec 55	320UNTS269	104647
USSR (Soviet Union)	Yugoslavia	19 Dec 55	378UNTS127	105423
New Zealand	UK Great Britain	20 Dec 55	268UNTS243	103860
Italy	Switzerland	22 Dec 55	260UNTS339	103717
USA (United States)	Yugoslavia	19 Jan 56	240UNTS121	103400
Denmark	Netherlands	31 Jan 56	286UNTS255	104172
USSR (Soviet Union)	Yugoslavia	02 Feb 56	259UNTS111	103685
Austria	Poland	08 Feb 56	334UNTS221	104770
Japan	USA (United States)	10 Feb 56	275UNTS105	103979
France	Italy	03 Mar 56	267UNTS181	103843
Burma	Yugoslavia	07 Mar 56	386UNTS207	105542
Canada	Hungary	08 Mar 56	305UNTS27	104409
Ceylon (Sri Lanka)	Romania	16 Mar 56	315UNTS51	104559
Ceylon (Sri Lanka)	Romania	16 Mar 56	315UNTS41	104558
Nicaragua	USA (United States)	19 Mar 56	275UNTS231	103984

PARTY ONE	PARTY TWO	DATE	CITATION	NUMBER
Payment schedules (Cont.)				
Austria	Italy	07 May 56	284UNTS351	104147
Denmark	Italy	12 May 56	260UNTS357	103720
Bulgaria	Yugoslavia	22 May 56	367UNTS119	105229
Netherlands	Yugoslavia	01 Jun 56	276UNTS319	103994
Sweden	UK Great Britain	09 Jun 56	309UNTS301	104479
Netherlands	UK Great Britain	12 Jun 56	250UNTS81	103519
Bulgaria	Ceylon (Sri Lanka)	19 Jun 56	315UNTS23	104556
Bulgaria	Ceylon (Sri Lanka)	19 Jun 56	315UNTS33	104557
France	Greece	25 Jun 56	251UNTS167	103540
Hungary	UK Great Britain	27 Jun 56	249UNTS19	103499
Italy	Switzerland	29 Jun 56	284UNTS299	104144
Italy	Netherlands	29 Jun 56	287UNTS193	104185
Burma	USA (United States)	30 Jun 56	281UNTS65	104070
Argentina	UK Great Britain	30 Jun 56	269UNTS235	103884
Denmark	UK Great Britain	09 Jul 56	264UNTS45	103787
Multilateral		09 Jul 56	314UNTS3	104539
France	UK Great Britain	10 Jul 56	326UNTS23	104708
Multilateral		13 Jul 56	281UNTS3	104066
Belgium	France	18 Jul 56	248UNTS121	103491
Greece	Romania	25 Aug 56	299UNTS231	104315
Multilateral		25 Sep 56	334UNTS89	104767
Multilateral		25 Sep 56	334UNTS13	104766
India	Poland	29 Sep 56	276UNTS305	103993
Germany, West	USA (United States)	08 Oct 56	278UNTS9	104018
Romania	Yugoslavia	27 Oct 56	389UNTS55	105592
Japan	USA (United States)	23 Nov 56	324UNTS177	104685
Belgium	Spain	28 Nov 56	308UNTS239	104464
Indonesia	Yugoslavia	14 Dec 56	378UNTS117	105422
Multilateral		19 Dec 56	427UNTS93	106148
Austria	Pakistan	24 Dec 56	316UNTS83	104579
Japan	Spain	08 Jan 57	318UNTS221	104615
Bulgaria	Czechoslovakia	25 Jan 57	501UNTS149	107316
Italy	UK Great Britain	29 Jan 57	326UNTS119	104710
Netherlands	USA (United States)	15 Feb 57	287UNTS239	104190
Burma	India	12 Mar 57	312UNTS131	104515
Liberia	USA (United States)	16 Mar 57	290UNTS59	104228
Saudi Arabia	USA (United States)	02 Apr 57	283UNTS97	104109
Canada	Netherlands	13 Apr 57	316UNTS223	104588
Netherlands	Paraguay	13 Apr 57	593UNTS85	108577
Colombia	USA (United States)	16 Apr 57	283UNTS245	104121
Canada	Norway	17 Apr 57	316UNTS215	104587
Canada	Denmark	17 Apr 57	316UNTS207	104586
Ceylon (Sri Lanka)	Italy	23 Apr 57	337UNTS115	104820
Argentina	Uruguay	27 Apr 57	635UNTS69	109072
Israel	UK Great Britain	29 Apr 57	280UNTS227	104062
Japan	USA (United States)	08 May 57	318UNTS257	104621
Denmark	Paraguay	18 May 57	286UNTS117	104163
Belgium	UK Great Britain	20 May 57	303UNTS53	104371
Czechoslovakia	Yugoslavia	22 May 57	391UNTS57	105617
Ceylon (Sri Lanka)	UK Great Britain	07 Jun 57	280UNTS107	104055
Italy	United Arab Rep	06 Jul 57	302UNTS147	104357
Denmark	Italy	12 Jul 57	291UNTS169	104251
Norway	UK Great Britain	25 Jul 57	313UNTS3	104528
Taiwan	USA (United States)	30 Jul 57	300UNTS61	104331
India	USA (United States)	19 Sep 57	290UNTS175	104236
Ceylon (Sri Lanka)	China People's Rep	19 Sep 57	337UNTS137	104821
Multilateral		03 Oct 57	366UNTS3	105215
Multilateral		03 Oct 57	365UNTS3	105213
Multilateral		03 Oct 57	365UNTS207	105214
Multilateral		03 Oct 57	366UNTS141	105217
Hungary	Yugoslavia	07 Oct 57	439UNTS61	106325
Taiwan	USA (United States)	08 Oct 57	304UNTS241	104400
USA (United States)	Vietnam, South	05 Nov 57	300UNTS23	104328
France	Italy	08 Nov 57	305UNTS393	104427
Argentina	Denmark	25 Nov 57	299UNTS83	104308

PARTY ONE	PARTY TWO	DATE	CITATION	NUMBER
Payment schedules (Cont.)				
Argentina	Italy	25 Nov 57	305UNTS275	104424
China People's Rep	Denmark	01 Dec 57	309UNTS241	104475
Italy	Monaco	06 Dec 57	363UNTS45	105198
Germany, West	USA (United States)	10 Dec 57	307UNTS59	104442
Italy	Yugoslavia	12 Dec 57	386UNTS293	105549
Bulgaria	Yugoslavia	18 Dec 57	376UNTS3	105372
Greece	USA (United States)	18 Dec 57	303UNTS159	104379
Poland	Yugoslavia	16 Jan 58	340UNTS137	104863
Indonesia	Japan	20 Jan 58	324UNTS247	104689
Indonesia	Japan	20 Jan 58	324UNTS227	104688
Italy	Romania	28 Jan 58	302UNTS231	104362
Australia	UK Great Britain	29 Jan 58	292UNTS233	104275
Iran	Italy	29 Jan 58	302UNTS181	104358
France	USA (United States)	30 Jan 58	304UNTS9	104388
Bulgaria	Netherlands	07 Feb 58	335UNTS45	104777
Ceylon (Sri Lanka)	USSR (Soviet Union)	08 Feb 58	348UNTS159	104999
Greece	India	14 Feb 58	609UNTS94	108827
Poland	USA (United States)	15 Feb 58	307UNTS217	104452
Canada	India	20 Feb 58	391UNTS231	105628
Bulgaria	Italy	25 Feb 58	362UNTS291	105194
Bulgaria	Italy	25 Feb 58	362UNTS279	105193
Bulgaria	Yugoslavia	21 Mar 58	386UNTS119	105541
Jordan	UK Great Britain	26 Mar 58	312UNTS373	104526
Belgium	Greece	01 Apr 58	388UNTS93	105574
Italy	Tunisia	08 Apr 58	378UNTS327	105430
Peru	USA (United States)	09 Apr 58	316UNTS37	104576
Belgium	Japan	30 Apr 58	303UNTS109	104373
Jordan	UK Great Britain	07 May 58	312UNTS379	104527
Albania	Italy	26 May 58	362UNTS259	105191
Multilateral		18 Jun 58	386UNTS345	105552
Multilateral		18 Jun 58	386UNTS355	105553
Italy	Morocco	24 Jun 58	363UNTS23	105197
Denmark	Romania	25 Jun 58	345UNTS231	104970
Ecuador	USA (United States)	27 Jun 58	317UNTS51	104593
Denmark	Hungary	17 Jul 58	344UNTS281	104954
Netherlands	Yugoslavia	22 Jul 58	386UNTS263	105546
Burma	USA (United States)	25 Aug 58	336UNTS3	104795
United Arab Rep	USSR (Soviet Union)	18 Sep 58	338UNTS29	104831
Australia	New Zealand	30 Sep 58	340UNTS61	104859
Germany, West	UK Great Britain	03 Oct 58	398UNTS293	105731
Iraq	USSR (Soviet Union)	11 Oct 58	328UNTS95	104730
Fed Rhod/Nyasaland	South Africa	11 Oct 58	373UNTS75	105315
Canada	India	22 Oct 58	392UNTS21	105635
Multilateral		27 Oct 58	351UNTS303	105031
Canada	USA (United States)	31 Oct 58	391UNTS219	105626
Canada	Ceylon (Sri Lanka)	05 Nov 58	391UNTS225	105627
Turkey	UK Great Britain	25 Nov 58	327UNTS35	104715
Netherlands	Turkey	29 Nov 58	335UNTS229	104790
Israel	Yugoslavia	11 Dec 58	386UNTS283	105548
Iraq	Romania	24 Dec 58	405UNTS243	105836
Portugal	USA (United States)	12 Jan 59	343UNTS49	104921
United Arab Rep	USA (United States)	13 Jan 59	358UNTS3	105122
Burma	UK Great Britain	06 Feb 59	343UNTS223	104927
Cambodia	Japan	02 Mar 59	341UNTS163	104882
India	USA (United States)	03 Mar 59	341UNTS235	104886
France	UK Great Britain	05 Mar 59	343UNTS277	104932
Austria	UK Great Britain	14 Mar 59	343UNTS263	104930
Germany, West	USA (United States)	20 Mar 59	341UNTS15	104874
Netherlands	Switzerland	14 Apr 59	486UNTS367	107086
Sweden	UK Great Britain	18 Apr 59	360UNTS89	105156
Belgium	UK Great Britain	23 Apr 59	343UNTS271	104931
Norway	UK Great Britain	23 Apr 59	343UNTS283	104933
Belgium	Netherlands	28 Apr 59	485UNTS123	107049
France	Netherlands	29 Apr 59	486UNTS379	107088
Italy	United Arab Rep	29 Apr 59	363UNTS91	105202

PARTY ONE	PARTY TWO	DATE	CITATION	NUMBER
Payment schedules (Cont.)				
Austria	Netherlands	29 Apr 59	486UNTS373	107087
Italy	Netherlands	29 Apr 59	486UNTS387	107089
Netherlands	Portugal	30 Apr 59	485UNTS129	107050
Iceland	Netherlands	30 Apr 59	487UNTS13	107091
Netherlands	Norway	30 Apr 59	487UNTS3	107090
Netherlands	Sweden	30 Apr 59	485UNTS147	107053
Greece	Netherlands	30 Apr 59	485UNTS135	107051
Denmark	Netherlands	30 Apr 59	487UNTS23	107092
Germany, West	Netherlands	30 Apr 59	485UNTS141	107052
Ceylon (Sri Lanka)	Yugoslavia	05 May 59	391UNTS101	105618
Switzerland	UK Great Britain	06 May 59	343UNTS315	104938
France	USA (United States)	07 May 59	354UNTS83	105055
Multilateral		11 May 59	527UNTS145	107623
Iceland	UK Great Britain	14 May 59	343UNTS301	104936
Greece	UK Great Britain	21 May 59	344UNTS3	104939
Denmark	Japan	25 May 59	341UNTS157	104881
Czechoslovakia	Switzerland	04 Jun 59	349UNTS121	105012
Ethiopia	Yugoslavia	06 Jun 59	386UNTS243	105544
Italy	Norway	12 Jun 59	428UNTS363	106187
Turkey	UK Great Britain	13 Jun 59	551UNTS59	108033
Greece	Yugoslavia	18 Jun 59	368UNTS125	105237
Greece	Yugoslavia	18 Jun 59	368UNTS3	105231
Greece	Yugoslavia	18 Jun 59	368UNTS27	105234
Ethiopia	Greece	22 Jun 59	534UNTS147	107759
Fed of Malaya	UK Great Britain	27 Jul 59	374UNTS21	105324
Finland	UK Great Britain	28 Jul 59	355UNTS31	105073
Germany, West	Norway	07 Aug 59	358UNTS185	105136
Multilateral		08 Sep 59	383UNTS203	105502
Turkey	UK Great Britain	09 Sep 59	424UNTS267	106113
India	Italy	06 Oct 59	378UNTS267	105427
Multilateral		09 Oct 59	376UNTS382	105391
Italy	Tunisia	31 Oct 59	378UNTS349	105431
Tunisia	UK Great Britain	16 Nov 59	354UNTS367	105070
Norway	Yugoslavia	18 Nov 59	383UNTS131	105499
Taiwan	USA (United States)	02 Dec 59	361UNTS115	105175
Canada	UK Great Britain	10 Dec 59	379UNTS201	105440
Multilateral		14 Dec 59	422UNTS75	106069
Denmark	Sweden	04 Jan 60	376UNTS375	105390
El Salvador	USA (United States)	29 Jan 60	372UNTS3	105283
Cuba	USSR (Soviet Union)	13 Feb 60	369UNTS17	105248
Korea, South	USA (United States)	19 Feb 60	372UNTS109	105291
Chile	USA (United States)	19 Feb 60	371UNTS255	105282
Greece	Tunisia	02 Mar 60	483UNTS89	107008
Multilateral		15 Mar 60	572UNTS133	108310
Austria	Guatemala	18 Mar 60	379UNTS89	105435
New Zealand	USA (United States)	23 Mar 60	371UNTS147	105276
Ireland	USA (United States)	24 Mar 60	371UNTS237	105280
Ireland	UK Great Britain	29 Mar 60	371UNTS3	105267
Multilateral		15 Apr 60	470UNTS239	106811
Germany, West	UK Great Britain	20 Apr 60	449UNTS77	106453
Germany, West	UK Great Britain	20 Apr 60	413UNTS236	105958
Germany, East	USSR (Soviet Union)	24 May 60	392UNTS205	105645
UN Special Fund	Thailand	04 Jun 60	360UNTS97	105157
Cuba	Czechoslovakia	10 Jun 60	447UNTS75	106412
Austria	Spain	17 Jun 60	390UNTS17	105600
Belgium	Netherlands	20 Jun 60	423UNTS19	106084
Somalia	UK Great Britain	26 Jun 60	374UNTS331	105346
Somalia	UK Great Britain	26 Jun 60	374UNTS339	105347
IAEA (Atom Energy)	USA (United States)	28 Jun 60	374UNTS133	105333
Peru	USA (United States)	15 Jul 60	384UNTS159	105517
Poland	USA (United States)	16 Jul 60	384UNTS169	105518
Spain	USA (United States)	21 Jul 60	393UNTS289	105663
Brazil	Greece	30 Jul 60	607UNTS245	108808
Ghana	USSR (Soviet Union)	04 Aug 60	421UNTS27	106050
Ghana	USSR (Soviet Union)	04 Aug 60	399UNTS61	105734

Payment schedules (Cont.)

PARTY ONE	PARTY TWO	DATE	CITATION	NUMBER
Cyprus	UK Great Britain	16 Aug 60	382UNTS239	105485
Korea, South	USA (United States)	17 Aug 60	400UNTS339	105757
United Arab Rep	USSR (Soviet Union)	27 Aug 60	399UNTS37	105733
Argentina	Bolivia	07 Sep 60	0UNTS0	109516
Austria	Czechoslovakia	14 Sep 60	495UNTS143	107243
Multilateral		19 Sep 60	419UNTS125	106032
Multilateral		19 Sep 60	444UNTS259	106371
Netherlands	Romania	30 Sep 60	479UNTS91	106948
Greece	Poland	08 Nov 60	483UNTS141	107011
Greece	Poland	08 Nov 60	483UNTS127	107010
Korea, South	USA (United States)	18 Nov 60	400UNTS49	105747
Israel	USA (United States)	19 Dec 60	401UNTS195	105772
Multilateral		30 Dec 60	395UNTS241	105689
Albania	Cuba	16 Jan 61	448UNTS67	106425
Canada	USA (United States)	17 Jan 61	542UNTS224	107894
Australia	Japan	07 Feb 61	450UNTS343	106478
Belgium	Netherlands	24 Feb 61	474UNTS167	106881
Japan	Pakistan	07 Mar 61	450UNTS359	106479
Philippines	USA (United States)	12 Mar 61	288UNTS285	104210
Brazil	USA (United States)	17 Mar 61	406UNTS241	105853
Multilateral		10 Apr 61	402UNTS281	105791
USA (United States)	Yugoslavia	19 Apr 61	409UNTS163	105883
Honduras	IDA (Devel Assoc)	12 May 61	414UNTS180	105973
Somalia	USSR (Soviet Union)	02 Jun 61	493UNTS173	107214
IDA (Devel Assoc)	Sudan	14 Jun 61	415UNTS50	105981
India	IDA (Devel Assoc)	21 Jun 61	418UNTS61	106017
Chile	IDA (Devel Assoc)	28 Jun 61	426UNTS89	106131
Indonesia	Japan	01 Jul 61	517UNTS107	107484
Bulgaria	Netherlands	07 Jul 61	489UNTS21	107133
Jordan	UK Great Britain	17 Jul 61	420UNTS53	106039
UK Great Britain	Yugoslavia	21 Jul 61	420UNTS61	106040
Brazil	UK Great Britain	21 Jul 61	414UNTS26	105962
Austria	Romania	21 Jul 61	421UNTS161	106057
Albania	Austria	27 Jul 61	407UNTS37	105858
Multilateral		28 Aug 61	416UNTS45	105994
Colombia	IDA (Devel Assoc)	28 Aug 61	416UNTS3	105992
Taiwan	IDA (Devel Assoc)	30 Aug 61	417UNTS227	106008
Taiwan	IDA (Devel Assoc)	30 Aug 61	416UNTS175	106003
Taiwan	IDA (Devel Assoc)	06 Sep 61	417UNTS253	106009
India	IDA (Devel Assoc)	06 Sep 61	418UNTS81	106018
Hungary	Romania	07 Sep 61	519UNTS141	107506
Pakistan	Philippines	29 Sep 61	422UNTS3	106065
Multilateral		04 Oct 61	412UNTS210	105934
Switzerland	UK Great Britain	20 Oct 61	431UNTS29	106206
Iraq	Syria	03 Nov 61	489UNTS45	107134
Ghana	USSR (Soviet Union)	04 Nov 61	437UNTS213	106308
Ghana	USSR (Soviet Union)	04 Nov 61	0UNTS0	109381
United Nations	USA (United States)	18 Nov 61	494UNTS213	107235
India	IDA (Devel Assoc)	22 Nov 61	427UNTS55	106146
India	IDA (Devel Assoc)	22 Nov 61	427UNTS29	106145
India	IDA (Devel Assoc)	22 Nov 61	427UNTS3	106144
Morocco	USA (United States)	30 Nov 61	451UNTS167	106492
Ivory Coast	USA (United States)	01 Dec 61	462UNTS221	106681
Taiwan	IDA (Devel Assoc)	01 Dec 61	426UNTS105	106132
IBRD (World Bank)	South Africa	01 Dec 61	425UNTS197	106125
Japan	USA (United States)	09 Jan 62	451UNTS97	106488
UK Great Britain	Zambia	30 Jan 62	590UNTS173	108553
Hungary	Yugoslavia	09 Feb 62	577UNTS3	108370
Bolivia	USA (United States)	12 Feb 62	451UNTS281	106499
Multilateral		20 Feb 62	597UNTS159	108644
Multilateral		23 Mar 62	434UNTS145	106262
Liberia	USA (United States)	12 Apr 62	445UNTS213	106390
Dominican Republic	USA (United States)	02 May 62	442UNTS99	106341
France	Romania	18 May 62	498UNTS115	107279
Jordan	UK Great Britain	30 May 62	449UNTS167	106458

Payment schedules (Cont.)

PARTY ONE	PARTY TWO	DATE	CITATION	NUMBER
Thailand	USA (United States)	31 May 62	459UNTS135	106619
Germany, West	Israel	01 Jun 62	448UNTS227	106435
United Arab Rep	USSR (Soviet Union)	23 Jun 62	472UNTS43	106836
United Arab Rep	USSR (Soviet Union)	23 Jun 62	472UNTS19	106835
Multilateral		27 Jun 62	463UNTS17	106690
Taiwan	Paraguay	11 Jul 62	458UNTS41	106591
Chile	USA (United States)	07 Aug 62	461UNTS61	106652
Ethiopia	USA (United States)	13 Aug 62	459UNTS31	106611
IAEA (Atom Energy)	USA (United States)	20 Aug 62	456UNTS447	106570
Cyprus	Greece	23 Aug 62	609UNTS15	108825
Israel	USA (United States)	28 Aug 62	448UNTS317	106445
Taiwan	USA (United States)	31 Aug 62	460UNTS247	106644
Morocco	USA (United States)	11 Sep 62	462UNTS207	106680
Belgium	Germany, West	21 Sep 62	502UNTS63	107326
Finland	USSR (Soviet Union)	27 Sep 62	479UNTS99	106949
Multilateral		28 Sep 62	469UNTS169	106791
Uganda	UK Great Britain	10 Oct 62	475UNTS177	106893
Multilateral		16 Oct 62	470UNTS291	106814
Germany, West	Ireland	17 Oct 62	604UNTS135	108749
Czechoslovakia	Yugoslavia	22 Oct 62	480UNTS267	106974
Japan	UK Great Britain	14 Nov 62	478UNTS29	106934
Czechoslovakia	Poland	16 Nov 62	526UNTS3	107597
Dominican Republic	USA (United States)	30 Nov 62	471UNTS25	106819
Laos	USSR (Soviet Union)	01 Dec 62	458UNTS21	106590
Laos	USSR (Soviet Union)	01 Dec 62	471UNTS181	106832
Multilateral		08 Dec 62	510UNTS235	107418
Austria	Yugoslavia	11 Dec 62	546UNTS3	107938
Hungary	USSR (Soviet Union)	20 Dec 62	577UNTS245	108381
Nigeria	USA (United States)	24 Dec 62	462UNTS180	106677
Brazil	Taiwan	28 Dec 62	500UNTS61	107307
Jamaica	USA (United States)	04 Jan 63	471UNTS119	106826
Greece	Pakistan	17 Jan 63	538UNTS175	107814
Bolivia	USA (United States)	04 Feb 63	473UNTS65	106856
Japan	USA (United States)	19 Feb 63	473UNTS107	106859
India	New Zealand	22 Feb 63	486UNTS19	107069
Colombia	USA (United States)	27 Mar 63	489UNTS289	107145
Burma	Japan	29 Mar 63	518UNTS3	107490
Multilateral		02 Apr 63	475UNTS121	106889
Burma	UK Great Britain	02 Apr 63	475UNTS139	106890
Ecuador	USA (United States)	05 Apr 63	477UNTS135	106919
Austria	Bulgaria	05 Apr 63	480UNTS3	106963
Gabon	USA (United States)	10 Apr 63	474UNTS113	106876
Belgium	USA (United States)	19 Apr 63	493UNTS83	107209
Brazil	USSR (Soviet Union)	20 Apr 63	0UNTS0	109256
Poland	USSR (Soviet Union)	22 Apr 63	493UNTS229	107217
Greece	Hungary	27 Apr 63	550UNTS197	108016
Jordan	UK Great Britain	27 Apr 63	475UNTS169	106892
Austria	Bulgaria	02 May 63	535UNTS143	107778
Belgium	Netherlands	13 May 63	540UNTS3	107843
Argentina	UK Great Britain	05 Jun 63	482UNTS353	107004
Finland	Poland	10 Jun 63	503UNTS179	107343
Ethiopia	USA (United States)	11 Jun 63	487UNTS269	107109
Japan	USA (United States)	14 Jun 63	479UNTS165	106951
Austria	IAEA (Atom Energy)	21 Jun 63	490UNTS351	107164
India	USA (United States)	27 Jun 63	479UNTS215	106955
United Arab Rep	USA (United States)	29 Jun 63	479UNTS207	106954
Finland	IAEA (Atom Energy)	02 Jul 63	490UNTS403	107167
Senegal	USA (United States)	03 Jul 63	527UNTS95	107620
Austria	Mongolia	15 Jul 63	496UNTS171	107251
Mali	Tunisia	24 Jul 63	602UNTS91	108708
New Zealand	USSR (Soviet Union)	01 Aug 63	486UNTS27	107070
France	USA (United States)	01 Aug 63	527UNTS89	107619
Argentina	Bolivia	02 Aug 63	0UNTS0	109517
Tanganyika	USSR (Soviet Union)	14 Aug 63	493UNTS195	107215
Iraq	USA (United States)	27 Aug 63	489UNTS271	107144

PARTY ONE	PARTY TWO	DATE	CITATION	NUMBER
Payment schedules (Cont.)				
Denmark	Norway	12 Sep 63	613UNTS289	108857
Paraguay	USA (United States)	16 Sep 63	494UNTS101	107229
Australia	UK Great Britain	23 Sep 63	483UNTS39	107006
Greece	Poland	30 Sep 63	534UNTS23	107751
Italy	IAEA (Atom Energy)	11 Oct 63	639UNTS25	109142
Multilateral		19 Oct 63	523UNTS249	107559
Multilateral		23 Oct 63	506UNTS197	107388
Multilateral		09 Nov 63	489UNTS209	107141
Multilateral		14 Nov 63	619UNTS299	108948
Syria	USA (United States)	18 Nov 63	494UNTS169	107232
Argentina	USA (United States)	30 Nov 63	505UNTS131	107369
IAEA (Atom Energy)	Yugoslavia	07 Dec 63	501UNTS273	107322
Multilateral		18 Dec 63	490UNTS383	107166
Netherlands	Poland	20 Dec 63	514UNTS169	107446
Greece	Poland	21 Dec 63	538UNTS155	107813
Romania	Yugoslavia	25 Dec 63	576UNTS95	108366
Kenya	UK Great Britain	16 Jan 64	502UNTS213	107332
Finland	IAEA (Atom Energy)	27 Jan 64	501UNTS213	107319
Australia	USA (United States)	05 Feb 64	511UNTS103	107430
Iceland	USA (United States)	13 Feb 64	511UNTS3	107421
Denmark	USSR (Soviet Union)	27 Feb 64	509UNTS285	107407
Multilateral		08 Apr 64	501UNTS221	107320
Liberia	USA (United States)	14 Apr 64	526UNTS221	107606
USA (United States)	Yugoslavia	27 Apr 64	526UNTS73	107601
USA (United States)	Yugoslavia	27 Apr 64	526UNTS89	107602
USA (United States)	Yugoslavia	28 Apr 64	526UNTS103	107603
Korea, South	USA (United States)	12 May 64	529UNTS299	107667
Norway	Romania	21 May 64	563UNTS45	108203
France	Italy	02 Jun 64	634UNTS117	109056
Taiwan	Ecuador	17 Jun 64	533UNTS141	107740
Ireland	USA (United States)	18 Jun 64	530UNTS217	107684
UK Great Britain	USA (United States)	19 Jun 64	530UNTS99	107675
Ireland	UK Great Britain	25 Jun 64	553UNTS221	108090
Malaysia	UK Great Britain	09 Jul 64	522UNTS189	107545
Malaysia	UK Great Britain	09 Jul 64	522UNTS201	107546
Malaysia	UK Great Britain	09 Jul 64	522UNTS213	107547
Multilateral		10 Jul 64	613UNTS193	108852
Multilateral		10 Jul 64	613UNTS3	108850
Austria	Spain	15 Jul 64	589UNTS169	108541
Germany, West	UK Great Britain	27 Jul 64	539UNTS243	107835
Jordan	UK Great Britain	31 Aug 64	541UNTS3	107856
Taiwan	Mexico	25 Sep 64	547UNTS233	107960
Israel	USSR (Soviet Union)	07 Oct 64	516UNTS59	107471
Brazil	UK Great Britain	14 Oct 64	539UNTS289	107840
Czechoslovakia	Hungary	17 Oct 64	545UNTS21	107924
Taiwan	Ecuador	23 Oct 64	543UNTS241	107904
USA (United States)	Yugoslavia	28 Oct 64	533UNTS3	107728
USA (United States)	Yugoslavia	29 Oct 64	533UNTS17	107729
Austria	Hungary	31 Oct 64	605UNTS3	108758
Austria	Hungary	31 Oct 64	605UNTS63	108759
Greece	Yugoslavia	05 Nov 64	539UNTS13	107820
USA (United States)	Yugoslavia	05 Nov 64	550UNTS31	108007
Taiwan	Guatemala	08 Nov 64	543UNTS227	107903
Iran	USA (United States)	16 Nov 64	532UNTS213	107719
Greece	USA (United States)	17 Nov 64	532UNTS107	107714
India	UK Great Britain	20 Nov 64	534UNTS85	107756
Iceland	USA (United States)	30 Dec 64	542UNTS37	107878
Iceland	USA (United States)	30 Dec 64	531UNTS287	107709
Taiwan	USA (United States)	31 Dec 64	532UNTS59	107712
Malta	Switzerland	20 Jan 65	548UNTS193	107978
Sierra Leone	USA (United States)	29 Jan 65	542UNTS87	107882
Benelux Econ Union	Poland	17 Feb 65	547UNTS165	107956
Belgium	United Nations	20 Feb 65	535UNTS197	107780
France	UK Great Britain	25 Feb 65	543UNTS157	107899
USA (United States)	Yugoslavia	16 Mar 65	542UNTS161	107887

PARTY ONE	PARTY TWO	DATE	CITATION	NUMBER
Payment schedules (Cont.)				
Dominican Republic	USA (United States)	18 Mar 65	542UNTS215	107892
Ivory Coast	USA (United States)	05 Apr 65	546UNTS143	107941
Israel	UK Great Britain	15 Apr 65	551UNTS19	108031
Australia	Germany, West	21 Apr 65	598UNTS25	108654
Philippines	USA (United States)	23 Apr 65	546UNTS157	107942
India	IBRD (World Bank)	28 May 65	552UNTS39	108049
Finland	USSR (Soviet Union)	04 Jun 65	560UNTS169	108173
Gambia	UK Great Britain	05 Jun 65	551UNTS193	108041
Jordan	UK Great Britain	08 Jun 65	552UNTS251	108057
Ecuador	USA (United States)	25 Jun 65	549UNTS23	107986
New Zealand	Poland	07 Jul 65	548UNTS19	107966
Australia	Germany, West	08 Jul 65	543UNTS305	107907
Malta	Yugoslavia	15 Jul 65	561UNTS223	108186
USA (United States)	Yugoslavia	16 Jul 65	549UNTS111	107994
Hungary	Poland	18 Jul 65	577UNTS161	108376
Israel	USA (United States)	26 Jul 65	549UNTS49	107988
Bolivia	USA (United States)	17 Aug 65	587UNTS289	108514
Ethiopia	USA (United States)	17 Aug 65	564UNTS119	108224
Australia	Korea, South	21 Sep 65	548UNTS163	107977
Multilateral		24 Sep 65	556UNTS141	108124
Australia	USSR (Soviet Union)	15 Oct 65	553UNTS239	108092
Turkey	UK Great Britain	21 Oct 65	561UNTS185	108180
Austria	Yugoslavia	19 Nov 65	591UNTS3	108556
USA (United States)	Yugoslavia	22 Nov 65	574UNTS211	108351
Chile	UK Great Britain	23 Nov 65	560UNTS215	108176
Ethiopia	USA (United States)	14 Dec 65	574UNTS115	108344
France	Israel	17 Dec 65	581UNTS311	108451
United Arab Rep	USA (United States)	03 Jan 66	579UNTS83	108400
Liberia	USA (United States)	06 Jan 66	592UNTS101	108570
Iran	USSR (Soviet Union)	13 Jan 66	633UNTS123	109037
Japan	USSR (Soviet Union)	21 Jan 66	633UNTS165	109038
Czechoslovakia	Poland	22 Jan 66	588UNTS175	108524
IAEA (Atom Energy)	Turkey	08 Feb 66	573UNTS75	108323
Multilateral		10 Feb 66	575UNTS129	108356
Algeria	USA (United States)	23 Feb 66	592UNTS117	108571
Multilateral		04 Mar 66	578UNTS57	108387
Singapore	USSR (Soviet Union)	02 Apr 66	631UNTS125	108992
Bulgaria	Turkey	18 Apr 66	631UNTS263	108999
Indonesia	USA (United States)	18 Apr 66	578UNTS106	108390
Paraguay	USA (United States)	27 Apr 66	578UNTS121	108391
Multilateral		04 May 66	575UNTS49	108354
Guyana	UK Great Britain	26 May 66	588UNTS143	108521
Burma	USA (United States)	01 Jun 66	580UNTS253	108428
Poland	Singapore	07 Jun 66	631UNTS189	108994
Bel-Lux Econ Union	Bulgaria	14 Jun 66	601UNTS167	108694
Greece	United Nations	20 Jun 66	565UNTS3	108230
Australia	Poland	20 Jun 66	638UNTS201	109136
Multilateral		20 Jun 66	573UNTS41	108322
Romania	USSR (Soviet Union)	21 Jun 66	604UNTS81	108746
Australia	Bulgaria	22 Jun 66	607UNTS69	108796
Denmark	Jordan	28 Jun 66	574UNTS3	108338
Indonesia	USA (United States)	28 Jun 66	593UNTS201	108585
Brazil	Denmark	08 Jul 66	581UNTS95	108435
Jordan	UK Great Britain	26 Jul 66	597UNTS219	108647
UK Great Britain	Zambia	28 Jul 66	590UNTS191	108554
Turkey	UK Great Britain	29 Jul 66	597UNTS241	108649
Denmark	Malawi	01 Sep 66	586UNTS3	108493
Argentina	UK Great Britain	15 Sep 66	603UNTS151	108732
UN Special Fund	UPU (Postal Union)	21 Sep 66	573UNTS259	200626
Multilateral		28 Sep 66	589UNTS41	108534
USSR (Soviet Union)	Yugoslavia	29 Sep 66	608UNTS219	108818
Botswana	UK Great Britain	30 Sep 66	633UNTS339	109044
Mauritania	USSR (Soviet Union)	17 Oct 66	633UNTS231	109040
UK Great Britain	USA (United States)	27 Oct 66	597UNTS265	108650
IBRD (World Bank)	IFC (Finance Corp)	28 Oct 66	586UNTS225	200628

PARTY ONE	PARTY TWO	DATE	CITATION	NUMBER
Payment schedules (Cont.)				
Romania	United Arab Rep	14 Nov 66	642UNTS141	109170
Romania	United Arab Rep	14 Nov 66	642UNTS129	109169
Ghana	Romania	23 Nov 66	642UNTS63	109165
Ghana	Romania	23 Nov 66	642UNTS79	109166
Guinea	Romania	01 Dec 66	642UNTS89	109167
India	IAEA (Atom Energy)	09 Dec 66	603UNTS35	108722
Syria	USSR (Soviet Union)	18 Dec 66	633UNTS247	109041
Philippines	USA (United States)	22 Dec 66	591UNTS219	108559
Kuwait	UK Great Britain	29 Dec 66	617UNTS203	108914
Korea, South	New Zealand	31 Jan 67	598UNTS91	108656
Czechoslovakia	USSR (Soviet Union)	03 Feb 67	617UNTS267	108917
Ghana	UK Great Britain	27 Feb 67	606UNTS133	108783
Guatemala	IBRD (World Bank)	10 Mar 67	616UNTS139	108894
Haiti	Israel	28 Mar 67	630UNTS293	108975
Bulgaria	USSR (Soviet Union)	27 Apr 67	631UNTS3	108983
Netherlands	Romania	08 May 67	607UNTS105	108800
Italy	USSR (Soviet Union)	16 May 67	608UNTS79	108814
USSR (Soviet Union)	Zambia	26 May 67	643UNTS179	109191
Liberia	IBRD (World Bank)	05 Jun 67	633UNTS13	109031
IAEA (Atom Energy)	USA (United States)	07 Jun 67	614UNTS109	108866
Cameroon	UK Great Britain	16 Jun 67	618UNTS329	108933
Multilateral		23 Jun 67	614UNTS185	108871
UK Great Britain	Yugoslavia	30 Jun 67	642UNTS325	109182
Israel	USA (United States)	04 Aug 67	0UNTS0	109351
Multilateral		23 Aug 67	614UNTS145	108869
IAEA (Atom Energy)	USA (United States)	16 Oct 67	630UNTS57	108965
Multilateral		19 Oct 67	630UNTS69	108966
Denmark	Tanzania	01 Nov 67	619UNTS47	108938
Denmark	Iran	02 Nov 67	638UNTS217	109138
Multilateral		05 Nov 67	630UNTS77	108967
Finland	Hungary	10 Nov 67	643UNTS95	109186
Australia	Hungary	05 Dec 67	638UNTS209	109137
Italy	United Nations	15 Jan 68	635UNTS11	109070
Austria	Canada	28 Feb 68	636UNTS141	109101
Denmark	Malaysia	29 Feb 68	640UNTS29	109153
Israel	Singapore	24 Apr 68	642UNTS235	109176
Guyana	WHO (World Health)	03 Jul 68	642UNTS13	109161
Inter-Am Devel Bnk	UN Special Fund	16 Jul 68	640UNTS305	200640
Purchase authorizations				
UK Great Britain	USA (United States)	06 Dec 45	126UNTS13	101679
Hungary	Yugoslavia	11 May 47	130UNTS171	101730
Czechoslovakia	Yugoslavia	24 May 48	112UNTS215	101544
UK Great Britain	Yugoslavia	28 Sep 51	117UNTS107	101587
UK Great Britain	USA (United States)	29 Jul 52	179UNTS129	102362
ECSC (Coal/Steel)	USA (United States)	23 Apr 54	229UNTS229	103170
Chile	USA (United States)	27 Jan 55	262UNTS3	103735
Argentina	USA (United States)	25 Apr 55	251UNTS283	103546
Thailand	USA (United States)	21 Jun 55	262UNTS87	103738
Israel	USA (United States)	10 Nov 55	240UNTS3	103390
United Arab Rep	USA (United States)	14 Dec 55	240UNTS37	103392
Germany, West	USA (United States)	23 Dec 55	240UNTS79	103395
Japan	USA (United States)	10 Feb 56	275UNTS105	103979
Italy	USA (United States)	27 Feb 56	291UNTS287	104260
Chile	USA (United States)	13 Mar 56	275UNTS49	103975
Peru	USA (United States)	07 May 56	268UNTS285	103862
Multilateral		06 Jul 56	312UNTS109	104514
Pakistan	USA (United States)	07 Aug 56	281UNTS75	104071
Netherlands	USA (United States)	07 Aug 56	281UNTS57	104069
Greece	USA (United States)	08 Aug 56	277UNTS203	104007
Taiwan	USA (United States)	14 Aug 56	281UNTS257	104083
India	USA (United States)	29 Aug 56	278UNTS25	104019
Israel	USA (United States)	11 Sep 56	277UNTS215	104008
Spain	USA (United States)	23 Oct 56	277UNTS105	104001
Ceylon (Sri Lanka)	USA (United States)	02 Nov 56	282UNTS93	104094

PARTY ONE	PARTY TWO	DATE	CITATION	NUMBER
Purchase authorizations (Cont.)				
USA (United States)	Yugoslavia	03 Nov 56	277UNTS119	104002
Turkey	USA (United States)	12 Nov 56	282UNTS77	104093
Korea, South	USA (United States)	30 Jan 57	278UNTS85	104024
Ecuador	USA (United States)	15 Feb 57	279UNTS155	104037
Thailand	USA (United States)	04 Mar 57	279UNTS235	104043
Iceland	USA (United States)	11 Apr 57	283UNTS107	104110
Peru	USA (United States)	02 May 57	283UNTS55	104106
Austria	USA (United States)	10 May 57	283UNTS15	104103
Poland	USA (United States)	07 Jun 57	291UNTS41	104243
Bolivia	USA (United States)	07 Jun 57	291UNTS77	104245
Philippines	USA (United States)	25 Jun 57	289UNTS279	104224
Mexico	USA (United States)	23 Oct 57	300UNTS35	104330
Colombia	USA (United States)	06 Oct 59	358UNTS145	105132
Denmark	Sweden	04 Jan 60	376UNTS375	105390
Iceland	USA (United States)	30 Dec 60	401UNTS43	105761
Ghana	USSR (Soviet Union)	04 Nov 61	437UNTS213	106308
Morocco	USA (United States)	09 Feb 62	442UNTS135	106345
Brazil	Germany, West	30 Nov 63	0UNTS0	109425
Morocco	USA (United States)	23 Apr 65	594UNTS3	108591
Congo (Zaire)	USA (United States)	19 Jul 65	593UNTS215	108586
Jordan	USA (United States)	05 Apr 66	593UNTS239	108587
Pakistan	USA (United States)	26 May 66	594UNTS27	108592
IBRD (World Bank)	IFC (Finance Corp)	28 Oct 66	586UNTS225	200628
Australia	Romania	18 May 67	642UNTS25	109162
Non-interest rates and fees				
Anglo-Egypt Sudan	Fr Equatorial Afri	02 Nov 39	2UNTS209	200012
Brazil	Paraguay	14 Jun 41	54UNTS289	200201
UK Great Britain	USSR (Soviet Union)	16 Aug 41	91UNTS341	200269
Multilateral		22 Apr 42	8UNTS237	200044
Brazil	Uruguay	18 May 42	54UNTS369	200207
Panama	USA (United States)	18 May 42	124UNTS221	200422
Brazil	Paraguay	08 Oct 42	65UNTS191	200211
Mexico	USA (United States)	23 Dec 42	13UNTS231	200081
Brazil	Paraguay	11 Aug 44	67UNTS303	200227
UK Great Britain	USSR (Soviet Union)	23 Sep 44	10UNTS171	200060
UK Great Britain	USA (United States)	16 Apr 45	6UNTS189	100076
UK Great Britain	USA (United States)	16 Apr 45	6UNTS359	200039
Argentina	USA (United States)	09 May 45	139UNTS227	200453
Poland	Yugoslavia	23 Nov 45	115UNTS3	101555
Multilateral		04 Dec 45	9UNTS101	100128
Greece	UK Great Britain	24 Jan 46	6UNTS45	100067
France	USA (United States)	07 Feb 46	3UNTS239	100034
Netherlands	USA (United States)	09 Feb 46	3UNTS247	100035
UK Great Britain	USA (United States)	01 Mar 46	3UNTS293	100037
France	Norway	06 Mar 46	15UNTS13	100227
France	Norway	26 Mar 46	31UNTS69	100468
Multilateral		17 Apr 46	27UNTS103	100402
Thailand	UK Great Britain	01 May 46	99UNTS169	101377
Thailand	UK Great Britain	01 May 46	99UNTS175	101378
Multilateral		06 May 46	99UNTS181	101379
France	USA (United States)	28 May 46	84UNTS151	101125
Canada	UK Great Britain	05 Jun 46	27UNTS207	100408
Romania	Yugoslavia	26 Jun 46	116UNTS21	101566
Paraguay	USA (United States)	12 Sep 46	125UNTS179	101677
Argentina	USA (United States)	19 Sep 46	7UNTS131	100095
Denmark	USA (United States)	01 Oct 46	42UNTS219	100650
India	USA (United States)	14 Nov 46	22UNTS55	100331
Albania	Yugoslavia	28 Nov 46	111UNTS127	101525
Hungary	Yugoslavia	23 Dec 46	113UNTS125	101549
Denmark	UK Great Britain	20 Jan 47	118UNTS73	101597
Australia	Netherlands	24 Jan 47	10UNTS77	100144
USSR (Soviet Union)	Yugoslavia	04 Feb 47	130UNTS235	101731
Czechoslovakia	Yugoslavia	25 Feb 47	112UNTS3	101539
Czechoslovakia	Turkey	05 Mar 47	14UNTS101	100214

PARTY ONE	PARTY TWO	DATE	CITATION	NUMBER
Non-interest rates and fees (Cont.)				
Muscat and Oman	UK Great Britain	05 Apr 47	27UNTS287	100412
Poland	Yugoslavia	24 May 47	115UNTS37	101557
Albania	Yugoslavia	22 Jun 47	111UNTS207	101536
France	India	16 Jul 47	27UNTS325	100415
Hungary	Yugoslavia	24 Jul 47	114UNTS3	101554
Czechoslovakia	Greece	30 Jul 47	185UNTS115	102463
Chile	UK Great Britain	16 Sep 47	133UNTS143	101786
Multilateral		02 Oct 47	193UNTS188	102616
Sweden	Yugoslavia	06 Oct 47	53UNTS107	100775
Cuba	USA (United States)	30 Oct 47	119UNTS163	101611
Poland	Yugoslavia	07 Nov 47	115UNTS137	101561
Belgium	UK Great Britain	14 Nov 47	25UNTS269	100367
Peru	UK Great Britain	22 Dec 47	72UNTS143	100932
Ethiopia	Pakistan	01 Jan 48	35UNTS3	100547
Philippines	UK Great Britain	07 Jan 48	28UNTS63	100420
Italy	USA (United States)	02 Feb 48	79UNTS171	101040
Hungary	Yugoslavia	18 Mar 48	113UNTS201	101551
Hungary	Yugoslavia	18 Mar 48	113UNTS141	101550
Hungary	Yugoslavia	18 Mar 48	113UNTS219	101552
Canada	USA (United States)	31 Mar 48	81UNTS285	101077
Norway	Sweden	29 Apr 48	26UNTS41	100376
Pakistan	Sweden	06 May 48	36UNTS3	100564
Ireland	Switzerland	06 May 48	334UNTS187	104768
India	Sweden	21 May 48	34UNTS285	100543
Czechoslovakia	Yugoslavia	24 May 48	112UNTS111	101542
Luxembourg	UK Great Britain	27 May 48	53UNTS115	100776
India	Pakistan	23 Jun 48	28UNTS143	100423
Italy	UK Great Britain	25 Jun 48	94UNTS239	101313
Greece	Sweden	25 Jun 48	267UNTS337	103849
France	Norway	05 Jul 48	30UNTS281	100463
Ireland	UK Great Britain	31 Jul 48	86UNTS37	101151
Multilateral		18 Aug 48	33UNTS181	100518
France	Spain	23 Aug 48	28UNTS173	100425
France	USA (United States)	19 Oct 48	98UNTS3	101355
Czechoslovakia	Poland	12 Nov 48	84UNTS347	101141
Argentina	Denmark	14 Dec 48	74UNTS41	100956
Ceylon (Sri Lanka)	India	21 Dec 48	28UNTS223	100427
USSR (Soviet Union)	Yugoslavia	27 Dec 48	116UNTS327	101579
Ceylon (Sri Lanka)	Pakistan	03 Jan 49	28UNTS247	100428
Switzerland	Turkey	16 Feb 49	72UNTS175	100933
Denmark	Greece	25 Feb 49	78UNTS325	101022
Czechoslovakia	Yugoslavia	01 Mar 49	113UNTS3	101547
Netherlands	Switzerland	07 Mar 49	35UNTS69	100551
Multilateral		23 Mar 49	203UNTS179	102746
Panama	USA (United States)	31 Mar 49	55UNTS125	100811
Italy	Spain	31 May 49	231UNTS251	103224
Australia	Pakistan	03 Jun 49	35UNTS23	100549
Ethiopia	India	07 Jun 49	35UNTS13	100548
Norway	Pakistan	23 Jun 49	35UNTS49	100550
India	Switzerland	24 Jun 49	95UNTS109	101319
Argentina	UK Great Britain	27 Jun 49	83UNTS217	101110
Czechoslovakia	Poland	02 Jul 49	260UNTS179	103709
Czechoslovakia	Poland	02 Jul 49	260UNTS149	103708
Australia	India	11 Jul 49	35UNTS83	100552
Pakistan	Philippines	16 Jul 49	35UNTS111	100553
Pakistan	UK Great Britain	27 Jul 49	44UNTS199	100685
Brazil	UK Great Britain	03 Aug 49	86UNTS113	101154
Ceylon (Sri Lanka)	UK Great Britain	05 Aug 49	35UNTS137	100554
Multilateral		12 Aug 49	87UNTS131	101169
Canada	UK Great Britain	19 Aug 49	44UNTS223	100686
Belgium	Canada	30 Aug 49	53UNTS221	100782
Argentina	Norway	09 Sep 49	42UNTS125	100646
Belgium	United Arab Rep	19 Sep 49	137UNTS189	101853
Greece	Philippines	08 Oct 49	187UNTS221	102515
India	Philippines	20 Oct 49	72UNTS191	100934

PARTY ONE	PARTY TWO	DATE	CITATION	NUMBER
Non-interest rates and fees (Cont.)				
Iran	Netherlands	31 Oct 49	254UNTS257	103596
Denmark	Pakistan	09 Nov 49	44UNTS255	100687
Italy	Turkey	25 Nov 49	192UNTS39	102594
Netherlands	United Arab Rep	08 Dec 49	95UNTS123	101320
Sweden	United Arab Rep	12 Dec 49	108UNTS15	101466
Afghanistan	India	14 Dec 49	53UNTS95	100774
Austria	Switzerland	19 Dec 49	254UNTS287	103597
Multilateral		18 Feb 50	123UNTS45	101654
Norway	United Arab Rep	11 Mar 50	95UNTS157	101321
Denmark	United Arab Rep	14 Mar 50	95UNTS197	101322
Sweden	UK Great Britain	05 Apr 50	99UNTS107	101374
Turkey	United Arab Rep	12 Apr 50	128UNTS3	101711
Greece	United Arab Rep	24 Apr 50	163UNTS229	102149
Switzerland	United Arab Rep	15 May 50	95UNTS255	101325
Iraq	Pakistan	20 Jun 50	77UNTS215	101001
Netherlands	Spain	20 Jun 50	95UNTS303	101327
Denmark	Italy	01 Jul 50	133UNTS181	101788
Spain	UK Great Britain	20 Jul 50	398UNTS101	105719
France	Pakistan	31 Jul 50	96UNTS23	101329
Canada	France	01 Aug 50	73UNTS21	100941
Spain	Switzerland	03 Aug 50	254UNTS365	103600
France	United Arab Rep	08 Aug 50	127UNTS293	101710
Brazil	UK Great Britain	18 Sep 50	88UNTS115	101188
Ceylon (Sri Lanka)	United Arab Rep	26 Sep 50	192UNTS53	102595
Germany, West	Netherlands	14 Dec 50	87UNTS257	101177
Colombia	Denmark	26 Jan 51	87UNTS161	101171
Israel	Turkey	05 Feb 51	193UNTS3	102607
Greece	Yugoslavia	15 Mar 51	187UNTS237	102516
Pakistan	UK Great Britain	02 Apr 51	168UNTS281	102219
Multilateral		18 Apr 51	261UNTS140	103729
Iraq	UK Great Britain	19 Apr 51	108UNTS121	101470
Ceylon (Sri Lanka)	India	30 Apr 51	196UNTS199	102625
Belgium	UK Great Britain	08 May 51	158UNTS451	102079
Ceylon (Sri Lanka)	USA (United States)	14 May 51	141UNTS159	101913
India	Netherlands	24 May 51	108UNTS151	101471
Israel	Philippines	07 Aug 51	192UNTS81	102596
Lebanon	UK Great Britain	15 Aug 51	160UNTS327	102116
Burma	India	29 Sep 51	132UNTS71	101752
New Zealand	UK Great Britain	28 Nov 51	127UNTS263	101707
India	UK Great Britain	01 Dec 51	128UNTS39	101712
El Salvador	Guatemala	14 Dec 51	131UNTS131	101740
Jordan	United Arab Rep	02 Jan 52	192UNTS157	102599
UK Great Britain	USA (United States)	18 Jan 52	184UNTS79	102440
Pakistan	Switzerland	17 Mar 52	192UNTS237	102603
Iraq	Switzerland	31 Mar 52	311UNTS43	104498
France	Mexico	17 Apr 52	163UNTS321	102153
France	Israel	29 Apr 52	189UNTS55	102542
Mexico	UK Great Britain	12 Jun 52	196UNTS149	102622
Australia	United Arab Rep	14 Jun 52	173UNTS241	102269
India	United Arab Rep	14 Jun 52	173UNTS209	102268
Belgium	Israel	30 Jun 52	183UNTS263	102435
Netherlands	Pakistan	17 Jul 52	150UNTS277	101980
Japan	USA (United States)	11 Aug 52	212UNTS27	102862
Ethiopia	Pakistan	29 Aug 52	150UNTS257	101979
Austria	Luxembourg	13 Oct 52	192UNTS291	102606
Iceland	Luxembourg	23 Oct 52	193UNTS39	102609
Burma	UK Great Britain	25 Oct 52	150UNTS237	101978
Chile	Sweden	27 Oct 52	311UNTS63	104499
Chile	Denmark	27 Oct 52	271UNTS93	103911
Luxembourg	Sweden	17 Nov 52	173UNTS277	102270
Luxembourg	Norway	17 Nov 52	311UNTS95	104500
Israel	Switzerland	19 Nov 52	232UNTS3	103226
South Africa	Sweden	09 Jan 53	173UNTS299	102271
Netherlands	Philippines	05 Feb 53	216UNTS99	102934
Japan	Netherlands	17 Feb 53	192UNTS215	102602

PARTY ONE	PARTY TWO	DATE	CITATION	NUMBER
Non-interest rates and fees (Cont.)				
Japan	Sweden	20 Feb 53	173UNTS307	102272
Libya	UK Great Britain	21 Feb 53	311UNTS115	104501
Japan	Norway	23 Feb 53	192UNTS191	102601
Denmark	Japan	26 Feb 53	173UNTS329	102273
Lebanon	Sweden	23 Mar 53	255UNTS83	103605
Turkey	Yugoslavia	16 Apr 53	255UNTS99	103606
Syria	Turkey	28 Apr 53	204UNTS255	102760
Denmark	South Africa	30 Apr 53	174UNTS19	102275
Israel	South Africa	05 May 53	192UNTS183	102600
Switzerland	Yugoslavia	28 May 53	232UNTS45	103228
Japan	Thailand	19 Jun 53	174UNTS29	102276
Canada	Mexico	27 Jul 53	192UNTS255	102604
Norway	South Africa	21 Sep 53	192UNTS105	102597
Multilateral		01 Oct 53	258UNTS153	103677
Austria	Yugoslavia	11 Nov 53	363UNTS149	105206
Belgium	Lebanon	24 Dec 53	219UNTS153	102972
Ethiopia	Greece	20 Jan 54	222UNTS281	103035
Syria	UK Great Britain	05 Feb 54	204UNTS267	102761
France	Sweden	16 Feb 54	228UNTS137	103147
Multilateral		01 Mar 54	256UNTS31	103622
Switzerland	Syria	26 May 54	255UNTS145	103609
Iran	Switzerland	27 May 54	496UNTS273	107257
Greece	Portugal	13 Jul 54	230UNTS19	103173
Ireland	Luxembourg	27 Jul 54	232UNTS91	103231
Norway	USA (United States)	06 Aug 54	222UNTS269	103034
Thailand	USA (United States)	11 Aug 54	234UNTS155	103281
Brazil	USA (United States)	20 Aug 54	410UNTS79	105898
Belgium	South Africa	13 Sep 54	201UNTS15	102707
France	South Africa	17 Sep 54	216UNTS29	102930
Denmark	Philippines	20 Oct 54	216UNTS3	102927
Netherlands	Venezuela	26 Oct 54	232UNTS103	103232
Canada	Ireland	28 Oct 54	305UNTS3	104407
Pakistan	United Arab Rep	13 Dec 54	255UNTS167	103610
Norway	Switzerland	30 Dec 54	311UNTS147	104502
Austria	Belgium	07 Jan 55	380UNTS219	105458
Canada	Japan	12 Jan 55	311UNTS167	104503
Philippines	UK Great Britain	31 Jan 55	216UNTS51	102932
United Arab Rep	Yugoslavia	20 Feb 55	255UNTS199	103611
Iraq	United Arab Rep	23 Mar 55	311UNTS199	104504
Syria	United Arab Rep	03 Jul 55	393UNTS67	105652
Germany, West	USA (United States)	07 Jul 55	275UNTS3	103973
Germany, West	UK Great Britain	22 Jul 55	269UNTS189	103881
USSR (Soviet Union)	Yugoslavia	03 Sep 55	240UNTS267	103408
Thailand	USA (United States)	09 Sep 55	264UNTS285	103799
Belgium	Ireland	10 Sep 55	255UNTS235	103612
Bulgaria	Yugoslavia	01 Oct 55	396UNTS223	105698
France	Germany, West	04 Oct 55	353UNTS203	105044
Denmark	Syria	20 Oct 55	250UNTS61	103518
Austria	Italy	22 Oct 55	260UNTS327	103716
Pakistan	Turkey	02 Nov 55	311UNTS217	104505
Australia	South Africa	04 Nov 55	232UNTS143	103234
Burma	China People's Rep	08 Nov 55	306UNTS11	104430
Austria	USSR (Soviet Union)	09 Nov 55	255UNTS247	103613
Thailand	USA (United States)	14 Nov 55	239UNTS201	103380
Bulgaria	Yugoslavia	15 Nov 55	396UNTS191	105697
Austria	Israel	17 Nov 55	232UNTS153	103235
India	Japan	26 Nov 55	311UNTS243	104506
Korea, North	Romania	05 Dec 55	362UNTS141	105186
Costa Rica	Guatemala	20 Dec 55	280UNTS121	104056
France	Japan	17 Jan 56	255UNTS275	103614
Australia	Japan	19 Jan 56	311UNTS291	104507
Austria	Italy	23 Jan 56	393UNTS97	105653
Romania	Yugoslavia	01 Feb 56	362UNTS203	105189
India	USA (United States)	03 Feb 56	272UNTS75	103932
Austria	Poland	08 Feb 56	334UNTS221	104770

PARTY ONE	PARTY TWO	DATE	CITATION	NUMBER
Non-interest rates and fees (Cont.)				
Netherlands	Sudan	12 Feb 56	311UNTS319	104508
Norway	Syria	25 Feb 56	463UNTS217	106706
Burma	Yugoslavia	07 Mar 56	386UNTS207	105542
Belgium	Germany, West	14 Apr 56	344UNTS103	104945
Multilateral		25 Apr 56	270UNTS103	103896
Germany, West	Switzerland	02 May 56	559UNTS157	108158
Italy	South Africa	21 May 56	255UNTS323	103616
Japan	Switzerland	24 May 56	312UNTS3	104509
Greece	Italy	26 May 56	496UNTS301	107258
Italy	Switzerland	04 Jun 56	378UNTS311	105429
Poland	Sweden	08 Jun 56	334UNTS257	104771
Germany, West	Ireland	12 Jun 56	353UNTS121	105040
Guatemala	Honduras	22 Aug 56	263UNTS49	103767
Germany, West	Netherlands	28 Sep 56	327UNTS185	104722
India	Poland	29 Sep 56	276UNTS305	103993
Switzerland	Thailand	13 Oct 56	312UNTS43	104510
Belgium	Poland	17 Oct 56	356UNTS279	105100
Austria	UK Great Britain	27 Oct 56	264UNTS67	103789
Albania	Yugoslavia	23 Nov 56	386UNTS73	105539
Peru	Switzerland	23 Nov 56	411UNTS97	105916
Belgium	Romania	04 Dec 56	317UNTS161	104602
Iran	USA (United States)	16 Jan 57	308UNTS147	104460
Iceland	Thailand	22 Jan 57	312UNTS63	104511
Denmark	Germany, West	29 Jan 57	302UNTS75	104354
Germany, West	Sweden	29 Jan 57	393UNTS113	105654
Germany, West	Norway	29 Jan 57	353UNTS39	105037
Canada	USA (United States)	26 Feb 57	279UNTS179	104039
Netherlands	Yugoslavia	13 Mar 57	327UNTS227	104723
Netherlands	USA (United States)	03 Apr 57	410UNTS193	105904
Denmark	Pakistan	10 Apr 57	302UNTS53	104353
Germany, West	Yugoslavia	10 Apr 57	463UNTS269	106708
Romania	Sweden	15 Apr 57	342UNTS325	104915
Bulgaria	Sweden	17 Apr 57	464UNTS3	106709
Belgium	Bulgaria	14 May 57	317UNTS81	104596
Australia	Germany, West	22 May 57	357UNTS45	105105
Belgium	Hungary	01 Jun 57	291UNTS17	104242
Afghanistan	Pakistan	13 Jun 57	327UNTS51	104717
Czechoslovakia	United Arab Rep	30 Jun 57	411UNTS126	105917
Pakistan	USA (United States)	01 Jul 57	344UNTS203	104951
Greece	Italy	02 Aug 57	533UNTS217	107744
Hungary	Sweden	02 Aug 57	334UNTS307	104774
Netherlands	Romania	27 Aug 57	342UNTS309	104914
Ceylon (Sri Lanka)	China People's Rep	19 Sep 57	337UNTS137	104821
Italy	Switzerland	19 Sep 57	363UNTS69	105200
Multilateral		03 Oct 57	366UNTS87	105216
Italy	Pakistan	05 Oct 57	353UNTS91	105039
Fed of Malaya	UK Great Britain	18 Oct 57	335UNTS3	104775
Belgium	Netherlands	24 Oct 57	489UNTS11	107132
France	Morocco	25 Oct 57	559UNTS95	108156
Argentina	Denmark	25 Nov 57	299UNTS83	104308
UK Great Britain	USSR (Soviet Union)	19 Dec 57	351UNTS235	105026
Australia	Ireland	30 Dec 57	497UNTS29	107260
Canada	Switzerland	10 Jan 58	464UNTS21	106710
Belgium	Morocco	20 Jan 58	288UNTS3	104192
Czechoslovakia	Poland	31 Jan 58	431UNTS99	106214
Bulgaria	Netherlands	07 Feb 58	335UNTS45	104777
Australia	UK Great Britain	07 Feb 58	335UNTS23	104776
Afghanistan	Turkey	08 Feb 58	464UNTS39	106711
Sudan	Sweden	17 Feb 58	393UNTS161	105655
Norway	Pakistan	05 Mar 58	334UNTS199	104769
Pakistan	Sweden	06 Mar 58	393UNTS181	105656
Bulgaria	Yugoslavia	21 Mar 58	386UNTS119	105541
Germany, West	Portugal	21 Mar 58	464UNTS71	106712
South Africa	Sweden	28 Mar 58	300UNTS95	104333
Denmark	South Africa	28 Mar 58	300UNTS107	104334

PARTY ONE	PARTY TWO	DATE	CITATION	NUMBER
Non-interest rates and fees (Cont.)				
Norway	South Africa	28 Mar 58	300UNTS83	104332
Morocco	Portugal	03 Apr 58	393UNTS203	105657
Belgium	Iran	14 Apr 58	381UNTS309	105473
Sweden	Yugoslavia	18 Apr 58	393UNTS225	105658
Bulgaria	Denmark	28 May 58	312UNTS235	104521
India	USSR (Soviet Union)	02 Jun 58	393UNTS3	105650
Pakistan	Portugal	07 Jun 58	320UNTS225	104645
Denmark	Luxembourg	10 Jun 58	356UNTS193	105096
Multilateral		10 Jun 58	454UNTS47	106539
Belgium	South Africa	11 Jun 58	335UNTS63	104778
Denmark	Romania	25 Jun 58	345UNTS231	104970
Belgium	Pakistan	04 Jul 58	387UNTS305	105569
Ethiopia	UK Great Britain	07 Jul 58	331UNTS3	104749
Austria	Romania	10 Jul 58	353UNTS155	105041
Denmark	Hungary	17 Jul 58	344UNTS281	104954
Romania	United Arab Rep	14 Aug 58	405UNTS189	105834
Austria	Bulgaria	12 Sep 58	353UNTS3	105036
Ghana	UK Great Britain	24 Sep 58	411UNTS146	105918
Australia	South Africa	26 Sep 58	335UNTS121	104780
Liberia	Netherlands	28 Nov 58	393UNTS55	105651
Multilateral		01 Dec 58	385UNTS137	105534
Multilateral		03 Dec 58	398UNTS9	105715
Multilateral		03 Dec 58	416UNTS51	105995
Finland	Switzerland	07 Jan 59	353UNTS173	105042
UK Great Britain	Yugoslavia	03 Feb 59	359UNTS339	105151
Japan	Philippines	02 Mar 59	341UNTS49	104877
Netherlands	Tunisia	19 Mar 59	497UNTS61	107262
Sweden	Tunisia	19 Mar 59	497UNTS43	107261
Norway	Tunisia	28 Mar 59	497UNTS77	107263
Poland	UK Great Britain	03 Apr 59	351UNTS295	105030
Multilateral		06 Apr 59	349UNTS167	105013
Denmark	Tunisia	14 Apr 59	340UNTS273	104870
Denmark	Sudan	11 May 59	445UNTS105	106380
Ceylon (Sri Lanka)	Norway	29 May 59	411UNTS165	105919
Ceylon (Sri Lanka)	Sweden	29 May 59	464UNTS109	106713
Ceylon (Sri Lanka)	Denmark	29 May 59	348UNTS225	105002
Greece	Yugoslavia	18 Jun 59	368UNTS27	105234
Belgium	Japan	20 Jun 59	411UNTS3	105911
Bulgaria	United Arab Rep	09 Jul 59	411UNTS187	105920
India	Italy	16 Jul 59	464UNTS129	106714
Afghanistan	Germany, West	22 Jul 59	464UNTS177	106715
Germany, West	Iceland	12 Aug 59	411UNTS224	105921
Canada	Germany, West	04 Sep 59	411UNTS260	105922
Australia	Fed of Malaya	29 Sep 59	357UNTS29	105104
South Africa	Switzerland	19 Oct 59	559UNTS257	108162
Czechoslovakia	Germany, East	25 Nov 59	374UNTS101	105331
Germany, West	Pakistan	25 Nov 59	457UNTS22	106575
Liberia	Sweden	09 Dec 59	464UNTS219	106716
Czechoslovakia	UK Great Britain	15 Jan 60	374UNTS207	105336
Multilateral		06 Feb 60	383UNTS3	105494
Germany, West	United Arab Rep	16 Feb 60	464UNTS233	106717
France	Thailand	26 Feb 60	392UNTS279	105648
Multilateral		26 Feb 60	418UNTS171	106022
Australia	Thailand	26 Feb 60	392UNTS255	105647
Guinea	Netherlands	09 Mar 60	392UNTS243	105646
Belgium	Switzerland	24 Mar 60	416UNTS81	105996
Luxembourg	Yugoslavia	09 Apr 60	464UNTS293	106719
Germany, West	Spain	28 Apr 60	465UNTS3	106720
Greece	Romania	02 May 60	485UNTS17	107043
Morocco	United Arab Rep	19 May 60	563UNTS121	108208
Switzerland	Tunisia	21 May 60	497UNTS109	107265
Kuwait	UK Great Britain	24 May 60	412UNTS4	105923
Afghanistan	Czechoslovakia	28 May 60	497UNTS129	107266
Cuba	Czechoslovakia	10 Jun 60	447UNTS75	106412
Luxembourg	Tunisia	13 Jun 60	497UNTS143	107267

PARTY ONE	PARTY TWO	DATE	CITATION	NUMBER
Non-interest rates and fees (Cont.)				
Belgium	Netherlands	20 Jun 60	423UNTS19	106084
Ireland	Portugal	24 Jun 60	412UNTS30	105924
Poland	UK Great Britain	02 Jul 60	385UNTS87	105532
Switzerland	United Arab Rep	14 Jul 60	497UNTS161	107268
Germany, West	Pakistan	20 Jul 60	465UNTS41	106721
Ghana	Netherlands	30 Jul 60	412UNTS51	105925
Mexico	USA (United States)	15 Aug 60	402UNTS177	105786
Belgium	Burma	17 Aug 60	540UNTS185	107850
Ghana	United Arab Rep	29 Aug 60	412UNTS71	105926
Multilateral		01 Sep 60	403UNTS3	105792
Belgium	Jordan	19 Oct 60	479UNTS277	106959
Hungary	UK Great Britain	25 Oct 60	419UNTS309	106034
Burma	Switzerland	31 Oct 60	465UNTS97	106723
Australia	Italy	10 Nov 60	497UNTS247	107271
Indonesia	UK Great Britain	23 Nov 60	398UNTS71	105718
Multilateral		13 Dec 60	455UNTS3	106543
Multilateral		13 Dec 60	523UNTS117	107557
Canada	Pakistan	21 Dec 60	465UNTS115	106724
Luxembourg	Thailand	29 Dec 60	465UNTS131	106725
Jordan	Sweden	09 Jan 61	465UNTS155	106726
Sudan	UK Great Britain	16 Jan 61	424UNTS233	106112
Albania	Cuba	16 Jan 61	448UNTS67	106425
Norway	Poland	17 Jan 61	412UNTS130	105928
Germany, West	Japan	18 Jan 61	465UNTS173	106727
Belgium	Netherlands	24 Feb 61	474UNTS167	106881
Cuba	Czechoslovakia	04 Mar 61	465UNTS209	106728
Turkey	USSR (Soviet Union)	27 Apr 61	420UNTS307	106047
Poland	Switzerland	18 May 61	559UNTS233	108161
Czechoslovakia	Morocco	08 Jun 61	497UNTS275	107272
New Zealand	UK Great Britain	13 Jun 61	497UNTS293	107273
Cameroon	France	16 Jun 61	412UNTS148	105929
Guinea	Sweden	17 Jun 61	465UNTS236	106729
Czechoslovakia	Ghana	02 Aug 61	465UNTS249	106730
Finland	Luxembourg	15 Aug 61	541UNTS45	107859
Jordan	Norway	21 Aug 61	465UNTS275	106731
Jordan	Netherlands	24 Aug 61	466UNTS3	106733
Mexico	Netherlands	24 Aug 61	465UNTS291	106732
Liberia	Switzerland	31 Aug 61	559UNTS215	108160
Ghana	Romania	30 Sep 61	467UNTS443	106769
Germany, West	Morocco	12 Oct 61	523UNTS289	107562
Japan	Pakistan	17 Oct 61	466UNTS17	106734
Ghana	USSR (Soviet Union)	04 Nov 61	437UNTS213	106308
Cyprus	Greece	23 Nov 61	497UNTS311	107274
Czechoslovakia	Mali	27 Nov 61	466UNTS41	106736
Czechoslovakia	Guinea	16 Dec 61	559UNTS49	108154
Netherlands	Sweden	08 Jan 62	466UNTS65	106737
Austria	Greece	15 Jan 62	498UNTS3	107275
Indonesia	Japan	23 Jan 62	559UNTS77	108155
Italy	Japan	31 Jan 62	498UNTS23	107276
Luxembourg	South Africa	31 Jan 62	563UNTS153	108209
Finland	Hungary	13 Feb 62	463UNTS61	106693
Germany, West	Thailand	05 Mar 62	563UNTS165	108210
Luxembourg	Spain	26 Mar 62	563UNTS205	108211
France	Luxembourg	29 Mar 62	563UNTS227	108212
Sierra Leone	UK Great Britain	05 Apr 62	434UNTS227	106265
Ghana	USSR (Soviet Union)	06 Apr 62	498UNTS41	107277
Japan	United Arab Rep	10 May 62	498UNTS69	107278
Multilateral		15 May 62	444UNTS3	106367
France	Romania	18 May 62	498UNTS115	107279
France	Senegal	15 Jun 62	524UNTS3	107563
Czechoslovakia	Senegal	20 Jun 62	498UNTS145	107280
Guinea	Norway	21 Jun 62	466UNTS81	106738
United Arab Rep	USSR (Soviet Union)	23 Jun 62	472UNTS43	106836
Liberia	Norway	29 Jun 62	466UNTS95	106739
Morocco	Switzerland	05 Jul 62	498UNTS171	107281

PARTY ONE	PARTY TWO	DATE	CITATION	NUMBER
Non-interest rates and fees (Cont.)				
Ecuador	Germany, West	20 Sep 62	498UNTS199	107283
Japan	Kuwait	06 Oct 62	498UNTS235	107284
Finland	France	12 Oct 62	498UNTS299	107285
Germany, West	Ireland	17 Oct 62	604UNTS135	108749
Netherlands	Norway	18 Oct 62	466UNTS145	106741
Hungary	Syria	18 Oct 62	491UNTS209	107178
France	Ivory Coast	19 Oct 62	498UNTS317	107286
Poland	Syria	10 Nov 62	491UNTS228	107179
Ivory Coast	Switzerland	17 Nov 62	499UNTS3	107289
Ghana	Tunisia	11 Dec 62	563UNTS243	108213
Ghana	Mali	09 Jan 63	466UNTS165	106742
Senegal	Switzerland	23 Jan 63	524UNTS23	107564
Guinea	Switzerland	01 Feb 63	499UNTS35	107291
Mali	Senegal	07 Feb 63	524UNTS41	107565
Sudan	Switzerland	18 Feb 63	563UNTS281	108215
Algeria	France	18 Feb 63	563UNTS263	108214
Multilateral		02 Apr 63	475UNTS121	106889
Burma	UK Great Britain	02 Apr 63	475UNTS139	106890
Cyprus	Denmark	27 Apr 63	529UNTS255	107664
Greece	Hungary	27 Apr 63	534UNTS3	107750
Algeria	Morocco	30 Apr 63	564UNTS3	108217
Portugal	South Africa	07 May 63	499UNTS49	107292
Finland	Poland	10 Jun 63	503UNTS179	107343
Guinea	Ivory Coast	26 Jun 63	499UNTS71	107293
Austria	Romania	03 Jul 63	588UNTS3	108516
Austria	France	12 Jul 63	499UNTS91	107294
Algeria	Mali	22 Jul 63	564UNTS29	108219
Mali	Tunisia	24 Jul 63	602UNTS91	108708
Cameroon	Israel	09 Aug 63	499UNTS121	107295
Tanganyika	USSR (Soviet Union)	14 Aug 63	493UNTS195	107215
Pakistan	USSR (Soviet Union)	07 Oct 63	499UNTS161	107297
Ivory Coast	Netherlands	09 Oct 63	499UNTS141	107296
Czechoslovakia	Hungary	20 Dec 63	538UNTS127	107812
Greece	Poland	21 Dec 63	538UNTS155	107813
Mali	Niger	15 Jan 64	499UNTS197	107299
Denmark	Yugoslavia	11 Feb 64	511UNTS241	107437
Cameroon	Mali	17 Mar 64	524UNTS61	107566
Portugal	UK Great Britain	07 Apr 64	539UNTS167	107830
Malaysia	Netherlands	07 Apr 64	524UNTS81	107567
Canada	UK Great Britain	15 Apr 64	515UNTS39	107452
Argentina	UK Great Britain	15 Apr 64	515UNTS3	107450
Australia	UK Great Britain	15 Apr 64	515UNTS23	107451
UK Great Britain	USA (United States)	15 Apr 64	515UNTS55	107453
United Arab Rep	USA (United States)	05 May 64	531UNTS229	107706
Multilateral		20 Jun 64	539UNTS3	107819
South Africa	UK Great Britain	22 Jun 64	515UNTS71	107454
New Zealand	USA (United States)	24 Jun 64	524UNTS101	107568
Ireland	UK Great Britain	25 Jun 64	553UNTS221	108090
Sweden	UK Great Britain	30 Jun 64	515UNTS83	107455
Cyprus	UK Great Britain	02 Jul 64	522UNTS129	107540
Ivory Coast	Mali	09 Jul 64	524UNTS121	107569
India	UK Great Britain	31 Jul 64	522UNTS153	107542
Multilateral		20 Aug 64	514UNTS25	107441
Kenya	UK Great Britain	25 Aug 64	522UNTS165	107543
Syria	UK Great Britain	31 Aug 64	539UNTS259	107837
Malawi	UK Great Britain	01 Sep 64	522UNTS117	107539
Tanganyika	UK Great Britain	02 Sep 64	522UNTS177	107544
Finland	UK Great Britain	12 Sep 64	535UNTS13	107773
Denmark	UK Great Britain	16 Sep 64	534UNTS427	107771
Morocco	USA (United States)	29 Dec 64	593UNTS185	108584
Argentina	UK Great Britain	12 Jan 65	597UNTS177	108645
Finland	UK Great Britain	25 Mar 65	539UNTS103	107826
Denmark	Malaysia	26 Mar 65	540UNTS205	107851
Jamaica	IBRD (World Bank)	08 Apr 65	539UNTS303	107841
Ghana	Malawi	04 May 65	541UNTS163	107869

PARTY ONE	PARTY TWO	DATE	CITATION	NUMBER
Non-interest rates and fees (Cont.)				
Denmark	Spain	05 May 65	543UNTS255	107905
Argentina	Yugoslavia	09 Jun 65	601UNTS3	108684
Laos	Thailand	12 Aug 65	547UNTS209	107958
Romania	UK Great Britain	22 Mar 66	571UNTS281	108307
Argentina	India	26 Mar 66	601UNTS201	108697
Netherlands	Norway	22 Sep 66	600UNTS227	108683
Denmark	Singapore	20 Dec 66	593UNTS125	108580
Kuwait	UK Great Britain	29 Dec 66	617UNTS203	108914
Multilateral		23 Jun 67	614UNTS185	108871
Sale of local currency				
USA (United States)	Vietnam, South	25 Mar 61	406UNTS187	105849
Dominican Republic	USA (United States)	11 Jan 62	433UNTS133	106236
Seizure funds				
Israel	USA (United States)	07 Dec 51	157UNTS53	102046
Jordan	USA (United States)	20 Dec 51	157UNTS69	102048
Italy	USA (United States)	28 Dec 51	157UNTS63	102047
Laos	USA (United States)	31 Dec 51	198UNTS243	102668
India	USA (United States)	05 Jan 52	157UNTS39	102045
Indonesia	USA (United States)	05 Jan 52	215UNTS121	102916
Dominican Republic	USA (United States)	07 Jan 52	174UNTS243	102289
El Salvador	USA (United States)	07 Jan 52	198UNTS231	102667
UK Great Britain	USA (United States)	08 Jan 52	126UNTS307	101696
Guatemala	USA (United States)	08 Jan 52	181UNTS31	102395
Iran	USA (United States)	20 Jan 52	200UNTS191	102703
Jordan	USA (United States)	12 Feb 52	168UNTS25	102211
Israel	USA (United States)	27 Feb 52	177UNTS123	102314
Honduras	USA (United States)	07 Mar 52	233UNTS151	103260
Israel	USA (United States)	09 May 52	177UNTS63	102309
Israel	USA (United States)	09 May 52	177UNTS269	102326
Korea, South	USA (United States)	24 May 52	179UNTS23	102353
Chile	USA (United States)	30 Jun 52	199UNTS241	102688
Panama	USA (United States)	30 Jun 52	181UNTS121	102404
United Arab Rep	USA (United States)	12 Mar 53	204UNTS3	102747
United Arab Rep	USA (United States)	19 Mar 53	215UNTS17	102909
El Salvador	USA (United States)	14 May 53	234UNTS71	103273
United Arab Rep	USA (United States)	21 May 53	204UNTS29	102748
Colombia	USA (United States)	09 Jun 53	213UNTS3	102877
United Arab Rep	USA (United States)	18 Jun 53	215UNTS45	102910
Liberia	USA (United States)	23 Jun 53	213UNTS37	102879
Spain	USA (United States)	26 Sep 53	207UNTS93	102802
Israel	USA (United States)	25 Nov 53	219UNTS205	102976
Bolivia	USA (United States)	15 Jan 54	229UNTS213	103168
United Arab Rep	USA (United States)	24 Feb 54	236UNTS61	103316
Ethiopia	USA (United States)	01 Jun 54	232UNTS311	103245
Ethiopia	USA (United States)	12 Jun 54	234UNTS25	103270
Italy	USA (United States)	28 Jun 54	237UNTS121	103340
Guatemala	USA (United States)	01 Sep 54	199UNTS51	102677
Peru	USA (United States)	30 Apr 55	263UNTS309	103780
Libya	USA (United States)	21 Jul 55	264UNTS247	103796
USA (United States)	Uruguay	23 Mar 56	376UNTS311	105386
Ceylon (Sri Lanka)	USA (United States)	28 Apr 56	274UNTS35	103956
Libya	USA (United States)	04 Apr 57	283UNTS181	104116
Ethiopia	USA (United States)	25 Apr 57	283UNTS205	104118
Ghana	USA (United States)	03 Jun 57	284UNTS63	104129
Argentina	USA (United States)	03 Jun 57	291UNTS61	104244
Multilateral		13 Dec 60	523UNTS117	107557
Togo	USA (United States)	22 Dec 60	401UNTS33	105760
Sierra Leone	USA (United States)	05 May 61	409UNTS194	105885
Senegal	USA (United States)	13 May 61	409UNTS232	105888
Ivory Coast	USA (United States)	17 May 61	409UNTS241	105889
Niger	USA (United States)	26 May 61	410UNTS213	105905
Cameroon	USA (United States)	26 May 61	413UNTS195	105953
Dahomey	USA (United States)	27 May 61	445UNTS23	106373
Madagascar	USA (United States)	22 Jun 61	413UNTS219	105956

PARTY ONE	PARTY TWO	DATE	CITATION	NUMBER
Seizure funds (Cont.)				
Iran	USA (United States)	21 Dec 61	433UNTS269	106249
Germany, West	Israel	09 Jul 62	630UNTS87	108968
Central Afri Rep	USA (United States)	10 Feb 63	473UNTS83	106857
Transportation costs				
UK Great Britain	USSR (Soviet Union)	16 Aug 41	91UNTS341	200269
UK Great Britain	USSR (Soviet Union)	22 Jun 42	91UNTS355	200270
Mexico	USA (United States)	23 Dec 42	13UNTS231	200081
Mexico	USA (United States)	26 Apr 43	21UNTS245	200127
Mexico	USA (United States)	29 Apr 43	105UNTS119	200327
Multilateral		15 Jan 44	161UNTS281	200489
Costa Rica	USA (United States)	29 May 44	124UNTS155	200417
Argentina	USA (United States)	09 May 45	139UNTS227	200453
Netherlands	Switzerland	24 Oct 45	3UNTS73	100025
Netherlands	Norway	06 Nov 45	2UNTS5	100017
Finland	Norway	27 Nov 45	17UNTS247	100279
India	USA (United States)	16 May 46	4UNTS183	100045
Taiwan	USA (United States)	14 Jun 46	4UNTS253	100049
Poland	UK Great Britain	24 Jun 46	11UNTS59	100149
Brazil	USA (United States)	28 Jun 46	6UNTS327	100085
Philippines	USA (United States)	11 Sep 46	43UNTS231	100670
Albania	Yugoslavia	28 Nov 46	111UNTS163	101529
Romania	Yugoslavia	23 Dec 46	116UNTS33	101567
Peru	USA (United States)	27 Dec 46	152UNTS93	102013
Denmark	UK Great Britain	04 Mar 48	77UNTS57	100992
India	Pakistan	31 Mar 48	54UNTS33	100793
Greece	USA (United States)	23 Apr 48	74UNTS107	100958
Taiwan	USA (United States)	18 Nov 48	198UNTS287	102672
Italy	USA (United States)	26 Nov 48	79UNTS71	101032
UK Great Britain	USA (United States)	01 Dec 48	81UNTS93	101066
Italy	Netherlands	04 Dec 48	46UNTS271	100716
Argentina	Denmark	14 Dec 48	74UNTS41	100956
Multilateral		16 Dec 48	79UNTS85	101033
France	USA (United States)	23 Dec 48	67UNTS171	100876
Netherlands	USA (United States)	17 Jan 49	32UNTS241	100502
France	USA (United States)	07 Feb 49	67UNTS189	100877
Greece	USA (United States)	09 Feb 49	79UNTS95	101034
Austria	USA (United States)	11 Feb 49	79UNTS113	101035
Trieste	USA (United States)	11 Feb 49	79UNTS123	101036
Belgium	Portugal	01 Mar 49	32UNTS49	100488
Panama	USA (United States)	31 Mar 49	55UNTS141	100812
Argentina	Norway	09 Sep 49	42UNTS125	100646
Norway	USA (United States)	31 Oct 49	68UNTS3	100879
Afghanistan	India	04 Apr 50	167UNTS105	102201
Netherlands	New Zealand	16 Oct 50	83UNTS269	101111
Austria	Sweden	31 Oct 50	197UNTS311	102645
Brazil	Netherlands	15 Dec 50	123UNTS101	101657
Australia	Netherlands	22 Feb 51	128UNTS115	101717
Australia	Italy	29 Mar 51	131UNTS187	101741
Germany, West	USA (United States)	07 Jun 51	238UNTS161	103360
Mexico	USA (United States)	11 Aug 51	162UNTS103	102133
Costa Rica	USA (United States)	11 Sep 51	234UNTS255	103288
Brazil	WHO (World Health)	12 Jun 52	151UNTS333	102003
Australia	Germany, West	29 Aug 52	184UNTS147	102446
Sweden	USA (United States)	20 Nov 52	177UNTS203	102319
USA (United States)	Yugoslavia	03 Dec 52	185UNTS183	102469
Germany, West	USA (United States)	27 Feb 53	205UNTS103	102771
Iran	USA (United States)	13 Oct 53	222UNTS67	103023
Czechoslovakia	Greece	01 Feb 54	225UNTS77	103091
France	Greece	13 May 54	222UNTS299	103036
Greece	Romania	19 May 54	225UNTS17	103083
Afghanistan	USA (United States)	29 May 54	234UNTS3	103268
Bolivia	USA (United States)	16 Jun 54	234UNTS35	103271
USA (United States)	Vietnam, South	26 Aug 54	234UNTS111	103276
Pakistan	USA (United States)	02 Oct 54	236UNTS187	103324

PARTY ONE	PARTY TWO	DATE	CITATION	NUMBER
Transportation costs (Cont.)				
Peru	USA (United States)	25 Oct 54	238UNTS247	103368
United Arab Rep	USA (United States)	30 Oct 54	234UNTS139	103279
Turkey	USA (United States)	15 Nov 54	238UNTS135	103358
USSR (Soviet Union)	Yugoslavia	05 Jan 55	240UNTS225	103405
Honduras	USA (United States)	21 Mar 55	253UNTS3	103572
Chile	USA (United States)	05 Apr 55	250UNTS253	103527
Israel	USA (United States)	29 Apr 55	261UNTS331	103731
Korea, South	USA (United States)	02 May 55	258UNTS3	103666
Finland	USA (United States)	06 May 55	251UNTS3	103529
Italy	USA (United States)	23 May 55	251UNTS303	103547
Multilateral		25 May 55	264UNTS117	103791
Korea, South	USA (United States)	31 May 55	251UNTS321	103548
Greece	USA (United States)	24 Jun 55	270UNTS351	103905
Greece	USA (United States)	24 Jun 55	270UNTS361	103906
France	USA (United States)	11 Aug 55	251UNTS15	103530
Ecuador	USA (United States)	06 Sep 55	256UNTS187	103628
Bulgaria	UK Great Britain	22 Sep 55	222UNTS349	103039
Libya	USA (United States)	22 Dec 55	240UNTS111	103399
Austria	USA (United States)	07 Feb 56	272UNTS117	103933
Iran	USA (United States)	20 Feb 56	272UNTS135	103934
Italy	USA (United States)	27 Feb 56	291UNTS287	104260
Indonesia	USA (United States)	02 Mar 56	271UNTS345	103925
Pakistan	USA (United States)	02 Mar 56	271UNTS371	103927
Spain	USA (United States)	05 Mar 56	271UNTS329	103924
Burma	Yugoslavia	07 Mar 56	386UNTS207	105542
Turkey	USA (United States)	12 Mar 56	272UNTS21	103929
Korea, South	USA (United States)	13 Mar 56	272UNTS3	103928
Paraguay	USA (United States)	02 May 56	268UNTS299	103863
Peru	USA (United States)	07 May 56	268UNTS285	103862
Portugal	USA (United States)	24 May 56	268UNTS323	103865
Australia	Netherlands	01 Aug 56	280UNTS3	104047
Pakistan	USA (United States)	07 Aug 56	281UNTS75	104071
Netherlands	USA (United States)	07 Aug 56	281UNTS57	104069
Greece	USA (United States)	08 Aug 56	277UNTS203	104007
Taiwan	USA (United States)	14 Aug 56	281UNTS257	104083
Multilateral		16 Aug 56	287UNTS223	104188
Guatemala	Honduras	22 Aug 56	263UNTS49	103767
India	USA (United States)	29 Aug 56	278UNTS25	104019
Israel	USA (United States)	11 Sep 56	277UNTS215	104008
Italy	USA (United States)	30 Oct 56	263UNTS221	103775
Turkey	USA (United States)	12 Nov 56	282UNTS77	104093
Belgium	Spain	28 Nov 56	308UNTS285	104465
Burma	USA (United States)	04 Dec 56	268UNTS189	103858
Brazil	USA (United States)	31 Dec 56	266UNTS151	103829
Korea, South	USA (United States)	30 Jan 57	278UNTS85	104024
Ecuador	USA (United States)	15 Feb 57	279UNTS155	104037
Thailand	USA (United States)	04 Mar 57	279UNTS235	104043
Australia	UK Great Britain	01 Apr 57	271UNTS235	103918
Iceland	USA (United States)	11 Apr 57	283UNTS107	104110
Colombia	USA (United States)	16 Apr 57	283UNTS245	104121
Peru	USA (United States)	02 May 57	283UNTS55	104106
Austria	USA (United States)	10 May 57	283UNTS15	104103
Austria	USA (United States)	10 May 57	283UNTS33	104104
Bolivia	USA (United States)	07 Jun 57	291UNTS77	104245
Poland	USA (United States)	07 Jun 57	291UNTS41	104243
Philippines	USA (United States)	25 Jun 57	289UNTS279	104224
Tunisia	USA (United States)	28 Jun 57	289UNTS301	104226
Mexico	USA (United States)	23 Oct 57	300UNTS35	104330
Israel	USA (United States)	07 Nov 57	302UNTS255	104365
Pakistan	USA (United States)	15 Nov 57	303UNTS173	104380
France	USA (United States)	27 Dec 57	307UNTS79	104444
Turkey	USA (United States)	20 Jan 58	304UNTS15	104389
Spain	USA (United States)	27 Jan 58	303UNTS247	104384
USA (United States)	Yugoslavia	03 Feb 58	304UNTS293	104404
UK Great Britain	USA (United States)	03 Feb 58	307UNTS199	104450

PARTY ONE	PARTY TWO	DATE	CITATION	NUMBER
Transportation costs (Cont.)				
Korea, South	USA (United States)	05 Feb 58	307UNTS121	104447
Finland	USA (United States)	21 Feb 58	304UNTS253	104401
France	USA (United States)	28 Feb 58	366UNTS343	105222
Colombia	USA (United States)	14 Mar 58	308UNTS115	104459
Peru	USA (United States)	09 Apr 58	316UNTS37	104576
Taiwan	USA (United States)	18 Apr 58	308UNTS179	104461
Iceland	USA (United States)	03 May 58	316UNTS137	104581
Burma	USA (United States)	27 May 58	315UNTS197	104569
Philippines	USA (United States)	03 Jun 58	316UNTS3	104573
Ceylon (Sri Lanka)	USA (United States)	18 Jun 58	316UNTS15	104574
Ecuador	USA (United States)	30 Jun 58	336UNTS11	104796
Australia	Germany, West	27 Aug 58	320UNTS303	104649
Haiti	USA (United States)	09 Sep 58	335UNTS257	104793
India	USA (United States)	26 Sep 58	336UNTS59	104798
Israel	USA (United States)	06 Nov 58	336UNTS275	104810
Pakistan	USA (United States)	26 Nov 58	337UNTS3	104812
USA (United States)	Yugoslavia	22 Dec 58	338UNTS243	104839
United Arab Rep	USA (United States)	24 Dec 58	338UNTS221	104837
Finland	USA (United States)	30 Dec 58	340UNTS259	104869
Spain	USA (United States)	13 Jan 59	341UNTS241	104887
Turkey	USA (United States)	13 Feb 59	340UNTS235	104867
Iceland	USA (United States)	03 Mar 59	341UNTS261	104889
Ceylon (Sri Lanka)	USA (United States)	13 Mar 59	342UNTS51	104900
France	USA (United States)	21 Mar 59	342UNTS71	104901
Indonesia	USA (United States)	29 May 59	347UNTS85	104992
Taiwan	USA (United States)	09 Jun 59	353UNTS257	105046
Poland	USA (United States)	10 Jun 59	347UNTS41	104989
Argentina	USA (United States)	12 Jun 59	347UNTS59	104990
USA (United States)	Yemen	30 Jun 59	357UNTS137	105112
Korea, South	USA (United States)	30 Jun 59	353UNTS297	105047
United Arab Rep	USA (United States)	29 Jul 59	357UNTS121	105111
Colombia	USA (United States)	06 Oct 59	358UNTS145	105132
USA (United States)	Vietnam, South	16 Oct 59	360UNTS271	105163
Japan	USA (United States)	12 Nov 59	361UNTS27	105171
India	USA (United States)	13 Nov 59	360UNTS287	105164
United Arab Rep	USA (United States)	14 Nov 59	360UNTS311	105165
Turkey	USA (United States)	30 Nov 59	361UNTS107	105174
Turkey	USA (United States)	22 Dec 59	367UNTS57	105225
Denmark	Sweden	04 Jan 60	376UNTS375	105390
Greece	USA (United States)	07 Jan 60	368UNTS221	105243
Australia	Canada	12 Feb 60	369UNTS89	105253
Peru	USA (United States)	12 Feb 60	372UNTS83	105290
Iceland	USA (United States)	06 Apr 60	372UNTS71	105289
Pakistan	USA (United States)	11 Apr 60	372UNTS251	105302
India	USA (United States)	04 May 60	376UNTS279	105384
Spain	USA (United States)	22 Jun 60	378UNTS3	105414
Poland	USA (United States)	21 Jul 60	380UNTS157	105456
Iran	USA (United States)	26 Jul 60	384UNTS141	105516
United Arab Rep	USA (United States)	01 Aug 60	384UNTS189	105519
United Arab Rep	USA (United States)	09 Aug 60	388UNTS271	105584
Taiwan	USA (United States)	30 Aug 60	388UNTS191	105579
Ecuador	USA (United States)	27 Sep 60	401UNTS115	105766
Ceylon (Sri Lanka)	USA (United States)	30 Sep 60	389UNTS221	105594
USA (United States)	Vietnam, South	28 Oct 60	401UNTS3	105758
France	USA (United States)	04 Nov 60	400UNTS323	105756
Indonesia	USA (United States)	05 Nov 60	400UNTS35	105746
Greece	USA (United States)	07 Nov 60	400UNTS57	105748
Chile	USA (United States)	08 Nov 60	405UNTS85	105825
Israel	USA (United States)	19 Dec 60	401UNTS195	105772
Korea, South	USA (United States)	28 Dec 60	402UNTS3	105773
Turkey	USA (United States)	11 Jan 61	405UNTS173	105833
Ecuador	USA (United States)	03 Apr 61	409UNTS140	105882
Iceland	USA (United States)	07 Apr 61	406UNTS203	105850
Bolivia	USA (United States)	07 Apr 61	433UNTS3	106227
USA (United States)	Yugoslavia	19 Apr 61	409UNTS163	105883

PARTY ONE	PARTY TWO	DATE	CITATION	NUMBER
Transportation costs (Cont.)				
USA (United States)	Yugoslavia	28 Apr 61	409UNTS172	105884
Brazil	USA (United States)	04 May 61	433UNTS91	106233
Israel	USA (United States)	10 May 61	409UNTS213	105887
Spain	USA (United States)	22 May 61	409UNTS260	105891
Finland	USA (United States)	16 Jun 61	413UNTS211	105955
Tunisia	USA (United States)	30 Jun 61	434UNTS85	106257
Paraguay	USA (United States)	07 Jul 61	433UNTS53	106231
USA (United States)	Vietnam, South	14 Jul 61	416UNTS133	105999
Taiwan	USA (United States)	21 Jul 61	416UNTS101	105998
Turkey	USA (United States)	29 Jul 61	416UNTS151	106001
Finland	USA (United States)	04 Aug 61	418UNTS19	106014
El Salvador	USA (United States)	21 Aug 61	418UNTS35	106015
UK Great Britain	USA (United States)	28 Aug 61	434UNTS103	106258
Denmark	Germany, West	12 Sep 61	516UNTS283	107478
Indonesia	USA (United States)	26 Oct 61	433UNTS249	106248
Iraq	Syria	03 Nov 61	489UNTS45	107134
Iceland	USA (United States)	06 Nov 61	426UNTS225	106140
Syria	USA (United States)	09 Nov 61	435UNTS75	106271
Sudan	USA (United States)	14 Nov 61	434UNTS51	106255
Bolivia	USA (United States)	15 Nov 61	456UNTS192	106557
Congo (Zaire)	USA (United States)	18 Nov 61	433UNTS207	106244
Philippines	USA (United States)	24 Nov 61	433UNTS315	106251
Portugal	USA (United States)	28 Nov 61	434UNTS31	106253
Poland	USA (United States)	15 Dec 61	434UNTS3	106252
USA (United States)	Vietnam, South	27 Dec 61	433UNTS185	106242
Cyprus	USA (United States)	15 Jan 62	435UNTS15	106267
United Arab Rep	USA (United States)	19 Jan 62	435UNTS107	106273
Iran	USA (United States)	29 Jan 62	435UNTS53	106270
Guinea	USA (United States)	02 Feb 62	435UNTS35	106269
Morocco	USA (United States)	09 Feb 62	442UNTS135	106345
Bolivia	USA (United States)	12 Feb 62	451UNTS281	106499
Tunisia	USA (United States)	16 Feb 62	442UNTS161	106347
Indonesia	USA (United States)	19 Feb 62	435UNTS137	106276
Korea, South	USA (United States)	02 Mar 62	442UNTS185	106349
Multilateral		05 Mar 62	425UNTS3	106114
Brazil	USA (United States)	15 Mar 62	456UNTS209	106558
Iceland	USA (United States)	16 Mar 62	445UNTS49	106376
Peru	USA (United States)	20 Mar 62	445UNTS61	106377
Taiwan	USA (United States)	27 Apr 62	436UNTS25	106287
USA (United States)	Uruguay	27 Apr 62	452UNTS25	106502
India	USA (United States)	01 May 62	451UNTS179	106493
Israel	USA (United States)	03 May 62	442UNTS83	106340
USA (United States)	Venezuela	17 May 62	456UNTS275	106562
Tunisia	USA (United States)	14 Sep 62	461UNTS31	106649
United Arab Rep	USA (United States)	08 Oct 62	462UNTS39	106670
Iran	USA (United States)	15 Oct 62	473UNTS291	106866
Greece	USA (United States)	22 Oct 62	462UNTS187	106678
Korea, South	USA (United States)	07 Nov 62	462UNTS129	106674
Burma	USA (United States)	09 Nov 62	461UNTS113	106655
Japan	UK Great Britain	14 Nov 62	478UNTS29	106934
Taiwan	USA (United States)	19 Nov 62	459UNTS263	106629
Paraguay	USA (United States)	24 Nov 62	471UNTS49	106821
India	USA (United States)	26 Nov 62	460UNTS203	106641
USA (United States)	Yugoslavia	28 Nov 62	460UNTS185	106640
India	USA (United States)	30 Nov 62	459UNTS231	106626
Dominican Republic	USA (United States)	30 Nov 62	471UNTS25	106819
Israel	USA (United States)	06 Dec 62	460UNTS151	106638
Bolivia	USA (United States)	17 Dec 62	469UNTS121	106788
Sudan	USA (United States)	31 Jan 63	494UNTS119	107230
India	USA (United States)	01 Feb 63	473UNTS37	106852
Poland	USA (United States)	01 Feb 63	487UNTS143	107100
Iceland	USA (United States)	06 Feb 63	473UNTS93	106858
Turkey	USA (United States)	21 Feb 63	473UNTS311	106867
Congo (Zaire)	USA (United States)	23 Feb 63	493UNTS17	107204
Congo (Zaire)	USA (United States)	23 Feb 63	493UNTS3	107203

PARTY ONE	PARTY TWO	DATE	CITATION	NUMBER
Transportation costs (Cont.)				
Austria	Czechoslovakia	08 Mar 63	495UNTS219	107245
Colombia	USA (United States)	27 Mar 63	489UNTS289	107145
Brazil	USA (United States)	29 Mar 63	476UNTS67	106904
India	USA (United States)	09 May 63	476UNTS43	106902
Laos	UK Great Britain	17 May 63	475UNTS155	106891
Guinea	USA (United States)	22 May 63	487UNTS251	107108
Ethiopia	USA (United States)	11 Jun 63	487UNTS269	107109
Cyprus	USA (United States)	18 Jun 63	479UNTS191	106953
India	USA (United States)	27 Jun 63	479UNTS215	106955
Tanganyika	USSR (Soviet Union)	14 Aug 63	493UNTS195	107215
Iraq	USA (United States)	27 Aug 63	489UNTS271	107144
Brazil	USA (United States)	11 Sep 63	493UNTS267	107220
Paraguay	USA (United States)	16 Sep 63	494UNTS101	107229
Greece	USA (United States)	30 Oct 63	493UNTS29	107205
Paraguay	USA (United States)	14 Nov 63	505UNTS87	107366
Argentina	USA (United States)	30 Nov 63	505UNTS131	107369
Brazil	Germany, West	30 Nov 63	0UNTS0	109425
USA (United States)	Vietnam, South	09 Jan 64	505UNTS173	107373
Finland	IAEA (Atom Energy)	27 Jan 64	501UNTS213	107319
Poland	USA (United States)	03 Feb 64	505UNTS245	107376
Poland	USA (United States)	03 Feb 64	505UNTS215	107375
Jordan	USA (United States)	11 Feb 64	511UNTS85	107429
Iceland	USA (United States)	13 Feb 64	510UNTS295	107420
Peru	USA (United States)	13 Feb 64	511UNTS119	107431
Sudan	USA (United States)	02 Mar 64	524UNTS217	107575
Ivory Coast	USA (United States)	10 Mar 64	526UNTS285	107611
Bolivia	USA (United States)	25 Mar 64	532UNTS3	107710
Tunisia	USA (United States)	07 Apr 64	527UNTS3	107613
USA (United States)	Yugoslavia	27 Apr 64	526UNTS89	107602
USA (United States)	Yugoslavia	27 Apr 64	526UNTS73	107601
USA (United States)	Yugoslavia	28 Apr 64	526UNTS103	107603
Congo (Zaire)	USA (United States)	28 Apr 64	526UNTS55	107600
Philippines	USA (United States)	14 May 64	526UNTS113	107604
Austria	Turkey	15 May 64	515UNTS109	107457
Taiwan	USA (United States)	03 Jun 64	526UNTS257	107610
Netherlands	Turkey	19 Aug 64	521UNTS197	107523
Paraguay	USA (United States)	05 Sep 64	530UNTS225	107685
USA (United States)	Vietnam, South	29 Sep 64	531UNTS183	107703
Iran	USA (United States)	29 Sep 64	531UNTS163	107702
India	USA (United States)	30 Sep 64	532UNTS321	107726
Colombia	USA (United States)	08 Oct 64	579UNTS3	108395
India	UK Great Britain	20 Oct 64	534UNTS77	107755
USA (United States)	Yugoslavia	28 Oct 64	533UNTS3	107728
USA (United States)	Yugoslavia	29 Oct 64	533UNTS17	107729
Iran	USA (United States)	16 Nov 64	532UNTS213	107719
Greece	USA (United States)	17 Nov 64	532UNTS107	107714
Kenya	USA (United States)	07 Dec 64	532UNTS263	107722
Congo (Zaire)	USA (United States)	09 Dec 64	531UNTS249	107707
India	Netherlands	11 Dec 64	570UNTS165	108292
Israel	USA (United States)	22 Dec 64	532UNTS231	107720
Morocco	USA (United States)	29 Dec 64	593UNTS185	108584
Iceland	USA (United States)	30 Dec 64	542UNTS37	107878
Taiwan	USA (United States)	31 Dec 64	532UNTS59	107712
Dahomey	USA (United States)	31 Dec 64	541UNTS117	107865
Korea, South	USA (United States)	31 Dec 64	535UNTS315	107787
Taiwan	USA (United States)	31 Dec 64	532UNTS29	107711
Sierra Leone	USA (United States)	29 Jan 65	542UNTS87	107882
Tunisia	USA (United States)	17 Feb 65	542UNTS125	107885
USA (United States)	Yugoslavia	16 Mar 65	542UNTS161	107887
Dominican Republic	USA (United States)	18 Mar 65	542UNTS215	107892
Morocco	USA (United States)	23 Apr 65	594UNTS3	108591
Philippines	USA (United States)	23 Apr 65	546UNTS157	107942
Bolivia	USA (United States)	12 May 65	564UNTS143	108226
Afghanistan	USA (United States)	22 May 65	579UNTS29	108396
USA (United States)	Vietnam, South	26 May 65	550UNTS3	108005

PARTY ONE	PARTY TWO	DATE	CITATION	NUMBER
Transportation costs (Cont.)				
Ecuador	USA (United States)	25 Jun 65	549UNTS23	107986
Mali	USA (United States)	14 Jul 65	564UNTS101	108223
USA (United States)	Yugoslavia	16 Jul 65	549UNTS111	107994
Congo (Zaire)	USA (United States)	19 Jul 65	593UNTS215	108586
Chile	USA (United States)	27 Jul 65	574UNTS83	108342
Ethiopia	USA (United States)	17 Aug 65	564UNTS119	108224
Netherlands	Nigeria	28 Oct 65	578UNTS15	108383
Austria	Yugoslavia	19 Nov 65	587UNTS239	108512
USA (United States)	Yugoslavia	22 Nov 65	574UNTS211	108351
Ethiopia	USA (United States)	14 Dec 65	574UNTS115	108344
United Arab Rep	USA (United States)	03 Jan 66	579UNTS63	108399
Liberia	USA (United States)	06 Jan 66	592UNTS101	108570
Guinea	USA (United States)	04 Feb 66	579UNTS213	108409
Algeria	USA (United States)	23 Feb 66	592UNTS117	108571
Korea, South	USA (United States)	07 Mar 66	579UNTS137	108404
Ceylon (Sri Lanka)	USA (United States)	12 Mar 66	579UNTS117	108403
Ghana	USA (United States)	01 Apr 66	579UNTS157	108405
Jordan	USA (United States)	05 Apr 66	593UNTS239	108587
USA (United States)	Yugoslavia	11 Apr 66	580UNTS239	108427
Sudan	USA (United States)	13 Apr 66	586UNTS39	108495
Bolivia	USA (United States)	22 Apr 66	578UNTS73	108388
Pakistan	USA (United States)	26 May 66	594UNTS27	108592
Israel	USA (United States)	06 Jun 66	593UNTS165	108583
Indonesia	USA (United States)	28 Jun 66	593UNTS201	108585
Philippines	USA (United States)	22 Dec 66	591UNTS219	108559
Israel	USA (United States)	04 Aug 67	0UNTS0	109351
Local currency				
Netherlands	UK Great Britain	14 Jun 40	2UNTS251	200018
Mexico	USA (United States)	19 Nov 41	148UNTS367	200474
France	USA (United States)	25 Sep 43	76UNTS183	200245
Belgium	UK Great Britain	22 Aug 44	90UNTS295	200267
Belgium	UK Great Britain	05 Oct 44	5UNTS227	200031
Canada	Czechoslovakia	01 Mar 45	45UNTS283	200185
Sweden	UK Great Britain	06 Mar 45	82UNTS219	101095
Sweden	UK Great Britain	06 Mar 45	5UNTS241	200032
Belgium	USA (United States)	19 Apr 45	139UNTS179	200455
Netherlands	USA (United States)	30 Apr 45	139UNTS319	200459
Canada	Norway	25 Jun 45	45UNTS297	200186
Belgium	Norway	23 Oct 45	16UNTS311	200107
Czechoslovakia	UK Great Britain	01 Nov 45	5UNTS15	100062
Netherlands	Norway	06 Nov 45	2UNTS5	100017
Finland	Norway	27 Nov 45	17UNTS247	100279
Czechoslovakia	Norway	13 Dec 45	17UNTS261	100280
Multilateral		27 Dec 45	2UNTS39	100020
Greece	UK Great Britain	24 Jan 46	6UNTS45	100067
Switzerland	UK Great Britain	12 Mar 46	6UNTS107	100070
Portugal	UK Great Britain	16 Apr 46	6UNTS119	100071
Poland	USA (United States)	22 Apr 46	406UNTS215	105851
Greece	USA (United States)	16 May 46	184UNTS230	102451
France	USA (United States)	28 May 46	84UNTS141	101124
France	USA (United States)	28 May 46	84UNTS121	101123
Romania	Yugoslavia	26 Jun 46	116UNTS21	101566
Italy	Norway	20 Jul 46	17UNTS273	100281
Norway	Yugoslavia	30 Aug 46	15UNTS163	100232
Norway	Sweden	22 Nov 46	15UNTS171	100233
Norway	Poland	03 Dec 46	15UNTS203	100234
Norway	USSR (Soviet Union)	27 Dec 46	17UNTS283	100282
Burma	USA (United States)	28 Feb 47	25UNTS27	100355
Spain	UK Great Britain	28 Mar 47	66UNTS91	100849
Poland	Yugoslavia	24 May 47	115UNTS69	101558
New Zealand	UK Great Britain	27 May 47	17UNTS211	100277
Netherlands	USA (United States)	28 May 47	17UNTS29	100267
Austria	USA (United States)	25 Jun 47	22UNTS141	100334
Haiti	USA (United States)	04 Jul 47	22UNTS165	100335

PARTY ONE	PARTY TWO	DATE	CITATION	NUMBER
Local currency (Cont.)				
Italy	USA (United States)	04 Jul 47	22UNTS173	100336
Greece	USA (United States)	08 Jul 47	16UNTS157	100256
UK Great Britain	Uruguay	15 Jul 47	71UNTS179	100918
Taiwan	Italy	30 Jul 47	12UNTS377	100194
Taiwan	USA (United States)	27 Oct 47	12UNTS11	100178
France	Lebanon	24 Jan 48	173UNTS99	102263
Denmark	Hungary	28 Feb 48	85UNTS35	101144
Poland	UK Great Britain	02 Mar 48	77UNTS47	100991
Hungary	Yugoslavia	18 Mar 48	113UNTS201	101551
India	Pakistan	31 Mar 48	54UNTS33	100793
Denmark	Norway	21 Apr 48	18UNTS139	100284
Brazil	UK Great Britain	21 May 48	66UNTS121	100851
Chile	UK Great Britain	24 Jun 48	77UNTS113	100995
Italy	USA (United States)	28 Jun 48	20UNTS43	100314
France	USA (United States)	28 Jun 48	19UNTS9	100302
Ireland	USA (United States)	28 Jun 48	24UNTS3	100349
Denmark	USA (United States)	29 Jun 48	22UNTS217	100338
India	Pakistan	30 Jun 48	29UNTS199	100441
Austria	USA (United States)	02 Jul 48	21UNTS29	100323
Greece	USA (United States)	02 Jul 48	23UNTS43	100342
Netherlands	USA (United States)	02 Jul 48	20UNTS91	100315
Belgium	USA (United States)	02 Jul 48	19UNTS127	100309
Taiwan	USA (United States)	03 Jul 48	17UNTS119	100273
Norway	USA (United States)	03 Jul 48	20UNTS185	100317
Luxembourg	USA (United States)	03 Jul 48	24UNTS35	100350
Iceland	USA (United States)	03 Jul 48	20UNTS141	100316
UK Great Britain	USA (United States)	06 Jul 48	22UNTS263	100339
France	USA (United States)	09 Jul 48	24UNTS103	100352
Multilateral		14 Jul 48	23UNTS3	100340
Trieste	USA (United States)	15 Oct 48	29UNTS249	100443
Taiwan	USA (United States)	18 Nov 48	198UNTS287	102672
Austria	Denmark	29 Nov 48	74UNTS257	100968
Argentina	Denmark	14 Dec 48	74UNTS41	100956
Denmark	Poland	14 Dec 48	81UNTS33	101060
Spain	UK Great Britain	15 Dec 48	87UNTS49	101165
Denmark	Sweden	08 Feb 49	33UNTS227	100519
Denmark	Greece	25 Feb 49	78UNTS335	101023
Belgium	Portugal	01 Mar 49	32UNTS49	100488
Greece	Norway	12 Mar 49	33UNTS13	100510
Belgium	Bolivia	26 Apr 49	34UNTS103	100530
Ethiopia	USA (United States)	20 May 49	89UNTS99	101211
UNICEF (Children)	UK Great Britain	17 Jun 49	65UNTS50	100820
Multilateral		10 Aug 49	45UNTS3	100689
Iran	USA (United States)	01 Sep 49	79UNTS155	101039
Argentina	Norway	09 Sep 49	42UNTS125	100646
Italy	Norway	19 Nov 49	47UNTS89	100724
Norway	Portugal	28 Nov 49	47UNTS117	100726
Germany, West	USA (United States)	15 Dec 49	92UNTS269	101277
Czechoslovakia	Denmark	17 Dec 49	74UNTS159	100962
Norway	Poland	21 Dec 49	47UNTS107	100725
Turkey	USA (United States)	27 Dec 49	98UNTS141	101361
Korea, South	USA (United States)	26 Jan 50	178UNTS97	102337
Luxembourg	USA (United States)	27 Jan 50	80UNTS187	101052
Netherlands	USA (United States)	27 Jan 50	80UNTS219	101054
France	USA (United States)	27 Jan 50	80UNTS171	101051
UK Great Britain	USA (United States)	27 Jan 50	80UNTS261	101056
Denmark	USA (United States)	27 Jan 50	48UNTS115	100740
Norway	USA (United States)	27 Jan 50	80UNTS241	101055
Italy	USA (United States)	27 Jan 50	80UNTS145	101050
Belgium	USA (United States)	27 Jan 50	51UNTS213	100767
Canada	Yugoslavia	29 Mar 50	230UNTS357	103195
Paraguay	UK Great Britain	03 Apr 50	99UNTS81	101372
Korea, South	USA (United States)	28 Jul 50	140UNTS57	101883
Indonesia	USA (United States)	15 Aug 50	134UNTS255	101804
Brazil	USA (United States)	16 Aug 50	140UNTS223	101890

PARTY ONE	PARTY TWO	DATE	CITATION	NUMBER
Local currency (Cont.)				
Denmark	Italy	04 Oct 50	78UNTS353	101025
Thailand	USA (United States)	17 Oct 50	79UNTS41	101030
Multilateral		02 Nov 50	81UNTS160	101071
Burma	USA (United States)	06 Nov 50	122UNTS81	101638
USA (United States)	Yugoslavia	21 Nov 50	93UNTS45	101286
Multilateral		24 Nov 50	81UNTS188	101072
Multilateral		15 Dec 50	76UNTS120	100985
Italy	UK Great Britain	21 Dec 50	175UNTS187	102301
Multilateral		23 Dec 50	185UNTS3	102456
Portugal	USA (United States)	05 Jan 51	133UNTS75	101782
United Nations	Yugoslavia	06 Jan 51	78UNTS165	101015
USA (United States)	Yugoslavia	06 Jan 51	122UNTS137	101643
Chile	USA (United States)	16 Jan 51	157UNTS3	102043
Multilateral		18 Jan 51	81UNTS233	101073
Ceylon (Sri Lanka)	ILO (Labor Org)	24 Jan 51	117UNTS355	200380
Ethiopia	ICAO (Civil Aviat)	02 Feb 51	96UNTS123	101333
Multilateral		15 Feb 51	81UNTS245	101074
Israel	ICAO (Civil Aviat)	19 Feb 51	96UNTS141	101334
Israel	ILO (Labor Org)	19 Feb 51	100UNTS105	101391
ILO (Labor Org)	Syria	03 Mar 51	110UNTS69	101502
Multilateral		05 Mar 51	81UNTS261	101075
Multilateral		28 Mar 51	181UNTS61	102399
Jordan	ILO (Labor Org)	29 Mar 51	100UNTS247	200287
Jordan	United Nations	29 Mar 51	137UNTS267	200448
Liberia	ILO (Labor Org)	02 Apr 51	100UNTS117	101392
Multilateral		05 Apr 51	84UNTS299	101139
Mexico	ILO (Labor Org)	06 Apr 51	100UNTS131	101393
Ceylon (Sri Lanka)	ILO (Labor Org)	06 Apr 51	100UNTS235	200286
Peru	ILO (Labor Org)	13 Apr 51	100UNTS31	101385
Guatemala	ILO (Labor Org)	13 Apr 51	126UNTS249	101692
USA (United States)	Yugoslavia	17 Apr 51	162UNTS173	102134
ICAO (Civil Aviat)	Thailand	19 Apr 51	96UNTS181	101336
Ecuador	ILO (Labor Org)	19 Apr 51	100UNTS77	101389
Cuba	ILO (Labor Org)	21 Apr 51	99UNTS205	101382
Greece	ILO (Labor Org)	25 Apr 51	100UNTS93	101390
India	ILO (Labor Org)	26 Apr 51	100UNTS19	101384
WHO (World Health)	Yugoslavia	02 May 51	103UNTS117	101429
Ethiopia	USA (United States)	02 May 51	139UNTS85	101877
Austria	USA (United States)	15 May 51	139UNTS79	101876
Iceland	ICAO (Civil Aviat)	07 Jun 51	96UNTS193	101337
Lebanon	WHO (World Health)	07 Jun 51	126UNTS221	101690
United Nations	Thailand	11 Jun 51	90UNTS45	101225
Dominican Republic	ILO (Labor Org)	18 Jun 51	100UNTS3	101383
Multilateral		19 Jun 51	199UNTS67	102678
Multilateral		25 Jun 51	92UNTS27	101258
Israel	United Nations	25 Jun 51	97UNTS21	101344
ILO (Labor Org)	Vietnam, South	26 Jun 51	100UNTS223	200285
Multilateral		28 Jun 51	118UNTS154	101604
Ethiopia	WHO (World Health)	02 Jul 51	103UNTS39	101422
Canada	France	04 Jul 51	233UNTS101	103253
ILO (Labor Org)	Thailand	11 Jul 51	100UNTS159	101395
Paraguay	ILO (Labor Org)	12 Jul 51	117UNTS155	101591
Portugal	UK Great Britain	20 Jul 51	105UNTS61	101453
Multilateral		27 Jul 51	97UNTS291	200273
Israel	WHO (World Health)	07 Aug 51	104UNTS213	101442
WHO (World Health)	Saudi Arabia	29 Aug 51	110UNTS277	101516
Japan	UK Great Britain	31 Aug 51	108UNTS273	101480
Multilateral		05 Sep 51	173UNTS15	102256
UNICEF (Children)	Turkey	05 Sep 51	193UNTS55	102610
Iraq	ICAO (Civil Aviat)	18 Sep 51	108UNTS219	101475
Paraguay	United Nations	27 Sep 51	120UNTS105	101617
Multilateral		01 Oct 51	104UNTS249	101446
Bolivia	United Nations	01 Oct 51	104UNTS263	101447
Pakistan	WHO (World Health)	07 Oct 51	126UNTS101	101684
United Nations	Uruguay	17 Oct 51	122UNTS29	101633

PARTY ONE	PARTY TWO	DATE	CITATION	NUMBER
Local currency (Cont.)				
ILO (Labor Org)	Venezuela	22 Oct 51	117UNTS139	101590
Panama	ILO (Labor Org)	10 Nov 51	126UNTS269	101693
USA (United States)	Yugoslavia	14 Nov 51	174UNTS201	102286
Turkey	USA (United States)	15 Nov 51	177UNTS315	102331
Israel	USA (United States)	07 Dec 51	157UNTS53	102046
Jordan	USA (United States)	20 Dec 51	157UNTS69	102048
Spain	UK Great Britain	20 Dec 51	123UNTS187	101660
Multilateral		24 Dec 51	118UNTS290	200383
India	USA (United States)	05 Jan 52	157UNTS39	102045
USA (United States)	Yugoslavia	08 Jan 52	152UNTS61	102011
India	United Nations	12 Jan 52	118UNTS175	101606
Iran	USA (United States)	20 Jan 52	200UNTS191	102703
Ceylon (Sri Lanka)	United Nations	21 Jan 52	118UNTS281	200382
WHO (World Health)	Spain	30 Jan 52	124UNTS259	200425
WHO (World Health)	UK Great Britain	07 Feb 52	121UNTS75	101627
Multilateral		11 Feb 52	165UNTS77	102169
Jordan	USA (United States)	12 Feb 52	168UNTS25	102211
Austria	USA (United States)	16 Feb 52	177UNTS299	102329
Philippines	USA (United States)	19 Feb 52	177UNTS307	102330
Ecuador	USA (United States)	20 Feb 52	177UNTS43	102308
Peru	USA (United States)	22 Feb 52	165UNTS31	102166
Israel	USA (United States)	27 Feb 52	177UNTS123	102314
Japan	USA (United States)	28 Feb 52	208UNTS255	102817
Greece	United Nations	05 Mar 52	123UNTS3	101650
ICAO (Civil Aviat)	United Arab Rep	06 Mar 52	151UNTS111	101986
Finland	WHO (World Health)	07 Mar 52	128UNTS269	200436
Cuba	USA (United States)	07 Mar 52	165UNTS11	102165
Brazil	USA (United States)	15 Mar 52	199UNTS221	102687
Norway	USA (United States)	01 Apr 52	177UNTS291	102328
India	United Nations	02 Apr 52	126UNTS145	101687
Greece	Switzerland	04 Apr 52	166UNTS271	102192
Chile	USA (United States)	09 Apr 52	186UNTS53	102482
Colombia	USA (United States)	17 Apr 52	174UNTS215	102287
Greece	USA (United States)	23 Apr 52	177UNTS283	102327
Belgium	Greece	24 Apr 52	166UNTS261	102191
Israel	USA (United States)	09 May 52	177UNTS269	102326
Israel	USA (United States)	09 May 52	177UNTS63	102309
Netherlands	USA (United States)	15 May 52	177UNTS233	102321
Belgium	UNICEF (Children)	17 Jun 52	171UNTS249	102228
Multilateral		19 Jun 52	133UNTS165	101787
WHO (World Health)	Syria	20 Jun 52	165UNTS219	102178
South Africa	USA (United States)	24 Jun 52	177UNTS241	102322
USA (United States)	Uruguay	30 Jun 52	207UNTS139	102804
Jordan	UNICEF (Children)	08 Jul 52	173UNTS353	200503
Chile	WHO (World Health)	11 Jul 52	137UNTS27	101846
Multilateral		11 Jul 52	171UNTS143	102226
India	WHO (World Health)	16 Jul 52	135UNTS291	101828
France	USA (United States)	22 Jul 52	181UNTS319	102420
Chile	ILO (Labor Org)	23 Jul 52	178UNTS323	102348
Brazil	United Nations	04 Aug 52	135UNTS185	101820
Israel	USA (United States)	08 Aug 52	181UNTS37	102396
Denmark	USA (United States)	08 Aug 52	181UNTS249	102414
USA (United States)	Yugoslavia	15 Aug 52	184UNTS97	102441
Panama	United Nations	20 Aug 52	136UNTS3	101829
UNICEF (Children)	Vietnam, South	29 Aug 52	161UNTS335	200492
Italy	ILO (Labor Org)	04 Sep 52	178UNTS371	200505
ILO (Labor Org)	Uruguay	20 Sep 52	187UNTS25	102499
United Nations	Trieste	30 Sep 52	140UNTS11	101881
Multilateral		15 Oct 52	141UNTS96	101909
Iraq	USA (United States)	23 Oct 52	212UNTS201	102872
Multilateral		16 Dec 52	158UNTS407	102074
Multilateral		29 Dec 52	151UNTS317	102002
Greece	Italy	04 Feb 53	189UNTS295	102552
Taiwan	ILO (Labor Org)	13 Feb 53	178UNTS337	102349
Germany, West	USA (United States)	27 Feb 53	205UNTS103	102771

PARTY ONE	PARTY TWO	DATE	CITATION	NUMBER
Local currency (Cont.)				
Multilateral		27 Feb 53	333UNTS3	104764
Costa Rica	United Nations	27 Feb 53	161UNTS45	102121
Nepal	United Nations	02 Mar 53	161UNTS347	200493
Dominican Republic	USA (United States)	06 Mar 53	199UNTS267	102689
United Arab Rep	USA (United States)	19 Mar 53	215UNTS17	102909
France	WHO (World Health)	02 Apr 53	174UNTS83	102279
United Nations	Yemen	07 Apr 53	163UNTS73	102142
Netherlands	United Nations	09 Apr 53	163UNTS89	102143
Czechoslovakia	Denmark	23 Apr 53	174UNTS107	102281
Ethiopia	UNICEF (Children)	27 Apr 53	213UNTS169	102885
France	WHO (World Health)	30 Apr 53	174UNTS71	102278
Israel	UK Great Britain	13 May 53	175UNTS179	102300
ICAO (Civil Aviat)	Syria	28 May 53	173UNTS199	102267
Ecuador	United Nations	16 Jun 53	166UNTS289	102194
Ethiopia	United Nations	22 Jun 53	172UNTS93	102241
Japan	United Nations	24 Jun 53	167UNTS249	200499
Cambodia	United Nations	24 Jun 53	168UNTS309	200500
UK Great Britain	USA (United States)	24 Jun 53	224UNTS141	103074
Pakistan	USA (United States)	25 Jun 53	205UNTS139	102773
Ethiopia	USA (United States)	25 Jun 53	212UNTS175	102869
Philippines	USA (United States)	26 Jun 53	213UNTS77	102881
Afghanistan	USA (United States)	30 Jun 53	215UNTS3	102908
India	UK Great Britain	20 Jul 53	196UNTS251	102628
Spain	USA (United States)	26 Sep 53	207UNTS61	102800
Spain	USA (United States)	26 Sep 53	207UNTS93	102802
Jordan	USA (United States)	21 Oct 53	222UNTS31	103020
Dominican Republic	United Nations	19 Nov 53	180UNTS45	102374
Czechoslovakia	Greece	01 Feb 54	225UNTS95	103092
Brazil	WHO (World Health)	04 Feb 54	233UNTS49	103250
Turkey	UK Great Britain	11 Feb 54	190UNTS343	102575
United Nations	Venezuela	05 Mar 54	187UNTS9	102498
Japan	USA (United States)	08 Mar 54	232UNTS227	103238
Japan	USA (United States)	08 Mar 54	232UNTS169	103236
Liberia	United Nations	09 Mar 54	187UNTS61	102501
Guatemala	United Nations	10 Mar 54	191UNTS271	102587
Afghanistan	USA (United States)	20 Mar 54	229UNTS7	103156
Multilateral		20 Apr 54	189UNTS11	102539
Iraq	USA (United States)	21 Apr 54	222UNTS251	103032
Pakistan	USA (United States)	01 May 54	237UNTS231	103349
UNICEF (Children)	Spain	07 May 54	190UNTS357	200515
Nepal	WHO (World Health)	13 May 54	204UNTS311	200522
Pakistan	USA (United States)	19 May 54	202UNTS301	102736
Mexico	UNICEF (Children)	20 May 54	192UNTS3	102591
Honduras	USA (United States)	20 May 54	222UNTS87	103025
Multilateral		31 May 54	192UNTS20	102592
Multilateral		01 Jun 54	200UNTS235	200520
Greece	Hungary	05 Jun 54	299UNTS295	104321
Netherlands	Norway	09 Jun 54	287UNTS179	104184
Jordan	USA (United States)	17 Jun 54	266UNTS137	103828
France	Netherlands	09 Jul 54	287UNTS169	104183
Multilateral		19 Aug 54	201UNTS51	102710
Pakistan	USA (United States)	23 Aug 54	234UNTS243	103287
Libya	USA (United States)	09 Sep 54	224UNTS217	103078
Multilateral		06 Oct 54	201UNTS75	102711
Multilateral		27 Oct 54	201UNTS95	102712
Multilateral		29 Oct 54	201UNTS115	102713
Turkey	USA (United States)	15 Nov 54	238UNTS135	103358
Guatemala	USA (United States)	13 Dec 54	237UNTS169	103343
Netherlands	USA (United States)	14 Dec 54	262UNTS35	103737
Belgium	Greece	16 Dec 54	223UNTS73	103056
Netherlands	UNICEF (Children)	31 Dec 54	202UNTS135	102729
USA (United States)	Yugoslavia	05 Jan 55	251UNTS29	103531
Pakistan	USA (United States)	11 Jan 55	251UNTS111	103537
Chile	USA (United States)	14 Jan 55	238UNTS191	103362
Pakistan	USA (United States)	18 Jan 55	239UNTS61	103372

PARTY ONE	PARTY TWO	DATE	CITATION	NUMBER
Local currency (Cont.)				
Chile	USA (United States)	27 Jan 55	262UNTS3	103735
Haiti	USA (United States)	28 Jan 55	270UNTS83	103894
Peru	USA (United States)	07 Feb 55	241UNTS63	103424
Italy	USA (United States)	11 Feb 55	240UNTS87	103396
Germany, West	USA (United States)	18 Feb 55	247UNTS257	103474
United Arab Rep	USA (United States)	07 Mar 55	252UNTS159	103565
Haiti	USA (United States)	01 Apr 55	261UNTS361	103734
Multilateral		04 Apr 55	208UNTS239	102816
Germany, West	USA (United States)	14 Apr 55	263UNTS351	103782
Taiwan	WHO (World Health)	21 Apr 55	210UNTS71	102835
Argentina	USA (United States)	25 Apr 55	251UNTS283	103546
Philippines	USA (United States)	27 Apr 55	261UNTS351	103733
Israel	USA (United States)	29 Apr 55	261UNTS331	103731
USA (United States)	Yugoslavia	12 May 55	251UNTS337	103550
Cambodia	USA (United States)	16 May 55	263UNTS273	103777
Italy	USA (United States)	19 May 55	269UNTS83	103876
Italy	USA (United States)	23 May 55	251UNTS303	103547
Korea, South	USA (United States)	31 May 55	251UNTS321	103548
UK Great Britain	USA (United States)	07 Jun 55	265UNTS27	103804
Multilateral		14 Jun 55	212UNTS263	200526
Austria	USA (United States)	14 Jun 55	258UNTS37	103668
Guatemala	USA (United States)	18 Jun 55	262UNTS105	103740
Thailand	USA (United States)	21 Jun 55	262UNTS87	103738
Colombia	USA (United States)	23 Jun 55	263UNTS337	103781
Greece	USA (United States)	24 Jun 55	270UNTS351	103905
Greece	USA (United States)	24 Jun 55	270UNTS361	103906
Germany, West	USA (United States)	30 Jun 55	240UNTS47	103393
Multilateral		04 Jul 55	214UNTS10	102897
Laos	USA (United States)	08 Jul 55	278UNTS59	104021
France	USA (United States)	11 Aug 55	251UNTS15	103530
Indonesia	USA (United States)	15 Sep 55	256UNTS293	103639
Israel	USA (United States)	10 Nov 55	240UNTS3	103390
Colombia	USA (United States)	18 Nov 55	239UNTS173	103377
Guatemala	UNICEF (Children)	22 Nov 55	221UNTS305	103012
United Arab Rep	USA (United States)	14 Dec 55	240UNTS37	103392
Colombia	USA (United States)	20 Dec 55	241UNTS25	103421
USA (United States)	Yugoslavia	19 Jan 56	240UNTS121	103400
Denmark	Netherlands	31 Jan 56	286UNTS255	104172
Multilateral		02 Feb 56	227UNTS153	103137
Austria	USA (United States)	07 Feb 56	272UNTS117	103933
Multilateral		10 Feb 56	228UNTS189	103151
Japan	USA (United States)	10 Feb 56	275UNTS105	103979
Multilateral		10 Feb 56	228UNTS167	103150
Iran	USA (United States)	20 Feb 56	272UNTS135	103934
Italy	USA (United States)	27 Feb 56	291UNTS287	104260
Indonesia	USA (United States)	02 Mar 56	271UNTS345	103925
Pakistan	USA (United States)	02 Mar 56	271UNTS371	103927
Spain	USA (United States)	05 Mar 56	271UNTS329	103924
Ethiopia	Italy	05 Mar 56	267UNTS189	103844
Bolivia	USA (United States)	10 Mar 56	270UNTS199	103897
Turkey	USA (United States)	12 Mar 56	272UNTS21	103929
Chile	USA (United States)	13 Mar 56	275UNTS49	103975
Korea, South	USA (United States)	13 Mar 56	272UNTS3	103928
Ceylon (Sri Lanka)	USA (United States)	28 Apr 56	274UNTS35	103956
Paraguay	USA (United States)	02 May 56	268UNTS299	103863
Peru	USA (United States)	03 May 56	272UNTS59	103931
Peru	USA (United States)	07 May 56	268UNTS285	103862
Austria	Italy	07 May 56	284UNTS351	104147
Portugal	USA (United States)	24 May 56	268UNTS323	103865
Multilateral		31 May 56	251UNTS181	103541
UK Great Britain	USA (United States)	05 Jun 56	247UNTS205	103470
Multilateral		14 Jun 56	265UNTS125	103809
Multilateral		26 Jun 56	253UNTS12	103573
Multilateral		26 Jun 56	321UNTS2	104650
Italy	Netherlands	29 Jun 56	287UNTS193	104185

PARTY ONE	PARTY TWO	DATE	CITATION	NUMBER
Local currency (Cont.)				
Burma	USA (United States)	30 Jun 56	281UNTS65	104070
Multilateral		02 Jul 56	248UNTS37	103484
Multilateral		02 Jul 56	540UNTS110	107846
Netherlands	USA (United States)	07 Aug 56	281UNTS57	104069
Pakistan	USA (United States)	07 Aug 56	281UNTS75	104071
Greece	USA (United States)	08 Aug 56	277UNTS203	104007
UNESCO (Educ/Cult)	UK Great Britain	09 Aug 56	256UNTS139	103624
Taiwan	USA (United States)	14 Aug 56	281UNTS257	104083
India	USA (United States)	29 Aug 56	278UNTS25	104019
Multilateral		31 Aug 56	249UNTS158	103506
Israel	USA (United States)	11 Sep 56	277UNTS215	104008
IBRD (World Bank)	Switzerland	17 Sep 56	340UNTS311	200560
Multilateral		05 Oct 56	251UNTS267	103545
Multilateral		05 Oct 56	251UNTS245	103544
Spain	USA (United States)	23 Oct 56	277UNTS105	104001
Burma	USA (United States)	23 Oct 56	282UNTS37	104091
Italy	USA (United States)	30 Oct 56	263UNTS221	103775
USA (United States)	Yugoslavia	03 Nov 56	277UNTS119	104002
Turkey	USA (United States)	12 Nov 56	282UNTS77	104093
Multilateral		21 Nov 56	253UNTS266	103588
Turkey	USA (United States)	23 Nov 56	290UNTS273	104239
Burma	USA (United States)	04 Dec 56	268UNTS189	103858
Brazil	USA (United States)	31 Dec 56	266UNTS151	103829
Multilateral		15 Jan 57	376UNTS122	105378
Multilateral		23 Jan 57	259UNTS426	103701
Korea, South	USA (United States)	30 Jan 57	278UNTS85	104024
Ecuador	USA (United States)	15 Feb 57	279UNTS155	104037
Multilateral		17 Feb 57	271UNTS2	103907
Multilateral		01 Mar 57	264UNTS94	103790
Thailand	USA (United States)	04 Mar 57	279UNTS235	104043
Tunisia	USA (United States)	26 Mar 57	283UNTS117	104111
Multilateral		28 Mar 57	271UNTS30	103908
Morocco	USA (United States)	02 Apr 57	288UNTS157	104203
Libya	USA (United States)	04 Apr 57	283UNTS181	104116
Multilateral		09 Apr 57	274UNTS172	103965
Iceland	USA (United States)	11 Apr 57	283UNTS107	104110
Netherlands	Paraguay	13 Apr 57	593UNTS85	108577
Ethiopia	USA (United States)	25 Apr 57	283UNTS205	104118
Peru	USA (United States)	02 May 57	283UNTS55	104106
Austria	USA (United States)	10 May 57	283UNTS33	104104
Austria	USA (United States)	10 May 57	283UNTS15	104103
Finland	USA (United States)	10 May 57	283UNTS43	104105
Denmark	Paraguay	18 May 57	286UNTS117	104163
Multilateral		24 May 57	268UNTS270	103861
Denmark	Uruguay	04 Jun 57	286UNTS107	104162
Poland	USA (United States)	07 Jun 57	291UNTS41	104243
Germany, West	USA (United States)	07 Jun 57	346UNTS241	104984
Bolivia	USA (United States)	07 Jun 57	291UNTS77	104245
Italy	USA (United States)	22 Jun 57	284UNTS51	104128
Philippines	USA (United States)	25 Jun 57	289UNTS279	104224
UK Great Britain	USA (United States)	27 Jun 57	290UNTS133	104232
Jordan	USA (United States)	27 Jun 57	288UNTS269	104209
Libya	USA (United States)	30 Jun 57	284UNTS177	104136
Italy	United Arab Rep	06 Jul 57	302UNTS147	104357
Multilateral		09 Jul 57	274UNTS300	103972
Peru	USA (United States)	19 Jul 57	289UNTS271	104223
Morocco	UNICEF (Children)	31 Jul 57	282UNTS99	104095
Mexico	USA (United States)	23 Oct 57	300UNTS35	104330
Multilateral		05 Nov 57	285UNTS301	104155
Israel	USA (United States)	07 Nov 57	302UNTS255	104365
Pakistan	USA (United States)	15 Nov 57	303UNTS173	104380
Finland	Italy	17 Dec 57	291UNTS133	104248
Greece	USA (United States)	18 Dec 57	303UNTS159	104379
France	USA (United States)	27 Dec 57	307UNTS79	104444
Turkey	USA (United States)	20 Jan 58	304UNTS15	104389

PARTY ONE	PARTY TWO	DATE	CITATION	NUMBER
Local currency (Cont.)				
Ghana	WHO (World Health)	21 Jan 58	307UNTS3	104437
Spain	USA (United States)	27 Jan 58	303UNTS247	104384
Italy	Romania	28 Jan 58	302UNTS231	104362
Iran	Italy	29 Jan 58	302UNTS181	104358
USA (United States)	Yugoslavia	03 Feb 58	304UNTS293	104404
UK Great Britain	USA (United States)	03 Feb 58	307UNTS199	104450
Indonesia	WHO (World Health)	05 Feb 58	307UNTS15	104438
Korea, South	USA (United States)	05 Feb 58	307UNTS121	104447
Poland	USA (United States)	12 Feb 58	304UNTS287	104403
Poland	USA (United States)	15 Feb 58	307UNTS217	104452
Finland	USA (United States)	21 Feb 58	304UNTS253	104401
Bulgaria	Italy	25 Feb 58	362UNTS279	105193
France	USA (United States)	28 Feb 58	366UNTS343	105222
Colombia	USA (United States)	14 Mar 58	308UNTS115	104459
Multilateral		15 Mar 58	292UNTS273	104276
USA (United States)	Yugoslavia	05 Apr 58	338UNTS233	104838
Peru	USA (United States)	09 Apr 58	316UNTS37	104576
Israel	WHO (World Health)	11 Apr 58	307UNTS27	104439
Taiwan	USA (United States)	18 Apr 58	308UNTS179	104461
Belgium	Japan	30 Apr 58	303UNTS109	104373
Iceland	USA (United States)	03 May 58	316UNTS137	104581
Albania	Italy	26 May 58	362UNTS259	105191
Burma	USA (United States)	27 May 58	315UNTS197	104569
Philippines	USA (United States)	03 Jun 58	316UNTS3	104573
Ceylon (Sri Lanka)	USA (United States)	18 Jun 58	316UNTS15	104574
Multilateral		18 Jun 58	386UNTS355	105553
Multilateral		19 Jun 58	306UNTS236	200550
WHO (World Health)	Sudan	21 Jun 58	307UNTS235	104453
Ecuador	USA (United States)	30 Jun 58	336UNTS11	104796
Turkey	USA (United States)	06 Sep 58	336UNTS85	104800
India	USA (United States)	26 Sep 58	336UNTS59	104798
Multilateral		27 Oct 58	351UNTS303	105031
Israel	USA (United States)	06 Nov 58	336UNTS275	104810
Pakistan	USA (United States)	26 Nov 58	337UNTS3	104812
Netherlands	Turkey	29 Nov 58	335UNTS229	104790
Korea, South	USA (United States)	18 Dec 58	325UNTS233	104702
USA (United States)	Yugoslavia	22 Dec 58	338UNTS243	104839
Taiwan	USA (United States)	24 Dec 58	340UNTS251	104868
United Arab Rep	USA (United States)	24 Dec 58	338UNTS221	104837
Finland	USA (United States)	30 Dec 58	340UNTS259	104869
Spain	USA (United States)	13 Jan 59	341UNTS241	104887
Turkey	USA (United States)	13 Feb 59	340UNTS235	104867
Iceland	USA (United States)	03 Mar 59	341UNTS261	104889
France	UK Great Britain	05 Mar 59	343UNTS277	104932
Ceylon (Sri Lanka)	USA (United States)	13 Mar 59	342UNTS51	104900
France	USA (United States)	21 Mar 59	342UNTS71	104901
Italy	UK Great Britain	14 Apr 59	343UNTS289	104934
Netherlands	Switzerland	14 Apr 59	486UNTS367	107086
Norway	UK Great Britain	23 Apr 59	343UNTS283	104933
Belgium	UK Great Britain	23 Apr 59	343UNTS271	104931
Iceland	Netherlands	30 Apr 59	487UNTS13	107091
Netherlands	Norway	30 Apr 59	487UNTS3	107090
Iceland	UK Great Britain	14 May 59	343UNTS301	104936
Indonesia	USA (United States)	29 May 59	347UNTS85	104992
Taiwan	USA (United States)	09 Jun 59	353UNTS257	105046
Poland	USA (United States)	10 Jun 59	347UNTS41	104989
Argentina	USA (United States)	12 Jun 59	347UNTS59	104990
Korea, South	USA (United States)	30 Jun 59	353UNTS297	105047
United Arab Rep	USA (United States)	29 Jul 59	357UNTS121	105111
Korea, South	USA (United States)	01 Oct 59	358UNTS115	105129
Colombia	USA (United States)	06 Oct 59	358UNTS145	105132
USA (United States)	Vietnam, South	16 Oct 59	360UNTS271	105163
USA (United States)	Yugoslavia	22 Oct 59	360UNTS259	105161
India	USA (United States)	13 Nov 59	360UNTS287	105164
United Arab Rep	USA (United States)	14 Nov 59	360UNTS311	105165

PARTY ONE	PARTY TWO	DATE	CITATION	NUMBER
Local currency (Cont.)				
Norway	Yugoslavia	18 Nov 59	383UNTS131	105499
Multilateral		03 Dec 59	348UNTS246	105003
Turkey	USA (United States)	22 Dec 59	367UNTS57	105225
Denmark	Sweden	04 Jan 60	376UNTS375	105390
Greece	USA (United States)	07 Jan 60	368UNTS221	105243
Peru	USA (United States)	12 Feb 60	372UNTS83	105290
Iceland	USA (United States)	06 Apr 60	372UNTS71	105289
Pakistan	USA (United States)	11 Apr 60	372UNTS251	105302
Multilateral		12 Apr 60	359UNTS323	105150
UK Great Britain	Yugoslavia	12 Apr 60	360UNTS79	105155
India	USA (United States)	04 May 60	376UNTS279	105384
Japan	USA (United States)	31 May 60	376UNTS301	105385
Multilateral		04 Jun 60	360UNTS208	105159
Spain	USA (United States)	22 Jun 60	378UNTS3	105414
Multilateral		08 Jul 60	366UNTS310	105220
Poland	USA (United States)	21 Jul 60	380UNTS157	105456
Iran	USA (United States)	26 Jul 60	384UNTS141	105516
United Arab Rep	USA (United States)	01 Aug 60	384UNTS189	105519
Jordan	WHO (World Health)	03 Aug 60	381UNTS133	105469
WHO (World Health)	United Arab Rep	03 Aug 60	385UNTS3	105524
WHO (World Health)	Tunisia	04 Aug 60	381UNTS335	105474
United Arab Rep	USA (United States)	09 Aug 60	388UNTS271	105584
Congo (Zaire)	United Nations	23 Aug 60	373UNTS327	200576
Taiwan	USA (United States)	30 Aug 60	388UNTS191	105579
WHO (World Health)	Saudi Arabia	06 Sep 60	395UNTS169	105684
Lebanon	WHO (World Health)	08 Sep 60	387UNTS49	105557
Brazil	UN Special Fund	16 Sep 60	375UNTS3	105351
Ecuador	USA (United States)	27 Sep 60	401UNTS115	105766
Ceylon (Sri Lanka)	USA (United States)	30 Sep 60	389UNTS221	105594
Chile	USA (United States)	28 Oct 60	401UNTS177	105770
USA (United States)	Vietnam, South	28 Oct 60	401UNTS3	105758
France	USA (United States)	04 Nov 60	400UNTS323	105756
Indonesia	USA (United States)	05 Nov 60	400UNTS35	105746
Greece	USA (United States)	07 Nov 60	400UNTS57	105748
Chile	USA (United States)	08 Nov 60	405UNTS85	105825
WHO (World Health)	Upper Volta	15 Nov 60	383UNTS91	105496
Fed of Malaya	WHO (World Health)	25 Nov 60	387UNTS37	105556
WHO (World Health)	Yemen	03 Dec 60	395UNTS187	105685
Dahomey	WHO (World Health)	07 Dec 60	387UNTS277	105567
Congo (Brazzaville)	WHO (World Health)	12 Dec 60	399UNTS105	105737
Togo	USA (United States)	22 Dec 60	401UNTS33	105760
Niger	WHO (World Health)	28 Dec 60	394UNTS195	105679
Korea, South	USA (United States)	28 Dec 60	402UNTS3	105773
Iceland	USA (United States)	30 Dec 60	401UNTS43	105761
Mali	USA (United States)	04 Jan 61	405UNTS165	105832
Turkey	USA (United States)	11 Jan 61	405UNTS173	105833
Korea, South	WHO (World Health)	20 Jan 61	406UNTS269	200589
Multilateral		28 Jan 61	387UNTS202	105563
Ivory Coast	WHO (World Health)	30 Jan 61	395UNTS205	105686
Chad	WHO (World Health)	03 Feb 61	394UNTS161	105676
WHO (World Health)	Togo	03 Feb 61	394UNTS207	105680
Central Afri Rep	WHO (World Health)	13 Feb 61	394UNTS149	105675
Afghanistan	USA (United States)	15 Feb 61	406UNTS235	105852
Kuwait	WHO (World Health)	16 Mar 61	397UNTS315	200588
USA (United States)	Vietnam, South	25 Mar 61	406UNTS187	105849
Ecuador	USA (United States)	03 Apr 61	409UNTS140	105882
Iceland	USA (United States)	07 Apr 61	406UNTS203	105850
Bolivia	USA (United States)	07 Apr 61	433UNTS3	106227
Mauritania	WHO (World Health)	17 Apr 61	396UNTS301	200587
Gabon	WHO (World Health)	27 Apr 61	397UNTS215	105707
Mali	WHO (World Health)	27 Apr 61	407UNTS66	105860
USA (United States)	Yugoslavia	28 Apr 61	409UNTS172	105884
Brazil	USA (United States)	04 May 61	433UNTS91	106233
Israel	USA (United States)	10 May 61	409UNTS213	105887
Spain	USA (United States)	22 May 61	409UNTS260	105891

PARTY ONE	PARTY TWO	DATE	CITATION	NUMBER
Local currency (Cont.)				
Somalia	USSR (Soviet Union)	02 Jun 61	457UNTS263	106587
Congo (Zaire)	United Nations	12 Jun 61	494UNTS205	107234
Tunisia	USA (United States)	30 Jun 61	434UNTS85	106257
Paraguay	USA (United States)	07 Jul 61	433UNTS53	106231
Bulgaria	Netherlands	07 Jul 61	489UNTS21	107133
USA (United States)	Vietnam, South	14 Jul 61	416UNTS133	105999
Taiwan	USA (United States)	21 Jul 61	416UNTS101	105998
Turkey	USA (United States)	29 Jul 61	416UNTS151	106001
Finland	USA (United States)	04 Aug 61	418UNTS19	106014
Morocco	WHO (World Health)	09 Aug 61	412UNTS192	105932
WHO (World Health)	Somalia	17 Aug 61	423UNTS111	106088
El Salvador	USA (United States)	21 Aug 61	418UNTS35	106015
Iraq	WHO (World Health)	13 Sep 61	419UNTS69	106030
Multilateral		20 Sep 61	407UNTS52	105859
Malagasy	WHO (World Health)	13 Oct 61	421UNTS273	106064
Multilateral		16 Oct 61	410UNTS242	105908
Indonesia	USA (United States)	26 Oct 61	433UNTS249	106248
Iceland	USA (United States)	06 Nov 61	426UNTS225	106140
Multilateral		07 Nov 61	412UNTS258	105937
Syria	USA (United States)	09 Nov 61	435UNTS75	106271
Sudan	USA (United States)	14 Nov 61	434UNTS51	106255
Bolivia	USA (United States)	15 Nov 61	456UNTS192	106557
Congo (Zaire)	USA (United States)	18 Nov 61	433UNTS207	106244
Philippines	USA (United States)	24 Nov 61	433UNTS315	106251
Portugal	USA (United States)	28 Nov 61	434UNTS31	106253
Poland	USA (United States)	15 Dec 61	434UNTS3	106252
Multilateral		27 Dec 61	425UNTS83	106120
USA (United States)	Vietnam, South	27 Dec 61	433UNTS185	106242
Japan	USA (United States)	09 Jan 62	451UNTS97	106488
Ethiopia	WHO (World Health)	11 Jan 62	423UNTS99	106087
Multilateral		17 Jan 62	419UNTS294	106033
United Arab Rep	USA (United States)	19 Jan 62	435UNTS107	106273
Multilateral		20 Jan 62	429UNTS230	200596
Iran	USA (United States)	29 Jan 62	435UNTS53	106270
Guinea	USA (United States)	02 Feb 62	435UNTS35	106269
Morocco	USA (United States)	09 Feb 62	442UNTS135	106345
Bolivia	USA (United States)	12 Feb 62	451UNTS281	106499
Multilateral		13 Feb 62	422UNTS288	200594
Tunisia	USA (United States)	16 Feb 62	442UNTS161	106347
Indonesia	USA (United States)	19 Feb 62	435UNTS137	106276
Multilateral		21 Feb 62	423UNTS151	106091
Multilateral		01 Mar 62	423UNTS122	106089
Korea, South	USA (United States)	02 Mar 62	442UNTS185	106349
WHO (World Health)	Sudan	11 Mar 62	432UNTS325	106226
Brazil	USA (United States)	15 Mar 62	456UNTS209	106558
Iceland	USA (United States)	16 Mar 62	445UNTS49	106376
Peru	USA (United States)	20 Mar 62	445UNTS61	106377
Nigeria	WHO (World Health)	27 Mar 62	429UNTS123	106194
Dahomey	UN Special Fund	28 Mar 62	424UNTS55	106099
Multilateral		10 Apr 62	429UNTS78	106192
Multilateral		18 Apr 62	463UNTS44	106692
Taiwan	USA (United States)	27 Apr 62	436UNTS25	106287
USA (United States)	Uruguay	27 Apr 62	452UNTS25	106502
India	USA (United States)	01 May 62	451UNTS179	106493
Israel	USA (United States)	03 May 62	442UNTS83	106340
Multilateral		17 May 62	429UNTS46	106189
USA (United States)	Venezuela	17 May 62	456UNTS275	106562
Libya	WHO (World Health)	16 Jun 62	437UNTS127	106301
WHO (World Health)	Sierra Leone	19 Jun 62	439UNTS151	106327
WHO (World Health)	Senegal	06 Aug 62	435UNTS179	106279
Multilateral		12 Aug 62	443UNTS266	106365
WHO (World Health)	Western Samoa	14 Aug 62	437UNTS317	200598
Multilateral		29 Aug 62	443UNTS280	106366
Morocco	USA (United States)	11 Sep 62	462UNTS207	106680
Tunisia	USA (United States)	14 Sep 62	461UNTS31	106649
Local currency (Cont.)				
United Arab Rep	USA (United States)	08 Oct 62	462UNTS39	106670
Iran	USA (United States)	15 Oct 62	473UNTS291	106866
Greece	USA (United States)	22 Oct 62	462UNTS187	106678
Guinea	USA (United States)	03 Nov 62	459UNTS259	106628
Korea, South	USA (United States)	07 Nov 62	462UNTS129	106674
Burma	USA (United States)	09 Nov 62	461UNTS113	106655
Multilateral		15 Nov 62	448UNTS50	106424
WHO (World Health)	Syria	18 Nov 62	480UNTS249	106972
Taiwan	USA (United States)	19 Nov 62	459UNTS263	106629
Paraguay	USA (United States)	24 Nov 62	471UNTS49	106821
India	USA (United States)	26 Nov 62	460UNTS203	106641
USA (United States)	Yugoslavia	28 Nov 62	460UNTS185	106640
India	USA (United States)	30 Nov 62	459UNTS231	106626
Dominican Republic	USA (United States)	30 Nov 62	471UNTS25	106819
Multilateral		06 Dec 62	450UNTS240	106471
Israel	USA (United States)	06 Dec 62	460UNTS151	106638
Cameroon	WHO (World Health)	08 Dec 62	451UNTS215	106496
Multilateral		12 Dec 62	457UNTS72	106578
Bolivia	USA (United States)	17 Dec 62	469UNTS121	106788
Algeria	WHO (World Health)	20 Dec 62	463UNTS135	106698
Multilateral		21 Jan 63	453UNTS20	106517
Sudan	USA (United States)	31 Jan 63	494UNTS119	107230
Poland	USA (United States)	01 Feb 63	487UNTS143	107100
Bolivia	USA (United States)	04 Feb 63	473UNTS65	106856
Multilateral		05 Feb 63	453UNTS36	106518
Iceland	USA (United States)	06 Feb 63	473UNTS93	106858
Central Afri Rep	USA (United States)	10 Feb 63	473UNTS83	106857
Multilateral		14 Feb 63	453UNTS168	106524
Turkey	USA (United States)	21 Feb 63	473UNTS311	106867
Congo (Zaire)	USA (United States)	23 Feb 63	493UNTS3	107203
Congo (Zaire)	USA (United States)	23 Feb 63	493UNTS17	107204
Multilateral		06 Mar 63	455UNTS386	106552
Multilateral		18 Apr 63	463UNTS121	106697
Multilateral		06 May 63	463UNTS78	106694
Multilateral		09 May 63	463UNTS159	106700
Multilateral		22 May 63	483UNTS72	107007
Guinea	USA (United States)	22 May 63	487UNTS251	107108
Multilateral		24 May 63	466UNTS346	106754
Ethiopia	USA (United States)	11 Jun 63	487UNTS269	107109
Cyprus	USA (United States)	18 Jun 63	479UNTS191	106953
Mongolia	WHO (World Health)	21 Jun 63	472UNTS373	106848
Senegal	USA (United States)	03 Jul 63	527UNTS95	107620
Multilateral		31 Jul 63	472UNTS220	106842
Burundi	WHO (World Health)	08 Aug 63	477UNTS346	106928
Multilateral		27 Aug 63	511UNTS210	107435
Multilateral		10 Sep 63	480UNTS100	106965
Brazil	USA (United States)	11 Sep 63	493UNTS267	107220
Jamaica	WHO (World Health)	25 Sep 63	481UNTS125	106980
UK Great Britain	USA (United States)	11 Oct 63	483UNTS3	107005
Greece	USA (United States)	30 Oct 63	493UNTS29	107205
Multilateral		30 Oct 63	480UNTS180	106968
WHO (World Health)	Tanganyika	05 Nov 63	496UNTS193	107252
Multilateral		07 Nov 63	480UNTS232	106971
Multilateral		08 Nov 63	482UNTS286	106999
Paraguay	USA (United States)	14 Nov 63	505UNTS87	107366
USA (United States)	Vietnam, South	09 Jan 64	505UNTS173	107373
Multilateral		28 Jan 64	502UNTS321	107336
Poland	USA (United States)	03 Feb 64	505UNTS245	107376
Poland	USA (United States)	03 Feb 64	505UNTS215	107375
Jordan	USA (United States)	11 Feb 64	511UNTS85	107429
Peru	USA (United States)	13 Feb 64	511UNTS119	107431
Iceland	USA (United States)	13 Feb 64	510UNTS295	107420
Multilateral		20 Feb 64	491UNTS30	107172
Sudan	USA (United States)	02 Mar 64	524UNTS217	107575
Ivory Coast	USA (United States)	10 Mar 64	526UNTS285	107611

PARTY ONE	PARTY TWO	DATE	CITATION	NUMBER
Local currency (Cont.)				
Spain	USA (United States)	18 Mar 64	535UNTS343	107789
Bolivia	USA (United States)	25 Mar 64	532UNTS3	107710
Cyprus	United Nations	31 Mar 64	492UNTS57	107187
Tunisia	USA (United States)	07 Apr 64	527UNTS3	107613
USA (United States)	Yugoslavia	27 Apr 64	526UNTS73	107601
Congo (Zaire)	USA (United States)	28 Apr 64	526UNTS55	107600
Philippines	USA (United States)	14 May 64	526UNTS113	107604
Taiwan	USA (United States)	03 Jun 64	526UNTS257	107610
Rwanda	WHO (World Health)	22 Jun 64	514UNTS11	107440
Rwanda	WHO (World Health)	23 Jun 64	514UNTS157	107445
Multilateral		23 Jun 64	506UNTS108	107383
WHO (World Health)	Trinidad/Tobago	23 Jun 64	503UNTS167	107342
Multilateral		28 Jun 64	519UNTS14	107499
Paraguay	USA (United States)	05 Sep 64	530UNTS225	107685
USA (United States)	Vietnam, South	29 Sep 64	531UNTS183	107703
Iran	USA (United States)	29 Sep 64	531UNTS163	107702
India	USA (United States)	30 Sep 64	532UNTS321	107726
Israel	USSR (Soviet Union)	07 Oct 64	516UNTS59	107471
Colombia	USA (United States)	08 Oct 64	579UNTS3	108395
Multilateral		24 Oct 64	514UNTS220	200608
Multilateral		11 Nov 64	515UNTS94	107456
Kenya	USA (United States)	07 Dec 64	532UNTS263	107722
Congo (Zaire)	USA (United States)	09 Dec 64	531UNTS249	107707
Israel	USA (United States)	22 Dec 64	532UNTS231	107720
Iceland	USA (United States)	30 Dec 64	542UNTS37	107878
Dahomey	USA (United States)	31 Dec 64	541UNTS117	107865
Korea, South	USA (United States)	31 Dec 64	535UNTS315	107787
Taiwan	USA (United States)	31 Dec 64	532UNTS29	107711
Malawi	WHO (World Health)	06 Jan 65	525UNTS165	107588
Malawi	WHO (World Health)	08 Jan 65	524UNTS281	107579
India	USA (United States)	13 Jan 65	541UNTS107	107864
Multilateral		27 Jan 65	523UNTS102	107556
Multilateral		02 Feb 65	523UNTS256	107560
Multilateral		12 Feb 65	525UNTS148	107587
Tunisia	USA (United States)	17 Feb 65	542UNTS125	107885
Philippines	USA (United States)	23 Apr 65	546UNTS157	107942
Morocco	USA (United States)	23 Apr 65	594UNTS3	108591
USA (United States)	Uruguay	17 May 65	564UNTS69	108221
Afghanistan	USA (United States)	22 May 65	579UNTS29	108396
USA (United States)	Vietnam, South	26 May 65	550UNTS3	108005
Multilateral		02 Jun 65	537UNTS348	200611
Mali	USA (United States)	14 Jul 65	564UNTS101	108223
Congo (Zaire)	USA (United States)	19 Jul 65	593UNTS215	108586
Israel	USA (United States)	20 Jul 65	549UNTS55	107989
Chile	USA (United States)	27 Jul 65	574UNTS83	108342
Bolivia	USA (United States)	17 Aug 65	587UNTS289	108514
Poland	WHO (World Health)	26 Aug 65	552UNTS3	108047
Multilateral		13 Sep 65	547UNTS264	107962
Multilateral		21 Oct 65	547UNTS216	107959
United Arab Rep	USA (United States)	03 Jan 66	579UNTS63	108399
United Arab Rep	USA (United States)	03 Jan 66	579UNTS83	108400
Guinea	USA (United States)	04 Feb 66	579UNTS213	108409
Korea, South	USA (United States)	07 Mar 66	579UNTS137	108404
Ceylon (Sri Lanka)	USA (United States)	12 Mar 66	579UNTS117	108403
WHO (World Health)	Singapore	28 Mar 66	562UNTS59	108195
Ghana	USA (United States)	01 Apr 66	579UNTS157	108405
Jordan	USA (United States)	05 Apr 66	593UNTS239	108587
USA (United States)	Yugoslavia	11 Apr 66	580UNTS239	108427
Sudan	USA (United States)	13 Apr 66	586UNTS39	108495
Bolivia	USA (United States)	22 Apr 66	578UNTS73	108388
Pakistan	USA (United States)	26 May 66	594UNTS27	108592
Burma	USA (United States)	01 Jun 66	580UNTS253	108428
Israel	USA (United States)	06 Jun 66	593UNTS165	108583
Claims, debts and assets				
Mexico	Netherlands	07 Feb 46	3UNTS13	100022
Greece	UK Great Britain	21 Mar 46	91UNTS149	101247
South Africa	USA (United States)	21 Mar 47	16UNTS47	100248
Multilateral		19 Jun 48	310UNTS151	104492
Canada	USA (United States)	31 Jan 49	43UNTS119	100666
Chile	USA (United States)	16 Jan 51	147UNTS11	101925
Belgium	UK Great Britain	30 Jun 52	199UNTS113	102679
Denmark	Poland	26 Feb 53	186UNTS301	102496
Netherlands	Yugoslavia	09 Feb 61	453UNTS221	106526
Argentina	Yugoslavia	09 Jun 65	601UNTS3	108684
Indonesia	UK Great Britain	01 Dec 66	606UNTS125	108782
Korea, South	USA (United States)	09 Feb 67	0UNTS0	109605
Ghana	UK Great Britain	27 Feb 67	606UNTS133	108783
Assets				
Brazil	Paraguay	14 Jun 41	54UNTS289	200201
Canada	USA (United States)	04 Mar 42	124UNTS271	200426
Greece	UK Great Britain	21 Mar 46	91UNTS149	101247
Belgium	Denmark	08 Apr 46	4UNTS429	100059
France	Greece	24 Apr 46	91UNTS83	101243
Denmark	Luxembourg	21 May 46	4UNTS435	100060
Denmark	New Zealand	18 Sep 46	10UNTS39	100141
Albania	Yugoslavia	03 Oct 46	111UNTS227	101537
Greece	USA (United States)	08 Oct 46	180UNTS119	102379
Belgium	Netherlands	12 Oct 46	23UNTS179	100347
Denmark	South Africa	14 Oct 46	10UNTS29	100140
Albania	Yugoslavia	28 Nov 46	111UNTS93	101520
Albania	Yugoslavia	28 Nov 46	111UNTS127	101525
Albania	Yugoslavia	28 Nov 46	111UNTS151	101528
Albania	Yugoslavia	28 Nov 46	111UNTS113	101523
Belgium	Sweden	30 Dec 46	23UNTS197	100348
Italy	UK Great Britain	17 Apr 47	54UNTS169	100802
New Zealand	UK Great Britain	27 May 47	17UNTS211	100277
Sweden	USA (United States)	24 Jun 47	36UNTS25	100565
Belgium	United Arab Rep	01 Jul 47	34UNTS93	100529
Belgium	South Africa	04 Jul 47	47UNTS9	100720
Iraq	UK Great Britain	13 Aug 47	9UNTS259	100136
Italy	USA (United States)	14 Aug 47	36UNTS105	100567
India	UK Great Britain	14 Aug 47	11UNTS371	100176
Czechoslovakia	Yugoslavia	04 Sep 47	112UNTS91	101540
France	Lebanon	24 Jan 48	173UNTS99	102263
India	Pakistan	31 Mar 48	54UNTS33	100793
Netherlands	USA (United States)	29 Apr 48	32UNTS167	100498
Denmark	USA (United States)	06 May 48	26UNTS55	100377
Australia	Greece	16 Jun 48	18UNTS211	100290
France	UK Great Britain	15 Jul 48	71UNTS215	100920
USA (United States)	Yugoslavia	19 Jul 48	89UNTS43	101208
Belgium	Netherlands	25 Sep 48	123UNTS81	101655
Australia	Denmark	08 Oct 48	22UNTS43	100330
Belgium	Luxembourg	09 Oct 48	123UNTS29	101652
Australia	Belgium	09 Dec 48	25UNTS159	100361
India	Pakistan	23 Apr 49	54UNTS51	100795
Greece	Turkey	21 Jul 49	78UNTS65	101012
Argentina	Norway	09 Sep 49	42UNTS125	100646
Norway	Portugal	28 Nov 49	47UNTS117	100726
Belgium	France	30 Dec 49	46UNTS111	100704
Australia	Yugoslavia	22 Feb 50	51UNTS201	100766
Australia	Netherlands	26 Apr 50	54UNTS83	100796
Switzerland	UK Great Britain	08 Dec 50	175UNTS55	102295
Chile	USA (United States)	16 Jan 51	157UNTS3	102043
Denmark	Switzerland	20 Jan 51	87UNTS223	101174
Jordan	UK Great Britain	01 May 51	117UNTS19	101582
Italy	USA (United States)	28 Dec 51	157UNTS63	102047
Libya	USA (United States)	21 Jan 52	183UNTS177	102427

PARTY ONE	PARTY TWO	DATE	CITATION	NUMBER
Assets (Cont.)				
Jordan	USA (United States)	12 Feb 52	168UNTS25	102211
Israel	USA (United States)	09 May 52	177UNTS63	102309
Panama	USA (United States)	30 Jun 52	181UNTS121	102404
Chile	USA (United States)	30 Jun 52	199UNTS241	102688
Ethiopia	USA (United States)	07 Nov 52	184UNTS285	102453
United Arab Rep	USA (United States)	12 Mar 53	204UNTS3	102747
United Arab Rep	USA (United States)	19 Mar 53	215UNTS17	102909
United Arab Rep	USA (United States)	21 May 53	204UNTS29	102748
Liberia	USA (United States)	23 Jun 53	213UNTS37	102879
Brazil	USA (United States)	26 Jun 53	336UNTS241	104808
Nicaragua	USA (United States)	30 Jun 53	215UNTS133	102917
Jordan	USA (United States)	21 Oct 53	222UNTS31	103020
Chile	USA (United States)	30 Dec 53	236UNTS41	103315
Czechoslovakia	Greece	01 Feb 54	225UNTS77	103091
Panama	USA (United States)	11 May 54	236UNTS107	103319
Ethiopia	USA (United States)	12 Jun 54	234UNTS25	103270
Italy	USA (United States)	28 Jun 54	237UNTS121	103340
Multilateral		30 Jun 54	193UNTS67	102611
Ecuador	USA (United States)	30 Jun 54	236UNTS163	103323
India	Netherlands	04 Dec 54	289UNTS221	104219
Austria	Yugoslavia	18 Jan 55	378UNTS31	105416
Mexico	USA (United States)	09 Mar 55	263UNTS247	103776
Haiti	USA (United States)	01 Apr 55	261UNTS361	103734
Peru	USA (United States)	30 Apr 55	263UNTS309	103780
Multilateral		10 May 55	273UNTS121	103948
Multilateral		15 May 55	217UNTS223	102949
Ceylon (Sri Lanka)	USA (United States)	28 Apr 56	274UNTS35	103956
Italy	Spain	05 Sep 56	302UNTS195	104359
Multilateral		29 Mar 57	283UNTS137	104113
Morocco	USA (United States)	02 Apr 57	288UNTS157	104203
Libya	USA (United States)	04 Apr 57	283UNTS181	104116
Ethiopia	USA (United States)	25 Apr 57	283UNTS205	104118
Jordan	USA (United States)	27 Jun 57	288UNTS269	104209
Peru	USA (United States)	19 Jul 57	289UNTS271	104223
France	Italy	08 Nov 57	305UNTS393	104427
Italy	Yugoslavia	12 Dec 57	386UNTS293	105549
USA (United States)	Yugoslavia	05 Apr 58	338UNTS233	104838
Italy	United Arab Rep	29 Apr 59	363UNTS91	105202
USA (United States)	Yugoslavia	22 Oct 59	360UNTS259	105161
Congo (Zaire)	United Nations	23 Aug 60	373UNTS327	200576
Mali	USA (United States)	04 Jan 61	405UNTS165	105832
Honduras	USA (United States)	12 Apr 61	413UNTS182	105952
Congo (Zaire)	United Nations	12 Jun 61	494UNTS205	107234
Inter-Am Devel Bnk	USA (United States)	19 Jun 61	410UNTS34	105895
Germany, West	Ireland	17 Oct 62	604UNTS135	108749
Bulgaria	USA (United States)	02 Jul 63	479UNTS245	106957
Canada	USA (United States)	22 Jan 64	530UNTS89	107674
Czechoslovakia	Netherlands	11 Jun 64	556UNTS89	108120
Netherlands	Norway	22 Sep 66	600UNTS227	108683
Kenya	IBRD (World Bank)	17 Feb 67	599UNTS233	108669
IBRD (World Bank)	Uganda	17 Feb 67	599UNTS321	108673
IBRD (World Bank)	Tanzania	17 Feb 67	599UNTS287	108671
Pakistan	IBRD (World Bank)	15 Mar 67	599UNTS245	108670
IBRD (World Bank)	Thailand	24 Mar 67	599UNTS299	108672
Claims and settlements				
Multilateral		29 Jun 33	39UNTS189	100618
Multilateral		29 Jun 33	39UNTS259	100621
Multilateral		29 Jun 33	39UNTS235	100620
Multilateral		29 Jun 33	39UNTS211	100619
Multilateral		29 Jun 33	39UNTS165	100617
Norway	USA (United States)	28 Mar 40	88UNTS365	200253
Mexico	USA (United States)	19 Nov 41	125UNTS287	200430
Canada	USA (United States)	04 Mar 42	124UNTS271	200426
Finland	Sweden	10 Mar 43	198UNTS333	200518
Claims and settlements (Cont.)				
Canada	USA (United States)	26 May 43	7UNTS345	200043
Mexico	USA (United States)	29 Sep 43	106UNTS265	200345
Liberia	USA (United States)	31 Dec 43	106UNTS199	200341
Mexico	USA (United States)	03 Feb 44	3UNTS313	200025
Canada	USA (United States)	23 Mar 44	125UNTS345	200432
UK Great Britain	USA (United States)	28 Mar 44	15UNTS413	200104
Australia	USA (United States)	10 May 44	106UNTS237	200343
Canada	USA (United States)	08 Jun 44	124UNTS297	200427
Multilateral		28 Oct 44	123UNTS223	200414
France	USA (United States)	28 Feb 45	76UNTS213	200247
Australia	USA (United States)	08 Mar 45	121UNTS205	200400
France	UK Great Britain	27 Mar 45	98UNTS227	200274
Norway	USA (United States)	29 May 45	34UNTS371	200180
Czechoslovakia	USSR (Soviet Union)	29 Jun 45	504UNTS299	200607
USA (United States)	USSR (Soviet Union)	15 Oct 45	278UNTS151	200547
USSR (Soviet Union)	Yugoslavia	13 Nov 45	116UNTS139	101573
Finland	Norway	27 Nov 45	17UNTS247	100279
Denmark	UK Great Britain	06 Dec 45	5UNTS3	100061
Greece	UK Great Britain	21 Mar 46	91UNTS149	101247
France	Norway	26 Mar 46	31UNTS69	100468
UK Great Britain	USA (United States)	27 Mar 46	4UNTS101	100040
UK Great Britain	USA (United States)	07 May 46	6UNTS285	100082
Canada	UK Great Britain	05 Jun 46	86UNTS3	101147
Taiwan	USA (United States)	14 Jun 46	4UNTS253	100049
Philippines	USA (United States)	04 Jul 46	7UNTS3	100088
Luxembourg	USA (United States)	12 Sep 46	149UNTS19	101947
Denmark	New Zealand	18 Sep 46	10UNTS39	100141
Belgium	USA (United States)	24 Sep 46	132UNTS80	101753
Denmark	South Africa	14 Oct 46	10UNTS29	100140
South Africa	UK Great Britain	14 Oct 46	86UNTS51	101152
France	USA (United States)	18 Oct 46	140UNTS23	101882
Canada	USA (United States)	15 Nov 46	7UNTS141	100096
Luxembourg	UK Great Britain	11 Dec 46	11UNTS167	100155
South Africa	USA (United States)	13 Dec 46	167UNTS171	102207
Thailand	UK Great Britain	06 Jan 47	99UNTS149	101376
Multilateral		10 Feb 47	42UNTS3	100645
Multilateral		10 Feb 47	49UNTS3	100747
Philippines	USA (United States)	14 Mar 47	43UNTS271	100673
Belgium	Czechoslovakia	19 Mar 47	23UNTS35	100341
Australia	Norway	24 Mar 47	18UNTS185	100288
South Africa	USA (United States)	10 Apr 47	167UNTS211	102208
Thailand	UK Great Britain	08 May 47	100UNTS47	101386
Albania	Yugoslavia	12 Jun 47	111UNTS189	101533
Austria	USA (United States)	21 Jun 47	67UNTS99	100869
Belgium	United Arab Rep	01 Jul 47	34UNTS93	100529
USSR (Soviet Union)	Yugoslavia	25 Jul 47	130UNTS315	101732
Italy	USA (United States)	14 Aug 47	36UNTS105	100567
Czechoslovakia	Yugoslavia	04 Sep 47	112UNTS91	101540
Multilateral		10 Oct 47	54UNTS193	100804
Multilateral		30 Oct 47	55UNTS188	100814
Greece	USA (United States)	03 Dec 47	89UNTS119	101213
France	Lebanon	24 Jan 48	173UNTS99	102263
New Zealand	USA (United States)	16 Mar 48	127UNTS133	101703
India	Pakistan	31 Mar 48	54UNTS33	100793
Netherlands	USA (United States)	29 Apr 48	32UNTS167	100498
Denmark	USA (United States)	06 May 48	26UNTS55	100377
Taiwan	UK Great Britain	18 May 48	66UNTS113	100850
Brazil	UK Great Britain	21 May 48	66UNTS121	100851
Australia	Greece	16 Jun 48	18UNTS211	100290
Multilateral		19 Jun 48	310UNTS151	104492
Burma	Pakistan	22 Jun 48	91UNTS197	101252
France	USA (United States)	28 Jun 48	19UNTS9	100302
New Zealand	Pakistan	28 Jun 48	91UNTS235	101253
Italy	USA (United States)	28 Jun 48	20UNTS43	100314
Ireland	USA (United States)	28 Jun 48	24UNTS3	100349

Claims and settlements (Cont.)

PARTY ONE	PARTY TWO	DATE	CITATION	NUMBER
Denmark	USA (United States)	29 Jun 48	22UNTS217	100338
Belgium	USA (United States)	02 Jul 48	19UNTS127	100309
Austria	USA (United States)	02 Jul 48	21UNTS29	100323
Netherlands	USA (United States)	02 Jul 48	20UNTS91	100315
Greece	USA (United States)	02 Jul 48	23UNTS43	100342
Taiwan	USA (United States)	03 Jul 48	17UNTS119	100273
Norway	USA (United States)	03 Jul 48	20UNTS185	100317
Iceland	USA (United States)	03 Jul 48	20UNTS141	100316
Luxembourg	USA (United States)	03 Jul 48	24UNTS35	100350
Sweden	USA (United States)	03 Jul 48	23UNTS101	100343
Turkey	USA (United States)	04 Jul 48	24UNTS67	100351
UK Great Britain	USA (United States)	06 Jul 48	22UNTS263	100339
UK Great Britain	Uruguay	12 Jul 48	71UNTS199	100919
USA (United States)	Yugoslavia	19 Jul 48	89UNTS43	101208
Philippines	USA (United States)	27 Aug 48	44UNTS13	100675
Korea, South	USA (United States)	11 Sep 48	89UNTS155	101216
Portugal	USA (United States)	28 Sep 48	29UNTS213	100442
Netherlands	UK Great Britain	15 Oct 48	73UNTS203	100954
Sweden	Switzerland	16 Oct 48	197UNTS55	102634
France	USA (United States)	22 Oct 48	84UNTS173	101128
Belgium	USA (United States)	28 Oct 48	173UNTS67	102262
Czechoslovakia	Poland	12 Nov 48	84UNTS347	101141
New Zealand	UK Great Britain	12 Nov 48	162UNTS197	102136
Australia	Belgium	09 Dec 48	25UNTS159	100361
Ceylon (Sri Lanka)	Pakistan	15 Dec 48	91UNTS303	101255
Canada	USA (United States)	31 Jan 49	43UNTS119	100666
Belgium	France	18 Feb 49	31UNTS173	100478
France	USA (United States)	14 Mar 49	84UNTS237	101133
Israel	Lebanon	23 Mar 49	42UNTS287	100655
Israel	Jordan	03 Apr 49	42UNTS303	100656
Japan	USA (United States)	14 Apr 49	89UNTS141	101215
India	Pakistan	23 Apr 49	54UNTS51	100795
Denmark	Poland	12 May 49	87UNTS179	101172
Norway	USA (United States)	13 Jun 49	127UNTS163	101704
Norway	USA (United States)	13 Jun 49	127UNTS189	101705
Czechoslovakia	Poland	02 Jul 49	260UNTS149	103708
Israel	Syria	20 Jul 49	42UNTS327	100657
Australia	Netherlands	12 Aug 49	34UNTS213	100539
Poland	UK Great Britain	22 Aug 49	404UNTS17	105801
Ireland	USA (United States)	13 Sep 49	127UNTS119	101702
UK Great Britain	USA (United States)	19 Sep 49	68UNTS31	100882
Czechoslovakia	UK Great Britain	28 Sep 49	86UNTS161	101157
Finland	USA (United States)	01 Nov 49	68UNTS11	100880
Norway	Sweden	17 Dec 49	197UNTS215	102641
Norway	Sweden	17 Dec 49	197UNTS197	102640
France	Netherlands	30 Dec 49	203UNTS85	102742
Australia	Ceylon (Sri Lanka)	12 Jan 50	53UNTS295	100789
Canada	USA (United States)	24 Jan 50	151UNTS171	101992
Panama	USA (United States)	26 Jan 50	132UNTS233	101763
Norway	USA (United States)	27 Jan 50	80UNTS241	101055
UK Great Britain	USA (United States)	27 Jan 50	80UNTS261	101056
Netherlands	USA (United States)	27 Jan 50	80UNTS219	101054
Denmark	USA (United States)	27 Jan 50	48UNTS115	100740
France	USA (United States)	27 Jan 50	80UNTS171	101051
Italy	USA (United States)	27 Jan 50	80UNTS145	101050
Belgium	USA (United States)	27 Jan 50	51UNTS213	100767
Greece	USA (United States)	20 Feb 50	196UNTS269	102629
Greece	USA (United States)	20 Feb 50	196UNTS291	102630
Israel	UK Great Britain	30 Mar 50	86UNTS231	101162
Finland	Sweden	31 Mar 50	197UNTS285	102643
Australia	Netherlands	26 Apr 50	54UNTS83	100796
Iran	USA (United States)	23 May 50	81UNTS3	101057
Canada	USA (United States)	12 Jun 50	127UNTS57	101699
Haiti	WHO (World Health)	27 Jun 50	110UNTS99	101504
UK Great Britain	USA (United States)	21 Jul 50	97UNTS193	101351
Korea, South	USA (United States)	28 Jul 50	140UNTS57	101883
WHO (World Health)	Venezuela	11 Sep 50	110UNTS237	101513
Iceland	WHO (World Health)	06 Oct 50	110UNTS127	101506
Thailand	USA (United States)	17 Oct 50	79UNTS41	101030
WHO (World Health)	Turkey	19 Oct 50	110UNTS215	101512
Philippines	USA (United States)	06 Nov 50	122UNTS63	101637
Nicaragua	WHO (World Health)	10 Nov 50	110UNTS155	101508
Peru	WHO (World Health)	10 Nov 50	110UNTS187	101510
Switzerland	UK Great Britain	08 Dec 50	175UNTS55	102295
Philippines	WHO (World Health)	28 Dec 50	110UNTS203	101511
Netherlands	Norway	29 Dec 50	134UNTS19	101795
Australia	Finland	04 Jan 51	80UNTS27	101042
Portugal	USA (United States)	05 Jan 51	133UNTS75	101782
Chile	USA (United States)	16 Jan 51	147UNTS11	101925
Canada	France	26 Jan 51	233UNTS65	103251
Ethiopia	ICAO (Civil Aviat)	02 Feb 51	96UNTS123	101333
Paraguay	WHO (World Health)	15 Feb 51	110UNTS171	101509
Israel	ICAO (Civil Aviat)	19 Feb 51	96UNTS141	101334
Multilateral		06 Mar 51	106UNTS141	101461
Canada	France	16 Mar 51	236UNTS267	103330
Canada	France	16 Mar 51	236UNTS297	103331
Indonesia	WHO (World Health)	28 Mar 51	103UNTS71	101425
Jordan	WHO (World Health)	03 Apr 51	110UNTS297	200367
Canada	Sweden	06 Apr 51	197UNTS393	102648
France	UK Great Britain	11 Apr 51	106UNTS3	101456
Honduras	WHO (World Health)	20 Apr 51	110UNTS111	101505
Ceylon (Sri Lanka)	India	30 Apr 51	196UNTS199	102625
Jordan	UK Great Britain	01 May 51	117UNTS19	101582
Colombia	WHO (World Health)	04 May 51	110UNTS83	101503
Germany, West	Norway	07 May 51	92UNTS51	101260
Switzerland	USA (United States)	24 May 51	127UNTS227	101706
Cambodia	WHO (World Health)	31 May 51	102UNTS279	200307
Liberia	WHO (World Health)	11 Jun 51	103UNTS83	101426
WHO (World Health)	Uruguay	11 Jun 51	128UNTS251	101724
Multilateral		19 Jun 51	199UNTS67	102678
Iraq	WHO (World Health)	01 Jul 51	110UNTS139	101507
Switzerland	USA (United States)	09 Jul 51	165UNTS51	102167
Mexico	USA (United States)	11 Aug 51	162UNTS103	102133
Multilateral		08 Sep 51	136UNTS45	101832
India	WHO (World Health)	11 Oct 51	118UNTS27	101594
India	WHO (World Health)	16 Oct 51	109UNTS49	101490
Netherlands	Switzerland	12 Nov 51	126UNTS157	101688
Netherlands	Switzerland	12 Nov 51	126UNTS173	101689
India	WHO (World Health)	20 Dec 51	124UNTS109	101669
Jordan	USA (United States)	20 Dec 51	157UNTS69	102048
Italy	USA (United States)	28 Dec 51	157UNTS63	102047
Denmark	Norway	14 Jan 52	120UNTS119	101618
UK Great Britain	USA (United States)	15 Jan 52	127UNTS3	101697
Belgium	Norway	21 Jan 52	123UNTS39	101653
ICAO (Civil Aviat)	Yugoslavia	06 Feb 52	128UNTS97	101715
Indonesia	United Nations	06 Feb 52	121UNTS3	101621
Lebanon	ICAO (Civil Aviat)	14 Feb 52	128UNTS83	101714
Austria	USA (United States)	16 Feb 52	177UNTS299	102329
Philippines	USA (United States)	19 Feb 52	177UNTS307	102330
Ecuador	USA (United States)	20 Feb 52	177UNTS43	102308
Peru	USA (United States)	22 Feb 52	165UNTS31	102166
Japan	USA (United States)	28 Feb 52	208UNTS255	102817
Finland	USA (United States)	03 Mar 52	177UNTS163	102317
Cuba	USA (United States)	07 Mar 52	165UNTS11	102165
Brazil	USA (United States)	15 Mar 52	199UNTS221	102687
Austria	Greece	22 Mar 52	187UNTS255	102517
Norway	USA (United States)	01 Apr 52	177UNTS291	102328
India	WHO (World Health)	17 Apr 52	131UNTS241	101744
Colombia	USA (United States)	17 Apr 52	174UNTS215	102287
India	WHO (World Health)	19 Apr 52	131UNTS253	101745

PARTY ONE	PARTY TWO	DATE	CITATION	NUMBER
Claims and settlements (Cont.)				
Greece	USA (United States)	23 Apr 52	177UNTS283	102327
Netherlands	Sweden	25 Apr 52	163UNTS195	102148
Netherlands	Sweden	25 Apr 52	163UNTS131	102147
India	ICAO (Civil Aviat)	29 Apr 52	151UNTS123	101987
Israel	USA (United States)	09 May 52	177UNTS269	102326
Norway	WHO (World Health)	09 May 52	131UNTS281	101747
Multilateral		10 May 52	439UNTS217	106331
Netherlands	USA (United States)	15 May 52	177UNTS233	102321
Iraq	UK Great Britain	22 May 52	175UNTS97	102298
Australia	USA (United States)	27 May 52	178UNTS113	102338
Multilateral		12 Jun 52	138UNTS183	101869
South Africa	USA (United States)	24 Jun 52	177UNTS241	102322
Taiwan	USA (United States)	25 Jun 52	136UNTS229	101837
Austria	UK Great Britain	30 Jun 52	138UNTS153	101867
USA (United States)	Uruguay	30 Jun 52	207UNTS139	102804
Multilateral		11 Jul 52	171UNTS3	102224
Multilateral		11 Jul 52	170UNTS3	102221
Multilateral		11 Jul 52	170UNTS269	102223
Multilateral		11 Jul 52	171UNTS89	102225
France	USA (United States)	22 Jul 52	181UNTS319	102420
Denmark	USA (United States)	08 Aug 52	181UNTS249	102414
Israel	USA (United States)	08 Aug 52	181UNTS37	102396
USA (United States)	Yugoslavia	15 Aug 52	184UNTS97	102441
Ethiopia	UK Great Britain	06 Sep 52	149UNTS57	101951
Multilateral		06 Sep 52	216UNTS132	102937
Mexico	ICAO (Civil Aviat)	28 Nov 52	164UNTS15	102156
Belgium	Germany, West	23 Dec 52	186UNTS69	102483
UK Great Britain	USA (United States)	19 Jan 53	161UNTS3	102117
India	WHO (World Health)	11 Feb 53	163UNTS43	102140
Denmark	Poland	26 Feb 53	186UNTS301	102496
Germany, West	USA (United States)	27 Feb 53	224UNTS13	103067
Germany, West	USA (United States)	27 Feb 53	223UNTS167	103065
Germany, West	UK Great Britain	27 Feb 53	330UNTS217	104747
Multilateral		27 Feb 53	333UNTS3	104764
Germany, West	USA (United States)	27 Feb 53	224UNTS31	103068
Germany, West	USA (United States)	27 Feb 53	205UNTS103	102771
Dominican Republic	USA (United States)	06 Mar 53	199UNTS267	102689
Haiti	USA (United States)	13 Mar 53	212UNTS143	102866
Japan	USA (United States)	23 Mar 53	185UNTS93	102461
Libya	UK Great Britain	25 Mar 53	172UNTS281	102252
Belgium	Sweden	01 Apr 53	185UNTS225	102473
Australia	USA (United States)	14 May 53	205UNTS253	102779
Australia	USA (United States)	14 May 53	205UNTS277	102780
Philippines	USA (United States)	26 Jun 53	213UNTS77	102881
Libya	UK Great Britain	29 Jul 53	186UNTS201	102492
Spain	USA (United States)	26 Sep 53	207UNTS93	102802
UNICEF (Children)	UK Great Britain	07 Oct 53	180UNTS59	102375
Denmark	Sweden	27 Oct 53	198UNTS71	102658
Denmark	Sweden	27 Oct 53	198UNTS129	102660
Denmark	Sweden	27 Oct 53	198UNTS111	102659
Czechoslovakia	Greece	01 Feb 54	225UNTS77	103091
Turkey	UK Great Britain	11 Feb 54	190UNTS343	102575
Belgium	Finland	11 Feb 54	211UNTS63	102848
Japan	USA (United States)	08 Mar 54	232UNTS251	103240
Finland	Netherlands	29 Mar 54	252UNTS239	103568
Japan	USA (United States)	16 Apr 54	238UNTS39	103354
Japan	USA (United States)	16 Apr 54	238UNTS3	103353
Japan	USA (United States)	14 May 54	247UNTS273	103476
Austria	Yugoslavia	25 May 54	227UNTS111	103135
Multilateral		01 Jun 54	200UNTS235	200520
Greece	Hungary	05 Jun 54	299UNTS285	104320
UK Great Britain	USA (United States)	19 Jul 54	250UNTS193	103523
UK Great Britain	USA (United States)	21 Jul 54	222UNTS243	103031
Indonesia	Netherlands	11 Aug 54	241UNTS129	103429
Germany, West	USA (United States)	17 Aug 54	233UNTS31	103248

PARTY ONE	PARTY TWO	DATE	CITATION	NUMBER
Claims and settlements (Cont.)				
Hungary	UK Great Britain	19 Aug 54	199UNTS149	102681
Thailand	USA (United States)	01 Sep 54	237UNTS209	103347
Multilateral		06 Oct 54	201UNTS75	102711
Multilateral		23 Oct 54	332UNTS157	104761
Canada	Ireland	28 Oct 54	305UNTS3	104407
Germany, West	Netherlands	29 Oct 54	237UNTS3	103335
Poland	UK Great Britain	11 Nov 54	204UNTS137	102755
India	Netherlands	04 Dec 54	289UNTS221	104219
Netherlands	UNICEF (Children)	31 Dec 54	202UNTS135	102729
Japan	USA (United States)	04 Jan 55	237UNTS197	103346
Korea, South	USA (United States)	29 Jan 55	239UNTS53	103371
Costa Rica	USA (United States)	26 Feb 55	252UNTS129	103562
Greece	UK Great Britain	07 Mar 55	211UNTS249	102856
Peru	USA (United States)	16 Mar 55	252UNTS151	103564
Guatemala	USA (United States)	23 Mar 55	252UNTS143	103563
Ecuador	USA (United States)	29 Mar 55	261UNTS343	103732
Italy	USA (United States)	30 Mar 55	257UNTS199	103655
Italy	USA (United States)	30 Mar 55	257UNTS169	103654
Norway	USA (United States)	06 Apr 55	269UNTS65	103874
Germany, West	USA (United States)	14 Apr 55	263UNTS351	103782
Iraq	UK Great Britain	30 Apr 55	226UNTS319	103126
Austria	Romania	11 May 55	342UNTS119	104904
Austria	UK Great Britain	15 May 55	344UNTS9	104940
Italy	Sweden	25 May 55	291UNTS235	104259
Pakistan	USA (United States)	26 May 55	257UNTS93	103652
Hungary	USSR (Soviet Union)	27 May 55	407UNTS156	105864
Honduras	USA (United States)	10 Jun 55	258UNTS51	103669
Japan	Thailand	09 Jul 55	230UNTS13	103172
Denmark	Finland	18 Jul 55	250UNTS167	103522
South Africa	Sweden	28 Jul 55	230UNTS287	103191
Japan	USA (United States)	24 Aug 55	257UNTS297	103662
Finland	USSR (Soviet Union)	19 Sep 55	226UNTS187	103113
Bulgaria	UK Great Britain	22 Sep 55	222UNTS349	103039
Austria	USA (United States)	26 Sep 55	272UNTS31	103930
Canada	Denmark	30 Sep 55	258UNTS115	103675
Paraguay	USA (United States)	28 Oct 55	273UNTS97	103946
Colombia	USA (United States)	18 Nov 55	239UNTS173	103377
Guatemala	UNICEF (Children)	22 Nov 55	221UNTS305	103012
Germany, West	USA (United States)	04 Jan 56	268UNTS143	103856
Belgium	Sweden	18 Jan 56	293UNTS23	104283
Czechoslovakia	Yugoslavia	11 Feb 56	397UNTS135	105703
Multilateral		01 Mar 56	343UNTS129	104923
Japan	Netherlands	13 Mar 56	252UNTS3	103554
Germany, West	Sweden	22 Mar 56	262UNTS361	103761
New Zealand	Sweden	16 Apr 56	274UNTS259	103971
Indonesia	United Nations	17 Apr 56	233UNTS267	103266
Brazil	France	04 May 56	323UNTS339	104675
Multilateral		19 May 56	399UNTS189	105742
Denmark	Norway	23 May 56	271UNTS49	103909
Sweden	UK Great Britain	09 Jun 56	309UNTS301	104479
Switzerland	UK Great Britain	12 Jun 56	269UNTS133	103879
Multilateral		20 Jun 56	268UNTS3	103850
UK Great Britain	USA (United States)	25 Jun 56	249UNTS59	103501
Poland	USA (United States)	28 Jun 56	273UNTS79	103944
Lebanon	UNICEF (Children)	03 Jul 56	324UNTS145	104683
Finland	Sweden	07 Jul 56	258UNTS83	103672
Austria	UK Great Britain	09 Jul 56	310UNTS61	104487
Multilateral		09 Jul 56	314UNTS3	104539
France	UK Great Britain	10 Jul 56	326UNTS23	104708
Multilateral		11 Sep 56	266UNTS221	103832
Multilateral		24 Sep 56	253UNTS171	103583
Jordan	USA (United States)	24 Sep 56	278UNTS51	104020
Canada	South Africa	28 Sep 56	299UNTS3	104303
Japan	USSR (Soviet Union)	19 Oct 56	263UNTS99	103768
Austria	USA (United States)	25 Oct 56	299UNTS123	104310

PARTY ONE	PARTY TWO	DATE	CITATION	NUMBER
Claims and settlements (Cont.)				
UK Great Britain	USA (United States)	01 Nov 56	264UNTS3	103785
Iceland	USA (United States)	23 Nov 56	281UNTS361	104088
UK Great Britain	USA (United States)	27 Nov 56	282UNTS43	104092
Belgium	Spain	28 Nov 56	308UNTS239	104464
Dominican Republic	USA (United States)	07 Dec 56	263UNTS193	103774
Germany, West	USA (United States)	12 Dec 56	280UNTS71	104052
Japan	Sweden	12 Dec 56	318UNTS309	104623
Germany, West	USA (United States)	12 Dec 56	280UNTS63	104051
Italy	Sweden	20 Dec 56	369UNTS357	105265
Italy	Sweden	20 Dec 56	369UNTS305	105263
UNESCO (Educ/Cult)	Tunisia	03 Jan 57	257UNTS21	103645
Japan	Spain	08 Jan 57	318UNTS221	104615
Italy	Netherlands	24 Jan 57	485UNTS67	107047
Germany, West	Netherlands	29 Jan 57	314UNTS173	104548
Multilateral		31 Jan 57	278UNTS105	104026
Denmark	Netherlands	20 Feb 57	287UNTS41	104179
Germany, East	USSR (Soviet Union)	12 Mar 57	285UNTS105	104150
Multilateral		29 Mar 57	283UNTS137	104113
Italy	USA (United States)	29 Mar 57	299UNTS157	104311
Philippines	USA (United States)	08 Apr 57	303UNTS227	104382
Other Unilat Decla	United Arab Rep	24 Apr 57	265UNTS299	103821
Israel	UK Great Britain	29 Apr 57	280UNTS227	104062
Ceylon (Sri Lanka)	Sweden	18 May 57	315UNTS85	104561
Belgium	UK Great Britain	20 May 57	303UNTS53	104371
Czechoslovakia	Yugoslavia	22 May 57	391UNTS57	105617
Germany, West	USA (United States)	07 Jun 57	346UNTS241	104984
Germany, West	Netherlands	10 Jul 57	339UNTS97	104848
Norway	UK Great Britain	25 Jul 57	313UNTS3	104528
Taiwan	USA (United States)	30 Jul 57	300UNTS61	104331
Morocco	UNICEF (Children)	31 Jul 57	282UNTS99	104095
Turkey	UK Great Britain	16 Aug 57	310UNTS21	104482
Multilateral		03 Oct 57	365UNTS207	105214
Multilateral		03 Oct 57	366UNTS3	105215
Hungary	Yugoslavia	07 Oct 57	439UNTS61	106325
Australia	Netherlands	09 Oct 57	312UNTS225	104520
Poland	USSR (Soviet Union)	26 Oct 57	432UNTS221	106223
UK Great Britain	USA (United States)	01 Nov 57	299UNTS167	104312
Philippines	USA (United States)	01 Nov 57	307UNTS39	104440
USA (United States)	Vietnam, South	05 Nov 57	300UNTS23	104328
Argentina	UNICEF (Children)	19 Nov 57	300UNTS229	104338
Italy	Monaco	06 Dec 57	363UNTS45	105198
Germany, West	USA (United States)	10 Dec 57	307UNTS59	104442
Bulgaria	Yugoslavia	18 Dec 57	376UNTS3	105372
Laos	UNICEF (Children)	11 Jan 58	287UNTS255	104191
Poland	Yugoslavia	16 Jan 58	340UNTS137	104863
Indonesia	Japan	20 Jan 58	325UNTS3	104690
Australia	UK Great Britain	29 Jan 58	292UNTS233	104275
Philippines	USA (United States)	20 Feb 58	303UNTS261	104385
Belgium	Greece	01 Apr 58	388UNTS93	105574
UK Great Britain	Yugoslavia	24 May 58	326UNTS69	104709
Denmark	Sweden	21 Jul 58	320UNTS163	104642
Netherlands	Yugoslavia	22 Jul 58	386UNTS263	105546
Lebanon	USA (United States)	06 Aug 58	366UNTS361	105223
Jordan	UNICEF (Children)	09 Aug 58	309UNTS297	104478
Ghana	UNICEF (Children)	12 Aug 58	309UNTS103	104469
United Arab Rep	USSR (Soviet Union)	18 Sep 58	338UNTS29	104831
Iraq	USSR (Soviet Union)	11 Oct 58	328UNTS117	104731
Finland	Sweden	16 Oct 58	428UNTS125	106171
Canada	USA (United States)	31 Oct 58	391UNTS219	105626
Germany, West	Norway	18 Nov 58	357UNTS205	105119
Portugal	USA (United States)	12 Jan 59	343UNTS49	104921
Multilateral		15 Jan 59	348UNTS13	104996
Belgium	France	20 Jan 59	361UNTS155	105178
Philippines	USA (United States)	21 Jan 59	341UNTS255	104888
Czechoslovakia	Hungary	30 Jan 59	351UNTS3	105016

PARTY ONE	PARTY TWO	DATE	CITATION	NUMBER
Claims and settlements (Cont.)				
Japan	Pakistan	17 Feb 59	341UNTS127	104880
Japan	Norway	21 Feb 59	356UNTS231	105098
Finland	USSR (Soviet Union)	21 Feb 59	338UNTS3	104830
Denmark	Japan	10 Mar 59	341UNTS55	104878
Sudan	USA (United States)	17 Mar 59	342UNTS13	104896
Tunisia	USA (United States)	18 Mar 59	344UNTS179	104948
Germany, West	USA (United States)	20 Mar 59	341UNTS15	104874
Canada	Finland	28 Mar 59	355UNTS3	105072
Morocco	UN Special Fund	04 Apr 59	354UNTS347	105069
Nicaragua	USA (United States)	14 Apr 59	343UNTS119	104922
Germany, West	Sweden	17 Apr 59	428UNTS155	106175
Fed of Malaya	USA (United States)	21 Apr 59	343UNTS3	104916
Austria	Sweden	14 May 59	428UNTS3	106167
Canada	USA (United States)	22 May 59	354UNTS63	105054
Czechoslovakia	Switzerland	04 Jun 59	349UNTS121	105012
Guinea	UNICEF (Children)	08 Jun 59	334UNTS277	104772
Italy	Norway	12 Jun 59	428UNTS363	106187
Germany, West	Netherlands	16 Jun 59	593UNTS3	108576
South Africa	UK Great Britain	18 Jun 59	380UNTS81	105451
Greece	Yugoslavia	18 Jun 59	368UNTS9	105232
South Africa	UK Great Britain	18 Jun 59	380UNTS103	105452
South Africa	UK Great Britain	18 Jun 59	380UNTS59	105450
Denmark	Yugoslavia	13 Jul 59	386UNTS251	105545
India	Norway	20 Jul 59	356UNTS257	105099
Finland	USA (United States)	22 Jul 59	354UNTS39	105051
Finland	UK Great Britain	28 Jul 59	355UNTS31	105073
Ghana	UN Special Fund	12 Aug 59	338UNTS203	104836
Netherlands	Turkey	12 Aug 59	527UNTS181	107624
Turkey	UK Great Britain	09 Sep 59	424UNTS267	106113
Austria	Netherlands	30 Sep 59	507UNTS111	107397
Germany, West	USA (United States)	01 Oct 59	358UNTS129	105130
Iran	UN Special Fund	06 Oct 59	342UNTS89	104902
Austria	France	08 Oct 59	453UNTS95	106521
Poland	UN Special Fund	15 Oct 59	344UNTS29	104941
India	UN Special Fund	20 Oct 59	344UNTS143	104946
UN Special Fund	Yugoslavia	27 Oct 59	344UNTS159	104947
Ecuador	UN Special Fund	10 Nov 59	345UNTS3	104955
Greece	UN Special Fund	13 Nov 59	345UNTS171	104966
UN Special Fund	Turkey	20 Nov 59	345UNTS105	104963
UN Special Fund	United Arab Rep	25 Nov 59	345UNTS125	104964
Israel	UN Special Fund	01 Dec 59	345UNTS197	104968
Guinea	UN Special Fund	02 Dec 59	345UNTS215	104969
Argentina	UN Special Fund	04 Dec 59	345UNTS263	104972
Norway	USSR (Soviet Union)	09 Dec 59	361UNTS93	105173
Jordan	UN Special Fund	15 Dec 59	346UNTS3	104974
Israel	Sweden	22 Dec 59	377UNTS277	105407
Argentina	USA (United States)	22 Dec 59	411UNTS42	105912
UN Special Fund	UK Great Britain	07 Jan 60	348UNTS177	105000
Japan	USA (United States)	19 Jan 60	373UNTS207	105321
Chile	UN Special Fund	22 Jan 60	351UNTS115	105020
India	Japan	25 Jan 60	384UNTS31	105508
El Salvador	USA (United States)	29 Jan 60	372UNTS3	105283
Colombia	UN Special Fund	04 Feb 60	355UNTS257	105080
Bolivia	UN Special Fund	09 Feb 60	351UNTS203	105024
Cuba	UNICEF (Children)	11 Feb 60	349UNTS277	105014
Spain	USA (United States)	13 Feb 60	371UNTS185	105279
Korea, South	USA (United States)	19 Feb 60	372UNTS109	105291
Afghanistan	UN Special Fund	21 Feb 60	351UNTS93	105019
Pakistan	UN Special Fund	25 Feb 60	351UNTS141	105021
Austria	Norway	25 Feb 60	376UNTS155	105380
Germany, West	USA (United States)	16 Mar 60	371UNTS101	105272
France	UN Special Fund	17 Mar 60	354UNTS119	105059
Ireland	UK Great Britain	29 Mar 60	371UNTS3	105267
Romania	USA (United States)	30 Mar 60	371UNTS163	105278
Italy	UN Special Fund	01 Apr 60	354UNTS261	105066

Claims and settlements (Cont.)

PARTY ONE	PARTY TWO	DATE	CITATION	NUMBER
UN Special Fund	Tunisia	12 Apr 60	355UNTS289	105082
Multilateral		15 Apr 60	470UNTS239	106811
Libya	UN Special Fund	19 Apr 60	356UNTS11	105090
Germany, West	UK Great Britain	20 Apr 60	413UNTS236	105958
Germany, West	UK Great Britain	20 Apr 60	449UNTS77	106453
UN Special Fund	Sudan	21 Apr 60	356UNTS213	105097
UN Special Fund	Vietnam, South	29 Apr 60	357UNTS311	200567
Nepal	USA (United States)	17 May 60	372UNTS313	105307
UN Special Fund	Thailand	04 Jun 60	360UNTS97	105157
Finland	USSR (Soviet Union)	23 Jun 60	379UNTS277	105443
UK Great Britain	USA (United States)	24 Jun 60	377UNTS63	105396
Poland	USA (United States)	16 Jul 60	384UNTS169	105518
Sweden	UK Great Britain	28 Jul 60	404UNTS85	105806
Chile	USA (United States)	29 Jul 60	405UNTS127	105829
Guatemala	USA (United States)	09 Aug 60	461UNTS15	106648
Cyprus	UK Great Britain	16 Aug 60	382UNTS231	105484
Germany, West	USA (United States)	16 Aug 60	418UNTS235	106024
Korea, South	USA (United States)	17 Aug 60	400UNTS339	105757
Sweden	Tunisia	06 Sep 60	427UNTS301	106162
Liberia	USA (United States)	06 Sep 60	389UNTS245	105596
United Nations	United Arab Rep	17 Oct 60	388UNTS143	105575
Romania	UK Great Britain	10 Nov 60	385UNTS113	105533
UNICEF (Children)	Upper Volta	15 Nov 60	402UNTS33	105776
Mali	UNICEF (Children)	17 Nov 60	402UNTS23	105775
Nepal	UNICEF (Children)	12 Dec 60	382UNTS273	105488
Panama	USA (United States)	23 Jan 61	445UNTS135	106382
Netherlands	Yugoslavia	09 Feb 61	453UNTS221	106526
Canada	USA (United States)	17 Feb 61	445UNTS143	106383
Morocco	Sweden	30 Mar 61	427UNTS185	106154
Morocco	USA (United States)	31 Mar 61	406UNTS249	105854
Japan	UK Great Britain	11 Apr 61	420UNTS75	106042
Sierra Leone	USA (United States)	19 May 61	409UNTS251	105890
South Africa	Sweden	29 May 61	442UNTS15	106335
Finland	India	23 Jun 61	421UNTS49	106051
Bulgaria	Hungary	30 Jun 61	438UNTS287	106320
UNICEF (Children)	Saudi Arabia	04 Jul 61	413UNTS122	105947
Bulgaria	Netherlands	07 Jul 61	489UNTS21	107133
Bulgaria	Poland	12 Jul 61	436UNTS147	106294
Cameroon	UNICEF (Children)	12 Aug 61	402UNTS235	105788
Central Afri Rep	UNICEF (Children)	21 Aug 61	413UNTS48	105939
Jordan	Norway	21 Aug 61	465UNTS275	106731
Poland	UNICEF (Children)	24 Aug 61	406UNTS95	105841
Italy	Norway	25 Aug 61	475UNTS269	106896
Canada	USA (United States)	01 Sep 61	421UNTS199	106058
Denmark	Pakistan	04 Sep 61	455UNTS305	106549
Multilateral		18 Sep 61	500UNTS31	107305
Philippines	USA (United States)	04 Oct 61	433UNTS83	106232
Sweden	Thailand	20 Oct 61	428UNTS275	106180
IBRD (World Bank)	South Africa	01 Dec 61	425UNTS197	106125
Ivory Coast	USA (United States)	01 Dec 61	462UNTS221	106681
Germany, West	Thailand	13 Dec 61	541UNTS181	107870
Canada	Ghana	08 Jan 62	528UNTS221	107645
Japan	USA (United States)	09 Jan 62	451UNTS97	106488
Dominican Republic	USA (United States)	08 Mar 62	527UNTS29	107615
Togo	USA (United States)	20 Mar 62	445UNTS79	106378
Norway	USSR (Soviet Union)	16 Apr 62	437UNTS175	106307
Greece	USA (United States)	24 Apr 62	459UNTS3	106609
Niger	USA (United States)	26 Apr 62	459UNTS129	106618
Israel	Sweden	15 May 62	484UNTS261	107036
Germany, West	Israel	01 Jun 62	448UNTS227	106435
Ethiopia	USA (United States)	03 Aug 62	459UNTS79	106613
Congo (Brazzaville)	USA (United States)	01 Sep 62	459UNTS117	106616
Austria	Czechoslovakia	22 Sep 62	495UNTS157	107244
Finland	Sweden	05 Nov 62	455UNTS289	106548
Czechoslovakia	Poland	16 Nov 62	526UNTS3	107597

Claims and settlements (Cont.)

PARTY ONE	PARTY TWO	DATE	CITATION	NUMBER
Congo (Zaire)	USA (United States)	17 Nov 62	474UNTS41	106870
Germany, West	USA (United States)	29 Nov 62	460UNTS169	106639
Multilateral		08 Dec 62	510UNTS235	107418
Austria	Yugoslavia	11 Dec 62	546UNTS3	107938
Luxembourg	USA (United States)	18 Dec 62	532UNTS277	107723
Nigeria	USA (United States)	24 Dec 62	462UNTS180	106677
Jamaica	USA (United States)	04 Jan 63	471UNTS119	106826
UK Great Britain	USA (United States)	15 Jan 63	466UNTS181	106743
Japan	Philippines	19 Jan 63	517UNTS281	107489
Japan	New Zealand	30 Jan 63	517UNTS183	107486
Austria	Netherlands	06 Feb 63	570UNTS101	108290
Netherlands	USA (United States)	06 Feb 63	487UNTS113	107098
United Nations	United Arab Rep	08 Feb 63	453UNTS79	106520
Ceylon (Sri Lanka)	Denmark	16 Feb 63	486UNTS285	107083
Norway	USA (United States)	01 Mar 63	524UNTS185	107573
Germany, West	USA (United States)	14 Mar 63	474UNTS71	106872
UK Great Britain	USA (United States)	06 Apr 63	474UNTS49	106871
Gabon	USA (United States)	10 Apr 63	474UNTS113	106876
Poland	USSR (Soviet Union)	22 Apr 63	493UNTS229	107217
Greece	Hungary	27 Apr 63	550UNTS197	108016
Austria	Bulgaria	02 May 63	535UNTS143	107778
Australia	USA (United States)	09 May 63	475UNTS331	106897
Australia	USA (United States)	09 May 63	469UNTS55	106784
Cyprus	USA (United States)	29 May 63	487UNTS283	107110
Hungary	Romania	13 Jun 63	576UNTS275	108369
France	UK Great Britain	21 Jun 63	540UNTS311	107855
United Arab Rep	USA (United States)	29 Jun 63	479UNTS207	106954
Bulgaria	USA (United States)	02 Jul 63	479UNTS245	106957
Austria	Romania	03 Jul 63	588UNTS3	108516
Canada	Nigeria	03 Jul 63	529UNTS57	107656
Malagasy	USA (United States)	26 Jul 63	487UNTS189	107104
Multilateral		31 Jul 63	550UNTS343	108029
France	Greece	21 Aug 63	533UNTS235	107746
Austria	India	24 Sep 63	545UNTS199	107935
Austria	Finland	08 Oct 63	490UNTS255	107160
UK Great Britain	USA (United States)	11 Oct 63	483UNTS3	107005
Czechoslovakia	Hungary	22 Oct 63	514UNTS95	107444
Multilateral		14 Nov 63	619UNTS299	108948
Austria	Belgium	14 Nov 63	544UNTS97	107912
Tanganyika	USA (United States)	14 Nov 63	493UNTS75	107208
Netherlands	Poland	20 Dec 63	514UNTS169	107446
Somalia	USA (United States)	08 Jan 64	505UNTS165	107372
Denmark	USSR (Soviet Union)	27 Feb 64	509UNTS285	107407
Argentina	Yugoslavia	21 Mar 64	635UNTS153	109078
Germany, West	Greece	16 Apr 64	609UNTS27	108826
Kenya	USA (United States)	20 Apr 64	524UNTS165	107571
Korea, South	USA (United States)	12 May 64	529UNTS299	107667
Norway	Romania	21 May 64	563UNTS45	108203
Mali	USA (United States)	09 Jun 64	530UNTS133	107678
Ceylon (Sri Lanka)	Norway	11 Jun 64	559UNTS23	108153
Czechoslovakia	Netherlands	11 Jun 64	556UNTS89	108120
Ireland	USA (United States)	18 Jun 64	530UNTS217	107684
UK Great Britain	USA (United States)	19 Jun 64	530UNTS99	107675
Denmark	USA (United States)	02 Jul 64	529UNTS277	107665
Sweden	USA (United States)	06 Jul 64	529UNTS287	107666
Spain	USA (United States)	16 Jul 64	529UNTS187	107661
Sweden	UK Great Britain	14 Oct 64	543UNTS135	107898
Austria	Hungary	31 Oct 64	605UNTS63	108759
Austria	Hungary	31 Oct 64	605UNTS77	108760
USA (United States)	Yugoslavia	05 Nov 64	550UNTS31	108007
Taiwan	USA (United States)	19 Dec 64	532UNTS313	107725
Laos	USA (United States)	29 Dec 64	542UNTS23	107876
Central Afri Rep	USA (United States)	31 Dec 64	542UNTS29	107877
Belgium	Luxembourg	14 Jan 65	620UNTS3	108949
USA (United States)	Vietnam, South	09 Feb 65	542UNTS175	107888

PARTY ONE	PARTY TWO	DATE	CITATION	NUMBER
Claims and settlements (Cont.)				
Belgium	United Nations	20 Feb 65	535UNTS191	107779
Belgium	United Nations	20 Feb 65	535UNTS197	107780
Dahomey	USA (United States)	13 Mar 65	549UNTS43	107987
Canada	USA (United States)	25 Mar 65	607UNTS141	108802
Israel	UK Great Britain	15 Apr 65	551UNTS19	108031
Australia	Germany, West	21 Apr 65	598UNTS25	108654
Chad	USA (United States)	12 May 65	546UNTS183	107944
Uganda	USA (United States)	29 May 65	546UNTS209	107948
Denmark	Thailand	01 Jun 65	551UNTS157	108040
Saudi Arabia	USA (United States)	05 Jun 65	548UNTS285	107984
Canada	USA (United States)	08 Jun 65	546UNTS201	107947
USA (United States)	Upper Volta	18 Jun 65	549UNTS133	107996
Japan	Korea, South	22 Jun 65	583UNTS173	108473
Hungary	Netherlands	02 Jul 65	564UNTS49	108220
Multilateral		05 Jul 65	563UNTS104	108207
China	USA (United States)	31 Aug 65	572UNTS3	108308
Multilateral		18 Nov 65	609UNTS115	108830
Saudi Arabia	USA (United States)	19 Nov 65	580UNTS35	108419
United Nations	United Arab Rep	26 Nov 65	551UNTS253	108046
Italy	USA (United States)	16 Dec 65	574UNTS139	108346
Malta	USA (United States)	15 Jan 66	579UNTS109	108402
Malaysia	Philippines	07 Feb 66	608UNTS3	108809
Panama	USA (United States)	15 Feb 66	586UNTS27	108494
Austria	Germany, West	17 Feb 66	614UNTS263	108875
Austria	Finland	21 Feb 66	597UNTS273	108651
Ceylon (Sri Lanka)	USA (United States)	23 Feb 66	586UNTS91	108498
Argentina	Uruguay	07 Mar 66	635UNTS275	109088
Brazil	UNICEF (Children)	28 Mar 66	607UNTS235	108807
Belgium	United Arab Rep	30 Mar 66	632UNTS237	109026
Argentina	Portugal	20 May 66	635UNTS301	109090
Guyana	UK Great Britain	26 May 66	595UNTS255	108621
Bulgaria	UN Special Fund	26 May 66	563UNTS71	108205
United Nations	Switzerland	03 Jun 66	564UNTS193	200621
Liberia	UNICEF (Children)	08 Jun 66	570UNTS31	108286
Greece	United Nations	20 Jun 66	565UNTS3	108230
USA (United States)	Zambia	11 Aug 66	616UNTS267	108901
Greece	Japan	20 Sep 66	609UNTS103	108828
UK Great Britain	USA (United States)	27 Oct 66	597UNTS265	108650
Indonesia	UK Great Britain	01 Dec 66	606UNTS125	108782
Guinea	UNICEF (Children)	22 Dec 66	585UNTS137	108486
Luxembourg	United Nations	28 Dec 66	585UNTS147	108487
UK Great Britain	USA (United States)	30 Dec 66	603UNTS245	108736
Italy	United Nations	18 Jan 67	588UNTS197	108525
Trinidad/Tobago	UK Great Britain	23 Jan 67	605UNTS277	108767
IBRD (World Bank)	UK Great Britain	24 Apr 67	600UNTS3	108674
Netherlands	Romania	08 May 67	607UNTS105	108800
Indonesia	UK Great Britain	01 Aug 67	638UNTS3	109128
Finland	France	27 Oct 67	643UNTS75	109185
Australia	UNICEF (Children)	21 Dec 67	614UNTS83	108864
UK Great Britain	USSR (Soviet Union)	05 Jan 68	638UNTS41	109130
Iran	United Nations	15 Feb 68	631UNTS103	108990
UK Great Britain	Zambia	21 Feb 68	0UNTS0	109264
Barbados	UNICEF (Children)	30 Mar 68	637UNTS0	109123
UN Special Fund	Syria	22 Apr 68	634UNTS207	109063
Botswana	UNICEF (Children)	25 Jun 68	639UNTS61	109144
State/IGO Group	Southern Yemen	04 Apr 69	0UNTS0	109455
State/IGO Group	Southern Yemen	04 Apr 69	0UNTS0	109454
State/IGO Group	Yemen	23 Apr 69	0UNTS0	109514
Lump sum settlements				
Mexico	USA (United States)	19 Nov 41	125UNTS287	200430
Mexico	USA (United States)	29 Sep 43	106UNTS265	200345
Turkey	UK Great Britain	23 Mar 44	2UNTS227	200015
Multilateral		08 Oct 44	45UNTS311	200187
Multilateral		20 Jan 45	140UNTS397	200471

PARTY ONE	PARTY TWO	DATE	CITATION	NUMBER
Lump sum settlements (Cont.)				
Czechoslovakia	USSR (Soviet Union)	29 Jun 45	504UNTS299	200607
Portugal	UK Great Britain	01 Jul 45	5UNTS263	200034
Canada	UK Great Britain	06 Mar 46	20UNTS3	100311
UK Great Britain	USA (United States)	27 Mar 46	4UNTS2	100039
Turkey	USA (United States)	07 May 46	6UNTS293	100083
Hungary	Yugoslavia	11 May 46	129UNTS3	101725
India	USA (United States)	16 May 46	4UNTS183	100045
France	USA (United States)	28 May 46	84UNTS113	101122
France	USA (United States)	28 May 46	84UNTS59	101119
France	USA (United States)	28 May 46	84UNTS93	101121
Australia	USA (United States)	07 Jun 46	4UNTS237	100048
Poland	UK Great Britain	24 Jun 46	11UNTS59	100149
New Zealand	USA (United States)	10 Jul 46	6UNTS341	100087
Belgium	Canada	13 Jul 46	230UNTS159	103181
Hungary	Yugoslavia	25 Jan 47	130UNTS3	101726
Netherlands	Thailand	30 Jan 47	247UNTS353	103480
Multilateral		10 Feb 47	41UNTS21	100643
Multilateral		10 Feb 47	41UNTS135	100644
South Africa	USA (United States)	21 Mar 47	16UNTS47	100248
Netherlands	USA (United States)	28 May 47	17UNTS29	100267
Austria	USA (United States)	21 Jun 47	67UNTS89	100868
Belgium	South Africa	04 Jul 47	47UNTS9	100720
France	Norway	15 Jul 47	15UNTS5	100226
Czechoslovakia	USA (United States)	25 Jul 47	90UNTS19	101223
Czechoslovakia	New Zealand	08 Aug 47	18UNTS161	100285
Italy	USA (United States)	14 Aug 47	36UNTS105	100567
Burma	UK Great Britain	17 Oct 47	70UNTS183	100904
Multilateral		04 Nov 47	93UNTS61	101288
Norway	USA (United States)	24 Feb 48	34UNTS155	100535
France	USA (United States)	27 Feb 48	84UNTS207	101131
Netherlands	UK Great Britain	11 Mar 48	77UNTS69	100993
UK Great Britain	Uruguay	12 Jul 48	71UNTS199	100919
USA (United States)	Yugoslavia	19 Jul 48	34UNTS195	100537
Czechoslovakia	USA (United States)	16 Sep 48	90UNTS35	101224
New Zealand	UK Great Britain	12 Nov 48	162UNTS197	102136
UK Great Britain	Yugoslavia	23 Dec 48	81UNTS121	101068
Canada	Netherlands	09 May 49	46UNTS263	100715
Ethiopia	USA (United States)	20 May 49	89UNTS99	101211
Italy	Yugoslavia	23 May 49	150UNTS179	101972
Portugal	USA (United States)	04 Aug 49	181UNTS15	102394
Australia	Netherlands	12 Aug 49	34UNTS213	100539
USSR (Soviet Union)	Yugoslavia	31 Aug 49	116UNTS345	101580
Switzerland	USA (United States)	21 Oct 49	132UNTS163	101757
France	New Zealand	13 Jan 50	150UNTS151	101969
Panama	USA (United States)	26 Jan 50	132UNTS233	101763
Canada	Norway	18 Mar 50	230UNTS349	103194
Canada	Denmark	25 Mar 50	230UNTS343	103193
Canada	Yugoslavia	29 Mar 50	230UNTS357	103195
Philippines	USA (United States)	06 Nov 50	122UNTS63	101637
Chile	USA (United States)	16 Jan 51	147UNTS11	101925
Canada	France	04 Jul 51	233UNTS101	103253
Canada	Italy	20 Sep 51	236UNTS251	103328
Germany, West	Netherlands	19 May 52	134UNTS3	101794
Multilateral		28 Jun 52	210UNTS132	102838
Multilateral		28 Aug 52	175UNTS69	102296
Germany, West	Israel	10 Sep 52	162UNTS205	102137
Germany, West	USA (United States)	27 Feb 53	224UNTS13	103067
Germany, West	UK Great Britain	27 Feb 53	330UNTS217	104747
Germany, West	USA (United States)	27 Feb 53	223UNTS167	103065
Germany, West	USA (United States)	30 Mar 53	235UNTS285	103310
Italy	UK Great Britain	13 Apr 53	172UNTS271	102251
Netherlands	Thailand	30 May 53	293UNTS17	104282
France	Netherlands	27 Nov 53	302UNTS245	104363
Turkey	UK Great Britain	11 Feb 54	190UNTS343	102575
Belgium	UK Great Britain	09 Jul 54	201UNTS299	102721

PARTY ONE	PARTY TWO	DATE	CITATION	NUMBER
Lump sum settlements (Cont.)				
Netherlands	UK Great Britain	09 Jul 54	199UNTS157	102682
Austria	UK Great Britain	09 Jul 54	201UNTS277	102720
Portugal	UK Great Britain	10 Jul 54	199UNTS169	102683
Germany, West	UK Great Britain	10 Jul 54	199UNTS135	102680
Sweden	UK Great Britain	28 Jul 54	199UNTS181	102684
Multilateral		28 Sep 54	207UNTS293	102812
Burma	Japan	05 Nov 54	251UNTS201	103542
Belgium	France	12 Nov 54	306UNTS85	104434
Japan	USA (United States)	04 Jan 55	237UNTS197	103346
Austria	UK Great Britain	15 May 55	344UNTS9	104940
Japan	Netherlands	13 Mar 56	252UNTS3	103554
Hungary	UK Great Britain	27 Jun 56	249UNTS19	103499
Poland	USA (United States)	28 Jun 56	273UNTS79	103944
Greece	Romania	25 Aug 56	299UNTS231	104315
Japan	Spain	08 Jan 57	318UNTS221	104615
France	Japan	27 Mar 57	318UNTS233	104617
Ceylon (Sri Lanka)	UK Great Britain	07 Jun 57	280UNTS107	104055
Japan	Sweden	20 Sep 57	325UNTS29	104693
Brazil	Italy	08 Jan 58	362UNTS273	105192
Indonesia	Japan	20 Jan 58	324UNTS247	104689
Indonesia	Japan	20 Jan 58	324UNTS227	104688
Denmark	USA (United States)	28 Aug 58	335UNTS133	104781
Multilateral		27 Oct 58	351UNTS303	105031
Canada	USA (United States)	31 Oct 58	391UNTS219	105626
Netherlands	Switzerland	14 Apr 59	486UNTS367	107086
Belgium	Netherlands	28 Apr 59	485UNTS123	107049
Austria	Netherlands	29 Apr 59	486UNTS373	107087
France	Netherlands	29 Apr 59	486UNTS379	107088
Finland	USSR (Soviet Union)	29 Apr 59	346UNTS209	104981
Italy	Netherlands	29 Apr 59	486UNTS387	107089
Greece	Netherlands	30 Apr 59	485UNTS135	107051
Netherlands	Sweden	30 Apr 59	485UNTS147	107053
Denmark	Netherlands	30 Apr 59	487UNTS23	107092
Iceland	Netherlands	30 Apr 59	487UNTS13	107091
Netherlands	Norway	30 Apr 59	487UNTS3	107090
Greece	UK Great Britain	14 May 59	360UNTS69	105154
Greece	UK Great Britain	21 May 59	344UNTS3	104939
Denmark	Japan	25 May 59	341UNTS157	104881
Greece	Yugoslavia	18 Jun 59	368UNTS3	105231
Denmark	Yugoslavia	13 Jul 59	386UNTS251	105545
Germany, West	Norway	07 Aug 59	358UNTS185	105136
Spain	USA (United States)	13 Feb 60	371UNTS185	105279
Romania	USA (United States)	30 Mar 60	371UNTS163	105278
Multilateral		15 Apr 60	470UNTS239	106811
Poland	USA (United States)	16 Jul 60	384UNTS169	105518
Japan	UK Great Britain	07 Oct 60	384UNTS89	105513
Romania	UK Great Britain	10 Nov 60	385UNTS113	105533
Japan	USA (United States)	08 Jun 61	410UNTS183	105903
Canada	Japan	05 Sep 61	451UNTS47	106483
Bulgaria	USA (United States)	02 Jul 63	479UNTS245	106957
Austria	Romania	03 Jul 63	588UNTS3	108516
Multilateral		14 Nov 63	619UNTS299	108948
Netherlands	Poland	20 Dec 63	514UNTS169	107446
Belgium	Netherlands	06 Jan 64	531UNTS119	107698
Australia	USA (United States)	05 Feb 64	511UNTS103	107430
Denmark	USSR (Soviet Union)	27 Feb 64	509UNTS285	107407
Argentina	Yugoslavia	21 Mar 64	635UNTS153	109078
Norway	Romania	21 May 64	563UNTS45	108203
Germany, West	UK Great Britain	09 Jun 64	539UNTS187	107831
Czechoslovakia	Netherlands	11 Jun 64	556UNTS89	108120
Austria	Hungary	31 Oct 64	605UNTS77	108760
Austria	Hungary	31 Oct 64	605UNTS63	108759
Austria	Hungary	31 Oct 64	605UNTS3	108758
Israel	UK Great Britain	15 Apr 65	551UNTS19	108031
Austria	Finland	21 Feb 66	597UNTS273	108651

PARTY ONE	PARTY TWO	DATE	CITATION	NUMBER
Lump sum settlements (Cont.)				
Greece	Japan	20 Sep 66	609UNTS103	108828
Italy	United Nations	18 Jan 67	588UNTS197	108525
Ghana	UK Great Britain	27 Feb 67	606UNTS133	108783
Netherlands	Romania	08 May 67	607UNTS105	108800
UK Great Britain	USSR (Soviet Union)	05 Jan 68	638UNTS41	109130
Debts				
Haiti	USA (United States)	13 Sep 41	103UNTS141	200311
Panama	USA (United States)	18 May 42	124UNTS221	200422
Canada	Czechoslovakia	01 Mar 45	45UNTS283	200185
Canada	Norway	25 Jun 45	45UNTS297	200186
Belgium	Canada	25 Oct 45	230UNTS127	103180
Netherlands	USA (United States)	11 Feb 46	3UNTS37	100023
Multilateral		17 Apr 46	27UNTS103	100402
Denmark	New Zealand	18 Sep 46	10UNTS39	100141
Belgium	USA (United States)	24 Sep 46	132UNTS80	101753
Greece	USA (United States)	08 Oct 46	180UNTS119	102379
Luxembourg	UK Great Britain	11 Dec 46	11UNTS167	100155
Australia	Norway	24 Mar 47	18UNTS185	100288
Italy	UK Great Britain	17 Apr 47	54UNTS169	100802
Belgium	United Arab Rep	01 Jul 47	34UNTS93	100529
Czechoslovakia	New Zealand	08 Aug 47	18UNTS161	100285
Multilateral		30 Oct 47	55UNTS188	100814
Hungary	Yugoslavia	18 Mar 48	113UNTS219	101552
Korea, South	USA (United States)	11 Sep 48	89UNTS155	101216
Czechoslovakia	Poland	21 Jan 49	31UNTS205	100480
France	USA (United States)	14 Mar 49	84UNTS237	101133
Denmark	Poland	12 May 49	87UNTS179	101172
Australia	Ceylon (Sri Lanka)	12 Jan 50	53UNTS295	100789
Canada	USA (United States)	12 Jun 50	127UNTS57	101699
Nicaragua	USA (United States)	31 Jan 51	160UNTS121	102105
Panama	USA (United States)	26 Feb 51	160UNTS153	102106
Multilateral		06 Mar 51	106UNTS141	101461
Austria	Greece	22 Mar 52	187UNTS255	102517
Greece	Switzerland	04 Apr 52	166UNTS271	102192
Netherlands	Sweden	25 Apr 52	163UNTS195	102148
Iraq	UK Great Britain	22 May 52	175UNTS97	102298
Belgium	UK Great Britain	30 Jun 52	199UNTS113	102679
Germany, West	UK Great Britain	27 Feb 53	330UNTS217	104747
Multilateral		27 Feb 53	333UNTS3	104764
Germany, West	USA (United States)	27 Feb 53	224UNTS31	103068
Germany, West	USA (United States)	27 Feb 53	205UNTS103	102771
Brazil	UK Great Britain	01 Oct 53	183UNTS207	102430
Denmark	Sweden	27 Oct 53	198UNTS111	102659
Multilateral		01 Mar 54	286UNTS265	104173
Finland	Netherlands	29 Mar 54	252UNTS239	103568
Lebanon	USSR (Soviet Union)	30 Apr 54	226UNTS109	103111
Switzerland	UK Great Britain	16 Jul 54	199UNTS197	102685
Austria	Netherlands	17 Nov 54	292UNTS45	104266
UK Great Britain	Yugoslavia	22 Dec 54	207UNTS227	102808
Germany, West	USA (United States)	14 Apr 55	263UNTS351	103782
Multilateral		15 May 55	217UNTS223	102949
Denmark	Finland	18 Jul 55	250UNTS149	103521
Austria	USSR (Soviet Union)	17 Oct 55	0UNTS0	109255
Belgium	Sweden	18 Jan 56	293UNTS23	104283
Denmark	Netherlands	31 Jan 56	286UNTS255	104172
Denmark	Norway	23 May 56	271UNTS75	103910
Italy	Sweden	20 Dec 56	369UNTS305	105263
Finland	Switzerland	27 Dec 56	277UNTS59	103997
Denmark	Switzerland	14 Jan 57	286UNTS85	104161
Argentina	UK Great Britain	25 Nov 57	313UNTS95	104531
Belgium	France	20 Jan 59	361UNTS155	105178
Denmark	IBRD (World Bank)	04 Feb 59	328UNTS143	104733
France	UK Great Britain	05 Mar 59	343UNTS277	104932
Austria	UK Great Britain	14 Mar 59	343UNTS263	104930

PARTY ONE	PARTY TWO	DATE	CITATION	NUMBER
Debts (Cont.)				
Netherlands	Switzerland	14 Apr 59	486UNTS367	107086
Italy	UK Great Britain	14 Apr 59	343UNTS289	104934
Norway	UK Great Britain	23 Apr 59	343UNTS283	104933
Belgium	UK Great Britain	23 Apr 59	343UNTS271	104931
France	Netherlands	29 Apr 59	486UNTS379	107088
Iceland	Netherlands	30 Apr 59	487UNTS13	107091
Denmark	Netherlands	30 Apr 59	487UNTS23	107092
Multilateral		11 May 59	527UNTS145	107623
Iceland	UK Great Britain	14 May 59	343UNTS301	104936
Turkey	UK Great Britain	13 Jun 59	551UNTS59	108033
Netherlands	Turkey	12 Aug 59	527UNTS181	107624
Austria	France	08 Oct 59	453UNTS95	106521
Belgium	Congo (Zaire)	15 Nov 60	394UNTS79	105670
Netherlands	Yugoslavia	09 Feb 61	453UNTS221	106526
South Africa	Sweden	29 May 61	442UNTS15	106335
Israel	Sweden	15 May 62	484UNTS261	107036
Philippines	IBRD (World Bank)	07 Nov 62	468UNTS281	106777
Multilateral		08 Dec 62	510UNTS235	107418
Austria	Bulgaria	02 May 63	535UNTS143	107778
Argentina	Bolivia	02 Aug 63	0UNTS0	109517
France	Greece	21 Aug 63	533UNTS235	107746
Belgium	France	10 Mar 64	557UNTS13	108127
Norway	Romania	21 May 64	563UNTS45	108203
Belgium	Congo (Zaire)	06 Feb 65	540UNTS227	107852
Japan	IBRD (World Bank)	10 Sep 65	566UNTS249	108246
Israel	IBRD (World Bank)	16 Sep 65	566UNTS212	108245
Morocco	IBRD (World Bank)	08 Nov 65	566UNTS279	108247
Denmark	Italy	10 Mar 66	643UNTS349	109201
Brazil	IBRD (World Bank)	15 Mar 66	599UNTS52	108664
Israel	UK Great Britain	05 Jul 66	630UNTS189	108971
East Afri Service	IBRD (World Bank)	17 Feb 67	599UNTS335	200629
IBRD (World Bank)	Yugoslavia	24 Feb 67	599UNTS27	108663
IBRD (World Bank)	UK Great Britain	24 Apr 67	600UNTS3	108674
Indonesia	UK Great Britain	01 Aug 67	638UNTS3	109128
Debt settlement				
Multilateral		10 Jun 25	38UNTS229	100600
UK Great Britain	USSR (Soviet Union)	16 Aug 41	91UNTS341	200269
Canada	Czechoslovakia	01 Mar 45	45UNTS283	200185
France	UK Great Britain	27 Mar 45	98UNTS227	200274
Canada	Norway	25 Jun 45	45UNTS297	200186
Belgium	Canada	25 Oct 45	230UNTS127	103180
Mexico	Netherlands	07 Feb 46	3UNTS13	100022
Greece	UK Great Britain	21 Mar 46	91UNTS149	101247
Philippines	USA (United States)	04 Jul 46	7UNTS3	100088
Italy	Norway	20 Jul 46	17UNTS273	100281
Denmark	New Zealand	18 Sep 46	10UNTS39	100141
Belgium	USA (United States)	24 Sep 46	132UNTS80	101753
Taiwan	USA (United States)	04 Nov 46	25UNTS69	100359
France	UK Great Britain	03 Dec 46	54UNTS117	100798
Hungary	Yugoslavia	23 Dec 46	113UNTS125	101549
Norway	USSR (Soviet Union)	27 Dec 46	17UNTS283	100282
Belgium	Sweden	30 Dec 46	23UNTS197	100348
Czechoslovakia	Yugoslavia	25 Feb 47	112UNTS3	101539
Greece	UK Great Britain	07 Apr 47	11UNTS201	100158
Italy	UK Great Britain	17 Apr 47	54UNTS169	100802
Poland	Yugoslavia	24 May 47	115UNTS37	101557
Czechoslovakia	Greece	30 Jul 47	185UNTS149	102466
Burma	UK Great Britain	17 Oct 47	70UNTS183	100904
France	Lebanon	24 Jan 48	173UNTS99	102263
Netherlands	UK Great Britain	11 Mar 48	77UNTS69	100993
Poland	Yugoslavia	12 Apr 48	115UNTS167	101563
Denmark	Norway	21 Apr 48	18UNTS139	100284
Czechoslovakia	Yugoslavia	24 May 48	112UNTS111	101542
Australia	Greece	16 Jun 48	18UNTS211	100290

PARTY ONE	PARTY TWO	DATE	CITATION	NUMBER
Debt settlement (Cont.)				
Burma	Pakistan	22 Jun 48	91UNTS197	101252
New Zealand	Pakistan	28 Jun 48	91UNTS235	101253
Korea, South	USA (United States)	11 Sep 48	89UNTS155	101216
France	USA (United States)	22 Oct 48	84UNTS173	101128
Australia	Belgium	09 Dec 48	25UNTS159	100361
USSR (Soviet Union)	Yugoslavia	27 Dec 48	116UNTS327	101579
Poland	UK Great Britain	14 Jan 49	83UNTS3	101100
Poland	Yugoslavia	16 Jan 49	115UNTS241	101564
Czechoslovakia	Yugoslavia	01 Mar 49	113UNTS3	101547
Greece	Turkey	21 Jul 49	78UNTS65	101012
Czechoslovakia	UK Great Britain	28 Sep 49	86UNTS175	101158
Czechoslovakia	UK Great Britain	28 Sep 49	86UNTS141	101156
Italy	Norway	19 Nov 49	47UNTS89	100724
Australia	Ceylon (Sri Lanka)	12 Jan 50	53UNTS295	100789
Denmark	WHO (World Health)	14 Feb 51	104UNTS243	101445
France	UK Great Britain	17 Feb 51	88UNTS199	101191
Jordan	UK Great Britain	01 May 51	117UNTS19	101582
Canada	Spain	29 Jan 52	233UNTS117	103255
Austria	Greece	22 Mar 52	187UNTS255	102517
Greece	Switzerland	04 Apr 52	166UNTS271	102192
Belgium	UK Great Britain	30 Jun 52	199UNTS113	102679
Japan	UK Great Britain	21 Nov 52	172UNTS303	102254
Denmark	Poland	26 Feb 53	186UNTS301	102496
Germany, West	UK Great Britain	27 Feb 53	330UNTS217	104747
Multilateral		27 Feb 53	333UNTS3	104764
Germany, West	USA (United States)	27 Feb 53	224UNTS31	103068
Germany, West	USA (United States)	27 Feb 53	224UNTS13	103067
Argentina	USSR (Soviet Union)	05 Aug 53	221UNTS99	103004
Germany, East	USSR (Soviet Union)	22 Aug 53	221UNTS129	103005
Brazil	UK Great Britain	01 Oct 53	183UNTS207	102430
Greece	Turkey	07 Nov 53	225UNTS163	103098
Bulgaria	Greece	05 Dec 53	225UNTS145	103096
Czechoslovakia	Greece	01 Feb 54	225UNTS95	103092
Czechoslovakia	Hungary	16 Apr 54	504UNTS231	107360
ECSC (Coal/Steel)	USA (United States)	23 Apr 54	229UNTS229	103170
Greece	Romania	19 May 54	225UNTS27	103084
Netherlands	Norway	09 Jun 54	287UNTS179	104184
France	Netherlands	09 Jul 54	287UNTS169	104183
Belgium	Italy	12 Jul 54	288UNTS59	104198
India	Netherlands	04 Dec 54	289UNTS221	104219
Australia	Taiwan	22 Mar 55	209UNTS3	102818
Australia	Czechoslovakia	01 Apr 55	213UNTS199	102888
Germany, West	USA (United States)	14 Apr 55	263UNTS351	103782
Netherlands	USA (United States)	25 May 55	289UNTS227	104220
Austria	USSR (Soviet Union)	17 Oct 55	0UNTS0	109255
Colombia	USA (United States)	18 Nov 55	239UNTS173	103377
Sweden	UK Great Britain	22 Dec 55	231UNTS179	103218
Germany, West	Sweden	17 Jan 56	262UNTS301	103758
Denmark	Netherlands	31 Jan 56	286UNTS255	104172
Germany, West	USA (United States)	02 Mar 56	273UNTS209	103952
Brazil	France	04 May 56	323UNTS339	104675
Italy	Netherlands	29 Jun 56	287UNTS193	104185
Italy	Switzerland	29 Jun 56	284UNTS299	104144
Greece	Romania	25 Aug 56	299UNTS231	104315
Multilateral		25 Mar 57	294UNTS2	104300
Germany, West	Italy	12 Jul 57	291UNTS181	104252
Denmark	IBRD (World Bank)	04 Feb 59	328UNTS143	104733
France	UK Great Britain	05 Mar 59	343UNTS277	104932
Germany, West	UK Great Britain	10 Apr 59	343UNTS295	104935
Italy	UK Great Britain	14 Apr 59	343UNTS289	104934
Sweden	UK Great Britain	18 Apr 59	360UNTS89	105156
Belgium	UK Great Britain	23 Apr 59	343UNTS271	104931
Norway	UK Great Britain	23 Apr 59	343UNTS283	104933
Denmark	UK Great Britain	28 Apr 59	343UNTS257	104929
Austria	Netherlands	29 Apr 59	486UNTS373	107087

PARTY ONE	PARTY TWO	DATE	CITATION	NUMBER
Debt settlement (Cont.)				
Italy	Netherlands	29 Apr 59	486UNTS387	107089
Netherlands	Portugal	30 Apr 59	485UNTS129	107050
Germany, West	Netherlands	30 Apr 59	485UNTS141	107052
Netherlands	UK Great Britain	30 Apr 59	343UNTS307	104937
Switzerland	UK Great Britain	06 May 59	343UNTS315	104938
Iceland	UK Great Britain	14 May 59	343UNTS301	104936
Greece	UK Great Britain	21 May 59	344UNTS3	104939
Greece	Yugoslavia	18 Jun 59	368UNTS9	105232
Australia	Austria	18 Dec 59	348UNTS201	105001
India	IBRD (World Bank)	29 Jul 60	377UNTS153	105399
Honduras	IDA (Devel Assoc)	12 May 61	414UNTS180	105973
IDA (Devel Assoc)	Sudan	14 Jun 61	415UNTS50	105981
India	IDA (Devel Assoc)	21 Jun 61	418UNTS61	106017
Chile	IDA (Devel Assoc)	28 Jun 61	426UNTS89	106131
Colombia	IDA (Devel Assoc)	28 Aug 61	416UNTS3	105992
Taiwan	IDA (Devel Assoc)	30 Aug 61	416UNTS175	106003
Taiwan	IDA (Devel Assoc)	30 Aug 61	417UNTS227	106008
India	IDA (Devel Assoc)	06 Sep 61	418UNTS81	106018
Taiwan	IDA (Devel Assoc)	06 Sep 61	417UNTS253	106009
India	IDA (Devel Assoc)	22 Nov 61	427UNTS55	106146
India	IDA (Devel Assoc)	22 Nov 61	427UNTS29	106145
India	IDA (Devel Assoc)	22 Nov 61	427UNTS3	106144
Taiwan	IDA (Devel Assoc)	01 Dec 61	426UNTS105	106132
Multilateral		08 Dec 62	510UNTS235	107418
Greece	Hungary	27 Apr 63	550UNTS197	108016
Austria	Bulgaria	02 May 63	535UNTS143	107778
Jamaica	IBRD (World Bank)	08 Apr 65	539UNTS303	107841
Denmark	Jordan	28 Jun 66	574UNTS3	108338
Brazil	Denmark	08 Jul 66	581UNTS95	108435
Denmark	Malawi	01 Sep 66	586UNTS3	108493
Ghana	UK Great Britain	27 Feb 67	606UNTS133	108783
Denmark	Paraguay	03 May 67	608UNTS55	108812
Cameroon	UK Great Britain	16 Jun 67	618UNTS329	108933
Assessment procedures				
Mexico	USA (United States)	19 Nov 41	148UNTS367	200474
Finland	Sweden	10 Mar 43	198UNTS333	200518
Mexico	UK Great Britain	07 Feb 46	6UNTS55	100068
Denmark	New Zealand	18 Sep 46	10UNTS39	100141
Greece	USA (United States)	08 Oct 46	180UNTS119	102379
Albania	Yugoslavia	28 Nov 46	111UNTS113	101523
Albania	Yugoslavia	28 Nov 46	111UNTS127	101525
Albania	Yugoslavia	28 Nov 46	111UNTS151	101528
Australia	Norway	24 Mar 47	18UNTS185	100288
Belgium	United Arab Rep	01 Jul 47	34UNTS93	100529
Belgium	South Africa	04 Jul 47	47UNTS9	100720
Czechoslovakia	New Zealand	08 Aug 47	18UNTS161	100285
India	UK Great Britain	14 Aug 47	11UNTS371	100176
Czechoslovakia	Yugoslavia	04 Sep 47	112UNTS91	101540
Australia	Greece	16 Jun 48	18UNTS211	100290
Australia	Belgium	09 Dec 48	25UNTS159	100361
France	USA (United States)	14 Mar 49	84UNTS237	101133
Australia	Netherlands	26 Apr 50	54UNTS83	100796
Australia	Finland	04 Jan 51	80UNTS27	101042
Denmark	Sweden	27 Oct 53	198UNTS129	102660
Hungary	UK Great Britain	27 Jun 56	249UNTS19	103499
Austria	USA (United States)	30 Jan 59	511UNTS145	107432
Turkey	UK Great Britain	13 Jun 59	551UNTS59	108033
Netherlands	Turkey	12 Aug 59	527UNTS181	107624
Germany, West	Ireland	17 Oct 62	604UNTS135	108749
Greece	India	11 Feb 65	606UNTS9	108771
Multilateral		17 Jan 66	592UNTS101	108573
Denmark	Netherlands	31 Mar 66	604UNTS209	108751
United Nations	Switzerland	03 Jun 66	564UNTS193	200621
Greece	United Nations	20 Jun 66	565UNTS3	108230

PARTY ONE	PARTY TWO	DATE	CITATION	NUMBER
Assessment procedures (Cont.)				
Singapore	UK Great Britain	01 Dec 66	605UNTS153	108763
Trinidad/Tobago	UK Great Britain	29 Dec 66	605UNTS237	108766
Private investment guarantee				
Taiwan	USA (United States)	04 Nov 46	25UNTS69	100359
El Salvador	Guatemala	14 Dec 51	131UNTS131	101740
Italy	USA (United States)	28 Dec 51	157UNTS63	102047
Belgium	USA (United States)	12 May 52	179UNTS15	102352
Japan	USA (United States)	08 Mar 54	232UNTS251	103240
Japan	USA (United States)	08 Mar 54	232UNTS267	103241
Thailand	USA (United States)	01 Sep 54	237UNTS209	103347
Costa Rica	USA (United States)	26 Feb 55	252UNTS129	103562
Peru	USA (United States)	16 Mar 55	252UNTS151	103564
Guatemala	USA (United States)	23 Mar 55	252UNTS143	103563
Ecuador	USA (United States)	29 Mar 55	261UNTS343	103732
Multilateral		10 May 55	273UNTS121	103948
Pakistan	USA (United States)	26 May 55	257UNTS93	103652
Honduras	USA (United States)	10 Jun 55	258UNTS51	103669
Bolivia	USA (United States)	23 Sep 55	256UNTS275	103637
Iceland	USA (United States)	05 Oct 55	256UNTS285	103638
Paraguay	USA (United States)	28 Oct 55	273UNTS97	103946
Italy	Lebanon	04 Nov 55	267UNTS147	103840
Colombia	USA (United States)	18 Nov 55	239UNTS173	103377
Costa Rica	Guatemala	20 Dec 55	280UNTS121	104056
Luxembourg	USA (United States)	07 Dec 56	265UNTS255	103817
Turkey	USA (United States)	15 Jan 57	280UNTS79	104053
India	USA (United States)	19 Sep 57	290UNTS175	104236
Iran	USA (United States)	21 Sep 57	293UNTS287	104296
USA (United States)	Vietnam, South	05 Nov 57	300UNTS23	104328
Multilateral		20 Aug 59	376UNTS99	105376
El Salvador	USA (United States)	29 Jan 60	372UNTS3	105283
Korea, South	USA (United States)	19 Feb 60	372UNTS109	105291
Nepal	USA (United States)	17 May 60	372UNTS313	105307
Guatemala	USA (United States)	09 Aug 60	461UNTS15	106648
Ivory Coast	USA (United States)	01 Dec 61	462UNTS221	106681
Germany, West	Thailand	13 Dec 61	541UNTS181	107870
Niger	USA (United States)	26 Apr 62	459UNTS129	106618
Dominican Republic	USA (United States)	02 May 62	442UNTS99	106341
Guinea	USA (United States)	09 May 62	451UNTS197	106494
Austria	IBRD (World Bank)	15 Jun 62	447UNTS127	106414
Ethiopia	USA (United States)	03 Aug 62	459UNTS79	106613
Congo (Brazzaville)	USA (United States)	01 Sep 62	459UNTS117	106616
Colombia	USA (United States)	05 Oct 62	459UNTS191	106621
Congo (Zaire)	USA (United States)	17 Nov 62	474UNTS41	106870
USA (United States)	Venezuela	29 Nov 62	474UNTS107	106875
Nigeria	USA (United States)	24 Dec 62	462UNTS180	106677
Jamaica	USA (United States)	04 Jan 63	471UNTS119	106826
Trinidad/Tobago	USA (United States)	15 Jan 63	471UNTS141	106829
Gabon	USA (United States)	10 Apr 63	474UNTS113	106876
Cyprus	USA (United States)	29 May 63	487UNTS283	107110
United Arab Rep	USA (United States)	29 Jun 63	479UNTS207	106954
Malagasy	USA (United States)	26 Jul 63	487UNTS189	107104
Tanganyika	USA (United States)	14 Nov 63	493UNTS75	107208
Somalia	USA (United States)	08 Jan 64	505UNTS165	107372
Kenya	USA (United States)	20 Apr 64	524UNTS165	107571
Mali	USA (United States)	09 Jun 64	530UNTS133	107678
Mauritania	USA (United States)	03 Jul 64	532UNTS307	107724
Laos	USA (United States)	29 Dec 64	542UNTS23	107876
Central Afri Rep	USA (United States)	31 Dec 64	542UNTS29	107877
Dahomey	USA (United States)	13 Mar 65	549UNTS43	107987
Chad	USA (United States)	12 May 65	546UNTS183	107944
Uganda	USA (United States)	29 May 65	546UNTS209	107948
USA (United States)	Upper Volta	18 Jun 65	549UNTS133	107996
Ceylon (Sri Lanka)	USA (United States)	23 Feb 66	586UNTS91	108498
Singapore	USA (United States)	25 Mar 66	580UNTS221	108425

PARTY ONE	PARTY TWO	DATE	CITATION	NUMBER
Liens				
Australia	Norway	24 Mar 47	18UNTS185	100288
United Nations	USA (United States)	23 Mar 48	19UNTS43	100303
Australia	Denmark	08 Oct 48	22UNTS43	100330
Australia	Belgium	09 Dec 48	25UNTS159	100361
Switzerland	UK Great Britain	08 Dec 50	175UNTS55	102295
ECSC (Coal/Steel)	USA (United States)	23 Apr 54	229UNTS229	103170
Denmark	IBRD (World Bank)	04 Feb 59	328UNTS143	104733
India	IBRD (World Bank)	29 Jul 60	377UNTS153	105399
Philippines	IBRD (World Bank)	07 Nov 62	468UNTS281	106777
IBRD (World Bank)	Spain	31 Jul 64	537UNTS81	107798
India	IBRD (World Bank)	28 May 65	552UNTS39	108049
Philippines	IBRD (World Bank)	23 Sep 66	596UNTS71	108629
IBRD (World Bank)	IFC (Finance Corp)	28 Oct 66	586UNTS225	200628
Brazil	IBRD (World Bank)	19 Dec 66	599UNTS107	108665
Brazil	IBRD (World Bank)	19 Dec 66	599UNTS177	108667
Brazil	IBRD (World Bank)	19 Dec 66	599UNTS205	108668
Brazil	IBRD (World Bank)	19 Dec 66	599UNTS149	108666
East Afri Service	IBRD (World Bank)	17 Feb 67	599UNTS335	200629
IBRD (World Bank)	Uganda	17 Feb 67	599UNTS321	108673
IBRD (World Bank)	Tanzania	17 Feb 67	599UNTS287	108671
Kenya	IBRD (World Bank)	17 Feb 67	599UNTS233	108669
Pakistan	IBRD (World Bank)	15 Mar 67	599UNTS245	108670
IBRD (World Bank)	Thailand	24 Mar 67	599UNTS299	108672
Assets transfer				
Multilateral		26 Mar 43	13UNTS427	200089
Peru	USA (United States)	20 May 43	100UNTS259	200288
Belgium	Norway	23 Oct 45	183UNTS337	200510
Multilateral		27 Dec 45	2UNTS39	100020
Netherlands	USA (United States)	11 Feb 46	3UNTS37	100023
Czechoslovakia	Poland	12 Feb 46	25UNTS207	100364
Canada	USA (United States)	03 Mar 46	6UNTS279	100081
Canada	France	22 Mar 46	230UNTS165	103182
Belgium	Denmark	08 Apr 46	4UNTS429	100059
New Zealand	Norway	03 May 46	16UNTS211	100262
Denmark	Luxembourg	21 May 46	4UNTS435	100060
Poland	UK Great Britain	24 Jun 46	11UNTS59	100149
Iceland	UK Great Britain	04 Jul 46	6UNTS223	100077
League of Nations	United Nations	19 Jul 46	1UNTS109	200002
League of Nations	United Nations	31 Jul 46	1UNTS119	200003
League of Nations	United Nations	01 Aug 46	1UNTS135	200005
League of Nations	United Nations	01 Aug 46	1UNTS131	200004
Greece	USA (United States)	08 Oct 46	180UNTS119	102379
Denmark	South Africa	14 Oct 46	10UNTS29	100140
Luxembourg	UK Great Britain	11 Dec 46	11UNTS167	100155
Denmark	India	20 Dec 46	7UNTS309	100107
Belgium	Sweden	30 Dec 46	23UNTS197	100348
Multilateral		10 Feb 47	41UNTS135	100644
Multilateral		10 Feb 47	41UNTS21	100643
Multilateral		10 Feb 47	48UNTS203	100746
Belgium	Czechoslovakia	19 Mar 47	23UNTS35	100341
Belgium	Poland	24 Mar 47	18UNTS279	100297
Australia	Norway	24 Mar 47	18UNTS185	100288
France	South Africa	18 Apr 47	225UNTS35	103085
Austria	USA (United States)	21 Jun 47	67UNTS89	100868
Sweden	USA (United States)	24 Jun 47	36UNTS25	100565
League of Nations	United Nations	27 Jun 47	5UNTS395	200037
League of Nations	United Nations	27 Jun 47	5UNTS389	200036
Belgium	United Arab Rep	01 Jul 47	34UNTS93	100529
Belgium	South Africa	04 Jul 47	47UNTS9	100720
France	Norway	15 Jul 47	15UNTS5	100226
Belgium	India	04 Aug 47	76UNTS23	100976
Czechoslovakia	New Zealand	08 Aug 47	18UNTS161	100285
Multilateral		14 Aug 47	138UNTS111	101863

PARTY ONE	PARTY TWO	DATE	CITATION	NUMBER
Assets transfer (Cont.)				
Italy	USA (United States)	14 Aug 47	36UNTS105	100567
Poland	UNICEF (Children)	23 Aug 47	65UNTS22	100815
Czechoslovakia	Yugoslavia	04 Sep 47	112UNTS91	101540
Norway	Sweden	22 Dec 47	22UNTS203	100337
Denmark	Sweden	23 Dec 47	14UNTS3	100207
Denmark	Norway	21 Jan 48	14UNTS307	100223
France	Lebanon	24 Jan 48	173UNTS99	102263
India	Pakistan	31 Mar 48	54UNTS33	100793
Multilateral		11 May 48	500UNTS267	107313
Denmark	Iceland	14 May 48	23UNTS163	100346
Australia	Greece	16 Jun 48	18UNTS211	100290
USA (United States)	Yugoslavia	19 Jul 48	89UNTS43	101208
Australia	Denmark	08 Oct 48	22UNTS43	100330
Norway	Sweden	18 Dec 48	30UNTS117	100450
UK Great Britain	Yugoslavia	23 Dec 48	81UNTS103	101067
Poland	UK Great Britain	14 Jan 49	83UNTS51	101101
Netherlands	UK Great Britain	17 Jan 49	83UNTS67	101102
Ceylon (Sri Lanka)	UK Great Britain	28 Feb 49	314UNTS269	104551
India	Pakistan	23 Apr 49	54UNTS51	100795
UNICEF (Children)	UK Great Britain	17 Jun 49	65UNTS50	100820
USSR (Soviet Union)	Yugoslavia	31 Aug 49	116UNTS345	101580
UNICEF (Children)	UK Great Britain	10 Feb 50	65UNTS86	100837
Australia	Yugoslavia	22 Feb 50	51UNTS201	100766
Canada	Denmark	25 Mar 50	230UNTS343	103193
Israel	UK Great Britain	30 Mar 50	86UNTS231	101162
Australia	Netherlands	26 Apr 50	54UNTS83	100796
Belgium	Iraq	05 Jul 50	68UNTS165	100893
Multilateral		23 Dec 50	185UNTS3	102456
Australia	Finland	04 Jan 51	80UNTS27	101042
Netherlands	USA (United States)	19 Jan 51	141UNTS221	101917
France	India	02 Feb 51	203UNTS155	102744
New Zealand	Yugoslavia	27 Feb 51	150UNTS165	101971
Ceylon (Sri Lanka)	USA (United States)	14 May 51	141UNTS159	101913
Italy	UK Great Britain	28 Jun 51	118UNTS115	101600
United Arab Rep	UK Great Britain	01 Jul 51	249UNTS125	103503
Multilateral		02 Jul 51	189UNTS137	102545
Canada	France	04 Jul 51	233UNTS101	103253
Canada	Italy	20 Sep 51	236UNTS251	103328
Paraguay	United Nations	27 Sep 51	120UNTS105	101617
United Nations	Uruguay	17 Oct 51	122UNTS29	101633
Italy	UK Great Britain	07 Nov 51	118UNTS133	101601
Turkey	USA (United States)	15 Nov 51	177UNTS315	102331
Italy	USA (United States)	28 Dec 51	157UNTS63	102047
Multilateral		04 Feb 52	124UNTS3	101662
Multilateral		11 Feb 52	165UNTS77	102169
Italy	UK Great Britain	12 Feb 52	126UNTS297	101695
Austria	USA (United States)	16 Feb 52	177UNTS299	102329
Philippines	USA (United States)	19 Feb 52	177UNTS307	102330
Norway	USA (United States)	01 Apr 52	177UNTS291	102328
Greece	USA (United States)	23 Apr 52	177UNTS283	102327
Jordan	WHO (World Health)	16 Jun 52	135UNTS323	200445
Germany, West	Netherlands	20 Jun 52	136UNTS221	101836
Norway	USA (United States)	21 Jun 52	236UNTS9	103313
Austria	UK Great Britain	30 Jun 52	138UNTS153	101867
France	USA (United States)	22 Jul 52	181UNTS319	102420
Israel	USA (United States)	08 Aug 52	181UNTS37	102396
Denmark	USA (United States)	08 Aug 52	181UNTS249	102414
USA (United States)	Yugoslavia	15 Aug 52	184UNTS97	102441
Multilateral		17 Oct 52	141UNTS121	101911
Greece	Spain	03 Feb 53	225UNTS3	103081
Multilateral		27 Feb 53	333UNTS3	104764
Haiti	USA (United States)	13 Mar 53	212UNTS143	102866
Chile	USA (United States)	27 Jun 53	229UNTS53	103160
India	UK Great Britain	20 Jul 53	196UNTS251	102628
Germany, East	USSR (Soviet Union)	22 Aug 53	221UNTS129	103005

PARTY ONE	PARTY TWO	DATE	CITATION	NUMBER
Assets transfer (Cont.)				
Spain	USA (United States)	26 Sep 53	207UNTS93	102802
Multilateral		28 Sep 54	360UNTS117	105158
Iran	UK Great Britain	25 Oct 54	204UNTS131	102754
Germany, West	USA (United States)	29 Oct 54	273UNTS3	103943
India	Netherlands	04 Dec 54	289UNTS221	104219
USA (United States)	Yugoslavia	05 Jan 55	251UNTS29	103531
Turkey	UK Great Britain	17 Jan 55	204UNTS195	102758
Multilateral		15 May 55	217UNTS223	102949
India	Pakistan	12 Jun 55	228UNTS211	103153
Libya	USA (United States)	21 Jul 55	264UNTS247	103796
Germany, West	USA (United States)	02 Aug 55	268UNTS121	103854
Austria	USA (United States)	26 Sep 55	272UNTS31	103930
Netherlands	USA (United States)	22 Jan 56	287UNTS121	104181
Ireland	USA (United States)	16 Mar 56	317UNTS195	104604
Austria	Italy	07 May 56	284UNTS351	104147
Costa Rica	USA (United States)	18 May 56	404UNTS237	105814
Argentina	Italy	23 May 56	267UNTS255	103846
Australia	USA (United States)	22 Jun 56	283UNTS275	104123
Cuba	USA (United States)	26 Jun 56	293UNTS257	104294
Guatemala	USA (United States)	15 Aug 56	288UNTS181	104205
Liberia	USA (United States)	22 Sep 56	278UNTS109	104027
Japan	USA (United States)	23 Nov 56	324UNTS177	104685
Multilateral		31 Jan 57	278UNTS105	104026
Cuba	USA (United States)	04 Feb 57	302UNTS273	104366
Netherlands	USA (United States)	15 Feb 57	287UNTS239	104190
Norway	USA (United States)	25 Feb 57	284UNTS19	104126
Iran	USA (United States)	05 Mar 57	342UNTS29	104898
Multilateral		29 Mar 57	283UNTS137	104113
Japan	USA (United States)	08 May 57	318UNTS257	104621
Ecuador	USA (United States)	31 May 57	304UNTS61	104391
Afghanistan	USA (United States)	09 Jun 57	307UNTS97	104445
Nicaragua	USA (United States)	11 Jun 57	304UNTS267	104402
Germany, West	USA (United States)	28 Jun 57	288UNTS339	104213
Germany, West	USA (United States)	03 Jul 57	288UNTS305	104212
South Africa	USA (United States)	08 Jul 57	290UNTS147	104234
Spain	USA (United States)	16 Aug 57	307UNTS169	104449
Czechoslovakia	USSR (Soviet Union)	31 Aug 57	308UNTS3	104456
Germany, East	Hungary	30 Oct 57	408UNTS4	105867
USA (United States)	Vietnam, South	05 Nov 57	300UNTS23	104328
Germany, East	USSR (Soviet Union)	28 Nov 57	305UNTS113	104419
Korea, North	USSR (Soviet Union)	16 Dec 57	301UNTS301	104349
Multilateral		31 Mar 58	320UNTS103	104639
Ceylon (Sri Lanka)	Sweden	22 May 58	428UNTS65	106168
Japan	USA (United States)	19 Jun 58	325UNTS143	104699
Albania	USSR (Soviet Union)	30 Jun 58	328UNTS3	104729
Germany, East	Romania	15 Jul 58	395UNTS3	105681
Mongolia	USSR (Soviet Union)	25 Aug 58	322UNTS105	104657
Ghana	USA (United States)	30 Sep 58	336UNTS169	104805
Hungary	Romania	07 Oct 58	416UNTS199	106004
USA (United States)	Venezuela	08 Oct 58	371UNTS69	105271
Czechoslovakia	Romania	25 Oct 58	417UNTS37	106006
Bulgaria	Romania	03 Dec 58	417UNTS133	106007
Finland	USA (United States)	30 Dec 58	340UNTS259	104869
Albania	Czechoslovakia	16 Jan 59	363UNTS195	105208
Austria	USA (United States)	30 Jan 59	511UNTS145	107432
Turkey	USA (United States)	13 Feb 59	340UNTS235	104867
Hungary	Poland	06 Mar 59	432UNTS3	106216
USA (United States)	Vietnam, South	22 Apr 59	347UNTS113	104993
Multilateral		11 May 59	527UNTS145	107623
Austria	USA (United States)	22 Jul 59	368UNTS199	105242
Austria	Netherlands	30 Sep 59	507UNTS111	107397
Ethiopia	France	12 Nov 59	381UNTS3	105465
Norway	Yugoslavia	18 Nov 59	383UNTS131	105499
Multilateral		04 Jan 60	370UNTS3	105266
Greece	USA (United States)	07 Jan 60	368UNTS221	105243

PARTY ONE	PARTY TWO	DATE	CITATION	NUMBER
Assets transfer (Cont.)				
Albania	Hungary	12 Jan 60	520UNTS3	107511
Spain	USA (United States)	18 Mar 60	372UNTS13	105284
Nepal	USA (United States)	17 May 60	372UNTS313	105307
Indonesia	USA (United States)	08 Jun 60	388UNTS287	105585
UK Great Britain	USA (United States)	24 Jun 60	377UNTS63	105396
Cyprus	UK Great Britain	16 Aug 60	382UNTS207	105481
Greece	Poland	08 Nov 60	483UNTS141	107011
Belgium	Congo (Zaire)	15 Nov 60	394UNTS79	105670
Libya	USA (United States)	11 Dec 60	445UNTS125	106381
Multilateral		10 Apr 61	402UNTS281	105791
Bulgaria	Hungary	30 Jun 61	438UNTS287	106320
Czechoslovakia	Poland	04 Jul 61	436UNTS189	106295
Bulgaria	Poland	12 Jul 61	436UNTS147	106294
Czechoslovakia	Hungary	02 Nov 61	438UNTS3	106313
Bulgaria	Poland	04 Dec 61	484UNTS3	107019
Germany, West	Thailand	13 Dec 61	541UNTS181	107870
Poland	Romania	25 Jan 62	468UNTS3	106770
USSR (Soviet Union)	Yugoslavia	24 Feb 62	471UNTS195	106833
United Arab Rep	USSR (Soviet Union)	23 Jun 62	472UNTS19	106835
Austria	Bulgaria	02 May 63	535UNTS143	107778
Greece	UK Great Britain	09 May 63	398UNTS179	105722
Netherlands	Tunisia	23 May 63	523UNTS237	107558
Austria	Belgium	14 Nov 63	544UNTS97	107912
Japan	UK Great Britain	06 Jan 64	502UNTS183	107329
Czechoslovakia	Yugoslavia	20 Jan 64	538UNTS197	107816
Israel	USSR (Soviet Union)	07 Oct 64	516UNTS59	107471
Malta	Switzerland	20 Jan 65	548UNTS193	107978
Belgium	Congo (Zaire)	06 Feb 65	540UNTS227	107852
Bel-Lux Econ Union	Morocco	28 Apr 65	620UNTS171	108954
Multilateral		24 Sep 65	556UNTS141	108124
Pakistan	IAEA (Atom Energy)	15 Mar 66	588UNTS261	108530
Commodity trade				
Multilateral		28 Nov 40	139UNTS159	200452
Canada	USA (United States)	13 Dec 40	117UNTS173	200368
Brazil	Paraguay	14 Apr 41	54UNTS269	200199
Multilateral		22 Apr 42	8UNTS237	200044
USA (United States)	Venezuela	13 Oct 42	138UNTS282	200451
Dominican Republic	USA (United States)	11 Feb 44	109UNTS251	200363
Argentina	USA (United States)	09 May 45	139UNTS227	200453
USSR (Soviet Union)	Yugoslavia	30 Nov 45	116UNTS153	101574
Greece	UK Great Britain	24 Jan 46	6UNTS45	100067
France	USA (United States)	07 Feb 46	3UNTS239	100034
Canada	Mexico	08 Feb 46	230UNTS183	103183
Netherlands	USA (United States)	09 Feb 46	3UNTS247	100035
UK Great Britain	USA (United States)	01 Mar 46	3UNTS293	100037
USSR (Soviet Union)	Yugoslavia	26 Apr 46	116UNTS163	101575
Thailand	UK Great Britain	01 May 46	99UNTS169	101377
Thailand	UK Great Britain	01 May 46	99UNTS175	101378
Multilateral		06 May 46	157UNTS85	102049
Thailand	UK Great Britain	06 May 46	99UNTS193	101380
Multilateral		06 May 46	99UNTS181	101379
Portugal	USA (United States)	17 May 46	126UNTS3	101678
France	USA (United States)	28 May 46	84UNTS167	101127
France	USA (United States)	28 May 46	84UNTS151	101125
Multilateral		03 Jun 46	7UNTS331	100109
Philippines	USA (United States)	04 Jul 46	43UNTS135	100668
Norway	Portugal	16 Aug 46	30UNTS215	100459
Multilateral		03 Sep 46	139UNTS3	101872
Australia	Sweden	16 Sep 46	10UNTS63	100143
Argentina	UK Great Britain	17 Sep 46	88UNTS47	101185
Argentina	USA (United States)	19 Sep 46	7UNTS131	100095
Multilateral		07 Dec 46	157UNTS103	102050
Multilateral		23 Dec 46	126UNTS47	101681
Czechoslovakia	Yugoslavia	25 Feb 47	112UNTS3	101539

PARTY ONE	PARTY TWO	DATE	CITATION	NUMBER
Commodity trade (Cont.)				
Czechoslovakia	Turkey	05 Mar 47	14UNTS101	100214
Canada	USA (United States)	18 Mar 47	117UNTS79	101584
France	USA (United States)	19 Apr 47	132UNTS135	101754
France	New Zealand	02 Jul 47	16UNTS219	100263
Hungary	USSR (Soviet Union)	15 Jul 47	216UNTS247	102940
Czechoslovakia	Greece	30 Jul 47	185UNTS143	102465
Czechoslovakia	USSR (Soviet Union)	11 Dec 47	217UNTS35	102943
Czechoslovakia	New Zealand	22 Jan 48	16UNTS229	100264
Czechoslovakia	Yugoslavia	10 Apr 48	112UNTS101	101541
Norway	Sweden	29 Apr 48	26UNTS41	100376
France	Ireland	06 May 48	558UNTS170	108141
Brazil	UK Great Britain	21 May 48	66UNTS121	100851
Ireland	UK Great Britain	31 Jul 48	86UNTS37	101151
Ireland	Netherlands	02 Sep 48	558UNTS249	108145
Canada	USA (United States)	23 Nov 48	81UNTS295	101078
South Africa	UK Great Britain	06 Dec 48	118UNTS183	101607
Italy	USSR (Soviet Union)	11 Dec 48	217UNTS181	102948
Argentina	Denmark	14 Dec 48	74UNTS41	100956
USSR (Soviet Union)	Yugoslavia	27 Dec 48	116UNTS327	101579
Austria	Norway	28 Jan 49	30UNTS145	100452
France	Norway	09 Feb 49	29UNTS13	100431
Denmark	Greece	25 Feb 49	78UNTS325	101022
Multilateral		23 Mar 49	203UNTS179	102746
Argentina	UK Great Britain	27 Jun 49	83UNTS217	101110
Allied Milit Occup	Norway	16 Sep 49	53UNTS3	100769
Ireland	Netherlands	25 Nov 49	558UNTS256	108146
UK Great Britain	Yugoslavia	26 Dec 49	87UNTS71	101167
Finland	Ireland	06 Jan 51	558UNTS120	108140
Colombia	Denmark	26 Jan 51	87UNTS161	101171
United Arab Rep	UK Great Britain	01 Jul 51	249UNTS125	103503
Cuba	UK Great Britain	10 Aug 51	108UNTS243	101478
Germany, West	USA (United States)	19 Sep 51	180UNTS161	102381
Burma	India	29 Sep 51	132UNTS71	101752
New Zealand	UK Great Britain	28 Nov 51	127UNTS263	101707
Multilateral		20 Dec 51	163UNTS293	102151
UK Great Britain	USA (United States)	18 Jan 52	184UNTS79	102440
Greece	Syria	02 Jun 52	183UNTS251	102434
Germany, West	Greece	28 Jul 52	182UNTS85	102424
Germany, West	Ireland	26 Sep 52	558UNTS27	108138
Multilateral		07 Nov 52	221UNTS255	103010
Denmark	Israel	14 Nov 52	160UNTS279	102113
Fed Rhod/Nyasaland	South Africa	28 Jun 53	267UNTS270	103848
Ireland	Italy	27 Jul 53	558UNTS237	108144
Multilateral		01 Oct 53	258UNTS153	103677
Denmark	Greece	19 Oct 53	225UNTS9	103082
Ceylon (Sri Lanka)	Ireland	20 Nov 53	345UNTS189	104967
Multilateral		01 Mar 54	256UNTS31	103622
Australia	Belgium	26 Mar 54	198UNTS305	102673
Canada	Spain	26 May 54	391UNTS273	105632
Canada	Portugal	28 May 54	391UNTS253	105631
Greece	Portugal	13 Jul 54	230UNTS19	103173
Finland	USSR (Soviet Union)	17 Jul 54	240UNTS173	103403
Thailand	USA (United States)	11 Aug 54	234UNTS155	103281
Brazil	USA (United States)	20 Aug 54	410UNTS79	105898
Greece	Netherlands	01 Nov 54	223UNTS79	103057
Turkey	USA (United States)	15 Nov 54	238UNTS135	103358
Multilateral		29 Nov 54	287UNTS209	104187
Turkey	UK Great Britain	17 Jan 55	204UNTS195	102758
Canada	South Africa	21 Mar 55	213UNTS291	102892
Argentina	UK Great Britain	31 Mar 55	210UNTS223	102840
France	Ireland	07 Jun 55	558UNTS217	108142
Greece	Netherlands	14 Jul 55	227UNTS27	103129
Greece	Sweden	30 Jul 55	225UNTS243	103102
Thailand	USA (United States)	09 Sep 55	264UNTS285	103799
Thailand	USA (United States)	14 Nov 55	239UNTS201	103380
Commodity trade (Cont.)				
Multilateral		21 Dec 55	292UNTS63	104267
Argentina	USA (United States)	21 Dec 55	240UNTS329	103411
Denmark	UK Great Britain	27 Feb 56	252UNTS83	103558
Iceland	USA (United States)	06 Mar 56	270UNTS205	103898
Burma	Yugoslavia	07 Mar 56	386UNTS207	105542
Canada	Hungary	08 Mar 56	305UNTS27	104409
Germany, West	Italy	19 Apr 56	281UNTS195	104080
Multilateral		25 Apr 56	270UNTS103	103896
Burma	UK Great Britain	18 Jun 56	256UNTS125	103623
Multilateral		08 Nov 56	470UNTS171	106809
Australia	UK Great Britain	26 Feb 57	265UNTS197	103813
UK Great Britain	USA (United States)	27 Jun 57	284UNTS75	104130
Ceylon (Sri Lanka)	India	13 Jan 58	315UNTS107	104562
Belgium	Luxembourg	28 Mar 58	303UNTS101	104372
Multilateral		03 Apr 58	302UNTS121	104355
Multilateral		03 Apr 58	336UNTS177	104806
Burma	USA (United States)	25 Aug 58	336UNTS3	104795
Australia	Fed of Malaya	26 Aug 58	325UNTS253	104703
Multilateral		01 Dec 58	385UNTS137	105534
Burma	UK Great Britain	20 Jan 59	343UNTS201	104926
Burma	UK Great Britain	06 Feb 59	343UNTS223	104927
Australia	Italy	12 Feb 59	328UNTS133	104732
Multilateral		06 Apr 59	349UNTS167	105013
UK Great Britain	USSR (Soviet Union)	24 May 59	374UNTS305	105344
New Zealand	UK Great Britain	12 Aug 59	354UNTS161	105062
India	Italy	06 Oct 59	378UNTS267	105427
Australia	Germany, West	14 Oct 59	345UNTS35	104957
Austria	Denmark	14 Nov 59	630UNTS29	108962
Argentina	Brazil	26 Nov 59	374UNTS45	105327
Australia	Indonesia	17 Dec 59	354UNTS109	105058
Denmark	Switzerland	21 Dec 59	633UNTS351	109045
Denmark	Sweden	04 Jan 60	376UNTS375	105390
Cuba	USSR (Soviet Union)	13 Feb 60	369UNTS17	105248
Cuba	USSR (Soviet Union)	13 Feb 60	369UNTS3	105247
Austria	Guatemala	18 Mar 60	379UNTS89	105435
Austria	El Salvador	23 Mar 60	390UNTS3	105599
Multilateral		01 Sep 60	403UNTS3	105792
Austria	Czechoslovakia	14 Sep 60	495UNTS143	107243
Belgium	Ireland	23 Sep 60	557UNTS180	108134
Denmark	Finland	27 Mar 61	630UNTS3	108961
Japan	USA (United States)	16 Oct 61	433UNTS287	106250
Ghana	USSR (Soviet Union)	04 Nov 61	437UNTS213	106308
Cyprus	USA (United States)	15 Jan 62	435UNTS15	106267
Multilateral		07 Mar 62	445UNTS199	106388
Multilateral		07 Mar 62	445UNTS205	106389
Japan	New Zealand	09 Mar 62	485UNTS351	107066
Taiwan	USA (United States)	16 Apr 62	445UNTS249	106392
India	USA (United States)	16 Apr 62	445UNTS257	106393
UK Great Britain	USA (United States)	26 Apr 62	445UNTS273	106395
Colombia	USA (United States)	15 May 62	445UNTS279	106396
El Salvador	USA (United States)	15 May 62	452UNTS49	106503
Multilateral		15 May 62	444UNTS3	106367
Guatemala	USA (United States)	21 May 62	451UNTS205	106495
Italy	USA (United States)	06 Jul 62	459UNTS123	106617
IAEA (Atom Energy)	USA (United States)	20 Aug 62	456UNTS447	106570
Japan	UK Great Britain	14 Nov 62	478UNTS29	106934
UK Great Britain	Yugoslavia	28 Nov 62	470UNTS65	106796
Multilateral		02 Apr 63	475UNTS121	106889
Burma	UK Great Britain	02 Apr 63	475UNTS139	106890
Denmark	Norway	11 May 63	613UNTS271	108856
New Zealand	UK Great Britain	15 May 63	486UNTS11	107068
Multilateral		09 Jun 63	538UNTS309	107818
Spain	USA (United States)	16 Jul 63	488UNTS77	107120
Japan	USA (United States)	27 Aug 63	487UNTS197	107105
Japan	USA (United States)	28 Aug 63	487UNTS237	107106

PARTY ONE	PARTY TWO	DATE	CITATION	NUMBER
Commodity trade (Cont.)				
Denmark	Norway	12 Sep 63	613UNTS289	108857
Jamaica	USA (United States)	01 Oct 63	488UNTS133	107124
Taiwan	USA (United States)	19 Oct 63	494UNTS27	107224
Canada	Poland	05 Nov 63	529UNTS81	107658
Israel	USA (United States)	22 Nov 63	494UNTS89	107228
United Arab Rep	USA (United States)	04 Dec 63	505UNTS117	107368
UK Great Britain	Yugoslavia	18 Dec 63	502UNTS177	107328
New Zealand	USA (United States)	17 Feb 64	511UNTS37	107424
Australia	USA (United States)	17 Feb 64	511UNTS17	107422
Philippines	USA (United States)	24 Feb 64	505UNTS283	107378
Ireland	USA (United States)	25 Feb 64	511UNTS27	107423
Portugal	USA (United States)	12 Mar 64	542UNTS3	107875
UK Great Britain	USA (United States)	15 Apr 64	515UNTS55	107453
Australia	UK Great Britain	15 Apr 64	515UNTS23	107451
India	USA (United States)	15 Apr 64	527UNTS19	107614
Canada	UK Great Britain	15 Apr 64	515UNTS39	107452
Argentina	UK Great Britain	15 Apr 64	515UNTS3	107450
Korea, South	USA (United States)	12 May 64	529UNTS299	107667
Mexico	USA (United States)	14 May 64	526UNTS228	107607
Multilateral		20 Jun 64	539UNTS3	107819
South Africa	UK Great Britain	22 Jun 64	515UNTS71	107454
Ireland	UK Great Britain	25 Jun 64	553UNTS221	108090
Sweden	UK Great Britain	30 Jun 64	515UNTS83	107455
Cyprus	UK Great Britain	02 Jul 64	522UNTS129	107540
Greece	USA (United States)	17 Jul 64	530UNTS13	107669
Turkey	USA (United States)	17 Jul 64	530UNTS25	107670
India	UK Great Britain	31 Jul 64	522UNTS153	107542
Multilateral		20 Aug 64	514UNTS25	107441
Kenya	UK Great Britain	25 Aug 64	522UNTS165	107543
Syria	UK Great Britain	31 Aug 64	539UNTS259	107837
Malawi	UK Great Britain	01 Sep 64	522UNTS117	107539
Tanganyika	UK Great Britain	02 Sep 64	522UNTS177	107544
Finland	UK Great Britain	12 Sep 64	535UNTS13	107773
Israel	UK Great Britain	15 Sep 64	539UNTS283	107839
Denmark	UK Great Britain	16 Sep 64	534UNTS427	107771
USA (United States)	Yugoslavia	05 Oct 64	531UNTS63	107693
Morocco	USA (United States)	29 Dec 64	593UNTS185	108584
Canada	USA (United States)	16 Jan 65	606UNTS31	108772
Korea, South	USA (United States)	26 Jan 65	541UNTS77	107862
Denmark	Portugal	20 Feb 65	639UNTS43	109143
Pakistan	USA (United States)	26 Feb 65	542UNTS103	107883
Colombia	USA (United States)	09 Jun 65	549UNTS3	107985
Argentina	United Arab Rep	21 Jun 65	634UNTS177	109059
Poland	USA (United States)	24 Jun 65	593UNTS147	108581
Ireland	UK Great Britain	14 Dec 65	565UNTS58	108235
UK Great Britain	Yugoslavia	02 Feb 66	571UNTS275	108306
France	Romania	14 Mar 66	604UNTS33	108741
Romania	UK Great Britain	22 Mar 66	571UNTS281	108307
Argentina	India	26 Mar 66	601UNTS201	108697
Singapore	USA (United States)	30 Aug 66	616UNTS242	108899
Denmark	Norway	23 Dec 66	613UNTS265	108855
UK Great Britain	Yugoslavia	05 Jan 67	604UNTS13	108739
Malta	USA (United States)	14 Jun 67	604UNTS231	108753
Israel	USA (United States)	04 Aug 67	0UNTS0	109351
Israel	USA (United States)	29 Mar 68	0UNTS0	109352
Delivery guarantees				
UK Great Britain	USSR (Soviet Union)	16 Aug 41	91UNTS341	200269
Multilateral		21 Dec 43	65UNTS231	200214
Dominican Republic	USA (United States)	11 Feb 44	109UNTS251	200363
Poland	Yugoslavia	23 Nov 45	115UNTS3	101555
Poland	Yugoslavia	18 Jan 46	115UNTS83	101559
United Arab Rep	UK Great Britain	30 Jun 47	93UNTS165	101299
Hungary	Yugoslavia	24 Jul 47	114UNTS3	101554
USSR (Soviet Union)	Yugoslavia	25 Jul 47	130UNTS315	101732

PARTY ONE	PARTY TWO	DATE	CITATION	NUMBER
Delivery guarantees (Cont.)				
Multilateral		30 Oct 47	55UNTS188	100814
Poland	Yugoslavia	07 Nov 47	115UNTS137	101561
Poland	Yugoslavia	16 Jan 49	115UNTS241	101564
Ireland	Spain	19 Dec 51	0UNTS0	109228
Thailand	USA (United States)	11 Aug 54	234UNTS155	103281
Thailand	USA (United States)	09 Sep 55	264UNTS285	103799
Multilateral		25 Apr 56	270UNTS103	103896
United Arab Rep	USSR (Soviet Union)	23 Jun 62	472UNTS43	106836
Bel-Lux Econ Union	Czechoslovakia	10 Oct 67	0UNTS0	109362
Delivery schedules				
Mexico	USA (United States)	03 Feb 44	3UNTS313	200025
Dominican Republic	USA (United States)	11 Feb 44	109UNTS251	200363
USA (United States)	USSR (Soviet Union)	15 Oct 45	278UNTS151	200547
Poland	Yugoslavia	23 Nov 45	115UNTS3	101555
USSR (Soviet Union)	Yugoslavia	26 Apr 46	116UNTS163	101575
Thailand	UK Great Britain	01 May 46	99UNTS169	101377
Hungary	Yugoslavia	11 May 46	129UNTS3	101725
Denmark	UK Great Britain	16 Aug 46	9UNTS163	100130
Norway	UK Great Britain	27 Sep 46	6UNTS259	100079
Netherlands	UK Great Britain	04 Dec 46	12UNTS241	100187
Norway	USSR (Soviet Union)	27 Dec 46	17UNTS283	100282
Belgium	UK Great Britain	16 Jan 47	54UNTS97	100797
Norway	USSR (Soviet Union)	19 Feb 47	30UNTS293	100464
Czechoslovakia	Yugoslavia	25 Feb 47	112UNTS3	101539
Poland	Sweden	18 Mar 47	12UNTS295	100190
Poland	Yugoslavia	24 May 47	115UNTS89	101560
Poland	Yugoslavia	24 May 47	115UNTS37	101557
Albania	Yugoslavia	22 Jun 47	111UNTS207	101536
Denmark	Yugoslavia	28 Jun 47	78UNTS242	101020
Hungary	Yugoslavia	24 Jul 47	114UNTS3	101554
USSR (Soviet Union)	Yugoslavia	25 Jul 47	130UNTS315	101732
USSR (Soviet Union)	Yugoslavia	23 Aug 47	116UNTS281	101577
Multilateral		30 Oct 47	55UNTS188	100814
Poland	Yugoslavia	07 Nov 47	115UNTS137	101561
Greece	USA (United States)	03 Dec 47	89UNTS119	101213
Taiwan	USA (United States)	08 Dec 47	70UNTS3	100895
Denmark	UK Great Britain	04 Mar 48	77UNTS57	100992
Poland	Yugoslavia	12 Apr 48	115UNTS167	101563
Hungary	Yugoslavia	17 Apr 48	130UNTS121	101729
Brazil	UK Great Britain	21 May 48	66UNTS121	100851
Czechoslovakia	Yugoslavia	24 May 48	112UNTS111	101542
Belgium	Greece	27 Dec 48	77UNTS265	101004
Allied Milit Occup	Norway	17 Feb 49	30UNTS137	100451
Denmark	Greece	25 Feb 49	78UNTS325	101022
Czechoslovakia	Yugoslavia	01 Mar 49	113UNTS3	101547
Finland	Greece	24 Mar 49	78UNTS3	101008
Argentina	UK Great Britain	27 Jun 49	83UNTS217	101110
France	Greece	06 Aug 49	91UNTS95	101244
Greece	Italy	31 Aug 49	78UNTS89	101014
UK Great Britain	Yugoslavia	26 Dec 49	87UNTS71	101167
Austria	Greece	11 May 50	184UNTS217	102450
Norway	USA (United States)	28 Dec 50	240UNTS391	103414
Cuba	UK Great Britain	10 Aug 51	108UNTS243	101478
Germany, West	USA (United States)	19 Sep 51	180UNTS161	102381
Denmark	USA (United States)	16 Nov 51	180UNTS275	102391
Greece	USA (United States)	07 Jan 52	177UNTS249	102323
UK Great Britain	USA (United States)	18 Jan 52	184UNTS79	102440
Denmark	Poland	09 Jun 52	135UNTS209	101822
Portugal	USA (United States)	09 Jul 52	180UNTS251	102389
Multilateral		11 Jul 52	170UNTS63	102222
Germany, West	Israel	10 Sep 52	162UNTS205	102137
Japan	Syria	08 Jun 53	184UNTS3	102436
Argentina	USSR (Soviet Union)	05 Aug 53	221UNTS99	103004
Germany, West	USA (United States)	20 Aug 53	224UNTS49	103069

PARTY ONE	PARTY TWO	DATE	CITATION	NUMBER
Delivery schedules (Cont.)				
France	USA (United States)	02 Sep 53	224UNTS153	103075
Belgium	USA (United States)	17 Nov 53	251UNTS105	103536
Belgium	Taiwan	13 Jan 54	223UNTS111	103059
Japan	USA (United States)	08 Mar 54	232UNTS215	103237
USA (United States)	USSR (Soviet Union)	26 Mar 54	247UNTS263	103475
Italy	USA (United States)	27 Apr 54	234UNTS103	103275
Japan	USA (United States)	14 May 54	247UNTS273	103476
Taiwan	USA (United States)	14 May 54	231UNTS165	103216
Honduras	USA (United States)	24 May 54	433UNTS155	106238
Turkey	USA (United States)	01 Jul 54	234UNTS147	103280
Luxembourg	USA (United States)	07 Jul 54	233UNTS23	103247
Finland	USSR (Soviet Union)	17 Jul 54	240UNTS173	103403
Thailand	USA (United States)	11 Aug 54	234UNTS155	103281
Multilateral		29 Nov 54	287UNTS209	104187
USA (United States)	USSR (Soviet Union)	22 Dec 54	251UNTS41	103532
Korea, South	USA (United States)	29 Jan 55	239UNTS53	103371
Haiti	USA (United States)	05 Apr 55	270UNTS97	103895
Dominican Republic	USA (United States)	22 Apr 55	239UNTS325	103389
USA (United States)	Vietnam, South	10 May 55	273UNTS157	103950
USA (United States)	USSR (Soviet Union)	26 May 55	270UNTS61	103892
Turkey	USA (United States)	26 May 55	262UNTS97	103739
Germany, West	USA (United States)	30 Jun 55	240UNTS69	103394
Thailand	USA (United States)	09 Sep 55	264UNTS285	103799
France	USA (United States)	23 Sep 55	270UNTS341	103904
Austria	USSR (Soviet Union)	09 Nov 55	255UNTS247	103613
Canada	Norway	20 Dec 55	305UNTS17	104408
Multilateral		21 Dec 55	292UNTS63	104267
Canada	Hungary	08 Mar 56	305UNTS27	104409
Taiwan	USA (United States)	03 Apr 56	268UNTS315	103864
Korea, South	USA (United States)	02 Jul 56	281UNTS41	104067
Ecuador	USA (United States)	19 Jul 56	372UNTS149	105295
Multilateral		16 Aug 56	287UNTS223	104188
Portugal	USA (United States)	07 Nov 56	277UNTS133	104003
Brazil	USA (United States)	16 Jan 57	266UNTS99	103824
Spain	USA (United States)	09 Mar 57	283UNTS89	104108
Germany, West	USA (United States)	01 May 57	284UNTS85	104131
Greece	USA (United States)	05 Aug 57	290UNTS167	104235
Albania	USSR (Soviet Union)	15 Feb 58	313UNTS261	104536
Turkey	USA (United States)	14 Oct 58	336UNTS145	104803
Greece	USA (United States)	15 Jan 59	357UNTS281	105120
Burma	UK Great Britain	06 Feb 59	343UNTS223	104927
Taiwan	USA (United States)	07 Feb 59	341UNTS225	104885
Multilateral		06 Apr 59	349UNTS167	105013
Thailand	USA (United States)	19 May 59	346UNTS271	104986
Peru	USA (United States)	15 Jun 59	346UNTS279	104987
Spain	USA (United States)	23 Jun 59	354UNTS11	105049
Taiwan	USA (United States)	08 Jul 59	354UNTS47	105052
Italy	USA (United States)	18 Aug 59	361UNTS11	105169
Brazil	USA (United States)	19 Oct 59	372UNTS131	105293
Ecuador	USA (United States)	11 Feb 60	372UNTS141	105294
Peru	USA (United States)	26 Feb 60	394UNTS141	105674
Argentina	USA (United States)	01 Apr 60	371UNTS245	105281
Colombia	USA (United States)	07 Apr 60	372UNTS27	105285
Canada	Norway	25 Apr 60	470UNTS109	106801
Haiti	USA (United States)	08 Jul 60	380UNTS135	105454
Canada	UK Great Britain	05 Aug 60	470UNTS133	106804
Canada	USA (United States)	31 Aug 60	393UNTS247	105659
Somalia	USSR (Soviet Union)	02 Jun 61	457UNTS263	106587
Austria	Romania	21 Jul 61	421UNTS161	106057
Portugal	USA (United States)	05 Mar 62	436UNTS101	106290
EEC (Econ Commnty)	USA (United States)	07 Mar 62	436UNTS49	106288
India	USA (United States)	16 Apr 62	445UNTS257	106393
UK Great Britain	USA (United States)	26 Apr 62	445UNTS273	106395
Ireland	USA (United States)	03 May 62	442UNTS117	106343
Colombia	USA (United States)	15 May 62	445UNTS279	106396

PARTY ONE	PARTY TWO	DATE	CITATION	NUMBER
Delivery schedules (Cont.)				
El Salvador	USA (United States)	15 May 62	452UNTS49	106503
Guatemala	USA (United States)	21 May 62	451UNTS205	106495
United Arab Rep	USSR (Soviet Union)	23 Jun 62	472UNTS43	106836
IAEA (Atom Energy)	USA (United States)	20 Aug 62	456UNTS447	106570
India	UK Great Britain	27 Nov 62	466UNTS189	106744
Pakistan	USA (United States)	16 Jan 63	471UNTS133	106828
Multilateral		02 Apr 63	475UNTS121	106889
Burma	UK Great Britain	02 Apr 63	475UNTS139	106890
UK Great Britain	USA (United States)	06 Apr 63	474UNTS49	106871
Spain	USA (United States)	16 Jul 63	488UNTS77	107120
Greece	Poland	30 Sep 63	534UNTS23	107751
Jamaica	USA (United States)	01 Oct 63	488UNTS133	107124
Netherlands	USA (United States)	26 Nov 63	388UNTS303	105586
United Arab Rep	USA (United States)	04 Dec 63	505UNTS117	107368
Philippines	USA (United States)	24 Feb 64	505UNTS283	107378
USA (United States)	Yugoslavia	05 Oct 64	531UNTS63	107693
Korea, South	USA (United States)	26 Jan 65	541UNTS77	107862
Benelux Econ Union	Poland	17 Feb 65	547UNTS165	107956
Malta	USA (United States)	14 Jun 67	604UNTS231	108753
Denmark	Netherlands	20 Jun 67	619UNTS67	108939
Quotas				
Multilateral		28 Nov 40	139UNTS159	200452
Canada	USA (United States)	13 Dec 40	117UNTS173	200368
Brazil	Canada	17 Oct 41	67UNTS263	200224
Peru	USA (United States)	07 May 42	103UNTS219	200316
USA (United States)	Uruguay	21 Jul 42	120UNTS211	200393
Canada	USA (United States)	19 Dec 42	26UNTS363	200156
Mexico	USA (United States)	23 Dec 42	13UNTS231	200081
Iceland	USA (United States)	27 Sep 43	29UNTS317	200170
Dominican Republic	USA (United States)	11 Feb 44	109UNTS251	200363
Argentina	USA (United States)	09 May 45	139UNTS227	200453
Poland	Yugoslavia	23 Nov 45	115UNTS3	101555
USSR (Soviet Union)	Yugoslavia	30 Nov 45	116UNTS153	101574
Romania	Yugoslavia	15 Dec 45	116UNTS3	101565
Multilateral		27 Dec 45	2UNTS39	100020
Belgium	Norway	21 Feb 46	31UNTS435	100485
Denmark	Norway	30 Mar 46	29UNTS163	100438
Thailand	UK Great Britain	01 May 46	99UNTS169	101377
France	USA (United States)	28 May 46	84UNTS151	101125
Bolivia	USA (United States)	10 Jun 46	13UNTS19	100197
Ethiopia	USA (United States)	04 Jul 46	13UNTS27	100198
Philippines	USA (United States)	04 Jul 46	43UNTS135	100668
Norway	USA (United States)	08 Jul 46	13UNTS35	100199
Spain	USA (United States)	11 Jul 46	13UNTS51	100201
Belgium	USA (United States)	11 Jul 46	13UNTS43	100200
Italy	Norway	20 Jul 46	30UNTS177	100456
United Arab Rep	USA (United States)	15 Aug 46	13UNTS59	100202
Portugal	USA (United States)	26 Aug 46	13UNTS67	100203
Denmark	USA (United States)	10 Sep 46	13UNTS75	100204
Paraguay	USA (United States)	12 Sep 46	125UNTS179	101677
Argentina	UK Great Britain	17 Sep 46	88UNTS47	101185
Argentina	USA (United States)	19 Sep 46	7UNTS131	100095
USA (United States)	Yugoslavia	03 Oct 46	13UNTS83	100205
Dominican Republic	USA (United States)	07 Oct 46	13UNTS91	100206
Multilateral		23 Dec 46	126UNTS47	101681
Multilateral		03 Mar 47	11UNTS43	100148
Poland	Sweden	18 Mar 47	12UNTS295	100190
Canada	USA (United States)	18 Mar 47	117UNTS79	101584
Poland	Yugoslavia	24 May 47	115UNTS89	101560
Poland	Yugoslavia	24 May 47	115UNTS37	101557
Sweden	USA (United States)	24 Jun 47	36UNTS25	100565
Denmark	Yugoslavia	28 Jun 47	78UNTS242	101020
Czechoslovakia	Greece	30 Jul 47	185UNTS115	102463
Multilateral		30 Oct 47	55UNTS188	100814

PARTY ONE	PARTY TWO	DATE	CITATION	NUMBER
Quotas (Cont.)				
Poland	Yugoslavia	07 Nov 47	115UNTS137	101561
Finland	Norway	15 Nov 47	29UNTS179	100439
Poland	Yugoslavia	21 Jan 48	115UNTS155	101562
France	Lebanon	24 Jan 48	173UNTS99	102263
Norway	Poland	04 Feb 48	30UNTS205	100458
Sweden	Switzerland	16 Mar 48	197UNTS39	102632
Switzerland	USSR (Soviet Union)	17 Mar 48	217UNTS73	102944
Hungary	Yugoslavia	18 Mar 48	113UNTS141	101550
Poland	Yugoslavia	12 Apr 48	115UNTS167	101563
Norway	Sweden	29 Apr 48	26UNTS33	100375
Norway	Sweden	29 Apr 48	26UNTS41	100376
Czechoslovakia	Yugoslavia	24 May 48	112UNTS111	101542
Greece	Sweden	25 Jun 48	267UNTS337	103849
Norway	Switzerland	26 Jun 48	29UNTS193	100440
Ireland	UK Great Britain	31 Jul 48	86UNTS37	101151
Ireland	Netherlands	02 Sep 48	558UNTS249	108145
Canada	USA (United States)	23 Nov 48	81UNTS295	101078
UK Great Britain	Yugoslavia	23 Dec 48	81UNTS133	101069
Belgium	Greece	27 Dec 48	77UNTS265	101004
Norway	Poland	31 Dec 48	29UNTS3	100430
Poland	UK Great Britain	14 Jan 49	83UNTS3	101100
Poland	Yugoslavia	16 Jan 49	115UNTS241	101564
Denmark	Greece	25 Feb 49	78UNTS325	101022
Netherlands	Norway	26 Feb 49	29UNTS33	100432
Czechoslovakia	Yugoslavia	01 Mar 49	113UNTS3	101547
Belgium	Norway	08 Mar 49	29UNTS83	100435
Greece	Norway	12 Mar 49	30UNTS161	100454
Multilateral		23 Mar 49	203UNTS179	102746
Finland	Greece	24 Mar 49	78UNTS3	101008
Denmark	Portugal	08 Apr 49	74UNTS209	100964
Multilateral		28 Apr 49	83UNTS105	101105
Netherlands	Sweden	06 Jul 49	197UNTS189	102639
Brazil	UK Great Britain	03 Aug 49	86UNTS113	101154
Allied Milit Occup	Norway	16 Sep 49	53UNTS3	100769
Czechoslovakia	UK Great Britain	28 Sep 49	86UNTS141	101156
France	Ireland	21 Nov 49	553UNTS59	108069
Denmark	Poland	07 Dec 49	81UNTS21	101059
Czechoslovakia	Denmark	17 Dec 49	74UNTS147	100961
UK Great Britain	Yugoslavia	26 Dec 49	87UNTS71	101167
Greece	Portugal	31 Dec 49	92UNTS71	101262
Austria	Denmark	23 Feb 50	74UNTS269	100969
Austria	Greece	11 May 50	184UNTS217	102450
Multilateral		31 May 50	74UNTS95	100957
Denmark	Portugal	02 Jun 50	74UNTS229	100966
Denmark	Spain	12 Jul 50	71UNTS135	100914
Germany, West	Ireland	12 Jul 50	557UNTS221	108136
Denmark	Poland	01 Oct 50	81UNTS43	101061
Denmark	Italy	04 Oct 50	78UNTS341	101024
Canada	Venezuela	11 Oct 50	231UNTS3	103198
Denmark	Hungary	10 Feb 51	85UNTS49	101145
Belgium	Finland	20 Mar 51	110UNTS27	101498
Denmark	Portugal	05 Jun 51	101UNTS61	101402
Denmark	Spain	03 Jul 51	101UNTS51	101401
Germany, West	Ireland	23 Jul 51	558UNTS3	108137
Cuba	UK Great Britain	10 Aug 51	108UNTS243	101478
Mexico	USA (United States)	11 Aug 51	162UNTS103	102133
Denmark	Switzerland	15 Sep 51	110UNTS55	101501
Belgium	Sweden	18 Sep 51	133UNTS187	101789
Germany, West	USA (United States)	19 Sep 51	180UNTS161	102381
Burma	India	29 Sep 51	132UNTS71	101752
UK Great Britain	USA (United States)	18 Jan 52	184UNTS79	102440
Czechoslovakia	Denmark	04 Apr 52	133UNTS245	101792
Denmark	Poland	09 Jun 52	135UNTS209	101822
Multilateral		11 Jul 52	170UNTS63	102222
Germany, West	Greece	28 Jul 52	182UNTS85	102424

PARTY ONE	PARTY TWO	DATE	CITATION	NUMBER
Quotas (Cont.)				
Denmark	Spain	28 Jul 52	135UNTS255	101825
France	Greece	31 Jul 52	187UNTS169	102510
Greece	Sweden	19 Aug 52	189UNTS117	102544
USA (United States)	Venezuela	28 Aug 52	178UNTS51	102336
Denmark	Portugal	29 Aug 52	149UNTS49	101950
Denmark	Greece	15 Sep 52	187UNTS207	102513
Austria	Greece	20 Sep 52	187UNTS191	102512
Denmark	Israel	14 Nov 52	160UNTS279	102113
Netherlands	Switzerland	20 Nov 52	163UNTS121	102146
France	Greece	23 Dec 52	187UNTS175	102511
Greece	Italy	04 Feb 53	189UNTS269	102551
Greece	Netherlands	05 Feb 53	263UNTS361	103783
Turkey	Yugoslavia	26 Feb 53	247UNTS54	103460
Greece	Yugoslavia	28 Feb 53	252UNTS27	103557
Czechoslovakia	Denmark	23 Apr 53	174UNTS95	102280
Germany, West	Sweden	15 May 53	227UNTS195	103139
Japan	Syria	08 Jun 53	184UNTS3	102436
Fed Rhod/Nyasaland	South Africa	28 Jun 53	267UNTS270	103848
Multilateral		01 Oct 53	258UNTS153	103677
Denmark	Greece	19 Oct 53	225UNTS9	103082
Greece	Turkey	07 Nov 53	225UNTS163	103098
Ceylon (Sri Lanka)	Ireland	20 Nov 53	345UNTS189	104967
Bulgaria	Greece	05 Dec 53	225UNTS135	103095
Multilateral		09 Dec 53	249UNTS197	103509
Denmark	Italy	10 Apr 54	196UNTS175	102623
France	Greece	13 May 54	222UNTS299	103036
Greece	Spain	15 May 54	299UNTS261	104318
Pakistan	Yugoslavia	15 May 54	286UNTS3	104158
Greece	Romania	19 May 54	225UNTS17	103083
France	Greece	30 Jun 54	257UNTS83	103651
Greece	Portugal	13 Jul 54	230UNTS19	103173
France	Greece	22 Jul 54	225UNTS199	103099
Austria	Denmark	07 Sep 54	201UNTS39	102709
Greece	Netherlands	01 Nov 54	223UNTS79	103057
Multilateral		29 Nov 54	287UNTS209	104187
USSR (Soviet Union)	Yugoslavia	05 Jan 55	240UNTS225	103405
USSR (Soviet Union)	Yugoslavia	05 Jan 55	240UNTS207	103404
Turkey	UK Great Britain	17 Jan 55	204UNTS195	102758
Greece	Japan	12 Mar 55	227UNTS33	103130
Bulgaria	Yugoslavia	16 Mar 55	397UNTS83	105702
Argentina	UK Great Britain	31 Mar 55	210UNTS223	102840
Ceylon (Sri Lanka)	Germany, West	01 Apr 55	369UNTS57	105251
France	Ireland	07 Jun 55	558UNTS217	108142
France	Greece	28 Jun 55	225UNTS219	103100
Greece	Sweden	30 Jul 55	225UNTS243	103102
Greece	USSR (Soviet Union)	23 Aug 55	233UNTS39	103249
Denmark	Greece	29 Aug 55	230UNTS25	103174
Thailand	USA (United States)	09 Sep 55	264UNTS285	103799
Austria	Sweden	03 Nov 55	262UNTS289	103757
Italy	Lebanon	04 Nov 55	267UNTS113	103838
Italy	Syria	10 Nov 55	267UNTS157	103841
Thailand	USA (United States)	14 Nov 55	239UNTS201	103380
Costa Rica	Guatemala	20 Dec 55	280UNTS121	104056
Multilateral		21 Dec 55	292UNTS63	104267
Austria	Belgium	20 Jan 56	248UNTS3	103481
Denmark	UK Great Britain	27 Feb 56	252UNTS83	103558
Germany, West	Italy	19 Apr 56	281UNTS195	104080
Multilateral		25 Apr 56	270UNTS103	103896
Austria	Italy	12 Jul 56	378UNTS249	105426
Guatemala	Honduras	22 Aug 56	263UNTS49	103767
Denmark	Greece	04 Sep 56	256UNTS319	103643
Italy	Spain	05 Sep 56	302UNTS195	104359
Canada	France	04 Oct 56	305UNTS65	104414
Taiwan	Philippines	18 Oct 56	541UNTS57	107860
Australia	UK Great Britain	26 Feb 57	265UNTS197	103813

PARTY ONE	PARTY TWO	DATE	CITATION	NUMBER
Quotas (Cont.)				
Multilateral		25 Mar 57	294UNTS2	104300
Ceylon (Sri Lanka)	Italy	23 Apr 57	337UNTS115	104820
France	Italy	01 Aug 57	302UNTS221	104360
Ceylon (Sri Lanka)	China People's Rep	19 Sep 57	337UNTS137	104821
Italy	Spain	25 Nov 57	378UNTS289	105428
Ireland	Sweden	05 Dec 57	428UNTS221	106176
Ceylon (Sri Lanka)	India	13 Jan 58	315UNTS107	104562
Bulgaria	Italy	25 Feb 58	362UNTS291	105194
Italy	Tunisia	08 Apr 58	378UNTS327	105430
Multilateral		10 Jun 58	454UNTS47	106539
Italy	Morocco	24 Jun 58	363UNTS23	105197
Germany, West	Netherlands	30 Jun 58	315UNTS179	104568
Australia	Fed of Malaya	26 Aug 58	325UNTS253	104703
Japan	New Zealand	09 Sep 58	325UNTS119	104698
Multilateral		01 Dec 58	385UNTS137	105534
Iraq	Romania	24 Dec 58	405UNTS243	105836
Germany, West	New Zealand	20 Apr 59	402UNTS125	105782
UK Great Britain	USSR (Soviet Union)	24 May 59	374UNTS305	105344
Ireland	Netherlands	28 May 59	344UNTS95	104944
India	Italy	06 Oct 59	378UNTS267	105427
Australia	Germany, West	14 Oct 59	345UNTS35	104957
Guinea	UK Great Britain	22 Oct 59	351UNTS341	105033
Italy	Tunisia	31 Oct 59	378UNTS349	105431
Tunisia	UK Great Britain	16 Nov 59	354UNTS367	105070
Denmark	Switzerland	21 Dec 59	633UNTS351	109045
Albania	Yugoslavia	29 Dec 59	396UNTS63	105693
Denmark	Sweden	04 Jan 60	376UNTS375	105390
Multilateral		06 Feb 60	383UNTS3	105494
Finland	USA (United States)	23 Mar 60	371UNTS117	105274
Germany, West	Ireland	11 May 60	553UNTS69	108070
Austria	Spain	17 Jun 60	390UNTS17	105600
Austria	Czechoslovakia	14 Sep 60	495UNTS143	107243
Belgium	Ireland	23 Sep 60	557UNTS180	108134
Greece	Poland	08 Nov 60	483UNTS127	107010
Multilateral		13 Dec 60	455UNTS3	106543
Tunisia	UK Great Britain	17 Jan 61	566UNTS2	108236
Finland	Italy	18 Feb 61	434UNTS199	106263
Austria	Romania	21 Jul 61	421UNTS161	106057
Denmark	Germany, West	12 Sep 61	516UNTS283	107478
Austria	Finland	01 Feb 62	425UNTS33	106116
Multilateral		07 Mar 62	445UNTS205	106389
Taiwan	USA (United States)	16 Apr 62	445UNTS249	106392
India	USA (United States)	16 Apr 62	445UNTS257	106393
UK Great Britain	USA (United States)	26 Apr 62	445UNTS273	106395
Ireland	USA (United States)	03 May 62	442UNTS117	106343
Colombia	USA (United States)	15 May 62	445UNTS279	106396
Multilateral		06 Jun 62	486UNTS263	107080
Multilateral		28 Sep 62	469UNTS169	106791
Japan	UK Great Britain	14 Nov 62	478UNTS29	106934
South Africa	Spain	08 Feb 63	458UNTS79	106593
New Zealand	UK Great Britain	15 May 63	486UNTS11	107068
Multilateral		09 Jun 63	538UNTS309	107818
Cameroon	UK Great Britain	29 Jul 63	478UNTS148	106935
New Zealand	USSR (Soviet Union)	01 Aug 63	486UNTS27	107070
Denmark	Greece	26 Sep 63	534UNTS43	107752
Greece	Poland	30 Sep 63	534UNTS23	107751
Jamaica	USA (United States)	01 Oct 63	488UNTS133	107124
Taiwan	USA (United States)	19 Oct 63	494UNTS27	107224
Canada	Poland	05 Nov 63	529UNTS81	107658
Israel	USA (United States)	22 Nov 63	494UNTS89	107228
United Arab Rep	USA (United States)	04 Dec 63	505UNTS117	107368
IAEA (Atom Energy)	Yugoslavia	07 Dec 63	501UNTS273	107322
Congo (Zaire)	UK Great Britain	03 Jan 64	534UNTS417	107770
New Zealand	USA (United States)	17 Feb 64	511UNTS37	107424
Australia	USA (United States)	17 Feb 64	511UNTS17	107422

PARTY ONE	PARTY TWO	DATE	CITATION	NUMBER
Quotas (Cont.)				
Philippines	USA (United States)	24 Feb 64	505UNTS283	107378
Ireland	USA (United States)	25 Feb 64	511UNTS27	107423
Portugal	USA (United States)	12 Mar 64	542UNTS3	107875
India	USA (United States)	15 Apr 64	527UNTS19	107614
Mexico	USA (United States)	14 May 64	526UNTS228	107607
Greece	USA (United States)	17 Jul 64	530UNTS13	107669
Israel	UK Great Britain	15 Sep 64	539UNTS283	107839
USA (United States)	Yugoslavia	05 Oct 64	531UNTS63	107693
Korea, South	USA (United States)	26 Jan 65	541UNTS77	107862
Colombia	USA (United States)	09 Jun 65	549UNTS3	107985
Poland	USA (United States)	24 Jun 65	593UNTS147	108581
Ireland	UK Great Britain	14 Dec 65	565UNTS58	108235
France	Romania	14 Mar 66	604UNTS33	108741
Romania	United Arab Rep	14 Nov 66	642UNTS129	109169
Malta	USA (United States)	14 Jun 67	604UNTS231	108753
Finland	France	27 Oct 67	643UNTS75	109185
Multilateral		24 Dec 68	0UNTS0	109369
Smuggling				
Norway	Yugoslavia	30 Aug 46	30UNTS187	100457
Poland	UK Great Britain	14 Jan 49	83UNTS3	101100
Greece	Netherlands	14 Jul 55	227UNTS27	103129
Italy	Lebanon	04 Nov 55	267UNTS147	103840
Ceylon (Sri Lanka)	Romania	16 Mar 56	315UNTS41	104558
Multilateral		16 Aug 56	287UNTS223	104188
Fed Rhod/Nyasaland	Portugal	29 Nov 58	354UNTS137	105060
New Zealand	UK Great Britain	12 Aug 59	354UNTS161	105062
Greece	Tunisia	02 Mar 60	483UNTS89	107008
Greece	Morocco	01 Nov 61	483UNTS113	107009
El Salvador	USA (United States)	15 May 62	452UNTS49	106503
Guatemala	USA (United States)	21 May 62	451UNTS205	106495
United Arab Rep	USSR (Soviet Union)	23 Jun 62	472UNTS43	106836
Austria	Bulgaria	05 Apr 63	480UNTS3	106963
Australia	New Zealand	31 Aug 65	554UNTS169	108101
Most favored nation clause				
Greece	Iran	09 Jan 31	166UNTS323	200496
Canada	France	12 May 33	253UNTS285	200545
Brazil	France	27 Jan 40	72UNTS77	100929
Brazil	Canada	17 Oct 41	67UNTS263	200224
Haiti	USA (United States)	19 Feb 42	105UNTS238	200336
Peru	USA (United States)	07 May 42	103UNTS219	200316
USA (United States)	Uruguay	21 Jul 42	120UNTS211	200393
Mexico	USA (United States)	12 Aug 42	125UNTS301	200431
Dominican Republic	USA (United States)	14 Nov 42	24UNTS233	200148
Mexico	USA (United States)	23 Dec 42	13UNTS231	200081
Iran	USA (United States)	08 Apr 43	106UNTS155	200340
Iceland	USA (United States)	27 Sep 43	29UNTS317	200170
Canada	Taiwan	14 Apr 44	14UNTS408	200097
Chile	UK Great Britain	01 Jul 44	2UNTS243	200017
Spain	USA (United States)	02 Dec 44	89UNTS345	200262
Denmark	USA (United States)	16 Dec 44	10UNTS213	200063
Sweden	USA (United States)	16 Dec 44	6UNTS397	200041
Iceland	USA (United States)	27 Jan 45	122UNTS293	200411
Ireland	USA (United States)	03 Feb 45	122UNTS305	200412
Canada	USA (United States)	17 Feb 45	122UNTS261	200409
Colombia	USA (United States)	17 Apr 45	139UNTS303	200457
Switzerland	USA (United States)	03 Aug 45	51UNTS233	200191
Norway	USA (United States)	06 Oct 45	122UNTS319	200413
South Africa	UK Great Britain	26 Oct 45	72UNTS41	100927
Greece	UK Great Britain	26 Nov 45	35UNTS161	100555
Portugal	UK Great Britain	06 Dec 45	6UNTS3	100065
Portugal	UK Great Britain	06 Dec 45	5UNTS37	100064
Canada	UK Great Britain	21 Dec 45	27UNTS155	100405
Multilateral		01 Jan 46	99UNTS131	101375
Poland	Yugoslavia	02 Jan 46	115UNTS21	101556

Most favored nation clause (Cont.)

PARTY ONE	PARTY TWO	DATE	CITATION	NUMBER
Czechoslovakia	USA (United States)	03 Jan 46	6UNTS309	100084
Czechoslovakia	Poland	24 Jan 46	25UNTS181	100363
Canada	Mexico	08 Feb 46	230UNTS183	103183
UK Great Britain	USA (United States)	11 Feb 46	3UNTS253	100036
Turkey	USA (United States)	12 Feb 46	13UNTS3	100196
Turkey	UK Great Britain	12 Feb 46	6UNTS79	100069
France	UK Great Britain	28 Feb 46	27UNTS173	100407
Taiwan	France	28 Feb 46	14UNTS137	100216
France	USA (United States)	27 Mar 46	139UNTS114	101879
Greece	USA (United States)	27 Mar 46	15UNTS233	100239
Ireland	UK Great Britain	05 Apr 46	72UNTS57	100928
Belgium	USA (United States)	05 Apr 46	4UNTS125	100041
Netherlands	Portugal	12 Apr 46	4UNTS317	100054
Argentina	UK Great Britain	17 Apr 46	164UNTS53	102159
USA (United States)	Yemen	04 May 46	4UNTS165	100043
France	Ireland	16 May 46	44UNTS105	100681
Taiwan	Denmark	20 May 46	12UNTS59	100180
Ireland	Sweden	29 May 46	35UNTS231	100557
Bolivia	USA (United States)	10 Jun 46	13UNTS19	100197
Australia	Canada	11 Jun 46	10UNTS47	100142
United Arab Rep	USA (United States)	15 Jun 46	71UNTS157	100917
Chile	UK Great Britain	25 Jun 46	91UNTS137	101246
Sweden	Turkey	26 Jun 46	14UNTS21	100208
Luxembourg	USA (United States)	03 Jul 46	32UNTS85	100491
Ethiopia	USA (United States)	04 Jul 46	13UNTS27	100198
Norway	USA (United States)	08 Jul 46	13UNTS35	100199
Spain	USA (United States)	11 Jul 46	13UNTS51	100201
Belgium	USA (United States)	11 Jul 46	13UNTS43	100200
Canada	Newfoundland	29 Jul 46	17UNTS169	100275
France	Sweden	02 Aug 46	27UNTS251	100410
Lebanon	USA (United States)	11 Aug 46	66UNTS211	100856
Netherlands	UK Great Britain	13 Aug 46	4UNTS367	100056
United Arab Rep	USA (United States)	15 Aug 46	13UNTS59	100202
Denmark	USSR (Soviet Union)	17 Aug 46	8UNTS201	100124
Portugal	USA (United States)	26 Aug 46	13UNTS67	100203
Norway	UK Great Britain	31 Aug 46	6UNTS235	100078
Denmark	USA (United States)	10 Sep 46	13UNTS75	100204
Paraguay	USA (United States)	12 Sep 46	125UNTS179	101677
Canada	Taiwan	26 Sep 46	14UNTS167	100219
USA (United States)	Yugoslavia	03 Oct 46	13UNTS83	100205
Dominican Republic	USA (United States)	07 Oct 46	13UNTS91	100206
France	Turkey	12 Oct 46	14UNTS33	100209
Denmark	South Africa	14 Oct 46	10UNTS29	100140
Belgium	Portugal	22 Oct 46	34UNTS49	100527
Brazil	UK Great Britain	31 Oct 46	11UNTS115	100152
India	USA (United States)	14 Nov 46	22UNTS55	100331
Czechoslovakia	USA (United States)	14 Nov 46	7UNTS119	100094
Taiwan	Saudi Arabia	15 Nov 46	18UNTS197	100289
Philippines	USA (United States)	16 Nov 46	7UNTS151	100097
Sweden	UK Great Britain	27 Nov 46	11UNTS229	100162
Australia	USA (United States)	03 Dec 46	7UNTS201	100100
New Zealand	USA (United States)	03 Dec 46	7UNTS175	100099
Portugal	Switzerland	09 Dec 46	310UNTS251	104495
Brazil	Portugal	10 Dec 46	200UNTS67	102695
USA (United States)	Uruguay	14 Dec 46	532UNTS87	107713
Canada	Nicaragua	19 Dec 46	236UNTS229	103326
Taiwan	USA (United States)	20 Dec 46	22UNTS87	100332
Peru	USA (United States)	27 Dec 46	26UNTS227	100390
Ecuador	USA (United States)	08 Jan 47	22UNTS119	100333
Czechoslovakia	Ireland	29 Jan 47	27UNTS267	100411
Multilateral		10 Feb 47	48UNTS203	100746
Multilateral		10 Feb 47	41UNTS21	100643
Multilateral		10 Feb 47	41UNTS135	100644
Romania	USSR (Soviet Union)	20 Feb 47	226UNTS79	103110
Thailand	USA (United States)	26 Feb 47	16UNTS17	100246

Most favored nation clause (Cont.)

PARTY ONE	PARTY TWO	DATE	CITATION	NUMBER
Paraguay	USA (United States)	28 Feb 47	44UNTS25	100676
Portugal	Sweden	06 Mar 47	35UNTS243	100558
Belgium	Turkey	12 Mar 47	37UNTS221	100579
Belgium	Czechoslovakia	19 Mar 47	23UNTS35	100341
Netherlands	Turkey	19 Mar 47	14UNTS59	100211
Greece	Switzerland	01 Apr 47	180UNTS115	102378
Greece	Sweden	08 Apr 47	94UNTS73	101307
Greece	Netherlands	17 Apr 47	32UNTS115	100494
France	South Africa	18 Apr 47	225UNTS35	103085
Taiwan	Philippines	18 Apr 47	11UNTS361	100175
Jordan	United Arab Rep	21 Apr 47	11UNTS3	100146
Canada	Portugal	25 Apr 47	94UNTS87	101308
Nepal	USA (United States)	25 Apr 47	16UNTS97	100251
Syria	USA (United States)	28 Apr 47	262UNTS121	103741
Austria	UK Great Britain	28 Apr 47	93UNTS53	101287
France	Greece	05 May 47	76UNTS61	100980
Bulgaria	Denmark	09 May 47	74UNTS131	100959
Chile	USA (United States)	10 May 47	55UNTS21	100807
Czechoslovakia	Denmark	14 May 47	27UNTS297	100413
South Africa	USA (United States)	23 May 47	66UNTS233	100857
Poland	Yugoslavia	24 May 47	115UNTS89	101560
Canada	Sweden	27 Jun 47	27UNTS313	100414
Denmark	Yugoslavia	28 Jun 47	78UNTS242	101020
Iraq	Turkey	30 Jun 47	72UNTS107	100930
Denmark	Turkey	30 Jun 47	32UNTS301	100504
Belgium	South Africa	04 Jul 47	47UNTS9	100720
Hungary	USSR (Soviet Union)	15 Jul 47	216UNTS247	102940
France	India	16 Jul 47	27UNTS325	100415
Canada	UK Great Britain	17 Jul 47	28UNTS3	100416
Netherlands	Thailand	18 Jul 47	28UNTS27	100417
Greece	Turkey	22 Jul 47	72UNTS131	100931
Netherlands	South Africa	22 Jul 47	12UNTS257	100188
Taiwan	UK Great Britain	23 Jul 47	9UNTS207	100135
Greece	South Africa	28 Jul 47	185UNTS161	102467
Canada	Greece	28 Jul 47	43UNTS111	100665
Czechoslovakia	Greece	30 Jul 47	185UNTS149	102466
Poland	Romania	09 Aug 47	12UNTS363	100193
Hungary	Poland	28 Aug 47	15UNTS145	100231
Czechoslovakia	Netherlands	01 Sep 47	32UNTS129	100495
Czechoslovakia	Switzerland	10 Sep 47	35UNTS275	100559
Lebanon	Turkey	16 Sep 47	44UNTS123	100682
Czechoslovakia	Sweden	15 Oct 47	44UNTS149	100683
Colombia	UK Great Britain	16 Oct 47	160UNTS297	102115
Cuba	USA (United States)	30 Oct 47	119UNTS163	101611
Brazil	Netherlands	06 Nov 47	53UNTS59	100773
Norway	Portugal	11 Nov 47	34UNTS257	100542
Brazil	Sweden	14 Nov 47	94UNTS139	101310
Brazil	Denmark	14 Nov 47	47UNTS39	100722
Brazil	Norway	14 Nov 47	44UNTS163	100684
Denmark	Greece	14 Nov 47	35UNTS295	100560
Denmark	Ireland	18 Nov 47	35UNTS309	100561
Ireland	Italy	21 Nov 47	353UNTS73	105038
Taiwan	Netherlands	06 Dec 47	43UNTS185	100669
Czechoslovakia	USSR (Soviet Union)	11 Dec 47	217UNTS35	102943
Denmark	Portugal	15 Dec 47	35UNTS329	100563
Italy	USA (United States)	02 Feb 48	79UNTS171	101040
Italy	USA (United States)	06 Feb 48	73UNTS113	100950
Denmark	Guatemala	04 Mar 48	96UNTS223	101339
Switzerland	USSR (Soviet Union)	17 Mar 48	217UNTS73	102944
Argentina	Denmark	18 Mar 48	94UNTS175	101311
Cuba	UK Great Britain	19 Mar 48	175UNTS23	102294
Bulgaria	USSR (Soviet Union)	01 Apr 48	217UNTS97	102946
Czechoslovakia	Poland	05 Apr 48	31UNTS325	100481
Canada	Italy	28 Apr 48	231UNTS69	103206
Ireland	Switzerland	06 May 48	334UNTS187	104768

PARTY ONE	PARTY TWO	DATE	CITATION	NUMBER
Most favored nation clause (Cont.)				
Pakistan	Sweden	06 May 48	36UNTS3	100564
Jordan	Turkey	07 May 48	32UNTS313	100505
Ireland	Netherlands	10 May 48	28UNTS121	100422
Norway	Turkey	20 May 48	26UNTS137	100384
India	Sweden	21 May 48	34UNTS285	100543
Greece	Switzerland	26 May 48	94UNTS217	101312
Australia	Greece	16 Jun 48	18UNTS211	100290
Ireland	Norway	21 Jun 48	34UNTS317	100545
India	Pakistan	23 Jun 48	28UNTS143	100423
Greece	Sweden	25 Jun 48	267UNTS337	103849
France	USA (United States)	28 Jun 48	31UNTS115	100472
Italy	USA (United States)	28 Jun 48	25UNTS45	100356
Denmark	USA (United States)	29 Jun 48	27UNTS35	100396
Netherlands	USA (United States)	02 Jul 48	32UNTS77	100490
Belgium	USA (United States)	02 Jul 48	27UNTS43	100397
Greece	USA (United States)	02 Jul 48	31UNTS131	100474
Austria	USA (United States)	02 Jul 48	25UNTS53	100357
Iceland	USA (United States)	03 Jul 48	27UNTS49	100398
Sweden	USA (United States)	03 Jul 48	27UNTS69	100400
Norway	USA (United States)	03 Jul 48	27UNTS59	100399
Turkey	USA (United States)	04 Jul 48	34UNTS185	100536
UK Great Britain	USA (United States)	06 Jul 48	25UNTS61	100358
France	USA (United States)	09 Jul 48	32UNTS93	100492
Multilateral		14 Jul 48	31UNTS123	100473
USA (United States)	Yugoslavia	19 Jul 48	89UNTS43	101208
Peru	UK Great Britain	20 Jul 48	66UNTS197	100855
Brazil	Switzerland	10 Aug 48	94UNTS269	101314
India	Switzerland	14 Aug 48	33UNTS3	100509
Greece	Lebanon	06 Sep 48	178UNTS37	102335
Korea, South	USA (United States)	11 Sep 48	89UNTS155	101216
Multilateral		14 Sep 48	18UNTS267	100296
Portugal	USA (United States)	28 Sep 48	31UNTS139	100475
Bolivia	USA (United States)	29 Sep 48	505UNTS139	107370
Greece	Lebanon	06 Oct 48	87UNTS351	101179
France	USA (United States)	19 Oct 48	98UNTS3	101355
Mexico	Portugal	22 Oct 48	34UNTS329	100546
Argentina	Netherlands	29 Oct 48	95UNTS21	101316
Canada	Finland	17 Nov 48	231UNTS75	103207
South Africa	UK Great Britain	06 Dec 48	118UNTS183	101607
Korea, South	USA (United States)	10 Dec 48	55UNTS157	100813
Italy	USSR (Soviet Union)	11 Dec 48	217UNTS181	102948
Ceylon (Sri Lanka)	Pakistan	03 Jan 49	28UNTS247	100428
Italy	Lebanon	24 Jan 49	231UNTS241	103223
Switzerland	Turkey	16 Feb 49	72UNTS175	100933
Belgium	France	18 Feb 49	31UNTS173	100478
Finland	Netherlands	25 Feb 49	53UNTS123	100777
Netherlands	Switzerland	07 Mar 49	35UNTS69	100551
Korea, North	USSR (Soviet Union)	17 Mar 49	221UNTS3	102999
Finland	USA (United States)	29 Mar 49	55UNTS59	100808
Panama	USA (United States)	31 Mar 49	55UNTS87	100810
Finland	Sweden	26 Apr 49	95UNTS83	101318
Denmark	Poland	12 May 49	87UNTS179	101172
Canada	USA (United States)	04 Jun 49	122UNTS237	101649
Belgium	Greece	21 Jun 49	137UNTS215	101854
Norway	Pakistan	23 Jun 49	35UNTS49	100550
India	Switzerland	24 Jun 49	95UNTS109	101319
Korea, South	USA (United States)	29 Jun 49	55UNTS79	100809
Greece	Syria	05 Jul 49	78UNTS71	101013
Iraq	Norway	12 Jul 49	53UNTS137	100778
Czechoslovakia	Finland	13 Jul 49	53UNTS153	100779
Pakistan	Philippines	16 Jul 49	35UNTS111	100553
Dominican Republic	USA (United States)	19 Jul 49	51UNTS145	100762
France	Netherlands	20 Jul 49	204UNTS287	102763
Multilateral		22 Jul 49	557UNTS211	108135
Pakistan	UK Great Britain	27 Jul 49	44UNTS199	100685

PARTY ONE	PARTY TWO	DATE	CITATION	NUMBER
Most favored nation clause (Cont.)				
Ceylon (Sri Lanka)	UK Great Britain	05 Aug 49	35UNTS137	100554
France	Greece	06 Aug 49	91UNTS95	101244
Multilateral		12 Aug 49	87UNTS131	101169
Canada	UK Great Britain	19 Aug 49	44UNTS223	100686
Finland	Norway	24 Aug 49	53UNTS167	100780
Denmark	Finland	26 Aug 49	53UNTS191	100781
Argentina	Norway	09 Sep 49	42UNTS125	100646
Lebanon	Netherlands	20 Sep 49	108UNTS205	101474
Burma	USA (United States)	28 Sep 49	55UNTS3	100806
Greece	Philippines	08 Oct 49	187UNTS221	102515
Denmark	Pakistan	09 Nov 49	44UNTS255	100687
Sweden	Thailand	23 Nov 49	72UNTS217	100935
Denmark	Thailand	23 Nov 49	53UNTS255	100786
Italy	Turkey	25 Nov 49	192UNTS39	102594
Norway	Thailand	26 Nov 49	53UNTS269	100787
Austria	Sweden	02 Dec 49	108UNTS3	101465
Austria	Norway	02 Dec 49	72UNTS230	100936
Austria	Denmark	02 Dec 49	53UNTS281	100788
Canada	Denmark	13 Dec 49	72UNTS247	100937
Austria	Switzerland	19 Dec 49	254UNTS287	103597
Greece	Portugal	31 Dec 49	92UNTS71	101262
Ireland	USA (United States)	21 Jan 50	206UNTS269	102792
Netherlands	Syria	13 Feb 50	108UNTS53	101467
Canada	Norway	14 Feb 50	53UNTS329	100790
Austria	Denmark	23 Feb 50	74UNTS269	100969
Ceylon (Sri Lanka)	Thailand	24 Feb 50	72UNTS261	100938
Iraq	Pakistan	26 Feb 50	214UNTS3	102896
Iceland	Netherlands	22 Mar 50	95UNTS237	101323
Denmark	Iceland	22 Mar 50	72UNTS273	100939
Canada	Yugoslavia	29 Mar 50	230UNTS357	103195
Paraguay	UK Great Britain	03 Apr 50	99UNTS81	101372
Afghanistan	India	04 Apr 50	167UNTS105	102201
Sweden	UK Great Britain	05 Apr 50	99UNTS107	101374
Austria	Greece	11 May 50	184UNTS217	102450
Israel	USA (United States)	13 Jun 50	212UNTS93	102863
Iraq	Pakistan	20 Jun 50	77UNTS215	101001
Burma	Ceylon (Sri Lanka)	29 Jun 50	73UNTS3	100940
Israel	Turkey	04 Jul 50	220UNTS3	102982
Germany, West	Ireland	12 Jul 50	557UNTS221	108136
Spain	UK Great Britain	20 Jul 50	398UNTS101	105719
France	Pakistan	31 Jul 50	96UNTS23	101329
Canada	France	01 Aug 50	73UNTS21	100941
Spain	Switzerland	03 Aug 50	254UNTS365	103600
Canada	New Zealand	16 Aug 50	77UNTS239	101002
Greece	Philippines	28 Aug 50	225UNTS155	103097
Burma	Sweden	14 Sep 50	96UNTS45	101330
Brazil	Turkey	21 Sep 50	150UNTS299	101981
Iran	Italy	24 Sep 50	281UNTS157	104077
Canada	Venezuela	11 Oct 50	231UNTS3	103198
Sweden	Switzerland	18 Oct 50	166UNTS49	102185
Luxembourg	Portugal	21 Oct 50	108UNTS67	101468
Israel	Netherlands	23 Oct 50	189UNTS89	102543
Canada	Ecuador	10 Nov 50	231UNTS15	103199
Canada	Costa Rica	18 Nov 50	231UNTS25	103200
Norway	UK Great Britain	15 Dec 50	106UNTS87	101459
Israel	Turkey	05 Feb 51	193UNTS3	102607
Germany, West	Greece	12 Feb 51	198UNTS193	102665
Colombia	Portugal	09 Mar 51	108UNTS87	101469
Greece	Yugoslavia	15 Mar 51	187UNTS237	102516
France	UK Great Britain	11 Apr 51	106UNTS3	101456
Greece	India	18 Apr 51	166UNTS305	102195
Iraq	UK Great Britain	19 Apr 51	108UNTS121	101470
Belgium	UK Great Britain	08 May 51	158UNTS451	102079
India	Netherlands	24 May 51	108UNTS151	101471
Greece	Norway	28 May 51	187UNTS141	102507

PARTY ONE	PARTY TWO	DATE	CITATION	NUMBER
Most favored nation clause (Cont.)				
Cuba	Portugal	26 Jun 51	192UNTS115	102598
Multilateral		02 Jul 51	189UNTS137	102545
Ireland	Norway	02 Jul 51	100UNTS53	101387
Iceland	Norway	14 Jul 51	163UNTS265	102150
Israel	Yugoslavia	29 Jul 51	220UNTS7	102983
Burma	Denmark	30 Jul 51	108UNTS167	101472
Greece	USA (United States)	03 Aug 51	224UNTS279	103080
Israel	Philippines	07 Aug 51	192UNTS81	102596
Lebanon	UK Great Britain	15 Aug 51	160UNTS327	102116
France	Italy	23 Aug 51	291UNTS143	104249
Israel	USA (United States)	23 Aug 51	219UNTS237	102979
Pakistan	United Arab Rep	28 Aug 51	214UNTS247	102902
France	USSR (Soviet Union)	03 Sep 51	221UNTS79	103003
France	Greece	03 Sep 51	187UNTS113	102505
Australia	Israel	06 Sep 51	188UNTS303	102534
Burma	Netherlands	06 Sep 51	108UNTS187	101473
Ethiopia	USA (United States)	07 Sep 51	206UNTS41	102785
Multilateral		08 Sep 51	136UNTS45	101832
Panama	UK Great Britain	15 Sep 51	560UNTS143	108172
Denmark	USA (United States)	01 Oct 51	421UNTS105	106056
Philippines	Spain	06 Oct 51	215UNTS193	102920
Greece	Luxembourg	22 Oct 51	187UNTS119	102506
Israel	Italy	08 Nov 51	219UNTS293	102980
Denmark	Iraq	18 Nov 51	232UNTS25	103227
Pakistan	Saudi Arabia	25 Nov 51	177UNTS3	102304
India	UK Great Britain	01 Dec 51	128UNTS39	101712
Colombia	Spain	11 Dec 51	216UNTS73	102933
El Salvador	Guatemala	14 Dec 51	131UNTS131	101740
Jordan	USA (United States)	20 Dec 51	157UNTS69	102048
Ecuador	USA (United States)	20 Feb 52	177UNTS43	102308
Peru	USA (United States)	22 Feb 52	165UNTS31	102166
Japan	USA (United States)	28 Feb 52	208UNTS255	102817
Cuba	USA (United States)	07 Mar 52	165UNTS11	102165
Belgium	Spain	10 Mar 52	178UNTS243	102342
Belgium	Pakistan	15 Mar 52	316UNTS65	104578
Brazil	USA (United States)	15 Mar 52	199UNTS221	102687
Norway	Uruguay	20 Mar 52	310UNTS279	104496
Chile	USA (United States)	09 Apr 52	186UNTS53	102482
Colombia	USA (United States)	17 Apr 52	174UNTS215	102287
France	Mexico	17 Apr 52	163UNTS321	102153
France	Israel	29 Apr 52	189UNTS55	102542
Israel	USA (United States)	09 May 52	177UNTS269	102326
Switzerland	UK Great Britain	13 May 52	164UNTS91	102160
Greece	Syria	02 Jun 52	183UNTS251	102434
India	United Arab Rep	14 Jun 52	173UNTS209	102268
Denmark	UK Great Britain	23 Jun 52	151UNTS3	101982
Multilateral		28 Jun 52	210UNTS132	102838
USA (United States)	Uruguay	30 Jun 52	207UNTS139	102804
Belgium	Israel	30 Jun 52	183UNTS263	102435
Netherlands	Pakistan	17 Jul 52	150UNTS277	101980
Greece	Israel	22 Jul 52	219UNTS231	102978
USA (United States)	Venezuela	28 Aug 52	178UNTS51	102336
Ethiopia	Pakistan	29 Aug 52	150UNTS257	101979
Austria	Luxembourg	13 Oct 52	192UNTS291	102606
Mexico	Netherlands	13 Oct 52	163UNTS341	102154
Iceland	Luxembourg	23 Oct 52	193UNTS39	102609
Burma	UK Great Britain	25 Oct 52	150UNTS237	101978
Chile	Sweden	27 Oct 52	311UNTS63	104499
Chile	Denmark	27 Oct 52	271UNTS93	103911
Australia	Iceland	13 Nov 52	161UNTS59	102122
Denmark	Israel	14 Nov 52	160UNTS275	102112
Luxembourg	Norway	17 Nov 52	311UNTS95	104500
Luxembourg	Sweden	17 Nov 52	173UNTS277	102270
Israel	Switzerland	19 Nov 52	232UNTS3	103226
Mexico	ICAO (Civil Aviat)	28 Nov 52	164UNTS15	102156

PARTY ONE	PARTY TWO	DATE	CITATION	NUMBER
Most favored nation clause (Cont.)				
Canada	United Arab Rep	03 Dec 52	233UNTS145	103259
France	Greece	23 Dec 52	187UNTS175	102511
Greece	South Africa	27 Jan 53	533UNTS303	107748
Japan	Netherlands	17 Feb 53	192UNTS215	102602
Japan	Sweden	20 Feb 53	173UNTS307	102272
Libya	UK Great Britain	21 Feb 53	311UNTS115	104501
Japan	Norway	23 Feb 53	192UNTS191	102601
Denmark	Japan	26 Feb 53	173UNTS329	102273
Greece	Yugoslavia	28 Feb 53	252UNTS27	103557
Denmark	Uruguay	04 Mar 53	250UNTS51	103517
Dominican Republic	USA (United States)	06 Mar 53	199UNTS267	102689
India	Muscat and Oman	15 Mar 53	190UNTS69	102559
Lebanon	Sweden	23 Mar 53	255UNTS83	103605
Belgium	Canada	30 Mar 53	181UNTS95	102401
Japan	USA (United States)	02 Apr 53	206UNTS143	102788
Turkey	Yugoslavia	16 Apr 53	255UNTS99	103606
Philippines	Thailand	27 Apr 53	174UNTS3	102274
Greece	United Arab Rep	21 May 53	256UNTS17	103620
Israel	Italy	22 May 53	219UNTS297	102981
Cuba	USA (United States)	26 May 53	224UNTS75	103070
Switzerland	Yugoslavia	28 May 53	232UNTS45	103228
Japan	Syria	08 Jun 53	184UNTS3	102436
Japan	Thailand	19 Jun 53	174UNTS29	102276
Burma	Norway	22 Jun 53	174UNTS49	102277
India	Yugoslavia	24 Jul 53	394UNTS13	105665
Canada	Mexico	27 Jul 53	192UNTS255	102604
Ceylon (Sri Lanka)	Yugoslavia	30 Jul 53	337UNTS103	104819
USA (United States)	Venezuela	14 Aug 53	213UNTS99	102883
Ethiopia	Yugoslavia	21 Aug 53	378UNTS105	105421
Austria	Yugoslavia	11 Nov 53	363UNTS149	105206
Belgium	Lebanon	24 Dec 53	219UNTS153	102972
Syria	UK Great Britain	30 Jan 54	449UNTS47	106452
France	Sweden	16 Feb 54	228UNTS137	103147
Canada	Peru	18 Feb 54	411UNTS64	105915
Canada	Japan	31 Mar 54	236UNTS329	103334
Peru	Spain	31 Mar 54	232UNTS65	103230
Lebanon	USSR (Soviet Union)	30 Apr 54	226UNTS109	103111
UNICEF (Children)	Spain	07 May 54	190UNTS357	200515
Pakistan	Yugoslavia	15 May 54	286UNTS3	104158
Honduras	USA (United States)	20 May 54	222UNTS87	103025
Canada	Spain	26 May 54	391UNTS273	105632
Canada	Portugal	28 May 54	391UNTS253	105631
France	USA (United States)	31 May 54	236UNTS141	103321
Haiti	Italy	14 Jun 54	267UNTS97	103837
UK Great Britain	USA (United States)	15 Jun 54	236UNTS133	103320
Italy	USA (United States)	24 Jun 54	235UNTS3	103290
Ireland	Luxembourg	27 Jul 54	232UNTS91	103231
Multilateral		28 Sep 54	360UNTS117	105158
Multilateral		28 Sep 54	207UNTS293	102812
Germany, West	USA (United States)	29 Oct 54	273UNTS3	103943
Ceylon (Sri Lanka)	United Arab Rep	17 Nov 54	315UNTS3	104554
Belgium	USA (United States)	23 Nov 54	235UNTS19	103292
Ecuador	Netherlands	14 Dec 54	232UNTS115	103233
India	Iran	15 Dec 54	327UNTS245	104724
Austria	Belgium	07 Jan 55	380UNTS219	105458
Canada	Japan	12 Jan 55	311UNTS167	104503
Haiti	USA (United States)	28 Jan 55	270UNTS83	103894
Philippines	UK Great Britain	31 Jan 55	216UNTS51	102932
Argentina	UK Great Britain	31 Mar 55	210UNTS223	102840
Austria	Romania	11 May 55	342UNTS119	104904
Multilateral		15 May 55	217UNTS223	102949
Ceylon (Sri Lanka)	Pakistan	23 May 55	286UNTS15	104159
Guatemala	USA (United States)	18 Jun 55	262UNTS105	103740
Israel	USSR (Soviet Union)	15 Jul 55	226UNTS253	103119
Germany, West	UK Great Britain	22 Jul 55	269UNTS189	103881

Most favored nation clause (Cont.)

PARTY ONE	PARTY TWO	DATE	CITATION	NUMBER
Iran	USA (United States)	15 Aug 55	284UNTS93	104132
Bolivia	USA (United States)	23 Sep 55	256UNTS275	103637
USA (United States)	Yugoslavia	30 Sep 55	269UNTS89	103877
Bulgaria	Yugoslavia	01 Oct 55	396UNTS223	105698
Iceland	USA (United States)	05 Oct 55	256UNTS285	103638
Austria	USSR (Soviet Union)	17 Oct 55	240UNTS289	103409
Denmark	Syria	20 Oct 55	250UNTS61	103518
Italy	Lebanon	04 Nov 55	267UNTS113	103838
Italy	Syria	10 Nov 55	267UNTS157	103841
Syria	USSR (Soviet Union)	16 Nov 55	259UNTS71	103683
Austria	Israel	17 Nov 55	232UNTS153	103235
Pakistan	Syria	18 Dec 55	320UNTS269	104647
Costa Rica	Guatemala	20 Dec 55	280UNTS121	104056
Australia	Japan	19 Jan 56	311UNTS291	104507
Nicaragua	USA (United States)	21 Jan 56	367UNTS3	105224
Austria	Italy	23 Jan 56	393UNTS97	105653
Argentina	Switzerland	25 Jan 56	559UNTS121	108157
Romania	Yugoslavia	01 Feb 56	362UNTS203	105189
India	USA (United States)	03 Feb 56	272UNTS75	103932
Norway	Syria	25 Feb 56	463UNTS217	106706
Canada	USSR (Soviet Union)	29 Feb 56	252UNTS165	103566
Ceylon (Sri Lanka)	Romania	16 Mar 56	315UNTS41	104558
Germany, West	Sweden	22 Mar 56	262UNTS401	103762
Netherlands	USA (United States)	27 Mar 56	285UNTS231	104154
Portugal	Venezuela	16 May 56	463UNTS239	106707
Japan	Switzerland	24 May 56	312UNTS3	104509
Ceylon (Sri Lanka)	Hungary	04 Jun 56	315UNTS13	104555
Bulgaria	Ceylon (Sri Lanka)	19 Jun 56	315UNTS23	104556
Argentina	UK Great Britain	30 Jun 56	269UNTS235	103884
Canada	Honduras	11 Jul 56	305UNTS39	104411
Guatemala	Honduras	22 Aug 56	263UNTS49	103767
Jordan	USA (United States)	24 Sep 56	278UNTS51	104020
Costa Rica	Denmark	26 Sep 56	341UNTS305	104893
Japan	USSR (Soviet Union)	19 Oct 56	263UNTS119	103769
Belgium	Turkey	25 Oct 56	380UNTS3	105447
Austria	UK Great Britain	27 Oct 56	264UNTS67	103789
Peru	Switzerland	23 Nov 56	411UNTS97	105916
Albania	Yugoslavia	23 Nov 56	386UNTS73	105539
Korea, South	USA (United States)	28 Nov 56	302UNTS281	104367
Luxembourg	USA (United States)	07 Dec 56	265UNTS255	103817
Indonesia	Yugoslavia	14 Dec 56	378UNTS117	105422
Japan	Norway	28 Feb 57	280UNTS87	104054
Morocco	UK Great Britain	01 Mar 57	310UNTS3	104480
Belgium	Czechoslovakia	12 Mar 57	312UNTS75	104512
Netherlands	Yugoslavia	13 Mar 57	327UNTS227	104723
Netherlands	USA (United States)	03 Apr 57	410UNTS193	105904
Denmark	Pakistan	10 Apr 57	302UNTS53	104353
Ceylon (Sri Lanka)	Italy	23 Apr 57	337UNTS115	104820
Other Unilat Decla	United Arab Rep	24 Apr 57	265UNTS299	103821
Belgium	Bulgaria	14 May 57	317UNTS81	104596
Denmark	Peru	10 Jun 57	406UNTS63	105839
Afghanistan	Pakistan	13 Jun 57	327UNTS51	104717
Austria	USSR (Soviet Union)	14 Jun 57	285UNTS169	104152
Iraq	USA (United States)	16 Jun 57	284UNTS39	104127
Czechoslovakia	United Arab Rep	30 Jun 57	411UNTS126	105917
Australia	Japan	06 Jul 57	318UNTS381	104627
Ceylon (Sri Lanka)	China People's Rep	19 Sep 57	337UNTS137	104821
France	USA (United States)	23 Sep 57	293UNTS297	104297
Germany, East	USSR (Soviet Union)	27 Sep 57	292UNTS75	104268
Italy	Pakistan	05 Oct 57	353UNTS91	105039
Fed of Malaya	UK Great Britain	18 Oct 57	335UNTS3	104775
USA (United States)	Vietnam, South	05 Nov 57	300UNTS23	104328
Ireland	Portugal	11 Nov 57	553UNTS141	108080
Japan	USSR (Soviet Union)	06 Dec 57	325UNTS35	104694
Canada	Switzerland	10 Jan 58	464UNTS21	106710

Most favored nation clause (Cont.)

PARTY ONE	PARTY TWO	DATE	CITATION	NUMBER
Indonesia	Japan	20 Jan 58	324UNTS227	104688
India	Japan	04 Feb 58	324UNTS215	104687
Afghanistan	Turkey	08 Feb 58	464UNTS39	106711
Ceylon (Sri Lanka)	USSR (Soviet Union)	08 Feb 58	348UNTS159	104999
Albania	USSR (Soviet Union)	15 Feb 58	313UNTS261	104536
Sudan	Sweden	17 Feb 58	393UNTS161	105655
Norway	Pakistan	05 Mar 58	334UNTS199	104769
Pakistan	Sweden	06 Mar 58	393UNTS181	105656
Belgium	Iran	14 Apr 58	381UNTS309	105473
Sweden	Yugoslavia	18 Apr 58	393UNTS225	105658
China People's Rep	USSR (Soviet Union)	23 Apr 58	313UNTS135	104534
Germany, West	USSR (Soviet Union)	25 Apr 58	346UNTS71	104978
Japan	Poland	26 Apr 58	340UNTS221	104866
Pakistan	Portugal	07 Jun 58	320UNTS225	104645
Multilateral		10 Jun 58	454UNTS47	106539
Denmark	Luxembourg	10 Jun 58	356UNTS193	105096
Belgium	Pakistan	04 Jul 58	387UNTS305	105569
Ethiopia	UK Great Britain	07 Jul 58	331UNTS3	104749
Denmark	El Salvador	09 Jul 58	341UNTS289	104892
Japan	Philippines	24 Jul 58	325UNTS103	104696
Australia	Fed of Malaya	26 Aug 58	325UNTS253	104703
Japan	New Zealand	09 Sep 58	325UNTS119	104698
United Arab Rep	USSR (Soviet Union)	18 Sep 58	338UNTS29	104831
Ghana	UK Great Britain	24 Sep 58	411UNTS146	105918
Iraq	USSR (Soviet Union)	11 Oct 58	328UNTS95	104730
Poland	Yugoslavia	17 Nov 58	432UNTS267	106225
Fed Rhod/Nyasaland	Portugal	29 Nov 58	354UNTS137	105060
Haiti	Japan	17 Dec 58	518UNTS91	107492
Muscat and Oman	USA (United States)	20 Dec 58	380UNTS181	105457
Iraq	Romania	24 Dec 58	405UNTS243	105836
Multilateral		30 Jan 59	0UNTS0	109234
Czechoslovakia	United Arab Rep	07 Feb 59	372UNTS243	105301
Japan	Yugoslavia	28 Feb 59	341UNTS179	104883
Netherlands	Tunisia	19 Mar 59	497UNTS61	107262
Sweden	Tunisia	19 Mar 59	497UNTS43	107261
Norway	Tunisia	28 Mar 59	497UNTS77	107263
Denmark	Tunisia	14 Apr 59	340UNTS273	104870
Italy	United Arab Rep	29 Apr 59	363UNTS91	105202
Denmark	Sudan	11 May 59	445UNTS105	106380
Ceylon (Sri Lanka)	Sweden	29 May 59	464UNTS109	106713
Ceylon (Sri Lanka)	Norway	29 May 59	411UNTS165	105919
Ceylon (Sri Lanka)	Denmark	29 May 59	348UNTS225	105002
Belgium	Japan	20 Jun 59	411UNTS3	105911
Ethiopia	Greece	22 Jun 59	534UNTS147	107759
India	Italy	06 Oct 59	378UNTS267	105427
Czechoslovakia	Germany, East	25 Nov 59	374UNTS101	105331
Czechoslovakia	Japan	15 Dec 59	383UNTS277	105505
Australia	Indonesia	17 Dec 59	354UNTS109	105058
Czechoslovakia	UK Great Britain	15 Jan 60	374UNTS207	105336
India	Japan	25 Jan 60	384UNTS31	105508
Cuba	USSR (Soviet Union)	13 Feb 60	369UNTS17	105248
Greece	USA (United States)	15 Feb 60	377UNTS95	105397
Korea, South	USA (United States)	19 Feb 60	372UNTS109	105291
France	Thailand	26 Feb 60	392UNTS279	105648
Turkey	USA (United States)	02 Mar 60	372UNTS37	105286
Greece	Tunisia	02 Mar 60	483UNTS89	107008
Finland	Iceland	10 Mar 60	497UNTS95	107264
Czechoslovakia	Iraq	11 Mar 60	464UNTS267	106718
Austria	Guatemala	18 Mar 60	379UNTS89	105435
Austria	El Salvador	23 Mar 60	390UNTS3	105599
Denmark	USA (United States)	12 Apr 60	373UNTS9	105311
Cuba	Japan	22 Apr 60	442UNTS261	106354
Nepal	USA (United States)	17 May 60	372UNTS313	105307
Switzerland	Tunisia	21 May 60	497UNTS109	107265
Afghanistan	Czechoslovakia	28 May 60	497UNTS129	107266

PARTY ONE	PARTY TWO	DATE	CITATION	NUMBER
Most favored nation clause (Cont.)				
Cuba	Czechoslovakia	10 Jun 60	447UNTS75	106412
Korea, North	USSR (Soviet Union)	22 Jun 60	399UNTS3	105732
Denmark	Peru	22 Jun 60	439UNTS113	106326
Italy	USA (United States)	07 Jul 60	380UNTS143	105455
Ghana	Netherlands	30 Jul 60	412UNTS51	105925
Ghana	USSR (Soviet Union)	04 Aug 60	421UNTS27	106050
Guatemala	USA (United States)	09 Aug 60	461UNTS15	106648
Belgium	Burma	17 Aug 60	540UNTS185	107850
New Zealand	Yugoslavia	09 Sep 60	402UNTS119	105781
Iran	Japan	12 Sep 60	384UNTS43	105509
Multilateral		08 Oct 60	450UNTS309	106476
Burma	Switzerland	31 Oct 60	465UNTS97	106723
Norway	Peru	02 Nov 60	497UNTS207	107270
Indonesia	UK Great Britain	23 Nov 60	398UNTS71	105718
Japan	Pakistan	18 Dec 60	423UNTS197	106093
Canada	Pakistan	21 Dec 60	465UNTS115	106724
Luxembourg	Thailand	29 Dec 60	465UNTS131	106725
Sudan	UK Great Britain	16 Jan 61	424UNTS233	106112
Albania	Cuba	16 Jan 61	448UNTS67	106425
Germany, West	Japan	18 Jan 61	465UNTS173	106727
Malaysia	New Zealand	03 Feb 61	447UNTS251	106418
Belgium	USA (United States)	21 Feb 61	480UNTS149	106967
Korea, South	Philippines	24 Feb 61	423UNTS217	106094
Cuba	Czechoslovakia	04 Mar 61	465UNTS209	106728
Japan	Peru	15 May 61	451UNTS3	106482
Somalia	USSR (Soviet Union)	02 Jun 61	493UNTS173	107214
Austria	Yugoslavia	30 Jun 61	443UNTS51	106358
Indonesia	Japan	01 Jul 61	517UNTS107	107484
Czechoslovakia	Ghana	02 Aug 61	465UNTS249	106730
Finland	Luxembourg	15 Aug 61	541UNTS45	107859
Mexico	Netherlands	24 Aug 61	465UNTS291	106732
Bulgaria	Poland	19 Sep 61	483UNTS249	107018
Pakistan	Philippines	29 Sep 61	422UNTS3	106065
Japan	Pakistan	17 Oct 61	466UNTS17	106734
Greece	Morocco	01 Nov 61	483UNTS113	107009
Ghana	USSR (Soviet Union)	04 Nov 61	437UNTS213	106308
Czechoslovakia	Mali	27 Nov 61	466UNTS41	106736
Germany, West	Thailand	13 Dec 61	541UNTS181	107870
Czechoslovakia	Guinea	16 Dec 61	559UNTS49	108154
Argentina	Japan	20 Dec 61	613UNTS323	108859
Indonesia	Japan	23 Jan 62	559UNTS77	108155
Dominican Republic	USA (United States)	08 Mar 62	527UNTS29	107615
Israel	Vietnam, South	11 Apr 62	448UNTS205	106432
Dominican Republic	USA (United States)	02 May 62	442UNTS99	106341
Greece	Tunisia	26 May 62	534UNTS163	107761
United Arab Rep	USSR (Soviet Union)	23 Jun 62	472UNTS19	106835
United Arab Rep	USSR (Soviet Union)	23 Jun 62	472UNTS43	106836
Morocco	Switzerland	05 Jul 62	498UNTS171	107281
Taiwan	Paraguay	11 Jul 62	458UNTS41	106591
Chile	Netherlands	13 Jul 62	466UNTS109	106740
Cyprus	Greece	23 Aug 62	609UNTS15	108825
Japan	Kuwait	06 Oct 62	498UNTS235	107284
Hungary	Syria	18 Oct 62	491UNTS209	107178
Poland	Syria	10 Nov 62	491UNTS228	107179
Brazil	Taiwan	28 Dec 62	500UNTS61	107307
Japan	USA (United States)	31 Dec 62	471UNTS83	106823
Greece	Pakistan	17 Jan 63	538UNTS175	107814
South Africa	Spain	08 Feb 63	458UNTS79	106593
Sudan	Switzerland	18 Feb 63	563UNTS281	108215
Austria	Czechoslovakia	08 Mar 63	495UNTS219	107245
Brazil	USSR (Soviet Union)	20 Apr 63	0UNTS0	109256
El Salvador	Japan	19 Jul 63	518UNTS135	107494
New Zealand	USSR (Soviet Union)	01 Aug 63	486UNTS27	107070
Tanganyika	USSR (Soviet Union)	14 Aug 63	493UNTS195	107215
Iran	USA (United States)	24 Oct 63	489UNTS303	107146

PARTY ONE	PARTY TWO	DATE	CITATION	NUMBER
Most favored nation clause (Cont.)				
Czechoslovakia	Romania	16 Dec 63	527UNTS285	107630
Czechoslovakia	Hungary	20 Dec 63	538UNTS127	107812
Greece	Poland	21 Dec 63	538UNTS155	107813
Denmark	Yugoslavia	11 Feb 64	511UNTS241	107437
Malaysia	Netherlands	07 Apr 64	524UNTS81	107567
Taiwan	Ecuador	17 Jun 64	533UNTS141	107740
Belgium	Tunisia	15 Jul 64	561UNTS297	108190
Taiwan	Mexico	25 Sep 64	547UNTS233	107960
Czechoslovakia	Yugoslavia	08 Oct 64	544UNTS129	107916
Taiwan	Ecuador	23 Oct 64	543UNTS241	107904
Taiwan	Guatemala	08 Nov 64	543UNTS227	107903
Ireland	Vietnam, South	01 Dec 64	553UNTS233	108091
Argentina	UK Great Britain	12 Jan 65	597UNTS177	108645
Malta	Switzerland	20 Jan 65	548UNTS193	107978
Denmark	Malaysia	26 Mar 65	540UNTS205	107851
Argentina	Yugoslavia	09 Jun 65	601UNTS3	108684
Australia	Philippines	16 Jun 65	541UNTS31	107858
Argentina	United Arab Rep	21 Jun 65	634UNTS161	109058
New Zealand	Poland	07 Jul 65	548UNTS19	107966
Malta	Yugoslavia	15 Jul 65	561UNTS223	108186
Australia	Korea, South	21 Sep 65	548UNTS163	107977
Australia	USSR (Soviet Union)	15 Oct 65	553UNTS239	108092
Argentina	India	26 Mar 66	601UNTS201	108697
Singapore	USSR (Soviet Union)	02 Apr 66	631UNTS125	108992
Poland	Singapore	07 Jun 66	631UNTS189	108994
Australia	Poland	20 Jun 66	638UNTS201	109136
Australia	Bulgaria	22 Jun 66	607UNTS69	108796
Argentina	Germany, West	13 Jul 66	636UNTS3	109091
Mauritania	USSR (Soviet Union)	17 Oct 66	633UNTS231	109040
Romania	United Arab Rep	14 Nov 66	642UNTS129	109169
Ghana	Romania	23 Nov 66	642UNTS63	109165
Guinea	Romania	01 Dec 66	642UNTS89	109167
Denmark	Singapore	20 Dec 66	593UNTS125	108580
Korea, South	New Zealand	31 Jan 67	598UNTS91	108656
Argentina	Uruguay	12 Feb 67	635UNTS125	109076
Haiti	Israel	28 Mar 67	630UNTS293	108975
Bulgaria	USSR (Soviet Union)	27 Apr 67	631UNTS3	108983
Denmark	Paraguay	03 May 67	608UNTS55	108812
Australia	Romania	18 May 67	642UNTS25	109162
Chad	USSR (Soviet Union)	22 Jun 67	643UNTS121	109188
Ecuador	Romania	10 Oct 67	642UNTS33	109163
Australia	Hungary	05 Dec 67	638UNTS209	109137
Israel	Singapore	24 Apr 68	642UNTS235	109176
Taxation				
France	USA (United States)	25 Jul 39	125UNTS259	200429
Panama	USA (United States)	28 Mar 41	103UNTS163	200312
Canada	USA (United States)	04 Mar 42	124UNTS271	200426
Finland	Sweden	10 Mar 43	198UNTS333	200518
Canada	USA (United States)	08 Jun 44	124UNTS297	200427
UK Great Britain	USA (United States)	16 Apr 45	6UNTS359	200039
UK Great Britain	USA (United States)	16 Apr 45	6UNTS189	100076
Canada	UK Great Britain	05 Jun 46	86UNTS3	101147
Canada	UK Great Britain	05 Jun 46	27UNTS207	100408
South Africa	UK Great Britain	14 Oct 46	86UNTS77	101153
South Africa	UK Great Britain	14 Oct 46	86UNTS51	101152
France	USA (United States)	18 Oct 46	140UNTS23	101882
Australia	UK Great Britain	29 Oct 46	17UNTS181	100276
South Africa	USA (United States)	13 Dec 46	167UNTS171	102207
France	UK Great Britain	14 Dec 46	105UNTS27	101452
Denmark	Norway	30 Dec 46	8UNTS21	100111
Finland	USA (United States)	07 Jan 47	15UNTS273	100243
Norway	Sweden	21 Jun 47	94UNTS107	101309
India	Pakistan	10 Dec 47	51UNTS173	100764
Canada	New Zealand	12 Mar 48	231UNTS219	103222

PARTY ONE	PARTY TWO	DATE	CITATION	NUMBER
Taxation (Cont.)				
New Zealand	USA (United States)	16 Mar 48	127UNTS133	101703
Belgium	Luxembourg	25 Mar 48	18UNTS323	100300
Netherlands	USA (United States)	29 Apr 48	32UNTS167	100498
Denmark	USA (United States)	06 May 48	26UNTS55	100377
Belgium	Netherlands	25 Sep 48	123UNTS81	101655
Belgium	Luxembourg	09 Oct 48	123UNTS29	101652
Netherlands	UK Great Britain	15 Oct 48	74UNTS3	100955
Netherlands	UK Great Britain	15 Oct 48	73UNTS203	100954
Sweden	Switzerland	16 Oct 48	197UNTS55	102634
Sweden	Switzerland	16 Oct 48	197UNTS101	102635
Belgium	USA (United States)	28 Oct 48	173UNTS67	102262
Argentina	Sweden	20 Nov 48	197UNTS47	102633
Argentina	Denmark	15 Dec 48	67UNTS71	100866
Argentina	Netherlands	15 Jan 49	46UNTS241	100713
Italy	Yugoslavia	03 Feb 49	33UNTS105	100517
Argentina	UK Great Britain	14 Mar 49	83UNTS193	101108
Sweden	UK Great Britain	30 Mar 49	209UNTS129	102826
France	Sweden	08 Apr 49	197UNTS177	102637
France	Sweden	08 Apr 49	197UNTS183	102638
Ireland	UK Great Britain	18 May 49	553UNTS209	108089
Norway	USA (United States)	13 Jun 49	127UNTS189	101705
Norway	USA (United States)	13 Jun 49	127UNTS163	101704
Argentina	Belgium	25 Jul 49	46UNTS103	100703
Argentina	Canada	06 Aug 49	231UNTS43	103202
Ireland	USA (United States)	13 Sep 49	127UNTS119	101702
Ireland	USA (United States)	13 Sep 49	127UNTS89	101701
Norway	Sweden	17 Dec 49	197UNTS215	102641
Norway	Sweden	17 Dec 49	197UNTS197	102640
Finland	Sweden	21 Dec 49	197UNTS243	102642
France	Netherlands	30 Dec 49	203UNTS85	102742
France	Netherlands	30 Dec 49	203UNTS133	102743
Belgium	France	30 Dec 49	46UNTS111	100704
Israel	UK Great Britain	10 Feb 50	86UNTS211	101161
Greece	USA (United States)	20 Feb 50	196UNTS291	102630
Greece	USA (United States)	20 Feb 50	196UNTS269	102629
Burma	UK Great Britain	13 Mar 50	131UNTS53	101735
Denmark	UK Great Britain	27 Mar 50	68UNTS117	100891
Finland	Sweden	31 Mar 50	197UNTS285	102643
Canada	USA (United States)	12 Jun 50	127UNTS57	101699
Canada	USA (United States)	12 Jun 50	127UNTS67	101700
Argentina	USA (United States)	20 Jul 50	89UNTS63	101209
Ceylon (Sri Lanka)	UK Great Britain	26 Jul 50	337UNTS77	104818
Greece	UK Great Britain	16 Nov 50	166UNTS281	102193
Denmark	South Africa	30 Nov 50	84UNTS51	101118
France	Greece	09 Dec 50	166UNTS315	102196
Finland	Sweden	29 Dec 50	197UNTS333	102646
Netherlands	Norway	29 Dec 50	134UNTS19	101795
Canada	France	16 Mar 51	236UNTS267	103330
Canada	France	16 Mar 51	236UNTS297	103331
Canada	Sweden	06 Apr 51	197UNTS393	102648
Norway	UK Great Britain	02 May 51	106UNTS101	101460
Switzerland	USA (United States)	24 May 51	127UNTS227	101706
South Africa	Sweden	25 May 51	197UNTS425	102649
Mexico	USA (United States)	27 Jun 51	141UNTS211	101916
Switzerland	USA (United States)	09 Jul 51	165UNTS51	102167
Austria	Sweden	19 Jul 51	198UNTS9	102652
Greece	USA (United States)	03 Aug 51	224UNTS279	103080
France	Italy	23 Aug 51	291UNTS143	104249
Denmark	USA (United States)	01 Oct 51	421UNTS105	106056
Netherlands	Switzerland	12 Nov 51	126UNTS173	101689
Netherlands	Switzerland	12 Nov 51	126UNTS157	101688
Canada	South Africa	26 Nov 51	248UNTS107	103489
Finland	UK Great Britain	12 Dec 51	172UNTS45	102239
El Salvador	Guatemala	14 Dec 51	131UNTS131	101740
France	Israel	24 Jan 52	220UNTS55	102988

PARTY ONE	PARTY TWO	DATE	CITATION	NUMBER
Taxation (Cont.)				
Belgium	Luxembourg	07 Feb 52	147UNTS3	101924
Finland	USA (United States)	03 Mar 52	177UNTS141	102316
Finland	USA (United States)	03 Mar 52	177UNTS163	102317
Canada	USA (United States)	19 Mar 52	174UNTS267	102291
Netherlands	Sweden	25 Apr 52	163UNTS131	102147
Netherlands	Sweden	25 Apr 52	163UNTS195	102148
Greece	Israel	22 Jul 52	215UNTS365	102924
Multilateral		25 Oct 52	241UNTS336	103442
Israel	South Africa	24 Dec 52	207UNTS303	102813
Belgium	Sweden	01 Apr 53	185UNTS225	102473
Japan	USA (United States)	02 Apr 53	206UNTS143	102788
Australia	USA (United States)	14 May 53	205UNTS277	102780
Australia	USA (United States)	14 May 53	205UNTS253	102779
Australia	USA (United States)	14 May 53	205UNTS237	102778
Greece	UK Great Britain	25 Jun 53	190UNTS281	102571
Italy	South Africa	26 Jun 53	211UNTS255	102857
Denmark	Sweden	27 Oct 53	198UNTS71	102658
Denmark	Sweden	27 Oct 53	198UNTS111	102659
Belgium	Finland	11 Feb 54	211UNTS63	102848
Finland	Netherlands	29 Mar 54	252UNTS239	103568
Finland	Netherlands	29 Mar 54	252UNTS185	103567
Japan	USA (United States)	16 Apr 54	238UNTS39	103354
Japan	USA (United States)	16 Apr 54	238UNTS3	103353
Netherlands	South Africa	22 Apr 54	211UNTS215	102853
Germany, West	USA (United States)	22 Jul 54	239UNTS3	103369
Switzerland	UK Great Britain	30 Sep 54	209UNTS197	102828
Ireland	Norway	18 Oct 54	553UNTS123	108077
Ireland	Sweden	18 Oct 54	262UNTS259	103753
Germany, West	UK Great Britain	18 Oct 54	218UNTS301	102960
Denmark	Ireland	18 Oct 54	218UNTS295	102959
Canada	Ireland	28 Oct 54	305UNTS3	104407
Canada	Ireland	28 Oct 54	304UNTS317	104406
Germany, West	USA (United States)	29 Oct 54	273UNTS3	103943
France	Sweden	05 Nov 54	262UNTS229	103748
France	South Africa	22 Nov 54	219UNTS35	102963
Switzerland	United Arab Rep	05 Jan 55	216UNTS41	102931
Italy	USA (United States)	30 Mar 55	257UNTS169	103654
Italy	USA (United States)	30 Mar 55	257UNTS199	103655
Pakistan	UK Great Britain	10 Jun 55	243UNTS15	103444
Israel	Italy	10 Jun 55	280UNTS219	104061
Denmark	Finland	18 Jul 55	250UNTS149	103521
South Africa	Sweden	28 Jul 55	230UNTS287	103191
Iran	USA (United States)	15 Aug 55	284UNTS93	104132
Iceland	Sweden	17 Sep 55	262UNTS273	103755
Canada	Denmark	30 Sep 55	258UNTS115	103675
Denmark	Iceland	10 Oct 55	230UNTS3	103171
Austria	Sweden	17 Oct 55	262UNTS283	103756
South Africa	Switzerland	07 Nov 55	230UNTS279	103190
Belgium	France	10 Dec 55	231UNTS101	103211
Belgium	Sweden	18 Jan 56	293UNTS23	104283
Nicaragua	USA (United States)	21 Jan 56	367UNTS3	105224
Netherlands	USA (United States)	27 Mar 56	285UNTS231	104154
New Zealand	Sweden	16 Apr 56	274UNTS259	103971
Fed Rhod/Nyasaland	South Africa	22 May 56	254UNTS227	103595
Denmark	Norway	23 May 56	271UNTS75	103910
Canada	Germany, West	04 Jun 56	316UNTS231	104589
Switzerland	UK Great Britain	12 Jun 56	269UNTS133	103879
France	USA (United States)	22 Jun 56	291UNTS101	104246
Honduras	USA (United States)	25 Jun 56	279UNTS113	104036
Austria	UK Great Britain	20 Jul 56	269UNTS147	103880
Ceylon (Sri Lanka)	India	10 Sep 56	315UNTS59	104560
Belgium	Germany, West	24 Sep 56	314UNTS195	104549
Norway	Sweden	27 Sep 56	261UNTS71	103726
Canada	South Africa	28 Sep 56	299UNTS17	104304
Canada	South Africa	28 Sep 56	299UNTS3	104303

PARTY ONE	PARTY TWO	DATE	CITATION	NUMBER
Taxation (Cont.)				
Germany, West	South Africa	28 Sep 56	327UNTS83	104718
Austria	USA (United States)	25 Oct 56	299UNTS123	104310
UK Great Britain	USA (United States)	01 Nov 56	264UNTS3	103785
UK Great Britain	USA (United States)	27 Nov 56	282UNTS43	104092
Korea, South	USA (United States)	28 Nov 56	302UNTS281	104367
Japan	Sweden	12 Dec 56	318UNTS309	104623
Italy	Sweden	20 Dec 56	369UNTS305	105263
Italy	Sweden	20 Dec 56	369UNTS357	105265
Finland	Switzerland	27 Dec 56	277UNTS7	103996
Finland	Switzerland	27 Dec 56	277UNTS59	103997
Denmark	Switzerland	14 Jan 57	286UNTS85	104161
Denmark	Switzerland	14 Jan 57	286UNTS27	104160
Italy	Netherlands	24 Jan 57	485UNTS67	107047
Denmark	Netherlands	20 Feb 57	287UNTS41	104179
Denmark	Norway	22 Feb 57	286UNTS127	104164
Japan	Norway	28 Feb 57	280UNTS87	104054
Paraguay	USA (United States)	04 Apr 57	283UNTS193	104117
Ceylon (Sri Lanka)	Sweden	18 May 57	315UNTS85	104561
Belgium	South Africa	11 Jun 57	292UNTS165	104272
Pakistan	USA (United States)	01 Jul 57	344UNTS203	104951
Australia	Canada	01 Oct 57	392UNTS41	105638
UK Great Britain	USA (United States)	01 Nov 57	299UNTS167	104312
Belgium	Switzerland	05 Dec 57	293UNTS317	104299
India	Japan	04 Feb 58	324UNTS215	104687
Ireland	South Africa	01 May 58	398UNTS3	105714
Ireland	Switzerland	18 Jun 58	553UNTS183	108086
Denmark	Sweden	21 Jul 58	320UNTS163	104642
Sweden	United Arab Rep	29 Jul 58	369UNTS323	105264
India	Sweden	30 Jul 58	369UNTS211	105259
Pakistan	Sweden	25 Aug 58	369UNTS183	105258
Germany, West	Norway	18 Nov 58	357UNTS205	105119
Muscat and Oman	USA (United States)	20 Dec 58	380UNTS181	105457
Belgium	France	20 Jan 59	361UNTS155	105178
Japan	Pakistan	17 Feb 59	341UNTS127	104880
Japan	Norway	21 Feb 59	356UNTS231	105098
Denmark	Japan	10 Mar 59	341UNTS55	104878
Canada	Finland	28 Mar 59	355UNTS3	105072
Germany, West	Sweden	17 Apr 59	428UNTS155	106175
Austria	Sweden	14 May 59	428UNTS3	106167
Germany, West	Netherlands	16 Jun 59	593UNTS3	108576
South Africa	UK Great Britain	18 Jun 59	380UNTS103	105452
South Africa	UK Great Britain	18 Jun 59	380UNTS59	105450
South Africa	UK Great Britain	18 Jun 59	380UNTS81	105451
India	Norway	20 Jul 59	356UNTS257	105099
Austria	France	08 Oct 59	453UNTS95	106521
Ireland	Sweden	06 Nov 59	428UNTS231	106177
Israel	Sweden	22 Dec 59	377UNTS277	105407
India	Japan	05 Jan 60	384UNTS3	105507
Austria	Norway	25 Feb 60	376UNTS155	105380
Iran	UK Great Britain	09 Apr 60	385UNTS63	105529
Australia	New Zealand	12 May 60	369UNTS119	105254
Italy	UK Great Britain	04 Jul 60	466UNTS195	106745
Sweden	UK Great Britain	28 Jul 60	404UNTS113	105808
Sweden	UK Great Britain	28 Jul 60	404UNTS85	105806
Sweden	Tunisia	06 Sep 60	427UNTS301	106162
Japan	Pakistan	18 Dec 60	423UNTS197	106093
Canada	USA (United States)	17 Feb 61	445UNTS143	106383
Belgium	USA (United States)	21 Feb 61	480UNTS149	106967
Morocco	Sweden	30 Mar 61	427UNTS185	106154
USA (United States)	Vietnam, South	03 Apr 61	424UNTS137	106106
Japan	UK Great Britain	11 Apr 61	420UNTS75	106042
Japan	Peru	15 May 61	451UNTS3	106482
South Africa	Sweden	29 May 61	442UNTS15	106335
Finland	India	23 Jun 61	421UNTS49	106051
Indonesia	Japan	01 Jul 61	517UNTS107	107484

PARTY ONE	PARTY TWO	DATE	CITATION	NUMBER
Taxation (Cont.)				
Belgium	France	07 Jul 61	406UNTS157	105846
Portugal	UK Great Britain	31 Jul 61	449UNTS119	106454
Colombia	USA (United States)	01 Aug 61	433UNTS123	106235
Italy	Norway	25 Aug 61	475UNTS269	106896
Denmark	Pakistan	04 Sep 61	455UNTS305	106549
Greece	Sweden	06 Oct 61	481UNTS137	106981
Sweden	Thailand	20 Oct 61	428UNTS275	106180
Austria	Denmark	23 Oct 61	425UNTS115	106122
Belgium	Denmark	23 Oct 61	425UNTS181	106123
Austria	Japan	20 Dec 61	517UNTS155	107485
Luxembourg	USA (United States)	23 Feb 62	474UNTS3	106868
Israel	Sweden	15 May 62	484UNTS261	107036
South Africa	UK Great Britain	28 May 62	443UNTS79	106361
Greece	Switzerland	12 Jun 62	492UNTS47	107186
Germany, West	Israel	09 Jul 62	630UNTS87	108968
Belgium	Luxembourg	30 Aug 62	485UNTS313	107062
Japan	UK Great Britain	04 Sep 62	475UNTS31	106888
Israel	UK Great Britain	26 Sep 62	474UNTS233	106885
Mali	USSR (Soviet Union)	10 Oct 62	493UNTS219	107216
Austria	United Arab Rep	16 Oct 62	491UNTS63	107174
Germany, West	Ireland	17 Oct 62	604UNTS135	108749
Austria	Luxembourg	18 Oct 62	496UNTS97	107248
Norway	Sweden	31 Oct 62	466UNTS361	106755
Ethiopia	Greece	07 Nov 62	550UNTS189	108015
Luxembourg	USA (United States)	18 Dec 62	532UNTS277	107723
Iceland	USA (United States)	27 Dec 62	469UNTS91	106785
Japan	New Zealand	30 Jan 63	517UNTS183	107486
Ceylon (Sri Lanka)	Denmark	16 Feb 63	486UNTS285	107083
Japan	Thailand	01 Mar 63	475UNTS233	106895
Norway	Spain	25 Apr 63	503UNTS41	107340
France	Monaco	18 May 63	0UNTS0	109438
Japan	Malaysia	04 Jun 63	517UNTS245	107488
France	UK Great Britain	21 Jun 63	540UNTS311	107855
France	Israel	20 Aug 63	515UNTS173	107460
France	Greece	21 Aug 63	533UNTS235	107746
Panama	USA (United States)	30 Aug 63	488UNTS11	107116
Austria	India	24 Sep 63	545UNTS199	107935
Austria	Finland	08 Oct 63	490UNTS255	107160
Lebanon	UK Great Britain	24 Oct 63	535UNTS3	107772
France	UK Great Britain	05 Nov 63	539UNTS277	107838
Norway	Thailand	09 Jan 64	522UNTS65	107537
Denmark	Ireland	04 Feb 64	525UNTS233	107596
Belgium	France	10 Mar 64	557UNTS13	108127
Denmark	Finland	07 Apr 64	525UNTS89	107586
Austria	Belgium	11 Jun 64	521UNTS157	107518
Ceylon (Sri Lanka)	Norway	11 Jun 64	559UNTS23	108153
Denmark	Tanganyika	04 Aug 64	544UNTS117	107914
Mexico	USA (United States)	07 Aug 64	530UNTS123	107677
Canada	Japan	05 Sep 64	569UNTS99	108282
Sweden	UK Great Britain	14 Oct 64	543UNTS135	107898
Norway	United Arab Rep	20 Oct 64	543UNTS3	107895
France	Japan	27 Nov 64	569UNTS157	108283
Finland	Israel	21 Jan 65	581UNTS275	108450
Greece	India	11 Feb 65	606UNTS9	108771
Belgium	Luxembourg	11 Mar 65	540UNTS297	107854
Finland	United Arab Rep	01 Apr 65	562UNTS3	108193
Jamaica	UK Great Britain	02 Apr 65	552UNTS219	108056
Denmark	Thailand	01 Jun 65	551UNTS157	108040
Belgium	Sweden	02 Jul 65	0UNTS0	109367
Cameroon	France	10 Jul 65	0UNTS0	109433
Finland	Ireland	15 Sep 65	0UNTS0	109372
France	Italy	29 Oct 65	0UNTS0	109445
Canada	UK Great Britain	06 Dec 65	572UNTS161	108311
Denmark	Italy	10 Mar 66	0UNTS0	109217
Iceland	Norway	30 Mar 66	566UNTS51	108240

PARTY ONE	PARTY TWO	DATE	CITATION	NUMBER
Taxation (Cont.)				
Denmark	Netherlands	31 Mar 66	604UNTS209	108751
Fed Rhod/Nyasaland	Norway	18 Jun 66	580UNTS9	108415
Denmark	Israel	27 Jun 66	581UNTS227	108448
New Zealand	UK Great Britain	13 Jul 66	598UNTS121	108658
Netherlands	Norway	22 Sep 66	600UNTS227	108683
Israel	Norway	02 Nov 66	630UNTS225	108972
Ireland	Switzerland	08 Nov 66	0UNTS0	109499
Canada	Norway	23 Nov 66	604UNTS295	108757
Canada	Israel	30 Nov 66	630UNTS267	108973
Singapore	UK Great Britain	01 Dec 66	605UNTS153	108763
France	Monaco	09 Dec 66	0UNTS0	109439
Austria	Spain	20 Dec 66	636UNTS197	109103
Trinidad/Tobago	UK Great Britain	29 Dec 66	605UNTS237	108766
UK Great Britain	USA (United States)	30 Dec 66	603UNTS245	108736
France	USSR (Soviet Union)	14 Mar 67	0UNTS0	109330
Denmark	Lebanon	29 Mar 67	602UNTS251	108717
South Africa	Switzerland	03 Jul 67	643UNTS3	109184
Malaysia	UK Great Britain	17 Jul 67	637UNTS0	109127
Netherlands	UK Great Britain	31 Oct 67	0UNTS0	109222
Argentina	Chile	06 Nov 67	636UNTS111	109097
Finland	Spain	15 Nov 67	0UNTS0	109375
Australia	UK Great Britain	07 Dec 67	0UNTS0	109458
Brazil	UK Great Britain	29 Dec 67	643UNTS217	109193
Denmark	Japan	03 Feb 68	0UNTS0	109405
Italy	UK Great Britain	15 Feb 68	0UNTS0	109263
Cyprus	Greece	30 Mar 68	0UNTS0	109465
Turkey	UK Great Britain	02 Apr 68	0UNTS0	109452
Malawi	UK Great Britain	02 Apr 68	0UNTS0	109450
Denmark	Yugoslavia	11 Apr 68	0UNTS0	109406
Gambia	UK Great Britain	19 Sep 68	0UNTS0	109799
Death duties				
Nicaragua	USA (United States)	27 Oct 42	99UNTS287	200283
Canada	USA (United States)	08 Jun 44	124UNTS297	200427
UK Great Britain	USA (United States)	16 Apr 45	6UNTS359	200039
Canada	UK Great Britain	05 Jun 46	86UNTS3	101147
South Africa	UK Great Britain	14 Oct 46	86UNTS51	101152
France	USA (United States)	18 Oct 46	140UNTS23	101882
South Africa	USA (United States)	10 Apr 47	167UNTS211	102208
Netherlands	UK Great Britain	15 Oct 48	73UNTS203	100954
Sweden	Switzerland	16 Oct 48	197UNTS101	102635
Sweden	UK Great Britain	30 Mar 49	209UNTS129	102826
France	Sweden	08 Apr 49	197UNTS183	102638
Norway	USA (United States)	13 Jun 49	127UNTS163	101704
Ireland	USA (United States)	13 Sep 49	127UNTS119	101702
Norway	Sweden	17 Dec 49	197UNTS197	102640
Finland	Sweden	21 Dec 49	197UNTS243	102642
Greece	USA (United States)	20 Feb 50	196UNTS269	102629
Finland	Sweden	31 Mar 50	197UNTS285	102643
Canada	USA (United States)	12 Jun 50	127UNTS57	101699
Finland	Sweden	29 Dec 50	197UNTS333	102646
Netherlands	Norway	29 Dec 50	134UNTS19	101795
Canada	France	16 Mar 51	236UNTS297	103331
Norway	UK Great Britain	02 May 51	106UNTS101	101460
Switzerland	USA (United States)	09 Jul 51	165UNTS51	102167
Netherlands	Switzerland	12 Nov 51	126UNTS157	101688
Finland	USA (United States)	03 Mar 52	177UNTS141	102316
Netherlands	Sweden	25 Apr 52	163UNTS195	102148
Australia	USA (United States)	14 May 53	205UNTS277	102780
Denmark	Sweden	27 Oct 53	198UNTS111	102659
Belgium	Finland	11 Feb 54	211UNTS63	102848
Finland	Netherlands	29 Mar 54	252UNTS239	103568
Finland	Netherlands	29 Mar 54	252UNTS185	103567
Japan	USA (United States)	16 Apr 54	238UNTS3	103353
Canada	Ireland	28 Oct 54	305UNTS3	104407

PARTY ONE	PARTY TWO	DATE	CITATION	NUMBER
Death duties (Cont.)				
Denmark	Finland	18 Jul 55	250UNTS149	103521
South Africa	Sweden	28 Jul 55	230UNTS287	103191
Belgium	Sweden	18 Jan 56	293UNTS23	104283
Denmark	Norway	23 May 56	271UNTS75	103910
Switzerland	UK Great Britain	12 Jun 56	269UNTS133	103879
Belgium	Germany, West	24 Sep 56	314UNTS195	104549
Norway	Sweden	27 Sep 56	261UNTS71	103726
Canada	South Africa	28 Sep 56	299UNTS3	104303
Italy	Sweden	20 Dec 56	369UNTS357	105265
Italy	Sweden	20 Dec 56	369UNTS305	105263
Finland	Switzerland	27 Dec 56	277UNTS59	103997
Denmark	Switzerland	14 Jan 57	286UNTS85	104161
Denmark	Norway	22 Feb 57	286UNTS127	104164
Denmark	Sweden	21 Jul 58	320UNTS163	104642
Sweden	United Arab Rep	29 Jul 58	369UNTS323	105264
Pakistan	Sweden	25 Aug 58	369UNTS183	105258
Germany, West	Norway	18 Nov 58	357UNTS205	105119
New Zealand	Switzerland	30 Dec 58	380UNTS313	105463
Belgium	France	20 Jan 59	361UNTS155	105178
Japan	Norway	21 Feb 59	356UNTS231	105098
Denmark	Japan	10 Mar 59	341UNTS55	104878
Germany, West	Sweden	17 Apr 59	428UNTS155	106175
Australia	Switzerland	21 May 59	341UNTS283	104891
Austria	France	08 Oct 59	453UNTS95	106521
Israel	Sweden	22 Dec 59	377UNTS277	105407
Sweden	UK Great Britain	28 Jul 60	404UNTS85	105806
Sweden	UK Great Britain	28 Jul 60	404UNTS113	105808
Canada	USA (United States)	17 Feb 61	445UNTS143	106383
South Africa	Sweden	29 May 61	442UNTS15	106335
Greece	Sweden	06 Oct 61	481UNTS137	106981
Austria	Denmark	23 Oct 61	425UNTS115	106122
Israel	Sweden	15 May 62	484UNTS261	107036
France	UK Great Britain	21 Jun 63	540UNTS311	107855
Hungary	Mongolia	10 Jul 63	519UNTS173	107508
Denmark	Finland	07 Apr 64	525UNTS89	107586
Sweden	UK Great Britain	14 Oct 64	543UNTS135	107898
Cameroon	France	10 Jul 65	0UNTS0	109433
Denmark	Yugoslavia	11 Apr 68	0UNTS0	109406
Tax credits				
France	USA (United States)	25 Jul 39	125UNTS259	200429
Canada	USA (United States)	04 Mar 42	124UNTS271	200426
UK Great Britain	USA (United States)	16 Apr 45	6UNTS359	200039
Canada	UK Great Britain	05 Jun 46	27UNTS207	100408
South Africa	UK Great Britain	14 Oct 46	86UNTS77	101153
France	USA (United States)	18 Oct 46	140UNTS23	101882
South Africa	USA (United States)	13 Dec 46	167UNTS171	102207
South Africa	USA (United States)	10 Apr 47	167UNTS211	102208
Canada	New Zealand	12 Mar 48	231UNTS219	103222
New Zealand	USA (United States)	16 Mar 48	127UNTS133	101703
Netherlands	UK Great Britain	15 Oct 48	74UNTS3	100955
Sweden	UK Great Britain	30 Mar 49	209UNTS129	102826
Ireland	UK Great Britain	18 May 49	553UNTS209	108089
Norway	USA (United States)	13 Jun 49	127UNTS163	101704
Ireland	USA (United States)	13 Sep 49	127UNTS119	101702
Ireland	USA (United States)	13 Sep 49	127UNTS89	101701
France	Netherlands	30 Dec 49	203UNTS85	102742
Greece	USA (United States)	20 Feb 50	196UNTS269	102629
Greece	USA (United States)	20 Feb 50	196UNTS291	102630
Burma	UK Great Britain	13 Mar 50	131UNTS53	101735
Denmark	UK Great Britain	27 Mar 50	68UNTS117	100891
Canada	USA (United States)	12 Jun 50	127UNTS57	101699
Ceylon (Sri Lanka)	UK Great Britain	26 Jul 50	337UNTS77	104818
Canada	France	16 Mar 51	236UNTS267	103330
Canada	France	16 Mar 51	236UNTS297	103331

PARTY ONE	PARTY TWO	DATE	CITATION	NUMBER
Tax credits (Cont.)				
Norway	UK Great Britain	02 May 51	106UNTS101	101460
Switzerland	USA (United States)	09 Jul 51	165UNTS51	102167
Finland	UK Great Britain	12 Dec 51	172UNTS45	102239
Finland	USA (United States)	03 Mar 52	177UNTS141	102316
Australia	USA (United States)	14 May 53	205UNTS277	102780
Denmark	Sweden	27 Oct 53	198UNTS71	102658
Japan	USA (United States)	16 Apr 54	238UNTS3	103353
Japan	USA (United States)	16 Apr 54	238UNTS39	103354
Switzerland	UK Great Britain	30 Sep 54	209UNTS197	102828
Germany, West	UK Great Britain	18 Oct 54	218UNTS301	102960
Canada	Ireland	28 Oct 54	304UNTS317	104406
Italy	USA (United States)	30 Mar 55	257UNTS199	103655
Italy	USA (United States)	30 Mar 55	257UNTS169	103654
Canada	Denmark	30 Sep 55	258UNTS115	103675
Fed Rhod/Nyasaland	South Africa	22 May 56	254UNTS227	103595
Denmark	Norway	23 May 56	271UNTS49	103909
Switzerland	UK Great Britain	12 Jun 56	269UNTS133	103879
Honduras	USA (United States)	25 Jun 56	279UNTS113	104036
Austria	UK Great Britain	20 Jul 56	269UNTS147	103880
Ceylon (Sri Lanka)	India	10 Sep 56	315UNTS59	104560
Canada	South Africa	28 Sep 56	299UNTS17	104304
Denmark	Switzerland	14 Jan 57	286UNTS27	104160
Italy	Netherlands	24 Jan 57	485UNTS67	107047
Denmark	Netherlands	20 Feb 57	287UNTS41	104179
Ceylon (Sri Lanka)	Sweden	18 May 57	315UNTS85	104561
Australia	Canada	01 Oct 57	392UNTS41	105638
Sweden	United Arab Rep	29 Jul 58	369UNTS323	105264
Pakistan	Sweden	25 Aug 58	369UNTS183	105258
Japan	Norway	21 Feb 59	356UNTS231	105098
Denmark	Japan	10 Mar 59	341UNTS55	104878
Canada	Finland	28 Mar 59	355UNTS3	105072
South Africa	UK Great Britain	18 Jun 59	380UNTS103	105452
South Africa	UK Great Britain	18 Jun 59	380UNTS81	105451
Israel	Sweden	22 Dec 59	377UNTS277	105407
India	Japan	05 Jan 60	384UNTS3	105507
Australia	New Zealand	12 May 60	369UNTS119	105254
Italy	UK Great Britain	04 Jul 60	466UNTS195	106745
Sweden	UK Great Britain	28 Jul 60	404UNTS85	105806
Sweden	UK Great Britain	28 Jul 60	404UNTS113	105808
Canada	USA (United States)	17 Feb 61	445UNTS143	106383
Japan	UK Great Britain	11 Apr 61	420UNTS75	106042
Denmark	Pakistan	04 Sep 61	455UNTS305	106549
Greece	Sweden	06 Oct 61	481UNTS137	106981
Austria	Japan	20 Dec 61	517UNTS155	107485
South Africa	UK Great Britain	28 May 62	443UNTS79	106361
Israel	UK Great Britain	26 Sep 62	474UNTS233	106885
Luxembourg	USA (United States)	18 Dec 62	532UNTS277	107723
Japan	New Zealand	30 Jan 63	517UNTS183	107486
France	Monaco	18 May 63	0UNTS0	109438
Japan	Malaysia	04 Jun 63	517UNTS245	107488
France	Israel	20 Aug 63	515UNTS173	107460
France	Greece	21 Aug 63	533UNTS235	107746
Panama	USA (United States)	30 Aug 63	488UNTS11	107116
Austria	Finland	08 Oct 63	490UNTS255	107160
Norway	Thailand	09 Jan 64	522UNTS65	107537
Belgium	France	10 Mar 64	557UNTS13	108127
Denmark	Finland	07 Apr 64	525UNTS89	107586
Sweden	UK Great Britain	14 Oct 64	543UNTS135	107898
Norway	United Arab Rep	20 Oct 64	543UNTS3	107895
Finland	United Arab Rep	01 Apr 65	562UNTS3	108193
Jamaica	UK Great Britain	02 Apr 65	552UNTS219	108056
Denmark	Thailand	01 Jun 65	551UNTS157	108040
Belgium	Sweden	02 Jul 65	0UNTS0	109367
Cameroon	France	10 Jul 65	0UNTS0	109433
Denmark	Israel	27 Jun 66	581UNTS227	108448
New Zealand	UK Great Britain	13 Jul 66	598UNTS121	108658
Ireland	Switzerland	08 Nov 66	0UNTS0	109499
Australia	UK Great Britain	07 Dec 67	0UNTS0	109458
Denmark	Japan	03 Feb 68	0UNTS0	109405
Denmark	Yugoslavia	11 Apr 68	0UNTS0	109406
Equitable taxes				
France	USA (United States)	25 Jul 39	125UNTS259	200429
Brazil	Canada	17 Oct 41	67UNTS263	200224
Iran	USA (United States)	08 Apr 43	106UNTS155	200340
UK Great Britain	USA (United States)	16 Apr 45	6UNTS189	100076
Greece	UK Great Britain	24 Jan 46	6UNTS45	100067
Canada	Mexico	08 Feb 46	230UNTS183	103183
Taiwan	France	28 Feb 46	14UNTS137	100216
South Africa	USA (United States)	13 Dec 46	167UNTS171	102207
France	UK Great Britain	14 Dec 46	105UNTS27	101452
Canada	Nicaragua	19 Dec 46	236UNTS229	103326
Multilateral		30 Oct 47	55UNTS188	100814
Switzerland	USSR (Soviet Union)	17 Mar 48	217UNTS73	102944
Netherlands	USA (United States)	29 Apr 48	32UNTS167	100498
Denmark	USA (United States)	06 May 48	26UNTS55	100377
Netherlands	UK Great Britain	15 Oct 48	74UNTS3	100955
Sweden	UK Great Britain	30 Mar 49	209UNTS129	102826
Ireland	UK Great Britain	18 May 49	553UNTS209	108089
Ireland	USA (United States)	13 Sep 49	127UNTS89	101701
France	Netherlands	30 Dec 49	203UNTS85	102742
Italy	Netherlands	04 Mar 50	254UNTS305	103598
Burma	UK Great Britain	13 Mar 50	131UNTS53	101735
Denmark	UK Great Britain	27 Mar 50	68UNTS117	100891
Afghanistan	India	04 Apr 50	167UNTS105	102201
Ceylon (Sri Lanka)	UK Great Britain	26 Jul 50	337UNTS77	104818
Netherlands	Norway	29 Dec 50	134UNTS19	101795
Canada	France	16 Mar 51	236UNTS267	103330
Canada	Sweden	06 Apr 51	197UNTS393	102648
Norway	UK Great Britain	02 May 51	106UNTS101	101460
Ireland	Norway	02 Jul 51	100UNTS53	101387
Netherlands	Switzerland	12 Nov 51	126UNTS157	101688
Finland	UK Great Britain	12 Dec 51	172UNTS45	102239
El Salvador	Guatemala	14 Dec 51	131UNTS131	101740
Finland	USA (United States)	03 Mar 52	177UNTS163	102317
Netherlands	Sweden	25 Apr 52	163UNTS131	102147
France	Israel	29 Apr 52	189UNTS55	102542
Belgium	UK Great Britain	27 Mar 53	188UNTS153	102526
Greece	UK Great Britain	25 Jun 53	190UNTS281	102571
Belgium	Finland	11 Feb 54	211UNTS63	102848
Finland	Netherlands	29 Mar 54	252UNTS185	103567
Switzerland	UK Great Britain	30 Sep 54	209UNTS197	102828
Germany, West	UK Great Britain	18 Oct 54	218UNTS301	102960
Pakistan	UK Great Britain	10 Jun 55	243UNTS15	103444
South Africa	Sweden	28 Jul 55	230UNTS287	103191
Belgium	Sweden	18 Jan 56	293UNTS23	104283
Canada	USSR (Soviet Union)	29 Feb 56	252UNTS165	103566
Honduras	USA (United States)	25 Jun 56	279UNTS113	104036
Costa Rica	Denmark	26 Sep 56	341UNTS305	104893
Norway	Sweden	27 Sep 56	261UNTS71	103726
Denmark	Netherlands	20 Feb 57	287UNTS41	104179
Denmark	Norway	22 Feb 57	286UNTS127	104164
Multilateral		25 Mar 57	294UNTS2	104300
Canada	Netherlands	02 Apr 57	285UNTS193	104153
Denmark	Peru	10 Jun 57	406UNTS63	105839
Pakistan	USA (United States)	01 Jul 57	344UNTS203	104951
Albania	USSR (Soviet Union)	15 Feb 58	313UNTS261	104536
Denmark	Sweden	21 Jul 58	320UNTS163	104642
Sweden	United Arab Rep	29 Jul 58	369UNTS323	105264
Germany, West	Norway	18 Nov 58	357UNTS205	105119

PARTY ONE	PARTY TWO	DATE	CITATION	NUMBER
Equitable taxes (Cont.)				
Belgium	France	20 Jan 59	361UNTS155	105178
Japan	Pakistan	17 Feb 59	341UNTS127	104880
Japan	Norway	21 Feb 59	356UNTS231	105098
Japan	Yugoslavia	28 Feb 59	341UNTS179	104883
Denmark	Japan	10 Mar 59	341UNTS55	104878
Canada	Finland	28 Mar 59	355UNTS3	105072
Germany, West	Sweden	17 Apr 59	428UNTS155	106175
Austria	France	08 Oct 59	453UNTS95	106521
Ireland	Sweden	06 Nov 59	428UNTS231	106177
Israel	Sweden	22 Dec 59	377UNTS277	105407
Multilateral		04 Jan 60	370UNTS3	105266
India	Japan	05 Jan 60	384UNTS3	105507
Multilateral		06 Feb 60	383UNTS3	105494
Austria	Norway	25 Feb 60	376UNTS155	105380
France	Thailand	26 Feb 60	392UNTS279	105648
Italy	UK Great Britain	04 Jul 60	466UNTS195	106745
Sweden	UK Great Britain	28 Jul 60	404UNTS113	105808
Japan	UK Great Britain	11 Apr 61	420UNTS75	106042
Czechoslovakia	Morocco	08 Jun 61	497UNTS275	107272
Italy	Norway	25 Aug 61	475UNTS269	106896
Denmark	Pakistan	04 Sep 61	455UNTS305	106549
Greece	Sweden	06 Oct 61	481UNTS137	106981
Sweden	Thailand	20 Oct 61	428UNTS275	106180
Austria	Japan	20 Dec 61	517UNTS155	107485
South Africa	UK Great Britain	28 May 62	443UNTS79	106361
Morocco	Switzerland	05 Jul 62	498UNTS171	107281
Japan	UK Great Britain	04 Sep 62	475UNTS31	106888
Israel	UK Great Britain	26 Sep 62	474UNTS233	106885
Austria	United Arab Rep	16 Oct 62	491UNTS63	107174
Austria	Luxembourg	18 Oct 62	496UNTS97	107248
Japan	UK Great Britain	14 Nov 62	478UNTS29	106934
Ceylon (Sri Lanka)	Denmark	16 Feb 63	486UNTS285	107083
Japan	Thailand	01 Mar 63	475UNTS233	106895
Norway	Spain	25 Apr 63	503UNTS41	107340
France	Japan	14 May 63	518UNTS111	107493
France	Monaco	18 May 63	0UNTS0	109438
Japan	Malaysia	04 Jun 63	517UNTS245	107488
El Salvador	Japan	19 Jul 63	518UNTS135	107494
Tanganyika	USSR (Soviet Union)	14 Aug 63	493UNTS195	107215
France	Israel	20 Aug 63	515UNTS173	107460
France	Greece	21 Aug 63	533UNTS235	107746
Austria	Finland	08 Oct 63	490UNTS255	107160
Norway	Thailand	09 Jan 64	522UNTS65	107537
Mali	Niger	15 Jan 64	499UNTS197	107299
Denmark	Ireland	04 Feb 64	525UNTS233	107596
Belgium	France	10 Mar 64	557UNTS13	108127
Denmark	Finland	07 Apr 64	525UNTS89	107586
Ceylon (Sri Lanka)	Norway	11 Jun 64	559UNTS23	108153
Canada	Japan	05 Sep 64	569UNTS99	108282
Norway	United Arab Rep	20 Oct 64	543UNTS3	107895
Germany, West	UK Great Britain	26 Nov 64	603UNTS183	108734
France	Japan	27 Nov 64	569UNTS157	108283
Finland	Israel	21 Jan 65	581UNTS275	108450
Greece	India	11 Feb 65	606UNTS9	108771
Finland	United Arab Rep	01 Apr 65	562UNTS3	108193
Denmark	Thailand	01 Jun 65	551UNTS157	108040
Belgium	Sweden	02 Jul 65	0UNTS0	109367
Cameroon	France	10 Jul 65	0UNTS0	109433
Finland	Ireland	15 Sep 65	0UNTS0	109372
France	Italy	29 Oct 65	0UNTS0	109445
Denmark	Italy	10 Mar 66	0UNTS0	109217
Iceland	Norway	30 Mar 66	566UNTS51	108240
Denmark	Netherlands	31 Mar 66	604UNTS209	108751
Denmark	Israel	27 Jun 66	581UNTS227	108448
Netherlands	Norway	22 Sep 66	600UNTS227	108683

PARTY ONE	PARTY TWO	DATE	CITATION	NUMBER
Equitable taxes (Cont.)				
Ireland	Switzerland	08 Nov 66	0UNTS0	109499
Singapore	UK Great Britain	01 Dec 66	605UNTS153	108763
Trinidad/Tobago	UK Great Britain	29 Dec 66	605UNTS237	108766
Netherlands	UK Great Britain	31 Oct 67	0UNTS0	109222
Finland	Spain	15 Nov 67	0UNTS0	109375
Australia	UK Great Britain	07 Dec 67	0UNTS0	109458
Denmark	Japan	03 Feb 68	0UNTS0	109405
Italy	UK Great Britain	15 Feb 68	0UNTS0	109263
Cyprus	Greece	30 Mar 68	0UNTS0	109465
Malawi	UK Great Britain	02 Apr 68	0UNTS0	109450
Denmark	Yugoslavia	11 Apr 68	0UNTS0	109406
General				
France	USA (United States)	25 Jul 39	125UNTS259	200429
Canada	USA (United States)	04 Mar 42	124UNTS271	200426
Peru	USA (United States)	07 May 42	103UNTS219	200316
Mexico	USA (United States)	23 Dec 42	13UNTS231	200081
Canada	USA (United States)	23 Feb 43	101UNTS243	200299
Finland	Sweden	10 Mar 43	198UNTS333	200518
Canada	USA (United States)	09 Aug 43	29UNTS295	200168
Canada	USA (United States)	08 Jun 44	124UNTS297	200427
UK Great Britain	USA (United States)	16 Apr 45	6UNTS189	100076
UK Great Britain	USA (United States)	16 Apr 45	6UNTS359	200039
Canada	UK Great Britain	05 Jun 46	27UNTS207	100408
Canada	UK Great Britain	05 Jun 46	86UNTS3	101147
Philippines	USA (United States)	04 Jul 46	43UNTS135	100668
Philippines	USA (United States)	11 Sep 46	43UNTS231	100670
Greece	USA (United States)	08 Oct 46	180UNTS119	102379
South Africa	UK Great Britain	14 Oct 46	86UNTS51	101152
South Africa	UK Great Britain	14 Oct 46	86UNTS77	101153
France	UK Great Britain	14 Dec 46	105UNTS27	101452
Denmark	Norway	30 Dec 46	8UNTS21	100111
France	USA (United States)	04 Apr 47	24UNTS133	100353
South Africa	USA (United States)	10 Apr 47	167UNTS211	102208
Belgium	South Africa	04 Jul 47	47UNTS9	100720
Canada	France	08 Sep 47	253UNTS259	103587
India	Pakistan	10 Dec 47	51UNTS173	100764
Italy	USA (United States)	02 Feb 48	79UNTS171	101040
Canada	New Zealand	12 Mar 48	231UNTS219	103222
Netherlands	USA (United States)	29 Apr 48	32UNTS167	100498
Philippines	USA (United States)	27 Aug 48	44UNTS13	100675
Belgium	Netherlands	25 Sep 48	123UNTS81	101655
Greece	Lebanon	06 Oct 48	87UNTS351	101179
Belgium	Luxembourg	09 Oct 48	123UNTS29	101652
Netherlands	UK Great Britain	15 Oct 48	74UNTS3	100955
Netherlands	UK Great Britain	15 Oct 48	73UNTS203	100954
Sweden	Switzerland	16 Oct 48	197UNTS55	102634
Belgium	USA (United States)	28 Oct 48	173UNTS67	102262
Australia	Belgium	09 Dec 48	25UNTS159	100361
Finland	Sweden	17 Feb 49	197UNTS123	102636
Greece	Norway	12 Mar 49	30UNTS161	100454
Sweden	UK Great Britain	30 Mar 49	209UNTS129	102826
Panama	USA (United States)	31 Mar 49	55UNTS125	100811
Norway	USA (United States)	13 Jun 49	127UNTS189	101705
Ireland	USA (United States)	13 Sep 49	127UNTS89	101701
Norway	Sweden	17 Dec 49	197UNTS215	102641
Finland	Sweden	21 Dec 49	197UNTS243	102642
France	Netherlands	30 Dec 49	203UNTS133	102743
France	Netherlands	30 Dec 49	203UNTS85	102742
Belgium	France	30 Dec 49	46UNTS111	100704
Greece	USA (United States)	20 Feb 50	196UNTS269	102629
Burma	UK Great Britain	13 Mar 50	131UNTS53	101735
Argentina	Greece	21 Mar 50	187UNTS213	102514
Denmark	UK Great Britain	27 Mar 50	68UNTS117	100891
Ceylon (Sri Lanka)	UK Great Britain	26 Jul 50	337UNTS77	104818

PARTY ONE	PARTY TWO	DATE	CITATION	NUMBER
General (Cont.)				
Italy	UK Great Britain	28 Jul 50	101UNTS25	101399
Netherlands	Norway	29 Dec 50	134UNTS19	101795
Australia	Finland	04 Jan 51	80UNTS27	101042
Canada	France	16 Mar 51	236UNTS267	103330
Canada	Sweden	06 Apr 51	197UNTS393	102648
Norway	UK Great Britain	02 May 51	106UNTS101	101460
Switzerland	USA (United States)	24 May 51	127UNTS227	101706
Multilateral		19 Jun 51	199UNTS67	102678
IBRD (World Bank)	Switzerland	29 Jun 51	216UNTS347	200529
Netherlands	Switzerland	12 Nov 51	126UNTS173	101689
Iran	USA (United States)	20 Jan 52	200UNTS191	102703
France	Israel	24 Jan 52	220UNTS55	102988
Belgium	Luxembourg	07 Feb 52	147UNTS3	101924
Japan	USA (United States)	28 Feb 52	208UNTS255	102817
Finland	USA (United States)	03 Mar 52	177UNTS163	102317
Finland	USA (United States)	03 Mar 52	177UNTS141	102316
Italy	USA (United States)	05 Mar 52	179UNTS3	102351
Netherlands	USA (United States)	07 Mar 52	135UNTS199	101821
Luxembourg	USA (United States)	13 Mar 52	168UNTS57	102212
Belgium	USA (United States)	07 Apr 52	205UNTS3	102765
Netherlands	Sweden	25 Apr 52	163UNTS131	102147
Korea, South	USA (United States)	24 May 52	179UNTS23	102353
France	USA (United States)	13 Jun 52	181UNTS3	102393
Multilateral		05 Sep 52	256UNTS3	103619
Denmark	Uruguay	04 Mar 53	250UNTS51	103517
Portugal	USA (United States)	01 Apr 53	205UNTS41	102769
Belgium	Sweden	01 Apr 53	185UNTS225	102473
Australia	USA (United States)	14 May 53	205UNTS237	102778
Australia	USA (United States)	14 May 53	205UNTS253	102779
Greece	UK Great Britain	25 Jun 53	190UNTS281	102571
Belgium	USA (United States)	18 Jul 53	180UNTS9	102371
UNICEF (Children)	UK Great Britain	07 Oct 53	180UNTS59	102375
Denmark	Sweden	27 Oct 53	198UNTS129	102660
Denmark	Sweden	27 Oct 53	198UNTS71	102658
Belgium	Finland	11 Feb 54	211UNTS63	102848
Finland	Netherlands	29 Mar 54	252UNTS185	103567
Canada	Japan	31 Mar 54	236UNTS329	103334
Japan	USA (United States)	16 Apr 54	238UNTS3	103353
Japan	USA (United States)	16 Apr 54	238UNTS39	103354
Netherlands	South Africa	22 Apr 54	211UNTS215	102853
Canada	Spain	26 May 54	391UNTS273	105632
Greece	Sweden	27 May 54	219UNTS147	102971
Canada	Portugal	28 May 54	391UNTS253	105631
Belgium	Greece	23 Jun 54	199UNTS43	102676
Germany, West	USA (United States)	22 Jul 54	239UNTS3	103369
Spain	USA (United States)	30 Jul 54	235UNTS45	103295
Libya	USA (United States)	09 Sep 54	224UNTS217	103078
Switzerland	UK Great Britain	30 Sep 54	209UNTS197	102828
Multilateral		23 Oct 54	332UNTS387	104763
Canada	Ireland	28 Oct 54	304UNTS317	104406
Germany, West	USA (United States)	18 Feb 55	247UNTS257	103474
Italy	USA (United States)	30 Mar 55	257UNTS169	103654
Austria	Romania	11 May 55	342UNTS119	104904
Israel	Norway	24 May 55	220UNTS71	102990
Pakistan	UK Great Britain	10 Jun 55	243UNTS15	103444
Denmark	Finland	18 Jul 55	250UNTS167	103522
South Africa	Sweden	28 Jul 55	230UNTS287	103191
Canada	Denmark	30 Sep 55	258UNTS115	103675
Italy	Syria	10 Nov 55	267UNTS157	103841
Argentina	Switzerland	25 Jan 56	559UNTS121	108157
New Zealand	Sweden	16 Apr 56	274UNTS259	103971
Multilateral		18 May 56	339UNTS3	104844
Fed Rhod/Nyasaland	South Africa	22 May 56	254UNTS227	103595
Denmark	Norway	23 May 56	271UNTS49	103909
Canada	Germany, West	04 Jun 56	316UNTS231	104589

PARTY ONE	PARTY TWO	DATE	CITATION	NUMBER
General (Cont.)				
France	USA (United States)	22 Jun 56	291UNTS101	104246
Austria	UK Great Britain	20 Jul 56	269UNTS147	103880
Guatemala	Honduras	22 Aug 56	263UNTS49	103767
Norway	Sweden	27 Sep 56	261UNTS71	103726
Austria	USA (United States)	25 Oct 56	299UNTS123	104310
Japan	Sweden	12 Dec 56	318UNTS309	104623
Multilateral		14 Dec 56	436UNTS131	106293
Multilateral		14 Dec 56	436UNTS115	106292
Finland	Switzerland	27 Dec 56	277UNTS7	103996
Denmark	Switzerland	14 Jan 57	286UNTS27	104160
Denmark	Netherlands	20 Feb 57	287UNTS41	104179
Dominican Republic	USA (United States)	09 Mar 57	279UNTS249	104044
Multilateral		25 Mar 57	294UNTS2	104300
Canada	Netherlands	02 Apr 57	285UNTS193	104153
Paraguay	USA (United States)	04 Apr 57	283UNTS193	104117
Austria	USSR (Soviet Union)	14 Jun 57	285UNTS169	104152
Pakistan	USA (United States)	01 Jul 57	344UNTS203	104951
Italy	Switzerland	19 Sep 57	363UNTS69	105200
Australia	Canada	01 Oct 57	392UNTS41	105638
France	Morocco	25 Oct 57	559UNTS95	108156
Japan	USSR (Soviet Union)	06 Dec 57	325UNTS35	104694
India	Japan	04 Feb 58	324UNTS215	104687
Multilateral		10 Jun 58	454UNTS47	106539
Denmark	Sweden	21 Jul 58	320UNTS163	104642
Sweden	United Arab Rep	29 Jul 58	369UNTS323	105264
Pakistan	Sweden	25 Aug 58	369UNTS183	105258
Nicaragua	USA (United States)	05 Sep 58	336UNTS33	104797
Iraq	USSR (Soviet Union)	11 Oct 58	328UNTS117	104731
France	UK Great Britain	28 Nov 58	351UNTS263	105027
Japan	Norway	21 Feb 59	356UNTS231	105098
Denmark	Japan	10 Mar 59	341UNTS55	104878
Canada	Finland	28 Mar 59	355UNTS3	105072
Germany, West	Sweden	17 Apr 59	428UNTS155	106175
Austria	Sweden	14 May 59	428UNTS3	106167
Argentina	Sweden	12 Jun 59	427UNTS337	106164
Germany, West	Netherlands	16 Jun 59	593UNTS3	108576
Taiwan	USA (United States)	22 Jul 59	357UNTS293	105121
Denmark	France	17 Sep 59	410UNTS141	105901
Canada	Switzerland	22 Sep 59	470UNTS101	106800
Korea, South	USA (United States)	01 Oct 59	358UNTS115	105129
Ireland	Sweden	06 Nov 59	428UNTS231	106177
Ethiopia	France	12 Nov 59	381UNTS3	105465
Czechoslovakia	Japan	15 Dec 59	383UNTS277	105505
Israel	Sweden	22 Dec 59	377UNTS277	105407
India	Japan	05 Jan 60	384UNTS3	105507
India	Japan	25 Jan 60	384UNTS31	105508
Cuba	USSR (Soviet Union)	13 Feb 60	369UNTS17	105248
Finland	Iceland	10 Mar 60	497UNTS95	107264
Cuba	Japan	22 Apr 60	442UNTS261	106354
Australia	New Zealand	12 May 60	369UNTS119	105254
Morocco	United Arab Rep	19 May 60	563UNTS121	108208
UK Great Britain	USA (United States)	24 Jun 60	377UNTS63	105396
Sweden	UK Great Britain	28 Jul 60	404UNTS113	105808
Iran	Japan	12 Sep 60	384UNTS43	105509
Multilateral		13 Dec 60	455UNTS3	106543
Canada	USA (United States)	17 Feb 61	445UNTS143	106383
Korea, South	Philippines	24 Feb 61	423UNTS217	106094
Congo (Zaire)	United Nations	12 Jun 61	494UNTS205	107234
Finland	India	23 Jun 61	421UNTS49	106051
Italy	Norway	25 Aug 61	475UNTS269	106896
Denmark	Pakistan	04 Sep 61	455UNTS305	106549
Austria	Japan	20 Dec 61	517UNTS155	107485
Canada	Ghana	08 Jan 62	528UNTS221	107645
South Africa	UK Great Britain	28 May 62	443UNTS79	106361
Pakistan	USA (United States)	31 May 62	460UNTS75	106631

PARTY ONE	PARTY TWO	DATE	CITATION	NUMBER
General (Cont.)				
Germany, West	Israel	09 Jul 62	630UNTS87	108968
Honduras	USA (United States)	20 Jul 62	460UNTS125	106635
Niger	USA (United States)	23 Jul 62	487UNTS325	107114
Ecuador	USA (United States)	03 Aug 62	460UNTS133	106636
UK Great Britain	USA (United States)	15 Aug 62	580UNTS189	108421
Cyprus	USA (United States)	23 Aug 62	461UNTS147	106658
Nepal	USA (United States)	24 Aug 62	460UNTS143	106637
Turkey	USA (United States)	27 Aug 62	461UNTS55	106651
Belgium	Luxembourg	30 Aug 62	485UNTS313	107062
Japan	UK Great Britain	04 Sep 62	475UNTS31	106888
Togo	USA (United States)	05 Sep 62	461UNTS47	106650
Belgium	Rwanda	13 Oct 62	456UNTS431	106569
Germany, West	Ireland	17 Oct 62	604UNTS135	108749
Hungary	Syria	18 Oct 62	491UNTS209	107178
Multilateral		25 Oct 62	457UNTS137	106583
Multilateral		25 Oct 62	457UNTS129	106582
Norway	Sweden	31 Oct 62	466UNTS361	106755
Japan	UK Great Britain	14 Nov 62	478UNTS29	106934
Ceylon (Sri Lanka)	USA (United States)	21 Nov 62	462UNTS237	106683
Multilateral		08 Dec 62	510UNTS235	107418
Austria	Yugoslavia	11 Dec 62	546UNTS3	107938
Ghana	Tunisia	11 Dec 62	563UNTS243	108213
Guinea	USA (United States)	14 Dec 62	462UNTS247	106684
Luxembourg	USA (United States)	18 Dec 62	532UNTS277	107723
Japan	New Zealand	30 Jan 63	517UNTS183	107486
South Africa	Spain	08 Feb 63	458UNTS79	106593
Japan	Thailand	01 Mar 63	475UNTS233	106895
Greece	Hungary	27 Apr 63	534UNTS3	107750
Australia	USA (United States)	09 May 63	469UNTS55	106784
France	Monaco	18 May 63	0UNTS0	109438
USA (United States)	Uruguay	31 Jul 63	488UNTS3	107115
France	USA (United States)	01 Aug 63	527UNTS89	107619
France	Israel	20 Aug 63	515UNTS173	107460
Sweden	USA (United States)	22 Oct 63	530UNTS247	107686
Czechoslovakia	Hungary	20 Dec 63	538UNTS127	107812
Belgium	France	10 Mar 64	557UNTS13	108127
Multilateral		25 May 64	620UNTS149	108953
Czechoslovakia	Netherlands	11 Jun 64	556UNTS89	108120
Belgium	Tunisia	15 Jul 64	560UNTS65	108169
Canada	Japan	05 Sep 64	569UNTS99	108282
Argentina	France	03 Oct 64	635UNTS155	109080
Multilateral		25 Nov 64	587UNTS19	108507
Germany, West	UK Great Britain	26 Nov 64	603UNTS183	108734
France	Japan	27 Nov 64	569UNTS157	108283
Greece	India	11 Feb 65	606UNTS9	108771
Belgium	Luxembourg	11 Mar 65	540UNTS297	107854
Malaysia	UK Great Britain	07 May 65	552UNTS259	108058
Netherlands	Senegal	12 Jun 65	602UNTS231	108715
Cameroon	France	10 Jul 65	0UNTS0	109433
UK Great Britain	USA (United States)	09 Aug 65	580UNTS181	108420
Australia	New Zealand	31 Aug 65	554UNTS169	108101
Finland	Ireland	15 Sep 65	0UNTS0	109372
Belgium	Denmark	20 Sep 65	549UNTS63	107990
France	Italy	29 Oct 65	0UNTS0	109445
UK Great Britain	USA (United States)	10 Nov 65	580UNTS197	108422
Saudi Arabia	USA (United States)	19 Nov 65	580UNTS35	108419
Canada	UK Great Britain	06 Dec 65	572UNTS161	108311
Ireland	UK Great Britain	14 Dec 65	565UNTS58	108235
Denmark	Italy	10 Mar 66	643UNTS349	109201
Denmark	Italy	10 Mar 66	0UNTS0	109217
Brazil	IBRD (World Bank)	15 Mar 66	599UNTS52	108664
Iceland	Norway	30 Mar 66	566UNTS51	108240
Denmark	Netherlands	31 Mar 66	604UNTS209	108751
Austria	Ireland	24 May 66	636UNTS149	109102
New Zealand	UK Great Britain	13 Jul 66	598UNTS121	108658

PARTY ONE	PARTY TWO	DATE	CITATION	NUMBER
General (Cont.)				
Argentina	Germany, West	13 Jul 66	636UNTS3	109091
Belgium	Spain	19 Jul 66	575UNTS3	108352
Israel	Norway	02 Nov 66	630UNTS225	108972
Ireland	Switzerland	08 Nov 66	0UNTS0	109499
Singapore	UK Great Britain	01 Dec 66	605UNTS153	108763
France	Monaco	09 Dec 66	0UNTS0	109439
Brazil	IBRD (World Bank)	19 Dec 66	599UNTS177	108667
Brazil	IBRD (World Bank)	19 Dec 66	599UNTS107	108665
Brazil	IBRD (World Bank)	19 Dec 66	599UNTS205	108668
Brazil	IBRD (World Bank)	19 Dec 66	599UNTS149	108666
Austria	Spain	20 Dec 66	636UNTS197	109103
Asian Devel Bank	Philippines	22 Dec 66	615UNTS375	108887
Trinidad/Tobago	UK Great Britain	29 Dec 66	605UNTS237	108766
Korea, South	USA (United States)	09 Feb 67	0UNTS0	109605
Kenya	IBRD (World Bank)	17 Feb 67	599UNTS233	108669
IBRD (World Bank)	Tanzania	17 Feb 67	599UNTS287	108671
East Afri Service	IBRD (World Bank)	17 Feb 67	599UNTS335	200629
IBRD (World Bank)	Yugoslavia	24 Feb 67	599UNTS27	108663
Pakistan	IBRD (World Bank)	15 Mar 67	599UNTS245	108670
Belgium	Hungary	20 Mar 67	601UNTS37	108686
South Africa	Switzerland	03 Jul 67	643UNTS3	109184
Malaysia	UK Great Britain	17 Jul 67	637UNTS0	109127
Netherlands	UK Great Britain	31 Oct 67	0UNTS0	109222
Argentina	Chile	06 Nov 67	636UNTS111	109097
Finland	Spain	15 Nov 67	0UNTS0	109375
Australia	UK Great Britain	07 Dec 67	0UNTS0	109458
Denmark	Japan	03 Feb 68	0UNTS0	109405
Austria	Poland	05 Feb 68	0UNTS0	109213
Italy	UK Great Britain	15 Feb 68	0UNTS0	109263
Cyprus	Greece	30 Mar 68	0UNTS0	109465
Denmark	Yugoslavia	11 Apr 68	0UNTS0	109406
Taxation of immovable property				
Canada	UK Great Britain	05 Jun 46	86UNTS3	101147
Norway	Spain	25 Apr 63	503UNTS41	107340
Belgium	Cyprus	08 Jun 63	601UNTS311	108703
Cyprus	Hungary	02 Jun 64	602UNTS3	108704
Cyprus	Syria	22 Dec 64	602UNTS25	108705
Income taxes				
Italy	Spain	31 May 49	231UNTS251	103224
Nicaragua	USA (United States)	02 Sep 53	215UNTS69	102911
Nicaragua	USA (United States)	21 Jan 56	367UNTS3	105224
Albania	USSR (Soviet Union)	30 Jun 58	328UNTS3	104729
Taxation of professional services				
Philippines	USA (United States)	27 Aug 48	44UNTS13	100675
Multilateral		24 Apr 63	596UNTS261	108638
Taxable items				
Kenya	USA (United States)	26 Aug 64	531UNTS51	107692
Tax exemptions				
Canada	France	12 May 33	253UNTS285	200545
Bolivia	Brazil	25 Feb 38	88UNTS379	200254
France	USA (United States)	25 Jul 39	125UNTS259	200429
Panama	USA (United States)	23 Mar 40	124UNTS195	200420
Panama	USA (United States)	06 Sep 40	124UNTS209	200421
Multilateral		27 Mar 41	67UNTS231	200222
Panama	USA (United States)	28 Mar 41	103UNTS163	200312
Haiti	USA (United States)	23 May 41	117UNTS191	200370
Brazil	Paraguay	14 Jun 41	54UNTS289	200201
Bolivia	USA (United States)	04 Sep 41	8UNTS345	200046
Canada	USA (United States)	04 Mar 42	124UNTS271	200426
Peru	USA (United States)	11 Mar 42	117UNTS266	200375
Canada	USA (United States)	18 Mar 42	101UNTS205	200294
Peru	USA (United States)	21 Apr 42	89UNTS317	200260
Brazil	USA (United States)	07 May 42	6UNTS377	200040

PARTY ONE	PARTY TWO	DATE	CITATION	NUMBER
Tax exemptions (Cont.)				
Colombia	USA (United States)	29 May 42	8UNTS365	200047
Canada	USA (United States)	27 Jun 42	99UNTS223	200276
Panama	USA (United States)	07 Jul 42	9UNTS289	200048
Brazil	USA (United States)	17 Jul 42	102UNTS203	200303
Ecuador	USA (United States)	29 Oct 42	89UNTS301	200259
Canada	USA (United States)	04 Nov 42	24UNTS217	200146
El Salvador	USA (United States)	02 Dec 42	122UNTS277	200410
Dominican Republic	USA (United States)	25 Jan 43	13UNTS399	200083
Colombia	USA (United States)	29 Mar 43	124UNTS139	200416
Guatemala	USA (United States)	17 Jul 43	28UNTS431	200166
Canada	USA (United States)	09 Aug 43	29UNTS295	200168
Paraguay	USA (United States)	27 Oct 43	29UNTS391	200174
Brazil	USA (United States)	25 Nov 43	102UNTS227	200305
Iran	USA (United States)	27 Nov 43	31UNTS451	200176
Paraguay	USA (United States)	10 Dec 43	21UNTS305	200131
Liberia	USA (United States)	31 Dec 43	106UNTS199	200341
USA (United States)	Venezuela	13 Jan 44	109UNTS171	200358
Multilateral		15 Jan 44	161UNTS281	200489
Peru	USA (United States)	15 Apr 44	150UNTS317	200479
Ecuador	USA (United States)	29 Jun 44	80UNTS283	200250
Peru	USA (United States)	10 Jul 44	117UNTS291	200377
Guatemala	USA (United States)	15 Jul 44	106UNTS285	200347
Brazil	Paraguay	11 Aug 44	67UNTS303	200227
Bolivia	USA (United States)	07 Sep 44	162UNTS315	200494
Guatemala	USA (United States)	16 Sep 44	135UNTS315	200444
Brazil	USA (United States)	29 Sep 44	65UNTS271	200216
Ecuador	USA (United States)	22 Jan 45	24UNTS273	200152
Guatemala	USA (United States)	21 Feb 45	121UNTS133	200396
UK Great Britain	USA (United States)	16 Apr 45	6UNTS189	100076
Guatemala	USA (United States)	21 May 45	121UNTS185	200399
Chile	USA (United States)	24 May 45	121UNTS219	200401
Dominican Republic	USA (United States)	13 Oct 45	149UNTS361	200477
USSR (Soviet Union)	Yugoslavia	13 Nov 45	116UNTS139	101573
Costa Rica	USA (United States)	10 Dec 45	3UNTS157	100029
Honduras	USA (United States)	28 Dec 45	3UNTS185	100031
Taiwan	France	28 Feb 46	14UNTS113	100215
Belgium	UK Great Britain	11 Mar 46	26UNTS167	100387
Brazil	USA (United States)	05 Apr 46	12UNTS131	100183
Portugal	USA (United States)	30 May 46	174UNTS187	102285
Canada	UK Great Britain	05 Jun 46	27UNTS207	100408
Hungary	USA (United States)	09 Aug 46	148UNTS313	101941
Albania	Yugoslavia	03 Oct 46	111UNTS227	101537
Peru	USA (United States)	07 Oct 46	7UNTS71	100092
Colombia	USA (United States)	14 Oct 46	7UNTS97	100093
South Africa	UK Great Britain	14 Oct 46	86UNTS77	101153
Australia	UK Great Britain	29 Oct 46	17UNTS181	100276
Albania	Yugoslavia	28 Nov 46	111UNTS151	101528
Albania	Yugoslavia	28 Nov 46	111UNTS93	101520
Albania	Yugoslavia	28 Nov 46	111UNTS113	101523
South Africa	USA (United States)	13 Dec 46	167UNTS171	102207
France	UK Great Britain	14 Dec 46	105UNTS27	101452
Finland	USA (United States)	07 Jan 47	15UNTS273	100243
USSR (Soviet Union)	Yugoslavia	04 Feb 47	130UNTS235	101731
USSR (Soviet Union)	Yugoslavia	04 Feb 47	116UNTS171	101576
Multilateral		10 Feb 47	41UNTS21	100643
Burma	USA (United States)	28 Feb 47	25UNTS27	100355
Philippines	USA (United States)	14 Mar 47	43UNTS271	100673
Austria	France	15 Mar 47	12UNTS109	100182
Netherlands	USA (United States)	11 Apr 47	148UNTS343	101943
France	IBRD (World Bank)	09 May 47	152UNTS111	102014
Hungary	Yugoslavia	11 May 47	130UNTS171	101730
Philippines	USA (United States)	12 May 47	16UNTS137	100254
Philippines	USA (United States)	12 May 47	16UNTS109	100252
Philippines	USA (United States)	12 May 47	16UNTS123	100253
Honduras	USA (United States)	13 May 47	166UNTS159	102189

PARTY ONE	PARTY TWO	DATE	CITATION	NUMBER
Tax exemptions (Cont.)				
Bulgaria	Czechoslovakia	20 Jun 47	46UNTS15	100698
Norway	Sweden	21 Jun 47	94UNTS107	101309
Ecuador	USA (United States)	21 Jun 47	26UNTS275	100391
Austria	USA (United States)	25 Jun 47	22UNTS141	100334
Italy	USA (United States)	04 Jul 47	22UNTS173	100336
Belgium	USA (United States)	23 Jul 47	33UNTS33	100512
Netherlands	IBRD (World Bank)	07 Aug 47	152UNTS165	102015
El Salvador	USA (United States)	19 Aug 47	51UNTS57	100752
Denmark	IBRD (World Bank)	22 Aug 47	152UNTS223	102016
Finland	UNICEF (Children)	23 Aug 47	68UNTS224	200233
Bulgaria	UNICEF (Children)	23 Aug 47	68UNTS223	200232
Romania	UNICEF (Children)	28 Aug 47	68UNTS228	200235
Luxembourg	IBRD (World Bank)	28 Aug 47	153UNTS3	102017
Hungary	UNICEF (Children)	28 Aug 47	68UNTS226	200234
Belgium	Netherlands	29 Aug 47	36UNTS349	100573
Canada	France	08 Sep 47	253UNTS259	103587
Iran	USA (United States)	06 Oct 47	11UNTS303	100171
Greece	UNICEF (Children)	14 Oct 47	102UNTS39	101409
Bolivia	USA (United States)	03 Nov 47	51UNTS33	100750
Italy	UNICEF (Children)	06 Nov 47	68UNTS240	200236
Austria	UNICEF (Children)	07 Nov 47	68UNTS252	200237
Ecuador	USA (United States)	14 Nov 47	149UNTS297	101959
UNICEF (Children)	Yugoslavia	20 Nov 47	65UNTS28	100817
Guatemala	USA (United States)	05 Jan 48	135UNTS104	101817
Costa Rica	USA (United States)	12 Jan 48	70UNTS27	100896
France	Lebanon	24 Jan 48	173UNTS99	102263
Greece	United Nations	12 Feb 48	47UNTS223	100732
France	United Nations	10 Mar 48	47UNTS203	100731
Paraguay	USA (United States)	12 Mar 48	162UNTS30	102131
Canada	New Zealand	12 Mar 48	231UNTS219	103222
New Zealand	USA (United States)	16 Mar 48	127UNTS133	101703
Philippines	USA (United States)	23 Mar 48	43UNTS247	100671
USA (United States)	Venezuela	24 Mar 48	44UNTS57	100678
Belgium	Netherlands	13 Apr 48	32UNTS153	100497
Belgium	France	13 Apr 48	31UNTS409	100483
Greece	USA (United States)	23 Apr 48	74UNTS107	100958
Netherlands	USA (United States)	29 Apr 48	32UNTS167	100498
Denmark	USA (United States)	06 May 48	26UNTS55	100377
Ecuador	USA (United States)	14 May 48	89UNTS71	101210
Guatemala	USA (United States)	18 May 48	67UNTS161	100875
Finland	United Nations	20 May 48	47UNTS319	200189
Netherlands	IBRD (World Bank)	15 Jul 48	153UNTS259	102021
Netherlands	IBRD (World Bank)	15 Jul 48	153UNTS259	102025
Netherlands	IBRD (World Bank)	15 Jul 48	153UNTS259	102023
Netherlands	IBRD (World Bank)	15 Jul 48	153UNTS259	102022
Netherlands	IBRD (World Bank)	15 Jul 48	153UNTS259	102024
Brazil	USA (United States)	29 Jul 48	80UNTS111	101047
Pakistan	United Nations	27 Aug 48	47UNTS269	100734
Belgium	Netherlands	25 Sep 48	123UNTS81	101655
United Nations	Thailand	05 Oct 48	47UNTS287	100735
Argentina	USA (United States)	06 Oct 48	80UNTS91	101046
United Nations	San Marino	07 Oct 48	47UNTS337	200190
Czechoslovakia	United Nations	07 Oct 48	47UNTS185	100730
Netherlands	UK Great Britain	15 Oct 48	74UNTS3	100955
Sweden	Switzerland	16 Oct 48	197UNTS55	102634
Belgium	USA (United States)	28 Oct 48	173UNTS67	102262
Argentina	Sweden	20 Nov 48	197UNTS47	102633
Brazil	USA (United States)	26 Nov 48	88UNTS3	101180
Argentina	Denmark	15 Dec 48	67UNTS71	100866
Italy	USA (United States)	18 Dec 48	79UNTS133	101037
Haiti	USA (United States)	04 Jan 49	44UNTS69	100679
Mexico	IBRD (World Bank)	06 Jan 49	154UNTS3	102027
Mexico	IBRD (World Bank)	06 Jan 49	154UNTS81	102028
Argentina	Netherlands	15 Jan 49	46UNTS241	100713
Brazil	IBRD (World Bank)	27 Jan 49	153UNTS264	102026

PARTY ONE	PARTY TWO	DATE	CITATION	NUMBER
Tax exemptions (Cont.)				
Finland	Sweden	17 Feb 49	197UNTS123	102636
Colombia	USA (United States)	21 Feb 49	44UNTS83	100680
Colombia	USA (United States)	21 Feb 49	92UNTS227	101275
Belgium	IBRD (World Bank)	01 Mar 49	154UNTS133	102029
Argentina	UK Great Britain	14 Mar 49	83UNTS193	101108
United Nations	UK Great Britain	18 Mar 49	47UNTS305	100736
Chile	IBRD (World Bank)	23 Mar 49	153UNTS141	102019
Austria	USA (United States)	23 Mar 49	43UNTS127	100667
Chile	IBRD (World Bank)	23 Mar 49	153UNTS61	102018
Peru	USA (United States)	25 Mar 49	89UNTS15	101205
Sweden	UK Great Britain	30 Mar 49	209UNTS129	102826
Panama	USA (United States)	31 Mar 49	55UNTS141	100812
Haiti	USA (United States)	14 Apr 49	80UNTS37	101043
Bulgaria	Poland	16 May 49	84UNTS313	101140
Netherlands	USA (United States)	17 May 49	46UNTS291	100717
Ireland	UK Great Britain	18 May 49	553UNTS209	108089
Norway	USA (United States)	25 May 49	32UNTS345	100507
Philippines	USA (United States)	07 Jun 49	45UNTS63	100692
Norway	USA (United States)	13 Jun 49	127UNTS189	101705
Norway	USA (United States)	13 Jun 49	127UNTS163	101704
Peru	USA (United States)	20 Jun 49	92UNTS249	101276
Mexico	USA (United States)	21 Jun 49	89UNTS3	101204
Mexico	USA (United States)	05 Jul 49	68UNTS55	100884
Argentina	Belgium	25 Jul 49	46UNTS103	100703
Netherlands	IBRD (World Bank)	26 Jul 49	154UNTS178	102030
Finland	IBRD (World Bank)	01 Aug 49	156UNTS289	200480
Argentina	Canada	06 Aug 49	231UNTS43	103202
WHO (World Health)	Thailand	12 Aug 49	178UNTS347	102350
India	IBRD (World Bank)	18 Aug 49	154UNTS269	102031
Colombia	IBRD (World Bank)	19 Aug 49	154UNTS329	102032
USSR (Soviet Union)	Yugoslavia	31 Aug 49	116UNTS345	101580
Ireland	USA (United States)	13 Sep 49	127UNTS89	101701
IBRD (World Bank)	Yugoslavia	17 Sep 49	155UNTS3	102034
India	IBRD (World Bank)	29 Sep 49	154UNTS393	102033
Finland	IBRD (World Bank)	17 Oct 49	156UNTS355	200481
Australia	USA (United States)	26 Nov 49	45UNTS133	100695
Afghanistan	WHO (World Health)	04 Dec 49	102UNTS117	101414
El Salvador	IBRD (World Bank)	14 Dec 49	155UNTS43	102035
Finland	Sweden	21 Dec 49	197UNTS243	102642
France	Netherlands	30 Dec 49	203UNTS85	102742
Korea, South	USA (United States)	26 Jan 50	178UNTS97	102337
Norway	USA (United States)	27 Jan 50	80UNTS241	101055
Netherlands	USA (United States)	27 Jan 50	80UNTS219	101054
Italy	USA (United States)	27 Jan 50	80UNTS145	101050
Luxembourg	USA (United States)	27 Jan 50	80UNTS187	101052
France	USA (United States)	27 Jan 50	80UNTS171	101051
Denmark	USA (United States)	27 Jan 50	48UNTS115	100740
Belgium	USA (United States)	27 Jan 50	51UNTS213	100767
India	USA (United States)	02 Feb 50	89UNTS127	101214
UNICEF (Children)	UK Great Britain	10 Feb 50	65UNTS86	100837
Ceylon (Sri Lanka)	WHO (World Health)	17 Feb 50	102UNTS309	200309
Greece	USA (United States)	20 Feb 50	196UNTS291	102630
Greece	USA (United States)	20 Feb 50	196UNTS269	102629
Chile	UNICEF (Children)	03 Mar 50	126UNTS119	101685
Honduras	USA (United States)	06 Mar 50	80UNTS51	101044
Honduras	USA (United States)	06 Mar 50	80UNTS71	101045
Burma	UK Great Britain	13 Mar 50	131UNTS53	101735
Indonesia	UNICEF (Children)	06 Apr 50	68UNTS254	200238
India	IBRD (World Bank)	18 Apr 50	155UNTS117	102036
Mexico	IBRD (World Bank)	28 Apr 50	155UNTS185	102037
Korea, South	USA (United States)	28 Apr 50	93UNTS21	101284
Iran	USA (United States)	23 May 50	81UNTS3	101057
Brazil	IBRD (World Bank)	26 May 50	301UNTS165	104345
Austria	USA (United States)	06 Jun 50	92UNTS201	101273
Ceylon (Sri Lanka)	UNICEF (Children)	07 Jun 50	68UNTS256	200239

PARTY ONE	PARTY TWO	DATE	CITATION	NUMBER
Tax exemptions (Cont.)				
Canada	USA (United States)	12 Jun 50	127UNTS57	101699
Canada	USA (United States)	12 Jun 50	127UNTS67	101700
Iraq	IBRD (World Bank)	15 Jun 50	155UNTS267	102038
Haiti	WHO (World Health)	27 Jun 50	110UNTS99	101504
Thailand	USA (United States)	01 Jul 50	81UNTS61	101063
IBRD (World Bank)	Turkey	07 Jul 50	156UNTS3	102039
IBRD (World Bank)	Turkey	07 Jul 50	156UNTS75	102040
Argentina	USA (United States)	20 Jul 50	89UNTS63	101209
UK Great Britain	USA (United States)	21 Jul 50	97UNTS193	101351
Ceylon (Sri Lanka)	UK Great Britain	26 Jul 50	337UNTS77	104818
USA (United States)	Venezuela	23 Aug 50	92UNTS341	101279
IBRD (World Bank)	Uruguay	25 Aug 50	156UNTS203	102042
WHO (World Health)	Venezuela	11 Sep 50	110UNTS237	101513
Ethiopia	IBRD (World Bank)	13 Sep 50	157UNTS233	102056
Ethiopia	IBRD (World Bank)	13 Sep 50	157UNTS213	102055
Pakistan	USA (United States)	23 Sep 50	82UNTS131	101088
Iceland	WHO (World Health)	06 Oct 50	110UNTS127	101506
Mexico	IBRD (World Bank)	18 Oct 50	157UNTS259	102057
IBRD (World Bank)	Turkey	19 Oct 50	157UNTS333	102058
Iran	USA (United States)	19 Oct 50	92UNTS135	101266
WHO (World Health)	Turkey	19 Oct 50	110UNTS215	101512
IBRD (World Bank)	Thailand	27 Oct 50	158UNTS3	102059
IBRD (World Bank)	Thailand	27 Oct 50	158UNTS43	102061
IBRD (World Bank)	Thailand	27 Oct 50	158UNTS25	102060
Ceylon (Sri Lanka)	USA (United States)	07 Nov 50	92UNTS125	101265
Peru	WHO (World Health)	10 Nov 50	110UNTS187	101510
Nicaragua	WHO (World Health)	10 Nov 50	110UNTS155	101508
Australia	IBRD (World Bank)	14 Nov 50	156UNTS147	102041
Greece	UK Great Britain	16 Nov 50	166UNTS281	102193
Colombia	USA (United States)	24 Nov 50	133UNTS49	101779
Denmark	South Africa	30 Nov 50	84UNTS51	101118
France	Greece	09 Dec 50	166UNTS315	102196
Brazil	USA (United States)	19 Dec 50	141UNTS3	101900
Panama	USA (United States)	20 Dec 50	92UNTS167	101269
Cuba	USA (United States)	22 Dec 50	122UNTS97	101640
Liberia	USA (United States)	22 Dec 50	92UNTS145	101267
Multilateral		23 Dec 50	185UNTS3	102456
Nicaragua	USA (United States)	23 Dec 50	92UNTS155	101268
Italy	Yugoslavia	23 Dec 50	171UNTS291	102233
Philippines	WHO (World Health)	28 Dec 50	110UNTS203	101511
Colombia	IBRD (World Bank)	28 Dec 50	158UNTS87	102063
India	USA (United States)	28 Dec 50	99UNTS39	101369
Netherlands	Norway	29 Dec 50	134UNTS19	101795
Paraguay	USA (United States)	29 Dec 50	122UNTS157	101645
Liberia	USA (United States)	11 Jan 51	122UNTS125	101642
Costa Rica	USA (United States)	11 Jan 51	92UNTS179	101270
Chile	USA (United States)	16 Jan 51	151UNTS147	101990
Costa Rica	USA (United States)	17 Jan 51	134UNTS215	101801
Saudi Arabia	USA (United States)	17 Jan 51	140UNTS335	101897
IBRD (World Bank)	South Africa	23 Jan 51	158UNTS115	102064
Nepal	USA (United States)	23 Jan 51	184UNTS65	102439
IBRD (World Bank)	South Africa	23 Jan 51	158UNTS135	102065
Panama	USA (United States)	26 Jan 51	137UNTS69	101849
Afghanistan	USA (United States)	07 Feb 51	132UNTS265	101766
Pakistan	USA (United States)	09 Feb 51	100UNTS67	101388
Chile	USA (United States)	15 Feb 51	133UNTS117	101784
Chile	USA (United States)	15 Feb 51	133UNTS95	101783
Paraguay	WHO (World Health)	15 Feb 51	110UNTS171	101509
Ethiopia	IBRD (World Bank)	19 Feb 51	186UNTS101	102486
Dominican Republic	USA (United States)	20 Feb 51	132UNTS305	101770
Israel	USA (United States)	26 Feb 51	137UNTS57	101848
Jordan	USA (United States)	27 Feb 51	141UNTS55	101905
Israel	USA (United States)	28 Feb 51	220UNTS79	102991
Colombia	USA (United States)	09 Mar 51	141UNTS15	101901
Bolivia	USA (United States)	14 Mar 51	132UNTS319	101771

PARTY ONE	PARTY TWO	DATE	CITATION	NUMBER
Tax exemptions (Cont.)				
Canada	France	16 Mar 51	236UNTS267	103330
El Salvador	USA (United States)	19 Mar 51	134UNTS245	101803
Indonesia	WHO (World Health)	28 Mar 51	103UNTS71	101425
Jordan	WHO (World Health)	03 Apr 51	110UNTS297	200367
Canada	Sweden	06 Apr 51	197UNTS393	102648
Colombia	IBRD (World Bank)	10 Apr 51	158UNTS155	102066
Iraq	USA (United States)	10 Apr 51	151UNTS179	101993
Nicaragua	USA (United States)	20 Apr 51	138UNTS57	101859
Honduras	WHO (World Health)	20 Apr 51	110UNTS111	101505
Honduras	USA (United States)	24 Apr 51	140UNTS287	101894
Ethiopia	USA (United States)	02 May 51	139UNTS85	101877
Haiti	USA (United States)	02 May 51	151UNTS191	101994
Norway	UK Great Britain	02 May 51	106UNTS101	101460
Belgium	Czechoslovakia	02 May 51	109UNTS3	101483
Ecuador	USA (United States)	03 May 51	141UNTS27	101902
Colombia	WHO (World Health)	04 May 51	110UNTS83	101503
United Arab Rep	USA (United States)	05 May 51	198UNTS265	102670
Ceylon (Sri Lanka)	USA (United States)	14 May 51	141UNTS159	101913
Switzerland	USA (United States)	24 May 51	127UNTS227	101706
South Africa	Sweden	25 May 51	197UNTS425	102649
Lebanon	USA (United States)	29 May 51	160UNTS49	102101
Cambodia	WHO (World Health)	31 May 51	102UNTS279	200307
Lebanon	WHO (World Health)	05 Jun 51	104UNTS225	101443
Nicaragua	IBRD (World Bank)	07 Jun 51	158UNTS215	102067
Nicaragua	IBRD (World Bank)	07 Jun 51	158UNTS277	102068
WHO (World Health)	Uruguay	11 Jun 51	128UNTS251	101724
Liberia	WHO (World Health)	11 Jun 51	103UNTS83	101426
Multilateral		15 Jun 51	148UNTS67	101936
UK Great Britain	USA (United States)	15 Jun 51	141UNTS79	101907
Ethiopia	USA (United States)	16 Jun 51	148UNTS39	101933
Multilateral		19 Jun 51	199UNTS67	102678
Iceland	IBRD (World Bank)	20 Jun 51	158UNTS301	102069
Cuba	USA (United States)	20 Jun 51	148UNTS3	101931
Mexico	USA (United States)	27 Jun 51	141UNTS211	101916
Iraq	WHO (World Health)	01 Jul 51	110UNTS139	101507
Switzerland	USA (United States)	09 Jul 51	165UNTS51	102167
Multilateral		10 Jul 51	108UNTS287	101481
UK Great Britain	USA (United States)	13 Jul 51	105UNTS71	101454
El Salvador	USA (United States)	19 Jul 51	140UNTS259	101892
Greece	Netherlands	26 Jul 51	109UNTS103	101495
Multilateral		29 Jul 51	117UNTS85	101585
Panama	USA (United States)	30 Jul 51	140UNTS321	101896
Austria	Sweden	01 Aug 51	198UNTS13	102653
Iran	UNICEF (Children)	02 Aug 51	247UNTS11	103457
USA (United States)	Venezuela	10 Aug 51	140UNTS345	101898
Jordan	UN Relief Palestin	20 Aug 51	120UNTS277	200394
Israel	USA (United States)	23 Aug 51	219UNTS237	102979
Cuba	USA (United States)	28 Aug 51	140UNTS239	101891
Cuba	USA (United States)	28 Aug 51	134UNTS225	101802
WHO (World Health)	Saudi Arabia	29 Aug 51	110UNTS277	101516
UNICEF (Children)	Turkey	05 Sep 51	193UNTS55	102610
Ethiopia	USA (United States)	07 Sep 51	206UNTS41	102785
Belgium	IBRD (World Bank)	13 Sep 51	158UNTS349	102071
Belgium	IBRD (World Bank)	13 Sep 51	158UNTS323	102070
WHO (World Health)	Vietnam, South	21 Sep 51	107UNTS63	200352
Netherlands	USA (United States)	26 Sep 51	158UNTS469	102080
UNICEF (Children)	UK Great Britain	02 Oct 51	104UNTS301	101448
Italy	IBRD (World Bank)	10 Oct 51	159UNTS383	200482
Chile	IBRD (World Bank)	10 Oct 51	158UNTS369	102072
IBRD (World Bank)	Yugoslavia	11 Oct 51	159UNTS3	102081
Colombia	IBRD (World Bank)	13 Oct 51	159UNTS75	102084
El Salvador	USA (United States)	23 Oct 51	137UNTS43	101847
Nicaragua	IBRD (World Bank)	29 Oct 51	159UNTS35	102082
Multilateral		31 Oct 51	172UNTS193	102247
Saudi Arabia	USA (United States)	10 Nov 51	180UNTS263	102390

PARTY ONE	PARTY TWO	DATE	CITATION	NUMBER
Tax exemptions (Cont.)				
Netherlands	Switzerland	12 Nov 51	126UNTS173	101689
Canada	South Africa	26 Nov 51	248UNTS107	103489
USA (United States)	Uruguay	04 Dec 51	152UNTS41	102010
Paraguay	IBRD (World Bank)	07 Dec 51	159UNTS103	102085
Iraq	UNICEF (Children)	10 Dec 51	126UNTS57	101682
El Salvador	USA (United States)	12 Dec 51	132UNTS287	101768
Multilateral		10 Jan 52	163UNTS27	102139
Colombia	USA (United States)	12 Jan 52	168UNTS109	102216
UK Great Britain	USA (United States)	15 Jan 52	127UNTS3	101697
Iran	USA (United States)	20 Jan 52	200UNTS191	102703
Libya	USA (United States)	21 Jan 52	183UNTS177	102427
Peru	IBRD (World Bank)	23 Jan 52	159UNTS163	102087
UNICEF (Children)	UK Great Britain	04 Feb 52	120UNTS147	101620
Dominican Republic	UNICEF (Children)	15 Feb 52	121UNTS43	101625
IBRD (World Bank)	UK Great Britain	27 Feb 52	159UNTS181	102088
Japan	USA (United States)	28 Feb 52	208UNTS255	102817
Finland	USA (United States)	03 Mar 52	177UNTS163	102317
France	USA (United States)	13 Mar 52	177UNTS21	102306
Iceland	USA (United States)	18 Mar 52	177UNTS263	102325
UK Great Britain	USA (United States)	18 Mar 52	177UNTS33	102307
Netherlands	IBRD (World Bank)	20 Mar 52	159UNTS207	102089
Pakistan	IBRD (World Bank)	27 Mar 52	159UNTS251	102090
El Salvador	USA (United States)	04 Apr 52	177UNTS219	102320
Libya	UNICEF (Children)	05 Apr 52	133UNTS287	200441
Belgium	USA (United States)	07 Apr 52	205UNTS3	102765
Denmark	USA (United States)	07 Apr 52	177UNTS257	102324
Chile	USA (United States)	09 Apr 52	186UNTS53	102482
Netherlands	Sweden	25 Apr 52	163UNTS195	102148
Netherlands	Sweden	25 Apr 52	163UNTS131	102147
Finland	IBRD (World Bank)	30 Apr 52	159UNTS408	200483
Norway	WHO (World Health)	09 May 52	131UNTS281	101747
Ethiopia	USA (United States)	15 May 52	180UNTS227	102388
UNICEF (Children)	United Arab Rep	18 May 52	324UNTS161	104684
Germany, West	Netherlands	19 May 52	134UNTS3	101794
Germany, West	USA (United States)	11 Jun 52	273UNTS105	103947
Pakistan	IBRD (World Bank)	13 Jun 52	191UNTS85	102578
Belgium	UNICEF (Children)	17 Jun 52	171UNTS249	102228
IBRD (World Bank)	Turkey	18 Jun 52	159UNTS269	102091
Brazil	IBRD (World Bank)	27 Jun 52	190UNTS115	102561
Brazil	IBRD (World Bank)	27 Jun 52	190UNTS85	102560
Norway	USA (United States)	27 Jun 52	184UNTS271	102452
USA (United States)	Uruguay	30 Jun 52	207UNTS139	102804
Belgium	France	30 Jun 52	137UNTS259	101857
Australia	FAO (Food Agri)	07 Jul 52	184UNTS209	102449
Jordan	UNICEF (Children)	08 Jul 52	173UNTS353	200503
Peru	IBRD (World Bank)	08 Jul 52	159UNTS321	102093
Australia	IBRD (World Bank)	08 Jul 52	159UNTS295	102092
UNICEF (Children)	Syria	10 Jul 52	136UNTS17	101830
Greece	Israel	22 Jul 52	215UNTS365	102924
Japan	USA (United States)	25 Jul 52	198UNTS281	102671
UNICEF (Children)	UK Great Britain	25 Jul 52	135UNTS37	101812
Japan	USA (United States)	11 Aug 52	212UNTS27	102862
Laos	UNICEF (Children)	15 Aug 52	161UNTS323	200491
Jordan	WHO (World Health)	21 Aug 52	141UNTS341	200472
Colombia	IBRD (World Bank)	26 Aug 52	159UNTS339	102094
Iceland	IBRD (World Bank)	26 Aug 52	159UNTS363	102095
UNICEF (Children)	Vietnam, South	29 Aug 52	161UNTS335	200492
Saudi Arabia	USA (United States)	10 Nov 52	.181UNTS307	102419
Japan	IBRD (World Bank)	12 Nov 52	354UNTS313	105068
Nicaragua	USA (United States)	19 Nov 52	186UNTS3	102478
Mexico	ICAO (Civil Aviat)	28 Nov 52	164UNTS15	102156
Canada	USA (United States)	05 Dec 52	206UNTS11	102783
India	WHO (World Health)	11 Dec 52	158UNTS391	102073
UNICEF (Children)	UK Great Britain	16 Dec 52	151UNTS359	102005
India	IBRD (World Bank)	18 Dec 52	201UNTS241	102719

PARTY ONE	PARTY TWO	DATE	CITATION	NUMBER
Tax exemptions (Cont.)				
Israel	South Africa	24 Dec 52	207UNTS303	102813
USA (United States)	Venezuela	16 Jan 53	199UNTS287	102690
India	IBRD (World Bank)	23 Jan 53	201UNTS145	102715
Greece	USA (United States)	04 Feb 53	189UNTS3	102538
IBRD (World Bank)	Yugoslavia	11 Feb 53	165UNTS231	102179
United Arab Rep	USA (United States)	12 Mar 53	204UNTS3	102747
Portugal	USA (United States)	01 Apr 53	205UNTS41	102769
Belgium	Sweden	01 Apr 53	185UNTS225	102473
Netherlands	United Nations	09 Apr 53	163UNTS89	102143
Ethiopia	UNICEF (Children)	27 Apr 53	213UNTS169	102885
Brazil	IBRD (World Bank)	30 Apr 53	190UNTS133	102562
El Salvador	USA (United States)	14 May 53	234UNTS71	103273
Australia	USA (United States)	14 May 53	205UNTS237	102778
Australia	USA (United States)	14 May 53	205UNTS253	102779
Australia	USA (United States)	14 May 53	205UNTS277	102780
El Salvador	USA (United States)	21 May 53	213UNTS15	102878
Ethiopia	USA (United States)	22 May 53	191UNTS59	102577
Brazil	USA (United States)	30 May 53	460UNTS89	106633
Colombia	USA (United States)	09 Jun 53	213UNTS3	102877
Liberia	USA (United States)	23 Jun 53	213UNTS37	102879
Greece	UK Great Britain	25 Jun 53	190UNTS281	102571
Brazil	USA (United States)	26 Jun 53	336UNTS241	104808
Panama	USA (United States)	26 Jun 53	215UNTS77	102912
Italy	South Africa	26 Jun 53	211UNTS255	102857
Philippines	USA (United States)	26 Jun 53	213UNTS77	102881
Nicaragua	USA (United States)	30 Jun 53	215UNTS133	102917
Italy	Switzerland	02 Jul 53	257UNTS99	103653
Brazil	IBRD (World Bank)	17 Jul 53	190UNTS149	102563
USA (United States)	Yugoslavia	23 Jul 53	221UNTS365	103018
Libya	UK Great Britain	29 Jul 53	186UNTS201	102492
IBRD (World Bank)	South Africa	28 Aug 53	180UNTS73	102376
IBRD (World Bank)	South Africa	28 Aug 53	180UNTS91	102377
Nicaragua	IBRD (World Bank)	04 Sep 53	186UNTS117	102487
Iceland	IBRD (World Bank)	04 Sep 53	188UNTS3	102519
Nicaragua	IBRD (World Bank)	04 Sep 53	186UNTS137	102488
Iceland	IBRD (World Bank)	04 Sep 53	178UNTS275	102344
Colombia	IBRD (World Bank)	10 Sep 53	203UNTS3	102738
IBRD (World Bank)	Turkey	10 Sep 53	187UNTS71	102502
Chile	IBRD (World Bank)	10 Sep 53	188UNTS25	102520
Panama	IBRD (World Bank)	25 Sep 53	188UNTS95	102522
Panama	IBRD (World Bank)	25 Sep 53	188UNTS71	102521
Spain	USA (United States)	26 Sep 53	207UNTS61	102800
Italy	IBRD (World Bank)	06 Oct 53	301UNTS135	104344
Greece	USA (United States)	12 Oct 53	191UNTS319	102589
Iran	USA (United States)	13 Oct 53	222UNTS67	103023
Japan	IBRD (World Bank)	15 Oct 53	187UNTS367	200513
Japan	IBRD (World Bank)	15 Oct 53	187UNTS321	200512
Japan	IBRD (World Bank)	15 Oct 53	187UNTS271	200511
Nicaragua	USA (United States)	19 Nov 53	206UNTS117	102787
Japan	UNICEF (Children)	21 Nov 53	183UNTS297	200507
Israel	USA (United States)	25 Nov 53	219UNTS205	102976
Brazil	IBRD (World Bank)	18 Dec 53	301UNTS229	104346
Brazil	IBRD (World Bank)	18 Dec 53	190UNTS179	102564
Bolivia	USA (United States)	15 Jan 54	229UNTS213	103168
UK Great Britain	USA (United States)	20 Jan 54	196UNTS95	102619
Netherlands	USA (United States)	22 Jan 54	190UNTS207	102565
Belgium	Finland	11 Feb 54	211UNTS63	102848
France	Sweden	16 Feb 54	228UNTS137	103147
Multilateral		19 Feb 54	214UNTS51	102899
Brazil	IBRD (World Bank)	24 Feb 54	301UNTS249	104347
United Arab Rep	USA (United States)	24 Feb 54	236UNTS61	103316
Australia	IBRD (World Bank)	02 Mar 54	191UNTS103	102579
Japan	USA (United States)	08 Mar 54	232UNTS169	103236
Finland	Netherlands	29 Mar 54	252UNTS185	103567
Finland	Netherlands	29 Mar 54	252UNTS239	103568

PARTY ONE	PARTY TWO	DATE	CITATION	NUMBER
Tax exemptions (Cont.)				
Mexico	USA (United States)	06 Apr 54	236UNTS69	103317
Mexico	USA (United States)	06 Apr 54	233UNTS163	103261
Norway	IBRD (World Bank)	08 Apr 54	201UNTS131	102714
Peru	IBRD (World Bank)	12 Apr 54	190UNTS231	102567
Japan	USA (United States)	16 Apr 54	238UNTS39	103354
Japan	USA (United States)	16 Apr 54	238UNTS3	103353
Luxembourg	USA (United States)	17 Apr 54	257UNTS255	103661
Ethiopia	USA (United States)	21 Apr 54	232UNTS299	103244
Iraq	USA (United States)	21 Apr 54	222UNTS251	103032
Lebanon	USSR (Soviet Union)	30 Apr 54	226UNTS109	103111
Canada	USA (United States)	03 May 54	221UNTS339	103015
UNICEF (Children)	Spain	07 May 54	190UNTS357	200515
Panama	USA (United States)	11 May 54	236UNTS107	103319
Pakistan	USA (United States)	19 May 54	202UNTS301	102736
Honduras	USA (United States)	20 May 54	222UNTS87	103025
Mexico	UNICEF (Children)	20 May 54	192UNTS3	102591
Greece	Sweden	27 May 54	219UNTS147	102971
Afghanistan	USA (United States)	29 May 54	234UNTS3	103268
Pakistan	IBRD (World Bank)	02 Jun 54	324UNTS59	104678
France	IBRD (World Bank)	10 Jun 54	210UNTS89	102836
Bolivia	USA (United States)	16 Jun 54	234UNTS35	103271
Mexico	USA (United States)	17 Jun 54	237UNTS275	103352
UK Great Britain	USA (United States)	21 Jun 54	209UNTS61	102821
Turkey	USA (United States)	23 Jun 54	233UNTS189	103263
Turkey	USA (United States)	23 Jun 54	222UNTS161	103027
Belgium	Greece	23 Jun 54	199UNTS43	102676
Italy	USA (United States)	28 Jun 54	237UNTS121	103340
Brazil	USA (United States)	30 Jun 54	237UNTS137	103341
Colombia	USA (United States)	30 Jun 54	237UNTS263	103351
Ecuador	USA (United States)	30 Jun 54	236UNTS163	103323
Costa Rica	USA (United States)	30 Jun 54	235UNTS35	103294
Ceylon (Sri Lanka)	IBRD (World Bank)	09 Jul 54	198UNTS313	200517
Belgium	Italy	12 Jul 54	288UNTS59	104198
El Salvador	USA (United States)	16 Jul 54	237UNTS237	103350
Germany, West	USA (United States)	22 Jul 54	239UNTS3	103369
Germany, West	USA (United States)	22 Jul 54	221UNTS351	103016
Netherlands	USA (United States)	13 Aug 54	251UNTS91	103535
Mexico	IBRD (World Bank)	24 Aug 54	286UNTS211	104168
USA (United States)	Vietnam, South	26 Aug 54	234UNTS111	103276
New Zealand	UNICEF (Children)	26 Aug 54	198UNTS173	102663
El Salvador	USA (United States)	31 Aug 54	237UNTS49	103336
Guatemala	USA (United States)	01 Sep 54	199UNTS51	102677
Libya	USA (United States)	09 Sep 54	224UNTS217	103078
El Salvador	USA (United States)	23 Sep 54	237UNTS91	103338
Switzerland	UK Great Britain	30 Sep 54	209UNTS197	102828
Pakistan	USA (United States)	02 Oct 54	236UNTS187	103324
Ethiopia	Sweden	13 Oct 54	202UNTS273	102734
Germany, West	USA (United States)	15 Oct 54	239UNTS135	103375
Ireland	Norway	18 Oct 54	553UNTS123	108077
USA (United States)	Yugoslavia	18 Oct 54	273UNTS163	103951
Germany, West	UK Great Britain	18 Oct 54	218UNTS301	102960
Denmark	Ireland	18 Oct 54	218UNTS295	102959
Canada	UK Great Britain	19 Oct 54	214UNTS309	102906
Multilateral		23 Oct 54	332UNTS3	104760
Multilateral		23 Oct 54	332UNTS387	104763
Peru	USA (United States)	25 Oct 54	238UNTS247	103368
Canada	Ireland	28 Oct 54	304UNTS317	104406
United Arab Rep	USA (United States)	30 Oct 54	234UNTS139	103279
Austria	IBRD (World Bank)	08 Nov 54	216UNTS305	200528
Peru	IBRD (World Bank)	12 Nov 54	209UNTS287	102831
India	IBRD (World Bank)	19 Nov 54	309UNTS159	104473
France	South Africa	22 Nov 54	219UNTS35	102963
Netherlands	USA (United States)	14 Dec 54	262UNTS35	103737
Belgium	IBRD (World Bank)	14 Dec 54	210UNTS113	102837
Colombia	IBRD (World Bank)	29 Dec 54	211UNTS135	102851

PARTY ONE	PARTY TWO	DATE	CITATION	NUMBER
Tax exemptions (Cont.)				
Netherlands	UNICEF (Children)	31 Dec 54	202UNTS135	102729
Switzerland	United Arab Rep	05 Jan 55	216UNTS41	102931
Belgium	Brazil	10 Jan 55	272UNTS181	103937
Haiti	USA (United States)	28 Jan 55	270UNTS83	103894
Germany, West	USA (United States)	18 Feb 55	247UNTS257	103474
Iraq	USA (United States)	02 Mar 55	250UNTS229	103526
Mexico	USA (United States)	09 Mar 55	263UNTS247	103776
India	IBRD (World Bank)	14 Mar 55	309UNTS129	104472
IBRD (World Bank)	UK Great Britain	15 Mar 55	265UNTS85	103808
Australia	IBRD (World Bank)	18 Mar 55	220UNTS131	102998
El Salvador	USA (United States)	21 Mar 55	250UNTS261	103528
Honduras	USA (United States)	21 Mar 55	253UNTS3	103572
Finland	IBRD (World Bank)	24 Mar 55	211UNTS305	200525
Colombia	IBRD (World Bank)	24 Mar 55	212UNTS217	102874
Italy	USA (United States)	30 Mar 55	257UNTS169	103654
Italy	USA (United States)	30 Mar 55	257UNTS199	103655
Chile	USA (United States)	31 Mar 55	262UNTS19	103736
Haiti	USA (United States)	01 Apr 55	261UNTS361	103734
Germany, West	USA (United States)	04 Apr 55	279UNTS73	104034
Denmark	Israel	04 Apr 55	213UNTS283	102891
Chile	USA (United States)	05 Apr 55	250UNTS253	103527
Peru	IBRD (World Bank)	05 Apr 55	211UNTS115	102850
Peru	IBRD (World Bank)	19 Apr 55	221UNTS153	103007
Norway	IBRD (World Bank)	19 Apr 55	211UNTS159	102852
Philippines	USA (United States)	27 Apr 55	261UNTS351	103733
Peru	USA (United States)	30 Apr 55	263UNTS309	103780
Korea, South	USA (United States)	02 May 55	258UNTS3	103666
Greece	Norway	25 May 55	423UNTS77	106085
Norway	Sweden	28 May 55	262UNTS151	103743
Italy	IBRD (World Bank)	01 Jun 55	358UNTS203	105137
Pakistan	Sweden	04 Jun 55	228UNTS121	103146
Pakistan	UK Great Britain	10 Jun 55	243UNTS15	103444
Austria	IBRD (World Bank)	14 Jun 55	221UNTS375	200531
Colombia	IBRD (World Bank)	15 Jun 55	248UNTS161	103494
Canada	USA (United States)	15 Jun 55	235UNTS201	103302
Guatemala	USA (United States)	18 Jun 55	262UNTS105	103740
Pakistan	IBRD (World Bank)	20 Jun 55	230UNTS41	103176
Turkey	USA (United States)	29 Jun 55	269UNTS97	103878
Dominican Republic	USA (United States)	30 Jun 55	257UNTS313	103664
Germany, West	USA (United States)	30 Jun 55	240UNTS47	103393
Nicaragua	IBRD (World Bank)	08 Jul 55	229UNTS123	103163
Nicaragua	IBRD (World Bank)	08 Jul 55	229UNTS97	103162
Panama	IBRD (World Bank)	12 Jul 55	219UNTS127	102970
Denmark	Finland	18 Jul 55	250UNTS149	103521
Libya	USA (United States)	21 Jul 55	264UNTS247	103796
South Africa	Sweden	28 Jul 55	230UNTS287	103191
Guatemala	IBRD (World Bank)	29 Jul 55	229UNTS167	103165
Brazil	USA (United States)	03 Aug 55	270UNTS71	103893
Pakistan	IBRD (World Bank)	04 Aug 55	230UNTS79	103177
Peru	IBRD (World Bank)	05 Aug 55	218UNTS3	102950
Pakistan	IBRD (World Bank)	06 Aug 55	236UNTS195	103325
IBRD (World Bank)	Thailand	09 Aug 55	221UNTS283	103011
Italy	Spain	11 Aug 55	267UNTS125	103839
Iran	USA (United States)	15 Aug 55	284UNTS93	104132
Lebanon	IBRD (World Bank)	25 Aug 55	230UNTS233	103188
France	IBRD (World Bank)	26 Aug 55	247UNTS305	103478
Nicaragua	IBRD (World Bank)	26 Aug 55	229UNTS145	103164
IBRD (World Bank)	Uruguay	29 Aug 55	243UNTS123	103450
Ecuador	USA (United States)	06 Sep 55	256UNTS187	103628
Germany, East	Hungary	10 Sep 55	407UNTS132	105863
Multilateral		21 Sep 55	269UNTS241	103885
Canada	Denmark	30 Sep 55	258UNTS115	103675
Liberia	USA (United States)	06 Oct 55	275UNTS93	103978
Denmark	Iceland	10 Oct 55	230UNTS3	103171
Czechoslovakia	Germany, East	24 Oct 55	504UNTS173	107358

PARTY ONE	PARTY TWO	DATE	CITATION	NUMBER
Tax exemptions (Cont.)				
Japan	IBRD (World Bank)	25 Oct 55	230UNTS379	200534
South Africa	Switzerland	07 Nov 55	230UNTS279	103190
Guatemala	UNICEF (Children)	22 Nov 55	221UNTS305	103012
IBRD (World Bank)	South Africa	28 Nov 55	230UNTS101	103178
Belgium	France	10 Dec 55	231UNTS101	103211
Italy	Vatican/Holy See	16 Dec 55	260UNTS319	103715
Costa Rica	Guatemala	20 Dec 55	280UNTS121	104056
Libya	USA (United States)	22 Dec 55	240UNTS111	103399
Honduras	IBRD (World Bank)	22 Dec 55	230UNTS262	103189
Czechoslovakia	Poland	13 Jan 56	265UNTS157	103811
Hungary	Romania	03 Feb 56	362UNTS233	105190
Japan	IBRD (World Bank)	21 Feb 56	248UNTS321	200543
Multilateral		05 Mar 56	326UNTS181	104712
Colombia	USA (United States)	14 Mar 56	271UNTS303	103922
USA (United States)	Uruguay	23 Mar 56	376UNTS311	105386
Ecuador	IBRD (World Bank)	26 Mar 56	292UNTS391	104277
Netherlands	USA (United States)	27 Mar 56	285UNTS231	104154
New Zealand	Sweden	16 Apr 56	274UNTS259	103971
Cambodia	UNICEF (Children)	28 Apr 56	136UNTS341	200446
Ceylon (Sri Lanka)	USA (United States)	28 Apr 56	274UNTS35	103956
Germany, West	Switzerland	02 May 56	559UNTS157	108158
Norway	IBRD (World Bank)	03 May 56	243UNTS281	103455
Burma	IBRD (World Bank)	04 May 56	253UNTS209	103585
Burma	IBRD (World Bank)	04 May 56	253UNTS179	103584
Haiti	IBRD (World Bank)	07 May 56	252UNTS279	103570
Japan	Philippines	09 May 56	285UNTS3	104148
Multilateral		18 May 56	339UNTS3	104844
Fed Rhod/Nyasaland	South Africa	22 May 56	254UNTS227	103595
Nicaragua	IBRD (World Bank)	22 May 56	253UNTS233	103586
Finland	IBRD (World Bank)	22 May 56	248UNTS57	103485
Pakistan	USA (United States)	28 May 56	269UNTS15	103868
Canada	Germany, West	04 Jun 56	316UNTS231	104589
Colombia	IBRD (World Bank)	06 Jun 56	248UNTS139	103493
Israel	Sweden	17 Jun 56	257UNTS47	103648
IBRD (World Bank)	UK Great Britain	21 Jun 56	285UNTS355	104157
Fed Rhod/Nyasaland	IBRD (World Bank)	21 Jun 56	285UNTS317	104156
France	USA (United States)	22 Jun 56	291UNTS101	104246
UK Great Britain	USA (United States)	25 Jun 56	249UNTS59	103501
India	IBRD (World Bank)	26 Jun 56	301UNTS3	104341
Israel	USA (United States)	26 Jun 56	257UNTS55	103649
Bolivia	USA (United States)	30 Jun 56	271UNTS243	103919
Lebanon	UNICEF (Children)	03 Jul 56	324UNTS145	104683
Austria	UK Great Britain	20 Jul 56	269UNTS147	103880
UNICEF (Children)	Sudan	07 Aug 56	248UNTS307	200542
Austria	Sweden	14 Aug 56	262UNTS355	103760
Guatemala	Honduras	22 Aug 56	263UNTS49	103767
Costa Rica	IBRD (World Bank)	18 Sep 56	260UNTS369	103721
Austria	IBRD (World Bank)	21 Sep 56	259UNTS17	103681
Austria	IBRD (World Bank)	21 Sep 56	259UNTS43	103682
Belgium	Germany, West	24 Sep 56	314UNTS195	104549
Germany, West	South Africa	28 Sep 56	327UNTS83	104718
Canada	South Africa	28 Sep 56	299UNTS17	104304
Argentina	USA (United States)	03 Oct 56	279UNTS13	104032
Italy	IBRD (World Bank)	11 Oct 56	359UNTS3	105138
IBRD (World Bank)	Thailand	12 Oct 56	261UNTS117	103728
Philippines	USA (United States)	18 Oct 56	280UNTS55	104050
Austria	USA (United States)	25 Oct 56	299UNTS123	104310
IBRD (World Bank)	Uruguay	25 Oct 56	265UNTS59	103807
Belgium	United Arab Rep	31 Oct 56	257UNTS235	103659
UK Great Britain	USA (United States)	01 Nov 56	264UNTS3	103785
Chile	IBRD (World Bank)	01 Nov 56	261UNTS27	103724
Belgium	Sweden	20 Nov 56	281UNTS239	104081
Taiwan	USA (United States)	21 Nov 56	265UNTS241	103816
UK Great Britain	USA (United States)	27 Nov 56	282UNTS43	104092
Dominican Republic	USA (United States)	07 Dec 56	263UNTS193	103774

PARTY ONE	PARTY TWO	DATE	CITATION	NUMBER
Tax exemptions (Cont.)				
Japan	Sweden	12 Dec 56	318UNTS309	104623
Multilateral		14 Dec 56	436UNTS115	106292
Multilateral		14 Dec 56	436UNTS131	106293
India	IBRD (World Bank)	19 Dec 56	310UNTS75	104489
Japan	IBRD (World Bank)	19 Dec 56	268UNTS203	103859
Japan	IBRD (World Bank)	19 Dec 56	264UNTS179	103793
Italy	Sweden	20 Dec 56	369UNTS357	105265
Italy	Sweden	20 Dec 56	369UNTS305	105263
Finland	Switzerland	27 Dec 56	277UNTS7	103996
UNESCO (Educ/Cult)	Tunisia	03 Jan 57	257UNTS21	103645
Denmark	Switzerland	14 Jan 57	286UNTS27	104160
Iran	IBRD (World Bank)	22 Jan 57	317UNTS129	104600
Italy	Netherlands	24 Jan 57	485UNTS67	107047
Ethiopia	IBRD (World Bank)	28 Jan 57	286UNTS307	104175
Germany, West	Sweden	29 Jan 57	393UNTS113	105654
Denmark	Germany, West	29 Jan 57	302UNTS75	104354
Denmark	Netherlands	20 Feb 57	287UNTS41	104179
Denmark	Norway	22 Feb 57	286UNTS127	104164
India	IBRD (World Bank)	05 Mar 57	272UNTS201	103939
Dominican Republic	USA (United States)	09 Mar 57	279UNTS249	104044
Peru	IBRD (World Bank)	13 Mar 57	274UNTS59	103958
Ethiopia	Sweden	16 Mar 57	304UNTS214	104398
Tunisia	USA (United States)	26 Mar 57	283UNTS117	104111
Canada	Netherlands	02 Apr 57	285UNTS193	104153
Morocco	USA (United States)	02 Apr 57	288UNTS157	104203
Paraguay	USA (United States)	04 Apr 57	283UNTS193	104117
Libya	USA (United States)	04 Apr 57	283UNTS181	104116
ICJ Option Clause	Sweden	06 Apr 57	264UNTS221	103794
Germany, West	Yugoslavia	10 Apr 57	463UNTS269	106708
Bulgaria	Yugoslavia	19 Apr 57	349UNTS3	105006
Ethiopia	USA (United States)	25 Apr 57	283UNTS205	104118
Netherlands	United Arab Rep	15 May 57	288UNTS29	104194
Netherlands	IBRD (World Bank)	15 May 57	274UNTS211	103967
Ceylon (Sri Lanka)	Sweden	18 May 57	315UNTS85	104561
Australia	Germany, West	22 May 57	357UNTS45	105105
India	IBRD (World Bank)	29 May 57	309UNTS201	104474
Argentina	USA (United States)	03 Jun 57	291UNTS61	104244
Ghana	USA (United States)	03 Jun 57	284UNTS63	104129
Finland	India	14 Jun 57	277UNTS327	104016
Iraq	USA (United States)	16 Jun 57	284UNTS39	104127
Belgium	IBRD (World Bank)	26 Jun 57	322UNTS301	104661
Jordan	USA (United States)	27 Jun 57	288UNTS269	104209
Libya	USA (United States)	30 Jun 57	284UNTS177	104136
Pakistan	USA (United States)	01 Jul 57	344UNTS203	104951
India	IBRD (World Bank)	12 Jul 57	288UNTS135	104202
Chile	IBRD (World Bank)	24 Jul 57	282UNTS139	104098
Chile	IBRD (World Bank)	24 Jul 57	282UNTS189	104099
Morocco	UNICEF (Children)	31 Jul 57	282UNTS99	104095
Greece	Italy	02 Aug 57	533UNTS217	107744
Japan	IBRD (World Bank)	09 Aug 57	293UNTS59	104286
Hungary	USSR (Soviet Union)	24 Aug 57	318UNTS35	104608
Romania	USSR (Soviet Union)	04 Sep 57	318UNTS89	104610
Belgium	IBRD (World Bank)	10 Sep 57	286UNTS291	104174
IBRD (World Bank)	Thailand	12 Sep 57	299UNTS349	104324
Ecuador	IBRD (World Bank)	20 Sep 57	293UNTS135	104291
Ecuador	IBRD (World Bank)	20 Sep 57	289UNTS237	104221
France	USA (United States)	23 Sep 57	293UNTS297	104297
Australia	Canada	01 Oct 57	392UNTS41	105638
IBRD (World Bank)	South Africa	01 Oct 57	280UNTS285	104065
Multilateral		03 Oct 57	366UNTS87	105216
Czechoslovakia	USSR (Soviet Union)	05 Oct 57	320UNTS111	104640
Austria	IBRD (World Bank)	10 Oct 57	301UNTS95	104343
Pakistan	IBRD (World Bank)	18 Oct 57	299UNTS303	104322
France	Morocco	25 Oct 57	559UNTS95	108156
UK Great Britain	USA (United States)	01 Nov 57	299UNTS167	104312

PARTY ONE	PARTY TWO	DATE	CITATION	NUMBER
Tax exemptions (Cont.)				
Argentina	UNICEF (Children)	19 Nov 57	300UNTS229	104338
India	IBRD (World Bank)	20 Nov 57	301UNTS47	104342
El Salvador	USA (United States)	21 Nov 57	303UNTS19	104369
Philippines	IBRD (World Bank)	22 Nov 57	293UNTS83	104287
Belgium	IBRD (World Bank)	27 Nov 57	292UNTS175	104273
Austria	IAEA (Atom Energy)	11 Dec 57	339UNTS110	104849
Bulgaria	USSR (Soviet Union)	12 Dec 57	302UNTS3	104351
Korea, North	USSR (Soviet Union)	16 Dec 57	292UNTS107	104269
Pakistan	IBRD (World Bank)	17 Dec 57	299UNTS321	104323
UK Great Britain	USSR (Soviet Union)	19 Dec 57	351UNTS235	105026
Mexico	IBRD (World Bank)	14 Jan 58	293UNTS167	104292
Indonesia	Japan	20 Jan 58	324UNTS247	104689
Poland	USSR (Soviet Union)	21 Jan 58	319UNTS277	104636
Brazil	IBRD (World Bank)	22 Jan 58	323UNTS99	104666
Czechoslovakia	Poland	31 Jan 58	431UNTS99	106214
Bulgaria	Yugoslavia	21 Mar 58	386UNTS119	105541
Bulgaria	Yugoslavia	21 Mar 58	349UNTS61	105009
Sudan	USA (United States)	31 Mar 58	308UNTS105	104458
Bulgaria	Yugoslavia	04 Apr 58	367UNTS89	105228
Pakistan	IBRD (World Bank)	23 Apr 58	323UNTS253	104672
Chile	IBRD (World Bank)	28 Apr 58	359UNTS89	105140
Austria	IBRD (World Bank)	28 Apr 58	359UNTS145	105142
Argentina	USA (United States)	28 Apr 58	315UNTS211	104570
Ireland	South Africa	01 May 58	398UNTS3	105714
Saudi Arabia	USA (United States)	01 May 58	315UNTS221	104571
IBRD (World Bank)	UK Great Britain	02 May 58	324UNTS25	104677
Mexico	IBRD (World Bank)	05 May 58	309UNTS3	104466
Ceylon (Sri Lanka)	Sweden	22 May 58	428UNTS65	106168
India	USSR (Soviet Union)	02 Jun 58	393UNTS3	105650
Japan	IBRD (World Bank)	13 Jun 58	312UNTS159	104518
IBRD (World Bank)	UK Great Britain	16 Jun 58	309UNTS35	104467
Ireland	Switzerland	18 Jun 58	553UNTS183	108086
India	IBRD (World Bank)	25 Jun 58	323UNTS157	104668
India	IBRD (World Bank)	25 Jun 58	323UNTS131	104667
Philippines	USA (United States)	30 Jun 58	321UNTS51	104653
Sweden	United Arab Rep	21 Jul 58	427UNTS285	106160
Denmark	Sweden	21 Jul 58	320UNTS163	104642
India	IBRD (World Bank)	23 Jul 58	317UNTS3	104590
Sweden	United Arab Rep	29 Jul 58	369UNTS323	105264
India	Sweden	30 Jul 58	369UNTS211	105259
Taiwan	USA (United States)	06 Aug 58	462UNTS3	106666
Lebanon	USA (United States)	06 Aug 58	366UNTS361	105223
Ghana	UNICEF (Children)	12 Aug 58	309UNTS103	104469
Japan	IBRD (World Bank)	18 Aug 58	323UNTS205	104670
Pakistan	Sweden	25 Aug 58	369UNTS183	105258
Haiti	USA (United States)	09 Sep 58	335UNTS257	104793
Japan	IBRD (World Bank)	10 Sep 58	323UNTS297	104673
Japan	IBRD (World Bank)	10 Sep 58	318UNTS133	104612
Peru	IBRD (World Bank)	17 Sep 58	323UNTS27	104663
Fed of Malaya	IBRD (World Bank)	22 Sep 58	323UNTS71	104665
Australia	New Zealand	30 Sep 58	340UNTS61	104859
Brazil	IBRD (World Bank)	03 Oct 58	337UNTS177	104823
Ecuador	IBRD (World Bank)	09 Oct 58	337UNTS299	104827
France	Italy	30 Oct 58	363UNTS3	105196
Germany, West	Norway	18 Nov 58	357UNTS205	105119
Denmark	United Arab Rep	01 Dec 58	337UNTS69	104817
Austria	IBRD (World Bank)	02 Dec 58	340UNTS3	104856
Colombia	IBRD (World Bank)	15 Dec 58	354UNTS233	105065
Korea, South	USA (United States)	18 Dec 58	325UNTS233	104702
United Nations	Tunisia	23 Dec 58	321UNTS23	104651
Haiti	USA (United States)	24 Dec 58	338UNTS265	104840
Colombia	IBRD (World Bank)	30 Jan 59	337UNTS327	104828
Costa Rica	IBRD (World Bank)	11 Feb 59	337UNTS245	104825
Japan	Pakistan	17 Feb 59	341UNTS127	104880
Japan	IBRD (World Bank)	17 Feb 59	337UNTS205	104824

PARTY ONE	PARTY TWO	DATE	CITATION	NUMBER
Tax exemptions (Cont.)				
El Salvador	IBRD (World Bank)	20 Feb 59	362UNTS75	105183
Japan	Norway	21 Feb 59	356UNTS231	105098
Ghana	United Nations	27 Feb 59	324UNTS133	104682
Denmark	Japan	10 Mar 59	341UNTS55	104878
Finland	IBRD (World Bank)	16 Mar 59	337UNTS269	104826
Canada	Finland	28 Mar 59	355UNTS3	105072
United Nations	Sudan	28 Mar 59	327UNTS95	104719
Morocco	UN Special Fund	04 Apr 59	354UNTS347	105069
India	IBRD (World Bank)	08 Apr 59	348UNTS131	104998
Ghana	USA (United States)	09 Apr 59	342UNTS21	104897
Germany, West	Sweden	17 Apr 59	428UNTS155	106175
Italy	IBRD (World Bank)	21 Apr 59	359UNTS191	105143
Colombia	USA (United States)	08 May 59	344UNTS193	104950
Austria	Sweden	14 May 59	428UNTS3	106167
Colombia	IBRD (World Bank)	20 May 59	344UNTS251	104953
Honduras	IBRD (World Bank)	20 May 59	359UNTS119	105141
Fed of Malaya	USA (United States)	22 May 59	346UNTS263	104985
Iran	IBRD (World Bank)	29 May 59	348UNTS103	104997
Guinea	UNICEF (Children)	08 Jun 59	334UNTS277	104772
Germany, West	Netherlands	16 Jun 59	593UNTS3	108576
Brazil	IBRD (World Bank)	17 Jun 59	377UNTS111	105398
South Africa	UK Great Britain	18 Jun 59	380UNTS59	105450
Greece	Yugoslavia	18 Jun 59	368UNTS27	105234
South Africa	UK Great Britain	18 Jun 59	380UNTS81	105451
Libya	United Nations	27 Jun 59	336UNTS291	104811
France	IBRD (World Bank)	30 Jun 59	452UNTS67	106505
Gabon	IBRD (World Bank)	30 Jun 59	452UNTS135	106507
Congo (Brazzaville)	IBRD (World Bank)	30 Jun 59	452UNTS123	106506
Laos	United Nations	06 Jul 59	337UNTS41	104814
Norway	IBRD (World Bank)	08 Jul 59	344UNTS229	104952
India	IBRD (World Bank)	15 Jul 59	346UNTS33	104976
India	IBRD (World Bank)	15 Jul 59	355UNTS95	105075
Pakistan	USA (United States)	18 Jul 59	355UNTS367	105087
India	Norway	20 Jul 59	356UNTS257	105099
Japan	Paraguay	22 Jul 59	373UNTS85	105316
Afghanistan	Germany, West	22 Jul 59	464UNTS177	106715
Taiwan	USA (United States)	22 Jul 59	357UNTS293	105121
Fed of Malaya	UK Great Britain	27 Jul 59	374UNTS21	105324
Paraguay	United Nations	01 Aug 59	341UNTS319	104894
Ghana	UN Special Fund	12 Aug 59	338UNTS203	104836
Liberia	USA (United States)	13 Aug 59	357UNTS181	105116
Pakistan	IBRD (World Bank)	13 Aug 59	355UNTS129	105076
Canada	Germany, West	04 Sep 59	411UNTS260	105922
Italy	IBRD (World Bank)	16 Sep 59	375UNTS159	105366
Denmark	France	17 Sep 59	410UNTS141	105901
Pakistan	IBRD (World Bank)	25 Sep 59	355UNTS169	105077
Iran	UN Special Fund	06 Oct 59	342UNTS89	104902
Poland	UN Special Fund	15 Oct 59	344UNTS29	104941
Guinea	United Nations	15 Oct 59	344UNTS47	104942
India	UN Special Fund	20 Oct 59	344UNTS143	104946
UN Special Fund	Yugoslavia	27 Oct 59	344UNTS159	104947
Korea, South	United Nations	06 Nov 59	346UNTS289	200565
Ireland	Sweden	06 Nov 59	428UNTS231	106177
Ecuador	UN Special Fund	10 Nov 59	345UNTS3	104955
Japan	IBRD (World Bank)	12 Nov 59	354UNTS279	105067
Ethiopia	France	12 Nov 59	381UNTS3	105465
Greece	UN Special Fund	13 Nov 59	345UNTS171	104966
Turkey	USA (United States)	13 Nov 59	361UNTS3	105168
UN Special Fund	Turkey	20 Nov 59	345UNTS105	104963
Iran	IBRD (World Bank)	23 Nov 59	380UNTS245	105459
Afghanistan	United Nations	24 Nov 59	397UNTS187	105705
UN Special Fund	United Arab Rep	25 Nov 59	345UNTS125	104964
Belgium	USA (United States)	27 Nov 59	366UNTS331	105221
Turkey	USA (United States)	30 Nov 59	361UNTS107	105174
Israel	UN Special Fund	01 Dec 59	345UNTS197	104968

PARTY ONE	PARTY TWO	DATE	CITATION	NUMBER
Tax exemptions (Cont.)				
Guinea	UN Special Fund	02 Dec 59	345UNTS215	104969
Argentina	UN Special Fund	04 Dec 59	345UNTS263	104972
France	IBRD (World Bank)	10 Dec 59	380UNTS319	105464
Jordan	UN Special Fund	15 Dec 59	346UNTS3	104974
Israel	Sweden	22 Dec 59	377UNTS277	105407
IBRD (World Bank)	United Arab Rep	22 Dec 59	354UNTS197	105063
IBRD (World Bank)	Uruguay	30 Dec 59	384UNTS275	105523
India	Japan	05 Jan 60	384UNTS3	105507
UN Special Fund	UK Great Britain	07 Jan 60	348UNTS177	105000
Czechoslovakia	UK Great Britain	15 Jan 60	374UNTS207	105336
Japan	USA (United States)	19 Jan 60	373UNTS207	105321
Colombia	IBRD (World Bank)	20 Jan 60	375UNTS49	105353
Chile	UN Special Fund	22 Jan 60	351UNTS115	105020
Colombia	UN Special Fund	04 Feb 60	355UNTS257	105080
Bolivia	UN Special Fund	09 Feb 60	351UNTS203	105024
Cuba	UNICEF (Children)	11 Feb 60	349UNTS277	105014
Afghanistan	UN Special Fund	21 Feb 60	351UNTS93	105019
Ecuador	USA (United States)	24 Feb 60	371UNTS55	105270
Austria	Norway	25 Feb 60	376UNTS155	105380
Pakistan	UN Special Fund	25 Feb 60	351UNTS141	105021
Multilateral		26 Feb 60	418UNTS171	106022
France	IBRD (World Bank)	17 Mar 60	452UNTS147	106508
Mauritania	IBRD (World Bank)	17 Mar 60	452UNTS211	106509
France	UN Special Fund	17 Mar 60	354UNTS119	105059
Japan	IBRD (World Bank)	17 Mar 60	362UNTS43	105182
Belgium	IBRD (World Bank)	30 Mar 60	379UNTS103	105437
Belgium	IBRD (World Bank)	30 Mar 60	379UNTS129	105438
Belgium	IBRD (World Bank)	30 Mar 60	379UNTS161	105439
IBRD (World Bank)	UK Great Britain	01 Apr 60	379UNTS397	105446
Italy	UN Special Fund	01 Apr 60	354UNTS261	105066
Germany, West	Netherlands	08 Apr 60	508UNTS14	107404
UN Special Fund	Tunisia	12 Apr 60	355UNTS289	105082
Libya	UN Special Fund	19 Apr 60	356UNTS11	105090
UN Special Fund	Sudan	21 Apr 60	356UNTS213	105097
UN Special Fund	Vietnam, South	29 Apr 60	357UNTS311	200567
Laos	UN Special Fund	30 Apr 60	361UNTS171	105179
Costa Rica	IBRD (World Bank)	04 May 60	390UNTS201	105609
United Nations	Togo	06 May 60	388UNTS53	105571
Lebanon	UN Special Fund	07 May 60	360UNTS225	105160
Colombia	IBRD (World Bank)	10 May 60	379UNTS218	105441
Australia	New Zealand	12 May 60	369UNTS119	105254
Morocco	United Arab Rep	19 May 60	563UNTS121	108208
IBRD (World Bank)	UK Great Britain	27 May 60	375UNTS201	105367
Afghanistan	Czechoslovakia	28 May 60	497UNTS129	107266
Peru	IBRD (World Bank)	01 Jun 60	380UNTS15	105448
Cuba	Czechoslovakia	10 Jun 60	447UNTS75	106412
Nicaragua	IBRD (World Bank)	22 Jun 60	384UNTS243	105522
UK Great Britain	USA (United States)	24 Jun 60	377UNTS63	105396
Ireland	Portugal	24 Jun 60	412UNTS30	105924
Peru	IBRD (World Bank)	29 Jun 60	400UNTS99	105750
Kuwait	UN Special Fund	29 Jun 60	369UNTS419	200575
Honduras	IBRD (World Bank)	29 Jun 60	400UNTS137	105751
Poland	UK Great Britain	02 Jul 60	385UNTS87	105532
Italy	UK Great Britain	04 Jul 60	466UNTS195	106745
Ethiopia	United Nations	13 Jul 60	368UNTS143	105239
Ethiopia	UN Special Fund	13 Jul 60	368UNTS159	105240
Germany, West	Pakistan	20 Jul 60	465UNTS41	106721
Sweden	UK Great Britain	28 Jul 60	404UNTS113	105808
El Salvador	IBRD (World Bank)	29 Jul 60	390UNTS101	105605
Argentina	USA (United States)	02 Aug 60	384UNTS105	105514
Mexico	USA (United States)	15 Aug 60	402UNTS177	105786
Panama	IBRD (World Bank)	19 Aug 60	390UNTS153	105607
El Salvador	Israel	05 Sep 60	413UNTS73	105941
Brazil	UN Special Fund	16 Sep 60	375UNTS3	105351
Pakistan	IBRD (World Bank)	19 Sep 60	444UNTS207	106370

PARTY ONE	PARTY TWO	DATE	CITATION	NUMBER
Tax exemptions (Cont.)				
Taiwan	UN Special Fund	20 Sep 60	375UNTS29	105352
Colombia	IBRD (World Bank)	20 Sep 60	390UNTS173	105608
Guinea	USA (United States)	30 Sep 60	394UNTS103	105671
Mexico	IBRD (World Bank)	18 Oct 60	422UNTS177	106075
Nigeria	USA (United States)	19 Oct 60	394UNTS113	105672
Hungary	UK Great Britain	25 Oct 60	419UNTS309	106034
India	IBRD (World Bank)	28 Oct 60	406UNTS27	105838
Czechoslovakia	Hungary	04 Nov 60	397UNTS227	105708
Belgium	Congo (Zaire)	15 Nov 60	394UNTS79	105670
UNICEF (Children)	Upper Volta	15 Nov 60	402UNTS33	105776
Pakistan	United Nations	17 Nov 60	380UNTS277	105460
Mali	UNICEF (Children)	17 Nov 60	402UNTS23	105775
Multilateral		26 Nov 60	500UNTS25	107304
Cambodia	United Nations	30 Nov 60	383UNTS147	105500
Norway	IBRD (World Bank)	02 Dec 60	390UNTS131	105606
Libya	USA (United States)	11 Dec 60	445UNTS125	106381
Nepal	UNICEF (Children)	12 Dec 60	382UNTS273	105488
Multilateral		13 Dec 60	523UNTS117	107557
Bolivia	United Nations	14 Dec 60	382UNTS283	105489
Peru	IBRD (World Bank)	19 Dec 60	417UNTS275	106010
Japan	IBRD (World Bank)	20 Dec 60	400UNTS167	105752
Japan	IBRD (World Bank)	20 Dec 60	400UNTS279	105754
Togo	USA (United States)	22 Dec 60	401UNTS33	105760
Jordan	Sweden	09 Jan 61	465UNTS155	106726
Burma	IBRD (World Bank)	16 Jan 61	400UNTS73	105749
Mexico	IBRD (World Bank)	16 Jan 61	422UNTS203	106076
UK Great Britain	USA (United States)	20 Jan 61	402UNTS153	105783
Costa Rica	IBRD (World Bank)	03 Feb 61	414UNTS314	105977
India	USA (United States)	07 Feb 61	462UNTS57	106671
IBRD (World Bank)	Yugoslavia	23 Feb 61	415UNTS92	105982
Cuba	Czechoslovakia	04 Mar 61	465UNTS209	106728
Denmark	Greece	04 Mar 61	534UNTS157	107760
Iraq	United Nations	05 Mar 61	409UNTS56	105878
Afghanistan	Japan	15 Mar 61	450UNTS373	106480
UK Great Britain	USA (United States)	15 Mar 61	404UNTS207	105811
Japan	IBRD (World Bank)	16 Mar 61	400UNTS201	105753
IBRD (World Bank)	UK Great Britain	29 Mar 61	415UNTS300	105990
Japan	UK Great Britain	11 Apr 61	420UNTS75	106042
Honduras	USA (United States)	12 Apr 61	413UNTS182	105952
Cyprus	UNICEF (Children)	19 Apr 61	394UNTS185	105678
Turkey	USSR (Soviet Union)	27 Apr 61	420UNTS307	106047
IBRD (World Bank)	Thailand	28 Apr 61	415UNTS121	105983
Japan	IBRD (World Bank)	02 May 61	415UNTS144	105984
Sierra Leone	USA (United States)	05 May 61	409UNTS194	105885
Australia	USA (United States)	09 May 61	409UNTS203	105886
Colombia	IBRD (World Bank)	12 May 61	415UNTS172	105985
Senegal	USA (United States)	13 May 61	409UNTS232	105888
Ivory Coast	USA (United States)	17 May 61	409UNTS241	105889
Niger	USA (United States)	26 May 61	410UNTS213	105905
Cameroon	USA (United States)	26 May 61	413UNTS195	105953
Dahomey	USA (United States)	27 May 61	445UNTS23	106373
Australia	USA (United States)	05 Jun 61	409UNTS279	105892
UK Great Britain	Yugoslavia	08 Jun 61	437UNTS111	106300
Cyprus	United Nations	15 Jun 61	398UNTS39	105716
Madagascar	USA (United States)	22 Jun 61	413UNTS219	105956
Finland	India	23 Jun 61	421UNTS49	106051
IBRD (World Bank)	UK Great Britain	23 Jun 61	415UNTS358	105991
Pakistan	IBRD (World Bank)	27 Jun 61	425UNTS241	106127
Haiti	United Nations	28 Jun 61	399UNTS159	105740
Argentina	IBRD (World Bank)	30 Jun 61	445UNTS85	106379
UNICEF (Children)	Saudi Arabia	04 Jul 61	413UNTS122	105947
Israel	IBRD (World Bank)	11 Jul 61	429UNTS3	106188
Ghana	USA (United States)	19 Jul 61	416UNTS167	106002
Tanganyika	USA (United States)	21 Jul 61	445UNTS33	106374
Philippines	IBRD (World Bank)	26 Jul 61	414UNTS253	105976

PARTY ONE	PARTY TWO	DATE	CITATION	NUMBER
Tax exemptions (Cont.)				
Colombia	USA (United States)	01 Aug 61	433UNTS123	106235
India	IBRD (World Bank)	09 Aug 61	417UNTS297	106011
Finland	IBRD (World Bank)	09 Aug 61	415UNTS204	105986
Cameroon	UNICEF (Children)	12 Aug 61	402UNTS235	105788
IBRD (World Bank)	UK Great Britain	16 Aug 61	426UNTS287	106143
India	IBRD (World Bank)	17 Aug 61	417UNTS319	106012
Jordan	Norway	21 Aug 61	465UNTS275	106731
Central Afri Rep	UNICEF (Children)	21 Aug 61	413UNTS48	105939
Poland	UNICEF (Children)	24 Aug 61	406UNTS95	105841
Italy	Norway	25 Aug 61	475UNTS269	106896
Chad	UNICEF (Children)	26 Aug 61	422UNTS231	106077
Lebanon	United Nations	26 Aug 61	406UNTS105	105842
Colombia	IBRD (World Bank)	28 Aug 61	416UNTS23	105993
Denmark	Pakistan	04 Sep 61	455UNTS305	106549
Fed of Malaya	USA (United States)	04 Sep 61	421UNTS215	106060
Costa Rica	IBRD (World Bank)	06 Sep 61	446UNTS345	106408
UK Great Britain	USA (United States)	08 Sep 61	418UNTS53	106016
Jordan	United Nations	11 Sep 61	406UNTS255	105855
China People's Rep	Denmark	23 Sep 61	446UNTS3	106397
Greece	Sweden	06 Oct 61	481UNTS137	106981
India	IBRD (World Bank)	13 Oct 61	418UNTS3	106013
Costa Rica	IDA (Devel Assoc)	13 Oct 61	431UNTS3	106204
Philippines	IBRD (World Bank)	13 Oct 61	415UNTS269	105989
Pakistan	IDA (Devel Assoc)	19 Oct 61	447UNTS161	106415
Sweden	Thailand	20 Oct 61	428UNTS275	106180
Austria	Denmark	23 Oct 61	425UNTS115	106122
Belgium	Denmark	23 Oct 61	425UNTS181	106123
Paraguay	IDA (Devel Assoc)	26 Oct 61	447UNTS277	106419
Philippines	USA (United States)	31 Oct 61	424UNTS129	106105
Gabon	UNICEF (Children)	02 Nov 61	422UNTS241	106078
Brazil	USA (United States)	11 Nov 61	433UNTS199	106243
Malagasy	UNICEF (Children)	16 Nov 61	422UNTS251	106079
El Salvador	USA (United States)	20 Nov 61	433UNTS221	106245
Pakistan	IDA (Devel Assoc)	22 Nov 61	447UNTS295	106420
Cyprus	Greece	23 Nov 61	497UNTS311	107274
Czechoslovakia	Mali	27 Nov 61	466UNTS41	106736
Thailand	USA (United States)	28 Nov 61	434UNTS77	106256
Japan	IBRD (World Bank)	29 Nov 61	426UNTS3	106128
IBRD (World Bank)	UK Great Britain	29 Nov 61	426UNTS49	106130
IBRD (World Bank)	South Africa	01 Dec 61	425UNTS215	106126
Ceylon (Sri Lanka)	United Nations	04 Dec 61	415UNTS236	105987
Panama	USA (United States)	11 Dec 61	445UNTS161	106384
IBRD (World Bank)	Venezuela	13 Dec 61	446UNTS371	106409
El Salvador	USA (United States)	19 Dec 61	445UNTS175	106385
Argentina	Japan	20 Dec 61	451UNTS91	106487
Austria	Japan	20 Dec 61	517UNTS155	107485
Iran	USA (United States)	21 Dec 61	433UNTS269	106249
Jordan	IDA (Devel Assoc)	22 Dec 61	448UNTS21	106423
India	IBRD (World Bank)	22 Dec 61	481UNTS85	106979
Costa Rica	USA (United States)	22 Dec 61	460UNTS277	106646
Sierra Leone	USA (United States)	29 Dec 61	434UNTS43	106254
Ghana	USA (United States)	03 Jan 62	433UNTS147	106237
Netherlands	Sweden	08 Jan 62	466UNTS65	106737
Ivory Coast	UNICEF (Children)	10 Jan 62	422UNTS261	106080
Dominican Republic	USA (United States)	11 Jan 62	433UNTS133	106236
Austria	Greece	15 Jan 62	498UNTS3	107275
Paraguay	USA (United States)	16 Jan 62	433UNTS169	106240
Argentina	IBRD (World Bank)	19 Jan 62	446UNTS305	106407
United Nations	Somalia	20 Jan 62	420UNTS133	106044
Australia	IBRD (World Bank)	23 Jan 62	430UNTS3	106201
Poland	Romania	25 Jan 62	468UNTS3	106770
Peru	USA (United States)	25 Jan 62	473UNTS57	106855
UK Great Britain	Zambia	30 Jan 62	590UNTS173	108553
UNICEF (Children)	Yemen	31 Jan 62	422UNTS271	106081
Ghana	IBRD (World Bank)	08 Feb 62	449UNTS207	106462

PARTY ONE	PARTY TWO	DATE	CITATION	NUMBER
Tax exemptions (Cont.)				
Hungary	Yugoslavia	09 Feb 62	577UNTS3	108370
Finland	Hungary	13 Feb 62	463UNTS61	106693
India	IDA (Devel Assoc)	14 Feb 62	468UNTS177	106773
Iceland	IBRD (World Bank)	14 Feb 62	447UNTS95	106413
UK Great Britain	USA (United States)	22 Feb 62	435UNTS127	106275
India	IBRD (World Bank)	28 Feb 62	447UNTS3	106410
Dominican Republic	USA (United States)	08 Mar 62	527UNTS29	107615
Liberia	USA (United States)	08 Mar 62	445UNTS41	106375
Argentina	USA (United States)	16 Mar 62	454UNTS3	106535
Dahomey	UN Special Fund	28 Mar 62	424UNTS55	106099
Brazil	Japan	28 Mar 62	451UNTS125	106489
Nicaragua	USA (United States)	30 Mar 62	456UNTS241	106559
India	Japan	31 Mar 62	451UNTS143	106490
UNICEF (Children)	Somalia	01 Apr 62	431UNTS75	106211
Ghana	USSR (Soviet Union)	06 Apr 62	498UNTS41	107277
Congo (Brazzaville)	UNICEF (Children)	09 Apr 62	431UNTS65	106210
UNICEF (Children)	Sierra Leone	11 Apr 62	431UNTS55	106209
Somalia	USA (United States)	17 Apr 62	436UNTS107	106291
Ecuador	USA (United States)	17 Apr 62	442UNTS69	106339
Ivory Coast	USA (United States)	21 Apr 62	526UNTS39	107598
India	Japan	23 Apr 62	451UNTS155	106491
Netherlands	USA (United States)	24 Apr 62	436UNTS93	106289
Dominican Republic	USA (United States)	02 May 62	442UNTS107	106342
Colombia	IBRD (World Bank)	23 May 62	447UNTS39	106411
Ethiopia	USA (United States)	23 May 62	456UNTS293	106563
Greece	Tunisia	26 May 62	534UNTS163	107761
South Africa	UK Great Britain	28 May 62	443UNTS79	106361
Pakistan	USA (United States)	31 May 62	460UNTS75	106631
Ethiopia	IBRD (World Bank)	31 May 62	467UNTS237	106765
Austria	IBRD (World Bank)	15 Jun 62	447UNTS127	106414
France	Senegal	15 Jun 62	524UNTS3	107563
Bolivia	USA (United States)	19 Jun 62	458UNTS239	106606
Mexico	IBRD (World Bank)	20 Jun 62	468UNTS109	106771
Mexico	IBRD (World Bank)	20 Jun 62	467UNTS205	106764
Israel	USA (United States)	22 Jun 62	448UNTS273	106440
Germany, West	Syria	25 Jun 62	489UNTS71	107135
Pakistan	IDA (Devel Assoc)	29 Jun 62	447UNTS325	106421
India	IDA (Devel Assoc)	29 Jun 62	447UNTS221	106417
Morocco	Switzerland	05 Jul 62	498UNTS171	107281
Germany, West	Israel	09 Jul 62	630UNTS87	108968
IBRD (World Bank)	Yugoslavia	11 Jul 62	468UNTS143	106772
India	IDA (Devel Assoc)	18 Jul 62	447UNTS191	106416
Honduras	USA (United States)	20 Jul 62	460UNTS125	106635
Colombia	USA (United States)	23 Jul 62	458UNTS123	106595
Niger	USA (United States)	23 Jul 62	487UNTS325	107114
Ecuador	USA (United States)	03 Aug 62	460UNTS133	106636
Nigeria	United Nations	07 Aug 62	435UNTS167	106278
Finland	IBRD (World Bank)	15 Aug 62	467UNTS177	106763
Korea, South	IDA (Devel Assoc)	17 Aug 62	468UNTS387	200603
Cyprus	USA (United States)	23 Aug 62	461UNTS147	106658
Nepal	USA (United States)	24 Aug 62	460UNTS143	106637
Turkey	USA (United States)	27 Aug 62	461UNTS55	106651
Cameroon	United Nations	29 Aug 62	442UNTS3	106334
Japan	UK Great Britain	04 Sep 62	475UNTS31	106888
Togo	USA (United States)	05 Sep 62	461UNTS47	106650
Nicaragua	IDA (Devel Assoc)	07 Sep 62	478UNTS313	106940
Afghanistan	USA (United States)	11 Sep 62	461UNTS169	106661
Pakistan	IBRD (World Bank)	14 Sep 62	467UNTS152	106762
Panama	IBRD (World Bank)	14 Sep 62	476UNTS153	106908
Pakistan	IBRD (World Bank)	14 Sep 62	467UNTS125	106761
India	IDA (Devel Assoc)	14 Sep 62	448UNTS3	106422
India	IDA (Devel Assoc)	14 Sep 62	467UNTS265	106766
IDA (Devel Assoc)	Tunisia	17 Sep 62	469UNTS33	106783
Ecuador	Germany, West	20 Sep 62	498UNTS199	107283
Austria	Czechoslovakia	22 Sep 62	495UNTS157	107244
Tax exemptions (Cont.)				
Israel	UK Great Britain	26 Sep 62	474UNTS233	106885
Niger	United Nations	01 Oct 62	439UNTS181	106329
Gabon	USA (United States)	04 Oct 62	459UNTS185	106620
India	USA (United States)	09 Oct 62	471UNTS39	106820
Austria	United Arab Rep	16 Oct 62	491UNTS63	107174
Germany, West	Ireland	17 Oct 62	604UNTS135	108749
Israel	IBRD (World Bank)	17 Oct 62	467UNTS107	106760
Netherlands	Norway	18 Oct 62	466UNTS145	106741
Czechoslovakia	Yugoslavia	22 Oct 62	480UNTS267	106974
Dominican Republic	USA (United States)	25 Oct 62	459UNTS247	106627
Czechoslovakia	Norway	25 Oct 62	498UNTS335	107287
Multilateral		25 Oct 62	457UNTS137	106583
Czechoslovakia	Denmark	25 Oct 62	456UNTS457	106571
Czechoslovakia	Sweden	25 Oct 62	498UNTS343	107288
Multilateral		25 Oct 62	457UNTS129	106582
IBRD (World Bank)	Uruguay	26 Oct 62	481UNTS39	106977
Pakistan	IDA (Devel Assoc)	02 Nov 62	468UNTS351	106781
El Salvador	IDA (Devel Assoc)	02 Nov 62	468UNTS331	106780
Haiti	IDA (Devel Assoc)	02 Nov 62	468UNTS205	106774
United Nations	Western Samoa	05 Nov 62	443UNTS297	200599
Ethiopia	Greece	07 Nov 62	550UNTS179	108014
Poland	Syria	10 Nov 62	491UNTS228	107179
Japan	UK Great Britain	14 Nov 62	478UNTS29	106934
Algeria	UN Special Fund	15 Nov 62	452UNTS243	106512
Algeria	UNICEF (Children)	20 Nov 62	453UNTS151	106522
Thailand	UK Great Britain	20 Nov 62	466UNTS243	106747
India	USA (United States)	21 Nov 62	462UNTS255	106685
Ceylon (Sri Lanka)	USA (United States)	21 Nov 62	462UNTS237	106683
IDA (Devel Assoc)	Turkey	23 Nov 62	469UNTS3	106782
Costa Rica	USA (United States)	23 Nov 62	541UNTS67	107861
Ecuador	United Nations	26 Nov 62	445UNTS3	106372
Rwanda	United Nations	28 Nov 62	450UNTS267	106473
Ivory Coast	United Nations	10 Dec 62	451UNTS269	106498
Nigeria	IBRD (World Bank)	10 Dec 62	468UNTS255	106776
Austria	Yugoslavia	11 Dec 62	546UNTS3	107938
Ghana	Tunisia	11 Dec 62	563UNTS243	108213
Guinea	USA (United States)	14 Dec 62	462UNTS247	106684
Luxembourg	USA (United States)	18 Dec 62	532UNTS277	107723
IBRD (World Bank)	Thailand	21 Dec 62	467UNTS43	106757
Morocco	IBRD (World Bank)	21 Dec 62	478UNTS205	106937
IBRD (World Bank)	Thailand	21 Dec 62	467UNTS63	106758
Syria	United Arab Rep	27 Dec 62	491UNTS245	107180
Canada	USA (United States)	28 Dec 62	471UNTS13	106818
Israel	United Nations	07 Jan 63	450UNTS229	106470
Ghana	Mali	09 Jan 63	466UNTS165	106742
Senegal	USA (United States)	17 Jan 63	493UNTS97	107210
Mauritania	UNICEF (Children)	19 Jan 63	452UNTS271	106514
UNICEF (Children)	Tanganyika	25 Jan 63	453UNTS249	106528
Japan	New Zealand	30 Jan 63	517UNTS183	107486
Central Afri Rep	USA (United States)	10 Feb 63	473UNTS83	106857
Pakistan	IBRD (World Bank)	13 Feb 63	467UNTS3	106756
Philippines	IBRD (World Bank)	15 Feb 63	478UNTS161	106936
Ceylon (Sri Lanka)	Denmark	16 Feb 63	486UNTS285	107083
Algeria	France	18 Feb 63	563UNTS263	108214
Ethiopia	IDA (Devel Assoc)	27 Feb 63	478UNTS289	106939
Nicaragua	IBRD (World Bank)	01 Mar 63	481UNTS15	106976
Japan	Thailand	01 Mar 63	475UNTS233	106895
IBRD (World Bank)	Thailand	07 Mar 63	467UNTS83	106759
Peru	IBRD (World Bank)	13 Mar 63	478UNTS245	106938
India	IDA (Devel Assoc)	22 Mar 63	477UNTS3	106911
Burma	Japan	29 Mar 63	518UNTS3	107490
Norway	Spain	25 Apr 63	503UNTS41	107340
Thailand	USA (United States)	25 Apr 63	476UNTS115	106906
Greece	Hungary	27 Apr 63	534UNTS3	107750
Cyprus	Denmark	27 Apr 63	529UNTS255	107664

Tax exemptions (Cont.)

PARTY ONE	PARTY TWO	DATE	CITATION	NUMBER
Mexico	IBRD (World Bank)	29 Apr 63	489UNTS151	107138
Algeria	Morocco	30 Apr 63	564UNTS3	108217
Philippines	USA (United States)	06 May 63	477UNTS67	106916
Australia	USA (United States)	09 May 63	475UNTS331	106897
Australia	USA (United States)	09 May 63	469UNTS55	106784
IBRD (World Bank)	UK Great Britain	16 May 63	476UNTS211	106910
IBRD (World Bank)	UK Great Britain	16 May 63	477UNTS361	106929
France	Monaco	18 May 63	0UNTS0	109438
India	IDA (Devel Assoc)	24 May 63	483UNTS205	107014
IDA (Devel Assoc)	Turkey	31 May 63	480UNTS127	106966
Colombia	IBRD (World Bank)	03 Jun 63	490UNTS199	107155
Japan	Malaysia	04 Jun 63	517UNTS245	107488
India	IBRD (World Bank)	05 Jun 63	481UNTS191	106983
Finland	Poland	10 Jun 63	503UNTS179	107343
IBRD (World Bank)	Thailand	11 Jun 63	481UNTS227	106984
El Salvador	IBRD (World Bank)	19 Jun 63	481UNTS59	106978
IBRD (World Bank)	Yugoslavia	21 Jun 63	482UNTS43	106990
Colombia	IBRD (World Bank)	21 Jun 63	482UNTS159	106994
Pakistan	IDA (Devel Assoc)	26 Jun 63	492UNTS115	107189
New Zealand	UN Special Fund	28 Jun 63	470UNTS3	106792
Colombia	IBRD (World Bank)	28 Jun 63	489UNTS113	107137
IBRD (World Bank)	Tunisia	03 Jul 63	480UNTS209	106970
Costa Rica	IBRD (World Bank)	10 Jul 63	482UNTS69	106991
Malaysia	IBRD (World Bank)	15 Jul 63	482UNTS123	106993
Colombia	IBRD (World Bank)	16 Jul 63	482UNTS256	106998
Congo (Zaire)	USA (United States)	19 Jul 63	511UNTS47	107425
Greece	Romania	20 Jul 63	609UNTS109	108829
Algeria	Mali	22 Jul 63	564UNTS29	108219
Denmark	IBRD (World Bank)	24 Jul 63	481UNTS171	106982
Pakistan	IDA (Devel Assoc)	26 Jul 63	492UNTS143	107190
USA (United States)	Uruguay	31 Jul 63	488UNTS3	107115
Malaysia	IBRD (World Bank)	07 Aug 63	485UNTS253	107060
Pakistan	IDA (Devel Assoc)	16 Aug 63	492UNTS205	107192
Pakistan	IDA (Devel Assoc)	16 Aug 63	492UNTS171	107191
France	Israel	20 Aug 63	515UNTS173	107460
France	Greece	21 Aug 63	533UNTS235	107746
IBRD (World Bank)	UK Great Britain	06 Sep 63	483UNTS173	107013
Finland	IBRD (World Bank)	18 Sep 63	491UNTS345	107183
Mexico	IBRD (World Bank)	20 Sep 63	491UNTS317	107182
IBRD (World Bank)	Venezuela	20 Sep 63	482UNTS227	106997
IBRD (World Bank)	UK Great Britain	23 Sep 63	503UNTS247	107348
Germany, West	Greece	26 Sep 63	550UNTS203	108017
Japan	IBRD (World Bank)	27 Sep 63	485UNTS283	107061
Taiwan	IBRD (World Bank)	27 Sep 63	483UNTS151	107012
El Salvador	IBRD (World Bank)	01 Oct 63	517UNTS3	107481
Guatemala	USA (United States)	03 Oct 63	493UNTS45	107206
Pakistan	USSR (Soviet Union)	07 Oct 63	499UNTS161	107297
Malagasy	USA (United States)	07 Oct 63	494UNTS3	107221
Austria	Finland	08 Oct 63	490UNTS255	107160
UK Great Britain	USA (United States)	11 Oct 63	483UNTS3	107005
Norway	IBRD (World Bank)	15 Oct 63	482UNTS103	106992
Czechoslovakia	Hungary	22 Oct 63	514UNTS95	107444
Lebanon	UK Great Britain	24 Oct 63	535UNTS3	107772
Iran	USA (United States)	24 Oct 63	489UNTS303	107146
Jamaica	USA (United States)	24 Oct 63	489UNTS337	107148
IBRD (World Bank)	Spain	25 Oct 63	491UNTS297	107181
IBRD (World Bank)	Yugoslavia	28 Oct 63	503UNTS289	107349
Panama	USA (United States)	30 Oct 63	530UNTS3	107668
France	UK Great Britain	05 Nov 63	539UNTS277	107838
Portugal	IBRD (World Bank)	06 Nov 63	491UNTS137	107176
Portugal	IBRD (World Bank)	06 Nov 63	492UNTS89	107188
New Zealand	IBRD (World Bank)	12 Nov 63	485UNTS233	107059
Tunisia	USA (United States)	18 Nov 63	494UNTS193	107233
Peru	IBRD (World Bank)	22 Nov 63	491UNTS101	107175
Jordan	IDA (Devel Assoc)	12 Dec 63	506UNTS51	107381

Tax exemptions (Cont.)

PARTY ONE	PARTY TWO	DATE	CITATION	NUMBER
Jordan	IDA (Devel Assoc)	12 Dec 63	492UNTS3	107184
Greece	USA (United States)	13 Dec 63	494UNTS55	107226
Chile	IBRD (World Bank)	18 Dec 63	504UNTS3	107351
Cameroon	Netherlands	18 Dec 63	521UNTS303	107527
Chile	IBRD (World Bank)	18 Dec 63	504UNTS29	107352
IDA (Devel Assoc)	Syria	24 Dec 63	534UNTS253	107764
Paraguay	IDA (Devel Assoc)	26 Dec 63	507UNTS3	107394
Multilateral		30 Dec 63	568UNTS233	108271
Multilateral		30 Dec 63	551UNTS119	108037
Multilateral		30 Dec 63	551UNTS75	108035
Multilateral		30 Dec 63	551UNTS105	108036
Multilateral		30 Dec 63	568UNTS215	108270
Multilateral		30 Dec 63	568UNTS243	108272
France	South Africa	06 Jan 64	601UNTS229	108699
Saudi Arabia	USA (United States)	06 Jan 64	531UNTS3	107689
Liberia	IBRD (World Bank)	08 Jan 64	504UNTS53	107353
Norway	Thailand	09 Jan 64	522UNTS65	107537
Hungary	Netherlands	11 Jan 64	522UNTS243	107550
Greece	Poland	21 Jan 64	533UNTS309	107749
Canada	USA (United States)	22 Jan 64	530UNTS89	107674
Denmark	Ireland	04 Feb 64	525UNTS233	107596
IDA (Devel Assoc)	Tanganyika	05 Feb 64	506UNTS91	107382
Colombia	IBRD (World Bank)	07 Feb 64	516UNTS99	107473
Mexico	USA (United States)	14 Feb 64	524UNTS197	107574
UNESCO (Educ/Cult)	Yugoslavia	27 Feb 64	489UNTS257	107143
Multilateral		28 Feb 64	501UNTS245	107321
Belgium	France	10 Mar 64	557UNTS13	108127
IBRD (World Bank)	Thailand	11 Mar 64	504UNTS73	107354
New Zealand	IBRD (World Bank)	12 Mar 64	505UNTS3	107362
Nigeria	IBRD (World Bank)	12 Mar 64	516UNTS325	107480
Pakistan	IDA (Devel Assoc)	25 Mar 64	534UNTS275	107765
Pakistan	IDA (Devel Assoc)	25 Mar 64	535UNTS43	107775
Germany, West	Thailand	02 Apr 64	503UNTS3	107338
Portugal	UK Great Britain	07 Apr 64	539UNTS167	107830
Denmark	Finland	07 Apr 64	525UNTS89	107586
Malaysia	Netherlands	07 Apr 64	524UNTS81	107567
Japan	IBRD (World Bank)	22 Apr 64	505UNTS21	107363
Peru	IBRD (World Bank)	22 Apr 64	519UNTS95	107503
United Arab Rep	USA (United States)	05 May 64	531UNTS229	107706
Ethiopia	IBRD (World Bank)	08 May 64	505UNTS51	107364
Germany, West	Ireland	13 May 64	553UNTS87	108071
Algeria	IBRD (World Bank)	14 May 64	522UNTS265	107552
Pakistan	IBRD (World Bank)	14 May 64	516UNTS145	107475
Multilateral		25 May 64	620UNTS149	108953
Netherlands	NATO (North Atlan)	25 May 64	544UNTS237	107920
Ecuador	IDA (Devel Assoc)	26 May 64	534UNTS93	107757
Ecuador	IBRD (World Bank)	26 May 64	534UNTS113	107758
IBRD (World Bank)	Tunisia	05 Jun 64	539UNTS129	107827
India	IDA (Devel Assoc)	09 Jun 64	506UNTS31	107380
Iran	IBRD (World Bank)	10 Jun 64	537UNTS111	107799
Pakistan	IDA (Devel Assoc)	11 Jun 64	534UNTS309	107766
Ceylon (Sri Lanka)	Norway	11 Jun 64	559UNTS23	108153
Pakistan	IDA (Devel Assoc)	11 Jun 64	506UNTS3	107379
Niger	IDA (Devel Assoc)	24 Jun 64	554UNTS93	108098
Pakistan	IDA (Devel Assoc)	24 Jun 64	533UNTS191	107743
Pakistan	IDA (Devel Assoc)	24 Jun 64	533UNTS165	107742
India	IDA (Devel Assoc)	06 Jul 64	534UNTS49	107753
Colombia	Netherlands	06 Jul 64	543UNTS289	107906
Nigeria	IBRD (World Bank)	07 Jul 64	537UNTS3	107795
Gabon	IBRD (World Bank)	10 Jul 64	537UNTS63	107797
Finland	IBRD (World Bank)	10 Jul 64	516UNTS125	107474
IDA (Devel Assoc)	Turkey	14 Jul 64	534UNTS339	107767
Belgium	Tunisia	15 Jul 64	560UNTS57	108168
Pakistan	IDA (Devel Assoc)	21 Jul 64	534UNTS373	107768
Philippines	IBRD (World Bank)	22 Jul 64	516UNTS171	107476

PARTY ONE	PARTY TWO	DATE	CITATION	NUMBER
Tax exemptions (Cont.)				
Bolivia	IDA (Devel Assoc)	24 Jul 64	534UNTS171	107762
Bolivia	IDA (Devel Assoc)	24 Jul 64	534UNTS203	107763
Mexico	USA (United States)	07 Aug 64	530UNTS123	107677
Kenya	IDA (Devel Assoc)	17 Aug 64	535UNTS79	107776
IBRD (World Bank)	Sierra Leone	18 Aug 64	516UNTS295	107479
Pakistan	IDA (Devel Assoc)	26 Aug 64	535UNTS263	107784
Morocco	IBRD (World Bank)	26 Aug 64	537UNTS193	107802
Kenya	USA (United States)	26 Aug 64	531UNTS51	107692
IBRD (World Bank)	Venezuela	28 Aug 64	537UNTS135	107800
IBRD (World Bank)	Venezuela	28 Aug 64	520UNTS97	107512
Dominican Republic	USA (United States)	28 Aug 64	531UNTS35	107691
Australia	USA (United States)	28 Aug 64	510UNTS201	107415
Ceylon (Sri Lanka)	USA (United States)	29 Aug 64	531UNTS93	107695
IDA (Devel Assoc)	Turkey	31 Aug 64	535UNTS111	107777
Canada	Japan	05 Sep 64	569UNTS99	108282
Pakistan	IDA (Devel Assoc)	22 Sep 64	594UNTS225	108605
Mali	IDA (Devel Assoc)	29 Sep 64	594UNTS187	108604
Czechoslovakia	Hungary	17 Oct 64	545UNTS21	107924
Norway	United Arab Rep	20 Oct 64	543UNTS3	107895
India	IDA (Devel Assoc)	26 Oct 64	535UNTS245	107783
Chile	USA (United States)	27 Oct 64	532UNTS347	107727
Philippines	IBRD (World Bank)	28 Oct 64	537UNTS165	107801
Ethiopia	Netherlands	28 Oct 64	541UNTS235	107872
Germany, West	Thailand	28 Oct 64	521UNTS311	107528
Germany, West	Thailand	28 Oct 64	521UNTS333	107529
Netherlands	Pakistan	30 Oct 64	541UNTS243	107873
Greece	Yugoslavia	05 Nov 64	539UNTS19	107821
Greece	South Africa	11 Nov 64	631UNTS319	109001
Afghanistan	IDA (Devel Assoc)	23 Nov 64	567UNTS155	108255
IBRD (World Bank)	Thailand	25 Nov 64	537UNTS273	107805
Germany, West	UK Great Britain	26 Nov 64	603UNTS183	108734
France	Japan	27 Nov 64	569UNTS157	108283
Netherlands	Nigeria	04 Dec 64	545UNTS155	107931
Japan	USA (United States)	04 Dec 64	532UNTS249	107721
India	Netherlands	11 Dec 64	570UNTS165	108292
IBRD (World Bank)	Yugoslavia	11 Dec 64	537UNTS321	107807
Denmark	Pakistan	12 Dec 64	636UNTS313	109107
Germany, West	Jamaica	16 Dec 64	531UNTS129	107699
Paraguay	IBRD (World Bank)	16 Dec 64	549UNTS173	107999
Taiwan	IBRD (World Bank)	17 Dec 64	538UNTS3	107808
Belgium	Germany, West	17 Dec 64	631UNTS229	108996
Japan	IBRD (World Bank)	23 Dec 64	538UNTS37	107809
Mauritania	IDA (Devel Assoc)	28 Dec 64	540UNTS163	107849
Kenya	IDA (Devel Assoc)	29 Dec 64	535UNTS225	107782
Japan	IBRD (World Bank)	13 Jan 65	537UNTS293	107806
Ecuador	Netherlands	14 Jan 65	551UNTS129	108038
Finland	Israel	21 Jan 65	581UNTS275	108450
Denmark	Thailand	25 Jan 65	530UNTS173	107680
Honduras	IDA (Devel Assoc)	02 Feb 65	561UNTS279	108189
Honduras	IBRD (World Bank)	02 Feb 65	561UNTS255	108188
Mexico	IBRD (World Bank)	04 Feb 65	549UNTS189	108000
Belgium	Congo (Zaire)	06 Feb 65	540UNTS275	107853
Greece	India	11 Feb 65	606UNTS9	108771
Chile	IBRD (World Bank)	12 Feb 65	537UNTS35	107796
Brazil	IBRD (World Bank)	26 Feb 65	567UNTS91	108253
Malaysia	IBRD (World Bank)	26 Feb 65	549UNTS239	108002
Brazil	IBRD (World Bank)	26 Feb 65	553UNTS3	108065
Nigeria	IDA (Devel Assoc)	01 Mar 65	563UNTS3	108201
Nigeria	IDA (Devel Assoc)	01 Mar 65	571UNTS3	108297
IBRD (World Bank)	Thailand	22 Mar 65	538UNTS63	107810
IDA (Devel Assoc)	Somalia	29 Mar 65	586UNTS101	108499
Poland	USSR (Soviet Union)	31 Mar 65	571UNTS217	108304
Finland	United Arab Rep	01 Apr 65	562UNTS3	108193
IDA (Devel Assoc)	Turkey	01 Apr 65	554UNTS137	108100
Hungary	Yugoslavia	08 Apr 65	587UNTS169	108511

PARTY ONE	PARTY TWO	DATE	CITATION	NUMBER
Tax exemptions (Cont.)				
Malawi	USA (United States)	20 Apr 65	546UNTS175	107943
Iran	IBRD (World Bank)	28 Apr 65	555UNTS45	108104
Taiwan	IBRD (World Bank)	28 Apr 65	549UNTS145	107998
Iran	IBRD (World Bank)	28 Apr 65	555UNTS21	108103
Portugal	IBRD (World Bank)	29 Apr 65	549UNTS69	107991
Ghana	Malawi	04 May 65	541UNTS163	107869
Denmark	Spain	05 May 65	543UNTS255	107905
UK Great Britain	USA (United States)	10 May 65	545UNTS181	107934
USA (United States)	Uruguay	17 May 65	564UNTS69	108221
Japan	IBRD (World Bank)	26 May 65	550UNTS95	108010
India	IBRD (World Bank)	28 May 65	552UNTS39	108049
Denmark	Thailand	01 Jun 65	551UNTS157	108040
Multilateral		02 Jun 65	551UNTS2	108030
Ivory Coast	Netherlands	03 Jun 65	634UNTS95	109054
Peru	IBRD (World Bank)	03 Jun 65	551UNTS227	108045
Saudi Arabia	USA (United States)	05 Jun 65	548UNTS285	107984
India	IBRD (World Bank)	11 Jun 65	557UNTS59	108128
India	IBRD (World Bank)	11 Jun 65	557UNTS101	108130
Peru	IBRD (World Bank)	18 Jun 65	568UNTS191	108269
Italy	IBRD (World Bank)	28 Jun 65	567UNTS127	108254
Guinea	USA (United States)	29 Jun 65	549UNTS139	107997
Finland	IBRD (World Bank)	30 Jun 65	550UNTS63	108009
Pakistan	IDA (Devel Assoc)	30 Jun 65	554UNTS111	108099
Kenya	IDA (Devel Assoc)	30 Jun 65	554UNTS75	108097
Belgium	Sweden	02 Jul 65	0UNTS0	109367
Multilateral		05 Jul 65	563UNTS104	108207
Cameroon	Netherlands	06 Jul 65	571UNTS75	108300
Pakistan	IBRD (World Bank)	09 Jul 65	554UNTS39	108096
Cameroon	France	10 Jul 65	0UNTS0	109433
Iran	IBRD (World Bank)	12 Jul 65	554UNTS3	108095
India	IDA (Devel Assoc)	11 Aug 65	562UNTS277	108199
Belgium	Denmark	20 Sep 65	549UNTS63	107990
Nigeria	IBRD (World Bank)	26 Sep 65	570UNTS233	108296
Nigeria	IBRD (World Bank)	26 Sep 65	571UNTS39	108298
IBRD (World Bank)	Spain	29 Sep 65	568UNTS49	108264
IBRD (World Bank)	Uganda	29 Sep 65	568UNTS317	108276
IBRD (World Bank)	Tanzania	29 Sep 65	568UNTS309	108275
East Afri Service	IBRD (World Bank)	29 Sep 65	568UNTS327	200623
Kenya	IBRD (World Bank)	29 Sep 65	568UNTS289	108274
Mexico	IBRD (World Bank)	01 Oct 65	589UNTS339	108542
Chile	IBRD (World Bank)	06 Oct 65	567UNTS293	108261
Morocco	IDA (Devel Assoc)	11 Oct 65	562UNTS299	108200
Netherlands	Nigeria	28 Oct 65	578UNTS15	108383
France	Italy	29 Oct 65	0UNTS0	109445
Philippines	IBRD (World Bank)	02 Nov 65	567UNTS3	108249
Malaysia	IBRD (World Bank)	17 Nov 65	568UNTS23	108263
Canada	UK Great Britain	06 Dec 65	572UNTS161	108311
IBRD (World Bank)	Venezuela	13 Dec 65	568UNTS77	108265
Mexico	IBRD (World Bank)	15 Dec 65	568UNTS125	108267
Paraguay	IBRD (World Bank)	16 Dec 65	568UNTS165	108268
New Zealand	IBRD (World Bank)	17 Dec 65	567UNTS275	108260
New Zealand	IBRD (World Bank)	17 Dec 65	567UNTS255	108259
IBRD (World Bank)	Sudan	27 Dec 65	567UNTS27	108250
Denmark	Syria	28 Dec 65	588UNTS163	108523
Ethiopia	IBRD (World Bank)	28 Dec 65	567UNTS229	108258
Austria	Tunisia	30 Dec 65	589UNTS119	108539
Pakistan	IDA (Devel Assoc)	13 Jan 66	567UNTS67	108252
IDA (Devel Assoc)	Tanzania	13 Jan 66	567UNTS177	108256
Multilateral		17 Jan 66	592UNTS101	108573
Norway	Eur Space Research	31 Jan 66	580UNTS3	108414
Pakistan	IDA (Devel Assoc)	10 Feb 66	575UNTS89	108355
Austria	Germany, West	17 Feb 66	614UNTS263	108875
Israel	Kenya	25 Feb 66	582UNTS23	108455
Brazil	Denmark	25 Feb 66	590UNTS95	108549
Argentina	Germany, West	01 Mar 66	635UNTS247	109087

PARTY ONE	PARTY TWO	DATE	CITATION	NUMBER
Tax exemptions (Cont.)				
Denmark	Italy	10 Mar 66	0UNTS0	109217
Iceland	Norway	30 Mar 66	566UNTS51	108240
Guinea	IBRD (World Bank)	30 Mar 66	568UNTS3	108262
Multilateral		30 Mar 66	593UNTS261	108588
Denmark	Netherlands	31 Mar 66	604UNTS209	108751
Paraguay	IDA (Devel Assoc)	04 Apr 66	582UNTS331	108469
Paraguay	IBRD (World Bank)	04 Apr 66	570UNTS41	108287
Spain	USA (United States)	14 Apr 66	579UNTS173	108406
Bulgaria	Turkey	18 Apr 66	631UNTS263	108999
IBRD (World Bank)	Venezuela	21 Apr 66	568UNTS257	108273
Finland	IBRD (World Bank)	27 Apr 66	568UNTS107	108266
Peru	IBRD (World Bank)	13 May 66	570UNTS61	108288
IBRD (World Bank)	Tunisia	16 May 66	584UNTS155	108477
Austria	Ireland	24 May 66	636UNTS149	109102
Mexico	IBRD (World Bank)	25 May 66	596UNTS3	108627
Bulgaria	UN Special Fund	26 May 66	563UNTS71	108205
Guyana	UK Great Britain	26 May 66	595UNTS255	108621
Portugal	IBRD (World Bank)	14 Jun 66	581UNTS3	108430
Portugal	IBRD (World Bank)	14 Jun 66	581UNTS29	108431
Denmark	Iran	14 Jun 66	597UNTS283	108652
Pakistan	IDA (Devel Assoc)	17 Jun 66	582UNTS297	108468
Jamaica	IBRD (World Bank)	20 Jun 66	582UNTS145	108462
IBRD (World Bank)	Thailand	24 Jun 66	582UNTS259	108466
Denmark	Israel	27 Jun 66	581UNTS227	108448
Denmark	Jordan	28 Jun 66	574UNTS3	108338
India	IDA (Devel Assoc)	29 Jun 66	582UNTS277	108467
India	IDA (Devel Assoc)	29 Jun 66	585UNTS101	108484
India	IBRD (World Bank)	07 Jul 66	595UNTS3	108610
Brazil	Denmark	08 Jul 66	581UNTS95	108435
New Zealand	UK Great Britain	13 Jul 66	598UNTS121	108658
Argentina	Germany, West	13 Jul 66	636UNTS3	109091
Iraq	IBRD (World Bank)	22 Jul 66	584UNTS233	108480
Malaysia	IBRD (World Bank)	26 Jul 66	586UNTS195	108504
Iran	IBRD (World Bank)	26 Jul 66	582UNTS107	108461
Ivory Coast	Netherlands	01 Aug 66	591UNTS245	108561
IDA (Devel Assoc)	Siam	02 Aug 66	585UNTS271	108492
IBRD (World Bank)	Turkey	10 Aug 66	585UNTS199	108490
IDA (Devel Assoc)	Turkey	10 Aug 66	585UNTS237	108491
IBRD (World Bank)	Singapore	11 Aug 66	585UNTS39	108482
Kenya	IDA (Devel Assoc)	19 Aug 66	585UNTS119	108485
India	IDA (Devel Assoc)	19 Aug 66	584UNTS193	108478
Honduras	IBRD (World Bank)	25 Aug 66	582UNTS79	108460
Denmark	Malawi	01 Sep 66	586UNTS3	108493
Peru	IBRD (World Bank)	07 Sep 66	585UNTS3	108481
Netherlands	Yugoslavia	08 Sep 66	597UNTS147	108643
IBRD (World Bank)	South Africa	08 Sep 66	585UNTS71	108483
Tunisia	USA (United States)	26 Sep 66	616UNTS259	108900
IDA (Devel Assoc)	Senegal	29 Sep 66	594UNTS277	108607
Botswana	UK Great Britain	30 Sep 66	597UNTS211	108646
Jamaica	IBRD (World Bank)	30 Sep 66	582UNTS179	108463
IBRD (World Bank)	Zambia	04 Oct 66	585UNTS181	108489
Malawi	IDA (Devel Assoc)	04 Oct 66	584UNTS215	108479
Nicaragua	IBRD (World Bank)	05 Oct 66	582UNTS231	108465
Mauritania	USSR (Soviet Union)	17 Oct 66	633UNTS231	109040
Israel	Norway	02 Nov 66	630UNTS225	108972
IBRD (World Bank)	Singapore	04 Nov 66	585UNTS155	108488
Ireland	Switzerland	08 Nov 66	0UNTS0	109499
Canada	Israel	30 Nov 66	630UNTS267	108973
Singapore	UK Great Britain	01 Dec 66	605UNTS153	108763
Australia	USA (United States)	09 Dec 66	607UNTS83	108798
France	Monaco	09 Dec 66	0UNTS0	109439
Denmark	Singapore	20 Dec 66	593UNTS125	108580
Austria	Spain	20 Dec 66	636UNTS197	109103
India	IDA (Devel Assoc)	23 Dec 66	594UNTS165	108603
Chile	IBRD (World Bank)	23 Dec 66	595UNTS141	108618

PARTY ONE	PARTY TWO	DATE	CITATION	NUMBER
Tax exemptions (Cont.)				
Pakistan	IDA (Devel Assoc)	23 Dec 66	594UNTS255	108606
Trinidad/Tobago	UK Great Britain	29 Dec 66	605UNTS237	108766
Jamaica	IBRD (World Bank)	23 Jan 67	594UNTS311	108608
IBRD (World Bank)	Venezuela	26 Jan 67	596UNTS35	108628
IBRD (World Bank)	Tanzania	17 Feb 67	599UNTS287	108671
IBRD (World Bank)	Uganda	17 Feb 67	599UNTS321	108673
Romania	Sweden	01 Mar 67	642UNTS163	109172
Guatemala	IBRD (World Bank)	10 Mar 67	616UNTS139	108894
France	USSR (Soviet Union)	14 Mar 67	0UNTS0	109330
IBRD (World Bank)	Thailand	24 Mar 67	599UNTS299	108672
Haiti	Israel	28 Mar 67	630UNTS293	108975
Denmark	Lebanon	29 Mar 67	602UNTS251	108717
Denmark	Tanzania	05 Apr 67	604UNTS19	108740
Austria	United Nations	13 Apr 67	600UNTS93	108679
Greece	Yugoslavia	15 Apr 67	633UNTS373	109046
Denmark	Netherlands	20 Jun 67	619UNTS67	108939
Multilateral		21 Jun 67	598UNTS2	108653
Malaysia	UK Great Britain	17 Jul 67	637UNTS0	109127
Netherlands	UK Great Britain	31 Oct 67	0UNTS0	109222
Australia	UK Great Britain	07 Dec 67	0UNTS0	109458
Brazil	UK Great Britain	29 Dec 67	643UNTS217	109193
Denmark	Japan	03 Feb 68	0UNTS0	109405
Sweden	UK Great Britain	12 Feb 68	0UNTS0	109449
Italy	UK Great Britain	15 Feb 68	0UNTS0	109263
Cyprus	Greece	30 Mar 68	0UNTS0	109465
Turkey	UK Great Britain	02 Apr 68	0UNTS0	109452
Denmark	Yugoslavia	11 Apr 68	0UNTS0	109406
Patents, copyrights and trademarks				
UK Great Britain	USA (United States)	27 Mar 46	4UNTS101	100040
USSR (Soviet Union)	Yugoslavia	25 Jul 47	130UNTS315	101732
Hungary	Poland	28 Aug 47	15UNTS145	100231
Denmark	Poland	12 May 49	87UNTS179	101172
Germany, West	Greece	28 Jul 52	182UNTS85	102424
UK Great Britain	USA (United States)	19 Jan 53	161UNTS3	102117
Spain	USA (United States)	30 Jul 54	235UNTS45	103295
India	USA (United States)	21 Oct 54	234UNTS119	103277
Bulgaria	Yugoslavia	02 Nov 54	375UNTS333	105371
Netherlands	USA (United States)	14 Dec 54	262UNTS35	103737
Norway	USA (United States)	06 Apr 55	269UNTS65	103874
Iran	USA (United States)	15 Aug 55	284UNTS93	104132
Italy	Lebanon	04 Nov 55	267UNTS147	103840
USSR (Soviet Union)	Yugoslavia	19 Dec 55	378UNTS127	105423
Germany, West	USA (United States)	04 Jan 56	268UNTS143	103856
Japan	USA (United States)	22 Mar 56	275UNTS195	103983
Czechoslovakia	Yugoslavia	03 Jul 56	397UNTS165	105704
Ceylon (Sri Lanka)	Yugoslavia	05 May 59	391UNTS101	105618
Germany, East	Hungary	12 Jan 60	409UNTS22	105875
IAEA (Atom Energy)	USA (United States)	28 Jun 60	374UNTS133	105333
Australia	USA (United States)	23 Aug 60	388UNTS237	105581
Norway	IAEA (Atom Energy)	10 Apr 61	402UNTS255	105790
IAEA (Atom Energy)	Yugoslavia	04 Oct 61	412UNTS226	105935
Pakistan	IAEA (Atom Energy)	05 Mar 62	425UNTS17	106115
Congo (Zaire)	IAEA (Atom Energy)	27 Jun 62	463UNTS31	106691
Cyprus	Greece	23 Aug 62	609UNTS15	108825
Sweden	USA (United States)	04 Oct 62	462UNTS31	106669
Australia	India	23 Jan 63	456UNTS185	106556
Czechoslovakia	Hungary	20 Dec 63	538UNTS127	107812
Germany, West	Greece	16 Apr 64	609UNTS27	108826
Compliance with domestic patent and copyright laws				
Australia	USA (United States)	23 Aug 60	388UNTS237	105581
Italy	USA (United States)	04 Aug 64	529UNTS205	107662
Literary and artistic copyrights				
Belgium	UK Great Britain	15 Mar 50	76UNTS85	100981

PARTY ONE	PARTY TWO	DATE	CITATION	NUMBER
Trademarks				
Multilateral		08 Feb 47	14UNTS287	100222
Belgium	Chile	11 Feb 47	76UNTS107	100983
Denmark	France	16 Jul 47	12UNTS3	100177
Multilateral		30 Oct 47	55UNTS188	100814
USA (United States)	Yugoslavia	19 Jul 48	89UNTS43	101208
Greece	Lebanon	06 Oct 48	87UNTS351	101179
Israel	UK Great Britain	10 Dec 50	88UNTS211	101193
Germany, West	Greece	28 Jul 52	182UNTS85	102424
Belgium	Iceland	10 Dec 52	158UNTS445	102078
Denmark	USA (United States)	15 Oct 53	215UNTS111	102915
Sweden	Switzerland	25 Sep 54	262UNTS205	103746
Denmark	Sweden	30 Sep 54	262UNTS199	103745
Bulgaria	Yugoslavia	02 Nov 54	375UNTS333	105371
USA (United States)	Vietnam, South	22 Nov 54	235UNTS11	103291
Multilateral		19 Dec 54	218UNTS51	102953
Norway	Sweden	10 Jan 55	204UNTS293	102764
Netherlands	Vietnam, South	05 Mar 55	288UNTS53	104197
Brazil	Sweden	29 Apr 55	228UNTS115	103145
Australia	Taiwan	29 Jul 55	213UNTS193	102887
UK Great Britain	Vietnam, South	14 Oct 55	231UNTS193	103220
Germany, West	Sweden	22 Mar 56	262UNTS423	103763
Multilateral		05 Jul 56	258UNTS371	103679
Belgium	Philippines	05 Feb 57	269UNTS49	103872
Multilateral		29 Mar 57	283UNTS137	104113
China People's Rep	Sweden	08 Apr 57	428UNTS267	106179
Multilateral		15 Jun 57	550UNTS45	108008
Czechoslovakia	Germany, East	26 Jun 58	504UNTS221	107359
Canada	Euratom	06 Oct 59	475UNTS187	106894
Germany, East	Hungary	12 Jan 60	409UNTS22	105875
Iceland	Israel	15 Jun 60	377UNTS261	105405
IAEA (Atom Energy)	Yugoslavia	07 Dec 63	501UNTS273	107322
Italy	Romania	16 Jun 64	558UNTS313	108150
Korea, South	Netherlands	08 Dec 65	571UNTS83	108301
Laws and formalities				
UK Great Britain	USA (United States)	01 Dec 43	3UNTS209	100033
UK Great Britain	USA (United States)	10 Mar 44	5UNTS205	200030
Multilateral		27 Jul 46	90UNTS229	101238
Canada	USA (United States)	27 Sep 46	21UNTS3	100320
Multilateral		08 Feb 47	14UNTS287	100222
France	USA (United States)	27 Mar 47	16UNTS65	100249
New Zealand	USA (United States)	24 Apr 47	16UNTS79	100250
Multilateral		06 Jun 47	46UNTS249	100714
Bulgaria	Czechoslovakia	20 Jun 47	46UNTS15	100698
Multilateral		30 Oct 47	55UNTS188	100814
Italy	USA (United States)	02 Feb 48	79UNTS171	101040
Czechoslovakia	Yugoslavia	14 Mar 48	28UNTS81	100421
Multilateral		26 Jun 48	331UNTS217	104757
Philippines	USA (United States)	23 Aug 48	82UNTS11	101080
Philippines	USA (United States)	21 Oct 48	77UNTS197	101000
Australia	USA (United States)	29 Dec 49	71UNTS45	100909
UNICEF (Children)	UK Great Britain	10 Feb 50	65UNTS86	100837
Belgium	UK Great Britain	15 Mar 50	76UNTS85	100981
Israel	USA (United States)	04 May 50	132UNTS189	101760
Denmark	Italy	01 Jul 50	133UNTS181	101788
Israel	UK Great Britain	10 Dec 50	88UNTS211	101193
Italy	UK Great Britain	16 Jun 51	172UNTS293	102253
Italy	USA (United States)	12 Dec 51	137UNTS175	101852
Multilateral		06 Sep 52	216UNTS132	102937
Monaco	USA (United States)	24 Sep 52	186UNTS43	102481
UK Great Britain	USA (United States)	19 Jan 53	161UNTS3	102117
Japan	USA (United States)	10 Nov 53	224UNTS161	103076
Multilateral		11 Dec 53	218UNTS27	102952
Japan	Sweden	31 Mar 54	262UNTS187	103744

PARTY ONE	PARTY TWO	DATE	CITATION	NUMBER
Laws and formalities (Cont.)				
Belgium	USA (United States)	12 Oct 54	202UNTS289	102735
Multilateral		19 Dec 54	218UNTS51	102953
Norway	USA (United States)	06 Apr 55	269UNTS65	103874
Netherlands	USA (United States)	29 Apr 55	219UNTS105	102969
Canada	USA (United States)	15 Jun 55	235UNTS176	103301
Belgium	USA (United States)	15 Jun 55	235UNTS133	103299
UK Great Britain	USA (United States)	15 Jun 55	229UNTS73	103161
Greece	USA (United States)	16 Jun 55	262UNTS137	103742
Belgium	UK Great Britain	18 Nov 55	222UNTS327	103038
Germany, West	USA (United States)	04 Jan 56	268UNTS143	103856
Germany, West	Sweden	22 Mar 56	262UNTS423	103763
Japan	USA (United States)	22 Mar 56	275UNTS195	103983
Canada	India	30 Aug 56	305UNTS59	104413
Multilateral		24 Sep 56	253UNTS171	103583
Multilateral		25 Sep 56	334UNTS89	104767
Italy	Norway	16 Dec 56	291UNTS207	104256
Brazil	USA (United States)	02 Apr 57	290UNTS119	104231
France	Italy	29 Jul 57	291UNTS163	104250
Italy	Spain	12 Oct 57	291UNTS229	104258
Canada	Pakistan	15 Jan 58	392UNTS35	105637
Australia	USA (United States)	24 Jan 58	307UNTS105	104446
Czechoslovakia	Germany, East	26 Jun 58	504UNTS221	107359
UK Great Britain	USA (United States)	03 Jul 58	326UNTS3	104707
Euratom	USA (United States)	08 Nov 58	338UNTS135	104835
Canada	USA (United States)	22 May 59	354UNTS63	105054
Austria	USA (United States)	15 Jun 60	376UNTS267	105383
Australia	USA (United States)	23 Aug 60	388UNTS237	105581
Italy	USA (United States)	03 Dec 60	410UNTS3	105893
Multilateral		05 Oct 61	527UNTS181	107625
Multilateral		26 Oct 61	496UNTS43	107247
Luxembourg	USA (United States)	23 Feb 62	474UNTS3	106868
Taiwan	Paraguay	11 Jul 62	458UNTS41	106591
Ivory Coast	Netherlands	26 Apr 65	634UNTS81	109053
Saudi Arabia	USA (United States)	19 Nov 65	580UNTS35	108419
Korea, South	Netherlands	08 Dec 65	571UNTS83	108301
Morocco	USSR (Soviet Union)	27 Oct 66	608UNTS197	108816
Post-war adjustment				
UK Great Britain	USA (United States)	10 Mar 44	5UNTS205	200030
France	UK Great Britain	29 Aug 45	11UNTS397	200069
UK Great Britain	USA (United States)	27 Mar 46	4UNTS101	100040
France	USA (United States)	28 May 46	84UNTS59	101119
Multilateral		08 Feb 47	14UNTS287	100222
France	USA (United States)	27 Mar 47	16UNTS65	100249
France	USA (United States)	04 Apr 47	24UNTS133	100353
New Zealand	USA (United States)	24 Apr 47	16UNTS79	100250
Netherlands	USA (United States)	28 May 47	17UNTS29	100267
Denmark	France	16 Jul 47	12UNTS3	100177
Denmark	UK Great Britain	19 Aug 47	9UNTS277	100137
Canada	France	05 May 48	231UNTS87	103209
France	USA (United States)	14 Mar 49	84UNTS237	101133
Australia	USA (United States)	29 Dec 49	71UNTS45	100909
Denmark	Italy	01 Jul 50	133UNTS181	101788
Multilateral		29 Nov 50	88UNTS221	101194
Finland	USA (United States)	16 Nov 51	140UNTS273	101893
Italy	USA (United States)	12 Dec 51	137UNTS175	101852
Austria	Greece	22 Mar 52	187UNTS255	102517
Italy	Netherlands	22 Sep 52	150UNTS113	101965
Japan	Sweden	31 Mar 54	262UNTS187	103744
Germany, West	Sweden	22 Mar 56	262UNTS423	103763
Poland	USA (United States)	28 Jun 56	273UNTS79	103944
Multilateral		05 Jul 56	258UNTS371	103679
Multilateral		24 Sep 56	253UNTS171	103583
Austria	USA (United States)	15 Jun 60	376UNTS267	105383

PARTY ONE	PARTY TWO	DATE	CITATION	NUMBER
Recognition				
Iceland	USA (United States)	21 Nov 41	124UNTS179	200418
USA (United States)	USSR (Soviet Union)	18 Apr 42	105UNTS285	200339
Taiwan	USA (United States)	02 Jun 42	14UNTS343	200092
Belgium	USA (United States)	16 Jun 42	105UNTS159	200329
Poland	USA (United States)	01 Jul 42	103UNTS267	200317
Netherlands	USA (United States)	08 Jul 42	103UNTS277	200318
Greece	USA (United States)	10 Jul 42	103UNTS289	200319
Czechoslovakia	USA (United States)	11 Jul 42	90UNTS257	200263
USA (United States)	Yugoslavia	24 Jul 42	34UNTS361	200179
Liberia	USA (United States)	08 Jun 43	117UNTS242	200373
Ethiopia	USA (United States)	09 Aug 43	29UNTS303	200169
UK Great Britain	USA (United States)	01 Dec 43	3UNTS209	100033
Iraq	USA (United States)	31 Jul 45	121UNTS239	200402
France	UK Great Britain	29 Aug 45	11UNTS397	200069
Belgium	France	22 Feb 46	68UNTS157	100892
France	USA (United States)	28 May 46	84UNTS151	101125
France	Netherlands	19 Nov 46	32UNTS101	100493
Albania	Yugoslavia	09 Jul 47	33UNTS91	100516
Czechoslovakia	Romania	05 Sep 47	46UNTS37	100699
Multilateral		30 Oct 47	55UNTS188	100814
Italy	USA (United States)	02 Feb 48	79UNTS171	101040
Multilateral		26 Jun 48	331UNTS217	104757
Korea, South	USA (United States)	26 Jan 50	80UNTS205	101053
France	USA (United States)	27 Jan 50	80UNTS171	101051
Luxembourg	USA (United States)	27 Jan 50	80UNTS187	101052
Italy	USA (United States)	27 Jan 50	80UNTS145	101050
UK Great Britain	USA (United States)	27 Jan 50	80UNTS261	101056
Denmark	USA (United States)	27 Jan 50	48UNTS115	100740
Norway	USA (United States)	27 Jan 50	80UNTS241	101055
Netherlands	USA (United States)	27 Jan 50	80UNTS219	101054
Belgium	USA (United States)	27 Jan 50	51UNTS213	100767
Iran	USA (United States)	23 May 50	81UNTS3	101057
Thailand	USA (United States)	17 Oct 50	79UNTS41	101030
Norway	UK Great Britain	15 Dec 50	106UNTS87	101459
Portugal	USA (United States)	05 Jan 51	133UNTS75	101782
Ethiopia	USA (United States)	07 Sep 51	206UNTS41	102785
Multilateral		08 Sep 51	136UNTS45	101832
USA (United States)	Yugoslavia	14 Nov 51	174UNTS201	102286
Denmark	USA (United States)	04 Feb 52	157UNTS25	102044
Ecuador	USA (United States)	20 Feb 52	177UNTS43	102308
Peru	USA (United States)	22 Feb 52	165UNTS31	102166
Cuba	USA (United States)	07 Mar 52	165UNTS11	102165
Brazil	USA (United States)	15 Mar 52	199UNTS221	102687
Chile	USA (United States)	09 Apr 52	186UNTS53	102482
Colombia	USA (United States)	17 Apr 52	174UNTS215	102287
USA (United States)	Uruguay	30 Jun 52	207UNTS139	102804
Austria	Belgium	17 Oct 52	162UNTS183	102135
Dominican Republic	USA (United States)	06 Mar 53	199UNTS267	102689
Japan	USA (United States)	02 Apr 53	206UNTS143	102788
Israel	Uruguay	30 Apr 53	280UNTS269	104064
Philippines	USA (United States)	26 Jun 53	213UNTS77	102881
Spain	USA (United States)	26 Sep 53	207UNTS61	102800
Japan	USA (United States)	21 Jan 54	223UNTS145	103063
Canada	Japan	31 Mar 54	236UNTS329	103334
Japan	Sweden	31 Mar 54	262UNTS187	103744
Iraq	USA (United States)	21 Apr 54	222UNTS251	103032
Pakistan	USA (United States)	19 May 54	202UNTS301	102736
Honduras	USA (United States)	20 May 54	222UNTS87	103025
Canada	Spain	26 May 54	391UNTS273	105632
Canada	Portugal	28 May 54	391UNTS253	105631
Multilateral		28 Sep 54	360UNTS117	105158
Germany, West	USA (United States)	29 Oct 54	273UNTS3	103943
Haiti	USA (United States)	28 Jan 55	270UNTS83	103894
Norway	USA (United States)	06 Apr 55	269UNTS65	103874

PARTY ONE	PARTY TWO	DATE	CITATION	NUMBER
Recognition (Cont.)				
Guatemala	USA (United States)	18 Jun 55	262UNTS105	103740
Germany, West	USA (United States)	30 Jun 55	240UNTS47	103393
Germany, West	USA (United States)	04 Jan 56	268UNTS143	103856
Nicaragua	USA (United States)	21 Jan 56	367UNTS3	105224
Netherlands	USA (United States)	27 Mar 56	285UNTS231	104154
Korea, South	USA (United States)	28 Nov 56	302UNTS281	104367
Multilateral		15 Jun 57	550UNTS45	108008
Libya	USA (United States)	30 Jun 57	284UNTS177	104136
Czechoslovakia	United Arab Rep	19 Oct 57	530UNTS181	107681
Czechoslovakia	Romania	25 Mar 58	339UNTS77	104846
Multilateral		03 Apr 58	336UNTS177	104806
Czechoslovakia	Romania	25 Oct 58	338UNTS301	104843
Belgium	Spain	27 Oct 58	327UNTS107	104720
Multilateral		15 Dec 58	546UNTS235	107950
Netherlands	USA (United States)	06 May 59	355UNTS327	105084
Canada	USA (United States)	22 May 59	354UNTS63	105054
Germany, East	Hungary	19 Dec 59	409UNTS4	105874
Germany, East	Hungary	12 Jan 60	409UNTS22	105875
Argentina	Mexico	26 Jan 60	635UNTS79	109073
UK Great Britain	Yugoslavia	12 Apr 60	360UNTS79	105155
Spain	USA (United States)	21 Jul 60	393UNTS289	105663
Australia	USA (United States)	23 Aug 60	388UNTS237	105581
Cambodia	Czechoslovakia	27 Nov 60	410UNTS263	105910
Czechoslovakia	Hungary	24 Feb 61	422UNTS15	106066
Japan	Peru	15 May 61	451UNTS3	106482
France	USA (United States)	27 Jul 61	433UNTS29	106229
Dominican Republic	USA (United States)	08 Mar 62	527UNTS29	107615
Belgium	USA (United States)	17 May 62	461UNTS3	106647
Multilateral		14 Jun 62	528UNTS33	107634
Israel	Peru	25 Jun 62	515UNTS263	107464
Taiwan	Paraguay	11 Jul 62	458UNTS41	106591
Canada	Greece	18 Jul 62	528UNTS265	107647
Sweden	USA (United States)	04 Oct 62	462UNTS31	106669
Australia	India	23 Jan 63	456UNTS185	106556
UK Great Britain	USA (United States)	06 Apr 63	474UNTS49	106871
Czechoslovakia	Tunisia	06 Apr 63	555UNTS111	108106
El Salvador	Japan	19 Jul 63	518UNTS135	107494
Hungary	Yugoslavia	15 Oct 63	577UNTS49	108372
Netherlands	UK Great Britain	30 Oct 63	490UNTS11	107151
Czechoslovakia	Hungary	20 Dec 63	538UNTS127	107812
Multilateral		28 Feb 64	501UNTS245	107321
Algeria	Czechoslovakia	14 May 64	538UNTS301	107817
Italy	Netherlands	29 May 64	541UNTS147	107867
Italy	USA (United States)	04 Aug 64	529UNTS205	107662
Czechoslovakia	Germany, East	06 Oct 64	545UNTS113	107927
Germany, East	Poland	06 Oct 64	552UNTS89	108051
Japan	USA (United States)	04 Dec 64	532UNTS249	107721
Bulgaria	Czechoslovakia	22 May 65	545UNTS65	107925
Bulgaria	Hungary	19 Aug 65	577UNTS67	108373
Czechoslovakia	Poland	22 Jan 66	588UNTS175	108524
Customs duties				
Greece	Iran	09 Jan 31	166UNTS331	200497
Argentina	Brazil	23 Jan 40	51UNTS281	200194
Brazil	Paraguay	14 Jun 41	54UNTS259	200198
Brazil	Uruguay	08 Jan 42	54UNTS359	200206
Haiti	USA (United States)	19 Feb 42	105UNTS238	200336
Peru	USA (United States)	07 May 42	103UNTS219	200316
Brazil	USA (United States)	07 May 42	6UNTS377	200040
USA (United States)	Uruguay	21 Jul 42	120UNTS211	200393
Canada	USA (United States)	09 Nov 42	101UNTS233	200298
Mexico	USA (United States)	23 Dec 42	13UNTS231	200081
Iran	USA (United States)	08 Apr 43	106UNTS155	200340
UK Great Britain	USA (United States)	10 May 43	147UNTS109	200473
Peru	USA (United States)	20 May 43	100UNTS259	200288

PARTY ONE	PARTY TWO	DATE	CITATION	NUMBER
Customs duties (Cont.)				
Iceland	USA (United States)	27 Sep 43	29UNTS317	200170
Turkey	USA (United States)	22 Apr 44	109UNTS279	200364
Multilateral		07 Dec 44	171UNTS345	200501
Multilateral		07 Dec 44	15UNTS295	200102
Canada	USA (United States)	17 Feb 45	122UNTS261	200409
Portugal	UK Great Britain	01 Jul 45	5UNTS263	200034
UK Great Britain	USA (United States)	06 Dec 45	126UNTS13	101679
United Arab Rep	USA (United States)	05 Jan 46	160UNTS27	102098
Taiwan	France	28 Feb 46	14UNTS137	100216
Portugal	USA (United States)	30 May 46	174UNTS187	102285
USA (United States)	Venezuela	03 Jun 46	4UNTS215	100047
Bolivia	USA (United States)	10 Jun 46	13UNTS19	100197
Luxembourg	USA (United States)	03 Jul 46	32UNTS85	100491
Ethiopia	USA (United States)	04 Jul 46	13UNTS27	100198
Norway	USA (United States)	08 Jul 46	13UNTS35	100199
Spain	USA (United States)	11 Jul 46	13UNTS51	100201
Belgium	USA (United States)	11 Jul 46	13UNTS43	100200
Ceylon (Sri Lanka)	India	12 Aug 46	196UNTS209	102626
United Arab Rep	USA (United States)	15 Aug 46	13UNTS59	100202
Denmark	USSR (Soviet Union)	17 Aug 46	8UNTS201	100124
Portugal	USA (United States)	26 Aug 46	13UNTS67	100203
Denmark	USA (United States)	10 Sep 46	13UNTS75	100204
Canada	Taiwan	26 Sep 46	14UNTS167	100219
USA (United States)	Yugoslavia	03 Oct 46	13UNTS83	100205
Dominican Republic	USA (United States)	07 Oct 46	13UNTS91	100206
Peru	USA (United States)	07 Oct 46	7UNTS71	100092
Netherlands	USA (United States)	21 Nov 46	12UNTS173	100185
USA (United States)	Uruguay	14 Dec 46	532UNTS87	107713
Canada	Nicaragua	19 Dec 46	236UNTS229	103326
Belgium	Turkey	12 Mar 47	37UNTS221	100579
Canada	USA (United States)	18 Mar 47	117UNTS79	101584
Hungary	USSR (Soviet Union)	15 Jul 47	216UNTS247	102940
Canada	Greece	28 Jul 47	43UNTS111	100665
Czechoslovakia	USSR (Soviet Union)	11 Dec 47	217UNTS35	102943
Multilateral		22 Dec 47	32UNTS143	100496
Taiwan	UK Great Britain	12 Jan 48	14UNTS74	100212
UK Great Britain	USA (United States)	24 Feb 48	73UNTS143	100951
Canada	Turkey	15 Mar 48	231UNTS63	103205
Bulgaria	USSR (Soviet Union)	01 Apr 48	217UNTS97	102946
Czechoslovakia	Poland	05 Apr 48	31UNTS325	100481
Czechoslovakia	Yugoslavia	10 Apr 48	112UNTS101	101541
Belgium	Netherlands	13 Apr 48	32UNTS153	100497
Canada	Italy	28 Apr 48	231UNTS69	103206
Burma	Pakistan	22 Jun 48	91UNTS197	101252
New Zealand	Pakistan	28 Jun 48	91UNTS235	101253
France	USA (United States)	28 Jun 48	31UNTS115	100472
Netherlands	USA (United States)	02 Jul 48	32UNTS77	100490
Greece	USA (United States)	02 Jul 48	31UNTS131	100474
Belgium	Czechoslovakia	03 Jul 48	77UNTS137	100997
Turkey	USA (United States)	04 Jul 48	34UNTS185	100536
Ireland	UK Great Britain	31 Jul 48	86UNTS37	101151
Portugal	USA (United States)	28 Sep 48	31UNTS139	100475
Bolivia	USA (United States)	29 Sep 48	505UNTS139	107370
Czechoslovakia	Poland	12 Nov 48	84UNTS347	101141
South Africa	UK Great Britain	06 Dec 48	118UNTS183	101607
Italy	USSR (Soviet Union)	11 Dec 48	217UNTS181	102948
Ceylon (Sri Lanka)	Pakistan	15 Dec 48	91UNTS303	101255
Multilateral		12 Feb 49	189UNTS33	102541
Korea, South	USA (United States)	17 Feb 49	74UNTS167	100963
Panama	USA (United States)	31 Mar 49	55UNTS87	100810
Chile	USA (United States)	09 Apr 49	122UNTS169	101646
Multilateral		28 Apr 49	83UNTS105	101105
Belgium	Netherlands	13 May 49	65UNTS133	100841
Italy	Spain	31 May 49	231UNTS251	103224
Canada	USA (United States)	04 Jun 49	122UNTS237	101649

PARTY ONE	PARTY TWO	DATE	CITATION	NUMBER
Customs duties (Cont.)				
Czechoslovakia	Poland	02 Jul 49	260UNTS149	103708
Czechoslovakia	Poland	02 Jul 49	260UNTS179	103709
Belgium	Canada	30 Aug 49	53UNTS221	100782
Australia	Philippines	01 Sep 49	46UNTS215	100711
Denmark	ICAO (Civil Aviat)	09 Sep 49	53UNTS341	100791
Multilateral		19 Sep 49	125UNTS3	101671
India	Philippines	20 Oct 49	72UNTS191	100934
Brazil	Spain	28 Nov 49	215UNTS303	102923
Canada	Denmark	13 Dec 49	72UNTS247	100937
USA (United States)	Yugoslavia	24 Dec 49	89UNTS209	101219
Ireland	USA (United States)	21 Jan 50	206UNTS269	102792
Canada	Norway	14 Feb 50	53UNTS329	100790
Spain	Sweden	18 Feb 50	166UNTS15	102184
Multilateral		18 Feb 50	123UNTS45	101654
Italy	Netherlands	04 Mar 50	254UNTS305	103598
Canada	USA (United States)	24 Mar 50	200UNTS211	102705
Paraguay	UK Great Britain	03 Apr 50	99UNTS81	101372
Afghanistan	India	04 Apr 50	167UNTS105	102201
Costa Rica	USA (United States)	04 Apr 50	132UNTS177	101759
Italy	Portugal	05 Apr 50	254UNTS329	103599
South Africa	UK Great Britain	12 Jun 50	93UNTS67	101290
Netherlands	Spain	20 Jun 50	95UNTS303	101327
Israel	Turkey	04 Jul 50	220UNTS3	102982
India	Nepal	31 Jul 50	104UNTS3	101430
USA (United States)	Yugoslavia	14 Aug 50	137UNTS131	101851
Canada	New Zealand	16 Aug 50	77UNTS239	101002
Belgium	Luxembourg	12 Sep 50	110UNTS21	101497
Czechoslovakia	USA (United States)	29 Sep 50	290UNTS3	104227
Multilateral		15 Dec 50	347UNTS127	104994
Multilateral		15 Dec 50	157UNTS129	102052
India	USA (United States)	28 Dec 50	99UNTS39	101369
UK Great Britain	Yemen	20 Jan 51	101UNTS39	101400
Nepal	USA (United States)	23 Jan 51	184UNTS65	102439
Pakistan	USA (United States)	09 Feb 51	100UNTS67	101388
Greece	Yugoslavia	15 Mar 51	187UNTS237	102516
Pakistan	UK Great Britain	02 Apr 51	168UNTS281	102219
Multilateral		18 Apr 51	261UNTS140	103729
Canada	USA (United States)	18 Apr 51	134UNTS205	101800
United Arab Rep	USA (United States)	05 May 51	198UNTS265	102670
Lebanon	USA (United States)	29 May 51	160UNTS49	102101
UK Great Britain	USA (United States)	03 Jun 51	137UNTS81	101850
Multilateral		19 Jun 51	199UNTS67	102678
Mexico	USA (United States)	27 Jun 51	141UNTS211	101916
Israel	Yugoslavia	29 Jul 51	220UNTS7	102983
Cuba	UK Great Britain	10 Aug 51	108UNTS243	101478
Burma	India	29 Sep 51	132UNTS71	101752
Cuba	USA (United States)	17 Dec 51	152UNTS87	102012
Multilateral		10 Jan 52	163UNTS3	102138
Australia	Pakistan	16 Jan 52	151UNTS281	102001
Iran	USA (United States)	20 Jan 52	200UNTS191	102703
Pakistan	Switzerland	17 Mar 52	192UNTS237	102603
Sweden	Uruguay	20 Mar 52	311UNTS3	104497
Iraq	Switzerland	31 Mar 52	311UNTS43	104498
Korea, South	USA (United States)	24 May 52	179UNTS23	102353
Australia	USA (United States)	27 May 52	178UNTS113	102338
Multilateral		11 Jul 52	170UNTS63	102222
Netherlands	Pakistan	17 Jul 52	150UNTS277	101980
Greece	Israel	22 Jul 52	219UNTS231	102978
USA (United States)	Venezuela	28 Aug 52	178UNTS51	102336
Multilateral		05 Sep 52	247UNTS329	103479
Denmark	Israel	14 Nov 52	160UNTS275	102112
Turkey	Yugoslavia	16 Apr 53	255UNTS99	103606
Switzerland	Yugoslavia	28 May 53	232UNTS45	103228
Fed Rhod/Nyasaland	South Africa	28 Jun 53	267UNTS270	103848
Ethiopia	Yugoslavia	21 Aug 53	378UNTS105	105421

PARTY ONE	PARTY TWO	DATE	CITATION	NUMBER
Customs duties (Cont.)				
UNICEF (Children)	UK Great Britain	07 Oct 53	180UNTS59	102375
Netherlands	Switzerland	03 Nov 53	293UNTS53	104285
Ceylon (Sri Lanka)	Ireland	20 Nov 53	345UNTS189	104967
Italy	South Africa	20 Dec 53	277UNTS293	104014
Multilateral		19 Feb 54	214UNTS51	102899
Lebanon	Switzerland	03 Mar 54	255UNTS127	103608
Chile	USA (United States)	10 May 54	247UNTS299	103477
Canada	Spain	26 May 54	391UNTS273	105632
Switzerland	Syria	26 May 54	255UNTS145	103609
Canada	Portugal	28 May 54	391UNTS253	105631
Multilateral		04 Jun 54	276UNTS191	103992
Haiti	Italy	14 Jun 54	267UNTS97	103837
India	USA (United States)	29 Jul 54	239UNTS69	103373
Libya	USA (United States)	09 Sep 54	224UNTS217	103078
Multilateral		23 Oct 54	332UNTS3	104760
India	Iran	15 Dec 54	327UNTS245	104724
Canada	Japan	12 Jan 55	311UNTS167	104503
United Arab Rep	Yugoslavia	20 Feb 55	255UNTS199	103611
Ceylon (Sri Lanka)	Germany, West	01 Apr 55	369UNTS57	105251
India	Pakistan	15 Apr 55	247UNTS25	103458
Austria	Romania	11 May 55	342UNTS119	104904
Canada	USA (United States)	08 Jun 55	247UNTS163	103466
Ceylon (Sri Lanka)	USA (United States)	18 Jul 55	281UNTS295	104086
USSR (Soviet Union)	Yugoslavia	03 Sep 55	240UNTS267	103408
Czechoslovakia	Germany, East	24 Oct 55	504UNTS173	107358
Italy	Syria	10 Nov 55	267UNTS157	103841
Multilateral		21 Dec 55	292UNTS63	104267
Austria	Italy	23 Jan 56	393UNTS97	105653
Argentina	Switzerland	25 Jan 56	559UNTS121	108157
Canada	USSR (Soviet Union)	29 Feb 56	252UNTS165	103566
Multilateral		01 Mar 56	343UNTS129	104923
Netherlands	USA (United States)	27 Mar 56	285UNTS231	104154
Bulgaria	Yugoslavia	22 May 56	367UNTS119	105229
India	Thailand	12 Jun 56	255UNTS341	103617
Canada	Honduras	11 Jul 56	305UNTS39	104411
Multilateral		16 Aug 56	287UNTS223	104188
Guatemala	Honduras	22 Aug 56	263UNTS49	103767
Peru	Switzerland	23 Nov 56	411UNTS97	105916
Poland	United Arab Rep	02 Feb 57	319UNTS221	104633
Australia	UK Great Britain	26 Feb 57	265UNTS197	103813
Japan	Norway	28 Feb 57	280UNTS87	104054
Turkey	UK Great Britain	28 Feb 57	310UNTS29	104483
Morocco	UK Great Britain	01 Mar 57	310UNTS3	104480
Belgium	Czechoslovakia	12 Mar 57	312UNTS75	104512
Liberia	USA (United States)	16 Mar 57	290UNTS59	104228
Multilateral		25 Mar 57	294UNTS2	104300
Denmark	Pakistan	10 Apr 57	302UNTS53	104353
Denmark	Peru	10 Jun 57	406UNTS63	105839
Austria	USSR (Soviet Union)	14 Jun 57	285UNTS169	104152
UK Great Britain	USA (United States)	27 Jun 57	284UNTS75	104130
Ceylon (Sri Lanka)	China People's Rep	19 Sep 57	337UNTS137	104821
Germany, East	USSR (Soviet Union)	27 Sep 57	292UNTS75	104268
Multilateral		03 Oct 57	364UNTS3	105211
Japan	USSR (Soviet Union)	06 Dec 57	325UNTS35	104694
China People's Rep	USSR (Soviet Union)	21 Dec 57	305UNTS213	104420
Canada	Switzerland	10 Jan 58	464UNTS21	106710
Multilateral		15 Jan 58	383UNTS229	105503
Belgium	Morocco	20 Jan 58	288UNTS3	104192
Czechoslovakia	Poland	31 Jan 58	431UNTS99	106214
India	Japan	04 Feb 58	324UNTS215	104687
Afghanistan	Turkey	08 Feb 58	464UNTS39	106711
Bulgaria	Yugoslavia	21 Mar 58	349UNTS61	105009
Japan	Poland	26 Apr 58	340UNTS221	104866
Czechoslovakia	Hungary	08 May 58	407UNTS92	105862
Italy	Switzerland	23 May 58	363UNTS81	105201

PARTY ONE	PARTY TWO	DATE	CITATION	NUMBER
Customs duties (Cont.)				
India	USSR (Soviet Union)	02 Jun 58	393UNTS3	105650
Multilateral		10 Jun 58	454UNTS47	106539
Hungary	USSR (Soviet Union)	21 Jul 58	408UNTS194	105871
Multilateral		25 Jul 58	352UNTS3	105035
Australia	Fed of Malaya	26 Aug 58	325UNTS253	104703
Nicaragua	USA (United States)	05 Sep 58	336UNTS33	104797
Iraq	USSR (Soviet Union)	11 Oct 58	328UNTS95	104730
Japan	USA (United States)	03 Nov 58	341UNTS83	104879
Czechoslovakia	Poland	25 Nov 58	372UNTS205	105299
Fed Rhod/Nyasaland	Portugal	29 Nov 58	354UNTS137	105060
Portugal	USA (United States)	12 Jan 59	343UNTS49	104921
United Arab Rep	USA (United States)	13 Jan 59	358UNTS3	105122
Netherlands	Tunisia	19 Mar 59	497UNTS61	107262
Sweden	Tunisia	19 Mar 59	497UNTS43	107261
Norway	Tunisia	28 Mar 59	497UNTS77	107263
India	Italy	16 Jul 59	464UNTS129	106714
Austria	Hungary	17 Jul 59	0UNTS0	109237
Taiwan	USA (United States)	22 Jul 59	357UNTS293	105121
Mexico	USA (United States)	05 Aug 59	356UNTS3	105089
New Zealand	UK Great Britain	12 Aug 59	354UNTS161	105062
Multilateral		01 Sep 59	454UNTS289	106542
Korea, South	USA (United States)	01 Oct 59	358UNTS115	105129
Norway	Sweden	28 Oct 59	427UNTS225	106157
Czechoslovakia	Japan	15 Dec 59	383UNTS277	105505
Japan	USA (United States)	19 Jan 60	373UNTS207	105321
India	Japan	25 Jan 60	384UNTS31	105508
Australia	Canada	12 Feb 60	369UNTS89	105253
Cuba	USSR (Soviet Union)	13 Feb 60	369UNTS17	105248
Finland	Iceland	10 Mar 60	497UNTS95	107264
Czechoslovakia	Iraq	11 Mar 60	464UNTS267	106718
Luxembourg	Yugoslavia	09 Apr 60	464UNTS293	106719
Iran	USA (United States)	12 Apr 60	372UNTS63	105288
Cuba	Japan	22 Apr 60	442UNTS261	106354
New Zealand	Philippines	09 May 60	486UNTS65	107073
Switzerland	Tunisia	21 May 60	497UNTS109	107265
Afghanistan	Czechoslovakia	28 May 60	497UNTS129	107266
Korea, North	USSR (Soviet Union)	22 Jun 60	399UNTS3	105732
Ghana	Netherlands	30 Jul 60	412UNTS51	105925
Cyprus	UK Great Britain	16 Aug 60	382UNTS215	105482
Iran	Japan	12 Sep 60	384UNTS43	105509
Czechoslovakia	India	19 Sep 60	465UNTS67	106722
Norway	Peru	02 Nov 60	497UNTS207	107270
Multilateral		09 Dec 60	429UNTS211	106200
Multilateral		13 Dec 60	455UNTS3	106543
Canada	Pakistan	21 Dec 60	465UNTS115	106724
Malaysia	New Zealand	03 Feb 61	447UNTS251	106418
Korea, South	Philippines	24 Feb 61	423UNTS217	106094
USA (United States)	Vietnam, South	03 Apr 61	424UNTS137	106106
Multilateral		08 Jun 61	473UNTS153	106862
Finland	USA (United States)	16 Jun 61	413UNTS211	105955
Indonesia	Japan	01 Jul 61	517UNTS107	107484
Finland	Luxembourg	15 Aug 61	541UNTS45	107859
Japan	Pakistan	17 Oct 61	466UNTS17	106734
Australia	UK Great Britain	14 Nov 61	466UNTS35	106735
Czechoslovakia	Mali	27 Nov 61	466UNTS41	106736
Czechoslovakia	Guinea	16 Dec 61	559UNTS49	108154
Hungary	Yugoslavia	09 Feb 62	577UNTS3	108370
Austria	Spain	19 Feb 62	0UNTS0	109238
Israel	USA (United States)	05 Mar 62	446UNTS29	106400
Finland	USA (United States)	05 Mar 62	446UNTS19	106399
Norway	USA (United States)	05 Mar 62	446UNTS47	106402
Denmark	USA (United States)	05 Mar 62	446UNTS9	106398
Pakistan	USA (United States)	05 Mar 62	446UNTS57	106403
New Zealand	USA (United States)	05 Mar 62	446UNTS39	106401
Peru	USA (United States)	05 Mar 62	446UNTS65	106404

PARTY ONE	PARTY TWO	DATE	CITATION	NUMBER
Customs duties (Cont.)				
EEC (Econ Commnty)	USA (United States)	07 Mar 62	446UNTS81	106405
UK Great Britain	USA (United States)	07 Mar 62	446UNTS231	106406
Japan	New Zealand	09 Mar 62	485UNTS351	107066
Israel	Vietnam, South	11 Apr 62	448UNTS205	106432
Ireland	USA (United States)	03 May 62	442UNTS117	106343
Thailand	USA (United States)	31 May 62	459UNTS135	106619
Nepal	USA (United States)	24 Aug 62	460UNTS143	106637
Mali	USSR (Soviet Union)	10 Oct 62	493UNTS219	107216
Multilateral		16 Oct 62	470UNTS336	106816
Hungary	Syria	18 Oct 62	491UNTS209	107178
Finland	Sweden	05 Nov 62	455UNTS289	106548
Poland	Syria	10 Nov 62	491UNTS228	107179
Japan	UK Great Britain	14 Nov 62	478UNTS29	106934
Ceylon (Sri Lanka)	USA (United States)	21 Nov 62	462UNTS237	106683
Laos	USSR (Soviet Union)	01 Dec 62	458UNTS21	106590
Japan	Philippines	19 Jan 63	517UNTS281	107489
Japan	South Africa	06 Apr 63	484UNTS319	107040
Australia	USA (United States)	09 May 63	469UNTS55	106784
Tanganyika	USSR (Soviet Union)	14 Aug 63	493UNTS195	107215
Algeria	Tunisia	01 Sep 63	601UNTS275	108701
Kuwait	USA (United States)	21 Oct 63	530UNTS281	107688
Czechoslovakia	Hungary	22 Oct 63	514UNTS95	107444
Nicaragua	United Nations	03 Dec 63	482UNTS329	107002
Czechoslovakia	Romania	16 Dec 63	527UNTS285	107630
Czechoslovakia	Hungary	20 Dec 63	538UNTS127	107812
Romania	Yugoslavia	25 Dec 63	576UNTS95	108366
France	South Africa	06 Jan 64	601UNTS229	108699
Denmark	Yugoslavia	11 Feb 64	511UNTS241	107437
Taiwan	USA (United States)	23 Apr 64	524UNTS141	107570
Netherlands	NATO (North Atlan)	25 May 64	544UNTS237	107920
Kenya	USA (United States)	26 Aug 64	531UNTS51	107692
Taiwan	Mexico	25 Sep 64	547UNTS233	107960
Multilateral		25 Nov 64	587UNTS19	108507
Cyprus	Syria	22 Dec 64	602UNTS25	108705
Argentina	UK Great Britain	12 Jan 65	597UNTS177	108645
Canada	USA (United States)	16 Jan 65	606UNTS31	108772
Denmark	Malaysia	26 Mar 65	540UNTS205	107851
Australia	France	13 Apr 65	601UNTS293	108702
Mauritania	Spain	11 May 65	602UNTS111	108709
Hungary	Yugoslavia	25 May 65	576UNTS145	108367
Malaysia	Norway	26 May 65	602UNTS157	108711
Multilateral		28 May 65	559UNTS273	108163
Argentina	Yugoslavia	09 Jun 65	601UNTS3	108684
New Zealand	Poland	07 Jul 65	548UNTS19	107966
Malta	Yugoslavia	15 Jul 65	561UNTS223	108186
Hungary	Poland	18 Jul 65	577UNTS161	108376
Australia	New Zealand	31 Aug 65	554UNTS169	108101
Belgium	Denmark	20 Sep 65	549UNTS63	107990
Australia	Korea, South	21 Sep 65	548UNTS163	107977
Nigeria	Switzerland	11 Oct 65	602UNTS137	108710
Australia	USSR (Soviet Union)	15 Oct 65	553UNTS239	108092
Multilateral		18 Nov 65	609UNTS115	108830
Ireland	UK Great Britain	14 Dec 65	565UNTS58	108235
Burma	Czechoslovakia	15 Dec 65	602UNTS71	108707
France	Romania	14 Mar 66	604UNTS33	108741
Argentina	India	26 Mar 66	601UNTS201	108697
Romania	USSR (Soviet Union)	21 Jun 66	604UNTS81	108746
Austria	USA (United States)	23 Jun 66	601UNTS51	108687
UK Great Britain	USA (United States)	30 Dec 66	603UNTS245	108736
UK Great Britain	USA (United States)	01 Jan 67	604UNTS3	108738
Philippines	USA (United States)	04 Jan 67	590UNTS51	108546
Trinidad/Tobago	UK Great Britain	23 Jan 67	605UNTS277	108767
Korea, South	USA (United States)	09 Feb 67	0UNTS0	109605
Trinidad/Tobago	UK Great Britain	01 Mar 67	606UNTS149	108784
Denmark	Tanzania	05 Apr 67	604UNTS19	108740

PARTY ONE	PARTY TWO	DATE	CITATION	NUMBER
Customs duties (Cont.)				
Denmark	Paraguay	03 May 67	608UNTS55	108812
Czechoslovakia	Yugoslavia	17 May 67	617UNTS305	108918
Customs declarations				
USA (United States)	Uruguay	21 Jul 42	120UNTS211	200393
Mexico	USA (United States)	23 Dec 42	13UNTS231	200081
Chile	USA (United States)	30 Jul 45	6UNTS409	200042
France	USA (United States)	08 Nov 45	76UNTS151	100986
UK Great Britain	USA (United States)	21 Feb 46	6UNTS137	100073
Taiwan	France	28 Feb 46	14UNTS137	100216
France	USA (United States)	28 May 46	84UNTS151	101125
Philippines	USA (United States)	04 Jul 46	43UNTS135	100668
Nepal	USA (United States)	25 Apr 47	16UNTS97	100251
Hungary	USSR (Soviet Union)	15 Jul 47	216UNTS247	102940
Cuba	USA (United States)	30 Oct 47	119UNTS163	101611
Multilateral		30 Oct 47	55UNTS188	100814
Czechoslovakia	USSR (Soviet Union)	11 Dec 47	217UNTS35	102943
Switzerland	USSR (Soviet Union)	17 Mar 48	217UNTS73	102944
Bulgaria	USSR (Soviet Union)	01 Apr 48	217UNTS97	102946
Czechoslovakia	Yugoslavia	10 Apr 48	112UNTS101	101541
Italy	USSR (Soviet Union)	11 Dec 48	217UNTS181	102948
Korea, South	USA (United States)	17 Feb 49	74UNTS167	100963
Bulgaria	Poland	16 May 49	84UNTS313	101140
Multilateral		15 Dec 50	171UNTS305	102234
Multilateral		18 Apr 51	261UNTS140	103729
France	USSR (Soviet Union)	03 Sep 51	221UNTS79	103003
Denmark	Italy	24 Oct 51	118UNTS91	101598
El Salvador	Guatemala	14 Dec 51	131UNTS131	101740
Muscat and Oman	UK Great Britain	20 Dec 51	149UNTS247	101956
Multilateral		10 Jan 52	163UNTS27	102139
Ceylon (Sri Lanka)	Ireland	20 Nov 53	345UNTS189	104967
Italy	South Africa	20 Dec 53	277UNTS293	104014
Australia	Belgium	26 Mar 54	198UNTS305	102673
Canada	South Africa	04 Aug 54	261UNTS3	103722
Israel	South Africa	31 Dec 54	220UNTS11	102984
Italy	Yugoslavia	31 Mar 55	386UNTS307	105550
Costa Rica	Guatemala	20 Dec 55	280UNTS121	104056
Canada	Japan	20 Mar 56	517UNTS33	107482
Multilateral		08 Nov 56	470UNTS171	106809
Australia	UK Great Britain	26 Feb 57	265UNTS197	103813
Multilateral		25 Mar 57	294UNTS2	104300
Austria	South Africa	26 Sep 57	287UNTS3	104176
Multilateral		03 Oct 57	364UNTS3	105211
Multilateral		25 Nov 57	403UNTS169	105795
Bulgaria	Yugoslavia	21 Mar 58	376UNTS53	105373
Germany, West	Netherlands	30 May 58	570UNTS127	108291
Multilateral		10 Jun 58	454UNTS47	106539
Fed Rhod/Nyasaland	Portugal	29 Nov 58	354UNTS137	105060
Japan	Yugoslavia	28 Feb 59	341UNTS179	104883
New Zealand	UK Great Britain	12 Aug 59	354UNTS161	105062
Czechoslovakia	Germany, East	18 Sep 59	363UNTS287	105209
Ethiopia	France	12 Nov 59	381UNTS3	105465
Argentina	Brazil	26 Nov 59	374UNTS45	105327
Multilateral		06 Feb 60	383UNTS3	105494
Ireland	South Africa	13 Apr 60	390UNTS307	105612
Multilateral		13 Dec 60	455UNTS3	106543
Canada	USA (United States)	13 Jan 61	410UNTS62	105897
Greece	Morocco	01 Nov 61	483UNTS113	107009
Iraq	Syria	03 Nov 61	489UNTS45	107134
Austria	Bulgaria	05 Apr 63	480UNTS3	106963
Japan	South Africa	06 Apr 63	484UNTS319	107040
Austria	Switzerland	02 Sep 63	548UNTS91	107973
Jamaica	USA (United States)	24 Oct 63	489UNTS337	107148
Brazil	Germany, West	30 Nov 63	0UNTS0	109423
Czechoslovakia	Hungary	20 Dec 63	538UNTS127	107812

PARTY ONE	PARTY TWO	DATE	CITATION	NUMBER
Customs declarations (Cont.)				
Argentina	France	03 Oct 64	635UNTS155	109080
Denmark	Germany, West	09 Jun 65	605UNTS95	108762
Ireland	UK Great Britain	14 Dec 65	565UNTS58	108235
Malaysia	Philippines	01 Sep 67	608UNTS13	108810
Customs exemptions				
Bolivia	Brazil	25 Feb 38	88UNTS379	200254
Brazil	France	27 Jan 40	72UNTS77	100929
Panama	USA (United States)	23 Mar 40	124UNTS195	200420
Panama	USA (United States)	06 Sep 40	124UNTS209	200421
Honduras	USA (United States)	28 Feb 41	117UNTS205	200371
Multilateral		27 Mar 41	67UNTS231	200222
Haiti	USA (United States)	23 May 41	117UNTS191	200370
Brazil	Paraguay	14 Jun 41	54UNTS289	200201
Bolivia	USA (United States)	04 Sep 41	8UNTS345	200046
Argentina	USA (United States)	14 Oct 41	119UNTS193	200384
Peru	USA (United States)	11 Mar 42	117UNTS266	200375
Canada	USA (United States)	18 Mar 42	101UNTS205	200294
Liberia	USA (United States)	31 Mar 42	23UNTS302	200137
Brazil	Portugal	30 Apr 42	65UNTS183	200210
Brazil	USA (United States)	07 May 42	6UNTS377	200040
Peru	USA (United States)	07 May 42	103UNTS219	200316
Colombia	USA (United States)	29 May 42	8UNTS365	200047
Panama	USA (United States)	07 Jul 42	9UNTS289	200048
Bolivia	USA (United States)	11 Aug 42	9UNTS309	200049
Canada	USA (United States)	09 Nov 42	101UNTS233	200298
Dominican Republic	USA (United States)	25 Jan 43	13UNTS399	200083
Colombia	USA (United States)	29 Mar 43	124UNTS139	200416
Canada	USA (United States)	10 Apr 43	21UNTS237	200126
USA (United States)	Venezuela	14 May 43	28UNTS359	200160
Guatemala	USA (United States)	17 Jul 43	28UNTS431	200166
Ecuador	USA (United States)	13 Sep 43	29UNTS349	200171
Brazil	USA (United States)	25 Nov 43	102UNTS227	200305
Iran	USA (United States)	27 Nov 43	31UNTS451	200176
Paraguay	USA (United States)	10 Dec 43	21UNTS305	200131
USA (United States)	Venezuela	13 Jan 44	109UNTS171	200358
Multilateral		15 Jan 44	161UNTS281	200489
Mexico	USA (United States)	03 Feb 44	3UNTS313	200025
Ecuador	USA (United States)	29 Jun 44	80UNTS283	200250
Peru	USA (United States)	10 Jul 44	117UNTS291	200377
Brazil	Paraguay	11 Aug 44	67UNTS303	200227
Bolivia	USA (United States)	07 Sep 44	162UNTS315	200494
Guatemala	USA (United States)	16 Sep 44	135UNTS315	200444
Brazil	USA (United States)	29 Sep 44	65UNTS271	200216
Brazil	Uruguay	22 Nov 44	65UNTS289	200217
Portugal	USA (United States)	28 Nov 44	183UNTS311	200508
Spain	USA (United States)	02 Dec 44	89UNTS345	200262
Sweden	USA (United States)	16 Dec 44	6UNTS397	200041
Denmark	USA (United States)	16 Dec 44	10UNTS213	200063
Ecuador	USA (United States)	22 Jan 45	24UNTS273	200152
Iceland	USA (United States)	27 Jan 45	122UNTS293	200411
Ireland	USA (United States)	03 Feb 45	122UNTS305	200412
Canada	USA (United States)	17 Feb 45	122UNTS261	200409
Guatemala	USA (United States)	21 Feb 45	121UNTS133	200396
Colombia	USA (United States)	17 Apr 45	139UNTS303	200457
Guatemala	USA (United States)	21 May 45	121UNTS185	200399
Chile	USA (United States)	24 May 45	121UNTS219	200401
Switzerland	USA (United States)	03 Aug 45	51UNTS233	200191
Norway	USA (United States)	06 Oct 45	122UNTS319	200413
Dominican Republic	USA (United States)	13 Oct 45	149UNTS361	200477
South Africa	UK Great Britain	26 Oct 45	72UNTS41	100927
Greece	UK Great Britain	26 Nov 45	35UNTS161	100555
Portugal	USA (United States)	06 Dec 45	3UNTS139	100028
Portugal	UK Great Britain	06 Dec 45	5UNTS37	100064
Portugal	UK Great Britain	06 Dec 45	6UNTS3	100065

PARTY ONE	PARTY TWO	DATE	CITATION	NUMBER
Customs exemptions (Cont.)				
Costa Rica	USA (United States)	10 Dec 45	3UNTS157	100029
Canada	UK Great Britain	21 Dec 45	27UNTS155	100405
Multilateral		27 Dec 45	2UNTS39	100020
Honduras	USA (United States)	28 Dec 45	3UNTS185	100031
Czechoslovakia	USA (United States)	03 Jan 46	6UNTS309	100084
Czechoslovakia	Poland	24 Jan 46	25UNTS181	100363
UK Great Britain	USA (United States)	11 Feb 46	3UNTS253	100036
Turkey	UK Great Britain	12 Feb 46	6UNTS79	100069
Turkey	USA (United States)	12 Feb 46	13UNTS3	100196
Multilateral		13 Feb 46	1UNTS15	100004
Belgium	France	22 Feb 46	68UNTS157	100892
France	UK Great Britain	28 Feb 46	27UNTS173	100407
Belgium	UK Great Britain	11 Mar 46	26UNTS167	100387
France	USA (United States)	27 Mar 46	139UNTS114	101879
Greece	USA (United States)	27 Mar 46	15UNTS233	100239
Ireland	UK Great Britain	05 Apr 46	72UNTS57	100928
Belgium	USA (United States)	05 Apr 46	4UNTS125	100041
Brazil	USA (United States)	05 Apr 46	12UNTS131	100183
Netherlands	Portugal	12 Apr 46	4UNTS317	100054
Argentina	UK Great Britain	17 Apr 46	164UNTS53	102159
France	Ireland	16 May 46	44UNTS105	100681
Ireland	Sweden	29 May 46	35UNTS231	100557
USA (United States)	Venezuela	03 Jun 46	4UNTS215	100047
Australia	Canada	11 Jun 46	10UNTS47	100142
United Arab Rep	USA (United States)	15 Jun 46	71UNTS157	100917
Sweden	Turkey	26 Jun 46	14UNTS21	100208
United Nations	Switzerland	01 Jul 46	1UNTS163	200008
Netherlands	Spain	13 Jul 46	4UNTS351	100055
Czechoslovakia	USSR (Soviet Union)	25 Jul 46	27UNTS231	100409
Canada	Newfoundland	29 Jul 46	17UNTS169	100275
France	Sweden	02 Aug 46	27UNTS251	100410
Lebanon	USA (United States)	11 Aug 46	66UNTS211	100856
Netherlands	UK Great Britain	13 Aug 46	4UNTS367	100056
Norway	UK Great Britain	31 Aug 46	6UNTS235	100078
Brazil	USA (United States)	06 Sep 46	54UNTS197	100805
Peru	USA (United States)	07 Oct 46	7UNTS71	100092
France	Turkey	12 Oct 46	14UNTS33	100209
Belgium	Portugal	22 Oct 46	34UNTS49	100527
Brazil	UK Great Britain	31 Oct 46	11UNTS115	100152
India	USA (United States)	14 Nov 46	22UNTS55	100331
Philippines	USA (United States)	16 Nov 46	7UNTS151	100097
France	Netherlands	19 Nov 46	32UNTS101	100493
Sweden	UK Great Britain	27 Nov 46	11UNTS229	100162
Australia	USA (United States)	03 Dec 46	7UNTS201	100100
New Zealand	USA (United States)	03 Dec 46	7UNTS175	100099
Portugal	Switzerland	09 Dec 46	310UNTS251	104495
Brazil	Portugal	10 Dec 46	200UNTS67	102695
Multilateral		13 Dec 46	8UNTS135	100119
USA (United States)	Uruguay	14 Dec 46	532UNTS87	107713
Taiwan	USA (United States)	20 Dec 46	22UNTS87	100332
Peru	USA (United States)	27 Dec 46	26UNTS227	100390
Peru	USA (United States)	27 Dec 46	152UNTS93	102013
Ecuador	USA (United States)	08 Jan 47	22UNTS119	100333
Czechoslovakia	Ireland	29 Jan 47	27UNTS267	100411
USSR (Soviet Union)	Yugoslavia	04 Feb 47	130UNTS235	101731
Philippines	USA (United States)	14 Feb 47	16UNTS3	100245
Thailand	USA (United States)	26 Feb 47	16UNTS17	100246
Burma	USA (United States)	28 Feb 47	25UNTS27	100355
Paraguay	USA (United States)	28 Feb 47	44UNTS25	100676
Portugal	Sweden	06 Mar 47	35UNTS243	100558
Philippines	USA (United States)	14 Mar 47	16UNTS31	100247
Philippines	USA (United States)	14 Mar 47	43UNTS271	100673
Austria	France	15 Mar 47	12UNTS109	100182
Netherlands	Turkey	19 Mar 47	14UNTS59	100211
Muscat and Oman	UK Great Britain	05 Apr 47	27UNTS287	100412

PARTY ONE	PARTY TWO	DATE	CITATION	NUMBER
Customs exemptions (Cont.)				
Greece	Sweden	08 Apr 47	94UNTS73	101307
Netherlands	USA (United States)	11 Apr 47	148UNTS343	101943
Greece	Netherlands	17 Apr 47	32UNTS115	100494
Canada	Portugal	25 Apr 47	94UNTS87	101308
Syria	USA (United States)	28 Apr 47	262UNTS121	103741
France	Greece	05 May 47	76UNTS61	100980
Chile	USA (United States)	10 May 47	55UNTS21	100807
Hungary	Yugoslavia	11 May 47	130UNTS171	101730
Honduras	USA (United States)	13 May 47	166UNTS159	102189
Czechoslovakia	Denmark	14 May 47	27UNTS297	100413
Austria	USA (United States)	25 Jun 47	22UNTS141	100334
Canada	Sweden	27 Jun 47	27UNTS313	100414
Romania	Yugoslavia	30 Jun 47	116UNTS57	101569
Denmark	Turkey	30 Jun 47	32UNTS301	100504
Iraq	Turkey	30 Jun 47	72UNTS107	100930
Italy	USA (United States)	04 Jul 47	22UNTS173	100336
Greece	USA (United States)	08 Jul 47	16UNTS157	100256
France	India	16 Jul 47	27UNTS325	100415
Canada	UK Great Britain	17 Jul 47	28UNTS3	100416
Netherlands	Thailand	18 Jul 47	28UNTS27	100417
Greece	Turkey	22 Jul 47	72UNTS131	100931
Netherlands	South Africa	22 Jul 47	12UNTS257	100188
Belgium	USA (United States)	23 Jul 47	33UNTS33	100512
Taiwan	UK Great Britain	23 Jul 47	9UNTS207	100135
Poland	Romania	09 Aug 47	12UNTS363	100193
El Salvador	USA (United States)	19 Aug 47	51UNTS57	100752
Hungary	Poland	28 Aug 47	15UNTS145	100231
Czechoslovakia	Netherlands	01 Sep 47	32UNTS129	100495
Czechoslovakia	Switzerland	10 Sep 47	35UNTS275	100559
Lebanon	Turkey	16 Sep 47	44UNTS123	100682
France	USA (United States)	01 Oct 47	148UNTS303	101940
Czechoslovakia	Sweden	15 Oct 47	44UNTS149	100683
Colombia	UK Great Britain	16 Oct 47	160UNTS297	102115
Taiwan	USA (United States)	27 Oct 47	12UNTS11	100178
Bolivia	USA (United States)	03 Nov 47	51UNTS33	100750
Brazil	Netherlands	06 Nov 47	53UNTS59	100773
Norway	Portugal	11 Nov 47	34UNTS257	100542
Ecuador	USA (United States)	14 Nov 47	149UNTS297	101959
Brazil	Sweden	14 Nov 47	94UNTS139	101310
Brazil	Denmark	14 Nov 47	47UNTS39	100722
Brazil	Norway	14 Nov 47	44UNTS163	100684
Denmark	Greece	14 Nov 47	35UNTS295	100560
Denmark	Ireland	18 Nov 47	35UNTS309	100561
UNICEF (Children)	Yugoslavia	20 Nov 47	65UNTS28	100817
Ireland	Italy	21 Nov 47	353UNTS73	105038
Taiwan	Netherlands	06 Dec 47	43UNTS185	100669
Denmark	Portugal	15 Dec 47	35UNTS329	100563
Multilateral		22 Dec 47	32UNTS143	100496
Guatemala	USA (United States)	05 Jan 48	135UNTS104	101817
Costa Rica	USA (United States)	12 Jan 48	70UNTS27	100896
Austria	Netherlands	22 Jan 48	17UNTS99	100270
Italy	USA (United States)	06 Feb 48	73UNTS113	100950
Paraguay	USA (United States)	12 Mar 48	162UNTS30	102131
Czechoslovakia	Yugoslavia	14 Mar 48	28UNTS81	100421
Argentina	Denmark	18 Mar 48	94UNTS175	101311
Cuba	UK Great Britain	19 Mar 48	175UNTS23	102294
USA (United States)	Venezuela	24 Mar 48	44UNTS57	100678
Belgium	Netherlands	13 Apr 48	32UNTS153	100497
Belgium	France	13 Apr 48	31UNTS409	100483
Ireland	Switzerland	06 May 48	334UNTS187	104768
Pakistan	Sweden	06 May 48	36UNTS3	100564
Jordan	Turkey	07 May 48	32UNTS313	100505
Ireland	Netherlands	10 May 48	28UNTS121	100422
Norway	Turkey	20 May 48	26UNTS137	100384
India	Sweden	21 May 48	34UNTS285	100543

PARTY ONE	PARTY TWO	DATE	CITATION	NUMBER
Customs exemptions (Cont.)				
Greece	Switzerland	26 May 48	94UNTS217	101312
Ireland	Norway	21 Jun 48	34UNTS317	100545
India	Pakistan	23 Jun 48	28UNTS143	100423
Poland	USSR (Soviet Union)	08 Jul 48	37UNTS25	100575
Liberia	USA (United States)	26 Jul 48	182UNTS73	102423
Brazil	USA (United States)	29 Jul 48	80UNTS111	101047
Taiwan	USA (United States)	05 Aug 48	82UNTS109	101087
Brazil	Switzerland	10 Aug 48	94UNTS269	101314
Multilateral		18 Aug 48	33UNTS181	100518
France	Spain	23 Aug 48	28UNTS173	100425
Greece	Lebanon	06 Sep 48	178UNTS37	102335
Bolivia	USA (United States)	29 Sep 48	505UNTS139	107370
Argentina	USA (United States)	06 Oct 48	80UNTS91	101046
Netherlands	Spain	08 Oct 48	28UNTS209	100426
France	USA (United States)	19 Oct 48	98UNTS3	101355
Mexico	Portugal	22 Oct 48	34UNTS329	100546
Argentina	Netherlands	29 Oct 48	95UNTS21	101316
Czechoslovakia	Poland	12 Nov 48	84UNTS347	101141
Taiwan	USA (United States)	18 Nov 48	198UNTS287	102672
Italy	USA (United States)	26 Nov 48	79UNTS71	101032
UK Great Britain	USA (United States)	01 Dec 48	81UNTS93	101066
South Africa	UK Great Britain	06 Dec 48	118UNTS183	101607
Multilateral		16 Dec 48	79UNTS85	101033
France	USA (United States)	23 Dec 48	67UNTS171	100876
Ceylon (Sri Lanka)	Pakistan	03 Jan 49	28UNTS247	100428
Haiti	USA (United States)	04 Jan 49	44UNTS69	100679
Netherlands	USA (United States)	17 Jan 49	32UNTS241	100502
Italy	Lebanon	24 Jan 49	231UNTS241	103223
France	USA (United States)	07 Feb 49	67UNTS189	100877
Greece	USA (United States)	09 Feb 49	79UNTS95	101034
Trieste	USA (United States)	11 Feb 49	79UNTS123	101036
Austria	USA (United States)	11 Feb 49	79UNTS113	101035
Switzerland	Turkey	16 Feb 49	72UNTS175	100933
Finland	Sweden	17 Feb 49	197UNTS123	102636
Colombia	USA (United States)	21 Feb 49	92UNTS227	101275
Colombia	USA (United States)	21 Feb 49	44UNTS83	100680
Finland	Netherlands	25 Feb 49	53UNTS123	100777
Netherlands	Switzerland	07 Mar 49	35UNTS69	100551
Austria	USA (United States)	23 Mar 49	43UNTS127	100667
Finland	USA (United States)	29 Mar 49	55UNTS59	100808
Panama	USA (United States)	31 Mar 49	55UNTS141	100812
Panama	USA (United States)	31 Mar 49	55UNTS87	100810
Haiti	USA (United States)	14 Apr 49	80UNTS37	101043
Finland	Sweden	26 Apr 49	95UNTS83	101318
Bulgaria	Poland	16 May 49	84UNTS313	101140
Netherlands	USA (United States)	17 May 49	46UNTS291	100717
Italy	Spain	31 May 49	231UNTS251	103224
Australia	Pakistan	03 Jun 49	35UNTS23	100549
Canada	USA (United States)	04 Jun 49	122UNTS237	101649
Philippines	USA (United States)	07 Jun 49	45UNTS63	100692
Peru	USA (United States)	20 Jun 49	92UNTS249	101276
Belgium	Greece	21 Jun 49	137UNTS215	101854
Norway	Pakistan	23 Jun 49	35UNTS49	100550
India	Switzerland	24 Jun 49	95UNTS109	101319
Korea, South	USA (United States)	29 Jun 49	55UNTS79	100809
Czechoslovakia	Poland	02 Jul 49	260UNTS179	103709
Czechoslovakia	Poland	02 Jul 49	260UNTS149	103708
Greece	Syria	05 Jul 49	78UNTS71	101013
Mexico	USA (United States)	05 Jul 49	68UNTS55	100884
Australia	India	11 Jul 49	35UNTS83	100552
Iraq	Norway	12 Jul 49	53UNTS137	100778
Czechoslovakia	Finland	13 Jul 49	53UNTS153	100779
Multilateral		15 Jul 49	197UNTS3	102631
Pakistan	Philippines	16 Jul 49	35UNTS111	100553
Dominican Republic	USA (United States)	19 Jul 49	51UNTS145	100762

PARTY ONE	PARTY TWO	DATE	CITATION	NUMBER
Customs exemptions (Cont.)				
Pakistan	UK Great Britain	27 Jul 49	44UNTS199	100685
Ceylon (Sri Lanka)	UK Great Britain	05 Aug 49	35UNTS137	100554
Finland	Norway	24 Aug 49	53UNTS167	100780
Denmark	Finland	26 Aug 49	53UNTS191	100781
Belgium	United Arab Rep	19 Sep 49	137UNTS189	101853
Lebanon	Netherlands	20 Sep 49	108UNTS205	101474
Burma	USA (United States)	28 Sep 49	55UNTS3	100806
Greece	Philippines	08 Oct 49	187UNTS221	102515
India	Philippines	20 Oct 49	72UNTS191	100934
Norway	USA (United States)	31 Oct 49	68UNTS3	100879
Denmark	Pakistan	09 Nov 49	44UNTS255	100687
Sweden	Thailand	23 Nov 49	72UNTS217	100935
Denmark	Thailand	23 Nov 49	53UNTS255	100786
Italy	Turkey	25 Nov 49	192UNTS39	102594
Norway	Thailand	26 Nov 49	53UNTS269	100787
Australia	USA (United States)	26 Nov 49	45UNTS133	100695
Brazil	Spain	28 Nov 49	215UNTS303	102923
Austria	Sweden	02 Dec 49	108UNTS3	101465
Austria	Norway	02 Dec 49	72UNTS230	100936
Austria	Denmark	02 Dec 49	53UNTS281	100788
Afghanistan	WHO (World Health)	04 Dec 49	102UNTS117	101414
Netherlands	United Arab Rep	08 Dec 49	95UNTS123	101320
Sweden	United Arab Rep	12 Dec 49	108UNTS15	101466
Canada	Denmark	13 Dec 49	72UNTS247	100937
Austria	Switzerland	19 Dec 49	254UNTS287	103597
USA (United States)	Yugoslavia	24 Dec 49	89UNTS209	101219
Korea, South	USA (United States)	26 Jan 50	178UNTS97	102337
Korea, South	USA (United States)	26 Jan 50	80UNTS205	101053
France	USA (United States)	27 Jan 50	80UNTS171	101051
Netherlands	USA (United States)	27 Jan 50	80UNTS219	101054
UK Great Britain	USA (United States)	27 Jan 50	80UNTS261	101056
Norway	USA (United States)	27 Jan 50	80UNTS241	101055
Luxembourg	USA (United States)	27 Jan 50	80UNTS187	101052
Italy	USA (United States)	27 Jan 50	80UNTS145	101050
Belgium	USA (United States)	27 Jan 50	51UNTS213	100767
Denmark	USA (United States)	27 Jan 50	48UNTS115	100740
India	USA (United States)	02 Feb 50	89UNTS127	101214
Netherlands	Syria	13 Feb 50	108UNTS53	101467
Canada	Norway	14 Feb 50	53UNTS329	100790
Ceylon (Sri Lanka)	WHO (World Health)	17 Feb 50	102UNTS309	200309
Spain	Sweden	18 Feb 50	166UNTS15	102184
Multilateral		18 Feb 50	123UNTS45	101654
Ceylon (Sri Lanka)	Thailand	24 Feb 50	72UNTS261	100938
Italy	Netherlands	04 Mar 50	254UNTS305	103598
Honduras	USA (United States)	06 Mar 50	80UNTS71	101045
Honduras	USA (United States)	06 Mar 50	80UNTS51	101044
Norway	United Arab Rep	11 Mar 50	95UNTS157	101321
Denmark	United Arab Rep	14 Mar 50	95UNTS197	101322
Iceland	Netherlands	22 Mar 50	95UNTS237	101323
Denmark	Iceland	22 Mar 50	72UNTS273	100939
Italy	Portugal	05 Apr 50	254UNTS329	103599
Sweden	UK Great Britain	05 Apr 50	99UNTS107	101374
Turkey	United Arab Rep	12 Apr 50	128UNTS3	101711
Greece	United Arab Rep	24 Apr 50	163UNTS229	102149
Switzerland	United Arab Rep	15 May 50	95UNTS255	101325
Iran	USA (United States)	23 May 50	81UNTS3	101057
South Africa	UK Great Britain	12 Jun 50	93UNTS67	101290
Israel	USA (United States)	13 Jun 50	212UNTS93	102863
Netherlands	Spain	20 Jun 50	95UNTS303	101327
Iraq	Pakistan	20 Jun 50	77UNTS215	101001
Haiti	WHO (World Health)	27 Jun 50	110UNTS99	101504
Burma	Ceylon (Sri Lanka)	29 Jun 50	73UNTS3	100940
Spain	UK Great Britain	20 Jul 50	398UNTS101	105719
UK Great Britain	USA (United States)	21 Jul 50	97UNTS193	101351
India	Nepal	31 Jul 50	104UNTS3	101430

PARTY ONE	PARTY TWO	DATE	CITATION	NUMBER
Customs exemptions (Cont.)				
France	Pakistan	31 Jul 50	96UNTS23	101329
Spain	Switzerland	03 Aug 50	254UNTS365	103600
France	United Arab Rep	08 Aug 50	127UNTS293	101710
Canada	New Zealand	16 Aug 50	77UNTS239	101002
USA (United States)	Venezuela	23 Aug 50	92UNTS341	101279
WHO (World Health)	Venezuela	11 Sep 50	110UNTS237	101513
Burma	Sweden	14 Sep 50	96UNTS45	101330
Brazil	Turkey	21 Sep 50	150UNTS299	101981
Pakistan	USA (United States)	23 Sep 50	82UNTS131	101088
Ceylon (Sri Lanka)	United Arab Rep	26 Sep 50	192UNTS53	102595
Czechoslovakia	USA (United States)	29 Sep 50	290UNTS3	104227
Iceland	WHO (World Health)	06 Oct 50	110UNTS127	101506
Thailand	USA (United States)	17 Oct 50	79UNTS41	101030
Sweden	Switzerland	18 Oct 50	166UNTS49	102185
WHO (World Health)	Turkey	19 Oct 50	110UNTS215	101512
Iran	USA (United States)	19 Oct 50	92UNTS135	101266
Luxembourg	Portugal	21 Oct 50	108UNTS67	101468
Israel	Netherlands	23 Oct 50	189UNTS89	102543
Peru	WHO (World Health)	10 Nov 50	110UNTS187	101510
Nicaragua	WHO (World Health)	10 Nov 50	110UNTS155	101508
Multilateral		22 Nov 50	131UNTS25	101734
Brazil	USA (United States)	19 Dec 50	141UNTS3	101900
Cuba	USA (United States)	22 Dec 50	122UNTS97	101640
Multilateral		23 Dec 50	185UNTS3	102456
Philippines	WHO (World Health)	28 Dec 50	110UNTS203	101511
India	USA (United States)	28 Dec 50	99UNTS39	101369
Paraguay	USA (United States)	29 Dec 50	122UNTS157	101645
Portugal	USA (United States)	05 Jan 51	133UNTS75	101782
Liberia	USA (United States)	11 Jan 51	122UNTS125	101642
Saudi Arabia	USA (United States)	17 Jan 51	140UNTS335	101897
Nepal	USA (United States)	23 Jan 51	184UNTS65	102439
Israel	Turkey	05 Feb 51	193UNTS3	102607
Pakistan	USA (United States)	09 Feb 51	100UNTS67	101388
Chile	USA (United States)	15 Feb 51	133UNTS95	101783
Chile	USA (United States)	15 Feb 51	133UNTS117	101784
Paraguay	WHO (World Health)	15 Feb 51	110UNTS171	101509
Colombia	Portugal	09 Mar 51	108UNTS87	101469
Greece	Yugoslavia	15 Mar 51	187UNTS237	102516
Indonesia	WHO (World Health)	28 Mar 51	103UNTS71	101425
Jordan	WHO (World Health)	03 Apr 51	110UNTS297	200367
Multilateral		18 Apr 51	261UNTS140	103729
Honduras	WHO (World Health)	20 Apr 51	110UNTS111	101505
Honduras	USA (United States)	24 Apr 51	140UNTS287	101894
Ethiopia	USA (United States)	02 May 51	139UNTS85	101877
Colombia	WHO (World Health)	04 May 51	110UNTS83	101503
United Arab Rep	USA (United States)	05 May 51	198UNTS265	102670
Ceylon (Sri Lanka)	USA (United States)	14 May 51	141UNTS159	101913
Greece	Norway	28 May 51	187UNTS141	102507
Lebanon	USA (United States)	29 May 51	160UNTS49	102101
Cambodia	WHO (World Health)	31 May 51	102UNTS279	200307
Germany, West	USA (United States)	07 Jun 51	238UNTS161	103360
WHO (World Health)	Uruguay	11 Jun 51	128UNTS251	101724
Liberia	WHO (World Health)	11 Jun 51	103UNTS83	101426
Saudi Arabia	USA (United States)	18 Jun 51	102UNTS73	101412
Cuba	USA (United States)	20 Jun 51	148UNTS3	101931
Cuba	Portugal	26 Jun 51	192UNTS115	102598
Iraq	WHO (World Health)	01 Jul 51	110UNTS139	101507
India	USA (United States)	09 Jul 51	147UNTS43	101927
UK Great Britain	USA (United States)	13 Jul 51	105UNTS71	101454
Iceland	Norway	14 Jul 51	163UNTS265	102150
Multilateral		29 Jul 51	117UNTS85	101585
Panama	USA (United States)	30 Jul 51	140UNTS321	101896
Burma	Denmark	30 Jul 51	108UNTS167	101472
Iran	UNICEF (Children)	02 Aug 51	247UNTS11	103457
Israel	Philippines	07 Aug 51	192UNTS81	102596

PARTY ONE	PARTY TWO	DATE	CITATION	NUMBER
Customs exemptions (Cont.)				
USA (United States)	Venezuela	10 Aug 51	140UNTS345	101898
Lebanon	UK Great Britain	15 Aug 51	160UNTS327	102116
Cuba	USA (United States)	28 Aug 51	140UNTS239	101891
Cuba	USA (United States)	28 Aug 51	134UNTS225	101802
WHO (World Health)	Saudi Arabia	29 Aug 51	110UNTS277	101516
UNICEF (Children)	Turkey	05 Sep 51	193UNTS55	102610
Burma	Netherlands	06 Sep 51	108UNTS187	101473
Ethiopia	USA (United States)	07 Sep 51	206UNTS41	102785
Panama	UK Great Britain	15 Sep 51	560UNTS143	108172
WHO (World Health)	Vietnam, South	21 Sep 51	107UNTS63	200352
UNICEF (Children)	UK Great Britain	02 Oct 51	104UNTS301	101448
Philippines	Spain	06 Oct 51	215UNTS193	102920
Greece	Luxembourg	22 Oct 51	187UNTS119	102506
El Salvador	USA (United States)	23 Oct 51	137UNTS43	101847
Denmark	Italy	24 Oct 51	118UNTS91	101598
Multilateral		31 Oct 51	172UNTS193	102247
USA (United States)	Yugoslavia	14 Nov 51	174UNTS201	102286
Denmark	Iraq	18 Nov 51	232UNTS25	103227
India	UK Great Britain	01 Dec 51	128UNTS39	101712
USA (United States)	Uruguay	04 Dec 51	152UNTS41	102010
Colombia	Spain	11 Dec 51	216UNTS73	102933
El Salvador	USA (United States)	12 Dec 51	132UNTS287	101768
Jordan	United Arab Rep	02 Jan 52	192UNTS157	102599
India	USA (United States)	05 Jan 52	157UNTS39	102045
USA (United States)	Yugoslavia	08 Jan 52	152UNTS61	102011
Multilateral		10 Jan 52	163UNTS3	102138
Colombia	USA (United States)	12 Jan 52	168UNTS109	102216
UK Great Britain	USA (United States)	15 Jan 52	127UNTS3	101697
Iran	USA (United States)	20 Jan 52	200UNTS191	102703
Dominican Republic	UNICEF (Children)	15 Feb 52	121UNTS43	101625
Ecuador	USA (United States)	20 Feb 52	177UNTS43	102308
Peru	USA (United States)	22 Feb 52	165UNTS31	102166
Japan	USA (United States)	28 Feb 52	208UNTS255	102817
Cuba	USA (United States)	07 Mar 52	165UNTS11	102165
Belgium	Spain	10 Mar 52	178UNTS243	102342
France	USA (United States)	13 Mar 52	177UNTS21	102306
Brazil	USA (United States)	15 Mar 52	199UNTS221	102687
Pakistan	Switzerland	17 Mar 52	192UNTS237	102603
Iceland	USA (United States)	18 Mar 52	177UNTS263	102325
UK Great Britain	USA (United States)	18 Mar 52	177UNTS33	102307
Canada	USA (United States)	19 Mar 52	174UNTS267	102291
Sweden	Uruguay	20 Mar 52	311UNTS3	104497
Norway	Uruguay	20 Mar 52	310UNTS279	104496
Iraq	Switzerland	31 Mar 52	311UNTS43	104498
Denmark	USA (United States)	07 Apr 52	177UNTS257	102324
Chile	USA (United States)	09 Apr 52	186UNTS53	102482
Colombia	USA (United States)	17 Apr 52	174UNTS215	102287
France	Mexico	17 Apr 52	163UNTS321	102153
France	Israel	29 Apr 52	189UNTS55	102542
Norway	WHO (World Health)	09 May 52	131UNTS281	101747
Ethiopia	USA (United States)	15 May 52	180UNTS227	102388
Germany, West	USA (United States)	11 Jun 52	273UNTS105	103947
Australia	United Arab Rep	14 Jun 52	173UNTS241	102269
India	United Arab Rep	14 Jun 52	173UNTS209	102268
Belgium	UNICEF (Children)	17 Jun 52	171UNTS249	102228
Denmark	UK Great Britain	23 Jun 52	151UNTS3	101982
Norway	USA (United States)	27 Jun 52	184UNTS271	102452
USA (United States)	Uruguay	30 Jun 52	207UNTS139	102804
Belgium	Israel	30 Jun 52	183UNTS263	102435
Belgium	France	30 Jun 52	137UNTS259	101857
Australia	FAO (Food Agri)	07 Jul 52	184UNTS209	102449
Jordan	UNICEF (Children)	08 Jul 52	173UNTS353	200503
UNICEF (Children)	Syria	10 Jul 52	136UNTS17	101830
Multilateral		11 Jul 52	169UNTS3	102220
UNICEF (Children)	UK Great Britain	25 Jul 52	135UNTS37	101812

PARTY ONE	PARTY TWO	DATE	CITATION	NUMBER
Customs exemptions (Cont.)				
Japan	USA (United States)	11 Aug 52	212UNTS27	102862
Laos	UNICEF (Children)	15 Aug 52	161UNTS323	200491
UNICEF (Children)	Vietnam, South	29 Aug 52	161UNTS335	200492
Ethiopia	Pakistan	29 Aug 52	150UNTS257	101979
France	Israel	15 Sep 52	220UNTS65	102989
Belgium	Italy	22 Sep 52	157UNTS121	102051
Austria	Luxembourg	13 Oct 52	192UNTS291	102606
Mexico	Netherlands	13 Oct 52	163UNTS341	102154
Iceland	Luxembourg	23 Oct 52	193UNTS39	102609
Burma	UK Great Britain	25 Oct 52	150UNTS237	101978
Chile	Sweden	27 Oct 52	311UNTS63	104499
Chile	Denmark	27 Oct 52	271UNTS93	103911
Multilateral		07 Nov 52	221UNTS255	103010
Saudi Arabia	USA (United States)	10 Nov 52	181UNTS307	102419
Luxembourg	Norway	17 Nov 52	311UNTS95	104500
Ceylon (Sri Lanka)	USA (United States)	17 Nov 52	180UNTS207	102386
Luxembourg	Sweden	17 Nov 52	173UNTS277	102270
Israel	Switzerland	19 Nov 52	232UNTS3	103226
Nicaragua	USA (United States)	19 Nov 52	186UNTS3	102478
Mexico	ICAO (Civil Aviat)	28 Nov 52	164UNTS15	102156
USA (United States)	Yugoslavia	03 Dec 52	185UNTS183	102469
UNICEF (Children)	UK Great Britain	16 Dec 52	151UNTS359	102005
USA (United States)	Venezuela	16 Jan 53	199UNTS287	102690
Japan	Netherlands	17 Feb 53	192UNTS215	102602
Japan	Sweden	20 Feb 53	173UNTS307	102272
Libya	UK Great Britain	21 Feb 53	311UNTS115	104501
Japan	Norway	23 Feb 53	192UNTS191	102601
Denmark	Japan	26 Feb 53	173UNTS329	102273
Dominican Republic	USA (United States)	06 Mar 53	199UNTS267	102689
United Arab Rep	USA (United States)	12 Mar 53	204UNTS3	102747
Austria	Yugoslavia	19 Mar 53	467UNTS323	106768
United Arab Rep	USA (United States)	19 Mar 53	215UNTS17	102909
Netherlands	United Nations	09 Apr 53	163UNTS89	102143
Ethiopia	UNICEF (Children)	27 Apr 53	213UNTS169	102885
Philippines	Thailand	27 Apr 53	174UNTS3	102274
Ethiopia	USA (United States)	29 Apr 53	224UNTS121	103073
El Salvador	USA (United States)	14 May 53	234UNTS71	103273
El Salvador	USA (United States)	21 May 53	213UNTS15	102878
United Arab Rep	USA (United States)	21 May 53	204UNTS29	102748
Ethiopia	USA (United States)	22 May 53	191UNTS59	102577
Cuba	USA (United States)	26 May 53	224UNTS75	103070
Switzerland	Yugoslavia	28 May 53	232UNTS45	103228
Brazil	USA (United States)	30 May 53	460UNTS89	106633
Colombia	USA (United States)	09 Jun 53	213UNTS3	102877
Belgium	USA (United States)	18 Jun 53	222UNTS3	103019
United Arab Rep	USA (United States)	18 Jun 53	215UNTS45	102910
United Arab Rep	USA (United States)	18 Jun 53	204UNTS55	102749
Japan	Thailand	19 Jun 53	174UNTS29	102276
Burma	Norway	22 Jun 53	174UNTS49	102277
Liberia	USA (United States)	23 Jun 53	213UNTS37	102879
Liberia	USA (United States)	23 Jun 53	213UNTS57	102880
Brazil	USA (United States)	26 Jun 53	336UNTS241	104808
Panama	USA (United States)	26 Jun 53	215UNTS77	102912
Philippines	USA (United States)	26 Jun 53	213UNTS77	102881
Fed Rhod/Nyasaland	South Africa	28 Jun 53	267UNTS270	103848
Nicaragua	USA (United States)	30 Jun 53	215UNTS133	102917
Italy	Switzerland	02 Jul 53	257UNTS99	103653
Libya	UK Great Britain	29 Jul 53	186UNTS201	102492
Sweden	Switzerland	12 Aug 53	232UNTS59	103229
USA (United States)	Venezuela	14 Aug 53	213UNTS99	102883
Luxembourg	USA (United States)	17 Aug 53	234UNTS219	103284
Ethiopia	Yugoslavia	21 Aug 53	378UNTS105	105421
Multilateral		27 Aug 53	213UNTS137	102884
Belgium	USA (United States)	02 Sep 53	200UNTS127	102700
Spain	USA (United States)	26 Sep 53	207UNTS61	102800

PARTY ONE	PARTY TWO	DATE	CITATION	NUMBER
Customs exemptions (Cont.)				
Greece	USA (United States)	12 Oct 53	191UNTS319	102589
Iran	USA (United States)	13 Oct 53	222UNTS67	103023
Netherlands	UK Great Britain	19 Oct 53	306UNTS99	104435
Austria	Yugoslavia	11 Nov 53	363UNTS149	105206
Nicaragua	USA (United States)	19 Nov 53	206UNTS117	102787
Japan	UNICEF (Children)	21 Nov 53	183UNTS297	200507
Italy	South Africa	20 Dec 53	277UNTS293	104014
Belgium	Lebanon	24 Dec 53	219UNTS153	102972
Bolivia	USA (United States)	15 Jan 54	229UNTS213	103168
Ethiopia	Greece	20 Jan 54	222UNTS281	103035
Netherlands	USA (United States)	22 Jan 54	190UNTS207	102565
Syria	UK Great Britain	30 Jan 54	449UNTS47	106452
France	Sweden	16 Feb 54	228UNTS137	103147
Multilateral		19 Feb 54	214UNTS51	102899
United Arab Rep	USA (United States)	24 Feb 54	236UNTS61	103316
Japan	USA (United States)	08 Mar 54	232UNTS169	103236
Australia	Belgium	26 Mar 54	198UNTS305	102673
Peru	Spain	31 Mar 54	232UNTS65	103230
Mexico	USA (United States)	06 Apr 54	236UNTS69	103317
Mexico	USA (United States)	06 Apr 54	233UNTS163	103261
Czechoslovakia	Hungary	16 Apr 54	504UNTS231	107360
Ethiopia	USA (United States)	21 Apr 54	232UNTS299	103244
Iraq	USA (United States)	21 Apr 54	222UNTS251	103032
Canada	USA (United States)	03 May 54	221UNTS339	103015
UNICEF (Children)	Spain	07 May 54	190UNTS357	200515
Netherlands	USA (United States)	07 May 54	213UNTS325	102895
Panama	USA (United States)	11 May 54	236UNTS107	103319
Pakistan	USA (United States)	19 May 54	202UNTS301	102736
Honduras	USA (United States)	20 May 54	222UNTS87	103025
Mexico	UNICEF (Children)	20 May 54	192UNTS3	102591
Afghanistan	USA (United States)	29 May 54	234UNTS3	103268
Multilateral		04 Jun 54	282UNTS249	104101
Multilateral		04 Jun 54	276UNTS191	103992
Bolivia	USA (United States)	16 Jun 54	234UNTS35	103271
Mexico	USA (United States)	17 Jun 54	237UNTS275	103352
Italy	USA (United States)	28 Jun 54	237UNTS121	103340
Jordan	USA (United States)	29 Jun 54	237UNTS111	103339
Brazil	USA (United States)	30 Jun 54	237UNTS137	103341
Ecuador	USA (United States)	30 Jun 54	236UNTS163	103323
Costa Rica	USA (United States)	30 Jun 54	235UNTS35	103294
El Salvador	USA (United States)	16 Jul 54	237UNTS237	103350
Ireland	Luxembourg	27 Jul 54	232UNTS91	103231
India	USA (United States)	29 Jul 54	239UNTS69	103373
Canada	South Africa	04 Aug 54	261UNTS3	103722
Netherlands	USA (United States)	13 Aug 54	251UNTS91	103535
Ceylon (Sri Lanka)	USA (United States)	23 Aug 54	314UNTS297	104553
USA (United States)	Vietnam, South	26 Aug 54	234UNTS111	103276
New Zealand	UNICEF (Children)	26 Aug 54	198UNTS173	102663
El Salvador	USA (United States)	31 Aug 54	237UNTS49	103336
Guatemala	USA (United States)	01 Sep 54	199UNTS51	102677
Libya	USA (United States)	09 Sep 54	224UNTS217	103078
El Salvador	USA (United States)	23 Sep 54	237UNTS91	103338
Pakistan	USA (United States)	02 Oct 54	236UNTS187	103324
Ethiopia	Sweden	13 Oct 54	202UNTS273	102734
Germany, West	USA (United States)	15 Oct 54	239UNTS135	103375
Canada	UK Great Britain	19 Oct 54	214UNTS309	102906
Multilateral		23 Oct 54	332UNTS3	104760
Multilateral		23 Oct 54	332UNTS387	104763
Peru	USA (United States)	25 Oct 54	238UNTS247	103368
United Arab Rep	USA (United States)	30 Oct 54	234UNTS139	103279
Netherlands	USA (United States)	14 Dec 54	262UNTS35	103737
Ecuador	Netherlands	14 Dec 54	232UNTS115	103233
Norway	Switzerland	30 Dec 54	311UNTS147	104502
Netherlands	UNICEF (Children)	31 Dec 54	202UNTS135	102729
Austria	Belgium	07 Jan 55	380UNTS219	105458

PARTY ONE	PARTY TWO	DATE	CITATION	NUMBER
Customs exemptions (Cont.)				
Haiti	USA (United States)	28 Jan 55	270UNTS83	103894
Philippines	UK Great Britain	31 Jan 55	216UNTS51	102932
Iraq	USA (United States)	02 Mar 55	250UNTS229	103526
Mexico	USA (United States)	09 Mar 55	263UNTS247	103776
El Salvador	USA (United States)	21 Mar 55	250UNTS261	103528
Honduras	USA (United States)	21 Mar 55	253UNTS3	103572
Chile	USA (United States)	31 Mar 55	262UNTS19	103736
Haiti	USA (United States)	01 Apr 55	261UNTS361	103734
Germany, West	USA (United States)	04 Apr 55	279UNTS73	104034
Chile	USA (United States)	05 Apr 55	250UNTS253	103527
Philippines	USA (United States)	27 Apr 55	261UNTS351	103733
Peru	USA (United States)	30 Apr 55	263UNTS309	103780
Korea, South	USA (United States)	02 May 55	258UNTS3	103666
Austria	Romania	11 May 55	342UNTS119	104904
Pakistan	Sweden	04 Jun 55	228UNTS121	103146
Guatemala	USA (United States)	18 Jun 55	262UNTS105	103740
Afghanistan	USSR (Soviet Union)	28 Jun 55	240UNTS253	103407
Dominican Republic	USA (United States)	30 Jun 55	257UNTS313	103664
Australia	Fed Rhod/Nyasaland	30 Jun 55	226UNTS215	103115
Syria	United Arab Rep	03 Jul 55	393UNTS67	105652
Germany, West	USA (United States)	07 Jul 55	275UNTS3	103973
Italy	USA (United States)	08 Jul 55	270UNTS29	103889
Ceylon (Sri Lanka)	USA (United States)	18 Jul 55	281UNTS295	104086
Libya	USA (United States)	21 Jul 55	264UNTS247	103796
Germany, West	UK Great Britain	22 Jul 55	269UNTS189	103881
Germany, East	Romania	28 Jul 55	342UNTS207	104909
El Salvador	USA (United States)	08 Aug 55	264UNTS301	103801
Iran	USA (United States)	15 Aug 55	284UNTS93	104132
USSR (Soviet Union)	Yugoslavia	03 Sep 55	240UNTS267	103408
Ecuador	USA (United States)	06 Sep 55	256UNTS187	103628
Germany, East	Hungary	10 Sep 55	407UNTS132	105863
Italy	Switzerland	17 Sep 55	291UNTS213	104257
Multilateral		21 Sep 55	269UNTS241	103885
Bulgaria	Yugoslavia	01 Oct 55	396UNTS223	105698
France	Germany, West	04 Oct 55	353UNTS203	105044
Liberia	USA (United States)	06 Oct 55	275UNTS93	103978
Multilateral		12 Oct 55	560UNTS3	108165
Denmark	Syria	20 Oct 55	250UNTS61	103518
Czechoslovakia	Germany, East	24 Oct 55	504UNTS173	107358
Pakistan	Turkey	02 Nov 55	311UNTS217	104505
Burma	China People's Rep	08 Nov 55	306UNTS11	104430
Austria	Israel	17 Nov 55	232UNTS153	103235
Guatemala	UNICEF (Children)	22 Nov 55	221UNTS305	103012
India	Japan	26 Nov 55	311UNTS243	104506
Korea, North	Romania	05 Dec 55	362UNTS163	105187
Costa Rica	Guatemala	20 Dec 55	280UNTS121	104056
Libya	USA (United States)	22 Dec 55	240UNTS111	103399
Czechoslovakia	Poland	13 Jan 56	265UNTS157	103811
Australia	Japan	19 Jan 56	311UNTS291	104507
Austria	Italy	23 Jan 56	393UNTS97	105653
Argentina	Switzerland	25 Jan 56	559UNTS121	108157
Romania	Yugoslavia	01 Feb 56	362UNTS203	105189
Hungary	Romania	03 Feb 56	362UNTS233	105190
India	USA (United States)	03 Feb 56	272UNTS75	103932
Austria	Poland	08 Feb 56	334UNTS221	104770
Netherlands	Sudan	12 Feb 56	311UNTS319	104508
Norway	Syria	25 Feb 56	463UNTS217	106706
Multilateral		05 Mar 56	326UNTS181	104712
Ethiopia	Italy	05 Mar 56	267UNTS189	103844
France	USA (United States)	23 Mar 56	278UNTS131	104029
Sweden	USSR (Soviet Union)	31 Mar 56	259UNTS239	103691
Norway	USSR (Soviet Union)	31 Mar 56	259UNTS205	103690
Denmark	USSR (Soviet Union)	31 Mar 56	259UNTS169	103689
Belgium	Germany, West	14 Apr 56	344UNTS103	104945
Cambodia	UNICEF (Children)	28 Apr 56	136UNTS341	200446

PARTY ONE	PARTY TWO	DATE	CITATION	NUMBER
Customs exemptions (Cont.)				
Ceylon (Sri Lanka)	USA (United States)	28 Apr 56	274UNTS35	103956
Germany, West	Switzerland	02 May 56	559UNTS157	108158
Portugal	Venezuela	16 May 56	463UNTS239	106707
Japan	Switzerland	24 May 56	312UNTS3	104509
Greece	Italy	26 May 56	496UNTS301	107258
Pakistan	USA (United States)	28 May 56	269UNTS15	103868
Italy	Switzerland	04 Jun 56	378UNTS311	105429
Poland	Sweden	08 Jun 56	334UNTS257	104771
Germany, West	Ireland	12 Jun 56	353UNTS121	105040
UK Great Britain	USA (United States)	25 Jun 56	249UNTS59	103501
Israel	USA (United States)	26 Jun 56	257UNTS55	103649
Bolivia	USA (United States)	30 Jun 56	271UNTS243	103919
Lebanon	UNICEF (Children)	03 Jul 56	324UNTS145	104683
UNICEF (Children)	Sudan	07 Aug 56	248UNTS307	200542
Netherlands	USA (United States)	16 Aug 56	279UNTS3	104031
Germany, West	Netherlands	28 Sep 56	327UNTS185	104722
Argentina	USA (United States)	03 Oct 56	279UNTS13	104032
Czechoslovakia	Germany, East	06 Oct 56	501UNTS109	107315
Switzerland	Thailand	13 Oct 56	312UNTS43	104510
Belgium	Poland	17 Oct 56	356UNTS279	105100
Colombia	USA (United States)	24 Oct 56	476UNTS77	106905
Belgium	Turkey	25 Oct 56	380UNTS3	105447
Austria	UK Great Britain	27 Oct 56	264UNTS67	103789
Taiwan	USA (United States)	21 Nov 56	265UNTS241	103816
Albania	Yugoslavia	23 Nov 56	386UNTS73	105539
Australia	Netherlands	29 Nov 56	302UNTS141	104356
Belgium	Romania	04 Dec 56	317UNTS161	104602
Dominican Republic	USA (United States)	07 Dec 56	263UNTS193	103774
UNESCO (Educ/Cult)	Tunisia	03 Jan 57	257UNTS21	103645
Iran	USA (United States)	16 Jan 57	308UNTS147	104460
Iceland	Thailand	22 Jan 57	312UNTS63	104511
Germany, West	Sweden	29 Jan 57	393UNTS113	105654
Germany, West	Norway	29 Jan 57	353UNTS39	105037
Denmark	Germany, West	29 Jan 57	302UNTS75	104354
Australia	UK Great Britain	26 Feb 57	265UNTS197	103813
Turkey	UK Great Britain	28 Feb 57	310UNTS29	104483
Belgium	Czechoslovakia	12 Mar 57	312UNTS75	104512
Netherlands	Yugoslavia	13 Mar 57	327UNTS227	104723
Ethiopia	Sweden	16 Mar 57	304UNTS214	104398
Liberia	USA (United States)	16 Mar 57	290UNTS59	104228
Multilateral		25 Mar 57	294UNTS2	104300
Tunisia	USA (United States)	26 Mar 57	283UNTS117	104111
Morocco	USA (United States)	02 Apr 57	288UNTS157	104203
Netherlands	USA (United States)	03 Apr 57	410UNTS193	105904
Libya	USA (United States)	04 Apr 57	283UNTS181	104116
Germany, West	Yugoslavia	10 Apr 57	463UNTS269	106708
Denmark	Pakistan	10 Apr 57	302UNTS53	104353
Romania	United Arab Rep	15 Apr 57	389UNTS21	105589
Romania	Sweden	15 Apr 57	342UNTS325	104915
Bulgaria	Sweden	17 Apr 57	464UNTS3	106709
Peru	USA (United States)	17 Apr 57	283UNTS3	104102
Bulgaria	Yugoslavia	19 Apr 57	349UNTS3	105006
Ceylon (Sri Lanka)	Italy	23 Apr 57	337UNTS115	104820
Ecuador	USA (United States)	24 Apr 57	284UNTS3	104124
Korea, South	USA (United States)	24 Apr 57	288UNTS219	104207
Ethiopia	USA (United States)	25 Apr 57	283UNTS205	104118
Austria	USA (United States)	10 May 57	283UNTS33	104104
Belgium	Bulgaria	14 May 57	317UNTS81	104596
Australia	Germany, West	22 May 57	357UNTS45	105105
Hungary	Netherlands	28 May 57	334UNTS291	104773
Belgium	Hungary	01 Jun 57	291UNTS17	104242
Argentina	USA (United States)	03 Jun 57	291UNTS61	104244
Ghana	USA (United States)	03 Jun 57	284UNTS63	104129
Austria	USSR (Soviet Union)	14 Jun 57	285UNTS169	104152
Finland	India	14 Jun 57	277UNTS327	104016

PARTY ONE	PARTY TWO	DATE	CITATION	NUMBER
Customs exemptions (Cont.)				
Iraq	USA (United States)	16 Jun 57	284UNTS39	104127
Italy	USA (United States)	22 Jun 57	284UNTS51	104128
Jordan	USA (United States)	27 Jun 57	288UNTS269	104209
Czechoslovakia	United Arab Rep	30 Jun 57	411UNTS126	105917
Libya	USA (United States)	30 Jun 57	284UNTS177	104136
Thailand	UK Great Britain	25 Jul 57	277UNTS81	103999
Morocco	UNICEF (Children)	31 Jul 57	282UNTS99	104095
Greece	Italy	02 Aug 57	533UNTS217	107744
Hungary	Sweden	02 Aug 57	334UNTS307	104774
Netherlands	Romania	27 Aug 57	342UNTS309	104914
Albania	Yugoslavia	29 Aug 57	391UNTS167	105622
France	USA (United States)	23 Sep 57	293UNTS297	104297
Austria	South Africa	26 Sep 57	287UNTS3	104176
Germany, East	USSR (Soviet Union)	27 Sep 57	292UNTS75	104268
Multilateral		03 Oct 57	364UNTS3	105211
Multilateral		03 Oct 57	366UNTS87	105216
Italy	Pakistan	05 Oct 57	353UNTS91	105039
Fed of Malaya	UK Great Britain	18 Oct 57	335UNTS3	104775
Belgium	Netherlands	24 Oct 57	489UNTS11	107132
Belgium	Netherlands	24 Oct 57	489UNTS3	107131
France	Morocco	25 Oct 57	559UNTS95	108156
Argentina	UNICEF (Children)	19 Nov 57	300UNTS229	104338
El Salvador	USA (United States)	21 Nov 57	303UNTS19	104369
Austria	IAEA (Atom Energy)	11 Dec 57	339UNTS110	104849
UK Great Britain	USSR (Soviet Union)	19 Dec 57	351UNTS235	105026
Ethiopia	USA (United States)	26 Dec 57	307UNTS71	104443
Australia	Ireland	30 Dec 57	497UNTS29	107260
Multilateral		06 Jan 58	304UNTS227	104399
Belgium	Morocco	20 Jan 58	288UNTS3	104192
Germany, West	Netherlands	28 Jan 58	453UNTS183	106525
Czechoslovakia	Poland	31 Jan 58	431UNTS99	106214
Multilateral		03 Feb 58	381UNTS165	105471
Bulgaria	Netherlands	07 Feb 58	335UNTS45	104777
Australia	UK Great Britain	07 Feb 58	335UNTS23	104776
Afghanistan	Turkey	08 Feb 58	464UNTS39	106711
Albania	USSR (Soviet Union)	15 Feb 58	313UNTS261	104536
Sudan	Sweden	17 Feb 58	393UNTS161	105655
Norway	Pakistan	05 Mar 58	334UNTS199	104769
Pakistan	Sweden	06 Mar 58	393UNTS181	105656
Czechoslovakia	Poland	21 Mar 58	538UNTS89	107811
Germany, West	Portugal	21 Mar 58	464UNTS71	106712
Bulgaria	Yugoslavia	21 Mar 58	386UNTS119	105541
Bulgaria	Yugoslavia	21 Mar 58	349UNTS61	105009
Sudan	USA (United States)	31 Mar 58	308UNTS105	104458
Morocco	Portugal	03 Apr 58	393UNTS203	105657
Bulgaria	Yugoslavia	04 Apr 58	367UNTS89	105228
Belgium	Iran	14 Apr 58	381UNTS309	105473
Sweden	Yugoslavia	18 Apr 58	393UNTS225	105658
China People's Rep	USSR (Soviet Union)	23 Apr 58	313UNTS135	104534
Japan	Poland	26 Apr 58	340UNTS221	104866
Argentina	USA (United States)	28 Apr 58	315UNTS211	104570
Saudi Arabia	USA (United States)	01 May 58	315UNTS221	104571
Ceylon (Sri Lanka)	Sweden	22 May 58	428UNTS65	106168
Bulgaria	Denmark	28 May 58	312UNTS235	104521
India	USSR (Soviet Union)	02 Jun 58	393UNTS3	105650
Belgium	USSR (Soviet Union)	05 Jun 58	345UNTS145	104965
Denmark	Luxembourg	10 Jun 58	356UNTS193	105096
Netherlands	USSR (Soviet Union)	17 Jun 58	335UNTS77	104779
Denmark	Romania	25 Jun 58	345UNTS231	104970
Philippines	USA (United States)	30 Jun 58	321UNTS51	104653
Ethiopia	UK Great Britain	07 Jul 58	331UNTS3	104749
Austria	Romania	10 Jul 58	353UNTS155	105041
Denmark	Hungary	17 Jul 58	344UNTS281	104954
Taiwan	USA (United States)	06 Aug 58	462UNTS3	106666
Lebanon	USA (United States)	06 Aug 58	366UNTS361	105223

PARTY ONE	PARTY TWO	DATE	CITATION	NUMBER
Customs exemptions (Cont.)				
Ghana	UNICEF (Children)	12 Aug 58	309UNTS103	104469
Romania	United Arab Rep	14 Aug 58	405UNTS189	105834
Nicaragua	USA (United States)	05 Sep 58	336UNTS33	104797
Haiti	USA (United States)	09 Sep 58	335UNTS257	104793
Austria	Bulgaria	12 Sep 58	353UNTS3	105036
Ghana	UK Great Britain	24 Sep 58	411UNTS146	105918
Australia	New Zealand	30 Sep 58	340UNTS61	104859
Japan	USA (United States)	03 Nov 58	341UNTS83	104879
Liberia	Netherlands	28 Nov 58	393UNTS55	105651
Multilateral		03 Dec 58	416UNTS51	105995
Multilateral		03 Dec 58	398UNTS9	105715
Multilateral		15 Dec 58	351UNTS159	105022
Korea, South	USA (United States)	18 Dec 58	325UNTS233	104702
United Nations	Tunisia	23 Dec 58	321UNTS23	104651
Haiti	USA (United States)	24 Dec 58	338UNTS265	104840
Finland	Switzerland	07 Jan 59	353UNTS173	105042
Portugal	USA (United States)	12 Jan 59	343UNTS49	104921
United Arab Rep	USA (United States)	13 Jan 59	358UNTS3	105122
Multilateral		15 Jan 59	348UNTS13	104996
UK Great Britain	Yugoslavia	03 Feb 59	359UNTS339	105151
Czechoslovakia	United Arab Rep	07 Feb 59	372UNTS243	105301
Ghana	United Nations	27 Feb 59	324UNTS133	104682
Japan	Yugoslavia	28 Feb 59	341UNTS179	104883
Indonesia	USA (United States)	02 Mar 59	357UNTS145	105113
Netherlands	Tunisia	19 Mar 59	497UNTS61	107262
Sweden	Tunisia	19 Mar 59	497UNTS43	107261
Norway	Tunisia	28 Mar 59	497UNTS77	107263
United Nations	Sudan	28 Mar 59	327UNTS95	104719
Poland	UK Great Britain	03 Apr 59	351UNTS295	105030
Ghana	USA (United States)	09 Apr 59	342UNTS21	104897
Denmark	Tunisia	14 Apr 59	340UNTS273	104870
USA (United States)	Venezuela	17 Apr 59	358UNTS83	105126
Colombia	USA (United States)	08 May 59	344UNTS193	104950
Denmark	Sudan	11 May 59	445UNTS105	106380
Fed of Malaya	USA (United States)	22 May 59	346UNTS263	104985
Ceylon (Sri Lanka)	Sweden	29 May 59	464UNTS109	106713
Ceylon (Sri Lanka)	Norway	29 May 59	411UNTS165	105919
Ceylon (Sri Lanka)	Denmark	29 May 59	348UNTS225	105002
Greece	Yugoslavia	18 Jun 59	368UNTS27	105234
Belgium	Japan	20 Jun 59	411UNTS3	105911
Libya	United Nations	27 Jun 59	336UNTS291	104811
Czechoslovakia	Poland	04 Jul 59	363UNTS333	105210
Laos	United Nations	06 Jul 59	337UNTS41	104814
Bulgaria	United Arab Rep	09 Jul 59	411UNTS187	105920
India	Italy	16 Jul 59	464UNTS129	106714
Pakistan	USA (United States)	18 Jul 59	355UNTS367	105087
Afghanistan	Germany, West	22 Jul 59	464UNTS177	106715
Japan	Paraguay	22 Jul 59	373UNTS85	105316
Taiwan	USA (United States)	22 Jul 59	357UNTS293	105121
Australia	Thailand	28 Jul 59	339UNTS91	104847
Paraguay	United Nations	01 Aug 59	341UNTS319	104894
Germany, West	Iceland	12 Aug 59	411UNTS224	105921
New Zealand	UK Great Britain	12 Aug 59	354UNTS161	105062
Ghana	UN Special Fund	12 Aug 59	338UNTS203	104836
Liberia	USA (United States)	13 Aug 59	357UNTS181	105116
Canada	Germany, West	04 Sep 59	411UNTS260	105922
Iran	UN Special Fund	06 Oct 59	342UNTS89	104902
Nicaragua	Peru	14 Oct 59	392UNTS303	105649
Guinea	United Nations	15 Oct 59	344UNTS47	104942
Poland	UN Special Fund	15 Oct 59	344UNTS29	104941
South Africa	Switzerland	19 Oct 59	559UNTS257	108162
India	UN Special Fund	20 Oct 59	344UNTS143	104946
UN Special Fund	Yugoslavia	27 Oct 59	344UNTS159	104947
Korea, South	United Nations	06 Nov 59	346UNTS289	200565
Ecuador	UN Special Fund	10 Nov 59	345UNTS3	104955

PARTY ONE	PARTY TWO	DATE	CITATION	NUMBER
Customs exemptions (Cont.)				
Ethiopia	France	12 Nov 59	381UNTS3	105465
Turkey	USA (United States)	13 Nov 59	361UNTS3	105168
Greece	UN Special Fund	13 Nov 59	345UNTS171	104966
UN Special Fund	Turkey	20 Nov 59	345UNTS105	104963
Afghanistan	United Nations	24 Nov 59	397UNTS187	105705
Czechoslovakia	Germany, East	25 Nov 59	374UNTS101	105331
UN Special Fund	United Arab Rep	25 Nov 59	345UNTS125	104964
Belgium	USA (United States)	27 Nov 59	366UNTS331	105221
Turkey	USA (United States)	30 Nov 59	361UNTS107	105174
Israel	UN Special Fund	01 Dec 59	345UNTS197	104968
Argentina	UN Special Fund	04 Dec 59	345UNTS263	104972
Liberia	Sweden	09 Dec 59	464UNTS219	106716
Jordan	UN Special Fund	15 Dec 59	346UNTS3	104974
New Zealand	Thailand	24 Dec 59	351UNTS197	105023
UN Special Fund	UK Great Britain	07 Jan 60	348UNTS177	105000
Czechoslovakia	UK Great Britain	15 Jan 60	374UNTS207	105336
Japan	USA (United States)	19 Jan 60	373UNTS207	105321
Chile	UN Special Fund	22 Jan 60	351UNTS115	105020
Multilateral		26 Jan 60	439UNTS249	106333
Multilateral		06 Feb 60	383UNTS3	105494
Cuba	UNICEF (Children)	11 Feb 60	349UNTS277	105014
Norway	USA (United States)	13 Feb 60	388UNTS255	105583
Greece	USA (United States)	15 Feb 60	377UNTS95	105397
Germany, West	United Arab Rep	16 Feb 60	464UNTS233	106717
Afghanistan	UN Special Fund	21 Feb 60	351UNTS93	105019
Multilateral		26 Feb 60	418UNTS171	106022
France	Thailand	26 Feb 60	392UNTS279	105648
Australia	Thailand	26 Feb 60	392UNTS255	105647
Australia	USA (United States)	26 Feb 60	354UNTS95	105056
Turkey	USA (United States)	02 Mar 60	372UNTS37	105286
Guinea	Netherlands	09 Mar 60	392UNTS243	105646
Finland	Iceland	10 Mar 60	497UNTS95	107264
Czechoslovakia	Iraq	11 Mar 60	464UNTS267	106718
Austria	Guatemala	18 Mar 60	379UNTS89	105435
Austria	El Salvador	23 Mar 60	390UNTS3	105599
Belgium	Switzerland	24 Mar 60	416UNTS81	105996
Netherlands	USA (United States)	24 Mar 60	406UNTS165	105847
Denmark	UK Great Britain	08 Apr 60	374UNTS233	105337
Luxembourg	Yugoslavia	09 Apr 60	464UNTS293	106719
Denmark	USA (United States)	12 Apr 60	373UNTS9	105311
Germany, West	Spain	28 Apr 60	465UNTS3	106720
Multilateral		28 Apr 60	376UNTS111	105377
Laos	UN Special Fund	30 Apr 60	361UNTS171	105179
Iran	UK Great Britain	02 May 60	566UNTS129	108241
Greece	Romania	02 May 60	485UNTS17	107043
United Nations	Togo	06 May 60	388UNTS53	105571
Lebanon	UN Special Fund	07 May 60	360UNTS225	105160
Morocco	United Arab Rep	19 May 60	563UNTS121	108208
Switzerland	Tunisia	21 May 60	497UNTS109	107265
Kuwait	UK Great Britain	24 May 60	412UNTS4	105923
Afghanistan	Czechoslovakia	28 May 60	497UNTS129	107266
Luxembourg	Tunisia	13 Jun 60	497UNTS143	107267
Denmark	Peru	22 Jun 60	439UNTS113	106326
Korea, North	USSR (Soviet Union)	22 Jun 60	399UNTS3	105732
Ireland	Portugal	24 Jun 60	412UNTS30	105924
UK Great Britain	USA (United States)	24 Jun 60	377UNTS63	105396
Kuwait	UN Special Fund	29 Jun 60	369UNTS419	200575
Poland	UK Great Britain	02 Jul 60	385UNTS87	105532
Italy	USA (United States)	07 Jul 60	380UNTS143	105455
Ethiopia	UN Special Fund	13 Jul 60	368UNTS159	105240
Ethiopia	United Nations	13 Jul 60	368UNTS143	105239
Switzerland	United Arab Rep	14 Jul 60	497UNTS161	107268
Germany, West	Pakistan	20 Jul 60	465UNTS41	106721
Multilateral		28 Jul 60	394UNTS37	105667
Argentina	USA (United States)	02 Aug 60	384UNTS105	105514

Customs exemptions (Cont.)

PARTY ONE	PARTY TWO	DATE	CITATION	NUMBER
Mexico	USA (United States)	15 Aug 60	402UNTS177	105786
Belgium	Burma	17 Aug 60	540UNTS185	107850
Japan	Thailand	24 Aug 60	384UNTS73	105512
Ghana	United Arab Rep	29 Aug 60	412UNTS71	105926
South Africa	USA (United States)	13 Sep 60	388UNTS65	105572
Brazil	UN Special Fund	16 Sep 60	375UNTS3	105351
Czechoslovakia	India	19 Sep 60	465UNTS67	106722
France	USA (United States)	19 Sep 60	400UNTS21	105745
Taiwan	UN Special Fund	20 Sep 60	375UNTS29	105352
Portugal	USA (United States)	26 Sep 60	393UNTS257	105660
Guinea	USA (United States)	30 Sep 60	394UNTS103	105671
Belgium	Jordan	19 Oct 60	479UNTS277	106959
Hungary	UK Great Britain	25 Oct 60	419UNTS309	106034
Burma	Switzerland	31 Oct 60	465UNTS97	106723
Norway	Peru	02 Nov 60	497UNTS207	107270
Australia	Italy	10 Nov 60	497UNTS247	107271
Brazil	Japan	14 Nov 60	518UNTS29	107491
UNICEF (Children)	Upper Volta	15 Nov 60	402UNTS33	105776
Mali	UNICEF (Children)	17 Nov 60	402UNTS23	105775
Pakistan	United Nations	17 Nov 60	380UNTS277	105460
Indonesia	UK Great Britain	23 Nov 60	398UNTS71	105718
Cambodia	United Nations	30 Nov 60	383UNTS147	105500
Multilateral		09 Dec 60	429UNTS211	106200
Nepal	UNICEF (Children)	12 Dec 60	382UNTS273	105488
Multilateral		13 Dec 60	523UNTS117	107557
Multilateral		13 Dec 60	455UNTS204	106544
Bolivia	United Nations	14 Dec 60	382UNTS283	105489
Japan	Pakistan	18 Dec 60	423UNTS197	106093
Canada	Pakistan	21 Dec 60	465UNTS115	106724
Togo	USA (United States)	22 Dec 60	401UNTS33	105760
Luxembourg	Thailand	29 Dec 60	465UNTS131	106725
Mali	USA (United States)	04 Jan 61	405UNTS165	105832
Jordan	Sweden	09 Jan 61	465UNTS155	106726
Sudan	UK Great Britain	16 Jan 61	424UNTS233	106112
Norway	Poland	17 Jan 61	412UNTS130	105928
Germany, West	Japan	18 Jan 61	465UNTS173	106727
Cuba	Czechoslovakia	04 Mar 61	465UNTS209	106728
Iraq	United Nations	05 Mar 61	409UNTS56	105878
Afghanistan	Japan	15 Mar 61	450UNTS373	106480
Honduras	USA (United States)	12 Apr 61	413UNTS182	105952
Cyprus	UNICEF (Children)	19 Apr 61	394UNTS185	105678
Turkey	USSR (Soviet Union)	27 Apr 61	420UNTS307	106047
Sierra Leone	USA (United States)	05 May 61	409UNTS194	105885
Senegal	USA (United States)	13 May 61	409UNTS232	105888
Ivory Coast	USA (United States)	17 May 61	409UNTS241	105889
Poland	Switzerland	18 May 61	559UNTS233	108161
Cameroon	USA (United States)	26 May 61	413UNTS195	105953
Niger	USA (United States)	26 May 61	410UNTS213	105905
Dahomey	USA (United States)	27 May 61	445UNTS23	106373
Czechoslovakia	Morocco	08 Jun 61	497UNTS275	107272
UK Great Britain	Yugoslavia	08 Jun 61	437UNTS111	106300
Nepal	USA (United States)	09 Jun 61	421UNTS223	106061
New Zealand	UK Great Britain	13 Jun 61	497UNTS293	107273
Cyprus	United Nations	15 Jun 61	398UNTS39	105716
Cameroon	France	16 Jun 61	412UNTS148	105929
Guinea	Sweden	17 Jun 61	465UNTS236	106729
Madagascar	USA (United States)	22 Jun 61	413UNTS219	105956
Haiti	United Nations	28 Jun 61	399UNTS159	105740
UNICEF (Children)	Saudi Arabia	04 Jul 61	413UNTS122	105947
Ghana	USA (United States)	19 Jul 61	416UNTS167	106002
Tanganyika	USA (United States)	21 Jul 61	445UNTS33	106374
Czechoslovakia	Ghana	02 Aug 61	465UNTS249	106730
Cameroon	UNICEF (Children)	12 Aug 61	402UNTS235	105788
Finland	Luxembourg	15 Aug 61	541UNTS45	107859
Central Afri Rep	UNICEF (Children)	21 Aug 61	413UNTS48	105939

Customs exemptions (Cont.)

PARTY ONE	PARTY TWO	DATE	CITATION	NUMBER
Jordan	Netherlands	24 Aug 61	466UNTS3	106733
Mexico	Netherlands	24 Aug 61	465UNTS291	106732
Poland	UNICEF (Children)	24 Aug 61	406UNTS95	105841
Chad	UNICEF (Children)	26 Aug 61	422UNTS231	106077
Lebanon	United Nations	26 Aug 61	406UNTS105	105842
Liberia	Switzerland	31 Aug 61	559UNTS215	108160
Fed of Malaya	USA (United States)	04 Sep 61	421UNTS215	106060
Jordan	United Nations	11 Sep 61	406UNTS255	105855
Paraguay	USA (United States)	26 Sep 61	461UNTS91	106653
Germany, West	UK Great Britain	26 Sep 61	424UNTS201	106108
Ghana	Romania	30 Sep 61	467UNTS443	106769
Germany, West	Morocco	12 Oct 61	523UNTS289	107562
Japan	Pakistan	17 Oct 61	466UNTS17	106734
Philippines	USA (United States)	31 Oct 61	424UNTS129	106105
Gabon	UNICEF (Children)	02 Nov 61	422UNTS241	106078
Iraq	Syria	03 Nov 61	489UNTS45	107134
Brazil	USA (United States)	11 Nov 61	433UNTS199	106243
Mexico	USA (United States)	15 Nov 61	460UNTS113	106634
Malagasy	UNICEF (Children)	16 Nov 61	422UNTS251	106079
El Salvador	USA (United States)	20 Nov 61	433UNTS221	106245
Cyprus	Greece	23 Nov 61	497UNTS311	107274
Czechoslovakia	Mali	27 Nov 61	466UNTS41	106736
Thailand	USA (United States)	28 Nov 61	434UNTS77	106256
Ceylon (Sri Lanka)	United Nations	04 Dec 61	415UNTS236	105987
Ethiopia	USA (United States)	06 Dec 61	433UNTS231	106246
Panama	USA (United States)	11 Dec 61	445UNTS161	106384
Czechoslovakia	Guinea	16 Dec 61	559UNTS49	108154
El Salvador	USA (United States)	19 Dec 61	445UNTS175	106385
Iran	USA (United States)	21 Dec 61	433UNTS269	106249
Costa Rica	USA (United States)	22 Dec 61	460UNTS277	106646
Sierra Leone	USA (United States)	29 Dec 61	434UNTS43	106254
Netherlands	Sweden	08 Jan 62	466UNTS65	106737
Ivory Coast	UNICEF (Children)	10 Jan 62	422UNTS261	106080
Dominican Republic	USA (United States)	11 Jan 62	433UNTS133	106236
Austria	Greece	15 Jan 62	498UNTS3	107275
Cyprus	USA (United States)	18 Jan 62	435UNTS3	106266
United Nations	Somalia	20 Jan 62	420UNTS133	106044
Indonesia	Japan	23 Jan 62	559UNTS77	108155
Peru	USA (United States)	25 Jan 62	473UNTS57	106855
Luxembourg	South Africa	31 Jan 62	563UNTS153	108209
Italy	Japan	31 Jan 62	498UNTS23	107276
UNICEF (Children)	Yemen	31 Jan 62	422UNTS271	106081
Hungary	Yugoslavia	09 Feb 62	577UNTS3	108370
Finland	Hungary	13 Feb 62	463UNTS61	106693
UK Great Britain	USA (United States)	22 Feb 62	435UNTS127	106275
Cyprus	USA (United States)	02 Mar 62	445UNTS189	106386
Germany, West	Thailand	05 Mar 62	563UNTS165	108210
Dominican Republic	USA (United States)	08 Mar 62	527UNTS29	107615
Liberia	USA (United States)	08 Mar 62	445UNTS41	106375
Luxembourg	Spain	26 Mar 62	563UNTS205	108211
Brazil	Japan	28 Mar 62	451UNTS125	106489
Dahomey	UN Special Fund	28 Mar 62	424UNTS55	106099
France	Luxembourg	29 Mar 62	563UNTS227	108212
Nicaragua	USA (United States)	30 Mar 62	456UNTS241	106559
India	Japan	31 Mar 62	451UNTS143	106490
UNICEF (Children)	Somalia	01 Apr 62	431UNTS75	106211
Sierra Leone	UK Great Britain	05 Apr 62	434UNTS227	106265
Ghana	USSR (Soviet Union)	06 Apr 62	498UNTS41	107277
Congo (Brazzaville)	UNICEF (Children)	09 Apr 62	431UNTS65	106210
UNICEF (Children)	Sierra Leone	11 Apr 62	431UNTS55	106209
Ecuador	USA (United States)	17 Apr 62	442UNTS69	106339
Somalia	USA (United States)	17 Apr 62	436UNTS107	106291
India	Japan	23 Apr 62	451UNTS155	106491
Netherlands	USA (United States)	24 Apr 62	436UNTS93	106289
Dominican Republic	USA (United States)	02 May 62	442UNTS107	106342

Customs exemptions (Cont.)

PARTY ONE	PARTY TWO	DATE	CITATION	NUMBER
Japan	United Arab Rep	10 May 62	498UNTS69	107278
France	Romania	18 May 62	498UNTS115	107279
Ethiopia	USA (United States)	23 May 62	456UNTS293	106563
Greece	Tunisia	26 May 62	534UNTS163	107761
Pakistan	USA (United States)	31 May 62	460UNTS75	106631
France	Senegal	15 Jun 62	524UNTS3	107563
Bolivia	USA (United States)	19 Jun 62	458UNTS239	106606
Czechoslovakia	Senegal	20 Jun 62	498UNTS145	107280
United Arab Rep	USSR (Soviet Union)	23 Jun 62	472UNTS43	106836
Germany, West	Syria	25 Jun 62	489UNTS71	107135
Liberia	Norway	29 Jun 62	466UNTS95	106739
Morocco	Switzerland	05 Jul 62	498UNTS171	107281
Honduras	USA (United States)	20 Jul 62	460UNTS125	106635
Niger	USA (United States)	23 Jul 62	487UNTS325	107114
Colombia	USA (United States)	23 Jul 62	458UNTS123	106595
Ecuador	USA (United States)	03 Aug 62	460UNTS133	106636
Nigeria	United Nations	07 Aug 62	435UNTS167	106278
Cyprus	USA (United States)	23 Aug 62	461UNTS147	106658
Nepal	USA (United States)	24 Aug 62	460UNTS143	106637
Turkey	USA (United States)	27 Aug 62	461UNTS55	106651
Cameroon	United Nations	29 Aug 62	442UNTS3	106334
Togo	USA (United States)	05 Sep 62	461UNTS47	106650
Multilateral		10 Sep 62	502UNTS3	107323
Ecuador	Germany, West	20 Sep 62	498UNTS199	107283
Austria	Czechoslovakia	22 Sep 62	495UNTS157	107244
Multilateral		28 Sep 62	469UNTS169	106791
Niger	United Nations	01 Oct 62	439UNTS181	106329
Gabon	USA (United States)	04 Oct 62	459UNTS185	106620
Japan	Kuwait	06 Oct 62	498UNTS235	107284
Finland	France	12 Oct 62	498UNTS299	107285
Czechoslovakia	Hungary	16 Oct 62	479UNTS301	106961
Hungary	Syria	18 Oct 62	491UNTS209	107178
Netherlands	Norway	18 Oct 62	466UNTS145	106741
France	Ivory Coast	19 Oct 62	498UNTS317	107286
Czechoslovakia	Yugoslavia	22 Oct 62	480UNTS267	106974
Multilateral		25 Oct 62	457UNTS137	106583
Multilateral		25 Oct 62	457UNTS129	106582
United Nations	Western Samoa	05 Nov 62	443UNTS297	200599
Poland	Syria	10 Nov 62	491UNTS228	107179
Algeria	UN Special Fund	15 Nov 62	452UNTS243	106512
Czechoslovakia	Poland	16 Nov 62	526UNTS3	107597
Ivory Coast	Switzerland	17 Nov 62	499UNTS3	107289
Thailand	UK Great Britain	20 Nov 62	466UNTS243	106747
Algeria	UNICEF (Children)	20 Nov 62	453UNTS151	106522
Ceylon (Sri Lanka)	USA (United States)	21 Nov 62	462UNTS237	106683
India	USA (United States)	21 Nov 62	462UNTS255	106685
Costa Rica	USA (United States)	23 Nov 62	541UNTS67	107861
Ecuador	United Nations	26 Nov 62	445UNTS3	106372
Rwanda	United Nations	28 Nov 62	450UNTS267	106473
Ivory Coast	United Nations	10 Dec 62	451UNTS269	106498
Austria	Yugoslavia	11 Dec 62	546UNTS3	107938
Ghana	Tunisia	11 Dec 62	563UNTS243	108213
Guinea	USA (United States)	14 Dec 62	462UNTS247	106684
Syria	United Arab Rep	27 Dec 62	491UNTS245	107180
Guatemala	USA (United States)	29 Dec 62	474UNTS31	106869
Israel	United Nations	07 Jan 63	450UNTS229	106470
Ghana	Mali	09 Jan 63	466UNTS165	106742
Senegal	USA (United States)	17 Jan 63	493UNTS97	107210
Mauritania	UNICEF (Children)	19 Jan 63	452UNTS271	106514
Senegal	Switzerland	23 Jan 63	524UNTS23	107564
New Zealand	Western Samoa	24 Jan 63	499UNTS21	107290
UNICEF (Children)	Tanganyika	25 Jan 63	453UNTS249	106528
Guinea	Switzerland	01 Feb 63	499UNTS35	107291
Mali	Senegal	07 Feb 63	524UNTS41	107565
Central Afri Rep	USA (United States)	10 Feb 63	473UNTS83	106857

Customs exemptions (Cont.)

PARTY ONE	PARTY TWO	DATE	CITATION	NUMBER
Sudan	Switzerland	18 Feb 63	563UNTS281	108215
Algeria	France	18 Feb 63	563UNTS263	108214
Burma	Japan	29 Mar 63	518UNTS3	107490
Japan	South Africa	06 Apr 63	484UNTS319	107040
Poland	USSR (Soviet Union)	22 Apr 63	493UNTS229	107217
Greece	Hungary	27 Apr 63	534UNTS3	107750
Cyprus	Denmark	27 Apr 63	529UNTS255	107664
Algeria	Morocco	30 Apr 63	564UNTS3	108217
Australia	USA (United States)	09 May 63	469UNTS55	106784
Australia	USA (United States)	09 May 63	475UNTS331	106897
Denmark	India	15 May 63	616UNTS23	108889
Denmark	India	15 May 63	616UNTS39	108890
Finland	Poland	10 Jun 63	503UNTS179	107343
Guinea	Ivory Coast	26 Jun 63	499UNTS71	107293
IBRD (World Bank)	Tunisia	03 Jul 63	480UNTS209	106970
Austria	France	12 Jul 63	499UNTS91	107294
Congo (Zaire)	USA (United States)	19 Jul 63	511UNTS47	107425
Algeria	Mali	22 Jul 63	564UNTS29	108219
USA (United States)	Uruguay	31 Jul 63	488UNTS3	107115
Cameroon	Israel	09 Aug 63	499UNTS121	107295
Germany, West	Greece	26 Sep 63	550UNTS203	108017
Guatemala	USA (United States)	03 Oct 63	493UNTS45	107206
Pakistan	USSR (Soviet Union)	07 Oct 63	499UNTS161	107297
Ivory Coast	Netherlands	09 Oct 63	499UNTS141	107296
Multilateral		19 Oct 63	523UNTS249	107559
Kuwait	USA (United States)	21 Oct 63	530UNTS281	107688
Czechoslovakia	Hungary	22 Oct 63	514UNTS95	107444
Iran	USA (United States)	24 Oct 63	489UNTS303	107146
Jamaica	USA (United States)	24 Oct 63	489UNTS337	107148
Panama	USA (United States)	30 Oct 63	530UNTS3	107668
Niger	United Nations	20 Nov 63	536UNTS3	107793
Brazil	Germany, West	30 Nov 63	0UNTS0	109423
Greece	USA (United States)	13 Dec 63	494UNTS55	107226
Czechoslovakia	Romania	16 Dec 63	527UNTS285	107630
Czechoslovakia	Hungary	20 Dec 63	538UNTS127	107812
France	Israel	20 Dec 63	515UNTS165	107459
Romania	Yugoslavia	25 Dec 63	576UNTS95	108366
Saudi Arabia	USA (United States)	06 Jan 64	531UNTS3	107689
France	South Africa	06 Jan 64	601UNTS229	108699
Mali	Niger	15 Jan 64	499UNTS197	107299
Canada	USA (United States)	22 Jan 64	530UNTS89	107674
Denmark	Yugoslavia	11 Feb 64	511UNTS241	107437
UNESCO (Educ/Cult)	Yugoslavia	27 Feb 64	489UNTS257	107143
Netherlands	Tunisia	03 Mar 64	533UNTS133	107739
Cameroon	Mali	17 Mar 64	524UNTS61	107566
Germany, West	Thailand	02 Apr 64	503UNTS3	107338
Malaysia	Netherlands	07 Apr 64	524UNTS81	107567
Finland	USSR (Soviet Union)	24 Apr 64	537UNTS231	107804
United Arab Rep	USA (United States)	05 May 64	531UNTS229	107706
Germany, West	Ireland	13 May 64	553UNTS87	108071
Netherlands	NATO (North Atlan)	25 May 64	544UNTS237	107920
New Zealand	USA (United States)	24 Jun 64	524UNTS101	107568
Colombia	Netherlands	06 Jul 64	543UNTS289	107906
Ivory Coast	Mali	09 Jul 64	524UNTS121	107569
Belgium	Tunisia	15 Jul 64	560UNTS57	108168
Kenya	USA (United States)	26 Aug 64	531UNTS51	107692
Australia	USA (United States)	28 Aug 64	510UNTS201	107415
Ceylon (Sri Lanka)	USA (United States)	29 Aug 64	531UNTS93	107695
Czechoslovakia	Hungary	17 Oct 64	545UNTS21	107924
India	UK Great Britain	20 Oct 64	534UNTS77	107755
Argentina	Paraguay	21 Oct 64	635UNTS189	109082
Chile	USA (United States)	27 Oct 64	532UNTS347	107727
Ethiopia	Netherlands	28 Oct 64	541UNTS235	107872
Netherlands	Pakistan	30 Oct 64	541UNTS243	107873
Greece	Yugoslavia	05 Nov 64	539UNTS19	107821

PARTY ONE	PARTY TWO	DATE	CITATION	NUMBER
Customs exemptions (Cont.)				
Multilateral		01 Dec 64	550UNTS133	108012
Netherlands	Nigeria	04 Dec 64	545UNTS155	107931
Japan	USA (United States)	04 Dec 64	532UNTS249	107721
Germany, West	Jamaica	16 Dec 64	531UNTS129	107699
Argentina	UK Great Britain	12 Jan 65	597UNTS177	108645
Ecuador	Netherlands	14 Jan 65	551UNTS129	108038
Canada	USA (United States)	16 Jan 65	606UNTS31	108772
Denmark	Thailand	25 Jan 65	530UNTS173	107680
Mexico	USA (United States)	27 Feb 65	542UNTS181	107889
Finland	UK Great Britain	25 Mar 65	539UNTS103	107826
Denmark	Malaysia	26 Mar 65	540UNTS205	107851
Hungary	Yugoslavia	08 Apr 65	587UNTS169	108511
Malawi	USA (United States)	20 Apr 65	546UNTS175	107943
Ghana	Malawi	04 May 65	541UNTS163	107869
Denmark	Spain	05 May 65	543UNTS255	107905
Spain	Sweden	05 May 65	0UNTS0	109239
Multilateral		02 Jun 65	551UNTS2	108030
Ivory Coast	Netherlands	03 Jun 65	634UNTS95	109054
Saudi Arabia	USA (United States)	05 Jun 65	548UNTS285	107984
Ivory Coast	Sweden	07 Jun 65	0UNTS0	109240
Canada	USA (United States)	08 Jun 65	546UNTS201	107947
Guinea	USA (United States)	29 Jun 65	549UNTS139	107997
Multilateral		02 Jul 65	592UNTS215	108575
Multilateral		05 Jul 65	563UNTS104	108207
Cameroon	Netherlands	06 Jul 65	571UNTS75	108300
Malta	Yugoslavia	15 Jul 65	561UNTS223	108186
Italy	UK Great Britain	01 Sep 65	0UNTS0	109283
Italy	UK Great Britain	01 Sep 65	0UNTS0	109284
Saudi Arabia	USA (United States)	19 Nov 65	580UNTS35	108419
Denmark	Syria	28 Dec 65	588UNTS163	108523
Ethiopia	USA (United States)	30 Dec 65	574UNTS129	108345
Austria	Tunisia	30 Dec 65	589UNTS119	108539
USA (United States)	Vietnam, South	03 Jan 66	579UNTS99	108401
Malta	USA (United States)	15 Jan 66	579UNTS109	108402
Norway	Eur Space Research	31 Jan 66	580UNTS3	108414
Austria	Germany, West	17 Feb 66	614UNTS263	108875
Israel	Kenya	25 Feb 66	582UNTS23	108455
Brazil	Denmark	25 Feb 66	590UNTS95	108549
Argentina	Germany, West	01 Mar 66	635UNTS247	109087
Spain	USA (United States)	14 Apr 66	579UNTS173	108406
Bulgaria	UN Special Fund	26 May 66	563UNTS71	108205
Guyana	UK Great Britain	26 May 66	595UNTS255	108621
Ivory Coast	Norway	07 Jun 66	0UNTS0	109249
Denmark	Iran	14 Jun 66	597UNTS283	108652
Netherlands	Yugoslavia	08 Sep 66	597UNTS147	108643
Tunisia	USA (United States)	26 Sep 66	616UNTS259	108900
Botswana	UK Great Britain	30 Sep 66	597UNTS211	108646
Mauritania	USSR (Soviet Union)	17 Oct 66	633UNTS231	109040
Romania	United Arab Rep	14 Nov 66	642UNTS129	109169
Ghana	Romania	23 Nov 66	642UNTS63	109165
Denmark	Singapore	20 Dec 66	593UNTS125	108580
Norway	Singapore	20 Dec 66	0UNTS0	109242
Romania	Spain	05 Jan 67	642UNTS103	109168
Trinidad/Tobago	UK Great Britain	23 Jan 67	605UNTS277	108767
Japan	Singapore	14 Feb 67	0UNTS0	109244
Denmark	France	15 Feb 67	604UNTS247	108754
Algeria	Ivory Coast	16 Feb 67	0UNTS0	109245
Romania	Sweden	01 Mar 67	642UNTS163	109172
Australia	Austria	22 Mar 67	0UNTS0	109246
Multilateral		04 May 67	595UNTS287	108623
Netherlands	Sierra Leone	13 Jun 67	0UNTS0	109247
Multilateral		21 Jun 67	598UNTS2	108653
Multilateral		03 Jul 67	0UNTS0	109248
Malta	UK Great Britain	10 Jul 67	619UNTS11	108936

PARTY ONE	PARTY TWO	DATE	CITATION	NUMBER
Customs and excise cooperation				
Multilateral		08 Sep 51	136UNTS45	101832
Temporary importation				
Peru	USA (United States)	07 May 42	103UNTS219	200316
Canada	USA (United States)	09 Nov 42	101UNTS233	200298
Philippines	USA (United States)	04 Jul 46	43UNTS135	100668
Australia	USA (United States)	03 Dec 46	7UNTS201	100100
New Zealand	USA (United States)	03 Dec 46	7UNTS175	100099
South Africa	USA (United States)	23 May 47	66UNTS233	100857
Hungary	USSR (Soviet Union)	15 Jul 47	216UNTS247	102940
Czechoslovakia	USSR (Soviet Union)	11 Dec 47	217UNTS35	102943
Bulgaria	USSR (Soviet Union)	01 Apr 48	217UNTS97	102946
South Africa	UK Great Britain	06 Dec 48	118UNTS183	101607
Italy	USSR (Soviet Union)	11 Dec 48	217UNTS181	102948
Pakistan	Philippines	16 Jul 49	35UNTS111	100553
Canada	New Zealand	16 Aug 50	77UNTS239	101002
Canada	Ecuador	10 Nov 50	231UNTS15	103199
Multilateral		18 Apr 51	261UNTS140	103729
Multilateral		19 Jun 51	199UNTS67	102678
Multilateral		07 Nov 52	221UNTS255	103010
USA (United States)	Venezuela	14 Aug 53	213UNTS99	102883
Multilateral		04 Jun 54	282UNTS249	104101
Austria	Yugoslavia	27 Nov 54	396UNTS75	105694
Austria	Italy	22 Oct 55	260UNTS327	103716
Czechoslovakia	Poland	13 Jan 56	265UNTS157	103811
Multilateral		01 Mar 56	343UNTS129	104923
Austria	Hungary	09 Apr 56	438UNTS123	106315
Multilateral		18 May 56	327UNTS123	104721
Multilateral		18 May 56	338UNTS103	104834
Multilateral		18 May 56	319UNTS21	104630
Multilateral		08 Nov 56	470UNTS171	106809
Multilateral		14 Dec 56	436UNTS115	106292
Multilateral		25 Mar 57	294UNTS2	104300
Multilateral		03 Oct 57	364UNTS3	105211
Italy	Pakistan	05 Oct 57	353UNTS91	105039
Japan	USSR (Soviet Union)	06 Dec 57	325UNTS35	104694
Bulgaria	Yugoslavia	21 Mar 58	349UNTS61	105009
UK Great Britain	Yugoslavia	03 Feb 59	359UNTS339	105151
Greece	Yugoslavia	18 Jun 59	363UNTS133	105205
India	Italy	16 Jul 59	464UNTS129	106714
Pakistan	USA (United States)	18 Jul 59	355UNTS367	105087
Czechoslovakia	Japan	15 Dec 59	383UNTS277	105505
Cuba	Czechoslovakia	10 Jun 60	447UNTS75	106412
Ghana	USSR (Soviet Union)	04 Aug 60	421UNTS27	106050
Multilateral		06 Oct 60	473UNTS131	106861
Turkey	USSR (Soviet Union)	27 Apr 61	420UNTS307	106047
Senegal	USA (United States)	13 May 61	409UNTS232	105888
Multilateral		08 Jun 61	473UNTS187	106863
Multilateral		08 Jun 61	473UNTS153	106862
Madagascar	USA (United States)	22 Jun 61	413UNTS219	105956
Ghana	USSR (Soviet Union)	04 Nov 61	437UNTS213	106308
Mexico	USA (United States)	15 Nov 61	460UNTS113	106634
Multilateral		06 Dec 61	473UNTS219	106864
Czechoslovakia	Yugoslavia	22 Oct 62	480UNTS267	106974
Austria	Czechoslovakia	08 Mar 63	495UNTS219	107245
Tanganyika	USSR (Soviet Union)	14 Aug 63	493UNTS195	107215
Romania	Yugoslavia	25 Dec 63	576UNTS95	108366
Czechoslovakia	Hungary	17 Oct 64	545UNTS21	107924
Hungary	Poland	18 Jul 65	577UNTS161	108376
Denmark	Norway	23 Dec 66	613UNTS265	108855
Multilateral		04 May 67	595UNTS287	108623
Aid and development				
Multilateral		11 Jul 47	218UNTS345	102961
Iceland	United Nations	19 Apr 48	47UNTS251	100733

PARTY ONE	PARTY TWO	DATE	CITATION	NUMBER
Aid and development (Cont.)				
Canada	United Nations	27 Aug 48	47UNTS167	100729
Israel	USA (United States)	27 Feb 52	177UNTS123	102314
Pakistan	USA (United States)	05 Mar 59	327UNTS285	104726
Iran	USA (United States)	05 Mar 59	327UNTS277	104725
UN Special Fund	Togo	08 Jun 60	369UNTS401	200574
Austria	USA (United States)	29 Mar 61	459UNTS45	106612
Chile	IBRD (World Bank)	28 Jun 61	426UNTS33	106129
Fed of Malaya	UN Special Fund	25 Jul 61	401UNTS159	105769
Pakistan	USA (United States)	25 Jul 62	459UNTS87	106614
Taiwan	USA (United States)	09 Apr 65	546UNTS81	107939
Multilateral		23 Sep 66	573UNTS148	108328
Multilateral		10 Jun 67	602UNTS212	108714
Multilateral		28 Sep 68	0UNTS0	109296
UN Special Fund	Southern Yemen	04 Apr 69	0UNTS0	109456
State/IGO Group	Southern Yemen	04 Apr 69	0UNTS0	109454
State/IGO Group	Southern Yemen	04 Apr 69	0UNTS0	109455
State/IGO Group	Yemen	23 Apr 69	0UNTS0	109514
Commodities and services				
France	USA (United States)	25 Sep 43	76UNTS183	200245
Netherlands	UK Great Britain	20 Dec 45	4UNTS303	100053
Albania	Yugoslavia	12 Jun 47	111UNTS177	101531
Poland	UNICEF (Children)	23 Aug 47	65UNTS22	100815
Italy	USA (United States)	28 Jun 48	20UNTS43	100314
Denmark	USA (United States)	29 Jun 48	22UNTS217	100338
Australia	Hungary	01 Jul 48	22UNTS3	100325
Netherlands	USA (United States)	02 Jul 48	20UNTS91	100315
Taiwan	USA (United States)	03 Jul 48	17UNTS119	100273
Australia	Italy	08 Jul 48	22UNTS11	100326
Australia	Yugoslavia	09 Jul 48	22UNTS17	100327
Australia	Austria	19 Jul 48	22UNTS25	100328
Chile	UNICEF (Children)	03 Mar 50	126UNTS119	101685
Burma	USA (United States)	13 Sep 50	92UNTS361	101280
USA (United States)	Yugoslavia	06 Jan 51	122UNTS137	101643
Austria	USA (United States)	15 May 51	139UNTS79	101876
Iran	UNICEF (Children)	02 Aug 51	247UNTS11	103457
USA (United States)	Vietnam, South	07 Sep 51	174UNTS165	102284
Cambodia	USA (United States)	08 Sep 51	174UNTS115	102282
Laos	USA (United States)	09 Sep 51	174UNTS141	102283
UNICEF (Children)	UK Great Britain	02 Oct 51	104UNTS301	101448
Iraq	UNICEF (Children)	10 Dec 51	126UNTS57	101682
Jordan	USA (United States)	20 Dec 51	157UNTS69	102048
USA (United States)	Yugoslavia	08 Jan 52	152UNTS61	102011
Israel	USA (United States)	27 Feb 52	177UNTS123	102314
Libya	UNICEF (Children)	05 Apr 52	133UNTS287	200441
Liberia	UNICEF (Children)	17 Apr 52	133UNTS3	101773
Israel	USA (United States)	09 May 52	177UNTS269	102326
Belgium	UNICEF (Children)	17 Jun 52	171UNTS249	102228
Panama	USA (United States)	30 Jun 52	181UNTS121	102404
Jordan	UNICEF (Children)	08 Jul 52	173UNTS353	200503
UNICEF (Children)	Syria	10 Jul 52	136UNTS17	101830
UNICEF (Children)	UK Great Britain	25 Jul 52	135UNTS37	101812
UNICEF (Children)	Vietnam, South	29 Aug 52	161UNTS335	200492
Germany, West	Israel	10 Sep 52	162UNTS205	102137
UNICEF (Children)	UK Great Britain	16 Dec 52	151UNTS359	102005
Netherlands	United Nations	09 Apr 53	163UNTS89	102143
Ethiopia	UNICEF (Children)	27 Apr 53	213UNTS169	102885
Pakistan	USA (United States)	25 Jun 53	205UNTS139	102773
UNICEF (Children)	UK Great Britain	07 Oct 53	180UNTS59	102375
Japan	UNICEF (Children)	21 Nov 53	183UNTS297	200507
Libya	USA (United States)	11 Jan 54	229UNTS15	103157
Japan	USA (United States)	08 Mar 54	232UNTS227	103238
Japan	USA (United States)	08 Mar 54	232UNTS243	103239
UNICEF (Children)	Spain	07 May 54	190UNTS357	200515
Mexico	UNICEF (Children)	20 May 54	192UNTS3	102591

PARTY ONE	PARTY TWO	DATE	CITATION	NUMBER
Commodities and services (Cont.)				
Jordan	USA (United States)	17 Jun 54	266UNTS137	103828
New Zealand	UNICEF (Children)	26 Aug 54	198UNTS173	102663
Libya	USA (United States)	09 Sep 54	238UNTS217	103365
Libya	USA (United States)	03 Nov 54	238UNTS227	103366
United Arab Rep	USA (United States)	06 Nov 54	237UNTS183	103344
Lebanon	UN Relief Palestin	26 Nov 54	202UNTS123	102728
Guatemala	USA (United States)	13 Dec 54	237UNTS169	103343
Netherlands	UNICEF (Children)	31 Dec 54	202UNTS135	102729
Philippines	USA (United States)	27 Apr 55	261UNTS351	103733
Guatemala	UNICEF (Children)	22 Nov 55	221UNTS305	103012
Japan	USA (United States)	10 Feb 56	275UNTS157	103980
Japan	USA (United States)	10 Feb 56	275UNTS181	103981
Italy	USA (United States)	27 Apr 56	273UNTS149	103949
Cambodia	UNICEF (Children)	28 Apr 56	136UNTS341	200446
Ceylon (Sri Lanka)	USA (United States)	28 Apr 56	274UNTS35	103956
Lebanon	UNICEF (Children)	03 Jul 56	324UNTS145	104683
UNICEF (Children)	Sudan	07 Aug 56	248UNTS307	200542
UNESCO (Educ/Cult)	Tunisia	03 Jan 57	257UNTS21	103645
Tunisia	USA (United States)	26 Mar 57	283UNTS117	104111
Morocco	USA (United States)	02 Apr 57	288UNTS157	104203
Libya	USA (United States)	04 Apr 57	283UNTS181	104116
Jordan	USA (United States)	27 Jun 57	288UNTS269	104209
Morocco	UNICEF (Children)	31 Jul 57	282UNTS99	104095
Ceylon (Sri Lanka)	China People's Rep	19 Sep 57	337UNTS169	104822
France	USA (United States)	23 Sep 57	293UNTS297	104297
Argentina	UNICEF (Children)	19 Nov 57	300UNTS229	104338
Multilateral		06 Jan 58	304UNTS227	104399
USA (United States)	Yugoslavia	05 Apr 58	338UNTS233	104838
Ghana	UNICEF (Children)	12 Aug 58	309UNTS103	104469
Japan	Laos	15 Oct 58	341UNTS25	104875
Italy	United Arab Rep	29 Apr 59	363UNTS91	105202
Guinea	UNICEF (Children)	08 Jun 59	334UNTS277	104772
Italy	USA (United States)	30 Jul 59	355UNTS393	105088
USA (United States)	Yugoslavia	22 Oct 59	360UNTS259	105161
Cuba	UNICEF (Children)	11 Feb 60	349UNTS277	105014
Italy	USA (United States)	19 Jul 60	389UNTS237	105595
Brazil	UN Special Fund	16 Sep 60	375UNTS3	105351
Taiwan	UN Special Fund	20 Sep 60	375UNTS29	105352
Guinea	USA (United States)	30 Sep 60	394UNTS103	105671
Togo	USA (United States)	22 Dec 60	401UNTS33	105760
Mali	USA (United States)	04 Jan 61	405UNTS165	105832
USA (United States)	Yugoslavia	19 Jan 61	402UNTS163	105784
Honduras	USA (United States)	12 Apr 61	413UNTS182	105952
Sierra Leone	USA (United States)	05 May 61	409UNTS194	105885
Senegal	USA (United States)	13 May 61	409UNTS232	105888
Ghana	Switzerland	17 May 61	559UNTS193	108159
Ivory Coast	USA (United States)	17 May 61	409UNTS241	105889
Niger	USA (United States)	26 May 61	410UNTS213	105905
Cameroon	USA (United States)	26 May 61	413UNTS195	105953
Dahomey	USA (United States)	27 May 61	445UNTS23	106373
Madagascar	USA (United States)	22 Jun 61	413UNTS219	105956
Central Afri Rep	UNICEF (Children)	21 Aug 61	413UNTS48	105939
Poland	UNICEF (Children)	24 Aug 61	406UNTS95	105841
Panama	USA (United States)	11 Dec 61	445UNTS161	106384
Iran	USA (United States)	21 Dec 61	433UNTS269	106249
Dominican Republic	USA (United States)	11 Jan 62	433UNTS133	106236
Cyprus	USA (United States)	02 Mar 62	445UNTS189	106386
Dahomey	UN Special Fund	28 Mar 62	424UNTS55	106099
United Nations	South Pacific Com	24 Jan 63	470UNTS361	200604
Central Afri Rep	USA (United States)	10 Feb 63	473UNTS83	106857
Burma	Japan	29 Mar 63	518UNTS3	107490
Multilateral		23 Jul 63	471UNTS158	106831
Niger	United Nations	20 Nov 63	536UNTS3	107793

PARTY ONE	PARTY TWO	DATE	CITATION	NUMBER
Domestic obligation				
Multilateral		05 Jun 25	38UNTS257	100602
Multilateral		10 Jun 25	38UNTS243	100601
Multilateral		10 Jun 25	38UNTS229	100600
Multilateral		26 Jun 28	39UNTS15	100610
Multilateral		21 Jun 29	39UNTS27	100611
Multilateral		20 Jun 36	40UNTS109	100630
Multilateral		24 Oct 36	40UNTS187	100634
Multilateral		23 Jun 37	40UNTS233	100637
Multilateral		12 May 40	101UNTS91	101405
Peru	USA (United States)	21 Apr 42	89UNTS317	200260
Peru	USA (United States)	11 May 42	136UNTS353	200447
Nicaragua	USA (United States)	27 Oct 42	99UNTS287	200283
Ecuador	USA (United States)	29 Oct 42	89UNTS301	200259
El Salvador	USA (United States)	02 Dec 42	122UNTS277	200410
Mexico	USA (United States)	14 Jun 43	66UNTS331	200220
Canada	Taiwan	22 Mar 44	14UNTS397	200096
Peru	USA (United States)	04 Apr 44	89UNTS291	200258
Multilateral		19 Apr 44	89UNTS279	200257
Norway	USA (United States)	16 May 44	67UNTS253	200223
Guatemala	USA (United States)	15 Jul 44	106UNTS285	200347
Multilateral		02 Aug 44	67UNTS221	200221
France	USA (United States)	20 Feb 45	76UNTS193	200246
Belgium	USA (United States)	19 Apr 45	139UNTS179	200455
UK Great Britain	USA (United States)	27 Mar 46	4UNTS2	100039
Mexico	USA (United States)	12 Apr 46	66UNTS293	100861
France	IBRD (World Bank)	09 May 47	152UNTS111	102014
Hungary	Yugoslavia	11 May 47	130UNTS171	101730
Greece	USA (United States)	20 Jun 47	7UNTS267	100105
Austria	USA (United States)	25 Jun 47	22UNTS141	100334
Italy	USA (United States)	04 Jul 47	22UNTS173	100336
Greece	USA (United States)	08 Jul 47	16UNTS157	100256
Turkey	USA (United States)	12 Jul 47	7UNTS299	100106
Netherlands	IBRD (World Bank)	07 Aug 47	152UNTS165	102015
Denmark	IBRD (World Bank)	22 Aug 47	152UNTS223	102016
Poland	UNICEF (Children)	23 Aug 47	65UNTS22	100815
Luxembourg	IBRD (World Bank)	28 Aug 47	153UNTS3	102017
Czechoslovakia	UNICEF (Children)	03 Oct 47	65UNTS26	100816
Greece	UNICEF (Children)	14 Oct 47	102UNTS39	101409
Taiwan	USA (United States)	27 Oct 47	12UNTS11	100178
Multilateral		12 Nov 47	53UNTS49	100772
UNICEF (Children)	Yugoslavia	20 Nov 47	65UNTS28	100817
France	USA (United States)	02 Jan 48	31UNTS97	100470
Italy	USA (United States)	03 Jan 48	31UNTS105	100471
Cuba	USA (United States)	27 Jan 48	67UNTS3	100862
Ecuador	USA (United States)	14 May 48	89UNTS71	101210
Ireland	USA (United States)	28 Jun 48	24UNTS3	100349
Italy	USA (United States)	28 Jun 48	20UNTS43	100314
France	USA (United States)	28 Jun 48	19UNTS9	100302
Denmark	USA (United States)	29 Jun 48	22UNTS217	100338
Greece	USA (United States)	02 Jul 48	23UNTS43	100342
Belgium	USA (United States)	02 Jul 48	19UNTS127	100309
Austria	USA (United States)	02 Jul 48	21UNTS29	100323
Netherlands	USA (United States)	02 Jul 48	20UNTS91	100315
Taiwan	USA (United States)	03 Jul 48	17UNTS119	100273
Luxembourg	USA (United States)	03 Jul 48	24UNTS35	100350
Sweden	USA (United States)	03 Jul 48	23UNTS101	100343
Norway	USA (United States)	03 Jul 48	20UNTS185	100317
Iceland	USA (United States)	03 Jul 48	20UNTS141	100316
Turkey	USA (United States)	04 Jul 48	24UNTS67	100351
UK Great Britain	USA (United States)	06 Jul 48	22UNTS263	100339
France	USA (United States)	09 Jul 48	24UNTS103	100352
Multilateral		14 Jul 48	23UNTS3	100340
Netherlands	IBRD (World Bank)	15 Jul 48	153UNTS259	102025
Netherlands	IBRD (World Bank)	15 Jul 48	153UNTS259	102022

PARTY ONE	PARTY TWO	DATE	CITATION	NUMBER
Domestic obligation (Cont.)				
Netherlands	IBRD (World Bank)	15 Jul 48	153UNTS259	102021
Netherlands	IBRD (World Bank)	15 Jul 48	153UNTS259	102024
Netherlands	IBRD (World Bank)	15 Jul 48	153UNTS259	102023
Portugal	USA (United States)	28 Sep 48	29UNTS213	100442
Trieste	USA (United States)	15 Oct 48	29UNTS249	100443
Brazil	USA (United States)	26 Nov 48	88UNTS3	101180
Korea, South	USA (United States)	10 Dec 48	55UNTS157	100813
Mexico	IBRD (World Bank)	06 Jan 49	154UNTS81	102028
Mexico	IBRD (World Bank)	06 Jan 49	154UNTS3	102027
Brazil	IBRD (World Bank)	27 Jan 49	153UNTS264	102026
Belgium	IBRD (World Bank)	01 Mar 49	154UNTS133	102029
Chile	IBRD (World Bank)	23 Mar 49	153UNTS61	102018
Chile	IBRD (World Bank)	23 Mar 49	153UNTS141	102019
Peru	USA (United States)	25 Mar 49	89UNTS15	101205
Philippines	USA (United States)	07 Jun 49	45UNTS63	100692
UNICEF (Children)	UK Great Britain	17 Jun 49	65UNTS50	100820
Netherlands	IBRD (World Bank)	26 Jul 49	154UNTS178	102030
India	IBRD (World Bank)	18 Aug 49	154UNTS269	102031
Colombia	IBRD (World Bank)	19 Aug 49	154UNTS329	102032
IBRD (World Bank)	Yugoslavia	17 Sep 49	155UNTS3	102034
India	IBRD (World Bank)	29 Sep 49	154UNTS393	102033
Finland	IBRD (World Bank)	17 Oct 49	156UNTS355	200481
El Salvador	IBRD (World Bank)	14 Dec 49	155UNTS43	102035
Germany, West	USA (United States)	15 Dec 49	92UNTS269	101277
UNICEF (Children)	UK Great Britain	19 Dec 49	65UNTS64	100828
Haiti	UNICEF (Children)	20 Dec 49	65UNTS68	100829
Costa Rica	UNICEF (Children)	14 Jan 50	65UNTS70	100830
Korea, South	USA (United States)	26 Jan 50	80UNTS205	101053
Netherlands	USA (United States)	27 Jan 50	80UNTS219	101054
UK Great Britain	USA (United States)	27 Jan 50	80UNTS261	101056
Luxembourg	USA (United States)	27 Jan 50	80UNTS187	101052
France	USA (United States)	27 Jan 50	80UNTS171	101051
Belgium	USA (United States)	27 Jan 50	51UNTS213	100767
Norway	USA (United States)	27 Jan 50	80UNTS241	101055
Italy	USA (United States)	27 Jan 50	80UNTS145	101050
Denmark	USA (United States)	27 Jan 50	48UNTS115	100740
UNICEF (Children)	UK Great Britain	10 Feb 50	65UNTS86	100837
Indonesia	USA (United States)	24 Mar 50	92UNTS387	101281
Mexico	IBRD (World Bank)	28 Apr 50	155UNTS185	102037
Iran	USA (United States)	23 May 50	81UNTS3	101057
Brazil	IBRD (World Bank)	26 May 50	301UNTS165	104345
Iraq	IBRD (World Bank)	15 Jun 50	155UNTS267	102038
Canada	USA (United States)	22 Jun 50	70UNTS115	100900
Afghanistan	UNICEF (Children)	04 Jul 50	71UNTS3	100906
IBRD (World Bank)	Turkey	07 Jul 50	156UNTS75	102040
IBRD (World Bank)	Turkey	07 Jul 50	156UNTS3	102039
Indonesia	USA (United States)	15 Aug 50	134UNTS255	101804
Brazil	USA (United States)	16 Aug 50	140UNTS223	101890
IBRD (World Bank)	Uruguay	25 Aug 50	156UNTS203	102042
Ethiopia	IBRD (World Bank)	13 Sep 50	157UNTS233	102056
Ethiopia	IBRD (World Bank)	13 Sep 50	157UNTS213	102055
Burma	USA (United States)	13 Sep 50	92UNTS361	101280
Thailand	USA (United States)	19 Sep 50	132UNTS199	101761
Indonesia	USA (United States)	16 Oct 50	281UNTS105	104074
Thailand	USA (United States)	17 Oct 50	79UNTS41	101030
Mexico	IBRD (World Bank)	18 Oct 50	157UNTS259	102057
IBRD (World Bank)	Turkey	19 Oct 50	157UNTS333	102058
Iran	USA (United States)	19 Oct 50	92UNTS135	101266
IBRD (World Bank)	Thailand	27 Oct 50	158UNTS25	102060
IBRD (World Bank)	Thailand	27 Oct 50	158UNTS3	102059
IBRD (World Bank)	Thailand	27 Oct 50	158UNTS43	102061
Multilateral		02 Nov 50	81UNTS160	101071
Burma	USA (United States)	06 Nov 50	122UNTS81	101638
Ceylon (Sri Lanka)	USA (United States)	07 Nov 50	92UNTS125	101265
Australia	IBRD (World Bank)	14 Nov 50	156UNTS147	102041

PARTY ONE	PARTY TWO	DATE	CITATION	NUMBER
Domestic obligation (Cont.)				
Multilateral		24 Nov 50	81UNTS188	101072
Colombia	USA (United States)	24 Nov 50	133UNTS49	101779
Multilateral		15 Dec 50	76UNTS120	100985
Brazil	USA (United States)	19 Dec 50	141UNTS3	101900
Liberia	USA (United States)	22 Dec 50	92UNTS145	101267
Liberia	USA (United States)	22 Dec 50	133UNTS69	101781
Nicaragua	USA (United States)	23 Dec 50	92UNTS155	101268
Multilateral		23 Dec 50	185UNTS3	102456
India	USA (United States)	28 Dec 50	99UNTS39	101369
Colombia	IBRD (World Bank)	28 Dec 50	158UNTS87	102063
Paraguay	USA (United States)	29 Dec 50	122UNTS157	101645
Portugal	USA (United States)	05 Jan 51	133UNTS75	101782
United Nations	Yugoslavia	06 Jan 51	78UNTS165	101015
USA (United States)	Yugoslavia	06 Jan 51	122UNTS137	101643
Chile	USA (United States)	16 Jan 51	151UNTS147	101990
Chile	USA (United States)	16 Jan 51	157UNTS3	102043
Saudi Arabia	USA (United States)	17 Jan 51	140UNTS335	101897
Multilateral		18 Jan 51	81UNTS233	101073
IBRD (World Bank)	South Africa	23 Jan 51	158UNTS135	102065
Nepal	USA (United States)	23 Jan 51	184UNTS65	102439
IBRD (World Bank)	South Africa	23 Jan 51	158UNTS115	102064
Ceylon (Sri Lanka)	ILO (Labor Org)	24 Jan 51	117UNTS355	200380
Ethiopia	ICAO (Civil Aviat)	02 Feb 51	96UNTS123	101333
Afghanistan	USA (United States)	07 Feb 51	132UNTS265	101766
Pakistan	USA (United States)	09 Feb 51	100UNTS67	101388
Multilateral		15 Feb 51	81UNTS245	101074
Israel	ILO (Labor Org)	19 Feb 51	100UNTS105	101391
Ethiopia	IBRD (World Bank)	19 Feb 51	186UNTS101	102486
Israel	ICAO (Civil Aviat)	19 Feb 51	96UNTS141	101334
Dominican Republic	USA (United States)	20 Feb 51	132UNTS305	101770
Australia	USA (United States)	20 Feb 51	132UNTS297	101769
Lebanon	USA (United States)	24 Feb 51	223UNTS121	103060
Israel	USA (United States)	26 Feb 51	137UNTS57	101848
Jordan	USA (United States)	27 Feb 51	141UNTS55	101905
ILO (Labor Org)	Syria	03 Mar 51	110UNTS69	101502
Multilateral		05 Mar 51	81UNTS261	101075
Colombia	USA (United States)	09 Mar 51	141UNTS15	101901
Bolivia	USA (United States)	14 Mar 51	132UNTS319	101771
Indonesia	WHO (World Health)	28 Mar 51	103UNTS71	101425
Multilateral		28 Mar 51	181UNTS61	102399
Jordan	ILO (Labor Org)	29 Mar 51	100UNTS247	200287
Jordan	United Nations	29 Mar 51	137UNTS267	200448
Liberia	ILO (Labor Org)	02 Apr 51	100UNTS117	101392
Multilateral		05 Apr 51	84UNTS299	101139
Mexico	ILO (Labor Org)	06 Apr 51	100UNTS131	101393
Ceylon (Sri Lanka)	ILO (Labor Org)	06 Apr 51	100UNTS235	200286
Iraq	USA (United States)	10 Apr 51	151UNTS179	101993
Colombia	IBRD (World Bank)	10 Apr 51	158UNTS155	102066
Peru	ILO (Labor Org)	13 Apr 51	100UNTS31	101385
Guatemala	ILO (Labor Org)	13 Apr 51	126UNTS249	101692
El Salvador	USA (United States)	18 Apr 51	141UNTS37	101903
Ecuador	ILO (Labor Org)	19 Apr 51	100UNTS77	101389
ICAO (Civil Aviat)	Thailand	19 Apr 51	96UNTS181	101336
Cuba	ILO (Labor Org)	21 Apr 51	99UNTS205	101382
India	ILO (Labor Org)	26 Apr 51	100UNTS19	101384
Philippines	USA (United States)	27 Apr 51	174UNTS251	102290
Mexico	WHO (World Health)	30 Apr 51	103UNTS95	101427
WHO (World Health)	Yugoslavia	02 May 51	103UNTS117	101429
Haiti	USA (United States)	02 May 51	151UNTS191	101994
Ecuador	USA (United States)	03 May 51	141UNTS27	101902
United Arab Rep	USA (United States)	05 May 51	198UNTS265	102670
Pakistan	ILO (Labor Org)	16 May 51	100UNTS147	101394
Lebanon	USA (United States)	29 May 51	160UNTS49	102101
Cambodia	WHO (World Health)	31 May 51	102UNTS279	200307
Multilateral		01 Jun 51	118UNTS57	101596

PARTY ONE	PARTY TWO	DATE	CITATION	NUMBER
Domestic obligation (Cont.)				
Lebanon	WHO (World Health)	05 Jun 51	104UNTS225	101443
Nicaragua	IBRD (World Bank)	07 Jun 51	158UNTS215	102067
Nicaragua	IBRD (World Bank)	07 Jun 51	158UNTS277	102068
Lebanon	WHO (World Health)	07 Jun 51	126UNTS221	101690
Iceland	ICAO (Civil Aviat)	07 Jun 51	96UNTS193	101337
USA (United States)	Venezuela	07 Jun 51	141UNTS273	101918
United Nations	Thailand	11 Jun 51	90UNTS45	101225
Costa Rica	WHO (World Health)	14 Jun 51	102UNTS151	101418
UK Great Britain	USA (United States)	15 Jun 51	141UNTS79	101907
Multilateral		15 Jun 51	148UNTS67	101936
Ethiopia	USA (United States)	16 Jun 51	148UNTS39	101933
Dominican Republic	ILO (Labor Org)	18 Jun 51	100UNTS3	101383
Cuba	USA (United States)	20 Jun 51	148UNTS3	101931
Iceland	IBRD (World Bank)	20 Jun 51	158UNTS301	102069
Israel	United Nations	25 Jun 51	97UNTS21	101344
ILO (Labor Org)	Vietnam, South	26 Jun 51	100UNTS223	200285
Mexico	USA (United States)	27 Jun 51	141UNTS211	101916
Multilateral		28 Jun 51	118UNTS154	101604
Ethiopia	WHO (World Health)	02 Jul 51	103UNTS39	101422
Burma	WHO (World Health)	09 Jul 51	102UNTS131	101416
ILO (Labor Org)	Thailand	11 Jul 51	100UNTS159	101395
Paraguay	ILO (Labor Org)	12 Jul 51	117UNTS155	101591
UK Great Britain	USA (United States)	13 Jul 51	105UNTS71	101454
Multilateral		18 Jul 51	102UNTS291	200308
El Salvador	USA (United States)	19 Jul 51	140UNTS259	101892
Multilateral		27 Jul 51	97UNTS291	200273
Panama	USA (United States)	30 Jul 51	140UNTS321	101896
Israel	WHO (World Health)	07 Aug 51	104UNTS213	101442
WHO (World Health)	Saudi Arabia	29 Aug 51	110UNTS277	101516
Multilateral		05 Sep 51	173UNTS15	102256
USA (United States)	Vietnam, South	07 Sep 51	174UNTS165	102284
Cambodia	USA (United States)	08 Sep 51	174UNTS115	102282
Laos	USA (United States)	09 Sep 51	174UNTS141	102283
Belgium	IBRD (World Bank)	13 Sep 51	158UNTS323	102070
Belgium	IBRD (World Bank)	13 Sep 51	158UNTS349	102071
Iraq	ICAO (Civil Aviat)	18 Sep 51	108UNTS219	101475
Paraguay	United Nations	27 Sep 51	120UNTS105	101617
Multilateral		01 Oct 51	104UNTS249	101446
Bolivia	United Nations	01 Oct 51	104UNTS263	101447
UNICEF (Children)	UK Great Britain	02 Oct 51	104UNTS301	101448
WHO (World Health)	Thailand	04 Oct 51	109UNTS85	101493
Pakistan	WHO (World Health)	07 Oct 51	126UNTS101	101684
Italy	IBRD (World Bank)	10 Oct 51	159UNTS383	200482
Chile	IBRD (World Bank)	10 Oct 51	158UNTS369	102072
IBRD (World Bank)	Yugoslavia	11 Oct 51	159UNTS3	102081
Colombia	IBRD (World Bank)	13 Oct 51	159UNTS75	102084
India	WHO (World Health)	16 Oct 51	109UNTS49	101490
United Nations	Uruguay	17 Oct 51	122UNTS29	101633
ILO (Labor Org)	Venezuela	22 Oct 51	117UNTS139	101590
El Salvador	USA (United States)	23 Oct 51	137UNTS43	101847
Nicaragua	IBRD (World Bank)	29 Oct 51	159UNTS35	102082
Iceland	IBRD (World Bank)	01 Nov 51	159UNTS55	102083
India	WHO (World Health)	01 Nov 51	118UNTS13	101593
Saudi Arabia	USA (United States)	10 Nov 51	180UNTS263	102390
Panama	ILO (Labor Org)	10 Nov 51	126UNTS269	101693
USA (United States)	Yugoslavia	14 Nov 51	174UNTS201	102286
Paraguay	IBRD (World Bank)	07 Dec 51	159UNTS103	102085
Libya	UK Great Britain	13 Dec 51	123UNTS167	101658
Mexico	WHO (World Health)	17 Dec 51	124UNTS121	101670
Jordan	USA (United States)	20 Dec 51	157UNTS69	102048
India	WHO (World Health)	20 Dec 51	124UNTS109	101669
Multilateral		24 Dec 51	118UNTS290	200383
Cambodia	USA (United States)	28 Dec 51	179UNTS97	102358
Thailand	USA (United States)	29 Dec 51	179UNTS113	102360
Taiwan	USA (United States)	02 Jan 52	181UNTS161	102407

Domestic obligation (Cont.)

PARTY ONE	PARTY TWO	DATE	CITATION	NUMBER
India	USA (United States)	05 Jan 52	157UNTS39	102045
Italy	USA (United States)	07 Jan 52	179UNTS165	102365
Belgium	USA (United States)	07 Jan 52	179UNTS81	102356
Turkey	USA (United States)	07 Jan 52	179UNTS121	102361
Korea, South	USA (United States)	07 Jan 52	179UNTS105	102359
Philippines	USA (United States)	07 Jan 52	179UNTS193	102368
Greece	USA (United States)	07 Jan 52	180UNTS171	102382
Dominican Republic	USA (United States)	07 Jan 52	174UNTS243	102289
Portugal	USA (United States)	08 Jan 52	207UNTS51	102799
UK Great Britain	USA (United States)	08 Jan 52	179UNTS201	102369
Iceland	USA (United States)	08 Jan 52	180UNTS183	102383
Luxembourg	USA (United States)	08 Jan 52	180UNTS191	102384
Netherlands	USA (United States)	08 Jan 52	179UNTS175	102366
Norway	USA (United States)	08 Jan 52	179UNTS185	102367
Denmark	USA (United States)	08 Jan 52	179UNTS65	102354
USA (United States)	Yugoslavia	08 Jan 52	152UNTS61	102011
UK Great Britain	USA (United States)	08 Jan 52	126UNTS307	101696
Mexico	IBRD (World Bank)	11 Jan 52	159UNTS129	102086
India	United Nations	12 Jan 52	118UNTS175	101606
USA (United States)	Vietnam, South	19 Jan 52	205UNTS127	102772
Iran	USA (United States)	20 Jan 52	200UNTS191	102703
Ceylon (Sri Lanka)	United Nations	21 Jan 52	118UNTS281	200382
Libya	USA (United States)	21 Jan 52	183UNTS177	102427
Peru	IBRD (World Bank)	23 Jan 52	159UNTS163	102087
Multilateral		23 Jan 52	127UNTS269	101708
WHO (World Health)	Spain	30 Jan 52	124UNTS259	200425
ICAO (Civil Aviat)	Yugoslavia	06 Feb 52	128UNTS97	101715
Indonesia	United Nations	06 Feb 52	121UNTS3	101621
WHO (World Health)	UK Great Britain	07 Feb 52	121UNTS75	101627
Lebanon	ICAO (Civil Aviat)	14 Feb 52	128UNTS83	101714
Multilateral		18 Feb 52	126UNTS319	200434
Burma	WHO (World Health)	18 Feb 52	127UNTS43	101698
Ecuador	USA (United States)	20 Feb 52	177UNTS43	102308
Peru	USA (United States)	22 Feb 52	165UNTS31	102166
IBRD (World Bank)	UK Great Britain	27 Feb 52	159UNTS181	102088
Japan	USA (United States)	28 Feb 52	208UNTS255	102817
Greece	United Nations	05 Mar 52	123UNTS3	101650
ICAO (Civil Aviat)	United Arab Rep	06 Mar 52	151UNTS111	101986
Finland	WHO (World Health)	07 Mar 52	128UNTS269	200436
Cuba	USA (United States)	07 Mar 52	165UNTS11	102165
Brazil	USA (United States)	15 Mar 52	199UNTS221	102687
Iraq	USA (United States)	18 Mar 52	223UNTS131	103061
Netherlands	IBRD (World Bank)	20 Mar 52	159UNTS207	102089
Pakistan	IBRD (World Bank)	27 Mar 52	159UNTS251	102090
India	United Nations	02 Apr 52	126UNTS145	101687
El Salvador	USA (United States)	04 Apr 52	177UNTS219	102320
Peru	USA (United States)	09 Apr 52	184UNTS295	102454
Chile	USA (United States)	09 Apr 52	186UNTS53	102482
United Nations	Yugoslavia	10 Apr 52	141UNTS89	101908
Multilateral		11 Apr 52	173UNTS2	102255
Colombia	USA (United States)	17 Apr 52	174UNTS215	102287
India	WHO (World Health)	17 Apr 52	131UNTS241	101744
India	WHO (World Health)	19 Apr 52	131UNTS253	101745
Pakistan	United Nations	28 Apr 52	128UNTS191	101720
India	ICAO (Civil Aviat)	29 Apr 52	151UNTS123	101987
Finland	IBRD (World Bank)	30 Apr 52	159UNTS408	200483
Israel	USA (United States)	09 May 52	177UNTS269	102326
Israel	USA (United States)	09 May 52	177UNTS63	102309
Libya	USA (United States)	20 May 52	178UNTS307	102346
Libya	USA (United States)	20 May 52	178UNTS155	102339
Libya	USA (United States)	20 May 52	177UNTS81	102310
Iraq	USA (United States)	21 May 52	212UNTS183	102870
Iraq	USA (United States)	21 May 52	205UNTS25	102767
Iraq	USA (United States)	21 May 52	205UNTS33	102768
Korea, South	USA (United States)	24 May 52	179UNTS23	102353

Domestic obligation (Cont.)

PARTY ONE	PARTY TWO	DATE	CITATION	NUMBER
Chile	WHO (World Health)	31 May 52	136UNTS323	101841
Brazil	USA (United States)	02 Jun 52	181UNTS109	102403
Iraq	USA (United States)	09 Jun 52	212UNTS193	102871
Pakistan	IBRD (World Bank)	13 Jun 52	191UNTS85	102578
Jordan	WHO (World Health)	16 Jun 52	135UNTS323	200445
Ethiopia	USA (United States)	18 Jun 52	181UNTS207	102410
IBRD (World Bank)	Turkey	18 Jun 52	159UNTS269	102091
Multilateral		19 Jun 52	133UNTS165	101787
WHO (World Health)	Syria	20 Jun 52	165UNTS219	102178
Ethiopia	USA (United States)	24 Jun 52	181UNTS215	102411
Brazil	IBRD (World Bank)	27 Jun 52	190UNTS115	102561
Brazil	IBRD (World Bank)	27 Jun 52	190UNTS85	102560
USA (United States)	Uruguay	30 Jun 52	207UNTS139	102804
Chile	USA (United States)	30 Jun 52	199UNTS241	102688
Panama	USA (United States)	30 Jun 52	181UNTS121	102404
Australia	FAO (Food Agri)	07 Jul 52	184UNTS209	102449
Peru	IBRD (World Bank)	08 Jul 52	159UNTS321	102093
Australia	IBRD (World Bank)	08 Jul 52	159UNTS295	102092
Chile	WHO (World Health)	11 Jul 52	137UNTS27	101846
India	WHO (World Health)	16 Jul 52	135UNTS291	101828
Colombia	United Nations	17 Jul 52	135UNTS61	101815
Chile	ILO (Labor Org)	23 Jul 52	178UNTS323	102348
Brazil	United Nations	04 Aug 52	135UNTS185	101820
Laos	UNICEF (Children)	15 Aug 52	161UNTS323	200491
Iraq	USA (United States)	18 Aug 52	184UNTS131	102444
Panama	United Nations	20 Aug 52	136UNTS3	101829
Jordan	WHO (World Health)	21 Aug 52	141UNTS341	200472
Multilateral		21 Aug 52	141UNTS129	101912
Colombia	IBRD (World Bank)	26 Aug 52	159UNTS339	102094
Australia	Germany, West	29 Aug 52	184UNTS147	102446
Italy	ILO (Labor Org)	04 Sep 52	178UNTS371	200505
ILO (Labor Org)	Uruguay	20 Sep 52	187UNTS25	102499
United Nations	Trieste	30 Sep 52	140UNTS11	101881
Multilateral		15 Oct 52	141UNTS96	101909
Iraq	USA (United States)	23 Oct 52	212UNTS201	102872
Ethiopia	USA (United States)	07 Nov 52	184UNTS285	102453
Saudi Arabia	USA (United States)	10 Nov 52	181UNTS307	102419
Japan	IBRD (World Bank)	12 Nov 52	354UNTS313	105068
Japan	WHO (World Health)	26 Nov 52	204UNTS301	200521
Mexico	ICAO (Civil Aviat)	28 Nov 52	164UNTS15	102156
Multilateral		16 Dec 52	158UNTS407	102074
India	IBRD (World Bank)	18 Dec 52	201UNTS241	102719
Multilateral		29 Dec 52	151UNTS317	102002
ILO (Labor Org)	UN Relief Palestin	31 Dec 52	182UNTS201	200506
India	IBRD (World Bank)	23 Jan 53	201UNTS145	102715
United Nations	Sweden	11 Feb 53	160UNTS3	102096
India	WHO (World Health)	11 Feb 53	163UNTS43	102140
IBRD (World Bank)	Yugoslavia	11 Feb 53	165UNTS231	102179
Taiwan	ILO (Labor Org)	13 Feb 53	178UNTS337	102349
UK Great Britain	USA (United States)	25 Feb 53	212UNTS157	102868
Multilateral		26 Feb 53	161UNTS31	102120
Costa Rica	United Nations	27 Feb 53	161UNTS45	102121
Nepal	United Nations	02 Mar 53	161UNTS347	200493
Dominican Republic	USA (United States)	06 Mar 53	199UNTS267	102689
IBRD (World Bank)	UK Great Britain	11 Mar 53	172UNTS115	102243
United Arab Rep	USA (United States)	12 Mar 53	204UNTS3	102747
United Arab Rep	USA (United States)	19 Mar 53	215UNTS17	102909
Jordan	UN Relief Palestin	30 Mar 53	165UNTS317	200495
France	WHO (World Health)	02 Apr 53	174UNTS83	102279
United Nations	Yemen	07 Apr 53	163UNTS73	102142
Brazil	IBRD (World Bank)	30 Apr 53	190UNTS133	102562
France	WHO (World Health)	30 Apr 53	174UNTS71	102278
El Salvador	USA (United States)	14 May 53	234UNTS71	103273
ICAO (Civil Aviat)	Syria	28 May 53	173UNTS199	102267
Ecuador	United Nations	16 Jun 53	166UNTS289	102194

PARTY ONE	PARTY TWO	DATE	CITATION	NUMBER
Domestic obligation (Cont.)				
Ethiopia	United Nations	22 Jun 53	172UNTS93	102241
Japan	United Nations	24 Jun 53	167UNTS249	200499
Cambodia	United Nations	24 Jun 53	168UNTS309	200500
Ethiopia	USA (United States)	25 Jun 53	212UNTS175	102869
Brazil	USA (United States)	26 Jun 53	336UNTS241	104808
Philippines	USA (United States)	26 Jun 53	213UNTS77	102881
Chile	USA (United States)	27 Jun 53	229UNTS53	103160
Chile	USA (United States)	27 Jun 53	229UNTS193	103167
Brazil	IBRD (World Bank)	17 Jul 53	190UNTS149	102563
IBRD (World Bank)	South Africa	28 Aug 53	180UNTS91	102377
IBRD (World Bank)	South Africa	28 Aug 53	180UNTS73	102376
Iceland	IBRD (World Bank)	04 Sep 53	188UNTS3	102519
Nicaragua	IBRD (World Bank)	04 Sep 53	186UNTS137	102488
Nicaragua	IBRD (World Bank)	04 Sep 53	186UNTS117	102487
Iceland	IBRD (World Bank)	04 Sep 53	178UNTS275	102344
Colombia	IBRD (World Bank)	10 Sep 53	203UNTS3	102738
Chile	IBRD (World Bank)	10 Sep 53	188UNTS25	102520
IBRD (World Bank)	Turkey	10 Sep 53	187UNTS71	102502
Panama	IBRD (World Bank)	25 Sep 53	188UNTS71	102521
Panama	IBRD (World Bank)	25 Sep 53	188UNTS95	102522
Spain	USA (United States)	26 Sep 53	207UNTS93	102802
Spain	USA (United States)	26 Sep 53	207UNTS61	102800
Italy	IBRD (World Bank)	06 Oct 53	301UNTS135	104344
UNICEF (Children)	UK Great Britain	07 Oct 53	180UNTS59	102375
Multilateral		09 Oct 53	190UNTS49	102557
UN Relief Palestin	United Arab Rep	14 Oct 53	190UNTS13	102555
Japan	IBRD (World Bank)	15 Oct 53	187UNTS367	200513
Japan	IBRD (World Bank)	15 Oct 53	187UNTS271	200511
Japan	IBRD (World Bank)	15 Oct 53	187UNTS321	200512
Jordan	USA (United States)	21 Oct 53	222UNTS31	103020
Netherlands	USA (United States)	27 Oct 53	221UNTS357	103017
Dominican Republic	United Nations	19 Nov 53	180UNTS45	102374
Thailand	USA (United States)	03 Dec 53	213UNTS91	102882
Brazil	IBRD (World Bank)	18 Dec 53	301UNTS229	104346
Brazil	IBRD (World Bank)	18 Dec 53	190UNTS179	102564
Chile	USA (United States)	30 Dec 53	236UNTS41	103315
UK Great Britain	USA (United States)	20 Jan 54	196UNTS95	102619
Netherlands	USA (United States)	22 Jan 54	190UNTS207	102565
Pakistan	United Nations	25 Jan 54	185UNTS213	102472
Brazil	WHO (World Health)	04 Feb 54	233UNTS49	103250
Brazil	IBRD (World Bank)	24 Feb 54	301UNTS249	104347
Australia	IBRD (World Bank)	02 Mar 54	191UNTS103	102579
United Nations	Venezuela	05 Mar 54	187UNTS9	102498
Japan	USA (United States)	08 Mar 54	232UNTS169	103236
Liberia	United Nations	09 Mar 54	187UNTS61	102501
Guatemala	United Nations	10 Mar 54	191UNTS271	102587
Mexico	USA (United States)	06 Apr 54	236UNTS69	103317
Norway	IBRD (World Bank)	08 Apr 54	201UNTS131	102714
Peru	IBRD (World Bank)	12 Apr 54	190UNTS231	102567
Multilateral		20 Apr 54	189UNTS11	102539
Iraq	USA (United States)	21 Apr 54	222UNTS251	103032
Nepal	WHO (World Health)	13 May 54	204UNTS311	200522
Jordan	USA (United States)	13 May 54	234UNTS225	103285
Pakistan	USA (United States)	19 May 54	202UNTS301	102736
Honduras	USA (United States)	20 May 54	222UNTS87	103025
Multilateral		31 May 54	192UNTS20	102592
Multilateral		01 Jun 54	200UNTS235	200520
Pakistan	IBRD (World Bank)	02 Jun 54	324UNTS59	104678
France	IBRD (World Bank)	10 Jun 54	210UNTS89	102836
Lebanon	USA (United States)	18 Jun 54	233UNTS177	103262
Italy	USA (United States)	28 Jun 54	237UNTS121	103340
Chile	USA (United States)	28 Jun 54	233UNTS3	103246
Ecuador	USA (United States)	30 Jun 54	236UNTS163	103323
Costa Rica	USA (United States)	30 Jun 54	235UNTS35	103294
Ceylon (Sri Lanka)	IBRD (World Bank)	09 Jul 54	198UNTS313	200517

PARTY ONE	PARTY TWO	DATE	CITATION	NUMBER
Domestic obligation (Cont.)				
Guatemala	USA (United States)	30 Jul 54	234UNTS235	103286
Multilateral		19 Aug 54	201UNTS51	102710
Mexico	IBRD (World Bank)	24 Aug 54	286UNTS211	104168
New Zealand	UNICEF (Children)	26 Aug 54	198UNTS173	102663
Guatemala	USA (United States)	01 Sep 54	199UNTS51	102677
Multilateral		02 Oct 54	201UNTS171	102716
Multilateral		02 Oct 54	201UNTS179	102717
Multilateral		06 Oct 54	201UNTS75	102711
El Salvador	IBRD (World Bank)	12 Oct 54	203UNTS37	102739
Ethiopia	Sweden	13 Oct 54	202UNTS273	102734
Canada	UK Great Britain	19 Oct 54	214UNTS309	102906
Multilateral		27 Oct 54	201UNTS95	102712
Multilateral		29 Oct 54	201UNTS115	102713
Burma	Japan	05 Nov 54	251UNTS215	103543
Austria	IBRD (World Bank)	08 Nov 54	216UNTS305	200528
Peru	IBRD (World Bank)	12 Nov 54	209UNTS287	102831
Korea, South	USA (United States)	17 Nov 54	256UNTS251	103635
India	IBRD (World Bank)	19 Nov 54	309UNTS159	104473
Guatemala	USA (United States)	13 Dec 54	237UNTS169	103343
Belgium	IBRD (World Bank)	14 Dec 54	210UNTS113	102837
Colombia	IBRD (World Bank)	29 Dec 54	211UNTS135	102851
Peru	USA (United States)	31 Dec 54	251UNTS51	103533
Pakistan	USA (United States)	11 Jan 55	251UNTS111	103537
Pakistan	USA (United States)	18 Jan 55	239UNTS61	103372
Haiti	USA (United States)	28 Jan 55	270UNTS83	103894
Mexico	USA (United States)	09 Mar 55	263UNTS247	103776
India	IBRD (World Bank)	14 Mar 55	309UNTS129	104472
IBRD (World Bank)	UK Great Britain	15 Mar 55	265UNTS85	103808
Australia	IBRD (World Bank)	18 Mar 55	220UNTS131	102998
Finland	IBRD (World Bank)	24 Mar 55	211UNTS305	200525
Colombia	IBRD (World Bank)	24 Mar 55	212UNTS217	102874
Haiti	USA (United States)	01 Apr 55	261UNTS361	103734
Multilateral		04 Apr 55	208UNTS239	102816
Peru	IBRD (World Bank)	05 Apr 55	211UNTS115	102850
Japan	USA (United States)	07 Apr 55	263UNTS285	103778
Peru	IBRD (World Bank)	19 Apr 55	221UNTS153	103007
Norway	IBRD (World Bank)	19 Apr 55	211UNTS159	102852
Taiwan	WHO (World Health)	21 Apr 55	210UNTS71	102835
Argentina	USA (United States)	25 Apr 55	251UNTS283	103546
Philippines	USA (United States)	27 Apr 55	261UNTS351	103733
Peru	USA (United States)	30 Apr 55	263UNTS309	103780
Norway	Sweden	28 May 55	262UNTS151	103743
Italy	IBRD (World Bank)	01 Jun 55	358UNTS203	105137
Pakistan	Sweden	04 Jun 55	228UNTS121	103146
Multilateral		14 Jun 55	212UNTS263	200526
Austria	IBRD (World Bank)	14 Jun 55	221UNTS375	200531
Colombia	IBRD (World Bank)	15 Jun 55	248UNTS161	103494
Belgium	USA (United States)	15 Jun 55	235UNTS133	103299
Guatemala	USA (United States)	18 Jun 55	262UNTS105	103740
Pakistan	IBRD (World Bank)	20 Jun 55	230UNTS41	103176
Multilateral		21 Jun 55	305UNTS265	104423
Germany, West	USA (United States)	30 Jun 55	240UNTS47	103393
Iran	WHO (World Health)	04 Jul 55	227UNTS65	103131
Multilateral		04 Jul 55	214UNTS10	102897
Nicaragua	IBRD (World Bank)	08 Jul 55	229UNTS123	103163
Nicaragua	IBRD (World Bank)	08 Jul 55	229UNTS97	103162
Panama	IBRD (World Bank)	12 Jul 55	219UNTS127	102970
Libya	USA (United States)	21 Jul 55	264UNTS247	103796
Argentina	USA (United States)	29 Jul 55	235UNTS121	103298
Guatemala	IBRD (World Bank)	29 Jul 55	229UNTS167	103165
Brazil	USA (United States)	03 Aug 55	270UNTS71	103893
Pakistan	IBRD (World Bank)	04 Aug 55	230UNTS79	103177
Peru	IBRD (World Bank)	05 Aug 55	218UNTS3	102950
Pakistan	IBRD (World Bank)	06 Aug 55	236UNTS195	103325
IBRD (World Bank)	Thailand	09 Aug 55	221UNTS283	103011

PARTY ONE	PARTY TWO	DATE	CITATION	NUMBER
Domestic obligation (Cont.)				
Lebanon	IBRD (World Bank)	25 Aug 55	230UNTS233	103188
France	IBRD (World Bank)	26 Aug 55	247UNTS305	103478
Nicaragua	IBRD (World Bank)	26 Aug 55	229UNTS145	103164
IBRD (World Bank)	Uruguay	29 Aug 55	243UNTS123	103450
USA (United States)	Yugoslavia	30 Sep 55	269UNTS89	103877
Liberia	USA (United States)	06 Oct 55	275UNTS93	103978
Japan	IBRD (World Bank)	25 Oct 55	230UNTS379	200534
Israel	USA (United States)	10 Nov 55	240UNTS3	103390
Belgium	UK Great Britain	18 Nov 55	222UNTS327	103038
IBRD (World Bank)	South Africa	28 Nov 55	230UNTS101	103178
United Arab Rep	USA (United States)	14 Dec 55	240UNTS37	103392
Honduras	IBRD (World Bank)	22 Dec 55	230UNTS262	103189
Germany, West	USA (United States)	23 Dec 55	240UNTS79	103395
Multilateral		02 Feb 56	227UNTS153	103137
Multilateral		10 Feb 56	228UNTS167	103150
Multilateral		10 Feb 56	228UNTS189	103151
Japan	IBRD (World Bank)	21 Feb 56	248UNTS321	200543
Multilateral		13 Mar 56	427UNTS245	106158
Chile	USA (United States)	13 Mar 56	275UNTS49	103975
USA (United States)	Uruguay	23 Mar 56	376UNTS311	105386
Ecuador	IBRD (World Bank)	26 Mar 56	292UNTS391	104277
Multilateral		30 Mar 56	604UNTS114	108748
Ceylon (Sri Lanka)	USA (United States)	28 Apr 56	274UNTS35	103956
Norway	IBRD (World Bank)	03 May 56	243UNTS281	103455
Burma	IBRD (World Bank)	04 May 56	253UNTS209	103585
Burma	IBRD (World Bank)	04 May 56	253UNTS179	103584
Haiti	IBRD (World Bank)	07 May 56	252UNTS279	103570
Nicaragua	IBRD (World Bank)	22 May 56	253UNTS233	103586
Finland	IBRD (World Bank)	22 May 56	248UNTS57	103485
Multilateral		31 May 56	251UNTS181	103541
Colombia	IBRD (World Bank)	06 Jun 56	248UNTS139	103493
Multilateral		08 Jun 56	247UNTS366	200541
Multilateral		14 Jun 56	265UNTS125	103809
Fed Rhod/Nyasaland	IBRD (World Bank)	21 Jun 56	285UNTS317	104156
IBRD (World Bank)	UK Great Britain	21 Jun 56	285UNTS355	104157
Multilateral		26 Jun 56	321UNTS2	104650
India	IBRD (World Bank)	26 Jun 56	301UNTS3	104341
Multilateral		26 Jun 56	253UNTS12	103573
Multilateral		02 Jul 56	540UNTS110	107846
Multilateral		02 Jul 56	248UNTS37	103484
Australia	Netherlands	01 Aug 56	280UNTS3	104047
Netherlands	USA (United States)	07 Aug 56	281UNTS57	104069
UNESCO (Educ/Cult)	UK Great Britain	09 Aug 56	256UNTS139	103624
Multilateral		31 Aug 56	249UNTS158	103506
Costa Rica	IBRD (World Bank)	18 Sep 56	260UNTS369	103721
Austria	IBRD (World Bank)	21 Sep 56	259UNTS43	103682
Austria	IBRD (World Bank)	21 Sep 56	259UNTS17	103681
Multilateral		05 Oct 56	251UNTS245	103544
Multilateral		05 Oct 56	251UNTS267	103545
Italy	IBRD (World Bank)	11 Oct 56	359UNTS3	105138
IBRD (World Bank)	Thailand	12 Oct 56	261UNTS117	103728
IBRD (World Bank)	Uruguay	25 Oct 56	265UNTS59	103807
UK Great Britain	USA (United States)	01 Nov 56	264UNTS3	103785
Chile	IBRD (World Bank)	01 Nov 56	261UNTS27	103724
Australia	IBRD (World Bank)	15 Nov 56	288UNTS117	104201
Multilateral		21 Nov 56	253UNTS266	103588
UK Great Britain	USA (United States)	27 Nov 56	282UNTS43	104092
Czechoslovakia	USSR (Soviet Union)	30 Nov 56	266UNTS243	103833
Australia	IBRD (World Bank)	03 Dec 56	288UNTS99	104200
India	IBRD (World Bank)	19 Dec 56	310UNTS75	104489
Japan	IBRD (World Bank)	19 Dec 56	264UNTS179	103793
Japan	IBRD (World Bank)	19 Dec 56	268UNTS203	103859
Mexico	ICAO (Civil Aviat)	20 Dec 56	497UNTS3	107259
Multilateral		15 Jan 57	376UNTS122	105378
Iran	IBRD (World Bank)	22 Jan 57	317UNTS129	104600

PARTY ONE	PARTY TWO	DATE	CITATION	NUMBER
Domestic obligation (Cont.)				
Multilateral		23 Jan 57	259UNTS426	103701
Ethiopia	IBRD (World Bank)	28 Jan 57	286UNTS307	104175
Multilateral		17 Feb 57	271UNTS2	103907
Multilateral		22 Feb 57	274UNTS93	103960
Multilateral		01 Mar 57	264UNTS94	103790
India	IBRD (World Bank)	05 Mar 57	272UNTS201	103939
Peru	IBRD (World Bank)	13 Mar 57	274UNTS59	103958
Ethiopia	Sweden	16 Mar 57	304UNTS214	104398
Burma	USA (United States)	21 Mar 57	300UNTS11	104327
Tunisia	USA (United States)	26 Mar 57	283UNTS117	104111
Multilateral		28 Mar 57	271UNTS30	103908
Morocco	USA (United States)	02 Apr 57	288UNTS157	104203
Libya	USA (United States)	04 Apr 57	283UNTS181	104116
Multilateral		09 Apr 57	274UNTS172	103965
Ethiopia	USA (United States)	25 Apr 57	283UNTS205	104118
Finland	USA (United States)	10 May 57	283UNTS43	104105
Netherlands	IBRD (World Bank)	15 May 57	274UNTS211	103967
Multilateral		24 May 57	268UNTS270	103861
India	IBRD (World Bank)	29 May 57	309UNTS201	104474
Ghana	USA (United States)	03 Jun 57	284UNTS63	104129
Argentina	USA (United States)	03 Jun 57	291UNTS61	104244
Lebanon	USA (United States)	06 Jun 57	284UNTS155	104134
Finland	India	14 Jun 57	277UNTS327	104016
Multilateral		26 Jun 57	325UNTS279	104704
Belgium	IBRD (World Bank)	26 Jun 57	322UNTS301	104661
Jordan	USA (United States)	27 Jun 57	288UNTS269	104209
Australia	FAO (Food Agri)	08 Jul 57	277UNTS315	104015
Multilateral		09 Jul 57	274UNTS300	103972
India	IBRD (World Bank)	12 Jul 57	288UNTS135	104202
Chile	IBRD (World Bank)	24 Jul 57	282UNTS189	104099
Chile	IBRD (World Bank)	24 Jul 57	282UNTS139	104098
Japan	IBRD (World Bank)	09 Aug 57	293UNTS59	104286
Belgium	IBRD (World Bank)	10 Sep 57	286UNTS291	104174
IBRD (World Bank)	Thailand	12 Sep 57	299UNTS349	104324
Ecuador	IBRD (World Bank)	20 Sep 57	293UNTS135	104291
Ecuador	IBRD (World Bank)	20 Sep 57	289UNTS237	104221
Burma	WHO (World Health)	20 Sep 57	282UNTS113	104096
IBRD (World Bank)	South Africa	01 Oct 57	280UNTS285	104065
Austria	IBRD (World Bank)	10 Oct 57	301UNTS95	104343
Pakistan	IBRD (World Bank)	18 Oct 57	299UNTS303	104322
IAEA (Atom Energy)	United Nations	23 Oct 57	281UNTS369	200548
Multilateral		05 Nov 57	285UNTS301	104155
India	IBRD (World Bank)	20 Nov 57	301UNTS47	104342
Philippines	IBRD (World Bank)	22 Nov 57	293UNTS83	104287
Belgium	IBRD (World Bank)	27 Nov 57	292UNTS175	104273
Pakistan	IBRD (World Bank)	17 Dec 57	299UNTS321	104323
Multilateral		06 Jan 58	304UNTS227	104399
Mexico	IBRD (World Bank)	14 Jan 58	293UNTS167	104292
Ghana	WHO (World Health)	21 Jan 58	307UNTS3	104437
Brazil	IBRD (World Bank)	22 Jan 58	323UNTS99	104666
Indonesia	WHO (World Health)	05 Feb 58	307UNTS15	104438
Multilateral		15 Mar 58	292UNTS273	104276
Sudan	USA (United States)	31 Mar 58	308UNTS105	104458
Israel	WHO (World Health)	11 Apr 58	307UNTS27	104439
Bolivia	USA (United States)	22 Apr 58	317UNTS209	104605
Pakistan	IBRD (World Bank)	23 Apr 58	323UNTS253	104672
Chile	IBRD (World Bank)	28 Apr 58	359UNTS89	105140
Austria	IBRD (World Bank)	28 Apr 58	359UNTS145	105142
Saudi Arabia	USA (United States)	01 May 58	315UNTS221	104571
IBRD (World Bank)	UK Great Britain	02 May 58	324UNTS25	104677
Mexico	IBRD (World Bank)	05 May 58	309UNTS3	104466
Italy	USA (United States)	08 May 58	316UNTS177	104584
Honduras	IBRD (World Bank)	09 May 58	323UNTS4	104662
Multilateral		13 May 58	389UNTS277	105598
Ceylon (Sri Lanka)	Sweden	22 May 58	428UNTS65	106168

Domestic obligation (Cont.)

PARTY ONE	PARTY TWO	DATE	CITATION	NUMBER
Japan	IBRD (World Bank)	13 Jun 58	312UNTS159	104518
IBRD (World Bank)	UK Great Britain	16 Jun 58	309UNTS35	104467
Multilateral		19 Jun 58	306UNTS236	200550
WHO (World Health)	Sudan	21 Jun 58	307UNTS235	104453
India	IBRD (World Bank)	25 Jun 58	323UNTS131	104667
India	IBRD (World Bank)	25 Jun 58	323UNTS157	104668
IBRD (World Bank)	Sudan	21 Jul 58	323UNTS183	104669
India	IBRD (World Bank)	23 Jul 58	317UNTS3	104590
Ghana	UNICEF (Children)	12 Aug 58	309UNTS103	104469
Nepal	United Nations	18 Aug 58	508UNTS3	107403
Japan	IBRD (World Bank)	18 Aug 58	323UNTS205	104670
Japan	IBRD (World Bank)	10 Sep 58	323UNTS297	104673
Japan	IBRD (World Bank)	10 Sep 58	318UNTS133	104612
India	IBRD (World Bank)	16 Sep 58	323UNTS235	104671
Ceylon (Sri Lanka)	IBRD (World Bank)	17 Sep 58	323UNTS51	104664
Peru	IBRD (World Bank)	17 Sep 58	323UNTS27	104663
Fed of Malaya	IBRD (World Bank)	22 Sep 58	323UNTS71	104665
Brazil	IBRD (World Bank)	03 Oct 58	337UNTS177	104823
Ecuador	IBRD (World Bank)	09 Oct 58	337UNTS299	104827
Multilateral		01 Dec 58	385UNTS137	105534
Austria	IBRD (World Bank)	02 Dec 58	340UNTS3	104856
IBRD (World Bank)	South Africa	02 Dec 58	324UNTS3	104676
Colombia	IBRD (World Bank)	15 Dec 58	354UNTS233	105065
Burma	United Nations	15 Dec 58	319UNTS3	104629
United Nations	Tunisia	23 Dec 58	321UNTS23	104651
El Salvador	IBRD (World Bank)	07 Jan 59	346UNTS51	104977
Colombia	IBRD (World Bank)	30 Jan 59	337UNTS327	104828
Costa Rica	IBRD (World Bank)	11 Feb 59	337UNTS245	104825
Japan	IBRD (World Bank)	17 Feb 59	337UNTS205	104824
El Salvador	IBRD (World Bank)	20 Feb 59	362UNTS75	105183
Ghana	United Nations	27 Feb 59	324UNTS133	104682
Pakistan	USA (United States)	05 Mar 59	327UNTS285	104726
Iran	USA (United States)	05 Mar 59	327UNTS277	104725
Iraq	USSR (Soviet Union)	16 Mar 59	346UNTS107	104979
Finland	IBRD (World Bank)	16 Mar 59	337UNTS269	104826
United Nations	Sudan	28 Mar 59	327UNTS95	104719
Morocco	UN Special Fund	04 Apr 59	354UNTS347	105069
India	IBRD (World Bank)	08 Apr 59	348UNTS131	104998
Italy	IBRD (World Bank)	21 Apr 59	359UNTS191	105143
Honduras	IBRD (World Bank)	20 May 59	359UNTS119	105141
Colombia	IBRD (World Bank)	20 May 59	344UNTS251	104953
Fed of Malaya	USA (United States)	22 May 59	346UNTS263	104985
Iran	IBRD (World Bank)	29 May 59	348UNTS103	104997
IBRD (World Bank)	South Africa	10 Jun 59	340UNTS33	104857
Brazil	IBRD (World Bank)	17 Jun 59	377UNTS111	105398
Panama	United Nations	24 Jun 59	507UNTS245	107402
Libya	United Nations	27 Jun 59	336UNTS291	104811
Gabon	IBRD (World Bank)	30 Jun 59	452UNTS135	106507
France	IBRD (World Bank)	30 Jun 59	452UNTS67	106505
Congo (Brazzaville)	IBRD (World Bank)	30 Jun 59	452UNTS123	106506
USA (United States)	Yemen	30 Jun 59	357UNTS137	105112
Laos	United Nations	06 Jul 59	337UNTS41	104814
Norway	IBRD (World Bank)	08 Jul 59	344UNTS229	104952
India	IBRD (World Bank)	15 Jul 59	355UNTS95	105075
Italy	USA (United States)	30 Jul 59	355UNTS393	105088
Paraguay	United Nations	01 Aug 59	341UNTS319	104894
Ghana	UN Special Fund	12 Aug 59	338UNTS203	104836
Pakistan	IBRD (World Bank)	13 Aug 59	355UNTS129	105076
Italy	IBRD (World Bank)	16 Sep 59	375UNTS159	105366
Pakistan	IBRD (World Bank)	25 Sep 59	355UNTS169	105077
Korea, South	USA (United States)	01 Oct 59	358UNTS115	105129
Iran	UN Special Fund	06 Oct 59	342UNTS89	104902
Guinea	United Nations	15 Oct 59	344UNTS47	104942
Poland	UN Special Fund	15 Oct 59	344UNTS29	104941
India	UN Special Fund	20 Oct 59	344UNTS143	104946

Domestic obligation (Cont.)

PARTY ONE	PARTY TWO	DATE	CITATION	NUMBER
UN Special Fund	Yugoslavia	27 Oct 59	344UNTS159	104947
Ecuador	UN Special Fund	10 Nov 59	345UNTS3	104955
Japan	USA (United States)	12 Nov 59	361UNTS27	105171
Japan	IBRD (World Bank)	12 Nov 59	354UNTS279	105067
Greece	UN Special Fund	13 Nov 59	345UNTS171	104966
UN Special Fund	Turkey	20 Nov 59	345UNTS105	104963
Iran	IBRD (World Bank)	23 Nov 59	380UNTS245	105459
Afghanistan	United Nations	24 Nov 59	397UNTS187	105705
UN Special Fund	United Arab Rep	25 Nov 59	345UNTS125	104964
Pakistan	IBRD (World Bank)	30 Nov 59	355UNTS203	105078
Israel	UN Special Fund	01 Dec 59	345UNTS197	104968
Guinea	UN Special Fund	02 Dec 59	345UNTS215	104969
Multilateral		03 Dec 59	348UNTS246	105003
Argentina	UN Special Fund	04 Dec 59	345UNTS263	104972
France	IBRD (World Bank)	10 Dec 59	380UNTS319	105464
Jordan	UN Special Fund	15 Dec 59	346UNTS3	104974
Ceylon (Sri Lanka)	WHO (World Health)	21 Dec 59	349UNTS109	105011
IBRD (World Bank)	United Arab Rep	22 Dec 59	354UNTS197	105063
IBRD (World Bank)	Uruguay	30 Dec 59	384UNTS275	105523
UN Special Fund	UK Great Britain	07 Jan 60	348UNTS177	105000
Colombia	USA (United States)	11 Jan 60	371UNTS37	105268
Peru	UN Special Fund	19 Jan 60	349UNTS83	105010
Colombia	IBRD (World Bank)	20 Jan 60	375UNTS49	105353
Pakistan	WHO (World Health)	20 Jan 60	351UNTS355	105034
Chile	UN Special Fund	22 Jan 60	351UNTS115	105020
Colombia	UN Special Fund	04 Feb 60	355UNTS257	105080
Bolivia	UN Special Fund	09 Feb 60	351UNTS203	105024
Cuba	UNICEF (Children)	11 Feb 60	349UNTS277	105014
India	USSR (Soviet Union)	12 Feb 60	392UNTS153	105642
Iran	IBRD (World Bank)	20 Feb 60	384UNTS213	105521
Afghanistan	UN Special Fund	21 Feb 60	351UNTS93	105019
Pakistan	UN Special Fund	25 Feb 60	351UNTS141	105021
France	IBRD (World Bank)	17 Mar 60	452UNTS147	106508
Mauritania	IBRD (World Bank)	17 Mar 60	452UNTS211	106509
Japan	IBRD (World Bank)	17 Mar 60	362UNTS43	105182
France	UN Special Fund	17 Mar 60	354UNTS119	105059
Belgium	IBRD (World Bank)	30 Mar 60	379UNTS103	105437
Belgium	IBRD (World Bank)	30 Mar 60	379UNTS161	105439
Belgium	IBRD (World Bank)	30 Mar 60	379UNTS129	105438
IBRD (World Bank)	UK Great Britain	01 Apr 60	379UNTS397	105446
Italy	UN Special Fund	01 Apr 60	354UNTS261	105066
Multilateral		12 Apr 60	359UNTS323	105150
UN Special Fund	Tunisia	12 Apr 60	355UNTS289	105082
Libya	UN Special Fund	19 Apr 60	356UNTS11	105090
UN Special Fund	Sudan	21 Apr 60	356UNTS213	105097
UN Special Fund	Vietnam, South	29 Apr 60	357UNTS311	200567
Laos	UN Special Fund	30 Apr 60	361UNTS171	105179
Costa Rica	IBRD (World Bank)	04 May 60	390UNTS201	105609
United Nations	Togo	06 May 60	388UNTS53	105571
Lebanon	UN Special Fund	07 May 60	360UNTS225	105160
Colombia	IBRD (World Bank)	10 May 60	379UNTS218	105441
Cambodia	WHO (World Health)	19 May 60	372UNTS193	105298
IBRD (World Bank)	UK Great Britain	27 May 60	375UNTS201	105367
Peru	IBRD (World Bank)	01 Jun 60	380UNTS15	105448
Multilateral		04 Jun 60	360UNTS208	105159
IBRD (World Bank)	Sudan	17 Jun 60	379UNTS253	105442
Multilateral		19 Jun 60	537UNTS214	107803
Iraq	UN Special Fund	19 Jun 60	376UNTS357	105389
Nicaragua	IBRD (World Bank)	22 Jun 60	384UNTS243	105522
Somalia	UK Great Britain	26 Jun 60	374UNTS347	105348
Peru	IBRD (World Bank)	29 Jun 60	400UNTS99	105750
Honduras	IBRD (World Bank)	29 Jun 60	400UNTS137	105751
Multilateral		08 Jul 60	366UNTS310	105220
Ethiopia	United Nations	13 Jul 60	368UNTS143	105239
Ethiopia	UN Special Fund	13 Jul 60	368UNTS159	105240

PARTY ONE	PARTY TWO	DATE	CITATION	NUMBER
Domestic obligation (Cont.)				
Italy	USA (United States)	19 Jul 60	389UNTS237	105595
El Salvador	IBRD (World Bank)	29 Jul 60	390UNTS101	105605
India	IBRD (World Bank)	29 Jul 60	377UNTS153	105399
WHO (World Health)	United Arab Rep	03 Aug 60	385UNTS3	105524
Jordan	WHO (World Health)	03 Aug 60	381UNTS133	105469
WHO (World Health)	Tunisia	04 Aug 60	381UNTS335	105474
Laos	WHO (World Health)	04 Aug 60	373UNTS313	105322
Panama	IBRD (World Bank)	19 Aug 60	390UNTS153	105607
Australia	USA (United States)	23 Aug 60	388UNTS237	105581
Haiti	USA (United States)	01 Sep 60	388UNTS249	105582
WHO (World Health)	Saudi Arabia	06 Sep 60	395UNTS169	105684
Lebanon	WHO (World Health)	08 Sep 60	387UNTS49	105557
Israel	IBRD (World Bank)	09 Sep 60	406UNTS3	105837
Multilateral		19 Sep 60	444UNTS259	106371
Pakistan	IBRD (World Bank)	19 Sep 60	444UNTS207	106370
Multilateral		19 Sep 60	419UNTS125	106032
Colombia	IBRD (World Bank)	20 Sep 60	390UNTS173	105608
Guinea	USA (United States)	30 Sep 60	394UNTS103	105671
Indonesia	UN Special Fund	07 Oct 60	378UNTS141	105424
Liberia	UN Special Fund	11 Oct 60	376UNTS341	105388
Mexico	IBRD (World Bank)	18 Oct 60	422UNTS177	106075
El Salvador	UN Special Fund	24 Oct 60	377UNTS171	105400
India	IBRD (World Bank)	28 Oct 60	406UNTS27	105838
Kuwait	United Nations	31 Oct 60	391UNTS295	200581
UNICEF (Children)	Upper Volta	15 Nov 60	402UNTS33	105776
WHO (World Health)	Upper Volta	15 Nov 60	383UNTS91	105496
Mali	UNICEF (Children)	17 Nov 60	402UNTS23	105775
Nepal	UN Special Fund	17 Nov 60	380UNTS289	105461
Pakistan	United Nations	17 Nov 60	380UNTS277	105460
Guatemala	UN Special Fund	17 Nov 60	383UNTS67	105495
Cambodia	UN Special Fund	24 Nov 60	382UNTS255	105487
Fed of Malaya	WHO (World Health)	25 Nov 60	387UNTS37	105556
Cambodia	United Nations	30 Nov 60	383UNTS147	105500
Norway	IBRD (World Bank)	02 Dec 60	390UNTS131	105606
WHO (World Health)	Yemen	03 Dec 60	395UNTS187	105685
Dahomey	WHO (World Health)	07 Dec 60	387UNTS277	105567
Cyprus	USA (United States)	08 Dec 60	405UNTS145	105831
Congo (Brazzaville)	WHO (World Health)	12 Dec 60	399UNTS105	105737
Bolivia	United Nations	14 Dec 60	382UNTS283	105489
Peru	IBRD (World Bank)	19 Dec 60	417UNTS275	106010
Japan	IBRD (World Bank)	20 Dec 60	400UNTS279	105754
Japan	IBRD (World Bank)	20 Dec 60	400UNTS167	105752
Honduras	UN Special Fund	20 Dec 60	383UNTS103	105497
Togo	USA (United States)	22 Dec 60	401UNTS33	105760
Niger	WHO (World Health)	28 Dec 60	394UNTS195	105679
Burma	UN Special Fund	03 Jan 61	387UNTS219	105564
Mali	USA (United States)	04 Jan 61	405UNTS165	105832
Costa Rica	UN Special Fund	10 Jan 61	389UNTS253	105597
Mexico	IBRD (World Bank)	16 Jan 61	422UNTS203	106076
Burma	IBRD (World Bank)	16 Jan 61	400UNTS73	105749
UN Special Fund	Saudi Arabia	19 Jan 61	396UNTS27	105692
Korea, South	WHO (World Health)	20 Jan 61	406UNTS269	200589
Nicaragua	UN Special Fund	20 Jan 61	387UNTS15	105555
Chad	UN Special Fund	23 Jan 61	390UNTS69	105603
UN Special Fund	Somalia	28 Jan 61	388UNTS75	105573
Multilateral		28 Jan 61	387UNTS202	105563
Ivory Coast	WHO (World Health)	30 Jan 61	395UNTS205	105686
Gabon	UN Special Fund	02 Feb 61	387UNTS289	105568
Costa Rica	IBRD (World Bank)	03 Feb 61	414UNTS314	105977
WHO (World Health)	Togo	03 Feb 61	394UNTS207	105680
Chad	WHO (World Health)	03 Feb 61	394UNTS161	105676
Nigeria	UN Special Fund	10 Feb 61	390UNTS85	105604
Central Afri Rep	WHO (World Health)	13 Feb 61	394UNTS149	105675
IBRD (World Bank)	Yugoslavia	23 Feb 61	415UNTS92	105982
Mexico	UN Special Fund	23 Feb 61	388UNTS151	105576

PARTY ONE	PARTY TWO	DATE	CITATION	NUMBER
Domestic obligation (Cont.)				
Cyprus	UN Special Fund	24 Feb 61	389UNTS3	105588
Iraq	United Nations	05 Mar 61	409UNTS56	105878
Panama	UN Special Fund	09 Mar 61	396UNTS3	105691
Cuba	UN Special Fund	10 Mar 61	390UNTS35	105601
Japan	United Nations	15 Mar 61	397UNTS199	105706
Kuwait	WHO (World Health)	16 Mar 61	397UNTS315	200588
Japan	IBRD (World Bank)	16 Mar 61	400UNTS201	105753
Austria	USA (United States)	29 Mar 61	459UNTS45	106612
IBRD (World Bank)	UK Great Britain	29 Mar 61	415UNTS300	105990
Norway	IAEA (Atom Energy)	10 Apr 61	402UNTS255	105790
Honduras	USA (United States)	12 Apr 61	413UNTS182	105952
Mauritania	WHO (World Health)	17 Apr 61	396UNTS301	200587
Cyprus	UNICEF (Children)	19 Apr 61	394UNTS185	105678
Korea, South	UN Special Fund	21 Apr 61	394UNTS231	200583
Mali	WHO (World Health)	27 Apr 61	407UNTS66	105860
Gabon	WHO (World Health)	27 Apr 61	397UNTS215	105707
IBRD (World Bank)	Thailand	28 Apr 61	415UNTS121	105983
Japan	IBRD (World Bank)	02 May 61	415UNTS144	105984
Ceylon (Sri Lanka)	UN Special Fund	03 May 61	395UNTS217	105687
Sierra Leone	USA (United States)	05 May 61	409UNTS194	105885
Colombia	IBRD (World Bank)	12 May 61	415UNTS172	105985
Senegal	USA (United States)	13 May 61	409UNTS232	105888
Ivory Coast	USA (United States)	17 May 61	409UNTS241	105889
Cameroon	USA (United States)	26 May 61	413UNTS195	105953
Niger	USA (United States)	26 May 61	410UNTS213	105905
Dahomey	USA (United States)	27 May 61	445UNTS23	106373
Somalia	USSR (Soviet Union)	02 Jun 61	457UNTS263	106587
Ceylon (Sri Lanka)	IBRD (World Bank)	06 Jun 61	414UNTS349	105978
Cameroon	UN Special Fund	13 Jun 61	397UNTS297	105713
IBRD (World Bank)	Sudan	14 Jun 61	415UNTS26	105980
Multilateral		14 Jun 61	415UNTS4	105979
Ethiopia	United Nations	14 Jun 61	406UNTS81	105840
Cyprus	United Nations	15 Jun 61	398UNTS39	105716
Madagascar	USA (United States)	22 Jun 61	413UNTS219	105956
Paraguay	UN Special Fund	22 Jun 61	399UNTS117	105738
IBRD (World Bank)	UK Great Britain	23 Jun 61	415UNTS358	105991
UN Special Fund	Upper Volta	26 Jun 61	400UNTS3	105744
Pakistan	IBRD (World Bank)	27 Jun 61	425UNTS241	106127
Philippines	UN Special Fund	28 Jun 61	399UNTS141	105739
Haiti	United Nations	28 Jun 61	399UNTS159	105740
Haiti	UN Special Fund	28 Jun 61	399UNTS171	105741
Argentina	IBRD (World Bank)	30 Jun 61	445UNTS85	106379
UNICEF (Children)	Saudi Arabia	04 Jul 61	413UNTS122	105947
Israel	IBRD (World Bank)	11 Jul 61	429UNTS3	106188
Mali	UN Special Fund	21 Jul 61	401UNTS141	105768
Netherlands	Euratom	25 Jul 61	462UNTS263	106686
Philippines	IBRD (World Bank)	26 Jul 61	414UNTS253	105976
UN Special Fund	Yemen	02 Aug 61	402UNTS43	105777
Finland	IBRD (World Bank)	09 Aug 61	415UNTS204	105986
Morocco	WHO (World Health)	09 Aug 61	412UNTS192	105932
India	IBRD (World Bank)	09 Aug 61	417UNTS297	106011
Cameroon	UNICEF (Children)	12 Aug 61	402UNTS235	105788
IBRD (World Bank)	UK Great Britain	16 Aug 61	426UNTS287	106143
WHO (World Health)	Somalia	17 Aug 61	423UNTS111	106088
India	IBRD (World Bank)	17 Aug 61	417UNTS319	106012
Mexico	United Nations	18 Aug 61	404UNTS297	105817
Central Afri Rep	UNICEF (Children)	21 Aug 61	413UNTS48	105939
Poland	UNICEF (Children)	24 Aug 61	406UNTS95	105841
Chad	UNICEF (Children)	26 Aug 61	422UNTS231	106077
Lebanon	United Nations	26 Aug 61	406UNTS105	105842
Colombia	IBRD (World Bank)	28 Aug 61	416UNTS23	105993
Ivory Coast	UN Special Fund	29 Aug 61	406UNTS129	105844
Ghana	United Nations	29 Aug 61	406UNTS117	105843
Tunisia	USSR (Soviet Union)	30 Aug 61	437UNTS243	106310
Fed of Malaya	USA (United States)	04 Sep 61	421UNTS215	106060

PARTY ONE	PARTY TWO	DATE	CITATION	NUMBER
Domestic obligation (Cont.)				
Costa Rica	IBRD (World Bank)	06 Sep 61	446UNTS345	106408
Jordan	United Nations	11 Sep 61	406UNTS255	105855
Iraq	WHO (World Health)	13 Sep 61	419UNTS69	106030
Multilateral		20 Sep 61	407UNTS52	105859
Paraguay	USA (United States)	26 Sep 61	461UNTS91	106653
UN Special Fund	Sierra Leone	02 Oct 61	422UNTS131	106073
Costa Rica	IBRD (World Bank)	13 Oct 61	430UNTS27	106202
Malagasy	WHO (World Health)	13 Oct 61	421UNTS273	106064
India	IBRD (World Bank)	13 Oct 61	418UNTS3	106013
Philippines	IBRD (World Bank)	13 Oct 61	415UNTS269	105989
Multilateral		16 Oct 61	410UNTS242	105908
Gabon	UNICEF (Children)	02 Nov 61	422UNTS241	106078
Peru	IBRD (World Bank)	03 Nov 61	430UNTS47	106203
Multilateral		07 Nov 61	412UNTS258	105937
Mauritania	UN Special Fund	07 Nov 61	412UNTS240	105936
Congo (Brazzaville)	UN Special Fund	09 Nov 61	413UNTS58	105940
Malagasy	UNICEF (Children)	16 Nov 61	422UNTS251	106079
El Salvador	USA (United States)	20 Nov 61	433UNTS221	106245
Thailand	USA (United States)	28 Nov 61	434UNTS77	106256
IBRD (World Bank)	UK Great Britain	29 Nov 61	426UNTS49	106130
Japan	IBRD (World Bank)	29 Nov 61	426UNTS3	106128
IBRD (World Bank)	South Africa	01 Dec 61	425UNTS215	106126
Ceylon (Sri Lanka)	United Nations	04 Dec 61	415UNTS236	105987
COMECON (Econ Aid)	USSR (Soviet Union)	07 Dec 61	506UNTS325	107392
Panama	USA (United States)	11 Dec 61	445UNTS161	106384
UN Special Fund	Venezuela	11 Dec 61	422UNTS149	106074
IBRD (World Bank)	Venezuela	13 Dec 61	446UNTS371	106409
UN Special Fund	Senegal	16 Dec 61	425UNTS97	106121
El Salvador	USA (United States)	19 Dec 61	445UNTS175	106385
Iran	USA (United States)	21 Dec 61	433UNTS269	106249
India	IBRD (World Bank)	22 Dec 61	481UNTS85	106979
Costa Rica	USA (United States)	22 Dec 61	460UNTS277	106646
Multilateral		27 Dec 61	425UNTS83	106120
Sierra Leone	USA (United States)	29 Dec 61	434UNTS43	106254
Malagasy	UN Special Fund	05 Jan 62	419UNTS29	106028
Ivory Coast	UNICEF (Children)	10 Jan 62	422UNTS261	106080
Dominican Republic	USA (United States)	11 Jan 62	433UNTS133	106236
Ethiopia	WHO (World Health)	11 Jan 62	423UNTS99	106087
Multilateral		17 Jan 62	419UNTS294	106033
Argentina	IBRD (World Bank)	19 Jan 62	446UNTS305	106407
Multilateral		20 Jan 62	429UNTS230	200596
United Nations	Somalia	20 Jan 62	420UNTS133	106044
Australia	IBRD (World Bank)	23 Jan 62	430UNTS3	106201
Peru	USA (United States)	25 Jan 62	473UNTS57	106855
UNICEF (Children)	Yemen	31 Jan 62	422UNTS271	106081
Ghana	IBRD (World Bank)	08 Feb 62	449UNTS207	106462
Multilateral		13 Feb 62	422UNTS288	200594
Iceland	IBRD (World Bank)	14 Feb 62	447UNTS95	106413
India	United Nations	19 Feb 62	423UNTS3	106082
Multilateral		21 Feb 62	423UNTS151	106091
Niger	UN Special Fund	26 Feb 62	423UNTS83	106086
India	IBRD (World Bank)	28 Feb 62	447UNTS3	106410
Multilateral		01 Mar 62	423UNTS122	106089
Cyprus	USA (United States)	02 Mar 62	445UNTS189	106386
Dominican Republic	USA (United States)	08 Mar 62	527UNTS29	107615
WHO (World Health)	Sudan	11 Mar 62	432UNTS325	106226
Nigeria	WHO (World Health)	27 Mar 62	429UNTS123	106194
Nicaragua	USA (United States)	30 Mar 62	456UNTS241	106559
UNICEF (Children)	Somalia	01 Apr 62	431UNTS75	106211
Congo (Brazzaville)	UNICEF (Children)	09 Apr 62	431UNTS65	106210
Multilateral		10 Apr 62	429UNTS78	106192
UNICEF (Children)	Sierra Leone	11 Apr 62	431UNTS55	106209
Somalia	USA (United States)	17 Apr 62	436UNTS107	106291
Ecuador	USA (United States)	17 Apr 62	442UNTS69	106339
Multilateral		18 Apr 62	463UNTS44	106692

PARTY ONE	PARTY TWO	DATE	CITATION	NUMBER
Domestic obligation (Cont.)				
Dominican Republic	USA (United States)	02 May 62	442UNTS107	106342
UN Special Fund	Uruguay	04 May 62	429UNTS143	106196
Multilateral		15 May 62	444UNTS3	106367
Multilateral		17 May 62	429UNTS46	106189
Ethiopia	USA (United States)	23 May 62	456UNTS293	106563
Colombia	IBRD (World Bank)	23 May 62	447UNTS39	106411
USA (United States)	Venezuela	28 May 62	458UNTS249	106607
Ethiopia	IBRD (World Bank)	31 May 62	467UNTS237	106765
Pakistan	USA (United States)	31 May 62	460UNTS75	106631
United Nations	Sweden	01 Jun 62	429UNTS135	106195
Dominican Republic	UN Special Fund	06 Jun 62	429UNTS169	106197
Libya	WHO (World Health)	16 Jun 62	437UNTS127	106301
Bolivia	USA (United States)	19 Jun 62	458UNTS239	106606
WHO (World Health)	Sierra Leone	19 Jun 62	439UNTS151	106327
Mexico	IBRD (World Bank)	20 Jun 62	468UNTS109	106771
Mexico	IBRD (World Bank)	20 Jun 62	467UNTS205	106764
Germany, West	Syria	25 Jun 62	489UNTS71	107135
Germany, West	United Nations	28 Jun 62	434UNTS249	200597
UN Special Fund	Syria	07 Jul 62	443UNTS3	106355
IBRD (World Bank)	Yugoslavia	11 Jul 62	468UNTS143	106772
UN Special Fund	Tanganyika	17 Jul 62	435UNTS237	106281
Czechoslovakia	COMECON (Econ Aid)	20 Jul 62	506UNTS345	107393
Honduras	USA (United States)	20 Jul 62	460UNTS125	106635
Niger	USA (United States)	23 Jul 62	487UNTS325	107114
Colombia	USA (United States)	23 Jul 62	458UNTS123	106595
Ecuador	USA (United States)	03 Aug 62	460UNTS133	106636
WHO (World Health)	Senegal	06 Aug 62	435UNTS179	106279
Nigeria	United Nations	07 Aug 62	435UNTS167	106278
Multilateral		12 Aug 62	443UNTS266	106365
WHO (World Health)	Western Samoa	14 Aug 62	437UNTS317	200598
Finland	IBRD (World Bank)	15 Aug 62	467UNTS177	106763
Cyprus	USA (United States)	23 Aug 62	461UNTS147	106658
Nepal	USA (United States)	24 Aug 62	460UNTS143	106637
Turkey	USA (United States)	27 Aug 62	461UNTS55	106651
Cameroon	United Nations	29 Aug 62	442UNTS3	106334
Multilateral		29 Aug 62	443UNTS280	106366
Togo	USA (United States)	05 Sep 62	461UNTS47	106650
Afghanistan	USA (United States)	11 Sep 62	461UNTS169	106661
Panama	IBRD (World Bank)	14 Sep 62	476UNTS153	106908
Pakistan	IBRD (World Bank)	14 Sep 62	467UNTS125	106761
Pakistan	IBRD (World Bank)	14 Sep 62	467UNTS152	106762
India	IDA (Devel Assoc)	14 Sep 62	467UNTS265	106766
Niger	United Nations	01 Oct 62	439UNTS181	106329
Chile	USA (United States)	04 Oct 62	461UNTS129	106656
Gabon	USA (United States)	04 Oct 62	459UNTS185	106620
Mali	USSR (Soviet Union)	10 Oct 62	493UNTS219	107216
Multilateral		25 Oct 62	457UNTS137	106583
Multilateral		25 Oct 62	457UNTS129	106582
IBRD (World Bank)	Uruguay	26 Oct 62	481UNTS39	106977
Tunisia	USA (United States)	29 Oct 62	462UNTS201	106679
Japan	UN Special Fund	31 Oct 62	444UNTS171	106368
United Nations	Western Samoa	05 Nov 62	443UNTS297	200599
Algeria	UN Special Fund	15 Nov 62	452UNTS243	106512
Multilateral		15 Nov 62	448UNTS50	106424
WHO (World Health)	Syria	18 Nov 62	480UNTS249	106972
Algeria	UNICEF (Children)	20 Nov 62	453UNTS151	106522
India	USA (United States)	21 Nov 62	462UNTS255	106685
Ceylon (Sri Lanka)	USA (United States)	21 Nov 62	462UNTS237	106683
Ecuador	United Nations	26 Nov 62	445UNTS3	106372
Rwanda	United Nations	28 Nov 62	450UNTS267	106473
Laos	USSR (Soviet Union)	01 Dec 62	472UNTS3	106834
Multilateral		06 Dec 62	450UNTS240	106471
Cameroon	WHO (World Health)	08 Dec 62	451UNTS215	106496
Nigeria	IBRD (World Bank)	10 Dec 62	468UNTS255	106776
Ivory Coast	United Nations	10 Dec 62	451UNTS269	106498

PARTY ONE	PARTY TWO	DATE	CITATION	NUMBER
Domestic obligation (Cont.)				
Multilateral		12 Dec 62	457UNTS72	106578
Guinea	USA (United States)	14 Dec 62	462UNTS247	106684
Algeria	WHO (World Health)	20 Dec 62	463UNTS135	106698
Morocco	IBRD (World Bank)	21 Dec 62	478UNTS205	106937
IBRD (World Bank)	Thailand	21 Dec 62	467UNTS43	106757
IBRD (World Bank)	Thailand	21 Dec 62	467UNTS63	106758
India	United Nations	27 Dec 62	450UNTS3	106464
Guatemala	USA (United States)	29 Dec 62	474UNTS31	106869
Israel	United Nations	07 Jan 63	450UNTS229	106470
Senegal	USA (United States)	17 Jan 63	493UNTS97	107210
Mauritania	UNICEF (Children)	19 Jan 63	452UNTS271	106514
Multilateral		21 Jan 63	453UNTS20	106517
United Nations	South Pacific Com	24 Jan 63	470UNTS361	200604
New Zealand	Western Samoa	24 Jan 63	499UNTS21	107290
UNICEF (Children)	Tanganyika	25 Jan 63	453UNTS249	106528
Multilateral		05 Feb 63	453UNTS36	106518
United Nations	United Arab Rep	08 Feb 63	453UNTS79	106520
Central Afri Rep	USA (United States)	10 Feb 63	473UNTS83	106857
Pakistan	IBRD (World Bank)	13 Feb 63	467UNTS3	106756
Multilateral		14 Feb 63	453UNTS168	106524
Philippines	IBRD (World Bank)	15 Feb 63	478UNTS161	106936
United Nations	South Pacific Com	20 Feb 63	453UNTS333	200600
Poland	COMECON (Econ Aid)	22 Feb 63	506UNTS303	107391
Hungary	COMECON (Econ Aid)	28 Feb 63	506UNTS281	107390
Nicaragua	IBRD (World Bank)	01 Mar 63	481UNTS15	106976
Multilateral		06 Mar 63	455UNTS386	106552
IBRD (World Bank)	Thailand	07 Mar 63	467UNTS83	106759
Peru	IBRD (World Bank)	13 Mar 63	478UNTS245	106938
UN Special Fund	Uganda	22 Mar 63	456UNTS466	106572
Multilateral		18 Apr 63	463UNTS121	106697
Thailand	USA (United States)	25 Apr 63	476UNTS115	106906
Mexico	IBRD (World Bank)	29 Apr 63	489UNTS151	107138
UN Special Fund	Trinidad/Tobago	06 May 63	463UNTS93	106695
Multilateral		06 May 63	463UNTS78	106694
Multilateral		09 May 63	463UNTS159	106700
IBRD (World Bank)	UK Great Britain	16 May 63	477UNTS361	106929
IBRD (World Bank)	UK Great Britain	16 May 63	476UNTS211	106910
Jamaica	UN Special Fund	22 May 63	489UNTS191	107140
Multilateral		22 May 63	483UNTS72	107007
Multilateral		24 May 63	466UNTS346	106754
Netherlands	UN Special Fund	24 May 63	466UNTS289	106750
Colombia	IBRD (World Bank)	03 Jun 63	490UNTS199	107155
UN Special Fund	Western Samoa	05 Jun 63	467UNTS463	200601
India	IBRD (World Bank)	05 Jun 63	481UNTS191	106983
IBRD (World Bank)	Thailand	11 Jun 63	481UNTS227	106984
El Salvador	IBRD (World Bank)	19 Jun 63	481UNTS59	106978
Colombia	IBRD (World Bank)	21 Jun 63	482UNTS159	106994
IBRD (World Bank)	Yugoslavia	21 Jun 63	482UNTS43	106990
Mongolia	WHO (World Health)	21 Jun 63	472UNTS373	106848
Colombia	IBRD (World Bank)	28 Jun 63	489UNTS113	107137
Costa Rica	IBRD (World Bank)	10 Jul 63	482UNTS69	106991
Malaysia	IBRD (World Bank)	15 Jul 63	482UNTS123	106993
Colombia	IBRD (World Bank)	16 Jul 63	482UNTS256	106998
Poland	United Nations	16 Jul 63	471UNTS3	106817
Denmark	IBRD (World Bank)	24 Jul 63	481UNTS171	106982
Italy	United Nations	26 Jul 63	472UNTS173	106840
USA (United States)	Uruguay	31 Jul 63	488UNTS3	107115
Multilateral		31 Jul 63	472UNTS220	106842
Malaysia	IBRD (World Bank)	07 Aug 63	485UNTS253	107060
Burundi	WHO (World Health)	08 Aug 63	477UNTS346	106928
Burundi	UN Special Fund	22 Aug 63	476UNTS49	106903
Multilateral		27 Aug 63	511UNTS210	107435
IBRD (World Bank)	UK Great Britain	06 Sep 63	483UNTS173	107013
Multilateral		10 Sep 63	480UNTS100	106965
Finland	IBRD (World Bank)	18 Sep 63	491UNTS345	107183

PARTY ONE	PARTY TWO	DATE	CITATION	NUMBER
Domestic obligation (Cont.)				
Mexico	IBRD (World Bank)	20 Sep 63	491UNTS317	107182
IBRD (World Bank)	Venezuela	20 Sep 63	482UNTS227	106997
IBRD (World Bank)	UK Great Britain	23 Sep 63	503UNTS247	107348
Jamaica	WHO (World Health)	25 Sep 63	481UNTS125	106980
Japan	IBRD (World Bank)	27 Sep 63	485UNTS283	107061
Taiwan	IBRD (World Bank)	27 Sep 63	483UNTS151	107012
El Salvador	IBRD (World Bank)	01 Oct 63	517UNTS3	107481
Italy	IAEA (Atom Energy)	11 Oct 63	639UNTS25	109142
Norway	IBRD (World Bank)	15 Oct 63	482UNTS103	106992
Multilateral		21 Oct 63	480UNTS197	106969
Jamaica	USA (United States)	24 Oct 63	489UNTS337	107148
IBRD (World Bank)	Spain	25 Oct 63	491UNTS297	107181
IBRD (World Bank)	Yugoslavia	28 Oct 63	503UNTS289	107349
Multilateral		30 Oct 63	480UNTS180	106968
Central Afri Rep	UN Special Fund	30 Oct 63	481UNTS247	106985
WHO (World Health)	Tanganyika	05 Nov 63	496UNTS193	107252
Portugal	IBRD (World Bank)	06 Nov 63	492UNTS89	107188
Portugal	IBRD (World Bank)	06 Nov 63	491UNTS137	107176
Multilateral		07 Nov 63	480UNTS232	106971
WHO (World Health)	Somalia	08 Nov 63	493UNTS243	107218
Multilateral		08 Nov 63	482UNTS286	106999
Multilateral		09 Nov 63	489UNTS209	107141
New Zealand	IBRD (World Bank)	12 Nov 63	485UNTS233	107059
Niger	United Nations	20 Nov 63	536UNTS3	107793
WHO (World Health)	Sierra Leone	22 Nov 63	493UNTS255	107219
Peru	IBRD (World Bank)	22 Nov 63	491UNTS101	107175
Cameroon	Netherlands	18 Dec 63	521UNTS303	107527
Chile	IBRD (World Bank)	18 Dec 63	504UNTS3	107351
Australia	Laos	24 Dec 63	503UNTS315	107350
Multilateral		30 Dec 63	568UNTS215	108270
Multilateral		30 Dec 63	568UNTS233	108271
Multilateral		30 Dec 63	568UNTS243	108272
Multilateral		30 Dec 63	551UNTS105	108036
Multilateral		30 Dec 63	551UNTS119	108037
New Zealand	Western Samoa	31 Dec 63	521UNTS163	107519
Liberia	IBRD (World Bank)	08 Jan 64	504UNTS53	107353
Multilateral		28 Jan 64	502UNTS321	107336
Colombia	IBRD (World Bank)	07 Feb 64	516UNTS99	107473
Mexico	USA (United States)	14 Feb 64	524UNTS197	107574
Multilateral		20 Feb 64	491UNTS30	107172
IBRD (World Bank)	Thailand	11 Mar 64	504UNTS73	107354
Nigeria	IBRD (World Bank)	12 Mar 64	516UNTS325	107480
New Zealand	IBRD (World Bank)	12 Mar 64	505UNTS3	107362
Germany, West	Thailand	02 Apr 64	503UNTS3	107338
Taiwan	UNICEF (Children)	08 Apr 64	500UNTS49	107306
Peru	IBRD (World Bank)	22 Apr 64	519UNTS95	107503
Japan	IBRD (World Bank)	22 Apr 64	505UNTS21	107363
Canada	USA (United States)	06 May 64	524UNTS173	107572
Ethiopia	IBRD (World Bank)	08 May 64	505UNTS51	107364
Algeria	IBRD (World Bank)	14 May 64	522UNTS265	107552
Pakistan	IBRD (World Bank)	14 May 64	516UNTS145	107475
Ecuador	IBRD (World Bank)	26 May 64	534UNTS113	107758
Ireland	UN Special Fund	03 Jun 64	496UNTS205	107253
IBRD (World Bank)	Tunisia	05 Jun 64	539UNTS129	107827
Iran	IBRD (World Bank)	10 Jun 64	537UNTS111	107799
Rwanda	WHO (World Health)	22 Jun 64	514UNTS11	107440
Rwanda	WHO (World Health)	23 Jun 64	514UNTS157	107445
Multilateral		23 Jun 64	506UNTS108	107383
WHO (World Health)	Trinidad/Tobago	23 Jun 64	503UNTS167	107342
Multilateral		28 Jun 64	519UNTS14	107499
Colombia	Netherlands	06 Jul 64	543UNTS289	107906
Nigeria	IBRD (World Bank)	07 Jul 64	537UNTS3	107795
Gabon	IBRD (World Bank)	10 Jul 64	537UNTS63	107797
Finland	IBRD (World Bank)	10 Jul 64	516UNTS125	107474
Iceland	UN Special Fund	10 Jul 64	502UNTS343	107337

PARTY ONE	PARTY TWO	DATE	CITATION	NUMBER
Domestic obligation (Cont.)				
Belgium	Tunisia	15 Jul 64	560UNTS57	108168
Philippines	IBRD (World Bank)	22 Jul 64	516UNTS171	107476
IBRD (World Bank)	Spain	31 Jul 64	537UNTS81	107798
IBRD (World Bank)	Sierra Leone	18 Aug 64	516UNTS295	107479
Morocco	IBRD (World Bank)	26 Aug 64	537UNTS193	107802
IBRD (World Bank)	Venezuela	28 Aug 64	537UNTS135	107800
Dominican Republic	USA (United States)	28 Aug 64	531UNTS35	107691
IBRD (World Bank)	Venezuela	28 Aug 64	520UNTS97	107512
Philippines	United Nations	15 Sep 64	510UNTS137	107410
Algeria	United Nations	23 Sep 64	510UNTS217	107416
Australia	UN Special Fund	30 Sep 64	510UNTS277	107419
Kenya	United Nations	01 Oct 64	511UNTS199	107434
Kenya	UN Special Fund	01 Oct 64	511UNTS181	107433
Multilateral		24 Oct 64	514UNTS220	200608
Malawi	UN Special Fund	24 Oct 64	514UNTS235	200609
Romania	UN Special Fund	24 Oct 64	519UNTS29	107500
Ethiopia	Netherlands	28 Oct 64	541UNTS235	107872
Philippines	IBRD (World Bank)	28 Oct 64	537UNTS165	107801
Netherlands	Pakistan	30 Oct 64	541UNTS243	107873
Multilateral		11 Nov 64	515UNTS94	107456
IBRD (World Bank)	Thailand	25 Nov 64	537UNTS273	107805
India	United Nations	25 Nov 64	519UNTS47	107501
Ghana	Israel	30 Nov 64	550UNTS231	108019
IBRD (World Bank)	Yugoslavia	11 Dec 64	537UNTS321	107807
Denmark	Pakistan	12 Dec 64	636UNTS313	109107
UN Special Fund	Zambia	15 Dec 64	522UNTS3	107532
Paraguay	IBRD (World Bank)	16 Dec 64	549UNTS173	107999
Taiwan	IBRD (World Bank)	17 Dec 64	538UNTS3	107808
Japan	IBRD (World Bank)	23 Dec 64	538UNTS37	107809
Germany, West	Thailand	23 Dec 64	525UNTS185	107590
Germany, West	Thailand	23 Dec 64	525UNTS177	107589
Mongolia	United Nations	06 Jan 65	522UNTS45	107535
Malawi	WHO (World Health)	06 Jan 65	525UNTS165	107588
United Nations	Yugoslavia	07 Jan 65	522UNTS55	107536
Malawi	WHO (World Health)	08 Jan 65	524UNTS281	107579
Japan	IBRD (World Bank)	13 Jan 65	537UNTS293	107806
Ethiopia	WHO (World Health)	27 Jan 65	541UNTS135	107866
Multilateral		27 Jan 65	523UNTS102	107556
Honduras	IBRD (World Bank)	02 Feb 65	561UNTS255	108188
Multilateral		02 Feb 65	523UNTS256	107560
Mexico	IBRD (World Bank)	04 Feb 65	549UNTS189	108000
UN Special Fund	Zambia	04 Feb 65	527UNTS115	107621
Chile	IBRD (World Bank)	12 Feb 65	537UNTS35	107796
Multilateral		12 Feb 65	525UNTS148	107587
Multilateral		23 Feb 65	527UNTS120	107622
Brazil	IBRD (World Bank)	26 Feb 65	567UNTS91	108253
Brazil	IBRD (World Bank)	26 Feb 65	553UNTS3	108065
Malaysia	IBRD (World Bank)	26 Feb 65	549UNTS239	108002
IBRD (World Bank)	Thailand	22 Mar 65	538UNTS63	107810
IBRD (World Bank)	Uruguay	30 Mar 65	567UNTS45	108251
Multilateral		08 Apr 65	533UNTS66	107733
Iran	IBRD (World Bank)	28 Apr 65	555UNTS45	108104
Iran	IBRD (World Bank)	28 Apr 65	555UNTS21	108103
Taiwan	IBRD (World Bank)	28 Apr 65	549UNTS145	107998
Portugal	IBRD (World Bank)	29 Apr 65	549UNTS69	107991
Multilateral		12 May 65	534UNTS390	107769
Multilateral		14 May 65	550UNTS310	108026
Multilateral		25 May 65	535UNTS374	107791
Japan	IBRD (World Bank)	26 May 65	550UNTS95	108010
Multilateral		02 Jun 65	537UNTS348	200611
Multilateral		02 Jun 65	551UNTS2	108030
Peru	IBRD (World Bank)	03 Jun 65	551UNTS227	108045
India	IBRD (World Bank)	11 Jun 65	557UNTS59	108128
India	IBRD (World Bank)	11 Jun 65	557UNTS101	108130
Peru	IBRD (World Bank)	18 Jun 65	568UNTS191	108269

PARTY ONE	PARTY TWO	DATE	CITATION	NUMBER
Domestic obligation (Cont.)				
Australia	Germany, West	21 Jun 65	542UNTS53	107879
Japan	Korea, South	22 Jun 65	584UNTS3	108474
Italy	IBRD (World Bank)	28 Jun 65	567UNTS127	108254
Finland	IBRD (World Bank)	30 Jun 65	550UNTS63	108009
UN Special Fund	Spain	30 Jun 65	544UNTS159	107918
Multilateral		05 Jul 65	563UNTS104	108207
Pakistan	IBRD (World Bank)	09 Jul 65	554UNTS39	108096
Iran	IBRD (World Bank)	12 Jul 65	554UNTS3	108095
Multilateral		20 Jul 65	541UNTS12	107857
Poland	WHO (World Health)	26 Aug 65	552UNTS3	108047
Multilateral		13 Sep 65	547UNTS248	107961
Multilateral		13 Sep 65	547UNTS264	107962
Multilateral		21 Sep 65	547UNTS280	107963
Nigeria	IBRD (World Bank)	26 Sep 65	571UNTS39	108298
Nigeria	IBRD (World Bank)	26 Sep 65	570UNTS233	108296
East Afri Service	IBRD (World Bank)	29 Sep 65	568UNTS327	200623
IBRD (World Bank)	Spain	29 Sep 65	568UNTS49	108264
Kenya	IBRD (World Bank)	29 Sep 65	568UNTS289	108274
IBRD (World Bank)	Uganda	29 Sep 65	568UNTS317	108276
IBRD (World Bank)	Tanzania	29 Sep 65	568UNTS309	108275
Mexico	IBRD (World Bank)	01 Oct 65	589UNTS339	108542
Chile	IBRD (World Bank)	06 Oct 65	567UNTS293	108261
Multilateral		21 Oct 65	547UNTS216	107959
Philippines	IBRD (World Bank)	02 Nov 65	567UNTS3	108249
Multilateral		12 Nov 65	550UNTS160	108013
Malaysia	IBRD (World Bank)	17 Nov 65	568UNTS23	108263
IBRD (World Bank)	Venezuela	13 Dec 65	568UNTS77	108265
Mexico	IBRD (World Bank)	15 Dec 65	568UNTS125	108267
Paraguay	IBRD (World Bank)	16 Dec 65	568UNTS165	108268
New Zealand	IBRD (World Bank)	17 Dec 65	567UNTS275	108260
New Zealand	IBRD (World Bank)	17 Dec 65	567UNTS255	108259
IBRD (World Bank)	Sudan	27 Dec 65	567UNTS27	108250
Denmark	Syria	28 Dec 65	588UNTS163	108523
Ethiopia	IBRD (World Bank)	28 Dec 65	567UNTS229	108258
Mongolia	UN Special Fund	26 Jan 66	552UNTS201	108055
Israel	Kenya	25 Feb 66	582UNTS23	108455
Hungary	United Nations	04 Mar 66	559UNTS3	108151
Brazil	UNICEF (Children)	28 Mar 66	607UNTS235	108807
WHO (World Health)	Singapore	28 Mar 66	562UNTS59	108195
Guinea	IBRD (World Bank)	30 Mar 66	568UNTS3	108262
Paraguay	IBRD (World Bank)	04 Apr 66	570UNTS41	108287
IBRD (World Bank)	Venezuela	21 Apr 66	568UNTS257	108273
Romania	IAEA (Atom Energy)	22 Apr 66	603UNTS23	108721
Finland	IBRD (World Bank)	27 Apr 66	568UNTS107	108266
Multilateral		04 May 66	575UNTS49	108354
Peru	IBRD (World Bank)	13 May 66	570UNTS61	108288
IBRD (World Bank)	Tunisia	16 May 66	584UNTS155	108477
Mexico	IBRD (World Bank)	25 May 66	596UNTS3	108627
Portugal	IBRD (World Bank)	14 Jun 66	581UNTS29	108431
Portugal	IBRD (World Bank)	14 Jun 66	581UNTS3	108430
Jamaica	IBRD (World Bank)	20 Jun 66	582UNTS145	108462
IBRD (World Bank)	Thailand	24 Jun 66	582UNTS259	108466
India	IBRD (World Bank)	07 Jul 66	595UNTS3	108610
Iraq	IBRD (World Bank)	22 Jul 66	584UNTS233	108480
Iran	IBRD (World Bank)	26 Jul 66	582UNTS107	108461
Malaysia	IBRD (World Bank)	26 Jul 66	586UNTS195	108504
Ivory Coast	Netherlands	01 Aug 66	591UNTS245	108561
IBRD (World Bank)	Turkey	10 Aug 66	585UNTS199	108490
IBRD (World Bank)	Singapore	11 Aug 66	585UNTS39	108482
Honduras	IBRD (World Bank)	25 Aug 66	582UNTS79	108460
Peru	IBRD (World Bank)	07 Sep 66	585UNTS3	108481
IBRD (World Bank)	South Africa	08 Sep 66	585UNTS71	108483
Multilateral		23 Sep 66	573UNTS132	108327
Jamaica	IBRD (World Bank)	30 Sep 66	582UNTS179	108463
IBRD (World Bank)	Zambia	04 Oct 66	585UNTS181	108489

PARTY ONE	PARTY TWO	DATE	CITATION	NUMBER
Domestic obligation (Cont.)				
Nicaragua	IBRD (World Bank)	05 Oct 66	582UNTS231	108465
IBRD (World Bank)	Singapore	04 Nov 66	585UNTS155	108488
United Nations	Sudan	08 Nov 66	576UNTS85	108365
Australia	USA (United States)	09 Dec 66	607UNTS83	108798
India	IAEA (Atom Energy)	09 Dec 66	603UNTS35	108722
Chile	IBRD (World Bank)	23 Dec 66	595UNTS141	108618
Jamaica	IBRD (World Bank)	23 Jan 67	594UNTS311	108608
IBRD (World Bank)	Venezuela	26 Jan 67	596UNTS35	108628
UNICEF (Children)	Zambia	02 Feb 67	589UNTS89	108536
Australia	UN Special Fund	06 Feb 67	590UNTS3	108543
Poland	United Nations	20 Feb 67	590UNTS71	108547
Multilateral		27 Feb 67	590UNTS156	108552
Denmark	Tanzania	05 Apr 67	603UNTS111	108728
Malta	WHO (World Health)	10 May 67	603UNTS99	108727
USSR (Soviet Union)	Zambia	26 May 67	643UNTS179	109191
Multilateral		10 Jun 67	602UNTS212	108714
Israel	UN Relief Palestin	14 Jun 67	620UNTS183	108955
Multilateral		14 Jun 67	603UNTS2	108719
Multilateral		21 Jun 67	598UNTS2	108653
Czechoslovakia	UN Special Fund	13 Jul 67	606UNTS71	108776
Barbados	WHO (World Health)	18 Jul 67	603UNTS87	108726
Multilateral		26 Jul 67	614UNTS217	108872
New Zealand	WHO (World Health)	29 Aug 67	607UNTS57	108795
Multilateral		12 Oct 67	607UNTS2	108792
Multilateral		12 Oct 67	607UNTS20	108793
Botswana	UN Special Fund	12 Oct 67	607UNTS37	108794
Multilateral		14 Nov 67	614UNTS2	108860
ILO (Labor Org)	Zambia	20 Dec 67	619UNTS293	108947
Austria	Canada	28 Feb 68	636UNTS141	109101
United Nations	Tunisia	18 Mar 68	633UNTS3	109030
State/IGO Group	Nigeria	20 Apr 68	636UNTS294	109106
State/IGO Group	Malaysia	10 May 68	636UNTS276	109105
State/IGO Group	Australia	21 May 68	636UNTS326	109108
India	United Nations	22 Jul 68	640UNTS121	109158
General technical assistance				
Mexico	USA (United States)	11 Apr 41	117UNTS323	200379
Brazil	USA (United States)	03 Mar 42	105UNTS99	200325
Mexico	USA (United States)	10 Nov 42	66UNTS307	200219
Liberia	USA (United States)	31 Dec 43	106UNTS199	200341
Greece	UK Great Britain	24 Jan 46	6UNTS45	100067
Brazil	USA (United States)	15 Feb 46	162UNTS21	102130
Mexico	USA (United States)	05 Mar 46	120UNTS3	101612
Multilateral		30 Oct 46	11UNTS107	100151
UNESCO (Educ/Cult)	United Nations	03 Feb 47	1UNTS233	200011
FAO (Food Agri)	United Nations	03 Feb 47	1UNTS207	200010
Poland	Yugoslavia	24 May 47	115UNTS89	101560
Turkey	USA (United States)	12 Jul 47	7UNTS299	100106
USSR (Soviet Union)	Yugoslavia	25 Jul 47	130UNTS315	101732
Romania	Yugoslavia	30 Sep 47	116UNTS71	101570
Multilateral		11 Oct 47	77UNTS143	100998
Multilateral		30 Oct 47	55UNTS188	100814
United Nations	UPU (Postal Union)	15 Nov 47	19UNTS219	200116
United Nations	WHO (World Health)	15 Nov 47	19UNTS193	200115
Greece	USA (United States)	03 Dec 47	89UNTS119	101213
Australia	Poland	03 Jun 48	16UNTS189	100258
IRO (Refugee Org)	United Nations	07 Feb 49	26UNTS299	200153
Panama	USA (United States)	31 Mar 49	55UNTS141	100812
ITU (Telecommun)	United Nations	26 Apr 49	30UNTS315	200175
Multilateral		24 Sep 49	126UNTS237	101691
Afghanistan	WHO (World Health)	04 Dec 49	102UNTS117	101414
Nicaragua	USA (United States)	01 Feb 50	99UNTS25	101368
Ceylon (Sri Lanka)	WHO (World Health)	17 Feb 50	102UNTS309	200309
Chile	UNICEF (Children)	03 Mar 50	126UNTS119	101685
Hungary	USSR (Soviet Union)	13 Jul 50	221UNTS35	103001

PARTY ONE	PARTY TWO	DATE	CITATION	NUMBER
General technical assistance (Cont.)				
Brazil	USA (United States)	16 Aug 50	140UNTS223	101890
WHO (World Health)	United Arab Rep	25 Aug 50	92UNTS39	101259
Bulgaria	USSR (Soviet Union)	25 Aug 50	221UNTS57	103002
Thailand	USA (United States)	19 Sep 50	132UNTS199	101761
Bulgaria	Romania	29 Sep 50	342UNTS141	104905
Indonesia	USA (United States)	16 Oct 50	281UNTS105	104074
Iran	USA (United States)	19 Oct 50	92UNTS135	101266
Multilateral		02 Nov 50	81UNTS160	101071
Ceylon (Sri Lanka)	USA (United States)	07 Nov 50	92UNTS125	101265
Multilateral		24 Nov 50	81UNTS188	101072
Multilateral		15 Dec 50	76UNTS120	100985
Brazil	USA (United States)	19 Dec 50	141UNTS3	101900
Panama	USA (United States)	20 Dec 50	92UNTS167	101269
Liberia	USA (United States)	22 Dec 50	92UNTS145	101267
Nicaragua	USA (United States)	23 Dec 50	92UNTS155	101268
India	USA (United States)	28 Dec 50	99UNTS39	101369
Paraguay	USA (United States)	29 Dec 50	122UNTS157	101645
United Nations	Yugoslavia	06 Jan 51	78UNTS165	101015
Costa Rica	USA (United States)	11 Jan 51	92UNTS179	101270
Chile	USA (United States)	16 Jan 51	151UNTS147	101990
Saudi Arabia	USA (United States)	17 Jan 51	140UNTS335	101897
Multilateral		18 Jan 51	81UNTS233	101073
Nepal	USA (United States)	23 Jan 51	184UNTS65	102439
Albania	Poland	25 Jan 51	260UNTS217	103710
Honduras	USA (United States)	26 Jan 51	99UNTS49	101370
Ethiopia	ICAO (Civil Aviat)	02 Feb 51	96UNTS123	101333
Afghanistan	USA (United States)	07 Feb 51	132UNTS265	101766
Pakistan	USA (United States)	09 Feb 51	100UNTS67	101388
Multilateral		15 Feb 51	81UNTS245	101074
Israel	ILO (Labor Org)	19 Feb 51	100UNTS105	101391
Israel	ICAO (Civil Aviat)	19 Feb 51	96UNTS141	101334
Dominican Republic	USA (United States)	20 Feb 51	132UNTS305	101770
Israel	USA (United States)	26 Feb 51	137UNTS57	101848
Jordan	USA (United States)	27 Feb 51	141UNTS55	101905
ILO (Labor Org)	Syria	03 Mar 51	110UNTS69	101502
Multilateral		05 Mar 51	81UNTS261	101075
Colombia	USA (United States)	09 Mar 51	141UNTS15	101901
Bolivia	USA (United States)	14 Mar 51	132UNTS319	101771
Multilateral		20 Mar 51	82UNTS172	101091
Multilateral		28 Mar 51	181UNTS61	102399
Jordan	ILO (Labor Org)	29 Mar 51	100UNTS247	200287
Jordan	United Nations	29 Mar 51	137UNTS267	200448
Multilateral		05 Apr 51	84UNTS299	101139
Mexico	ILO (Labor Org)	06 Apr 51	100UNTS131	101393
Ceylon (Sri Lanka)	ILO (Labor Org)	06 Apr 51	100UNTS235	200286
United Nations	WMO (Meteorology)	10 Apr 51	103UNTS245	200415
Iraq	USA (United States)	10 Apr 51	151UNTS179	101993
Peru	ILO (Labor Org)	13 Apr 51	100UNTS31	101385
Guatemala	ILO (Labor Org)	13 Apr 51	126UNTS249	101692
El Salvador	USA (United States)	18 Apr 51	141UNTS37	101903
ICAO (Civil Aviat)	Thailand	19 Apr 51	96UNTS181	101336
Ecuador	ILO (Labor Org)	19 Apr 51	100UNTS77	101389
Cuba	ILO (Labor Org)	21 Apr 51	99UNTS205	101382
Honduras	USA (United States)	24 Apr 51	140UNTS287	101894
Greece	ILO (Labor Org)	25 Apr 51	100UNTS93	101390
India	ILO (Labor Org)	26 Apr 51	100UNTS19	101384
Philippines	USA (United States)	27 Apr 51	174UNTS251	102290
Haiti	USA (United States)	02 May 51	151UNTS191	101994
WHO (World Health)	Yugoslavia	02 May 51	103UNTS117	101429
Ecuador	USA (United States)	03 May 51	141UNTS27	101902
United Arab Rep	USA (United States)	05 May 51	198UNTS265	102670
Austria	USA (United States)	15 May 51	139UNTS79	101876
Pakistan	ILO (Labor Org)	16 May 51	100UNTS147	101394
Norway	Pakistan	21 May 51	318UNTS163	104613
Lebanon	USA (United States)	29 May 51	160UNTS49	102101

PARTY ONE	PARTY TWO	DATE	CITATION	NUMBER
General technical assistance (Cont.)				
Cambodia	WHO (World Health)	31 May 51	102UNTS279	200307
Iceland	ICAO (Civil Aviat)	07 Jun 51	96UNTS193	101337
Lebanon	WHO (World Health)	07 Jun 51	126UNTS221	101690
USA (United States)	Venezuela	07 Jun 51	141UNTS273	101918
United Nations	Thailand	11 Jun 51	90UNTS45	101225
Multilateral		15 Jun 51	148UNTS67	101936
UK Great Britain	USA (United States)	15 Jun 51	141UNTS79	101907
Ethiopia	USA (United States)	16 Jun 51	148UNTS39	101933
Saudi Arabia	USA (United States)	18 Jun 51	102UNTS73	101412
Dominican Republic	ILO (Labor Org)	18 Jun 51	100UNTS3	101383
Cuba	USA (United States)	20 Jun 51	148UNTS3	101931
Multilateral		25 Jun 51	92UNTS27	101258
Israel	United Nations	25 Jun 51	97UNTS21	101344
ILO (Labor Org)	Vietnam, South	26 Jun 51	100UNTS223	200285
Mexico	USA (United States)	27 Jun 51	141UNTS211	101916
Multilateral		28 Jun 51	118UNTS154	101604
Ethiopia	WHO (World Health)	02 Jul 51	103UNTS39	101422
ILO (Labor Org)	Thailand	11 Jul 51	100UNTS159	101395
Paraguay	ILO (Labor Org)	12 Jul 51	117UNTS155	101591
UK Great Britain	USA (United States)	13 Jul 51	105UNTS71	101454
Burma	WHO (World Health)	17 Jul 51	102UNTS127	101415
Multilateral		18 Jul 51	102UNTS291	200308
El Salvador	USA (United States)	19 Jul 51	140UNTS259	101892
Multilateral		27 Jul 51	97UNTS291	200273
Israel	WHO (World Health)	07 Aug 51	104UNTS213	101442
WHO (World Health)	Saudi Arabia	29 Aug 51	110UNTS277	101516
Multilateral		05 Sep 51	173UNTS15	102256
Portugal	USA (United States)	06 Sep 51	237UNTS217	103348
USA (United States)	Vietnam, South	07 Sep 51	174UNTS165	102284
Cambodia	USA (United States)	08 Sep 51	174UNTS115	102282
Laos	USA (United States)	09 Sep 51	174UNTS141	102283
Colombia	WHO (World Health)	18 Sep 51	109UNTS45	101489
Iraq	ICAO (Civil Aviat)	18 Sep 51	108UNTS219	101475
Paraguay	United Nations	27 Sep 51	120UNTS105	101617
Multilateral		01 Oct 51	104UNTS249	101446
Bolivia	United Nations	01 Oct 51	104UNTS263	101447
United Nations	Uruguay	17 Oct 51	122UNTS29	101633
ILO (Labor Org)	Venezuela	22 Oct 51	117UNTS139	101590
Panama	ILO (Labor Org)	10 Nov 51	126UNTS269	101693
Saudi Arabia	USA (United States)	10 Nov 51	180UNTS263	102390
Australia	USA (United States)	16 Nov 51	168UNTS75	102214
Council of Europe	ILO (Labor Org)	23 Nov 51	126UNTS331	200435
Israel	USA (United States)	07 Dec 51	157UNTS53	102046
El Salvador	USA (United States)	12 Dec 51	132UNTS287	101768
Multilateral		24 Dec 51	118UNTS290	200383
Laos	USA (United States)	31 Dec 51	198UNTS243	102668
India	USA (United States)	05 Jan 52	157UNTS39	102045
Lebanon	USA (United States)	05 Jan 52	180UNTS199	102385
Indonesia	USA (United States)	05 Jan 52	215UNTS121	102916
El Salvador	USA (United States)	07 Jan 52	198UNTS231	102667
Guatemala	USA (United States)	08 Jan 52	181UNTS31	102395
Austria	WHO (World Health)	10 Jan 52	131UNTS295	200438
Iran	USA (United States)	20 Jan 52	200UNTS191	102703
Libya	USA (United States)	21 Jan 52	183UNTS177	102427
Ceylon (Sri Lanka)	United Nations	21 Jan 52	118UNTS281	200382
Multilateral		23 Jan 52	127UNTS269	101708
WHO (World Health)	Spain	30 Jan 52	124UNTS259	200425
Greece	Yugoslavia	02 Feb 52	188UNTS311	102535
ICAO (Civil Aviat)	Yugoslavia	06 Feb 52	128UNTS97	101715
Indonesia	United Nations	06 Feb 52	121UNTS3	101621
Jordan	USA (United States)	12 Feb 52	168UNTS25	102211
Lebanon	ICAO (Civil Aviat)	14 Feb 52	128UNTS83	101714
Multilateral		18 Feb 52	126UNTS319	200434
Iraq	USA (United States)	21 Feb 52	198UNTS225	102666
OAS (Am States)	USA (United States)	03 Mar 52	165UNTS67	102168

PARTY ONE	PARTY TWO	DATE	CITATION	NUMBER
General technical assistance (Cont.)				
Ceylon (Sri Lanka)	WHO (World Health)	04 Mar 52	128UNTS281	200437
Greece	United Nations	05 Mar 52	123UNTS3	101650
ICAO (Civil Aviat)	United Arab Rep	06 Mar 52	151UNTS111	101986
Finland	WHO (World Health)	07 Mar 52	128UNTS269	200436
India	United Nations	02 Apr 52	126UNTS145	101687
El Salvador	USA (United States)	04 Apr 52	177UNTS219	102320
United Nations	Yugoslavia	10 Apr 52	141UNTS89	101908
Multilateral		11 Apr 52	173UNTS2	102255
India	WHO (World Health)	14 Apr 52	131UNTS265	101746
India	WHO (World Health)	17 Apr 52	131UNTS241	101744
India	WHO (World Health)	19 Apr 52	131UNTS253	101745
Pakistan	United Nations	28 Apr 52	128UNTS191	101720
India	ICAO (Civil Aviat)	29 Apr 52	151UNTS123	101987
Israel	USA (United States)	09 May 52	177UNTS269	102326
Israel	USA (United States)	09 May 52	177UNTS63	102309
Norway	WHO (World Health)	09 May 52	131UNTS281	101747
Libya	USA (United States)	20 May 52	177UNTS81	102310
Libya	USA (United States)	20 May 52	178UNTS155	102339
Libya	USA (United States)	20 May 52	178UNTS307	102346
Iraq	USA (United States)	21 May 52	206UNTS3	102782
Multilateral		22 May 52	131UNTS115	101739
Chile	WHO (World Health)	31 May 52	136UNTS323	101841
Jordan	WHO (World Health)	16 Jun 52	135UNTS323	200445
Ethiopia	USA (United States)	18 Jun 52	181UNTS207	102410
Multilateral		19 Jun 52	133UNTS165	101787
WHO (World Health)	Syria	20 Jun 52	165UNTS219	102178
Lebanon	USA (United States)	26 Jun 52	181UNTS187	102409
Chile	USA (United States)	30 Jun 52	199UNTS241	102688
Brazil	USA (United States)	30 Jun 52	185UNTS79	102460
Australia	FAO (Food Agri)	07 Jul 52	184UNTS209	102449
Chile	WHO (World Health)	11 Jul 52	137UNTS27	101846
India	WHO (World Health)	16 Jul 52	135UNTS291	101828
Panama	USA (United States)	21 Jul 52	181UNTS285	102417
Chile	ILO (Labor Org)	23 Jul 52	178UNTS323	102348
Brazil	United Nations	04 Aug 52	135UNTS185	101820
Panama	United Nations	20 Aug 52	136UNTS3	101829
Multilateral		21 Aug 52	141UNTS129	101912
Mexico	USA (United States)	26 Aug 52	264UNTS269	103797
Haiti	USA (United States)	29 Aug 52	186UNTS35	102480
Italy	ILO (Labor Org)	04 Sep 52	178UNTS371	200505
ILO (Labor Org)	Uruguay	20 Sep 52	187UNTS25	102499
USA (United States)	Venezuela	29 Sep 52	186UNTS23	102479
United Nations	Trieste	30 Sep 52	140UNTS11	101881
USA (United States)	Yugoslavia	11 Oct 52	235UNTS277	103309
Multilateral		15 Oct 52	141UNTS96	101909
Multilateral		17 Oct 52	141UNTS121	101911
Burma	USA (United States)	24 Oct 52	222UNTS55	103022
Saudi Arabia	USA (United States)	10 Nov 52	181UNTS235	102413
Ceylon (Sri Lanka)	USA (United States)	17 Nov 52	180UNTS207	102386
Japan	WHO (World Health)	26 Nov 52	204UNTS301	200521
Mexico	ICAO (Civil Aviat)	28 Nov 52	164UNTS15	102156
Multilateral		16 Dec 52	158UNTS407	102074
Multilateral		29 Dec 52	151UNTS317	102002
ILO (Labor Org)	UN Relief Palestin	31 Dec 52	182UNTS201	200506
UK Great Britain	USA (United States)	19 Jan 53	161UNTS3	102117
Saudi Arabia	USA (United States)	25 Jan 53	201UNTS3	102706
India	WHO (World Health)	11 Feb 53	163UNTS43	102140
United Nations	Sweden	11 Feb 53	160UNTS3	102096
Taiwan	ILO (Labor Org)	13 Feb 53	178UNTS337	102349
Multilateral		26 Feb 53	161UNTS31	102120
Costa Rica	United Nations	27 Feb 53	161UNTS45	102121
Nepal	United Nations	02 Mar 53	161UNTS347	200493
France	WHO (World Health)	02 Apr 53	174UNTS83	102279
United Nations	Yemen	07 Apr 53	163UNTS73	102142
Ethiopia	USA (United States)	29 Apr 53	224UNTS121	103073

PARTY ONE	PARTY TWO	DATE	CITATION	NUMBER
General technical assistance (Cont.)				
France	WHO (World Health)	30 Apr 53	174UNTS71	102278
ICAO (Civil Aviat)	Syria	28 May 53	173UNTS199	102267
Ecuador	United Nations	16 Jun 53	166UNTS289	102194
United Arab Rep	USA (United States)	18 Jun 53	204UNTS55	102749
Ethiopia	United Nations	22 Jun 53	172UNTS93	102241
Liberia	USA (United States)	23 Jun 53	213UNTS57	102880
Cambodia	United Nations	24 Jun 53	168UNTS309	200500
Japan	United Nations	24 Jun 53	167UNTS249	200499
UK Great Britain	USA (United States)	24 Jun 53	224UNTS141	103074
Afghanistan	USA (United States)	30 Jun 53	215UNTS3	102908
UN Relief Palestin	United Arab Rep	30 Jun 53	190UNTS3	102554
Multilateral		01 Jul 53	200UNTS149	102701
ECSC (Coal/Steel)	ILO (Labor Org)	16 Jul 53	412UNTS273	200591
Spain	USA (United States)	26 Sep 53	207UNTS93	102802
Multilateral		09 Oct 53	190UNTS49	102557
Dominican Republic	United Nations	19 Nov 53	180UNTS45	102374
Thailand	USA (United States)	03 Dec 53	213UNTS91	102882
USA (United States)	Yugoslavia	05 Jan 54	234UNTS267	103289
Bolivia	USA (United States)	15 Jan 54	229UNTS213	103168
UK Great Britain	USA (United States)	20 Jan 54	196UNTS95	102619
Netherlands	USA (United States)	22 Jan 54	190UNTS207	102565
Pakistan	United Nations	25 Jan 54	185UNTS213	102472
United Arab Rep	USA (United States)	24 Feb 54	236UNTS61	103316
United Nations	Venezuela	05 Mar 54	187UNTS9	102498
Liberia	United Nations	09 Mar 54	187UNTS61	102501
Guatemala	United Nations	10 Mar 54	191UNTS271	102587
United Nations	Vietnam, South	24 Mar 54	188UNTS345	200514
Mexico	USA (United States)	06 Apr 54	233UNTS163	103261
Mexico	USA (United States)	06 Apr 54	236UNTS69	103317
Peru	USA (United States)	13 Apr 54	236UNTS87	103318
Multilateral		20 Apr 54	189UNTS11	102539
Panama	USA (United States)	11 May 54	236UNTS107	103319
Nepal	WHO (World Health)	13 May 54	204UNTS311	200522
Jordan	USA (United States)	13 May 54	234UNTS225	103285
Spain	USA (United States)	19 May 54	235UNTS87	103296
Multilateral		31 May 54	192UNTS20	102592
Multilateral		01 Jun 54	200UNTS235	200520
Mexico	USA (United States)	07 Jun 54	234UNTS11	103269
Lebanon	USA (United States)	18 Jun 54	233UNTS177	103262
Italy	USA (United States)	24 Jun 54	235UNTS3	103290
Multilateral		30 Jun 54	193UNTS67	102611
Colombia	USA (United States)	30 Jun 54	237UNTS263	103351
Brazil	USA (United States)	30 Jun 54	237UNTS137	103341
UK Great Britain	USA (United States)	12 Jul 54	204UNTS123	102753
Multilateral		29 Jul 54	249UNTS45	103500
El Salvador	USA (United States)	31 Aug 54	237UNTS49	103336
Guatemala	USA (United States)	01 Sep 54	199UNTS51	102677
Multilateral		06 Oct 54	201UNTS75	102711
Ethiopia	Sweden	13 Oct 54	202UNTS273	102734
Multilateral		27 Oct 54	201UNTS95	102712
Multilateral		29 Oct 54	201UNTS115	102713
Belgium	USA (United States)	23 Nov 54	235UNTS19	103292
UK Great Britain	Yugoslavia	31 Dec 54	209UNTS81	102824
Iraq	USA (United States)	02 Mar 55	250UNTS229	103526
Mexico	USA (United States)	09 Mar 55	263UNTS247	103776
Ceylon (Sri Lanka)	Germany, West	01 Apr 55	369UNTS57	105251
Multilateral		04 Apr 55	208UNTS239	102816
Norway	USA (United States)	06 Apr 55	269UNTS65	103874
Haiti	USA (United States)	27 Apr 55	240UNTS17	103391
Czechoslovakia	Hungary	28 Apr 55	477UNTS197	106923
Greece	USA (United States)	27 May 55	251UNTS349	103552
Colombia	USA (United States)	14 Jun 55	256UNTS211	103630
Multilateral		14 Jun 55	212UNTS263	200526
Multilateral		04 Jul 55	214UNTS10	102897
Libya	WHO (World Health)	05 Jul 55	219UNTS305	200530

PARTY ONE	PARTY TWO	DATE	CITATION	NUMBER
General technical assistance (Cont.)				
Libya	USA (United States)	21 Jul 55	264UNTS247	103796
USA (United States)	Yugoslavia	30 Sep 55	269UNTS89	103877
Liberia	USA (United States)	06 Oct 55	275UNTS93	103978
Italy	Lebanon	04 Nov 55	267UNTS147	103840
Colombia	USA (United States)	28 Nov 55	241UNTS39	103422
Multilateral		13 Dec 55	407UNTS8	105857
Multilateral		13 Dec 55	529UNTS141	107660
USSR (Soviet Union)	Yugoslavia	19 Dec 55	378UNTS127	105423
Germany, West	USA (United States)	04 Jan 56	268UNTS143	103856
Multilateral		02 Feb 56	227UNTS153	103137
Multilateral		10 Feb 56	228UNTS189	103151
Bulgaria	Yugoslavia	10 Feb 56	349UNTS21	105007
Multilateral		10 Feb 56	228UNTS167	103150
Ethiopia	WHO (World Health)	17 Feb 56	243UNTS91	103448
Multilateral		26 Mar 56	259UNTS125	103686
Multilateral		30 Mar 56	604UNTS114	108748
Indonesia	United Nations	17 Apr 56	233UNTS267	103266
Germany, East	USSR (Soviet Union)	30 May 56	263UNTS143	103771
Multilateral		31 May 56	251UNTS181	103541
Multilateral		08 Jun 56	247UNTS366	200541
Multilateral		14 Jun 56	265UNTS125	103809
Multilateral		26 Jun 56	253UNTS12	103573
Multilateral		26 Jun 56	321UNTS2	104650
Multilateral		02 Jul 56	540UNTS110	107846
Multilateral		02 Jul 56	248UNTS37	103484
Multilateral		31 Aug 56	249UNTS158	103506
Denmark	WHO (World Health)	03 Sep 56	258UNTS103	103674
Multilateral		05 Oct 56	251UNTS245	103544
Multilateral		05 Oct 56	251UNTS267	103545
Germany, West	Thailand	09 Oct 56	258UNTS143	103676
Multilateral		26 Oct 56	276UNTS3	103988
Romania	Yugoslavia	27 Oct 56	389UNTS55	105592
Multilateral		21 Nov 56	253UNTS266	103588
Multilateral		15 Jan 57	376UNTS122	105378
Multilateral		23 Jan 57	259UNTS426	103701
Multilateral		17 Feb 57	271UNTS2	103907
Multilateral		22 Feb 57	274UNTS93	103960
Multilateral		01 Mar 57	264UNTS94	103790
Tunisia	USA (United States)	26 Mar 57	283UNTS117	104111
Multilateral		28 Mar 57	271UNTS30	103908
Morocco	USA (United States)	02 Apr 57	288UNTS157	104203
Multilateral		09 Apr 57	274UNTS172	103965
Czechoslovakia	United Arab Rep	06 May 57	292UNTS317	104278
Finland	USA (United States)	10 May 57	283UNTS43	104105
Albania	Yugoslavia	20 May 57	363UNTS99	105203
Multilateral		24 May 57	268UNTS270	103861
Ghana	USA (United States)	03 Jun 57	284UNTS63	104129
Argentina	USA (United States)	03 Jun 57	291UNTS61	104244
Czechoslovakia	Yugoslavia	11 Jun 57	504UNTS107	107355
Finland	India	14 Jun 57	277UNTS327	104016
Jordan	USA (United States)	27 Jun 57	288UNTS269	104209
Multilateral		09 Jul 57	274UNTS300	103972
Burma	WHO (World Health)	20 Sep 57	282UNTS113	104096
Germany, East	Hungary	25 Oct 57	408UNTS156	105869
Multilateral		05 Nov 57	285UNTS301	104155
Argentina	Italy	25 Nov 57	305UNTS275	104424
Hungary	Romania	17 Dec 57	477UNTS303	106926
Brazil	Ecuador	05 Mar 58	369UNTS43	105250
Multilateral		15 Mar 58	292UNTS273	104276
Sudan	USA (United States)	31 Mar 58	308UNTS105	104458
USA (United States)	Yugoslavia	05 Apr 58	338UNTS233	104838
Brazil	Colombia	28 May 58	369UNTS141	105255
Multilateral		19 Jun 58	306UNTS236	200550
Romania	Vietnam, North	30 Jun 58	389UNTS43	105591
EEC (Econ Commnty)	ILO (Labor Org)	07 Jul 58	312UNTS387	200551

General technical assistance (Cont.)

PARTY ONE	PARTY TWO	DATE	CITATION	NUMBER
FAO (Food Agri)	IAEA (Atom Energy)	01 Oct 58	361UNTS211	200571
IAEA (Atom Energy)	UNESCO (Educ/Cult)	01 Oct 58	339UNTS373	200558
Iran	Japan	09 Dec 58	325UNTS221	104701
Afghanistan	WHO (World Health)	18 Dec 58	324UNTS121	104681
Iraq	Romania	24 Dec 58	405UNTS243	105836
IMCO (Maritime Org)	United Nations	13 Jan 59	324UNTS273	200553
ILO (Labor Org)	UK Great Britain	14 Jan 59	355UNTS283	105081
Iraq	USSR (Soviet Union)	16 Mar 59	346UNTS107	104979
IAEA (Atom Energy)	Thailand	18 Mar 59	339UNTS307	104850
Bulgaria	Hungary	03 Apr 59	438UNTS269	106319
Morocco	UN Special Fund	04 Apr 59	354UNTS347	105069
Hungary	USSR (Soviet Union)	17 Apr 59	439UNTS41	106324
India	Netherlands	27 Apr 59	506UNTS141	107385
Italy	United Arab Rep	29 Apr 59	363UNTS91	105202
Ceylon (Sri Lanka)	Yugoslavia	05 May 59	391UNTS101	105618
Colombia	USA (United States)	08 May 59	344UNTS193	104950
IAEA (Atom Energy)	ILO (Labor Org)	08 May 59	328UNTS273	200555
IAEA (Atom Energy)	WHO (World Health)	28 May 59	339UNTS387	200559
United Nations	Vietnam, South	03 Jun 59	337UNTS361	200557
Greece	Yugoslavia	18 Jun 59	368UNTS125	105237
Ghana	UN Special Fund	12 Aug 59	338UNTS203	104836
IAEA (Atom Energy)	WMO (Meteorology)	12 Aug 59	341UNTS341	200561
IAEA (Atom Energy)	ICAO (Civil Aviat)	01 Oct 59	361UNTS193	200570
Iran	UN Special Fund	06 Oct 59	342UNTS89	104902
Multilateral		09 Oct 59	376UNTS382	105391
Poland	UN Special Fund	15 Oct 59	344UNTS29	104941
India	UN Special Fund	20 Oct 59	344UNTS143	104946
USA (United States)	Yugoslavia	22 Oct 59	360UNTS259	105161
UN Special Fund	Yugoslavia	27 Oct 59	344UNTS159	104947
Ecuador	UN Special Fund	10 Nov 59	345UNTS3	104955
Greece	UN Special Fund	13 Nov 59	345UNTS171	104966
Multilateral		19 Nov 59	410UNTS156	105902
UN Special Fund	Turkey	20 Nov 59	345UNTS105	104963
UN Special Fund	United Arab Rep	25 Nov 59	345UNTS125	104964
Turkey	USA (United States)	30 Nov 59	361UNTS107	105174
Israel	UN Special Fund	01 Dec 59	345UNTS197	104968
Multilateral		03 Dec 59	345UNTS251	104971
Multilateral		03 Dec 59	348UNTS246	105003
Argentina	UN Special Fund	04 Dec 59	345UNTS263	104972
Czechoslovakia	Ethiopia	11 Dec 59	386UNTS45	105536
Multilateral		14 Dec 59	368UNTS253	105245
Multilateral		14 Dec 59	422UNTS33	106067
Jordan	UN Special Fund	15 Dec 59	346UNTS3	104974
UN Special Fund	UK Great Britain	07 Jan 60	348UNTS177	105000
Peru	UN Special Fund	19 Jan 60	349UNTS83	105010
Chile	UN Special Fund	22 Jan 60	351UNTS115	105020
India	Japan	25 Jan 60	384UNTS31	105508
Colombia	UN Special Fund	04 Feb 60	355UNTS257	105080
Bolivia	UN Special Fund	09 Feb 60	351UNTS203	105024
Cuba	USSR (Soviet Union)	13 Feb 60	369UNTS3	105247
Greece	USA (United States)	15 Feb 60	377UNTS95	105397
Afghanistan	UN Special Fund	21 Feb 60	351UNTS93	105019
Pakistan	UN Special Fund	25 Feb 60	351UNTS141	105021
Indonesia	USSR (Soviet Union)	28 Feb 60	392UNTS173	105643
Turkey	USA (United States)	02 Mar 60	372UNTS37	105286
France	UN Special Fund	17 Mar 60	354UNTS119	105059
Japan	USA (United States)	23 Mar 60	372UNTS289	105305
Italy	UN Special Fund	01 Apr 60	354UNTS261	105066
UN Special Fund	Tunisia	12 Apr 60	355UNTS289	105082
Denmark	USA (United States)	12 Apr 60	373UNTS9	105311
Multilateral		12 Apr 60	359UNTS323	105150
Libya	UN Special Fund	19 Apr 60	356UNTS11	105090
UN Special Fund	Sudan	21 Apr 60	356UNTS213	105097
UN Special Fund	Vietnam, South	29 Apr 60	357UNTS311	200567
Laos	UN Special Fund	30 Apr 60	361UNTS171	105179

General technical assistance (Cont.)

PARTY ONE	PARTY TWO	DATE	CITATION	NUMBER
Lebanon	UN Special Fund	07 May 60	360UNTS225	105160
Multilateral		04 Jun 60	360UNTS208	105159
Iraq	UN Special Fund	19 Jun 60	376UNTS357	105389
Multilateral		19 Jun 60	537UNTS214	107803
Italy	USA (United States)	07 Jul 60	380UNTS143	105455
Multilateral		08 Jul 60	366UNTS310	105220
Ethiopia	UN Special Fund	13 Jul 60	368UNTS159	105240
France	Greece	25 Jul 60	533UNTS227	107745
Ghana	USSR (Soviet Union)	04 Aug 60	399UNTS61	105734
Japan	Thailand	24 Aug 60	384UNTS73	105512
Brazil	UN Special Fund	16 Sep 60	375UNTS3	105351
Taiwan	UN Special Fund	20 Sep 60	375UNTS29	105352
Guinea	USA (United States)	30 Sep 60	394UNTS103	105671
Indonesia	UN Special Fund	07 Oct 60	378UNTS141	105424
Liberia	UN Special Fund	11 Oct 60	376UNTS341	105388
El Salvador	UN Special Fund	24 Oct 60	377UNTS171	105400
Nepal	UN Special Fund	17 Nov 60	380UNTS289	105461
Czechoslovakia	Ghana	23 Nov 60	431UNTS85	106212
Cambodia	UN Special Fund	24 Nov 60	382UNTS255	105487
Israel	Mali	24 Nov 60	413UNTS95	105944
Honduras	UN Special Fund	20 Dec 60	383UNTS103	105497
Inter-Am Nuc Energ	IAEA (Atom Energy)	22 Dec 60	396UNTS285	200586
Togo	USA (United States)	22 Dec 60	401UNTS33	105760
Burma	UN Special Fund	03 Jan 61	387UNTS219	105564
Mali	USA (United States)	04 Jan 61	405UNTS165	105832
Costa Rica	UN Special Fund	10 Jan 61	389UNTS253	105597
UN Special Fund	Saudi Arabia	19 Jan 61	396UNTS27	105692
USA (United States)	Yugoslavia	19 Jan 61	402UNTS163	105784
Nicaragua	UN Special Fund	20 Jan 61	387UNTS15	105555
Chad	UN Special Fund	23 Jan 61	390UNTS69	105603
Euratom	ILO (Labor Org)	26 Jan 61	390UNTS323	200580
UN Special Fund	Somalia	28 Jan 61	388UNTS75	105573
Multilateral		28 Jan 61	387UNTS202	105563
Gabon	UN Special Fund	02 Feb 61	387UNTS289	105568
Somalia	USA (United States)	04 Feb 61	433UNTS179	106241
Korea, South	USA (United States)	08 Feb 61	405UNTS37	105821
Nigeria	UN Special Fund	10 Feb 61	390UNTS85	105604
Mexico	UN Special Fund	23 Feb 61	388UNTS151	105576
Cyprus	UN Special Fund	24 Feb 61	389UNTS3	105588
Panama	UN Special Fund	09 Mar 61	396UNTS3	105691
Cuba	UN Special Fund	10 Mar 61	390UNTS35	105601
Afghanistan	Japan	15 Mar 61	450UNTS373	106480
Ceylon (Sri Lanka)	Japan	20 Mar 61	450UNTS385	106481
Cuba	Czechoslovakia	05 Apr 61	442UNTS201	106350
Honduras	USA (United States)	12 Apr 61	413UNTS182	105952
Korea, South	UN Special Fund	21 Apr 61	394UNTS231	200583
Ceylon (Sri Lanka)	UN Special Fund	03 May 61	395UNTS217	105687
Sierra Leone	USA (United States)	05 May 61	409UNTS194	105885
Senegal	USA (United States)	13 May 61	409UNTS232	105888
Ivory Coast	USA (United States)	17 May 61	409UNTS241	105889
Niger	USA (United States)	26 May 61	410UNTS213	105905
Cameroon	USA (United States)	26 May 61	413UNTS195	105953
Dahomey	USA (United States)	27 May 61	445UNTS23	106373
USA (United States)	Upper Volta	01 Jun 61	410UNTS223	105906
Somalia	USSR (Soviet Union)	02 Jun 61	457UNTS263	106587
Czechoslovakia	Somalia	04 Jun 61	480UNTS261	106973
Israel	Upper Volta	11 Jun 61	413UNTS113	105946
Cameroon	UN Special Fund	13 Jun 61	397UNTS297	105713
Ethiopia	United Nations	14 Jun 61	406UNTS81	105840
Inter-Am Devel Bnk	USA (United States)	19 Jun 61	410UNTS34	105895
Paraguay	UN Special Fund	22 Jun 61	399UNTS117	105738
Madagascar	USA (United States)	22 Jun 61	413UNTS219	105956
UN Special Fund	Upper Volta	26 Jun 61	400UNTS3	105744
Philippines	UN Special Fund	28 Jun 61	399UNTS141	105739
Haiti	UN Special Fund	28 Jun 61	399UNTS171	105741

PARTY ONE	PARTY TWO	DATE	CITATION	NUMBER
General technical assistance (Cont.)				
Cyprus	USA (United States)	29 Jun 61	411UNTS56	105914
Mali	UN Special Fund	21 Jul 61	401UNTS141	105768
UN Special Fund	Yemen	02 Aug 61	402UNTS43	105777
Israel	Malagasy	27 Aug 61	413UNTS86	105943
Ivory Coast	UN Special Fund	29 Aug 61	406UNTS129	105844
Tunisia	USSR (Soviet Union)	30 Aug 61	437UNTS243	106310
Multilateral		20 Sep 61	407UNTS52	105859
Paraguay	USA (United States)	26 Sep 61	461UNTS91	106653
Dahomey	Israel	28 Sep 61	448UNTS151	106429
UN Special Fund	Sierra Leone	02 Oct 61	422UNTS131	106073
Japan	United Nations	04 Oct 61	410UNTS133	105900
Multilateral		16 Oct 61	410UNTS242	105908
Multilateral		07 Nov 61	412UNTS258	105937
Mauritania	UN Special Fund	07 Nov 61	412UNTS240	105936
Congo (Brazzaville)	UN Special Fund	09 Nov 61	413UNTS58	105940
Mexico	USA (United States)	15 Nov 61	460UNTS113	106634
Panama	USA (United States)	11 Dec 61	445UNTS161	106384
UN Special Fund	Venezuela	11 Dec 61	422UNTS149	106074
UN Special Fund	Senegal	16 Dec 61	425UNTS97	106121
El Salvador	USA (United States)	19 Dec 61	445UNTS175	106385
Argentina	Japan	20 Dec 61	451UNTS77	106486
Iran	USA (United States)	21 Dec 61	433UNTS269	106249
Costa Rica	USA (United States)	22 Dec 61	460UNTS277	106646
Multilateral		27 Dec 61	425UNTS83	106120
Malagasy	UN Special Fund	05 Jan 62	419UNTS29	106028
Dominican Republic	USA (United States)	11 Jan 62	433UNTS133	106236
Multilateral		17 Jan 62	419UNTS294	106033
Multilateral		20 Jan 62	429UNTS230	200596
Multilateral		13 Feb 62	422UNTS288	200594
Multilateral		21 Feb 62	423UNTS151	106091
Niger	UN Special Fund	26 Feb 62	423UNTS83	106086
Multilateral		01 Mar 62	423UNTS122	106089
United Nations	Saudi Arabia	16 Mar 62	456UNTS379	106566
Dahomey	UN Special Fund	28 Mar 62	424UNTS55	106099
Brazil	Japan	28 Mar 62	451UNTS125	106489
Nicaragua	USA (United States)	30 Mar 62	456UNTS241	106559
India	Japan	31 Mar 62	451UNTS143	106490
Multilateral		10 Apr 62	429UNTS78	106192
Ecuador	USA (United States)	17 Apr 62	442UNTS69	106339
Multilateral		18 Apr 62	463UNTS44	106692
India	Japan	23 Apr 62	451UNTS155	106491
UN Special Fund	Uruguay	04 May 62	429UNTS143	106196
Gabon	Israel	15 May 62	448UNTS211	106433
Multilateral		17 May 62	429UNTS46	106189
Ghana	Israel	25 May 62	515UNTS237	107461
Greece	Tunisia	26 May 62	534UNTS163	107761
Dominican Republic	UN Special Fund	06 Jun 62	429UNTS169	106197
Central Afri Rep	Israel	13 Jun 62	448UNTS265	106439
Multilateral		14 Jun 62	528UNTS33	107634
Israel	Liberia	25 Jun 62	448UNTS287	106441
Germany, West	Syria	25 Jun 62	489UNTS71	107135
Algeria	France	03 Jul 62	507UNTS25	107395
UN Special Fund	Syria	07 Jul 62	443UNTS3	106355
Taiwan	Paraguay	11 Jul 62	458UNTS41	106591
UN Special Fund	Tanganyika	17 Jul 62	435UNTS237	106281
Multilateral		23 Jul 62	456UNTS302	106564
Colombia	USA (United States)	23 Jul 62	458UNTS123	106595
Multilateral		12 Aug 62	443UNTS266	106365
Italy	USA (United States)	28 Aug 62	461UNTS137	106657
Multilateral		29 Aug 62	443UNTS280	106366
Multilateral		11 Sep 62	455UNTS402	106553
Algeria	France	24 Sep 62	0UNTS0	109507
Mali	USSR (Soviet Union)	10 Oct 62	493UNTS219	107216
Israel	OAS (Am States)	11 Oct 62	484UNTS241	107035
Belgium	Rwanda	13 Oct 62	456UNTS425	106568

PARTY ONE	PARTY TWO	DATE	CITATION	NUMBER
General technical assistance (Cont.)				
Israel	Rwanda	23 Oct 62	515UNTS291	107466
Multilateral		15 Nov 62	448UNTS50	106424
Algeria	UN Special Fund	15 Nov 62	452UNTS243	106512
Laos	USSR (Soviet Union)	01 Dec 62	472UNTS3	106834
Multilateral		06 Dec 62	450UNTS240	106471
Multilateral		12 Dec 62	457UNTS72	106578
Multilateral		15 Jan 63	456UNTS409	106567
Multilateral		21 Jan 63	453UNTS20	106517
Israel	Tanganyika	28 Jan 63	516UNTS39	107468
Israel	Uganda	04 Feb 63	484UNTS273	107037
Multilateral		05 Feb 63	453UNTS36	106518
United Nations	United Arab Rep	08 Feb 63	453UNTS79	106520
Central Afri Rep	USA (United States)	10 Feb 63	473UNTS83	106857
Multilateral		14 Feb 63	453UNTS168	106524
Multilateral		06 Mar 63	455UNTS386	106552
Austria	Czechoslovakia	08 Mar 63	495UNTS219	107245
Israel	USA (United States)	21 Mar 63	476UNTS131	106907
UN Special Fund	Uganda	22 Mar 63	456UNTS466	106572
Burma	Japan	29 Mar 63	518UNTS3	107490
Israel	Peru	02 Apr 63	515UNTS279	107465
Multilateral		18 Apr 63	463UNTS121	106697
Multilateral		06 May 63	463UNTS78	106694
Multilateral		09 May 63	463UNTS159	106700
Jamaica	UN Special Fund	22 May 63	489UNTS191	107140
Multilateral		22 May 63	483UNTS72	107007
Netherlands	UN Special Fund	24 May 63	466UNTS289	106750
Multilateral		24 May 63	466UNTS346	106754
Multilateral		24 May 63	470UNTS208	106810
Afromalagasy Org	ILO (Labor Org)	30 May 63	467UNTS482	200602
UN Special Fund	Western Samoa	05 Jun 63	467UNTS463	200601
Multilateral		23 Jul 63	471UNTS158	106831
Multilateral		31 Jul 63	472UNTS220	106842
Burundi	UN Special Fund	22 Aug 63	476UNTS49	106903
Multilateral		27 Aug 63	511UNTS210	107435
Multilateral		10 Sep 63	480UNTS100	106965
Guatemala	USA (United States)	03 Oct 63	493UNTS45	107206
Multilateral		21 Oct 63	480UNTS197	106969
Jamaica	USA (United States)	24 Oct 63	489UNTS337	107148
Multilateral		30 Oct 63	480UNTS180	106968
Central Afri Rep	UN Special Fund	30 Oct 63	481UNTS247	106985
Multilateral		07 Nov 63	480UNTS232	106971
Multilateral		08 Nov 63	482UNTS286	106999
Brazil	Germany, West	30 Nov 63	0UNTS0	109421
Multilateral		03 Dec 63	529UNTS217	107663
Tanganyika	USA (United States)	09 Dec 63	526UNTS301	107612
Czechoslovakia	Hungary	20 Dec 63	538UNTS127	107812
Dominican Republic	Israel	25 Dec 63	550UNTS221	108018
Multilateral		28 Jan 64	502UNTS321	107336
Subsahara Tech Com	IAEA (Atom Energy)	06 Feb 64	501UNTS285	200606
Multilateral		20 Feb 64	491UNTS30	107172
Israel	Philippines	16 Mar 64	550UNTS269	108021
Germany, West	Thailand	02 Apr 64	503UNTS3	107338
Indonesia	Netherlands	03 Apr 64	566UNTS45	108239
Morocco	UNESCO (Educ/Cult)	13 May 64	0UNTS0	109220
Chad	France	19 May 64	0UNTS0	109441
Cuba	Czechoslovakia	03 Jun 64	527UNTS205	107626
Ireland	UN Special Fund	03 Jun 64	496UNTS205	107253
Italy	Romania	16 Jun 64	558UNTS313	108150
Multilateral		23 Jun 64	506UNTS108	107383
Multilateral		28 Jun 64	519UNTS14	107499
Belgium	Tunisia	15 Jul 64	560UNTS57	108168
Multilateral		15 Jul 64	610UNTS143	108840
Taiwan	Philippines	25 Aug 64	511UNTS233	107436
Pakistan	IBRD (World Bank)	26 Aug 64	632UNTS201	109023
Kenya	UN Special Fund	01 Oct 64	511UNTS181	107433

PARTY ONE	PARTY TWO	DATE	CITATION	NUMBER
General technical assistance (Cont.)				
Argentina	France	03 Oct 64	635UNTS155	109080
Chad	Israel	07 Oct 64	630UNTS175	108969
Romania	UN Special Fund	24 Oct 64	519UNTS29	107500
Malawi	UN Special Fund	24 Oct 64	514UNTS235	200609
Multilateral		24 Oct 64	514UNTS220	200608
Asian Productivity	ILO (Labor Org)	27 Oct 64	516UNTS367	200610
Ethiopia	Netherlands	28 Oct 64	541UNTS235	107872
Netherlands	Pakistan	30 Oct 64	541UNTS243	107873
Multilateral		11 Nov 64	515UNTS94	107456
Israel	Turkey	13 Nov 64	550UNTS303	108025
Denmark	Pakistan	12 Dec 64	636UNTS313	109107
UN Special Fund	Zambia	15 Dec 64	522UNTS3	107532
Multilateral		15 Dec 64	522UNTS20	107533
Germany, West	Jamaica	16 Dec 64	531UNTS129	107699
Germany, West	Thailand	23 Dec 64	525UNTS177	107589
Denmark	Peru	30 Dec 64	595UNTS47	108611
Colombia	Israel	15 Jan 65	581UNTS173	108441
Malta	Switzerland	20 Jan 65	548UNTS193	107978
Denmark	Thailand	25 Jan 65	530UNTS173	107680
Multilateral		27 Jan 65	523UNTS102	107556
WHO (World Health)	Tunisia	27 Jan 65	528UNTS209	107644
Multilateral		02 Feb 65	523UNTS256	107560
Germany, West	Jamaica	03 Feb 65	531UNTS143	107700
Multilateral		12 Feb 65	525UNTS148	107587
Peru	IBRD (World Bank)	15 Mar 65	632UNTS209	109024
Ivory Coast	Netherlands	26 Apr 65	634UNTS81	109053
Netherlands	Tanzania	27 Apr 65	594UNTS123	108599
Multilateral		02 Jun 65	551UNTS2	108030
Multilateral		02 Jun 65	537UNTS348	200611
Canada	USA (United States)	08 Jun 65	546UNTS201	107947
Gambia	UN Special Fund	09 Jun 65	538UNTS321	200612
Netherlands	Senegal	12 Jun 65	602UNTS231	108715
UN Special Fund	Spain	30 Jun 65	544UNTS159	107918
Multilateral		02 Jul 65	592UNTS215	108575
ILO (Labor Org)	LAFTA (Free Trade)	02 Jul 65	563UNTS327	200619
ILO (Labor Org)	Org Ctrl Am States	26 Jul 65	563UNTS341	200620
Israel	Sierra Leone	22 Aug 65	550UNTS285	108023
Multilateral		13 Sep 65	547UNTS264	107962
Norway	Eur Space Research	21 Sep 65	579UNTS251	108413
Multilateral		21 Oct 65	547UNTS216	107959
Multilateral		04 Dec 65	571UNTS123	108303
Multilateral		31 Dec 65	552UNTS292	108060
Mongolia	UN Special Fund	26 Jan 66	552UNTS201	108055
Israel	Kenya	25 Feb 66	582UNTS23	108455
Argentina	Germany, West	01 Mar 66	635UNTS247	109087
Guinea	IBRD (World Bank)	30 Mar 66	568UNTS3	108262
Algeria	France	08 Apr 66	0UNTS0	109508
Romania	Tunisia	21 Apr 66	604UNTS65	108744
Maldive Islands	WHO (World Health)	23 May 66	566UNTS19	108237
France	USSR (Soviet Union)	30 Jun 66	589UNTS109	108538
Netherlands	Tunisia	08 Jul 66	591UNTS235	108560
Israel	Mexico	11 Jul 66	0UNTS0	109348
FAO (Food Agri)	IMCO (Maritime Org)	11 Jul 66	575UNTS238	200627
Colombia	Netherlands	19 Jul 66	591UNTS201	108558
Ivory Coast	Netherlands	01 Aug 66	591UNTS245	108561
Multilateral		22 Aug 66	571UNTS298	200624
Romania	United Arab Rep	03 Sep 66	604UNTS73	108745
Multilateral		23 Sep 66	573UNTS148	108328
Multilateral		23 Sep 66	573UNTS132	108327
Multilateral		30 Sep 66	576UNTS8	108361
Chile	UK Great Britain	07 Oct 66	603UNTS167	108733
Multilateral		17 Nov 66	580UNTS22	108417
Malawi	UK Great Britain	21 Nov 66	637UNTS0	109126
Afghanistan	IBRD (World Bank)	22 Nov 66	632UNTS171	109019
Syria	USSR (Soviet Union)	18 Dec 66	633UNTS247	109041

PARTY ONE	PARTY TWO	DATE	CITATION	NUMBER
General technical assistance (Cont.)				
Argentina	Bolivia	19 Dec 66	636UNTS75	109092
Multilateral		25 Jan 67	588UNTS212	108527
Bulgaria	United Arab Rep	12 Feb 67	630UNTS363	108982
Bulgaria	United Arab Rep	12 Feb 67	630UNTS353	108981
France	Niger	25 Feb 67	0UNTS0	109261
Nicaragua	IBRD (World Bank)	13 Mar 67	632UNTS177	109020
Denmark	Tanzania	05 Apr 67	604UNTS19	108740
Romania	Somalia	20 Apr 67	642UNTS155	109171
Malta	WHO (World Health)	10 May 67	603UNTS99	108727
Congo (Brazzaville)	IBRD (World Bank)	10 May 67	632UNTS185	109021
IBRD (World Bank)	Turkey	11 May 67	632UNTS193	109022
Bulgaria	USSR (Soviet Union)	12 May 67	631UNTS239	108997
USSR (Soviet Union)	Zambia	26 May 67	643UNTS179	109191
Liberia	IBRD (World Bank)	05 Jun 67	633UNTS13	109031
Multilateral		14 Jun 67	603UNTS2	108719
Multilateral		20 Jun 67	0UNTS0	109290
Multilateral		21 Jun 67	598UNTS2	108653
Barbados	WHO (World Health)	18 Jul 67	603UNTS87	108726
Multilateral		20 Jul 67	0UNTS0	109259
Germany, West	Romania	03 Aug 67	642UNTS47	109164
Netherlands	Poland	22 Aug 67	0UNTS0	109276
Ceylon (Sri Lanka)	IBRD (World Bank)	24 Aug 67	632UNTS217	109025
New Zealand	WHO (World Health)	29 Aug 67	607UNTS57	108795
Bulgaria	Germany, East	07 Sep 67	631UNTS81	108988
Multilateral		22 Sep 67	0UNTS0	109258
Cyprus	WHO (World Health)	07 Oct 67	608UNTS327	108821
Bel-Lux Econ Union	Czechoslovakia	10 Oct 67	0UNTS0	109362
Multilateral		12 Oct 67	607UNTS2	108792
Multilateral		12 Oct 67	607UNTS20	108793
Botswana	UN Special Fund	12 Oct 67	607UNTS37	108794
Denmark	Pakistan	21 Oct 67	632UNTS105	109012
Lesotho	WHO (World Health)	07 Nov 67	632UNTS143	109016
Denmark	Poland	15 Nov 67	643UNTS383	109203
Czechoslovakia	USSR (Soviet Union)	23 Nov 67	0UNTS0	109224
Chile	Denmark	15 Dec 67	643UNTS293	109199
Austria	Canada	28 Feb 68	636UNTS141	109101
Cyprus	UK Great Britain	11 Mar 68	0UNTS0	109285
Mauritius	UK Great Britain	12 Mar 68	0UNTS0	109270
Mauritius	UK Great Britain	12 Mar 68	0UNTS0	109268
Netherlands	Yugoslavia	13 Mar 68	0UNTS0	109297
Czechoslovakia	UK Great Britain	26 Mar 68	0UNTS0	109278
State/IGO Group	Nigeria	20 Apr 68	636UNTS294	109106
Denmark	Morocco	22 Apr 68	0UNTS0	109218
State/IGO Group	Malaysia	10 May 68	636UNTS276	109105
Hungary	Poland	16 May 68	0UNTS0	109292
Korea, South	Netherlands	16 May 68	0UNTS0	109260
State/IGO Group	Australia	21 May 68	636UNTS326	109108
Congo (Zaire)	Denmark	25 May 68	0UNTS0	109289
Denmark	India	10 Jun 68	0UNTS0	109219
Denmark	Uganda	03 Jul 68	0UNTS0	109467
Denmark	Uganda	03 Jul 68	0UNTS0	109466
Denmark	Malawi	03 Sep 68	0UNTS0	109414
Denmark	Thailand	16 Oct 68	0UNTS0	109463
Australia	UK Great Britain	16 Oct 68	0UNTS0	109459
State/IGO Group	Southern Yemen	04 Apr 69	0UNTS0	109454
State/IGO Group	Southern Yemen	04 Apr 69	0UNTS0	109455
UN Special Fund	Southern Yemen	04 Apr 69	0UNTS0	109456
State/IGO Group	Yemen	23 Apr 69	0UNTS0	109514
Agriculture				
Mexico	USA (United States)	11 Apr 41	117UNTS323	200379
Peru	USA (United States)	21 Apr 42	89UNTS317	200260
Brazil	USA (United States)	03 Sep 42	13UNTS109	200073
Nicaragua	USA (United States)	27 Oct 42	99UNTS287	200283
Ecuador	USA (United States)	29 Oct 42	89UNTS301	200259

PARTY ONE	PARTY TWO	DATE	CITATION	NUMBER
Agriculture (Cont.)				
El Salvador	USA (United States)	02 Dec 42	122UNTS277	200410
Multilateral		15 Jan 44	161UNTS281	200489
Guatemala	USA (United States)	15 Jul 44	106UNTS285	200347
Greece	UK Great Britain	24 Jan 46	6UNTS45	100067
Multilateral		30 Oct 46	27UNTS77	100401
United Arab Rep	UK Great Britain	10 Dec 46	105UNTS15	101451
Romania	Yugoslavia	23 Dec 46	116UNTS33	101567
Paraguay	USA (United States)	03 Mar 47	135UNTS156	101819
Bolivia	USA (United States)	16 May 47	168UNTS89	102215
Haiti	USA (United States)	19 Dec 47	135UNTS130	101818
Paraguay	USA (United States)	01 Jan 48	89UNTS191	101217
Costa Rica	USA (United States)	27 Feb 48	135UNTS74	101816
Poland	USSR (Soviet Union)	08 Apr 48	26UNTS191	100388
France	Ireland	06 May 48	558UNTS170	108141
Ecuador	USA (United States)	14 May 48	89UNTS71	101210
Taiwan	USA (United States)	05 Aug 48	82UNTS109	101087
Multilateral		29 Nov 48	120UNTS13	101613
Czechoslovakia	Poland	22 Jan 49	85UNTS3	101142
Korea, North	USSR (Soviet Union)	17 Mar 49	221UNTS3	102999
Austria	Czechoslovakia	30 Mar 50	495UNTS85	107240
Romania	USSR (Soviet Union)	27 May 50	221UNTS13	103000
Germany, East	Poland	23 Jun 50	304UNTS91	104393
Hungary	USSR (Soviet Union)	13 Jul 50	221UNTS35	103001
Bulgaria	USSR (Soviet Union)	25 Aug 50	221UNTS57	103002
Iran	USA (United States)	19 Oct 50	92UNTS135	101266
Chile	USA (United States)	16 Jan 51	157UNTS3	102043
Honduras	USA (United States)	30 Jan 51	124UNTS63	101667
El Salvador	USA (United States)	11 May 51	141UNTS191	101915
Multilateral		28 Jun 51	172UNTS159	102244
Panama	USA (United States)	30 Jul 51	140UNTS321	101896
India	WHO (World Health)	11 Oct 51	118UNTS27	101594
Dominican Republic	USA (United States)	07 Jan 52	174UNTS243	102289
Colombia	USA (United States)	12 Jan 52	168UNTS109	102216
Iran	USA (United States)	20 Jan 52	200UNTS191	102703
Jordan	USA (United States)	12 Feb 52	168UNTS25	102211
UNICEF (Children)	UK Great Britain	15 Feb 52	121UNTS63	101626
Iraq	USA (United States)	18 Mar 52	223UNTS131	103061
Peru	USA (United States)	09 Apr 52	184UNTS295	102454
Ethiopia	USA (United States)	15 May 52	180UNTS227	102388
Ecuador	USA (United States)	29 May 52	185UNTS203	102471
Bolivia	USA (United States)	18 Jun 52	199UNTS211	102686
Panama	USA (United States)	30 Jun 52	181UNTS121	102404
Czechoslovakia	Romania	31 Jul 52	362UNTS123	105185
Pakistan	USA (United States)	17 Sep 52	227UNTS77	103132
USA (United States)	Yugoslavia	11 Oct 52	235UNTS277	103309
Saudi Arabia	USA (United States)	10 Nov 52	181UNTS295	102418
Saudi Arabia	USA (United States)	15 Dec 52	185UNTS67	102459
Saudi Arabia	USA (United States)	25 Jan 53	201UNTS3	102706
UK Great Britain	USA (United States)	25 Feb 53	212UNTS157	102868
United Arab Rep	USA (United States)	12 Mar 53	204UNTS3	102747
United Arab Rep	USA (United States)	19 Mar 53	215UNTS17	102909
Multilateral		11 May 53	456UNTS3	106555
United Arab Rep	USA (United States)	21 May 53	204UNTS29	102748
Colombia	USA (United States)	09 Jun 53	213UNTS3	102877
Liberia	USA (United States)	23 Jun 53	213UNTS37	102879
UK Great Britain	USA (United States)	24 Jun 53	224UNTS141	103074
Brazil	USA (United States)	26 Jun 53	336UNTS241	104808
Chile	USA (United States)	27 Jun 53	229UNTS53	103160
Ethiopia	USA (United States)	30 Jun 53	212UNTS135	102865
Nicaragua	USA (United States)	30 Jun 53	215UNTS133	102917
Afghanistan	USA (United States)	30 Jun 53	215UNTS3	102908
Panama	IBRD (World Bank)	25 Sep 53	188UNTS71	102521
Panama	IBRD (World Bank)	25 Sep 53	188UNTS95	102522
Hungary	Romania	14 Dec 53	342UNTS151	104906
Chile	USA (United States)	30 Dec 53	236UNTS41	103315

PARTY ONE	PARTY TWO	DATE	CITATION	NUMBER
Agriculture (Cont.)				
USA (United States)	Yugoslavia	05 Jan 54	234UNTS267	103289
UK Great Britain	USA (United States)	20 Jan 54	196UNTS95	102619
Mexico	USA (United States)	17 Jun 54	237UNTS275	103352
Costa Rica	USA (United States)	30 Jun 54	235UNTS35	103294
El Salvador	USA (United States)	16 Jul 54	237UNTS237	103350
Bulgaria	Romania	22 Jul 54	362UNTS101	105184
Multilateral		29 Jul 54	249UNTS45	103500
El Salvador	USA (United States)	21 Mar 55	250UNTS261	103528
Canada	USA (United States)	15 Jun 55	235UNTS201	103302
Dominican Republic	USA (United States)	30 Jun 55	257UNTS313	103664
Libya	USA (United States)	28 Jul 55	270UNTS317	103903
Germany, East	Romania	05 Aug 55	342UNTS229	104910
Bulgaria	Greece	19 Apr 56	594UNTS131	108600
Romania	Yugoslavia	25 Sep 56	395UNTS147	105683
Japan	IBRD (World Bank)	19 Dec 56	268UNTS203	103859
Multilateral		25 Mar 57	294UNTS2	104300
Albania	Yugoslavia	20 May 57	363UNTS99	105203
Bulgaria	Yugoslavia	04 Jun 57	349UNTS35	105008
Germany, East	Hungary	25 Oct 57	408UNTS156	105869
Hungary	Yugoslavia	06 Dec 57	519UNTS215	107509
Multilateral		03 Feb 58	381UNTS165	105471
Multilateral		24 Jun 58	348UNTS275	105005
Muscat and Oman	UK Great Britain	25 Jul 58	312UNTS347	104524
India	Netherlands	27 Apr 59	506UNTS141	107385
USA (United States)	USSR (Soviet Union)	21 Nov 59	361UNTS35	105172
Multilateral		14 Dec 59	422UNTS33	106067
IBRD (World Bank)	Uruguay	30 Dec 59	384UNTS275	105523
Indonesia	USSR (Soviet Union)	28 Feb 60	392UNTS173	105643
Belgium	IBRD (World Bank)	30 Mar 60	379UNTS103	105437
IBRD (World Bank)	UK Great Britain	27 May 60	375UNTS201	105367
Peru	IBRD (World Bank)	01 Jun 60	380UNTS15	105448
Japan	Pakistan	30 Jul 60	384UNTS63	105511
Ghana	USSR (Soviet Union)	04 Aug 60	399UNTS61	105734
United Arab Rep	USSR (Soviet Union)	27 Aug 60	399UNTS37	105733
Libya	USA (United States)	11 Dec 60	445UNTS125	106381
Multilateral		13 Dec 60	455UNTS204	106544
Multilateral		30 Mar 61	520UNTS151	107515
Somalia	USSR (Soviet Union)	02 Jun 61	457UNTS263	106587
Jordan	UK Great Britain	17 Jul 61	420UNTS53	106039
USA (United States)	USSR (Soviet Union)	08 Mar 62	460UNTS3	106630
Jordan	UK Great Britain	30 May 62	449UNTS167	106458
Germany, West	Syria	25 Jun 62	489UNTS71	107135
Mali	USSR (Soviet Union)	10 Oct 62	493UNTS219	107216
Israel	Rwanda	23 Oct 62	515UNTS291	107466
Cameroon	Israel	24 Oct 62	449UNTS3	106446
Israel	Tanganyika	28 Jan 63	516UNTS39	107468
Israel	Uganda	04 Feb 63	484UNTS273	107037
Chile	IBRD (World Bank)	18 Dec 63	504UNTS3	107351
Dominican Republic	Israel	25 Dec 63	550UNTS221	108018
Multilateral		30 Dec 63	568UNTS243	108272
USA (United States)	USSR (Soviet Union)	22 Feb 64	526UNTS131	107605
Netherlands	Tunisia	03 Mar 64	533UNTS133	107739
Taiwan	Philippines	25 Aug 64	511UNTS233	107436
Morocco	IBRD (World Bank)	26 Aug 64	537UNTS193	107802
Ghana	Israel	30 Nov 64	550UNTS231	108019
Germany, West	Thailand	23 Dec 64	525UNTS201	107592
UK Great Britain	USSR (Soviet Union)	06 Jan 65	543UNTS77	107897
IBRD (World Bank)	Uruguay	30 Mar 65	567UNTS45	108251
Peru	IBRD (World Bank)	03 Jun 65	551UNTS227	108045
Jordan	UK Great Britain	08 Jun 65	552UNTS251	108057
Cameroon	Netherlands	06 Jul 65	571UNTS75	108300
Israel	Sierra Leone	22 Aug 65	550UNTS285	108023
Mexico	IBRD (World Bank)	01 Oct 65	589UNTS339	108542
Denmark	Syria	28 Dec 65	588UNTS163	108523
Austria	Tunisia	30 Dec 65	589UNTS119	108539

PARTY ONE	PARTY TWO	DATE	CITATION	NUMBER
Agriculture (Cont.)				
IDA (Devel Assoc)	Tanzania	13 Jan 66	567UNTS177	108256
Denmark	Iran	14 Jun 66	597UNTS283	108652
Multilateral		02 Aug 66	582UNTS59	108457
Romania	United Arab Rep	03 Sep 66	604UNTS73	108745
UK Great Britain	USSR (Soviet Union)	24 Feb 67	606UNTS171	108785
Conservation				
UK Great Britain	USA (United States)	20 Jan 54	196UNTS95	102619
Guatemala	Honduras	22 Aug 56	263UNTS49	103767
Multilateral		19 Sep 60	419UNTS125	106032
Israel	Mexico	11 Jul 66	0UNTS0	109348
Economic development				
Canada	UK Great Britain	18 Oct 58	392UNTS61	105639
Assistance				
Mexico	USA (United States)	11 Apr 41	117UNTS323	200379
Honduras	USA (United States)	08 May 42	166UNTS351	200498
Paraguay	USA (United States)	22 May 42	124UNTS243	200423
Multilateral		04 Dec 42	24UNTS247	200150
Chile	USA (United States)	11 May 43	139UNTS295	200456
USA (United States)	Venezuela	14 May 43	28UNTS359	200160
Australia	New Zealand	21 Jan 44	18UNTS357	200113
France	UK Great Britain	27 Mar 45	98UNTS227	200274
Colombia	USA (United States)	19 Feb 46	166UNTS104	102187
Brazil	USA (United States)	05 Apr 46	12UNTS131	100183
USA (United States)	Uruguay	23 Apr 46	160UNTS103	102104
Multilateral		22 Jul 46	14UNTS185	100221
Peru	USA (United States)	27 Dec 46	152UNTS93	102013
Mexico	USA (United States)	17 Mar 47	167UNTS30	102200
Honduras	USA (United States)	13 May 47	166UNTS159	102189
USA (United States)	Venezuela	30 Jun 47	166UNTS198	102190
Poland	UNICEF (Children)	23 Aug 47	65UNTS22	100815
Czechoslovakia	UNICEF (Children)	03 Oct 47	65UNTS26	100816
Ecuador	USA (United States)	27 Oct 47	44UNTS45	100677
UNICEF (Children)	Yugoslavia	20 Nov 47	65UNTS28	100817
Haiti	USA (United States)	19 Dec 47	135UNTS130	101818
Costa Rica	USA (United States)	27 Feb 48	135UNTS74	101816
Taiwan	UNICEF (Children)	21 May 48	65UNTS38	100818
Paraguay	USA (United States)	30 Jun 48	124UNTS34	101665
Taiwan	USA (United States)	05 Aug 48	82UNTS109	101087
Philippines	UNICEF (Children)	20 Nov 48	65UNTS48	100819
Chile	USA (United States)	21 Jan 49	160UNTS185	102107
Mexico	USA (United States)	14 Feb 49	160UNTS75	102103
UNICEF (Children)	UK Great Britain	13 Jun 49	65UNTS58	100825
UNICEF (Children)	UK Great Britain	17 Jun 49	65UNTS54	100822
UNICEF (Children)	UK Great Britain	17 Jun 49	65UNTS56	100824
UNICEF (Children)	UK Great Britain	17 Jun 49	65UNTS50	100820
UNICEF (Children)	UK Great Britain	17 Jun 49	65UNTS54	100821
UNICEF (Children)	UK Great Britain	17 Jun 49	65UNTS56	100823
Pakistan	UNICEF (Children)	20 Jun 49	65UNTS60	100826
USA (United States)	Uruguay	27 Jul 49	151UNTS199	101995
El Salvador	USA (United States)	27 Jul 49	180UNTS219	102387
WHO (World Health)	Thailand	12 Aug 49	178UNTS347	102350
Ecuador	UNICEF (Children)	12 Oct 49	65UNTS62	100827
UNICEF (Children)	UK Great Britain	19 Dec 49	65UNTS64	100828
Haiti	UNICEF (Children)	20 Dec 49	65UNTS68	100829
Costa Rica	UNICEF (Children)	14 Jan 50	65UNTS70	100830
Honduras	UNICEF (Children)	17 Jan 50	65UNTS74	100831
Nicaragua	UNICEF (Children)	17 Jan 50	65UNTS76	100832
El Salvador	UNICEF (Children)	18 Jan 50	65UNTS78	100833
Peru	UNICEF (Children)	31 Jan 50	65UNTS80	100834
Bolivia	UNICEF (Children)	03 Feb 50	65UNTS82	100835
Guatemala	UNICEF (Children)	09 Feb 50	65UNTS84	100836
UNICEF (Children)	UK Great Britain	10 Feb 50	65UNTS86	100837
Colombia	UNICEF (Children)	15 Mar 50	65UNTS104	100838
United Arab Rep	UK Great Britain	20 Mar 50	226UNTS287	103123

PARTY ONE	PARTY TWO	DATE	CITATION	NUMBER
Assistance (Cont.)				
Haiti	USA (United States)	28 Sep 50	162UNTS85	102132
Guatemala	WHO (World Health)	28 Nov 50	103UNTS51	101423
El Salvador	USA (United States)	13 Dec 50	166UNTS149	102188
Brazil	USA (United States)	27 Dec 50	147UNTS33	101926
El Salvador	WHO (World Health)	02 Jan 51	103UNTS29	101421
Nicaragua	WHO (World Health)	02 Jan 51	103UNTS107	101428
Honduras	USA (United States)	26 Jan 51	99UNTS49	101370
Honduras	USA (United States)	30 Jan 51	124UNTS63	101667
Nicaragua	USA (United States)	31 Jan 51	150UNTS3	101960
Nicaragua	USA (United States)	31 Jan 51	160UNTS121	102105
Costa Rica	USA (United States)	13 Feb 51	141UNTS169	101914
Lebanon	USA (United States)	24 Feb 51	223UNTS121	103060
Panama	USA (United States)	26 Feb 51	160UNTS153	102106
USA (United States)	Uruguay	07 Mar 51	165UNTS113	102173
Multilateral		20 Mar 51	82UNTS172	101091
Costa Rica	WHO (World Health)	13 Apr 51	103UNTS3	101419
Brazil	USA (United States)	29 Jun 51	184UNTS303	102455
Multilateral		01 Aug 51	107UNTS19	101464
Iran	UNICEF (Children)	02 Aug 51	247UNTS11	103457
India	United Nations	14 Aug 51	98UNTS115	101359
UNICEF (Children)	Turkey	05 Sep 51	193UNTS55	102610
Costa Rica	USA (United States)	11 Sep 51	234UNTS255	103288
UNICEF (Children)	UK Great Britain	02 Oct 51	104UNTS301	101448
WHO (World Health)	Thailand	04 Oct 51	109UNTS77	101492
India	WHO (World Health)	11 Oct 51	118UNTS27	101594
Taiwan	WHO (World Health)	25 Oct 51	126UNTS77	101683
Panama	WHO (World Health)	09 Nov 51	118UNTS43	101595
Iraq	UNICEF (Children)	10 Dec 51	126UNTS57	101682
Guatemala	WHO (World Health)	17 Dec 51	120UNTS133	101619
Guatemala	WHO (World Health)	29 Dec 51	124UNTS89	101668
Costa Rica	WHO (World Health)	23 Jan 52	135UNTS265	101826
UNICEF (Children)	UK Great Britain	04 Feb 52	120UNTS147	101620
Dominican Republic	UNICEF (Children)	15 Feb 52	121UNTS43	101625
Pakistan	WHO (World Health)	21 Feb 52	131UNTS221	101742
Ceylon (Sri Lanka)	WHO (World Health)	04 Mar 52	128UNTS281	200437
Taiwan	WHO (World Health)	07 Mar 52	128UNTS233	101723
Iraq	USA (United States)	18 Mar 52	223UNTS131	103061
India	WHO (World Health)	02 Apr 52	131UNTS227	101743
Libya	UNICEF (Children)	05 Apr 52	133UNTS287	200441
Peru	USA (United States)	09 Apr 52	184UNTS295	102454
Liberia	UNICEF (Children)	17 Apr 52	133UNTS3	101773
Libya	USA (United States)	20 May 52	178UNTS307	102346
Libya	USA (United States)	20 May 52	178UNTS155	102339
Iraq	USA (United States)	21 May 52	205UNTS25	102767
Iraq	USA (United States)	21 May 52	205UNTS33	102768
Iraq	USA (United States)	21 May 52	206UNTS3	102782
Iraq	USA (United States)	21 May 52	212UNTS183	102870
Ecuador	USA (United States)	29 May 52	185UNTS203	102471
India	WHO (World Health)	04 Jun 52	135UNTS279	101827
Iraq	USA (United States)	09 Jun 52	212UNTS193	102871
Burma	WHO (World Health)	09 Jun 52	134UNTS273	101806
Belgium	UNICEF (Children)	17 Jun 52	171UNTS249	102228
Ethiopia	USA (United States)	18 Jun 52	181UNTS207	102410
India	WHO (World Health)	19 Jun 52	134UNTS307	101809
Ethiopia	USA (United States)	24 Jun 52	181UNTS215	102411
Lebanon	USA (United States)	26 Jun 52	181UNTS187	102409
Norway	USA (United States)	27 Jun 52	184UNTS271	102452
Chile	USA (United States)	30 Jun 52	199UNTS241	102688
Brazil	USA (United States)	30 Jun 52	185UNTS79	102460
Jordan	UNICEF (Children)	08 Jul 52	173UNTS353	200503
UNICEF (Children)	Syria	10 Jul 52	136UNTS17	101830
UNICEF (Children)	UK Great Britain	25 Jul 52	135UNTS37	101812
Panama	USA (United States)	08 Aug 52	181UNTS257	102415
Laos	UNICEF (Children)	15 Aug 52	161UNTS323	200491
Iraq	USA (United States)	18 Aug 52	184UNTS131	102444

PARTY ONE	PARTY TWO	DATE	CITATION	NUMBER
Assistance (Cont.)				
Multilateral		21 Aug 52	141UNTS129	101912
UNICEF (Children)	Vietnam, South	29 Aug 52	161UNTS335	200492
USA (United States)	Venezuela	29 Sep 52	186UNTS23	102479
Iraq	USA (United States)	23 Oct 52	212UNTS201	102872
Burma	USA (United States)	24 Oct 52	222UNTS55	103022
Chile	WHO (World Health)	24 Oct 52	151UNTS339	102004
Chile	WHO (World Health)	04 Nov 52	150UNTS119	101966
Ethiopia	USA (United States)	07 Nov 52	184UNTS285	102453
Saudi Arabia	USA (United States)	10 Nov 52	181UNTS307	102419
Saudi Arabia	USA (United States)	10 Nov 52	181UNTS225	102412
Saudi Arabia	USA (United States)	10 Nov 52	181UNTS295	102418
Saudi Arabia	USA (United States)	10 Nov 52	181UNTS235	102413
Ceylon (Sri Lanka)	WHO (World Health)	21 Nov 52	161UNTS315	200490
Japan	WHO (World Health)	26 Nov 52	204UNTS301	200521
India	WHO (World Health)	11 Dec 52	158UNTS391	102073
Saudi Arabia	USA (United States)	15 Dec 52	185UNTS55	102458
Saudi Arabia	USA (United States)	15 Dec 52	185UNTS67	102459
UNICEF (Children)	UK Great Britain	16 Dec 52	151UNTS359	102005
United Arab Rep	USA (United States)	12 Mar 53	204UNTS3	102747
Japan	USA (United States)	18 Mar 53	212UNTS149	102867
United Arab Rep	USA (United States)	19 Mar 53	215UNTS17	102909
Netherlands	United Nations	09 Apr 53	163UNTS89	102143
Ethiopia	UNICEF (Children)	27 Apr 53	213UNTS169	102885
El Salvador	USA (United States)	14 May 53	234UNTS71	103273
United Arab Rep	USA (United States)	21 May 53	204UNTS29	102748
Brazil	USA (United States)	30 May 53	460UNTS89	106633
Colombia	USA (United States)	09 Jun 53	213UNTS3	102877
United Arab Rep	USA (United States)	18 Jun 53	215UNTS45	102910
Liberia	USA (United States)	23 Jun 53	213UNTS37	102879
Ethiopia	USA (United States)	25 Jun 53	212UNTS175	102869
Brazil	USA (United States)	26 Jun 53	336UNTS241	104808
Chile	USA (United States)	27 Jun 53	229UNTS193	103167
Chile	USA (United States)	27 Jun 53	229UNTS53	103160
Saudi Arabia	USA (United States)	29 Jun 53	206UNTS23	102784
Nicaragua	USA (United States)	30 Jun 53	215UNTS133	102917
Ethiopia	USA (United States)	30 Jun 53	212UNTS135	102865
UN Relief Palestin	United Arab Rep	30 Jun 53	190UNTS3	102554
UNICEF (Children)	UK Great Britain	07 Oct 53	180UNTS59	102375
UN Relief Palestin	United Arab Rep	14 Oct 53	190UNTS13	102555
Bolivia	USA (United States)	06 Nov 53	222UNTS41	103021
Japan	UNICEF (Children)	21 Nov 53	183UNTS297	200507
Chile	USA (United States)	30 Dec 53	236UNTS41	103315
Taiwan	United Nations	05 Feb 54	186UNTS85	102485
Japan	USA (United States)	08 Mar 54	232UNTS267	103241
United Nations	Vietnam, South	24 Mar 54	188UNTS345	200514
Mexico	USA (United States)	06 Apr 54	236UNTS69	103317
Peru	USA (United States)	13 Apr 54	236UNTS87	103318
UNICEF (Children)	Spain	07 May 54	190UNTS357	200515
Norway	USA (United States)	07 May 54	231UNTS157	103215
Mexico	UNICEF (Children)	20 May 54	192UNTS3	102591
Haiti	USA (United States)	28 May 54	233UNTS281	103267
Ethiopia	USA (United States)	01 Jun 54	232UNTS311	103245
Mexico	USA (United States)	07 Jun 54	234UNTS11	103269
Ethiopia	USA (United States)	12 Jun 54	234UNTS25	103270
Italy	USA (United States)	28 Jun 54	237UNTS121	103340
Chile	USA (United States)	28 Jun 54	233UNTS3	103246
Costa Rica	USA (United States)	30 Jun 54	235UNTS35	103294
Ecuador	USA (United States)	30 Jun 54	236UNTS163	103323
UK Great Britain	USA (United States)	12 Jul 54	204UNTS123	102753
United Arab Rep	USA (United States)	06 Nov 54	237UNTS183	103344
Netherlands	UNICEF (Children)	31 Dec 54	202UNTS135	102729
Mexico	USA (United States)	09 Mar 55	263UNTS247	103776
Japan	USA (United States)	07 Apr 55	263UNTS285	103778
Netherlands	USA (United States)	29 Apr 55	251UNTS357	103553
Canada	USA (United States)	15 Jun 55	235UNTS201	103302

PARTY ONE	PARTY TWO	DATE	CITATION	NUMBER
Assistance (Cont.)				
Libya	WHO (World Health)	05 Jul 55	219UNTS305	200530
USA (United States)	Yugoslavia	30 Sep 55	269UNTS89	103877
Italy	Lebanon	04 Nov 55	267UNTS147	103840
Guatemala	UNICEF (Children)	22 Nov 55	221UNTS305	103012
Multilateral		13 Dec 55	407UNTS8	105857
Japan	USA (United States)	10 Feb 56	275UNTS181	103981
Japan	USA (United States)	10 Feb 56	275UNTS157	103980
Ethiopia	WHO (World Health)	17 Feb 56	243UNTS91	103448
USA (United States)	Uruguay	23 Mar 56	376UNTS311	105386
Colombia	USA (United States)	27 Mar 56	273UNTS235	103954
Cambodia	UNICEF (Children)	28 Apr 56	136UNTS341	200446
Multilateral		10 May 56	243UNTS103	103449
Italy	UNICEF (Children)	28 May 56	243UNTS43	103445
Multilateral		12 Jun 56	243UNTS187	103453
Cambodia	UNICEF (Children)	25 Jun 56	249UNTS153	103505
Lebanon	UNICEF (Children)	03 Jul 56	324UNTS145	104683
UNICEF (Children)	Sudan	07 Aug 56	248UNTS307	200542
India	USA (United States)	29 Aug 56	278UNTS25	104019
UNESCO (Educ/Cult)	Tunisia	03 Jan 57	257UNTS21	103645
Tunisia	USA (United States)	28 Jun 57	289UNTS301	104226
Multilateral		30 Jun 57	286UNTS171	104165
Morocco	UNICEF (Children)	31 Jul 57	282UNTS99	104095
USA (United States)	Venezuela	24 Sep 57	293UNTS307	104298
Argentina	UNICEF (Children)	19 Nov 57	300UNTS229	104338
Multilateral		06 Jan 58	304UNTS227	104399
Italy	USA (United States)	08 May 58	316UNTS177	104584
Ceylon (Sri Lanka)	Sweden	22 May 58	428UNTS65	106168
Jordan	UNICEF (Children)	09 Aug 58	309UNTS297	104478
Ghana	UNICEF (Children)	12 Aug 58	309UNTS103	104469
Cambodia	Japan	02 Mar 59	341UNTS163	104882
Germany, West	USA (United States)	05 May 59	355UNTS307	105083
Fed of Malaya	USA (United States)	22 May 59	346UNTS263	104985
Italy	USA (United States)	30 Jul 59	355UNTS393	105088
Guinea	UN Special Fund	02 Dec 59	345UNTS215	104969
Cuba	UNICEF (Children)	11 Feb 60	349UNTS277	105014
Ecuador	USA (United States)	24 Feb 60	371UNTS55	105270
Italy	USA (United States)	19 Jul 60	389UNTS237	105595
United Arab Rep	USSR (Soviet Union)	27 Aug 60	399UNTS37	105733
Multilateral		19 Sep 60	444UNTS259	106371
UNICEF (Children)	Upper Volta	15 Nov 60	402UNTS33	105776
Mali	UNICEF (Children)	17 Nov 60	402UNTS23	105775
Nepal	UNICEF (Children)	12 Dec 60	382UNTS273	105488
Korea, South	USA (United States)	08 Feb 61	405UNTS37	105821
Guinea	WHO (World Health)	11 Feb 61	394UNTS173	105677
Cyprus	UNICEF (Children)	19 Apr 61	394UNTS185	105678
USA (United States)	Upper Volta	01 Jun 61	410UNTS223	105906
Cyprus	USA (United States)	29 Jun 61	411UNTS56	105914
UNICEF (Children)	Saudi Arabia	04 Jul 61	413UNTS122	105947
Cameroon	UNICEF (Children)	12 Aug 61	402UNTS235	105788
Central Afri Rep	UNICEF (Children)	21 Aug 61	413UNTS48	105939
Poland	UNICEF (Children)	24 Aug 61	406UNTS95	105841
Chad	UNICEF (Children)	26 Aug 61	422UNTS231	106077
Austria	USA (United States)	03 Oct 61	426UNTS187	106137
Gabon	UNICEF (Children)	02 Nov 61	422UNTS241	106078
Malagasy	UNICEF (Children)	16 Nov 61	422UNTS251	106079
Ivory Coast	UNICEF (Children)	10 Jan 62	422UNTS261	106080
UNICEF (Children)	Yemen	31 Jan 62	422UNTS271	106081
Cyprus	USA (United States)	02 Mar 62	445UNTS189	106386
United Nations	Saudi Arabia	16 Mar 62	456UNTS379	106566
UNICEF (Children)	Somalia	01 Apr 62	431UNTS75	106211
Congo (Brazzaville)	UNICEF (Children)	09 Apr 62	431UNTS65	106210
UNICEF (Children)	Sierra Leone	11 Apr 62	431UNTS55	106209
Brazil	USA (United States)	13 Apr 62	445UNTS227	106391
Greece	United Nations	18 May 62	429UNTS61	106190
United Nations	Tanganyika	01 Jun 62	479UNTS3	106944

PARTY ONE	PARTY TWO	DATE	CITATION	NUMBER
Assistance (Cont.)				
UK Great Britain	USA (United States)	15 Aug 62	580UNTS189	108421
Cameroon	USA (United States)	10 Sep 62	461UNTS177	106662
Multilateral		11 Sep 62	455UNTS402	106553
Algeria	France	24 Sep 62	0UNTS0	109507
Japan	UN Special Fund	31 Oct 62	444UNTS171	106368
Algeria	UNICEF (Children)	20 Nov 62	453UNTS151	106522
Burundi	United Nations	29 Dec 62	450UNTS279	106474
Mauritania	UNICEF (Children)	19 Jan 63	452UNTS271	106514
New Zealand	Western Samoa	24 Jan 63	499UNTS21	107290
UNICEF (Children)	Tanganyika	25 Jan 63	453UNTS249	106528
Mali	United Nations	09 May 63	463UNTS147	106699
Multilateral		24 May 63	470UNTS208	106810
United Nations	United Arab Rep	27 Aug 63	474UNTS221	106884
Brazil	Germany, West	30 Nov 63	0UNTS0	109421
Israel	Philippines	16 Mar 64	550UNTS269	108021
Indonesia	Netherlands	03 Apr 64	566UNTS45	108239
Morocco	UNESCO (Educ/Cult)	13 May 64	0UNTS0	109220
Chad	France	19 May 64	0UNTS0	109441
Belgium	Tunisia	15 Jul 64	560UNTS65	108169
Pakistan	IBRD (World Bank)	26 Aug 64	632UNTS201	109023
Israel	Turkey	13 Nov 64	550UNTS303	108025
Uganda	USA (United States)	16 Nov 64	586UNTS143	108501
Denmark	Pakistan	12 Dec 64	636UNTS313	109107
Multilateral		15 Dec 64	522UNTS20	107533
WMO (Meteorology)	UK Great Britain	16 Dec 64	548UNTS57	107969
Germany, West	Thailand	23 Dec 64	525UNTS193	107591
IAEA (Atom Energy)	United Arab Rep	14 Jan 65	603UNTS45	108723
Colombia	Israel	15 Jan 65	581UNTS173	108441
Peru	IBRD (World Bank)	15 Mar 65	632UNTS209	109024
Multilateral		02 Jun 65	551UNTS2	108030
Netherlands	Senegal	12 Jun 65	602UNTS231	108715
Multilateral		05 Jul 65	563UNTS104	108207
Cameroon	Netherlands	06 Jul 65	571UNTS63	108299
UK Great Britain	USA (United States)	09 Aug 65	580UNTS181	108420
UK Great Britain	USA (United States)	10 Nov 65	580UNTS197	108422
Denmark	Zambia	12 Dec 65	574UNTS21	108339
Denmark	Syria	28 Dec 65	588UNTS163	108523
Iran	USSR (Soviet Union)	13 Jan 66	633UNTS123	109037
Netherlands	Philippines	02 Mar 66	631UNTS325	109002
Algeria	France	08 Apr 66	0UNTS0	109508
Maldive Islands	WHO (World Health)	23 May 66	566UNTS19	108237
Bulgaria	UN Special Fund	26 May 66	563UNTS71	108205
Netherlands	Tunisia	08 Jul 66	591UNTS235	108560
Colombia	Netherlands	19 Jul 66	591UNTS201	108558
Multilateral		06 Aug 66	570UNTS178	108294
Multilateral		23 Sep 66	573UNTS148	108328
Botswana	United Nations	30 Sep 66	576UNTS17	108362
Chile	UK Great Britain	07 Oct 66	603UNTS167	108733
Netherlands	Nigeria	18 Oct 66	603UNTS53	108724
Malawi	UK Great Britain	21 Nov 66	637UNTS0	109126
Afghanistan	IBRD (World Bank)	22 Nov 66	632UNTS171	109019
France	Niger	25 Feb 67	0UNTS0	109261
Barbados	UN Special Fund	03 Mar 67	594UNTS91	108596
Nicaragua	IBRD (World Bank)	13 Mar 67	632UNTS177	109020
Multilateral		17 Mar 67	594UNTS105	108598
Netherlands	Vietnam, South	24 Mar 67	610UNTS0	108834
Multilateral		19 Apr 67	595UNTS120	108617
Romania	Somalia	20 Apr 67	642UNTS155	109171
Congo (Brazzaville)	IBRD (World Bank)	10 May 67	632UNTS185	109021
Iran	IAEA (Atom Energy)	10 May 67	614UNTS93	108865
IBRD (World Bank)	Turkey	11 May 67	632UNTS193	109022
Multilateral		20 Jun 67	0UNTS0	109290
Multilateral		21 Jun 67	598UNTS2	108653
IAEA (Atom Energy)	Spain	23 Jun 67	614UNTS169	108870
Mexico	IAEA (Atom Energy)	23 Aug 67	614UNTS133	108868

PARTY ONE	PARTY TWO	DATE	CITATION	NUMBER
Assistance (Cont.)				
Ceylon (Sri Lanka)	IBRD (World Bank)	24 Aug 67	632UNTS217	109025
Multilateral		22 Sep 67	0UNTS0	109258
Denmark	Zambia	17 Oct 67	620UNTS239	108960
Denmark	Pakistan	21 Oct 67	632UNTS105	109012
Multilateral		27 Oct 67	608UNTS37	108811
Lesotho	WHO (World Health)	07 Nov 67	632UNTS143	109016
Multilateral		14 Nov 67	614UNTS2	108860
Australia	UNICEF (Children)	21 Dec 67	614UNTS83	108864
Mauritius	UK Great Britain	12 Mar 68	0UNTS0	109268
Mauritius	UK Great Britain	12 Mar 68	0UNTS0	109269
Germany, West	Thailand	29 Mar 68	637UNTS0	109122
Denmark	Morocco	22 Apr 68	0UNTS0	109218
Korea, South	Netherlands	16 May 68	0UNTS0	109260
Congo (Zaire)	Denmark	25 May 68	0UNTS0	109289
State/IGO Group	Sierra Leone	29 May 68	637UNTS0	109120
Denmark	India	10 Jun 68	0UNTS0	109219
Botswana	UNICEF (Children)	25 Jun 68	639UNTS61	109144
UK Great Britain	USA (United States)	25 Jun 68	0UNTS0	109271
Nigeria	United Nations	02 Jul 68	639UNTS81	109146
Denmark	Uganda	03 Jul 68	0UNTS0	109466
Denmark	Uganda	03 Jul 68	0UNTS0	109467
Guyana	WHO (World Health)	03 Jul 68	642UNTS13	109161
Inter-Am Devel Bnk	UN Special Fund	16 Jul 68	640UNTS305	200640
Denmark	Malawi	03 Sep 68	0UNTS0	109414
Multilateral		28 Sep 68	0UNTS0	109296
Denmark	Thailand	16 Oct 68	0UNTS0	109463
UN Special Fund	Southern Yemen	04 Apr 69	0UNTS0	109456
Mutual exchange of technical knowledge				
Peru	USA (United States)	09 Apr 52	184UNTS295	102454
Multilateral		25 May 55	264UNTS117	103791
Multilateral		21 Jun 60	418UNTS109	106019
Special projects				
Panama	USA (United States)	23 Mar 40	124UNTS195	200420
Brazil	Paraguay	14 Jun 41	54UNTS259	200198
Brazil	USA (United States)	03 Mar 42	105UNTS91	200324
Honduras	USA (United States)	08 May 42	166UNTS351	200498
Nicaragua	USA (United States)	27 Oct 42	99UNTS287	200283
Mexico	USA (United States)	10 Nov 42	66UNTS307	200219
Mexico	USA (United States)	18 Nov 42	120UNTS183	200392
Brazil	USA (United States)	10 Feb 43	102UNTS217	200304
Panama	USA (United States)	07 Jun 43	21UNTS269	200128
Multilateral		15 Jan 44	161UNTS281	200489
Canada	USA (United States)	05 Aug 44	121UNTS299	200408
Bolivia	USA (United States)	07 Sep 44	162UNTS315	200494
United Arab Rep	USA (United States)	15 Jun 46	151UNTS135	101988
Mexico	USA (United States)	17 Mar 47	167UNTS30	102200
Hungary	Yugoslavia	11 May 47	130UNTS171	101730
Honduras	USA (United States)	13 May 47	166UNTS159	102189
USA (United States)	Venezuela	30 Jun 47	166UNTS198	102190
USSR (Soviet Union)	Yugoslavia	25 Jul 47	130UNTS315	101732
Bolivia	USA (United States)	03 Nov 47	51UNTS33	100750
USA (United States)	Venezuela	24 Mar 48	44UNTS57	100678
Ecuador	USA (United States)	14 May 48	89UNTS71	101210
Austria	USA (United States)	23 Mar 49	43UNTS127	100667
Panama	USA (United States)	31 Mar 49	55UNTS87	100810
UNICEF (Children)	UK Great Britain	10 Feb 50	65UNTS86	100837
Philippines	USA (United States)	16 Mar 50	89UNTS199	101218
El Salvador	WHO (World Health)	21 Apr 50	103UNTS13	101420
Haiti	WHO (World Health)	27 Jun 50	110UNTS99	101504
Brazil	USA (United States)	16 Aug 50	140UNTS223	101890
WHO (World Health)	Venezuela	11 Sep 50	110UNTS237	101513
Haiti	USA (United States)	28 Sep 50	162UNTS85	102132
Iceland	WHO (World Health)	06 Oct 50	110UNTS127	101506
WHO (World Health)	Turkey	19 Oct 50	110UNTS215	101512

PARTY ONE	PARTY TWO	DATE	CITATION	NUMBER
Special projects (Cont.)				
Iran	USA (United States)	19 Oct 50	92UNTS135	101266
Peru	WHO (World Health)	10 Nov 50	110UNTS187	101510
Nicaragua	WHO (World Health)	10 Nov 50	110UNTS155	101508
El Salvador	USA (United States)	13 Dec 50	166UNTS149	102188
Brazil	USA (United States)	27 Dec 50	147UNTS33	101926
Philippines	WHO (World Health)	28 Dec 50	110UNTS203	101511
Ceylon (Sri Lanka)	ILO (Labor Org)	24 Jan 51	117UNTS355	200380
Nicaragua	USA (United States)	31 Jan 51	160UNTS121	102105
Nicaragua	USA (United States)	31 Jan 51	150UNTS3	101960
Costa Rica	USA (United States)	13 Feb 51	141UNTS169	101914
Paraguay	WHO (World Health)	15 Feb 51	110UNTS171	101509
Panama	USA (United States)	26 Feb 51	160UNTS153	102106
USA (United States)	Uruguay	07 Mar 51	165UNTS113	102173
Indonesia	WHO (World Health)	28 Mar 51	103UNTS71	101425
Jordan	WHO (World Health)	03 Apr 51	110UNTS297	200367
Belgium	UK Great Britain	06 Apr 51	110UNTS3	101496
Honduras	WHO (World Health)	20 Apr 51	110UNTS111	101505
Mexico	WHO (World Health)	30 Apr 51	103UNTS95	101427
Colombia	WHO (World Health)	04 May 51	110UNTS83	101503
Cambodia	WHO (World Health)	31 May 51	102UNTS279	200307
Multilateral		01 Jun 51	118UNTS57	101596
Liberia	WHO (World Health)	11 Jun 51	103UNTS83	101426
WHO (World Health)	Uruguay	11 Jun 51	128UNTS251	101724
Burma	WHO (World Health)	13 Jun 51	117UNTS115	101588
Iraq	WHO (World Health)	01 Jul 51	110UNTS139	101507
Burma	WHO (World Health)	09 Jul 51	107UNTS9	101463
Burma	WHO (World Health)	17 Jul 51	102UNTS127	101415
El Salvador	USA (United States)	19 Jul 51	140UNTS259	101892
WHO (World Health)	Saudi Arabia	29 Aug 51	110UNTS277	101516
WHO (World Health)	Vietnam, South	21 Sep 51	107UNTS63	200352
Pakistan	WHO (World Health)	07 Oct 51	126UNTS101	101684
Ecuador	WHO (World Health)	16 Oct 51	110UNTS263	101515
India	WHO (World Health)	16 Oct 51	109UNTS49	101490
Mexico	WHO (World Health)	17 Dec 51	124UNTS121	101670
India	WHO (World Health)	20 Dec 51	124UNTS109	101669
Austria	WHO (World Health)	10 Jan 52	131UNTS295	200438
WHO (World Health)	UK Great Britain	07 Feb 52	121UNTS75	101627
Jordan	USA (United States)	12 Feb 52	168UNTS25	102211
Multilateral		18 Feb 52	126UNTS319	200434
Ceylon (Sri Lanka)	WHO (World Health)	04 Mar 52	128UNTS281	200437
Taiwan	WHO (World Health)	07 Mar 52	128UNTS233	101723
Honduras	USA (United States)	07 Mar 52	233UNTS151	103260
United Nations	Yugoslavia	10 Apr 52	141UNTS89	101908
India	WHO (World Health)	17 Apr 52	131UNTS241	101744
India	WHO (World Health)	19 Apr 52	131UNTS253	101745
Norway	WHO (World Health)	09 May 52	131UNTS281	101747
Multilateral		22 May 52	131UNTS115	101739
Burma	WHO (World Health)	09 Jun 52	134UNTS273	101806
Australia	FAO (Food Agri)	07 Jul 52	184UNTS209	102449
Chile	WHO (World Health)	11 Jul 52	137UNTS27	101846
India	WHO (World Health)	16 Jul 52	135UNTS291	101828
Ethiopia	USA (United States)	07 Nov 52	184UNTS285	102453
India	WHO (World Health)	11 Dec 52	158UNTS391	102073
India	WHO (World Health)	11 Feb 53	163UNTS43	102140
United Nations	Sweden	11 Feb 53	160UNTS3	102096
Multilateral		26 Feb 53	161UNTS31	102120
France	WHO (World Health)	02 Apr 53	174UNTS83	102279
Ethiopia	USA (United States)	29 Apr 53	224UNTS121	103073
France	WHO (World Health)	30 Apr 53	174UNTS71	102278
United Arab Rep	USA (United States)	18 Jun 53	215UNTS45	102910
Liberia	USA (United States)	23 Jun 53	213UNTS37	102879
Japan	United Nations	24 Jun 53	167UNTS249	200499
Panama	USA (United States)	26 Jun 53	215UNTS77	102912
Saudi Arabia	USA (United States)	29 Jun 53	206UNTS23	102784
Thailand	USA (United States)	03 Dec 53	213UNTS91	102882

PARTY ONE	PARTY TWO	DATE	CITATION	NUMBER
Special projects (Cont.)				
UK Great Britain	USA (United States)	20 Jan 54	196UNTS95	102619
Brazil	WHO (World Health)	04 Feb 54	233UNTS49	103250
Peru	USA (United States)	13 Apr 54	236UNTS87	103318
Ethiopia	USA (United States)	21 Apr 54	232UNTS299	103244
Nepal	WHO (World Health)	13 May 54	204UNTS311	200522
Multilateral		30 Jun 54	193UNTS67	102611
Taiwan	WHO (World Health)	21 Apr 55	210UNTS71	102835
Pakistan	Sweden	04 Jun 55	228UNTS121	103146
Iran	WHO (World Health)	04 Jul 55	227UNTS65	103131
UK Great Britain	USA (United States)	15 Nov 55	231UNTS185	103219
Burma	USA (United States)	30 Jun 56	281UNTS65	104070
UK Great Britain	USA (United States)	01 Nov 56	264UNTS3	103785
UK Great Britain	USA (United States)	27 Nov 56	282UNTS43	104092
Ethiopia	Sweden	16 Mar 57	304UNTS214	104398
Iraq	USA (United States)	16 Jun 57	284UNTS39	104127
Cambodia	USA (United States)	17 Oct 57	299UNTS203	104313
UK Great Britain	USA (United States)	01 Nov 57	299UNTS167	104312
Ghana	WHO (World Health)	21 Jan 58	307UNTS3	104437
Indonesia	WHO (World Health)	05 Feb 58	307UNTS15	104438
Australia	USA (United States)	25 Feb 58	317UNTS153	104601
Israel	WHO (World Health)	11 Apr 58	307UNTS27	104439
WHO (World Health)	Sudan	21 Jun 58	307UNTS235	104453
Ecuador	USA (United States)	27 Jun 58	317UNTS51	104593
Burma	United Nations	15 Dec 58	319UNTS3	104629
United Nations	Tunisia	23 Dec 58	321UNTS23	104651
Ghana	United Nations	27 Feb 59	324UNTS133	104682
United Nations	Sudan	28 Mar 59	327UNTS95	104719
India	Netherlands	27 Apr 59	506UNTS141	107385
Libya	United Nations	27 Jun 59	336UNTS291	104811
Laos	United Nations	06 Jul 59	337UNTS41	104814
Paraguay	United Nations	01 Aug 59	341UNTS319	104894
Guinea	United Nations	15 Oct 59	344UNTS47	104942
Afghanistan	United Nations	24 Nov 59	397UNTS187	105705
Ceylon (Sri Lanka)	WHO (World Health)	21 Dec 59	349UNTS109	105011
Pakistan	WHO (World Health)	20 Jan 60	351UNTS355	105034
Indonesia	USSR (Soviet Union)	28 Feb 60	392UNTS173	105643
United Nations	Togo	06 May 60	388UNTS53	105571
Cambodia	WHO (World Health)	19 May 60	372UNTS193	105298
Canada	USA (United States)	14 Jun 60	377UNTS365	105413
Ethiopia	United Nations	13 Jul 60	368UNTS143	105239
Jordan	WHO (World Health)	03 Aug 60	381UNTS133	105469
WHO (World Health)	United Arab Rep	03 Aug 60	385UNTS3	105524
Laos	WHO (World Health)	04 Aug 60	373UNTS313	105322
Ghana	USSR (Soviet Union)	04 Aug 60	399UNTS61	105734
WHO (World Health)	Tunisia	04 Aug 60	381UNTS335	105474
WHO (World Health)	Saudi Arabia	06 Sep 60	395UNTS169	105684
Lebanon	WHO (World Health)	08 Sep 60	387UNTS49	105557
Multilateral		19 Sep 60	419UNTS125	106032
UK Great Britain	USA (United States)	14 Oct 60	398UNTS165	105721
Kuwait	United Nations	31 Oct 60	391UNTS295	200581
WHO (World Health)	Upper Volta	15 Nov 60	383UNTS91	105496
Pakistan	United Nations	17 Nov 60	380UNTS277	105460
Argentina	Uruguay	23 Nov 60	0UNTS0	109519
Fed of Malaya	WHO (World Health)	25 Nov 60	387UNTS37	105556
Cambodia	United Nations	30 Nov 60	383UNTS147	105500
WHO (World Health)	Yemen	03 Dec 60	395UNTS187	105685
Dahomey	WHO (World Health)	07 Dec 60	387UNTS277	105567
Congo (Brazzaville)	WHO (World Health)	12 Dec 60	399UNTS105	105737
Bolivia	United Nations	14 Dec 60	382UNTS283	105489
Niger	WHO (World Health)	28 Dec 60	394UNTS195	105679
UK Great Britain	USA (United States)	20 Jan 61	402UNTS153	105783
Korea, South	WHO (World Health)	20 Jan 61	406UNTS269	200589
Ivory Coast	WHO (World Health)	30 Jan 61	395UNTS205	105686
WHO (World Health)	Togo	03 Feb 61	394UNTS207	105680
Chad	WHO (World Health)	03 Feb 61	394UNTS161	105676

PARTY ONE	PARTY TWO	DATE	CITATION	NUMBER
Special projects (Cont.)				
Central Afri Rep	WHO (World Health)	13 Feb 61	394UNTS149	105675
Iraq	United Nations	05 Mar 61	409UNTS56	105878
Kuwait	WHO (World Health)	16 Mar 61	397UNTS315	200588
Mauritania	WHO (World Health)	17 Apr 61	396UNTS301	200587
Gabon	WHO (World Health)	27 Apr 61	397UNTS215	105707
Mali	WHO (World Health)	27 Apr 61	407UNTS66	105860
Australia	USA (United States)	05 Jun 61	409UNTS279	105892
Cyprus	United Nations	15 Jun 61	398UNTS39	105716
Haiti	United Nations	28 Jun 61	399UNTS159	105740
Cyprus	USA (United States)	29 Jun 61	411UNTS56	105914
Morocco	WHO (World Health)	09 Aug 61	412UNTS192	105932
Chile	USA (United States)	12 Aug 61	421UNTS209	106059
WHO (World Health)	Somalia	17 Aug 61	423UNTS111	106088
Lebanon	United Nations	26 Aug 61	406UNTS105	105842
Tunisia	USSR (Soviet Union)	30 Aug 61	437UNTS243	106310
Jordan	United Nations	11 Sep 61	406UNTS255	105855
Iraq	WHO (World Health)	13 Sep 61	419UNTS69	106030
UK Great Britain	USA (United States)	26 Sep 61	421UNTS99	106055
Malagasy	WHO (World Health)	13 Oct 61	421UNTS273	106064
Ceylon (Sri Lanka)	United Nations	04 Dec 61	415UNTS236	105987
Ethiopia	WHO (World Health)	11 Jan 62	423UNTS99	106087
United Nations	Somalia	20 Jan 62	420UNTS133	106044
WHO (World Health)	Sudan	11 Mar 62	432UNTS325	106226
Nigeria	WHO (World Health)	27 Mar 62	429UNTS123	106194
Multilateral		29 Mar 62	507UNTS177	107401
Multilateral		25 May 62	486UNTS103	107075
Libya	WHO (World Health)	16 Jun 62	437UNTS127	106301
WHO (World Health)	Sierra Leone	19 Jun 62	439UNTS151	106327
WHO (World Health)	Senegal	06 Aug 62	435UNTS179	106279
Nigeria	United Nations	07 Aug 62	435UNTS167	106278
WHO (World Health)	Western Samoa	14 Aug 62	437UNTS317	200598
Cameroon	United Nations	29 Aug 62	442UNTS3	106334
Algeria	France	24 Sep 62	0UNTS0	109507
Niger	United Nations	01 Oct 62	439UNTS181	106329
Belgium	Rwanda	13 Oct 62	456UNTS431	106569
Czechoslovakia	Yugoslavia	22 Oct 62	480UNTS267	106974
United Nations	Western Samoa	05 Nov 62	443UNTS297	200599
WHO (World Health)	Syria	18 Nov 62	480UNTS249	106972
Ecuador	United Nations	26 Nov 62	445UNTS3	106372
Rwanda	United Nations	28 Nov 62	450UNTS267	106473
Cameroon	WHO (World Health)	08 Dec 62	451UNTS215	106496
Ivory Coast	United Nations	10 Dec 62	451UNTS269	106498
Algeria	WHO (World Health)	20 Dec 62	463UNTS135	106698
Israel	United Nations	07 Jan 63	450UNTS229	106470
India	USA (United States)	01 Feb 63	473UNTS37	106852
United Nations	South Pacific Com	20 Feb 63	453UNTS333	200600
Mongolia	WHO (World Health)	21 Jun 63	472UNTS373	106848
Burundi	WHO (World Health)	08 Aug 63	477UNTS346	106928
Jamaica	WHO (World Health)	25 Sep 63	481UNTS125	106980
UK Great Britain	USA (United States)	11 Oct 63	483UNTS3	107005
WHO (World Health)	Tanganyika	05 Nov 63	496UNTS193	107252
Finland	IAEA (Atom Energy)	27 Jan 64	501UNTS213	107319
Mexico	USA (United States)	14 Feb 64	524UNTS197	107574
Morocco	UNESCO (Educ/Cult)	13 May 64	0UNTS0	109220
Rwanda	WHO (World Health)	22 Jun 64	514UNTS11	107440
WHO (World Health)	Trinidad/Tobago	23 Jun 64	503UNTS167	107342
Rwanda	WHO (World Health)	23 Jun 64	514UNTS157	107445
Pakistan	IBRD (World Bank)	26 Aug 64	632UNTS201	109023
Germany, West	Thailand	23 Dec 64	525UNTS201	107592
Germany, West	Thailand	23 Dec 64	525UNTS185	107590
Malawi	WHO (World Health)	06 Jan 65	525UNTS165	107588
Malawi	WHO (World Health)	08 Jan 65	524UNTS281	107579
Peru	IBRD (World Bank)	15 Mar 65	632UNTS209	109024
Saudi Arabia	USA (United States)	05 Jun 65	548UNTS285	107984
Netherlands	Senegal	12 Jun 65	602UNTS231	108715
Special projects (Cont.)				
Cameroon	Netherlands	06 Jul 65	571UNTS63	108299
Poland	WHO (World Health)	26 Aug 65	552UNTS3	108047
East Afri Service	United Nations	27 Nov 65	550UNTS375	200616
Argentina	Uruguay	12 Feb 66	0UNTS0	109520
Panama	USA (United States)	15 Feb 66	586UNTS27	108494
WHO (World Health)	Singapore	28 Mar 66	562UNTS59	108195
Multilateral		12 May 66	563UNTS54	108204
Malawi	UK Great Britain	21 Nov 66	637UNTS0	109126
France	Niger	25 Feb 67	0UNTS0	109261
Nicaragua	IBRD (World Bank)	13 Mar 67	632UNTS177	109020
Denmark	Tanzania	05 Apr 67	604UNTS19	108740
Congo (Brazzaville)	IBRD (World Bank)	10 May 67	632UNTS185	109021
IBRD (World Bank)	Turkey	11 May 67	632UNTS193	109022
Argentina	Uruguay	30 May 67	0UNTS0	109521
Ceylon (Sri Lanka)	IBRD (World Bank)	24 Aug 67	632UNTS217	109025
Multilateral		22 Sep 67	0UNTS0	109258
Denmark	Pakistan	21 Oct 67	632UNTS105	109012
Eur Space Research	UK Great Britain	24 Nov 67	638UNTS17	109129
Cyprus	UK Great Britain	11 Mar 68	0UNTS0	109285
Mauritius	UK Great Britain	12 Mar 68	0UNTS0	109270
Mauritius	UK Great Britain	12 Mar 68	0UNTS0	109268
Korea, South	Netherlands	16 May 68	0UNTS0	109260
Denmark	Uganda	03 Jul 68	0UNTS0	109467
Multilateral		28 Sep 68	0UNTS0	109296
Denmark	Thailand	16 Oct 68	0UNTS0	109463
Specific technical assistance				
Ecuador	USA (United States)	24 Feb 42	26UNTS379	200157
Brazil	USA (United States)	14 Mar 42	102UNTS195	200302
Haiti	USA (United States)	07 Apr 42	106UNTS319	200349
El Salvador	USA (United States)	05 May 42	21UNTS215	200124
Nicaragua	USA (United States)	22 May 42	105UNTS141	200328
Bolivia	USA (United States)	16 Jul 42	13UNTS101	200072
Brazil	USA (United States)	17 Jul 42	102UNTS203	200303
Colombia	USA (United States)	23 Oct 42	105UNTS109	200326
Panama	USA (United States)	02 Mar 43	107UNTS55	200351
Chile	USA (United States)	11 May 43	139UNTS295	200456
Mexico	USA (United States)	01 Jul 43	28UNTS407	200164
Dominican Republic	USA (United States)	07 Jul 43	28UNTS419	200165
USA (United States)	Uruguay	01 Nov 43	106UNTS311	200348
Brazil	USA (United States)	25 Nov 43	102UNTS227	200305
Multilateral		15 Jan 44	161UNTS281	200489
Mexico	USA (United States)	27 Jan 44	106UNTS275	200346
Colombia	USA (United States)	19 Feb 46	166UNTS104	102187
USA (United States)	Uruguay	23 Apr 46	160UNTS103	102104
Multilateral		22 Jul 46	14UNTS185	100221
USA (United States)	Venezuela	30 Jun 47	166UNTS198	102190
Paraguay	USA (United States)	30 Jun 48	124UNTS34	101665
Multilateral		29 Nov 48	120UNTS13	101613
Czechoslovakia	Poland	22 Jan 49	85UNTS3	101142
WHO (World Health)	Thailand	12 Aug 49	178UNTS347	102350
Multilateral		17 Apr 50	131UNTS99	101738
El Salvador	WHO (World Health)	21 Apr 50	103UNTS13	101420
Haiti	WHO (World Health)	21 Jun 50	103UNTS61	101424
Peru	WHO (World Health)	26 Sep 50	104UNTS233	101444
Haiti	USA (United States)	28 Sep 50	162UNTS85	102132
Brazil	USA (United States)	27 Dec 50	147UNTS33	101926
Colombia	WHO (World Health)	05 Jan 51	102UNTS139	101417
Nicaragua	USA (United States)	31 Jan 51	160UNTS121	102105
Costa Rica	USA (United States)	13 Feb 51	141UNTS169	101914
Panama	USA (United States)	26 Feb 51	160UNTS153	102106
USA (United States)	Uruguay	07 Mar 51	165UNTS113	102173
Costa Rica	WHO (World Health)	13 Apr 51	103UNTS3	101419
Burma	WHO (World Health)	09 Jul 51	104UNTS175	101439
Burma	WHO (World Health)	09 Jul 51	104UNTS187	101440

PARTY ONE	PARTY TWO	DATE	CITATION	NUMBER
Specific technical assistance (Cont.)				
Burma	WHO (World Health)	09 Jul 51	107UNTS9	101463
Multilateral		01 Aug 51	107UNTS19	101464
Multilateral		04 Aug 51	104UNTS197	101441
Korea, South	WHO (World Health)	19 Sep 51	109UNTS297	200366
WHO (World Health)	Thailand	04 Oct 51	109UNTS77	101492
India	WHO (World Health)	23 Oct 51	109UNTS59	101491
Taiwan	WHO (World Health)	25 Oct 51	126UNTS77	101683
Panama	WHO (World Health)	09 Nov 51	118UNTS43	101595
Guatemala	WHO (World Health)	17 Dec 51	120UNTS133	101619
Guatemala	WHO (World Health)	29 Dec 51	124UNTS89	101668
Costa Rica	WHO (World Health)	23 Jan 52	135UNTS265	101826
Dominican Republic	WHO (World Health)	15 Feb 52	134UNTS291	101808
Taiwan	WHO (World Health)	07 Mar 52	128UNTS233	101723
India	WHO (World Health)	02 Apr 52	131UNTS227	101743
Mexico	WHO (World Health)	28 May 52	134UNTS319	101810
India	WHO (World Health)	04 Jun 52	135UNTS279	101827
Burma	WHO (World Health)	09 Jun 52	134UNTS273	101806
Chile	WHO (World Health)	24 Oct 52	151UNTS339	102004
Chile	WHO (World Health)	04 Nov 52	150UNTS119	101966
Ethiopia	USA (United States)	05 Nov 52	184UNTS139	102445
Ceylon (Sri Lanka)	WHO (World Health)	21 Nov 52	161UNTS315	200490
India	WHO (World Health)	11 Dec 52	158UNTS391	102073
United Arab Rep	USA (United States)	18 Jun 53	215UNTS45	102910
Czechoslovakia	Yugoslavia	16 Jun 56	552UNTS325	108064
Greece	Yugoslavia	11 Sep 56	552UNTS311	108063
USA (United States)	USSR (Soviet Union)	08 Mar 62	460UNTS3	106630
USA (United States)	USSR (Soviet Union)	22 Feb 64	526UNTS131	107605
Indonesia	Netherlands	03 Apr 64	566UNTS45	108239
Ecuador	Netherlands	14 Jan 65	551UNTS129	108038
East Afri Service	United Nations	27 Nov 65	550UNTS375	200616
Technical cooperation				
Colombia	USA (United States)	23 Oct 42	105UNTS109	200326
Colombia	WHO (World Health)	05 Jan 51	102UNTS139	101417
Panama	USA (United States)	26 Feb 51	160UNTS153	102106
USA (United States)	Venezuela	07 Jun 51	141UNTS273	101918
India	WHO (World Health)	11 Dec 52	158UNTS391	102073
Turkey	USA (United States)	12 Nov 56	282UNTS77	104093
Panama	USA (United States)	11 Dec 61	445UNTS161	106384
Cameroon	Israel	24 Oct 62	449UNTS3	106446
Ecuador	Netherlands	14 Jan 65	551UNTS129	108038
Technical education				
Mexico	USA (United States)	27 Jan 44	106UNTS275	200346
Canada	USA (United States)	06 Dec 46	149UNTS3	101945
Multilateral		08 Apr 50	66UNTS285	100860
IAEA (Atom Energy)	Yugoslavia	07 Dec 63	501UNTS273	107322
General aid				
France	USA (United States)	25 Sep 43	76UNTS183	200245
Turkey	USA (United States)	23 Feb 45	121UNTS165	200398
Netherlands	UK Great Britain	20 Dec 45	4UNTS303	100053
Greece	USA (United States)	20 Jun 47	7UNTS267	100105
Greece	USA (United States)	08 Jul 47	16UNTS157	100256
Turkey	USA (United States)	12 Jul 47	7UNTS299	100106
Taiwan	USA (United States)	27 Oct 47	12UNTS11	100178
Australia	Poland	03 Jun 48	16UNTS189	100258
Australia	Hungary	01 Jul 48	22UNTS3	100325
Australia	Italy	08 Jul 48	22UNTS11	100326
Australia	Yugoslavia	09 Jul 48	22UNTS17	100327
Australia	Austria	19 Jul 48	22UNTS25	100328
Korea, South	USA (United States)	10 Dec 48	55UNTS157	100813
Chile	UNICEF (Children)	03 Mar 50	126UNTS119	101685
Multilateral		09 Jan 51	197UNTS341	102647
Jordan	UK Great Britain	01 May 51	117UNTS19	101582
Iran	UNICEF (Children)	02 Aug 51	247UNTS11	103457
UNICEF (Children)	UK Great Britain	02 Oct 51	104UNTS301	101448

PARTY ONE	PARTY TWO	DATE	CITATION	NUMBER
General aid (Cont.)				
Panama	USA (United States)	23 Oct 51	140UNTS3	101880
Iraq	UNICEF (Children)	10 Dec 51	126UNTS57	101682
Libya	UK Great Britain	13 Dec 51	123UNTS167	101658
Libya	UNICEF (Children)	05 Apr 52	133UNTS287	200441
Liberia	UNICEF (Children)	17 Apr 52	133UNTS3	101773
Belgium	UNICEF (Children)	17 Jun 52	171UNTS249	102228
Jordan	UNICEF (Children)	08 Jul 52	173UNTS353	200503
UNICEF (Children)	Syria	10 Jul 52	136UNTS17	101830
UNICEF (Children)	UK Great Britain	25 Jul 52	135UNTS37	101812
Laos	UNICEF (Children)	15 Aug 52	161UNTS323	200491
UNICEF (Children)	Vietnam, South	29 Aug 52	161UNTS335	200492
UNICEF (Children)	UK Great Britain	16 Dec 52	151UNTS359	102005
Jordan	UN Relief Palestin	30 Mar 53	165UNTS317	200495
Netherlands	United Nations	09 Apr 53	163UNTS89	102143
Ethiopia	UNICEF (Children)	27 Apr 53	213UNTS169	102885
UK Great Britain	USA (United States)	24 Jun 53	224UNTS141	103074
Pakistan	USA (United States)	25 Jun 53	205UNTS139	102773
Japan	UNICEF (Children)	21 Nov 53	183UNTS297	200507
Brazil	WHO (World Health)	04 Feb 54	233UNTS49	103250
Japan	USA (United States)	08 Mar 54	232UNTS243	103239
UNICEF (Children)	Spain	07 May 54	190UNTS357	200515
Mexico	UNICEF (Children)	20 May 54	192UNTS3	102591
Jordan	USA (United States)	29 Jun 54	237UNTS111	103339
New Zealand	UNICEF (Children)	26 Aug 54	198UNTS173	102663
Netherlands	UNICEF (Children)	31 Dec 54	202UNTS135	102729
Pakistan	USA (United States)	11 Jan 55	251UNTS111	103537
Ceylon (Sri Lanka)	Germany, West	01 Apr 55	369UNTS57	105251
Ecuador	USA (United States)	07 Oct 55	256UNTS197	103629
Guatemala	UNICEF (Children)	22 Nov 55	221UNTS305	103012
Japan	USA (United States)	10 Feb 56	275UNTS181	103981
Japan	USA (United States)	10 Feb 56	275UNTS157	103980
Cambodia	UNICEF (Children)	28 Apr 56	136UNTS341	200446
Italy	UNICEF (Children)	28 May 56	243UNTS43	103445
Lebanon	UNICEF (Children)	03 Jul 56	324UNTS145	104683
Australia	Netherlands	01 Aug 56	280UNTS3	104047
UNICEF (Children)	Sudan	07 Aug 56	248UNTS307	200542
UNESCO (Educ/Cult)	UK Great Britain	09 Aug 56	256UNTS139	103624
UNESCO (Educ/Cult)	Tunisia	03 Jan 57	257UNTS21	103645
Australia	UK Great Britain	01 Apr 57	271UNTS235	103918
Tunisia	USA (United States)	28 Jun 57	289UNTS301	104226
Morocco	UNICEF (Children)	31 Jul 57	282UNTS99	104095
Argentina	UNICEF (Children)	19 Nov 57	300UNTS229	104338
Canada	India	20 Feb 58	391UNTS231	105628
Italy	USA (United States)	08 May 58	316UNTS177	104584
Ecuador	USA (United States)	27 Jun 58	317UNTS51	104593
Ghana	UNICEF (Children)	12 Aug 58	309UNTS103	104469
Australia	Germany, West	27 Aug 58	320UNTS303	104649
Canada	India	22 Oct 58	392UNTS21	105635
Canada	Ceylon (Sri Lanka)	05 Nov 58	391UNTS225	105627
Italy	USA (United States)	30 Jul 59	355UNTS393	105088
Guinea	UN Special Fund	02 Dec 59	345UNTS215	104969
Cuba	UNICEF (Children)	11 Feb 60	349UNTS277	105014
Italy	USA (United States)	19 Jul 60	389UNTS237	105595
Cyprus	UK Great Britain	16 Aug 60	382UNTS231	105484
Congo (Zaire)	United Nations	23 Aug 60	373UNTS327	200576
UNICEF (Children)	Upper Volta	15 Nov 60	402UNTS33	105776
Mali	UNICEF (Children)	17 Nov 60	402UNTS23	105775
Nepal	UNICEF (Children)	12 Dec 60	382UNTS273	105488
USA (United States)	Yugoslavia	19 Apr 61	409UNTS163	105883
Cyprus	UNICEF (Children)	19 Apr 61	394UNTS185	105678
UNICEF (Children)	Saudi Arabia	04 Jul 61	413UNTS122	105947
Cameroon	UNICEF (Children)	12 Aug 61	402UNTS235	105788
Central Afri Rep	UNICEF (Children)	21 Aug 61	413UNTS48	105939
Poland	UNICEF (Children)	24 Aug 61	406UNTS95	105841
Chad	UNICEF (Children)	26 Aug 61	422UNTS231	106077

PARTY ONE	PARTY TWO	DATE	CITATION	NUMBER
General aid (Cont.)				
UK Great Britain	USA (United States)	28 Aug 61	434UNTS103	106258
Gabon	UNICEF (Children)	02 Nov 61	422UNTS241	106078
Malagasy	UNICEF (Children)	16 Nov 61	422UNTS251	106079
Ivory Coast	UNICEF (Children)	10 Jan 62	422UNTS261	106080
Cyprus	USA (United States)	15 Jan 62	435UNTS15	106267
UNICEF (Children)	Yemen	31 Jan 62	422UNTS271	106081
UNICEF (Children)	Somalia	01 Apr 62	431UNTS75	106211
Congo (Brazzaville)	UNICEF (Children)	09 Apr 62	431UNTS65	106210
UNICEF (Children)	Sierra Leone	11 Apr 62	431UNTS55	106209
Tunisia	USA (United States)	29 Oct 62	462UNTS201	106679
Algeria	UNICEF (Children)	20 Nov 62	453UNTS151	106522
Laos	USSR (Soviet Union)	01 Dec 62	472UNTS3	106834
Mauritania	UNICEF (Children)	19 Jan 63	452UNTS271	106514
UNICEF (Children)	Tanganyika	25 Jan 63	453UNTS249	106528
Burma	UK Great Britain	02 Apr 63	475UNTS139	106890
Multilateral		02 Apr 63	475UNTS121	106889
Morocco	USA (United States)	29 Dec 64	593UNTS185	108584
New Zealand	Western Samoa	29 Jul 66	598UNTS115	108657
UN Special Fund	Singapore	23 Sep 66	573UNTS115	108326
Lesotho	UN Special Fund	17 Nov 66	580UNTS17	108416
State/IGO Group	Jordan	03 Apr 68	632UNTS66	109009
State/IGO Group	Nigeria	20 Apr 68	636UNTS294	109106
State/IGO Group	Malaysia	10 May 68	636UNTS276	109105
Agricultural commodities				
Multilateral		04 Dec 42	24UNTS247	200150
Dominican Republic	USA (United States)	11 Feb 44	109UNTS251	200363
Multilateral		01 Jan 46	99UNTS131	101375
Greece	UK Great Britain	24 Jan 46	6UNTS45	100067
Romania	Yugoslavia	23 Dec 46	116UNTS33	101567
USSR (Soviet Union)	Yugoslavia	23 Aug 47	116UNTS281	101577
USA (United States)	Yugoslavia	21 Nov 50	93UNTS45	101286
USA (United States)	Yugoslavia	17 Apr 51	162UNTS173	102134
Pakistan	USA (United States)	17 Sep 52	227UNTS77	103132
Denmark	Israel	14 Nov 52	160UNTS279	102113
Ethiopia	USA (United States)	12 Jun 54	234UNTS25	103270
Jordan	USA (United States)	29 Jun 54	237UNTS111	103339
Pakistan	USA (United States)	18 Jan 55	241UNTS53	103423
Germany, West	USA (United States)	18 Feb 55	247UNTS257	103474
Ceylon (Sri Lanka)	Pakistan	23 May 55	286UNTS15	104159
Japan	USA (United States)	31 May 55	241UNTS243	103435
Japan	USA (United States)	31 May 55	241UNTS197	103434
Libya	USA (United States)	18 Jul 55	241UNTS305	103437
Ecuador	USA (United States)	07 Oct 55	256UNTS197	103629
Multilateral		25 Mar 57	294UNTS2	104300
Canada	India	20 Feb 58	391UNTS231	105628
Italy	USA (United States)	07 Mar 58	303UNTS205	104381
India	USA (United States)	23 Jun 58	317UNTS181	104603
Muscat and Oman	UK Great Britain	25 Jul 58	312UNTS347	104524
Canada	Ceylon (Sri Lanka)	05 Nov 58	391UNTS225	105627
USA (United States)	Uruguay	20 Feb 59	341UNTS201	104884
Australia	Thailand	28 Jul 59	339UNTS91	104847
New Zealand	UK Great Britain	12 Aug 59	354UNTS161	105062
New Zealand	Thailand	24 Dec 59	351UNTS197	105023
Denmark	Sweden	04 Jan 60	376UNTS375	105390
Israel	USA (United States)	07 Jan 60	368UNTS181	105241
Finland	USA (United States)	23 Mar 60	371UNTS117	105274
Denmark	UK Great Britain	08 Apr 60	374UNTS233	105337
Canada	Norway	25 Apr 60	470UNTS109	106801
Chile	USA (United States)	02 Jun 60	377UNTS11	105393
USA (United States)	Yugoslavia	03 Jun 60	376UNTS243	105382
Canada	UK Great Britain	05 Aug 60	470UNTS133	106804
Libya	USA (United States)	11 Dec 60	445UNTS125	106381
Korea, South	USA (United States)	08 Feb 61	405UNTS37	105821
UK Great Britain	USA (United States)	28 Aug 61	434UNTS103	106258
Agricultural commodities (Cont.)				
United Arab Rep	USA (United States)	02 Sep 61	421UNTS251	106063
Pakistan	USA (United States)	14 Oct 61	426UNTS237	106141
Greece	USA (United States)	18 Oct 61	426UNTS209	106139
USA (United States)	Yugoslavia	28 Dec 61	434UNTS111	106259
Cyprus	USA (United States)	15 Jan 62	435UNTS15	106267
India	USA (United States)	16 Apr 62	445UNTS257	106393
Taiwan	USA (United States)	16 Apr 62	445UNTS249	106392
Colombia	USA (United States)	15 May 62	445UNTS279	106396
Ceylon (Sri Lanka)	USA (United States)	19 Jul 62	454UNTS31	106538
USA (United States)	Vietnam, South	21 Nov 62	469UNTS101	106786
Australia	Fed of Malaya	26 Nov 62	453UNTS161	106523
Israel	USA (United States)	21 Mar 63	476UNTS131	106907
Burma	UK Great Britain	02 Apr 63	475UNTS139	106890
Multilateral		02 Apr 63	475UNTS121	106889
Denmark	Norway	11 May 63	613UNTS271	108856
Japan	USA (United States)	14 Jun 63	479UNTS165	106951
Denmark	Norway	12 Sep 63	613UNTS289	108857
Iran	USA (United States)	17 Nov 63	530UNTS41	107671
Jordan	IDA (Devel Assoc)	12 Dec 63	492UNTS3	107184
Korea, South	USA (United States)	18 Mar 64	524UNTS263	107578
Guinea	USA (United States)	13 Jun 64	531UNTS263	107708
Kenya	IDA (Devel Assoc)	17 Aug 64	535UNTS79	107776
Morocco	USA (United States)	29 Dec 64	593UNTS185	108584
Denmark	Portugal	20 Feb 65	639UNTS43	109143
Bolivia	USA (United States)	17 Aug 65	587UNTS289	108514
Pakistan	IDA (Devel Assoc)	10 Feb 66	575UNTS89	108355
USA (United States)	Vietnam, South	21 Mar 66	578UNTS165	108394
Paraguay	IDA (Devel Assoc)	04 Apr 66	582UNTS331	108469
Brazil	USA (United States)	23 Apr 66	607UNTS117	108801
Paraguay	USA (United States)	27 Apr 66	578UNTS121	108391
Israel	USA (United States)	06 Jun 66	578UNTS143	108392
Denmark	Norway	23 Dec 66	613UNTS265	108855
Economic assistance				
Canada	USA (United States)	27 Jun 41	103UNTS205	200315
Brazil	USA (United States)	03 Mar 42	105UNTS91	200324
Brazil	USA (United States)	03 Mar 42	105UNTS99	200325
Canada	USA (United States)	30 Nov 42	119UNTS305	200387
Liberia	USA (United States)	08 Jun 43	117UNTS242	200373
France	USA (United States)	28 Feb 45	76UNTS213	200247
South Africa	USA (United States)	17 Apr 45	90UNTS275	200265
Taiwan	USSR (Soviet Union)	14 Aug 45	10UNTS300	200068
Greece	UK Great Britain	24 Jan 46	6UNTS45	100067
Brazil	USA (United States)	05 Apr 46	12UNTS131	100183
Poland	USA (United States)	24 Apr 46	4UNTS155	100042
France	USA (United States)	28 May 46	84UNTS167	101127
France	UK Great Britain	04 Mar 47	9UNTS187	100132
Czechoslovakia	Poland	04 Apr 47	85UNTS62	101146
Hungary	Yugoslavia	11 May 47	130UNTS171	101730
Albania	Yugoslavia	12 Jun 47	111UNTS177	101531
Multilateral		11 Jul 47	218UNTS345	102961
Multilateral		17 Mar 48	19UNTS51	100304
Ceylon (Sri Lanka)	UK Great Britain	30 Apr 48	182UNTS2	102421
Hungary	Poland	13 May 48	25UNTS301	100369
Ireland	USA (United States)	28 Jun 48	24UNTS3	100349
France	USA (United States)	28 Jun 48	19UNTS9	100302
Italy	USA (United States)	28 Jun 48	20UNTS43	100314
Denmark	USA (United States)	29 Jun 48	22UNTS217	100338
Austria	USA (United States)	02 Jul 48	21UNTS29	100323
Belgium	USA (United States)	02 Jul 48	19UNTS127	100309
Greece	USA (United States)	02 Jul 48	23UNTS43	100342
Netherlands	USA (United States)	02 Jul 48	20UNTS91	100315
Norway	USA (United States)	03 Jul 48	20UNTS185	100317
Luxembourg	USA (United States)	03 Jul 48	24UNTS35	100350
Sweden	USA (United States)	03 Jul 48	23UNTS101	100343

PARTY ONE	PARTY TWO	DATE	CITATION	NUMBER
Economic assistance (Cont.)				
Taiwan	USA (United States)	03 Jul 48	17UNTS119	100273
Iceland	USA (United States)	03 Jul 48	20UNTS141	100316
Turkey	USA (United States)	04 Jul 48	24UNTS67	100351
UK Great Britain	USA (United States)	06 Jul 48	22UNTS263	100339
France	USA (United States)	09 Jul 48	24UNTS103	100352
Multilateral		14 Jul 48	23UNTS3	100340
Portugal	USA (United States)	28 Sep 48	29UNTS213	100442
Trieste	USA (United States)	15 Oct 48	29UNTS249	100443
Belgium	Luxembourg	14 Jan 49	36UNTS339	100572
Germany, West	USA (United States)	15 Dec 49	92UNTS269	101277
Indonesia	USA (United States)	24 Mar 50	92UNTS387	101281
Burma	USA (United States)	13 Sep 50	92UNTS361	101280
Thailand	USA (United States)	19 Sep 50	132UNTS199	101761
Haiti	USA (United States)	28 Sep 50	162UNTS85	102132
Indonesia	USA (United States)	16 Oct 50	281UNTS105	104074
Canada	USA (United States)	26 Oct 50	132UNTS247	101764
Paraguay	USA (United States)	27 Nov 50	122UNTS147	101644
Brazil	USA (United States)	19 Dec 50	140UNTS365	101899
Liberia	USA (United States)	22 Dec 50	133UNTS69	101781
Brazil	USA (United States)	27 Dec 50	147UNTS33	101926
Multilateral		06 Mar 51	106UNTS141	101461
USA (United States)	Uruguay	07 Mar 51	165UNTS113	102173
Multilateral		18 Apr 51	261UNTS140	103729
Philippines	USA (United States)	27 Apr 51	174UNTS251	102290
Austria	USA (United States)	15 May 51	139UNTS79	101876
UK Great Britain	USA (United States)	18 Jul 51	117UNTS49	101583
Brazil	USA (United States)	24 Jul 51	134UNTS195	101799
USA (United States)	Vietnam, South	07 Sep 51	174UNTS165	102284
Cambodia	USA (United States)	08 Sep 51	174UNTS115	102282
Laos	USA (United States)	09 Sep 51	174UNTS141	102283
Canada	Pakistan	10 Sep 51	122UNTS21	101632
Canada	India	10 Sep 51	391UNTS237	105629
Multilateral		14 Oct 51	122UNTS3	101631
El Salvador	USA (United States)	23 Oct 51	137UNTS43	101847
Turkey	USA (United States)	15 Nov 51	177UNTS315	102331
Israel	USA (United States)	07 Dec 51	157UNTS53	102046
Libya	UK Great Britain	13 Dec 51	123UNTS167	101658
Jordan	USA (United States)	20 Dec 51	157UNTS69	102048
Germany, West	USA (United States)	28 Dec 51	181UNTS45	102397
Laos	USA (United States)	31 Dec 51	198UNTS243	102668
France	USA (United States)	05 Jan 52	181UNTS177	102408
Indonesia	USA (United States)	05 Jan 52	215UNTS121	102916
USA (United States)	Yugoslavia	08 Jan 52	152UNTS61	102011
Portugal	USA (United States)	08 Jan 52	207UNTS51	102799
UK Great Britain	USA (United States)	08 Jan 52	126UNTS307	101696
Multilateral		11 Feb 52	165UNTS77	102169
Jordan	USA (United States)	12 Feb 52	168UNTS25	102211
Austria	USA (United States)	16 Feb 52	177UNTS299	102329
Philippines	USA (United States)	19 Feb 52	177UNTS307	102330
Norway	USA (United States)	01 Apr 52	177UNTS291	102328
Greece	USA (United States)	23 Apr 52	177UNTS283	102327
Israel	USA (United States)	01 May 52	177UNTS89	102311
Israel	USA (United States)	09 May 52	177UNTS269	102326
Ethiopia	USA (United States)	15 May 52	180UNTS227	102388
Korea, South	USA (United States)	24 May 52	179UNTS23	102353
Brazil	WHO (World Health)	12 Jun 52	151UNTS333	102003
Taiwan	USA (United States)	25 Jun 52	136UNTS229	101837
Lebanon	USA (United States)	26 Jun 52	181UNTS187	102409
Canada	Ceylon (Sri Lanka)	11 Jul 52	391UNTS245	105630
France	USA (United States)	22 Jul 52	181UNTS319	102420
Denmark	USA (United States)	08 Aug 52	181UNTS249	102414
Israel	USA (United States)	08 Aug 52	181UNTS37	102396
USA (United States)	Yugoslavia	15 Aug 52	184UNTS97	102441
USA (United States)	Yugoslavia	11 Oct 52	235UNTS277	103309
Multilateral		17 Oct 52	141UNTS121	101911

PARTY ONE	PARTY TWO	DATE	CITATION	NUMBER
Economic assistance (Cont.)				
Iraq	USA (United States)	23 Oct 52	212UNTS201	102872
Chile	WHO (World Health)	24 Oct 52	151UNTS339	102004
India	WHO (World Health)	11 Dec 52	158UNTS391	102073
Liberia	USA (United States)	15 Dec 52	185UNTS45	102457
UK Great Britain	USA (United States)	25 Feb 53	212UNTS157	102868
Germany, West	UK Great Britain	27 Feb 53	330UNTS217	104747
Germany, West	USA (United States)	27 Feb 53	205UNTS103	102771
Multilateral		27 Feb 53	333UNTS3	104764
Germany, West	USA (United States)	27 Feb 53	224UNTS13	103067
Haiti	USA (United States)	13 Mar 53	212UNTS143	102866
Libya	UK Great Britain	21 Mar 53	172UNTS85	102240
Jordan	UN Relief Palestin	30 Mar 53	165UNTS317	200495
El Salvador	USA (United States)	14 May 53	234UNTS71	103273
Brazil	USA (United States)	30 May 53	460UNTS89	106633
UK Great Britain	USA (United States)	24 Jun 53	224UNTS141	103074
UK Great Britain	USA (United States)	26 Jun 53	183UNTS225	102432
Panama	USA (United States)	26 Jun 53	215UNTS77	102912
Afghanistan	USA (United States)	30 Jun 53	215UNTS3	102908
Spain	USA (United States)	26 Sep 53	207UNTS93	102802
Bolivia	USA (United States)	06 Nov 53	222UNTS41	103021
Israel	USA (United States)	25 Nov 53	219UNTS205	102976
USA (United States)	Yugoslavia	05 Jan 54	234UNTS267	103289
Japan	USA (United States)	08 Mar 54	232UNTS267	103241
USA (United States)	Yugoslavia	16 Apr 54	237UNTS77	103337
Ethiopia	USA (United States)	21 Apr 54	232UNTS299	103244
ECSC (Coal/Steel)	USA (United States)	23 Apr 54	229UNTS229	103170
Panama	USA (United States)	11 May 54	236UNTS107	103319
Jordan	USA (United States)	13 May 54	234UNTS225	103285
Italy	USA (United States)	16 Jun 54	236UNTS149	103322
Jordan	USA (United States)	17 Jun 54	266UNTS137	103828
Lebanon	USA (United States)	18 Jun 54	233UNTS177	103262
Libya	USA (United States)	09 Sep 54	238UNTS217	103365
United Arab Rep	USA (United States)	06 Nov 54	237UNTS183	103344
Korea, South	USA (United States)	17 Nov 54	256UNTS251	103635
Guatemala	USA (United States)	13 Dec 54	237UNTS169	103343
Peru	USA (United States)	31 Dec 54	251UNTS51	103533
USA (United States)	Yugoslavia	09 Feb 55	241UNTS13	103419
USA (United States)	Vietnam, South	07 Mar 55	277UNTS285	104013
Ceylon (Sri Lanka)	Germany, West	01 Apr 55	369UNTS57	105251
Haiti	USA (United States)	27 Apr 55	240UNTS17	103391
Philippines	USA (United States)	27 Apr 55	261UNTS351	103733
USA (United States)	Yugoslavia	12 May 55	251UNTS337	103550
USA (United States)	Yugoslavia	12 May 55	251UNTS343	103551
Libya	USA (United States)	30 May 55	270UNTS43	103890
Burma	Yugoslavia	14 Jun 55	378UNTS93	105419
Canada	USA (United States)	15 Jun 55	235UNTS201	103302
Laos	USA (United States)	08 Jul 55	278UNTS59	104021
Japan	Thailand	09 Jul 55	230UNTS13	103172
Bolivia	USA (United States)	23 Sep 55	256UNTS275	103637
Iceland	USA (United States)	05 Oct 55	256UNTS285	103638
Liberia	USA (United States)	06 Oct 55	275UNTS93	103978
Liberia	USA (United States)	06 Oct 55	275UNTS87	103977
Italy	Lebanon	04 Nov 55	267UNTS147	103840
Multilateral		05 Nov 55	250UNTS201	103524
Multilateral		13 Dec 55	529UNTS141	107660
USSR (Soviet Union)	Yugoslavia	19 Dec 55	378UNTS127	105423
Haiti	USA (United States)	28 Dec 55	240UNTS95	103397
USA (United States)	Yugoslavia	19 Jan 56	240UNTS121	103400
Burma	Israel	05 Mar 56	280UNTS209	104060
Burma	Yugoslavia	07 Mar 56	386UNTS207	105542
Burma	Yugoslavia	07 Mar 56	386UNTS235	105543
Burma	Yugoslavia	07 Mar 56	378UNTS99	105420
Ceylon (Sri Lanka)	USA (United States)	28 Apr 56	274UNTS35	103956
Peru	USA (United States)	08 May 56	278UNTS117	104028
Multilateral		07 Jun 56	381UNTS145	105470

PARTY ONE	PARTY TWO	DATE	CITATION	NUMBER
Economic assistance (Cont.)				
Afghanistan	USA (United States)	23 Jun 56	271UNTS295	103921
Cambodia	UNICEF (Children)	25 Jun 56	249UNTS153	103505
Libya	USA (United States)	27 Jun 56	273UNTS89	103945
Germany, West	Thailand	09 Oct 56	258UNTS143	103676
Romania	Yugoslavia	27 Oct 56	389UNTS55	105592
Luxembourg	USA (United States)	07 Dec 56	265UNTS255	103817
Burma	USA (United States)	21 Mar 57	300UNTS11	104327
Multilateral		25 Mar 57	294UNTS2	104300
Multilateral		25 Mar 57	294UNTS259	104301
Tunisia	USA (United States)	26 Mar 57	283UNTS117	104111
Morocco	USA (United States)	02 Apr 57	288UNTS157	104203
Libya	USA (United States)	04 Apr 57	283UNTS181	104116
Czechoslovakia	Mongolia	08 Apr 57	501UNTS171	107317
Ethiopia	USA (United States)	25 Apr 57	283UNTS205	104118
Jordan	USA (United States)	29 Apr 57	290UNTS111	104230
Iraq	USA (United States)	22 May 57	284UNTS13	104125
Jordan	USA (United States)	27 Jun 57	288UNTS269	104209
Jordan	USA (United States)	29 Jun 57	288UNTS263	104208
Ceylon (Sri Lanka)	China People's Rep	19 Sep 57	337UNTS169	104822
IAEA (Atom Energy)	United Nations	23 Oct 57	281UNTS369	200548
Multilateral		06 Jan 58	304UNTS227	104399
Indonesia	Japan	20 Jan 58	325UNTS13	104691
Multilateral		03 Feb 58	381UNTS165	105471
India	Japan	04 Feb 58	324UNTS215	104687
Poland	USA (United States)	15 Feb 58	307UNTS217	104452
Brazil	Ecuador	05 Mar 58	369UNTS43	105250
Czechoslovakia	Hungary	12 Mar 58	408UNTS178	105870
Sudan	USA (United States)	31 Mar 58	308UNTS105	104458
Saudi Arabia	USA (United States)	01 May 58	315UNTS221	104571
Brazil	Colombia	28 May 58	369UNTS141	105255
Romania	Vietnam, North	30 Jun 58	389UNTS43	105591
Multilateral		28 Jul 58	335UNTS205	104788
Lebanon	USA (United States)	03 Sep 58	336UNTS91	104801
Japan	Laos	15 Oct 58	341UNTS25	104875
Canada	UK Great Britain	18 Oct 58	392UNTS61	105639
Iran	Japan	09 Dec 58	325UNTS221	104701
Taiwan	USA (United States)	24 Dec 58	340UNTS251	104868
USA (United States)	Uruguay	20 Feb 59	341UNTS201	104884
Iraq	USSR (Soviet Union)	16 Mar 59	346UNTS107	104979
Germany, West	USA (United States)	20 Mar 59	341UNTS15	104874
Morocco	UN Special Fund	04 Apr 59	354UNTS347	105069
Italy	United Arab Rep	29 Apr 59	363UNTS91	105202
Ceylon (Sri Lanka)	Yugoslavia	05 May 59	391UNTS101	105618
Japan	Vietnam, South	13 May 59	373UNTS149	105318
Libya	USA (United States)	21 May 59	361UNTS123	105176
Greece	Yugoslavia	18 Jun 59	368UNTS125	105237
Burma	USA (United States)	24 Jun 59	358UNTS91	105127
Ghana	UN Special Fund	12 Aug 59	338UNTS203	104836
Iran	UN Special Fund	06 Oct 59	342UNTS89	104902
Canada	Euratom	06 Oct 59	475UNTS187	106894
Poland	UN Special Fund	15 Oct 59	344UNTS29	104941
India	UN Special Fund	20 Oct 59	344UNTS143	104946
USA (United States)	Yugoslavia	22 Oct 59	360UNTS259	105161
UN Special Fund	Yugoslavia	27 Oct 59	344UNTS159	104947
Ecuador	UN Special Fund	10 Nov 59	345UNTS3	104955
Greece	UN Special Fund	13 Nov 59	345UNTS171	104966
UN Special Fund	Turkey	20 Nov 59	345UNTS105	104963
UN Special Fund	United Arab Rep	25 Nov 59	345UNTS125	104964
Israel	UN Special Fund	01 Dec 59	345UNTS197	104968
Guinea	UN Special Fund	02 Dec 59	345UNTS215	104969
Argentina	UN Special Fund	04 Dec 59	345UNTS263	104972
Czechoslovakia	Ethiopia	11 Dec 59	386UNTS45	105536
Czechoslovakia	Ethiopia	11 Dec 59	386UNTS51	105537
Multilateral		14 Dec 59	368UNTS253	105245
Multilateral		14 Dec 59	422UNTS33	106067

PARTY ONE	PARTY TWO	DATE	CITATION	NUMBER
Economic assistance (Cont.)				
Jordan	UN Special Fund	15 Dec 59	346UNTS3	104974
UN Special Fund	UK Great Britain	07 Jan 60	348UNTS177	105000
Israel	USA (United States)	07 Jan 60	368UNTS181	105241
Peru	UN Special Fund	19 Jan 60	349UNTS83	105010
Chile	UN Special Fund	22 Jan 60	351UNTS115	105020
Colombia	UN Special Fund	04 Feb 60	355UNTS257	105080
Bolivia	UN Special Fund	09 Feb 60	351UNTS203	105024
Afghanistan	UN Special Fund	21 Feb 60	351UNTS93	105019
Pakistan	UN Special Fund	25 Feb 60	351UNTS141	105021
Indonesia	USSR (Soviet Union)	28 Feb 60	392UNTS173	105643
France	UN Special Fund	17 Mar 60	354UNTS119	105059
Chile	USA (United States)	28 Mar 60	401UNTS105	105765
Italy	UN Special Fund	01 Apr 60	354UNTS261	105066
UN Special Fund	Tunisia	12 Apr 60	355UNTS289	105082
Libya	UN Special Fund	19 Apr 60	356UNTS11	105090
UN Special Fund	Sudan	21 Apr 60	356UNTS213	105097
UN Special Fund	Vietnam, South	29 Apr 60	357UNTS311	200567
UN Special Fund	Togo	08 Jun 60	369UNTS401	200574
Iraq	UN Special Fund	19 Jun 60	376UNTS357	105389
Ghana	USSR (Soviet Union)	04 Aug 60	399UNTS61	105734
Cyprus	UK Great Britain	16 Aug 60	382UNTS239	105485
United Arab Rep	USSR (Soviet Union)	27 Aug 60	399UNTS37	105733
Guinea	USA (United States)	30 Sep 60	394UNTS103	105671
Indonesia	UN Special Fund	07 Oct 60	378UNTS141	105424
Liberia	UN Special Fund	11 Oct 60	376UNTS341	105388
UK Great Britain	USA (United States)	14 Oct 60	398UNTS165	105721
El Salvador	UN Special Fund	24 Oct 60	377UNTS171	105400
Nepal	UN Special Fund	17 Nov 60	380UNTS289	105461
Cambodia	UN Special Fund	24 Nov 60	382UNTS255	105487
Multilateral		13 Dec 60	455UNTS204	106544
Honduras	UN Special Fund	20 Dec 60	383UNTS103	105497
Togo	USA (United States)	22 Dec 60	401UNTS33	105760
Iceland	USA (United States)	30 Dec 60	401UNTS43	105761
Burma	UN Special Fund	03 Jan 61	387UNTS219	105564
Mali	USA (United States)	04 Jan 61	405UNTS165	105832
Costa Rica	UN Special Fund	10 Jan 61	389UNTS253	105597
USA (United States)	Yugoslavia	19 Jan 61	402UNTS163	105784
UN Special Fund	Saudi Arabia	19 Jan 61	396UNTS27	105692
Nicaragua	UN Special Fund	20 Jan 61	387UNTS15	105555
Chad	UN Special Fund	23 Jan 61	390UNTS69	105603
UN Special Fund	Somalia	28 Jan 61	388UNTS75	105573
Gabon	UN Special Fund	02 Feb 61	387UNTS289	105568
India	USA (United States)	07 Feb 61	462UNTS57	106671
Nigeria	UN Special Fund	10 Feb 61	390UNTS85	105604
Mexico	UN Special Fund	23 Feb 61	388UNTS151	105576
Cyprus	UN Special Fund	24 Feb 61	389UNTS3	105588
Panama	UN Special Fund	09 Mar 61	396UNTS3	105691
Cuba	UN Special Fund	10 Mar 61	390UNTS35	105601
UK Great Britain	USA (United States)	15 Mar 61	404UNTS207	105811
Austria	USA (United States)	29 Mar 61	459UNTS45	106612
Colombia	USA (United States)	04 Apr 61	405UNTS55	105822
UK Great Britain	USA (United States)	06 Apr 61	404UNTS215	105812
Honduras	USA (United States)	12 Apr 61	413UNTS182	105952
Korea, South	UN Special Fund	21 Apr 61	394UNTS231	200583
Ceylon (Sri Lanka)	UN Special Fund	03 May 61	395UNTS217	105687
Sierra Leone	USA (United States)	05 May 61	409UNTS194	105885
Australia	USA (United States)	09 May 61	409UNTS203	105886
Senegal	USA (United States)	13 May 61	409UNTS232	105888
Ivory Coast	USA (United States)	17 May 61	409UNTS241	105889
Australia	USA (United States)	22 May 61	419UNTS3	106026
Cameroon	USA (United States)	26 May 61	413UNTS195	105953
Niger	USA (United States)	26 May 61	410UNTS213	105905
Dahomey	USA (United States)	27 May 61	445UNTS23	106373
Somalia	USSR (Soviet Union)	02 Jun 61	457UNTS263	106587
Congo (Zaire)	United Nations	12 Jun 61	494UNTS205	107234

PARTY ONE	PARTY TWO	DATE	CITATION	NUMBER
Economic assistance (Cont.)				
Cameroon	UN Special Fund	13 Jun 61	397UNTS297	105713
Ecuador	USA (United States)	17 Jun 61	411UNTS49	105913
Inter-Am Devel Bnk	USA (United States)	19 Jun 61	410UNTS34	105895
Madagascar	USA (United States)	22 Jun 61	413UNTS219	105956
Paraguay	UN Special Fund	22 Jun 61	399UNTS117	105738
UN Special Fund	Upper Volta	26 Jun 61	400UNTS3	105744
Haiti	UN Special Fund	28 Jun 61	399UNTS171	105741
Philippines	UN Special Fund	28 Jun 61	399UNTS141	105739
Indonesia	UK Great Britain	29 Jun 61	443UNTS255	106364
Mali	UN Special Fund	21 Jul 61	401UNTS141	105768
UN Special Fund	Yemen	02 Aug 61	402UNTS43	105777
Ivory Coast	UN Special Fund	29 Aug 61	406UNTS129	105844
UK Great Britain	USA (United States)	08 Sep 61	418UNTS53	106016
Paraguay	USA (United States)	26 Sep 61	461UNTS91	106653
UN Special Fund	Sierra Leone	02 Oct 61	422UNTS131	106073
Mauritania	UN Special Fund	07 Nov 61	412UNTS240	105936
Congo (Brazzaville)	UN Special Fund	09 Nov 61	413UNTS58	105940
UN Special Fund	Venezuela	11 Dec 61	422UNTS149	106074
Panama	USA (United States)	11 Dec 61	445UNTS161	106384
UN Special Fund	Senegal	16 Dec 61	425UNTS97	106121
El Salvador	USA (United States)	19 Dec 61	445UNTS175	106385
Iran	USA (United States)	21 Dec 61	433UNTS269	106249
Costa Rica	USA (United States)	22 Dec 61	460UNTS277	106646
Malagasy	UN Special Fund	05 Jan 62	419UNTS29	106028
Japan	USA (United States)	09 Jan 62	451UNTS97	106488
Dominican Republic	USA (United States)	11 Jan 62	433UNTS133	106236
Paraguay	USA (United States)	16 Jan 62	433UNTS169	106240
Niger	UN Special Fund	26 Feb 62	423UNTS83	106086
Argentina	USA (United States)	16 Mar 62	454UNTS3	106535
Multilateral		23 Mar 62	434UNTS145	106262
Multilateral		29 Mar 62	507UNTS177	107401
Nicaragua	USA (United States)	30 Mar 62	456UNTS241	106559
Brazil	USA (United States)	13 Apr 62	445UNTS227	106391
Ecuador	USA (United States)	17 Apr 62	442UNTS69	106339
UN Special Fund	Uruguay	04 May 62	429UNTS143	106196
Greece	Tunisia	26 May 62	534UNTS163	107761
Dominican Republic	UN Special Fund	06 Jun 62	429UNTS169	106197
Multilateral		22 Jun 62	494UNTS249	107237
Algeria	France	03 Jul 62	507UNTS25	107395
UN Special Fund	Syria	07 Jul 62	443UNTS3	106355
Taiwan	Paraguay	11 Jul 62	458UNTS41	106591
UN Special Fund	Tanganyika	17 Jul 62	435UNTS237	106281
Colombia	USA (United States)	23 Jul 62	458UNTS123	106595
Italy	USA (United States)	05 Sep 62	461UNTS185	106663
Mali	USSR (Soviet Union)	10 Oct 62	493UNTS219	107216
Cameroon	Israel	24 Oct 62	449UNTS3	106446
Multilateral		12 Dec 62	552UNTS15	108048
Central Afri Rep	USA (United States)	10 Feb 63	473UNTS83	106857
Japan	USA (United States)	19 Feb 63	473UNTS107	106859
Austria	Czechoslovakia	08 Mar 63	495UNTS219	107245
UN Special Fund	Uganda	22 Mar 63	456UNTS466	106572
Burma	Japan	29 Mar 63	518UNTS3	107490
Bulgaria	COMECON (Econ Aid)	30 Mar 63	506UNTS257	107389
Multilateral		20 Apr 63	495UNTS3	107239
Denmark	India	15 May 63	616UNTS39	108890
Laos	UK Great Britain	17 May 63	475UNTS155	106891
Jamaica	UN Special Fund	22 May 63	489UNTS191	107140
Netherlands	UN Special Fund	24 May 63	466UNTS289	106750
Argentina	UK Great Britain	05 Jun 63	482UNTS353	107004
UN Special Fund	Western Samoa	05 Jun 63	467UNTS463	200601
Congo (Zaire)	UN Special Fund	26 Jul 63	474UNTS137	106878
Burundi	UN Special Fund	22 Aug 63	476UNTS49	106903
Dahomey	UNICEF (Children)	28 Aug 63	507UNTS101	107396
Jamaica	USA (United States)	24 Oct 63	489UNTS337	107148
Central Afri Rep	UN Special Fund	30 Oct 63	481UNTS247	106985

PARTY ONE	PARTY TWO	DATE	CITATION	NUMBER
Economic assistance (Cont.)				
Czechoslovakia	Romania	16 Dec 63	527UNTS285	107630
Rwanda	UN Special Fund	18 Mar 64	491UNTS3	107170
Taiwan	UNICEF (Children)	08 Apr 64	500UNTS49	107306
Japan	USA (United States)	25 Apr 64	530UNTS61	107672
Ireland	UN Special Fund	03 Jun 64	496UNTS205	107253
Malaysia	UNICEF (Children)	01 Jul 64	503UNTS229	107346
Colombia	Netherlands	06 Jul 64	543UNTS289	107906
France	Eur Space Research	10 Aug 64	528UNTS135	107637
Rwanda	UNICEF (Children)	11 Sep 64	510UNTS127	107409
Malta	UK Great Britain	21 Sep 64	588UNTS125	108519
Kenya	UN Special Fund	01 Oct 64	511UNTS181	107433
Asian Productivity	ILO (Labor Org)	27 Oct 64	516UNTS367	200610
Malta	Switzerland	20 Jan 65	548UNTS193	107978
Benelux Econ Union	Poland	17 Feb 65	547UNTS165	107956
Multilateral		28 May 65	559UNTS273	108163
UN Special Fund	Spain	30 Jun 65	544UNTS159	107918
ILO (Labor Org)	LAFTA (Free Trade)	02 Jul 65	563UNTS327	200619
Turkey	UK Great Britain	21 Oct 65	561UNTS185	108180
Denmark	Syria	28 Dec 65	588UNTS163	108523
Mongolia	UN Special Fund	26 Jan 66	552UNTS201	108055
USA (United States)	Vietnam, South	21 Mar 66	578UNTS165	108394
Denmark	Iran	14 Jun 66	597UNTS283	108652
France	USSR (Soviet Union)	30 Jun 66	589UNTS109	108538
Malawi	UK Great Britain	19 Jul 66	637UNTS0	109125
Turkey	UK Great Britain	29 Jul 66	597UNTS241	108649
USSR (Soviet Union)	Yugoslavia	29 Sep 66	608UNTS219	108818
Multilateral		04 May 67	595UNTS287	108623
Multilateral		27 Oct 67	608UNTS37	108811
Turkey	UK Great Britain	04 Mar 68	0UNTS0	109266
New Zealand	UK Great Britain	02 Apr 68	0UNTS0	109206
Multilateral		28 Sep 68	0UNTS0	109296
Use restrictions				
Peru	USA (United States)	22 Nov 46	100UNTS170	101396
Philippines	USA (United States)	14 Feb 47	16UNTS3	100245
Greece	USA (United States)	20 Jun 47	7UNTS267	100105
Turkey	USA (United States)	12 Jul 47	7UNTS299	100106
Australia	Poland	03 Jun 48	16UNTS189	100258
Australia	Hungary	01 Jul 48	22UNTS3	100325
Australia	Greece	01 Jul 48	22UNTS33	100329
Australia	Italy	08 Jul 48	22UNTS11	100326
Australia	Yugoslavia	09 Jul 48	22UNTS17	100327
Australia	Austria	19 Jul 48	22UNTS25	100328
India	WHO (World Health)	11 Oct 51	118UNTS27	101594
Jordan	USA (United States)	17 Jun 54	266UNTS137	103828
Brazil	USA (United States)	30 Jun 54	237UNTS137	103341
El Salvador	USA (United States)	31 Aug 54	237UNTS49	103336
Lebanon	USA (United States)	03 Sep 58	336UNTS91	104801
USA (United States)	Uruguay	20 Feb 59	341UNTS201	104884
Iraq	USSR (Soviet Union)	16 Mar 59	346UNTS107	104979
Turkey	USA (United States)	26 May 59	354UNTS57	105053
Italy	USA (United States)	30 Jul 59	355UNTS393	105088
Congo (Zaire)	United Nations	23 Aug 60	373UNTS327	200576
Austria	USA (United States)	29 Mar 61	459UNTS45	106612
OAS (Am States)	USA (United States)	29 Nov 61	424UNTS119	106104
Iran	USA (United States)	17 Nov 63	530UNTS41	107671
Guinea	USA (United States)	13 Jun 64	531UNTS263	107708
Malta	UK Great Britain	21 Sep 64	588UNTS125	108519
USA (United States)	Vietnam, South	21 Mar 66	578UNTS165	108394
Sweden	USA (United States)	28 Jul 66	603UNTS61	108725
IDA (Devel Assoc)	Tunisia	16 Sep 66	616UNTS285	108903
Peru	UK Great Britain	03 Dec 66	617UNTS231	108915
Syria	USSR (Soviet Union)	18 Dec 66	633UNTS247	109041
IDA (Devel Assoc)	Tunisia	21 Feb 67	618UNTS69	108924
IBRD (World Bank)	Tunisia	21 Feb 67	618UNTS39	108923

PARTY ONE	PARTY TWO	DATE	CITATION	NUMBER
Use restrictions (Cont.)				
Cameroon	IDA (Devel Assoc)	28 Mar 67	618UNTS133	108926
Denmark	Tanzania	05 Apr 67	603UNTS111	108728
IDA (Devel Assoc)	Uganda	21 Apr 67	617UNTS161	108911
Malawi	IDA (Devel Assoc)	04 May 67	617UNTS141	108910
Jordan	IDA (Devel Assoc)	09 May 67	617UNTS47	108907
Kenya	IDA (Devel Assoc)	11 May 67	617UNTS111	108909
Kenya	IDA (Devel Assoc)	11 May 67	617UNTS91	108908
Bolivia	IDA (Devel Assoc)	26 May 67	618UNTS159	108927
Honduras	IBRD (World Bank)	26 May 67	615UNTS145	108879
Multilateral		12 Jun 67	615UNTS321	108885
China	IBRD (World Bank)	14 Jun 67	615UNTS243	108882
Malaysia	IBRD (World Bank)	15 Jun 67	618UNTS235	108930
Cameroon	UK Great Britain	16 Jun 67	618UNTS329	108933
Other Party Combin	Ecuador	19 Jun 67	615UNTS75	108878
IDA (Devel Assoc)	Uganda	28 Jul 67	617UNTS177	108912
Argentina	IBRD (World Bank)	31 Jul 67	633UNTS289	109042
Madagascar	IBRD (World Bank)	23 Aug 67	618UNTS215	108929
IDA (Devel Assoc)	Uganda	15 Sep 67	639UNTS115	109148
IBRD (World Bank)	Thailand	19 Sep 67	619UNTS275	108946
Brazil	IBRD (World Bank)	23 Sep 67	620UNTS77	108951
Botswana	UN Special Fund	12 Oct 67	607UNTS37	108794
Denmark	Tanzania	01 Nov 67	619UNTS47	108938
Denmark	Iran	02 Nov 67	638UNTS217	109138
Korea, South	IDA (Devel Assoc)	18 Dec 67	639UNTS303	200639
Denmark	Malaysia	29 Feb 68	640UNTS29	109153
Materials, equipment and services				
Panama	USA (United States)	23 Mar 40	124UNTS195	200420
Panama	USA (United States)	06 Sep 40	124UNTS209	200421
Honduras	USA (United States)	28 Feb 41	117UNTS205	200371
Costa Rica	USA (United States)	18 Jun 41	103UNTS173	200313
Iceland	USA (United States)	01 Jul 41	12UNTS405	200071
Costa Rica	USA (United States)	16 Jan 42	23UNTS285	200135
Brazil	USA (United States)	03 Mar 42	105UNTS99	200325
Nicaragua	USA (United States)	08 Apr 42	24UNTS145	200138
USA (United States)	USSR (Soviet Union)	18 Apr 42	105UNTS285	200339
Peru	USA (United States)	21 Apr 42	89UNTS317	200260
Peru	USA (United States)	07 May 42	103UNTS219	200316
Peru	USA (United States)	11 May 42	136UNTS353	200447
Taiwan	USA (United States)	02 Jun 42	14UNTS343	200092
Belgium	USA (United States)	16 Jun 42	105UNTS159	200329
Canada	USA (United States)	27 Jun 42	99UNTS223	200276
Poland	USA (United States)	01 Jul 42	103UNTS267	200317
Netherlands	USA (United States)	08 Jul 42	103UNTS277	200318
Greece	USA (United States)	10 Jul 42	103UNTS289	200319
Czechoslovakia	USA (United States)	11 Jul 42	90UNTS257	200263
USA (United States)	Yugoslavia	24 Jul 42	34UNTS361	200179
Norway	USA (United States)	28 Aug 42	139UNTS361	200461
France	USA (United States)	03 Sep 42	24UNTS177	200141
Australia	USA (United States)	03 Sep 42	24UNTS195	200143
Brazil	USA (United States)	03 Sep 42	13UNTS109	200073
New Zealand	USA (United States)	03 Sep 42	24UNTS185	200142
Colombia	USA (United States)	23 Oct 42	105UNTS109	200326
Mexico	USA (United States)	24 Oct 42	21UNTS189	200123
Nicaragua	USA (United States)	27 Oct 42	99UNTS287	200283
Ecuador	USA (United States)	29 Oct 42	89UNTS301	200259
Belgium	USA (United States)	30 Jan 43	13UNTS371	200084
Colombia	USA (United States)	29 Mar 43	124UNTS139	200416
Mexico	USA (United States)	14 Jun 43	66UNTS331	200220
France	USA (United States)	25 Sep 43	76UNTS183	200245
Canada	Taiwan	22 Mar 44	14UNTS397	200096
Guatemala	USA (United States)	15 Jul 44	106UNTS285	200347
Multilateral		02 Aug 44	67UNTS221	200221
Haiti	USA (United States)	08 Jan 45	121UNTS153	200397
France	USA (United States)	20 Feb 45	76UNTS223	200248

PARTY ONE	PARTY TWO	DATE	CITATION	NUMBER
Materials, equipment and services (Cont.)				
France	USA (United States)	20 Feb 45	76UNTS193	200246
Turkey	USA (United States)	23 Feb 45	121UNTS165	200398
France	USA (United States)	28 Feb 45	76UNTS213	200247
Belgium	USA (United States)	17 Apr 45	139UNTS253	200454
Belgium	USA (United States)	19 Apr 45	139UNTS179	200455
Netherlands	USA (United States)	30 Apr 45	139UNTS319	200459
Netherlands	USA (United States)	30 Apr 45	139UNTS341	200460
Iraq	USA (United States)	31 Jul 45	121UNTS239	200402
Dominican Republic	USA (United States)	13 Oct 45	149UNTS361	200477
Netherlands	UK Great Britain	20 Dec 45	4UNTS303	100053
Greece	UK Great Britain	24 Jan 46	6UNTS45	100067
Brazil	USA (United States)	05 Apr 46	12UNTS131	100183
Mexico	USA (United States)	12 Apr 46	66UNTS293	100861
Multilateral		17 Apr 46	27UNTS103	100402
France	USA (United States)	28 May 46	84UNTS141	101124
France	USA (United States)	28 May 46	84UNTS121	101123
United Nations	Switzerland	01 Jul 46	1UNTS153	200007
Belgium	Canada	13 Jul 46	230UNTS159	103181
Multilateral		22 Jul 46	14UNTS185	100221
League of Nations	United Nations	31 Jul 46	1UNTS119	200003
Denmark	USA (United States)	01 Oct 46	42UNTS219	100650
Norway	USA (United States)	12 Nov 46	42UNTS227	100651
Albania	Yugoslavia	28 Nov 46	111UNTS139	101526
Austria	UK Great Britain	23 Dec 46	88UNTS93	101186
Philippines	USA (United States)	14 Feb 47	16UNTS3	100245
Burma	USA (United States)	28 Feb 47	25UNTS27	100355
Philippines	USA (United States)	14 Mar 47	16UNTS31	100247
Mexico	USA (United States)	17 Mar 47	167UNTS30	102200
South Africa	USA (United States)	21 Mar 47	16UNTS47	100248
Philippines	USA (United States)	21 Mar 47	45UNTS47	100691
Thailand	USA (United States)	08 May 47	42UNTS241	100653
Philippines	USA (United States)	12 May 47	16UNTS109	100252
Philippines	USA (United States)	12 May 47	16UNTS137	100254
Albania	Yugoslavia	12 Jun 47	111UNTS177	101531
Czechoslovakia	USA (United States)	25 Jul 47	90UNTS19	101223
France	USA (United States)	01 Oct 47	148UNTS303	101940
Austria	USA (United States)	08 Oct 47	25UNTS3	100354
UK Great Britain	USA (United States)	09 Oct 47	34UNTS129	100533
Greece	UNICEF (Children)	14 Oct 47	102UNTS39	101409
Ecuador	USA (United States)	14 Nov 47	149UNTS297	101959
Albania	UNICEF (Children)	20 Nov 47	65UNTS163	200208
Greece	USA (United States)	03 Dec 47	89UNTS119	101213
Taiwan	USA (United States)	08 Dec 47	70UNTS3	100895
Poland	Yugoslavia	21 Jan 48	115UNTS155	101562
Cuba	USA (United States)	27 Jan 48	67UNTS3	100862
ICJ Option Clause	Honduras	02 Feb 48	15UNTS217	100236
France	UNICEF (Children)	19 Feb 48	68UNTS75	100885
UK Great Britain	USA (United States)	24 Feb 48	73UNTS143	100951
USA (United States)	Venezuela	24 Mar 48	44UNTS57	100678
Ceylon (Sri Lanka)	UK Great Britain	30 Apr 48	182UNTS2	102421
Czechoslovakia	Yugoslavia	24 May 48	112UNTS215	101544
Greece	UK Great Britain	07 Sep 48	180UNTS144	102380
Israel	UNICEF (Children)	20 Sep 48	71UNTS17	100907
UNICEF (Children)	Thailand	01 Dec 48	68UNTS94	100886
Austria	USA (United States)	23 Mar 49	43UNTS127	100667
Panama	USA (United States)	31 Mar 49	55UNTS141	100812
India	UNICEF (Children)	10 May 49	68UNTS96	100887
Philippines	USA (United States)	07 Jun 49	45UNTS63	100692
Italy	UK Great Britain	14 Jun 49	135UNTS49	101813
UNICEF (Children)	UK Great Britain	17 Jun 49	65UNTS50	100820
Bulgaria	Poland	26 Sep 49	260UNTS227	103711
Hungary	Poland	29 Oct 49	260UNTS91	103705
Afghanistan	WHO (World Health)	04 Dec 49	102UNTS117	101414
UNICEF (Children)	UK Great Britain	19 Dec 49	65UNTS64	100828
Haiti	UNICEF (Children)	20 Dec 49	65UNTS68	100829

PARTY ONE	PARTY TWO	DATE	CITATION	NUMBER
Materials, equipment and services (Cont.)				
Belgium	UK Great Britain	23 Dec 49	99UNTS61	101371
Korea, South	USA (United States)	26 Jan 50	80UNTS205	101053
Norway	USA (United States)	27 Jan 50	80UNTS241	101055
Italy	USA (United States)	27 Jan 50	80UNTS145	101050
Netherlands	USA (United States)	27 Jan 50	80UNTS219	101054
Luxembourg	USA (United States)	27 Jan 50	80UNTS187	101052
France	USA (United States)	27 Jan 50	80UNTS171	101051
UK Great Britain	USA (United States)	27 Jan 50	80UNTS261	101056
Denmark	USA (United States)	27 Jan 50	48UNTS115	100740
Belgium	USA (United States)	27 Jan 50	51UNTS213	100767
UNICEF (Children)	UK Great Britain	10 Feb 50	65UNTS86	100837
China People's Rep	USSR (Soviet Union)	14 Feb 50	226UNTS21	103104
Ceylon (Sri Lanka)	WHO (World Health)	17 Feb 50	102UNTS309	200309
Multilateral		17 Apr 50	131UNTS99	101738
El Salvador	WHO (World Health)	21 Apr 50	103UNTS13	101420
Burma	UNICEF (Children)	22 Apr 50	68UNTS96	100888
Iran	USA (United States)	23 May 50	81UNTS3	101057
Romania	USSR (Soviet Union)	27 May 50	221UNTS13	103000
Brazil	UNICEF (Children)	09 Jun 50	66UNTS75	100848
Haiti	WHO (World Health)	27 Jun 50	110UNTS99	101504
Afghanistan	UNICEF (Children)	04 Jul 50	71UNTS3	100906
Hungary	USSR (Soviet Union)	13 Jul 50	221UNTS35	103001
Taiwan	UNICEF (Children)	19 Jul 50	94UNTS21	101304
Indonesia	USA (United States)	15 Aug 50	134UNTS255	101804
WHO (World Health)	United Arab Rep	25 Aug 50	92UNTS39	101259
Bulgaria	USSR (Soviet Union)	25 Aug 50	221UNTS57	103002
WHO (World Health)	Venezuela	11 Sep 50	110UNTS237	101513
UN Relief Palestin	WHO (World Health)	23 Sep 50	103UNTS129	200310
Peru	WHO (World Health)	26 Sep 50	104UNTS233	101444
Iceland	WHO (World Health)	06 Oct 50	110UNTS127	101506
Thailand	USA (United States)	17 Oct 50	79UNTS41	101030
Iran	USA (United States)	19 Oct 50	92UNTS135	101266
WHO (World Health)	Turkey	19 Oct 50	110UNTS215	101512
Multilateral		02 Nov 50	81UNTS160	101071
Ceylon (Sri Lanka)	USA (United States)	07 Nov 50	92UNTS125	101265
Nicaragua	WHO (World Health)	10 Nov 50	110UNTS155	101508
Peru	WHO (World Health)	10 Nov 50	110UNTS187	101510
Czechoslovakia	Poland	17 Nov 50	530UNTS195	107682
Multilateral		24 Nov 50	81UNTS188	101072
Multilateral		15 Dec 50	76UNTS120	100985
Brazil	USA (United States)	19 Dec 50	141UNTS3	101900
Panama	USA (United States)	20 Dec 50	92UNTS167	101269
Liberia	USA (United States)	22 Dec 50	92UNTS145	101267
Multilateral		23 Dec 50	185UNTS3	102456
India	USA (United States)	28 Dec 50	99UNTS39	101369
Philippines	WHO (World Health)	28 Dec 50	110UNTS203	101511
Paraguay	USA (United States)	29 Dec 50	122UNTS157	101645
Brazil	USA (United States)	04 Jan 51	165UNTS97	102171
Chile	USA (United States)	04 Jan 51	165UNTS105	102172
Portugal	USA (United States)	05 Jan 51	133UNTS75	101782
Colombia	WHO (World Health)	05 Jan 51	102UNTS139	101417
United Nations	Yugoslavia	06 Jan 51	78UNTS165	101015
Argentina	USA (United States)	08 Jan 51	165UNTS89	102170
Costa Rica	USA (United States)	11 Jan 51	92UNTS179	101270
Chile	USA (United States)	16 Jan 51	151UNTS147	101990
Chile	USA (United States)	16 Jan 51	157UNTS3	102043
Costa Rica	USA (United States)	17 Jan 51	134UNTS215	101801
Saudi Arabia	USA (United States)	17 Jan 51	140UNTS335	101897
Nepal	USA (United States)	23 Jan 51	184UNTS65	102439
Paraguay	UNICEF (Children)	25 Jan 51	79UNTS9	101027
Panama	USA (United States)	26 Jan 51	137UNTS69	101849
Honduras	USA (United States)	30 Jan 51	124UNTS63	101667
Ethiopia	ICAO (Civil Aviat)	02 Feb 51	96UNTS123	101333
Afghanistan	USA (United States)	07 Feb 51	132UNTS265	101766
Pakistan	USA (United States)	09 Feb 51	100UNTS67	101388

PARTY ONE	PARTY TWO	DATE	CITATION	NUMBER
Materials, equipment and services (Cont.)				
Denmark	WHO (World Health)	14 Feb 51	104UNTS243	101445
Multilateral		15 Feb 51	81UNTS245	101074
Paraguay	WHO (World Health)	15 Feb 51	110UNTS171	101509
Israel	ICAO (Civil Aviat)	19 Feb 51	96UNTS141	101334
Israel	ILO (Labor Org)	19 Feb 51	100UNTS105	101391
Dominican Republic	USA (United States)	20 Feb 51	132UNTS305	101770
Lebanon	USA (United States)	24 Feb 51	223UNTS121	103060
Israel	USA (United States)	26 Feb 51	137UNTS57	101848
Jordan	USA (United States)	27 Feb 51	141UNTS55	101905
ILO (Labor Org)	Syria	03 Mar 51	110UNTS69	101502
Multilateral		06 Mar 51	138UNTS67	101860
Colombia	USA (United States)	09 Mar 51	141UNTS15	101901
Bolivia	USA (United States)	14 Mar 51	132UNTS319	101771
India	USA (United States)	16 Mar 51	141UNTS47	101904
El Salvador	USA (United States)	19 Mar 51	134UNTS245	101803
Canada	USA (United States)	27 Mar 51	132UNTS333	101772
Multilateral		28 Mar 51	181UNTS61	102399
Jordan	ILO (Labor Org)	29 Mar 51	100UNTS247	200287
Jordan	United Nations	29 Mar 51	137UNTS267	200448
Liberia	ILO (Labor Org)	02 Apr 51	100UNTS117	101392
Jordan	WHO (World Health)	03 Apr 51	110UNTS297	200367
Multilateral		05 Apr 51	84UNTS299	101139
Ceylon (Sri Lanka)	ILO (Labor Org)	06 Apr 51	100UNTS235	200286
Mexico	ILO (Labor Org)	06 Apr 51	100UNTS131	101393
Belgium	UK Great Britain	06 Apr 51	110UNTS3	101496
Iraq	USA (United States)	10 Apr 51	151UNTS179	101993
Peru	ILO (Labor Org)	13 Apr 51	100UNTS31	101385
ICAO (Civil Aviat)	Thailand	19 Apr 51	96UNTS181	101336
Ecuador	ILO (Labor Org)	19 Apr 51	100UNTS77	101389
Honduras	WHO (World Health)	20 Apr 51	110UNTS111	101505
Nicaragua	USA (United States)	20 Apr 51	138UNTS57	101859
Cuba	ILO (Labor Org)	21 Apr 51	99UNTS205	101382
Greece	ILO (Labor Org)	25 Apr 51	100UNTS93	101390
UK Great Britain	USA (United States)	25 Apr 51	99UNTS97	101373
India	ILO (Labor Org)	26 Apr 51	100UNTS19	101384
Mexico	WHO (World Health)	30 Apr 51	103UNTS95	101427
Haiti	USA (United States)	02 May 51	151UNTS191	101994
WHO (World Health)	Yugoslavia	02 May 51	103UNTS117	101429
Ecuador	USA (United States)	03 May 51	141UNTS27	101902
Colombia	WHO (World Health)	04 May 51	110UNTS83	101503
Iceland	USA (United States)	05 May 51	205UNTS173	102776
United Arab Rep	USA (United States)	05 May 51	198UNTS265	102670
Lebanon	USA (United States)	29 May 51	160UNTS49	102101
Cambodia	WHO (World Health)	31 May 51	102UNTS279	200307
Multilateral		01 Jun 51	118UNTS57	101596
Lebanon	WHO (World Health)	05 Jun 51	104UNTS225	101443
Lebanon	WHO (World Health)	07 Jun 51	126UNTS221	101690
Iceland	ICAO (Civil Aviat)	07 Jun 51	96UNTS193	101337
WHO (World Health)	Uruguay	11 Jun 51	128UNTS251	101724
United Nations	Thailand	11 Jun 51	90UNTS45	101225
Liberia	WHO (World Health)	11 Jun 51	103UNTS83	101426
Burma	WHO (World Health)	13 Jun 51	117UNTS115	101588
Costa Rica	WHO (World Health)	14 Jun 51	102UNTS151	101418
UK Great Britain	USA (United States)	15 Jun 51	141UNTS79	101907
Multilateral		15 Jun 51	148UNTS67	101936
Ethiopia	USA (United States)	16 Jun 51	148UNTS39	101933
Dominican Republic	ILO (Labor Org)	18 Jun 51	100UNTS3	101383
Cuba	USA (United States)	20 Jun 51	148UNTS3	101931
Israel	United Nations	25 Jun 51	97UNTS21	101344
Multilateral		25 Jun 51	92UNTS27	101258
ILO (Labor Org)	Vietnam, South	26 Jun 51	100UNTS223	200285
Sweden	USA (United States)	27 Jun 51	148UNTS77	101937
Mexico	USA (United States)	27 Jun 51	141UNTS211	101916
Multilateral		28 Jun 51	118UNTS154	101604
Iraq	WHO (World Health)	01 Jul 51	110UNTS139	101507

Materials, equipment and services (Cont.)

PARTY ONE	PARTY TWO	DATE	CITATION	NUMBER
Ethiopia	WHO (World Health)	02 Jul 51	103UNTS39	101422
Burma	WHO (World Health)	09 Jul 51	104UNTS187	101440
ILO (Labor Org)	Thailand	11 Jul 51	100UNTS159	101395
Paraguay	ILO (Labor Org)	12 Jul 51	117UNTS155	101591
UK Great Britain	USA (United States)	13 Jul 51	105UNTS71	101454
Multilateral		18 Jul 51	102UNTS291	200308
Multilateral		27 Jul 51	97UNTS291	200273
Panama	USA (United States)	30 Jul 51	140UNTS321	101896
Multilateral		01 Aug 51	107UNTS19	101464
Canada	USA (United States)	01 Aug 51	233UNTS109	103254
Israel	WHO (World Health)	07 Aug 51	104UNTS213	101442
WHO (World Health)	Saudi Arabia	29 Aug 51	110UNTS277	101516
Multilateral		05 Sep 51	173UNTS15	102256
Japan	USA (United States)	08 Sep 51	136UNTS203	101834
Costa Rica	USA (United States)	11 Sep 51	234UNTS255	103288
Norway	USA (United States)	17 Sep 51	140UNTS313	101895
Iraq	ICAO (Civil Aviat)	18 Sep 51	108UNTS219	101475
Korea, South	WHO (World Health)	19 Sep 51	109UNTS297	200366
WHO (World Health)	Vietnam, South	21 Sep 51	107UNTS63	200352
Paraguay	United Nations	27 Sep 51	120UNTS105	101617
Bolivia	United Nations	01 Oct 51	104UNTS263	101447
Multilateral		01 Oct 51	104UNTS249	101446
Pakistan	WHO (World Health)	07 Oct 51	126UNTS101	101684
Ecuador	WHO (World Health)	16 Oct 51	110UNTS263	101515
United Nations	Uruguay	17 Oct 51	122UNTS29	101633
ILO (Labor Org)	Venezuela	22 Oct 51	117UNTS139	101590
India	WHO (World Health)	23 Oct 51	109UNTS59	101491
Taiwan	WHO (World Health)	25 Oct 51	126UNTS77	101683
South Africa	USA (United States)	09 Nov 51	160UNTS41	102100
Panama	ILO (Labor Org)	10 Nov 51	126UNTS269	101693
Italy	UK Great Britain	12 Nov 51	135UNTS55	101814
USA (United States)	Yugoslavia	14 Nov 51	174UNTS201	102286
Australia	USA (United States)	16 Nov 51	168UNTS75	102214
Mexico	WHO (World Health)	17 Dec 51	124UNTS121	101670
India	WHO (World Health)	20 Dec 51	124UNTS109	101669
Multilateral		24 Dec 51	118UNTS290	200383
Guatemala	WHO (World Health)	29 Dec 51	124UNTS89	101668
Indonesia	USA (United States)	05 Jan 52	215UNTS121	102916
Austria	WHO (World Health)	10 Jan 52	131UNTS295	200438
Colombia	USA (United States)	12 Jan 52	168UNTS109	102216
Iran	USA (United States)	20 Jan 52	200UNTS191	102703
Libya	USA (United States)	21 Jan 52	183UNTS177	102427
Ceylon (Sri Lanka)	United Nations	21 Jan 52	118UNTS281	200382
Costa Rica	WHO (World Health)	23 Jan 52	135UNTS265	101826
Multilateral		23 Jan 52	127UNTS269	101708
WHO (World Health)	Spain	30 Jan 52	124UNTS259	200425
UNICEF (Children)	UK Great Britain	04 Feb 52	120UNTS147	101620
ICAO (Civil Aviat)	Yugoslavia	06 Feb 52	128UNTS97	101715
WHO (World Health)	UK Great Britain	07 Feb 52	121UNTS75	101627
Jordan	USA (United States)	12 Feb 52	168UNTS25	102211
Lebanon	ICAO (Civil Aviat)	14 Feb 52	128UNTS83	101714
Dominican Republic	UNICEF (Children)	15 Feb 52	121UNTS43	101625
UNICEF (Children)	UK Great Britain	15 Feb 52	121UNTS63	101626
Ecuador	USA (United States)	20 Feb 52	177UNTS43	102308
Peru	USA (United States)	22 Feb 52	165UNTS31	102166
Multilateral		01 Mar 52	168UNTS9	102210
Greece	United Nations	05 Mar 52	123UNTS3	101650
ICAO (Civil Aviat)	United Arab Rep	06 Mar 52	151UNTS111	101986
Cuba	USA (United States)	07 Mar 52	165UNTS11	102165
Finland	WHO (World Health)	07 Mar 52	128UNTS269	200436
Taiwan	WHO (World Health)	07 Mar 52	128UNTS233	101723
Brazil	USA (United States)	15 Mar 52	199UNTS221	102687
Iraq	USA (United States)	18 Mar 52	223UNTS131	103061
India	United Nations	02 Apr 52	126UNTS145	101687
El Salvador	USA (United States)	04 Apr 52	177UNTS219	102320

Materials, equipment and services (Cont.)

PARTY ONE	PARTY TWO	DATE	CITATION	NUMBER
Chile	USA (United States)	09 Apr 52	186UNTS53	102482
Peru	USA (United States)	09 Apr 52	184UNTS295	102454
United Nations	Yugoslavia	10 Apr 52	141UNTS89	101908
Colombia	USA (United States)	17 Apr 52	174UNTS215	102287
India	WHO (World Health)	19 Apr 52	131UNTS253	101745
Pakistan	United Nations	28 Apr 52	128UNTS191	101720
India	ICAO (Civil Aviat)	29 Apr 52	151UNTS123	101987
Norway	WHO (World Health)	09 May 52	131UNTS281	101747
Israel	USA (United States)	09 May 52	177UNTS63	102309
Netherlands	USA (United States)	15 May 52	177UNTS233	102321
Libya	USA (United States)	20 May 52	178UNTS155	102339
Iraq	USA (United States)	21 May 52	212UNTS183	102870
Korea, South	USA (United States)	24 May 52	179UNTS23	102353
Mexico	WHO (World Health)	28 May 52	134UNTS319	101810
Chile	WHO (World Health)	31 May 52	136UNTS323	101841
Brazil	USA (United States)	02 Jun 52	181UNTS109	102403
India	WHO (World Health)	04 Jun 52	135UNTS279	101827
Ethiopia	USA (United States)	13 Jun 52	205UNTS17	102766
Jordan	WHO (World Health)	16 Jun 52	135UNTS323	200445
India	WHO (World Health)	19 Jun 52	134UNTS307	101809
Multilateral		19 Jun 52	133UNTS165	101787
WHO (World Health)	Syria	20 Jun 52	165UNTS219	102178
South Africa	USA (United States)	24 Jun 52	177UNTS241	102322
Lebanon	USA (United States)	26 Jun 52	181UNTS187	102409
Panama	USA (United States)	30 Jun 52	181UNTS121	102404
Chile	USA (United States)	30 Jun 52	199UNTS241	102688
USA (United States)	Uruguay	30 Jun 52	207UNTS139	102804
Sweden	USA (United States)	01 Jul 52	187UNTS3	102497
India	WHO (World Health)	16 Jul 52	135UNTS291	101828
Chile	ILO (Labor Org)	23 Jul 52	178UNTS323	102348
Japan	USA (United States)	25 Jul 52	198UNTS281	102671
Czechoslovakia	Romania	31 Jul 52	362UNTS123	105185
Panama	USA (United States)	08 Aug 52	181UNTS257	102415
Panama	United Nations	20 Aug 52	136UNTS3	101829
Jordan	WHO (World Health)	21 Aug 52	141UNTS341	200472
Multilateral		21 Aug 52	141UNTS129	101912
Italy	ILO (Labor Org)	04 Sep 52	178UNTS371	200505
ILO (Labor Org)	Uruguay	20 Sep 52	187UNTS25	102499
United Nations	Trieste	30 Sep 52	140UNTS11	101881
Multilateral		15 Oct 52	141UNTS96	101909
Multilateral		17 Oct 52	141UNTS121	101911
Chile	WHO (World Health)	24 Oct 52	151UNTS339	102004
Chile	WHO (World Health)	04 Nov 52	150UNTS119	101966
Ethiopia	USA (United States)	05 Nov 52	184UNTS139	102445
Saudi Arabia	USA (United States)	10 Nov 52	181UNTS225	102412
Saudi Arabia	USA (United States)	10 Nov 52	181UNTS307	102419
Saudi Arabia	USA (United States)	10 Nov 52	181UNTS295	102418
Ceylon (Sri Lanka)	WHO (World Health)	21 Nov 52	161UNTS315	200490
Japan	WHO (World Health)	26 Nov 52	204UNTS301	200521
Mexico	ICAO (Civil Aviat)	28 Nov 52	164UNTS15	102156
Canada	USA (United States)	05 Dec 52	206UNTS11	102783
India	WHO (World Health)	11 Dec 52	158UNTS391	102073
Saudi Arabia	USA (United States)	15 Dec 52	185UNTS67	102459
Saudi Arabia	USA (United States)	15 Dec 52	185UNTS55	102458
Multilateral		16 Dec 52	158UNTS407	102074
Multilateral		29 Dec 52	151UNTS317	102002
ILO (Labor Org)	UN Relief Palestin	31 Dec 52	182UNTS201	200506
Saudi Arabia	USA (United States)	25 Jan 53	201UNTS3	102706
Greece	USA (United States)	04 Feb 53	189UNTS3	102538
India	WHO (World Health)	11 Feb 53	163UNTS43	102140
Taiwan	ILO (Labor Org)	13 Feb 53	178UNTS337	102349
Multilateral		26 Feb 53	161UNTS31	102120
Costa Rica	United Nations	27 Feb 53	161UNTS45	102121
Nepal	United Nations	02 Mar 53	161UNTS347	200493
Dominican Republic	USA (United States)	06 Mar 53	199UNTS267	102689

PARTY ONE	PARTY TWO	DATE	CITATION	NUMBER
Materials, equipment and services (Cont.)				
United Arab Rep	USA (United States)	19 Mar 53	215UNTS17	102909
Lebanon	USA (United States)	23 Mar 53	239UNTS45	103370
France	WHO (World Health)	02 Apr 53	174UNTS83	102279
United Nations	Yemen	07 Apr 53	163UNTS73	102142
France	WHO (World Health)	30 Apr 53	174UNTS71	102278
El Salvador	USA (United States)	14 May 53	234UNTS71	103273
United Arab Rep	USA (United States)	21 May 53	204UNTS29	102748
Ethiopia	USA (United States)	22 May 53	191UNTS59	102577
ICAO (Civil Aviat)	Syria	28 May 53	173UNTS199	102267
Brazil	USA (United States)	30 May 53	460UNTS89	106633
Jordan	Syria	04 Jun 53	184UNTS15	102437
Colombia	USA (United States)	09 Jun 53	213UNTS3	102877
Ecuador	United Nations	16 Jun 53	166UNTS289	102194
Ethiopia	United Nations	22 Jun 53	172UNTS93	102241
Liberia	USA (United States)	23 Jun 53	213UNTS37	102879
Cambodia	United Nations	24 Jun 53	168UNTS309	200500
Panama	USA (United States)	26 Jun 53	215UNTS77	102912
Brazil	USA (United States)	26 Jun 53	336UNTS241	104808
Philippines	USA (United States)	26 Jun 53	213UNTS77	102881
Chile	USA (United States)	27 Jun 53	229UNTS193	103167
Chile	USA (United States)	27 Jun 53	229UNTS53	103160
Saudi Arabia	USA (United States)	29 Jun 53	206UNTS23	102784
Nicaragua	USA (United States)	30 Jun 53	215UNTS133	102917
Afghanistan	USA (United States)	30 Jun 53	215UNTS3	102908
Canada	USA (United States)	30 Jun 53	206UNTS93	102786
Nicaragua	USA (United States)	02 Sep 53	215UNTS69	102911
Belgium	USA (United States)	02 Sep 53	200UNTS127	102700
Spain	USA (United States)	26 Sep 53	207UNTS83	102801
Spain	USA (United States)	26 Sep 53	207UNTS61	102800
Multilateral		09 Oct 53	190UNTS49	102557
Greece	USA (United States)	12 Oct 53	191UNTS319	102589
UN Relief Palestin	United Arab Rep	14 Oct 53	190UNTS13	102555
Dominican Republic	United Nations	19 Nov 53	180UNTS45	102374
Germany, West	USA (United States)	23 Nov 53	224UNTS107	103071
Thailand	USA (United States)	03 Dec 53	213UNTS91	102882
Hungary	Romania	14 Dec 53	342UNTS151	104906
Chile	USA (United States)	30 Dec 53	236UNTS41	103315
Bolivia	USA (United States)	15 Jan 54	229UNTS213	103168
UK Great Britain	USA (United States)	20 Jan 54	196UNTS95	102619
Netherlands	USA (United States)	22 Jan 54	190UNTS207	102565
Pakistan	United Nations	25 Jan 54	185UNTS213	102472
Brazil	WHO (World Health)	04 Feb 54	233UNTS49	103250
Germany, West	USA (United States)	12 Feb 54	223UNTS153	103064
Multilateral		19 Feb 54	214UNTS51	102899
United Arab Rep	USA (United States)	24 Feb 54	236UNTS61	103316
United Nations	Venezuela	05 Mar 54	187UNTS9	102498
Japan	USA (United States)	08 Mar 54	232UNTS169	103236
Liberia	United Nations	09 Mar 54	187UNTS61	102501
Guatemala	United Nations	10 Mar 54	191UNTS271	102587
Belgium	Norway	24 Mar 54	219UNTS73	102967
Panama	USA (United States)	25 Mar 54	232UNTS289	103243
Italy	USA (United States)	31 Mar 54	235UNTS293	103311
Mexico	USA (United States)	06 Apr 54	236UNTS69	103317
Czechoslovakia	Hungary	16 Apr 54	504UNTS231	107360
Luxembourg	USA (United States)	17 Apr 54	257UNTS255	103661
Multilateral		20 Apr 54	189UNTS11	102539
Iraq	USA (United States)	21 Apr 54	222UNTS251	103032
Ethiopia	USA (United States)	21 Apr 54	232UNTS299	103244
Netherlands	USA (United States)	07 May 54	213UNTS325	102895
Norway	USA (United States)	07 May 54	231UNTS157	103215
Panama	USA (United States)	11 May 54	236UNTS107	103319
Nepal	WHO (World Health)	13 May 54	204UNTS311	200522
Japan	USA (United States)	14 May 54	247UNTS273	103476
Pakistan	USA (United States)	19 May 54	202UNTS301	102736
Spain	USA (United States)	19 May 54	235UNTS87	103296

PARTY ONE	PARTY TWO	DATE	CITATION	NUMBER
Materials, equipment and services (Cont.)				
Honduras	USA (United States)	20 May 54	222UNTS87	103025
Haiti	USA (United States)	28 May 54	233UNTS281	103267
Multilateral		31 May 54	192UNTS20	102592
France	USA (United States)	31 May 54	236UNTS141	103321
Multilateral		01 Jun 54	200UNTS235	200520
Ethiopia	USA (United States)	01 Jun 54	232UNTS311	103245
Ethiopia	USA (United States)	12 Jun 54	234UNTS25	103270
UK Great Britain	USA (United States)	15 Jun 54	236UNTS133	103320
Jordan	USA (United States)	17 Jun 54	266UNTS137	103828
Italy	USA (United States)	24 Jun 54	235UNTS3	103290
Chile	USA (United States)	28 Jun 54	233UNTS3	103246
Italy	USA (United States)	28 Jun 54	237UNTS121	103340
Costa Rica	USA (United States)	30 Jun 54	235UNTS35	103294
Ecuador	USA (United States)	30 Jun 54	236UNTS163	103323
Brazil	USA (United States)	30 Jun 54	237UNTS137	103341
El Salvador	USA (United States)	16 Jul 54	237UNTS237	103350
Bulgaria	Romania	22 Jul 54	362UNTS101	105184
Guatemala	USA (United States)	30 Jul 54	234UNTS235	103286
Multilateral		19 Aug 54	201UNTS51	102710
Guatemala	USA (United States)	01 Sep 54	199UNTS51	102677
Multilateral		06 Oct 54	201UNTS75	102711
Ethiopia	Sweden	13 Oct 54	202UNTS273	102734
Germany, West	USA (United States)	15 Oct 54	239UNTS135	103375
USA (United States)	Yugoslavia	18 Oct 54	273UNTS163	103951
Canada	UK Great Britain	19 Oct 54	214UNTS309	102906
Multilateral		23 Oct 54	332UNTS157	104761
Multilateral		23 Oct 54	332UNTS3	104760
Peru	USA (United States)	25 Oct 54	238UNTS247	103368
Multilateral		27 Oct 54	201UNTS95	102712
Multilateral		29 Oct 54	201UNTS115	102713
Burma	Japan	05 Nov 54	251UNTS215	103543
Japan	USA (United States)	19 Nov 54	238UNTS207	103364
Belgium	USA (United States)	23 Nov 54	235UNTS19	103292
Austria	Yugoslavia	27 Nov 54	396UNTS75	105694
Pakistan	USA (United States)	11 Jan 55	251UNTS111	103537
Haiti	USA (United States)	28 Jan 55	270UNTS83	103894
Korea, South	USA (United States)	29 Jan 55	239UNTS53	103371
Iraq	USA (United States)	02 Mar 55	250UNTS229	103526
Netherlands	USA (United States)	21 Mar 55	289UNTS129	104217
El Salvador	USA (United States)	21 Mar 55	250UNTS261	103528
Honduras	USA (United States)	21 Mar 55	253UNTS3	103572
Ceylon (Sri Lanka)	Germany, West	01 Apr 55	369UNTS57	105251
Germany, West	USA (United States)	04 Apr 55	279UNTS73	104034
Multilateral		04 Apr 55	208UNTS239	102816
Haiti	USA (United States)	05 Apr 55	270UNTS97	103895
Chile	USA (United States)	05 Apr 55	250UNTS253	103527
Japan	USA (United States)	07 Apr 55	263UNTS285	103778
Taiwan	WHO (World Health)	21 Apr 55	210UNTS71	102835
Dominican Republic	USA (United States)	22 Apr 55	239UNTS325	103389
Turkey	USA (United States)	25 Apr 55	263UNTS299	103779
Philippines	USA (United States)	27 Apr 55	261UNTS351	103733
Czechoslovakia	Hungary	28 Apr 55	477UNTS197	106923
Korea, South	USA (United States)	02 May 55	258UNTS3	103666
USA (United States)	Vietnam, South	10 May 55	273UNTS157	103950
Turkey	USA (United States)	26 May 55	262UNTS97	103739
Greece	USA (United States)	27 May 55	251UNTS349	103552
Korea, South	USA (United States)	29 May 55	256UNTS263	103636
Japan	USA (United States)	03 Jun 55	270UNTS51	103891
Pakistan	Sweden	04 Jun 55	228UNTS121	103146
Multilateral		14 Jun 55	212UNTS263	200526
Canada	USA (United States)	15 Jun 55	235UNTS201	103302
Bulgaria	Yugoslavia	17 Jun 55	375UNTS287	105370
Guatemala	USA (United States)	18 Jun 55	262UNTS105	103740
Turkey	USA (United States)	29 Jun 55	269UNTS97	103878
Germany, West	USA (United States)	30 Jun 55	240UNTS47	103393

Materials, equipment and services (Cont.)

PARTY ONE	PARTY TWO	DATE	CITATION	NUMBER
Iran	WHO (World Health)	04 Jul 55	227UNTS65	103131
Multilateral		04 Jul 55	214UNTS10	102897
Libya	WHO (World Health)	05 Jul 55	219UNTS305	200530
Italy	USA (United States)	08 Jul 55	270UNTS29	103889
Ecuador	USA (United States)	08 Jul 55	265UNTS49	103806
Belgium	USA (United States)	15 Jul 55	223UNTS3	103040
Libya	USA (United States)	21 Jul 55	264UNTS247	103796
Brazil	USA (United States)	03 Aug 55	270UNTS71	103893
Germany, East	Romania	05 Aug 55	342UNTS229	104910
Czechoslovakia	Germany, East	30 Aug 55	504UNTS279	107361
Ecuador	USA (United States)	06 Sep 55	256UNTS187	103628
France	USA (United States)	23 Sep 55	270UNTS341	103904
Liberia	USA (United States)	06 Oct 55	275UNTS93	103978
Italy	Lebanon	04 Nov 55	267UNTS147	103840
Bulgaria	Yugoslavia	11 Dec 55	378UNTS49	105417
Libya	USA (United States)	22 Dec 55	240UNTS111	103399
Cuba	USA (United States)	10 Jan 56	240UNTS101	103398
Multilateral		02 Feb 56	227UNTS153	103137
Multilateral		10 Feb 56	228UNTS189	103151
Multilateral		10 Feb 56	228UNTS167	103150
Multilateral		13 Mar 56	427UNTS245	106158
USA (United States)	Uruguay	23 Mar 56	376UNTS311	105386
Colombia	USA (United States)	27 Mar 56	273UNTS235	103954
Taiwan	USA (United States)	03 Apr 56	268UNTS315	103864
Japan	USA (United States)	13 Apr 56	273UNTS223	103953
Bulgaria	Greece	19 Apr 56	594UNTS131	108600
Ceylon (Sri Lanka)	USA (United States)	28 Apr 56	274UNTS35	103956
Peru	USA (United States)	03 May 56	272UNTS59	103931
Pakistan	USA (United States)	28 May 56	269UNTS15	103868
Germany, East	USSR (Soviet Union)	30 May 56	263UNTS143	103771
Multilateral		31 May 56	251UNTS181	103541
Multilateral		08 Jun 56	247UNTS366	200541
Multilateral		14 Jun 56	265UNTS125	103809
Multilateral		26 Jun 56	321UNTS2	104650
Multilateral		26 Jun 56	253UNTS12	103573
Multilateral		02 Jul 56	540UNTS110	107846
Korea, South	USA (United States)	02 Jul 56	281UNTS41	104067
Multilateral		02 Jul 56	248UNTS37	103484
Czechoslovakia	Yugoslavia	03 Jul 56	397UNTS165	105704
UNESCO (Educ/Cult)	UK Great Britain	09 Aug 56	256UNTS139	103624
Multilateral		31 Aug 56	249UNTS158	103506
Pakistan	USA (United States)	10 Sep 56	277UNTS259	104010
Romania	Yugoslavia	25 Sep 56	395UNTS147	105683
Multilateral		05 Oct 56	251UNTS245	103544
Multilateral		05 Oct 56	251UNTS267	103545
Czechoslovakia	Germany, East	06 Oct 56	501UNTS109	107315
Portugal	USA (United States)	07 Nov 56	277UNTS133	104003
Taiwan	USA (United States)	21 Nov 56	265UNTS241	103816
Multilateral		21 Nov 56	253UNTS266	103588
Germany, East	Romania	08 Dec 56	362UNTS189	105188
Germany, West	USA (United States)	12 Dec 56	280UNTS71	104052
Germany, West	USA (United States)	12 Dec 56	280UNTS63	104051
Australia	USA (United States)	31 Dec 56	266UNTS89	103823
Multilateral		15 Jan 57	376UNTS122	105378
Multilateral		23 Jan 57	259UNTS426	103701
Multilateral		17 Feb 57	271UNTS2	103907
Multilateral		01 Mar 57	264UNTS94	103790
Tunisia	USA (United States)	26 Mar 57	283UNTS117	104111
Multilateral		28 Mar 57	271UNTS30	103908
Morocco	USA (United States)	02 Apr 57	288UNTS157	104203
Libya	USA (United States)	04 Apr 57	283UNTS181	104116
Multilateral		09 Apr 57	274UNTS172	103965
Ethiopia	USA (United States)	25 Apr 57	283UNTS205	104118
Finland	USA (United States)	10 May 57	283UNTS43	104105
Multilateral		24 May 57	268UNTS270	103861

Materials, equipment and services (Cont.)

PARTY ONE	PARTY TWO	DATE	CITATION	NUMBER
Argentina	USA (United States)	03 Jun 57	291UNTS61	104244
Ghana	USA (United States)	03 Jun 57	284UNTS63	104129
Bulgaria	Yugoslavia	04 Jun 57	349UNTS35	105008
Lebanon	USA (United States)	06 Jun 57	284UNTS155	104134
Czechoslovakia	Yugoslavia	11 Jun 57	504UNTS107	107355
Iraq	USA (United States)	16 Jun 57	284UNTS39	104127
Jordan	USA (United States)	27 Jun 57	288UNTS269	104209
Libya	USA (United States)	30 Jun 57	284UNTS177	104136
Multilateral		09 Jul 57	274UNTS300	103972
Austria	USA (United States)	09 Aug 57	288UNTS299	104211
Burma	WHO (World Health)	20 Sep 57	282UNTS113	104096
France	USA (United States)	23 Sep 57	293UNTS297	104297
USA (United States)	Venezuela	24 Sep 57	293UNTS307	104298
Cambodia	USA (United States)	17 Oct 57	299UNTS203	104313
United Arab Rep	USSR (Soviet Union)	19 Oct 57	292UNTS151	104271
Multilateral		05 Nov 57	285UNTS301	104155
Germany, East	Hungary	13 Nov 57	407UNTS216	105866
Hungary	Yugoslavia	06 Dec 57	519UNTS215	107509
Germany, West	USA (United States)	10 Dec 57	307UNTS59	104442
Hungary	Romania	17 Dec 57	477UNTS303	106926
Norway	USSR (Soviet Union)	18 Dec 57	312UNTS257	104522
Ethiopia	USA (United States)	26 Dec 57	307UNTS71	104443
Multilateral		06 Jan 58	304UNTS227	104399
Indonesia	Japan	20 Jan 58	325UNTS13	104691
Ghana	WHO (World Health)	21 Jan 58	307UNTS3	104437
Japan	USA (United States)	25 Jan 58	304UNTS81	104392
Indonesia	WHO (World Health)	05 Feb 58	307UNTS15	104438
UK Great Britain	USA (United States)	22 Feb 58	307UNTS207	104451
Bulgaria	Hungary	13 Mar 58	438UNTS173	106316
Multilateral		15 Mar 58	292UNTS273	104276
Czechoslovakia	Poland	21 Mar 58	538UNTS89	107811
Sudan	USA (United States)	31 Mar 58	308UNTS105	104458
Israel	WHO (World Health)	11 Apr 58	307UNTS27	104439
Bolivia	USA (United States)	22 Apr 58	317UNTS209	104605
Argentina	USA (United States)	28 Apr 58	315UNTS211	104570
Saudi Arabia	USA (United States)	01 May 58	315UNTS221	104571
Lebanon	UK Great Britain	19 May 58	327UNTS43	104716
Ceylon (Sri Lanka)	Sweden	22 May 58	428UNTS65	106168
Multilateral		19 Jun 58	306UNTS236	200550
WHO (World Health)	Sudan	21 Jun 58	307UNTS235	104453
Burma	USA (United States)	24 Jun 58	335UNTS193	104786
Indonesia	USA (United States)	13 Aug 58	335UNTS187	104785
India	USA (United States)	17 Dec 58	358UNTS77	105125
Afghanistan	WHO (World Health)	18 Dec 58	324UNTS121	104681
Taiwan	USA (United States)	07 Feb 59	341UNTS225	104885
Cambodia	Japan	02 Mar 59	341UNTS163	104882
Bulgaria	Hungary	03 Apr 59	438UNTS269	106319
Morocco	UN Special Fund	04 Apr 59	354UNTS347	105069
Greece	Netherlands	30 Apr 59	485UNTS135	107051
Greece	USA (United States)	06 May 59	357UNTS163	105115
Panama	USA (United States)	20 May 59	346UNTS235	104983
Turkey	USA (United States)	26 May 59	354UNTS57	105053
Panama	USA (United States)	24 Jun 59	479UNTS145	106950
Iraq	USA (United States)	07 Jul 59	357UNTS153	105114
Ghana	UN Special Fund	12 Aug 59	338UNTS203	104836
USA (United States)	Yugoslavia	25 Aug 59	357UNTS77	105106
USA (United States)	Yugoslavia	25 Aug 59	357UNTS87	105107
Lebanon	USA (United States)	16 Sep 59	358UNTS175	105135
Germany, West	USA (United States)	01 Oct 59	358UNTS129	105130
Iran	UN Special Fund	06 Oct 59	342UNTS89	104902
Canada	Euratom	06 Oct 59	475UNTS187	106894
Multilateral		09 Oct 59	376UNTS382	105391
Poland	UN Special Fund	15 Oct 59	344UNTS29	104941
India	UN Special Fund	20 Oct 59	344UNTS143	104946
USA (United States)	Yugoslavia	22 Oct 59	360UNTS259	105161

Materials, equipment and services (Cont.)

PARTY ONE	PARTY TWO	DATE	CITATION	NUMBER
UN Special Fund	Yugoslavia	27 Oct 59	344UNTS159	104947
Ecuador	UN Special Fund	10 Nov 59	345UNTS3	104955
Greece	UN Special Fund	13 Nov 59	345UNTS171	104966
UN Special Fund	Turkey	20 Nov 59	345UNTS105	104963
UN Special Fund	United Arab Rep	25 Nov 59	345UNTS125	104964
Belgium	USA (United States)	27 Nov 59	366UNTS331	105221
Turkey	USA (United States)	30 Nov 59	361UNTS107	105174
Israel	UN Special Fund	01 Dec 59	345UNTS197	104968
Guinea	UN Special Fund	02 Dec 59	345UNTS215	104969
Taiwan	USA (United States)	02 Dec 59	361UNTS115	105175
Multilateral		03 Dec 59	348UNTS246	105003
Argentina	UN Special Fund	04 Dec 59	345UNTS263	104972
Czechoslovakia	Ethiopia	11 Dec 59	386UNTS45	105536
Multilateral		14 Dec 59	422UNTS57	106068
Jordan	UN Special Fund	15 Dec 59	346UNTS3	104974
Ceylon (Sri Lanka)	WHO (World Health)	21 Dec 59	349UNTS109	105011
UN Special Fund	UK Great Britain	07 Jan 60	348UNTS177	105000
Peru	UN Special Fund	19 Jan 60	349UNTS83	105010
Japan	USA (United States)	19 Jan 60	373UNTS207	105321
Pakistan	WHO (World Health)	20 Jan 60	351UNTS355	105034
Chile	UN Special Fund	22 Jan 60	351UNTS115	105020
India	Japan	25 Jan 60	384UNTS31	105508
Colombia	UN Special Fund	04 Feb 60	355UNTS257	105080
Bolivia	UN Special Fund	09 Feb 60	351UNTS203	105024
Cuba	USSR (Soviet Union)	13 Feb 60	369UNTS3	105247
Norway	USA (United States)	13 Feb 60	388UNTS255	105583
Greece	USA (United States)	15 Feb 60	377UNTS95	105397
Chile	USA (United States)	19 Feb 60	371UNTS255	105282
Afghanistan	UN Special Fund	21 Feb 60	351UNTS93	105019
Ecuador	USA (United States)	24 Feb 60	371UNTS55	105270
Pakistan	UN Special Fund	25 Feb 60	351UNTS141	105021
Multilateral		26 Feb 60	418UNTS171	106022
Indonesia	USSR (Soviet Union)	28 Feb 60	392UNTS173	105643
Turkey	USA (United States)	02 Mar 60	372UNTS37	105286
Germany, West	USA (United States)	16 Mar 60	371UNTS101	105272
France	UN Special Fund	17 Mar 60	354UNTS119	105059
New Zealand	USA (United States)	23 Mar 60	371UNTS147	105276
Ireland	USA (United States)	24 Mar 60	371UNTS237	105280
Netherlands	USA (United States)	24 Mar 60	406UNTS165	105847
Italy	UN Special Fund	01 Apr 60	354UNTS261	105066
Multilateral		12 Apr 60	359UNTS323	105150
Denmark	USA (United States)	12 Apr 60	373UNTS9	105311
UN Special Fund	Tunisia	12 Apr 60	355UNTS289	105082
Japan	USA (United States)	15 Apr 60	372UNTS267	105303
Libya	UN Special Fund	19 Apr 60	356UNTS11	105090
UN Special Fund	Sudan	21 Apr 60	356UNTS213	105097
Guatemala	USA (United States)	23 Apr 60	373UNTS23	105312
Multilateral		28 Apr 60	376UNTS111	105377
UN Special Fund	Vietnam, South	29 Apr 60	357UNTS311	200567
Laos	UN Special Fund	30 Apr 60	361UNTS171	105179
Lebanon	UN Special Fund	07 May 60	360UNTS225	105160
Cambodia	WHO (World Health)	19 May 60	372UNTS193	105298
Argentina	USA (United States)	23 May 60	377UNTS3	105392
Multilateral		04 Jun 60	360UNTS208	105159
Iraq	UN Special Fund	19 Jun 60	376UNTS357	105389
Belgium	Netherlands	20 Jun 60	423UNTS19	106084
Denmark	USA (United States)	07 Jul 60	380UNTS39	105449
Italy	USA (United States)	07 Jul 60	380UNTS143	105455
Multilateral		08 Jul 60	366UNTS310	105220
Ethiopia	UN Special Fund	13 Jul 60	368UNTS159	105240
Japan	Pakistan	30 Jul 60	384UNTS63	105511
Jordan	WHO (World Health)	03 Aug 60	381UNTS133	105469
WHO (World Health)	United Arab Rep	03 Aug 60	385UNTS3	105524
WHO (World Health)	Tunisia	04 Aug 60	381UNTS335	105474
Ghana	USSR (Soviet Union)	04 Aug 60	399UNTS61	105734

Materials, equipment and services (Cont.)

PARTY ONE	PARTY TWO	DATE	CITATION	NUMBER
Laos	WHO (World Health)	04 Aug 60	373UNTS313	105322
Cyprus	UK Great Britain	16 Aug 60	382UNTS239	105485
Japan	Thailand	24 Aug 60	384UNTS73	105512
United Arab Rep	USSR (Soviet Union)	27 Aug 60	399UNTS37	105733
Haiti	USA (United States)	01 Sep 60	388UNTS249	105582
WHO (World Health)	Saudi Arabia	06 Sep 60	395UNTS169	105684
Lebanon	WHO (World Health)	08 Sep 60	387UNTS49	105557
Iran	Japan	12 Sep 60	384UNTS43	105509
South Africa	USA (United States)	13 Sep 60	388UNTS65	105572
Brazil	UN Special Fund	16 Sep 60	375UNTS3	105351
France	USA (United States)	19 Sep 60	400UNTS21	105745
Multilateral		19 Sep 60	444UNTS259	106371
Taiwan	UN Special Fund	20 Sep 60	375UNTS29	105352
Portugal	USA (United States)	26 Sep 60	393UNTS257	105660
Guinea	USA (United States)	30 Sep 60	394UNTS103	105671
Indonesia	UN Special Fund	07 Oct 60	378UNTS141	105424
Liberia	UN Special Fund	11 Oct 60	376UNTS341	105388
El Salvador	UN Special Fund	24 Oct 60	377UNTS171	105400
WHO (World Health)	Upper Volta	15 Nov 60	383UNTS91	105496
UNICEF (Children)	Upper Volta	15 Nov 60	402UNTS33	105776
Nepal	UN Special Fund	17 Nov 60	380UNTS289	105461
Guatemala	UN Special Fund	17 Nov 60	383UNTS67	105495
Mali	UNICEF (Children)	17 Nov 60	402UNTS23	105775
Cambodia	UN Special Fund	24 Nov 60	382UNTS255	105487
Fed of Malaya	WHO (World Health)	25 Nov 60	387UNTS37	105556
WHO (World Health)	Yemen	03 Dec 60	395UNTS187	105685
Dahomey	WHO (World Health)	07 Dec 60	387UNTS277	105567
Congo (Brazzaville)	WHO (World Health)	12 Dec 60	399UNTS105	105737
Nepal	UNICEF (Children)	12 Dec 60	382UNTS273	105488
Honduras	UN Special Fund	20 Dec 60	383UNTS103	105497
Togo	USA (United States)	22 Dec 60	401UNTS33	105760
Niger	WHO (World Health)	28 Dec 60	394UNTS195	105679
Burma	UN Special Fund	03 Jan 61	387UNTS219	105564
Mali	USA (United States)	04 Jan 61	405UNTS165	105832
Costa Rica	UN Special Fund	10 Jan 61	389UNTS253	105597
UN Special Fund	Saudi Arabia	19 Jan 61	396UNTS27	105692
UK Great Britain	USA (United States)	20 Jan 61	402UNTS153	105783
Nicaragua	UN Special Fund	20 Jan 61	387UNTS15	105555
Korea, South	WHO (World Health)	20 Jan 61	406UNTS269	200589
Chad	UN Special Fund	23 Jan 61	390UNTS69	105603
UN Special Fund	Somalia	28 Jan 61	388UNTS75	105573
Multilateral		28 Jan 61	387UNTS202	105563
Ivory Coast	WHO (World Health)	30 Jan 61	395UNTS205	105686
Gabon	UN Special Fund	02 Feb 61	387UNTS289	105568
WHO (World Health)	Togo	03 Feb 61	394UNTS207	105680
Chad	WHO (World Health)	03 Feb 61	394UNTS161	105676
Bolivia	USA (United States)	09 Feb 61	405UNTS113	105827
Nigeria	UN Special Fund	10 Feb 61	390UNTS85	105604
Central Afri Rep	WHO (World Health)	13 Feb 61	394UNTS149	105675
Mexico	UN Special Fund	23 Feb 61	388UNTS151	105576
Cyprus	UN Special Fund	24 Feb 61	389UNTS3	105588
Panama	UN Special Fund	09 Mar 61	396UNTS3	105691
Cuba	UN Special Fund	10 Mar 61	390UNTS35	105601
Afghanistan	Japan	15 Mar 61	450UNTS373	106480
Kuwait	WHO (World Health)	16 Mar 61	397UNTS315	200588
Ceylon (Sri Lanka)	Japan	20 Mar 61	450UNTS385	106481
Colombia	USA (United States)	03 Apr 61	407UNTS3	105856
Cuba	Czechoslovakia	05 Apr 61	442UNTS201	106350
Honduras	USA (United States)	12 Apr 61	413UNTS182	105952
Mauritania	WHO (World Health)	17 Apr 61	396UNTS301	200587
Cyprus	UNICEF (Children)	19 Apr 61	394UNTS185	105678
Korea, South	UN Special Fund	21 Apr 61	394UNTS231	200583
Gabon	WHO (World Health)	27 Apr 61	397UNTS215	105707
Mali	WHO (World Health)	27 Apr 61	407UNTS66	105860
Ceylon (Sri Lanka)	UN Special Fund	03 May 61	395UNTS217	105687

PARTY ONE	PARTY TWO	DATE	CITATION	NUMBER
Materials, equipment and services (Cont.)				
Sierra Leone	USA (United States)	05 May 61	409UNTS194	105885
Senegal	USA (United States)	13 May 61	409UNTS232	105888
Ivory Coast	USA (United States)	17 May 61	409UNTS241	105889
Mali	USA (United States)	20 May 61	413UNTS205	105954
Niger	USA (United States)	26 May 61	410UNTS213	105905
Cameroon	USA (United States)	26 May 61	413UNTS195	105953
Dahomey	USA (United States)	27 May 61	445UNTS23	106373
Somalia	USSR (Soviet Union)	02 Jun 61	457UNTS263	106587
Cameroon	UN Special Fund	13 Jun 61	397UNTS297	105713
Ethiopia	United Nations	14 Jun 61	406UNTS81	105840
Liberia	USA (United States)	17 Jun 61	410UNTS233	105907
Paraguay	UN Special Fund	22 Jun 61	399UNTS117	105738
Madagascar	USA (United States)	22 Jun 61	413UNTS219	105956
UN Special Fund	Upper Volta	26 Jun 61	400UNTS3	105744
Mexico	USA (United States)	26 Jun 61	413UNTS229	105957
Haiti	UN Special Fund	28 Jun 61	399UNTS171	105741
Philippines	UN Special Fund	28 Jun 61	399UNTS141	105739
UNICEF (Children)	Saudi Arabia	04 Jul 61	413UNTS122	105947
Ghana	USA (United States)	19 Jul 61	416UNTS167	106002
Tanganyika	USA (United States)	21 Jul 61	445UNTS33	106374
Mali	UN Special Fund	21 Jul 61	401UNTS141	105768
UN Special Fund	Yemen	02 Aug 61	402UNTS43	105777
Morocco	WHO (World Health)	09 Aug 61	412UNTS192	105932
Cameroon	UNICEF (Children)	12 Aug 61	402UNTS235	105788
WHO (World Health)	Somalia	17 Aug 61	423UNTS111	106088
Chad	UNICEF (Children)	26 Aug 61	422UNTS231	106077
Ghana	United Nations	29 Aug 61	406UNTS117	105843
Ivory Coast	UN Special Fund	29 Aug 61	406UNTS129	105844
Fed of Malaya	USA (United States)	04 Sep 61	421UNTS215	106060
Iraq	WHO (World Health)	13 Sep 61	419UNTS69	106030
Multilateral		20 Sep 61	407UNTS52	105859
Germany, West	UK Great Britain	26 Sep 61	424UNTS201	106108
Paraguay	USA (United States)	26 Sep 61	461UNTS91	106653
UN Special Fund	Sierra Leone	02 Oct 61	422UNTS131	106073
Malagasy	WHO (World Health)	13 Oct 61	421UNTS273	106064
Multilateral		16 Oct 61	410UNTS242	105908
Philippines	USA (United States)	31 Oct 61	424UNTS129	106105
Gabon	UNICEF (Children)	02 Nov 61	422UNTS241	106078
Mauritania	UN Special Fund	07 Nov 61	412UNTS240	105936
Multilateral		07 Nov 61	412UNTS258	105937
Congo (Brazzaville)	UN Special Fund	09 Nov 61	413UNTS58	105940
Brazil	USA (United States)	11 Nov 61	433UNTS199	106243
Malagasy	UNICEF (Children)	16 Nov 61	422UNTS251	106079
El Salvador	USA (United States)	20 Nov 61	433UNTS221	106245
Thailand	USA (United States)	28 Nov 61	434UNTS77	106256
Panama	USA (United States)	11 Dec 61	445UNTS161	106384
UN Special Fund	Venezuela	11 Dec 61	422UNTS149	106074
UN Special Fund	Senegal	16 Dec 61	425UNTS97	106121
El Salvador	USA (United States)	19 Dec 61	445UNTS175	106385
Multilateral		27 Dec 61	425UNTS83	106120
Sierra Leone	USA (United States)	29 Dec 61	434UNTS43	106254
Malagasy	UN Special Fund	05 Jan 62	419UNTS29	106028
Ivory Coast	UNICEF (Children)	10 Jan 62	422UNTS261	106080
Dominican Republic	USA (United States)	11 Jan 62	433UNTS133	106236
Ethiopia	WHO (World Health)	11 Jan 62	423UNTS99	106087
Multilateral		17 Jan 62	419UNTS294	106033
Multilateral		20 Jan 62	429UNTS230	200596
Peru	USA (United States)	25 Jan 62	473UNTS57	106855
UNICEF (Children)	Yemen	31 Jan 62	422UNTS271	106081
Multilateral		13 Feb 62	422UNTS288	200594
Multilateral		21 Feb 62	423UNTS151	106091
UK Great Britain	USA (United States)	22 Feb 62	435UNTS127	106275
Niger	UN Special Fund	26 Feb 62	423UNTS83	106086
Multilateral		01 Mar 62	423UNTS122	106089
Dominican Republic	USA (United States)	08 Mar 62	527UNTS29	107615

PARTY ONE	PARTY TWO	DATE	CITATION	NUMBER
Materials, equipment and services (Cont.)				
Liberia	USA (United States)	08 Mar 62	445UNTS41	106375
WHO (World Health)	Sudan	11 Mar 62	432UNTS325	106226
Nigeria	WHO (World Health)	27 Mar 62	429UNTS123	106194
Brazil	Japan	28 Mar 62	451UNTS125	106489
Dahomey	UN Special Fund	28 Mar 62	424UNTS55	106099
Nicaragua	USA (United States)	30 Mar 62	456UNTS241	106559
India	Japan	31 Mar 62	451UNTS143	106490
UNICEF (Children)	Somalia	01 Apr 62	431UNTS75	106211
Congo (Brazzaville)	UNICEF (Children)	09 Apr 62	431UNTS65	106210
Colombia	USA (United States)	09 Apr 62	476UNTS9	106899
Multilateral		10 Apr 62	429UNTS78	106192
UNICEF (Children)	Sierra Leone	11 Apr 62	431UNTS55	106209
El Salvador	USA (United States)	13 Apr 62	451UNTS307	106500
Ecuador	USA (United States)	17 Apr 62	442UNTS69	106339
Somalia	USA (United States)	17 Apr 62	436UNTS107	106291
Multilateral		18 Apr 62	463UNTS44	106692
India	Japan	23 Apr 62	451UNTS155	106491
Bolivia	USA (United States)	26 Apr 62	461UNTS105	106654
Dominican Republic	USA (United States)	02 May 62	442UNTS107	106342
UN Special Fund	Uruguay	04 May 62	429UNTS143	106196
Multilateral		17 May 62	429UNTS46	106189
Panama	USA (United States)	23 May 62	458UNTS225	106604
Ethiopia	USA (United States)	23 May 62	456UNTS293	106563
Greece	Tunisia	26 May 62	534UNTS163	107761
USA (United States)	Venezuela	28 May 62	458UNTS249	106607
Pakistan	USA (United States)	31 May 62	460UNTS75	106631
Dominican Republic	UN Special Fund	06 Jun 62	429UNTS169	106197
Dahomey	USA (United States)	13 Jun 62	458UNTS219	106603
Niger	USA (United States)	14 Jun 62	458UNTS233	106605
Libya	WHO (World Health)	16 Jun 62	437UNTS127	106301
Costa Rica	USA (United States)	18 Jun 62	461UNTS155	106659
Bolivia	USA (United States)	19 Jun 62	458UNTS239	106606
WHO (World Health)	Sierra Leone	19 Jun 62	439UNTS151	106327
Germany, West	Syria	25 Jun 62	489UNTS71	107135
UN Special Fund	Syria	07 Jul 62	443UNTS3	106355
UN Special Fund	Tanganyika	17 Jul 62	435UNTS237	106281
Senegal	USA (United States)	20 Jul 62	458UNTS137	106596
Honduras	USA (United States)	20 Jul 62	460UNTS125	106635
Niger	USA (United States)	23 Jul 62	487UNTS325	107114
Guatemala	USA (United States)	02 Aug 62	461UNTS199	106664
Ecuador	USA (United States)	03 Aug 62	460UNTS133	106636
WHO (World Health)	Senegal	06 Aug 62	435UNTS179	106279
Multilateral		12 Aug 62	443UNTS266	106365
WHO (World Health)	Western Samoa	14 Aug 62	437UNTS317	200598
Cyprus	USA (United States)	23 Aug 62	461UNTS147	106658
Nepal	USA (United States)	24 Aug 62	460UNTS143	106637
Paraguay	USA (United States)	25 Aug 62	461UNTS207	106665
Multilateral		29 Aug 62	443UNTS280	106366
Togo	USA (United States)	05 Sep 62	461UNTS47	106650
Afghanistan	USA (United States)	11 Sep 62	461UNTS169	106661
Finland	USSR (Soviet Union)	27 Sep 62	479UNTS99	106949
Sweden	USA (United States)	04 Oct 62	462UNTS31	106669
Gabon	USA (United States)	04 Oct 62	459UNTS185	106620
Mali	USSR (Soviet Union)	10 Oct 62	493UNTS219	107216
Honduras	USA (United States)	24 Oct 62	459UNTS211	106624
Multilateral		25 Oct 62	457UNTS137	106583
Multilateral		25 Oct 62	457UNTS129	106582
Japan	UN Special Fund	31 Oct 62	444UNTS171	106368
Multilateral		15 Nov 62	448UNTS50	106424
Algeria	UN Special Fund	15 Nov 62	452UNTS243	106512
WHO (World Health)	Syria	18 Nov 62	480UNTS249	106972
Algeria	UNICEF (Children)	20 Nov 62	453UNTS151	106522
Ceylon (Sri Lanka)	USA (United States)	21 Nov 62	462UNTS237	106683
India	USA (United States)	21 Nov 62	462UNTS255	106685
Costa Rica	USA (United States)	23 Nov 62	541UNTS67	107861

PARTY ONE	PARTY TWO	DATE	CITATION	NUMBER
Materials, equipment and services (Cont.)				
Laos	USSR (Soviet Union)	01 Dec 62	472UNTS3	106834
Multilateral		06 Dec 62	450UNTS240	106471
Cameroon	WHO (World Health)	08 Dec 62	451UNTS215	106496
Multilateral		12 Dec 62	457UNTS72	106578
Guinea	USA (United States)	14 Dec 62	462UNTS247	106684
Multilateral		17 Dec 62	486UNTS119	107076
Algeria	WHO (World Health)	20 Dec 62	463UNTS135	106698
Guatemala	USA (United States)	29 Dec 62	474UNTS31	106869
UK Great Britain	USA (United States)	15 Jan 63	466UNTS181	106743
Senegal	USA (United States)	17 Jan 63	493UNTS97	107210
Mauritania	UNICEF (Children)	19 Jan 63	452UNTS271	106514
Multilateral		21 Jan 63	453UNTS20	106517
New Zealand	Western Samoa	24 Jan 63	499UNTS21	107290
UNICEF (Children)	Tanganyika	25 Jan 63	453UNTS249	106528
Ethiopia	USA (United States)	25 Jan 63	473UNTS27	106851
India	USA (United States)	01 Feb 63	473UNTS37	106852
Multilateral		05 Feb 63	453UNTS36	106518
Central Afri Rep	USA (United States)	10 Feb 63	473UNTS83	106857
Multilateral		14 Feb 63	453UNTS168	106524
Multilateral		06 Mar 63	455UNTS386	106552
UN Special Fund	Uganda	22 Mar 63	456UNTS466	106572
Brazil	USA (United States)	29 Mar 63	476UNTS67	106904
Multilateral		18 Apr 63	463UNTS121	106697
Japan	USA (United States)	26 Apr 63	477UNTS37	106914
Multilateral		06 May 63	463UNTS78	106694
Australia	USA (United States)	09 May 63	469UNTS55	106784
Australia	USA (United States)	09 May 63	475UNTS331	106897
Multilateral		09 May 63	463UNTS159	106700
Multilateral		22 May 63	483UNTS72	107007
Jamaica	UN Special Fund	22 May 63	489UNTS191	107140
Netherlands	UN Special Fund	24 May 63	466UNTS289	106750
Multilateral		24 May 63	466UNTS346	106754
UN Special Fund	Western Samoa	05 Jun 63	467UNTS463	200601
Mongolia	WHO (World Health)	21 Jun 63	472UNTS373	106848
UNICEF (Children)	Togo	27 Jun 63	540UNTS135	107847
Multilateral		23 Jul 63	471UNTS158	106831
Multilateral		31 Jul 63	472UNTS220	106842
USA (United States)	Uruguay	31 Jul 63	488UNTS3	107115
India	USA (United States)	08 Aug 63	488UNTS21	107117
Burundi	WHO (World Health)	08 Aug 63	477UNTS346	106928
Burundi	UN Special Fund	22 Aug 63	476UNTS49	106903
Multilateral		27 Aug 63	511UNTS210	107435
Multilateral		10 Sep 63	480UNTS100	106965
Multilateral		23 Sep 63	488UNTS99	107122
Jamaica	WHO (World Health)	25 Sep 63	481UNTS125	106980
Multilateral		19 Oct 63	523UNTS249	107559
Jamaica	USA (United States)	24 Oct 63	489UNTS337	107148
Central Afri Rep	UN Special Fund	30 Oct 63	481UNTS247	106985
Multilateral		30 Oct 63	480UNTS180	106968
Panama	USA (United States)	30 Oct 63	530UNTS3	107668
WHO (World Health)	Tanganyika	05 Nov 63	496UNTS193	107252
Multilateral		07 Nov 63	480UNTS232	106971
Multilateral		08 Nov 63	482UNTS286	106999
Iran	UNICEF (Children)	21 Nov 63	485UNTS35	107044
Argentina	USA (United States)	30 Nov 63	505UNTS131	107369
Cameroon	Netherlands	18 Dec 63	521UNTS303	107527
New Zealand	Western Samoa	31 Dec 63	521UNTS163	107519
Multilateral		28 Jan 64	502UNTS321	107336
Paraguay	USA (United States)	10 Feb 64	511UNTS53	107426
Mexico	USA (United States)	14 Feb 64	524UNTS197	107574
Multilateral		20 Feb 64	491UNTS30	107172
Netherlands	Tunisia	03 Mar 64	533UNTS133	107739
Germany, West	Thailand	02 Apr 64	503UNTS3	107338
Portugal	UK Great Britain	07 Apr 64	539UNTS167	107830
Japan	USA (United States)	25 Apr 64	530UNTS61	107672

PARTY ONE	PARTY TWO	DATE	CITATION	NUMBER
Materials, equipment and services (Cont.)				
Canada	USA (United States)	06 May 64	524UNTS173	107572
Argentina	USA (United States)	10 May 64	527UNTS77	107618
Multilateral		26 May 64	541UNTS271	200613
Ireland	UN Special Fund	03 Jun 64	496UNTS205	107253
Cuba	Czechoslovakia	03 Jun 64	527UNTS205	107626
Rwanda	WHO (World Health)	22 Jun 64	514UNTS11	107440
Multilateral		23 Jun 64	506UNTS108	107383
WHO (World Health)	Trinidad/Tobago	23 Jun 64	503UNTS167	107342
Rwanda	WHO (World Health)	23 Jun 64	514UNTS157	107445
Multilateral		28 Jun 64	519UNTS14	107499
Colombia	Netherlands	06 Jul 64	543UNTS289	107906
Belgium	Tunisia	15 Jul 64	560UNTS57	108168
Multilateral		28 Jul 64	555UNTS183	108113
Kenya	USA (United States)	26 Aug 64	531UNTS51	107692
Dominican Republic	USA (United States)	28 Aug 64	531UNTS35	107691
Multilateral		18 Sep 64	556UNTS25	108117
Multilateral		18 Sep 64	555UNTS205	108114
Multilateral		21 Sep 64	555UNTS227	108115
Australia	UN Special Fund	30 Sep 64	510UNTS277	107419
Multilateral		30 Sep 64	556UNTS3	108116
Czechoslovakia	Mongolia	21 Oct 64	545UNTS91	107926
Multilateral		24 Oct 64	514UNTS220	200608
Ethiopia	Netherlands	28 Oct 64	541UNTS235	107872
Netherlands	Pakistan	30 Oct 64	541UNTS243	107873
Multilateral		11 Nov 64	515UNTS94	107456
India	United Nations	25 Nov 64	519UNTS47	107501
Czechoslovakia	United Arab Rep	26 Nov 64	545UNTS11	107923
Ghana	Israel	30 Nov 64	550UNTS231	108019
Multilateral		02 Dec 64	572UNTS229	108317
Netherlands	Nigeria	04 Dec 64	545UNTS155	107931
Japan	USA (United States)	04 Dec 64	532UNTS249	107721
India	Netherlands	11 Dec 64	570UNTS165	108292
Germany, West	Thailand	23 Dec 64	525UNTS193	107591
Germany, West	Thailand	23 Dec 64	525UNTS185	107590
Germany, West	Thailand	23 Dec 64	525UNTS177	107589
Malawi	WHO (World Health)	06 Jan 65	525UNTS165	107588
Malawi	WHO (World Health)	08 Jan 65	524UNTS281	107579
Denmark	Thailand	25 Jan 65	530UNTS173	107680
Multilateral		27 Jan 65	523UNTS102	107556
WHO (World Health)	Tunisia	27 Jan 65	528UNTS209	107644
Multilateral		02 Feb 65	523UNTS256	107560
Multilateral		12 Feb 65	525UNTS148	107587
Belgium	United Nations	20 Feb 65	535UNTS191	107779
Multilateral		24 Feb 65	556UNTS47	108118
Multilateral		26 Feb 65	556UNTS69	108119
Hungary	Yugoslavia	08 Apr 65	587UNTS169	108511
Malawi	USA (United States)	20 Apr 65	546UNTS175	107943
Malta	UNICEF (Children)	22 Apr 65	533UNTS107	107737
Netherlands	Tanzania	27 Apr 65	594UNTS123	108599
Gambia	UNICEF (Children)	29 May 65	547UNTS29	107954
Multilateral		02 Jun 65	537UNTS348	200611
Canada	USA (United States)	08 Jun 65	546UNTS201	107947
Netherlands	Senegal	12 Jun 65	602UNTS231	108715
Mongolia	UNICEF (Children)	23 Jun 65	540UNTS83	107844
Canada	USA (United States)	29 Jun 65	549UNTS273	108003
Guinea	USA (United States)	29 Jun 65	549UNTS139	107997
UN Special Fund	Spain	30 Jun 65	544UNTS159	107918
Multilateral		02 Jul 65	592UNTS215	108575
Cameroon	Netherlands	06 Jul 65	571UNTS75	108300
Israel	USA (United States)	20 Jul 65	549UNTS55	107989
Laos	Thailand	12 Aug 65	547UNTS209	107958
Poland	WHO (World Health)	26 Aug 65	552UNTS3	108047
Multilateral		13 Sep 65	547UNTS264	107962
Multilateral		21 Oct 65	547UNTS216	107959
Netherlands	Nigeria	28 Oct 65	578UNTS15	108383

PARTY ONE	PARTY TWO	DATE	CITATION	NUMBER
Materials, equipment and services (Cont.)				
Saudi Arabia	USA (United States)	19 Nov 65	580UNTS35	108419
Denmark	Syria	28 Dec 65	588UNTS163	108523
Ethiopia	USA (United States)	30 Dec 65	574UNTS129	108345
Austria	Tunisia	30 Dec 65	589UNTS119	108539
Iran	USSR (Soviet Union)	13 Jan 66	633UNTS123	109037
Mongolia	UN Special Fund	26 Jan 66	552UNTS201	108055
Panama	USA (United States)	15 Feb 66	586UNTS27	108494
Brazil	Denmark	25 Feb 66	590UNTS95	108549
Bulgaria	UNICEF (Children)	10 Mar 66	559UNTS13	108152
WHO (World Health)	Singapore	28 Mar 66	562UNTS59	108195
Brazil	UNICEF (Children)	28 Mar 66	607UNTS235	108807
Bulgaria	UN Special Fund	26 May 66	563UNTS71	108205
Multilateral		20 Jun 66	572UNTS263	108318
Ivory Coast	Netherlands	01 Aug 66	591UNTS245	108561
Mexico	USA (United States)	24 Aug 66	606UNTS251	108789
UN Special Fund	Singapore	23 Sep 66	573UNTS115	108326
Netherlands	Nigeria	18 Oct 66	603UNTS53	108724
Indonesia	UNICEF (Children)	17 Nov 66	578UNTS47	108386
Australia	USA (United States)	09 Dec 66	607UNTS83	108798
Syria	USSR (Soviet Union)	18 Dec 66	633UNTS247	109041
UNICEF (Children)	Zambia	02 Feb 67	589UNTS89	108536
Kenya	Netherlands	09 Feb 67	610UNTS0	108833
Multilateral		17 Mar 67	594UNTS105	108598
Netherlands	Vietnam, South	24 Mar 67	610UNTS0	108834
Denmark	Pakistan	21 Oct 67	632UNTS105	109012
India	United Nations	04 Nov 67	609UNTS3	108824
United Nations	Senegal	08 Nov 67	613UNTS255	108854
Australia	UNICEF (Children)	21 Dec 67	614UNTS83	108864
UN Special Fund	Syria	22 Apr 68	634UNTS207	109063
Niger	United Nations	07 May 68	639UNTS71	109145
Botswana	UNICEF (Children)	25 Jun 68	639UNTS61	109144
Aid missions				
Dominican Republic	USA (United States)	13 Oct 45	149UNTS361	200477
Brazil	USA (United States)	15 Feb 46	162UNTS21	102130
Brazil	USA (United States)	05 Apr 46	12UNTS131	100183
Peru	USA (United States)	27 Dec 46	152UNTS93	102013
Greece	USA (United States)	20 Jun 47	7UNTS267	100105
Austria	USA (United States)	25 Jun 47	22UNTS141	100334
Italy	USA (United States)	04 Jul 47	22UNTS173	100336
Turkey	USA (United States)	12 Jul 47	7UNTS299	100106
Poland	UNICEF (Children)	23 Aug 47	65UNTS22	100815
Bolivia	USA (United States)	03 Nov 47	51UNTS33	100750
Ecuador	USA (United States)	14 Nov 47	149UNTS297	101959
UNICEF (Children)	Yugoslavia	20 Nov 47	65UNTS28	100817
USA (United States)	Venezuela	24 Mar 48	44UNTS57	100678
Ireland	USA (United States)	28 Jun 48	24UNTS3	100349
Italy	USA (United States)	28 Jun 48	20UNTS43	100314
France	USA (United States)	28 Jun 48	19UNTS9	100302
Denmark	USA (United States)	29 Jun 48	22UNTS217	100338
Austria	USA (United States)	02 Jul 48	21UNTS29	100323
Greece	USA (United States)	02 Jul 48	23UNTS43	100342
Netherlands	USA (United States)	02 Jul 48	20UNTS91	100315
Belgium	USA (United States)	02 Jul 48	19UNTS127	100309
Norway	USA (United States)	03 Jul 48	20UNTS185	100317
Sweden	USA (United States)	03 Jul 48	23UNTS101	100343
Taiwan	USA (United States)	03 Jul 48	17UNTS119	100273
Iceland	USA (United States)	03 Jul 48	20UNTS141	100316
Luxembourg	USA (United States)	03 Jul 48	24UNTS35	100350
Turkey	USA (United States)	04 Jul 48	24UNTS67	100351
UK Great Britain	USA (United States)	06 Jul 48	22UNTS263	100339
France	USA (United States)	09 Jul 48	24UNTS103	100352
Multilateral		14 Jul 48	23UNTS3	100340
Portugal	USA (United States)	28 Sep 48	29UNTS213	100442
Trieste	USA (United States)	15 Oct 48	29UNTS249	100443

PARTY ONE	PARTY TWO	DATE	CITATION	NUMBER
Aid missions (Cont.)				
Afghanistan	UNESCO (Educ/Cult)	08 Dec 48	46UNTS3	100697
Korea, South	USA (United States)	10 Dec 48	55UNTS157	100813
Austria	USA (United States)	23 Mar 49	43UNTS127	100667
Panama	USA (United States)	31 Mar 49	55UNTS141	100812
Panama	USA (United States)	31 Mar 49	55UNTS87	100810
WHO (World Health)	Thailand	12 Aug 49	178UNTS347	102350
Germany, West	USA (United States)	15 Dec 49	92UNTS269	101277
Korea, South	USA (United States)	26 Jan 50	80UNTS205	101053
Luxembourg	USA (United States)	27 Jan 50	80UNTS187	101052
France	USA (United States)	27 Jan 50	80UNTS171	101051
Italy	USA (United States)	27 Jan 50	80UNTS145	101050
Netherlands	USA (United States)	27 Jan 50	80UNTS219	101054
UK Great Britain	USA (United States)	27 Jan 50	80UNTS261	101056
Norway	USA (United States)	27 Jan 50	80UNTS241	101055
Belgium	USA (United States)	27 Jan 50	51UNTS213	100767
Denmark	USA (United States)	27 Jan 50	48UNTS115	100740
Iran	USA (United States)	23 May 50	81UNTS3	101057
Burma	USA (United States)	13 Sep 50	92UNTS361	101280
Thailand	USA (United States)	19 Sep 50	132UNTS199	101761
Indonesia	USA (United States)	16 Oct 50	281UNTS105	104074
Thailand	USA (United States)	17 Oct 50	79UNTS41	101030
Portugal	USA (United States)	05 Jan 51	133UNTS75	101782
Honduras	USA (United States)	30 Jan 51	124UNTS63	101667
Nicaragua	USA (United States)	31 Jan 51	150UNTS3	101960
Taiwan	USA (United States)	09 Feb 51	132UNTS273	101767
USA (United States)	Yugoslavia	17 Apr 51	162UNTS173	102134
Philippines	USA (United States)	27 Apr 51	174UNTS251	102290
Saudi Arabia	USA (United States)	18 Jun 51	102UNTS73	101412
Burma	WHO (World Health)	09 Jul 51	104UNTS175	101439
El Salvador	USA (United States)	23 Jul 51	138UNTS127	101865
Japan	USA (United States)	28 Aug 51	147UNTS81	101930
Portugal	USA (United States)	06 Sep 51	237UNTS217	103348
USA (United States)	Vietnam, South	07 Sep 51	174UNTS165	102284
Cambodia	USA (United States)	08 Sep 51	174UNTS115	102282
Laos	USA (United States)	09 Sep 51	174UNTS141	102283
Costa Rica	USA (United States)	11 Sep 51	234UNTS255	103288
El Salvador	USA (United States)	23 Oct 51	137UNTS43	101847
El Salvador	USA (United States)	12 Dec 51	132UNTS287	101768
Iran	USA (United States)	20 Jan 52	200UNTS191	102703
Libya	USA (United States)	21 Jan 52	183UNTS177	102427
Jordan	USA (United States)	12 Feb 52	168UNTS25	102211
Dominican Republic	WHO (World Health)	15 Feb 52	134UNTS291	101808
Ecuador	USA (United States)	20 Feb 52	177UNTS43	102308
Peru	USA (United States)	22 Feb 52	165UNTS31	102166
Honduras	USA (United States)	07 Mar 52	233UNTS151	103260
Cuba	USA (United States)	07 Mar 52	165UNTS11	102165
Brazil	USA (United States)	15 Mar 52	199UNTS221	102687
India	WHO (World Health)	02 Apr 52	131UNTS227	101743
Israel	USA (United States)	09 May 52	177UNTS63	102309
USA (United States)	Uruguay	30 Jun 52	207UNTS139	102804
Chile	USA (United States)	30 Jun 52	199UNTS241	102688
Panama	USA (United States)	30 Jun 52	181UNTS121	102404
Panama	USA (United States)	08 Aug 52	181UNTS257	102415
Ceylon (Sri Lanka)	USA (United States)	17 Nov 52	180UNTS207	102386
Dominican Republic	USA (United States)	06 Mar 53	199UNTS267	102689
United Arab Rep	USA (United States)	12 Mar 53	204UNTS3	102747
United Arab Rep	USA (United States)	19 Mar 53	215UNTS17	102909
El Salvador	USA (United States)	14 May 53	234UNTS71	103273
United Arab Rep	USA (United States)	21 May 53	204UNTS29	102748
Brazil	USA (United States)	30 May 53	460UNTS89	106633
United Arab Rep	USA (United States)	18 Jun 53	215UNTS45	102910
United Arab Rep	USA (United States)	18 Jun 53	204UNTS55	102749
Liberia	USA (United States)	23 Jun 53	213UNTS57	102880
Liberia	USA (United States)	23 Jun 53	213UNTS37	102879
Pakistan	USA (United States)	25 Jun 53	205UNTS139	102773

PARTY ONE	PARTY TWO	DATE	CITATION	NUMBER
Aid missions (Cont.)				
Brazil	USA (United States)	26 Jun 53	336UNTS241	104808
Philippines	USA (United States)	26 Jun 53	213UNTS77	102881
Nicaragua	USA (United States)	30 Jun 53	215UNTS133	102917
Spain	USA (United States)	26 Sep 53	207UNTS61	102800
Spain	USA (United States)	26 Sep 53	207UNTS93	102802
Bolivia	USA (United States)	15 Jan 54	229UNTS213	103168
Japan	USA (United States)	21 Jan 54	223UNTS145	103063
United Arab Rep	USA (United States)	24 Feb 54	236UNTS61	103316
Japan	USA (United States)	08 Mar 54	232UNTS169	103236
Belgium	Norway	24 Mar 54	219UNTS73	102967
Ethiopia	USA (United States)	21 Apr 54	232UNTS299	103244
Iraq	USA (United States)	21 Apr 54	222UNTS251	103032
Panama	USA (United States)	11 May 54	236UNTS107	103319
Pakistan	USA (United States)	19 May 54	202UNTS301	102736
Honduras	USA (United States)	20 May 54	222UNTS87	103025
Ecuador	USA (United States)	30 Jun 54	236UNTS163	103323
El Salvador	USA (United States)	16 Jul 54	237UNTS237	103350
El Salvador	USA (United States)	31 Aug 54	237UNTS49	103336
Guatemala	USA (United States)	01 Sep 54	199UNTS51	102677
Haiti	USA (United States)	28 Jan 55	270UNTS83	103894
El Salvador	USA (United States)	21 Mar 55	250UNTS261	103528
Cambodia	USA (United States)	16 May 55	263UNTS273	103777
Canada	USA (United States)	15 Jun 55	235UNTS201	103302
Guatemala	USA (United States)	18 Jun 55	262UNTS105	103740
Haiti	USA (United States)	24 Jun 55	264UNTS291	103800
Germany, West	USA (United States)	30 Jun 55	240UNTS47	103393
Libya	USA (United States)	21 Jul 55	264UNTS247	103796
Libya	USA (United States)	28 Jul 55	270UNTS245	103900
Libya	USA (United States)	28 Jul 55	270UNTS269	103901
Libya	USA (United States)	28 Jul 55	270UNTS317	103903
Liberia	USA (United States)	06 Oct 55	275UNTS93	103978
USA (United States)	Uruguay	23 Mar 56	376UNTS311	105386
Colombia	USA (United States)	27 Mar 56	273UNTS235	103954
Tunisia	USA (United States)	26 Mar 57	283UNTS117	104111
Morocco	USA (United States)	02 Apr 57	288UNTS157	104203
Ghana	USA (United States)	03 Jun 57	284UNTS63	104129
Argentina	USA (United States)	03 Jun 57	291UNTS61	104244
Jordan	USA (United States)	27 Jun 57	288UNTS269	104209
Libya	USA (United States)	30 Jun 57	284UNTS177	104136
Fed of Malaya	UK Great Britain	12 Oct 57	285UNTS59	104149
Sudan	USA (United States)	31 Mar 58	308UNTS105	104458
Iran	Japan	09 Dec 58	325UNTS221	104701
Guinea	USA (United States)	30 Sep 60	394UNTS103	105671
Togo	USA (United States)	22 Dec 60	401UNTS33	105760
Colombia	USA (United States)	04 Apr 61	405UNTS55	105822
Honduras	USA (United States)	12 Apr 61	413UNTS182	105952
Sierra Leone	USA (United States)	05 May 61	409UNTS194	105885
Senegal	USA (United States)	13 May 61	409UNTS232	105888
Ivory Coast	USA (United States)	17 May 61	409UNTS241	105889
Cameroon	USA (United States)	26 May 61	413UNTS195	105953
Niger	USA (United States)	26 May 61	410UNTS213	105905
Dahomey	USA (United States)	27 May 61	445UNTS23	106373
Ecuador	USA (United States)	17 Jun 61	411UNTS49	105913
Madagascar	USA (United States)	22 Jun 61	413UNTS219	105956
Paraguay	USA (United States)	26 Sep 61	461UNTS91	106653
Philippines	USA (United States)	31 Oct 61	424UNTS129	106105
Panama	USA (United States)	11 Dec 61	445UNTS161	106384
El Salvador	USA (United States)	19 Dec 61	445UNTS175	106385
Iran	USA (United States)	21 Dec 61	433UNTS269	106249
Costa Rica	USA (United States)	22 Dec 61	460UNTS277	106646
Dominican Republic	USA (United States)	11 Jan 62	433UNTS133	106236
Peru	USA (United States)	25 Jan 62	473UNTS57	106855
Dominican Republic	USA (United States)	08 Mar 62	527UNTS29	107615
Nicaragua	USA (United States)	30 Mar 62	456UNTS241	106559
Ecuador	USA (United States)	17 Apr 62	442UNTS69	106339

PARTY ONE	PARTY TWO	DATE	CITATION	NUMBER
Aid missions (Cont.)				
Ivory Coast	USA (United States)	21 Apr 62	526UNTS39	107598
USA (United States)	Venezuela	28 May 62	458UNTS249	106607
Pakistan	USA (United States)	31 May 62	460UNTS75	106631
Bolivia	USA (United States)	19 Jun 62	458UNTS239	106606
Honduras	USA (United States)	20 Jul 62	460UNTS125	106635
Niger	USA (United States)	23 Jul 62	487UNTS325	107114
Colombia	USA (United States)	23 Jul 62	458UNTS123	106595
Ecuador	USA (United States)	03 Aug 62	460UNTS133	106636
Cyprus	USA (United States)	23 Aug 62	461UNTS147	106658
Togo	USA (United States)	05 Sep 62	461UNTS47	106650
Afghanistan	USA (United States)	11 Sep 62	461UNTS169	106661
Gabon	USA (United States)	04 Oct 62	459UNTS185	106620
Belgium	Rwanda	13 Oct 62	456UNTS425	106568
Multilateral		25 Oct 62	457UNTS137	106583
Multilateral		25 Oct 62	457UNTS129	106582
Ceylon (Sri Lanka)	USA (United States)	21 Nov 62	462UNTS237	106683
India	USA (United States)	21 Nov 62	462UNTS255	106685
Costa Rica	USA (United States)	23 Nov 62	541UNTS67	107861
Guinea	USA (United States)	14 Dec 62	462UNTS247	106684
Guatemala	USA (United States)	29 Dec 62	474UNTS31	106869
Senegal	USA (United States)	17 Jan 63	493UNTS97	107210
Indonesia	USA (United States)	14 Mar 63	505UNTS79	107365
Burma	Japan	29 Mar 63	518UNTS3	107490
Jamaica	USA (United States)	06 Jun 63	477UNTS29	106913
USA (United States)	Uruguay	31 Jul 63	488UNTS3	107115
UK Great Britain	USA (United States)	11 Oct 63	483UNTS3	107005
Jamaica	USA (United States)	24 Oct 63	489UNTS337	107148
Panama	USA (United States)	30 Oct 63	530UNTS3	107668
Czechoslovakia	Hungary	20 Dec 63	538UNTS127	107812
Kenya	USA (United States)	26 Aug 64	531UNTS51	107692
Netherlands	Norway	17 Nov 64	579UNTS243	108412
Malawi	USA (United States)	20 Apr 65	546UNTS175	107943
Volunteer programs				
Ecuador	USA (United States)	30 Jun 54	236UNTS163	103323
Turkey	UK Great Britain	25 Nov 58	327UNTS35	104715
Ghana	USA (United States)	19 Jul 61	416UNTS167	106002
Tanganyika	USA (United States)	21 Jul 61	445UNTS33	106374
Fed of Malaya	USA (United States)	04 Sep 61	421UNTS215	106060
Jordan	United Nations	11 Sep 61	406UNTS255	105855
Philippines	USA (United States)	31 Oct 61	424UNTS129	106105
Brazil	USA (United States)	11 Nov 61	433UNTS199	106243
El Salvador	USA (United States)	20 Nov 61	433UNTS221	106245
Thailand	USA (United States)	28 Nov 61	434UNTS77	106256
Sierra Leone	USA (United States)	29 Dec 61	434UNTS43	106254
Peru	USA (United States)	25 Jan 62	473UNTS57	106855
UK Great Britain	USA (United States)	22 Feb 62	435UNTS127	106275
Liberia	USA (United States)	08 Mar 62	445UNTS41	106375
Somalia	USA (United States)	17 Apr 62	436UNTS107	106291
Ivory Coast	USA (United States)	21 Apr 62	526UNTS39	107598
Dominican Republic	USA (United States)	02 May 62	442UNTS107	106342
Ethiopia	USA (United States)	23 May 62	456UNTS293	106563
USA (United States)	Venezuela	28 May 62	458UNTS249	106607
Pakistan	USA (United States)	31 May 62	460UNTS75	106631
Bolivia	USA (United States)	19 Jun 62	458UNTS239	106606
Honduras	USA (United States)	20 Jul 62	460UNTS125	106635
Niger	USA (United States)	23 Jul 62	487UNTS325	107114
Ecuador	USA (United States)	03 Aug 62	460UNTS133	106636
Cyprus	USA (United States)	23 Aug 62	461UNTS147	106658
Nepal	USA (United States)	24 Aug 62	460UNTS143	106637
Turkey	USA (United States)	27 Aug 62	461UNTS55	106651
Togo	USA (United States)	05 Sep 62	461UNTS47	106650
Afghanistan	USA (United States)	11 Sep 62	461UNTS169	106661
Chile	USA (United States)	04 Oct 62	461UNTS129	106656
Gabon	USA (United States)	04 Oct 62	459UNTS185	106620

PARTY ONE	PARTY TWO	DATE	CITATION	NUMBER
Volunteer programs (Cont.)				
Multilateral		25 Oct 62	457UNTS137	106583
Multilateral		25 Oct 62	457UNTS129	106582
India	USA (United States)	21 Nov 62	462UNTS255	106685
Ceylon (Sri Lanka)	USA (United States)	21 Nov 62	462UNTS237	106683
Costa Rica	USA (United States)	23 Nov 62	541UNTS67	107861
Guinea	USA (United States)	14 Dec 62	462UNTS247	106684
Guatemala	USA (United States)	29 Dec 62	474UNTS31	106869
Senegal	USA (United States)	17 Jan 63	493UNTS97	107210
Indonesia	USA (United States)	14 Mar 63	505UNTS79	107365
USA (United States)	Uruguay	31 Jul 63	488UNTS3	107115
Cameroon	Netherlands	18 Dec 63	521UNTS303	107527
Colombia	Netherlands	06 Jul 64	543UNTS289	107906
Kenya	USA (United States)	26 Aug 64	531UNTS51	107692
Uganda	USA (United States)	16 Nov 64	586UNTS143	108501
Malawi	USA (United States)	20 Apr 65	546UNTS175	107943
Ivory Coast	Netherlands	03 Jun 65	634UNTS95	109054
Netherlands	Zambia	17 Dec 65	631UNTS311	109000
Chad	USA (United States)	31 Aug 66	606UNTS47	108773
Korea, South	USA (United States)	14 Sep 66	606UNTS55	108774
Botswana	UN Special Fund	30 Sep 66	576UNTS3	108360
Kenya	Netherlands	09 Feb 67	610UNTS0	108833
Denmark	Tanzania	05 Apr 67	603UNTS111	108728
Denmark	India	01 Sep 67	616UNTS69	108892
UK Great Britain	USA (United States)	25 Jun 68	0UNTS0	109271
Surplus property				
Canada	USA (United States)	07 Jun 44	99UNTS259	200280
Belgium	USA (United States)	17 Apr 45	139UNTS253	200454
Netherlands	USA (United States)	30 Apr 45	139UNTS341	200460
UK Great Britain	USA (United States)	27 Mar 46	4UNTS2	100039
Canada	USA (United States)	30 Mar 46	7UNTS15	100089
Poland	USA (United States)	24 Apr 46	4UNTS155	100042
Greece	USA (United States)	16 May 46	184UNTS230	102451
France	USA (United States)	28 May 46	84UNTS141	101124
France	USA (United States)	28 May 46	84UNTS167	101127
Philippines	USA (United States)	11 Sep 46	43UNTS231	100670
Canada	USA (United States)	09 Jan 47	11UNTS341	100173
Burma	USA (United States)	28 Feb 47	25UNTS27	100355
Canada	USA (United States)	06 Mar 47	11UNTS325	100172
Greece	USA (United States)	23 Apr 48	74UNTS107	100958
Korea, South	USA (United States)	11 Sep 48	89UNTS155	101216
Philippines	USA (United States)	16 May 49	67UNTS199	100878
Netherlands	USA (United States)	17 May 49	46UNTS291	100717
Iran	USA (United States)	01 Sep 49	79UNTS155	101039
Turkey	USA (United States)	27 Dec 49	98UNTS141	101361
Norway	USA (United States)	28 Dec 50	240UNTS391	103414
Canada	USA (United States)	18 Apr 51	134UNTS205	101800
Denmark	USA (United States)	16 Nov 51	180UNTS275	102391
Greece	USA (United States)	07 Jan 52	177UNTS249	102323
Greece	USA (United States)	25 Jun 52	181UNTS53	102398
Portugal	USA (United States)	09 Jul 52	180UNTS251	102389
Germany, West	USA (United States)	27 Feb 53	205UNTS103	102771
Belgium	USA (United States)	17 Nov 53	251UNTS105	103536
Japan	USA (United States)	08 Mar 54	232UNTS215	103237
Honduras	USA (United States)	24 May 54	433UNTS155	106238
Luxembourg	USA (United States)	07 Jul 54	233UNTS23	103247
Germany, West	USA (United States)	17 Aug 54	233UNTS31	103248
Multilateral		23 Oct 54	332UNTS3	104760
Haiti	USA (United States)	05 Apr 55	270UNTS97	103895
Germany, West	USA (United States)	14 Apr 55	263UNTS351	103782
Dominican Republic	USA (United States)	22 Apr 55	239UNTS325	103389
USA (United States)	Vietnam, South	10 May 55	273UNTS157	103950
Cambodia	USA (United States)	16 May 55	263UNTS273	103777
Turkey	USA (United States)	26 May 55	262UNTS97	103739
Germany, West	USA (United States)	30 Jun 55	240UNTS69	103394

PARTY ONE	PARTY TWO	DATE	CITATION	NUMBER
Surplus property (Cont.)				
Italy	USA (United States)	08 Jul 55	270UNTS29	103889
France	USA (United States)	23 Sep 55	270UNTS341	103904
Taiwan	USA (United States)	03 Apr 56	268UNTS315	103864
Korea, South	USA (United States)	02 Jul 56	281UNTS41	104067
Ecuador	USA (United States)	19 Jul 56	372UNTS149	105295
Italy	USA (United States)	22 Jun 57	284UNTS51	104128
Taiwan	USA (United States)	22 Jul 59	357UNTS293	105121
Korea, South	USA (United States)	01 Oct 59	358UNTS115	105129
Turkey	USA (United States)	13 Nov 59	361UNTS3	105168
Canada	Italy	18 Dec 61	470UNTS153	106807
Netherlands	USA (United States)	26 Nov 63	388UNTS303	105586
Relief supplies				
Austria	USA (United States)	25 Jun 47	22UNTS141	100334
Italy	USA (United States)	04 Jul 47	22UNTS173	100336
Greece	USA (United States)	08 Jul 47	16UNTS157	100256
Taiwan	USA (United States)	27 Oct 47	12UNTS11	100178
Austria	USA (United States)	02 Jan 48	34UNTS141	100534
France	USA (United States)	02 Jan 48	31UNTS97	100470
Italy	USA (United States)	03 Jan 48	31UNTS105	100471
Italy	USA (United States)	28 Jun 48	20UNTS43	100314
France	USA (United States)	28 Jun 48	19UNTS9	100302
Ireland	USA (United States)	28 Jun 48	24UNTS3	100349
Australia	Greece	01 Jul 48	22UNTS33	100329
Greece	USA (United States)	02 Jul 48	23UNTS43	100342
Belgium	USA (United States)	02 Jul 48	19UNTS127	100309
Netherlands	USA (United States)	02 Jul 48	20UNTS91	100315
Austria	USA (United States)	02 Jul 48	21UNTS29	100323
Luxembourg	USA (United States)	03 Jul 48	24UNTS35	100350
UK Great Britain	USA (United States)	06 Jul 48	22UNTS263	100339
France	USA (United States)	09 Jul 48	24UNTS103	100352
Multilateral		14 Jul 48	23UNTS3	100340
Portugal	USA (United States)	28 Sep 48	29UNTS213	100442
Trieste	USA (United States)	15 Oct 48	29UNTS249	100443
Taiwan	USA (United States)	18 Nov 48	198UNTS287	102672
Italy	USA (United States)	26 Nov 48	79UNTS71	101032
UK Great Britain	USA (United States)	01 Dec 48	81UNTS93	101066
Multilateral		16 Dec 48	79UNTS85	101033
France	USA (United States)	23 Dec 48	67UNTS171	100876
Netherlands	USA (United States)	17 Jan 49	32UNTS241	100502
France	USA (United States)	07 Feb 49	67UNTS189	100877
Greece	USA (United States)	09 Feb 49	79UNTS95	101034
Austria	USA (United States)	11 Feb 49	79UNTS113	101035
Trieste	USA (United States)	11 Feb 49	79UNTS123	101036
India	UNICEF (Children)	10 May 49	68UNTS96	100887
Norway	USA (United States)	31 Oct 49	68UNTS3	100879
UN Relief Palestin	United Arab Rep	12 Sep 50	121UNTS107	101630
USA (United States)	Yugoslavia	21 Nov 50	93UNTS39	101285
USA (United States)	Yugoslavia	06 Jan 51	122UNTS137	101643
Germany, West	USA (United States)	07 Jun 51	238UNTS161	103360
India	USA (United States)	09 Jul 51	147UNTS43	101927
UNICEF (Children)	Turkey	05 Sep 51	193UNTS55	102610
USA (United States)	Yugoslavia	08 Jan 52	152UNTS61	102011
USA (United States)	Yugoslavia	03 Dec 52	185UNTS183	102469
Iran	USA (United States)	13 Oct 53	222UNTS67	103023
Jordan	USA (United States)	21 Oct 53	222UNTS31	103020
Libya	USA (United States)	11 Jan 54	229UNTS15	103157
Afghanistan	USA (United States)	20 Mar 54	229UNTS7	103156
Afghanistan	USA (United States)	29 May 54	234UNTS3	103268
Bolivia	USA (United States)	16 Jun 54	234UNTS35	103271
Pakistan	USA (United States)	23 Aug 54	234UNTS243	103287
USA (United States)	Vietnam, South	26 Aug 54	234UNTS111	103276
Pakistan	USA (United States)	02 Oct 54	236UNTS187	103324
Peru	USA (United States)	25 Oct 54	238UNTS247	103368
United Arab Rep	USA (United States)	30 Oct 54	234UNTS139	103279

PARTY ONE	PARTY TWO	DATE	CITATION	NUMBER
Relief supplies (Cont.)				
Libya	USA (United States)	03 Nov 54	238UNTS227	103366
Guatemala	USA (United States)	13 Dec 54	237UNTS169	103343
Pakistan	USA (United States)	18 Jan 55	241UNTS53	103423
Honduras	USA (United States)	21 Mar 55	253UNTS3	103572
Haiti	USA (United States)	01 Apr 55	261UNTS361	103734
Chile	USA (United States)	05 Apr 55	250UNTS253	103527
Korea, South	USA (United States)	02 May 55	258UNTS3	103666
Ecuador	USA (United States)	06 Sep 55	256UNTS187	103628
India	USA (United States)	04 Oct 55	268UNTS115	103853
Libya	USA (United States)	22 Dec 55	240UNTS111	103399
Italy	USA (United States)	27 Apr 56	273UNTS149	103949
Peru	USA (United States)	08 May 56	278UNTS117	104028
India	USA (United States)	27 Sep 56	281UNTS289	104085
Israel	UN Relief Palestin	09 Nov 56	280UNTS261	104063
Haiti	USA (United States)	28 Dec 56	279UNTS107	104035
Austria	USA (United States)	10 May 57	283UNTS33	104104
Peru	USA (United States)	19 Jul 57	289UNTS271	104223
Haiti	USA (United States)	09 Sep 58	335UNTS257	104793
Ghana	USA (United States)	09 Apr 59	342UNTS21	104897
Japan	USA (United States)	12 Nov 59	361UNTS27	105171
Japan	USA (United States)	31 May 60	376UNTS301	105385
Chile	USA (United States)	29 Jun 60	377UNTS355	105411
Chile	USA (United States)	28 Oct 60	401UNTS177	105770
Cyprus	USA (United States)	08 Dec 60	405UNTS145	105831
Chile	USA (United States)	03 Aug 61	433UNTS21	106228
India	UK Great Britain	20 Oct 64	534UNTS77	107755
New Zealand	Western Samoa	29 Jul 66	598UNTS115	108657
Grants				
Ecuador	USA (United States)	24 Feb 42	26UNTS379	200157
Brazil	USA (United States)	14 Mar 42	102UNTS195	200302
Haiti	USA (United States)	07 Apr 42	106UNTS319	200349
El Salvador	USA (United States)	05 May 42	21UNTS215	200124
Honduras	USA (United States)	08 May 42	166UNTS351	200498
Paraguay	USA (United States)	22 May 42	124UNTS243	200423
Bolivia	USA (United States)	16 Jul 42	13UNTS101	200072
Colombia	USA (United States)	23 Oct 42	105UNTS109	200326
USA (United States)	Venezuela	18 Feb 43	21UNTS225	200125
Panama	USA (United States)	02 Mar 43	107UNTS55	200351
Chile	USA (United States)	11 May 43	139UNTS295	200456
Mexico	USA (United States)	01 Jul 43	28UNTS407	200164
USA (United States)	Uruguay	01 Nov 43	106UNTS311	200348
USA (United States)	Uruguay	23 Apr 46	160UNTS103	102104
Austria	UK Great Britain	23 Dec 46	88UNTS93	101186
Paraguay	USA (United States)	30 Jun 48	124UNTS34	101665
Taiwan	USA (United States)	03 Jul 48	17UNTS119	100273
Korea, South	USA (United States)	10 Dec 48	55UNTS157	100813
Belgium	Luxembourg	14 Jan 49	36UNTS339	100572
Mexico	USA (United States)	14 Feb 49	160UNTS75	102103
Denmark	Poland	12 May 49	87UNTS179	101172
Philippines	USA (United States)	07 Jun 49	45UNTS63	100692
USA (United States)	Uruguay	27 Jul 49	151UNTS199	101995
El Salvador	USA (United States)	18 Apr 51	141UNTS37	101903
Austria	USA (United States)	15 May 51	139UNTS79	101876
UK Great Britain	Yugoslavia	28 Sep 51	117UNTS107	101587
India	USA (United States)	05 Jan 52	157UNTS39	102045
Israel	USA (United States)	01 May 52	177UNTS89	102311
Multilateral		21 Aug 52	141UNTS129	101912
Libya	UK Great Britain	29 Jul 53	186UNTS277	102493
Japan	USA (United States)	08 Mar 54	232UNTS267	103241
Ireland	USA (United States)	17 Jun 54	241UNTS173	103432
USA (United States)	Yugoslavia	19 Jan 56	240UNTS121	103400
Japan	USA (United States)	10 Feb 56	275UNTS181	103981
Japan	USA (United States)	10 Feb 56	275UNTS157	103980
Afghanistan	USA (United States)	23 Jun 56	271UNTS295	103921

PARTY ONE	PARTY TWO	DATE	CITATION	NUMBER
Grants (Cont.)				
Denmark	WHO (World Health)	03 Sep 56	258UNTS103	103674
Haiti	USA (United States)	28 Dec 56	279UNTS107	104035
Tunisia	USA (United States)	26 Mar 57	283UNTS117	104111
Morocco	USA (United States)	02 Apr 57	288UNTS157	104203
Libya	USA (United States)	04 Apr 57	283UNTS181	104116
Austria	USA (United States)	10 May 57	283UNTS33	104104
Tunisia	USA (United States)	28 Jun 57	289UNTS301	104226
Peru	USA (United States)	19 Jul 57	289UNTS271	104223
Multilateral		06 Jan 58	304UNTS227	104399
Philippines	USA (United States)	30 Jun 58	321UNTS51	104653
Japan	Laos	15 Oct 58	341UNTS25	104875
SEATO (SE Asia)	USA (United States)	29 May 59	347UNTS77	104991
Burma	USA (United States)	24 Jun 59	358UNTS91	105127
Brazil	USA (United States)	27 Feb 60	384UNTS131	105515
Cyprus	UK Great Britain	16 Aug 60	382UNTS231	105484
Guinea	USA (United States)	30 Sep 60	394UNTS103	105671
Chile	USA (United States)	28 Oct 60	401UNTS177	105770
Korea, South	USA (United States)	18 Nov 60	400UNTS49	105747
Cyprus	USA (United States)	08 Dec 60	405UNTS145	105831
Israel	USA (United States)	19 Dec 60	401UNTS195	105772
Togo	USA (United States)	22 Dec 60	401UNTS33	105760
Iceland	USA (United States)	30 Dec 60	401UNTS43	105761
Mali	USA (United States)	04 Jan 61	405UNTS165	105832
Honduras	USA (United States)	12 Apr 61	413UNTS182	105952
USA (United States)	Yugoslavia	19 Apr 61	409UNTS163	105883
Sierra Leone	USA (United States)	05 May 61	409UNTS194	105885
Senegal	USA (United States)	13 May 61	409UNTS232	105888
Ghana	Switzerland	17 May 61	559UNTS193	108159
Ivory Coast	USA (United States)	17 May 61	409UNTS241	105889
Cameroon	USA (United States)	26 May 61	413UNTS195	105953
Niger	USA (United States)	26 May 61	410UNTS213	105905
Dahomey	USA (United States)	27 May 61	445UNTS23	106373
Madagascar	USA (United States)	22 Jun 61	413UNTS219	105956
Fed of Malaya	UN Special Fund	25 Jul 61	401UNTS159	105769
Panama	USA (United States)	11 Dec 61	445UNTS161	106384
Iran	USA (United States)	21 Dec 61	433UNTS269	106249
Dominican Republic	USA (United States)	11 Jan 62	433UNTS133	106236
UNESCO (Educ/Cult)	USA (United States)	19 Jan 62	435UNTS99	106272
Cyprus	USA (United States)	02 Mar 62	445UNTS189	106386
Italy	USA (United States)	28 Aug 62	461UNTS137	106657
Central Afri Rep	USA (United States)	10 Feb 63	473UNTS83	106857
Burma	Japan	29 Mar 63	518UNTS3	107490
USA (United States)	Vietnam, South	21 Mar 66	578UNTS165	108394
New Zealand	Western Samoa	29 Jul 66	598UNTS115	108657
Withdrawal conditions				
Greece	USA (United States)	20 Jun 47	7UNTS267	100105
Austria	USA (United States)	25 Jun 47	22UNTS141	100334
Italy	USA (United States)	04 Jul 47	22UNTS173	100336
Greece	USA (United States)	08 Jul 47	16UNTS157	100256
Taiwan	USA (United States)	27 Oct 47	12UNTS11	100178
Taiwan	USA (United States)	03 Jul 48	17UNTS119	100273
Korea, South	USA (United States)	10 Dec 48	55UNTS157	100813
USA (United States)	Yugoslavia	06 Jan 51	122UNTS137	101643
Pakistan	USA (United States)	25 Jun 53	205UNTS139	102773
Jordan	USA (United States)	21 Oct 53	222UNTS31	103020
Libya	USA (United States)	11 Jan 54	229UNTS15	103157
Libya	USA (United States)	03 Nov 54	238UNTS227	103366
Ceylon (Sri Lanka)	USA (United States)	28 Apr 56	274UNTS35	103956
Ethiopia	USA (United States)	25 Apr 57	283UNTS205	104118
USA (United States)	Uruguay	20 Feb 59	341UNTS201	104884
Honduras	USA (United States)	12 Apr 61	413UNTS182	105952
Ghana	USA (United States)	19 Jul 61	416UNTS167	106002
Germany, West	Thailand	23 Dec 64	525UNTS193	107591
East Afri Service	IBRD (World Bank)	17 Feb 67	599UNTS335	200629

PARTY ONE	PARTY TWO	DATE	CITATION	NUMBER
Withdrawal conditions (Cont.)				
Czechoslovakia	UN Special Fund	13 Jul 67	606UNTS71	108776
Procurement				
France	USA (United States)	25 Sep 43	76UNTS183	200245
Belgium	UK Great Britain	22 Aug 44	90UNTS295	200267
South Africa	USA (United States)	17 Apr 45	90UNTS267	200264
Austria	USA (United States)	25 Jun 47	22UNTS141	100334
Italy	USA (United States)	04 Jul 47	22UNTS173	100336
Greece	USA (United States)	08 Jul 47	16UNTS157	100256
Taiwan	USA (United States)	27 Oct 47	12UNTS11	100178
Austria	USA (United States)	02 Jan 48	34UNTS141	100534
France	USA (United States)	02 Jan 48	31UNTS97	100470
Italy	USA (United States)	03 Jan 48	31UNTS105	100471
Ireland	USA (United States)	28 Jun 48	24UNTS3	100349
France	USA (United States)	28 Jun 48	19UNTS9	100302
Italy	USA (United States)	28 Jun 48	20UNTS43	100314
Denmark	USA (United States)	29 Jun 48	22UNTS217	100338
Australia	Greece	01 Jul 48	22UNTS33	100329
Greece	USA (United States)	02 Jul 48	23UNTS43	100342
Belgium	USA (United States)	02 Jul 48	19UNTS127	100309
Austria	USA (United States)	02 Jul 48	21UNTS29	100323
Netherlands	USA (United States)	02 Jul 48	20UNTS91	100315
Iceland	USA (United States)	03 Jul 48	20UNTS141	100316
Sweden	USA (United States)	03 Jul 48	23UNTS101	100343
Luxembourg	USA (United States)	03 Jul 48	24UNTS35	100350
Taiwan	USA (United States)	03 Jul 48	17UNTS119	100273
Norway	USA (United States)	03 Jul 48	20UNTS185	100317
Turkey	USA (United States)	04 Jul 48	24UNTS67	100351
UK Great Britain	USA (United States)	06 Jul 48	22UNTS263	100339
France	USA (United States)	09 Jul 48	24UNTS103	100352
Multilateral		14 Jul 48	23UNTS3	100340
Portugal	USA (United States)	28 Sep 48	29UNTS213	100442
Trieste	USA (United States)	15 Oct 48	29UNTS249	100443
Korea, South	USA (United States)	10 Dec 48	55UNTS157	100813
Germany, West	USA (United States)	15 Dec 49	92UNTS269	101277
Chile	UNICEF (Children)	03 Mar 50	126UNTS119	101685
Burma	USA (United States)	13 Sep 50	92UNTS361	101280
Thailand	USA (United States)	19 Sep 50	132UNTS199	101761
Indonesia	USA (United States)	16 Oct 50	281UNTS105	104074
USA (United States)	Yugoslavia	06 Jan 51	122UNTS137	101643
USA (United States)	Vietnam, South	07 Sep 51	174UNTS165	102284
Cambodia	USA (United States)	08 Sep 51	174UNTS115	102282
Laos	USA (United States)	09 Sep 51	174UNTS141	102283
Iraq	UNICEF (Children)	10 Dec 51	126UNTS57	101682
USA (United States)	Yugoslavia	08 Jan 52	152UNTS61	102011
Libya	UNICEF (Children)	05 Apr 52	133UNTS287	200441
Liberia	UNICEF (Children)	17 Apr 52	133UNTS3	101773
Korea, South	USA (United States)	24 May 52	179UNTS23	102353
Jordan	UNICEF (Children)	08 Jul 52	173UNTS353	200503
UNICEF (Children)	UK Great Britain	25 Jul 52	135UNTS37	101812
Spain	USA (United States)	26 Sep 53	207UNTS93	102802
Afghanistan	USA (United States)	20 Mar 54	229UNTS7	103156
Jordan	USA (United States)	13 May 54	234UNTS225	103285
Jordan	USA (United States)	17 Jun 54	266UNTS137	103828
Lebanon	USA (United States)	18 Jun 54	233UNTS177	103262
Guatemala	USA (United States)	13 Dec 54	237UNTS169	103343
Haiti	USA (United States)	01 Apr 55	261UNTS361	103734
Philippines	USA (United States)	27 Apr 55	261UNTS351	103733
Thailand	USA (United States)	21 Jun 55	262UNTS87	103738
Italy	USA (United States)	27 Feb 56	291UNTS287	104260
Ceylon (Sri Lanka)	USA (United States)	28 Apr 56	274UNTS35	103956
Burma	USA (United States)	21 Mar 57	300UNTS11	104327
Ethiopia	USA (United States)	25 Apr 57	283UNTS205	104118
Iraq	USSR (Soviet Union)	16 Mar 59	346UNTS107	104979
Cuba	USSR (Soviet Union)	13 Feb 60	369UNTS3	105247
Procurement (Cont.)				
Brazil	USA (United States)	27 Feb 60	384UNTS131	105515
Japan	USA (United States)	31 May 60	376UNTS301	105385
Israel	USA (United States)	19 Dec 60	401UNTS195	105772
Togo	USA (United States)	22 Dec 60	401UNTS33	105760
USA (United States)	Yugoslavia	19 Apr 61	409UNTS163	105883
Tunisia	USA (United States)	29 Oct 62	462UNTS201	106679
Malta	UK Great Britain	21 Sep 64	588UNTS125	108519
Trinidad/Tobago	UK Great Britain	23 Jan 67	605UNTS277	108767
Distribution				
Austria	USA (United States)	25 Jun 47	22UNTS141	100334
Italy	USA (United States)	04 Jul 47	22UNTS173	100336
Greece	USA (United States)	08 Jul 47	16UNTS157	100256
Taiwan	USA (United States)	27 Oct 47	12UNTS11	100178
Austria	USA (United States)	02 Jan 48	34UNTS141	100534
Australia	Hungary	01 Jul 48	22UNTS3	100325
Taiwan	USA (United States)	03 Jul 48	17UNTS119	100273
Australia	Italy	08 Jul 48	22UNTS11	100326
Australia	Yugoslavia	09 Jul 48	22UNTS17	100327
Australia	Austria	19 Jul 48	22UNTS25	100328
Belgium	Luxembourg	14 Jan 49	36UNTS339	100572
India	UNICEF (Children)	10 May 49	68UNTS96	100887
Chile	UNICEF (Children)	03 Mar 50	126UNTS119	101685
Burma	USA (United States)	13 Sep 50	92UNTS361	101280
Thailand	USA (United States)	19 Sep 50	132UNTS199	101761
Indonesia	USA (United States)	16 Oct 50	281UNTS105	104074
USA (United States)	Yugoslavia	21 Nov 50	93UNTS39	101285
Multilateral		20 Mar 51	82UNTS172	101091
Brazil	USA (United States)	24 Jul 51	134UNTS195	101799
Iran	UNICEF (Children)	02 Aug 51	247UNTS11	103457
UNICEF (Children)	Turkey	05 Sep 51	193UNTS55	102610
USA (United States)	Vietnam, South	07 Sep 51	174UNTS165	102284
Cambodia	USA (United States)	08 Sep 51	174UNTS115	102282
Laos	USA (United States)	09 Sep 51	174UNTS141	102283
UNICEF (Children)	UK Great Britain	02 Oct 51	104UNTS301	101448
Iraq	UNICEF (Children)	10 Dec 51	126UNTS57	101682
UNICEF (Children)	UK Great Britain	15 Feb 52	121UNTS63	101626
Libya	UNICEF (Children)	05 Apr 52	133UNTS287	200441
Liberia	UNICEF (Children)	17 Apr 52	133UNTS3	101773
Korea, South	USA (United States)	24 May 52	179UNTS23	102353
Belgium	UNICEF (Children)	17 Jun 52	171UNTS249	102228
UNICEF (Children)	Syria	10 Jul 52	136UNTS17	101830
UNICEF (Children)	UK Great Britain	25 Jul 52	135UNTS37	101812
UNICEF (Children)	Vietnam, South	29 Aug 52	161UNTS335	200492
UNICEF (Children)	UK Great Britain	16 Dec 52	151UNTS359	102005
Netherlands	United Nations	09 Apr 53	163UNTS89	102143
Ethiopia	UNICEF (Children)	27 Apr 53	213UNTS169	102885
Pakistan	USA (United States)	25 Jun 53	205UNTS139	102773
Jordan	USA (United States)	21 Oct 53	222UNTS31	103020
Japan	UNICEF (Children)	21 Nov 53	183UNTS297	200507
Libya	USA (United States)	11 Jan 54	229UNTS15	103157
Afghanistan	USA (United States)	20 Mar 54	229UNTS7	103156
UNICEF (Children)	Spain	07 May 54	190UNTS357	200515
Jordan	USA (United States)	13 May 54	234UNTS225	103285
Mexico	UNICEF (Children)	20 May 54	192UNTS3	102591
Lebanon	USA (United States)	18 Jun 54	233UNTS177	103262
Pakistan	USA (United States)	23 Aug 54	234UNTS243	103287
New Zealand	UNICEF (Children)	26 Aug 54	198UNTS173	102663
Netherlands	UNICEF (Children)	31 Dec 54	202UNTS135	102729
Haiti	USA (United States)	01 Apr 55	261UNTS361	103734
Ecuador	USA (United States)	07 Oct 55	256UNTS197	103629
Guatemala	UNICEF (Children)	22 Nov 55	221UNTS305	103012
Italy	USA (United States)	27 Apr 56	273UNTS149	103949
Cambodia	UNICEF (Children)	28 Apr 56	136UNTS341	200446
Ceylon (Sri Lanka)	USA (United States)	28 Apr 56	274UNTS35	103956

PARTY ONE	PARTY TWO	DATE	CITATION	NUMBER
Distribution (Cont.)				
Lebanon	UNICEF (Children)	03 Jul 56	324UNTS145	104683
UNICEF (Children)	Sudan	07 Aug 56	248UNTS307	200542
UNESCO (Educ/Cult)	Tunisia	03 Jan 57	257UNTS21	103645
Tunisia	USA (United States)	28 Jun 57	289UNTS301	104226
Peru	USA (United States)	19 Jul 57	289UNTS271	104223
Morocco	UNICEF (Children)	31 Jul 57	282UNTS99	104095
Argentina	UNICEF (Children)	19 Nov 57	300UNTS229	104338
Ghana	UNICEF (Children)	12 Aug 58	309UNTS103	104469
USA (United States)	Uruguay	20 Feb 59	341UNTS201	104884
Cuba	UNICEF (Children)	11 Feb 60	349UNTS277	105014
UNICEF (Children)	Upper Volta	15 Nov 60	402UNTS33	105776
Mali	UNICEF (Children)	17 Nov 60	402UNTS23	105775
Cyprus	USA (United States)	08 Dec 60	405UNTS145	105831
Cyprus	UNICEF (Children)	19 Apr 61	394UNTS185	105678
UNICEF (Children)	Saudi Arabia	04 Jul 61	413UNTS122	105947
Cameroon	UNICEF (Children)	12 Aug 61	402UNTS235	105788
Central Afri Rep	UNICEF (Children)	21 Aug 61	413UNTS48	105939
Poland	UNICEF (Children)	24 Aug 61	406UNTS95	105841
Chad	UNICEF (Children)	26 Aug 61	422UNTS231	106077
Gabon	UNICEF (Children)	02 Nov 61	422UNTS241	106078
Malagasy	UNICEF (Children)	16 Nov 61	422UNTS251	106079
Ivory Coast	UNICEF (Children)	10 Jan 62	422UNTS261	106080
UNICEF (Children)	Yemen	31 Jan 62	422UNTS271	106081
UNICEF (Children)	Somalia	01 Apr 62	431UNTS75	106211
Congo (Brazzaville)	UNICEF (Children)	09 Apr 62	431UNTS65	106210
UNICEF (Children)	Sierra Leone	11 Apr 62	431UNTS55	106209
Algeria	UNICEF (Children)	20 Nov 62	453UNTS151	106522
Mauritania	UNICEF (Children)	19 Jan 63	452UNTS271	106514
UNICEF (Children)	Tanganyika	25 Jan 63	453UNTS249	106528
Access to materials				
Turkey	USA (United States)	23 Feb 45	121UNTS165	200398
Ireland	USA (United States)	28 Jun 48	24UNTS3	100349
France	USA (United States)	28 Jun 48	19UNTS9	100302
Italy	USA (United States)	28 Jun 48	20UNTS43	100314
Denmark	USA (United States)	29 Jun 48	22UNTS217	100338
Belgium	USA (United States)	02 Jul 48	19UNTS127	100309
Greece	USA (United States)	02 Jul 48	23UNTS43	100342
Netherlands	USA (United States)	02 Jul 48	20UNTS91	100315
Norway	USA (United States)	03 Jul 48	20UNTS185	100317
Luxembourg	USA (United States)	03 Jul 48	24UNTS35	100350
Sweden	USA (United States)	03 Jul 48	23UNTS101	100343
Iceland	USA (United States)	03 Jul 48	20UNTS141	100316
UK Great Britain	USA (United States)	06 Jul 48	22UNTS263	100339
France	USA (United States)	09 Jul 48	24UNTS103	100352
Multilateral		14 Jul 48	23UNTS3	100340
Portugal	USA (United States)	28 Sep 48	29UNTS213	100442
Korea, South	USA (United States)	10 Dec 48	55UNTS157	100813
Germany, West	USA (United States)	15 Dec 49	92UNTS269	101277
Indonesia	USA (United States)	24 Mar 50	92UNTS387	101281
USA (United States)	Yugoslavia	08 Jan 52	152UNTS61	102011
Spain	USA (United States)	26 Sep 53	207UNTS93	102802
Haiti	USA (United States)	01 Apr 55	261UNTS361	103734
Burma	USA (United States)	21 Mar 57	300UNTS11	104327
Loan and credit				
Multilateral		28 Nov 40	139UNTS159	200452
Brazil	Paraguay	14 Apr 41	54UNTS269	200199
Brazil	Paraguay	14 Jun 41	54UNTS313	200203
Costa Rica	USA (United States)	16 Jan 42	23UNTS285	200135
El Salvador	USA (United States)	13 Feb 42	23UNTS293	200136
Brazil	USA (United States)	03 Mar 42	105UNTS99	200325
Nicaragua	USA (United States)	08 Apr 42	24UNTS145	200138
Haiti	USA (United States)	30 Sep 42	24UNTS205	200144
Honduras	USA (United States)	26 Oct 42	24UNTS209	200145
Canada	Czechoslovakia	01 Mar 45	45UNTS283	200185

PARTY ONE	PARTY TWO	DATE	CITATION	NUMBER
Loan and credit (Cont.)				
France	UK Great Britain	27 Mar 45	98UNTS227	200274
Canada	Norway	25 Jun 45	45UNTS297	200186
Belgium	Canada	25 Oct 45	230UNTS127	103180
UK Great Britain	USA (United States)	06 Dec 45	126UNTS13	101679
Greece	UK Great Britain	24 Jan 46	6UNTS45	100067
Canada	Netherlands	05 Feb 46	43UNTS3	100658
Canada	Taiwan	07 Feb 46	43UNTS23	100659
Canada	UK Great Britain	06 Mar 46	20UNTS13	100312
Canada	France	09 Apr 46	43UNTS43	100660
Multilateral		17 Apr 46	27UNTS103	100402
Poland	USA (United States)	22 Apr 46	406UNTS215	105851
France	USA (United States)	28 May 46	84UNTS167	101127
Canada	Norway	06 Jun 46	43UNTS67	100661
Romania	Yugoslavia	26 Jun 46	116UNTS21	101566
Taiwan	USA (United States)	28 Jun 46	34UNTS121	100532
Albania	Yugoslavia	01 Jul 46	111UNTS81	101518
Albania	Yugoslavia	03 Oct 46	111UNTS87	101519
Albania	Yugoslavia	28 Nov 46	111UNTS143	101527
Romania	Yugoslavia	23 Dec 46	116UNTS33	101567
Albania	Yugoslavia	12 Jun 47	111UNTS189	101533
Albania	Yugoslavia	12 Jun 47	111UNTS177	101531
United Arab Rep	UK Great Britain	30 Jun 47	93UNTS165	101299
Romania	Yugoslavia	30 Sep 47	116UNTS71	101570
South Africa	UK Great Britain	09 Oct 47	17UNTS239	100278
Greece	Norway	08 Dec 47	30UNTS171	100455
Austria	USA (United States)	02 Jan 48	34UNTS141	100534
United Arab Rep	UK Great Britain	05 Jan 48	77UNTS3	100988
United Nations	USA (United States)	23 Mar 48	19UNTS43	100303
Greece	USA (United States)	01 Nov 48	185UNTS169	102468
Belgium	Luxembourg	14 Jan 49	36UNTS339	100572
United Arab Rep	UK Great Britain	31 Mar 49	83UNTS139	101106
Greece	UK Great Britain	29 Jun 49	86UNTS203	101160
Multilateral		10 Aug 49	45UNTS3	100689
Belgium	France	07 Sep 49	123UNTS13	101651
Belgium	Netherlands	07 Sep 49	117UNTS3	101581
Belgium	UK Great Britain	07 Sep 49	106UNTS61	101457
Italy	Norway	19 Nov 49	47UNTS89	100724
Turkey	USA (United States)	27 Dec 49	98UNTS141	101361
Sweden	UK Great Britain	30 Dec 49	87UNTS59	101166
Australia	Ceylon (Sri Lanka)	12 Jan 50	53UNTS295	100789
Multilateral		28 Jun 50	87UNTS153	101170
UK Great Britain	Yugoslavia	28 Dec 50	88UNTS329	101201
UK Great Britain	Yugoslavia	10 May 51	102UNTS29	101408
United Arab Rep	UK Great Britain	01 Jul 51	249UNTS125	103503
UK Great Britain	USA (United States)	18 Jul 51	117UNTS49	101583
India	USA (United States)	05 Jan 52	157UNTS39	102045
UNICEF (Children)	United Arab Rep	18 May 52	324UNTS161	104684
Lebanon	USA (United States)	26 Jun 52	181UNTS187	102409
Pakistan	USA (United States)	17 Sep 52	227UNTS77	103132
USA (United States)	Yugoslavia	11 Oct 52	235UNTS277	103309
UK Great Britain	USA (United States)	25 Feb 53	212UNTS157	102868
Libya	UK Great Britain	25 Mar 53	172UNTS281	102252
UK Great Britain	USA (United States)	26 Jun 53	183UNTS225	102432
Argentina	USSR (Soviet Union)	05 Aug 53	221UNTS99	103004
Denmark	Uruguay	09 Sep 53	256UNTS149	103625
USA (United States)	Yugoslavia	05 Jan 54	234UNTS267	103289
Finland	USSR (Soviet Union)	06 Feb 54	221UNTS143	103006
Ecuador	IBRD (World Bank)	10 Feb 54	209UNTS261	102830
ECSC (Coal/Steel)	USA (United States)	23 Apr 54	229UNTS229	103170
Italy	USA (United States)	16 Jun 54	236UNTS149	103322
Turkey	USA (United States)	15 Nov 54	238UNTS135	103358
Finland	USSR (Soviet Union)	24 Jan 55	240UNTS243	103406
Argentina	UK Great Britain	31 Mar 55	210UNTS223	102840
Argentina	USA (United States)	25 Apr 55	251UNTS283	103546
Israel	USA (United States)	10 Nov 55	240UNTS3	103390

PARTY ONE	PARTY TWO	DATE	CITATION	NUMBER
Loan and credit (Cont.)				
United Arab Rep	USA (United States)	14 Dec 55	240UNTS37	103392
USSR (Soviet Union)	Yugoslavia	02 Feb 56	259UNTS111	103685
Japan	USA (United States)	10 Feb 56	275UNTS105	103979
Canada	Hungary	08 Mar 56	305UNTS27	104409
Chile	USA (United States)	13 Mar 56	275UNTS49	103975
Peru	USA (United States)	08 May 56	278UNTS117	104028
Ecuador	USA (United States)	15 Feb 57	279UNTS155	104037
Burma	India	12 Mar 57	312UNTS131	104515
Burma	USA (United States)	21 Mar 57	300UNTS11	104327
Indonesia	Japan	20 Jan 58	325UNTS13	104691
Japan	IBRD (World Bank)	29 Jan 58	310UNTS111	104490
Canada	India	20 Feb 58	391UNTS231	105628
Italy	IBRD (World Bank)	28 Feb 58	359UNTS47	105139
Jordan	UK Great Britain	26 Mar 58	312UNTS373	104526
Jordan	UK Great Britain	07 May 58	312UNTS379	104527
USA (United States)	Vietnam, South	17 Jun 58	321UNTS35	104652
Japan	IBRD (World Bank)	27 Jun 58	312UNTS193	104519
Burma	USA (United States)	25 Aug 58	336UNTS3	104795
Canada	India	22 Oct 58	392UNTS21	105635
Canada	Ceylon (Sri Lanka)	05 Nov 58	391UNTS225	105627
Turkey	UK Great Britain	25 Nov 58	327UNTS35	104715
UK Great Britain	Yugoslavia	03 Feb 59	343UNTS153	104924
Iraq	USSR (Soviet Union)	16 Mar 59	346UNTS107	104979
Multilateral		08 Apr 59	389UNTS69	105593
Fed of Malaya	UK Great Britain	01 May 59	345UNTS57	104958
Japan	Vietnam, South	13 May 59	373UNTS149	105318
Japan	Vietnam, South	13 May 59	373UNTS173	105319
Ethiopia	Yugoslavia	06 Jun 59	386UNTS243	105544
Jordan	UK Great Britain	11 Jun 59	351UNTS283	105028
Iceland	USA (United States)	23 Jun 59	354UNTS3	105048
Ethiopia	France	12 Nov 59	381UNTS3	105465
Cuba	USSR (Soviet Union)	13 Feb 60	369UNTS3	105247
Multilateral		26 Feb 60	418UNTS171	106022
Jordan	UK Great Britain	04 May 60	385UNTS81	105531
United Arab Rep	USSR (Soviet Union)	27 Aug 60	399UNTS37	105733
Chile	UK Great Britain	21 Oct 60	385UNTS15	105525
Multilateral		13 Dec 60	523UNTS117	107557
Multilateral		13 Dec 60	455UNTS3	106543
Austria	USA (United States)	29 Mar 61	459UNTS45	106612
Ghana	Switzerland	17 May 61	559UNTS193	108159
Inter-Am Devel Bnk	USA (United States)	19 Jun 61	410UNTS34	105895
India	IDA (Devel Assoc)	21 Jun 61	418UNTS61	106017
Chile	IDA (Devel Assoc)	28 Jun 61	426UNTS89	106131
Jordan	UK Great Britain	17 Jul 61	420UNTS53	106039
UK Great Britain	Yugoslavia	21 Jul 61	420UNTS61	106040
Brazil	UK Great Britain	21 Jul 61	414UNTS26	105962
Chile	USA (United States)	03 Aug 61	433UNTS21	106228
UK Great Britain	USA (United States)	28 Aug 61	434UNTS103	106258
Colombia	IDA (Devel Assoc)	28 Aug 61	416UNTS3	105992
Taiwan	IDA (Devel Assoc)	30 Aug 61	416UNTS175	106003
Taiwan	IDA (Devel Assoc)	30 Aug 61	417UNTS227	106008
India	IDA (Devel Assoc)	06 Sep 61	418UNTS81	106018
Taiwan	IDA (Devel Assoc)	06 Sep 61	417UNTS253	106009
Costa Rica	IDA (Devel Assoc)	13 Oct 61	431UNTS3	106204
Pakistan	IDA (Devel Assoc)	19 Oct 61	447UNTS161	106415
Switzerland	UK Great Britain	20 Oct 61	431UNTS29	106206
Ghana	USSR (Soviet Union)	04 Nov 61	0UNTS0	109381
India	IDA (Devel Assoc)	22 Nov 61	427UNTS29	106145
India	IDA (Devel Assoc)	22 Nov 61	427UNTS3	106144
India	IDA (Devel Assoc)	22 Nov 61	427UNTS55	106146
Taiwan	IDA (Devel Assoc)	01 Dec 61	426UNTS105	106132
El Salvador	USA (United States)	15 May 62	452UNTS49	106503
Jordan	UK Great Britain	30 May 62	449UNTS167	106458
United Arab Rep	USSR (Soviet Union)	23 Jun 62	472UNTS19	106835
Pakistan	USA (United States)	25 Jul 62	459UNTS87	106614

PARTY ONE	PARTY TWO	DATE	CITATION	NUMBER
Loan and credit (Cont.)				
India	IDA (Devel Assoc)	08 Aug 62	478UNTS335	106941
Philippines	IBRD (World Bank)	07 Nov 62	468UNTS281	106777
Laos	USSR (Soviet Union)	01 Dec 62	472UNTS3	106834
IDA (Devel Assoc)	Turkey	01 Feb 63	468UNTS223	106775
India	New Zealand	22 Feb 63	486UNTS19	107069
Cyprus	IBRD (World Bank)	17 Apr 63	476UNTS185	106909
Jordan	UK Great Britain	27 Apr 63	475UNTS169	106892
Austria	Bulgaria	02 May 63	535UNTS143	107778
Canada	India	14 May 63	529UNTS31	107653
Argentina	UK Great Britain	05 Jun 63	482UNTS353	107004
New Zealand	UN Special Fund	28 Jun 63	470UNTS3	106792
Congo (Zaire)	UN Special Fund	26 Jul 63	474UNTS137	106878
Belgium	Turkey	23 Sep 63	566UNTS195	108244
Canada	Poland	05 Nov 63	529UNTS81	107658
Brazil	Germany, West	30 Nov 63	0UNTS0	109425
Congo (Zaire)	UK Great Britain	03 Jan 64	534UNTS417	107770
Jordan	UK Great Britain	31 Aug 64	541UNTS3	107856
Malta	UK Great Britain	21 Sep 64	588UNTS125	108519
Brazil	UK Great Britain	14 Oct 64	539UNTS289	107840
Germany, West	Thailand	28 Oct 64	521UNTS311	107528
Germany, West	Thailand	28 Oct 64	521UNTS333	107529
Morocco	USA (United States)	29 Dec 64	593UNTS185	108584
Taiwan	USA (United States)	09 Apr 65	546UNTS81	107939
Jordan	UK Great Britain	08 Jun 65	552UNTS251	108057
Japan	IBRD (World Bank)	10 Sep 65	566UNTS249	108246
Israel	IBRD (World Bank)	16 Sep 65	566UNTS212	108245
Peru	IBRD (World Bank)	17 Sep 65	566UNTS311	108248
Turkey	UK Great Britain	21 Oct 65	561UNTS185	108180
Philippines	IBRD (World Bank)	02 Nov 65	567UNTS3	108249
Morocco	IBRD (World Bank)	08 Nov 65	566UNTS279	108247
Chile	UK Great Britain	23 Nov 65	560UNTS215	108176
Iran	USSR (Soviet Union)	13 Jan 66	633UNTS123	109037
Ethiopia	IDA (Devel Assoc)	16 Feb 66	569UNTS43	108278
Burundi	IDA (Devel Assoc)	31 Mar 66	569UNTS3	108277
Burma	USA (United States)	01 Jun 66	580UNTS253	108428
Denmark	Jordan	28 Jun 66	574UNTS3	108338
Brazil	Denmark	08 Jul 66	581UNTS95	108435
Jordan	UK Great Britain	26 Jul 66	597UNTS219	108647
Turkey	UK Great Britain	29 Jul 66	597UNTS241	108649
New Zealand	Western Samoa	29 Jul 66	598UNTS115	108657
Denmark	Malawi	01 Sep 66	586UNTS3	108493
Iceland	IBRD (World Bank)	14 Sep 66	598UNTS223	108660
Argentina	UK Great Britain	15 Sep 66	603UNTS151	108732
IDA (Devel Assoc)	Tunisia	16 Sep 66	616UNTS285	108903
IBRD (World Bank)	Thailand	19 Oct 66	594UNTS347	108609
IBRD (World Bank)	IFC (Finance Corp)	28 Oct 66	586UNTS225	200628
Peru	UK Great Britain	03 Dec 66	617UNTS231	108915
Syria	USSR (Soviet Union)	18 Dec 66	633UNTS247	109041
Congo (Brazzaville)	IBRD (World Bank)	09 Jan 67	598UNTS161	108659
IDA (Devel Assoc)	Tunisia	21 Feb 67	618UNTS69	108924
IBRD (World Bank)	Tunisia	21 Feb 67	618UNTS39	108923
Cameroon	IDA (Devel Assoc)	28 Mar 67	618UNTS133	108926
Multilateral		19 Apr 67	595UNTS120	108617
IDA (Devel Assoc)	Uganda	21 Apr 67	617UNTS161	108911
Turkey	UK Great Britain	21 Apr 67	610UNTS0	108838
Hungary	UN Special Fund	28 Apr 67	595UNTS171	108619
Jordan	UK Great Britain	02 May 67	610UNTS0	108837
Malawi	IDA (Devel Assoc)	04 May 67	617UNTS141	108910
Jordan	IDA (Devel Assoc)	09 May 67	617UNTS47	108907
Kenya	IDA (Devel Assoc)	11 May 67	617UNTS111	108909
Kenya	IDA (Devel Assoc)	11 May 67	617UNTS91	108908
Bolivia	IDA (Devel Assoc)	26 May 67	618UNTS159	108927
Malaysia	IBRD (World Bank)	15 Jun 67	618UNTS235	108930
Cameroon	UK Great Britain	16 Jun 67	618UNTS329	108933
Denmark	Peru	20 Jun 67	0UNTS0	109446

PARTY ONE	PARTY TWO	DATE	CITATION	NUMBER
Loan and credit (Cont.)				
IDA (Devel Assoc)	Uganda	28 Jul 67	617UNTS177	108912
Argentina	IBRD (World Bank)	31 Jul 67	633UNTS289	109042
Denmark	Ghana	09 Aug 67	610UNTS0	108842
Jordan	UK Great Britain	15 Aug 67	632UNTS269	109028
Madagascar	IBRD (World Bank)	23 Aug 67	618UNTS215	108929
IDA (Devel Assoc)	Uganda	15 Sep 67	639UNTS115	109148
IBRD (World Bank)	Thailand	19 Sep 67	619UNTS275	108946
Brazil	IBRD (World Bank)	23 Sep 67	620UNTS77	108951
Iran	IBRD (World Bank)	17 Oct 67	0UNTS0	109331
Denmark	Zambia	18 Oct 67	637UNTS0	109116
Denmark	Tanzania	01 Nov 67	619UNTS47	108938
Denmark	Iran	02 Nov 67	638UNTS217	109138
El Salvador	IBRD (World Bank)	07 Dec 67	0UNTS0	109299
Korea, South	IDA (Devel Assoc)	18 Dec 67	639UNTS303	200639
Peru	UK Great Britain	19 Dec 67	0UNTS0	109447
Mexico	IBRD (World Bank)	26 Jan 68	0UNTS0	109511
Cameroon	IDA (Devel Assoc)	29 Jan 68	0UNTS0	109325
Denmark	Malaysia	29 Feb 68	640UNTS29	109153
Turkey	UK Great Britain	04 Mar 68	0UNTS0	109265
IDA (Devel Assoc)	Tanzania	21 Mar 68	0UNTS0	109327
Denmark	India	25 Mar 68	0UNTS0	109229
Turkey	UK Great Britain	29 Mar 68	0UNTS0	109286
Germany, West	Thailand	29 Mar 68	637UNTS0	109122
Denmark	Uganda	01 Apr 68	0UNTS0	109209
Nicaragua	IBRD (World Bank)	10 Apr 68	0UNTS0	109300
Denmark	India	29 Apr 68	0UNTS0	109230
IBRD (World Bank)	Thailand	23 May 68	0UNTS0	109332
Colombia	IBRD (World Bank)	03 Jun 68	0UNTS0	109333
Colombia	IBRD (World Bank)	03 Jun 68	0UNTS0	109334
Denmark	Tunisia	07 Jun 68	0UNTS0	109407
Honduras	IDA (Devel Assoc)	12 Jun 68	0UNTS0	109409
Denmark	Kenya	26 Jun 68	0UNTS0	109210
Ecuador	IDA (Devel Assoc)	27 Jun 68	0UNTS0	109321
Honduras	IBRD (World Bank)	12 Jul 68	0UNTS0	109408
Turkey	UK Great Britain	06 Aug 68	0UNTS0	109451
Denmark	Morocco	05 Nov 68	0UNTS0	109415
Denmark	Malawi	16 Dec 68	0UNTS0	109461
Finland	IBRD (World Bank)	24 Jan 69	0UNTS0	109596
Credit provisions				
Brazil	Paraguay	14 Apr 41	54UNTS269	200199
Brazil	USA (United States)	17 Jul 42	102UNTS203	200303
Haiti	USA (United States)	21 Sep 42	120UNTS177	200391
Canada	Norway	25 Jun 45	45UNTS297	200186
UK Great Britain	USA (United States)	06 Dec 45	126UNTS13	101679
Canada	UK Great Britain	06 Mar 46	20UNTS13	100312
Poland	USA (United States)	22 Apr 46	406UNTS215	105851
Poland	USA (United States)	24 Apr 46	4UNTS155	100042
Romania	Yugoslavia	26 Jun 46	116UNTS21	101566
Albania	Yugoslavia	01 Jul 46	111UNTS81	101518
Albania	Yugoslavia	03 Oct 46	111UNTS87	101519
Austria	UK Great Britain	23 Dec 46	88UNTS93	101186
Australia	Netherlands	24 Jan 47	10UNTS77	100144
Albania	Yugoslavia	12 Jun 47	111UNTS195	101534
Albania	Yugoslavia	12 Jun 47	111UNTS189	101533
Ecuador	USA (United States)	21 Jun 47	26UNTS275	100391
France	New Zealand	02 Jul 47	16UNTS219	100263
USSR (Soviet Union)	Yugoslavia	25 Jul 47	130UNTS315	101732
Greece	Norway	08 Dec 47	30UNTS171	100455
Czechoslovakia	New Zealand	22 Jan 48	16UNTS229	100264
France	Lebanon	24 Jan 48	173UNTS99	102263
Denmark	Hungary	28 Feb 48	85UNTS35	101144
Greece	USA (United States)	23 Apr 48	74UNTS107	100958
Netherlands	IBRD (World Bank)	15 Jul 48	153UNTS211	102020
Turkey	UK Great Britain	16 Oct 48	83UNTS85	101103

PARTY ONE	PARTY TWO	DATE	CITATION	NUMBER
Credit provisions (Cont.)				
Poland	UK Great Britain	14 Jan 49	83UNTS3	101100
Denmark	Sweden	08 Feb 49	33UNTS227	100519
Norway	Turkey	24 Feb 49	30UNTS151	100453
Greece	Norway	12 Mar 49	33UNTS13	100510
United Arab Rep	UK Great Britain	31 Mar 49	83UNTS139	101106
Norway	USA (United States)	25 May 49	32UNTS345	100507
Greece	UK Great Britain	29 Jun 49	86UNTS203	101160
Multilateral		10 Aug 49	45UNTS3	100689
Belgium	UK Great Britain	07 Sep 49	106UNTS61	101457
Belgium	France	07 Sep 49	123UNTS13	101651
Belgium	Netherlands	07 Sep 49	117UNTS3	101581
Argentina	Norway	09 Sep 49	42UNTS125	100646
Czechoslovakia	UK Great Britain	28 Sep 49	86UNTS175	101158
UK Great Britain	Yugoslavia	26 Dec 49	87UNTS71	101167
China People's Rep	USSR (Soviet Union)	14 Feb 50	226UNTS21	103104
Denmark	Poland	01 Oct 50	81UNTS43	101061
Netherlands	USA (United States)	07 Oct 50	79UNTS33	101029
Colombia	IBRD (World Bank)	02 Nov 50	158UNTS59	102062
UK Great Britain	Yugoslavia	28 Dec 50	88UNTS329	101201
Honduras	USA (United States)	30 Jan 51	124UNTS63	101667
France	UK Great Britain	11 Apr 51	106UNTS3	101456
UK Great Britain	Yugoslavia	10 May 51	102UNTS29	101408
United Arab Rep	UK Great Britain	01 Jul 51	249UNTS125	103503
UK Great Britain	USA (United States)	18 Jul 51	117UNTS49	101583
UK Great Britain	Yugoslavia	28 Sep 51	117UNTS107	101587
Israel	USA (United States)	09 May 52	177UNTS269	102326
Sweden	USA (United States)	20 Nov 52	177UNTS203	102319
Multilateral		27 Feb 53	333UNTS3	104764
Libya	UK Great Britain	25 Mar 53	172UNTS281	102252
Denmark	Uruguay	09 Sep 53	256UNTS149	103625
Bulgaria	Greece	05 Dec 53	225UNTS145	103096
Ecuador	IBRD (World Bank)	10 Feb 54	209UNTS261	102830
ECSC (Coal/Steel)	USA (United States)	23 Apr 54	229UNTS229	103170
Greece	Romania	19 May 54	225UNTS27	103084
Greece	Hungary	05 Jun 54	299UNTS295	104321
Italy	USA (United States)	16 Jun 54	236UNTS149	103322
Jordan	USA (United States)	17 Jun 54	266UNTS137	103828
Argentina	UK Great Britain	31 Mar 55	210UNTS223	102840
Austria	USSR (Soviet Union)	17 Oct 55	0UNTS0	109254
Canada	Hungary	08 Mar 56	305UNTS27	104409
Ceylon (Sri Lanka)	Romania	16 Mar 56	315UNTS51	104559
Paraguay	USA (United States)	02 May 56	268UNTS299	103863
Italy	IBRD (World Bank)	28 Feb 58	359UNTS47	105139
Ecuador	USA (United States)	27 Jun 58	317UNTS51	104593
Japan	IBRD (World Bank)	27 Jun 58	312UNTS193	104519
Japan	IBRD (World Bank)	11 Jul 58	318UNTS103	104611
Israel	Yugoslavia	11 Dec 58	386UNTS283	105548
UK Great Britain	Yugoslavia	03 Feb 59	343UNTS153	104924
Multilateral		08 Apr 59	389UNTS69	105593
Ethiopia	Yugoslavia	06 Jun 59	386UNTS243	105544
Cuba	USSR (Soviet Union)	13 Feb 60	369UNTS3	105247
UN Special Fund	Togo	08 Jun 60	369UNTS401	200574
Ghana	USSR (Soviet Union)	04 Aug 60	399UNTS61	105734
Korea, South	USA (United States)	08 Feb 61	405UNTS37	105821
Honduras	IDA (Devel Assoc)	12 May 61	414UNTS180	105973
Somalia	USSR (Soviet Union)	02 Jun 61	493UNTS173	107214
IDA (Devel Assoc)	Sudan	14 Jun 61	415UNTS50	105981
India	IDA (Devel Assoc)	21 Jun 61	418UNTS61	106017
Chile	IDA (Devel Assoc)	28 Jun 61	426UNTS89	106131
Jordan	UK Great Britain	17 Jul 61	420UNTS53	106039
UK Great Britain	Yugoslavia	21 Jul 61	420UNTS61	106040
Colombia	IDA (Devel Assoc)	28 Aug 61	416UNTS3	105992
Taiwan	IDA (Devel Assoc)	30 Aug 61	417UNTS227	106008
Taiwan	IDA (Devel Assoc)	30 Aug 61	416UNTS175	106003
India	IDA (Devel Assoc)	06 Sep 61	418UNTS81	106018

PARTY ONE	PARTY TWO	DATE	CITATION	NUMBER
Credit provisions (Cont.)				
Taiwan	IDA (Devel Assoc)	06 Sep 61	417UNTS253	106009
Costa Rica	IDA (Devel Assoc)	13 Oct 61	431UNTS3	106204
Pakistan	IDA (Devel Assoc)	19 Oct 61	447UNTS161	106415
Paraguay	IDA (Devel Assoc)	26 Oct 61	447UNTS277	106419
Pakistan	IDA (Devel Assoc)	22 Nov 61	447UNTS295	106420
India	IDA (Devel Assoc)	22 Nov 61	427UNTS29	106145
India	IDA (Devel Assoc)	22 Nov 61	427UNTS3	106144
India	IDA (Devel Assoc)	22 Nov 61	427UNTS55	106146
Taiwan	IDA (Devel Assoc)	01 Dec 61	426UNTS105	106132
Jordan	IDA (Devel Assoc)	22 Dec 61	448UNTS21	106423
India	IDA (Devel Assoc)	14 Feb 62	468UNTS177	106773
India	USA (United States)	16 Apr 62	445UNTS257	106393
Austria	IBRD (World Bank)	15 Jun 62	447UNTS127	106414
United Arab Rep	USSR (Soviet Union)	23 Jun 62	472UNTS19	106835
Pakistan	IDA (Devel Assoc)	29 Jun 62	447UNTS325	106421
India	IDA (Devel Assoc)	29 Jun 62	447UNTS221	106417
India	IDA (Devel Assoc)	18 Jul 62	447UNTS191	106416
Pakistan	USA (United States)	25 Jul 62	459UNTS87	106614
India	IDA (Devel Assoc)	08 Aug 62	478UNTS335	106941
Korea, South	IDA (Devel Assoc)	17 Aug 62	468UNTS387	200603
Nicaragua	IDA (Devel Assoc)	07 Sep 62	478UNTS313	106940
India	IDA (Devel Assoc)	14 Sep 62	448UNTS3	106422
IDA (Devel Assoc)	Tunisia	17 Sep 62	469UNTS33	106783
Mali	USSR (Soviet Union)	10 Oct 62	493UNTS219	107216
Haiti	IDA (Devel Assoc)	02 Nov 62	468UNTS205	106774
Pakistan	IDA (Devel Assoc)	02 Nov 62	468UNTS351	106781
El Salvador	IDA (Devel Assoc)	02 Nov 62	468UNTS331	106780
Philippines	IBRD (World Bank)	07 Nov 62	468UNTS281	106777
IDA (Devel Assoc)	Turkey	23 Nov 62	469UNTS3	106782
IDA (Devel Assoc)	Turkey	01 Feb 63	468UNTS223	106775
India	New Zealand	22 Feb 63	486UNTS19	107069
Ethiopia	IDA (Devel Assoc)	27 Feb 63	478UNTS289	106939
India	IDA (Devel Assoc)	22 Mar 63	477UNTS3	106911
Cyprus	IBRD (World Bank)	17 Apr 63	476UNTS185	106909
India	IDA (Devel Assoc)	24 May 63	483UNTS205	107014
IDA (Devel Assoc)	Turkey	31 May 63	480UNTS127	106966
Pakistan	IDA (Devel Assoc)	26 Jun 63	492UNTS115	107189
Pakistan	IDA (Devel Assoc)	26 Jul 63	492UNTS143	107190
Pakistan	IDA (Devel Assoc)	16 Aug 63	492UNTS171	107191
Pakistan	IDA (Devel Assoc)	16 Aug 63	492UNTS205	107192
Belgium	Turkey	23 Sep 63	566UNTS195	108244
Multilateral		23 Oct 63	506UNTS197	107388
Jordan	IDA (Devel Assoc)	12 Dec 63	506UNTS51	107381
Jordan	IDA (Devel Assoc)	12 Dec 63	492UNTS3	107184
Canada	India	16 Dec 63	529UNTS45	107655
IDA (Devel Assoc)	Tanganyika	19 Dec 63	492UNTS241	107193
IDA (Devel Assoc)	Syria	24 Dec 63	534UNTS253	107764
Paraguay	IDA (Devel Assoc)	26 Dec 63	507UNTS3	107394
IDA (Devel Assoc)	Tanganyika	05 Feb 64	506UNTS91	107382
Pakistan	IDA (Devel Assoc)	25 Mar 64	535UNTS43	107775
Pakistan	IDA (Devel Assoc)	25 Mar 64	534UNTS275	107765
Ecuador	IDA (Devel Assoc)	26 May 64	534UNTS93	107757
India	IDA (Devel Assoc)	09 Jun 64	506UNTS31	107380
Pakistan	IDA (Devel Assoc)	11 Jun 64	534UNTS309	107766
Pakistan	IDA (Devel Assoc)	11 Jun 64	506UNTS3	107379
Niger	IDA (Devel Assoc)	24 Jun 64	554UNTS93	108098
Pakistan	IDA (Devel Assoc)	24 Jun 64	533UNTS191	107743
Pakistan	IDA (Devel Assoc)	24 Jun 64	533UNTS165	107742
Pakistan	IBRD (World Bank)	30 Jun 64	519UNTS57	107502
India	IDA (Devel Assoc)	06 Jul 64	534UNTS49	107753
IDA (Devel Assoc)	Turkey	14 Jul 64	534UNTS339	107767
Pakistan	IDA (Devel Assoc)	21 Jul 64	534UNTS373	107768
Bolivia	IDA (Devel Assoc)	24 Jul 64	534UNTS171	107762
Bolivia	IDA (Devel Assoc)	24 Jul 64	534UNTS203	107763
Kenya	IDA (Devel Assoc)	17 Aug 64	535UNTS79	107776

PARTY ONE	PARTY TWO	DATE	CITATION	NUMBER
Credit provisions (Cont.)				
Pakistan	IDA (Devel Assoc)	26 Aug 64	535UNTS263	107784
IDA (Devel Assoc)	Turkey	31 Aug 64	535UNTS111	107777
Pakistan	IDA (Devel Assoc)	22 Sep 64	594UNTS225	108605
Mali	IDA (Devel Assoc)	29 Sep 64	594UNTS187	108604
India	IDA (Devel Assoc)	26 Oct 64	535UNTS245	107783
Afghanistan	IDA (Devel Assoc)	23 Nov 64	567UNTS155	108255
Mauritania	IDA (Devel Assoc)	28 Dec 64	540UNTS163	107849
Kenya	IDA (Devel Assoc)	29 Dec 64	535UNTS225	107782
Honduras	IDA (Devel Assoc)	02 Feb 65	561UNTS279	108189
Nigeria	IDA (Devel Assoc)	01 Mar 65	571UNTS3	108297
Nigeria	IDA (Devel Assoc)	01 Mar 65	563UNTS3	108201
IDA (Devel Assoc)	Somalia	29 Mar 65	586UNTS101	108499
Multilateral		29 Mar 65	540UNTS145	107848
IDA (Devel Assoc)	Turkey	01 Apr 65	554UNTS137	108100
Multilateral		29 Apr 65	586UNTS123	108500
Kenya	IDA (Devel Assoc)	30 Jun 65	554UNTS75	108097
India	IDA (Devel Assoc)	11 Aug 65	562UNTS277	108199
Japan	IBRD (World Bank)	10 Sep 65	566UNTS249	108246
Israel	IBRD (World Bank)	16 Sep 65	566UNTS212	108245
Peru	IBRD (World Bank)	17 Sep 65	566UNTS311	108248
Morocco	IDA (Devel Assoc)	11 Oct 65	562UNTS299	108200
Morocco	IBRD (World Bank)	08 Nov 65	566UNTS279	108247
Saudi Arabia	USA (United States)	19 Nov 65	580UNTS35	108419
Liberia	USA (United States)	06 Jan 66	592UNTS101	108570
IDA (Devel Assoc)	Tanzania	13 Jan 66	567UNTS177	108256
Pakistan	IDA (Devel Assoc)	13 Jan 66	567UNTS67	108252
Pakistan	IDA (Devel Assoc)	10 Feb 66	575UNTS89	108355
Multilateral		10 Feb 66	575UNTS129	108356
Ethiopia	IDA (Devel Assoc)	16 Feb 66	569UNTS43	108278
Algeria	USA (United States)	23 Feb 66	592UNTS117	108571
Burundi	IDA (Devel Assoc)	31 Mar 66	569UNTS3	108277
Paraguay	IDA (Devel Assoc)	04 Apr 66	582UNTS331	108469
Brazil	USA (United States)	23 Apr 66	607UNTS117	108801
Israel	USA (United States)	06 Jun 66	578UNTS143	108392
Pakistan	IDA (Devel Assoc)	17 Jun 66	582UNTS297	108468
Indonesia	USA (United States)	28 Jun 66	593UNTS201	108585
India	IDA (Devel Assoc)	29 Jun 66	585UNTS101	108484
India	IDA (Devel Assoc)	29 Jun 66	582UNTS277	108467
Brazil	Denmark	08 Jul 66	581UNTS95	108435
IDA (Devel Assoc)	Siam	02 Aug 66	585UNTS271	108492
IDA (Devel Assoc)	Turkey	10 Aug 66	585UNTS237	108491
India	IDA (Devel Assoc)	19 Aug 66	584UNTS193	108478
Kenya	IDA (Devel Assoc)	19 Aug 66	585UNTS119	108485
Denmark	Malawi	01 Sep 66	586UNTS3	108493
Iceland	IBRD (World Bank)	14 Sep 66	598UNTS223	108660
Argentina	UK Great Britain	15 Sep 66	603UNTS151	108732
IDA (Devel Assoc)	Tunisia	16 Sep 66	616UNTS285	108903
IDA (Devel Assoc)	Senegal	29 Sep 66	594UNTS277	108607
Indonesia	USA (United States)	30 Sep 66	616UNTS199	108897
Malawi	IDA (Devel Assoc)	04 Oct 66	584UNTS215	108479
IBRD (World Bank)	Thailand	19 Oct 66	594UNTS347	108609
Philippines	USA (United States)	22 Dec 66	591UNTS219	108559
India	IDA (Devel Assoc)	23 Dec 66	594UNTS165	108603
Pakistan	IDA (Devel Assoc)	23 Dec 66	594UNTS255	108606
Congo (Brazzaville)	IBRD (World Bank)	09 Jan 67	598UNTS161	108659
East Afri Service	IBRD (World Bank)	17 Feb 67	599UNTS335	200629
IBRD (World Bank)	Tanzania	17 Feb 67	599UNTS287	108671
Kenya	IBRD (World Bank)	17 Feb 67	599UNTS233	108669
IBRD (World Bank)	Uganda	17 Feb 67	599UNTS321	108673
IDA (Devel Assoc)	Tunisia	21 Feb 67	618UNTS69	108924
IBRD (World Bank)	Trinidad/Tobago	10 Mar 67	599UNTS3	108662
IBRD (World Bank)	Thailand	24 Mar 67	599UNTS299	108672
Cameroon	IDA (Devel Assoc)	28 Mar 67	618UNTS133	108926
Philippines	IBRD (World Bank)	05 Apr 67	598UNTS261	108661
IDA (Devel Assoc)	Uganda	21 Apr 67	617UNTS161	108911

PARTY ONE	PARTY TWO	DATE	CITATION	NUMBER
Credit provisions (Cont.)				
Hungary	UN Special Fund	28 Apr 67	595UNTS171	108619
Malawi	IDA (Devel Assoc)	04 May 67	617UNTS141	108910
Jordan	IDA (Devel Assoc)	09 May 67	617UNTS47	108907
Kenya	IDA (Devel Assoc)	11 May 67	617UNTS111	108909
Kenya	IDA (Devel Assoc)	11 May 67	617UNTS91	108908
Bolivia	IDA (Devel Assoc)	26 May 67	618UNTS159	108927
Denmark	Peru	20 Jun 67	0UNTS0	109446
IDA (Devel Assoc)	Uganda	28 Jul 67	617UNTS177	108912
Denmark	Ghana	09 Aug 67	610UNTS0	108842
IDA (Devel Assoc)	Uganda	15 Sep 67	639UNTS115	109148
IBRD (World Bank)	Thailand	19 Sep 67	619UNTS275	108946
Brazil	IBRD (World Bank)	23 Sep 67	620UNTS77	108951
Iran	IBRD (World Bank)	17 Oct 67	0UNTS0	109331
Denmark	Zambia	18 Oct 67	637UNTS0	109116
El Salvador	IBRD (World Bank)	07 Dec 67	0UNTS0	109299
Korea, South	IDA (Devel Assoc)	18 Dec 67	639UNTS303	200639
Peru	UK Great Britain	19 Dec 67	0UNTS0	109447
Mexico	IBRD (World Bank)	26 Jan 68	0UNTS0	109511
Cameroon	IDA (Devel Assoc)	29 Jan 68	0UNTS0	109325
Turkey	UK Great Britain	04 Mar 68	0UNTS0	109266
Turkey	UK Great Britain	04 Mar 68	0UNTS0	109265
IDA (Devel Assoc)	Tanzania	21 Mar 68	0UNTS0	109327
Denmark	India	25 Mar 68	0UNTS0	109229
Germany, West	Thailand	29 Mar 68	637UNTS0	109122
Turkey	UK Great Britain	29 Mar 68	0UNTS0	109286
Denmark	Uganda	01 Apr 68	0UNTS0	109209
Nicaragua	IBRD (World Bank)	10 Apr 68	0UNTS0	109300
Malaysia	IBRD (World Bank)	17 Apr 68	0UNTS0	109360
Denmark	India	29 Apr 68	0UNTS0	109230
Turkey	UK Great Britain	22 May 68	0UNTS0	109287
IBRD (World Bank)	Thailand	23 May 68	0UNTS0	109332
Colombia	IBRD (World Bank)	03 Jun 68	0UNTS0	109333
Colombia	IBRD (World Bank)	03 Jun 68	0UNTS0	109334
Iran	IBRD (World Bank)	05 Jun 68	0UNTS0	109373
Denmark	Tunisia	07 Jun 68	0UNTS0	109407
Honduras	IDA (Devel Assoc)	12 Jun 68	0UNTS0	109409
Ivory Coast	IBRD (World Bank)	21 Jun 68	0UNTS0	109412
Ecuador	IDA (Devel Assoc)	27 Jun 68	0UNTS0	109321
IBRD (World Bank)	Singapore	03 Jul 68	0UNTS0	109364
Gabon	IBRD (World Bank)	07 Jul 68	0UNTS0	109361
Honduras	IBRD (World Bank)	12 Jul 68	0UNTS0	109408
Denmark	Senegal	03 Aug 68	0UNTS0	109282
Turkey	UK Great Britain	06 Aug 68	0UNTS0	109451
Denmark	Morocco	05 Nov 68	0UNTS0	109415
Denmark	Malawi	16 Dec 68	0UNTS0	109461
Finland	IBRD (World Bank)	24 Jan 69	0UNTS0	109596
Internal loans				
Norway	Poland	31 Dec 48	29UNTS3	100430
Paraguay	USA (United States)	02 May 56	268UNTS299	103863
Germany, West	Thailand	29 Mar 68	637UNTS0	109122
Purchase authorization				
Brazil	Paraguay	14 Jun 41	54UNTS313	200203
Canada	Czechoslovakia	01 Mar 45	45UNTS283	200185
France	UK Great Britain	27 Mar 45	98UNTS227	200274
Canada	Norway	25 Jun 45	45UNTS297	200186
Belgium	Canada	25 Oct 45	230UNTS127	103180
UK Great Britain	USA (United States)	06 Dec 45	126UNTS13	101679
Poland	USA (United States)	22 Apr 46	406UNTS215	105851
Albania	Yugoslavia	01 Jul 46	111UNTS81	101518
Albania	Yugoslavia	12 Jun 47	111UNTS189	101533
United Arab Rep	UK Great Britain	30 Jun 47	93UNTS165	101299
South Africa	UK Great Britain	09 Oct 47	17UNTS239	100278
Greece	Norway	08 Dec 47	30UNTS171	100455
Multilateral		10 Aug 49	45UNTS3	100689

PARTY ONE	PARTY TWO	DATE	CITATION	NUMBER
Purchase authorization (Cont.)				
Argentina	Norway	09 Sep 49	42UNTS125	100646
UK Great Britain	Yugoslavia	26 Dec 49	87UNTS71	101167
UK Great Britain	Yugoslavia	28 Dec 50	88UNTS329	101201
UK Great Britain	Yugoslavia	10 May 51	102UNTS29	101408
UK Great Britain	USA (United States)	18 Jul 51	117UNTS49	101583
Iraq	USA (United States)	16 Aug 51	147UNTS65	101929
Denmark	USA (United States)	23 Aug 51	147UNTS49	101928
Pakistan	USA (United States)	17 Sep 52	227UNTS77	103132
Germany, West	UK Great Britain	27 Feb 53	330UNTS217	104747
Germany, West	USA (United States)	27 Feb 53	224UNTS13	103067
Germany, West	USA (United States)	27 Feb 53	205UNTS103	102771
Multilateral		11 May 53	456UNTS3	106555
Argentina	USSR (Soviet Union)	05 Aug 53	221UNTS99	103004
France	Netherlands	09 Jul 54	287UNTS169	104183
Belgium	Greece	16 Dec 54	223UNTS73	103056
Iceland	Netherlands	28 Dec 54	287UNTS159	104182
Argentina	UK Great Britain	31 Mar 55	210UNTS223	102840
Japan	Netherlands	13 Mar 56	252UNTS3	103554
Paraguay	USA (United States)	02 May 56	268UNTS299	103863
Hungary	UK Great Britain	27 Jun 56	249UNTS19	103499
Sweden	UK Great Britain	08 Dec 56	264UNTS61	103788
Multilateral		29 Mar 57	283UNTS137	104113
Argentina	UK Great Britain	25 Nov 57	313UNTS95	104531
Austria	UK Great Britain	14 Mar 59	343UNTS263	104930
Italy	UK Great Britain	14 Apr 59	343UNTS289	104934
Netherlands	UK Great Britain	30 Apr 59	343UNTS307	104937
Switzerland	UK Great Britain	06 May 59	343UNTS315	104938
Japan	Vietnam, South	13 May 59	373UNTS149	105318
Ethiopia	Yugoslavia	06 Jun 59	386UNTS243	105544
Cuba	USSR (Soviet Union)	13 Feb 60	369UNTS3	105247
India	IDA (Devel Assoc)	21 Jun 61	418UNTS61	106017
Chile	IDA (Devel Assoc)	28 Jun 61	426UNTS89	106131
Colombia	IDA (Devel Assoc)	28 Aug 61	416UNTS3	105992
Taiwan	IDA (Devel Assoc)	30 Aug 61	417UNTS227	106008
Taiwan	IDA (Devel Assoc)	30 Aug 61	416UNTS175	106003
India	IDA (Devel Assoc)	06 Sep 61	418UNTS81	106018
Taiwan	IDA (Devel Assoc)	06 Sep 61	417UNTS253	106009
India	IDA (Devel Assoc)	22 Nov 61	427UNTS3	106144
India	IDA (Devel Assoc)	22 Nov 61	427UNTS55	106146
India	IDA (Devel Assoc)	22 Nov 61	427UNTS29	106145
Taiwan	IDA (Devel Assoc)	01 Dec 61	426UNTS105	106132
Liberia	USA (United States)	12 Apr 62	445UNTS213	106390
India	USA (United States)	16 Apr 62	445UNTS257	106393
UK Great Britain	USA (United States)	26 Apr 62	445UNTS273	106395
USA (United States)	Venezuela	17 May 62	456UNTS275	106562
Chile	USA (United States)	07 Aug 62	461UNTS61	106652
Ethiopia	USA (United States)	13 Aug 62	459UNTS31	106611
Israel	USA (United States)	28 Aug 62	448UNTS317	106445
Taiwan	USA (United States)	31 Aug 62	460UNTS247	106644
Morocco	USA (United States)	11 Sep 62	462UNTS207	106680
Dominican Republic	USA (United States)	30 Nov 62	471UNTS25	106819
Bolivia	USA (United States)	04 Feb 63	473UNTS65	106856
India	New Zealand	22 Feb 63	486UNTS19	107069
Colombia	USA (United States)	27 Mar 63	489UNTS289	107145
Burma	UK Great Britain	02 Apr 63	475UNTS139	106890
Multilateral		02 Apr 63	475UNTS121	106889
Ecuador	USA (United States)	05 Apr 63	477UNTS135	106919
India	USA (United States)	09 May 63	476UNTS43	106902
Senegal	USA (United States)	03 Jul 63	527UNTS95	107620
Iraq	USA (United States)	27 Aug 63	489UNTS271	107144
Paraguay	USA (United States)	16 Sep 63	494UNTS101	107229
Syria	USA (United States)	18 Nov 63	494UNTS169	107232
Congo (Zaire)	UK Great Britain	03 Jan 64	534UNTS417	107770
Iceland	USA (United States)	13 Feb 64	511UNTS3	107421
USA (United States)	Yugoslavia	27 Apr 64	526UNTS89	107602

PARTY ONE	PARTY TWO	DATE	CITATION	NUMBER
Purchase authorization (Cont.)				
USA (United States)	Yugoslavia	28 Apr 64	526UNTS103	107603
USA (United States)	Yugoslavia	28 Oct 64	533UNTS3	107728
USA (United States)	Yugoslavia	29 Oct 64	533UNTS17	107729
Iran	USA (United States)	16 Nov 64	532UNTS213	107719
Greece	USA (United States)	17 Nov 64	532UNTS107	107714
Kenya	USA (United States)	07 Dec 64	532UNTS263	107722
Morocco	USA (United States)	29 Dec 64	593UNTS185	108584
Iceland	USA (United States)	30 Dec 64	531UNTS287	107709
Taiwan	USA (United States)	31 Dec 64	532UNTS59	107712
Sierra Leone	USA (United States)	29 Jan 65	542UNTS87	107882
Ivory Coast	USA (United States)	05 Apr 65	546UNTS143	107941
Taiwan	USA (United States)	09 Apr 65	546UNTS81	107939
Philippines	USA (United States)	23 Apr 65	546UNTS157	107942
Ecuador	USA (United States)	25 Jun 65	549UNTS23	107986
USA (United States)	Yugoslavia	16 Jul 65	549UNTS111	107994
Bolivia	USA (United States)	17 Aug 65	587UNTS289	108514
Ethiopia	USA (United States)	17 Aug 65	564UNTS119	108224
USA (United States)	Yugoslavia	22 Nov 65	574UNTS211	108351
Ethiopia	USA (United States)	14 Dec 65	574UNTS115	108344
United Arab Rep	USA (United States)	03 Jan 66	579UNTS83	108400
Liberia	USA (United States)	06 Jan 66	592UNTS101	108570
Algeria	USA (United States)	23 Feb 66	592UNTS117	108571
Multilateral		04 Mar 66	578UNTS57	108387
Indonesia	USA (United States)	18 Apr 66	578UNTS106	108390
Paraguay	USA (United States)	27 Apr 66	578UNTS121	108391
Indonesia	USA (United States)	28 Jun 66	593UNTS201	108585
Denmark	Jordan	28 Jun 66	574UNTS3	108338
Brazil	Denmark	08 Jul 66	581UNTS95	108435
Turkey	UK Great Britain	29 Jul 66	597UNTS241	108649
Denmark	Malawi	01 Sep 66	586UNTS3	108493
Philippines	USA (United States)	22 Dec 66	591UNTS219	108559
Iran	IBRD (World Bank)	17 Oct 67	0UNTS0	109331
Denmark	Zambia	18 Oct 67	637UNTS0	109116
Peru	UK Great Britain	19 Dec 67	0UNTS0	109447
Cameroon	IDA (Devel Assoc)	29 Jan 68	0UNTS0	109325
Turkey	UK Great Britain	04 Mar 68	0UNTS0	109266
IDA (Devel Assoc)	Tanzania	21 Mar 68	0UNTS0	109327
Denmark	India	25 Mar 68	0UNTS0	109229
Denmark	Uganda	01 Apr 68	0UNTS0	109209
Denmark	India	29 Apr 68	0UNTS0	109230
Turkey	UK Great Britain	22 May 68	0UNTS0	109287
Denmark	Tunisia	07 Jun 68	0UNTS0	109407
Denmark	Kenya	26 Jun 68	0UNTS0	109210
Ecuador	IDA (Devel Assoc)	27 Jun 68	0UNTS0	109321
Honduras	IBRD (World Bank)	12 Jul 68	0UNTS0	109408
Denmark	Senegal	03 Aug 68	0UNTS0	109282
Denmark	Malawi	16 Dec 68	0UNTS0	109461
Loan repayment				
Mexico	USA (United States)	19 Nov 41	125UNTS287	200430
Canada	Czechoslovakia	01 Mar 45	45UNTS283	200185
France	UK Great Britain	27 Mar 45	98UNTS227	200274
Belgium	Canada	25 Oct 45	230UNTS127	103180
Greece	UK Great Britain	24 Jan 46	6UNTS45	100067
Canada	Netherlands	05 Feb 46	43UNTS3	100658
Canada	Taiwan	07 Feb 46	43UNTS23	100659
Poland	USA (United States)	22 Apr 46	406UNTS215	105851
France	UK Great Britain	29 Apr 46	98UNTS123	101360
Poland	UK Great Britain	24 Jun 46	11UNTS59	100149
Canada	Czechoslovakia	28 Jun 46	43UNTS81	100662
Albania	Yugoslavia	01 Jul 46	111UNTS81	101518
Belgium	USA (United States)	24 Sep 46	132UNTS80	101753
Netherlands	IBRD (World Bank)	07 Aug 47	152UNTS165	102015
Denmark	IBRD (World Bank)	22 Aug 47	152UNTS223	102016
Luxembourg	IBRD (World Bank)	28 Aug 47	153UNTS3	102017

PARTY ONE	PARTY TWO	DATE	CITATION	NUMBER
Loan repayment (Cont.)				
Greece	Norway	08 Dec 47	30UNTS171	100455
United Nations	USA (United States)	23 Mar 48	19UNTS43	100303
France	USA (United States)	22 Oct 48	84UNTS173	101128
Belgium	IBRD (World Bank)	01 Mar 49	154UNTS133	102029
Greece	Norway	12 Mar 49	33UNTS13	100510
Germany, West	Greece	16 Mar 49	77UNTS327	101007
Australia	Netherlands	12 Aug 49	34UNTS213	100539
India	IBRD (World Bank)	18 Aug 49	154UNTS269	102031
Belgium	France	07 Sep 49	123UNTS13	101651
Belgium	Netherlands	07 Sep 49	117UNTS3	101581
Belgium	UK Great Britain	07 Sep 49	106UNTS61	101457
IBRD (World Bank)	Yugoslavia	17 Sep 49	155UNTS3	102034
Czechoslovakia	UK Great Britain	28 Sep 49	86UNTS175	101158
India	IBRD (World Bank)	29 Sep 49	154UNTS393	102033
Finland	IBRD (World Bank)	17 Oct 49	156UNTS355	200481
Italy	Norway	19 Nov 49	47UNTS89	100724
Australia	Ceylon (Sri Lanka)	12 Jan 50	53UNTS295	100789
China People's Rep	USSR (Soviet Union)	14 Feb 50	226UNTS21	103104
India	IBRD (World Bank)	18 Apr 50	155UNTS117	102036
Iraq	IBRD (World Bank)	15 Jun 50	155UNTS267	102038
Multilateral		28 Jun 50	87UNTS153	101170
IBRD (World Bank)	Turkey	07 Jul 50	156UNTS75	102040
IBRD (World Bank)	Turkey	07 Jul 50	156UNTS3	102039
Netherlands	USA (United States)	07 Oct 50	79UNTS33	101029
Denmark	Germany, West	26 Feb 53	178UNTS3	102332
Germany, West	USA (United States)	27 Feb 53	224UNTS31	103068
Libya	UK Great Britain	25 Mar 53	172UNTS281	102252
UK Great Britain	USA (United States)	26 Jun 53	183UNTS225	102432
Finland	USSR (Soviet Union)	06 Feb 54	221UNTS143	103006
ECSC (Coal/Steel)	USA (United States)	23 Apr 54	229UNTS229	103170
Netherlands	Norway	09 Jun 54	287UNTS179	104184
Italy	USA (United States)	16 Jun 54	236UNTS149	103322
Germany, West	Italy	28 Jun 54	288UNTS83	104199
Belgium	Italy	12 Jul 54	288UNTS59	104198
Switzerland	UK Great Britain	16 Jul 54	199UNTS197	102685
Finland	USSR (Soviet Union)	24 Jan 55	240UNTS243	103406
Chile	USA (United States)	27 Jan 55	262UNTS3	103735
Italy	USA (United States)	11 Feb 55	241UNTS91	103426
Argentina	UK Great Britain	31 Mar 55	210UNTS223	102840
Italy	Switzerland	23 Jul 55	284UNTS279	104142
USA (United States)	Yugoslavia	19 Jan 56	240UNTS121	103400
Denmark	Netherlands	31 Jan 56	286UNTS255	104172
USSR (Soviet Union)	Yugoslavia	02 Feb 56	259UNTS111	103685
Japan	USA (United States)	10 Feb 56	275UNTS105	103979
Chile	USA (United States)	13 Mar 56	275UNTS49	103975
Afghanistan	USA (United States)	23 Jun 56	271UNTS295	103921
Italy	Switzerland	29 Jun 56	284UNTS299	104144
Italy	Netherlands	29 Jun 56	287UNTS193	104185
IBRD (World Bank)	Switzerland	17 Sep 56	340UNTS311	200560
Burma	India	12 Mar 57	312UNTS131	104515
Germany, West	Italy	12 Jul 57	291UNTS181	104252
Canada	India	20 Feb 58	391UNTS231	105628
Jordan	UK Great Britain	26 Mar 58	312UNTS373	104526
Jordan	UK Great Britain	07 May 58	312UNTS379	104527
Turkey	USA (United States)	06 Sep 58	336UNTS85	104800
Canada	India	22 Oct 58	392UNTS21	105635
Canada	Ceylon (Sri Lanka)	05 Nov 58	391UNTS225	105627
Turkey	UK Great Britain	25 Nov 58	327UNTS35	104715
Netherlands	Turkey	29 Nov 58	335UNTS229	104790
Taiwan	USA (United States)	24 Dec 58	340UNTS251	104868
UK Great Britain	Yugoslavia	03 Feb 59	343UNTS153	104924
France	UK Great Britain	05 Mar 59	343UNTS277	104932
Iraq	USSR (Soviet Union)	16 Mar 59	346UNTS107	104979
Norway	UK Great Britain	23 Apr 59	343UNTS283	104933
Belgium	UK Great Britain	23 Apr 59	343UNTS271	104931

PARTY ONE	PARTY TWO	DATE	CITATION	NUMBER
Loan repayment (Cont.)				
France	Netherlands	29 Apr 59	486UNTS379	107088
Iceland	Netherlands	30 Apr 59	487UNTS13	107091
Netherlands	Portugal	30 Apr 59	485UNTS129	107050
Germany, West	Netherlands	30 Apr 59	485UNTS141	107052
Netherlands	Norway	30 Apr 59	487UNTS3	107090
Fed of Malaya	UK Great Britain	01 May 59	345UNTS57	104958
Japan	Vietnam, South	13 May 59	373UNTS149	105318
Iceland	UK Great Britain	14 May 59	343UNTS301	104936
Ethiopia	Yugoslavia	06 Jun 59	386UNTS243	105544
Jordan	UK Great Britain	11 Jun 59	351UNTS283	105028
Iceland	USA (United States)	23 Jun 59	354UNTS3	105048
Austria	IBRD (World Bank)	25 Sep 59	355UNTS223	105079
Denmark	Sweden	04 Jan 60	376UNTS375	105390
Indonesia	USSR (Soviet Union)	28 Feb 60	392UNTS173	105643
Romania	USA (United States)	30 Mar 60	371UNTS163	105278
Multilateral		28 Apr 60	376UNTS111	105377
Jordan	UK Great Britain	04 May 60	385UNTS81	105531
India	IBRD (World Bank)	29 Jul 60	377UNTS153	105399
United Arab Rep	USSR (Soviet Union)	27 Aug 60	399UNTS37	105733
Chile	UK Great Britain	21 Oct 60	385UNTS15	105525
Romania	UK Great Britain	10 Nov 60	385UNTS113	105533
Somalia	USSR (Soviet Union)	02 Jun 61	457UNTS263	106587
Inter-Am Devel Bnk	USA (United States)	19 Jun 61	410UNTS34	105895
India	IDA (Devel Assoc)	21 Jun 61	418UNTS61	106017
Chile	IDA (Devel Assoc)	28 Jun 61	426UNTS89	106131
Bulgaria	Netherlands	07 Jul 61	489UNTS21	107133
Jordan	UK Great Britain	17 Jul 61	420UNTS53	106039
Brazil	UK Great Britain	21 Jul 61	414UNTS26	105962
UK Great Britain	Yugoslavia	21 Jul 61	420UNTS61	106040
Colombia	IDA (Devel Assoc)	28 Aug 61	416UNTS3	105992
Taiwan	IDA (Devel Assoc)	30 Aug 61	417UNTS227	106008
Tunisia	USSR (Soviet Union)	30 Aug 61	437UNTS243	106310
Taiwan	IDA (Devel Assoc)	30 Aug 61	416UNTS175	106003
India	IDA (Devel Assoc)	06 Sep 61	418UNTS81	106018
Taiwan	IDA (Devel Assoc)	06 Sep 61	417UNTS253	106009
Costa Rica	IDA (Devel Assoc)	13 Oct 61	431UNTS3	106204
Pakistan	IDA (Devel Assoc)	19 Oct 61	447UNTS161	106415
Switzerland	UK Great Britain	20 Oct 61	431UNTS29	106206
Paraguay	IDA (Devel Assoc)	26 Oct 61	447UNTS277	106419
Ghana	USSR (Soviet Union)	04 Nov 61	0UNTS0	109381
India	IDA (Devel Assoc)	22 Nov 61	427UNTS29	106145
India	IDA (Devel Assoc)	22 Nov 61	427UNTS55	106146
Pakistan	IDA (Devel Assoc)	22 Nov 61	447UNTS295	106420
India	IDA (Devel Assoc)	22 Nov 61	427UNTS3	106144
Taiwan	IDA (Devel Assoc)	01 Dec 61	426UNTS105	106132
Jordan	IDA (Devel Assoc)	22 Dec 61	448UNTS21	106423
India	IDA (Devel Assoc)	14 Feb 62	468UNTS177	106773
Jordan	UK Great Britain	30 May 62	449UNTS167	106458
Pakistan	IDA (Devel Assoc)	29 Jun 62	447UNTS325	106421
India	IDA (Devel Assoc)	29 Jun 62	447UNTS221	106417
India	IDA (Devel Assoc)	18 Jul 62	447UNTS191	106416
Korea, South	IDA (Devel Assoc)	17 Aug 62	468UNTS387	200603
Nicaragua	IDA (Devel Assoc)	07 Sep 62	478UNTS313	106940
India	IDA (Devel Assoc)	14 Sep 62	448UNTS3	106422
IDA (Devel Assoc)	Tunisia	17 Sep 62	469UNTS33	106783
El Salvador	IDA (Devel Assoc)	02 Nov 62	468UNTS331	106780
Pakistan	IDA (Devel Assoc)	02 Nov 62	468UNTS351	106781
Haiti	IDA (Devel Assoc)	02 Nov 62	468UNTS205	106774
IDA (Devel Assoc)	Turkey	23 Nov 62	469UNTS3	106782
Laos	USSR (Soviet Union)	01 Dec 62	472UNTS3	106834
India	New Zealand	22 Feb 63	486UNTS19	107069
Ethiopia	IDA (Devel Assoc)	27 Feb 63	478UNTS289	106939
India	IDA (Devel Assoc)	22 Mar 63	477UNTS3	106911
Jordan	UK Great Britain	27 Apr 63	475UNTS169	106892
Greece	Hungary	27 Apr 63	550UNTS197	108016

PARTY ONE	PARTY TWO	DATE	CITATION	NUMBER
Loan repayment (Cont.)				
Canada	India	14 May 63	529UNTS31	107653
India	IDA (Devel Assoc)	24 May 63	483UNTS205	107014
IDA (Devel Assoc)	Turkey	31 May 63	480UNTS127	106966
Argentina	UK Great Britain	05 Jun 63	482UNTS353	107004
Pakistan	IDA (Devel Assoc)	26 Jun 63	492UNTS115	107189
Denmark	India	12 Jul 63	616UNTS3	108888
Pakistan	IDA (Devel Assoc)	26 Jul 63	492UNTS143	107190
Pakistan	IDA (Devel Assoc)	16 Aug 63	492UNTS171	107191
Pakistan	IDA (Devel Assoc)	16 Aug 63	492UNTS205	107192
Multilateral		23 Oct 63	506UNTS197	107388
Jordan	IDA (Devel Assoc)	12 Dec 63	492UNTS3	107184
Jordan	IDA (Devel Assoc)	12 Dec 63	506UNTS51	107381
Chile	IBRD (World Bank)	18 Dec 63	504UNTS29	107352
IDA (Devel Assoc)	Syria	24 Dec 63	534UNTS253	107764
Paraguay	IDA (Devel Assoc)	26 Dec 63	507UNTS3	107394
IDA (Devel Assoc)	Tanganyika	05 Feb 64	506UNTS91	107382
Pakistan	IDA (Devel Assoc)	25 Mar 64	535UNTS43	107775
Pakistan	IDA (Devel Assoc)	25 Mar 64	534UNTS275	107765
Ecuador	IDA (Devel Assoc)	26 May 64	534UNTS93	107757
India	IDA (Devel Assoc)	09 Jun 64	506UNTS31	107380
Pakistan	IDA (Devel Assoc)	11 Jun 64	534UNTS309	107766
Czechoslovakia	Netherlands	11 Jun 64	556UNTS89	108120
Pakistan	IDA (Devel Assoc)	11 Jun 64	506UNTS3	107379
Pakistan	IDA (Devel Assoc)	24 Jun 64	533UNTS165	107742
Pakistan	IDA (Devel Assoc)	24 Jun 64	533UNTS191	107743
Niger	IDA (Devel Assoc)	24 Jun 64	554UNTS93	108098
India	IDA (Devel Assoc)	06 Jul 64	534UNTS49	107753
IDA (Devel Assoc)	Turkey	14 Jul 64	534UNTS339	107767
Pakistan	IDA (Devel Assoc)	21 Jul 64	534UNTS373	107768
New Zealand	Western Samoa	23 Jul 64	521UNTS173	107520
Bolivia	IDA (Devel Assoc)	24 Jul 64	534UNTS171	107762
Bolivia	IDA (Devel Assoc)	24 Jul 64	534UNTS203	107763
Kenya	IDA (Devel Assoc)	17 Aug 64	535UNTS79	107776
Pakistan	IDA (Devel Assoc)	26 Aug 64	535UNTS263	107784
Jordan	UK Great Britain	31 Aug 64	541UNTS3	107856
IDA (Devel Assoc)	Turkey	31 Aug 64	535UNTS111	107777
Pakistan	IDA (Devel Assoc)	22 Sep 64	594UNTS225	108605
Mali	IDA (Devel Assoc)	29 Sep 64	594UNTS187	108604
Brazil	UK Great Britain	14 Oct 64	539UNTS289	107840
India	IDA (Devel Assoc)	26 Oct 64	535UNTS245	107783
Afghanistan	IDA (Devel Assoc)	23 Nov 64	567UNTS155	108255
Mauritania	IDA (Devel Assoc)	28 Dec 64	540UNTS163	107849
Kenya	IDA (Devel Assoc)	29 Dec 64	535UNTS225	107782
Honduras	IDA (Devel Assoc)	02 Feb 65	561UNTS279	108189
Nigeria	IDA (Devel Assoc)	01 Mar 65	563UNTS3	108201
Nigeria	IDA (Devel Assoc)	01 Mar 65	571UNTS3	108297
IDA (Devel Assoc)	Somalia	29 Mar 65	586UNTS101	108499
IDA (Devel Assoc)	Turkey	01 Apr 65	554UNTS137	108100
India	IBRD (World Bank)	28 May 65	552UNTS39	108049
Jordan	UK Great Britain	08 Jun 65	552UNTS251	108057
Pakistan	IDA (Devel Assoc)	30 Jun 65	554UNTS111	108099
Kenya	IDA (Devel Assoc)	30 Jun 65	554UNTS75	108097
India	IDA (Devel Assoc)	11 Aug 65	562UNTS277	108199
Japan	IBRD (World Bank)	10 Sep 65	566UNTS249	108246
Israel	IBRD (World Bank)	16 Sep 65	566UNTS212	108245
Morocco	IDA (Devel Assoc)	11 Oct 65	562UNTS299	108200
Turkey	UK Great Britain	21 Oct 65	561UNTS185	108180
Morocco	IBRD (World Bank)	08 Nov 65	566UNTS279	108247
Chile	UK Great Britain	23 Nov 65	560UNTS215	108176
Pakistan	IDA (Devel Assoc)	13 Jan 66	567UNTS67	108252
IDA (Devel Assoc)	Tanzania	13 Jan 66	567UNTS177	108256
Multilateral		10 Feb 66	575UNTS129	108356
Pakistan	IDA (Devel Assoc)	10 Feb 66	575UNTS89	108355
Ethiopia	IDA (Devel Assoc)	16 Feb 66	569UNTS43	108278
Brazil	IBRD (World Bank)	15 Mar 66	599UNTS52	108664

PARTY ONE	PARTY TWO	DATE	CITATION	NUMBER
Loan repayment (Cont.)				
Burundi	IDA (Devel Assoc)	31 Mar 66	569UNTS3	108277
Paraguay	IDA (Devel Assoc)	04 Apr 66	582UNTS331	108469
Colombia	IBRD (World Bank)	16 May 66	608UNTS249	108819
Argentina	Bolivia	15 Jun 66	0UNTS0	109518
Pakistan	IDA (Devel Assoc)	17 Jun 66	582UNTS297	108468
Denmark	Jordan	28 Jun 66	574UNTS3	108338
India	IDA (Devel Assoc)	29 Jun 66	582UNTS277	108467
India	IDA (Devel Assoc)	29 Jun 66	585UNTS101	108484
Brazil	Denmark	08 Jul 66	581UNTS95	108435
Jordan	UK Great Britain	26 Jul 66	597UNTS219	108647
New Zealand	Western Samoa	29 Jul 66	598UNTS115	108657
Turkey	UK Great Britain	29 Jul 66	597UNTS241	108649
IDA (Devel Assoc)	Siam	02 Aug 66	585UNTS271	108492
IDA (Devel Assoc)	Turkey	10 Aug 66	585UNTS237	108491
Kenya	IDA (Devel Assoc)	19 Aug 66	585UNTS119	108485
India	IDA (Devel Assoc)	19 Aug 66	584UNTS193	108478
Denmark	Malawi	01 Sep 66	586UNTS3	108493
Argentina	UK Great Britain	15 Sep 66	603UNTS151	108732
IDA (Devel Assoc)	Senegal	29 Sep 66	594UNTS277	108607
Malawi	IDA (Devel Assoc)	04 Oct 66	584UNTS215	108479
IBRD (World Bank)	Thailand	19 Oct 66	594UNTS347	108609
IBRD (World Bank)	IFC (Finance Corp)	28 Oct 66	586UNTS225	200628
Peru	UK Great Britain	03 Dec 66	617UNTS231	108915
India	IDA (Devel Assoc)	23 Dec 66	594UNTS165	108603
Pakistan	IDA (Devel Assoc)	23 Dec 66	594UNTS255	108606
Kenya	IBRD (World Bank)	17 Feb 67	599UNTS233	108669
East Afri Service	IBRD (World Bank)	17 Feb 67	599UNTS335	200629
IBRD (World Bank)	Yugoslavia	24 Feb 67	599UNTS27	108663
IBRD (World Bank)	Trinidad/Tobago	10 Mar 67	599UNTS3	108662
Turkey	UK Great Britain	21 Apr 67	610UNTS0	108838
IBRD (World Bank)	UK Great Britain	24 Apr 67	600UNTS3	108674
Argentina	Uruguay	30 May 67	0UNTS0	109521
Denmark	Peru	20 Jun 67	0UNTS0	109446
Jordan	UK Great Britain	15 Aug 67	632UNTS269	109028
Iran	IBRD (World Bank)	17 Oct 67	0UNTS0	109331
Denmark	Zambia	18 Oct 67	637UNTS0	109116
El Salvador	IBRD (World Bank)	07 Dec 67	0UNTS0	109299
Mexico	IBRD (World Bank)	26 Jan 68	0UNTS0	109511
Turkey	UK Great Britain	04 Mar 68	0UNTS0	109265
IDA (Devel Assoc)	Tanzania	21 Mar 68	0UNTS0	109327
Denmark	India	25 Mar 68	0UNTS0	109229
Turkey	UK Great Britain	29 Mar 68	0UNTS0	109286
Denmark	Uganda	01 Apr 68	0UNTS0	109209
Nicaragua	IBRD (World Bank)	10 Apr 68	0UNTS0	109300
Malaysia	IBRD (World Bank)	17 Apr 68	0UNTS0	109360
Denmark	India	29 Apr 68	0UNTS0	109230
Turkey	UK Great Britain	22 May 68	0UNTS0	109287
IBRD (World Bank)	Thailand	23 May 68	0UNTS0	109332
Colombia	IBRD (World Bank)	03 Jun 68	0UNTS0	109333
Colombia	IBRD (World Bank)	03 Jun 68	0UNTS0	109334
Iran	IBRD (World Bank)	05 Jun 68	0UNTS0	109373
Denmark	Tunisia	07 Jun 68	0UNTS0	109407
Ivory Coast	IBRD (World Bank)	21 Jun 68	0UNTS0	109412
Denmark	Kenya	26 Jun 68	0UNTS0	109210
IBRD (World Bank)	Singapore	03 Jul 68	0UNTS0	109364
Gabon	IBRD (World Bank)	07 Jul 68	0UNTS0	109361
Honduras	IBRD (World Bank)	12 Jul 68	0UNTS0	109408
Denmark	Senegal	03 Aug 68	0UNTS0	109282
Turkey	UK Great Britain	06 Aug 68	0UNTS0	109451
Denmark	Morocco	05 Nov 68	0UNTS0	109415
Denmark	Malawi	16 Dec 68	0UNTS0	109461
Finland	IBRD (World Bank)	24 Jan 69	0UNTS0	109596
Refinance of loan				
Czechoslovakia	UK Great Britain	28 Sep 49	86UNTS175	101158
Refinance of loan (Cont.)				
Australia	Ceylon (Sri Lanka)	12 Jan 50	53UNTS295	100789
Sweden	UK Great Britain	22 Dec 55	231UNTS179	103218
Argentina	UK Great Britain	05 Jun 63	482UNTS353	107004
Brazil	UK Great Britain	14 Oct 64	539UNTS289	107840
Turkey	UK Great Britain	21 Oct 65	561UNTS185	108180
Chile	UK Great Britain	23 Nov 65	560UNTS215	108176
Argentina	Bolivia	15 Jun 66	0UNTS0	109518
Argentina	Uruguay	30 May 67	0UNTS0	109521
Terms of loan				
Netherlands	UK Great Britain	13 Jun 39	5UNTS65	200028
Costa Rica	USA (United States)	16 Jan 42	23UNTS285	200135
Honduras	USA (United States)	26 Oct 42	24UNTS209	200145
Canada	Czechoslovakia	01 Mar 45	45UNTS283	200185
Canada	Norway	25 Jun 45	45UNTS297	200186
Belgium	Canada	25 Oct 45	230UNTS127	103180
Greece	UK Great Britain	24 Jan 46	6UNTS45	100067
Canada	Netherlands	05 Feb 46	43UNTS3	100658
Canada	Taiwan	07 Feb 46	43UNTS23	100659
Canada	UK Great Britain	06 Mar 46	20UNTS13	100312
Canada	France	09 Apr 46	43UNTS43	100660
Poland	USA (United States)	22 Apr 46	406UNTS215	105851
Taiwan	USA (United States)	28 Jun 46	34UNTS121	100532
United Arab Rep	UK Great Britain	30 Jun 47	93UNTS165	101299
France	New Zealand	02 Jul 47	16UNTS219	100263
United Arab Rep	UK Great Britain	05 Jan 48	77UNTS3	100988
Czechoslovakia	New Zealand	22 Jan 48	16UNTS229	100264
United Nations	USA (United States)	23 Mar 48	19UNTS43	100303
Belgium	France	07 Sep 49	123UNTS13	101651
Belgium	Netherlands	07 Sep 49	117UNTS3	101581
Australia	Ceylon (Sri Lanka)	12 Jan 50	53UNTS295	100789
Brazil	IBRD (World Bank)	26 May 50	301UNTS165	104345
Ethiopia	IBRD (World Bank)	13 Sep 50	157UNTS233	102056
Ethiopia	IBRD (World Bank)	13 Sep 50	157UNTS213	102055
IBRD (World Bank)	Thailand	27 Oct 50	158UNTS25	102060
IBRD (World Bank)	Thailand	27 Oct 50	158UNTS3	102059
IBRD (World Bank)	Thailand	27 Oct 50	158UNTS43	102061
Australia	IBRD (World Bank)	14 Nov 50	156UNTS147	102041
IBRD (World Bank)	South Africa	23 Jan 51	158UNTS115	102064
Ethiopia	IBRD (World Bank)	19 Feb 51	186UNTS101	102486
Colombia	IBRD (World Bank)	10 Apr 51	158UNTS155	102066
Nicaragua	IBRD (World Bank)	07 Jun 51	158UNTS277	102068
Iceland	IBRD (World Bank)	20 Jun 51	158UNTS301	102069
UK Great Britain	USA (United States)	18 Jul 51	117UNTS49	101583
Belgium	IBRD (World Bank)	13 Sep 51	158UNTS323	102070
IBRD (World Bank)	Yugoslavia	11 Oct 51	159UNTS3	102081
Nicaragua	IBRD (World Bank)	29 Oct 51	159UNTS35	102082
Iceland	IBRD (World Bank)	01 Nov 51	159UNTS55	102083
Paraguay	IBRD (World Bank)	07 Dec 51	159UNTS103	102085
Peru	IBRD (World Bank)	23 Jan 52	159UNTS163	102087
Pakistan	IBRD (World Bank)	27 Mar 52	159UNTS251	102090
Pakistan	IBRD (World Bank)	13 Jun 52	191UNTS85	102578
IBRD (World Bank)	Turkey	18 Jun 52	159UNTS269	102091
Brazil	IBRD (World Bank)	27 Jun 52	190UNTS85	102560
Brazil	IBRD (World Bank)	27 Jun 52	190UNTS115	102561
Peru	IBRD (World Bank)	08 Jul 52	159UNTS321	102093
Australia	IBRD (World Bank)	08 Jul 52	159UNTS295	102092
Colombia	IBRD (World Bank)	26 Aug 52	159UNTS339	102094
Iceland	IBRD (World Bank)	26 Aug 52	159UNTS363	102095
Pakistan	USA (United States)	17 Sep 52	227UNTS77	103132
Japan	IBRD (World Bank)	12 Nov 52	354UNTS313	105068
India	IBRD (World Bank)	18 Dec 52	201UNTS241	102719
IBRD (World Bank)	Yugoslavia	11 Feb 53	165UNTS231	102179
IBRD (World Bank)	UK Great Britain	11 Mar 53	172UNTS115	102243
Brazil	IBRD (World Bank)	30 Apr 53	190UNTS133	102562

PARTY ONE	PARTY TWO	DATE	CITATION	NUMBER
Terms of loan (Cont.)				
UK Great Britain	USA (United States)	24 Jun 53	224UNTS141	103074
Brazil	IBRD (World Bank)	17 Jul 53	190UNTS149	102563
IBRD (World Bank)	South Africa	28 Aug 53	180UNTS91	102377
IBRD (World Bank)	South Africa	28 Aug 53	180UNTS73	102376
Nicaragua	IBRD (World Bank)	04 Sep 53	186UNTS117	102487
Nicaragua	IBRD (World Bank)	04 Sep 53	186UNTS137	102488
Iceland	IBRD (World Bank)	04 Sep 53	188UNTS3	102519
Iceland	IBRD (World Bank)	04 Sep 53	178UNTS275	102344
Colombia	IBRD (World Bank)	10 Sep 53	203UNTS3	102738
Chile	IBRD (World Bank)	10 Sep 53	188UNTS25	102520
IBRD (World Bank)	Turkey	10 Sep 53	187UNTS71	102502
Panama	IBRD (World Bank)	25 Sep 53	188UNTS71	102521
Panama	IBRD (World Bank)	25 Sep 53	188UNTS95	102522
Italy	IBRD (World Bank)	06 Oct 53	301UNTS135	104344
Japan	IBRD (World Bank)	15 Oct 53	187UNTS367	200513
Japan	IBRD (World Bank)	15 Oct 53	187UNTS321	200512
Japan	IBRD (World Bank)	15 Oct 53	187UNTS271	200511
Brazil	IBRD (World Bank)	18 Dec 53	301UNTS229	104346
Brazil	IBRD (World Bank)	18 Dec 53	190UNTS179	102564
Finland	USSR (Soviet Union)	06 Feb 54	221UNTS143	103006
Ecuador	IBRD (World Bank)	10 Feb 54	209UNTS261	102830
Australia	IBRD (World Bank)	02 Mar 54	191UNTS103	102579
Norway	IBRD (World Bank)	08 Apr 54	201UNTS131	102714
Peru	IBRD (World Bank)	12 Apr 54	190UNTS231	102567
ECSC (Coal/Steel)	USA (United States)	23 Apr 54	229UNTS229	103170
Pakistan	IBRD (World Bank)	02 Jun 54	324UNTS59	104678
France	IBRD (World Bank)	10 Jun 54	210UNTS89	102836
Italy	USA (United States)	16 Jun 54	236UNTS149	103322
Ceylon (Sri Lanka)	IBRD (World Bank)	09 Jul 54	198UNTS313	200517
Mexico	IBRD (World Bank)	24 Aug 54	286UNTS211	104168
El Salvador	IBRD (World Bank)	12 Oct 54	203UNTS37	102739
Austria	IBRD (World Bank)	08 Nov 54	216UNTS305	200528
Peru	IBRD (World Bank)	12 Nov 54	209UNTS287	102831
India	IBRD (World Bank)	19 Nov 54	309UNTS159	104473
Belgium	IBRD (World Bank)	14 Dec 54	210UNTS113	102837
Colombia	IBRD (World Bank)	29 Dec 54	211UNTS135	102851
Finland	USSR (Soviet Union)	24 Jan 55	240UNTS243	103406
Italy	USA (United States)	11 Feb 55	241UNTS91	103426
India	IBRD (World Bank)	14 Mar 55	309UNTS129	104472
IBRD (World Bank)	UK Great Britain	15 Mar 55	265UNTS85	103808
Australia	IBRD (World Bank)	18 Mar 55	220UNTS131	102998
Finland	IBRD (World Bank)	24 Mar 55	211UNTS305	200525
Colombia	IBRD (World Bank)	24 Mar 55	212UNTS217	102874
Peru	IBRD (World Bank)	05 Apr 55	211UNTS115	102850
Peru	IBRD (World Bank)	19 Apr 55	221UNTS153	103007
Norway	IBRD (World Bank)	19 Apr 55	211UNTS159	102852
Italy	IBRD (World Bank)	01 Jun 55	358UNTS203	105137
Austria	IBRD (World Bank)	14 Jun 55	221UNTS375	200531
Colombia	IBRD (World Bank)	15 Jun 55	248UNTS161	103494
Pakistan	IBRD (World Bank)	20 Jun 55	230UNTS41	103176
Nicaragua	IBRD (World Bank)	08 Jul 55	229UNTS97	103162
Nicaragua	IBRD (World Bank)	08 Jul 55	229UNTS123	103163
Panama	IBRD (World Bank)	12 Jul 55	219UNTS127	102970
Italy	Switzerland	23 Jul 55	284UNTS279	104142
Guatemala	IBRD (World Bank)	29 Jul 55	229UNTS167	103165
Pakistan	IBRD (World Bank)	04 Aug 55	230UNTS79	103177
Peru	IBRD (World Bank)	05 Aug 55	218UNTS3	102950
Pakistan	IBRD (World Bank)	06 Aug 55	236UNTS195	103325
IBRD (World Bank)	Thailand	09 Aug 55	221UNTS283	103011
Lebanon	IBRD (World Bank)	25 Aug 55	230UNTS233	103188
France	IBRD (World Bank)	26 Aug 55	247UNTS305	103478
Nicaragua	IBRD (World Bank)	26 Aug 55	229UNTS145	103164
IBRD (World Bank)	Uruguay	29 Aug 55	243UNTS123	103450
Japan	IBRD (World Bank)	25 Oct 55	230UNTS379	200534
IBRD (World Bank)	South Africa	28 Nov 55	230UNTS101	103178

PARTY ONE	PARTY TWO	DATE	CITATION	NUMBER
Terms of loan (Cont.)				
USA (United States)	Yugoslavia	19 Jan 56	240UNTS121	103400
USSR (Soviet Union)	Yugoslavia	02 Feb 56	259UNTS111	103685
Japan	IBRD (World Bank)	21 Feb 56	248UNTS321	200543
Ecuador	IBRD (World Bank)	26 Mar 56	292UNTS391	104277
Norway	IBRD (World Bank)	03 May 56	243UNTS281	103455
Burma	IBRD (World Bank)	04 May 56	253UNTS179	103584
Burma	IBRD (World Bank)	04 May 56	253UNTS209	103585
Haiti	IBRD (World Bank)	07 May 56	252UNTS279	103570
Nicaragua	IBRD (World Bank)	22 May 56	253UNTS233	103586
Finland	IBRD (World Bank)	22 May 56	248UNTS57	103485
Colombia	IBRD (World Bank)	06 Jun 56	248UNTS139	103493
Fed Rhod/Nyasaland	IBRD (World Bank)	21 Jun 56	285UNTS317	104156
IBRD (World Bank)	UK Great Britain	21 Jun 56	285UNTS355	104157
India	IBRD (World Bank)	26 Jun 56	301UNTS3	104341
IBRD (World Bank)	Switzerland	17 Sep 56	340UNTS311	200560
Costa Rica	IBRD (World Bank)	18 Sep 56	260UNTS369	103721
Austria	IBRD (World Bank)	21 Sep 56	259UNTS43	103682
Austria	IBRD (World Bank)	21 Sep 56	259UNTS17	103681
Italy	IBRD (World Bank)	11 Oct 56	359UNTS3	105138
IBRD (World Bank)	Thailand	12 Oct 56	261UNTS117	103728
IBRD (World Bank)	Uruguay	25 Oct 56	265UNTS59	103807
Chile	IBRD (World Bank)	01 Nov 56	261UNTS27	103724
Australia	IBRD (World Bank)	15 Nov 56	288UNTS117	104201
Australia	IBRD (World Bank)	03 Dec 56	288UNTS99	104200
India	IBRD (World Bank)	19 Dec 56	310UNTS75	104489
Japan	IBRD (World Bank)	19 Dec 56	268UNTS203	103859
Japan	IBRD (World Bank)	19 Dec 56	264UNTS179	103793
Iran	IBRD (World Bank)	22 Jan 57	317UNTS129	104600
Ethiopia	IBRD (World Bank)	28 Jan 57	286UNTS307	104175
India	IBRD (World Bank)	05 Mar 57	272UNTS201	103939
Burma	India	12 Mar 57	312UNTS131	104515
Peru	IBRD (World Bank)	13 Mar 57	274UNTS59	103958
Netherlands	IBRD (World Bank)	15 May 57	274UNTS211	103967
India	IBRD (World Bank)	29 May 57	309UNTS201	104474
Belgium	IBRD (World Bank)	26 Jun 57	322UNTS301	104661
India	IBRD (World Bank)	12 Jul 57	288UNTS135	104202
Chile	IBRD (World Bank)	24 Jul 57	282UNTS139	104098
Chile	IBRD (World Bank)	24 Jul 57	282UNTS189	104099
Japan	IBRD (World Bank)	09 Aug 57	293UNTS59	104286
Turkey	UK Great Britain	16 Aug 57	310UNTS21	104482
Belgium	IBRD (World Bank)	10 Sep 57	286UNTS291	104174
IBRD (World Bank)	Thailand	12 Sep 57	299UNTS349	104324
Ecuador	IBRD (World Bank)	20 Sep 57	293UNTS135	104291
Ecuador	IBRD (World Bank)	20 Sep 57	289UNTS237	104221
IBRD (World Bank)	South Africa	01 Oct 57	280UNTS285	104065
Austria	IBRD (World Bank)	10 Oct 57	301UNTS95	104343
Pakistan	IBRD (World Bank)	18 Oct 57	299UNTS303	104322
India	IBRD (World Bank)	20 Nov 57	301UNTS47	104342
Philippines	IBRD (World Bank)	22 Nov 57	293UNTS83	104287
Belgium	IBRD (World Bank)	27 Nov 57	292UNTS175	104273
Pakistan	IBRD (World Bank)	17 Dec 57	299UNTS321	104323
Mexico	IBRD (World Bank)	14 Jan 58	293UNTS167	104292
Indonesia	Japan	20 Jan 58	325UNTS13	104691
Brazil	IBRD (World Bank)	22 Jan 58	323UNTS99	104666
Canada	India	20 Feb 58	391UNTS231	105628
Jordan	UK Great Britain	26 Mar 58	312UNTS373	104526
Pakistan	IBRD (World Bank)	23 Apr 58	323UNTS253	104672
Chile	IBRD (World Bank)	28 Apr 58	359UNTS89	105140
Austria	IBRD (World Bank)	28 Apr 58	359UNTS145	105142
IBRD (World Bank)	UK Great Britain	02 May 58	324UNTS25	104677
Jordan	UK Great Britain	07 May 58	312UNTS379	104527
Honduras	IBRD (World Bank)	09 May 58	323UNTS4	104662
Japan	IBRD (World Bank)	13 Jun 58	312UNTS159	104518
IBRD (World Bank)	UK Great Britain	16 Jun 58	309UNTS35	104467
India	IBRD (World Bank)	25 Jun 58	323UNTS157	104668

PARTY ONE	PARTY TWO	DATE	CITATION	NUMBER
Terms of loan (Cont.)				
India	IBRD (World Bank)	25 Jun 58	323UNTS131	104667
IBRD (World Bank)	Sudan	21 Jul 58	323UNTS183	104669
India	IBRD (World Bank)	23 Jul 58	317UNTS3	104590
Japan	IBRD (World Bank)	18 Aug 58	323UNTS205	104670
Japan	IBRD (World Bank)	10 Sep 58	323UNTS297	104673
Japan	IBRD (World Bank)	10 Sep 58	318UNTS133	104612
India	IBRD (World Bank)	16 Sep 58	323UNTS235	104671
Ceylon (Sri Lanka)	IBRD (World Bank)	17 Sep 58	323UNTS51	104664
Peru	IBRD (World Bank)	17 Sep 58	323UNTS27	104663
Fed of Malaya	IBRD (World Bank)	22 Sep 58	323UNTS71	104665
Brazil	IBRD (World Bank)	03 Oct 58	337UNTS177	104823
Ecuador	IBRD (World Bank)	09 Oct 58	337UNTS299	104827
Canada	India	22 Oct 58	392UNTS21	105635
Canada	Ceylon (Sri Lanka)	05 Nov 58	391UNTS225	105627
Austria	IBRD (World Bank)	02 Dec 58	340UNTS3	104856
IBRD (World Bank)	South Africa	02 Dec 58	324UNTS3	104676
Colombia	IBRD (World Bank)	15 Dec 58	354UNTS233	105065
El Salvador	IBRD (World Bank)	07 Jan 59	346UNTS51	104977
Colombia	IBRD (World Bank)	30 Jan 59	337UNTS327	104828
UK Great Britain	Yugoslavia	03 Feb 59	343UNTS153	104924
Costa Rica	IBRD (World Bank)	11 Feb 59	337UNTS245	104825
El Salvador	IBRD (World Bank)	20 Feb 59	362UNTS75	105183
Finland	IBRD (World Bank)	16 Mar 59	337UNTS269	104826
India	IBRD (World Bank)	08 Apr 59	348UNTS131	104998
Italy	IBRD (World Bank)	21 Apr 59	359UNTS191	105143
Fed of Malaya	UK Great Britain	01 May 59	345UNTS57	104958
Japan	Vietnam, South	13 May 59	373UNTS149	105318
Honduras	IBRD (World Bank)	20 May 59	359UNTS119	105141
Colombia	IBRD (World Bank)	20 May 59	344UNTS251	104953
Iran	IBRD (World Bank)	29 May 59	348UNTS103	104997
Ethiopia	Yugoslavia	06 Jun 59	386UNTS243	105544
IBRD (World Bank)	South Africa	10 Jun 59	340UNTS33	104857
Jordan	UK Great Britain	11 Jun 59	351UNTS283	105028
Brazil	IBRD (World Bank)	17 Jun 59	377UNTS111	105398
Congo (Brazzaville)	IBRD (World Bank)	30 Jun 59	452UNTS123	106506
Gabon	IBRD (World Bank)	30 Jun 59	452UNTS135	106507
France	IBRD (World Bank)	30 Jun 59	452UNTS67	106505
Norway	IBRD (World Bank)	08 Jul 59	344UNTS229	104952
India	IBRD (World Bank)	15 Jul 59	355UNTS95	105075
India	IBRD (World Bank)	15 Jul 59	346UNTS33	104976
Pakistan	IBRD (World Bank)	13 Aug 59	355UNTS129	105076
Italy	IBRD (World Bank)	16 Sep 59	375UNTS159	105366
Pakistan	IBRD (World Bank)	25 Sep 59	355UNTS169	105077
Japan	IBRD (World Bank)	12 Nov 59	354UNTS279	105067
Iran	IBRD (World Bank)	23 Nov 59	380UNTS245	105459
Pakistan	IBRD (World Bank)	30 Nov 59	355UNTS203	105078
France	IBRD (World Bank)	10 Dec 59	380UNTS319	105464
IBRD (World Bank)	United Arab Rep	22 Dec 59	354UNTS197	105063
IBRD (World Bank)	Uruguay	30 Dec 59	384UNTS275	105523
Denmark	Sweden	04 Jan 60	376UNTS375	105390
Colombia	IBRD (World Bank)	20 Jan 60	375UNTS49	105353
Iran	IBRD (World Bank)	20 Feb 60	384UNTS213	105521
Indonesia	USSR (Soviet Union)	28 Feb 60	392UNTS173	105643
France	IBRD (World Bank)	17 Mar 60	452UNTS147	106508
Mauritania	IBRD (World Bank)	17 Mar 60	452UNTS211	106509
Japan	IBRD (World Bank)	17 Mar 60	362UNTS43	105182
Belgium	IBRD (World Bank)	30 Mar 60	379UNTS129	105438
Belgium	IBRD (World Bank)	30 Mar 60	379UNTS161	105439
Belgium	IBRD (World Bank)	30 Mar 60	379UNTS103	105437
IBRD (World Bank)	UK Great Britain	01 Apr 60	379UNTS397	105446
Costa Rica	IBRD (World Bank)	04 May 60	390UNTS201	105609
Colombia	IBRD (World Bank)	10 May 60	379UNTS218	105441
IBRD (World Bank)	UK Great Britain	27 May 60	375UNTS201	105367
Peru	IBRD (World Bank)	01 Jun 60	380UNTS15	105448
IBRD (World Bank)	Sudan	17 Jun 60	379UNTS253	105442

PARTY ONE	PARTY TWO	DATE	CITATION	NUMBER
Terms of loan (Cont.)				
Nicaragua	IBRD (World Bank)	22 Jun 60	384UNTS243	105522
Peru	IBRD (World Bank)	29 Jun 60	400UNTS99	105750
Honduras	IBRD (World Bank)	29 Jun 60	400UNTS137	105751
El Salvador	IBRD (World Bank)	29 Jul 60	390UNTS101	105605
India	IBRD (World Bank)	29 Jul 60	377UNTS153	105399
Israel	IBRD (World Bank)	09 Sep 60	406UNTS3	105837
Pakistan	IBRD (World Bank)	19 Sep 60	444UNTS207	106370
Colombia	IBRD (World Bank)	20 Sep 60	390UNTS173	105608
Mexico	IBRD (World Bank)	18 Oct 60	422UNTS177	106075
India	IBRD (World Bank)	28 Oct 60	406UNTS27	105838
Norway	IBRD (World Bank)	02 Dec 60	390UNTS131	105606
Peru	IBRD (World Bank)	19 Dec 60	417UNTS275	106010
Japan	IBRD (World Bank)	20 Dec 60	400UNTS167	105752
Japan	IBRD (World Bank)	20 Dec 60	400UNTS279	105754
Mexico	IBRD (World Bank)	16 Jan 61	422UNTS203	106076
Burma	IBRD (World Bank)	16 Jan 61	400UNTS73	105749
Costa Rica	IBRD (World Bank)	03 Feb 61	414UNTS314	105977
IBRD (World Bank)	Yugoslavia	23 Feb 61	415UNTS92	105982
Japan	IBRD (World Bank)	16 Mar 61	400UNTS201	105753
Austria	USA (United States)	29 Mar 61	459UNTS45	106612
IBRD (World Bank)	UK Great Britain	29 Mar 61	415UNTS300	105990
IBRD (World Bank)	Thailand	28 Apr 61	415UNTS121	105983
Japan	IBRD (World Bank)	02 May 61	415UNTS144	105984
Colombia	IBRD (World Bank)	12 May 61	415UNTS172	105985
Ceylon (Sri Lanka)	IBRD (World Bank)	06 Jun 61	414UNTS349	105978
IBRD (World Bank)	Sudan	14 Jun 61	415UNTS26	105980
Multilateral		14 Jun 61	415UNTS4	105979
India	IDA (Devel Assoc)	21 Jun 61	418UNTS61	106017
IBRD (World Bank)	UK Great Britain	23 Jun 61	415UNTS358	105991
Pakistan	IBRD (World Bank)	27 Jun 61	425UNTS241	106127
Chile	IDA (Devel Assoc)	28 Jun 61	426UNTS89	106131
Chile	IBRD (World Bank)	28 Jun 61	426UNTS33	106129
Argentina	IBRD (World Bank)	30 Jun 61	445UNTS85	106379
Israel	IBRD (World Bank)	11 Jul 61	429UNTS3	106188
Jordan	UK Great Britain	17 Jul 61	420UNTS53	106039
Brazil	UK Great Britain	21 Jul 61	414UNTS26	105962
Philippines	IBRD (World Bank)	26 Jul 61	414UNTS253	105976
Finland	IBRD (World Bank)	09 Aug 61	415UNTS204	105986
India	IBRD (World Bank)	09 Aug 61	417UNTS297	106011
IBRD (World Bank)	UK Great Britain	16 Aug 61	426UNTS287	106143
India	IBRD (World Bank)	17 Aug 61	417UNTS319	106012
UK Great Britain	USA (United States)	28 Aug 61	434UNTS103	106258
Colombia	IDA (Devel Assoc)	28 Aug 61	416UNTS3	105992
Colombia	IBRD (World Bank)	28 Aug 61	416UNTS23	105993
Tunisia	USSR (Soviet Union)	30 Aug 61	437UNTS243	106310
Taiwan	IDA (Devel Assoc)	30 Aug 61	417UNTS227	106008
Taiwan	IDA (Devel Assoc)	30 Aug 61	416UNTS175	106003
Costa Rica	IBRD (World Bank)	06 Sep 61	446UNTS345	106408
India	IDA (Devel Assoc)	06 Sep 61	418UNTS81	106018
Taiwan	IDA (Devel Assoc)	06 Sep 61	417UNTS253	106009
Costa Rica	IBRD (World Bank)	13 Oct 61	430UNTS27	106202
Costa Rica	IDA (Devel Assoc)	13 Oct 61	431UNTS3	106204
India	IBRD (World Bank)	13 Oct 61	418UNTS3	106013
Philippines	IBRD (World Bank)	13 Oct 61	415UNTS269	105989
Pakistan	IDA (Devel Assoc)	19 Oct 61	447UNTS161	106415
Switzerland	UK Great Britain	20 Oct 61	431UNTS29	106206
Paraguay	IDA (Devel Assoc)	26 Oct 61	447UNTS277	106419
Peru	IBRD (World Bank)	03 Nov 61	430UNTS47	106203
Ghana	USSR (Soviet Union)	04 Nov 61	0UNTS0	109381
Pakistan	IDA (Devel Assoc)	22 Nov 61	447UNTS295	106420
India	IDA (Devel Assoc)	22 Nov 61	427UNTS55	106146
India	IDA (Devel Assoc)	22 Nov 61	427UNTS3	106144
India	IDA (Devel Assoc)	22 Nov 61	427UNTS29	106145
IBRD (World Bank)	UK Great Britain	29 Nov 61	426UNTS49	106130
Japan	IBRD (World Bank)	29 Nov 61	426UNTS3	106128

PARTY ONE	PARTY TWO	DATE	CITATION	NUMBER
Terms of loan (Cont.)				
Taiwan	IDA (Devel Assoc)	01 Dec 61	426UNTS105	106132
IBRD (World Bank)	South Africa	01 Dec 61	425UNTS215	106126
IBRD (World Bank)	Venezuela	13 Dec 61	446UNTS371	106409
Jordan	IDA (Devel Assoc)	22 Dec 61	448UNTS21	106423
Argentina	IBRD (World Bank)	19 Jan 62	446UNTS305	106407
Australia	IBRD (World Bank)	23 Jan 62	430UNTS3	106201
Ghana	IBRD (World Bank)	08 Feb 62	449UNTS207	106462
India	IDA (Devel Assoc)	14 Feb 62	468UNTS177	106773
Iceland	IBRD (World Bank)	14 Feb 62	447UNTS95	106413
India	IBRD (World Bank)	28 Feb 62	447UNTS3	106410
Colombia	IBRD (World Bank)	23 May 62	447UNTS39	106411
Jordan	UK Great Britain	30 May 62	449UNTS167	106458
Ethiopia	IBRD (World Bank)	31 May 62	467UNTS237	106765
New Zealand	USA (United States)	08 Jun 62	458UNTS209	106602
Austria	IBRD (World Bank)	15 Jun 62	447UNTS127	106414
Mexico	IBRD (World Bank)	20 Jun 62	468UNTS109	106771
Mexico	IBRD (World Bank)	20 Jun 62	467UNTS205	106764
Pakistan	IDA (Devel Assoc)	29 Jun 62	447UNTS325	106421
India	IDA (Devel Assoc)	29 Jun 62	447UNTS221	106417
India	IDA (Devel Assoc)	18 Jul 62	447UNTS191	106416
Finland	IBRD (World Bank)	15 Aug 62	467UNTS177	106763
Korea, South	IDA (Devel Assoc)	17 Aug 62	468UNTS387	200603
Nicaragua	IDA (Devel Assoc)	07 Sep 62	478UNTS313	106940
Panama	IBRD (World Bank)	14 Sep 62	476UNTS153	106908
Pakistan	IBRD (World Bank)	14 Sep 62	467UNTS152	106762
India	IDA (Devel Assoc)	14 Sep 62	467UNTS265	106766
Pakistan	IBRD (World Bank)	14 Sep 62	467UNTS125	106761
India	IDA (Devel Assoc)	14 Sep 62	448UNTS3	106422
IDA (Devel Assoc)	Tunisia	17 Sep 62	469UNTS33	106783
Israel	IBRD (World Bank)	17 Oct 62	467UNTS107	106760
IBRD (World Bank)	Uruguay	26 Oct 62	481UNTS39	106977
El Salvador	IDA (Devel Assoc)	02 Nov 62	468UNTS331	106780
Pakistan	IDA (Devel Assoc)	02 Nov 62	468UNTS351	106781
Haiti	IDA (Devel Assoc)	02 Nov 62	468UNTS205	106774
Saudi Arabia	USA (United States)	13 Nov 62	488UNTS175	107127
IDA (Devel Assoc)	Turkey	23 Nov 62	469UNTS3	106782
Nigeria	IBRD (World Bank)	10 Dec 62	468UNTS255	106776
Morocco	IBRD (World Bank)	21 Dec 62	478UNTS205	106937
IBRD (World Bank)	Thailand	21 Dec 62	467UNTS43	106757
IBRD (World Bank)	Thailand	21 Dec 62	467UNTS63	106758
IDA (Devel Assoc)	Turkey	01 Feb 63	468UNTS223	106775
Pakistan	IBRD (World Bank)	13 Feb 63	467UNTS3	106756
Philippines	IBRD (World Bank)	15 Feb 63	478UNTS161	106936
India	New Zealand	22 Feb 63	486UNTS19	107069
Ethiopia	IDA (Devel Assoc)	27 Feb 63	478UNTS289	106939
Nicaragua	IBRD (World Bank)	01 Mar 63	481UNTS15	106976
IBRD (World Bank)	Thailand	07 Mar 63	467UNTS83	106759
Peru	IBRD (World Bank)	13 Mar 63	478UNTS245	106938
India	IDA (Devel Assoc)	22 Mar 63	477UNTS3	106911
Thailand	USA (United States)	25 Apr 63	476UNTS115	106906
Jordan	UK Great Britain	27 Apr 63	475UNTS169	106892
Mexico	IBRD (World Bank)	29 Apr 63	489UNTS151	107138
Canada	India	14 May 63	529UNTS31	107653
IBRD (World Bank)	UK Great Britain	16 May 63	477UNTS361	106929
IBRD (World Bank)	UK Great Britain	16 May 63	476UNTS211	106910
India	IDA (Devel Assoc)	24 May 63	483UNTS205	107014
IDA (Devel Assoc)	Turkey	31 May 63	480UNTS127	106966
Colombia	IBRD (World Bank)	03 Jun 63	490UNTS199	107155
India	IBRD (World Bank)	05 Jun 63	481UNTS191	106983
IBRD (World Bank)	Thailand	11 Jun 63	481UNTS227	106984
El Salvador	IBRD (World Bank)	19 Jun 63	481UNTS59	106978
IBRD (World Bank)	Yugoslavia	21 Jun 63	482UNTS43	106990
Colombia	IBRD (World Bank)	21 Jun 63	482UNTS159	106994
Pakistan	IDA (Devel Assoc)	26 Jun 63	492UNTS115	107189
Colombia	IBRD (World Bank)	28 Jun 63	489UNTS113	107137

PARTY ONE	PARTY TWO	DATE	CITATION	NUMBER
Terms of loan (Cont.)				
Costa Rica	IBRD (World Bank)	10 Jul 63	482UNTS69	106991
Denmark	India	12 Jul 63	616UNTS3	108888
Malaysia	IBRD (World Bank)	15 Jul 63	482UNTS123	106993
Colombia	IBRD (World Bank)	16 Jul 63	482UNTS256	106998
Denmark	IBRD (World Bank)	24 Jul 63	481UNTS171	106982
Pakistan	IDA (Devel Assoc)	26 Jul 63	492UNTS143	107190
Malaysia	IBRD (World Bank)	07 Aug 63	485UNTS253	107060
Pakistan	IDA (Devel Assoc)	16 Aug 63	492UNTS205	107192
Pakistan	IDA (Devel Assoc)	16 Aug 63	492UNTS171	107191
IBRD (World Bank)	UK Great Britain	06 Sep 63	483UNTS173	107013
Finland	IBRD (World Bank)	18 Sep 63	491UNTS345	107183
Mexico	IBRD (World Bank)	20 Sep 63	491UNTS317	107182
IBRD (World Bank)	Venezuela	20 Sep 63	482UNTS227	106997
IBRD (World Bank)	UK Great Britain	23 Sep 63	503UNTS247	107348
Japan	IBRD (World Bank)	27 Sep 63	485UNTS283	107061
Taiwan	IBRD (World Bank)	27 Sep 63	483UNTS151	107012
El Salvador	IBRD (World Bank)	01 Oct 63	517UNTS3	107481
Norway	IBRD (World Bank)	15 Oct 63	482UNTS103	106992
IBRD (World Bank)	Spain	25 Oct 63	491UNTS297	107181
IBRD (World Bank)	Yugoslavia	28 Oct 63	503UNTS289	107349
Portugal	IBRD (World Bank)	06 Nov 63	491UNTS137	107176
Portugal	IBRD (World Bank)	06 Nov 63	492UNTS89	107188
New Zealand	IBRD (World Bank)	12 Nov 63	485UNTS233	107059
Peru	IBRD (World Bank)	22 Nov 63	491UNTS101	107175
Jordan	IDA (Devel Assoc)	12 Dec 63	506UNTS51	107381
Jordan	IDA (Devel Assoc)	12 Dec 63	492UNTS3	107184
Chile	IBRD (World Bank)	18 Dec 63	504UNTS3	107351
Chile	IBRD (World Bank)	18 Dec 63	504UNTS29	107352
IDA (Devel Assoc)	Syria	24 Dec 63	534UNTS253	107764
Paraguay	IDA (Devel Assoc)	26 Dec 63	507UNTS3	107394
Multilateral		30 Dec 63	568UNTS233	108271
Multilateral		30 Dec 63	568UNTS243	108272
Multilateral		30 Dec 63	568UNTS215	108270
Multilateral		30 Dec 63	551UNTS105	108036
Multilateral		30 Dec 63	551UNTS119	108037
Congo (Zaire)	UK Great Britain	03 Jan 64	534UNTS417	107770
Liberia	IBRD (World Bank)	08 Jan 64	504UNTS53	107353
IDA (Devel Assoc)	Tanganyika	05 Feb 64	506UNTS91	107382
Colombia	IBRD (World Bank)	07 Feb 64	516UNTS99	107473
IBRD (World Bank)	Thailand	11 Mar 64	504UNTS73	107354
Nigeria	IBRD (World Bank)	12 Mar 64	516UNTS325	107480
New Zealand	IBRD (World Bank)	12 Mar 64	505UNTS3	107362
Pakistan	IDA (Devel Assoc)	25 Mar 64	534UNTS275	107765
Pakistan	IDA (Devel Assoc)	25 Mar 64	535UNTS43	107775
Japan	IBRD (World Bank)	22 Apr 64	505UNTS21	107363
Ethiopia	IBRD (World Bank)	08 May 64	505UNTS51	107364
Algeria	IBRD (World Bank)	14 May 64	522UNTS265	107552
Pakistan	IBRD (World Bank)	14 May 64	516UNTS145	107475
Multilateral		26 May 64	541UNTS271	200613
Ecuador	IBRD (World Bank)	26 May 64	534UNTS113	107758
Ecuador	IDA (Devel Assoc)	26 May 64	534UNTS93	107757
IBRD (World Bank)	Tunisia	05 Jun 64	539UNTS129	107827
India	IDA (Devel Assoc)	09 Jun 64	506UNTS31	107380
Iran	IBRD (World Bank)	10 Jun 64	537UNTS111	107799
Pakistan	IDA (Devel Assoc)	11 Jun 64	534UNTS309	107766
Pakistan	IDA (Devel Assoc)	11 Jun 64	506UNTS3	107379
Niger	IDA (Devel Assoc)	24 Jun 64	554UNTS93	108098
Pakistan	IDA (Devel Assoc)	24 Jun 64	533UNTS191	107743
Pakistan	IDA (Devel Assoc)	24 Jun 64	533UNTS165	107742
India	IDA (Devel Assoc)	06 Jul 64	534UNTS49	107753
Nigeria	IBRD (World Bank)	07 Jul 64	537UNTS3	107795
Gabon	IBRD (World Bank)	10 Jul 64	537UNTS63	107797
Finland	IBRD (World Bank)	10 Jul 64	516UNTS125	107474
IDA (Devel Assoc)	Turkey	14 Jul 64	534UNTS339	107767
Pakistan	IDA (Devel Assoc)	21 Jul 64	534UNTS373	107768

PARTY ONE	PARTY TWO	DATE	CITATION	NUMBER
Terms of loan (Cont.)				
Philippines	IBRD (World Bank)	22 Jul 64	516UNTS171	107476
New Zealand	Western Samoa	23 Jul 64	521UNTS173	107520
Bolivia	IDA (Devel Assoc)	24 Jul 64	534UNTS203	107763
Bolivia	IDA (Devel Assoc)	24 Jul 64	534UNTS171	107762
IBRD (World Bank)	Spain	31 Jul 64	537UNTS81	107798
Kenya	IDA (Devel Assoc)	17 Aug 64	535UNTS79	107776
IBRD (World Bank)	Sierra Leone	18 Aug 64	516UNTS295	107479
Pakistan	IDA (Devel Assoc)	26 Aug 64	535UNTS263	107784
Morocco	IBRD (World Bank)	26 Aug 64	537UNTS193	107802
IBRD (World Bank)	Venezuela	28 Aug 64	537UNTS135	107800
IBRD (World Bank)	Venezuela	28 Aug 64	520UNTS97	107512
IDA (Devel Assoc)	Turkey	31 Aug 64	535UNTS111	107777
Jordan	UK Great Britain	31 Aug 64	541UNTS3	107856
Pakistan	IDA (Devel Assoc)	22 Sep 64	594UNTS225	108605
Mali	IDA (Devel Assoc)	29 Sep 64	594UNTS187	108604
Brazil	UK Great Britain	14 Oct 64	539UNTS289	107840
India	IDA (Devel Assoc)	26 Oct 64	535UNTS245	107783
Philippines	IBRD (World Bank)	28 Oct 64	537UNTS165	107801
Germany, West	Thailand	28 Oct 64	521UNTS311	107528
Germany, West	Thailand	28 Oct 64	521UNTS333	107529
Afghanistan	IDA (Devel Assoc)	23 Nov 64	567UNTS155	108255
IBRD (World Bank)	Thailand	25 Nov 64	537UNTS273	107805
IBRD (World Bank)	Yugoslavia	11 Dec 64	537UNTS321	107807
Paraguay	IBRD (World Bank)	16 Dec 64	549UNTS173	107999
Taiwan	IBRD (World Bank)	17 Dec 64	538UNTS3	107808
Japan	IBRD (World Bank)	23 Dec 64	538UNTS37	107809
Mauritania	IDA (Devel Assoc)	28 Dec 64	540UNTS163	107849
Kenya	IDA (Devel Assoc)	29 Dec 64	535UNTS225	107782
Japan	IBRD (World Bank)	13 Jan 65	537UNTS293	107806
Honduras	IBRD (World Bank)	02 Feb 65	561UNTS255	108188
Honduras	IDA (Devel Assoc)	02 Feb 65	561UNTS279	108189
Mexico	IBRD (World Bank)	04 Feb 65	549UNTS189	108000
Belgium	Congo (Zaire)	06 Feb 65	540UNTS227	107852
Chile	IBRD (World Bank)	12 Feb 65	537UNTS35	107796
Brazil	IBRD (World Bank)	26 Feb 65	567UNTS91	108253
Brazil	IBRD (World Bank)	26 Feb 65	553UNTS3	108065
Malaysia	IBRD (World Bank)	26 Feb 65	549UNTS239	108002
Nigeria	IDA (Devel Assoc)	01 Mar 65	571UNTS3	108297
Nigeria	IDA (Devel Assoc)	01 Mar 65	563UNTS3	108201
IBRD (World Bank)	Thailand	22 Mar 65	538UNTS63	107810
IDA (Devel Assoc)	Somalia	29 Mar 65	586UNTS101	108499
Multilateral		29 Mar 65	540UNTS145	107848
IBRD (World Bank)	Uruguay	30 Mar 65	567UNTS45	108251
IDA (Devel Assoc)	Turkey	01 Apr 65	554UNTS137	108100
Jamaica	IBRD (World Bank)	08 Apr 65	539UNTS303	107841
Malta	UNICEF (Children)	22 Apr 65	533UNTS107	107737
Iran	IBRD (World Bank)	28 Apr 65	555UNTS45	108104
Iran	IBRD (World Bank)	28 Apr 65	555UNTS21	108103
Taiwan	IBRD (World Bank)	28 Apr 65	549UNTS145	107998
Multilateral		29 Apr 65	586UNTS123	108500
Portugal	IBRD (World Bank)	29 Apr 65	549UNTS69	107991
Japan	IBRD (World Bank)	26 May 65	550UNTS95	108010
Peru	IBRD (World Bank)	03 Jun 65	551UNTS227	108045
Jordan	UK Great Britain	08 Jun 65	552UNTS251	108057
India	IBRD (World Bank)	11 Jun 65	557UNTS59	108128
India	IBRD (World Bank)	11 Jun 65	557UNTS101	108130
Peru	IBRD (World Bank)	18 Jun 65	568UNTS191	108269
Italy	IBRD (World Bank)	28 Jun 65	567UNTS127	108254
Kenya	IDA (Devel Assoc)	30 Jun 65	554UNTS75	108097
Pakistan	IDA (Devel Assoc)	30 Jun 65	554UNTS111	108099
Finland	IBRD (World Bank)	30 Jun 65	550UNTS63	108009
Pakistan	IBRD (World Bank)	09 Jul 65	554UNTS39	108096
Iran	IBRD (World Bank)	12 Jul 65	554UNTS3	108095
India	IDA (Devel Assoc)	11 Aug 65	562UNTS277	108199
Nigeria	IBRD (World Bank)	26 Sep 65	571UNTS39	108298

PARTY ONE	PARTY TWO	DATE	CITATION	NUMBER
Terms of loan (Cont.)				
Nigeria	IBRD (World Bank)	26 Sep 65	570UNTS233	108296
East Afri Service	IBRD (World Bank)	29 Sep 65	568UNTS327	200623
IBRD (World Bank)	Tanzania	29 Sep 65	568UNTS309	108275
IBRD (World Bank)	Spain	29 Sep 65	568UNTS49	108264
IBRD (World Bank)	Uganda	29 Sep 65	568UNTS317	108276
Kenya	IBRD (World Bank)	29 Sep 65	568UNTS289	108274
Mexico	IBRD (World Bank)	01 Oct 65	589UNTS339	108542
Chile	IBRD (World Bank)	06 Oct 65	567UNTS293	108261
Morocco	IDA (Devel Assoc)	11 Oct 65	562UNTS299	108200
Philippines	IBRD (World Bank)	02 Nov 65	567UNTS3	108249
Malaysia	IBRD (World Bank)	17 Nov 65	568UNTS23	108263
Chile	UK Great Britain	23 Nov 65	560UNTS215	108176
IBRD (World Bank)	Venezuela	13 Dec 65	568UNTS77	108265
Mexico	IBRD (World Bank)	15 Dec 65	568UNTS125	108267
Paraguay	IBRD (World Bank)	16 Dec 65	568UNTS165	108268
New Zealand	IBRD (World Bank)	17 Dec 65	567UNTS275	108260
New Zealand	IBRD (World Bank)	17 Dec 65	567UNTS255	108259
Italy	USA (United States)	27 Dec 65	574UNTS145	108347
IBRD (World Bank)	Sudan	27 Dec 65	567UNTS27	108250
Ethiopia	IBRD (World Bank)	28 Dec 65	567UNTS229	108258
IDA (Devel Assoc)	Tanzania	13 Jan 66	567UNTS177	108256
Pakistan	IDA (Devel Assoc)	13 Jan 66	567UNTS67	108252
Pakistan	IDA (Devel Assoc)	10 Feb 66	575UNTS89	108355
Multilateral		10 Feb 66	575UNTS129	108356
Brazil	IBRD (World Bank)	15 Mar 66	599UNTS52	108664
Guinea	IBRD (World Bank)	30 Mar 66	568UNTS3	108262
Paraguay	IDA (Devel Assoc)	04 Apr 66	582UNTS331	108469
Paraguay	IBRD (World Bank)	04 Apr 66	570UNTS41	108287
IBRD (World Bank)	Venezuela	21 Apr 66	568UNTS257	108273
Finland	IBRD (World Bank)	27 Apr 66	568UNTS107	108266
Peru	IBRD (World Bank)	13 May 66	570UNTS61	108288
IBRD (World Bank)	Tunisia	16 May 66	584UNTS155	108477
Mexico	IBRD (World Bank)	25 May 66	596UNTS3	108627
Portugal	IBRD (World Bank)	14 Jun 66	581UNTS29	108431
Portugal	IBRD (World Bank)	14 Jun 66	581UNTS3	108430
Pakistan	IDA (Devel Assoc)	17 Jun 66	582UNTS297	108468
Jamaica	IBRD (World Bank)	20 Jun 66	582UNTS145	108462
IBRD (World Bank)	Thailand	24 Jun 66	582UNTS259	108466
India	IDA (Devel Assoc)	29 Jun 66	582UNTS277	108467
India	IDA (Devel Assoc)	29 Jun 66	585UNTS101	108484
India	IBRD (World Bank)	07 Jul 66	595UNTS3	108610
Brazil	Denmark	08 Jul 66	581UNTS95	108435
Iraq	IBRD (World Bank)	22 Jul 66	584UNTS233	108480
Jordan	UK Great Britain	26 Jul 66	597UNTS219	108647
Iran	IBRD (World Bank)	26 Jul 66	582UNTS107	108461
Malaysia	IBRD (World Bank)	26 Jul 66	586UNTS195	108504
New Zealand	Western Samoa	29 Jul 66	598UNTS115	108657
Turkey	UK Great Britain	29 Jul 66	597UNTS241	108649
IDA (Devel Assoc)	Siam	02 Aug 66	585UNTS271	108492
IDA (Devel Assoc)	Turkey	10 Aug 66	585UNTS237	108491
IBRD (World Bank)	Turkey	10 Aug 66	585UNTS199	108490
IBRD (World Bank)	Singapore	11 Aug 66	585UNTS39	108482
India	IDA (Devel Assoc)	19 Aug 66	584UNTS193	108478
Kenya	IDA (Devel Assoc)	19 Aug 66	585UNTS119	108485
Honduras	IBRD (World Bank)	25 Aug 66	582UNTS79	108460
Denmark	Malawi	01 Sep 66	586UNTS3	108493
Peru	IBRD (World Bank)	07 Sep 66	585UNTS3	108481
IBRD (World Bank)	South Africa	08 Sep 66	585UNTS71	108483
IDA (Devel Assoc)	Senegal	29 Sep 66	594UNTS277	108607
Jamaica	IBRD (World Bank)	30 Sep 66	582UNTS179	108463
IBRD (World Bank)	Zambia	04 Oct 66	585UNTS181	108489
Malawi	IDA (Devel Assoc)	04 Oct 66	584UNTS215	108479
Nicaragua	IBRD (World Bank)	05 Oct 66	582UNTS231	108465
IBRD (World Bank)	Thailand	19 Oct 66	594UNTS347	108609
IBRD (World Bank)	IFC (Finance Corp)	28 Oct 66	586UNTS225	200628

PARTY ONE	PARTY TWO	DATE	CITATION	NUMBER
Terms of loan (Cont.)				
IBRD (World Bank)	Singapore	04 Nov 66	585UNTS155	108488
Syria	USSR (Soviet Union)	18 Dec 66	633UNTS247	109041
Chile	IBRD (World Bank)	23 Dec 66	595UNTS141	108618
India	IDA (Devel Assoc)	23 Dec 66	594UNTS165	108603
Pakistan	IDA (Devel Assoc)	23 Dec 66	594UNTS255	108606
Jamaica	IBRD (World Bank)	23 Jan 67	594UNTS311	108608
IBRD (World Bank)	Venezuela	26 Jan 67	596UNTS35	108628
East Afri Service	IBRD (World Bank)	17 Feb 67	599UNTS335	200629
IBRD (World Bank)	Yugoslavia	24 Feb 67	599UNTS27	108663
IBRD (World Bank)	Trinidad/Tobago	10 Mar 67	599UNTS3	108662
Turkey	UK Great Britain	21 Apr 67	610UNTS0	108838
Honduras	IBRD (World Bank)	26 May 67	615UNTS145	108879
Multilateral		12 Jun 67	615UNTS321	108885
China	IBRD (World Bank)	14 Jun 67	615UNTS243	108882
Other Party Combin	Ecuador	19 Jun 67	615UNTS75	108878
Denmark	Peru	20 Jun 67	0UNTS0	109446
Colombia	IBRD (World Bank)	29 Jun 67	619UNTS99	108941
Argentina	IBRD (World Bank)	31 Jul 67	633UNTS289	109042
IBRD (World Bank)	Spain	04 Aug 67	619UNTS209	108944
Taiwan	IBRD (World Bank)	07 Aug 67	620UNTS113	108952
Denmark	Ghana	09 Aug 67	610UNTS0	108842
Jordan	UK Great Britain	15 Aug 67	632UNTS269	109028
Peru	IBRD (World Bank)	11 Sep 67	619UNTS171	108943
Iran	IBRD (World Bank)	17 Oct 67	0UNTS0	109331
Denmark	Zambia	18 Oct 67	637UNTS0	109116
Israel	IBRD (World Bank)	15 Nov 67	619UNTS129	108942
El Salvador	IBRD (World Bank)	07 Dec 67	0UNTS0	109299
IBRD (World Bank)	Tanzania	13 Dec 67	619UNTS239	108945
Peru	UK Great Britain	19 Dec 67	0UNTS0	109447
Mexico	IBRD (World Bank)	26 Jan 68	0UNTS0	109511
Mexico	IBRD (World Bank)	26 Jan 68	640UNTS3	109152
Cameroon	IDA (Devel Assoc)	29 Jan 68	0UNTS0	109325
Turkey	UK Great Britain	04 Mar 68	0UNTS0	109265
IDA (Devel Assoc)	Tanzania	21 Mar 68	0UNTS0	109327
Denmark	India	25 Mar 68	0UNTS0	109229
Turkey	UK Great Britain	29 Mar 68	0UNTS0	109286
Denmark	Uganda	01 Apr 68	0UNTS0	109209
Nicaragua	IBRD (World Bank)	10 Apr 68	0UNTS0	109300
Malaysia	IBRD (World Bank)	17 Apr 68	0UNTS0	109360
Denmark	India	29 Apr 68	0UNTS0	109230
Turkey	UK Great Britain	22 May 68	0UNTS0	109287
Honduras	IDA (Devel Assoc)	12 Jun 68	0UNTS0	109409
Denmark	Kenya	26 Jun 68	0UNTS0	109210
Ecuador	IDA (Devel Assoc)	27 Jun 68	0UNTS0	109321
IBRD (World Bank)	Singapore	03 Jul 68	0UNTS0	109364
Gabon	IBRD (World Bank)	07 Jul 68	0UNTS0	109361
Denmark	Senegal	03 Aug 68	0UNTS0	109282
Turkey	UK Great Britain	06 Aug 68	0UNTS0	109451
Denmark	Morocco	05 Nov 68	0UNTS0	109415
Denmark	Malawi	16 Dec 68	0UNTS0	109461
Finland	IBRD (World Bank)	24 Jan 69	0UNTS0	109596
Agricultural commodities assistance				
Israel	USA (United States)	29 Apr 55	261UNTS331	103731
Colombia	USA (United States)	23 Jun 55	263UNTS337	103781
France	USA (United States)	08 Nov 56	280UNTS189	104058
Japan	USA (United States)	18 Feb 60	372UNTS117	105292
India	USA (United States)	27 Jun 63	479UNTS215	106955
Colombia	USA (United States)	10 Mar 66	0UNTS0	109604
Israel	USA (United States)	06 Jun 66	593UNTS165	108583
Tunisia	USA (United States)	30 Jul 66	601UNTS133	108692
Jordan	USA (United States)	25 Aug 66	606UNTS237	108788
Commodities schedule				
Jordan	USA (United States)	17 Jun 54	266UNTS137	103828
Chile	USA (United States)	27 Jan 55	262UNTS3	103735

PARTY ONE	PARTY TWO	DATE	CITATION	NUMBER
Commodities schedule (Cont.)				
Argentina	USA (United States)	25 Apr 55	251UNTS283	103546
Israel	USA (United States)	29 Apr 55	261UNTS331	103731
Finland	USA (United States)	06 May 55	251UNTS3	103529
Italy	USA (United States)	23 May 55	251UNTS303	103547
Korea, South	USA (United States)	31 May 55	251UNTS321	103548
Austria	USA (United States)	14 Jun 55	258UNTS37	103668
Thailand	USA (United States)	21 Jun 55	262UNTS87	103738
Colombia	USA (United States)	23 Jun 55	263UNTS337	103781
Greece	USA (United States)	24 Jun 55	270UNTS361	103906
Greece	USA (United States)	24 Jun 55	270UNTS351	103905
Italy	USA (United States)	30 Jun 55	258UNTS15	103667
France	USA (United States)	11 Aug 55	251UNTS15	103530
Israel	USA (United States)	10 Nov 55	240UNTS3	103390
United Arab Rep	USA (United States)	14 Dec 55	240UNTS37	103392
Germany, West	USA (United States)	23 Dec 55	240UNTS79	103395
Austria	USA (United States)	07 Feb 56	272UNTS117	103933
Japan	USA (United States)	10 Feb 56	275UNTS105	103979
Japan	USA (United States)	10 Feb 56	275UNTS157	103980
Iran	USA (United States)	20 Feb 56	272UNTS135	103934
Pakistan	USA (United States)	02 Mar 56	271UNTS371	103927
Indonesia	USA (United States)	02 Mar 56	271UNTS345	103925
Spain	USA (United States)	05 Mar 56	271UNTS329	103924
Turkey	USA (United States)	12 Mar 56	272UNTS21	103929
Korea, South	USA (United States)	13 Mar 56	272UNTS3	103928
Chile	USA (United States)	13 Mar 56	275UNTS49	103975
Italy	USA (United States)	27 Apr 56	273UNTS149	103949
Peru	USA (United States)	07 May 56	268UNTS285	103862
Peru	USA (United States)	08 May 56	278UNTS117	104028
Portugal	USA (United States)	24 May 56	268UNTS323	103865
Pakistan	USA (United States)	07 Aug 56	281UNTS75	104071
Greece	USA (United States)	08 Aug 56	277UNTS203	104007
Taiwan	USA (United States)	14 Aug 56	281UNTS257	104083
Israel	USA (United States)	11 Sep 56	277UNTS215	104008
Spain	USA (United States)	23 Oct 56	277UNTS105	104001
Italy	USA (United States)	30 Oct 56	263UNTS221	103775
USA (United States)	Yugoslavia	03 Nov 56	277UNTS119	104002
Turkey	USA (United States)	12 Nov 56	282UNTS77	104093
Burma	USA (United States)	04 Dec 56	268UNTS189	103858
Brazil	USA (United States)	31 Dec 56	266UNTS151	103829
Korea, South	USA (United States)	30 Jan 57	278UNTS85	104024
Ecuador	USA (United States)	15 Feb 57	279UNTS155	104037
Thailand	USA (United States)	04 Mar 57	279UNTS235	104043
Iceland	USA (United States)	11 Apr 57	283UNTS107	104110
Colombia	USA (United States)	16 Apr 57	283UNTS245	104121
Peru	USA (United States)	02 May 57	283UNTS55	104106
Austria	USA (United States)	10 May 57	283UNTS15	104103
Bolivia	USA (United States)	07 Jun 57	291UNTS77	104245
Poland	USA (United States)	07 Jun 57	291UNTS41	104243
Philippines	USA (United States)	25 Jun 57	289UNTS279	104224
Mexico	USA (United States)	23 Oct 57	300UNTS35	104330
Israel	USA (United States)	07 Nov 57	302UNTS255	104365
Pakistan	USA (United States)	15 Nov 57	303UNTS173	104380
Greece	USA (United States)	18 Dec 57	303UNTS159	104379
France	USA (United States)	27 Dec 57	307UNTS79	104444
Turkey	USA (United States)	20 Jan 58	304UNTS15	104389
Spain	USA (United States)	27 Jan 58	303UNTS247	104384
UK Great Britain	USA (United States)	03 Feb 58	307UNTS199	104450
USA (United States)	Yugoslavia	03 Feb 58	304UNTS293	104404
Korea, South	USA (United States)	05 Feb 58	307UNTS121	104447
Poland	USA (United States)	15 Feb 58	307UNTS217	104452
Finland	USA (United States)	21 Feb 58	304UNTS253	104401
France	USA (United States)	28 Feb 58	366UNTS343	105222
Colombia	USA (United States)	14 Mar 58	308UNTS115	104459
Peru	USA (United States)	09 Apr 58	316UNTS37	104576
Taiwan	USA (United States)	18 Apr 58	308UNTS179	104461

Commodities schedule (Cont.)

PARTY ONE	PARTY TWO	DATE	CITATION	NUMBER
Iceland	USA (United States)	03 May 58	316UNTS137	104581
Italy	USA (United States)	08 May 58	316UNTS177	104584
Burma	USA (United States)	27 May 58	315UNTS197	104569
Philippines	USA (United States)	03 Jun 58	316UNTS3	104573
Ceylon (Sri Lanka)	USA (United States)	18 Jun 58	316UNTS15	104574
Ecuador	USA (United States)	30 Jun 58	336UNTS11	104796
India	USA (United States)	26 Sep 58	336UNTS59	104798
Israel	USA (United States)	06 Nov 58	336UNTS275	104810
Pakistan	USA (United States)	26 Nov 58	337UNTS3	104812
USA (United States)	Yugoslavia	22 Dec 58	338UNTS243	104839
United Arab Rep	USA (United States)	24 Dec 58	338UNTS221	104837
Finland	USA (United States)	30 Dec 58	340UNTS259	104869
Spain	USA (United States)	13 Jan 59	341UNTS241	104887
Turkey	USA (United States)	13 Feb 59	340UNTS235	104867
India	USA (United States)	03 Mar 59	341UNTS235	104886
Iceland	USA (United States)	03 Mar 59	341UNTS261	104889
Ceylon (Sri Lanka)	USA (United States)	13 Mar 59	342UNTS51	104900
France	USA (United States)	21 Mar 59	342UNTS71	104901
Indonesia	USA (United States)	29 May 59	347UNTS85	104992
Taiwan	USA (United States)	09 Jun 59	353UNTS257	105046
Poland	USA (United States)	10 Jun 59	347UNTS41	104989
Argentina	USA (United States)	12 Jun 59	347UNTS59	104990
Korea, South	USA (United States)	30 Jun 59	353UNTS297	105047
United Arab Rep	USA (United States)	29 Jul 59	357UNTS121	105111
Colombia	USA (United States)	06 Oct 59	358UNTS145	105132
USA (United States)	Vietnam, South	16 Oct 59	360UNTS271	105163
India	USA (United States)	13 Nov 59	360UNTS287	105164
United Arab Rep	USA (United States)	14 Nov 59	360UNTS311	105165
Turkey	USA (United States)	22 Dec 59	367UNTS57	105225
Greece	USA (United States)	07 Jan 60	368UNTS221	105243
Peru	USA (United States)	12 Feb 60	372UNTS83	105290
IBRD (World Bank)	UK Great Britain	01 Apr 60	379UNTS397	105446
Iceland	USA (United States)	06 Apr 60	372UNTS71	105289
Pakistan	USA (United States)	11 Apr 60	372UNTS251	105302
India	USA (United States)	04 May 60	376UNTS279	105384
Spain	USA (United States)	22 Jun 60	378UNTS3	105414
Poland	USA (United States)	21 Jul 60	380UNTS157	105456
Iran	USA (United States)	26 Jul 60	384UNTS141	105516
United Arab Rep	USA (United States)	01 Aug 60	384UNTS189	105519
United Arab Rep	USA (United States)	09 Aug 60	388UNTS271	105584
Taiwan	USA (United States)	30 Aug 60	388UNTS191	105579
Ecuador	USA (United States)	27 Sep 60	401UNTS115	105766
Ceylon (Sri Lanka)	USA (United States)	30 Sep 60	389UNTS221	105594
USA (United States)	Vietnam, South	28 Oct 60	401UNTS3	105758
France	USA (United States)	04 Nov 60	400UNTS323	105756
Indonesia	USA (United States)	05 Nov 60	400UNTS35	105746
Greece	USA (United States)	07 Nov 60	400UNTS57	105748
Chile	USA (United States)	08 Nov 60	405UNTS85	105825
Korea, South	USA (United States)	28 Dec 60	402UNTS3	105773
Turkey	USA (United States)	11 Jan 61	405UNTS173	105833
USA (United States)	Vietnam, South	25 Mar 61	406UNTS187	105849
Ecuador	USA (United States)	03 Apr 61	409UNTS140	105882
Bolivia	USA (United States)	07 Apr 61	433UNTS3	106227
Iceland	USA (United States)	07 Apr 61	406UNTS203	105850
USA (United States)	Yugoslavia	28 Apr 61	409UNTS172	105884
Brazil	USA (United States)	04 May 61	433UNTS91	106233
Israel	USA (United States)	10 May 61	409UNTS213	105887
Spain	USA (United States)	22 May 61	409UNTS260	105891
Tunisia	USA (United States)	30 Jun 61	434UNTS85	106257
Paraguay	USA (United States)	07 Jul 61	433UNTS53	106231
USA (United States)	Vietnam, South	14 Jul 61	416UNTS133	105999
Taiwan	USA (United States)	21 Jul 61	416UNTS101	105998
Turkey	USA (United States)	29 Jul 61	416UNTS151	106001
Finland	USA (United States)	04 Aug 61	418UNTS19	106014
El Salvador	USA (United States)	21 Aug 61	418UNTS35	106015
Indonesia	USA (United States)	26 Oct 61	433UNTS249	106248
Iceland	USA (United States)	06 Nov 61	426UNTS225	106140
Syria	USA (United States)	09 Nov 61	435UNTS75	106271
Sudan	USA (United States)	14 Nov 61	434UNTS51	106255
Bolivia	USA (United States)	15 Nov 61	456UNTS192	106557
United Nations	USA (United States)	18 Nov 61	494UNTS213	107235
Congo (Zaire)	USA (United States)	18 Nov 61	433UNTS207	106244
Philippines	USA (United States)	24 Nov 61	433UNTS315	106251
Portugal	USA (United States)	28 Nov 61	434UNTS31	106253
Poland	USA (United States)	15 Dec 61	434UNTS3	106252
USA (United States)	Vietnam, South	27 Dec 61	433UNTS185	106242
United Arab Rep	USA (United States)	19 Jan 62	435UNTS107	106273
Iran	USA (United States)	29 Jan 62	435UNTS53	106270
Guinea	USA (United States)	02 Feb 62	435UNTS35	106269
Morocco	USA (United States)	09 Feb 62	442UNTS135	106345
Bolivia	USA (United States)	12 Feb 62	451UNTS281	106499
Tunisia	USA (United States)	16 Feb 62	442UNTS161	106347
Indonesia	USA (United States)	19 Feb 62	435UNTS137	106276
Korea, South	USA (United States)	02 Mar 62	442UNTS185	106349
Brazil	USA (United States)	15 Mar 62	456UNTS209	106558
Iceland	USA (United States)	16 Mar 62	445UNTS49	106376
Peru	USA (United States)	20 Mar 62	445UNTS61	106377
Liberia	USA (United States)	12 Apr 62	445UNTS213	106390
Taiwan	USA (United States)	27 Apr 62	436UNTS25	106287
USA (United States)	Uruguay	27 Apr 62	452UNTS25	106502
India	USA (United States)	01 May 62	451UNTS179	106493
Israel	USA (United States)	03 May 62	442UNTS83	106340
USA (United States)	Venezuela	17 May 62	456UNTS275	106562
Chile	USA (United States)	07 Aug 62	461UNTS61	106652
Ethiopia	USA (United States)	13 Aug 62	459UNTS31	106611
Taiwan	USA (United States)	31 Aug 62	460UNTS247	106644
Tunisia	USA (United States)	14 Sep 62	461UNTS31	106649
United Arab Rep	USA (United States)	08 Oct 62	462UNTS39	106670
Iran	USA (United States)	15 Oct 62	473UNTS291	106866
Greece	USA (United States)	22 Oct 62	462UNTS187	106678
Korea, South	USA (United States)	07 Nov 62	462UNTS129	106674
Burma	USA (United States)	09 Nov 62	461UNTS113	106655
Taiwan	USA (United States)	19 Nov 62	459UNTS263	106629
Paraguay	USA (United States)	24 Nov 62	471UNTS49	106821
India	USA (United States)	26 Nov 62	460UNTS203	106641
USA (United States)	Yugoslavia	28 Nov 62	460UNTS185	106640
India	USA (United States)	30 Nov 62	459UNTS231	106626
Dominican Republic	USA (United States)	30 Nov 62	471UNTS25	106819
Israel	USA (United States)	06 Dec 62	460UNTS151	106638
Bolivia	USA (United States)	17 Dec 62	469UNTS121	106788
Sudan	USA (United States)	31 Jan 63	494UNTS119	107230
Poland	USA (United States)	01 Feb 63	487UNTS143	107100
Bolivia	USA (United States)	04 Feb 63	473UNTS65	106856
Iceland	USA (United States)	06 Feb 63	473UNTS93	106858
Turkey	USA (United States)	21 Feb 63	473UNTS311	106867
Congo (Zaire)	USA (United States)	23 Feb 63	493UNTS17	107204
Congo (Zaire)	USA (United States)	23 Feb 63	493UNTS3	107203
Colombia	USA (United States)	27 Mar 63	489UNTS289	107145
Ecuador	USA (United States)	05 Apr 63	477UNTS135	106919
Guinea	USA (United States)	22 May 63	487UNTS251	107108
Ethiopia	USA (United States)	11 Jun 63	487UNTS269	107109
Cyprus	USA (United States)	18 Jun 63	479UNTS191	106953
Senegal	USA (United States)	03 Jul 63	527UNTS95	107620
Iraq	USA (United States)	27 Aug 63	489UNTS271	107144
Brazil	USA (United States)	11 Sep 63	493UNTS267	107220
Paraguay	USA (United States)	16 Sep 63	494UNTS101	107229
Greece	USA (United States)	30 Oct 63	493UNTS29	107205
Paraguay	USA (United States)	14 Nov 63	505UNTS87	107366
Syria	USA (United States)	18 Nov 63	494UNTS169	107232
USA (United States)	Vietnam, South	09 Jan 64	505UNTS173	107373

PARTY ONE	PARTY TWO	DATE	CITATION	NUMBER
Commodities schedule (Cont.)				
Poland	USA (United States)	03 Feb 64	505UNTS245	107376
Poland	USA (United States)	03 Feb 64	505UNTS215	107375
Jordan	USA (United States)	11 Feb 64	511UNTS85	107429
Iceland	USA (United States)	13 Feb 64	511UNTS3	107421
Peru	USA (United States)	13 Feb 64	511UNTS119	107431
Iceland	USA (United States)	13 Feb 64	510UNTS295	107420
Sudan	USA (United States)	02 Mar 64	524UNTS217	107575
Ivory Coast	USA (United States)	10 Mar 64	526UNTS285	107611
Bolivia	USA (United States)	25 Mar 64	532UNTS3	107710
Tunisia	USA (United States)	07 Apr 64	527UNTS3	107613
USA (United States)	Yugoslavia	27 Apr 64	526UNTS73	107601
USA (United States)	Yugoslavia	27 Apr 64	526UNTS89	107602
USA (United States)	Yugoslavia	28 Apr 64	526UNTS103	107603
Congo (Zaire)	USA (United States)	28 Apr 64	526UNTS55	107600
Philippines	USA (United States)	14 May 64	526UNTS113	107604
Taiwan	USA (United States)	03 Jun 64	526UNTS257	107610
Paraguay	USA (United States)	05 Sep 64	530UNTS225	107685
USA (United States)	Vietnam, South	29 Sep 64	531UNTS183	107703
Iran	USA (United States)	29 Sep 64	531UNTS163	107702
India	USA (United States)	30 Sep 64	532UNTS321	107726
Colombia	USA (United States)	08 Oct 64	579UNTS3	108395
USA (United States)	Yugoslavia	28 Oct 64	533UNTS3	107728
USA (United States)	Yugoslavia	29 Oct 64	533UNTS17	107729
Iran	USA (United States)	16 Nov 64	532UNTS213	107719
Greece	USA (United States)	17 Nov 64	532UNTS107	107714
Kenya	USA (United States)	07 Dec 64	532UNTS263	107722
Congo (Zaire)	USA (United States)	09 Dec 64	531UNTS249	107707
Israel	USA (United States)	22 Dec 64	532UNTS231	107720
Iceland	USA (United States)	30 Dec 64	531UNTS287	107709
Iceland	USA (United States)	30 Dec 64	542UNTS37	107878
Korea, South	USA (United States)	31 Dec 64	535UNTS315	107787
Taiwan	USA (United States)	31 Dec 64	532UNTS59	107712
Dahomey	USA (United States)	31 Dec 64	541UNTS117	107865
Taiwan	USA (United States)	31 Dec 64	532UNTS29	107711
Sierra Leone	USA (United States)	29 Jan 65	542UNTS87	107882
Tunisia	USA (United States)	17 Feb 65	542UNTS125	107885
Dominican Republic	USA (United States)	18 Mar 65	542UNTS215	107892
Ivory Coast	USA (United States)	05 Apr 65	546UNTS143	107941
Philippines	USA (United States)	23 Apr 65	546UNTS157	107942
Morocco	USA (United States)	23 Apr 65	594UNTS3	108591
Bolivia	USA (United States)	12 May 65	564UNTS143	108226
USA (United States)	Vietnam, South	26 May 65	550UNTS3	108005
Ecuador	USA (United States)	25 Jun 65	549UNTS23	107986
Mali	USA (United States)	14 Jul 65	564UNTS101	108223
USA (United States)	Yugoslavia	16 Jul 65	549UNTS111	107994
Congo (Zaire)	USA (United States)	19 Jul 65	593UNTS215	108586
Chile	USA (United States)	27 Jul 65	574UNTS83	108342
Ethiopia	USA (United States)	17 Aug 65	564UNTS119	108224
USA (United States)	Yugoslavia	22 Nov 65	574UNTS211	108351
Ethiopia	USA (United States)	14 Dec 65	574UNTS115	108344
United Arab Rep	USA (United States)	03 Jan 66	579UNTS83	108400
United Arab Rep	USA (United States)	03 Jan 66	579UNTS63	108399
Liberia	USA (United States)	06 Jan 66	592UNTS101	108570
Guinea	USA (United States)	04 Feb 66	579UNTS213	108409
Algeria	USA (United States)	23 Feb 66	592UNTS117	108571
Multilateral		04 Mar 66	578UNTS57	108387
Korea, South	USA (United States)	07 Mar 66	579UNTS137	108404
Colombia	USA (United States)	10 Mar 66	OUNTSO	109604
Ceylon (Sri Lanka)	USA (United States)	12 Mar 66	579UNTS117	108403
Ghana	USA (United States)	01 Apr 66	579UNTS157	108405
Jordan	USA (United States)	05 Apr 66	593UNTS239	108587
USA (United States)	Yugoslavia	11 Apr 66	580UNTS239	108427
Sudan	USA (United States)	13 Apr 66	586UNTS39	108495
Indonesia	USA (United States)	18 Apr 66	578UNTS106	108390
Bolivia	USA (United States)	22 Apr 66	578UNTS73	108388

PARTY ONE	PARTY TWO	DATE	CITATION	NUMBER
Commodities schedule (Cont.)				
Pakistan	USA (United States)	26 May 66	594UNTS27	108592
Israel	USA (United States)	06 Jun 66	593UNTS165	108583
Indonesia	USA (United States)	28 Jun 66	593UNTS201	108585
Philippines	USA (United States)	22 Dec 66	591UNTS219	108559
Purchase authorization				
Dominican Republic	USA (United States)	10 Jun 43	21UNTS277	200129
Belgium	Netherlands	24 May 46	31UNTS169	100477
UK Great Britain	USA (United States)	30 Sep 48	71UNTS241	100922
Pakistan	USA (United States)	18 Jan 55	241UNTS53	103423
Peru	USA (United States)	07 Feb 55	241UNTS63	103424
Israel	USA (United States)	29 Apr 55	261UNTS331	103731
Finland	USA (United States)	06 May 55	251UNTS3	103529
USA (United States)	Yugoslavia	12 May 55	251UNTS331	103549
Italy	USA (United States)	23 May 55	251UNTS303	103547
Korea, South	USA (United States)	31 May 55	251UNTS321	103548
UK Great Britain	USA (United States)	07 Jun 55	265UNTS27	103804
Austria	USA (United States)	14 Jun 55	258UNTS37	103668
Colombia	USA (United States)	23 Jun 55	263UNTS337	103781
Greece	USA (United States)	24 Jun 55	270UNTS361	103906
Greece	USA (United States)	24 Jun 55	270UNTS351	103905
France	USA (United States)	11 Aug 55	251UNTS15	103530
Belgium	UK Great Britain	18 Nov 55	222UNTS327	103038
Colombia	USA (United States)	20 Dec 55	241UNTS25	103421
Austria	USA (United States)	07 Feb 56	272UNTS117	103933
Iran	USA (United States)	20 Feb 56	272UNTS135	103934
Pakistan	USA (United States)	02 Mar 56	271UNTS371	103927
Indonesia	USA (United States)	02 Mar 56	271UNTS345	103925
Spain	USA (United States)	05 Mar 56	271UNTS329	103924
Turkey	USA (United States)	12 Mar 56	272UNTS21	103929
Korea, South	USA (United States)	13 Mar 56	272UNTS3	103928
Portugal	USA (United States)	24 May 56	268UNTS323	103865
UK Great Britain	USA (United States)	05 Jun 56	247UNTS205	103470
Italy	USA (United States)	30 Oct 56	263UNTS221	103775
Burma	USA (United States)	04 Dec 56	268UNTS189	103858
Brazil	USA (United States)	31 Dec 56	266UNTS151	103829
Israel	USA (United States)	07 Nov 57	302UNTS255	104365
Pakistan	USA (United States)	15 Nov 57	303UNTS173	104380
Greece	USA (United States)	18 Dec 57	303UNTS159	104379
France	USA (United States)	27 Dec 57	307UNTS79	104444
Turkey	USA (United States)	20 Jan 58	304UNTS15	104389
Spain	USA (United States)	27 Jan 58	303UNTS247	104384
UK Great Britain	USA (United States)	03 Feb 58	307UNTS199	104450
USA (United States)	Yugoslavia	03 Feb 58	304UNTS293	104404
Korea, South	USA (United States)	05 Feb 58	307UNTS121	104447
Finland	USA (United States)	21 Feb 58	304UNTS253	104401
France	USA (United States)	28 Feb 58	366UNTS343	105222
Colombia	USA (United States)	14 Mar 58	308UNTS115	104459
Peru	USA (United States)	09 Apr 58	316UNTS37	104576
Taiwan	USA (United States)	18 Apr 58	308UNTS179	104461
Iceland	USA (United States)	03 May 58	316UNTS137	104581
Burma	USA (United States)	27 May 58	315UNTS197	104569
Philippines	USA (United States)	03 Jun 58	316UNTS3	104573
USA (United States)	Vietnam, South	17 Jun 58	321UNTS35	104652
Ceylon (Sri Lanka)	USA (United States)	18 Jun 58	316UNTS15	104574
Ecuador	USA (United States)	30 Jun 58	336UNTS11	104796
India	USA (United States)	26 Sep 58	336UNTS59	104798
Israel	USA (United States)	06 Nov 58	336UNTS275	104810
Euratom	USA (United States)	08 Nov 58	338UNTS135	104835
Pakistan	USA (United States)	26 Nov 58	337UNTS3	104812
USA (United States)	Yugoslavia	22 Dec 58	338UNTS243	104839
United Arab Rep	USA (United States)	24 Dec 58	338UNTS221	104837
Finland	USA (United States)	30 Dec 58	340UNTS259	104869
Spain	USA (United States)	13 Jan 59	341UNTS241	104887
Euratom	UK Great Britain	04 Feb 59	331UNTS125	104752

PARTY ONE	PARTY TWO	DATE	CITATION	NUMBER
Purchase authorization (Cont.)				
Turkey	USA (United States)	13 Feb 59	340UNTS235	104867
Iceland	USA (United States)	03 Mar 59	341UNTS261	104889
Ceylon (Sri Lanka)	USA (United States)	13 Mar 59	342UNTS51	104900
France	USA (United States)	21 Mar 59	342UNTS71	104901
Indonesia	USA (United States)	29 May 59	347UNTS85	104992
Taiwan	USA (United States)	09 Jun 59	353UNTS257	105046
Poland	USA (United States)	10 Jun 59	347UNTS41	104989
Korea, South	USA (United States)	30 Jun 59	353UNTS297	105047
United Arab Rep	USA (United States)	29 Jul 59	357UNTS121	105111
USA (United States)	Vietnam, South	16 Oct 59	360UNTS271	105163
India	USA (United States)	13 Nov 59	360UNTS287	105164
United Arab Rep	USA (United States)	14 Nov 59	360UNTS311	105165
Turkey	USA (United States)	22 Dec 59	367UNTS57	105225
Greece	USA (United States)	07 Jan 60	368UNTS221	105243
Peru	USA (United States)	12 Feb 60	372UNTS83	105290
Iceland	USA (United States)	06 Apr 60	372UNTS71	105289
Pakistan	USA (United States)	11 Apr 60	372UNTS251	105302
India	USA (United States)	04 May 60	376UNTS279	105384
Spain	USA (United States)	22 Jun 60	378UNTS3	105414
Poland	USA (United States)	21 Jul 60	380UNTS157	105456
Iran	USA (United States)	26 Jul 60	384UNTS141	105516
United Arab Rep	USA (United States)	01 Aug 60	384UNTS189	105519
United Arab Rep	USA (United States)	09 Aug 60	388UNTS271	105584
Taiwan	USA (United States)	30 Aug 60	388UNTS191	105579
Ecuador	USA (United States)	27 Sep 60	401UNTS115	105766
Ceylon (Sri Lanka)	USA (United States)	30 Sep 60	389UNTS221	105594
USA (United States)	Vietnam, South	28 Oct 60	401UNTS3	105758
France	USA (United States)	04 Nov 60	400UNTS323	105756
Indonesia	USA (United States)	05 Nov 60	400UNTS35	105746
Greece	USA (United States)	07 Nov 60	400UNTS57	105748
Chile	USA (United States)	08 Nov 60	405UNTS85	105825
Korea, South	USA (United States)	28 Dec 60	402UNTS3	105773
Turkey	USA (United States)	11 Jan 61	405UNTS173	105833
USA (United States)	Vietnam, South	25 Mar 61	406UNTS187	105849
Ecuador	USA (United States)	03 Apr 61	409UNTS140	105882
Bolivia	USA (United States)	07 Apr 61	433UNTS3	106227
Iceland	USA (United States)	07 Apr 61	406UNTS203	105850
USA (United States)	Yugoslavia	28 Apr 61	409UNTS172	105884
Brazil	USA (United States)	04 May 61	433UNTS91	106233
Israel	USA (United States)	10 May 61	409UNTS213	105887
Spain	USA (United States)	22 May 61	409UNTS260	105891
Tunisia	USA (United States)	30 Jun 61	434UNTS85	106257
Paraguay	USA (United States)	07 Jul 61	433UNTS53	106231
USA (United States)	Vietnam, South	14 Jul 61	416UNTS133	105999
Taiwan	USA (United States)	21 Jul 61	416UNTS101	105998
Turkey	USA (United States)	29 Jul 61	416UNTS151	106001
Finland	USA (United States)	04 Aug 61	418UNTS19	106014
El Salvador	USA (United States)	21 Aug 61	418UNTS35	106015
Indonesia	USA (United States)	26 Oct 61	433UNTS249	106248
Iceland	USA (United States)	06 Nov 61	426UNTS225	106140
Syria	USA (United States)	09 Nov 61	435UNTS75	106271
Sudan	USA (United States)	14 Nov 61	434UNTS51	106255
Bolivia	USA (United States)	15 Nov 61	456UNTS192	106557
United Nations	USA (United States)	18 Nov 61	494UNTS213	107235
Congo (Zaire)	USA (United States)	18 Nov 61	433UNTS207	106244
Philippines	USA (United States)	24 Nov 61	433UNTS315	106251
Portugal	USA (United States)	28 Nov 61	434UNTS31	106253
Poland	USA (United States)	15 Dec 61	434UNTS3	106252
USA (United States)	Vietnam, South	27 Dec 61	433UNTS185	106242
United Arab Rep	USA (United States)	19 Jan 62	435UNTS107	106273
Iran	USA (United States)	29 Jan 62	435UNTS53	106270
Guinea	USA (United States)	02 Feb 62	435UNTS35	106269
Bolivia	USA (United States)	12 Feb 62	451UNTS281	106499
Tunisia	USA (United States)	16 Feb 62	442UNTS161	106347
Indonesia	USA (United States)	19 Feb 62	435UNTS137	106276

PARTY ONE	PARTY TWO	DATE	CITATION	NUMBER
Purchase authorization (Cont.)				
Korea, South	USA (United States)	02 Mar 62	442UNTS185	106349
Brazil	USA (United States)	15 Mar 62	456UNTS209	106558
Iceland	USA (United States)	16 Mar 62	445UNTS49	106376
Peru	USA (United States)	20 Mar 62	445UNTS61	106377
Liberia	USA (United States)	12 Apr 62	445UNTS213	106390
USA (United States)	Uruguay	27 Apr 62	452UNTS25	106502
Taiwan	USA (United States)	27 Apr 62	436UNTS25	106287
India	USA (United States)	01 May 62	451UNTS179	106493
Israel	USA (United States)	03 May 62	442UNTS83	106340
USA (United States)	Venezuela	17 May 62	456UNTS275	106562
Chile	USA (United States)	07 Aug 62	461UNTS61	106652
Ethiopia	USA (United States)	13 Aug 62	459UNTS31	106611
Taiwan	USA (United States)	31 Aug 62	460UNTS247	106644
Tunisia	USA (United States)	14 Sep 62	461UNTS31	106649
United Arab Rep	USA (United States)	08 Oct 62	462UNTS39	106670
Iran	USA (United States)	15 Oct 62	473UNTS291	106866
Greece	USA (United States)	22 Oct 62	462UNTS187	106678
Korea, South	USA (United States)	07 Nov 62	462UNTS129	106674
Burma	USA (United States)	09 Nov 62	461UNTS113	106655
Taiwan	USA (United States)	19 Nov 62	459UNTS263	106629
Paraguay	USA (United States)	24 Nov 62	471UNTS49	106821
India	USA (United States)	26 Nov 62	460UNTS203	106641
USA (United States)	Yugoslavia	28 Nov 62	460UNTS185	106640
Dominican Republic	USA (United States)	30 Nov 62	471UNTS25	106819
India	USA (United States)	30 Nov 62	459UNTS231	106626
Israel	USA (United States)	06 Dec 62	460UNTS151	106638
Bolivia	USA (United States)	17 Dec 62	469UNTS121	106788
Sudan	USA (United States)	31 Jan 63	494UNTS119	107230
Poland	USA (United States)	01 Feb 63	487UNTS143	107100
Bolivia	USA (United States)	04 Feb 63	473UNTS65	106856
Iceland	USA (United States)	06 Feb 63	473UNTS93	106858
Turkey	USA (United States)	21 Feb 63	473UNTS311	106867
Congo (Zaire)	USA (United States)	23 Feb 63	493UNTS17	107204
Congo (Zaire)	USA (United States)	23 Feb 63	493UNTS3	107203
Colombia	USA (United States)	27 Mar 63	489UNTS289	107145
Ecuador	USA (United States)	05 Apr 63	477UNTS135	106919
El Salvador	USA (United States)	07 May 63	476UNTS35	106901
India	USA (United States)	09 May 63	476UNTS43	106902
Guinea	USA (United States)	22 May 63	487UNTS251	107108
Ethiopia	USA (United States)	11 Jun 63	487UNTS269	107109
Cyprus	USA (United States)	18 Jun 63	479UNTS191	106953
Senegal	USA (United States)	03 Jul 63	527UNTS95	107620
Iraq	USA (United States)	27 Aug 63	489UNTS271	107144
Brazil	USA (United States)	11 Sep 63	493UNTS267	107220
Paraguay	USA (United States)	16 Sep 63	494UNTS101	107229
Peru	USA (United States)	23 Sep 63	488UNTS91	107121
Greece	USA (United States)	30 Oct 63	493UNTS29	107205
Paraguay	USA (United States)	14 Nov 63	505UNTS87	107366
Syria	USA (United States)	18 Nov 63	494UNTS169	107232
USA (United States)	Vietnam, South	09 Jan 64	505UNTS173	107373
Poland	USA (United States)	03 Feb 64	505UNTS245	107376
Poland	USA (United States)	03 Feb 64	505UNTS215	107375
Jordan	USA (United States)	11 Feb 64	511UNTS85	107429
Peru	USA (United States)	13 Feb 64	511UNTS119	107431
Iceland	USA (United States)	13 Feb 64	511UNTS3	107421
Iceland	USA (United States)	13 Feb 64	510UNTS295	107420
Sudan	USA (United States)	02 Mar 64	524UNTS217	107575
Ivory Coast	USA (United States)	10 Mar 64	526UNTS285	107611
Bolivia	USA (United States)	25 Mar 64	532UNTS3	107710
Tunisia	USA (United States)	07 Apr 64	527UNTS3	107613
USA (United States)	Yugoslavia	27 Apr 64	526UNTS73	107601
USA (United States)	Yugoslavia	27 Apr 64	526UNTS89	107602
USA (United States)	Yugoslavia	28 Apr 64	526UNTS103	107603
Philippines	USA (United States)	14 May 64	526UNTS113	107604
Taiwan	USA (United States)	03 Jun 64	526UNTS257	107610

PARTY ONE	PARTY TWO	DATE	CITATION	NUMBER
Purchase authorization (Cont.)				
Paraguay	USA (United States)	05 Sep 64	530UNTS225	107685
USA (United States)	Vietnam, South	29 Sep 64	531UNTS183	107703
Iran	USA (United States)	29 Sep 64	531UNTS163	107702
India	USA (United States)	30 Sep 64	532UNTS321	107726
Colombia	USA (United States)	08 Oct 64	579UNTS3	108395
USA (United States)	Yugoslavia	28 Oct 64	533UNTS3	107728
USA (United States)	Yugoslavia	29 Oct 64	533UNTS17	107729
Iran	USA (United States)	16 Nov 64	532UNTS213	107719
Greece	USA (United States)	17 Nov 64	532UNTS107	107714
Kenya	USA (United States)	07 Dec 64	532UNTS263	107722
Congo (Zaire)	USA (United States)	09 Dec 64	531UNTS249	107707
Israel	USA (United States)	22 Dec 64	532UNTS231	107720
Iceland	USA (United States)	30 Dec 64	542UNTS37	107878
Iceland	USA (United States)	30 Dec 64	531UNTS287	107709
Taiwan	USA (United States)	31 Dec 64	532UNTS59	107712
Korea, South	USA (United States)	31 Dec 64	535UNTS315	107787
Dahomey	USA (United States)	31 Dec 64	541UNTS117	107865
Taiwan	USA (United States)	31 Dec 64	532UNTS29	107711
Sierra Leone	USA (United States)	29 Jan 65	542UNTS87	107882
Tunisia	USA (United States)	17 Feb 65	542UNTS125	107885
USA (United States)	Yugoslavia	16 Mar 65	542UNTS161	107887
Dominican Republic	USA (United States)	18 Mar 65	542UNTS215	107892
Ivory Coast	USA (United States)	05 Apr 65	546UNTS143	107941
Philippines	USA (United States)	23 Apr 65	546UNTS157	107942
Bolivia	USA (United States)	12 May 65	564UNTS143	108226
Afghanistan	USA (United States)	22 May 65	579UNTS29	108396
USA (United States)	Vietnam, South	26 May 65	550UNTS3	108005
Ecuador	USA (United States)	25 Jun 65	549UNTS23	107986
Mali	USA (United States)	14 Jul 65	564UNTS101	108223
USA (United States)	Yugoslavia	16 Jul 65	549UNTS111	107994
Chile	USA (United States)	27 Jul 65	574UNTS83	108342
Ethiopia	USA (United States)	17 Aug 65	564UNTS119	108224
USA (United States)	Yugoslavia	22 Nov 65	574UNTS211	108351
Ethiopia	USA (United States)	14 Dec 65	574UNTS115	108344
United Arab Rep	USA (United States)	03 Jan 66	579UNTS63	108399
Guinea	USA (United States)	04 Feb 66	579UNTS213	108409
Multilateral		04 Mar 66	578UNTS57	108387
Korea, South	USA (United States)	07 Mar 66	579UNTS137	108404
Ceylon (Sri Lanka)	USA (United States)	12 Mar 66	579UNTS117	108403
Ghana	USA (United States)	01 Apr 66	579UNTS157	108405
USA (United States)	Yugoslavia	11 Apr 66	580UNTS239	108427
Sudan	USA (United States)	13 Apr 66	586UNTS39	108495
Bolivia	USA (United States)	22 Apr 66	578UNTS73	108388
Israel	USA (United States)	06 Jun 66	593UNTS165	108583
Tunisia	USA (United States)	30 Jul 66	601UNTS133	108692
Jordan	USA (United States)	25 Aug 66	606UNTS237	108788
Surplus commodities				
Dominican Republic	USA (United States)	10 Jun 43	21UNTS277	200129
Burma	WHO (World Health)	09 Jul 51	104UNTS175	101439
USA (United States)	Yugoslavia	05 Jan 55	251UNTS29	103531
Pakistan	USA (United States)	18 Jan 55	239UNTS61	103372
Chile	USA (United States)	27 Jan 55	262UNTS3	103735
Peru	USA (United States)	07 Feb 55	241UNTS63	103424
Spain	USA (United States)	20 Apr 55	239UNTS117	103374
Argentina	USA (United States)	25 Apr 55	251UNTS283	103546
Israel	USA (United States)	29 Apr 55	261UNTS331	103731
USA (United States)	Yugoslavia	12 May 55	251UNTS337	103550
USA (United States)	Yugoslavia	12 May 55	251UNTS331	103549
Italy	USA (United States)	19 May 55	269UNTS83	103876
Italy	USA (United States)	23 May 55	251UNTS303	103547
Austria	USA (United States)	14 Jun 55	258UNTS37	103668
Thailand	USA (United States)	21 Jun 55	262UNTS87	103738
Colombia	USA (United States)	23 Jun 55	263UNTS337	103781
Greece	USA (United States)	24 Jun 55	270UNTS361	103906

PARTY ONE	PARTY TWO	DATE	CITATION	NUMBER
Surplus commodities (Cont.)				
Greece	USA (United States)	24 Jun 55	270UNTS351	103905
Italy	USA (United States)	30 Jun 55	258UNTS15	103667
Israel	USA (United States)	10 Nov 55	240UNTS3	103390
United Arab Rep	USA (United States)	14 Dec 55	240UNTS37	103392
Colombia	USA (United States)	20 Dec 55	241UNTS25	103421
Germany, West	USA (United States)	23 Dec 55	240UNTS79	103395
Austria	USA (United States)	07 Feb 56	272UNTS117	103933
Japan	USA (United States)	10 Feb 56	275UNTS157	103980
Japan	USA (United States)	10 Feb 56	275UNTS105	103979
Iran	USA (United States)	20 Feb 56	272UNTS135	103934
Italy	USA (United States)	27 Feb 56	291UNTS287	104260
Indonesia	USA (United States)	02 Mar 56	271UNTS345	103925
Pakistan	USA (United States)	02 Mar 56	271UNTS371	103927
Spain	USA (United States)	05 Mar 56	271UNTS329	103924
Turkey	USA (United States)	12 Mar 56	272UNTS21	103929
Chile	USA (United States)	13 Mar 56	275UNTS49	103975
Korea, South	USA (United States)	13 Mar 56	272UNTS3	103928
Peru	USA (United States)	07 May 56	268UNTS285	103862
Peru	USA (United States)	08 May 56	278UNTS117	104028
Portugal	USA (United States)	24 May 56	268UNTS323	103865
UK Great Britain	USA (United States)	05 Jun 56	247UNTS205	103470
Netherlands	USA (United States)	07 Aug 56	281UNTS57	104069
Pakistan	USA (United States)	07 Aug 56	281UNTS75	104071
Greece	USA (United States)	08 Aug 56	277UNTS203	104007
Taiwan	USA (United States)	14 Aug 56	281UNTS257	104083
India	USA (United States)	29 Aug 56	278UNTS25	104019
Israel	USA (United States)	11 Sep 56	277UNTS215	104008
Spain	USA (United States)	23 Oct 56	277UNTS105	104001
Italy	USA (United States)	30 Oct 56	263UNTS221	103775
USA (United States)	Yugoslavia	03 Nov 56	277UNTS119	104002
Turkey	USA (United States)	12 Nov 56	282UNTS77	104093
Turkey	USA (United States)	23 Nov 56	290UNTS273	104239
Burma	USA (United States)	04 Dec 56	268UNTS189	103858
Brazil	USA (United States)	31 Dec 56	266UNTS151	103829
Korea, South	USA (United States)	30 Jan 57	278UNTS85	104024
Ecuador	USA (United States)	15 Feb 57	279UNTS155	104037
Thailand	USA (United States)	04 Mar 57	279UNTS235	104043
Iceland	USA (United States)	11 Apr 57	283UNTS107	104110
Colombia	USA (United States)	16 Apr 57	283UNTS245	104121
Peru	USA (United States)	02 May 57	283UNTS55	104106
Austria	USA (United States)	10 May 57	283UNTS15	104103
Poland	USA (United States)	07 Jun 57	291UNTS41	104243
Bolivia	USA (United States)	07 Jun 57	291UNTS77	104245
Philippines	USA (United States)	25 Jun 57	289UNTS279	104224
UK Great Britain	USA (United States)	27 Jun 57	290UNTS133	104232
Tunisia	USA (United States)	28 Jun 57	289UNTS301	104226
Mexico	USA (United States)	23 Oct 57	300UNTS35	104330
Israel	USA (United States)	07 Nov 57	302UNTS255	104365
Pakistan	USA (United States)	15 Nov 57	303UNTS173	104380
Greece	USA (United States)	18 Dec 57	303UNTS159	104379
France	USA (United States)	27 Dec 57	307UNTS79	104444
Turkey	USA (United States)	20 Jan 58	304UNTS15	104389
Spain	USA (United States)	27 Jan 58	303UNTS247	104384
UK Great Britain	USA (United States)	03 Feb 58	307UNTS199	104450
USA (United States)	Yugoslavia	03 Feb 58	304UNTS293	104404
Korea, South	USA (United States)	05 Feb 58	307UNTS121	104447
Finland	USA (United States)	21 Feb 58	304UNTS253	104401
France	USA (United States)	28 Feb 58	366UNTS343	105222
Colombia	USA (United States)	14 Mar 58	308UNTS115	104459
Peru	USA (United States)	09 Apr 58	316UNTS37	104576
Taiwan	USA (United States)	18 Apr 58	308UNTS179	104461
Iceland	USA (United States)	03 May 58	316UNTS137	104581
Italy	USA (United States)	08 May 58	316UNTS177	104584
Burma	USA (United States)	27 May 58	315UNTS197	104569
Ceylon (Sri Lanka)	USA (United States)	18 Jun 58	316UNTS15	104574

Surplus commodities (Cont.)

PARTY ONE	PARTY TWO	DATE	CITATION	NUMBER
Ecuador	USA (United States)	30 Jun 58	336UNTS11	104796
India	USA (United States)	26 Sep 58	336UNTS59	104798
Israel	USA (United States)	06 Nov 58	336UNTS275	104810
Pakistan	USA (United States)	26 Nov 58	337UNTS3	104812
USA (United States)	Yugoslavia	22 Dec 58	338UNTS243	104839
United Arab Rep	USA (United States)	24 Dec 58	338UNTS221	104837
Finland	USA (United States)	30 Dec 58	340UNTS259	104869
Spain	USA (United States)	13 Jan 59	341UNTS241	104887
Turkey	USA (United States)	13 Feb 59	340UNTS235	104867
Iceland	USA (United States)	03 Mar 59	341UNTS261	104889
Ceylon (Sri Lanka)	USA (United States)	13 Mar 59	342UNTS51	104900
France	USA (United States)	21 Mar 59	342UNTS71	104901
Indonesia	USA (United States)	29 May 59	347UNTS85	104992
Taiwan	USA (United States)	09 Jun 59	353UNTS257	105046
Poland	USA (United States)	10 Jun 59	347UNTS41	104989
Argentina	USA (United States)	12 Jun 59	347UNTS59	104990
Korea, South	USA (United States)	30 Jun 59	353UNTS297	105047
United Arab Rep	USA (United States)	29 Jul 59	357UNTS121	105111
Colombia	USA (United States)	06 Oct 59	358UNTS145	105132
USA (United States)	Vietnam, South	16 Oct 59	360UNTS271	105163
India	USA (United States)	13 Nov 59	360UNTS287	105164
United Arab Rep	USA (United States)	14 Nov 59	360UNTS311	105165
Turkey	USA (United States)	22 Dec 59	367UNTS57	105225
Greece	USA (United States)	07 Jan 60	368UNTS221	105243
Peru	USA (United States)	12 Feb 60	372UNTS83	105290
Japan	USA (United States)	18 Feb 60	372UNTS117	105292
Iceland	USA (United States)	06 Apr 60	372UNTS71	105289
Pakistan	USA (United States)	11 Apr 60	372UNTS251	105302
India	USA (United States)	04 May 60	376UNTS279	105384
Spain	USA (United States)	22 Jun 60	378UNTS3	105414
Poland	USA (United States)	21 Jul 60	380UNTS157	105456
Iran	USA (United States)	26 Jul 60	384UNTS141	105516
United Arab Rep	USA (United States)	01 Aug 60	384UNTS189	105519
United Arab Rep	USA (United States)	09 Aug 60	388UNTS271	105584
Taiwan	USA (United States)	30 Aug 60	388UNTS191	105579
Ecuador	USA (United States)	27 Sep 60	401UNTS115	105766
Ceylon (Sri Lanka)	USA (United States)	30 Sep 60	389UNTS221	105594
USA (United States)	Vietnam, South	28 Oct 60	401UNTS3	105758
France	USA (United States)	04 Nov 60	400UNTS323	105756
Indonesia	USA (United States)	05 Nov 60	400UNTS35	105746
Greece	USA (United States)	07 Nov 60	400UNTS57	105748
Chile	USA (United States)	08 Nov 60	405UNTS85	105825
Korea, South	USA (United States)	28 Dec 60	402UNTS3	105773
Turkey	USA (United States)	11 Jan 61	405UNTS173	105833
USA (United States)	Vietnam, South	25 Mar 61	406UNTS187	105849
Ecuador	USA (United States)	03 Apr 61	409UNTS140	105882
Bolivia	USA (United States)	07 Apr 61	433UNTS3	106227
Iceland	USA (United States)	07 Apr 61	406UNTS203	105850
USA (United States)	Yugoslavia	28 Apr 61	409UNTS172	105884
Brazil	USA (United States)	04 May 61	433UNTS91	106233
Israel	USA (United States)	10 May 61	409UNTS213	105887
Spain	USA (United States)	22 May 61	409UNTS260	105891
Tunisia	USA (United States)	30 Jun 61	434UNTS85	106257
Paraguay	USA (United States)	07 Jul 61	433UNTS53	106231
USA (United States)	Vietnam, South	14 Jul 61	416UNTS133	105999
Turkey	USA (United States)	29 Jul 61	416UNTS151	106001
Finland	USA (United States)	04 Aug 61	418UNTS19	106014
El Salvador	USA (United States)	21 Aug 61	418UNTS35	106015
UK Great Britain	USA (United States)	28 Aug 61	434UNTS103	106258
Austria	USA (United States)	03 Oct 61	426UNTS187	106137
Indonesia	USA (United States)	26 Oct 61	433UNTS249	106248
Iceland	USA (United States)	06 Nov 61	426UNTS225	106140
Syria	USA (United States)	09 Nov 61	435UNTS75	106271
Sudan	USA (United States)	14 Nov 61	434UNTS51	106255
Bolivia	USA (United States)	15 Nov 61	456UNTS192	106557

Surplus commodities (Cont.)

PARTY ONE	PARTY TWO	DATE	CITATION	NUMBER
Congo (Zaire)	USA (United States)	18 Nov 61	433UNTS207	106244
Philippines	USA (United States)	24 Nov 61	433UNTS315	106251
Portugal	USA (United States)	28 Nov 61	434UNTS31	106253
Poland	USA (United States)	15 Dec 61	434UNTS3	106252
USA (United States)	Vietnam, South	27 Dec 61	433UNTS185	106242
United Arab Rep	USA (United States)	19 Jan 62	435UNTS107	106273
Iran	USA (United States)	29 Jan 62	435UNTS53	106270
Guinea	USA (United States)	02 Feb 62	435UNTS35	106269
Morocco	USA (United States)	09 Feb 62	442UNTS135	106345
Bolivia	USA (United States)	12 Feb 62	451UNTS281	106499
Tunisia	USA (United States)	16 Feb 62	442UNTS161	106347
Indonesia	USA (United States)	19 Feb 62	435UNTS137	106276
Korea, South	USA (United States)	02 Mar 62	442UNTS185	106349
Brazil	USA (United States)	15 Mar 62	456UNTS209	106558
Iceland	USA (United States)	16 Mar 62	445UNTS49	106376
Peru	USA (United States)	20 Mar 62	445UNTS61	106377
USA (United States)	Uruguay	27 Apr 62	452UNTS25	106502
Taiwan	USA (United States)	27 Apr 62	436UNTS25	106287
India	USA (United States)	01 May 62	451UNTS179	106493
Israel	USA (United States)	03 May 62	442UNTS83	106340
Israel	USA (United States)	28 Aug 62	448UNTS317	106445
Tunisia	USA (United States)	14 Sep 62	461UNTS31	106649
United Arab Rep	USA (United States)	08 Oct 62	462UNTS39	106670
Greece	USA (United States)	22 Oct 62	462UNTS187	106678
Korea, South	USA (United States)	07 Nov 62	462UNTS129	106674
Burma	USA (United States)	09 Nov 62	461UNTS113	106655
Taiwan	USA (United States)	19 Nov 62	459UNTS263	106629
Paraguay	USA (United States)	24 Nov 62	471UNTS49	106821
India	USA (United States)	26 Nov 62	460UNTS203	106641
USA (United States)	Yugoslavia	28 Nov 62	460UNTS185	106640
India	USA (United States)	30 Nov 62	459UNTS231	106626
Israel	USA (United States)	06 Dec 62	460UNTS151	106638
Bolivia	USA (United States)	17 Dec 62	469UNTS121	106788
Sudan	USA (United States)	31 Jan 63	494UNTS119	107230
Poland	USA (United States)	01 Feb 63	487UNTS143	107100
Iceland	USA (United States)	06 Feb 63	473UNTS93	106858
Turkey	USA (United States)	21 Feb 63	473UNTS311	106867
Congo (Zaire)	USA (United States)	23 Feb 63	493UNTS17	107204
Congo (Zaire)	USA (United States)	23 Feb 63	493UNTS3	107203
Guinea	USA (United States)	22 May 63	487UNTS251	107108
Ethiopia	USA (United States)	11 Jun 63	487UNTS269	107109
Cyprus	USA (United States)	18 Jun 63	479UNTS191	106953
Brazil	USA (United States)	11 Sep 63	493UNTS267	107220
Greece	USA (United States)	30 Oct 63	493UNTS29	107205
Paraguay	USA (United States)	14 Nov 63	505UNTS87	107366
USA (United States)	Vietnam, South	09 Jan 64	505UNTS173	107373
Poland	USA (United States)	03 Feb 64	505UNTS215	107375
Poland	USA (United States)	03 Feb 64	505UNTS245	107376
Jordan	USA (United States)	11 Feb 64	511UNTS85	107429
Peru	USA (United States)	13 Feb 64	511UNTS119	107431
Iceland	USA (United States)	13 Feb 64	510UNTS295	107420
Sudan	USA (United States)	02 Mar 64	524UNTS217	107575
Ivory Coast	USA (United States)	10 Mar 64	526UNTS285	107611
Bolivia	USA (United States)	25 Mar 64	532UNTS3	107710
Tunisia	USA (United States)	07 Apr 64	527UNTS3	107613
USA (United States)	Yugoslavia	27 Apr 64	526UNTS73	107601
Congo (Zaire)	USA (United States)	28 Apr 64	526UNTS55	107600
Philippines	USA (United States)	14 May 64	526UNTS113	107604
Taiwan	USA (United States)	03 Jun 64	526UNTS257	107610
Paraguay	USA (United States)	05 Sep 64	530UNTS225	107685
Iran	USA (United States)	29 Sep 64	531UNTS163	107702
USA (United States)	Vietnam, South	29 Sep 64	531UNTS183	107703
India	USA (United States)	30 Sep 64	532UNTS321	107726
Kenya	USA (United States)	07 Dec 64	532UNTS263	107722
Congo (Zaire)	USA (United States)	09 Dec 64	531UNTS249	107707

PARTY ONE	PARTY TWO	DATE	CITATION	NUMBER
Surplus commodities (Cont.)				
Israel	USA (United States)	22 Dec 64	532UNTS231	107720
Korea, South	USA (United States)	31 Dec 64	535UNTS315	107787
Dahomey	USA (United States)	31 Dec 64	541UNTS117	107865
Taiwan	USA (United States)	31 Dec 64	532UNTS29	107711
USA (United States)	Yugoslavia	16 Mar 65	542UNTS161	107887
Morocco	USA (United States)	23 Apr 65	594UNTS3	108591
Bolivia	USA (United States)	12 May 65	564UNTS143	108226
USA (United States)	Uruguay	17 May 65	564UNTS69	108221
Congo (Zaire)	USA (United States)	19 Jul 65	593UNTS215	108586
Liberia	USA (United States)	06 Jan 66	592UNTS101	108570
Algeria	USA (United States)	23 Feb 66	592UNTS117	108571
Colombia	USA (United States)	10 Mar 66	0UNTS0	109604
Jordan	USA (United States)	05 Apr 66	593UNTS239	108587
Pakistan	USA (United States)	26 May 66	594UNTS27	108592
Israel	USA (United States)	06 Jun 66	593UNTS165	108583
Indonesia	USA (United States)	28 Jun 66	593UNTS201	108585
Jordan	USA (United States)	25 Aug 66	606UNTS237	108788
Philippines	USA (United States)	22 Dec 66	591UNTS219	108559
Israel	USA (United States)	04 Aug 67	0UNTS0	109351
Israel	USA (United States)	29 Mar 68	0UNTS0	109352
Atomic energy assistance				
Multilateral		26 Oct 56	276UNTS3	103988
Australia	USA (United States)	12 Jul 57	290UNTS139	104233
Germany, West	USA (United States)	05 May 59	355UNTS307	105083
Greece	USA (United States)	06 May 59	357UNTS163	105115
France	USA (United States)	07 May 59	354UNTS83	105055
Canada	USA (United States)	22 May 59	354UNTS63	105054
Lebanon	USA (United States)	16 Sep 59	358UNTS175	105135
Taiwan	USA (United States)	02 Dec 59	361UNTS115	105175
Colombia	USA (United States)	11 Jan 60	371UNTS37	105268
Chile	USA (United States)	19 Feb 60	371UNTS255	105282
Brazil	USA (United States)	27 Feb 60	384UNTS131	105515
Indonesia	USSR (Soviet Union)	28 Feb 60	392UNTS173	105643
New Zealand	USA (United States)	23 Mar 60	371UNTS147	105276
Ireland	USA (United States)	24 Mar 60	371UNTS237	105280
Guatemala	USA (United States)	23 Apr 60	373UNTS23	105312
Argentina	USA (United States)	23 May 60	377UNTS3	105392
Korea, South	USA (United States)	18 Nov 60	400UNTS49	105747
Israel	USA (United States)	19 Dec 60	401UNTS195	105772
USA (United States)	Yugoslavia	19 Apr 61	409UNTS163	105883
Australia	USA (United States)	09 May 61	409UNTS203	105886
Multilateral		27 Jun 62	463UNTS11	106689
Pakistan	UK Great Britain	13 Mar 63	482UNTS347	107003
Multilateral		28 Feb 64	501UNTS245	107321
Multilateral		08 Apr 64	501UNTS221	107320
Multilateral		18 Jun 64	542UNTS145	107886
Multilateral		28 Jul 64	555UNTS183	108113
Multilateral		18 Sep 64	556UNTS25	108117
Multilateral		18 Sep 64	555UNTS205	108114
Multilateral		21 Sep 64	555UNTS227	108115
Multilateral		30 Sep 64	556UNTS3	108116
State/IGO Group	IAEA (Atom Energy)	04 Dec 64	637UNTS0	109111
Multilateral		24 Feb 65	556UNTS47	108118
Multilateral		26 Feb 65	556UNTS69	108119
Brazil	USA (United States)	08 Jul 65	0UNTS0	109603
Romania	IAEA (Atom Energy)	22 Apr 66	603UNTS23	108721
State/IGO Group	IAEA (Atom Energy)	19 Jun 67	637UNTS0	109112
Iraq	IAEA (Atom Energy)	21 Sep 67	630UNTS41	108963
Multilateral		26 Sep 67	633UNTS73	109035
Burma	IAEA (Atom Energy)	11 Oct 67	630UNTS49	108964
State/IGO Group	IAEA (Atom Energy)	05 Jan 68	637UNTS0	109114
State/IGO Group	IAEA (Atom Energy)	28 Feb 68	637UNTS0	109115
Israel	Philippines	14 Jan 69	0UNTS0	109437

PARTY ONE	PARTY TWO	DATE	CITATION	NUMBER
Acceptance of delivery				
Sweden	USA (United States)	18 Jan 56	240UNTS413	103416
Japan	USA (United States)	23 Nov 56	324UNTS177	104685
Japan	USA (United States)	08 May 57	318UNTS257	104621
Japan	IAEA (Atom Energy)	24 Mar 59	339UNTS327	104852
Canada	IAEA (Atom Energy)	24 Mar 59	339UNTS315	104851
IAEA (Atom Energy)	UK Great Britain	11 May 59	339UNTS351	104854
Canada	Euratom	06 Oct 59	475UNTS187	106894
Netherlands	Euratom	25 Jul 61	462UNTS263	106686
Multilateral		04 Oct 61	412UNTS210	105934
Multilateral		05 Mar 62	425UNTS3	106114
Pakistan	IAEA (Atom Energy)	05 Mar 62	425UNTS17	106115
Argentina	USA (United States)	22 Jun 62	458UNTS97	106594
IAEA (Atom Energy)	Yugoslavia	04 Jun 63	490UNTS343	107163
Multilateral		08 Apr 64	501UNTS221	107320
Multilateral		28 Jul 64	555UNTS183	108113
Multilateral		18 Sep 64	556UNTS25	108117
Multilateral		18 Sep 64	555UNTS205	108114
Multilateral		21 Sep 64	555UNTS227	108115
Multilateral		30 Sep 64	556UNTS3	108116
Multilateral		02 Dec 64	572UNTS229	108317
Multilateral		24 Feb 65	556UNTS47	108118
Multilateral		26 Feb 65	556UNTS69	108119
Brazil	USA (United States)	08 Jul 65	0UNTS0	109603
Morocco	IAEA (Atom Energy)	24 Sep 65	556UNTS109	108122
IAEA (Atom Energy)	Turkey	08 Feb 66	573UNTS75	108323
Multilateral		20 Jun 66	572UNTS263	108318
Multilateral		28 Sep 66	589UNTS41	108534
Multilateral		23 Jun 67	614UNTS185	108871
Multilateral		23 Aug 67	614UNTS145	108869
Iraq	IAEA (Atom Energy)	21 Sep 67	630UNTS41	108963
Burma	IAEA (Atom Energy)	11 Oct 67	630UNTS49	108964
General				
UK Great Britain	USA (United States)	19 Aug 43	214UNTS341	200527
Multilateral		15 Feb 52	132UNTS51	101751
Multilateral		01 Jul 53	200UNTS149	102701
Norway	UK Great Britain	12 Jul 57	310UNTS41	104485
Italy	IBRD (World Bank)	16 Sep 59	375UNTS159	105366
Multilateral		22 Jun 60	431UNTS41	106208
Netherlands	Euratom	25 Jul 61	462UNTS263	106686
IAEA (Atom Energy)	Yugoslavia	04 Oct 61	412UNTS226	105935
Multilateral		05 Mar 62	425UNTS3	106114
Pakistan	IAEA (Atom Energy)	05 Mar 62	425UNTS17	106115
USA (United States)	USSR (Soviet Union)	08 Mar 62	460UNTS3	106630
IAEA (Atom Energy)	USA (United States)	30 Mar 62	442UNTS49	106338
Australia	Japan	07 Aug 62	435UNTS261	106283
India	USA (United States)	01 Feb 63	473UNTS37	106852
Pakistan	UK Great Britain	13 Mar 63	482UNTS347	107003
Brazil	USA (United States)	29 Mar 63	476UNTS67	106904
Multilateral		05 Aug 63	480UNTS43	106964
Multilateral		23 Sep 63	488UNTS99	107122
IAEA (Atom Energy)	Yugoslavia	07 Dec 63	501UNTS273	107322
Finland	IAEA (Atom Energy)	27 Jan 64	501UNTS213	107319
USA (United States)	USSR (Soviet Union)	22 Feb 64	526UNTS131	107605
Multilateral		28 Jul 64	555UNTS183	108113
Multilateral		18 Sep 64	555UNTS205	108114
Multilateral		18 Sep 64	556UNTS25	108117
Multilateral		21 Sep 64	555UNTS227	108115
Multilateral		30 Sep 64	556UNTS3	108116
Multilateral		02 Dec 64	572UNTS229	108317
Multilateral		24 Feb 65	556UNTS47	108118
Multilateral		26 Feb 65	556UNTS69	108119
Brazil	USA (United States)	08 Jul 65	0UNTS0	109603
Multilateral		07 Oct 65	556UNTS175	108125

PARTY ONE	PARTY TWO	DATE	CITATION	NUMBER
General (Cont.)				
Multilateral		20 Jun 66	572UNTS263	108318
Multilateral		28 Sep 66	589UNTS41	108534
Israel	Philippines	20 Feb 67	597UNTS139	108642
Israel	Philippines	14 Jan 69	0UNTS0	109437
Nuclear materials				
UK Great Britain	USA (United States)	19 Aug 43	214UNTS341	200527
Belgium	Netherlands	24 May 46	31UNTS169	100477
Turkey	USA (United States)	10 Jun 55	238UNTS149	103359
Canada	USA (United States)	15 Jun 55	235UNTS176	103301
Belgium	USA (United States)	15 Jun 55	235UNTS133	103299
UK Great Britain	USA (United States)	15 Jun 55	229UNTS73	103161
Israel	USA (United States)	12 Jul 55	219UNTS185	102974
Lebanon	USA (United States)	18 Jul 55	239UNTS247	103383
Taiwan	USA (United States)	18 Jul 55	235UNTS221	103304
Switzerland	USA (United States)	18 Jul 55	239UNTS311	103388
Netherlands	USA (United States)	18 Jul 55	240UNTS347	103412
Colombia	USA (United States)	19 Jul 55	235UNTS233	103305
Spain	USA (United States)	19 Jul 55	239UNTS299	103387
Portugal	USA (United States)	21 Jul 55	239UNTS283	103386
USA (United States)	Venezuela	21 Jul 55	238UNTS121	103357
Denmark	USA (United States)	25 Jul 55	235UNTS245	103306
Philippines	USA (United States)	27 Jul 55	239UNTS271	103385
Italy	USA (United States)	28 Jul 55	239UNTS235	103382
Argentina	USA (United States)	29 Jul 55	235UNTS121	103298
Brazil	USA (United States)	03 Aug 55	235UNTS159	103300
Brazil	USA (United States)	03 Aug 55	270UNTS71	103893
Greece	USA (United States)	04 Aug 55	235UNTS257	103307
Chile	USA (United States)	08 Aug 55	235UNTS209	103303
Pakistan	USA (United States)	11 Aug 55	239UNTS259	103384
Japan	USA (United States)	14 Nov 55	240UNTS361	103413
Belgium	UK Great Britain	18 Nov 55	222UNTS327	103038
USA (United States)	Uruguay	13 Jan 56	240UNTS401	103415
Sweden	USA (United States)	18 Jan 56	240UNTS413	103416
Netherlands	USA (United States)	22 Jan 56	287UNTS121	104181
Peru	USA (United States)	25 Jan 56	240UNTS425	103417
Korea, South	USA (United States)	03 Feb 56	240UNTS129	103401
Germany, West	USA (United States)	13 Feb 56	253UNTS119	103580
Thailand	USA (United States)	13 Mar 56	253UNTS105	103579
Ireland	USA (United States)	16 Mar 56	317UNTS195	104604
Chile	USA (United States)	20 Apr 56	293UNTS277	104295
Costa Rica	USA (United States)	18 May 56	404UNTS237	105814
Austria	USA (United States)	08 Jun 56	253UNTS139	103581
New Zealand	USA (United States)	13 Jun 56	253UNTS155	103582
Dominican Republic	USA (United States)	15 Jun 56	265UNTS227	103815
France	USA (United States)	19 Jun 56	281UNTS341	104087
Switzerland	USA (United States)	21 Jun 56	279UNTS41	104033
Australia	USA (United States)	22 Jun 56	283UNTS275	104123
Cuba	USA (United States)	26 Jun 56	293UNTS257	104294
Germany, West	UK Great Britain	31 Jul 56	252UNTS93	103559
Guatemala	USA (United States)	15 Aug 56	288UNTS181	104205
Multilateral		26 Oct 56	276UNTS3	103988
Japan	USA (United States)	23 Nov 56	324UNTS177	104685
Netherlands	USA (United States)	15 Feb 57	287UNTS239	104190
Norway	USA (United States)	25 Feb 57	284UNTS19	104126
Iran	USA (United States)	05 Mar 57	342UNTS29	104898
Japan	USA (United States)	08 May 57	318UNTS257	104621
Ecuador	USA (United States)	31 May 57	304UNTS61	104391
Nicaragua	USA (United States)	11 Jun 57	304UNTS267	104402
Germany, West	USA (United States)	28 Jun 57	288UNTS339	104213
Italy	USA (United States)	03 Jul 57	308UNTS195	104462
Germany, West	USA (United States)	03 Jul 57	288UNTS305	104212
South Africa	USA (United States)	08 Jul 57	290UNTS147	104234
Spain	USA (United States)	16 Aug 57	307UNTS169	104449
Sweden	UK Great Britain	20 Sep 57	310UNTS49	104486

PARTY ONE	PARTY TWO	DATE	CITATION	NUMBER
Nuclear materials (Cont.)				
Italy	UK Great Britain	28 Dec 57	305UNTS357	104425
Japan	UK Great Britain	16 Jun 58	325UNTS185	104700
Japan	USA (United States)	19 Jun 58	325UNTS143	104699
UK Great Britain	USA (United States)	03 Jul 58	326UNTS3	104707
Portugal	UK Great Britain	18 Jul 58	313UNTS109	104532
USA (United States)	Venezuela	08 Oct 58	371UNTS69	105271
Euratom	USA (United States)	08 Nov 58	338UNTS135	104835
Euratom	UK Great Britain	04 Feb 59	331UNTS125	104752
Japan	IAEA (Atom Energy)	24 Mar 59	339UNTS327	104852
Canada	IAEA (Atom Energy)	24 Mar 59	339UNTS315	104851
USA (United States)	Vietnam, South	22 Apr 59	347UNTS113	104993
France	USA (United States)	07 May 59	354UNTS83	105055
IAEA (Atom Energy)	USA (United States)	11 May 59	339UNTS359	104855
IAEA (Atom Energy)	UK Great Britain	11 May 59	339UNTS351	104854
IAEA (Atom Energy)	USSR (Soviet Union)	11 May 59	339UNTS341	104853
Canada	Pakistan	14 May 59	426UNTS129	106133
Panama	USA (United States)	24 Jun 59	479UNTS145	106950
Canada	Japan	02 Jul 59	383UNTS243	105504
Austria	USA (United States)	22 Jul 59	368UNTS199	105242
Australia	Canada	04 Aug 59	391UNTS191	105623
Lebanon	USA (United States)	16 Sep 59	358UNTS175	105135
Taiwan	USA (United States)	02 Dec 59	361UNTS115	105175
Colombia	USA (United States)	11 Jan 60	371UNTS37	105268
Spain	UK Great Britain	19 Jan 60	404UNTS41	105804
Chile	USA (United States)	19 Feb 60	371UNTS255	105282
New Zealand	USA (United States)	23 Mar 60	371UNTS147	105276
Ireland	USA (United States)	24 Mar 60	371UNTS237	105280
Guatemala	USA (United States)	23 Apr 60	373UNTS23	105312
Denmark	UK Great Britain	20 May 60	374UNTS245	105338
Argentina	USA (United States)	23 May 60	377UNTS3	105392
Indonesia	USA (United States)	08 Jun 60	388UNTS287	105585
India	USA (United States)	13 Jun 60	377UNTS37	105394
Multilateral		30 Dec 60	395UNTS241	105689
Finland	IAEA (Atom Energy)	30 Dec 60	395UNTS257	105690
Brazil	USA (United States)	17 Mar 61	406UNTS241	105853
Norway	IAEA (Atom Energy)	10 Apr 61	402UNTS255	105790
Multilateral		10 Apr 61	402UNTS281	105791
Multilateral		04 Oct 61	412UNTS210	105934
IAEA (Atom Energy)	Yugoslavia	04 Oct 61	412UNTS226	105935
Pakistan	IAEA (Atom Energy)	05 Mar 62	425UNTS17	106115
IAEA (Atom Energy)	USA (United States)	30 Mar 62	442UNTS49	106338
Colombia	USA (United States)	09 Apr 62	476UNTS9	106899
Argentina	USA (United States)	22 Jun 62	458UNTS97	106594
Congo (Zaire)	IAEA (Atom Energy)	27 Jun 62	463UNTS31	106691
Multilateral		27 Jun 62	463UNTS17	106690
Multilateral		27 Jun 62	463UNTS3	106688
Australia	Japan	07 Aug 62	435UNTS261	106283
Canada	Sweden	11 Sep 62	529UNTS9	107651
IAEA (Atom Energy)	Yugoslavia	04 Mar 63	490UNTS333	107162
Pakistan	UK Great Britain	13 Mar 63	482UNTS347	107003
IAEA (Atom Energy)	Yugoslavia	04 Jun 63	490UNTS343	107163
Austria	IAEA (Atom Energy)	21 Jun 63	490UNTS351	107164
Finland	IAEA (Atom Energy)	02 Jul 63	490UNTS403	107167
Finland	IAEA (Atom Energy)	30 Jul 63	490UNTS413	107168
Multilateral		05 Aug 63	480UNTS43	106964
India	USA (United States)	08 Aug 63	488UNTS21	107117
Multilateral		23 Sep 63	488UNTS99	107122
IAEA (Atom Energy)	Yugoslavia	07 Dec 63	501UNTS273	107322
Canada	India	16 Dec 63	529UNTS45	107655
Multilateral		18 Dec 63	490UNTS383	107166
Mexico	IAEA (Atom Energy)	18 Dec 63	490UNTS361	107165
Finland	IAEA (Atom Energy)	27 Jan 64	501UNTS213	107319
Multilateral		28 Feb 64	501UNTS245	107321
Multilateral		08 Apr 64	501UNTS221	107320
IAEA (Atom Energy)	USA (United States)	15 Jun 64	525UNTS3	107580

PARTY ONE	PARTY TWO	DATE	CITATION	NUMBER
Nuclear materials (Cont.)				
Multilateral		15 Jun 64	573UNTS85	108324
Multilateral		28 Jul 64	555UNTS183	108113
Switzerland	UK Great Britain	11 Aug 64	552UNTS271	108059
IAEA (Atom Energy)	United Arab Rep	17 Sep 64	525UNTS19	107581
Multilateral		18 Sep 64	555UNTS205	108114
Multilateral		21 Sep 64	555UNTS227	108115
Multilateral		30 Sep 64	556UNTS3	108116
Pakistan	UK Great Britain	13 Oct 64	534UNTS71	107754
Multilateral		02 Dec 64	525UNTS51	107583
Multilateral		02 Dec 64	572UNTS229	108317
Argentina	IAEA (Atom Energy)	02 Dec 64	525UNTS29	107582
State/IGO Group	IAEA (Atom Energy)	04 Dec 64	637UNTS0	109111
Switzerland	USA (United States)	30 Jan 65	594UNTS55	108594
Multilateral		24 Feb 65	556UNTS47	108118
Multilateral		26 Feb 65	556UNTS69	108119
Multilateral		18 Jun 65	573UNTS3	108320
Multilateral		23 Jun 65	548UNTS241	107981
Brazil	USA (United States)	08 Jul 65	0UNTS0	109603
Multilateral		24 Sep 65	556UNTS141	108124
IAEA (Atom Energy)	Uruguay	24 Sep 65	556UNTS117	108123
Multilateral		30 Dec 65	557UNTS3	108126
IAEA (Atom Energy)	Turkey	08 Feb 66	573UNTS75	108323
Romania	IAEA (Atom Energy)	22 Apr 66	603UNTS23	108721
UK Great Britain	USA (United States)	02 Jun 66	573UNTS229	108336
Multilateral		20 Jun 66	572UNTS263	108318
Mexico	IAEA (Atom Energy)	20 Jun 66	573UNTS25	108321
Multilateral		20 Jun 66	573UNTS41	108322
Sweden	USA (United States)	28 Jul 66	603UNTS61	108725
Philippines	IAEA (Atom Energy)	28 Sep 66	589UNTS25	108533
Multilateral		28 Sep 66	589UNTS41	108534
IAEA (Atom Energy)	USA (United States)	09 Dec 66	589UNTS55	108535
Iran	IAEA (Atom Energy)	10 May 67	614UNTS93	108865
IAEA (Atom Energy)	USA (United States)	07 Jun 67	614UNTS109	108866
State/IGO Group	IAEA (Atom Energy)	19 Jun 67	637UNTS0	109112
IAEA (Atom Energy)	Spain	23 Jun 67	614UNTS169	108870
Multilateral		23 Jun 67	614UNTS185	108871
Mexico	IAEA (Atom Energy)	23 Aug 67	614UNTS133	108868
Multilateral		23 Aug 67	614UNTS145	108869
IAEA (Atom Energy)	USA (United States)	16 Oct 67	630UNTS57	108965
IAEA (Atom Energy)	Vietnam, South	16 Oct 67	630UNTS379	200636
Multilateral		19 Oct 67	630UNTS69	108966
Multilateral		05 Nov 67	630UNTS77	108967
State/IGO Group	IAEA (Atom Energy)	05 Jan 68	637UNTS0	109114
State/IGO Group	IAEA (Atom Energy)	28 Feb 68	637UNTS0	109115
Israel	Philippines	14 Jan 69	0UNTS0	109437
Non-nuclear materials				
Belgium	Netherlands	24 May 46	31UNTS169	100477
Turkey	USA (United States)	10 Jun 55	238UNTS149	103359
Belgium	USA (United States)	15 Jun 55	235UNTS133	103299
Canada	USA (United States)	15 Jun 55	235UNTS176	103301
Israel	USA (United States)	12 Jul 55	219UNTS185	102974
Switzerland	USA (United States)	18 Jul 55	239UNTS311	103388
Netherlands	USA (United States)	18 Jul 55	240UNTS347	103412
Taiwan	USA (United States)	18 Jul 55	235UNTS221	103304
Lebanon	USA (United States)	18 Jul 55	239UNTS247	103383
Spain	USA (United States)	19 Jul 55	239UNTS299	103387
Colombia	USA (United States)	19 Jul 55	235UNTS233	103305
Portugal	USA (United States)	21 Jul 55	239UNTS283	103386
USA (United States)	Venezuela	21 Jul 55	238UNTS121	103357
Denmark	USA (United States)	25 Jul 55	235UNTS245	103306
Philippines	USA (United States)	27 Jul 55	239UNTS271	103385
Italy	USA (United States)	28 Jul 55	239UNTS235	103382
Argentina	USA (United States)	29 Jul 55	235UNTS121	103298
Brazil	USA (United States)	03 Aug 55	235UNTS159	103300
Non-nuclear materials (Cont.)				
Greece	USA (United States)	04 Aug 55	235UNTS257	103307
Chile	USA (United States)	08 Aug 55	235UNTS209	103303
Pakistan	USA (United States)	11 Aug 55	239UNTS259	103384
Japan	USA (United States)	14 Nov 55	240UNTS361	103413
Belgium	UK Great Britain	18 Nov 55	222UNTS327	103038
USA (United States)	Uruguay	13 Jan 56	240UNTS401	103415
Peru	USA (United States)	25 Jan 56	240UNTS425	103417
Korea, South	USA (United States)	03 Feb 56	240UNTS129	103401
Germany, West	USA (United States)	13 Feb 56	253UNTS119	103580
Thailand	USA (United States)	13 Mar 56	253UNTS105	103579
Ireland	USA (United States)	16 Mar 56	317UNTS195	104604
Costa Rica	USA (United States)	18 May 56	404UNTS237	105814
Austria	USA (United States)	08 Jun 56	253UNTS139	103581
New Zealand	USA (United States)	13 Jun 56	253UNTS155	103582
Dominican Republic	USA (United States)	15 Jun 56	265UNTS227	103815
France	USA (United States)	19 Jun 56	281UNTS341	104087
Switzerland	USA (United States)	21 Jun 56	279UNTS41	104033
Australia	USA (United States)	22 Jun 56	283UNTS275	104123
Cuba	USA (United States)	26 Jun 56	293UNTS257	104294
Germany, West	UK Great Britain	31 Jul 56	252UNTS93	103559
Guatemala	USA (United States)	15 Aug 56	288UNTS181	104205
Multilateral		26 Oct 56	276UNTS3	103988
Iran	USA (United States)	05 Mar 57	342UNTS29	104898
Ecuador	USA (United States)	31 May 57	304UNTS61	104391
Nicaragua	USA (United States)	11 Jun 57	304UNTS267	104402
Germany, West	USA (United States)	28 Jun 57	288UNTS339	104213
Germany, West	USA (United States)	03 Jul 57	288UNTS305	104212
Italy	USA (United States)	03 Jul 57	308UNTS195	104462
South Africa	USA (United States)	08 Jul 57	290UNTS147	104234
Spain	USA (United States)	16 Aug 57	307UNTS169	104449
Italy	UK Great Britain	28 Dec 57	305UNTS357	104425
Japan	USA (United States)	19 Jun 58	325UNTS143	104699
USA (United States)	Venezuela	08 Oct 58	371UNTS69	105271
Euratom	USA (United States)	08 Nov 58	338UNTS135	104835
Euratom	UK Great Britain	04 Feb 59	331UNTS125	104752
USA (United States)	Vietnam, South	22 Apr 59	347UNTS113	104993
Greece	USA (United States)	06 May 59	357UNTS163	105115
Netherlands	USA (United States)	06 May 59	355UNTS327	105084
Canada	USA (United States)	22 May 59	354UNTS63	105054
Panama	USA (United States)	24 Jun 59	479UNTS145	106950
Austria	USA (United States)	22 Jul 59	368UNTS199	105242
Australia	Canada	04 Aug 59	391UNTS191	105623
Peru	USA (United States)	22 Aug 59	357UNTS99	105109
Lebanon	USA (United States)	16 Sep 59	358UNTS175	105135
Taiwan	USA (United States)	02 Dec 59	361UNTS115	105175
Colombia	USA (United States)	11 Jan 60	371UNTS37	105268
Chile	USA (United States)	19 Feb 60	371UNTS255	105282
Brazil	USA (United States)	27 Feb 60	384UNTS131	105515
New Zealand	USA (United States)	23 Mar 60	371UNTS147	105276
Ireland	USA (United States)	24 Mar 60	371UNTS237	105280
Guatemala	USA (United States)	23 Apr 60	373UNTS23	105312
Argentina	USA (United States)	23 May 60	377UNTS3	105392
Indonesia	USA (United States)	08 Jun 60	388UNTS287	105585
Korea, South	USA (United States)	18 Nov 60	400UNTS49	105747
Italy	USA (United States)	03 Dec 60	410UNTS3	105893
Israel	USA (United States)	19 Dec 60	401UNTS195	105772
USA (United States)	Yugoslavia	19 Apr 61	409UNTS163	105883
France	USA (United States)	27 Jul 61	433UNTS29	106229
Colombia	USA (United States)	09 Apr 62	476UNTS9	106899
Belgium	USA (United States)	17 May 62	461UNTS3	106647
Argentina	USA (United States)	22 Jun 62	458UNTS97	106594
India	USA (United States)	08 Aug 63	488UNTS21	107117
Canada	India	16 Dec 63	529UNTS45	107655
Multilateral		28 Feb 64	501UNTS245	107321
Multilateral		15 Jun 64	573UNTS85	108324

PARTY ONE	PARTY TWO	DATE	CITATION	NUMBER
Non-nuclear materials (Cont.)				
Multilateral		28 Jul 64	555UNTS183	108113
Multilateral		18 Sep 64	555UNTS205	108114
Multilateral		18 Sep 64	556UNTS25	108117
Multilateral		21 Sep 64	555UNTS227	108115
Multilateral		30 Sep 64	556UNTS3	108116
Multilateral		02 Dec 64	572UNTS229	108317
Switzerland	USA (United States)	30 Jan 65	594UNTS55	108594
Multilateral		24 Feb 65	556UNTS47	108118
Multilateral		26 Feb 65	556UNTS69	108119
Multilateral		18 Jun 65	573UNTS3	108320
Brazil	USA (United States)	08 Jul 65	0UNTS0	109603
Multilateral		24 Sep 65	556UNTS141	108124
Morocco	IAEA (Atom Energy)	24 Sep 65	556UNTS109	108122
Afghanistan	IAEA (Atom Energy)	24 Sep 65	556UNTS101	108121
Pakistan	IAEA (Atom Energy)	15 Mar 66	588UNTS261	108530
Romania	IAEA (Atom Energy)	22 Apr 66	603UNTS23	108721
Multilateral		20 Jun 66	572UNTS263	108318
Multilateral		20 Jun 66	573UNTS41	108322
Multilateral		08 Jul 66	572UNTS283	108319
Sweden	USA (United States)	28 Jul 66	603UNTS61	108725
IAEA (Atom Energy)	USA (United States)	09 Dec 66	589UNTS55	108535
Mexico	IAEA (Atom Energy)	18 Aug 67	614UNTS123	108867
Ivory Coast	IBRD (World Bank)	21 Jun 68	0UNTS0	109412
Research facilities				
Portugal	UK Great Britain	18 Jul 58	313UNTS109	104532
Peaceful use				
Multilateral		15 Nov 45	3UNTS123	100026
Belgium	Netherlands	24 May 46	31UNTS169	100477
Multilateral		15 Feb 52	132UNTS51	101751
Multilateral		01 Jul 53	200UNTS149	102701
UK Great Britain	USA (United States)	15 Jun 55	229UNTS73	103161
Belgium	USA (United States)	15 Jun 55	235UNTS133	103299
Switzerland	USA (United States)	18 Jul 55	239UNTS311	103388
Belgium	UK Great Britain	18 Nov 55	222UNTS327	103038
Netherlands	USA (United States)	22 Jan 56	287UNTS121	104181
Ireland	USA (United States)	16 Mar 56	317UNTS195	104604
Austria	USA (United States)	08 Jun 56	253UNTS139	103581
New Zealand	USA (United States)	13 Jun 56	253UNTS155	103582
Dominican Republic	USA (United States)	15 Jun 56	265UNTS227	103815
France	USA (United States)	19 Jun 56	281UNTS341	104087
Switzerland	USA (United States)	21 Jun 56	279UNTS41	104033
Australia	USA (United States)	22 Jun 56	283UNTS275	104123
Germany, West	UK Great Britain	31 Jul 56	252UNTS93	103559
Multilateral		26 Oct 56	276UNTS3	103988
Norway	USA (United States)	25 Feb 57	284UNTS19	104126
Ecuador	USA (United States)	31 May 57	304UNTS61	104391
Nicaragua	USA (United States)	11 Jun 57	304UNTS267	104402
Germany, West	USA (United States)	28 Jun 57	288UNTS339	104213
Italy	USA (United States)	03 Jul 57	308UNTS195	104462
Germany, West	USA (United States)	03 Jul 57	288UNTS305	104212
South Africa	USA (United States)	08 Jul 57	290UNTS147	104234
Norway	UK Great Britain	12 Jul 57	310UNTS41	104485
Spain	USA (United States)	16 Aug 57	307UNTS169	104449
Sweden	UK Great Britain	20 Sep 57	310UNTS49	104486
Italy	UK Great Britain	28 Dec 57	305UNTS357	104425
Euratom	USA (United States)	29 May 58	335UNTS161	104783
Japan	UK Great Britain	16 Jun 58	325UNTS185	104700
Japan	USA (United States)	19 Jun 58	325UNTS143	104699
USA (United States)	Venezuela	08 Oct 58	371UNTS69	105271
Euratom	USA (United States)	08 Nov 58	338UNTS135	104835
Euratom	UK Great Britain	04 Feb 59	331UNTS125	104752
Japan	IAEA (Atom Energy)	24 Mar 59	339UNTS327	104852
IAEA (Atom Energy)	USSR (Soviet Union)	11 May 59	339UNTS341	104853
IAEA (Atom Energy)	USA (United States)	11 May 59	339UNTS359	104855

PARTY ONE	PARTY TWO	DATE	CITATION	NUMBER
Peaceful use (Cont.)				
Canada	Pakistan	14 May 59	426UNTS129	106133
Panama	USA (United States)	24 Jun 59	479UNTS145	106950
Canada	Japan	02 Jul 59	383UNTS243	105504
Austria	USA (United States)	22 Jul 59	368UNTS199	105242
Australia	Canada	04 Aug 59	391UNTS191	105623
Peru	USA (United States)	22 Aug 59	357UNTS99	105109
Lebanon	USA (United States)	16 Sep 59	358UNTS175	105135
Italy	IBRD (World Bank)	16 Sep 59	375UNTS159	105366
Canada	Euratom	06 Oct 59	475UNTS187	106894
USA (United States)	USSR (Soviet Union)	21 Nov 59	361UNTS35	105172
Taiwan	USA (United States)	02 Dec 59	361UNTS115	105175
Colombia	USA (United States)	11 Jan 60	371UNTS37	105268
Spain	UK Great Britain	19 Jan 60	404UNTS41	105804
Chile	USA (United States)	19 Feb 60	371UNTS255	105282
Brazil	USA (United States)	27 Feb 60	384UNTS131	105515
Indonesia	USSR (Soviet Union)	28 Feb 60	392UNTS173	105643
New Zealand	USA (United States)	23 Mar 60	371UNTS147	105276
Ireland	USA (United States)	24 Mar 60	371UNTS237	105280
Denmark	UK Great Britain	20 May 60	374UNTS245	105338
Argentina	USA (United States)	23 May 60	377UNTS3	105392
Indonesia	USA (United States)	08 Jun 60	388UNTS287	105585
India	USA (United States)	13 Jun 60	377UNTS37	105394
Korea, South	USA (United States)	18 Nov 60	400UNTS49	105747
Israel	USA (United States)	19 Dec 60	401UNTS195	105772
Finland	IAEA (Atom Energy)	30 Dec 60	395UNTS257	105690
Brazil	USA (United States)	17 Mar 61	406UNTS241	105853
Norway	IAEA (Atom Energy)	10 Apr 61	402UNTS255	105790
USA (United States)	Yugoslavia	19 Apr 61	409UNTS163	105883
Multilateral		04 Oct 61	412UNTS210	105934
Multilateral		05 Mar 62	425UNTS3	106114
Colombia	USA (United States)	09 Apr 62	476UNTS9	106899
Greece	USA (United States)	24 Apr 62	459UNTS3	106609
Argentina	USA (United States)	22 Jun 62	458UNTS97	106594
Multilateral		27 Jun 62	463UNTS17	106690
Australia	Japan	07 Aug 62	435UNTS261	106283
Denmark	USSR (Soviet Union)	11 Sep 62	458UNTS3	106589
Canada	Sweden	11 Sep 62	529UNTS9	107651
Germany, West	USA (United States)	29 Nov 62	460UNTS169	106639
Israel	Philippines	10 Jan 63	588UNTS205	108526
Norway	USA (United States)	01 Mar 63	524UNTS185	107573
IAEA (Atom Energy)	Yugoslavia	04 Mar 63	490UNTS333	107162
Brazil	USA (United States)	29 Mar 63	476UNTS67	106904
Belgium	USA (United States)	19 Apr 63	493UNTS83	107209
IAEA (Atom Energy)	Yugoslavia	04 Jun 63	490UNTS343	107163
Austria	IAEA (Atom Energy)	21 Jun 63	490UNTS351	107164
Finland	IAEA (Atom Energy)	02 Jul 63	490UNTS403	107167
Finland	IAEA (Atom Energy)	30 Jul 63	490UNTS413	107168
Multilateral		05 Aug 63	480UNTS43	106964
India	USA (United States)	08 Aug 63	488UNTS21	107117
Multilateral		23 Sep 63	488UNTS99	107122
Multilateral		17 Oct 63	525UNTS75	107585
Argentina	USA (United States)	30 Nov 63	505UNTS131	107369
Canada	India	16 Dec 63	529UNTS45	107655
Finland	IAEA (Atom Energy)	27 Jan 64	501UNTS213	107319
Multilateral		28 Feb 64	501UNTS245	107321
Multilateral		08 Apr 64	501UNTS221	107320
Multilateral		11 Jun 64	525UNTS61	107584
IAEA (Atom Energy)	USA (United States)	15 Jun 64	525UNTS3	107580
Multilateral		15 Jun 64	573UNTS85	108324
Denmark	USA (United States)	02 Jul 64	529UNTS277	107665
Sweden	USA (United States)	06 Jul 64	529UNTS287	107666
Spain	USA (United States)	16 Jul 64	529UNTS187	107661
Multilateral		28 Jul 64	555UNTS183	108113
Switzerland	UK Great Britain	11 Aug 64	552UNTS271	108059
IAEA (Atom Energy)	United Arab Rep	17 Sep 64	525UNTS19	107581

PARTY ONE	PARTY TWO	DATE	CITATION	NUMBER
Peaceful use (Cont.)				
Multilateral		18 Sep 64	556UNTS25	108117
Multilateral		18 Sep 64	555UNTS205	108114
Multilateral		21 Sep 64	555UNTS227	108115
Multilateral		30 Sep 64	556UNTS3	108116
Pakistan	UK Great Britain	13 Oct 64	534UNTS71	107754
USA (United States)	USSR (Soviet Union)	18 Nov 64	535UNTS307	107786
Italy	USA (United States)	23 Nov 64	532UNTS133	107716
Argentina	IAEA (Atom Energy)	02 Dec 64	525UNTS29	107582
Multilateral		02 Dec 64	572UNTS229	108317
State/IGO Group	IAEA (Atom Energy)	04 Dec 64	637UNTS0	109111
IAEA (Atom Energy)	United Arab Rep	14 Jan 65	603UNTS45	108723
Switzerland	USA (United States)	30 Jan 65	594UNTS55	108594
Multilateral		24 Feb 65	556UNTS47	108118
Multilateral		26 Feb 65	556UNTS69	108119
Multilateral		18 Jun 65	573UNTS3	108320
Multilateral		23 Jun 65	548UNTS241	107981
Brazil	USA (United States)	08 Jul 65	0UNTS0	109603
IAEA (Atom Energy)	Uruguay	24 Sep 65	556UNTS117	108123
Afghanistan	IAEA (Atom Energy)	24 Sep 65	556UNTS101	108121
Morocco	IAEA (Atom Energy)	24 Sep 65	556UNTS109	108122
IAEA (Atom Energy)	Turkey	08 Feb 66	573UNTS75	108323
Pakistan	IAEA (Atom Energy)	15 Mar 66	588UNTS261	108530
UK Great Britain	USA (United States)	02 Jun 66	573UNTS229	108336
Multilateral		20 Jun 66	572UNTS263	108318
Sweden	USA (United States)	28 Jul 66	603UNTS61	108725
IAEA (Atom Energy)	USA (United States)	26 Sep 66	589UNTS3	108532
IAEA (Atom Energy)	Turkey	08 Dec 66	608UNTS69	108813
IAEA (Atom Energy)	USA (United States)	09 Dec 66	589UNTS55	108535
India	IAEA (Atom Energy)	09 Dec 66	603UNTS35	108722
Multilateral		14 Feb 67	634UNTS281	109068
Israel	Philippines	20 Feb 67	597UNTS139	108642
Bulgaria	USSR (Soviet Union)	27 Apr 67	631UNTS3	108983
State/IGO Group	IAEA (Atom Energy)	19 Jun 67	637UNTS0	109112
Multilateral		26 Sep 67	633UNTS73	109035
State/IGO Group	IAEA (Atom Energy)	05 Jan 68	637UNTS0	109114
State/IGO Group	IAEA (Atom Energy)	28 Feb 68	637UNTS0	109115
Israel	Philippines	14 Jan 69	0UNTS0	109437
IAEA (Atom Energy)	OAU (Afri Unity)	26 Mar 69	0UNTS0	200646
Rights of supplier				
Turkey	USA (United States)	10 Jun 55	238UNTS149	103359
Canada	USA (United States)	15 Jun 55	235UNTS176	103301
UK Great Britain	USA (United States)	15 Jun 55	229UNTS73	103161
Belgium	USA (United States)	15 Jun 55	235UNTS133	103299
UK Great Britain	USA (United States)	15 Jun 55	214UNTS301	102905
Multilateral		22 Jun 55	249UNTS3	103498
Israel	USA (United States)	12 Jul 55	219UNTS185	102974
Taiwan	USA (United States)	18 Jul 55	235UNTS221	103304
Lebanon	USA (United States)	18 Jul 55	239UNTS247	103383
Netherlands	USA (United States)	18 Jul 55	240UNTS347	103412
Colombia	USA (United States)	19 Jul 55	235UNTS233	103305
Spain	USA (United States)	19 Jul 55	239UNTS299	103387
Portugal	USA (United States)	21 Jul 55	239UNTS283	103386
USA (United States)	Venezuela	21 Jul 55	238UNTS121	103357
Denmark	USA (United States)	25 Jul 55	235UNTS245	103306
Philippines	USA (United States)	27 Jul 55	239UNTS271	103385
Italy	USA (United States)	28 Jul 55	239UNTS235	103382
Argentina	USA (United States)	29 Jul 55	235UNTS121	103298
Brazil	USA (United States)	03 Aug 55	270UNTS71	103893
Brazil	USA (United States)	03 Aug 55	235UNTS159	103300
Greece	USA (United States)	04 Aug 55	235UNTS257	103307
Chile	USA (United States)	08 Aug 55	235UNTS209	103303
Pakistan	USA (United States)	11 Aug 55	239UNTS259	103384
Japan	USA (United States)	14 Nov 55	240UNTS361	103413
Belgium	UK Great Britain	18 Nov 55	222UNTS327	103038

PARTY ONE	PARTY TWO	DATE	CITATION	NUMBER
Rights of supplier (Cont.)				
USA (United States)	Uruguay	13 Jan 56	240UNTS401	103415
Sweden	USA (United States)	18 Jan 56	240UNTS413	103416
Peru	USA (United States)	25 Jan 56	240UNTS425	103417
Korea, South	USA (United States)	03 Feb 56	240UNTS129	103401
Germany, West	USA (United States)	13 Feb 56	253UNTS119	103580
Thailand	USA (United States)	13 Mar 56	253UNTS105	103579
Austria	USA (United States)	08 Jun 56	253UNTS139	103581
New Zealand	USA (United States)	13 Jun 56	253UNTS155	103582
Dominican Republic	USA (United States)	15 Jun 56	265UNTS227	103815
France	USA (United States)	19 Jun 56	281UNTS341	104087
Switzerland	USA (United States)	21 Jun 56	279UNTS41	104033
Multilateral		26 Oct 56	276UNTS3	103988
Canada	USA (United States)	22 May 59	354UNTS63	105054
Panama	USA (United States)	24 Jun 59	479UNTS145	106950
Canada	Euratom	06 Oct 59	475UNTS187	106894
Netherlands	Euratom	25 Jul 61	462UNTS263	106686
Multilateral		04 Oct 61	412UNTS210	105934
IAEA (Atom Energy)	Yugoslavia	04 Oct 61	412UNTS226	105935
India	United Nations	19 Feb 62	423UNTS3	106082
Colombia	USA (United States)	09 Apr 62	476UNTS9	106899
Argentina	USA (United States)	22 Jun 62	458UNTS97	106594
India	USA (United States)	08 Aug 63	488UNTS21	107117
Multilateral		23 Sep 63	488UNTS99	107122
Multilateral		08 Apr 64	501UNTS221	107320
Brazil	USA (United States)	08 Jul 65	0UNTS0	109603
Israel	Philippines	14 Jan 69	0UNTS0	109437
Samples and testing				
Multilateral		26 Oct 56	276UNTS3	103988
Canada	IAEA (Atom Energy)	24 Mar 59	339UNTS315	104851
Japan	IAEA (Atom Energy)	24 Mar 59	339UNTS327	104852
Panama	USA (United States)	24 Jun 59	479UNTS145	106950
Multilateral		04 Oct 61	412UNTS210	105934
Pakistan	IAEA (Atom Energy)	05 Mar 62	425UNTS17	106115
Multilateral		05 Mar 62	425UNTS3	106114
Colombia	USA (United States)	09 Apr 62	476UNTS9	106899
Multilateral		05 Aug 63	480UNTS43	106964
India	USA (United States)	08 Aug 63	488UNTS21	107117
Multilateral		23 Sep 63	488UNTS99	107122
Finland	IAEA (Atom Energy)	27 Jan 64	501UNTS213	107319
Multilateral		08 Apr 64	501UNTS221	107320
UK Great Britain	USA (United States)	19 Jun 64	530UNTS99	107675
World Bank projects				
Ethiopia	USA (United States)	02 May 51	139UNTS85	101877
Austria	USSR (Soviet Union)	17 Oct 55	0UNTS0	109254
IBRD (World Bank)	Switzerland	17 Sep 56	340UNTS311	200560
Denmark	IBRD (World Bank)	04 Feb 59	328UNTS143	104733
India	IBRD (World Bank)	29 Jul 60	377UNTS153	105399
Multilateral		28 Aug 61	416UNTS45	105994
Chile	IBRD (World Bank)	18 Dec 63	504UNTS29	107352
Belgium	Congo (Zaire)	06 Feb 65	540UNTS227	107852
Jamaica	IBRD (World Bank)	08 Apr 65	539UNTS303	107841
India	IBRD (World Bank)	28 May 65	552UNTS39	108049
Peru	IBRD (World Bank)	17 Sep 65	566UNTS311	108248
IBRD (World Bank)	IFC (Finance Corp)	28 Oct 66	586UNTS225	200628
Greece	IBRD (World Bank)	18 Mar 68	0UNTS0	109326
Malaysia	IBRD (World Bank)	17 Apr 68	0UNTS0	109360
State/IGO Group	IBRD (World Bank)	02 May 68	637UNTS0	109110
Iran	IBRD (World Bank)	05 Jun 68	0UNTS0	109373
IBRD (World Bank)	Singapore	03 Jul 68	0UNTS0	109364
Gabon	IBRD (World Bank)	07 Jul 68	0UNTS0	109361
Colombia	IBRD (World Bank)	31 Jul 68	0UNTS0	109512
Malaysia	IBRD (World Bank)	27 Sep 68	0UNTS0	109506
Malaysia	IBRD (World Bank)	27 Sep 68	0UNTS0	109505

PARTY ONE	PARTY TWO	DATE	CITATION	NUMBER
Loan regulations				
France	IBRD (World Bank)	09 May 47	152UNTS111	102014
Netherlands	IBRD (World Bank)	07 Aug 47	152UNTS165	102015
Denmark	IBRD (World Bank)	22 Aug 47	152UNTS223	102016
Luxembourg	IBRD (World Bank)	28 Aug 47	153UNTS3	102017
Netherlands	IBRD (World Bank)	15 Jul 48	153UNTS259	102025
Netherlands	IBRD (World Bank)	15 Jul 48	153UNTS259	102022
Netherlands	IBRD (World Bank)	15 Jul 48	153UNTS259	102023
Netherlands	IBRD (World Bank)	15 Jul 48	153UNTS259	102024
Netherlands	IBRD (World Bank)	15 Jul 48	153UNTS259	102021
Mexico	IBRD (World Bank)	06 Jan 49	154UNTS81	102028
Mexico	IBRD (World Bank)	06 Jan 49	154UNTS3	102027
Brazil	IBRD (World Bank)	27 Jan 49	153UNTS264	102026
Belgium	IBRD (World Bank)	01 Mar 49	154UNTS133	102029
Chile	IBRD (World Bank)	23 Mar 49	153UNTS61	102018
Chile	IBRD (World Bank)	23 Mar 49	153UNTS141	102019
Netherlands	IBRD (World Bank)	26 Jul 49	154UNTS178	102030
Finland	IBRD (World Bank)	01 Aug 49	156UNTS289	200480
India	IBRD (World Bank)	18 Aug 49	154UNTS269	102031
Colombia	IBRD (World Bank)	19 Aug 49	154UNTS329	102032
IBRD (World Bank)	Yugoslavia	17 Sep 49	155UNTS3	102034
Finland	IBRD (World Bank)	17 Oct 49	156UNTS355	200481
El Salvador	IBRD (World Bank)	14 Dec 49	155UNTS43	102035
India	IBRD (World Bank)	18 Apr 50	155UNTS117	102036
Mexico	IBRD (World Bank)	28 Apr 50	155UNTS185	102037
Brazil	IBRD (World Bank)	26 May 50	301UNTS165	104345
Iraq	IBRD (World Bank)	15 Jun 50	155UNTS267	102038
IBRD (World Bank)	Turkey	07 Jul 50	156UNTS75	102040
IBRD (World Bank)	Turkey	07 Jul 50	156UNTS3	102039
IBRD (World Bank)	Uruguay	25 Aug 50	156UNTS203	102042
Ethiopia	IBRD (World Bank)	13 Sep 50	157UNTS233	102056
Ethiopia	IBRD (World Bank)	13 Sep 50	157UNTS213	102055
Mexico	IBRD (World Bank)	18 Oct 50	157UNTS259	102057
IBRD (World Bank)	Turkey	19 Oct 50	157UNTS333	102058
IBRD (World Bank)	Thailand	27 Oct 50	158UNTS3	102059
IBRD (World Bank)	Thailand	27 Oct 50	158UNTS43	102061
IBRD (World Bank)	Thailand	27 Oct 50	158UNTS25	102060
Australia	IBRD (World Bank)	14 Nov 50	156UNTS147	102041
Colombia	IBRD (World Bank)	28 Dec 50	158UNTS87	102063
IBRD (World Bank)	South Africa	23 Jan 51	158UNTS135	102065
IBRD (World Bank)	South Africa	23 Jan 51	158UNTS115	102064
Ethiopia	IBRD (World Bank)	19 Feb 51	186UNTS101	102486
Colombia	IBRD (World Bank)	10 Apr 51	158UNTS155	102066
Nicaragua	IBRD (World Bank)	07 Jun 51	158UNTS215	102067
Nicaragua	IBRD (World Bank)	07 Jun 51	158UNTS277	102068
Iceland	IBRD (World Bank)	20 Jun 51	158UNTS301	102069
Belgium	IBRD (World Bank)	13 Sep 51	158UNTS349	102071
Belgium	IBRD (World Bank)	13 Sep 51	158UNTS323	102070
Chile	IBRD (World Bank)	10 Oct 51	158UNTS369	102072
Italy	IBRD (World Bank)	10 Oct 51	159UNTS383	200482
Colombia	IBRD (World Bank)	13 Oct 51	159UNTS75	102084
Nicaragua	IBRD (World Bank)	29 Oct 51	159UNTS35	102082
Iceland	IBRD (World Bank)	01 Nov 51	159UNTS55	102083
Paraguay	IBRD (World Bank)	07 Dec 51	159UNTS103	102085
Mexico	IBRD (World Bank)	11 Jan 52	159UNTS129	102086
Peru	IBRD (World Bank)	23 Jan 52	159UNTS163	102087
IBRD (World Bank)	UK Great Britain	27 Feb 52	159UNTS181	102088
Netherlands	IBRD (World Bank)	20 Mar 52	159UNTS207	102089
Pakistan	IBRD (World Bank)	27 Mar 52	159UNTS251	102090
Finland	IBRD (World Bank)	30 Apr 52	159UNTS408	200483
Pakistan	IBRD (World Bank)	13 Jun 52	191UNTS85	102578
IBRD (World Bank)	Turkey	18 Jun 52	159UNTS269	102091
Brazil	IBRD (World Bank)	27 Jun 52	190UNTS85	102560
Brazil	IBRD (World Bank)	27 Jun 52	190UNTS115	102561
Peru	IBRD (World Bank)	08 Jul 52	159UNTS321	102093

PARTY ONE	PARTY TWO	DATE	CITATION	NUMBER
Loan regulations (Cont.)				
Australia	IBRD (World Bank)	08 Jul 52	159UNTS295	102092
Iceland	IBRD (World Bank)	26 Aug 52	159UNTS363	102095
Colombia	IBRD (World Bank)	26 Aug 52	159UNTS339	102094
Japan	IBRD (World Bank)	12 Nov 52	354UNTS313	105068
India	IBRD (World Bank)	18 Dec 52	201UNTS241	102719
India	IBRD (World Bank)	23 Jan 53	201UNTS145	102715
IBRD (World Bank)	Yugoslavia	11 Feb 53	165UNTS231	102179
IBRD (World Bank)	UK Great Britain	11 Mar 53	172UNTS115	102243
Brazil	IBRD (World Bank)	30 Apr 53	190UNTS133	102562
Brazil	IBRD (World Bank)	17 Jul 53	190UNTS149	102563
IBRD (World Bank)	South Africa	28 Aug 53	180UNTS73	102376
IBRD (World Bank)	South Africa	28 Aug 53	180UNTS91	102377
Nicaragua	IBRD (World Bank)	04 Sep 53	186UNTS137	102488
Iceland	IBRD (World Bank)	04 Sep 53	178UNTS275	102344
Nicaragua	IBRD (World Bank)	04 Sep 53	186UNTS117	102487
Iceland	IBRD (World Bank)	04 Sep 53	188UNTS3	102519
IBRD (World Bank)	Turkey	10 Sep 53	187UNTS71	102502
Colombia	IBRD (World Bank)	10 Sep 53	203UNTS3	102738
Chile	IBRD (World Bank)	10 Sep 53	188UNTS25	102520
Panama	IBRD (World Bank)	25 Sep 53	188UNTS71	102521
Panama	IBRD (World Bank)	25 Sep 53	188UNTS95	102522
Italy	IBRD (World Bank)	06 Oct 53	301UNTS135	104344
Japan	IBRD (World Bank)	15 Oct 53	187UNTS271	200511
Japan	IBRD (World Bank)	15 Oct 53	187UNTS367	200513
Japan	IBRD (World Bank)	15 Oct 53	187UNTS321	200512
Brazil	IBRD (World Bank)	18 Dec 53	301UNTS229	104346
Brazil	IBRD (World Bank)	18 Dec 53	190UNTS179	102564
Brazil	IBRD (World Bank)	24 Feb 54	301UNTS249	104347
Australia	IBRD (World Bank)	02 Mar 54	191UNTS103	102579
Norway	IBRD (World Bank)	08 Apr 54	201UNTS131	102714
Peru	IBRD (World Bank)	12 Apr 54	190UNTS231	102567
Pakistan	IBRD (World Bank)	02 Jun 54	324UNTS59	104678
France	IBRD (World Bank)	10 Jun 54	210UNTS89	102836
Ceylon (Sri Lanka)	IBRD (World Bank)	09 Jul 54	198UNTS313	200517
Mexico	IBRD (World Bank)	24 Aug 54	286UNTS211	104168
Multilateral		02 Oct 54	201UNTS171	102716
Multilateral		02 Oct 54	201UNTS179	102717
El Salvador	IBRD (World Bank)	12 Oct 54	203UNTS37	102739
Austria	IBRD (World Bank)	08 Nov 54	216UNTS305	200528
Peru	IBRD (World Bank)	12 Nov 54	209UNTS287	102831
India	IBRD (World Bank)	19 Nov 54	309UNTS159	104473
Belgium	IBRD (World Bank)	14 Dec 54	210UNTS113	102837
Colombia	IBRD (World Bank)	29 Dec 54	211UNTS135	102851
India	IBRD (World Bank)	14 Mar 55	309UNTS129	104472
IBRD (World Bank)	UK Great Britain	15 Mar 55	265UNTS85	103808
Australia	IBRD (World Bank)	18 Mar 55	220UNTS131	102998
Colombia	IBRD (World Bank)	24 Mar 55	212UNTS217	102874
Finland	IBRD (World Bank)	24 Mar 55	211UNTS305	200525
Peru	IBRD (World Bank)	05 Apr 55	211UNTS115	102850
Norway	IBRD (World Bank)	19 Apr 55	211UNTS159	102852
Peru	IBRD (World Bank)	19 Apr 55	221UNTS153	103007
Italy	IBRD (World Bank)	01 Jun 55	358UNTS203	105137
Austria	IBRD (World Bank)	14 Jun 55	221UNTS375	200531
Colombia	IBRD (World Bank)	15 Jun 55	248UNTS161	103494
Pakistan	IBRD (World Bank)	20 Jun 55	230UNTS41	103176
Nicaragua	IBRD (World Bank)	08 Jul 55	229UNTS97	103162
Panama	IBRD (World Bank)	12 Jul 55	219UNTS127	102970
Guatemala	IBRD (World Bank)	29 Jul 55	229UNTS167	103165
Pakistan	IBRD (World Bank)	04 Aug 55	230UNTS79	103177
Peru	IBRD (World Bank)	05 Aug 55	218UNTS3	102950
Pakistan	IBRD (World Bank)	06 Aug 55	236UNTS195	103325
IBRD (World Bank)	Thailand	09 Aug 55	221UNTS283	103011
Lebanon	IBRD (World Bank)	25 Aug 55	230UNTS233	103188
France	IBRD (World Bank)	26 Aug 55	247UNTS305	103478
Nicaragua	IBRD (World Bank)	26 Aug 55	229UNTS145	103164

PARTY ONE	PARTY TWO	DATE	CITATION	NUMBER
Loan regulations (Cont.)				
IBRD (World Bank)	Uruguay	29 Aug 55	243UNTS123	103450
Austria	USSR (Soviet Union)	17 Oct 55	0UNTS0	109254
Japan	IBRD (World Bank)	25 Oct 55	230UNTS379	200534
IBRD (World Bank)	South Africa	28 Nov 55	230UNTS101	103178
Honduras	IBRD (World Bank)	22 Dec 55	230UNTS262	103189
Japan	IBRD (World Bank)	21 Feb 56	248UNTS321	200543
Ecuador	IBRD (World Bank)	26 Mar 56	292UNTS391	104277
Norway	IBRD (World Bank)	03 May 56	243UNTS281	103455
Burma	IBRD (World Bank)	04 May 56	253UNTS179	103584
Burma	IBRD (World Bank)	04 May 56	253UNTS209	103585
Haiti	IBRD (World Bank)	07 May 56	252UNTS279	103570
Finland	IBRD (World Bank)	22 May 56	248UNTS57	103485
Nicaragua	IBRD (World Bank)	22 May 56	253UNTS233	103586
Colombia	IBRD (World Bank)	06 Jun 56	248UNTS139	103493
IBRD (World Bank)	UK Great Britain	21 Jun 56	285UNTS355	104157
Fed Rhod/Nyasaland	IBRD (World Bank)	21 Jun 56	285UNTS317	104156
India	IBRD (World Bank)	26 Jun 56	301UNTS3	104341
Costa Rica	IBRD (World Bank)	18 Sep 56	260UNTS369	103721
Austria	IBRD (World Bank)	21 Sep 56	259UNTS43	103682
Austria	IBRD (World Bank)	21 Sep 56	259UNTS17	103681
Italy	IBRD (World Bank)	11 Oct 56	359UNTS3	105138
IBRD (World Bank)	Thailand	12 Oct 56	261UNTS117	103728
IBRD (World Bank)	Uruguay	25 Oct 56	265UNTS59	103807
Chile	IBRD (World Bank)	01 Nov 56	261UNTS27	103724
Australia	IBRD (World Bank)	15 Nov 56	288UNTS117	104201
Australia	IBRD (World Bank)	03 Dec 56	288UNTS99	104200
India	IBRD (World Bank)	19 Dec 56	310UNTS75	104489
Japan	IBRD (World Bank)	19 Dec 56	264UNTS179	103793
Japan	IBRD (World Bank)	19 Dec 56	268UNTS203	103859
Iran	IBRD (World Bank)	22 Jan 57	317UNTS129	104600
Ethiopia	IBRD (World Bank)	28 Jan 57	286UNTS307	104175
India	IBRD (World Bank)	05 Mar 57	272UNTS201	103939
Peru	IBRD (World Bank)	13 Mar 57	274UNTS59	103958
Netherlands	IBRD (World Bank)	15 May 57	274UNTS211	103967
India	IBRD (World Bank)	29 May 57	309UNTS201	104474
Belgium	IBRD (World Bank)	26 Jun 57	322UNTS301	104661
India	IBRD (World Bank)	12 Jul 57	288UNTS135	104202
Chile	IBRD (World Bank)	24 Jul 57	282UNTS189	104099
Chile	IBRD (World Bank)	24 Jul 57	282UNTS139	104098
Japan	IBRD (World Bank)	09 Aug 57	293UNTS59	104286
Belgium	IBRD (World Bank)	10 Sep 57	286UNTS291	104174
IBRD (World Bank)	Thailand	12 Sep 57	299UNTS349	104324
Ecuador	IBRD (World Bank)	20 Sep 57	293UNTS135	104291
Ecuador	IBRD (World Bank)	20 Sep 57	289UNTS237	104221
IBRD (World Bank)	South Africa	01 Oct 57	280UNTS285	104065
Austria	IBRD (World Bank)	10 Oct 57	301UNTS95	104343
Pakistan	IBRD (World Bank)	18 Oct 57	299UNTS303	104322
India	IBRD (World Bank)	20 Nov 57	301UNTS47	104342
Philippines	IBRD (World Bank)	22 Nov 57	293UNTS83	104287
Belgium	IBRD (World Bank)	27 Nov 57	292UNTS175	104273
Pakistan	IBRD (World Bank)	17 Dec 57	299UNTS321	104323
Mexico	IBRD (World Bank)	14 Jan 58	293UNTS167	104292
Brazil	IBRD (World Bank)	22 Jan 58	323UNTS99	104666
Pakistan	IBRD (World Bank)	23 Apr 58	323UNTS253	104672
Chile	IBRD (World Bank)	28 Apr 58	359UNTS89	105140
Austria	IBRD (World Bank)	28 Apr 58	359UNTS145	105142
IBRD (World Bank)	UK Great Britain	02 May 58	324UNTS25	104677
Mexico	IBRD (World Bank)	05 May 58	309UNTS3	104466
Honduras	IBRD (World Bank)	09 May 58	323UNTS4	104662
Japan	IBRD (World Bank)	13 Jun 58	312UNTS159	104518
IBRD (World Bank)	UK Great Britain	16 Jun 58	309UNTS35	104467
India	IBRD (World Bank)	25 Jun 58	323UNTS131	104667
India	IBRD (World Bank)	25 Jun 58	323UNTS157	104668
IBRD (World Bank)	Sudan	21 Jul 58	323UNTS183	104669
India	IBRD (World Bank)	23 Jul 58	317UNTS3	104590

PARTY ONE	PARTY TWO	DATE	CITATION	NUMBER
Loan regulations (Cont.)				
Japan	IBRD (World Bank)	18 Aug 58	323UNTS205	104670
Japan	IBRD (World Bank)	10 Sep 58	323UNTS297	104673
Japan	IBRD (World Bank)	10 Sep 58	318UNTS133	104612
India	IBRD (World Bank)	16 Sep 58	323UNTS235	104671
Peru	IBRD (World Bank)	17 Sep 58	323UNTS27	104663
Ceylon (Sri Lanka)	IBRD (World Bank)	17 Sep 58	323UNTS51	104664
Fed of Malaya	IBRD (World Bank)	22 Sep 58	323UNTS71	104665
Brazil	IBRD (World Bank)	03 Oct 58	337UNTS177	104823
Ecuador	IBRD (World Bank)	09 Oct 58	337UNTS299	104827
Austria	IBRD (World Bank)	02 Dec 58	340UNTS3	104856
IBRD (World Bank)	South Africa	02 Dec 58	324UNTS3	104676
Colombia	IBRD (World Bank)	15 Dec 58	354UNTS233	105065
El Salvador	IBRD (World Bank)	07 Jan 59	346UNTS51	104977
Colombia	IBRD (World Bank)	30 Jan 59	337UNTS327	104828
Denmark	IBRD (World Bank)	04 Feb 59	328UNTS143	104733
Costa Rica	IBRD (World Bank)	11 Feb 59	337UNTS245	104825
Japan	IBRD (World Bank)	17 Feb 59	337UNTS205	104824
El Salvador	IBRD (World Bank)	20 Feb 59	362UNTS75	105183
Finland	IBRD (World Bank)	16 Mar 59	337UNTS269	104826
India	IBRD (World Bank)	08 Apr 59	348UNTS131	104998
Italy	IBRD (World Bank)	21 Apr 59	359UNTS191	105143
Honduras	IBRD (World Bank)	20 May 59	359UNTS119	105141
Colombia	IBRD (World Bank)	20 May 59	344UNTS251	104953
Iran	IBRD (World Bank)	29 May 59	348UNTS103	104997
IBRD (World Bank)	South Africa	10 Jun 59	340UNTS33	104857
Brazil	IBRD (World Bank)	17 Jun 59	377UNTS111	105398
Gabon	IBRD (World Bank)	30 Jun 59	452UNTS135	106507
Congo (Brazzaville)	IBRD (World Bank)	30 Jun 59	452UNTS123	106506
France	IBRD (World Bank)	30 Jun 59	452UNTS67	106505
Norway	IBRD (World Bank)	08 Jul 59	344UNTS229	104952
India	IBRD (World Bank)	15 Jul 59	355UNTS95	105075
India	IBRD (World Bank)	15 Jul 59	346UNTS33	104976
Pakistan	IBRD (World Bank)	13 Aug 59	355UNTS129	105076
Italy	IBRD (World Bank)	16 Sep 59	375UNTS159	105366
Pakistan	IBRD (World Bank)	25 Sep 59	355UNTS169	105077
Japan	IBRD (World Bank)	12 Nov 59	354UNTS279	105067
Iran	IBRD (World Bank)	23 Nov 59	380UNTS245	105459
Pakistan	IBRD (World Bank)	30 Nov 59	355UNTS203	105078
France	IBRD (World Bank)	10 Dec 59	380UNTS319	105464
IBRD (World Bank)	United Arab Rep	22 Dec 59	354UNTS197	105063
IBRD (World Bank)	Uruguay	30 Dec 59	384UNTS275	105523
Colombia	IBRD (World Bank)	20 Jan 60	375UNTS49	105353
Iran	IBRD (World Bank)	20 Feb 60	384UNTS213	105521
Mauritania	IBRD (World Bank)	17 Mar 60	452UNTS211	106509
France	IBRD (World Bank)	17 Mar 60	452UNTS147	106508
Japan	IBRD (World Bank)	17 Mar 60	362UNTS43	105182
Belgium	IBRD (World Bank)	30 Mar 60	379UNTS129	105438
Belgium	IBRD (World Bank)	30 Mar 60	379UNTS103	105437
Belgium	IBRD (World Bank)	30 Mar 60	379UNTS161	105439
IBRD (World Bank)	UK Great Britain	01 Apr 60	379UNTS397	105446
Costa Rica	IBRD (World Bank)	04 May 60	390UNTS201	105609
Colombia	IBRD (World Bank)	10 May 60	379UNTS218	105441
IBRD (World Bank)	UK Great Britain	27 May 60	375UNTS201	105367
Peru	IBRD (World Bank)	01 Jun 60	380UNTS15	105448
IBRD (World Bank)	Sudan	17 Jun 60	379UNTS253	105442
Nicaragua	IBRD (World Bank)	22 Jun 60	384UNTS243	105522
Peru	IBRD (World Bank)	29 Jun 60	400UNTS99	105750
Honduras	IBRD (World Bank)	29 Jun 60	400UNTS137	105751
El Salvador	IBRD (World Bank)	29 Jul 60	390UNTS101	105605
India	IBRD (World Bank)	29 Jul 60	377UNTS153	105399
Panama	IBRD (World Bank)	19 Aug 60	390UNTS153	105607
Israel	IBRD (World Bank)	09 Sep 60	406UNTS3	105837
Pakistan	IBRD (World Bank)	19 Sep 60	444UNTS207	106370
Multilateral		19 Sep 60	444UNTS259	106371
Colombia	IBRD (World Bank)	20 Sep 60	390UNTS173	105608

Loan regulations (Cont.)

PARTY ONE	PARTY TWO	DATE	CITATION	NUMBER
Mexico	IBRD (World Bank)	18 Oct 60	422UNTS177	106075
India	IBRD (World Bank)	28 Oct 60	406UNTS27	105838
Norway	IBRD (World Bank)	02 Dec 60	390UNTS131	105606
Peru	IBRD (World Bank)	19 Dec 60	417UNTS275	106010
Japan	IBRD (World Bank)	20 Dec 60	400UNTS279	105754
Japan	IBRD (World Bank)	20 Dec 60	400UNTS167	105752
Mexico	IBRD (World Bank)	16 Jan 61	422UNTS203	106076
Burma	IBRD (World Bank)	16 Jan 61	400UNTS73	105749
Costa Rica	IBRD (World Bank)	03 Feb 61	414UNTS314	105977
IBRD (World Bank)	Yugoslavia	23 Feb 61	415UNTS92	105982
Japan	IBRD (World Bank)	16 Mar 61	400UNTS201	105753
IBRD (World Bank)	UK Great Britain	29 Mar 61	415UNTS300	105990
IBRD (World Bank)	Thailand	28 Apr 61	415UNTS121	105983
Japan	IBRD (World Bank)	02 May 61	415UNTS144	105984
Colombia	IBRD (World Bank)	12 May 61	415UNTS172	105985
Honduras	IDA (Devel Assoc)	12 May 61	414UNTS180	105973
Ceylon (Sri Lanka)	IBRD (World Bank)	06 Jun 61	414UNTS349	105978
Multilateral		14 Jun 61	415UNTS4	105979
IBRD (World Bank)	Sudan	14 Jun 61	415UNTS26	105980
IDA (Devel Assoc)	Sudan	14 Jun 61	415UNTS50	105981
IBRD (World Bank)	UK Great Britain	23 Jun 61	415UNTS358	105991
Pakistan	IBRD (World Bank)	27 Jun 61	425UNTS241	106127
Chile	IBRD (World Bank)	28 Jun 61	426UNTS33	106129
Argentina	IBRD (World Bank)	30 Jun 61	445UNTS85	106379
Israel	IBRD (World Bank)	11 Jul 61	429UNTS3	106188
Philippines	IBRD (World Bank)	26 Jul 61	414UNTS253	105976
India	IBRD (World Bank)	09 Aug 61	417UNTS297	106011
Finland	IBRD (World Bank)	09 Aug 61	415UNTS204	105986
IBRD (World Bank)	UK Great Britain	16 Aug 61	426UNTS287	106143
India	IBRD (World Bank)	17 Aug 61	417UNTS319	106012
Colombia	IBRD (World Bank)	28 Aug 61	416UNTS23	105993
Costa Rica	IBRD (World Bank)	06 Sep 61	446UNTS345	106408
IBRD (World Bank)	Switzerland	11 Oct 61	415UNTS396	200592
Costa Rica	IDA (Devel Assoc)	13 Oct 61	431UNTS3	106204
Costa Rica	IBRD (World Bank)	13 Oct 61	430UNTS27	106202
India	IBRD (World Bank)	13 Oct 61	418UNTS3	106013
Philippines	IBRD (World Bank)	13 Oct 61	415UNTS269	105989
Pakistan	IDA (Devel Assoc)	19 Oct 61	447UNTS161	106415
Paraguay	IDA (Devel Assoc)	26 Oct 61	447UNTS277	106419
Peru	IBRD (World Bank)	03 Nov 61	430UNTS47	106203
Pakistan	IDA (Devel Assoc)	22 Nov 61	447UNTS295	106420
Japan	IBRD (World Bank)	29 Nov 61	426UNTS3	106128
IBRD (World Bank)	UK Great Britain	29 Nov 61	426UNTS49	106130
IBRD (World Bank)	South Africa	01 Dec 61	425UNTS215	106126
IBRD (World Bank)	Venezuela	13 Dec 61	446UNTS371	106409
India	IBRD (World Bank)	22 Dec 61	481UNTS85	106979
Jordan	IDA (Devel Assoc)	22 Dec 61	448UNTS21	106423
Argentina	IBRD (World Bank)	19 Jan 62	446UNTS305	106407
Australia	IBRD (World Bank)	23 Jan 62	430UNTS3	106201
Ghana	IBRD (World Bank)	08 Feb 62	449UNTS207	106462
India	IDA (Devel Assoc)	14 Feb 62	468UNTS177	106773
Iceland	IBRD (World Bank)	14 Feb 62	447UNTS95	106413
India	IBRD (World Bank)	28 Feb 62	447UNTS3	106410
Colombia	IBRD (World Bank)	23 May 62	447UNTS39	106411
Ethiopia	IBRD (World Bank)	31 May 62	467UNTS237	106765
Mexico	IBRD (World Bank)	20 Jun 62	468UNTS109	106771
Mexico	IBRD (World Bank)	20 Jun 62	467UNTS205	106764
Pakistan	IDA (Devel Assoc)	29 Jun 62	447UNTS325	106421
India	IDA (Devel Assoc)	29 Jun 62	447UNTS221	106417
IBRD (World Bank)	Yugoslavia	11 Jul 62	468UNTS143	106772
India	IDA (Devel Assoc)	18 Jul 62	447UNTS191	106416
Finland	IBRD (World Bank)	15 Aug 62	467UNTS177	106763
Panama	IBRD (World Bank)	14 Sep 62	476UNTS153	106908
India	IDA (Devel Assoc)	14 Sep 62	467UNTS265	106766
Pakistan	IBRD (World Bank)	14 Sep 62	467UNTS152	106762

Loan regulations (Cont.)

PARTY ONE	PARTY TWO	DATE	CITATION	NUMBER
Pakistan	IBRD (World Bank)	14 Sep 62	467UNTS125	106761
India	IDA (Devel Assoc)	14 Sep 62	448UNTS3	106422
Israel	IBRD (World Bank)	17 Oct 62	467UNTS107	106760
IBRD (World Bank)	Uruguay	26 Oct 62	481UNTS39	106977
Haiti	IDA (Devel Assoc)	02 Nov 62	468UNTS205	106774
Nigeria	IBRD (World Bank)	10 Dec 62	468UNTS255	106776
Morocco	IBRD (World Bank)	21 Dec 62	478UNTS205	106937
IBRD (World Bank)	Thailand	21 Dec 62	467UNTS63	106758
IBRD (World Bank)	Thailand	21 Dec 62	467UNTS43	106757
Pakistan	IBRD (World Bank)	13 Feb 63	467UNTS3	106756
Philippines	IBRD (World Bank)	15 Feb 63	478UNTS161	106936
Nicaragua	IBRD (World Bank)	01 Mar 63	481UNTS15	106976
IBRD (World Bank)	Thailand	07 Mar 63	467UNTS83	106759
Peru	IBRD (World Bank)	13 Mar 63	478UNTS245	106938
Thailand	USA (United States)	25 Apr 63	476UNTS115	106906
Mexico	IBRD (World Bank)	29 Apr 63	489UNTS151	107138
IBRD (World Bank)	UK Great Britain	16 May 63	476UNTS211	106910
IBRD (World Bank)	UK Great Britain	16 May 63	477UNTS361	106929
Colombia	IBRD (World Bank)	03 Jun 63	490UNTS199	107155
India	IBRD (World Bank)	05 Jun 63	481UNTS191	106983
IBRD (World Bank)	Thailand	11 Jun 63	481UNTS227	106984
El Salvador	IBRD (World Bank)	19 Jun 63	481UNTS59	106978
IBRD (World Bank)	Yugoslavia	21 Jun 63	482UNTS43	106990
Colombia	IBRD (World Bank)	21 Jun 63	482UNTS159	106994
Colombia	IBRD (World Bank)	28 Jun 63	489UNTS113	107137
Costa Rica	IBRD (World Bank)	10 Jul 63	482UNTS69	106991
Malaysia	IBRD (World Bank)	15 Jul 63	482UNTS123	106993
Colombia	IBRD (World Bank)	16 Jul 63	482UNTS256	106998
Denmark	IBRD (World Bank)	24 Jul 63	481UNTS171	106982
Malaysia	IBRD (World Bank)	07 Aug 63	485UNTS253	107060
IBRD (World Bank)	UK Great Britain	06 Sep 63	483UNTS173	107013
Finland	IBRD (World Bank)	18 Sep 63	491UNTS345	107183
Mexico	IBRD (World Bank)	20 Sep 63	491UNTS317	107182
IBRD (World Bank)	Venezuela	20 Sep 63	482UNTS227	106997
IBRD (World Bank)	UK Great Britain	23 Sep 63	503UNTS247	107348
Japan	IBRD (World Bank)	27 Sep 63	485UNTS283	107061
Taiwan	IBRD (World Bank)	27 Sep 63	483UNTS151	107012
El Salvador	IBRD (World Bank)	01 Oct 63	517UNTS3	107481
Norway	IBRD (World Bank)	15 Oct 63	482UNTS103	106992
IBRD (World Bank)	Spain	25 Oct 63	491UNTS297	107181
IBRD (World Bank)	Yugoslavia	28 Oct 63	503UNTS289	107349
Portugal	IBRD (World Bank)	06 Nov 63	491UNTS137	107176
Portugal	IBRD (World Bank)	06 Nov 63	492UNTS89	107188
New Zealand	IBRD (World Bank)	12 Nov 63	485UNTS233	107059
Peru	IBRD (World Bank)	22 Nov 63	491UNTS101	107175
Chile	IBRD (World Bank)	18 Dec 63	504UNTS29	107352
Chile	IBRD (World Bank)	18 Dec 63	504UNTS3	107351
Multilateral		30 Dec 63	568UNTS215	108270
Multilateral		30 Dec 63	568UNTS243	108272
Multilateral		30 Dec 63	568UNTS233	108271
Multilateral		30 Dec 63	551UNTS75	108035
Multilateral		30 Dec 63	551UNTS119	108037
Multilateral		30 Dec 63	551UNTS105	108036
Liberia	IBRD (World Bank)	08 Jan 64	504UNTS53	107353
Colombia	IBRD (World Bank)	07 Feb 64	516UNTS99	107473
IBRD (World Bank)	Thailand	11 Mar 64	504UNTS73	107354
Nigeria	IBRD (World Bank)	12 Mar 64	516UNTS325	107480
New Zealand	IBRD (World Bank)	12 Mar 64	505UNTS3	107362
Peru	IBRD (World Bank)	22 Apr 64	519UNTS95	107503
Japan	IBRD (World Bank)	22 Apr 64	505UNTS21	107363
Ethiopia	IBRD (World Bank)	08 May 64	505UNTS51	107364
Algeria	IBRD (World Bank)	14 May 64	522UNTS265	107552
Pakistan	IBRD (World Bank)	14 May 64	516UNTS145	107475
Ecuador	IBRD (World Bank)	26 May 64	534UNTS113	107758
IBRD (World Bank)	Tunisia	05 Jun 64	539UNTS129	107827

PARTY ONE	PARTY TWO	DATE	CITATION	NUMBER
Loan regulations (Cont.)				
Iran	IBRD (World Bank)	10 Jun 64	537UNTS111	107799
Nigeria	IBRD (World Bank)	07 Jul 64	537UNTS3	107795
Gabon	IBRD (World Bank)	10 Jul 64	537UNTS63	107797
Finland	IBRD (World Bank)	10 Jul 64	516UNTS125	107474
Philippines	IBRD (World Bank)	22 Jul 64	516UNTS171	107476
IBRD (World Bank)	Spain	31 Jul 64	537UNTS81	107798
IBRD (World Bank)	Sierra Leone	18 Aug 64	516UNTS295	107479
Morocco	IBRD (World Bank)	26 Aug 64	537UNTS193	107802
IBRD (World Bank)	Venezuela	28 Aug 64	537UNTS135	107800
IBRD (World Bank)	Venezuela	28 Aug 64	520UNTS97	107512
Philippines	IBRD (World Bank)	28 Oct 64	537UNTS165	107801
IBRD (World Bank)	Thailand	25 Nov 64	537UNTS273	107805
IBRD (World Bank)	Yugoslavia	11 Dec 64	537UNTS321	107807
Paraguay	IBRD (World Bank)	16 Dec 64	549UNTS173	107999
Taiwan	IBRD (World Bank)	17 Dec 64	538UNTS3	107808
Japan	IBRD (World Bank)	23 Dec 64	538UNTS37	107809
Japan	IBRD (World Bank)	13 Jan 65	537UNTS293	107806
Honduras	IBRD (World Bank)	02 Feb 65	561UNTS255	108188
Mexico	IBRD (World Bank)	04 Feb 65	549UNTS189	108000
Chile	IBRD (World Bank)	12 Feb 65	537UNTS35	107796
Brazil	IBRD (World Bank)	26 Feb 65	567UNTS91	108253
Brazil	IBRD (World Bank)	26 Feb 65	553UNTS3	108065
Malaysia	IBRD (World Bank)	26 Feb 65	549UNTS239	108002
IBRD (World Bank)	Thailand	22 Mar 65	538UNTS63	107810
IBRD (World Bank)	Uruguay	30 Mar 65	567UNTS45	108251
Jamaica	IBRD (World Bank)	08 Apr 65	539UNTS303	107841
Iran	IBRD (World Bank)	28 Apr 65	555UNTS45	108104
Iran	IBRD (World Bank)	28 Apr 65	555UNTS21	108103
Taiwan	IBRD (World Bank)	28 Apr 65	549UNTS145	107998
Portugal	IBRD (World Bank)	29 Apr 65	549UNTS69	107991
Japan	IBRD (World Bank)	26 May 65	550UNTS95	108010
India	IBRD (World Bank)	28 May 65	552UNTS39	108049
Peru	IBRD (World Bank)	03 Jun 65	551UNTS227	108045
India	IBRD (World Bank)	11 Jun 65	557UNTS101	108130
India	IBRD (World Bank)	11 Jun 65	557UNTS59	108128
Peru	IBRD (World Bank)	18 Jun 65	568UNTS191	108269
Italy	IBRD (World Bank)	28 Jun 65	567UNTS127	108254
Finland	IBRD (World Bank)	30 Jun 65	550UNTS63	108009
Pakistan	IBRD (World Bank)	09 Jul 65	554UNTS39	108096
Iran	IBRD (World Bank)	12 Jul 65	554UNTS3	108095
Multilateral		22 Jul 65	561UNTS333	200618
Peru	IBRD (World Bank)	17 Sep 65	566UNTS311	108248
Nigeria	IBRD (World Bank)	26 Sep 65	571UNTS39	108298
Nigeria	IBRD (World Bank)	26 Sep 65	570UNTS233	108296
East Afri Service	IBRD (World Bank)	29 Sep 65	568UNTS327	200623
IBRD (World Bank)	Tanzania	29 Sep 65	568UNTS309	108275
IBRD (World Bank)	Uganda	29 Sep 65	568UNTS317	108276
Kenya	IBRD (World Bank)	29 Sep 65	568UNTS289	108274
IBRD (World Bank)	Spain	29 Sep 65	568UNTS49	108264
Mexico	IBRD (World Bank)	01 Oct 65	589UNTS339	108542
Chile	IBRD (World Bank)	06 Oct 65	567UNTS293	108261
Philippines	IBRD (World Bank)	02 Nov 65	567UNTS3	108249
Malaysia	IBRD (World Bank)	17 Nov 65	568UNTS23	108263
IBRD (World Bank)	Venezuela	13 Dec 65	568UNTS77	108265
Mexico	IBRD (World Bank)	15 Dec 65	568UNTS125	108267
Paraguay	IBRD (World Bank)	16 Dec 65	568UNTS165	108268
New Zealand	IBRD (World Bank)	17 Dec 65	567UNTS255	108259
New Zealand	IBRD (World Bank)	17 Dec 65	567UNTS275	108260
Ethiopia	IBRD (World Bank)	28 Dec 65	567UNTS229	108258
Brazil	IBRD (World Bank)	15 Mar 66	599UNTS52	108664
Guinea	IBRD (World Bank)	30 Mar 66	568UNTS3	108262
Paraguay	IBRD (World Bank)	04 Apr 66	570UNTS41	108287
IBRD (World Bank)	Venezuela	21 Apr 66	568UNTS257	108273
Finland	IBRD (World Bank)	27 Apr 66	568UNTS107	108266
Multilateral		04 May 66	575UNTS49	108354

PARTY ONE	PARTY TWO	DATE	CITATION	NUMBER
Loan regulations (Cont.)				
Peru	IBRD (World Bank)	13 May 66	570UNTS61	108288
Colombia	IBRD (World Bank)	16 May 66	608UNTS249	108819
IBRD (World Bank)	Tunisia	16 May 66	584UNTS155	108477
Mexico	IBRD (World Bank)	25 May 66	596UNTS3	108627
Morocco	IBRD (World Bank)	13 Jun 66	615UNTS205	108881
Portugal	IBRD (World Bank)	14 Jun 66	581UNTS3	108430
Portugal	IBRD (World Bank)	14 Jun 66	581UNTS29	108431
Jamaica	IBRD (World Bank)	20 Jun 66	582UNTS145	108462
IBRD (World Bank)	Thailand	24 Jun 66	582UNTS259	108466
India	IBRD (World Bank)	07 Jul 66	595UNTS3	108610
Iraq	IBRD (World Bank)	22 Jul 66	584UNTS233	108480
Malaysia	IBRD (World Bank)	26 Jul 66	586UNTS195	108504
Iran	IBRD (World Bank)	26 Jul 66	582UNTS107	108461
Japan	IBRD (World Bank)	29 Jul 66	582UNTS209	108464
IBRD (World Bank)	Turkey	10 Aug 66	585UNTS199	108490
IBRD (World Bank)	Singapore	11 Aug 66	585UNTS39	108482
Honduras	IBRD (World Bank)	25 Aug 66	582UNTS79	108460
Peru	IBRD (World Bank)	07 Sep 66	585UNTS3	108481
IBRD (World Bank)	South Africa	08 Sep 66	585UNTS71	108483
Jamaica	IBRD (World Bank)	30 Sep 66	582UNTS179	108463
IBRD (World Bank)	Zambia	04 Oct 66	585UNTS181	108489
Nicaragua	IBRD (World Bank)	05 Oct 66	582UNTS231	108465
IBRD (World Bank)	Singapore	04 Nov 66	585UNTS155	108488
Brazil	IBRD (World Bank)	19 Dec 66	599UNTS177	108667
Brazil	IBRD (World Bank)	19 Dec 66	599UNTS107	108665
Brazil	IBRD (World Bank)	19 Dec 66	599UNTS149	108666
Brazil	IBRD (World Bank)	19 Dec 66	599UNTS205	108668
Chile	IBRD (World Bank)	23 Dec 66	595UNTS141	108618
Jamaica	IBRD (World Bank)	23 Jan 67	594UNTS311	108608
IBRD (World Bank)	Venezuela	26 Jan 67	596UNTS35	108628
East Afri Service	IBRD (World Bank)	17 Feb 67	599UNTS335	200629
IBRD (World Bank)	Tanzania	17 Feb 67	599UNTS287	108671
IBRD (World Bank)	Uganda	17 Feb 67	599UNTS321	108673
Kenya	IBRD (World Bank)	17 Feb 67	599UNTS233	108669
IBRD (World Bank)	Tunisia	21 Feb 67	618UNTS39	108923
IBRD (World Bank)	Yugoslavia	24 Feb 67	599UNTS27	108663
Guatemala	IBRD (World Bank)	10 Mar 67	616UNTS139	108894
IBRD (World Bank)	Trinidad/Tobago	10 Mar 67	599UNTS3	108662
Pakistan	IBRD (World Bank)	15 Mar 67	599UNTS245	108670
IBRD (World Bank)	Thailand	24 Mar 67	599UNTS299	108672
Cameroon	IBRD (World Bank)	28 Mar 67	618UNTS89	108925
IBRD (World Bank)	Senegal	01 May 67	615UNTS267	108883
Cyprus	IBRD (World Bank)	16 May 67	617UNTS21	108906
Pakistan	IBRD (World Bank)	26 May 67	616UNTS167	108895
Honduras	IBRD (World Bank)	26 May 67	615UNTS145	108879
Multilateral		12 Jun 67	615UNTS321	108885
China	IBRD (World Bank)	14 Jun 67	615UNTS243	108882
Malaysia	IBRD (World Bank)	15 Jun 67	618UNTS235	108930
Colombia	IBRD (World Bank)	15 Jun 67	615UNTS47	108877
Other Party Combin	Ecuador	19 Jun 67	615UNTS75	108878
Colombia	IBRD (World Bank)	29 Jun 67	619UNTS99	108941
IBRD (World Bank)	Singapore	05 Jul 67	618UNTS189	108928
IBRD (World Bank)	Yugoslavia	18 Jul 67	615UNTS343	108886
Argentina	IBRD (World Bank)	31 Jul 67	633UNTS289	109042
Taiwan	IBRD (World Bank)	02 Aug 67	618UNTS301	108932
IBRD (World Bank)	Spain	04 Aug 67	619UNTS209	108944
Taiwan	IBRD (World Bank)	07 Aug 67	620UNTS113	108952
Pakistan	IBRD (World Bank)	10 Aug 67	618UNTS261	108931
Madagascar	IBRD (World Bank)	23 Aug 67	618UNTS215	108929
Peru	IBRD (World Bank)	11 Sep 67	619UNTS171	108943
IBRD (World Bank)	Tunisia	14 Sep 67	639UNTS147	109149
IBRD (World Bank)	Singapore	15 Sep 67	615UNTS295	108884
India	IBRD (World Bank)	19 Sep 67	615UNTS165	108880
Iran	IBRD (World Bank)	17 Oct 67	0UNTS0	109331
Israel	IBRD (World Bank)	15 Nov 67	619UNTS129	108942

PARTY ONE	PARTY TWO	DATE	CITATION	NUMBER
Loan regulations (Cont.)				
Ceylon (Sri Lanka)	IBRD (World Bank)	22 Nov 67	639UNTS221	109151
IBRD (World Bank)	Tanzania	13 Dec 67	619UNTS239	108945
Argentina	IBRD (World Bank)	25 Jan 68	639UNTS187	109150
Mexico	IBRD (World Bank)	26 Jan 68	640UNTS3	109152
Korea, South	IBRD (World Bank)	31 Jan 68	639UNTS263	200638
Greece	IBRD (World Bank)	18 Mar 68	0UNTS0	109326
Malaysia	IBRD (World Bank)	17 Apr 68	0UNTS0	109360
State/IGO Group	IBRD (World Bank)	02 May 68	637UNTS0	109110
IBRD (World Bank)	Thailand	23 May 68	0UNTS0	109332
Colombia	IBRD (World Bank)	03 Jun 68	0UNTS0	109333
Colombia	IBRD (World Bank)	03 Jun 68	0UNTS0	109334
IBRD (World Bank)	Singapore	03 Jul 68	0UNTS0	109364
Gabon	IBRD (World Bank)	07 Jul 68	0UNTS0	109361
Colombia	IBRD (World Bank)	31 Jul 68	0UNTS0	109512
Malaysia	IBRD (World Bank)	27 Sep 68	0UNTS0	109506
Malaysia	IBRD (World Bank)	27 Sep 68	0UNTS0	109505
Loan guarantee				
France	IBRD (World Bank)	09 May 47	152UNTS111	102014
Netherlands	IBRD (World Bank)	07 Aug 47	152UNTS165	102015
Denmark	IBRD (World Bank)	22 Aug 47	152UNTS223	102016
Luxembourg	IBRD (World Bank)	28 Aug 47	153UNTS3	102017
Netherlands	IBRD (World Bank)	15 Jul 48	153UNTS259	102024
Netherlands	IBRD (World Bank)	15 Jul 48	153UNTS259	102023
Netherlands	IBRD (World Bank)	15 Jul 48	153UNTS259	102025
Netherlands	IBRD (World Bank)	15 Jul 48	153UNTS259	102021
Mexico	IBRD (World Bank)	06 Jan 49	154UNTS81	102028
Mexico	IBRD (World Bank)	06 Jan 49	154UNTS3	102027
Brazil	IBRD (World Bank)	27 Jan 49	153UNTS264	102026
Belgium	IBRD (World Bank)	01 Mar 49	154UNTS133	102029
Chile	IBRD (World Bank)	23 Mar 49	153UNTS61	102018
Chile	IBRD (World Bank)	23 Mar 49	153UNTS141	102019
Netherlands	IBRD (World Bank)	26 Jul 49	154UNTS178	102030
Finland	IBRD (World Bank)	01 Aug 49	156UNTS289	200480
India	IBRD (World Bank)	18 Aug 49	154UNTS269	102031
Colombia	IBRD (World Bank)	19 Aug 49	154UNTS329	102032
IBRD (World Bank)	Yugoslavia	17 Sep 49	155UNTS3	102034
India	IBRD (World Bank)	29 Sep 49	154UNTS393	102033
Finland	IBRD (World Bank)	17 Oct 49	156UNTS355	200481
El Salvador	IBRD (World Bank)	14 Dec 49	155UNTS43	102035
India	IBRD (World Bank)	18 Apr 50	155UNTS117	102036
Mexico	IBRD (World Bank)	28 Apr 50	155UNTS185	102037
Brazil	IBRD (World Bank)	26 May 50	301UNTS165	104345
Iraq	IBRD (World Bank)	15 Jun 50	155UNTS267	102038
IBRD (World Bank)	Turkey	07 Jul 50	156UNTS3	102039
IBRD (World Bank)	Turkey	07 Jul 50	156UNTS75	102040
IBRD (World Bank)	Uruguay	25 Aug 50	156UNTS203	102042
Ethiopia	IBRD (World Bank)	13 Sep 50	157UNTS213	102055
Ethiopia	IBRD (World Bank)	13 Sep 50	157UNTS233	102056
Mexico	IBRD (World Bank)	18 Oct 50	157UNTS259	102057
IBRD (World Bank)	Turkey	19 Oct 50	157UNTS333	102058
IBRD (World Bank)	Thailand	27 Oct 50	158UNTS3	102059
IBRD (World Bank)	Thailand	27 Oct 50	158UNTS43	102061
IBRD (World Bank)	Thailand	27 Oct 50	158UNTS25	102060
Australia	IBRD (World Bank)	14 Nov 50	156UNTS147	102041
Colombia	IBRD (World Bank)	28 Dec 50	158UNTS87	102063
IBRD (World Bank)	South Africa	23 Jan 51	158UNTS135	102065
IBRD (World Bank)	South Africa	23 Jan 51	158UNTS115	102064
Ethiopia	IBRD (World Bank)	19 Feb 51	186UNTS101	102486
Colombia	IBRD (World Bank)	10 Apr 51	158UNTS155	102066
Nicaragua	IBRD (World Bank)	07 Jun 51	158UNTS215	102067
Nicaragua	IBRD (World Bank)	07 Jun 51	158UNTS277	102068
Iceland	IBRD (World Bank)	20 Jun 51	158UNTS301	102069
Belgium	IBRD (World Bank)	13 Sep 51	158UNTS323	102070
Belgium	IBRD (World Bank)	13 Sep 51	158UNTS349	102071

PARTY ONE	PARTY TWO	DATE	CITATION	NUMBER
Loan guarantee (Cont.)				
Chile	IBRD (World Bank)	10 Oct 51	158UNTS369	102072
Italy	IBRD (World Bank)	10 Oct 51	159UNTS383	200482
Colombia	IBRD (World Bank)	13 Oct 51	159UNTS75	102084
Nicaragua	IBRD (World Bank)	29 Oct 51	159UNTS35	102082
Iceland	IBRD (World Bank)	01 Nov 51	159UNTS55	102083
Paraguay	IBRD (World Bank)	07 Dec 51	159UNTS103	102085
Mexico	IBRD (World Bank)	11 Jan 52	159UNTS129	102086
Peru	IBRD (World Bank)	23 Jan 52	159UNTS163	102087
IBRD (World Bank)	UK Great Britain	27 Feb 52	159UNTS181	102088
Netherlands	IBRD (World Bank)	20 Mar 52	159UNTS207	102089
Pakistan	IBRD (World Bank)	27 Mar 52	159UNTS251	102090
Finland	IBRD (World Bank)	30 Apr 52	159UNTS408	200483
Pakistan	IBRD (World Bank)	13 Jun 52	191UNTS85	102578
IBRD (World Bank)	Turkey	18 Jun 52	159UNTS269	102091
Brazil	IBRD (World Bank)	27 Jun 52	190UNTS115	102561
Brazil	IBRD (World Bank)	27 Jun 52	190UNTS85	102560
Australia	IBRD (World Bank)	08 Jul 52	159UNTS295	102092
Peru	IBRD (World Bank)	08 Jul 52	159UNTS321	102093
Colombia	IBRD (World Bank)	26 Aug 52	159UNTS339	102094
Iceland	IBRD (World Bank)	26 Aug 52	159UNTS363	102095
Japan	IBRD (World Bank)	12 Nov 52	354UNTS313	105068
India	IBRD (World Bank)	18 Dec 52	201UNTS241	102719
India	IBRD (World Bank)	23 Jan 53	201UNTS145	102715
IBRD (World Bank)	Yugoslavia	11 Feb 53	165UNTS231	102179
IBRD (World Bank)	UK Great Britain	11 Mar 53	172UNTS115	102243
Brazil	IBRD (World Bank)	30 Apr 53	190UNTS133	102562
Brazil	IBRD (World Bank)	17 Jul 53	190UNTS149	102563
IBRD (World Bank)	South Africa	28 Aug 53	180UNTS91	102377
IBRD (World Bank)	South Africa	28 Aug 53	180UNTS73	102376
Nicaragua	IBRD (World Bank)	04 Sep 53	186UNTS117	102487
Iceland	IBRD (World Bank)	04 Sep 53	188UNTS3	102519
Nicaragua	IBRD (World Bank)	04 Sep 53	186UNTS137	102488
Iceland	IBRD (World Bank)	04 Sep 53	178UNTS275	102344
Chile	IBRD (World Bank)	10 Sep 53	188UNTS25	102520
IBRD (World Bank)	Turkey	10 Sep 53	187UNTS71	102502
Colombia	IBRD (World Bank)	10 Sep 53	203UNTS3	102738
Panama	IBRD (World Bank)	25 Sep 53	188UNTS71	102521
Panama	IBRD (World Bank)	25 Sep 53	188UNTS95	102522
Italy	IBRD (World Bank)	06 Oct 53	301UNTS135	104344
Japan	IBRD (World Bank)	15 Oct 53	187UNTS367	200513
Japan	IBRD (World Bank)	15 Oct 53	187UNTS271	200511
Japan	IBRD (World Bank)	15 Oct 53	187UNTS321	200512
Brazil	IBRD (World Bank)	18 Dec 53	190UNTS179	102564
Brazil	IBRD (World Bank)	18 Dec 53	301UNTS229	104346
Brazil	IBRD (World Bank)	24 Feb 54	301UNTS249	104347
Australia	IBRD (World Bank)	02 Mar 54	191UNTS103	102579
Norway	IBRD (World Bank)	08 Apr 54	201UNTS131	102714
Peru	IBRD (World Bank)	12 Apr 54	190UNTS231	102567
Pakistan	IBRD (World Bank)	02 Jun 54	324UNTS59	104678
France	IBRD (World Bank)	10 Jun 54	210UNTS89	102836
Ceylon (Sri Lanka)	IBRD (World Bank)	09 Jul 54	198UNTS313	200517
Mexico	IBRD (World Bank)	24 Aug 54	286UNTS211	104168
El Salvador	IBRD (World Bank)	12 Oct 54	203UNTS37	102739
Austria	IBRD (World Bank)	08 Nov 54	216UNTS305	200528
Peru	IBRD (World Bank)	12 Nov 54	209UNTS287	102831
India	IBRD (World Bank)	19 Nov 54	309UNTS159	104473
Belgium	IBRD (World Bank)	14 Dec 54	210UNTS113	102837
Colombia	IBRD (World Bank)	29 Dec 54	211UNTS135	102851
India	IBRD (World Bank)	14 Mar 55	309UNTS129	104472
IBRD (World Bank)	UK Great Britain	15 Mar 55	265UNTS85	103808
Australia	IBRD (World Bank)	18 Mar 55	220UNTS131	102998
Colombia	IBRD (World Bank)	24 Mar 55	212UNTS217	102874
Finland	IBRD (World Bank)	24 Mar 55	211UNTS305	200525
Peru	IBRD (World Bank)	05 Apr 55	211UNTS115	102850
Norway	IBRD (World Bank)	19 Apr 55	211UNTS159	102852

PARTY ONE	PARTY TWO	DATE	CITATION	NUMBER
Loan guarantee (Cont.)				
Peru	IBRD (World Bank)	19 Apr 55	221UNTS153	103007
Italy	IBRD (World Bank)	01 Jun 55	358UNTS203	105137
Austria	IBRD (World Bank)	14 Jun 55	221UNTS375	200531
Colombia	IBRD (World Bank)	15 Jun 55	248UNTS161	103494
Pakistan	IBRD (World Bank)	20 Jun 55	230UNTS41	103176
Nicaragua	IBRD (World Bank)	08 Jul 55	229UNTS97	103162
Nicaragua	IBRD (World Bank)	08 Jul 55	229UNTS123	103163
Panama	IBRD (World Bank)	12 Jul 55	219UNTS127	102970
Guatemala	IBRD (World Bank)	29 Jul 55	229UNTS167	103165
Pakistan	IBRD (World Bank)	04 Aug 55	230UNTS79	103177
Peru	IBRD (World Bank)	05 Aug 55	218UNTS3	102950
Pakistan	IBRD (World Bank)	06 Aug 55	236UNTS195	103325
IBRD (World Bank)	Thailand	09 Aug 55	221UNTS283	103011
Lebanon	IBRD (World Bank)	25 Aug 55	230UNTS233	103188
France	IBRD (World Bank)	26 Aug 55	247UNTS305	103478
Nicaragua	IBRD (World Bank)	26 Aug 55	229UNTS145	103164
IBRD (World Bank)	Uruguay	29 Aug 55	243UNTS123	103450
Austria	USSR (Soviet Union)	17 Oct 55	0UNTS0	109254
Japan	IBRD (World Bank)	25 Oct 55	230UNTS379	200534
IBRD (World Bank)	South Africa	28 Nov 55	230UNTS101	103178
Honduras	IBRD (World Bank)	22 Dec 55	230UNTS262	103189
Japan	IBRD (World Bank)	21 Feb 56	248UNTS321	200543
Ecuador	IBRD (World Bank)	26 Mar 56	292UNTS391	104277
Norway	IBRD (World Bank)	03 May 56	243UNTS281	103455
Burma	IBRD (World Bank)	04 May 56	253UNTS179	103584
Burma	IBRD (World Bank)	04 May 56	253UNTS209	103585
Haiti	IBRD (World Bank)	07 May 56	252UNTS279	103570
Finland	IBRD (World Bank)	22 May 56	248UNTS57	103485
Nicaragua	IBRD (World Bank)	22 May 56	253UNTS233	103586
Colombia	IBRD (World Bank)	06 Jun 56	248UNTS139	103493
Fed Rhod/Nyasaland	IBRD (World Bank)	21 Jun 56	285UNTS317	104156
IBRD (World Bank)	UK Great Britain	21 Jun 56	285UNTS355	104157
India	IBRD (World Bank)	26 Jun 56	301UNTS3	104341
Costa Rica	IBRD (World Bank)	18 Sep 56	260UNTS369	103721
Austria	IBRD (World Bank)	21 Sep 56	259UNTS43	103682
Austria	IBRD (World Bank)	21 Sep 56	259UNTS17	103681
Italy	IBRD (World Bank)	11 Oct 56	359UNTS3	105138
IBRD (World Bank)	Thailand	12 Oct 56	261UNTS117	103728
IBRD (World Bank)	Uruguay	25 Oct 56	265UNTS59	103807
Chile	IBRD (World Bank)	01 Nov 56	261UNTS27	103724
Australia	IBRD (World Bank)	15 Nov 56	288UNTS117	104201
Australia	IBRD (World Bank)	03 Dec 56	288UNTS99	104200
Japan	IBRD (World Bank)	19 Dec 56	268UNTS203	103859
India	IBRD (World Bank)	19 Dec 56	310UNTS75	104489
Japan	IBRD (World Bank)	19 Dec 56	264UNTS179	103793
Iran	IBRD (World Bank)	22 Jan 57	317UNTS129	104600
Ethiopia	IBRD (World Bank)	28 Jan 57	286UNTS307	104175
India	IBRD (World Bank)	05 Mar 57	272UNTS201	103939
Peru	IBRD (World Bank)	13 Mar 57	274UNTS59	103958
Netherlands	IBRD (World Bank)	15 May 57	274UNTS211	103967
India	IBRD (World Bank)	29 May 57	309UNTS201	104474
Belgium	IBRD (World Bank)	26 Jun 57	322UNTS301	104661
India	IBRD (World Bank)	12 Jul 57	288UNTS135	104202
Chile	IBRD (World Bank)	24 Jul 57	282UNTS189	104099
Chile	IBRD (World Bank)	24 Jul 57	282UNTS139	104098
Japan	IBRD (World Bank)	09 Aug 57	293UNTS59	104286
Belgium	IBRD (World Bank)	10 Sep 57	286UNTS291	104174
IBRD (World Bank)	Thailand	12 Sep 57	299UNTS349	104324
Ecuador	IBRD (World Bank)	20 Sep 57	293UNTS135	104291
Ecuador	IBRD (World Bank)	20 Sep 57	289UNTS237	104221
IBRD (World Bank)	South Africa	01 Oct 57	280UNTS285	104065
Austria	IBRD (World Bank)	10 Oct 57	301UNTS95	104343
Pakistan	IBRD (World Bank)	18 Oct 57	299UNTS303	104322
India	IBRD (World Bank)	20 Nov 57	301UNTS47	104342
Philippines	IBRD (World Bank)	22 Nov 57	293UNTS83	104287

PARTY ONE	PARTY TWO	DATE	CITATION	NUMBER
Loan guarantee (Cont.)				
Belgium	IBRD (World Bank)	27 Nov 57	292UNTS175	104273
Pakistan	IBRD (World Bank)	17 Dec 57	299UNTS321	104323
Mexico	IBRD (World Bank)	14 Jan 58	293UNTS167	104292
Brazil	IBRD (World Bank)	22 Jan 58	323UNTS99	104666
Pakistan	IBRD (World Bank)	23 Apr 58	323UNTS253	104672
Austria	IBRD (World Bank)	28 Apr 58	359UNTS145	105142
Chile	IBRD (World Bank)	28 Apr 58	359UNTS89	105140
IBRD (World Bank)	UK Great Britain	02 May 58	324UNTS25	104677
Mexico	IBRD (World Bank)	05 May 58	309UNTS3	104466
Honduras	IBRD (World Bank)	09 May 58	323UNTS4	104662
Japan	IBRD (World Bank)	13 Jun 58	312UNTS159	104518
IBRD (World Bank)	UK Great Britain	16 Jun 58	309UNTS35	104467
India	IBRD (World Bank)	25 Jun 58	323UNTS157	104668
India	IBRD (World Bank)	25 Jun 58	323UNTS131	104667
IBRD (World Bank)	Sudan	21 Jul 58	323UNTS183	104669
India	IBRD (World Bank)	23 Jul 58	317UNTS3	104590
Japan	IBRD (World Bank)	18 Aug 58	323UNTS205	104670
Japan	IBRD (World Bank)	10 Sep 58	318UNTS133	104612
Japan	IBRD (World Bank)	10 Sep 58	323UNTS297	104673
India	IBRD (World Bank)	16 Sep 58	323UNTS235	104671
Ceylon (Sri Lanka)	IBRD (World Bank)	17 Sep 58	323UNTS51	104664
Peru	IBRD (World Bank)	17 Sep 58	323UNTS27	104663
Fed of Malaya	IBRD (World Bank)	22 Sep 58	323UNTS71	104665
Brazil	IBRD (World Bank)	03 Oct 58	337UNTS177	104823
Ecuador	IBRD (World Bank)	09 Oct 58	337UNTS299	104827
IBRD (World Bank)	South Africa	02 Dec 58	324UNTS3	104676
Austria	IBRD (World Bank)	02 Dec 58	340UNTS3	104856
Colombia	IBRD (World Bank)	15 Dec 58	354UNTS233	105065
El Salvador	IBRD (World Bank)	07 Jan 59	346UNTS51	104977
Colombia	IBRD (World Bank)	30 Jan 59	337UNTS327	104828
Costa Rica	IBRD (World Bank)	11 Feb 59	337UNTS245	104825
Japan	IBRD (World Bank)	17 Feb 59	337UNTS205	104824
El Salvador	IBRD (World Bank)	20 Feb 59	362UNTS75	105183
Finland	IBRD (World Bank)	16 Mar 59	337UNTS269	104826
India	IBRD (World Bank)	08 Apr 59	348UNTS131	104998
Italy	IBRD (World Bank)	21 Apr 59	359UNTS191	105143
Colombia	IBRD (World Bank)	20 May 59	344UNTS251	104953
Honduras	IBRD (World Bank)	20 May 59	359UNTS119	105141
Iran	IBRD (World Bank)	29 May 59	348UNTS103	104997
IBRD (World Bank)	South Africa	10 Jun 59	340UNTS33	104857
Brazil	IBRD (World Bank)	17 Jun 59	377UNTS111	105398
Congo (Brazzaville)	IBRD (World Bank)	30 Jun 59	452UNTS123	106506
Gabon	IBRD (World Bank)	30 Jun 59	452UNTS135	106507
France	IBRD (World Bank)	30 Jun 59	452UNTS67	106505
Norway	IBRD (World Bank)	08 Jul 59	344UNTS229	104952
India	IBRD (World Bank)	15 Jul 59	346UNTS33	104976
India	IBRD (World Bank)	15 Jul 59	355UNTS95	105075
Pakistan	IBRD (World Bank)	13 Aug 59	355UNTS129	105076
Italy	IBRD (World Bank)	16 Sep 59	375UNTS159	105366
Pakistan	IBRD (World Bank)	25 Sep 59	355UNTS169	105077
Japan	IBRD (World Bank)	12 Nov 59	354UNTS279	105067
Iran	IBRD (World Bank)	23 Nov 59	380UNTS245	105459
Pakistan	IBRD (World Bank)	30 Nov 59	355UNTS203	105078
France	IBRD (World Bank)	10 Dec 59	380UNTS319	105464
IBRD (World Bank)	United Arab Rep	22 Dec 59	354UNTS197	105063
IBRD (World Bank)	Uruguay	30 Dec 59	384UNTS275	105523
Colombia	IBRD (World Bank)	20 Jan 60	375UNTS49	105353
Iran	IBRD (World Bank)	20 Feb 60	384UNTS213	105521
France	IBRD (World Bank)	17 Mar 60	452UNTS147	106508
Mauritania	IBRD (World Bank)	17 Mar 60	452UNTS211	106509
Japan	IBRD (World Bank)	17 Mar 60	362UNTS43	105182
Belgium	IBRD (World Bank)	30 Mar 60	379UNTS161	105439
Belgium	IBRD (World Bank)	30 Mar 60	379UNTS129	105438
Belgium	IBRD (World Bank)	30 Mar 60	379UNTS103	105437
IBRD (World Bank)	UK Great Britain	01 Apr 60	379UNTS397	105446

PARTY ONE	PARTY TWO	DATE	CITATION	NUMBER
Loan guarantee (Cont.)				
Costa Rica	IBRD (World Bank)	04 May 60	390UNTS201	105609
Colombia	IBRD (World Bank)	10 May 60	379UNTS218	105441
IBRD (World Bank)	UK Great Britain	27 May 60	375UNTS201	105367
Peru	IBRD (World Bank)	01 Jun 60	380UNTS15	105448
IBRD (World Bank)	Sudan	17 Jun 60	379UNTS253	105442
Nicaragua	IBRD (World Bank)	22 Jun 60	384UNTS243	105522
Honduras	IBRD (World Bank)	29 Jun 60	400UNTS137	105751
Peru	IBRD (World Bank)	29 Jun 60	400UNTS99	105750
El Salvador	IBRD (World Bank)	29 Jul 60	390UNTS101	105605
Panama	IBRD (World Bank)	19 Aug 60	390UNTS153	105607
Israel	IBRD (World Bank)	09 Sep 60	406UNTS3	105837
Pakistan	IBRD (World Bank)	19 Sep 60	444UNTS207	106370
Colombia	IBRD (World Bank)	20 Sep 60	390UNTS173	105608
Mexico	IBRD (World Bank)	18 Oct 60	422UNTS177	106075
India	IBRD (World Bank)	28 Oct 60	406UNTS27	105838
Norway	IBRD (World Bank)	02 Dec 60	390UNTS131	105606
Peru	IBRD (World Bank)	19 Dec 60	417UNTS275	106010
Japan	IBRD (World Bank)	20 Dec 60	400UNTS167	105752
Japan	IBRD (World Bank)	20 Dec 60	400UNTS279	105754
Burma	IBRD (World Bank)	16 Jan 61	400UNTS73	105749
Mexico	IBRD (World Bank)	16 Jan 61	422UNTS203	106076
Costa Rica	IBRD (World Bank)	03 Feb 61	414UNTS314	105977
IBRD (World Bank)	Yugoslavia	23 Feb 61	415UNTS92	105982
Japan	IBRD (World Bank)	16 Mar 61	400UNTS201	105753
IBRD (World Bank)	UK Great Britain	29 Mar 61	415UNTS300	105990
IBRD (World Bank)	Thailand	28 Apr 61	415UNTS121	105983
Japan	IBRD (World Bank)	02 May 61	415UNTS144	105984
Colombia	IBRD (World Bank)	12 May 61	415UNTS172	105985
Ceylon (Sri Lanka)	IBRD (World Bank)	06 Jun 61	414UNTS349	105978
Multilateral		14 Jun 61	415UNTS4	105979
IBRD (World Bank)	Sudan	14 Jun 61	415UNTS26	105980
IBRD (World Bank)	UK Great Britain	23 Jun 61	415UNTS358	105991
Pakistan	IBRD (World Bank)	27 Jun 61	425UNTS241	106127
Chile	IBRD (World Bank)	28 Jun 61	426UNTS33	106129
Argentina	IBRD (World Bank)	30 Jun 61	445UNTS85	106379
Israel	IBRD (World Bank)	11 Jul 61	429UNTS3	106188
Philippines	IBRD (World Bank)	26 Jul 61	414UNTS253	105976
India	IBRD (World Bank)	09 Aug 61	417UNTS297	106011
Finland	IBRD (World Bank)	09 Aug 61	415UNTS204	105986
IBRD (World Bank)	UK Great Britain	16 Aug 61	426UNTS287	106143
India	IBRD (World Bank)	17 Aug 61	417UNTS319	106012
Colombia	IBRD (World Bank)	28 Aug 61	416UNTS23	105993
Costa Rica	IBRD (World Bank)	06 Sep 61	446UNTS345	106408
India	IBRD (World Bank)	13 Oct 61	418UNTS3	106013
Costa Rica	IBRD (World Bank)	13 Oct 61	430UNTS27	106202
Philippines	IBRD (World Bank)	13 Oct 61	415UNTS269	105989
Peru	IBRD (World Bank)	03 Nov 61	430UNTS47	106203
Ethiopia	IBRD (World Bank)	22 Nov 61	426UNTS255	106142
Japan	IBRD (World Bank)	29 Nov 61	426UNTS3	106128
IBRD (World Bank)	UK Great Britain	29 Nov 61	426UNTS49	106130
IBRD (World Bank)	South Africa	01 Dec 61	425UNTS215	106126
IBRD (World Bank)	Venezuela	13 Dec 61	446UNTS371	106409
India	IBRD (World Bank)	22 Dec 61	481UNTS85	106979
Argentina	IBRD (World Bank)	19 Jan 62	446UNTS305	106407
Australia	IBRD (World Bank)	23 Jan 62	430UNTS3	106201
Ghana	IBRD (World Bank)	08 Feb 62	449UNTS207	106462
Iceland	IBRD (World Bank)	14 Feb 62	447UNTS95	106413
India	IBRD (World Bank)	28 Feb 62	447UNTS3	106410
Colombia	IBRD (World Bank)	23 May 62	447UNTS39	106411
Ethiopia	IBRD (World Bank)	31 May 62	467UNTS237	106765
Mexico	IBRD (World Bank)	20 Jun 62	467UNTS205	106764
Mexico	IBRD (World Bank)	20 Jun 62	468UNTS109	106771
IBRD (World Bank)	Yugoslavia	11 Jul 62	468UNTS143	106772
Finland	IBRD (World Bank)	15 Aug 62	467UNTS177	106763
Pakistan	IBRD (World Bank)	14 Sep 62	467UNTS152	106762

PARTY ONE	PARTY TWO	DATE	CITATION	NUMBER
Loan guarantee (Cont.)				
Pakistan	IBRD (World Bank)	14 Sep 62	467UNTS125	106761
India	IDA (Devel Assoc)	14 Sep 62	467UNTS265	106766
Panama	IBRD (World Bank)	14 Sep 62	476UNTS153	106908
Israel	IBRD (World Bank)	17 Oct 62	467UNTS107	106760
IBRD (World Bank)	Uruguay	26 Oct 62	481UNTS39	106977
Nigeria	IBRD (World Bank)	10 Dec 62	468UNTS255	106776
IBRD (World Bank)	Thailand	21 Dec 62	467UNTS43	106757
Morocco	IBRD (World Bank)	21 Dec 62	478UNTS205	106937
IBRD (World Bank)	Thailand	21 Dec 62	467UNTS63	106758
Pakistan	IBRD (World Bank)	13 Feb 63	467UNTS3	106756
Philippines	IBRD (World Bank)	15 Feb 63	478UNTS161	106936
Nicaragua	IBRD (World Bank)	01 Mar 63	481UNTS15	106976
IBRD (World Bank)	Thailand	07 Mar 63	467UNTS83	106759
Peru	IBRD (World Bank)	13 Mar 63	478UNTS245	106938
Thailand	USA (United States)	25 Apr 63	476UNTS115	106906
Mexico	IBRD (World Bank)	29 Apr 63	489UNTS151	107138
IBRD (World Bank)	UK Great Britain	16 May 63	476UNTS211	106910
IBRD (World Bank)	UK Great Britain	16 May 63	477UNTS361	106929
Colombia	IBRD (World Bank)	03 Jun 63	490UNTS199	107155
India	IBRD (World Bank)	05 Jun 63	481UNTS191	106983
IBRD (World Bank)	Thailand	11 Jun 63	481UNTS227	106984
El Salvador	IBRD (World Bank)	19 Jun 63	481UNTS59	106978
Colombia	IBRD (World Bank)	21 Jun 63	482UNTS159	106994
IBRD (World Bank)	Yugoslavia	21 Jun 63	482UNTS43	106990
Colombia	IBRD (World Bank)	28 Jun 63	489UNTS113	107137
Costa Rica	IBRD (World Bank)	10 Jul 63	482UNTS69	106991
Malaysia	IBRD (World Bank)	15 Jul 63	482UNTS123	106993
Colombia	IBRD (World Bank)	16 Jul 63	482UNTS256	106998
Denmark	IBRD (World Bank)	24 Jul 63	481UNTS171	106982
Malaysia	IBRD (World Bank)	07 Aug 63	485UNTS253	107060
IBRD (World Bank)	UK Great Britain	06 Sep 63	483UNTS173	107013
Finland	IBRD (World Bank)	18 Sep 63	491UNTS345	107183
IBRD (World Bank)	Venezuela	20 Sep 63	482UNTS227	106997
Mexico	IBRD (World Bank)	20 Sep 63	491UNTS317	107182
IBRD (World Bank)	UK Great Britain	23 Sep 63	503UNTS247	107348
Japan	IBRD (World Bank)	27 Sep 63	485UNTS283	107061
Taiwan	IBRD (World Bank)	27 Sep 63	483UNTS151	107012
El Salvador	IBRD (World Bank)	01 Oct 63	517UNTS3	107481
Norway	IBRD (World Bank)	15 Oct 63	482UNTS103	106992
IBRD (World Bank)	Spain	25 Oct 63	491UNTS297	107181
IBRD (World Bank)	Yugoslavia	28 Oct 63	503UNTS289	107349
Portugal	IBRD (World Bank)	06 Nov 63	491UNTS137	107176
Portugal	IBRD (World Bank)	06 Nov 63	492UNTS89	107188
New Zealand	IBRD (World Bank)	12 Nov 63	485UNTS233	107059
Peru	IBRD (World Bank)	22 Nov 63	491UNTS101	107175
Chile	IBRD (World Bank)	18 Dec 63	504UNTS3	107351
Chile	IBRD (World Bank)	18 Dec 63	504UNTS29	107352
Multilateral		30 Dec 63	568UNTS215	108270
Multilateral		30 Dec 63	551UNTS105	108036
Multilateral		30 Dec 63	568UNTS233	108271
Multilateral		30 Dec 63	551UNTS119	108037
Multilateral		30 Dec 63	551UNTS75	108035
Multilateral		30 Dec 63	568UNTS243	108272
Liberia	IBRD (World Bank)	08 Jan 64	504UNTS53	107353
Colombia	IBRD (World Bank)	07 Feb 64	516UNTS99	107473
IBRD (World Bank)	Thailand	11 Mar 64	504UNTS73	107354
New Zealand	IBRD (World Bank)	12 Mar 64	505UNTS3	107362
Nigeria	IBRD (World Bank)	12 Mar 64	516UNTS325	107480
Japan	IBRD (World Bank)	22 Apr 64	505UNTS21	107363
Peru	IBRD (World Bank)	22 Apr 64	519UNTS95	107503
Ethiopia	IBRD (World Bank)	08 May 64	505UNTS51	107364
Algeria	IBRD (World Bank)	14 May 64	522UNTS265	107552
Pakistan	IBRD (World Bank)	14 May 64	516UNTS145	107475
Ecuador	IBRD (World Bank)	26 May 64	534UNTS113	107758
IBRD (World Bank)	Tunisia	05 Jun 64	539UNTS129	107827

PARTY ONE	PARTY TWO	DATE	CITATION	NUMBER
Loan guarantee (Cont.)				
Iran	IBRD (World Bank)	10 Jun 64	537UNTS111	107799
Nigeria	IBRD (World Bank)	07 Jul 64	537UNTS3	107795
Finland	IBRD (World Bank)	10 Jul 64	516UNTS125	107474
Gabon	IBRD (World Bank)	10 Jul 64	537UNTS63	107797
Philippines	IBRD (World Bank)	22 Jul 64	516UNTS171	107476
IBRD (World Bank)	Spain	31 Jul 64	537UNTS81	107798
IBRD (World Bank)	Sierra Leone	18 Aug 64	516UNTS295	107479
Morocco	IBRD (World Bank)	26 Aug 64	537UNTS193	107802
IBRD (World Bank)	Venezuela	28 Aug 64	537UNTS135	107800
IBRD (World Bank)	Venezuela	28 Aug 64	520UNTS97	107512
Philippines	IBRD (World Bank)	28 Oct 64	537UNTS165	107801
IBRD (World Bank)	Thailand	25 Nov 64	537UNTS273	107805
IBRD (World Bank)	Yugoslavia	11 Dec 64	537UNTS321	107807
Paraguay	IBRD (World Bank)	16 Dec 64	549UNTS173	107999
Taiwan	IBRD (World Bank)	17 Dec 64	538UNTS3	107808
Japan	IBRD (World Bank)	23 Dec 64	538UNTS37	107809
Japan	IBRD (World Bank)	13 Jan 65	537UNTS293	107806
Honduras	IBRD (World Bank)	02 Feb 65	561UNTS255	108188
Mexico	IBRD (World Bank)	04 Feb 65	549UNTS189	108000
Chile	IBRD (World Bank)	12 Feb 65	537UNTS35	107796
Malaysia	IBRD (World Bank)	26 Feb 65	549UNTS239	108002
Brazil	IBRD (World Bank)	26 Feb 65	567UNTS91	108253
Brazil	IBRD (World Bank)	26 Feb 65	553UNTS3	108065
IBRD (World Bank)	Thailand	22 Mar 65	538UNTS63	107810
IBRD (World Bank)	Uruguay	30 Mar 65	567UNTS45	108251
Iran	IBRD (World Bank)	28 Apr 65	555UNTS21	108103
Iran	IBRD (World Bank)	28 Apr 65	555UNTS45	108104
Taiwan	IBRD (World Bank)	28 Apr 65	549UNTS145	107998
Portugal	IBRD (World Bank)	29 Apr 65	549UNTS69	107991
Japan	IBRD (World Bank)	26 May 65	550UNTS95	108010
Peru	IBRD (World Bank)	03 Jun 65	551UNTS227	108045
India	IBRD (World Bank)	11 Jun 65	557UNTS101	108130
India	IBRD (World Bank)	11 Jun 65	557UNTS59	108128
Peru	IBRD (World Bank)	18 Jun 65	568UNTS191	108269
Italy	IBRD (World Bank)	28 Jun 65	567UNTS127	108254
Finland	IBRD (World Bank)	30 Jun 65	550UNTS63	108009
Pakistan	IBRD (World Bank)	09 Jul 65	554UNTS39	108096
Iran	IBRD (World Bank)	12 Jul 65	554UNTS3	108095
Nigeria	IBRD (World Bank)	26 Sep 65	571UNTS39	108298
Nigeria	IBRD (World Bank)	26 Sep 65	570UNTS233	108296
IBRD (World Bank)	Tanzania	29 Sep 65	568UNTS309	108275
East Afri Service	IBRD (World Bank)	29 Sep 65	568UNTS327	200623
Kenya	IBRD (World Bank)	29 Sep 65	568UNTS289	108274
IBRD (World Bank)	Spain	29 Sep 65	568UNTS49	108264
IBRD (World Bank)	Uganda	29 Sep 65	568UNTS317	108276
Mexico	IBRD (World Bank)	01 Oct 65	589UNTS339	108542
Chile	IBRD (World Bank)	06 Oct 65	567UNTS293	108261
Philippines	IBRD (World Bank)	02 Nov 65	567UNTS3	108249
Malaysia	IBRD (World Bank)	17 Nov 65	568UNTS23	108263
IBRD (World Bank)	Venezuela	13 Dec 65	568UNTS77	108265
Mexico	IBRD (World Bank)	15 Dec 65	568UNTS125	108267
Paraguay	IBRD (World Bank)	16 Dec 65	568UNTS165	108268
New Zealand	IBRD (World Bank)	17 Dec 65	567UNTS255	108259
New Zealand	IBRD (World Bank)	17 Dec 65	567UNTS275	108260
IBRD (World Bank)	Sudan	27 Dec 65	567UNTS27	108250
Ethiopia	IBRD (World Bank)	28 Dec 65	567UNTS229	108258
Brazil	IBRD (World Bank)	15 Mar 66	599UNTS52	108664
Guinea	IBRD (World Bank)	30 Mar 66	568UNTS3	108262
Paraguay	IBRD (World Bank)	04 Apr 66	570UNTS41	108287
IBRD (World Bank)	Venezuela	21 Apr 66	568UNTS257	108273
Finland	IBRD (World Bank)	27 Apr 66	568UNTS107	108266
Multilateral		04 May 66	575UNTS49	108354
Peru	IBRD (World Bank)	13 May 66	570UNTS61	108288
IBRD (World Bank)	Tunisia	16 May 66	584UNTS155	108477
Mexico	IBRD (World Bank)	25 May 66	596UNTS3	108627

PARTY ONE	PARTY TWO	DATE	CITATION	NUMBER
Loan guarantee (Cont.)				
Colombia	IBRD (World Bank)	31 May 66	608UNTS279	108820
Morocco	IBRD (World Bank)	13 Jun 66	615UNTS205	108881
Portugal	IBRD (World Bank)	14 Jun 66	581UNTS29	108431
Portugal	IBRD (World Bank)	14 Jun 66	581UNTS3	108430
Jamaica	IBRD (World Bank)	20 Jun 66	582UNTS145	108462
IBRD (World Bank)	Thailand	24 Jun 66	582UNTS259	108466
India	IBRD (World Bank)	07 Jul 66	595UNTS3	108610
Iraq	IBRD (World Bank)	22 Jul 66	584UNTS233	108480
Malaysia	IBRD (World Bank)	26 Jul 66	586UNTS195	108504
Iran	IBRD (World Bank)	26 Jul 66	582UNTS107	108461
IBRD (World Bank)	Turkey	10 Aug 66	585UNTS199	108490
IBRD (World Bank)	Singapore	11 Aug 66	585UNTS39	108482
Honduras	IBRD (World Bank)	25 Aug 66	582UNTS79	108460
Peru	IBRD (World Bank)	07 Sep 66	585UNTS3	108481
IBRD (World Bank)	South Africa	08 Sep 66	585UNTS71	108483
Philippines	IBRD (World Bank)	23 Sep 66	596UNTS71	108629
USSR (Soviet Union)	Yugoslavia	29 Sep 66	608UNTS219	108818
Jamaica	IBRD (World Bank)	30 Sep 66	582UNTS179	108463
IBRD (World Bank)	Zambia	04 Oct 66	585UNTS181	108489
Nicaragua	IBRD (World Bank)	05 Oct 66	582UNTS231	108465
IBRD (World Bank)	Singapore	04 Nov 66	585UNTS155	108488
Brazil	IBRD (World Bank)	19 Dec 66	599UNTS205	108668
Brazil	IBRD (World Bank)	19 Dec 66	599UNTS107	108665
Brazil	IBRD (World Bank)	19 Dec 66	599UNTS149	108666
Brazil	IBRD (World Bank)	19 Dec 66	599UNTS177	108667
Chile	IBRD (World Bank)	23 Dec 66	595UNTS141	108618
Jamaica	IBRD (World Bank)	23 Jan 67	594UNTS311	108608
IBRD (World Bank)	Venezuela	26 Jan 67	596UNTS35	108628
Kenya	IBRD (World Bank)	17 Feb 67	599UNTS233	108669
IBRD (World Bank)	Tanzania	17 Feb 67	599UNTS287	108671
IBRD (World Bank)	Uganda	17 Feb 67	599UNTS321	108673
IBRD (World Bank)	Yugoslavia	24 Feb 67	599UNTS27	108663
Guatemala	IBRD (World Bank)	10 Mar 67	616UNTS139	108894
Pakistan	IBRD (World Bank)	15 Mar 67	599UNTS245	108670
IBRD (World Bank)	Thailand	24 Mar 67	599UNTS299	108672
Cameroon	IBRD (World Bank)	28 Mar 67	618UNTS89	108925
IBRD (World Bank)	Senegal	01 May 67	615UNTS267	108883
Cyprus	IBRD (World Bank)	16 May 67	617UNTS21	108906
Colombia	IBRD (World Bank)	15 Jun 67	615UNTS47	108877
Colombia	IBRD (World Bank)	29 Jun 67	619UNTS99	108941
IBRD (World Bank)	Singapore	05 Jul 67	618UNTS189	108928
IBRD (World Bank)	Yugoslavia	18 Jul 67	615UNTS343	108886
Argentina	IBRD (World Bank)	31 Jul 67	633UNTS289	109042
Taiwan	IBRD (World Bank)	02 Aug 67	618UNTS301	108932
IBRD (World Bank)	Spain	04 Aug 67	619UNTS209	108944
Taiwan	IBRD (World Bank)	07 Aug 67	620UNTS113	108952
Pakistan	IBRD (World Bank)	10 Aug 67	618UNTS261	108931
Peru	IBRD (World Bank)	11 Sep 67	619UNTS171	108943
IBRD (World Bank)	Tunisia	14 Sep 67	639UNTS147	109149
IBRD (World Bank)	Singapore	15 Sep 67	615UNTS295	108884
India	IBRD (World Bank)	19 Sep 67	615UNTS165	108880
Iran	IBRD (World Bank)	17 Oct 67	0UNTS0	109331
Israel	IBRD (World Bank)	15 Nov 67	619UNTS129	108942
Ceylon (Sri Lanka)	IBRD (World Bank)	22 Nov 67	639UNTS221	109151
IBRD (World Bank)	Tanzania	13 Dec 67	619UNTS239	108945
Argentina	IBRD (World Bank)	25 Jan 68	639UNTS187	109150
Mexico	IBRD (World Bank)	26 Jan 68	640UNTS3	109152
Korea, South	IBRD (World Bank)	31 Jan 68	639UNTS263	200638
Greece	IBRD (World Bank)	18 Mar 68	0UNTS0	109326
Malaysia	IBRD (World Bank)	17 Apr 68	0UNTS0	109360
IBRD (World Bank)	Thailand	23 May 68	0UNTS0	109332
Colombia	IBRD (World Bank)	03 Jun 68	0UNTS0	109334
Colombia	IBRD (World Bank)	03 Jun 68	0UNTS0	109333
Costa Rica	IBRD (World Bank)	05 Jun 68	0UNTS0	109365
Iran	IBRD (World Bank)	05 Jun 68	0UNTS0	109373

PARTY ONE	PARTY TWO	DATE	CITATION	NUMBER
Loan guarantee (Cont.)				
Nicaragua	IBRD (World Bank)	21 Jun 68	0UNTS0	109366
IBRD (World Bank)	Singapore	03 Jul 68	0UNTS0	109364
Gabon	IBRD (World Bank)	07 Jul 68	0UNTS0	109361
Colombia	IBRD (World Bank)	31 Jul 68	0UNTS0	109512
Ireland	UK Great Britain	23 Sep 68	0UNTS0	109374
Malaysia	IBRD (World Bank)	27 Sep 68	0UNTS0	109505
Malaysia	IBRD (World Bank)	27 Sep 68	0UNTS0	109506
Guarantor non-interference				
France	IBRD (World Bank)	09 May 47	152UNTS111	102014
Netherlands	IBRD (World Bank)	07 Aug 47	152UNTS165	102015
Denmark	IBRD (World Bank)	22 Aug 47	152UNTS223	102016
Luxembourg	IBRD (World Bank)	28 Aug 47	153UNTS3	102017
Netherlands	IBRD (World Bank)	15 Jul 48	153UNTS259	102023
Netherlands	IBRD (World Bank)	15 Jul 48	153UNTS259	102022
Netherlands	IBRD (World Bank)	15 Jul 48	153UNTS259	102021
Netherlands	IBRD (World Bank)	15 Jul 48	153UNTS259	102024
Netherlands	IBRD (World Bank)	15 Jul 48	153UNTS259	102025
Mexico	IBRD (World Bank)	06 Jan 49	154UNTS81	102028
Mexico	IBRD (World Bank)	06 Jan 49	154UNTS3	102027
Belgium	IBRD (World Bank)	01 Mar 49	154UNTS133	102029
Chile	IBRD (World Bank)	23 Mar 49	153UNTS61	102018
Chile	IBRD (World Bank)	23 Mar 49	153UNTS141	102019
Netherlands	IBRD (World Bank)	26 Jul 49	154UNTS178	102030
Finland	IBRD (World Bank)	01 Aug 49	156UNTS289	200480
India	IBRD (World Bank)	18 Aug 49	154UNTS269	102031
Colombia	IBRD (World Bank)	19 Aug 49	154UNTS329	102032
IBRD (World Bank)	Yugoslavia	17 Sep 49	155UNTS3	102034
India	IBRD (World Bank)	29 Sep 49	154UNTS393	102033
Finland	IBRD (World Bank)	17 Oct 49	156UNTS355	200481
El Salvador	IBRD (World Bank)	14 Dec 49	155UNTS43	102035
India	IBRD (World Bank)	18 Apr 50	155UNTS117	102036
Mexico	IBRD (World Bank)	28 Apr 50	155UNTS185	102037
Brazil	IBRD (World Bank)	26 May 50	301UNTS165	104345
Iraq	IBRD (World Bank)	15 Jun 50	155UNTS267	102038
IBRD (World Bank)	Turkey	07 Jul 50	156UNTS3	102039
IBRD (World Bank)	Turkey	07 Jul 50	156UNTS75	102040
IBRD (World Bank)	Uruguay	25 Aug 50	156UNTS203	102042
Ethiopia	IBRD (World Bank)	13 Sep 50	157UNTS213	102055
Ethiopia	IBRD (World Bank)	13 Sep 50	157UNTS233	102056
Mexico	IBRD (World Bank)	18 Oct 50	157UNTS259	102057
IBRD (World Bank)	Turkey	19 Oct 50	157UNTS333	102058
IBRD (World Bank)	Thailand	27 Oct 50	158UNTS3	102059
IBRD (World Bank)	Thailand	27 Oct 50	158UNTS25	102060
IBRD (World Bank)	Thailand	27 Oct 50	158UNTS43	102061
Australia	IBRD (World Bank)	14 Nov 50	156UNTS147	102041
Colombia	IBRD (World Bank)	28 Dec 50	158UNTS87	102063
IBRD (World Bank)	South Africa	23 Jan 51	158UNTS135	102065
IBRD (World Bank)	South Africa	23 Jan 51	158UNTS115	102064
Ethiopia	IBRD (World Bank)	19 Feb 51	186UNTS101	102486
Colombia	IBRD (World Bank)	10 Apr 51	158UNTS155	102066
Nicaragua	IBRD (World Bank)	07 Jun 51	158UNTS277	102068
Nicaragua	IBRD (World Bank)	07 Jun 51	158UNTS215	102067
Iceland	IBRD (World Bank)	20 Jun 51	158UNTS301	102069
Belgium	IBRD (World Bank)	13 Sep 51	158UNTS349	102071
Italy	IBRD (World Bank)	10 Oct 51	159UNTS383	200482
Chile	IBRD (World Bank)	10 Oct 51	158UNTS369	102072
Colombia	IBRD (World Bank)	13 Oct 51	159UNTS75	102084
Nicaragua	IBRD (World Bank)	29 Oct 51	159UNTS35	102082
Iceland	IBRD (World Bank)	01 Nov 51	159UNTS55	102083
Paraguay	IBRD (World Bank)	07 Dec 51	159UNTS103	102085
Mexico	IBRD (World Bank)	11 Jan 52	159UNTS129	102086
Peru	IBRD (World Bank)	23 Jan 52	159UNTS163	102087
IBRD (World Bank)	UK Great Britain	27 Feb 52	159UNTS181	102088
Netherlands	IBRD (World Bank)	20 Mar 52	159UNTS207	102089

PARTY ONE	PARTY TWO	DATE	CITATION	NUMBER
Guarantor non-interference (Cont.)				
Pakistan	IBRD (World Bank)	27 Mar 52	159UNTS251	102090
Finland	IBRD (World Bank)	30 Apr 52	159UNTS408	200483
Pakistan	IBRD (World Bank)	13 Jun 52	191UNTS85	102578
IBRD (World Bank)	Turkey	18 Jun 52	159UNTS269	102091
Brazil	IBRD (World Bank)	27 Jun 52	190UNTS115	102561
Brazil	IBRD (World Bank)	27 Jun 52	190UNTS85	102560
Peru	IBRD (World Bank)	08 Jul 52	159UNTS321	102093
Australia	IBRD (World Bank)	08 Jul 52	159UNTS295	102092
Colombia	IBRD (World Bank)	26 Aug 52	159UNTS339	102094
Iceland	IBRD (World Bank)	26 Aug 52	159UNTS363	102095
Japan	IBRD (World Bank)	12 Nov 52	354UNTS313	105068
India	IBRD (World Bank)	18 Dec 52	201UNTS241	102719
India	IBRD (World Bank)	23 Jan 53	201UNTS145	102715
IBRD (World Bank)	Yugoslavia	11 Feb 53	165UNTS231	102179
IBRD (World Bank)	UK Great Britain	11 Mar 53	172UNTS115	102243
Brazil	IBRD (World Bank)	30 Apr 53	190UNTS133	102562
Brazil	IBRD (World Bank)	17 Jul 53	190UNTS149	102563
IBRD (World Bank)	South Africa	28 Aug 53	180UNTS73	102376
IBRD (World Bank)	South Africa	28 Aug 53	180UNTS91	102377
Nicaragua	IBRD (World Bank)	04 Sep 53	186UNTS137	102488
Iceland	IBRD (World Bank)	04 Sep 53	188UNTS3	102519
Nicaragua	IBRD (World Bank)	04 Sep 53	186UNTS117	102487
Iceland	IBRD (World Bank)	04 Sep 53	178UNTS275	102344
Colombia	IBRD (World Bank)	10 Sep 53	203UNTS3	102738
IBRD (World Bank)	Turkey	10 Sep 53	187UNTS71	102502
Chile	IBRD (World Bank)	10 Sep 53	188UNTS25	102520
Panama	IBRD (World Bank)	25 Sep 53	188UNTS95	102522
Panama	IBRD (World Bank)	25 Sep 53	188UNTS71	102521
Italy	IBRD (World Bank)	06 Oct 53	301UNTS135	104344
Japan	IBRD (World Bank)	15 Oct 53	187UNTS321	200512
Japan	IBRD (World Bank)	15 Oct 53	187UNTS367	200513
Japan	IBRD (World Bank)	15 Oct 53	187UNTS271	200511
Brazil	IBRD (World Bank)	18 Dec 53	301UNTS229	104346
Brazil	IBRD (World Bank)	18 Dec 53	190UNTS179	102564
Brazil	IBRD (World Bank)	24 Feb 54	301UNTS249	104347
Australia	IBRD (World Bank)	02 Mar 54	191UNTS103	102579
Norway	IBRD (World Bank)	08 Apr 54	201UNTS131	102714
Peru	IBRD (World Bank)	12 Apr 54	190UNTS231	102567
Pakistan	IBRD (World Bank)	02 Jun 54	324UNTS59	104678
France	IBRD (World Bank)	10 Jun 54	210UNTS89	102836
Ceylon (Sri Lanka)	IBRD (World Bank)	09 Jul 54	198UNTS313	200517
Mexico	IBRD (World Bank)	24 Aug 54	286UNTS211	104168
El Salvador	IBRD (World Bank)	12 Oct 54	203UNTS37	102739
Austria	IBRD (World Bank)	08 Nov 54	216UNTS305	200528
Peru	IBRD (World Bank)	12 Nov 54	209UNTS287	102831
India	IBRD (World Bank)	19 Nov 54	309UNTS159	104473
Belgium	IBRD (World Bank)	14 Dec 54	210UNTS113	102837
Colombia	IBRD (World Bank)	29 Dec 54	211UNTS135	102851
India	IBRD (World Bank)	14 Mar 55	309UNTS129	104472
IBRD (World Bank)	UK Great Britain	15 Mar 55	265UNTS85	103808
Australia	IBRD (World Bank)	18 Mar 55	220UNTS131	102998
Finland	IBRD (World Bank)	24 Mar 55	211UNTS305	200525
Colombia	IBRD (World Bank)	24 Mar 55	212UNTS217	102874
Peru	IBRD (World Bank)	05 Apr 55	211UNTS115	102850
Norway	IBRD (World Bank)	19 Apr 55	211UNTS159	102852
Peru	IBRD (World Bank)	19 Apr 55	221UNTS153	103007
Italy	IBRD (World Bank)	01 Jun 55	358UNTS203	105137
Austria	IBRD (World Bank)	14 Jun 55	221UNTS375	200531
Colombia	IBRD (World Bank)	15 Jun 55	248UNTS161	103494
Pakistan	IBRD (World Bank)	20 Jun 55	230UNTS41	103176
Nicaragua	IBRD (World Bank)	08 Jul 55	229UNTS123	103163
Nicaragua	IBRD (World Bank)	08 Jul 55	229UNTS97	103162
Panama	IBRD (World Bank)	12 Jul 55	219UNTS127	102970
Guatemala	IBRD (World Bank)	29 Jul 55	229UNTS167	103165
Pakistan	IBRD (World Bank)	04 Aug 55	230UNTS79	103177

PARTY ONE	PARTY TWO	DATE	CITATION	NUMBER
Guarantor non-interference (Cont.)				
Peru	IBRD (World Bank)	05 Aug 55	218UNTS3	102950
Pakistan	IBRD (World Bank)	06 Aug 55	236UNTS195	103325
IBRD (World Bank)	Thailand	09 Aug 55	221UNTS283	103011
Lebanon	IBRD (World Bank)	25 Aug 55	230UNTS233	103188
France	IBRD (World Bank)	26 Aug 55	247UNTS305	103478
Nicaragua	IBRD (World Bank)	26 Aug 55	229UNTS145	103164
IBRD (World Bank)	Uruguay	29 Aug 55	243UNTS123	103450
Austria	USSR (Soviet Union)	17 Oct 55	0UNTS0	109254
Japan	IBRD (World Bank)	25 Oct 55	230UNTS379	200534
IBRD (World Bank)	South Africa	28 Nov 55	230UNTS101	103178
Honduras	IBRD (World Bank)	22 Dec 55	230UNTS262	103189
Japan	IBRD (World Bank)	21 Feb 56	248UNTS321	200543
Ecuador	IBRD (World Bank)	26 Mar 56	292UNTS391	104277
Norway	IBRD (World Bank)	03 May 56	243UNTS281	103455
Burma	IBRD (World Bank)	04 May 56	253UNTS209	103585
Burma	IBRD (World Bank)	04 May 56	253UNTS179	103584
Haiti	IBRD (World Bank)	07 May 56	252UNTS279	103570
Finland	IBRD (World Bank)	22 May 56	248UNTS57	103485
Nicaragua	IBRD (World Bank)	22 May 56	253UNTS233	103586
Colombia	IBRD (World Bank)	06 Jun 56	248UNTS139	103493
IBRD (World Bank)	UK Great Britain	21 Jun 56	285UNTS355	104157
Fed Rhod/Nyasaland	IBRD (World Bank)	21 Jun 56	285UNTS317	104156
India	IBRD (World Bank)	26 Jun 56	301UNTS3	104341
Costa Rica	IBRD (World Bank)	18 Sep 56	260UNTS369	103721
Austria	IBRD (World Bank)	21 Sep 56	259UNTS17	103681
Austria	IBRD (World Bank)	21 Sep 56	259UNTS43	103682
Italy	IBRD (World Bank)	11 Oct 56	359UNTS3	105138
IBRD (World Bank)	Thailand	12 Oct 56	261UNTS117	103728
IBRD (World Bank)	Uruguay	25 Oct 56	265UNTS59	103807
Chile	IBRD (World Bank)	01 Nov 56	261UNTS27	103724
Australia	IBRD (World Bank)	15 Nov 56	288UNTS117	104201
Australia	IBRD (World Bank)	03 Dec 56	288UNTS99	104200
India	IBRD (World Bank)	19 Dec 56	310UNTS75	104489
Japan	IBRD (World Bank)	19 Dec 56	264UNTS179	103793
Japan	IBRD (World Bank)	19 Dec 56	268UNTS203	103859
Iran	IBRD (World Bank)	22 Jan 57	317UNTS129	104600
Ethiopia	IBRD (World Bank)	28 Jan 57	286UNTS307	104175
India	IBRD (World Bank)	05 Mar 57	272UNTS201	103939
Peru	IBRD (World Bank)	13 Mar 57	274UNTS59	103958
Netherlands	IBRD (World Bank)	15 May 57	274UNTS211	103967
India	IBRD (World Bank)	29 May 57	309UNTS201	104474
Belgium	IBRD (World Bank)	26 Jun 57	322UNTS301	104661
India	IBRD (World Bank)	12 Jul 57	288UNTS135	104202
Chile	IBRD (World Bank)	24 Jul 57	282UNTS139	104098
Chile	IBRD (World Bank)	24 Jul 57	282UNTS189	104099
Japan	IBRD (World Bank)	09 Aug 57	293UNTS59	104286
Belgium	IBRD (World Bank)	10 Sep 57	286UNTS291	104174
IBRD (World Bank)	Thailand	12 Sep 57	299UNTS349	104324
Ecuador	IBRD (World Bank)	20 Sep 57	293UNTS135	104291
Ecuador	IBRD (World Bank)	20 Sep 57	289UNTS237	104221
IBRD (World Bank)	South Africa	01 Oct 57	280UNTS285	104065
Austria	IBRD (World Bank)	10 Oct 57	301UNTS95	104343
Pakistan	IBRD (World Bank)	18 Oct 57	299UNTS303	104322
India	IBRD (World Bank)	20 Nov 57	301UNTS47	104342
Philippines	IBRD (World Bank)	22 Nov 57	293UNTS83	104287
Belgium	IBRD (World Bank)	27 Nov 57	292UNTS175	104273
Pakistan	IBRD (World Bank)	17 Dec 57	299UNTS321	104323
Mexico	IBRD (World Bank)	14 Jan 58	293UNTS167	104292
Brazil	IBRD (World Bank)	22 Jan 58	323UNTS99	104666
Pakistan	IBRD (World Bank)	23 Apr 58	323UNTS253	104672
Chile	IBRD (World Bank)	28 Apr 58	359UNTS89	105140
Austria	IBRD (World Bank)	28 Apr 58	359UNTS145	105142
IBRD (World Bank)	UK Great Britain	02 May 58	324UNTS25	104677
Mexico	IBRD (World Bank)	05 May 58	309UNTS3	104466
Honduras	IBRD (World Bank)	09 May 58	323UNTS4	104662

PARTY ONE	PARTY TWO	DATE	CITATION	NUMBER
Guarantor non-interference (Cont.)				
Japan	IBRD (World Bank)	13 Jun 58	312UNTS159	104518
IBRD (World Bank)	UK Great Britain	16 Jun 58	309UNTS35	104467
India	IBRD (World Bank)	25 Jun 58	323UNTS131	104667
India	IBRD (World Bank)	25 Jun 58	323UNTS157	104668
IBRD (World Bank)	Sudan	21 Jul 58	323UNTS183	104669
India	IBRD (World Bank)	23 Jul 58	317UNTS3	104590
Japan	IBRD (World Bank)	18 Aug 58	323UNTS205	104670
Japan	IBRD (World Bank)	10 Sep 58	318UNTS133	104612
Japan	IBRD (World Bank)	10 Sep 58	323UNTS297	104673
India	IBRD (World Bank)	16 Sep 58	323UNTS235	104671
Peru	IBRD (World Bank)	17 Sep 58	323UNTS27	104663
Ceylon (Sri Lanka)	IBRD (World Bank)	17 Sep 58	323UNTS51	104664
Fed of Malaya	IBRD (World Bank)	22 Sep 58	323UNTS71	104665
Brazil	IBRD (World Bank)	03 Oct 58	337UNTS177	104823
Ecuador	IBRD (World Bank)	09 Oct 58	337UNTS299	104827
Austria	IBRD (World Bank)	02 Dec 58	340UNTS3	104856
IBRD (World Bank)	South Africa	02 Dec 58	324UNTS3	104676
Colombia	IBRD (World Bank)	15 Dec 58	354UNTS233	105065
El Salvador	IBRD (World Bank)	07 Jan 59	346UNTS51	104977
Colombia	IBRD (World Bank)	30 Jan 59	337UNTS327	104828
Denmark	IBRD (World Bank)	04 Feb 59	328UNTS143	104733
Costa Rica	IBRD (World Bank)	11 Feb 59	337UNTS245	104825
Japan	IBRD (World Bank)	17 Feb 59	337UNTS205	104824
El Salvador	IBRD (World Bank)	20 Feb 59	362UNTS75	105183
Finland	IBRD (World Bank)	16 Mar 59	337UNTS269	104826
India	IBRD (World Bank)	08 Apr 59	348UNTS131	104998
Italy	IBRD (World Bank)	21 Apr 59	359UNTS191	105143
Honduras	IBRD (World Bank)	20 May 59	359UNTS119	105141
Colombia	IBRD (World Bank)	20 May 59	344UNTS251	104953
Iran	IBRD (World Bank)	29 May 59	348UNTS103	104997
IBRD (World Bank)	South Africa	10 Jun 59	340UNTS33	104857
Brazil	IBRD (World Bank)	17 Jun 59	377UNTS111	105398
Gabon	IBRD (World Bank)	30 Jun 59	452UNTS135	106507
Congo (Brazzaville)	IBRD (World Bank)	30 Jun 59	452UNTS123	106506
France	IBRD (World Bank)	30 Jun 59	452UNTS67	106505
Norway	IBRD (World Bank)	08 Jul 59	344UNTS229	104952
India	IBRD (World Bank)	15 Jul 59	355UNTS95	105075
India	IBRD (World Bank)	15 Jul 59	346UNTS33	104976
Pakistan	IBRD (World Bank)	13 Aug 59	355UNTS129	105076
Italy	IBRD (World Bank)	16 Sep 59	375UNTS159	105366
Pakistan	IBRD (World Bank)	25 Sep 59	355UNTS169	105077
Japan	IBRD (World Bank)	12 Nov 59	354UNTS279	105067
Iran	IBRD (World Bank)	23 Nov 59	380UNTS245	105459
Pakistan	IBRD (World Bank)	30 Nov 59	355UNTS203	105078
France	IBRD (World Bank)	10 Dec 59	380UNTS319	105464
IBRD (World Bank)	United Arab Rep	22 Dec 59	354UNTS197	105063
IBRD (World Bank)	Uruguay	30 Dec 59	384UNTS275	105523
Colombia	IBRD (World Bank)	20 Jan 60	375UNTS49	105353
Iran	IBRD (World Bank)	20 Feb 60	384UNTS213	105521
France	IBRD (World Bank)	17 Mar 60	452UNTS147	106508
Mauritania	IBRD (World Bank)	17 Mar 60	452UNTS211	106509
Japan	IBRD (World Bank)	17 Mar 60	362UNTS43	105182
Belgium	IBRD (World Bank)	30 Mar 60	379UNTS161	105439
Belgium	IBRD (World Bank)	30 Mar 60	379UNTS129	105438
Belgium	IBRD (World Bank)	30 Mar 60	379UNTS103	105437
IBRD (World Bank)	UK Great Britain	01 Apr 60	379UNTS397	105446
Costa Rica	IBRD (World Bank)	04 May 60	390UNTS201	105609
Colombia	IBRD (World Bank)	10 May 60	379UNTS218	105441
IBRD (World Bank)	UK Great Britain	27 May 60	375UNTS201	105367
Peru	IBRD (World Bank)	01 Jun 60	380UNTS15	105448
IBRD (World Bank)	Sudan	17 Jun 60	379UNTS253	105442
Nicaragua	IBRD (World Bank)	22 Jun 60	384UNTS243	105522
Peru	IBRD (World Bank)	29 Jun 60	400UNTS99	105750
Honduras	IBRD (World Bank)	29 Jun 60	400UNTS137	105751
El Salvador	IBRD (World Bank)	29 Jul 60	390UNTS101	105605

Guarantor non-interference (Cont.)

PARTY ONE	PARTY TWO	DATE	CITATION	NUMBER
Panama	IBRD (World Bank)	19 Aug 60	390UNTS153	105607
Israel	IBRD (World Bank)	09 Sep 60	406UNTS3	105837
Pakistan	IBRD (World Bank)	19 Sep 60	444UNTS207	106370
Colombia	IBRD (World Bank)	20 Sep 60	390UNTS173	105608
Mexico	IBRD (World Bank)	18 Oct 60	422UNTS177	106075
India	IBRD (World Bank)	28 Oct 60	406UNTS27	105838
Norway	IBRD (World Bank)	02 Dec 60	390UNTS131	105606
Peru	IBRD (World Bank)	19 Dec 60	417UNTS275	106010
Japan	IBRD (World Bank)	20 Dec 60	400UNTS167	105752
Japan	IBRD (World Bank)	20 Dec 60	400UNTS279	105754
Mexico	IBRD (World Bank)	16 Jan 61	422UNTS203	106076
Burma	IBRD (World Bank)	16 Jan 61	400UNTS73	105749
Costa Rica	IBRD (World Bank)	03 Feb 61	414UNTS314	105977
IBRD (World Bank)	Yugoslavia	23 Feb 61	415UNTS92	105982
Japan	IBRD (World Bank)	16 Mar 61	400UNTS201	105753
IBRD (World Bank)	UK Great Britain	29 Mar 61	415UNTS300	105990
IBRD (World Bank)	Thailand	28 Apr 61	415UNTS121	105983
Japan	IBRD (World Bank)	02 May 61	415UNTS144	105984
Colombia	IBRD (World Bank)	12 May 61	415UNTS172	105985
Ceylon (Sri Lanka)	IBRD (World Bank)	06 Jun 61	414UNTS349	105978
IBRD (World Bank)	Sudan	14 Jun 61	415UNTS26	105980
Multilateral		14 Jun 61	415UNTS4	105979
IBRD (World Bank)	UK Great Britain	23 Jun 61	415UNTS358	105991
Pakistan	IBRD (World Bank)	27 Jun 61	425UNTS241	106127
Chile	IBRD (World Bank)	28 Jun 61	426UNTS33	106129
Argentina	IBRD (World Bank)	30 Jun 61	445UNTS85	106379
Israel	IBRD (World Bank)	11 Jul 61	429UNTS3	106188
Philippines	IBRD (World Bank)	26 Jul 61	414UNTS253	105976
India	IBRD (World Bank)	09 Aug 61	417UNTS297	106011
Finland	IBRD (World Bank)	09 Aug 61	415UNTS204	105986
IBRD (World Bank)	UK Great Britain	16 Aug 61	426UNTS287	106143
India	IBRD (World Bank)	17 Aug 61	417UNTS319	106012
Colombia	IBRD (World Bank)	28 Aug 61	416UNTS23	105993
Costa Rica	IBRD (World Bank)	06 Sep 61	446UNTS345	106408
Costa Rica	IBRD (World Bank)	13 Oct 61	430UNTS27	106202
Philippines	IBRD (World Bank)	13 Oct 61	415UNTS269	105989
India	IBRD (World Bank)	13 Oct 61	418UNTS3	106013
Peru	IBRD (World Bank)	03 Nov 61	430UNTS47	106203
IBRD (World Bank)	UK Great Britain	29 Nov 61	426UNTS49	106130
Japan	IBRD (World Bank)	29 Nov 61	426UNTS3	106128
IBRD (World Bank)	South Africa	01 Dec 61	425UNTS215	106126
IBRD (World Bank)	Venezuela	13 Dec 61	446UNTS371	106409
India	IBRD (World Bank)	22 Dec 61	481UNTS85	106979
Argentina	IBRD (World Bank)	19 Jan 62	446UNTS305	106407
Australia	IBRD (World Bank)	23 Jan 62	430UNTS3	106201
Ghana	IBRD (World Bank)	08 Feb 62	449UNTS207	106462
Iceland	IBRD (World Bank)	14 Feb 62	447UNTS95	106413
India	IBRD (World Bank)	28 Feb 62	447UNTS3	106410
Colombia	IBRD (World Bank)	23 May 62	447UNTS39	106411
Ethiopia	IBRD (World Bank)	31 May 62	467UNTS237	106765
Mexico	IBRD (World Bank)	20 Jun 62	468UNTS109	106771
Mexico	IBRD (World Bank)	20 Jun 62	467UNTS205	106764
IBRD (World Bank)	Yugoslavia	11 Jul 62	468UNTS143	106772
Finland	IBRD (World Bank)	15 Aug 62	467UNTS177	106763
Panama	IBRD (World Bank)	14 Sep 62	476UNTS153	106908
India	IDA (Devel Assoc)	14 Sep 62	467UNTS265	106766
Pakistan	IBRD (World Bank)	14 Sep 62	467UNTS125	106761
Pakistan	IBRD (World Bank)	14 Sep 62	467UNTS152	106762
Israel	IBRD (World Bank)	17 Oct 62	467UNTS107	106760
IBRD (World Bank)	Uruguay	26 Oct 62	481UNTS39	106977
Nigeria	IBRD (World Bank)	10 Dec 62	468UNTS255	106776
Morocco	IBRD (World Bank)	21 Dec 62	478UNTS205	106937
IBRD (World Bank)	Thailand	21 Dec 62	467UNTS63	106758
IBRD (World Bank)	Thailand	21 Dec 62	467UNTS43	106757
Pakistan	IBRD (World Bank)	13 Feb 63	467UNTS3	106756

Guarantor non-interference (Cont.)

PARTY ONE	PARTY TWO	DATE	CITATION	NUMBER
Philippines	IBRD (World Bank)	15 Feb 63	478UNTS161	106936
Nicaragua	IBRD (World Bank)	01 Mar 63	481UNTS15	106976
IBRD (World Bank)	Thailand	07 Mar 63	467UNTS83	106759
Peru	IBRD (World Bank)	13 Mar 63	478UNTS245	106938
Thailand	USA (United States)	25 Apr 63	476UNTS115	106906
Mexico	IBRD (World Bank)	29 Apr 63	489UNTS151	107138
IBRD (World Bank)	UK Great Britain	16 May 63	476UNTS211	106910
IBRD (World Bank)	UK Great Britain	16 May 63	477UNTS361	106929
Colombia	IBRD (World Bank)	03 Jun 63	490UNTS199	107155
India	IBRD (World Bank)	05 Jun 63	481UNTS191	106983
IBRD (World Bank)	Thailand	11 Jun 63	481UNTS227	106984
El Salvador	IBRD (World Bank)	19 Jun 63	481UNTS59	106978
Colombia	IBRD (World Bank)	21 Jun 63	482UNTS159	106994
IBRD (World Bank)	Yugoslavia	21 Jun 63	482UNTS43	106990
Colombia	IBRD (World Bank)	28 Jun 63	489UNTS113	107137
Costa Rica	IBRD (World Bank)	10 Jul 63	482UNTS69	106991
Malaysia	IBRD (World Bank)	15 Jul 63	482UNTS123	106993
Colombia	IBRD (World Bank)	16 Jul 63	482UNTS256	106998
Denmark	IBRD (World Bank)	24 Jul 63	481UNTS171	106982
Malaysia	IBRD (World Bank)	07 Aug 63	485UNTS253	107060
IBRD (World Bank)	UK Great Britain	06 Sep 63	483UNTS173	107013
Finland	IBRD (World Bank)	18 Sep 63	491UNTS345	107183
Mexico	IBRD (World Bank)	20 Sep 63	491UNTS317	107182
IBRD (World Bank)	Venezuela	20 Sep 63	482UNTS227	106997
IBRD (World Bank)	UK Great Britain	23 Sep 63	503UNTS247	107348
Japan	IBRD (World Bank)	27 Sep 63	485UNTS283	107061
Taiwan	IBRD (World Bank)	27 Sep 63	483UNTS151	107012
El Salvador	IBRD (World Bank)	01 Oct 63	517UNTS3	107481
IBRD (World Bank)	Spain	25 Oct 63	491UNTS297	107181
Portugal	IBRD (World Bank)	06 Nov 63	491UNTS137	107176
Portugal	IBRD (World Bank)	06 Nov 63	492UNTS89	107188
New Zealand	IBRD (World Bank)	12 Nov 63	485UNTS233	107059
Peru	IBRD (World Bank)	22 Nov 63	491UNTS101	107175
Chile	IBRD (World Bank)	18 Dec 63	504UNTS29	107352
Chile	IBRD (World Bank)	18 Dec 63	504UNTS3	107351
Multilateral		30 Dec 63	568UNTS215	108270
Multilateral		30 Dec 63	568UNTS233	108271
Multilateral		30 Dec 63	568UNTS243	108272
Multilateral		30 Dec 63	551UNTS105	108036
Multilateral		30 Dec 63	551UNTS119	108037
Liberia	IBRD (World Bank)	08 Jan 64	504UNTS53	107353
Colombia	IBRD (World Bank)	07 Feb 64	516UNTS99	107473
IBRD (World Bank)	Thailand	11 Mar 64	504UNTS73	107354
Nigeria	IBRD (World Bank)	12 Mar 64	516UNTS325	107480
New Zealand	IBRD (World Bank)	12 Mar 64	505UNTS3	107362
Peru	IBRD (World Bank)	22 Apr 64	519UNTS95	107503
Japan	IBRD (World Bank)	22 Apr 64	505UNTS21	107363
Ethiopia	IBRD (World Bank)	08 May 64	505UNTS51	107364
Algeria	IBRD (World Bank)	14 May 64	522UNTS265	107552
Pakistan	IBRD (World Bank)	14 May 64	516UNTS145	107475
Ecuador	IBRD (World Bank)	26 May 64	534UNTS113	107758
IBRD (World Bank)	Tunisia	05 Jun 64	539UNTS129	107827
Iran	IBRD (World Bank)	10 Jun 64	537UNTS111	107799
Nigeria	IBRD (World Bank)	07 Jul 64	537UNTS3	107795
Finland	IBRD (World Bank)	10 Jul 64	516UNTS125	107474
Gabon	IBRD (World Bank)	10 Jul 64	537UNTS63	107797
Philippines	IBRD (World Bank)	22 Jul 64	516UNTS171	107476
IBRD (World Bank)	Spain	31 Jul 64	537UNTS81	107798
IBRD (World Bank)	Sierra Leone	18 Aug 64	516UNTS295	107479
Morocco	IBRD (World Bank)	26 Aug 64	537UNTS193	107802
IBRD (World Bank)	Venezuela	28 Aug 64	520UNTS97	107512
IBRD (World Bank)	Venezuela	28 Aug 64	537UNTS135	107800
Philippines	IBRD (World Bank)	28 Oct 64	537UNTS165	107801
IBRD (World Bank)	Thailand	25 Nov 64	537UNTS273	107805
IBRD (World Bank)	Yugoslavia	11 Dec 64	537UNTS321	107807

PARTY ONE	PARTY TWO	DATE	CITATION	NUMBER
Guarantor non-interference (Cont.)				
Paraguay	IBRD (World Bank)	16 Dec 64	549UNTS173	107999
Taiwan	IBRD (World Bank)	17 Dec 64	538UNTS3	107808
Japan	IBRD (World Bank)	23 Dec 64	538UNTS37	107809
Japan	IBRD (World Bank)	13 Jan 65	537UNTS293	107806
Honduras	IBRD (World Bank)	02 Feb 65	561UNTS255	108188
Mexico	IBRD (World Bank)	04 Feb 65	549UNTS189	108000
Chile	IBRD (World Bank)	12 Feb 65	537UNTS35	107796
Brazil	IBRD (World Bank)	26 Feb 65	553UNTS3	108065
Brazil	IBRD (World Bank)	26 Feb 65	567UNTS91	108253
Malaysia	IBRD (World Bank)	26 Feb 65	549UNTS239	108002
IBRD (World Bank)	Thailand	22 Mar 65	538UNTS63	107810
IBRD (World Bank)	Uruguay	30 Mar 65	567UNTS45	108251
Iran	IBRD (World Bank)	28 Apr 65	555UNTS21	108103
Taiwan	IBRD (World Bank)	28 Apr 65	549UNTS145	107998
Iran	IBRD (World Bank)	28 Apr 65	555UNTS45	108104
Portugal	IBRD (World Bank)	29 Apr 65	549UNTS69	107991
Japan	IBRD (World Bank)	26 May 65	550UNTS95	108010
Peru	IBRD (World Bank)	03 Jun 65	551UNTS227	108045
India	IBRD (World Bank)	11 Jun 65	557UNTS59	108128
India	IBRD (World Bank)	11 Jun 65	557UNTS101	108130
Peru	IBRD (World Bank)	18 Jun 65	568UNTS191	108269
Italy	IBRD (World Bank)	28 Jun 65	567UNTS127	108254
Finland	IBRD (World Bank)	30 Jun 65	550UNTS63	108009
Pakistan	IBRD (World Bank)	09 Jul 65	554UNTS39	108096
Iran	IBRD (World Bank)	12 Jul 65	554UNTS3	108095
Nigeria	IBRD (World Bank)	26 Sep 65	570UNTS233	108296
Nigeria	IBRD (World Bank)	26 Sep 65	571UNTS39	108298
East Afri Service	IBRD (World Bank)	29 Sep 65	568UNTS327	200623
IBRD (World Bank)	Uganda	29 Sep 65	568UNTS317	108276
IBRD (World Bank)	Spain	29 Sep 65	568UNTS49	108264
IBRD (World Bank)	Tanzania	29 Sep 65	568UNTS309	108275
Kenya	IBRD (World Bank)	29 Sep 65	568UNTS289	108274
Mexico	IBRD (World Bank)	01 Oct 65	589UNTS339	108542
Chile	IBRD (World Bank)	06 Oct 65	567UNTS293	108261
Philippines	IBRD (World Bank)	02 Nov 65	567UNTS3	108249
Malaysia	IBRD (World Bank)	17 Nov 65	568UNTS23	108263
IBRD (World Bank)	Venezuela	13 Dec 65	568UNTS77	108265
Mexico	IBRD (World Bank)	15 Dec 65	568UNTS125	108267
Paraguay	IBRD (World Bank)	16 Dec 65	568UNTS165	108268
New Zealand	IBRD (World Bank)	17 Dec 65	567UNTS275	108260
New Zealand	IBRD (World Bank)	17 Dec 65	567UNTS255	108259
IBRD (World Bank)	Sudan	27 Dec 65	567UNTS27	108250
Ethiopia	IBRD (World Bank)	28 Dec 65	567UNTS229	108258
Guinea	IBRD (World Bank)	30 Mar 66	568UNTS3	108262
Paraguay	IBRD (World Bank)	04 Apr 66	570UNTS41	108287
IBRD (World Bank)	Venezuela	21 Apr 66	568UNTS257	108273
Finland	IBRD (World Bank)	27 Apr 66	568UNTS107	108266
Peru	IBRD (World Bank)	13 May 66	570UNTS61	108288
IBRD (World Bank)	Tunisia	16 May 66	584UNTS155	108477
Mexico	IBRD (World Bank)	25 May 66	596UNTS3	108627
Morocco	IBRD (World Bank)	13 Jun 66	615UNTS205	108881
Portugal	IBRD (World Bank)	14 Jun 66	581UNTS29	108431
Portugal	IBRD (World Bank)	14 Jun 66	581UNTS3	108430
Jamaica	IBRD (World Bank)	20 Jun 66	582UNTS145	108462
IBRD (World Bank)	Thailand	24 Jun 66	582UNTS259	108466
India	IBRD (World Bank)	07 Jul 66	595UNTS3	108610
Iraq	IBRD (World Bank)	22 Jul 66	584UNTS233	108480
Malaysia	IBRD (World Bank)	26 Jul 66	586UNTS195	108504
Iran	IBRD (World Bank)	26 Jul 66	582UNTS107	108461
IBRD (World Bank)	Turkey	10 Aug 66	585UNTS199	108490
IBRD (World Bank)	Singapore	11 Aug 66	585UNTS39	108482
Honduras	IBRD (World Bank)	25 Aug 66	582UNTS79	108460
Peru	IBRD (World Bank)	07 Sep 66	585UNTS3	108481
IBRD (World Bank)	South Africa	08 Sep 66	585UNTS71	108483
Jamaica	IBRD (World Bank)	30 Sep 66	582UNTS179	108463

PARTY ONE	PARTY TWO	DATE	CITATION	NUMBER
Guarantor non-interference (Cont.)				
IBRD (World Bank)	Zambia	04 Oct 66	585UNTS181	108489
Nicaragua	IBRD (World Bank)	05 Oct 66	582UNTS231	108465
IBRD (World Bank)	Singapore	04 Nov 66	585UNTS155	108488
Chile	IBRD (World Bank)	23 Dec 66	595UNTS141	108618
Jamaica	IBRD (World Bank)	23 Jan 67	594UNTS311	108608
IBRD (World Bank)	Venezuela	26 Jan 67	596UNTS35	108628
Guatemala	IBRD (World Bank)	10 Mar 67	616UNTS139	108894
Cameroon	IBRD (World Bank)	28 Mar 67	618UNTS89	108925
IBRD (World Bank)	Senegal	01 May 67	615UNTS267	108883
Colombia	IBRD (World Bank)	15 Jun 67	615UNTS47	108877
Colombia	IBRD (World Bank)	29 Jun 67	619UNTS99	108941
IBRD (World Bank)	Singapore	05 Jul 67	618UNTS189	108928
IBRD (World Bank)	Yugoslavia	18 Jul 67	615UNTS343	108886
Taiwan	IBRD (World Bank)	02 Aug 67	618UNTS301	108932
IBRD (World Bank)	Spain	04 Aug 67	619UNTS209	108944
Pakistan	IBRD (World Bank)	10 Aug 67	618UNTS261	108931
Peru	IBRD (World Bank)	11 Sep 67	619UNTS171	108943
IBRD (World Bank)	Tunisia	14 Sep 67	639UNTS147	109149
IBRD (World Bank)	Singapore	15 Sep 67	615UNTS295	108884
India	IBRD (World Bank)	19 Sep 67	615UNTS165	108880
Iran	IBRD (World Bank)	17 Oct 67	0UNTS0	109331
Israel	IBRD (World Bank)	15 Nov 67	619UNTS129	108942
Ceylon (Sri Lanka)	IBRD (World Bank)	22 Nov 67	639UNTS221	109151
IBRD (World Bank)	Tanzania	13 Dec 67	619UNTS239	108945
Argentina	IBRD (World Bank)	25 Jan 68	639UNTS187	109150
Mexico	IBRD (World Bank)	26 Jan 68	640UNTS3	109152
Korea, South	IBRD (World Bank)	31 Jan 68	639UNTS263	200638
IBRD (World Bank)	Thailand	23 May 68	0UNTS0	109332
Colombia	IBRD (World Bank)	03 Jun 68	0UNTS0	109333
Colombia	IBRD (World Bank)	03 Jun 68	0UNTS0	109334
Costa Rica	IBRD (World Bank)	05 Jun 68	0UNTS0	109365
Iran	IBRD (World Bank)	05 Jun 68	0UNTS0	109373
Nicaragua	IBRD (World Bank)	21 Jun 68	0UNTS0	109366
Plans and standards				
Costa Rica	USA (United States)	18 Jun 41	103UNTS173	200313
Brazil	USA (United States)	03 Sep 42	13UNTS109	200073
USA (United States)	Venezuela	14 May 43	28UNTS359	200160
Peru	USA (United States)	20 May 43	100UNTS259	200288
Philippines	USA (United States)	14 Feb 47	16UNTS3	100245
Philippines	USA (United States)	14 Mar 47	16UNTS31	100247
Poland	Yugoslavia	21 Jan 48	115UNTS155	101562
United Arab Rep	UK Great Britain	31 May 49	226UNTS273	103122
Czechoslovakia	Hungary	16 Apr 54	504UNTS231	107360
Austria	USSR (Soviet Union)	17 Oct 55	0UNTS0	109254
Norway	Sweden	29 Jun 56	262UNTS335	103759
Norway	USSR (Soviet Union)	18 Dec 57	312UNTS257	104522
Denmark	IBRD (World Bank)	04 Feb 59	328UNTS143	104733
Canada	USA (United States)	27 Feb 59	341UNTS3	104873
Multilateral		26 Jan 60	439UNTS249	106333
India	IBRD (World Bank)	29 Jul 60	377UNTS153	105399
Multilateral		19 Sep 60	444UNTS259	106371
Honduras	IDA (Devel Assoc)	12 May 61	414UNTS180	105973
IDA (Devel Assoc)	Sudan	14 Jun 61	415UNTS50	105981
India	IDA (Devel Assoc)	21 Jun 61	418UNTS61	106017
Chile	IDA (Devel Assoc)	28 Jun 61	426UNTS89	106131
Jordan	UK Great Britain	17 Jul 61	420UNTS53	106039
Taiwan	IDA (Devel Assoc)	30 Aug 61	417UNTS227	106008
India	IDA (Devel Assoc)	06 Sep 61	418UNTS81	106018
Taiwan	IDA (Devel Assoc)	06 Sep 61	417UNTS253	106009
India	IDA (Devel Assoc)	22 Nov 61	427UNTS29	106145
India	IDA (Devel Assoc)	22 Nov 61	427UNTS3	106144
India	IDA (Devel Assoc)	22 Nov 61	427UNTS55	106146
Taiwan	IDA (Devel Assoc)	01 Dec 61	426UNTS105	106132
Korea, South	IDA (Devel Assoc)	17 Aug 62	468UNTS387	200603

PARTY ONE	PARTY TWO	DATE	CITATION	NUMBER
Plans and standards (Cont.)				
Nicaragua	IDA (Devel Assoc)	07 Sep 62	478UNTS313	106940
IDA (Devel Assoc)	Tunisia	17 Sep 62	469UNTS33	106783
El Salvador	IDA (Devel Assoc)	02 Nov 62	468UNTS331	106780
Pakistan	IDA (Devel Assoc)	02 Nov 62	468UNTS351	106781
Saudi Arabia	USA (United States)	13 Nov 62	488UNTS175	107127
IDA (Devel Assoc)	Turkey	23 Nov 62	469UNTS3	106782
Ethiopia	IDA (Devel Assoc)	27 Feb 63	478UNTS289	106939
India	IDA (Devel Assoc)	22 Mar 63	477UNTS3	106911
Denmark	India	15 May 63	616UNTS23	108889
India	IDA (Devel Assoc)	24 May 63	483UNTS205	107014
IDA (Devel Assoc)	Turkey	31 May 63	480UNTS127	106966
Pakistan	IDA (Devel Assoc)	26 Jun 63	492UNTS115	107189
Pakistan	IDA (Devel Assoc)	26 Jul 63	492UNTS143	107190
Pakistan	IDA (Devel Assoc)	16 Aug 63	492UNTS205	107192
Pakistan	IDA (Devel Assoc)	16 Aug 63	492UNTS171	107191
Guatemala	USA (United States)	03 Oct 63	493UNTS45	107206
Jordan	IDA (Devel Assoc)	12 Dec 63	492UNTS3	107184
Jordan	IDA (Devel Assoc)	12 Dec 63	506UNTS51	107381
Canada	India	16 Dec 63	529UNTS45	107655
Chile	IBRD (World Bank)	18 Dec 63	504UNTS29	107352
IDA (Devel Assoc)	Syria	24 Dec 63	534UNTS253	107764
Paraguay	IDA (Devel Assoc)	26 Dec 63	507UNTS3	107394
Congo (Zaire)	UK Great Britain	03 Jan 64	534UNTS417	107770
IDA (Devel Assoc)	Tanganyika	05 Feb 64	506UNTS91	107382
Pakistan	IDA (Devel Assoc)	25 Mar 64	534UNTS275	107765
Ecuador	IDA (Devel Assoc)	26 May 64	534UNTS93	107757
India	IDA (Devel Assoc)	09 Jun 64	506UNTS31	107380
Pakistan	IDA (Devel Assoc)	11 Jun 64	506UNTS3	107379
Pakistan	IDA (Devel Assoc)	11 Jun 64	534UNTS309	107766
Pakistan	IDA (Devel Assoc)	24 Jun 64	533UNTS165	107742
Niger	IDA (Devel Assoc)	24 Jun 64	554UNTS93	108098
Pakistan	IDA (Devel Assoc)	24 Jun 64	533UNTS191	107743
India	IDA (Devel Assoc)	06 Jul 64	534UNTS49	107753
IDA (Devel Assoc)	Turkey	14 Jul 64	534UNTS339	107767
Pakistan	IDA (Devel Assoc)	21 Jul 64	534UNTS373	107768
Bolivia	IDA (Devel Assoc)	24 Jul 64	534UNTS171	107762
Bolivia	IDA (Devel Assoc)	24 Jul 64	534UNTS203	107763
Kenya	IDA (Devel Assoc)	17 Aug 64	535UNTS79	107776
Pakistan	IBRD (World Bank)	26 Aug 64	632UNTS201	109023
Pakistan	IDA (Devel Assoc)	26 Aug 64	535UNTS263	107784
IDA (Devel Assoc)	Turkey	31 Aug 64	535UNTS111	107777
Pakistan	IDA (Devel Assoc)	22 Sep 64	594UNTS225	108605
Mali	IDA (Devel Assoc)	29 Sep 64	594UNTS187	108604
India	IDA (Devel Assoc)	26 Oct 64	535UNTS245	107783
Afghanistan	IDA (Devel Assoc)	23 Nov 64	567UNTS155	108255
Mauritania	IDA (Devel Assoc)	28 Dec 64	540UNTS163	107849
Kenya	IDA (Devel Assoc)	29 Dec 64	535UNTS225	107782
Honduras	IDA (Devel Assoc)	02 Feb 65	561UNTS279	108189
Nigeria	IDA (Devel Assoc)	01 Mar 65	563UNTS3	108201
Nigeria	IDA (Devel Assoc)	01 Mar 65	571UNTS3	108297
Peru	IBRD (World Bank)	15 Mar 65	632UNTS209	109024
IDA (Devel Assoc)	Somalia	29 Mar 65	586UNTS101	108499
IDA (Devel Assoc)	Turkey	01 Apr 65	554UNTS137	108100
Jamaica	IBRD (World Bank)	08 Apr 65	539UNTS303	107841
Kenya	IDA (Devel Assoc)	30 Jun 65	554UNTS75	108097
Pakistan	IDA (Devel Assoc)	30 Jun 65	554UNTS111	108099
India	IDA (Devel Assoc)	11 Aug 65	562UNTS277	108199
Peru	IBRD (World Bank)	17 Sep 65	566UNTS311	108248
Morocco	IDA (Devel Assoc)	11 Oct 65	562UNTS299	108200
Pakistan	IDA (Devel Assoc)	13 Jan 66	567UNTS67	108252
IDA (Devel Assoc)	Tanzania	13 Jan 66	567UNTS177	108256
Pakistan	IDA (Devel Assoc)	10 Feb 66	575UNTS89	108355
Multilateral		10 Feb 66	575UNTS129	108356
Brazil	IBRD (World Bank)	15 Mar 66	599UNTS52	108664
Paraguay	IDA (Devel Assoc)	04 Apr 66	582UNTS331	108469
Plans and standards (Cont.)				
Pakistan	IDA (Devel Assoc)	17 Jun 66	582UNTS297	108468
Denmark	Jordan	28 Jun 66	574UNTS3	108338
India	IDA (Devel Assoc)	29 Jun 66	585UNTS101	108484
India	IDA (Devel Assoc)	29 Jun 66	582UNTS277	108467
Brazil	Denmark	08 Jul 66	581UNTS95	108435
IDA (Devel Assoc)	Siam	02 Aug 66	585UNTS271	108492
IDA (Devel Assoc)	Turkey	10 Aug 66	585UNTS237	108491
India	IDA (Devel Assoc)	19 Aug 66	584UNTS193	108478
Kenya	IDA (Devel Assoc)	19 Aug 66	585UNTS119	108485
Denmark	Malawi	01 Sep 66	586UNTS3	108493
IDA (Devel Assoc)	Senegal	29 Sep 66	594UNTS277	108607
Malawi	IDA (Devel Assoc)	04 Oct 66	584UNTS215	108479
IBRD (World Bank)	IFC (Finance Corp)	28 Oct 66	586UNTS225	200628
Afghanistan	IBRD (World Bank)	22 Nov 66	632UNTS171	109019
India	IDA (Devel Assoc)	23 Dec 66	594UNTS165	108603
Pakistan	IDA (Devel Assoc)	23 Dec 66	594UNTS255	108606
Morocco	IBRD (World Bank)	26 Jan 67	642UNTS3	109160
Guatemala	IBRD (World Bank)	10 Mar 67	616UNTS139	108894
Nicaragua	IBRD (World Bank)	13 Mar 67	632UNTS177	109020
Congo (Brazzaville)	IBRD (World Bank)	10 May 67	632UNTS185	109021
IBRD (World Bank)	Turkey	11 May 67	632UNTS193	109022
Czechoslovakia	UN Special Fund	13 Jul 67	606UNTS71	108776
Ceylon (Sri Lanka)	IBRD (World Bank)	24 Aug 67	632UNTS217	109025
Botswana	UN Special Fund	12 Oct 67	607UNTS37	108794
Iran	IBRD (World Bank)	17 Oct 67	0UNTS0	109331
Greece	IBRD (World Bank)	18 Mar 68	0UNTS0	109326
State/IGO Group	IBRD (World Bank)	02 May 68	637UNTS0	109110
IBRD (World Bank)	Thailand	23 May 68	0UNTS0	109332
Colombia	IBRD (World Bank)	03 Jun 68	0UNTS0	109333
Colombia	IBRD (World Bank)	03 Jun 68	0UNTS0	109334
Non-bank projects				
Brazil	USA (United States)	03 Sep 42	13UNTS109	200073
Mexico	USA (United States)	24 Oct 42	21UNTS189	200123
USA (United States)	Venezuela	14 May 43	28UNTS359	200160
Mexico	USA (United States)	22 Oct 46	21UNTS13	100321
Peru	USA (United States)	22 Nov 46	100UNTS170	101396
Albania	Yugoslavia	28 Nov 46	111UNTS127	101525
Philippines	USA (United States)	14 Mar 47	16UNTS31	100247
Portugal	UK Great Britain	21 Jan 53	175UNTS13	102293
Mexico	USA (United States)	17 Jun 54	237UNTS275	103352
Brazil	USA (United States)	30 Jun 54	237UNTS137	103341
El Salvador	USA (United States)	16 Jul 54	237UNTS237	103350
El Salvador	USA (United States)	31 Aug 54	237UNTS49	103336
Iraq	USA (United States)	02 Mar 55	250UNTS229	103526
El Salvador	USA (United States)	21 Mar 55	250UNTS261	103528
Honduras	USA (United States)	12 May 55	270UNTS3	103886
Colombia	USA (United States)	14 Jun 55	256UNTS211	103630
Haiti	USA (United States)	24 Jun 55	264UNTS291	103800
Dominican Republic	USA (United States)	30 Jun 55	257UNTS313	103664
Libya	USA (United States)	28 Jul 55	270UNTS317	103903
Libya	USA (United States)	28 Jul 55	270UNTS269	103901
Libya	USA (United States)	28 Jul 55	270UNTS245	103900
Bolivia	USA (United States)	03 Aug 55	264UNTS225	103795
El Salvador	USA (United States)	08 Aug 55	264UNTS301	103801
Haiti	USA (United States)	28 Dec 55	240UNTS95	103397
Finland	Norway	28 Jun 57	272UNTS191	103938
Argentina	Brazil	19 Sep 58	374UNTS57	105329
Sudan	United Arab Rep	08 Nov 59	453UNTS51	106519
Mexico	USA (United States)	24 Oct 60	401UNTS137	105767
Multilateral		26 Nov 60	500UNTS25	107304
Costa Rica	IDA (Devel Assoc)	13 Oct 61	431UNTS3	106204
Paraguay	IDA (Devel Assoc)	26 Oct 61	447UNTS277	106419
Pakistan	IDA (Devel Assoc)	22 Nov 61	447UNTS295	106420
Israel	Uganda	04 Feb 63	484UNTS273	107037

PARTY ONE	PARTY TWO	DATE	CITATION	NUMBER
Non-bank projects (Cont.)				
New Zealand	UN Special Fund	28 Jun 63	470UNTS3	106792
Guatemala	USA (United States)	03 Oct 63	493UNTS45	107206
Germany, West	Thailand	23 Dec 64	525UNTS193	107591
Saudi Arabia	USA (United States)	19 Nov 65	580UNTS35	108419
IDA (Devel Assoc)	UK Great Britain	08 Feb 66	567UNTS207	108257
Pakistan	IDA (Devel Assoc)	10 Feb 66	575UNTS89	108355
Canada	USA (United States)	09 Jun 66	580UNTS263	108429
Guyana	UN Special Fund	11 Jun 66	564UNTS201	200622
UN Special Fund	UPU (Postal Union)	21 Sep 66	573UNTS259	200626
Czechoslovakia	UN Special Fund	13 Jul 67	606UNTS71	108776
UN Special Fund	Syria	22 Apr 68	634UNTS207	109063
Agricultural development/credit				
Philippines	USA (United States)	14 Feb 47	16UNTS3	100245
Colombia	USA (United States)	30 Jun 54	237UNTS263	103351
New Zealand	Western Samoa	23 Jul 64	521UNTS173	107520
IDA development project				
Honduras	IDA (Devel Assoc)	12 May 61	414UNTS180	105973
IDA (Devel Assoc)	Sudan	14 Jun 61	415UNTS50	105981
India	IDA (Devel Assoc)	21 Jun 61	418UNTS61	106017
Chile	IDA (Devel Assoc)	28 Jun 61	426UNTS89	106131
Colombia	IDA (Devel Assoc)	28 Aug 61	416UNTS3	105992
Taiwan	IDA (Devel Assoc)	30 Aug 61	416UNTS175	106003
Taiwan	IDA (Devel Assoc)	30 Aug 61	417UNTS227	106008
India	IDA (Devel Assoc)	06 Sep 61	418UNTS81	106018
Taiwan	IDA (Devel Assoc)	06 Sep 61	417UNTS253	106009
Costa Rica	IDA (Devel Assoc)	13 Oct 61	431UNTS3	106204
Pakistan	IDA (Devel Assoc)	19 Oct 61	447UNTS161	106415
Paraguay	IDA (Devel Assoc)	26 Oct 61	447UNTS277	106419
India	IDA (Devel Assoc)	22 Nov 61	427UNTS3	106144
Pakistan	IDA (Devel Assoc)	22 Nov 61	447UNTS295	106420
India	IDA (Devel Assoc)	22 Nov 61	427UNTS29	106145
India	IDA (Devel Assoc)	22 Nov 61	427UNTS55	106146
Taiwan	IDA (Devel Assoc)	01 Dec 61	426UNTS105	106132
Jordan	IDA (Devel Assoc)	22 Dec 61	448UNTS21	106423
India	IDA (Devel Assoc)	14 Feb 62	468UNTS177	106773
IDA (Devel Assoc)	UK Great Britain	13 Mar 62	466UNTS331	106753
India	IDA (Devel Assoc)	18 Jul 62	447UNTS191	106416
Korea, South	IDA (Devel Assoc)	17 Aug 62	468UNTS387	200603
Nicaragua	IDA (Devel Assoc)	07 Sep 62	478UNTS313	106940
India	IDA (Devel Assoc)	14 Sep 62	448UNTS3	106422
IDA (Devel Assoc)	Tunisia	17 Sep 62	469UNTS33	106783
El Salvador	IDA (Devel Assoc)	02 Nov 62	468UNTS331	106780
Haiti	IDA (Devel Assoc)	02 Nov 62	468UNTS205	106774
Pakistan	IDA (Devel Assoc)	02 Nov 62	468UNTS351	106781
IDA (Devel Assoc)	Turkey	23 Nov 62	469UNTS3	106782
Ethiopia	IDA (Devel Assoc)	27 Feb 63	478UNTS289	106939
India	IDA (Devel Assoc)	22 Mar 63	477UNTS3	106911
India	IDA (Devel Assoc)	24 May 63	483UNTS205	107014
IDA (Devel Assoc)	Turkey	31 May 63	480UNTS127	106966
Pakistan	IDA (Devel Assoc)	26 Jun 63	492UNTS115	107189
Pakistan	IDA (Devel Assoc)	26 Jul 63	492UNTS143	107190
Pakistan	IDA (Devel Assoc)	16 Aug 63	492UNTS171	107191
Pakistan	IDA (Devel Assoc)	16 Aug 63	492UNTS205	107192
Jordan	IDA (Devel Assoc)	12 Dec 63	506UNTS51	107381
Jordan	IDA (Devel Assoc)	12 Dec 63	492UNTS3	107184
IDA (Devel Assoc)	Syria	24 Dec 63	534UNTS253	107764
Paraguay	IDA (Devel Assoc)	26 Dec 63	507UNTS3	107394
IDA (Devel Assoc)	Tanganyika	05 Feb 64	506UNTS91	107382
Pakistan	IDA (Devel Assoc)	25 Mar 64	535UNTS43	107775
Pakistan	IDA (Devel Assoc)	25 Mar 64	534UNTS275	107765
Ecuador	IDA (Devel Assoc)	26 May 64	534UNTS93	107757
India	IDA (Devel Assoc)	09 Jun 64	506UNTS31	107380
Pakistan	IDA (Devel Assoc)	11 Jun 64	534UNTS309	107766
Pakistan	IDA (Devel Assoc)	11 Jun 64	506UNTS3	107379

PARTY ONE	PARTY TWO	DATE	CITATION	NUMBER
IDA development project (Cont.)				
Niger	IDA (Devel Assoc)	24 Jun 64	554UNTS93	108098
Pakistan	IDA (Devel Assoc)	24 Jun 64	533UNTS165	107742
Pakistan	IDA (Devel Assoc)	24 Jun 64	533UNTS191	107743
India	IDA (Devel Assoc)	06 Jul 64	534UNTS49	107753
IDA (Devel Assoc)	Turkey	14 Jul 64	534UNTS339	107767
Pakistan	IDA (Devel Assoc)	21 Jul 64	534UNTS373	107768
Bolivia	IDA (Devel Assoc)	24 Jul 64	534UNTS203	107763
Bolivia	IDA (Devel Assoc)	24 Jul 64	534UNTS171	107762
IDA (Devel Assoc)	UK Great Britain	31 Jul 64	535UNTS205	107781
Kenya	IDA (Devel Assoc)	17 Aug 64	535UNTS79	107776
Pakistan	IDA (Devel Assoc)	26 Aug 64	535UNTS263	107784
IDA (Devel Assoc)	Turkey	31 Aug 64	535UNTS111	107777
Pakistan	IDA (Devel Assoc)	22 Sep 64	594UNTS225	108605
Mali	IDA (Devel Assoc)	29 Sep 64	594UNTS187	108604
India	IDA (Devel Assoc)	26 Oct 64	535UNTS245	107783
Afghanistan	IDA (Devel Assoc)	23 Nov 64	567UNTS155	108255
Mauritania	IDA (Devel Assoc)	28 Dec 64	540UNTS163	107849
Kenya	IDA (Devel Assoc)	29 Dec 64	535UNTS225	107782
Honduras	IDA (Devel Assoc)	02 Feb 65	561UNTS279	108189
Nigeria	IDA (Devel Assoc)	01 Mar 65	571UNTS3	108297
Nigeria	IDA (Devel Assoc)	01 Mar 65	563UNTS3	108201
IDA (Devel Assoc)	Somalia	29 Mar 65	586UNTS101	108499
Multilateral		29 Mar 65	540UNTS145	107848
IDA (Devel Assoc)	Turkey	01 Apr 65	554UNTS137	108100
Multilateral		29 Apr 65	586UNTS123	108500
Pakistan	IDA (Devel Assoc)	30 Jun 65	554UNTS111	108099
Kenya	IDA (Devel Assoc)	30 Jun 65	554UNTS75	108097
India	IDA (Devel Assoc)	11 Aug 65	562UNTS277	108199
Morocco	IDA (Devel Assoc)	11 Oct 65	562UNTS299	108200
IDA (Devel Assoc)	Tanzania	13 Jan 66	567UNTS177	108256
Pakistan	IDA (Devel Assoc)	13 Jan 66	567UNTS67	108252
Multilateral		10 Feb 66	575UNTS129	108356
Paraguay	IDA (Devel Assoc)	04 Apr 66	582UNTS331	108469
Pakistan	IDA (Devel Assoc)	17 Jun 66	582UNTS297	108468
India	IDA (Devel Assoc)	29 Jun 66	585UNTS101	108484
India	IDA (Devel Assoc)	29 Jun 66	582UNTS277	108467
IDA (Devel Assoc)	Siam	02 Aug 66	585UNTS271	108492
IDA (Devel Assoc)	Turkey	10 Aug 66	585UNTS237	108491
India	IDA (Devel Assoc)	19 Aug 66	584UNTS193	108478
Kenya	IDA (Devel Assoc)	19 Aug 66	585UNTS119	108485
IDA (Devel Assoc)	Senegal	29 Sep 66	594UNTS277	108607
Malawi	IDA (Devel Assoc)	04 Oct 66	584UNTS215	108479
Pakistan	IDA (Devel Assoc)	23 Dec 66	594UNTS255	108606
India	IDA (Devel Assoc)	23 Dec 66	594UNTS165	108603
Industry				
Hungary	Yugoslavia	11 May 47	130UNTS171	101730
Philippines	USA (United States)	12 May 47	16UNTS123	100253
Poland	Yugoslavia	21 Jan 48	115UNTS155	101562
Jordan	USA (United States)	12 Feb 52	168UNTS25	102211
Chile	USA (United States)	30 Jun 52	199UNTS241	102688
Japan	IBRD (World Bank)	12 Nov 52	354UNTS313	105068
UK Great Britain	USA (United States)	25 Feb 53	212UNTS157	102868
United Arab Rep	USA (United States)	19 Mar 53	215UNTS17	102909
UK Great Britain	USA (United States)	24 Jun 53	224UNTS141	103074
Afghanistan	USA (United States)	30 Jun 53	215UNTS3	102908
Ecuador	USA (United States)	30 Jun 54	236UNTS163	103323
Mexico	USA (United States)	09 Mar 55	263UNTS247	103776
Philippines	USA (United States)	27 Apr 55	261UNTS351	103733
Peru	USA (United States)	30 Apr 55	263UNTS309	103780
Italy	IBRD (World Bank)	01 Jun 55	358UNTS203	105137
Pakistan	Sweden	04 Jun 55	228UNTS121	103146
Italy	Lebanon	04 Nov 55	267UNTS147	103840
Burma	Yugoslavia	07 Mar 56	378UNTS99	105420
Germany, West	Netherlands	28 Jan 58	453UNTS183	106525

PARTY ONE	PARTY TWO	DATE	CITATION	NUMBER
Industry (Cont.)				
Multilateral		10 Jun 58	454UNTS47	106539
Japan	IBRD (World Bank)	18 Aug 58	323UNTS205	104670
Japan	IBRD (World Bank)	10 Sep 58	318UNTS133	104612
Congo (Brazzaville)	IBRD (World Bank)	30 Jun 59	452UNTS123	106506
Gabon	IBRD (World Bank)	30 Jun 59	452UNTS135	106507
Japan	IBRD (World Bank)	12 Nov 59	354UNTS279	105067
Iran	IBRD (World Bank)	23 Nov 59	380UNTS245	105459
India	Japan	25 Jan 60	384UNTS31	105508
Indonesia	USSR (Soviet Union)	28 Feb 60	392UNTS173	105643
Mauritania	IBRD (World Bank)	17 Mar 60	452UNTS211	106509
France	IBRD (World Bank)	17 Mar 60	452UNTS147	106508
Iran	Japan	12 Sep 60	384UNTS43	105509
Multilateral		13 Dec 60	455UNTS3	106543
India	IBRD (World Bank)	09 Aug 61	417UNTS297	106011
Costa Rica	IBRD (World Bank)	06 Sep 61	446UNTS345	106408
Mexico	USA (United States)	15 Nov 61	460UNTS113	106634
Taiwan	IDA (Devel Assoc)	01 Dec 61	426UNTS105	106132
India	IBRD (World Bank)	22 Dec 61	481UNTS85	106979
India	IBRD (World Bank)	28 Feb 62	447UNTS3	106410
Pakistan	IDA (Devel Assoc)	02 Nov 62	468UNTS351	106781
IDA (Devel Assoc)	Turkey	23 Nov 62	469UNTS3	106782
Pakistan	IBRD (World Bank)	13 Feb 63	467UNTS3	106756
United Nations	South Pacific Com	20 Feb 63	453UNTS333	200600
El Salvador	IBRD (World Bank)	19 Jun 63	481UNTS59	106978
India	IDA (Devel Assoc)	09 Jun 64	506UNTS31	107380
India	IDA (Devel Assoc)	11 Aug 65	562UNTS277	108199
Iran	USSR (Soviet Union)	13 Jan 66	633UNTS123	109037
India	IBRD (World Bank)	07 Jul 66	595UNTS3	108610
Jordan	UK Great Britain	26 Jul 66	597UNTS219	108647
IDA (Devel Assoc)	Turkey	10 Aug 66	585UNTS237	108491
India	IDA (Devel Assoc)	19 Aug 66	584UNTS193	108478
India	IDA (Devel Assoc)	23 Dec 66	594UNTS165	108603
Pakistan	IDA (Devel Assoc)	23 Dec 66	594UNTS255	108606
Irrigation				
Liberia	USA (United States)	31 Dec 43	106UNTS199	200341
Iraq	USA (United States)	21 May 52	212UNTS183	102870
Denmark	Israel	14 Nov 52	160UNTS279	102113
United Arab Rep	USA (United States)	12 Mar 53	204UNTS3	102747
Chile	USA (United States)	27 Jun 53	229UNTS193	103167
Chile	USA (United States)	27 Jun 53	229UNTS53	103160
UN Relief Palestin	United Arab Rep	14 Oct 53	190UNTS13	102555
Peru	USA (United States)	30 Apr 55	263UNTS309	103780
Italy	IBRD (World Bank)	01 Jun 55	358UNTS203	105137
IBRD (World Bank)	Sudan	17 Jun 60	379UNTS253	105442
United Arab Rep	USSR (Soviet Union)	27 Aug 60	399UNTS37	105733
Multilateral		19 Sep 60	419UNTS125	106032
Multilateral		19 Sep 60	444UNTS259	106371
Mexico	USA (United States)	24 Oct 60	401UNTS137	105767
Multilateral		26 Nov 60	500UNTS25	107304
Mexico	IBRD (World Bank)	16 Jan 61	422UNTS203	106076
Multilateral		14 Jun 61	415UNTS4	105979
IBRD (World Bank)	Sudan	14 Jun 61	415UNTS26	105980
India	IDA (Devel Assoc)	06 Sep 61	418UNTS81	106018
Pakistan	IDA (Devel Assoc)	19 Oct 61	447UNTS161	106415
India	IDA (Devel Assoc)	22 Nov 61	427UNTS29	106145
India	IDA (Devel Assoc)	22 Nov 61	427UNTS55	106146
India	IDA (Devel Assoc)	22 Nov 61	427UNTS3	106144
India	IDA (Devel Assoc)	29 Jun 62	447UNTS221	106417
India	IDA (Devel Assoc)	18 Jul 62	447UNTS191	106416
IBRD (World Bank)	Thailand	21 Dec 62	467UNTS63	106758
Nicaragua	IBRD (World Bank)	01 Mar 63	481UNTS15	106976
Mexico	IBRD (World Bank)	29 Apr 63	489UNTS151	107138
IDA (Devel Assoc)	Turkey	31 May 63	480UNTS127	106966
Pakistan	IDA (Devel Assoc)	26 Jun 63	492UNTS115	107189

PARTY ONE	PARTY TWO	DATE	CITATION	NUMBER
Irrigation (Cont.)				
Pakistan	IDA (Devel Assoc)	26 Jul 63	492UNTS143	107190
Jordan	UK Great Britain	31 Aug 64	541UNTS3	107856
IBRD (World Bank)	Thailand	25 Nov 64	537UNTS273	107805
Malaysia	IBRD (World Bank)	26 Feb 65	549UNTS239	108002
Malaysia	IBRD (World Bank)	17 Nov 65	568UNTS23	108263
Mexico	IBRD (World Bank)	25 May 66	596UNTS3	108627
Jordan	UK Great Britain	26 Jul 66	597UNTS219	108647
Mexico	USA (United States)	24 Aug 66	606UNTS251	108789
Natural resources				
Bolivia	Brazil	25 Feb 38	51UNTS245	200192
Canada	USA (United States)	27 Jun 42	99UNTS223	200276
Canada	USA (United States)	15 Aug 42	99UNTS233	200277
Canada	USA (United States)	28 Dec 42	99UNTS241	200278
Canada	USA (United States)	13 Mar 43	99UNTS249	200279
Liberia	USA (United States)	31 Dec 43	106UNTS199	200341
Canada	USA (United States)	26 Feb 45	99UNTS273	200281
Canada	USA (United States)	06 Sep 45	99UNTS281	200282
Albania	Yugoslavia	28 Nov 46	111UNTS105	101521
Albania	Yugoslavia	28 Nov 46	111UNTS151	101528
Albania	Yugoslavia	28 Nov 46	111UNTS93	101520
Brazil	USA (United States)	26 Nov 48	88UNTS3	101180
UK Great Britain	USA (United States)	18 Jul 51	117UNTS49	101583
Libya	USA (United States)	20 May 52	178UNTS307	102346
United Arab Rep	USA (United States)	12 Mar 53	204UNTS3	102747
Colombia	USA (United States)	09 Jun 53	213UNTS3	102877
Liberia	USA (United States)	23 Jun 53	213UNTS37	102879
Brazil	USA (United States)	26 Jun 53	336UNTS241	104808
Chile	USA (United States)	27 Jun 53	229UNTS193	103167
Afghanistan	USA (United States)	30 Jun 53	215UNTS3	102908
Chile	USA (United States)	30 Dec 53	236UNTS41	103315
Libya	USA (United States)	28 Jul 55	270UNTS293	103902
Burma	Yugoslavia	07 Mar 56	378UNTS99	105420
Finland	India	14 Jun 57	277UNTS327	104016
France	IBRD (World Bank)	10 Dec 59	380UNTS319	105464
Jordan	UK Great Britain	17 Jul 61	420UNTS53	106039
Taiwan	IDA (Devel Assoc)	30 Aug 61	417UNTS227	106008
Taiwan	IDA (Devel Assoc)	06 Sep 61	417UNTS253	106009
Jordan	IDA (Devel Assoc)	22 Dec 61	448UNTS21	106423
Jordan	UK Great Britain	30 May 62	449UNTS167	106458
Pakistan	IDA (Devel Assoc)	29 Jun 62	447UNTS325	106421
Nicaragua	IDA (Devel Assoc)	07 Sep 62	478UNTS313	106940
ILO (Labor Org)	USA (United States)	22 Feb 63	489UNTS347	107149
Pakistan	IDA (Devel Assoc)	16 Aug 63	492UNTS205	107192
Pakistan	IDA (Devel Assoc)	16 Aug 63	492UNTS171	107191
Jordan	IDA (Devel Assoc)	12 Dec 63	506UNTS51	107381
Algeria	IBRD (World Bank)	14 May 64	522UNTS265	107552
Pakistan	IDA (Devel Assoc)	21 Jul 64	534UNTS373	107768
Pakistan	IDA (Devel Assoc)	26 Aug 64	535UNTS263	107784
Jordan	UK Great Britain	31 Aug 64	541UNTS3	107856
Jordan	UK Great Britain	08 Jun 65	552UNTS251	108057
Saudi Arabia	USA (United States)	19 Nov 65	580UNTS35	108419
Multilateral		17 Mar 67	594UNTS105	108598
Liberia	IBRD (World Bank)	05 Jun 67	633UNTS13	109031
Hydro-electric power				
Canada	USA (United States)	10 Nov 41	23UNTS275	200134
Canada	USA (United States)	27 Nov 41	103UNTS193	200314
Panama	USA (United States)	18 May 42	124UNTS221	200422
Mexico	USA (United States)	03 Feb 44	3UNTS313	200025
Albania	Yugoslavia	28 Nov 46	111UNTS109	101522
Albania	Yugoslavia	28 Nov 46	111UNTS123	101524
Albania	Yugoslavia	28 Nov 46	111UNTS113	101523
United Arab Rep	UK Great Britain	31 May 49	226UNTS273	103122
India	WHO (World Health)	11 Oct 51	118UNTS27	101594
Australia	USA (United States)	16 Nov 51	168UNTS75	102214

PARTY ONE	PARTY TWO	DATE	CITATION	NUMBER
Hydro-electric power (Cont.)				
United Arab Rep	USA (United States)	12 Mar 53	204UNTS3	102747
Jordan	Syria	04 Jun 53	184UNTS15	102437
Canada	USA (United States)	12 Nov 53	234UNTS97	103274
Brazil	IBRD (World Bank)	24 Feb 54	301UNTS249	104347
Czechoslovakia	Hungary	16 Apr 54	504UNTS231	107360
Austria	Yugoslavia	25 May 54	227UNTS111	103135
Italy	IBRD (World Bank)	01 Jun 55	358UNTS203	105137
Colombia	Italy	20 Dec 55	260UNTS315	103714
Burma	Yugoslavia	07 Mar 56	378UNTS99	105420
Ecuador	IBRD (World Bank)	26 Mar 56	292UNTS391	104277
Norway	USSR (Soviet Union)	18 Dec 57	312UNTS257	104522
Mexico	IBRD (World Bank)	14 Jan 58	293UNTS167	104292
Brazil	IBRD (World Bank)	22 Jan 58	323UNTS99	104666
Mexico	IBRD (World Bank)	05 May 58	309UNTS3	104466
Ceylon (Sri Lanka)	IBRD (World Bank)	17 Sep 58	323UNTS51	104664
Brazil	IBRD (World Bank)	03 Oct 58	337UNTS177	104823
El Salvador	IBRD (World Bank)	20 Feb 59	362UNTS75	105183
India	IBRD (World Bank)	08 Apr 59	348UNTS131	104998
Honduras	IBRD (World Bank)	20 May 59	359UNTS119	105141
Brazil	IBRD (World Bank)	17 Jun 59	377UNTS111	105398
Greece	Yugoslavia	18 Jun 59	363UNTS133	105205
Pakistan	IBRD (World Bank)	13 Aug 59	355UNTS129	105076
Colombia	IBRD (World Bank)	20 Jan 60	375UNTS49	105353
Colombia	IBRD (World Bank)	10 May 60	379UNTS218	105441
El Salvador	IBRD (World Bank)	29 Jul 60	390UNTS101	105605
United Arab Rep	USSR (Soviet Union)	27 Aug 60	399UNTS37	105733
Multilateral		19 Sep 60	444UNTS259	106371
Mexico	USA (United States)	24 Oct 60	401UNTS137	105767
Canada	USA (United States)	17 Jan 61	542UNTS224	107894
Costa Rica	IBRD (World Bank)	03 Feb 61	414UNTS314	105977
IBRD (World Bank)	Yugoslavia	23 Feb 61	415UNTS92	105982
Japan	IBRD (World Bank)	16 Mar 61	400UNTS201	105753
IBRD (World Bank)	UK Great Britain	29 Mar 61	415UNTS300	105990
Somalia	USSR (Soviet Union)	02 Jun 61	457UNTS263	106587
Ceylon (Sri Lanka)	IBRD (World Bank)	06 Jun 61	414UNTS349	105978
IBRD (World Bank)	UK Great Britain	16 Aug 61	426UNTS287	106143
Ghana	IBRD (World Bank)	08 Feb 62	449UNTS207	106462
Mexico	IBRD (World Bank)	20 Jun 62	468UNTS109	106771
IBRD (World Bank)	Yugoslavia	11 Jul 62	468UNTS143	106772
Multilateral		25 Jul 62	506UNTS177	107387
Finland	IBRD (World Bank)	15 Aug 62	467UNTS177	106763
Panama	IBRD (World Bank)	14 Sep 62	476UNTS153	106908
Laos	USSR (Soviet Union)	01 Dec 62	472UNTS3	106834
Thailand	USA (United States)	25 Apr 63	476UNTS115	106906
IBRD (World Bank)	UK Great Britain	16 May 63	476UNTS211	106910
IBRD (World Bank)	UK Great Britain	16 May 63	477UNTS361	106929
India	IDA (Devel Assoc)	24 May 63	483UNTS205	107014
Colombia	IBRD (World Bank)	03 Jun 63	490UNTS199	107155
Costa Rica	IBRD (World Bank)	10 Jul 63	482UNTS69	106991
Colombia	IBRD (World Bank)	16 Jul 63	482UNTS256	106998
Denmark	IBRD (World Bank)	24 Jul 63	481UNTS171	106982
IBRD (World Bank)	UK Great Britain	06 Sep 63	483UNTS173	107013
IBRD (World Bank)	Venezuela	20 Sep 63	482UNTS227	106997
IBRD (World Bank)	UK Great Britain	23 Sep 63	503UNTS247	107348
Portugal	IBRD (World Bank)	06 Nov 63	491UNTS137	107176
Portugal	IBRD (World Bank)	06 Nov 63	492UNTS89	107188
Romania	Yugoslavia	30 Nov 63	512UNTS2	107438
Canada	India	16 Dec 63	529UNTS45	107655
New Zealand	IBRD (World Bank)	12 Mar 64	505UNTS3	107362
Ethiopia	IBRD (World Bank)	08 May 64	505UNTS51	107364
IDA (Devel Assoc)	Turkey	14 Jul 64	534UNTS339	107767
Bolivia	IDA (Devel Assoc)	24 Jul 64	534UNTS171	107762
Bolivia	IDA (Devel Assoc)	24 Jul 64	534UNTS203	107763
IBRD (World Bank)	Sierra Leone	18 Aug 64	516UNTS295	107479
IBRD (World Bank)	Venezuela	28 Aug 64	537UNTS135	107800

PARTY ONE	PARTY TWO	DATE	CITATION	NUMBER
Hydro-electric power (Cont.)				
Germany, West	Thailand	28 Oct 64	521UNTS311	107528
Chile	IBRD (World Bank)	12 Feb 65	537UNTS35	107796
Brazil	IBRD (World Bank)	26 Feb 65	553UNTS3	108065
Brazil	IBRD (World Bank)	26 Feb 65	567UNTS91	108253
Portugal	IBRD (World Bank)	29 Apr 65	549UNTS69	107991
India	IBRD (World Bank)	11 Jun 65	557UNTS59	108128
India	IBRD (World Bank)	11 Jun 65	557UNTS101	108130
Italy	IBRD (World Bank)	28 Jun 65	567UNTS127	108254
Laos	Thailand	12 Aug 65	547UNTS209	107958
Multilateral		07 Oct 65	556UNTS175	108125
Multilateral		04 Dec 65	571UNTS123	108303
Mexico	IBRD (World Bank)	15 Dec 65	568UNTS125	108267
New Zealand	IBRD (World Bank)	17 Dec 65	567UNTS255	108259
UK Great Britain	USA (United States)	02 Jun 66	573UNTS229	108336
Portugal	IBRD (World Bank)	14 Jun 66	581UNTS3	108430
Portugal	IBRD (World Bank)	14 Jun 66	581UNTS29	108431
Jamaica	IBRD (World Bank)	20 Jun 66	582UNTS145	108462
Malaysia	IBRD (World Bank)	26 Jul 66	586UNTS195	108504
Jordan	UK Great Britain	26 Jul 66	597UNTS219	108647
Peru	IBRD (World Bank)	07 Sep 66	585UNTS3	108481
Nicaragua	IBRD (World Bank)	05 Oct 66	582UNTS231	108465
IBRD (World Bank)	Singapore	04 Nov 66	585UNTS155	108488
Syria	USSR (Soviet Union)	18 Dec 66	633UNTS247	109041
Chile	IBRD (World Bank)	23 Dec 66	595UNTS141	108618
IBRD (World Bank)	Venezuela	26 Jan 67	596UNTS35	108628
IBRD (World Bank)	Turkey	11 May 67	632UNTS193	109022
Czechoslovakia	Hungary	27 Feb 68	640UNTS49	109154
Malaysia	IBRD (World Bank)	27 Sep 68	0UNTS0	109505
General transportation				
Multilateral		20 Jun 36	40UNTS109	100630
Mexico	USA (United States)	23 Dec 42	13UNTS231	200081
Multilateral		22 Mar 45	70UNTS237	200241
Argentina	USA (United States)	09 May 45	139UNTS227	200453
Hungary	USSR (Soviet Union)	15 Jul 47	216UNTS247	102940
Poland	Yugoslavia	07 Nov 47	115UNTS137	101561
Czechoslovakia	USSR (Soviet Union)	11 Dec 47	217UNTS35	102943
Switzerland	USSR (Soviet Union)	17 Mar 48	217UNTS73	102944
Bulgaria	USSR (Soviet Union)	01 Apr 48	217UNTS97	102946
Multilateral		10 Jun 48	164UNTS113	102163
Philippines	USA (United States)	27 Aug 48	44UNTS13	100675
Italy	USSR (Soviet Union)	11 Dec 48	217UNTS181	102948
Multilateral		12 Aug 49	75UNTS287	100973
Spain	UK Great Britain	20 Jul 50	398UNTS101	105719
UN Relief Palestin	WHO (World Health)	23 Sep 50	103UNTS129	200310
Canada	Venezuela	11 Oct 50	231UNTS3	103198
Canada	Ecuador	10 Nov 50	231UNTS15	103199
Canada	Costa Rica	18 Nov 50	231UNTS25	103200
Multilateral		18 Apr 51	261UNTS140	103729
Burma	WHO (World Health)	13 Jun 51	117UNTS115	101588
Burma	WHO (World Health)	09 Jul 51	104UNTS187	101440
Burma	WHO (World Health)	09 Jul 51	104UNTS175	101439
Burma	WHO (World Health)	09 Jul 51	107UNTS9	101463
India	WHO (World Health)	23 Oct 51	109UNTS59	101491
El Salvador	Guatemala	14 Dec 51	131UNTS131	101740
Guatemala	WHO (World Health)	29 Dec 51	124UNTS89	101668
Jordan	USA (United States)	12 Feb 52	168UNTS25	102211
Pakistan	Turkey	29 Jun 53	211UNTS225	102854
Afghanistan	USA (United States)	30 Jun 53	215UNTS3	102908
India	Iran	15 Dec 54	327UNTS245	104724
Peru	USA (United States)	30 Apr 55	263UNTS309	103780
Austria	USSR (Soviet Union)	17 Oct 55	240UNTS289	103409
Syria	USSR (Soviet Union)	16 Nov 55	259UNTS71	103683
Costa Rica	Guatemala	20 Dec 55	280UNTS121	104056
Burma	Sweden	06 Mar 56	369UNTS275	105261

PARTY ONE	PARTY TWO	DATE	CITATION	NUMBER
General transportation (Cont.)				
Ceylon (Sri Lanka)	Hungary	04 Jun 56	315UNTS13	104555
Finland	Sweden	07 Jul 56	258UNTS83	103672
Guatemala	Honduras	22 Aug 56	263UNTS49	103767
Japan	Norway	28 Feb 57	280UNTS87	104054
Ceylon (Sri Lanka)	China People's Rep	19 Sep 57	337UNTS137	104821
Argentina	Italy	25 Nov 57	305UNTS275	104424
Japan	USSR (Soviet Union)	06 Dec 57	325UNTS35	104694
Multilateral		06 Jan 58	304UNTS227	104399
Albania	USSR (Soviet Union)	15 Feb 58	313UNTS261	104536
China People's Rep	USSR (Soviet Union)	23 Apr 58	313UNTS135	104534
Multilateral		10 Jun 58	454UNTS47	106539
Iraq	USSR (Soviet Union)	11 Oct 58	328UNTS95	104730
Japan	Yugoslavia	28 Feb 59	341UNTS179	104883
Greece	Yugoslavia	18 Jun 59	368UNTS17	105233
India	Italy	06 Oct 59	378UNTS267	105427
USA (United States)	USSR (Soviet Union)	21 Nov 59	361UNTS35	105172
Czechoslovakia	Germany, East	25 Nov 59	374UNTS101	105331
Greece	Tunisia	02 Mar 60	483UNTS89	107008
Cuba	Czechoslovakia	10 Jun 60	447UNTS75	106412
Korea, North	USSR (Soviet Union)	22 Jun 60	399UNTS3	105732
Multilateral		08 Oct 60	450UNTS309	106476
USA (United States)	USSR (Soviet Union)	08 Mar 62	460UNTS3	106630
Israel	Rwanda	23 Oct 62	515UNTS291	107466
UK Great Britain	USSR (Soviet Union)	21 Jan 63	475UNTS3	106887
Israel	Tanganyika	28 Jan 63	516UNTS39	107468
Israel	Uganda	04 Feb 63	484UNTS273	107037
Austria	Mongolia	15 Jul 63	496UNTS171	107251
USA (United States)	USSR (Soviet Union)	22 Feb 64	526UNTS131	107605
UNESCO (Educ/Cult)	Yugoslavia	27 Feb 64	489UNTS257	107143
Italy	United Nations	18 Mar 64	491UNTS21	107171
Afghanistan	United Nations	28 Apr 64	494UNTS77	107227
UK Great Britain	USSR (Soviet Union)	13 Feb 65	543UNTS43	107896
Denmark	Germany, West	09 Jun 65	605UNTS95	108762
Netherlands	Senegal	12 Jun 65	602UNTS231	108715
United Nations	United Arab Rep	26 Nov 65	551UNTS253	108046
Philippines	United Nations	05 Apr 66	560UNTS191	108174
Finland	United Nations	16 Jan 67	588UNTS153	108522
Denmark	Lebanon	29 Mar 67	602UNTS251	108717
Austria	United Nations	13 Apr 67	600UNTS93	108679
Competency certificate				
Multilateral		24 Oct 36	40UNTS153	100632
Brazil	France	27 Jan 40	72UNTS77	100929
Spain	USA (United States)	02 Dec 44	89UNTS345	200262
Multilateral		07 Dec 44	171UNTS345	200501
Sweden	USA (United States)	16 Dec 44	6UNTS397	200041
Denmark	USA (United States)	16 Dec 44	10UNTS213	200063
Iceland	USA (United States)	27 Jan 45	122UNTS293	200411
Ireland	USA (United States)	03 Feb 45	122UNTS305	200412
Switzerland	USA (United States)	03 Aug 45	51UNTS233	200191
Norway	USA (United States)	06 Oct 45	122UNTS319	200413
South Africa	UK Great Britain	26 Oct 45	72UNTS41	100927
Greece	UK Great Britain	26 Nov 45	35UNTS161	100555
Portugal	USA (United States)	06 Dec 45	3UNTS139	100028
Portugal	UK Great Britain	06 Dec 45	6UNTS3	100065
Portugal	UK Great Britain	06 Dec 45	5UNTS37	100064
Canada	UK Great Britain	21 Dec 45	27UNTS155	100405
Czechoslovakia	USA (United States)	03 Jan 46	6UNTS309	100084
Czechoslovakia	Poland	24 Jan 46	25UNTS181	100363
UK Great Britain	USA (United States)	11 Feb 46	3UNTS253	100036
Turkey	USA (United States)	12 Feb 46	13UNTS3	100196
Turkey	UK Great Britain	12 Feb 46	6UNTS79	100069
France	UK Great Britain	28 Feb 46	27UNTS173	100407
France	USA (United States)	27 Mar 46	139UNTS114	101879
Greece	USA (United States)	27 Mar 46	15UNTS233	100239
Competency certificate (Cont.)				
Ireland	UK Great Britain	05 Apr 46	72UNTS57	100928
Belgium	USA (United States)	05 Apr 46	4UNTS125	100041
Netherlands	Portugal	12 Apr 46	4UNTS317	100054
Argentina	UK Great Britain	17 Apr 46	164UNTS53	102159
France	Ireland	16 May 46	44UNTS105	100681
Ireland	Sweden	29 May 46	35UNTS231	100557
Australia	Canada	11 Jun 46	10UNTS47	100142
United Arab Rep	USA (United States)	15 Jun 46	71UNTS157	100917
Sweden	Turkey	26 Jun 46	14UNTS21	100208
Multilateral		27 Jun 46	164UNTS37	102157
Multilateral		29 Jun 46	94UNTS11	101303
Netherlands	Spain	13 Jul 46	4UNTS351	100055
France	Sweden	02 Aug 46	27UNTS251	100410
Lebanon	USA (United States)	11 Aug 46	66UNTS211	100856
Netherlands	UK Great Britain	13 Aug 46	4UNTS367	100056
Norway	UK Great Britain	31 Aug 46	6UNTS235	100078
Brazil	USA (United States)	06 Sep 46	54UNTS197	100805
France	Turkey	12 Oct 46	14UNTS33	100209
Belgium	Portugal	22 Oct 46	34UNTS49	100527
Brazil	UK Great Britain	31 Oct 46	11UNTS115	100152
Philippines	USA (United States)	16 Nov 46	7UNTS151	100097
Sweden	UK Great Britain	27 Nov 46	11UNTS229	100162
New Zealand	USA (United States)	03 Dec 46	7UNTS175	100099
Australia	USA (United States)	03 Dec 46	7UNTS201	100100
Portugal	Switzerland	09 Dec 46	310UNTS251	104495
Brazil	Portugal	10 Dec 46	200UNTS67	102695
USA (United States)	Uruguay	14 Dec 46	532UNTS87	107713
Taiwan	USA (United States)	20 Dec 46	22UNTS87	100332
Peru	USA (United States)	27 Dec 46	26UNTS227	100390
Ecuador	USA (United States)	08 Jan 47	22UNTS119	100333
Czechoslovakia	Ireland	29 Jan 47	27UNTS267	100411
USSR (Soviet Union)	Yugoslavia	04 Feb 47	130UNTS235	101731
Thailand	USA (United States)	26 Feb 47	16UNTS17	100246
Paraguay	USA (United States)	28 Feb 47	44UNTS25	100676
Portugal	Sweden	06 Mar 47	35UNTS243	100558
Netherlands	Turkey	19 Mar 47	14UNTS59	100211
Greece	Sweden	08 Apr 47	94UNTS73	101307
Greece	Netherlands	17 Apr 47	32UNTS115	100494
Canada	Portugal	25 Apr 47	94UNTS87	101308
Syria	USA (United States)	28 Apr 47	262UNTS121	103741
France	Greece	05 May 47	76UNTS61	100980
Chile	USA (United States)	10 May 47	55UNTS21	100807
Czechoslovakia	Denmark	14 May 47	27UNTS297	100413
South Africa	USA (United States)	23 May 47	66UNTS233	100857
Canada	Sweden	27 Jun 47	27UNTS313	100414
Romania	Yugoslavia	30 Jun 47	116UNTS57	101569
Iraq	Turkey	30 Jun 47	72UNTS107	100930
Denmark	Turkey	30 Jun 47	32UNTS301	100504
Canada	UK Great Britain	17 Jul 47	28UNTS3	100416
Netherlands	Thailand	18 Jul 47	28UNTS27	100417
Greece	Turkey	22 Jul 47	72UNTS131	100931
Netherlands	South Africa	22 Jul 47	12UNTS257	100188
Taiwan	UK Great Britain	23 Jul 47	9UNTS207	100135
Poland	Romania	09 Aug 47	12UNTS363	100193
Hungary	Poland	28 Aug 47	15UNTS145	100231
Czechoslovakia	Netherlands	01 Sep 47	32UNTS129	100495
Czechoslovakia	Switzerland	10 Sep 47	35UNTS275	100559
Lebanon	Turkey	16 Sep 47	44UNTS123	100682
Czechoslovakia	Sweden	15 Oct 47	44UNTS149	100683
Colombia	UK Great Britain	16 Oct 47	160UNTS297	102115
Norway	Portugal	11 Nov 47	34UNTS257	100542
Denmark	Greece	14 Nov 47	35UNTS295	100560
Denmark	Ireland	18 Nov 47	35UNTS309	100561
Ireland	Italy	21 Nov 47	353UNTS73	105038
Taiwan	Netherlands	06 Dec 47	43UNTS185	100669

Competency certificate (Cont.)

PARTY ONE	PARTY TWO	DATE	CITATION	NUMBER
Denmark	Portugal	15 Dec 47	35UNTS329	100563
Austria	Netherlands	22 Jan 48	17UNTS99	100270
Italy	USA (United States)	06 Feb 48	73UNTS113	100950
Czechoslovakia	Yugoslavia	14 Mar 48	28UNTS81	100421
Argentina	Denmark	18 Mar 48	94UNTS175	101311
Cuba	UK Great Britain	19 Mar 48	175UNTS23	102294
Ireland	Switzerland	06 May 48	334UNTS187	104768
Jordan	Turkey	07 May 48	32UNTS313	100505
Ireland	Netherlands	10 May 48	28UNTS121	100422
Norway	Turkey	20 May 48	26UNTS137	100384
Greece	Switzerland	26 May 48	94UNTS217	101312
Ireland	Norway	21 Jun 48	34UNTS317	100545
France	Spain	23 Aug 48	28UNTS173	100425
Greece	Lebanon	06 Sep 48	178UNTS37	102335
Bolivia	USA (United States)	29 Sep 48	505UNTS139	107370
Netherlands	Spain	08 Oct 48	28UNTS209	100426
Mexico	Portugal	22 Oct 48	34UNTS329	100546
Belgium	France	28 Oct 48	25UNTS151	100360
Argentina	Netherlands	29 Oct 48	95UNTS21	101316
Argentina	Chile	14 Dec 48	635UNTS21	109071
Belgium	Sweden	16 Dec 48	26UNTS3	100372
Belgium	Italy	01 Jan 49	26UNTS151	100385
Italy	Lebanon	24 Jan 49	231UNTS241	103223
Switzerland	Turkey	16 Feb 49	72UNTS175	100933
Finland	Netherlands	25 Feb 49	53UNTS123	100777
Netherlands	Switzerland	07 Mar 49	35UNTS69	100551
Finland	USA (United States)	29 Mar 49	55UNTS59	100808
Panama	USA (United States)	31 Mar 49	55UNTS87	100810
Finland	Sweden	26 Apr 49	95UNTS83	101318
Bulgaria	Poland	16 May 49	84UNTS313	101140
Italy	Spain	31 May 49	231UNTS251	103224
Belgium	Denmark	31 May 49	32UNTS337	100506
Canada	USA (United States)	04 Jun 49	122UNTS237	101649
Belgium	Greece	21 Jun 49	137UNTS215	101854
Korea, South	USA (United States)	29 Jun 49	55UNTS79	100809
Greece	Syria	05 Jul 49	78UNTS71	101013
Iraq	Norway	12 Jul 49	53UNTS137	100778
Czechoslovakia	Finland	13 Jul 49	53UNTS153	100779
Dominican Republic	USA (United States)	19 Jul 49	51UNTS145	100762
Finland	Norway	24 Aug 49	53UNTS167	100780
Denmark	Finland	26 Aug 49	53UNTS191	100781
Belgium	Canada	30 Aug 49	53UNTS221	100782
Lebanon	Netherlands	20 Sep 49	108UNTS205	101474
Burma	USA (United States)	28 Sep 49	55UNTS3	100806
Greece	Philippines	08 Oct 49	187UNTS221	102515
Sweden	Thailand	23 Nov 49	72UNTS217	100935
Denmark	Thailand	23 Nov 49	53UNTS255	100786
Italy	Turkey	25 Nov 49	192UNTS39	102594
Norway	Thailand	26 Nov 49	53UNTS269	100787
Brazil	Spain	28 Nov 49	215UNTS303	102923
Austria	Sweden	02 Dec 49	108UNTS3	101465
Austria	Norway	02 Dec 49	72UNTS230	100936
Austria	Denmark	02 Dec 49	53UNTS281	100788
Austria	Switzerland	19 Dec 49	254UNTS287	103597
USA (United States)	Yugoslavia	24 Dec 49	89UNTS209	101219
Netherlands	Syria	13 Feb 50	108UNTS53	101467
Canada	Norway	14 Feb 50	53UNTS329	100790
Spain	Sweden	18 Feb 50	166UNTS15	102184
Ceylon (Sri Lanka)	Thailand	24 Feb 50	72UNTS261	100938
Italy	Netherlands	04 Mar 50	254UNTS305	103598
Iceland	Netherlands	22 Mar 50	95UNTS237	101323
Denmark	Iceland	22 Mar 50	72UNTS273	100939
Italy	Portugal	05 Apr 50	254UNTS329	103599
Israel	USA (United States)	13 Jun 50	212UNTS93	102863
Netherlands	Spain	20 Jun 50	95UNTS303	101327

Competency certificate (Cont.)

PARTY ONE	PARTY TWO	DATE	CITATION	NUMBER
Iraq	Pakistan	20 Jun 50	77UNTS215	101001
Burma	Ceylon (Sri Lanka)	29 Jun 50	73UNTS3	100940
Spain	UK Great Britain	20 Jul 50	398UNTS101	105719
Spain	Switzerland	03 Aug 50	254UNTS365	103600
Canada	New Zealand	16 Aug 50	77UNTS239	101002
Burma	Sweden	14 Sep 50	96UNTS45	101330
Brazil	Turkey	21 Sep 50	150UNTS299	101981
Sweden	Switzerland	18 Oct 50	166UNTS49	102185
Luxembourg	Portugal	21 Oct 50	108UNTS67	101468
Israel	Netherlands	23 Oct 50	189UNTS89	102543
Israel	Turkey	05 Feb 51	193UNTS3	102607
Colombia	Portugal	09 Mar 51	108UNTS87	101469
Greece	Yugoslavia	15 Mar 51	187UNTS237	102516
Greece	Norway	28 May 51	187UNTS141	102507
Cuba	Portugal	26 Jun 51	192UNTS115	102598
Iceland	Norway	14 Jul 51	163UNTS265	102150
Burma	Denmark	30 Jul 51	108UNTS167	101472
Burma	Netherlands	06 Sep 51	108UNTS187	101473
Panama	UK Great Britain	15 Sep 51	560UNTS143	108172
Philippines	Spain	06 Oct 51	215UNTS193	102920
Greece	Luxembourg	22 Oct 51	187UNTS119	102506
Denmark	Iraq	18 Nov 51	232UNTS25	103227
Colombia	Spain	11 Dec 51	216UNTS73	102933
Belgium	Spain	10 Mar 52	178UNTS243	102342
Norway	Uruguay	20 Mar 52	310UNTS279	104496
Sweden	Uruguay	20 Mar 52	311UNTS3	104497
Iraq	Switzerland	31 Mar 52	311UNTS43	104498
France	Mexico	17 Apr 52	163UNTS321	102153
France	Israel	29 Apr 52	189UNTS55	102542
Switzerland	UK Great Britain	13 May 52	164UNTS91	102160
Denmark	UK Great Britain	23 Jun 52	151UNTS3	101982
Japan	USA (United States)	11 Aug 52	212UNTS27	102862
Austria	Luxembourg	13 Oct 52	192UNTS291	102606
Mexico	Netherlands	13 Oct 52	163UNTS341	102154
Iceland	Luxembourg	23 Oct 52	193UNTS39	102609
Chile	Sweden	27 Oct 52	311UNTS63	104499
Chile	Denmark	27 Oct 52	271UNTS93	103911
Luxembourg	Norway	17 Nov 52	311UNTS95	104500
Luxembourg	Sweden	17 Nov 52	173UNTS277	102270
Israel	Switzerland	19 Nov 52	232UNTS3	103226
Philippines	Thailand	27 Apr 53	174UNTS3	102274
Cuba	USA (United States)	26 May 53	224UNTS75	103070
Switzerland	Yugoslavia	28 May 53	232UNTS45	103228
Burma	Norway	22 Jun 53	174UNTS49	102277
USA (United States)	Venezuela	14 Aug 53	213UNTS99	102883
Austria	Yugoslavia	11 Nov 53	363UNTS149	105206
Syria	UK Great Britain	30 Jan 54	449UNTS47	106452
Peru	Spain	31 Mar 54	232UNTS65	103230
Ireland	Luxembourg	27 Jul 54	232UNTS91	103231
Belgium	UK Great Britain	05 Nov 54	209UNTS69	102822
Ecuador	Netherlands	14 Dec 54	232UNTS115	103233
Norway	Switzerland	30 Dec 54	311UNTS147	104502
Austria	Belgium	07 Jan 55	380UNTS219	105458
Germany, West	USA (United States)	07 Jul 55	275UNTS3	103973
France	Germany, West	04 Oct 55	353UNTS203	105044
Denmark	Syria	20 Oct 55	250UNTS61	103518
Austria	Israel	17 Nov 55	232UNTS153	103235
Austria	Italy	23 Jan 56	393UNTS97	105653
Argentina	Switzerland	25 Jan 56	559UNTS121	108157
Hungary	Romania	03 Feb 56	362UNTS233	105190
Austria	Poland	08 Feb 56	334UNTS221	104770
Norway	Syria	25 Feb 56	463UNTS217	106706
Belgium	Germany, West	14 Apr 56	344UNTS103	104945
Germany, West	Switzerland	02 May 56	559UNTS157	108158
Portugal	Venezuela	16 May 56	463UNTS239	106707

PARTY ONE	PARTY TWO	DATE	CITATION	NUMBER
Competency certificate (Cont.)				
Greece	Italy	26 May 56	496UNTS301	107258
Italy	Switzerland	04 Jun 56	378UNTS311	105429
Germany, West	Ireland	12 Jun 56	353UNTS121	105040
Switzerland	Thailand	13 Oct 56	312UNTS43	104510
Colombia	USA (United States)	24 Oct 56	476UNTS77	106905
Belgium	Turkey	25 Oct 56	380UNTS3	105447
Peru	Switzerland	23 Nov 56	411UNTS97	105916
Iran	USA (United States)	16 Jan 57	308UNTS147	104460
Iceland	Thailand	22 Jan 57	312UNTS63	104511
Germany, West	Sweden	29 Jan 57	393UNTS113	105654
Germany, West	Norway	29 Jan 57	353UNTS39	105037
Denmark	Germany, West	29 Jan 57	302UNTS75	104354
Belgium	Czechoslovakia	12 Mar 57	312UNTS75	104512
Netherlands	Yugoslavia	13 Mar 57	327UNTS227	104723
Netherlands	USA (United States)	03 Apr 57	410UNTS193	105904
Germany, West	Yugoslavia	10 Apr 57	463UNTS269	106708
Korea, South	USA (United States)	24 Apr 57	288UNTS219	104207
Afghanistan	Pakistan	13 Jun 57	327UNTS51	104717
Czechoslovakia	United Arab Rep	30 Jun 57	411UNTS126	105917
Greece	Italy	02 Aug 57	533UNTS217	107744
Italy	Pakistan	05 Oct 57	353UNTS91	105039
France	Morocco	25 Oct 57	559UNTS95	108156
Belgium	Morocco	20 Jan 58	288UNTS3	104192
Afghanistan	Turkey	08 Feb 58	464UNTS39	106711
Morocco	Portugal	03 Apr 58	393UNTS203	105657
Multilateral		29 Apr 58	450UNTS11	106465
Denmark	Luxembourg	10 Jun 58	356UNTS193	105096
Romania	United Arab Rep	14 Aug 58	405UNTS189	105834
Austria	Bulgaria	12 Sep 58	353UNTS3	105036
UK Great Britain	Yugoslavia	03 Feb 59	359UNTS339	105151
Indonesia	USA (United States)	02 Mar 59	357UNTS145	105113
Sweden	Tunisia	19 Mar 59	497UNTS43	107261
Norway	Tunisia	28 Mar 59	497UNTS77	107263
Denmark	Tunisia	14 Apr 59	340UNTS273	104870
Ceylon (Sri Lanka)	Sweden	29 May 59	464UNTS109	106713
Ceylon (Sri Lanka)	Norway	29 May 59	411UNTS165	105919
Ceylon (Sri Lanka)	Denmark	29 May 59	348UNTS225	105002
Bulgaria	United Arab Rep	09 Jul 59	411UNTS187	105920
Multilateral		06 Feb 60	383UNTS3	105494
France	Thailand	26 Feb 60	392UNTS279	105648
Finland	Iceland	10 Mar 60	497UNTS95	107264
Greece	Romania	02 May 60	485UNTS17	107043
Morocco	United Arab Rep	19 May 60	563UNTS121	108208
Switzerland	Tunisia	21 May 60	497UNTS109	107265
Afghanistan	Czechoslovakia	28 May 60	497UNTS129	107266
Luxembourg	Tunisia	13 Jun 60	497UNTS143	107267
Denmark	Peru	22 Jun 60	439UNTS113	106326
Mexico	USA (United States)	15 Aug 60	402UNTS177	105786
Belgium	Burma	17 Aug 60	540UNTS185	107850
Burma	Switzerland	31 Oct 60	465UNTS97	106723
Norway	Peru	02 Nov 60	497UNTS207	107270
Luxembourg	Thailand	29 Dec 60	465UNTS131	106725
Czechoslovakia	Morocco	08 Jun 61	497UNTS275	107272
Cameroon	France	16 Jun 61	412UNTS148	105929
Finland	Luxembourg	15 Aug 61	541UNTS45	107859
Mexico	Netherlands	24 Aug 61	465UNTS291	106732
Liberia	Switzerland	31 Aug 61	559UNTS215	108160
Ghana	Romania	30 Sep 61	467UNTS443	106769
Finland	Hungary	13 Feb 62	463UNTS61	106693
France	Senegal	15 Jun 62	524UNTS3	107563
Morocco	Switzerland	05 Jul 62	498UNTS171	107281
Finland	France	12 Oct 62	498UNTS299	107285
France	Ivory Coast	19 Oct 62	498UNTS317	107286
Ivory Coast	Switzerland	17 Nov 62	499UNTS3	107289
Ghana	Tunisia	11 Dec 62	563UNTS243	108213

PARTY ONE	PARTY TWO	DATE	CITATION	NUMBER
Competency certificate (Cont.)				
Ghana	Mali	09 Jan 63	466UNTS165	106742
Senegal	Switzerland	23 Jan 63	524UNTS23	107564
Mali	Senegal	07 Feb 63	524UNTS41	107565
Algeria	France	18 Feb 63	563UNTS263	108214
Algeria	Morocco	30 Apr 63	564UNTS3	108217
Belgium	Cyprus	08 Jun 63	601UNTS311	108703
Guinea	Ivory Coast	26 Jun 63	499UNTS71	107293
Algeria	Mali	22 Jul 63	564UNTS29	108219
Cameroon	Israel	09 Aug 63	499UNTS121	107295
Algeria	Tunisia	01 Sep 63	601UNTS275	108701
Ivory Coast	Netherlands	09 Oct 63	499UNTS141	107296
Mali	Niger	15 Jan 64	499UNTS197	107299
Cameroon	Mali	17 Mar 64	524UNTS61	107566
United Arab Rep	USA (United States)	05 May 64	531UNTS229	107706
Cyprus	Hungary	02 Jun 64	602UNTS3	108704
New Zealand	USA (United States)	24 Jun 64	524UNTS101	107568
Ivory Coast	Mali	09 Jul 64	524UNTS121	107569
Cyprus	Syria	22 Dec 64	602UNTS25	108705
Australia	France	13 Apr 65	601UNTS293	108702
Mauritania	Spain	11 May 65	602UNTS111	108709
Malaysia	Norway	26 May 65	602UNTS157	108711
Nigeria	Switzerland	11 Oct 65	602UNTS137	108710
Burma	Czechoslovakia	15 Dec 65	602UNTS71	108707
Belgium	Spain	19 Jul 66	575UNTS3	108352
Denmark	Singapore	20 Dec 66	593UNTS125	108580
Registration certificate				
Multilateral		07 Dec 44	171UNTS345	200501
Czechoslovakia	USSR (Soviet Union)	25 Jul 46	27UNTS231	100409
Romania	Yugoslavia	30 Jun 47	116UNTS57	101569
Hungary	Poland	28 Aug 47	15UNTS145	100231
Burma	Pakistan	18 Nov 47	35UNTS321	100562
Czechoslovakia	Yugoslavia	14 Mar 48	28UNTS81	100421
USA (United States)	Venezuela	24 Mar 48	44UNTS57	100678
Multilateral		10 Jun 48	164UNTS113	102163
Multilateral		19 Jun 48	310UNTS151	104492
Austria	USA (United States)	23 Mar 49	43UNTS127	100667
Multilateral		12 Aug 49	75UNTS31	100970
Multilateral		12 Aug 49	75UNTS85	100971
Multilateral		19 Sep 49	125UNTS3	101671
Iraq	Pakistan	20 Jun 50	77UNTS215	101001
France	UK Great Britain	06 Oct 50	96UNTS63	101331
Costa Rica	USA (United States)	17 Jan 51	134UNTS215	101801
Panama	USA (United States)	26 Jan 51	137UNTS69	101849
Greece	Yugoslavia	15 Mar 51	187UNTS237	102516
El Salvador	USA (United States)	19 Mar 51	134UNTS245	101803
Nicaragua	USA (United States)	20 Apr 51	138UNTS57	101859
Netherlands	UK Great Britain	17 May 51	118UNTS103	101599
Italy	UK Great Britain	24 Oct 51	118UNTS143	101602
Multilateral		20 Dec 51	163UNTS293	102151
Canada	USA (United States)	21 Feb 52	205UNTS293	102781
Belgium	Sweden	21 Apr 52	166UNTS9	102183
Belgium	France	30 Jun 52	137UNTS259	101857
Switzerland	Yugoslavia	28 May 53	232UNTS45	103228
Nicaragua	USA (United States)	02 Sep 53	215UNTS69	102911
Austria	Yugoslavia	11 Nov 53	363UNTS149	105206
Cuba	USA (United States)	26 Nov 53	205UNTS213	102777
France	Sweden	16 Feb 54	228UNTS137	103147
Lebanon	Yugoslavia	17 Apr 54	602UNTS199	108713
Sweden	USA (United States)	22 Dec 54	228UNTS85	103143
Italy	USA (United States)	26 Jan 55	238UNTS179	103361
South Africa	USA (United States)	22 Feb 55	247UNTS247	103473
USSR (Soviet Union)	Yugoslavia	03 Sep 55	240UNTS267	103408
Germany, East	Hungary	10 Sep 55	407UNTS132	105863
Bulgaria	Yugoslavia	01 Oct 55	396UNTS223	105698

PARTY ONE	PARTY TWO	DATE	CITATION	NUMBER
Registration certificate (Cont.)				
Finland	USSR (Soviet Union)	19 Oct 55	353UNTS185	105043
Netherlands	USA (United States)	04 Nov 55	269UNTS3	103867
Burma	China People's Rep	08 Nov 55	306UNTS11	104430
Romania	Yugoslavia	01 Feb 56	362UNTS203	105189
Hungary	Romania	03 Feb 56	362UNTS233	105190
Austria	Poland	08 Feb 56	334UNTS221	104770
Denmark	USSR (Soviet Union)	31 Mar 56	259UNTS169	103689
Sweden	USSR (Soviet Union)	31 Mar 56	259UNTS239	103691
Norway	USSR (Soviet Union)	31 Mar 56	259UNTS205	103690
Poland	Sweden	08 Jun 56	334UNTS257	104771
Denmark	Finland	15 Sep 56	254UNTS3	103589
Denmark	Sweden	15 Sep 56	263UNTS3	103764
Belgium	Poland	17 Oct 56	356UNTS279	105100
Albania	Yugoslavia	23 Nov 56	386UNTS73	105539
Belgium	Romania	04 Dec 56	317UNTS161	104602
France	USA (United States)	14 Dec 56	266UNTS117	103826
Norway	USA (United States)	05 Feb 57	279UNTS169	104038
Netherlands	Yugoslavia	13 Mar 57	327UNTS227	104723
Germany, West	Yugoslavia	10 Apr 57	463UNTS269	106708
Romania	Sweden	15 Apr 57	342UNTS325	104915
Bulgaria	Sweden	17 Apr 57	464UNTS3	106709
Belgium	Bulgaria	14 May 57	317UNTS81	104596
Hungary	Netherlands	28 May 57	334UNTS291	104773
Belgium	Hungary	01 Jun 57	291UNTS17	104242
Hungary	Sweden	02 Aug 57	334UNTS307	104774
Netherlands	Romania	27 Aug 57	342UNTS309	104914
Spain	USA (United States)	23 Sep 57	290UNTS261	104238
Netherlands	UK Great Britain	22 Oct 57	313UNTS309	104538
Belgium	USA (United States)	03 Dec 57	303UNTS45	104370
UK Great Britain	USSR (Soviet Union)	19 Dec 57	351UNTS235	105026
Bulgaria	Netherlands	07 Feb 58	335UNTS45	104777
Bulgaria	Yugoslavia	21 Mar 58	386UNTS119	105541
Sweden	Yugoslavia	18 Apr 58	393UNTS225	105658
Germany, West	USSR (Soviet Union)	25 Apr 58	346UNTS71	104978
Bulgaria	Denmark	28 May 58	312UNTS235	104521
India	USSR (Soviet Union)	02 Jun 58	393UNTS3	105650
Belgium	USSR (Soviet Union)	05 Jun 58	345UNTS145	104965
Multilateral		10 Jun 58	454UNTS115	106540
Multilateral		10 Jun 58	454UNTS47	106539
Netherlands	USSR (Soviet Union)	17 Jun 58	335UNTS77	104779
Denmark	Romania	25 Jun 58	345UNTS231	104970
Austria	Romania	10 Jul 58	353UNTS155	105041
Denmark	Hungary	17 Jul 58	344UNTS281	104954
Romania	United Arab Rep	14 Aug 58	405UNTS189	105834
Austria	Bulgaria	12 Sep 58	353UNTS3	105036
Germany, West	USA (United States)	11 Dec 58	337UNTS31	104813
UK Great Britain	Yugoslavia	03 Feb 59	359UNTS339	105151
Austria	USA (United States)	30 Apr 59	343UNTS41	104920
Greece	Yugoslavia	18 Jun 59	368UNTS27	105234
Bulgaria	United Arab Rep	09 Jul 59	411UNTS187	105920
Australia	USA (United States)	20 Nov 59	349UNTS293	105015
Luxembourg	Yugoslavia	09 Apr 60	464UNTS293	106719
Greece	Romania	02 May 60	485UNTS17	107043
Multilateral		17 Jun 60	536UNTS27	107794
Hungary	UK Great Britain	25 Oct 60	419UNTS309	106034
Norway	Poland	17 Jan 61	412UNTS130	105928
Switzerland	USA (United States)	13 Oct 61	459UNTS219	106625
Australia	UK Great Britain	14 Nov 61	466UNTS35	106735
Finland	Hungary	13 Feb 62	463UNTS61	106693
Ghana	USSR (Soviet Union)	06 Apr 62	498UNTS41	107277
France	Romania	18 May 62	498UNTS115	107279
Hungary	Syria	18 Oct 62	491UNTS209	107178
Finland	New Zealand	12 Nov 62	485UNTS331	107064
Syria	United Arab Rep	27 Dec 62	491UNTS245	107180
Japan	USA (United States)	01 Feb 63	473UNTS49	106854

PARTY ONE	PARTY TWO	DATE	CITATION	NUMBER
Registration certificate (Cont.)				
Austria	Czechoslovakia	08 Mar 63	495UNTS219	107245
Greece	Hungary	27 Apr 63	534UNTS3	107750
Canada	Finland	05 Jun 63	472UNTS345	106846
Pakistan	USSR (Soviet Union)	07 Oct 63	499UNTS161	107297
Romania	Yugoslavia	25 Dec 63	576UNTS95	108366
Ceylon (Sri Lanka)	Finland	08 Jan 64	492UNTS285	107198
Denmark	Yugoslavia	11 Feb 64	511UNTS241	107437
Norway	Yugoslavia	15 Apr 64	602UNTS177	108712
Finland	South Africa	12 Jun 64	505UNTS107	107367
Canada	Denmark	15 Oct 64	525UNTS227	107595
Denmark	India	06 Feb 65	531UNTS23	107690
Finland	Ireland	15 Sep 65	604UNTS199	108750
France	Romania	14 Mar 66	604UNTS33	108741
Multilateral		05 Apr 66	640UNTS133	109159
Belgium	Spain	19 Jul 66	575UNTS3	108352
Romania	Sweden	01 Mar 67	642UNTS163	109172
Denmark	Pakistan	01 Jun 67	620UNTS217	108958
Finland	France	27 Oct 67	643UNTS75	109185
Passenger transport				
Spain	USA (United States)	02 Dec 44	89UNTS345	200262
Iceland	USA (United States)	11 Apr 45	16UNTS241	200105
Sweden	USA (United States)	04 Dec 45	6UNTS273	100080
Sweden	Yugoslavia	06 Oct 47	53UNTS107	100775
Peru	UK Great Britain	22 Dec 47	72UNTS143	100932
Philippines	UK Great Britain	07 Jan 48	28UNTS63	100420
Luxembourg	UK Great Britain	27 May 48	53UNTS115	100776
Multilateral		10 Jun 48	164UNTS113	102163
Luxembourg	Netherlands	23 Jun 48	32UNTS229	100500
Czechoslovakia	Poland	12 Nov 48	84UNTS347	101141
Czechoslovakia	Poland	02 Jul 49	260UNTS179	103709
Multilateral		19 Sep 49	125UNTS3	101671
USA (United States)	Yugoslavia	24 Dec 49	89UNTS209	101219
France	UK Great Britain	06 Oct 50	96UNTS63	101331
Brazil	Netherlands	15 Dec 50	123UNTS101	101657
Greece	Israel	22 Jul 52	219UNTS231	102978
Multilateral		25 Oct 52	241UNTS336	103442
Lebanon	Sweden	23 Mar 53	255UNTS83	103605
Lebanon	Switzerland	03 Mar 54	255UNTS127	103608
Pakistan	United Arab Rep	13 Dec 54	255UNTS167	103610
United Arab Rep	Yugoslavia	20 Feb 55	255UNTS199	103611
Multilateral		12 Mar 55	211UNTS3	102844
Austria	USSR (Soviet Union)	09 Nov 55	255UNTS247	103613
France	Japan	17 Jan 56	255UNTS275	103614
Italy	South Africa	21 May 56	255UNTS323	103616
Italy	Switzerland	19 Sep 57	363UNTS69	105200
Netherlands	Sweden	23 Oct 57	306UNTS75	104433
Denmark	Netherlands	13 Nov 57	306UNTS67	104432
India	Japan	04 Feb 58	324UNTS215	104687
Austria	Sweden	18 Feb 58	427UNTS349	106166
Bulgaria	Yugoslavia	21 Mar 58	386UNTS119	105541
Multilateral		10 Jun 58	454UNTS47	106539
Multilateral		05 Nov 58	428UNTS73	106169
Greece	Yugoslavia	18 Jun 59	368UNTS27	105234
India	Italy	06 Oct 59	378UNTS267	105427
Czechoslovakia	Germany, East	25 Nov 59	374UNTS101	105331
Italy	Netherlands	08 Dec 59	484UNTS309	107039
Argentina	Mexico	26 Jan 60	635UNTS79	109073
Cuba	Japan	22 Apr 60	442UNTS261	106354
Korea, North	USSR (Soviet Union)	22 Jun 60	399UNTS3	105732
Turkey	USSR (Soviet Union)	27 Apr 61	420UNTS307	106047
Morocco	Switzerland	05 Jul 62	498UNTS189	107282
Czechoslovakia	Yugoslavia	22 Oct 62	480UNTS267	106974
Japan	UK Great Britain	14 Nov 62	478UNTS29	106934
Czechoslovakia	Poland	16 Nov 62	526UNTS3	107597

PARTY ONE	PARTY TWO	DATE	CITATION	NUMBER
Passenger transport (Cont.)				
Austria	Yugoslavia	11 Dec 62	546UNTS3	107938
Poland	USSR (Soviet Union)	22 Apr 63	493UNTS229	107217
Belgium	Cyprus	08 Jun 63	601UNTS311	108703
El Salvador	Japan	19 Jul 63	518UNTS135	107494
Algeria	Tunisia	01 Sep 63	601UNTS275	108701
Romania	Yugoslavia	25 Dec 63	576UNTS95	108366
Austria	Belgium	20 Jan 64	509UNTS275	107406
Cyprus	Hungary	02 Jun 64	602UNTS3	108704
Czechoslovakia	Hungary	17 Oct 64	545UNTS21	107924
Cyprus	Syria	22 Dec 64	602UNTS25	108705
Australia	France	13 Apr 65	601UNTS293	108702
Hungary	Poland	18 Jul 65	577UNTS161	108376
Burma	Czechoslovakia	15 Dec 65	602UNTS71	108707
Belgium	Denmark	04 Feb 66	561UNTS233	108187
Austria	Germany, West	17 Feb 66	614UNTS263	108875
Bulgaria	Turkey	18 Apr 66	631UNTS263	108999
Belgium	Spain	19 Jul 66	575UNTS3	108352
Netherlands	Yugoslavia	08 Sep 66	597UNTS147	108643
Argentina	Uruguay	12 Feb 67	635UNTS125	109076
Belgium	Hungary	20 Mar 67	601UNTS37	108686
Austria	Czechoslovakia	19 Oct 67	634UNTS19	109048
Finland	France	27 Oct 67	643UNTS75	109185
India	United Nations	04 Nov 67	609UNTS3	108824
United Nations	Senegal	08 Nov 67	613UNTS255	108854
Finland	Hungary	10 Nov 67	643UNTS95	109186
Iran	United Nations	15 Feb 68	631UNTS103	108990
Finland	USSR (Soviet Union)	07 Mar 68	643UNTS107	109187
United Nations	Tunisia	18 Mar 68	633UNTS3	109030
Germany, West	Thailand	29 Mar 68	637UNTS0	109122
Niger	United Nations	07 May 68	639UNTS71	109145
Belgium	Poland	30 Oct 68	0UNTS0	109597
Dangerous goods				
Netherlands	Turkey	19 Mar 47	14UNTS59	100211
Iran	USA (United States)	06 Oct 47	11UNTS303	100171
Netherlands	UK Great Britain	17 May 51	118UNTS103	101599
Italy	UK Great Britain	24 Oct 51	118UNTS143	101602
Multilateral		19 May 56	399UNTS189	105742
Multilateral		30 Sep 57	619UNTS77	108940
Multilateral		15 Mar 60	572UNTS133	108310
Belgium	Luxembourg	29 Nov 61	486UNTS37	107071
Routes and logistics				
Bolivia	Brazil	25 Feb 38	88UNTS379	200254
Brazil	France	27 Jan 40	72UNTS77	100929
Panama	USA (United States)	23 Mar 40	124UNTS195	200420
Panama	USA (United States)	06 Sep 40	124UNTS209	200421
Brazil	Paraguay	14 Jun 41	54UNTS289	200201
Canada	USA (United States)	18 Mar 42	101UNTS205	200294
Nicaragua	USA (United States)	08 Apr 42	24UNTS145	200138
Saudi Arabia	UK Great Britain	20 Apr 42	10UNTS151	200058
Canada	USA (United States)	07 Dec 42	101UNTS227	200297
Canada	USA (United States)	04 Mar 43	13UNTS411	200087
Brazil	Paraguay	11 Aug 44	67UNTS303	200227
Spain	USA (United States)	02 Dec 44	89UNTS345	200262
Multilateral		07 Dec 44	171UNTS387	200502
Multilateral		07 Dec 44	84UNTS389	200252
Denmark	USA (United States)	16 Dec 44	10UNTS213	200063
Sweden	USA (United States)	16 Dec 44	6UNTS397	200041
Iceland	USA (United States)	27 Jan 45	122UNTS293	200411
Ireland	USA (United States)	03 Feb 45	122UNTS305	200412
Canada	USA (United States)	17 Feb 45	122UNTS261	200409
Iceland	USA (United States)	11 Apr 45	16UNTS241	200105
Switzerland	USA (United States)	03 Aug 45	51UNTS233	200191
Norway	USA (United States)	06 Oct 45	122UNTS319	200413
South Africa	UK Great Britain	26 Oct 45	72UNTS41	100927

PARTY ONE	PARTY TWO	DATE	CITATION	NUMBER
Routes and logistics (Cont.)				
Greece	UK Great Britain	26 Nov 45	35UNTS161	100555
Sweden	USA (United States)	04 Dec 45	6UNTS273	100080
Portugal	UK Great Britain	06 Dec 45	5UNTS37	100064
Portugal	USA (United States)	06 Dec 45	3UNTS139	100028
Portugal	UK Great Britain	06 Dec 45	6UNTS3	100065
Canada	UK Great Britain	21 Dec 45	27UNTS155	100405
France	USA (United States)	29 Dec 45	139UNTS105	101878
Czechoslovakia	USA (United States)	03 Jan 46	6UNTS309	100084
Denmark	France	04 Jan 46	27UNTS169	100406
Czechoslovakia	Poland	24 Jan 46	25UNTS181	100363
UK Great Britain	USA (United States)	11 Feb 46	3UNTS253	100036
Turkey	USA (United States)	12 Feb 46	13UNTS3	100196
Turkey	UK Great Britain	12 Feb 46	6UNTS79	100069
France	UK Great Britain	28 Feb 46	27UNTS173	100407
Denmark	USA (United States)	21 Mar 46	3UNTS301	100038
France	USA (United States)	27 Mar 46	139UNTS114	101879
Greece	USA (United States)	27 Mar 46	15UNTS233	100239
Ireland	UK Great Britain	05 Apr 46	72UNTS57	100928
Belgium	USA (United States)	05 Apr 46	4UNTS125	100041
Netherlands	Portugal	12 Apr 46	4UNTS317	100054
Multilateral		17 Apr 46	27UNTS103	100402
Argentina	UK Great Britain	17 Apr 46	164UNTS53	102159
France	Ireland	16 May 46	44UNTS105	100681
Ireland	Sweden	29 May 46	35UNTS231	100557
United Arab Rep	USA (United States)	15 Jun 46	71UNTS157	100917
Sweden	Turkey	26 Jun 46	14UNTS21	100208
Netherlands	Spain	13 Jul 46	4UNTS351	100055
Czechoslovakia	USSR (Soviet Union)	25 Jul 46	27UNTS231	100409
France	Sweden	02 Aug 46	27UNTS251	100410
Lebanon	USA (United States)	11 Aug 46	66UNTS211	100856
Netherlands	UK Great Britain	13 Aug 46	4UNTS367	100056
Norway	UK Great Britain	31 Aug 46	6UNTS235	100078
Brazil	USA (United States)	06 Sep 46	54UNTS197	100805
Sweden	USA (United States)	30 Sep 46	42UNTS213	100649
Denmark	USA (United States)	01 Oct 46	42UNTS219	100650
France	Turkey	12 Oct 46	14UNTS33	100209
Belgium	Portugal	22 Oct 46	34UNTS49	100527
Brazil	UK Great Britain	31 Oct 46	11UNTS115	100152
Norway	USA (United States)	12 Nov 46	42UNTS227	100651
India	USA (United States)	14 Nov 46	22UNTS55	100331
Philippines	USA (United States)	16 Nov 46	7UNTS151	100097
Sweden	UK Great Britain	27 Nov 46	11UNTS229	100162
Australia	USA (United States)	03 Dec 46	7UNTS201	100100
New Zealand	USA (United States)	03 Dec 46	7UNTS175	100099
Portugal	Switzerland	09 Dec 46	310UNTS251	104495
Brazil	Portugal	10 Dec 46	200UNTS67	102695
USA (United States)	Uruguay	14 Dec 46	532UNTS87	107713
Taiwan	USA (United States)	20 Dec 46	22UNTS87	100332
Peru	USA (United States)	27 Dec 46	26UNTS227	100390
Ecuador	USA (United States)	08 Jan 47	22UNTS119	100333
Czechoslovakia	Ireland	29 Jan 47	27UNTS267	100411
Greece	UK Great Britain	21 Feb 47	70UNTS215	100905
Thailand	USA (United States)	26 Feb 47	16UNTS17	100246
Paraguay	USA (United States)	28 Feb 47	44UNTS25	100676
Portugal	Sweden	06 Mar 47	35UNTS243	100558
Australia	USA (United States)	10 Mar 47	10UNTS89	100145
Netherlands	Turkey	19 Mar 47	14UNTS59	100211
Greece	Sweden	08 Apr 47	94UNTS73	101307
Greece	Netherlands	17 Apr 47	32UNTS115	100494
Canada	Portugal	25 Apr 47	94UNTS87	101308
Syria	USA (United States)	28 Apr 47	262UNTS121	103741
France	Greece	05 May 47	76UNTS61	100980
Thailand	USA (United States)	08 May 47	42UNTS241	100653
Chile	USA (United States)	10 May 47	55UNTS21	100807
Czechoslovakia	Denmark	14 May 47	27UNTS297	100413

PARTY ONE	PARTY TWO	DATE	CITATION	NUMBER
Routes and logistics (Cont.)				
South Africa	USA (United States)	23 May 47	66UNTS233	100857
Ireland	USA (United States)	03 Jun 47	16UNTS151	100255
Italy	USA (United States)	09 Jun 47	104UNTS157	101437
Canada	Sweden	27 Jun 47	27UNTS313	100414
Romania	Yugoslavia	30 Jun 47	116UNTS57	101569
Denmark	Turkey	30 Jun 47	32UNTS301	100504
Iraq	Turkey	30 Jun 47	72UNTS107	100930
France	India	16 Jul 47	27UNTS325	100415
Canada	UK Great Britain	17 Jul 47	28UNTS3	100416
Netherlands	Thailand	18 Jul 47	28UNTS27	100417
Greece	Turkey	22 Jul 47	72UNTS131	100931
Netherlands	South Africa	22 Jul 47	12UNTS257	100188
Canada	Ireland	08 Aug 47	28UNTS47	100419
Poland	Romania	09 Aug 47	12UNTS363	100193
Hungary	Poland	28 Aug 47	15UNTS145	100231
Czechoslovakia	Netherlands	01 Sep 47	32UNTS129	100495
Czechoslovakia	Switzerland	10 Sep 47	35UNTS275	100559
Lebanon	Turkey	16 Sep 47	44UNTS123	100682
Chile	UK Great Britain	16 Sep 47	133UNTS143	101786
Sweden	Yugoslavia	06 Oct 47	53UNTS107	100775
Czechoslovakia	Sweden	15 Oct 47	44UNTS149	100683
Colombia	UK Great Britain	16 Oct 47	160UNTS297	102115
Brazil	Netherlands	06 Nov 47	53UNTS59	100773
Norway	Portugal	11 Nov 47	34UNTS257	100542
Brazil	Sweden	14 Nov 47	94UNTS139	101310
Brazil	Norway	14 Nov 47	44UNTS163	100684
Brazil	Denmark	14 Nov 47	47UNTS39	100722
Denmark	Greece	14 Nov 47	35UNTS295	100560
Burma	Pakistan	18 Nov 47	35UNTS321	100562
Denmark	Ireland	18 Nov 47	35UNTS309	100561
Ireland	Italy	21 Nov 47	353UNTS73	105038
Taiwan	Netherlands	06 Dec 47	43UNTS185	100669
Denmark	Portugal	15 Dec 47	35UNTS329	100563
Peru	UK Great Britain	22 Dec 47	72UNTS143	100932
Ethiopia	Pakistan	01 Jan 48	35UNTS3	100547
Philippines	UK Great Britain	07 Jan 48	28UNTS63	100420
Austria	Netherlands	22 Jan 48	17UNTS99	100270
Italy	USA (United States)	06 Feb 48	73UNTS113	100950
Czechoslovakia	Yugoslavia	14 Mar 48	28UNTS81	100421
Argentina	Denmark	18 Mar 48	94UNTS175	101311
Cuba	UK Great Britain	19 Mar 48	175UNTS23	102294
Ireland	Switzerland	06 May 48	334UNTS187	104768
Jordan	Turkey	07 May 48	32UNTS313	100505
Ireland	Netherlands	10 May 48	28UNTS121	100422
Norway	Turkey	20 May 48	26UNTS137	100384
India	Sweden	21 May 48	34UNTS285	100543
Greece	Switzerland	26 May 48	94UNTS217	101312
Luxembourg	UK Great Britain	27 May 48	53UNTS115	100776
Canada	Netherlands	02 Jun 48	32UNTS215	100499
Ireland	Norway	21 Jun 48	34UNTS317	100545
India	Pakistan	23 Jun 48	28UNTS143	100423
Italy	UK Great Britain	25 Jun 48	94UNTS239	101313
Australia	Italy	02 Aug 48	28UNTS165	100424
Brazil	Switzerland	10 Aug 48	94UNTS269	101314
France	Spain	23 Aug 48	28UNTS173	100425
Greece	Lebanon	06 Sep 48	178UNTS37	102335
Bolivia	USA (United States)	29 Sep 48	505UNTS139	107370
Netherlands	Spain	08 Oct 48	28UNTS209	100426
France	USA (United States)	19 Oct 48	98UNTS3	101355
Mexico	Portugal	22 Oct 48	34UNTS329	100546
Argentina	Netherlands	29 Oct 48	95UNTS21	101316
Argentina	Chile	14 Dec 48	635UNTS21	109071
Ceylon (Sri Lanka)	India	21 Dec 48	28UNTS223	100427
Ceylon (Sri Lanka)	Pakistan	03 Jan 49	28UNTS247	100428
Italy	Lebanon	24 Jan 49	231UNTS241	103223

PARTY ONE	PARTY TWO	DATE	CITATION	NUMBER
Routes and logistics (Cont.)				
Switzerland	Turkey	16 Feb 49	72UNTS175	100933
Belgium	Sweden	21 Feb 49	95UNTS73	101317
Finland	Netherlands	25 Feb 49	53UNTS123	100777
Netherlands	Switzerland	07 Mar 49	35UNTS69	100551
Finland	USA (United States)	29 Mar 49	55UNTS59	100808
Panama	USA (United States)	31 Mar 49	55UNTS87	100810
Finland	Sweden	26 Apr 49	95UNTS83	101318
Belgium	Netherlands	13 May 49	65UNTS133	100841
Bulgaria	Poland	16 May 49	84UNTS313	101140
Italy	Spain	31 May 49	231UNTS251	103224
Australia	Pakistan	03 Jun 49	35UNTS23	100549
Canada	USA (United States)	04 Jun 49	122UNTS237	101649
Ethiopia	India	07 Jun 49	35UNTS13	100548
Belgium	Greece	21 Jun 49	137UNTS215	101854
Norway	Pakistan	23 Jun 49	35UNTS49	100550
India	Switzerland	24 Jun 49	95UNTS109	101319
Czechoslovakia	Poland	02 Jul 49	260UNTS179	103709
Czechoslovakia	Poland	02 Jul 49	260UNTS149	103708
Greece	Syria	05 Jul 49	78UNTS71	101013
Australia	India	11 Jul 49	35UNTS83	100552
Iraq	Norway	12 Jul 49	53UNTS137	100778
Czechoslovakia	Finland	13 Jul 49	53UNTS153	100779
Pakistan	Philippines	16 Jul 49	35UNTS111	100553
Dominican Republic	USA (United States)	19 Jul 49	51UNTS145	100762
Pakistan	UK Great Britain	27 Jul 49	44UNTS199	100685
Ceylon (Sri Lanka)	UK Great Britain	05 Aug 49	35UNTS137	100554
Multilateral		12 Aug 49	75UNTS85	100971
Canada	UK Great Britain	19 Aug 49	44UNTS223	100686
Finland	Norway	24 Aug 49	53UNTS167	100780
Denmark	Finland	26 Aug 49	53UNTS191	100781
Belgium	Canada	30 Aug 49	53UNTS221	100782
Multilateral		15 Sep 49	53UNTS235	100783
Belgium	United Arab Rep	19 Sep 49	137UNTS189	101853
Lebanon	Netherlands	20 Sep 49	108UNTS205	101474
Burma	USA (United States)	28 Sep 49	55UNTS3	100806
Greece	Philippines	08 Oct 49	187UNTS221	102515
India	Philippines	20 Oct 49	72UNTS191	100934
Multilateral		27 Oct 49	53UNTS241	100784
Iran	Netherlands	31 Oct 49	254UNTS257	103596
Denmark	Pakistan	09 Nov 49	44UNTS255	100687
Denmark	Thailand	23 Nov 49	53UNTS255	100786
Sweden	Thailand	23 Nov 49	72UNTS217	100935
Italy	Turkey	25 Nov 49	192UNTS39	102594
Norway	Thailand	26 Nov 49	53UNTS269	100787
Brazil	Spain	28 Nov 49	215UNTS303	102923
Austria	Sweden	02 Dec 49	108UNTS3	101465
Austria	Denmark	02 Dec 49	53UNTS281	100788
Austria	Norway	02 Dec 49	72UNTS230	100936
Netherlands	United Arab Rep	08 Dec 49	95UNTS123	101320
Sweden	United Arab Rep	12 Dec 49	108UNTS15	101466
Canada	Denmark	13 Dec 49	72UNTS247	100937
Austria	Switzerland	19 Dec 49	254UNTS287	103597
USA (United States)	Yugoslavia	24 Dec 49	89UNTS209	101219
Netherlands	Syria	13 Feb 50	108UNTS53	101467
Canada	Norway	14 Feb 50	53UNTS329	100790
Spain	Sweden	18 Feb 50	166UNTS15	102184
Ceylon (Sri Lanka)	Thailand	24 Feb 50	72UNTS261	100938
Italy	Netherlands	04 Mar 50	254UNTS305	103598
Norway	United Arab Rep	11 Mar 50	95UNTS157	101321
Denmark	United Arab Rep	14 Mar 50	95UNTS197	101322
Philippines	USA (United States)	16 Mar 50	89UNTS199	101218
Iceland	Netherlands	22 Mar 50	95UNTS237	101323
Denmark	Iceland	22 Mar 50	72UNTS273	100939
Italy	Portugal	05 Apr 50	254UNTS329	103599
Sweden	UK Great Britain	05 Apr 50	99UNTS107	101374

PARTY ONE	PARTY TWO	DATE	CITATION	NUMBER
Routes and logistics (Cont.)				
Turkey	United Arab Rep	12 Apr 50	128UNTS3	101711
Australia	Philippines	14 Apr 50	127UNTS281	101709
Greece	United Arab Rep	24 Apr 50	163UNTS229	102149
Switzerland	United Arab Rep	15 May 50	95UNTS255	101325
Israel	USA (United States)	13 Jun 50	212UNTS93	102863
Netherlands	Spain	20 Jun 50	95UNTS303	101327
Iraq	Pakistan	20 Jun 50	77UNTS215	101001
Burma	Ceylon (Sri Lanka)	29 Jun 50	73UNTS3	100940
France	Pakistan	31 Jul 50	96UNTS23	101329
Spain	Switzerland	03 Aug 50	254UNTS365	103600
France	United Arab Rep	08 Aug 50	127UNTS293	101710
Canada	New Zealand	16 Aug 50	77UNTS239	101002
Panama	USA (United States)	14 Sep 50	241UNTS159	103431
Burma	Sweden	14 Sep 50	96UNTS45	101330
Multilateral		16 Sep 50	92UNTS91	101264
Brazil	Turkey	21 Sep 50	150UNTS299	101981
Ceylon (Sri Lanka)	United Arab Rep	26 Sep 50	192UNTS53	102595
France	UK Great Britain	06 Oct 50	96UNTS63	101331
Sweden	Switzerland	18 Oct 50	166UNTS49	102185
Luxembourg	Portugal	21 Oct 50	108UNTS67	101468
Taiwan	Philippines	23 Oct 50	215UNTS159	102918
Israel	Netherlands	23 Oct 50	189UNTS89	102543
Israel	Turkey	05 Feb 51	193UNTS3	102607
Germany, West	Greece	12 Feb 51	198UNTS193	102665
Colombia	Portugal	09 Mar 51	108UNTS87	101469
Greece	Yugoslavia	15 Mar 51	187UNTS237	102516
Iraq	UK Great Britain	19 Apr 51	108UNTS121	101470
France	UK Great Britain	20 Apr 51	106UNTS81	101458
Belgium	UK Great Britain	08 May 51	158UNTS451	102079
India	Netherlands	24 May 51	108UNTS151	101471
Greece	Norway	28 May 51	187UNTS141	102507
Cuba	Portugal	26 Jun 51	192UNTS115	102598
Iceland	Norway	14 Jul 51	163UNTS265	102150
Burma	Denmark	30 Jul 51	108UNTS167	101472
Israel	Philippines	07 Aug 51	192UNTS81	102596
Lebanon	UK Great Britain	15 Aug 51	160UNTS327	102116
Burma	Netherlands	06 Sep 51	108UNTS187	101473
Panama	UK Great Britain	15 Sep 51	560UNTS143	108172
Taiwan	Thailand	29 Sep 51	215UNTS166	102919
Philippines	Spain	06 Oct 51	215UNTS193	102920
Greece	Luxembourg	22 Oct 51	187UNTS119	102506
Denmark	Iraq	18 Nov 51	232UNTS25	103227
India	UK Great Britain	01 Dec 51	128UNTS39	101712
Colombia	Spain	11 Dec 51	216UNTS73	102933
El Salvador	Guatemala	14 Dec 51	131UNTS131	101740
Jordan	United Arab Rep	02 Jan 52	192UNTS157	102599
Norway	Uruguay	20 Mar 52	310UNTS279	104496
Sweden	Uruguay	20 Mar 52	311UNTS3	104497
Iraq	Switzerland	31 Mar 52	311UNTS43	104498
France	Mexico	17 Apr 52	163UNTS321	102153
Belgium	Sweden	21 Apr 52	166UNTS9	102183
France	Israel	29 Apr 52	189UNTS55	102542
Switzerland	UK Great Britain	13 May 52	164UNTS91	102160
Greece	Syria	02 Jun 52	183UNTS251	102434
Australia	United Arab Rep	14 Jun 52	173UNTS241	102269
India	United Arab Rep	14 Jun 52	173UNTS209	102268
Denmark	UK Great Britain	23 Jun 52	151UNTS3	101982
Greece	USA (United States)	25 Jun 52	181UNTS53	102398
Belgium	Israel	30 Jun 52	183UNTS263	102435
Netherlands	Pakistan	17 Jul 52	150UNTS277	101980
Japan	USA (United States)	11 Aug 52	212UNTS27	102862
Burma	Philippines	15 Aug 52	200UNTS97	102696
Ethiopia	Pakistan	29 Aug 52	150UNTS257	101979
Mexico	Netherlands	13 Oct 52	163UNTS341	102154
Austria	Luxembourg	13 Oct 52	192UNTS291	102606

PARTY ONE	PARTY TWO	DATE	CITATION	NUMBER
Routes and logistics (Cont.)				
Iceland	Luxembourg	23 Oct 52	193UNTS39	102609
Burma	UK Great Britain	25 Oct 52	150UNTS237	101978
Chile	Denmark	27 Oct 52	271UNTS93	103911
Chile	Sweden	27 Oct 52	311UNTS63	104499
Luxembourg	Sweden	17 Nov 52	173UNTS277	102270
Luxembourg	Norway	17 Nov 52	311UNTS95	104500
Israel	Switzerland	19 Nov 52	232UNTS3	103226
South Africa	Sweden	09 Jan 53	173UNTS299	102271
Netherlands	Philippines	05 Feb 53	216UNTS99	102934
Japan	Netherlands	17 Feb 53	192UNTS215	102602
India	Pakistan	20 Feb 53	164UNTS3	102155
Japan	Sweden	20 Feb 53	173UNTS307	102272
Libya	UK Great Britain	21 Feb 53	311UNTS115	104501
Japan	Norway	23 Feb 53	192UNTS191	102601
Denmark	Japan	26 Feb 53	173UNTS329	102273
Philippines	Thailand	27 Apr 53	174UNTS3	102274
Denmark	South Africa	30 Apr 53	174UNTS19	102275
Israel	South Africa	05 May 53	192UNTS183	102600
Cuba	USA (United States)	26 May 53	224UNTS75	103070
Switzerland	Yugoslavia	28 May 53	232UNTS45	103228
Japan	Thailand	19 Jun 53	174UNTS29	102276
Burma	Norway	22 Jun 53	174UNTS49	102277
Canada	Mexico	27 Jul 53	192UNTS255	102604
USA (United States)	Venezuela	14 Aug 53	213UNTS99	102883
Ceylon (Sri Lanka)	Netherlands	14 Sep 53	193UNTS21	102608
Norway	South Africa	21 Sep 53	192UNTS105	102597
Korea, South	Netherlands	26 Oct 53	200UNTS103	102697
Belgium	Lebanon	24 Dec 53	219UNTS153	102972
Ethiopia	Greece	20 Jan 54	222UNTS281	103035
Syria	UK Great Britain	30 Jan 54	449UNTS47	106452
Canada	Peru	18 Feb 54	411UNTS64	105915
Peru	Spain	31 Mar 54	232UNTS65	103230
China People's Rep	India	29 Apr 54	299UNTS57	104307
France	South Africa	05 May 54	215UNTS401	102926
Belgium	Ireland	30 Jun 54	212UNTS255	102876
Laos	Thailand	07 Jul 54	200UNTS115	102698
Ireland	Luxembourg	27 Jul 54	232UNTS91	103231
Sweden	USA (United States)	06 Aug 54	221UNTS331	103014
Norway	USA (United States)	06 Aug 54	222UNTS261	103033
Denmark	USA (United States)	06 Aug 54	222UNTS235	103030
Philippines	Sweden	20 Aug 54	200UNTS121	102699
Belgium	South Africa	13 Sep 54	201UNTS15	102707
France	South Africa	17 Sep 54	216UNTS29	102930
Denmark	Philippines	20 Oct 54	216UNTS3	102927
Norway	Philippines	20 Oct 54	216UNTS11	102928
Netherlands	Venezuela	26 Oct 54	232UNTS103	103232
Ecuador	Netherlands	14 Dec 54	232UNTS115	103233
Norway	Switzerland	30 Dec 54	311UNTS147	104502
Austria	Belgium	07 Jan 55	380UNTS219	105458
Canada	Japan	12 Jan 55	311UNTS167	104503
Philippines	UK Great Britain	31 Jan 55	216UNTS51	102932
Iraq	United Arab Rep	23 Mar 55	311UNTS199	104504
India	Pakistan	15 Apr 55	247UNTS25	103458
Syria	United Arab Rep	03 Jul 55	393UNTS67	105652
Germany, West	USA (United States)	07 Jul 55	275UNTS3	103973
Germany, West	UK Great Britain	22 Jul 55	269UNTS189	103881
Italy	Switzerland	23 Jul 55	284UNTS279	104142
USSR (Soviet Union)	Yugoslavia	03 Sep 55	240UNTS267	103408
Germany, East	Hungary	10 Sep 55	407UNTS132	105863
Bulgaria	Yugoslavia	01 Oct 55	396UNTS223	105698
France	Germany, West	04 Oct 55	353UNTS203	105044
Finland	USSR (Soviet Union)	19 Oct 55	353UNTS185	105043
Denmark	Syria	20 Oct 55	250UNTS61	103518
Czechoslovakia	Germany, East	24 Oct 55	504UNTS173	107358
Pakistan	Turkey	02 Nov 55	311UNTS217	104505

PARTY ONE	PARTY TWO	DATE	CITATION	NUMBER
Routes and logistics (Cont.)				
Australia	South Africa	04 Nov 55	232UNTS143	103234
Burma	China People's Rep	08 Nov 55	306UNTS11	104430
Syria	USSR (Soviet Union)	16 Nov 55	259UNTS71	103683
Austria	Israel	17 Nov 55	232UNTS153	103235
India	Japan	26 Nov 55	311UNTS243	104506
Costa Rica	Guatemala	20 Dec 55	280UNTS121	104056
Multilateral		04 Jan 56	256UNTS171	103627
Australia	Japan	19 Jan 56	311UNTS291	104507
Austria	Italy	23 Jan 56	393UNTS97	105653
Romania	Yugoslavia	01 Feb 56	362UNTS203	105189
India	USA (United States)	03 Feb 56	272UNTS75	103932
Hungary	Romania	03 Feb 56	362UNTS233	105190
Austria	Poland	08 Feb 56	334UNTS221	104770
Netherlands	Sudan	12 Feb 56	311UNTS319	104508
Norway	Sweden	09 Mar 56	369UNTS285	105262
Denmark	USSR (Soviet Union)	31 Mar 56	259UNTS169	103689
Sweden	USSR (Soviet Union)	31 Mar 56	259UNTS239	103691
Norway	USSR (Soviet Union)	31 Mar 56	259UNTS205	103690
Bulgaria	Yugoslavia	04 Apr 56	391UNTS47	105616
Belgium	Germany, West	14 Apr 56	344UNTS103	104945
Germany, West	Switzerland	02 May 56	559UNTS157	108158
Portugal	Venezuela	16 May 56	463UNTS239	106707
Bulgaria	Yugoslavia	22 May 56	367UNTS119	105229
Japan	Switzerland	24 May 56	312UNTS3	104509
Greece	Italy	26 May 56	496UNTS301	107258
Poland	Sweden	08 Jun 56	334UNTS257	104771
Germany, West	Ireland	12 Jun 56	353UNTS121	105040
Guatemala	Honduras	22 Aug 56	263UNTS49	103767
Germany, West	Netherlands	28 Sep 56	327UNTS185	104722
Switzerland	Thailand	13 Oct 56	312UNTS43	104510
Belgium	Poland	17 Oct 56	356UNTS279	105100
Colombia	USA (United States)	24 Oct 56	476UNTS77	106905
Belgium	Turkey	25 Oct 56	380UNTS3	105447
Austria	UK Great Britain	27 Oct 56	264UNTS67	103789
Albania	Yugoslavia	23 Nov 56	363UNTS123	105204
Albania	Yugoslavia	23 Nov 56	386UNTS73	105539
Peru	Switzerland	23 Nov 56	411UNTS97	105916
Belgium	Romania	04 Dec 56	317UNTS161	104602
Iran	USA (United States)	16 Jan 57	308UNTS147	104460
Iceland	Thailand	22 Jan 57	312UNTS63	104511
Denmark	Germany, West	29 Jan 57	302UNTS75	104354
Germany, West	Sweden	29 Jan 57	393UNTS113	105654
Germany, West	Norway	29 Jan 57	353UNTS39	105037
Mexico	USA (United States)	07 Mar 57	279UNTS205	104042
Dominican Republic	USA (United States)	09 Mar 57	279UNTS249	104044
Netherlands	Yugoslavia	13 Mar 57	327UNTS227	104723
Netherlands	USA (United States)	03 Apr 57	410UNTS193	105904
Denmark	Pakistan	10 Apr 57	302UNTS53	104353
Germany, West	Yugoslavia	10 Apr 57	463UNTS269	106708
Romania	Sweden	15 Apr 57	342UNTS325	104915
Bulgaria	Sweden	17 Apr 57	464UNTS3	106709
Korea, South	USA (United States)	24 Apr 57	288UNTS219	104207
Belgium	Bulgaria	14 May 57	317UNTS81	104596
Australia	Germany, West	22 May 57	357UNTS45	105105
Hungary	Netherlands	28 May 57	334UNTS291	104773
Belgium	Hungary	01 Jun 57	291UNTS17	104242
Afghanistan	Pakistan	13 Jun 57	327UNTS51	104717
Czechoslovakia	United Arab Rep	30 Jun 57	411UNTS126	105917
Greece	Italy	02 Aug 57	533UNTS217	107744
Netherlands	Romania	27 Aug 57	342UNTS309	104914
Multilateral		03 Oct 57	366UNTS87	105216
Italy	Pakistan	05 Oct 57	353UNTS91	105039
Fed of Malaya	UK Great Britain	18 Oct 57	335UNTS3	104775
France	Morocco	25 Oct 57	559UNTS95	108156
UK Great Britain	USSR (Soviet Union)	19 Dec 57	351UNTS235	105026

PARTY ONE	PARTY TWO	DATE	CITATION	NUMBER
Routes and logistics (Cont.)				
Australia	Ireland	30 Dec 57	497UNTS29	107260
Canada	Switzerland	10 Jan 58	464UNTS21	106710
Belgium	Morocco	20 Jan 58	288UNTS3	104192
Bulgaria	Netherlands	07 Feb 58	335UNTS45	104777
Australia	UK Great Britain	07 Feb 58	335UNTS23	104776
Afghanistan	Turkey	08 Feb 58	464UNTS39	106711
Sudan	Sweden	17 Feb 58	393UNTS161	105655
Norway	Pakistan	05 Mar 58	334UNTS199	104769
Pakistan	Sweden	06 Mar 58	393UNTS181	105656
Bulgaria	Yugoslavia	21 Mar 58	386UNTS119	105541
Germany, West	Portugal	21 Mar 58	464UNTS71	106712
South Africa	Sweden	28 Mar 58	300UNTS95	104333
Denmark	South Africa	28 Mar 58	300UNTS107	104334
Norway	South Africa	28 Mar 58	300UNTS83	104332
Morocco	Portugal	03 Apr 58	393UNTS203	105657
Belgium	Iran	14 Apr 58	381UNTS309	105473
Sweden	Yugoslavia	18 Apr 58	393UNTS225	105658
Italy	Switzerland	23 May 58	363UNTS81	105201
Bulgaria	Denmark	28 May 58	312UNTS235	104521
India	USSR (Soviet Union)	02 Jun 58	393UNTS3	105650
Belgium	USSR (Soviet Union)	05 Jun 58	345UNTS145	104965
Pakistan	Portugal	07 Jun 58	320UNTS225	104645
Belgium	South Africa	11 Jun 58	335UNTS63	104778
Netherlands	USSR (Soviet Union)	17 Jun 58	335UNTS77	104779
Denmark	Romania	25 Jun 58	345UNTS231	104970
Belgium	Pakistan	04 Jul 58	387UNTS305	105569
Ethiopia	UK Great Britain	07 Jul 58	331UNTS3	104749
Austria	Romania	10 Jul 58	353UNTS155	105041
Denmark	Hungary	17 Jul 58	344UNTS281	104954
Romania	United Arab Rep	14 Aug 58	405UNTS189	105834
Austria	Bulgaria	12 Sep 58	353UNTS3	105036
United Arab Rep	USSR (Soviet Union)	18 Sep 58	338UNTS29	104831
Ghana	UK Great Britain	24 Sep 58	411UNTS146	105918
Australia	South Africa	26 Sep 58	335UNTS121	104780
France	Italy	30 Oct 58	363UNTS3	105196
Multilateral		05 Nov 58	428UNTS73	106169
Liberia	Netherlands	28 Nov 58	393UNTS55	105651
Finland	Switzerland	07 Jan 59	353UNTS173	105042
UK Great Britain	Yugoslavia	03 Feb 59	359UNTS339	105151
Japan	Philippines	02 Mar 59	341UNTS49	104877
Netherlands	Tunisia	19 Mar 59	497UNTS61	107262
Sweden	Tunisia	19 Mar 59	497UNTS43	107261
Norway	Tunisia	28 Mar 59	497UNTS77	107263
Poland	UK Great Britain	03 Apr 59	351UNTS295	105030
Denmark	Tunisia	14 Apr 59	340UNTS273	104870
Denmark	Sudan	11 May 59	445UNTS105	106380
Ceylon (Sri Lanka)	Norway	29 May 59	411UNTS165	105919
Ceylon (Sri Lanka)	Sweden	29 May 59	464UNTS109	106713
Ceylon (Sri Lanka)	Denmark	29 May 59	348UNTS225	105002
Greece	Yugoslavia	18 Jun 59	368UNTS27	105234
Greece	Yugoslavia	18 Jun 59	368UNTS17	105233
Belgium	Japan	20 Jun 59	411UNTS3	105911
Bulgaria	United Arab Rep	09 Jul 59	411UNTS187	105920
India	Italy	16 Jul 59	464UNTS129	106714
Afghanistan	Germany, West	22 Jul 59	464UNTS177	106715
Germany, West	Iceland	12 Aug 59	411UNTS224	105921
Canada	Germany, West	04 Sep 59	411UNTS260	105922
Australia	Fed of Malaya	29 Sep 59	357UNTS29	105104
Nicaragua	Peru	14 Oct 59	392UNTS303	105649
South Africa	Switzerland	19 Oct 59	559UNTS257	108162
Liberia	Sweden	09 Dec 59	464UNTS219	106716
Czechoslovakia	Japan	15 Dec 59	383UNTS277	105505
Czechoslovakia	UK Great Britain	15 Jan 60	374UNTS207	105336
Germany, West	United Arab Rep	16 Feb 60	464UNTS233	106717
France	Thailand	26 Feb 60	392UNTS279	105648

PARTY ONE	PARTY TWO	DATE	CITATION	NUMBER
Routes and logistics (Cont.)				
Australia	Thailand	26 Feb 60	392UNTS255	105647
Guinea	Netherlands	09 Mar 60	392UNTS243	105646
Czechoslovakia	Iraq	11 Mar 60	464UNTS267	106718
Belgium	Switzerland	24 Mar 60	416UNTS81	105996
Luxembourg	Yugoslavia	09 Apr 60	464UNTS293	106719
Germany, West	Spain	28 Apr 60	465UNTS3	106720
Greece	Romania	02 May 60	485UNTS17	107043
Morocco	United Arab Rep	19 May 60	563UNTS121	108208
Switzerland	Tunisia	21 May 60	497UNTS109	107265
Kuwait	UK Great Britain	24 May 60	412UNTS4	105923
Afghanistan	Czechoslovakia	28 May 60	497UNTS129	107266
Luxembourg	Tunisia	13 Jun 60	497UNTS143	107267
Denmark	Peru	22 Jun 60	439UNTS113	106326
Ireland	Portugal	24 Jun 60	412UNTS30	105924
Poland	UK Great Britain	02 Jul 60	385UNTS87	105532
Switzerland	United Arab Rep	14 Jul 60	497UNTS161	107268
Germany, West	Pakistan	20 Jul 60	465UNTS41	106721
Ghana	Netherlands	30 Jul 60	412UNTS51	105925
Mexico	USA (United States)	15 Aug 60	402UNTS177	105786
Belgium	Burma	17 Aug 60	540UNTS185	107850
Ghana	United Arab Rep	29 Aug 60	412UNTS71	105926
Czechoslovakia	India	19 Sep 60	465UNTS67	106722
Belgium	Jordan	19 Oct 60	479UNTS277	106959
Hungary	UK Great Britain	25 Oct 60	419UNTS309	106034
Burma	Switzerland	31 Oct 60	465UNTS97	106723
Norway	Peru	02 Nov 60	497UNTS207	107270
Australia	Italy	10 Nov 60	497UNTS247	107271
Indonesia	UK Great Britain	23 Nov 60	398UNTS71	105718
Multilateral		13 Dec 60	455UNTS3	106543
Multilateral		13 Dec 60	523UNTS117	107557
Canada	Pakistan	21 Dec 60	465UNTS115	106724
Luxembourg	Thailand	29 Dec 60	465UNTS131	106725
Jordan	Sweden	09 Jan 61	465UNTS155	106726
Sudan	UK Great Britain	16 Jan 61	424UNTS233	106112
Norway	Poland	17 Jan 61	412UNTS130	105928
Germany, West	Japan	18 Jan 61	465UNTS173	106727
Cuba	Czechoslovakia	04 Mar 61	465UNTS209	106728
Poland	Switzerland	18 May 61	559UNTS233	108161
Czechoslovakia	Morocco	08 Jun 61	497UNTS275	107272
New Zealand	UK Great Britain	13 Jun 61	497UNTS293	107273
Cameroon	France	16 Jun 61	412UNTS148	105929
Guinea	Sweden	17 Jun 61	465UNTS236	106729
Czechoslovakia	Ghana	02 Aug 61	465UNTS249	106730
Mexico	Netherlands	24 Aug 61	465UNTS291	106732
Jordan	Netherlands	24 Aug 61	466UNTS3	106733
Liberia	Switzerland	31 Aug 61	559UNTS215	108160
Ghana	Romania	30 Sep 61	467UNTS443	106769
Germany, West	Morocco	12 Oct 61	523UNTS289	107562
Japan	Pakistan	17 Oct 61	466UNTS17	106734
Cyprus	Greece	23 Nov 61	497UNTS311	107274
Czechoslovakia	Mali	27 Nov 61	466UNTS41	106736
Denmark	Jordan	07 Dec 61	631UNTS333	109003
Czechoslovakia	Guinea	16 Dec 61	559UNTS49	108154
Netherlands	Sweden	08 Jan 62	466UNTS65	106737
Austria	Greece	15 Jan 62	498UNTS3	107275
Indonesia	Japan	23 Jan 62	559UNTS77	108155
Italy	Japan	31 Jan 62	498UNTS23	107276
Luxembourg	South Africa	31 Jan 62	563UNTS153	108209
Finland	Hungary	13 Feb 62	463UNTS61	106693
Germany, West	Thailand	05 Mar 62	563UNTS165	108210
Luxembourg	Spain	26 Mar 62	563UNTS205	108211
France	Luxembourg	29 Mar 62	563UNTS227	108212
Sierra Leone	UK Great Britain	05 Apr 62	434UNTS227	106265
Ghana	USSR (Soviet Union)	06 Apr 62	498UNTS41	107277
Japan	United Arab Rep	10 May 62	498UNTS69	107278

PARTY ONE	PARTY TWO	DATE	CITATION	NUMBER
Routes and logistics (Cont.)				
France	Romania	18 May 62	498UNTS115	107279
France	Senegal	15 Jun 62	524UNTS3	107563
Czechoslovakia	Senegal	20 Jun 62	498UNTS145	107280
Guinea	Norway	21 Jun 62	466UNTS81	106738
Liberia	Norway	29 Jun 62	466UNTS95	106739
Morocco	Switzerland	05 Jul 62	498UNTS171	107281
Ecuador	Germany, West	20 Sep 62	498UNTS199	107283
Austria	Czechoslovakia	22 Sep 62	495UNTS157	107244
Japan	Kuwait	06 Oct 62	498UNTS235	107284
Trinidad/Tobago	USA (United States)	08 Oct 62	462UNTS145	106675
Finland	France	12 Oct 62	498UNTS299	107285
Netherlands	Norway	18 Oct 62	466UNTS145	106741
Hungary	Syria	18 Oct 62	491UNTS209	107178
France	Ivory Coast	19 Oct 62	498UNTS317	107286
Poland	Syria	10 Nov 62	491UNTS228	107179
Japan	UK Great Britain	14 Nov 62	478UNTS29	106934
Czechoslovakia	Poland	16 Nov 62	526UNTS3	107597
Ivory Coast	Switzerland	17 Nov 62	499UNTS3	107289
Germany, West	USA (United States)	29 Nov 62	460UNTS169	106639
Austria	Yugoslavia	11 Dec 62	546UNTS3	107938
Ghana	Tunisia	11 Dec 62	563UNTS243	108213
Syria	United Arab Rep	27 Dec 62	491UNTS245	107180
Ghana	Mali	09 Jan 63	466UNTS165	106742
Senegal	Switzerland	23 Jan 63	524UNTS23	107564
Mali	Senegal	07 Feb 63	524UNTS41	107565
Sudan	Switzerland	18 Feb 63	563UNTS281	108215
Algeria	France	18 Feb 63	563UNTS263	108214
Poland	USSR (Soviet Union)	22 Apr 63	493UNTS229	107217
Cyprus	Denmark	27 Apr 63	529UNTS255	107664
Greece	Hungary	27 Apr 63	534UNTS3	107750
Algeria	Morocco	30 Apr 63	564UNTS3	108217
Portugal	South Africa	07 May 63	499UNTS49	107292
Finland	Poland	10 Jun 63	503UNTS179	107343
Guinea	Ivory Coast	26 Jun 63	499UNTS71	107293
Austria	France	12 Jul 63	499UNTS91	107294
Taiwan	Luxembourg	19 Jul 63	564UNTS23	108218
Algeria	Mali	22 Jul 63	564UNTS29	108219
Mali	Tunisia	24 Jul 63	602UNTS91	108708
Cameroon	Israel	09 Aug 63	499UNTS121	107295
Multilateral		02 Sep 63	548UNTS129	107974
Pakistan	USSR (Soviet Union)	07 Oct 63	499UNTS161	107297
Ivory Coast	Netherlands	09 Oct 63	499UNTS141	107296
Czechoslovakia	Hungary	22 Oct 63	514UNTS95	107444
Romania	Yugoslavia	25 Dec 63	576UNTS95	108366
Mali	Niger	15 Jan 64	499UNTS197	107299
Lebanon	Pakistan	04 Feb 64	614UNTS55	108863
Argentina	Paraguay	07 Feb 64	634UNTS127	109057
Denmark	Yugoslavia	11 Feb 64	511UNTS241	107437
France	New Zealand	27 Feb 64	499UNTS191	107298
Cameroon	Mali	17 Mar 64	524UNTS61	107566
Malaysia	Netherlands	07 Apr 64	524UNTS81	107567
Portugal	UK Great Britain	07 Apr 64	539UNTS167	107830
United Arab Rep	USA (United States)	05 May 64	531UNTS229	107706
UK Great Britain	USA (United States)	19 Jun 64	530UNTS99	107675
New Zealand	USA (United States)	24 Jun 64	524UNTS101	107568
Ivory Coast	Mali	09 Jul 64	524UNTS121	107569
Germany, West	Jamaica	07 Oct 64	514UNTS187	107447
Czechoslovakia	Hungary	17 Oct 64	545UNTS21	107924
Greece	Yugoslavia	05 Nov 64	539UNTS19	107821
Argentina	UK Great Britain	12 Jan 65	597UNTS177	108645
Finland	UK Great Britain	25 Mar 65	539UNTS103	107826
Denmark	Malaysia	26 Mar 65	540UNTS205	107851
Ghana	Malawi	04 May 65	541UNTS163	107869
Denmark	Spain	05 May 65	543UNTS255	107905
Hungary	Poland	18 Jul 65	577UNTS161	108376

PARTY ONE	PARTY TWO	DATE	CITATION	NUMBER
Routes and logistics (Cont.)				
Burma	Czechoslovakia	15 Dec 65	602UNTS71	108707
Belgium	Denmark	04 Feb 66	561UNTS233	108187
Portugal	UK Great Britain	17 Apr 66	573UNTS223	108335
Bulgaria	Turkey	18 Apr 66	631UNTS263	108999
Romania	USSR (Soviet Union)	21 Jun 66	604UNTS81	108746
Austria	USA (United States)	23 Jun 66	601UNTS51	108687
Netherlands	Yugoslavia	08 Sep 66	597UNTS147	108643
Denmark	Singapore	20 Dec 66	593UNTS125	108580
Trinidad/Tobago	UK Great Britain	01 Mar 67	606UNTS149	108784
Malta	UK Great Britain	10 Jul 67	619UNTS11	108936
Malaysia	UK Great Britain	01 Aug 67	633UNTS93	109036
Singapore	UK Great Britain	01 Aug 67	619UNTS29	108937
Denmark	Malaysia	14 Dec 67	614UNTS26	108862
Finland	Sweden	07 Oct 68	0UNTS0	109376
Navigational conditions				
Brazil	France	27 Jan 40	72UNTS77	100929
Multilateral		07 Dec 44	171UNTS345	200501
Denmark	USA (United States)	16 Dec 44	10UNTS213	200063
Sweden	USA (United States)	16 Dec 44	6UNTS397	200041
Iceland	USA (United States)	27 Jan 45	122UNTS293	200411
Ireland	USA (United States)	03 Feb 45	122UNTS305	200412
Canada	USA (United States)	17 Feb 45	122UNTS261	200409
Australia	USA (United States)	08 Mar 45	121UNTS205	200400
Belgium	France	30 Mar 45	20UNTS297	200122
Switzerland	USA (United States)	03 Aug 45	51UNTS233	200191
Norway	USA (United States)	06 Oct 45	122UNTS319	200413
South Africa	UK Great Britain	26 Oct 45	72UNTS41	100927
Greece	UK Great Britain	26 Nov 45	35UNTS161	100555
Portugal	UK Great Britain	06 Dec 45	5UNTS37	100064
Portugal	UK Great Britain	06 Dec 45	6UNTS3	100065
Portugal	USA (United States)	06 Dec 45	3UNTS139	100028
Canada	UK Great Britain	21 Dec 45	27UNTS155	100405
Czechoslovakia	USA (United States)	03 Jan 46	6UNTS309	100084
Czechoslovakia	Poland	24 Jan 46	25UNTS181	100363
UK Great Britain	USA (United States)	11 Feb 46	3UNTS253	100036
Turkey	USA (United States)	12 Feb 46	13UNTS3	100196
Turkey	UK Great Britain	12 Feb 46	6UNTS79	100069
France	UK Great Britain	28 Feb 46	27UNTS173	100407
France	USA (United States)	27 Mar 46	139UNTS114	101879
Greece	USA (United States)	27 Mar 46	15UNTS233	100239
Ireland	UK Great Britain	05 Apr 46	72UNTS57	100928
Belgium	USA (United States)	05 Apr 46	4UNTS125	100041
Netherlands	Portugal	12 Apr 46	4UNTS317	100054
Argentina	UK Great Britain	17 Apr 46	164UNTS53	102159
France	Ireland	16 May 46	44UNTS105	100681
Ireland	Sweden	29 May 46	35UNTS231	100557
Australia	Canada	11 Jun 46	10UNTS47	100142
United Arab Rep	USA (United States)	15 Jun 46	71UNTS157	100917
Sweden	Turkey	26 Jun 46	14UNTS21	100208
Netherlands	Spain	13 Jul 46	4UNTS351	100055
UK Great Britain	USA (United States)	31 Jul 46	42UNTS199	100648
France	Sweden	02 Aug 46	27UNTS251	100410
Lebanon	USA (United States)	11 Aug 46	66UNTS211	100856
Netherlands	UK Great Britain	13 Aug 46	4UNTS367	100056
Norway	UK Great Britain	31 Aug 46	6UNTS235	100078
Brazil	USA (United States)	06 Sep 46	54UNTS197	100805
France	Turkey	12 Oct 46	14UNTS33	100209
Belgium	Portugal	22 Oct 46	34UNTS49	100527
Brazil	UK Great Britain	31 Oct 46	11UNTS115	100152
Philippines	USA (United States)	16 Nov 46	7UNTS151	100097
Sweden	UK Great Britain	27 Nov 46	11UNTS229	100162
New Zealand	USA (United States)	03 Dec 46	7UNTS175	100099
Portugal	Switzerland	09 Dec 46	310UNTS251	104495
Brazil	Portugal	10 Dec 46	200UNTS67	102695
Navigational conditions (Cont.)				
USA (United States)	Uruguay	14 Dec 46	532UNTS87	107713
Taiwan	USA (United States)	20 Dec 46	22UNTS87	100332
Peru	USA (United States)	27 Dec 46	26UNTS227	100390
Ecuador	USA (United States)	08 Jan 47	22UNTS119	100333
Czechoslovakia	Ireland	29 Jan 47	27UNTS267	100411
Thailand	USA (United States)	26 Feb 47	16UNTS17	100246
Paraguay	USA (United States)	28 Feb 47	44UNTS25	100676
Portugal	Sweden	06 Mar 47	35UNTS243	100558
Australia	USA (United States)	10 Mar 47	10UNTS89	100145
Belgium	Turkey	12 Mar 47	37UNTS221	100579
Netherlands	Turkey	19 Mar 47	14UNTS59	100211
Greece	Switzerland	01 Apr 47	180UNTS115	102378
Greece	Sweden	08 Apr 47	94UNTS73	101307
Canada	Portugal	25 Apr 47	94UNTS87	101308
Syria	USA (United States)	28 Apr 47	262UNTS121	103741
France	Greece	05 May 47	76UNTS61	100980
Thailand	USA (United States)	08 May 47	42UNTS241	100653
Chile	USA (United States)	10 May 47	55UNTS21	100807
Czechoslovakia	Denmark	14 May 47	27UNTS297	100413
South Africa	USA (United States)	23 May 47	66UNTS233	100857
Canada	Sweden	27 Jun 47	27UNTS313	100414
Romania	Yugoslavia	30 Jun 47	116UNTS57	101569
Iraq	Turkey	30 Jun 47	72UNTS107	100930
Denmark	Turkey	30 Jun 47	32UNTS301	100504
Hungary	USSR (Soviet Union)	15 Jul 47	216UNTS247	102940
Canada	UK Great Britain	17 Jul 47	28UNTS3	100416
Netherlands	Thailand	18 Jul 47	28UNTS27	100417
Greece	Turkey	22 Jul 47	72UNTS131	100931
Netherlands	South Africa	22 Jul 47	12UNTS257	100188
Taiwan	UK Great Britain	23 Jul 47	9UNTS207	100135
Poland	Romania	09 Aug 47	12UNTS363	100193
Hungary	Poland	28 Aug 47	15UNTS145	100231
Czechoslovakia	Switzerland	10 Sep 47	35UNTS275	100559
Chile	UK Great Britain	16 Sep 47	133UNTS143	101786
Lebanon	Turkey	16 Sep 47	44UNTS123	100682
Czechoslovakia	Sweden	15 Oct 47	44UNTS149	100683
Colombia	UK Great Britain	16 Oct 47	160UNTS297	102115
Norway	Portugal	11 Nov 47	34UNTS257	100542
Denmark	Greece	14 Nov 47	35UNTS295	100560
Denmark	Ireland	18 Nov 47	35UNTS309	100561
Ireland	Italy	21 Nov 47	353UNTS73	105038
Taiwan	Netherlands	06 Dec 47	43UNTS185	100669
Czechoslovakia	USSR (Soviet Union)	11 Dec 47	217UNTS35	102943
Denmark	Portugal	15 Dec 47	35UNTS329	100563
Austria	Netherlands	22 Jan 48	17UNTS99	100270
Italy	USA (United States)	02 Feb 48	79UNTS171	101040
Italy	USA (United States)	06 Feb 48	73UNTS113	100950
Denmark	Guatemala	04 Mar 48	96UNTS223	101339
Argentina	Denmark	18 Mar 48	94UNTS175	101311
Cuba	UK Great Britain	19 Mar 48	175UNTS23	102294
Bulgaria	USSR (Soviet Union)	01 Apr 48	217UNTS97	102946
Ireland	Switzerland	06 May 48	334UNTS187	104768
Jordan	Turkey	07 May 48	32UNTS313	100505
Ireland	Netherlands	10 May 48	28UNTS121	100422
Norway	Turkey	20 May 48	26UNTS137	100384
Greece	Switzerland	26 May 48	94UNTS217	101312
Multilateral		19 Jun 48	310UNTS151	104492
Ireland	Norway	21 Jun 48	34UNTS317	100545
Multilateral		18 Aug 48	33UNTS181	100518
Greece	Lebanon	06 Sep 48	178UNTS37	102335
Bolivia	USA (United States)	29 Sep 48	505UNTS139	107370
Greece	Lebanon	06 Oct 48	87UNTS351	101179
Netherlands	Spain	08 Oct 48	28UNTS209	100426
Mexico	Portugal	22 Oct 48	34UNTS329	100546
Argentina	Netherlands	29 Oct 48	95UNTS21	101316

Navigational conditions (Cont.)

PARTY ONE	PARTY TWO	DATE	CITATION	NUMBER
Argentina	Denmark	14 Dec 48	74UNTS41	100956
Italy	Lebanon	24 Jan 49	231UNTS241	103223
Switzerland	Turkey	16 Feb 49	72UNTS175	100933
Finland	Netherlands	25 Feb 49	53UNTS123	100777
Netherlands	Switzerland	07 Mar 49	35UNTS69	100551
Finland	USA (United States)	29 Mar 49	55UNTS59	100808
Panama	USA (United States)	31 Mar 49	55UNTS87	100810
Finland	Sweden	26 Apr 49	95UNTS83	101318
Bulgaria	Poland	16 May 49	84UNTS313	101140
Italy	Spain	31 May 49	231UNTS251	103224
Canada	USA (United States)	04 Jun 49	200UNTS201	102704
Canada	USA (United States)	04 Jun 49	122UNTS237	101649
Belgium	Greece	21 Jun 49	137UNTS215	101854
Korea, South	USA (United States)	29 Jun 49	55UNTS79	100809
Greece	Syria	05 Jul 49	78UNTS71	101013
Iraq	Norway	12 Jul 49	53UNTS137	100778
Czechoslovakia	Finland	13 Jul 49	53UNTS153	100779
Dominican Republic	USA (United States)	19 Jul 49	51UNTS145	100762
Finland	Norway	24 Aug 49	53UNTS167	100780
Denmark	Finland	26 Aug 49	53UNTS191	100781
Denmark	ICAO (Civil Aviat)	09 Sep 49	53UNTS341	100791
Belgium	United Arab Rep	19 Sep 49	137UNTS189	101853
Lebanon	Netherlands	20 Sep 49	108UNTS205	101474
Burma	USA (United States)	28 Sep 49	55UNTS3	100806
Greece	Philippines	08 Oct 49	187UNTS221	102515
Sweden	Thailand	23 Nov 49	72UNTS217	100935
Denmark	Thailand	23 Nov 49	53UNTS255	100786
Italy	Turkey	25 Nov 49	192UNTS39	102594
Norway	Thailand	26 Nov 49	53UNTS269	100787
Brazil	Spain	28 Nov 49	215UNTS303	102923
Austria	Sweden	02 Dec 49	108UNTS3	101465
Austria	Norway	02 Dec 49	72UNTS230	100936
Austria	Denmark	02 Dec 49	53UNTS281	100788
Netherlands	United Arab Rep	08 Dec 49	95UNTS123	101320
Sweden	United Arab Rep	12 Dec 49	108UNTS15	101466
Austria	Switzerland	19 Dec 49	254UNTS287	103597
USA (United States)	Yugoslavia	24 Dec 49	89UNTS209	101219
Netherlands	Syria	13 Feb 50	108UNTS53	101467
Canada	Norway	14 Feb 50	53UNTS329	100790
Belgium	Netherlands	17 Feb 50	51UNTS101	100756
Spain	Sweden	18 Feb 50	166UNTS15	102184
Ceylon (Sri Lanka)	Thailand	24 Feb 50	72UNTS261	100938
Italy	Netherlands	04 Mar 50	254UNTS305	103598
Norway	United Arab Rep	11 Mar 50	95UNTS157	101321
Denmark	United Arab Rep	14 Mar 50	95UNTS197	101322
Philippines	USA (United States)	16 Mar 50	89UNTS199	101218
Iceland	Netherlands	22 Mar 50	95UNTS237	101323
Denmark	Iceland	22 Mar 50	72UNTS273	100939
Italy	Portugal	05 Apr 50	254UNTS329	103599
Turkey	United Arab Rep	12 Apr 50	128UNTS3	101711
Greece	United Arab Rep	24 Apr 50	163UNTS229	102149
Switzerland	United Arab Rep	15 May 50	95UNTS255	101325
Israel	USA (United States)	13 Jun 50	212UNTS93	102863
Netherlands	Spain	20 Jun 50	95UNTS303	101327
Burma	Ceylon (Sri Lanka)	29 Jun 50	73UNTS3	100940
Israel	Turkey	04 Jul 50	220UNTS3	102982
Germany, West	Ireland	12 Jul 50	557UNTS221	108136
Spain	UK Great Britain	20 Jul 50	398UNTS101	105719
Spain	Switzerland	03 Aug 50	254UNTS365	103600
France	United Arab Rep	08 Aug 50	127UNTS293	101710
Canada	New Zealand	16 Aug 50	77UNTS239	101002
Burma	Sweden	14 Sep 50	96UNTS45	101330
Brazil	Turkey	21 Sep 50	150UNTS299	101981
Ceylon (Sri Lanka)	United Arab Rep	26 Sep 50	192UNTS53	102595
Sweden	Switzerland	18 Oct 50	166UNTS49	102185

Navigational conditions (Cont.)

PARTY ONE	PARTY TWO	DATE	CITATION	NUMBER
Luxembourg	Portugal	21 Oct 50	108UNTS67	101468
Israel	Netherlands	23 Oct 50	189UNTS89	102543
Germany, West	Netherlands	14 Dec 50	87UNTS257	101177
Israel	Turkey	05 Feb 51	193UNTS3	102607
Germany, West	Greece	12 Feb 51	198UNTS193	102665
Colombia	Portugal	09 Mar 51	108UNTS87	101469
Greece	Yugoslavia	15 Mar 51	187UNTS237	102516
Greece	Norway	28 May 51	187UNTS141	102507
Denmark	Iran	18 Jun 51	255UNTS3	103602
Cuba	Portugal	26 Jun 51	192UNTS115	102598
Iceland	Norway	14 Jul 51	163UNTS265	102150
Israel	Yugoslavia	29 Jul 51	220UNTS7	102983
Burma	Denmark	30 Jul 51	108UNTS167	101472
Israel	Philippines	07 Aug 51	192UNTS81	102596
France	Greece	03 Sep 51	187UNTS113	102505
Burma	Netherlands	06 Sep 51	108UNTS187	101473
Panama	UK Great Britain	15 Sep 51	560UNTS143	108172
Denmark	USA (United States)	01 Oct 51	421UNTS105	106056
Philippines	Spain	06 Oct 51	215UNTS193	102920
Greece	Luxembourg	22 Oct 51	187UNTS119	102506
Denmark	Iraq	18 Nov 51	232UNTS25	103227
Colombia	Spain	11 Dec 51	216UNTS73	102933
El Salvador	Guatemala	14 Dec 51	131UNTS131	101740
Jordan	United Arab Rep	02 Jan 52	192UNTS157	102599
Germany, East	Poland	06 Feb 52	304UNTS131	104395
Japan	USA (United States)	28 Feb 52	208UNTS255	102817
Taiwan	Korea, South	01 Mar 52	255UNTS35	103603
Belgium	Spain	10 Mar 52	178UNTS243	102342
Norway	Uruguay	20 Mar 52	310UNTS279	104496
Sweden	Uruguay	20 Mar 52	311UNTS3	104497
Iraq	Switzerland	31 Mar 52	311UNTS43	104498
France	Mexico	17 Apr 52	163UNTS321	102153
France	Israel	29 Apr 52	189UNTS55	102542
Multilateral		10 May 52	439UNTS217	106331
Multilateral		10 May 52	439UNTS193	106330
India	United Arab Rep	14 Jun 52	173UNTS209	102268
Denmark	UK Great Britain	23 Jun 52	151UNTS3	101982
Japan	USA (United States)	11 Aug 52	212UNTS27	102862
Netherlands	Peru	22 Sep 52	255UNTS49	103604
Austria	Luxembourg	13 Oct 52	192UNTS291	102606
Mexico	Netherlands	13 Oct 52	163UNTS341	102154
Iceland	Luxembourg	23 Oct 52	193UNTS39	102609
Chile	Sweden	27 Oct 52	311UNTS63	104499
Chile	Denmark	27 Oct 52	271UNTS93	103911
Denmark	Israel	14 Nov 52	160UNTS275	102112
Luxembourg	Norway	17 Nov 52	311UNTS95	104500
Luxembourg	Sweden	17 Nov 52	173UNTS277	102270
Israel	Switzerland	19 Nov 52	232UNTS3	103226
Greece	South Africa	27 Jan 53	533UNTS303	107748
India	Pakistan	20 Feb 53	164UNTS3	102155
Denmark	Uruguay	04 Mar 53	250UNTS51	103517
Lebanon	Sweden	23 Mar 53	255UNTS83	103605
Philippines	Thailand	27 Apr 53	174UNTS3	102274
Israel	Italy	22 May 53	219UNTS297	102981
Cuba	USA (United States)	26 May 53	224UNTS75	103070
Switzerland	Yugoslavia	28 May 53	232UNTS45	103228
Burma	Norway	22 Jun 53	174UNTS49	102277
Ceylon (Sri Lanka)	Yugoslavia	30 Jul 53	337UNTS103	104819
Argentina	USSR (Soviet Union)	05 Aug 53	221UNTS99	103004
USA (United States)	Venezuela	14 Aug 53	213UNTS99	102883
Austria	Yugoslavia	11 Nov 53	363UNTS149	105206
India	USSR (Soviet Union)	02 Dec 53	240UNTS143	103402
Ethiopia	Greece	20 Jan 54	222UNTS281	103035
Syria	UK Great Britain	30 Jan 54	449UNTS47	106452
France	Sweden	16 Feb 54	228UNTS137	103147

Navigational conditions (Cont.)

PARTY ONE	PARTY TWO	DATE	CITATION	NUMBER
Multilateral		25 Feb 54	215UNTS249	102922
Peru	Spain	31 Mar 54	232UNTS65	103230
Pakistan	Yugoslavia	15 May 54	286UNTS3	104158
Ireland	Luxembourg	27 Jul 54	232UNTS91	103231
Germany, West	USA (United States)	29 Oct 54	273UNTS3	103943
Ceylon (Sri Lanka)	United Arab Rep	17 Nov 54	315UNTS3	104554
Ecuador	Netherlands	14 Dec 54	232UNTS115	103233
Norway	Switzerland	30 Dec 54	311UNTS147	104502
Austria	Belgium	07 Jan 55	380UNTS219	105458
Iraq	United Arab Rep	23 Mar 55	311UNTS199	104504
Argentina	UK Great Britain	31 Mar 55	210UNTS223	102840
Austria	Romania	11 May 55	342UNTS119	104904
Ceylon (Sri Lanka)	Pakistan	23 May 55	286UNTS15	104159
Germany, West	USA (United States)	07 Jul 55	275UNTS3	103973
Iran	USA (United States)	15 Aug 55	284UNTS93	104132
USSR (Soviet Union)	Yugoslavia	03 Sep 55	240UNTS267	103408
Belgium	Ireland	10 Sep 55	255UNTS235	103612
France	Germany, West	04 Oct 55	353UNTS203	105044
Finland	USSR (Soviet Union)	19 Oct 55	353UNTS185	105043
Denmark	Syria	20 Oct 55	250UNTS61	103518
Pakistan	Turkey	02 Nov 55	311UNTS217	104505
Austria	Israel	17 Nov 55	232UNTS153	103235
Czechoslovakia	Poland	13 Jan 56	265UNTS157	103811
Nicaragua	USA (United States)	21 Jan 56	367UNTS3	105224
Austria	Italy	23 Jan 56	393UNTS97	105653
Argentina	Switzerland	25 Jan 56	559UNTS121	108157
Romania	Yugoslavia	01 Feb 56	362UNTS203	105189
Austria	Poland	08 Feb 56	334UNTS221	104770
Norway	Syria	25 Feb 56	463UNTS217	106706
Canada	USSR (Soviet Union)	29 Feb 56	252UNTS165	103566
Netherlands	USA (United States)	27 Mar 56	285UNTS231	104154
Sweden	USSR (Soviet Union)	31 Mar 56	259UNTS239	103691
Norway	USSR (Soviet Union)	31 Mar 56	259UNTS205	103690
Denmark	USSR (Soviet Union)	31 Mar 56	259UNTS169	103689
Belgium	Germany, West	14 Apr 56	344UNTS103	104945
Portugal	Venezuela	16 May 56	463UNTS239	106707
Greece	Italy	26 May 56	496UNTS301	107258
Italy	Switzerland	04 Jun 56	378UNTS311	105429
Poland	Sweden	08 Jun 56	334UNTS257	104771
Germany, West	Ireland	12 Jun 56	353UNTS121	105040
Bulgaria	Ceylon (Sri Lanka)	19 Jun 56	315UNTS23	104556
Argentina	UK Great Britain	30 Jun 56	269UNTS235	103884
Finland	Sweden	07 Jul 56	258UNTS83	103672
Germany, West	Netherlands	20 Sep 56	509UNTS269	107405
Multilateral		25 Sep 56	334UNTS89	104767
Multilateral		25 Sep 56	334UNTS13	104766
Switzerland	Thailand	13 Oct 56	312UNTS43	104510
Belgium	Poland	17 Oct 56	356UNTS279	105100
Colombia	USA (United States)	24 Oct 56	476UNTS77	106905
Belgium	Turkey	25 Oct 56	380UNTS3	105447
Peru	Switzerland	23 Nov 56	411UNTS97	105916
Korea, South	USA (United States)	28 Nov 56	302UNTS281	104367
Belgium	Romania	04 Dec 56	317UNTS161	104602
Iran	USA (United States)	16 Jan 57	308UNTS147	104460
Iceland	Thailand	22 Jan 57	312UNTS63	104511
Germany, West	Sweden	29 Jan 57	393UNTS113	105654
Germany, West	Norway	29 Jan 57	353UNTS39	105037
Denmark	Germany, West	29 Jan 57	302UNTS75	104354
USA (United States)	Venezuela	21 Feb 57	279UNTS199	104041
Canada	USA (United States)	26 Feb 57	279UNTS179	104039
Japan	Norway	28 Feb 57	280UNTS87	104054
Dominican Republic	USA (United States)	09 Mar 57	279UNTS249	104044
Belgium	Czechoslovakia	12 Mar 57	312UNTS75	104512
Netherlands	Yugoslavia	13 Mar 57	327UNTS227	104723
Netherlands	USA (United States)	03 Apr 57	410UNTS193	105904

Navigational conditions (Cont.)

PARTY ONE	PARTY TWO	DATE	CITATION	NUMBER
Canada	USA (United States)	09 Apr 57	283UNTS217	104119
Germany, West	Yugoslavia	10 Apr 57	463UNTS269	106708
Romania	Sweden	15 Apr 57	342UNTS325	104915
Bulgaria	Sweden	17 Apr 57	464UNTS3	106709
Bulgaria	Yugoslavia	19 Apr 57	349UNTS3	105006
Ceylon (Sri Lanka)	Italy	23 Apr 57	337UNTS115	104820
Korea, South	USA (United States)	24 Apr 57	288UNTS219	104207
Belgium	Bulgaria	14 May 57	317UNTS81	104596
Hungary	Netherlands	28 May 57	334UNTS291	104773
Denmark	Peru	10 Jun 57	406UNTS63	105839
Afghanistan	Pakistan	13 Jun 57	327UNTS51	104717
Austria	USSR (Soviet Union)	14 Jun 57	285UNTS169	104152
Czechoslovakia	United Arab Rep	30 Jun 57	411UNTS126	105917
Greece	Italy	02 Aug 57	533UNTS217	107744
Hungary	Sweden	02 Aug 57	334UNTS307	104774
Panama	USA (United States)	05 Aug 57	299UNTS113	104309
Netherlands	Romania	27 Aug 57	342UNTS309	104914
Italy	Pakistan	05 Oct 57	353UNTS91	105039
Belgium	Netherlands	24 Oct 57	489UNTS11	107132
Belgium	Netherlands	24 Oct 57	489UNTS3	107131
France	Morocco	25 Oct 57	559UNTS95	108156
Ireland	Portugal	11 Nov 57	553UNTS141	108080
Japan	USSR (Soviet Union)	06 Dec 57	325UNTS35	104694
China People's Rep	USSR (Soviet Union)	21 Dec 57	305UNTS213	104420
Belgium	Morocco	20 Jan 58	288UNTS3	104192
Multilateral		03 Feb 58	381UNTS165	105471
India	Japan	04 Feb 58	324UNTS215	104687
Bulgaria	Netherlands	07 Feb 58	335UNTS45	104777
Afghanistan	Turkey	08 Feb 58	464UNTS39	106711
Ceylon (Sri Lanka)	USSR (Soviet Union)	08 Feb 58	348UNTS159	104999
Albania	USSR (Soviet Union)	15 Feb 58	313UNTS261	104536
Morocco	Portugal	03 Apr 58	393UNTS203	105657
Sweden	Yugoslavia	18 Apr 58	393UNTS225	105658
Japan	Poland	26 Apr 58	340UNTS221	104866
Multilateral		29 Apr 58	450UNTS11	106465
Bulgaria	Denmark	28 May 58	312UNTS235	104521
India	USSR (Soviet Union)	02 Jun 58	393UNTS3	105650
Belgium	USSR (Soviet Union)	05 Jun 58	345UNTS145	104965
Multilateral		10 Jun 58	454UNTS47	106539
Denmark	Luxembourg	10 Jun 58	356UNTS193	105096
Netherlands	USSR (Soviet Union)	17 Jun 58	335UNTS77	104779
Denmark	Romania	25 Jun 58	345UNTS231	104970
Austria	Romania	10 Jul 58	353UNTS155	105041
Denmark	Hungary	17 Jul 58	344UNTS281	104954
Romania	United Arab Rep	14 Aug 58	405UNTS189	105834
Austria	Bulgaria	12 Sep 58	353UNTS3	105036
United Arab Rep	USSR (Soviet Union)	18 Sep 58	338UNTS29	104831
Iraq	USSR (Soviet Union)	11 Oct 58	328UNTS95	104730
Muscat and Oman	USA (United States)	20 Dec 58	380UNTS181	105457
Iraq	Romania	24 Dec 58	405UNTS243	105836
Finland	Switzerland	07 Jan 59	353UNTS173	105042
UK Great Britain	Yugoslavia	03 Feb 59	359UNTS339	105151
Netherlands	Tunisia	19 Mar 59	497UNTS61	107262
Sweden	Tunisia	19 Mar 59	497UNTS43	107261
Norway	Tunisia	28 Mar 59	497UNTS77	107263
Denmark	Tunisia	14 Apr 59	340UNTS273	104870
Ceylon (Sri Lanka)	Sweden	29 May 59	464UNTS109	106713
Ceylon (Sri Lanka)	Norway	29 May 59	411UNTS165	105919
Ceylon (Sri Lanka)	Denmark	29 May 59	348UNTS225	105002
India	Italy	16 Jul 59	464UNTS129	106714
Germany, West	USA (United States)	01 Oct 59	358UNTS129	105130
Nicaragua	Peru	14 Oct 59	392UNTS303	105649
South Africa	Switzerland	19 Oct 59	559UNTS257	108162
Czechoslovakia	Japan	15 Dec 59	383UNTS277	105505
Czechoslovakia	UK Great Britain	15 Jan 60	374UNTS207	105336

PARTY ONE	PARTY TWO	DATE	CITATION	NUMBER
Navigational conditions (Cont.)				
Multilateral		26 Feb 60	418UNTS171	106022
France	Thailand	26 Feb 60	392UNTS279	105648
Guinea	Netherlands	09 Mar 60	392UNTS243	105646
Finland	Iceland	10 Mar 60	497UNTS95	107264
Czechoslovakia	Iraq	11 Mar 60	464UNTS267	106718
Belgium	Switzerland	24 Mar 60	416UNTS81	105996
Luxembourg	Yugoslavia	09 Apr 60	464UNTS293	106719
Greece	Romania	02 May 60	485UNTS17	107043
Morocco	United Arab Rep	19 May 60	563UNTS121	108208
Switzerland	Tunisia	21 May 60	497UNTS109	107265
Afghanistan	Czechoslovakia	28 May 60	497UNTS129	107266
Cuba	Czechoslovakia	10 Jun 60	447UNTS75	106412
Luxembourg	Tunisia	13 Jun 60	497UNTS143	107267
Multilateral		17 Jun 60	536UNTS27	107794
Denmark	Peru	22 Jun 60	439UNTS113	106326
UK Great Britain	USA (United States)	24 Jun 60	377UNTS63	105396
Poland	UK Great Britain	02 Jul 60	385UNTS87	105532
Denmark	USA (United States)	07 Jul 60	380UNTS39	105449
Switzerland	United Arab Rep	14 Jul 60	497UNTS161	107268
Multilateral		29 Jul 60	392UNTS69	105640
Mexico	USA (United States)	15 Aug 60	402UNTS177	105786
Belgium	Burma	17 Aug 60	540UNTS185	107850
Ghana	United Arab Rep	29 Aug 60	412UNTS71	105926
Czechoslovakia	India	19 Sep 60	465UNTS67	106722
Multilateral		19 Sep 60	419UNTS125	106032
Belgium	Jordan	19 Oct 60	479UNTS277	106959
Hungary	UK Great Britain	25 Oct 60	419UNTS309	106034
Burma	Switzerland	31 Oct 60	465UNTS97	106723
Norway	Peru	02 Nov 60	497UNTS207	107270
Multilateral		13 Dec 60	523UNTS117	107557
Luxembourg	Thailand	29 Dec 60	465UNTS131	106725
Jordan	Sweden	09 Jan 61	465UNTS155	106726
Norway	Poland	17 Jan 61	412UNTS130	105928
Poland	USSR (Soviet Union)	05 Feb 61	420UNTS161	106046
Belgium	USA (United States)	21 Feb 61	480UNTS149	106967
Cuba	Czechoslovakia	04 Mar 61	465UNTS209	106728
USA (United States)	Vietnam, South	03 Apr 61	424UNTS137	106106
Argentina	Uruguay	07 Apr 61	635UNTS91	109074
Poland	Switzerland	18 May 61	559UNTS233	108161
Somalia	USSR (Soviet Union)	02 Jun 61	493UNTS173	107214
Czechoslovakia	Morocco	08 Jun 61	497UNTS275	107272
Cameroon	France	16 Jun 61	412UNTS148	105929
Guinea	Sweden	17 Jun 61	465UNTS236	106729
Finland	Luxembourg	15 Aug 61	541UNTS45	107859
Jordan	Norway	21 Aug 61	465UNTS275	106731
Jordan	Netherlands	24 Aug 61	466UNTS3	106733
Mexico	Netherlands	24 Aug 61	465UNTS291	106732
Liberia	Switzerland	31 Aug 61	559UNTS215	108160
Ghana	USSR (Soviet Union)	04 Nov 61	437UNTS213	106308
Czechoslovakia	Mali	27 Nov 61	466UNTS41	106736
Czechoslovakia	Guinea	16 Dec 61	559UNTS49	108154
Argentina	Japan	20 Dec 61	613UNTS323	108859
Luxembourg	South Africa	31 Jan 62	563UNTS153	108209
Finland	Hungary	13 Feb 62	463UNTS61	106693
Multilateral		20 Feb 62	597UNTS159	108644
USA (United States)	USSR (Soviet Union)	08 Mar 62	460UNTS3	106630
Ghana	USSR (Soviet Union)	06 Apr 62	498UNTS41	107277
Greece	USA (United States)	24 Apr 62	459UNTS3	106609
France	Romania	18 May 62	498UNTS115	107279
France	Senegal	15 Jun 62	524UNTS3	107563
Czechoslovakia	Senegal	20 Jun 62	498UNTS145	107280
Guinea	Norway	21 Jun 62	466UNTS81	106738
Morocco	Switzerland	05 Jul 62	498UNTS171	107281
Multilateral		18 Sep 62	442UNTS215	106351
Finland	USSR (Soviet Union)	27 Sep 62	479UNTS99	106949

PARTY ONE	PARTY TWO	DATE	CITATION	NUMBER
Navigational conditions (Cont.)				
Finland	France	12 Oct 62	498UNTS299	107285
Hungary	Syria	18 Oct 62	491UNTS209	107178
France	Ivory Coast	19 Oct 62	498UNTS317	107286
Czechoslovakia	Norway	25 Oct 62	498UNTS335	107287
Czechoslovakia	Sweden	25 Oct 62	498UNTS343	107288
Poland	Syria	10 Nov 62	491UNTS228	107179
Japan	UK Great Britain	14 Nov 62	478UNTS29	106934
Ivory Coast	Switzerland	17 Nov 62	499UNTS3	107289
Germany, West	USA (United States)	29 Nov 62	460UNTS169	106639
Syria	United Arab Rep	27 Dec 62	491UNTS245	107180
Senegal	Switzerland	23 Jan 63	524UNTS23	107564
New Zealand	Western Samoa	24 Jan 63	499UNTS21	107290
Guinea	Switzerland	01 Feb 63	499UNTS35	107291
Mali	Senegal	07 Feb 63	524UNTS41	107565
Algeria	France	18 Feb 63	563UNTS263	108214
Norway	USA (United States)	01 Mar 63	524UNTS185	107573
Austria	Czechoslovakia	08 Mar 63	495UNTS219	107245
Belgium	USA (United States)	19 Apr 63	493UNTS83	107209
Greece	Hungary	27 Apr 63	534UNTS3	107750
Algeria	Morocco	30 Apr 63	564UNTS3	108217
Multilateral		07 Jun 63	472UNTS95	106837
Finland	Poland	10 Jun 63	503UNTS179	107343
Guinea	Ivory Coast	26 Jun 63	499UNTS71	107293
Algeria	Mali	22 Jul 63	564UNTS29	108219
Cameroon	Israel	09 Aug 63	499UNTS121	107295
Tanganyika	USSR (Soviet Union)	14 Aug 63	493UNTS195	107215
Ivory Coast	Netherlands	09 Oct 63	499UNTS141	107296
UK Great Britain	USA (United States)	11 Oct 63	483UNTS3	107005
Canada	Denmark	28 Nov 63	496UNTS223	107254
Canada	USA (United States)	27 Dec 63	494UNTS21	107223
Mali	Niger	15 Jan 64	499UNTS197	107299
USA (United States)	USSR (Soviet Union)	22 Feb 64	526UNTS131	107605
Cameroon	Mali	17 Mar 64	524UNTS61	107566
United Arab Rep	USA (United States)	05 May 64	531UNTS229	107706
UK Great Britain	USA (United States)	19 Jun 64	530UNTS99	107675
New Zealand	USA (United States)	24 Jun 64	524UNTS101	107568
Denmark	USA (United States)	02 Jul 64	529UNTS277	107665
Ivory Coast	Mali	09 Jul 64	524UNTS121	107569
Spain	USA (United States)	16 Jul 64	529UNTS187	107661
Multilateral		25 Nov 64	587UNTS19	108507
Argentina	UK Great Britain	12 Jan 65	597UNTS177	108645
Multilateral		05 Apr 66	640UNTS133	109159
Denmark	Singapore	20 Dec 66	593UNTS125	108580
Haiti	Israel	28 Mar 67	630UNTS293	108975
Denmark	Malaysia	14 Dec 67	614UNTS26	108862
Denmark	Poland	26 Feb 68	643UNTS371	109202
Czechoslovakia	Hungary	27 Feb 68	640UNTS49	109154
Finland	USSR (Soviet Union)	07 Mar 68	643UNTS107	109187
Navigational equipment				
Multilateral		07 Dec 44	171UNTS345	200501
United Arab Rep	USA (United States)	15 Jun 46	151UNTS135	101988
USSR (Soviet Union)	Yugoslavia	04 Feb 47	130UNTS235	101731
Romania	Yugoslavia	30 Jun 47	116UNTS57	101569
UK Great Britain	USA (United States)	13 Oct 47	66UNTS269	100858
France	USA (United States)	19 Oct 48	98UNTS3	101355
Netherlands	Norway	26 Feb 49	29UNTS33	100432
Philippines	Spain	06 Oct 51	215UNTS193	102920
Greece	USA (United States)	25 Jun 52	181UNTS53	102398
India	Pakistan	20 Feb 53	164UNTS3	102155
Multilateral		25 Feb 54	215UNTS249	102922
Canada	Japan	12 Jan 55	311UNTS167	104503
Netherlands	USA (United States)	21 Mar 55	289UNTS129	104217
Germany, West	USA (United States)	02 Aug 55	268UNTS121	103854
Burma	China People's Rep	08 Nov 55	306UNTS11	104430

PARTY ONE	PARTY TWO	DATE	CITATION	NUMBER
Navigational equipment (Cont.)				
Multilateral		25 Sep 56	334UNTS13	104766
Multilateral		25 Sep 56	334UNTS89	104767
UK Great Britain	USA (United States)	01 Nov 56	264UNTS3	103785
UK Great Britain	USA (United States)	27 Nov 56	282UNTS43	104092
Dominican Republic	USA (United States)	09 Mar 57	279UNTS249	104044
Belgium	Hungary	01 Jun 57	291UNTS17	104242
UK Great Britain	USA (United States)	01 Nov 57	299UNTS167	104312
Czechoslovakia	Poland	31 Jan 58	431UNTS99	106214
Albania	USSR (Soviet Union)	15 Feb 58	313UNTS261	104536
Germany, West	USSR (Soviet Union)	25 Apr 58	346UNTS71	104978
Belgium	USSR (Soviet Union)	05 Jun 58	345UNTS145	104965
Finland	Sweden	22 Sep 58	428UNTS119	106170
Germany, West	USA (United States)	01 Oct 59	358UNTS129	105130
Multilateral		26 Feb 60	418UNTS171	106022
Denmark	USA (United States)	07 Jul 60	380UNTS39	105449
Multilateral		13 Dec 60	523UNTS117	107557
Argentina	Uruguay	07 Apr 61	635UNTS91	109074
Australia	USA (United States)	05 Jun 61	409UNTS279	105892
Multilateral		20 Feb 62	597UNTS159	108644
New Zealand	Western Samoa	24 Jan 63	499UNTS21	107290
Cyprus	Denmark	27 Apr 63	529UNTS255	107664
Pakistan	USSR (Soviet Union)	07 Oct 63	499UNTS161	107297
UK Great Britain	USA (United States)	11 Oct 63	483UNTS3	107005
Canada	USA (United States)	08 Jun 65	546UNTS201	107947
Malta	Yugoslavia	15 Jul 65	561UNTS223	108186
Permit designation				
Brazil	France	27 Jan 40	72UNTS77	100929
Spain	USA (United States)	02 Dec 44	89UNTS345	200262
Multilateral		07 Dec 44	84UNTS389	200252
Sweden	USA (United States)	16 Dec 44	6UNTS397	200041
Denmark	USA (United States)	16 Dec 44	10UNTS213	200063
Iceland	USA (United States)	27 Jan 45	122UNTS293	200411
Ireland	USA (United States)	03 Feb 45	122UNTS305	200412
Switzerland	USA (United States)	03 Aug 45	51UNTS233	200191
Norway	USA (United States)	06 Oct 45	122UNTS319	200413
South Africa	UK Great Britain	26 Oct 45	72UNTS41	100927
Greece	UK Great Britain	26 Nov 45	35UNTS161	100555
Portugal	UK Great Britain	06 Dec 45	6UNTS3	100065
Portugal	USA (United States)	06 Dec 45	3UNTS139	100028
Portugal	UK Great Britain	06 Dec 45	5UNTS37	100064
Canada	UK Great Britain	21 Dec 45	27UNTS155	100405
Czechoslovakia	USA (United States)	03 Jan 46	6UNTS309	100084
Czechoslovakia	Poland	24 Jan 46	25UNTS181	100363
UK Great Britain	USA (United States)	11 Feb 46	3UNTS253	100036
Turkey	UK Great Britain	12 Feb 46	6UNTS79	100069
Turkey	USA (United States)	12 Feb 46	13UNTS3	100196
France	UK Great Britain	28 Feb 46	27UNTS173	100407
Greece	USA (United States)	27 Mar 46	15UNTS233	100239
France	USA (United States)	27 Mar 46	139UNTS114	101879
Ireland	UK Great Britain	05 Apr 46	72UNTS57	100928
Belgium	USA (United States)	05 Apr 46	4UNTS125	100041
Netherlands	Portugal	12 Apr 46	4UNTS317	100054
Argentina	UK Great Britain	17 Apr 46	164UNTS53	102159
France	Ireland	16 May 46	44UNTS105	100681
Ireland	Sweden	29 May 46	35UNTS231	100557
United Arab Rep	USA (United States)	15 Jun 46	71UNTS157	100917
Sweden	Turkey	26 Jun 46	14UNTS21	100208
Netherlands	Spain	13 Jul 46	4UNTS351	100055
France	Sweden	02 Aug 46	27UNTS251	100410
Lebanon	USA (United States)	11 Aug 46	66UNTS211	100856
Netherlands	UK Great Britain	13 Aug 46	4UNTS367	100056
Norway	UK Great Britain	31 Aug 46	6UNTS235	100078
Brazil	USA (United States)	06 Sep 46	54UNTS197	100805
France	Turkey	12 Oct 46	14UNTS33	100209

PARTY ONE	PARTY TWO	DATE	CITATION	NUMBER
Permit designation (Cont.)				
Belgium	Portugal	22 Oct 46	34UNTS49	100527
Brazil	UK Great Britain	31 Oct 46	11UNTS115	100152
India	USA (United States)	14 Nov 46	22UNTS55	100331
Philippines	USA (United States)	16 Nov 46	7UNTS151	100097
Sweden	UK Great Britain	27 Nov 46	11UNTS229	100162
Australia	USA (United States)	03 Dec 46	7UNTS201	100100
New Zealand	USA (United States)	03 Dec 46	7UNTS175	100099
Portugal	Switzerland	09 Dec 46	310UNTS251	104495
Brazil	Portugal	10 Dec 46	200UNTS67	102695
USA (United States)	Uruguay	14 Dec 46	532UNTS87	107713
Taiwan	USA (United States)	20 Dec 46	22UNTS87	100332
Peru	USA (United States)	27 Dec 46	26UNTS227	100390
Ecuador	USA (United States)	08 Jan 47	22UNTS119	100333
Czechoslovakia	Ireland	29 Jan 47	27UNTS267	100411
Greece	UK Great Britain	21 Feb 47	70UNTS215	100905
Thailand	USA (United States)	26 Feb 47	16UNTS17	100246
Paraguay	USA (United States)	28 Feb 47	44UNTS25	100676
Portugal	Sweden	06 Mar 47	35UNTS243	100558
Netherlands	Turkey	19 Mar 47	14UNTS59	100211
Greece	Sweden	08 Apr 47	94UNTS73	101307
Greece	Netherlands	17 Apr 47	32UNTS115	100494
Canada	Portugal	25 Apr 47	94UNTS87	101308
Syria	USA (United States)	28 Apr 47	262UNTS121	103741
France	Greece	05 May 47	76UNTS61	100980
Czechoslovakia	Denmark	14 May 47	27UNTS297	100413
South Africa	USA (United States)	23 May 47	66UNTS233	100857
Iraq	Turkey	30 Jun 47	72UNTS107	100930
Romania	Yugoslavia	30 Jun 47	116UNTS57	101569
Denmark	Turkey	30 Jun 47	32UNTS301	100504
France	India	16 Jul 47	27UNTS325	100415
Canada	UK Great Britain	17 Jul 47	28UNTS3	100416
Netherlands	Thailand	18 Jul 47	28UNTS27	100417
Netherlands	South Africa	22 Jul 47	12UNTS257	100188
Greece	Turkey	22 Jul 47	72UNTS131	100931
Taiwan	UK Great Britain	23 Jul 47	9UNTS207	100135
Canada	Ireland	08 Aug 47	28UNTS47	100419
Poland	Romania	09 Aug 47	12UNTS363	100193
Hungary	Poland	28 Aug 47	15UNTS145	100231
Czechoslovakia	Netherlands	01 Sep 47	32UNTS129	100495
Czechoslovakia	Switzerland	10 Sep 47	35UNTS275	100559
Lebanon	Turkey	16 Sep 47	44UNTS123	100682
Chile	UK Great Britain	16 Sep 47	133UNTS143	101786
Czechoslovakia	Sweden	15 Oct 47	44UNTS149	100683
Colombia	UK Great Britain	16 Oct 47	160UNTS297	102115
Brazil	Netherlands	06 Nov 47	53UNTS59	100773
Norway	Portugal	11 Nov 47	34UNTS257	100542
Brazil	Norway	14 Nov 47	44UNTS163	100684
Brazil	Sweden	14 Nov 47	94UNTS139	101310
Denmark	Greece	14 Nov 47	35UNTS295	100560
Denmark	Ireland	18 Nov 47	35UNTS309	100561
Ireland	Italy	21 Nov 47	353UNTS73	105038
Taiwan	Netherlands	06 Dec 47	43UNTS185	100669
Denmark	Portugal	15 Dec 47	35UNTS329	100563
Peru	UK Great Britain	22 Dec 47	72UNTS143	100932
Ethiopia	Pakistan	01 Jan 48	35UNTS3	100547
Philippines	UK Great Britain	07 Jan 48	28UNTS63	100420
Austria	Netherlands	22 Jan 48	17UNTS99	100270
Italy	USA (United States)	06 Feb 48	73UNTS113	100950
Czechoslovakia	Yugoslavia	14 Mar 48	28UNTS81	100421
Argentina	Denmark	18 Mar 48	94UNTS175	101311
Cuba	UK Great Britain	19 Mar 48	175UNTS23	102294
Ireland	Switzerland	06 May 48	334UNTS187	104768
Pakistan	Sweden	06 May 48	36UNTS3	100564
Jordan	Turkey	07 May 48	32UNTS313	100505
Ireland	Netherlands	10 May 48	28UNTS121	100422

PARTY ONE	PARTY TWO	DATE	CITATION	NUMBER
Permit designation (Cont.)				
Norway	Turkey	20 May 48	26UNTS137	100384
India	Sweden	21 May 48	34UNTS285	100543
Greece	Switzerland	26 May 48	94UNTS217	101312
Canada	Netherlands	02 Jun 48	32UNTS215	100499
Ireland	Norway	21 Jun 48	34UNTS317	100545
India	Pakistan	23 Jun 48	28UNTS143	100423
Italy	UK Great Britain	25 Jun 48	94UNTS239	101313
France	Spain	23 Aug 48	28UNTS173	100425
Greece	Lebanon	06 Sep 48	178UNTS37	102335
Bolivia	USA (United States)	29 Sep 48	505UNTS139	107370
Netherlands	Spain	08 Oct 48	28UNTS209	100426
France	USA (United States)	19 Oct 48	98UNTS3	101355
Mexico	Portugal	22 Oct 48	34UNTS329	100546
Argentina	Netherlands	29 Oct 48	95UNTS21	101316
Ceylon (Sri Lanka)	India	21 Dec 48	28UNTS223	100427
Ceylon (Sri Lanka)	Pakistan	03 Jan 49	28UNTS247	100428
Italy	Lebanon	24 Jan 49	231UNTS241	103223
Switzerland	Turkey	16 Feb 49	72UNTS175	100933
Belgium	Sweden	21 Feb 49	95UNTS73	101317
Finland	Netherlands	25 Feb 49	53UNTS123	100777
Netherlands	Switzerland	07 Mar 49	35UNTS69	100551
Finland	USA (United States)	29 Mar 49	55UNTS59	100808
Panama	USA (United States)	31 Mar 49	55UNTS87	100810
Finland	Sweden	26 Apr 49	95UNTS83	101318
Bulgaria	Poland	16 May 49	84UNTS313	101140
Italy	Spain	31 May 49	231UNTS251	103224
Australia	Pakistan	03 Jun 49	35UNTS23	100549
Canada	USA (United States)	04 Jun 49	122UNTS237	101649
Ethiopia	India	07 Jun 49	35UNTS13	100548
Belgium	Greece	21 Jun 49	137UNTS215	101854
Norway	Pakistan	23 Jun 49	35UNTS49	100550
India	Switzerland	24 Jun 49	95UNTS109	101319
Greece	Syria	05 Jul 49	78UNTS71	101013
Australia	India	11 Jul 49	35UNTS83	100552
Iraq	Norway	12 Jul 49	53UNTS137	100778
Czechoslovakia	Finland	13 Jul 49	53UNTS153	100779
Pakistan	Philippines	16 Jul 49	35UNTS111	100553
Dominican Republic	USA (United States)	19 Jul 49	51UNTS145	100762
Pakistan	UK Great Britain	27 Jul 49	44UNTS199	100685
Ceylon (Sri Lanka)	UK Great Britain	05 Aug 49	35UNTS137	100554
Canada	UK Great Britain	19 Aug 49	44UNTS223	100686
Finland	Norway	24 Aug 49	53UNTS167	100780
Denmark	Finland	26 Aug 49	53UNTS191	100781
Belgium	Canada	30 Aug 49	53UNTS221	100782
Belgium	United Arab Rep	19 Sep 49	137UNTS189	101853
Lebanon	Netherlands	20 Sep 49	108UNTS205	101474
Burma	USA (United States)	28 Sep 49	55UNTS3	100806
India	Philippines	20 Oct 49	72UNTS191	100934
Multilateral		27 Oct 49	53UNTS241	100784
Iran	Netherlands	31 Oct 49	254UNTS257	103596
Denmark	Pakistan	09 Nov 49	44UNTS255	100687
Denmark	Thailand	23 Nov 49	53UNTS255	100786
Sweden	Thailand	23 Nov 49	72UNTS217	100935
Italy	Turkey	25 Nov 49	192UNTS39	102594
Norway	Thailand	26 Nov 49	53UNTS269	100787
Brazil	Spain	28 Nov 49	215UNTS303	102923
Austria	Denmark	02 Dec 49	53UNTS281	100788
Austria	Norway	02 Dec 49	72UNTS230	100936
Austria	Sweden	02 Dec 49	108UNTS3	101465
Netherlands	United Arab Rep	08 Dec 49	95UNTS123	101320
Sweden	United Arab Rep	12 Dec 49	108UNTS15	101466
Canada	Denmark	13 Dec 49	72UNTS247	100937
Austria	Switzerland	19 Dec 49	254UNTS287	103597
USA (United States)	Yugoslavia	24 Dec 49	89UNTS209	101219
Netherlands	Syria	13 Feb 50	108UNTS53	101467

PARTY ONE	PARTY TWO	DATE	CITATION	NUMBER
Permit designation (Cont.)				
Canada	Norway	14 Feb 50	53UNTS329	100790
Spain	Sweden	18 Feb 50	166UNTS15	102184
Ceylon (Sri Lanka)	Thailand	24 Feb 50	72UNTS261	100938
Italy	Netherlands	04 Mar 50	254UNTS305	103598
Norway	United Arab Rep	11 Mar 50	95UNTS157	101321
Denmark	United Arab Rep	14 Mar 50	95UNTS197	101322
Denmark	Iceland	22 Mar 50	72UNTS273	100939
Iceland	Netherlands	22 Mar 50	95UNTS237	101323
Sweden	UK Great Britain	05 Apr 50	99UNTS107	101374
Italy	Portugal	05 Apr 50	254UNTS329	103599
Turkey	United Arab Rep	12 Apr 50	128UNTS3	101711
Australia	Philippines	14 Apr 50	127UNTS281	101709
Greece	United Arab Rep	24 Apr 50	163UNTS229	102149
Switzerland	United Arab Rep	15 May 50	95UNTS255	101325
Israel	USA (United States)	13 Jun 50	212UNTS93	102863
Iraq	Pakistan	20 Jun 50	77UNTS215	101001
Netherlands	Spain	20 Jun 50	95UNTS303	101327
Burma	Ceylon (Sri Lanka)	29 Jun 50	73UNTS3	100940
Spain	UK Great Britain	20 Jul 50	398UNTS101	105719
France	Pakistan	31 Jul 50	96UNTS23	101329
Canada	France	01 Aug 50	73UNTS21	100941
Spain	Switzerland	03 Aug 50	254UNTS365	103600
France	United Arab Rep	08 Aug 50	127UNTS293	101710
Canada	New Zealand	16 Aug 50	77UNTS239	101002
Burma	Sweden	14 Sep 50	96UNTS45	101330
Brazil	Turkey	21 Sep 50	150UNTS299	101981
Ceylon (Sri Lanka)	United Arab Rep	26 Sep 50	192UNTS53	102595
Sweden	Switzerland	18 Oct 50	166UNTS49	102185
Luxembourg	Portugal	21 Oct 50	108UNTS67	101468
Taiwan	Philippines	23 Oct 50	215UNTS159	102918
Israel	Netherlands	23 Oct 50	189UNTS89	102543
Israel	Turkey	05 Feb 51	193UNTS3	102607
Colombia	Portugal	09 Mar 51	108UNTS87	101469
Greece	Yugoslavia	15 Mar 51	187UNTS237	102516
Iraq	UK Great Britain	19 Apr 51	108UNTS121	101470
Belgium	UK Great Britain	08 May 51	158UNTS451	102079
Netherlands	UK Great Britain	17 May 51	118UNTS103	101599
India	Netherlands	24 May 51	108UNTS151	101471
Greece	Norway	28 May 51	187UNTS141	102507
Cuba	Portugal	26 Jun 51	192UNTS115	102598
Iceland	Norway	14 Jul 51	163UNTS265	102150
Burma	Denmark	30 Jul 51	108UNTS167	101472
Israel	Philippines	07 Aug 51	192UNTS81	102596
Lebanon	UK Great Britain	15 Aug 51	160UNTS327	102116
Burma	Netherlands	06 Sep 51	108UNTS187	101473
Panama	UK Great Britain	15 Sep 51	560UNTS143	108172
Taiwan	Thailand	29 Sep 51	215UNTS166	102919
Philippines	Spain	06 Oct 51	215UNTS193	102920
Greece	Luxembourg	22 Oct 51	187UNTS119	102506
Italy	UK Great Britain	24 Oct 51	118UNTS143	101602
Denmark	Iraq	18 Nov 51	232UNTS25	103227
India	UK Great Britain	01 Dec 51	128UNTS39	101712
Colombia	Spain	11 Dec 51	216UNTS73	102933
Jordan	United Arab Rep	02 Jan 52	192UNTS157	102599
Belgium	Spain	10 Mar 52	178UNTS243	102342
Pakistan	Switzerland	17 Mar 52	192UNTS237	102603
Norway	Uruguay	20 Mar 52	310UNTS279	104496
Sweden	Uruguay	20 Mar 52	311UNTS3	104497
Iraq	Switzerland	31 Mar 52	311UNTS43	104498
France	Mexico	17 Apr 52	163UNTS321	102153
Belgium	Sweden	21 Apr 52	166UNTS9	102183
France	Israel	29 Apr 52	189UNTS55	102542
India	United Arab Rep	14 Jun 52	173UNTS209	102268
Australia	United Arab Rep	14 Jun 52	173UNTS241	102269
Denmark	UK Great Britain	23 Jun 52	151UNTS3	101982

PARTY ONE	PARTY TWO	DATE	CITATION	NUMBER
Permit designation (Cont.)				
Belgium	Israel	30 Jun 52	183UNTS263	102435
Netherlands	Pakistan	17 Jul 52	150UNTS277	101980
Japan	USA (United States)	11 Aug 52	212UNTS27	102862
Burma	Philippines	15 Aug 52	200UNTS97	102696
Ethiopia	Pakistan	29 Aug 52	150UNTS257	101979
Mexico	Netherlands	13 Oct 52	163UNTS341	102154
Austria	Luxembourg	13 Oct 52	192UNTS291	102606
Iceland	Luxembourg	23 Oct 52	193UNTS39	102609
Burma	UK Great Britain	25 Oct 52	150UNTS237	101978
Chile	Denmark	27 Oct 52	271UNTS93	103911
Chile	Sweden	27 Oct 52	311UNTS63	104499
Luxembourg	Sweden	17 Nov 52	173UNTS277	102270
Luxembourg	Norway	17 Nov 52	311UNTS95	104500
Israel	Switzerland	19 Nov 52	232UNTS3	103226
Japan	Netherlands	17 Feb 53	192UNTS215	102602
Japan	Sweden	20 Feb 53	173UNTS307	102272
Libya	UK Great Britain	21 Feb 53	311UNTS115	104501
Japan	Norway	23 Feb 53	192UNTS191	102601
Denmark	Japan	26 Feb 53	173UNTS329	102273
Philippines	Thailand	27 Apr 53	174UNTS3	102274
Cuba	USA (United States)	26 May 53	224UNTS75	103070
Switzerland	Yugoslavia	28 May 53	232UNTS45	103228
Japan	Thailand	19 Jun 53	174UNTS29	102276
Burma	Norway	22 Jun 53	174UNTS49	102277
Canada	Mexico	27 Jul 53	192UNTS255	102604
USA (United States)	Venezuela	14 Aug 53	213UNTS99	102883
Ceylon (Sri Lanka)	Netherlands	14 Sep 53	193UNTS21	102608
Korea, South	Netherlands	26 Oct 53	200UNTS103	102697
Austria	Yugoslavia	11 Nov 53	363UNTS149	105206
Belgium	Lebanon	24 Dec 53	219UNTS153	102972
Ethiopia	Greece	20 Jan 54	222UNTS281	103035
Syria	UK Great Britain	30 Jan 54	449UNTS47	106452
Canada	Peru	18 Feb 54	411UNTS64	105915
Peru	Spain	31 Mar 54	232UNTS65	103230
France	South Africa	05 May 54	215UNTS401	102926
Iran	Switzerland	27 May 54	496UNTS273	107257
Ireland	Luxembourg	27 Jul 54	232UNTS91	103231
Norway	USA (United States)	06 Aug 54	222UNTS261	103033
Denmark	USA (United States)	06 Aug 54	222UNTS235	103030
Sweden	USA (United States)	06 Aug 54	221UNTS331	103014
Philippines	Sweden	20 Aug 54	200UNTS121	102699
Belgium	South Africa	13 Sep 54	201UNTS15	102707
France	South Africa	17 Sep 54	216UNTS29	102930
Norway	Philippines	20 Oct 54	216UNTS11	102928
Denmark	Philippines	20 Oct 54	216UNTS3	102927
Ecuador	Netherlands	14 Dec 54	232UNTS115	103233
Norway	Switzerland	30 Dec 54	311UNTS147	104502
Austria	Belgium	07 Jan 55	380UNTS219	105458
Canada	Japan	12 Jan 55	311UNTS167	104503
Philippines	UK Great Britain	31 Jan 55	216UNTS51	102932
Iraq	United Arab Rep	23 Mar 55	311UNTS199	104504
Syria	United Arab Rep	03 Jul 55	393UNTS67	105652
Germany, West	USA (United States)	07 Jul 55	275UNTS3	103973
Germany, West	UK Great Britain	22 Jul 55	269UNTS189	103881
Germany, East	Hungary	10 Sep 55	407UNTS132	105863
Bulgaria	Yugoslavia	01 Oct 55	396UNTS223	105698
France	Germany, West	04 Oct 55	353UNTS203	105044
Finland	USSR (Soviet Union)	19 Oct 55	353UNTS185	105043
Denmark	Syria	20 Oct 55	250UNTS61	103518
Pakistan	Turkey	02 Nov 55	311UNTS217	104505
Australia	South Africa	04 Nov 55	232UNTS143	103234
Burma	China People's Rep	08 Nov 55	306UNTS11	104430
Austria	Israel	17 Nov 55	232UNTS153	103235
India	Japan	26 Nov 55	311UNTS243	104506
Australia	Japan	19 Jan 56	311UNTS291	104507

PARTY ONE	PARTY TWO	DATE	CITATION	NUMBER
Permit designation (Cont.)				
Austria	Italy	23 Jan 56	393UNTS97	105653
Argentina	Switzerland	25 Jan 56	559UNTS121	108157
Romania	Yugoslavia	01 Feb 56	362UNTS203	105189
Hungary	Romania	03 Feb 56	362UNTS233	105190
India	USA (United States)	03 Feb 56	272UNTS75	103932
Austria	Poland	08 Feb 56	334UNTS221	104770
Netherlands	Sudan	12 Feb 56	311UNTS319	104508
Norway	Syria	25 Feb 56	463UNTS217	106706
Denmark	USSR (Soviet Union)	31 Mar 56	259UNTS169	103689
Sweden	USSR (Soviet Union)	31 Mar 56	259UNTS239	103691
Norway	USSR (Soviet Union)	31 Mar 56	259UNTS205	103690
Belgium	Germany, West	14 Apr 56	344UNTS103	104945
Portugal	Venezuela	16 May 56	463UNTS239	106707
Japan	Switzerland	24 May 56	312UNTS3	104509
Greece	Italy	26 May 56	496UNTS301	107258
Italy	Switzerland	04 Jun 56	378UNTS311	105429
Poland	Sweden	08 Jun 56	334UNTS257	104771
Germany, West	Ireland	12 Jun 56	353UNTS121	105040
Germany, West	Netherlands	28 Sep 56	327UNTS185	104722
Switzerland	Thailand	13 Oct 56	312UNTS43	104510
Belgium	Poland	17 Oct 56	356UNTS279	105100
Colombia	USA (United States)	24 Oct 56	476UNTS77	106905
Belgium	Turkey	25 Oct 56	380UNTS3	105447
Austria	UK Great Britain	27 Oct 56	264UNTS67	103789
Peru	Switzerland	23 Nov 56	411UNTS97	105916
Belgium	Romania	04 Dec 56	317UNTS161	104602
Iran	USA (United States)	16 Jan 57	308UNTS147	104460
Iceland	Thailand	22 Jan 57	312UNTS63	104511
Germany, West	Norway	29 Jan 57	353UNTS39	105037
Germany, West	Sweden	29 Jan 57	393UNTS113	105654
Denmark	Germany, West	29 Jan 57	302UNTS75	104354
Mexico	USA (United States)	07 Mar 57	279UNTS205	104042
Belgium	Czechoslovakia	12 Mar 57	312UNTS75	104512
Netherlands	Yugoslavia	13 Mar 57	327UNTS227	104723
Netherlands	USA (United States)	03 Apr 57	410UNTS193	105904
Denmark	Pakistan	10 Apr 57	302UNTS53	104353
Germany, West	Yugoslavia	10 Apr 57	463UNTS269	106708
Romania	Sweden	15 Apr 57	342UNTS325	104915
Bulgaria	Sweden	17 Apr 57	464UNTS3	106709
Korea, South	USA (United States)	24 Apr 57	288UNTS219	104207
Belgium	Bulgaria	14 May 57	317UNTS81	104596
Australia	Germany, West	22 May 57	357UNTS45	105105
Hungary	Netherlands	28 May 57	334UNTS291	104773
Belgium	Hungary	01 Jun 57	291UNTS17	104242
Afghanistan	Pakistan	13 Jun 57	327UNTS51	104717
Czechoslovakia	United Arab Rep	30 Jun 57	411UNTS126	105917
Greece	Italy	02 Aug 57	533UNTS217	107744
Hungary	Sweden	02 Aug 57	334UNTS307	104774
Netherlands	Romania	27 Aug 57	342UNTS309	104914
Multilateral		03 Oct 57	366UNTS87	105216
Italy	Pakistan	05 Oct 57	353UNTS91	105039
Fed of Malaya	UK Great Britain	18 Oct 57	335UNTS3	104775
France	Morocco	25 Oct 57	559UNTS95	108156
UK Great Britain	USSR (Soviet Union)	19 Dec 57	351UNTS235	105026
Australia	Ireland	30 Dec 57	497UNTS29	107260
Canada	Switzerland	10 Jan 58	464UNTS21	106710
Belgium	Morocco	20 Jan 58	288UNTS3	104192
Australia	UK Great Britain	07 Feb 58	335UNTS23	104776
Bulgaria	Netherlands	07 Feb 58	335UNTS45	104777
Afghanistan	Turkey	08 Feb 58	464UNTS39	106711
Sudan	Sweden	17 Feb 58	393UNTS161	105655
Norway	Pakistan	05 Mar 58	334UNTS199	104769
Pakistan	Sweden	06 Mar 58	393UNTS181	105656
Germany, West	Portugal	21 Mar 58	464UNTS71	106712
Denmark	South Africa	28 Mar 58	300UNTS107	104334

PARTY ONE	PARTY TWO	DATE	CITATION	NUMBER
Permit designation (Cont.)				
South Africa	Sweden	28 Mar 58	300UNTS95	104333
Norway	South Africa	28 Mar 58	300UNTS83	104332
Morocco	Portugal	03 Apr 58	393UNTS203	105657
Belgium	Iran	14 Apr 58	381UNTS309	105473
Sweden	Yugoslavia	18 Apr 58	393UNTS225	105658
Bulgaria	Denmark	28 May 58	312UNTS235	104521
India	USSR (Soviet Union)	02 Jun 58	393UNTS3	105650
Belgium	USSR (Soviet Union)	05 Jun 58	345UNTS145	104965
Pakistan	Portugal	07 Jun 58	320UNTS225	104645
Denmark	Luxembourg	10 Jun 58	356UNTS193	105096
Belgium	South Africa	11 Jun 58	335UNTS63	104778
Netherlands	USSR (Soviet Union)	17 Jun 58	335UNTS77	104779
Denmark	Romania	25 Jun 58	345UNTS231	104970
Belgium	Pakistan	04 Jul 58	387UNTS305	105569
Ethiopia	UK Great Britain	07 Jul 58	331UNTS3	104749
Austria	Romania	10 Jul 58	353UNTS155	105041
Denmark	Hungary	17 Jul 58	344UNTS281	104954
Romania	United Arab Rep	14 Aug 58	405UNTS189	105834
Austria	Bulgaria	12 Sep 58	353UNTS3	105036
United Arab Rep	USSR (Soviet Union)	18 Sep 58	338UNTS29	104831
Ghana	UK Great Britain	24 Sep 58	411UNTS146	105918
Australia	South Africa	26 Sep 58	335UNTS121	104780
Liberia	Netherlands	28 Nov 58	393UNTS55	105651
Finland	Switzerland	07 Jan 59	353UNTS173	105042
UK Great Britain	Yugoslavia	03 Feb 59	359UNTS339	105151
Japan	Philippines	02 Mar 59	341UNTS49	104877
Sweden	Tunisia	19 Mar 59	497UNTS43	107261
Netherlands	Tunisia	19 Mar 59	497UNTS61	107262
Norway	Tunisia	28 Mar 59	497UNTS77	107263
Poland	UK Great Britain	03 Apr 59	351UNTS295	105030
Denmark	Tunisia	14 Apr 59	340UNTS273	104870
Denmark	Sudan	11 May 59	445UNTS105	106380
Ceylon (Sri Lanka)	Denmark	29 May 59	348UNTS225	105002
Ceylon (Sri Lanka)	Sweden	29 May 59	464UNTS109	106713
Ceylon (Sri Lanka)	Norway	29 May 59	411UNTS165	105919
Belgium	Japan	20 Jun 59	411UNTS3	105911
Bulgaria	United Arab Rep	09 Jul 59	411UNTS187	105920
India	Italy	16 Jul 59	464UNTS129	106714
Afghanistan	Germany, West	22 Jul 59	464UNTS177	106715
Germany, West	Iceland	12 Aug 59	411UNTS224	105921
Canada	Germany, West	04 Sep 59	411UNTS260	105922
Australia	Fed of Malaya	29 Sep 59	357UNTS29	105104
South Africa	Switzerland	19 Oct 59	559UNTS257	108162
Liberia	Sweden	09 Dec 59	464UNTS219	106716
Czechoslovakia	UK Great Britain	15 Jan 60	374UNTS207	105336
Germany, West	United Arab Rep	16 Feb 60	464UNTS233	106717
France	Thailand	26 Feb 60	392UNTS279	105648
Australia	Thailand	26 Feb 60	392UNTS255	105647
Guinea	Netherlands	09 Mar 60	392UNTS243	105646
Finland	Iceland	10 Mar 60	497UNTS95	107264
Czechoslovakia	Iraq	11 Mar 60	464UNTS267	106718
Belgium	Switzerland	24 Mar 60	416UNTS81	105996
Luxembourg	Yugoslavia	09 Apr 60	464UNTS293	106719
Germany, West	Spain	28 Apr 60	465UNTS3	106720
Greece	Romania	02 May 60	485UNTS17	107043
Morocco	United Arab Rep	19 May 60	563UNTS121	108208
Switzerland	Tunisia	21 May 60	497UNTS109	107265
Kuwait	UK Great Britain	24 May 60	412UNTS4	105923
Afghanistan	Czechoslovakia	28 May 60	497UNTS129	107266
Luxembourg	Tunisia	13 Jun 60	497UNTS143	107267
Denmark	Peru	22 Jun 60	439UNTS113	106326
Ireland	Portugal	24 Jun 60	412UNTS30	105924
Poland	UK Great Britain	02 Jul 60	385UNTS87	105532
Switzerland	United Arab Rep	14 Jul 60	497UNTS161	107268
Germany, West	Pakistan	20 Jul 60	465UNTS41	106721

PARTY ONE	PARTY TWO	DATE	CITATION	NUMBER
Permit designation (Cont.)				
Ghana	Netherlands	30 Jul 60	412UNTS51	105925
Mexico	USA (United States)	15 Aug 60	402UNTS177	105786
Belgium	Burma	17 Aug 60	540UNTS185	107850
Ghana	United Arab Rep	29 Aug 60	412UNTS71	105926
Czechoslovakia	India	19 Sep 60	465UNTS67	106722
Belgium	Jordan	19 Oct 60	479UNTS277	106959
Hungary	UK Great Britain	25 Oct 60	419UNTS309	106034
Burma	Switzerland	31 Oct 60	465UNTS97	106723
Norway	Peru	02 Nov 60	497UNTS207	107270
Australia	Italy	10 Nov 60	497UNTS247	107271
Indonesia	UK Great Britain	23 Nov 60	398UNTS71	105718
Canada	Pakistan	21 Dec 60	465UNTS115	106724
Luxembourg	Thailand	29 Dec 60	465UNTS131	106725
Jordan	Sweden	09 Jan 61	465UNTS155	106726
Sudan	UK Great Britain	16 Jan 61	424UNTS233	106112
Norway	Poland	17 Jan 61	412UNTS130	105928
Germany, West	Japan	18 Jan 61	465UNTS173	106727
Cuba	Czechoslovakia	04 Mar 61	465UNTS209	106728
Poland	Switzerland	18 May 61	559UNTS233	108161
Czechoslovakia	Morocco	08 Jun 61	497UNTS275	107272
New Zealand	UK Great Britain	13 Jun 61	497UNTS293	107273
Cameroon	France	16 Jun 61	412UNTS148	105929
Guinea	Sweden	17 Jun 61	465UNTS236	106729
Czechoslovakia	Ghana	02 Aug 61	465UNTS249	106730
Finland	Luxembourg	15 Aug 61	541UNTS45	107859
Jordan	Norway	21 Aug 61	465UNTS275	106731
Mexico	Netherlands	24 Aug 61	465UNTS291	106732
Jordan	Netherlands	24 Aug 61	466UNTS3	106733
Liberia	Switzerland	31 Aug 61	559UNTS215	108160
Ghana	Romania	30 Sep 61	467UNTS443	106769
Germany, West	Morocco	12 Oct 61	523UNTS289	107562
Cyprus	Greece	23 Nov 61	497UNTS311	107274
Czechoslovakia	Mali	27 Nov 61	466UNTS41	106736
Czechoslovakia	Guinea	16 Dec 61	559UNTS49	108154
Netherlands	Sweden	08 Jan 62	466UNTS65	106737
Austria	Greece	15 Jan 62	498UNTS3	107275
Indonesia	Japan	23 Jan 62	559UNTS77	108155
Italy	Japan	31 Jan 62	498UNTS23	107276
Luxembourg	South Africa	31 Jan 62	563UNTS153	108209
Finland	Hungary	13 Feb 62	463UNTS61	106693
Germany, West	Thailand	05 Mar 62	563UNTS165	108210
Luxembourg	Spain	26 Mar 62	563UNTS205	108211
France	Luxembourg	29 Mar 62	563UNTS227	108212
Sierra Leone	UK Great Britain	05 Apr 62	434UNTS227	106265
Ghana	USSR (Soviet Union)	06 Apr 62	498UNTS41	107277
Japan	United Arab Rep	10 May 62	498UNTS69	107278
France	Romania	18 May 62	498UNTS115	107279
France	Senegal	15 Jun 62	524UNTS3	107563
Czechoslovakia	Senegal	20 Jun 62	498UNTS145	107280
Guinea	Norway	21 Jun 62	466UNTS81	106738
Liberia	Norway	29 Jun 62	466UNTS95	106739
Morocco	Switzerland	05 Jul 62	498UNTS171	107281
Ecuador	Germany, West	20 Sep 62	498UNTS199	107283
Japan	Kuwait	06 Oct 62	498UNTS235	107284
Finland	France	12 Oct 62	498UNTS299	107285
Hungary	Syria	18 Oct 62	491UNTS209	107178
Netherlands	Norway	18 Oct 62	466UNTS145	106741
France	Ivory Coast	19 Oct 62	498UNTS317	107286
Poland	Syria	10 Nov 62	491UNTS228	107179
Ivory Coast	Switzerland	17 Nov 62	499UNTS3	107289
Ghana	Tunisia	11 Dec 62	563UNTS243	108213
Syria	United Arab Rep	27 Dec 62	491UNTS245	107180
Ghana	Mali	09 Jan 63	466UNTS165	106742
Senegal	Switzerland	23 Jan 63	524UNTS23	107564
Guinea	Switzerland	01 Feb 63	499UNTS35	107291

PARTY ONE	PARTY TWO	DATE	CITATION	NUMBER
Permit designation (Cont.)				
Mali	Senegal	07 Feb 63	524UNTS41	107565
Algeria	France	18 Feb 63	563UNTS263	108214
Sudan	Switzerland	18 Feb 63	563UNTS281	108215
Cyprus	Denmark	27 Apr 63	529UNTS255	107664
Greece	Hungary	27 Apr 63	534UNTS3	107750
Algeria	Morocco	30 Apr 63	564UNTS3	108217
Portugal	South Africa	07 May 63	499UNTS49	107292
Finland	Poland	10 Jun 63	503UNTS179	107343
Guinea	Ivory Coast	26 Jun 63	499UNTS71	107293
Austria	France	12 Jul 63	499UNTS91	107294
Taiwan	Luxembourg	19 Jul 63	564UNTS23	108218
Algeria	Mali	22 Jul 63	564UNTS29	108219
Cameroon	Israel	09 Aug 63	499UNTS121	107295
Pakistan	USSR (Soviet Union)	07 Oct 63	499UNTS161	107297
Ivory Coast	Netherlands	09 Oct 63	499UNTS141	107296
Mali	Niger	15 Jan 64	499UNTS197	107299
Denmark	Yugoslavia	11 Feb 64	511UNTS241	107437
France	New Zealand	27 Feb 64	499UNTS191	107298
Cameroon	Mali	17 Mar 64	524UNTS61	107566
Malaysia	Netherlands	07 Apr 64	524UNTS81	107567
United Arab Rep	USA (United States)	05 May 64	531UNTS229	107706
New Zealand	USA (United States)	24 Jun 64	524UNTS101	107568
Ivory Coast	Mali	09 Jul 64	524UNTS121	107569
Argentina	UK Great Britain	12 Jan 65	597UNTS177	108645
Finland	UK Great Britain	25 Mar 65	539UNTS103	107826
Denmark	Malaysia	26 Mar 65	540UNTS205	107851
Ghana	Malawi	04 May 65	541UNTS163	107869
Denmark	Spain	05 May 65	543UNTS255	107905
Portugal	UK Great Britain	17 Apr 66	573UNTS223	108335
Romania	USSR (Soviet Union)	21 Jun 66	604UNTS81	108746
Denmark	Singapore	20 Dec 66	593UNTS125	108580
Belgium	Hungary	20 Mar 67	601UNTS37	108686
Goods in transit				
Saudi Arabia	UK Great Britain	20 Apr 42	10UNTS151	200058
Denmark	Yugoslavia	28 Jun 47	78UNTS242	101020
Multilateral		19 May 56	399UNTS189	105742
Multilateral		14 Dec 59	422UNTS75	106069
Czechoslovakia	Yugoslavia	22 Oct 62	480UNTS267	106974
Transport of goods				
Canada	France	12 May 33	253UNTS285	200545
Bolivia	Brazil	25 Feb 38	51UNTS245	200192
UK Great Britain	USSR (Soviet Union)	16 Aug 41	91UNTS341	200269
Saudi Arabia	UK Great Britain	20 Apr 42	10UNTS151	200058
UK Great Britain	USSR (Soviet Union)	22 Jun 42	91UNTS355	200270
Mexico	USA (United States)	18 Nov 42	120UNTS183	200392
Spain	USA (United States)	02 Dec 44	89UNTS345	200262
Australia	USA (United States)	08 Mar 45	121UNTS205	200400
France	UK Great Britain	27 Mar 45	98UNTS227	200274
Iceland	USA (United States)	11 Apr 45	16UNTS241	200105
Argentina	USA (United States)	09 May 45	139UNTS227	200453
Norway	USA (United States)	29 May 45	34UNTS371	200180
Poland	Yugoslavia	23 Nov 45	115UNTS3	101555
Sweden	USA (United States)	04 Dec 45	6UNTS273	100080
France	USA (United States)	07 Feb 46	3UNTS239	100034
Netherlands	USA (United States)	09 Feb 46	3UNTS247	100035
UK Great Britain	USA (United States)	01 Mar 46	3UNTS293	100037
Albania	Yugoslavia	01 Jul 46	111UNTS3	101517
Denmark	USSR (Soviet Union)	17 Aug 46	8UNTS201	100124
Romania	USSR (Soviet Union)	20 Feb 47	226UNTS79	103110
Poland	Yugoslavia	24 May 47	115UNTS37	101557
Albania	Yugoslavia	22 Jun 47	111UNTS207	101536
Sweden	USA (United States)	24 Jun 47	36UNTS25	100565
Hungary	USSR (Soviet Union)	15 Jul 47	216UNTS247	102940
Multilateral		30 Oct 47	55UNTS188	100814

PARTY ONE	PARTY TWO	DATE	CITATION	NUMBER
Transport of goods (Cont.)				
Poland	Yugoslavia	07 Nov 47	115UNTS137	101561
Finland	USSR (Soviet Union)	01 Dec 47	217UNTS3	102942
Czechoslovakia	USSR (Soviet Union)	11 Dec 47	217UNTS35	102943
Peru	UK Great Britain	22 Dec 47	72UNTS143	100932
Philippines	UK Great Britain	07 Jan 48	28UNTS63	100420
Multilateral		06 Mar 48	289UNTS3	104214
Switzerland	USSR (Soviet Union)	17 Mar 48	217UNTS73	102944
Hungary	Yugoslavia	18 Mar 48	113UNTS141	101550
Bulgaria	USSR (Soviet Union)	01 Apr 48	217UNTS97	102946
Poland	Yugoslavia	12 Apr 48	115UNTS167	101563
Czechoslovakia	Yugoslavia	24 May 48	112UNTS111	101542
Luxembourg	UK Great Britain	27 May 48	53UNTS115	100776
Luxembourg	Netherlands	23 Jun 48	32UNTS229	100500
Multilateral		18 Aug 48	33UNTS181	100518
Czechoslovakia	Poland	12 Nov 48	84UNTS347	101141
Italy	USSR (Soviet Union)	11 Dec 48	217UNTS181	102948
Argentina	Denmark	14 Dec 48	74UNTS41	100956
Poland	UK Great Britain	14 Jan 49	83UNTS3	101100
Poland	Yugoslavia	16 Jan 49	115UNTS241	101564
Czechoslovakia	Yugoslavia	01 Mar 49	113UNTS3	101547
Italy	Spain	31 May 49	231UNTS251	103224
Multilateral		16 Jun 49	45UNTS149	100696
Czechoslovakia	Poland	02 Jul 49	260UNTS179	103709
Czechoslovakia	Poland	02 Jul 49	260UNTS149	103708
Multilateral		19 Sep 49	125UNTS3	101671
USA (United States)	Yugoslavia	24 Dec 49	89UNTS209	101219
Afghanistan	India	04 Apr 50	167UNTS105	102201
Multilateral		13 May 50	128UNTS171	101719
India	Nepal	31 Jul 50	104UNTS3	101430
Denmark	Poland	01 Oct 50	81UNTS43	101061
France	UK Great Britain	06 Oct 50	96UNTS63	101331
Iceland	Ireland	02 Dec 50	558UNTS231	108143
Norway	UK Great Britain	15 Dec 50	106UNTS87	101459
Finland	Ireland	06 Jan 51	558UNTS120	108140
India	USA (United States)	09 Jul 51	147UNTS43	101927
El Salvador	Guatemala	14 Dec 51	131UNTS131	101740
Ireland	Switzerland	26 Dec 51	558UNTS305	108149
Multilateral		10 Jan 52	163UNTS27	102139
Ireland	Portugal	06 Feb 52	558UNTS289	108147
Belgium	France	21 Mar 52	137UNTS249	101856
Belgium	France	30 Jun 52	137UNTS259	101857
Greece	Israel	22 Jul 52	219UNTS231	102978
Germany, West	Greece	28 Jul 52	182UNTS85	102424
Netherlands	Peru	22 Sep 52	255UNTS49	103604
Multilateral		25 Oct 52	241UNTS336	103442
Lebanon	Sweden	23 Mar 53	255UNTS83	103605
Turkey	Yugoslavia	16 Apr 53	255UNTS99	103606
France	Netherlands	20 Jun 53	187UNTS97	102503
Pakistan	USA (United States)	25 Jun 53	205UNTS139	102773
Ireland	Italy	27 Jul 53	558UNTS237	108144
Ceylon (Sri Lanka)	Ireland	20 Nov 53	345UNTS189	104967
Lebanon	Switzerland	03 Mar 54	255UNTS127	103608
Canada	Japan	31 Mar 54	236UNTS329	103334
Canada	Spain	26 May 54	391UNTS273	105632
Canada	Portugal	28 May 54	391UNTS253	105631
Peru	USA (United States)	07 Feb 55	241UNTS63	103424
Multilateral		12 Mar 55	211UNTS3	102844
Haiti	USA (United States)	01 Apr 55	261UNTS361	103734
Austria	Romania	11 May 55	342UNTS119	104904
Afghanistan	USSR (Soviet Union)	28 Jun 55	240UNTS253	103407
Italy	USA (United States)	30 Jun 55	258UNTS15	103667
Thailand	USA (United States)	09 Sep 55	264UNTS285	103799
Austria	USSR (Soviet Union)	17 Oct 55	240UNTS289	103409
Austria	Italy	22 Oct 55	260UNTS327	103716
Burma	China People's Rep	08 Nov 55	306UNTS11	104430

Transport of goods (Cont.)

PARTY ONE	PARTY TWO	DATE	CITATION	NUMBER
Austria	USSR (Soviet Union)	09 Nov 55	255UNTS247	103613
Syria	USSR (Soviet Union)	16 Nov 55	259UNTS71	103683
Costa Rica	Guatemala	20 Dec 55	280UNTS121	104056
Multilateral		21 Dec 55	292UNTS63	104267
France	Japan	17 Jan 56	255UNTS275	103614
Japan	USA (United States)	10 Feb 56	275UNTS105	103979
Italy	USA (United States)	27 Feb 56	291UNTS287	104260
Canada	USSR (Soviet Union)	29 Feb 56	252UNTS165	103566
Norway	Sweden	09 Mar 56	369UNTS285	105262
Italy	USA (United States)	27 Apr 56	273UNTS149	103949
Peru	USA (United States)	08 May 56	278UNTS117	104028
Multilateral		19 May 56	399UNTS189	105742
Italy	South Africa	21 May 56	255UNTS323	103616
Ceylon (Sri Lanka)	Hungary	04 Jun 56	315UNTS13	104555
Multilateral		16 Aug 56	287UNTS223	104188
Guatemala	Honduras	22 Aug 56	263UNTS49	103767
Finland	USSR (Soviet Union)	14 Sep 56	255UNTS365	103618
Japan	USA (United States)	23 Nov 56	324UNTS177	104685
Multilateral		14 Dec 56	436UNTS131	106293
Austria	USSR (Soviet Union)	14 Jun 57	285UNTS169	104152
Peru	USA (United States)	19 Jul 57	289UNTS271	104223
Italy	Switzerland	19 Sep 57	363UNTS69	105200
Germany, East	USSR (Soviet Union)	27 Sep 57	292UNTS75	104268
Multilateral		30 Sep 57	619UNTS77	108940
Netherlands	Sweden	23 Oct 57	306UNTS75	104433
Denmark	Netherlands	13 Nov 57	306UNTS67	104432
Japan	USSR (Soviet Union)	06 Dec 57	325UNTS35	104694
India	Japan	04 Feb 58	324UNTS215	104687
Greece	India	14 Feb 58	609UNTS94	108827
Albania	USSR (Soviet Union)	15 Feb 58	313UNTS261	104536
Austria	Sweden	18 Feb 58	427UNTS349	106166
Bulgaria	Yugoslavia	21 Mar 58	386UNTS119	105541
China People's Rep	USSR (Soviet Union)	23 Apr 58	313UNTS135	104534
Japan	Poland	26 Apr 58	340UNTS221	104866
Belgium	Sweden	08 May 58	312UNTS145	104516
Austria	Belgium	20 Jun 58	312UNTS95	104513
Denmark	El Salvador	09 Jul 58	341UNTS289	104892
United Arab Rep	USSR (Soviet Union)	18 Sep 58	338UNTS29	104831
Iraq	USSR (Soviet Union)	11 Oct 58	328UNTS95	104730
Multilateral		05 Nov 58	428UNTS73	106169
Czechoslovakia	Poland	25 Nov 58	372UNTS205	105299
Multilateral		15 Jan 59	348UNTS13	104996
Greece	Yugoslavia	18 Jun 59	368UNTS27	105234
India	Italy	06 Oct 59	378UNTS267	105427
Czechoslovakia	Germany, East	25 Nov 59	374UNTS101	105331
Italy	Netherlands	08 Dec 59	484UNTS309	107039
Multilateral		14 Dec 59	422UNTS75	106069
Czechoslovakia	Japan	15 Dec 59	383UNTS277	105505
Australia	Canada	12 Feb 60	369UNTS89	105253
Brazil	USA (United States)	27 Feb 60	384UNTS131	105515
Cuba	Japan	22 Apr 60	442UNTS261	106354
Belgium	Netherlands	20 Jun 60	423UNTS19	106084
Korea, South	USA (United States)	18 Nov 60	400UNTS49	105747
Cyprus	USA (United States)	08 Dec 60	405UNTS145	105831
Multilateral		09 Dec 60	429UNTS211	106200
Israel	USA (United States)	19 Dec 60	401UNTS195	105772
Multilateral		30 Dec 60	395UNTS241	105689
Finland	IAEA (Atom Energy)	30 Dec 60	395UNTS257	105690
Brazil	USA (United States)	17 Mar 61	406UNTS241	105853
Multilateral		10 Apr 61	402UNTS281	105791
USA (United States)	Yugoslavia	19 Apr 61	409UNTS163	105883
Turkey	USSR (Soviet Union)	27 Apr 61	420UNTS307	106047
Somalia	USSR (Soviet Union)	02 Jun 61	493UNTS173	107214
Iraq	Syria	03 Nov 61	489UNTS45	107134
Ghana	USSR (Soviet Union)	04 Nov 61	437UNTS213	106308

Transport of goods (Cont.)

PARTY ONE	PARTY TWO	DATE	CITATION	NUMBER
Cyprus	USA (United States)	15 Jan 62	435UNTS15	106267
Hungary	Yugoslavia	09 Feb 62	577UNTS3	108370
Germany, West	Greece	08 Mar 62	533UNTS269	107747
Congo (Zaire)	IAEA (Atom Energy)	27 Jun 62	463UNTS31	106691
Multilateral		27 Jun 62	463UNTS17	106690
Morocco	Switzerland	05 Jul 62	498UNTS189	107282
IAEA (Atom Energy)	USA (United States)	20 Aug 62	456UNTS447	106570
Czechoslovakia	Yugoslavia	22 Oct 62	480UNTS267	106974
Japan	UK Great Britain	14 Nov 62	478UNTS29	106934
Czechoslovakia	Poland	16 Nov 62	526UNTS3	107597
Poland	USSR (Soviet Union)	22 Apr 63	493UNTS229	107217
IAEA (Atom Energy)	Yugoslavia	04 Jun 63	490UNTS343	107163
Austria	IAEA (Atom Energy)	21 Jun 63	490UNTS351	107164
Finland	IAEA (Atom Energy)	02 Jul 63	490UNTS403	107167
El Salvador	Japan	19 Jul 63	518UNTS135	107494
Finland	IAEA (Atom Energy)	30 Jul 63	490UNTS413	107168
Tanganyika	USSR (Soviet Union)	14 Aug 63	493UNTS195	107215
Algeria	Tunisia	01 Sep 63	601UNTS275	108701
Brazil	Germany, West	30 Nov 63	0UNTS0	109426
Multilateral		18 Dec 63	490UNTS383	107166
Mexico	IAEA (Atom Energy)	18 Dec 63	490UNTS361	107165
Romania	Yugoslavia	25 Dec 63	576UNTS95	108366
Austria	Romania	27 May 64	588UNTS29	108517
Multilateral		15 Jun 64	573UNTS85	108324
IAEA (Atom Energy)	United Arab Rep	17 Sep 64	525UNTS19	107581
Czechoslovakia	Hungary	17 Oct 64	545UNTS21	107924
Greece	Yugoslavia	05 Nov 64	539UNTS19	107821
Hungary	Poland	18 Jul 65	577UNTS161	108376
IAEA (Atom Energy)	Uruguay	24 Sep 65	556UNTS117	108123
Morocco	IAEA (Atom Energy)	24 Sep 65	556UNTS109	108122
Afghanistan	IAEA (Atom Energy)	24 Sep 65	556UNTS101	108121
Multilateral		24 Sep 65	556UNTS141	108124
Multilateral		18 Nov 65	609UNTS115	108830
Burma	Czechoslovakia	15 Dec 65	602UNTS71	108707
Belgium	Denmark	04 Feb 66	561UNTS233	108187
IAEA (Atom Energy)	Turkey	08 Feb 66	573UNTS75	108323
France	Romania	14 Mar 66	604UNTS33	108741
Austria	Spain	24 Mar 66	590UNTS203	108555
Romania	IAEA (Atom Energy)	22 Apr 66	603UNTS23	108721
UK Great Britain	USA (United States)	02 Jun 66	573UNTS229	108336
Bel-Lux Econ Union	Bulgaria	14 Jun 66	601UNTS167	108694
Belgium	Bulgaria	14 Jun 66	607UNTS183	108806
Multilateral		20 Jun 66	573UNTS41	108322
Mexico	IAEA (Atom Energy)	20 Jun 66	573UNTS25	108321
Romania	USSR (Soviet Union)	21 Jun 66	604UNTS81	108746
Belgium	Spain	19 Jul 66	575UNTS3	108352
Bulgaria	United Arab Rep	29 Aug 66	630UNTS325	108980
Netherlands	Yugoslavia	08 Sep 66	597UNTS147	108643
Philippines	IAEA (Atom Energy)	28 Sep 66	589UNTS25	108533
India	IAEA (Atom Energy)	09 Dec 66	603UNTS35	108722
UK Great Britain	USA (United States)	30 Dec 66	603UNTS245	108736
Czechoslovakia	USSR (Soviet Union)	03 Feb 67	617UNTS267	108917
Argentina	Uruguay	12 Feb 67	635UNTS125	109076
Romania	Sweden	01 Mar 67	642UNTS163	109172
Belgium	Hungary	20 Mar 67	601UNTS37	108686
Austria	Yugoslavia	26 Apr 67	603UNTS143	108731
Iran	IAEA (Atom Energy)	10 May 67	614UNTS93	108865
IAEA (Atom Energy)	USA (United States)	07 Jun 67	614UNTS109	108866
Mexico	IAEA (Atom Energy)	18 Aug 67	614UNTS123	108867
Mexico	IAEA (Atom Energy)	23 Aug 67	614UNTS133	108868
Denmark	Romania	29 Aug 67	0UNTS0	109231
Austria	Czechoslovakia	19 Oct 67	634UNTS19	109048
Finland	France	27 Oct 67	643UNTS75	109185
Finland	Hungary	10 Nov 67	643UNTS95	109186
Eur Space Research	UK Great Britain	24 Nov 67	638UNTS17	109129

PARTY ONE	PARTY TWO	DATE	CITATION	NUMBER
Transport of goods (Cont.)				
Belgium	Poland	30 Oct 68	0UNTS0	109597
Air transport				
Brazil	France	27 Jan 40	72UNTS77	100929
Canada	USA (United States)	04 Mar 42	124UNTS271	200426
Canada	USA (United States)	10 Sep 42	101UNTS221	200296
Canada	USA (United States)	04 Mar 43	13UNTS411	200087
Spain	USA (United States)	02 Dec 44	89UNTS345	200262
Multilateral		07 Dec 44	171UNTS345	200501
Multilateral		07 Dec 44	171UNTS387	200502
Multilateral		15 Dec 44	16UNTS247	200106
Denmark	USA (United States)	16 Dec 44	10UNTS213	200063
Sweden	USA (United States)	16 Dec 44	6UNTS397	200041
Ethiopia	UK Great Britain	19 Dec 44	93UNTS303	200272
Iceland	USA (United States)	27 Jan 45	122UNTS293	200411
Ireland	USA (United States)	03 Feb 45	122UNTS305	200412
Canada	USA (United States)	17 Feb 45	122UNTS261	200409
Iceland	USA (United States)	11 Apr 45	16UNTS241	200105
Switzerland	USA (United States)	03 Aug 45	51UNTS233	200191
Norway	USA (United States)	06 Oct 45	122UNTS319	200413
Sweden	USA (United States)	04 Dec 45	6UNTS273	100080
Portugal	USA (United States)	06 Dec 45	3UNTS139	100028
France	USA (United States)	29 Dec 45	139UNTS105	101878
Multilateral		01 Jan 46	99UNTS131	101375
Czechoslovakia	USA (United States)	03 Jan 46	6UNTS309	100084
Denmark	France	04 Jan 46	27UNTS169	100406
Turkey	USA (United States)	12 Feb 46	13UNTS3	100196
France	UK Great Britain	28 Feb 46	27UNTS173	100407
Denmark	USA (United States)	21 Mar 46	3UNTS301	100038
Greece	USA (United States)	27 Mar 46	15UNTS233	100239
France	USA (United States)	27 Mar 46	139UNTS114	101879
Belgium	USA (United States)	05 Apr 46	4UNTS125	100041
Netherlands	Portugal	12 Apr 46	4UNTS317	100054
Argentina	UK Great Britain	17 Apr 46	164UNTS53	102159
Ireland	Sweden	29 May 46	35UNTS231	100557
Portugal	USA (United States)	30 May 46	174UNTS187	102285
United Arab Rep	USA (United States)	15 Jun 46	71UNTS157	100917
United Arab Rep	USA (United States)	15 Jun 46	151UNTS135	101988
Sweden	Turkey	26 Jun 46	14UNTS21	100208
Canada	Newfoundland	29 Jul 46	17UNTS169	100275
France	Sweden	02 Aug 46	27UNTS251	100410
Lebanon	USA (United States)	11 Aug 46	66UNTS211	100856
Brazil	USA (United States)	06 Sep 46	54UNTS197	100805
Belgium	Portugal	22 Oct 46	34UNTS49	100527
Brazil	UK Great Britain	31 Oct 46	11UNTS115	100152
Philippines	USA (United States)	16 Nov 46	7UNTS151	100097
Sweden	UK Great Britain	27 Nov 46	11UNTS229	100162
Australia	USA (United States)	03 Dec 46	7UNTS201	100100
New Zealand	USA (United States)	03 Dec 46	7UNTS175	100099
Portugal	Switzerland	09 Dec 46	310UNTS251	104495
Brazil	Portugal	10 Dec 46	200UNTS67	102695
USA (United States)	Uruguay	14 Dec 46	532UNTS87	107713
Taiwan	USA (United States)	20 Dec 46	22UNTS87	100332
Peru	USA (United States)	27 Dec 46	152UNTS93	102013
Ecuador	USA (United States)	08 Jan 47	22UNTS119	100333
Czechoslovakia	Ireland	29 Jan 47	27UNTS267	100411
Netherlands	Thailand	30 Jan 47	247UNTS353	103480
USSR (Soviet Union)	Yugoslavia	04 Feb 47	130UNTS235	101731
Thailand	USA (United States)	26 Feb 47	16UNTS17	100246
Portugal	Sweden	06 Mar 47	35UNTS243	100558
Canada	USA (United States)	12 Apr 47	122UNTS229	101648
Syria	USA (United States)	28 Apr 47	262UNTS121	103741
Chile	USA (United States)	10 May 47	55UNTS21	100807
Multilateral		27 May 47	418UNTS161	106021
Ireland	USA (United States)	03 Jun 47	16UNTS151	100255

PARTY ONE	PARTY TWO	DATE	CITATION	NUMBER
Air transport (Cont.)				
Italy	USA (United States)	09 Jun 47	104UNTS157	101437
France	UK Great Britain	18 Jun 47	9UNTS203	100134
Norway	Sweden	21 Jun 47	94UNTS107	101309
Iraq	Turkey	30 Jun 47	72UNTS107	100930
Romania	Yugoslavia	30 Jun 47	116UNTS57	101569
France	India	16 Jul 47	27UNTS325	100415
Greece	Turkey	22 Jul 47	72UNTS131	100931
Taiwan	UK Great Britain	23 Jul 47	9UNTS207	100135
Multilateral		04 Aug 47	28UNTS41	100418
Hungary	Poland	28 Aug 47	15UNTS145	100231
Czechoslovakia	Switzerland	10 Sep 47	35UNTS275	100559
Sweden	Yugoslavia	06 Oct 47	53UNTS107	100775
Ecuador	USA (United States)	27 Oct 47	44UNTS45	100677
Bolivia	USA (United States)	03 Nov 47	51UNTS33	100750
Brazil	Netherlands	06 Nov 47	53UNTS59	100773
Norway	Portugal	11 Nov 47	34UNTS257	100542
Brazil	Denmark	14 Nov 47	47UNTS39	100722
Brazil	Sweden	14 Nov 47	94UNTS139	101310
Burma	Pakistan	18 Nov 47	35UNTS321	100562
Denmark	Ireland	18 Nov 47	35UNTS309	100561
Austria	Netherlands	22 Jan 48	17UNTS99	100270
Canada	New Zealand	12 Mar 48	231UNTS219	103222
Czechoslovakia	Yugoslavia	14 Mar 48	28UNTS81	100421
New Zealand	USA (United States)	16 Mar 48	127UNTS133	101703
Argentina	Denmark	18 Mar 48	94UNTS175	101311
USA (United States)	Venezuela	24 Mar 48	44UNTS57	100678
Pakistan	Sweden	06 May 48	36UNTS3	100564
Ireland	Switzerland	06 May 48	334UNTS187	104768
Denmark	USA (United States)	06 May 48	26UNTS55	100377
Jordan	Turkey	07 May 48	32UNTS313	100505
Ireland	Netherlands	10 May 48	28UNTS121	100422
India	Sweden	21 May 48	34UNTS285	100543
Luxembourg	UK Great Britain	27 May 48	53UNTS115	100776
Argentina	Brazil	02 Jun 48	0UNTS0	109515
Pakistan	USA (United States)	16 Jun 48	235UNTS29	103293
Multilateral		19 Jun 48	310UNTS151	104492
Australia	Italy	02 Aug 48	28UNTS165	100424
Brazil	Switzerland	10 Aug 48	94UNTS269	101314
Iceland	ICAO (Civil Aviat)	16 Sep 48	28UNTS267	100429
Bolivia	USA (United States)	29 Sep 48	505UNTS139	107370
Netherlands	Spain	08 Oct 48	28UNTS209	100426
Netherlands	UK Great Britain	15 Oct 48	74UNTS3	100955
Belgium	USA (United States)	28 Oct 48	173UNTS67	102262
Argentina	Sweden	20 Nov 48	197UNTS47	102633
Argentina	Chile	14 Dec 48	635UNTS21	109071
Argentina	Denmark	15 Dec 48	67UNTS71	100866
Argentina	Netherlands	15 Jan 49	46UNTS241	100713
Italy	Lebanon	24 Jan 49	231UNTS241	103223
Switzerland	Turkey	16 Feb 49	72UNTS175	100933
Finland	Netherlands	25 Feb 49	53UNTS123	100777
Netherlands	Switzerland	07 Mar 49	35UNTS69	100551
Argentina	UK Great Britain	14 Mar 49	83UNTS193	101108
Austria	USA (United States)	23 Mar 49	43UNTS127	100667
Finland	USA (United States)	29 Mar 49	55UNTS59	100808
Sweden	UK Great Britain	30 Mar 49	209UNTS129	102826
Finland	Sweden	26 Apr 49	95UNTS83	101318
Canada	USA (United States)	04 Jun 49	122UNTS237	101649
Canada	USA (United States)	04 Jun 49	200UNTS201	102704
Norway	USA (United States)	13 Jun 49	127UNTS189	101705
Belgium	Greece	21 Jun 49	137UNTS215	101854
Korea, South	USA (United States)	29 Jun 49	55UNTS79	100809
Iraq	Norway	12 Jul 49	53UNTS137	100778
Czechoslovakia	Finland	13 Jul 49	53UNTS153	100779
Dominican Republic	USA (United States)	19 Jul 49	51UNTS145	100762
Pakistan	UK Great Britain	27 Jul 49	44UNTS199	100685

PARTY ONE	PARTY TWO	DATE	CITATION	NUMBER
Air transport (Cont.)				
Argentina	Canada	06 Aug 49	231UNTS43	103202
Multilateral		12 Aug 49	75UNTS31	100970
Canada	UK Great Britain	19 Aug 49	44UNTS223	100686
Finland	Norway	24 Aug 49	53UNTS167	100780
Denmark	Finland	26 Aug 49	53UNTS191	100781
Ireland	USA (United States)	13 Sep 49	127UNTS89	101701
Multilateral		15 Sep 49	53UNTS235	100783
Belgium	United Arab Rep	19 Sep 49	137UNTS189	101853
Lebanon	Netherlands	20 Sep 49	108UNTS205	101474
Greece	Philippines	08 Oct 49	187UNTS221	102515
Multilateral		27 Oct 49	53UNTS241	100784
Iran	Netherlands	31 Oct 49	254UNTS257	103596
Denmark	Pakistan	09 Nov 49	44UNTS255	100687
Denmark	Thailand	23 Nov 49	53UNTS255	100786
Sweden	Thailand	23 Nov 49	72UNTS217	100935
Norway	Thailand	26 Nov 49	53UNTS269	100787
Brazil	Spain	28 Nov 49	215UNTS303	102923
Austria	Denmark	02 Dec 49	53UNTS281	100788
Austria	Norway	02 Dec 49	72UNTS230	100936
Netherlands	United Arab Rep	08 Dec 49	95UNTS123	101320
Sweden	United Arab Rep	12 Dec 49	108UNTS15	101466
Austria	Switzerland	19 Dec 49	254UNTS287	103597
Finland	Sweden	21 Dec 49	197UNTS243	102642
USA (United States)	Yugoslavia	24 Dec 49	89UNTS209	101219
Greece	USA (United States)	20 Feb 50	196UNTS291	102630
Ceylon (Sri Lanka)	Thailand	24 Feb 50	72UNTS261	100938
Italy	Netherlands	04 Mar 50	254UNTS305	103598
Norway	United Arab Rep	11 Mar 50	95UNTS157	101321
Denmark	United Arab Rep	14 Mar 50	95UNTS197	101322
Philippines	USA (United States)	16 Mar 50	89UNTS199	101218
Iceland	Netherlands	22 Mar 50	95UNTS237	101323
Denmark	UK Great Britain	27 Mar 50	68UNTS117	100891
Italy	Portugal	05 Apr 50	254UNTS329	103599
Sweden	UK Great Britain	05 Apr 50	99UNTS107	101374
Turkey	United Arab Rep	12 Apr 50	128UNTS3	101711
Australia	Philippines	14 Apr 50	127UNTS281	101709
Greece	United Arab Rep	24 Apr 50	163UNTS229	102149
Switzerland	United Arab Rep	15 May 50	95UNTS255	101325
Israel	USA (United States)	13 Jun 50	212UNTS93	102863
Netherlands	Spain	20 Jun 50	95UNTS303	101327
Denmark	Switzerland	22 Jun 50	96UNTS3	101328
Argentina	USA (United States)	20 Jul 50	89UNTS63	101209
Ceylon (Sri Lanka)	UK Great Britain	26 Jul 50	337UNTS77	104818
Spain	Switzerland	03 Aug 50	254UNTS365	103600
France	United Arab Rep	08 Aug 50	127UNTS293	101710
Burma	Sweden	14 Sep 50	96UNTS45	101330
Brazil	Turkey	21 Sep 50	150UNTS299	101981
Ceylon (Sri Lanka)	United Arab Rep	26 Sep 50	192UNTS53	102595
France	UK Great Britain	06 Oct 50	96UNTS63	101331
Luxembourg	Portugal	21 Oct 50	108UNTS67	101468
Israel	Netherlands	23 Oct 50	189UNTS89	102543
Taiwan	Philippines	23 Oct 50	215UNTS159	102918
Thailand	UK Great Britain	10 Nov 50	96UNTS77	101332
Greece	UK Great Britain	16 Nov 50	166UNTS281	102193
Denmark	South Africa	30 Nov 50	84UNTS51	101118
France	Greece	09 Dec 50	166UNTS315	102196
Israel	Turkey	05 Feb 51	193UNTS3	102607
Colombia	Portugal	09 Mar 51	108UNTS87	101469
Greece	Yugoslavia	15 Mar 51	187UNTS237	102516
Canada	France	16 Mar 51	236UNTS267	103330
Canada	Sweden	06 Apr 51	197UNTS393	102648
Luxembourg	Switzerland	09 Apr 51	254UNTS389	103601
France	UK Great Britain	20 Apr 51	106UNTS81	101458
Netherlands	UK Great Britain	17 May 51	118UNTS103	101599
Switzerland	USA (United States)	24 May 51	127UNTS227	101706

PARTY ONE	PARTY TWO	DATE	CITATION	NUMBER
Air transport (Cont.)				
India	Netherlands	24 May 51	108UNTS151	101471
South Africa	Sweden	25 May 51	197UNTS425	102649
Denmark	Iran	18 Jun 51	255UNTS3	103602
Iceland	Norway	14 Jul 51	163UNTS265	102150
Greece	Netherlands	26 Jul 51	109UNTS103	101495
Burma	Denmark	30 Jul 51	108UNTS167	101472
Burma	Netherlands	06 Sep 51	108UNTS187	101473
Multilateral		08 Sep 51	136UNTS45	101832
Costa Rica	USA (United States)	11 Sep 51	234UNTS255	103288
Philippines	Spain	06 Oct 51	215UNTS193	102920
Greece	Luxembourg	22 Oct 51	187UNTS119	102506
Italy	UK Great Britain	24 Oct 51	118UNTS143	101602
Denmark	Iraq	18 Nov 51	232UNTS25	103227
Canada	South Africa	26 Nov 51	248UNTS107	103489
Colombia	Spain	11 Dec 51	216UNTS73	102933
Multilateral		20 Dec 51	163UNTS309	102152
Multilateral		20 Dec 51	163UNTS293	102151
Jordan	United Arab Rep	02 Jan 52	192UNTS157	102599
Taiwan	Korea, South	01 Mar 52	255UNTS35	103603
Finland	USA (United States)	03 Mar 52	177UNTS163	102317
Philippines	Switzerland	08 Mar 52	231UNTS301	103225
Belgium	Spain	10 Mar 52	178UNTS243	102342
Norway	Uruguay	20 Mar 52	310UNTS279	104496
Sweden	Uruguay	20 Mar 52	311UNTS3	104497
Libya	UK Great Britain	31 Mar 52	151UNTS69	101984
Iraq	Switzerland	31 Mar 52	311UNTS43	104498
France	Mexico	17 Apr 52	163UNTS321	102153
Belgium	Sweden	21 Apr 52	166UNTS9	102183
Netherlands	Sweden	25 Apr 52	163UNTS131	102147
Taiwan	Japan	28 Apr 52	138UNTS3	101858
Denmark	Japan	28 Apr 52	166UNTS3	102182
Switzerland	UK Great Britain	13 May 52	164UNTS91	102160
Iceland	Sweden	03 Jun 52	215UNTS223	102921
Australia	United Arab Rep	14 Jun 52	173UNTS241	102269
India	United Arab Rep	14 Jun 52	173UNTS209	102268
Denmark	UK Great Britain	23 Jun 52	151UNTS3	101982
Norway	UK Great Britain	23 Jun 52	151UNTS81	101985
Mexico	USA (United States)	15 Jul 52	181UNTS263	102416
Netherlands	Pakistan	17 Jul 52	150UNTS277	101980
Greece	Israel	22 Jul 52	215UNTS365	102924
Panama	USA (United States)	08 Aug 52	181UNTS257	102415
Japan	USA (United States)	11 Aug 52	212UNTS27	102862
Burma	Philippines	15 Aug 52	200UNTS97	102696
Netherlands	Peru	22 Sep 52	255UNTS49	103604
Mexico	Netherlands	13 Oct 52	163UNTS341	102154
Austria	Luxembourg	13 Oct 52	192UNTS291	102606
Iceland	Luxembourg	23 Oct 52	193UNTS39	102609
Burma	UK Great Britain	25 Oct 52	150UNTS237	101978
Luxembourg	Sweden	17 Nov 52	173UNTS277	102270
Israel	Switzerland	19 Nov 52	232UNTS3	103226
Israel	South Africa	24 Dec 52	207UNTS303	102813
Japan	UK Great Britain	29 Dec 52	175UNTS129	102299
South Africa	Sweden	09 Jan 53	173UNTS299	102271
Japan	Sweden	20 Feb 53	173UNTS307	102272
Japan	Norway	23 Feb 53	192UNTS191	102601
Denmark	Japan	26 Feb 53	173UNTS329	102273
Lebanon	Sweden	23 Mar 53	255UNTS83	103605
Turkey	Yugoslavia	16 Apr 53	255UNTS99	103606
Philippines	Thailand	27 Apr 53	174UNTS3	102274
Denmark	South Africa	30 Apr 53	174UNTS19	102275
Israel	UK Great Britain	13 May 53	175UNTS179	102300
Australia	USA (United States)	14 May 53	205UNTS253	102779
Cuba	USA (United States)	26 May 53	224UNTS75	103070
Japan	Thailand	19 Jun 53	174UNTS29	102276
Burma	Norway	22 Jun 53	174UNTS49	102277

PARTY ONE	PARTY TWO	DATE	CITATION	NUMBER
Air transport (Cont.)				
Greece	UK Great Britain	25 Jun 53	190UNTS281	102571
Italy	South Africa	26 Jun 53	211UNTS255	102857
USA (United States)	Venezuela	14 Aug 53	213UNTS99	102883
Belgium	New Zealand	01 Sep 53	192UNTS283	102605
Australia	Thailand	26 Oct 53	255UNTS117	103607
Korea, South	Netherlands	26 Oct 53	200UNTS103	102697
Netherlands	Switzerland	03 Nov 53	293UNTS53	104285
Cuba	USA (United States)	26 Nov 53	205UNTS213	102777
Italy	Netherlands	21 Dec 53	189UNTS25	102540
Ethiopia	Greece	20 Jan 54	222UNTS281	103035
Syria	UK Great Britain	30 Jan 54	449UNTS47	106452
Belgium	Finland	11 Feb 54	211UNTS63	102848
Lebanon	Switzerland	03 Mar 54	255UNTS127	103608
Finland	Netherlands	29 Mar 54	252UNTS185	103567
Peru	Spain	31 Mar 54	232UNTS65	103230
Japan	USA (United States)	16 Apr 54	238UNTS39	103354
Lebanon	Yugoslavia	17 Apr 54	602UNTS199	108713
France	South Africa	05 May 54	215UNTS401	102926
Switzerland	Syria	26 May 54	255UNTS145	103609
Greece	Sweden	27 May 54	219UNTS147	102971
Multilateral		14 Jun 54	320UNTS217	104644
Belgium	Greece	23 Jun 54	199UNTS43	102676
Laos	Thailand	07 Jul 54	200UNTS115	102698
Germany, West	USA (United States)	22 Jul 54	221UNTS351	103016
Germany, West	USA (United States)	22 Jul 54	239UNTS3	103369
Ireland	Luxembourg	27 Jul 54	232UNTS91	103231
Sweden	USA (United States)	06 Aug 54	221UNTS331	103014
Denmark	USA (United States)	06 Aug 54	222UNTS235	103030
Norway	USA (United States)	06 Aug 54	222UNTS261	103033
Norway	USA (United States)	06 Aug 54	222UNTS269	103034
Philippines	Sweden	20 Aug 54	200UNTS121	102699
South Africa	Switzerland	26 Aug 54	216UNTS19	102929
France	South Africa	17 Sep 54	216UNTS29	102930
Sweden	USSR (Soviet Union)	29 Sep 54	202UNTS259	102733
Switzerland	UK Great Britain	30 Sep 54	209UNTS197	102828
Ireland	Sweden	18 Oct 54	262UNTS259	103753
Denmark	Ireland	18 Oct 54	218UNTS295	102959
Ireland	Norway	18 Oct 54	553UNTS123	108077
Germany, West	UK Great Britain	18 Oct 54	218UNTS301	102960
Denmark	Philippines	20 Oct 54	216UNTS3	102927
Norway	Philippines	20 Oct 54	216UNTS11	102928
Canada	Ireland	28 Oct 54	304UNTS317	104406
France	South Africa	22 Nov 54	219UNTS35	102963
Pakistan	United Arab Rep	13 Dec 54	255UNTS167	103610
Ecuador	Netherlands	14 Dec 54	232UNTS115	103233
Norway	Switzerland	30 Dec 54	311UNTS147	104502
Switzerland	United Arab Rep	05 Jan 55	216UNTS41	102931
United Arab Rep	Yugoslavia	20 Feb 55	255UNTS199	103611
Iraq	United Arab Rep	23 Mar 55	311UNTS199	104504
Italy	USA (United States)	30 Mar 55	257UNTS169	103654
Denmark	Israel	04 Apr 55	213UNTS283	102891
Israel	Norway	24 May 55	220UNTS71	102990
Greece	Norway	25 May 55	423UNTS77	106085
Israel	Italy	10 Jun 55	280UNTS219	104061
Syria	United Arab Rep	03 Jul 55	393UNTS67	105652
Germany, West	UK Great Britain	22 Jul 55	269UNTS223	103882
Germany, East	Romania	28 Jul 55	342UNTS207	104909
USSR (Soviet Union)	Yugoslavia	03 Sep 55	240UNTS267	103408
Belgium	Ireland	10 Sep 55	255UNTS235	103612
Germany, East	Hungary	10 Sep 55	407UNTS132	105863
Iceland	Sweden	17 Sep 55	262UNTS273	103755
Multilateral		28 Sep 55	478UNTS371	106943
Multilateral		29 Sep 55	222UNTS313	103037
Canada	Denmark	30 Sep 55	258UNTS115	103675
France	Germany, West	04 Oct 55	353UNTS203	105044

PARTY ONE	PARTY TWO	DATE	CITATION	NUMBER
Air transport (Cont.)				
Denmark	Iceland	10 Oct 55	230UNTS3	103171
Finland	USSR (Soviet Union)	19 Oct 55	353UNTS185	105043
Denmark	Syria	20 Oct 55	250UNTS61	103518
Pakistan	Turkey	02 Nov 55	311UNTS217	104505
Australia	South Africa	04 Nov 55	232UNTS143	103234
South Africa	Switzerland	07 Nov 55	230UNTS279	103190
Austria	USSR (Soviet Union)	09 Nov 55	255UNTS247	103613
Austria	Israel	17 Nov 55	232UNTS153	103235
Belgium	France	10 Dec 55	231UNTS101	103211
France	Japan	17 Jan 56	255UNTS275	103614
Austria	Italy	23 Jan 56	393UNTS97	105653
Argentina	Switzerland	25 Jan 56	559UNTS121	108157
India	USA (United States)	03 Feb 56	272UNTS75	103932
Hungary	Romania	03 Feb 56	362UNTS233	105190
Austria	Poland	08 Feb 56	334UNTS221	104770
Netherlands	Sudan	12 Feb 56	311UNTS319	104508
Norway	Syria	25 Feb 56	463UNTS217	106706
Colombia	USA (United States)	27 Mar 56	273UNTS235	103954
Sweden	USSR (Soviet Union)	31 Mar 56	259UNTS239	103691
Norway	USSR (Soviet Union)	31 Mar 56	259UNTS205	103690
Bulgaria	Yugoslavia	04 Apr 56	391UNTS47	105616
Multilateral		30 Apr 56	310UNTS229	104494
Germany, West	Switzerland	02 May 56	559UNTS157	108158
Portugal	Venezuela	16 May 56	463UNTS239	106707
Italy	South Africa	21 May 56	255UNTS323	103616
Greece	Italy	26 May 56	496UNTS301	107258
Fed Rhod/Nyasaland	South Africa	30 May 56	255UNTS317	103615
Italy	Switzerland	04 Jun 56	378UNTS311	105429
Poland	Sweden	08 Jun 56	334UNTS257	104771
India	Thailand	12 Jun 56	255UNTS341	103617
Germany, West	Ireland	12 Jun 56	353UNTS121	105040
Israel	Sweden	17 Jun 56	257UNTS47	103648
Honduras	USA (United States)	25 Jun 56	279UNTS113	104036
Austria	UK Great Britain	20 Jul 56	269UNTS147	103880
Norway	Sweden	27 Sep 56	261UNTS71	103726
Germany, West	South Africa	28 Sep 56	327UNTS83	104718
Canada	South Africa	28 Sep 56	299UNTS17	104304
Switzerland	Thailand	13 Oct 56	312UNTS43	104510
Belgium	Poland	17 Oct 56	356UNTS279	105100
Colombia	USA (United States)	24 Oct 56	476UNTS77	106905
Austria	USA (United States)	25 Oct 56	299UNTS123	104310
Belgium	Turkey	25 Oct 56	380UNTS3	105447
Belgium	United Arab Rep	31 Oct 56	257UNTS235	103659
Australia	Netherlands	29 Nov 56	302UNTS141	104356
Belgium	Romania	04 Dec 56	317UNTS161	104602
Finland	USSR (Soviet Union)	07 Dec 56	258UNTS89	103673
Iceland	Thailand	22 Jan 57	312UNTS63	104511
Sweden	USSR (Soviet Union)	28 Jan 57	428UNTS315	106183
Denmark	Norway	22 Feb 57	286UNTS127	104164
Mexico	USA (United States)	07 Mar 57	279UNTS205	104042
Netherlands	USA (United States)	03 Apr 57	410UNTS193	105904
Paraguay	USA (United States)	04 Apr 57	283UNTS193	104117
Denmark	Pakistan	10 Apr 57	302UNTS53	104353
Germany, West	Yugoslavia	10 Apr 57	463UNTS269	106708
Romania	Sweden	15 Apr 57	342UNTS325	104915
Bulgaria	Sweden	17 Apr 57	464UNTS3	106709
Netherlands	United Arab Rep	15 May 57	288UNTS29	104194
Ceylon (Sri Lanka)	Sweden	18 May 57	315UNTS85	104561
Hungary	Netherlands	28 May 57	334UNTS291	104773
Belgium	Hungary	01 Jun 57	291UNTS17	104242
Belgium	South Africa	11 Jun 57	292UNTS165	104272
Afghanistan	Pakistan	13 Jun 57	327UNTS51	104717
Czechoslovakia	United Arab Rep	30 Jun 57	411UNTS126	105917
Greece	Italy	02 Aug 57	533UNTS217	107744
Hungary	Sweden	02 Aug 57	334UNTS307	104774

PARTY ONE	PARTY TWO	DATE	CITATION	NUMBER
Air transport (Cont.)				
Netherlands	Romania	27 Aug 57	342UNTS309	104914
Australia	Canada	01 Oct 57	392UNTS41	105638
Multilateral		03 Oct 57	366UNTS87	105216
Italy	Pakistan	05 Oct 57	353UNTS91	105039
France	Morocco	25 Oct 57	559UNTS95	108156
Belgium	Switzerland	05 Dec 57	293UNTS317	104299
Australia	Ireland	30 Dec 57	497UNTS29	107260
Belgium	Morocco	20 Jan 58	288UNTS3	104192
USA (United States)	USSR (Soviet Union)	27 Jan 58	301UNTS405	104350
Bulgaria	Netherlands	07 Feb 58	335UNTS45	104777
Afghanistan	Turkey	08 Feb 58	464UNTS39	106711
Norway	Pakistan	05 Mar 58	334UNTS199	104769
Pakistan	Sweden	06 Mar 58	393UNTS181	105656
Germany, West	Portugal	21 Mar 58	464UNTS71	106712
Morocco	Portugal	03 Apr 58	393UNTS203	105657
Sweden	Yugoslavia	18 Apr 58	393UNTS225	105658
Ireland	South Africa	01 May 58	398UNTS3	105714
Bulgaria	Denmark	28 May 58	312UNTS235	104521
Belgium	USSR (Soviet Union)	05 Jun 58	345UNTS145	104965
Pakistan	Portugal	07 Jun 58	320UNTS225	104645
Denmark	Luxembourg	10 Jun 58	356UNTS193	105096
Norway	Romania	16 Jun 58	405UNTS223	105835
Ireland	Switzerland	18 Jun 58	553UNTS183	108086
Belgium	Pakistan	04 Jul 58	387UNTS305	105569
Denmark	Hungary	17 Jul 58	344UNTS281	104954
Sweden	United Arab Rep	21 Jul 58	427UNTS285	106160
Afghanistan	Austria	21 Jul 58	0UNTS0	109236
Denmark	Sweden	21 Jul 58	320UNTS163	104642
India	Sweden	30 Jul 58	369UNTS211	105259
Romania	United Arab Rep	14 Aug 58	405UNTS189	105834
Pakistan	Sweden	25 Aug 58	369UNTS183	105258
Austria	Bulgaria	12 Sep 58	353UNTS3	105036
Germany, West	Norway	18 Nov 58	357UNTS205	105119
Liberia	Netherlands	28 Nov 58	393UNTS55	105651
Denmark	United Arab Rep	01 Dec 58	337UNTS69	104817
Finland	Switzerland	07 Jan 59	353UNTS173	105042
Belgium	France	20 Jan 59	361UNTS155	105178
Japan	Norway	21 Feb 59	356UNTS231	105098
Indonesia	USA (United States)	02 Mar 59	357UNTS145	105113
Denmark	Japan	10 Mar 59	341UNTS55	104878
Sweden	Tunisia	19 Mar 59	497UNTS43	107261
Netherlands	Tunisia	19 Mar 59	497UNTS61	107262
Norway	Tunisia	28 Mar 59	497UNTS77	107263
Canada	Finland	28 Mar 59	355UNTS3	105072
Denmark	Tunisia	14 Apr 59	340UNTS273	104870
Germany, West	Sweden	17 Apr 59	428UNTS155	106175
Austria	Sweden	14 May 59	428UNTS3	106167
Germany, West	Netherlands	16 Jun 59	593UNTS3	108576
Bulgaria	United Arab Rep	09 Jul 59	411UNTS187	105920
Austria	Hungary	17 Jul 59	0UNTS0	109237
India	Norway	20 Jul 59	356UNTS257	105099
Afghanistan	Germany, West	22 Jul 59	464UNTS177	106715
Germany, West	Iceland	12 Aug 59	411UNTS224	105921
Multilateral		20 Aug 59	376UNTS99	105376
Canada	Switzerland	22 Sep 59	470UNTS101	106800
Germany, West	USA (United States)	01 Oct 59	358UNTS129	105130
India	Italy	06 Oct 59	378UNTS267	105427
Austria	France	08 Oct 59	453UNTS95	106521
Nicaragua	Peru	14 Oct 59	392UNTS303	105649
South Africa	Switzerland	19 Oct 59	559UNTS257	108162
USA (United States)	USSR (Soviet Union)	21 Nov 59	361UNTS35	105172
Liberia	Sweden	09 Dec 59	464UNTS219	106716
Israel	Sweden	22 Dec 59	377UNTS277	105407
India	Japan	05 Jan 60	384UNTS3	105507
Germany, West	United Arab Rep	16 Feb 60	464UNTS233	106717

PARTY ONE	PARTY TWO	DATE	CITATION	NUMBER
Air transport (Cont.)				
Austria	Norway	25 Feb 60	376UNTS155	105380
France	Thailand	26 Feb 60	392UNTS279	105648
Australia	Thailand	26 Feb 60	392UNTS255	105647
Guinea	Netherlands	09 Mar 60	392UNTS243	105646
Finland	Iceland	10 Mar 60	497UNTS95	107264
Czechoslovakia	Iraq	11 Mar 60	464UNTS267	106718
Belgium	Switzerland	24 Mar 60	416UNTS81	105996
Iran	UK Great Britain	09 Apr 60	385UNTS63	105529
Luxembourg	Yugoslavia	09 Apr 60	464UNTS293	106719
Germany, West	Spain	28 Apr 60	465UNTS3	106720
Morocco	United Arab Rep	19 May 60	563UNTS121	108208
Switzerland	Tunisia	21 May 60	497UNTS109	107265
Afghanistan	Czechoslovakia	28 May 60	497UNTS129	107266
Luxembourg	Tunisia	13 Jun 60	497UNTS143	107267
Denmark	Peru	22 Jun 60	439UNTS113	106326
Ireland	Portugal	24 Jun 60	412UNTS30	105924
Poland	UK Great Britain	02 Jul 60	385UNTS87	105532
Italy	UK Great Britain	04 Jul 60	466UNTS195	106745
Denmark	USA (United States)	07 Jul 60	380UNTS39	105449
Switzerland	United Arab Rep	14 Jul 60	497UNTS161	107268
Germany, West	Pakistan	20 Jul 60	465UNTS41	106721
Sweden	UK Great Britain	28 Jul 60	404UNTS113	105808
Mexico	USA (United States)	15 Aug 60	402UNTS177	105786
Belgium	Burma	17 Aug 60	540UNTS185	107850
Sweden	Tunisia	06 Sep 60	427UNTS301	106162
Belgium	Jordan	19 Oct 60	479UNTS277	106959
Burma	Switzerland	31 Oct 60	465UNTS97	106723
Norway	Peru	02 Nov 60	497UNTS207	107270
Australia	Italy	10 Nov 60	497UNTS247	107271
Multilateral		13 Dec 60	523UNTS117	107557
Luxembourg	Thailand	29 Dec 60	465UNTS131	106725
Denmark	Poland	17 Jan 61	412UNTS111	105927
Norway	Poland	17 Jan 61	412UNTS130	105928
Denmark	Greece	04 Mar 61	534UNTS157	107760
Cuba	Czechoslovakia	04 Mar 61	465UNTS209	106728
Morocco	Sweden	30 Mar 61	427UNTS185	106154
Japan	UK Great Britain	11 Apr 61	420UNTS75	106042
Poland	Switzerland	18 May 61	559UNTS233	108161
Czechoslovakia	Morocco	08 Jun 61	497UNTS275	107272
Cameroon	France	16 Jun 61	412UNTS148	105929
Guinea	Sweden	17 Jun 61	465UNTS236	106729
Finland	India	23 Jun 61	421UNTS49	106051
Australia	New Zealand	25 Jul 61	523UNTS271	107561
Portugal	UK Great Britain	31 Jul 61	449UNTS119	106454
Colombia	USA (United States)	01 Aug 61	433UNTS123	106235
Finland	Luxembourg	15 Aug 61	541UNTS45	107859
Mexico	Netherlands	24 Aug 61	465UNTS291	106732
Jordan	Netherlands	24 Aug 61	466UNTS3	106733
Italy	Norway	25 Aug 61	475UNTS269	106896
Liberia	Switzerland	31 Aug 61	559UNTS215	108160
Denmark	Pakistan	04 Sep 61	455UNTS305	106549
Multilateral		18 Sep 61	500UNTS31	107305
Greece	Sweden	06 Oct 61	481UNTS137	106981
Germany, West	Morocco	12 Oct 61	523UNTS289	107562
Sweden	Thailand	20 Oct 61	428UNTS275	106180
Austria	Denmark	23 Oct 61	425UNTS115	106122
Belgium	Denmark	23 Oct 61	425UNTS181	106123
Australia	UK Great Britain	14 Nov 61	466UNTS35	106735
Cyprus	Greece	23 Nov 61	497UNTS311	107274
Czechoslovakia	Mali	27 Nov 61	466UNTS41	106736
Czechoslovakia	Guinea	16 Dec 61	559UNTS49	108154
Austria	Japan	20 Dec 61	517UNTS155	107485
Netherlands	Sweden	08 Jan 62	466UNTS65	106737
Austria	Greece	15 Jan 62	498UNTS3	107275
Indonesia	Japan	23 Jan 62	559UNTS77	108155

PARTY ONE	PARTY TWO	DATE	CITATION	NUMBER
Air transport (Cont.)				
Finland	Hungary	13 Feb 62	463UNTS61	106693
Austria	Spain	19 Feb 62	0UNTS0	109238
Germany, West	Thailand	05 Mar 62	563UNTS165	108210
Luxembourg	Spain	26 Mar 62	563UNTS205	108211
France	Luxembourg	29 Mar 62	563UNTS227	108212
Ghana	USSR (Soviet Union)	06 Apr 62	498UNTS41	107277
France	Romania	18 May 62	498UNTS115	107279
South Africa	UK Great Britain	28 May 62	443UNTS79	106361
Greece	Switzerland	12 Jun 62	492UNTS47	107186
France	Senegal	15 Jun 62	524UNTS3	107563
Czechoslovakia	Senegal	20 Jun 62	498UNTS145	107280
Guinea	Norway	21 Jun 62	466UNTS81	106738
Liberia	Norway	29 Jun 62	466UNTS95	106739
Morocco	Switzerland	05 Jul 62	498UNTS171	107281
Germany, West	Israel	09 Jul 62	630UNTS87	108968
Japan	UK Great Britain	04 Sep 62	475UNTS31	106888
Israel	UK Great Britain	26 Sep 62	474UNTS233	106885
Trinidad/Tobago	USA (United States)	08 Oct 62	462UNTS145	106675
Finland	France	12 Oct 62	498UNTS299	107285
Austria	United Arab Rep	16 Oct 62	491UNTS63	107174
Netherlands	Norway	18 Oct 62	466UNTS145	106741
Austria	Luxembourg	18 Oct 62	496UNTS97	107248
Hungary	Syria	18 Oct 62	491UNTS209	107178
France	Ivory Coast	19 Oct 62	498UNTS317	107286
Czechoslovakia	Denmark	25 Oct 62	456UNTS457	106571
Czechoslovakia	Sweden	25 Oct 62	498UNTS343	107288
Czechoslovakia	Norway	25 Oct 62	498UNTS335	107287
Ethiopia	Greece	07 Nov 62	550UNTS189	108015
Poland	Syria	10 Nov 62	491UNTS228	107179
Ivory Coast	Switzerland	17 Nov 62	499UNTS3	107289
Jamaica	USA (United States)	29 Nov 62	462UNTS229	106682
Ghana	Tunisia	11 Dec 62	563UNTS243	108213
Luxembourg	USA (United States)	18 Dec 62	532UNTS277	107723
Iceland	USA (United States)	27 Dec 62	469UNTS91	106785
Ghana	Mali	09 Jan 63	466UNTS165	106742
Senegal	Switzerland	23 Jan 63	524UNTS23	107564
New Zealand	Western Samoa	24 Jan 63	499UNTS21	107290
Japan	New Zealand	30 Jan 63	517UNTS183	107486
Guinea	Switzerland	01 Feb 63	499UNTS35	107291
Mali	Senegal	07 Feb 63	524UNTS41	107565
UK Great Britain	Yugoslavia	16 Feb 63	507UNTS171	107400
Ceylon (Sri Lanka)	Denmark	16 Feb 63	486UNTS285	107083
Algeria	France	18 Feb 63	563UNTS263	108214
Japan	Thailand	01 Mar 63	475UNTS233	106895
Japan	South Africa	06 Apr 63	484UNTS319	107040
Norway	Spain	25 Apr 63	503UNTS41	107340
Cyprus	Denmark	27 Apr 63	529UNTS255	107664
Greece	Hungary	27 Apr 63	534UNTS3	107750
Algeria	Morocco	30 Apr 63	564UNTS3	108217
Canada	India	14 May 63	529UNTS31	107653
Japan	Malaysia	04 Jun 63	517UNTS245	107488
Belgium	Cyprus	08 Jun 63	601UNTS311	108703
Finland	Poland	10 Jun 63	503UNTS179	107343
Guinea	Ivory Coast	26 Jun 63	499UNTS71	107293
Austria	France	12 Jul 63	499UNTS91	107294
Taiwan	Luxembourg	19 Jul 63	564UNTS23	108218
Greece	Romania	20 Jul 63	609UNTS109	108829
Algeria	Mali	22 Jul 63	564UNTS29	108219
Mali	Tunisia	24 Jul 63	602UNTS91	108708
Cameroon	Israel	09 Aug 63	499UNTS121	107295
France	Israel	20 Aug 63	515UNTS173	107460
France	Greece	21 Aug 63	533UNTS235	107746
Algeria	Tunisia	01 Sep 63	601UNTS275	108701
Austria	India	24 Sep 63	545UNTS199	107935
Ivory Coast	Netherlands	09 Oct 63	499UNTS141	107296

PARTY ONE	PARTY TWO	DATE	CITATION	NUMBER
Air transport (Cont.)				
Lebanon	UK Great Britain	24 Oct 63	535UNTS3	107772
France	UK Great Britain	05 Nov 63	539UNTS277	107838
Canada	Denmark	28 Nov 63	496UNTS223	107254
Canada	USA (United States)	27 Dec 63	494UNTS21	107223
Norway	Thailand	09 Jan 64	522UNTS65	107537
Mali	Niger	15 Jan 64	499UNTS197	107299
Greece	Poland	21 Jan 64	533UNTS309	107749
Denmark	Yugoslavia	11 Feb 64	511UNTS241	107437
France	New Zealand	27 Feb 64	499UNTS191	107298
Cyprus	USSR (Soviet Union)	29 Feb 64	602UNTS45	108706
Algeria	Czechoslovakia	09 Mar 64	601UNTS247	108700
Cameroon	Mali	17 Mar 64	524UNTS61	107566
Denmark	Finland	07 Apr 64	525UNTS89	107586
Norway	Yugoslavia	15 Apr 64	602UNTS177	108712
United Arab Rep	USA (United States)	05 May 64	531UNTS229	107706
Cyprus	Hungary	02 Jun 64	602UNTS3	108704
Austria	Belgium	11 Jun 64	521UNTS157	107518
Ceylon (Sri Lanka)	Norway	11 Jun 64	559UNTS23	108153
New Zealand	USA (United States)	24 Jun 64	524UNTS101	107568
Ivory Coast	Mali	09 Jul 64	524UNTS121	107569
Mexico	USA (United States)	07 Aug 64	530UNTS123	107677
Germany, West	Jamaica	07 Oct 64	514UNTS187	107447
France	Trinidad/Tobago	12 Oct 64	535UNTS25	107774
Norway	United Arab Rep	20 Oct 64	543UNTS3	107895
Greece	South Africa	11 Nov 64	631UNTS319	109001
Cyprus	Syria	22 Dec 64	602UNTS25	108705
Argentina	UK Great Britain	12 Jan 65	597UNTS177	108645
Finland	Israel	21 Jan 65	581UNTS275	108450
Greece	India	11 Feb 65	606UNTS9	108771
Finland	United Arab Rep	01 Apr 65	562UNTS3	108193
Jamaica	UK Great Britain	02 Apr 65	552UNTS219	108056
Australia	France	13 Apr 65	601UNTS293	108702
Ivory Coast	Netherlands	26 Apr 65	634UNTS81	109053
Ghana	Malawi	04 May 65	541UNTS163	107869
Mauritania	Spain	11 May 65	602UNTS111	108709
Denmark	Thailand	01 Jun 65	551UNTS157	108040
Netherlands	Senegal	12 Jun 65	602UNTS231	108715
Nigeria	Switzerland	11 Oct 65	602UNTS137	108710
Burma	Czechoslovakia	15 Dec 65	602UNTS71	108707
Canada	USA (United States)	17 Jan 66	586UNTS151	108502
Denmark	Netherlands	31 Mar 66	604UNTS209	108751
Portugal	UK Great Britain	17 Apr 66	573UNTS223	108335
Fed Rhod/Nyasaland	Norway	18 Jun 66	580UNTS9	108415
Austria	USA (United States)	23 Jun 66	601UNTS51	108687
Denmark	Israel	27 Jun 66	581UNTS227	108448
Taiwan	Vietnam, South	19 Aug 66	0UNTS0	109241
Denmark	Nigeria	08 Sep 66	591UNTS177	108557
Netherlands	Norway	22 Sep 66	600UNTS227	108683
Israel	Norway	02 Nov 66	630UNTS225	108972
Canada	Israel	30 Nov 66	630UNTS267	108973
Singapore	UK Great Britain	01 Dec 66	605UNTS153	108763
Trinidad/Tobago	UK Great Britain	29 Dec 66	605UNTS237	108766
Trinidad/Tobago	UK Great Britain	01 Mar 67	606UNTS149	108784
Greece	Yugoslavia	15 Apr 67	633UNTS373	109046
South Africa	Switzerland	03 Jul 67	643UNTS3	109184
Brazil	UK Great Britain	29 Dec 67	643UNTS217	109193
Airport facilities				
Brazil	France	27 Jan 40	72UNTS77	100929
Canada	USA (United States)	18 Mar 42	101UNTS205	200294
Spain	USA (United States)	02 Dec 44	89UNTS345	200262
Multilateral		07 Dec 44	84UNTS389	200252
Multilateral		07 Dec 44	171UNTS387	200502
Multilateral		07 Dec 44	171UNTS345	200501
Multilateral		07 Dec 44	15UNTS295	200102

PARTY ONE	PARTY TWO	DATE	CITATION	NUMBER
Airport facilities (Cont.)				
Denmark	USA (United States)	16 Dec 44	10UNTS213	200063
Sweden	USA (United States)	16 Dec 44	6UNTS397	200041
Iceland	USA (United States)	27 Jan 45	122UNTS293	200411
Ireland	USA (United States)	03 Feb 45	122UNTS305	200412
Canada	USA (United States)	13 Feb 45	200UNTS219	200519
Canada	USA (United States)	17 Feb 45	122UNTS261	200409
Iceland	USA (United States)	11 Apr 45	16UNTS241	200105
Switzerland	USA (United States)	03 Aug 45	51UNTS233	200191
Norway	USA (United States)	06 Oct 45	122UNTS319	200413
South Africa	UK Great Britain	26 Oct 45	72UNTS41	100927
Greece	UK Great Britain	26 Nov 45	35UNTS161	100555
Portugal	USA (United States)	06 Dec 45	3UNTS139	100028
Portugal	UK Great Britain	06 Dec 45	6UNTS3	100065
Portugal	UK Great Britain	06 Dec 45	5UNTS37	100064
Canada	UK Great Britain	21 Dec 45	27UNTS155	100405
Czechoslovakia	USA (United States)	03 Jan 46	6UNTS309	100084
Czechoslovakia	Poland	24 Jan 46	25UNTS181	100363
UK Great Britain	USA (United States)	11 Feb 46	3UNTS253	100036
Turkey	UK Great Britain	12 Feb 46	6UNTS79	100069
Turkey	USA (United States)	12 Feb 46	13UNTS3	100196
France	UK Great Britain	28 Feb 46	27UNTS173	100407
Greece	USA (United States)	27 Mar 46	15UNTS233	100239
France	USA (United States)	27 Mar 46	139UNTS114	101879
Multilateral		31 Mar 46	17UNTS159	100274
Ireland	UK Great Britain	05 Apr 46	72UNTS57	100928
Belgium	USA (United States)	05 Apr 46	4UNTS125	100041
Netherlands	Portugal	12 Apr 46	4UNTS317	100054
Argentina	UK Great Britain	17 Apr 46	164UNTS53	102159
France	Ireland	16 May 46	44UNTS105	100681
Ireland	Sweden	29 May 46	35UNTS231	100557
Portugal	USA (United States)	30 May 46	174UNTS187	102285
Australia	Canada	11 Jun 46	10UNTS47	100142
United Arab Rep	USA (United States)	15 Jun 46	151UNTS135	101988
United Arab Rep	USA (United States)	15 Jun 46	71UNTS157	100917
France	USA (United States)	18 Jun 46	42UNTS183	100647
Sweden	Turkey	26 Jun 46	14UNTS21	100208
Iceland	UK Great Britain	04 Jul 46	6UNTS223	100077
Albania	Yugoslavia	11 Jul 46	4UNTS407	100058
Netherlands	Spain	13 Jul 46	4UNTS351	100055
Czechoslovakia	USSR (Soviet Union)	25 Jul 46	27UNTS231	100409
Canada	Newfoundland	29 Jul 46	17UNTS169	100275
UK Great Britain	USA (United States)	31 Jul 46	42UNTS199	100648
France	Sweden	02 Aug 46	27UNTS251	100410
Lebanon	USA (United States)	11 Aug 46	66UNTS211	100856
Netherlands	UK Great Britain	13 Aug 46	4UNTS367	100056
Brazil	USA (United States)	06 Sep 46	54UNTS197	100805
Sweden	USA (United States)	30 Sep 46	42UNTS213	100649
Denmark	USA (United States)	01 Oct 46	42UNTS219	100650
France	Turkey	12 Oct 46	14UNTS33	100209
Belgium	Portugal	22 Oct 46	34UNTS49	100527
Brazil	UK Great Britain	31 Oct 46	11UNTS115	100152
Norway	USA (United States)	12 Nov 46	42UNTS227	100651
India	USA (United States)	14 Nov 46	22UNTS55	100331
Philippines	USA (United States)	16 Nov 46	7UNTS151	100097
Sweden	UK Great Britain	27 Nov 46	11UNTS229	100162
New Zealand	USA (United States)	03 Dec 46	7UNTS175	100099
Australia	USA (United States)	03 Dec 46	7UNTS201	100100
Portugal	Switzerland	09 Dec 46	310UNTS251	104495
Brazil	Portugal	10 Dec 46	200UNTS67	102695
USA (United States)	Uruguay	14 Dec 46	532UNTS87	107713
Taiwan	USA (United States)	20 Dec 46	22UNTS87	100332
Peru	USA (United States)	27 Dec 46	26UNTS227	100390
Peru	USA (United States)	27 Dec 46	152UNTS93	102013
Ecuador	USA (United States)	08 Jan 47	22UNTS119	100333
Czechoslovakia	Ireland	29 Jan 47	27UNTS267	100411

PARTY ONE	PARTY TWO	DATE	CITATION	NUMBER
Airport facilities (Cont.)				
USSR (Soviet Union)	Yugoslavia	04 Feb 47	130UNTS235	101731
Thailand	USA (United States)	26 Feb 47	16UNTS17	100246
Paraguay	USA (United States)	28 Feb 47	44UNTS25	100676
Portugal	Sweden	06 Mar 47	35UNTS243	100558
Australia	USA (United States)	10 Mar 47	10UNTS89	100145
Netherlands	Turkey	19 Mar 47	14UNTS59	100211
Muscat and Oman	UK Great Britain	05 Apr 47	27UNTS287	100412
Greece	Sweden	08 Apr 47	94UNTS73	101307
Greece	Netherlands	17 Apr 47	32UNTS115	100494
Canada	Portugal	25 Apr 47	94UNTS87	101308
Syria	USA (United States)	28 Apr 47	262UNTS121	103741
Switzerland	USA (United States)	30 Apr 47	42UNTS235	100652
France	Greece	05 May 47	76UNTS61	100980
Thailand	USA (United States)	08 May 47	42UNTS241	100653
Chile	USA (United States)	10 May 47	55UNTS21	100807
Czechoslovakia	Denmark	14 May 47	27UNTS297	100413
South Africa	USA (United States)	23 May 47	66UNTS233	100857
India	Netherlands	31 May 47	17UNTS65	100268
Greece	UK Great Britain	05 Jun 47	9UNTS197	100133
Italy	USA (United States)	09 Jun 47	104UNTS157	101437
Canada	Sweden	27 Jun 47	27UNTS313	100414
Iraq	Turkey	30 Jun 47	72UNTS107	100930
Romania	Yugoslavia	30 Jun 47	116UNTS57	101569
Denmark	Turkey	30 Jun 47	32UNTS301	100504
France	India	16 Jul 47	27UNTS325	100415
Canada	UK Great Britain	17 Jul 47	28UNTS3	100416
Netherlands	Thailand	18 Jul 47	28UNTS27	100417
Netherlands	South Africa	22 Jul 47	12UNTS257	100188
Greece	Turkey	22 Jul 47	72UNTS131	100931
Taiwan	UK Great Britain	23 Jul 47	9UNTS207	100135
Poland	Romania	09 Aug 47	12UNTS363	100193
Hungary	Poland	28 Aug 47	15UNTS145	100231
Czechoslovakia	Netherlands	01 Sep 47	32UNTS129	100495
Czechoslovakia	Switzerland	10 Sep 47	35UNTS275	100559
Lebanon	Turkey	16 Sep 47	44UNTS123	100682
Sweden	Yugoslavia	06 Oct 47	53UNTS107	100775
Czechoslovakia	Sweden	15 Oct 47	44UNTS149	100683
Colombia	UK Great Britain	16 Oct 47	160UNTS297	102115
Brazil	Netherlands	06 Nov 47	53UNTS59	100773
Norway	Portugal	11 Nov 47	34UNTS257	100542
Brazil	Norway	14 Nov 47	44UNTS163	100684
Brazil	Sweden	14 Nov 47	94UNTS139	101310
Brazil	Denmark	14 Nov 47	47UNTS39	100722
Denmark	Greece	14 Nov 47	35UNTS295	100560
Denmark	Ireland	18 Nov 47	35UNTS309	100561
Burma	Pakistan	18 Nov 47	35UNTS321	100562
Ireland	Italy	21 Nov 47	353UNTS73	105038
Taiwan	Netherlands	06 Dec 47	43UNTS185	100669
Denmark	Portugal	15 Dec 47	35UNTS329	100563
Austria	Netherlands	22 Jan 48	17UNTS99	100270
Italy	USA (United States)	06 Feb 48	73UNTS113	100950
UK Great Britain	USA (United States)	24 Feb 48	73UNTS143	100951
Czechoslovakia	Yugoslavia	14 Mar 48	28UNTS81	100421
Argentina	Denmark	18 Mar 48	94UNTS175	101311
Cuba	UK Great Britain	19 Mar 48	175UNTS23	102294
Pakistan	Sweden	06 May 48	36UNTS3	100564
Ireland	Switzerland	06 May 48	334UNTS187	104768
Jordan	Turkey	07 May 48	32UNTS313	100505
Ireland	Netherlands	10 May 48	28UNTS121	100422
Norway	Turkey	20 May 48	26UNTS137	100384
India	Sweden	21 May 48	34UNTS285	100543
Greece	Switzerland	26 May 48	94UNTS217	101312
Ireland	Norway	21 Jun 48	34UNTS317	100545
India	Pakistan	23 Jun 48	28UNTS143	100423
Australia	Italy	02 Aug 48	28UNTS165	100424

Airport facilities (Cont.)

PARTY ONE	PARTY TWO	DATE	CITATION	NUMBER
Brazil	Switzerland	10 Aug 48	94UNTS269	101314
France	Spain	23 Aug 48	28UNTS173	100425
Greece	Lebanon	06 Sep 48	178UNTS37	102335
Iceland	ICAO (Civil Aviat)	16 Sep 48	28UNTS267	100429
Bolivia	USA (United States)	29 Sep 48	505UNTS139	107370
Netherlands	Spain	08 Oct 48	28UNTS209	100426
Mexico	Portugal	22 Oct 48	34UNTS329	100546
Argentina	Netherlands	29 Oct 48	95UNTS21	101316
Argentina	Chile	14 Dec 48	635UNTS21	109071
Ceylon (Sri Lanka)	Pakistan	03 Jan 49	28UNTS247	100428
Italy	Lebanon	24 Jan 49	231UNTS241	103223
Switzerland	Turkey	16 Feb 49	72UNTS175	100933
Belgium	Sweden	21 Feb 49	95UNTS73	101317
Finland	Netherlands	25 Feb 49	53UNTS123	100777
Netherlands	Switzerland	07 Mar 49	35UNTS69	100551
Finland	USA (United States)	29 Mar 49	55UNTS59	100808
Panama	USA (United States)	31 Mar 49	55UNTS87	100810
Finland	Sweden	26 Apr 49	95UNTS83	101318
Bulgaria	Poland	16 May 49	84UNTS313	101140
Italy	Spain	31 May 49	231UNTS251	103224
Australia	Pakistan	03 Jun 49	35UNTS23	100549
Canada	USA (United States)	04 Jun 49	122UNTS237	101649
Canada	USA (United States)	04 Jun 49	200UNTS201	102704
Ethiopia	India	07 Jun 49	35UNTS13	100548
Belgium	Greece	21 Jun 49	137UNTS215	101854
Norway	Pakistan	23 Jun 49	35UNTS49	100550
India	Switzerland	24 Jun 49	95UNTS109	101319
Korea, South	USA (United States)	29 Jun 49	55UNTS79	100809
India	USA (United States)	04 Jul 49	200UNTS181	102702
Greece	Syria	05 Jul 49	78UNTS71	101013
Iraq	Norway	12 Jul 49	53UNTS137	100778
Czechoslovakia	Finland	13 Jul 49	53UNTS153	100779
Pakistan	Philippines	16 Jul 49	35UNTS111	100553
Dominican Republic	USA (United States)	19 Jul 49	51UNTS145	100762
Pakistan	UK Great Britain	27 Jul 49	44UNTS199	100685
Finland	Norway	24 Aug 49	53UNTS167	100780
Denmark	Finland	26 Aug 49	53UNTS191	100781
Lebanon	Netherlands	20 Sep 49	108UNTS205	101474
Burma	USA (United States)	28 Sep 49	55UNTS3	100806
Greece	Philippines	08 Oct 49	187UNTS221	102515
Denmark	Pakistan	09 Nov 49	44UNTS255	100687
Sweden	Thailand	23 Nov 49	72UNTS217	100935
Denmark	Thailand	23 Nov 49	53UNTS255	100786
Italy	Turkey	25 Nov 49	192UNTS39	102594
Norway	Thailand	26 Nov 49	53UNTS269	100787
Brazil	Spain	28 Nov 49	215UNTS303	102923
Austria	Norway	02 Dec 49	72UNTS230	100936
Austria	Sweden	02 Dec 49	108UNTS3	101465
Austria	Denmark	02 Dec 49	53UNTS281	100788
Canada	Denmark	13 Dec 49	72UNTS247	100937
Austria	Switzerland	19 Dec 49	254UNTS287	103597
Guatemala	USA (United States)	20 Dec 49	70UNTS71	100897
USA (United States)	Yugoslavia	24 Dec 49	89UNTS209	101219
Netherlands	Syria	13 Feb 50	108UNTS53	101467
Canada	Norway	14 Feb 50	53UNTS329	100790
Spain	Sweden	18 Feb 50	166UNTS15	102184
Ceylon (Sri Lanka)	Thailand	24 Feb 50	72UNTS261	100938
Italy	Netherlands	04 Mar 50	254UNTS305	103598
Philippines	USA (United States)	16 Mar 50	89UNTS199	101218
Denmark	Iceland	22 Mar 50	72UNTS273	100939
Iceland	Netherlands	22 Mar 50	95UNTS237	101323
Italy	Portugal	05 Apr 50	254UNTS329	103599
Iceland	UK Great Britain	26 May 50	95UNTS277	101326
Israel	USA (United States)	13 Jun 50	212UNTS93	102863
Iraq	Pakistan	20 Jun 50	77UNTS215	101001

Airport facilities (Cont.)

PARTY ONE	PARTY TWO	DATE	CITATION	NUMBER
Netherlands	Spain	20 Jun 50	95UNTS303	101327
Denmark	Switzerland	22 Jun 50	96UNTS3	101328
Burma	Ceylon (Sri Lanka)	29 Jun 50	73UNTS3	100940
Spain	UK Great Britain	20 Jul 50	398UNTS101	105719
France	Pakistan	31 Jul 50	96UNTS23	101329
Spain	Switzerland	03 Aug 50	254UNTS365	103600
Canada	New Zealand	16 Aug 50	77UNTS239	101002
Burma	Sweden	14 Sep 50	96UNTS45	101330
Brazil	Turkey	21 Sep 50	150UNTS299	101981
Sweden	Switzerland	18 Oct 50	166UNTS49	102185
Luxembourg	Portugal	21 Oct 50	108UNTS67	101468
Israel	Netherlands	23 Oct 50	189UNTS89	102543
Thailand	UK Great Britain	10 Nov 50	96UNTS77	101332
Israel	UK Great Britain	06 Dec 50	151UNTS33	101983
Israel	Turkey	05 Feb 51	193UNTS3	102607
Colombia	Portugal	09 Mar 51	108UNTS87	101469
Greece	Yugoslavia	15 Mar 51	187UNTS237	102516
Canada	ICAO (Civil Aviat)	14 Apr 51	96UNTS155	101335
Multilateral		25 May 51	175UNTS215	102303
Greece	Norway	28 May 51	187UNTS141	102507
Saudi Arabia	USA (United States)	18 Jun 51	102UNTS73	101412
Cuba	Portugal	26 Jun 51	192UNTS115	102598
Iceland	Norway	14 Jul 51	163UNTS265	102150
Burma	Denmark	30 Jul 51	108UNTS167	101472
Israel	Philippines	07 Aug 51	192UNTS81	102596
Burma	Netherlands	06 Sep 51	108UNTS187	101473
Panama	UK Great Britain	15 Sep 51	560UNTS143	108172
Philippines	Spain	06 Oct 51	215UNTS193	102920
Greece	Luxembourg	22 Oct 51	187UNTS119	102506
Denmark	Iraq	18 Nov 51	232UNTS25	103227
Colombia	Spain	11 Dec 51	216UNTS73	102933
Belgium	Spain	10 Mar 52	178UNTS243	102342
Pakistan	Switzerland	17 Mar 52	192UNTS237	102603
Sweden	Uruguay	20 Mar 52	311UNTS3	104497
Norway	Uruguay	20 Mar 52	310UNTS279	104496
Libya	UK Great Britain	31 Mar 52	151UNTS69	101984
Iraq	Switzerland	31 Mar 52	311UNTS43	104498
France	Mexico	17 Apr 52	163UNTS321	102153
Honduras	USA (United States)	23 Apr 52	198UNTS251	102669
Denmark	Japan	28 Apr 52	166UNTS3	102182
France	Israel	29 Apr 52	189UNTS55	102542
Norway	UK Great Britain	23 Jun 52	151UNTS81	101985
Greece	USA (United States)	25 Jun 52	181UNTS53	102398
Ethiopia	UK Great Britain	03 Jul 52	151UNTS207	101996
Mexico	USA (United States)	15 Jul 52	181UNTS263	102416
Japan	USA (United States)	11 Aug 52	212UNTS27	102862
Ethiopia	Pakistan	29 Aug 52	150UNTS257	101979
Netherlands	Peru	22 Sep 52	255UNTS49	103604
Austria	Luxembourg	13 Oct 52	192UNTS291	102606
Mexico	Netherlands	13 Oct 52	163UNTS341	102154
Iceland	Luxembourg	23 Oct 52	193UNTS39	102609
Chile	Denmark	27 Oct 52	271UNTS93	103911
Chile	Sweden	27 Oct 52	311UNTS63	104499
Luxembourg	Sweden	17 Nov 52	173UNTS277	102270
Luxembourg	Norway	17 Nov 52	311UNTS95	104500
Israel	Switzerland	19 Nov 52	232UNTS3	103226
Netherlands	Philippines	05 Feb 53	216UNTS99	102934
Japan	Netherlands	17 Feb 53	192UNTS215	102602
Japan	Sweden	20 Feb 53	173UNTS307	102272
Japan	Norway	23 Feb 53	192UNTS191	102601
Denmark	Japan	26 Feb 53	173UNTS329	102273
Philippines	Thailand	27 Apr 53	174UNTS3	102274
Ethiopia	USA (United States)	22 May 53	191UNTS59	102577
Cuba	USA (United States)	26 May 53	224UNTS75	103070
Switzerland	Yugoslavia	28 May 53	232UNTS45	103228

PARTY ONE	PARTY TWO	DATE	CITATION	NUMBER
Airport facilities (Cont.)				
Japan	Thailand	19 Jun 53	174UNTS29	102276
Burma	Norway	22 Jun 53	174UNTS49	102277
USA (United States)	Venezuela	14 Aug 53	213UNTS99	102883
Austria	Yugoslavia	11 Nov 53	363UNTS149	105206
Cuba	USA (United States)	26 Nov 53	205UNTS213	102777
Syria	UK Great Britain	30 Jan 54	449UNTS47	106452
Peru	Spain	31 Mar 54	232UNTS65	103230
Lebanon	Yugoslavia	17 Apr 54	602UNTS199	108713
Belgium	Ireland	30 Jun 54	212UNTS255	102876
Ireland	Luxembourg	27 Jul 54	232UNTS91	103231
Ecuador	Netherlands	14 Dec 54	232UNTS115	103233
Norway	Switzerland	30 Dec 54	311UNTS147	104502
Austria	Belgium	07 Jan 55	380UNTS219	105458
Canada	Japan	12 Jan 55	311UNTS167	104503
United Arab Rep	Yugoslavia	20 Feb 55	255UNTS199	103611
Germany, West	USA (United States)	07 Jul 55	275UNTS3	103973
Germany, West	UK Great Britain	22 Jul 55	269UNTS189	103881
Germany, East	Romania	28 Jul 55	342UNTS207	104909
USSR (Soviet Union)	Yugoslavia	03 Sep 55	240UNTS267	103408
Belgium	Ireland	10 Sep 55	255UNTS235	103612
Bulgaria	Yugoslavia	01 Oct 55	396UNTS223	105698
France	Germany, West	04 Oct 55	353UNTS203	105044
Denmark	Syria	20 Oct 55	250UNTS61	103518
Denmark	Lebanon	21 Oct 55	248UNTS17	103482
Burma	China People's Rep	08 Nov 55	306UNTS11	104430
Austria	USSR (Soviet Union)	09 Nov 55	255UNTS247	103613
Austria	Israel	17 Nov 55	232UNTS153	103235
India	Japan	26 Nov 55	311UNTS243	104506
France	Japan	17 Jan 56	255UNTS275	103614
Australia	Japan	19 Jan 56	311UNTS291	104507
Austria	Italy	23 Jan 56	393UNTS97	105653
Argentina	Switzerland	25 Jan 56	559UNTS121	108157
Romania	Yugoslavia	01 Feb 56	362UNTS203	105189
Hungary	Romania	03 Feb 56	362UNTS233	105190
India	USA (United States)	03 Feb 56	272UNTS75	103932
Austria	Poland	08 Feb 56	334UNTS221	104770
Norway	Syria	25 Feb 56	463UNTS217	106706
Norway	USSR (Soviet Union)	31 Mar 56	259UNTS205	103690
Sweden	USSR (Soviet Union)	31 Mar 56	259UNTS239	103691
Denmark	USSR (Soviet Union)	31 Mar 56	259UNTS169	103689
Belgium	Germany, West	14 Apr 56	344UNTS103	104945
Germany, West	Switzerland	02 May 56	559UNTS157	108158
Portugal	Venezuela	16 May 56	463UNTS239	106707
Japan	Switzerland	24 May 56	312UNTS3	104509
Greece	Italy	26 May 56	496UNTS301	107258
Italy	Switzerland	04 Jun 56	378UNTS311	105429
Poland	Sweden	08 Jun 56	334UNTS257	104771
Germany, West	Ireland	12 Jun 56	353UNTS121	105040
Germany, West	Netherlands	28 Sep 56	327UNTS185	104722
Switzerland	Thailand	13 Oct 56	312UNTS43	104510
Belgium	Poland	17 Oct 56	356UNTS279	105100
Colombia	USA (United States)	24 Oct 56	476UNTS77	106905
Belgium	Turkey	25 Oct 56	380UNTS3	105447
Peru	Switzerland	23 Nov 56	411UNTS97	105916
Albania	Yugoslavia	23 Nov 56	386UNTS73	105539
Belgium	Romania	04 Dec 56	317UNTS161	104602
Iran	USA (United States)	16 Jan 57	308UNTS147	104460
Iceland	Thailand	22 Jan 57	312UNTS63	104511
Denmark	Germany, West	29 Jan 57	302UNTS75	104354
Germany, West	Sweden	29 Jan 57	393UNTS113	105654
Germany, West	Norway	29 Jan 57	353UNTS39	105037
Netherlands	Yugoslavia	13 Mar 57	327UNTS227	104723
Netherlands	USA (United States)	03 Apr 57	410UNTS193	105904
Germany, West	Yugoslavia	10 Apr 57	463UNTS269	106708
Romania	Sweden	15 Apr 57	342UNTS325	104915

PARTY ONE	PARTY TWO	DATE	CITATION	NUMBER
Airport facilities (Cont.)				
Bulgaria	Sweden	17 Apr 57	464UNTS3	106709
Korea, South	USA (United States)	24 Apr 57	288UNTS219	104207
Australia	Germany, West	22 May 57	357UNTS45	105105
Hungary	Netherlands	28 May 57	334UNTS291	104773
Czechoslovakia	United Arab Rep	30 Jun 57	411UNTS126	105917
Hungary	Sweden	02 Aug 57	334UNTS307	104774
Greece	Italy	02 Aug 57	533UNTS217	107744
Netherlands	Romania	27 Aug 57	342UNTS309	104914
Multilateral		03 Oct 57	366UNTS87	105216
France	Morocco	25 Oct 57	559UNTS95	108156
Canada	Switzerland	10 Jan 58	464UNTS21	106710
Belgium	Morocco	20 Jan 58	288UNTS3	104192
Bulgaria	Netherlands	07 Feb 58	335UNTS45	104777
Norway	Pakistan	05 Mar 58	334UNTS199	104769
Pakistan	Sweden	06 Mar 58	393UNTS181	105656
Germany, West	Portugal	21 Mar 58	464UNTS71	106712
Morocco	Portugal	03 Apr 58	393UNTS203	105657
Belgium	Iran	14 Apr 58	381UNTS309	105473
Sweden	Yugoslavia	18 Apr 58	393UNTS225	105658
Bulgaria	Denmark	28 May 58	312UNTS235	104521
India	USSR (Soviet Union)	02 Jun 58	393UNTS3	105650
Denmark	Luxembourg	10 Jun 58	356UNTS193	105096
Norway	Romania	16 Jun 58	405UNTS223	105835
Denmark	Romania	25 Jun 58	345UNTS231	104970
Austria	Romania	10 Jul 58	353UNTS155	105041
Denmark	Hungary	17 Jul 58	344UNTS281	104954
Afghanistan	Austria	21 Jul 58	0UNTS0	109236
Muscat and Oman	UK Great Britain	25 Jul 58	312UNTS347	104524
Romania	United Arab Rep	14 Aug 58	405UNTS189	105834
Austria	Bulgaria	12 Sep 58	353UNTS3	105036
Finland	Switzerland	07 Jan 59	353UNTS173	105042
UK Great Britain	Yugoslavia	03 Feb 59	359UNTS339	105151
Indonesia	USA (United States)	02 Mar 59	357UNTS145	105113
Netherlands	Tunisia	19 Mar 59	497UNTS61	107262
Sweden	Tunisia	19 Mar 59	497UNTS43	107261
Norway	Tunisia	28 Mar 59	497UNTS77	107263
Denmark	Tunisia	14 Apr 59	340UNTS273	104870
Ceylon (Sri Lanka)	Denmark	29 May 59	348UNTS225	105002
Ceylon (Sri Lanka)	Sweden	29 May 59	464UNTS109	106713
Ceylon (Sri Lanka)	Norway	29 May 59	411UNTS165	105919
Belgium	Japan	20 Jun 59	411UNTS3	105911
Bulgaria	United Arab Rep	09 Jul 59	411UNTS187	105920
Austria	Hungary	17 Jul 59	0UNTS0	109237
Afghanistan	Germany, West	22 Jul 59	464UNTS177	106715
Germany, West	Iceland	12 Aug 59	411UNTS224	105921
Canada	Germany, West	04 Sep 59	411UNTS260	105922
Nicaragua	Peru	14 Oct 59	392UNTS303	105649
France	Thailand	26 Feb 60	392UNTS279	105648
Finland	Iceland	10 Mar 60	497UNTS95	107264
Czechoslovakia	Iraq	11 Mar 60	464UNTS267	106718
Luxembourg	Yugoslavia	09 Apr 60	464UNTS293	106719
Germany, West	Spain	28 Apr 60	465UNTS3	106720
Iran	UK Great Britain	02 May 60	566UNTS129	108241
Greece	Romania	02 May 60	485UNTS17	107043
Morocco	United Arab Rep	19 May 60	563UNTS121	108208
Switzerland	Tunisia	21 May 60	497UNTS109	107265
Afghanistan	Czechoslovakia	28 May 60	497UNTS129	107266
Luxembourg	Tunisia	13 Jun 60	497UNTS143	107267
Denmark	Peru	22 Jun 60	439UNTS113	106326
Germany, West	Pakistan	20 Jul 60	465UNTS41	106721
Netherlands	Poland	21 Jul 60	497UNTS189	107269
Mexico	USA (United States)	15 Aug 60	402UNTS177	105786
Belgium	Burma	17 Aug 60	540UNTS185	107850
Czechoslovakia	India	19 Sep 60	465UNTS67	106722
Hungary	UK Great Britain	25 Oct 60	419UNTS309	106034

PARTY ONE	PARTY TWO	DATE	CITATION	NUMBER
Airport facilities (Cont.)				
Burma	Switzerland	31 Oct 60	465UNTS97	106723
Norway	Peru	02 Nov 60	497UNTS207	107270
Luxembourg	Thailand	29 Dec 60	465UNTS131	106725
Denmark	Poland	17 Jan 61	412UNTS111	105927
Norway	Poland	17 Jan 61	412UNTS130	105928
Germany, West	Japan	18 Jan 61	465UNTS173	106727
Cuba	Czechoslovakia	04 Mar 61	465UNTS209	106728
Czechoslovakia	Morocco	08 Jun 61	497UNTS275	107272
Australia	New Zealand	25 Jul 61	523UNTS271	107561
Finland	Luxembourg	15 Aug 61	541UNTS45	107859
Mexico	Netherlands	24 Aug 61	465UNTS291	106732
Ghana	Romania	30 Sep 61	467UNTS443	106769
Germany, West	Morocco	12 Oct 61	523UNTS289	107562
Cyprus	Greece	23 Nov 61	497UNTS311	107274
Czechoslovakia	Mali	27 Nov 61	466UNTS41	106736
Denmark	Jordan	07 Dec 61	631UNTS333	109003
Czechoslovakia	Guinea	16 Dec 61	559UNTS49	108154
Austria	Greece	15 Jan 62	498UNTS3	107275
Indonesia	Japan	23 Jan 62	559UNTS77	108155
Finland	Hungary	13 Feb 62	463UNTS61	106693
Austria	Spain	19 Feb 62	0UNTS0	109238
Germany, West	Thailand	05 Mar 62	563UNTS165	108210
Netherlands	USA (United States)	24 Apr 62	436UNTS93	106289
France	Romania	18 May 62	498UNTS115	107279
Morocco	Switzerland	05 Jul 62	498UNTS171	107281
Ecuador	Germany, West	20 Sep 62	498UNTS199	107283
Japan	Kuwait	06 Oct 62	498UNTS235	107284
Finland	France	12 Oct 62	498UNTS299	107285
Hungary	Syria	18 Oct 62	491UNTS209	107178
Poland	Syria	10 Nov 62	491UNTS228	107179
New Zealand	Western Samoa	24 Jan 63	499UNTS21	107290
Mali	Senegal	07 Feb 63	524UNTS41	107565
Cyprus	Denmark	27 Apr 63	529UNTS255	107664
Greece	Hungary	27 Apr 63	534UNTS3	107750
Jordan	UK Great Britain	27 Apr 63	475UNTS169	106892
Algeria	Morocco	30 Apr 63	564UNTS3	108217
Algeria	Mali	22 Jul 63	564UNTS29	108219
Pakistan	USSR (Soviet Union)	07 Oct 63	499UNTS161	107297
Lebanon	Pakistan	04 Feb 64	614UNTS55	108863
Argentina	Paraguay	07 Feb 64	634UNTS127	109057
Denmark	Yugoslavia	11 Feb 64	511UNTS241	107437
Norway	Yugoslavia	15 Apr 64	602UNTS177	108712
United Arab Rep	USA (United States)	05 May 64	531UNTS229	107706
New Zealand	USA (United States)	24 Jun 64	524UNTS101	107568
France	Trinidad/Tobago	12 Oct 64	535UNTS25	107774
Argentina	UK Great Britain	12 Jan 65	597UNTS177	108645
Spain	Sweden	05 May 65	0UNTS0	109239
Denmark	Spain	05 May 65	543UNTS255	107905
Ivory Coast	Sweden	07 Jun 65	0UNTS0	109240
Canada	USA (United States)	17 Jan 66	586UNTS151	108502
Bulgaria	Turkey	18 Apr 66	631UNTS263	108999
Ivory Coast	Norway	07 Jun 66	0UNTS0	109249
Denmark	Ivory Coast	07 Jun 66	595UNTS313	108626
Denmark	Nigeria	08 Sep 66	591UNTS177	108557
Norway	Singapore	20 Dec 66	0UNTS0	109242
Denmark	Singapore	20 Dec 66	593UNTS125	108580
Japan	Singapore	14 Feb 67	0UNTS0	109244
Algeria	Ivory Coast	16 Feb 67	0UNTS0	109245
Congo (Brazzaville)	Denmark	27 Feb 67	600UNTS189	108681
Australia	Austria	22 Mar 67	0UNTS0	109246
Netherlands	Sierra Leone	13 Jun 67	0UNTS0	109247
Multilateral		03 Jul 67	0UNTS0	109248
Singapore	UK Great Britain	01 Aug 67	619UNTS29	108937
Malaysia	UK Great Britain	01 Aug 67	633UNTS93	109036
Denmark	Malaysia	14 Dec 67	614UNTS26	108862

PARTY ONE	PARTY TWO	DATE	CITATION	NUMBER
Airport equipment				
Multilateral		07 Dec 44	15UNTS295	200102
United Arab Rep	USA (United States)	15 Jun 46	151UNTS135	101988
France	USA (United States)	18 Jun 46	42UNTS183	100647
Iceland	UK Great Britain	04 Jul 46	6UNTS223	100077
Canada	Newfoundland	29 Jul 46	17UNTS169	100275
UK Great Britain	USA (United States)	31 Jul 46	42UNTS199	100648
Sweden	USA (United States)	30 Sep 46	42UNTS213	100649
Brazil	UK Great Britain	31 Oct 46	11UNTS115	100152
Norway	USA (United States)	12 Nov 46	42UNTS227	100651
Australia	USA (United States)	03 Dec 46	7UNTS201	100100
New Zealand	USA (United States)	03 Dec 46	7UNTS175	100099
USSR (Soviet Union)	Yugoslavia	04 Feb 47	130UNTS235	101731
Muscat and Oman	UK Great Britain	05 Apr 47	27UNTS287	100412
Switzerland	USA (United States)	30 Apr 47	42UNTS235	100652
Thailand	USA (United States)	08 May 47	42UNTS241	100653
Philippines	USA (United States)	12 May 47	16UNTS137	100254
India	Netherlands	31 May 47	17UNTS65	100268
UK Great Britain	USA (United States)	13 Oct 47	66UNTS269	100858
Ecuador	USA (United States)	27 Oct 47	44UNTS45	100677
France	USA (United States)	19 Oct 48	98UNTS3	101355
Argentina	Chile	14 Dec 48	635UNTS21	109071
Belgium	Sweden	21 Feb 49	95UNTS73	101317
Korea, South	USA (United States)	29 Jun 49	55UNTS79	100809
Guatemala	USA (United States)	20 Dec 49	70UNTS71	100897
Iceland	UK Great Britain	26 May 50	95UNTS277	101326
Israel	UK Great Britain	06 Dec 50	151UNTS33	101983
Saudi Arabia	USA (United States)	18 Jun 51	102UNTS73	101412
Libya	UK Great Britain	31 Mar 52	151UNTS69	101984
Norway	UK Great Britain	23 Jun 52	151UNTS81	101985
Greece	USA (United States)	25 Jun 52	181UNTS53	102398
Sweden	Switzerland	12 Aug 53	232UNTS59	103229
Lebanon	Yugoslavia	17 Apr 54	602UNTS199	108713
Switzerland	Syria	26 May 54	255UNTS145	103609
Pakistan	United Arab Rep	13 Dec 54	255UNTS167	103610
United Arab Rep	Yugoslavia	20 Feb 55	255UNTS199	103611
Germany, West	USA (United States)	02 Aug 55	268UNTS121	103854
USSR (Soviet Union)	Yugoslavia	03 Sep 55	240UNTS267	103408
Belgium	Ireland	10 Sep 55	255UNTS235	103612
Denmark	Lebanon	21 Oct 55	248UNTS17	103482
France	Japan	17 Jan 56	255UNTS275	103614
Denmark	USSR (Soviet Union)	31 Mar 56	259UNTS169	103689
Sweden	USSR (Soviet Union)	31 Mar 56	259UNTS239	103691
Norway	USSR (Soviet Union)	31 Mar 56	259UNTS205	103690
India	Thailand	12 Jun 56	255UNTS341	103617
Norway	Romania	16 Jun 58	405UNTS223	105835
Afghanistan	Austria	21 Jul 58	0UNTS0	109236
Austria	Hungary	17 Jul 59	0UNTS0	109237
Iran	UK Great Britain	02 May 60	566UNTS129	108241
Denmark	Poland	17 Jan 61	412UNTS111	105927
Australia	New Zealand	25 Jul 61	523UNTS271	107561
Denmark	Jordan	07 Dec 61	631UNTS333	109003
Austria	Spain	19 Feb 62	0UNTS0	109238
Cyprus	Norway	05 Mar 63	563UNTS305	108216
Belgium	Cyprus	08 Jun 63	601UNTS311	108703
Algeria	Tunisia	01 Sep 63	601UNTS275	108701
Lebanon	Pakistan	04 Feb 64	614UNTS55	108863
Argentina	Paraguay	07 Feb 64	634UNTS127	109057
Cyprus	USSR (Soviet Union)	29 Feb 64	602UNTS45	108706
Norway	Yugoslavia	15 Apr 64	602UNTS177	108712
Cyprus	Hungary	02 Jun 64	602UNTS3	108704
France	Trinidad/Tobago	12 Oct 64	535UNTS25	107774
Cyprus	Syria	22 Dec 64	602UNTS25	108705
Australia	France	13 Apr 65	601UNTS293	108702
Spain	Sweden	05 May 65	0UNTS0	109239

PARTY ONE	PARTY TWO	DATE	CITATION	NUMBER
Airport equipment (Cont.)				
Ivory Coast	Sweden	07 Jun 65	0UNTS0	109240
Burma	Czechoslovakia	15 Dec 65	602UNTS71	108707
Canada	USA (United States)	17 Jan 66	586UNTS151	108502
Bulgaria	Turkey	18 Apr 66	631UNTS263	108999
Ivory Coast	Norway	07 Jun 66	0UNTS0	109249
Denmark	Ivory Coast	07 Jun 66	595UNTS313	108626
Denmark	Nigeria	08 Sep 66	591UNTS177	108557
Norway	Singapore	20 Dec 66	0UNTS0	109242
Japan	Singapore	14 Feb 67	0UNTS0	109244
Algeria	Ivory Coast	16 Feb 67	0UNTS0	109245
Congo (Brazzaville)	Denmark	27 Feb 67	600UNTS189	108681
Australia	Austria	22 Mar 67	0UNTS0	109246
Netherlands	Sierra Leone	13 Jun 67	0UNTS0	109247
Multilateral		03 Jul 67	0UNTS0	109248
Malaysia	UK Great Britain	01 Aug 67	633UNTS93	109036
Singapore	UK Great Britain	01 Aug 67	619UNTS29	108937
Denmark	Malaysia	14 Dec 67	614UNTS26	108862
Airworthiness certificates				
Brazil	France	27 Jan 40	72UNTS77	100929
Spain	USA (United States)	02 Dec 44	89UNTS345	200262
Multilateral		07 Dec 44	171UNTS345	200501
Multilateral		07 Dec 44	15UNTS295	200102
Denmark	USA (United States)	16 Dec 44	10UNTS213	200063
Sweden	USA (United States)	16 Dec 44	6UNTS397	200041
Iceland	USA (United States)	27 Jan 45	122UNTS293	200411
Ireland	USA (United States)	03 Feb 45	122UNTS305	200412
Canada	USA (United States)	17 Feb 45	122UNTS261	200409
Norway	USA (United States)	06 Oct 45	122UNTS319	200413
South Africa	UK Great Britain	26 Oct 45	72UNTS41	100927
Greece	UK Great Britain	26 Nov 45	35UNTS161	100555
Portugal	UK Great Britain	06 Dec 45	6UNTS3	100065
Portugal	UK Great Britain	06 Dec 45	5UNTS37	100064
Portugal	USA (United States)	06 Dec 45	3UNTS139	100028
Canada	UK Great Britain	21 Dec 45	27UNTS155	100405
Czechoslovakia	USA (United States)	03 Jan 46	6UNTS309	100084
Czechoslovakia	Poland	24 Jan 46	25UNTS181	100363
UK Great Britain	USA (United States)	11 Feb 46	3UNTS253	100036
Turkey	UK Great Britain	12 Feb 46	6UNTS79	100069
Turkey	USA (United States)	12 Feb 46	13UNTS3	100196
France	UK Great Britain	28 Feb 46	27UNTS173	100407
France	USA (United States)	27 Mar 46	139UNTS114	101879
Greece	USA (United States)	27 Mar 46	15UNTS233	100239
Multilateral		31 Mar 46	17UNTS159	100274
Belgium	USA (United States)	05 Apr 46	4UNTS125	100041
Ireland	UK Great Britain	05 Apr 46	72UNTS57	100928
Netherlands	Portugal	12 Apr 46	4UNTS317	100054
Argentina	UK Great Britain	17 Apr 46	164UNTS53	102159
France	Ireland	16 May 46	44UNTS105	100681
Ireland	Sweden	29 May 46	35UNTS231	100557
Australia	Canada	11 Jun 46	10UNTS47	100142
United Arab Rep	USA (United States)	15 Jun 46	71UNTS157	100917
France	USA (United States)	18 Jun 46	42UNTS183	100647
Sweden	Turkey	26 Jun 46	14UNTS21	100208
Albania	Yugoslavia	11 Jul 46	4UNTS407	100058
Netherlands	Spain	13 Jul 46	4UNTS351	100055
Czechoslovakia	USSR (Soviet Union)	25 Jul 46	27UNTS231	100409
France	Sweden	02 Aug 46	27UNTS251	100410
Lebanon	USA (United States)	11 Aug 46	66UNTS211	100856
Netherlands	UK Great Britain	13 Aug 46	4UNTS367	100056
Norway	UK Great Britain	31 Aug 46	6UNTS235	100078
Brazil	USA (United States)	06 Sep 46	54UNTS197	100805
France	Turkey	12 Oct 46	14UNTS33	100209
Belgium	Portugal	22 Oct 46	34UNTS49	100527
Brazil	UK Great Britain	31 Oct 46	11UNTS115	100152

PARTY ONE	PARTY TWO	DATE	CITATION	NUMBER
Airworthiness certificates (Cont.)				
Philippines	USA (United States)	16 Nov 46	7UNTS151	100097
Sweden	UK Great Britain	27 Nov 46	11UNTS229	100162
Australia	USA (United States)	03 Dec 46	7UNTS201	100100
New Zealand	USA (United States)	03 Dec 46	7UNTS175	100099
Portugal	Switzerland	09 Dec 46	310UNTS251	104495
Brazil	Portugal	10 Dec 46	200UNTS67	102695
USA (United States)	Uruguay	14 Dec 46	532UNTS87	107713
Taiwan	USA (United States)	20 Dec 46	22UNTS87	100332
Peru	USA (United States)	27 Dec 46	26UNTS227	100390
Ecuador	USA (United States)	08 Jan 47	22UNTS119	100333
Czechoslovakia	Ireland	29 Jan 47	27UNTS267	100411
Thailand	USA (United States)	26 Feb 47	16UNTS17	100246
Paraguay	USA (United States)	28 Feb 47	44UNTS25	100676
Portugal	Sweden	06 Mar 47	35UNTS243	100558
Netherlands	Turkey	19 Mar 47	14UNTS59	100211
Greece	Sweden	08 Apr 47	94UNTS73	101307
Greece	Netherlands	17 Apr 47	32UNTS115	100494
Canada	Portugal	25 Apr 47	94UNTS87	101308
Syria	USA (United States)	28 Apr 47	262UNTS121	103741
France	Greece	05 May 47	76UNTS61	100980
Chile	USA (United States)	10 May 47	55UNTS21	100807
Czechoslovakia	Denmark	14 May 47	27UNTS297	100413
South Africa	USA (United States)	23 May 47	66UNTS233	100857
India	Netherlands	31 May 47	17UNTS65	100268
Canada	Sweden	27 Jun 47	27UNTS313	100414
Iraq	Turkey	30 Jun 47	72UNTS107	100930
Romania	Yugoslavia	30 Jun 47	116UNTS57	101569
Denmark	Turkey	30 Jun 47	32UNTS301	100504
Canada	UK Great Britain	17 Jul 47	28UNTS3	100416
Netherlands	Thailand	18 Jul 47	28UNTS27	100417
Greece	Turkey	22 Jul 47	72UNTS131	100931
Netherlands	South Africa	22 Jul 47	12UNTS257	100188
Taiwan	UK Great Britain	23 Jul 47	9UNTS207	100135
Poland	Romania	09 Aug 47	12UNTS363	100193
Hungary	Poland	28 Aug 47	15UNTS145	100231
Czechoslovakia	Netherlands	01 Sep 47	32UNTS129	100495
Czechoslovakia	Switzerland	10 Sep 47	35UNTS275	100559
Lebanon	Turkey	16 Sep 47	44UNTS123	100682
Czechoslovakia	Sweden	15 Oct 47	44UNTS149	100683
Colombia	UK Great Britain	16 Oct 47	160UNTS297	102115
Norway	Portugal	11 Nov 47	34UNTS257	100542
Denmark	Greece	14 Nov 47	35UNTS295	100560
Denmark	Ireland	18 Nov 47	35UNTS309	100561
Ireland	Italy	21 Nov 47	353UNTS73	105038
Taiwan	Netherlands	06 Dec 47	43UNTS185	100669
Denmark	Portugal	15 Dec 47	35UNTS329	100563
Austria	Netherlands	22 Jan 48	17UNTS99	100270
Italy	USA (United States)	06 Feb 48	73UNTS113	100950
Czechoslovakia	Yugoslavia	14 Mar 48	28UNTS81	100421
Argentina	Denmark	18 Mar 48	94UNTS175	101311
Cuba	UK Great Britain	19 Mar 48	175UNTS23	102294
Ireland	Switzerland	06 May 48	334UNTS187	104768
Jordan	Turkey	07 May 48	32UNTS313	100505
Ireland	Netherlands	10 May 48	28UNTS121	100422
Norway	Turkey	20 May 48	26UNTS137	100384
Greece	Switzerland	26 May 48	94UNTS217	101312
Argentina	Brazil	02 Jun 48	0UNTS0	109515
Ireland	Norway	21 Jun 48	34UNTS317	100545
France	Spain	23 Aug 48	28UNTS173	100425
Greece	Lebanon	06 Sep 48	178UNTS37	102335
Bolivia	USA (United States)	29 Sep 48	505UNTS139	107370
Netherlands	Spain	08 Oct 48	28UNTS209	100426
Mexico	Portugal	22 Oct 48	34UNTS329	100546
Argentina	Netherlands	29 Oct 48	95UNTS21	101316
Argentina	Chile	14 Dec 48	635UNTS21	109071

Airworthiness certificates (Cont.)

PARTY ONE	PARTY TWO	DATE	CITATION	NUMBER
Italy	Lebanon	24 Jan 49	231UNTS241	103223
Switzerland	Turkey	16 Feb 49	72UNTS175	100933
Finland	Netherlands	25 Feb 49	53UNTS123	100777
Netherlands	Switzerland	07 Mar 49	35UNTS69	100551
Finland	USA (United States)	29 Mar 49	55UNTS59	100808
Panama	USA (United States)	31 Mar 49	55UNTS87	100810
Finland	Sweden	26 Apr 49	95UNTS83	101318
Bulgaria	Poland	16 May 49	84UNTS313	101140
Italy	Spain	31 May 49	231UNTS251	103224
Canada	USA (United States)	04 Jun 49	122UNTS237	101649
Belgium	Greece	21 Jun 49	137UNTS215	101854
India	Switzerland	24 Jun 49	95UNTS109	101319
Korea, South	USA (United States)	29 Jun 49	55UNTS79	100809
Greece	Syria	05 Jul 49	78UNTS71	101013
Iraq	Norway	12 Jul 49	53UNTS137	100778
Czechoslovakia	Finland	13 Jul 49	53UNTS153	100779
Finland	Norway	24 Aug 49	53UNTS167	100780
Denmark	Finland	26 Aug 49	53UNTS191	100781
Lebanon	Netherlands	20 Sep 49	108UNTS205	101474
Burma	USA (United States)	28 Sep 49	55UNTS3	100806
Greece	Philippines	08 Oct 49	187UNTS221	102515
Sweden	Thailand	23 Nov 49	72UNTS217	100935
Denmark	Thailand	23 Nov 49	53UNTS255	100786
Italy	Turkey	25 Nov 49	192UNTS39	102594
Norway	Thailand	26 Nov 49	53UNTS269	100787
Brazil	Spain	28 Nov 49	215UNTS303	102923
Austria	Norway	02 Dec 49	72UNTS230	100936
Austria	Sweden	02 Dec 49	108UNTS3	101465
Austria	Denmark	02 Dec 49	53UNTS281	100788
Austria	Switzerland	19 Dec 49	254UNTS287	103597
Finland	Sweden	21 Dec 49	197UNTS243	102642
USA (United States)	Yugoslavia	24 Dec 49	89UNTS209	101219
Netherlands	Syria	13 Feb 50	108UNTS53	101467
Canada	Norway	14 Feb 50	53UNTS329	100790
Spain	Sweden	18 Feb 50	166UNTS15	102184
Ceylon (Sri Lanka)	Thailand	24 Feb 50	72UNTS261	100938
Italy	Netherlands	04 Mar 50	254UNTS305	103598
Iceland	Netherlands	22 Mar 50	95UNTS237	101323
Denmark	Iceland	22 Mar 50	72UNTS273	100939
Italy	Portugal	05 Apr 50	254UNTS329	103599
Iceland	UK Great Britain	26 May 50	95UNTS277	101326
Israel	USA (United States)	13 Jun 50	212UNTS93	102863
Netherlands	Spain	20 Jun 50	95UNTS303	101327
Burma	Ceylon (Sri Lanka)	29 Jun 50	73UNTS3	100940
Spain	UK Great Britain	20 Jul 50	398UNTS101	105719
Spain	Switzerland	03 Aug 50	254UNTS365	103600
Canada	New Zealand	16 Aug 50	77UNTS239	101002
Burma	Sweden	14 Sep 50	96UNTS45	101330
Brazil	Turkey	21 Sep 50	150UNTS299	101981
Sweden	Switzerland	18 Oct 50	166UNTS49	102185
Luxembourg	Portugal	21 Oct 50	108UNTS67	101468
Israel	Netherlands	23 Oct 50	189UNTS89	102543
Israel	UK Great Britain	06 Dec 50	151UNTS33	101983
Israel	Turkey	05 Feb 51	193UNTS3	102607
Colombia	Portugal	09 Mar 51	108UNTS87	101469
Greece	Yugoslavia	15 Mar 51	187UNTS237	102516
Greece	Norway	28 May 51	187UNTS141	102507
Cuba	Portugal	26 Jun 51	192UNTS115	102598
Iceland	Norway	14 Jul 51	163UNTS265	102150
Burma	Denmark	30 Jul 51	108UNTS167	101472
Burma	Netherlands	06 Sep 51	108UNTS187	101473
Panama	UK Great Britain	15 Sep 51	560UNTS143	108172
Philippines	Spain	06 Oct 51	215UNTS193	102920
Greece	Luxembourg	22 Oct 51	187UNTS119	102506
Denmark	Iraq	18 Nov 51	232UNTS25	103227

Airworthiness certificates (Cont.)

PARTY ONE	PARTY TWO	DATE	CITATION	NUMBER
Colombia	Spain	11 Dec 51	216UNTS73	102933
Belgium	Spain	10 Mar 52	178UNTS243	102342
Norway	Uruguay	20 Mar 52	310UNTS279	104496
Sweden	Uruguay	20 Mar 52	311UNTS3	104497
Iraq	Switzerland	31 Mar 52	311UNTS43	104498
France	Mexico	17 Apr 52	163UNTS321	102153
France	Israel	29 Apr 52	189UNTS55	102542
Denmark	UK Great Britain	23 Jun 52	151UNTS3	101982
Norway	UK Great Britain	23 Jun 52	151UNTS81	101985
Japan	USA (United States)	11 Aug 52	212UNTS27	102862
Netherlands	Peru	22 Sep 52	255UNTS49	103604
Mexico	Netherlands	13 Oct 52	163UNTS341	102154
Austria	Luxembourg	13 Oct 52	192UNTS291	102606
Iceland	Luxembourg	23 Oct 52	193UNTS39	102609
Chile	Denmark	27 Oct 52	271UNTS93	103911
Chile	Sweden	27 Oct 52	311UNTS63	104499
Luxembourg	Norway	17 Nov 52	311UNTS95	104500
Luxembourg	Sweden	17 Nov 52	173UNTS277	102270
Israel	Switzerland	19 Nov 52	232UNTS3	103226
Lebanon	Sweden	23 Mar 53	255UNTS83	103605
Turkey	Yugoslavia	16 Apr 53	255UNTS99	103606
Philippines	Thailand	27 Apr 53	174UNTS3	102274
Cuba	USA (United States)	26 May 53	224UNTS75	103070
Switzerland	Yugoslavia	28 May 53	232UNTS45	103228
Burma	Norway	22 Jun 53	174UNTS49	102277
USA (United States)	Venezuela	14 Aug 53	213UNTS99	102883
Austria	Yugoslavia	11 Nov 53	363UNTS149	105206
Syria	UK Great Britain	30 Jan 54	449UNTS47	106452
Lebanon	Switzerland	03 Mar 54	255UNTS127	103608
Peru	Spain	31 Mar 54	232UNTS65	103230
Lebanon	Yugoslavia	17 Apr 54	602UNTS199	108713
Switzerland	Syria	26 May 54	255UNTS145	103609
Ireland	Luxembourg	27 Jul 54	232UNTS91	103231
Ecuador	Netherlands	14 Dec 54	232UNTS115	103233
Denmark	USA (United States)	15 Dec 54	213UNTS273	102890
Sweden	USA (United States)	22 Dec 54	228UNTS85	103143
Norway	Switzerland	30 Dec 54	311UNTS147	104502
Austria	Belgium	07 Jan 55	380UNTS219	105458
Italy	USA (United States)	26 Jan 55	238UNTS179	103361
South Africa	USA (United States)	22 Feb 55	247UNTS247	103473
Germany, West	USA (United States)	07 Jul 55	275UNTS3	103973
Germany, East	Romania	28 Jul 55	342UNTS207	104909
USSR (Soviet Union)	Yugoslavia	03 Sep 55	240UNTS267	103408
Belgium	Ireland	10 Sep 55	255UNTS235	103612
Germany, East	Hungary	10 Sep 55	407UNTS132	105863
Bulgaria	Yugoslavia	01 Oct 55	396UNTS223	105698
France	Germany, West	04 Oct 55	353UNTS203	105044
Finland	USSR (Soviet Union)	19 Oct 55	353UNTS185	105043
Denmark	Syria	20 Oct 55	250UNTS61	103518
Denmark	Lebanon	21 Oct 55	248UNTS17	103482
Netherlands	USA (United States)	04 Nov 55	269UNTS3	103867
Burma	China People's Rep	08 Nov 55	306UNTS11	104430
Austria	Israel	17 Nov 55	232UNTS153	103235
Austria	Italy	23 Jan 56	393UNTS97	105653
Argentina	Switzerland	25 Jan 56	559UNTS121	108157
Romania	Yugoslavia	01 Feb 56	362UNTS203	105189
Hungary	Romania	03 Feb 56	362UNTS233	105190
Austria	Poland	08 Feb 56	334UNTS221	104770
Norway	Syria	25 Feb 56	463UNTS217	106706
Denmark	USSR (Soviet Union)	31 Mar 56	259UNTS169	103689
Sweden	USSR (Soviet Union)	31 Mar 56	259UNTS239	103691
Norway	USSR (Soviet Union)	31 Mar 56	259UNTS205	103690
Belgium	Germany, West	14 Apr 56	344UNTS103	104945
Germany, West	Switzerland	02 May 56	559UNTS157	108158
Portugal	Venezuela	16 May 56	463UNTS239	106707

Airworthiness certificates (Cont.)

PARTY ONE	PARTY TWO	DATE	CITATION	NUMBER
Greece	Italy	26 May 56	496UNTS301	107258
Italy	Switzerland	04 Jun 56	378UNTS311	105429
Poland	Sweden	08 Jun 56	334UNTS257	104771
Germany, West	Ireland	12 Jun 56	353UNTS121	105040
Switzerland	Thailand	13 Oct 56	312UNTS43	104510
Belgium	Poland	17 Oct 56	356UNTS279	105100
Colombia	USA (United States)	24 Oct 56	476UNTS77	106905
Belgium	Turkey	25 Oct 56	380UNTS3	105447
Albania	Yugoslavia	23 Nov 56	386UNTS73	105539
Peru	Switzerland	23 Nov 56	411UNTS97	105916
France	USA (United States)	14 Dec 56	266UNTS117	103826
Iran	USA (United States)	16 Jan 57	308UNTS147	104460
Iceland	Thailand	22 Jan 57	312UNTS63	104511
Denmark	Germany, West	29 Jan 57	302UNTS75	104354
Germany, West	Norway	29 Jan 57	353UNTS39	105037
Germany, West	Sweden	29 Jan 57	393UNTS113	105654
Norway	USA (United States)	05 Feb 57	279UNTS169	104038
Belgium	Czechoslovakia	12 Mar 57	312UNTS75	104512
Netherlands	Yugoslavia	13 Mar 57	327UNTS227	104723
Netherlands	USA (United States)	03 Apr 57	410UNTS193	105904
Germany, West	Yugoslavia	10 Apr 57	463UNTS269	106708
Romania	Sweden	15 Apr 57	342UNTS325	104915
Bulgaria	Sweden	17 Apr 57	464UNTS3	106709
Korea, South	USA (United States)	24 Apr 57	288UNTS219	104207
Belgium	Bulgaria	14 May 57	317UNTS81	104596
Hungary	Netherlands	28 May 57	334UNTS291	104773
Belgium	Hungary	01 Jun 57	291UNTS17	104242
Afghanistan	Pakistan	13 Jun 57	327UNTS51	104717
Czechoslovakia	United Arab Rep	30 Jun 57	411UNTS126	105917
Hungary	Sweden	02 Aug 57	334UNTS307	104774
Greece	Italy	02 Aug 57	533UNTS217	107744
Netherlands	Romania	27 Aug 57	342UNTS309	104914
Spain	USA (United States)	23 Sep 57	290UNTS261	104238
Italy	Pakistan	05 Oct 57	353UNTS91	105039
Netherlands	UK Great Britain	22 Oct 57	313UNTS309	104538
France	Morocco	25 Oct 57	559UNTS95	108156
Belgium	USA (United States)	03 Dec 57	303UNTS45	104370
UK Great Britain	USSR (Soviet Union)	19 Dec 57	351UNTS235	105026
Belgium	Morocco	20 Jan 58	288UNTS3	104192
Bulgaria	Netherlands	07 Feb 58	335UNTS45	104777
Afghanistan	Turkey	08 Feb 58	464UNTS39	106711
Morocco	Portugal	03 Apr 58	393UNTS203	105657
Sweden	Yugoslavia	18 Apr 58	393UNTS225	105658
Bulgaria	Denmark	28 May 58	312UNTS235	104521
India	USSR (Soviet Union)	02 Jun 58	393UNTS3	105650
Belgium	USSR (Soviet Union)	05 Jun 58	345UNTS145	104965
Denmark	Luxembourg	10 Jun 58	356UNTS193	105096
Norway	Romania	16 Jun 58	405UNTS223	105835
Netherlands	USSR (Soviet Union)	17 Jun 58	335UNTS77	104779
Denmark	Romania	25 Jun 58	345UNTS231	104970
Austria	Romania	10 Jul 58	353UNTS155	105041
Denmark	Hungary	17 Jul 58	344UNTS281	104954
Afghanistan	Austria	21 Jul 58	0UNTS0	109236
Romania	United Arab Rep	14 Aug 58	405UNTS189	105834
Austria	Bulgaria	12 Sep 58	353UNTS3	105036
Germany, West	USA (United States)	11 Dec 58	337UNTS31	104813
UK Great Britain	Yugoslavia	03 Feb 59	359UNTS339	105151
Indonesia	USA (United States)	02 Mar 59	357UNTS145	105113
Sweden	Tunisia	19 Mar 59	497UNTS43	107261
Norway	Tunisia	28 Mar 59	497UNTS77	107263
Denmark	Tunisia	14 Apr 59	340UNTS273	104870
Austria	USA (United States)	30 Apr 59	343UNTS41	104920
Ceylon (Sri Lanka)	Norway	29 May 59	411UNTS165	105919
Ceylon (Sri Lanka)	Sweden	29 May 59	464UNTS109	106713
Ceylon (Sri Lanka)	Denmark	29 May 59	348UNTS225	105002

Airworthiness certificates (Cont.)

PARTY ONE	PARTY TWO	DATE	CITATION	NUMBER
Bulgaria	United Arab Rep	09 Jul 59	411UNTS187	105920
Austria	Hungary	17 Jul 59	0UNTS0	109237
Australia	USA (United States)	20 Nov 59	349UNTS293	105015
France	Thailand	26 Feb 60	392UNTS279	105648
Finland	Iceland	10 Mar 60	497UNTS95	107264
Luxembourg	Yugoslavia	09 Apr 60	464UNTS293	106719
Multilateral		22 Apr 60	418UNTS211	106023
Greece	Romania	02 May 60	485UNTS17	107043
Iran	UK Great Britain	02 May 60	566UNTS129	108241
Morocco	United Arab Rep	19 May 60	563UNTS121	108208
Switzerland	Tunisia	21 May 60	497UNTS109	107265
Afghanistan	Czechoslovakia	28 May 60	497UNTS129	107266
Luxembourg	Tunisia	13 Jun 60	497UNTS143	107267
Denmark	Peru	22 Jun 60	439UNTS113	106326
Netherlands	Poland	21 Jul 60	497UNTS189	107269
Mexico	USA (United States)	15 Aug 60	402UNTS177	105786
Belgium	Burma	17 Aug 60	540UNTS185	107850
Hungary	UK Great Britain	25 Oct 60	419UNTS309	106034
Burma	Switzerland	31 Oct 60	465UNTS97	106723
Norway	Peru	02 Nov 60	497UNTS207	107270
Luxembourg	Thailand	29 Dec 60	465UNTS131	106725
Norway	Poland	17 Jan 61	412UNTS130	105928
Denmark	Poland	17 Jan 61	412UNTS111	105927
Czechoslovakia	Morocco	08 Jun 61	497UNTS275	107272
Cameroon	France	16 Jun 61	412UNTS148	105929
Mexico	USA (United States)	19 Jul 61	433UNTS43	106230
Finland	Luxembourg	15 Aug 61	541UNTS45	107859
Mexico	Netherlands	24 Aug 61	465UNTS291	106732
Liberia	Switzerland	31 Aug 61	559UNTS215	108160
Ghana	Romania	30 Sep 61	467UNTS443	106769
Switzerland	USA (United States)	13 Oct 61	459UNTS219	106625
Finland	Hungary	13 Feb 62	463UNTS61	106693
Austria	Spain	19 Feb 62	0UNTS0	109238
Ghana	USSR (Soviet Union)	06 Apr 62	498UNTS41	107277
France	Romania	18 May 62	498UNTS115	107279
France	Senegal	15 Jun 62	524UNTS3	107563
Morocco	Switzerland	05 Jul 62	498UNTS171	107281
Finland	France	12 Oct 62	498UNTS299	107285
Hungary	Syria	18 Oct 62	491UNTS209	107178
France	Ivory Coast	19 Oct 62	498UNTS317	107286
Ivory Coast	Switzerland	17 Nov 62	499UNTS3	107289
Ghana	Tunisia	11 Dec 62	563UNTS243	108213
Syria	United Arab Rep	27 Dec 62	491UNTS245	107180
Ghana	Mali	09 Jan 63	466UNTS165	106742
Senegal	Switzerland	23 Jan 63	524UNTS23	107564
Japan	USA (United States)	01 Feb 63	473UNTS49	106854
Mali	Senegal	07 Feb 63	524UNTS41	107565
Algeria	France	18 Feb 63	563UNTS263	108214
Cyprus	Norway	05 Mar 63	563UNTS305	108216
Greece	Hungary	27 Apr 63	534UNTS3	107750
Algeria	Morocco	30 Apr 63	564UNTS3	108217
Guinea	Ivory Coast	26 Jun 63	499UNTS71	107293
Algeria	Mali	22 Jul 63	564UNTS29	108219
Cameroon	Israel	09 Aug 63	499UNTS121	107295
Pakistan	USSR (Soviet Union)	07 Oct 63	499UNTS161	107297
Ivory Coast	Netherlands	09 Oct 63	499UNTS141	107296
Mali	Niger	15 Jan 64	499UNTS197	107299
Denmark	Yugoslavia	11 Feb 64	511UNTS241	107437
Cameroon	Mali	17 Mar 64	524UNTS61	107566
Norway	Yugoslavia	15 Apr 64	602UNTS177	108712
United Arab Rep	USA (United States)	05 May 64	531UNTS229	107706
Cyprus	Hungary	02 Jun 64	602UNTS3	108704
New Zealand	USA (United States)	24 Jun 64	524UNTS101	107568
Ivory Coast	Mali	09 Jul 64	524UNTS121	107569
France	Trinidad/Tobago	12 Oct 64	535UNTS25	107774

PARTY ONE	PARTY TWO	DATE	CITATION	NUMBER
Airworthiness certificates (Cont.)				
Cyprus	Syria	22 Dec 64	602UNTS25	108705
Spain	Sweden	05 May 65	0UNTS0	109239
Mauritania	Spain	11 May 65	602UNTS111	108709
Malaysia	Norway	26 May 65	602UNTS157	108711
Ivory Coast	Sweden	07 Jun 65	0UNTS0	109240
Poland	USA (United States)	27 Sep 65	564UNTS169	108227
Nigeria	Switzerland	11 Oct 65	602UNTS137	108710
Finland	USA (United States)	03 Nov 65	573UNTS175	108330
Burma	Czechoslovakia	15 Dec 65	602UNTS71	108707
Canada	USA (United States)	17 Jan 66	586UNTS151	108502
Bulgaria	Turkey	18 Apr 66	631UNTS263	108999
Denmark	Ivory Coast	07 Jun 66	595UNTS313	108626
Ivory Coast	Norway	07 Jun 66	0UNTS0	109249
Denmark	Nigeria	08 Sep 66	591UNTS177	108557
Denmark	Singapore	20 Dec 66	593UNTS125	108580
Norway	Singapore	20 Dec 66	0UNTS0	109242
Japan	Singapore	14 Feb 67	0UNTS0	109244
Algeria	Ivory Coast	16 Feb 67	0UNTS0	109245
Congo (Brazzaville)	Denmark	27 Feb 67	600UNTS189	108681
Australia	Austria	22 Mar 67	0UNTS0	109246
Netherlands	Sierra Leone	13 Jun 67	0UNTS0	109247
Multilateral		03 Jul 67	0UNTS0	109248
Malaysia	UK Great Britain	01 Aug 67	633UNTS93	109036
Israel	USA (United States)	23 Jul 68	0UNTS0	109358
Conditions of airlines operating permission				
Brazil	France	27 Jan 40	72UNTS77	100929
Spain	USA (United States)	02 Dec 44	89UNTS345	200262
Multilateral		07 Dec 44	171UNTS387	200502
Multilateral		07 Dec 44	171UNTS345	200501
Multilateral		07 Dec 44	15UNTS295	200102
Multilateral		07 Dec 44	84UNTS389	200252
Sweden	USA (United States)	16 Dec 44	6UNTS397	200041
Denmark	USA (United States)	16 Dec 44	10UNTS213	200063
Iceland	USA (United States)	27 Jan 45	122UNTS293	200411
Ireland	USA (United States)	03 Feb 45	122UNTS305	200412
Switzerland	USA (United States)	03 Aug 45	51UNTS233	200191
Norway	USA (United States)	06 Oct 45	122UNTS319	200413
South Africa	UK Great Britain	26 Oct 45	72UNTS41	100927
Greece	UK Great Britain	26 Nov 45	35UNTS161	100555
Portugal	UK Great Britain	06 Dec 45	5UNTS37	100064
Portugal	USA (United States)	06 Dec 45	3UNTS139	100028
Portugal	UK Great Britain	06 Dec 45	6UNTS3	100065
Canada	UK Great Britain	21 Dec 45	27UNTS155	100405
Czechoslovakia	USA (United States)	03 Jan 46	6UNTS309	100084
Spain	USA (United States)	15 Jan 46	89UNTS241	101221
Czechoslovakia	Poland	24 Jan 46	25UNTS181	100363
UK Great Britain	USA (United States)	11 Feb 46	3UNTS253	100036
Turkey	USA (United States)	12 Feb 46	13UNTS3	100196
Turkey	UK Great Britain	12 Feb 46	6UNTS79	100069
France	UK Great Britain	28 Feb 46	27UNTS173	100407
France	USA (United States)	27 Mar 46	139UNTS114	101879
Greece	USA (United States)	27 Mar 46	15UNTS233	100239
Ireland	UK Great Britain	05 Apr 46	72UNTS57	100928
Belgium	USA (United States)	05 Apr 46	4UNTS125	100041
Netherlands	Portugal	12 Apr 46	4UNTS317	100054
Argentina	UK Great Britain	17 Apr 46	164UNTS53	102159
France	Ireland	16 May 46	44UNTS105	100681
Ireland	Sweden	29 May 46	35UNTS231	100557
Australia	Canada	11 Jun 46	10UNTS47	100142
United Arab Rep	USA (United States)	15 Jun 46	71UNTS157	100917
France	USA (United States)	18 Jun 46	42UNTS183	100647
Sweden	Turkey	26 Jun 46	14UNTS21	100208
Albania	Yugoslavia	11 Jul 46	4UNTS407	100058
Netherlands	Spain	13 Jul 46	4UNTS351	100055

PARTY ONE	PARTY TWO	DATE	CITATION	NUMBER
Conditions of airlines operating permission (Cont.)				
France	Sweden	02 Aug 46	27UNTS251	100410
Lebanon	USA (United States)	11 Aug 46	66UNTS211	100856
Netherlands	UK Great Britain	13 Aug 46	4UNTS367	100056
Norway	UK Great Britain	31 Aug 46	6UNTS235	100078
Brazil	USA (United States)	06 Sep 46	54UNTS197	100805
France	Turkey	12 Oct 46	14UNTS33	100209
Belgium	Portugal	22 Oct 46	34UNTS49	100527
Brazil	UK Great Britain	31 Oct 46	11UNTS115	100152
India	USA (United States)	14 Nov 46	22UNTS55	100331
Philippines	USA (United States)	16 Nov 46	7UNTS151	100097
Sweden	UK Great Britain	27 Nov 46	11UNTS229	100162
Australia	USA (United States)	03 Dec 46	7UNTS201	100100
New Zealand	USA (United States)	03 Dec 46	7UNTS175	100099
Portugal	Switzerland	09 Dec 46	310UNTS251	104495
Brazil	Portugal	10 Dec 46	200UNTS67	102695
USA (United States)	Uruguay	14 Dec 46	532UNTS87	107713
Taiwan	USA (United States)	20 Dec 46	22UNTS87	100332
Peru	USA (United States)	27 Dec 46	26UNTS227	100390
Ecuador	USA (United States)	08 Jan 47	22UNTS119	100333
Czechoslovakia	Ireland	29 Jan 47	27UNTS267	100411
Greece	UK Great Britain	21 Feb 47	70UNTS215	100905
Thailand	USA (United States)	26 Feb 47	16UNTS17	100246
Paraguay	USA (United States)	28 Feb 47	44UNTS25	100676
Portugal	Sweden	06 Mar 47	35UNTS243	100558
Greece	Sweden	08 Apr 47	94UNTS73	101307
Canada	USA (United States)	12 Apr 47	122UNTS229	101648
Greece	Netherlands	17 Apr 47	32UNTS115	100494
Canada	Portugal	25 Apr 47	94UNTS87	101308
Syria	USA (United States)	28 Apr 47	262UNTS121	103741
France	Greece	05 May 47	76UNTS61	100980
Chile	USA (United States)	10 May 47	55UNTS21	100807
Czechoslovakia	Denmark	14 May 47	27UNTS297	100413
South Africa	USA (United States)	23 May 47	66UNTS233	100857
India	Netherlands	31 May 47	17UNTS65	100268
Canada	Sweden	27 Jun 47	27UNTS313	100414
Romania	Yugoslavia	30 Jun 47	116UNTS57	101569
Iraq	Turkey	30 Jun 47	72UNTS107	100930
Denmark	Turkey	30 Jun 47	32UNTS301	100504
France	India	16 Jul 47	27UNTS325	100415
Canada	UK Great Britain	17 Jul 47	28UNTS3	100416
Netherlands	Thailand	18 Jul 47	28UNTS27	100417
Greece	Turkey	22 Jul 47	72UNTS131	100931
Netherlands	South Africa	22 Jul 47	12UNTS257	100188
Taiwan	UK Great Britain	23 Jul 47	9UNTS207	100135
Canada	Ireland	08 Aug 47	28UNTS47	100419
Poland	Romania	09 Aug 47	12UNTS363	100193
Hungary	Poland	28 Aug 47	15UNTS145	100231
Czechoslovakia	Netherlands	01 Sep 47	32UNTS129	100495
Czechoslovakia	Switzerland	10 Sep 47	35UNTS275	100559
Chile	UK Great Britain	16 Sep 47	133UNTS143	101786
Lebanon	Turkey	16 Sep 47	44UNTS123	100682
Czechoslovakia	Sweden	15 Oct 47	44UNTS149	100683
Colombia	UK Great Britain	16 Oct 47	160UNTS297	102115
Brazil	Netherlands	06 Nov 47	53UNTS59	100773
Norway	Portugal	11 Nov 47	34UNTS257	100542
Brazil	Sweden	14 Nov 47	94UNTS139	101310
Brazil	Denmark	14 Nov 47	47UNTS39	100722
Brazil	Norway	14 Nov 47	44UNTS163	100684
Denmark	Greece	14 Nov 47	35UNTS295	100560
Denmark	Ireland	18 Nov 47	35UNTS309	100561
Ireland	Italy	21 Nov 47	353UNTS73	105038
Taiwan	Netherlands	06 Dec 47	43UNTS185	100669
Denmark	Portugal	15 Dec 47	35UNTS329	100563
Peru	UK Great Britain	22 Dec 47	72UNTS143	100932
Ethiopia	Pakistan	01 Jan 48	35UNTS3	100547

PARTY ONE	PARTY TWO	DATE	CITATION	NUMBER
Conditions of airlines operating permission (Cont.)				
Philippines	UK Great Britain	07 Jan 48	28UNTS63	100420
Austria	Netherlands	22 Jan 48	17UNTS99	100270
Italy	USA (United States)	06 Feb 48	73UNTS113	100950
Czechoslovakia	Yugoslavia	14 Mar 48	28UNTS81	100421
Argentina	Denmark	18 Mar 48	94UNTS175	101311
Cuba	UK Great Britain	19 Mar 48	175UNTS23	102294
Ireland	Switzerland	06 May 48	334UNTS187	104768
Pakistan	Sweden	06 May 48	36UNTS3	100564
Jordan	Turkey	07 May 48	32UNTS313	100505
Ireland	Netherlands	10 May 48	28UNTS121	100422
Norway	Turkey	20 May 48	26UNTS137	100384
India	Sweden	21 May 48	34UNTS285	100543
Greece	Switzerland	26 May 48	94UNTS217	101312
Argentina	Brazil	02 Jun 48	0UNTS0	109515
Canada	Netherlands	02 Jun 48	32UNTS215	100499
Ireland	Norway	21 Jun 48	34UNTS317	100545
India	Pakistan	23 Jun 48	28UNTS143	100423
Italy	UK Great Britain	25 Jun 48	94UNTS239	101313
Brazil	Switzerland	10 Aug 48	94UNTS269	101314
France	Spain	23 Aug 48	28UNTS173	100425
Greece	Lebanon	06 Sep 48	178UNTS37	102335
Bolivia	USA (United States)	29 Sep 48	505UNTS139	107370
Netherlands	Spain	08 Oct 48	28UNTS209	100426
France	USA (United States)	19 Oct 48	98UNTS3	101355
Mexico	Portugal	22 Oct 48	34UNTS329	100546
Argentina	Netherlands	29 Oct 48	95UNTS21	101316
Argentina	Chile	14 Dec 48	635UNTS21	109071
Ceylon (Sri Lanka)	India	21 Dec 48	28UNTS223	100427
Ceylon (Sri Lanka)	Pakistan	03 Jan 49	28UNTS247	100428
Italy	Lebanon	24 Jan 49	231UNTS241	103223
Switzerland	Turkey	16 Feb 49	72UNTS175	100933
Finland	Netherlands	25 Feb 49	53UNTS123	100777
Netherlands	Switzerland	07 Mar 49	35UNTS69	100551
Finland	USA (United States)	29 Mar 49	55UNTS59	100808
Panama	USA (United States)	31 Mar 49	55UNTS87	100810
Finland	Sweden	26 Apr 49	95UNTS83	101318
Bulgaria	Poland	16 May 49	84UNTS313	101140
Italy	Spain	31 May 49	231UNTS251	103224
Australia	Pakistan	03 Jun 49	35UNTS23	100549
Canada	USA (United States)	04 Jun 49	200UNTS201	102704
Canada	USA (United States)	04 Jun 49	122UNTS237	101649
Ethiopia	India	07 Jun 49	35UNTS13	100548
Belgium	Greece	21 Jun 49	137UNTS215	101854
Norway	Pakistan	23 Jun 49	35UNTS49	100550
India	Switzerland	24 Jun 49	95UNTS109	101319
Greece	Syria	05 Jul 49	78UNTS71	101013
Australia	India	11 Jul 49	35UNTS83	100552
Iraq	Norway	12 Jul 49	53UNTS137	100778
Czechoslovakia	Finland	13 Jul 49	53UNTS153	100779
Pakistan	Philippines	16 Jul 49	35UNTS111	100553
Dominican Republic	USA (United States)	19 Jul 49	51UNTS145	100762
Pakistan	UK Great Britain	27 Jul 49	44UNTS199	100685
Ceylon (Sri Lanka)	UK Great Britain	05 Aug 49	35UNTS137	100554
Canada	UK Great Britain	19 Aug 49	44UNTS223	100686
Finland	Norway	24 Aug 49	53UNTS167	100780
Denmark	Finland	26 Aug 49	53UNTS191	100781
Belgium	Canada	30 Aug 49	53UNTS221	100782
Belgium	United Arab Rep	19 Sep 49	137UNTS189	101853
Lebanon	Netherlands	20 Sep 49	108UNTS205	101474
Burma	USA (United States)	28 Sep 49	55UNTS3	100806
Greece	Philippines	08 Oct 49	187UNTS221	102515
India	Philippines	20 Oct 49	72UNTS191	100934
Iran	Netherlands	31 Oct 49	254UNTS257	103596
Denmark	Pakistan	09 Nov 49	44UNTS255	100687
France	New Zealand	15 Nov 49	53UNTS247	100785

PARTY ONE	PARTY TWO	DATE	CITATION	NUMBER
Conditions of airlines operating permission (Cont.)				
Sweden	Thailand	23 Nov 49	72UNTS217	100935
Denmark	Thailand	23 Nov 49	53UNTS255	100786
Italy	Turkey	25 Nov 49	192UNTS39	102594
Norway	Thailand	26 Nov 49	53UNTS269	100787
Brazil	Spain	28 Nov 49	215UNTS303	102923
Austria	Sweden	02 Dec 49	108UNTS3	101465
Austria	Norway	02 Dec 49	72UNTS230	100936
Austria	Denmark	02 Dec 49	53UNTS281	100788
Netherlands	United Arab Rep	08 Dec 49	95UNTS123	101320
Sweden	United Arab Rep	12 Dec 49	108UNTS15	101466
Canada	Denmark	13 Dec 49	72UNTS247	100937
Austria	Switzerland	19 Dec 49	254UNTS287	103597
Netherlands	Syria	13 Feb 50	108UNTS53	101467
Canada	Norway	14 Feb 50	53UNTS329	100790
Spain	Sweden	18 Feb 50	166UNTS15	102184
Ceylon (Sri Lanka)	Thailand	24 Feb 50	72UNTS261	100938
Italy	Netherlands	04 Mar 50	254UNTS305	103598
Norway	United Arab Rep	11 Mar 50	95UNTS157	101321
Denmark	United Arab Rep	14 Mar 50	95UNTS197	101322
Iceland	Netherlands	22 Mar 50	95UNTS237	101323
Denmark	Iceland	22 Mar 50	72UNTS273	100939
Italy	Portugal	05 Apr 50	254UNTS329	103599
Sweden	UK Great Britain	05 Apr 50	99UNTS107	101374
Turkey	United Arab Rep	12 Apr 50	128UNTS3	101711
Greece	United Arab Rep	24 Apr 50	163UNTS229	102149
Switzerland	United Arab Rep	15 May 50	95UNTS255	101325
Israel	USA (United States)	13 Jun 50	212UNTS93	102863
Netherlands	Spain	20 Jun 50	95UNTS303	101327
Iraq	Pakistan	20 Jun 50	77UNTS215	101001
Denmark	Switzerland	22 Jun 50	96UNTS3	101328
Burma	Ceylon (Sri Lanka)	29 Jun 50	73UNTS3	100940
Spain	UK Great Britain	20 Jul 50	398UNTS101	105719
France	Pakistan	31 Jul 50	96UNTS23	101329
Canada	France	01 Aug 50	73UNTS21	100941
Spain	Switzerland	03 Aug 50	254UNTS365	103600
France	United Arab Rep	08 Aug 50	127UNTS293	101710
Canada	New Zealand	16 Aug 50	77UNTS239	101002
Burma	Sweden	14 Sep 50	96UNTS45	101330
Brazil	Turkey	21 Sep 50	150UNTS299	101981
Ceylon (Sri Lanka)	United Arab Rep	26 Sep 50	192UNTS53	102595
France	UK Great Britain	06 Oct 50	96UNTS63	101331
Sweden	Switzerland	18 Oct 50	166UNTS49	102185
Luxembourg	Portugal	21 Oct 50	108UNTS67	101468
Israel	Netherlands	23 Oct 50	189UNTS89	102543
Thailand	UK Great Britain	10 Nov 50	96UNTS77	101332
Israel	UK Great Britain	06 Dec 50	151UNTS33	101983
Israel	Turkey	05 Feb 51	193UNTS3	102607
Colombia	Portugal	09 Mar 51	108UNTS87	101469
Greece	Yugoslavia	15 Mar 51	187UNTS237	102516
Iraq	UK Great Britain	19 Apr 51	108UNTS121	101470
Belgium	UK Great Britain	08 May 51	158UNTS451	102079
India	Netherlands	24 May 51	108UNTS151	101471
Greece	Norway	28 May 51	187UNTS141	102507
Cuba	Portugal	26 Jun 51	192UNTS115	102598
Iceland	Norway	14 Jul 51	163UNTS265	102150
Burma	Denmark	30 Jul 51	108UNTS167	101472
Israel	Philippines	07 Aug 51	192UNTS81	102596
Lebanon	UK Great Britain	15 Aug 51	160UNTS327	102116
Burma	Netherlands	06 Sep 51	108UNTS187	101473
Panama	UK Great Britain	15 Sep 51	560UNTS143	108172
Philippines	Spain	06 Oct 51	215UNTS193	102920
Greece	Luxembourg	22 Oct 51	187UNTS119	102506
Denmark	Iraq	18 Nov 51	232UNTS25	103227
India	UK Great Britain	01 Dec 51	128UNTS39	101712
Colombia	Spain	11 Dec 51	216UNTS73	102933

Conditions of airlines operating permission (Cont.)

PARTY ONE	PARTY TWO	DATE	CITATION	NUMBER
Jordan	United Arab Rep	02 Jan 52	192UNTS157	102599
Belgium	Spain	10 Mar 52	178UNTS243	102342
Pakistan	Switzerland	17 Mar 52	192UNTS237	102603
Norway	Uruguay	20 Mar 52	310UNTS279	104496
Sweden	Uruguay	20 Mar 52	311UNTS3	104497
Iraq	Switzerland	31 Mar 52	311UNTS43	104498
France	Mexico	17 Apr 52	163UNTS321	102153
France	Israel	29 Apr 52	189UNTS55	102542
Switzerland	UK Great Britain	13 May 52	164UNTS91	102160
India	United Arab Rep	14 Jun 52	173UNTS209	102268
Australia	United Arab Rep	14 Jun 52	173UNTS241	102269
Norway	UK Great Britain	23 Jun 52	151UNTS81	101985
Denmark	UK Great Britain	23 Jun 52	151UNTS3	101982
Belgium	Israel	30 Jun 52	183UNTS263	102435
Netherlands	Pakistan	17 Jul 52	150UNTS277	101980
Japan	USA (United States)	11 Aug 52	212UNTS27	102862
Ethiopia	Pakistan	29 Aug 52	150UNTS257	101979
Netherlands	Peru	22 Sep 52	255UNTS49	103604
Austria	Luxembourg	13 Oct 52	192UNTS291	102606
Mexico	Netherlands	13 Oct 52	163UNTS341	102154
Iceland	Luxembourg	23 Oct 52	193UNTS39	102609
Burma	UK Great Britain	25 Oct 52	150UNTS237	101978
Chile	Sweden	27 Oct 52	311UNTS63	104499
Chile	Denmark	27 Oct 52	271UNTS93	103911
Luxembourg	Norway	17 Nov 52	311UNTS95	104500
Luxembourg	Sweden	17 Nov 52	173UNTS277	102270
Israel	Switzerland	19 Nov 52	232UNTS3	103226
Japan	Netherlands	17 Feb 53	192UNTS215	102602
Japan	Sweden	20 Feb 53	173UNTS307	102272
Libya	UK Great Britain	21 Feb 53	311UNTS115	104501
Japan	Norway	23 Feb 53	192UNTS191	102601
Denmark	Japan	26 Feb 53	173UNTS329	102273
Lebanon	Sweden	23 Mar 53	255UNTS83	103605
Turkey	Yugoslavia	16 Apr 53	255UNTS99	103606
Philippines	Thailand	27 Apr 53	174UNTS3	102274
Cuba	USA (United States)	26 May 53	224UNTS75	103070
Switzerland	Yugoslavia	28 May 53	232UNTS45	103228
Japan	Thailand	19 Jun 53	174UNTS29	102276
Burma	Norway	22 Jun 53	174UNTS49	102277
Canada	Mexico	27 Jul 53	192UNTS255	102604
USA (United States)	Venezuela	14 Aug 53	213UNTS99	102883
Ceylon (Sri Lanka)	Netherlands	14 Sep 53	193UNTS21	102608
Australia	Thailand	26 Oct 53	255UNTS117	103607
Austria	Yugoslavia	11 Nov 53	363UNTS149	105206
Belgium	Lebanon	24 Dec 53	219UNTS153	102972
Ethiopia	Greece	20 Jan 54	222UNTS281	103035
Syria	UK Great Britain	30 Jan 54	449UNTS47	106452
Canada	Peru	18 Feb 54	411UNTS64	105915
Lebanon	Switzerland	03 Mar 54	255UNTS127	103608
Peru	Spain	31 Mar 54	232UNTS65	103230
Lebanon	Yugoslavia	17 Apr 54	602UNTS199	108713
Iran	Switzerland	27 May 54	496UNTS273	107257
Ireland	Luxembourg	27 Jul 54	232UNTS91	103231
Belgium	South Africa	13 Sep 54	201UNTS15	102707
France	South Africa	17 Sep 54	216UNTS29	102930
Pakistan	United Arab Rep	13 Dec 54	255UNTS167	103610
Ecuador	Netherlands	14 Dec 54	232UNTS115	103233
Norway	Switzerland	30 Dec 54	311UNTS147	104502
Austria	Belgium	07 Jan 55	380UNTS219	105458
Canada	Japan	12 Jan 55	311UNTS167	104503
Philippines	UK Great Britain	31 Jan 55	216UNTS51	102932
United Arab Rep	Yugoslavia	20 Feb 55	255UNTS199	103611
Iraq	United Arab Rep	23 Mar 55	311UNTS199	104504
Syria	United Arab Rep	03 Jul 55	393UNTS67	105652
Germany, West	USA (United States)	07 Jul 55	275UNTS3	103973

Conditions of airlines operating permission (Cont.)

PARTY ONE	PARTY TWO	DATE	CITATION	NUMBER
Germany, West	UK Great Britain	22 Jul 55	269UNTS189	103881
Germany, East	Romania	28 Jul 55	342UNTS207	104909
Belgium	Ireland	10 Sep 55	255UNTS235	103612
France	Germany, West	04 Oct 55	353UNTS203	105044
Finland	USSR (Soviet Union)	19 Oct 55	353UNTS185	105043
Denmark	Syria	20 Oct 55	250UNTS61	103518
Denmark	Lebanon	21 Oct 55	248UNTS17	103482
Pakistan	Turkey	02 Nov 55	311UNTS217	104505
Australia	South Africa	04 Nov 55	232UNTS143	103234
Burma	China People's Rep	08 Nov 55	306UNTS11	104430
Austria	USSR (Soviet Union)	09 Nov 55	255UNTS247	103613
Austria	Israel	17 Nov 55	232UNTS153	103235
India	Japan	26 Nov 55	311UNTS243	104506
France	Japan	17 Jan 56	255UNTS275	103614
Australia	Japan	19 Jan 56	311UNTS291	104507
Austria	Italy	23 Jan 56	393UNTS97	105653
Argentina	Switzerland	25 Jan 56	559UNTS121	108157
Austria	Poland	08 Feb 56	334UNTS221	104770
Netherlands	Sudan	12 Feb 56	311UNTS319	104508
Norway	Syria	25 Feb 56	463UNTS217	106706
Denmark	USSR (Soviet Union)	31 Mar 56	259UNTS169	103689
Sweden	USSR (Soviet Union)	31 Mar 56	259UNTS239	103691
Norway	USSR (Soviet Union)	31 Mar 56	259UNTS205	103690
Belgium	Germany, West	14 Apr 56	344UNTS103	104945
Multilateral		30 Apr 56	310UNTS229	104494
Germany, West	Switzerland	02 May 56	559UNTS157	108158
Portugal	Venezuela	16 May 56	463UNTS239	106707
Italy	South Africa	21 May 56	255UNTS323	103616
Japan	Switzerland	24 May 56	312UNTS3	104509
Greece	Italy	26 May 56	496UNTS301	107258
Fed Rhod/Nyasaland	South Africa	30 May 56	255UNTS317	103615
Italy	Switzerland	04 Jun 56	378UNTS311	105429
Poland	Sweden	08 Jun 56	334UNTS257	104771
Germany, West	Ireland	12 Jun 56	353UNTS121	105040
India	Thailand	12 Jun 56	255UNTS341	103617
Germany, West	Netherlands	28 Sep 56	327UNTS185	104722
Switzerland	Thailand	13 Oct 56	312UNTS43	104510
Belgium	Poland	17 Oct 56	356UNTS279	105100
Colombia	USA (United States)	24 Oct 56	476UNTS77	106905
Belgium	Turkey	25 Oct 56	380UNTS3	105447
Austria	UK Great Britain	27 Oct 56	264UNTS67	103789
Peru	Switzerland	23 Nov 56	411UNTS97	105916
Belgium	Romania	04 Dec 56	317UNTS161	104602
Iran	USA (United States)	16 Jan 57	308UNTS147	104460
Iceland	Thailand	22 Jan 57	312UNTS63	104511
Germany, West	Sweden	29 Jan 57	393UNTS113	105654
Germany, West	Norway	29 Jan 57	353UNTS39	105037
Denmark	Germany, West	29 Jan 57	302UNTS75	104354
Belgium	Czechoslovakia	12 Mar 57	312UNTS75	104512
Netherlands	Yugoslavia	13 Mar 57	327UNTS227	104723
Netherlands	USA (United States)	03 Apr 57	410UNTS193	105904
Germany, West	Yugoslavia	10 Apr 57	463UNTS269	106708
Denmark	Pakistan	10 Apr 57	302UNTS53	104353
Romania	Sweden	15 Apr 57	342UNTS325	104915
Bulgaria	Sweden	17 Apr 57	464UNTS3	106709
Korea, South	USA (United States)	24 Apr 57	288UNTS219	104207
Belgium	Bulgaria	14 May 57	317UNTS81	104596
Australia	Germany, West	22 May 57	357UNTS45	105105
Hungary	Netherlands	28 May 57	334UNTS291	104773
Belgium	Hungary	01 Jun 57	291UNTS17	104242
Afghanistan	Pakistan	13 Jun 57	327UNTS51	104717
Czechoslovakia	United Arab Rep	30 Jun 57	411UNTS126	105917
Greece	Italy	02 Aug 57	533UNTS217	107744
Hungary	Sweden	02 Aug 57	334UNTS307	104774
Netherlands	Romania	27 Aug 57	342UNTS309	104914

Conditions of airlines operating permission (Cont.)

PARTY ONE	PARTY TWO	DATE	CITATION	NUMBER
Multilateral		03 Oct 57	366UNTS87	105216
Italy	Pakistan	05 Oct 57	353UNTS91	105039
Fed of Malaya	UK Great Britain	18 Oct 57	335UNTS3	104775
Netherlands	UK Great Britain	22 Oct 57	313UNTS309	104538
France	Morocco	25 Oct 57	559UNTS95	108156
UK Great Britain	USSR (Soviet Union)	19 Dec 57	351UNTS235	105026
Australia	Ireland	30 Dec 57	497UNTS29	107260
Belgium	Morocco	20 Jan 58	288UNTS3	104192
Bulgaria	Netherlands	07 Feb 58	335UNTS45	104777
Australia	UK Great Britain	07 Feb 58	335UNTS23	104776
Afghanistan	Turkey	08 Feb 58	464UNTS39	106711
Sudan	Sweden	17 Feb 58	393UNTS161	105655
Norway	Pakistan	05 Mar 58	334UNTS199	104769
Pakistan	Sweden	06 Mar 58	393UNTS181	105656
Germany, West	Portugal	21 Mar 58	464UNTS71	106712
South Africa	Sweden	28 Mar 58	300UNTS95	104333
Norway	South Africa	28 Mar 58	300UNTS83	104332
Denmark	South Africa	28 Mar 58	300UNTS107	104334
Morocco	Portugal	03 Apr 58	393UNTS203	105657
Belgium	Iran	14 Apr 58	381UNTS309	105473
Sweden	Yugoslavia	18 Apr 58	393UNTS225	105658
Bulgaria	Denmark	28 May 58	312UNTS235	104521
India	USSR (Soviet Union)	02 Jun 58	393UNTS3	105650
Belgium	USSR (Soviet Union)	05 Jun 58	345UNTS145	104965
Pakistan	Portugal	07 Jun 58	320UNTS225	104645
Denmark	Luxembourg	10 Jun 58	356UNTS193	105096
Belgium	South Africa	11 Jun 58	335UNTS63	104778
Norway	Romania	16 Jun 58	405UNTS223	105835
Netherlands	USSR (Soviet Union)	17 Jun 58	335UNTS77	104779
Denmark	Romania	25 Jun 58	345UNTS231	104970
Belgium	Pakistan	04 Jul 58	387UNTS305	105569
Ethiopia	UK Great Britain	07 Jul 58	331UNTS3	104749
Austria	Romania	10 Jul 58	353UNTS155	105041
Denmark	Hungary	17 Jul 58	344UNTS281	104954
Afghanistan	Austria	21 Jul 58	0UNTS0	109236
Romania	United Arab Rep	14 Aug 58	405UNTS189	105834
Austria	Bulgaria	12 Sep 58	353UNTS3	105036
Ghana	UK Great Britain	24 Sep 58	411UNTS146	105918
Australia	South Africa	26 Sep 58	335UNTS121	104780
Liberia	Netherlands	28 Nov 58	393UNTS55	105651
Finland	Switzerland	07 Jan 59	353UNTS173	105042
UK Great Britain	Yugoslavia	03 Feb 59	359UNTS339	105151
Japan	Philippines	02 Mar 59	341UNTS49	104877
Sweden	Tunisia	19 Mar 59	497UNTS43	107261
Netherlands	Tunisia	19 Mar 59	497UNTS61	107262
Norway	Tunisia	28 Mar 59	497UNTS77	107263
Denmark	Tunisia	14 Apr 59	340UNTS273	104870
Denmark	Sudan	11 May 59	445UNTS105	106380
Ceylon (Sri Lanka)	Sweden	29 May 59	464UNTS109	106713
Ceylon (Sri Lanka)	Norway	29 May 59	411UNTS165	105919
Ceylon (Sri Lanka)	Denmark	29 May 59	348UNTS225	105002
Belgium	Japan	20 Jun 59	411UNTS3	105911
Bulgaria	United Arab Rep	09 Jul 59	411UNTS187	105920
India	Italy	16 Jul 59	464UNTS129	106714
Austria	Hungary	17 Jul 59	0UNTS0	109237
Afghanistan	Germany, West	22 Jul 59	464UNTS177	106715
Germany, West	Iceland	12 Aug 59	411UNTS224	105921
Canada	Germany, West	04 Sep 59	411UNTS260	105922
Nicaragua	Peru	14 Oct 59	392UNTS303	105649
South Africa	Switzerland	19 Oct 59	559UNTS257	108162
Liberia	Sweden	09 Dec 59	464UNTS219	106716
Czechoslovakia	UK Great Britain	15 Jan 60	374UNTS207	105336
Germany, West	United Arab Rep	16 Feb 60	464UNTS233	106717
France	Thailand	26 Feb 60	392UNTS279	105648
Australia	Thailand	26 Feb 60	392UNTS255	105647

Conditions of airlines operating permission (Cont.)

PARTY ONE	PARTY TWO	DATE	CITATION	NUMBER
Guinea	Netherlands	09 Mar 60	392UNTS243	105646
Finland	Iceland	10 Mar 60	497UNTS95	107264
Czechoslovakia	Iraq	11 Mar 60	464UNTS267	106718
Belgium	Switzerland	24 Mar 60	416UNTS81	105996
Luxembourg	Yugoslavia	09 Apr 60	464UNTS293	106719
Germany, West	Spain	28 Apr 60	465UNTS3	106720
Iran	UK Great Britain	02 May 60	566UNTS129	108241
Greece	Romania	02 May 60	485UNTS17	107043
Morocco	United Arab Rep	19 May 60	563UNTS121	108208
Switzerland	Tunisia	21 May 60	497UNTS109	107265
Kuwait	UK Great Britain	24 May 60	412UNTS4	105923
Afghanistan	Czechoslovakia	28 May 60	497UNTS129	107266
Luxembourg	Tunisia	13 Jun 60	497UNTS143	107267
Denmark	Peru	22 Jun 60	439UNTS113	106326
Ireland	Portugal	24 Jun 60	412UNTS30	105924
Poland	UK Great Britain	02 Jul 60	385UNTS87	105532
Switzerland	United Arab Rep	14 Jul 60	497UNTS161	107268
Germany, West	Pakistan	20 Jul 60	465UNTS41	106721
Netherlands	Poland	21 Jul 60	497UNTS189	107269
Ghana	Netherlands	30 Jul 60	412UNTS51	105925
Mexico	USA (United States)	15 Aug 60	402UNTS177	105786
Belgium	Burma	17 Aug 60	540UNTS185	107850
Ghana	United Arab Rep	29 Aug 60	412UNTS71	105926
Czechoslovakia	India	19 Sep 60	465UNTS67	106722
Belgium	Jordan	19 Oct 60	479UNTS277	106959
Hungary	UK Great Britain	25 Oct 60	419UNTS309	106034
Burma	Switzerland	31 Oct 60	465UNTS97	106723
Norway	Peru	02 Nov 60	497UNTS207	107270
Australia	Italy	10 Nov 60	497UNTS247	107271
Indonesia	UK Great Britain	23 Nov 60	398UNTS71	105718
Canada	Pakistan	21 Dec 60	465UNTS115	106724
Luxembourg	Thailand	29 Dec 60	465UNTS131	106725
Jordan	Sweden	09 Jan 61	465UNTS155	106726
Sudan	UK Great Britain	16 Jan 61	424UNTS233	106112
Norway	Poland	17 Jan 61	412UNTS130	105928
Denmark	Poland	17 Jan 61	412UNTS111	105927
Germany, West	Japan	18 Jan 61	465UNTS173	106727
Cuba	Czechoslovakia	04 Mar 61	465UNTS209	106728
Poland	Switzerland	18 May 61	559UNTS233	108161
Czechoslovakia	Morocco	08 Jun 61	497UNTS275	107272
New Zealand	UK Great Britain	13 Jun 61	497UNTS293	107273
Cameroon	France	16 Jun 61	412UNTS148	105929
Guinea	Sweden	17 Jun 61	465UNTS236	106729
Australia	New Zealand	25 Jul 61	523UNTS271	107561
Fed of Malaya	UN Special Fund	25 Jul 61	401UNTS159	105769
Czechoslovakia	Ghana	02 Aug 61	465UNTS249	106730
Finland	Luxembourg	15 Aug 61	541UNTS45	107859
Jordan	Norway	21 Aug 61	465UNTS275	106731
Jordan	Netherlands	24 Aug 61	466UNTS3	106733
Mexico	Netherlands	24 Aug 61	465UNTS291	106732
Liberia	Switzerland	31 Aug 61	559UNTS215	108160
Ghana	Romania	30 Sep 61	467UNTS443	106769
Germany, West	Morocco	12 Oct 61	523UNTS289	107562
Japan	Pakistan	17 Oct 61	466UNTS17	106734
Cyprus	Greece	23 Nov 61	497UNTS311	107274
Czechoslovakia	Mali	27 Nov 61	466UNTS41	106736
Denmark	Jordan	07 Dec 61	631UNTS333	109003
Czechoslovakia	Guinea	16 Dec 61	559UNTS49	108154
Netherlands	Sweden	08 Jan 62	466UNTS65	106737
Austria	Greece	15 Jan 62	498UNTS3	107275
Indonesia	Japan	23 Jan 62	559UNTS77	108155
Luxembourg	South Africa	31 Jan 62	563UNTS153	108209
Italy	Japan	31 Jan 62	498UNTS23	107276
Finland	Hungary	13 Feb 62	463UNTS61	106693
Austria	Spain	19 Feb 62	0UNTS0	109238

PARTY ONE	PARTY TWO	DATE	CITATION	NUMBER
Conditions of airlines operating permission (Cont.)				
Germany, West	Thailand	05 Mar 62	563UNTS165	108210
Luxembourg	Spain	26 Mar 62	563UNTS205	108211
France	Luxembourg	29 Mar 62	563UNTS227	108212
Sierra Leone	UK Great Britain	05 Apr 62	434UNTS227	106265
Ghana	USSR (Soviet Union)	06 Apr 62	498UNTS41	107277
Japan	United Arab Rep	10 May 62	498UNTS69	107278
France	Romania	18 May 62	498UNTS115	107279
France	Senegal	15 Jun 62	524UNTS3	107563
Czechoslovakia	Senegal	20 Jun 62	498UNTS145	107280
Guinea	Norway	21 Jun 62	466UNTS81	106738
Liberia	Norway	29 Jun 62	466UNTS95	106739
Morocco	Switzerland	05 Jul 62	498UNTS189	107282
Morocco	Switzerland	05 Jul 62	498UNTS171	107281
Ecuador	Germany, West	20 Sep 62	498UNTS199	107283
Japan	Kuwait	06 Oct 62	498UNTS235	107284
Finland	France	12 Oct 62	498UNTS299	107285
Hungary	Syria	18 Oct 62	491UNTS209	107178
Netherlands	Norway	18 Oct 62	466UNTS145	106741
France	Ivory Coast	19 Oct 62	498UNTS317	107286
Poland	Syria	10 Nov 62	491UNTS228	107179
Ghana	Tunisia	11 Dec 62	563UNTS243	108213
Syria	United Arab Rep	27 Dec 62	491UNTS245	107180
Ghana	Mali	09 Jan 63	466UNTS165	106742
Senegal	Switzerland	23 Jan 63	524UNTS23	107564
Guinea	Switzerland	01 Feb 63	499UNTS35	107291
Mali	Senegal	07 Feb 63	524UNTS41	107565
Algeria	France	18 Feb 63	563UNTS263	108214
Sudan	Switzerland	18 Feb 63	563UNTS281	108215
Cyprus	Norway	05 Mar 63	563UNTS305	108216
Greece	Hungary	27 Apr 63	534UNTS3	107750
Cyprus	Denmark	27 Apr 63	529UNTS255	107664
Algeria	Morocco	30 Apr 63	564UNTS3	108217
Portugal	South Africa	07 May 63	499UNTS49	107292
Finland	Poland	10 Jun 63	503UNTS179	107343
Guinea	Ivory Coast	26 Jun 63	499UNTS71	107293
Austria	France	12 Jul 63	499UNTS91	107294
Algeria	Mali	22 Jul 63	564UNTS29	108219
Cameroon	Israel	09 Aug 63	499UNTS121	107295
Pakistan	USSR (Soviet Union)	07 Oct 63	499UNTS161	107297
Ivory Coast	Netherlands	09 Oct 63	499UNTS141	107296
Mali	Niger	15 Jan 64	499UNTS197	107299
Lebanon	Pakistan	04 Feb 64	614UNTS55	108863
Argentina	Paraguay	07 Feb 64	634UNTS127	109057
Denmark	Yugoslavia	11 Feb 64	511UNTS241	107437
Cyprus	USSR (Soviet Union)	29 Feb 64	602UNTS45	108706
Cameroon	Mali	17 Mar 64	524UNTS61	107566
Malaysia	Netherlands	07 Apr 64	524UNTS81	107567
Norway	Yugoslavia	15 Apr 64	602UNTS177	108712
United Arab Rep	USA (United States)	05 May 64	531UNTS229	107706
New Zealand	USA (United States)	24 Jun 64	524UNTS101	107568
Ivory Coast	Mali	09 Jul 64	524UNTS121	107569
France	Trinidad/Tobago	12 Oct 64	535UNTS25	107774
Argentina	UK Great Britain	12 Jan 65	597UNTS177	108645
Finland	UK Great Britain	25 Mar 65	539UNTS103	107826
Denmark	Malaysia	26 Mar 65	540UNTS205	107851
Ghana	Malawi	04 May 65	541UNTS163	107869
Spain	Sweden	05 May 65	0UNTS0	109239
Denmark	Spain	05 May 65	543UNTS255	107905
Mauritania	Spain	11 May 65	602UNTS111	108709
Malaysia	Norway	26 May 65	602UNTS157	108711
Ivory Coast	Sweden	07 Jun 65	0UNTS0	109240
Nigeria	Switzerland	11 Oct 65	602UNTS137	108710
Canada	USA (United States)	17 Jan 66	586UNTS151	108502
Bulgaria	Turkey	18 Apr 66	631UNTS263	108999
Ivory Coast	Norway	07 Jun 66	0UNTS0	109249

PARTY ONE	PARTY TWO	DATE	CITATION	NUMBER
Conditions of airlines operating permission (Cont.)				
Denmark	Ivory Coast	07 Jun 66	595UNTS313	108626
Austria	USA (United States)	23 Jun 66	601UNTS51	108687
Taiwan	Vietnam, South	19 Aug 66	0UNTS0	109241
Denmark	Nigeria	08 Sep 66	591UNTS177	108557
Norway	Singapore	20 Dec 66	0UNTS0	109242
Singapore	Sweden	20 Dec 66	0UNTS0	109243
Denmark	Singapore	20 Dec 66	593UNTS125	108580
Japan	Singapore	14 Feb 67	0UNTS0	109244
Algeria	Ivory Coast	16 Feb 67	0UNTS0	109245
Congo (Brazzaville)	Denmark	27 Feb 67	600UNTS189	108681
Trinidad/Tobago	UK Great Britain	01 Mar 67	606UNTS149	108784
Australia	Austria	22 Mar 67	0UNTS0	109246
Netherlands	Sierra Leone	13 Jun 67	0UNTS0	109247
Multilateral		03 Jul 67	0UNTS0	109248
Malta	UK Great Britain	10 Jul 67	619UNTS11	108936
Malaysia	UK Great Britain	01 Aug 67	633UNTS93	109036
Denmark	Malaysia	14 Dec 67	614UNTS26	108862
Algeria	France	26 Dec 67	0UNTS0	109509
Overflights and technical stops				
Multilateral		07 Dec 44	84UNTS389	200252
Multilateral		07 Dec 44	171UNTS387	200502
Multilateral		07 Dec 44	15UNTS295	200102
Sweden	USA (United States)	16 Dec 44	6UNTS397	200041
Denmark	USA (United States)	16 Dec 44	10UNTS213	200063
Canada	USA (United States)	17 Feb 45	122UNTS261	200409
Sweden	USA (United States)	04 Dec 45	6UNTS273	100080
UK Great Britain	USA (United States)	11 Feb 46	3UNTS253	100036
Denmark	USA (United States)	21 Mar 46	3UNTS301	100038
France	USA (United States)	27 Mar 46	139UNTS114	101879
Multilateral		31 Mar 46	17UNTS159	100274
Portugal	USA (United States)	30 May 46	174UNTS187	102285
Ecuador	USA (United States)	11 Jun 46	167UNTS135	102203
France	USA (United States)	18 Jun 46	42UNTS183	100647
Iceland	UK Great Britain	04 Jul 46	6UNTS223	100077
Albania	Yugoslavia	11 Jul 46	4UNTS407	100058
Czechoslovakia	USSR (Soviet Union)	25 Jul 46	27UNTS231	100409
Canada	Newfoundland	29 Jul 46	17UNTS169	100275
Muscat and Oman	UK Great Britain	05 Apr 47	27UNTS287	100412
India	Netherlands	31 May 47	17UNTS65	100268
Ireland	USA (United States)	03 Jun 47	16UNTS151	100255
Taiwan	UK Great Britain	23 Jul 47	9UNTS207	100135
Chile	UK Great Britain	16 Sep 47	133UNTS143	101786
Peru	UK Great Britain	22 Dec 47	72UNTS143	100932
Ethiopia	Pakistan	01 Jan 48	35UNTS3	100547
Philippines	UK Great Britain	07 Jan 48	28UNTS63	100420
UK Great Britain	USA (United States)	24 Feb 48	73UNTS143	100951
Czechoslovakia	Yugoslavia	14 Mar 48	28UNTS81	100421
France	UK Great Britain	19 Apr 48	83UNTS201	101109
Pakistan	Sweden	06 May 48	36UNTS3	100564
Portugal	UK Great Britain	25 May 48	34UNTS311	100544
Argentina	Brazil	02 Jun 48	0UNTS0	109515
Luxembourg	Netherlands	23 Jun 48	32UNTS229	100500
India	Pakistan	23 Jun 48	28UNTS143	100423
Italy	UK Great Britain	25 Jun 48	94UNTS239	101313
Australia	Italy	02 Aug 48	28UNTS165	100424
France	Spain	23 Aug 48	28UNTS173	100425
France	USA (United States)	19 Oct 48	98UNTS3	101355
Ceylon (Sri Lanka)	India	21 Dec 48	28UNTS223	100427
Ceylon (Sri Lanka)	Pakistan	03 Jan 49	28UNTS247	100428
Canada	USA (United States)	31 Jan 49	43UNTS119	100666
Italy	Spain	31 May 49	231UNTS251	103224
Australia	Pakistan	03 Jun 49	35UNTS23	100549
Ethiopia	India	07 Jun 49	35UNTS13	100548
Norway	Pakistan	23 Jun 49	35UNTS49	100550

Overflights and technical stops (Cont.)

PARTY ONE	PARTY TWO	DATE	CITATION	NUMBER
Korea, South	USA (United States)	29 Jun 49	55UNTS79	100809
India	USA (United States)	04 Jul 49	200UNTS181	102702
Pakistan	Philippines	16 Jul 49	35UNTS111	100553
Pakistan	UK Great Britain	27 Jul 49	44UNTS199	100685
Ceylon (Sri Lanka)	UK Great Britain	05 Aug 49	35UNTS137	100554
Multilateral		12 Aug 49	75UNTS31	100970
Multilateral		12 Aug 49	75UNTS85	100971
Canada	UK Great Britain	19 Aug 49	44UNTS223	100686
Belgium	United Arab Rep	19 Sep 49	137UNTS189	101853
India	Philippines	20 Oct 49	72UNTS191	100934
Iran	Netherlands	31 Oct 49	254UNTS257	103596
Sweden	United Arab Rep	12 Dec 49	108UNTS15	101466
Guatemala	USA (United States)	20 Dec 49	70UNTS71	100897
USA (United States)	Yugoslavia	24 Dec 49	89UNTS209	101219
Spain	Sweden	18 Feb 50	166UNTS15	102184
Australia	Philippines	14 Apr 50	127UNTS281	101709
Iraq	Pakistan	20 Jun 50	77UNTS215	101001
Spain	UK Great Britain	20 Jul 50	398UNTS101	105719
India	Nepal	31 Jul 50	104UNTS3	101430
Canada	France	01 Aug 50	73UNTS21	100941
Spain	Switzerland	03 Aug 50	254UNTS365	103600
France	United Arab Rep	08 Aug 50	127UNTS293	101710
Dominican Republic	USA (United States)	11 Aug 50	92UNTS329	101278
France	UK Great Britain	06 Oct 50	96UNTS63	101331
Israel	UK Great Britain	06 Dec 50	151UNTS33	101983
Iraq	UK Great Britain	19 Apr 51	108UNTS121	101470
France	UK Great Britain	20 Apr 51	106UNTS81	101458
Belgium	UK Great Britain	08 May 51	158UNTS451	102079
Saudi Arabia	USA (United States)	18 Jun 51	102UNTS73	101412
Denmark	Iran	18 Jun 51	255UNTS3	103602
Israel	Philippines	07 Aug 51	192UNTS81	102596
Lebanon	UK Great Britain	15 Aug 51	160UNTS327	102116
Portugal	USA (United States)	06 Sep 51	237UNTS217	103348
India	UK Great Britain	01 Dec 51	128UNTS39	101712
Nicaragua	USA (United States)	12 Dec 51	167UNTS151	102205
Costa Rica	USA (United States)	25 Feb 52	174UNTS233	102288
Pakistan	Switzerland	17 Mar 52	192UNTS237	102603
France	Mexico	17 Apr 52	163UNTS321	102153
Honduras	USA (United States)	23 Apr 52	198UNTS251	102669
France	Israel	29 Apr 52	189UNTS55	102542
Switzerland	UK Great Britain	13 May 52	164UNTS91	102160
Australia	United Arab Rep	14 Jun 52	173UNTS241	102269
India	United Arab Rep	14 Jun 52	173UNTS209	102268
Norway	UK Great Britain	23 Jun 52	151UNTS81	101985
Belgium	Israel	30 Jun 52	183UNTS263	102435
Ethiopia	UK Great Britain	03 Jul 52	151UNTS207	101996
Netherlands	Pakistan	17 Jul 52	150UNTS277	101980
Japan	USA (United States)	11 Aug 52	212UNTS27	102862
Burma	UK Great Britain	25 Oct 52	150UNTS237	101978
Chile	Denmark	27 Oct 52	271UNTS93	103911
Chile	Sweden	27 Oct 52	311UNTS63	104499
South Africa	Sweden	09 Jan 53	173UNTS299	102271
Japan	Netherlands	17 Feb 53	192UNTS215	102602
India	Pakistan	20 Feb 53	164UNTS3	102155
Japan	Sweden	20 Feb 53	173UNTS307	102272
Libya	UK Great Britain	21 Feb 53	311UNTS115	104501
Japan	Norway	23 Feb 53	192UNTS191	102601
Denmark	Japan	26 Feb 53	173UNTS329	102273
India	Muscat and Oman	15 Mar 53	190UNTS69	102559
Lebanon	Sweden	23 Mar 53	255UNTS83	103605
Turkey	Yugoslavia	16 Apr 53	255UNTS99	103606
Denmark	South Africa	30 Apr 53	174UNTS19	102275
Ethiopia	USA (United States)	22 May 53	191UNTS59	102577
Japan	Thailand	19 Jun 53	174UNTS29	102276
Canada	Mexico	27 Jul 53	192UNTS255	102604

Overflights and technical stops (Cont.)

PARTY ONE	PARTY TWO	DATE	CITATION	NUMBER
Ceylon (Sri Lanka)	Netherlands	14 Sep 53	193UNTS21	102608
Belgium	Lebanon	24 Dec 53	219UNTS153	102972
Canada	Peru	18 Feb 54	411UNTS64	105915
Switzerland	Syria	26 May 54	255UNTS145	103609
Iran	Switzerland	27 May 54	496UNTS273	107257
Laos	Thailand	07 Jul 54	200UNTS115	102698
Libya	USA (United States)	09 Sep 54	224UNTS217	103078
United Arab Rep	UK Great Britain	19 Oct 54	210UNTS3	102833
Multilateral		23 Oct 54	332UNTS3	104760
Canada	Japan	12 Jan 55	311UNTS167	104503
Philippines	UK Great Britain	31 Jan 55	216UNTS51	102932
Syria	United Arab Rep	03 Jul 55	393UNTS67	105652
Germany, West	USA (United States)	07 Jul 55	275UNTS3	103973
Germany, West	UK Great Britain	22 Jul 55	269UNTS189	103881
Germany, East	Romania	28 Jul 55	342UNTS207	104909
France	Germany, West	04 Oct 55	353UNTS203	105044
Denmark	Syria	20 Oct 55	250UNTS61	103518
Austria	USSR (Soviet Union)	09 Nov 55	255UNTS247	103613
India	Japan	26 Nov 55	311UNTS243	104506
France	Japan	17 Jan 56	255UNTS275	103614
Australia	Japan	19 Jan 56	311UNTS291	104507
India	USA (United States)	03 Feb 56	272UNTS75	103932
Netherlands	Sudan	12 Feb 56	311UNTS319	104508
Norway	Syria	25 Feb 56	463UNTS217	106706
Belgium	Germany, West	14 Apr 56	344UNTS103	104945
Multilateral		30 Apr 56	310UNTS229	104494
Germany, West	Switzerland	02 May 56	559UNTS157	108158
Japan	Switzerland	24 May 56	312UNTS3	104509
Germany, West	Ireland	12 Jun 56	353UNTS121	105040
Germany, West	Netherlands	28 Sep 56	327UNTS185	104722
Colombia	USA (United States)	24 Oct 56	476UNTS77	106905
Austria	UK Great Britain	27 Oct 56	264UNTS67	103789
Peru	Switzerland	23 Nov 56	411UNTS97	105916
Iran	USA (United States)	16 Jan 57	308UNTS147	104460
Denmark	Germany, West	29 Jan 57	302UNTS75	104354
Germany, West	Sweden	29 Jan 57	393UNTS113	105654
Germany, West	Norway	29 Jan 57	353UNTS39	105037
Netherlands	USA (United States)	03 Apr 57	410UNTS193	105904
Denmark	Pakistan	10 Apr 57	302UNTS53	104353
Korea, South	USA (United States)	24 Apr 57	288UNTS219	104207
Australia	Germany, West	22 May 57	357UNTS45	105105
Ceylon (Sri Lanka)	UK Great Britain	07 Jun 57	280UNTS107	104055
Afghanistan	Pakistan	13 Jun 57	327UNTS51	104717
Czechoslovakia	United Arab Rep	30 Jun 57	411UNTS126	105917
Multilateral		03 Oct 57	366UNTS87	105216
Italy	Pakistan	05 Oct 57	353UNTS91	105039
Fed of Malaya	UK Great Britain	18 Oct 57	335UNTS3	104775
Australia	Ireland	30 Dec 57	497UNTS29	107260
Canada	Switzerland	10 Jan 58	464UNTS21	106710
Lebanon	United Nations	20 Jan 58	286UNTS189	104166
Belgium	Morocco	20 Jan 58	288UNTS3	104192
Australia	UK Great Britain	07 Feb 58	335UNTS23	104776
Afghanistan	Turkey	08 Feb 58	464UNTS39	106711
Sudan	Sweden	17 Feb 58	393UNTS161	105655
Norway	Pakistan	05 Mar 58	334UNTS199	104769
Pakistan	Sweden	06 Mar 58	393UNTS181	105656
Germany, West	Portugal	21 Mar 58	464UNTS71	106712
Morocco	Portugal	03 Apr 58	393UNTS203	105657
Belgium	Iran	14 Apr 58	381UNTS309	105473
Pakistan	Portugal	07 Jun 58	320UNTS225	104645
Norway	Romania	16 Jun 58	405UNTS223	105835
Netherlands	USSR (Soviet Union)	17 Jun 58	335UNTS77	104779
Belgium	Pakistan	04 Jul 58	387UNTS305	105569
Ethiopia	UK Great Britain	07 Jul 58	331UNTS3	104749
Germany, East	Romania	15 Jul 58	387UNTS133	105561

PARTY ONE	PARTY TWO	DATE	CITATION	NUMBER
Overflights and technical stops (Cont.)				
Afghanistan	Austria	21 Jul 58	0UNTSO	109236
Romania	United Arab Rep	14 Aug 58	405UNTS189	105834
Ghana	UK Great Britain	24 Sep 58	411UNTS146	105918
Liberia	Netherlands	28 Nov 58	393UNTS55	105651
Finland	Switzerland	07 Jan 59	353UNTS173	105042
Indonesia	USA (United States)	02 Mar 59	357UNTS145	105113
Sweden	Tunisia	19 Mar 59	497UNTS43	107261
Netherlands	Tunisia	19 Mar 59	497UNTS61	107262
Norway	Tunisia	28 Mar 59	497UNTS77	107263
Denmark	Tunisia	14 Apr 59	340UNTS273	104870
Ghana	UK Great Britain	17 Apr 59	337UNTS353	104829
Denmark	Sudan	11 May 59	445UNTS105	106380
Belgium	Japan	20 Jun 59	411UNTS3	105911
Bulgaria	United Arab Rep	09 Jul 59	411UNTS187	105920
India	Italy	16 Jul 59	464UNTS129	106714
Austria	Hungary	17 Jul 59	0UNTSO	109237
Afghanistan	Germany, West	22 Jul 59	464UNTS177	106715
Germany, West	Iceland	12 Aug 59	411UNTS224	105921
Canada	Germany, West	04 Sep 59	411UNTS260	105922
Australia	Fed of Malaya	29 Sep 59	357UNTS29	105104
Liberia	Sweden	09 Dec 59	464UNTS219	106716
Czechoslovakia	UK Great Britain	15 Jan 60	374UNTS207	105336
Australia	Thailand	26 Feb 60	392UNTS255	105647
Belgium	Switzerland	24 Mar 60	416UNTS81	105996
Germany, West	Spain	28 Apr 60	465UNTS3	106720
Iran	UK Great Britain	02 May 60	566UNTS129	108241
Switzerland	Tunisia	21 May 60	497UNTS109	107265
Kuwait	UK Great Britain	24 May 60	412UNTS4	105923
Luxembourg	Tunisia	13 Jun 60	497UNTS143	107267
Ireland	Portugal	24 Jun 60	412UNTS30	105924
Poland	UK Great Britain	02 Jul 60	385UNTS87	105532
Germany, West	Pakistan	20 Jul 60	465UNTS41	106721
Netherlands	Poland	21 Jul 60	497UNTS189	107269
Ghana	Netherlands	30 Jul 60	412UNTS51	105925
Mexico	USA (United States)	15 Aug 60	402UNTS177	105786
Ghana	United Arab Rep	29 Aug 60	412UNTS71	105926
Australia	Italy	10 Nov 60	497UNTS247	107271
Indonesia	UK Great Britain	23 Nov 60	398UNTS71	105718
Canada	Pakistan	21 Dec 60	465UNTS115	106724
Luxembourg	Thailand	29 Dec 60	465UNTS131	106725
Jordan	Sweden	09 Jan 61	465UNTS155	106726
Sudan	UK Great Britain	16 Jan 61	424UNTS233	106112
Denmark	Poland	17 Jan 61	412UNTS111	105927
Germany, West	Japan	18 Jan 61	465UNTS173	106727
Poland	Switzerland	18 May 61	559UNTS233	108161
New Zealand	UK Great Britain	13 Jun 61	497UNTS293	107273
Australia	New Zealand	25 Jul 61	523UNTS271	107561
Czechoslovakia	Ghana	02 Aug 61	465UNTS249	106730
Jordan	Norway	21 Aug 61	465UNTS275	106731
Mexico	Netherlands	24 Aug 61	465UNTS291	106732
Ghana	Romania	30 Sep 61	467UNTS443	106769
Germany, West	Morocco	12 Oct 61	523UNTS289	107562
Japan	Pakistan	17 Oct 61	466UNTS17	106734
Cyprus	Greece	23 Nov 61	497UNTS311	107274
Denmark	Jordan	07 Dec 61	631UNTS333	109003
Czechoslovakia	Guinea	16 Dec 61	559UNTS49	108154
Netherlands	Sweden	08 Jan 62	466UNTS65	106737
Austria	Greece	15 Jan 62	498UNTS3	107275
Indonesia	Japan	23 Jan 62	559UNTS77	108155
Italy	Japan	31 Jan 62	498UNTS23	107276
Austria	Spain	19 Feb 62	0UNTSO	109238
Germany, West	Thailand	05 Mar 62	563UNTS165	108210
Luxembourg	Spain	26 Mar 62	563UNTS205	108211
France	Luxembourg	29 Mar 62	563UNTS227	108212
Sierra Leone	UK Great Britain	05 Apr 62	434UNTS227	106265

PARTY ONE	PARTY TWO	DATE	CITATION	NUMBER
Overflights and technical stops (Cont.)				
Japan	United Arab Rep	10 May 62	498UNTS69	107278
Liberia	Norway	29 Jun 62	466UNTS95	106739
Morocco	Switzerland	05 Jul 62	498UNTS171	107281
UK Great Britain	USA (United States)	29 Aug 62	449UNTS177	106459
Ecuador	Germany, West	20 Sep 62	498UNTS199	107283
Japan	Kuwait	06 Oct 62	498UNTS235	107284
Finland	France	12 Oct 62	498UNTS299	107285
Netherlands	Norway	18 Oct 62	466UNTS145	106741
Poland	Syria	10 Nov 62	491UNTS228	107179
Ivory Coast	Switzerland	17 Nov 62	499UNTS3	107289
Ghana	Tunisia	11 Dec 62	563UNTS243	108213
Ghana	Mali	09 Jan 63	466UNTS165	106742
Senegal	Switzerland	23 Jan 63	524UNTS23	107564
Guinea	Switzerland	01 Feb 63	499UNTS35	107291
Sudan	Switzerland	18 Feb 63	563UNTS281	108215
Cyprus	Norway	05 Mar 63	563UNTS305	108216
Cyprus	Denmark	27 Apr 63	529UNTS255	107664
Belgium	Cyprus	08 Jun 63	601UNTS311	108703
Finland	Poland	10 Jun 63	503UNTS179	107343
Hungary	Mongolia	10 Jul 63	519UNTS173	107508
Austria	France	12 Jul 63	499UNTS91	107294
Mali	Tunisia	24 Jul 63	602UNTS91	108708
Algeria	Tunisia	01 Sep 63	601UNTS275	108701
Argentina	Paraguay	07 Feb 64	634UNTS127	109057
Cyprus	USSR (Soviet Union)	29 Feb 64	602UNTS45	108706
Malaysia	Netherlands	07 Apr 64	524UNTS81	107567
United Arab Rep	USA (United States)	05 May 64	531UNTS229	107706
Cyprus	Hungary	02 Jun 64	602UNTS3	108704
New Zealand	USA (United States)	24 Jun 64	524UNTS101	107568
France	Trinidad/Tobago	12 Oct 64	535UNTS25	107774
Cyprus	Syria	22 Dec 64	602UNTS25	108705
Argentina	UK Great Britain	12 Jan 65	597UNTS177	108645
Finland	UK Great Britain	25 Mar 65	539UNTS103	107826
Denmark	Malaysia	26 Mar 65	540UNTS205	107851
Australia	France	13 Apr 65	601UNTS293	108702
Ghana	Malawi	04 May 65	541UNTS163	107869
Spain	Sweden	05 May 65	0UNTSO	109239
Denmark	Spain	05 May 65	543UNTS255	107905
Mauritania	Spain	11 May 65	602UNTS111	108709
Malaysia	Norway	26 May 65	602UNTS157	108711
Saudi Arabia	USA (United States)	05 Jun 65	548UNTS285	107984
Ivory Coast	Sweden	07 Jun 65	0UNTSO	109240
Nigeria	Switzerland	11 Oct 65	602UNTS137	108710
Canada	USA (United States)	17 Jan 66	586UNTS151	108502
Bulgaria	Turkey	18 Apr 66	631UNTS263	108999
Ivory Coast	Norway	07 Jun 66	0UNTSO	109249
Denmark	Ivory Coast	07 Jun 66	595UNTS313	108626
Denmark	Nigeria	08 Sep 66	591UNTS177	108557
Norway	Singapore	20 Dec 66	0UNTSO	109242
Denmark	Singapore	20 Dec 66	593UNTS125	108580
Japan	Singapore	14 Feb 67	0UNTSO	109244
Algeria	Ivory Coast	16 Feb 67	0UNTSO	109245
Australia	Austria	22 Mar 67	0UNTSO	109246
Netherlands	Sierra Leone	13 Jun 67	0UNTSO	109247
Multilateral		03 Jul 67	0UNTSO	109248
Malaysia	UK Great Britain	01 Aug 67	633UNTS93	109036
Operating authorizations and regulations				
Brazil	France	27 Jan 40	72UNTS77	100929
Liberia	USA (United States)	31 Mar 42	23UNTS302	200137
Spain	USA (United States)	02 Dec 44	89UNTS345	200262
Multilateral		07 Dec 44	171UNTS345	200501
Multilateral		07 Dec 44	171UNTS387	200502
Multilateral		07 Dec 44	84UNTS389	200252
Multilateral		07 Dec 44	15UNTS295	200102

PARTY ONE	PARTY TWO	DATE	CITATION	NUMBER
Operating authorizations and regulations (Cont.)				
Denmark	USA (United States)	16 Dec 44	10UNTS213	200063
Sweden	USA (United States)	16 Dec 44	6UNTS397	200041
Iceland	USA (United States)	27 Jan 45	122UNTS293	200411
Ireland	USA (United States)	03 Feb 45	122UNTS305	200412
Canada	USA (United States)	17 Feb 45	122UNTS261	200409
Belgium	France	30 Mar 45	20UNTS297	200122
Switzerland	USA (United States)	03 Aug 45	51UNTS233	200191
Norway	USA (United States)	06 Oct 45	122UNTS319	200413
South Africa	UK Great Britain	26 Oct 45	72UNTS41	100927
Greece	UK Great Britain	26 Nov 45	35UNTS161	100555
Portugal	UK Great Britain	06 Dec 45	6UNTS3	100065
Portugal	UK Great Britain	06 Dec 45	5UNTS37	100064
Canada	UK Great Britain	21 Dec 45	27UNTS155	100405
France	USA (United States)	29 Dec 45	139UNTS105	101878
Czechoslovakia	USA (United States)	03 Jan 46	6UNTS309	100084
Spain	USA (United States)	15 Jan 46	89UNTS241	101221
Czechoslovakia	Poland	24 Jan 46	25UNTS181	100363
UK Great Britain	USA (United States)	11 Feb 46	3UNTS253	100036
Turkey	USA (United States)	12 Feb 46	13UNTS3	100196
Turkey	UK Great Britain	12 Feb 46	6UNTS79	100069
France	USA (United States)	27 Mar 46	139UNTS114	101879
Greece	USA (United States)	27 Mar 46	15UNTS233	100239
Ireland	UK Great Britain	05 Apr 46	72UNTS57	100928
Netherlands	Portugal	12 Apr 46	4UNTS317	100054
Argentina	UK Great Britain	17 Apr 46	164UNTS53	102159
Ireland	Sweden	29 May 46	35UNTS231	100557
Portugal	USA (United States)	30 May 46	174UNTS187	102285
Australia	Canada	11 Jun 46	10UNTS47	100142
United Arab Rep	USA (United States)	15 Jun 46	151UNTS135	101988
United Arab Rep	USA (United States)	15 Jun 46	71UNTS157	100917
France	USA (United States)	18 Jun 46	42UNTS183	100647
Sweden	Turkey	26 Jun 46	14UNTS21	100208
Albania	Yugoslavia	11 Jul 46	4UNTS407	100058
Netherlands	Spain	13 Jul 46	4UNTS351	100055
Czechoslovakia	USSR (Soviet Union)	25 Jul 46	27UNTS231	100409
Canada	Newfoundland	29 Jul 46	17UNTS169	100275
UK Great Britain	USA (United States)	31 Jul 46	42UNTS199	100648
Lebanon	USA (United States)	11 Aug 46	66UNTS211	100856
Netherlands	UK Great Britain	13 Aug 46	4UNTS367	100056
Norway	UK Great Britain	31 Aug 46	6UNTS235	100078
Brazil	USA (United States)	06 Sep 46	54UNTS197	100805
Sweden	USA (United States)	30 Sep 46	42UNTS213	100649
Denmark	USA (United States)	01 Oct 46	42UNTS219	100650
France	Turkey	12 Oct 46	14UNTS33	100209
Brazil	UK Great Britain	31 Oct 46	11UNTS115	100152
Norway	USA (United States)	12 Nov 46	42UNTS227	100651
India	USA (United States)	14 Nov 46	22UNTS55	100331
Philippines	USA (United States)	16 Nov 46	7UNTS151	100097
Sweden	UK Great Britain	27 Nov 46	11UNTS229	100162
Australia	USA (United States)	03 Dec 46	7UNTS201	100100
New Zealand	USA (United States)	03 Dec 46	7UNTS175	100099
Portugal	Switzerland	09 Dec 46	310UNTS251	104495
Brazil	Portugal	10 Dec 46	200UNTS67	102695
USA (United States)	Uruguay	14 Dec 46	532UNTS87	107713
Taiwan	USA (United States)	20 Dec 46	22UNTS87	100332
Peru	USA (United States)	27 Dec 46	26UNTS227	100390
Ecuador	USA (United States)	08 Jan 47	22UNTS119	100333
Czechoslovakia	Ireland	29 Jan 47	27UNTS267	100411
USSR (Soviet Union)	Yugoslavia	04 Feb 47	130UNTS235	101731
Greece	UK Great Britain	21 Feb 47	70UNTS215	100905
Thailand	USA (United States)	26 Feb 47	16UNTS17	100246
Paraguay	USA (United States)	28 Feb 47	44UNTS25	100676
Portugal	Sweden	06 Mar 47	35UNTS243	100558
Australia	USA (United States)	10 Mar 47	10UNTS89	100145
Netherlands	Turkey	19 Mar 47	14UNTS59	100211

PARTY ONE	PARTY TWO	DATE	CITATION	NUMBER
Operating authorizations and regulations (Cont.)				
Muscat and Oman	UK Great Britain	05 Apr 47	27UNTS287	100412
Greece	Sweden	08 Apr 47	94UNTS73	101307
Canada	USA (United States)	12 Apr 47	122UNTS229	101648
Greece	Netherlands	17 Apr 47	32UNTS115	100494
Canada	Portugal	25 Apr 47	94UNTS87	101308
Syria	USA (United States)	28 Apr 47	262UNTS121	103741
France	Greece	05 May 47	76UNTS61	100980
Thailand	USA (United States)	08 May 47	42UNTS241	100653
Chile	USA (United States)	10 May 47	55UNTS21	100807
Czechoslovakia	Denmark	14 May 47	27UNTS297	100413
South Africa	USA (United States)	23 May 47	66UNTS233	100857
UK Great Britain	USA (United States)	23 May 47	11UNTS211	100159
India	Netherlands	31 May 47	17UNTS65	100268
Norway	UK Great Britain	05 Jun 47	54UNTS181	100803
Italy	USA (United States)	09 Jun 47	104UNTS157	101437
Canada	Sweden	27 Jun 47	27UNTS313	100414
Romania	Yugoslavia	30 Jun 47	116UNTS57	101569
Iraq	Turkey	30 Jun 47	72UNTS107	100930
Denmark	Turkey	30 Jun 47	32UNTS301	100504
France	India	16 Jul 47	27UNTS325	100415
Canada	UK Great Britain	17 Jul 47	28UNTS3	100416
Netherlands	Thailand	18 Jul 47	28UNTS27	100417
Greece	Turkey	22 Jul 47	72UNTS131	100931
Netherlands	South Africa	22 Jul 47	12UNTS257	100188
Taiwan	UK Great Britain	23 Jul 47	9UNTS207	100135
Canada	Ireland	08 Aug 47	28UNTS47	100419
Poland	Romania	09 Aug 47	12UNTS363	100193
Hungary	Poland	28 Aug 47	15UNTS145	100231
Czechoslovakia	Netherlands	01 Sep 47	32UNTS129	100495
Czechoslovakia	Switzerland	10 Sep 47	35UNTS275	100559
Chile	UK Great Britain	16 Sep 47	133UNTS143	101786
Sweden	Yugoslavia	06 Oct 47	53UNTS107	100775
Colombia	UK Great Britain	16 Oct 47	160UNTS297	102115
Brazil	Netherlands	06 Nov 47	53UNTS59	100773
Norway	Portugal	11 Nov 47	34UNTS257	100542
Brazil	Sweden	14 Nov 47	94UNTS139	101310
Brazil	Norway	14 Nov 47	44UNTS163	100684
Brazil	Denmark	14 Nov 47	47UNTS39	100722
Denmark	Greece	14 Nov 47	35UNTS295	100560
Denmark	Ireland	18 Nov 47	35UNTS309	100561
Ireland	Italy	21 Nov 47	353UNTS73	105038
Taiwan	Netherlands	06 Dec 47	43UNTS185	100669
Denmark	Portugal	15 Dec 47	35UNTS329	100563
Peru	UK Great Britain	22 Dec 47	72UNTS143	100932
Ethiopia	Pakistan	01 Jan 48	35UNTS3	100547
Philippines	UK Great Britain	07 Jan 48	28UNTS63	100420
Austria	Netherlands	22 Jan 48	17UNTS99	100270
Italy	USA (United States)	06 Feb 48	73UNTS113	100950
Multilateral		06 Mar 48	289UNTS3	104214
Argentina	Denmark	18 Mar 48	94UNTS175	101311
Cuba	UK Great Britain	19 Mar 48	175UNTS23	102294
France	UK Great Britain	19 Apr 48	83UNTS201	101109
Ireland	Switzerland	06 May 48	334UNTS187	104768
Pakistan	Sweden	06 May 48	36UNTS3	100564
Jordan	Turkey	07 May 48	32UNTS313	100505
Ireland	Netherlands	10 May 48	28UNTS121	100422
Norway	Turkey	20 May 48	26UNTS137	100384
India	Sweden	21 May 48	34UNTS285	100543
Greece	Switzerland	26 May 48	94UNTS217	101312
Luxembourg	UK Great Britain	27 May 48	53UNTS115	100776
Argentina	Brazil	02 Jun 48	0UNTS0	109515
Canada	Netherlands	02 Jun 48	32UNTS215	100499
Ireland	Norway	21 Jun 48	34UNTS317	100545
India	Pakistan	23 Jun 48	28UNTS143	100423
Luxembourg	Netherlands	23 Jun 48	32UNTS229	100500

Operating authorizations and regulations (Cont.)

PARTY ONE	PARTY TWO	DATE	CITATION	NUMBER
Italy	UK Great Britain	25 Jun 48	94UNTS239	101313
Brazil	Switzerland	10 Aug 48	94UNTS269	101314
Multilateral		18 Aug 48	33UNTS181	100518
France	Spain	23 Aug 48	28UNTS173	100425
Greece	Lebanon	06 Sep 48	178UNTS37	102335
Bolivia	USA (United States)	29 Sep 48	505UNTS139	107370
Netherlands	Spain	08 Oct 48	28UNTS209	100426
France	USA (United States)	19 Oct 48	98UNTS3	101355
Mexico	Portugal	22 Oct 48	34UNTS329	100546
Argentina	Netherlands	29 Oct 48	95UNTS21	101316
Czechoslovakia	Poland	12 Nov 48	84UNTS347	101141
Argentina	Chile	14 Dec 48	635UNTS21	109071
Ceylon (Sri Lanka)	India	21 Dec 48	28UNTS223	100427
Ceylon (Sri Lanka)	Pakistan	03 Jan 49	28UNTS247	100428
Italy	Lebanon	24 Jan 49	231UNTS241	103223
Canada	USA (United States)	31 Jan 49	43UNTS119	100666
Switzerland	Turkey	16 Feb 49	72UNTS175	100933
Belgium	Sweden	21 Feb 49	95UNTS73	101317
Finland	Netherlands	25 Feb 49	53UNTS123	100777
Netherlands	Switzerland	07 Mar 49	35UNTS69	100551
Finland	USA (United States)	29 Mar 49	55UNTS59	100808
Panama	USA (United States)	31 Mar 49	55UNTS87	100810
Finland	Sweden	26 Apr 49	95UNTS83	101318
Bulgaria	Poland	16 May 49	84UNTS313	101140
Italy	Spain	31 May 49	231UNTS251	103224
Australia	Pakistan	03 Jun 49	35UNTS23	100549
Canada	USA (United States)	04 Jun 49	200UNTS201	102704
Canada	USA (United States)	04 Jun 49	122UNTS237	101649
Ethiopia	India	07 Jun 49	35UNTS13	100548
Belgium	Greece	21 Jun 49	137UNTS215	101854
Norway	Pakistan	23 Jun 49	35UNTS49	100550
India	Switzerland	24 Jun 49	95UNTS109	101319
Greece	Syria	05 Jul 49	78UNTS71	101013
Australia	India	11 Jul 49	35UNTS83	100552
Pakistan	Philippines	16 Jul 49	35UNTS111	100553
Dominican Republic	USA (United States)	19 Jul 49	51UNTS145	100762
Pakistan	UK Great Britain	27 Jul 49	44UNTS199	100685
Ceylon (Sri Lanka)	UK Great Britain	05 Aug 49	35UNTS137	100554
Canada	UK Great Britain	19 Aug 49	44UNTS223	100686
Finland	Norway	24 Aug 49	53UNTS167	100780
Denmark	Finland	26 Aug 49	53UNTS191	100781
Belgium	Canada	30 Aug 49	53UNTS221	100782
Denmark	ICAO (Civil Aviat)	09 Sep 49	53UNTS341	100791
Multilateral		15 Sep 49	53UNTS235	100783
Belgium	United Arab Rep	19 Sep 49	137UNTS189	101853
Lebanon	Netherlands	20 Sep 49	108UNTS205	101474
Burma	USA (United States)	28 Sep 49	55UNTS3	100806
Greece	Philippines	08 Oct 49	187UNTS221	102515
India	Philippines	20 Oct 49	72UNTS191	100934
Multilateral		27 Oct 49	53UNTS241	100784
Iran	Netherlands	31 Oct 49	254UNTS257	103596
Denmark	Pakistan	09 Nov 49	44UNTS255	100687
France	New Zealand	15 Nov 49	53UNTS247	100785
Italy	Turkey	25 Nov 49	192UNTS39	102594
Brazil	Spain	28 Nov 49	215UNTS303	102923
Austria	Sweden	02 Dec 49	108UNTS3	101465
Austria	Norway	02 Dec 49	72UNTS230	100936
Austria	Denmark	02 Dec 49	53UNTS281	100788
Netherlands	United Arab Rep	08 Dec 49	95UNTS123	101320
Sweden	United Arab Rep	12 Dec 49	108UNTS15	101466
Canada	Denmark	13 Dec 49	72UNTS247	100937
Austria	Switzerland	19 Dec 49	254UNTS287	103597
USA (United States)	Yugoslavia	24 Dec 49	89UNTS209	101219
Netherlands	Syria	13 Feb 50	108UNTS53	101467
Canada	Norway	14 Feb 50	53UNTS329	100790

Operating authorizations and regulations (Cont.)

PARTY ONE	PARTY TWO	DATE	CITATION	NUMBER
Spain	Sweden	18 Feb 50	166UNTS15	102184
Italy	Netherlands	04 Mar 50	254UNTS305	103598
Norway	United Arab Rep	11 Mar 50	95UNTS157	101321
Denmark	United Arab Rep	14 Mar 50	95UNTS197	101322
Philippines	USA (United States)	16 Mar 50	89UNTS199	101218
Iceland	Netherlands	22 Mar 50	95UNTS237	101323
Denmark	Iceland	22 Mar 50	72UNTS273	100939
Italy	Portugal	05 Apr 50	254UNTS329	103599
Sweden	UK Great Britain	05 Apr 50	99UNTS107	101374
Turkey	United Arab Rep	12 Apr 50	128UNTS3	101711
Australia	Philippines	14 Apr 50	127UNTS281	101709
Greece	United Arab Rep	24 Apr 50	163UNTS229	102149
Multilateral		13 May 50	128UNTS171	101719
Switzerland	United Arab Rep	15 May 50	95UNTS255	101325
Iceland	UK Great Britain	26 May 50	95UNTS277	101326
Israel	USA (United States)	13 Jun 50	212UNTS93	102863
Netherlands	Spain	20 Jun 50	95UNTS303	101327
Iraq	Pakistan	20 Jun 50	77UNTS215	101001
Denmark	Switzerland	22 Jun 50	96UNTS3	101328
Burma	Ceylon (Sri Lanka)	29 Jun 50	73UNTS3	100940
Spain	UK Great Britain	20 Jul 50	398UNTS101	105719
France	Pakistan	31 Jul 50	96UNTS23	101329
Canada	France	01 Aug 50	73UNTS21	100941
Spain	Switzerland	03 Aug 50	254UNTS365	103600
France	United Arab Rep	08 Aug 50	127UNTS293	101710
Dominican Republic	USA (United States)	11 Aug 50	92UNTS329	101278
Canada	New Zealand	16 Aug 50	77UNTS239	101002
Burma	Sweden	14 Sep 50	96UNTS45	101330
Brazil	Turkey	21 Sep 50	150UNTS299	101981
Ceylon (Sri Lanka)	United Arab Rep	26 Sep 50	192UNTS53	102595
France	UK Great Britain	06 Oct 50	96UNTS63	101331
Sweden	Switzerland	18 Oct 50	166UNTS49	102185
Luxembourg	Portugal	21 Oct 50	108UNTS67	101468
Taiwan	Philippines	23 Oct 50	215UNTS159	102918
Israel	Netherlands	23 Oct 50	189UNTS89	102543
Thailand	UK Great Britain	10 Nov 50	96UNTS77	101332
Israel	UK Great Britain	06 Dec 50	151UNTS33	101983
Israel	Turkey	05 Feb 51	193UNTS3	102607
Canada	USA (United States)	08 Feb 51	207UNTS17	102797
Colombia	Portugal	09 Mar 51	108UNTS87	101469
Greece	Yugoslavia	15 Mar 51	187UNTS237	102516
Iraq	UK Great Britain	19 Apr 51	108UNTS121	101470
France	UK Great Britain	20 Apr 51	106UNTS81	101458
UK Great Britain	USA (United States)	25 Apr 51	99UNTS97	101373
Belgium	UK Great Britain	08 May 51	158UNTS451	102079
India	Netherlands	24 May 51	108UNTS151	101471
Greece	Norway	28 May 51	187UNTS141	102507
Denmark	Iran	18 Jun 51	255UNTS3	103602
Cuba	Portugal	26 Jun 51	192UNTS115	102598
Iceland	Norway	14 Jul 51	163UNTS265	102150
Burma	Denmark	30 Jul 51	108UNTS167	101472
Israel	Philippines	07 Aug 51	192UNTS81	102596
Lebanon	UK Great Britain	15 Aug 51	160UNTS327	102116
Burma	Netherlands	06 Sep 51	108UNTS187	101473
Panama	UK Great Britain	15 Sep 51	560UNTS143	108172
Taiwan	Thailand	29 Sep 51	215UNTS166	102919
Philippines	Spain	06 Oct 51	215UNTS193	102920
Greece	Luxembourg	22 Oct 51	187UNTS119	102506
India	UK Great Britain	01 Dec 51	128UNTS39	101712
Colombia	Spain	11 Dec 51	216UNTS73	102933
Multilateral		20 Dec 51	163UNTS293	102151
Jordan	United Arab Rep	02 Jan 52	192UNTS157	102599
Japan	USA (United States)	28 Feb 52	208UNTS255	102817
Taiwan	Korea, South	01 Mar 52	255UNTS35	103603
Belgium	Spain	10 Mar 52	178UNTS243	102342

Operating authorizations and regulations (Cont.)

PARTY ONE	PARTY TWO	DATE	CITATION	NUMBER
Pakistan	Switzerland	17 Mar 52	192UNTS237	102603
Norway	Uruguay	20 Mar 52	310UNTS279	104496
Sweden	Uruguay	20 Mar 52	311UNTS3	104497
Iraq	Switzerland	31 Mar 52	311UNTS43	104498
Libya	UK Great Britain	31 Mar 52	151UNTS69	101984
France	Mexico	17 Apr 52	163UNTS321	102153
Belgium	Sweden	21 Apr 52	166UNTS9	102183
Denmark	Japan	28 Apr 52	166UNTS3	102182
France	Israel	29 Apr 52	189UNTS55	102542
Switzerland	UK Great Britain	13 May 52	164UNTS91	102160
Australia	United Arab Rep	14 Jun 52	173UNTS241	102269
India	United Arab Rep	14 Jun 52	173UNTS209	102268
Denmark	UK Great Britain	23 Jun 52	151UNTS3	101982
Greece	USA (United States)	25 Jun 52	181UNTS53	102398
Belgium	Israel	30 Jun 52	183UNTS263	102435
Mexico	USA (United States)	15 Jul 52	181UNTS263	102416
Netherlands	Pakistan	17 Jul 52	150UNTS277	101980
Japan	USA (United States)	11 Aug 52	212UNTS27	102862
Ethiopia	Pakistan	29 Aug 52	150UNTS257	101979
Netherlands	Peru	22 Sep 52	255UNTS49	103604
Austria	Luxembourg	13 Oct 52	192UNTS291	102606
Mexico	Netherlands	13 Oct 52	163UNTS341	102154
Iceland	Luxembourg	23 Oct 52	193UNTS39	102609
Burma	UK Great Britain	25 Oct 52	150UNTS237	101978
Chile	Sweden	27 Oct 52	311UNTS63	104499
Chile	Denmark	27 Oct 52	271UNTS93	103911
Luxembourg	Norway	17 Nov 52	311UNTS95	104500
Luxembourg	Sweden	17 Nov 52	173UNTS277	102270
Israel	Switzerland	19 Nov 52	232UNTS3	103226
South Africa	Sweden	09 Jan 53	173UNTS299	102271
Netherlands	Philippines	05 Feb 53	216UNTS99	102934
Japan	Netherlands	17 Feb 53	192UNTS215	102602
Japan	Sweden	20 Feb 53	173UNTS307	102272
India	Pakistan	20 Feb 53	164UNTS3	102155
Libya	UK Great Britain	21 Feb 53	311UNTS115	104501
Japan	Norway	23 Feb 53	192UNTS191	102601
Denmark	Japan	26 Feb 53	173UNTS329	102273
Lebanon	Sweden	23 Mar 53	255UNTS83	103605
Turkey	Yugoslavia	16 Apr 53	255UNTS99	103606
Philippines	Thailand	27 Apr 53	174UNTS3	102274
Denmark	South Africa	30 Apr 53	174UNTS19	102275
Israel	South Africa	05 May 53	192UNTS183	102600
Cuba	USA (United States)	26 May 53	224UNTS75	103070
Switzerland	Yugoslavia	28 May 53	232UNTS45	103228
Japan	Thailand	19 Jun 53	174UNTS29	102276
Burma	Norway	22 Jun 53	174UNTS49	102277
Canada	Mexico	27 Jul 53	192UNTS255	102604
USA (United States)	Venezuela	14 Aug 53	213UNTS99	102883
Belgium	New Zealand	01 Sep 53	192UNTS283	102605
Ceylon (Sri Lanka)	Netherlands	14 Sep 53	193UNTS21	102608
Norway	South Africa	21 Sep 53	192UNTS105	102597
Korea, South	Netherlands	26 Oct 53	200UNTS103	102697
Austria	Yugoslavia	11 Nov 53	363UNTS149	105206
Cuba	USA (United States)	26 Nov 53	205UNTS213	102777
Belgium	Lebanon	24 Dec 53	219UNTS153	102972
Ethiopia	Greece	20 Jan 54	222UNTS281	103035
Syria	UK Great Britain	30 Jan 54	449UNTS47	106452
Canada	Peru	18 Feb 54	411UNTS64	105915
Multilateral		19 Feb 54	214UNTS51	102899
Multilateral		25 Feb 54	215UNTS249	102922
Lebanon	Switzerland	03 Mar 54	255UNTS127	103608
Peru	Spain	31 Mar 54	232UNTS65	103230
France	South Africa	05 May 54	215UNTS401	102926
Switzerland	Syria	26 May 54	255UNTS145	103609
Iran	Switzerland	27 May 54	496UNTS273	107257

Operating authorizations and regulations (Cont.)

PARTY ONE	PARTY TWO	DATE	CITATION	NUMBER
Ireland	Luxembourg	27 Jul 54	232UNTS91	103231
Norway	USA (United States)	06 Aug 54	222UNTS261	103033
Denmark	USA (United States)	06 Aug 54	222UNTS235	103030
Sweden	USA (United States)	06 Aug 54	221UNTS331	103014
Philippines	Sweden	20 Aug 54	200UNTS121	102699
Belgium	South Africa	13 Sep 54	201UNTS15	102707
France	South Africa	17 Sep 54	216UNTS29	102930
Denmark	Philippines	20 Oct 54	216UNTS3	102927
Norway	Philippines	20 Oct 54	216UNTS11	102928
Multilateral		23 Oct 54	332UNTS219	104762
Netherlands	Venezuela	26 Oct 54	232UNTS103	103232
Pakistan	United Arab Rep	13 Dec 54	255UNTS167	103610
Ecuador	Netherlands	14 Dec 54	232UNTS115	103233
Norway	Switzerland	30 Dec 54	311UNTS147	104502
Austria	Belgium	07 Jan 55	380UNTS219	105458
Canada	Japan	12 Jan 55	311UNTS167	104503
Philippines	UK Great Britain	31 Jan 55	216UNTS51	102932
United Arab Rep	Yugoslavia	20 Feb 55	255UNTS199	103611
Iraq	United Arab Rep	23 Mar 55	311UNTS199	104504
Austria	Romania	11 May 55	342UNTS119	104904
Syria	United Arab Rep	03 Jul 55	393UNTS67	105652
Germany, West	USA (United States)	07 Jul 55	275UNTS3	103973
Germany, West	UK Great Britain	22 Jul 55	269UNTS189	103881
Germany, East	Romania	28 Jul 55	342UNTS207	104909
USSR (Soviet Union)	Yugoslavia	03 Sep 55	240UNTS267	103408
Germany, East	Hungary	10 Sep 55	407UNTS132	105863
Belgium	Ireland	10 Sep 55	255UNTS235	103612
Bulgaria	Yugoslavia	01 Oct 55	396UNTS223	105698
France	Germany, West	04 Oct 55	353UNTS203	105044
Finland	USSR (Soviet Union)	19 Oct 55	353UNTS185	105043
Denmark	Syria	20 Oct 55	250UNTS61	103518
Denmark	Lebanon	21 Oct 55	248UNTS17	103482
Czechoslovakia	Germany, East	24 Oct 55	504UNTS173	107358
Pakistan	Turkey	02 Nov 55	311UNTS217	104505
Australia	South Africa	04 Nov 55	232UNTS143	103234
Burma	China People's Rep	08 Nov 55	306UNTS11	104430
Austria	USSR (Soviet Union)	09 Nov 55	255UNTS247	103613
Austria	Israel	17 Nov 55	232UNTS153	103235
India	Japan	26 Nov 55	311UNTS243	104506
France	Japan	17 Jan 56	255UNTS275	103614
Australia	Japan	19 Jan 56	311UNTS291	104507
Austria	Italy	23 Jan 56	393UNTS97	105653
Argentina	Switzerland	25 Jan 56	559UNTS121	108157
Romania	Yugoslavia	01 Feb 56	362UNTS203	105189
Hungary	Romania	03 Feb 56	362UNTS233	105190
India	USA (United States)	03 Feb 56	272UNTS75	103932
Austria	Poland	08 Feb 56	334UNTS221	104770
Netherlands	Sudan	12 Feb 56	311UNTS319	104508
Norway	Syria	25 Feb 56	463UNTS217	106706
Denmark	USSR (Soviet Union)	31 Mar 56	259UNTS169	103689
Norway	USSR (Soviet Union)	31 Mar 56	259UNTS205	103690
Sweden	USSR (Soviet Union)	31 Mar 56	259UNTS239	103691
Bulgaria	Yugoslavia	04 Apr 56	391UNTS47	105616
Belgium	Germany, West	14 Apr 56	344UNTS103	104945
Multilateral		30 Apr 56	310UNTS229	104494
Portugal	Venezuela	16 May 56	463UNTS239	106707
Italy	South Africa	21 May 56	255UNTS323	103616
Japan	Switzerland	24 May 56	312UNTS3	104509
Greece	Italy	26 May 56	496UNTS301	107258
Fed Rhod/Nyasaland	South Africa	30 May 56	255UNTS317	103615
Italy	Switzerland	04 Jun 56	378UNTS311	105429
Poland	Sweden	08 Jun 56	334UNTS257	104771
Germany, West	Ireland	12 Jun 56	353UNTS121	105040
India	Thailand	12 Jun 56	255UNTS341	103617
Multilateral		25 Sep 56	334UNTS89	104767

Operating authorizations and regulations (Cont.)

PARTY ONE	PARTY TWO	DATE	CITATION	NUMBER
Multilateral		25 Sep 56	334UNTS13	104766
Germany, West	Netherlands	28 Sep 56	327UNTS185	104722
Switzerland	Thailand	13 Oct 56	312UNTS43	104510
Belgium	Poland	17 Oct 56	356UNTS279	105100
Colombia	USA (United States)	24 Oct 56	476UNTS77	106905
Belgium	Turkey	25 Oct 56	380UNTS3	105447
Austria	UK Great Britain	27 Oct 56	264UNTS67	103789
Peru	Switzerland	23 Nov 56	411UNTS97	105916
Albania	Yugoslavia	23 Nov 56	386UNTS73	105539
Belgium	Romania	04 Dec 56	317UNTS161	104602
Iran	USA (United States)	16 Jan 57	308UNTS147	104460
Iceland	Thailand	22 Jan 57	312UNTS63	104511
Germany, West	Sweden	29 Jan 57	393UNTS113	105654
Germany, West	Norway	29 Jan 57	353UNTS39	105037
Denmark	Germany, West	29 Jan 57	302UNTS75	104354
Mexico	USA (United States)	07 Mar 57	279UNTS205	104042
Belgium	Czechoslovakia	12 Mar 57	312UNTS75	104512
Netherlands	Yugoslavia	13 Mar 57	327UNTS227	104723
Netherlands	USA (United States)	03 Apr 57	410UNTS193	105904
Germany, West	Yugoslavia	10 Apr 57	463UNTS269	106708
Denmark	Pakistan	10 Apr 57	302UNTS53	104353
Romania	Sweden	15 Apr 57	342UNTS325	104915
Bulgaria	Sweden	17 Apr 57	464UNTS3	106709
Korea, South	USA (United States)	24 Apr 57	288UNTS219	104207
Belgium	Bulgaria	14 May 57	317UNTS81	104596
Australia	Germany, West	22 May 57	357UNTS45	105105
Hungary	Netherlands	28 May 57	334UNTS291	104773
Belgium	Hungary	01 Jun 57	291UNTS17	104242
Afghanistan	Pakistan	13 Jun 57	327UNTS51	104717
Czechoslovakia	United Arab Rep	30 Jun 57	411UNTS126	105917
Greece	Italy	02 Aug 57	533UNTS217	107744
Hungary	Sweden	02 Aug 57	334UNTS307	104774
Netherlands	Romania	27 Aug 57	342UNTS309	104914
Multilateral		30 Sep 57	619UNTS77	108940
Multilateral		03 Oct 57	366UNTS87	105216
Italy	Pakistan	05 Oct 57	353UNTS91	105039
Fed of Malaya	UK Great Britain	18 Oct 57	335UNTS3	104775
France	Morocco	25 Oct 57	559UNTS95	108156
UK Great Britain	USSR (Soviet Union)	19 Dec 57	351UNTS235	105026
Australia	Ireland	30 Dec 57	497UNTS29	107260
Canada	Switzerland	10 Jan 58	464UNTS21	106710
Lebanon	United Nations	20 Jan 58	286UNTS189	104166
Belgium	Morocco	20 Jan 58	288UNTS3	104192
Australia	UK Great Britain	07 Feb 58	335UNTS23	104776
Bulgaria	Netherlands	07 Feb 58	335UNTS45	104777
Afghanistan	Turkey	08 Feb 58	464UNTS39	106711
Sudan	Sweden	17 Feb 58	393UNTS161	105655
Austria	Sweden	19 Feb 58	427UNTS211	106155
Norway	Pakistan	05 Mar 58	334UNTS199	104769
Pakistan	Sweden	06 Mar 58	393UNTS181	105656
Germany, West	Portugal	21 Mar 58	464UNTS71	106712
Denmark	South Africa	28 Mar 58	300UNTS107	104334
South Africa	Sweden	28 Mar 58	300UNTS95	104333
Norway	South Africa	28 Mar 58	300UNTS83	104332
Morocco	Portugal	03 Apr 58	393UNTS203	105657
Belgium	Iran	14 Apr 58	381UNTS309	105473
Sweden	Yugoslavia	18 Apr 58	393UNTS225	105658
Japan	Poland	26 Apr 58	340UNTS221	104866
Multilateral		29 Apr 58	450UNTS11	106465
Bulgaria	Denmark	28 May 58	312UNTS235	104521
India	USSR (Soviet Union)	02 Jun 58	393UNTS3	105650
Belgium	USSR (Soviet Union)	05 Jun 58	345UNTS145	104965
Pakistan	Portugal	07 Jun 58	320UNTS225	104645
Belgium	South Africa	11 Jun 58	335UNTS63	104778
Norway	Romania	16 Jun 58	405UNTS223	105835

Operating authorizations and regulations (Cont.)

PARTY ONE	PARTY TWO	DATE	CITATION	NUMBER
Netherlands	USSR (Soviet Union)	17 Jun 58	335UNTS77	104779
Austria	Belgium	20 Jun 58	312UNTS95	104513
Denmark	Romania	25 Jun 58	345UNTS231	104970
Belgium	Pakistan	04 Jul 58	387UNTS305	105569
Ethiopia	UK Great Britain	07 Jul 58	331UNTS3	104749
Austria	Romania	10 Jul 58	353UNTS155	105041
Denmark	Hungary	17 Jul 58	344UNTS281	104954
Afghanistan	Austria	21 Jul 58	0UNTS0	109236
Romania	United Arab Rep	14 Aug 58	405UNTS189	105834
Austria	Bulgaria	12 Sep 58	353UNTS3	105036
Ghana	UK Great Britain	24 Sep 58	411UNTS146	105918
Australia	South Africa	26 Sep 58	335UNTS121	104780
Liberia	Netherlands	28 Nov 58	393UNTS55	105651
Finland	Switzerland	07 Jan 59	353UNTS173	105042
UK Great Britain	Yugoslavia	03 Feb 59	359UNTS339	105151
Indonesia	USA (United States)	02 Mar 59	357UNTS145	105113
Japan	Philippines	02 Mar 59	341UNTS49	104877
Netherlands	Tunisia	19 Mar 59	497UNTS61	107262
Sweden	Tunisia	19 Mar 59	497UNTS43	107261
Norway	Tunisia	28 Mar 59	497UNTS77	107263
Poland	UK Great Britain	03 Apr 59	351UNTS295	105030
Denmark	Tunisia	14 Apr 59	340UNTS273	104870
Austria	Netherlands	06 May 59	485UNTS175	107055
Denmark	Sudan	11 May 59	445UNTS105	106380
Ceylon (Sri Lanka)	Norway	29 May 59	411UNTS165	105919
Ceylon (Sri Lanka)	Denmark	29 May 59	348UNTS225	105002
Belgium	Japan	20 Jun 59	411UNTS3	105911
Bulgaria	United Arab Rep	09 Jul 59	411UNTS187	105920
India	Italy	16 Jul 59	464UNTS129	106714
Austria	Hungary	17 Jul 59	0UNTS0	109237
Afghanistan	Germany, West	22 Jul 59	464UNTS177	106715
Germany, West	Iceland	12 Aug 59	411UNTS224	105921
Canada	Germany, West	04 Sep 59	411UNTS260	105922
Australia	Fed of Malaya	29 Sep 59	357UNTS29	105104
Germany, West	USA (United States)	01 Oct 59	358UNTS129	105130
Nicaragua	Peru	14 Oct 59	392UNTS303	105649
South Africa	Switzerland	19 Oct 59	559UNTS257	108162
Italy	Netherlands	08 Dec 59	484UNTS309	107039
Liberia	Sweden	09 Dec 59	464UNTS219	106716
Czechoslovakia	UK Great Britain	15 Jan 60	374UNTS207	105336
Germany, West	United Arab Rep	16 Feb 60	464UNTS233	106717
Multilateral		26 Feb 60	418UNTS171	106022
Australia	Thailand	26 Feb 60	392UNTS255	105647
France	Thailand	26 Feb 60	392UNTS279	105648
Guinea	Netherlands	09 Mar 60	392UNTS243	105646
Finland	Iceland	10 Mar 60	497UNTS95	107264
Czechoslovakia	Iraq	11 Mar 60	464UNTS267	106718
Belgium	Switzerland	24 Mar 60	416UNTS81	105996
Luxembourg	Yugoslavia	09 Apr 60	464UNTS293	106719
Multilateral		22 Apr 60	418UNTS211	106023
Germany, West	Spain	28 Apr 60	465UNTS3	106720
Iran	UK Great Britain	02 May 60	566UNTS129	108241
Greece	Romania	02 May 60	485UNTS17	107043
Morocco	United Arab Rep	19 May 60	563UNTS121	108208
Switzerland	Tunisia	21 May 60	497UNTS109	107265
Kuwait	UK Great Britain	24 May 60	412UNTS4	105923
Afghanistan	Czechoslovakia	28 May 60	497UNTS129	107266
Luxembourg	Tunisia	13 Jun 60	497UNTS143	107267
Denmark	Peru	22 Jun 60	439UNTS113	106326
Ireland	Portugal	24 Jun 60	412UNTS30	105924
Poland	UK Great Britain	02 Jul 60	385UNTS87	105532
Switzerland	United Arab Rep	14 Jul 60	497UNTS161	107268
Germany, West	Pakistan	20 Jul 60	465UNTS41	106721
Netherlands	Poland	21 Jul 60	497UNTS189	107269
Ghana	Netherlands	30 Jul 60	412UNTS51	105925

PARTY ONE	PARTY TWO	DATE	CITATION	NUMBER
Operating authorizations and regulations (Cont.)				
Mexico	USA (United States)	15 Aug 60	402UNTS177	105786
Belgium	Burma	17 Aug 60	540UNTS185	107850
Ghana	United Arab Rep	29 Aug 60	412UNTS71	105926
Czechoslovakia	India	19 Sep 60	465UNTS67	106722
Belgium	Jordan	19 Oct 60	479UNTS277	106959
Hungary	UK Great Britain	25 Oct 60	419UNTS309	106034
Burma	Switzerland	31 Oct 60	465UNTS97	106723
Norway	Peru	02 Nov 60	497UNTS207	107270
Australia	Italy	10 Nov 60	497UNTS247	107271
Indonesia	UK Great Britain	23 Nov 60	398UNTS71	105718
Canada	Pakistan	21 Dec 60	465UNTS115	106724
Luxembourg	Thailand	29 Dec 60	465UNTS131	106725
Jordan	Sweden	09 Jan 61	465UNTS155	106726
Sudan	UK Great Britain	16 Jan 61	424UNTS233	106112
Norway	Poland	17 Jan 61	412UNTS130	105928
Denmark	Poland	17 Jan 61	412UNTS111	105927
Germany, West	Japan	18 Jan 61	465UNTS173	106727
Cuba	Czechoslovakia	04 Mar 61	465UNTS209	106728
Turkey	USSR (Soviet Union)	27 Apr 61	420UNTS307	106047
Poland	Switzerland	18 May 61	559UNTS233	108161
Czechoslovakia	Morocco	08 Jun 61	497UNTS275	107272
New Zealand	UK Great Britain	13 Jun 61	497UNTS293	107273
Cameroon	France	16 Jun 61	412UNTS148	105929
Guinea	Sweden	17 Jun 61	465UNTS236	106729
Czechoslovakia	Ghana	02 Aug 61	465UNTS249	106730
Jordan	Norway	21 Aug 61	465UNTS275	106731
Jordan	Netherlands	24 Aug 61	466UNTS3	106733
Mexico	Netherlands	24 Aug 61	465UNTS291	106732
Liberia	Switzerland	31 Aug 61	559UNTS215	108160
Multilateral		18 Sep 61	500UNTS31	107305
Ghana	Romania	30 Sep 61	467UNTS443	106769
Germany, West	Morocco	12 Oct 61	523UNTS289	107562
Japan	Pakistan	17 Oct 61	466UNTS17	106734
Cyprus	Greece	23 Nov 61	497UNTS311	107274
Czechoslovakia	Mali	27 Nov 61	466UNTS41	106736
Denmark	Jordan	07 Dec 61	631UNTS333	109003
Czechoslovakia	Guinea	16 Dec 61	559UNTS49	108154
Netherlands	Sweden	08 Jan 62	466UNTS65	106737
Austria	Greece	15 Jan 62	498UNTS3	107275
Indonesia	Japan	23 Jan 62	559UNTS77	108155
Italy	Japan	31 Jan 62	498UNTS23	107276
Finland	Hungary	13 Feb 62	463UNTS61	106693
Austria	Spain	19 Feb 62	0UNTS0	109238
Germany, West	Thailand	05 Mar 62	563UNTS165	108210
Luxembourg	Spain	26 Mar 62	563UNTS205	108211
France	Luxembourg	29 Mar 62	563UNTS227	108212
Sierra Leone	UK Great Britain	05 Apr 62	434UNTS227	106265
Ghana	USSR (Soviet Union)	06 Apr 62	498UNTS41	107277
Netherlands	USA (United States)	24 Apr 62	436UNTS93	106289
Japan	United Arab Rep	10 May 62	498UNTS69	107278
France	Romania	18 May 62	498UNTS115	107279
France	Senegal	15 Jun 62	524UNTS3	107563
Czechoslovakia	Senegal	20 Jun 62	498UNTS145	107280
Guinea	Norway	21 Jun 62	466UNTS81	106738
Liberia	Norway	29 Jun 62	466UNTS95	106739
Morocco	Switzerland	05 Jul 62	498UNTS189	107282
Morocco	Switzerland	05 Jul 62	498UNTS171	107281
Ecuador	Germany, West	20 Sep 62	498UNTS199	107283
Austria	Czechoslovakia	22 Sep 62	495UNTS157	107244
Japan	Kuwait	06 Oct 62	498UNTS235	107284
Trinidad/Tobago	USA (United States)	08 Oct 62	462UNTS145	106675
Finland	France	12 Oct 62	498UNTS299	107285
Hungary	Syria	18 Oct 62	491UNTS209	107178
Netherlands	Norway	18 Oct 62	466UNTS145	106741
France	Ivory Coast	19 Oct 62	498UNTS317	107286

PARTY ONE	PARTY TWO	DATE	CITATION	NUMBER
Operating authorizations and regulations (Cont.)				
Poland	Syria	10 Nov 62	491UNTS228	107179
Czechoslovakia	Poland	16 Nov 62	526UNTS3	107597
Ivory Coast	Switzerland	17 Nov 62	499UNTS3	107289
Jamaica	USA (United States)	29 Nov 62	462UNTS229	106682
Austria	Yugoslavia	11 Dec 62	546UNTS3	107938
Syria	United Arab Rep	27 Dec 62	491UNTS245	107180
Ghana	Mali	09 Jan 63	466UNTS165	106742
Senegal	Switzerland	23 Jan 63	524UNTS23	107564
Guinea	Switzerland	01 Feb 63	499UNTS35	107291
Mali	Senegal	07 Feb 63	524UNTS41	107565
UK Great Britain	Yugoslavia	16 Feb 63	507UNTS171	107400
Sudan	Switzerland	18 Feb 63	563UNTS281	108215
Algeria	France	18 Feb 63	563UNTS263	108214
Cyprus	Norway	05 Mar 63	563UNTS305	108216
Poland	USSR (Soviet Union)	22 Apr 63	493UNTS229	107217
Cyprus	Denmark	27 Apr 63	529UNTS255	107664
Greece	Hungary	27 Apr 63	534UNTS3	107750
Algeria	Morocco	30 Apr 63	564UNTS3	108217
Portugal	South Africa	07 May 63	499UNTS49	107292
Belgium	Cyprus	08 Jun 63	601UNTS311	108703
Finland	Poland	10 Jun 63	503UNTS179	107343
Guinea	Ivory Coast	26 Jun 63	499UNTS71	107293
Austria	France	12 Jul 63	499UNTS91	107294
Taiwan	Luxembourg	19 Jul 63	564UNTS23	108218
Algeria	Mali	22 Jul 63	564UNTS29	108219
Cameroon	Israel	09 Aug 63	499UNTS121	107295
Algeria	Tunisia	01 Sep 63	601UNTS275	108701
Pakistan	USSR (Soviet Union)	07 Oct 63	499UNTS161	107297
Ivory Coast	Netherlands	09 Oct 63	499UNTS141	107296
Canada	Denmark	28 Nov 63	496UNTS223	107254
Canada	USA (United States)	27 Dec 63	494UNTS21	107223
Mali	Niger	15 Jan 64	499UNTS197	107299
Lebanon	Pakistan	04 Feb 64	614UNTS55	108863
Denmark	Yugoslavia	11 Feb 64	511UNTS241	107437
France	New Zealand	27 Feb 64	499UNTS191	107298
Cyprus	USSR (Soviet Union)	29 Feb 64	602UNTS45	108706
Algeria	Czechoslovakia	09 Mar 64	601UNTS247	108700
Cameroon	Mali	17 Mar 64	524UNTS61	107566
Portugal	UK Great Britain	07 Apr 64	539UNTS167	107830
Malaysia	Netherlands	07 Apr 64	524UNTS81	107567
United Arab Rep	USA (United States)	05 May 64	531UNTS229	107706
Cyprus	Hungary	02 Jun 64	602UNTS3	108704
New Zealand	USA (United States)	24 Jun 64	524UNTS101	107568
Sweden	USA (United States)	06 Jul 64	529UNTS287	107666
Ivory Coast	Mali	09 Jul 64	524UNTS121	107569
Germany, West	Jamaica	07 Oct 64	514UNTS187	107447
France	Trinidad/Tobago	12 Oct 64	535UNTS25	107774
Greece	Yugoslavia	05 Nov 64	539UNTS19	107821
Italy	USA (United States)	23 Nov 64	532UNTS133	107716
Cyprus	Syria	22 Dec 64	602UNTS25	108705
Argentina	UK Great Britain	12 Jan 65	597UNTS177	108645
Finland	UK Great Britain	25 Mar 65	539UNTS103	107826
Denmark	Malaysia	26 Mar 65	540UNTS205	107851
Australia	France	13 Apr 65	601UNTS293	108702
Ghana	Malawi	04 May 65	541UNTS163	107869
Spain	Sweden	05 May 65	0UNTS0	109239
Denmark	Spain	05 May 65	543UNTS255	107905
Ivory Coast	Sweden	07 Jun 65	0UNTS0	109240
Burma	Czechoslovakia	15 Dec 65	602UNTS71	108707
Canada	USA (United States)	17 Jan 66	586UNTS151	108502
Portugal	UK Great Britain	17 Apr 66	573UNTS223	108335
Bulgaria	Turkey	18 Apr 66	631UNTS263	108999
Ivory Coast	Norway	07 Jun 66	0UNTS0	109249
Denmark	Ivory Coast	07 Jun 66	595UNTS313	108626
Austria	USA (United States)	23 Jun 66	601UNTS51	108687

PARTY ONE	PARTY TWO	DATE	CITATION	NUMBER
Operating authorizations and regulations (Cont.)				
Taiwan	Vietnam, South	19 Aug 66	0UNTS0	109241
Denmark	Nigeria	08 Sep 66	591UNTS177	108557
Norway	Singapore	20 Dec 66	0UNTS0	109242
Singapore	Sweden	20 Dec 66	0UNTS0	109243
Denmark	Singapore	20 Dec 66	593UNTS125	108580
Japan	Singapore	14 Feb 67	0UNTS0	109244
Algeria	Ivory Coast	16 Feb 67	0UNTS0	109245
Congo (Brazzaville)	Denmark	27 Feb 67	600UNTS189	108681
Trinidad/Tobago	UK Great Britain	01 Mar 67	606UNTS149	108784
Australia	Austria	22 Mar 67	0UNTS0	109246
Netherlands	Sierra Leone	13 Jun 67	0UNTS0	109247
Multilateral		03 Jul 67	0UNTS0	109248
Malta	UK Great Britain	10 Jul 67	619UNTS11	108936
Singapore	UK Great Britain	01 Aug 67	619UNTS29	108937
Malaysia	UK Great Britain	01 Aug 67	633UNTS93	109036
Denmark	Malaysia	14 Dec 67	614UNTS26	108862
Algeria	France	26 Dec 67	0UNTS0	109509
Licenses and certificates of nationality				
Brazil	France	27 Jan 40	72UNTS77	100929
Multilateral		07 Dec 44	15UNTS295	200102
Sweden	USA (United States)	16 Dec 44	6UNTS397	200041
Denmark	USA (United States)	16 Dec 44	10UNTS213	200063
Iceland	USA (United States)	27 Jan 45	122UNTS293	200411
Ireland	USA (United States)	03 Feb 45	122UNTS305	200412
Switzerland	USA (United States)	03 Aug 45	51UNTS233	200191
Norway	USA (United States)	06 Oct 45	122UNTS319	200413
South Africa	UK Great Britain	26 Oct 45	72UNTS41	100927
Greece	UK Great Britain	26 Nov 45	35UNTS161	100555
Portugal	UK Great Britain	06 Dec 45	6UNTS3	100065
Portugal	USA (United States)	06 Dec 45	3UNTS139	100028
Portugal	UK Great Britain	06 Dec 45	5UNTS37	100064
Canada	UK Great Britain	21 Dec 45	27UNTS155	100405
Czechoslovakia	USA (United States)	03 Jan 46	6UNTS309	100084
Czechoslovakia	Poland	24 Jan 46	25UNTS181	100363
UK Great Britain	USA (United States)	11 Feb 46	3UNTS253	100036
Turkey	USA (United States)	12 Feb 46	13UNTS3	100196
Turkey	UK Great Britain	12 Feb 46	6UNTS79	100069
France	UK Great Britain	28 Feb 46	27UNTS173	100407
France	USA (United States)	27 Mar 46	139UNTS114	101879
Greece	USA (United States)	27 Mar 46	15UNTS233	100239
Ireland	UK Great Britain	05 Apr 46	72UNTS57	100928
Belgium	USA (United States)	05 Apr 46	4UNTS125	100041
Netherlands	Portugal	12 Apr 46	4UNTS317	100054
Argentina	UK Great Britain	17 Apr 46	164UNTS53	102159
France	Ireland	16 May 46	44UNTS105	100681
Ireland	Sweden	29 May 46	35UNTS231	100557
Australia	Canada	11 Jun 46	10UNTS47	100142
United Arab Rep	USA (United States)	15 Jun 46	71UNTS157	100917
France	USA (United States)	18 Jun 46	42UNTS183	100647
Sweden	Turkey	26 Jun 46	14UNTS21	100208
Albania	Yugoslavia	11 Jul 46	4UNTS407	100058
Netherlands	Spain	13 Jul 46	4UNTS351	100055
France	Sweden	02 Aug 46	27UNTS251	100410
Lebanon	USA (United States)	11 Aug 46	66UNTS211	100856
Netherlands	UK Great Britain	13 Aug 46	4UNTS367	100056
Norway	UK Great Britain	31 Aug 46	6UNTS235	100078
Brazil	USA (United States)	06 Sep 46	54UNTS197	100805
France	Turkey	12 Oct 46	14UNTS33	100209
Belgium	Portugal	22 Oct 46	34UNTS49	100527
Brazil	UK Great Britain	31 Oct 46	11UNTS115	100152
Philippines	USA (United States)	16 Nov 46	7UNTS151	100097
Sweden	UK Great Britain	27 Nov 46	11UNTS229	100162
Australia	USA (United States)	03 Dec 46	7UNTS201	100100
New Zealand	USA (United States)	03 Dec 46	7UNTS175	100099

PARTY ONE	PARTY TWO	DATE	CITATION	NUMBER
Licenses and certificates of nationality (Cont.)				
Portugal	Switzerland	09 Dec 46	310UNTS251	104495
Brazil	Portugal	10 Dec 46	200UNTS67	102695
USA (United States)	Uruguay	14 Dec 46	532UNTS87	107713
Taiwan	USA (United States)	20 Dec 46	22UNTS87	100332
Peru	USA (United States)	27 Dec 46	26UNTS227	100390
Ecuador	USA (United States)	08 Jan 47	22UNTS119	100333
Czechoslovakia	Ireland	29 Jan 47	27UNTS267	100411
Thailand	USA (United States)	26 Feb 47	16UNTS17	100246
Paraguay	USA (United States)	28 Feb 47	44UNTS25	100676
Portugal	Sweden	06 Mar 47	35UNTS243	100558
Netherlands	Turkey	19 Mar 47	14UNTS59	100211
Greece	Sweden	08 Apr 47	94UNTS73	101307
Greece	Netherlands	17 Apr 47	32UNTS115	100494
Canada	Portugal	25 Apr 47	94UNTS87	101308
Syria	USA (United States)	28 Apr 47	262UNTS121	103741
France	Greece	05 May 47	76UNTS61	100980
Chile	USA (United States)	10 May 47	55UNTS21	100807
Czechoslovakia	Denmark	14 May 47	27UNTS297	100413
South Africa	USA (United States)	23 May 47	66UNTS233	100857
India	Netherlands	31 May 47	17UNTS65	100268
Canada	Sweden	27 Jun 47	27UNTS313	100414
Romania	Yugoslavia	30 Jun 47	116UNTS57	101569
Iraq	Turkey	30 Jun 47	72UNTS107	100930
Denmark	Turkey	30 Jun 47	32UNTS301	100504
Hungary	USSR (Soviet Union)	15 Jul 47	216UNTS247	102940
Canada	UK Great Britain	17 Jul 47	28UNTS3	100416
Netherlands	Thailand	18 Jul 47	28UNTS27	100417
Greece	Turkey	22 Jul 47	72UNTS131	100931
Netherlands	South Africa	22 Jul 47	12UNTS257	100188
Taiwan	UK Great Britain	23 Jul 47	9UNTS207	100135
Poland	Romania	09 Aug 47	12UNTS363	100193
Hungary	Poland	28 Aug 47	15UNTS145	100231
Czechoslovakia	Netherlands	01 Sep 47	32UNTS129	100495
Czechoslovakia	Switzerland	10 Sep 47	35UNTS275	100559
Lebanon	Turkey	16 Sep 47	44UNTS123	100682
Czechoslovakia	Sweden	15 Oct 47	44UNTS149	100683
Colombia	UK Great Britain	16 Oct 47	160UNTS297	102115
Norway	Portugal	11 Nov 47	34UNTS257	100542
Denmark	Greece	14 Nov 47	35UNTS295	100560
Denmark	Ireland	18 Nov 47	35UNTS309	100561
Ireland	Italy	21 Nov 47	353UNTS73	105038
Taiwan	Netherlands	06 Dec 47	43UNTS185	100669
Denmark	Portugal	15 Dec 47	35UNTS329	100563
Austria	Netherlands	22 Jan 48	17UNTS99	100270
Italy	USA (United States)	06 Feb 48	73UNTS113	100950
Czechoslovakia	Yugoslavia	14 Mar 48	28UNTS81	100421
Argentina	Denmark	18 Mar 48	94UNTS175	101311
Cuba	UK Great Britain	19 Mar 48	175UNTS23	102294
Ireland	Switzerland	06 May 48	334UNTS187	104768
Jordan	Turkey	07 May 48	32UNTS313	100505
Ireland	Netherlands	10 May 48	28UNTS121	100422
Norway	Turkey	20 May 48	26UNTS137	100384
Greece	Switzerland	26 May 48	94UNTS217	101312
Ireland	Norway	21 Jun 48	34UNTS317	100545
France	Spain	23 Aug 48	28UNTS173	100425
Greece	Lebanon	06 Sep 48	178UNTS37	102335
Bolivia	USA (United States)	29 Sep 48	505UNTS139	107370
Netherlands	Spain	08 Oct 48	28UNTS209	100426
Mexico	Portugal	22 Oct 48	34UNTS329	100546
Argentina	Netherlands	29 Oct 48	95UNTS21	101316
Italy	USSR (Soviet Union)	11 Dec 48	217UNTS181	102948
Italy	Lebanon	24 Jan 49	231UNTS241	103223
Switzerland	Turkey	16 Feb 49	72UNTS175	100933
Finland	Netherlands	25 Feb 49	53UNTS123	100777
Netherlands	Switzerland	07 Mar 49	35UNTS69	100551

PARTY ONE	PARTY TWO	DATE	CITATION	NUMBER
Licenses and certificates of nationality (Cont.)				
Finland	USA (United States)	29 Mar 49	55UNTS59	100808
Panama	USA (United States)	31 Mar 49	55UNTS87	100810
Finland	Sweden	26 Apr 49	95UNTS83	101318
Bulgaria	Poland	16 May 49	84UNTS313	101140
Italy	Spain	31 May 49	231UNTS251	103224
Canada	USA (United States)	04 Jun 49	122UNTS237	101649
Belgium	Greece	21 Jun 49	137UNTS215	101854
India	Switzerland	24 Jun 49	95UNTS109	101319
Greece	Syria	05 Jul 49	78UNTS71	101013
Iraq	Norway	12 Jul 49	53UNTS137	100778
Czechoslovakia	Finland	13 Jul 49	53UNTS153	100779
Dominican Republic	USA (United States)	19 Jul 49	51UNTS145	100762
Finland	Norway	24 Aug 49	53UNTS167	100780
Denmark	Finland	26 Aug 49	53UNTS191	100781
Lebanon	Netherlands	20 Sep 49	108UNTS205	101474
Burma	USA (United States)	28 Sep 49	55UNTS3	100806
Greece	Philippines	08 Oct 49	187UNTS221	102515
Sweden	Thailand	23 Nov 49	72UNTS217	100935
Denmark	Thailand	23 Nov 49	53UNTS255	100786
Italy	Turkey	25 Nov 49	192UNTS39	102594
Norway	Thailand	26 Nov 49	53UNTS269	100787
Brazil	Spain	28 Nov 49	215UNTS303	102923
Austria	Sweden	02 Dec 49	108UNTS3	101465
Austria	Norway	02 Dec 49	72UNTS230	100936
Austria	Denmark	02 Dec 49	53UNTS281	100788
Austria	Switzerland	19 Dec 49	254UNTS287	103597
USA (United States)	Yugoslavia	24 Dec 49	89UNTS209	101219
Netherlands	Syria	13 Feb 50	108UNTS53	101467
Canada	Norway	14 Feb 50	53UNTS329	100790
Spain	Sweden	18 Feb 50	166UNTS15	102184
Ceylon (Sri Lanka)	Thailand	24 Feb 50	72UNTS261	100938
Italy	Netherlands	04 Mar 50	254UNTS305	103598
Iceland	Netherlands	22 Mar 50	95UNTS237	101323
Denmark	Iceland	22 Mar 50	72UNTS273	100939
Italy	Portugal	05 Apr 50	254UNTS329	103599
Australia	UK Great Britain	28 Apr 50	95UNTS249	101324
Israel	USA (United States)	13 Jun 50	212UNTS93	102863
Netherlands	Spain	20 Jun 50	95UNTS303	101327
Denmark	Switzerland	22 Jun 50	96UNTS3	101328
Burma	Ceylon (Sri Lanka)	29 Jun 50	73UNTS3	100940
Spain	Switzerland	03 Aug 50	254UNTS365	103600
Canada	New Zealand	16 Aug 50	77UNTS239	101002
Burma	Sweden	14 Sep 50	96UNTS45	101330
Brazil	Turkey	21 Sep 50	150UNTS299	101981
Sweden	Switzerland	18 Oct 50	166UNTS49	102185
Luxembourg	Portugal	21 Oct 50	108UNTS67	101468
Israel	Netherlands	23 Oct 50	189UNTS89	102543
Thailand	UK Great Britain	10 Nov 50	96UNTS77	101332
Israel	UK Great Britain	06 Dec 50	151UNTS33	101983
Israel	Turkey	05 Feb 51	193UNTS3	102607
Colombia	Portugal	09 Mar 51	108UNTS87	101469
Greece	Yugoslavia	15 Mar 51	187UNTS237	102516
Greece	Norway	28 May 51	187UNTS141	102507
Cuba	Portugal	26 Jun 51	192UNTS115	102598
Iceland	Norway	14 Jul 51	163UNTS265	102150
Burma	Denmark	30 Jul 51	108UNTS167	101472
France	USSR (Soviet Union)	03 Sep 51	221UNTS79	103003
Burma	Netherlands	06 Sep 51	108UNTS187	101473
Panama	UK Great Britain	15 Sep 51	560UNTS143	108172
Philippines	Spain	06 Oct 51	215UNTS193	102920
Greece	Luxembourg	22 Oct 51	187UNTS119	102506
Denmark	Iraq	18 Nov 51	232UNTS25	103227
Colombia	Spain	11 Dec 51	216UNTS73	102933
Multilateral		20 Dec 51	163UNTS293	102151
Belgium	Spain	10 Mar 52	178UNTS243	102342

PARTY ONE	PARTY TWO	DATE	CITATION	NUMBER
Licenses and certificates of nationality (Cont.)				
Sweden	Uruguay	20 Mar 52	311UNTS3	104497
Iraq	Switzerland	31 Mar 52	311UNTS43	104498
France	Mexico	17 Apr 52	163UNTS321	102153
Denmark	UK Great Britain	23 Jun 52	151UNTS3	101982
Japan	USA (United States)	11 Aug 52	212UNTS27	102862
Austria	Luxembourg	13 Oct 52	192UNTS291	102606
Mexico	Netherlands	13 Oct 52	163UNTS341	102154
Iceland	Luxembourg	23 Oct 52	193UNTS39	102609
Chile	Denmark	27 Oct 52	271UNTS93	103911
Luxembourg	Norway	17 Nov 52	311UNTS95	104500
Luxembourg	Sweden	17 Nov 52	173UNTS277	102270
Israel	Switzerland	19 Nov 52	232UNTS3	103226
Philippines	Thailand	27 Apr 53	174UNTS3	102274
Cuba	USA (United States)	26 May 53	224UNTS75	103070
Switzerland	Yugoslavia	28 May 53	232UNTS45	103228
Burma	Norway	22 Jun 53	174UNTS49	102277
USA (United States)	Venezuela	14 Aug 53	213UNTS99	102883
Austria	Yugoslavia	11 Nov 53	363UNTS149	105206
Peru	Spain	31 Mar 54	232UNTS65	103230
Lebanon	Yugoslavia	17 Apr 54	602UNTS199	108713
Ireland	Luxembourg	27 Jul 54	232UNTS91	103231
Ecuador	Netherlands	14 Dec 54	232UNTS115	103233
Norway	Switzerland	30 Dec 54	311UNTS147	104502
Austria	Belgium	07 Jan 55	380UNTS219	105458
Germany, West	USA (United States)	07 Jul 55	275UNTS3	103973
Germany, East	Romania	28 Jul 55	342UNTS207	104909
France	Germany, West	04 Oct 55	353UNTS203	105044
Austria	USSR (Soviet Union)	17 Oct 55	240UNTS289	103409
Denmark	Syria	20 Oct 55	250UNTS61	103518
Austria	Israel	17 Nov 55	232UNTS153	103235
Austria	Italy	23 Jan 56	393UNTS97	105653
Argentina	Switzerland	25 Jan 56	559UNTS121	108157
India	USA (United States)	03 Feb 56	272UNTS75	103932
Austria	Poland	08 Feb 56	334UNTS221	104770
Norway	Syria	25 Feb 56	463UNTS217	106706
Belgium	Germany, West	14 Apr 56	344UNTS103	104945
Germany, West	Switzerland	02 May 56	559UNTS157	108158
Portugal	Venezuela	16 May 56	463UNTS239	106707
Greece	Italy	26 May 56	496UNTS301	107258
Italy	Switzerland	04 Jun 56	378UNTS311	105429
Germany, West	Ireland	12 Jun 56	353UNTS121	105040
Switzerland	Thailand	13 Oct 56	312UNTS43	104510
Colombia	USA (United States)	24 Oct 56	476UNTS77	106905
Belgium	Turkey	25 Oct 56	380UNTS3	105447
Peru	Switzerland	23 Nov 56	411UNTS97	105916
Iran	USA (United States)	16 Jan 57	308UNTS147	104460
Iceland	Thailand	22 Jan 57	312UNTS63	104511
Germany, West	Sweden	29 Jan 57	393UNTS113	105654
Germany, West	Norway	29 Jan 57	353UNTS39	105037
Denmark	Germany, West	29 Jan 57	302UNTS75	104354
Netherlands	Yugoslavia	13 Mar 57	327UNTS227	104723
Netherlands	USA (United States)	03 Apr 57	410UNTS193	105904
Germany, West	Yugoslavia	10 Apr 57	463UNTS269	106708
Korea, South	USA (United States)	24 Apr 57	288UNTS219	104207
Hungary	Netherlands	28 May 57	334UNTS291	104773
Afghanistan	Pakistan	13 Jun 57	327UNTS51	104717
Czechoslovakia	United Arab Rep	30 Jun 57	411UNTS126	105917
Greece	Italy	02 Aug 57	533UNTS217	107744
Netherlands	Romania	27 Aug 57	342UNTS309	104914
Germany, East	USSR (Soviet Union)	27 Sep 57	292UNTS75	104268
Italy	Pakistan	05 Oct 57	353UNTS91	105039
France	Morocco	25 Oct 57	559UNTS95	108156
Japan	USSR (Soviet Union)	06 Dec 57	325UNTS35	104694
Belgium	Morocco	20 Jan 58	288UNTS3	104192
Bulgaria	Netherlands	07 Feb 58	335UNTS45	104777

PARTY ONE	PARTY TWO	DATE	CITATION	NUMBER
Licenses and certificates of nationality (Cont.)				
Afghanistan	Turkey	08 Feb 58	464UNTS39	106711
Albania	USSR (Soviet Union)	15 Feb 58	313UNTS261	104536
Morocco	Portugal	03 Apr 58	393UNTS203	105657
Sweden	Yugoslavia	18 Apr 58	393UNTS225	105658
Germany, West	USSR (Soviet Union)	25 Apr 58	346UNTS71	104978
Denmark	Luxembourg	10 Jun 58	356UNTS193	105096
Norway	Romania	16 Jun 58	405UNTS223	105835
Austria	Bulgaria	12 Sep 58	353UNTS3	105036
UK Great Britain	Yugoslavia	03 Feb 59	359UNTS339	105151
Japan	Yugoslavia	28 Feb 59	341UNTS179	104883
Sweden	Tunisia	19 Mar 59	497UNTS43	107261
Norway	Tunisia	28 Mar 59	497UNTS77	107263
Denmark	Tunisia	14 Apr 59	340UNTS273	104870
Ceylon (Sri Lanka)	Sweden	29 May 59	464UNTS109	106713
Ceylon (Sri Lanka)	Norway	29 May 59	411UNTS165	105919
Ceylon (Sri Lanka)	Denmark	29 May 59	348UNTS225	105002
Denmark	Pakistan	05 Sep 59	354UNTS377	105071
Czechoslovakia	Germany, East	25 Nov 59	374UNTS101	105331
France	Thailand	26 Feb 60	392UNTS279	105648
Finland	Iceland	10 Mar 60	497UNTS95	107264
Luxembourg	Yugoslavia	09 Apr 60	464UNTS293	106719
Iran	UK Great Britain	02 May 60	566UNTS129	108241
Greece	Romania	02 May 60	485UNTS17	107043
Switzerland	Tunisia	21 May 60	497UNTS109	107265
Afghanistan	Czechoslovakia	28 May 60	497UNTS129	107266
Luxembourg	Tunisia	13 Jun 60	497UNTS143	107267
Denmark	Peru	22 Jun 60	439UNTS113	106326
Korea, North	USSR (Soviet Union)	22 Jun 60	399UNTS3	105732
Netherlands	Poland	21 Jul 60	497UNTS189	107269
Mexico	USA (United States)	15 Aug 60	402UNTS177	105786
Belgium	Burma	17 Aug 60	540UNTS185	107850
Hungary	UK Great Britain	25 Oct 60	419UNTS309	106034
Burma	Switzerland	31 Oct 60	465UNTS97	106723
Norway	Peru	02 Nov 60	497UNTS207	107270
Luxembourg	Thailand	29 Dec 60	465UNTS131	106725
Czechoslovakia	Morocco	08 Jun 61	497UNTS275	107272
Cameroon	France	16 Jun 61	412UNTS148	105929
Finland	Luxembourg	15 Aug 61	541UNTS45	107859
Mexico	Netherlands	24 Aug 61	465UNTS291	106732
Liberia	Switzerland	31 Aug 61	559UNTS215	108160
Ghana	Romania	30 Sep 61	467UNTS443	106769
France	Romania	18 May 62	498UNTS115	107279
France	Senegal	15 Jun 62	524UNTS3	107563
Morocco	Switzerland	05 Jul 62	498UNTS171	107281
Finland	France	12 Oct 62	498UNTS299	107285
Hungary	Syria	18 Oct 62	491UNTS209	107178
France	Ivory Coast	19 Oct 62	498UNTS317	107286
Ivory Coast	Switzerland	17 Nov 62	499UNTS3	107289
Syria	United Arab Rep	27 Dec 62	491UNTS245	107180
Senegal	Switzerland	23 Jan 63	524UNTS23	107564
Mali	Senegal	07 Feb 63	524UNTS41	107565
Algeria	France	18 Feb 63	563UNTS263	108214
Greece	Hungary	27 Apr 63	534UNTS3	107750
Algeria	Morocco	30 Apr 63	564UNTS3	108217
Guinea	Ivory Coast	26 Jun 63	499UNTS71	107293
Algeria	Mali	22 Jul 63	564UNTS29	108219
Cameroon	Israel	09 Aug 63	499UNTS121	107295
Ivory Coast	Netherlands	09 Oct 63	499UNTS141	107296
Czechoslovakia	Romania	16 Dec 63	527UNTS285	107630
Czechoslovakia	Hungary	20 Dec 63	538UNTS127	107812
Mali	Niger	15 Jan 64	499UNTS197	107299
Denmark	Yugoslavia	11 Feb 64	511UNTS241	107437
Cyprus	USSR (Soviet Union)	29 Feb 64	602UNTS45	108706
Cameroon	Mali	17 Mar 64	524UNTS61	107566
Norway	Yugoslavia	15 Apr 64	602UNTS177	108712

PARTY ONE	PARTY TWO	DATE	CITATION	NUMBER
Licenses and certificates of nationality (Cont.)				
United Arab Rep	USA (United States)	05 May 64	531UNTS229	107706
New Zealand	USA (United States)	24 Jun 64	524UNTS101	107568
Ivory Coast	Mali	09 Jul 64	524UNTS121	107569
Mauritania	Spain	11 May 65	602UNTS111	108709
Malaysia	Norway	26 May 65	602UNTS157	108711
Nigeria	Switzerland	11 Oct 65	602UNTS137	108710
Canada	USA (United States)	17 Jan 66	586UNTS151	108502
Ivory Coast	Norway	07 Jun 66	0UNTS0	109249
Denmark	Ivory Coast	07 Jun 66	595UNTS313	108626
Denmark	Nigeria	08 Sep 66	591UNTS177	108557
Denmark	Singapore	20 Dec 66	593UNTS125	108580
Japan	Singapore	14 Feb 67	0UNTS0	109244
Algeria	Ivory Coast	16 Feb 67	0UNTS0	109245
Australia	Austria	22 Mar 67	0UNTS0	109246
Netherlands	Sierra Leone	13 Jun 67	0UNTS0	109247
Multilateral		03 Jul 67	0UNTS0	109248
Water transport				
Saudi Arabia	UK Great Britain	20 Apr 42	10UNTS151	200058
Australia	USA (United States)	08 Mar 45	121UNTS205	200400
Norway	USA (United States)	29 May 45	34UNTS371	200180
UK Great Britain	USA (United States)	07 May 46	6UNTS285	100082
France	USA (United States)	28 May 46	84UNTS167	101127
Denmark	USSR (Soviet Union)	17 Aug 46	8UNTS201	100124
Australia	Sweden	16 Sep 46	10UNTS63	100143
Czechoslovakia	Turkey	05 Mar 47	14UNTS101	100214
Hungary	USSR (Soviet Union)	15 Jul 47	216UNTS247	102940
Czechoslovakia	USSR (Soviet Union)	11 Dec 47	217UNTS35	102943
Multilateral		06 Mar 48	289UNTS3	104214
Switzerland	USSR (Soviet Union)	17 Mar 48	217UNTS73	102944
Multilateral		10 Jun 48	164UNTS113	102163
Italy	USSR (Soviet Union)	11 Dec 48	217UNTS181	102948
Argentina	Denmark	14 Dec 48	74UNTS41	100956
UK Great Britain	Yugoslavia	23 Dec 48	81UNTS133	101069
Multilateral		18 Jun 49	605UNTS295	108768
Multilateral		12 Aug 49	75UNTS85	100971
Argentina	Norway	09 Sep 49	42UNTS125	100646
UK Great Britain	Yugoslavia	26 Dec 49	87UNTS71	101167
Ireland	USA (United States)	21 Jan 50	206UNTS269	102792
Finland	Ireland	06 Jan 51	558UNTS120	108140
Japan	USA (United States)	02 Apr 53	206UNTS143	102788
India	Yugoslavia	24 Jul 53	394UNTS13	105665
Ceylon (Sri Lanka)	Ireland	20 Nov 53	345UNTS189	104967
India	USSR (Soviet Union)	02 Dec 53	240UNTS143	103402
Multilateral		25 Feb 54	215UNTS249	102922
USSR (Soviet Union)	Yugoslavia	05 Jan 55	240UNTS225	103405
IBRD (World Bank)	UK Great Britain	15 Mar 55	265UNTS85	103808
Burma	Sweden	06 Mar 56	369UNTS275	105261
IBRD (World Bank)	Thailand	12 Oct 56	261UNTS117	103728
Belgium	IBRD (World Bank)	26 Jun 57	322UNTS301	104661
Belgium	IBRD (World Bank)	10 Sep 57	286UNTS291	104174
Bulgaria	Yugoslavia	04 Apr 58	367UNTS89	105228
India	IBRD (World Bank)	25 Jun 58	323UNTS157	104668
India	IBRD (World Bank)	25 Jun 58	323UNTS131	104667
Peru	IBRD (World Bank)	17 Sep 58	323UNTS27	104663
United Arab Rep	USSR (Soviet Union)	18 Sep 58	338UNTS29	104831
Finland	Sweden	22 Sep 58	428UNTS119	106170
Ecuador	IBRD (World Bank)	09 Oct 58	337UNTS299	104827
Haiti	Japan	17 Dec 58	518UNTS91	107492
Czechoslovakia	United Arab Rep	07 Feb 59	372UNTS243	105301
UK Great Britain	USSR (Soviet Union)	24 May 59	374UNTS305	105344
Czechoslovakia	Germany, East	18 Sep 59	363UNTS287	105209
Multilateral		14 Dec 59	422UNTS75	106069
Australia	Indonesia	17 Dec 59	354UNTS109	105058
Israel	IBRD (World Bank)	09 Sep 60	406UNTS3	105837

PARTY ONE	PARTY TWO	DATE	CITATION	NUMBER
Water transport (Cont.)				
Indonesia	UK Great Britain	29 Jun 61	443UNTS255	106364
India	IBRD (World Bank)	17 Aug 61	417UNTS319	106012
Pakistan	Philippines	29 Sep 61	422UNTS3	106065
Multilateral		20 Feb 62	597UNTS159	108644
Mexico	IBRD (World Bank)	20 Jun 62	467UNTS205	106764
Germany, West	Israel	09 Jul 62	630UNTS87	108968
India	IDA (Devel Assoc)	14 Sep 62	467UNTS265	106766
Multilateral		18 Sep 62	442UNTS215	106351
Nigeria	IBRD (World Bank)	10 Dec 62	468UNTS255	106776
Japan	South Africa	06 Apr 63	484UNTS319	107040
Greece	Romania	20 Jul 63	609UNTS109	108829
Cameroon	UK Great Britain	29 Jul 63	478UNTS148	106935
New Zealand	USSR (Soviet Union)	01 Aug 63	486UNTS27	107070
New Zealand	IBRD (World Bank)	12 Nov 63	485UNTS233	107059
Pakistan	IBRD (World Bank)	14 May 64	516UNTS145	107475
IBRD (World Bank)	Tunisia	05 Jun 64	539UNTS129	107827
Greece	South Africa	11 Nov 64	631UNTS319	109001
Greece	India	11 Feb 65	606UNTS9	108771
Denmark	Germany, West	09 Jun 65	605UNTS95	108762
Argentina	Yugoslavia	09 Jun 65	601UNTS3	108684
Finland	Ireland	15 Sep 65	604UNTS199	108750
East Afri Service	IBRD (World Bank)	29 Sep 65	568UNTS327	200623
Kenya	IBRD (World Bank)	29 Sep 65	568UNTS289	108274
IBRD (World Bank)	Tanzania	29 Sep 65	568UNTS309	108275
IBRD (World Bank)	Uganda	29 Sep 65	568UNTS317	108276
IBRD (World Bank)	Spain	29 Sep 65	568UNTS49	108264
Cuba	USA (United States)	06 Nov 65	601UNTS81	108688
Paraguay	IBRD (World Bank)	16 Dec 65	568UNTS165	108268
Argentina	India	26 Mar 66	601UNTS201	108697
Denmark	Netherlands	31 Mar 66	604UNTS209	108751
Peru	IBRD (World Bank)	13 May 66	570UNTS61	108288
Canada	USA (United States)	10 Jun 66	639UNTS13	109141
IBRD (World Bank)	Singapore	11 Aug 66	585UNTS39	108482
Israel	Norway	02 Nov 66	630UNTS225	108972
Canada	Israel	30 Nov 66	630UNTS267	108973
Singapore	UK Great Britain	01 Dec 66	605UNTS153	108763
Trinidad/Tobago	UK Great Britain	29 Dec 66	605UNTS237	108766
Argentina	Uruguay	12 Feb 67	635UNTS125	109076
Greece	Yugoslavia	15 Apr 67	633UNTS373	109046
South Africa	Switzerland	03 Jul 67	643UNTS3	109184
Brazil	UK Great Britain	29 Dec 67	643UNTS217	109193
Finland	USSR (Soviet Union)	07 Mar 68	643UNTS107	109187
Argentina	Brazil	27 Sep 68	0UNTS0	109420
Canal improvement				
Belgium	Netherlands	17 Feb 50	51UNTS101	100756
Czechoslovakia	Poland	17 Nov 50	530UNTS195	107682
UK Great Britain	Yugoslavia	28 Dec 50	88UNTS329	101201
Canada	USA (United States)	30 Jun 52	234UNTS199	103283
UK Great Britain	USA (United States)	26 Jun 53	183UNTS225	102432
Italy	Switzerland	17 Sep 55	291UNTS213	104257
Canada	USA (United States)	26 Feb 57	279UNTS179	104039
Canada	USA (United States)	09 Apr 57	283UNTS217	104119
Albania	Yugoslavia	20 May 57	363UNTS99	105203
Belgium	Netherlands	24 Oct 57	489UNTS3	107131
Belgium	Netherlands	24 Oct 57	489UNTS11	107132
Germany, East	Hungary	25 Oct 57	408UNTS156	105869
Bulgaria	Yugoslavia	04 Apr 58	367UNTS89	105228
Canada	USA (United States)	27 Feb 59	341UNTS3	104873
Belgium	Netherlands	24 Feb 61	474UNTS167	106881
Taiwan	IDA (Devel Assoc)	30 Aug 61	416UNTS175	106003
Canada	USA (United States)	17 Oct 61	424UNTS101	106102
Multilateral		20 Dec 61	419UNTS79	106031
Canada	USA (United States)	13 Jul 62	460UNTS83	106632
Finland	USSR (Soviet Union)	27 Sep 62	479UNTS99	106949

PARTY ONE	PARTY TWO	DATE	CITATION	NUMBER
Canal improvement (Cont.)				
Belgium	Netherlands	13 May 63	540UNTS3	107843
Multilateral		25 Nov 64	587UNTS19	108507
Innocent passage				
Philippines	USA (United States)	14 Mar 47	43UNTS271	100673
UK Great Britain	USA (United States)	06 Mar 51	97UNTS137	101347
Other Unilat Decla	United Arab Rep	24 Apr 57	265UNTS299	103821
Multilateral		29 Apr 58	516UNTS205	107477
Merchant vessels				
Multilateral		09 Jul 20	38UNTS109	100590
Multilateral		09 Jul 20	38UNTS119	100591
Multilateral		11 Nov 21	38UNTS217	100599
Multilateral		11 Nov 21	38UNTS203	100598
Multilateral		23 Jun 26	38UNTS315	100606
Multilateral		24 Jun 26	38UNTS295	100605
Panama	USA (United States)	28 Mar 41	103UNTS163	200312
Brazil	Paraguay	14 Jun 41	54UNTS303	200202
Canada	USA (United States)	04 Mar 42	124UNTS271	200426
UK Great Britain	USSR (Soviet Union)	22 Jun 42	91UNTS355	200270
Canada	Taiwan	22 Mar 44	14UNTS397	200096
Australia	USA (United States)	08 Mar 45	121UNTS205	200400
Norway	USA (United States)	29 May 45	34UNTS371	200180
Multilateral		14 Jan 46	555UNTS69	108105
France	USA (United States)	07 Feb 46	3UNTS239	100034
Netherlands	USA (United States)	09 Feb 46	3UNTS247	100035
UK Great Britain	USA (United States)	01 Mar 46	3UNTS293	100037
UK Great Britain	USA (United States)	27 Mar 46	4UNTS2	100039
Multilateral		27 Jun 46	264UNTS163	103792
Multilateral		29 Jun 46	214UNTS233	102901
Denmark	USSR (Soviet Union)	17 Aug 46	8UNTS201	100124
Canada	USA (United States)	15 Nov 46	7UNTS141	100096
Finland	USA (United States)	07 Jan 47	15UNTS273	100243
Multilateral		20 Jan 47	87UNTS247	101176
Multilateral		03 Mar 47	11UNTS43	100148
Norway	Sweden	21 Jun 47	94UNTS107	101309
Italy	USA (United States)	14 Aug 47	36UNTS105	100567
Finland	USSR (Soviet Union)	01 Dec 47	217UNTS3	102942
Multilateral		06 Mar 48	289UNTS3	104214
Canada	New Zealand	12 Mar 48	231UNTS219	103222
New Zealand	USA (United States)	16 Mar 48	127UNTS133	101703
Bulgaria	USSR (Soviet Union)	01 Apr 48	217UNTS97	102946
Denmark	USA (United States)	06 May 48	26UNTS55	100377
Multilateral		10 Jun 48	164UNTS113	102163
Netherlands	IBRD (World Bank)	15 Jul 48	153UNTS259	102021
Netherlands	IBRD (World Bank)	15 Jul 48	153UNTS259	102023
Netherlands	IBRD (World Bank)	15 Jul 48	153UNTS259	102024
Netherlands	IBRD (World Bank)	15 Jul 48	153UNTS259	102025
Netherlands	IBRD (World Bank)	15 Jul 48	153UNTS259	102022
Multilateral		18 Aug 48	33UNTS181	100518
Netherlands	UK Great Britain	15 Oct 48	74UNTS3	100955
Belgium	USA (United States)	28 Oct 48	173UNTS67	102262
Argentina	Sweden	20 Nov 48	197UNTS47	102633
Argentina	Denmark	15 Dec 48	67UNTS71	100866
Argentina	Netherlands	15 Jan 49	46UNTS241	100713
France	Norway	09 Feb 49	29UNTS13	100431
Argentina	UK Great Britain	14 Mar 49	83UNTS193	101108
Sweden	UK Great Britain	30 Mar 49	209UNTS129	102826
Japan	USA (United States)	14 Apr 49	89UNTS141	101215
Multilateral		14 Apr 49	141UNTS281	101919
Ireland	UK Great Britain	18 May 49	553UNTS209	108089
Norway	USA (United States)	13 Jun 49	127UNTS189	101705
Multilateral		18 Jun 49	160UNTS223	102109
Argentina	Belgium	25 Jul 49	46UNTS103	100703
Argentina	Canada	06 Aug 49	231UNTS43	103202
Ireland	USA (United States)	13 Sep 49	127UNTS89	101701

PARTY ONE	PARTY TWO	DATE	CITATION	NUMBER
Merchant vessels (Cont.)				
Multilateral		22 Nov 49	185UNTS307	102477
Greece	USA (United States)	20 Feb 50	196UNTS291	102630
Argentina	Greece	21 Mar 50	187UNTS213	102514
Denmark	UK Great Britain	27 Mar 50	68UNTS117	100891
Germany, West	Ireland	12 Jul 50	557UNTS221	108136
Argentina	USA (United States)	20 Jul 50	89UNTS63	101209
Ceylon (Sri Lanka)	UK Great Britain	26 Jul 50	337UNTS77	104818
Greece	UK Great Britain	16 Nov 50	166UNTS281	102193
Denmark	South Africa	30 Nov 50	84UNTS51	101118
Iceland	Ireland	02 Dec 50	558UNTS231	108143
France	Greece	09 Dec 50	166UNTS315	102196
Germany, West	Netherlands	14 Dec 50	87UNTS257	101177
Netherlands	Norway	29 Dec 50	134UNTS19	101795
Canada	France	16 Mar 51	236UNTS267	103330
Multilateral		03 Apr 51	141UNTS303	101920
Canada	Sweden	06 Apr 51	197UNTS393	102648
Norway	UK Great Britain	02 May 51	106UNTS101	101460
Switzerland	USA (United States)	24 May 51	127UNTS227	101706
South Africa	Sweden	25 May 51	197UNTS425	102649
Greece	Netherlands	26 Jul 51	109UNTS103	101495
Canada	South Africa	26 Nov 51	248UNTS107	103489
Ireland	Switzerland	26 Dec 51	558UNTS305	108149
Ireland	Portugal	06 Feb 52	558UNTS289	108147
Canada	USA (United States)	21 Feb 52	205UNTS293	102781
Finland	USA (United States)	03 Mar 52	177UNTS163	102317
Netherlands	Sweden	25 Apr 52	163UNTS131	102147
Greece	Israel	22 Jul 52	215UNTS365	102924
Israel	South Africa	24 Dec 52	207UNTS303	102813
Denmark	Uruguay	04 Mar 53	250UNTS51	103517
Australia	USA (United States)	14 May 53	205UNTS253	102779
Greece	UK Great Britain	25 Jun 53	190UNTS281	102571
Italy	South Africa	26 Jun 53	211UNTS255	102857
Ireland	Italy	27 Jul 53	558UNTS237	108144
Belgium	Finland	11 Feb 54	211UNTS63	102848
Belgium	Norway	24 Mar 54	219UNTS73	102967
Finland	Netherlands	29 Mar 54	252UNTS185	103567
Japan	USA (United States)	16 Apr 54	238UNTS39	103354
Lebanon	USSR (Soviet Union)	30 Apr 54	226UNTS109	103111
Multilateral		12 May 54	327UNTS3	104714
Haiti	Italy	14 Jun 54	267UNTS97	103837
Belgium	Greece	23 Jun 54	199UNTS43	102676
Germany, West	USA (United States)	22 Jul 54	239UNTS3	103369
Sweden	USSR (Soviet Union)	29 Sep 54	202UNTS259	102733
Switzerland	UK Great Britain	30 Sep 54	209UNTS197	102828
Ireland	Sweden	18 Oct 54	262UNTS259	103753
Denmark	Ireland	18 Oct 54	218UNTS295	102959
Ireland	Norway	18 Oct 54	553UNTS123	108077
Germany, West	UK Great Britain	18 Oct 54	218UNTS301	102960
Canada	Ireland	28 Oct 54	304UNTS317	104406
France	South Africa	22 Nov 54	219UNTS35	102963
India	Iran	15 Dec 54	327UNTS245	104724
USA (United States)	Yugoslavia	05 Jan 55	251UNTS29	103531
Netherlands	USA (United States)	21 Mar 55	289UNTS129	104217
Italy	USA (United States)	30 Mar 55	257UNTS169	103654
Denmark	Israel	04 Apr 55	213UNTS283	102891
Finland	USA (United States)	06 May 55	251UNTS3	103529
Ceylon (Sri Lanka)	Pakistan	23 May 55	286UNTS15	104159
Israel	Norway	24 May 55	220UNTS71	102990
Israel	Italy	10 Jun 55	280UNTS219	104061
Italy	USA (United States)	30 Jun 55	258UNTS15	103667
Israel	USSR (Soviet Union)	15 Jul 55	226UNTS253	103119
Iceland	Sweden	17 Sep 55	262UNTS273	103755
Canada	Denmark	30 Sep 55	258UNTS115	103675
Denmark	Iceland	10 Oct 55	230UNTS3	103171
South Africa	Switzerland	07 Nov 55	230UNTS279	103190

PARTY ONE	PARTY TWO	DATE	CITATION	NUMBER
Merchant vessels (Cont.)				
Syria	USSR (Soviet Union)	16 Nov 55	259UNTS71	103683
Czechoslovakia	Poland	13 Jan 56	265UNTS157	103811
Canada	USSR (Soviet Union)	29 Feb 56	252UNTS165	103566
Israel	Sweden	17 Jun 56	257UNTS47	103648
Honduras	USA (United States)	25 Jun 56	279UNTS113	104036
Austria	UK Great Britain	20 Jul 56	269UNTS147	103880
Costa Rica	Denmark	26 Sep 56	341UNTS305	104893
Norway	Sweden	27 Sep 56	261UNTS71	103726
Germany, West	South Africa	28 Sep 56	327UNTS83	104718
Canada	South Africa	28 Sep 56	299UNTS17	104304
Austria	USA (United States)	25 Oct 56	299UNTS123	104310
Finland	USSR (Soviet Union)	07 Dec 56	258UNTS89	103673
USA (United States)	Venezuela	21 Feb 57	279UNTS199	104041
Denmark	Norway	22 Feb 57	286UNTS127	104164
Japan	Norway	28 Feb 57	280UNTS87	104054
Paraguay	USA (United States)	04 Apr 57	283UNTS193	104117
Bulgaria	Yugoslavia	19 Apr 57	349UNTS3	105006
Ceylon (Sri Lanka)	Sweden	18 May 57	315UNTS85	104561
Denmark	Peru	10 Jun 57	406UNTS63	105839
Belgium	South Africa	11 Jun 57	292UNTS165	104272
Austria	USSR (Soviet Union)	14 Jun 57	285UNTS169	104152
Germany, East	USSR (Soviet Union)	27 Sep 57	292UNTS75	104268
Australia	Canada	01 Oct 57	392UNTS41	105638
Belgium	Switzerland	05 Dec 57	293UNTS317	104299
India	Japan	04 Feb 58	324UNTS215	104687
Ceylon (Sri Lanka)	USSR (Soviet Union)	08 Feb 58	348UNTS159	104999
Poland	USA (United States)	15 Feb 58	307UNTS217	104452
Germany, West	USSR (Soviet Union)	25 Apr 58	346UNTS71	104978
Japan	Poland	26 Apr 58	340UNTS221	104866
Multilateral		29 Apr 58	450UNTS11	106465
Multilateral		29 Apr 58	516UNTS205	107477
Ireland	South Africa	01 May 58	398UNTS3	105714
Multilateral		13 May 58	389UNTS277	105598
Ireland	Switzerland	18 Jun 58	553UNTS183	108086
Denmark	El Salvador	09 Jul 58	341UNTS289	104892
Denmark	Sweden	21 Jul 58	320UNTS163	104642
India	Sweden	30 Jul 58	369UNTS211	105259
Germany, West	Norway	18 Nov 58	357UNTS205	105119
Haiti	Japan	17 Dec 58	518UNTS91	107492
Iraq	Romania	24 Dec 58	405UNTS243	105836
Belgium	France	20 Jan 59	361UNTS155	105178
Japan	Norway	21 Feb 59	356UNTS231	105098
Denmark	Japan	10 Mar 59	341UNTS55	104878
Germany, West	Sweden	17 Apr 59	428UNTS155	106175
Austria	Sweden	14 May 59	428UNTS3	106167
UK Great Britain	USSR (Soviet Union)	24 May 59	374UNTS305	105344
Germany, West	Netherlands	16 Jun 59	593UNTS3	108576
India	Norway	20 Jul 59	356UNTS257	105099
Canada	Switzerland	22 Sep 59	470UNTS101	106800
Austria	France	08 Oct 59	453UNTS95	106521
Czechoslovakia	Germany, East	25 Nov 59	374UNTS101	105331
Czechoslovakia	Japan	15 Dec 59	383UNTS277	105505
Israel	Sweden	22 Dec 59	377UNTS277	105407
India	Japan	05 Jan 60	384UNTS3	105507
Cuba	USSR (Soviet Union)	13 Feb 60	369UNTS17	105248
Austria	Norway	25 Feb 60	376UNTS155	105380
Cuba	Japan	22 Apr 60	442UNTS261	106354
Cuba	Czechoslovakia	10 Jun 60	447UNTS75	106412
Multilateral		17 Jun 60	536UNTS27	107794
Korea, North	USSR (Soviet Union)	22 Jun 60	399UNTS3	105732
Italy	UK Great Britain	04 Jul 60	466UNTS195	106745
Sweden	UK Great Britain	28 Jul 60	404UNTS113	105808
Multilateral		29 Jul 60	392UNTS69	105640
Ghana	USSR (Soviet Union)	04 Aug 60	421UNTS27	106050
Sweden	Tunisia	06 Sep 60	427UNTS301	106162

PARTY ONE	PARTY TWO	DATE	CITATION	NUMBER
Merchant vessels (Cont.)				
Albania	Cuba	16 Jan 61	448UNTS67	106425
Denmark	Greece	04 Mar 61	534UNTS157	107760
Morocco	Sweden	30 Mar 61	427UNTS185	106154
Japan	UK Great Britain	11 Apr 61	420UNTS75	106042
Finland	USA (United States)	16 Jun 61	413UNTS211	105955
Finland	India	23 Jun 61	421UNTS49	106051
Indonesia	UK Great Britain	29 Jun 61	443UNTS255	106364
Portugal	UK Great Britain	31 Jul 61	449UNTS119	106454
Colombia	USA (United States)	01 Aug 61	433UNTS123	106235
Italy	Norway	25 Aug 61	475UNTS269	106896
Philippines	USA (United States)	04 Oct 61	433UNTS83	106232
Greece	Sweden	06 Oct 61	481UNTS137	106981
Austria	Denmark	23 Oct 61	425UNTS115	106122
Ghana	USSR (Soviet Union)	04 Nov 61	437UNTS213	106308
Finland	UK Great Britain	05 Dec 61	424UNTS217	106110
Argentina	Japan	20 Dec 61	451UNTS91	106487
Austria	Japan	20 Dec 61	517UNTS155	107485
Argentina	Japan	20 Dec 61	613UNTS323	108859
South Africa	UK Great Britain	28 May 62	443UNTS79	106361
Greece	Switzerland	12 Jun 62	492UNTS47	107186
Cyprus	Greece	23 Aug 62	609UNTS15	108825
Israel	USA (United States)	28 Aug 62	448UNTS317	106445
Japan	UK Great Britain	04 Sep 62	475UNTS31	106888
Israel	UK Great Britain	26 Sep 62	474UNTS233	106885
Austria	United Arab Rep	16 Oct 62	491UNTS63	107174
Austria	Luxembourg	18 Oct 62	496UNTS97	107248
Ethiopia	Greece	07 Nov 62	550UNTS179	108014
Finland	New Zealand	12 Nov 62	485UNTS331	107064
Japan	UK Great Britain	14 Nov 62	478UNTS29	106934
Luxembourg	USA (United States)	18 Dec 62	532UNTS277	107723
Iceland	USA (United States)	27 Dec 62	469UNTS91	106785
Greece	Pakistan	17 Jan 63	538UNTS175	107814
United Nations	South Pacific Com	24 Jan 63	470UNTS361	200604
Japan	New Zealand	30 Jan 63	517UNTS183	107486
Bolivia	USA (United States)	04 Feb 63	473UNTS65	106856
Netherlands	USA (United States)	06 Feb 63	487UNTS113	107098
Ceylon (Sri Lanka)	Denmark	16 Feb 63	486UNTS285	107083
Japan	Thailand	01 Mar 63	475UNTS233	106895
Ecuador	USA (United States)	05 Apr 63	477UNTS135	106919
Norway	Spain	25 Apr 63	503UNTS41	107340
Netherlands	USA (United States)	20 May 63	487UNTS123	107099
Japan	Malaysia	04 Jun 63	517UNTS245	107488
Canada	Finland	05 Jun 63	472UNTS345	106846
El Salvador	Japan	19 Jul 63	518UNTS135	107494
Tanganyika	USSR (Soviet Union)	14 Aug 63	493UNTS195	107215
France	Israel	20 Aug 63	515UNTS173	107460
France	Greece	21 Aug 63	533UNTS235	107746
Lebanon	UK Great Britain	24 Oct 63	535UNTS3	107772
France	UK Great Britain	05 Nov 63	539UNTS277	107838
Brazil	Germany, West	30 Nov 63	0UNTS0	109426
Czechoslovakia	Romania	16 Dec 63	527UNTS285	107630
Greece	Poland	21 Dec 63	538UNTS155	107813
Ceylon (Sri Lanka)	Finland	08 Jan 64	492UNTS285	107198
Norway	Thailand	09 Jan 64	522UNTS65	107537
Greece	Poland	21 Jan 64	533UNTS309	107749
Denmark	Finland	07 Apr 64	525UNTS89	107586
USA (United States)	Yugoslavia	27 Apr 64	526UNTS73	107601
Ceylon (Sri Lanka)	Norway	11 Jun 64	559UNTS23	108153
Finland	South Africa	12 Jun 64	505UNTS107	107367
Ireland	USA (United States)	18 Jun 64	530UNTS217	107684
Denmark	UK Great Britain	30 Jun 64	539UNTS203	107833
Mexico	USA (United States)	07 Aug 64	530UNTS123	107677
Canada	Denmark	15 Oct 64	525UNTS227	107595
Norway	United Arab Rep	20 Oct 64	543UNTS3	107895
Multilateral		01 Dec 64	550UNTS133	108012
Iceland	USA (United States)	30 Dec 64	531UNTS287	107709
Finland	Israel	21 Jan 65	581UNTS275	108450
Denmark	India	06 Feb 65	531UNTS23	107690
Multilateral		09 Mar 65	591UNTS265	108564
Finland	United Arab Rep	01 Apr 65	562UNTS3	108193
Jamaica	UK Great Britain	02 Apr 65	552UNTS219	108056
Denmark	Thailand	01 Jun 65	551UNTS157	108040
Argentina	Yugoslavia	09 Jun 65	601UNTS3	108684
Ecuador	USA (United States)	25 Jun 65	549UNTS23	107986
Malta	Yugoslavia	15 Jul 65	561UNTS223	108186
Finland	Ireland	15 Sep 65	604UNTS199	108750
Italy	USA (United States)	16 Dec 65	574UNTS139	108346
Italy	USA (United States)	27 Dec 65	574UNTS145	108347
Singapore	USSR (Soviet Union)	02 Apr 66	631UNTS125	108992
Poland	Singapore	07 Jun 66	631UNTS189	108994
Fed Rhod/Nyasaland	Norway	18 Jun 66	580UNTS9	108415
Denmark	Israel	27 Jun 66	581UNTS227	108448
Mauritania	USSR (Soviet Union)	17 Oct 66	633UNTS231	109040
Belgium	Hungary	20 Mar 67	601UNTS37	108686
Bulgaria	USSR (Soviet Union)	27 Apr 67	631UNTS3	108983
Finland	Pakistan	11 Dec 67	631UNTS99	108989
Argentina	Brazil	27 Sep 68	0UNTS0	109420
Inland and territorial waters				
Canada	France	12 May 33	253UNTS285	200545
Brazil	Paraguay	14 Jun 41	54UNTS303	200202
Belgium	Taiwan	20 Oct 43	14UNTS376	200095
Belgium	France	30 Mar 45	20UNTS297	200122
UK Great Britain	USA (United States)	05 Nov 45	138UNTS75	101861
Taiwan	Denmark	20 May 46	12UNTS59	100180
Multilateral		20 Jan 47	87UNTS247	101176
Philippines	USA (United States)	14 Mar 47	16UNTS31	100247
Philippines	USA (United States)	12 May 47	16UNTS109	100252
Italy	USA (United States)	02 Feb 48	79UNTS171	101040
Multilateral		18 Aug 48	33UNTS181	100518
Ireland	USA (United States)	21 Jan 50	206UNTS269	102792
Germany, West	Ireland	12 Jul 50	557UNTS221	108136
Germany, West	Netherlands	14 Dec 50	87UNTS257	101177
Germany, West	Greece	12 Feb 51	198UNTS193	102665
UK Great Britain	USA (United States)	06 Mar 51	97UNTS137	101347
Greece	USA (United States)	03 Aug 51	224UNTS279	103080
Israel	USA (United States)	23 Aug 51	219UNTS237	102979
Ethiopia	USA (United States)	07 Sep 51	206UNTS41	102785
Multilateral		10 May 52	439UNTS233	106332
Canada	USA (United States)	30 Jun 52	234UNTS199	103283
Greece	Israel	22 Jul 52	219UNTS231	102978
India	Muscat and Oman	15 Mar 53	190UNTS69	102559
Japan	USA (United States)	02 Apr 53	206UNTS143	102788
Ceylon (Sri Lanka)	Yugoslavia	30 Jul 53	337UNTS103	104819
United Arab Rep	UK Great Britain	19 Oct 54	210UNTS3	102833
Germany, West	USA (United States)	29 Oct 54	273UNTS3	103943
India	Iran	15 Dec 54	327UNTS245	104724
Austria	Romania	11 May 55	342UNTS119	104904
Czechoslovakia	Poland	13 Jan 56	265UNTS157	103811
Nicaragua	USA (United States)	21 Jan 56	367UNTS3	105224
Germany, West	Netherlands	20 Sep 56	509UNTS269	107405
Costa Rica	Denmark	26 Sep 56	341UNTS305	104893
Canada	USA (United States)	26 Feb 57	279UNTS179	104039
Japan	Norway	28 Feb 57	280UNTS87	104054
Canada	USA (United States)	09 Apr 57	283UNTS217	104119
Bulgaria	Yugoslavia	19 Apr 57	349UNTS3	105006
Denmark	Peru	10 Jun 57	406UNTS63	105839
Japan	USSR (Soviet Union)	06 Dec 57	325UNTS35	104694
India	Japan	04 Feb 58	324UNTS215	104687
Ceylon (Sri Lanka)	USSR (Soviet Union)	08 Feb 58	348UNTS159	104999

PARTY ONE	PARTY TWO	DATE	CITATION	NUMBER
Inland and territorial waters (Cont.)				
Albania	USSR (Soviet Union)	15 Feb 58	313UNTS261	104536
Poland	USSR (Soviet Union)	18 Mar 58	340UNTS89	104861
Bulgaria	Yugoslavia	04 Apr 58	367UNTS89	105228
China People's Rep	USSR (Soviet Union)	23 Apr 58	313UNTS135	104534
Japan	Poland	26 Apr 58	340UNTS221	104866
Multilateral		29 Apr 58	450UNTS11	106465
Norway	Sweden	09 Jun 58	427UNTS221	106156
Finland	Sweden	22 Sep 58	428UNTS119	106170
Finland	USSR (Soviet Union)	21 Feb 59	338UNTS3	104830
Australia	Germany, West	14 Oct 59	345UNTS35	104957
Czechoslovakia	Japan	15 Dec 59	383UNTS277	105505
Cuba	Czechoslovakia	10 Jun 60	447UNTS75	106412
Belgium	Netherlands	20 Jun 60	423UNTS19	106084
Multilateral		19 Sep 60	419UNTS125	106032
Albania	Cuba	16 Jan 61	448UNTS67	106425
Poland	USSR (Soviet Union)	05 Feb 61	420UNTS161	106046
Belgium	USA (United States)	21 Feb 61	480UNTS149	106967
Canada	USA (United States)	05 May 61	419UNTS9	106027
Pakistan	Philippines	29 Sep 61	422UNTS3	106065
Greece	USA (United States)	24 Apr 62	459UNTS3	106609
Multilateral		18 Sep 62	442UNTS215	106351
Finland	USSR (Soviet Union)	27 Sep 62	479UNTS99	106949
Japan	UK Great Britain	14 Nov 62	478UNTS29	106934
Germany, West	USA (United States)	29 Nov 62	460UNTS169	106639
Norway	USA (United States)	01 Mar 63	524UNTS185	107573
Austria	Czechoslovakia	08 Mar 63	495UNTS219	107245
Belgium	USA (United States)	19 Apr 63	493UNTS83	107209
Belgium	Netherlands	13 May 63	540UNTS3	107843
Netherlands	USA (United States)	20 May 63	487UNTS123	107099
Hungary	Romania	13 Jun 63	576UNTS275	108369
Tanganyika	USSR (Soviet Union)	14 Aug 63	493UNTS195	107215
Multilateral		26 Oct 63	587UNTS9	108506
Czechoslovakia	Romania	16 Dec 63	527UNTS285	107630
Czechoslovakia	Hungary	20 Dec 63	538UNTS127	107812
UK Great Britain	USA (United States)	19 Jun 64	530UNTS99	107675
Denmark	USA (United States)	02 Jul 64	529UNTS277	107665
Sweden	USA (United States)	06 Jul 64	529UNTS287	107666
Spain	USA (United States)	16 Jul 64	529UNTS187	107661
Denmark	Germany, West	09 Jun 65	581UNTS141	108439
Argentina	Paraguay	23 Jan 67	634UNTS181	109060
Argentina	Uruguay	12 Feb 67	635UNTS125	109076
Multilateral		22 Sep 67	0UNTS0	109258
Denmark	Poland	26 Feb 68	643UNTS371	109202
Argentina	Brazil	27 Sep 68	0UNTS0	109420
Tonnage				
Panama	USA (United States)	18 May 42	124UNTS221	200422
Denmark	USSR (Soviet Union)	17 Aug 46	8UNTS201	100124
Multilateral		10 Jun 47	208UNTS3	102814
Hungary	USSR (Soviet Union)	15 Jul 47	216UNTS247	102940
Czechoslovakia	USSR (Soviet Union)	11 Dec 47	217UNTS35	102943
Bulgaria	USSR (Soviet Union)	01 Apr 48	217UNTS97	102946
Multilateral		10 Jun 48	164UNTS113	102163
Italy	USSR (Soviet Union)	11 Dec 48	217UNTS181	102948
Germany, West	USA (United States)	29 Oct 54	273UNTS3	103943
USA (United States)	Venezuela	21 Feb 57	279UNTS199	104041
Sweden	Venezuela	13 Mar 57	428UNTS351	106185
Netherlands	Venezuela	11 Apr 57	288UNTS23	104193
Germany, East	USSR (Soviet Union)	27 Sep 57	292UNTS75	104268
Fed of Malaya	Japan	10 May 60	383UNTS293	105506
Multilateral		20 Feb 62	597UNTS159	108644
Finland	New Zealand	12 Nov 62	485UNTS331	107064
Canada	Finland	05 Jun 63	472UNTS345	106846
Czechoslovakia	Romania	16 Dec 63	527UNTS285	107630
Ceylon (Sri Lanka)	Finland	08 Jan 64	492UNTS285	107198

PARTY ONE	PARTY TWO	DATE	CITATION	NUMBER
Tonnage (Cont.)				
Finland	South Africa	12 Jun 64	505UNTS107	107367
Canada	Denmark	15 Oct 64	525UNTS227	107595
Denmark	India	06 Feb 65	531UNTS23	107690
Mauritania	Spain	11 May 65	602UNTS111	108709
Malaysia	Norway	26 May 65	602UNTS157	108711
Finland	Ireland	15 Sep 65	604UNTS199	108750
Nigeria	Switzerland	11 Oct 65	602UNTS137	108710
Multilateral		05 Apr 66	640UNTS133	109159
Denmark	Pakistan	01 Jun 67	620UNTS217	108958
Finland	Pakistan	11 Dec 67	631UNTS99	108989
Use of ports and territorial waters				
Italy	USA (United States)	02 Feb 48	79UNTS171	101040
Greece	Lebanon	06 Oct 48	87UNTS351	101179
Multilateral		03 Feb 58	381UNTS165	105471
Ports and pilotage				
Greece	Iran	09 Jan 31	166UNTS331	200497
Multilateral		27 Apr 32	39UNTS103	100614
Canada	France	12 May 33	253UNTS285	200545
Bolivia	Brazil	25 Feb 38	88UNTS379	200254
Canada	USA (United States)	19 Dec 42	26UNTS363	200156
Taiwan	Denmark	20 May 46	12UNTS59	100180
Denmark	USSR (Soviet Union)	17 Aug 46	8UNTS201	100124
Philippines	USA (United States)	14 Mar 47	43UNTS271	100673
Philippines	USA (United States)	12 May 47	16UNTS109	100252
Poland	Yugoslavia	24 May 47	115UNTS89	101560
Hungary	USSR (Soviet Union)	15 Jul 47	216UNTS247	102940
Czechoslovakia	USSR (Soviet Union)	11 Dec 47	217UNTS35	102943
Italy	USA (United States)	02 Feb 48	79UNTS171	101040
Bulgaria	USSR (Soviet Union)	01 Apr 48	217UNTS97	102946
Hungary	Poland	13 May 48	25UNTS301	100369
Multilateral		18 Aug 48	33UNTS181	100518
Italy	USSR (Soviet Union)	11 Dec 48	217UNTS181	102948
UK Great Britain	Yugoslavia	23 Dec 48	81UNTS133	101069
Argentina	Norway	09 Sep 49	42UNTS125	100646
USA (United States)	USSR (Soviet Union)	27 Sep 49	149UNTS23	101948
UK Great Britain	Yugoslavia	26 Dec 49	87UNTS71	101167
Canada	USA (United States)	24 Mar 50	200UNTS211	102705
Germany, West	Ireland	12 Jul 50	557UNTS221	108136
UK Great Britain	USA (United States)	21 Jul 50	97UNTS193	101351
Germany, West	Greece	12 Feb 51	198UNTS193	102665
Belgium	UK Great Britain	06 Apr 51	110UNTS3	101496
France	USSR (Soviet Union)	03 Sep 51	221UNTS79	103003
Ethiopia	USA (United States)	07 Sep 51	206UNTS41	102785
Belgium	Netherlands	14 Nov 51	123UNTS91	101656
Cuba	USA (United States)	17 Dec 51	152UNTS87	102012
UK Great Britain	USA (United States)	15 Jan 52	127UNTS3	101697
Germany, East	Poland	06 Feb 52	304UNTS131	104395
Japan	USA (United States)	28 Feb 52	208UNTS255	102817
Greece	Israel	22 Jul 52	219UNTS231	102978
Germany, West	Greece	28 Jul 52	182UNTS85	102424
Denmark	Uruguay	04 Mar 53	250UNTS51	103517
Japan	USA (United States)	02 Apr 53	206UNTS143	102788
Libya	UK Great Britain	29 Jul 53	186UNTS201	102492
France	Sweden	16 Feb 54	228UNTS137	103147
Multilateral		19 Feb 54	214UNTS51	102899
USA (United States)	USSR (Soviet Union)	26 Mar 54	247UNTS263	103475
Multilateral		12 May 54	327UNTS3	104714
Haiti	Italy	14 Jun 54	267UNTS97	103837
Germany, West	USA (United States)	29 Oct 54	273UNTS3	103943
India	Iran	15 Dec 54	327UNTS245	104724
USA (United States)	USSR (Soviet Union)	22 Dec 54	251UNTS41	103532
Peru	USA (United States)	07 Jan 55	261UNTS321	103730
Argentina	UK Great Britain	31 Mar 55	210UNTS223	102840
USA (United States)	USSR (Soviet Union)	26 May 55	270UNTS61	103892

PARTY ONE	PARTY TWO	DATE	CITATION	NUMBER
Ports and pilotage (Cont.)				
Ecuador	USA (United States)	08 Jul 55	265UNTS49	103806
Austria	USSR (Soviet Union)	17 Oct 55	240UNTS289	103409
Austria	Italy	22 Oct 55	260UNTS327	103716
Syria	USSR (Soviet Union)	16 Nov 55	259UNTS71	103683
Cuba	USA (United States)	10 Jan 56	240UNTS101	103398
Czechoslovakia	Poland	13 Jan 56	265UNTS157	103811
Canada	USSR (Soviet Union)	29 Feb 56	252UNTS165	103566
Norway	Sweden	09 Mar 56	369UNTS285	105262
Netherlands	USA (United States)	27 Mar 56	285UNTS231	104154
UK Great Britain	USA (United States)	25 Jun 56	249UNTS59	103501
Argentina	UK Great Britain	30 Jun 56	269UNTS235	103884
UK Great Britain	Venezuela	20 Jul 56	351UNTS289	105029
Multilateral		16 Aug 56	287UNTS223	104188
Pakistan	USA (United States)	10 Sep 56	277UNTS259	104010
Costa Rica	Denmark	26 Sep 56	341UNTS305	104893
Japan	USSR (Soviet Union)	19 Oct 56	263UNTS119	103769
Australia	USA (United States)	31 Dec 56	266UNTS89	103823
USA (United States)	Venezuela	21 Feb 57	279UNTS199	104041
Bulgaria	Yugoslavia	19 Apr 57	349UNTS3	105006
Ceylon (Sri Lanka)	Italy	23 Apr 57	337UNTS115	104820
Denmark	Peru	10 Jun 57	406UNTS63	105839
Austria	USSR (Soviet Union)	14 Jun 57	285UNTS169	104152
Germany, East	USSR (Soviet Union)	27 Sep 57	292UNTS75	104268
Belgium	Netherlands	24 Oct 57	489UNTS3	107131
Belgium	Netherlands	24 Oct 57	489UNTS11	107132
Belgium	Netherlands	24 Oct 57	292UNTS199	104274
Argentina	Denmark	25 Nov 57	299UNTS83	104308
Japan	USSR (Soviet Union)	06 Dec 57	325UNTS35	104694
China People's Rep	USSR (Soviet Union)	21 Dec 57	305UNTS213	104420
Belgium	Netherlands	03 Feb 58	381UNTS305	105472
Ceylon (Sri Lanka)	USSR (Soviet Union)	08 Feb 58	348UNTS159	104999
Albania	USSR (Soviet Union)	15 Feb 58	313UNTS261	104536
China People's Rep	USSR (Soviet Union)	23 Apr 58	313UNTS135	104534
Germany, West	USSR (Soviet Union)	25 Apr 58	346UNTS71	104978
Japan	Poland	26 Apr 58	340UNTS221	104866
Multilateral		29 Apr 58	450UNTS11	106465
Denmark	El Salvador	09 Jul 58	341UNTS289	104892
United Arab Rep	USSR (Soviet Union)	18 Sep 58	338UNTS29	104831
Iraq	USSR (Soviet Union)	11 Oct 58	328UNTS95	104730
Iraq	Romania	24 Dec 58	405UNTS243	105836
Czechoslovakia	United Arab Rep	07 Feb 59	372UNTS243	105301
Multilateral		07 Jul 59	377UNTS203	105402
India	Italy	06 Oct 59	378UNTS267	105427
Australia	Germany, West	14 Oct 59	345UNTS35	104957
Ethiopia	France	12 Nov 59	381UNTS3	105465
Czechoslovakia	Germany, East	25 Nov 59	374UNTS101	105331
Multilateral		14 Dec 59	422UNTS75	106069
Multilateral		06 Feb 60	383UNTS3	105494
Cuba	USSR (Soviet Union)	13 Feb 60	369UNTS17	105248
Cuba	Japan	22 Apr 60	442UNTS261	106354
Cuba	Czechoslovakia	10 Jun 60	447UNTS75	106412
Belgium	Netherlands	20 Jun 60	423UNTS19	106084
Korea, North	USSR (Soviet Union)	22 Jun 60	399UNTS3	105732
Multilateral		29 Jul 60	392UNTS69	105640
Albania	Cuba	16 Jan 61	448UNTS67	106425
Canada	USA (United States)	05 May 61	419UNTS9	106027
Ghana	USSR (Soviet Union)	04 Nov 61	437UNTS213	106308
Pakistan	IDA (Devel Assoc)	22 Nov 61	447UNTS295	106420
Greece	USA (United States)	24 Apr 62	459UNTS3	106609
Finland	USSR (Soviet Union)	27 Sep 62	479UNTS99	106949
Germany, West	USA (United States)	29 Nov 62	460UNTS169	106639
Greece	Pakistan	17 Jan 63	538UNTS175	107814
Norway	USA (United States)	01 Mar 63	524UNTS185	107573
Belgium	USA (United States)	19 Apr 63	493UNTS83	107209
Netherlands	USA (United States)	20 May 63	487UNTS123	107099

PARTY ONE	PARTY TWO	DATE	CITATION	NUMBER
Ports and pilotage (Cont.)				
Multilateral		07 Jun 63	472UNTS95	106837
El Salvador	Japan	19 Jul 63	518UNTS135	107494
Tanganyika	USSR (Soviet Union)	14 Aug 63	493UNTS195	107215
Czechoslovakia	Romania	16 Dec 63	527UNTS285	107630
Portugal	UK Great Britain	07 Apr 64	539UNTS167	107830
Liberia	USA (United States)	14 Apr 64	526UNTS221	107606
UK Great Britain	USA (United States)	19 Jun 64	530UNTS99	107675
Denmark	USA (United States)	02 Jul 64	529UNTS277	107665
Sweden	USA (United States)	06 Jul 64	529UNTS287	107666
Spain	USA (United States)	16 Jul 64	529UNTS187	107661
Portugal	USA (United States)	12 Nov 64	541UNTS251	107874
Italy	USA (United States)	23 Nov 64	532UNTS133	107716
Multilateral		01 Dec 64	550UNTS133	108012
Malta	Yugoslavia	15 Jul 65	561UNTS223	108186
Argentina	Uruguay	12 Feb 67	635UNTS125	109076
Malaysia	Philippines	01 Sep 67	608UNTS13	108810
Argentina	Brazil	27 Sep 68	0UNTS0	109420
Shipwreck and salvage				
Greece	Iran	09 Jan 31	166UNTS331	200497
Australia	USA (United States)	08 Mar 45	121UNTS205	200400
Norway	USA (United States)	29 May 45	34UNTS371	200180
Denmark	USSR (Soviet Union)	17 Aug 46	8UNTS201	100124
Romania	USSR (Soviet Union)	20 Feb 47	226UNTS79	103110
Philippines	USA (United States)	14 Mar 47	45UNTS23	100690
Hungary	USSR (Soviet Union)	15 Jul 47	216UNTS247	102940
Czechoslovakia	USSR (Soviet Union)	11 Dec 47	217UNTS35	102943
Costa Rica	USA (United States)	12 Jan 48	70UNTS27	100896
Multilateral		06 Mar 48	289UNTS3	104214
Bulgaria	USSR (Soviet Union)	01 Apr 48	217UNTS97	102946
Philippines	Spain	20 May 48	70UNTS143	100903
Greece	Lebanon	06 Oct 48	87UNTS351	101179
Italy	USSR (Soviet Union)	11 Dec 48	217UNTS181	102948
Greece	USA (United States)	03 Aug 51	224UNTS279	103080
Multilateral		10 May 52	439UNTS233	106332
Italy	UK Great Britain	06 Nov 52	158UNTS431	102076
India	Muscat and Oman	15 Mar 53	190UNTS69	102559
France	Sweden	16 Feb 54	228UNTS137	103147
Germany, West	USA (United States)	29 Oct 54	273UNTS3	103943
Turkey	USA (United States)	12 Mar 56	272UNTS21	103929
Netherlands	USA (United States)	27 Mar 56	285UNTS231	104154
Multilateral		11 Sep 56	266UNTS221	103832
Japan	Norway	28 Feb 57	280UNTS87	104054
Germany, East	USSR (Soviet Union)	27 Sep 57	292UNTS75	104268
Japan	USSR (Soviet Union)	06 Dec 57	325UNTS35	104694
India	Japan	04 Feb 58	324UNTS215	104687
Albania	USSR (Soviet Union)	15 Feb 58	313UNTS261	104536
Germany, West	USSR (Soviet Union)	25 Apr 58	346UNTS71	104978
Japan	Poland	26 Apr 58	340UNTS221	104866
Germany, East	Romania	15 Jul 58	387UNTS133	105561
Fed of Malaya	Japan	10 May 60	383UNTS293	105506
Korea, North	USSR (Soviet Union)	22 Jun 60	399UNTS3	105732
Belgium	USA (United States)	21 Feb 61	480UNTS149	106967
Japan	UK Great Britain	14 Nov 62	478UNTS29	106934
Austria	Czechoslovakia	08 Mar 63	495UNTS219	107245
Czechoslovakia	Romania	16 Dec 63	527UNTS285	107630
Czechoslovakia	Hungary	20 Dec 63	538UNTS127	107812
Denmark	UK Great Britain	30 Jun 64	539UNTS203	107833
Argentina	Uruguay	12 Feb 67	635UNTS125	109076
Denmark	Poland	26 Feb 68	643UNTS371	109202
Collision				
Canada	USA (United States)	26 May 43	7UNTS345	200043
Ceylon (Sri Lanka)	Sweden	29 May 59	464UNTS109	106713

PARTY ONE	PARTY TWO	DATE	CITATION	NUMBER
Land transport				
Mexico	USA (United States)	18 Nov 42	120UNTS183	200392
Multilateral		27 Sep 45	5UNTS327	200035
Multilateral		30 Oct 46	27UNTS77	100401
Hungary	USSR (Soviet Union)	15 Jul 47	216UNTS247	102940
Czechoslovakia	USSR (Soviet Union)	11 Dec 47	217UNTS35	102943
UK Great Britain	USA (United States)	19 Sep 49	68UNTS31	100882
Multilateral		17 Oct 53	184UNTS42	102438
Finland	USSR (Soviet Union)	14 Sep 56	255UNTS365	103618
Multilateral		08 Nov 56	470UNTS171	106809
Austria	Sweden	19 Feb 58	427UNTS211	106155
Multilateral		16 Mar 61	638UNTS235	109139
Austria	Hungary	09 Apr 65	638UNTS53	109131
Denmark	Germany, West	09 Jun 65	605UNTS95	108762
France	Romania	14 Mar 66	604UNTS33	108741
Romania	USSR (Soviet Union)	21 Jun 66	604UNTS81	108746
Belgium	Spain	19 Jul 66	575UNTS3	108352
Czechoslovakia	USSR (Soviet Union)	03 Feb 67	617UNTS267	108917
Czechoslovakia	Netherlands	15 Nov 67	0UNTS0	109223
Agricultural vehicles and construction				
Bulgaria	Yugoslavia	22 May 56	367UNTS119	105229
Thailand	UK Great Britain	25 Jul 57	277UNTS81	103999
Multilateral		10 Jun 58	454UNTS115	106540
Australia	Thailand	28 Jul 59	339UNTS91	104847
New Zealand	Thailand	24 Dec 59	351UNTS197	105023
Austria	Spain	24 Mar 66	590UNTS203	108555
Belgium	Spain	19 Jul 66	575UNTS3	108352
Commercial road vehicles				
Multilateral		28 Jun 39	209UNTS39	102820
Multilateral		27 Sep 45	5UNTS327	200035
Multilateral		16 Jun 49	45UNTS149	100696
El Salvador	Guatemala	14 Dec 51	131UNTS131	101740
Belgium	France	30 Jun 52	137UNTS259	101857
Multilateral		05 Sep 52	256UNTS3	103619
Multilateral		18 May 56	327UNTS123	104721
Multilateral		19 May 56	399UNTS189	105742
Belgium	Sweden	20 Nov 56	281UNTS239	104081
Netherlands	Sweden	23 Oct 57	306UNTS75	104433
Denmark	Netherlands	13 Nov 57	306UNTS67	104432
Bulgaria	Yugoslavia	21 Mar 58	386UNTS119	105541
Bulgaria	Yugoslavia	21 Mar 58	349UNTS61	105009
Bulgaria	Yugoslavia	21 Mar 58	376UNTS53	105373
Multilateral		05 Nov 58	428UNTS73	106169
Austria	Netherlands	06 May 59	485UNTS153	107054
Austria	Netherlands	06 May 59	485UNTS175	107055
Greece	Yugoslavia	18 Jun 59	368UNTS27	105234
Iraq	Syria	03 Nov 61	489UNTS45	107134
Germany, West	Greece	08 Mar 62	533UNTS269	107747
Czechoslovakia	Yugoslavia	22 Oct 62	480UNTS267	106974
Romania	Yugoslavia	25 Dec 63	576UNTS95	108366
Hungary	Netherlands	11 Jan 64	522UNTS243	107550
Austria	Belgium	20 Jan 64	509UNTS275	107406
Czechoslovakia	Hungary	17 Oct 64	545UNTS21	107924
Greece	Yugoslavia	05 Nov 64	539UNTS19	107821
Hungary	Yugoslavia	25 May 65	576UNTS145	108367
Pakistan	IDA (Devel Assoc)	13 Jan 66	567UNTS67	108252
Belgium	Denmark	04 Feb 66	561UNTS233	108187
Austria	Spain	24 Mar 66	590UNTS203	108555
Belgium	Spain	19 Jul 66	575UNTS3	108352
Netherlands	Yugoslavia	08 Sep 66	597UNTS147	108643
Belgium	Hungary	20 Mar 67	601UNTS37	108686
Denmark	Romania	29 Aug 67	0UNTS0	109231
Belgium	Romania	22 Sep 67	637UNTS0	109109
Czechoslovakia	Netherlands	15 Nov 67	0UNTS0	109223

PARTY ONE	PARTY TWO	DATE	CITATION	NUMBER
Commercial road vehicles (Cont.)				
Sweden	UK Great Britain	12 Feb 68	0UNTS0	109449
Driving permits				
Multilateral		19 Sep 49	125UNTS3	101671
Belgium	Czechoslovakia	02 May 51	109UNTS3	101483
Belgium	France	21 Mar 52	137UNTS249	101856
France	Netherlands	20 Jun 53	187UNTS97	102503
Multilateral		19 Feb 54	214UNTS51	102899
Multilateral		23 Oct 54	332UNTS3	104760
Multilateral		12 Mar 55	211UNTS3	102844
Italy	Yugoslavia	31 Mar 55	386UNTS307	105550
Germany, West	Sweden	05 Aug 55	262UNTS265	103754
Denmark	Norway	15 Sep 56	259UNTS3	103680
Finland	Norway	15 Sep 56	254UNTS17	103590
Norway	Sweden	15 Sep 56	263UNTS17	103765
Denmark	Finland	15 Sep 56	254UNTS3	103589
Denmark	Sweden	15 Sep 56	263UNTS3	103764
Finland	Sweden	15 Sep 56	254UNTS31	103591
Germany, West	Sweden	13 Feb 57	428UNTS149	106174
Luxembourg	Sweden	06 Apr 57	427UNTS173	106152
Austria	Sweden	10 Apr 57	427UNTS343	106165
France	Sweden	10 May 57	427UNTS127	106149
Netherlands	Sweden	21 May 57	286UNTS237	104169
Italy	Switzerland	19 Sep 57	363UNTS69	105200
Luxembourg	Sweden	12 Mar 58	427UNTS179	106153
Bulgaria	Yugoslavia	21 Mar 58	386UNTS119	105541
Italy	Sweden	14 Apr 58	427UNTS167	106151
Sweden	Switzerland	30 Apr 58	427UNTS295	106161
Belgium	Sweden	08 May 58	312UNTS145	104516
Multilateral		10 Jun 58	454UNTS115	106540
Austria	Belgium	20 Jun 58	312UNTS95	104513
Multilateral		05 Nov 58	428UNTS73	106169
Austria	Netherlands	19 Mar 59	485UNTS117	107048
Austria	Netherlands	06 May 59	485UNTS153	107054
Greece	Yugoslavia	18 Jun 59	368UNTS27	105234
Germany, West	Greece	08 Mar 62	533UNTS269	107747
Romania	Yugoslavia	25 Dec 63	576UNTS95	108366
Austria	Romania	27 May 64	588UNTS29	108517
Belgium	Denmark	04 Feb 66	561UNTS233	108187
Trinidad/Tobago	UK Great Britain	23 Jan 67	605UNTS277	108767
Czechoslovakia	USSR (Soviet Union)	03 Feb 67	617UNTS267	108917
Belgium	Romania	22 Sep 67	637UNTS0	109109
Czechoslovakia	Netherlands	15 Nov 67	0UNTS0	109223
Railway border crossing				
Multilateral		27 Sep 45	5UNTS327	200035
Czechoslovakia	Poland	12 Nov 48	84UNTS347	101141
Multilateral		10 Jan 52	163UNTS3	102138
Multilateral		10 Jan 52	163UNTS27	102139
Czechoslovakia	Germany, East	24 Oct 55	504UNTS173	107358
Czechoslovakia	Poland	13 Jan 56	265UNTS157	103811
Norway	Sweden	09 Mar 56	369UNTS285	105262
Bulgaria	Yugoslavia	22 May 56	367UNTS119	105229
Multilateral		08 Nov 56	470UNTS171	106809
Albania	Yugoslavia	29 Aug 57	391UNTS127	105621
Czechoslovakia	Poland	31 Jan 58	431UNTS99	106214
Germany, West	Netherlands	30 May 58	570UNTS127	108291
Germany, West	Netherlands	08 Apr 60	508UNTS14	107404
Poland	USSR (Soviet Union)	05 Feb 61	420UNTS161	106046
Turkey	USSR (Soviet Union)	27 Apr 61	420UNTS307	106047
Belgium	Luxembourg	29 Nov 61	486UNTS37	107071
Belgium	France	30 Mar 62	502UNTS297	107335
Austria	Czechoslovakia	22 Sep 62	495UNTS157	107244
Czechoslovakia	Poland	16 Nov 62	526UNTS3	107597
Austria	Yugoslavia	11 Dec 62	546UNTS3	107938
Poland	USSR (Soviet Union)	22 Apr 63	493UNTS229	107217

PARTY ONE	PARTY TWO	DATE	CITATION	NUMBER
Railway border crossing (Cont.)				
Czechoslovakia	Hungary	22 Oct 63	514UNTS95	107444
Denmark	Germany, West	09 Jun 65	605UNTS95	108762
Austria	Germany, West	17 Feb 66	614UNTS263	108875
Germany, West	Netherlands	22 Sep 66	0UNTS0	109226
Austria	Yugoslavia	08 Apr 67	0UNTS0	109216
Motor vehicles and combinations				
Chile	USA (United States)	09 Apr 49	122UNTS169	101646
Multilateral		19 Sep 49	125UNTS3	101671
Multilateral		13 May 50	128UNTS171	101719
Belgium	Czechoslovakia	02 May 51	109UNTS3	101483
Austria	Sweden	01 Aug 51	198UNTS13	102653
Belgium	France	21 Mar 52	137UNTS249	101856
Chile	USA (United States)	10 May 54	247UNTS299	103477
Multilateral		04 Jun 54	282UNTS249	104101
Multilateral		12 Mar 55	211UNTS3	102844
Italy	Yugoslavia	31 Mar 55	386UNTS307	105550
Italy	Switzerland	23 Jul 55	284UNTS279	104142
Austria	Sweden	17 Oct 55	262UNTS283	103756
Multilateral		18 May 56	339UNTS3	104844
Denmark	Finland	15 Sep 56	254UNTS3	103589
Denmark	Sweden	15 Sep 56	263UNTS3	103764
Belgium	Sweden	20 Nov 56	281UNTS239	104081
Multilateral		14 Dec 56	436UNTS115	106292
Sweden	Switzerland	30 Apr 58	427UNTS295	106161
Belgium	Sweden	08 May 58	312UNTS145	104516
Multilateral		10 Jun 58	454UNTS115	106540
Austria	Belgium	20 Jun 58	312UNTS95	104513
Multilateral		05 Nov 58	428UNTS73	106169
Iraq	Syria	03 Nov 61	489UNTS45	107134
Hungary	Yugoslavia	09 Feb 62	577UNTS3	108370
Germany, West	Greece	08 Mar 62	533UNTS269	107747
Romania	Yugoslavia	25 Dec 63	576UNTS95	108366
Hungary	Netherlands	11 Jan 64	522UNTS243	107550
Belgium	Germany, West	17 Dec 64	631UNTS229	108996
Hungary	Poland	18 Jul 65	577UNTS161	108376
Belgium	Denmark	20 Sep 65	549UNTS63	107990
Austria	Germany, West	17 Feb 66	615UNTS3	108876
France	Romania	14 Mar 66	604UNTS33	108741
Austria	Spain	24 Mar 66	590UNTS203	108555
Romania	USSR (Soviet Union)	21 Jun 66	604UNTS81	108746
Belgium	Spain	19 Jul 66	575UNTS3	108352
Czechoslovakia	USSR (Soviet Union)	03 Feb 67	617UNTS267	108917
Denmark	Romania	29 Aug 67	0UNTS0	109231
Belgium	Romania	22 Sep 67	637UNTS0	109109
Czechoslovakia	Netherlands	15 Nov 67	0UNTS0	109223
Sweden	UK Great Britain	12 Feb 68	0UNTS0	109449
Railways				
Bolivia	Brazil	25 Feb 38	88UNTS379	200254
Panama	USA (United States)	23 Mar 40	124UNTS195	200420
Brazil	Paraguay	14 Jun 41	54UNTS289	200201
Panama	USA (United States)	18 May 42	124UNTS221	200422
Panama	USA (United States)	18 May 42	124UNTS221	200422
Mexico	USA (United States)	18 Nov 42	120UNTS183	200392
Canada	USA (United States)	23 Feb 43	101UNTS243	200299
Brazil	Paraguay	11 Aug 44	67UNTS303	200227
Ethiopia	UK Great Britain	19 Dec 44	93UNTS303	200272
Multilateral		27 Sep 45	5UNTS327	200035
Mexico	USA (United States)	05 Mar 46	120UNTS3	101612
Multilateral		17 Apr 46	27UNTS103	100402
Argentina	UK Great Britain	17 Sep 46	88UNTS47	101185
Albania	Yugoslavia	28 Nov 46	111UNTS139	101526
Albania	Yugoslavia	28 Nov 46	111UNTS127	101525
Hungary	USSR (Soviet Union)	15 Jul 47	216UNTS247	102940
Czechoslovakia	USSR (Soviet Union)	11 Dec 47	217UNTS35	102943

PARTY ONE	PARTY TWO	DATE	CITATION	NUMBER
Railways (Cont.)				
Bulgaria	USSR (Soviet Union)	01 Apr 48	217UNTS97	102946
Czechoslovakia	Poland	12 Nov 48	84UNTS347	101141
Czechoslovakia	Poland	02 Jul 49	260UNTS149	103708
Czechoslovakia	Poland	02 Jul 49	260UNTS179	103709
Multilateral		13 May 50	128UNTS171	101719
Saudi Arabia	USA (United States)	18 Jun 51	102UNTS73	101412
UK Great Britain	USA (United States)	18 Jul 51	117UNTS49	101583
Saudi Arabia	USA (United States)	10 Nov 52	181UNTS307	102419
Pakistan	United Nations	25 Jan 54	185UNTS213	102472
IBRD (World Bank)	UK Great Britain	15 Mar 55	265UNTS85	103808
India	Pakistan	15 Apr 55	247UNTS25	103458
Italy	Switzerland	23 Jul 55	284UNTS279	104142
Multilateral		20 Oct 55	378UNTS159	105425
Austria	Italy	22 Oct 55	260UNTS327	103716
Czechoslovakia	Germany, East	24 Oct 55	504UNTS173	107358
Czechoslovakia	Poland	13 Jan 56	265UNTS157	103811
Norway	Sweden	09 Mar 56	369UNTS285	105262
Burma	IBRD (World Bank)	04 May 56	253UNTS179	103584
Bulgaria	Yugoslavia	22 May 56	367UNTS119	105229
Finland	USSR (Soviet Union)	14 Sep 56	255UNTS365	103618
Greece	Yugoslavia	22 Apr 57	391UNTS109	105619
India	IBRD (World Bank)	12 Jul 57	288UNTS135	104202
Multilateral		26 Jul 57	386UNTS3	105535
Multilateral		15 Jan 58	383UNTS229	105503
Czechoslovakia	Poland	31 Jan 58	431UNTS99	106214
IBRD (World Bank)	UK Great Britain	02 May 58	324UNTS25	104677
Multilateral		10 Jun 58	454UNTS115	106540
IBRD (World Bank)	Sudan	21 Jul 58	323UNTS183	104669
India	IBRD (World Bank)	16 Sep 58	323UNTS235	104671
India	IBRD (World Bank)	15 Jul 59	346UNTS33	104976
Pakistan	IBRD (World Bank)	30 Nov 59	355UNTS203	105078
Multilateral		14 Dec 59	422UNTS75	106069
Germany, West	Netherlands	08 Apr 60	508UNTS14	107404
Belgium	Netherlands	20 Jun 60	423UNTS19	106084
Argentina	Bolivia	07 Sep 60	0UNTS0	109516
Colombia	IBRD (World Bank)	20 Sep 60	390UNTS173	105608
Burma	IBRD (World Bank)	16 Jan 61	400UNTS73	105749
Poland	USSR (Soviet Union)	05 Feb 61	420UNTS161	106046
Turkey	USSR (Soviet Union)	27 Apr 61	420UNTS307	106047
IBRD (World Bank)	Thailand	28 Apr 61	415UNTS121	105983
Japan	IBRD (World Bank)	02 May 61	415UNTS144	105984
India	IBRD (World Bank)	13 Oct 61	418UNTS3	106013
Pakistan	IBRD (World Bank)	14 Sep 62	467UNTS152	106762
Austria	Czechoslovakia	22 Sep 62	495UNTS157	107244
Czechoslovakia	Poland	16 Nov 62	526UNTS3	107597
Multilateral		08 Dec 62	510UNTS235	107418
Austria	Yugoslavia	11 Dec 62	546UNTS3	107938
Peru	IBRD (World Bank)	13 Mar 63	478UNTS245	106938
India	IDA (Devel Assoc)	22 Mar 63	477UNTS3	106911
Poland	USSR (Soviet Union)	22 Apr 63	493UNTS229	107217
Colombia	IBRD (World Bank)	21 Jun 63	482UNTS159	106994
Czechoslovakia	Hungary	22 Oct 63	514UNTS95	107444
IBRD (World Bank)	Yugoslavia	28 Oct 63	503UNTS289	107349
Multilateral		30 Dec 63	568UNTS233	108271
Multilateral		30 Dec 63	568UNTS215	108270
Portugal	UK Great Britain	07 Apr 64	539UNTS167	107830
Ecuador	IDA (Devel Assoc)	26 May 64	534UNTS93	107757
Pakistan	IDA (Devel Assoc)	24 Jun 64	533UNTS191	107743
IBRD (World Bank)	Spain	31 Jul 64	537UNTS81	107798
Mali	IDA (Devel Assoc)	29 Sep 64	594UNTS187	108604
Multilateral		25 Nov 64	587UNTS19	108507
IBRD (World Bank)	Yugoslavia	11 Dec 64	537UNTS321	107807
Taiwan	IBRD (World Bank)	28 Apr 65	549UNTS145	107998
Denmark	Germany, West	09 Jun 65	605UNTS95	108762
East Afri Service	IBRD (World Bank)	29 Sep 65	568UNTS327	200623

PARTY ONE	PARTY TWO	DATE	CITATION	NUMBER
Railways (Cont.)				
IBRD (World Bank)	Uganda	29 Sep 65	568UNTS317	108276
IBRD (World Bank)	Tanzania	29 Sep 65	568UNTS309	108275
Kenya	IBRD (World Bank)	29 Sep 65	568UNTS289	108274
New Zealand	IBRD (World Bank)	17 Dec 65	567UNTS275	108260
IBRD (World Bank)	Sudan	27 Dec 65	567UNTS27	108250
India	IDA (Devel Assoc)	29 Jun 66	582UNTS277	108467
IDA (Devel Assoc)	Senegal	29 Sep 66	594UNTS277	108607
Austria	Yugoslavia	08 Apr 67	0UNTS0	109216
Roads and highways				
Panama	USA (United States)	06 Sep 40	124UNTS209	200421
Jordan	UK Great Britain	19 Jul 41	9UNTS381	200054
Costa Rica	USA (United States)	16 Jan 42	23UNTS285	200135
El Salvador	USA (United States)	13 Feb 42	23UNTS293	200136
Canada	USA (United States)	18 Mar 42	101UNTS205	200294
Nicaragua	USA (United States)	08 Apr 42	24UNTS145	200138
Nicaragua	USA (United States)	08 Apr 42	132UNTS343	200439
Canada	USA (United States)	09 May 42	101UNTS215	200295
Panama	USA (United States)	18 May 42	124UNTS221	200422
Canada	USA (United States)	10 Sep 42	101UNTS221	200296
Honduras	USA (United States)	26 Oct 42	24UNTS209	200145
Canada	USA (United States)	07 Dec 42	101UNTS227	200297
Guatemala	USA (United States)	19 May 43	28UNTS377	200161
Panama	USA (United States)	07 Jun 43	21UNTS269	200128
Canada	USA (United States)	19 Jul 43	29UNTS289	200167
Brazil	Uruguay	22 Nov 44	65UNTS289	200217
Guatemala	USA (United States)	18 May 48	67UNTS161	100875
Multilateral		16 Jun 49	45UNTS149	100696
Multilateral		19 Sep 49	125UNTS3	101671
Norway	Sweden	28 Jan 50	202UNTS151	102730
Panama	USA (United States)	14 Sep 50	124UNTS25	101664
Multilateral		16 Sep 50	92UNTS91	101264
Costa Rica	USA (United States)	17 Jan 51	134UNTS215	101801
Panama	USA (United States)	26 Jan 51	137UNTS69	101849
El Salvador	USA (United States)	19 Mar 51	134UNTS245	101803
Nicaragua	USA (United States)	20 Apr 51	138UNTS57	101859
El Salvador	Guatemala	14 Dec 51	131UNTS131	101740
Jordan	USA (United States)	12 Feb 52	168UNTS25	102211
Belgium	France	21 Mar 52	137UNTS249	101856
Saudi Arabia	USA (United States)	15 Dec 52	185UNTS67	102459
France	Italy	14 Mar 53	284UNTS221	104140
France	Netherlands	20 Jun 53	187UNTS97	102503
Nicaragua	USA (United States)	02 Sep 53	215UNTS69	102911
Nicaragua	IBRD (World Bank)	04 Sep 53	186UNTS117	102487
Colombia	IBRD (World Bank)	10 Sep 53	203UNTS3	102738
El Salvador	IBRD (World Bank)	12 Oct 54	203UNTS37	102739
Multilateral		23 Oct 54	332UNTS3	104760
Honduras	USA (United States)	12 May 55	270UNTS3	103886
Bolivia	USA (United States)	03 Aug 55	264UNTS225	103795
Honduras	IBRD (World Bank)	22 Dec 55	230UNTS262	103189
Norway	Sweden	09 Mar 56	369UNTS285	105262
Multilateral		19 May 56	399UNTS189	105742
Colombia	IBRD (World Bank)	06 Jun 56	248UNTS139	103493
Nicaragua	USA (United States)	02 Aug 56	281UNTS99	104073
Ethiopia	IBRD (World Bank)	28 Jan 57	286UNTS307	104175
Belgium	IBRD (World Bank)	26 Jun 57	322UNTS301	104661
Ecuador	IBRD (World Bank)	20 Sep 57	289UNTS237	104221
Netherlands	Sweden	23 Oct 57	306UNTS75	104433
Denmark	Netherlands	13 Nov 57	306UNTS67	104432
Belgium	IBRD (World Bank)	27 Nov 57	292UNTS175	104273
Multilateral		13 Dec 57	372UNTS159	105296
Austria	Sweden	18 Feb 58	427UNTS349	106166
Bulgaria	Yugoslavia	21 Mar 58	386UNTS119	105541
Belgium	Sweden	08 May 58	312UNTS145	104516
Honduras	IBRD (World Bank)	09 May 58	323UNTS4	104662

PARTY ONE	PARTY TWO	DATE	CITATION	NUMBER
Roads and highways (Cont.)				
Italy	Switzerland	23 May 58	363UNTS81	105201
Multilateral		10 Jun 58	454UNTS211	106541
Austria	Belgium	20 Jun 58	312UNTS95	104513
Finland	Sweden	22 Sep 58	428UNTS119	106170
Multilateral		05 Nov 58	428UNTS73	106169
El Salvador	IBRD (World Bank)	07 Jan 59	346UNTS51	104977
Iran	IBRD (World Bank)	29 May 59	348UNTS103	104997
Greece	Yugoslavia	18 Jun 59	368UNTS27	105234
Italy	Netherlands	08 Dec 59	484UNTS309	107039
Japan	IBRD (World Bank)	17 Mar 60	362UNTS43	105182
Belgium	Netherlands	20 Jun 60	423UNTS19	106084
Panama	IBRD (World Bank)	19 Aug 60	390UNTS153	105607
Mexico	IBRD (World Bank)	18 Oct 60	422UNTS177	106075
Peru	IBRD (World Bank)	19 Dec 60	417UNTS275	106010
India	IDA (Devel Assoc)	21 Jun 61	418UNTS61	106017
Chile	IDA (Devel Assoc)	28 Jun 61	426UNTS89	106131
Chile	IBRD (World Bank)	28 Jun 61	426UNTS33	106129
Argentina	IBRD (World Bank)	30 Jun 61	445UNTS85	106379
Jordan	UK Great Britain	17 Jul 61	420UNTS53	106039
Colombia	IBRD (World Bank)	28 Aug 61	416UNTS23	105993
Colombia	IDA (Devel Assoc)	28 Aug 61	416UNTS3	105992
Costa Rica	IDA (Devel Assoc)	13 Oct 61	431UNTS3	106204
Costa Rica	IBRD (World Bank)	13 Oct 61	430UNTS27	106202
Paraguay	IDA (Devel Assoc)	26 Oct 61	447UNTS277	106419
Peru	IBRD (World Bank)	03 Nov 61	430UNTS47	106203
Japan	IBRD (World Bank)	29 Nov 61	426UNTS3	106128
IBRD (World Bank)	Venezuela	13 Dec 61	446UNTS371	106409
Hungary	Yugoslavia	09 Feb 62	577UNTS3	108370
Germany, West	Greece	08 Mar 62	533UNTS269	107747
Jordan	UK Great Britain	30 May 62	449UNTS167	106458
Israel	IBRD (World Bank)	17 Oct 62	467UNTS107	106760
IBRD (World Bank)	Uruguay	26 Oct 62	481UNTS39	106977
Haiti	IDA (Devel Assoc)	02 Nov 62	468UNTS205	106774
El Salvador	IDA (Devel Assoc)	02 Nov 62	468UNTS331	106780
Jordan	UK Great Britain	27 Apr 63	475UNTS169	106892
IBRD (World Bank)	Thailand	11 Jun 63	481UNTS227	106984
IBRD (World Bank)	Yugoslavia	21 Jun 63	482UNTS43	106990
Mexico	IBRD (World Bank)	20 Sep 63	491UNTS317	107182
Japan	IBRD (World Bank)	27 Sep 63	485UNTS283	107061
IBRD (World Bank)	Spain	25 Oct 63	491UNTS297	107181
IDA (Devel Assoc)	Syria	24 Dec 63	534UNTS253	107764
Romania	Yugoslavia	25 Dec 63	576UNTS95	108366
Liberia	IBRD (World Bank)	08 Jan 64	504UNTS53	107353
Austria	Belgium	20 Jan 64	509UNTS275	107406
IDA (Devel Assoc)	Tanganyika	05 Feb 64	506UNTS91	107382
Canada	USA (United States)	06 Mar 64	524UNTS255	107577
Japan	IBRD (World Bank)	22 Apr 64	505UNTS21	107363
Multilateral		26 May 64	541UNTS271	200613
Ecuador	IBRD (World Bank)	26 May 64	534UNTS113	107758
Austria	Romania	27 May 64	588UNTS29	108517
Iran	IBRD (World Bank)	10 Jun 64	537UNTS111	107799
Pakistan	IDA (Devel Assoc)	11 Jun 64	534UNTS309	107766
Pakistan	IDA (Devel Assoc)	11 Jun 64	506UNTS3	107379
Pakistan	IDA (Devel Assoc)	24 Jun 64	533UNTS165	107742
Niger	IDA (Devel Assoc)	24 Jun 64	554UNTS93	108098
Gabon	IBRD (World Bank)	10 Jul 64	537UNTS63	107797
Finland	IBRD (World Bank)	10 Jul 64	516UNTS125	107474
IDA (Devel Assoc)	UK Great Britain	31 Jul 64	535UNTS205	107781
IBRD (World Bank)	Venezuela	28 Aug 64	520UNTS97	107512
Pakistan	IDA (Devel Assoc)	22 Sep 64	594UNTS225	108605
Czechoslovakia	Hungary	17 Oct 64	545UNTS21	107924
Greece	Yugoslavia	05 Nov 64	539UNTS19	107821
Multilateral		25 Nov 64	587UNTS19	108507
Paraguay	IBRD (World Bank)	16 Dec 64	549UNTS173	107999
Japan	IBRD (World Bank)	23 Dec 64	538UNTS37	107809

PARTY ONE	PARTY TWO	DATE	CITATION	NUMBER
Roads and highways (Cont.)				
Mauritania	IDA (Devel Assoc)	28 Dec 64	540UNTS163	107849
Kenya	IDA (Devel Assoc)	29 Dec 64	535UNTS225	107782
Honduras	IBRD (World Bank)	02 Feb 65	561UNTS255	108188
Honduras	IDA (Devel Assoc)	02 Feb 65	561UNTS279	108189
Nigeria	IDA (Devel Assoc)	01 Mar 65	563UNTS3	108201
IDA (Devel Assoc)	Somalia	29 Mar 65	586UNTS101	108499
Jamaica	IBRD (World Bank)	08 Apr 65	539UNTS303	107841
Iran	IBRD (World Bank)	28 Apr 65	555UNTS21	108103
Iran	IBRD (World Bank)	28 Apr 65	555UNTS45	108104
Multilateral		29 Apr 65	586UNTS123	108500
Japan	IBRD (World Bank)	26 May 65	550UNTS95	108010
Jordan	UK Great Britain	08 Jun 65	552UNTS251	108057
Kenya	IDA (Devel Assoc)	30 Jun 65	554UNTS75	108097
Hungary	Poland	18 Jul 65	577UNTS161	108376
Multilateral		22 Jul 65	561UNTS333	200618
Nigeria	IBRD (World Bank)	26 Sep 65	571UNTS39	108298
Nigeria	IBRD (World Bank)	26 Sep 65	570UNTS233	108296
IDA (Devel Assoc)	UK Great Britain	08 Feb 66	567UNTS207	108257
Austria	Germany, West	17 Feb 66	615UNTS3	108876
Austria	Germany, West	17 Feb 66	614UNTS263	108875
Paraguay	IBRD (World Bank)	04 Apr 66	570UNTS41	108287
Finland	IBRD (World Bank)	27 Apr 66	568UNTS107	108266
IBRD (World Bank)	Thailand	24 Jun 66	582UNTS259	108466
Iraq	IBRD (World Bank)	22 Jul 66	584UNTS233	108480
Japan	IBRD (World Bank)	29 Jul 66	582UNTS209	108464
IDA (Devel Assoc)	Siam	02 Aug 66	585UNTS271	108492
Netherlands	Yugoslavia	08 Sep 66	597UNTS147	108643
Malawi	IDA (Devel Assoc)	04 Oct 66	584UNTS215	108479
IBRD (World Bank)	Zambia	04 Oct 66	585UNTS181	108489
Denmark	Romania	29 Aug 67	0UNTS0	109231
Czechoslovakia	Netherlands	15 Nov 67	0UNTS0	109223
Road rules				
Canada	USA (United States)	23 Mar 44	125UNTS345	200432
Multilateral		19 Sep 49	125UNTS3	101671
El Salvador	Guatemala	14 Dec 51	131UNTS131	101740
Belgium	France	21 Mar 52	137UNTS249	101856
France	Italy	14 Mar 53	284UNTS221	104140
United Arab Rep	USA (United States)	19 Mar 53	215UNTS17	102909
France	Netherlands	20 Jun 53	187UNTS97	102503
Multilateral		12 Mar 55	211UNTS3	102844
Italy	Yugoslavia	31 Mar 55	386UNTS307	105550
Germany, West	Sweden	05 Aug 55	262UNTS265	103754
Multilateral		19 May 56	399UNTS189	105742
Norway	Sweden	15 Sep 56	263UNTS17	103765
Finland	Sweden	15 Sep 56	254UNTS31	103591
Multilateral		08 Nov 56	470UNTS171	106809
Italy	Switzerland	19 Sep 57	363UNTS69	105200
Netherlands	Sweden	23 Oct 57	306UNTS75	104433
Denmark	Netherlands	13 Nov 57	306UNTS67	104432
Multilateral		13 Dec 57	372UNTS159	105296
Multilateral		03 Feb 58	381UNTS165	105471
Bulgaria	Yugoslavia	21 Mar 58	386UNTS119	105541
Bulgaria	Yugoslavia	21 Mar 58	349UNTS61	105009
Belgium	Sweden	08 May 58	312UNTS145	104516
Multilateral		10 Jun 58	454UNTS211	106541
Multilateral		10 Jun 58	454UNTS115	106540
Austria	Belgium	20 Jun 58	312UNTS95	104513
Multilateral		05 Nov 58	428UNTS73	106169
Austria	Netherlands	06 May 59	485UNTS153	107054
Greece	Yugoslavia	18 Jun 59	368UNTS27	105234
Italy	Netherlands	08 Dec 59	484UNTS309	107039
Multilateral		14 Dec 59	422UNTS75	106069
Poland	USSR (Soviet Union)	05 Feb 61	420UNTS161	106046
Italy	UK Great Britain	23 Oct 61	424UNTS225	106111

PARTY ONE	PARTY TWO	DATE	CITATION	NUMBER
Road rules (Cont.)				
Hungary	Yugoslavia	09 Feb 62	577UNTS3	108370
Germany, West	Greece	08 Mar 62	533UNTS269	107747
Czechoslovakia	Yugoslavia	22 Oct 62	480UNTS267	106974
Romania	Yugoslavia	25 Dec 63	576UNTS95	108366
Austria	Belgium	20 Jan 64	509UNTS275	107406
Austria	Romania	27 May 64	588UNTS29	108517
Czechoslovakia	Hungary	17 Oct 64	545UNTS21	107924
Greece	Yugoslavia	05 Nov 64	539UNTS19	107821
Hungary	Yugoslavia	08 Apr 65	587UNTS169	108511
Hungary	Poland	18 Jul 65	577UNTS161	108376
Belgium	Denmark	04 Feb 66	561UNTS233	108187
Austria	Germany, West	17 Feb 66	615UNTS3	108876
Austria	Germany, West	17 Feb 66	614UNTS263	108875
Austria	Spain	24 Mar 66	590UNTS203	108555
Belgium	Spain	19 Jul 66	575UNTS3	108352
Netherlands	Yugoslavia	08 Sep 66	597UNTS147	108643
Czechoslovakia	USSR (Soviet Union)	03 Feb 67	617UNTS267	108917
Finland	Hungary	10 Nov 67	643UNTS95	109186
Austria	Poland	05 Feb 68	0UNTS0	109213
Belgium	Poland	30 Oct 68	0UNTS0	109597
General communications				
Multilateral		22 Mar 45	70UNTS237	200241
Multilateral		10 Jun 58	454UNTS47	106539
Nigeria	USA (United States)	19 Oct 60	394UNTS113	105672
Multilateral		23 Mar 62	434UNTS145	106262
Israel	Uganda	04 Feb 63	484UNTS273	107037
Bulgaria	United Arab Rep	12 Feb 67	630UNTS363	108982
Bulgaria	United Arab Rep	12 Feb 67	630UNTS353	108981
UK Great Britain	USSR (Soviet Union)	24 Feb 67	606UNTS171	108785
Canada	Israel	05 Apr 67	0UNTS0	109350
Amateur radio				
Multilateral		12 May 40	101UNTS91	101405
Canada	USA (United States)	01 Apr 48	82UNTS99	101086
Multilateral		09 Jul 49	168UNTS143	102218
Liberia	USA (United States)	10 Jan 51	132UNTS255	101765
Canada	USA (United States)	08 Feb 51	207UNTS17	102797
Cuba	USA (United States)	27 Feb 52	168UNTS3	102209
Ecuador	USA (United States)	17 Mar 52	177UNTS115	102313
Canada	USA (United States)	17 Mar 53	236UNTS259	103329
Panama	USA (United States)	01 Aug 56	281UNTS49	104068
Nicaragua	USA (United States)	16 Oct 56	282UNTS29	104090
Costa Rica	USA (United States)	19 Oct 56	278UNTS65	104022
Mexico	USA (United States)	29 Jan 57	418UNTS253	106025
Germany, West	Netherlands	30 Jan 58	315UNTS117	104563
Mexico	USA (United States)	31 Jul 59	357UNTS187	105117
USA (United States)	Venezuela	12 Nov 59	367UNTS81	105227
Haiti	USA (United States)	06 Jan 60	367UNTS75	105226
Honduras	USA (United States)	19 Feb 60	371UNTS109	105273
Paraguay	USA (United States)	06 Oct 60	393UNTS281	105662
USA (United States)	Uruguay	12 Sep 61	607UNTS175	108805
Bolivia	USA (United States)	23 Oct 61	424UNTS93	106101
Canada	Venezuela	22 Nov 61	470UNTS148	106806
El Salvador	USA (United States)	05 Apr 62	442UNTS41	106337
Canada	Mexico	30 Jul 62	528UNTS257	107646
Canada	Chile	14 Oct 62	528UNTS273	107648
Canada	El Salvador	11 Mar 63	529UNTS25	107652
Dominican Republic	USA (United States)	22 Apr 63	487UNTS169	107101
Bolivia	Canada	31 May 63	529UNTS37	107654
Colombia	USA (United States)	29 Nov 63	494UNTS49	107225
Costa Rica	USA (United States)	24 Aug 64	531UNTS107	107696
Dominican Republic	USA (United States)	02 Feb 65	542UNTS117	107884
Bolivia	USA (United States)	16 Mar 65	542UNTS209	107891
Ecuador	USA (United States)	26 Mar 65	542UNTS237	107893
Portugal	USA (United States)	26 May 65	546UNTS189	107945

PARTY ONE	PARTY TWO	DATE	CITATION	NUMBER
Amateur radio (Cont.)				
Brazil	USA (United States)	01 Jun 65	546UNTS195	107946
Belgium	USA (United States)	18 Jun 65	549UNTS95	107992
Australia	USA (United States)	25 Jun 65	541UNTS155	107868
Israel	USA (United States)	07 Jul 65	549UNTS281	108004
Luxembourg	USA (United States)	29 Jul 65	573UNTS197	108332
Peru	USA (United States)	11 Aug 65	564UNTS135	108225
Sierra Leone	USA (United States)	16 Aug 65	579UNTS55	108398
Colombia	USA (United States)	28 Oct 65	574UNTS109	108343
UK Great Britain	USA (United States)	26 Nov 65	561UNTS193	108181
Paraguay	USA (United States)	18 Apr 66	586UNTS189	108503
France	USA (United States)	05 May 66	593UNTS279	108589
India	USA (United States)	25 May 66	593UNTS157	108582
Israel	USA (United States)	15 Jun 66	578UNTS159	108393
Netherlands	USA (United States)	22 Jun 66	590UNTS109	108550
Germany, West	USA (United States)	30 Jun 66	601UNTS107	108689
Kuwait	USA (United States)	24 Jul 66	593UNTS289	108590
Canada	Israel	12 Sep 66	581UNTS167	108440
Nicaragua	USA (United States)	20 Sep 66	607UNTS167	108804
Argentina	USA (United States)	31 Mar 67	636UNTS95	109095
Argentina	USA (United States)	31 Mar 67	636UNTS103	109096
Austria	Israel	03 Apr 67	630UNTS301	108976
Canada	Israel	05 Apr 67	0UNTS0	109350
Norway	USA (United States)	01 Jun 67	631UNTS119	108991
New Zealand	USA (United States)	21 Jun 67	0UNTS0	109205
Switzerland	UK Great Britain	29 Jun 67	617UNTS261	108916
Austria	USA (United States)	21 Nov 67	634UNTS43	109049
France	UK Great Britain	22 Nov 67	643UNTS225	109194
Commercial and public radio				
Canada	USA (United States)	17 Jan 44	109UNTS199	200360
Ceylon (Sri Lanka)	UK Great Britain	28 Feb 49	314UNTS269	104551
Ceylon (Sri Lanka)	USA (United States)	14 May 51	141UNTS159	101913
Germany, West	USA (United States)	11 Jun 52	273UNTS105	103947
Mexico	UK Great Britain	12 Jun 52	196UNTS149	102622
Syria	UK Great Britain	05 Feb 54	204UNTS267	102761
Iceland	USA (United States)	20 Jul 55	256UNTS245	103634
Mexico	USA (United States)	29 Jan 57	418UNTS253	106025
Cyprus	USA (United States)	23 Apr 63	487UNTS291	107111
Israel	USA (United States)	21 May 63	487UNTS319	107113
Saudi Arabia	USA (United States)	06 Jan 64	531UNTS3	107689
USA (United States)	Vietnam, South	03 Jan 66	579UNTS99	108401
Amateur third party message				
Multilateral		09 Jul 49	168UNTS143	102218
Liberia	USA (United States)	10 Jan 51	132UNTS255	101765
Cuba	USA (United States)	27 Feb 52	168UNTS3	102209
Ecuador	USA (United States)	17 Mar 52	177UNTS115	102313
Mexico	UK Great Britain	12 Jun 52	196UNTS149	102622
Panama	USA (United States)	01 Aug 56	281UNTS49	104068
Nicaragua	USA (United States)	16 Oct 56	282UNTS29	104090
Costa Rica	USA (United States)	19 Oct 56	278UNTS65	104022
Mexico	USA (United States)	31 Jul 59	357UNTS187	105117
USA (United States)	Venezuela	12 Nov 59	367UNTS81	105227
Haiti	USA (United States)	06 Jan 60	367UNTS75	105226
Honduras	USA (United States)	19 Feb 60	371UNTS109	105273
Paraguay	USA (United States)	06 Oct 60	393UNTS281	105662
USA (United States)	Uruguay	12 Sep 61	607UNTS175	108805
Bolivia	USA (United States)	23 Oct 61	424UNTS93	106101
Canada	Venezuela	22 Nov 61	470UNTS148	106806
El Salvador	USA (United States)	05 Apr 62	442UNTS41	106337
Canada	Mexico	30 Jul 62	528UNTS257	107646
Canada	Chile	14 Oct 62	528UNTS273	107648
Dominican Republic	USA (United States)	22 Apr 63	487UNTS169	107101
Bolivia	Canada	31 May 63	529UNTS37	107654
Colombia	USA (United States)	29 Nov 63	494UNTS49	107225
Brazil	USA (United States)	01 Jun 65	546UNTS195	107946

PARTY ONE	PARTY TWO	DATE	CITATION	NUMBER
Amateur third party message (Cont.)				
Belgium	USA (United States)	18 Jun 65	549UNTS95	107992
Israel	USA (United States)	07 Jul 65	549UNTS281	108004
Luxembourg	USA (United States)	29 Jul 65	573UNTS197	108332
Peru	USA (United States)	11 Aug 65	564UNTS135	108225
UK Great Britain	USA (United States)	26 Nov 65	561UNTS193	108181
Argentina	USA (United States)	31 Mar 67	636UNTS103	109096
Bands and frequency allocation				
Canada	USA (United States)	17 Jan 44	109UNTS199	200360
Belgium	UK Great Britain	11 Mar 46	26UNTS167	100387
Sweden	USA (United States)	30 Sep 46	42UNTS213	100649
Norway	USA (United States)	12 Nov 46	42UNTS227	100651
Australia	USA (United States)	10 Mar 47	10UNTS89	100145
Thailand	USA (United States)	08 May 47	42UNTS241	100653
Italy	USA (United States)	09 Jun 47	104UNTS157	101437
Multilateral		02 Oct 47	193UNTS188	102616
UK Great Britain	USA (United States)	13 Oct 47	66UNTS269	100858
Canada	USA (United States)	15 Oct 47	82UNTS53	101085
Canada	USA (United States)	01 Apr 48	82UNTS99	101086
Multilateral		17 Sep 48	97UNTS31	101345
France	USA (United States)	19 Oct 48	98UNTS3	101355
Panama	USA (United States)	31 Mar 49	55UNTS87	100810
Multilateral		09 Jul 49	168UNTS143	102218
Philippines	USA (United States)	16 Mar 50	89UNTS199	101218
Spain	Sweden	12 Oct 50	197UNTS305	102644
Ceylon (Sri Lanka)	USA (United States)	14 May 51	141UNTS159	101913
Mexico	USA (United States)	10 Aug 51	152UNTS27	102009
Cuba	USA (United States)	18 Dec 51	165UNTS3	102164
Canada	USA (United States)	21 Feb 52	205UNTS293	102781
Denmark	USA (United States)	04 Apr 52	177UNTS13	102305
Greece	USA (United States)	25 Jun 52	181UNTS53	102398
Canada	USA (United States)	03 May 54	221UNTS339	103015
Sweden	USSR (Soviet Union)	29 Sep 54	202UNTS259	102733
Multilateral		23 Oct 54	332UNTS3	104760
UK Great Britain	USA (United States)	15 Nov 55	231UNTS185	103219
UK Great Britain	USA (United States)	25 Jun 56	249UNTS59	103501
Multilateral		11 Sep 56	266UNTS221	103832
Norway	USSR (Soviet Union)	19 Oct 56	257UNTS3	103644
Finland	USSR (Soviet Union)	07 Dec 56	258UNTS89	103673
Mexico	USA (United States)	29 Jan 57	418UNTS253	106025
Mexico	USA (United States)	16 Jul 58	335UNTS139	104782
Canada	USA (United States)	07 Jan 59	391UNTS207	105624
Nigeria	USA (United States)	19 Oct 60	394UNTS113	105672
Multilateral		13 Dec 60	523UNTS117	107557
UK Great Britain	USA (United States)	20 Jan 61	402UNTS153	105783
UK Great Britain	USA (United States)	06 Apr 61	404UNTS215	105812
Mexico	USA (United States)	18 Apr 62	452UNTS3	106501
Canada	USA (United States)	24 Oct 62	462UNTS67	106672
Philippines	USA (United States)	06 May 63	477UNTS67	106916
USA (United States)	USSR (Soviet Union)	14 Dec 64	531UNTS213	107705
Multilateral		22 Jan 65	634UNTS239	109066
Mexico	USA (United States)	27 Feb 65	542UNTS181	107889
Spain	USA (United States)	14 Apr 66	579UNTS173	108406
Facilities and equipment				
Multilateral		12 May 40	101UNTS91	101405
Multilateral		02 Aug 44	67UNTS221	200221
Denmark	Norway	07 Aug 45	10UNTS203	200062
Mexico	USA (United States)	12 Apr 46	66UNTS293	100861
USA (United States)	USSR (Soviet Union)	24 May 46	4UNTS201	100046
UK Great Britain	USA (United States)	31 Jul 46	42UNTS199	100648
Sweden	USA (United States)	30 Sep 46	42UNTS213	100649
Denmark	USA (United States)	01 Oct 46	42UNTS219	100650
Philippines	USA (United States)	19 Oct 46	43UNTS263	100672
Norway	USA (United States)	12 Nov 46	42UNTS227	100651
Peru	USA (United States)	27 Dec 46	152UNTS93	102013

PARTY ONE	PARTY TWO	DATE	CITATION	NUMBER
Facilities and equipment (Cont.)				
Denmark	UK Great Britain	20 Jan 47	118UNTS73	101597
USSR (Soviet Union)	Yugoslavia	04 Feb 47	130UNTS235	101731
Australia	USA (United States)	10 Mar 47	10UNTS89	100145
Philippines	USA (United States)	14 Mar 47	43UNTS271	100673
Muscat and Oman	UK Great Britain	05 Apr 47	27UNTS287	100412
Thailand	USA (United States)	08 May 47	42UNTS241	100653
Norway	UK Great Britain	05 Jun 47	54UNTS181	100803
Italy	USA (United States)	09 Jun 47	104UNTS157	101437
UK Great Britain	USA (United States)	13 Oct 47	66UNTS269	100858
Cuba	USA (United States)	27 Jan 48	67UNTS3	100862
Canada	USA (United States)	31 Mar 48	81UNTS285	101077
Hungary	Poland	13 May 48	25UNTS301	100369
Multilateral		10 Jun 48	164UNTS113	102163
Multilateral		18 Aug 48	33UNTS181	100518
France	USA (United States)	19 Oct 48	98UNTS3	101355
Multilateral		28 Feb 49	29UNTS53	100434
Ceylon (Sri Lanka)	UK Great Britain	28 Feb 49	314UNTS269	104551
Panama	USA (United States)	31 Mar 49	55UNTS125	100811
Panama	USA (United States)	31 Mar 49	55UNTS87	100810
Czechoslovakia	Poland	02 Jul 49	260UNTS149	103708
Czechoslovakia	Poland	02 Jul 49	260UNTS179	103709
Multilateral		09 Jul 49	168UNTS143	102218
Philippines	USA (United States)	16 Mar 50	89UNTS199	101218
UK Great Britain	USA (United States)	21 Jul 50	97UNTS193	101351
Canada	USA (United States)	08 Feb 51	207UNTS17	102797
Ceylon (Sri Lanka)	USA (United States)	14 May 51	141UNTS159	101913
Mexico	USA (United States)	10 Aug 51	152UNTS27	102009
UK Great Britain	USA (United States)	15 Jan 52	127UNTS3	101697
Canada	USA (United States)	21 Feb 52	205UNTS293	102781
Germany, West	USA (United States)	11 Jun 52	273UNTS105	103947
Canada	USA (United States)	23 Jun 52	207UNTS25	102798
Greece	USA (United States)	25 Jun 52	181UNTS53	102398
Mexico	USA (United States)	15 Jul 52	181UNTS263	102416
Canada	USA (United States)	08 Nov 52	207UNTS3	102796
Canada	USA (United States)	05 Dec 52	206UNTS11	102783
Syria	Turkey	28 Apr 53	204UNTS255	102760
Ethiopia	USA (United States)	22 May 53	191UNTS59	102577
Libya	UK Great Britain	29 Jul 53	186UNTS201	102492
Luxembourg	USA (United States)	17 Aug 53	234UNTS219	103284
Iceland	IBRD (World Bank)	04 Sep 53	188UNTS3	102519
Cuba	USA (United States)	26 Nov 53	205UNTS213	102777
Greece	USA (United States)	18 Aug 54	234UNTS161	103282
Ceylon (Sri Lanka)	USA (United States)	23 Aug 54	314UNTS297	104553
Multilateral		23 Oct 54	332UNTS3	104760
Netherlands	USA (United States)	21 Mar 55	289UNTS129	104217
UK Great Britain	USA (United States)	15 Nov 55	231UNTS185	103219
Norway	USSR (Soviet Union)	31 Mar 56	259UNTS205	103690
Denmark	USSR (Soviet Union)	31 Mar 56	259UNTS169	103689
Sweden	USSR (Soviet Union)	31 Mar 56	259UNTS239	103691
France	USA (United States)	06 Sep 56	335UNTS173	104784
Dominican Republic	USA (United States)	09 Mar 57	279UNTS249	104044
Greece	Italy	02 Aug 57	533UNTS217	107744
Austria	IAEA (Atom Energy)	11 Dec 57	339UNTS110	104849
Czechoslovakia	Poland	31 Jan 58	431UNTS99	106214
Canada	USA (United States)	07 Jan 59	391UNTS207	105624
Canada	USA (United States)	13 Apr 59	342UNTS43	104899
Canada	USA (United States)	13 Jul 59	353UNTS237	105045
Pakistan	USA (United States)	18 Jul 59	355UNTS367	105087
Liberia	USA (United States)	13 Aug 59	357UNTS181	105116
Japan	USA (United States)	19 Jan 60	373UNTS207	105321
Multilateral		26 Feb 60	418UNTS171	106022
Spain	USA (United States)	18 Mar 60	372UNTS13	105284
Mexico	USA (United States)	12 Apr 60	372UNTS47	105287
UK Great Britain	USA (United States)	24 Jun 60	377UNTS63	105396
Denmark	USA (United States)	07 Jul 60	380UNTS39	105449

PARTY ONE	PARTY TWO	DATE	CITATION	NUMBER
Facilities and equipment (Cont.)				
South Africa	USA (United States)	13 Sep 60	388UNTS65	105572
UK Great Britain	USA (United States)	14 Oct 60	398UNTS165	105721
Nigeria	USA (United States)	19 Oct 60	394UNTS113	105672
Finland	Sweden	21 Nov 60	383UNTS125	105498
UK Great Britain	USA (United States)	20 Jan 61	402UNTS153	105783
UK Great Britain	USA (United States)	15 Mar 61	404UNTS207	105811
UK Great Britain	USA (United States)	29 Mar 61	405UNTS107	105826
France	USA (United States)	31 Mar 61	409UNTS136	105881
UK Great Britain	USA (United States)	06 Apr 61	404UNTS215	105812
Australia	USA (United States)	09 May 61	409UNTS203	105886
Australia	USA (United States)	05 Jun 61	409UNTS279	105892
Germany, West	USA (United States)	29 Sep 61	424UNTS113	106103
Brazil	USA (United States)	27 Oct 61	433UNTS113	106234
Mexico	USA (United States)	18 Apr 62	452UNTS3	106501
Czechoslovakia	Poland	16 Nov 62	526UNTS3	107597
Philippines	USA (United States)	11 Jan 63	473UNTS43	106853
New Zealand	Western Samoa	24 Jan 63	499UNTS21	107290
Belgium	USA (United States)	19 Apr 63	476UNTS29	106900
Philippines	USA (United States)	06 May 63	477UNTS67	106916
Australia	USA (United States)	09 May 63	475UNTS331	106897
Malagasy	USA (United States)	07 Oct 63	494UNTS3	107221
UK Great Britain	USA (United States)	11 Oct 63	483UNTS3	107005
Czechoslovakia	Hungary	22 Oct 63	514UNTS95	107444
Australia	USA (United States)	03 Jan 64	505UNTS159	107371
Mexico	USA (United States)	14 Feb 64	524UNTS197	107574
Mexico	USA (United States)	14 Feb 64	524UNTS197	107574
Nigeria	IBRD (World Bank)	12 Mar 64	516UNTS325	107480
Netherlands	NATO (North Atlan)	25 May 64	544UNTS237	107920
Canada	USA (United States)	16 Sep 64	530UNTS267	107687
Mexico	USA (United States)	27 Feb 65	542UNTS181	107889
Saudi Arabia	USA (United States)	05 Jun 65	548UNTS285	107984
USA (United States)	Vietnam, South	03 Jan 66	579UNTS99	108401
Spain	USA (United States)	14 Apr 66	579UNTS173	108406
Asian Devel Bank	Philippines	22 Dec 66	615UNTS375	108887
Indonesia	Philippines	21 Feb 67	593UNTS109	108578
Communications linkage				
Multilateral		27 Dec 45	2UNTS39	100020
Canada	USA (United States)	31 Mar 48	81UNTS285	101077
Multilateral		12 Aug 49	87UNTS131	101169
Sweden	USSR (Soviet Union)	29 Sep 54	202UNTS259	102733
Finland	USSR (Soviet Union)	07 Dec 56	258UNTS89	103673
Canada	USA (United States)	13 Jul 59	353UNTS237	105045
Pakistan	USA (United States)	18 Jul 59	355UNTS367	105087
USA (United States)	USSR (Soviet Union)	20 Jun 63	472UNTS163	106839
Argentina	Bolivia	19 Dec 66	636UNTS89	109094
Indonesia	Philippines	21 Feb 67	593UNTS109	108578
UK Great Britain	USSR (Soviet Union)	24 Feb 67	606UNTS171	108785
Interference of broadcasts				
Multilateral		02 Oct 47	193UNTS188	102616
Canada	USA (United States)	15 Oct 47	82UNTS53	101085
Multilateral		09 Jul 49	168UNTS143	102218
Mexico	USA (United States)	29 Jan 57	418UNTS253	106025
Malagasy	USA (United States)	07 Oct 63	494UNTS3	107221
Mail and money orders				
India	UK Great Britain	07 Dec 49	281UNTS245	104082
Ceylon (Sri Lanka)	India	30 Apr 51	196UNTS199	102625
Australia	USA (United States)	20 Jun 58	336UNTS97	104802
Multilateral		10 Jul 64	612UNTS361	108849
Multilateral		10 Jul 64	611UNTS105	108845
Multilateral		10 Jul 64	612UNTS233	108848
Japan	UK Great Britain	22 Feb 65	560UNTS123	108171
India	Japan	24 Feb 65	570UNTS3	108284
Korea, South	USA (United States)	09 Feb 67	0UNTS0	109605
Czechoslovakia	USSR (Soviet Union)	23 Nov 67	0UNTS0	109224

PARTY ONE	PARTY TWO	DATE	CITATION	NUMBER
Postal services				
Brazil	Portugal	30 Apr 42	65UNTS183	200210
UK Great Britain	USA (United States)	10 May 43	147UNTS109	200473
Multilateral		15 Jan 44	161UNTS281	200489
Canada	USA (United States)	17 Feb 45	122UNTS261	200409
Portugal	UK Great Britain	01 Jul 45	5UNTS263	200034
Guatemala	USA (United States)	25 Oct 45	139UNTS45	101875
Lebanon	USA (United States)	21 Jan 46	140UNTS73	101884
Belgium	UK Great Britain	11 Mar 46	26UNTS167	100387
Czechoslovakia	USSR (Soviet Union)	25 Jul 46	27UNTS231	100409
Canada	Newfoundland	29 Jul 46	17UNTS169	100275
Ceylon (Sri Lanka)	India	12 Aug 46	196UNTS209	102626
Philippines	USA (United States)	14 Mar 47	43UNTS271	100673
Hungary	Poland	28 Aug 47	15UNTS145	100231
Czechoslovakia	Netherlands	01 Sep 47	32UNTS129	100495
Philippines	USA (United States)	17 Sep 47	206UNTS249	102790
Sweden	Yugoslavia	06 Oct 47	53UNTS107	100775
Burma	UK Great Britain	17 Oct 47	70UNTS183	100904
Luxembourg	UK Great Britain	27 May 48	53UNTS115	100776
Burma	Pakistan	22 Jun 48	91UNTS197	101252
Luxembourg	Netherlands	23 Jun 48	32UNTS229	100500
New Zealand	Pakistan	28 Jun 48	91UNTS235	101253
France	UK Great Britain	12 Jul 48	90UNTS83	101230
France	Spain	23 Aug 48	28UNTS173	100425
Italy	USSR (Soviet Union)	11 Dec 48	217UNTS181	102948
Ceylon (Sri Lanka)	Pakistan	15 Dec 48	91UNTS303	101255
Korea, South	USA (United States)	17 Feb 49	74UNTS167	100963
Italy	Spain	31 May 49	231UNTS251	103224
Lebanon	UK Great Britain	20 Jun 49	90UNTS137	101232
Multilateral		12 Aug 49	75UNTS287	100973
Australia	Philippines	01 Sep 49	46UNTS215	100711
United Nations	Switzerland	14 Sep 49	43UNTS327	200183
Greece	UK Great Britain	17 Oct 49	93UNTS185	101300
Colombia	UK Great Britain	13 Dec 49	88UNTS133	101189
UK Great Britain	Yugoslavia	09 Feb 50	88UNTS287	101200
UK Great Britain	USA (United States)	21 Jul 50	97UNTS193	101351
Spain	Switzerland	03 Aug 50	254UNTS365	103600
USA (United States)	Yugoslavia	14 Aug 50	137UNTS131	101851
Czechoslovakia	USA (United States)	29 Sep 50	290UNTS3	104227
Sweden	UK Great Britain	17 Jan 51	93UNTS225	101301
United Nations	USA (United States)	28 Mar 51	108UNTS231	101476
Ceylon (Sri Lanka)	India	30 Apr 51	196UNTS199	102625
India	UK Great Britain	05 Jun 51	135UNTS3	101811
Pakistan	UK Great Britain	26 Sep 51	118UNTS221	101608
Philippines	Spain	06 Oct 51	215UNTS193	102920
Netherlands	UK Great Britain	30 Nov 51	123UNTS177	101659
Colombia	Spain	11 Dec 51	216UNTS73	102933
UK Great Britain	USA (United States)	15 Jan 52	127UNTS3	101697
Japan	USA (United States)	28 Feb 52	208UNTS255	102817
Belgium	Spain	10 Mar 52	178UNTS243	102342
Canada	USA (United States)	19 Mar 52	174UNTS267	102291
Australia	USA (United States)	27 May 52	178UNTS113	102338
Multilateral		11 Jul 52	171UNTS3	102224
Multilateral		11 Jul 52	170UNTS269	102223
Multilateral		11 Jul 52	171UNTS191	102227
Multilateral		11 Jul 52	170UNTS3	102221
Multilateral		11 Jul 52	170UNTS63	102222
Multilateral		11 Jul 52	169UNTS3	102220
Multilateral		11 Jul 52	171UNTS143	102226
Pakistan	UK Great Britain	22 Jul 52	157UNTS185	102054
Ethiopia	USA (United States)	22 May 53	191UNTS59	102577
Libya	UK Great Britain	29 Jul 53	186UNTS201	102492
Greece	USA (United States)	12 Oct 53	191UNTS319	102589
Australia	Netherlands	22 Oct 53	184UNTS193	102448
Italy	South Africa	20 Dec 53	277UNTS293	104014

PARTY ONE	PARTY TWO	DATE	CITATION	NUMBER
Postal services (Cont.)				
Peru	Spain	31 Mar 54	232UNTS65	103230
Australia	Greece	24 May 54	191UNTS255	102586
Australia	Israel	18 Jun 54	220UNTS29	102985
India	USA (United States)	29 Jul 54	239UNTS69	103373
Canada	South Africa	04 Aug 54	261UNTS3	103722
Libya	USA (United States)	09 Sep 54	224UNTS217	103078
Multilateral		23 Oct 54	332UNTS3	104760
Australia	Poland	25 Nov 54	521UNTS281	107526
Australia	Austria	20 Dec 54	205UNTS157	102775
Israel	South Africa	31 Dec 54	220UNTS11	102984
Australia	Hungary	10 Feb 55	207UNTS173	102806
Australia	Taiwan	22 Mar 55	209UNTS3	102818
Australia	Czechoslovakia	01 Apr 55	213UNTS199	102888
Spain	USA (United States)	16 Jul 55	270UNTS211	103899
Ceylon (Sri Lanka)	USA (United States)	18 Jul 55	281UNTS295	104086
Pakistan	USA (United States)	20 Jul 55	241UNTS255	103436
Bulgaria	Yugoslavia	15 Nov 55	396UNTS191	105697
Korea, North	Romania	05 Dec 55	362UNTS163	105187
Romania	Yugoslavia	13 Jan 56	342UNTS265	104912
Australia	Yugoslavia	28 Feb 56	243UNTS53	103446
Nicaragua	USA (United States)	19 Mar 56	275UNTS231	103984
Canada	Japan	20 Mar 56	517UNTS33	107482
Bulgaria	Yugoslavia	22 May 56	367UNTS119	105229
Canada	UK Great Britain	21 Jun 56	381UNTS111	105467
UK Great Britain	USA (United States)	25 Jun 56	249UNTS59	103501
Canada	UK Great Britain	20 Oct 56	381UNTS99	105466
UK Great Britain	USA (United States)	01 Nov 56	264UNTS3	103785
Canada	UK Great Britain	16 Nov 56	412UNTS166	105930
UK Great Britain	USA (United States)	27 Nov 56	282UNTS43	104092
Liberia	USA (United States)	16 Mar 57	290UNTS59	104228
Greece	Yugoslavia	22 Apr 57	391UNTS109	105619
Taiwan	USA (United States)	30 Jul 57	300UNTS61	104331
Albania	Yugoslavia	29 Aug 57	391UNTS167	105622
Albania	Yugoslavia	29 Aug 57	391UNTS127	105621
Austria	South Africa	26 Sep 57	287UNTS3	104176
Multilateral		03 Oct 57	365UNTS3	105213
Multilateral		03 Oct 57	366UNTS141	105217
Multilateral		03 Oct 57	365UNTS207	105214
Multilateral		03 Oct 57	366UNTS193	105218
Multilateral		03 Oct 57	364UNTS3	105211
Multilateral		03 Oct 57	366UNTS255	105219
Taiwan	USA (United States)	08 Oct 57	304UNTS241	104400
UK Great Britain	USA (United States)	01 Nov 57	299UNTS167	104312
Lebanon	United Nations	20 Jan 58	286UNTS189	104166
Lebanon	United Nations	20 Jan 58	286UNTS199	104167
Australia	USA (United States)	20 Jun 58	336UNTS97	104802
Australia	Netherlands	23 Jul 58	328UNTS227	104736
Japan	USA (United States)	03 Nov 58	341UNTS83	104879
Portugal	USA (United States)	12 Jan 59	343UNTS49	104921
United Arab Rep	USA (United States)	13 Jan 59	358UNTS3	105122
Japan	USA (United States)	19 Jan 60	373UNTS207	105321
France	Thailand	26 Feb 60	392UNTS279	105648
Ireland	South Africa	13 Apr 60	390UNTS307	105612
New Zealand	Philippines	09 May 60	486UNTS65	107073
UK Great Britain	USA (United States)	24 Jun 60	377UNTS63	105396
Australia	USSR (Soviet Union)	29 Jun 60	392UNTS131	105641
Korea, South	USA (United States)	17 Aug 60	400UNTS339	105757
Canada	USA (United States)	13 Jan 61	410UNTS62	105897
Multilateral		23 Jan 61	530UNTS141	107679
Japan	Pakistan	07 Mar 61	450UNTS359	106479
Philippines	USA (United States)	12 Mar 61	288UNTS285	104210
Thailand	USA (United States)	12 Jan 62	459UNTS95	106615
Jordan	UK Great Britain	28 Feb 62	466UNTS249	106748
Australia	Japan	01 Mar 62	517UNTS81	107483
Australia	Germany, West	19 Mar 62	488UNTS203	107130

PARTY ONE	PARTY TWO	DATE	CITATION	NUMBER
Postal services (Cont.)				
Israel	Netherlands	28 May 62	448UNTS219	106434
Thailand	USA (United States)	31 May 62	459UNTS135	106619
Multilateral		16 Oct 62	470UNTS321	106815
Multilateral		16 Oct 62	470UNTS336	106816
Multilateral		16 Oct 62	470UNTS291	106814
Australia	UK Great Britain	06 Dec 62	457UNTS145	106584
Japan	Philippines	19 Jan 63	517UNTS281	107489
Japan	New Zealand	15 Mar 63	517UNTS229	107487
Japan	South Africa	06 Apr 63	484UNTS319	107040
Australia	USA (United States)	09 May 63	469UNTS55	106784
Congo (Zaire)	USA (United States)	19 Jul 63	511UNTS47	107425
UK Great Britain	USA (United States)	11 Oct 63	483UNTS3	107005
Kuwait	USA (United States)	21 Oct 63	530UNTS281	107688
Multilateral		10 Jul 64	612UNTS3	108847
Multilateral		10 Jul 64	613UNTS3	108851
Multilateral		10 Jul 64	611UNTS105	108845
Multilateral		10 Jul 64	613UNTS193	108852
Philippines	USA (United States)	12 Nov 64	574UNTS159	108349
Japan	UK Great Britain	22 Feb 65	560UNTS123	108171
Multilateral		16 Dec 65	570UNTS201	108295
United Nations	Senegal	12 Jan 66	551UNTS147	108039
Guyana	UK Great Britain	26 May 66	595UNTS255	108621
UK Great Britain	USA (United States)	30 Dec 66	603UNTS245	108736
Finland	United Nations	16 Jan 67	588UNTS153	108522
Czechoslovakia	USSR (Soviet Union)	23 Nov 67	0UNTS0	109224
Regulations				
UK Great Britain	USA (United States)	10 May 43	147UNTS109	200473
Multilateral		15 Jan 44	161UNTS281	200489
Portugal	UK Great Britain	01 Jul 45	5UNTS263	200034
Guatemala	USA (United States)	25 Oct 45	139UNTS45	101875
Lebanon	USA (United States)	21 Jan 46	140UNTS73	101884
Ceylon (Sri Lanka)	India	12 Aug 46	196UNTS209	102626
South Africa	UK Great Britain	24 Aug 46	51UNTS187	100765
Philippines	USA (United States)	17 Sep 47	206UNTS249	102790
Philippines	UK Great Britain	07 Jan 48	28UNTS63	100420
New Zealand	Pakistan	17 Sep 48	91UNTS275	101254
Czechoslovakia	Poland	12 Nov 48	84UNTS347	101141
Korea, South	USA (United States)	17 Feb 49	74UNTS167	100963
Czechoslovakia	Poland	02 Jul 49	260UNTS179	103709
Australia	Philippines	01 Sep 49	46UNTS215	100711
USA (United States)	Yugoslavia	14 Aug 50	137UNTS131	101851
Czechoslovakia	USA (United States)	29 Sep 50	290UNTS3	104227
Ceylon (Sri Lanka)	India	30 Apr 51	196UNTS199	102625
UK Great Britain	USA (United States)	03 Jun 51	137UNTS81	101850
India	UK Great Britain	05 Jun 51	135UNTS3	101811
Netherlands	UK Great Britain	30 Nov 51	123UNTS177	101659
Australia	Pakistan	16 Jan 52	151UNTS281	102001
Australia	USA (United States)	27 May 52	178UNTS113	102338
Multilateral		11 Jul 52	171UNTS3	102224
Multilateral		11 Jul 52	171UNTS143	102226
Multilateral		11 Jul 52	170UNTS269	102223
Multilateral		11 Jul 52	170UNTS63	102222
Multilateral		11 Jul 52	171UNTS191	102227
Multilateral		11 Jul 52	169UNTS3	102220
Multilateral		11 Jul 52	171UNTS89	102225
Multilateral		11 Jul 52	170UNTS3	102221
Israel	Switzerland	01 Jul 53	220UNTS41	102986
Australia	Netherlands	22 Oct 53	184UNTS193	102448
Italy	South Africa	20 Dec 53	277UNTS293	104014
Australia	Greece	24 May 54	191UNTS255	102586
Australia	Israel	18 Jun 54	220UNTS29	102985
India	USA (United States)	29 Jul 54	239UNTS69	103373
Canada	South Africa	04 Aug 54	261UNTS3	103722
Australia	Poland	25 Nov 54	521UNTS281	107526

PARTY ONE	PARTY TWO	DATE	CITATION	NUMBER
Regulations (Cont.)				
Australia	Austria	20 Dec 54	205UNTS157	102775
Israel	South Africa	31 Dec 54	220UNTS11	102984
Australia	Hungary	10 Feb 55	207UNTS173	102806
Australia	Taiwan	22 Mar 55	209UNTS3	102818
Australia	Czechoslovakia	01 Apr 55	213UNTS199	102888
Spain	USA (United States)	16 Jul 55	270UNTS211	103899
Ceylon (Sri Lanka)	USA (United States)	18 Jul 55	281UNTS295	104086
Pakistan	USA (United States)	20 Jul 55	241UNTS255	103436
Czechoslovakia	Germany, East	24 Oct 55	504UNTS173	107358
Bulgaria	Yugoslavia	15 Nov 55	396UNTS191	105697
Korea, North	Romania	05 Dec 55	362UNTS163	105187
Romania	Yugoslavia	13 Jan 56	342UNTS265	104912
Australia	Yugoslavia	28 Feb 56	243UNTS53	103446
Nicaragua	USA (United States)	19 Mar 56	275UNTS231	103984
Canada	Japan	20 Mar 56	517UNTS33	107482
Canada	UK Great Britain	16 Nov 56	412UNTS166	105930
Liberia	USA (United States)	16 Mar 57	290UNTS59	104228
Taiwan	USA (United States)	30 Jul 57	300UNTS61	104331
Albania	Yugoslavia	29 Aug 57	391UNTS127	105621
Austria	South Africa	26 Sep 57	287UNTS3	104176
Multilateral		03 Oct 57	365UNTS3	105213
Multilateral		03 Oct 57	364UNTS3	105211
Taiwan	USA (United States)	08 Oct 57	304UNTS241	104400
Czechoslovakia	Poland	31 Jan 58	431UNTS99	106214
USA (United States)	Yugoslavia	16 Jun 58	317UNTS31	104591
Australia	Netherlands	23 Jul 58	328UNTS227	104736
United Arab Rep	USA (United States)	31 Oct 58	355UNTS355	105086
Japan	USA (United States)	03 Nov 58	341UNTS83	104879
Ireland	South Africa	13 Apr 60	390UNTS307	105612
New Zealand	Philippines	09 May 60	486UNTS65	107073
Korea, South	USA (United States)	17 Aug 60	400UNTS339	105757
Australia	Japan	07 Feb 61	450UNTS343	106478
Japan	Pakistan	07 Mar 61	450UNTS359	106479
Philippines	USA (United States)	12 Mar 61	288UNTS285	104210
Morocco	USA (United States)	30 Nov 61	451UNTS167	106492
Thailand	USA (United States)	12 Jan 62	459UNTS95	106615
Australia	Japan	01 Mar 62	517UNTS81	107483
Australia	Germany, West	19 Mar 62	488UNTS203	107130
Thailand	USA (United States)	31 May 62	459UNTS135	106619
Austria	Czechoslovakia	22 Sep 62	495UNTS157	107244
Multilateral		16 Oct 62	470UNTS336	106816
Multilateral		16 Oct 62	470UNTS291	106814
Czechoslovakia	Poland	16 Nov 62	526UNTS3	107597
Australia	UK Great Britain	06 Dec 62	457UNTS145	106584
Austria	Yugoslavia	11 Dec 62	546UNTS3	107938
Japan	Philippines	19 Jan 63	517UNTS281	107489
Japan	New Zealand	15 Mar 63	517UNTS229	107487
Japan	South Africa	06 Apr 63	484UNTS319	107040
Australia	UK Great Britain	23 Sep 63	483UNTS39	107006
Kuwait	USA (United States)	21 Oct 63	530UNTS281	107688
Czechoslovakia	Hungary	22 Oct 63	514UNTS95	107444
Multilateral		10 Jul 64	611UNTS387	108846
Multilateral		10 Jul 64	613UNTS3	108851
Philippines	USA (United States)	12 Nov 64	574UNTS159	108349
Japan	UK Great Britain	22 Feb 65	560UNTS123	108171
India	Japan	24 Feb 65	570UNTS3	108284
Multilateral		16 Dec 65	570UNTS201	108295
Kuwait	UK Great Britain	29 Dec 66	617UNTS203	108914
Insured letters and boxes				
UK Great Britain	USA (United States)	10 May 43	147UNTS109	200473
Portugal	UK Great Britain	01 Jul 45	5UNTS263	200034
Guatemala	USA (United States)	25 Oct 45	139UNTS45	101875
Ceylon (Sri Lanka)	India	12 Aug 46	196UNTS209	102626
Burma	Pakistan	22 Jun 48	91UNTS197	101252

PARTY ONE	PARTY TWO	DATE	CITATION	NUMBER
Insured letters and boxes (Cont.)				
New Zealand	Pakistan	28 Jun 48	91UNTS235	101253
Ceylon (Sri Lanka)	Pakistan	15 Dec 48	91UNTS303	101255
USA (United States)	Yugoslavia	14 Aug 50	137UNTS131	101851
Czechoslovakia	USA (United States)	29 Sep 50	290UNTS3	104227
UK Great Britain	USA (United States)	03 Jun 51	137UNTS81	101850
Netherlands	UK Great Britain	30 Nov 51	123UNTS177	101659
Australia	Pakistan	16 Jan 52	151UNTS281	102001
Australia	USA (United States)	27 May 52	178UNTS113	102338
Multilateral		11 Jul 52	170UNTS3	102221
Multilateral		11 Jul 52	170UNTS63	102222
Multilateral		11 Jul 52	171UNTS89	102225
Israel	Switzerland	01 Jul 53	220UNTS41	102986
Australia	Netherlands	22 Oct 53	184UNTS193	102448
Australia	Greece	24 May 54	191UNTS255	102586
Australia	Israel	18 Jun 54	220UNTS29	102985
India	USA (United States)	29 Jul 54	239UNTS69	103373
Australia	Poland	25 Nov 54	521UNTS281	107526
Australia	Austria	20 Dec 54	205UNTS157	102775
Israel	South Africa	31 Dec 54	220UNTS11	102984
Australia	Hungary	10 Feb 55	207UNTS173	102806
Australia	Taiwan	22 Mar 55	209UNTS3	102818
Australia	Czechoslovakia	01 Apr 55	213UNTS199	102888
Spain	USA (United States)	16 Jul 55	270UNTS211	103899
Ceylon (Sri Lanka)	USA (United States)	18 Jul 55	281UNTS295	104086
Pakistan	USA (United States)	20 Jul 55	241UNTS255	103436
Bulgaria	Yugoslavia	15 Nov 55	396UNTS191	105697
Romania	Yugoslavia	13 Jan 56	342UNTS265	104912
Australia	Yugoslavia	28 Feb 56	243UNTS53	103446
Nicaragua	USA (United States)	19 Mar 56	275UNTS231	103984
Canada	Japan	20 Mar 56	517UNTS33	107482
Liberia	USA (United States)	16 Mar 57	290UNTS59	104228
Taiwan	USA (United States)	30 Jul 57	300UNTS61	104331
Albania	Yugoslavia	29 Aug 57	391UNTS167	105622
Multilateral		03 Oct 57	364UNTS3	105211
Multilateral		03 Oct 57	365UNTS3	105213
Multilateral		03 Oct 57	364UNTS331	105212
Japan	USA (United States)	03 Nov 58	341UNTS83	104879
Portugal	USA (United States)	12 Jan 59	343UNTS49	104921
United Arab Rep	USA (United States)	13 Jan 59	358UNTS3	105122
Hungary	Poland	06 Mar 59	432UNTS3	106216
Canada	Finland	28 Mar 59	355UNTS3	105072
Australia	USSR (Soviet Union)	29 Jun 60	392UNTS131	105641
Korea, South	USA (United States)	17 Aug 60	400UNTS339	105757
Canada	USA (United States)	13 Jan 61	410UNTS62	105897
Czechoslovakia	Poland	04 Jul 61	436UNTS189	106295
Czechoslovakia	Hungary	02 Nov 61	438UNTS3	106313
Australia	Japan	01 Mar 62	517UNTS81	107483
Australia	Germany, West	19 Mar 62	488UNTS203	107130
Thailand	USA (United States)	31 May 62	459UNTS135	106619
Japan	New Zealand	15 Mar 63	517UNTS229	107487
Kuwait	USA (United States)	21 Oct 63	530UNTS281	107688
Philippines	USA (United States)	12 Nov 64	574UNTS159	108349
Multilateral		16 Dec 65	570UNTS201	108295
Conveyance in transit				
Bolivia	Brazil	25 Feb 38	54UNTS333	200205
Brazil	Portugal	30 Apr 42	65UNTS183	200210
Portugal	UK Great Britain	01 Jul 45	5UNTS263	200034
Belgium	Netherlands	25 Mar 47	18UNTS309	100299
Burma	Pakistan	22 Jun 48	91UNTS197	101252
New Zealand	Pakistan	28 Jun 48	91UNTS235	101253
Korea, South	USA (United States)	17 Feb 49	74UNTS167	100963
Australia	Philippines	01 Sep 49	46UNTS215	100711
Afghanistan	India	14 Dec 49	53UNTS95	100774
USA (United States)	Yugoslavia	14 Aug 50	137UNTS131	101851

PARTY ONE	PARTY TWO	DATE	CITATION	NUMBER
Conveyance in transit (Cont.)				
Czechoslovakia	USA (United States)	29 Sep 50	290UNTS3	104227
UK Great Britain	USA (United States)	03 Jun 51	137UNTS81	101850
Australia	Pakistan	16 Jan 52	151UNTS281	102001
Australia	Netherlands	22 Oct 53	184UNTS193	102448
Bulgaria	Czechoslovakia	13 Apr 54	501UNTS3	107314
Australia	Greece	24 May 54	191UNTS255	102586
Australia	Israel	18 Jun 54	220UNTS29	102985
Canada	South Africa	04 Aug 54	261UNTS3	103722
Australia	Poland	25 Nov 54	521UNTS281	107526
Israel	South Africa	31 Dec 54	220UNTS11	102984
Australia	Hungary	10 Feb 55	207UNTS173	102806
Australia	Taiwan	22 Mar 55	209UNTS3	102818
Australia	Czechoslovakia	01 Apr 55	213UNTS199	102888
Israel	Italy	24 Feb 56	316UNTS97	104580
Bulgaria	Yugoslavia	23 Mar 56	367UNTS213	105230
Belgium	Israel	26 Mar 56	260UNTS3	103702
Israel	Luxembourg	26 Jul 56	550UNTS239	108020
Germany, East	Poland	01 Feb 57	319UNTS115	104632
Liberia	USA (United States)	16 Mar 57	290UNTS59	104228
Greece	Yugoslavia	22 Apr 57	391UNTS109	105619
Czechoslovakia	USSR (Soviet Union)	31 Aug 57	308UNTS3	104456
Austria	South Africa	26 Sep 57	287UNTS3	104176
Multilateral		03 Oct 57	364UNTS3	105211
Germany, East	Hungary	30 Oct 57	408UNTS4	105867
Germany, East	USSR (Soviet Union)	28 Nov 57	305UNTS113	104419
Bulgaria	USSR (Soviet Union)	12 Dec 57	317UNTS217	104606
Multilateral		13 Dec 57	359UNTS273	105146
Korea, North	USSR (Soviet Union)	16 Dec 57	301UNTS301	104349
Poland	USSR (Soviet Union)	28 Dec 57	320UNTS3	104638
Belgium	Germany, West	17 Jan 58	328UNTS173	104735
Romania	USSR (Soviet Union)	03 Apr 58	313UNTS167	104535
Albania	USSR (Soviet Union)	30 Jun 58	328UNTS3	104729
Hungary	USSR (Soviet Union)	15 Jul 58	322UNTS3	104656
Germany, East	Romania	15 Jul 58	395UNTS3	105681
Mongolia	USSR (Soviet Union)	25 Aug 58	322UNTS105	104657
Hungary	Romania	07 Oct 58	416UNTS199	106004
Czechoslovakia	Romania	25 Oct 58	417UNTS37	106006
Japan	USA (United States)	03 Nov 58	341UNTS83	104879
Bulgaria	Romania	03 Dec 58	417UNTS133	106007
Israel	Switzerland	31 Dec 58	377UNTS305	105408
Portugal	USA (United States)	12 Jan 59	343UNTS49	104921
United Arab Rep	USA (United States)	13 Jan 59	358UNTS3	105122
Albania	Czechoslovakia	16 Jan 59	363UNTS195	105208
Belgium	Morocco	27 Feb 59	390UNTS275	105611
Greece	Yugoslavia	18 Jun 59	368UNTS81	105236
Albania	Hungary	12 Jan 60	520UNTS3	107511
Poland	Yugoslavia	06 Feb 60	521UNTS37	107517
Hungary	Yugoslavia	07 May 60	519UNTS237	107510
Canada	USA (United States)	13 Jan 61	410UNTS62	105897
Brazil	USA (United States)	13 Jan 61	532UNTS177	107718
Argentina	Brazil	06 Jul 61	0UNTS0	109410
Sweden	USA (United States)	24 Oct 61	494UNTS141	107231
Bulgaria	Poland	04 Dec 61	484UNTS3	107019
Poland	Romania	25 Jan 62	468UNTS3	106770
Australia	Japan	01 Mar 62	517UNTS81	107483
Thailand	USA (United States)	31 May 62	459UNTS135	106619
Multilateral		27 Jun 62	616UNTS79	108893
Multilateral		16 Oct 62	470UNTS321	106815
Israel	USA (United States)	10 Dec 62	484UNTS283	107038
Japan	New Zealand	15 Mar 63	517UNTS229	107487
Japan	South Africa	06 Apr 63	484UNTS319	107040
Kuwait	USA (United States)	21 Oct 63	530UNTS281	107688
Czechoslovakia	Yugoslavia	20 Jan 64	538UNTS197	107816
Multilateral		03 Dec 65	572UNTS105	108309
Multilateral		16 Dec 65	570UNTS201	108295

PARTY ONE	PARTY TWO	DATE	CITATION	NUMBER
Conveyance in transit (Cont.)				
Czechoslovakia	USSR (Soviet Union)	23 Nov 67	0UNTS0	109224
Money orders and postal checks				
Australia	New Zealand	21 Jan 44	18UNTS357	200113
Lebanon	USA (United States)	21 Jan 46	140UNTS73	101884
USA (United States)	USSR (Soviet Union)	24 May 46	4UNTS201	100046
South Africa	UK Great Britain	24 Aug 46	51UNTS187	100765
Belgium	Netherlands	25 Mar 47	18UNTS309	100299
Multilateral		02 Oct 47	193UNTS188	102616
Bulgaria	UK Great Britain	13 Mar 48	104UNTS25	101432
France	UK Great Britain	12 Jul 48	90UNTS83	101230
New Zealand	Pakistan	17 Sep 48	91UNTS275	101254
Lebanon	UK Great Britain	20 Jun 49	90UNTS137	101232
Greece	UK Great Britain	17 Oct 49	93UNTS185	101300
India	UK Great Britain	07 Dec 49	281UNTS245	104082
Colombia	UK Great Britain	13 Dec 49	88UNTS133	101189
UK Great Britain	Yugoslavia	09 Feb 50	88UNTS287	101200
Sweden	UK Great Britain	17 Jan 51	93UNTS225	101301
India	UK Great Britain	05 Jun 51	135UNTS3	101811
Pakistan	United Arab Rep	08 Sep 51	133UNTS257	101793
Pakistan	UK Great Britain	26 Sep 51	118UNTS221	101608
Multilateral		11 Jul 52	171UNTS3	102224
Multilateral		11 Jul 52	171UNTS89	102225
Multilateral		11 Jul 52	170UNTS269	102223
Multilateral		11 Jul 52	171UNTS143	102226
Pakistan	UK Great Britain	22 Jul 52	157UNTS185	102054
Libya	UK Great Britain	29 Jul 53	186UNTS201	102492
Korea, North	Romania	05 Dec 55	362UNTS163	105187
Canada	UK Great Britain	21 Jun 56	381UNTS111	105467
Canada	UK Great Britain	20 Oct 56	381UNTS99	105466
Canada	UK Great Britain	16 Nov 56	412UNTS166	105930
Multilateral		03 Oct 57	366UNTS3	105215
Multilateral		03 Oct 57	365UNTS207	105214
Multilateral		03 Oct 57	366UNTS141	105217
Multilateral		03 Oct 57	366UNTS193	105218
Taiwan	USA (United States)	08 Oct 57	304UNTS241	104400
Australia	Netherlands	23 Jul 58	328UNTS227	104736
United Arab Rep	USA (United States)	31 Oct 58	355UNTS355	105086
Australia	Japan	07 Feb 61	450UNTS343	106478
Japan	Pakistan	07 Mar 61	450UNTS359	106479
Philippines	USA (United States)	12 Mar 61	288UNTS285	104210
Morocco	USA (United States)	30 Nov 61	451UNTS167	106492
Thailand	USA (United States)	12 Jan 62	459UNTS95	106615
Jordan	UK Great Britain	28 Feb 62	466UNTS249	106748
Multilateral		16 Oct 62	470UNTS321	106815
Multilateral		16 Oct 62	470UNTS291	106814
Australia	UK Great Britain	06 Dec 62	457UNTS145	106584
Australia	UK Great Britain	23 Sep 63	483UNTS39	107006
Multilateral		10 Jul 64	612UNTS361	108849
Multilateral		10 Jul 64	612UNTS233	108848
Philippines	USA (United States)	12 Nov 64	574UNTS159	108349
Japan	UK Great Britain	22 Feb 65	560UNTS123	108171
India	Japan	24 Feb 65	570UNTS3	108284
Australia	Germany, West	08 Jul 65	543UNTS305	107907
Multilateral		16 Dec 65	570UNTS201	108295
Kuwait	UK Great Britain	29 Dec 66	617UNTS203	108914
UK Great Britain	Yugoslavia	30 Jun 67	642UNTS325	109182
Parcel post				
UK Great Britain	USA (United States)	10 May 43	147UNTS109	200473
Portugal	UK Great Britain	01 Jul 45	5UNTS263	200034
Guatemala	USA (United States)	25 Oct 45	139UNTS45	101875
USA (United States)	USSR (Soviet Union)	24 May 46	4UNTS201	100046
Ceylon (Sri Lanka)	India	12 Aug 46	196UNTS209	102626
Philippines	USA (United States)	17 Sep 47	206UNTS249	102790
Burma	Pakistan	22 Jun 48	91UNTS197	101252

PARTY ONE	PARTY TWO	DATE	CITATION	NUMBER
Parcel post (Cont.)				
New Zealand	Pakistan	28 Jun 48	91UNTS235	101253
Ceylon (Sri Lanka)	Pakistan	15 Dec 48	91UNTS303	101255
Korea, South	USA (United States)	17 Feb 49	74UNTS167	100963
Australia	Philippines	01 Sep 49	46UNTS215	100711
USA (United States)	Yugoslavia	14 Aug 50	137UNTS131	101851
Czechoslovakia	USA (United States)	29 Sep 50	290UNTS3	104227
UK Great Britain	USA (United States)	03 Jun 51	137UNTS81	101850
Australia	Pakistan	16 Jan 52	151UNTS281	102001
Australia	USA (United States)	27 May 52	178UNTS113	102338
Multilateral		11 Jul 52	170UNTS63	102222
Israel	Switzerland	01 Jul 53	220UNTS41	102986
Australia	Netherlands	22 Oct 53	184UNTS193	102448
Italy	South Africa	20 Dec 53	277UNTS293	104014
Australia	Greece	24 May 54	191UNTS255	102586
Australia	Israel	18 Jun 54	220UNTS29	102985
India	USA (United States)	29 Jul 54	239UNTS69	103373
Canada	South Africa	04 Aug 54	261UNTS3	103722
Australia	Poland	25 Nov 54	521UNTS281	107526
Australia	Austria	20 Dec 54	205UNTS157	102775
Israel	South Africa	31 Dec 54	220UNTS11	102984
Australia	Hungary	10 Feb 55	207UNTS173	102806
Australia	Taiwan	22 Mar 55	209UNTS3	102818
Australia	Czechoslovakia	01 Apr 55	213UNTS199	102888
Spain	USA (United States)	16 Jul 55	270UNTS211	103899
Ceylon (Sri Lanka)	USA (United States)	18 Jul 55	281UNTS295	104086
Pakistan	USA (United States)	20 Jul 55	241UNTS255	103436
Bulgaria	Yugoslavia	15 Nov 55	396UNTS191	105697
Korea, North	Romania	05 Dec 55	362UNTS163	105187
Romania	Yugoslavia	13 Jan 56	342UNTS265	104912
Australia	Yugoslavia	28 Feb 56	243UNTS53	103446
Nicaragua	USA (United States)	19 Mar 56	275UNTS231	103984
Canada	Japan	20 Mar 56	517UNTS33	107482
Liberia	USA (United States)	16 Mar 57	290UNTS59	104228
Taiwan	USA (United States)	30 Jul 57	300UNTS61	104331
Austria	South Africa	26 Sep 57	287UNTS3	104176
Multilateral		03 Oct 57	365UNTS3	105213
Japan	USA (United States)	03 Nov 58	341UNTS83	104879
Portugal	USA (United States)	12 Jan 59	343UNTS49	104921
United Arab Rep	USA (United States)	13 Jan 59	358UNTS3	105122
Ireland	South Africa	13 Apr 60	390UNTS307	105612
New Zealand	Philippines	09 May 60	486UNTS65	107073
Australia	USSR (Soviet Union)	29 Jun 60	392UNTS131	105641
Canada	USA (United States)	13 Jan 61	410UNTS62	105897
Australia	Japan	01 Mar 62	517UNTS81	107483
Australia	Germany, West	19 Mar 62	488UNTS203	107130
Israel	Netherlands	28 May 62	448UNTS219	106434
Thailand	USA (United States)	31 May 62	459UNTS135	106619
Israel	Liberia	18 Sep 62	484UNTS209	107031
Multilateral		16 Oct 62	470UNTS321	106815
Multilateral		16 Oct 62	470UNTS336	106816
Japan	Philippines	19 Jan 63	517UNTS281	107489
Japan	New Zealand	15 Mar 63	517UNTS229	107487
Japan	South Africa	06 Apr 63	484UNTS319	107040
Kuwait	USA (United States)	21 Oct 63	530UNTS281	107688
Multilateral		10 Jul 64	612UNTS3	108847
Philippines	USA (United States)	12 Nov 64	574UNTS159	108349
Rates and charges				
Brazil	Portugal	30 Apr 42	65UNTS183	200210
UK Great Britain	USA (United States)	10 May 43	147UNTS109	200473
Portugal	UK Great Britain	01 Jul 45	5UNTS263	200034
Guatemala	USA (United States)	25 Oct 45	139UNTS45	101875
Lebanon	USA (United States)	21 Jan 46	140UNTS73	101884
Ceylon (Sri Lanka)	India	12 Aug 46	196UNTS209	102626
South Africa	UK Great Britain	24 Aug 46	51UNTS187	100765

PARTY ONE	PARTY TWO	DATE	CITATION	NUMBER
Rates and charges (Cont.)				
Belgium	Netherlands	25 Mar 47	18UNTS309	100299
Philippines	USA (United States)	17 Sep 47	206UNTS249	102790
Burma	Pakistan	22 Jun 48	91UNTS197	101252
New Zealand	Pakistan	28 Jun 48	91UNTS235	101253
France	UK Great Britain	12 Jul 48	90UNTS83	101230
New Zealand	Pakistan	17 Sep 48	91UNTS275	101254
Ceylon (Sri Lanka)	Pakistan	15 Dec 48	91UNTS303	101255
Korea, South	USA (United States)	17 Feb 49	74UNTS167	100963
Belgium	Luxembourg	07 Jun 49	34UNTS117	100531
Lebanon	UK Great Britain	20 Jun 49	90UNTS137	101232
Australia	Philippines	01 Sep 49	46UNTS215	100711
Greece	UK Great Britain	17 Oct 49	93UNTS185	101300
Colombia	UK Great Britain	13 Dec 49	88UNTS133	101189
UK Great Britain	Yugoslavia	09 Feb 50	88UNTS287	101200
USA (United States)	Yugoslavia	14 Aug 50	137UNTS131	101851
Czechoslovakia	USA (United States)	29 Sep 50	290UNTS3	104227
Sweden	UK Great Britain	17 Jan 51	93UNTS225	101301
United Nations	USA (United States)	28 Mar 51	108UNTS231	101476
Ceylon (Sri Lanka)	India	30 Apr 51	196UNTS199	102625
India	UK Great Britain	05 Jun 51	135UNTS3	101811
Pakistan	United Arab Rep	08 Sep 51	133UNTS257	101793
Pakistan	UK Great Britain	26 Sep 51	118UNTS221	101608
Netherlands	UK Great Britain	30 Nov 51	123UNTS177	101659
Australia	Pakistan	16 Jan 52	151UNTS281	102001
Australia	USA (United States)	27 May 52	178UNTS113	102338
Multilateral		11 Jul 52	170UNTS63	102222
Multilateral		11 Jul 52	170UNTS269	102223
Multilateral		11 Jul 52	171UNTS191	102227
Multilateral		11 Jul 52	171UNTS143	102226
Multilateral		11 Jul 52	170UNTS3	102221
Multilateral		11 Jul 52	171UNTS3	102224
Multilateral		11 Jul 52	171UNTS89	102225
Australia	Netherlands	22 Oct 53	184UNTS193	102448
Italy	South Africa	20 Dec 53	277UNTS293	104014
Australia	Greece	24 May 54	191UNTS255	102586
Australia	Israel	18 Jun 54	220UNTS29	102985
India	USA (United States)	29 Jul 54	239UNTS69	103373
Canada	South Africa	04 Aug 54	261UNTS3	103722
Australia	Poland	25 Nov 54	521UNTS281	107526
Australia	Austria	20 Dec 54	205UNTS157	102775
Israel	South Africa	31 Dec 54	220UNTS11	102984
Australia	Hungary	10 Feb 55	207UNTS173	102806
Australia	Taiwan	22 Mar 55	209UNTS3	102818
Australia	Czechoslovakia	01 Apr 55	213UNTS199	102888
Ceylon (Sri Lanka)	USA (United States)	18 Jul 55	281UNTS295	104086
Pakistan	USA (United States)	20 Jul 55	241UNTS255	103436
Bulgaria	Yugoslavia	15 Nov 55	396UNTS191	105697
Korea, North	Romania	05 Dec 55	362UNTS163	105187
Romania	Yugoslavia	13 Jan 56	342UNTS265	104912
Australia	Yugoslavia	28 Feb 56	243UNTS53	103446
Canada	Japan	20 Mar 56	517UNTS33	107482
Canada	UK Great Britain	21 Jun 56	381UNTS111	105467
Dominican Republic	UK Great Britain	09 Aug 56	252UNTS127	103561
Canada	UK Great Britain	20 Oct 56	381UNTS99	105466
Canada	UK Great Britain	16 Nov 56	412UNTS166	105930
Liberia	USA (United States)	16 Mar 57	290UNTS59	104228
Albania	Yugoslavia	29 Aug 57	391UNTS167	105622
Austria	South Africa	26 Sep 57	287UNTS3	104176
Multilateral		03 Oct 57	366UNTS3	105215
Multilateral		03 Oct 57	366UNTS255	105219
Multilateral		03 Oct 57	365UNTS3	105213
Multilateral		03 Oct 57	364UNTS331	105212
Multilateral		03 Oct 57	364UNTS3	105211
Multilateral		03 Oct 57	365UNTS207	105214
Multilateral		03 Oct 57	366UNTS141	105217

PARTY ONE	PARTY TWO	DATE	CITATION	NUMBER
Rates and charges (Cont.)				
Taiwan	USA (United States)	08 Oct 57	304UNTS241	104400
United Arab Rep	USA (United States)	31 Oct 58	355UNTS355	105086
Japan	USA (United States)	03 Nov 58	341UNTS83	104879
Portugal	USA (United States)	12 Jan 59	343UNTS49	104921
United Arab Rep	USA (United States)	13 Jan 59	358UNTS3	105122
Ireland	South Africa	13 Apr 60	390UNTS307	105612
New Zealand	Philippines	09 May 60	486UNTS65	107073
Australia	USSR (Soviet Union)	29 Jun 60	392UNTS131	105641
Canada	USA (United States)	13 Jan 61	410UNTS62	105897
Multilateral		23 Jan 61	530UNTS141	107679
Australia	Japan	07 Feb 61	450UNTS343	106478
Japan	Pakistan	07 Mar 61	450UNTS359	106479
Philippines	USA (United States)	12 Mar 61	288UNTS285	104210
Morocco	USA (United States)	30 Nov 61	451UNTS167	106492
Thailand	USA (United States)	12 Jan 62	459UNTS95	106615
Jordan	UK Great Britain	28 Feb 62	466UNTS249	106748
Australia	Japan	01 Mar 62	517UNTS81	107483
Australia	Germany, West	19 Mar 62	488UNTS203	107130
Israel	Netherlands	28 May 62	448UNTS219	106434
Thailand	USA (United States)	31 May 62	459UNTS135	106619
Israel	Liberia	18 Sep 62	484UNTS209	107031
Multilateral		16 Oct 62	470UNTS321	106815
Multilateral		16 Oct 62	470UNTS336	106816
Multilateral		16 Oct 62	470UNTS291	106814
Japan	Philippines	19 Jan 63	517UNTS281	107489
Japan	New Zealand	15 Mar 63	517UNTS229	107487
Japan	South Africa	06 Apr 63	484UNTS319	107040
Australia	UK Great Britain	23 Sep 63	483UNTS39	107006
Multilateral		10 Jul 64	613UNTS3	108850
Multilateral		10 Jul 64	611UNTS387	108846
Japan	UK Great Britain	22 Feb 65	560UNTS123	108171
Australia	Germany, West	08 Jul 65	543UNTS305	107907
Multilateral		16 Dec 65	570UNTS201	108295
UK Great Britain	Yugoslavia	30 Jun 67	642UNTS325	109182
Czechoslovakia	USSR (Soviet Union)	23 Nov 67	0UNTS0	109224
Advice lists and orders				
Ethiopia	UK Great Britain	19 Dec 44	93UNTS303	200272
Lebanon	USA (United States)	21 Jan 46	140UNTS73	101884
South Africa	UK Great Britain	24 Aug 46	51UNTS187	100765
New Zealand	Pakistan	17 Sep 48	91UNTS275	101254
Greece	UK Great Britain	17 Oct 49	93UNTS185	101300
Colombia	UK Great Britain	13 Dec 49	88UNTS133	101189
UK Great Britain	Yugoslavia	09 Feb 50	88UNTS287	101200
Sweden	UK Great Britain	17 Jan 51	93UNTS225	101301
India	UK Great Britain	05 Jun 51	135UNTS3	101811
Pakistan	United Arab Rep	08 Sep 51	133UNTS257	101793
Pakistan	UK Great Britain	26 Sep 51	118UNTS221	101608
Multilateral		11 Jul 52	171UNTS3	102224
Pakistan	UK Great Britain	22 Jul 52	157UNTS185	102054
Pakistan	USA (United States)	20 Jul 55	241UNTS255	103436
Australia	Yugoslavia	28 Feb 56	243UNTS53	103446
Taiwan	USA (United States)	08 Oct 57	304UNTS241	104400
Guatemala	USA (United States)	23 Apr 60	373UNTS23	105312
Japan	Pakistan	07 Mar 61	450UNTS359	106479
Philippines	USA (United States)	12 Mar 61	288UNTS285	104210
Jordan	UK Great Britain	28 Feb 62	466UNTS249	106748
Multilateral		16 Oct 62	470UNTS291	106814
Australia	UK Great Britain	23 Sep 63	483UNTS39	107006
Philippines	USA (United States)	12 Nov 64	574UNTS159	108349
Australia	Germany, West	08 Jul 65	543UNTS305	107907
Multilateral		16 Dec 65	570UNTS201	108295
Kuwait	UK Great Britain	29 Dec 66	617UNTS203	108914
UK Great Britain	Yugoslavia	30 Jun 67	642UNTS325	109182

PARTY ONE	PARTY TWO	DATE	CITATION	NUMBER
Telecommunications				
France	Lebanon	24 Jan 48	173UNTS99	102263
Ethiopia	IBRD (World Bank)	19 Feb 51	186UNTS101	102486
Mexico	USA (United States)	10 Aug 51	152UNTS27	102009
Japan	USA (United States)	28 Feb 52	208UNTS255	102817
Canada	USA (United States)	23 Jun 52	207UNTS25	102798
India	Poland	29 Sep 56	276UNTS305	103993
Multilateral		10 Jun 58	454UNTS47	106539
Mexico	USA (United States)	16 Jul 58	335UNTS139	104782
Canada	USA (United States)	07 Jan 59	391UNTS207	105624
Multilateral		22 Jun 60	546UNTS247	107951
Japan	Thailand	24 Aug 60	384UNTS73	105512
Mexico	USA (United States)	18 Apr 62	452UNTS3	106501
Ethiopia	IBRD (World Bank)	31 May 62	467UNTS237	106765
Canada	USA (United States)	28 Dec 62	471UNTS13	106818
Belgium	USA (United States)	19 Apr 63	476UNTS29	106900
Costa Rica	IBRD (World Bank)	10 Jul 63	482UNTS69	106991
El Salvador	IBRD (World Bank)	01 Oct 63	517UNTS3	107481
Saudi Arabia	USA (United States)	06 Jan 64	531UNTS3	107689
India	IDA (Devel Assoc)	06 Jul 64	534UNTS49	107753
IBRD (World Bank)	Venezuela	13 Dec 65	568UNTS77	108265
Ethiopia	IBRD (World Bank)	28 Dec 65	567UNTS229	108258
USA (United States)	Vietnam, South	03 Jan 66	579UNTS99	108401
Jamaica	IBRD (World Bank)	23 Jan 67	594UNTS311	108608
Czechoslovakia	USSR (Soviet Union)	23 Nov 67	0UNTS0	109224
Cable				
Denmark	Norway	07 Aug 45	10UNTS203	200062
Multilateral		04 Dec 45	9UNTS101	100128
Panama	USA (United States)	31 Mar 49	55UNTS125	100811
Multilateral		12 Aug 49	87UNTS131	101169
Satellites				
Spain	USA (United States)	18 Mar 60	372UNTS13	105284
Mexico	USA (United States)	12 Apr 60	372UNTS47	105287
UK Great Britain	USA (United States)	29 Mar 61	405UNTS107	105826
France	USA (United States)	31 Mar 61	409UNTS136	105881
Australia	USA (United States)	05 Jun 61	409UNTS279	105892
Japan	USA (United States)	06 Nov 62	459UNTS203	106623
Italy	USA (United States)	14 Nov 62	459UNTS197	106622
Canada	USA (United States)	23 Aug 63	494UNTS13	107222
Multilateral		14 Sep 63	488UNTS121	107123
Malagasy	USA (United States)	07 Oct 63	494UNTS3	107221
UK Great Britain	USA (United States)	01 Jan 67	604UNTS3	108738
Eur Space Research	UK Great Britain	24 Nov 67	638UNTS17	109129
Services				
Multilateral		04 Dec 45	9UNTS101	100128
Multilateral		02 Oct 47	193UNTS188	102616
New Zealand	USA (United States)	16 Mar 48	127UNTS133	101703
France	UK Great Britain	12 Jul 48	90UNTS83	101230
Denmark	USA (United States)	04 Apr 52	177UNTS13	102305
Mexico	UK Great Britain	12 Jun 52	196UNTS149	102622
Czechoslovakia	Germany, East	24 Oct 55	504UNTS173	107358
Bulgaria	Yugoslavia	15 Nov 55	396UNTS191	105697
India	Poland	29 Sep 56	276UNTS305	103993
Albania	Yugoslavia	29 Aug 57	391UNTS167	105622
Austria	IAEA (Atom Energy)	11 Dec 57	339UNTS110	104849
Czechoslovakia	Poland	31 Jan 58	431UNTS99	106214
Multilateral		26 Feb 60	418UNTS171	106022
India	IDA (Devel Assoc)	14 Sep 62	448UNTS3	106422
Austria	Czechoslovakia	22 Sep 62	495UNTS157	107244
Czechoslovakia	Poland	16 Nov 62	526UNTS3	107597
Austria	Yugoslavia	11 Dec 62	546UNTS3	107938
Czechoslovakia	Hungary	22 Oct 63	514UNTS95	107444
Australia	USA (United States)	03 Jan 64	505UNTS159	107371
IBRD (World Bank)	UK Great Britain	24 Apr 67	600UNTS3	108674

PARTY ONE	PARTY TWO	DATE	CITATION	NUMBER
Services (Cont.)				
UK Great Britain	USSR (Soviet Union)	25 Aug 67	632UNTS49	109007
Czechoslovakia	USSR (Soviet Union)	23 Nov 67	0UNTS0	109224
Eur Space Research	UK Great Britain	24 Nov 67	638UNTS17	109129
Telegrams				
Brazil	Paraguay	08 Oct 42	65UNTS191	200211
Denmark	UK Great Britain	20 Jan 47	118UNTS73	101597
Multilateral		11 May 48	500UNTS267	107313
France	UK Great Britain	12 Jul 48	90UNTS83	101230
New Zealand	Pakistan	17 Sep 48	91UNTS275	101254
Greece	UK Great Britain	17 Oct 49	93UNTS185	101300
Afghanistan	India	14 Dec 49	53UNTS95	100774
Sweden	UK Great Britain	17 Jan 51	93UNTS225	101301
Pakistan	UK Great Britain	26 Sep 51	118UNTS221	101608
Mexico	UK Great Britain	12 Jun 52	196UNTS149	102622
Syria	Turkey	28 Apr 53	204UNTS255	102760
Syria	UK Great Britain	05 Feb 54	204UNTS267	102761
Czechoslovakia	Germany, East	24 Oct 55	504UNTS173	107358
Multilateral		03 Oct 57	366UNTS3	105215
Japan	Pakistan	07 Mar 61	450UNTS359	106479
Multilateral		16 Oct 62	470UNTS291	106814
Australia	UK Great Britain	23 Sep 63	483UNTS39	107006
Czechoslovakia	USSR (Soviet Union)	23 Nov 67	0UNTS0	109224
Radio-telephone-telegraphic communications				
Anglo-Egypt Sudan	Fr Equatorial Afri	02 Nov 39	2UNTS209	200012
Brazil	Uruguay	18 May 42	54UNTS369	200207
Brazil	Paraguay	08 Oct 42	65UNTS191	200211
Canada	USA (United States)	17 Jan 44	109UNTS199	200360
UK Great Britain	USSR (Soviet Union)	23 Sep 44	10UNTS171	200060
Multilateral		04 Dec 45	9UNTS101	100128
Belgium	UK Great Britain	11 Mar 46	26UNTS167	100387
South Africa	UK Great Britain	24 Aug 46	51UNTS187	100765
Philippines	USA (United States)	19 Oct 46	43UNTS263	100672
Denmark	UK Great Britain	20 Jan 47	118UNTS73	101597
Canada	USA (United States)	20 Aug 47	27UNTS3	100392
Multilateral		02 Oct 47	193UNTS188	102616
Multilateral		17 Sep 48	97UNTS31	101345
Multilateral		09 Jul 49	168UNTS143	102218
Multilateral		12 Aug 49	87UNTS131	101169
Afghanistan	India	14 Dec 49	53UNTS95	100774
Liberia	USA (United States)	10 Jan 51	132UNTS255	101765
Canada	USA (United States)	08 Feb 51	207UNTS17	102797
Canada	USA (United States)	21 Feb 52	205UNTS293	102781
Cuba	USA (United States)	27 Feb 52	168UNTS3	102209
Ecuador	USA (United States)	17 Mar 52	177UNTS115	102313
Germany, West	USA (United States)	11 Jun 52	273UNTS105	103947
Multilateral		11 Jul 52	171UNTS3	102224
Canada	USA (United States)	17 Mar 53	236UNTS259	103329
Syria	Turkey	28 Apr 53	204UNTS255	102760
Luxembourg	USA (United States)	17 Aug 53	234UNTS219	103284
Syria	UK Great Britain	05 Feb 54	204UNTS267	102761
Greece	USA (United States)	18 Aug 54	234UNTS161	103282
Ceylon (Sri Lanka)	USA (United States)	23 Aug 54	314UNTS297	104553
Bulgaria	Yugoslavia	15 Nov 55	396UNTS191	105697
Korea, North	Romania	05 Dec 55	362UNTS141	105186
Panama	USA (United States)	01 Aug 56	281UNTS49	104068
Nicaragua	USA (United States)	16 Oct 56	282UNTS29	104090
Costa Rica	USA (United States)	19 Oct 56	278UNTS65	104022
Mexico	USA (United States)	29 Jan 57	418UNTS253	106025
Dominican Republic	USA (United States)	09 Mar 57	279UNTS249	104044
Nicaragua	USA (United States)	05 Sep 58	336UNTS33	104797
Chile	USA (United States)	19 Feb 59	343UNTS17	104918
Pakistan	USA (United States)	18 Jul 59	355UNTS367	105087
Mexico	USA (United States)	31 Jul 59	357UNTS187	105117
Liberia	USA (United States)	13 Aug 59	357UNTS181	105116

PARTY ONE	PARTY TWO	DATE	CITATION	NUMBER
Radio-telephone-telegraphic communications (Cont.)				
USA (United States)	Venezuela	12 Nov 59	367UNTS81	105227
Haiti	USA (United States)	06 Jan 60	367UNTS75	105226
Honduras	USA (United States)	19 Feb 60	371UNTS109	105273
UK Great Britain	USA (United States)	24 Jun 60	377UNTS63	105396
Paraguay	USA (United States)	06 Oct 60	393UNTS281	105662
Cambodia	Thailand	15 Dec 60	382UNTS301	105490
Bolivia	USA (United States)	23 Oct 61	424UNTS93	106101
Canada	Venezuela	22 Nov 61	470UNTS148	106806
El Salvador	USA (United States)	05 Apr 62	442UNTS41	106337
Turkey	USSR (Soviet Union)	09 Jun 62	493UNTS155	107213
Canada	USA (United States)	24 Oct 62	462UNTS67	106672
Dominican Republic	USA (United States)	22 Apr 63	487UNTS169	107101
Cyprus	USA (United States)	23 Apr 63	487UNTS291	107111
Philippines	USA (United States)	06 May 63	477UNTS67	106916
Israel	USA (United States)	21 May 63	487UNTS319	107113
Colombia	USA (United States)	29 Nov 63	494UNTS49	107225
Sierra Leone	USA (United States)	16 Aug 65	579UNTS55	108398
Colombia	USA (United States)	28 Oct 65	574UNTS109	108343
Philippines	United Nations	05 Apr 66	560UNTS191	108174
Netherlands	USA (United States)	22 Jun 66	590UNTS109	108550
Austria	United Nations	13 Apr 67	600UNTS93	108679
UK Great Britain	USSR (Soviet Union)	25 Aug 67	632UNTS49	109007
Czechoslovakia	USSR (Soviet Union)	23 Nov 67	0UNTS0	109224
Mass media				
USA (United States)	Yugoslavia	06 Jan 51	122UNTS137	101643
Mexico	USA (United States)	10 Aug 51	152UNTS27	102009
Italy	UK Great Britain	30 Sep 67	642UNTS271	109180
Publications exchange				
Brazil	Paraguay	14 Jun 41	54UNTS249	200197
Brazil	Chile	18 Nov 41	67UNTS279	200225
Brazil	Venezuela	22 Oct 42	65UNTS203	200212
El Salvador	USA (United States)	02 Dec 42	122UNTS277	200410
Brazil	Ecuador	24 May 44	73UNTS223	200242
Brazil	Canada	24 May 44	65UNTS265	200215
Brazil	Dominican Republic	09 Apr 45	67UNTS293	200226
Czechoslovakia	France	08 Dec 45	46UNTS77	100701
Belgium	France	22 Feb 46	68UNTS157	100892
Belgium	UK Great Britain	17 Apr 46	6UNTS177	100075
France	Netherlands	19 Nov 46	32UNTS101	100493
France	USA (United States)	10 Dec 46	15UNTS265	100242
Belgium	Czechoslovakia	06 Mar 47	34UNTS77	100528
Czechoslovakia	Yugoslavia	27 Apr 47	33UNTS49	100514
France	Poland	19 May 47	12UNTS95	100181
Bulgaria	Czechoslovakia	20 Jun 47	46UNTS15	100698
Romania	Yugoslavia	26 Jun 47	116UNTS39	101568
Czechoslovakia	Poland	04 Jul 47	25UNTS249	100366
Albania	Yugoslavia	09 Jul 47	33UNTS91	100516
Czechoslovakia	Romania	05 Sep 47	46UNTS37	100699
Hungary	Yugoslavia	15 Oct 47	33UNTS73	100515
Colombia	USA (United States)	22 Dec 47	51UNTS45	100751
Hungary	Poland	31 Jan 48	25UNTS283	100368
Norway	UK Great Britain	19 Feb 48	34UNTS33	100526
Belgium	Norway	20 Feb 48	32UNTS39	100487
Poland	Romania	27 Feb 48	46UNTS143	100707
Belgium	Luxembourg	27 Mar 48	178UNTS265	102343
Hungary	Poland	18 Jun 48	25UNTS319	100370
Netherlands	UK Great Britain	07 Jul 48	82UNTS259	101099
Belgium	Italy	29 Nov 48	41UNTS3	100641
Luxembourg	Netherlands	26 Apr 49	182UNTS187	102425
Greece	Lebanon	10 Jun 49	178UNTS29	102334
Hungary	Poland	29 Oct 49	260UNTS113	103706
Luxembourg	UK Great Britain	27 Jun 50	183UNTS217	102431
Spain	Sweden	12 Oct 50	197UNTS305	102644
Multilateral		22 Nov 50	131UNTS25	101734

PARTY ONE	PARTY TWO	DATE	CITATION	NUMBER
Publications exchange (Cont.)				
Albania	Poland	25 Jan 51	260UNTS217	103710
China People's Rep	Poland	03 Apr 51	304UNTS187	104396
Greece	Turkey	20 Apr 51	178UNTS17	102333
Netherlands	South Africa	31 May 51	188UNTS289	102533
India	Turkey	29 Jun 51	213UNTS183	102886
Greece	UK Great Britain	29 Sep 51	190UNTS260	102570
Italy	UK Great Britain	28 Nov 51	172UNTS27	102238
Germany, East	Poland	08 Jan 52	304UNTS113	104394
Burma	WHO (World Health)	18 Feb 52	127UNTS43	101698
Multilateral		11 Jul 52	171UNTS191	102227
Austria	Belgium	17 Oct 52	162UNTS183	102135
Austria	UK Great Britain	12 Dec 52	172UNTS9	102237
Bolivia	Italy	31 Jan 53	281UNTS181	104079
Albania	Romania	14 Feb 53	342UNTS107	104903
Greece	Netherlands	29 Apr 53	191UNTS235	102583
Israel	Uruguay	30 Apr 53	280UNTS269	104064
Pakistan	Turkey	29 Jun 53	211UNTS225	102854
Saudi Arabia	USA (United States)	29 Jun 53	206UNTS23	102784
Pakistan	United Arab Rep	14 Nov 53	485UNTS55	107046
UK Great Britain	Yugoslavia	31 Dec 53	190UNTS335	102574
Belgium	South Africa	01 Jun 54	201UNTS25	102708
Greece	Italy	11 Sep 54	284UNTS313	104145
Belgium	Greece	09 Dec 54	257UNTS243	103660
UK Great Britain	Yugoslavia	31 Dec 54	209UNTS81	102824
Japan	Thailand	06 Apr 55	230UNTS219	103187
Czechoslovakia	Hungary	28 Apr 55	477UNTS197	106923
Netherlands	Norway	18 May 55	252UNTS269	103569
Belgium	Portugal	30 Jul 55	250UNTS213	103525
Italy	Spain	11 Aug 55	267UNTS125	103839
Czechoslovakia	Germany, East	30 Aug 55	504UNTS279	107361
Bulgaria	Yugoslavia	11 Dec 55	378UNTS49	105417
Bulgaria	Yugoslavia	10 Feb 56	349UNTS21	105007
Iran	Pakistan	09 Mar 56	449UNTS183	106460
Turkey	UK Great Britain	12 Mar 56	313UNTS73	104530
Romania	USSR (Soviet Union)	07 Apr 56	259UNTS377	103698
Bulgaria	Greece	19 Apr 56	594UNTS131	108600
Mongolia	USSR (Soviet Union)	24 Apr 56	259UNTS297	103693
Bulgaria	USSR (Soviet Union)	28 Apr 56	259UNTS363	103697
Albania	USSR (Soviet Union)	03 May 56	259UNTS391	103699
Mongolia	Romania	08 May 56	342UNTS291	104913
Korea, North	Poland	11 May 56	432UNTS161	106219
Korea, North	Romania	12 May 56	342UNTS189	104908
USSR (Soviet Union)	Yugoslavia	17 May 56	259UNTS145	103687
Czechoslovakia	USSR (Soviet Union)	01 Jun 56	259UNTS341	103696
China People's Rep	USSR (Soviet Union)	05 Jul 56	263UNTS129	103770
Poland	Yugoslavia	06 Jul 56	281UNTS143	104076
Greece	United Arab Rep	04 Sep 56	299UNTS253	104317
Korea, North	USSR (Soviet Union)	05 Sep 56	259UNTS329	103695
Belgium	Germany, West	24 Sep 56	263UNTS31	103766
Romania	Vietnam, North	12 Oct 56	342UNTS173	104907
Romania	Yugoslavia	27 Oct 56	389UNTS33	105590
India	Japan	29 Oct 56	318UNTS289	104622
Germany, East	Romania	08 Dec 56	362UNTS189	105188
Bulgaria	Yugoslavia	24 Dec 56	397UNTS3	105699
Czechoslovakia	Yugoslavia	29 Jan 57	300UNTS249	104339
Belgium	Yugoslavia	05 Feb 57	276UNTS143	103990
Taiwan	Turkey	12 Feb 57	282UNTS125	104097
USSR (Soviet Union)	Vietnam, North	15 Feb 57	274UNTS115	103962
Japan	United Arab Rep	20 Mar 57	318UNTS345	104625
India	Poland	27 Mar 57	319UNTS263	104635
Poland	Vietnam, North	06 Apr 57	432UNTS255	106224
Iran	Japan	16 Apr 57	325UNTS113	104697
India	Romania	30 Apr 57	342UNTS251	104911
Czechoslovakia	Yugoslavia	22 May 57	391UNTS33	105615
Argentina	Israel	23 May 57	280UNTS199	104059

Publications exchange (Cont.)

PARTY ONE	PARTY TWO	DATE	CITATION	NUMBER
Japan	Pakistan	27 May 57	325UNTS21	104692
Bulgaria	Czechoslovakia	03 Jun 57	292UNTS3	104261
Czechoslovakia	Yugoslavia	11 Jun 57	504UNTS107	107355
Czechoslovakia	Syria	18 Jun 57	303UNTS119	104374
Czechoslovakia	United Arab Rep	19 Oct 57	530UNTS181	107681
United Arab Rep	USSR (Soviet Union)	19 Oct 57	292UNTS151	104271
Germany, East	Hungary	13 Nov 57	407UNTS216	105866
Hungary	Yugoslavia	20 Nov 57	477UNTS267	106925
Argentina	Italy	25 Nov 57	305UNTS275	104424
Czechoslovakia	USSR (Soviet Union)	04 Dec 57	313UNTS291	104537
Hungary	Yugoslavia	06 Dec 57	519UNTS215	107509
Hungary	Romania	17 Dec 57	477UNTS303	106926
Belgium	Denmark	31 Dec 57	305UNTS247	104422
USA (United States)	USSR (Soviet Union)	27 Jan 58	301UNTS405	104350
Bulgaria	Hungary	13 Mar 58	438UNTS173	106316
Germany, West	UK Great Britain	18 Apr 58	343UNTS241	104928
Hungary	Poland	08 May 58	408UNTS212	105872
Poland	USA (United States)	30 May 58	315UNTS231	104572
Germany, East	Hungary	14 Jun 58	407UNTS78	105861
Germany, East	Romania	15 Jul 58	387UNTS115	105560
Czechoslovakia	Romania	25 Oct 58	338UNTS301	104843
Belgium	Spain	27 Oct 58	327UNTS107	104720
Multilateral		15 Dec 58	546UNTS235	107950
Mongolia	Poland	23 Dec 58	432UNTS177	106220
Belgium	Turkey	29 Dec 58	357UNTS195	105118
Bulgaria	Hungary	03 Apr 59	438UNTS269	106319
Hungary	Iraq	11 Apr 59	439UNTS25	106323
Hungary	USSR (Soviet Union)	17 Apr 59	439UNTS41	106324
Iraq	USSR (Soviet Union)	05 May 59	356UNTS179	105095
Iran	UK Great Britain	06 May 59	398UNTS51	105717
Israel	Mexico	15 Jun 59	377UNTS267	105406
Brazil	Israel	24 Jun 59	515UNTS151	107458
Czechoslovakia	India	07 Jul 59	359UNTS259	105145
Iraq	Romania	04 Aug 59	502UNTS17	107324
Korea, South	USA (United States)	25 Sep 59	358UNTS163	105133
USA (United States)	USSR (Soviet Union)	21 Nov 59	361UNTS35	105172
Czechoslovakia	Guinea	30 Nov 59	386UNTS63	105538
France	Israel	30 Nov 59	377UNTS237	105404
Czechoslovakia	Ethiopia	11 Dec 59	399UNTS93	105736
Multilateral		14 Dec 59	422UNTS57	106068
Germany, East	Hungary	19 Dec 59	409UNTS4	105874
Belgium	Brazil	06 Jan 60	531UNTS149	107701
Guinea	Hungary	12 Jan 60	519UNTS131	107505
Italy	USSR (Soviet Union)	09 Feb 60	399UNTS75	105735
India	USSR (Soviet Union)	12 Feb 60	392UNTS153	105642
Indonesia	USSR (Soviet Union)	28 Feb 60	392UNTS191	105644
UK Great Britain	Yugoslavia	12 Apr 60	360UNTS79	105155
Belgium	Iran	14 May 60	522UNTS249	107551
Finland	USSR (Soviet Union)	27 May 60	379UNTS381	105444
Spain	UK Great Britain	12 Jul 60	414UNTS123	105971
Cuba	Korea, North	29 Aug 60	473UNTS117	106860
Israel	UK Great Britain	31 Aug 60	385UNTS71	105530
Cuba	Romania	28 Oct 60	457UNTS9	106574
Czechoslovakia	Ghana	23 Nov 60	431UNTS91	106213
Israel	Mali	24 Nov 60	413UNTS104	105945
Cambodia	Czechoslovakia	27 Nov 60	410UNTS263	105910
Japan	UK Great Britain	03 Dec 60	414UNTS61	105966
Romania	USA (United States)	09 Dec 60	401UNTS19	105759
Cuba	Czechoslovakia	22 Dec 60	426UNTS145	106134
UK Great Britain	USSR (Soviet Union)	12 Jan 61	398UNTS157	105720
Ethiopia	USSR (Soviet Union)	13 Jan 61	421UNTS13	106049
Czechoslovakia	Hungary	24 Feb 61	422UNTS15	106066
Cuba	Poland	06 Mar 61	484UNTS123	107020
Cuba	Czechoslovakia	05 Apr 61	442UNTS201	106350
India	Norway	19 Apr 61	404UNTS307	105818

Publications exchange (Cont.)

PARTY ONE	PARTY TWO	DATE	CITATION	NUMBER
Afghanistan	Czechoslovakia	23 Apr 61	437UNTS25	106297
Germany, West	Netherlands	27 Apr 61	487UNTS77	107095
Ghana	Hungary	27 Apr 61	439UNTS17	106322
Taiwan	Uruguay	03 May 61	596UNTS121	108630
Somalia	USSR (Soviet Union)	02 Jun 61	528UNTS147	107638
Czechoslovakia	Somalia	04 Jun 61	479UNTS291	106960
Austria	Yugoslavia	30 Jun 61	443UNTS51	106358
Pakistan	Philippines	15 Aug 61	522UNTS35	107534
Ghana	Romania	30 Sep 61	457UNTS3	106573
Taiwan	Jordan	17 Oct 61	435UNTS267	106284
United Arab Rep	UK Great Britain	14 Nov 61	449UNTS129	106455
Guatemala	Israel	27 Nov 61	448UNTS191	106431
Taiwan	El Salvador	27 Nov 61	437UNTS161	106306
IBRD (World Bank)	South Africa	01 Dec 61	425UNTS197	106125
UK Great Britain	Yugoslavia	13 Feb 62	431UNTS35	106207
USA (United States)	USSR (Soviet Union)	08 Mar 62	460UNTS3	106630
Hungary	India	30 Mar 62	519UNTS119	107504
United Arab Rep	USA (United States)	21 May 62	458UNTS197	106601
Senegal	USSR (Soviet Union)	14 Jun 62	437UNTS233	106309
Israel	Peru	25 Jun 62	515UNTS263	107464
Israel	Liberia	25 Jun 62	448UNTS295	106442
Costa Rica	Israel	31 Jul 62	484UNTS155	107024
Syria	USSR (Soviet Union)	19 Aug 62	457UNTS285	106588
Denmark	USSR (Soviet Union)	11 Sep 62	458UNTS3	106589
Cameroon	Israel	24 Oct 62	449UNTS15	106447
Belgium	Tunisia	21 Dec 62	482UNTS3	106987
Thailand	UK Great Britain	09 Jan 63	470UNTS59	106795
Iraq	USA (United States)	23 Jan 63	488UNTS163	107126
Dahomey	USSR (Soviet Union)	20 Mar 63	528UNTS181	107641
Hungary	Korea, North	29 Mar 63	577UNTS219	108379
Romania	USA (United States)	02 Apr 63	474UNTS95	106874
Czechoslovakia	Tunisia	06 Apr 63	555UNTS111	108106
Belgium	Venezuela	15 May 63	470UNTS259	106812
Mali	Romania	26 Sep 63	528UNTS193	107642
Hungary	Yugoslavia	15 Oct 63	577UNTS49	108372
Tanganyika	USSR (Soviet Union)	06 Nov 63	528UNTS157	107639
Belgium	Romania	13 Nov 63	520UNTS119	107513
Belgium	Pakistan	14 Nov 63	535UNTS393	107792
Belgium	Poland	09 Dec 63	514UNTS195	107448
USA (United States)	USSR (Soviet Union)	22 Feb 64	526UNTS131	107605
Mexico	Netherlands	08 Apr 64	575UNTS35	108353
Algeria	Czechoslovakia	14 May 64	538UNTS301	107817
Cuba	Czechoslovakia	03 Jun 64	527UNTS205	107626
Multilateral		10 Jul 64	613UNTS127	108853
Germany, East	Poland	06 Oct 64	552UNTS89	108051
Czechoslovakia	Germany, East	06 Oct 64	545UNTS113	107927
Czechoslovakia	Mongolia	21 Oct 64	545UNTS91	107926
Belgium	Mexico	19 Nov 64	546UNTS217	107949
Ethiopia	USA (United States)	25 Nov 64	532UNTS125	107715
Czechoslovakia	United Arab Rep	26 Nov 64	545UNTS11	107923
Belgium	Sweden	11 Jan 65	533UNTS157	107741
Belgium	Hungary	11 Feb 65	544UNTS3	107908
UK Great Britain	USSR (Soviet Union)	13 Feb 65	543UNTS43	107896
Bulgaria	Czechoslovakia	22 May 65	545UNTS65	107925
China People's Rep	Romania	27 May 65	592UNTS3	108566
Pakistan	USSR (Soviet Union)	05 Jun 65	593UNTS115	108579
Uganda	USSR (Soviet Union)	24 Jul 65	596UNTS199	108633
Israel	Sierra Leone	22 Aug 65	550UNTS275	108022
Czechoslovakia	Poland	22 Jan 66	588UNTS175	108524
Rwanda	USSR (Soviet Union)	06 May 66	633UNTS217	109039
Bulgaria	Poland	03 Oct 66	618UNTS3	108921
Belgium	Israel	23 Mar 67	630UNTS275	108974
Austria	United Nations	13 Apr 67	600UNTS93	108679
Belgium	Bulgaria	17 May 67	631UNTS215	108995
Italy	Romania	08 Aug 67	642UNTS191	109174

PARTY ONE	PARTY TWO	DATE	CITATION	NUMBER
Mass media exchange				
Brazil	Chile	18 Nov 41	67UNTS279	200225
Brazil	Canada	24 May 44	65UNTS265	200215
Multilateral		16 Nov 45	4UNTS275	100052
Czechoslovakia	France	08 Dec 45	46UNTS77	100701
Belgium	Netherlands	16 May 46	17UNTS13	100266
France	USA (United States)	28 May 46	84UNTS161	101126
Multilateral		22 Jul 46	14UNTS185	100221
France	Netherlands	19 Nov 46	32UNTS101	100493
Belgium	Czechoslovakia	06 Mar 47	34UNTS77	100528
Austria	France	15 Mar 47	12UNTS109	100182
Czechoslovakia	Yugoslavia	27 Apr 47	33UNTS49	100514
France	Poland	19 May 47	12UNTS95	100181
Czechoslovakia	UK Great Britain	16 Jun 47	46UNTS61	100700
Bulgaria	Czechoslovakia	20 Jun 47	46UNTS15	100698
Romania	Yugoslavia	26 Jun 47	116UNTS39	101568
Czechoslovakia	Poland	04 Jul 47	25UNTS249	100366
Albania	Yugoslavia	09 Jul 47	33UNTS91	100516
Czechoslovakia	Romania	05 Sep 47	46UNTS37	100699
Hungary	Yugoslavia	15 Oct 47	33UNTS73	100515
Colombia	USA (United States)	22 Dec 47	51UNTS45	100751
Hungary	Poland	31 Jan 48	25UNTS283	100368
Norway	UK Great Britain	19 Feb 48	34UNTS33	100526
Belgium	Norway	20 Feb 48	32UNTS39	100487
Poland	Romania	27 Feb 48	46UNTS143	100707
New Zealand	USA (United States)	16 Mar 48	127UNTS133	101703
Belgium	Luxembourg	27 Mar 48	178UNTS265	102343
Hungary	Poland	18 Jun 48	25UNTS319	100370
Netherlands	UK Great Britain	07 Jul 48	82UNTS259	101099
France	USA (United States)	16 Sep 48	84UNTS185	101129
Belgium	Italy	29 Nov 48	41UNTS3	100641
Luxembourg	Netherlands	26 Apr 49	182UNTS187	102425
Bulgaria	Poland	26 Sep 49	260UNTS227	103711
Bulgaria	Poland	26 Sep 49	260UNTS249	103712
Hungary	Poland	29 Oct 49	260UNTS113	103706
Haiti	WHO (World Health)	21 Jun 50	103UNTS61	101424
Germany, East	Poland	23 Jun 50	304UNTS91	104393
Luxembourg	UK Great Britain	27 Jun 50	183UNTS217	102431
Multilateral		22 Nov 50	131UNTS25	101734
China People's Rep	Poland	03 Apr 51	304UNTS187	104396
Greece	Turkey	20 Apr 51	178UNTS17	102333
Netherlands	South Africa	31 May 51	188UNTS289	102533
India	Turkey	29 Jun 51	213UNTS183	102886
Greece	UK Great Britain	29 Sep 51	190UNTS260	102570
Italy	UK Great Britain	28 Nov 51	172UNTS27	102238
Germany, East	Poland	08 Jan 52	304UNTS113	104394
Netherlands	Sweden	25 Apr 52	163UNTS131	102147
Ethiopia	USA (United States)	15 May 52	180UNTS227	102388
Austria	Belgium	17 Oct 52	162UNTS183	102135
Chile	WHO (World Health)	24 Oct 52	151UNTS339	102004
Austria	UK Great Britain	12 Dec 52	172UNTS9	102237
Bolivia	Italy	31 Jan 53	281UNTS181	104079
Albania	Romania	14 Feb 53	342UNTS107	104903
Greece	Netherlands	29 Apr 53	191UNTS235	102583
Israel	Uruguay	30 Apr 53	280UNTS269	104064
Pakistan	Turkey	29 Jun 53	211UNTS225	102854
Belgium	South Africa	01 Jun 54	201UNTS25	102708
Bulgaria	Romania	22 Jul 54	362UNTS101	105184
Greece	Italy	11 Sep 54	284UNTS313	104145
Belgium	Greece	09 Dec 54	257UNTS243	103660
Austria	Yugoslavia	18 Jan 55	378UNTS31	105416
Japan	Thailand	06 Apr 55	230UNTS219	103187
Netherlands	Norway	18 May 55	252UNTS269	103569
Belgium	Portugal	30 Jul 55	250UNTS213	103525
Germany, East	Romania	05 Aug 55	342UNTS229	104910

PARTY ONE	PARTY TWO	DATE	CITATION	NUMBER
Mass media exchange (Cont.)				
Italy	Spain	11 Aug 55	267UNTS125	103839
USA (United States)	USSR (Soviet Union)	05 Sep 55	256UNTS307	103641
Iran	Pakistan	09 Mar 56	449UNTS183	106460
Turkey	UK Great Britain	12 Mar 56	313UNTS73	104530
Romania	USSR (Soviet Union)	07 Apr 56	259UNTS377	103698
Mongolia	USSR (Soviet Union)	24 Apr 56	259UNTS297	103693
Germany, West	USA (United States)	26 Apr 56	283UNTS267	104122
Bulgaria	USSR (Soviet Union)	28 Apr 56	259UNTS363	103697
Albania	USSR (Soviet Union)	03 May 56	259UNTS391	103699
Mongolia	Romania	08 May 56	342UNTS291	104913
Korea, North	Poland	11 May 56	432UNTS161	106219
Korea, North	Romania	12 May 56	342UNTS189	104908
USSR (Soviet Union)	Yugoslavia	17 May 56	259UNTS145	103687
Czechoslovakia	USSR (Soviet Union)	01 Jun 56	259UNTS341	103696
China People's Rep	USSR (Soviet Union)	05 Jul 56	263UNTS129	103770
Poland	Yugoslavia	06 Jul 56	281UNTS143	104076
Syria	USSR (Soviet Union)	20 Aug 56	274UNTS105	103961
Greece	United Arab Rep	04 Sep 56	299UNTS253	104317
Italy	Spain	05 Sep 56	302UNTS195	104359
Korea, North	USSR (Soviet Union)	05 Sep 56	259UNTS329	103695
Belgium	Germany, West	24 Sep 56	263UNTS31	103766
Norway	Sweden	27 Sep 56	261UNTS71	103726
Romania	Vietnam, North	12 Oct 56	342UNTS173	104907
Denmark	Italy	26 Oct 56	267UNTS261	103847
Romania	Yugoslavia	27 Oct 56	389UNTS33	105590
India	Japan	29 Oct 56	318UNTS289	104622
Bulgaria	Yugoslavia	24 Dec 56	397UNTS3	105699
Poland	United Arab Rep	02 Feb 57	319UNTS221	104633
Belgium	Yugoslavia	05 Feb 57	276UNTS143	103990
Taiwan	Turkey	12 Feb 57	282UNTS125	104097
USSR (Soviet Union)	Vietnam, North	15 Feb 57	274UNTS115	103962
Japan	United Arab Rep	20 Mar 57	318UNTS345	104625
India	Poland	27 Mar 57	319UNTS263	104635
Poland	Vietnam, North	06 Apr 57	432UNTS255	106224
Romania	United Arab Rep	15 Apr 57	389UNTS21	105589
Iran	Japan	16 Apr 57	325UNTS113	104697
Argentina	Israel	23 May 57	280UNTS199	104059
Japan	Pakistan	27 May 57	325UNTS21	104692
Czechoslovakia	Syria	18 Jun 57	303UNTS119	104374
Czechoslovakia	United Arab Rep	19 Oct 57	530UNTS181	107681
United Arab Rep	USSR (Soviet Union)	19 Oct 57	292UNTS151	104271
Germany, East	Hungary	25 Oct 57	408UNTS156	105869
France	Italy	08 Nov 57	305UNTS393	104427
Taiwan	Iran	11 Nov 57	563UNTS31	108202
Argentina	Italy	25 Nov 57	305UNTS275	104424
Italy	Yugoslavia	12 Dec 57	386UNTS293	105549
Belgium	Denmark	31 Dec 57	305UNTS247	104422
Ceylon (Sri Lanka)	USSR (Soviet Union)	15 Jan 58	305UNTS235	104421
USA (United States)	USSR (Soviet Union)	27 Jan 58	301UNTS405	104350
Czechoslovakia	Hungary	12 Mar 58	408UNTS178	105870
Taiwan	Costa Rica	10 Apr 58	315UNTS165	104567
Germany, West	UK Great Britain	18 Apr 58	343UNTS241	104928
Germany, East	Romania	15 Jul 58	387UNTS115	105560
Czechoslovakia	Romania	25 Oct 58	338UNTS301	104843
Belgium	Spain	27 Oct 58	327UNTS107	104720
El Salvador	Israel	14 Nov 58	345UNTS67	104959
Multilateral		15 Dec 58	546UNTS235	107950
Mongolia	Poland	23 Dec 58	432UNTS177	106220
Belgium	Turkey	29 Dec 58	357UNTS195	105118
Hungary	Iraq	11 Apr 59	439UNTS25	106323
Hungary	USSR (Soviet Union)	17 Apr 59	439UNTS41	106324
Iraq	USSR (Soviet Union)	05 May 59	356UNTS179	105095
Iran	UK Great Britain	06 May 59	398UNTS51	105717
Iran	Netherlands	22 May 59	474UNTS195	106882
Finland	Hungary	10 Jun 59	439UNTS3	106321

PARTY ONE	PARTY TWO	DATE	CITATION	NUMBER
Mass media exchange (Cont.)				
Taiwan	Ecuador	12 Jun 59	387UNTS3	105554
Argentina	Sweden	12 Jun 59	427UNTS337	106164
Israel	Mexico	15 Jun 59	377UNTS267	105406
Greece	Yugoslavia	18 Jun 59	368UNTS137	105238
Brazil	Israel	24 Jun 59	515UNTS151	107458
Czechoslovakia	India	07 Jul 59	359UNTS259	105145
Iraq	Romania	04 Aug 59	502UNTS17	107324
Bulgaria	Czechoslovakia	19 Sep 59	355UNTS77	105074
Korea, South	USA (United States)	25 Sep 59	358UNTS163	105133
USA (United States)	USSR (Soviet Union)	21 Nov 59	361UNTS35	105172
France	Israel	30 Nov 59	377UNTS237	105404
Czechoslovakia	Guinea	30 Nov 59	386UNTS63	105538
Czechoslovakia	Ethiopia	11 Dec 59	399UNTS93	105736
Germany, East	Hungary	19 Dec 59	409UNTS4	105874
Belgium	Brazil	06 Jan 60	531UNTS149	107701
Guinea	Hungary	12 Jan 60	519UNTS131	107505
Italy	USSR (Soviet Union)	09 Feb 60	399UNTS75	105735
Taiwan	Panama	26 Feb 60	435UNTS281	106285
Indonesia	USSR (Soviet Union)	28 Feb 60	392UNTS191	105644
UK Great Britain	Yugoslavia	12 Apr 60	360UNTS79	105155
Netherlands	Turkey	12 May 60	463UNTS207	106704
Belgium	Iran	14 May 60	522UNTS249	107551
Finland	USSR (Soviet Union)	27 May 60	379UNTS381	105444
Multilateral		22 Jun 60	431UNTS41	106208
Spain	UK Great Britain	12 Jul 60	414UNTS123	105971
Cuba	Korea, North	29 Aug 60	473UNTS117	106860
Israel	UK Great Britain	31 Aug 60	385UNTS71	105530
Cuba	Romania	28 Oct 60	457UNTS9	106574
Czechoslovakia	Ghana	23 Nov 60	431UNTS91	106213
Israel	Mali	24 Nov 60	413UNTS104	105945
Cambodia	Czechoslovakia	27 Nov 60	410UNTS263	105910
Japan	UK Great Britain	03 Dec 60	414UNTS61	105966
Romania	USA (United States)	09 Dec 60	401UNTS19	105759
Cuba	USSR (Soviet Union)	12 Dec 60	421UNTS3	106048
Cuba	Czechoslovakia	22 Dec 60	426UNTS145	106134
UK Great Britain	USSR (Soviet Union)	09 Jan 61	404UNTS175	105810
Ethiopia	USSR (Soviet Union)	13 Jan 61	421UNTS13	106049
Czechoslovakia	Hungary	24 Feb 61	422UNTS15	106066
Cuba	Poland	06 Mar 61	484UNTS123	107020
Cuba	Germany, East	29 Mar 61	448UNTS81	106426
India	Norway	19 Apr 61	404UNTS307	105818
Afghanistan	Czechoslovakia	23 Apr 61	437UNTS25	106297
Taiwan	Nicaragua	25 Apr 61	423UNTS139	106090
Germany, West	Netherlands	27 Apr 61	487UNTS77	107095
Ghana	Hungary	27 Apr 61	439UNTS17	106322
Taiwan	Uruguay	03 May 61	596UNTS121	108630
Somalia	USSR (Soviet Union)	02 Jun 61	528UNTS147	107638
Czechoslovakia	Somalia	04 Jun 61	479UNTS291	106960
Pakistan	Philippines	15 Aug 61	522UNTS35	107534
Taiwan	Paraguay	18 Aug 61	438UNTS109	106314
Ghana	Romania	30 Sep 61	457UNTS3	106573
Hungary	Iraq	11 Oct 61	577UNTS231	108380
Taiwan	Jordan	17 Oct 61	435UNTS267	106284
Brazil	Poland	19 Oct 61	552UNTS75	108050
Belgium	Italy	28 Oct 61	429UNTS199	106199
Guatemala	Israel	27 Nov 61	448UNTS191	106431
Taiwan	El Salvador	27 Nov 61	437UNTS161	106306
UK Great Britain	Yugoslavia	13 Feb 62	431UNTS35	106207
USA (United States)	USSR (Soviet Union)	08 Mar 62	460UNTS3	106630
Hungary	India	30 Mar 62	519UNTS119	107504
United Arab Rep	USA (United States)	21 May 62	458UNTS197	106601
Senegal	USSR (Soviet Union)	14 Jun 62	437UNTS233	106309
Israel	Liberia	25 Jun 62	448UNTS295	106442
Israel	Peru	25 Jun 62	515UNTS263	107464
Costa Rica	Israel	31 Jul 62	484UNTS155	107024

PARTY ONE	PARTY TWO	DATE	CITATION	NUMBER
Mass media exchange (Cont.)				
Syria	USSR (Soviet Union)	19 Aug 62	457UNTS285	106588
Denmark	USSR (Soviet Union)	11 Sep 62	458UNTS3	106589
Cameroon	Israel	24 Oct 62	449UNTS15	106447
Belgium	Tunisia	21 Dec 62	482UNTS3	106987
UK Great Britain	USSR (Soviet Union)	21 Jan 63	475UNTS3	106887
Iraq	USA (United States)	23 Jan 63	488UNTS163	107126
Dahomey	USSR (Soviet Union)	20 Mar 63	528UNTS181	107641
Romania	USA (United States)	02 Apr 63	474UNTS95	106874
Czechoslovakia	Tunisia	06 Apr 63	555UNTS111	108106
Belgium	Venezuela	15 May 63	470UNTS259	106812
Cameroon	UK Great Britain	20 Aug 63	539UNTS233	107834
Canada	France	11 Oct 63	529UNTS71	107657
Hungary	Yugoslavia	15 Oct 63	577UNTS49	108372
Tanganyika	USSR (Soviet Union)	06 Nov 63	528UNTS157	107639
Belgium	Romania	13 Nov 63	520UNTS119	107513
Belgium	Pakistan	14 Nov 63	535UNTS393	107792
Belgium	Poland	09 Dec 63	514UNTS195	107448
USA (United States)	USSR (Soviet Union)	22 Feb 64	526UNTS131	107605
Mexico	Netherlands	08 Apr 64	575UNTS35	108353
Algeria	Czechoslovakia	14 May 64	538UNTS301	107817
Argentina	France	03 Oct 64	635UNTS155	109080
Czechoslovakia	Germany, East	06 Oct 64	545UNTS113	107927
Germany, East	Poland	06 Oct 64	552UNTS89	108051
Belgium	Mexico	19 Nov 64	546UNTS217	107949
Poland	Romania	26 Nov 64	552UNTS157	108053
Belgium	Sweden	11 Jan 65	533UNTS157	107741
Belgium	Hungary	11 Feb 65	544UNTS3	107908
UK Great Britain	USSR (Soviet Union)	13 Feb 65	543UNTS43	107896
Bulgaria	Czechoslovakia	22 May 65	545UNTS65	107925
Ethiopia	Hungary	25 May 65	577UNTS193	108377
China People's Rep	Romania	27 May 65	592UNTS3	108566
Pakistan	USSR (Soviet Union)	05 Jun 65	593UNTS115	108579
Uganda	USSR (Soviet Union)	24 Jul 65	596UNTS199	108633
Israel	Sierra Leone	22 Aug 65	550UNTS275	108022
France	UK Great Britain	21 Sep 65	561UNTS3	108177
Argentina	Belgium	05 Nov 65	635UNTS229	109086
Czechoslovakia	Poland	22 Jan 66	588UNTS175	108524
UK Great Britain	Yugoslavia	27 Jan 66	573UNTS243	108337
Brazil	Chile	18 Mar 66	0UNTS0	109418
Argentina	Taiwan	19 Mar 66	635UNTS281	109089
Rwanda	USSR (Soviet Union)	06 May 66	633UNTS217	109039
Morocco	USSR (Soviet Union)	27 Oct 66	608UNTS207	108817
France	Niger	25 Feb 67	0UNTS0	109261
France	USSR (Soviet Union)	08 Jul 67	0UNTS0	109378
Italy	Romania	08 Aug 67	642UNTS213	109175
Czechoslovakia	France	06 Mar 68	0UNTS0	109379
Information agency				
Multilateral		16 Nov 45	4UNTS275	100052
Multilateral		27 Jun 46	164UNTS37	102157
Bulgaria	Poland	28 Jun 47	15UNTS123	100230
Iran	USA (United States)	19 Oct 50	92UNTS135	101266
Multilateral		31 Mar 53	435UNTS191	106280
Ceylon (Sri Lanka)	USA (United States)	23 Aug 54	314UNTS297	104553
Multilateral		15 Jun 57	583UNTS3	108470
Germany, East	Hungary	19 Dec 59	409UNTS4	105874
UK Great Britain	Yugoslavia	08 Jun 61	437UNTS111	106300
Austria	Yugoslavia	30 Jun 61	443UNTS51	106358
Media guaranty				
Israel	USA (United States)	09 Jun 52	178UNTS297	102345
Pakistan	USA (United States)	01 May 54	237UNTS231	103349
Chile	USA (United States)	14 Jan 55	238UNTS191	103362
United Arab Rep	USA (United States)	07 Mar 55	252UNTS159	103565
Indonesia	USA (United States)	15 Sep 55	256UNTS293	103639
USA (United States)	Vietnam, South	03 Nov 55	239UNTS195	103379

PARTY ONE	PARTY TWO	DATE	CITATION	NUMBER
Media guaranty (Cont.)				
Bolivia	USA (United States)	10 Mar 56	270UNTS199	103897
Poland	USSR (Soviet Union)	30 Jun 56	259UNTS311	103694
Burma	USA (United States)	23 Oct 56	282UNTS37	104091
Poland	USA (United States)	12 Feb 58	304UNTS287	104403
Bulgaria	Hungary	13 Mar 58	438UNTS173	106316
Korea, South	USA (United States)	25 Sep 59	358UNTS163	105133
Afghanistan	USA (United States)	15 Feb 61	406UNTS235	105852
Guinea	USA (United States)	03 Nov 62	459UNTS259	106628
Press and wire services				
Multilateral		04 Dec 45	9UNTS101	100128
France	Poland	19 May 47	12UNTS95	100181
Bulgaria	Czechoslovakia	20 Jun 47	46UNTS15	100698
Austria	USA (United States)	25 Jun 47	22UNTS141	100334
Italy	USA (United States)	04 Jul 47	22UNTS173	100336
Czechoslovakia	Romania	05 Sep 47	46UNTS37	100699
Hungary	Yugoslavia	15 Oct 47	33UNTS73	100515
Taiwan	USA (United States)	27 Oct 47	12UNTS11	100178
Colombia	USA (United States)	22 Dec 47	51UNTS45	100751
Poland	Romania	27 Feb 48	46UNTS143	100707
Korea, South	USA (United States)	10 Dec 48	55UNTS157	100813
USA (United States)	Yugoslavia	21 Nov 50	93UNTS39	101285
Albania	Poland	02 Dec 50	260UNTS131	103707
USA (United States)	Yugoslavia	06 Jan 51	122UNTS137	101643
China People's Rep	Poland	03 Apr 51	304UNTS187	104396
Germany, East	Poland	08 Jan 52	304UNTS113	104394
Japan	USA (United States)	28 Feb 52	208UNTS255	102817
Multilateral		11 Jul 52	171UNTS191	102227
Albania	Romania	14 Feb 53	342UNTS107	104903
Multilateral		31 Mar 53	435UNTS191	106280
Israel	Uruguay	30 Apr 53	280UNTS269	104064
India	USA (United States)	21 Oct 54	234UNTS119	103277
Romania	USSR (Soviet Union)	07 Apr 56	259UNTS377	103698
Albania	USSR (Soviet Union)	03 May 56	259UNTS391	103699
Mongolia	Romania	08 May 56	342UNTS291	104913
Korea, North	Romania	12 May 56	342UNTS189	104908
Turkey	USA (United States)	18 May 56	283UNTS167	104115
Czechoslovakia	USSR (Soviet Union)	01 Jun 56	259UNTS341	103696
Poland	USSR (Soviet Union)	30 Jun 56	259UNTS311	103694
China People's Rep	USSR (Soviet Union)	05 Jul 56	263UNTS129	103770
Poland	Yugoslavia	06 Jul 56	281UNTS143	104076
Romania	Vietnam, North	12 Oct 56	342UNTS173	104907
Romania	Yugoslavia	27 Oct 56	389UNTS33	105590
Czechoslovakia	Yugoslavia	29 Jan 57	300UNTS249	104339
USSR (Soviet Union)	Vietnam, North	15 Feb 57	274UNTS115	103962
France	USA (United States)	12 Mar 57	279UNTS275	104045
India	Poland	27 Mar 57	319UNTS263	104635
Poland	Vietnam, North	06 Apr 57	432UNTS255	106224
Romania	United Arab Rep	15 Apr 57	389UNTS21	105589
India	Romania	30 Apr 57	342UNTS251	104911
Multilateral		03 Oct 57	366UNTS255	105219
USA (United States)	USSR (Soviet Union)	27 Jan 58	301UNTS405	104350
Germany, East	Romania	15 Jul 58	387UNTS115	105560
Czechoslovakia	Romania	25 Oct 58	338UNTS301	104843
Mongolia	Poland	23 Dec 58	432UNTS177	106220
Iraq	USSR (Soviet Union)	05 May 59	356UNTS179	105095
Brazil	Israel	24 Jun 59	515UNTS151	107458
Iraq	Romania	04 Aug 59	502UNTS17	107324
Czechoslovakia	Guinea	30 Nov 59	386UNTS63	105538
Germany, East	Hungary	19 Dec 59	409UNTS4	105874
Guinea	Hungary	12 Jan 60	519UNTS131	107505
Denmark	USA (United States)	19 Feb 60	354UNTS151	105061
Taiwan	Panama	26 Feb 60	435UNTS281	106285
Greece	USA (United States)	26 Apr 60	372UNTS299	105306
Belgium	USA (United States)	18 May 60	373UNTS31	105313

PARTY ONE	PARTY TWO	DATE	CITATION	NUMBER
Press and wire services (Cont.)				
Cuba	Korea, North	29 Aug 60	473UNTS117	106860
Multilateral		21 Sep 60	394UNTS3	105664
Cuba	Romania	28 Oct 60	457UNTS9	106574
Portugal	USA (United States)	31 Oct 60	394UNTS127	105673
Cuba	USSR (Soviet Union)	12 Dec 60	421UNTS3	106048
Cambodia	Thailand	15 Dec 60	382UNTS301	105490
Cuba	Czechoslovakia	22 Dec 60	426UNTS145	106134
Czechoslovakia	Hungary	24 Feb 61	422UNTS15	106066
Cuba	Poland	06 Mar 61	484UNTS123	107020
Cuba	Germany, East	29 Mar 61	448UNTS81	106426
India	Norway	19 Apr 61	404UNTS307	105818
Taiwan	Nicaragua	25 Apr 61	423UNTS139	106090
Taiwan	Paraguay	18 Aug 61	438UNTS109	106314
Ghana	Romania	30 Sep 61	457UNTS3	106573
Taiwan	Jordan	17 Oct 61	435UNTS267	106284
Brazil	Poland	19 Oct 61	552UNTS75	108050
Taiwan	El Salvador	27 Nov 61	437UNTS161	106306
USA (United States)	USSR (Soviet Union)	08 Mar 62	460UNTS3	106630
Israel	Peru	25 Jun 62	515UNTS263	107464
Denmark	USSR (Soviet Union)	11 Sep 62	458UNTS3	106589
Australia	India	23 Jan 63	456UNTS185	106556
Czechoslovakia	Tunisia	06 Apr 63	555UNTS111	108106
Denmark	Netherlands	06 Jun 63	484UNTS137	107021
Mali	Romania	26 Sep 63	528UNTS193	107642
USA (United States)	USSR (Soviet Union)	22 Feb 64	526UNTS131	107605
Algeria	Czechoslovakia	14 May 64	538UNTS301	107817
France	Norway	16 Jul 64	510UNTS229	107417
Germany, East	Poland	06 Oct 64	552UNTS89	108051
Czechoslovakia	Germany, East	06 Oct 64	545UNTS113	107927
Belgium	Hungary	11 Feb 65	544UNTS3	107908
Bulgaria	Czechoslovakia	22 May 65	545UNTS65	107925
China People's Rep	Romania	27 May 65	592UNTS3	108566
Uganda	USSR (Soviet Union)	24 Jul 65	596UNTS199	108633
Bulgaria	Hungary	19 Aug 65	577UNTS67	108373
United Nations	Senegal	12 Jan 66	551UNTS147	108039
Czechoslovakia	Poland	22 Jan 66	588UNTS175	108524
Philippines	United Nations	05 Apr 66	560UNTS191	108174
Morocco	USSR (Soviet Union)	27 Oct 66	608UNTS207	108817
Television				
Canada	USA (United States)	23 Jun 52	207UNTS25	102798
Saudi Arabia	USA (United States)	29 Jun 53	206UNTS23	102784
Argentina	France	03 Oct 64	635UNTS155	109080
General military				
Canada	USA (United States)	27 Jun 42	99UNTS223	200276
Canada	USA (United States)	15 Aug 42	99UNTS233	200277
Canada	USA (United States)	28 Dec 42	99UNTS241	200278
Canada	USA (United States)	13 Mar 43	99UNTS249	200279
Norway	USA (United States)	16 May 44	67UNTS253	200223
Ethiopia	UK Great Britain	19 Dec 44	93UNTS303	200272
Canada	USA (United States)	26 Feb 45	99UNTS273	200281
Multilateral		22 Mar 45	70UNTS237	200241
Poland	USSR (Soviet Union)	21 Apr 45	12UNTS391	200070
Multilateral		09 Jun 45	139UNTS381	200464
Canada	USA (United States)	06 Sep 45	99UNTS281	200282
Multilateral		28 Jun 46	138UNTS85	101862
Netherlands	Thailand	30 Jan 47	247UNTS353	103480
Germany, West	Greece	16 Mar 49	77UNTS327	101007
USA (United States)	Yugoslavia	24 Dec 49	89UNTS209	101219
Multilateral		08 Sep 51	136UNTS165	101833
Austria	USA (United States)	05 Jan 52	179UNTS73	102355
Multilateral		09 May 52	168UNTS65	102213
Philippines	Vatican/Holy See	18 Jun 52	543UNTS165	107900
Multilateral		23 Oct 54	332UNTS219	104762
Greece	UK Great Britain	07 Mar 55	211UNTS249	102856

PARTY ONE	PARTY TWO	DATE	CITATION	NUMBER
General military (Cont.)				
Iceland	USA (United States)	20 Jul 55	256UNTS245	103634
Germany, West	UK Great Britain	07 Jun 57	398UNTS275	105730
Post-war reconstruction				
France	USA (United States)	25 Aug 44	138UNTS247	200449
Belgium	UK Great Britain	11 Mar 46	26UNTS167	100387
Multilateral		28 Jun 46	138UNTS85	101862
UK Great Britain	USA (United States)	02 Dec 46	7UNTS163	100098
Multilateral		10 Feb 47	42UNTS3	100645
Korea, South	USA (United States)	11 Sep 48	89UNTS155	101216
Italy	USA (United States)	29 Mar 57	299UNTS157	104311
Burial arrangements				
Multilateral		12 Aug 49	75UNTS287	100973
Multilateral		23 Dec 50	185UNTS3	102456
Germany, West	New Zealand	05 Mar 56	402UNTS103	105779
Multilateral		05 Mar 56	326UNTS181	104712
Australia	Germany, West	05 Mar 56	328UNTS241	104737
Canada	France	04 Sep 56	305UNTS79	104415
Italy	Yugoslavia	12 Feb 60	379UNTS77	105434
New Zealand	USA (United States)	08 Jun 62	458UNTS209	106602
Multilateral		10 Sep 62	502UNTS3	107323
Denmark	Germany, West	03 Oct 62	450UNTS291	106475
Netherlands	UK Great Britain	27 Aug 63	490UNTS3	107150
Germany, West	Greece	26 Sep 63	550UNTS203	108017
Germany, West	Ireland	13 May 64	553UNTS87	108071
Multilateral		26 Apr 65	533UNTS50	107732
Greece	UK Great Britain	12 Oct 66	578UNTS33	108385
Repatriation of combatants				
Multilateral		10 Feb 47	42UNTS3	100645
Israel	United Arab Rep	24 Feb 49	42UNTS251	100654
Multilateral		12 Aug 49	75UNTS287	100973
South Africa	UK Great Britain	30 Jun 55	248UNTS191	103495
Bulgaria	Germany, East	07 Sep 67	631UNTS81	108988
Joint defense				
Multilateral		29 Jan 42	93UNTS279	200271
Norway	USA (United States)	28 Aug 42	139UNTS361	200461
Australia	New Zealand	21 Jan 44	18UNTS357	200113
France	USA (United States)	25 Aug 44	138UNTS247	200449
Canada	USA (United States)	06 Dec 46	149UNTS3	101945
Philippines	USA (United States)	14 Mar 47	43UNTS271	100673
Denmark	UK Great Britain	22 Apr 47	8UNTS3	100110
Norway	UK Great Britain	05 Jun 47	54UNTS181	100803
Multilateral		04 Apr 49	34UNTS243	100541
Canada	USA (United States)	12 Apr 49	206UNTS241	102789
Belgium	UK Great Britain	23 Dec 49	99UNTS61	101371
Korea, South	USA (United States)	26 Jan 50	80UNTS205	101053
Luxembourg	USA (United States)	27 Jan 50	80UNTS187	101052
France	USA (United States)	27 Jan 50	80UNTS171	101051
Netherlands	USA (United States)	27 Jan 50	80UNTS219	101054
UK Great Britain	USA (United States)	27 Jan 50	80UNTS261	101056
Belgium	USA (United States)	27 Jan 50	51UNTS213	100767
Norway	USA (United States)	27 Jan 50	80UNTS241	101055
Denmark	USA (United States)	27 Jan 50	48UNTS115	100740
Italy	USA (United States)	27 Jan 50	80UNTS145	101050
Thailand	USA (United States)	17 Oct 50	79UNTS41	101030
Portugal	USA (United States)	05 Jan 51	133UNTS75	101782
France	USA (United States)	27 Feb 51	0UNTS0	109598
Canada	USA (United States)	27 Mar 51	132UNTS333	101772
Canada	USA (United States)	01 Aug 51	233UNTS109	103254
Portugal	USA (United States)	06 Sep 51	237UNTS217	103348
Ecuador	USA (United States)	20 Feb 52	177UNTS43	102308
Peru	USA (United States)	22 Feb 52	165UNTS31	102166
Cuba	USA (United States)	07 Mar 52	165UNTS11	102165
Brazil	USA (United States)	15 Mar 52	199UNTS221	102687

PARTY ONE	PARTY TWO	DATE	CITATION	NUMBER
Joint defense (Cont.)				
Chile	USA (United States)	09 Apr 52	186UNTS53	102482
Colombia	USA (United States)	17 Apr 52	174UNTS215	102287
Korea, South	USA (United States)	24 May 52	179UNTS23	102353
USA (United States)	Uruguay	30 Jun 52	207UNTS139	102804
France	USA (United States)	04 Oct 52	0UNTS0	109599
Dominican Republic	USA (United States)	06 Mar 53	199UNTS267	102689
Philippines	USA (United States)	26 Jun 53	213UNTS77	102881
Libya	UK Great Britain	29 Jul 53	186UNTS201	102492
Korea, South	USA (United States)	01 Oct 53	238UNTS199	103363
Japan	USA (United States)	08 Mar 54	232UNTS169	103236
Honduras	USA (United States)	20 May 54	222UNTS87	103025
Korea, South	USA (United States)	17 Nov 54	256UNTS251	103635
Netherlands	USA (United States)	14 Dec 54	262UNTS35	103737
Haiti	USA (United States)	28 Jan 55	270UNTS83	103894
Iraq	Turkey	24 Feb 55	233UNTS199	103264
Canada	USA (United States)	05 May 55	241UNTS179	103433
Multilateral		14 May 55	219UNTS3	102962
Guatemala	USA (United States)	18 Jun 55	262UNTS105	103740
South Africa	UK Great Britain	30 Jun 55	248UNTS191	103495
Germany, West	USA (United States)	30 Jun 55	240UNTS47	103393
Syria	United Arab Rep	20 Oct 55	247UNTS117	103461
New Zealand	UK Great Britain	04 Jul 57	402UNTS109	105780
Greece	USA (United States)	05 Aug 57	290UNTS167	104235
Fed of Malaya	UK Great Britain	12 Oct 57	285UNTS59	104149
Ghana	WHO (World Health)	21 Jan 58	307UNTS3	104437
UK Great Britain	USA (United States)	22 Feb 58	307UNTS207	104451
Canada	USA (United States)	12 May 58	316UNTS151	104582
Philippines	USA (United States)	15 May 58	316UNTS163	104583
Muscat and Oman	UK Great Britain	25 Jul 58	312UNTS347	104524
Taiwan	USA (United States)	06 Aug 58	462UNTS3	106666
Canada	USA (United States)	02 Sep 58	335UNTS249	104792
Canada	USA (United States)	22 May 59	354UNTS63	105054
Canada	USA (United States)	13 Jul 59	353UNTS237	105045
Turkey	USA (United States)	02 Mar 60	372UNTS37	105286
Denmark	USA (United States)	02 Dec 60	402UNTS245	105789
Canada	USA (United States)	12 Jun 61	410UNTS21	105894
France	USA (United States)	27 Jul 61	433UNTS29	106229
Canada	USA (United States)	23 Sep 61	421UNTS79	106053
Canada	USA (United States)	27 Sep 61	421UNTS85	106054
Belgium	USA (United States)	17 May 62	461UNTS3	106647
UK Great Britain	USA (United States)	06 Apr 63	474UNTS49	106871
Canada	USA (United States)	15 Nov 63	493UNTS67	107207
Multilateral		14 Dec 63	507UNTS149	107399
Taiwan	USA (United States)	19 Dec 63	527UNTS69	107617
Brazil	USA (United States)	30 Jan 64	511UNTS77	107428
Netherlands	NATO (North Atlan)	25 May 64	544UNTS237	107920
Japan	USA (United States)	04 Dec 64	532UNTS249	107721
Canada	USA (United States)	01 Dec 65	574UNTS37	108340
UK Great Britain	USA (United States)	30 Dec 66	603UNTS245	108736
Defense and security				
Netherlands	USA (United States)	17 Jan 33	474UNTS119	106877
Iceland	USA (United States)	01 Jul 41	12UNTS405	200071
Multilateral		29 Jan 42	93UNTS279	200271
Liberia	USA (United States)	31 Mar 42	23UNTS302	200137
Nicaragua	USA (United States)	08 Apr 42	132UNTS343	200439
USA (United States)	USSR (Soviet Union)	18 Apr 42	105UNTS285	200339
Taiwan	USA (United States)	02 Jun 42	14UNTS343	200092
Belgium	USA (United States)	16 Jun 42	105UNTS159	200329
Poland	USA (United States)	01 Jul 42	103UNTS267	200317
Netherlands	USA (United States)	08 Jul 42	103UNTS277	200318
Greece	USA (United States)	10 Jul 42	103UNTS289	200319
Czechoslovakia	USA (United States)	11 Jul 42	90UNTS257	200263
USA (United States)	Yugoslavia	24 Jul 42	34UNTS361	200179
Norway	USA (United States)	28 Aug 42	139UNTS361	200461

Defense and security (Cont.)

PARTY ONE	PARTY TWO	DATE	CITATION	NUMBER
Australia	USA (United States)	03 Sep 42	24UNTS195	200143
New Zealand	USA (United States)	03 Sep 42	24UNTS185	200142
France	USA (United States)	03 Sep 42	24UNTS177	200141
Belgium	USA (United States)	30 Jan 43	13UNTS371	200084
USA (United States)	Venezuela	18 Feb 43	21UNTS225	200125
Colombia	USA (United States)	29 Mar 43	124UNTS139	200416
Chile	USA (United States)	11 May 43	139UNTS295	200456
Panama	USA (United States)	07 Jun 43	21UNTS269	200128
Liberia	USA (United States)	08 Jun 43	117UNTS242	200373
Netherlands	USA (United States)	14 Jun 43	28UNTS397	200163
Dominican Republic	USA (United States)	07 Jul 43	28UNTS419	200165
Ethiopia	USA (United States)	09 Aug 43	29UNTS303	200169
UK Great Britain	USA (United States)	19 Aug 43	214UNTS341	200527
Liberia	USA (United States)	31 Dec 43	106UNTS199	200341
Australia	New Zealand	21 Jan 44	18UNTS357	200113
Canada	Taiwan	22 Mar 44	14UNTS397	200096
Albania	Yugoslavia	23 Mar 44	1UNTS81	100015
Portugal	USA (United States)	28 Nov 44	183UNTS311	200508
Ethiopia	UK Great Britain	19 Dec 44	93UNTS303	200272
France	USA (United States)	20 Feb 45	76UNTS193	200246
France	USA (United States)	28 Feb 45	76UNTS213	200247
South Africa	USA (United States)	17 Apr 45	90UNTS267	200264
Poland	USSR (Soviet Union)	21 Apr 45	12UNTS391	200070
Canada	USA (United States)	15 May 45	125UNTS353	200433
Iraq	USA (United States)	31 Jul 45	121UNTS239	200402
Taiwan	USSR (Soviet Union)	14 Aug 45	10UNTS300	200068
United Arab Rep	Yemen	27 Sep 45	9UNTS373	200053
Denmark	UK Great Britain	24 Oct 45	93UNTS143	101297
Mongolia	USSR (Soviet Union)	27 Feb 46	48UNTS177	100744
Jordan	UK Great Britain	22 Mar 46	6UNTS143	100074
Czechoslovakia	Yugoslavia	09 May 46	1UNTS67	100014
Taiwan	USA (United States)	28 Jun 46	34UNTS121	100532
Philippines	USA (United States)	04 Jul 46	7UNTS3	100088
Canada	USA (United States)	06 Dec 46	149UNTS3	101945
France	UK Great Britain	04 Mar 47	9UNTS187	100132
Czechoslovakia	Poland	10 Mar 47	25UNTS231	100365
Philippines	USA (United States)	14 Mar 47	43UNTS271	100673
Guatemala	USA (United States)	29 Aug 47	27UNTS11	100393
Multilateral		02 Sep 47	21UNTS77	100324
Ceylon (Sri Lanka)	UK Great Britain	11 Nov 47	86UNTS19	101148
Romania	Yugoslavia	19 Dec 47	116UNTS89	101571
Hungary	Romania	24 Jan 48	477UNTS155	106920
Romania	USSR (Soviet Union)	04 Feb 48	48UNTS189	100745
Hungary	USSR (Soviet Union)	18 Feb 48	48UNTS163	100743
Jordan	UK Great Britain	15 Mar 48	77UNTS77	100994
Multilateral		17 Mar 48	19UNTS51	100304
Bulgaria	USSR (Soviet Union)	18 Mar 48	48UNTS135	100741
Finland	USSR (Soviet Union)	06 Apr 48	48UNTS149	100742
Multilateral		30 Apr 48	119UNTS3	101609
Bulgaria	Poland	29 May 48	26UNTS213	100389
Bulgaria	Hungary	16 Jul 48	477UNTS169	106921
Korea, South	USA (United States)	24 Aug 48	79UNTS57	101031
Greece	UK Great Britain	07 Sep 48	180UNTS144	102380
Poland	Romania	26 Jan 49	85UNTS21	101143
Multilateral		04 Apr 49	34UNTS243	100541
Canada	USA (United States)	12 Apr 49	206UNTS241	102789
Czechoslovakia	Hungary	16 Apr 49	477UNTS183	106922
Ecuador	Italy	24 Aug 49	72UNTS35	100926
Belgium	UK Great Britain	23 Dec 49	99UNTS61	101371
Korea, South	USA (United States)	26 Jan 50	178UNTS97	102337
Korea, South	USA (United States)	26 Jan 50	80UNTS205	101053
France	USA (United States)	27 Jan 50	80UNTS171	101051
Norway	USA (United States)	27 Jan 50	80UNTS241	101055
Netherlands	USA (United States)	27 Jan 50	80UNTS219	101054
Italy	USA (United States)	27 Jan 50	80UNTS145	101050

Defense and security (Cont.)

PARTY ONE	PARTY TWO	DATE	CITATION	NUMBER
Denmark	USA (United States)	27 Jan 50	48UNTS115	100740
UK Great Britain	USA (United States)	27 Jan 50	80UNTS261	101056
Luxembourg	USA (United States)	27 Jan 50	80UNTS187	101052
Belgium	USA (United States)	27 Jan 50	51UNTS213	100767
India	Nepal	31 Jul 50	94UNTS3	101302
Canada	USA (United States)	26 Oct 50	132UNTS247	101764
Burma	USA (United States)	06 Nov 50	122UNTS81	101638
USA (United States)	Yugoslavia	21 Nov 50	93UNTS45	101286
Pakistan	USA (United States)	15 Dec 50	122UNTS89	101639
Brazil	USA (United States)	04 Jan 51	165UNTS97	102171
Chile	USA (United States)	04 Jan 51	165UNTS105	102172
Argentina	USA (United States)	08 Jan 51	165UNTS89	102170
Taiwan	USA (United States)	09 Feb 51	132UNTS273	101767
Australia	USA (United States)	20 Feb 51	132UNTS297	101769
Multilateral		06 Mar 51	138UNTS67	101860
Canada	USA (United States)	27 Mar 51	132UNTS333	101772
USA (United States)	Yugoslavia	17 Apr 51	162UNTS173	102134
Iceland	USA (United States)	05 May 51	205UNTS173	102776
Canada	USA (United States)	01 Aug 51	233UNTS109	103254
Philippines	USA (United States)	30 Aug 51	177UNTS133	102315
Multilateral		01 Sep 51	131UNTS83	101736
Japan	USA (United States)	08 Sep 51	136UNTS211	101835
Japan	USA (United States)	08 Sep 51	136UNTS203	101834
Cuba	USA (United States)	18 Dec 51	165UNTS3	102164
Germany, West	USA (United States)	28 Dec 51	181UNTS45	102397
Cambodia	USA (United States)	28 Dec 51	179UNTS97	102358
Thailand	USA (United States)	29 Dec 51	179UNTS113	102360
Laos	USA (United States)	31 Dec 51	198UNTS243	102668
Taiwan	USA (United States)	02 Jan 52	181UNTS161	102407
Greece	USA (United States)	07 Jan 52	180UNTS171	102382
Italy	USA (United States)	07 Jan 52	179UNTS165	102365
Belgium	USA (United States)	07 Jan 52	179UNTS81	102356
Korea, South	USA (United States)	07 Jan 52	179UNTS105	102359
Philippines	USA (United States)	07 Jan 52	179UNTS193	102368
Turkey	USA (United States)	07 Jan 52	179UNTS121	102361
Denmark	USA (United States)	08 Jan 52	179UNTS65	102354
Netherlands	USA (United States)	08 Jan 52	179UNTS175	102366
Iceland	USA (United States)	08 Jan 52	180UNTS183	102383
Luxembourg	USA (United States)	08 Jan 52	180UNTS191	102384
UK Great Britain	USA (United States)	08 Jan 52	179UNTS201	102369
Norway	USA (United States)	08 Jan 52	179UNTS185	102367
USA (United States)	Vietnam, South	19 Jan 52	205UNTS127	102772
Burma	USA (United States)	09 Feb 52	179UNTS91	102357
Ecuador	USA (United States)	20 Feb 52	177UNTS43	102308
Peru	USA (United States)	22 Feb 52	165UNTS31	102166
Japan	USA (United States)	28 Feb 52	208UNTS255	102817
Cuba	USA (United States)	07 Mar 52	165UNTS11	102165
Brazil	USA (United States)	15 Mar 52	199UNTS221	102687
Chile	USA (United States)	09 Apr 52	186UNTS53	102482
Colombia	USA (United States)	17 Apr 52	174UNTS215	102287
Netherlands	USA (United States)	15 May 52	177UNTS233	102321
Ethiopia	USA (United States)	13 Jun 52	205UNTS17	102766
New Zealand	USA (United States)	19 Jun 52	178UNTS315	102347
South Africa	USA (United States)	24 Jun 52	177UNTS241	102322
USA (United States)	Uruguay	30 Jun 52	207UNTS139	102804
Israel	USA (United States)	23 Jul 52	179UNTS139	102363
China People's Rep	USSR (Soviet Union)	15 Sep 52	226UNTS45	103106
France	USA (United States)	04 Oct 52	0UNTS0	109599
Belgium	UK Great Britain	12 Nov 52	180UNTS15	102372
Nicaragua	USA (United States)	19 Nov 52	186UNTS3	102478
Portugal	UK Great Britain	21 Nov 52	404UNTS27	105802
Canada	USA (United States)	05 Dec 52	206UNTS11	102783
UK Great Britain	USA (United States)	19 Jan 53	161UNTS3	102117
Greece	USA (United States)	04 Feb 53	189UNTS3	102538
Dominican Republic	USA (United States)	06 Mar 53	199UNTS267	102689

PARTY ONE	PARTY TWO	DATE	CITATION	NUMBER
Defense and security (Cont.)				
Libya	UK Great Britain	21 Mar 53	172UNTS85	102240
Lebanon	USA (United States)	23 Mar 53	239UNTS45	103370
Belgium	Canada	30 Mar 53	181UNTS95	102401
Ethiopia	USA (United States)	22 May 53	207UNTS127	102803
Ethiopia	USA (United States)	22 May 53	191UNTS59	102577
Belgium	USA (United States)	18 Jun 53	222UNTS3	103019
Belgium	USA (United States)	02 Sep 53	200UNTS127	102700
Spain	USA (United States)	26 Sep 53	207UNTS83	102801
Korea, South	USA (United States)	01 Oct 53	238UNTS199	103363
Greece	USA (United States)	12 Oct 53	191UNTS319	102589
Japan	USA (United States)	21 Jan 54	223UNTS145	103063
Japan	USA (United States)	08 Mar 54	232UNTS169	103236
Japan	USA (United States)	08 Mar 54	232UNTS227	103238
Afghanistan	USA (United States)	20 Mar 54	229UNTS7	103156
Italy	USA (United States)	31 Mar 54	235UNTS293	103311
Luxembourg	USA (United States)	17 Apr 54	257UNTS255	103661
Iraq	USA (United States)	21 Apr 54	222UNTS251	103032
ECSC (Coal/Steel)	USA (United States)	23 Apr 54	229UNTS229	103170
Canada	USA (United States)	03 May 54	221UNTS339	103015
Norway	USA (United States)	07 May 54	231UNTS157	103215
Netherlands	USA (United States)	07 May 54	213UNTS325	102895
Spain	USA (United States)	19 May 54	235UNTS87	103296
Honduras	USA (United States)	20 May 54	222UNTS87	103025
France	USA (United States)	31 May 54	236UNTS141	103321
UK Great Britain	USA (United States)	15 Jun 54	236UNTS133	103320
Italy	USA (United States)	24 Jun 54	235UNTS3	103290
Multilateral		09 Aug 54	211UNTS237	102855
Netherlands	USA (United States)	13 Aug 54	251UNTS91	103535
Multilateral		08 Sep 54	209UNTS23	102819
Libya	USA (United States)	09 Sep 54	224UNTS217	103078
China People's Rep	USSR (Soviet Union)	12 Oct 54	226UNTS51	103107
Germany, West	USA (United States)	15 Oct 54	239UNTS135	103375
Canada	UK Great Britain	19 Oct 54	214UNTS309	102906
Multilateral		23 Oct 54	332UNTS3	104760
Multilateral		23 Oct 54	334UNTS3	104765
Korea, South	USA (United States)	17 Nov 54	256UNTS251	103635
Belgium	USA (United States)	23 Nov 54	235UNTS19	103292
Iceland	USA (United States)	10 Dec 54	237UNTS191	103345
Taiwan	USA (United States)	10 Dec 54	248UNTS213	103496
Netherlands	USA (United States)	14 Dec 54	262UNTS35	103737
Pakistan	USA (United States)	11 Jan 55	251UNTS111	103537
Haiti	USA (United States)	28 Jan 55	270UNTS83	103894
Iraq	Turkey	24 Feb 55	233UNTS199	103264
Germany, West	USA (United States)	04 Apr 55	279UNTS73	104034
Norway	USA (United States)	06 Apr 55	269UNTS65	103874
Turkey	USA (United States)	25 Apr 55	263UNTS299	103779
Netherlands	USA (United States)	29 Apr 55	251UNTS357	103553
Multilateral		14 May 55	219UNTS3	102962
Greece	USA (United States)	27 May 55	251UNTS349	103552
UK Great Britain	USA (United States)	15 Jun 55	214UNTS301	102905
Multilateral		22 Jun 55	249UNTS3	103498
Turkey	USA (United States)	29 Jun 55	269UNTS97	103878
South Africa	UK Great Britain	30 Jun 55	248UNTS191	103495
Brazil	USA (United States)	20 Sep 55	257UNTS349	103665
Germany, West	USA (United States)	04 Jan 56	268UNTS143	103856
Iceland	USA (United States)	06 Dec 56	265UNTS261	103818
Poland	USSR (Soviet Union)	17 Dec 56	266UNTS179	103830
Brazil	USA (United States)	21 Jan 57	278UNTS97	104025
Canada	Netherlands	13 Apr 57	316UNTS223	104588
Romania	USSR (Soviet Union)	15 Apr 57	274UNTS143	103964
Canada	Norway	17 Apr 57	316UNTS215	104587
Canada	Denmark	17 Apr 57	316UNTS207	104586
Iraq	USA (United States)	16 Jun 57	284UNTS39	104127
Greece	USA (United States)	05 Aug 57	290UNTS167	104235
France	USA (United States)	23 Sep 57	293UNTS297	104297

PARTY ONE	PARTY TWO	DATE	CITATION	NUMBER
Defense and security (Cont.)				
Fed of Malaya	UK Great Britain	12 Oct 57	285UNTS59	104149
Ethiopia	USA (United States)	26 Dec 57	307UNTS71	104443
UK Great Britain	USA (United States)	22 Feb 58	307UNTS207	104451
Canada	USA (United States)	12 May 58	316UNTS151	104582
Canada	USA (United States)	20 Jun 58	317UNTS37	104592
Muscat and Oman	UK Great Britain	25 Jul 58	312UNTS347	104524
Multilateral		28 Jul 58	335UNTS205	104788
Canada	USA (United States)	02 Sep 58	335UNTS249	104792
Germany, West	UK Great Britain	03 Oct 58	398UNTS293	105731
Turkey	USA (United States)	14 Oct 58	336UNTS145	104803
Turkey	USA (United States)	05 Mar 59	327UNTS293	104727
Pakistan	USA (United States)	05 Mar 59	327UNTS285	104726
Iran	USA (United States)	05 Mar 59	327UNTS277	104725
Netherlands	USA (United States)	06 May 59	355UNTS327	105084
Greece	USA (United States)	06 May 59	357UNTS163	105115
Canada	USA (United States)	22 May 59	354UNTS63	105054
Liberia	USA (United States)	08 Jul 59	357UNTS93	105108
Canada	USA (United States)	13 Jul 59	353UNTS237	105045
Turkey	USA (United States)	28 Oct 59	360UNTS265	105162
Turkey	USA (United States)	30 Nov 59	361UNTS107	105174
Japan	USA (United States)	19 Jan 60	373UNTS179	105320
Turkey	USA (United States)	02 Mar 60	372UNTS37	105286
Denmark	USA (United States)	12 Apr 60	373UNTS9	105311
Japan	USA (United States)	15 Apr 60	372UNTS267	105303
Norway	USA (United States)	06 Jul 60	378UNTS25	105415
Italy	USA (United States)	07 Jul 60	380UNTS143	105455
Spain	USA (United States)	21 Jul 60	393UNTS289	105663
Multilateral		16 Aug 60	382UNTS8	105476
Australia	USA (United States)	23 Aug 60	388UNTS237	105581
France	USA (United States)	19 Sep 60	400UNTS21	105745
Norway	USA (United States)	29 Nov 60	404UNTS251	105815
Denmark	USA (United States)	02 Dec 60	402UNTS245	105789
UK Great Britain	USA (United States)	10 Feb 61	409UNTS68	105879
Colombia	USA (United States)	03 Apr 61	407UNTS3	105856
Canada	USA (United States)	12 Jun 61	410UNTS21	105894
Liberia	USA (United States)	17 Jun 61	410UNTS233	105907
Korea, North	USSR (Soviet Union)	06 Jul 61	420UNTS145	106045
France	USA (United States)	27 Jul 61	433UNTS29	106229
Canada	USA (United States)	27 Sep 61	421UNTS85	106054
Canada	Greece	18 Jul 62	528UNTS265	107647
Multilateral		23 Jul 62	456UNTS302	106564
Japan	USA (United States)	28 Aug 62	460UNTS267	106645
Saudi Arabia	USA (United States)	13 Nov 62	488UNTS175	107127
Multilateral		12 Dec 62	552UNTS15	108048
Peru	USA (United States)	20 Dec 62	471UNTS75	106822
Japan	USA (United States)	26 Apr 63	477UNTS37	106914
Canada	USA (United States)	15 Nov 63	493UNTS67	107207
Multilateral		14 Dec 63	507UNTS149	107399
Taiwan	USA (United States)	19 Dec 63	527UNTS69	107617
Brazil	USA (United States)	30 Jan 64	511UNTS77	107428
Germany, East	USSR (Soviet Union)	12 Jun 64	553UNTS249	108093
Italy	USA (United States)	04 Aug 64	529UNTS205	107662
Malta	UK Great Britain	21 Sep 64	588UNTS55	108518
Japan	USA (United States)	04 Dec 64	532UNTS249	107721
Taiwan	USA (United States)	19 Dec 64	532UNTS313	107725
Poland	USSR (Soviet Union)	08 Apr 65	540UNTS97	107845
Canada	USA (United States)	01 Dec 65	574UNTS37	108340
Mongolia	USSR (Soviet Union)	15 Jan 66	562UNTS43	108194
Germany, East	Poland	15 Mar 67	618UNTS21	108922
Czechoslovakia	Germany, East	17 Mar 67	609UNTS187	108831
Bulgaria	Poland	06 Apr 67	617UNTS327	108920
Bulgaria	USSR (Soviet Union)	12 May 67	631UNTS239	108997
Bulgaria	Germany, East	07 Sep 67	631UNTS81	108988
Mauritius	UK Great Britain	12 Mar 68	0UNTS0	109267

PARTY ONE	PARTY TWO	DATE	CITATION	NUMBER
Prisoners of war				
Germany, West	USA (United States)	30 Mar 42	105UNTS219	200334
Multilateral		28 Oct 44	123UNTS223	200414
Multilateral		20 Jan 45	140UNTS397	200471
USA (United States)	USSR (Soviet Union)	11 Feb 45	68UNTS175	200229
Multilateral		05 Jun 45	68UNTS189	200230
Multilateral		02 Sep 45	139UNTS387	200465
Taiwan	France	28 Feb 46	14UNTS151	100217
Belgium	UK Great Britain	11 Mar 46	26UNTS167	100387
Thailand	UK Great Britain	06 Jan 47	99UNTS149	101376
France	USA (United States)	11 Mar 47	151UNTS159	101991
Israel	United Arab Rep	24 Feb 49	42UNTS251	100654
Multilateral		12 Aug 49	75UNTS287	100973
Multilateral		12 Aug 49	75UNTS85	100971
Multilateral		12 Aug 49	75UNTS135	100972
Multilateral		12 Aug 49	75UNTS31	100970
Nicaragua	USA (United States)	01 Feb 50	99UNTS25	101368
France	USA (United States)	05 Jan 52	181UNTS177	102408
France	USA (United States)	02 Feb 52	247UNTS223	103472
Multilateral		11 Jul 52	170UNTS63	102222
Rearmament restrictions and controls				
Finland	USSR (Soviet Union)	11 Oct 40	67UNTS139	100872
Multilateral		20 Jan 45	140UNTS397	200471
Taiwan	USSR (Soviet Union)	14 Aug 45	10UNTS300	200068
Multilateral		10 Feb 47	48UNTS203	100746
Multilateral		10 Feb 47	49UNTS3	100747
Multilateral		10 Feb 47	42UNTS3	100645
Multilateral		10 Feb 47	41UNTS135	100644
Multilateral		10 Feb 47	41UNTS21	100643
Multilateral		20 Jun 49	128UNTS141	101718
Pakistan	Turkey	04 Feb 54	211UNTS263	102858
Multilateral		15 May 55	217UNTS223	102949
Repatriation of civilians				
Multilateral		12 May 40	101UNTS91	101405
Cuba	USA (United States)	27 Jan 48	67UNTS3	100862
Italy	USA (United States)	02 Feb 48	79UNTS171	101040
Greece	Lebanon	06 Oct 48	87UNTS351	101179
Multilateral		28 Feb 49	29UNTS53	100434
Peru	USA (United States)	25 Mar 49	89UNTS15	101205
Multilateral		12 Aug 49	75UNTS287	100973
Multilateral		12 Aug 49	75UNTS135	100972
WHO (World Health)	Thailand	04 Oct 51	109UNTS85	101493
Brazil	USA (United States)	03 Aug 55	270UNTS71	103893
Multilateral		13 Dec 55	250UNTS3	103514
Multilateral		17 Jun 60	536UNTS27	107794
Withdrawal or relief of occupation forces				
Poland	USA (United States)	24 Apr 46	4UNTS155	100042
Military assistance				
France	UK Great Britain	31 Aug 45	98UNTS249	200275
Peru	USA (United States)	07 Oct 46	7UNTS71	100092
Czechoslovakia	UK Great Britain	19 Feb 47	9UNTS173	100131
Colombia	USA (United States)	21 Feb 49	44UNTS83	100680
Multilateral		23 Dec 50	185UNTS3	102456
Liberia	USA (United States)	19 Nov 51	167UNTS141	102204
Belgium	USA (United States)	07 Apr 52	205UNTS3	102765
Greece	USA (United States)	24 Dec 52	185UNTS193	102470
Portugal	USA (United States)	01 Apr 53	205UNTS41	102769
Nicaragua	USA (United States)	23 Apr 54	229UNTS37	103159
Canada	USA (United States)	21 Jul 55	269UNTS53	103873
Bolivia	USA (United States)	22 Apr 58	317UNTS209	104605
Turkey	USA (United States)	05 May 59	355UNTS341	105085
Chad	France	19 May 64	0UNTS0	109443

PARTY ONE	PARTY TWO	DATE	CITATION	NUMBER
Atomic weapons				
UK Great Britain	USA (United States)	03 Jul 58	326UNTS3	104707
Turkey	USA (United States)	05 May 59	355UNTS341	105085
Canada	USA (United States)	22 May 59	354UNTS63	105054
Turkey	USA (United States)	28 Oct 59	360UNTS265	105162
Italy	USA (United States)	03 Dec 60	410UNTS3	105893
France	USA (United States)	27 Jul 61	433UNTS29	106229
Belgium	USA (United States)	17 May 62	461UNTS3	106647
UK Great Britain	USA (United States)	06 Apr 63	474UNTS49	106871
Multilateral		27 Jan 67	610UNTS205	108843
Multilateral		14 Feb 67	634UNTS281	109068
Self-defense				
Israel	Lebanon	23 Mar 49	42UNTS287	100655
Israel	Jordan	03 Apr 49	42UNTS303	100656
Israel	Syria	20 Jul 49	42UNTS327	100657
Denmark	USA (United States)	27 Jan 50	48UNTS115	100740
Belgium	USA (United States)	27 Jan 50	51UNTS213	100767
Taiwan	USA (United States)	09 Feb 51	132UNTS273	101767
South Africa	USA (United States)	09 Nov 51	160UNTS41	102100
USA (United States)	Yugoslavia	14 Nov 51	174UNTS201	102286
Cambodia	USA (United States)	28 Dec 51	179UNTS97	102358
Thailand	USA (United States)	29 Dec 51	179UNTS113	102360
Italy	USA (United States)	07 Jan 52	179UNTS165	102365
Korea, South	USA (United States)	07 Jan 52	179UNTS105	102359
Greece	USA (United States)	07 Jan 52	180UNTS171	102382
Turkey	USA (United States)	07 Jan 52	179UNTS121	102361
Philippines	USA (United States)	07 Jan 52	179UNTS193	102368
Belgium	USA (United States)	07 Jan 52	179UNTS81	102356
UK Great Britain	USA (United States)	08 Jan 52	179UNTS201	102369
Iceland	USA (United States)	08 Jan 52	180UNTS183	102383
Netherlands	USA (United States)	08 Jan 52	179UNTS175	102366
Norway	USA (United States)	08 Jan 52	179UNTS185	102367
Luxembourg	USA (United States)	08 Jan 52	180UNTS191	102384
Denmark	USA (United States)	08 Jan 52	179UNTS65	102354
USA (United States)	Vietnam, South	19 Jan 52	205UNTS127	102772
Ecuador	USA (United States)	20 Feb 52	177UNTS43	102308
Peru	USA (United States)	22 Feb 52	165UNTS31	102166
Cuba	USA (United States)	07 Mar 52	165UNTS11	102165
Colombia	USA (United States)	17 Apr 52	174UNTS215	102287
Ethiopia	USA (United States)	13 Jun 52	205UNTS17	102766
Norway	USA (United States)	27 Jun 52	184UNTS271	102452
USA (United States)	Uruguay	30 Jun 52	207UNTS139	102804
Sweden	USA (United States)	01 Jul 52	187UNTS3	102497
Israel	USA (United States)	23 Jul 52	179UNTS139	102363
Dominican Republic	USA (United States)	06 Mar 53	199UNTS267	102689
Lebanon	USA (United States)	23 Mar 53	239UNTS45	103370
Philippines	USA (United States)	26 Jun 53	213UNTS77	102881
Spain	USA (United States)	26 Sep 53	207UNTS61	102800
Iraq	USA (United States)	21 Apr 54	222UNTS251	103032
Nicaragua	USA (United States)	23 Apr 54	229UNTS37	103159
Pakistan	USA (United States)	19 May 54	202UNTS301	102736
Honduras	USA (United States)	20 May 54	222UNTS87	103025
Guatemala	USA (United States)	30 Jul 54	234UNTS235	103286
Pakistan	USA (United States)	11 Jan 55	251UNTS111	103537
Germany, West	USA (United States)	04 Apr 55	279UNTS73	104034
Cambodia	USA (United States)	16 May 55	263UNTS273	103777
Japan	USA (United States)	03 Jun 55	270UNTS51	103891
Guatemala	USA (United States)	18 Jun 55	262UNTS105	103740
Germany, West	USA (United States)	30 Jun 55	240UNTS47	103393
Japan	USA (United States)	13 Apr 56	273UNTS223	103953
Ceylon (Sri Lanka)	USA (United States)	02 Nov 56	282UNTS93	104094
Libya	USA (United States)	30 Jun 57	284UNTS177	104136
Austria	USA (United States)	09 Aug 57	288UNTS299	104211
Japan	USA (United States)	25 Jan 58	304UNTS81	104392

PARTY ONE	PARTY TWO	DATE	CITATION	NUMBER
Self-defense (Cont.)				
Bolivia	USA (United States)	22 Apr 58	317UNTS209	104605
Burma	USA (United States)	24 Jun 58	335UNTS193	104786
Fed of Malaya	USA (United States)	09 Jul 58	336UNTS79	104799
Indonesia	USA (United States)	13 Aug 58	335UNTS187	104785
Canada	USA (United States)	13 Apr 59	342UNTS43	104899
Panama	USA (United States)	20 May 59	346UNTS235	104983
Iraq	USA (United States)	07 Jul 59	357UNTS153	105114
USA (United States)	Yugoslavia	25 Aug 59	357UNTS87	105107
USA (United States)	Yugoslavia	25 Aug 59	357UNTS77	105106
New Zealand	UK Great Britain	21 Sep 59	401UNTS51	105762
Argentina	USA (United States)	01 Apr 60	371UNTS245	105281
Japan	USA (United States)	15 Apr 60	372UNTS267	105303
Canada	USA (United States)	31 Aug 60	393UNTS247	105659
Haiti	USA (United States)	01 Sep 60	388UNTS249	105582
Colombia	USA (United States)	03 Apr 61	407UNTS3	105856
Mali	USA (United States)	20 May 61	413UNTS205	105954
Liberia	USA (United States)	17 Jun 61	410UNTS233	105907
Dominican Republic	USA (United States)	08 Mar 62	527UNTS29	107615
Bolivia	USA (United States)	26 Apr 62	461UNTS105	106654
Panama	USA (United States)	23 May 62	458UNTS225	106604
Dahomey	USA (United States)	13 Jun 62	458UNTS219	106603
Niger	USA (United States)	14 Jun 62	458UNTS233	106605
Costa Rica	USA (United States)	18 Jun 62	461UNTS155	106659
Senegal	USA (United States)	20 Jul 62	458UNTS137	106596
Guatemala	USA (United States)	02 Aug 62	461UNTS199	106664
Jamaica	USA (United States)	06 Jun 63	477UNTS29	106913
Congo (Zaire)	USA (United States)	19 Jul 63	511UNTS47	107425
Korea, South	USA (United States)	12 May 64	529UNTS299	107667
India	USA (United States)	13 Jan 65	541UNTS107	107864
Australia	USA (United States)	09 Dec 66	607UNTS83	108798
UK Great Britain	USA (United States)	30 Dec 66	603UNTS273	108737
Germany, East	Hungary	18 May 67	617UNTS3	108905
Mauritius	UK Great Britain	12 Mar 68	0UNTS0	109267
Payment for war supplies				
Iceland	USA (United States)	21 Nov 41	124UNTS179	200418
Norway	USA (United States)	28 Aug 42	139UNTS361	200461
France	USA (United States)	20 Feb 45	76UNTS223	200248
Belgium	USA (United States)	17 Apr 45	139UNTS253	200454
Netherlands	USA (United States)	30 Apr 45	139UNTS341	200460
UK Great Britain	USA (United States)	27 Mar 46	4UNTS2	100039
Canada	USA (United States)	30 Mar 46	7UNTS15	100089
UK Great Britain	USA (United States)	07 May 46	6UNTS285	100082
India	USA (United States)	16 May 46	4UNTS183	100045
France	USA (United States)	28 May 46	84UNTS167	101127
France	USA (United States)	28 May 46	84UNTS93	101121
France	USA (United States)	28 May 46	84UNTS59	101119
France	USA (United States)	28 May 46	84UNTS113	101122
Australia	USA (United States)	07 Jun 46	4UNTS237	100048
Taiwan	USA (United States)	14 Jun 46	4UNTS253	100049
Poland	UK Great Britain	24 Jun 46	11UNTS59	100149
Brazil	USA (United States)	28 Jun 46	6UNTS327	100085
Taiwan	USA (United States)	28 Jun 46	34UNTS121	100532
New Zealand	USA (United States)	10 Jul 46	6UNTS341	100087
Denmark	UK Great Britain	16 Aug 46	9UNTS163	100130
Philippines	USA (United States)	11 Sep 46	43UNTS231	100670
Norway	UK Great Britain	27 Sep 46	6UNTS259	100079
Netherlands	UK Great Britain	04 Dec 46	12UNTS241	100187
Belgium	UK Great Britain	16 Jan 47	54UNTS97	100797
Australia	Netherlands	24 Jan 47	10UNTS77	100144
Czechoslovakia	UK Great Britain	19 Feb 47	9UNTS173	100131
Denmark	UK Great Britain	22 Apr 47	8UNTS3	100110
Multilateral		29 Sep 47	45UNTS125	100694
UK Great Britain	USA (United States)	09 Oct 47	34UNTS129	100533
Norway	USA (United States)	24 Feb 48	34UNTS155	100535

PARTY ONE	PARTY TWO	DATE	CITATION	NUMBER
Payment for war supplies (Cont.)				
France	USA (United States)	27 Feb 48	84UNTS207	101131
Denmark	UK Great Britain	04 Mar 48	77UNTS57	100992
Netherlands	UK Great Britain	11 Mar 48	77UNTS69	100993
USA (United States)	Yugoslavia	19 Jul 48	34UNTS195	100537
Korea, South	USA (United States)	11 Sep 48	89UNTS155	101216
Czechoslovakia	USA (United States)	16 Sep 48	90UNTS35	101224
France	USA (United States)	22 Oct 48	84UNTS173	101128
New Zealand	UK Great Britain	12 Nov 48	162UNTS197	102136
Canada	USA (United States)	14 Mar 49	82UNTS3	101079
Ethiopia	USA (United States)	20 May 49	89UNTS99	101211
France	New Zealand	13 Jan 50	150UNTS151	101969
Canada	USSR (Soviet Union)	29 Sep 50	230UNTS371	103197
Burma	USA (United States)	06 Nov 50	122UNTS81	101638
Brazil	USA (United States)	04 Jan 51	165UNTS97	102171
Chile	USA (United States)	04 Jan 51	165UNTS105	102172
Argentina	USA (United States)	08 Jan 51	165UNTS89	102170
Greece	USA (United States)	07 Jan 52	177UNTS249	102323
Ecuador	USA (United States)	20 Feb 52	177UNTS43	102308
Netherlands	USA (United States)	15 May 52	177UNTS233	102321
Ethiopia	USA (United States)	13 Jun 52	205UNTS17	102766
Belgium	UK Great Britain	30 Jun 52	199UNTS113	102679
Japan	USA (United States)	12 Nov 52	184UNTS111	102443
Canada	USA (United States)	05 Dec 52	206UNTS11	102783
France	Greece	08 Feb 54	225UNTS107	103093
France	Greece	08 Feb 54	225UNTS121	103094
Turkey	UK Great Britain	11 Feb 54	190UNTS343	102575
Multilateral		23 Oct 54	332UNTS157	104761
Iceland	USA (United States)	10 Dec 54	237UNTS191	103345
Netherlands	USA (United States)	29 Apr 55	251UNTS357	103553
Belgium	USA (United States)	31 Aug 55	223UNTS111	103041
Iraq	USA (United States)	03 Dec 55	241UNTS19	103420
Bolivia	USA (United States)	30 Jun 56	271UNTS269	103920
Peru	USA (United States)	06 Sep 56	277UNTS231	104009
Pakistan	USA (United States)	10 Sep 56	277UNTS259	104010
Canada	Germany, West	10 Dec 56	392UNTS3	105633
Germany, West	USA (United States)	07 Jun 57	346UNTS241	104984
Turkey	UK Great Britain	16 Aug 57	310UNTS21	104482
Burma	USA (United States)	24 Jun 58	335UNTS193	104786
Indonesia	USA (United States)	13 Aug 58	335UNTS187	104785
Germany, West	UK Great Britain	03 Oct 58	398UNTS293	105731
Panama	USA (United States)	20 May 59	346UNTS235	104983
New Zealand	UK Great Britain	21 Sep 59	401UNTS51	105762
Germany, West	USA (United States)	25 May 62	458UNTS259	106608
UK Great Britain	USA (United States)	06 Apr 63	474UNTS49	106871
Japan	USA (United States)	26 Apr 63	477UNTS37	106914
Japan	USA (United States)	14 Jun 63	479UNTS165	106951
Cyprus	United Nations	31 Mar 64	492UNTS57	107187
India	UK Great Britain	20 Nov 64	534UNTS85	107756
Israel	USA (United States)	20 Jul 65	549UNTS55	107989
Germany, West	UK Great Britain	11 Apr 68	0UNTS0	109288
Lease of military property				
Taiwan	USA (United States)	02 Jun 42	14UNTS343	200092
New Zealand	USA (United States)	03 Sep 42	24UNTS185	200142
Australia	USA (United States)	03 Sep 42	24UNTS195	200143
France	USA (United States)	03 Sep 42	24UNTS177	200141
Belgium	USA (United States)	30 Jan 43	13UNTS371	200084
Canada	Taiwan	22 Mar 44	14UNTS397	200096
UK Great Britain	USA (United States)	27 Mar 46	4UNTS2	100039
India	USA (United States)	16 May 46	4UNTS183	100045
Australia	USA (United States)	07 Jun 46	4UNTS237	100048
Taiwan	USA (United States)	14 Jun 46	4UNTS253	100049
Brazil	USA (United States)	28 Jun 46	6UNTS327	100085
New Zealand	USA (United States)	10 Jul 46	6UNTS341	100087
Philippines	USA (United States)	21 Mar 47	45UNTS47	100691

PARTY ONE	PARTY TWO	DATE	CITATION	NUMBER
Lease of military property (Cont.)				
Denmark	UK Great Britain	04 Mar 48	77UNTS57	100992
Taiwan	UK Great Britain	18 May 48	66UNTS113	100850
UK Great Britain	Uruguay	12 Jul 48	71UNTS199	100919
Korea, South	USA (United States)	11 Sep 48	89UNTS155	101216
Multilateral		08 Oct 48	19UNTS113	100308
UK Great Britain	USA (United States)	06 Mar 51	97UNTS137	101347
Sweden	USA (United States)	01 Jul 52	187UNTS3	102497
UK Great Britain	USA (United States)	29 Jul 52	179UNTS129	102362
Canada	USA (United States)	08 Nov 52	207UNTS3	102796
Japan	USA (United States)	12 Nov 52	184UNTS111	102443
Ethiopia	USA (United States)	22 May 53	191UNTS59	102577
France	USA (United States)	02 Sep 53	224UNTS153	103075
Belgium	Taiwan	13 Jan 54	223UNTS111	103059
Italy	USA (United States)	27 Apr 54	234UNTS103	103275
Japan	USA (United States)	14 May 54	247UNTS273	103476
Taiwan	USA (United States)	14 May 54	231UNTS165	103216
Turkey	USA (United States)	01 Jul 54	234UNTS147	103280
Korea, South	USA (United States)	29 Jan 55	239UNTS53	103371
Canada	Norway	20 Dec 55	305UNTS17	104408
Portugal	USA (United States)	07 Nov 56	277UNTS133	104003
Brazil	USA (United States)	16 Jan 57	266UNTS99	103824
New Zealand	UK Great Britain	04 Jul 57	402UNTS109	105780
Greece	USA (United States)	05 Aug 57	290UNTS167	104235
Greece	USA (United States)	15 Jan 59	357UNTS281	105120
Taiwan	USA (United States)	07 Feb 59	341UNTS225	104885
Thailand	USA (United States)	19 May 59	346UNTS271	104986
Peru	USA (United States)	15 Jun 59	346UNTS279	104987
Spain	USA (United States)	23 Jun 59	354UNTS11	105049
Taiwan	USA (United States)	08 Jul 59	354UNTS47	105052
Japan	USA (United States)	31 Jul 59	357UNTS107	105110
Italy	USA (United States)	18 Aug 59	361UNTS11	105169
New Zealand	UK Great Britain	21 Sep 59	401UNTS51	105762
Brazil	USA (United States)	19 Oct 59	372UNTS131	105293
Ecuador	USA (United States)	11 Feb 60	372UNTS141	105294
Peru	USA (United States)	26 Feb 60	394UNTS141	105674
Argentina	USA (United States)	01 Apr 60	371UNTS245	105281
Colombia	USA (United States)	07 Apr 60	372UNTS27	105285
Haiti	USA (United States)	08 Jul 60	380UNTS135	105454
Chile	USA (United States)	16 Jul 60	393UNTS271	105661
Canada	USA (United States)	31 Aug 60	393UNTS247	105659
New Zealand	USA (United States)	08 Jun 62	458UNTS209	106602
Taiwan	USA (United States)	15 Aug 62	460UNTS237	106643
Japan	USA (United States)	28 Aug 62	460UNTS267	106645
Saudi Arabia	USA (United States)	13 Nov 62	488UNTS175	107127
Pakistan	USA (United States)	16 Jan 63	471UNTS133	106828
Pakistan	USA (United States)	29 Jun 63	487UNTS243	107107
Spain	USA (United States)	21 Apr 66	580UNTS231	108426
Malta	USA (United States)	03 Aug 66	601UNTS125	108691
Military assistance				
Multilateral		27 Mar 41	67UNTS231	200222
Haiti	USA (United States)	23 May 41	117UNTS191	200370
Iceland	USA (United States)	01 Jul 41	12UNTS405	200071
Bolivia	USA (United States)	04 Sep 41	8UNTS345	200046
Multilateral		29 Jan 42	93UNTS279	200271
Peru	USA (United States)	11 Mar 42	117UNTS266	200375
Liberia	USA (United States)	31 Mar 42	23UNTS302	200137
USA (United States)	USSR (Soviet Union)	18 Apr 42	105UNTS285	200339
Brazil	USA (United States)	07 May 42	6UNTS377	200040
Colombia	USA (United States)	29 May 42	8UNTS365	200047
Taiwan	USA (United States)	02 Jun 42	14UNTS343	200092
Belgium	USA (United States)	16 Jun 42	105UNTS159	200329
Poland	USA (United States)	01 Jul 42	103UNTS267	200317
Panama	USA (United States)	07 Jul 42	9UNTS289	200048
Netherlands	USA (United States)	08 Jul 42	103UNTS277	200318

PARTY ONE	PARTY TWO	DATE	CITATION	NUMBER
Military assistance (Cont.)				
Greece	USA (United States)	10 Jul 42	103UNTS289	200319
Czechoslovakia	USA (United States)	11 Jul 42	90UNTS257	200263
USA (United States)	Yugoslavia	24 Jul 42	34UNTS361	200179
Bolivia	USA (United States)	11 Aug 42	9UNTS309	200049
Norway	USA (United States)	28 Aug 42	139UNTS361	200461
Australia	USA (United States)	03 Sep 42	24UNTS195	200143
France	USA (United States)	03 Sep 42	24UNTS177	200141
New Zealand	USA (United States)	03 Sep 42	24UNTS185	200142
El Salvador	USA (United States)	24 Nov 42	24UNTS241	200149
Dominican Republic	USA (United States)	25 Jan 43	13UNTS399	200083
Belgium	USA (United States)	30 Jan 43	13UNTS371	200084
Liberia	USA (United States)	08 Jun 43	117UNTS242	200373
Netherlands	USA (United States)	14 Jun 43	28UNTS397	200163
Guatemala	USA (United States)	17 Jul 43	28UNTS431	200166
Ethiopia	USA (United States)	09 Aug 43	29UNTS303	200169
Ecuador	USA (United States)	13 Sep 43	29UNTS349	200171
France	USA (United States)	25 Sep 43	76UNTS183	200245
Paraguay	USA (United States)	27 Oct 43	29UNTS391	200174
Iran	USA (United States)	27 Nov 43	31UNTS451	200176
Paraguay	USA (United States)	10 Dec 43	21UNTS305	200131
USA (United States)	Venezuela	13 Jan 44	109UNTS171	200358
Canada	Taiwan	22 Mar 44	14UNTS397	200096
Ecuador	USA (United States)	29 Jun 44	80UNTS283	200250
Peru	USA (United States)	10 Jul 44	117UNTS291	200377
Belgium	UK Great Britain	22 Aug 44	90UNTS295	200267
Ethiopia	UK Great Britain	19 Dec 44	93UNTS303	200272
Multilateral		20 Jan 45	140UNTS397	200471
France	USA (United States)	20 Feb 45	76UNTS223	200248
France	USA (United States)	20 Feb 45	76UNTS193	200246
Guatemala	USA (United States)	21 Feb 45	121UNTS133	200396
Turkey	USA (United States)	23 Feb 45	121UNTS165	200398
France	USA (United States)	28 Feb 45	76UNTS213	200247
South Africa	USA (United States)	17 Apr 45	90UNTS267	200264
Netherlands	USA (United States)	30 Apr 45	139UNTS319	200459
Guatemala	USA (United States)	21 May 45	121UNTS185	200399
Chile	USA (United States)	24 May 45	121UNTS219	200401
Iraq	USA (United States)	31 Jul 45	121UNTS239	200402
Denmark	UK Great Britain	24 Oct 45	93UNTS143	101297
Costa Rica	USA (United States)	10 Dec 45	3UNTS157	100029
Netherlands	UK Great Britain	20 Dec 45	4UNTS303	100053
Honduras	USA (United States)	28 Dec 45	3UNTS185	100031
Mongolia	USSR (Soviet Union)	27 Feb 46	48UNTS177	100744
UK Great Britain	USA (United States)	27 Mar 46	4UNTS2	100039
France	UK Great Britain	29 Apr 46	98UNTS123	101360
Czechoslovakia	Yugoslavia	09 May 46	1UNTS67	100014
USA (United States)	Venezuela	03 Jun 46	4UNTS215	100047
Taiwan	USA (United States)	28 Jun 46	34UNTS121	100532
Peru	USA (United States)	07 Oct 46	7UNTS71	100092
Colombia	USA (United States)	14 Oct 46	7UNTS97	100093
Australia	Netherlands	24 Jan 47	10UNTS77	100144
Philippines	USA (United States)	21 Mar 47	45UNTS47	100691
Iraq	Jordan	14 Apr 47	23UNTS148	100345
India	USA (United States)	05 Jul 47	185UNTS293	102476
El Salvador	USA (United States)	19 Aug 47	51UNTS57	100752
Iran	USA (United States)	06 Oct 47	11UNTS303	100171
UK Great Britain	USA (United States)	09 Oct 47	34UNTS129	100533
Ceylon (Sri Lanka)	UK Great Britain	11 Nov 47	86UNTS19	101148
Greece	USA (United States)	03 Dec 47	89UNTS119	101213
Romania	USSR (Soviet Union)	04 Feb 48	48UNTS189	100745
Hungary	USSR (Soviet Union)	18 Feb 48	48UNTS163	100743
Denmark	UK Great Britain	04 Mar 48	77UNTS57	100992
Multilateral		17 Mar 48	19UNTS51	100304
Bulgaria	USSR (Soviet Union)	18 Mar 48	48UNTS135	100741
Finland	USSR (Soviet Union)	06 Apr 48	48UNTS149	100742
Taiwan	UK Great Britain	18 May 48	66UNTS113	100850

PARTY ONE	PARTY TWO	DATE	CITATION	NUMBER
Military assistance (Cont.)				
Brazil	USA (United States)	29 Jul 48	80UNTS111	101047
Korea, South	USA (United States)	24 Aug 48	79UNTS57	101031
Argentina	USA (United States)	06 Oct 48	80UNTS91	101046
New Zealand	UK Great Britain	12 Nov 48	162UNTS197	102136
Haiti	USA (United States)	04 Jan 49	44UNTS69	100679
Poland	Romania	26 Jan 49	85UNTS21	101143
Colombia	USA (United States)	21 Feb 49	44UNTS83	100680
Colombia	USA (United States)	21 Feb 49	92UNTS227	101275
Haiti	USA (United States)	14 Apr 49	80UNTS37	101043
Peru	USA (United States)	20 Jun 49	92UNTS249	101276
Mexico	USA (United States)	05 Jul 49	68UNTS55	100884
Korea, South	USA (United States)	26 Jan 50	80UNTS205	101053
Korea, South	USA (United States)	26 Jan 50	178UNTS97	102337
France	USA (United States)	27 Jan 50	80UNTS171	101051
Norway	USA (United States)	27 Jan 50	80UNTS241	101055
UK Great Britain	USA (United States)	27 Jan 50	80UNTS261	101056
Italy	USA (United States)	27 Jan 50	80UNTS145	101050
Luxembourg	USA (United States)	27 Jan 50	80UNTS187	101052
Denmark	USA (United States)	27 Jan 50	48UNTS115	100740
Netherlands	USA (United States)	27 Jan 50	80UNTS219	101054
Belgium	USA (United States)	27 Jan 50	51UNTS213	100767
Honduras	USA (United States)	06 Mar 50	80UNTS71	101045
Honduras	USA (United States)	06 Mar 50	80UNTS51	101044
Indonesia	USA (United States)	15 Aug 50	134UNTS255	101804
USA (United States)	Venezuela	23 Aug 50	92UNTS341	101279
Thailand	USA (United States)	17 Oct 50	79UNTS41	101030
Burma	USA (United States)	06 Nov 50	122UNTS81	101638
Pakistan	USA (United States)	15 Dec 50	122UNTS89	101639
Cuba	USA (United States)	22 Dec 50	122UNTS97	101640
Liberia	USA (United States)	11 Jan 51	122UNTS125	101642
Taiwan	USA (United States)	09 Feb 51	132UNTS273	101767
Chile	USA (United States)	15 Feb 51	133UNTS95	101783
Chile	USA (United States)	15 Feb 51	133UNTS117	101784
Australia	USA (United States)	20 Feb 51	132UNTS297	101769
Multilateral		06 Mar 51	138UNTS67	101860
India	USA (United States)	16 Mar 51	141UNTS47	101904
Iceland	USA (United States)	05 May 51	205UNTS173	102776
Saudi Arabia	USA (United States)	18 Jun 51	141UNTS67	101906
USA (United States)	Venezuela	10 Aug 51	140UNTS345	101898
Cuba	USA (United States)	28 Aug 51	134UNTS225	101802
Cuba	USA (United States)	28 Aug 51	140UNTS239	101891
Philippines	USA (United States)	30 Aug 51	177UNTS133	102315
Multilateral		01 Sep 51	131UNTS83	101736
Japan	USA (United States)	08 Sep 51	136UNTS211	101835
South Africa	USA (United States)	09 Nov 51	160UNTS41	102100
Liberia	USA (United States)	19 Nov 51	167UNTS141	102204
USA (United States)	Uruguay	04 Dec 51	152UNTS41	102010
Cambodia	USA (United States)	28 Dec 51	179UNTS97	102358
Thailand	USA (United States)	29 Dec 51	179UNTS113	102360
Laos	USA (United States)	31 Dec 51	198UNTS243	102668
Taiwan	USA (United States)	02 Jan 52	181UNTS161	102407
Turkey	USA (United States)	07 Jan 52	179UNTS121	102361
Italy	USA (United States)	C7 Jan 52	179UNTS165	102365
Belgium	USA (United States)	07 Jan 52	179UNTS81	102356
Greece	USA (United States)	07 Jan 52	180UNTS171	102382
Philippines	USA (United States)	07 Jan 52	179UNTS193	102368
Korea, South	USA (United States)	07 Jan 52	179UNTS105	102359
Denmark	USA (United States)	08 Jan 52	179UNTS65	102354
Netherlands	USA (United States)	08 Jan 52	179UNTS175	102366
Portugal	USA (United States)	08 Jan 52	207UNTS51	102799
Iceland	USA (United States)	08 Jan 52	180UNTS183	102383
Norway	USA (United States)	08 Jan 52	179UNTS185	102367
Luxembourg	USA (United States)	08 Jan 52	180UNTS191	102384
Ecuador	USA (United States)	20 Feb 52	177UNTS43	102308
Peru	USA (United States)	22 Feb 52	165UNTS31	102166

PARTY ONE	PARTY TWO	DATE	CITATION	NUMBER
Military assistance (Cont.)				
Cuba	USA (United States)	07 Mar 52	165UNTS11	102165
Brazil	USA (United States)	15 Mar 52	199UNTS221	102687
Chile	USA (United States)	09 Apr 52	186UNTS53	102482
Colombia	USA (United States)	17 Apr 52	174UNTS215	102287
United Arab Rep	USA (United States)	29 Apr 52	241UNTS3	103418
Ethiopia	USA (United States)	13 Jun 52	205UNTS17	102766
USA (United States)	Uruguay	30 Jun 52	207UNTS139	102804
Israel	USA (United States)	23 Jul 52	179UNTS139	102363
Japan	USA (United States)	25 Jul 52	198UNTS281	102671
Portugal	UK Great Britain	21 Nov 52	404UNTS27	105802
USA (United States)	Venezuela	16 Jan 53	199UNTS287	102690
Dominican Republic	USA (United States)	06 Mar 53	199UNTS267	102689
Lebanon	USA (United States)	23 Mar 53	239UNTS45	103370
El Salvador	USA (United States)	21 May 53	213UNTS15	102878
Ethiopia	USA (United States)	22 May 53	207UNTS127	102803
Philippines	USA (United States)	26 Jun 53	213UNTS77	102881
Libya	UK Great Britain	29 Jul 53	186UNTS201	102492
France	USA (United States)	02 Sep 53	224UNTS153	103075
Spain	USA (United States)	26 Sep 53	207UNTS83	102801
Korea, South	USA (United States)	01 Oct 53	238UNTS199	103363
Nicaragua	USA (United States)	19 Nov 53	206UNTS117	102787
Belgium	Taiwan	13 Jan 54	223UNTS111	103059
Japan	USA (United States)	08 Mar 54	232UNTS169	103236
Iraq	USA (United States)	21 Apr 54	222UNTS251	103032
Italy	USA (United States)	27 Apr 54	234UNTS103	103275
Norway	USA (United States)	07 May 54	231UNTS157	103215
Pakistan	USA (United States)	19 May 54	202UNTS301	102736
Honduras	USA (United States)	20 May 54	222UNTS87	103025
France	USA (United States)	31 May 54	236UNTS141	103321
UK Great Britain	USA (United States)	15 Jun 54	236UNTS133	103320
Italy	USA (United States)	24 Jun 54	235UNTS3	103290
Turkey	USA (United States)	01 Jul 54	234UNTS147	103280
Multilateral		08 Sep 54	209UNTS23	102819
El Salvador	USA (United States)	23 Sep 54	237UNTS91	103338
United Arab Rep	UK Great Britain	19 Oct 54	210UNTS3	102833
Turkey	USA (United States)	15 Nov 54	238UNTS135	103358
Korea, South	USA (United States)	17 Nov 54	256UNTS251	103635
Japan	USA (United States)	19 Nov 54	238UNTS207	103364
Taiwan	USA (United States)	10 Dec 54	248UNTS213	103496
Pakistan	USA (United States)	11 Jan 55	251UNTS111	103537
Haiti	USA (United States)	28 Jan 55	270UNTS83	103894
Korea, South	USA (United States)	29 Jan 55	239UNTS53	103371
Italy	USA (United States)	11 Feb 55	240UNTS87	103396
Iraq	Turkey	24 Feb 55	233UNTS199	103264
USA (United States)	Vietnam, South	23 Apr 55	277UNTS279	104012
Turkey	USA (United States)	25 Apr 55	263UNTS299	103779
Philippines	USA (United States)	27 Apr 55	261UNTS351	103733
USA (United States)	Yugoslavia	12 May 55	251UNTS343	103551
Cambodia	USA (United States)	16 May 55	263UNTS273	103777
Greece	USA (United States)	27 May 55	251UNTS349	103552
Japan	USA (United States)	03 Jun 55	270UNTS51	103891
South Africa	UK Great Britain	30 Jun 55	248UNTS191	103495
Belgium	USA (United States)	31 Aug 55	223UNTS111	103041
Brazil	USA (United States)	20 Sep 55	257UNTS349	103665
USA (United States)	Yugoslavia	30 Sep 55	269UNTS89	103877
Syria	United Arab Rep	20 Oct 55	247UNTS117	103461
Iraq	USA (United States)	03 Dec 55	241UNTS19	103420
Multilateral		13 Dec 55	407UNTS8	105857
Canada	Norway	20 Dec 55	305UNTS17	104408
Japan	USA (United States)	13 Apr 56	273UNTS223	103953
Bolivia	USA (United States)	30 Jun 56	271UNTS269	103920
Bolivia	USA (United States)	30 Jun 56	271UNTS243	103919
Peru	USA (United States)	06 Sep 56	277UNTS231	104009
Argentina	USA (United States)	03 Oct 56	279UNTS13	104032
Germany, West	USA (United States)	08 Oct 56	278UNTS9	104018

PARTY ONE	PARTY TWO	DATE	CITATION	NUMBER
Military assistance (Cont.)				
Chile	USA (United States)	15 Nov 56	282UNTS3	104089
Iceland	USA (United States)	06 Dec 56	265UNTS261	103818
Dominican Republic	USA (United States)	07 Dec 56	263UNTS193	103774
Saudi Arabia	USA (United States)	02 Apr 57	283UNTS97	104109
Germany, West	USA (United States)	07 Jun 57	346UNTS241	104984
Iraq	USA (United States)	16 Jun 57	284UNTS39	104127
New Zealand	UK Great Britain	04 Jul 57	402UNTS109	105780
France	USA (United States)	23 Sep 57	293UNTS297	104297
Fed of Malaya	UK Great Britain	12 Oct 57	285UNTS59	104149
El Salvador	USA (United States)	21 Nov 57	303UNTS19	104369
Japan	USA (United States)	25 Jan 58	304UNTS81	104392
UK Great Britain	USA (United States)	22 Feb 58	307UNTS207	104451
Lebanon	UK Great Britain	19 May 58	327UNTS43	104716
Burma	USA (United States)	24 Jun 58	335UNTS193	104786
Muscat and Oman	UK Great Britain	25 Jul 58	312UNTS347	104524
Multilateral		28 Jul 58	335UNTS205	104788
Indonesia	USA (United States)	13 Aug 58	335UNTS187	104785
Canada	USA (United States)	02 Sep 58	335UNTS249	104792
Haiti	USA (United States)	24 Dec 58	338UNTS265	104840
Iran	USA (United States)	05 Mar 59	327UNTS277	104725
Pakistan	USA (United States)	05 Mar 59	327UNTS285	104726
Greece	USA (United States)	06 May 59	357UNTS163	105115
Denmark	USA (United States)	08 May 59	344UNTS185	104949
Liberia	USA (United States)	08 Jul 59	357UNTS93	105108
USA (United States)	Yugoslavia	25 Aug 59	357UNTS87	105107
USA (United States)	Yugoslavia	25 Aug 59	357UNTS77	105106
Turkey	USA (United States)	30 Nov 59	361UNTS107	105174
Argentina	USA (United States)	02 Aug 60	384UNTS105	105514
Australia	USA (United States)	23 Aug 60	388UNTS237	105581
Haiti	USA (United States)	01 Sep 60	388UNTS249	105582
Italy	USA (United States)	03 Dec 60	410UNTS3	105893
Bolivia	USA (United States)	09 Feb 61	405UNTS113	105827
Mali	USA (United States)	20 May 61	413UNTS205	105954
Canada	USA (United States)	12 Jun 61	410UNTS21	105894
Liberia	USA (United States)	17 Jun 61	410UNTS233	105907
Congo (Zaire)	United Nations	27 Nov 61	414UNTS229	105975
Bolivia	USA (United States)	26 Apr 62	461UNTS105	106654
Panama	USA (United States)	23 May 62	458UNTS225	106604
Germany, West	USA (United States)	25 May 62	458UNTS259	106608
Dahomey	USA (United States)	13 Jun 62	458UNTS219	106603
Niger	USA (United States)	14 Jun 62	458UNTS233	106605
Costa Rica	USA (United States)	18 Jun 62	461UNTS155	106659
Canada	Greece	18 Jul 62	528UNTS265	107647
Senegal	USA (United States)	20 Jul 62	458UNTS137	106596
Guatemala	USA (United States)	02 Aug 62	461UNTS199	106664
Honduras	USA (United States)	24 Oct 62	459UNTS211	106624
India	UK Great Britain	27 Nov 62	466UNTS189	106744
Peru	USA (United States)	20 Dec 62	471UNTS75	106822
UK Great Britain	USA (United States)	06 Apr 63	474UNTS49	106871
Jamaica	USA (United States)	06 Jun 63	477UNTS29	106913
Canada	Nigeria	03 Jul 63	529UNTS57	107656
Congo (Zaire)	USA (United States)	19 Jul 63	511UNTS47	107425
Australia	India	03 Dec 63	486UNTS279	107082
Brazil	USA (United States)	30 Jan 64	511UNTS77	107428
Paraguay	USA (United States)	10 Feb 64	511UNTS53	107426
Argentina	USA (United States)	10 May 64	527UNTS77	107618
Chad	France	19 May 64	0UNTS0	109443
Malta	UK Great Britain	21 Sep 64	588UNTS55	108518
Chile	USA (United States)	27 Oct 64	532UNTS347	107727
India	USA (United States)	13 Jan 65	541UNTS107	107864
Jamaica	UK Great Britain	31 Mar 65	539UNTS59	107824
Guinea	USA (United States)	29 Jun 65	549UNTS139	107997
Germany, West	USA (United States)	18 Dec 65	579UNTS193	108407
Paraguay	USA (United States)	11 Apr 66	578UNTS99	108389
New Zealand	UK Great Britain	02 Apr 68	0UNTS0	109206

PARTY ONE	PARTY TWO	DATE	CITATION	NUMBER
Lend lease				
Iceland	USA (United States)	21 Nov 41	124UNTS179	200418
Taiwan	USA (United States)	02 Jun 42	14UNTS343	200092
New Zealand	USA (United States)	03 Sep 42	24UNTS185	200142
Australia	USA (United States)	03 Sep 42	24UNTS195	200143
France	USA (United States)	03 Sep 42	24UNTS177	200141
Netherlands	USA (United States)	14 Jun 43	28UNTS397	200163
Canada	Taiwan	22 Mar 44	14UNTS397	200096
Belgium	USA (United States)	17 Apr 45	139UNTS253	200454
Netherlands	USA (United States)	30 Apr 45	139UNTS341	200460
USA (United States)	USSR (Soviet Union)	15 Oct 45	278UNTS151	200547
UK Great Britain	USA (United States)	27 Mar 46	4UNTS2	100039
UK Great Britain	USA (United States)	27 Mar 46	4UNTS101	100040
Turkey	USA (United States)	07 May 46	6UNTS293	100083
India	USA (United States)	16 May 46	4UNTS183	100045
France	USA (United States)	28 May 46	84UNTS59	101119
France	USA (United States)	28 May 46	84UNTS93	101121
Australia	USA (United States)	07 Jun 46	4UNTS237	100048
Taiwan	USA (United States)	14 Jun 46	4UNTS253	100049
Brazil	USA (United States)	28 Jun 46	6UNTS327	100085
New Zealand	USA (United States)	10 Jul 46	6UNTS341	100087
Czechoslovakia	UK Great Britain	19 Feb 47	9UNTS173	100131
South Africa	USA (United States)	21 Mar 47	16UNTS47	100248
Norway	USA (United States)	24 Feb 48	34UNTS155	100535
UK Great Britain	Uruguay	12 Jul 48	71UNTS199	100919
New Zealand	USA (United States)	14 Sep 48	18UNTS251	100295
Czechoslovakia	USA (United States)	16 Sep 48	90UNTS35	101224
UK Great Britain	USA (United States)	22 Sep 48	71UNTS64	100910
Multilateral		08 Oct 48	19UNTS113	100308
France	USA (United States)	19 Oct 48	98UNTS3	101355
France	USA (United States)	14 Mar 49	84UNTS237	101133
Netherlands	USA (United States)	17 May 49	46UNTS291	100717
Ethiopia	USA (United States)	20 May 49	89UNTS99	101211
South Africa	USA (United States)	24 Jun 52	177UNTS241	102322
USA (United States)	USSR (Soviet Union)	26 Mar 54	247UNTS263	103475
USA (United States)	USSR (Soviet Union)	22 Dec 54	251UNTS41	103532
Netherlands	USA (United States)	25 May 55	289UNTS227	104220
USA (United States)	USSR (Soviet Union)	26 May 55	270UNTS61	103892
Spain	USA (United States)	09 Mar 57	283UNTS89	104108
Germany, West	USA (United States)	01 May 57	284UNTS85	104131
Turkey	UK Great Britain	16 Aug 57	310UNTS21	104482
Philippines	USA (United States)	04 Oct 61	433UNTS83	106232
Canada	Greece	18 Jul 62	528UNTS265	107647
Naval vessels				
Canada	USA (United States)	10 Jun 39	149UNTS332	200476
Australia	USA (United States)	10 May 44	106UNTS237	200343
Brazil	USA (United States)	29 Sep 44	65UNTS271	200216
Multilateral		05 Jun 45	68UNTS189	200230
UK Great Britain	USA (United States)	15 Jun 45	89UNTS327	200261
Greece	UK Great Britain	11 Oct 45	183UNTS329	200509
Greece	UK Great Britain	30 Nov 45	183UNTS197	102428
France	UK Great Britain	26 Jan 46	91UNTS183	101251
UK Great Britain	USA (United States)	27 Mar 46	4UNTS2	100039
France	USA (United States)	28 May 46	84UNTS59	101119
France	USA (United States)	28 May 46	84UNTS113	101122
France	USA (United States)	28 May 46	84UNTS93	101121
New Zealand	USA (United States)	10 Jul 46	6UNTS341	100087
Philippines	USA (United States)	11 Sep 46	43UNTS231	100670
Canada	USA (United States)	15 Nov 46	7UNTS141	100096
Canada	USA (United States)	06 Dec 46	149UNTS3	101945
Multilateral		10 Feb 47	140UNTS111	101886
South Africa	USA (United States)	21 Mar 47	16UNTS47	100248
Netherlands	USA (United States)	28 May 47	17UNTS29	100267
Greece	USA (United States)	03 Dec 47	89UNTS119	101213

PARTY ONE	PARTY TWO	DATE	CITATION	NUMBER
Naval vessels (Cont.)				
Taiwan	UK Great Britain	18 May 48	66UNTS113	100850
USA (United States)	Yugoslavia	19 Jul 48	34UNTS195	100537
Cuba	USA (United States)	21 Feb 49	231UNTS108	103212
Multilateral		12 Aug 49	75UNTS85	100971
USA (United States)	USSR (Soviet Union)	27 Sep 49	149UNTS23	101948
Burma	USA (United States)	06 Nov 50	122UNTS81	101638
Brazil	USA (United States)	04 Jan 51	165UNTS97	102171
Chile	USA (United States)	04 Jan 51	165UNTS105	102172
Argentina	USA (United States)	08 Jan 51	165UNTS89	102170
UK Great Britain	USA (United States)	06 Mar 51	97UNTS137	101347
Canada	France	04 Jul 51	233UNTS101	103253
Canada	USA (United States)	21 Feb 52	205UNTS293	102781
Italy	UK Great Britain	06 Nov 52	158UNTS431	102076
Japan	USA (United States)	12 Nov 52	184UNTS111	102443
Germany, West	USA (United States)	20 Aug 53	224UNTS49	103069
France	USA (United States)	02 Sep 53	224UNTS153	103075
France	Netherlands	27 Nov 53	302UNTS245	104363
Belgium	Taiwan	13 Jan 54	223UNTS111	103059
USA (United States)	USSR (Soviet Union)	26 Mar 54	247UNTS263	103475
Italy	USA (United States)	27 Apr 54	234UNTS103	103275
Multilateral		12 May 54	327UNTS3	104714
Japan	USA (United States)	14 May 54	247UNTS273	103476
Taiwan	USA (United States)	14 May 54	231UNTS165	103216
Turkey	USA (United States)	01 Jul 54	234UNTS147	103280
USA (United States)	USSR (Soviet Union)	22 Dec 54	251UNTS41	103532
Peru	USA (United States)	07 Jan 55	261UNTS321	103730
Korea, South	USA (United States)	29 Jan 55	239UNTS53	103371
USA (United States)	USSR (Soviet Union)	26 May 55	270UNTS61	103892
South Africa	UK Great Britain	30 Jun 55	248UNTS191	103495
Ecuador	USA (United States)	08 Jul 55	265UNTS49	103806
Canada	Norway	20 Dec 55	305UNTS17	104408
Cuba	USA (United States)	10 Jan 56	240UNTS101	103398
Portugal	USA (United States)	07 Nov 56	277UNTS133	104003
Australia	USA (United States)	31 Dec 56	266UNTS89	103823
Brazil	USA (United States)	16 Jan 57	266UNTS99	103824
Spain	USA (United States)	09 Mar 57	283UNTS89	104108
Germany, West	USA (United States)	01 May 57	284UNTS85	104131
Greece	USA (United States)	05 Aug 57	290UNTS167	104235
Turkey	UK Great Britain	16 Aug 57	310UNTS21	104482
Multilateral		29 Apr 58	516UNTS205	107477
Denmark	USA (United States)	28 Aug 58	335UNTS133	104781
Turkey	USA (United States)	14 Oct 58	336UNTS145	104803
Greece	USA (United States)	15 Jan 59	357UNTS281	105120
Taiwan	USA (United States)	07 Feb 59	341UNTS225	104885
Denmark	USA (United States)	08 May 59	344UNTS185	104949
Thailand	USA (United States)	19 May 59	346UNTS271	104986
Spain	USA (United States)	23 Jun 59	354UNTS11	105049
Taiwan	USA (United States)	08 Jul 59	354UNTS47	105052
Japan	USA (United States)	31 Jul 59	357UNTS107	105110
Italy	USA (United States)	18 Aug 59	361UNTS11	105169
Brazil	USA (United States)	19 Oct 59	372UNTS131	105293
Ecuador	USA (United States)	11 Feb 60	372UNTS141	105294
Peru	USA (United States)	26 Feb 60	394UNTS141	105674
Argentina	USA (United States)	01 Apr 60	371UNTS245	105281
Colombia	USA (United States)	07 Apr 60	372UNTS27	105285
Norway	USA (United States)	06 Jul 60	378UNTS25	105415
Haiti	USA (United States)	08 Jul 60	380UNTS135	105454
Chile	USA (United States)	16 Jul 60	393UNTS271	105661
Canada	USA (United States)	31 Aug 60	393UNTS247	105659
Norway	USA (United States)	29 Nov 60	404UNTS251	105815
Greece	USA (United States)	24 Apr 62	459UNTS3	106609
New Zealand	USA (United States)	08 Jun 62	458UNTS209	106602
Taiwan	USA (United States)	15 Aug 62	460UNTS237	106643
Philippines	USA (United States)	21 Aug 62	461UNTS163	106660
Japan	USA (United States)	28 Aug 62	460UNTS267	106645

PARTY ONE	PARTY TWO	DATE	CITATION	NUMBER
Naval vessels (Cont.)				
Saudi Arabia	USA (United States)	13 Nov 62	488UNTS175	107127
Germany, West	USA (United States)	29 Nov 62	460UNTS169	106639
Pakistan	USA (United States)	16 Jan 63	471UNTS133	106828
Norway	USA (United States)	01 Mar 63	524UNTS185	107573
Belgium	USA (United States)	19 Apr 63	493UNTS83	107209
Pakistan	USA (United States)	29 Jun 63	487UNTS243	107107
Ireland	USA (United States)	18 Jun 64	530UNTS217	107684
UK Great Britain	USA (United States)	19 Jun 64	530UNTS99	107675
Denmark	USA (United States)	02 Jul 64	529UNTS277	107665
Sweden	USA (United States)	06 Jul 64	529UNTS287	107666
Spain	USA (United States)	16 Jul 64	529UNTS187	107661
Italy	USA (United States)	23 Nov 64	532UNTS133	107716
Malta	USA (United States)	15 Jan 66	579UNTS109	108402
Spain	USA (United States)	21 Apr 66	580UNTS231	108426
Malta	USA (United States)	03 Aug 66	601UNTS125	108691
Return of equipment and recapture				
USA (United States)	USSR (Soviet Union)	18 Apr 42	105UNTS285	200339
Taiwan	USA (United States)	02 Jun 42	14UNTS343	200092
Belgium	USA (United States)	16 Jun 42	105UNTS159	200329
Poland	USA (United States)	01 Jul 42	103UNTS267	200317
Netherlands	USA (United States)	08 Jul 42	103UNTS277	200318
Greece	USA (United States)	10 Jul 42	103UNTS289	200319
Czechoslovakia	USA (United States)	11 Jul 42	90UNTS257	200263
USA (United States)	Yugoslavia	24 Jul 42	34UNTS361	200179
Liberia	USA (United States)	08 Jun 43	117UNTS242	200373
Ethiopia	USA (United States)	09 Aug 43	29UNTS303	200169
France	USA (United States)	25 Sep 43	76UNTS183	200245
Canada	Taiwan	22 Mar 44	14UNTS397	200096
Belgium	UK Great Britain	22 Aug 44	90UNTS295	200267
France	USA (United States)	20 Feb 45	76UNTS193	200246
Turkey	USA (United States)	23 Feb 45	121UNTS165	200398
UK Great Britain	USA (United States)	15 Jun 45	89UNTS327	200261
Iraq	USA (United States)	31 Jul 45	121UNTS239	200402
Denmark	UK Great Britain	24 Oct 45	93UNTS143	101297
Greece	UK Great Britain	30 Nov 45	183UNTS197	102428
Netherlands	UK Great Britain	20 Dec 45	4UNTS303	100053
UK Great Britain	USA (United States)	27 Mar 46	4UNTS2	100039
Canada	USA (United States)	30 Mar 46	7UNTS15	100089
Turkey	USA (United States)	07 May 46	6UNTS293	100083
India	USA (United States)	16 May 46	4UNTS183	100045
France	USA (United States)	28 May 46	84UNTS59	101119
Australia	USA (United States)	07 Jun 46	4UNTS237	100048
Taiwan	USA (United States)	14 Jun 46	4UNTS253	100049
New Zealand	USA (United States)	10 Jul 46	6UNTS341	100087
Philippines	USA (United States)	11 Sep 46	43UNTS231	100670
Multilateral		10 Feb 47	42UNTS3	100645
South Africa	USA (United States)	21 Mar 47	16UNTS47	100248
Netherlands	USA (United States)	28 May 47	17UNTS29	100267
Italy	USA (United States)	14 Aug 47	36UNTS53	100566
Norway	USA (United States)	24 Feb 48	34UNTS155	100535
Taiwan	UK Great Britain	18 May 48	66UNTS113	100850
USA (United States)	Yugoslavia	19 Jul 48	34UNTS195	100537
Czechoslovakia	USA (United States)	16 Sep 48	90UNTS35	101224
France	USA (United States)	19 Oct 48	98UNTS3	101355
Ethiopia	USA (United States)	20 May 49	89UNTS99	101211
USA (United States)	USSR (Soviet Union)	27 Sep 49	149UNTS23	101948
Norway	USA (United States)	28 Dec 50	240UNTS391	103414
Sweden	USA (United States)	27 Jun 51	148UNTS77	101937
Norway	USA (United States)	17 Sep 51	140UNTS313	101895
Denmark	USA (United States)	16 Nov 51	180UNTS275	102391
Cambodia	USA (United States)	28 Dec 51	179UNTS97	102358
Thailand	USA (United States)	29 Dec 51	179UNTS113	102360
Laos	USA (United States)	31 Dec 51	198UNTS243	102668
Taiwan	USA (United States)	02 Jan 52	181UNTS161	102407

PARTY ONE	PARTY TWO	DATE	CITATION	NUMBER
Return of equipment and recapture (Cont.)				
Indonesia	USA (United States)	05 Jan 52	215UNTS121	102916
Philippines	USA (United States)	07 Jan 52	179UNTS193	102368
Italy	USA (United States)	07 Jan 52	179UNTS165	102365
Belgium	USA (United States)	07 Jan 52	179UNTS81	102356
Greece	USA (United States)	07 Jan 52	180UNTS171	102382
Korea, South	USA (United States)	07 Jan 52	179UNTS105	102359
Greece	USA (United States)	07 Jan 52	177UNTS249	102323
Portugal	USA (United States)	08 Jan 52	207UNTS51	102799
Norway	USA (United States)	08 Jan 52	179UNTS185	102367
Denmark	USA (United States)	08 Jan 52	179UNTS65	102354
Luxembourg	USA (United States)	08 Jan 52	180UNTS191	102384
UK Great Britain	USA (United States)	08 Jan 52	179UNTS201	102369
Netherlands	USA (United States)	08 Jan 52	179UNTS175	102366
UK Great Britain	USA (United States)	08 Jan 52	126UNTS307	101696
USA (United States)	Vietnam, South	19 Jan 52	205UNTS127	102772
Ecuador	USA (United States)	20 Feb 52	177UNTS43	102308
Peru	USA (United States)	22 Feb 52	165UNTS31	102166
Japan	USA (United States)	28 Feb 52	208UNTS255	102817
Cuba	USA (United States)	07 Mar 52	165UNTS11	102165
Brazil	USA (United States)	15 Mar 52	199UNTS221	102687
Chile	USA (United States)	09 Apr 52	186UNTS53	102482
Colombia	USA (United States)	17 Apr 52	174UNTS215	102287
Netherlands	USA (United States)	15 May 52	177UNTS233	102321
South Africa	USA (United States)	24 Jun 52	177UNTS241	102322
USA (United States)	Uruguay	30 Jun 52	207UNTS139	102804
Portugal	USA (United States)	09 Jul 52	180UNTS251	102389
Japan	USA (United States)	12 Nov 52	184UNTS111	102443
Dominican Republic	USA (United States)	06 Mar 53	199UNTS267	102689
Philippines	USA (United States)	09 Mar 53	227UNTS101	103134
Philippines	USA (United States)	26 Jun 53	213UNTS77	102881
France	USA (United States)	02 Sep 53	224UNTS153	103075
Spain	USA (United States)	26 Sep 53	207UNTS61	102800
Belgium	USA (United States)	17 Nov 53	251UNTS105	103536
Belgium	Taiwan	13 Jan 54	223UNTS111	103059
Germany, West	USA (United States)	12 Feb 54	223UNTS153	103064
Japan	USA (United States)	08 Mar 54	232UNTS215	103237
Japan	USA (United States)	08 Mar 54	232UNTS169	103236
USA (United States)	USSR (Soviet Union)	26 Mar 54	247UNTS263	103475
Iraq	USA (United States)	21 Apr 54	222UNTS251	103032
Italy	USA (United States)	27 Apr 54	234UNTS103	103275
Japan	USA (United States)	14 May 54	247UNTS273	103476
Taiwan	USA (United States)	14 May 54	231UNTS165	103216
Pakistan	USA (United States)	19 May 54	202UNTS301	102736
Honduras	USA (United States)	20 May 54	222UNTS87	103025
Turkey	USA (United States)	01 Jul 54	234UNTS147	103280
Luxembourg	USA (United States)	07 Jul 54	233UNTS23	103247
USA (United States)	USSR (Soviet Union)	22 Dec 54	251UNTS41	103532
Haiti	USA (United States)	28 Jan 55	270UNTS83	103894
Haiti	USA (United States)	05 Apr 55	270UNTS97	103895
Dominican Republic	USA (United States)	22 Apr 55	239UNTS325	103389
USA (United States)	Vietnam, South	10 May 55	273UNTS157	103950
Cambodia	USA (United States)	16 May 55	263UNTS273	103777
USA (United States)	USSR (Soviet Union)	26 May 55	270UNTS61	103892
Turkey	USA (United States)	26 May 55	262UNTS97	103739
Guatemala	USA (United States)	18 Jun 55	262UNTS105	103740
Germany, West	USA (United States)	30 Jun 55	240UNTS69	103394
Germany, West	USA (United States)	30 Jun 55	240UNTS47	103393
Belgium	USA (United States)	15 Jul 55	223UNTS3	103040
France	USA (United States)	23 Sep 55	270UNTS341	103904
Canada	Norway	20 Dec 55	305UNTS17	104408
Taiwan	USA (United States)	03 Apr 56	268UNTS315	103864
Poland	USA (United States)	28 Jun 56	273UNTS79	103944
Korea, South	USA (United States)	02 Jul 56	281UNTS41	104067
Portugal	USA (United States)	07 Nov 56	277UNTS133	104003
Brazil	USA (United States)	16 Jan 57	266UNTS99	103824
Return of equipment and recapture (Cont.)				
Spain	USA (United States)	09 Mar 57	283UNTS89	104108
Germany, West	USA (United States)	01 May 57	284UNTS85	104131
Libya	USA (United States)	30 Jun 57	284UNTS177	104136
Greece	USA (United States)	05 Aug 57	290UNTS167	104235
Bolivia	USA (United States)	22 Apr 58	317UNTS209	104605
Lebanon	UK Great Britain	19 May 58	327UNTS43	104716
Turkey	USA (United States)	14 Oct 58	336UNTS145	104803
Greece	USA (United States)	15 Jan 59	357UNTS281	105120
Taiwan	USA (United States)	07 Feb 59	341UNTS225	104885
France	USA (United States)	07 May 59	354UNTS83	105055
Thailand	USA (United States)	19 May 59	346UNTS271	104986
Peru	USA (United States)	15 Jun 59	346UNTS279	104987
Spain	USA (United States)	23 Jun 59	354UNTS11	105049
Iraq	USA (United States)	07 Jul 59	357UNTS153	105114
Taiwan	USA (United States)	08 Jul 59	354UNTS47	105052
Japan	USA (United States)	31 Jul 59	357UNTS107	105110
Italy	USA (United States)	18 Aug 59	361UNTS11	105169
Brazil	USA (United States)	19 Oct 59	372UNTS131	105293
Japan	USA (United States)	19 Jan 60	373UNTS207	105321
Ecuador	USA (United States)	11 Feb 60	372UNTS141	105294
Peru	USA (United States)	26 Feb 60	394UNTS141	105674
Argentina	USA (United States)	01 Apr 60	371UNTS245	105281
Colombia	USA (United States)	07 Apr 60	372UNTS27	105285
Haiti	USA (United States)	08 Jul 60	380UNTS135	105454
Canada	USA (United States)	31 Aug 60	393UNTS247	105659
Nepal	UNICEF (Children)	12 Dec 60	382UNTS273	105488
Mali	USA (United States)	20 May 61	413UNTS205	105954
Liberia	USA (United States)	17 Jun 61	410UNTS233	105907
Canada	USA (United States)	01 Sep 61	421UNTS199	106058
Dominican Republic	USA (United States)	08 Mar 62	527UNTS29	107615
El Salvador	USA (United States)	13 Apr 62	451UNTS307	106500
Bolivia	USA (United States)	26 Apr 62	461UNTS105	106654
Panama	USA (United States)	23 May 62	458UNTS225	106604
Germany, West	USA (United States)	25 May 62	458UNTS259	106608
Dahomey	USA (United States)	13 Jun 62	458UNTS219	106603
Niger	USA (United States)	14 Jun 62	458UNTS233	106605
Costa Rica	USA (United States)	18 Jun 62	461UNTS155	106659
Senegal	USA (United States)	20 Jul 62	458UNTS137	106596
Guatemala	USA (United States)	02 Aug 62	461UNTS199	106664
Paraguay	USA (United States)	25 Aug 62	461UNTS207	106665
Honduras	USA (United States)	24 Oct 62	459UNTS211	106624
India	UK Great Britain	27 Nov 62	466UNTS189	106744
Peru	USA (United States)	20 Dec 62	471UNTS75	106822
Philippines	USA (United States)	11 Jan 63	473UNTS43	106853
Pakistan	USA (United States)	16 Jan 63	471UNTS133	106828
Jamaica	USA (United States)	06 Jun 63	477UNTS29	106913
Congo (Zaire)	USA (United States)	19 Jul 63	511UNTS47	107425
Netherlands	USA (United States)	26 Nov 63	388UNTS303	105586
Paraguay	USA (United States)	10 Feb 64	511UNTS53	107426
Cyprus	United Nations	31 Mar 64	492UNTS57	107187
Guinea	USA (United States)	29 Jun 65	549UNTS139	107997
Spain	USA (United States)	21 Apr 66	580UNTS231	108426
Canada	USA (United States)	30 Sep 66	616UNTS193	108896
Military training				
Multilateral		27 Mar 41	67UNTS231	200222
Haiti	USA (United States)	23 May 41	117UNTS191	200370
Bolivia	USA (United States)	04 Sep 41	8UNTS345	200046
Peru	USA (United States)	11 Mar 42	117UNTS266	200375
Brazil	USA (United States)	07 May 42	6UNTS377	200040
Colombia	USA (United States)	29 May 42	8UNTS365	200047
Bolivia	USA (United States)	11 Aug 42	9UNTS309	200049
Dominican Republic	USA (United States)	25 Jan 43	13UNTS399	200083
Guatemala	USA (United States)	17 Jul 43	28UNTS431	200166
Ecuador	USA (United States)	13 Sep 43	29UNTS349	200171

PARTY ONE	PARTY TWO	DATE	CITATION	NUMBER
Military training (Cont.)				
Paraguay	USA (United States)	27 Oct 43	29UNTS391	200174
Iran	USA (United States)	27 Nov 43	31UNTS451	200176
Paraguay	USA (United States)	10 Dec 43	21UNTS305	200131
USA (United States)	Venezuela	13 Jan 44	109UNTS171	200358
Ecuador	USA (United States)	29 Jun 44	80UNTS283	200250
Peru	USA (United States)	10 Jul 44	117UNTS291	200377
Guatemala	USA (United States)	21 Feb 45	121UNTS133	200396
Guatemala	USA (United States)	21 May 45	121UNTS185	200399
Chile	USA (United States)	24 May 45	121UNTS219	200401
Costa Rica	USA (United States)	10 Dec 45	3UNTS157	100029
Honduras	USA (United States)	28 Dec 45	3UNTS185	100031
Canada	USA (United States)	30 Mar 46	7UNTS15	100089
USA (United States)	Venezuela	03 Jun 46	4UNTS215	100047
Taiwan	USA (United States)	28 Jun 46	34UNTS121	100532
Peru	USA (United States)	07 Oct 46	7UNTS71	100092
Colombia	USA (United States)	14 Oct 46	7UNTS97	100093
Philippines	USA (United States)	14 Mar 47	43UNTS271	100673
Philippines	USA (United States)	21 Mar 47	45UNTS47	100691
Denmark	UK Great Britain	22 Apr 47	8UNTS3	100110
Norway	UK Great Britain	05 Jun 47	54UNTS181	100803
El Salvador	USA (United States)	19 Aug 47	51UNTS57	100752
Iran	USA (United States)	06 Oct 47	11UNTS303	100171
Brazil	USA (United States)	29 Jul 48	80UNTS111	101047
Argentina	USA (United States)	06 Oct 48	80UNTS91	101046
Haiti	USA (United States)	04 Jan 49	44UNTS69	100679
Colombia	USA (United States)	21 Feb 49	92UNTS227	101275
Greece	USA (United States)	21 Feb 49	88UNTS29	101182
Colombia	USA (United States)	21 Feb 49	44UNTS83	100680
Haiti	USA (United States)	14 Apr 49	80UNTS37	101043
Peru	USA (United States)	20 Jun 49	92UNTS249	101276
Mexico	USA (United States)	05 Jul 49	68UNTS55	100884
Belgium	UK Great Britain	23 Dec 49	99UNTS61	101371
Korea, South	USA (United States)	26 Jan 50	178UNTS97	102337
Honduras	USA (United States)	06 Mar 50	80UNTS71	101045
Honduras	USA (United States)	06 Mar 50	80UNTS51	101044
USA (United States)	Venezuela	23 Aug 50	92UNTS341	101279
Liberia	USA (United States)	11 Jan 51	122UNTS125	101642
Chile	USA (United States)	15 Feb 51	133UNTS95	101783
Chile	USA (United States)	15 Feb 51	133UNTS117	101784
Canada	USA (United States)	27 Mar 51	132UNTS333	101772
Saudi Arabia	USA (United States)	18 Jun 51	141UNTS67	101906
Saudi Arabia	USA (United States)	18 Jun 51	102UNTS73	101412
USA (United States)	Venezuela	10 Aug 51	140UNTS345	101898
Cuba	USA (United States)	28 Aug 51	140UNTS239	101891
Cuba	USA (United States)	28 Aug 51	134UNTS225	101802
Liberia	USA (United States)	19 Nov 51	167UNTS141	102204
USA (United States)	Uruguay	04 Dec 51	152UNTS41	102010
Nicaragua	USA (United States)	19 Nov 52	186UNTS3	102478
USA (United States)	Venezuela	16 Jan 53	199UNTS287	102690
El Salvador	USA (United States)	21 May 53	213UNTS15	102878
Libya	UK Great Britain	29 Jul 53	186UNTS201	102492
Nicaragua	USA (United States)	19 Nov 53	206UNTS117	102787
Japan	USA (United States)	21 Jan 54	223UNTS145	103063
Nicaragua	USA (United States)	23 Apr 54	229UNTS37	103159
Libya	USA (United States)	09 Sep 54	224UNTS217	103078
El Salvador	USA (United States)	23 Sep 54	237UNTS91	103338
Multilateral		23 Oct 54	332UNTS3	104760
Multilateral		23 Oct 54	334UNTS3	104765
Hungary	USSR (Soviet Union)	27 May 55	407UNTS156	105864
Bolivia	USA (United States)	30 Jun 56	271UNTS243	103919
Argentina	USA (United States)	03 Oct 56	279UNTS13	104032
Dominican Republic	USA (United States)	07 Dec 56	263UNTS193	103774
Canada	Germany, West	10 Dec 56	392UNTS3	105633
Germany, West	USA (United States)	12 Dec 56	280UNTS71	104052
Germany, West	USA (United States)	12 Dec 56	280UNTS63	104051

PARTY ONE	PARTY TWO	DATE	CITATION	NUMBER
Military training (Cont.)				
Poland	USSR (Soviet Union)	17 Dec 56	266UNTS179	103830
Germany, East	USSR (Soviet Union)	12 Mar 57	285UNTS105	104150
Saudi Arabia	USA (United States)	02 Apr 57	283UNTS97	104109
Canada	Netherlands	13 Apr 57	316UNTS223	104588
Canada	Denmark	17 Apr 57	316UNTS207	104586
Canada	Norway	17 Apr 57	316UNTS215	104587
New Zealand	UK Great Britain	04 Jul 57	402UNTS109	105780
Australia	USA (United States)	12 Jul 57	290UNTS139	104233
Fed of Malaya	UK Great Britain	12 Oct 57	285UNTS59	104149
Poland	USSR (Soviet Union)	26 Oct 57	432UNTS221	106223
El Salvador	USA (United States)	21 Nov 57	303UNTS19	104369
Germany, West	USA (United States)	10 Dec 57	307UNTS59	104442
UK Great Britain	USA (United States)	22 Feb 58	307UNTS207	104451
Nicaragua	USA (United States)	05 Sep 58	336UNTS33	104797
Haiti	USA (United States)	24 Dec 58	338UNTS265	104840
Philippines	USA (United States)	21 Jan 59	341UNTS255	104888
Netherlands	USA (United States)	06 May 59	355UNTS327	105084
Canada	USA (United States)	22 May 59	354UNTS63	105054
Argentina	USA (United States)	02 Aug 60	384UNTS105	105514
Canada	USA (United States)	31 Aug 60	393UNTS247	105659
France	USA (United States)	27 Jul 61	433UNTS29	106229
Germany, West	UK Great Britain	26 Sep 61	424UNTS201	106108
Belgium	USA (United States)	17 May 62	461UNTS3	106647
UK Great Britain	USA (United States)	06 Apr 63	474UNTS49	106871
Japan	USA (United States)	26 Apr 63	477UNTS37	106914
Canada	Nigeria	03 Jul 63	529UNTS57	107656
Jamaica	UK Great Britain	20 Feb 64	496UNTS239	107256
Malta	UK Great Britain	21 Sep 64	588UNTS55	108518
Chile	USA (United States)	27 Oct 64	532UNTS347	107727
Jamaica	UK Great Britain	31 Mar 65	539UNTS59	107824
Canada	Jamaica	16 Jul 65	548UNTS265	107982
Guyana	UK Great Britain	15 Jun 67	632UNTS15	109005
Kenya	UK Great Britain	14 Jul 67	643UNTS254	109196
Cyprus	UK Great Britain	11 Mar 68	0UNTS0	109285
Security of information				
Multilateral		27 Mar 41	67UNTS231	200222
Haiti	USA (United States)	23 May 41	117UNTS191	200370
Bolivia	USA (United States)	04 Sep 41	8UNTS345	200046
Peru	USA (United States)	11 Mar 42	117UNTS266	200375
Brazil	USA (United States)	07 May 42	6UNTS377	200040
Colombia	USA (United States)	29 May 42	8UNTS365	200047
Panama	USA (United States)	07 Jul 42	9UNTS289	200048
Bolivia	USA (United States)	11 Aug 42	9UNTS309	200049
Dominican Republic	USA (United States)	25 Jan 43	13UNTS399	200083
Guatemala	USA (United States)	17 Jul 43	28UNTS431	200166
UK Great Britain	USA (United States)	19 Aug 43	214UNTS341	200527
Ecuador	USA (United States)	13 Sep 43	29UNTS349	200171
Paraguay	USA (United States)	27 Oct 43	29UNTS391	200174
Iran	USA (United States)	27 Nov 43	31UNTS451	200176
UK Great Britain	USA (United States)	01 Dec 43	3UNTS209	100033
Paraguay	USA (United States)	10 Dec 43	21UNTS305	200131
USA (United States)	Venezuela	13 Jan 44	109UNTS171	200358
Ecuador	USA (United States)	29 Jun 44	80UNTS283	200250
Peru	USA (United States)	10 Jul 44	117UNTS291	200377
France	USA (United States)	20 Feb 45	76UNTS193	200246
Guatemala	USA (United States)	21 Feb 45	121UNTS133	200396
Turkey	USA (United States)	23 Feb 45	121UNTS165	200398
Belgium	USA (United States)	19 Apr 45	139UNTS179	200455
Guatemala	USA (United States)	21 May 45	121UNTS185	200399
Chile	USA (United States)	24 May 45	121UNTS219	200401
Multilateral		15 Nov 45	3UNTS123	100026
Costa Rica	USA (United States)	10 Dec 45	3UNTS157	100029
Honduras	USA (United States)	28 Dec 45	3UNTS185	100031
UK Great Britain	USA (United States)	27 Mar 46	4UNTS101	100040

Security of information (Cont.)

PARTY ONE	PARTY TWO	DATE	CITATION	NUMBER
Belgium	Netherlands	24 May 46	31UNTS169	100477
USA (United States)	Venezuela	03 Jun 46	4UNTS215	100047
Colombia	USA (United States)	14 Oct 46	7UNTS97	100093
Philippines	USA (United States)	14 Mar 47	43UNTS271	100673
Philippines	USA (United States)	21 Mar 47	45UNTS47	100691
El Salvador	USA (United States)	19 Aug 47	51UNTS57	100752
Iran	USA (United States)	06 Oct 47	11UNTS303	100171
Greece	USA (United States)	03 Dec 47	89UNTS119	101213
Taiwan	USA (United States)	08 Dec 47	70UNTS3	100895
UK Great Britain	USA (United States)	24 Feb 48	73UNTS143	100951
Brazil	USA (United States)	29 Jul 48	80UNTS111	101047
Argentina	USA (United States)	06 Oct 48	80UNTS91	101046
Haiti	USA (United States)	04 Jan 49	44UNTS69	100679
Colombia	USA (United States)	21 Feb 49	92UNTS227	101275
Haiti	USA (United States)	14 Apr 49	80UNTS37	101043
Peru	USA (United States)	20 Jun 49	92UNTS249	101276
Mexico	USA (United States)	05 Jul 49	68UNTS55	100884
Philippines	USA (United States)	08 Aug 49	163UNTS103	102144
Korea, South	USA (United States)	26 Jan 50	80UNTS205	101053
Korea, South	USA (United States)	26 Jan 50	178UNTS97	102337
UK Great Britain	USA (United States)	27 Jan 50	80UNTS261	101056
Italy	USA (United States)	27 Jan 50	80UNTS145	101050
Netherlands	USA (United States)	27 Jan 50	80UNTS219	101054
Norway	USA (United States)	27 Jan 50	80UNTS241	101055
Denmark	USA (United States)	27 Jan 50	48UNTS115	100740
Luxembourg	USA (United States)	27 Jan 50	80UNTS187	101052
France	USA (United States)	27 Jan 50	80UNTS171	101051
Belgium	USA (United States)	27 Jan 50	51UNTS213	100767
Honduras	USA (United States)	06 Mar 50	80UNTS51	101044
Honduras	USA (United States)	06 Mar 50	80UNTS71	101045
Iran	USA (United States)	23 May 50	81UNTS3	101057
UK Great Britain	USA (United States)	21 Jul 50	97UNTS193	101351
USA (United States)	Venezuela	23 Aug 50	92UNTS341	101279
Thailand	USA (United States)	17 Oct 50	79UNTS41	101030
Pakistan	USA (United States)	15 Dec 50	122UNTS89	101639
Cuba	USA (United States)	22 Dec 50	122UNTS97	101640
Brazil	USA (United States)	04 Jan 51	165UNTS97	102171
Chile	USA (United States)	04 Jan 51	165UNTS105	102172
Portugal	USA (United States)	05 Jan 51	133UNTS75	101782
Liberia	USA (United States)	11 Jan 51	122UNTS125	101642
Taiwan	USA (United States)	09 Feb 51	132UNTS273	101767
Chile	USA (United States)	15 Feb 51	133UNTS117	101784
Chile	USA (United States)	15 Feb 51	133UNTS95	101783
Australia	USA (United States)	20 Feb 51	132UNTS297	101769
Saudi Arabia	USA (United States)	18 Jun 51	102UNTS73	101412
Multilateral		19 Jun 51	199UNTS67	102678
USA (United States)	Venezuela	10 Aug 51	140UNTS345	101898
Cuba	USA (United States)	28 Aug 51	134UNTS225	101802
Cuba	USA (United States)	28 Aug 51	140UNTS239	101891
South Africa	USA (United States)	09 Nov 51	160UNTS41	102100
USA (United States)	Yugoslavia	14 Nov 51	174UNTS201	102286
USA (United States)	Uruguay	04 Dec 51	152UNTS41	102010
UK Great Britain	USA (United States)	15 Jan 52	127UNTS3	101697
Ecuador	USA (United States)	20 Feb 52	177UNTS43	102308
Peru	USA (United States)	22 Feb 52	165UNTS31	102166
Cuba	USA (United States)	07 Mar 52	165UNTS11	102165
Brazil	USA (United States)	15 Mar 52	199UNTS221	102687
Chile	USA (United States)	09 Apr 52	186UNTS53	102482
Colombia	USA (United States)	17 Apr 52	174UNTS215	102287
United Arab Rep	USA (United States)	29 Apr 52	241UNTS3	103418
Ethiopia	USA (United States)	13 Jun 52	205UNTS17	102766
USA (United States)	Uruguay	30 Jun 52	207UNTS139	102804
Sweden	USA (United States)	01 Jul 52	187UNTS3	102497
Israel	USA (United States)	23 Jul 52	179UNTS139	102363
Nicaragua	USA (United States)	19 Nov 52	186UNTS3	102478

Security of information (Cont.)

PARTY ONE	PARTY TWO	DATE	CITATION	NUMBER
Canada	USA (United States)	05 Dec 52	206UNTS11	102783
USA (United States)	Venezuela	16 Jan 53	199UNTS287	102690
UK Great Britain	USA (United States)	19 Jan 53	161UNTS3	102117
Dominican Republic	USA (United States)	06 Mar 53	199UNTS267	102689
Lebanon	USA (United States)	23 Mar 53	239UNTS45	103370
El Salvador	USA (United States)	21 May 53	213UNTS15	102878
Ethiopia	USA (United States)	22 May 53	191UNTS59	102577
Philippines	USA (United States)	26 Jun 53	213UNTS77	102881
Libya	UK Great Britain	29 Jul 53	186UNTS201	102492
Belgium	USA (United States)	02 Sep 53	200UNTS127	102700
Spain	USA (United States)	26 Sep 53	207UNTS61	102800
Nicaragua	USA (United States)	19 Nov 53	206UNTS117	102787
Germany, West	USA (United States)	23 Nov 53	224UNTS107	103071
Multilateral		19 Feb 54	214UNTS51	102899
Japan	USA (United States)	08 Mar 54	232UNTS169	103236
Italy	USA (United States)	31 Mar 54	235UNTS293	103311
Luxembourg	USA (United States)	17 Apr 54	257UNTS255	103661
Iraq	USA (United States)	21 Apr 54	222UNTS251	103032
Netherlands	USA (United States)	07 May 54	213UNTS325	102895
Japan	USA (United States)	14 May 54	247UNTS273	103476
Pakistan	USA (United States)	19 May 54	202UNTS301	102736
Honduras	USA (United States)	20 May 54	222UNTS87	103025
Greece	USA (United States)	30 Jul 54	234UNTS43	103272
El Salvador	USA (United States)	23 Sep 54	237UNTS91	103338
USA (United States)	Yugoslavia	18 Oct 54	273UNTS163	103951
Multilateral		23 Oct 54	332UNTS3	104760
Iceland	USA (United States)	10 Dec 54	237UNTS191	103345
Netherlands	USA (United States)	14 Dec 54	262UNTS35	103737
Haiti	USA (United States)	28 Jan 55	270UNTS83	103894
Korea, South	USA (United States)	29 Jan 55	239UNTS53	103371
Germany, West	USA (United States)	04 Apr 55	279UNTS73	104034
Norway	USA (United States)	06 Apr 55	269UNTS65	103874
Cambodia	USA (United States)	16 May 55	263UNTS273	103777
Turkey	USA (United States)	10 Jun 55	238UNTS149	103359
Belgium	USA (United States)	15 Jun 55	235UNTS133	103299
UK Great Britain	USA (United States)	15 Jun 55	214UNTS301	102905
Canada	USA (United States)	15 Jun 55	235UNTS176	103301
UK Great Britain	USA (United States)	15 Jun 55	229UNTS73	103161
Guatemala	USA (United States)	18 Jun 55	262UNTS105	103740
Turkey	USA (United States)	29 Jun 55	269UNTS97	103878
Germany, West	USA (United States)	30 Jun 55	240UNTS47	103393
Israel	USA (United States)	12 Jul 55	219UNTS185	102974
Netherlands	USA (United States)	18 Jul 55	240UNTS347	103412
Lebanon	USA (United States)	18 Jul 55	239UNTS247	103383
Taiwan	USA (United States)	18 Jul 55	235UNTS221	103304
Colombia	USA (United States)	19 Jul 55	235UNTS233	103305
Spain	USA (United States)	19 Jul 55	239UNTS299	103387
Portugal	USA (United States)	21 Jul 55	239UNTS283	103386
USA (United States)	Venezuela	21 Jul 55	238UNTS121	103357
Denmark	USA (United States)	25 Jul 55	235UNTS245	103306
Philippines	USA (United States)	27 Jul 55	239UNTS271	103385
Italy	USA (United States)	28 Jul 55	239UNTS235	103382
Argentina	USA (United States)	29 Jul 55	235UNTS121	103298
Brazil	USA (United States)	03 Aug 55	235UNTS159	103300
Greece	USA (United States)	04 Aug 55	235UNTS257	103307
Chile	USA (United States)	08 Aug 55	235UNTS209	103303
Pakistan	USA (United States)	11 Aug 55	239UNTS259	103384
Japan	USA (United States)	14 Nov 55	240UNTS361	103413
Belgium	UK Great Britain	18 Nov 55	222UNTS327	103038
Canada	Norway	20 Dec 55	305UNTS17	104408
Germany, West	USA (United States)	04 Jan 56	268UNTS143	103856
USA (United States)	Uruguay	13 Jan 56	240UNTS401	103415
Sweden	USA (United States)	18 Jan 56	240UNTS413	103416
Netherlands	USA (United States)	22 Jan 56	287UNTS121	104181
Peru	USA (United States)	25 Jan 56	240UNTS425	103417

PARTY ONE	PARTY TWO	DATE	CITATION	NUMBER
Security of information (Cont.)				
Korea, South	USA (United States)	03 Feb 56	240UNTS129	103401
Germany, West	USA (United States)	13 Feb 56	253UNTS119	103580
Thailand	USA (United States)	13 Mar 56	253UNTS105	103579
Ireland	USA (United States)	16 Mar 56	317UNTS195	104604
Turkey	USA (United States)	18 May 56	283UNTS167	104115
Costa Rica	USA (United States)	18 May 56	404UNTS237	105814
Austria	USA (United States)	08 Jun 56	253UNTS139	103581
New Zealand	USA (United States)	13 Jun 56	253UNTS155	103582
Dominican Republic	USA (United States)	15 Jun 56	265UNTS227	103815
France	USA (United States)	19 Jun 56	281UNTS341	104087
Switzerland	USA (United States)	21 Jun 56	279UNTS41	104033
Australia	USA (United States)	22 Jun 56	283UNTS275	104123
UK Great Britain	USA (United States)	25 Jun 56	249UNTS59	103501
Cuba	USA (United States)	26 Jun 56	293UNTS257	104294
Bolivia	USA (United States)	30 Jun 56	271UNTS243	103919
Germany, West	UK Great Britain	31 Jul 56	252UNTS93	103559
Guatemala	USA (United States)	15 Aug 56	288UNTS181	104205
Argentina	USA (United States)	03 Oct 56	279UNTS13	104032
UK Great Britain	USA (United States)	01 Nov 56	264UNTS3	103785
Ceylon (Sri Lanka)	USA (United States)	02 Nov 56	282UNTS93	104094
Taiwan	USA (United States)	21 Nov 56	265UNTS241	103816
UK Great Britain	USA (United States)	27 Nov 56	282UNTS43	104092
Dominican Republic	USA (United States)	07 Dec 56	263UNTS193	103774
Norway	USA (United States)	25 Feb 57	284UNTS19	104126
Iran	USA (United States)	05 Mar 57	342UNTS29	104898
France	USA (United States)	12 Mar 57	279UNTS275	104045
Multilateral		25 Mar 57	294UNTS2	104300
Ecuador	USA (United States)	31 May 57	304UNTS61	104391
Nicaragua	USA (United States)	11 Jun 57	304UNTS267	104402
Iraq	USA (United States)	16 Jun 57	284UNTS39	104127
Germany, West	USA (United States)	28 Jun 57	288UNTS339	104213
Libya	USA (United States)	30 Jun 57	284UNTS177	104136
Germany, West	USA (United States)	03 Jul 57	288UNTS305	104212
South Africa	USA (United States)	08 Jul 57	290UNTS147	104234
Australia	USA (United States)	12 Jul 57	290UNTS139	104233
Norway	UK Great Britain	12 Jul 57	310UNTS41	104485
Austria	USA (United States)	09 Aug 57	288UNTS299	104211
Spain	USA (United States)	16 Aug 57	307UNTS169	104449
Sweden	UK Great Britain	20 Sep 57	310UNTS49	104486
France	USA (United States)	23 Sep 57	293UNTS297	104297
UK Great Britain	USA (United States)	01 Nov 57	299UNTS167	104312
El Salvador	USA (United States)	21 Nov 57	303UNTS19	104369
Ethiopia	USA (United States)	26 Dec 57	307UNTS71	104443
Italy	UK Great Britain	28 Dec 57	305UNTS357	104425
Australia	USA (United States)	24 Jan 58	307UNTS105	104446
Canada	USA (United States)	12 May 58	316UNTS151	104582
Japan	USA (United States)	19 Jun 58	325UNTS143	104699
UK Great Britain	USA (United States)	03 Jul 58	326UNTS3	104707
Fed of Malaya	USA (United States)	09 Jul 58	336UNTS79	104799
Portugal	UK Great Britain	18 Jul 58	313UNTS109	104532
Lebanon	USA (United States)	06 Aug 58	366UNTS361	105223
Nicaragua	USA (United States)	05 Sep 58	336UNTS33	104797
USA (United States)	Venezuela	08 Oct 58	371UNTS69	105271
Euratom	USA (United States)	08 Nov 58	338UNTS135	104835
Haiti	USA (United States)	24 Dec 58	338UNTS265	104840
Japan	IAEA (Atom Energy)	24 Mar 59	339UNTS327	104852
USA (United States)	Vietnam, South	22 Apr 59	347UNTS113	104993
Netherlands	USA (United States)	06 May 59	355UNTS327	105084
Greece	USA (United States)	06 May 59	357UNTS163	105115
IAEA (Atom Energy)	USA (United States)	11 May 59	339UNTS359	104855
Canada	Pakistan	14 May 59	426UNTS129	106133
Panama	USA (United States)	20 May 59	346UNTS235	104983
Canada	USA (United States)	22 May 59	354UNTS63	105054
Panama	USA (United States)	24 Jun 59	479UNTS145	106950
Canada	Japan	02 Jul 59	383UNTS243	105504

PARTY ONE	PARTY TWO	DATE	CITATION	NUMBER
Security of information (Cont.)				
Austria	USA (United States)	22 Jul 59	368UNTS199	105242
Australia	Canada	04 Aug 59	391UNTS191	105623
USA (United States)	Yugoslavia	25 Aug 59	357UNTS87	105107
USA (United States)	Yugoslavia	25 Aug 59	357UNTS77	105106
Japan	USA (United States)	19 Jan 60	373UNTS207	105321
Spain	UK Great Britain	19 Jan 60	404UNTS41	105804
Norway	USA (United States)	13 Feb 60	388UNTS255	105583
Denmark	USA (United States)	19 Feb 60	354UNTS151	105061
Netherlands	USA (United States)	24 Mar 60	406UNTS165	105847
Denmark	UK Great Britain	20 May 60	374UNTS245	105338
Indonesia	USA (United States)	08 Jun 60	388UNTS287	105585
UK Great Britain	USA (United States)	24 Jun 60	377UNTS63	105396
Spain	USA (United States)	21 Jul 60	393UNTS289	105663
Argentina	USA (United States)	02 Aug 60	384UNTS105	105514
Cyprus	UK Great Britain	16 Aug 60	382UNTS177	105477
Australia	USA (United States)	23 Aug 60	388UNTS237	105581
Haiti	USA (United States)	01 Sep 60	388UNTS249	105582
France	USA (United States)	19 Sep 60	400UNTS21	105745
Multilateral		21 Sep 60	394UNTS3	105664
Portugal	USA (United States)	31 Oct 60	394UNTS127	105673
Italy	USA (United States)	03 Dec 60	410UNTS3	105893
Finland	IAEA (Atom Energy)	30 Dec 60	395UNTS257	105690
Liberia	USA (United States)	17 Jun 61	410UNTS233	105907
France	USA (United States)	27 Jul 61	433UNTS29	106229
India	United Nations	19 Feb 62	423UNTS3	106082
Dominican Republic	USA (United States)	08 Mar 62	527UNTS29	107615
Colombia	USA (United States)	09 Apr 62	476UNTS9	106899
El Salvador	USA (United States)	13 Apr 62	451UNTS307	106500
Bolivia	USA (United States)	26 Apr 62	461UNTS105	106654
Belgium	USA (United States)	17 May 62	461UNTS3	106647
Panama	USA (United States)	23 May 62	458UNTS225	106604
Canada	France	25 May 62	470UNTS163	106808
New Zealand	USA (United States)	08 Jun 62	458UNTS209	106602
Dahomey	USA (United States)	13 Jun 62	458UNTS219	106603
Niger	USA (United States)	14 Jun 62	458UNTS233	106605
Costa Rica	USA (United States)	18 Jun 62	461UNTS155	106659
Argentina	USA (United States)	22 Jun 62	458UNTS97	106594
Canada	Greece	18 Jul 62	528UNTS265	107647
Senegal	USA (United States)	20 Jul 62	458UNTS137	106596
Australia	Japan	07 Aug 62	435UNTS261	106283
Paraguay	USA (United States)	25 Aug 62	461UNTS207	106665
Canada	Sweden	11 Sep 62	529UNTS9	107651
Sweden	USA (United States)	04 Oct 62	462UNTS31	106669
Ethiopia	USA (United States)	25 Jan 63	473UNTS27	106851
IAEA (Atom Energy)	Yugoslavia	04 Mar 63	490UNTS333	107162
UK Great Britain	USA (United States)	06 Apr 63	474UNTS49	106871
Australia	USA (United States)	09 May 63	469UNTS55	106784
IAEA (Atom Energy)	Yugoslavia	04 Jun 63	490UNTS343	107163
Jamaica	USA (United States)	06 Jun 63	477UNTS29	106913
Denmark	Netherlands	06 Jun 63	484UNTS137	107021
Austria	IAEA (Atom Energy)	21 Jun 63	490UNTS351	107164
Canada	Nigeria	03 Jul 63	529UNTS57	107656
Congo (Zaire)	USA (United States)	19 Jul 63	511UNTS47	107425
India	USA (United States)	08 Aug 63	488UNTS21	107117
UK Great Britain	USA (United States)	11 Oct 63	483UNTS3	107005
Multilateral		17 Oct 63	525UNTS75	107585
Netherlands	UK Great Britain	30 Oct 63	490UNTS11	107151
Mexico	IAEA (Atom Energy)	18 Dec 63	490UNTS361	107165
Paraguay	USA (United States)	10 Feb 64	511UNTS53	107426
Italy	Netherlands	29 May 64	541UNTS147	107867
Multilateral		15 Jun 64	573UNTS85	108324
IAEA (Atom Energy)	USA (United States)	15 Jun 64	525UNTS3	107580
Multilateral		18 Jun 64	542UNTS145	107886
Italy	USA (United States)	04 Aug 64	529UNTS205	107662
Switzerland	UK Great Britain	11 Aug 64	552UNTS271	108059

PARTY ONE	PARTY TWO	DATE	CITATION	NUMBER
Security of information (Cont.)				
Dominican Republic	USA (United States)	28 Aug 64	531UNTS35	107691
IAEA (Atom Energy)	United Arab Rep	17 Sep 64	525UNTS19	107581
Chile	USA (United States)	27 Oct 64	532UNTS347	107727
Trinidad/Tobago	USA (United States)	05 Dec 64	535UNTS331	107788
Switzerland	USA (United States)	30 Jan 65	594UNTS55	108594
Multilateral		18 Jun 65	573UNTS3	108320
Multilateral		23 Jun 65	548UNTS241	107981
Guinea	USA (United States)	29 Jun 65	549UNTS139	107997
United Nations	United Arab Rep	26 Nov 65	551UNTS253	108046
IAEA (Atom Energy)	Turkey	08 Feb 66	573UNTS75	108323
Paraguay	USA (United States)	11 Apr 66	578UNTS99	108389
UK Great Britain	USA (United States)	02 Jun 66	573UNTS229	108336
Mexico	IAEA (Atom Energy)	20 Jun 66	573UNTS25	108321
Philippines	USA (United States)	26 Aug 66	606UNTS259	108790
IAEA (Atom Energy)	USA (United States)	26 Sep 66	589UNTS3	108532
Philippines	IAEA (Atom Energy)	28 Sep 66	589UNTS25	108533
IAEA (Atom Energy)	USA (United States)	09 Dec 66	589UNTS55	108535
Sweden	UK Great Britain	26 Oct 67	632UNTS277	109029
Surplus war property				
Canada	USA (United States)	27 Jan 43	101UNTS257	200300
Colombia	USA (United States)	29 Mar 43	124UNTS139	200416
Multilateral		28 Oct 44	123UNTS223	200414
Multilateral		20 Jan 45	140UNTS397	200471
France	USA (United States)	20 Feb 45	76UNTS223	200248
France	UK Great Britain	27 Mar 45	98UNTS227	200274
Canada	USA (United States)	15 May 45	125UNTS353	200433
UK Great Britain	USA (United States)	15 Jun 45	89UNTS327	200261
USA (United States)	USSR (Soviet Union)	15 Oct 45	278UNTS151	200547
France	UK Great Britain	26 Jan 46	91UNTS183	101251
Canada	USA (United States)	03 Mar 46	6UNTS279	100081
Belgium	UK Great Britain	11 Mar 46	26UNTS167	100387
UK Great Britain	USA (United States)	27 Mar 46	4UNTS2	100039
Canada	USA (United States)	30 Mar 46	7UNTS15	100089
Poland	USA (United States)	24 Apr 46	4UNTS155	100042
France	UK Great Britain	29 Apr 46	98UNTS123	101360
India	USA (United States)	16 May 46	4UNTS183	100045
France	USA (United States)	28 May 46	84UNTS59	101119
France	USA (United States)	28 May 46	84UNTS79	101120
France	USA (United States)	28 May 46	84UNTS167	101127
Australia	USA (United States)	07 Jun 46	4UNTS237	100048
Poland	UK Great Britain	24 Jun 46	11UNTS59	100149
New Zealand	USA (United States)	10 Jul 46	6UNTS341	100087
UK Great Britain	USA (United States)	31 Jul 46	42UNTS199	100648
Denmark	UK Great Britain	16 Aug 46	9UNTS163	100130
Philippines	USA (United States)	11 Sep 46	43UNTS231	100670
Norway	UK Great Britain	27 Sep 46	6UNTS259	100079
Denmark	USA (United States)	01 Oct 46	42UNTS219	100650
Norway	USA (United States)	12 Nov 46	42UNTS227	100651
Netherlands	UK Great Britain	04 Dec 46	12UNTS241	100187
Belgium	UK Great Britain	16 Jan 47	54UNTS97	100797
South Africa	USA (United States)	21 Mar 47	16UNTS47	100248
Thailand	USA (United States)	08 May 47	42UNTS241	100653
Netherlands	USA (United States)	28 May 47	17UNTS29	100267
Italy	USA (United States)	09 Jun 47	104UNTS157	101437
Italy	USA (United States)	14 Aug 47	36UNTS105	100567
USSR (Soviet Union)	Yugoslavia	23 Aug 47	116UNTS281	101577
Burma	UK Great Britain	17 Oct 47	70UNTS183	100904
Taiwan	USA (United States)	08 Dec 47	70UNTS3	100895
France	Lebanon	24 Jan 48	173UNTS99	102263
Philippines	USA (United States)	23 Mar 48	43UNTS247	100671
UK Great Britain	Uruguay	12 Jul 48	71UNTS199	100919
New Zealand	USA (United States)	14 Sep 48	18UNTS251	100295
UK Great Britain	USA (United States)	30 Sep 48	71UNTS241	100922
Multilateral		08 Oct 48	19UNTS113	100308
Surplus war property (Cont.)				
France	USA (United States)	22 Oct 48	84UNTS173	101128
Canada	Netherlands	28 Oct 48	231UNTS95	103210
France	USA (United States)	14 Mar 49	84UNTS237	101133
Philippines	USA (United States)	16 May 49	67UNTS199	100878
Australia	Netherlands	12 Aug 49	34UNTS213	100539
Denmark	USA (United States)	16 Nov 51	180UNTS275	102391
Greece	USA (United States)	07 Jan 52	177UNTS249	102323
Portugal	USA (United States)	09 Jul 52	180UNTS251	102389
Sweden	USA (United States)	20 Nov 52	177UNTS203	102319
Libya	UK Great Britain	25 Mar 53	172UNTS281	102252
Turkey	UK Great Britain	11 Feb 54	190UNTS343	102575
Honduras	USA (United States)	24 May 54	433UNTS155	106238
Multilateral		23 Oct 54	332UNTS3	104760
Japan	USA (United States)	19 Nov 54	238UNTS207	103364
Iceland	USA (United States)	10 Dec 54	237UNTS191	103345
Germany, West	USA (United States)	14 Apr 55	263UNTS351	103782
Multilateral		15 May 55	217UNTS223	102949
Germany, West	USA (United States)	30 Jun 55	240UNTS69	103394
Ecuador	USA (United States)	19 Jul 56	372UNTS149	105295
Italy	USA (United States)	22 Jun 57	284UNTS51	104128
Turkey	UK Great Britain	16 Aug 57	310UNTS21	104482
Taiwan	USA (United States)	22 Jul 59	357UNTS293	105121
USA (United States)	Yugoslavia	25 Aug 59	357UNTS77	105106
New Zealand	UK Great Britain	21 Sep 59	401UNTS51	105762
Turkey	USA (United States)	13 Nov 59	361UNTS3	105168
Canada	USA (United States)	01 Sep 61	421UNTS199	106058
Netherlands	USA (United States)	26 Nov 63	388UNTS303	105586
Chad	France	19 May 64	0UNTS0	109443
Military assistance missions				
Colombia	USA (United States)	19 Feb 42	117UNTS185	200369
Guatemala	USA (United States)	21 Jul 42	103UNTS299	200320
Colombia	USA (United States)	05 Nov 42	24UNTS227	200147
El Salvador	USA (United States)	25 Mar 43	13UNTS419	200088
Chile	USA (United States)	14 Apr 43	9UNTS331	200050
El Salvador	USA (United States)	21 May 43	9UNTS341	200051
Argentina	USA (United States)	02 Sep 43	9UNTS363	200052
Nicaragua	USA (United States)	25 Oct 43	29UNTS383	200173
Peru	USA (United States)	20 Dec 43	117UNTS285	200376
Peru	USA (United States)	31 Mar 44	109UNTS165	200357
Peru	USA (United States)	02 May 44	109UNTS211	200361
Colombia	USA (United States)	03 Dec 45	107UNTS3	101462
Iran	USA (United States)	08 Aug 46	31UNTS423	100484
Peru	USA (United States)	19 Aug 46	109UNTS15	101485
Brazil	USA (United States)	17 Sep 46	7UNTS49	100091
Denmark	UK Great Britain	20 Jan 47	118UNTS73	101597
Philippines	USA (United States)	21 Mar 47	45UNTS47	100691
UK Great Britain	USA (United States)	09 Oct 47	34UNTS129	100533
Greece	USA (United States)	03 Dec 47	89UNTS119	101213
USA (United States)	Venezuela	30 Jan 48	109UNTS25	101486
Peru	USA (United States)	02 Mar 48	109UNTS9	101484
Ecuador	USA (United States)	21 Sep 48	80UNTS127	101048
Guatemala	USA (United States)	08 Oct 48	121UNTS37	101624
Guatemala	USA (United States)	08 Oct 48	121UNTS31	101623
Ecuador	USA (United States)	04 Feb 49	80UNTS137	101049
Ecuador	USA (United States)	17 May 49	66UNTS3	100845
Indonesia	USA (United States)	15 Aug 50	134UNTS255	101804
Burma	USA (United States)	06 Nov 50	122UNTS81	101638
Iceland	USA (United States)	05 May 51	205UNTS173	102776
Saudi Arabia	USA (United States)	18 Jun 51	141UNTS67	101906
Paraguay	USA (United States)	30 Jul 51	178UNTS163	102340
USA (United States)	Uruguay	30 Jun 52	207UNTS139	102804
Dominican Republic	USA (United States)	06 Mar 53	199UNTS267	102689
Philippines	USA (United States)	26 Jun 53	213UNTS77	102881
Spain	USA (United States)	26 Sep 53	207UNTS61	102800

PARTY ONE	PARTY TWO	DATE	CITATION	NUMBER
Military assistance missions (Cont.)				
Spain	USA (United States)	26 Sep 53	207UNTS83	102801
Japan	USA (United States)	08 Mar 54	232UNTS169	103236
Pakistan	USA (United States)	19 May 54	202UNTS301	102736
Honduras	USA (United States)	20 May 54	222UNTS87	103025
USA (United States)	Vietnam, South	23 Apr 55	277UNTS279	104012
Cambodia	USA (United States)	16 May 55	263UNTS273	103777
Germany, West	USA (United States)	30 Jun 55	240UNTS47	103393
Paraguay	USA (United States)	22 Jul 55	265UNTS3	103802
Paraguay	USA (United States)	22 Jul 55	265UNTS15	103803
Bolivia	USA (United States)	09 Sep 55	256UNTS239	103633
Nicaragua	USA (United States)	09 Feb 57	279UNTS191	104040
Dominican Republic	USA (United States)	09 Mar 57	279UNTS249	104044
Saudi Arabia	USA (United States)	02 Apr 57	283UNTS97	104109
Fed of Malaya	UK Great Britain	12 Oct 57	285UNTS59	104149
Germany, West	USA (United States)	10 Dec 57	307UNTS59	104442
Muscat and Oman	UK Great Britain	25 Jul 58	312UNTS347	104524
Haiti	USA (United States)	27 Oct 58	336UNTS235	104807
Peru	USA (United States)	15 Jul 60	384UNTS159	105517
Canada	Ghana	08 Jan 62	528UNTS221	107645
Congo (Zaire)	USA (United States)	19 Jul 63	511UNTS47	107425
Guinea	USA (United States)	29 Jun 65	549UNTS139	107997
Malaysia	UK Great Britain	05 Dec 67	642UNTS293	109181
UK Great Britain	Zambia	21 Feb 68	0UNTS0	109264
Airforce-army-navy personnel ratio				
Multilateral		27 Mar 41	67UNTS231	200222
Haiti	USA (United States)	23 May 41	117UNTS191	200370
Bolivia	USA (United States)	04 Sep 41	8UNTS345	200046
Peru	USA (United States)	11 Mar 42	117UNTS266	200375
Brazil	USA (United States)	07 May 42	6UNTS377	200040
Colombia	USA (United States)	29 May 42	8UNTS365	200047
Panama	USA (United States)	07 Jul 42	9UNTS289	200048
Bolivia	USA (United States)	11 Aug 42	9UNTS309	200049
Dominican Republic	USA (United States)	25 Jan 43	13UNTS399	200083
El Salvador	USA (United States)	21 May 43	9UNTS341	200051
Guatemala	USA (United States)	17 Jul 43	28UNTS431	200166
Ecuador	USA (United States)	13 Sep 43	29UNTS349	200171
Paraguay	USA (United States)	27 Oct 43	29UNTS391	200174
Iran	USA (United States)	27 Nov 43	31UNTS451	200176
Paraguay	USA (United States)	10 Dec 43	21UNTS305	200131
USA (United States)	Venezuela	13 Jan 44	109UNTS171	200358
Ecuador	USA (United States)	29 Jun 44	80UNTS283	200250
Peru	USA (United States)	10 Jul 44	117UNTS291	200377
Brazil	USA (United States)	29 Sep 44	65UNTS271	200216
Guatemala	USA (United States)	21 Feb 45	121UNTS133	200396
Guatemala	USA (United States)	21 May 45	121UNTS185	200399
Chile	USA (United States)	24 May 45	121UNTS219	200401
Costa Rica	USA (United States)	10 Dec 45	3UNTS157	100029
Honduras	USA (United States)	28 Dec 45	3UNTS185	100031
France	USA (United States)	28 May 46	84UNTS141	101124
USA (United States)	Venezuela	03 Jun 46	4UNTS215	100047
Peru	USA (United States)	07 Oct 46	7UNTS71	100092
Colombia	USA (United States)	14 Oct 46	7UNTS97	100093
Philippines	USA (United States)	21 Mar 47	45UNTS47	100691
Greece	UK Great Britain	05 Jun 47	9UNTS197	100133
El Salvador	USA (United States)	19 Aug 47	51UNTS57	100752
Guatemala	USA (United States)	29 Aug 47	27UNTS11	100393
Taiwan	USA (United States)	03 Sep 47	9UNTS91	100126
Iran	USA (United States)	06 Oct 47	11UNTS303	100171
UK Great Britain	USA (United States)	09 Oct 47	34UNTS129	100533
Brazil	USA (United States)	02 Feb 48	67UNTS109	100870
France	UK Great Britain	19 Apr 48	83UNTS201	101109
Brazil	USA (United States)	29 Jul 48	80UNTS111	101047
Argentina	USA (United States)	06 Oct 48	80UNTS91	101046
Haiti	USA (United States)	04 Jan 49	44UNTS69	100679

PARTY ONE	PARTY TWO	DATE	CITATION	NUMBER
Airforce-army-navy personnel ratio (Cont.)				
Colombia	USA (United States)	21 Feb 49	44UNTS83	100680
Colombia	USA (United States)	21 Feb 49	92UNTS227	101275
Haiti	USA (United States)	14 Apr 49	80UNTS37	101043
Peru	USA (United States)	20 Jun 49	92UNTS249	101276
Mexico	USA (United States)	05 Jul 49	68UNTS55	100884
Guatemala	USA (United States)	20 Dec 49	70UNTS71	100897
Korea, South	USA (United States)	26 Jan 50	178UNTS97	102337
China People's Rep	USSR (Soviet Union)	14 Feb 50	226UNTS31	103105
Honduras	USA (United States)	06 Mar 50	80UNTS51	101044
Honduras	USA (United States)	06 Mar 50	80UNTS71	101045
Bolivia	USA (United States)	30 Mar 50	241UNTS77	103425
Dominican Republic	USA (United States)	11 Aug 50	92UNTS329	101278
USA (United States)	Venezuela	23 Aug 50	92UNTS341	101279
Cuba	USA (United States)	22 Dec 50	122UNTS97	101640
Liberia	USA (United States)	11 Jan 51	122UNTS125	101642
Chile	USA (United States)	15 Feb 51	133UNTS117	101784
Chile	USA (United States)	15 Feb 51	133UNTS95	101783
UK Great Britain	USA (United States)	06 Mar 51	97UNTS137	101347
USA (United States)	Venezuela	10 Aug 51	140UNTS345	101898
Cuba	USA (United States)	28 Aug 51	140UNTS239	101891
Cuba	USA (United States)	28 Aug 51	134UNTS225	101802
USA (United States)	Uruguay	04 Dec 51	152UNTS41	102010
Nicaragua	USA (United States)	12 Dec 51	167UNTS151	102205
Costa Rica	USA (United States)	25 Feb 52	174UNTS233	102288
Honduras	USA (United States)	23 Apr 52	198UNTS251	102669
Nicaragua	USA (United States)	19 Nov 52	186UNTS3	102478
USA (United States)	Venezuela	16 Jan 53	199UNTS287	102690
El Salvador	USA (United States)	21 May 53	213UNTS15	102878
Ethiopia	USA (United States)	22 May 53	207UNTS127	102803
Nicaragua	USA (United States)	19 Nov 53	206UNTS117	102787
El Salvador	USA (United States)	23 Sep 54	237UNTS91	103338
Iraq	UK Great Britain	04 Apr 55	233UNTS118	103265
Cuba	USA (United States)	03 Aug 55	265UNTS41	103805
Ecuador	USA (United States)	24 Aug 55	256UNTS299	103640
Colombia	USA (United States)	16 Sep 55	256UNTS221	103631
Brazil	USA (United States)	20 Sep 55	257UNTS349	103665
Peru	USA (United States)	28 Oct 55	239UNTS181	103378
Honduras	USA (United States)	25 Apr 56	269UNTS25	103869
Bolivia	USA (United States)	30 Jun 56	271UNTS269	103920
Bolivia	USA (United States)	30 Jun 56	271UNTS243	103919
Peru	USA (United States)	06 Sep 56	277UNTS231	104009
Argentina	USA (United States)	03 Oct 56	279UNTS13	104032
Taiwan	USA (United States)	21 Nov 56	265UNTS241	103816
Dominican Republic	USA (United States)	07 Dec 56	263UNTS193	103774
Denmark	USA (United States)	12 Dec 56	304UNTS311	104405
El Salvador	USA (United States)	21 Nov 57	303UNTS19	104369
Haiti	USA (United States)	27 Oct 58	336UNTS235	104807
Haiti	USA (United States)	24 Dec 58	338UNTS265	104840
Argentina	USA (United States)	02 Aug 60	384UNTS105	105514
Canada	USA (United States)	23 Sep 61	421UNTS79	106053
Canada	Ghana	08 Jan 62	528UNTS221	107645
Congo (Zaire)	USA (United States)	19 Jul 63	511UNTS47	107425
Jamaica	UK Great Britain	20 Feb 64	496UNTS239	107256
Chad	France	19 May 64	0UNTS0	109443
Malta	UK Great Britain	21 Sep 64	588UNTS55	108518
Chile	USA (United States)	27 Oct 64	532UNTS347	107727
Jamaica	UK Great Britain	31 Mar 65	539UNTS59	107824
Saudi Arabia	USA (United States)	05 Jun 65	548UNTS285	107984
Guyana	UK Great Britain	26 May 66	595UNTS255	108621
Guyana	UK Great Britain	15 Jun 67	632UNTS15	109005
Malaysia	UK Great Britain	05 Dec 67	642UNTS293	109181
UK Great Britain	Zambia	21 Feb 68	0UNTS0	109264
Ranks and privileges				
Multilateral		27 Mar 41	67UNTS231	200222

PARTY ONE	PARTY TWO	DATE	CITATION	NUMBER
Ranks and privileges (Cont.)				
Haiti	USA (United States)	23 May 41	117UNTS191	200370
Bolivia	USA (United States)	04 Sep 41	8UNTS345	200046
Peru	USA (United States)	11 Mar 42	117UNTS266	200375
Brazil	USA (United States)	07 May 42	6UNTS377	200040
Colombia	USA (United States)	29 May 42	8UNTS365	200047
Panama	USA (United States)	07 Jul 42	9UNTS289	200048
Bolivia	USA (United States)	11 Aug 42	9UNTS309	200049
Dominican Republic	USA (United States)	25 Jan 43	13UNTS399	200083
El Salvador	USA (United States)	21 May 43	9UNTS341	200051
Guatemala	USA (United States)	17 Jul 43	28UNTS431	200166
Ecuador	USA (United States)	13 Sep 43	29UNTS349	200171
Paraguay	USA (United States)	27 Oct 43	29UNTS391	200174
Iran	USA (United States)	27 Nov 43	31UNTS451	200176
Paraguay	USA (United States)	10 Dec 43	21UNTS305	200131
USA (United States)	Venezuela	13 Jan 44	109UNTS171	200358
Ecuador	USA (United States)	29 Jun 44	80UNTS283	200250
Peru	USA (United States)	10 Jul 44	117UNTS291	200377
Guatemala	USA (United States)	21 Feb 45	121UNTS133	200396
Guatemala	USA (United States)	21 May 45	121UNTS185	200399
Chile	USA (United States)	24 May 45	121UNTS219	200401
Costa Rica	USA (United States)	10 Dec 45	3UNTS157	100029
Honduras	USA (United States)	28 Dec 45	3UNTS185	100031
USA (United States)	Venezuela	03 Jun 46	4UNTS215	100047
Peru	USA (United States)	07 Oct 46	7UNTS71	100092
Colombia	USA (United States)	14 Oct 46	7UNTS97	100093
Philippines	USA (United States)	21 Mar 47	45UNTS47	100691
El Salvador	USA (United States)	19 Aug 47	51UNTS57	100752
Iran	USA (United States)	06 Oct 47	11UNTS303	100171
Brazil	USA (United States)	29 Jul 48	80UNTS111	101047
Argentina	USA (United States)	06 Oct 48	80UNTS91	101046
Belgium	USA (United States)	26 Oct 48	84UNTS265	101135
Haiti	USA (United States)	04 Jan 49	44UNTS69	100679
Colombia	USA (United States)	21 Feb 49	44UNTS83	100680
Colombia	USA (United States)	21 Feb 49	92UNTS227	101275
Haiti	USA (United States)	14 Apr 49	80UNTS37	101043
Peru	USA (United States)	20 Jun 49	92UNTS249	101276
Mexico	USA (United States)	05 Jul 49	68UNTS55	100884
Multilateral		12 Aug 49	75UNTS135	100972
Guatemala	USA (United States)	20 Dec 49	70UNTS71	100897
Korea, South	USA (United States)	26 Jan 50	178UNTS97	102337
Honduras	USA (United States)	06 Mar 50	80UNTS71	101045
Honduras	USA (United States)	06 Mar 50	80UNTS51	101044
USA (United States)	Venezuela	23 Aug 50	92UNTS341	101279
Cuba	USA (United States)	22 Dec 50	122UNTS97	101640
Liberia	USA (United States)	11 Jan 51	122UNTS125	101642
Chile	USA (United States)	15 Feb 51	133UNTS117	101784
Chile	USA (United States)	15 Feb 51	133UNTS95	101783
Multilateral		19 Jun 51	199UNTS67	102678
USA (United States)	Venezuela	10 Aug 51	140UNTS345	101898
Cuba	USA (United States)	28 Aug 51	140UNTS239	101891
Cuba	USA (United States)	28 Aug 51	134UNTS225	101802
USA (United States)	Uruguay	04 Dec 51	152UNTS41	102010
Nicaragua	USA (United States)	12 Dec 51	167UNTS151	102205
Costa Rica	USA (United States)	25 Feb 52	174UNTS233	102288
Japan	USA (United States)	28 Feb 52	208UNTS255	102817
Honduras	USA (United States)	23 Apr 52	198UNTS251	102669
Nicaragua	USA (United States)	19 Nov 52	186UNTS3	102478
USA (United States)	Venezuela	16 Jan 53	199UNTS287	102690
El Salvador	USA (United States)	21 May 53	213UNTS15	102878
Nicaragua	USA (United States)	19 Nov 53	206UNTS117	102787
Multilateral		19 Feb 54	214UNTS51	102899
El Salvador	USA (United States)	23 Sep 54	237UNTS91	103338
Cambodia	USA (United States)	16 May 55	263UNTS273	103777
Cuba	USA (United States)	03 Aug 55	265UNTS41	103805
Ecuador	USA (United States)	24 Aug 55	256UNTS299	103640

PARTY ONE	PARTY TWO	DATE	CITATION	NUMBER
Ranks and privileges (Cont.)				
Colombia	USA (United States)	16 Sep 55	256UNTS221	103631
Taiwan	USA (United States)	14 Oct 55	268UNTS165	103857
Peru	USA (United States)	28 Oct 55	239UNTS181	103378
Honduras	USA (United States)	25 Apr 56	269UNTS25	103869
Bolivia	USA (United States)	30 Jun 56	271UNTS269	103920
Bolivia	USA (United States)	30 Jun 56	271UNTS243	103919
Peru	USA (United States)	06 Sep 56	277UNTS231	104009
Argentina	USA (United States)	03 Oct 56	279UNTS13	104032
Dominican Republic	USA (United States)	07 Dec 56	263UNTS193	103774
Denmark	USA (United States)	12 Dec 56	304UNTS311	104405
Nicaragua	USA (United States)	09 Feb 57	279UNTS191	104040
Dominican Republic	USA (United States)	09 Mar 57	279UNTS249	104044
El Salvador	USA (United States)	21 Nov 57	303UNTS19	104369
Haiti	USA (United States)	24 Dec 58	338UNTS265	104840
Argentina	USA (United States)	02 Aug 60	384UNTS105	105514
Pakistan	United Nations	18 Apr 63	503UNTS25	107339
Congo (Zaire)	USA (United States)	19 Jul 63	511UNTS47	107425
Chad	France	19 May 64	0UNTS0	109443
Chile	USA (United States)	27 Oct 64	532UNTS347	107727
Jamaica	UK Great Britain	31 Mar 65	539UNTS59	107824
Saudi Arabia	USA (United States)	05 Jun 65	548UNTS285	107984
Denmark	United Nations	21 Feb 66	555UNTS151	108108
Canada	United Nations	21 Feb 66	555UNTS119	108107
New Zealand	United Nations	21 Feb 66	555UNTS163	108110
Finland	United Nations	21 Feb 66	555UNTS157	108109
United Nations	Sweden	21 Feb 66	555UNTS169	108111
UK Great Britain	Zambia	21 Feb 68	0UNTS0	109264
Conditions for assistance missions				
Canada	USA (United States)	29 May 40	119UNTS285	200385
Multilateral		27 Mar 41	67UNTS231	200222
Haiti	USA (United States)	23 May 41	117UNTS191	200370
Bolivia	USA (United States)	04 Sep 41	8UNTS345	200046
Peru	USA (United States)	11 Mar 42	117UNTS266	200375
Brazil	USA (United States)	07 May 42	6UNTS377	200040
Colombia	USA (United States)	29 May 42	8UNTS365	200047
Panama	USA (United States)	07 Jul 42	9UNTS289	200048
Bolivia	USA (United States)	11 Aug 42	9UNTS309	200049
Dominican Republic	USA (United States)	25 Jan 43	13UNTS399	200083
El Salvador	USA (United States)	21 May 43	9UNTS341	200051
Guatemala	USA (United States)	17 Jul 43	28UNTS431	200166
Ecuador	USA (United States)	13 Sep 43	29UNTS349	200171
Paraguay	USA (United States)	27 Oct 43	29UNTS391	200174
Iran	USA (United States)	27 Nov 43	31UNTS451	200176
Paraguay	USA (United States)	10 Dec 43	21UNTS305	200131
USA (United States)	Venezuela	13 Jan 44	109UNTS171	200358
Ecuador	USA (United States)	29 Jun 44	80UNTS283	200250
Peru	USA (United States)	10 Jul 44	117UNTS291	200377
Brazil	USA (United States)	29 Sep 44	65UNTS271	200216
Guatemala	USA (United States)	21 Feb 45	121UNTS133	200396
Guatemala	USA (United States)	21 May 45	121UNTS185	200399
Chile	USA (United States)	24 May 45	121UNTS219	200401
France	UK Great Britain	31 Aug 45	98UNTS249	200275
Costa Rica	USA (United States)	10 Dec 45	3UNTS157	100029
Honduras	USA (United States)	28 Dec 45	3UNTS185	100031
USA (United States)	Venezuela	03 Jun 46	4UNTS215	100047
Colombia	USA (United States)	14 Oct 46	7UNTS97	100093
Philippines	USA (United States)	21 Mar 47	45UNTS47	100691
El Salvador	USA (United States)	19 Aug 47	51UNTS57	100752
Iran	USA (United States)	06 Oct 47	11UNTS303	100171
Brazil	USA (United States)	29 Jul 48	80UNTS111	101047
Argentina	USA (United States)	06 Oct 48	80UNTS91	101046
Haiti	USA (United States)	04 Jan 49	44UNTS69	100679
Colombia	USA (United States)	21 Feb 49	44UNTS83	100680
Colombia	USA (United States)	21 Feb 49	92UNTS227	101275

PARTY ONE	PARTY TWO	DATE	CITATION	NUMBER
Conditions for assistance missions (Cont.)				
Haiti	USA (United States)	14 Apr 49	80UNTS37	101043
Peru	USA (United States)	20 Jun 49	92UNTS249	101276
India	USA (United States)	04 Jul 49	200UNTS181	102702
Mexico	USA (United States)	05 Jul 49	68UNTS55	100884
Korea, South	USA (United States)	26 Jan 50	178UNTS97	102337
Honduras	USA (United States)	06 Mar 50	80UNTS71	101045
Honduras	USA (United States)	06 Mar 50	80UNTS51	101044
USA (United States)	Venezuela	23 Aug 50	92UNTS341	101279
Thailand	USA (United States)	17 Oct 50	79UNTS41	101030
Cuba	USA (United States)	22 Dec 50	122UNTS97	101640
Liberia	USA (United States)	11 Jan 51	122UNTS125	101642
Chile	USA (United States)	15 Feb 51	133UNTS95	101783
Chile	USA (United States)	15 Feb 51	133UNTS117	101784
USA (United States)	Venezuela	10 Aug 51	140UNTS345	101898
Cuba	USA (United States)	28 Aug 51	140UNTS239	101891
Cuba	USA (United States)	28 Aug 51	134UNTS225	101802
USA (United States)	Uruguay	04 Dec 51	152UNTS41	102010
Japan	USA (United States)	28 Feb 52	208UNTS255	102817
Nicaragua	USA (United States)	19 Nov 52	186UNTS3	102478
USA (United States)	Venezuela	16 Jan 53	199UNTS287	102690
El Salvador	USA (United States)	21 May 53	213UNTS15	102878
Luxembourg	USA (United States)	17 Aug 53	234UNTS219	103284
Nicaragua	USA (United States)	19 Nov 53	206UNTS117	102787
El Salvador	USA (United States)	23 Sep 54	237UNTS91	103338
Iraq	UK Great Britain	04 Apr 55	233UNTS118	103265
Cuba	USA (United States)	03 Aug 55	265UNTS41	103805
Honduras	USA (United States)	25 Apr 56	269UNTS25	103869
Bolivia	USA (United States)	30 Jun 56	271UNTS243	103919
Bolivia	USA (United States)	30 Jun 56	271UNTS269	103920
Peru	USA (United States)	06 Sep 56	277UNTS231	104009
Argentina	USA (United States)	03 Oct 56	279UNTS13	104032
Dominican Republic	USA (United States)	07 Dec 56	263UNTS193	103774
El Salvador	USA (United States)	21 Nov 57	303UNTS19	104369
Germany, West	USA (United States)	10 Dec 57	307UNTS59	104442
Haiti	USA (United States)	24 Dec 58	338UNTS265	104840
Argentina	USA (United States)	02 Aug 60	384UNTS105	105514
Netherlands	NATO (North Atlan)	25 May 64	544UNTS237	107920
Chile	USA (United States)	27 Oct 64	532UNTS347	107727
Jamaica	UK Great Britain	31 Mar 65	539UNTS59	107824
Saudi Arabia	USA (United States)	05 Jun 65	548UNTS285	107984
Guyana	UK Great Britain	26 May 66	595UNTS255	108621
UK Great Britain	Zambia	21 Feb 68	0UNTS0	109264
Cyprus	UK Great Britain	11 Mar 68	0UNTS0	109285
Third country military personnel				
Multilateral		27 Mar 41	67UNTS231	200222
Haiti	USA (United States)	23 May 41	117UNTS191	200370
Bolivia	USA (United States)	04 Sep 41	8UNTS345	200046
Peru	USA (United States)	11 Mar 42	117UNTS266	200375
Brazil	USA (United States)	07 May 42	6UNTS377	200040
Colombia	USA (United States)	29 May 42	8UNTS365	200047
Panama	USA (United States)	07 Jul 42	9UNTS289	200048
Bolivia	USA (United States)	11 Aug 42	9UNTS309	200049
Dominican Republic	USA (United States)	25 Jan 43	13UNTS399	200083
El Salvador	USA (United States)	21 May 43	9UNTS341	200051
Guatemala	USA (United States)	17 Jul 43	28UNTS431	200166
Ecuador	USA (United States)	13 Sep 43	29UNTS349	200171
Paraguay	USA (United States)	27 Oct 43	29UNTS391	200174
Iran	USA (United States)	27 Nov 43	31UNTS451	200176
USA (United States)	Venezuela	13 Jan 44	109UNTS171	200358
Ecuador	USA (United States)	29 Jun 44	80UNTS283	200250
Peru	USA (United States)	10 Jul 44	117UNTS291	200377
Brazil	USA (United States)	29 Sep 44	65UNTS271	200216
Guatemala	USA (United States)	21 Feb 45	121UNTS133	200396
Guatemala	USA (United States)	21 May 45	121UNTS185	200399

PARTY ONE	PARTY TWO	DATE	CITATION	NUMBER
Third country military personnel (Cont.)				
Chile	USA (United States)	24 May 45	121UNTS219	200401
Costa Rica	USA (United States)	10 Dec 45	3UNTS157	100029
Honduras	USA (United States)	28 Dec 45	3UNTS185	100031
USA (United States)	Venezuela	03 Jun 46	4UNTS215	100047
Peru	USA (United States)	07 Oct 46	7UNTS71	100092
Colombia	USA (United States)	14 Oct 46	7UNTS97	100093
El Salvador	USA (United States)	19 Aug 47	51UNTS57	100752
Iran	USA (United States)	06 Oct 47	11UNTS303	100171
Brazil	USA (United States)	29 Jul 48	80UNTS111	101047
Argentina	USA (United States)	06 Oct 48	80UNTS91	101046
Haiti	USA (United States)	04 Jan 49	44UNTS69	100679
Colombia	USA (United States)	21 Feb 49	44UNTS83	100680
Colombia	USA (United States)	21 Feb 49	92UNTS227	101275
Haiti	USA (United States)	14 Apr 49	80UNTS37	101043
Peru	USA (United States)	20 Jun 49	92UNTS249	101276
Mexico	USA (United States)	05 Jul 49	68UNTS55	100884
Korea, South	USA (United States)	26 Jan 50	178UNTS97	102337
Honduras	USA (United States)	06 Mar 50	80UNTS51	101044
Honduras	USA (United States)	06 Mar 50	80UNTS71	101045
USA (United States)	Venezuela	23 Aug 50	92UNTS341	101279
Cuba	USA (United States)	22 Dec 50	122UNTS97	101640
Liberia	USA (United States)	11 Jan 51	122UNTS125	101642
Chile	USA (United States)	15 Feb 51	133UNTS117	101784
Chile	USA (United States)	15 Feb 51	133UNTS95	101783
USA (United States)	Venezuela	10 Aug 51	140UNTS345	101898
Cuba	USA (United States)	28 Aug 51	140UNTS239	101891
Cuba	USA (United States)	28 Aug 51	134UNTS225	101802
USA (United States)	Uruguay	04 Dec 51	152UNTS41	102010
USA (United States)	Venezuela	16 Jan 53	199UNTS287	102690
El Salvador	USA (United States)	21 May 53	213UNTS15	102878
Nicaragua	USA (United States)	19 Nov 53	206UNTS117	102787
El Salvador	USA (United States)	23 Sep 54	237UNTS91	103338
Bolivia	USA (United States)	30 Jun 56	271UNTS243	103919
Argentina	USA (United States)	03 Oct 56	279UNTS13	104032
Dominican Republic	USA (United States)	07 Dec 56	263UNTS193	103774
El Salvador	USA (United States)	21 Nov 57	303UNTS19	104369
Nicaragua	USA (United States)	05 Sep 58	336UNTS33	104797
Haiti	USA (United States)	24 Dec 58	338UNTS265	104840
Argentina	USA (United States)	02 Aug 60	384UNTS105	105514
Status of military forces				
Canada	USA (United States)	29 May 40	119UNTS285	200385
Multilateral		29 Jan 42	93UNTS279	200271
Netherlands	USA (United States)	16 May 44	132UNTS355	200440
Multilateral		09 Jun 45	139UNTS381	200464
France	USA (United States)	28 May 46	84UNTS121	101123
Portugal	USA (United States)	30 May 46	174UNTS187	102285
Ecuador	USA (United States)	11 Jun 46	167UNTS135	102203
UK Great Britain	USA (United States)	23 Jan 47	15UNTS281	100244
Multilateral		10 Feb 47	49UNTS3	100747
Greece	UK Great Britain	05 Jun 47	9UNTS197	100133
Brazil	USA (United States)	02 Feb 48	67UNTS109	100870
Portugal	UK Great Britain	25 May 48	34UNTS311	100544
Greece	UK Great Britain	07 Sep 48	180UNTS144	102380
Cuba	USA (United States)	21 Feb 49	231UNTS108	103212
Greece	USA (United States)	21 Feb 49	88UNTS29	101182
India	USA (United States)	04 Jul 49	200UNTS181	102702
UK Great Britain	USA (United States)	06 Mar 51	97UNTS137	101347
Canada	USA (United States)	01 Aug 51	233UNTS109	103254
Nicaragua	USA (United States)	12 Dec 51	167UNTS151	102205
Costa Rica	USA (United States)	25 Feb 52	174UNTS233	102288
Canada	USA (United States)	30 Apr 52	235UNTS269	103308
Ethiopia	UK Great Britain	03 Jul 52	151UNTS207	101996
China People's Rep	USSR (Soviet Union)	15 Sep 52	226UNTS45	103106
Korea, South	USA (United States)	01 Oct 53	238UNTS199	103363

PARTY ONE	PARTY TWO	DATE	CITATION	NUMBER
Status of military forces (Cont.)				
Multilateral		26 Oct 53	207UNTS237	102809
Norway	USA (United States)	13 Apr 54	229UNTS223	103169
Turkey	USA (United States)	23 Jun 54	233UNTS189	103263
UK Great Britain	USA (United States)	21 Jul 54	222UNTS243	103031
Netherlands	USA (United States)	13 Aug 54	251UNTS91	103535
Multilateral		28 Sep 54	207UNTS293	102812
Multilateral		23 Oct 54	332UNTS387	104763
Canada	UK Great Britain	09 Jan 56	331UNTS192	104755
Canada	USA (United States)	26 Jan 56	241UNTS115	103428
Netherlands	UK Great Britain	11 Jun 56	306UNTS107	104436
Canada	Germany, West	10 Dec 56	392UNTS3	105633
Germany, West	UK Great Britain	11 Apr 57	331UNTS173	104753
Germany, West	Netherlands	10 Jul 57	339UNTS97	104848
Philippines	USA (United States)	01 Nov 57	307UNTS39	104440
Philippines	USA (United States)	20 Feb 58	303UNTS261	104385
Ghana	UK Great Britain	17 Apr 59	337UNTS353	104829
Germany, West	USA (United States)	03 Aug 59	490UNTS28	107153
USA (United States)	Yugoslavia	21 Apr 62	442UNTS123	106344
Germany, West	UK Great Britain	06 Jun 62	437UNTS39	106298
Germany, West	USA (United States)	14 Mar 63	474UNTS71	106872
Taiwan	USA (United States)	19 Dec 63	527UNTS69	107617
Canada	UK Great Britain	11 Sep 64	522UNTS99	107538
Taiwan	USA (United States)	19 Dec 64	532UNTS313	107725
China	USA (United States)	31 Aug 65	572UNTS3	108308
Germany, West	USA (United States)	18 Dec 65	579UNTS193	108407
Korea, South	USA (United States)	09 Feb 67	OUNTSO	109605
Kenya	UK Great Britain	14 Jul 67	643UNTS231	109195
Jurisdiction				
Netherlands	USA (United States)	17 Jan 33	474UNTS119	106877
Iceland	USA (United States)	01 Jul 41	12UNTS405	200071
UK Great Britain	USA (United States)	27 Jul 42	117UNTS311	200378
Norway	USA (United States)	28 Aug 42	139UNTS361	200461
Taiwan	USA (United States)	21 May 43	14UNTS353	200093
Canada	USA (United States)	23 Mar 44	125UNTS345	200432
UK Great Britain	USA (United States)	28 Mar 44	15UNTS413	200104
Norway	USA (United States)	16 May 44	67UNTS253	200223
Multilateral		09 Jun 45	139UNTS381	200464
Taiwan	UK Great Britain	07 Jul 45	14UNTS455	200100
United Arab Rep	USA (United States)	05 Jan 46	160UNTS27	102098
Poland	USA (United States)	29 Aug 46	160UNTS11	102097
UK Great Britain	USA (United States)	23 Jan 47	15UNTS281	100244
Philippines	USA (United States)	14 Mar 47	43UNTS271	100673
Denmark	UK Great Britain	22 Apr 47	8UNTS3	100110
Norway	UK Great Britain	05 Jun 47	54UNTS181	100803
Italy	USA (United States)	03 Sep 47	67UNTS15	100863
Ceylon (Sri Lanka)	UK Great Britain	11 Nov 47	86UNTS19	101148
Korea, South	USA (United States)	24 Aug 48	79UNTS57	101031
Multilateral		20 Jun 49	128UNTS141	101718
Multilateral		12 Aug 49	75UNTS135	100972
Belgium	UK Great Britain	23 Dec 49	99UNTS61	101371
Korea, South	USA (United States)	12 Jul 50	222UNTS229	103029
UK Great Britain	USA (United States)	21 Jul 50	97UNTS193	101351
Denmark	USA (United States)	27 Apr 51	94UNTS35	101305
Saudi Arabia	USA (United States)	18 Jun 51	102UNTS73	101412
Multilateral		19 Jun 51	199UNTS67	102678
Portugal	USA (United States)	06 Sep 51	237UNTS217	103348
UK Great Britain	USA (United States)	15 Jan 52	127UNTS3	101697
Japan	USA (United States)	28 Feb 52	208UNTS255	102817
Canada	USA (United States)	19 Mar 52	174UNTS267	102291
Nicaragua	USA (United States)	19 Nov 52	186UNTS3	102478
Canada	USA (United States)	05 Dec 52	206UNTS11	102783
Ethiopia	USA (United States)	22 May 53	191UNTS59	102577
Libya	UK Great Britain	29 Jul 53	186UNTS201	102492
Multilateral		26 Oct 53	207UNTS237	102809

PARTY ONE	PARTY TWO	DATE	CITATION	NUMBER
Jurisdiction (Cont.)				
Multilateral		19 Feb 54	214UNTS51	102899
Norway	USA (United States)	13 Apr 54	229UNTS223	103169
Turkey	USA (United States)	23 Jun 54	233UNTS189	103263
Libya	USA (United States)	09 Sep 54	224UNTS217	103078
Multilateral		23 Oct 54	332UNTS3	104760
Multilateral		23 Oct 54	334UNTS3	104765
Hungary	USSR (Soviet Union)	27 May 55	407UNTS156	105864
UK Great Britain	USA (United States)	15 Nov 55	231UNTS185	103219
UK Great Britain	USA (United States)	25 Jun 56	249UNTS59	103501
UK Great Britain	USA (United States)	25 Jun 56	249UNTS91	103502
Greece	USA (United States)	07 Sep 56	278UNTS141	104030
UK Great Britain	USA (United States)	01 Nov 56	264UNTS3	103785
UK Great Britain	USA (United States)	27 Nov 56	282UNTS43	104092
Poland	USSR (Soviet Union)	17 Dec 56	266UNTS179	103830
Germany, West	Netherlands	29 Jan 57	314UNTS173	104548
United Nations	United Arab Rep	08 Feb 57	260UNTS61	103704
Dominican Republic	USA (United States)	09 Mar 57	279UNTS249	104044
Germany, East	USSR (Soviet Union)	12 Mar 57	285UNTS105	104150
Romania	USSR (Soviet Union)	15 Apr 57	274UNTS143	103964
Finland	United Nations	27 Jun 57	271UNTS135	103913
United Nations	Sweden	01 Jul 57	271UNTS187	103914
Norway	United Nations	09 Jul 57	271UNTS223	103917
Denmark	United Nations	16 Jul 57	274UNTS81	103959
Canada	United Nations	29 Jul 57	274UNTS47	103957
Brazil	United Nations	13 Aug 57	274UNTS199	103966
India	United Nations	14 Aug 57	274UNTS233	103968
United Nations	Yugoslavia	01 Oct 57	277UNTS191	104006
Poland	USSR (Soviet Union)	26 Oct 57	432UNTS221	106223
UK Great Britain	USA (United States)	01 Nov 57	299UNTS167	104312
Hungary	USSR (Soviet Union)	24 Apr 58	408UNTS118	105868
Argentina	USA (United States)	28 Apr 58	315UNTS211	104570
Lebanon	USA (United States)	06 Aug 58	366UNTS361	105223
Nicaragua	USA (United States)	05 Sep 58	336UNTS33	104797
Haiti	USA (United States)	27 Oct 58	336UNTS235	104807
Ghana	UK Great Britain	17 Apr 59	337UNTS353	104829
Japan	USA (United States)	19 Jan 60	373UNTS207	105321
UK Great Britain	USA (United States)	24 Jun 60	377UNTS63	105396
UK Great Britain	USA (United States)	10 Feb 61	409UNTS68	105879
Congo (Zaire)	United Nations	27 Nov 61	414UNTS229	105975
Canada	Ghana	08 Jan 62	528UNTS221	107645
USA (United States)	Yugoslavia	21 Apr 62	442UNTS123	106344
Algeria	France	03 Jul 62	507UNTS25	107395
Pakistan	United Nations	18 Apr 63	503UNTS25	107339
Australia	USA (United States)	09 May 63	469UNTS55	106784
UK Great Britain	USA (United States)	11 Oct 63	483UNTS3	107005
Cyprus	United Nations	31 Mar 64	492UNTS57	107187
Philippines	USA (United States)	16 Mar 65	542UNTS199	107890
Guatemala	USA (United States)	04 May 65	545UNTS163	107932
Saudi Arabia	USA (United States)	05 Jun 65	548UNTS285	107984
Canada	Jamaica	16 Jul 65	548UNTS265	107982
China	USA (United States)	31 Aug 65	572UNTS3	108308
United Nations	Sweden	21 Feb 66	555UNTS169	108111
Denmark	United Nations	21 Feb 66	555UNTS151	108108
Canada	United Nations	21 Feb 66	555UNTS119	108107
Finland	United Nations	21 Feb 66	555UNTS157	108109
New Zealand	United Nations	21 Feb 66	555UNTS163	108110
Austria	United Nations	24 Feb 66	557UNTS129	108131
Australia	United Nations	25 Feb 66	557UNTS85	108129
Guyana	UK Great Britain	26 May 66	595UNTS255	108621
Botswana	UK Great Britain	30 Sep 66	597UNTS211	108646
Korea, South	USA (United States)	09 Feb 67	OUNTSO	109605
Procurement and logistics				
Liberia	USA (United States)	31 Mar 42	23UNTS302	200137
Netherlands	USA (United States)	16 May 44	132UNTS355	200440

PARTY ONE	PARTY TWO	DATE	CITATION	NUMBER
Procurement and logistics (Cont.)				
Multilateral		28 Oct 44	123UNTS223	200414
Multilateral		20 Jan 45	140UNTS397	200471
Netherlands	UK Great Britain	20 Dec 45	4UNTS303	100053
Belgium	UK Great Britain	11 Mar 46	26UNTS167	100387
France	USA (United States)	28 May 46	84UNTS121	101123
Multilateral		10 Feb 47	48UNTS203	100746
Denmark	UK Great Britain	22 Apr 47	8UNTS3	100110
Norway	UK Great Britain	05 Jun 47	54UNTS181	100803
France	UK Great Britain	19 Apr 48	83UNTS201	101109
Guatemala	USA (United States)	20 Dec 49	70UNTS71	100897
Australia	Philippines	14 Apr 50	127UNTS281	101709
Dominican Republic	USA (United States)	11 Aug 50	92UNTS329	101278
Denmark	USA (United States)	27 Apr 51	94UNTS35	101305
Nicaragua	USA (United States)	12 Dec 51	167UNTS151	102205
UK Great Britain	USA (United States)	15 Jan 52	127UNTS3	101697
Costa Rica	USA (United States)	25 Feb 52	174UNTS233	102288
Japan	USA (United States)	28 Feb 52	208UNTS255	102817
Honduras	USA (United States)	23 Apr 52	198UNTS251	102669
Belgium	UK Great Britain	12 Nov 52	180UNTS15	102372
Canada	USA (United States)	05 Dec 52	206UNTS11	102783
Belgium	Canada	30 Mar 53	181UNTS95	102401
Ethiopia	USA (United States)	22 May 53	191UNTS59	102577
Libya	UK Great Britain	29 Jul 53	186UNTS201	102492
Belgium	USA (United States)	02 Sep 53	200UNTS127	102700
Greece	USA (United States)	12 Oct 53	191UNTS319	102589
Libya	USA (United States)	09 Sep 54	224UNTS217	103078
Multilateral		23 Oct 54	332UNTS157	104761
Multilateral		23 Oct 54	334UNTS3	104765
Multilateral		23 Oct 54	332UNTS3	104760
Hungary	USSR (Soviet Union)	27 May 55	407UNTS156	105864
South Africa	UK Great Britain	30 Jun 55	248UNTS191	103495
UK Great Britain	USA (United States)	25 Jun 56	249UNTS91	103502
UK Great Britain	USA (United States)	25 Jun 56	249UNTS59	103501
Taiwan	USA (United States)	21 Nov 56	265UNTS241	103816
Poland	USSR (Soviet Union)	17 Dec 56	266UNTS179	103830
Greece	USA (United States)	19 Jan 57	280UNTS45	104049
United Nations	United Arab Rep	08 Feb 57	260UNTS61	103704
Germany, East	USSR (Soviet Union)	12 Mar 57	285UNTS105	104150
Romania	USSR (Soviet Union)	15 Apr 57	274UNTS143	103964
Poland	USSR (Soviet Union)	26 Oct 57	432UNTS221	106223
Lebanon	USA (United States)	06 Aug 58	366UNTS361	105223
Taiwan	USA (United States)	06 Aug 58	462UNTS3	106666
France	USA (United States)	08 Dec 58	0UNTS0	109602
Germany, West	USA (United States)	03 Aug 59	490UNTS28	107153
Germany, West	USA (Uni‘ed States)	27 May 60	377UNTS45	105395
UK Great Britain	USA (United States)	10 Feb 61	409UNTS68	105879
Congo (Zaire)	United Nations	27 Nov 61	414UNTS229	105975
Canada	Ghana	08 Jan 62	528UNTS221	107645
Australia	USA (United States)	09 May 63	475UNTS331	106897
Cyprus	United Nations	31 Mar 64	492UNTS57	107187
Netherlands	NATO (North Atlan)	25 May 64	544UNTS237	107920
Saudi Arabia	USA (United States)	05 Jun 65	548UNTS285	107984
Israel	USA (United States)	26 Jul 65	549UNTS49	107988
China	USA (United States)	31 Aug 65	572UNTS3	108308
Malta	USA (United States)	03 Aug 66	601UNTS125	108691
Korea, South	USA (United States)	09 Feb 67	0UNTS0	109605
Withdrawal of forces				
Multilateral		29 Jan 42	93UNTS279	200271
Norway	USA (United States)	28 Aug 42	139UNTS361	200461
Netherlands	USA (United States)	16 May 44	132UNTS355	200440
Multilateral		28 Oct 44	123UNTS223	200414
Ethiopia	UK Great Britain	19 Dec 44	93UNTS303	200272
France	UK Great Britain	31 Aug 45	98UNTS249	200275
Multilateral		01 Jan 46	99UNTS131	101375

PARTY ONE	PARTY TWO	DATE	CITATION	NUMBER
Withdrawal of forces (Cont.)				
Mongolia	USSR (Soviet Union)	27 Feb 46	48UNTS177	100744
Belgium	UK Great Britain	11 Mar 46	26UNTS167	100387
Thailand	USA (United States)	08 May 47	42UNTS241	100653
Czechoslovakia	USA (United States)	25 Jul 47	90UNTS19	101223
Taiwan	USA (United States)	03 Sep 47	9UNTS91	100126
Israel	United Arab Rep	24 Feb 49	42UNTS251	100654
Israel	Lebanon	23 Mar 49	42UNTS287	100655
Israel	Jordan	03 Apr 49	42UNTS303	100656
Israel	Syria	20 Jul 49	42UNTS327	100657
United Arab Rep	UK Great Britain	12 Feb 53	161UNTS157	102127
China People's Rep	USSR (Soviet Union)	12 Oct 54	226UNTS51	103107
United Arab Rep	UK Great Britain	19 Oct 54	210UNTS3	102833
Ethiopia	UK Great Britain	29 Nov 54	207UNTS283	102811
Multilateral		15 May 55	217UNTS223	102949
Finland	USSR (Soviet Union)	19 Sep 55	226UNTS187	103113
Ceylon (Sri Lanka)	UK Great Britain	07 Jun 57	280UNTS107	104055
Denmark	United Nations	16 Jul 57	274UNTS81	103959
Canada	United Nations	29 Jul 57	274UNTS47	103957
Brazil	United Nations	13 Aug 57	274UNTS199	103966
India	United Nations	14 Aug 57	274UNTS233	103968
United Nations	Yugoslavia	01 Oct 57	277UNTS191	104006
Algeria	France	03 Jul 62	507UNTS25	107395
Multilateral		23 Jul 62	456UNTS302	106564
China	USA (United States)	31 Aug 65	572UNTS3	108308
India	Pakistan	10 Jan 66	560UNTS39	108166
Korea, South	USA (United States)	09 Feb 67	0UNTS0	109605
Status of forces				
Netherlands	USA (United States)	17 Jan 33	474UNTS119	106877
Multilateral		27 Mar 41	67UNTS231	200222
Haiti	USA (United States)	23 May 41	117UNTS191	200370
Bolivia	USA (United States)	04 Sep 41	8UNTS345	200046
Multilateral		29 Jan 42	93UNTS279	200271
Peru	USA (United States)	11 Mar 42	117UNTS266	200375
Liberia	USA (United States)	31 Mar 42	23UNTS302	200137
Brazil	USA (United States)	07 May 42	6UNTS377	200040
Colombia	USA (United States)	29 May 42	8UNTS365	200047
Panama	USA (United States)	07 Jul 42	9UNTS289	200048
Bolivia	USA (United States)	11 Aug 42	9UNTS309	200049
Norway	USA (United States)	28 Aug 42	139UNTS361	200461
India	USA (United States)	16 Oct 42	109UNTS111	200353
Dominican Republic	USA (United States)	25 Jan 43	13UNTS399	200083
Taiwan	USA (United States)	21 May 43	14UNTS353	200093
Guatemala	USA (United States)	17 Jul 43	28UNTS431	200166
Belgium	USA (United States)	04 Aug 43	109UNTS149	200356
Ecuador	USA (United States)	13 Sep 43	29UNTS349	200171
Paraguay	USA (United States)	27 Oct 43	29UNTS391	200174
Iran	USA (United States)	27 Nov 43	31UNTS451	200176
Paraguay	USA (United States)	10 Dec 43	21UNTS305	200131
USA (United States)	Venezuela	13 Jan 44	109UNTS171	200358
Canada	USA (United States)	23 Mar 44	125UNTS345	200432
Netherlands	USA (United States)	16 May 44	132UNTS355	200440
Ecuador	USA (United States)	29 Jun 44	80UNTS283	200250
Peru	USA (United States)	10 Jul 44	117UNTS291	200377
Brazil	USA (United States)	29 Sep 44	65UNTS271	200216
Guatemala	USA (United States)	21 Feb 45	121UNTS133	200396
Guatemala	USA (United States)	21 May 45	121UNTS185	200399
Chile	USA (United States)	24 May 45	121UNTS219	200401
Taiwan	UK Great Britain	07 Jul 45	14UNTS455	200100
United Arab Rep	USA (United States)	05 Jan 46	160UNTS27	102098
Belgium	UK Great Britain	11 Mar 46	26UNTS167	100387
Multilateral		31 Mar 46	17UNTS159	100274
USA (United States)	Venezuela	03 Jun 46	4UNTS215	100047
Poland	USA (United States)	29 Aug 46	160UNTS11	102097
Peru	USA (United States)	07 Oct 46	7UNTS71	100092

Status of forces (Cont.)

PARTY ONE	PARTY TWO	DATE	CITATION	NUMBER
Colombia	USA (United States)	14 Oct 46	7UNTS97	100093
Philippines	USA (United States)	14 Mar 47	43UNTS271	100673
El Salvador	USA (United States)	19 Aug 47	51UNTS57	100752
Guatemala	USA (United States)	29 Aug 47	27UNTS11	100393
Italy	USA (United States)	03 Sep 47	67UNTS15	100863
Iran	USA (United States)	06 Oct 47	11UNTS303	100171
Brazil	USA (United States)	29 Jul 48	80UNTS111	101047
Korea, South	USA (United States)	24 Aug 48	79UNTS57	101031
Argentina	USA (United States)	06 Oct 48	80UNTS91	101046
Haiti	USA (United States)	04 Jan 49	44UNTS69	100679
Colombia	USA (United States)	21 Feb 49	44UNTS83	100680
Colombia	USA (United States)	21 Feb 49	92UNTS227	101275
Haiti	USA (United States)	14 Apr 49	80UNTS37	101043
Peru	USA (United States)	20 Jun 49	92UNTS249	101276
Mexico	USA (United States)	05 Jul 49	68UNTS55	100884
Multilateral		12 Aug 49	75UNTS287	100973
Belgium	UK Great Britain	23 Dec 49	99UNTS61	101371
Honduras	USA (United States)	06 Mar 50	80UNTS71	101045
Honduras	USA (United States)	06 Mar 50	80UNTS51	101044
Korea, South	USA (United States)	12 Jul 50	222UNTS229	103029
UK Great Britain	USA (United States)	21 Jul 50	97UNTS193	101351
USA (United States)	Venezuela	23 Aug 50	92UNTS341	101279
Cuba	USA (United States)	22 Dec 50	122UNTS97	101640
Liberia	USA (United States)	11 Jan 51	122UNTS125	101642
Chile	USA (United States)	15 Feb 51	133UNTS117	101784
Chile	USA (United States)	15 Feb 51	133UNTS95	101783
Saudi Arabia	USA (United States)	18 Jun 51	102UNTS73	101412
Multilateral		19 Jun 51	199UNTS67	102678
USA (United States)	Venezuela	10 Aug 51	140UNTS345	101898
Cuba	USA (United States)	28 Aug 51	134UNTS225	101802
Cuba	USA (United States)	28 Aug 51	140UNTS239	101891
USA (United States)	Uruguay	04 Dec 51	152UNTS41	102010
UK Great Britain	USA (United States)	15 Jan 52	127UNTS3	101697
Japan	USA (United States)	28 Feb 52	208UNTS255	102817
Canada	USA (United States)	19 Mar 52	174UNTS267	102291
France	USA (United States)	04 Oct 52	0UNTS0	109599
Belgium	UK Great Britain	12 Nov 52	180UNTS15	102372
USA (United States)	Venezuela	16 Jan 53	199UNTS287	102690
El Salvador	USA (United States)	21 May 53	213UNTS15	102878
Ethiopia	USA (United States)	22 May 53	191UNTS59	102577
France	USA (United States)	17 Jun 53	0UNTS0	109600
Libya	UK Great Britain	29 Jul 53	186UNTS201	102492
Multilateral		26 Oct 53	207UNTS237	102809
Nicaragua	USA (United States)	19 Nov 53	206UNTS117	102787
Multilateral		19 Feb 54	214UNTS51	102899
Turkey	USA (United States)	23 Jun 54	233UNTS189	103263
Netherlands	USA (United States)	13 Aug 54	251UNTS91	103535
Libya	USA (United States)	09 Sep 54	224UNTS217	103078
El Salvador	USA (United States)	23 Sep 54	237UNTS91	103338
Multilateral		23 Oct 54	334UNTS3	104765
Multilateral		23 Oct 54	332UNTS157	104761
Multilateral		23 Oct 54	332UNTS3	104760
Hungary	USSR (Soviet Union)	27 May 55	407UNTS156	105864
Germany, East	USSR (Soviet Union)	20 Sep 55	226UNTS201	103114
Belgium	UK Great Britain	10 Nov 55	331UNTS209	104756
Canada	USA (United States)	26 Jan 56	241UNTS115	103428
UK Great Britain	USA (United States)	25 Jun 56	249UNTS91	103502
UK Great Britain	USA (United States)	25 Jun 56	249UNTS59	103501
Bolivia	USA (United States)	30 Jun 56	271UNTS243	103919
Greece	USA (United States)	07 Sep 56	278UNTS141	104030
Argentina	USA (United States)	03 Oct 56	279UNTS13	104032
Iceland	USA (United States)	06 Dec 56	265UNTS261	103818
Dominican Republic	USA (United States)	07 Dec 56	263UNTS193	103774
Poland	USSR (Soviet Union)	17 Dec 56	266UNTS179	103830
United Nations	United Arab Rep	08 Feb 57	260UNTS61	103704

PARTY ONE	PARTY TWO	DATE	CITATION	NUMBER
Germany, East	USSR (Soviet Union)	12 Mar 57	285UNTS105	104150
Romania	USSR (Soviet Union)	15 Apr 57	274UNTS143	103964
Finland	United Nations	27 Jun 57	271UNTS135	103913
United Nations	Sweden	01 Jul 57	271UNTS187	103914
Norway	United Nations	09 Jul 57	271UNTS223	103917
Poland	USSR (Soviet Union)	26 Oct 57	432UNTS221	106223
El Salvador	USA (United States)	21 Nov 57	303UNTS19	104369
Australia	USA (United States)	25 Feb 58	317UNTS153	104601
Argentina	USA (United States)	28 Apr 58	315UNTS211	104570
Canada	USA (United States)	12 May 58	316UNTS151	104582
Lebanon	USA (United States)	06 Aug 58	366UNTS361	105223
Nicaragua	USA (United States)	05 Sep 58	336UNTS33	104797
France	USA (United States)	08 Dec 58	0UNTS0	109602
Haiti	USA (United States)	24 Dec 58	338UNTS265	104840
Germany, West	USA (United States)	03 Aug 59	490UNTS28	107153
Japan	USA (United States)	19 Jan 60	373UNTS207	105321
UK Great Britain	USA (United States)	24 Jun 60	377UNTS63	105396
Argentina	USA (United States)	02 Aug 60	384UNTS105	105514
Multilateral		16 Aug 60	382UNTS8	105476
UK Great Britain	USA (United States)	10 Feb 61	409UNTS68	105879
Germany, West	UK Great Britain	12 Jul 61	424UNTS211	106109
Congo (Zaire)	United Nations	27 Nov 61	414UNTS229	105975
Canada	Ghana	08 Jan 62	528UNTS221	107645
Belgium	USA (United States)	19 Apr 63	476UNTS29	106900
Australia	USA (United States)	09 May 63	469UNTS55	106784
UK Great Britain	USA (United States)	11 Oct 63	483UNTS3	107005
Cyprus	United Nations	31 Mar 64	492UNTS57	107187
Chile	USA (United States)	27 Oct 64	532UNTS347	107727
Guatemala	USA (United States)	04 May 65	545UNTS163	107932
Saudi Arabia	USA (United States)	05 Jun 65	548UNTS285	107984
China	USA (United States)	31 Aug 65	572UNTS3	108308
United Nations	UK Great Britain	21 Feb 66	555UNTS177	108112
Guyana	UK Great Britain	26 May 66	595UNTS255	108621
Botswana	UK Great Britain	30 Sep 66	597UNTS211	108646
Korea, South	USA (United States)	09 Feb 67	0UNTS0	109605

Military installations and equipment

PARTY ONE	PARTY TWO	DATE	CITATION	NUMBER
Panama	USA (United States)	23 Mar 40	124UNTS195	200420
Panama	USA (United States)	06 Sep 40	124UNTS209	200421
Canada	USA (United States)	18 Mar 42	101UNTS205	200294
Canada	USA (United States)	07 Dec 42	101UNTS227	200297
Canada	USA (United States)	27 Jun 44	101UNTS273	200301
France	UK Great Britain	04 Dec 45	9UNTS121	100129
Multilateral		31 Mar 46	17UNTS159	100274
Multilateral		02 Oct 47	193UNTS188	102616
Italy	UK Great Britain	21 Jan 48	77UNTS23	100989
UK Great Britain	USA (United States)	01 Aug 50	88UNTS273	101199
Iceland	USA (United States)	05 May 51	205UNTS173	102776
Dominican Republic	UK Great Britain	26 Nov 51	133UNTS205	101791
Italy	USA (United States)	05 Mar 52	179UNTS3	102351
Netherlands	USA (United States)	07 Mar 52	135UNTS199	101821
Luxembourg	USA (United States)	13 Mar 52	168UNTS57	102212
Belgium	USA (United States)	07 Apr 52	205UNTS3	102765
United Arab Rep	USA (United States)	29 Apr 52	241UNTS3	103418
France	USA (United States)	13 Jun 52	181UNTS3	102393
Greece	USA (United States)	25 Jun 52	181UNTS53	102398
Norway	USA (United States)	27 Jun 52	184UNTS271	102452
Portugal	USA (United States)	01 Apr 53	205UNTS41	102769
France	USA (United States)	30 Jun 53	0UNTS0	109601
Denmark	USA (United States)	08 Jun 54	307UNTS133	104448
Spain	USA (United States)	30 Jul 54	235UNTS45	103295
UK Great Britain	USA (United States)	24 Sep 54	300UNTS3	104326
Canada	USA (United States)	05 May 55	241UNTS179	103433
Canada	USA (United States)	13 Jun 55	268UNTS87	103851
Canada	USA (United States)	15 Jun 55	268UNTS101	103852

PARTY ONE	PARTY TWO	DATE	CITATION	NUMBER
Military installations and equipment (Cont.)				
Philippines	USA (United States)	18 Jun 57	289UNTS289	104225
Greece	Italy	02 Aug 57	533UNTS217	107744
Fed of Malaya	UK Great Britain	12 Oct 57	285UNTS59	104149
Norway	USSR (Soviet Union)	18 Dec 57	312UNTS257	104522
Philippines	USA (United States)	17 Jul 58	335UNTS199	104787
France	USA (United States)	08 Dec 58	0UNTS0	109602
Turkey	USA (United States)	30 Nov 59	361UNTS107	105174
Taiwan	USA (United States)	15 Apr 60	462UNTS19	106667
Canada	Norway	25 Apr 60	470UNTS109	106801
Canada	Norway	24 May 60	470UNTS125	106803
Canada	UK Great Britain	05 Aug 60	470UNTS133	106804
Denmark	USA (United States)	02 Dec 60	402UNTS245	105789
UK Great Britain	USA (United States)	10 Feb 61	409UNTS129	105880
Taiwan	USA (United States)	28 Feb 62	462UNTS25	106668
Philippines	USA (United States)	11 Jan 63	473UNTS43	106853
Japan	USA (United States)	26 Apr 63	477UNTS37	106914
Philippines	USA (United States)	16 Oct 67	632UNTS113	109013
Philippines	USA (United States)	28 Dec 68	0UNTS0	109436
Exchange of defense information				
Canada	USA (United States)	10 Jun 39	149UNTS332	200476
USA (United States)	USSR (Soviet Union)	18 Apr 42	105UNTS285	200339
Belgium	USA (United States)	16 Jun 42	105UNTS159	200329
Poland	USA (United States)	01 Jul 42	103UNTS267	200317
Netherlands	USA (United States)	08 Jul 42	103UNTS277	200318
Greece	USA (United States)	10 Jul 42	103UNTS289	200319
Czechoslovakia	USA (United States)	11 Jul 42	90UNTS257	200263
Liberia	USA (United States)	08 Jun 43	117UNTS242	200373
France	USA (United States)	20 Feb 45	76UNTS193	200246
Turkey	USA (United States)	23 Feb 45	121UNTS165	200398
France	USA (United States)	28 Feb 45	76UNTS213	200247
Belgium	USA (United States)	19 Apr 45	139UNTS179	200455
Iraq	USA (United States)	31 Jul 45	121UNTS239	200402
UK Great Britain	USA (United States)	27 Mar 46	4UNTS101	100040
Canada	USA (United States)	06 Dec 46	149UNTS3	101945
Philippines	USA (United States)	21 Mar 47	45UNTS47	100691
Greece	USA (United States)	03 Dec 47	89UNTS119	101213
Korea, South	USA (United States)	26 Jan 50	80UNTS205	101053
Korea, South	USA (United States)	26 Jan 50	178UNTS97	102337
UK Great Britain	USA (United States)	27 Jan 50	80UNTS261	101056
Norway	USA (United States)	27 Jan 50	80UNTS241	101055
France	USA (United States)	27 Jan 50	80UNTS171	101051
Italy	USA (United States)	27 Jan 50	80UNTS145	101050
Belgium	USA (United States)	27 Jan 50	51UNTS213	100767
Netherlands	USA (United States)	27 Jan 50	80UNTS219	101054
Luxembourg	USA (United States)	27 Jan 50	80UNTS187	101052
Denmark	USA (United States)	27 Jan 50	48UNTS115	100740
Iran	USA (United States)	23 May 50	81UNTS3	101057
Thailand	USA (United States)	17 Oct 50	79UNTS41	101030
Pakistan	USA (United States)	15 Dec 50	122UNTS89	101639
Chile	USA (United States)	04 Jan 51	165UNTS105	102172
Brazil	USA (United States)	04 Jan 51	165UNTS97	102171
Portugal	USA (United States)	05 Jan 51	133UNTS75	101782
Argentina	USA (United States)	08 Jan 51	165UNTS89	102170
Taiwan	USA (United States)	09 Feb 51	132UNTS273	101767
Australia	USA (United States)	20 Feb 51	132UNTS297	101769
Denmark	USA (United States)	27 Apr 51	94UNTS35	101305
South Africa	USA (United States)	09 Nov 51	160UNTS41	102100
USA (United States)	Yugoslavia	14 Nov 51	174UNTS201	102286
Ecuador	USA (United States)	20 Feb 52	177UNTS43	102308
Peru	USA (United States)	22 Feb 52	165UNTS31	102166
Cuba	USA (United States)	07 Mar 52	165UNTS11	102165
Brazil	USA (United States)	15 Mar 52	199UNTS221	102687
Colombia	USA (United States)	17 Apr 52	174UNTS215	102287
Ethiopia	USA (United States)	13 Jun 52	205UNTS17	102766

PARTY ONE	PARTY TWO	DATE	CITATION	NUMBER
Exchange of defense information (Cont.)				
USA (United States)	Uruguay	30 Jun 52	207UNTS139	102804
Sweden	USA (United States)	01 Jul 52	187UNTS3	102497
Israel	USA (United States)	23 Jul 52	179UNTS139	102363
UK Great Britain	USA (United States)	19 Jan 53	161UNTS3	102117
Dominican Republic	USA (United States)	06 Mar 53	199UNTS267	102689
Lebanon	USA (United States)	23 Mar 53	239UNTS45	103370
Philippines	USA (United States)	26 Jun 53	213UNTS77	102881
Belgium	USA (United States)	02 Sep 53	200UNTS127	102700
Spain	USA (United States)	26 Sep 53	207UNTS61	102800
Spain	USA (United States)	26 Sep 53	207UNTS83	102801
Pakistan	Turkey	04 Feb 54	211UNTS263	102858
Japan	USA (United States)	08 Mar 54	232UNTS169	103236
Italy	USA (United States)	31 Mar 54	235UNTS293	103311
Luxembourg	USA (United States)	17 Apr 54	257UNTS255	103661
Iraq	USA (United States)	21 Apr 54	222UNTS251	103032
Netherlands	USA (United States)	07 May 54	213UNTS325	102895
Japan	USA (United States)	14 May 54	247UNTS273	103476
Pakistan	USA (United States)	19 May 54	202UNTS301	102736
Honduras	USA (United States)	20 May 54	222UNTS87	103025
Greece	USA (United States)	30 Jul 54	234UNTS43	103272
Belgium	USA (United States)	12 Oct 54	202UNTS289	102735
USA (United States)	Yugoslavia	18 Oct 54	273UNTS163	103951
Netherlands	USA (United States)	14 Dec 54	262UNTS35	103737
Haiti	USA (United States)	28 Jan 55	270UNTS83	103894
Korea, South	USA (United States)	29 Jan 55	239UNTS53	103371
Germany, West	USA (United States)	04 Apr 55	279UNTS73	104034
Norway	USA (United States)	06 Apr 55	269UNTS65	103874
Netherlands	USA (United States)	29 Apr 55	219UNTS105	102969
Cambodia	USA (United States)	16 May 55	263UNTS273	103777
Japan	USA (United States)	03 Jun 55	270UNTS51	103891
Guatemala	USA (United States)	18 Jun 55	262UNTS105	103740
Turkey	USA (United States)	29 Jun 55	269UNTS97	103878
Germany, West	USA (United States)	30 Jun 55	240UNTS47	103393
South Africa	UK Great Britain	30 Jun 55	248UNTS191	103495
USA (United States)	Yugoslavia	30 Sep 55	269UNTS89	103877
Syria	United Arab Rep	20 Oct 55	247UNTS117	103461
Canada	Norway	20 Dec 55	305UNTS17	104408
Germany, West	USA (United States)	04 Jan 56	268UNTS143	103856
Turkey	USA (United States)	18 May 56	283UNTS167	104115
France	USA (United States)	06 Sep 56	335UNTS173	104784
Ceylon (Sri Lanka)	USA (United States)	02 Nov 56	282UNTS93	104094
France	USA (United States)	12 Mar 57	279UNTS275	104045
Libya	USA (United States)	30 Jun 57	284UNTS177	104136
Australia	USA (United States)	12 Jul 57	290UNTS139	104233
Austria	USA (United States)	09 Aug 57	288UNTS299	104211
Australia	USA (United States)	24 Jan 58	307UNTS105	104446
Canada	USA (United States)	12 May 58	316UNTS151	104582
Fed of Malaya	USA (United States)	09 Jul 58	336UNTS79	104799
India	USA (United States)	17 Dec 58	358UNTS77	105125
Netherlands	USA (United States)	06 May 59	355UNTS327	105084
Greece	USA (United States)	06 May 59	357UNTS163	105115
Panama	USA (United States)	20 May 59	346UNTS235	104983
Canada	USA (United States)	22 May 59	354UNTS63	105054
Norway	USA (United States)	13 Feb 60	388UNTS255	105583
Denmark	USA (United States)	19 Feb 60	354UNTS151	105061
Turkey	USA (United States)	02 Mar 60	372UNTS37	105286
Netherlands	USA (United States)	24 Mar 60	406UNTS165	105847
Denmark	USA (United States)	12 Apr 60	373UNTS9	105311
Canada	Norway	24 May 60	470UNTS125	106803
Italy	USA (United States)	07 Jul 60	380UNTS143	105455
Spain	USA (United States)	21 Jul 60	393UNTS289	105663
Australia	USA (United States)	23 Aug 60	388UNTS237	105581
France	USA (United States)	19 Sep 60	400UNTS21	105745
Portugal	USA (United States)	26 Sep 60	393UNTS257	105660
Portugal	USA (United States)	31 Oct 60	394UNTS127	105673

PARTY ONE	PARTY TWO	DATE	CITATION	NUMBER
Exchange of defense information (Cont.)				
Liberia	USA (United States)	17 Jun 61	410UNTS233	105907
France	USA (United States)	27 Jul 61	433UNTS29	106229
Canada	USA (United States)	27 Sep 61	421UNTS85	106054
Dominican Republic	USA (United States)	08 Mar 62	527UNTS29	107615
El Salvador	USA (United States)	13 Apr 62	451UNTS307	106500
Bolivia	USA (United States)	26 Apr 62	461UNTS105	106654
Belgium	USA (United States)	17 May 62	461UNTS3	106647
Panama	USA (United States)	23 May 62	458UNTS225	106604
Canada	France	25 May 62	470UNTS163	106808
Dahomey	USA (United States)	13 Jun 62	458UNTS219	106603
Niger	USA (United States)	14 Jun 62	458UNTS233	106605
Costa Rica	USA (United States)	18 Jun 62	461UNTS155	106659
Canada	Greece	18 Jul 62	528UNTS265	107647
Sweden	USA (United States)	04 Oct 62	462UNTS31	106669
UK Great Britain	USA (United States)	06 Apr 63	474UNTS49	106871
Denmark	Netherlands	06 Jun 63	484UNTS137	107021
Jamaica	USA (United States)	06 Jun 63	477UNTS29	106913
Netherlands	UK Great Britain	30 Oct 63	490UNTS11	107151
Canada	USA (United States)	15 Nov 63	493UNTS67	107207
Italy	Netherlands	29 May 64	541UNTS147	107867
Italy	USA (United States)	04 Aug 64	529UNTS205	107662
Sweden	UK Great Britain	26 Oct 67	632UNTS277	109029
Testing ranges and sites				
UK Great Britain	USA (United States)	21 Jul 50	97UNTS193	101351
Japan	USA (United States)	28 Feb 52	208UNTS255	102817
Haiti	USA (United States)	29 Aug 52	186UNTS35	102480
Germany, West	UK Great Britain	09 Sep 52	151UNTS215	101997
UK Great Britain	USA (United States)	02 Mar 53	172UNTS257	102249
UK Great Britain	USA (United States)	25 Jun 56	249UNTS91	103502
UK Great Britain	USA (United States)	25 Jun 56	249UNTS59	103501
Brazil	USA (United States)	21 Jan 57	278UNTS97	104025
UK Great Britain	USA (United States)	22 Feb 58	307UNTS207	104451
Spain	USA (United States)	29 Jan 64	511UNTS61	107427
Canada	USA (United States)	12 May 65	545UNTS169	107933
Bases and facilities				
Netherlands	USA (United States)	17 Jan 33	474UNTS119	106877
Liberia	USA (United States)	31 Mar 42	23UNTS302	200137
Nicaragua	USA (United States)	08 Apr 42	132UNTS343	200439
Canada	USA (United States)	27 Jan 43	101UNTS257	200300
Colombia	USA (United States)	29 Mar 43	124UNTS139	200416
Canada	USA (United States)	09 Aug 43	29UNTS295	200168
Liberia	USA (United States)	31 Dec 43	106UNTS199	200341
Canada	USA (United States)	27 Jun 44	101UNTS273	200301
Portugal	USA (United States)	28 Nov 44	183UNTS311	200508
Belgium	UK Great Britain	11 Mar 46	26UNTS167	100387
UK Great Britain	USA (United States)	27 Mar 46	4UNTS2	100039
Multilateral		31 Mar 46	17UNTS159	100274
United Nations	Switzerland	01 Jul 46	1UNTS153	200007
Philippines	USA (United States)	04 Jul 46	7UNTS3	100088
UK Great Britain	USA (United States)	31 Jul 46	42UNTS199	100648
Denmark	USA (United States)	01 Oct 46	42UNTS219	100650
Philippines	USA (United States)	14 Mar 47	43UNTS271	100673
Thailand	USA (United States)	08 May 47	42UNTS241	100653
Italy	USA (United States)	09 Jun 47	104UNTS157	101437
Ceylon (Sri Lanka)	UK Great Britain	11 Nov 47	86UNTS19	101148
UK Great Britain	USA (United States)	24 Feb 48	73UNTS143	100951
UK Great Britain	Uruguay	12 Jul 48	71UNTS199	100919
Korea, South	USA (United States)	24 Aug 48	79UNTS57	101031
Philippines	USA (United States)	16 May 49	67UNTS199	100878
Canada	USA (United States)	04 Jun 49	200UNTS201	102704
Philippines	USA (United States)	08 Aug 49	163UNTS103	102144
UK Great Britain	USA (United States)	19 Sep 49	68UNTS31	100882
China People's Rep	USSR (Soviet Union)	14 Feb 50	226UNTS31	103105
France	USA (United States)	27 Feb 51	0UNTS0	109598

PARTY ONE	PARTY TWO	DATE	CITATION	NUMBER
Bases and facilities (Cont.)				
Denmark	USA (United States)	27 Apr 51	94UNTS35	101305
Multilateral		19 Jun 51	199UNTS67	102678
Canada	USA (United States)	01 Aug 51	233UNTS109	103254
Portugal	USA (United States)	06 Sep 51	237UNTS217	103348
Dominican Republic	USA (United States)	26 Nov 51	150UNTS227	101976
UK Great Britain	USA (United States)	15 Jan 52	127UNTS3	101697
Japan	USA (United States)	28 Feb 52	208UNTS255	102817
Canada	USA (United States)	19 Mar 52	174UNTS267	102291
UK Great Britain	USA (United States)	29 Jul 52	179UNTS129	102362
France	USA (United States)	04 Oct 52	0UNTS0	109599
Canada	USA (United States)	05 Dec 52	206UNTS11	102783
Ethiopia	USA (United States)	22 May 53	191UNTS59	102577
France	USA (United States)	17 Jun 53	0UNTS0	109600
France	USA (United States)	30 Jun 53	0UNTS0	109601
Libya	UK Great Britain	29 Jul 53	186UNTS201	102492
Spain	USA (United States)	26 Sep 53	207UNTS83	102801
Greece	USA (United States)	12 Oct 53	191UNTS319	102589
Canada	USA (United States)	03 May 54	221UNTS339	103015
Libya	USA (United States)	09 Sep 54	224UNTS217	103078
United Arab Rep	UK Great Britain	19 Oct 54	221UNTS227	103008
United Arab Rep	UK Great Britain	19 Oct 54	210UNTS3	102833
Multilateral		23 Oct 54	332UNTS3	104760
Germany, West	USA (United States)	18 Feb 55	247UNTS257	103474
Philippines	USA (United States)	27 Apr 55	261UNTS351	103733
Canada	USA (United States)	05 May 55	241UNTS179	103433
Hungary	USSR (Soviet Union)	27 May 55	407UNTS156	105864
Korea, South	USA (United States)	29 May 55	256UNTS263	103636
UK Great Britain	USA (United States)	07 Jun 55	265UNTS27	103804
Italy	USA (United States)	08 Jul 55	270UNTS29	103889
Finland	USSR (Soviet Union)	19 Sep 55	226UNTS187	103113
Philippines	USA (United States)	28 Oct 55	239UNTS165	103376
Canada	USA (United States)	19 Apr 56	274UNTS3	103955
Pakistan	USA (United States)	28 May 56	269UNTS15	103868
UK Great Britain	USA (United States)	05 Jun 56	247UNTS205	103470
UK Great Britain	USA (United States)	25 Jun 56	249UNTS59	103501
France	USA (United States)	06 Sep 56	335UNTS173	104784
Taiwan	USA (United States)	21 Nov 56	265UNTS241	103816
Poland	USSR (Soviet Union)	17 Dec 56	266UNTS179	103830
Brazil	USA (United States)	21 Jan 57	278UNTS97	104025
Germany, East	USSR (Soviet Union)	12 Mar 57	285UNTS105	104150
Saudi Arabia	USA (United States)	02 Apr 57	283UNTS97	104109
Romania	USSR (Soviet Union)	15 Apr 57	274UNTS143	103964
Ceylon (Sri Lanka)	UK Great Britain	07 Jun 57	280UNTS107	104055
New Zealand	UK Great Britain	04 Jul 57	402UNTS109	105780
Fed of Malaya	UK Great Britain	12 Oct 57	285UNTS59	104149
Poland	USSR (Soviet Union)	26 Oct 57	432UNTS221	106223
Germany, West	USA (United States)	10 Dec 57	307UNTS59	104442
Muscat and Oman	UK Great Britain	25 Jul 58	312UNTS347	104524
Taiwan	USA (United States)	06 Aug 58	462UNTS3	106666
Nicaragua	USA (United States)	05 Sep 58	336UNTS33	104797
France	USA (United States)	08 Dec 58	0UNTS0	109602
Canada	USA (United States)	01 May 59	343UNTS27	104919
Philippines	USA (United States)	07 Dec 59	359UNTS227	105144
Japan	USA (United States)	19 Jan 60	373UNTS207	105321
Spain	USA (United States)	13 Feb 60	371UNTS185	105279
UK Great Britain	USA (United States)	15 Feb 60	371UNTS45	105269
Taiwan	USA (United States)	15 Apr 60	462UNTS19	106667
Belgium	USA (United States)	22 Apr 60	372UNTS277	105304
UK Great Britain	USA (United States)	18 Jul 61	404UNTS227	105813
Canada	USA (United States)	23 Sep 61	421UNTS79	106053
Germany, West	UK Great Britain	26 Sep 61	424UNTS201	106108
Canada	USA (United States)	27 Sep 61	421UNTS85	106054
Taiwan	USA (United States)	28 Feb 62	462UNTS25	106668
Algeria	France	03 Jul 62	507UNTS25	107395
UK Great Britain	USA (United States)	29 Aug 62	449UNTS177	106459

PARTY ONE	PARTY TWO	DATE	CITATION	NUMBER
Bases and facilities (Cont.)				
Australia	USA (United States)	09 May 63	475UNTS331	106897
Multilateral		15 Feb 64	533UNTS98	107736
Congo (Zaire)	United Nations	02 Mar 64	533UNTS93	107735
Belgium	United Nations	20 Mar 64	533UNTS83	107734
Chad	France	19 May 64	0UNTS0	109443
Netherlands	NATO (North Atlan)	25 May 64	544UNTS237	107920
Canada	USA (United States)	25 May 64	526UNTS251	107609
Malta	UK Great Britain	21 Sep 64	588UNTS55	108518
Japan	USA (United States)	04 Dec 64	532UNTS249	107721
Trinidad/Tobago	USA (United States)	05 Dec 64	535UNTS331	107788
Philippines	USA (United States)	16 Mar 65	542UNTS199	107890
Canada	USA (United States)	12 May 65	545UNTS169	107933
Saudi Arabia	USA (United States)	05 Jun 65	548UNTS285	107984
Guinea	USA (United States)	29 Jun 65	549UNTS139	107997
Philippines	USA (United States)	12 Aug 65	579UNTS47	108397
China	USA (United States)	31 Aug 65	572UNTS3	108308
Philippines	USA (United States)	15 Nov 65	574UNTS205	108350
Canada	USA (United States)	01 Dec 65	574UNTS37	108340
Ethiopia	USA (United States)	30 Dec 65	574UNTS129	108345
Guyana	UK Great Britain	26 May 66	595UNTS255	108621
Canada	USA (United States)	15 Jun 66	594UNTS83	108595
Philippines	USA (United States)	16 Oct 67	632UNTS113	109013
New Zealand	UK Great Britain	02 Apr 68	0UNTS0	109206
Equipment and supplies				
Canada	USA (United States)	27 Jun 41	103UNTS205	200315
Netherlands	USA (United States)	30 Apr 45	139UNTS319	200459
Multilateral		10 Feb 47	42UNTS3	100645
Multilateral		20 Jun 49	128UNTS141	101718
France	USA (United States)	27 Feb 51	0UNTS0	109598
Luxembourg	USA (United States)	17 Aug 53	234UNTS219	103284
Norway	USA (United States)	07 May 54	231UNTS157	103215
Spain	USA (United States)	19 May 54	235UNTS87	103296
France	USA (United States)	31 May 54	236UNTS141	103321
UK Great Britain	USA (United States)	15 Jun 54	236UNTS133	103320
Italy	USA (United States)	24 Jun 54	235UNTS3	103290
Belgium	USA (United States)	12 Oct 54	202UNTS289	102735
Belgium	USA (United States)	23 Nov 54	235UNTS19	103292
Turkey	USA (United States)	25 Apr 55	263UNTS299	103779
Netherlands	USA (United States)	29 Apr 55	219UNTS105	102969
Greece	USA (United States)	27 May 55	251UNTS349	103552
Korea, South	USA (United States)	29 May 55	256UNTS263	103636
Japan	USA (United States)	03 Jun 55	270UNTS51	103891
Italy	USA (United States)	08 Jul 55	270UNTS29	103889
USA (United States)	Yugoslavia	30 Sep 55	269UNTS89	103877
Japan	USA (United States)	13 Apr 56	273UNTS223	103953
Pakistan	USA (United States)	28 May 56	269UNTS15	103868
Dominican Republic	USA (United States)	09 Mar 57	279UNTS249	104044
Iraq	USA (United States)	16 Jun 57	284UNTS39	104127
France	USA (United States)	23 Sep 57	293UNTS297	104297
Ethiopia	USA (United States)	26 Dec 57	307UNTS71	104443
UK Great Britain	USA (United States)	03 Jul 58	326UNTS3	104707
Denmark	USA (United States)	08 May 59	344UNTS185	104949
Norway	USA (United States)	13 Feb 60	388UNTS255	105583
Greece	USA (United States)	15 Feb 60	377UNTS95	105397
Turkey	USA (United States)	02 Mar 60	372UNTS37	105286
Netherlands	USA (United States)	24 Mar 60	406UNTS165	105847
Denmark	USA (United States)	12 Apr 60	373UNTS9	105311
Japan	USA (United States)	15 Apr 60	372UNTS267	105303
Italy	USA (United States)	07 Jul 60	380UNTS143	105455
France	USA (United States)	19 Sep 60	400UNTS21	105745
Portugal	USA (United States)	26 Sep 60	393UNTS257	105660
Norway	USA (United States)	29 Nov 60	404UNTS251	105815

PARTY ONE	PARTY TWO	DATE	CITATION	NUMBER
Restrictions on transfer				
Iceland	USA (United States)	21 Nov 41	124UNTS179	200418
USA (United States)	USSR (Soviet Union)	18 Apr 42	105UNTS285	200339
Taiwan	USA (United States)	02 Jun 42	14UNTS343	200092
Belgium	USA (United States)	16 Jun 42	105UNTS159	200329
Poland	USA (United States)	01 Jul 42	103UNTS267	200317
Netherlands	USA (United States)	08 Jul 42	103UNTS277	200318
Greece	USA (United States)	10 Jul 42	103UNTS289	200319
Czechoslovakia	USA (United States)	11 Jul 42	90UNTS257	200263
Liberia	USA (United States)	08 Jun 43	117UNTS242	200373
Ethiopia	USA (United States)	09 Aug 43	29UNTS303	200169
Canada	Taiwan	22 Mar 44	14UNTS397	200096
France	USA (United States)	20 Feb 45	76UNTS193	200246
Iraq	USA (United States)	31 Jul 45	121UNTS239	200402
Turkey	USA (United States)	07 May 46	6UNTS293	100083
India	USA (United States)	16 May 46	4UNTS183	100045
France	USA (United States)	28 May 46	84UNTS79	101120
France	USA (United States)	28 May 46	84UNTS59	101119
Australia	USA (United States)	07 Jun 46	4UNTS237	100048
Brazil	USA (United States)	28 Jun 46	6UNTS327	100085
New Zealand	USA (United States)	10 Jul 46	6UNTS341	100087
Philippines	USA (United States)	11 Sep 46	43UNTS231	100670
Norway	UK Great Britain	27 Sep 46	6UNTS259	100079
Netherlands	UK Great Britain	04 Dec 46	12UNTS241	100187
Belgium	UK Great Britain	16 Jan 47	54UNTS97	100797
Multilateral		10 Feb 47	42UNTS3	100645
Philippines	USA (United States)	21 Mar 47	45UNTS47	100691
South Africa	USA (United States)	21 Mar 47	16UNTS47	100248
Italy	USA (United States)	14 Aug 47	36UNTS53	100566
Greece	USA (United States)	03 Dec 47	89UNTS119	101213
Taiwan	USA (United States)	08 Dec 47	70UNTS3	100895
Norway	USA (United States)	24 Feb 48	34UNTS155	100535
Denmark	UK Great Britain	04 Mar 48	77UNTS57	100992
Korea, South	USA (United States)	11 Sep 48	89UNTS155	101216
Czechoslovakia	USA (United States)	16 Sep 48	90UNTS35	101224
Ethiopia	USA (United States)	20 May 49	89UNTS99	101211
Korea, South	USA (United States)	26 Jan 50	80UNTS205	101053
UK Great Britain	USA (United States)	27 Jan 50	80UNTS261	101056
Italy	USA (United States)	27 Jan 50	80UNTS145	101050
Luxembourg	USA (United States)	27 Jan 50	80UNTS187	101052
France	USA (United States)	27 Jan 50	80UNTS171	101051
Norway	USA (United States)	27 Jan 50	80UNTS241	101055
Belgium	USA (United States)	27 Jan 50	51UNTS213	100767
Netherlands	USA (United States)	27 Jan 50	80UNTS219	101054
Denmark	USA (United States)	27 Jan 50	48UNTS115	100740
Iran	USA (United States)	23 May 50	81UNTS3	101057
Thailand	USA (United States)	17 Oct 50	79UNTS41	101030
Burma	USA (United States)	06 Nov 50	122UNTS81	101638
USA (United States)	Yugoslavia	21 Nov 50	93UNTS45	101286
Pakistan	USA (United States)	15 Dec 50	122UNTS89	101639
Chile	USA (United States)	04 Jan 51	165UNTS105	102172
Brazil	USA (United States)	04 Jan 51	165UNTS97	102171
Portugal	USA (United States)	05 Jan 51	133UNTS75	101782
Argentina	USA (United States)	08 Jan 51	165UNTS89	102170
Taiwan	USA (United States)	09 Feb 51	132UNTS273	101767
Australia	USA (United States)	20 Feb 51	132UNTS297	101769
India	USA (United States)	16 Mar 51	141UNTS47	101904
USA (United States)	Yugoslavia	17 Apr 51	162UNTS173	102134
Denmark	USA (United States)	27 Apr 51	94UNTS35	101305
Saudi Arabia	USA (United States)	18 Jun 51	141UNTS67	101906
South Africa	USA (United States)	09 Nov 51	160UNTS41	102100
USA (United States)	Yugoslavia	14 Nov 51	174UNTS201	102286
Ecuador	USA (United States)	20 Feb 52	177UNTS43	102308
Peru	USA (United States)	22 Feb 52	165UNTS31	102166
Cuba	USA (United States)	07 Mar 52	165UNTS11	102165

Restrictions on transfer (Cont.)

PARTY ONE	PARTY TWO	DATE	CITATION	NUMBER
Brazil	USA (United States)	15 Mar 52	199UNTS221	102687
Chile	USA (United States)	09 Apr 52	186UNTS53	102482
Colombia	USA (United States)	17 Apr 52	174UNTS215	102287
Ethiopia	USA (United States)	13 Jun 52	205UNTS17	102766
USA (United States)	Uruguay	30 Jun 52	207UNTS139	102804
Sweden	USA (United States)	01 Jul 52	187UNTS3	102497
Israel	USA (United States)	23 Jul 52	179UNTS139	102363
Japan	USA (United States)	12 Nov 52	184UNTS111	102443
UK Great Britain	USA (United States)	19 Jan 53	161UNTS3	102117
Dominican Republic	USA (United States)	06 Mar 53	199UNTS267	102689
Lebanon	USA (United States)	23 Mar 53	239UNTS45	103370
Ethiopia	USA (United States)	22 May 53	191UNTS59	102577
Philippines	USA (United States)	26 Jun 53	213UNTS77	102881
Germany, West	USA (United States)	20 Aug 53	224UNTS49	103069
France	USA (United States)	02 Sep 53	224UNTS153	103075
Spain	USA (United States)	26 Sep 53	207UNTS61	102800
Germany, West	USA (United States)	23 Nov 53	224UNTS107	103071
Belgium	Taiwan	13 Jan 54	223UNTS111	103059
Japan	USA (United States)	08 Mar 54	232UNTS169	103236
Iraq	USA (United States)	21 Apr 54	222UNTS251	103032
Italy	USA (United States)	27 Apr 54	234UNTS103	103275
Netherlands	USA (United States)	07 May 54	213UNTS325	102895
Taiwan	USA (United States)	14 May 54	231UNTS165	103216
Japan	USA (United States)	14 May 54	247UNTS273	103476
Pakistan	USA (United States)	19 May 54	202UNTS301	102736
Honduras	USA (United States)	20 May 54	222UNTS87	103025
Turkey	USA (United States)	01 Jul 54	234UNTS147	103280
Greece	USA (United States)	30 Jul 54	234UNTS43	103272
Guatemala	USA (United States)	30 Jul 54	234UNTS235	103286
Iceland	USA (United States)	10 Dec 54	237UNTS191	103345
Haiti	USA (United States)	28 Jan 55	270UNTS83	103894
Korea, South	USA (United States)	29 Jan 55	239UNTS53	103371
Cambodia	USA (United States)	16 May 55	263UNTS273	103777
UK Great Britain	USA (United States)	07 Jun 55	265UNTS27	103804
Guatemala	USA (United States)	18 Jun 55	262UNTS105	103740
Germany, West	USA (United States)	30 Jun 55	240UNTS47	103393
Italy	USA (United States)	08 Jul 55	270UNTS29	103889
UK Great Britain	USA (United States)	05 Jun 56	247UNTS205	103470
Iraq	USA (United States)	16 Jun 57	284UNTS39	104127
Australia	USA (United States)	12 Jul 57	290UNTS139	104233
Greece	USA (United States)	05 Aug 57	290UNTS167	104235
Austria	USA (United States)	09 Aug 57	288UNTS299	104211
France	USA (United States)	23 Sep 57	293UNTS297	104297
Ethiopia	USA (United States)	26 Dec 57	307UNTS71	104443
Lebanon	UK Great Britain	19 May 58	327UNTS43	104716
Burma	USA (United States)	24 Jun 58	335UNTS193	104786
Fed of Malaya	USA (United States)	09 Jul 58	336UNTS79	104799
Indonesia	USA (United States)	13 Aug 58	335UNTS187	104785
Turkey	USA (United States)	14 Oct 58	336UNTS145	104803
Taiwan	USA (United States)	07 Feb 59	341UNTS225	104885
Netherlands	USA (United States)	06 May 59	355UNTS327	105084
France	USA (United States)	07 May 59	354UNTS83	105055
Thailand	USA (United States)	19 May 59	346UNTS271	104986
Panama	USA (United States)	20 May 59	346UNTS235	104983
Canada	USA (United States)	22 May 59	354UNTS63	105054
Spain	USA (United States)	23 Jun 59	354UNTS11	105049
Iraq	USA (United States)	07 Jul 59	357UNTS153	105114
Italy	USA (United States)	18 Aug 59	361UNTS11	105169
USA (United States)	Yugoslavia	25 Aug 59	357UNTS77	105106
USA (United States)	Yugoslavia	25 Aug 59	357UNTS87	105107
Brazil	USA (United States)	19 Oct 59	372UNTS131	105293
Norway	USA (United States)	13 Feb 60	388UNTS255	105583
Netherlands	USA (United States)	24 Mar 60	406UNTS165	105847
Argentina	USA (United States)	01 Apr 60	371UNTS245	105281
Colombia	USA (United States)	07 Apr 60	372UNTS27	105285

Restrictions on transfer (Cont.)

PARTY ONE	PARTY TWO	DATE	CITATION	NUMBER
Haiti	USA (United States)	08 Jul 60	380UNTS135	105454
Australia	USA (United States)	23 Aug 60	388UNTS237	105581
Haiti	USA (United States)	01 Sep 60	388UNTS249	105582
France	USA (United States)	19 Sep 60	400UNTS21	105745
Portugal	USA (United States)	26 Sep 60	393UNTS257	105660
Mali	USA (United States)	20 May 61	413UNTS205	105954
Liberia	USA (United States)	17 Jun 61	410UNTS233	105907
France	USA (United States)	27 Jul 61	433UNTS29	106229
Dominican Republic	USA (United States)	08 Mar 62	527UNTS29	107615
El Salvador	USA (United States)	13 Apr 62	451UNTS307	106500
Bolivia	USA (United States)	26 Apr 62	461UNTS105	106654
Belgium	USA (United States)	17 May 62	461UNTS3	106647
Panama	USA (United States)	23 May 62	458UNTS225	106604
Canada	France	25 May 62	470UNTS163	106808
Dahomey	USA (United States)	13 Jun 62	458UNTS219	106603
Niger	USA (United States)	14 Jun 62	458UNTS233	106605
Costa Rica	USA (United States)	18 Jun 62	461UNTS155	106659
Canada	Greece	18 Jul 62	528UNTS265	107647
Senegal	USA (United States)	20 Jul 62	458UNTS137	106596
Paraguay	USA (United States)	25 Aug 62	461UNTS207	106665
India	UK Great Britain	27 Nov 62	466UNTS189	106744
Pakistan	USA (United States)	16 Jan 63	471UNTS133	106828
UK Great Britain	USA (United States)	06 Apr 63	474UNTS49	106871
Jamaica	USA (United States)	06 Jun 63	477UNTS29	106913
Congo (Zaire)	USA (United States)	19 Jul 63	511UNTS47	107425
Australia	India	03 Dec 63	486UNTS279	107082
Paraguay	USA (United States)	10 Feb 64	511UNTS53	107426
Italy	Netherlands	29 May 64	541UNTS147	107867
Italy	USA (United States)	04 Aug 64	529UNTS205	107662
Guinea	USA (United States)	29 Jun 65	549UNTS139	107997
Philippines	USA (United States)	12 Aug 65	579UNTS47	108397
Paraguay	USA (United States)	11 Apr 66	578UNTS99	108389
UK Great Britain	USA (United States)	27 Oct 66	597UNTS265	108650

Military service and citizenship

PARTY ONE	PARTY TWO	DATE	CITATION	NUMBER
Greece	Iran	09 Jan 31	166UNTS331	200497
USA (United States)	Yugoslavia	30 Mar 42	13UNTS199	200079
India	USA (United States)	30 Sep 42	13UNTS185	200078
Brazil	UK Great Britain	27 May 44	2UNTS235	200016
India	Iran	15 Dec 54	327UNTS245	104724
Italy	Netherlands	24 Jan 61	450UNTS207	106468
Argentina	UK Great Britain	12 Sep 63	601UNTS213	108698

Dual nationality

PARTY ONE	PARTY TWO	DATE	CITATION	NUMBER
Canada	USA (United States)	20 Mar 42	105UNTS169	200330
Canada	USA (United States)	08 Apr 42	105UNTS179	200331
France	USA (United States)	25 Feb 48	67UNTS33	100864
Denmark	France	22 Jun 49	48UNTS3	100737
Belgium	France	29 Aug 49	93UNTS87	101293
France	UK Great Britain	21 Dec 49	264UNTS37	103786
Chile	Denmark	22 Oct 53	348UNTS261	105004
France	Italy	28 Dec 53	267UNTS89	103836
Belgium	Netherlands	09 Jun 54	216UNTS121	102936
Denmark	Italy	15 Jul 54	250UNTS43	103516
Chile	UK Great Britain	31 Jul 54	618UNTS353	108934
Multilateral		03 Mar 56	243UNTS169	103452
Chile	Italy	04 Jun 56	362UNTS309	105195
Argentina	Sweden	16 Jan 59	427UNTS327	106163
France	Israel	30 Jun 59	448UNTS107	106428
Italy	Netherlands	24 Jan 61	450UNTS207	106468
Argentina	Denmark	28 Nov 62	455UNTS429	106554
Multilateral		06 May 63	634UNTS221	109065
Argentina	Finland	08 May 63	482UNTS309	107000
Denmark	France	06 Jun 63	600UNTS213	108682

PARTY ONE	PARTY TWO	DATE	CITATION	NUMBER
Certificates of service				
Canada	USA (United States)	20 Mar 42	105UNTS169	200330
Canada	USA (United States)	08 Apr 42	105UNTS179	200331
Chile	UK Great Britain	27 Oct 47	82UNTS209	101094
France	USA (United States)	25 Feb 48	67UNTS33	100864
Denmark	France	22 Jun 49	48UNTS3	100737
Belgium	France	29 Aug 49	93UNTS87	101293
France	UK Great Britain	21 Dec 49	264UNTS37	103786
Chile	Denmark	22 Oct 53	348UNTS261	105004
France	Italy	28 Dec 53	267UNTS89	103836
Belgium	Netherlands	09 Jun 54	216UNTS121	102936
Denmark	Italy	15 Jul 54	250UNTS43	103516
Chile	UK Great Britain	31 Jul 54	618UNTS353	108934
Denmark	UK Great Britain	20 Jan 55	210UNTS303	102842
Brazil	UK Great Britain	05 Apr 55	403UNTS139	105793
Multilateral		03 Mar 56	243UNTS169	103452
Chile	Italy	04 Jun 56	362UNTS309	105195
Argentina	Sweden	16 Jan 59	427UNTS327	106163
France	Israel	30 Jun 59	448UNTS107	106428
Argentina	Denmark	28 Nov 62	455UNTS429	106554
Argentina	Finland	08 May 63	482UNTS309	107000
Argentina	UK Great Britain	12 Sep 63	601UNTS213	108698
Cyprus	United Nations	31 Mar 64	492UNTS57	107187
Foreign nationals				
Greece	Iran	09 Jan 31	166UNTS331	200497
Canada	France	12 May 33	253UNTS285	200545
Canada	USA (United States)	20 Mar 42	105UNTS169	200330
USA (United States)	Yugoslavia	30 Mar 42	13UNTS199	200079
Canada	USA (United States)	08 Apr 42	105UNTS179	200331
Mexico	USA (United States)	12 Aug 42	125UNTS301	200431
New Zealand	USA (United States)	30 Sep 42	13UNTS139	200075
Netherlands	USA (United States)	30 Sep 42	13UNTS151	200076
UK Great Britain	USA (United States)	30 Sep 42	13UNTS169	200077
Australia	USA (United States)	30 Sep 42	13UNTS125	200074
India	USA (United States)	30 Sep 42	13UNTS185	200078
Belgium	USA (United States)	16 Oct 42	13UNTS211	200080
South Africa	USA (United States)	31 Oct 42	105UNTS269	200338
Norway	USA (United States)	16 Jan 43	13UNTS335	200082
Mexico	USA (United States)	22 Jan 43	105UNTS259	200337
Cuba	USA (United States)	01 Feb 43	13UNTS379	200085
Poland	USA (United States)	25 Feb 43	13UNTS395	200086
Greece	USA (United States)	16 Mar 43	105UNTS227	200335
Mexico	USA (United States)	26 Apr 43	21UNTS245	200127
Mexico	USA (United States)	29 Apr 43	105UNTS119	200327
Brazil	USA (United States)	24 May 43	28UNTS385	200162
El Salvador	USA (United States)	31 May 43	105UNTS205	200333
Czechoslovakia	USA (United States)	21 Oct 43	29UNTS369	200172
Colombia	USA (United States)	12 Feb 44	109UNTS287	200365
Brazil	UK Great Britain	27 May 44	2UNTS235	200016
Taiwan	USA (United States)	13 Jun 44	107UNTS43	200350
Belgium	USSR (Soviet Union)	13 Mar 45	19UNTS235	200117
Ecuador	USA (United States)	05 Apr 45	121UNTS265	200404
USA (United States)	Venezuela	11 May 45	121UNTS273	200405
Chile	USA (United States)	11 Jun 45	121UNTS291	200407
Peru	USA (United States)	12 Jun 45	121UNTS283	200406
Poland	Yugoslavia	02 Jan 46	115UNTS21	101556
Multilateral		10 Feb 47	42UNTS3	100645
Philippines	USA (United States)	14 Mar 47	45UNTS23	100690
Chile	UK Great Britain	27 Oct 47	82UNTS209	101094
Costa Rica	USA (United States)	12 Jan 48	70UNTS27	100896
Philippines	Spain	20 May 48	70UNTS143	100903
Multilateral		12 Aug 49	75UNTS85	100971
Belgium	France	29 Aug 49	93UNTS87	101293
Mexico	USA (United States)	11 Aug 51	162UNTS103	102133

PARTY ONE	PARTY TWO	DATE	CITATION	NUMBER
Foreign nationals (Cont.)				
France	Italy	23 Aug 51	291UNTS143	104249
Finland	Norway	22 Sep 53	183UNTS245	102433
France	Sweden	16 Feb 54	228UNTS137	103147
Belgium	Netherlands	09 Jun 54	216UNTS121	102936
France	Norway	06 Dec 54	202UNTS313	102737
Denmark	UK Great Britain	20 Jan 55	210UNTS303	102842
Multilateral		15 May 55	217UNTS223	102949
Multilateral		03 Mar 56	243UNTS169	103452
Japan	Norway	28 Feb 57	280UNTS87	104054
Japan	Yugoslavia	28 Feb 59	341UNTS179	104883
Japan	Pakistan	18 Dec 60	423UNTS197	106093
Italy	Netherlands	24 Jan 61	450UNTS207	106468
Japan	UK Great Britain	14 Nov 62	478UNTS29	106934
Denmark	France	06 Jun 63	600UNTS213	108682
Argentina	Belgium	11 Jun 63	635UNTS135	109077
Argentina	UK Great Britain	12 Sep 63	601UNTS213	108698
Austria	United Nations	24 Feb 66	557UNTS129	108131
Australia	United Nations	25 Feb 66	557UNTS85	108129
Service in foreign army				
Canada	USA (United States)	20 Mar 42	105UNTS169	200330
USA (United States)	Yugoslavia	30 Mar 42	13UNTS199	200079
Canada	USA (United States)	08 Apr 42	105UNTS179	200331
Netherlands	USA (United States)	30 Sep 42	13UNTS151	200076
Australia	USA (United States)	30 Sep 42	13UNTS125	200074
India	USA (United States)	30 Sep 42	13UNTS185	200078
UK Great Britain	USA (United States)	30 Sep 42	13UNTS169	200077
New Zealand	USA (United States)	30 Sep 42	13UNTS139	200075
Belgium	USA (United States)	16 Oct 42	13UNTS211	200080
South Africa	USA (United States)	31 Oct 42	105UNTS269	200338
Norway	USA (United States)	16 Jan 43	13UNTS335	200082
Mexico	USA (United States)	22 Jan 43	105UNTS259	200337
Cuba	USA (United States)	01 Feb 43	13UNTS379	200085
Poland	USA (United States)	25 Feb 43	13UNTS395	200086
Greece	USA (United States)	16 Mar 43	105UNTS227	200335
Brazil	USA (United States)	24 May 43	28UNTS385	200162
El Salvador	USA (United States)	31 May 43	105UNTS205	200333
Czechoslovakia	USA (United States)	21 Oct 43	29UNTS369	200172
Colombia	USA (United States)	12 Feb 44	109UNTS287	200365
Norway	USA (United States)	16 May 44	67UNTS253	200223
Brazil	UK Great Britain	27 May 44	2UNTS235	200016
Taiwan	USA (United States)	13 Jun 44	107UNTS43	200350
Ecuador	USA (United States)	05 Apr 45	121UNTS265	200404
USA (United States)	Venezuela	11 May 45	121UNTS273	200405
Chile	USA (United States)	11 Jun 45	121UNTS291	200407
Peru	USA (United States)	12 Jun 45	121UNTS283	200406
France	Poland	11 Feb 47	12UNTS287	100189
Philippines	USA (United States)	14 Mar 47	43UNTS271	100673
Chile	UK Great Britain	27 Oct 47	82UNTS209	101094
Denmark	France	22 Jun 49	48UNTS3	100737
Belgium	France	29 Aug 49	93UNTS87	101293
France	UK Great Britain	21 Dec 49	264UNTS37	103786
Ireland	USA (United States)	21 Jan 50	206UNTS269	102792
Philippines	USA (United States)	09 Mar 53	227UNTS101	103134
Chile	Denmark	22 Oct 53	348UNTS261	105004
France	Italy	28 Dec 53	267UNTS89	103836
Denmark	Italy	15 Jul 54	250UNTS43	103516
Chile	UK Great Britain	31 Jul 54	618UNTS353	108934
Denmark	UK Great Britain	20 Jan 55	210UNTS303	102842
Brazil	UK Great Britain	05 Apr 55	403UNTS139	105793
Multilateral		03 Mar 56	243UNTS169	103452
Chile	Italy	04 Jun 56	362UNTS309	105195
Argentina	Sweden	16 Jan 59	427UNTS327	106163
France	Israel	30 Jun 59	448UNTS107	106428
Italy	Netherlands	24 Jan 61	450UNTS207	106468

PARTY ONE	PARTY TWO	DATE	CITATION	NUMBER
Service in foreign army (Cont.)				
Indonesia	Japan	01 Jul 61	517UNTS107	107484
Argentina	Denmark	28 Nov 62	455UNTS429	106554
Argentina	Finland	08 May 63	482UNTS309	107000
Denmark	France	06 Jun 63	600UNTS213	108682
Peace and disarmament				
Multilateral		04 Feb 52	124UNTS3	101662
Japan	Pakistan	24 Apr 53	221UNTS325	103013
Reconversion to normalcy				
Canada	USA (United States)	30 Nov 42	119UNTS305	200387
South Africa	USA (United States)	17 Apr 45	90UNTS275	200265
Canada	USA (United States)	15 May 45	125UNTS353	200433
Netherlands	Thailand	30 Jan 47	247UNTS353	103480
Multilateral		10 Feb 47	42UNTS3	100645
Multilateral		10 Feb 47	49UNTS3	100747
Thailand	UK Great Britain	08 May 47	100UNTS47	101386
France	Norway	15 Jul 47	15UNTS5	100226
Italy	USA (United States)	03 Sep 47	67UNTS15	100863
France	USA (United States)	25 Oct 47	89UNTS111	101212
Multilateral		08 Apr 49	140UNTS196	101889
Multilateral		22 Nov 49	185UNTS307	102477
Finland	UK Great Britain	28 Dec 49	86UNTS191	101159
Japan	Pakistan	24 Apr 53	221UNTS325	103013
Austria	UK Great Britain	09 Jul 56	310UNTS61	104487
Armistice and peace				
Multilateral		28 Oct 44	123UNTS223	200414
Multilateral		20 Jan 45	140UNTS397	200471
Multilateral		05 Jun 45	68UNTS189	200230
Multilateral		02 Sep 45	139UNTS387	200465
Multilateral		26 Dec 45	20UNTS259	100319
Multilateral		01 Jan 46	99UNTS131	101375
Multilateral		10 Feb 47	41UNTS21	100643
Multilateral		10 Feb 47	49UNTS3	100747
Multilateral		10 Feb 47	41UNTS135	100644
Multilateral		10 Feb 47	48UNTS203	100746
Israel	United Arab Rep	24 Feb 49	42UNTS251	100654
Israel	Lebanon	23 Mar 49	42UNTS287	100655
Israel	Jordan	03 Apr 49	42UNTS303	100656
Israel	Syria	20 Jul 49	42UNTS327	100657
India	Pakistan	27 Jul 49	81UNTS273	101076
Guatemala	Italy	10 Sep 49	102UNTS53	101410
Multilateral		08 Sep 51	136UNTS45	101832
Multilateral		08 Sep 51	136UNTS165	101833
Australia	Italy	20 Dec 51	190UNTS223	102566
Italy	New Zealand	20 Dec 51	150UNTS157	101970
Italy	USA (United States)	21 Dec 51	167UNTS163	102206
Italy	UK Great Britain	21 Dec 51	121UNTS89	101628
Taiwan	Japan	28 Apr 52	138UNTS3	101858
Multilateral		30 Jul 53	215UNTS97	102913
Burma	Japan	05 Nov 54	251UNTS201	103542
Japan	Poland	08 Feb 57	318UNTS251	104620
Indonesia	Japan	20 Jan 58	324UNTS227	104688
Japan	Thailand	01 Mar 63	475UNTS233	106895
Finland	Israel	21 Jan 65	581UNTS275	108450
India	Pakistan	30 Jun 65	548UNTS277	107983
Arms limitations				
Multilateral		13 Dec 46	8UNTS91	100116
Multilateral		13 Dec 46	8UNTS71	100115
Multilateral		13 Dec 46	8UNTS105	100117
Multilateral		10 Feb 47	42UNTS3	100645
Thailand	UK Great Britain	08 May 47	100UNTS47	101386
Philippines	USA (United States)	26 Jun 53	213UNTS77	102881
Spain	USA (United States)	26 Sep 53	207UNTS61	102800
Multilateral		14 May 55	219UNTS3	102962

PARTY ONE	PARTY TWO	DATE	CITATION	NUMBER
Arms limitations (Cont.)				
Multilateral		15 May 55	217UNTS223	102949
Multilateral		01 May 57	284UNTS201	104138
Brazil	USA (United States)	27 Oct 61	433UNTS113	106234
Multilateral		05 Aug 63	480UNTS43	106964
War claims and reparations				
Multilateral		08 Oct 44	45UNTS311	200187
France	UK Great Britain	27 Mar 45	98UNTS227	200274
Belgium	UK Great Britain	25 Jun 45	90UNTS307	200268
Luxembourg	USA (United States)	29 Aug 46	140UNTS101	101885
Luxembourg	USA (United States)	12 Sep 46	149UNTS19	101947
Denmark	South Africa	14 Oct 46	10UNTS29	100140
Multilateral		10 Feb 47	42UNTS3	100645
Belgium	South Africa	04 Jul 47	47UNTS9	100720
Italy	USA (United States)	14 Feb 48	67UNTS115	100871
Australia	Greece	16 Jun 48	18UNTS211	100290
Philippines	USA (United States)	27 Aug 48	44UNTS13	100675
Netherlands	UK Great Britain	17 Jan 49	83UNTS67	101102
France	USA (United States)	14 Mar 49	84UNTS237	101133
Italy	Yugoslavia	23 Dec 50	150UNTS213	101975
Japan	USA (United States)	24 Dec 53	222UNTS193	103028
Philippines	USA (United States)	06 Feb 57	303UNTS237	104383
Japan	Vietnam, South	13 May 59	373UNTS101	105317
Korea, South	USA (United States)	19 Feb 60	372UNTS109	105291
Nepal	USA (United States)	17 May 60	372UNTS313	105307
Loss and/or damage				
Belgium	France	30 Oct 45	19UNTS87	100306
Multilateral		14 Jan 46	555UNTS69	108105
Hungary	Yugoslavia	11 May 46	129UNTS3	101725
Belgium	Canada	13 Jul 46	230UNTS159	103181
France	Thailand	17 Nov 46	344UNTS59	104943
France	UK Great Britain	03 Dec 46	54UNTS127	100799
Multilateral		10 Feb 47	49UNTS3	100747
France	Poland	11 Feb 47	12UNTS287	100189
Canada	France	05 May 47	231UNTS81	103208
Austria	USA (United States)	21 Jun 47	67UNTS89	100868
Czechoslovakia	USA (United States)	25 Jul 47	90UNTS19	101223
Greece	South Africa	28 Jul 47	185UNTS161	102467
Belgium	India	04 Aug 47	76UNTS23	100976
Netherlands	UK Great Britain	08 Oct 47	252UNTS19	103556
Taiwan	USA (United States)	17 Mar 48	76UNTS157	100987
Belgium	UK Great Britain	07 Jun 48	20UNTS33	100313
Australia	Greece	16 Jun 48	18UNTS211	100290
USA (United States)	Yugoslavia	19 Jul 48	89UNTS43	101208
Israel	United Arab Rep	24 Feb 49	42UNTS251	100654
France	USA (United States)	14 Mar 49	84UNTS237	101133
United Arab Rep	UK Great Britain	17 Apr 49	83UNTS183	101107
Canada	Netherlands	09 May 49	46UNTS263	100715
Portugal	USA (United States)	04 Aug 49	181UNTS15	102394
Australia	Netherlands	12 Aug 49	34UNTS213	100539
Belgium	Canada	16 Nov 49	51UNTS3	100748
France	UK Great Britain	23 Jan 50	97UNTS149	101348
Belgium	Netherlands	15 Mar 51	93UNTS97	101294
Belgium	USA (United States)	16 Mar 51	93UNTS109	101295
Italy	USA (United States)	16 May 51	206UNTS325	102795
Belgium	Netherlands	14 Jun 51	101UNTS3	101397
Australia	France	28 Sep 51	161UNTS185	102128
Denmark	Netherlands	08 May 52	131UNTS91	101737
Austria	UK Great Britain	30 Jun 52	138UNTS153	101867
Belgium	France	11 Mar 53	191UNTS329	102590
Germany, West	USA (United States)	30 Mar 53	235UNTS285	103310
Italy	UK Great Britain	13 Apr 53	172UNTS271	102251
Multilateral		30 Jul 53	215UNTS97	102913
Luxembourg	UK Great Britain	18 Jun 54	192UNTS33	102593
Multilateral		23 Oct 54	332UNTS219	104762

PARTY ONE	PARTY TWO	DATE	CITATION	NUMBER
Loss and/or damage (Cont.)				
Burma	Japan	05 Nov 54	251UNTS215	103543
Belgium	France	12 Nov 54	306UNTS85	104434
Austria	UK Great Britain	15 May 55	344UNTS9	104940
Luxembourg	USA (United States)	15 Jun 55	264UNTS279	103798
Bulgaria	UK Great Britain	22 Sep 55	222UNTS349	103039
Belgium	Switzerland	05 Jan 56	228UNTS159	103149
Germany, West	Sweden	22 Mar 56	262UNTS401	103762
Greece	Romania	25 Aug 56	299UNTS231	104315
Philippines	USA (United States)	06 Feb 57	303UNTS237	104383
Italy	UK Great Britain	29 Mar 57	310UNTS11	104481
Belgium	UK Great Britain	03 Oct 57	394UNTS69	105669
USA (United States)	Vietnam, South	05 Nov 57	300UNTS23	104328
Brazil	Italy	08 Jan 58	362UNTS273	105192
Indonesia	Japan	20 Jan 58	324UNTS247	104689
Czechoslovakia	Poland	29 Mar 58	340UNTS199	104865
Netherlands	Norway	30 Jun 58	346UNTS217	104982
Nicaragua	USA (United States)	05 Sep 58	336UNTS33	104797
Belgium	France	20 Sep 58	376UNTS331	105387
Korea, South	USA (United States)	18 Dec 58	325UNTS233	104702
Philippines	USA (United States)	21 Jan 59	341UNTS255	104888
Japan	Vietnam, South	13 May 59	373UNTS101	105317
Austria	USA (United States)	22 May 59	347UNTS3	104988
Denmark	Japan	25 May 59	341UNTS157	104881
Germany, West	Norway	07 Aug 59	358UNTS185	105136
Japan	UK Great Britain	07 Oct 60	384UNTS89	105513
Japan	USA (United States)	08 Jun 61	410UNTS183	105903
San Marino	UK Great Britain	22 Jul 61	420UNTS3	106035
Canada	Japan	05 Sep 61	451UNTS47	106483
Belgium	Germany, West	21 Sep 62	502UNTS63	107326
Germany, West	UK Great Britain	09 Jun 64	539UNTS187	107831
Claims arising from occupation of territories				
Multilateral		10 Feb 47	49UNTS3	100747
Enemy financial interests				
Belgium	Norway	23 Oct 45	183UNTS337	200510
Multilateral		14 Jan 46	555UNTS69	108105
Netherlands	USA (United States)	11 Feb 46	3UNTS37	100023
Belgium	Denmark	08 Apr 46	4UNTS429	100059
Hungary	Yugoslavia	11 May 46	129UNTS3	101725
Denmark	Luxembourg	21 May 46	4UNTS435	100060
France	USA (United States)	18 Jul 46	125UNTS165	101675
Multilateral		18 Jul 46	125UNTS119	101674
Denmark	New Zealand	18 Sep 46	10UNTS39	100141
Greece	USA (United States)	08 Oct 46	180UNTS119	102379
Denmark	South Africa	14 Oct 46	10UNTS29	100140
Hungary	Yugoslavia	25 Jan 47	130UNTS3	101726
Multilateral		10 Feb 47	42UNTS3	100645
Australia	Norway	24 Mar 47	18UNTS185	100288
Belgium	South Africa	04 Jul 47	47UNTS9	100720
Greece	South Africa	28 Jul 47	185UNTS161	102467
Multilateral		14 Aug 47	138UNTS111	101863
Italy	USA (United States)	14 Aug 47	36UNTS105	100567
Multilateral		04 Nov 47	93UNTS61	101288
Multilateral		16 Dec 47	82UNTS237	101096
Hungary	Yugoslavia	17 Apr 48	130UNTS101	101727
Hungary	Yugoslavia	17 Apr 48	130UNTS121	101729
Hungary	Yugoslavia	17 Apr 48	130UNTS111	101728
Multilateral		10 May 48	140UNTS129	101887
Multilateral		13 May 48	140UNTS187	101888
Australia	Greece	16 Jun 48	18UNTS211	100290
USA (United States)	Yugoslavia	19 Jul 48	89UNTS43	101208
Australia	Denmark	08 Oct 48	22UNTS43	100330
Australia	Belgium	09 Dec 48	25UNTS159	100361
Poland	UK Great Britain	14 Jan 49	83UNTS3	101100
France	USA (United States)	14 Mar 49	84UNTS237	101133

PARTY ONE	PARTY TWO	DATE	CITATION	NUMBER
Enemy financial interests (Cont.)				
Multilateral		31 Mar 49	122UNTS57	101636
Nicaragua	USA (United States)	01 Feb 50	99UNTS25	101368
Australia	Yugoslavia	22 Feb 50	51UNTS201	100766
Israel	UK Great Britain	30 Mar 50	86UNTS231	101162
Australia	Netherlands	26 Apr 50	54UNTS83	100796
Italy	USA (United States)	16 May 51	206UNTS325	102795
Germany, West	Netherlands	19 May 52	134UNTS3	101794
Austria	UK Great Britain	30 Jun 52	138UNTS153	101867
Italy	Netherlands	22 Sep 52	150UNTS113	101965
Belgium	Luxembourg	26 Sep 52	141UNTS111	101910
Multilateral		30 Jul 53	215UNTS97	102913
Multilateral		23 Oct 54	332UNTS219	104762
India	Netherlands	04 Dec 54	289UNTS221	104219
Multilateral		10 May 55	273UNTS121	103948
Germany, West	Sweden	22 Mar 56	262UNTS361	103761
Japan	Philippines	09 May 56	285UNTS3	104148
Multilateral		31 Jan 57	278UNTS105	104026
Multilateral		29 Mar 57	283UNTS137	104113
Netherlands	Norway	30 Jun 58	348UNTS3	104995
Multilateral		27 Oct 58	351UNTS303	105031
Austria	USA (United States)	22 May 59	347UNTS3	104988
Australia	Austria	18 Dec 59	348UNTS201	105001
Reparations and restrictions				
Multilateral		20 Jan 45	140UNTS397	200471
Multilateral		14 Jan 46	555UNTS69	108105
Greece	UK Great Britain	24 Jan 46	6UNTS45	100067
Hungary	Yugoslavia	11 May 46	129UNTS3	101725
France	USA (United States)	28 May 46	84UNTS151	101125
Multilateral		18 Jul 46	125UNTS119	101674
France	USA (United States)	18 Jul 46	125UNTS165	101675
Hungary	Yugoslavia	25 Jan 47	130UNTS3	101726
Multilateral		10 Feb 47	49UNTS3	100747
Multilateral		10 Feb 47	140UNTS111	101886
Multilateral		10 Feb 47	42UNTS3	100645
Multilateral		10 Feb 47	41UNTS21	100643
Multilateral		10 Feb 47	48UNTS203	100746
Czechoslovakia	Norway	20 Mar 47	30UNTS223	100460
Multilateral		14 Aug 47	138UNTS111	101863
Multilateral		04 Nov 47	93UNTS61	101288
Multilateral		16 Dec 47	82UNTS237	101096
Hungary	Yugoslavia	17 Apr 48	130UNTS121	101729
Hungary	Yugoslavia	17 Apr 48	130UNTS101	101727
Hungary	Yugoslavia	17 Apr 48	130UNTS111	101728
Multilateral		10 May 48	140UNTS129	101887
Multilateral		13 May 48	140UNTS187	101888
France	USA (United States)	22 Oct 48	84UNTS173	101128
Multilateral		31 Mar 49	122UNTS57	101636
Multilateral		20 Jun 49	128UNTS141	101718
Multilateral		12 Aug 49	75UNTS135	100972
Greece	Italy	31 Aug 49	78UNTS89	101014
Guatemala	Italy	10 Sep 49	102UNTS53	101410
Germany, West	Netherlands	14 Dec 50	87UNTS257	101177
Multilateral		08 Sep 51	136UNTS45	101832
Australia	France	28 Sep 51	161UNTS185	102128
Germany, West	Netherlands	20 Jun 52	136UNTS221	101836
Germany, West	Greece	28 Jul 52	182UNTS85	102424
Germany, West	Israel	10 Sep 52	162UNTS205	102137
Italy	Netherlands	22 Sep 52	150UNTS113	101965
Belgium	Luxembourg	26 Sep 52	141UNTS111	101910
Belgium	France	11 Mar 53	191UNTS329	102590
Italy	UK Great Britain	13 Apr 53	172UNTS271	102251
Multilateral		30 Jul 53	215UNTS97	102913
Germany, East	USSR (Soviet Union)	22 Aug 53	221UNTS129	103005
Multilateral		23 Oct 54	332UNTS219	104762

PARTY ONE	PARTY TWO	DATE	CITATION	NUMBER
Reparations and restrictions (Cont.)				
Burma	Japan	05 Nov 54	251UNTS215	103543
Ethiopia	Italy	05 Mar 56	267UNTS189	103844
Japan	Philippines	09 May 56	285UNTS3	104148
Belgium	Germany, West	24 Sep 56	314UNTS195	104549
Japan	USSR (Soviet Union)	19 Oct 56	263UNTS99	103768
Japan	Sweden	20 Sep 57	325UNTS29	104693
Indonesia	Japan	20 Jan 58	324UNTS247	104689
Indonesia	Japan	20 Jan 58	324UNTS227	104688
Netherlands	Norway	30 Jun 58	348UNTS3	104995
Austria	USA (United States)	22 May 59	347UNTS3	104988
Denmark	Japan	25 May 59	341UNTS157	104881
Germany, West	Norway	07 Aug 59	358UNTS185	105136
Australia	Austria	18 Dec 59	348UNTS201	105001
Germany, West	Netherlands	08 Apr 60	508UNTS14	107404
Japan	UK Great Britain	07 Oct 60	384UNTS89	105513
Canada	Japan	05 Sep 61	451UNTS47	106483
Finland	USSR (Soviet Union)	24 Apr 64	537UNTS231	107804
Germany, West	UK Great Britain	09 Jun 64	539UNTS187	107831
Multilateral		30 Apr 66	620UNTS191	108956
Post-war claims settlement				
Multilateral		20 Jan 45	140UNTS397	200471
Belgium	UK Great Britain	25 Jun 45	90UNTS307	200268
Greece	UK Great Britain	11 Oct 45	183UNTS329	200509
Belgium	France	30 Oct 45	19UNTS87	100306
Multilateral		01 Jan 46	99UNTS131	101375
Czechoslovakia	Poland	12 Feb 46	25UNTS207	100364
Canada	UK Great Britain	06 Mar 46	20UNTS3	100311
Canada	France	22 Mar 46	230UNTS165	103182
UK Great Britain	USA (United States)	27 Mar 46	4UNTS2	100039
Greece	United Arab Rep	30 Mar 46	187UNTS263	102518
Turkey	USA (United States)	07 May 46	6UNTS293	100083
Hungary	Yugoslavia	11 May 46	129UNTS3	101725
India	USA (United States)	16 May 46	4UNTS183	100045
France	USA (United States)	28 May 46	84UNTS59	101119
France	USA (United States)	28 May 46	84UNTS121	101123
France	USA (United States)	28 May 46	84UNTS113	101122
France	USA (United States)	28 May 46	84UNTS93	101121
Australia	USA (United States)	07 Jun 46	4UNTS237	100048
Poland	UK Great Britain	24 Jun 46	11UNTS59	100149
New Zealand	USA (United States)	10 Jul 46	6UNTS341	100087
Belgium	Canada	13 Jul 46	230UNTS159	103181
France	USA (United States)	18 Jul 46	125UNTS165	101675
Philippines	USA (United States)	11 Sep 46	43UNTS231	100670
France	Thailand	17 Nov 46	344UNTS59	104943
France	UK Great Britain	03 Dec 46	54UNTS127	100799
Denmark	India	20 Dec 46	7UNTS309	100107
Canada	Netherlands	30 Dec 46	230UNTS205	103185
Hungary	Yugoslavia	25 Jan 47	130UNTS3	101726
Multilateral		10 Feb 47	41UNTS135	100644
Multilateral		10 Feb 47	48UNTS203	100746
Multilateral		10 Feb 47	42UNTS3	100645
Multilateral		10 Feb 47	41UNTS21	100643
South Africa	USA (United States)	21 Mar 47	16UNTS47	100248
France	South Africa	18 Apr 47	225UNTS35	103085
Austria	UK Great Britain	28 Apr 47	93UNTS53	101287
Canada	France	05 May 47	231UNTS81	103208
Netherlands	USA (United States)	28 May 47	17UNTS29	100267
Austria	USA (United States)	21 Jun 47	67UNTS89	100868
France	Norway	15 Jul 47	15UNTS5	100226
Czechoslovakia	USA (United States)	25 Jul 47	90UNTS19	101223
Greece	South Africa	28 Jul 47	185UNTS161	102467
Australia	France	28 Jul 47	97UNTS271	101353
Czechoslovakia	Greece	30 Jul 47	185UNTS149	102466
Belgium	India	04 Aug 47	76UNTS23	100976

PARTY ONE	PARTY TWO	DATE	CITATION	NUMBER
Post-war claims settlement (Cont.)				
Italy	USA (United States)	14 Aug 47	36UNTS105	100567
Italy	USA (United States)	14 Aug 47	36UNTS53	100566
Denmark	UK Great Britain	19 Aug 47	9UNTS277	100137
Netherlands	UK Great Britain	08 Oct 47	252UNTS19	103556
Multilateral		10 Oct 47	54UNTS193	100804
Denmark	UK Great Britain	01 Dec 47	93UNTS151	101298
Italy	USA (United States)	14 Feb 48	67UNTS115	100871
Norway	USA (United States)	24 Feb 48	34UNTS155	100535
France	USA (United States)	27 Feb 48	84UNTS207	101131
Netherlands	UK Great Britain	11 Mar 48	77UNTS69	100993
Taiwan	USA (United States)	17 Mar 48	76UNTS157	100987
Hungary	Yugoslavia	17 Apr 48	130UNTS121	101729
Hungary	Yugoslavia	17 Apr 48	130UNTS111	101728
Hungary	Yugoslavia	17 Apr 48	130UNTS101	101727
Spain	USA (United States)	03 May 48	132UNTS155	101756
Canada	France	05 May 48	231UNTS87	103209
Multilateral		10 May 48	140UNTS129	101887
Multilateral		13 May 48	140UNTS187	101888
Taiwan	UK Great Britain	18 May 48	66UNTS113	100850
Belgium	UK Great Britain	07 Jun 48	20UNTS33	100313
USA (United States)	Yugoslavia	19 Jul 48	34UNTS195	100537
Philippines	USA (United States)	27 Aug 48	44UNTS13	100675
Netherlands	UK Great Britain	06 Sep 48	32UNTS235	100501
Korea, South	USA (United States)	11 Sep 48	89UNTS155	101216
Czechoslovakia	USA (United States)	16 Sep 48	90UNTS35	101224
France	USA (United States)	22 Oct 48	84UNTS173	101128
Canada	Netherlands	28 Oct 48	231UNTS95	103210
UK Great Britain	Yugoslavia	23 Dec 48	81UNTS103	101067
UK Great Britain	Yugoslavia	23 Dec 48	81UNTS121	101068
Poland	UK Great Britain	14 Jan 49	83UNTS51	101101
Netherlands	UK Great Britain	17 Jan 49	83UNTS67	101102
Canada	USA (United States)	14 Mar 49	82UNTS3	101079
France	USA (United States)	14 Mar 49	84UNTS237	101133
United Arab Rep	UK Great Britain	17 Apr 49	83UNTS183	101107
Canada	Netherlands	09 May 49	46UNTS263	100715
Ethiopia	USA (United States)	20 May 49	89UNTS99	101211
Italy	Yugoslavia	23 May 49	150UNTS179	101972
Multilateral		20 Jun 49	128UNTS141	101718
Portugal	USA (United States)	04 Aug 49	181UNTS15	102394
Australia	Netherlands	12 Aug 49	34UNTS213	100539
Greece	Italy	31 Aug 49	78UNTS89	101014
Czechoslovakia	UK Great Britain	28 Sep 49	86UNTS161	101157
Switzerland	USA (United States)	21 Oct 49	132UNTS163	101757
Belgium	Canada	16 Nov 49	51UNTS3	100748
France	UK Great Britain	23 Jan 50	97UNTS149	101348
Canada	Norway	18 Mar 50	230UNTS349	103194
Canada	Denmark	25 Mar 50	230UNTS343	103193
Canada	Yugoslavia	29 Mar 50	230UNTS357	103195
Canada	USSR (Soviet Union)	29 Sep 50	230UNTS371	103197
Netherlands	USA (United States)	19 Jan 51	141UNTS221	101917
New Zealand	Yugoslavia	27 Feb 51	150UNTS165	101971
Belgium	Netherlands	15 Mar 51	93UNTS97	101294
Belgium	USA (United States)	16 Mar 51	93UNTS109	101295
Greece	India	18 Apr 51	166UNTS305	102195
Multilateral		25 Apr 51	91UNTS21	101240
Italy	USA (United States)	16 May 51	206UNTS325	102795
Belgium	Netherlands	14 Jun 51	101UNTS3	101397
Italy	Netherlands	15 Jun 51	150UNTS103	101964
Canada	France	04 Jul 51	233UNTS101	103253
Multilateral		08 Sep 51	136UNTS45	101832
Multilateral		08 Sep 51	136UNTS165	101833
Canada	Italy	20 Sep 51	236UNTS251	103328
Australia	France	28 Sep 51	161UNTS185	102128
France	USA (United States)	02 Feb 52	247UNTS223	103472
Austria	Greece	22 Mar 52	187UNTS255	102517

PARTY ONE	PARTY TWO	DATE	CITATION	NUMBER
Post-war claims settlement (Cont.)				
Canada	Netherlands	10 Apr 52	233UNTS129	103257
Taiwan	Japan	28 Apr 52	138UNTS3	101858
Denmark	Netherlands	08 May 52	131UNTS91	101737
Germany, West	Netherlands	19 May 52	134UNTS3	101794
Australia	Italy	24 May 52	161UNTS65	102123
Norway	USA (United States)	21 Jun 52	236UNTS9	103313
Austria	UK Great Britain	30 Jun 52	138UNTS153	101867
Italy	Netherlands	22 Sep 52	150UNTS113	101965
Belgium	Luxembourg	26 Sep 52	141UNTS111	101910
Japan	UK Great Britain	04 Nov 52	164UNTS107	102162
Japan	UK Great Britain	04 Nov 52	164UNTS101	102161
Japan	UK Great Britain	21 Nov 52	172UNTS303	102254
Multilateral		27 Feb 53	333UNTS3	104764
Belgium	France	11 Mar 53	191UNTS329	102590
Germany, West	USA (United States)	30 Mar 53	235UNTS285	103310
Netherlands	Thailand	30 May 53	293UNTS17	104282
Greece	UK Great Britain	05 Oct 53	243UNTS73	103447
France	Netherlands	27 Nov 53	302UNTS245	104363
France	Netherlands	30 Apr 54	202UNTS115	102727
Luxembourg	UK Great Britain	18 Jun 54	192UNTS33	102593
Burma	Japan	05 Nov 54	251UNTS215	103543
Burma	Japan	05 Nov 54	251UNTS201	103542
Belgium	France	12 Nov 54	306UNTS85	104434
Iran	USSR (Soviet Union)	02 Dec 54	451UNTS227	106497
France	Netherlands	15 Dec 54	288UNTS37	104195
Italy	Yugoslavia	18 Dec 54	284UNTS239	104141
Luxembourg	USA (United States)	15 Jun 55	264UNTS279	103798
Bulgaria	UK Great Britain	22 Sep 55	222UNTS349	103039
Belgium	Switzerland	05 Jan 56	228UNTS159	103149
Germany, West	Sweden	17 Jan 56	262UNTS301	103758
Luxembourg	Netherlands	06 Feb 56	261UNTS17	103723
Ethiopia	Italy	05 Mar 56	267UNTS189	103844
Germany, West	Sweden	22 Mar 56	262UNTS401	103762
Poland	USA (United States)	28 Jun 56	273UNTS79	103944
Greece	Romania	25 Aug 56	299UNTS231	104315
Japan	Spain	08 Jan 57	318UNTS221	104615
Japan	Poland	08 Feb 57	318UNTS251	104620
Czechoslovakia	Japan	13 Feb 57	300UNTS119	104335
Italy	UK Great Britain	29 Mar 57	310UNTS11	104481
Japan	Sweden	20 Sep 57	325UNTS29	104693
Belgium	UK Great Britain	03 Oct 57	394UNTS69	105669
Brazil	Italy	08 Jan 58	362UNTS273	105192
Czechoslovakia	Poland	29 Mar 58	340UNTS199	104865
Netherlands	Norway	30 Jun 58	346UNTS217	104982
Denmark	USA (United States)	28 Aug 58	335UNTS133	104781
Belgium	France	20 Sep 58	376UNTS331	105387
Multilateral		27 Oct 58	351UNTS303	105031
Korea, South	USA (United States)	18 Dec 58	325UNTS233	104702
Germany, West	USA (United States)	20 Mar 59	341UNTS15	104874
Netherlands	UK Great Britain	30 Apr 59	343UNTS307	104937
Austria	USA (United States)	22 May 59	347UNTS3	104988
Denmark	Japan	25 May 59	341UNTS157	104881
Germany, West	Norway	07 Aug 59	358UNTS185	105136
Australia	Austria	18 Dec 59	348UNTS201	105001
Germany, West	UK Great Britain	28 Jan 60	420UNTS29	106038
Japan	UK Great Britain	07 Oct 60	384UNTS89	105513
Japan	USA (United States)	08 Jun 61	410UNTS183	105903
San Marino	UK Great Britain	22 Jul 61	420UNTS3	106035
Canada	Japan	05 Sep 61	451UNTS47	106483
Germany, West	Israel	01 Jun 62	448UNTS227	106435
Belgium	Germany, West	21 Sep 62	502UNTS63	107326
Greece	Hungary	27 Apr 63	550UNTS197	108016
Belgium	Netherlands	06 Jan 64	531UNTS119	107698
Germany, West	UK Great Britain	09 Jun 64	539UNTS187	107831
Japan	Korea, South	22 Jun 65	583UNTS173	108473

PARTY ONE	PARTY TWO	DATE	CITATION	NUMBER
Post-war claims settlement (Cont.)				
Italy	USA (United States)	12 Jan 66	587UNTS309	108515
Occupation regime				
Australia	New Zealand	21 Jan 44	18UNTS357	200113
Multilateral		09 Jul 45	160UNTS359	200484
Multilateral		26 Jul 45	227UNTS297	200533
Luxembourg	USA (United States)	03 Jul 46	32UNTS85	100491
Austria	USA (United States)	21 Jun 47	67UNTS99	100869
Czechoslovakia	Poland	05 Apr 48	31UNTS325	100481
France	USA (United States)	28 Jun 48	31UNTS115	100472
Denmark	USA (United States)	29 Jun 48	27UNTS35	100396
Greece	USA (United States)	02 Jul 48	31UNTS131	100474
Netherlands	USA (United States)	02 Jul 48	32UNTS77	100490
Belgium	USA (United States)	02 Jul 48	27UNTS43	100397
Turkey	USA (United States)	04 Jul 48	34UNTS185	100536
France	USA (United States)	09 Jul 48	32UNTS93	100492
France	USA (United States)	09 Jul 48	24UNTS103	100352
Multilateral		14 Jul 48	31UNTS123	100473
Multilateral		14 Jul 48	23UNTS3	100340
Portugal	USA (United States)	28 Sep 48	31UNTS139	100475
Trieste	USA (United States)	15 Oct 48	29UNTS249	100443
Multilateral		16 Dec 48	79UNTS85	101033
France	USA (United States)	07 Feb 49	67UNTS189	100877
Trieste	USA (United States)	11 Feb 49	79UNTS123	101036
Multilateral		09 May 52	168UNTS65	102213
Multilateral		05 Oct 54	235UNTS99	103297
Disarmament and demilitarization				
Multilateral		28 Oct 44	123UNTS223	200414
Multilateral		20 Jan 45	140UNTS397	200471
Multilateral		05 Jun 45	68UNTS189	200230
Taiwan	USA (United States)	28 Jun 46	34UNTS121	100532
Multilateral		10 Feb 47	49UNTS3	100747
Multilateral		10 Feb 47	48UNTS203	100746
Multilateral		10 Feb 47	41UNTS21	100643
Multilateral		10 Feb 47	41UNTS135	100644
Multilateral		08 Apr 49	140UNTS196	101889
Multilateral		14 Apr 49	141UNTS281	101919
Multilateral		20 Jun 49	128UNTS141	101718
India	Pakistan	27 Jul 49	81UNTS273	101076
Multilateral		22 Nov 49	185UNTS307	102477
Multilateral		03 Apr 51	141UNTS303	101920
Multilateral		23 Oct 54	331UNTS327	104759
Multilateral		23 Oct 54	331UNTS253	104758
Multilateral		23 Oct 54	332UNTS219	104762
Industrial controls				
Multilateral		05 Jun 45	68UNTS189	200230
UK Great Britain	USA (United States)	02 Dec 46	7UNTS163	100098
Multilateral		10 Feb 47	49UNTS3	100747
Multilateral		31 Mar 49	122UNTS57	101636
Multilateral		08 Apr 49	140UNTS196	101889
Multilateral		14 Apr 49	141UNTS281	101919
Multilateral		20 Jun 49	128UNTS141	101718
Multilateral		03 Apr 51	141UNTS303	101920
Multilateral		09 May 52	168UNTS65	102213
Turkey	USA (United States)	23 Jun 54	233UNTS189	103263
Multilateral		23 Oct 54	332UNTS219	104762
Control and occupation machinery				
France	USA (United States)	25 Aug 44	138UNTS247	200449
Multilateral		12 Sep 44	227UNTS279	200532
Multilateral		14 Nov 44	236UNTS359	200539
Multilateral		05 Jun 45	68UNTS189	200230
Multilateral		09 Jun 45	139UNTS381	200464
Multilateral		09 Jul 45	160UNTS359	200484
Multilateral		02 Sep 45	139UNTS387	200465

PARTY ONE	PARTY TWO	DATE	CITATION	NUMBER
Control and occupation machinery (Cont.)				
USA (United States)	USSR (Soviet Union)	17 Sep 45	235UNTS346	200538
Taiwan	USA (United States)	28 Jun 46	34UNTS121	100532
UK Great Britain	USA (United States)	02 Dec 46	7UNTS163	100098
Multilateral		10 Feb 47	49UNTS3	100747
Denmark	UK Great Britain	22 Apr 47	8UNTS3	100110
Norway	UK Great Britain	05 Jun 47	54UNTS181	100803
Italy	USA (United States)	28 Jun 48	25UNTS45	100356
Austria	USA (United States)	02 Jul 48	25UNTS53	100357
Norway	USA (United States)	03 Jul 48	27UNTS59	100399
Sweden	USA (United States)	03 Jul 48	27UNTS69	100400
Iceland	USA (United States)	03 Jul 48	27UNTS49	100398
UK Great Britain	USA (United States)	06 Jul 48	25UNTS61	100358
Multilateral		14 Sep 48	18UNTS267	100296
Allied Milit Occup	Norway	17 Feb 49	30UNTS137	100451
Multilateral		08 Apr 49	140UNTS196	101889
Multilateral		04 May 49	138UNTS123	101864
Multilateral		20 Jun 49	128UNTS141	101718
Multilateral		09 May 52	168UNTS65	102213
Multilateral		23 Oct 54	331UNTS327	104759
Austria	United Nations	24 Feb 66	557UNTS129	108131
Australia	United Nations	25 Feb 66	557UNTS85	108129
Withdrawal of occupation				
France	UK Great Britain	31 Aug 45	98UNTS249	200275
Taiwan	France	28 Feb 46	14UNTS151	100217
Multilateral		10 Feb 47	48UNTS203	100746
Multilateral		10 Feb 47	49UNTS3	100747
Multilateral		10 Feb 47	41UNTS21	100643
Multilateral		10 Feb 47	41UNTS135	100644
Italy	USA (United States)	03 Sep 47	67UNTS15	100863
Multilateral		08 Apr 49	140UNTS196	101889
Portugal	USA (United States)	06 Sep 51	237UNTS217	103348
Multilateral		23 Oct 54	331UNTS327	104759
Multilateral		23 Oct 54	331UNTS253	104758
Denmark	United Nations	21 Feb 66	555UNTS151	108108
United Nations	Sweden	21 Feb 66	555UNTS169	108111
New Zealand	United Nations	21 Feb 66	555UNTS163	108110
Canada	United Nations	21 Feb 66	555UNTS119	108107
Finland	United Nations	21 Feb 66	555UNTS157	108109
War graves				
Multilateral		08 Jun 52	210UNTS317	102843
Multilateral		15 May 55	217UNTS223	102949
Multilateral		05 Mar 56	326UNTS169	104711
France	USA (United States)	19 Mar 56	275UNTS37	103974
Australia	Austria	05 Jul 67	636UNTS117	109098
Multilateral		06 Nov 67	640UNTS87	109155
Austria	South Africa	08 Nov 67	636UNTS125	109099
Austria	Pakistan	10 Jan 68	636UNTS133	109100
Austria	Canada	28 Feb 68	636UNTS141	109101
Austria	India	10 Jul 68	0UNTS0	109227
Responsibility for war dead				
Romania	USA (United States)	28 Jun 46	148UNTS355	101944
Hungary	USA (United States)	09 Aug 46	148UNTS313	101941
Netherlands	USA (United States)	11 Apr 47	148UNTS343	101943
Czechoslovakia	UK Great Britain	03 Mar 49	83UNTS95	101104
Multilateral		12 Aug 49	75UNTS287	100973
Multilateral		12 Aug 49	75UNTS85	100971
Multilateral		12 Aug 49	75UNTS135	100972
Multilateral		12 Aug 49	75UNTS31	100970
Netherlands	USA (United States)	26 Sep 51	158UNTS469	102080
Multilateral		22 Feb 54	188UNTS273	102531
UK Great Britain	USA (United States)	21 Jun 54	209UNTS61	102821
Multilateral		24 Aug 54	247UNTS213	103471
Germany, West	Netherlands	11 Oct 54	291UNTS9	104241
France	USA (United States)	01 Jul 55	270UNTS19	103888

PARTY ONE	PARTY TWO	DATE	CITATION	NUMBER
Responsibility for war dead (Cont.)				
France	USA (United States)	19 Mar 56	275UNTS37	103974
Germany, West	UK Great Britain	16 Oct 59	385UNTS21	105526
Korea, South	United Nations	06 Nov 59	346UNTS289	200565
Italy	Yugoslavia	12 Feb 60	379UNTS77	105434
Multilateral		10 Sep 62	502UNTS3	107323
Denmark	Germany, West	03 Oct 62	450UNTS291	106475
Germany, West	Greece	26 Sep 63	550UNTS203	108017
Cyprus	United Nations	31 Mar 64	492UNTS57	107187
Germany, West	Ireland	13 May 64	553UNTS87	108071
Greece	UK Great Britain	12 Oct 66	578UNTS33	108385
Multilateral		06 Nov 67	640UNTS87	109155
Austria	India	10 Jul 68	0UNTS0	109227
Upkeep of war graves				
Multilateral		01 Jan 46	99UNTS131	101375
Netherlands	Thailand	30 Jan 47	247UNTS353	103480
Philippines	USA (United States)	14 Mar 47	43UNTS271	100673
Netherlands	USA (United States)	11 Apr 47	148UNTS343	101943
Belgium	USA (United States)	23 Jul 47	33UNTS33	100512
France	USA (United States)	01 Oct 47	148UNTS303	101940
Czechoslovakia	UK Great Britain	03 Mar 49	83UNTS95	101104
Multilateral		12 Aug 49	75UNTS287	100973
Multilateral		12 Aug 49	75UNTS85	100971
Multilateral		12 Aug 49	75UNTS31	100970
Luxembourg	USA (United States)	20 Mar 51	180UNTS283	102392
Multilateral		10 Jul 51	108UNTS287	101481
Multilateral		29 Jul 51	117UNTS85	101585
Netherlands	USA (United States)	26 Sep 51	158UNTS469	102080
India	Italy	27 Aug 53	275UNTS279	103987
Australia	Italy	27 Aug 53	225UNTS47	103086
Multilateral		27 Aug 53	213UNTS137	102884
Multilateral		18 Feb 54	226UNTS297	103124
Multilateral		22 Feb 54	188UNTS273	102531
UK Great Britain	USA (United States)	21 Jun 54	209UNTS61	102821
France	USA (United States)	01 Jul 55	270UNTS19	103888
Multilateral		21 Sep 55	269UNTS241	103885
Germany, West	New Zealand	05 Mar 56	402UNTS103	105779
Australia	Germany, West	05 Mar 56	328UNTS241	104737
Multilateral		05 Mar 56	326UNTS181	104712
Multilateral		05 Mar 56	326UNTS169	104711
France	USA (United States)	19 Mar 56	275UNTS37	103974
ICJ Option Clause	Sweden	06 Apr 57	264UNTS221	103794
Germany, West	UK Great Britain	16 Oct 59	385UNTS21	105526
Korea, South	United Nations	06 Nov 59	346UNTS289	200565
Multilateral		10 Sep 62	502UNTS3	107323
Denmark	Germany, West	03 Oct 62	450UNTS291	106475
Netherlands	UK Great Britain	27 Aug 63	490UNTS3	107150
Germany, West	Greece	26 Sep 63	550UNTS203	108017
Germany, West	Ireland	13 May 64	553UNTS87	108071
Multilateral		09 Mar 67	603UNTS135	108730
Australia	Austria	05 Jul 67	636UNTS117	109098
Multilateral		06 Nov 67	640UNTS87	109155
Austria	South Africa	08 Nov 67	636UNTS125	109099
Austria	Pakistan	10 Jan 68	636UNTS133	109100
Austria	Canada	28 Feb 68	636UNTS141	109101
Establishment of war cemeteries				
Romania	USA (United States)	28 Jun 46	148UNTS355	101944
Hungary	USA (United States)	09 Aug 46	148UNTS313	101941
Italy	USA (United States)	24 Sep 46	148UNTS323	101942
Philippines	USA (United States)	14 Mar 47	43UNTS271	100673
Netherlands	USA (United States)	11 Apr 47	148UNTS343	101943
Belgium	USA (United States)	23 Jul 47	33UNTS33	100512
France	USA (United States)	01 Oct 47	148UNTS303	101940
Czechoslovakia	UK Great Britain	03 Mar 49	83UNTS95	101104
Multilateral		12 Aug 49	75UNTS135	100972

PARTY ONE	PARTY TWO	DATE	CITATION	NUMBER
Establishment of war cemeteries (Cont.)				
Luxembourg	USA (United States)	20 Mar 51	180UNTS283	102392
Multilateral		10 Jul 51	108UNTS287	101481
Multilateral		29 Jul 51	117UNTS85	101585
Multilateral		31 Oct 51	172UNTS193	102247
Italy	South Africa	27 Aug 53	212UNTS211	102873
Multilateral		27 Aug 53	213UNTS137	102884
Multilateral		18 Feb 54	226UNTS297	103124
Multilateral		22 Feb 54	188UNTS273	102531
UK Great Britain	USA (United States)	21 Jun 54	209UNTS61	102821
Multilateral		24 Aug 54	247UNTS213	103471
France	USA (United States)	01 Jul 55	270UNTS19	103888
Multilateral		05 Mar 56	326UNTS181	104712
Multilateral		05 Mar 56	326UNTS169	104711
France	USA (United States)	19 Mar 56	275UNTS37	103974
ICJ Option Clause	Sweden	06 Apr 57	264UNTS221	103794
Germany, West	UK Great Britain	16 Oct 59	385UNTS21	105526
Korea, South	United Nations	06 Nov 59	346UNTS289	200565
Belgium	USA (United States)	27 Nov 59	366UNTS331	105221
Multilateral		10 Sep 62	502UNTS3	107323
Denmark	Germany, West	03 Oct 62	450UNTS291	106475
Netherlands	UK Great Britain	27 Aug 63	490UNTS3	107150
Germany, West	Greece	26 Sep 63	550UNTS203	108017
Germany, West	Ireland	13 May 64	553UNTS87	108071
Philippines	USA (United States)	22 Dec 66	579UNTS203	108408
Multilateral		06 Nov 67	640UNTS87	109155
Austria	India	10 Jul 68	0UNTS0	109227
International organizations				
Multilateral		27 Sep 45	5UNTS327	200035
Multilateral		02 Oct 47	193UNTS188	102616
Denmark	ICAO (Civil Aviat)	09 Sep 49	53UNTS341	100791
United Nations	Switzerland	14 Sep 49	43UNTS327	200183
Mexico	USA (United States)	30 Jul 54	269UNTS39	103871
Multilateral		03 Oct 57	364UNTS3	105211
Germany, West	Netherlands	08 Apr 60	508UNTS14	107404
UK Great Britain	USSR (Soviet Union)	21 Jan 63	475UNTS3	106887
State/IGO Group	Jordan	03 Apr 68	632UNTS66	109009
IGO constitution				
Multilateral		27 Sep 45	5UNTS327	200035
Multilateral		27 Dec 45	2UNTS39	100020
Multilateral		15 Dec 46	18UNTS3	100283
Accept UN Charter	Thailand	16 Dec 46	1UNTS47	100011
Albania	Yugoslavia	12 Jun 47	111UNTS201	101535
Multilateral		11 May 48	500UNTS267	107313
Multilateral		29 Nov 48	120UNTS13	101613
Mexico	USA (United States)	25 Jan 49	99UNTS3	101367
India	WHO (World Health)	11 Oct 51	118UNTS27	101594
Colombia	United Nations	17 Jul 52	135UNTS61	101815
Canada	USA (United States)	12 Nov 53	234UNTS97	103274
Multilateral		18 Jan 54	330UNTS121	104743
Multilateral		25 Mar 57	294UNTS2	104300
Thailand	USA (United States)	23 Dec 60	405UNTS135	105830
Multilateral		27 Mar 61	420UNTS109	106043
Japan	United Nations	11 Apr 62	425UNTS45	106117
ILO (Labor Org)	Tanganyika	03 May 62	429UNTS73	106191
Greece	United Nations	18 May 62	429UNTS61	106190
Other Unilat Decla	United Nations	31 Aug 65	557UNTS143	108132
Austria	United Nations	12 Mar 68	632UNTS131	109015
Multilateral		18 Mar 68	0UNTS0	109262
Admission				
Multilateral		07 Dec 44	171UNTS345	200501
UK Great Britain	USA (United States)	05 Nov 45	138UNTS75	101861
Multilateral		07 Nov 45	2UNTS17	100018
Multilateral		27 Dec 45	2UNTS39	100020
Multilateral		22 Jul 46	14UNTS185	100221

PARTY ONE	PARTY TWO	DATE	CITATION	NUMBER
Admission (Cont.)				
Multilateral		22 Jul 46	9UNTS3	100125
Multilateral		30 Oct 46	27UNTS77	100401
Accept UN Charter	Thailand	16 Dec 46	1UNTS47	100011
UNESCO (Educ/Cult)	United Nations	03 Feb 47	1UNTS233	200011
Multilateral		02 Oct 47	193UNTS188	102616
Multilateral		11 Oct 47	77UNTS143	100998
Multilateral		30 Apr 48	119UNTS3	101609
Multilateral		10 Jun 48	191UNTS3	102576
Multilateral		05 May 49	87UNTS103	101168
Pan Am Health Org	WHO (World Health)	24 May 49	32UNTS387	200178
Multilateral		22 Nov 49	185UNTS307	102477
Multilateral		08 Apr 50	66UNTS285	100860
Italy	USA (United States)	13 Feb 51	148UNTS57	101935
Multilateral		09 Oct 51	220UNTS121	102997
Multilateral		14 Oct 51	122UNTS3	101631
Multilateral		11 Jul 52	169UNTS3	102220
Multilateral		19 Oct 53	207UNTS189	102807
Multilateral		25 May 55	264UNTS117	103791
Multilateral		06 Jun 55	219UNTS79	102968
Multilateral		22 Jun 55	249UNTS3	103498
Multilateral		12 Oct 55	560UNTS3	108165
Multilateral		20 Oct 55	378UNTS159	105425
Multilateral		26 Mar 56	259UNTS125	103686
Multilateral		26 Oct 56	276UNTS3	103988
Accept UN Charter	Ghana	01 Mar 57	261UNTS113	103727
Multilateral		25 Mar 57	294UNTS2	104300
Multilateral		19 Nov 59	410UNTS156	105902
Multilateral		14 Dec 59	368UNTS253	105245
Multilateral		26 Jan 60	439UNTS249	106333
Multilateral		28 Jul 60	394UNTS37	105667
Multilateral		14 Sep 60	443UNTS247	106363
Multilateral		13 Dec 60	523UNTS117	107557
Multilateral		13 Dec 60	455UNTS204	106544
Multilateral		23 Jan 61	530UNTS141	107679
Multilateral		14 Apr 61	422UNTS101	106071
Multilateral		21 Jun 61	514UNTS209	107449
Multilateral		26 Mar 62	539UNTS67	107825
Multilateral		29 Mar 62	507UNTS177	107401
Multilateral		14 Jun 62	528UNTS33	107634
Multilateral		28 Sep 62	469UNTS169	106791
Multilateral		05 Oct 62	502UNTS225	107333
Multilateral		12 Dec 62	552UNTS15	108048
Multilateral		20 Apr 63	495UNTS3	107239
Multilateral		03 Dec 63	529UNTS217	107663
Multilateral		14 Dec 63	507UNTS149	107399
Multilateral		02 Jul 65	592UNTS215	108575
Multilateral		04 Dec 65	571UNTS123	108303
Hungary	United Nations	04 Mar 66	559UNTS3	108151
Multilateral		12 May 66	563UNTS54	108204
United Nations	Tunisia	04 Aug 66	576UNTS23	108363
Multilateral		04 May 67	595UNTS287	108623
Multilateral		18 Mar 68	0UNTS0	109262
Multilateral		24 Dec 68	0UNTS0	109369
Constitutional amendment				
Multilateral		04 Jan 46	6UNTS35	100066
Multilateral		22 Jul 46	14UNTS185	100221
Multilateral		09 Oct 46	15UNTS35	100229
Multilateral		27 May 47	418UNTS161	106021
Multilateral		18 Mar 68	0UNTS0	109262
Decisions				
Mexico	USA (United States)	03 Feb 44	3UNTS313	200025
Multilateral		07 Dec 44	84UNTS389	200252
Multilateral		22 Mar 45	70UNTS237	200241
Multilateral		02 Oct 47	193UNTS188	102616

PARTY ONE	PARTY TWO	DATE	CITATION	NUMBER
Decisions (Cont.)				
Philippines	USA (United States)	27 Aug 48	44UNTS13	100675
Greece	USA (United States)	25 Oct 48	185UNTS103	102462
Multilateral		13 May 50	128UNTS171	101719
Multilateral		01 Oct 53	258UNTS153	103677
Multilateral		01 Mar 54	256UNTS31	103622
Costa Rica	Guatemala	20 Dec 55	280UNTS121	104056
Multilateral		25 Apr 56	270UNTS103	103896
Multilateral		03 Oct 57	365UNTS3	105213
Multilateral		01 Dec 58	385UNTS137	105534
Multilateral		06 Apr 59	349UNTS167	105013
Multilateral		08 Apr 59	389UNTS69	105593
Czechoslovakia	Germany, East	16 Jun 60	415UNTS248	105988
Multilateral		13 Dec 60	455UNTS3	106543
Multilateral		13 Dec 60	523UNTS117	107557
Multilateral		20 Apr 63	495UNTS3	107239
Romania	Yugoslavia	20 Dec 63	527UNTS245	107629
Brazil	United Nations	24 Mar 66	560UNTS47	108167
Multilateral		18 Mar 68	0UNTS0	109262
Multilateral		24 Dec 68	0UNTS0	109369
Subsidiary organ				
Multilateral		30 Jul 40	161UNTS253	200488
Brazil	Paraguay	14 Jun 41	54UNTS303	200202
Brazil	Paraguay	14 Jun 41	54UNTS323	200204
Brazil	USA (United States)	17 Jul 42	102UNTS203	200303
UK Great Britain	USA (United States)	19 Aug 43	214UNTS341	200527
Multilateral		15 Jan 44	161UNTS281	200489
Australia	New Zealand	21 Jan 44	18UNTS357	200113
Multilateral		07 Dec 44	15UNTS295	200102
Multilateral		22 Mar 45	70UNTS237	200241
Multilateral		16 Nov 45	4UNTS275	100052
Multilateral		22 Jul 46	14UNTS185	100221
Multilateral		30 Oct 46	27UNTS77	100401
Multilateral		15 Dec 46	18UNTS3	100283
Bulgaria	UNICEF (Children)	23 Aug 47	68UNTS223	200232
Finland	UNICEF (Children)	23 Aug 47	68UNTS224	200233
Romania	UNICEF (Children)	28 Aug 47	68UNTS228	200235
Hungary	UNICEF (Children)	28 Aug 47	68UNTS226	200234
Multilateral		02 Oct 47	193UNTS188	102616
Multilateral		11 Oct 47	77UNTS143	100998
Italy	UNICEF (Children)	06 Nov 47	68UNTS240	200236
Austria	UNICEF (Children)	07 Nov 47	68UNTS252	200237
Belgium	Netherlands	13 Apr 48	32UNTS153	100497
Multilateral		30 Apr 48	119UNTS3	101609
Multilateral		11 May 48	500UNTS267	107313
Multilateral		10 Jun 48	191UNTS3	102576
Multilateral		15 Nov 48	120UNTS59	101615
Multilateral		22 Feb 49	93UNTS129	101296
Multilateral		04 Apr 49	34UNTS243	100541
Multilateral		28 Apr 49	83UNTS105	101105
Multilateral		05 May 49	87UNTS103	101168
Multilateral		20 Jun 49	128UNTS141	101718
Korea, South	UNICEF (Children)	25 Mar 50	65UNTS171	200209
Multilateral		06 Apr 50	119UNTS99	101610
Indonesia	UNICEF (Children)	06 Apr 50	68UNTS254	200238
Multilateral		08 Apr 50	66UNTS285	100860
Multilateral		13 May 50	128UNTS171	101719
Ceylon (Sri Lanka)	UNICEF (Children)	07 Jun 50	68UNTS256	200239
Iran	USA (United States)	19 Oct 50	92UNTS135	101266
Multilateral		15 Dec 50	347UNTS127	104994
Nicaragua	UK Great Britain	25 May 51	101UNTS77	101404
Multilateral		01 Sep 51	131UNTS83	101736
Multilateral		14 Oct 51	122UNTS3	101631
Multilateral		06 Dec 51	150UNTS67	101963
Multilateral		11 Jul 52	169UNTS3	102220

PARTY ONE	PARTY TWO	DATE	CITATION	NUMBER
Subsidiary organ (Cont.)				
Multilateral		06 Sep 52	216UNTS132	102937
Multilateral		24 Jul 53	250UNTS108	103520
Multilateral		19 Oct 53	207UNTS189	102807
Canada	USA (United States)	12 Nov 53	223UNTS139	103062
Canada	USA (United States)	12 Nov 53	234UNTS97	103274
Multilateral		11 Dec 53	191UNTS285	102588
Multilateral		18 Jan 54	330UNTS121	104743
Multilateral		01 Mar 54	256UNTS31	103622
Multilateral		21 Dec 54	258UNTS322	103678
Multilateral		14 May 55	219UNTS3	102962
Multilateral		13 Dec 55	529UNTS141	107660
Multilateral		25 Apr 56	270UNTS103	103896
Turkey	USA (United States)	18 May 56	283UNTS167	104115
Multilateral		18 May 56	339UNTS3	104844
United Nations	Venezuela	18 Nov 56	588UNTS243	108529
France	USA (United States)	12 Mar 57	279UNTS275	104045
Multilateral		25 Mar 57	294UNTS259	104301
Multilateral		25 Mar 57	294UNTS2	104300
Multilateral		12 Apr 57	443UNTS128	106362
Multilateral		03 Oct 57	364UNTS3	105211
Australia	USA (United States)	24 Jan 58	307UNTS105	104446
Multilateral		03 Feb 58	381UNTS165	105471
Multilateral		03 Apr 58	336UNTS177	104806
FAO (Food Agri)	UK Great Britain	24 Apr 58	642UNTS245	109177
Multilateral		01 Dec 58	385UNTS137	105534
Multilateral		06 Apr 59	349UNTS167	105013
Mexico	United Nations	07 Apr 59	381UNTS123	105468
Subsahara Tech Com	ILO (Labor Org)	25 Jul 59	409UNTS290	200590
Multilateral		18 Nov 59	390UNTS227	105610
Multilateral		19 Nov 59	410UNTS156	105902
Multilateral		14 Dec 59	368UNTS253	105245
Denmark	USA (United States)	19 Feb 60	354UNTS151	105061
Multilateral		01 Sep 60	403UNTS3	105792
Portugal	USA (United States)	31 Oct 60	394UNTS127	105673
Council of Europe	ILO (Labor Org)	08 Dec 60	389UNTS291	200579
Multilateral		13 Dec 60	523UNTS117	107557
FAO (Food Agri)	UK Great Britain	20 Feb 61	642UNTS253	109178
Multilateral		27 Mar 61	420UNTS109	106043
IDA (Devel Assoc)	United Nations	10 Apr 61	394UNTS221	200582
Romania	United Nations	29 May 61	406UNTS147	105845
Multilateral		09 May 62	453UNTS299	106531
Multilateral		15 May 62	444UNTS3	106367
Multilateral		14 Jun 62	528UNTS33	107634
Germany, West	United Nations	28 Jun 62	434UNTS249	200597
Multilateral		25 May 63	479UNTS39	106947
Poland	United Nations	16 Jul 63	471UNTS3	106817
Multilateral		04 Aug 63	510UNTS3	107408
Multilateral		23 Oct 63	506UNTS197	107388
Chad	France	19 May 64	0UNTS0	109440
Austria	United Nations	11 Jun 64	500UNTS85	107309
Mexico	United Nations	17 Jul 64	533UNTS117	107738
Multilateral		11 Dec 64	547UNTS297	107964
United Nations	Sweden	16 Jun 65	539UNTS45	107823
Multilateral		02 Jul 65	592UNTS215	108575
Monaco	United Nations	17 Dec 65	550UNTS365	200615
Multilateral		31 Dec 65	616UNTS317	108904
Multilateral		17 Jan 66	592UNTS101	108573
Brazil	United Nations	24 Mar 66	560UNTS47	108167
Italy	United Nations	23 May 66	565UNTS11	108231
Liberia	UNICEF (Children)	08 Jun 66	570UNTS31	108286
United Nations	Tunisia	04 Aug 66	576UNTS23	108363
Nigeria	United Nations	07 Feb 67	590UNTS25	108544
Multilateral		14 Feb 67	634UNTS281	109068
Morocco	UNESCO (Educ/Cult)	18 Dec 67	0UNTS0	109221
Italy	United Nations	15 Jan 68	635UNTS11	109070

PARTY ONE	PARTY TWO	DATE	CITATION	NUMBER
Subsidiary organ (Cont.)				
Multilateral		07 Feb 68	0UNTS0	109513
Austria	United Nations	12 Mar 68	632UNTS131	109015
United Nations	UK Great Britain	12 Mar 68	632UNTS121	109014
Congo (Brazzaville)	United Nations	13 Mar 68	632UNTS161	109018
Multilateral		18 Mar 68	0UNTS0	109262
Denmark	Int Coun Expl Sea	24 Jul 68	0UNTS0	109413
Multilateral		01 Aug 68	0UNTS0	109368
Ghana	United Nations	19 Sep 68	0UNTS0	109250
Austria	United Nations	24 Sep 68	0UNTS0	109253
United Nations	United Arab Rep	14 Nov 68	0UNTS0	109371
Int Wheat Coun	UK Great Britain	28 Nov 68	0UNTS0	109498
Multilateral		24 Dec 68	0UNTS0	109369
IAEA (Atom Energy)	OAU (Afri Unity)	26 Mar 69	0UNTS0	200646
Establishment				
Canada	USA (United States)	27 Jun 41	103UNTS205	200315
Multilateral		15 Jan 44	161UNTS281	200489
Mexico	USA (United States)	27 Jan 44	106UNTS275	200346
Brazil	UNRRA (Relief)	12 Oct 44	67UNTS321	200228
Multilateral		07 Dec 44	171UNTS345	200501
Multilateral		22 Mar 45	70UNTS237	200241
France	UK Great Britain	31 Aug 45	98UNTS249	200275
Multilateral		27 Sep 45	5UNTS327	200035
Multilateral		07 Nov 45	2UNTS17	100018
Multilateral		16 Nov 45	4UNTS275	100052
UK Great Britain	USA (United States)	10 Dec 45	3UNTS177	100030
Multilateral		27 Dec 45	2UNTS39	100020
Multilateral		04 Jan 46	6UNTS35	100066
Multilateral		22 Jul 46	9UNTS3	100125
Multilateral		22 Jul 46	14UNTS185	100221
Philippines	USA (United States)	17 Sep 46	15UNTS249	100240
Multilateral		30 Oct 46	11UNTS107	100151
Multilateral		30 Oct 46	27UNTS77	100401
Multilateral		15 Dec 46	18UNTS3	100283
Multilateral		06 Jun 47	46UNTS249	100714
Multilateral		02 Oct 47	193UNTS188	102616
Multilateral		11 Oct 47	77UNTS143	100998
Multilateral		06 Mar 48	289UNTS3	104214
Multilateral		30 Apr 48	119UNTS3	101609
Multilateral		11 May 48	500UNTS267	107313
Taiwan	USA (United States)	05 Aug 48	82UNTS109	101087
Multilateral		18 Aug 48	33UNTS181	100518
Multilateral		15 Nov 48	120UNTS59	101615
Multilateral		29 Nov 48	120UNTS13	101613
Multilateral		28 Apr 49	83UNTS105	101105
Multilateral		05 May 49	87UNTS103	101168
Costa Rica	USA (United States)	31 May 49	80UNTS3	101041
Multilateral		20 Jun 49	128UNTS141	101718
Mexico	USA (United States)	30 Aug 49	98UNTS183	101364
Multilateral		24 Sep 49	126UNTS237	101691
Multilateral		08 Apr 50	66UNTS285	100860
Multilateral		18 Apr 51	261UNTS140	103729
Multilateral		09 Oct 51	220UNTS121	102997
Multilateral		14 Oct 51	122UNTS3	101631
Multilateral		06 Dec 51	425UNTS61	106119
Multilateral		11 Jul 52	169UNTS3	102220
Mexico	USA (United States)	26 Aug 52	264UNTS269	103797
Multilateral		01 Jul 53	200UNTS149	102701
Multilateral		24 Jul 53	250UNTS108	103520
Multilateral		01 Oct 53	258UNTS153	103677
Multilateral		17 Oct 53	184UNTS42	102438
Multilateral		19 Oct 53	207UNTS189	102807
NATO (North Atlan)	USA (United States)	22 Oct 54	249UNTS175	103507
Multilateral		02 Mar 55	225UNTS233	103101
Haiti	USA (United States)	27 Apr 55	240UNTS17	103391

PARTY ONE	PARTY TWO	DATE	CITATION	NUMBER
Establishment (Cont.)				
Multilateral		06 Jun 55	219UNTS79	102968
Multilateral		12 Oct 55	560UNTS3	108165
Multilateral		20 Oct 55	378UNTS159	105425
Multilateral		05 Nov 55	250UNTS201	103524
Multilateral		26 Mar 56	259UNTS125	103686
Multilateral		26 Oct 56	276UNTS3	103988
Multilateral		25 Mar 57	294UNTS2	104300
Multilateral		25 Mar 57	294UNTS259	104301
Multilateral		03 Oct 57	364UNTS3	105211
Multilateral		03 Feb 58	381UNTS165	105471
Multilateral		24 Jan 59	486UNTS157	107078
Multilateral		08 Apr 59	389UNTS69	105593
Greece	Yugoslavia	18 Jun 59	368UNTS17	105233
Multilateral		14 Dec 59	368UNTS253	105245
Multilateral		04 Jan 60	370UNTS3	105266
Multilateral		26 Jan 60	439UNTS249	106333
Multilateral		28 Jul 60	485UNTS3	107042
Multilateral		14 Sep 60	443UNTS247	106363
Multilateral		13 Dec 60	523UNTS117	107557
Multilateral		13 Dec 60	455UNTS204	106544
Multilateral		23 Jan 61	530UNTS141	107679
Multilateral		14 Apr 61	422UNTS101	106071
Multilateral		18 Oct 61	529UNTS89	107659
Tanganyika	UK Great Britain	09 Dec 61	437UNTS47	106299
Multilateral		26 Mar 62	539UNTS67	107825
Multilateral		29 Mar 62	507UNTS177	107401
Multilateral		25 May 62	486UNTS103	107075
Multilateral		14 Jun 62	528UNTS33	107634
Multilateral		28 Sep 62	469UNTS169	106791
Multilateral		05 Oct 62	502UNTS225	107333
Multilateral		12 Dec 62	552UNTS15	108048
Multilateral		20 Apr 63	495UNTS3	107239
Multilateral		25 May 63	479UNTS39	106947
Multilateral		26 Oct 63	587UNTS9	108506
Multilateral		03 Dec 63	529UNTS217	107663
Multilateral		14 Dec 63	507UNTS149	107399
Multilateral		15 Jul 64	610UNTS143	108840
Australia	USA (United States)	28 Aug 64	510UNTS201	107415
Multilateral		25 Nov 64	587UNTS19	108507
Multilateral		28 May 65	559UNTS273	108163
Multilateral		02 Jul 65	592UNTS215	108575
Multilateral		04 Dec 65	571UNTS123	108303
Multilateral		27 May 66	637UNTS0	109121
Multilateral		04 May 67	595UNTS287	108623
Multilateral		18 Mar 68	0UNTS0	109262
Regional offices				
Multilateral		15 Jan 44	161UNTS281	200489
Multilateral		27 Dec 45	2UNTS39	100020
Multilateral		22 Jul 46	14UNTS185	100221
France	ICAO (Civil Aviat)	14 Mar 47	94UNTS59	101306
Multilateral		11 Oct 47	77UNTS143	100998
Greece	UNICEF (Children)	14 Oct 47	102UNTS39	101409
United Nations	WHO (World Health)	15 Nov 47	19UNTS193	200115
ICJ Option Clausé	Honduras	02 Feb 48	15UNTS217	100236
UNESCO (Educ/Cult)	WHO (World Health)	15 Jul 48	44UNTS323	200184
FAO (Food Agri)	WHO (World Health)	17 Jul 48	76UNTS171	200244
Israel	UNICEF (Children)	20 Sep 48	71UNTS17	100907
Peru	ICAO (Civil Aviat)	22 Oct 48	95UNTS3	101315
IRO (Refugee Org)	United Nations	07 Feb 49	26UNTS299	200153
Burma	UNICEF (Children)	22 Apr 50	68UNTS96	100888
Korea, South	United Nations	21 Sep 51	104UNTS323	200322
Council of Europe	ILO (Labor Org)	23 Nov 51	126UNTS331	200435
UNICEF (Children)	UK Great Britain	04 Feb 52	120UNTS147	101620
Dominican Republic	UNICEF (Children)	15 Feb 52	121UNTS43	101625

PARTY ONE	PARTY TWO	DATE	CITATION	NUMBER
Regional offices (Cont.)				
Lebanon	United Nations	01 May 57	266UNTS125	103827
ILO (Labor Org)	UK Great Britain	14 Jan 59	355UNTS283	105081
UNESCO (Educ/Cult)	Thailand	25 Aug 61	410UNTS125	105899
COMECON (Econ Aid)	USSR (Soviet Union)	07 Dec 61	506UNTS325	107392
ILO (Labor Org)	Tanganyika	03 May 62	429UNTS73	106191
Czechoslovakia	COMECON (Econ Aid)	20 Jul 62	506UNTS345	107393
Multilateral		14 Sep 62	494UNTS219	107236
Ceylon (Sri Lanka)	ILO (Labor Org)	21 Nov 62	449UNTS263	106463
Poland	COMECON (Econ Aid)	22 Feb 63	506UNTS303	107391
Pakistan	United Nations	18 Apr 63	503UNTS25	107339
Niger	United Nations	20 Nov 63	536UNTS3	107793
UNICEF (Children)	Senegal	22 Jan 64	486UNTS91	107074
Philippines	United Nations	15 Sep 64	510UNTS137	107410
Lebanon	ILO (Labor Org)	14 May 66	600UNTS69	108676
ILO (Labor Org)	Senegal	09 Feb 67	600UNTS75	108677
Algeria	ILO (Labor Org)	06 Apr 67	595UNTS99	108614
Cameroon	ILO (Labor Org)	07 May 67	596UNTS209	108634
ILO (Labor Org)	Zambia	20 Dec 67	619UNTS293	108947
ILO (Labor Org)	Trinidad/Tobago	14 Mar 69	0UNTS0	109500
Procedure				
Multilateral		07 Dec 44	171UNTS345	200501
Multilateral		07 Dec 44	84UNTS389	200252
Multilateral		22 Mar 45	70UNTS237	200241
Multilateral		06 Mar 48	289UNTS3	104214
Multilateral		30 Apr 48	119UNTS3	101609
Greece	USA (United States)	25 Oct 48	185UNTS103	102462
Multilateral		05 May 49	87UNTS103	101168
Multilateral		14 Oct 51	122UNTS3	101631
Multilateral		01 Oct 53	258UNTS153	103677
Multilateral		02 Mar 55	225UNTS233	103101
Multilateral		26 Mar 56	259UNTS125	103686
Multilateral		25 Mar 57	294UNTS259	104301
Multilateral		03 Feb 58	381UNTS165	105471
Multilateral		14 Dec 59	368UNTS253	105245
Multilateral		13 Dec 60	523UNTS117	107557
Japan	United Nations	15 Mar 61	397UNTS199	105706
Japan	United Nations	11 Apr 62	425UNTS45	106117
Gabon	United Nations	11 Jan 63	450UNTS257	106472
Multilateral		23 Oct 63	506UNTS197	107388
Multilateral		25 Nov 64	587UNTS19	108507
Argentina	Brazil	23 Apr 65	0UNTS0	109411
Multilateral		02 Jul 65	592UNTS215	108575
Multilateral		12 May 66	563UNTS54	108204
Multilateral		27 May 66	637UNTS0	109121
Jamaica	United Nations	06 Dec 66	580UNTS211	108424
IAEA (Atom Energy)	Turkey	08 Dec 66	608UNTS69	108813
Multilateral		07 Feb 68	0UNTS0	109513
Congo (Brazzaville)	United Nations	13 Mar 68	632UNTS161	109018
Multilateral		18 Mar 68	0UNTS0	109262
State/IGO Group	Sierra Leone	29 May 68	637UNTS0	109120
Denmark	Int Coun Expl Sea	24 Jul 68	0UNTS0	109413
Multilateral		24 Dec 68	0UNTS0	109369
Headquarters and facilities				
Multilateral		15 Jan 44	161UNTS281	200489
Multilateral		07 Dec 44	171UNTS345	200501
Multilateral		27 Sep 45	5UNTS327	200035
Multilateral		04 Jan 46	6UNTS35	100066
Multilateral		05 Apr 46	231UNTS199	103221
League of Nations	ILO (Labor Org)	04 May 46	19UNTS187	200114
Multilateral		19 Jul 46	1UNTS97	200001
Multilateral		22 Jul 46	14UNTS185	100221
Multilateral		30 Oct 46	27UNTS77	100401
ILO (Labor Org)	United Nations	19 Dec 46	1UNTS183	200009
Multilateral		06 Jun 47	46UNTS249	100714

PARTY ONE	PARTY TWO	DATE	CITATION	NUMBER
Headquarters and facilities (Cont.)				
United Nations	USA (United States)	26 Jun 47	11UNTS11	100147
Multilateral		02 Oct 47	193UNTS188	102616
United Nations	WHO (World Health)	15 Nov 47	19UNTS193	200115
UNICEF (Children)	Yugoslavia	20 Nov 47	65UNTS28	100817
United Nations	USA (United States)	18 Dec 47	11UNTS347	100174
Multilateral		06 Mar 48	289UNTS3	104214
Multilateral		30 Apr 48	119UNTS3	101609
Multilateral		18 Aug 48	33UNTS181	100518
Multilateral		15 Nov 48	120UNTS59	101615
Multilateral		28 Apr 49	83UNTS105	101105
Multilateral		05 May 49	87UNTS103	101168
Multilateral		20 Jun 49	128UNTS141	101718
Mexico	USA (United States)	30 Aug 49	98UNTS183	101364
UNICEF (Children)	UK Great Britain	19 Dec 49	65UNTS64	100828
Haiti	UNICEF (Children)	20 Dec 49	65UNTS68	100829
Costa Rica	UNICEF (Children)	14 Jan 50	65UNTS70	100830
Peru	UNICEF (Children)	31 Jan 50	65UNTS80	100834
Bolivia	UNICEF (Children)	03 Feb 50	65UNTS82	100835
United Nations	WHO (World Health)	10 Feb 50	46UNTS327	200188
Colombia	UNICEF (Children)	15 Mar 50	65UNTS104	100838
Korea, South	UNICEF (Children)	25 Mar 50	65UNTS171	200209
Multilateral		15 Dec 50	157UNTS129	102052
United Nations	USA (United States)	28 Mar 51	108UNTS231	101476
United Nations	WMO (Meteorology)	10 Apr 51	103UNTS245	200415
Multilateral		09 Oct 51	220UNTS121	102997
Multilateral		14 Oct 51	122UNTS3	101631
Multilateral		06 Dec 51	425UNTS61	106119
Multilateral		18 Feb 52	126UNTS319	200434
Multilateral		09 May 52	205UNTS65	102770
Multilateral		22 May 52	131UNTS115	101739
Multilateral		11 Jul 52	169UNTS3	102220
Panama	USA (United States)	08 Aug 52	181UNTS257	102415
UNICEF (Children)	UK Great Britain	07 Oct 53	180UNTS59	102375
Multilateral		17 Oct 53	184UNTS42	102438
Multilateral		19 Oct 53	207UNTS189	102807
France	UNESCO (Educ/Cult)	02 Jul 54	357UNTS3	105103
Multilateral		25 May 55	264UNTS117	103791
Multilateral		06 Jun 55	219UNTS79	102968
Multilateral		12 Oct 55	560UNTS3	108165
Multilateral		20 Oct 55	378UNTS159	105425
Multilateral		26 Mar 56	259UNTS125	103686
Peru	USA (United States)	03 May 56	272UNTS59	103931
Multilateral		12 Apr 57	443UNTS128	106362
Austria	IAEA (Atom Energy)	11 Dec 57	339UNTS110	104849
Multilateral		03 Feb 58	381UNTS165	105471
France	Italy	30 Oct 58	363UNTS3	105196
Multilateral		08 Apr 59	389UNTS69	105593
Multilateral		19 Nov 59	410UNTS156	105902
Multilateral		14 Dec 59	368UNTS253	105245
Multilateral		28 Jul 60	485UNTS3	107042
Multilateral		13 Dec 60	455UNTS204	106544
Multilateral		13 Dec 60	523UNTS117	107557
Multilateral		23 Jan 61	530UNTS141	107679
Multilateral		26 Mar 62	539UNTS67	107825
Multilateral		29 Mar 62	507UNTS177	107401
Multilateral		25 May 62	486UNTS103	107075
Multilateral		14 Jun 62	528UNTS33	107634
Multilateral		28 Sep 62	469UNTS169	106791
Multilateral		05 Oct 62	502UNTS225	107333
Multilateral		12 Dec 62	552UNTS15	108048
Korea, South	USA (United States)	08 Jan 63	493UNTS105	107211
Bulgaria	COMECON (Econ Aid)	30 Mar 63	506UNTS257	107389
Multilateral		23 Oct 63	506UNTS197	107388
Multilateral		03 Dec 63	529UNTS217	107663
Multilateral		14 Dec 63	507UNTS149	107399

PARTY ONE	PARTY TWO	DATE	CITATION	NUMBER
Headquarters and facilities (Cont.)				
Multilateral		25 Nov 64	587UNTS19	108507
Multilateral		28 May 65	559UNTS273	108163
Austria	Petrol Export Org	24 Jun 65	589UNTS135	108540
Norway	Eur Space Research	21 Sep 65	579UNTS251	108413
United Nations	Zambia	23 Oct 65	549UNTS101	107993
Multilateral		08 Dec 65	600UNTS161	108680
Multilateral		27 May 66	637UNTS0	109121
Jamaica	United Nations	06 Dec 66	580UNTS211	108424
Asian Devel Bank	Philippines	22 Dec 66	615UNTS375	108887
Austria	United Nations	13 Apr 67	600UNTS93	108679
Cyprus	WHO (World Health)	07 Oct 67	608UNTS327	108821
Eur Space Research	UK Great Britain	24 Nov 67	638UNTS17	109129
Morocco	UNESCO (Educ/Cult)	18 Dec 67	0UNTS0	109221
Czechoslovakia	Hungary	27 Feb 68	640UNTS49	109154
Int Wheat Coun	UK Great Britain	28 Nov 68	0UNTS0	109498
Extension of functions				
Multilateral		04 Dec 45	9UNTS101	100128
Multilateral		04 Jan 46	6UNTS35	100066
Multilateral		23 Apr 46	16UNTS179	100257
Multilateral		11 Dec 46	12UNTS179	100186
Multilateral		15 Dec 46	18UNTS3	100283
Finland	UNICEF (Children)	23 Aug 47	68UNTS224	200233
Bulgaria	UNICEF (Children)	23 Aug 47	68UNTS223	200232
Hungary	UNICEF (Children)	28 Aug 47	68UNTS226	200234
Romania	UNICEF (Children)	28 Aug 47	68UNTS228	200235
Italy	UNICEF (Children)	06 Nov 47	68UNTS240	200236
Austria	UNICEF (Children)	07 Nov 47	68UNTS252	200237
Multilateral		11 May 48	500UNTS267	107313
India	UNICEF (Children)	10 May 49	68UNTS96	100887
Korea, South	UNICEF (Children)	25 Mar 50	65UNTS171	200209
Indonesia	UNICEF (Children)	06 Apr 50	68UNTS254	200238
Ceylon (Sri Lanka)	UNICEF (Children)	07 Jun 50	68UNTS256	200239
Multilateral		20 May 52	219UNTS55	102966
Denmark	WHO (World Health)	03 Sep 56	258UNTS103	103674
IAEA (Atom Energy)	IMCO (Maritime Org)	13 Apr 61	425UNTS281	200595
Multilateral		23 Oct 63	506UNTS197	107388
ILO (Labor Org)	OAU (Afri Unity)	25 Nov 65	550UNTS389	200617
Guinea	UNICEF (Children)	22 Dec 66	585UNTS137	108486
Barbados	UNICEF (Children)	30 Mar 68	637UNTS0	109123
State/IGO Group	Sierra Leone	29 May 68	637UNTS0	109120
Multilateral		24 Dec 68	0UNTS0	109369
Liaison with other IGO's				
Multilateral		16 Nov 45	4UNTS275	100052
Multilateral		22 Jul 46	14UNTS185	100221
Multilateral		30 Oct 46	27UNTS77	100401
Multilateral		30 Oct 46	11UNTS107	100151
ILO (Labor Org)	United Nations	19 Dec 46	1UNTS183	200009
UNESCO (Educ/Cult)	United Nations	03 Feb 47	1UNTS233	200011
FAO (Food Agri)	United Nations	03 Feb 47	1UNTS207	200010
Multilateral		06 Jun 47	46UNTS249	100714
FAO (Food Agri)	ILO (Labor Org)	11 Sep 47	18UNTS335	200111
Multilateral		02 Oct 47	193UNTS188	102616
Multilateral		11 Oct 47	77UNTS143	100998
Multilateral		10 Jun 48	191UNTS3	102576
Multilateral		15 Nov 48	120UNTS59	101615
Multilateral		29 Nov 48	120UNTS13	101613
Multilateral		08 Feb 49	157UNTS157	102053
Multilateral		24 Sep 49	126UNTS237	101691
United Nations	WHO (World Health)	20 Apr 50	139UNTS445	200470
Canada	USA (United States)	22 Jun 50	70UNTS115	100900
Multilateral		15 Dec 50	157UNTS129	102052
Multilateral		15 Feb 52	132UNTS51	101751
Multilateral		06 Sep 52	216UNTS132	102937
Multilateral		01 Oct 53	258UNTS153	103677

PARTY ONE	PARTY TWO	DATE	CITATION	NUMBER
Liaison with other IGO's (Cont.)				
Multilateral		19 Oct 53	207UNTS189	102807
Multilateral		25 May 55	264UNTS117	103791
Multilateral		25 Apr 56	270UNTS103	103896
Multilateral		26 Oct 56	276UNTS3	103988
Multilateral		03 Oct 57	364UNTS3	105211
Multilateral		03 Apr 58	336UNTS177	104806
Multilateral		01 Dec 58	385UNTS137	105534
Multilateral		06 Apr 59	349UNTS167	105013
Multilateral		08 Apr 59	389UNTS69	105593
IAEA (Atom Energy)	WHO (World Health)	28 May 59	339UNTS387	200559
Multilateral		14 Dec 59	368UNTS253	105245
Multilateral		26 Jan 60	439UNTS249	106333
IAEA (Atom Energy)	OECD (Econ Coop)	24 Nov 60	396UNTS273	200585
IDA (Devel Assoc)	United Nations	10 Apr 61	394UNTS221	200582
IAEA (Atom Energy)	IMCO (Maritime Org)	13 Apr 61	425UNTS281	200595
Multilateral		14 Apr 61	422UNTS101	106071
Multilateral		29 Mar 62	507UNTS177	107401
Multilateral		15 May 62	444UNTS3	106367
Multilateral		28 Sep 62	469UNTS169	106791
Multilateral		20 Apr 63	495UNTS3	107239
Multilateral		03 Dec 63	529UNTS217	107663
Iraq	UNICEF (Children)	03 Dec 63	482UNTS319	107001
Multilateral		23 Feb 65	527UNTS120	107622
Multilateral		05 Mar 65	527UNTS221	107627
ILO (Labor Org)	OAU (Afri Unity)	25 Nov 65	550UNTS389	200617
Multilateral		12 May 66	563UNTS54	108204
Multilateral		27 May 66	637UNTS0	109121
Multilateral		25 Jan 67	588UNTS212	108527
Turkey	USSR (Soviet Union)	24 Feb 67	643UNTS153	109190
Morocco	UNESCO (Educ/Cult)	18 Dec 67	0UNTS0	109221
Czechoslovakia	Hungary	27 Feb 68	640UNTS49	109154
Multilateral		18 Mar 68	0UNTS0	109262
Multilateral		24 Dec 68	0UNTS0	109369
IAEA (Atom Energy)	OAU (Afri Unity)	26 Mar 69	0UNTS0	200646
Internal structure				
Multilateral		15 Jan 44	161UNTS281	200489
Brazil	UNRRA (Relief)	12 Oct 44	67UNTS321	200228
France	UK Great Britain	31 Aug 45	98UNTS249	200275
Multilateral		16 Nov 45	4UNTS275	100052
UK Great Britain	USA (United States)	10 Dec 45	3UNTS177	100030
Multilateral		27 Dec 45	2UNTS39	100020
Multilateral		04 Jan 46	6UNTS35	100066
Multilateral		14 Jan 46	555UNTS69	108105
Multilateral		05 Apr 46	231UNTS199	103221
Multilateral		22 Jul 46	14UNTS185	100221
Taiwan	USA (United States)	30 Aug 46	12UNTS39	100179
Multilateral		09 Oct 46	15UNTS35	100229
Multilateral		30 Oct 46	11UNTS107	100151
Multilateral		30 Oct 46	27UNTS77	100401
Multilateral		02 Dec 46	161UNTS72	102124
Burma	USA (United States)	28 Feb 47	25UNTS27	100355
Multilateral		06 Jun 47	46UNTS249	100714
Multilateral		02 Oct 47	193UNTS188	102616
Multilateral		11 Oct 47	77UNTS143	100998
Multilateral		30 Apr 48	119UNTS3	101609
Multilateral		11 May 48	500UNTS267	107313
Greece	USA (United States)	25 Oct 48	185UNTS103	102462
Multilateral		15 Nov 48	120UNTS59	101615
Multilateral		29 Nov 48	120UNTS13	101613
Multilateral		28 Apr 49	83UNTS105	101105
Multilateral		05 May 49	87UNTS103	101168
Costa Rica	USA (United States)	31 May 49	80UNTS3	101041
Iran	USA (United States)	01 Sep 49	79UNTS155	101039
Multilateral		24 Sep 49	126UNTS237	101691

PARTY ONE	PARTY TWO	DATE	CITATION	NUMBER
Internal structure (Cont.)				
Turkey	USA (United States)	27 Dec 49	98UNTS141	101361
Multilateral		08 Apr 50	66UNTS285	100860
United Nations	WHO (World Health)	20 Apr 50	139UNTS445	200470
Paraguay	USA (United States)	27 Nov 50	122UNTS147	101644
Multilateral		15 Dec 50	157UNTS129	102052
Multilateral		18 Apr 51	261UNTS140	103729
Multilateral		18 Jul 51	102UNTS291	200308
Multilateral		09 Oct 51	220UNTS121	102997
Multilateral		14 Oct 51	122UNTS3	101631
Multilateral		06 Dec 51	425UNTS61	106119
Multilateral		09 May 52	205UNTS65	102770
Multilateral		11 Jul 52	169UNTS3	102220
Multilateral		06 Sep 52	216UNTS132	102937
Multilateral		01 Oct 53	258UNTS153	103677
Libya	UK Great Britain	19 Oct 53	186UNTS285	102494
Multilateral		19 Oct 53	207UNTS189	102807
Multilateral		01 Mar 54	256UNTS31	103622
Multilateral		01 Dec 54	210UNTS197	102839
Multilateral		02 Mar 55	225UNTS233	103101
Haiti	USA (United States)	27 Apr 55	240UNTS17	103391
Multilateral		25 May 55	264UNTS117	103791
Multilateral		12 Oct 55	560UNTS3	108165
Multilateral		05 Nov 55	250UNTS201	103524
Multilateral		26 Mar 56	259UNTS125	103686
Multilateral		25 Apr 56	270UNTS103	103896
Peru	USA (United States)	03 May 56	272UNTS59	103931
Multilateral		26 Oct 56	276UNTS3	103988
Multilateral		25 Mar 57	294UNTS259	104301
Multilateral		25 Mar 57	294UNTS411	104302
Multilateral		25 Mar 57	294UNTS2	104300
Multilateral		03 Oct 57	364UNTS3	105211
Multilateral		03 Feb 58	381UNTS165	105471
Multilateral		03 Apr 58	336UNTS177	104806
Multilateral		01 Dec 58	385UNTS137	105534
Multilateral		06 Apr 59	349UNTS167	105013
Multilateral		08 Apr 59	389UNTS69	105593
Multilateral		18 Nov 59	390UNTS227	105610
Multilateral		14 Dec 59	368UNTS253	105245
Multilateral		26 Jan 60	439UNTS249	106333
Multilateral		01 Sep 60	403UNTS3	105792
Multilateral		13 Dec 60	455UNTS204	106544
Multilateral		23 Jan 61	530UNTS141	107679
Multilateral		14 Apr 61	422UNTS101	106071
Romania	United Nations	29 May 61	406UNTS147	105845
Ethiopia	United Nations	14 Jun 61	406UNTS81	105840
Mexico	United Nations	18 Aug 61	404UNTS297	105817
Ghana	United Nations	29 Aug 61	406UNTS117	105843
India	United Nations	19 Feb 62	423UNTS3	106082
Multilateral		26 Mar 62	539UNTS67	107825
Multilateral		15 May 62	444UNTS3	106367
Multilateral		25 May 62	486UNTS103	107075
Multilateral		14 Jun 62	528UNTS33	107634
Multilateral		28 Sep 62	469UNTS169	106791
Multilateral		05 Oct 62	502UNTS225	107333
Multilateral		12 Dec 62	552UNTS15	108048
Multilateral		15 Jan 63	456UNTS409	106567
United Nations	United Arab Rep	08 Feb 63	453UNTS79	106520
Multilateral		20 Apr 63	495UNTS3	107239
Multilateral		25 May 63	479UNTS39	106947
Poland	United Nations	16 Jul 63	471UNTS3	106817
Multilateral		03 Dec 63	529UNTS217	107663
Multilateral		14 Dec 63	507UNTS149	107399
Italy	Eur Space Research	23 May 64	528UNTS75	107635
Multilateral		10 Jul 64	611UNTS7	108844
Belgium	Luxembourg	14 Jan 65	620UNTS3	108949

PARTY ONE	PARTY TWO	DATE	CITATION	NUMBER
Internal structure (Cont.)				
Multilateral		18 Mar 65	575UNTS159	108359
Multilateral		28 May 65	559UNTS273	108163
Other Unilat Decla	United Nations	31 Aug 65	557UNTS143	108132
Multilateral		04 Dec 65	571UNTS123	108303
Multilateral		08 Dec 65	600UNTS161	108680
Multilateral		31 Dec 65	616UNTS317	108904
Multilateral		12 May 66	563UNTS54	108204
Multilateral		27 May 66	637UNTS0	109121
Multilateral		14 Feb 67	634UNTS281	109068
Multilateral		27 Feb 67	590UNTS156	108552
Multilateral		04 May 67	595UNTS287	108623
Multilateral		27 Oct 67	608UNTS37	108811
Morocco	UNESCO (Educ/Cult)	18 Dec 67	0UNTS0	109221
Italy	United Nations	15 Jan 68	635UNTS11	109070
Czechoslovakia	Hungary	27 Feb 68	640UNTS49	109154
Multilateral		18 Mar 68	0UNTS0	109262
Multilateral		01 Aug 68	0UNTS0	109368
IGO status				
Multilateral		15 Jan 44	161UNTS281	200489
Multilateral		13 Feb 46	1UNTS15	100004
ILO (Labor Org)	Switzerland	11 Mar 46	15UNTS377	200103
Netherlands	ICJ (Int Court)	26 Jun 46	8UNTS61	100114
United Nations	Switzerland	01 Jul 46	1UNTS163	200008
Multilateral		06 Feb 47	97UNTS227	101352
France	ICAO (Civil Aviat)	14 Mar 47	94UNTS59	101306
Bulgaria	UNICEF (Children)	23 Aug 47	68UNTS223	200232
Finland	UNICEF (Children)	23 Aug 47	68UNTS224	200233
Hungary	UNICEF (Children)	28 Aug 47	68UNTS226	200234
Romania	UNICEF (Children)	28 Aug 47	68UNTS228	200235
Italy	UNICEF (Children)	06 Nov 47	68UNTS240	200236
Austria	UNICEF (Children)	07 Nov 47	68UNTS252	200237
Multilateral		06 Mar 48	289UNTS3	104214
Peru	ICAO (Civil Aviat)	22 Oct 48	95UNTS3	101315
WHO (World Health)	Switzerland	12 Jan 49	26UNTS331	200155
India	UNICEF (Children)	10 May 49	68UNTS96	100887
Pakistan	UNICEF (Children)	20 Jun 49	65UNTS60	100826
Afghanistan	WHO (World Health)	04 Dec 49	102UNTS117	101414
UNICEF (Children)	UK Great Britain	10 Feb 50	65UNTS86	100837
Ceylon (Sri Lanka)	WHO (World Health)	17 Feb 50	102UNTS309	200309
Chile	UNICEF (Children)	03 Mar 50	126UNTS119	101685
Korea, South	UNICEF (Children)	25 Mar 50	65UNTS171	200209
Indonesia	UNICEF (Children)	06 Apr 50	68UNTS254	200238
Ceylon (Sri Lanka)	UNICEF (Children)	07 Jun 50	68UNTS256	200239
Haiti	WHO (World Health)	27 Jun 50	110UNTS99	101504
WHO (World Health)	Venezuela	11 Sep 50	110UNTS237	101513
Iceland	WHO (World Health)	06 Oct 50	110UNTS127	101506
WHO (World Health)	Turkey	19 Oct 50	110UNTS215	101512
Multilateral		02 Nov 50	81UNTS160	101071
Peru	WHO (World Health)	10 Nov 50	110UNTS187	101510
Nicaragua	WHO (World Health)	10 Nov 50	110UNTS155	101508
Multilateral		24 Nov 50	81UNTS188	101072
Multilateral		15 Dec 50	76UNTS120	100985
Philippines	WHO (World Health)	28 Dec 50	110UNTS203	101511
United Nations	Yugoslavia	06 Jan 51	78UNTS165	101015
Multilateral		18 Jan 51	81UNTS233	101073
Ethiopia	ICAO (Civil Aviat)	02 Feb 51	96UNTS123	101333
Multilateral		15 Feb 51	81UNTS245	101074
Paraguay	WHO (World Health)	15 Feb 51	110UNTS171	101509
Israel	ICAO (Civil Aviat)	19 Feb 51	96UNTS141	101334
Israel	ILO (Labor Org)	19 Feb 51	100UNTS105	101391
ILO (Labor Org)	Syria	03 Mar 51	110UNTS69	101502
Multilateral		05 Mar 51	81UNTS261	101075
Indonesia	WHO (World Health)	28 Mar 51	103UNTS71	101425
Multilateral		28 Mar 51	181UNTS61	102399

PARTY ONE	PARTY TWO	DATE	CITATION	NUMBER
IGO status (Cont.)				
Jordan	ILO (Labor Org)	29 Mar 51	100UNTS247	200287
Jordan	United Nations	29 Mar 51	137UNTS267	200448
Jordan	WHO (World Health)	03 Apr 51	110UNTS297	200367
Multilateral		05 Apr 51	84UNTS299	101139
Mexico	ILO (Labor Org)	06 Apr 51	100UNTS131	101393
Ceylon (Sri Lanka)	ILO (Labor Org)	06 Apr 51	100UNTS235	200286
Peru	ILO (Labor Org)	13 Apr 51	100UNTS31	101385
Canada	ICAO (Civil Aviat)	14 Apr 51	96UNTS155	101335
ICAO (Civil Aviat)	Thailand	19 Apr 51	96UNTS181	101336
Ecuador	ILO (Labor Org)	19 Apr 51	100UNTS77	101389
Honduras	WHO (World Health)	20 Apr 51	110UNTS111	101505
Cuba	ILO (Labor Org)	21 Apr 51	99UNTS205	101382
Greece	ILO (Labor Org)	25 Apr 51	100UNTS93	101390
India	ILO (Labor Org)	26 Apr 51	100UNTS19	101384
WHO (World Health)	Yugoslavia	02 May 51	103UNTS117	101429
Colombia	WHO (World Health)	04 May 51	110UNTS83	101503
Pakistan	ILO (Labor Org)	16 May 51	100UNTS147	101394
Cambodia	WHO (World Health)	31 May 51	102UNTS279	200307
Iceland	ICAO (Civil Aviat)	07 Jun 51	96UNTS193	101337
United Nations	Thailand	11 Jun 51	90UNTS45	101225
Liberia	WHO (World Health)	11 Jun 51	103UNTS83	101426
WHO (World Health)	Uruguay	11 Jun 51	128UNTS251	101724
Multilateral		25 Jun 51	92UNTS27	101258
Israel	United Nations	25 Jun 51	97UNTS21	101344
ILO (Labor Org)	Vietnam, South	26 Jun 51	100UNTS223	200285
Multilateral		28 Jun 51	118UNTS154	101604
IBRD (World Bank)	Switzerland	29 Jun 51	216UNTS347	200529
Iraq	WHO (World Health)	01 Jul 51	110UNTS139	101507
Ethiopia	WHO (World Health)	02 Jul 51	103UNTS39	101422
ILO (Labor Org)	Thailand	11 Jul 51	100UNTS159	101395
Multilateral		27 Jul 51	97UNTS291	200273
Iran	UNICEF (Children)	02 Aug 51	247UNTS11	103457
Israel	WHO (World Health)	07 Aug 51	104UNTS213	101442
Jordan	UN Relief Palestin	20 Aug 51	120UNTS277	200394
Multilateral		05 Sep 51	173UNTS15	102256
UNICEF (Children)	Turkey	05 Sep 51	193UNTS55	102610
Iraq	ICAO (Civil Aviat)	18 Sep 51	108UNTS219	101475
WHO (World Health)	Vietnam, South	21 Sep 51	107UNTS63	200352
Korea, South	United Nations	21 Sep 51	104UNTS323	200322
Paraguay	United Nations	27 Sep 51	120UNTS105	101617
Bolivia	United Nations	01 Oct 51	104UNTS263	101447
Multilateral		01 Oct 51	104UNTS249	101446
UNICEF (Children)	UK Great Britain	02 Oct 51	104UNTS301	101448
Pakistan	WHO (World Health)	07 Oct 51	126UNTS101	101684
India	WHO (World Health)	11 Oct 51	118UNTS27	101594
Ecuador	WHO (World Health)	16 Oct 51	110UNTS263	101515
India	WHO (World Health)	16 Oct 51	109UNTS49	101490
United Nations	Uruguay	17 Oct 51	122UNTS29	101633
Iraq	UNICEF (Children)	10 Dec 51	126UNTS57	101682
Mexico	WHO (World Health)	17 Dec 51	124UNTS121	101670
India	WHO (World Health)	20 Dec 51	124UNTS109	101669
Multilateral		24 Dec 51	118UNTS290	200383
Austria	WHO (World Health)	10 Jan 52	131UNTS295	200438
Ceylon (Sri Lanka)	United Nations	21 Jan 52	118UNTS281	200382
Multilateral		23 Jan 52	127UNTS269	101708
WHO (World Health)	Spain	30 Jan 52	124UNTS259	200425
ICAO (Civil Aviat)	Yugoslavia	06 Feb 52	128UNTS97	101715
WHO (World Health)	UK Great Britain	07 Feb 52	121UNTS75	101627
Lebanon	ICAO (Civil Aviat)	14 Feb 52	128UNTS83	101714
Greece	United Nations	05 Mar 52	123UNTS3	101650
ICAO (Civil Aviat)	United Arab Rep	06 Mar 52	151UNTS111	101986
India	United Nations	02 Apr 52	126UNTS145	101687
Libya	UNICEF (Children)	05 Apr 52	133UNTS287	200441
India	WHO (World Health)	17 Apr 52	131UNTS241	101744
Liberia	UNICEF (Children)	17 Apr 52	133UNTS3	101773

PARTY ONE	PARTY TWO	DATE	CITATION	NUMBER
IGO status (Cont.)				
India	WHO (World Health)	19 Apr 52	131UNTS253	101745
Pakistan	United Nations	28 Apr 52	128UNTS191	101720
India	ICAO (Civil Aviat)	29 Apr 52	151UNTS123	101987
Norway	WHO (World Health)	09 May 52	131UNTS281	101747
UNICEF (Children)	United Arab Rep	18 May 52	324UNTS161	104684
Belgium	UNICEF (Children)	17 Jun 52	171UNTS249	102228
Multilateral		19 Jun 52	133UNTS165	101787
OAS (Am States)	USA (United States)	22 Jun 52	181UNTS147	102405
Australia	FAO (Food Agri)	07 Jul 52	184UNTS209	102449
Jordan	UNICEF (Children)	08 Jul 52	173UNTS353	200503
UNICEF (Children)	Syria	10 Jul 52	136UNTS17	101830
Chile	WHO (World Health)	11 Jul 52	137UNTS27	101846
India	WHO (World Health)	16 Jul 52	135UNTS291	101828
UNICEF (Children)	UK Great Britain	25 Jul 52	135UNTS37	101812
Japan	United Nations	25 Jul 52	135UNTS305	200443
Brazil	United Nations	04 Aug 52	135UNTS185	101820
Laos	UNICEF (Children)	15 Aug 52	161UNTS323	200491
Panama	United Nations	20 Aug 52	136UNTS3	101829
Multilateral		21 Aug 52	141UNTS129	101912
Jordan	WHO (World Health)	21 Aug 52	141UNTS341	200472
UNICEF (Children)	Vietnam, South	29 Aug 52	161UNTS335	200492
Italy	ILO (Labor Org)	04 Sep 52	178UNTS371	200505
ILO (Labor Org)	Uruguay	20 Sep 52	187UNTS25	102499
United Nations	Trieste	30 Sep 52	140UNTS11	101881
Multilateral		15 Oct 52	141UNTS96	101909
Japan	WHO (World Health)	26 Nov 52	204UNTS301	200521
Mexico	ICAO (Civil Aviat)	28 Nov 52	164UNTS15	102156
UNICEF (Children)	UK Great Britain	16 Dec 52	151UNTS359	102005
Multilateral		16 Dec 52	158UNTS407	102074
Multilateral		29 Dec 52	151UNTS317	102002
United Nations	Sweden	11 Feb 53	160UNTS3	102096
India	WHO (World Health)	11 Feb 53	163UNTS43	102140
Multilateral		26 Feb 53	161UNTS31	102120
Costa Rica	United Nations	27 Feb 53	161UNTS45	102121
Nepal	United Nations	02 Mar 53	161UNTS347	200493
United Nations	Yemen	07 Apr 53	163UNTS73	102142
Netherlands	United Nations	09 Apr 53	163UNTS89	102143
France	WHO (World Health)	30 Apr 53	174UNTS71	102278
ICAO (Civil Aviat)	Syria	28 May 53	173UNTS199	102267
Ecuador	United Nations	16 Jun 53	166UNTS289	102194
Ethiopia	United Nations	22 Jun 53	172UNTS93	102241
Cambodia	United Nations	24 Jun 53	168UNTS309	200500
UNICEF (Children)	UK Great Britain	07 Oct 53	180UNTS59	102375
Multilateral		09 Oct 53	190UNTS49	102557
Dominican Republic	United Nations	19 Nov 53	180UNTS45	102374
Japan	UNICEF (Children)	21 Nov 53	183UNTS297	200507
Pakistan	United Nations	25 Jan 54	185UNTS213	102472
United Nations	Venezuela	05 Mar 54	187UNTS9	102498
Liberia	United Nations	09 Mar 54	187UNTS61	102501
Guatemala	United Nations	10 Mar 54	191UNTS271	102587
Multilateral		20 Apr 54	189UNTS11	102539
UNICEF (Children)	Spain	07 May 54	190UNTS357	200515
Nepal	WHO (World Health)	13 May 54	204UNTS311	200522
Mexico	UNICEF (Children)	20 May 54	192UNTS3	102591
Multilateral		31 May 54	192UNTS20	102592
Multilateral		01 Jun 54	200UNTS235	200520
Multilateral		19 Aug 54	201UNTS51	102710
New Zealand	UNICEF (Children)	26 Aug 54	198UNTS173	102663
Multilateral		06 Oct 54	201UNTS75	102711
Multilateral		27 Oct 54	201UNTS95	102712
Multilateral		29 Oct 54	201UNTS115	102713
Lebanon	UN Relief Palestin	26 Nov 54	202UNTS123	102728
Multilateral		04 Apr 55	208UNTS239	102816
Taiwan	WHO (World Health)	21 Apr 55	210UNTS71	102835
Multilateral		25 May 55	264UNTS117	103791

PARTY ONE	PARTY TWO	DATE	CITATION	NUMBER
IGO status (Cont.)				
Multilateral		14 Jun 55	212UNTS263	200526
Multilateral		04 Jul 55	214UNTS10	102897
Iran	WHO (World Health)	04 Jul 55	227UNTS65	103131
Guatemala	UNICEF (Children)	22 Nov 55	221UNTS305	103012
Multilateral		02 Feb 56	227UNTS153	103137
Multilateral		10 Feb 56	228UNTS167	103150
Multilateral		10 Feb 56	228UNTS189	103151
Cambodia	UNICEF (Children)	28 Apr 56	136UNTS341	200446
Multilateral		31 May 56	251UNTS181	103541
Multilateral		08 Jun 56	247UNTS366	200541
Multilateral		14 Jun 56	265UNTS125	103809
Multilateral		26 Jun 56	253UNTS12	103573
Multilateral		26 Jun 56	321UNTS2	104650
Multilateral		02 Jul 56	248UNTS37	103484
Multilateral		02 Jul 56	540UNTS110	107846
Lebanon	UNICEF (Children)	03 Jul 56	324UNTS145	104683
UNICEF (Children)	Sudan	07 Aug 56	248UNTS307	200542
UNESCO (Educ/Cult)	UK Great Britain	09 Aug 56	256UNTS139	103624
Multilateral		05 Oct 56	251UNTS245	103544
Multilateral		05 Oct 56	251UNTS267	103545
Multilateral		21 Nov 56	253UNTS266	103588
UNESCO (Educ/Cult)	Tunisia	03 Jan 57	257UNTS21	103645
United Nations	United Arab Rep	08 Jan 57	257UNTS75	103650
Multilateral		23 Jan 57	259UNTS426	103701
Multilateral		17 Feb 57	271UNTS2	103907
Multilateral		01 Mar 57	264UNTS94	103790
Multilateral		28 Mar 57	271UNTS30	103908
Multilateral		09 Apr 57	274UNTS172	103965
Finland	USA (United States)	10 May 57	283UNTS43	104105
Multilateral		24 May 57	268UNTS270	103861
Finland	United Nations	27 Jun 57	271UNTS135	103913
United Nations	Sweden	01 Jul 57	271UNTS187	103914
Australia	FAO (Food Agri)	08 Jul 57	277UNTS315	104015
Norway	United Nations	09 Jul 57	271UNTS223	103917
Multilateral		09 Jul 57	274UNTS300	103972
Morocco	UNICEF (Children)	31 Jul 57	282UNTS99	104095
Burma	WHO (World Health)	20 Sep 57	282UNTS113	104096
Multilateral		05 Nov 57	285UNTS301	104155
Argentina	UNICEF (Children)	19 Nov 57	300UNTS229	104338
Lebanon	United Nations	20 Jan 58	286UNTS189	104166
Ghana	WHO (World Health)	21 Jan 58	307UNTS3	104437
Indonesia	WHO (World Health)	05 Feb 58	307UNTS15	104438
Multilateral		15 Mar 58	292UNTS273	104276
Israel	WHO (World Health)	11 Apr 58	307UNTS27	104439
Multilateral		19 Jun 58	306UNTS236	200550
WHO (World Health)	Sudan	21 Jun 58	307UNTS235	104453
Ghana	UNICEF (Children)	12 Aug 58	309UNTS103	104469
Germany, West	Norway	18 Nov 58	357UNTS205	105119
IAEA (Atom Energy)	Thailand	18 Mar 59	339UNTS307	104850
Morocco	UN Special Fund	04 Apr 59	354UNTS347	105069
Ghana	UN Special Fund	12 Aug 59	338UNTS203	104836
Iran	UN Special Fund	06 Oct 59	342UNTS89	104902
Poland	UN Special Fund	15 Oct 59	344UNTS29	104941
India	UN Special Fund	20 Oct 59	344UNTS143	104946
UN Special Fund	Yugoslavia	27 Oct 59	344UNTS159	104947
Ecuador	UN Special Fund	10 Nov 59	345UNTS3	104955
Greece	UN Special Fund	13 Nov 59	345UNTS171	104966
UN Special Fund	Turkey	20 Nov 59	345UNTS105	104963
UN Special Fund	United Arab Rep	25 Nov 59	345UNTS125	104964
Israel	UN Special Fund	01 Dec 59	345UNTS197	104968
Hague Private IL	Netherlands	01 Dec 59	510UNTS191	107414
Multilateral		03 Dec 59	348UNTS246	105003
Argentina	UN Special Fund	04 Dec 59	345UNTS263	104972
Jordan	UN Special Fund	15 Dec 59	346UNTS3	104974
Ceylon (Sri Lanka)	WHO (World Health)	21 Dec 59	349UNTS109	105011

PARTY ONE	PARTY TWO	DATE	CITATION	NUMBER
IGO status (Cont.)				
UN Special Fund	UK Great Britain	07 Jan 60	348UNTS177	105000
Peru	UN Special Fund	19 Jan 60	349UNTS83	105010
Pakistan	WHO (World Health)	20 Jan 60	351UNTS355	105034
Chile	UN Special Fund	22 Jan 60	351UNTS115	105020
Colombia	UN Special Fund	04 Feb 60	355UNTS257	105080
Bolivia	UN Special Fund	09 Feb 60	351UNTS203	105024
Cuba	UNICEF (Children)	11 Feb 60	349UNTS277	105014
Afghanistan	UN Special Fund	21 Feb 60	351UNTS93	105019
France	UN Special Fund	17 Mar 60	354UNTS119	105059
Italy	UN Special Fund	01 Apr 60	354UNTS261	105066
UN Special Fund	Tunisia	12 Apr 60	355UNTS289	105082
Libya	UN Special Fund	19 Apr 60	356UNTS11	105090
UN Special Fund	Sudan	21 Apr 60	356UNTS213	105097
UN Special Fund	Vietnam, South	29 Apr 60	357UNTS311	200567
Laos	UN Special Fund	30 Apr 60	361UNTS171	105179
Lebanon	UN Special Fund	07 May 60	360UNTS225	105160
Cambodia	WHO (World Health)	19 May 60	372UNTS193	105298
Multilateral		04 Jun 60	360UNTS208	105159
Iraq	UN Special Fund	19 Jun 60	376UNTS357	105389
Peru	ILO (Labor Org)	22 Jun 60	423UNTS165	106092
Kuwait	UN Special Fund	29 Jun 60	369UNTS419	200575
Multilateral		08 Jul 60	366UNTS310	105220
Ethiopia	UN Special Fund	13 Jul 60	368UNTS159	105240
WHO (World Health)	United Arab Rep	03 Aug 60	385UNTS3	105524
Jordan	WHO (World Health)	03 Aug 60	381UNTS133	105469
Laos	WHO (World Health)	04 Aug 60	373UNTS313	105322
WHO (World Health)	Tunisia	04 Aug 60	381UNTS335	105474
WHO (World Health)	Saudi Arabia	06 Sep 60	395UNTS169	105684
Lebanon	WHO (World Health)	08 Sep 60	387UNTS49	105557
Brazil	UN Special Fund	16 Sep 60	375UNTS3	105351
Taiwan	UN Special Fund	20 Sep 60	375UNTS29	105352
Indonesia	UN Special Fund	07 Oct 60	378UNTS141	105424
Liberia	UN Special Fund	11 Oct 60	376UNTS341	105388
El Salvador	UN Special Fund	24 Oct 60	377UNTS171	105400
WHO (World Health)	Upper Volta	15 Nov 60	383UNTS91	105496
UNICEF (Children)	Upper Volta	15 Nov 60	402UNTS33	105776
Nepal	UN Special Fund	17 Nov 60	380UNTS289	105461
Mali	UNICEF (Children)	17 Nov 60	402UNTS23	105775
Guatemala	UN Special Fund	17 Nov 60	383UNTS67	105495
Cambodia	UN Special Fund	24 Nov 60	382UNTS255	105487
Fed of Malaya	WHO (World Health)	25 Nov 60	387UNTS37	105556
WHO (World Health)	Yemen	03 Dec 60	395UNTS187	105685
Dahomey	WHO (World Health)	07 Dec 60	387UNTS277	105567
Congo (Brazzaville)	WHO (World Health)	12 Dec 60	399UNTS105	105737
Nepal	UNICEF (Children)	12 Dec 60	382UNTS273	105488
Honduras	UN Special Fund	20 Dec 60	383UNTS103	105497
Niger	WHO (World Health)	28 Dec 60	394UNTS195	105679
Burma	UN Special Fund	03 Jan 61	387UNTS219	105564
Costa Rica	UN Special Fund	10 Jan 61	389UNTS253	105597
UN Special Fund	Saudi Arabia	19 Jan 61	396UNTS27	105692
Nicaragua	UN Special Fund	20 Jan 61	387UNTS15	105555
Korea, South	WHO (World Health)	20 Jan 61	406UNTS269	200589
Chad	UN Special Fund	23 Jan 61	390UNTS69	105603
Multilateral		28 Jan 61	387UNTS202	105563
UN Special Fund	Somalia	28 Jan 61	388UNTS75	105573
Ivory Coast	WHO (World Health)	30 Jan 61	395UNTS205	105686
Gabon	UN Special Fund	02 Feb 61	387UNTS289	105568
WHO (World Health)	Togo	03 Feb 61	394UNTS207	105680
Chad	WHO (World Health)	03 Feb 61	394UNTS161	105676
Nigeria	UN Special Fund	10 Feb 61	390UNTS85	105604
Central Afri Rep	WHO (World Health)	13 Feb 61	394UNTS149	105675
Mexico	UN Special Fund	23 Feb 61	388UNTS151	105576
Cyprus	UN Special Fund	24 Feb 61	389UNTS3	105588
Austria	United Nations	27 Feb 61	394UNTS27	105666
Panama	UN Special Fund	09 Mar 61	396UNTS3	105691

PARTY ONE	PARTY TWO	DATE	CITATION	NUMBER
IGO status (Cont.)				
Cuba	UN Special Fund	10 Mar 61	390UNTS35	105601
Kuwait	WHO (World Health)	16 Mar 61	397UNTS315	200588
IDA (Devel Assoc)	United Nations	10 Apr 61	394UNTS221	200582
Mauritania	WHO (World Health)	17 Apr 61	396UNTS301	200587
Cyprus	UNICEF (Children)	19 Apr 61	394UNTS185	105678
Korea, South	UN Special Fund	21 Apr 61	394UNTS231	200583
Mali	WHO (World Health)	27 Apr 61	407UNTS66	105860
Gabon	WHO (World Health)	27 Apr 61	397UNTS215	105707
Ceylon (Sri Lanka)	UN Special Fund	03 May 61	395UNTS217	105687
Cameroon	UN Special Fund	13 Jun 61	397UNTS297	105713
Paraguay	UN Special Fund	22 Jun 61	399UNTS117	105738
UN Special Fund	Upper Volta	26 Jun 61	400UNTS3	105744
Philippines	UN Special Fund	28 Jun 61	399UNTS141	105739
Haiti	UN Special Fund	28 Jun 61	399UNTS171	105741
UNICEF (Children)	Saudi Arabia	04 Jul 61	413UNTS122	105947
Mali	UN Special Fund	21 Jul 61	401UNTS141	105768
Netherlands	Euratom	25 Jul 61	462UNTS313	106687
UN Special Fund	Yemen	02 Aug 61	402UNTS43	105777
Morocco	WHO (World Health)	09 Aug 61	412UNTS192	105932
Cameroon	UNICEF (Children)	12 Aug 61	402UNTS235	105788
WHO (World Health)	Somalia	17 Aug 61	423UNTS111	106088
Central Afri Rep	UNICEF (Children)	21 Aug 61	413UNTS48	105939
Poland	UNICEF (Children)	24 Aug 61	406UNTS95	105841
Chad	UNICEF (Children)	26 Aug 61	422UNTS231	106077
Ivory Coast	UN Special Fund	29 Aug 61	406UNTS129	105844
Iraq	WHO (World Health)	13 Sep 61	419UNTS69	106030
Multilateral		20 Sep 61	407UNTS52	105859
UN Special Fund	Sierra Leone	02 Oct 61	422UNTS131	106073
Malagasy	WHO (World Health)	13 Oct 61	421UNTS273	106064
Multilateral		16 Oct 61	410UNTS242	105908
Gabon	UNICEF (Children)	02 Nov 61	422UNTS241	106078
Multilateral		07 Nov 61	412UNTS258	105937
Mauritania	UN Special Fund	07 Nov 61	412UNTS240	105936
Congo (Brazzaville)	UN Special Fund	09 Nov 61	413UNTS58	105940
Malagasy	UNICEF (Children)	16 Nov 61	422UNTS251	106079
UN Special Fund	Venezuela	11 Dec 61	422UNTS149	106074
UN Special Fund	Senegal	16 Dec 61	425UNTS97	106121
Multilateral		27 Dec 61	425UNTS83	106120
Malagasy	UN Special Fund	05 Jan 62	419UNTS29	106028
Ivory Coast	UNICEF (Children)	10 Jan 62	422UNTS261	106080
Ethiopia	WHO (World Health)	11 Jan 62	423UNTS99	106087
Multilateral		17 Jan 62	419UNTS294	106033
Multilateral		20 Jan 62	429UNTS230	200596
UNICEF (Children)	Yemen	31 Jan 62	422UNTS271	106081
Multilateral		13 Feb 62	422UNTS288	200594
Multilateral		21 Feb 62	423UNTS151	106091
Niger	UN Special Fund	26 Feb 62	423UNTS83	106086
Multilateral		01 Mar 62	423UNTS122	106089
WHO (World Health)	Sudan	11 Mar 62	432UNTS325	106226
Nigeria	WHO (World Health)	27 Mar 62	429UNTS123	106194
Dahomey	UN Special Fund	28 Mar 62	424UNTS55	106099
UNICEF (Children)	Somalia	01 Apr 62	431UNTS75	106211
Congo (Brazzaville)	UNICEF (Children)	09 Apr 62	431UNTS65	106210
Multilateral		10 Apr 62	429UNTS78	106192
UNICEF (Children)	Sierra Leone	11 Apr 62	431UNTS55	106209
Multilateral		18 Apr 62	463UNTS44	106692
UN Special Fund	Uruguay	04 May 62	429UNTS143	106196
Multilateral		17 May 62	429UNTS46	106189
Dominican Republic	UN Special Fund	06 Jun 62	429UNTS169	106197
Libya	WHO (World Health)	16 Jun 62	437UNTS127	106301
WHO (World Health)	Sierra Leone	19 Jun 62	439UNTS151	106327
UN Special Fund	Syria	07 Jul 62	443UNTS3	106355
UN Special Fund	Tanganyika	17 Jul 62	435UNTS237	106281
WHO (World Health)	Senegal	06 Aug 62	435UNTS179	106279
Multilateral		12 Aug 62	443UNTS266	106365

PARTY ONE	PARTY TWO	DATE	CITATION	NUMBER
IGO status (Cont.)				
WHO (World Health)	Western Samoa	14 Aug 62	437UNTS317	200598
Indonesia	Netherlands	15 Aug 62	437UNTS273	106311
Multilateral		29 Aug 62	443UNTS280	106366
Iran	United Nations	05 Sep 62	442UNTS249	106353
Japan	UN Special Fund	31 Oct 62	444UNTS171	106368
Algeria	UN Special Fund	15 Nov 62	452UNTS243	106512
Multilateral		15 Nov 62	448UNTS50	106424
WHO (World Health)	Syria	18 Nov 62	480UNTS249	106972
Algeria	UNICEF (Children)	20 Nov 62	453UNTS151	106522
Multilateral		06 Dec 62	450UNTS240	106471
Cameroon	WHO (World Health)	08 Dec 62	451UNTS215	106496
Multilateral		12 Dec 62	457UNTS72	106578
Algeria	WHO (World Health)	20 Dec 62	463UNTS135	106698
Mauritania	UNICEF (Children)	19 Jan 63	452UNTS271	106514
Multilateral		21 Jan 63	453UNTS20	106517
UNICEF (Children)	Tanganyika	25 Jan 63	453UNTS249	106528
Multilateral		05 Feb 63	453UNTS36	106518
Multilateral		14 Feb 63	453UNTS168	106524
Multilateral		06 Mar 63	455UNTS386	106552
UN Special Fund	Uganda	22 Mar 63	456UNTS466	106572
Multilateral		18 Apr 63	463UNTS121	106697
Multilateral		06 May 63	463UNTS78	106694
Multilateral		09 May 63	463UNTS159	106700
Multilateral		22 May 63	483UNTS72	107007
Jamaica	UN Special Fund	22 May 63	489UNTS191	107140
Multilateral		24 May 63	466UNTS346	106754
Netherlands	UN Special Fund	24 May 63	466UNTS289	106750
UN Special Fund	Western Samoa	05 Jun 63	467UNTS463	200601
Mongolia	WHO (World Health)	21 Jun 63	472UNTS373	106848
Multilateral		23 Jul 63	471UNTS158	106831
Multilateral		31 Jul 63	472UNTS220	106842
Burundi	WHO (World Health)	08 Aug 63	477UNTS346	106928
Burundi	UN Special Fund	22 Aug 63	476UNTS49	106903
Multilateral		27 Aug 63	511UNTS210	107435
Multilateral		10 Sep 63	480UNTS100	106965
Jamaica	WHO (World Health)	25 Sep 63	481UNTS125	106980
Central Afri Rep	UN Special Fund	30 Oct 63	481UNTS247	106985
Multilateral		30 Oct 63	480UNTS180	106968
WHO (World Health)	Tanganyika	05 Nov 63	496UNTS193	107252
Multilateral		07 Nov 63	480UNTS232	106971
Multilateral		08 Nov 63	482UNTS286	106999
Multilateral		28 Jan 64	502UNTS321	107336
Multilateral		20 Feb 64	491UNTS30	107172
Netherlands	United Nations	27 May 64	548UNTS79	107971
Ireland	UN Special Fund	03 Jun 64	496UNTS205	107253
Rwanda	WHO (World Health)	22 Jun 64	514UNTS11	107440
WHO (World Health)	Trinidad/Tobago	23 Jun 64	503UNTS167	107342
Rwanda	WHO (World Health)	23 Jun 64	514UNTS157	107445
Multilateral		23 Jun 64	506UNTS108	107383
Multilateral		28 Jun 64	519UNTS14	107499
Multilateral		24 Oct 64	514UNTS220	200608
Multilateral		11 Nov 64	515UNTS94	107456
Malawi	WHO (World Health)	06 Jan 65	525UNTS165	107588
Malawi	WHO (World Health)	08 Jan 65	524UNTS281	107579
Multilateral		27 Jan 65	523UNTS102	107556
Multilateral		02 Feb 65	523UNTS256	107560
Multilateral		12 Feb 65	525UNTS148	107587
Multilateral		02 Jun 65	537UNTS348	200611
UN Special Fund	Spain	30 Jun 65	544UNTS159	107918
Poland	WHO (World Health)	26 Aug 65	552UNTS3	108047
Multilateral		13 Sep 65	547UNTS264	107962
Multilateral		21 Oct 65	547UNTS216	107959
United Nations	Zambia	23 Oct 65	549UNTS101	107993
Mongolia	UN Special Fund	26 Jan 66	552UNTS201	108055
WHO (World Health)	Singapore	28 Mar 66	562UNTS59	108195

PARTY ONE	PARTY TWO	DATE	CITATION	NUMBER
IGO status (Cont.)				
Bulgaria	UN Special Fund	26 May 66	563UNTS71	108205
Cyprus	WHO (World Health)	07 Oct 67	608UNTS327	108821
Barbados	UNICEF (Children)	30 Mar 68	637UNTS0	109123
Multilateral		24 Dec 68	0UNTS0	109369
Freedom of action				
Ethiopia	UNICEF (Children)	27 Apr 53	213UNTS169	102885
Multilateral		26 Oct 56	276UNTS3	103988
UNICEF (Children)	Trinidad/Tobago	08 Aug 63	473UNTS281	106865
Freedom of meeting				
Multilateral		06 Dec 51	425UNTS61	106119
France	WHO (World Health)	23 Jul 52	209UNTS231	102829
Multilateral		03 Feb 58	381UNTS165	105471
Multilateral		26 Jan 60	439UNTS249	106333
Multilateral		13 Dec 60	455UNTS204	106544
Multilateral		28 Sep 62	469UNTS169	106791
Niger	UNICEF (Children)	05 Dec 62	503UNTS195	107344
Jamaica	UNICEF (Children)	19 May 64	500UNTS75	107308
IGO obligations				
Colombia	WHO (World Health)	05 Jan 51	102UNTS139	101417
Multilateral		06 Dec 51	425UNTS61	106119
Multilateral		14 Dec 59	368UNTS237	105244
Multilateral		26 Jan 60	439UNTS249	106333
Multilateral		19 Jun 60	537UNTS214	107803
Multilateral		13 Dec 60	455UNTS204	106544
Security of the government				
UNICEF (Children)	Trinidad/Tobago	08 Aug 63	473UNTS281	106865
Iraq	UNICEF (Children)	03 Dec 63	482UNTS319	107001
Special status				
Multilateral		27 Dec 45	2UNTS39	100020
Multilateral		13 Feb 46	1UNTS15	100004
Netherlands	ICJ (Int Court)	26 Jun 46	8UNTS61	100114
United Nations	Switzerland	01 Jul 46	1UNTS163	200008
Multilateral		22 Jul 46	14UNTS185	100221
France	ICAO (Civil Aviat)	14 Mar 47	94UNTS59	101306
United Nations	USA (United States)	26 Jun 47	11UNTS11	100147
Bulgaria	UNICEF (Children)	23 Aug 47	68UNTS223	200232
Finland	UNICEF (Children)	23 Aug 47	68UNTS224	200233
Hungary	UNICEF (Children)	28 Aug 47	68UNTS226	200234
Romania	UNICEF (Children)	28 Aug 47	68UNTS228	200235
Multilateral		11 Oct 47	77UNTS143	100998
Italy	UNICEF (Children)	06 Nov 47	68UNTS240	200236
Austria	UNICEF (Children)	07 Nov 47	68UNTS252	200237
ICJ Option Clause	Honduras	02 Feb 48	15UNTS217	100236
Multilateral		06 Mar 48	289UNTS3	104214
Multilateral		30 Apr 48	119UNTS3	101609
Taiwan	USA (United States)	05 Aug 48	82UNTS109	101087
Greece	Italy	21 Sep 48	77UNTS259	101003
Peru	ICAO (Civil Aviat)	22 Oct 48	95UNTS3	101315
WHO (World Health)	Switzerland	12 Jan 49	26UNTS331	200155
Multilateral		28 Apr 49	83UNTS105	101105
Multilateral		05 May 49	87UNTS103	101168
Pan Am Health Org	WHO (World Health)	24 May 49	32UNTS387	200178
Multilateral		12 Aug 49	75UNTS31	100970
Multilateral		12 Aug 49	75UNTS85	100971
Multilateral		02 Sep 49	250UNTS12	103515
India	WHO (World Health)	09 Nov 49	67UNTS43	100865
Indonesia	UNICEF (Children)	06 Apr 50	68UNTS254	200238
Ceylon (Sri Lanka)	UNICEF (Children)	07 Jun 50	68UNTS256	200239
WHO (World Health)	United Arab Rep	25 Aug 50	92UNTS39	101259
WHO (World Health)	United Arab Rep	25 Mar 51	223UNTS87	103058
IBRD (World Bank)	Switzerland	29 Jun 51	216UNTS347	200529
Multilateral		20 Sep 51	200UNTS3	102691
UNICEF (Children)	United Arab Rep	18 May 52	324UNTS161	104684

PARTY ONE	PARTY TWO	DATE	CITATION	NUMBER
Special status (Cont.)				
Japan	United Nations	25 Jul 52	135UNTS305	200443
Chile	United Nations	16 Feb 53	314UNTS49	104541
ICAO (Civil Aviat)	United Arab Rep	27 Aug 53	215UNTS371	102925
Multilateral		19 Oct 53	207UNTS189	102807
Multilateral		11 Dec 53	191UNTS285	102588
United Nations	Thailand	26 May 54	260UNTS35	103703
France	UNESCO (Educ/Cult)	02 Jul 54	357UNTS3	105103
Mexico	ILO (Labor Org)	05 Jan 55	208UNTS225	102815
Multilateral		25 May 55	264UNTS117	103791
CERN (Nuc Resrch)	Switzerland	11 Jun 55	249UNTS405	200544
Denmark	WHO (World Health)	29 Jun 55	247UNTS168	103467
Multilateral		12 Oct 55	560UNTS3	108165
Multilateral		26 Oct 56	276UNTS3	103988
Mexico	ICAO (Civil Aviat)	20 Dec 56	497UNTS3	107259
Colombia	USA (United States)	09 Jan 57	462UNTS151	106676
Austria	IAEA (Atom Energy)	11 Dec 57	339UNTS110	104849
Ethiopia	United Nations	18 Jun 58	317UNTS101	104597
Jordan	United Nations	18 Nov 58	315UNTS125	104564
UK Great Britain	USA (United States)	16 Apr 59	343UNTS11	104917
United Nations	Vietnam, South	03 Jun 59	337UNTS361	200557
Multilateral		01 Jul 59	374UNTS147	105334
Multilateral		14 Dec 59	368UNTS253	105245
Multilateral		14 Dec 59	368UNTS237	105244
ICAO (Civil Aviat)	UN Special Fund	21 Apr 60	360UNTS367	200569
Peru	ILO (Labor Org)	22 Jun 60	423UNTS165	106092
Multilateral		28 Jul 60	394UNTS37	105667
Multilateral		13 Dec 60	523UNTS117	107557
Nepal	USA (United States)	09 Jun 61	421UNTS223	106061
ILO (Labor Org)	Thailand	30 Aug 61	422UNTS125	106072
Congo (Zaire)	United Nations	27 Nov 61	414UNTS229	105975
IAEA (Atom Energy)	UN Special Fund	29 Nov 61	415UNTS408	200593
Ethiopia	USA (United States)	06 Dec 61	433UNTS231	106246
Cyprus	USA (United States)	18 Jan 62	435UNTS3	106266
Ghana	USA (United States)	24 Jan 62	435UNTS23	106268
Multilateral		26 Mar 62	539UNTS67	107825
Denmark	USA (United States)	28 May 62	450UNTS215	106469
Multilateral		14 Jun 62	528UNTS33	107634
Germany, West	United Nations	28 Jun 62	434UNTS249	200597
Germany, West	USA (United States)	20 Nov 62	505UNTS263	107377
Ceylon (Sri Lanka)	ILO (Labor Org)	21 Nov 62	449UNTS263	106463
Malaysia	USA (United States)	28 Jan 63	473UNTS15	106850
Bulgaria	COMECON (Econ Aid)	30 Mar 63	506UNTS257	107389
Pakistan	United Nations	18 Apr 63	503UNTS25	107339
UN Special Fund	Trinidad/Tobago	06 May 63	463UNTS93	106695
Australia	United Nations	13 May 63	463UNTS187	106702
Thailand	USA (United States)	24 May 63	477UNTS123	106918
New Zealand	UN Special Fund	28 Jun 63	470UNTS3	106792
Italy	United Nations	26 Jul 63	472UNTS173	106840
UNICEF (Children)	Trinidad/Tobago	08 Aug 63	473UNTS281	106865
United Nations	Saudi Arabia	23 Aug 63	474UNTS155	106879
Colombia	United Nations	27 Aug 63	481UNTS3	106975
Mexico	IAEA (Atom Energy)	18 Dec 63	490UNTS361	107165
Iceland	USA (United States)	13 Feb 64	524UNTS235	107576
UNESCO (Educ/Cult)	Yugoslavia	27 Feb 64	489UNTS257	107143
Cyprus	United Nations	31 Mar 64	492UNTS57	107187
Taiwan	UNICEF (Children)	08 Apr 64	500UNTS49	107306
Jamaica	UNICEF (Children)	19 May 64	500UNTS75	107308
Netherlands	United Nations	27 May 64	548UNTS79	107971
IAEA (Atom Energy)	USA (United States)	15 Jun 64	525UNTS3	107580
Multilateral		15 Jun 64	573UNTS85	108324
Iceland	UN Special Fund	10 Jul 64	502UNTS343	107337
Rwanda	UNICEF (Children)	11 Sep 64	510UNTS127	107409
IAEA (Atom Energy)	United Arab Rep	17 Sep 64	525UNTS19	107581
Multilateral		25 Nov 64	587UNTS19	108507
Argentina	IAEA (Atom Energy)	02 Dec 64	525UNTS29	107582

PARTY ONE	PARTY TWO	DATE	CITATION	NUMBER
Special status (Cont.)				
Multilateral		08 Apr 65	533UNTS66	107733
Multilateral		26 Apr 65	533UNTS50	107732
Multilateral		12 May 65	534UNTS390	107769
Multilateral		25 May 65	535UNTS374	107791
Multilateral		18 Jun 65	573UNTS3	108320
Multilateral		23 Jun 65	548UNTS241	107981
Austria	Petrol Export Org	24 Jun 65	589UNTS135	108540
Morocco	IAEA (Atom Energy)	24 Sep 65	556UNTS109	108122
Afghanistan	IAEA (Atom Energy)	24 Sep 65	556UNTS101	108121
IAEA (Atom Energy)	Uruguay	24 Sep 65	556UNTS117	108123
IAEA (Atom Energy)	Turkey	08 Feb 66	573UNTS75	108323
Bulgaria	UNICEF (Children)	10 Mar 66	559UNTS13	108152
IAEA (Atom Energy)	USA (United States)	26 Sep 66	589UNTS3	108532
Philippines	IAEA (Atom Energy)	28 Sep 66	589UNTS25	108533
IAEA (Atom Energy)	USA (United States)	09 Dec 66	589UNTS55	108535
Multilateral		25 Jan 67	588UNTS212	108527
Greece	United Nations	14 Apr 67	595UNTS83	108613
Morocco	UNESCO (Educ/Cult)	18 Dec 67	0UNTS0	109221
Barbados	UNICEF (Children)	30 Mar 68	637UNTS0	109123
State/IGO Group	Sierra Leone	29 May 68	637UNTS0	109120
United Nations	United Arab Rep	14 Nov 68	0UNTS0	109371
Status of experts				
Mexico	USA (United States)	03 Feb 44	3UNTS313	200025
Multilateral		16 Nov 45	4UNTS275	100052
Multilateral		27 Dec 45	2UNTS39	100020
Multilateral		14 Jan 46	555UNTS69	108105
Multilateral		13 Feb 46	1UNTS15	100004
ILO (Labor Org)	Switzerland	11 Mar 46	15UNTS377	200103
Netherlands	ICJ (Int Court)	26 Jun 46	8UNTS61	100114
United Nations	Switzerland	01 Jul 46	1UNTS163	200008
Multilateral		22 Jul 46	14UNTS185	100221
FAO (Food Agri)	United Nations	03 Feb 47	1UNTS207	200010
France	ICAO (Civil Aviat)	14 Mar 47	94UNTS59	101306
Bulgaria	UNICEF (Children)	23 Aug 47	68UNTS223	200232
Finland	UNICEF (Children)	23 Aug 47	68UNTS224	200233
Poland	UNICEF (Children)	23 Aug 47	65UNTS22	100815
Hungary	UNICEF (Children)	28 Aug 47	68UNTS226	200234
Romania	UNICEF (Children)	28 Aug 47	68UNTS228	200235
Multilateral		11 Oct 47	77UNTS143	100998
Greece	UNICEF (Children)	14 Oct 47	102UNTS39	101409
Italy	UNICEF (Children)	06 Nov 47	68UNTS240	200236
Austria	UNICEF (Children)	07 Nov 47	68UNTS252	200237
UNICEF (Children)	Yugoslavia	20 Nov 47	65UNTS28	100817
Multilateral		21 Nov 47	33UNTS261	100521
Multilateral		30 Apr 48	119UNTS3	101609
Taiwan	UNICEF (Children)	21 May 48	65UNTS38	100818
Taiwan	USA (United States)	05 Aug 48	82UNTS109	101087
Philippines	USA (United States)	27 Aug 48	44UNTS13	100675
Korea, South	USA (United States)	11 Sep 48	89UNTS155	101216
Peru	ICAO (Civil Aviat)	22 Oct 48	95UNTS3	101315
Greece	USA (United States)	25 Oct 48	185UNTS103	102462
WHO (World Health)	Switzerland	12 Jan 49	26UNTS331	200155
Multilateral		28 Apr 49	83UNTS105	101105
Multilateral		05 May 49	87UNTS103	101168
India	UNICEF (Children)	10 May 49	68UNTS96	100887
Multilateral		02 Sep 49	250UNTS12	103515
Denmark	ICAO (Civil Aviat)	09 Sep 49	53UNTS341	100791
Korea, South	UNICEF (Children)	25 Mar 50	65UNTS171	200209
Indonesia	UNICEF (Children)	06 Apr 50	68UNTS254	200238
Ceylon (Sri Lanka)	UNICEF (Children)	07 Jun 50	68UNTS256	200239
WHO (World Health)	United Arab Rep	25 Mar 51	223UNTS87	103058
Multilateral		18 Apr 51	261UNTS140	103729
IBRD (World Bank)	Switzerland	29 Jun 51	216UNTS347	200529
Philippines	WHO (World Health)	22 Jul 51	149UNTS197	101953

PARTY ONE	PARTY TWO	DATE	CITATION	NUMBER
Status of experts (Cont.)				
India	United Nations	14 Aug 51	98UNTS115	101359
France	United Nations	17 Aug 51	122UNTS191	101647
Multilateral		20 Sep 51	200UNTS3	102691
Korea, South	United Nations	21 Sep 51	104UNTS323	200322
India	WHO (World Health)	11 Oct 51	118UNTS27	101594
UNICEF (Children)	UK Great Britain	04 Feb 52	120UNTS147	101620
Dominican Republic	UNICEF (Children)	15 Feb 52	121UNTS43	101625
Pakistan	WHO (World Health)	21 Feb 52	131UNTS221	101742
UNICEF (Children)	United Arab Rep	18 May 52	324UNTS161	104684
OAS (Am States)	USA (United States)	22 Jun 52	181UNTS147	102405
France	WHO (World Health)	23 Jul 52	209UNTS231	102829
Japan	United Nations	25 Jul 52	135UNTS305	200443
India	WHO (World Health)	11 Dec 52	158UNTS391	102073
Chile	United Nations	16 Feb 53	314UNTS49	104541
ICAO (Civil Aviat)	United Arab Rep	27 Aug 53	215UNTS371	102925
Multilateral		19 Oct 53	207UNTS189	102807
United Nations	Thailand	26 May 54	260UNTS35	103703
France	UNESCO (Educ/Cult)	02 Jul 54	357UNTS3	105103
Mexico	ILO (Labor Org)	05 Jan 55	208UNTS225	102815
WMO (Meteorology)	Switzerland	10 Mar 55	211UNTS277	200524
Multilateral		25 May 55	264UNTS117	103791
CERN (Nuc Resrch)	Switzerland	11 Jun 55	249UNTS405	200544
Denmark	WHO (World Health)	29 Jun 55	247UNTS168	103467
Libya	WHO (World Health)	05 Jul 55	219UNTS305	200530
Multilateral		12 Oct 55	560UNTS3	108165
Indonesia	United Nations	17 Apr 56	233UNTS267	103266
Mexico	ICAO (Civil Aviat)	20 Dec 56	497UNTS3	107259
Multilateral		12 Apr 57	443UNTS128	106362
Ethiopia	United Nations	18 Jun 58	317UNTS101	104597
Burma	United Nations	15 Dec 58	319UNTS3	104629
United Nations	Tunisia	23 Dec 58	321UNTS23	104651
Ghana	United Nations	27 Feb 59	324UNTS133	104682
United Nations	Sudan	28 Mar 59	327UNTS95	104719
Libya	United Nations	27 Jun 59	336UNTS291	104811
Multilateral		01 Jul 59	374UNTS147	105334
Paraguay	United Nations	01 Aug 59	341UNTS319	104894
Guinea	United Nations	15 Oct 59	344UNTS47	104942
Afghanistan	United Nations	24 Nov 59	397UNTS187	105705
Guinea	UN Special Fund	02 Dec 59	345UNTS215	104969
Multilateral		14 Dec 59	368UNTS253	105245
United Nations	Togo	06 May 60	388UNTS53	105571
Peru	ILO (Labor Org)	22 Jun 60	423UNTS165	106092
Ethiopia	United Nations	13 Jul 60	368UNTS143	105239
Multilateral		28 Jul 60	394UNTS37	105667
Multilateral		19 Sep 60	419UNTS125	106032
Kuwait	United Nations	31 Oct 60	391UNTS295	200581
Pakistan	United Nations	17 Nov 60	380UNTS277	105460
Cambodia	United Nations	30 Nov 60	383UNTS147	105500
Multilateral		13 Dec 60	523UNTS117	107557
Bolivia	United Nations	14 Dec 60	382UNTS283	105489
Iraq	United Nations	05 Mar 61	409UNTS56	105878
Multilateral		14 Apr 61	422UNTS101	106071
Cyprus	United Nations	15 Jun 61	398UNTS39	105716
Haiti	United Nations	28 Jun 61	399UNTS159	105740
Mexico	United Nations	18 Aug 61	404UNTS297	105817
Lebanon	United Nations	26 Aug 61	406UNTS105	105842
Ceylon (Sri Lanka)	United Nations	04 Dec 61	415UNTS236	105987
United Nations	Somalia	20 Jan 62	420UNTS133	106044
India	United Nations	19 Feb 62	423UNTS3	106082
United Nations	Saudi Arabia	16 Mar 62	456UNTS379	106566
Greece	United Nations	18 May 62	429UNTS61	106190
Multilateral		14 Jun 62	528UNTS33	107634
Germany, West	United Nations	28 Jun 62	434UNTS249	200597
Nigeria	United Nations	07 Aug 62	435UNTS167	106278
Cameroon	United Nations	29 Aug 62	442UNTS3	106334

PARTY ONE	PARTY TWO	DATE	CITATION	NUMBER
Status of experts (Cont.)				
Iran	United Nations	05 Sep 62	442UNTS249	106353
Multilateral		11 Sep 62	455UNTS402	106553
Niger	United Nations	01 Oct 62	439UNTS181	106329
United Nations	Western Samoa	05 Nov 62	443UNTS297	200599
United Nations	Syria	17 Nov 62	456UNTS359	106565
Germany, West	USA (United States)	20 Nov 62	505UNTS263	107377
Ceylon (Sri Lanka)	ILO (Labor Org)	21 Nov 62	449UNTS263	106463
Ecuador	United Nations	26 Nov 62	445UNTS3	106372
Rwanda	United Nations	28 Nov 62	450UNTS267	106473
Ivory Coast	United Nations	10 Dec 62	451UNTS269	106498
Israel	United Nations	07 Jan 63	450UNTS229	106470
United Nations	Trinidad/Tobago	06 May 63	463UNTS109	106696
Jamaica	United Nations	22 May 63	479UNTS19	106945
United Nations	Uganda	29 May 63	466UNTS311	106751
New Zealand	UN Special Fund	28 Jun 63	470UNTS3	106792
Dominican Republic	United Nations	05 Aug 63	472UNTS353	106847
Burundi	WHO (World Health)	30 Aug 63	490UNTS423	107169
Niger	United Nations	20 Nov 63	536UNTS3	107793
Nicaragua	United Nations	03 Dec 63	482UNTS329	107002
Mexico	IAEA (Atom Energy)	18 Dec 63	490UNTS361	107165
Cyprus	United Nations	30 Mar 64	492UNTS261	107194
Cyprus	United Nations	31 Mar 64	492UNTS57	107187
Greece	United Nations	31 Mar 64	492UNTS267	107195
United Nations	Turkey	31 Mar 64	492UNTS273	107196
United Nations	UK Great Britain	02 Apr 64	492UNTS279	107197
Austria	United Nations	11 Jun 64	500UNTS85	107309
Multilateral		15 Jun 64	573UNTS85	108324
Argentina	IAEA (Atom Energy)	02 Dec 64	525UNTS29	107582
Multilateral		11 Dec 64	547UNTS297	107964
Multilateral		02 Jun 65	551UNTS2	108030
Multilateral		18 Jun 65	573UNTS3	108320
Multilateral		23 Jun 65	548UNTS241	107981
Austria	Petrol Export Org	24 Jun 65	589UNTS135	108540
IAEA (Atom Energy)	Uruguay	24 Sep 65	556UNTS117	108123
Afghanistan	IAEA (Atom Energy)	24 Sep 65	556UNTS101	108121
Morocco	IAEA (Atom Energy)	24 Sep 65	556UNTS109	108122
Chile	UNICEF (Children)	30 Nov 65	596UNTS215	108635
United Nations	Senegal	12 Jan 66	551UNTS147	108039
IAEA (Atom Energy)	Turkey	08 Feb 66	573UNTS75	108323
Canada	United Nations	21 Feb 66	555UNTS119	108107
Denmark	United Nations	21 Feb 66	555UNTS151	108108
New Zealand	United Nations	21 Feb 66	555UNTS163	108110
Finland	United Nations	21 Feb 66	555UNTS157	108109
UN Special Fund	Singapore	23 Sep 66	573UNTS115	108326
IAEA (Atom Energy)	USA (United States)	26 Sep 66	589UNTS3	108532
Philippines	IAEA (Atom Energy)	28 Sep 66	589UNTS25	108533
IAEA (Atom Energy)	USA (United States)	09 Dec 66	589UNTS55	108535
Finland	United Nations	16 Jan 67	588UNTS153	108522
Multilateral		25 Jan 67	588UNTS212	108527
Nigeria	United Nations	07 Feb 67	590UNTS25	108544
Greece	United Nations	14 Apr 67	595UNTS83	108613
Multilateral		20 Jun 67	0UNTS0	109290
Multilateral		21 Jun 67	598UNTS2	108653
Multilateral		27 Oct 67	608UNTS37	108811
Barbados	UNICEF (Children)	30 Mar 68	637UNTS0	109123
Austria	United Nations	25 May 68	637UNTS0	109117
Austria	United Nations	25 May 68	637UNTS0	109118
Ghana	United Nations	19 Sep 68	0UNTS0	109250
Austria	United Nations	24 Sep 68	0UNTS0	109253
United Nations	United Arab Rep	14 Nov 68	0UNTS0	109371
Multilateral		24 Dec 68	0UNTS0	109369
IGO operations				
Multilateral		07 Dec 44	171UNTS345	200501
Multilateral		15 Dec 50	160UNTS267	102111

PARTY ONE	PARTY TWO	DATE	CITATION	NUMBER
IGO operations (Cont.)				
Netherlands	IRO (Refugee Org)	13 Feb 51	87UNTS239	101175
Multilateral		20 Mar 51	82UNTS172	101091
Mexico	United Nations	20 May 51	102UNTS103	101413
Colombia	United Nations	17 Jul 52	135UNTS61	101815
Brazil	United Nations	04 Aug 52	135UNTS185	101820
ICJ Option Clause	Laos	24 Oct 52	149UNTS285	101957
Multilateral		01 Jul 53	200UNTS149	102701
Guinea	UN Special Fund	02 Dec 59	345UNTS215	104969
Multilateral		23 Mar 62	434UNTS145	106262
Multilateral		19 Oct 63	523UNTS249	107559
IAEA (Atom Energy)	UK Great Britain	20 Jun 66	588UNTS269	108531
Guyana	United Nations	22 Aug 66	571UNTS305	200625
Multilateral		30 Sep 66	576UNTS8	108361
Romania	United Nations	08 Apr 67	594UNTS159	108602
FAO (Food Agri)	UK Great Britain	13 Jul 67	642UNTS263	109179
State/IGO Group	Sierra Leone	29 May 68	637UNTS0	109120
Conformity with IGO decisions				
Brazil	Paraguay	08 Oct 42	65UNTS191	200211
UK Great Britain	USSR (Soviet Union)	23 Sep 44	10UNTS171	200060
South Africa	UK Great Britain	24 Aug 46	51UNTS187	100765
Multilateral		13 Dec 46	8UNTS119	100118
Multilateral		13 Dec 46	8UNTS71	100115
Greece	UNICEF (Children)	14 Oct 47	102UNTS39	101409
Multilateral		17 Sep 48	97UNTS31	101345
Multilateral		08 Feb 49	157UNTS157	102053
Multilateral		20 Jun 49	128UNTS141	101718
Belgium	UK Great Britain	07 Sep 49	106UNTS61	101457
Afghanistan	WHO (World Health)	04 Dec 49	102UNTS117	101414
Afghanistan	India	14 Dec 49	53UNTS95	100774
Ceylon (Sri Lanka)	WHO (World Health)	17 Feb 50	102UNTS309	200309
Canada	USA (United States)	12 Jun 50	127UNTS67	101700
FAO (Food Agri)	United Nations	02 Aug 50	139UNTS407	200467
ILO (Labor Org)	United Nations	12 Oct 50	139UNTS395	200466
Multilateral		02 Nov 50	81UNTS160	101071
Multilateral		24 Nov 50	81UNTS188	101072
Multilateral		15 Dec 50	76UNTS120	100985
United Nations	Yugoslavia	06 Jan 51	78UNTS165	101015
Ceylon (Sri Lanka)	ILO (Labor Org)	24 Jan 51	117UNTS355	200380
Ethiopia	ICAO (Civil Aviat)	02 Feb 51	96UNTS123	101333
Multilateral		15 Feb 51	81UNTS245	101074
Israel	ICAO (Civil Aviat)	19 Feb 51	96UNTS141	101334
Israel	ILO (Labor Org)	19 Feb 51	100UNTS105	101391
ICAO (Civil Aviat)	United Nations	28 Feb 51	139UNTS429	200469
ILO (Labor Org)	Syria	03 Mar 51	110UNTS69	101502
Multilateral		05 Mar 51	81UNTS261	101075
UNESCO (Educ/Cult)	United Nations	07 Mar 51	139UNTS417	200468
Multilateral		28 Mar 51	181UNTS61	102399
Jordan	ILO (Labor Org)	29 Mar 51	100UNTS247	200287
Jordan	United Nations	29 Mar 51	137UNTS267	200448
Liberia	ILO (Labor Org)	02 Apr 51	100UNTS117	101392
Multilateral		05 Apr 51	84UNTS299	101139
Mexico	ILO (Labor Org)	06 Apr 51	100UNTS131	101393
Ceylon (Sri Lanka)	ILO (Labor Org)	06 Apr 51	100UNTS235	200286
Guatemala	ILO (Labor Org)	13 Apr 51	126UNTS249	101692
Peru	ILO (Labor Org)	13 Apr 51	100UNTS31	101385
ICAO (Civil Aviat)	Thailand	19 Apr 51	96UNTS181	101336
Ecuador	ILO (Labor Org)	19 Apr 51	100UNTS77	101389
Cuba	ILO (Labor Org)	21 Apr 51	99UNTS205	101382
Greece	ILO (Labor Org)	25 Apr 51	100UNTS93	101390
India	ILO (Labor Org)	26 Apr 51	100UNTS19	101384
Mexico	WHO (World Health)	30 Apr 51	103UNTS95	101427
WHO (World Health)	Yugoslavia	02 May 51	103UNTS117	101429
Pakistan	ILO (Labor Org)	16 May 51	100UNTS147	101394
Iceland	ICAO (Civil Aviat)	07 Jun 51	96UNTS193	101337

Conformity with IGO decisions (Cont.)

PARTY ONE	PARTY TWO	DATE	CITATION	NUMBER
Lebanon	WHO (World Health)	07 Jun 51	126UNTS221	101690
United Nations	Thailand	11 Jun 51	90UNTS45	101225
Dominican Republic	ILO (Labor Org)	18 Jun 51	100UNTS3	101383
Multilateral		25 Jun 51	92UNTS27	101258
Israel	United Nations	25 Jun 51	97UNTS21	101344
ILO (Labor Org)	Vietnam, South	26 Jun 51	100UNTS223	200285
Multilateral		28 Jun 51	118UNTS154	101604
Ethiopia	WHO (World Health)	02 Jul 51	103UNTS39	101422
ILO (Labor Org)	Thailand	11 Jul 51	100UNTS159	101395
Paraguay	ILO (Labor Org)	12 Jul 51	117UNTS155	101591
Multilateral		27 Jul 51	97UNTS291	200273
Israel	WHO (World Health)	07 Aug 51	104UNTS213	101442
WHO (World Health)	Saudi Arabia	29 Aug 51	110UNTS277	101516
Multilateral		05 Sep 51	173UNTS15	102256
Iraq	ICAO (Civil Aviat)	18 Sep 51	108UNTS219	101475
Paraguay	United Nations	27 Sep 51	120UNTS105	101617
Bolivia	United Nations	01 Oct 51	104UNTS263	101447
Multilateral		01 Oct 51	104UNTS249	101446
Pakistan	WHO (World Health)	07 Oct 51	126UNTS101	101684
India	WHO (World Health)	16 Oct 51	109UNTS49	101490
United Nations	Uruguay	17 Oct 51	122UNTS29	101633
ILO (Labor Org)	Venezuela	22 Oct 51	117UNTS139	101590
Panama	ILO (Labor Org)	10 Nov 51	126UNTS269	101693
Multilateral		24 Dec 51	118UNTS290	200383
Austria	WHO (World Health)	10 Jan 52	131UNTS295	200438
Ceylon (Sri Lanka)	United Nations	21 Jan 52	118UNTS281	200382
Multilateral		23 Jan 52	127UNTS269	101708
WHO (World Health)	Spain	30 Jan 52	124UNTS259	200425
UNICEF (Children)	UK Great Britain	04 Feb 52	120UNTS147	101620
ICAO (Civil Aviat)	Yugoslavia	06 Feb 52	128UNTS97	101715
WHO (World Health)	UK Great Britain	07 Feb 52	121UNTS75	101627
Lebanon	ICAO (Civil Aviat)	14 Feb 52	128UNTS83	101714
Dominican Republic	UNICEF (Children)	15 Feb 52	121UNTS43	101625
Multilateral		18 Feb 52	126UNTS319	200434
Greece	United Nations	05 Mar 52	123UNTS3	101650
ICAO (Civil Aviat)	United Arab Rep	06 Mar 52	151UNTS111	101986
India	United Nations	02 Apr 52	126UNTS145	101687
Denmark	USA (United States)	04 Apr 52	177UNTS13	102305
Multilateral		11 Apr 52	173UNTS2	102255
India	WHO (World Health)	17 Apr 52	131UNTS241	101744
India	WHO (World Health)	19 Apr 52	131UNTS253	101745
Pakistan	United Nations	28 Apr 52	128UNTS191	101720
India	ICAO (Civil Aviat)	29 Apr 52	151UNTS123	101987
Multilateral		22 May 52	131UNTS115	101739
Germany, West	USA (United States)	11 Jun 52	273UNTS105	103947
Mexico	UK Great Britain	12 Jun 52	196UNTS149	102622
Multilateral		19 Jun 52	133UNTS165	101787
Multilateral		11 Jul 52	171UNTS89	102225
Multilateral		11 Jul 52	169UNTS3	102220
Multilateral		11 Jul 52	171UNTS191	102227
Multilateral		11 Jul 52	171UNTS3	102224
Multilateral		11 Jul 52	171UNTS143	102226
Chile	WHO (World Health)	11 Jul 52	137UNTS27	101846
India	WHO (World Health)	16 Jul 52	135UNTS291	101828
Chile	ILO (Labor Org)	23 Jul 52	178UNTS323	102348
Panama	United Nations	20 Aug 52	136UNTS3	101829
Italy	ILO (Labor Org)	04 Sep 52	178UNTS371	200505
ILO (Labor Org)	Uruguay	20 Sep 52	187UNTS25	102499
United Nations	Trieste	30 Sep 52	140UNTS11	101881
Multilateral		15 Oct 52	141UNTS96	101909
Multilateral		17 Oct 52	141UNTS121	101911
Mexico	ICAO (Civil Aviat)	28 Nov 52	164UNTS15	102156
Multilateral		16 Dec 52	158UNTS407	102074
Multilateral		29 Dec 52	151UNTS317	102002
ILO (Labor Org)	UN Relief Palestin	31 Dec 52	182UNTS201	200506

Conformity with IGO decisions (Cont.)

PARTY ONE	PARTY TWO	DATE	CITATION	NUMBER
Taiwan	ILO (Labor Org)	13 Feb 53	178UNTS337	102349
Costa Rica	United Nations	27 Feb 53	161UNTS45	102121
Germany, West	USA (United States)	27 Feb 53	223UNTS167	103065
Nepal	United Nations	02 Mar 53	161UNTS347	200493
United Nations	WMO (Meteorology)	27 Mar 53	178UNTS361	200504
France	WHO (World Health)	02 Apr 53	174UNTS83	102279
United Nations	Yemen	07 Apr 53	163UNTS73	102142
Syria	Turkey	28 Apr 53	204UNTS255	102760
France	WHO (World Health)	30 Apr 53	174UNTS71	102278
ICAO (Civil Aviat)	Syria	28 May 53	173UNTS199	102267
Ecuador	United Nations	16 Jun 53	166UNTS289	102194
Ethiopia	United Nations	22 Jun 53	172UNTS93	102241
Cambodia	United Nations	24 Jun 53	168UNTS309	200500
Japan	United Nations	24 Jun 53	167UNTS249	200499
Multilateral		09 Oct 53	190UNTS49	102557
Multilateral		19 Oct 53	207UNTS189	102807
Dominican Republic	United Nations	19 Nov 53	180UNTS45	102374
Brazil	WHO (World Health)	04 Feb 54	233UNTS49	103250
Syria	UK Great Britain	05 Feb 54	204UNTS267	102761
United Nations	Venezuela	05 Mar 54	187UNTS9	102498
Liberia	United Nations	09 Mar 54	187UNTS61	102501
Guatemala	United Nations	10 Mar 54	191UNTS271	102587
Multilateral		20 Apr 54	189UNTS11	102539
Nepal	WHO (World Health)	13 May 54	204UNTS311	200522
United Nations	Thailand	26 May 54	260UNTS35	103703
Multilateral		31 May 54	192UNTS20	102592
Multilateral		01 Jun 54	200UNTS235	200520
Multilateral		30 Jun 54	193UNTS67	102611
Multilateral		19 Aug 54	201UNTS51	102710
Multilateral		06 Oct 54	201UNTS75	102711
Multilateral		27 Oct 54	201UNTS95	102712
Multilateral		29 Oct 54	201UNTS115	102713
Multilateral		16 Dec 54	204UNTS323	200523
Multilateral		04 Apr 55	208UNTS239	102816
Multilateral		25 May 55	264UNTS117	103791
Multilateral		14 Jun 55	212UNTS263	200526
Multilateral		04 Jul 55	214UNTS10	102897
Iran	WHO (World Health)	04 Jul 55	227UNTS65	103131
Germany, East	Romania	28 Jul 55	342UNTS207	104909
Multilateral		20 Oct 55	378UNTS159	105425
Multilateral		13 Dec 55	529UNTS141	107660
Multilateral		02 Feb 56	227UNTS153	103137
Multilateral		10 Feb 56	228UNTS189	103151
Multilateral		10 Feb 56	228UNTS167	103150
Indonesia	United Nations	17 Apr 56	233UNTS267	103266
Multilateral		31 May 56	251UNTS181	103541
Multilateral		08 Jun 56	247UNTS366	200541
Multilateral		14 Jun 56	265UNTS125	103809
Multilateral		26 Jun 56	253UNTS12	103573
Multilateral		26 Jun 56	321UNTS2	104650
Multilateral		02 Jul 56	540UNTS110	107846
Multilateral		02 Jul 56	248UNTS37	103484
Multilateral		31 Aug 56	249UNTS158	103506
India	Poland	29 Sep 56	276UNTS305	103993
Multilateral		05 Oct 56	251UNTS267	103545
Multilateral		05 Oct 56	251UNTS245	103544
Multilateral		21 Nov 56	253UNTS266	103588
Multilateral		15 Jan 57	376UNTS122	105378
Multilateral		23 Jan 57	259UNTS426	103701
Multilateral		17 Feb 57	271UNTS2	103907
IBRD (World Bank)	United Nations	20 Feb 57	265UNTS312	200546
Multilateral		01 Mar 57	264UNTS94	103790
Multilateral		28 Mar 57	271UNTS30	103908
Multilateral		09 Apr 57	274UNTS172	103965
Finland	USA (United States)	10 May 57	283UNTS43	104105

Conformity with IGO decisions (Cont.)

PARTY ONE	PARTY TWO	DATE	CITATION	NUMBER
Multilateral		24 May 57	268UNTS270	103861
Italy	USA (United States)	03 Jul 57	308UNTS195	104462
Multilateral		09 Jul 57	274UNTS300	103972
Burma	WHO (World Health)	20 Sep 57	282UNTS113	104096
Multilateral		03 Oct 57	366UNTS255	105219
Multilateral		03 Oct 57	366UNTS193	105218
Multilateral		03 Oct 57	366UNTS141	105217
Multilateral		03 Oct 57	366UNTS3	105215
Multilateral		03 Oct 57	365UNTS207	105214
Multilateral		03 Oct 57	365UNTS3	105213
Multilateral		05 Nov 57	285UNTS301	104155
Ghana	WHO (World Health)	21 Jan 58	307UNTS3	104437
Multilateral		03 Feb 58	381UNTS165	105471
Indonesia	WHO (World Health)	05 Feb 58	307UNTS15	104438
Multilateral		15 Mar 58	292UNTS273	104276
Israel	WHO (World Health)	11 Apr 58	307UNTS27	104439
WHO (World Health)	Sudan	21 Jun 58	307UNTS235	104453
IAEA (Atom Energy)	United Nations	22 Sep 58	313UNTS323	200552
Burma	United Nations	15 Dec 58	319UNTS3	104629
United Nations	Tunisia	23 Dec 58	321UNTS23	104651
IMCO (Maritime Org)	United Nations	13 Jan 59	324UNTS273	200553
Ghana	United Nations	27 Feb 59	324UNTS133	104682
IAEA (Atom Energy)	Thailand	18 Mar 59	339UNTS307	104850
United Nations	Sudan	28 Mar 59	327UNTS95	104719
Libya	United Nations	27 Jun 59	336UNTS291	104811
Laos	United Nations	06 Jul 59	337UNTS41	104814
Paraguay	United Nations	01 Aug 59	341UNTS319	104894
Guinea	United Nations	15 Oct 59	344UNTS47	104942
Afghanistan	United Nations	24 Nov 59	397UNTS187	105705
Multilateral		03 Dec 59	348UNTS246	105003
Multilateral		14 Dec 59	368UNTS253	105245
Ceylon (Sri Lanka)	WHO (World Health)	21 Dec 59	349UNTS109	105011
Pakistan	WHO (World Health)	20 Jan 60	351UNTS355	105034
Multilateral		12 Apr 60	359UNTS323	105150
Laos	UN Special Fund	30 Apr 60	361UNTS171	105179
United Nations	Togo	06 May 60	388UNTS53	105571
Lebanon	UN Special Fund	07 May 60	360UNTS225	105160
Cambodia	WHO (World Health)	19 May 60	372UNTS193	105298
Multilateral		04 Jun 60	360UNTS208	105159
Multilateral		08 Jul 60	366UNTS310	105220
Ethiopia	United Nations	13 Jul 60	368UNTS143	105239
Ethiopia	UN Special Fund	13 Jul 60	368UNTS159	105240
WHO (World Health)	United Arab Rep	03 Aug 60	385UNTS3	105524
Jordan	WHO (World Health)	03 Aug 60	381UNTS133	105469
Laos	WHO (World Health)	04 Aug 60	373UNTS313	105322
WHO (World Health)	Tunisia	04 Aug 60	381UNTS335	105474
WHO (World Health)	Saudi Arabia	06 Sep 60	395UNTS169	105684
Lebanon	WHO (World Health)	08 Sep 60	387UNTS49	105557
Brazil	UN Special Fund	16 Sep 60	375UNTS3	105351
Taiwan	UN Special Fund	20 Sep 60	375UNTS29	105352
WHO (World Health)	Upper Volta	15 Nov 60	383UNTS91	105496
Pakistan	United Nations	17 Nov 60	380UNTS277	105460
Fed of Malaya	WHO (World Health)	25 Nov 60	387UNTS37	105556
Cambodia	United Nations	30 Nov 60	383UNTS147	105500
WHO (World Health)	Yemen	03 Dec 60	395UNTS187	105685
Dahomey	WHO (World Health)	07 Dec 60	387UNTS277	105567
Congo (Brazzaville)	WHO (World Health)	12 Dec 60	399UNTS105	105737
Bolivia	United Nations	14 Dec 60	382UNTS283	105489
Niger	WHO (World Health)	28 Dec 60	394UNTS195	105679
Korea, South	WHO (World Health)	20 Jan 61	406UNTS269	200589
Multilateral		23 Jan 61	530UNTS141	107679
Multilateral		28 Jan 61	387UNTS202	105563
Ivory Coast	WHO (World Health)	30 Jan 61	395UNTS205	105686
WHO (World Health)	Togo	03 Feb 61	394UNTS207	105680
Chad	WHO (World Health)	03 Feb 61	394UNTS161	105676

Conformity with IGO decisions (Cont.)

PARTY ONE	PARTY TWO	DATE	CITATION	NUMBER
Central Afri Rep	WHO (World Health)	13 Feb 61	394UNTS149	105675
Iraq	United Nations	05 Mar 61	409UNTS56	105878
Kuwait	WHO (World Health)	16 Mar 61	397UNTS315	200588
Multilateral		27 Mar 61	420UNTS109	106043
Mauritania	WHO (World Health)	17 Apr 61	396UNTS301	200587
Gabon	WHO (World Health)	27 Apr 61	397UNTS215	105707
Mali	WHO (World Health)	27 Apr 61	407UNTS66	105860
Ethiopia	United Nations	14 Jun 61	406UNTS81	105840
Cyprus	United Nations	15 Jun 61	398UNTS39	105716
Haiti	United Nations	28 Jun 61	399UNTS159	105740
Morocco	WHO (World Health)	09 Aug 61	412UNTS192	105932
WHO (World Health)	Somalia	17 Aug 61	423UNTS111	106088
Lebanon	United Nations	26 Aug 61	406UNTS105	105842
Ghana	United Nations	29 Aug 61	406UNTS117	105843
Jordan	United Nations	11 Sep 61	406UNTS255	105855
Iraq	WHO (World Health)	13 Sep 61	419UNTS69	106030
Multilateral		20 Sep 61	407UNTS52	105859
Malagasy	WHO (World Health)	13 Oct 61	421UNTS273	106064
Multilateral		16 Oct 61	410UNTS242	105908
Multilateral		18 Oct 61	529UNTS89	107659
Multilateral		07 Nov 61	412UNTS258	105937
Ceylon (Sri Lanka)	United Nations	04 Dec 61	415UNTS236	105987
Multilateral		27 Dec 61	425UNTS83	106120
Ethiopia	WHO (World Health)	11 Jan 62	423UNTS99	106087
Multilateral		17 Jan 62	419UNTS294	106033
United Nations	Somalia	20 Jan 62	420UNTS133	106044
Multilateral		20 Jan 62	429UNTS230	200596
Multilateral		13 Feb 62	422UNTS288	200594
Multilateral		21 Feb 62	423UNTS151	106091
Multilateral		01 Mar 62	423UNTS122	106089
WHO (World Health)	Sudan	11 Mar 62	432UNTS325	106226
Nigeria	WHO (World Health)	27 Mar 62	429UNTS123	106194
Dahomey	UN Special Fund	28 Mar 62	424UNTS55	106099
Multilateral		29 Mar 62	507UNTS177	107401
Multilateral		10 Apr 62	429UNTS78	106192
Multilateral		18 Apr 62	463UNTS44	106692
Multilateral		17 May 62	429UNTS46	106189
Libya	WHO (World Health)	16 Jun 62	437UNTS127	106301
WHO (World Health)	Sierra Leone	19 Jun 62	439UNTS151	106327
WHO (World Health)	Senegal	06 Aug 62	435UNTS179	106279
Nigeria	United Nations	07 Aug 62	435UNTS167	106278
Multilateral		12 Aug 62	443UNTS266	106365
WHO (World Health)	Western Samoa	14 Aug 62	437UNTS317	200598
Multilateral		29 Aug 62	443UNTS280	106366
Cameroon	United Nations	29 Aug 62	442UNTS3	106334
Multilateral		28 Sep 62	469UNTS169	106791
Niger	United Nations	01 Oct 62	439UNTS181	106329
Japan	UN Special Fund	31 Oct 62	444UNTS171	106368
United Nations	Western Samoa	05 Nov 62	443UNTS297	200599
Multilateral		15 Nov 62	448UNTS50	106424
Algeria	UN Special Fund	15 Nov 62	452UNTS243	106512
WHO (World Health)	Syria	18 Nov 62	480UNTS249	106972
Ecuador	United Nations	26 Nov 62	445UNTS3	106372
Rwanda	United Nations	28 Nov 62	450UNTS267	106473
Multilateral		06 Dec 62	450UNTS240	106471
Cameroon	WHO (World Health)	08 Dec 62	451UNTS215	106496
Ivory Coast	United Nations	10 Dec 62	451UNTS269	106498
Multilateral		12 Dec 62	457UNTS72	106578
Multilateral		12 Dec 62	552UNTS15	108048
Algeria	WHO (World Health)	20 Dec 62	463UNTS135	106698
Israel	United Nations	07 Jan 63	450UNTS229	106470
Multilateral		21 Jan 63	453UNTS20	106517
United Nations	South Pacific Com	24 Jan 63	470UNTS361	200604
Multilateral		05 Feb 63	453UNTS36	106518
United Nations	United Arab Rep	08 Feb 63	453UNTS79	106520

PARTY ONE	PARTY TWO	DATE	CITATION	NUMBER
Conformity with IGO decisions (Cont.)				
Multilateral		14 Feb 63	453UNTS168	106524
Multilateral		06 Mar 63	455UNTS386	106552
Multilateral		18 Apr 63	463UNTS121	106697
Multilateral		06 May 63	463UNTS78	106694
Multilateral		09 May 63	463UNTS159	106700
Multilateral		22 May 63	483UNTS72	107007
Multilateral		24 May 63	466UNTS346	106754
Multilateral		25 May 63	479UNTS39	106947
Mongolia	WHO (World Health)	21 Jun 63	472UNTS373	106848
Multilateral		23 Jul 63	471UNTS158	106831
Multilateral		31 Jul 63	472UNTS220	106842
Burundi	WHO (World Health)	08 Aug 63	477UNTS346	106928
Multilateral		27 Aug 63	511UNTS210	107435
Multilateral		10 Sep 63	480UNTS100	106965
Jamaica	WHO (World Health)	25 Sep 63	481UNTS125	106980
Multilateral		30 Oct 63	480UNTS180	106968
WHO (World Health)	Tanganyika	05 Nov 63	496UNTS193	107252
Multilateral		07 Nov 63	480UNTS232	106971
Multilateral		08 Nov 63	482UNTS286	106999
UNESCO (Educ/Cult)	United Arab Rep	09 Nov 63	489UNTS233	107142
Multilateral		28 Jan 64	502UNTS321	107336
Multilateral		20 Feb 64	491UNTS30	107172
Rwanda	WHO (World Health)	22 Jun 64	514UNTS11	107440
Multilateral		23 Jun 64	506UNTS108	107383
WHO (World Health)	Trinidad/Tobago	23 Jun 64	503UNTS167	107342
Rwanda	WHO (World Health)	23 Jun 64	514UNTS157	107445
Multilateral		28 Jun 64	519UNTS14	107499
Multilateral		28 Jul 64	555UNTS183	108113
Multilateral		18 Sep 64	555UNTS205	108114
Multilateral		18 Sep 64	556UNTS25	108117
Multilateral		21 Sep 64	555UNTS227	108115
Australia	UN Special Fund	30 Sep 64	510UNTS277	107419
Multilateral		30 Sep 64	556UNTS3	108116
Multilateral		24 Oct 64	514UNTS220	200608
Multilateral		11 Nov 64	515UNTS94	107456
Multilateral		02 Dec 64	572UNTS229	108317
Malawi	WHO (World Health)	06 Jan 65	525UNTS165	107588
Malawi	WHO (World Health)	08 Jan 65	524UNTS281	107579
Multilateral		27 Jan 65	523UNTS102	107556
Multilateral		02 Feb 65	523UNTS256	107560
Multilateral		12 Feb 65	525UNTS148	107587
Multilateral		24 Feb 65	556UNTS47	108118
Multilateral		26 Feb 65	556UNTS69	108119
Multilateral		02 Jun 65	537UNTS348	200611
Poland	WHO (World Health)	26 Aug 65	552UNTS3	108047
Multilateral		13 Sep 65	547UNTS264	107962
Belgium	Denmark	20 Sep 65	549UNTS63	107990
Multilateral		21 Oct 65	547UNTS216	107959
Multilateral		07 Mar 66	0UNTS0	109464
WHO (World Health)	Singapore	28 Mar 66	562UNTS59	108195
Multilateral		20 Jun 66	572UNTS263	108318
Assistance to United Nations				
Multilateral		22 Jul 46	14UNTS185	100221
Multilateral		13 Dec 46	8UNTS119	100118
UNESCO (Educ/Cult)	United Nations	03 Feb 47	1UNTS233	200011
FAO (Food Agri)	United Nations	03 Feb 47	1UNTS207	200010
United Nations	WHO (World Health)	15 Nov 47	19UNTS193	200115
United Nations	UPU (Postal Union)	15 Nov 47	19UNTS219	200116
Albania	UNICEF (Children)	20 Nov 47	65UNTS163	200208
Greece	United Nations	12 Feb 48	47UNTS223	100732
France	UNICEF (Children)	19 Feb 48	68UNTS75	100885
France	United Nations	10 Mar 48	47UNTS203	100731
Multilateral		30 Apr 48	119UNTS3	101609
Finland	United Nations	20 May 48	47UNTS319	200189

PARTY ONE	PARTY TWO	DATE	CITATION	NUMBER
Assistance to United Nations (Cont.)				
Pakistan	United Nations	27 Aug 48	47UNTS269	100734
United Nations	Thailand	05 Oct 48	47UNTS287	100735
Czechoslovakia	United Nations	07 Oct 48	47UNTS185	100730
United Nations	San Marino	07 Oct 48	47UNTS337	200190
UNICEF (Children)	Thailand	01 Dec 48	68UNTS94	100886
United Nations	UK Great Britain	18 Mar 49	47UNTS305	100736
ITU (Telecommun)	United Nations	26 Apr 49	30UNTS315	200175
Burma	UNICEF (Children)	22 Apr 50	68UNTS96	100888
Brazil	UNICEF (Children)	09 Jun 50	66UNTS75	100848
Taiwan	UNICEF (Children)	19 Jul 50	94UNTS21	101304
FAO (Food Agri)	United Nations	02 Aug 50	139UNTS407	200467
ILO (Labor Org)	United Nations	12 Oct 50	139UNTS395	200466
Paraguay	UNICEF (Children)	25 Jan 51	79UNTS9	101027
ICAO (Civil Aviat)	United Nations	28 Feb 51	139UNTS429	200469
UNESCO (Educ/Cult)	United Nations	07 Mar 51	139UNTS417	200468
United Nations	WMO (Meteorology)	10 Apr 51	103UNTS245	200415
Panama	UNICEF (Children)	14 Jun 51	97UNTS3	101343
Multilateral		06 Jun 55	219UNTS79	102968
Multilateral		03 Oct 57	364UNTS3	105211
Nepal	United Nations	18 Aug 58	508UNTS3	107403
IMCO (Maritime Org)	United Nations	13 Jan 59	324UNTS273	200553
Panama	United Nations	24 Jun 59	507UNTS245	107402
Japan	United Nations	04 Oct 61	410UNTS133	105900
Niger	UNICEF (Children)	05 Dec 62	503UNTS195	107344
ILO (Labor Org)	USA (United States)	22 Feb 63	489UNTS347	107149
United Nations	UK Great Britain	27 Jun 63	469UNTS145	106789
UNICEF (Children)	Togo	27 Jun 63	540UNTS135	107847
Dahomey	UNICEF (Children)	28 Aug 63	507UNTS101	107396
Taiwan	UNICEF (Children)	08 Apr 64	500UNTS49	107306
Jamaica	UNICEF (Children)	19 May 64	500UNTS75	107308
Malaysia	UNICEF (Children)	01 Jul 64	503UNTS229	107346
Rwanda	UNICEF (Children)	11 Sep 64	510UNTS127	107409
Kenya	UN Special Fund	01 Oct 64	511UNTS181	107433
Ethiopia	WHO (World Health)	27 Jan 65	541UNTS135	107866
Malta	UNICEF (Children)	22 Apr 65	533UNTS107	107737
Multilateral		12 May 65	534UNTS390	107769
Multilateral		14 May 65	550UNTS310	108026
Multilateral		25 May 65	535UNTS374	107791
Gambia	UNICEF (Children)	29 May 65	547UNTS29	107954
Mongolia	UNICEF (Children)	23 Jun 65	540UNTS83	107844
Multilateral		02 Jul 65	592UNTS215	108575
Multilateral		20 Jul 65	541UNTS12	107857
Multilateral		13 Sep 65	547UNTS248	107961
Multilateral		21 Sep 65	547UNTS280	107963
Multilateral		12 Nov 65	550UNTS160	108013
Hungary	United Nations	04 Mar 66	559UNTS3	108151
Bulgaria	UNICEF (Children)	10 Mar 66	559UNTS13	108152
Liberia	UNICEF (Children)	08 Jun 66	570UNTS31	108286
Botswana	UN Special Fund	30 Sep 66	576UNTS3	108360
Indonesia	UNICEF (Children)	17 Nov 66	578UNTS47	108386
UNICEF (Children)	Zambia	02 Feb 67	589UNTS89	108536
Multilateral		27 Feb 67	590UNTS156	108552
United Nations	Senegal	08 Nov 67	613UNTS255	108854
United Nations	Switzerland	13 May 68	636UNTS353	200637
Conferences				
Multilateral		22 Apr 42	8UNTS237	200044
Australia	New Zealand	21 Jan 44	18UNTS357	200113
Panama	USA (United States)	14 Nov 44	139UNTS367	200462
Multilateral		22 Mar 45	70UNTS237	200241
Czechoslovakia	France	08 Dec 45	46UNTS77	100701
Multilateral		19 Jul 46	1UNTS97	200001
Multilateral		28 Aug 46	1UNTS139	200006
Czechoslovakia	UK Great Britain	16 Jun 47	46UNTS61	100700
Bulgaria	Czechoslovakia	20 Jun 47	46UNTS15	100698

PARTY ONE	PARTY TWO	DATE	CITATION	NUMBER
Conferences (Cont.)				
Czechoslovakia	Romania	05 Sep 47	46UNTS37	100699
Multilateral		02 Oct 47	193UNTS188	102616
Czechoslovakia	USSR (Soviet Union)	28 Nov 47	216UNTS285	102941
Multilateral		06 Mar 48	289UNTS3	104214
Bulgaria	Poland	26 Sep 49	260UNTS249	103712
Hungary	Poland	29 Oct 49	260UNTS113	103706
Austria	Czechoslovakia	30 Mar 50	495UNTS85	107240
Romania	USSR (Soviet Union)	27 May 50	221UNTS13	103000
Germany, East	Poland	23 Jun 50	304UNTS91	104393
Hungary	USSR (Soviet Union)	13 Jul 50	221UNTS35	103001
Bulgaria	USSR (Soviet Union)	25 Aug 50	221UNTS57	103002
China People's Rep	Poland	03 Apr 51	304UNTS187	104396
Germany, East	Poland	08 Jan 52	304UNTS113	104394
India	United Nations	12 Jan 52	118UNTS175	101606
Colombia	United Nations	17 Jul 52	135UNTS61	101815
Czechoslovakia	Romania	31 Jul 52	362UNTS123	105185
Brazil	United Nations	04 Aug 52	135UNTS185	101820
Hungary	Romania	14 Dec 53	342UNTS151	104906
Multilateral		25 Feb 54	215UNTS249	102922
Bulgaria	Romania	22 Jul 54	362UNTS101	105184
Greece	Italy	11 Sep 54	284UNTS313	104145
Italy	Yugoslavia	26 Mar 55	379UNTS3	105432
Germany, East	Romania	05 Aug 55	342UNTS229	104910
Bulgaria	Yugoslavia	11 Dec 55	378UNTS49	105417
Germany, East	USSR (Soviet Union)	30 May 56	263UNTS143	103771
Romania	Yugoslavia	04 Aug 56	395UNTS99	105682
Romania	Yugoslavia	25 Sep 56	395UNTS147	105683
Germany, East	Romania	08 Dec 56	362UNTS189	105188
Albania	Yugoslavia	20 May 57	363UNTS99	105203
Bulgaria	Czechoslovakia	03 Jun 57	292UNTS3	104261
Bulgaria	Yugoslavia	04 Jun 57	349UNTS35	105008
Czechoslovakia	Yugoslavia	11 Jun 57	504UNTS107	107355
New Zealand	UK Great Britain	20 Sep 57	287UNTS105	104180
Germany, East	Hungary	25 Oct 57	408UNTS156	105869
Czechoslovakia	USSR (Soviet Union)	04 Dec 57	313UNTS291	104537
Hungary	Yugoslavia	06 Dec 57	519UNTS215	107509
Belgium	Denmark	31 Dec 57	305UNTS247	104422
Ceylon (Sri Lanka)	USSR (Soviet Union)	15 Jan 58	305UNTS235	104421
Bulgaria	Hungary	13 Mar 58	438UNTS173	106316
Czechoslovakia	Romania	25 Mar 58	339UNTS77	104846
Hungary	Poland	08 May 58	408UNTS212	105872
Germany, East	Hungary	14 Jun 58	407UNTS78	105861
Multilateral		11 May 59	527UNTS145	107623
Greece	Yugoslavia	18 Jun 59	368UNTS125	105237
Bulgaria	Czechoslovakia	19 Sep 59	355UNTS77	105074
Multilateral		14 Dec 59	422UNTS33	106067
Austria	Czechoslovakia	23 Jan 60	495UNTS99	107241
Italy	United Nations	23 Aug 61	405UNTS3	105819
Belgium	Yugoslavia	31 Oct 61	426UNTS165	106136
United Nations	Sweden	01 Jun 62	429UNTS135	106195
Iran	United Nations	05 Sep 62	442UNTS249	106353
Italy	United Nations	26 Jul 63	472UNTS173	106840
UNESCO (Educ/Cult)	Yugoslavia	27 Feb 64	489UNTS257	107143
Afghanistan	United Nations	28 Apr 64	494UNTS77	107227
Netherlands	United Nations	27 May 64	548UNTS79	107971
United Nations	Togo	03 Jul 64	502UNTS287	107334
Czechoslovakia	Germany, East	06 Oct 64	545UNTS113	107927
Multilateral		07 Nov 64	548UNTS3	107965
UK Great Britain	USSR (Soviet Union)	06 Jan 65	543UNTS77	107897
Mongolia	United Nations	06 Jan 65	522UNTS45	107535
United Nations	Yugoslavia	07 Jan 65	522UNTS55	107536
Iran	United Nations	16 Feb 65	525UNTS211	107593
Multilateral		14 May 65	550UNTS310	108026
Bulgaria	Czechoslovakia	22 May 65	545UNTS65	107925
Austria	Bulgaria	12 Jul 65	587UNTS51	108510

PARTY ONE	PARTY TWO	DATE	CITATION	NUMBER
Conferences (Cont.)				
United Nations	Zambia	23 Oct 65	549UNTS101	107993
United Nations	United Arab Rep	26 Nov 65	551UNTS253	108046
Multilateral		31 Dec 65	616UNTS317	108904
United Nations	Senegal	12 Jan 66	551UNTS147	108039
Jamaica	United Nations	06 Dec 66	580UNTS211	108424
Finland	United Nations	16 Jan 67	588UNTS153	108522
Multilateral		14 Feb 67	634UNTS281	109068
Romania	United Nations	08 Apr 67	594UNTS159	108602
Ghana	United Nations	08 Apr 67	594UNTS149	108601
United Nations	Zambia	06 Jul 67	600UNTS81	108678
India	United Nations	04 Nov 67	609UNTS3	108824
Iran	United Nations	15 Feb 68	631UNTS103	108990
United Nations	Tunisia	18 Mar 68	633UNTS3	109030
Niger	United Nations	07 May 68	639UNTS71	109145
Austria	United Nations	25 May 68	637UNTS0	109118
Austria	United Nations	25 May 68	637UNTS0	109117
India	United Nations	22 Jul 68	640UNTS121	109158
Ghana	United Nations	19 Sep 68	0UNTS0	109250
Austria	United Nations	24 Sep 68	0UNTS0	109253
Membership				
Multilateral		31 Dec 65	616UNTS317	108904
UN administrative tribunal				
Multilateral		15 Dec 44	16UNTS247	200106
Multilateral		15 Dec 44	17UNTS305	200110
Multilateral		23 Apr 46	17UNTS3	100265
Multilateral		19 Jul 46	1UNTS97	200001
Multilateral		28 Aug 46	1UNTS139	200006
UNESCO (Educ/Cult)	United Nations	03 Feb 47	1UNTS233	200011
FAO (Food Agri)	United Nations	03 Feb 47	1UNTS207	200010
France	UNICEF (Children)	19 Feb 48	68UNTS75	100885
Multilateral		29 Nov 48	120UNTS13	101613
Multilateral		19 Nov 59	410UNTS156	105902
Multilateral		26 Jan 60	439UNTS249	106333
Multilateral		18 Oct 61	529UNTS89	107659
Inter-agency agreements				
Multilateral		16 Nov 45	4UNTS275	100052
Multilateral		27 Dec 45	2UNTS39	100020
Multilateral		22 Jul 46	14UNTS185	100221
Multilateral		30 Oct 46	27UNTS77	100401
ILO (Labor Org)	United Nations	19 Dec 46	1UNTS183	200009
FAO (Food Agri)	United Nations	03 Feb 47	1UNTS207	200010
UNESCO (Educ/Cult)	United Nations	03 Feb 47	1UNTS233	200011
FAO (Food Agri)	ILO (Labor Org)	11 Sep 47	18UNTS335	200111
Multilateral		11 Oct 47	77UNTS143	100998
United Nations	WHO (World Health)	15 Nov 47	19UNTS193	200115
United Nations	UPU (Postal Union)	15 Nov 47	19UNTS219	200116
Multilateral		06 Mar 48	289UNTS3	104214
ILO (Labor Org)	WHO (World Health)	10 Jul 48	19UNTS269	200121
FAO (Food Agri)	WHO (World Health)	17 Jul 48	76UNTS171	200244
FAO (Food Agri)	UNESCO (Educ/Cult)	23 Aug 48	18UNTS345	200112
Multilateral		29 Nov 48	120UNTS13	101613
IRO (Refugee Org)	United Nations	07 Feb 49	26UNTS299	200153
ITU (Telecommun)	United Nations	26 Apr 49	30UNTS315	200175
Multilateral		28 Apr 49	83UNTS105	101105
Multilateral		20 Jun 49	128UNTS141	101718
United Nations	WMO (Meteorology)	10 Apr 51	103UNTS245	200415
Multilateral		06 Dec 51	425UNTS61	106119
Multilateral		11 Jul 52	169UNTS3	102220
Multilateral		17 Oct 53	184UNTS42	102438
Multilateral		19 Oct 53	207UNTS189	102807
Multilateral		25 Feb 54	215UNTS249	102922
Multilateral		02 Mar 55	225UNTS233	103101
Multilateral		25 May 55	264UNTS117	103791
Multilateral		06 Jun 55	219UNTS79	102968

PARTY ONE	PARTY TWO	DATE	CITATION	NUMBER
Inter-agency agreements (Cont.)				
Multilateral		26 Oct 56	276UNTS3	103988
IBRD (World Bank)	United Nations	20 Feb 57	265UNTS312	200546
EEC (Econ Commnty)	ILO (Labor Org)	07 Jul 58	312UNTS387	200551
Nepal	United Nations	18 Aug 58	508UNTS3	107403
IMCO (Maritime Org)	United Nations	13 Jan 59	324UNTS273	200553
Japan	Vietnam, South	13 May 59	373UNTS173	105319
IAEA (Atom Energy)	WHO (World Health)	28 May 59	339UNTS387	200559
Laos	United Nations	06 Jul 59	337UNTS41	104814
FAO (Food Agri)	UN Special Fund	28 Sep 59	341UNTS353	200562
ILO (Labor Org)	UN Special Fund	12 Oct 59	343UNTS325	200563
UN Special Fund	WMO (Meteorology)	17 Nov 59	345UNTS311	200564
Multilateral		18 Nov 59	390UNTS227	105610
Multilateral		26 Jan 60	439UNTS249	106333
UN Special Fund	WHO (World Health)	25 May 60	359UNTS375	200568
Multilateral		19 Jun 60	537UNTS214	107803
Multilateral		13 Dec 60	523UNTS117	107557
Multilateral		14 Apr 61	422UNTS101	106071
FAO (Food Agri)	USA (United States)	29 Mar 62	454UNTS13	106536
Multilateral		28 Sep 62	469UNTS169	106791
Niger	UNICEF (Children)	05 Dec 62	503UNTS195	107344
Ethiopia	UNICEF (Children)	01 Apr 63	457UNTS103	106579
UN Special Fund	Trinidad/Tobago	06 May 63	463UNTS93	106695
UNICEF (Children)	Togo	27 Jun 63	540UNTS135	107847
Poland	United Nations	16 Jul 63	471UNTS3	106817
UNICEF (Children)	Trinidad/Tobago	08 Aug 63	473UNTS281	106865
Dahomey	UNICEF (Children)	28 Aug 63	507UNTS101	107396
Iran	UNICEF (Children)	21 Nov 63	485UNTS35	107044
Iraq	UNICEF (Children)	03 Dec 63	482UNTS319	107001
Burundi	UNICEF (Children)	08 Jan 64	485UNTS45	107045
Subsahara Tech Com	IAEA (Atom Energy)	06 Feb 64	501UNTS285	200606
IMCO (Maritime Org)	United Nations	11 Feb 64	489UNTS357	200605
Taiwan	UNICEF (Children)	08 Apr 64	500UNTS49	107306
Jamaica	UNICEF (Children)	19 May 64	500UNTS75	107308
Malaysia	UNICEF (Children)	01 Jul 64	503UNTS229	107346
Rwanda	UNICEF (Children)	11 Sep 64	510UNTS127	107409
WHO (World Health)	Tunisia	27 Jan 65	528UNTS209	107644
Multilateral		23 Feb 65	527UNTS120	107622
Multilateral		05 Mar 65	527UNTS221	107627
Multilateral		12 May 65	534UNTS390	107769
Multilateral		25 May 65	535UNTS374	107791
Gambia	UNICEF (Children)	29 May 65	547UNTS29	107954
Mongolia	UNICEF (Children)	23 Jun 65	540UNTS83	107844
Australia	Eur Space Vehicle	13 Jul 65	543UNTS183	107902
Multilateral		20 Jul 65	541UNTS12	107857
ILO (Labor Org)	Org Ctrl Am States	26 Jul 65	563UNTS341	200620
Multilateral		13 Sep 65	547UNTS248	107961
Multilateral		21 Sep 65	547UNTS280	107963
Multilateral		12 Nov 65	550UNTS160	108013
OAU (Afri Unity)	United Nations	15 Nov 65	548UNTS315	200614
Hungary	United Nations	04 Mar 66	559UNTS3	108151
Bulgaria	UNICEF (Children)	10 Mar 66	559UNTS13	108152
FAO (Food Agri)	IMCO (Maritime Org)	11 Jul 66	575UNTS238	200627
Botswana	UN Special Fund	30 Sep 66	576UNTS3	108360
Indonesia	UNICEF (Children)	17 Nov 66	578UNTS47	108386
Multilateral		27 Feb 67	590UNTS156	108552
Multilateral		04 May 67	595UNTS287	108623
Peace-keeping force				
Finland	United Nations	27 Jun 57	271UNTS135	103913
United Nations	Sweden	01 Jul 57	271UNTS187	103914
Norway	United Nations	09 Jul 57	271UNTS223	103917
Denmark	United Nations	16 Jul 57	274UNTS81	103959
Canada	United Nations	29 Jul 57	274UNTS47	103957
Brazil	United Nations	13 Aug 57	274UNTS199	103966
India	United Nations	14 Aug 57	274UNTS233	103968

PARTY ONE	PARTY TWO	DATE	CITATION	NUMBER
Peace-keeping force (Cont.)				
United Nations	Yugoslavia	01 Oct 57	277UNTS191	104006
Lebanon	United Nations	20 Jan 58	286UNTS189	104166
Belgium	United Nations	20 Feb 65	535UNTS197	107780
United Nations	UK Great Britain	21 Feb 66	555UNTS177	108112
Greece	United Nations	20 Jun 66	565UNTS3	108230
Recognition of specialized agency				
ILO (Labor Org)	United Nations	19 Dec 46	1UNTS183	200009
FAO (Food Agri)	United Nations	03 Feb 47	1UNTS207	200010
UNESCO (Educ/Cult)	United Nations	03 Feb 47	1UNTS233	200011
United Nations	UPU (Postal Union)	15 Nov 47	19UNTS219	200116
United Nations	WHO (World Health)	15 Nov 47	19UNTS193	200115
IRO (Refugee Org)	United Nations	07 Feb 49	26UNTS299	200153
ILO (Labor Org)	United Nations	17 Feb 49	26UNTS323	200154
ITU (Telecommun)	United Nations	26 Apr 49	30UNTS315	200175
FAO (Food Agri)	United Nations	02 Aug 50	139UNTS407	200467
ILO (Labor Org)	United Nations	12 Oct 50	139UNTS395	200466
ICAO (Civil Aviat)	United Nations	28 Feb 51	139UNTS429	200469
UNESCO (Educ/Cult)	United Nations	07 Mar 51	139UNTS417	200468
United Nations	WMO (Meteorology)	10 Apr 51	103UNTS245	200415
IMCO (Maritime Org)	United Nations	13 Jan 59	324UNTS273	200553
ILO (Labor Org)	UK Great Britain	14 Jan 59	355UNTS283	105081
IMCO (Maritime Org)	United Nations	23 Jun 59	336UNTS317	200556
Multilateral		25 May 62	486UNTS103	107075
Interagency requests				
ITU (Telecommun)	UN Special Fund	13 Jul 60	368UNTS329	200573
OAU (Afri Unity)	United Nations	15 Nov 65	548UNTS315	200614
Mutual consultation				
France	UK Great Britain	27 Mar 45	98UNTS227	200274
FAO (Food Agri)	ILO (Labor Org)	11 Sep 47	18UNTS335	200111
UNESCO (Educ/Cult)	WHO (World Health)	15 Jul 48	44UNTS323	200184
FAO (Food Agri)	WHO (World Health)	17 Jul 48	76UNTS171	200244
FAO (Food Agri)	UNESCO (Educ/Cult)	09 Feb 49	43UNTS315	200182
ILO (Labor Org)	OAS (Am States)	07 Jun 50	70UNTS223	200240
Council of Europe	ILO (Labor Org)	23 Nov 51	126UNTS331	200435
ECSC (Coal/Steel)	ILO (Labor Org)	16 Jul 53	412UNTS273	200591
UNESCO (Educ/Cult)	UN Special Fund	29 Sep 54	363UNTS367	200572
Italy	USA (United States)	23 May 55	251UNTS303	103547
Austria	USA (United States)	14 Jun 55	258UNTS37	103668
Greece	USA (United States)	24 Jun 55	270UNTS361	103906
France	USA (United States)	11 Aug 55	251UNTS15	103530
Austria	USA (United States)	07 Feb 56	272UNTS117	103933
Iran	USA (United States)	20 Feb 56	272UNTS135	103934
Indonesia	USA (United States)	02 Mar 56	271UNTS345	103925
Spain	USA (United States)	05 Mar 56	271UNTS329	103924
Turkey	USA (United States)	12 Mar 56	272UNTS21	103929
Korea, South	USA (United States)	13 Mar 56	272UNTS3	103928
Paraguay	USA (United States)	02 May 56	268UNTS299	103863
Portugal	USA (United States)	24 May 56	268UNTS323	103865
Italy	USA (United States)	30 Oct 56	263UNTS221	103775
Burma	USA (United States)	04 Dec 56	268UNTS189	103858
Brazil	USA (United States)	31 Dec 56	266UNTS151	103829
Israel	USA (United States)	07 Nov 57	302UNTS255	104365
Pakistan	USA (United States)	15 Nov 57	303UNTS173	104380
Greece	USA (United States)	18 Dec 57	303UNTS159	104379
France	USA (United States)	27 Dec 57	307UNTS79	104444
Turkey	USA (United States)	20 Jan 58	304UNTS15	104389
Spain	USA (United States)	27 Jan 58	303UNTS247	104384
USA (United States)	Yugoslavia	03 Feb 58	304UNTS293	104404
UK Great Britain	USA (United States)	03 Feb 58	307UNTS199	104450
Korea, South	USA (United States)	05 Feb 58	307UNTS121	104447
Poland	USA (United States)	15 Feb 58	307UNTS217	104452
Finland	USA (United States)	21 Feb 58	304UNTS253	104401
France	USA (United States)	28 Feb 58	366UNTS343	105222
Colombia	USA (United States)	14 Mar 58	308UNTS115	104459

PARTY ONE	PARTY TWO	DATE	CITATION	NUMBER
Mutual consultation (Cont.)				
Peru	USA (United States)	09 Apr 58	316UNTS37	104576
Taiwan	USA (United States)	18 Apr 58	308UNTS179	104461
Iceland	USA (United States)	03 May 58	316UNTS137	104581
Burma	USA (United States)	27 May 58	315UNTS197	104569
Philippines	USA (United States)	03 Jun 58	316UNTS3	104573
Ceylon (Sri Lanka)	USA (United States)	18 Jun 58	316UNTS15	104574
Ecuador	USA (United States)	30 Jun 58	336UNTS11	104796
Nepal	United Nations	18 Aug 58	508UNTS3	107403
India	USA (United States)	26 Sep 58	336UNTS59	104798
IAEA (Atom Energy)	UNESCO (Educ/Cult)	01 Oct 58	339UNTS373	200558
FAO (Food Agri)	IAEA (Atom Energy)	01 Oct 58	361UNTS211	200571
Israel	USA (United States)	06 Nov 58	336UNTS275	104810
Pakistan	USA (United States)	26 Nov 58	337UNTS3	104812
USA (United States)	Yugoslavia	22 Dec 58	338UNTS243	104839
United Arab Rep	USA (United States)	24 Dec 58	338UNTS221	104837
Spain	USA (United States)	13 Jan 59	341UNTS241	104887
ILO (Labor Org)	IMCO (Maritime Org)	16 Jan 59	327UNTS309	200554
Iceland	USA (United States)	03 Mar 59	341UNTS261	104889
Ceylon (Sri Lanka)	USA (United States)	13 Mar 59	342UNTS51	104900
France	USA (United States)	21 Mar 59	342UNTS71	104901
IAEA (Atom Energy)	ILO (Labor Org)	08 May 59	328UNTS273	200555
IAEA (Atom Energy)	WHO (World Health)	28 May 59	339UNTS387	200559
Indonesia	USA (United States)	29 May 59	347UNTS85	104992
Taiwan	USA (United States)	09 Jun 59	353UNTS257	105046
Poland	USA (United States)	10 Jun 59	347UNTS41	104989
Argentina	USA (United States)	12 Jun 59	347UNTS59	104990
Panama	United Nations	24 Jun 59	507UNTS245	107402
Korea, South	USA (United States)	30 Jun 59	353UNTS297	105047
Subsahara Tech Com	ILO (Labor Org)	25 Jul 59	409UNTS290	200590
United Arab Rep	USA (United States)	29 Jul 59	357UNTS121	105111
IAEA (Atom Energy)	WMO (Meteorology)	12 Aug 59	341UNTS341	200561
IAEA (Atom Energy)	ICAO (Civil Aviat)	01 Oct 59	361UNTS193	200570
USA (United States)	Vietnam, South	16 Oct 59	360UNTS271	105163
India	USA (United States)	13 Nov 59	360UNTS287	105164
Turkey	USA (United States)	22 Dec 59	367UNTS57	105225
Peru	USA (United States)	12 Feb 60	372UNTS83	105290
Iceland	USA (United States)	06 Apr 60	372UNTS71	105289
Pakistan	USA (United States)	11 Apr 60	372UNTS251	105302
India	USA (United States)	04 May 60	376UNTS279	105384
Spain	USA (United States)	22 Jun 60	378UNTS3	105414
Poland	USA (United States)	21 Jul 60	380UNTS157	105456
Iran	USA (United States)	26 Jul 60	384UNTS141	105516
United Arab Rep	USA (United States)	01 Aug 60	384UNTS189	105519
United Arab Rep	USA (United States)	09 Aug 60	388UNTS271	105584
Taiwan	USA (United States)	30 Aug 60	388UNTS191	105579
Ecuador	USA (United States)	27 Sep 60	401UNTS115	105766
Ceylon (Sri Lanka)	USA (United States)	30 Sep 60	389UNTS221	105594
USA (United States)	Vietnam, South	28 Oct 60	401UNTS3	105758
France	USA (United States)	04 Nov 60	400UNTS323	105756
Indonesia	USA (United States)	05 Nov 60	400UNTS35	105746
Greece	USA (United States)	07 Nov 60	400UNTS57	105748
Chile	USA (United States)	08 Nov 60	405UNTS85	105825
Inter-Am Nuc Energ	IAEA (Atom Energy)	22 Dec 60	396UNTS285	200586
Korea, South	USA (United States)	28 Dec 60	402UNTS3	105773
Turkey	USA (United States)	11 Jan 61	405UNTS173	105833
Euratom	ILO (Labor Org)	26 Jan 61	390UNTS323	200580
USA (United States)	Vietnam, South	25 Mar 61	406UNTS187	105849
Ecuador	USA (United States)	03 Apr 61	409UNTS140	105882
Iceland	USA (United States)	07 Apr 61	406UNTS203	105850
Bolivia	USA (United States)	07 Apr 61	433UNTS3	106227
USA (United States)	Yugoslavia	28 Apr 61	409UNTS172	105884
Brazil	USA (United States)	04 May 61	433UNTS91	106233
Israel	USA (United States)	10 May 61	409UNTS213	105887
Spain	USA (United States)	22 May 61	409UNTS260	105891
Tunisia	USA (United States)	30 Jun 61	434UNTS85	106257

PARTY ONE	PARTY TWO	DATE	CITATION	NUMBER
Mutual consultation (Cont.)				
Paraguay	USA (United States)	07 Jul 61	433UNTS53	106231
USA (United States)	Vietnam, South	14 Jul 61	416UNTS133	105999
Taiwan	USA (United States)	21 Jul 61	416UNTS101	105998
Turkey	USA (United States)	29 Jul 61	416UNTS151	106001
Finland	USA (United States)	04 Aug 61	418UNTS19	106014
El Salvador	USA (United States)	21 Aug 61	418UNTS35	106015
Indonesia	USA (United States)	26 Oct 61	433UNTS249	106248
Iceland	USA (United States)	06 Nov 61	426UNTS225	106140
Syria	USA (United States)	09 Nov 61	435UNTS75	106271
Sudan	USA (United States)	14 Nov 61	434UNTS51	106255
Bolivia	USA (United States)	15 Nov 61	456UNTS192	106557
Congo (Zaire)	USA (United States)	18 Nov 61	433UNTS207	106244
Philippines	USA (United States)	24 Nov 61	433UNTS315	106251
Portugal	USA (United States)	28 Nov 61	434UNTS31	106253
COMECON (Econ Aid)	USSR (Soviet Union)	07 Dec 61	506UNTS325	107392
Poland	USA (United States)	15 Dec 61	434UNTS3	106252
USA (United States)	Vietnam, South	27 Dec 61	433UNTS185	106242
United Arab Rep	USA (United States)	19 Jan 62	435UNTS107	106273
Iran	USA (United States)	29 Jan 62	435UNTS53	106270
Guinea	USA (United States)	02 Feb 62	435UNTS35	106269
Bolivia	USA (United States)	12 Feb 62	451UNTS281	106499
Tunisia	USA (United States)	16 Feb 62	442UNTS161	106347
Indonesia	USA (United States)	19 Feb 62	435UNTS137	106276
Korea, South	USA (United States)	02 Mar 62	442UNTS185	106349
Brazil	USA (United States)	15 Mar 62	456UNTS209	106558
Iceland	USA (United States)	16 Mar 62	445UNTS49	106376
Peru	USA (United States)	20 Mar 62	445UNTS61	106377
Liberia	USA (United States)	12 Apr 62	445UNTS213	106390
Taiwan	USA (United States)	27 Apr 62	436UNTS25	106287
USA (United States)	Uruguay	27 Apr 62	452UNTS25	106502
India	USA (United States)	01 May 62	451UNTS179	106493
Israel	USA (United States)	03 May 62	442UNTS83	106340
USA (United States)	Venezuela	17 May 62	456UNTS275	106562
Czechoslovakia	COMECON (Econ Aid)	20 Jul 62	506UNTS345	107393
Chile	USA (United States)	07 Aug 62	461UNTS61	106652
Ethiopia	USA (United States)	13 Aug 62	459UNTS31	106611
Taiwan	USA (United States)	31 Aug 62	460UNTS247	106644
Morocco	USA (United States)	11 Sep 62	462UNTS207	106680
Tunisia	USA (United States)	14 Sep 62	461UNTS31	106649
United Arab Rep	USA (United States)	08 Oct 62	462UNTS39	106670
Iran	USA (United States)	15 Oct 62	473UNTS291	106866
Greece	USA (United States)	22 Oct 62	462UNTS187	106678
Korea, South	USA (United States)	07 Nov 62	462UNTS129	106674
Burma	USA (United States)	09 Nov 62	461UNTS113	106655
Taiwan	USA (United States)	19 Nov 62	459UNTS263	106629
Paraguay	USA (United States)	24 Nov 62	471UNTS49	106821
India	USA (United States)	26 Nov 62	460UNTS203	106641
India	USA (United States)	30 Nov 62	459UNTS231	106626
Israel	USA (United States)	06 Dec 62	460UNTS151	106638
Bolivia	USA (United States)	17 Dec 62	469UNTS121	106788
Sudan	USA (United States)	31 Jan 63	494UNTS119	107230
Poland	USA (United States)	01 Feb 63	487UNTS143	107100
Bolivia	USA (United States)	04 Feb 63	473UNTS65	106856
Turkey	USA (United States)	21 Feb 63	473UNTS311	106867
Poland	COMECON (Econ Aid)	22 Feb 63	506UNTS303	107391
Congo (Zaire)	USA (United States)	23 Feb 63	493UNTS3	107203
Colombia	USA (United States)	27 Mar 63	489UNTS289	107145
Ethiopia	UNICEF (Children)	01 Apr 63	457UNTS103	106579
Ecuador	USA (United States)	05 Apr 63	477UNTS135	106919
El Salvador	USA (United States)	07 May 63	476UNTS35	106901
India	USA (United States)	09 May 63	476UNTS43	106902
Guinea	USA (United States)	22 May 63	487UNTS251	107108
Afromalagasy Org	ILO (Labor Org)	30 May 63	467UNTS482	200602
Ethiopia	USA (United States)	11 Jun 63	487UNTS269	107109
Cyprus	USA (United States)	18 Jun 63	479UNTS191	106953

PARTY ONE	PARTY TWO	DATE	CITATION	NUMBER
Mutual consultation (Cont.)				
Senegal	USA (United States)	03 Jul 63	527UNTS95	107620
Dominican Republic	USA (United States)	13 Aug 63	492UNTS327	107202
Iraq	USA (United States)	27 Aug 63	489UNTS271	107144
Brazil	USA (United States)	11 Sep 63	493UNTS267	107220
Paraguay	USA (United States)	16 Sep 63	494UNTS101	107229
Peru	USA (United States)	23 Sep 63	488UNTS91	107121
Greece	USA (United States)	30 Oct 63	493UNTS29	107205
Paraguay	USA (United States)	14 Nov 63	505UNTS87	107366
Syria	USA (United States)	18 Nov 63	494UNTS169	107232
USA (United States)	Vietnam, South	09 Jan 64	505UNTS173	107373
Poland	USA (United States)	03 Feb 64	505UNTS215	107375
Poland	USA (United States)	03 Feb 64	505UNTS245	107376
Subsahara Tech Com	IAEA (Atom Energy)	06 Feb 64	501UNTS285	200606
Jordan	USA (United States)	11 Feb 64	511UNTS85	107429
Peru	USA (United States)	13 Feb 64	511UNTS119	107431
Iceland	USA (United States)	13 Feb 64	510UNTS295	107420
Iceland	USA (United States)	13 Feb 64	511UNTS3	107421
Sudan	USA (United States)	02 Mar 64	524UNTS217	107575
Ivory Coast	USA (United States)	10 Mar 64	526UNTS285	107611
Bolivia	USA (United States)	25 Mar 64	532UNTS3	107710
Tunisia	USA (United States)	07 Apr 64	527UNTS3	107613
USA (United States)	Yugoslavia	27 Apr 64	526UNTS73	107601
USA (United States)	Yugoslavia	27 Apr 64	526UNTS89	107602
USA (United States)	Yugoslavia	28 Apr 64	526UNTS103	107603
Congo (Zaire)	USA (United States)	28 Apr 64	526UNTS55	107600
Philippines	USA (United States)	14 May 64	526UNTS113	107604
Taiwan	USA (United States)	03 Jun 64	526UNTS257	107610
Paraguay	USA (United States)	05 Sep 64	530UNTS225	107685
USA (United States)	Vietnam, South	29 Sep 64	531UNTS183	107703
Iran	USA (United States)	29 Sep 64	531UNTS163	107702
India	USA (United States)	30 Sep 64	532UNTS321	107726
USA (United States)	Yugoslavia	28 Oct 64	533UNTS3	107728
Iran	USA (United States)	16 Nov 64	532UNTS213	107719
Greece	USA (United States)	17 Nov 64	532UNTS107	107714
Kenya	USA (United States)	07 Dec 64	532UNTS263	107722
Congo (Zaire)	USA (United States)	09 Dec 64	531UNTS249	107707
Israel	USA (United States)	22 Dec 64	532UNTS231	107720
Iceland	USA (United States)	30 Dec 64	542UNTS37	107878
Iceland	USA (United States)	30 Dec 64	531UNTS287	107709
Taiwan	USA (United States)	31 Dec 64	532UNTS29	107711
Taiwan	USA (United States)	31 Dec 64	532UNTS59	107712
Korea, South	USA (United States)	31 Dec 64	535UNTS315	107787
Dahomey	USA (United States)	31 Dec 64	541UNTS117	107865
Sierra Leone	USA (United States)	29 Jan 65	542UNTS87	107882
Tunisia	USA (United States)	17 Feb 65	542UNTS125	107885
USA (United States)	Yugoslavia	16 Mar 65	542UNTS161	107887
Dominican Republic	USA (United States)	18 Mar 65	542UNTS215	107892
Ivory Coast	USA (United States)	05 Apr 65	546UNTS143	107941
Multilateral		08 Apr 65	533UNTS66	107733
Philippines	USA (United States)	23 Apr 65	546UNTS157	107942
Multilateral		26 Apr 65	533UNTS50	107732
Bolivia	USA (United States)	12 May 65	564UNTS143	108226
USA (United States)	Vietnam, South	26 May 65	550UNTS3	108005
Ecuador	USA (United States)	25 Jun 65	549UNTS23	107986
Mali	USA (United States)	14 Jul 65	564UNTS101	108223
USA (United States)	Yugoslavia	16 Jul 65	549UNTS111	107994
ILO (Labor Org)	Org Ctrl Am States	26 Jul 65	563UNTS341	200620
Chile	USA (United States)	27 Jul 65	574UNTS83	108342
Ethiopia	USA (United States)	17 Aug 65	564UNTS119	108224
USA (United States)	Yugoslavia	22 Nov 65	574UNTS211	108351
Ethiopia	USA (United States)	14 Dec 65	574UNTS115	108344
Brazil	UNICEF (Children)	28 Mar 66	607UNTS235	108807
Bolivia	USA (United States)	22 Apr 66	578UNTS73	108388
Liberia	UNICEF (Children)	08 Jun 66	570UNTS31	108286
FAO (Food Agri)	IMCO (Maritime Org)	11 Jul 66	575UNTS238	200627

PARTY ONE	PARTY TWO	DATE	CITATION	NUMBER
Mutual consultation (Cont.)				
Multilateral		23 Sep 66	573UNTS132	108327
UN recommendations				
Multilateral		22 Jul 46	9UNTS3	100125
FAO (Food Agri)	United Nations	03 Feb 47	1UNTS207	200010
UNESCO (Educ/Cult)	United Nations	03 Feb 47	1UNTS233	200011
United Nations	WHO (World Health)	15 Nov 47	19UNTS193	200115
United Nations	UPU (Postal Union)	15 Nov 47	19UNTS219	200116
Greece	United Nations	12 Feb 48	47UNTS223	100732
France	United Nations	10 Mar 48	47UNTS203	100731
Finland	United Nations	20 May 48	47UNTS319	200189
Multilateral		10 Jun 48	191UNTS3	102576
Pakistan	United Nations	27 Aug 48	47UNTS269	100734
United Nations	Thailand	05 Oct 48	47UNTS287	100735
Czechoslovakia	United Nations	07 Oct 48	47UNTS185	100730
United Nations	San Marino	07 Oct 48	47UNTS337	200190
IRO (Refugee Org)	United Nations	07 Feb 49	26UNTS299	200153
United Nations	UK Great Britain	18 Mar 49	47UNTS305	100736
ITU (Telecommun)	United Nations	26 Apr 49	30UNTS315	200175
Poland	United Nations	16 Jul 63	471UNTS3	106817
IGO obligations				
Afghanistan	UNICEF (Children)	04 Jul 50	71UNTS3	100906
WHO (World Health)	Thailand	04 Oct 51	109UNTS85	101493
India	WHO (World Health)	01 Nov 51	118UNTS13	101593
Burma	WHO (World Health)	18 Feb 52	127UNTS43	101698
Chile	WHO (World Health)	31 May 52	136UNTS323	101841
Greece	USA (United States)	24 Jun 55	270UNTS351	103905
Pakistan	USA (United States)	02 Mar 56	271UNTS371	103927
Multilateral		25 Mar 57	294UNTS2	104300
IAEA (Atom Energy)	United Nations	23 Oct 57	281UNTS369	200548
Multilateral		03 Dec 58	398UNTS9	105715
Multilateral		03 Dec 58	416UNTS51	105995
Japan	United Nations	15 Mar 61	397UNTS199	105706
Norway	IAEA (Atom Energy)	10 Apr 61	402UNTS255	105790
Netherlands	Euratom	25 Jul 61	462UNTS263	106686
India	United Nations	19 Feb 62	423UNTS3	106082
United Nations	Sweden	01 Jun 62	429UNTS135	106195
India	United Nations	27 Dec 62	450UNTS3	106464
Hungary	COMECON (Econ Aid)	28 Feb 63	506UNTS281	107390
UNICEF (Children)	Togo	27 Jun 63	540UNTS135	107847
Italy	IAEA (Atom Energy)	11 Oct 63	639UNTS25	109142
WHO (World Health)	Somalia	08 Nov 63	493UNTS243	107218
WHO (World Health)	Sierra Leone	22 Nov 63	493UNTS255	107219
Nicaragua	United Nations	03 Dec 63	482UNTS329	107002
Algeria	United Nations	23 Sep 64	510UNTS217	107416
Australia	UN Special Fund	30 Sep 64	510UNTS277	107419
Kenya	United Nations	01 Oct 64	511UNTS199	107434
Romania	UN Special Fund	24 Oct 64	519UNTS29	107500
India	United Nations	25 Nov 64	519UNTS47	107501
UN Special Fund	Zambia	15 Dec 64	522UNTS3	107532
Mongolia	United Nations	06 Jan 65	522UNTS45	107535
United Nations	Yugoslavia	07 Jan 65	522UNTS55	107536
Ethiopia	WHO (World Health)	27 Jan 65	541UNTS135	107866
WHO (World Health)	Tunisia	27 Jan 65	528UNTS209	107644
Multilateral		23 Feb 65	527UNTS120	107622
Multilateral		05 Mar 65	527UNTS221	107627
Multilateral		12 May 65	534UNTS390	107769
Multilateral		14 May 65	550UNTS310	108026
Multilateral		25 May 65	535UNTS374	107791
Australia	Eur Space Vehicle	13 Jul 65	543UNTS183	107902
Multilateral		20 Jul 65	541UNTS12	107857
Multilateral		13 Sep 65	547UNTS248	107961
Multilateral		21 Sep 65	547UNTS280	107963
Multilateral		12 Nov 65	550UNTS160	108013
Hungary	United Nations	04 Mar 66	559UNTS3	108151

PARTY ONE	PARTY TWO	DATE	CITATION	NUMBER
IGO obligations (Cont.)				
Multilateral		12 May 66	563UNTS54	108204
Multilateral		23 Sep 66	573UNTS132	108327
United Nations	Sudan	08 Nov 66	576UNTS85	108365
IAEA (Atom Energy)	Turkey	08 Dec 66	608UNTS69	108813
India	IAEA (Atom Energy)	09 Dec 66	603UNTS35	108722
UNICEF (Children)	Zambia	02 Feb 67	589UNTS89	108536
Poland	United Nations	20 Feb 67	590UNTS71	108547
Multilateral		27 Feb 67	590UNTS156	108552
Multilateral		13 Apr 67	595UNTS60	108612
Malta	WHO (World Health)	10 May 67	603UNTS99	108727
Multilateral		14 Jun 67	603UNTS2	108719
Barbados	WHO (World Health)	18 Jul 67	603UNTS87	108726
Multilateral		26 Jul 67	614UNTS217	108872
New Zealand	WHO (World Health)	29 Aug 67	607UNTS57	108795
Cyprus	WHO (World Health)	07 Oct 67	608UNTS327	108821
Multilateral		12 Oct 67	607UNTS20	108793
Multilateral		12 Oct 67	607UNTS2	108792
Multilateral		27 Oct 67	608UNTS37	108811
Multilateral		14 Nov 67	614UNTS2	108860
State/IGO Group	Nigeria	20 Apr 68	636UNTS294	109106
State/IGO Group	Malaysia	10 May 68	636UNTS276	109105
State/IGO Group	Australia	21 May 68	636UNTS326	109108
Guyana	WHO (World Health)	03 Jul 68	642UNTS13	109161
India	United Nations	22 Jul 68	640UNTS121	109158
Adherence to UN Charter				
Accept UN Charter	Pakistan	30 Sep 47	8UNTS57	100112
Accept UN Charter	Bulgaria	09 Oct 48	223UNTS31	103045
UK Great Britain	Yemen	20 Jan 51	101UNTS39	101400
Accept UN Charter	Austria	06 Aug 52	223UNTS27	103044
ICJ Option Clause	Laos	24 Oct 52	149UNTS285	101957
ICJ Option Clause	Finland	26 Feb 54	189UNTS223	102546
Accept UN Charter	Jordan	11 Oct 55	223UNTS43	103048
ICJ Option Clause	UK Great Britain	31 Oct 55	219UNTS179	102973
Accept UN Charter	Romania	15 Dec 55	223UNTS69	103055
Burma	Yugoslavia	07 Mar 56	378UNTS99	105420
Accept UN Charter	Ghana	01 Mar 57	261UNTS113	103727
Accept UN Charter	Cameroon	13 Jan 60	375UNTS79	105354
Accept UN Charter	Malagasy	26 Jun 60	375UNTS87	105356
Accept UN Charter	Dahomey	02 Aug 60	375UNTS91	105357
Accept UN Charter	Niger	07 Aug 60	375UNTS95	105358
Accept UN Charter	Upper Volta	07 Aug 60	375UNTS99	105359
Accept UN Charter	Ivory Coast	07 Aug 60	375UNTS103	105360
Accept UN Charter	Chad	12 Aug 60	375UNTS107	105361
Accept UN Charter	Congo (Brazzaville)	12 Aug 60	375UNTS111	105362
Accept UN Charter	Central Afri Rep	13 Aug 60	375UNTS115	105363
Accept UN Charter	Senegal	20 Sep 60	376UNTS79	105374
Accept UN Charter	Gabon	02 Nov 60	379UNTS99	105436
Accept UN Charter	Somalia	11 Feb 61	388UNTS179	105577
Accept UN Charter	Congo (Zaire)	31 Oct 61	418UNTS157	106020
Accept UN Charter	Mongolia	04 Dec 61	434UNTS141	106261
Accept UN Charter	Rwanda	01 Jul 62	437UNTS145	106302
Accept UN Charter	Burundi	04 Jul 62	437UNTS149	106303
Accept UN Charter	Jamaica	06 Aug 62	437UNTS153	106304
Accept UN Charter	Trinidad/Tobago	06 Sep 62	437UNTS157	106305
Accept UN Charter	Algeria	30 Sep 62	442UNTS37	106336
Accept UN Charter	Uganda	09 Oct 62	443UNTS47	106357
Accept UN Charter	Zanzibar	10 Dec 63	483UNTS237	107016
Accept UN Charter	Kenya	12 Dec 63	483UNTS233	107015
Accept UN Charter	Malawi	04 Aug 64	519UNTS3	107496
Accept UN Charter	Zambia	26 Oct 64	519UNTS11	107498
Accept UN Charter	Mauritius	12 Mar 68	634UNTS217	109064
ICJ Option Clause	Swaziland	06 Sep 68	0UNTS0	109252

PARTY ONE	PARTY TWO	DATE	CITATION	NUMBER
Acceptance of UN obligations				
Accept UN Charter	Afghanistan	19 Nov 46	1UNTS39	100007
Accept UN Charter	Iceland	19 Nov 46	1UNTS41	100008
Accept UN Charter	Sweden	19 Nov 46	1UNTS43	100009
Accept UN Charter	Pakistan	30 Sep 47	8UNTS57	100112
Accept UN Charter	Yemen	30 Sep 47	8UNTS59	100113
Multilateral		06 Mar 48	289UNTS3	104214
Multilateral		30 Apr 48	119UNTS3	101609
Italy	UK Great Britain	21 Mar 50	128UNTS225	101722
Accept UN Charter	Libya	24 Dec 51	223UNTS51	103050
Accept UN Charter	Cambodia	15 Jun 52	223UNTS35	103046
Accept UN Charter	Austria	06 Aug 52	223UNTS27	103044
Ethiopia	UK Great Britain	29 Aug 52	190UNTS329	102573
Libya	UK Great Britain	29 Jul 53	186UNTS185	102491
ICJ Option Clause	San Marino	11 Jan 54	186UNTS295	102495
ICJ Option Clause	Japan	25 Mar 54	188UNTS137	102524
Accept UN Charter	Jordan	11 Oct 55	223UNTS43	103048
Accept UN Charter	Nepal	15 Dec 55	223UNTS65	103054
Accept UN Charter	Romania	15 Dec 55	223UNTS69	103055
Accept UN Charter	Malagasy	26 Jun 60	375UNTS87	105356
Accept UN Charter	Dahomey	02 Aug 60	375UNTS91	105357
Accept UN Charter	Upper Volta	07 Aug 60	375UNTS99	105359
Accept UN Charter	Niger	07 Aug 60	375UNTS95	105358
Accept UN Charter	Ivory Coast	07 Aug 60	375UNTS103	105360
Accept UN Charter	Chad	12 Aug 60	375UNTS107	105361
Accept UN Charter	Congo (Brazzaville)	12 Aug 60	375UNTS111	105362
Accept UN Charter	Central Afri Rep	13 Aug 60	375UNTS115	105363
Accept UN Charter	Mali	22 Oct 60	377UNTS361	105412
Accept UN Charter	Gabon	02 Nov 60	379UNTS99	105436
Accept UN Charter	Somalia	11 Feb 61	388UNTS179	105577
Accept UN Charter	Sierra Leone	27 Apr 61	409UNTS44	105876
Accept UN Charter	Congo (Zaire)	31 Oct 61	418UNTS157	106020
Accept UN Charter	Tanganyika	09 Dec 61	416UNTS147	106000
Accept UN Charter	Rwanda	01 Jul 62	437UNTS145	106302
Accept UN Charter	Burundi	04 Jul 62	437UNTS149	106303
Accept UN Charter	Jamaica	06 Aug 62	437UNTS153	106304
Accept UN Charter	Trinidad/Tobago	06 Sep 62	437UNTS157	106305
Accept UN Charter	Algeria	30 Sep 62	442UNTS37	106336
Accept UN Charter	Uganda	09 Oct 62	443UNTS47	106357
Accept UN Charter	Mauritania	20 Mar 63	457UNTS59	106576
Accept UN Charter	Kuwait	20 Apr 63	463UNTS213	106705
Multilateral		25 May 63	479UNTS39	106947
Accept UN Charter	Zanzibar	10 Dec 63	483UNTS237	107016
Accept UN Charter	Kenya	12 Dec 63	483UNTS233	107015
Accept UN Charter	Malawi	04 Aug 64	519UNTS3	107496
Accept UN Charter	Malta	29 Sep 64	519UNTS7	107497
Accept UN Charter	Zambia	26 Oct 64	519UNTS11	107498
Ethiopia	ILO (Labor Org)	10 Dec 64	521UNTS217	107524
Accept UN Charter	Gambia	18 Feb 65	545UNTS143	107928
Japan	Korea, South	22 Jun 65	583UNTS33	108471
Accept UN Charter	Maldive Islands	26 Aug 65	545UNTS147	107929
Accept UN Charter	Singapore	04 Sep 65	545UNTS151	107930
Accept UN Charter	Guyana	04 Jun 66	572UNTS225	108316
Accept UN Charter	Botswana	30 Sep 66	575UNTS151	108357
Accept UN Charter	Lesotho	04 Oct 66	575UNTS155	108358
Accept UN Charter	United Arab Rep	30 Nov 66	581UNTS131	108437
Accept UN Charter	Southern Yemen	30 Nov 67	614UNTS21	108861
ICJ Option Clause	Swaziland	06 Sep 68	0UNTS0	109252
Acceptance of obligations upon admittance to UN				
Accept UN Charter	Pakistan	30 Sep 47	8UNTS57	100112
Accept UN Charter	Burma	17 Mar 48	15UNTS3	100225
Accept UN Charter	Ceylon (Sri Lanka)	16 Jun 48	223UNTS39	103047
Accept UN Charter	Bulgaria	09 Oct 48	223UNTS31	103045
Accept UN Charter	Israel	29 Nov 48	30UNTS53	100448

PARTY ONE	PARTY TWO	DATE	CITATION	NUMBER
Acceptance of obligations upon admittance to UN (Cont.)				
Accept UN Charter	Albania	02 Dec 48	223UNTS23	103043
Accept UN Charter	Hungary	10 Mar 49	223UNTS55	103051
Accept UN Charter	Indonesia	25 Sep 50	71UNTS153	100916
Accept UN Charter	Japan	16 Jun 52	256UNTS167	103626
Accept UN Charter	Laos	30 Jun 52	223UNTS47	103049
Accept UN Charter	Austria	06 Aug 52	223UNTS27	103044
Accept UN Charter	Spain	23 Sep 55	223UNTS63	103053
Accept UN Charter	Jordan	11 Oct 55	223UNTS43	103048
Accept UN Charter	Romania	14 Dec 55	223UNTS59	103052
Accept UN Charter	Romania	15 Dec 55	223UNTS69	103055
Accept UN Charter	Sudan	12 Jan 56	253UNTS81	103576
Accept UN Charter	Portugal	04 Feb 56	229UNTS3	103155
Accept UN Charter	Italy	22 Feb 56	231UNTS175	103217
Accept UN Charter	Tunisia	14 Jul 56	253UNTS85	103577
Accept UN Charter	Morocco	17 Jul 56	253UNTS77	103575
Accept UN Charter	Ireland	06 Nov 56	254UNTS223	103594
Accept UN Charter	Fed of Malaya	31 Aug 57	277UNTS3	103995
Accept UN Charter	Guinea	03 Dec 58	317UNTS77	104595
Accept UN Charter	Togo	21 May 60	375UNTS83	105355
Accept UN Charter	Dahomey	02 Aug 60	375UNTS91	105357
Accept UN Charter	Nigeria	21 Mar 61	395UNTS237	105688
Accept UN Charter	Sierra Leone	27 Apr 61	409UNTS44	105876
Accept UN Charter	Cyprus	29 May 61	397UNTS283	105711
Accept UN Charter	Mongolia	04 Dec 61	434UNTS141	106261
Accept UN Charter	Tanganyika	09 Dec 61	416UNTS147	106000
Accept UN Charter	Gambia	18 Feb 65	545UNTS143	107928
UK Great Britain	Venezuela	17 Feb 66	561UNTS321	108192
Accept UN Charter	Guinea	25 Oct 68	0UNTS0	109295
Optional clause ICJ				
Multilateral		17 Apr 46	27UNTS103	100402
ICJ Option Clause	Sweden	05 Apr 47	2UNTS3	100016
ICJ Option Clause	Brazil	12 Feb 48	15UNTS221	100237
Multilateral		06 Mar 48	289UNTS3	104214
ICJ Option Clause	Bolivia	05 Jul 48	16UNTS207	100261
ICJ Option Clause	Switzerland	06 Jul 48	17UNTS111	100271
ICJ Option Clause	Liechtenstein	10 Mar 50	51UNTS115	100758
Israel	USA (United States)	09 May 52	177UNTS269	102326
France	Sweden	16 Feb 54	228UNTS137	103147
ICJ Option Clause	India	07 Jan 56	226UNTS235	103116
ICJ Option Clause	Norway	17 Dec 56	256UNTS315	103642
India	Italy	16 Jul 59	464UNTS129	106714
Liberia	Sweden	09 Dec 59	464UNTS219	106716
Multilateral		15 Mar 60	572UNTS133	108310
Jordan	Netherlands	24 Aug 61	466UNTS3	106733
Guinea	Norway	21 Jun 62	466UNTS81	106738
Liberia	Norway	29 Jun 62	466UNTS95	106739
Algeria	France	03 Jul 62	507UNTS25	107395
ICJ Option Clause	Mauritius	23 Sep 68	0UNTS0	109251
ICJ Option Clause	UK Great Britain	01 Jan 69	0UNTS0	109370
Compulsory jurisdiction				
ICJ Option Clause	UK Great Britain	13 Feb 46	1UNTS3	100001
ICJ Option Clause	Netherlands	05 Aug 46	1UNTS7	100002
ICJ Option Clause	USA (United States)	14 Aug 46	1UNTS9	100003
ICJ Option Clause	Taiwan	26 Oct 46	1UNTS35	100005
ICJ Option Clause	Norway	16 Nov 46	1UNTS37	100006
ICJ Option Clause	Denmark	10 Dec 46	1UNTS45	100010
ICJ Option Clause	Guatemala	27 Jan 47	1UNTS49	100012
ICJ Option Clause	France	18 Feb 47	26UNTS91	100378
ICJ Option Clause	Sweden	05 Apr 47	2UNTS3	100016
ICJ Option Clause	Turkey	22 May 47	4UNTS265	100050
Italy	Philippines	09 Jul 47	44UNTS3	100674
ICJ Option Clause	Philippines	12 Jul 47	7UNTS229	100101
ICJ Option Clause	Mexico	23 Oct 47	9UNTS97	100127
ICJ Option Clause	Belgium	10 Jun 48	16UNTS203	100260

PARTY ONE	PARTY TWO	DATE	CITATION	NUMBER
Compulsory jurisdiction (Cont.)				
ICJ Option Clause	Pakistan	22 Jun 48	16UNTS197	100259
ICJ Option Clause	Bolivia	05 Jul 48	16UNTS207	100261
ICJ Option Clause	Switzerland	06 Jul 48	17UNTS115	100272
Belgium	Canada	30 Aug 49	53UNTS221	100782
ICJ Option Clause	Liechtenstein	10 Mar 50	51UNTS115	100758
ICJ Option Clause	Liechtenstein	10 Mar 50	51UNTS119	100759
ICJ Option Clause	Thailand	20 May 50	65UNTS157	100844
ICJ Option Clause	Israel	04 Sep 50	108UNTS239	101477
ICJ Option Clause	Japan	24 Nov 51	137UNTS3	101842
ICJ Option Clause	Liberia	03 Mar 52	163UNTS117	102145
ICJ Option Clause	Ceylon (Sri Lanka)	23 Apr 52	137UNTS7	101843
ICJ Option Clause	Cambodia	17 Jul 52	137UNTS11	101844
Multilateral		06 Sep 52	216UNTS132	102937
ICJ Option Clause	Vietnam, South	05 Nov 52	150UNTS147	101968
Multilateral		19 Oct 53	207UNTS189	102807
ICJ Option Clause	San Marino	11 Jan 54	186UNTS295	102495
ICJ Option Clause	Australia	06 Feb 54	186UNTS77	102484
ICJ Option Clause	UK Great Britain	02 Jun 55	211UNTS109	102849
ICJ Option Clause	South Africa	12 Sep 55	216UNTS115	102935
ICJ Option Clause	UK Great Britain	31 Oct 55	219UNTS179	102973
ICJ Option Clause	Portugal	19 Dec 55	224UNTS275	103079
ICJ Option Clause	India	07 Jan 56	226UNTS235	103116
ICJ Option Clause	Netherlands	01 Aug 56	248UNTS33	103483
ICJ Option Clause	Israel	03 Oct 56	252UNTS301	103571
ICJ Option Clause	Denmark	10 Dec 56	257UNTS35	103646
ICJ Option Clause	Norway	17 Dec 56	256UNTS315	103642
ICJ Option Clause	UK Great Britain	18 Apr 57	265UNTS221	103814
Other Unilat Decla	United Arab Rep	24 Apr 57	265UNTS299	103821
Multilateral		29 Apr 57	320UNTS243	104646
ICJ Option Clause	Pakistan	23 May 57	269UNTS77	103875
Special Decla ICJ	United Arab Rep	18 Jun 57	272UNTS225	103940
ICJ Option Clause	Cambodia	09 Sep 57	277UNTS77	103998
ICJ Option Clause	Sudan	30 Dec 57	284UNTS215	104139
ICJ Option Clause	Belgium	03 Apr 58	302UNTS251	104364
ICJ Option Clause	Finland	25 Jun 58	303UNTS137	104376
ICJ Option Clause	Japan	15 Sep 58	312UNTS155	104517
ICJ Option Clause	UK Great Britain	26 Nov 58	316UNTS59	104577
ICJ Option Clause	France	10 Jul 59	337UNTS65	104816
ICJ Option Clause	India	14 Sep 59	340UNTS289	104871
Multilateral		01 Dec 59	402UNTS71	105778
ICJ Option Clause	Pakistan	12 Sep 60	374UNTS127	105332
Multilateral		21 Apr 61	484UNTS349	107041
Germany, West	Iceland	19 Jul 61	409UNTS47	105877
ICJ Option Clause	Somalia	25 Mar 63	458UNTS143	106597
ICJ Option Clause	Uganda	03 Oct 63	479UNTS35	106946
ICJ Option Clause	UK Great Britain	27 Nov 63	482UNTS187	106995
Ethiopia	ILO (Labor Org)	10 Dec 64	521UNTS217	107524
ICJ Option Clause	Kenya	12 Apr 65	531UNTS113	107697
ICJ Option Clause	Nigeria	14 Aug 65	544UNTS113	107913
ICJ Option Clause	France	16 May 66	562UNTS299	108196
ICJ Option Clause	Gambia	14 Jun 66	565UNTS21	108232
ICJ Option Clause	Malawi	22 Nov 66	581UNTS135	108438
ICJ Option Clause	Malta	29 Nov 66	580UNTS205	108423
ICJ Option Clause	Mauritius	23 Sep 68	0UNTS0	109251
ICJ Option Clause	UK Great Britain	01 Jan 69	0UNTS0	109370
Paragraph 2, Article 36				
Multilateral		17 Mar 48	19UNTS51	100304
France	USA (United States)	28 Jun 48	19UNTS9	100302
Italy	USA (United States)	28 Jun 48	20UNTS43	100314
Ireland	USA (United States)	28 Jun 48	24UNTS3	100349
Denmark	USA (United States)	29 Jun 48	22UNTS217	100338
Austria	USA (United States)	02 Jul 48	21UNTS29	100323
Greece	USA (United States)	02 Jul 48	23UNTS43	100342
Belgium	USA (United States)	02 Jul 48	19UNTS127	100309

PARTY ONE	PARTY TWO	DATE	CITATION	NUMBER
Paragraph 2, Article 36 (Cont.)				
Netherlands	USA (United States)	02 Jul 48	20UNTS91	100315
Norway	USA (United States)	03 Jul 48	20UNTS185	100317
Iceland	USA (United States)	03 Jul 48	20UNTS141	100316
Sweden	USA (United States)	03 Jul 48	23UNTS101	100343
Luxembourg	USA (United States)	03 Jul 48	24UNTS35	100350
Taiwan	USA (United States)	03 Jul 48	17UNTS119	100273
Turkey	USA (United States)	04 Jul 48	24UNTS67	100351
UK Great Britain	USA (United States)	06 Jul 48	22UNTS263	100339
Portugal	USA (United States)	28 Sep 48	29UNTS213	100442
Multilateral		19 Sep 49	125UNTS3	101671
France	India	02 Feb 51	203UNTS155	102744
Germany, West	USA (United States)	11 Jun 52	273UNTS105	103947
Spain	USA (United States)	26 Sep 53	207UNTS93	102802
Italy	Switzerland	17 Sep 55	291UNTS213	104257
Multilateral		19 May 56	399UNTS189	105742
Multilateral		17 Oct 63	525UNTS75	107585
OAU (Afri Unity)	United Nations	15 Nov 65	548UNTS315	200614
Trusteeship				
Multilateral		02 Apr 47	8UNTS189	100123
Multilateral		02 Oct 47	193UNTS188	102616
Multilateral		02 Dec 50	118UNTS255	200381
Jordan	UK Great Britain	01 May 51	117UNTS19	101582
Multilateral		25 Jun 51	92UNTS27	101258
Multilateral		27 Jul 51	97UNTS291	200273
Indonesia	Netherlands	15 Aug 62	437UNTS273	106311
Israel	UK Great Britain	15 Apr 65	551UNTS19	108031
Basic freedoms				
Multilateral		02 Dec 50	118UNTS255	200381
Multilateral		24 Jun 58	348UNTS275	105005
Multilateral		18 Oct 61	529UNTS89	107659
Administering authority				
Multilateral		13 Dec 46	8UNTS71	100115
Multilateral		13 Dec 46	8UNTS105	100117
Multilateral		13 Dec 46	8UNTS91	100116
Multilateral		13 Dec 46	8UNTS135	100119
Multilateral		13 Dec 46	8UNTS181	100122
Multilateral		13 Dec 46	8UNTS165	100121
Multilateral		13 Dec 46	8UNTS119	100118
Multilateral		02 Apr 47	8UNTS189	100123
Multilateral		11 Jul 47	218UNTS345	102961
Multilateral		01 Nov 47	10UNTS3	100138
Multilateral		29 Jun 49	138UNTS207	101870
Multilateral		02 Dec 50	118UNTS255	200381
Multilateral		31 May 54	192UNTS20	102592
Indonesia	Netherlands	15 Aug 62	437UNTS273	106311
Multilateral		10 Dec 62	521UNTS231	107525
United Nations	UK Great Britain	27 Jun 63	469UNTS145	106789
Disposition of territory				
Multilateral		13 Dec 46	8UNTS181	100122
Multilateral		13 Dec 46	8UNTS119	100118
Multilateral		13 Dec 46	8UNTS165	100121
Multilateral		13 Dec 46	8UNTS91	100116
Multilateral		13 Dec 46	8UNTS135	100119
Multilateral		13 Dec 46	8UNTS151	100120
Multilateral		13 Dec 46	8UNTS105	100117
Multilateral		13 Dec 46	8UNTS71	100115
Multilateral		02 Apr 47	8UNTS189	100123
Multilateral		01 Nov 47	10UNTS3	100138
Italy	UK Great Britain	20 Mar 50	128UNTS201	101721
Italy	UK Great Britain	21 Mar 50	128UNTS225	101722
Multilateral		02 Dec 50	118UNTS255	200381
Multilateral		08 Sep 51	136UNTS45	101832
Ethiopia	UK Great Britain	29 Aug 52	190UNTS329	102573

PARTY ONE	PARTY TWO	DATE	CITATION	NUMBER
Disposition of territory (Cont.)				
Canada	UK Great Britain	10 Dec 59	379UNTS201	105440
Multilateral		15 Aug 62	437UNTS292	106312
Definition of territory				
Multilateral		13 Dec 46	8UNTS105	100117
Multilateral		13 Dec 46	8UNTS71	100115
Multilateral		13 Dec 46	8UNTS91	100116
Multilateral		13 Dec 46	8UNTS151	100120
Multilateral		13 Dec 46	8UNTS181	100122
Multilateral		13 Dec 46	8UNTS119	100118
Multilateral		13 Dec 46	8UNTS165	100121
Multilateral		13 Dec 46	8UNTS135	100119
Multilateral		02 Apr 47	8UNTS189	100123
Greece	UK Great Britain	07 Apr 47	11UNTS201	100158
Multilateral		01 Nov 47	10UNTS3	100138
South Africa	UK Great Britain	22 Feb 49	93UNTS75	101291
Italy	UK Great Britain	20 Mar 50	128UNTS201	101721
Italy	UK Great Britain	21 Mar 50	128UNTS225	101722
Multilateral		02 Dec 50	118UNTS255	200381
Australia	UK Great Britain	19 Dec 50	93UNTS81	101292
Multilateral		08 Sep 51	136UNTS45	101832
UK Great Britain	USA (United States)	06 Apr 61	404UNTS215	105812
Socio-economic development				
Multilateral		13 Dec 46	8UNTS165	100121
Multilateral		13 Dec 46	8UNTS105	100117
Multilateral		13 Dec 46	8UNTS151	100120
Multilateral		13 Dec 46	8UNTS71	100115
Multilateral		13 Dec 46	8UNTS181	100122
Multilateral		13 Dec 46	8UNTS91	100116
Multilateral		13 Dec 46	8UNTS135	100119
Multilateral		13 Dec 46	8UNTS119	100118
Multilateral		02 Apr 47	8UNTS189	100123
Multilateral		11 Jul 47	218UNTS345	102961
Multilateral		01 Nov 47	10UNTS3	100138
Multilateral		02 Dec 50	118UNTS255	200381
Multilateral		25 May 55	264UNTS117	103791
Multilateral		26 Jun 57	328UNTS247	104738
Multilateral		22 Jun 62	494UNTS249	107237
Multilateral		13 Jul 64	569UNTS65	108279
Asian Productivity	ILO (Labor Org)	27 Oct 64	516UNTS367	200610
ILO (Labor Org)	LAFTA (Free Trade)	02 Jul 65	563UNTS327	200619
Barbados	UNICEF (Children)	30 Mar 68	637UNTS0	109123
Respect for local customs				
Multilateral		13 Dec 46	8UNTS105	100117
Multilateral		13 Dec 46	8UNTS71	100115
Multilateral		13 Dec 46	8UNTS151	100120
Multilateral		13 Dec 46	8UNTS165	100121
Multilateral		13 Dec 46	8UNTS181	100122
Multilateral		13 Dec 46	8UNTS119	100118
Multilateral		13 Dec 46	8UNTS135	100119
Multilateral		01 Nov 47	10UNTS3	100138
Multilateral		02 Dec 50	118UNTS255	200381
Internal travel				
Multilateral		13 Dec 46	8UNTS151	100120
Multilateral		13 Dec 46	8UNTS91	100116
Multilateral		02 Apr 47	8UNTS189	100123
Multilateral		02 Dec 50	118UNTS255	200381
Ecuador	USA (United States)	05 Apr 63	477UNTS135	106919
UNICEF (Children)	Trinidad/Tobago	08 Aug 63	473UNTS281	106865
Paraguay	USA (United States)	16 Sep 63	494UNTS101	107229
Rwanda	UNICEF (Children)	11 Sep 64	510UNTS127	107409
India	USA (United States)	30 Sep 64	532UNTS321	107726
Denmark	Netherlands	20 Jun 67	619UNTS67	108939

PARTY ONE	PARTY TWO	DATE	CITATION	NUMBER
Disposition of particulars				
Panama	USA (United States)	25 Jan 55	243UNTS211	103454
UNESCO (Educ/Cult)	USA (United States)	19 Jan 62	435UNTS99	106272
Netherlands	USA (United States)	06 Feb 63	487UNTS113	107098
Specific claims or waivers				
Norway	USA (United States)	28 Mar 40	88UNTS365	200253
Mexico	USA (United States)	19 Nov 41	148UNTS367	200474
Mexico	USA (United States)	29 Sep 43	106UNTS265	200345
Turkey	UK Great Britain	23 Mar 44	2UNTS227	200015
Mexico	Netherlands	07 Feb 46	3UNTS13	100022
UK Great Britain	USA (United States)	07 May 46	6UNTS285	100082
Canada	USA (United States)	15 Nov 46	7UNTS141	100096
Multilateral		19 Oct 48	84UNTS201	101130
Japan	USA (United States)	14 Apr 49	89UNTS141	101215
Canada	USA (United States)	24 Jan 50	151UNTS171	101992
Panama	USA (United States)	26 Jan 50	132UNTS233	101763
Germany, West	Netherlands	14 Dec 50	87UNTS257	101177
Canada	France	26 Jan 51	233UNTS65	103251
France	UK Great Britain	11 Apr 51	106UNTS3	101456
Germany, West	Norway	07 May 51	92UNTS51	101260
Denmark	Norway	14 Jan 52	120UNTS119	101618
Italy	UK Great Britain	06 Nov 52	158UNTS431	102076
Denmark	Germany, West	26 Feb 53	178UNTS3	102332
Germany, West	UK Great Britain	27 Feb 53	330UNTS217	104747
Multilateral		27 Feb 53	333UNTS3	104764
Germany, West	USA (United States)	27 Feb 53	205UNTS103	102771
Australia	Japan	24 May 54	191UNTS125	102580
Japan	USA (United States)	04 Jan 55	237UNTS197	103346
Greece	UK Great Britain	24 Feb 55	209UNTS187	102827
Multilateral		10 May 55	273UNTS121	103948
Japan	USA (United States)	24 Aug 55	257UNTS297	103662
Iceland	USA (United States)	23 Nov 56	281UNTS361	104088
France	Japan	27 Mar 57	318UNTS233	104617
Multilateral		29 Mar 57	283UNTS137	104113
Honduras	Nicaragua	22 Jun 57	277UNTS159	104005
France	USA (United States)	30 Jan 58	304UNTS9	104388
Philippines	USA (United States)	21 Jan 59	341UNTS255	104888
Finland	USSR (Soviet Union)	29 Apr 59	346UNTS209	104981
Greece	UK Great Britain	14 May 59	360UNTS69	105154
Norway	USSR (Soviet Union)	09 Dec 59	361UNTS93	105173
Poland	USA (United States)	16 Jul 60	384UNTS169	105518
United Nations	United Arab Rep	17 Oct 60	388UNTS143	105575
Denmark	USSR (Soviet Union)	27 Feb 64	509UNTS285	107407
Canada	Jamaica	16 Jul 65	548UNTS265	107982
Italy	USA (United States)	16 Dec 65	574UNTS139	108346
Italy	United Nations	18 Jan 67	588UNTS197	108525
Facilities and property				
Bolivia	Brazil	25 Feb 38	51UNTS245	200192
Brazil	Paraguay	14 Jun 41	54UNTS259	200198
Panama	USA (United States)	07 Jun 43	21UNTS269	200128
Mexico	USA (United States)	03 Feb 44	3UNTS313	200025
Canada	USA (United States)	07 Jun 44	99UNTS259	200280
Brazil	Paraguay	11 Aug 44	67UNTS303	200227
Canada	USA (United States)	03 Mar 46	6UNTS279	100081
Portugal	USA (United States)	30 May 46	174UNTS187	102285
United Nations	Switzerland	01 Jul 46	1UNTS153	200007
Iceland	UK Great Britain	04 Jul 46	6UNTS223	100077
League of Nations	United Nations	19 Jul 46	1UNTS109	200002
League of Nations	United Nations	31 Jul 46	1UNTS119	200003
League of Nations	United Nations	01 Aug 46	1UNTS131	200004
League of Nations	United Nations	01 Aug 46	1UNTS135	200005
Sweden	USA (United States)	30 Sep 46	42UNTS213	100649
Norway	USA (United States)	12 Nov 46	42UNTS227	100651
Canada	USA (United States)	09 Jan 47	11UNTS341	100173

PARTY ONE	PARTY TWO	DATE	CITATION	NUMBER
Facilities and property (Cont.)				
Canada	USA (United States)	06 Mar 47	11UNTS325	100172
Australia	USA (United States)	10 Mar 47	10UNTS89	100145
Switzerland	USA (United States)	30 Apr 47	42UNTS235	100652
UK Great Britain	USA (United States)	23 May 47	11UNTS211	100159
League of Nations	United Nations	27 Jun 47	5UNTS395	200037
League of Nations	United Nations	27 Jun 47	5UNTS389	200036
Multilateral		10 Jul 47	5UNTS401	200038
France	Norway	15 Jul 47	15UNTS5	100226
Ceylon (Sri Lanka)	UK Great Britain	28 Feb 49	314UNTS269	104551
United Arab Rep	UK Great Britain	31 May 49	226UNTS273	103122
Italy	UK Great Britain	14 Jun 49	135UNTS49	101813
China People's Rep	USSR (Soviet Union)	14 Feb 50	226UNTS31	103105
Belgium	UK Great Britain	06 Apr 51	110UNTS3	101496
UK Great Britain	USA (United States)	25 Apr 51	99UNTS97	101373
Italy	UK Great Britain	12 Nov 51	135UNTS55	101814
Japan	USA (United States)	28 Feb 52	208UNTS255	102817
Japan	UK Great Britain	04 Nov 52	164UNTS101	102161
Japan	UK Great Britain	04 Nov 52	164UNTS107	102162
United Arab Rep	UK Great Britain	05 Jan 53	207UNTS277	102810
Jordan	Syria	04 Jun 53	184UNTS15	102437
Canada	USA (United States)	30 Jun 53	206UNTS93	102786
Panama	USA (United States)	25 Mar 54	232UNTS289	103243
Canada	USA (United States)	22 Sep 55	256UNTS227	103632
Austria	USA (United States)	26 Sep 55	272UNTS31	103930
Austria	Italy	22 Oct 55	260UNTS327	103716
France	USA (United States)	23 Mar 56	278UNTS131	104029
Netherlands	USA (United States)	16 Aug 56	279UNTS3	104031
Germany, West	Netherlands	20 Sep 56	509UNTS269	107405
Liberia	USA (United States)	22 Sep 56	278UNTS109	104027
United Nations	United Arab Rep	08 Jan 57	257UNTS75	103650
Peru	USA (United States)	17 Apr 57	283UNTS3	104102
Ecuador	USA (United States)	24 Apr 57	284UNTS3	104124
UK Great Britain	USA (United States)	20 Jan 58	304UNTS3	104387
Germany, West	Netherlands	28 Jan 58	453UNTS183	106525
Multilateral		31 Mar 58	320UNTS103	104639
Philippines	USA (United States)	17 Jul 58	335UNTS199	104787
UK Great Britain	USA (United States)	30 Dec 58	338UNTS281	104841
Chile	USA (United States)	19 Feb 59	343UNTS17	104918
Multilateral		29 Apr 59	346UNTS167	104980
Canada	USA (United States)	01 May 59	343UNTS27	104919
Greece	Yugoslavia	18 Jun 59	363UNTS133	105205
Norway	South Africa	30 Oct 59	346UNTS21	104975
Sudan	United Arab Rep	08 Nov 59	453UNTS51	106519
Ethiopia	France	12 Nov 59	381UNTS3	105465
Australia	USA (United States)	26 Feb 60	354UNTS95	105056
Germany, West	USA (United States)	16 Mar 60	371UNTS101	105272
Spain	USA (United States)	18 Mar 60	372UNTS13	105284
Canada	USA (United States)	31 Mar 60	400UNTS315	105755
Mexico	USA (United States)	12 Apr 60	372UNTS47	105287
Belgium	Netherlands	20 Jun 60	423UNTS19	106084
Cyprus	UK Great Britain	16 Aug 60	382UNTS201	105480
Cyprus	UK Great Britain	16 Aug 60	382UNTS189	105479
Cyprus	UK Great Britain	16 Aug 60	382UNTS207	105481
Cyprus	UK Great Britain	16 Aug 60	382UNTS177	105477
South Africa	USA (United States)	13 Sep 60	388UNTS65	105572
Mexico	USA (United States)	24 Oct 60	401UNTS137	105767
Canada	USA (United States)	17 Jan 61	542UNTS224	107894
Canada	USA (United States)	17 Oct 61	426UNTS201	106138
Canada	USA (United States)	19 Apr 62	445UNTS265	106394
Germany, West	Israel	01 Jun 62	448UNTS227	106435
Multilateral		25 Jul 62	506UNTS177	107387
Philippines	USA (United States)	11 Jan 63	473UNTS43	106853
Greece	UK Great Britain	09 May 63	398UNTS179	105722
Netherlands	USA (United States)	20 May 63	487UNTS123	107099
Malagasy	USA (United States)	07 Oct 63	494UNTS3	107221

PARTY ONE	PARTY TWO	DATE	CITATION	NUMBER
Facilities and property (Cont.)				
Canada	USA (United States)	22 Jan 64	530UNTS89	107674
Spain	USA (United States)	29 Jan 64	511UNTS61	107427
Liberia	USA (United States)	14 Apr 64	526UNTS221	107606
UK Great Britain	USA (United States)	20 Aug 64	531UNTS85	107694
Poland	UK Great Britain	26 Sep 64	539UNTS153	107828
Norway	UK Great Britain	28 Sep 64	548UNTS63	107970
UK Great Britain	USSR (Soviet Union)	30 Sep 64	539UNTS159	107829
UNESCO (Educ/Cult)	USA (United States)	16 Oct 64	550UNTS23	108006
Portugal	USA (United States)	12 Nov 64	541UNTS251	107874
USA (United States)	USSR (Soviet Union)	14 Dec 64	531UNTS213	107705
UK Great Britain	USA (United States)	07 Jul 65	551UNTS221	108044
Laos	Thailand	12 Aug 65	547UNTS209	107958
Norway	Eur Space Research	31 Jan 66	580UNTS3	108414
Spain	USA (United States)	14 Apr 66	579UNTS173	108406
Burma	USA (United States)	01 Jun 66	580UNTS253	108428
Nigeria	United Nations	07 Feb 67	590UNTS25	108544
Aquisition of property				
Finland	Norway	20 May 53	173UNTS163	102265
Multilateral		24 Feb 56	243UNTS147	103451
Boundaries of territory				
Czechoslovakia	USSR (Soviet Union)	29 Jun 45	504UNTS299	200607
Norway	USSR (Soviet Union)	18 Dec 47	52UNTS3	100768
Liberia	USA (United States)	26 Jul 48	182UNTS73	102423
Australia	New Zealand	26 Nov 49	198UNTS161	102662
Pakistan	Saudi Arabia	25 Nov 51	177UNTS3	102304
Belgium	France	21 Mar 52	137UNTS249	101856
Japan	USA (United States)	24 Dec 53	222UNTS193	103028
UK Great Britain	USA (United States)	19 Jul 54	250UNTS193	103523
Multilateral		12 Mar 55	211UNTS3	102844
Norway	Sweden	09 Mar 56	369UNTS285	105262
Czechoslovakia	Hungary	13 Oct 56	300UNTS177	104337
Czechoslovakia	USSR (Soviet Union)	30 Nov 56	266UNTS243	103833
Belgium	Netherlands	03 Feb 58	381UNTS305	105472
Italy	Switzerland	23 May 58	363UNTS81	105201
Multilateral		05 Nov 58	428UNTS73	106169
Multilateral		01 Dec 59	402UNTS71	105778
Austria	Switzerland	02 Sep 63	548UNTS91	107973
Canada	USA (United States)	27 Dec 63	494UNTS21	107223
Canada	USA (United States)	06 Mar 64	524UNTS255	107577
Denmark	Netherlands	31 Mar 66	604UNTS209	108751
UK Great Britain	USA (United States)	30 Dec 66	603UNTS273	108737
Muscat and Oman	UK Great Britain	15 Nov 67	617UNTS319	108919
Pasturage in frontier zones				
France	Norway	26 Mar 46	31UNTS69	100468
Finland	Norway	10 Sep 48	32UNTS3	100486
Italy	Yugoslavia	03 Feb 49	33UNTS105	100517
Finland	Norway	18 Mar 52	188UNTS187	102527
Austria	Yugoslavia	19 Mar 53	467UNTS323	106768
Italy	Switzerland	02 Jul 53	257UNTS99	103653
Ethiopia	UK Great Britain	29 Nov 54	207UNTS283	102811
Turkey	USSR (Soviet Union)	24 Feb 67	643UNTS153	109190
Changes of territory				
Haiti	USA (United States)	19 Oct 42	120UNTS171	200390
Taiwan	France	18 Aug 45	14UNTS477	200101
Finland	USSR (Soviet Union)	03 Feb 47	216UNTS231	102939
Greece	UK Great Britain	07 Apr 47	11UNTS201	100158
South Africa	UK Great Britain	22 Feb 49	93UNTS75	101291
China People's Rep	USSR (Soviet Union)	14 Feb 50	226UNTS31	103105
France	India	02 Feb 51	203UNTS155	102744
Poland	USSR (Soviet Union)	15 Feb 51	432UNTS199	106222
Japan	USA (United States)	24 Dec 53	222UNTS193	103028
UK Great Britain	USA (United States)	19 Jul 54	250UNTS193	103523
Multilateral		05 Oct 54	235UNTS99	103297

PARTY ONE	PARTY TWO	DATE	CITATION	NUMBER
Changes of territory (Cont.)				
Ethiopia	UK Great Britain	12 Aug 55	227UNTS3	103127
Multilateral		29 Oct 56	263UNTS165	103772
Germany, West	Netherlands	08 Apr 60	508UNTS14	107404
Austria	Belgium	14 Nov 63	544UNTS97	107912
Greece	Yugoslavia	05 Nov 64	539UNTS13	107820
Philippines	USA (United States)	16 Oct 67	632UNTS113	109013
Muscat and Oman	UK Great Britain	15 Nov 67	617UNTS319	108919
Fish, wildlife, and natural resources				
Canada	USA (United States)	05 Aug 44	121UNTS299	200408
Multilateral		30 Oct 46	27UNTS77	100401
Multilateral		03 Mar 47	11UNTS43	100148
Denmark	Norway	09 Jul 47	7UNTS321	100108
Poland	USSR (Soviet Union)	08 Jul 48	37UNTS25	100575
Finland	Norway	10 Sep 48	32UNTS3	100486
Finland	USSR (Soviet Union)	09 Dec 48	217UNTS135	102947
Norway	Sweden	28 Jan 49	196UNTS3	102617
Italy	Yugoslavia	13 Apr 49	171UNTS279	102232
Norway	Sweden	14 Dec 49	196UNTS19	102618
Norway	USSR (Soviet Union)	29 Dec 49	83UNTS291	101112
Italy	UK Great Britain	20 Mar 50	128UNTS201	101721
Italy	UK Great Britain	21 Mar 50	128UNTS225	101722
Belgium	Netherlands	23 Oct 50	136UNTS31	101831
Australia	UK Great Britain	19 Dec 50	93UNTS81	101292
Greece	Yugoslavia	02 Feb 52	188UNTS311	102535
Finland	Norway	18 Mar 52	188UNTS187	102527
Italy	Switzerland	02 Jul 53	257UNTS99	103653
Iran	USSR (Soviet Union)	02 Dec 54	451UNTS227	106497
Norway	Sweden	29 Jun 56	262UNTS335	103759
Czechoslovakia	Hungary	13 Oct 56	300UNTS125	104336
Czechoslovakia	USSR (Soviet Union)	30 Nov 56	266UNTS243	103833
Afghanistan	USSR (Soviet Union)	18 Jan 58	321UNTS77	104655
Multilateral		29 Apr 58	559UNTS285	108164
Multilateral		29 Apr 58	499UNTS311	107302
Finland	USSR (Soviet Union)	21 Feb 59	338UNTS3	104830
Czechoslovakia	Poland	04 Jul 59	363UNTS333	105210
Finland	USSR (Soviet Union)	23 Jun 60	379UNTS277	105443
Poland	USSR (Soviet Union)	05 Feb 61	420UNTS161	106046
Argentina	Chile	29 Dec 61	635UNTS111	109075
Hungary	Romania	13 Jun 63	576UNTS275	108369
Finland	USSR (Soviet Union)	24 Apr 64	537UNTS231	107804
Finland	Norway	09 Jun 64	503UNTS205	107345
Poland	UK Great Britain	26 Sep 64	539UNTS153	107828
Norway	UK Great Britain	28 Sep 64	548UNTS63	107970
UK Great Britain	USSR (Soviet Union)	30 Sep 64	539UNTS159	107829
Austria	Hungary	31 Oct 64	545UNTS241	107937
Finland	USSR (Soviet Union)	20 May 65	566UNTS31	108238
Finland	USSR (Soviet Union)	04 Jun 65	560UNTS169	108173
Denmark	Germany, West	30 Nov 67	632UNTS153	109017
Denmark	Norway	26 Apr 68	0UNTS0	109211
Denmark	Netherlands	30 May 68	0UNTS0	109233
Markers and definitions				
Argentina	Brazil	27 Dec 27	51UNTS271	200193
Brazil	UK Great Britain	15 Mar 40	5UNTS71	200029
Finland	USSR (Soviet Union)	11 Oct 40	67UNTS139	100872
Brazil	Paraguay	14 Jun 41	88UNTS401	200255
Taiwan	UK Great Britain	18 Jun 41	10UNTS227	200064
Multilateral		12 Sep 44	227UNTS279	200532
Belgium	France	21 May 45	23UNTS215	200133
Czechoslovakia	USSR (Soviet Union)	29 Jun 45	504UNTS299	200607
Multilateral		09 Jul 45	160UNTS359	200484
Multilateral		26 Jul 45	227UNTS297	200533
Poland	USSR (Soviet Union)	16 Aug 45	10UNTS193	200061
USA (United States)	USSR (Soviet Union)	17 Sep 45	235UNTS346	200538
France	Norway	26 Mar 46	31UNTS69	100468

Markers and definitions (Cont.)

PARTY ONE	PARTY TWO	DATE	CITATION	NUMBER
Afghanistan	USSR (Soviet Union)	13 Jun 46	31UNTS147	100476
Finland	USSR (Soviet Union)	03 Feb 47	216UNTS231	102939
Multilateral		10 Feb 47	48UNTS203	100746
Multilateral		10 Feb 47	41UNTS135	100644
Multilateral		10 Feb 47	49UNTS3	100747
Multilateral		10 Feb 47	41UNTS21	100643
Panama	USA (United States)	26 May 47	138UNTS137	101866
Denmark	Norway	09 Jul 47	7UNTS321	100108
Ethiopia	UK Great Britain	29 Sep 47	82UNTS191	101092
UK Great Britain	USA (United States)	23 Oct 47	66UNTS277	100859
Norway	USSR (Soviet Union)	18 Dec 47	52UNTS3	100768
Belgium	Luxembourg	25 Mar 48	18UNTS323	100300
Belgium	France	13 Apr 48	31UNTS409	100483
Belgium	France	23 Apr 48	19UNTS95	100307
Poland	USSR (Soviet Union)	08 Jul 48	37UNTS25	100575
Finland	USSR (Soviet Union)	09 Dec 48	217UNTS135	102947
Italy	Yugoslavia	03 Feb 49	33UNTS105	100517
Israel	Lebanon	23 Mar 49	42UNTS287	100655
Israel	Jordan	03 Apr 49	42UNTS303	100656
Belgium	UK Great Britain	14 Apr 49	65UNTS117	100840
Israel	Syria	20 Jul 49	42UNTS327	100657
India	Pakistan	27 Jul 49	81UNTS273	101076
Norway	Sweden	14 Dec 49	196UNTS19	102618
Norway	USSR (Soviet Union)	29 Dec 49	83UNTS291	101112
Panama	USA (United States)	24 May 50	241UNTS139	103430
Germany, East	Poland	06 Jul 50	319UNTS93	104631
Belgium	Netherlands	23 Oct 50	136UNTS31	101831
Poland	USSR (Soviet Union)	15 Feb 51	432UNTS199	106222
Germany, West	Netherlands	18 Jan 52	179UNTS147	102364
Germany, East	Poland	06 Feb 52	304UNTS131	104395
India	Pakistan	21 Aug 52	207UNTS161	102805
Belgium	France	30 Jan 53	188UNTS141	102525
Multilateral		07 Feb 53	173UNTS143	102264
Italy	Switzerland	02 Jul 53	257UNTS99	103653
Bulgaria	Yugoslavia	20 Feb 54	397UNTS13	105700
Belgium	Netherlands	28 Jun 54	272UNTS235	103942
Multilateral		05 Oct 54	235UNTS99	103297
Portugal	UK Great Britain	18 Nov 54	210UNTS265	102841
Portugal	UK Great Britain	18 Nov 54	325UNTS307	104706
Austria	Yugoslavia	27 Nov 54	396UNTS75	105694
Iran	USSR (Soviet Union)	02 Dec 54	451UNTS227	106497
Multilateral		15 May 55	217UNTS223	102949
USA (United States)	USSR (Soviet Union)	25 Jun 55	270UNTS15	103887
Czechoslovakia	Germany, East	24 Oct 55	504UNTS173	107358
Bulgaria	Yugoslavia	22 May 56	367UNTS119	105229
Bulgaria	Yugoslavia	16 Jun 56	375UNTS235	105368
Bulgaria	Yugoslavia	16 Jun 56	391UNTS3	105613
Belgium	Germany, West	24 Sep 56	314UNTS195	104549
Czechoslovakia	Hungary	13 Oct 56	300UNTS125	104336
Czechoslovakia	USSR (Soviet Union)	30 Nov 56	266UNTS243	103833
France	Libya	26 Dec 56	300UNTS263	104340
Norway	USSR (Soviet Union)	15 Feb 57	312UNTS289	104523
Poland	USSR (Soviet Union)	05 Mar 57	274UNTS133	103963
Iran	USSR (Soviet Union)	14 May 57	457UNTS161	106586
Bulgaria	Yugoslavia	04 Jun 57	349UNTS35	105008
Bulgaria	Yugoslavia	17 Jun 57	375UNTS249	105369
Norway	Sweden	16 Sep 57	428UNTS263	106178
Afghanistan	USSR (Soviet Union)	18 Jan 58	321UNTS77	104655
Czechoslovakia	Poland	31 Jan 58	431UNTS99	106214
Poland	USSR (Soviet Union)	18 Mar 58	340UNTS89	104861
Multilateral		29 Apr 58	516UNTS205	107477
Italy	Switzerland	23 May 58	363UNTS81	105201
Czechoslovakia	Poland	13 Jun 58	354UNTS221	105064
India	Pakistan	10 Sep 58	369UNTS81	105252
France	Italy	30 Oct 58	363UNTS3	105196

Markers and definitions (Cont.)

PARTY ONE	PARTY TWO	DATE	CITATION	NUMBER
Multilateral		20 Apr 59	376UNTS85	105375
Czechoslovakia	Poland	04 Jul 59	363UNTS333	105210
India	Pakistan	23 Oct 59	362UNTS3	105180
Norway	Sweden	28 Oct 59	427UNTS225	106157
India	Pakistan	11 Jan 60	375UNTS119	105364
Germany, West	Netherlands	08 Apr 60	508UNTS14	107404
Germany, West	Netherlands	03 Jun 60	487UNTS37	107094
Finland	USSR (Soviet Union)	23 Jun 60	379UNTS277	105443
Norway	UK Great Britain	17 Nov 60	398UNTS189	105723
Poland	USSR (Soviet Union)	05 Feb 61	420UNTS161	106046
Iceland	UK Great Britain	11 Mar 61	397UNTS275	105710
Argentina	Uruguay	07 Apr 61	635UNTS91	109074
Germany, West	Iceland	19 Jul 61	409UNTS47	105877
Belgium	Luxembourg	29 Nov 61	486UNTS37	107071
Argentina	Chile	29 Dec 61	635UNTS111	109075
Belgium	France	30 Mar 62	502UNTS297	107335
Norway	USSR (Soviet Union)	16 Apr 62	437UNTS175	106307
Czechoslovakia	Hungary	16 Oct 62	479UNTS301	106961
Hungary	Romania	13 Jun 63	576UNTS275	108369
Mexico	USA (United States)	29 Aug 63	505UNTS185	107374
Austria	Switzerland	02 Sep 63	548UNTS91	107973
Czechoslovakia	Hungary	22 Oct 63	514UNTS95	107444
Romania	Yugoslavia	20 Dec 63	527UNTS245	107629
Multilateral		09 Mar 64	581UNTS57	108432
France	Luxembourg	16 Jul 64	0UNTS0	109225
Argentina	Paraguay	21 Oct 64	635UNTS177	109081
Austria	Hungary	31 Oct 64	545UNTS241	107937
Germany, West	Netherlands	01 Dec 64	550UNTS123	108011
Norway	UK Great Britain	10 Mar 65	551UNTS213	108043
Hungary	Yugoslavia	08 Apr 65	587UNTS169	108511
Finland	USSR (Soviet Union)	20 May 65	566UNTS31	108238
Denmark	Germany, West	09 Jun 65	570UNTS91	108289
Japan	Korea, South	22 Jun 65	583UNTS51	108472
India	Pakistan	30 Jun 65	548UNTS277	107983
Hungary	Yugoslavia	09 Aug 65	577UNTS103	108375
Denmark	Norway	08 Dec 65	634UNTS71	109052
UK Great Britain	Venezuela	17 Feb 66	561UNTS321	108192
Denmark	Netherlands	31 Mar 66	604UNTS209	108751
Denmark	Norway	19 Dec 66	606UNTS3	108770
Multilateral		19 Dec 66	605UNTS313	108769
Germany, West	Netherlands	02 Feb 67	606UNTS105	108779
Denmark	Germany, West	02 Feb 67	606UNTS97	108778
Multilateral		02 Feb 67	606UNTS89	108777
Finland	USSR (Soviet Union)	05 May 67	640UNTS111	109157
Belgium	Denmark	29 Jun 67	606UNTS113	108780
Philippines	USA (United States)	16 Oct 67	632UNTS113	109013
Denmark	Germany, West	30 Nov 67	632UNTS153	109017

Frontier peoples and personnel

PARTY ONE	PARTY TWO	DATE	CITATION	NUMBER
Saudi Arabia	UK Great Britain	20 Apr 42	10UNTS117	200057
Belgium	France	21 May 45	23UNTS215	200133
Czechoslovakia	USSR (Soviet Union)	29 Jun 45	504UNTS299	200607
Multilateral		10 Feb 47	49UNTS3	100747
Belgium	Netherlands	28 Apr 47	37UNTS199	100577
Belgium	France	23 Apr 48	19UNTS95	100307
Romania	Yugoslavia	31 Dec 48	116UNTS103	101572
Belgium	France	08 Jan 49	36UNTS151	100569
Italy	Yugoslavia	03 Feb 49	33UNTS105	100517
Belgium	UK Great Britain	14 Apr 49	65UNTS117	100840
Belgium	Netherlands	20 Aug 49	46UNTS133	100706
Norway	USSR (Soviet Union)	29 Dec 49	83UNTS291	101112
Multilateral		10 Jan 52	163UNTS27	102139
Belgium	Germany, West	18 Jan 52	243UNTS3	103443
Belgium	France	30 Jan 53	188UNTS141	102525
Austria	Yugoslavia	19 Mar 53	467UNTS323	106768

PARTY ONE	PARTY TWO	DATE	CITATION	NUMBER
Frontier peoples and personnel (Cont.)				
Italy	Switzerland	02 Jul 53	257UNTS99	103653
Ethiopia	UK Great Britain	29 Nov 54	207UNTS283	102811
Bulgaria	Yugoslavia	22 May 56	367UNTS119	105229
Czechoslovakia	Germany, East	06 Oct 56	501UNTS109	107315
Czechoslovakia	USSR (Soviet Union)	30 Nov 56	266UNTS243	103833
Iran	USSR (Soviet Union)	14 May 57	457UNTS161	106586
France	Italy	27 Mar 58	305UNTS387	104426
Czechoslovakia	Poland	04 Jul 59	363UNTS333	105210
Germany, West	Netherlands	03 Jun 60	487UNTS37	107094
Cyprus	UK Great Britain	16 Aug 60	382UNTS177	105477
Argentina	Uruguay	07 Apr 61	635UNTS91	109074
Belgium	Luxembourg	29 Nov 61	486UNTS37	107071
Finland	USSR (Soviet Union)	27 Sep 62	479UNTS99	106949
Czechoslovakia	Hungary	16 Oct 62	479UNTS301	106961
Hungary	Romania	13 Jun 63	576UNTS275	108369
Austria	Switzerland	02 Sep 63	548UNTS91	107973
Romania	Yugoslavia	20 Dec 63	527UNTS245	107629
Austria	Hungary	31 Oct 64	545UNTS241	107937
Hungary	Yugoslavia	09 Aug 65	577UNTS103	108375
Austria	Yugoslavia	10 Oct 66	595UNTS273	108622
Frontier waterways				
Mexico	USA (United States)	03 Feb 44	3UNTS313	200025
Poland	USSR (Soviet Union)	08 Jul 48	37UNTS25	100575
Finland	USSR (Soviet Union)	09 Dec 48	217UNTS135	102947
Finland	Sweden	17 Feb 49	197UNTS123	102636
Norway	USSR (Soviet Union)	29 Dec 49	83UNTS291	101112
Germany, East	Poland	06 Feb 52	304UNTS131	104395
Portugal	UK Great Britain	21 Jan 53	175UNTS13	102293
Belgium	France	30 Jan 53	188UNTS141	102525
Czechoslovakia	Hungary	16 Apr 54	504UNTS231	107360
Portugal	UK Great Britain	18 Nov 54	325UNTS307	104706
Multilateral		24 Feb 56	243UNTS147	103451
Austria	Hungary	09 Apr 56	438UNTS123	106315
Czechoslovakia	Hungary	13 Oct 56	300UNTS125	104336
Czechoslovakia	USSR (Soviet Union)	30 Nov 56	266UNTS243	103833
Iran	USSR (Soviet Union)	14 May 57	457UNTS161	106586
Finland	Norway	28 Jun 57	272UNTS191	103938
China People's Rep	USSR (Soviet Union)	21 Dec 57	305UNTS213	104420
Afghanistan	USSR (Soviet Union)	18 Jan 58	321UNTS77	104655
Poland	USSR (Soviet Union)	18 Mar 58	340UNTS89	104861
Czechoslovakia	Poland	21 Mar 58	538UNTS89	107811
Multilateral		29 Apr 58	516UNTS205	107477
Australia	New Zealand	30 Sep 58	340UNTS61	104859
Canada	USA (United States)	27 Feb 59	341UNTS3	104873
Canada	USA (United States)	09 Mar 59	340UNTS295	104872
Greece	Yugoslavia	18 Jun 59	363UNTS133	105205
Germany, West	Netherlands	08 Apr 60	508UNTS14	107404
Finland	USSR (Soviet Union)	23 Jun 60	379UNTS277	105443
Finland	Sweden	21 Nov 60	383UNTS125	105498
Canada	USA (United States)	17 Jan 61	542UNTS224	107894
Poland	USSR (Soviet Union)	05 Feb 61	420UNTS161	106046
Germany, West	Iceland	19 Jul 61	409UNTS47	105877
Canada	USA (United States)	17 Oct 61	426UNTS201	106138
Finland	USSR (Soviet Union)	27 Sep 62	479UNTS99	106949
Belgium	Netherlands	13 May 63	540UNTS3	107843
Hungary	Romania	13 Jun 63	576UNTS275	108369
Mexico	USA (United States)	29 Aug 63	505UNTS185	107374
Romania	Yugoslavia	30 Nov 63	512UNTS2	107438
Finland	USSR (Soviet Union)	24 Apr 64	537UNTS231	107804
Poland	USSR (Soviet Union)	17 Jul 64	552UNTS175	108054
Argentina	Paraguay	21 Oct 64	635UNTS177	109081
Argentina	Paraguay	21 Oct 64	635UNTS189	109082
Austria	Hungary	31 Oct 64	545UNTS241	107937
Hungary	Yugoslavia	08 Apr 65	587UNTS169	108511

PARTY ONE	PARTY TWO	DATE	CITATION	NUMBER
Frontier waterways (Cont.)				
Austria	Hungary	09 Apr 65	638UNTS53	109131
Multilateral		30 Apr 66	620UNTS191	108956
Mexico	USA (United States)	24 Aug 66	606UNTS251	108789
Finland	Sweden	07 Oct 68	0UNTS0	109376
Frontier crossing points				
Netherlands	USA (United States)	17 Jan 33	474UNTS119	106877
Jordan	UK Great Britain	19 Jul 41	9UNTS381	200054
Canada	USA (United States)	10 Apr 43	21UNTS237	200126
France	Norway	26 Mar 46	31UNTS69	100468
Norway	USSR (Soviet Union)	18 Dec 47	52UNTS3	100768
Belgium	Netherlands	13 Apr 48	32UNTS153	100497
Belgium	France	13 Apr 48	31UNTS409	100483
Poland	USSR (Soviet Union)	08 Jul 48	37UNTS25	100575
Poland	USSR (Soviet Union)	08 Jul 48	37UNTS107	100576
Finland	Norway	10 Sep 48	32UNTS3	100486
Germany, East	Poland	06 Jul 50	319UNTS93	104631
Jordan	Syria	04 Jun 53	184UNTS15	102437
Ethiopia	UK Great Britain	29 Nov 54	207UNTS283	102811
Austria	Hungary	09 Apr 56	438UNTS123	106315
Indonesia	Philippines	04 Jul 56	401UNTS59	105763
Belgium	Germany, West	24 Sep 56	314UNTS195	104549
Czechoslovakia	Hungary	13 Oct 56	300UNTS177	104337
Czechoslovakia	Hungary	08 May 58	407UNTS92	105862
Hungary	USSR (Soviet Union)	21 Jul 58	408UNTS194	105871
Germany, West	Netherlands	10 Oct 58	486UNTS345	107085
Finland	USSR (Soviet Union)	21 Feb 59	338UNTS3	104830
Greece	Yugoslavia	18 Jun 59	388UNTS3	105570
Mexico	USA (United States)	05 Aug 59	356UNTS3	105089
Germany, West	Netherlands	08 Apr 60	508UNTS14	107404
Germany, West	Netherlands	03 Jun 60	487UNTS37	107094
Belgium	France	30 Mar 62	502UNTS297	107335
Finland	Sweden	05 Nov 62	455UNTS289	106548
Hungary	Romania	13 Jun 63	576UNTS275	108369
Romania	Yugoslavia	30 Nov 63	512UNTS2	107438
Multilateral		14 May 64	528UNTS13	107632
UK Great Britain	USSR (Soviet Union)	30 Sep 64	539UNTS159	107829
Czechoslovakia	Yugoslavia	08 Oct 64	544UNTS129	107916
Hungary	Yugoslavia	08 Apr 65	587UNTS169	108511
Austria	Hungary	09 Apr 65	638UNTS53	109131
Hungary	Yugoslavia	25 May 65	576UNTS145	108367
Hungary	Yugoslavia	23 Nov 65	577UNTS89	108374
Germany, West	Netherlands	22 Sep 66	0UNTS0	109226
Belgium	France	23 Sep 66	588UNTS227	108528
Finland	Sweden	07 Oct 68	0UNTS0	109376
Continental shelf				
Multilateral		29 Apr 58	499UNTS311	107302
Germany, West	Netherlands	01 Dec 64	550UNTS123	108011
Norway	UK Great Britain	10 Mar 65	551UNTS213	108043
Denmark	Germany, West	09 Jun 65	570UNTS91	108289
Netherlands	UK Great Britain	06 Oct 65	595UNTS105	108615
Netherlands	UK Great Britain	06 Oct 65	595UNTS113	108616
Denmark	Norway	08 Dec 65	634UNTS71	109052
Denmark	UK Great Britain	03 Mar 66	592UNTS207	108574
Germany, West	Netherlands	02 Feb 67	606UNTS105	108779
Denmark	Germany, West	02 Feb 67	606UNTS97	108778
Multilateral		02 Feb 67	606UNTS89	108777
Finland	USSR (Soviet Union)	05 May 67	640UNTS111	109157
Specific goods and equipment				
Brazil	Uruguay	22 Nov 44	65UNTS289	200217
Czechoslovakia	Yugoslavia	24 May 48	112UNTS215	101544
Multilateral		08 Apr 50	68UNTS99	100889
Canada	USA (United States)	13 Jun 55	268UNTS87	103851
Canada	USA (United States)	15 Jun 55	268UNTS101	103852
Germany, West	USA (United States)	02 Aug 55	268UNTS121	103854

PARTY ONE	PARTY TWO	DATE	CITATION	NUMBER
Specific goods and equipment (Cont.)				
Colombia	Italy	20 Dec 55	260UNTS315	103714
Canada	USA (United States)	24 Oct 56	281UNTS281	104084
Canada	USA (United States)	17 Jan 57	266UNTS109	103825
Finland	Norway	28 Jun 57	272UNTS191	103938
Philippines	USA (United States)	04 Oct 61	433UNTS83	106232
Australia	Fed of Malaya	26 Nov 62	453UNTS161	106523
Malta	USA (United States)	15 Jan 66	579UNTS109	108402
Conservation of specific resources				
UK Great Britain	USA (United States)	30 Apr 43	28UNTS341	200159
El Salvador	Guatemala	14 Dec 51	131UNTS131	101740
Libya	USA (United States)	28 Jul 55	270UNTS293	103902
Libya	USA (United States)	11 Dec 60	445UNTS125	106381
Multilateral		25 Nov 64	587UNTS19	108507
Multilateral		19 Dec 66	605UNTS313	108769
Denmark	Norway	19 Dec 66	606UNTS3	108770
Ocean resources				
Mexico	USA (United States)	24 Oct 42	21UNTS189	200123
Canada	USA (United States)	19 Dec 42	26UNTS363	200156
Multilateral		05 Apr 46	231UNTS199	103221
Mexico	USA (United States)	22 Oct 46	21UNTS13	100321
Multilateral		03 Mar 47	11UNTS43	100148
Philippines	USA (United States)	14 Mar 47	16UNTS31	100247
Multilateral		15 Nov 48	120UNTS59	101615
Norway	Sweden	28 Jan 49	196UNTS3	102617
Multilateral		08 Feb 49	157UNTS157	102053
Costa Rica	USA (United States)	31 May 49	80UNTS3	101041
Multilateral		24 Sep 49	126UNTS237	101691
Multilateral		08 Sep 51	136UNTS45	101832
Multilateral		01 Mar 52	168UNTS9	102210
Multilateral		07 Mar 52	175UNTS205	102302
Taiwan	Japan	28 Apr 52	138UNTS3	101858
Canada	USA (United States)	02 Mar 53	222UNTS77	103024
Finland	Norway	20 May 53	173UNTS163	102265
United Arab Rep	USA (United States)	21 May 53	204UNTS29	102748
Liberia	USA (United States)	23 Jun 53	213UNTS37	102879
Australia	Japan	24 May 54	191UNTS125	102580
Japan	USSR (Soviet Union)	19 Oct 56	263UNTS99	103768
Multilateral		09 Feb 57	314UNTS105	104546
Norway	USSR (Soviet Union)	22 Nov 57	309UNTS269	104476
Multilateral		29 Jan 58	339UNTS23	104845
Multilateral		29 Apr 58	559UNTS285	108164
Multilateral		29 Apr 58	450UNTS11	106465
Multilateral		29 Apr 58	450UNTS169	106466
Cuba	USA (United States)	15 Aug 58	358UNTS63	105124
Multilateral		24 Jan 59	486UNTS157	107078
Finland	USSR (Soviet Union)	21 Feb 59	338UNTS3	104830
Germany, West	Iceland	19 Jul 61	409UNTS47	105877
Greece	USA (United States)	24 Apr 62	459UNTS3	106609
Germany, West	USA (United States)	29 Nov 62	460UNTS169	106639
Norway	USA (United States)	01 Mar 63	524UNTS185	107573
Belgium	USA (United States)	19 Apr 63	493UNTS83	107209
Belgium	Netherlands	13 May 63	540UNTS3	107843
Taiwan	IBRD (World Bank)	27 Sep 63	483UNTS151	107012
Japan	UK Great Britain	06 Jan 64	502UNTS183	107329
Multilateral		09 Mar 64	581UNTS57	108432
France	UK Great Britain	10 Apr 64	0UNTS0	109272
UK Great Britain	USA (United States)	19 Jun 64	530UNTS99	107675
Denmark	USA (United States)	02 Jul 64	529UNTS277	107665
Spain	USA (United States)	16 Jul 64	529UNTS187	107661
Norway	UK Great Britain	28 Sep 64	548UNTS63	107970
Italy	USA (United States)	23 Nov 64	532UNTS133	107716
USA (United States)	USSR (Soviet Union)	14 Dec 64	531UNTS213	107705
USA (United States)	USSR (Soviet Union)	05 Feb 65	541UNTS97	107863
Japan	Korea, South	22 Jun 65	583UNTS51	108472

PARTY ONE	PARTY TWO	DATE	CITATION	NUMBER
Ocean resources (Cont.)				
Belgium	France	23 Sep 66	588UNTS227	108528
Denmark	Sweden	05 Dec 67	631UNTS257	108998
Multilateral		08 Dec 67	620UNTS225	108959
Wildlife				
Multilateral		12 Oct 40	161UNTS193	200485
Canada	USA (United States)	19 Dec 42	26UNTS363	200156
Finland	USSR (Soviet Union)	09 Dec 48	217UNTS135	102947
Multilateral		18 Oct 50	638UNTS185	109134
Multilateral		01 Mar 52	168UNTS9	102210
Finland	Norway	18 Mar 52	188UNTS187	102527
Canada	USA (United States)	03 May 54	221UNTS339	103015
Multilateral		23 Oct 54	332UNTS3	104760
Norway	Sweden	29 Jun 56	262UNTS335	103759
Norway	USSR (Soviet Union)	22 Nov 57	309UNTS269	104476
Finland	USSR (Soviet Union)	23 Jun 60	379UNTS277	105443
Hungary	Romania	13 Jun 63	576UNTS275	108369
Poland	UK Great Britain	26 Sep 64	539UNTS153	107828
Japan	USA (United States)	25 Nov 64	533UNTS31	107730
Finland	USSR (Soviet Union)	04 Jun 65	560UNTS169	108173
Fisheries and fishing				
Multilateral		05 Apr 46	231UNTS199	103221
IMF (Fund)	United Nations	15 Apr 48	16UNTS325	200108
Multilateral		09 May 52	205UNTS65	102770
Canada	USA (United States)	02 Mar 53	222UNTS77	103024
Denmark	UK Great Britain	23 Jul 54	213UNTS313	102894
Canada	USA (United States)	10 Sep 54	238UNTS97	103355
Multilateral		03 Jun 55	310UNTS145	104491
UK Great Britain	USSR (Soviet Union)	25 May 56	266UNTS209	103831
Canada	USA (United States)	28 Dec 56	290UNTS103	104229
Multilateral		29 Jan 58	339UNTS23	104845
Multilateral		29 Apr 58	559UNTS285	108164
Cuba	USA (United States)	15 Aug 58	358UNTS63	105124
Multilateral		07 Jul 59	377UNTS203	105402
Fed of Malaya	UK Great Britain	07 Jun 60	375UNTS141	105365
Finland	Norway	15 Nov 60	383UNTS159	105501
Norway	UK Great Britain	17 Nov 60	398UNTS189	105723
Germany, West	Iceland	19 Jul 61	409UNTS47	105877
Denmark	Iceland	01 Aug 61	425UNTS191	106124
Norway	USSR (Soviet Union)	16 Apr 62	437UNTS175	106307
Multilateral		28 Jul 62	460UNTS219	106642
Japan	UK Great Britain	06 Jan 64	502UNTS183	107329
Multilateral		09 Mar 64	581UNTS57	108432
Multilateral		09 Mar 64	581UNTS83	108433
Multilateral		09 Mar 64	581UNTS89	108434
USA (United States)	USSR (Soviet Union)	05 Feb 65	541UNTS97	107863
Japan	Korea, South	22 Jun 65	583UNTS51	108472
Multilateral		19 Dec 66	605UNTS313	108769
Denmark	Norway	19 Dec 66	606UNTS3	108770
UK Great Britain	USSR (Soviet Union)	24 Feb 67	606UNTS171	108785
Denmark	Norway	20 Apr 67	604UNTS103	108747
Belgium	Denmark	29 Jun 67	606UNTS113	108780
Regulation of natural resources				
Bolivia	Brazil	25 Feb 38	51UNTS245	200192
Canada	USA (United States)	10 Nov 41	23UNTS275	200134
Canada	USA (United States)	27 Nov 41	103UNTS193	200314
Mexico	USA (United States)	03 Feb 44	3UNTS313	200025
Canada	USA (United States)	03 Mar 44	109UNTS191	200359
Multilateral		04 Jan 46	6UNTS35	100066
Multilateral		02 Dec 46	161UNTS72	102124
Multilateral		13 Dec 46	8UNTS71	100115
Multilateral		13 Dec 46	8UNTS91	100116
Multilateral		13 Dec 46	8UNTS105	100117
Finland	USSR (Soviet Union)	09 Dec 48	217UNTS135	102947
Finland	Sweden	17 Feb 49	197UNTS123	102636

PARTY ONE	PARTY TWO	DATE	CITATION	NUMBER
Regulation of natural resources (Cont.)				
Australia	New Zealand	26 Nov 49	198UNTS161	102662
Canada	USA (United States)	27 Feb 50	132UNTS223	101762
France	UK Great Britain	30 Jan 51	121UNTS97	101629
Saudi Arabia	USA (United States)	10 Nov 51	180UNTS263	102390
Jordan	USA (United States)	12 Feb 52	168UNTS25	102211
Iraq	USA (United States)	21 May 52	212UNTS183	102870
Ethiopia	USA (United States)	24 Jun 52	181UNTS215	102411
Saudi Arabia	USA (United States)	10 Nov 52	181UNTS225	102412
Portugal	UK Great Britain	21 Jan 53	175UNTS13	102293
United Arab Rep	USA (United States)	12 Mar 53	204UNTS3	102747
United Arab Rep	USA (United States)	19 Mar 53	215UNTS17	102909
Jordan	Syria	04 Jun 53	184UNTS15	102437
UN Relief Palestin	United Arab Rep	14 Oct 53	190UNTS13	102555
Austria	Yugoslavia	25 May 54	227UNTS111	103135
Denmark	UK Great Britain	23 Jul 54	213UNTS313	102894
Austria	Yugoslavia	27 Nov 54	396UNTS75	105694
Brazil	USA (United States)	03 Aug 55	270UNTS71	103893
Italy	Switzerland	17 Sep 55	291UNTS213	104257
Austria	Hungary	09 Apr 56	438UNTS123	106315
Czechoslovakia	Hungary	13 Oct 56	300UNTS125	104336
Czechoslovakia	USSR (Soviet Union)	30 Nov 56	266UNTS243	103833
Norway	USSR (Soviet Union)	18 Dec 57	312UNTS257	104522
Germany, West	Netherlands	28 Jan 58	453UNTS183	106525
Multilateral		29 Jan 58	339UNTS23	104845
Czechoslovakia	Poland	21 Mar 58	538UNTS89	107811
Bulgaria	Yugoslavia	04 Apr 58	367UNTS89	105228
Australia	New Zealand	30 Sep 58	340UNTS61	104859
Italy	Yugoslavia	20 Nov 58	379UNTS23	105433
Finland	USSR (Soviet Union)	21 Feb 59	338UNTS3	104830
Multilateral		29 Apr 59	346UNTS167	104980
Sudan	United Arab Rep	08 Nov 59	453UNTS51	106519
Austria	Czechoslovakia	23 Jan 60	495UNTS99	107241
Germany, West	Netherlands	08 Apr 60	508UNTS14	107404
Belgium	Netherlands	20 Jun 60	423UNTS19	106084
Finland	USSR (Soviet Union)	23 Jun 60	379UNTS277	105443
United Arab Rep	USSR (Soviet Union)	27 Aug 60	399UNTS37	105733
Canada	USA (United States)	17 Jan 61	542UNTS224	107894
Argentina	Uruguay	07 Apr 61	635UNTS91	109074
Tunisia	USSR (Soviet Union)	30 Aug 61	437UNTS243	106310
Belgium	Netherlands	13 May 63	540UNTS3	107843
Hungary	Romania	13 Jun 63	576UNTS275	108369
Multilateral		09 Mar 64	581UNTS57	108432
Finland	USSR (Soviet Union)	24 Apr 64	537UNTS231	107804
Poland	USSR (Soviet Union)	17 Jul 64	552UNTS175	108054
Japan	Korea, South	22 Jun 65	583UNTS51	108472
Netherlands	UK Great Britain	06 Oct 65	595UNTS105	108615
Mexico	USA (United States)	24 Aug 66	606UNTS251	108789
Multilateral		08 Dec 67	620UNTS225	108959
Raw materials				
Nicaragua	USA (United States)	11 Jan 41	117UNTS253	200374
Honduras	USA (United States)	28 Feb 41	117UNTS205	200371
Costa Rica	USA (United States)	18 Jun 41	103UNTS173	200313
Taiwan	UK Great Britain	18 Jun 41	10UNTS227	200064
Brazil	USA (United States)	03 Mar 42	105UNTS91	200324
Brazil	USA (United States)	03 Mar 42	105UNTS99	200325
Mexico	USA (United States)	18 Nov 42	120UNTS183	200392
Belgium	USA (United States)	30 Jan 43	13UNTS371	200084
Multilateral		26 Mar 43	13UNTS427	200089
Colombia	USA (United States)	29 Mar 43	124UNTS139	200416
Haiti	USA (United States)	08 Jan 45	121UNTS153	200397
France	USA (United States)	07 Feb 46	3UNTS239	100034

PARTY ONE	PARTY TWO	DATE	CITATION	NUMBER
Raw materials (Cont.)				
Netherlands	USA (United States)	09 Feb 46	3UNTS247	100035
UK Great Britain	USA (United States)	01 Mar 46	3UNTS293	100037
UK Great Britain	USA (United States)	27 Mar 46	4UNTS2	100039
USA (United States)	Venezuela	29 Mar 46	124UNTS57	101666
Albania	Yugoslavia	28 Nov 46	111UNTS151	101528
Haiti	USA (United States)	11 Feb 48	149UNTS11	101946
Taiwan	USA (United States)	03 Jul 48	17UNTS119	100273
UK Great Britain	USA (United States)	30 Sep 48	71UNTS241	100922
Multilateral		28 Apr 49	83UNTS105	101105
Greece	Turkey	21 Jul 49	78UNTS55	101011
Greece	Italy	31 Aug 49	78UNTS89	101014
Korea, South	USA (United States)	26 Jan 50	80UNTS205	101053
Luxembourg	USA (United States)	27 Jan 50	80UNTS187	101052
France	USA (United States)	27 Jan 50	80UNTS171	101051
Netherlands	USA (United States)	27 Jan 50	80UNTS219	101054
Belgium	USA (United States)	27 Jan 50	51UNTS213	100767
Iran	USA (United States)	23 May 50	81UNTS3	101057
Thailand	USA (United States)	17 Oct 50	79UNTS41	101030
USA (United States)	Yugoslavia	21 Nov 50	93UNTS45	101286
Multilateral		23 Dec 50	185UNTS3	102456
Portugal	USA (United States)	05 Jan 51	133UNTS75	101782
Multilateral		06 Mar 51	138UNTS67	101860
USA (United States)	Yugoslavia	17 Apr 51	162UNTS173	102134
Multilateral		08 Sep 51	136UNTS45	101832
USA (United States)	Yugoslavia	14 Nov 51	174UNTS201	102286
Germany, West	Netherlands	18 Jan 52	179UNTS147	102364
UK Great Britain	USA (United States)	18 Jan 52	184UNTS79	102440
Ecuador	USA (United States)	20 Feb 52	177UNTS43	102308
Peru	USA (United States)	22 Feb 52	165UNTS31	102166
Cuba	USA (United States)	07 Mar 52	165UNTS11	102165
Chile	USA (United States)	09 Apr 52	186UNTS53	102482
Israel	USA (United States)	09 May 52	177UNTS269	102326
Philippines	USA (United States)	26 Jun 53	213UNTS77	102881
Greece	Turkey	07 Nov 53	225UNTS163	103098
Japan	USA (United States)	08 Mar 54	232UNTS169	103236
Iraq	USA (United States)	21 Apr 54	222UNTS251	103032
Pakistan	USA (United States)	19 May 54	202UNTS301	102736
Greece	Romania	19 May 54	225UNTS17	103083
Honduras	USA (United States)	20 May 54	222UNTS87	103025
Haiti	USA (United States)	28 Jan 55	270UNTS83	103894
France	Ireland	07 Jun 55	558UNTS217	108142
Germany, West	USA (United States)	30 Jun 55	240UNTS47	103393
Ethiopia	Italy	05 Mar 56	267UNTS189	103844
Philippines	USA (United States)	08 Apr 57	303UNTS227	104382
Finland	India	14 Jun 57	277UNTS327	104016
Libya	USA (United States)	30 Jun 57	284UNTS177	104136
Germany, West	Netherlands	28 Jan 58	453UNTS183	106525
Denmark	El Salvador	09 Jul 58	341UNTS289	104892
Austria	Czechoslovakia	23 Jan 60	495UNTS125	107242
Canada	Italy	18 Dec 61	470UNTS153	106807
Algeria	France	03 Jul 62	507UNTS25	107395
Iran	United Nations	05 Sep 62	442UNTS249	106353
Belgium	Netherlands	27 Apr 65	596UNTS235	108636
Ireland	UK Great Britain	14 Dec 65	565UNTS58	108235
Philippines	USA (United States)	26 Aug 66	606UNTS259	108790
Control of internal finance				
Haiti	USA (United States)	13 Sep 41	103UNTS141	200311
Haiti	USA (United States)	21 Sep 42	120UNTS177	200391
Haiti	USA (United States)	30 Sep 42	24UNTS205	200144
Haiti	USA (United States)	30 Sep 46	15UNTS257	100241
Haiti	USA (United States)	01 Oct 47	102UNTS67	101411